How to use Volume I

This book provides in-depth information about prescription and over-the-counter medicines and nutritional supplements. Its clinically relevant nature makes it a valuable reference guide for health care professionals.

On this page, you'll find general information about how to use this book. Illustrations showing how the monographs and indexes are organized appear on the next two pages.

About the monographs

The drug monographs are arranged alphabetically like an encyclopedia. ***If you already know which monograph the drug belongs to,*** you can turn directly to it.

If you know only the drug's generic or brand name, the best way to find your information is to use the General Index at the back of this book. It will tell you which monograph includes that drug and the page number on which the monograph starts.

For more information

For more detailed information about this book's content, see *Preface.* In addition to the monographs, this book has an Indications Index plus the following supplemental appendixes:

- *Selected List of Drug-induced Effects*
- *Therapeutic Guidelines*
- *Poison Control Center Listing*
- *The Medicine Chart*
- *Combination Product Cross-Reference Listing*
- *VA Medication Classification System*
- *Excluded Monograph Listing*
- *Off-Label Use Indices*

Monograph sample

Indications: lists both FDA- and Health Canada-approved indications, in addition to off-label uses.

Category: lists the category of therapeutic use for the drug.

Title section: tells the drug's VA classification codes, whether it is a controlled substance in the U.S. or Canada, and what its commonly used brand and generic names are.

Side/Adverse Effects: lists common and rare side effects of the drug, with presenting symptoms noted in parentheses, and tells whether the side effects require medical attention.

General Dosing Information: provides general information, including affect on diet and nutrition and treatment of overdose.

GEMCITABINE Systemic

VA CLASSIFICATION (Primary): AN300
Commonly used brand name(s): Gemzar.

Note: For a listing of dosage forms and brand names by country availability, see *Dosage Forms* section(s).

Category: Antineoplastic.

Indications

Note: Bracketed information in the *Indications* section refers to uses that are not included in U.S. product labeling.

Accepted

Carcinoma, pancreatic (treatment)óGemcitabine is indicated as first-line therapy for locally advanced (nonresectable Stage II or III) or metastatic (Stage IV) adenocarcinoma of the pancreas. It is also indicated as second-line therapy for patients who have previously been treated with fluorouracil. Treatment with gemcitabine is primarily palliative.

Carcinoma, lung, nonfismall cellóGemcitabine is indicated in combination with cisplatin as first-line therapy for inoperable, locally advanced (Stage IIIA or IIIB) or metastatic (Stage IV) nonfismall cell lung carcinoma.

[Carcinoma, biliary tract (treatment)][1] or
[Carcinoma, gallbladder (treatment)][1]óGemcitabine is indicated for the treatment of locally advanced, unresectable, or metastatic biliary tract (i.e., cholangiocarcinoma, biliary tree carcinoma, bile duct carcinoma) and gallbladder carcinomas.

Acceptance not established

Use of gemcitabine for the treatment of primary breast carcinoma has not been established, due to insufficient efficacy data.

Use of gemcitabine for the treatment of mesotheliomas has not been established. Although case reports state objective and subjective benefit in few patients, most phase II trials of an adequate sample size do not demonstrate an established benefit of gemcitabine therapy.

[1] Not included in Canadian product labeling.

Pharmacology/Pharmacokinetics

Physicochemical characteristics:

Chemical groupóGemcitabine is a nucleoside (deoxycytidine) analog.
Molecular weightóGemcitabine hydrochloride: 299.66.
pHó2.7 to 3.3 (after reconstitution).
pKaó3.6.
SolubilityóPractically insoluble in ethanol and polar organic solvents; soluble in water.

Mechanism of action/Effect:
Gemcitabine is an antimetabolite of the pyrimidine analog type. Gemcitabine is cell cyclefispecific for the S phase and for the G_1/S phase boundary of cell division.

Other actions/effects: Gemcitabine is a potent radiation sensitizer. In *in vitro* studies, it produced significant radiosensitization even in lower-than-cytotoxic concentrations.

Distribution: The volume of distribution is significantly affected by the duration of the gemcitabine infusion and the gender of the patient.

Protein binding: Very low (< 10%).

Biotransformation: Gemcitabine undergoes intracellular metabolism, via nucleoside kinases, to produce two active metabolites.

Half-life:
Gemcitabine triphosphate metaboliteóTerminal (from peripheral blood mononuclear cells): 1.7 to 19.4 hours.

Elimination: Renaló92 to 98% of a single dose of radiolabeled gemcitabine was recovered within 1 week.

Precautions to Consider

Carcinogenicity
Secondary malignancies are potential delayed effects of many antineoplastic agents, although it is not clear whether the effect is related to their mutagenic or immunosuppressive action. The effect of dose and duration of therapy is also unknown, although risk seems to increase with long-term use. The risk of secondary malignancies developing after gemcitabine therapy is not known.

Mutagenicity
Gemcitabine was mutagenic in *in vitro* (mouse lymphoma assay) and *in vivo* (mouse micronucleus assay) mammalian test systems. However, it was not mutagenic in the Ames test, *in vivo* sister chromatid exchange, or in *in vitro* (chromosomal aberration assays and unscheduled DNA synthesis) test systems.

Pregnancy/Reproduction
FertilityóIntraperitoneal administration to male mice of 0.5 mg per kg of body weight (mg/kg) per day resulted in moderate to severe hypospermatogenesis.
PregnancyóStudies in humans have not been done.
Other potential hazards to the fetus include adverse reactions seen in adults.
FDA Pregnancy Category D.

Breast-feeding
Little information is available regarding distribution of antineoplastic agents into breast milk.

Pediatrics
Appropriate studies on the relationship of age to the effects of gemcitabine have not been performed in the pediatric population. Safety and efficacy have not been established.

Geriatrics
Appropriate studies performed to date have not demonstrated geriatrics-specific problems that would limit the usefulness of gemcitabine in the elderly.

Dental
The bone marrow depressant effects of gemcitabine may result in an increased incidence of microbial infection, delayed healing, and gingival bleeding.

Drug interactions and/or related problems
The following drug interactions and/or related problems have been selected on the basis of their potential clinical significance (possible mechanism in parentheses where appropriate)ónot necessarily inclusive (» = major clinical significance):

Blood dyscrasiaficausing medications (see *Appendix II*)
(leukopenic and/or thrombocytopenic effects of gemcitabine may be increased with concurrent or recent therapy if these medications cause the same effects; dosage adjustment of gemcitabine, if necessary, should be based on blood counts)

» Bone marrow depressants, other (see *Appendix II*) or
» Radiation therapy
(additive bone marrow depression may occur; dosage reduction may be required when two or more bone marrow depressants, including radiation, are used concurrently or consecutively)

Laboratory value alterations
With physiology/laboratory test values
Alanine aminotransferase (ALT [SGPT])
(values may be increased. However, continuation of gemcitabine therapy despite these elevations produced no evidence of increasing hepatotoxicity)
Blood urea nitrogen (BUN)
(concentrations may be increased)

Medical considerations/Contraindications
The medical considerations/contraindications included have been selected on the basis of their potential clinical significance (reasons given in parentheses where appropriate)ónot necessarily inclusive (» = major clinical significance).

Risk-benefit should be considered when the following medical problems exist:

» Bone marrow depression
(will be exacerbated; reduction, delay, or omission of a gemcitabine dose may be necessary)
» Herpes zoster
(risk of severe generalized disease)

Patient monitoring
The following may be especially important in patient monitoring (other tests may be warranted in some patients, depending on condition; » = major clinical significance):
Alanine aminotransferase (ALT [SGPT])

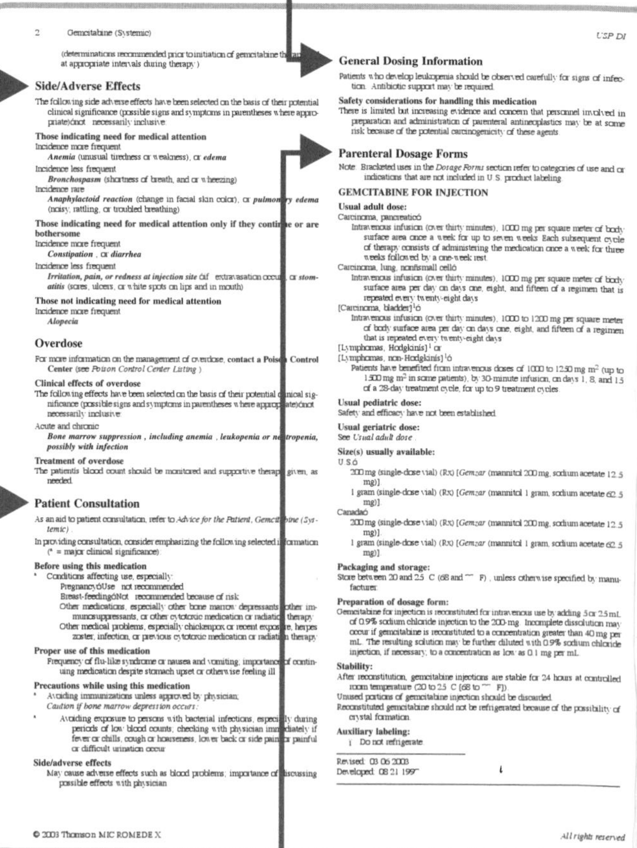

(determinations recommended prior to initiation of gemcitabine therapy and at appropriate intervals during therapy)

Side/Adverse Effects

The following side/adverse effects have been selected on the basis of their potential clinical significance (possible signs and symptoms in parentheses where appropriate)ónot necessarily inclusive:

Those indicating need for medical attention
Incidence more frequent
Anemia (unusual tiredness or weakness), or ***edema***
Incidence less frequent
Bronchospasm (shortness of breath, and/or wheezing)
Incidence rare
Anaphylactoid reaction (change in facial skin color), or ***pulmonary edema*** (noisy, rattling, or troubled breathing)

Those indicating need for medical attention only if they continue or are bothersome
Incidence more frequent
Constipation, or ***diarrhea***
Incidence less frequent
Irritation, pain, or redness at injection site óif extravasation occurs, or ***stomatitis*** (sores, ulcers, or white spots on lips and in mouth)

Those not indicating need for medical attention
Incidence more frequent
Alopecia

Overdose

For more information on the management of overdose, **contact a Poison Control Center** (see *Poison Control Center Listing*).

Clinical effects of overdose
The following effects have been selected on the basis of their potential clinical significance (possible signs and symptoms in parentheses where appropriate)ónot necessarily inclusive:
Acute and chronic
Bone marrow suppression, including anemia, leukopenia or neutropenia, possibly with infection

Treatment of overdose
The patientís blood count should be monitored and supportive therapy given, as needed.

Patient Consultation

As an aid to patient consultation, refer to *Advice for the Patient, Gemcitabine (Systemic)*.

In providing consultation, consider emphasizing the following selected information (» = major clinical significance):

Before using this medication
» Conditions affecting use, especially:
PregnancyóUse not recommended
Breast-feedingóNot recommended because of risk
Other medications, especially other bone marrow depressants, other immunosuppressants, or other cytotoxic medication or radiation therapy
Other medical problems, especially chickenpox or recent exposure, herpes zoster, infection, or previous cytotoxic medication or radiation therapy

Proper use of this medication
Frequency of flu-like syndrome or nausea and vomiting; importance of continuing medication despite stomach upset or otherwise feeling ill

Precautions while using this medication
» Avoiding immunizations unless approved by physician;
Caution if bone marrow depression occurs:
» Avoiding exposure to persons with bacterial infections, especially during periods of low blood counts; checking with physician immediately if fever or chills, cough or hoarseness, lower back or side pain, or painful or difficult urination occur

Side/adverse effects
May cause adverse effects such as blood problems; importance of discussing possible effects with physician

General Dosing Information

Patients who develop leukopenia should be observed carefully for signs of infection. Antibiotic support may be required.

Safety considerations for handling this medication
There is limited but increasing evidence and concern that personnel involved in preparation and administration of parenteral antineoplastics may be at some risk because of the potential carcinogenicity of these agents.

Parenteral Dosage Forms

Note: Bracketed uses in the *Dosage Forms* section refer to categories of use and/or indications that are not included in U.S. product labeling.

GEMCITABINE FOR INJECTION

Usual adult dose:
Carcinoma, pancreaticó
Intravenous infusion (over thirty minutes), 1000 mg per square meter of body surface area once a week for up to seven weeks. Each subsequent cycle of therapy consists of administering the medication once a week for three weeks followed by a one-week rest.
Carcinoma, lung, nonfismall celló
Intravenous infusion (over thirty minutes), 1000 mg per square meter of body surface area per day on days one, eight, and fifteen of a regimen that is repeated every twenty-eight days.
[Carcinoma, bladder][1]ó
Intravenous infusion (over thirty minutes), 1000 to 1200 mg per square meter of body surface area per day on days one, eight, and fifteen of a regimen that is repeated every twenty-eight days.
[Lymphomas, Hodgkinís][1] or
[Lymphomas, non-Hodgkinís][1]ó
Patients have benefited from intravenous doses of 1000 to 1250 mg/m^2 (up to 1500 mg/m^2 in some patients), by 30-minute infusion, on days 1, 8, and 15 of a 28-day treatment cycle, for up to 9 treatment cycles.

Usual pediatric dose:
Safety and efficacy have not been established.

Usual geriatric dose:
See *Usual adult dose*.

Size(s) usually available:
U.S.ó
200 mg (single-dose vial) (Rx) [*Gemzar* (mannitol 200 mg, sodium acetate 12.5 mg)].
1 gram (single-dose vial) (Rx) [*Gemzar* (mannitol 1 gram, sodium acetate 62.5 mg)].
Canadaó
200 mg (single-dose vial) (Rx) [*Gemzar* (mannitol 200 mg, sodium acetate 12.5 mg)].
1 gram (single-dose vial) (Rx) [*Gemzar* (mannitol 1 gram, sodium acetate 62.5 mg)].

Packaging and storage:
Store between 20 and 25 °C (68 and 77 °F), unless otherwise specified by manufacturer.

Preparation of dosage form:
Gemcitabine for injection is reconstituted for intravenous use by adding 5 or 25 mL of 0.9% sodium chloride injection to the 200-mg. Incomplete dissolution may occur if gemcitabine is reconstituted to a concentration greater than 40 mg per mL. The resulting solution may be further diluted with 0.9% sodium chloride injection, if necessary, to a concentration as low as 0.1 mg per mL.

Stability:
After reconstitution, gemcitabine injections are stable for 24 hours at controlled room temperature (20 to 25 °C [68 to 77 °F]).
Unused portions of gemcitabine injection should be discarded.
Reconstituted gemcitabine should not be refrigerated because of the possibility of crystal formation.

Auxiliary labeling:
1. Do not refrigerate.

Revised: 03/06/2003
Developed: 08/21/1997

Precautions: explains significant clinical considerations, such as drug interactions, medical considerations, laboratory value alterations, recommended patient monitoring, use in pediatric or geriatric patients, cancer-causing potential, and special concerns relating to surgery and in dental practice.

Pharmacology/Pharmacokinetics: provides information on pharmacologic actions and pharmacokinetics.

Dosage forms: gives recommended dosages, prescribing limits, packaging and storage guidelines, and other specific information for each available dosage form.

Patient Consultation: highlights details you may want to discuss with a patient. The most important information is marked with a chevron (»).

A Premier Source for Off-label Uses

Volume I

Drug Information for the Health Care Professional

NOTICE AND WARNING

Read the section, Description and Limitations of Information Included, of the "Preface" before consulting individual monographs.

The inclusion in *USP Dispensing Information (USP DI®)* of a monograph on any drug in respect to which patent or trademark rights may exist shall not be deemed, and is not intended as, a grant of, or authority to exercise, any rights or privilege protected by such patent or trademark. All such rights and privileges are vested in the patent or trademark owner, and no other person may exercise the same without express permission, authority, or license secured from such patent or trademark owner.

The listing of selected brand names is intended only for ease of reference. The inclusion of a brand name does not mean the authors have any particular knowledge that the brand listed has properties different from other brands of the same drug, nor should it be interpreted as an endorsement. Similarly, the fact that a particular brand has not been included does not indicate that the product has been judged to be unsatisfactory or unacceptable.

Attention is called to the fact that all volumes of *USP Dispensing Information* are fully copyrighted: Volume I—*Drug Information for the Health Care Professional;* Volume II—*Advice for the Patient®*; Volume III—*Approved Drug Products and Legal Requirements.*

For permission to copy or utilize limited excerpts of this text, address inquiries to *USP DI* Reprint Requests, Thomson Micromedex, 6200 S. Syracuse Way, Suite 300, Greenwood Village, CO 80111.

Physicians, pharmacists, nurses, and other health practitioners are hereby given permission to reproduce a limited number of one or more pages of advice from the *Advice for the Patient* volume of *USP DI* but only when for direct distribution, without charge, to their patients or clients receiving the prescribed drug, provided that such reproduction shall include the copyright notice appearing on the pages from which it was copied.

Library of Congress Catalog Card Number 81-640842

ISBN 1-56363-574-7
ISSN 0740-4174

Printed by Quebecor World, Taunton, Massachusetts, 02780.
Published & distributed by Thomson Micromedex, 6200 S. Syracuse Way, Suite 300, Greenwood Village, CO 80111.

Contents

USP DI–Volume I
Drug Information for the Health Care Professional

Preface

The *USP DI*, originally developed by the United States Pharmacopeia (USP), was created in response to unmet information needs of both professionals and patients in terms of the safe and effective use of medication once it was prescribed. The first edition was published in 1980. From one book in 1980, it grew to two volumes in 1983, and three volumes in 1989. On September 17, 1998, the USP Board of Trustees entered into agreements with Thomson MICROMEDEX for the sale of the *USP DI* Volume I and Volume II databases and licensing of the *USP DI* trademarks. At that time, USP continued to have editorial involvement in the creation of content for Volume I and Volume II.

In May of 2004, Thomson MICROMEDEX and USP modified their relationship. As a result of this modification, USP no longer has editorial review responsibilities with regard to Volume I and Volume II content. Thomson MICROMEDEX now entirely creates and maintains the drug monographs contained in the Volumes.

USP DI is, and always will be, a work in progress. The information is under constant revision. This twenty-seventh edition incorporates the experiences and comments provided by previous editions. New drug monographs and information have been added, and the existing text has been reviewed for changes and revised accordingly.

Development of the 2007 *USP DI*

The USP DI is a comprehensive collection of clinically relevant, established information about each drug. However, it is far more than that. It is also a premier source for off-label use information. The information included represents generally accepted facts about each medication as well as information that represents the clinical judgments of professionals based on the best available evidence placed in the context of medical practice concerns.

For further information about *USP DI* or to comment on how information published in this volume might better meet your information needs, please contact:

Thomson MICROMEDEX
6200 S. Syracuse Way
Suite 300
Greenwood Village, CO 80111-4740
Telephone: (303) 486-6400
Telefax: (303) 486-6464
http://www.micromedex.com/support/request

Organization of *USP DI*

USP DI comprises three distinct volumes. The first volume, *Drug Information for the Health Care Professional,* includes the drug information monographs arranged in alphabetical order. The Volume I general index includes established names, cross-references by brand names (both U.S. and Canadian), and older nonproprietary names. In addition, an indications index, off-label use indices and appendices presenting categories of use and other useful information are included. The second volume, *Advice for the Patient®,* includes the lay language versions of the patient consultation guidelines found in Volume I. These lay language versions are intended to be used at the discretion of the health care provider as an aid to patient consultation if written information would be of benefit or if it is requested by the prescriber. Brand and generic names are cross-referenced in the index of *Advice for the Patient.* The third volume, *Approved Drug Products and Legal Requirements* is owned and published by USP and Thomson MICROMEDEX is a distributor of that volume. It reproduces information from the Food and Drug Administration on therapeutic equivalence and other requirements relating to drug product selection. The third volume includes USP and NF legal requirements for labeling, storage, packaging, and quality for drugs. It also contains those portions of the Federal Controlled Substances Act Regulations, the Poison Prevention Packaging Act and Regulations, and the FD&C Act provisions relating to drugs for human use, and the Current Good Manufacturing Practice Regulations that are most relevant to the physician, pharmacist, nurse, and other health care professionals. However, the reader should review all applicable laws and regulations in the decision-making process.

The individual Volume I monograph covers the basic information that is applicable to that substance when used for a specific area of effect (e.g., Systemic). Information that is unique to a specific dosage form of the base substance is then included under that specific dosage form heading. To illustrate this approach, assume that DRUG X is used for its systemic effects and its topical effects. Also assume that the drug is available in the following dosage forms: cream, injection, ointment, syrup, and tablet. The *USP DI* Volume I monographs for DRUG X would be organized as follows:

DRUG X (Systemic)
[General information applicable to Drug X's systemic use.]
- Drug X Syrup
- Drug X Tablets
- Drug X Injection
- [Specific information applicable to each of the systemic dosage forms.]

DRUG X (Topical)
[General information applicable to Drug X's topical use.]
- Drug X Cream
- Drug X Ointment
- [Specific information applicable to each of the topical dosage forms.]

Examples of other major headings based on specific area of effect are Dental, Inhalation-Local, Intracavernosal, Mucosal-Local, Nasal-Local, Ophthalmic, Oral-Local, Otic, Parenteral-Local, Rectal-Local, Transdermal-Systemic, or Vaginal use.

Whenever feasible, monographs are grouped under family headings. This permits a sizable saving of space and also allows the practitioner to readily identify differences among agents of the same family. Significant differences are addressed in charts and in Summary of Differences sections.

The following headings and subheadings are employed, where appropriate, in organizing the information for each Volume I monograph:

Category
Indications
- General considerations
- Accepted
- Acceptance not established
- Unaccepted

Pharmacology/Pharmacokinetics
- Physicochemical characteristics
  - Source
  - Molecular weight
  - pKa
  - Solubility
  - Partition coefficient
  - Other characteristics
- Mechanism of action/Effect
- Other actions/effects
- Absorption
- Distribution
- Protein binding
- Biotransformation
- Half-life

Onset of action
Time to peak concentration
Peak serum concentration
Time to peak effect
Duration of action
Elimination
In dialysis

Precautions to Consider
Cross-sensitivity and/or related problems
Carcinogenicity
Tumorigenicity
Mutagenicity
Pregnancy/Reproduction
Fertility
Pregnancy
Labor
Delivery
Postpartum
Breast-feeding
Pediatrics
Adolescents
Geriatrics
Pharmacogenetics
Dental
Surgical
Critical/Emergency care
Drug interactions and/or related problems
Laboratory value alterations
With diagnostic test results
With physiology/laboratory test values
Medical considerations/Contraindications
Patient monitoring

Side/Adverse Effects
Those indicating need for medical attention
Those indicating need for medical attention only if they continue or are bothersome
Those not indicating need for medical attention
Those indicating need for medical attention if they occur after medication is discontinued

Overdose
Clinical effects of overdose
Treatment of overdose

Patient Consultation
Before using this medication
Proper use of this medication
Precautions while using this medication
Side/adverse effects

General Dosing Information
Diet/Nutrition
Bioequivalence information
Safety considerations for handling this medication
For treatment of adverse effects

Dosage forms (each separate)
Usual adult dose
Usual adult prescribing limits
Usual pediatric dose
Usual pediatric prescribing limits
Usual geriatric dose
Strengths usually available
Packaging and storage
Preparation of dosage form
Stability
Incompatibilities
Auxiliary labeling
Caution
Additional information

Selected Bibliography

Description and Limitations of Information Included

USP DI contains selected information and takes into account practice concerns. It is meant to aid the health care professional and the patient in minimizing the risks and enhancing the benefits of the drugs used. Collectively, the *USP DI* is valuable when assessing quality of care. Ultimately, the information required is defined by the practice standards of medicine, pharmacy, nursing, dentistry, and the other health professions as well as by the information needs of the patient.

USP DI is not intended to be "full disclosure" information.

Readers are advised that the information in *USP DI* may contain statements that differ from those in the "full disclosure" information labeling approved or required by the United States or Canadian governments. Readers should also remember that FDA-approved full disclosure information can differ from brand to brand of the same generic drug product. It should not be inferred that the inclusion of information that is not in the approved labeling has been sought or agreed to by the manufacturer.

Selected brand names are included in the monographs as well as in the indexes of both Volumes I and II, for ease of reference purposes only. The inclusion of a brand name is not intended as an endorsement of a particular product. The omission of a particular brand name does not indicate that the agent was judged to be inferior or inadequate. The inclusion of various brands in Volumes I and II bears no relationship to, and is not intended to affect, any applicable brand interchange requirements.

The Veterans Administration medication classification codes (primary and secondary assignments) are included at the beginning of each monograph. See the VA Medication Classification System appendix in *USP DI* Volume I for a detailed description as well as a complete listing of primary and secondary classifications.

Where appropriate, controlled substance classifications are included at the beginning of the monograph. United States schedules include:

Schedule I–No legal medical use is recognized by the U.S. Controlled Substances Act. Use of Schedule I substances for research purposes is permitted with proper registration. Schedule I substances are not included in *USP DI*.
Examples: Heroin, LSD, peyote.

Schedule II–The most stringent classification for drugs recognized by the U.S. Controlled Substances Act as having a legitimate medical use; these drugs are characterized by a very high abuse potential and/or potential for severe physical and psychic dependency. Distribution and inventory are highly controlled; prescriptions are non-refillable. Emergency telephone orders for limited quantities of these drugs are authorized but the prescriber must provide a written, signed prescription order to the pharmacy within 72 hours.
Examples: Amphetamines, anabolic steroids, meperidine, morphine, short-acting barbiturates.

Schedule III–Includes drugs having significant abuse potential, but to a lesser degree than Schedule II substances. Prescriptions can be refilled up to five times within six months after the date of issue if authorized by the prescriber. Telephone orders are permitted.
Examples: Certain barbiturates not included in Schedule II, opiates in combination with other substances such as acetaminophen or aspirin.

Schedule IV–Includes drugs having a low abuse potential. Prescriptions can be refilled up to five times within six months after the date of issue if authorized by the prescriber. Telephone orders are permitted.
Examples: Benzodiazepines, certain long-acting barbiturates, chloral hydrate, pentazocine, propoxyphene.

Schedule V– Includes products having the lowest abuse potential of the controlled substances. No limitations on refills other than those imposed by the prescriber. Some Schedule V products may be available without a prescription (for example, certain cough preparations and antidiarrheal preparations containing limited amounts of an opiate).

In addition to the Federal Controlled Substances Act, most states have controlled substances acts similar to the federal requirements. In some instances, the state regulations may be more restrictive. These differences are not addressed in *USP DI* monographs.

Canadian controlled substance classifications (and the designations used in this publication) include:

Narcotics (N)–Includes products containing a narcotic. Within this broad classification, there are several levels of regulatory control. These levels range from strict controls for the most abusable of the substances (for example, single-entity narcotics; products containing a narcotic with one active non-narcotic ingredient; any preparation containing heroin, hydrocodone, or oxycodone) to lesser controls for preparations containing one narcotic and two active non-narcotic ingredients and exempt codeine preparations (those containing a limited amount of codeine plus two active non-narcotic ingredients).

Controlled Drugs–Includes non-narcotic preparations with abuse potential. As with narcotics, different regulations apply depending on specific content.

Examples: Amphetamines, barbiturates.

Category/Indications–Statements of categories of use and indications are provided for each agent.

The category of use indicates the area of therapeutic utility for which the drug was intended and generally represents an application of the best known pharmacologic action of the agent or its active ingredient. The statement is not intended to be all-inclusive nor to indicate that the agent may have no other activity or utility.

Indications for use stated in manufacturers' labeling and approved by the U.S. Food and Drug Administration (FDA) or Health Canada's Therapeutic Products Directorate are generally included. These indications are included under an *Accepted* subheading.

New uses for approved products that are not reflected in a product's labeling are often discovered after marketing. Before a pharmaceutical manufacturer may include any new indications in the labeling for a particular drug (and to promote the product for those uses), it must obtain the government's approval for the uses. Such approval requires the completion of adequate and well-controlled clinical trials to document the drug's safety and efficacy for the new uses. Since the clinical trials required for approval may take considerable time and effort, manufacturers, in some cases, may not seek or obtain approval for new uses since there may not be sufficient economic incentive for the product sponsor to perform the necessary research or to make application to the agency. In other cases, of course, the manufacturer may have carried out the research but the new proposed use was found to be unsupported.

Medically accepted off-label indications are identified in the *Indications* section, by brackets for the U.S. products and a superscript 1 for Canadian products. A brief explanatory statement may follow the off-label indication. These indications are included under an *Accepted* subheading.

The legality of prescribing approved drugs for uses not included in their official labeling is sometimes a cause for concern and confusion among practitioners. In the U.S., the Federal Food, Drug, and Cosmetic Act does not prohibit practitioners from prescribing nor pharmacists from dispensing a drug product for a particular patient for an indication not contained in its approved labeling. During recent years, U.S. federal and state officials have scrutinized the sales and marketing practices of pharmaceutical manufacturers and the resulting utilization in the health care industry of approved drugs for uses not included in their official labeling. Practitioners and pharmacists may want to stay abreast of the evolving legal and regulatory environment. Further, the appropriateness of prescribing or dispensing an approved drug for an off-label indication would ultimately be judged in accordance with accepted legal principles governing professional activities (such as negligence or strict liability) in the event of a question of liability to an injured patient.

Another point of concern to practitioners relates to differences in approved labeled indications for different brands of the same generic drug product. Because of the legalities involved, it is possible for different manufactured products of the same generic product to have in their labeling different indications (as well as different precautions, side effects, dosage schedules, etc.). *USP DI* indications are not directed to a specific brand product unless a particular characteristic of a brand must be taken into account.

An *Unaccepted* indications section identifies uses of a drug that are considered to be inappropriate, obsolete, or unproven. For certain drugs whose place in therapy has not been determined and the use does not clearly fall into the "Accepted" or "Unaccepted" categorization, information is included under an *Acceptance not established* subheading.

A *General considerations* subsection is included in the Indications section for some drugs, such as antibiotics, to give the reader more complete information about the use of the drug (e.g., the activity spectrum of antibiotics).

Evidence ratings—Evidence ratings based on study design and strength of endpoints are included in selected monographs (primarily oncology agents) to support off-label use recommendations. Once an off-label indication has been approved, the evidence rating supporting that use is placed in parentheses in Roman type (e.g. Evidence rating: IA) in the text after the paragraph that discusses the indication, or after each indication, if they are listed in a string within a statement. Ratings are assigned based on the following scheme:

Grade level (ranked in descending order of strength)—

I: Evidence from randomized, controlled trials or meta-analyses of a group of randomized, controlled trials.

II: Evidence from well-designed, internally controlled clinical trials without randomization, from cohort or case-controlled analytic studies, preferably from more than one center, from multiple time series, or from dramatic results in uncontrolled experiments.

III: Evidence from clinical trials with low power, preliminary reports of trials in progress, opinions of respected authorities on the basis of clinical experience, descriptive studies such as case reports or series, or reports of expert committees.

Strength of Endpoints (ranked in descending order of strength) for oncology agents—

A. Total Mortality (or overall survival from a defined point in time, such as the time of randomization).

B. Cause-Specific Mortality (or cause-specific mortality from a defined point in time).

C. Carefully Assessed Quality of Life (does not include reports of symptoms or toxicity).

D. Indirect Surrogates (includes disease-free survival, progression free survival, tumor response rate).

Pharmacology/Pharmacokinetics—A brief statement of physicochemical characteristics and pharmacologic actions includes, whenever appropriate and available, source, molecular weight, pKa, solubility, partition coefficient, mechanism of action, actions other than the therapeutic actions, absorption, distribution in the body, protein-binding characteristics, biotransformation, half-life, onset of action, time to peak concentration, peak serum concentration, time to peak effect, duration of action, and elimination. The information is not intended to be all inclusive. In some cases, protein binding is expressed in general terms with ranges as follows, rather than in terms of specific percentages:

Very high: >90%
High: 65-90%
Moderate: 35-64%
Low: 10-34%
Very low: <10%

Precautions to Consider—The precautions to consider in using a specific drug, as listed under this heading, are not intended to provide "full disclosure" information. Instead, precautions have been selected on the basis of their common or usual clinical significance to the population as a whole. It cannot be assumed that the omission of a precaution in *USP DI* means that such a precaution may not be of clinical significance for a specific patient. In many cases, there is a lack of scientifically valid information to support inclusion in *USP DI*. As in all aspects of medical care, risk benefit considerations must be made on an individual basis, which may, in fact, supersede general precautions to the use of any medication.

Cross-sensitivity and/or related problems—Where known, potential for cross-sensitivity with other drugs is included.

Carcinogenicity—Where known, reference is made to the cancer-causing potential of a drug. Not all such precautions may necessarily be listed.

Tumorigenicity—Where known, reference is made to the tumor-causing potential of a drug. Not all such precautions may necessarily be listed.

Mutagenicity—Where known, reference is made to the mutagenic potential of a drug. Not all such precautions may necessarily be listed.

Pregnancy/Reproduction—Documented problems in humans with the use of a drug during pregnancy are included. Where appropriate, information is included on fertility, pregnancy, labor, delivery, and postpartum effects. In addition, reference is made to problems documented in animal studies even though the significance of such findings to humans may not be known. FDA-assigned pregnancy categories are included whenever available. These categories are:

A: Adequate and well-controlled studies have failed to demonstrate a risk to the fetus in the first trimester of pregnancy (and there is no evidence of risk in later trimesters).

B: Animal reproduction studies have failed to demonstrate a risk to the fetus and there are no adequate and well-controlled studies in pregnant women.

C: Animal reproduction studies have shown an adverse effect on the fetus and there are no adequate and well-controlled studies in humans, but potential benefits may warrant use of the drug in pregnant women despite potential risks.

D: There is positive evidence of human fetal risk based on adverse reaction data from investigational or marketing experience or studies in humans, but potential benefits may warrant use of the drug in pregnant women despite potential risks, if the drug is needed in a life-threatening situation or for a serious disease for which safer drugs cannot be used or are ineffective.

X: Studies in animals or humans have demonstrated fetal abnormalities and/or there is positive evidence of human fetal risk based on adverse reaction data from investigational or marketing experience, and the risks involved in use of the drug in pregnant women clearly outweigh potential benefits.

Breast-feeding—Documented problems in humans associated with the use of a drug while breast-feeding are included. Where appropriate, reference is also made to problems documented in animal studies even though the significance of such findings to humans may not be known.

Pediatrics—Selected precautions relating to use of an agent in the pediatric patient are included. Not all precautions relevant to such use may necessarily be listed. If no information about the use of a drug in the pediatric patient is known, this is so stated.

Adolescents—Selected precautions relating to use of an agent in the adolescent patient are included. Not all precautions relevant to such use may necessarily be listed.

Geriatrics—Selected precautions relating to use of an agent in the geriatric patient are included. Not all precautions relevant to such use may necessarily be listed. If no information about the use of a drug in the geriatric patient is known, this is so stated.

Pharmacogenetics—Selected precautions relating to genetic factors and potential responses to drugs are included. Not all such potential effects may necessarily be listed.

Dental—Selected precautions relating to potential dental effects of an agent are included. Not all such potential effects may necessarily be listed.

Surgical—Selected precautions relating to potential effects of an agent on surgery are included. Not all precautions relevant to surgery may necessarily be listed.

Critical/Emergency care—Selected precautions relating to potential effects of an agent in a critical/emergency care situation are included. Not all such precautions may necessarily be listed.

Drug interactions and/or related problems—Drug and/or food interactions have been selected on the basis of their potential clinical significance. Those considered to have greater significance are identified with a chevron (») to the left of the drug entry. In some cases, an interaction appearing in one monograph may not be cross-referenced in the corresponding monograph. Since each monograph is finalized individually, such inconsistencies are constantly in the process of resolution in preparation for the next revision of the monograph.

Laboratory value alterations—This section includes effects of the drug on laboratory test values. No attempt has been made to provide a complete listing of effects on the normal or diseased body or interferences with other tests that may be required if proper diagnosis is to be expected. The information included in this section is broken down into two subsections:

With diagnostic test results—Includes changes in laboratory test values caused by effects of the drug in the body or on the test materials or procedure that may produce inaccurate results (e.g., diagnostic tests for which the results may be false-positive or false-negative in patients receiving the drug).

With physiology/laboratory test values—Includes changes in laboratory test values that may occur because of the physiologic effects of the drug (for example, increases or decreases in serum electrolytes).

Effects listed have been selected on the basis of potential clinical significance. The list is not necessarily inclusive.

Medical considerations/Contraindications—Some medical conditions, the presence of which may alter the decision to prescribe a drug for a given patient or may affect the dosage, are listed. As a general rule, the list is compiled from the approved labeling and covers precautions, warnings, and contraindications. Those conditions considered to be of greater importance are identified by a chevron (») to the left of the specific medical problem. Contraindications that are considered to be absolute, except under special circumstances, are listed first. Relative contraindications are included for those problems requiring risk-benefit consideration.

Patient monitoring—To exercise judgment in refilling prescriptions and to monitor continuing use of a medication, patient examinations that may be particularly important are listed. The list is not meant to be a complete listing of the check-ups a patient may require nor is it meant to imply that all check-ups listed are necessarily required for every patient taking the medication.

Side/Adverse Effects–Selected side effects are listed. Selection is based on seriousness (e.g., agranulocytosis), frequency of occurrence, effect on life style (e.g., drowsiness), and/or likelihood that a non-threatening side effect might cause concern to the patient if he or she were not aware that the effect might occur (e.g., rapid pulse). Wherever possible, side effects are grouped according to reported incidence—i.e., incidence more frequent, incidence less frequent, or incidence rare; or by percentages, if available. Not all such side/adverse effects may necessarily be listed. The side effects are listed by effect with presenting symptom(s) in parentheses.

Overdose—This section includes selected information on therapeutic and toxic concentrations of the drug, time to onset of overdose symptoms, clinical effects of overdose, and treatment of overdose.

Patient Consultation—Current medical practice embraces the belief that patient compliance and the effectiveness of therapy can be advanced in certain clinical situations if the prescriber provides, or asks the dispenser to provide, written drug use information of the type contained in *USP DI.* To help ensure patient understanding, the prescriber and dispenser should, in turn, translate the essence of this information in words suitable to the ability of the individual patient to understand.

Prior to providing oral consultation, health care professionals should apprise themselves of the entire monograph for the indicated medication. The patient consultation section is provided as a reminder, highlighting a limited, selected number of items peculiar to the medication for oral discussion and, in general, assumes more complete written information can be made available.

Suggested guidelines for patient consultation are listed. The statements marked with a chevron (») are considered to be of greatest importance. If written information is desired, the health care provider may refer to the corresponding lay language monograph in *Advice for the Patient.*

The information provided is intended to aid efforts to advance patient compliance and the effectiveness of the therapy selected by the prescriber. The information provided is not complete, but is intended to serve as a basic reminder or general guide to the health care provider who may vary or omit it in accordance with professional judgment taking into account the best interests of the patient, the request of the prescriber, or the particular circumstances involved. It is not intended as a substitute for professional judgment or to modify any legal requirements imposed on the dispenser. It serves also as a general reminder to the prescriber of the concerns of the dispenser in the dispenser-patient relationship.

Some drugs are not amenable to general rules since they may be prescribed for various purposes not necessarily known to the dispenser, to the person administering the drug, or to other physicians caring for the patient; also, the differences in their utilization might affect the advice to be given. However, where it is clear how a drug is being utilized, it may be helpful to reinforce the prescriber's instructions or to provide such additional advice as would assist the patient.

Occasionally, a dispenser or person administering a drug may have particular knowledge of problems peculiar to the patient that justifies giving exceptional instructions. The fact that *USP DI* makes no mention of such unusual or exceptional circumstances is not intended to limit or influence professional judgment in conveying to the patient information that is deemed to be correct and proper under the circumstances.

General Dosing Information—Dosing information of a general nature that may be applicable to the usual dispensing or administration situation and guidelines relating to diet/nutrition and bioequivalence are included, where appropriate. The information is meant to supplement the dosing information included under each specific dosage form, and the two sets of information must be used together.

Information relating to safety considerations for handling a medication and the treatment of adverse effects is also included in this section.

Dosage Forms—The following information is listed separately for each dosage form, whenever appropriate:

Summary of differences—In family monographs, a summary of differences for each individual family member is included. Not all differences are necessarily included. The fact that this section does not include certain information does not necessarily indicate that the point in question does not occur with that particular family member. It may, instead, reflect a lack of information. Users of *USP DI* must exercise caution and not use the information included in family monographs as the sole basis of comparison between agents.

Usual adult dose—The usual adult dose given for each agent is that which may ordinarily be expected to produce in adults with normal renal/hepatic function, following administration in the manner indicated, at such time intervals as may be specified, the diagnostic, therapeutic, prophylactic, or other effect for which the agent is recognized. The usual adult dose is intended to serve only as a guide, it may be varied in the best interests of the patient, and in accordance with the variables that affect the action of the drug. Where appropriate, information relating to dosing in a patient who has renal/hepatic function impairment is included.

The statements of dosage in the case of capsules and tablets are in terms of the content of active ingredient and rarely represent the total weight of the capsule contents or of the tablets.

In some instances, the dosage may be stated in terms of the pharmacologically active portion (moiety) of the molecule in order to permit the prescriber or dispenser to correlate the weight equivalent for salts, esters, or other chemical forms of the drug moiety. However, it is not to be inferred that all chemical forms in which the active moiety may be presented are therapeutically equivalent. Neither are different dosage forms administered by the same route always therapeutically equivalent, e.g., tablets vs. syrups or creams vs. ointments.

Usual adult prescribing limits—The usual adult prescribing limits subsection is intended primarily to guide the dispenser with respect to seeking confirmation of prescription orders calling for unusually small or large doses. In some cases, it may take into account some uses in addition to those implied in the statement of category. The time schedule and route of administration where given for the usual adult dose apply also to the usual adult prescribing limits unless otherwise specified.

The limits statement does not address the issue of toxicity levels but instead focuses on the generally accepted lower and/or upper ranges of dosage believed to be used in medical practice.

Usual pediatric dose—The usual pediatric dose generally given in the monograph is that which may ordinarily be expected to produce in infants and children with normal renal/hepatic function (following administration in the manner indicated, at such time intervals as may be designated) the diagnostic, therapeutic, or prophylactic effect for which the agent is recognized. Where appropriate, information relating to dosing in a patient who has renal/hepatic function impairment is included.

The provision of the usual pediatric dose is not a recommendation or indication that the drug should be utilized in the pediatric patient, but is intended to serve only as a guide. It should be emphasized that metabolism and elimination of many drugs, including the "inactive" ingredients in the dosage forms, are markedly different in full-term newborn infants, and even more so in premature infants, from those in older children and adults.

Usual pediatric prescribing limits—The usual pediatric prescribing limits subsection is intended primarily to guide the dispenser with respect to seeking confirmation of prescription orders calling for unusually small or large doses. In some cases, it may take into account some uses in addition to those implied in the statement of category. The time schedule and route of administration where given for the usual pediatric dose apply also to the usual pediatric prescribing limits unless otherwise specified.

Usual geriatric dose—A usual geriatric dose statement is included if current knowledge allows. It is to be emphasized that metabolism and elimination of many drugs, including the "inactive" ingredients in the dosage forms, may be markedly different in the geriatric patient.

The provision of the usual geriatric dose is not a recommendation or indication that the drug should be utilized in the geriatric patient. It is intended to serve only as a guide and it may be varied in the best interests of the patient and in accordance with the variables that affect the action of the drug.

Strength(s) usually available—The statement on strengths usually available for a dosage form, given in the individual monograph, is not necessarily complete and is intended solely as information to physicians, pharmacists, nurses, and others concerned with the manner in which dosage forms are commercially supplied.

If a specific drug product is known to contain sulfites, large amounts of lactose, or other inactive ingredients known to cause allergic reactions in large numbers of patients, this information has been included for selected medications. The inactive ingredient listings are not all inclusive. The fact that a product listing does not include identification of inactive ingredients does not necessarily mean that the product is free of potentially offending inactive ingredients.

Packaging and storage—Information concerning packaging and storage of medications as applicable to the dispenser is provided in this section. The labeling of the brand product selected may contain additional or other packaging and storage information specific to that product.

The information included in this section is not intended to replace more definitive requirements that may be contained in the official *USP* monographs.

For those dosage forms included in USP, compendial requirements for packaging and storage apply to the dispenser.

For those products not covered by *USP,* the packaging and storage recommendations found in *USP DI* are usually those recommended by the manufacturer(s).

Preparation of dosage form—Instructions on constitution and/or dilution of a dosage form for administration are included. Information on the extemporaneous preparation of certain drugs, for example, for pediatric use, is also included, where deemed appropriate.

Stability—Included is information concerning beyond-use dates for reconstituted solutions or suspensions, along with special stability problems associated with certain drug products (for example, nitroglycerin tablets). The labeling of the brand product selected may contain specific stability information that differs from information stated in *USP DI.*

Incompatibilities—Chemical and physical incompatibilities of certain admixtures (e.g., intravenous preparations) are included, where deemed appropriate.

Auxiliary labeling—Auxiliary information that is suggested for consideration of placement on the actual prescription container (in addition to the prescription labeling) in accordance with applicable practice requirements is specified in this section.

Recommended labeling that relates to physical properties of the product (e.g., "shake well" for suspensions) can be considered to be universally applicable.

Suggested labeling that relates to therapy (e.g., take on an empty stomach) and would be appropriate for most, but not necessarily all patients, must be considered on an individual basis by the dispenser.

Caution—Information on potential medication errors, where known, and steps to help minimize occurrence of such errors are included where deemed appropriate.

Additional information—Additional information relating to the specific drug product is included if necessary, especially as this information relates to the act of dispensing the medication.

Advice for the Patient (Volume II)—*Advice for the Patient* (Volume II) presents in lay language the concepts listed in the Patient Consultation guidelines of Volume I. It is meant to reinforce the oral consultation and to be provided in written form at the discretion of the health care provider.

The information presented under the section entitled Uses for This Medicine includes information related to medically accepted off-label uses of the drug. This section is intended for use where the health care provider has knowledge that the medication has been prescribed for a particular purpose referred to therein. It is intended as an aid to providing individualized patient education and is not for use when providing the general population with information about the drug. Since the section may contain information that may be or seem to be contradictory or confusing to the patient receiving the drug for its labeled purposes, the health care provider should consider not including this section if photocopies of the information are given to patients routinely.

Approved Drug Products and Legal Requirements (Volume III)—The United States Pharmacopeial Convention is the publisher of the *United States Pharmacopeia* and the *National Formulary.* These texts are recognized as official compendia by the pharmacy and medical professions. They contain standards, specifications, and other requirements relating to drugs and other agents used in medical and pharmacy practice that may be enforceable under various statutes. These requirements are applicable not only when drugs are in the possession of the manufacturer, but at the practice level as well.

Although the standards continue to be applicable when drugs are dispensed or sold, it must also be recognized that most prescriptions today are filled with manufactured products and for the most part physicians and pharmacists no longer routinely compound or analyze drug products. On the other hand, dispensers need to be aware of the quality attributes of products, their packaging and storage requirements, and the other applicable standards to which legal consequences may attach.

In recognition of this need, Volume III provides abstracts of *USP-NF* standards. Similarly, selected portions of the *USP-NF* General Notices and Chapters that are deemed to be especially relevant are reprinted in Volume III.

The incorporation of these official *USP-NF* materials into *USP DI* is for informational purposes only. Because of varying publication schedules, there may occasionally be a time difference between publication of revisions in the *USP-NF* and the appearance of these changes in *USP DI.*

Readers are advised that only the standards as written in the USP-NF are regarded as official. The *USP-NF* material included in *USP DI* is not intended to represent nor shall it be interpreted to be the equivalent of or a substitute for the official *United States Pharmacopeia* and/or *National Formulary.* In the event of any difference or discrepancy between the current official *USP* or *NF* standards and the information contained herein, the context and effect of the official compendia shall prevail.

Volume III also contains federal requirements relevant to the dispensing situation, including:

- the entire text of FDA's "Orange Book," *Approved Drug Products with Therapeutic Equivalence Evaluations;*
- separate listings of B-rated drugs from the FDA "Orange Book" and pre-1938 drugs ("grandfathered" drugs not included in the "Orange Book");
- selected portions of the federal Controlled Substance Act Regulations;
- the Federal Food, Drug and Cosmetic Act requirements as they relate to human drugs, including the recent drug diversion and sampling amendments;
- FDA's Current Good Manufacturing Practice Regulations for Finished Pharmaceuticals.

Appendixes

To help the user of *USP DI,* numerous appendices have been included in both Volume I and Volume II.

Volume I—Volume I includes the following additional material as appendixes:

Selected List of Drug-induced Effects (Appendix I)—A list of selected drug-induced side effects has been compiled for use primarily in conjunction with the drug interactions section of *USP DI* monographs. The listing of drugs is not meant to be inclusive.

Therapeutic Guidelines (Appendix II)—This appendix provides selected general therapeutic guidelines for the health care professional.

Combination Product Cross-reference Listing (Appendix III)—This appendix provides a listing of the therapeutically active ingredients found in combination products included in the 2005 edition of *USP DI* along with a cross-reference to the title of the monograph where the specific combination product can be found.

VA Medication Classification System (Appendix IV)—The Veterans Administration Medication Classification system was developed to provide a systematic and management approach to the classification of medications, investigational drugs, prosthetic items, and expendable supplies for hospital patients. Primary and secondary VA codes are included in each *USP DI* monograph and in this appendix.

The Medicine Chart (Appendix V)—The Medicine Chart presents photographs of many of the most frequently prescribed medicines in the United States. In general, commonly used brand names and a representative sampling of generic products have been included. Only solid oral dosage forms (tablets and capsules) have been included. Since color and size variations may exist and since product changes may have subsequently been adopted by a manufacturer, the chart should be used only as an initial guide, with verification of product identity being made before any further actions are taken.

Poison Control Center Listing (Appendix VI)—Includes a listing of certified regional U.S. poison control centers.

Excluded Monographs (Appendix VII)—This appendix provides a listing of monographs that are not included in this printed edition of *USP DI* Volume I. These monographs are still available by accessing the *USP DI* Updates Online website. See the front cover for details on how to access the website.

Volume II—As in Volume I, The Medicine Chart is included in Volume II in the front of the book. Also included are sections on General Information about Use of Medicines, Avoiding Medicine Mishaps, Getting the Most Out of Your Medicines, and About the Medicines You Are Taking.

In addition, Volume II includes:

Excluded Monographs (Appendix I)—This appendix provides a listing of monographs that are not included in this printed edition of *USP DI* Volume I. These monographs are still available by accessing the *USP DI* Updates Online website. See the front cover for details on how to access the website.

Poison Control Center Listing (Appendix II)—Includes a listing of certified regional U.S. poison control centers.

Categories of Use (Appendix III)—A listing of drugs by their category of use is included in this appendix only as a useful reference. It should not be used to make decisions concerning the appropriateness of therapy. In addition, the drugs included under each entry should not be considered interchangeable for any given patient since in many instances the drugs will differ significantly with regard to effectiveness, seriousness of side effects, and other critical considerations.

Pregnancy Precaution Listing (Appendix IV)—To assist the user of the *USP DI* database, this appendix provides a list of those *USP DI* monographs that have a specific precaution included as to use during pregnancy. Since the clinical significance of the precaution varies from drug to drug, the individual monograph should be consulted for additional information. The absence of a drug from the list is not meant to imply that the drug is necessarily known to be safe for use in pregnant patients.

Breast-feeding Precaution Listing (Appendix V)—This appendix provides a list of those *USP DI* monographs that have a specific precaution included as to use of a drug while breast-feeding. Since the clinical significance of the precaution varies from drug to drug, the individual monograph should be consulted for additional information. The absence of a drug from the list is not meant to imply that the drug is necessarily known to be safe for use in women who are breast-feeding.

Volume II also includes a glossary of drug and medical terminology to help the consumer better understand the information presented in the *Advice for the Patient* monographs.

ABACAVIR Systemic

VA CLASSIFICATION (Primary): AM840

Commonly used brand name(s): *Ziagen*.

Another commonly used name isABC

Note: For a listing of dosage forms and brand names by country availability, see *Dosage Forms* section(s).

Category

Antiviral (systemic).

Indications

General Considerations

Human immunodeficiency virus (HIV-1) isolates with reduced susceptibility to abacavir have been recovered *in vitro*, as well as from some patients treated with this medication. Genetic analysis of isolates from patients treated with abacavir alone has found point mutations in the reverse transcriptase gene that resulted in amino acid substitutions at positions K65R, L74V, Y115F, and M184V; M184V and L74V mutations were observed most frequently in clinical isolates. Phenotypic analysis of HIV-1 isolates with abacavir-associated mutations from 17 patients after 12 weeks of monotherapy with abacavir found a threefold decrease in susceptibility to abacavir *in vitro*. However, the clinical significance of these genotypic and phenotypic findings has not been established.

In vitro, cross-resistance has been observed with other nucleoside reverse transcriptase inhibitors; recombinant laboratory strains of HIV-1 (HXB2) containing multiple reverse transcriptase mutations conferring abacavir resistance exhibited cross-resistance to lamivudine, didanosine, and zalcitabine.

Cross-resistance between abacavir and HIV-protease inhibitors is unlikely because the enzyme targets involved are different. Cross-resistance between abacavir and non-nucleoside reverse transcriptase inhibitors is unlikely because the binding sites on reverse transcriptase are different.

Accepted

Human immunodeficiency virus (HIV) infection (treatment)—Abacavir is indicated, in combination with other agents, for treatment of HIV-1 infection.

Note: This indication is based on analyses of surrogate markers in controlled studies of up to 24 weeks duration. Currently, there are no data from controlled clinical trials evaluating long-term suppression of HIV RNA or disease progression with abacavir therapy.

Patients may continue to experience illness associated with HIV infection, including opportunistic infections.

Treatment with abacavir does not reduce the risk of transmission of HIV to others through sexual contact or blood contamination.

Pharmacology/Pharmacokinetics

Physicochemical characteristics

Source—Synthetic.

Chemical Group—Carbocyclic synthetic nucleoside analog.

Molecular weight—670.76 daltons.

Mechanism of action/Effect

Reverse transcriptase inhibitor. Activity follows intracellular conversion by cellular enzymes to the active metabolite, carbovir triphosphate, which is an analog of deoxyguanosine-5′-triphosphate (dGTP). Carbovir triphosphate competes with the natural substrate dGTP and is incorporated into viral DNA, inhibiting the activity of HIV-1 reverse transcriptase. The incorporated nucleoside analog lacks a 3′-OH group, and thus prevents formation of the 5′ to 3′ phosphodiester linkage that is essential for DNA chain elongation, terminating viral DNA growth.

Absorption

Rapid and extensive. The geometric absolute bioavailability of the tablet is 83% and is not affected by food; systemic exposure to the oral solution is comparable.

Distribution

Vol_D = 0.86 ± 0.15 liter per kg (L/kg), following intravenous administration.

Concentrations in cerebrospinal fluid (CSF) range from 27 to 33% of those in plasma. Readily distributed into erythrocytes, as indicated by identical total blood and plasma drug-related radioactivity concentrations.

Protein binding

Moderate (approximately 50%); unrelated to concentration.

Biotransformation

Hepatic, by alcohol dehydrogenase (to the 5′-carboxylic acid metabolite) and glucuronosyltransferase (to the 5′-glucuronide metabolite). Metabolites do not have antiviral activity. Not significantly metabolized by cytochrome P450 enzymes.

Half-life

Elimination—1.54 ± 0.63 hours.

Steady-state

Adults—3 ± 0.89 mcg per mL following oral administration of 300 mg twice daily.

Children—3.71 ± 1.36 mcg per mL following oral administration of 8 mg per kg of body weight (mg/kg) twice daily.

Elimination

Renal, 1.2% as abacavir, 30% as the 5′-carboxylic acid metabolite, 36% as the 5′-glucuronide metabolite, and 15% as other unidentified minor metabolites.

Fecal, 16%.

In dialysis—

It is not known whether abacavir is removable by hemodialysis or peritoneal dialysis.

Note: Total clearance after intravenous administration is 0.8 ± 0.24 liters per hour per kg of body weight (L/hr/kg) (mean ± SD).

Precautions to Consider

Mutagenicity

Abacavir was found to induce chromosomal aberrations both in the presence and absence of metabolic activation in an *in vitro* cytogenicity study in human lymphocytes. It was mutagenic in the absence of metabolic activation, although it was not mutagenic in the presence of metabolic activation in an L5178Y mouse lymphoma assay. Abacavir was clastogenic in males and not clastogenic in females in an *in vivo* mouse bone marrow micronucleus assay at systemic exposures approximately nine times higher than that in humans at the therapeutic dose. Abacavir was not found to be mutagenic in bacterial mutagenicity assays in either the presence or the absence of metabolic activation.

Pregnancy/Reproduction

Fertility—No adverse effects on the mating performance or fertility of male and female rats were observed with abacavir at doses of up to 500 mg per kg of body weight (mg/kg) per day (producing exposures approximately eightfold higher than that in humans at the therapeutic dose based on body surface area comparisons).

Pregnancy—Adequate and well-controlled studies in humans have not been done.

Studies in rats revealed that abacavir crosses the placenta. At doses of 1000 mg/kg (35 times the human exposure, based on area under the curve [AUC]) during organogenesis, developmental toxicity (depressed fetal body weight and reduced crown-rump length) and increased incidences of fetal anasarca and skeletal malformations were found. In a fertility study, doses of 500 mg/kg per day were associated with evidence of toxicity to the developing embryos and fetuses (increased resorptions and decreased fetal body weights). Studies in female rats at doses of 500 mg/kg (beginning at embryo implantation and ending at weaning) showed an increased incidence of stillbirths and lower body weights throughout life. Studies in rabbits at doses of up to 700 mg/kg (8.5 times the human exposure at the recommended dose, based on AUC) found no evidence of drug-related developmental toxicity or increases in fetal malformations.

Risk-benefit should be considered before use of abacavir during pregnancy.

An Antiretroviral Pregnancy Registry has been established to monitor the outcomes of pregnant women exposed to abacavir. Physicians are encouraged by the manufacturer to register patients by calling (800) 258-4263.

FDA Pregnancy Category C.

Breast-feeding

It is not known whether abacavir is distributed into human breast milk. However, it is distributed into the milk in lactating rats. In addition, the Centers for Disease Control and Prevention recommends that HIV-infected mothers refrain from breast-feeding their infants to avoid risking postnatal transmission of HIV. Because of both the potential for HIV transmission and the potential for serious adverse reactions in nursing infants, mothers should be instructed not to breast-feed if they are receiving abacavir.

Pediatrics

Safety and efficacy in children between the ages of 3 months and 13 years have been established in adequate and well-controlled studies.

Geriatrics

No information is available on the relationship of age to the effects of abacavir in geriatric patients. In general, dose selection should be cautious, reflecting the greater frequency of decreased hepatic, renal, or cardiac function, and of concomitant disease or other drug therapy.

Drug interactions and/or related problems

The following drug interactions and/or related problems have been selected on the basis of their potential clinical significance (possible mechanism in parentheses where appropriate)—not necessarily inclusive (» = major clinical significance):

Note: Combinations containing the following medication, depending on the amount present, may also interact with this medication.

Ethanol
(concurrent use with abacavir may result in increased concentrations and half-life of abacavir as a result of competition for common metabolic pathways via alcohol dehydrogenase)

Methadone
(methadone clearance increased 22% in patients stabilized on oral methadone maintenance therapy who started abacavir therapy with 600 mg twice daily; increase in clearance will not be clinically significant in the majority of patients; methadone dosage increase may be required in a small number of patients)

Laboratory value alterations

The following have been selected on the basis of their potential clinical significance (possible effect in parentheses where appropriate)—not necessarily inclusive (» = major clinical significance).

With physiology/laboratory test values

Alanine aminotransferase (ALT [SGPT]) and
Aspartate aminotransferase (AST [SGOT]) and
Gamma-glutamyltransferase (GGT)
(values may be increased)

Creatine kinase (CK) or
Creatinine
(serum values may be increased)

Glucose and
Triglycerides
(mild increases in blood concentrations have been reported)

Hemoglobin and
Leukocytes
(blood concentrations may be decreased)

Lactate, serum
(plasma concentrations may be increased, indicating lactic acidosis, which has been reported in association with severe hepatomegaly with steatosis)

Lymphocytes
(blood concentrations may be decreased)

Medical considerations/Contraindications

The medical considerations/contraindications included have been selected on the basis of their potential clinical significance (reasons given in parentheses where appropriate)—not necessarily inclusive (» = major clinical significance).

Except under special circumstances, this medication should not be used when the following medical problem exists:

» Hepatic impairment, moderate or severe
(safety, efficacy, and pharmacokinetics of abacavir have not been studied in these patients; use is contraindicated)

» Hypersensitivity reaction to abacavir or any other component of the product
(discontinue abacavir as soon as a hypersensitivity reaction is suspected; permanently discontinue if hypersensitivity cannot be ruled out, even when other diagnoses are possible; fatal rechallenge reactions [including life-threatening hypotension and death] have been associated with readministration of abacavir to patients with a prior history of a hypersensitivity reaction to abacavir; following a hypersensitivity reaction to abacavir, ***never*** restart any abacavir-containing product because more severe symptoms can occur within hours)

Risk-benefit should be considered when the following medical problems exist:

» Risk factors for hepatic disease such as
Obesity or
Prolonged nucleoside exposure
(caution should be exercised when administering abacavir to any patient with known risk factors; abacavir treatment should be suspended in any patient who develops clinical or laboratory findings suggestive of lactic acidosis or pronounced hepatotoxicity which may include hepatomegaly and steatosis even in the absence of marked transaminase elevations)

Patient monitoring

The following may be especially important in patient monitoring (other tests may be warranted in some patients, depending on condition; » = major clinical significance):

Note: To facilitate reporting of hypersensitivity reactions and collection of information on each case, an Abacavir Hypersensitivity Registry has been established. Physicians should register patients by calling 1-800-270-0425.

» Signs and symptoms of hypersensitivity
(usually characterized by a sign or symptom in 2 or more of the following groups:
- Group 1: Fever
- Group 2: Rash
- Group 3: Gastrointestinal (including nausea, vomiting, diarrhea, or abdominal pain)
- Group 4: Constitutional (including generalized malaise, fatigue, or achiness)
- Group 5: Respiratory (including dyspnea, cough, or pharyngitis.

(abacavir should be permanently discontinued if hypersensitivity can not be ruled out, even when other diagnoses are possible (e.g., acute onset respiratory diseases such as pneumonia, bronchitis, pharyngitis, or influenza; gastroenteritis; or reactions to other medications)

Side/Adverse Effects

Lactic acidosis and severe hepatomegaly with steatosis, including fatal cases, have been reported with the use of antiretroviral nucleoside analogs, including abacavir, alone or in combination.

The redistribution or accumulation of body fat, including central obesity, dorsocervical fat enlargement (buffalo hump), peripheral wasting, breast enlargement, and "cushingoid appearance" have been reported in patients on protease inhibitor therapy. The mechanism and long-term consequences of these events are currently unknown. A causal relationship has not been established.

The following side/adverse effects have been selected on the basis of their potential clinical significance (possible signs and symptoms in parentheses where appropriate)—not necessarily inclusive:

Those indicating need for medical attention

Incidence more frequent

Hypersensitivity reaction (abdominal or stomach pain; cough; diarrhea; difficult or labored breathing; fever; headache; joint or muscle pain; nausea; numbness or tingling of face, hands, or feet; redness and soreness of eyes; skin rash; shortness of breath; sore throat; sores in mouth; swelling of feet or lower legs; vomiting; unusual feeling of discomfort or illness; unusual tiredness)

Note: Symptoms of the *hypersensitivity reaction* usually occur within the first 6 weeks of treatment, although they may occur at any time, and indicate multi-organ/body involvement. The reaction may be severe, progressing to anaphylaxis, hepatic failure, renal failure, adult respiratory distress syndrome, respiratory failure, hypotension, and death. Symptoms worsen with continued therapy but frequently resolve on withdrawal of abacavir. However, following a hypersensitivity reaction to abacavir, ***never*** restart any abacavir-containing product because more severe symptoms can occur within hours, possibly including life-threatening hypotension and death.

The *skin rash* is usually maculopapular or urticarial, but the appearance varies and hypersensitivity reactions have occurred without skin rash.

The diagnosis of hypersensitivity reaction should be carefully considered for patients presenting with acute onset respiratory disease symptoms, even if alternative respiratory diagnoses (pneumonia, bronchitis, pharyngitis, or flu-like illness) are possible.

Other physical findings with the *hypersensitivity reaction* include lymphadenopathy and mucous membrane lesions. Laboratory value alterations may include elevated hepatic function values, creatine kinase, or creatinine, and lymphopenia.

An Abacavir Hypersensitivity Registry has been established to facilitate the reporting of *hypersensitivity reactions* and to collect information about each case. Physicians are encouraged by the manufacturer to register patients by calling (800) 270-0425.

A warning card which provides information about recognition of abacavir hypersensitivity reactions should be dispensed to the patient with each new prescription and refill.

Incidence rare

Hepatotoxicity, including lactic acidosis (abdominal discomfort; nausea; decreased appetite; general feeling of discomfort; diarrhea; fast, shallow breathing; muscle pain or cramping; shortness of breath; sleepiness; unusual tiredness or weakness); ***pancreatitis*** (abdominal pain and distention; fever; nausea; vomiting)

Note: *Hepatotoxicity*, consisting of *lactic acidosis* and severe hepatomegaly with steatosis, has been reported with nucleoside therapy (including abacavir), alone or in combination. Fatalities have occurred. The majority of cases have occurred in women. Possible risk factors include obesity and prolonged nucleoside exposure, as well as other risk factors for liver disease, although cases have occurred in the absence of any known risk factors.

Incidence not determined—Observed during clinical practice; estimates of frequency cannot be determined

Erythema multiforme, Stevens-Johnson syndrome, or toxic epidermal necrolysis (blistering, peeling, loosening of skin; chills; cough; diarrhea; itching; joint or muscle pain; red, irritated eyes; red skin lesions, often with a purple center; sore throat; sores, ulcers, or white spots in mouth or on lips; unusual tiredness or weakness); ***hepatic steatosis*** (dark urine; light-colored stools; nausea and vomiting; upper right abdominal pain; yellow eyes and skin)

Those indicating need for medical attention only if they continue or are bothersome

Incidence more frequent

Diarrhea; fatigue; headache; loss of appetite; nausea or vomiting

Incidence less frequent

Insomnia (trouble in sleeping)

Incidence not determined—Observed during clinical practice; estimates of frequency cannot be determined

Accumulation/redistribution of body fat (breast enlargement; buffalo hump; central obesity; facial wasting; peripheral wasting)

Overdose

There is no specific information on overdose with abacavir.

There is no known antidote for abacavir. It is not known whether abacavir can be removed by peritoneal dialysis or hemodialysis.

For information on the management of overdose or unintentional ingestion, **contact a Poison Control Center** (see *Poison Control Center Listing*).

Patient Consultation

As an aid to patient consultation, refer to *Advice for the Patient, Abacavir (Systemic)*.

In providing consultation, consider emphasizing the following selected information (» = major clinical significance):

Before using this medication

» Conditions affecting use, especially:
- Sensitivity to abacavir
- Pregnancy—Causes birth defects and slowed growth in animals; risk-benefit should be considered
- Breast-feeding—Nursing mothers should be instructed not to breast-feed because of the potential for postnatal transmission of HIV and for adverse effects.
- Use in the elderly—Dose selection should be cautious in the elderly.
- Other medical problems, especially hypersensitivity reaction to abacavir or any other component of the product, moderate or severe hepatic impairment, or risk factors for hepatic disease such as obesity or prolonged nucleoside exposure

Proper use of this medication

» Compliance with therapy

» Proper dosing

Missed dose: Taking as soon as possible; not taking if almost time for next dose; not doubling doses

» Proper storage

Precautions while using this medication

» Checking with physician immediately if signs or symptoms of a hypersensitivity reaction (cough, dyspnea, fever, skin rash, fatigue, gastrointestinal symptoms, or pharyngitis) occur

(Carrying warning card for recognition of hypersensitivity reaction)

Side/adverse effects

Signs of potential side effects, especially hypersensitivity reaction, hepatotoxicity, including lactic acidosis, and pancreatitis

Signs of potential side effects observed during clinical practice, especially erythema multiforme, hepatic steatosis, Stevens-Johnson syndrome, or toxic epidermal necrolysis

General Dosing Information

Abacavir therapy should be permanently withdrawn at the first sign of a hypersensitivity reaction or if hypersensitivity cannot be ruled out, even when other diagnoses are possible. Therapy with abacavir should never be restarted because more severe symptoms will recur within hours, possibly including life-threatening hypotension and death.

Treatment with abacavir should be suspended if clinical or laboratory findings suggestive of lactic acidosis or pronounced hepatotoxicity (possibly including hepatomegaly and steatosis, with or without marked transaminase elevations) occur.

Abacavir should always be used in combination with other antiretroviral agents. Abacavir should not be added as a single agent when antiretroviral regimens are changed due to loss of virologic response.

Oral Dosage Forms

Note: Dosing and strengths of the dosage forms available are expressed in terms of abacavir base (not the sulfate salt).

ABACAVIR SULFATE ORAL SOLUTION

Usual adult and adolescent dose

Human immunodeficiency virus (HIV) infection—

Oral, 300 mg (base) twice daily or 600 mg (base) once daily, in combination with other antiretroviral agents.

Note: Patients with mild hepatic impairment (Child-Pugh score 5 to 6)—Oral, 200 mg (10 mL) twice daily. To enable dose reduction, oral solution should be used for the treatment of these patients.

Abacavir use is contraindicated in patients with moderate to severe hepatic impairment.

Usual pediatric dose

Human immunodeficiency virus (HIV) infection—

Children up to 3 months of age: Safety and efficacy have not been established.

Children 3 months to 16 years of age: Oral, 8 mg (base) per kg of body weight (up to 300 mg) two times a day, in combination with other antiretroviral agents.

Children 16 years of age and older: See *Usual adult and adolescent dose*.

Usual pediatric prescribing limits

600 mg per day.

Strength(s) usually available

U.S.—

20 mg per mL (Rx) [*Ziagen* (artificial strawberry and banana flavors; citric acid anhydrous; methylparaben and propylparaben; propylene glycol; saccharin sodium; sodium citrate dihydrate; sorbitol solution; water)].

Packaging and storage

Store between 20 and 25 °C (68 and 77 °F), unless otherwise specified by manufacturer. Protect from freezing. May be refrigerated.

Auxiliary labeling

- This medication can be taken with or without food.

ABACAVIR SULFATE TABLETS

Usual adult and adolescent dose

Human immunodeficiency virus (HIV) infection—

See *Abacavir Sulfate Oral Solution*.

Usual pediatric dose

Human immunodeficiency virus (HIV) infection—

See *Abacavir Sulfate Oral Solution*.

Strength(s) usually available

U.S.—

300 mg (base) (Rx) [*Ziagen* (colloidal silicon dioxide; magnesium stearate; microcrystalline cellulose; sodium starch glycolate; hypromellose; polysorbate 80; synthetic yellow iron oxide; titanium dioxide; triacetin)].

Packaging and storage

Store between 20 and 25 °C (68 and 77 °F), unless otherwise specified by manufacturer.

Auxiliary labeling

- This medication can be taken with or without food.

Revised: 11/09/2004
Developed: 06/14/1999

ABACAVIR AND LAMIVUDINE Systemic†

VA CLASSIFICATION (Primary): AM480

Commonly used brand name(s): *Epzicom*.

Note: For a listing of dosage forms and brand names by country availability, see *Dosage Forms* section(s).

†Not commercially available in Canada.

Category

Antiviral (systemic).

Indications

General Considerations

Human immunodeficiency virus (HIV-1) isolates with reduced susceptibility to the combination of abacavir and lamivudine have been recovered *in vitro*, as well as from some patients treated with this medication. Genotypic characterization of abacavir/lamivudine-resistant viruses selected in vitro identified amino acid substitutions at positions M184V/I, K65R, L74V, and Y115F in HIV-RT.

Cross-resistance has been observed with other nucleoside reverse transcriptase inhibitors. Viruses containing multiple reverse transcriptase mutations conferring abacavir and lamivudine resistance exhibited cross-resistance to didanosine, emtricitabine, lamivudine, tenofovir, and zalcitabine. The K65R mutation can confer resistance to abacavir, didanosine, emtricitabine, lamivudine, stavudine, tenofovir, and zalcitabine; and the M184V mutation can confer resistance to abacavir, didanosine, emtricitabine, lamivudine and zalcitabine.

The combination of abacavir/lamivudine has demonstrated decreased susceptibility to viruses with mutations K65R with or without the M184V/I mutation, viruses with L74V plus the M184V/I mutation, and viruses with thymidine analog mutations (TAMs: M41L, D67N, K70R, L210W, T215Y/F, K219 E/R/H/Q/N) plus M184V. An increasing number of TAMs is associated with a progressive reduction in abacavir susceptibility.

Accepted

Human immunodeficiency virus infection (treatment)—Abacavir and lamivudine in combination with other antiviral agents is indicated for the treatment of HIV-1 infection.

Pharmacology/Pharmacokinetics

Physicochemical characteristics

Molecular weight—

Abacavir: 670.76 daltons.

Lamivudine: 229.3 daltons.

Solubility—

Abacavir—Approximately 77 mg/mL in distilled water at 25°C.

Lamivudine—Approximately 70 mg/mL in water at 20°C.

Mechanism of action/Effect

Abacavir, and lamivudine are synthetic nucleoside analogs. Intracellularly, abacavir and lamivudine are phosphorylated to their respective active metabolites, carbovir triphosphate and lamivudine triphosphate. HIV reverse transcriptase utilizes these nucleotide analogs when transcribing viral RNA to DNA. Incorporation of carbovir triphosphate, and lamivudine triphosphate into the growing chain of viral DNA results in termination of reverse transcriptase and thus inhibition of HIV reverse transcription.

Absorption

Abacavir—Rapidly absorbed; oral bioavailability is 86 ± 25% (mean ± SD).

Lamivudine—Rapidly absorbed; oral bioavailability is 86 ± 16% (mean ± SD).

Food had no effects on lamivudine, however food decreases the rate of absorption approximately 24% for abacavir.

AUC—

Abacavir: 11.95 ± 2.51 mcg hr per mL

Lamivudine: 8.87 ± 1.83 mcg hr per mL

Distribution

Abacavir—Vol_D is approximately 0.86 ± 0.15 L per kg.

Lamivudine—Vol_D is approximately 1.3 ± 0.4 L per kg.

Protein binding

Abacavir—Moderate (approximately 50%).

Lamivudine—Low.

Biotransformation

Abacavir—Hepatic, by alcohol dehydrogenase (to the 5′-carboxylic acid metabolite) and glucuronyl transferase (to the 5′-glucuronide metabolite).

Lamivudine—In humans, the only known metabolite is the trans-sulfoxide metabolite, which accounts for approximately 5% of an oral dose after 12 hours.

Half-life

Elimination—

Abacavir: 1.45 ± 0.32 hours.

Lamivudine: 5 to 7 hours.

Peak plasma concentration

Lamivudine (steady state)—2.04 ± 0.54 mcg/mL following 300 mg lamivudine once daily for 7 days.

Elimination

Abacavir—Primarily hepatic via metabolism.

Lamivudine—Renal; approximately 70% of an intravenous dose is recovered unchanged in the urine.

Precautions to Consider

Carcinogenicity

Abacavir—

In two-year carcinogenicity studies in mice and rats given systemic doses (6 to 32 times the human exposure at the recommended dose) results showed an increase in the incidence of malignant and non-malignant tumors. Malignant tumors occurred in the preputial gland of males and the clitoral gland of females of both species, and in the liver of female rats.

Lamivudine—

Long term carcinogenicity studies in mice and rats given up to 10 times (mice) and 58 times (rats) the human recommended therapeutic dose for HIV infection showed no evidence of carcinogenic potential.

It is not known how predictive these studies may be for humans.

Mutagenicity

Abacavir—

Abacavir was found to induce chromosomal aberrations both in the presence and absence of metabolic activation in an *in vitro* cytogenicity study in human lymphocytes. It was mutagenic in the absence of metabolic activation, although it was not mutagenic in the presence of metabolic activation in an L5178Y mouse lymphoma assay. Abacavir was clastogenic in males and not clastogenic in females in an *in vivo* mouse bone marrow micronucleus assay. Abacavir was not found to be mutagenic in bacterial mutagenicity assays in either the presence or the absence of metabolic activation.

Lamivudine—

Lamivudine was mutagenic in the L5178Y mouse lymphoma assay and clastogenic in a cytogenetic assay using cultured human lymphocytes. Lamivudine was not mutagenic in a microbial mutagenicity screen, an *in vitro* cell transformation assay, the rat micronucleus test, a rat bone marrow cytogenetic assay, or the unscheduled DNA synthesis test in rat liver.

Pregnancy/Reproduction

Fertility—No adverse effects on the mating performance or fertility of male and female rats were observed with abacavir or lamivudine at systemic exposure levels (approximately 8 to 130 times higher than that in humans at the therapeutic dose based on body surface area comparisons).

Pregnancy—Adequate and well-controlled studies with abacavir and lamivudine have not been done in humans. However, both abacavir and lamivudine have been shown to cross the placenta. Abacavir and lamivudine should be used during pregnancy only if the potential benefits outweigh the risks.

Abacavir—

Studies in rats revealed that abacavir crosses the placenta. At doses (35 times the human exposure, based on area under the curve [AUC]) during organogenesis, developmental toxicity (depressed fetal body weight and reduced crown-rump length) and increased incidences of fetal anasarca and skeletal malformations were found. In a fertility study, with doses half the above mentioned dose evidence of toxicity to the developing embryos and fetuses (increased resorptions and decreased fetal body weights) occurred in rats. Studies in rabbits given doses (8.5 times the human exposure at the recommended dose, based on AUC) found no evidence of drug-related developmental toxicity or increases in fetal malformations.

Lamivudine—
Lamivudine crosses the placenta in rats. Reproduction studies performed in rats producing plasma levels up to 35 times that for the recommended adult HIV dose found no evidence of teratogenicity. Evidence of early embryolethality was seen in rabbits at similar exposure levels. However, there was no indication of this effect in rat at exposure levels up to 35 times that in humans.

FDA Pregnancy Category C

Note: An Antiretroviral Pregnancy Registry has been established to monitor the outcomes of pregnant women exposed to antiretroviral agents. Physicians are encouraged by the manufacturer to register patients by calling (800) 258-4263.

Breast-feeding

Both abacavir and lamivudine are distributed into the milk of lactating rats. Lamivudine is distributed into human breast milk. Because of the potential for HIV transmission and the potential for serious adverse reactions in nursing infants, **mothers should be instructed not to breast-feed if they are receiving these medicines.**

Pediatrics

Safety and effectiveness of abacavir and lamivudine in pediatric patients have not been established.

Geriatrics

Appropriate studies on the relationship of age to the effects of abacavir and lamivudine combination have not been performed in the geriatric population. Dose selection should be done with caution. Elderly patients are more likely to have age related problems such as decreased hepatic, renal or cardiac function, and concomitant diseases or other drug therapy.

Pharmacogenetics

There are no significant differences between blacks and Caucasians in abacavir or lamivudine pharmacokinetics.

Drug interactions and/or related problems

The following drug interactions and/or related problems have been selected on the basis of their potential clinical significance (possible mechanism in parentheses where appropriate)—not necessarily inclusive (» = major clinical significance):

Note: No drug interaction studies have been conducted using abacavir and lamivudine combination.

Combinations containing any of the following medications, depending on the amount present, may also interact with this medication. The drug interactions described are based on studies conducted using the individual medications.

» Abacavir or
» Lamivudine
(abacavir and lamivudine combination is a fixed-dose product; concurrent use of other products containing abacavir or lamivudine with the combination product is not recommended)

Alcohol
(concurrent use with abacavir decreases the elimination of abacavir resulting in an increase in overall exposure)

Methadone
(methadone clearance increased 22% in patients stabilized on oral methadone maintenance therapy who started abacavir therapy with 600 mg twice daily; increase in clearance will not be clinically significant in the majority of patients; methadone dosage increase may be required in a small number of patients)

Nelfinavir or
Trimethoprim/Sulfamethoxazole
(may increases lamivudine exposure [AUC])

» Zalcitabine
(use with abacavir and lamivudine combination is not recommended; lamivudine and zalcitabine may inhibit the intracellular phosphorylation of one another)

Laboratory value alterations

The following have been selected on the basis of their potential clinical significance (possible effect in parentheses where appropriate)—not necessarily inclusive (» = major clinical significance).

With physiology/laboratory test values
» Alanine aminotransferase (ALT [SGPT]) and
Amylase and
Aspartate aminotransferase (AST [SGOT]) and
Creatine kinase and
Gamma glutamyl transferase (GGT) and
Lipase
(values may be increased)

Bilirubin and
Glucose, blood and
Triglycerides
(concentrations may be increased)

Creatine kinase (CK) or
Creatinine
(serum values may be increased)

Hemoglobin and
Leukocytes
(blood concentrations may be decreased)

Lactate, serum
(plasma concentrations may be increased, indicating lactic acidosis, which has been reported in association with severe hepatomegaly with steatosis)

Lymphocytes
(blood concentrations may be decreased)

Medical considerations/Contraindications

The medical considerations/contraindications included have been selected on the basis of their potential clinical significance (reasons given in parentheses where appropriate)—not necessarily inclusive (» = major clinical significance).

Except under special circumstances, this medication should not be used when the following medical problem exists:

» Hypersensitivity reaction to abacavir or lamivudine or any other component of the product
(fatal rechallenge reactions [including life-threatening hypotension and death] have been associated with readministration of abacavir to patients with a prior history of a hypersensitivity reaction to abacavir; following a hypersensitivity reaction to abacavir, ***never*** restart any abacavir-containing product because more severe symptoms can occur within hours)

» Hepatic function impairment
(use is contraindicated since abacavir and lamivudine combination is a fixed-dose tablet and the dosage of the individual components can not be altered)

Risk-benefit should be considered when the following medical problems exist:

» Renal function impairment
(patients with creatinine clearance ≤ 50 mL per minute should not receive abacavir, and lamivudine, combination as it is a fixed-dose tablet)

» Hepatitis B
(severe acute exacerbations of hepatitis B and HIV have been reported upon discontinuation of lamivudine; hepatic function should be monitored closely with both clinical and laboratory follow up for at least several months; if appropriate, initiation of anti-hepatitis B therapy may be warranted)

» Human immunodeficiency virus (HIV) and hepatitis B virus co-infection
(emergence of hepatitis B virus variants associated with resistance to lamivudine have been reported in HIV-infected patients who have lamivudine-containing antiretroviral regimens in the presence of concurrent infection with hepatitis B virus)

» Risk factors for hepatic disease such as
Obesity or
Prolonged nucleoside exposure
(caution should be exercised when administering abacavir and lamivudine to any patient with known risk factors; abacavir and lamivudine treatment should be suspended in any patient who develops clinical or laboratory findings suggestive of lactic acidosis or pronounced hepatotoxicity which may include hepatomegaly and steatosis even in the absence of marked transaminase elevations)

Stevens-Johnson syndrome, suspected and
Toxic epidermal necrolysis
(due to overlap of clinical signs and symptoms between hypersensitivity to abacavir and SJS and TEN, and the possibility of multiple drug sensitivity, abacavir should be discontinued and not restarted in such cases)

Patient monitoring

The following may be especially important in patient monitoring (other tests may be warranted in some patients, depending on condition; » = major clinical significance):

Note: To facilitate reporting of hypersensitivity reactions and collection of information on each case, an Abacavir Hypersensitivity Registry has been established. Physicians should register patients by calling 1–800–270–0425.

» Signs and symptoms of hypersensitivity
(usually characterized by a sign or symptom in 2 or more of the following groups:
- Group 1: Fever
- Group 2: Rash
- Group 3: Gastrointestinal (including nausea, vomiting, diarrhea, or abdominal pain)
- Group 4: Constitutional (including generalized malaise, fatigue, or achiness)
- Group 5: Respiratory (including dyspnea, cough, or pharyngitis)

(abacavir should be permanently discontinued if hypersensitivity can not be ruled out, even when other diagnoses are possible (e.g., acute onset respiratory diseases such as pneumonia, bronchitis, pharyngitis, or influenza; gastroenteritis; or reactions to other medications)

Side/Adverse Effects

The following side/adverse effects have been selected on the basis of their potential clinical significance (possible signs and symptoms in parentheses where appropriate)—not necessarily inclusive:

Those indicating need for medical attention

Incidence more frequent

Hypersensitivity (fast heartbeat; fever; hives; itching; irritation; hoarseness; joint pain stiffness or swelling; rash; redness of skin; shortness of breath; swelling of eyelids, face, lips, hands, or feet; tightness in chest; troubled breathing or swallowing; wheezing)

Observed during clinical practice

Anemia (pale skin; troubled breathing with exertion; unusual bleeding or bruising; unusual tiredness or weakness); ***anemia, aplastic*** (chest pain; chills; cough; fever; headache; shortness of breath; sores, ulcers, or white spots on lips or in mouth; swollen or painful glands; tightness in chest, unusual bleeding or bruising; unusual tiredness or weakness; wheezing); ***anaphylaxis*** (cough; difficulty swallowing; dizziness; fast heartbeat; hives; itching; puffiness or swelling of the eyelids or around the eyes, face, lips or tongue; shortness of breath; skin rash; tightness in chest; unusual tiredness or weakness; wheezing); ***creatine phosphokinase (CPK) elevations; erythema multiforme*** (blistering, peeling, loosening of skin; chills; cough; diarrhea; fever; itching; joint or muscle pain; red irritated eyes; sore throat; sores, ulcers, or white spots in mouth or on lips; unusual tiredness or weakness); ***hepatic steatosis*** (dark urine; light-colored stools; nausea and vomiting; upper right abdominal pain; yellow eyes and skin); ***hepatitis B, exacerbation*** (dark urine; general tiredness and weakness; light-colored stools; nausea and vomiting; upper right abdominal pain; yellow eyes and skin); ***lactic acidosis*** (abdominal discomfort; decreased appetite; diarrhea; fast, shallow breathing; general feeling of discomfort; muscle pain or cramping; nausea; shortness of breath; sleepiness; unusual tiredness or weakness); ***lymphadenopathy*** (swollen, painful, or tender lymph glands in neck, armpit, or groin); ***pancreatitis*** (bloating; chills; constipation; darkened urine; fast heartbeat; fever; indigestion; loss of appetite; nausea; pains in stomach, side, or abdomen, possibly radiating to the back; vomiting; yellow eyes or skin); ***peripheral neuropathy*** (burning, numbness, tingling, or painful sensations weakness in arms, hands, legs, or feet; unsteadiness or awkwardness); ***rhabdomyolysis*** (dark-colored urine; fever; muscle cramps or spasms; muscle pain or stiffness; unusual tiredness or weakness); ***seizure*** (convulsions; muscle spasm or jerking of all extremities; sudden loss of consciousness; loss of bladder control); ***splenomegaly*** (abdominal pain; feeling of fullness); ***Stevens-Johnson syndrome*** (blistering, peeling, loosening of skin; chills; cough; diarrhea; itching; joint or muscle pain; red irritated eyes; red skin lesions, often with a purple center; sore throat; sores, ulcers, or white spots in mouth or on lips; unusual tiredness or weakness); ***toxic epidermal necrolysis*** (blistering, peeling, loosening of skin; chills; cough; diarrhea; itching; joint or muscle pain; red irritated eyes; red skin lesions, often with a purple center; sore throat; sores, ulcers, or white spots in mouth or on lips; unusual tiredness or weakness); ***urticaria*** (hives or welts; itching; redness of skin; skin rash)

Those indicating need for medical attention only if they continue or are bothersome

Incidence more frequent

Abdominal pain (stomach pain); ***abnormal dreams; anxiety*** (fear, nervousness); ***diarrhea; dizziness; gastritis*** (burning feeling in chest or stomach; tenderness in stomach area; stomach upset; indigestion); ***headache; insomnia*** (sleeplessness; trouble sleeping; unable to sleep); ***malaise and/or fatigue*** (general feeling of discomfort or illness; unusual tiredness or weakness); ***migraine*** (headache, severe and throbbing); ***nausea; rash, mild; vertigo*** (dizziness or lightheadedness; feeling of constant movement of self or surroundings; sensation of spinning)

Incidence less frequent

Pyrexia (fever)

Observed during clinical practice

Alopecia (hair loss; thinning of hair); ***hyperglycemia*** (abdominal pain; blurred vision; dry mouth; fatigue; flushed; dry skin; fruit-like breath odor; increased hunger; increased thirst; increased urination; nausea; sweating; troubled breathing; unexplained weight loss; vomiting); ***muscle weakness; paresthesias*** (burning, crawling, itching, numbness, prickling, "pins and needles", or tingling feelings); ***redistribution/accumulation of body fat; stomatitis*** (swelling or inflammation of the mouth); ***weakness; wheezing or abnormal breathing sounds***

Overdose

For more information on the management of overdose or unintentional ingestion, **contact a poison control center** (see *Poison Control Center Listing*).

Clinical effects of overdose

For lamivudine, one case of an adult ingesting 6 grams has been reported. There were no clinical signs or symptoms noted, and hematologic tests remained normal.

Treatment of overdose

To enhance elimination—

It is not known whether abacavir or lamivudine can be removed by hemodialysis or peritoneal dialysis.

Supportive care—

Treatment should be symptomatic and supportive.

Patients in whom intentional overdose is confirmed or suspected should be referred for psychiatric consultation.

Patient Consultation

As an aid to patient consultation, refer to *Advice for the Patient, Abacavir and Lamivudine (Systemic).*

In providing consultation, consider emphasizing the following selected information (» = major clinical significance):

Before using this medication

» Conditions affecting use, especially:

Hypersensitivity to abacavir or lamivudine.

An increase in the incidence of malignant and non-malignant tumors occurred in rats given doses 6 to 32 times the human exposure at the recommended dose.

Pregnancy—Abacavir caused birth defects and slowed growth in animals given doses equivalent to 8.5 to 35 times the human exposure; risk-benefit should be considered.

Lamivudine crosses the placenta.

Breast-feeding—Both abacavir and lamivudine are distributed into the breast milk of rats and lamivudine is distributed into human breast milk; it is recommended that HIV-infected mothers do not breast-feed their infants to avoid potential postnatal transmission of HIV.

Use in children—Safety and effectiveness of abacavir and lamivudine in pediatric patients have not been established.

Use in the elderly—Dose selection should be cautious in the elderly.

Other medications, especially abacavir, lamivudine, or zalcitabine.

Other medical problems, especially hepatic function impairment, hepatitis B virus and HIV co-infection, renal function impairment, or risk factors for hepatic disease such as obesity or prolonged nucleoside exposure or renal function impairment

Proper use of this medication

» Compliance with therapy

» Proper dosing

Missed dose: Taking as soon as possible; not taking if almost time for next scheduled dose; not doubling doses

Proper storage

Precautions while using this medication

» Regular visits to physician for blood tests

» Checking with physician immediately if signs or symptoms of a hypersensitivity reaction (cough, dyspnea, fever, skin rash, fatigue, gastrointestinal symptoms, or pharyngitis) occur.

» Carrying warning card for recognition of hypersensitivity reaction

Side/adverse effects

Signs of potential side effects, especially hypersensitivity reaction

Signs of potential side effects observed during clinical practice, especially anemia, aplastic anemia, anaphylaxis, creatine phosphokinase elevations, erythema multiforme, hepatic steatosis, hepatitis B, exacerbation, lactic acidosis, lymphadenopathy, pancreatitis, peripheral neuropathy, rhabdomyolysis, seizure, splenomegaly, Stevens-Johnson, syndrome, toxic epidermal necrolysis, or urticaria

General Dosing Information

A Medication Guide and Warning Card that provide information about the recognition of hypersensitivity reactions should be dispensed with each new prescription and refill.

Abacavir and lamivudine can be taken with or without food.

Patients with prolonged prior NRTI exposure or who had HIV-1 isolates that contained multiple mutations conferring resistance to NRTIs had limited response to abacavir. Therefore, the potential for cross-resistance between abacavir and other NRTIs should be considered when choosing new therapeutic regimens in therapy-experienced patients.

Treatment with abacavir should be suspended if clinical or laboratory findings suggestive of lactic acidosis or pronounced hepatotoxicity (possibly including hepatomegaly and steatosis, with or without marked transaminase elevations) occur.

Discontinue use of abacavir and lamivudine as soon as hypersensitivity reaction is suspected. To minimize the risk of a life-threatening hypersensitivity reaction, permanently discontinue if hypersensitivity cannot be ruled out even when other diagnoses are possible. If abacavir and lamivudine therapy have been discontinued for reasons other than hypersensitivity reaction, and if re-initiation is under consideration, careful evaluation of the reason for discontinuation to ensure the patient had no symptoms of hypersensitivity is recommended. If hypersensitivity cannot be ruled out NEVER reintroduce abacavir and lamivudine combination or any other product containing abacavir. If reintroduction is necessary, only do so if medical care can be readily accessed by the patient or others.

Oral Dosage Forms

ABACAVIR SULFATE AND LAMIVUDINE TABLETS

Usual adult dose

Human immunodeficiency virus (HIV-1) infection—

Oral, one tablet daily, in combination with other antiretroviral agents.

Note: Because abacavir and lamivudine is a fixed dose tablet it should not be administered to patients requiring dosage adjustment such as those with creatinine clearance <50 mL/min, those with hepatic impairment, or those experiencing dose limiting adverse events. Use of abacavir and lamivudine oral solution may be considered.

Usual pediatric dose

Safety and effectiveness in pediatric patients have not been established.

Usual geriatric dose

See *Usual adult dose*.

Strength(s) usually available

U.S.—

600 mg of abacavir (base), and 300 mg lamivudine (Rx) [*Epzicom* (FD&C Yellow #6; hypromellose; magnesium stearate; microcrystalline cellulose; polyethylene glycol 400; polysorbate 80; sodium starch glycolate; titanium dioxide)].

Packaging and storage

Store at 25 °C (77 °F); excursions permitted to 15° to 30°C (59° to 86°C).

Auxiliary labeling

- Please read patient information leaflet enclosed

Developed: 10/26/2004

ABACAVIR, LAMIVUDINE, AND ZIDOVUDINE Systemic

VA CLASSIFICATION (Primary): AM840

Commonly used brand name(s): *Trizivir*.

NOTE: The *Abacavir, Lamivudine, and Zidovudine (Systemic)* monograph is maintained on the *USP DI* electronic data base. A copy of the most recent revision of the complete monograph can be accessed on the *USP DI* Updates Online website. See the front cover of book for details on accessing the site.

For information on the specific components of this combination, see the *USP DI* monographs for *Abacavir (Systemic)*, *Lamivudine (Systemic)*, and *Zidovudine (Systemic)*.

The information that follows is selectively abstracted from the complete monograph and is provided to facilitate drug use review and patient counseling.

Note: For a listing of dosage forms and brand names by country availability, see *Dosage Forms* section(s).

Category

Antiviral (systemic).

Indications

General Considerations

Human immunodeficiency virus (HIV-1) isolates with reduced susceptibility to abacavir, lamivudine, or zidovudine have been recovered *in vitro*, as well as from some patients treated with this combination and with lamivudine and zidovudine combination. After 16 to 48 weeks of therapy with abacavir, lamivudine, and zidovudine combination, genetic analysis of HIV-1 isolates from 21 previously antiretroviral therapy–naive patients with confirmed virologic failure revealed that 16 of the 21 isolates had developed an abacavir/lamivudine-associated mutation, either alone or in combination with abacavir- or zidovudine-associated mutations. Available phenotypic data revealed that *in vitro* susceptibility to lamivudine had decreased 25- to 86-fold in 7 of 10 isolates. In addition, *in vitro* susceptibility to abacavir had decreased 7- to 10-fold in 2 of the 7 isolates.

In vitro, cross-resistance has been observed with other nucleoside reverse transcriptase inhibitors; recombinant laboratory strains of HIV-1 (HXB2) containing multiple reverse transcriptase mutations conferring abacavir resistance exhibited cross-resistance to lamivudine, didanosine, and zalcitabine.

Cross-resistance among certain reverse transcriptase inhibitors has been recognized. However, cross-resistance between lamivudine and zidovudine has not been reported.

Accepted

Human immunodeficiency virus type 1 (HIV-1) infection (treatment)—Abacavir, lamivudine, and zidovudine combination is indicated for concurrent use with other nucleoside analogs or alone for the treatment of HIV-1 infection.

There are limited data on the use of abacavir, lamivudine, and zidovudine combination in patients who have baseline viral load concentrations > 100,000 copies per mL.

Patient Consultation

As an aid to patient consultation, refer to *Advice for the Patient, Abacavir, Lamivudine, and Zidovudine (Systemic)*.

In providing consultation, consider emphasizing the following selected information (» = major clinical significance):

Before using this medication

» Conditions affecting use, especially:

Hypersensitivity to abacavir, lamivudine, or zidovudine

Pregnancy—Abacavir caused birth defects and slowed growth in animals given doses equivalent to 8.5 to 35 times the human exposure; risk-benefit should be considered

Zidovudine crosses the placenta; it caused birth defects in animals given doses equivalent to 350 times the human exposure

Breast-feeding—Zidovudine is distributed into breast milk; it is recommended that HIV-infected mothers do not breast-feed their infants to avoid potential postnatal transmission of HIV

Use in children—Because this is a fixed-dose combination and the dosage cannot be adjusted, use is not recommended in patients weighing less than 40 kg (88 lbs)

Other medications, especially abacavir, alpha interferons, doxorubicin, ganciclovir, lamivudine, other bone marrow depressants, ribavirin, stavudine, or zidovudine

Other medical problems, especially bone marrow depression, hepatic function impairment, hepatitis B virus and HIV co-infection, or renal function impairment

Proper use of this medication

» Importance of not taking more medication than prescribed; importance of not discontinuing medication without checking with physician

» Importance of not missing doses and of taking at evenly spaced times

Not sharing medication with others

» Proper dosing

Missed dose: Taking as soon as possible; not taking if almost time for next dose; not doubling doses

Proper storage

Precautions while using this medication

» Regular visits to physician for blood tests

» Checking with physician immediately if signs or symptoms of a hypersensitivity reaction (cough, dyspnea, fever, skin rash, fatigue, gastrointestinal symptoms, or pharyngitis) occur

(Carrying warning card for recognition of hypersensitivity reaction)

Side/adverse effects
Signs of potential side effects, especially neutropenia; anemia; hepatotoxicity, including lactic acidosis; hypersensitivity reaction; myopathy or myositis; pancreatitis; and thrombocytopenia

Oral Dosage Forms

ABACAVIR SULFATE, LAMIVUDINE, AND ZIDOVUDINE TABLETS

Usual adult and adolescent dose
Human immunodeficiency virus (HIV-1) infection—
Adults and adolescents 40 kg of body weight and over: Oral, 300 mg of abacavir, 150 mg of lamivudine, and 300 mg of zidovudine two times a day.
Adults and adolescents up to 40 kg of body weight: Use is not recommended.

Usual pediatric dose
Human immunodeficiency virus (HIV-1) infection—
Children up to 40 kg of body weight: Use is not recommended.
Children 40 kg of body weight and over: See *Usual adult and adolescent dose*.

Usual geriatric dose
Dose selection for elderly patients should be cautious due to the greater frequency of geriatric-specific problems.

Strength(s) usually available
U.S.—
300 mg of abacavir, 150 mg of lamivudine, and 300 mg of zidovudine (Rx) [*Trizivir* (magnesium stearate; microcrystalline cellulose; sodium starch glycolate)].

Revised: 10/22/2001
Developed: 06/28/2001

ABARELIX Systemic†

VA CLASSIFICATION (Primary): AN500

Commonly used brand name(s): *Plenaxis*.

Note: For a listing of dosage forms and brand names by country availability, see *Dosage Forms* section(s).

†Not commercially available in Canada.

Category
Antineoplastic.

Indications

Accepted
Carcinoma, prostate—Abarelix is indicated for palliative treatment of men with advanced symptomatic prostate cancer, in whom LHRH agonist therapy is not appropriate and who refuse surgical castration, and have one or more of the following: risk of neurological compromise due to metastases; ureteral or bladder outlet obstruction due to local encroachment or metastatic disease; or severe bone pain from skeletal metastases persisting on narcotic analgesia.

Pharmacology/Pharmacokinetics

Physicochemical characteristics
Source—Synthetic.
Chemical Group—Decapeptide; potent antagonistic activity against naturally occurring gonadotropin releasing-hormone (GnRH)
Molecular weight—1416.06 (anhydrous free base).
pH—Reconstituted: 5 ± 1

Mechanism of action/Effect
Abarelix exerts its pharmacological action by directly suppressing luteinizing hormone (LH) and follicle stimulating hormone (FSH) secretion and thereby reducing the secretion of testosterone by the testes. Due to the direct inhibition of the secretion of LH by abarelix, there is no initial increase in serum testosterone concentrations.
Saturation binding studies revealed that [^{125}I]-abarelix has a very high affinity (K_D = 0.1 nM) for the rat pituitary LHRH receptor.

Absorption
Slow absorption
AUC: 500 ± 96 ng day per mL

Distribution
Vol_D: 4040 ± 1607 liters; implying extensive distribution

Protein binding
Highly bound to plasma proteins—96 to 99%

Biotransformation
In vitro hepatocyte (rat, monkey, human) studies and *in vivo* studies in rats and monkeys showed that the major metabolites of abarelix were formed via hydrolysis of peptide bonds. No significant oxidative or conjugated metabolites of abarelix were found either *in vitro* or *in vivo*. There is no evidence of cytochrome P-450 involvement in the metabolism of abarelix.

Half-life
Terminal: 13.2 ± 3.2 days

Time to peak concentration
T_{max}: 3 ± 2.9 days

Peak concentration:
C_{max}: 43.4 ± 32.3 ng per mL

Time to peak effect
Medical castration (serum testosterone ≤ 50 ng per dL) was attained in 94% of patients by day 29 of clinical studies.

Elimination
In humans, approximately 13% of unchanged abarelix was recovered in urine after a 15 μg per kg IM injection; there were no detectable metabolites in urine. Renal clearance of abarelix was 14.4 L/day (or 10 mL/min) after administration of 100 mg abarelix.

Special populations
Race: Data from Hispanics, Blacks and Caucasians demonstrated that race appeared to have no influence on the pharmacokinetics of abarelix

Renal and Hepatic Insufficiency: The pharmacokinetics of abarelix in hepatically and/or renally impaired patients have not been determined

Precautions to Consider

Carcinogenicity
Abarelix was not carcinogenic to mice or rats when administered as a subcutaneous depot every 28 days for 2 years at doses up to 300 mg per kg in mice and 100 mg per kg in rats. Systemic drug exposures, as measured by mean C_{max}, were approximately 210- to 278-fold, for mice, and 21- to 32-fold, for rats, the human exposure following subcutaneous depot administration of 100 mg.

Mutagenicity
Abarelix was not mutagenic in the *in vitro* bacterial Ames assay or forward mutation assay in mouse lymphoma, or clastogenic in the *in vivo* mouse micronucleus assay.

Pregnancy/Reproduction
Fertility—No effects on mating or fertility in male and female rats given 1 mg per kg subcutaneous abarelix, a dose 0.114-fold the human therapeutic dose of 100 mg based on body surface area. Mating and fertility were significantly decreased at doses of 3 and 10 mg per kg (0.34-fold and 1.135-fold, respectively, the human therapeutic dose of 100 mg based on body surface area), but the effects were reversible.

Pregnancy—Abarelix is not indicated for use in women. Abarelix may cause fetal harm if administered to pregnant women.

Embryolethality occurred in pregnant rats administered a single subcutaneous dose of abarelix up to 3 mg per kg (0.228-fold the human therapeutic dose of 100 mg based on body surface area). In rabbits a dose-related increase in fetal resorptions and reduced viability was observed at doses up to 30 mg per kg (6.81-fold the human therapeutic dose of 100 mg based on body surface area).

No teratogenic effects were observed in rats or rabbits up to doses of 3 mg per kg or 30 mg per kg, respectively. A no-observable-adverse-effect-level (NOAEL) dose was 0.3 mg per kg (approximately 0.034-fold the human therapeutic dose of 100 mg based on body surface area) in rats and <0.01 mg per kg (<0.0023-fold the human therapeutic dose of 100 mg based on body surface area) in rabbits.

FDA Pregnancy Category X

Breast-feeding
It is not known whether abarelix is distributed in human milk. Because many drugs are distributed in human milk, and because the effects of abarelix on lactation and/or the breast-fed child have not been determined, abarelix should not be used by nursing mothers.

Pediatrics
Abarelix is not indicated for use in pediatric patients. Safety and effectiveness of abarelix in pediatric patients have not been studied.

Geriatrics
Appropriate studies performed to date have not demonstrated geriatrics-specific problems that would limit the usefulness of abarelix in the elderly. Prostate cancer occurs primarily in an older patient population.

Clinical studies with abarelix have been conducted primarily in patients ≥ 65 years of age. No difference in the safety profile, when examined as a function of age, was apparent.

Drug interactions and/or related problems

The following drug interactions and/or related problems have been selected on the basis of their potential clinical significance (possible mechanism in parentheses where appropriate)—not necessarily inclusive (» = major clinical significance):

Note: Combinations containing any of the following medications, depending on the amount present, may also interact with this medication.

» Class IA antiarrhythmic medications, such as
Procainamide or
Quinidine or
» Class III antiarrhythmic medications, such as
Amiodarone or
Sotalol
(abarelix may prolong the QTc interval; these medications should be used with caution)

Laboratory value alterations

The following have been selected on the basis of their potential clinical significance (possible effect in parentheses where appropriate)—not necessarily inclusive (» = major clinical significance).

With diagnostic test results
Serum transaminase
(clinically meaningful increases in serum transaminases (serum ALT or AST > 2.5 times upper limit of normal [ULN] or > 200 U/L) were seen in a small percentage of patients)
Hemoglobin
(slight decreases were seen, which is a pharmacological consequence of castration)
Triglycerides, serum
(mean increases in serum triglycerides of approximately 10% were seen in abarelix treated patients)

Medical considerations/Contraindications

The medical considerations/contraindications included have been selected on the basis of their potential clinical significance (reasons given in parentheses where appropriate)—not necessarily inclusive (» = major clinical significance).

Except under special circumstances, this medication should not be used when the following medical problem exists:

» Hypersensitivity to any of the components in abarelix for injectable suspension

Risk-benefit should be considered when the following medical problems exist:

Osteoporosis
(abarelix may exacerbate this condition)
» QTc prolongation
(may prolong the QT interval; physicians should carefully consider whether the risks of abarelix outweigh the benefits in patients with baseline QTc values >450 msec [e.g. congenital QT prolongation])

Patient monitoring

The following may be especially important in patient monitoring (other tests may be warranted in some patients, depending on condition; » = major clinical significance):

» Allergic reactions, immediate onset
(immediate-onset systemic allergic reactions, some resulting in hypotension and syncope, have occurred after administration of abarelix; may occur following any administration of abarelix, including after the initial dose; the cumulative risk increases with the duration of treatment; following each injection of abarelix, patients should be observed for at least 30 minutes in the office and in the event of an allergic reaction, managed appropriately)
Bone mineral density
(extended treatment may result in a decrease in bone mineral density; patients should be monitored)
PSA, serum
(periodic measurement of serum PSA levels may also be considered)
» Testosterone, total, serum
(response to abarelix should be monitored by measuring serum total testosterone concentrations just prior to administration on Day 29 and every 8 weeks thereafter; effectiveness beyond 12 months has not been established)
(successful response was defined as attainment of medical castration on day 29 and maintenance of medical castration through day 85, where no two consecutive serum testosterone concentrations were greater than 50 ng/dL; effectiveness beyond 12 months has not been established)
(the decrease in overall effectiveness of abarelix with increased duration of treatment is greater in patients who weigh more than 225 pounds; strict monitoring of serum testosterone in these patients is warranted)
» Transaminases, serum
(serum transaminase levels should be obtained before starting treatment and periodically during treatment; clinically meaningful transaminase elevations (serum ALT or AST > 2.5 times ULN or > 200 U/L) were observed in some patients who received abarelix or comparator drugs)

Side/Adverse Effects

The following side/adverse effects have been selected on the basis of their potential clinical significance (possible signs and symptoms in parentheses where appropriate)—not necessarily inclusive:

Immediate-Onset Systemic Allergic Reactions: In the clinical trial of patients with advanced, symptomatic prostate cancer, 3 of 81 (3.7%) patients experienced an immediate-onset systemic allergic reaction within minutes of receiving abarelix. The allergic reactions were urticaria (Day 15), urticaria and pruritus (Day 29), and hypotension and syncope (Day 141). From all the prostate cancer clinical trials with abarelix (mostly in men without advanced, symptomatic disease), immediate-onset systemic allergic reactions (occurring within 30 minutes of dosing), were observed in 1.1% (15/1397) of patients dosed with abarelix. In 14/15 patients who experienced an allergic reaction, each developed symptoms within 8 minutes of injection. The cumulative risk of such a reaction increased with duration of treatment. The cumulative rates (and 95% confidence intervals) on Days 56, 141, 365 and 676 were 0.51%, (0.13%, 0.88%) 0.80% (0.30%, 1.29%), 1.24% (0.43%, 2.04%) and 2.91% (0.87, 4.95%), respectively. Seven patients experienced hypotension or syncope as part of their allergic reaction, representing 0.5% of all patients. The cumulative rates (and 95% confidence intervals) for these types of reactions on Days 56, 141, 365, and 617 after the initial dose were 0.22% (0.0%, 0.46%), 0.32% (0.0%, 0.64%), 0.61% (0.0%, 1.24%) and 1.67% (0.07, 3.28%), respectively.

Note: Adverse events are listed without regard to causality. Causality is often difficult to assess in elderly patients with multiple co-morbidities and prostate cancer.

Those indicating need for medical attention

Incidence less frequent

Allergic reactions, severe (fainting or loss of consciousness; fast or irregular breathing; swelling of eyes or eyelids; trouble in breathing; tightness in chest and/or wheezing; skin rash; itching)—immediate onset; ***pruritus*** (itching skin); ***urticaria*** (hives or welts; itching; redness of skin; skin rash)

Those indicating need for medical attention only if they continue or are bothersome

Incidence more frequent

Back pain; breast enlargement—pharmacological consequence of androgen deprivation; ***breast pain/nipple enlargement***—pharmacological consequence of androgen deprivation; ***constipation*** (difficulty having a bowel movement (stool)); ***diarrhea; dizziness; dysuria*** (difficult or painful urination; burning while urinating); ***fatigue*** (unusual tiredness or weakness); ***headache; hot flushes*** (feeling of warmth; redness of the face, neck, arms and occasionally upper chest; sudden sweating)—pharmacological consequence of androgen deprivation; ***micturition frequency*** (trouble in holding or releasing urine; painful urination); ***nausea; pain; peripheral edema*** (bloating or swelling of face, arms, hands, lower legs, or feet; rapid weight gain; tingling of hands or feet; unusual weight gain or loss); ***sleep disturbance*** (trouble in sleeping)—pharmacological consequence of androgen deprivation; ***upper respiratory tract infection*** (ear congestion; nasal congestion; chills; cough; fever; sneezing; sore throat; body aches or pain; headache; loss of voice; runny nose; unusual tiredness or weakness; difficulty in breathing); ***urinary retention*** (decrease in urine volume; decrease in frequency of urination; difficulty in passing urine [dribbling]; painful urination); ***urinary tract infection*** (bladder pain; bloody or cloudy urine; difficult, burning, or painful urination; frequent urge to urinate; lower back or side pain)

Overdose

For more information on the management of overdose or unintentional ingestion, **contact a poison control center** (see *Poison Control Center Listing*).

The maximum tolerated dose of abarelix has not been determined. The maximum dose used in clinical studies was 150 mg. There have been no reports of accidental overdose with abarelix.

Patient Consultation

As an aid to patient consultation, refer to *Abarelix (Systemic)*.

In providing consultation, consider emphasizing the following selected information (» = major clinical significance):

Before using this medication

» Conditions affecting use, especially:

Hypersensitivity to any of the components in abarelix for injectable suspension.

Pregnancy—Abarelix is not indicated in women. Abarelix may cause fetal harm if administered to pregnant women

FDA Pregnancy Category X

Use in children—Abarelix is not indicated for use in children.

Other medications, especially Class IA antiarrhythmic medications and Class III antiarrhythmic medications

Other medical problems, especially heart condition called prolongation of the QTc interval

Proper use of this medication

» Proper dosing

Proper storage

» Importance of reading the patient information before treatment with abarelix begins. Your doctor will ask you to sign a form stating that you understand the risks and benefits of treatment and that you agree to treatment with abarelix.

Precautions while using this medication

» Importance of monitoring patient for 30 minutes following each administration for any signs or symptoms of an immediate-onset systemic allergic event

» Regular visits to physician to receive injection (shot). Your doctor will do blood tests periodically to make sure abarelix is working for you and check for liver function side effects.

Potential loss in bone mineral density with extended treatment and potential for QTc prolongation

Side/adverse effects

Signs of potential side effects, especially severe allergic reactions, pruritus, or urticaria

General Dosing Information

For parenteral dosing forms:

For safety reasons, abarelix is approved with marketing restrictions. Only physicians who attest to the following qualifications and accept the following responsibilities, and on that basis enroll in Praecis Pharmaceuticals Incorporated Plenaxis™ Plus Program should prescribe abarelix. Praecis Pharmaceuticals Incorporated and its agents will provide abarelix to physicians enrolled in the Plenaxis™ PLUS Program.

To enroll, physicians must attest that they are able and willing to:

- Diagnose and manage advanced symptomatic prostate cancer
- Diagnose and treat allergic reactions, including anaphylaxis
- Have access to medication and equipment necessary to treat allergic reactions, including anaphylaxis
- Have patients observed for development of allergic reactions for 30 minutes following each administration of abarelix
- Understand the risks and benefits of palliative treatment with abarelix, including information from the Package Insert, Patient Information, and the Physician Attestation
- Educate the patients on the risks and benefits of treatment with abarelix and obtain the patient's signature on the Patient Information signature page, sign it, and place the original signed form in the patient's medical record, and give a copy of the Patient Information leaflet with the signed page to the patient
- Report serious adverse events, such as any immediate-onset systemic allergic event (including anaphylaxis, hypotension, and syncope) as soon as possible to Praecis Pharmaceuticals Incorporated at 1-866-PLENAXIS (1-866-753-6294) or to the Food and Drug Administration's MedWatch Program at 1-800-FDA-1088
- Understand that they may withdraw their enrollment in the Plenaxis™ Prescribing Program by a written statement submitted to Praecis Pharmaceuticals Incorporated (contact information below) or that Praecis Pharmaceuticals Incorporated may withdraw physicians from the Plenaxis™ PLUS Program if they do not meet the agreed upon responsibilities
- To enroll in the Plenaxis™ Prescribing Program call 1-866-PLENAXIS (1-866-753-6294) or visit www.plenaxisplus.com

Extended treatment with GnRH antagonists and LHRH antagonists may result in a decrease in bone mineral density.

A decrease in overall effectiveness with increased duration of treatment, as measured by failure to maintain suppression of serum testosterone below 50 ng per dL, was noted. Treatment failure can be detected by measuring total serum testosterone concentrations just prior to administration of the dose on day 29 (after the initial dose) and every 8 weeks thereafter.

Immediate-Onset Systemic Allergic Reactions

Patients should be monitored for at least 30 minutes after each injection of abarelix. In the event of an allergic reaction associated with hypotension and/or syncope, appropriate supportive measures such as leg elevation, oxygen, IV fluids, antihistamines, corticosteroids, and epinephrine (alone or in combination) should be employed.Clinical observation should continue until event has resolved.

Parenteral Dosage Forms

Note: Only physicians who have enrolled in the Plenaxis™ PLUS Program (Plenaxis™ User Safety Program), based on their attestation of qualifications and acceptance of prescribing responsibilities, may prescribe abarelix. Praecis Pharmaceuticals Incorporated and its agents will only provide abarelix to physicians enrolled in the Plenaxis™ Prescribing Program. Abarelix vials are not to be resold or redistributed.

ABARELIX FOR INJECTION

Usual adult dose

Prostate cancer—

Intramuscular, 100 milligrams in the buttock on Day 1, 15, 29 (week 4) and every 4 weeks thereafter.

Treatment failure can be detected by measuring serum testosterone concentrations just prior to abarelix administration, beginning on Day 29 and every 8 weeks thereafter.

Usual geriatric dose

See *Usual adult dose*.

Strength(s) usually available

U.S.—

100 mg vial (anhydrous abarelix free base peptide 113 mg) (Rx) [*Plenaxis*].

Canada—

Not commercially available

Packaging and storage

Store at 25°C (77°F), excursions permitted to 15-30 C° (59-86 F°), USP Controlled Room Temperature.

Preparation of dosage form

Reconstitution Instructions for 1 Vial of abarelix to provide a 100 mg (50 mg/mL) Dose as a Single IM Injection— Use aseptic technique throughout. Prior to reconstitution, gently shake the vial of abarelix (abarelix for injectable suspension). Hold the vial at an angle (45 degrees) and tap lightly on table to break up any caking. Withdraw 2.2 mL of 0.9% Sodium Chloride Inj., USP using the enclosed 18 G x 1½" needle and a 3 cc syringe. Discard the remaining diluent. Keeping the vial **upright**, insert the needle all the way into the vial and inject the diluent **quickly**. Before withdrawing the needle, remove **2.2 mL** of air. Shake immediately. **Shake** for approximately 15 seconds. Allow the vial to stand for approximately 2 minutes. Tap the vial to **reduce foaming** and swirl the vial occasionally. Again, **shake** for approximately 15 seconds. Allow the vial to stand for approximately 2 minutes. Tap the vial to **reduce foaming** and swirl the vial occasionally. **Do not reinject the air into the vial. Locate a second injection spot on the stopper**, and then insert the 18 Gauge needle. Invert the vial and draw up some of the suspension into the syringe and ***without removing the needle from the vial reinject it at any remaining solids in the vial. Repeat the process until all solids are dispersed.*** Swirl the vial before withdrawal and withdraw **the entire contents (at least 2 mL)** by positioning the needle at a 45 degree angle. Pull the plunger back to recover the residual suspension in the 18 G x 1½" needle. Exchange the 18 G x 1½" needle with the enclosed 22 G x 1½" Safety Glide injection needle. Insert the needle at the desired injection site, pull the plunger back to check for back-flow of blood. If blood flows into the syringe, do not inject at this site. Select another injection site. Deliver the entire reconstituted suspension intramuscularly ***immediately***.

Stability

Abarelix does not contain a preservative and should be administered within 1 hour following reconstitution.

Revised: 02/01/2006
Developed: 03/15/2004

ACAMPROSATE Systemic†

VA CLASSIFICATION (Primary): AD100

Commonly used brand name(s): *Campral*.

Note: For a listing of dosage forms and brand names by country availability, see *Dosage Forms* section(s).

†Not commercially available in Canada.

Category

Alcohol-abuse deterrent.

Indications

Accepted

Alcoholism (treatment)—Acamprosate is indicated for the maintenance of sobriety in patients with alcohol dependence who are abstinent at treatment initiation. Acamprosate treatment should be part of a comprehensive management program including psychosocial support.

Unaccepted

Acamprosate is not indicated for use in promoting abstinence in patients who have not undergone detoxification and not achieved alcohol abstinence prior to the beginning of acamprosate treatment. Nor has the efficacy of acamprosate in promoting abstinence from alcohol in polysubstance abusers been established.

Pharmacology/Pharmacokinetics

Physicochemical characteristics

Source—Acamprosate calcium is a synthetic compound with a chemical structure similar to that of the endogenous amino acid homotaurine, which is a structural analogue of the amino acid neurotransmitter γ-aminobutyric acid and the amino acid neuromodulator taurine.

Molecular weight—Acamprosate: 400.48.

Solubility—Acamprosate is freely soluble in water, and practically insoluble in absolute ethanol and dichloromethane.

Mechanism of action/Effect

The mechanism of action is not completely understood. Studies in animals suggest acamprosate may interact with glutamate and GABA neurotransmitter systems centrally. This has led to the hypothesis that acamprosate restores the balance between neuronal excitation and inhibition which are hypothesized to be altered in chronic alcohol exposure.

Studies have also shown that acamprosate calcium reduces alcohol intake in alcohol-dependent animals in a dose-dependent manner and that this effect appears to be specific to alcohol and the mechanisms of alcohol dependence.

Absorption

The absolute bioavailability following oral administration is about 11%. Food decreases bioavailability as measured by C_{max} and AUC, 42% and 23% respectively. The effect of food on absorption is not clinically significant.

Distribution

Volume of distribution (Vol_D)—72 to 109 liters (approximately 1 L/kg) following intravenous administration.

Protein binding

Negligible.

Biotransformation

Acamprosate does not undergo metabolism.

Half-life

Terminal—20 to 33 hours following oral dosing of 2 x 333 mg.

Time to peak concentration

3 to 8 hours post dose.

Peak plasma concentration:

350 ng/mL following doses of 2 x 333 mg, three times daily.

Elimination

Via the kidneys as unchanged drug.

Precautions to Consider

Carcinogenicity

Studies in rats given doses of 0.2, 0.7 or 2.5-fold the maximum recommended human dose (based on an AUC comparison) showed no evidence of increased incidence of tumors. Adequate carcinogenicity studies in mice have not been done.

Mutagenicity

Acamprosate showed no evidence of genotoxicity in an *in vitro* bacterial reverse point mutation assay or in the *in vitro* mammalian cell gene mutation test in Chinese Hamster Lung V79 cells. Acamprosate was also negative for clastogenicity in the *in vitro* chromosomal aberration assay in human lymphocytes and negative for chromosomal damage in an *in vivo* mouse micronucleus assay.

Pregnancy/Reproduction

Fertility—Acamprosate had no effect on fertility in rats or mice given oral doses (4 and 5 times the maximum recommended human daily oral dose on a mg/m^2 basis) prior to mating and throughout gestation in females.

Pregnancy—Adequate and well controlled studies in humans have not been done. Studies in animals have shown that acamprosate causes adverse effects in the fetus. Acamprosate should be used during pregnancy only if the potential benefit justifies the potential risk to the fetus.

Studies done in rats given doses equal to the human dose and in rabbits given doses approximately 3 times the human dose have been shown to be teratogenic. In rats acamprosate produced a dose-related increase in the number of fetuses with malformations The malformations included hydronephrosis, malformed iris, retinal dysplasia and retroesophageal subclavin artery. The no effect levels were one-fifth the maximum recommended human daily oral dose. No developmental effects were observed in New Zealand white rabbits at doses 8 times the maximum recommended human daily oral dose. These findings should be considered in relation to known developmental effects of ethyl alcohol, including fetal alcohol syndrome and milder forms of neurological and behavioral disorders in humans.

Other studies in pregnant mice given oral doses starting on Day 15 of gestation through the end of lactation on postnatal day 28 demonstrated increased incidence of stillborn fetuses at doses approximately 2 times the maximum recommended human daily dose.

FDA Pregnancy Category C

Labor and delivery—Unknown

Breast-feeding

It is not known whether acamprosate is distributed into breast milk. However, acamprosate is distributed into the milk of lactating rats. Because many drugs are distributed in human milk, caution should be exercised when acamprosate is administered to a nursing woman.

Pediatrics

Safety and efficacy in pediatric patients have not been established.

Geriatrics

Appropriate studies performed to date have not demonstrated geriatric-specific problems that would limit the usefulness of acamprosate in the elderly. Because elderly patients are more likely to have decreased renal function, care should be taken in dose selection and renal monitoring may be useful.

Pharmacogenetics

Acamprosate has not shown any significant pharmacokinetic differences between male and female subjects.

Drug interactions and/or related problems

The following drug interactions and/or related problems have been selected on the basis of their potential clinical significance (possible mechanism in parentheses where appropriate)—not necessarily inclusive (» = major clinical significance):

Note: Combinations containing any of the following medications, depending on the amount present, may also interact with this medication.

Naltrexone
(coadministration increases C_{max} 33% and AUC 25% of acamprosate; however no adjustment of dosage is recommended; naltrexone and its major metabolite 6-beta-naltrexol are unaffected by coadministration with acamprosate)

Medical considerations/Contraindications

The medical considerations/contraindications included have been selected on the basis of their potential clinical significance (reasons given in parentheses where appropriate)—not necessarily inclusive (» = major clinical significance).

Except under special circumstances, this medication should not be used when the following medical problem exists:

» Hypersensitivity to acamprosate calcium, or any of its components or sulfites.

Note: Patients sensitive to sulfites may be sensitive to acamprosate also. Sulfites were used in the synthesis and traces of residual sulfites may be present.

» Renal function impairment, severe
(use is contraindicated in patients with creatinine clearance ≤30 mL/min)

Risk-benefit should be considered when the following medical problems exist:

» Renal function impairment, moderate
(patients with creatinine clearance 30 to 50 mL/min require a dose reduction)

Patient monitoring

The following may be especially important in patient monitoring (other tests may be warranted in some patients, depending on condition; » = major clinical significance):

» Depression, development of or
» Suicidal thinking
(families and care givers of patients being treated with acamprosate should be alerted to the need to monitor patients for the emergence of symptoms of depression or suicide, and report symptoms to the patient's health care provider)

Side/Adverse Effects

The following side/adverse effects have been selected on the basis of their potential clinical significance (possible signs and symptoms in parentheses where appropriate)—not necessarily inclusive:

Note: Although no causal relationship has been found, the serious adverse event of acute kidney failure has been reported in at least 3 patients and is not described elsewhere in the labeling.

Those indicating need for medical attention

Incidence unknown—Observed during Non-US postmarketing evaluation

Kidney failure, acute (agitation; coma; confusion; decreased urine output; depression; dizziness; headache; hostility; irritability; lethargy; muscle twitching; nausea; rapid weight gain; seizures; stupor; swelling of face, ankles, or hands; unusual tiredness or weakness)

Those indicating need for medical attention only if they continue or are bothersome

Incidence more frequent

Asthenia (lack or loss of strength); ***depression*** (discouragement; feeling sad or empty; irritability; lack of appetite; loss of interest or pleasure; tiredness; trouble concentrating; trouble sleeping); ***diarrhea; insomnia*** (sleeplessness; trouble sleeping; unable to sleep)

Incidence less frequent

Accidental injury; pain; anorexia (loss of appetite; weight loss); ***anxiety*** (fear; nervousness); ***dizziness; dry mouth; flatulence*** (bloated full feeling; excess air or gas in stomach or intestines; passing gas); ***nausea; paresthesias*** (burning, crawling, itching, numbness, prickling, "pins and needles", or tingling feelings); ***pruritus*** (itching skin); ***sweating***

Overdose

For more information on the management of overdose or unintentional ingestion, **contact a poison control center** (see *Poison Control Center Listing*).

Clinical effects of overdose

The following effects have been selected on the basis of their potential clinical significance (possible signs and symptoms in parentheses where appropriate)—not necessarily inclusive:

Acute

Diarrhea

Chronic

Hypercalcemia, risk of (abdominal pain; confusion; constipation; depression; dry mouth; headache; incoherent speech; increased urination; loss of appetite; metallic taste; muscle weakness; nausea; thirst; unusual tiredness; vomiting; weight loss)

Treatment of overdose

Treatment of overdose should be symptomatic and supportive.

Patients in whom intentional overdose is confirmed or suspected should be referred for psychiatric consultation.

Patient Consultation

As an aid to patient consultation, refer to *Advice for the Patient, Acamprosate (Systemic).*

In providing consultation, consider emphasizing the following selected information (» = major clinical significance):

Before using this medication

» Conditions affecting use, especially:
Hypersensitivity to acamprosate calcium or any of its components or sulfite
Pregnancy—Not recommended for use during pregnancy
Breast-feeding—Acamprosate is distributed into the milk of lactating rats. Because many drugs are distributed in human milk, caution should be exercised when acamprosate is administered to a nursing woman.
Other medical problems, especially severe renal function impairment

Proper use of this medication

» Beginning treatment as soon as possible after the period of alcohol withdrawal, when the patient has achieved abstinence.
» Using acamprosate as part of a comprehensive psychosocial treatment program.
» Compliance with therapy, even in the event of a relapse
» Proper dosing
Missed dose: Taking as soon as possible; not taking if almost time for next scheduled dose; not doubling doses
Proper storage

Precautions while using this medication

» Regular visits to physician to check progress
» Caution when driving or operating hazardous machinery

Side/adverse effects

Signs of potential side effects, especially acute kidney failure.

General Dosing Information

Acamprosate does not eliminate or diminish withdrawal symptoms.

The use of acamprosate in animals has not demonstrated central nervous system (CNS) activity outside of its effects on alcohol dependence, exhibiting no anticonvulsant, antidepressant, or anxiolytic activity.

Acamprosate calcium is not associated with the development of tolerance or dependence.

Acamprosate dose not cause alcohol aversion or a disulfiram-like reaction as a result of ethanol ingestion.

Acamprosate has not shown evidence of producing withdrawal symptoms in patients.

Oral Dosage Forms

Note: Bracketed information in the *Indications* section refers to uses that are not included in U.S. product labeling.

ACAMPROSATE TABLETS

Usual adult dose

Alcohol abuse deterrent—
Oral, two 333-milligram tablets (666-mg dose) taken three times daily.

Note: For patients with moderate renal impairment (creatinine clearance of 30 to 50 mL/min), a starting dose of one 333-mg tablet taken three times daily is recommended. Patients with severe renal impairment (creatinine clearance of ≤30 mL/min) should not be given acamprosate.

Usual pediatric dose

Safety and efficacy have not been established.

Usual geriatric dose

See *Usual adult dose.*

Strength(s) usually available

U.S.—

Note: Sulfites were used in the synthesis of acamprosate; therefore, trace amounts of residual sulfites may be present.

333 mg (Rx) [*Campral* (colloidal anhydrous silica; crospovidone; Eudragit® L 30 D or equivalent; magnesium silicate; magnesium stearate; microcrystalline cellulose; propylene glycol; sodium starch glycolate; talc)].

Packaging and storage

Store at 25 °C (77 °F), excursions permitted to 15 °C to 30 °C (59° to 86 °F)

Auxiliary labeling

- May cause drowsiness. Be careful while driving or operating machinery. Use caution until you become familiar with its effects.
- Avoid alcohol while on this medication.
- Products contains sulfites which may cause allergic reactions in some asthmatic patients. Contact you doctor or pharmacist.

Developed: 09/15/2004

ACARBOSE Systemic

VA CLASSIFICATION (Primary): HS504

Commonly used brand name(s): *Precose*.

Note: For a listing of dosage forms and brand names by country availability, see *Dosage Forms* section(s).

Category

Antidiabetic agent.

Indications

Accepted

Diabetes, type 2 (treatment)—Acarbose is indicated as an adjunctive therapy to diet in the treatment of patients with type 2 diabetes (previously referred to as non-insulin-dependent diabetes mellitus [NIDDM]) whose blood glucose cannot be controlled by diet alone. It may be used as monotherapy or in combination with a sulfonylurea.

Pharmacology/Pharmacokinetics

Physicochemical characteristics

Source—Acarbose is an oligosaccharide obtained from fermentation processes of the microorganism *Actinoplanes utahensis*.

Molecular weight—645.6.

pKa—5.1.

Mechanism of action/Effect

Acarbose lowers postprandial blood glucose concentrations in patients with diabetes by competitive, reversible inhibition of pancreatic alpha-amylase and membrane-bound intestinal alpha-glucoside hydrolases. These enzymes inhibit hydrolysis of complex starches to oligosaccharides in the lumen of the small intestine and hydrolysis of oligosaccharides, trisaccharides, and disaccharides to glucose and other monosaccharides in the brush border of the small intestine. Acarbose does not enhance insulin secretion and, when used as monotherapy, should not cause hypoglycemia.

Other actions/effects

Although the antihyperglycemic effect of acarbose is additive to that of sulfonylureas (which act via a different mechanism), acarbose decreases the insulinotropic and weight-increasing effects of sulfonylureas when used concurrently.

Acarbose does not inhibit lactase and would not be expected to cause lactose intolerance.

Absorption

Studies with radiolabeled acarbose indicate that less than 2% of an oral dose is absorbed in active form. Because the medication acts within the gastrointestinal tract, low systemic bioavailability is therapeutically desirable. However, approximately 35% of a dose is absorbed on a delayed basis, probably as metabolites formed in the gastrointestinal tract.

Biotransformation

Gastrointestinal, primarily by intestinal bacteria and, to a lesser extent, by digestive enzymes. At least 13 metabolites have been identified. One of these, formed by cleavage of a glucose molecule from acarbose, has alpha-glucosidase inhibitory activity. Other major metabolites are primarily sulfate, methyl, and glucuronide conjugates.

Half-life

Approximately 2 hours.

Time to peak concentration

In plasma—

Acarbose: 1 hour.

Metabolites: 14 to 24 hours.

Elimination

Fecal, as unabsorbed acarbose, approximately 51% of an oral dose within 96 hours.

Renal, approximately 34% of an oral dose as absorbed metabolites. Less than 2% of an oral dose is excreted in the urine as acarbose and its active metabolite.

Precautions to Consider

Carcinogenicity/Tumorigenicity

Up to 500 mg per kg of body weight (mg/kg) of acarbose administered orally to Sprague-Dawley rats for 104 weeks resulted in a significant increase in the incidence of renal adenomas and adenocarcinomas and benign Leydig cell tumors. The study was repeated with similar results. However, an increase in renal tumors did not occur in Sprague-Dawley rats when carbohydrate malnutrition was prevented by glucose supplementation or by administration of acarbose by daily postprandial gavage. Also, no evidence of tumorigenicity or carcinogenicity was found in two studies in Wistar rats receiving acarbose by postprandial gavage or two studies in hamsters given oral acarbose with or without glucose supplementation.

Mutagenicity

No evidence of mutagenicity was noted in six *in vitro* and in three *in vivo* assays.

Pregnancy/Reproduction

Fertility—Oral administration of acarbose to rats produced no impairment of fertility or overall reproductive capacity.

Pregnancy—Adequate and well-controlled studies have not been done in humans, and safety has not been established. Insulin is usually recommended for pregnant patients with diabetes.

Animal studies failed to show an adverse effect on the fetus in rats given up to 480 mg/kg (approximately 9 times the human exposure, based on blood concentrations) or in rabbits given up to 32 times the human dose (based on body surface area). In rabbit studies, high doses of acarbose caused a reduction in maternal weight gain, which may have been responsible for a slight increase in embryonic losses. However, no embryotoxicity occurred in rabbits given 160 mg/kg (corresponding to 10 times the human dose, based on body surface area).

FDA Pregnancy Category B.

Breast-feeding

It is not known whether acarbose is distributed into human breast milk. In animal studies, administration of radiolabeled acarbose resulted in detection of a small quantity of radioactivity in the milk of lactating rats. Acarbose is not recommended for use by nursing women.

Pediatrics

Safety and efficacy in pediatric patients have not been established.

Geriatrics

In pharmacokinetic studies, maximum plasma concentrations of acarbose and the area under the acarbose concentration-time curve (AUC) were approximately 1.5 times higher in geriatric individuals than in younger adults, but the differences were not statistically significant.

Drug interactions and/or related problems

The following drug interactions and/or related problems have been selected on the basis of their potential clinical significance (possible mechanism in parentheses where appropriate)—not necessarily inclusive (» = major clinical significance):

Note: Combinations containing any of the following medications, depending on the amount present, may also interact with this medication.

» Adsorbents, intestinal, such as activated charcoal or

» Digestive enzyme preparations containing carbohydrate-splitting enzymes, such as amylase or pancreatin
(these medications may decrease the efficacy of acarbose; concurrent use is not recommended)

Antidiabetic agents, other
(antihyperglycemic effects of acarbose are additive to those of other antidiabetic agents; although this effect is used for therapeutic benefit, the risk of hypoglycemia may be increased with concurrent use; a reduction in dosage of the other antidiabetic agent may be necessary)

Hyperglycemia-inducing medications, such as:
- Calcium channel blocking agents
- Corticosteroids
- Diuretics, especially thiazide diuretics
- Estrogens
- Estrogen and progestin–containing oral contraceptives
- Isoniazid
- Niacin
- Phenothiazines
- Phenytoin
- Sympathomimetic agents
- Thyroid hormones

(these agents may cause loss of glycemic control; patients should be monitored for evidence of hyperglycemia and the dosage of the antidiabetic agent adjusted if necessary; also, patients receiving combined therapy with acarbose and another antidiabetic agent should be monitored for evidence of hypoglycemia after treatment with one of these agents is discontinued)

Laboratory value alterations

The following have been selected on the basis of their potential clinical significance (possible effect in parentheses where appropriate)—not necessarily inclusive (» = major clinical significance).

With physiology/laboratory test values

Bilirubin, serum
(elevations have been reported rarely)

Transaminases, serum
(transaminase elevations occurred in 15% of acarbose-treated patients in clinical trials; in patients receiving a total of 150 to 300 mg of acarbose a day, elevations did not occur more often than in placebo controls, but elevations to more than three times the upper limit of normal occurred two to three times more often in patients receiving more than 300 mg per day than in placebo controls. The elevations were more common in female patients, reversible, and not associated with other evidence of liver injury. In postmarketing surveillance of more than 500,000 patients, 19 cases of transaminase elevations to 500 IU per L or higher have been reported, 12 of which were associated with jaundice. Of these 19 patients, 15 had been receiving total doses of 300 mg or more of acarbose per day, and 13 of the 16 patients for whom weights were reported weighed less than 60 kg. Hepatic abnormalities improved or resolved after treatment was discontinued in the 18 patients for whom follow-up information is available)

Medical considerations/Contraindications

The medical considerations/contraindications included have been selected on the basis of their potential clinical significance (reasons given in parentheses where appropriate)—not necessarily inclusive (» = major clinical significance).

Except under special circumstances, this medication should not be used when the following medical problems exist:

» Diabetic ketoacidosis

» Hepatic cirrhosis
(acarbose may cause transaminase elevations and, rarely, jaundice)

Intestinal disorders, including:

» Chronic conditions leading to marked disorders of absorption or digestion

» Conditions that would be affected adversely by increased intestinal gas formation

» Inflammatory or ulcerative intestinal disease

» Obstructive intestinal disease or predisposition to

» Renal function impairment, severe (serum creatinine higher than 2 mg/dL)
(although long-term studies in patients with severe renal function impairment have not been done, use of acarbose is not recommended; pharmacokinetic studies have shown that plasma concentrations of acarbose increase in proportion to the degree of renal function impairment, with maximum concentrations being approximately five times higher and the area under the acarbose concentration-time curve [AUC] being approximately six times higher in patients with creatinine clearances of less than 25 mL per minute per 1.73 square meters of body surface area than in patients with normal renal function)

Risk-benefit should be considered when the following medical problems exist:

Fever or
Infection or
Surgery or
Trauma
(these conditions may cause loss of glycemic control; temporary insulin therapy may be necessary)

Sensitivity to acarbose

Patient monitoring

The following may be especially important in patient monitoring (other tests may be warranted in some patients, depending on condition; » = major clinical significance):

» Glucose concentrations, blood and/or urine
(monitoring essential as a guide to efficacy of treatment)

» Glycosylated hemoglobin determinations
(recommended at 3-month intervals for monitoring long-term glycemic control)

» Transaminase values
(monitoring recommended at 3-month intervals during the first year of treatment and periodically thereafter; a reduction of acarbose dosage or discontinuation of therapy may be necessary, especially if elevations persist)

Side/Adverse Effects

The following side/adverse effects have been selected on the basis of their potential clinical significance (possible signs and symptoms in parentheses where appropriate)—not necessarily inclusive:

Those indicating need for medical attention

Incidence rare
Jaundice (yellow eyes or skin)

Those indicating need for medical attention only if they continue or are bothersome

Incidence more frequent
Abdominal pain—incidence 21%; ***diarrhea***—incidence 33%; ***flatulence*** (bloated feeling or passing of gas)—incidence 77%

Note: These effects are related to the presence of undigested carbohydrates in the lower gastrointestinal tract, a result of acarbose's mechanism of action. In clinical trials, *abdominal pain* and *diarrhea* tended to return to pretreatment levels, and the frequency and severity of *flatulence* tended to abate, over time. Rarely, gastrointestinal effects may be severe enough to be confused with paralytic ileus.

Overdose

For more information on the management of overdose or unintentional ingestion, **contact a Poison Control Center** (see *Poison Control Center Listing*).

Clinical effects of overdose

The most likely effects are increases in abdominal discomfort, diarrhea, and flatulence, which should subside without treatment. Hypoglycemia should not occur with an overdose of acarbose alone, but can occur if the patient is receiving combined therapy with other antidiabetic agents.

Patient Consultation

As an aid to patient consultation, refer to *Advice for the Patient, Acarbose (Systemic)*.

In providing consultation, consider emphasizing the following selected information (» = major clinical significance):

Before using this medication

» Conditions affecting use, especially:
Sensitivity to acarbose
Pregnancy—Insulin is usually recommended
Breast-feeding—Use of acarbose is not recommended
Other medications, especially digestive enzyme preparations, or intestinal adsorbents
Other medical problems, especially diabetic ketoacidosis, hepatic cirrhosis, intestinal disorders, or renal function impairment

Proper use of this medication

» Importance of adherence to recommended regimens for diet, exercise, and glucose monitoring

» Taking medication at the beginning of each main meal

» Proper dosing
Missed dose (if meal completed without having taken medication): Skipping missed dose; taking next dose with next meal; not doubling doses

» Proper storage

Precautions while using this medication

» Regular visits to physician to check progress

» *Carefully following special instructions of health care team:*
Discussing use of alcohol and tobacco
Not taking other medications unless discussed with physician
Getting counseling for family members to help them assist the diabetic patient; also, special counseling for pregnancy planning and contraception
Making travel plans to include preparedness for diabetic emergencies and keeping meal times near the usual times with changing time zones

» Preparing for and understanding what to do in case of emergency; carrying medical history and current medication list and wearing medical identification

» Recognizing what brings on symptoms of hypoglycemia, such as using other antidiabetic medication; delaying or missing a meal; exercising more than usual; drinking significant amounts of alcohol; illness, including vomiting or diarrhea

» Recognizing symptoms of hypoglycemia: anxiety; behavior change similar to drunkenness; blurred vision; cold sweats; confusion; cool, pale skin; difficulty in concentrating; drowsiness; excessive hunger; fast heartbeat; headache; nausea; nervousness; nightmares; restless sleep; shakiness; slurred speech; and unusual tiredness or weakness

» Knowing what to do if symptoms of hypoglycemia occur, such as ingesting a source of dextrose (not sucrose) or, if severe, injecting glucagon

» Recognizing what brings on symptoms of hyperglycemia, such as not taking enough or skipping a dose of antidiabetic medication, overeating or not following meal plan, fever or infection, exercising less than usual

» Recognizing symptoms of hyperglycemia and ketoacidosis: blurred vision; drowsiness; dry mouth; flushed, dry skin; fruit-like breath odor; increased urination (frequency and volume); ketones in urine; loss of appetite; stomachache, nausea, or vomiting; tiredness; troubled breathing (rapid and deep); unconsciousness; unusual thirst

» Knowing what to do if symptoms of hyperglycemia occur, such as checking blood glucose and contacting a member of the health care team

Side/adverse effects

Signs of potential side effects, especially jaundice

General Dosing Information

Dosage must be individualized on the basis of 1-hour postprandial blood glucose determinations and patient tolerance. The goal of treatment is to reduce postprandial plasma glucose concentrations and glycosylated hemoglobin concentrations to normal or near normal using the lowest effective dose of acarbose, alone or in conjunction with a sulfonylurea.

Starting treatment with a low dose that is increased gradually to the maximally effective dose is recommended to reduce gastrointestinal side effects as well as to facilitate identification of the lowest effective dose for the individual patient.

Acarbose is taken three times a day, at the beginning (with the first bite) of each main meal.

For treatment of hypoglycemia

Hypoglycemia should not occur as a result of acarbose monotherapy, but may occur during combined therapy with a sulfonylurea or insulin. Because acarbose inhibits hydrolysis of sucrose to glucose and fructose, sucrose is not recommended for treatment of mild to moderate hypoglycemia in acarbose-treated patients. A simple sugar, such as dextrose (glucose), should be ingested instead. Intravenous infusion of dextrose or administration of glucagon may be required for severe hypoglycemia.

Oral Dosage Forms

ACARBOSE TABLETS

Usual adult dose

Antidiabetic agent—

Oral, 25 mg three times a day, at the start of each main meal. Dosage may be adjusted, at four- to eight-week intervals, first to 50 mg three times a day, then, if necessary and appropriate, to 100 mg three times a day.

Note: If an increase in dosage to 100 mg three times a day fails to produce a further reduction in postprandial glucose concentration, consideration should be given to lowering the dose.

Usual adult prescribing limits

Antidiabetic agent—

Patients weighing 60 kg or less: 50 mg three times a day.

Patients weighing more than 60 kg: 100 mg three times a day.

Usual pediatric dose

Safety and efficacy have not been established.

Usual geriatric dose

Antidiabetic agent—

See *Usual adult dose*

Usual geriatric prescribing limits

Antidiabetic agent—

See *Usual adult prescribing limits*.

Strength(s) usually available

U.S.—

50 mg (Rx) [*Precose* (scored; starch; microcrystalline cellulose; magnesium stearate; colloidal silicon dioxide)].

100 mg (Rx) [*Precose* (starch; microcrystalline cellulose; magnesium stearate; colloidal silicon dioxide)].

Packaging and storage

Store below 25 °C (77 °F), protected from moisture, unless otherwise directed by manufacturer.

Revised: 07/31/1998

ACEBUTOLOL—See *Beta-adrenergic Blocking Agents (Systemic)*

ACENOCOUMAROL—See *Anticoagulants (Systemic)*

ACETAMINOPHEN Systemic

INN: Paracetamol

VA CLASSIFICATION (Primary/Secondary): CN103/CN850

Note: For information on acetaminophen combinations that are used for antacid as well as analgesic effects, see *Acetaminophen, Sodium Bicarbonate, and Citric Acid (Systemic)*.

Commonly used brand name(s): *Tempra Caplets; Abenol; Aceta Elixir; Aceta Tablets; Acetaminophen Uniserts; Actamin; Actamin Extra; Actamin Super; Actimol Chewable Tablets; Actimol Children's Suspension; Actimol Infants' Suspension; Actimol Junior Strength Caplets; Aminofen; Aminofen Max; Anacin-3; Anacin-3 Extra Strength; Apacet Capsules; Apacet Elixir; Apacet Extra Strength Caplets; Apacet Extra Strength Tablets; Apacet, Infants; Apacet Regular Strength Tablets; Apo-Acetaminophen; Aspirin Free Anacin Maximum Strength Caplets; Aspirin Free Anacin Maximum Strength Gel Caplets; Aspirin Free Anacin Maximum Strength Tablets; Aspirin-Free Excedrin Caplets; Atasol Caplets; Atasol Drops; Atasol Forte Caplets; Atasol Forte Tablets; Atasol Oral Solution; Atasol Tablets; Banesin; Bayer Select Maximum Strength Headache Pain Relief Formula; Dapa; Dapa X-S; Datril Extra-Strength; Excedrin Caplets; Excedrin Extra Strength Caplets; Exdol; Exdol Strong; Feverall, Children's; Feverall, Infants"; Feverall Junior Strength; Feverall Sprinkle Caps, Children's; Feverall Sprinkle Caps Junior Strength; Genapap Children's Elixir; Genapap Children's Tablets; Genapap Extra Strength Caplets; Genapap Extra Strength Tablets; Genapap, Infants; Genapap Regular Strength Tablets; Genebs Extra Strength Caplets; Genebs Regular Strength Tablets; Genebs X-Tra; Liquiprin Children's Elixir; Liquiprin Infants" Drops; Neopap; Oraphen-PD; Panadol; Panadol, Children's; Panadol Extra Strength; Panadol, Infants; Panadol Junior Strength Caplets; Panadol Maximum Strength Caplets; Panadol Maximum Strength Tablets; Phenaphen Caplets; Redutemp; Robigesic; Rounox; Snaplets-FR; St. Joseph Aspirin-Free Fever Reducer for Children; Suppap-120; Suppap-325; Suppap-650; Tapanol Extra Strength Caplets; Tapanol Extra Strength Tablets; Tempra; Tempra Chewable Tablets; Tempra D.S; Tempra Drops; Tempra, Infants; Tempra Syrup; Tylenol Arthritis Extended Relief; Tylenol Caplets; Tylenol Children's Chewable Tablets; Tylenol Children's Elixir; Tylenol Children's Suspension Liquid; Tylenol Drops; Tylenol Elixir; Tylenol Extra Strength Adult Liquid Pain Reliever; Tylenol Extra Strength Caplets; Tylenol Extra Strength Gelcaps; Tylenol Extra Strength Tablets; Tylenol Gelcaps; Tylenol Infants Drops; Tylenol Infants" Suspension Drops; Tylenol Junior Strength Caplets; Tylenol Junior Strength Chewable Tablets; Tylenol Regular Strength Caplets; Tylenol Regular Strength Tablets; Tylenol Tablets; Valorin; Valorin Extra.*

Other commonly used names are APAP and paracetamol.

Note: For a listing of dosage forms and brand names by country availability, see *Dosage Forms* section(s).

Category

Analgesic; antipyretic.

Indications

Accepted

Pain (treatment);

Pain, arthritic, mild (treatment); or

Fever (treatment)—Acetaminophen is indicated to relieve mild to moderate pain and reduce fever. It provides symptomatic relief only; additional therapy to treat the cause of the pain or fever should be instituted when necessary.

Acetaminophen has minimal anti-inflammatory activity and does not relieve redness, swelling, or stiffness due to arthritis; it cannot be used in place of aspirin or other salicylates or other nonsteroidal anti-inflammatory drugs (NSAIDs) in the treatment of rheumatoid arthritis. However, it may be used to relieve pain due to mild osteoarthritis.

Acetaminophen may be used when aspirin therapy is contraindicated or inadvisable, e.g., in patients receiving anticoagulants or uricosuric agents, patients with hemophilia or other bleeding problems, and those with upper gastrointestinal disease or intolerance or hypersensitivity to aspirin. However, chronic, high-dose acetaminophen therapy may require adjustment of anticoagulant dosage based on increased monitoring of prothrombin time in patients receiving a coumarin- or indandione-derivative anticoagulant.

Note: The FDA has proposed that caffeine (present as an analgesic adjuvant in some products) be classified as a Category III ingredient (i.e., lacking documentation of efficacy) in OTC products containing acetaminophen as the sole analgesic/antipyretic agent.

Pharmacology/Pharmacokinetics

Physicochemical characteristics
Molecular weight—151.16.

Mechanism of action/Effect
For acetaminophen—

Analgesic:

The mechanism of analgesic action has not been fully determined. Acetaminophen may act predominantly by inhibiting prostaglandin synthesis in the central nervous system (CNS) and, to a lesser extent, through a peripheral action by blocking pain-impulse generation. The peripheral action may also be due to inhibition of prostaglandin synthesis or to inhibition of the synthesis or actions of other substances that sensitize pain receptors to mechanical or chemical stimulation.

Antipyretic:

Acetaminophen probably produces antipyresis by acting centrally on the hypothalamic heat-regulating center to produce peripheral vasodilation resulting in increased blood flow through the skin, sweating, and heat loss. The central action probably involves inhibition of prostaglandin synthesis in the hypothalamus.

For caffeine—

Caffeine is a mild CNS stimulant. Caffeine-induced constriction of cerebral blood vessels, which leads to a decrease in cerebral blood flow and in the oxygen tension of the brain, may contribute to relief of some types of headache.

It has been suggested that the addition of caffeine to acetaminophen may provide a more rapid onset of action and/or enhanced pain relief with lower doses of the analgesic. However, the FDA has determined that studies performed to date have not demonstrated that caffeine is an effective analgesic adjuvant or that it does not interfere with acetaminophen's efficacy as an antipyretic.

Absorption
Oral—Rapid and almost complete; may be decreased if acetaminophen is taken following a high-carbohydrate meal.

Rectal—The rate and extent of absorption from the suppository dosage form may vary, depending on the composition of the base.

Distribution
In breast milk—Peak concentrations of 10 to 15 mcg per mL (66.2 to 99.3 micromoles/L) have been measured 1 to 2 hours following maternal ingestion of a single 650-mg dose. The half-life in breast milk is 1.35 to 3.5 hours.

Protein binding
Not significant with doses producing plasma concentrations below 60 mcg per mL (397.2 micromoles/L); may reach moderate levels with high or toxic doses.

Biotransformation
Approximately 90 to 95% of a dose is metabolized in the liver, primarily by conjugation with glucuronic acid, sulfuric acid, and cysteine. An intermediate metabolite, which may accumulate in overdosage after the primary metabolic pathways become saturated, is hepatotoxic and possibly nephrotoxic.

Half-life
1 to 4 hours; does not change with renal failure but may be prolonged in acute overdosage, in some forms of hepatic disease, in the elderly, and in the neonate; may be somewhat shortened in children.

Time to peak concentration
0.5 to 2 hours

Peak plasma concentration
5 to 20 mcg per mL (33.1 to 132.4 micromoles/L), with doses up to 650 mg.

Time to peak effect:
1 to 3 hours

Duration of action
3 to 4 hours

Elimination
Renal, as metabolites, primarily conjugates; 3% of a dose may be excreted unchanged.

In dialysis—

Hemodialysis: 120 mL per minute (for unmetabolized drug); metabolites are also cleared rapidly.

Hemoperfusion: 200 mL per minute.

Peritoneal dialysis: <10 mL per minute.

Precautions to Consider

Cross-sensitivity and/or related problems
Patients sensitive to aspirin may not be sensitive to acetaminophen; however, mild bronchospastic reactions with acetaminophen have been reported in some aspirin-sensitive asthmatics (less than 5% of those tested).

Pregnancy/Reproduction
Fertility—Chronic toxicity studies in animals have shown that high doses of acetaminophen cause testicular atrophy and inhibition of spermatogenesis; the relevance of this finding to use in humans is not known.

Pregnancy—Problems in humans have not been documented. Although controlled studies have not been done, it has been shown that acetaminophen crosses the placenta.

Breast-feeding
Problems in humans have not been documented. Although peak concentrations of 10 to 15 mcg per mL (66.2 to 99.3 micromoles/L) have been measured in breast milk 1 to 2 hours following maternal ingestion of a single 650-mg dose, neither acetaminophen nor its metabolites were detected in the urine of the nursing infants. The half-life in breast milk is 1.35 to 3.5 hours.

Pediatrics
Studies performed to date have not demonstrated pediatrics-specific problems that would limit the usefulness of acetaminophen in children. However, some products intended for pediatric use contain aspartame, which is metabolized to phenylalanine, and must be used with caution, if at all, in children with phenylketonuria.

Geriatrics
Appropriate studies performed to date have not demonstrated geriatrics-specific problems that would limit the usefulness of acetaminophen in the elderly.

Drug interactions and/or related problems
The following drug interactions and/or related problems have been selected on the basis of their potential clinical significance (possible mechanism in parentheses where appropriate)—not necessarily inclusive (» = major clinical significance):

Note: Combinations containing any of the following medications, depending on the amount present, may also interact with this medication.

For acetaminophen

» Alcohol, especially chronic abuse of or
Hepatic enzyme inducers (See *Appendix II*) or
Hepatotoxic medications, other (See *Appendix II*)

(risk of hepatotoxicity with single toxic doses or prolonged use of high doses of acetaminophen may be increased in alcoholics or in patients regularly taking other hepatotoxic medications or hepatic enzyme inducers)

(chronic use of barbiturates [except butalbital] or primidone has been reported to decrease the therapeutic effects of acetaminophen, probably because of increased metabolism resulting from induction of hepatic microsomal enzyme activity; the possibility should be considered that similar effects may occur with other hepatic enzyme inducers)

Anticoagulants, coumarin- or indandione-derivative

(concurrent chronic, high-dose administration of acetaminophen may increase the anticoagulant effect, possibly by decreasing hepatic synthesis of procoagulant factors; anticoagulant dosage adjustment based on increased monitoring of prothrombin time may be necessary when chronic, high-dose acetaminophen therapy is initiated or discontinued; however, this does not apply to occasional use, or to chronic use of doses below 2 grams per day, of acetaminophen)

Anti-inflammatory drugs, nonsteroidal (NSAIDs) or
Aspirin or other salicylates
(prolonged concurrent use of acetaminophen and a salicylate is not recommended because recent evidence suggests that chronic, high-dose administration of the combined analgesics [1.35 grams daily, or cumulative ingestion of 1 kg annually, for 3 years or longer] significantly increases the risk of analgesic nephropathy, renal papillary necrosis, end-stage renal disease, and cancer of the kidney or urinary bladder; also, it is recommended that for short-term use, the combined dose of acetaminophen plus salicylate not exceed that recommended for acetaminophen or a salicylate given alone)

(prolonged concurrent use of acetaminophen and NSAIDs other than aspirin may also increase the risk of adverse renal effects; it is recommended that patients be under close medical supervision while receiving such combined therapy)

(diflunisal may increase the plasma concentration of acetaminophen by 50%, leading to increased risk of acetaminophen-induced hepatotoxicity)

For formulations containing caffeine (in addition to those interactions listed above)

CNS stimulation-producing medications, other (See *Appendix II*)
(concurrent use with caffeine may result in excessive CNS stimulation, leading to unwanted effects such as nervousness, irritability, insomnia, or possibly convulsions or cardiac arrhythmias; close observation is recommended)

Lithium
(caffeine increases urinary excretion of lithium, and may thereby reduce its therapeutic effect)

Monoamine oxidase (MAO) inhibitors, including furazolidone, procarbazine, and selegiline
(the sympathomimetic side effects of caffeine may produce dangerous cardiac arrhythmias or severe hypertension when large doses of caffeine are used concurrently with MAO inhibitors)

Laboratory value alterations

The following have been selected on the basis of their potential clinical significance (possible effect in parentheses where appropriate)—not necessarily inclusive (» = major clinical significance).

With diagnostic test results

Glucose, blood, determinations
(acetaminophen may cause falsely decreased values when the glucose oxidase/peroxidase method is used, but probably not when the hexokinase/glucose-6-phosphate dehydrogenase [G6PD] method is used)

(values may be falsely increased when certain instruments are used in glucose analysis if high acetaminophen concentrations are present; instrument manufacturer's instruction manual should be consulted)

5-Hydroxyindoleacetic acid (5-HIAA), serum, determinations
(acetaminophen may cause false-positive results in qualitative screening tests using nitrosonaphthol reagent; the quantitative test is unaffected)

Myocardial perfusion imaging, radionuclide, when adenosine or dipyridamole is used as an adjunct to the radiopharmaceutical
(the caffeine in specific formulations may reverse the effects of adenosine or dipyridamole on myocardial blood flow, thereby interfering with test results; patients should be advised to avoid caffeine for 8 to 12 hours prior to the test)

Pancreatic function test using bentiromide
(administration of acetaminophen prior to the bentiromide test will invalidate test results because acetaminophen is also metabolized to an arylamine and will thus increase the apparent quantity of para-aminobenzoic acid [PABA] recovered; it is recommended that acetaminophen be discontinued at least 3 days prior to administration of bentiromide)

Uric acid, serum, determinations
(acetaminophen may cause falsely increased values when the phosphotungstate uric acid test method is used)

With physiology/laboratory test values

Bilirubin concentrations, serum and
Lactate dehydrogenase activity, serum and
Prothrombin time and
Transaminase activity, serum
(may be increased, indicating hepatotoxicity, especially in alcoholics, patients taking other hepatic enzyme inducers, or patients with pre-existing hepatic disease, when single toxic doses [> 8 to 10 grams] of acetaminophen are taken or with prolonged use of lower doses [> 3 to 5 grams a day])

Medical considerations/Contraindications

The medical considerations/contraindications included have been selected on the basis of their potential clinical significance (reasons given in parentheses where appropriate)—not necessarily inclusive (» = major clinical significance).

Risk-benefit should be considered when the following medical problems exist:

» Alcoholism, active or
» Hepatic disease or
» Viral hepatitis
(increased risk of hepatotoxicity)

Phenylketonuria
(products that contain aspartame, which is metabolized to phenylalanine, may be hazardous to patients with phenylketonuria, especially young children; caution is recommended)

Renal function impairment, severe
(risk of adverse renal effects may be increased with prolonged use of high doses; occasional use is acceptable)

Sensitivity to acetaminophen or aspirin
(increased risk of allergic reaction)

Patient monitoring

The following may be especially important in patient monitoring (other tests may be warranted in some patients, depending on condition; » = major clinical significance):

Hepatic function determinations
(may be required at periodic intervals during high-dose or long-term therapy, especially in patients with pre-existing hepatic disease)

Side/Adverse Effects

The following side/adverse effects have been selected on the basis of their potential clinical significance (possible signs and symptoms in parentheses where appropriate)—not necessarily inclusive:

Those indicating need for medical attention

Incidence rare

Agranulocytosis (fever with or without chills; sores, ulcers or white spots on lips or in mouth; sore throat); ***anemia*** (unusual tiredness or weakness); ***dermatitis, allergic*** (skin rash, hives or, itching); ***hepatitis*** (yellow eyes or skin); ***renal colic*** (pain, severe and/or sharp, in lower back and/or side)—with prolonged use of high doses in patients with severe renal function impairment; ***renal failure*** (sudden decrease in amount of urine); ***sterile pyuria*** (cloudy urine); ***thrombocytopenia*** (rarely, unusual bleeding or bruising; black, tarry stools; blood in urine or stools; pinpoint red spots on skin)—usually asymptomatic

Note: Acetaminophen-induced *renal function impairment* may be sufficiently severe to result in *uremia*, especially with prolonged use of high doses in patients with pre-existing renal impairment. Also, although a causal association has not been established, a retrospective study has suggested that long-term daily use of acetaminophen may be associated with an increased risk of *chronic renal failure* (analgesic nephropathy) in individuals without pre-existing renal function impairment.

Overdose

For specific information on the agents used in the management of acetaminophen overdose, see:

- *Acetylcysteine (Systemic)* monograph; and/or
- *Charcoal, Activated (Oral-Local)* monograph.

For more information on the management of overdose or unintentional ingestion, **contact a Poison Control Center** (see *Poison Control Center Listing*).

Clinical effects of overdose

The following effects have been selected on the basis of their potential clinical significance (possible signs and symptoms in parentheses where appropriate)—not necessarily inclusive:

Acute

Gastrointestinal upset (diarrhea, loss of appetite, nausea or vomiting, stomach cramps or pain)***increased sweating***

Note: Although *gastrointestinal upset* and *increased sweating* often do not occur, they sometimes occur within 6 to 14 hours after ingestion of an overdose and persist for about 24 hours.

Chronic

Hepatotoxicity (pain, tenderness, and/or swelling in upper abdominal area)—may occur 2 to 4 days after the overdose is ingested

Note: The first indications of overdosage may be signs and symptoms of possible *liver damage* and abnormalities in liver function tests, which may not occur until 2 to 4 days after ingestion of the overdose. Maximal changes in liver function tests usually occur 3 to 5 days after ingestion of the overdose.

Overt *hepatic disease or failure* may occur 4 to 6 days after ingestion of the overdose. *Hepatic encephalopathy* (with mental changes, confusion, agitation, or stupor), *convulsions, respiratory depression, coma, cerebral edema, coagulation defects, gastrointestinal bleeding, disseminated intravascular coagulation, hypoglycemia, metabolic acidosis, cardiac arrhythmias,* and *cardiovascular collapse* may occur.

Renal tubular necrosis leading to *renal failure* (signs may include bloody or cloudy urine and sudden decrease in amount of urine) has also been reported in acetaminophen overdose, usually, but not exclusively, in conjunction with acetaminophen-induced *hepatotoxicity.*

Treatment of overdose

To decrease absorption—May include emptying the stomach via induction of emesis or gastric lavage.

Removing activated charcoal (if used) by gastric lavage may be advisable. Although activated charcoal is recommended in cases of mixed drug overdose, it may interfere with absorption of orally administered acetylcysteine (antidote used to protect against acetaminophen-induced hepatotoxicity) and decrease its efficacy.

To enhance elimination—Instituting hemodialysis or hemoperfusion to remove acetaminophen from the circulation may be beneficial if acetylcysteine administration cannot be instituted within 24 hours following ingestion of a massive acetaminophen overdose. However, the efficacy of such treatment in preventing acetaminophen-induced hepatotoxicity is not known.

Specific treatment—Use of acetylcysteine. *It is recommended that acetylcysteine administration be instituted as soon as possible after ingestion of an overdose has been reported,* without waiting for the results of plasma acetaminophen determinations or other laboratory tests. Acetylcysteine is most effective if treatment is started within 10 to 12 hours after ingestion of the overdose; however it may be of some benefit if treatment is started within 24 hours. See the package insert or *Acetylcysteine (Systemic)* monograph for specific dosing guidelines for use of this product.

Monitoring—May include determining plasma acetaminophen concentration at least 4 hours following ingestion of the overdose. Determinations performed prior to this time are not reliable for assessing potential hepatotoxicity. Initial plasma concentrations above 150 mcg per mL (993 micromoles/L) at 4 hours, 100 mcg per mL (662 micromoles/L) at 6 hours, 70 mcg per mL (463.4 micromoles/L) at 8 hours, 50 mcg per mL (331 micromoles/L) at 10 hours, 20 mcg per mL (132.4 micromoles/L) at 15 hours, 8 mcg per mL (53 micromoles/L) at 20 hours, or 3.5 mcg per mL (23.2 micromoles/L) at 24 hours postingestion indicate possible hepatotoxicity and the need for completing the full course of acetylcysteine treatment. If the initial determination indicates a plasma concentration below those listed at the times indicated, cessation of acetylcysteine therapy can be considered. However, some clinicians advise that more than one determination should be performed to ascertain peak absorption and half-life of acetaminophen prior to considering discontinuation of acetylcysteine.

Performing liver function tests (serum aspartate aminotransferase [AST; SGOT], serum alanine aminotransferase [ALT; SGPT], prothrombin time, and bilirubin) at 24-hour intervals for at least 96 hours postingestion if the plasma acetaminophen concentration indicates potential hepatotoxicity. If no abnormalities are detected within 96 hours, further determinations are not needed.

Monitoring renal and cardiac function and administering appropriate therapy as required.

Supportive care—May include maintaining fluid and electrolyte balance, correcting hypoglycemia, and administering vitamin K_1 (if prothrombin time ratio exceeds 1.5) and fresh frozen plasma or clotting factor concentrate (if prothrombin time ratio exceeds 3.0). Patients in whom intentional overdose is known or suspected should be referred for psychiatric consultation.

Patient Consultation

As an aid to patient consultation, refer to *Advice for the Patient, Acetaminophen (Systemic).*

In providing consultation, consider emphasizing the following selected information (» = major clinical significance):

Before using this medication

» Conditions affecting use, especially:
  Sensitivity to acetaminophen or aspirin
  Use in children—Aspartame-containing chewable tablets must be used with caution, if at all, in children with phenylketonuria
  Other medical problems, especially alcoholism (active), hepatic disease, or viral hepatitis

Proper use of this medication

» Importance of not taking more medication than the amount recommended because acetaminophen may cause kidney or liver damage with long-term use or greater-than-recommended doses

» Unless otherwise directed by physician, children should not receive more than 5 doses per day

» *Proper administration of:*
  Acetaminophen oral granules
  Acetaminophen oral powders
  Acetaminophen suppositories

» Proper dosing

» Proper storage

Precautions while using this medication

Regular visits to physician to check progress if long-term therapy is prescribed

Checking with physician because additional treatment may be needed:
  —if taking for pain, including arthritic pain, and pain persists for longer than 10 days for adults or 5 days for children, condition becomes worse, new symptoms occur, or the painful area is red or swollen
  —if taking for fever, and fever persists for longer than 3 days, condition becomes worse, or new symptoms occur
  —if taking for sore throat, and sore throat is severe, persists for longer than 2 days, or occurs together with or is followed by fever, headache, rash, nausea, or vomiting

» Risk of overdose if other medications containing acetaminophen are used

» Avoiding use of alcohol if taking more than an occasional 1 or 2 doses of this medication; increased risk of liver toxicity, especially in alcoholics, with high doses or prolonged use

Not using a salicylate or a nonsteroidal anti-inflammatory drug together with acetaminophen for more than a few days, unless directed by physician

Possible interference with some laboratory tests; preferably discussing use of the medication with physician in charge 3 to 4 days ahead of time; if this is not possible, informing physician in charge if acetaminophen taken within the past 3 or 4 days

Diabetics: Possible false results with blood glucose tests; checking with physician, nurse, or pharmacist if changes in test results noted

Not taking caffeine-containing formulations for 8 to 12 hours prior to adenosine- or dipyridamole-assisted myocardial perfusion imaging test

» Suspected overdose: Getting emergency help at once even if no symptoms apparent; symptoms of severe overdosage may be delayed, but treatment must be begun as soon as possible; treatment started 24 hours or more after the overdose may be ineffective in preventing liver damage or fatality

Side/adverse effects

Signs and symptoms of potential side effects, especially adverse renal effects, allergic dermatitis, hepatotoxicity, agranulocytosis, and thrombocytopenia

General Dosing Information

The doses are based on the FDA's proposed labeling requirements for over-the-counter (OTC) internal analgesic, antipyretic, and antirheumatic products. The dosage unit of 80 mg (1.23 grains) is used for pediatric doses; the dosage unit of 325 mg (5 grains) is used for adult doses. The conversion factor of 1 grain equal to 65 mg is used. The doses recommended by manufacturers of individual products, and the strengths of individual products, may not conform to the recommended doses.

One retrospective study has suggested that long-term daily use of acetaminophen may be associated with an increased risk of chronic renal disease (analgesic nephropathy). The results of this study are not considered conclusive, and further investigation is required to establish a causal association. However, until more definitive information is available, prolonged daily administration of acetaminophen should probably be limited to patients who are receiving appropriate medical supervision.

Oral Dosage Forms

ACETAMINOPHEN CAPSULES USP

Usual adult and adolescent dose

Analgesic and
Antipyretic—
Oral, 325 to 500 mg every three hours, 325 to 650 mg every four hours, 650 mg to 1 gram every six hours as needed, or 1300 mg every 8 hours, while symptoms persist.

Note: For patient self-medication, it is recommended that a physician be consulted if pain is not relieved within ten days, fever within three days, or sore throat within two days.

Usual adult prescribing limits

Up to 4 grams daily

Usual pediatric dose

Analgesic and
Antipyretic—
Oral, 1.5 grams per square meter of body surface a day in divided doses; or for
Infants up to 3 months of age—Oral, 40 mg every four hours as needed.
Infants 4 to 12 months of age—Oral, 80 mg every four hours as needed.
Children 1 to 2 years of age—Oral, 120 mg every four hours as needed.
Children 2 to 4 years of age—Oral, 160 mg every four hours as needed, while symptoms persist.
Children 4 to 6 years of age—Oral, 240 mg every four hours as needed, while symptoms persist.
Children 6 to 9 years of age—Oral, 320 mg every four hours as needed, while symptoms persist.
Children 9 to 11 years of age—Oral, 320 to 400 mg every four hours as needed, while symptoms persist.
Children 11 to 12 years of age—Oral, 320 to 480 mg every four hours as needed, while symptoms persist.

Note: It is recommended that children up to 12 years of age receive no more than five doses in each twenty-four-hour period, unless otherwise directed by a physician, and that a physician be consulted if pain is not relieved within five days, fever within three days, or sore throat within two days.

Dosage recommendations for children younger than 2 years of age do not appear on OTC packaging.

Administration of an individual product to a pediatric patient depends upon ability to achieve suitable dosage for the age of the child. Liquid dosage forms (oral solution or suspension), granules, powders, or chewable tablets are usually used.

Strength(s) usually available

U.S.—
325 mg (OTC) [GENERIC].
500 mg (OTC) [*Apacet Capsules; Dapa X-S;* GENERIC].
Canada—
Not commercially available.

Packaging and storage

Store below 40 °C (104 °F), preferably between 15 and 30 °C (59 and 86 °F), unless otherwise specified by manufacturer. Store in a tight container.

Auxiliary labeling

- Avoid alcoholic beverages.

ACETAMINOPHEN ORAL GRANULES

Usual adult and adolescent dose

See *Acetaminophen Capsules USP*.

Usual pediatric dose

See *Acetaminophen Capsules USP*.

Strength(s) usually available

U.S.—
80 mg (in individual packets) (OTC) [*Snaplets-FR*].
Canada—
Not commercially available.

Packaging and storage

Store below 40 °C (104 °F), preferably between 15 and 30 °C (59 and 86 °F), unless otherwise specified by manufacturer.

Preparation of dosage form

Single dose—The contents of the packets are to be mixed with a small quantity of soft food, such as applesauce, ice cream, or jam immediately prior to ingestion.

ACETAMINOPHEN ORAL POWDERS

Usual adult and adolescent dose

See *Acetaminophen Capsules USP*.

Usual pediatric dose

See *Acetaminophen Capsules USP*.

Strength(s) usually available

U.S.—
80 mg (in capsules) (OTC) [*Feverall Sprinkle Caps, Children's*].
160 mg (in capsules) (OTC) [*Feverall Sprinkle Caps Junior Strength*].
Canada—
Not commercially available.

Packaging and storage

Store below 40 °C (104 °F), preferably between 15 and 30 °C (59 and 86 °F), unless otherwise specified by manufacturer.

Preparation of dosage form

Single dose—The capsules are not intended to be swallowed whole. They are to be opened and the contents sprinkled over a small quantity (< 5 mL) of water or other liquid immediately prior to ingestion. Alternatively, the contents of the capsules may be mixed with a small quantity of soft food, such as applesauce, ice cream, or jam, immediately prior to ingestion.

ACETAMINOPHEN ORAL SOLUTION USP

Usual adult and adolescent dose

See *Acetaminophen Capsules USP*.

Usual adult prescribing limits

See *Acetaminophen Capsules USP*.

Usual pediatric dose

See *Acetaminophen Capsules USP*.

Strength(s) usually available

U.S.—
100 mg per mL (80 mg per 0.8-mL dropperful) (OTC) [*Apacet, Infants; Genapap, Infants; Panadol, Infants; St. Joseph Aspirin-Free Fever Reducer for Children; Tempra, Infants; Tylenol Infants Drops;* GENERIC].
80 mg per 5 mL (OTC) [GENERIC].
120 mg per 5 mL (OTC) [*Aceta Elixir* (alcohol 7%); *Oraphen-PD* (alcohol 5%); GENERIC].
130 mg per 5 mL (OTC) [GENERIC].
160 mg per 5 mL (OTC) [*Apacet Elixir; Genapap Children's Elixir; Liquiprin Children's Elixir; Panadol, Children's; St. Joseph Aspirin-Free Fever Reducer for Children; Tempra Syrup; Tylenol Children's Elixir* (sugar); GENERIC].

Note: Also available generically in unit-dose cups containing 325 mg per 10.15 mL and 650 mg per 20.3 mL.

500 mg per 15 mL (OTC) [*Tylenol Extra Strength Adult Liquid Pain Reliever* (alcohol 7%)].
Canada—
80 mg per mL (OTC) [*Atasol Drops; Panadol; Tempra Drops* (alcohol 10%); *Tylenol Drops;* GENERIC].
80 mg per 5 mL (OTC) [*Atasol Oral Solution; Panadol* (sodium); *Robigesic* (alcohol 8.5%); *Tempra Syrup*].
160 mg per 5 mL (OTC) [*Tempra Syrup; Tylenol Elixir;* GENERIC].

Note: The strengths of specific products may not conform to some of the recommended pediatric dosages.

Packaging and storage

Store below 40 °C (104 °F), preferably between 15 and 30 °C (59 and 86 °F), unless otherwise specified by manufacturer. Store in a tight container. Protect from freezing.

Auxiliary labeling

- Avoid alcoholic beverages.

ACETAMINOPHEN ORAL SUSPENSION USP

Usual adult and adolescent dose

See *Acetaminophen Capsules USP*.

Usual pediatric dose

See *Acetaminophen Capsules USP*.

Strength(s) usually available

U.S.—
48 mg per mL (120 mg per 2.5-mL dropperful) (OTC) [*Liquiprin Infants" Drops*].
100 mg per mL (80 mL per 0.8-mL dropperful) (OTC) [*Tylenol Infants" Suspension Drops*].
160 mg per 5 mL (OTC) [*Tylenol Children's Suspension Liquid*].

Note: It is recommended that children up to 12 years of age receive no more than five doses in each twenty-four-hour period, unless otherwise directed by a physician, and that a physician be consulted if pain is not relieved within five days, fever within three days, or sore throat within two days.

Strength(s) usually available

U.S.—
- 80 mg (OTC) [*Feverall, Infants'*].
- 120 mg (OTC) [*Acetaminophen Uniserts; Feverall, Children's; Neopap* (scored); *Suppap-120;* GENERIC].
- 300 mg (OTC) [GENERIC].
- 325 mg (OTC) [*Acetaminophen Uniserts; Feverall Junior Strength; Suppap-325*].
- 650 mg (OTC) [*Acetaminophen Uniserts; Suppap-650;* GENERIC].

Canada—
- 120 mg (OTC) [*Abenol*].
- 325 mg (OTC) [*Abenol*].
- 650 mg (OTC) [*Abenol*].

Note: The strengths of the specific products may not conform to the recommended pediatric doses.

Packaging and storage

Store below 40 °C (104 °F), preferably between 15 and 30 °C (59 and 86 °F), in a well-closed container, unless otherwise specified by manufacturer. Protect from freezing.

Auxiliary labeling

- Avoid alcoholic beverages.

Revised: 11/07/2002

ACETAZOLAMIDE—See *Carbonic Anhydrase Inhibitors (Systemic)*

ACETOHEXAMIDE—See *Antidiabetic Agents, Sulfonylurea (Systemic)*

ACETYLCYSTEINE Inhalation

JAN: *N*-Acetyl-L-Cysteine

VA CLASSIFICATION (Primary/Secondary): RE400/DX900

Commonly used brand name(s): *Mucomyst; Mucomyst-10; Mucosil.*

Another commonly used name is *N*-acetylcysteine.

Note: For a listing of dosage forms and brand names by country availability, see *Dosage Forms* section(s).

Category

Mucolytic; diagnostic aid (bronchoscopy).

Indications

Acceptance not established

Acetylcysteine is used in current medical practice in conjunction with chest physiotherapy as a *mucolytic* in patients who have viscid or thickened airway mucus. When administered via direct instillation, it is used to loosen impacted mucus plugs during bronchoscopy. Acetylcysteine can irritate the airways and induce bronchospasm when given by inhalation; therefore, it should be administered simultaneously with or following administration of an inhaled beta-adrenergic bronchodilator.

There are no controlled clinical studies showing that the drug improves mucus clearance. Early reports indicating efficacy in clinical practice presented cases or used subjective information or nonspecific tests, such as sputum volume. Additionally, there are other sources concluding that acetylcysteine is ineffective.

Pharmacology/Pharmacokinetics

Physicochemical characteristics

Molecular weight—163.2.

Mechanism of action/Effect

Acetylcysteine exerts its mucolytic action through its free sulfhydryl group, which opens the disulfide bonds and lowers mucus viscosity. This action increases with increasing pH and is most significant at pH 7 to 9. The mucolytic action of acetylcysteine is not affected by the presence of DNA.

Biotransformation

Hepatic. Acetylcysteine undergoes rapid deacetylation *in vivo* to yield cysteine or oxidation to yield diacetylcystine.

Onset of action

In vitro—Within 1 minute.

Time to peak effect

In vitro—5 to 10 minutes.

Precautions to Consider

Carcinogenicity

Studies have not been done to determine the carcinogenic potential of acetylcysteine.

Mutagenicity

In the Ames test, both with and without metabolic activation, acetylcysteine was not shown to be mutagenic.

Pregnancy/Reproduction

Fertility—A reproduction toxicity study in rats given acetylcysteine with isoproterenol by inhalation showed no adverse effects on fertility. In reproduction toxicity studies in rats given acetylcysteine orally at doses up to 5.2 times the human dose, one study showed only a slight non–dose-related reduction in fertility.

Pregnancy—Adequate and well-controlled studies in humans have not been done.

Reproduction studies in rats given acetylcysteine with isoproterenol and in rabbits given acetylcysteine alone at doses up to 2.6 times the human dose have shown no evidence of teratogenicity or harm to the fetus.

FDA Pregnancy Category B.

Breast-feeding

It is not known whether acetylcysteine is distributed into breast milk. However, problems in humans have not been documented.

Pediatrics

Appropriate studies on the relationship of age to the effects of acetylcysteine inhalation have not been performed in the pediatric population. However, no pediatrics-specific problems have been documented to date.

Geriatrics

Appropriate studies on the relationship of age to the effects of acetylcysteine inhalation have not been performed in the geriatric population. However, no geriatrics-specific problems have been documented to date.

Medical considerations/Contraindications

The medical considerations/contraindications included have been selected on the basis of their potential clinical significance (reasons given in parentheses where appropriate)—not necessarily inclusive (» = major clinical significance).

Risk-benefit should be considered when the following medical problems exist:

» Asthma
(asthmatics may experience bronchospasm associated with the administration of nebulized acetylcysteine; therefore, it should be administered simultaneously with or following administration of an inhaled beta-adrenergic bronchodilator)

» Cough, inadequate ability to
(after treatment with acetylcysteine, an increased mobilization of bronchial secretions may develop; when the ability to cough is inadequate, mechanical suctioning may be required to maintain open airways)

Sensitivity to acetylcysteine

Side/Adverse Effects

The following side/adverse effects have been selected on the basis of their potential clinical significance (possible signs and symptoms in parentheses where appropriate)—not necessarily inclusive:

Those indicating need for medical attention

Incidence less frequent

Increased airways obstruction, (difficulty in breathing; tightness in chest; wheezing)—especially in asthma patients

Note: *Increased airways obstruction* of varying and unpredictable severity has been reported following administration of acetylcysteine; however, it is not possible to identify those who will react. Patients who have developed increased airways obstruction following administration do not necessarily react to a subsequent administration, and vice versa.

Incidence rare

Sensitization (skin rash or other irritation)—with frequent and prolonged exposure

Those indicating need for medical attention only if they continue or are bothersome

Incidence less frequent

Clammy skin; fever; increase in bronchial secretions; irritation of throat or lungs—more frequent with a 20% solution; ***nausea; rhinorrhea*** (runny nose); ***stomatitis*** (irritation or soreness of mouth); ***vomiting***

Those not indicating need for medical attention

Incidence more frequent

Stickiness on face, after nebulization using a face mask; unpleasant odor during administration, transient

Patient Consultation

As an aid to patient consultation, refer to *Advice for the Patient, Acetylcysteine (Inhalation).*

In providing consultation, consider emphasizing the following selected information (» = major clinical significance):

Before using this medication

» Conditions affecting use, especially:
- Sensitivity to acetylcysteine
- Other medical problems, especially asthma or decreased ability to cough

Proper use of this medication

» Importance of not using more medication than the amount prescribed

Proper administration: Knowing correct administration technique; checking with physician if necessary

After using medication, coughing up loosened mucus to prevent excessive accumulation in lungs; mechanical suction may be necessary if cough inadequate to remove mucus

» Proper dosing

Missed dose: Using as soon as possible; using any remaining doses for that day at regularly spaced intervals

» Proper storage

Precautions while using this medication

» Checking with physician if condition does not improve or if it becomes worse

Side/adverse effects

Signs of potential side effects, especially increased airways obstruction and sensitization

Possibility of stickiness on face after nebulization using a face mask; removing by washing with water

Possibility of acetylcysteine having a transient unpleasant odor during administration

General Dosing Information

The method of acetylcysteine administration depends on the condition being treated. Acetylcysteine, usually as a 10 to 20% solution, may be administered by nebulization or direct instillation.

Acetylcysteine usually is administered by nebulization, using conventional nebulizers made of plastic or glass. Certain materials used in nebulization equipment react with acetylcysteine, especially iron, copper, and rubber.

Acetylcysteine should not be placed directly into the chamber of a heated (hot pot) nebulizer. A heated nebulizer may be part of the nebulization assembly to provide a warm saturated atmosphere if the acetylcysteine aerosol is introduced by means of a separate unheated nebulizer. The usual precautions for administration of warm saturated nebulae should be followed.

The nebulizing equipment should be cleaned immediately after use because the residues may clog the smaller orifices or corrode metal parts.

Hand bulb nebulizers are not recommended for nebulizing acetylcysteine because their output is generally too small and some deliver particles that are larger than optimum for inhalation therapy.

Nebulization with a face mask may leave a sticky residue on the face. This can be removed by washing with water.

For treatment of adverse effects

Bronchospasm may be relieved by the administration of a bronchodilator by nebulization. If bronchospasm continues, acetylcysteine should be discontinued.

Inhalation or Direct Instillation Dosage Forms

ACETYLCYSTEINE SOLUTION USP

Usual adult and adolescent dose

Mucolytic—

Nebulization via face mask, mouthpiece, or tracheostomy—

Inhalation, 3 to 5 (range, 1 to 10) mL of a 20% solution or 6 to 10 (range, 2 to 20) mL of a 10% solution three or four times a day (range, every two to six hours).

Nebulization via tent or croupette—

Inhalation, a sufficient volume of a 10 or 20% solution to maintain a very heavy mist in the tent or croupette for the period of time necessary.

Note: The method of nebulization, via tent or croupette, must be individualized according to the available equipment and the patient's condition. Very large volumes of the solution are required, occasionally as much as 300 mL during a single treatment period.

Instillation, direct—

1 to 2 mL of a 10 to 20% solution every hour, if necessary.

For routine care of patients with tracheostomy—Intratracheal, 1 to 2 mL of a 10 to 20% solution every one to four hours.

For instillation into a particular segment of bronchopulmonary tree via small plastic catheter into trachea—Intratracheal, 2 to 5 mL of a 20% solution instilled by means of a syringe connected to the catheter.

For instillation via percutaneous intratracheal catheter—Intratracheal, 2 to 4 mL of a 10% solution or 1 to 2 mL of a 20% solution every one to four hours administered by a syringe attached to the catheter.

Diagnostic aid (bronchoscopy)—

Inhalation or intratracheal instillation, 1 to 2 mL of a 20% solution or 2 to 4 mL of a 10% solution for two or three doses prior to the procedure.

Note: Acetylcysteine can irritate the airways and induce bronchospasm when given by inhalation; therefore, it should be administered simultaneously with or following administration of an inhaled beta-adrenergic bronchodilator.

Usual pediatric dose

See *Usual adult and adolescent dose.*

Usual geriatric dose

See *Usual adult and adolescent dose.*

Strength(s) usually available

U.S.—

10% (Rx) [*Mucomyst-10; Mucosil;* GENERIC].

20% (Rx) [*Mucomyst; Mucosil;* GENERIC].

Canada—

20% (Rx) [*Mucomyst*].

Packaging and storage

Store below 40 °C (104 °F), preferably between 15 and 30 °C (59 and 86 °F), unless otherwise specified by manufacturer. Store in a tight container.

Preparation of dosage form

The 10% solution may be used undiluted.

The 20% solution may be used undiluted or diluted to a lesser concentration with 0.9% sodium chloride injection, sodium chloride inhalation solution, sterile water for injection, or sterile water for inhalation.

Stability

Acetylcysteine solution does not contain an antimicrobial agent; therefore, care must be taken to minimize contamination of the sterile solution.

After opening, the vial should be stored in the refrigerator; the opened vial should be discarded after 96 hours.

A color change may occur in acetylcysteine after the bottle has been opened. The light purple color results from a chemical reaction that does not significantly affect the safety or mucolytic efficacy of acetylcysteine.

Acetylcysteine has been shown to be physically and chemically compatible with cromolyn sodium inhalation solution for up to 60 minutes and with isoproterenol. Although the admixture of albuterol inhalation solution and acetylcysteine is common medical practice, there is no information about the stability of this combination. If an admixture with acetylcysteine is necessary, it should be administered as soon as possible after preparation; unused admixtures should not be stored.

Incompatibilities

Acetylcysteine reacts with certain materials, such as iron, copper, and rubber, used in nebulization equipment. Where materials may come into contact with acetylcysteine solution, parts made of the following materials should be used: glass, plastic, aluminum, anodized aluminum, chromed metal, tantalum, sterling silver, or stainless steel. Silver may become tarnished after exposure but this does not affect the efficacy of acetylcysteine or harm the patient.

Auxiliary labeling
- Store in refrigerator after opening.
- Discard opened vial after 96 hours.

Revised: 05/14/1997

ACITRETIN Systemic

VA CLASSIFICATION (Primary): DE801

Commonly used brand name(s): *Soriatane*.

Other commonly used names are 13-cis-acitretin, etretin, and isoetretin.

Note: For a listing of dosage forms and brand names by country availability, see *Dosage Forms* section(s).

Category

Antipsoriatic (systemic); keratinization stabilizer (systemic).

Indications

Note: Bracketed information in the *Indications* section refers to uses that are not included in U.S. product labeling.

General Considerations

Note: **FOR INFORMATION REGARDING PROBLEMS THAT HAVE OCCURRED DURING PREGNANCY SEE THE *PREGNANCY/REPRODUCTION* SECTION OF *PRECAUTIONS TO CONSIDER*.**

Since **acitretin is a teratogen in pregnant females** and can cause serious and severe side effects in both males and females, it should be prescribed only by physicians experienced in its use. It is not known if the concentration of acitretin in seminal fluid is sufficient to pose a risk to a fetus. Acitretin should not be used in females of childbearing potential, unless the patient is unresponsive to or intolerant of other treatments, and can accept routine clinical monitoring and the strict criteria for avoiding use of alcohol and preventing pregnancy before and after treatment is discontinued.

FOR FEMALES OF CHILDBEARING POTENTIAL:

- **The duration of teratogenic risk has not been determined. The minimum plasma concentration of acitretin and its active metabolite etretinate that is associated with teratogenicity is not known.** The sensitivity of tests to detect plasma concentrations of acitretin and its metabolites, 13-cis acitretin and etretinate, is inadequate. Also, testing for acitretin and its metabolites in plasma poorly predicts the presence or absence of these teratogens in subcutaneous tissue after acitretin treatment is stopped.
- **Use of acitretin is contraindicated in females of childbearing potential, unless all of the following criteria have been met**:
  —Patient shows severe, disfiguring, recalcitrant psoriasis or one of the accepted indications.
  —Patient understands treatment instructions and intends to follow them.
  —Patient is capable of complying with the mandatory contraceptive measures. Two effective forms of contraception should be used at least 1 month before therapy begins, during therapy, and for an undetermined amount of time following discontinuation of therapy, at least 2 years, according to Canadian labeling, or 3 years, according to U.S. labeling. A planned pregnancy should be discussed with the physician for a recommendation of timing.
  —Patient receives both verbal and written warnings of the hazards associated with pregnancy during and following acitretin therapy and she acknowledges in writing her responsibility to avoid pregnancy.
  —Patient is not pregnant, as concluded from a negative pregnancy test. The pregnancy test should be performed after normal menstrual cycles are achieved and within 1 week prior to initiation of acitretin therapy. If acitretin therapy is initiated, it should begin within the same week as the pregnancy test, on Day 2 or Day 3 of the menstrual period.

For males and females:

- During treatment and for 2 months after acitretin treatment discontinuation—*Patients should not drink alcohol-containing beverages* to avoid the prolonged effects of etretinate, an active metabolite of acitretin, that may accumulate from alcohol-induced transesterification. Alcohol is a major factor for inducing the conversion of acitretin to etretinate. It is not known what other substances may also induce this conversion.
- During treatment and for several years after acitretin treatment discontinuation—*Patients should not donate blood* intended for transfusion purposes for 2 years, according to Canadian labeling, or for 3 years, according to U.S. labeling. Although the risk is small, a blood transfusion from such donors to pregnant women during their first trimester may expose the fetus to the medication.

Accepted

Psoriasis, severe (treatment)—Acitretin is indicated to treat symptoms of severe erythrodermic and generalized pustular psoriasis that involve more than 10% of the patient's body surface area, especially when psoriasis is physically, occupationally, or psychologically disabling. Acitretin is indicated for the treatment of localized palmoplantar pustulosis, but the localized condition is more recalcitrant to treatment than is generalized, severe psoriasis.

When treating severe plaque psoriasis, other therapies that have been added to a regimen of acitretin monotherapy after 1 or 2 months include ultraviolet B (UVB) light or psoralen plus ultraviolet A (UVA) light (PUVA), topical corticosteroids, or anthralin ointments.

[Keratinization disorders (treatment)]
[Erythroderma, ichthyosiform][1]
[Ichthyosis, lamellar][1]
[Keratosis follicularis][1]
—Acitretin is indicated to treat inherited disorders of keratinization, such as bullous or nonbullous ichthyosiform erythroderma, keratosis follicularis, and lamellar ichthyosis. Best results are obtained in treatment of keratosis follicularis (also called Darier's disease), severe recessive X-linked ichthyosis, and nonbullous congenital ichthyosis, such as erythrodermic or nonerythrodermic lamellar ichthyosis. Patients with bullous ichthyosiform erythroderma may experience improvement of their condition under less aggressive treatment with a low-dose regimen.

Acceptance not established

There are published case reports of using the retinoids, acitretin or etretinate, in the treatment of *other disorders of keratinization*, including *cutaneous lichen planus*, *erythrokeratodermia variabilis*, *palmoplantar keratoses* (including *mal de Meleda* and *Papillon-Lefevre syndrome*), *pityriasis rubra pilaris*, and *Sjogren-Larsson syndrome*. Other studies are needed to evaluate fully acitretin's efficacy in the treatment of these conditions. Some children with *Netherton's syndrome* and *keratosis pilaris* experienced a worsening of their condition when treated with acitretin for several weeks; acitretin therapy was withdrawn.

Acitretin has been used in conjunction with interferon-alpha 2a to treat *cutaneous T-cell lymphoma* when there was no known internal organ involvement.

Small studies have been done using acitretin prophylactically in the treatment of *keratotic skin lesions* or *skin cancer*. Acitretin prevented development of new keratotic skin lesions in renal transplant patients who had a history of extensive keratotic skin lesions and/or recurrent squamous cell and basal cell carcinomas. Additional studies are needed.

Acitretin has been used as monotherapy in the treatment of *psoriasis associated with human immunodeficiency virus (HIV)* infection. Although acitretin does not appear to have immunosuppressive properties capable of worsening a compromised immune system, additional studies are needed to assess acitretin's immunosuppressive properties in HIV-positive patients.

Unaccepted

An *in vitro* study reported that acitretin was totally ineffective in the treatment of acute myelocytic leukemia.

Mild disorders of keratinization, including autosomal dominant ichthyosis vulgaris and mild recessive X-linked ichthyosis that can be controlled with topical medications generally should not be treated with acitretin because of risk-benefit issues. Also, acitretin treatment may cause skin erosions and exacerbate the epidermolytic form of palmoplantar keratoderma.

Acitretin is not efficacious and is not used to treat severe nodulocystic acne.

[1]Not included in Canadian product labeling.

Pharmacology/Pharmacokinetics

Note: The length of time that etretinate (a metabolite of acitretin) remains in the blood has not been determined.

Physicochemical characteristics

Chemical Group—Acitretin is considered a second-generation retinoid and a synthetic aromatic analog of vitamin A.

Molecular weight—326.44.
pKa—5.

Mechanism of action/Effect
The exact mechanism of action for acitretin is not known. One possible explanation is altered gene expression through nuclear retinoic acid receptors (RARs) and binding to DNA to cause transcription or transrepression changes in protein synthesis. Although acitretin binds to all three classes of RARs (alpha, beta, and gamma receptors), it binds selectively to beta and gamma receptors to modify gene expression.

Antipsoriatic—Studies suggest that acitretin affects immune response, epidermal proliferation, and glycoprotein synthesis in the skin. Specifically, acitretin helps to normalize cell differentiation and thin the cornified layer by directly reducing the keratinocytes' rate of proliferation. Acitretin's anti-inflammatory and antiproliferative actions in the skin decrease epidermal and dermal inflammation and reduce the scaling, erythema, and thickness of psoriatic lesions.

Keratolytic (systemic)—Acitretin is thought to interfere with the terminal differentiation of keratinocytes.

Absorption
The mean absolute bioavailability of acitretin is 59% (range, 36 to 95%). The dose absorbed is linear up to 50 mg a day, but may become nonproportional or nonlinear for doses greater than 50 mg a day. The rate and extent of acitretin absorption are doubled when 50 mg of acitretin is given with food when compared with the absorption of the same dose given under fasting conditions.

As judged from the area under the plasma concentration-time curve (AUC), the amount absorbed, corrected for body weight and dose, shows a six-fold systemic interindividual variation for the metabolite etretinate.

Distribution
The mean accumulation ratio is 1.2 for acitretin and 6.6 for the cis-metabolite. Acitretin has not been shown to accumulate in any particular organ; however, etretinate (an active metabolite) does accumulate in fat and, to a lesser degree, in the liver; lower tissue concentrations are found in the kidneys, brain, and testes. Five hours after acitretin administration, etretinate concentrations in the subcutaneous fat exceed those found in the plasma; however, accumulation does not occur. In one patient given acitretin orally, the concentration of etretinate in the adrenal glands exceeded that found in the fat tissue.

Patients receiving 30 mg of acitretin once a day for 30 days showed skin concentrations of acitretin that were 10 times higher than those observed in the plasma and 3 to 5 times higher than the skin concentrations of its metabolite, 13-cis acitretin. Concentrations of acitretin and 13-cis acitretin are higher in lesional skin than in uninvolved skin.

Protein binding
Acitretin and its metabolite etretinate are highly bound to plasma proteins (> 99%). Acitretin is primarily bound to albumin (91%) and etretinate is primarily bound to low-density lipoprotein (48%).

Biotransformation
Acitretin is metabolized to other active metabolites, including 13-cis acitretin and etretinate, following oral administration. No detectable etretinate was formed when a single dose of 100 mg of acitretin was administered without ingestion of alcohol, but the potential for its formation cannot be ruled out. Other metabolites are likely to occur.

The relative formation of the 13-cis acitretin does not change regardless of acitretin dose, dose formulation (capsules versus solution), and ingestion with or without food. Ingestion of alcohol increases the conversion of acitretin to etretinate (an active metabolite), even after discontinuation of treatment.

One crossover study of 10 healthy volunteers who took 100 mg of acitretin and 1.4 grams per kg of body weight of ethanol over approximately 3 hours showed a mean peak plasma concentration of 59 nanograms of etretinate per mL (range, 22 to 105 nanograms per mL), a concentration that is comparable to receiving a 5-mg dose of etretinate. In another study where protocol did not restrict patients from drinking alcohol, 57.5% of 240 patients taking 5 to 60 mg of acitretin a day for treatment of psoriasis had plasma etretinate concentrations of 5 to 62 nanograms per mL; 27% of patients showed a measurable trace of etretinate in their plasma.

Half-life
Elimination—
- Acitretin: 49 hours (range, 33 to 96 hours; some studies have shown the upper limit of the half-life to be as high as 120 hours).
- 13-cis acitretin (active metabolite): 63 hours (range, 28 to 157 hours).
- Etretinate (active metabolite): 120 days, mean (range, up to 168 days).

Peak serum concentration
Single dose of 50 mg acitretin—196 to 728 nanograms per mL.

At multiple doses of 10 to 50 mg acitretin a day—The dose-related trough steady-state plasma concentrations are between 6 and 25 nanograms per mL for acitretin; the serum concentration for the 13-cis metabolite is about five times higher than that of acitretin.

Time to peak effect
Single dose of 50 mg acitretin: 2 to 5 hours.

At doses of 10 to 50 mg acitretin a day, steady-state plasma concentrations are reached within 2 weeks.

Elimination
For acitretin or 13-cis acitretin conjugates, 34 to 54% fecal and 16 to 53% renal. No acitretin or 13-cis acitretin (active metabolite) was recovered in the urine.

If alcohol is taken during treatment with acitretin, more than 98% of etretinate would be eliminated after 2 years, assuming a mean half-life of 120 days. Using the upper limit of the half-life of 168 days, more than 98% of etretinate would be eliminated after 3 years. One woman who ingested alcohol sporadically during acitretin therapy showed detectable plasma and subcutaneous fat concentrations of etretinate 52 months after discontinuing acitretin treatment.

In dialysis—

For patients taking a single 50-mg dose of acitretin, the mean AUC values of acitretin and 13-cis acitretin (active metabolite) were about 50% less in patients undergoing hemodialysis compared to patients without renal failure. No retinoids were detectable in the dialysate.

Precautions to Consider

Cross-sensitivity and/or related problems
Patients sensitive to isotretinoin, tretinoin, or vitamin A derivatives may be sensitive to this medication also, since acitretin is related to both retinoic acid and retinol (vitamin A). Also, allergy to parabens should be considered.

Carcinogenicity
Male and female Wistar rats given acitretin in doses up to 2 mg per kg of body weight (mg/kg) a day for 104 weeks showed a greater incidence of non-neoplastic bone lesions compared to two control groups not given acitretin. Neoplastic lesions that developed in the endocrine and reproductive organs and the skin were consistent with those that developed in the control rats, and were not associated with use of acitretin. An 80-week carcinogenesis study in mice has been completed with etretinate, the ethyl ester of acitretin. Blood level data obtained during this study demonstrated that etretinate was metabolized to acitretin and that blood levels of acitretin exceeded those of etretinate at all times. In the etretinate study, an increased incidence of blood vessel tumors (hemangiomas and hemangiosarcomas at several different sites) was noted in male, but not female, mice at doses approximately one half the maximum recommended human therapeutic dose based on a mg per m^2 comparison.

Mutagenicity
Acitretin is not mutagenic according to the following *in vitro* tests: Ames test, hamster HGPRT assay, unscheduled DNA synthesis in rat hepatocytes, induction of chromosomal aberrations in human lymphocytes, and mouse micronucleus assay.

Pregnancy/Reproduction
The inability to detect plasma acitretin and its metabolite etretinate is a poor predictor of the absence of these teratogens in tissue after discontinuation of acitretin treatment.

Fertility—A fertility study of 31 men given 30 to 50 mg per day of acitretin for at least 12 weeks showed no decreases in sperm count or concentration, no changes in sperm motility or morphology, and no deleterious effects on either testosterone production, LH, FSH or the hypothalamic-pituitary axis. In a fertility study in rats, the fertility of treated rats was not impaired at the highest dosage of acitretin tested, 3 mg per kg of body weight per day (approximately one half the maximum recommended therapeutic dose based on a mg per m^2 comparison. However, one study of dogs given doses of acitretin greater than 30 mg per kg of body weight per day showed testicular changes including reversible mild to moderate spermatogenic arrest and appearance of multinucleated giant cells.

Pregnancy—The manufacturer has established a Pregnancy Prevention Program to monitor the outcomes of pregnant women exposed to acitretin. Physicians are encouraged by the manufacturer to report all cases of pregnancy while the patient is taking acitretin or at any time within 3 years after discontinuation to a Roche Pregnancy Prevention Program Specialist by calling 1-800-526-6367 or prescribers may contact the Food and Drug Administration MedWatch Program by calling 1-800-526-6367.

Acitretin is teratogenic in humans and is contraindicated during pregnancy. Unless abstinence is the chosen method or if the patient has undergone a hysterectomy or is postmenopausal, it is recommended that the patient use two forms of effective contraception with at least one being a primary form to prevent pregnancy during treatment and for at least 2 years, according to Canadian labeling, or for at least 3 years, according to U.S. labeling, after acitretin has been discontinued.

A small study of acitretin's effect in eight men showed no changes in sperm concentrations. However, for male patients taking acitretin, it is not known whether residual acitretin in seminal fluid during treatment or after treatment has been discontinued poses a risk to a fetus. The maximum acitretin concentration observed in human seminal fluid from systemic use of acitretin or etretinate was 12.5 nanograms per mL, which would transfer approximately 125 nanograms of acitretin per 10 mL of ejaculate. Of the 13 reported cases with known fetal outcomes in pregnant women whose male partner took acitretin, five infants were normal, five spontaneous abortions occurred, and one fetus had bilateral cystic hygromas and multiple cardiopulmonary malformations. Therefore, although it appears that residual acitretin in seminal fluid poses little, if any, risk to a fetus while a male patient is taking the drug or after it is discontinued, the no-effect limit for teratogenicity is unknown and there is no registry for birth defects associated with acitretin.

The duration of teratogenic risk is not known. Teratogenic risk may continue longer if the mother has ingested alcoholic beverages during acitretin treatment. Whenever an unexpected pregnancy occurs during the time of teratogenic risk, the risk-benefit ratio of continuing the pregnancy must be considered. Major human fetal abnormalities associated with the use of acitretin or its metabolite etretinate include:

- Anophthalmia;
- Heart defects;
- Microcephalus; and
- Skeletal or connective tissue abnormalities, including absence of terminal phalanges, alterations of the skull and cervical vertebra, and malformations of hip, ankle, and forearm; facial dysmorphia; high palate; low-set ears; meningomyelocele; multiple synostoses; and syndactyly.

In one study of pregnant rats given acitretin in doses of 0 (control group), 0.3, 1, and 3 mg/kg a day, no drug-related parental mortality and no signs of parental toxicity were noted; however, in the 3 mg/kg group, fewer offspring survived (24% mortality compared to 8.8% for the control group). In addition, developmental tests showed hair growth, ear opening, auditory startle, pupillary contraction, and memory retention were affected. According to another study in rats, 7.5 mg/kg of acitretin per day was the highest dose that did not show teratogenic effects. Pregnant rats given 7.5 mg/kg of acitretin or higher produced fewer pups and, at doses greater than 7.5 mg/kg, their fetuses developed skeletal adverse effects, such as a cleft palate and abnormally shaped long bones.

In one study of pregnant mice given acitretin in doses of 0 (control group), 1, 3, and 10 mg/kg of acitretin per day, no drug-related maternal mortality and no signs of parental toxicity were noted. No teratogenic effects were seen in fetuses whose mothers received 1 mg/kg of acitretin per day. However, maternal doses of 3 and 10 mg/kg of acitretin per day caused fetal skeletal malformations (cervical, neural arches, and long bones) and soft tissue malformations (exencephaly, cleft palate, unilateral kidney agenesis, and enlarged renal pelvis).

In one study of pregnant rabbits given acitretin in doses of 0 (control group), 0.2, 0.6, and 2 mg/kg of acitretin per day, no drug-related parental mortality and no signs of parental toxicity were noted. No teratogenic effects were seen in fetuses whose mothers received 0.2 mg/kg of acitretin per day. However, maternal doses of 0.6 mg/kg of acitretin per day resulted in a low incidence of cleft palate and brain anomalies in fetuses. Maternal doses of 2 mg/kg of acitretin per day caused teratogenic effects in fetuses, including open eyes, ectrodactyly, spina bifida, ectopia of abdominal viscera, and bilateral apical deficiencies of the distal phalanges of forelimbs and hind limbs.

FDA Pregnancy Category X

Breast-feeding

It is not known if acitretin is distributed into human breast milk. However, there is one prospective case report where acitretin is reported to be distributed into human breast milk. Additionally, studies on lactating rats have shown that etretinate is distributed in the milk. Therefore, nursing mothers should not receive acitretin prior to or during nursing because of the potential for serious adverse reactions in nursing infants.

Pediatrics

Safety and efficacy have not been established. Acitretin is not routinely recommended for use in children because of its potential side/adverse effects, including skeletal hyperostosis and skeletal growth retardation resulting from premature epiphyseal closure and ossification of bones and tendons. Although it is not known that these occurrences are more severe or more frequent in children, there is special concern in pediatric patients because of the implications for growth potential.

If acitretin is used in children with severe forms of keratinization unresponsive to alternative therapies, bone age should be evaluated before treatment initiation and annually during treatment. In children, radiographic studies to determine bone age, including radiographs (x-rays) of the knees, should be done before acitretin therapy is initiated, followed by annual monitoring of bone by scintigraphy (bone scans) and/or radiography. Special attention should be given to any child experiencing pain or limitation of motion.

Geriatrics

Steady-state trough concentrations of acitretin for males 64 to 72 years of age were double compared with those for healthy males 24 to 32 years of age. Although the harmonic mean for the terminal half-life was similar at 53 and 54 hours in these age groups, the range was greater in older patients (37 to 96 hours compared with 39 to 70 hours in the younger adults), potentially making some older patients more sensitive to acitretin's effect.

Reported clinical experience has not identified differences in responses between the elderly and younger patients. However, dose selection should be cautious, usually starting at the low end of the dosing range, reflecting the greater frequency of decreased hepatic, renal, or cardiac function, and of concomitant disease or other drug therapy.

Dental

Acitretin can increase or decrease saliva production. Continuing dryness of the mouth may increase the risk of dental disease, including tooth decay, gum disease, and fungal infection. Having regular dental checkups and using artificial saliva or dissolving sugarless candy or ice in the mouth may help to reduce the incidence of dental problems.

Drug interactions and/or related problems

The following drug interactions and/or related problems have been selected on the basis of their potential clinical significance (possible mechanism in parentheses where appropriate)—not necessarily inclusive (» = major clinical significance):

Note: Combinations containing any of the following medications, depending on the amount present, may also interact with this medication.

» Alcoholic beverages
(concurrent use with acitretin causes increased metabolic conversion of acitretin to etretinate, which accumulates in the body. This increase in accumulation of etretinate increases the potential for teratogenicity in females using acitretin and for side/adverse effects in males and females, since etretinate is eliminated from the body much more slowly than acitretin)

» Cyclosporine
(etretinate has been shown to inhibit the metabolism of cyclosporine and its metabolites by 33 to 45% via cytochrome P450 enzymes; acitretin may have a similar effect. Etretinate has been used therapeutically to reduce the needed dose of cyclosporine; however, some studies have failed to show a clear advantage to this use of etretinate)

» Methotrexate
(increased risk of hepatitis has been reported with concomitant use of methotrexate and etretinate; coadministration of methotrexate and acitretin is **contraindicated**)

» Oral contraceptives, progestin-only
(contraceptive effect of microdosed "minipill" progestins may be diminished with concurrent use of acitretin; it is not known if acitretin reduces the effect of other progestational contraceptives, such as implants or injections. Acitretin has not been shown to reduce the efficacy of estrogen and progestin oral contraceptives)

» Phenytoin
(may reduce the protein binding of phenytoin when given concomitantly with acitretin)

Phototherapy
(significantly lower doses of phototherapy are required with concomitant use because acitretin-induced affects on the stratum corneum can increase risk of erythema)

Retinoids, other, systemic, such as:
» Etretinate

» Isotretinoin
» Tretinoin, oral
Vitamin A and its derivatives, including vitamin supplements containing vitamin A or
Retinoids, topical, such as adapalene and tretinoin
(concurrent use of retinoids or doses of vitamin A larger than the minimum recommended daily allowance (RDA) increases risk of clinical symptoms resembling those of excessive vitamin A intake or toxicity, also called hypervitaminosis A)
Sensitivity to retinoids, vitamin A (also called retinol), or their derivatives
» Tetracycline, oral
(can increase intracranial pressure; concomitant use with acitretin is **contraindicated**)

Laboratory value alterations

The following have been selected on the basis of their potential clinical significance (possible effect in parentheses where appropriate)—not necessarily inclusive (» = major clinical significance).

With physiology/laboratory test values
Alanine aminotransferase (ALT [SGPT]) and
Aspartate aminotransferase (AST [SGOT]) and
Lactate dehydrogenase (LDH)
(serum values increase in about 33% of patients taking acitretin; this effect is considered dose-related and may be transient)
Blood cell counts including:
Bands or
Basophils or
Eosinophils or
Haptoglobin or
Hematocrit or
Hemoglobin or
Lymphocytes or
Monocytes or
Neutrophils or
Platelets or
Red blood cells or
Reticulocytes or
White blood cells
(may be increased or decreased; bands, basophils, eosinophils, and monocytes may be increased)
Cholesterol, total, serum and
Triglyceride, serum
(increased serum total cholesterol concentrations occur in 33% of patients. Although triglyceride levels associated with pancreatitis are rare, hypertriglyceridemia occurs in about 66% of patients. These effects may be reversible upon reduction of dose or upon discontinuation of this medication)
Creatine phosphokinase [CPK]
(may be increased)
Electrolytes including:
Calcium or
Chloride or
Magnesium or
Phosphorus or
Potassium or
Sodium
(may be increased or decreased)
Fasting blood sugar
(may be increased or decreased)
High-density lipoprotein (HDL)
(decreased serum HDL concentrations occur in 40% of patients and are reversible upon dose reduction for many patients or upon discontinuation of this medication)
High occult blood
(value may be decreased)
Iron
(may be increased or decreased)
Liver values including:
Alanine aminotransferase (ALT[SGPT]), serum or
Alkaline phosphatase or
Aspartate aminotransferase (AST[SGOT]), serum or
Bilirubin, total or direct, or
GGTP or
Globulin or
Lactate dehydrogenase (LDH), serum or
Protein, total, or
Serum albumin
(may be increased; serum albumin may be increased or decreased)
Renal and urinary values including:
Acetonuria or
BUN or
Glycosuria or
Hematuria or
Proteinuria or
Red blood cells in urine or
Serum creatinine or
Uric acid or
White blood cells in urine
(may be increased)

Medical considerations/Contraindications

The medical considerations/contraindications included have been selected on the basis of their potential clinical significance (reasons given in parentheses where appropriate)—not necessarily inclusive (» = major clinical significance).

Except under special circumstances, this medication should not be used when the following medical problems exist:
» Hepatic disease, severe or
» Renal disease, severe
(acitretin use is contraindicated in these patients)
(severe renal or hepatic function impairment can delay the elimination of acitretin and its metabolites, and, if a significant amount of drug accumulates, it potentially can make these conditions worse)
(a preliminary study of a single dose of 50 mg of acitretin in patients with end-stage renal failure showed that the pharmacokinetics of acitretin remain unaltered; however, there is concern that if acitretin is metabolized to etretinate, it may accumulate in fat tissues and prolong drug elimination)
» Hyperlipidemia, intractable, or history of or
» Pancreatitis
(66% of patients receiving acitretin in the clinical trials experienced an elevation in serum triglycerides 33% of patients experienced elevated serum cholesterol, and 40% of patients developed a decrease in high-density lipoproteins; these trends reversed upon treatment discontinuation. If serum lipid levels cannot be controlled, acitretin treatment should be withdrawn to avoid increasing the patient's risk of cardiovascular disease and pancreatitis. Patients likely to develop intractable hyperlipidemia include those with diabetes mellitus, obesity, increased alcohol intake, or familial history of these conditions)
» Hypersensitivity to acitretin or any of its components or to other retinoids
(acitretin use contraindicated in these patients)
» Hypervitaminosis A, or history of
(this condition may be exacerbated with use of acitretin)

Risk-benefit should be considered when the following medical problems exist:
Diabetes mellitus, type 1 or 2 or
Pancreatitis, history of
(acitretin may mildly increase or decrease glucose tolerance or increase serum lipid levels in these patients; pancreatitis may be exacerbated in patients with a history of pancreatitis; some patients with diabetes mellitus may require dose adjustment in their diabetes therapy regimens)

Patient monitoring

The following may be especially important in patient monitoring (other tests may be warranted in some patients, depending on condition; » = major clinical significance):

Blood sugar
(patients receiving retinoids have experienced problems with blood sugar control; monitor very carefully in diabetic patients)
Bone-age determinations or
Bone radiography (x-rays), including x-rays of the knees
(recommended in children prior to therapy and yearly during therapy to determine effects on epiphyseal centers and as recommended by physician for older patients to evaluate the possibility of hyperostosis during long-term or recurrent courses of acitretin therapy. Some physicians recommend baseline evaluation for older patients if long-term therapy is anticipated and repeat bone tests only if patient becomes symptomatic)
» Contraceptive counseling and
» Pregnancy testing
(within 1 week before initiating treatment with acitretin, a negative pregnancy test should be obtained after a normal menstrual cycle has been established. Then acitretin treatment should be initiated on Day 2 or 3 of the menstrual cycle. Regularly testing for possible pregnancy is recommended, as well as counseling on importance

of beginning contraception 1 month before treatment initiation and continuing the contraception counseling for as long as needed or appropriate; these measures should include patients with a history of infertility or tubal ligation)

» Hepatic function tests
(recommended before initiation, every 1 to 2 weeks during the first 2 months after treatment initiation, and then every 3 months during treatment or as clinically indicated. Weekly checking is recommended if liver test results are abnormal and medication should be withdrawn if results worsen. If liver test results do not return to normal after withdrawal of acitretin treatment, continued monitoring for at least 3 months is advised)

» Lipoprotein profile, serum
(determinations recommended in patients under fasting conditions prior to therapy and at 1- to 2-week intervals during therapy until the lipid response is established, usually within 4 to 8 weeks. Following consumption of alcohol, 36 hours should elapse before blood lipid determination)
(restricting dietary fat and alcohol intake and, when appropriate, lowering body weight are ways that patients can control significant serum concentration increases in triglycerides and decreases in high-density lipoproteins; discontinuation of retinoid should be considered if abnormal lipid or lipoprotein serum concentrations persist)

Monitoring etretinate concentrations, plasma
(some clinicians monitor plasma concentrations of etretinate, an active metabolite, to help assess patients taking acitretin and advise them in planning a future pregnancy; however, most studies have found that the absence of etretinate in plasma does not predict its absence in tissues and most clinicians do not monitor etretinate concentrations, even in cases of pregnancy)

Ophthalmologic examinations
(regular monitoring may be indicated since 29% of patients taking acitretin experience medication-related ophthalmic effects from acitretin; medication should be discontinued and neurological diagnosis and care considered for patients developing early symptoms of pseudotumor cerebri [benign intracranial hypertension], such as severe or continuing headache, nausea and vomiting, or blurred vision or other changes in vision. Also, medication should be discontinued and ophthalmologic examination should be done when any changes in vision occur)

Side/Adverse Effects

The following side/adverse effects have been selected on the basis of their potential clinical significance (possible signs and symptoms in parentheses where appropriate)—not necessarily inclusive:

Those indicating need for medical attention

Incidence more frequent

Anorexia (loss of appetite; weight loss); ***arthralgia; hypertonia; myalgia; or spinal hyperostosis*** (back pain; bone or joint pain; difficulty in moving or walking; stiff, painful muscles)—progression of existing lesions; ***headache; nausea; vomiting***

Incidence less frequent

Ophthalmologic effects, including blepharitis; conjunctivitis; eye irritation; photophobia; or other visual problems (blurred vision; eye pain; loss of eyebrows or lashes; redness or swelling of the eyelid; redness of the eyes; sensitivity of eyes to light; watery eyes); ***paronychia*** (loosening of the fingernails; redness or soreness around fingernails)

Incidence rare

Bleeding time increased; chest pain; Dermatologic effects, such as abnormal skin odor; dermatitis; or psoriasiform rash (skin irritation or rash, including rash that looks like psoriasis); ***fissuring; hypertrophy; infection; or ulceration of skin*** (cracking of skin; redness of skin); ***otitis externa*** (itchy or painful ears); ***paresthesia*** (abnormal sensation of burning or stinging of skin); ***pyogenic granuloma; or purpura*** (small spots in skin where bleeding occurred); ***hemorrhage*** (bleeding gums; coughing up blood; difficulty in breathing or swallowing; dizziness; headache; increased menstrual flow; or vaginal bleeding; nosebleeds; paralysis; prolonged bleeding from cuts; red or dark brown urine; red or black, tarry stools; shortness of breath); ***hepatic function abnormal l*** (abdominal or stomach pain; chills; light-colored stools; dark urine; diarrhea; dizziness; fever; headache; itching; loss of appetite; nausea; rash; unpleasant breath odor; unusual tiredness or weakness; vomiting of blood; yellow eyes or skin); ***hepatitis; jaundice; or pancreatitis*** (abdominal pain; darkened urine; yellowing of the skin or eyes); ***influenza-like symptoms; laryngitis; or pharyngitis*** (coughing; hoarseness; trouble in speaking); ***ophthalmologic effects, such as cortical, nuclear, and posterior subcapsular cataracts, pannus, or subepithelial corneal lesions*** (eye pain; trouble in seeing); ***decreased night vision*** (decreased vision after sunset and before sunrise); ***pseudotumor cerebri*** (blurred or double vision; continuing severe headache, nausea, and vomiting); ***or recurring stye*** (sore on the edge of the eyelid); ***peripheral ischemia*** (abdominal pain; chest pain; itching of skin; numbness and tingling of fingers, toes, or face; pain in arms, legs, or lower back; pale or cold hands or feet; weakness in legs); ***vulvovaginitis*** (thick, white, curd-like vaginal discharge; vaginal itching or irritation)—due to *Candida albicans*

Incidence not determined—Observed during clinical practice, estimates of frequency cannot be determined

Acute myocardial infarction (chest pain or discomfort, pain or discomfort in arms, jaw, back or neck, shortness of breath, nausea, sweating, vomiting); ***aggressive feelings*** (attack, assault, force); ***peripheral neuropathy*** (burning, numbness, tingling, or painful sensations, weakness in arms, hands, legs, or feet, unsteadiness or awkwardness)—condition improved with discontinuation of the drug; ***self-injurious behavior*** (doing things to injure oneself); ***stroke*** (confusion, difficulty in speaking, slow speech, inability to speak, inability to move arms, legs, or facial muscles, double vision, headache); ***suicidal thoughts*** (thoughts of killing oneself); ***thromboembolism*** (pain in chest, groin, or legs, especially the calves, difficulty breathing, severe, sudden headache slurred speech, sudden, unexplained shortness of breath sudden loss of coordination, sudden, severe weakness or numbness in arm or leg, vision changes)

Those indicating need for medical attention only if they continue or are bothersome

Incidence more frequent

Abdominal pain; alopecia (loss of hair)—may be reversible after treatment discontinuation; ***appetite increased; arthritis*** (pain, swelling, or redness in joints; muscle pain or stiffness; difficulty in moving); ***arthrosis*** (degenerative disease of the joint); ***dermatologic effects, such as ceruminosis*** (increased amount of ear wax); ***chapped lips or cheilitis*** (chapped, red, or swollen lips); ***dry, irritated mucous membranes of nose or rhinitis*** (dry or runny nose; nosebleeds); ***pruritus*** (itching skin); ***scaling and peeling of eyelids, fingertips, palms, or soles of feet; and sticky skin; difficulty in wearing contact lenses; dry mouth; earache; edema*** (swelling); ***epistaxis*** (bloody nose); ***erythematous rash*** (redness of skin); ***flushing*** (feeling of warmth redness of the face, neck, arms and occasionally, upper chest); ***gingivitis or stomatitis*** (irritation in mouth or swollen gums; mouth ulcers); ***hot flashes; hyperesthesia*** (increased sensitivity to pain, increased sensitivity to touch, tingling in the hands and feet); ***hypertonia*** (excessive muscle tone; muscle tension or tightness; muscle stiffness); ***insomnia*** (sleeplessness; trouble sleeping; unable to sleep); ***osteodynia*** (bone pain); ***photosensitivity*** (increased ability to sunburn); ***skin atrophy*** (thinning of skin with easy bruising); ***taste perversion*** (change in taste; bad, unusual or unpleasant (after)taste); ***tinnitus*** (continuing ringing or buzzing or other unexplained noise in ears; hearing loss); ***tongue disorder*** (tongue irritation); ***xerophthalmia*** (dryness of eyes)—23%; ***unusual thirst***

Incidence less frequent

Breast pain; Constipation; diarrhea; dizziness; dyspepsia (acid or sour stomach; belching; heartburn; indigestion; stomach discomfort upset or pain;); ***eczema*** (skin rash encrusted, scaly and oozing); ***fever*** (elevated body temperature); ***fatigue; herpes simplex*** (burning or stinging of skin; painful cold sores or blisters on lips, nose, eyes, or genitals); ***hypertrichosis*** (increased hair growth on forehead, back, arms, and legs); ***increased sweating; malaise*** (general feeling of discomfort or illness; unusual tiredness or weakness); ***moniliasis*** (sore mouth or tongue; white patches in mouth and/or on tongue); ***otitis media*** (earache; redness or swelling in ear); ***urticaria*** (hives or welts; itching; redness of skin; skin rash); ***vaginitis, atrophic*** (itching of the vagina or genital area; pain during sexual intercourse; thick, white vaginal discharge with no odor or with a mild odor); ***verrucae***

Incidence not determined—Observed during clinical practice, estimates of frequency cannot be determined

Myopathy (muscular pain, tenderness, wasting or weakness)—improved with discontinuation of drug; ***nail fragility*** (cracking fingernails, fingernails break easily)

Overdose

For more information on the management of overdose or unintentional ingestion, **contact a Poison Control Center** (see *Poison Control Center Listing*).

Clinical effects of overdose

The following effects have been selected on the basis of their potential clinical significance (possible signs and symptoms in parentheses where appropriate)—not necessarily inclusive:

Acute and/or chronic
Headache; vertigo (dizziness or lightheadedness; feeling of constant movement of self or surroundings, sensation of spinning)

Treatment of overdose

Treatment is symptomatic and supportive.

To decrease absorption—Evacuation of stomach should be considered within 2 hours of ingestion of acute overdose. Caution is advised when selecting a method of evacuation due to the risk of vomiting associated with acitretin overdose.Medication should be discontinued in patients with symptoms of overdose who were given therapeutic doses.

Monitoring—Monitor for increased intracranial pressure. All female patients of childbearing potential must have a pregnancy test at time of overdose and be counseled as per the precautions and contraindications regarding birth defects and contraceptive use for at least 3 years' duration after the overdose.

Supportive care—Patients in whom intentional overdose is confirmed or suspected should be referred for psychiatric consultation.

Patient Consultation

As an aid to patient consultation, refer to *Advice for the Patient, Acitretin (Systemic)*.

In providing consultation, consider emphasizing the following selected information (» = major clinical significance):

Before using this medication

» Conditions affecting use, especially:

Hypersensitivity to acitretin, etretinate, isotretinoin, tretinoin, or vitamin A or its derivatives

Pregnancy—Contraindicated for use during pregnancy; can cause birth defects of skeletal, heart, and connective tissue. Pregnancy is not recommended for at least 2 or 3 years after discontinuation of acitretin. Use of alcohol and alcohol products is prohibited; recommended waiting period may be longer if alcohol is consumed during treatment. Also, for women of childbearing potential, two effective forms of birth control should be used at least 1 month prior to initiating acitretin therapy, and continued for at least 2 to 3 years after acitretin therapy is stopped

Acitretin is distributed in the semen of male patients taking acitretin. Amount transferred to the female partner is 125 nanograms of acitretin per 10 mL of ejaculate.

FDA Pregnancy Category X

Breast-feeding—It is not known whether this drug is distributed into human breast milk. Because of the potential for adverse effects, nursing mothers should not receive acitretin prior to or during nursing.

Use in children—Safety and efficacy not established; not routinely recommended for use in children; children may be more sensitive to medication; special concern should be given to the implications for growth potential due to skeletal side effects

Use in the elderly—Geriatric patients may be more sensitive to medication since some patients, when compared to younger adults, may have higher acitretin serum concentrations resulting from slower elimination; dose selection should be cautious

Other medications, especially alcoholic beverages; cyclosporine; methotrexate; phenytoin; progestin-only oral contraceptives; retinoids, other (systemic and topical); or tetracyclines

Other medical problems, especially intractable hyperlipidemia (or history of), pancreatitis, hypersensitivity to acitretin or any of its components or other retinoid, hypervitaminosis A (or history of), severe hepatic disease, or severe renal disease

Proper use of this medication

» Reading accompanying patient information before using this medication

» Missed dose: Taking acitretin dose with a main meal or with a glass of milk

» For women—Special precautions are needed before beginning treatment to ensure that the patient is not pregnant, such as using an effective form of birth control for 30 days before initiating treatment, obtaining a negative pregnancy test after a normal menstrual period pattern has been established and within 1 week before initiating treatment, then starting medication on Day 2 or 3 of menstrual period. Women of reproductive age or potential are required to use two forms of contraception during treatment, beginning at least 1 month before initiation of treatment with acitretin. These women are required to continue contraception for an indeterminate time after medication is discontinued, for at least 2 years per Canadian labeling or for at least 3 years per U.S. labeling

» Importance of not sharing medication with anyone else because of the risk of birth defects and other serious side effects.

» Importance of checking with your doctor before taking any medications including vitamins, herbal products, or over-the-counter (OTC) medicines. Some of these medicines or nutritional supplements (e.g., St. John's wort) may make your birth control pills not work.

» Proper dosing

Missed dose: Taking as soon as possible; not taking if almost time for next dose; not doubling doses.

» Proper storage

Precautions while using this medication

» Regular visits to physician to check progress during therapy and for up to 2 years after treatment is discontinued, especially in women wanting to become pregnant, children, and the elderly

» Checking with physician if skin condition does not improve within 8 to 12 weeks; expecting that skin irritation may occur or skin condition may worsen within the first several weeks of treatment but will lessen in severity with continued use

» Importance of not drinking alcoholic beverages or products containing alcohol during treatment and for 2 months after treatment discontinuation. Teratogenic risk may continue for longer periods of time if alcohol was consumed during acitretin treatment

» Importance of not donating blood for transfusion purposes during treatment and for at least 2 or 3 years after discontinuing treatment with acitretin as specified by physician

» Understanding that vision impairment can occur, including sudden night vision impairment, photophobia, blurred vision, or dryness of eyes. Vision problems can make driving a car or operating machinery dangerous

Checking with physician anytime vision problems occur; wearing contact lenses may be uncomfortable

» Understanding that mood or behavior problems can occur, including having aggressive feelings or thought of self-harm; check with you doctor right away if unusual mood or behavior problems occur.

Understanding that dental problems can occur resulting from dryness of mouth and may increase dental disease, including tooth decay, gum disease, and fungus infections; regular dental appointments are needed and use of sugarless candy or saliva substitute or melting ice in mouth may be necessary to lessen dental problems

Minimizing exposure of skin to wind, cold temperatures, and sunlight, including on cloudy days, to avoid sunburn, dryness, or irritation, especially during the first months of treatment. Also, not using artificial sunlight or sunlamp, unless directed otherwise by physician

Using sunscreen preparations (minimum sun protection factor [SPF] of 15) and wearing protective clothing over exposed areas and UV-blocking sunglasses when sunlight exposure cannot be avoided; avoiding direct sunlight between 10 a.m. and 3 p.m.; checking with physician at any time skin becomes too dry or irritated; choosing proper skin products to reduce skin dryness or irritation

Either checking with health care professional before using or avoiding use of topical acne or skin products containing a peeling agent (benzoyl peroxide, resorcinol, salicylic acid, or sulfur), irritating hair products (permanents or hair removal products), sun-sensitizing skin products (including products containing limes or spices), alcohol-containing skin products, or drying or abrasive skin products (some cosmetics, soaps, or skin cleansers)

Not using vitamin A or vitamin A-containing supplement in doses that exceed the minimum recommended daily allowances (RDA)

Side/adverse effects

Signs of potential side effects, especially arthralgia, hypertonia, myalgia, or spinal hyperostosis; headache; nausea; vomiting; ophthalmologic effects, including blepharitis, conjunctivitis, eye irritation, photophobia, or other visual problems; paronychia; dermatologic effects, such as abnormal skin odor, dermatitis or psoriasiform rash, fissuring, hypertrophy, infection, or ulceration of skin, otitis externa, paresthesia, pyogenic granuloma, or purpura; hepatitis, jaundice, or pancreatitis; influenza-like symptoms, laryngitis, or pharyngitis; ophthalmologic effects such as cortical, nuclear, and posterior subcapsular cataracts, pannus, or subepithelial corneal lesions, decreased night vision, pseudotumor cerebri, or recurring stye; vulvovaginitis

Signs of potential side effects observed during clinical practice, especially, acute myocardial infarction, aggressive feelings, peripheral neuropathy, self-injurious behavior, stroke, suicidal thoughts, and thromboembolism

General Dosing Information

Acitretin should be prescribed only by those who have special competence in the diagnosis and treatment of severe psoriasis, are experienced in the use of systemic retinoids, and understand the risk of teratogenicity

Females of childbearing potential must sign a patient agreement/informed consent that contains warnings about the risk of potential birth defects if the fetus is exposed to acitretin, about contraceptive failure, and about the fact that they must not ingest beverages or products containing ethanol while taking acitretin and for 2 months after acitretin treatment has been discontinued. In addition, *all patients* must receive an acitretin medication guide each time acitretin is dispensed, as required by law

Some medications may decrease effectiveness of birth control products. St. John's Wort, an over-the-counter herbal supplement for depression, should not be used concomitantly with hormonal contraceptives based on reports of breakthrough bleeding and pregnancies. Prescribers should consult the package insert of medication administered concomitantly with hormonal contraceptives and/or see *Estrogens and Progestins Oral Contraceptives (Systemic)* for specific drug interactions with hormonal contraceptives.

Patients previously taking etretinate should continue to follow the contraception recommendations for etretinate.

There is a significant interpatient variation in absorption and metabolism of acitretin, of treatment efficacy, ability to tolerate treatment, and progress of psoriasis or keratinization condition. The dosage of acitretin should be individualized to achieve the maximal therapeutic response possible with a tolerable level of side effects.

Transient worsening of psoriasis commonly occurs on initiation of acitretin treatment. The full effect of acitretin may take 2 to 3 months, and its action can continue after treatment is discontinued. Treatment should be discontinued when psoriatic lesions are sufficiently resolved, and treatment reinstituted at initiation doses for relapses as needed.

Patients unresponsive to treatment with acitretin may be responsive to etretinate. When switching from etretinate to acitretin, a 20% reduction is recommended if the etretinate dose is greater than 0.75 mg per kg of body weight (mg/kg) a day or if side effects are dose-limiting. Otherwise the same dose can be used.

Other treatments that have been added to a patient's regimen after 1 or 2 months of acitretin monotherapy include ultraviolet B (UVB) light, PUVA (8-methoxypsoralen plus ultraviolet A [UVA] light), bath PUVA (trimethylpsoralen bath plus UVA), topical corticosteroids, or anthralin ointments. Dose reduction of acitretin may be required before beginning these other treatments.

Diet/Nutrition

Take with main meal of the day or with milk. Patient should follow a cholesterol-free diet for best results to lower serum cholesterol.

Oral Dosage Forms

Note: Bracketed uses in the Dosage Forms section refer to categories of use and/or indications that are not included in U.S. product labeling.

ACITRETIN CAPSULES

Usual adult dose

Antipsoriatic (systemic)—

Initial: Oral, 25 to 50 mg a day, given as a single dose with the main meal.

Maintenance: Oral, 25 to 50 mg a day, dependent upon an individual patient's response to initial treatment.

Note: Lower doses of acitretin are used when initiating combination therapy in the treatment of severe plaque psoriasis.

[Keratinization stabilizer (systemic)]—

Initial: Oral, 25 mg a day; dose may be increased up to 75 mg a day after four weeks, if needed and tolerated.

Maintenance: Oral, 10 to 50 mg a day.

Usual pediatric dose

Antipsoriatic—

Safety and efficacy have not been established.

[Keratinization stabilizer (systemic)]—

Initial: Oral, 0.5 mg per kg of body weight once a day. May be increased to 1 mg per kg a day for limited periods of time as needed, not to exceed a total dose of 35 mg a day.

Maintenance: Oral, 20 mg or lower once a day for prolonged treatment.

Usual pediatric prescribing limits

Oral, 35 mg a day.

Usual geriatric dose

See *Usual adult dose*.

Strength(s) usually available

U.S.—

10 mg (Rx) [*Soriatane* (microcrystalline cellulose; sodium ascorbate; gelatin; black monogramming ink; maltodextrin (a mixture of polysaccharides))].

25 mg (Rx) [*Soriatane* (microcrystalline cellulose; sodium ascorbate; gelatin; black monogramming ink; maltodextrin (a mixture of polysaccharides))].

Canada—

10 mg (Rx) [*Soriatane*].

25 mg (Rx) [*Soriatane* (gelatin; maltodextrin; microcrystalline cellulose; sodium ascorbate; yellow, black and red iron oxide; titanium dioxide)].

Packaging and storage

Store between 15 and 25 °C (59 and 77 °F), unless otherwise specified by manufacturer. Protect from light. Keep in a tightly closed container. Avoid exposure to high temperatures and humidity after the bottle is opened

Auxiliary labeling

- Do not take this medication if you become pregnant.
- Take with food.
- Do not drink alcoholic beverages when taking this medication.
- Avoid extended exposure to sunlight or tanning beds while taking this drug. Severe burns may result.
- May cause dizziness or blurred vision.
- This medication may impair your ability to drive or operate machinery. Use care until you become familiar with its effects.
- Ask your doctor or pharmacist before using nonprescription drugs.
- Vitamin A supplements should not be taken with this medication.
- Dry mouth may occur when taking this medication.
- Keep out of reach of children.
- Caution: Federal law prohibits the transfer of this drug to any person other than the patient for whom it was prescribed.

Note

Include patient directions when dispensing.

Counsel female patients about using two forms of birth control 1 month before starting treatment, during treatment, and for at least 2 years, according to Canadian labeling, or for at least 3 years, according to U.S. labeling, after discontinuing treatment.

Counsel male and female patients:

- Not to donate blood for transfusion during treatment and for at least 2 years, according to Canadian labeling, or for at least 3 years, according to U.S. labeling, after discontinuing treatment.
- Not to drink alcoholic beverages during treatment and for at least 2 months after discontinuing treatment.
- To be aware that sudden night vision inadequacies can occur, which can be hazardous when operating a vehicle.
- To be advised that decreased tolerance to contact lenses may occur during the treatment period and sometimes after treatment has stopped.

Selected Bibliography

Geiger JM, Saurat JH. Acitretin and etretinate. How and when they should be used. Dermatol Clin 1993 Jan; 11(1): 117-29.

Product Information: Soriatane®, acitretin. Roche Laboratories, Nutley, NJ, (PI revised 04/2003) reviewed 03/2004.

Revised: 10/26/2004
Developed: 04/24/1998

ACYCLOVIR Systemic

INN: Aciclovir

VA CLASSIFICATION (Primary): AM820

Commonly used brand name(s): *Alti-Acyclovir; Avirax; Zovirax; Zovirax Wellstat Pac; Zovirax Zostab Pac.*

Note: For a listing of dosage forms and brand names by country availability, see *Dosage Forms* section(s).

Category

Antiviral (systemic).

Indications

Note: Bracketed information in the *Indications* section refers to uses that are not included in U.S. product labeling.

General Considerations

Acyclovir is a synthetic purine analog that has antiviral activity against herpes simplex virus (HSV-1 and HSV-2) and varicella-zoster virus (VZV). Resistance of HSV and VZV to acyclovir has been reported to develop with prolonged treatment or repeated therapy with acyclovir in severely immunocompromised patients. Resistance may occasionally develop as quickly as within a few weeks of beginning treatment. If lesions due to herpes simplex virus fail to respond to acyclovir therapy, especially with continued viral shedding, viral isolates should be tested for susceptibility to acyclovir.

This resistance of HSV and VZV to antiviral nucleoside analogs can result from qualitative or quantitative changes in the viral thymidine kinase (TK) or deoxyribonucleic acid (DNA) polymerase. Most of the acyclovir-resistant mutants isolated from immunocompromised patients, such as those from patients with advanced human immunodeficiency virus (HIV) infections, have been found to be TK-deficient mutants; however, other mutants involving the viral TK gene (TK-partial and TK-altered) and DNA polymerase also have been isolated. TK-negative mutants of HSV and VZV may cause severe disease in infants and immunocompromised adults.

Accepted

Herpes genitalis, initial episode (treatment)—Oral acyclovir is indicated in the treatment of initial episodes of genital herpes infection in immunocompetent and immunocompromised patients. Parenteral acyclovir is indicated in the treatment of severe initial episodes of genital herpes infection in immunocompetent patients and in patients who are unable to take (or absorb) oral acyclovir.

Herpes genitalis, recurrent episodes (treatment)—Oral acyclovir is indicated in the treatment of frequently recurrent (≥ 6 episodes per year) or intermittent episodes of genital herpes infection in immunocompetent and immunocompromised patients.

Herpes simplex (treatment)—Parenteral [and oral][1] acyclovir are indicated in the treatment of initial and recurrent mucocutaneous herpes simplex (HSV-1 and HSV-2) infections in immunocompromised patients.

Herpes simplex, neonatal infection (treatment)[1]—Parenteral acyclovir is indicated in the treatment of neonatal herpes simplex virus infections.

Herpes simplex encephalitis (treatment)[1]—Parenteral acyclovir is indicated in the treatment of herpes simplex encephalitis in immunocompetent patients.

Herpes zoster (treatment)—Oral acyclovir is indicated in the treatment of herpes zoster infections (shingles) caused by varicella-zoster virus (VZV) in any adult patient with herpes zoster. Therapy is most effective when started within 48 hours of the onset of rash. Parenteral acyclovir is indicated in the treatment of herpes zoster infections (shingles) caused by VZV in immunocompromised patients [and disseminated herpes zoster in immunocompetent patients].

Varicella (treatment)—Oral acyclovir is indicated in the treatment of varicella infections (chickenpox) in immunocompetent patients when started within 24 hours of the onset of a typical chickenpox rash. [Parenteral acyclovir is used in the treatment of varicella infections (chickenpox) caused by VZV in immunocompromised patients].[1]

Although acyclovir is indicated for the treatment of varicella infections in immunocompetent patients, the American Academy of Pediatrics does not recommend its use for the treatment of uncomplicated chickenpox in healthy children. It is recommended for certain groups at increased risk of severe varicella or its complications, such as otherwise healthy, nonpregnant persons 13 years of age or older; children older than 12 months of age with a chronic cutaneous or pulmonary disorder; and children receiving short, intermittent, or aerosolized courses of corticosteroids. If possible, steroids should be discontinued after known exposure to varicella.

[Herpes simplex (prophylaxis)][1]—Parenteral and oral acyclovir are used in the prophylaxis of herpes simplex virus (HSV) infections in patients who are immunocompromised, including transplant patients receiving immunosuppressant therapy, human immunodeficiency virus (HIV)-infected patients, and patients receiving chemotherapy.

[Herpes zoster (prophylaxis)][1]—Oral acyclovir is used in the prophylaxis of herpes zoster infections (shingles) caused by VZV, after an initial period of treatment with parenteral acyclovir, in any immunocompromised patient, including transplant patients receiving immunosuppressant therapy, HIV-infected patients, and patients receiving chemotherapy.

[Herpes zoster ophthalmicus (treatment)][1]—Oral and parenteral acyclovir are indicated in the treatment of herpes zoster ophthalmicus.

[1]Not included in Canadian product labeling.

Pharmacology/Pharmacokinetics

Physicochemical characteristics

Molecular weight—
- Acyclovir: 225.21.
- Acyclovir sodium: 247.19.

pH—Reconstituted acyclovir (50 mg per mL): Approximately 11.

Mechanism of action/Effect

Acyclovir is a synthetic purine nucleoside analog that possesses *in vitro* and *in vivo* inhibitory activity against herpes virus types HSV-1, HSV-2, and VZV. The inhibitory activity of acyclovir is highly selective due to its affinity for the enzyme thymidine kinase encoded by HSV and VZV. *In vitro*, acyclovir exhibits stronger antiviral activity against HSV-1, followed by HSV-2 and VZV in decreasing order of potency. The reason for greater antiviral activity against HSV compared to that against VZV is more efficient phosphorylation of acyclovir by HSV thymidine kinase.

Acyclovir is converted to the nucleotide analog acyclovir monophosphate by the viral thymidine kinases of herpes simplex virus (HSV-1 and HSV-2) and varicella-zoster virus (VZV). Acyclovir monophosphate is converted to the diphosphate by cellular guanylate kinase and to the triphosphate by a number of cellular enzymes. The antiviral activity of acyclovir is achieved by the prevention of viral DNA replication by acyclovir triphosphate. Viral DNA replication is prevented through three mechanisms: competitive inhibition of viral DNA polymerase, incorporation into and termination of the growing viral DNA chain, and inactivation of viral DNA polymerase.

Absorption

Oral—Bioavailability 10 to 20%; the bioavailability decreases with increasing dose. Poorly absorbed from the gastrointestinal tract. Not significantly affected by food.

Distribution

Widely distributed into tissues and body fluids, including brain, kidneys, lungs, liver, aqueous humor, tears, intestines, muscle, spleen, breast milk, uterus, vaginal mucosa, vaginal secretions, semen, amniotic fluid, cerebrospinal fluid (CSF), and herpetic vesicular fluid. Highest concentrations are found in kidneys, liver, and intestines. CSF concentrations are approximately 50% of plasma concentrations. Crosses the placenta, also.

Vol_D (steady state)—
- Adults: Approximately 48 liters (L) per square meter of body surface area (m^2) (range, 37 to 57 L per m^2).
- Children and adolescents (1 to 18 years old): Approximately 45 L per m^2.
- Neonates (0 to 28 daysold): Approximately 28 L per m^2 (range, 24 to 30 L per m^2).
- End-stage renal disease: Approximately 41 L per m^2.

Protein binding

Low (9 to 33%).

Biotransformation

Hepatic; the only major urinary metabolite that has been detected is 9-carboxymethoxymethylguanine, which accounts for up to 14.1% of the acyclovir dose in patients who have normal renal function. This metabolite has no known antiviral activity.

Half-life

Elimination of parenteral acyclovir—
- Adults with normal renal function: Approximately 2.5 hours.
- Children (29 days to 12 years old): Approximately 2.3 hours.
- Neonates (0 to 28 daysold): Approximately 3.8 hours.
- Adults with renal function impairment:

Creatinine clearance (mL/min)/(mL/sec)	Half-life (hr)
> 80/1.33	2.5
50–80/0.83–1.33	3
15–50/0.25–0.83	3.5
Anuric	19.5
During hemodialysis	5.7
Continuous ambulatory peritoneal dialysis	14–18

Oral acyclovir—2.5 to 3.3 hours.

Time to peak serum concentration

Intravenous—End of infusion (approximately 1 hour).
Oral—1.7 hours.

Mean peak serum concentration (steady-state)

Oral—
- Adults:
  - 200 mg every 4 hours—0.83 mcg/mL (3.68 micromoles/L).
  - 400 mg every 4 hours—1.2 mcg/mL (5.3 micromoles/L).
  - 800 mg every 4 hours—1.6 mcg/mL (6.9 micromoles/L).

Intravenous—
Adults:
5 mg per kg (over 1 hour) every 8 hours—9.8 mcg/mL (43.5 micromoles/L).
10 mg per kg (over 1 hour) every 8 hours—22.9 mcg/mL (101.7 micromoles/L).
Children (1 to 18 years old):
250 mg per m² (over 1 hour) every 8 hours—10.3 mcg/mL (45.8 micromoles/L).
500 mg per m² (over 1 hour) every 8 hours—20.7 mcg/mL (91.9 micromoles/L).
Neonates (0 to 28 days old):
5 mg per kg (over 1 hour) every 8 hours—6.8 mcg/mL (30 micromoles/L).
10 mg per kg (over 1 hour) every 8 hours—13.8 mcg/mL (61.2 micromoles/L).

Elimination

Renal—
Excreted by both glomerular filtration and tubular secretion.
Oral: Approximately 14% of total dose excreted unchanged in urine.
Intravenous: Approximately 62 to 91% excreted unchanged in urine.
Fecal—
Insignificant amounts (< 2%).
Lungs—
Trace amounts in exhaled CO_2.
Dialysis—
Hemodialysis: A single 6-hour period of hemodialysis reduces plasma acyclovir concentrations by approximately 60%.
Peritoneal dialysis: Peritoneal dialysis does not substantially alter acyclovir clearance.

Precautions to Consider

Cross-sensitivity and/or related problems

Patients allergic to valacyclovir may also be allergic to acyclovir.

Tumorigenicity

Lifetime bioassays in rats and mice given daily doses of up to 450 mg per kg of body weight (mg/kg) by gavage did not increase the incidence of tumors or shorten the latency of tumor formation. Maximum plasma concentrations were three to six times the human plasma concentration in the mouse bioassay and one to two times the human plasma concentration in the rat bioassay. However, one of two *in vitro* cell transformation assays resulted in morphologically transformed cells that formed tumors when inoculated into immunosuppressed, syngeneic, weanling mice.

Mutagenicity

Acyclovir has been shown to be mutagenic in some *in vitro* cytogenetic assay systems (human lymphocytes and one mouse lymphoma cell line). However, acyclovir was not mutagenic in other *in vitro* cytogenetic assay systems (three Chinese hamster ovary cell lines and two mouse lymphoma cell lines) or in four microbial assays. Acyclovir was clastogenic in Chinese hamster cells at 380 to 760 times the human plasma concentration. No mutagenicity was reported in a dominant lethal study in mice (36 to 73 times the human plasma concentration).

Pregnancy/Reproduction

Fertility—Impairment of spermatogenesis, sperm motility, or morphology has not been documented in humans given the recommended doses of acyclovir.

High doses of parenteral acyclovir have caused testicular atrophy in rats and dogs. However, no testicular abnormalities were observed in dogs given intravenous acyclovir at doses of 50 mg/kg per day for 1 month (resulting in plasma concentrations one to three times the human plasma concentration) or in dogs given oral acyclovir at doses of 60 mg/kg per day for 1 year (resulting in plasma concentrations 6 to 12 times the human plasma concentration). Studies in mice given oral doses of 450 mg/kg per day or rats given subcutaneous doses of 25 mg/kg per day have shown that acyclovir does not impair fertility or reproduction. Studies in female rats and rabbits given acyclovir subcutaneously subsequent to mating have shown a significant decrease in implantation efficiency, but no decrease in litter size, at doses of 50 mg/kg per day.

Pregnancy—Acyclovir crosses the placenta. Acyclovir has been used in all stages of pregnancy, and no adverse fetal effects have been reported. One small, controlled study found that pre-partum treatment of women with recurrent genital herpes helped prevent symptomatic recurrences and viral shedding at the time of delivery, reducing the risk of the infant being exposed to the virus. Also, a prospective epidemiological registry of acyclovir was established in 1984 and completed in 1999. The registry had 756 outcomes in 749 women exposed to systemic acyclovir during the first trimester of pregnancy. The occurrence rate of birth defects approximates the rate found in the general population. However, the small size of the registry is insufficient to evaluate the risk of less common defects or to permit reliable and definitive conclusions regarding the safety of acyclovir use in pregnant women and their developing fetuses. Adequate and well-controlled studies in humans have not been done. During pregnancy, acyclovir should be used only if the potential benefit to the mother outweighs the potential risk to the fetus.

Acyclovir was not teratogenic in mice given oral doses of 450 mg/kg per day (resulting in plasma concentrations 9 to 18 times the human plasma concentration), rabbits given subcutaneous or intravenous doses of 50 mg/kg per day (resulting in plasma concentrations 16 to 106 times the human plasma concentration), or rats given subcutaneous doses of 50 mg/kg per day (resulting in plasma concentrations 11 to 22 times the human plasma concentration).

FDA Pregnancy Category B.

Breast-feeding

Acyclovir was distributed into the breast milk of two patients at concentrations from 0.6 to 4.1 times the corresponding plasma concentration. These concentrations would potentially expose the nursing infant to a dose as high as 0.3 mg/kg per day. A very small amount of acyclovir has been measured in one nursing infant's urine; no toxicity was observed.

Pediatrics

Limited data are available about the use of oral acyclovir in children younger than 2 years of age. However, no unusual toxicity or pediatrics-specific problems have been observed in studies done in children using doses of up to 3000 mg per square meter of body surface area (mg/m²) per day and 80 mg/kg per day. Intravenous acyclovir should be used with greater caution in neonates due to their age-related decrease in clearance. The half-life and clearance of intravenous acyclovir in children older than 1 year of age is similar to that seen in adults with normal renal function.

Geriatrics

Geriatric patients may be more sensitive to the central nervous system effects of acyclovir. In addition, acyclovir plasma concentrations are higher in geriatric patients compared to younger adults, in part due to age-related changes in renal function impairment. Dosage adjustment may be required in geriatric patients with underlying renal function impairment.

Drug interactions and/or related problems

The following drug interactions and/or related problems have been selected on the basis of their potential clinical significance (possible mechanism in parentheses where appropriate)—not necessarily inclusive (» = major clinical significance):

Note: Combinations containing any of the following medications, depending on the amount present, may also interact with this medication.

» Nephrotoxic medications, other (see *Appendix II*)
(concurrent use with oral or parenteral acyclovir may increase the potential for nephrotoxicity, especially in the presence of renal function impairment)

Probenecid
(may decrease renal tubular secretion of intravenous acyclovir when used concurrently, resulting in increased acyclovir serum and cerebrospinal fluid [CSF] concentrations, prolonged elimination half-life in the serum and CSF, and, potentially, increased toxicity)

Laboratory value alterations

The following have been selected on the basis of their potential clinical significance (possible effect in parentheses where appropriate)—not necessarily inclusive (» = major clinical significance).

With physiology/laboratory test values
» Blood urea nitrogen (BUN) and
» Creatinine, serum
(concentrations may be increased because of renal tubular obstruction caused by intravenous acyclovir; no increase generally occurs with proper dosage and adequate hydration)

Liver function tests
(serum values may be increased with either oral or parenteral acyclovir)

Medical considerations/Contraindications

The medical considerations/contraindications included have been selected on the basis of their potential clinical significance (reasons given in parentheses where appropriate)—not necessarily inclusive (» = major clinical significance).

Risk-benefit should be considered when the following medical problems exist:

» Dehydration or
» Renal function impairment, pre-existing
(the potential for nephrotoxicity may be increased; it is recommended that acyclovir be administered in a reduced dosage to patients with impaired renal function)

Hypersensitivity to acyclovir or valacyclovir

Neurological abnormalities or
Prior neurologic reactions to cytotoxic medications
(the potential for neurologic side effects may be increased)

Patient monitoring

The following may be especially important in patient monitoring (other tests may be warranted in some patients, depending on condition; » = major clinical significance):

» Blood urea nitrogen (BUN) and
» Creatinine, serum
(concentrations required prior to and during therapy since intravenous acyclovir may be nephrotoxic; if acyclovir is given by rapid intravenous injection or its urine solubility is exceeded, precipitation of acyclovir crystals may occur in renal tubules; renal tubular damage may occur and may progress to acute renal failure)

Side/Adverse Effects

Note: Acute renal insufficiency may occur due to precipitation of acyclovir in the renal tubules. It is most likely to occur if acyclovir is given by rapid intravenous injection, concurrently with known nephrotoxic medications, to patients who are inadequately hydrated, or to patients with renal function impairment without appropriate dosage reduction. However, acute renal failure has also been reported in patients receiving oral acyclovir.

Thrombotic thrombocytopenic purpura/hemolytic uremic syndrome (TTP/HUS) has occurred in immunocompromised patients with high exposures to parenteral acyclovir and has resulted in death.

Neuropsychiatric toxicity has been associated with high plasma acyclovir concentrations—which may occur when high doses are used, or when patients with renal function impairment are not given an appropriately lowered dose. Neuropsychiatric toxicity may also be more likely to occur in immunocompromised patients and geriatric patients.

The following side/adverse effects have been selected on the basis of their potential clinical significance (possible signs and symptoms in parentheses where appropriate)—not necessarily inclusive:

Those indicating need for medical attention

Incidence more frequent

Phlebitis or inflammation at the injection site (pain, swelling, or redness at site of injection)—with parenteral acyclovir

Incidence less frequent

Acute renal failure (abdominal pain; decreased frequency of urination or amount of urine; increased thirst; loss of appetite; nausea; vomiting; unusual tiredness or weakness)

Incidence rare

Encephalopathic changes (coma; confusion; hallucinations; seizures; tremors); ***hematologic abnormalities, such as anemia*** (unusual tiredness or weakness); ***leukocytosis, neutropenia or neutrophilia*** (chills, fever, or sore throat); ***or thrombocytopenia or thrombocytosis*** (black, tarry stools; blood in urine or stools; pinpoint red spots on skin; unusual bleeding or bruising)—usually asymptomatic; ***hematuria*** (blood in urine); ***urticaria*** (hives)

Incidence not determined—Observed during clinical practice; estimates of frequency cannot be determined

Delirium; disseminated intravascular coagulation (DIC) (cyanosis [bluish coloring], especially of the hands and feet; bruising at the injection site; persistent bleeding or oozing from puncture sites or mucous membranes [bowel, mouth, nose, or urinary bladder]); ***hemolysis; hypotension*** (faintness or lightheadedness); ***mental obtundation*** (mental changes); ***psychosis*** (mood or mental changes, severe)

Note: *Delirium, mental obtundation*, and *psychosis* may be marked, particularly in older adults.

Anaphylaxis (changes in facial skin color; coughing; difficulty in breathing or swallowing; dizziness or feeling faint, severe; fast heartbeat; rash, itching, or hives; sense of agitation or uneasiness; swelling of eyelids, face, or lips); ***anemia*** (pale skin; unusual tiredness or weakness); ***angioedema*** (large, hive-like swelling on face, eyelids, lips, tongue, throat, hands, legs, feet, sex organs); ***ataxia*** (shakiness and unsteady walk; clumsiness, unsteadiness, or other problems with muscle control or coordination); ***confusion; consciousness, decreased; elevated liver function tests***—asymptomatic; ***encephalopathy*** (blurred vision; confusion; dizziness; mood or mental changes; seizures; unusual tiredness or weakness); ***fever; hallucinations*** (seeing, hearing, or feeling things that are not there); ***hyperbilirubinemia*** (yellow eyes or skin); ***leukopenia*** (chills, fever, or sore throat)—usually asymptomatic; ***lymphadenopathy*** (swollen, painful, or tender lymph nodes [glands] in neck, armpit, or groin); ***peripheral edema*** (swelling of hands, feet, or lower legs); ***seizures; skin reactions, such as erythema multiforme, pruritus, rash, Stevens-Johnson syndrome, toxic epidermal necrolysis, or urticaria*** (blistering, peeling, or loosening of skin; muscle cramps, pain, or weakness; red or irritated eyes; skin rash, itching, or hives; sore throat, fever, or chills; sores, ulcers, or white spots in mouth or on lips); ***tremors*** (shakiness); ***visual abnormalities*** (changes in vision)

Those indicating need for medical attention only if they continue or are bothersome

Incidence more frequent—especially with high doses

Gastrointestinal disturbances (nausea or vomiting)—incidence approximately 7% with parenteral acyclovir; ***malaise*** (general feeling of discomfort or illness)—incidence 11%

Incidence less frequent—with long-term use or high doses

Gastrointestinal disturbances (diarrhea; nausea or vomiting)—with oral acyclovir; ***headache; lightheadedness***

Incidence not determined—Observed during clinical practice; estimates of frequency cannot be determined

Agitation; alopecia (loss of hair); ***dizziness; myalgia*** (muscle pain); ***paresthesia*** (burning, prickling, or tingling sensations); ***somnolence*** (drowsiness)

Note: *Agitation, dizziness, paresthesia*, and *somnolence* may be marked, particularly in older adults.

Overdose

In general, acyclovir has a broad therapeutic index and excessive doses of acyclovir are well-tolerated. There are limited data in the medical literature regarding acyclovir intoxication, and there are no reports in peer-reviewed literature on serious toxic effects following an overdose of acyclovir. The inadvertent infusion of acyclovir at a dose ten times higher than the normal dose to two neonates (65 and 100 mg per kg of body weight, respectively) did not produce any adverse renal or neurological effects.

For more information on the management of overdose or unintentional ingestion, **contact a Poison Control Center** (see *Poison Control Center Listing*).

Clinical effects of overdose

The following effects have been selected on the basis of their potential clinical significance (possible signs and symptoms in parentheses where appropriate)—not necessarily inclusive:

Nephrotoxicity (crystallization of acyclovir within renal tubules; elevation of serum creatinine, transient); ***neurotoxicity*** (coma; hallucinations; lethargy; seizures; tremors)

Note: *Nephrotoxicity* and *neurotoxicity* usually resolve after cessation of acyclovir therapy. However, there is no well-defined relationship between acyclovir concentrations in the blood and these adverse effects. Therefore, additional factors other than elevated acyclovir concentrations may account for these effects.

Treatment of overdose

There are no clinical data to guide management of acyclovir overdose. Treatment is supportive. Adequate urine flow should be maintained to prevent precipitation of acyclovir in the renal tubules. Hemodialysis is generally not recommended because even very large overdoses do not usually result in major toxicity.

Supportive care—Patients in whom intentional overdose is confirmed or suspected should be referred for psychiatric consultation.

Patient Consultation

As an aid to patient consultation, refer to *Advice for the Patient, Acyclovir (Systemic)*.

In providing consultation, consider emphasizing the following selected information (» = major clinical significance):

Before using this medication

» Conditions affecting use, especially:
Hypersensitivity to acyclovir or valacyclovir
Pregnancy—Acyclovir crosses the placenta; acyclovir should be used only if the potential benefit to the mother outweighs the potential risk to the fetus
Breast-feeding—Acyclovir is distributed into breast milk

Use in children—Neonates have an age-related decrease in acyclovir clearance
Use in the elderly—Elderly patients may be more sensitive to the central nervous system effects of acyclovir
Other medications, especially nephrotoxic medications
Other medical problems, especially dehydration or pre-existing renal function impairment

Proper use of this medication

Supplying patient information about herpes simplex or varicella-zoster infections
» For treatment of herpes zoster (shingles) or recurrent herpes simplex infections, initiating use of the medication as soon as possible after symptoms of recurrence begin to appear
» For treatment of chickenpox (varicella), initiating use of oral acyclovir at the earliest sign or symptom; it is most effective when started within 24 hours of the onset of a typical chickenpox rash
Capsules, tablets, and oral suspension may be taken with meals or on an empty stomach
Taking with full glass of water
Proper administration technique for oral liquids
» Compliance with full course of therapy; not using more often or for longer than prescribed
» Advising patient to drink plenty of fluids while taking capsules, tablets, or oral suspension
» Proper dosing
Missed dose: Taking as soon as possible; not taking if almost time for next dose; not doubling doses
» Proper storage

Precautions while using this medication

Checking with physician if no improvement within a few days
Keeping affected areas as clean and dry as possible; wearing loose-fitting clothing to avoid irritation of lesions
» Use of acyclovir has not been shown to prevent the transmission of herpes simplex virus to sexual partners
» Herpes genitalis may be sexually transmitted even if partner is asymptomatic; sexual activity should be avoided if either partner has signs and symptoms of herpes genitalis; use of a condom may help prevent transmission of herpes; however, spermicidal jellies or diaphragms probably will not be adequately protective

Side/adverse effects

Signs of potential side effects, especially phlebitis or inflammation at site of injection; acute renal failure; encephalopathic changes; hematologic abnormalities, such as anemia, leukocytosis, neutropenia or neutrophilia, thrombocytopenia or thrombocytosis; hematuria; and urticaria
(Signs of potential side effects observed during clinical practice, especially delirium; disseminated intravascular coagulation (DIC); hemolysis; hypotension; mental obtundation; psychosis; anaphylaxis; anemia; angioedema; ataxia; confusion; decreased consciousness; encephalopathy; fever; hallucinations; hyperbilirubinemia; leukopenia; lymphadenopathy; peripheral edema; seizures; skin reactions, such as erythema multiforme, pruritus, rash, Stevens-Johnson syndrome, toxic epidermal necrolysis, or urticaria; tremors; and visual abnormalities)

General Dosing Information

Therapy should be initiated as soon as possible following the onset of signs and symptoms of herpes simplex or varicella zoster infections.

Because it may take longer for lesions to heal in immunocompromised patients (an average of 2 weeks of therapy for herpes simplex infections), the duration of therapy may need to be prolonged beyond the recommended number of days until the lesions are crusted over or epithelialized.

The frequency and severity of episodes of untreated genital herpes may change over time. It is recommended by the manufacturer that the frequency and severity of the patient's genital herpes infection be re-evaluated following 1 year of treatment with acyclovir, to assess the need for continued acyclovir treatment.

For oral dosage forms only

Acyclovir capsules, tablets, and oral suspension may be taken with meals since absorption has not been shown to be significantly affected by food; however, they may be taken on an empty stomach.

Patients should be advised to maintain adequate hydration while taking acyclovir.

Intermittent short-term treatment of recurrent herpes genitalis infections may be effective for some patients, especially when treatment is patient-initiated during the prodrome or first sign of lesion formation.

For parenteral dosage forms only

Acyclovir for injection should be administered by intravenous infusion only. It should not be administered topically, intramuscularly, orally, subcutaneously, or ophthalmically.

Intravenous infusions of acyclovir should be administered at a constant rate over at least a 1-hour period to avoid renal tubular damage. Rapid or bolus injection must be avoided since precipitation of acyclovir crystals in the renal tubules may occur and may result in acute renal failure. Also, precipitation of acyclovir crystals in renal tubules and resulting renal damage may occur if the maximum water solubility of free acyclovir (2.5 mg/mL at 37 °C) is exceeded.

Obese patients should be dosed based on ideal body weight.

Patients receiving parenteral acyclovir should be adequately hydrated to reduce the risk of renal damage. Since maximum urinary concentrations of acyclovir are achieved within 2 hours, patients receiving intravenous infusions and high oral doses must be adequately hydrated during this period to prevent precipitation of acyclovir in renal tubules.

Abnormal renal function (decreased creatinine clearance) can occur as a result of acyclovir administration and depends on the patient's state of hydration, other treatments and the rate of drug administration. Concomitant use of other nephrotoxic drugs, pre-existing renal disease, and dehydration make further renal impairment more likely.

The dose of acyclovir should be adjusted so that a dose is repeated after hemodialysis, since each 6-hour hemodialysis period results in approximately a 60% reduction in acyclovir plasma concentrations.

Bioequivalence information

Bioequivalence informationThe capsule, oral suspension, and tablet dosage forms are bioequivalent.

Oral Dosage Forms

Note: Bracketed uses in the *Dosage Forms* section refer to categories of use and/or indications that are not included in U.S. product labeling.

ACYCLOVIR CAPSULES USP

Usual adult and adolescent dose

Genital herpes infection—
Initial episode: Oral, 200 mg every four hours while awake, five times a day, for ten days.
Recurrent infections, intermittent therapy (< 6 episodes per year): Oral, 200 mg every four hours while awake, five times a day, for five days.
Recurrent infections, chronic suppressive therapy (≥ 6 episodes per year): Oral, 400 mg twice a day, or 200 mg three to five times a day, for up to twelve months.
[Herpes simplex, mucocutaneous (treatment)][1]—
Oral, 200 to 400 mg five times a day for seven to ten days in immunocompromised patients.
[Herpes simplex, mucocutaneous (prophylaxis)][1]—
Oral, 400 mg every twelve or twenty-four hours.
Herpes zoster (shingles)—
Oral, 800 mg every four hours while awake, five times a day, for seven to ten days.
Varicella (chickenpox)—
Oral, 800 mg four times a day for five days. Treatment should be initiated at the earliest sign or symptom of chickenpox.

Note: Adults with acute or chronic renal impairment may require a reduction in dose as follows:

Normal dosing regimen	Creatinine clearance (mL/min)/(mL/sec)	Adjusted dosing regimen
200 mg every 4 hours, 5 times daily while awake	> 10/0.17	200 mg every 4 hours, 5 times daily while awake
	0–10/0–0.17	200 mg every 12 hours
400 mg every 12 hours	> 10/0.17	400 mg every 12 hours
	0–10/0–0.17	200 mg every 12 hours
800 mg every 4 hours, 5 times daily while awake	> 25/0.42	800 mg every 4 hours, 5 times daily while awake
	10–25/0.17–0.42	800 mg every 8 hours
	0–10/0–0.17	800 mg every 12 hours

Hemodialysis patients: A dose should be administered after each dialysis session.

Usual pediatric dose
Varicella (chickenpox)—
Children up to 2 years of age: Safety and efficacy have not been established. However, no unusual toxicity or pediatrics-specific problems have been observed in studies done in children given 3000 mg per square meter of body surface area per day or 80 mg per kg of body weight per day.
Children 2 to 12 years of age, up to 40 kg of body weight: Oral, 20 mg per kg of body weight, up to 800 mg per dose, four times a day for five days. Treatment should be initiated at the earliest sign or symptom of chickenpox.
Children 2 to 12 years of age, 40 kg of body weight and over: See *Usual adult and adolescent dose*.

Strength(s) usually available
U.S.—
200 mg (Rx) [*Zovirax* (lactose; may contain one or more parabens)].
Canada—
Not commercially available.

Packaging and storage
Store between 15 and 25 °C (59 and 77 °F), in a tight container. Protect from light and moisture.

Auxiliary labeling
- Continue medicine for full time of treatment.
- Drink plenty of fluids while taking this medication.

ACYCLOVIR ORAL SUSPENSION USP

Usual adult and adolescent dose
See *Acyclovir Capsules USP*.

Usual pediatric dose
See *Acyclovir Capsules USP*.

Strength(s) usually available
U.S.—
200 mg per 5 mL (Rx) [*Zovirax* (methylparaben 0.1%; propylparaben 0.02%; sorbitol)].
Canada—
200 mg per 5 mL (Rx) [*Zovirax* (sodium)].

Note: The acyclovir suspension products are banana-flavored.

Packaging and storage
Store between 15 and 25 °C (59 and 77 °F), in a tight container. Protect from light.

Stability
Suspension retains its potency for 24 months from date of manufacture. Does not require reconstitution or refrigeration.

Auxiliary labeling
- Continue medicine for full time of treatment.
- Shake well.
- Take with water.
- Drink plenty of fluids while taking this medication.
- Beyond-use date.

Note
When dispensing, include a calibrated liquid-measuring device.

ACYCLOVIR TABLETS USP

Usual adult and adolescent dose
See *Acyclovir Capsules USP*.

Usual pediatric dose
See *Acyclovir Capsules USP*.

Strength(s) usually available
U.S.—
400 mg (Rx) [*Zovirax*].
800 mg (Rx) [*Zovirax*].
Canada—
200 mg (Rx) [*Alti-Acyclovir* (lactose); *Avirax* (scored; lactose); *Zovirax* (lactose)].
400 mg (Rx) [*Alti-Acyclovir* (scored); *Avirax* (scored); *Zovirax Wellstat Pac*].
800 mg (Rx) [*Alti-Acyclovir* (scored); *Avirax* (scored); *Zovirax Zostab Pac*].

Packaging and storage
Store between 15 and 25 °C (59 and 77 °F), in a tight container. Protect from light.

Auxiliary labeling
- Continue medicine for full time of treatment.
- Drink plenty of fluids while taking this medication.

Parenteral Dosage Forms

Note: Bracketed uses in the *Dosage Forms* section refer to categories of use and/or indications that are not included in U.S. product labeling.
The dosing and strength of the dosage forms available are expressed in terms of acyclovir base.

ACYCLOVIR FOR INJECTION USP

Usual adult and adolescent dose
Genital herpes infections, severe, initial episode—
Intravenous infusion, 5 mg (base) per kg of body weight every eight hours for five days. Administer at a constant rate over at least a one-hour period.
Herpes simplex (HSV-1 and HSV-2) infections, mucocutaneous, in immunocompromised patients—
Intravenous infusion, 5 mg (base) per kg of body weight every eight hours for seven days. Administer at a constant rate over at least a one-hour period.
Herpes simplex encephalitis[1]—
Intravenous infusion, 10 mg (base) per kg of body weight every eight hours for ten days. Administer at a constant rate over at least a one-hour period.
Herpes zoster, caused by varicella zoster virus, in immunocompromised patients—
Intravenous infusion, 10 mg (base) per kg of body weight every eight hours for seven days. Administer at a constant rate over at least a one-hour period.

Note: Adults with acute or chronic renal impairment require a reduction in dose and/or dosing interval as follows:

Creatinine clearance (mL/min)/(mL/sec)	Dose (base)	Dosing interval (hr)
> 50/0.83	100%	8
25–50/0.42–0.83	100%	12
10–25/0.17–0.42	100%	24
0–10/0–0.17	50%	24

Hemodialysis patients require administration of an additional dose following each hemodialysis session.
No additional dosing is required for peritoneal dialysis patients.
Obese patients should be dosed at the recommended adult dosing using Ideal Body Weight.

Usual adult prescribing limits
20 mg per kg of body weight, every 8 hours.

Usual pediatric dose
Genital herpes infections, severe, initial episode—
[Infants and children up to 12 years of age: Intravenous infusion, 250 mg (base) per square meter of body surface area every eight hours for five days. Administer at a constant rate over at least a one-hour period.]
Children 12 years of age and over: See *Usual adult and adolescent dose*.
Herpes simplex (HSV-1 and HSV-2) infections, mucocutaneous, in immunocompromised patients—
Infants and children up to 12 years of age: Intravenous infusion, 10 mg (base) per kg of body weight every eight hours for seven days. Administer at a constant rate over at least a one-hour period.
Children 12 years of age and over: See *Usual adult and adolescent dose*.
Herpes simplex infections, neonatal[1]—
Infants from birth to 3 months of age: Intravenous infusion, 10 mg (base) per kg of body weight every eight hours for ten days. Administer at a constant rate over at least a one-hour period.
Note: Intravenous doses of 15 or 20 mg (base) per kg of body weight every eight hours, administered at a constant rate over at least a one-hour period, have been used; however, the safety and efficacy of these doses have not been established.
Herpes simplex encephalitis[1]—
Infants 3 months and older and children up to 12 years of age: Intravenous infusion, 20 mg (base) per kg of body weight every eight hours for ten days. Administer at a constant rate over at least a one-hour period.
Children 12 years of age and older: See *Usual adult and adolescent dose*.
Herpes zoster, caused by varicella zoster virus, in immunocompromised patients—
Children up to 12 years of age: Intravenous infusion, 20 mg (base) per kg of body weight every eight hours for seven days. Administer at a constant rate over at least a one-hour period.

Children 12 years of age and older: See *Usual adult and adolescent dose*.

Note: Patients with acute or chronic renal impairment require a reduction in dose and/or dosing interval as follows:

Creatinine clearance (mL/min)/(mL/sec)	Dose (base)	Dosing interval (hr)
> 50/0.83	100%	8
25–50/0.42–0.83	100%	12
10–25/0.17–0.42	100%	24
0–10/0–0.17	50%	24

Hemodialysis patients require administration of an additional dose following each hemodialysis session.

No additional dosing is required for peritoneal dialysis patients.

Usual pediatric prescribing limits
20 mg per kg of body weight every eight hours.

Strength(s) usually available
U.S.—
500 mg (base) (Rx) [*Zovirax* (49 mg sodium)].
1 gram (base) (Rx) [*Zovirax* (98 mg sodium)].

Canada—
500 mg (base) (Rx) [*Zovirax* (sodium hydroxide)].
1 gram (base) (Rx) [*Zovirax* (sodium hydroxide)].

Packaging and storage
Prior to reconstitution, store between 15 and 25 °C (59 and 77 °F).

Preparation of dosage form
To prepare initial dilution for intravenous infusion, add 10 or 20 mL of sterile water for injection to each 500-mg or 1-gram vial, respectively, to provide a concentration of 50 mg per mL. **Do not use bacteriostatic water for injection containing benzyl alcohol or parabens.** To ensure complete dissolution, shake vial well until solution is clear. The resulting solution should be further diluted with a suitable diluent (standard electrolyte- and glucose-containing solutions [see manufacturer's package insert]) to at least 100 mL. Final concentrations of 7 mg per mL or less are recommended. Higher concentrations (e.g., 10 mg per mL) may cause phlebitis or inflammation at the injection site upon inadvertent extravasation.

Stability
After reconstitution with sterile water for injection, solutions at concentrations of 50 mg per mL retain their potency for 12 hours at controlled room temperature (15 to 25 °C [59 to 77 °F]).

After further dilution with standard electrolyte- and dextrose-containing solutions for intravenous infusion, solutions retain their potency for 24 hours at controlled room temperature (15 to 25 °C [59 to 77 °F]).

Refrigeration of reconstituted solutions may result in the formation of a precipitate, which will redissolve when warmed to room temperature.

Incompatibilities
Acyclovir for injection is incompatible with biological or colloidal solutions (e.g., blood products, protein-containing solutions).

Parabens are incompatible with acyclovir for injection and may cause precipitation.

[1]Not included in Canadian product labeling.

Selected Bibliography

Wagstaff AJ, Faulds D, Goa KL. Aciclovir: a reappraisal of its antiviral activity, pharmacokinetic properties, and therapeutic efficacy. Drugs 1994; 47(1): 153-205.

Whitley RJ, Gnann JW. Acyclovir: a decade later. N Engl J Med 1992; 327(11): 782-9.

Revised: 05/12/2006

ACYCLOVIR Topical

INN: Aciclovir

VA CLASSIFICATION (Primary): DE103

Commonly used brand name(s): *Zovirax*.

A commonly used name is acycloguanosine.

Note: For a listing of dosage forms and brand names by country availability, see *Dosage Forms* section(s).

Category
Antiviral (topical).

Indications
Note: Bracketed information in the *Indications* section refers to uses that are not included in U.S. product labeling.

General Considerations
Acyclovir is a synthetic purine analog that has antiviral activity against herpes simplex virus (HSV-1 and HSV-2) and varicella-zoster virus (VZV). Resistance of HSV and VZV to acyclovir have been reported, especially in severely immunocompromised patients such as those with advanced HIV infection. The possibility of viral resistance to acyclovir should be considered in patients who show poor clinical response to therapy.

This resistance of HSV and VZV to antiviral nucleoside analogs can result from qualitative or quantitative changes in the viral thymidine kinase (TK) or deoxyribonucleic acid (DNA) polymerase. Most of the acyclovir-resistant mutants isolated from immunocompromised patients, such as those from patients with advanced human immunodeficiency virus (HIV) infections, have been found to be TK-deficient mutants; however, other mutants involving the viral TK gene (TK-partial and TK-altered) and DNA polymerase also have been isolated. TK-negative mutants of HSV and VZV may cause severe disease in infants and immunocompromised adults.

Accepted
Herpes simplex (treatment)—Topical acyclovir is indicated in the treatment of initial episodes of genital herpes simplex virus infections and limited non-life-threatening mucocutaneous[1] herpes simplex virus (HSV-1 and HSV-2) infections in immunocompromised patients; however, systemic acyclovir is more effective and may be preferred.

Note: Canadian manufacturer states that cream and ointment preparation are indicated in the topical management of initial herpes simplex virus (HSV-1 and HSV-2 infections). Acyclovir ointment is also indicated for limited non-life-threatening cutaneous HSV infections in immunocompromised patients. Cream and ointment preparations are not indicated for mucosal use.

[Herpes zoster (treatment adjunct)][1]—Topical acyclovir is used as adjunctive therapy to improve cutaneous healing of localized herpes zoster in immunosuppressed persons being treated systemically with other treatment regimens for herpes zoster.

Resistance to acyclovir, although currently of minor clinical significance, has been reported to develop with prolonged treatment in immunocompromised patients. Resistance does not appear to be significant in patients with normal immune function.

Unaccepted
Herpes genitalis (treatment)—Although topical acyclovir is FDA-approved for the treatment of *initial* herpes genitalis infections caused by herpes simplex virus (HSV), the Centers for Disease Control (CDC) and USP medical experts do not recommend it for use, because oral acyclovir is considerably more effective.

Topical acyclovir is not effective in the treatment of *recurrent* herpes genitalis or herpes febrilis (labialis) infections in non-immunocompromised patients, although topical acyclovir may cause some reduction in the duration of viral shedding. Also, there is no evidence that topical acyclovir will prevent the transmission of herpes infection to others or that it will prevent recurrent infections in the absence of signs and symptoms of infection.

[1]Not included in Canadian product labeling.

Pharmacology/Pharmacokinetics

Physicochemical characteristics
Molecular weight—225.21.

Mechanism of action/Effect
Acyclovir is converted to acyclovir monophosphate, a nucleotide, by herpes simplex virus (HSV)-coded thymidine kinase. Acyclovir monophosphate is converted to the diphosphate by cellular guanylate kinase and to the triphosphate by a number of cellular enzymes. Acyclovir triphosphate interferes with HSV DNA polymerase and inhibits viral DNA replication. The triphosphate can be incorporated into growing chains of DNA by viral DNA polymerase, resulting in termination of the DNA chain. Since acyclovir is preferentially taken up and selectively converted to the active triphosphate form by HSV-infected cells, it is much less toxic to normal uninfected cells.

Absorption
Intact skin—Minimal; acyclovir not detected in blood or urine.

Diseased skin (herpes zoster)—Moderate; serum concentrations up to 0.28 mcg per mL have been reported in patients with normal renal function and up to 0.78 mcg per mL in patients with impaired renal function.

Elimination
Renal—Up to 9.4% of the total daily dose may be excreted in the urine.

Precautions to Consider
Note: Systemic exposure following topical administration of acyclovir is minimal.

Carcinogenicity
Lifetime bioassays in rats and mice given daily doses of 50, 150, and 450 mg per kg of body weight (mg/kg) by gavage have not shown any evidence of carcinogenicity. However, *in vitro* cell transformation assays have given conflicting results, being positive at the highest dose used in one system. The resulting morphologically transformed cells induced tumors when inoculated into immunosuppressed, syngeneic, weanling mice, although results were negative in another animal system.

Note: Dermal carcinogenicity studies were not conducted.

Tumorigenicity
Studies in rats and mice have not shown any statistically significant difference between the incidence of benign and malignant tumors produced in drug-treated animals and that produced in control animals.

Mutagenicity
No chromosomal damage was noted at maximum tolerated parenteral doses (100 mg/kg) in rats or Chinese hamsters. Higher doses (500 and I000 mg/kg) were clastogenic in Chinese hamsters. No problems were reported in dominant lethal studies in mice. Also, there was no evidence of mutagenicity in 9 out of 11 microbial and mammalian cell assays. In 2 of the mammalian cell assays, a positive response for mutagenicity and chromosomal damage was noted, but only at concentrations at least 1000 times the usual plasma concentrations in humans following topical application.

Pregnancy/Reproduction
Fertility—Studies in mice given oral doses of up to 450 mg/kg or in rats given subcutaneous doses of up to 25 mg/kg per day have not shown that acyclovir impairs fertility or reproduction. Female rabbits given acyclovir subcutaneously at a dose of 50 mg/kg per day displayed a significant decrease in implantation efficiency.

Pregnancy—Adequate and well-controlled studies in humans have not been done.

Studies done in rats (given subcutaneous doses) and rabbits (given subcutaneous or intravenous doses) of up to 50 mg/kg daily and in mice given oral doses of up to 450 mg/kg daily have not shown that acyclovir causes adverse effects on the fetus. In a nonstandard test in rats, fetal abnormalities, such as head and tail anomalies, were observed following subcutaneous administration of acyclovir at a very high dose, which was associated with toxicity in the maternal rat.

A prospective epidemiological registry of systemic acyclovir used during pregnancy was completed in April 1999. There were 749 pregnancies followed, with 756 outcomes. The occurrence rate of birth defects approximates that found in the general population. The small size of the registry is insufficient to evaluate the risk for less common defects or to permit reliable or definitive conclusions regarding safety and use in pregnant women.

FDA Pregnancy Category B.

Breast-feeding
It is not known whether topical acyclovir is distributed into breast milk. After oral administration of acyclovir, concentrations that ranged from 0.6 to 4.1 times the corresponding plasma levels have been documented in the breast milk of two women. These concentrations could potentially expose the infant to a dose of acyclovir up to 0.3 mg/kg per day. However, acyclovir is unlikely to be distributed into breast milk in significant amounts following topical administration, since the total daily dose is small, even though absorption through diseased skin is moderate.If the mother has active herpatic lesions in the breast area should avoid nursing.

Pediatrics
Appropriate studies on the relationship of age to the effects of topical acyclovir have not been performed in the pediatric population. Safety and efficacy have not been established. However, limited data are available about the use of oral acyclovir in the pediatric population, and no unusual toxicity or pediatrics-specific problems have been observed in studies done in children using doses of up to 3000 mg per square meter of body surface per day and 80 mg/kg per day.

Geriatrics
Appropriate studies on the relationship of age to the effects of topical acyclovir have not been performed in the geriatric population. However, no geriatrics-specific problems have been documented to date. Reported clinical experience has not found there to be differences in responses between geriatric patients and other patients.

Medical considerations/Contraindications
The medical considerations/contraindications included have been selected on the basis of their potential clinical significance (reasons given in parentheses where appropriate)—not necessarily inclusive (» = major clinical significance).

Risk-benefit should be considered when the following medical problem exists:

Hypersensitivity to topical acyclovir

Recurrent herpes simplex virus HSV-1 and HSV-2
(Topical acyclovir should not be used for the prevention of recurrent HSV infections; possibility of viral resistance to acyclovir should be considered in patients who show poor clinical response during therapy)

Patient monitoring
The following may be especially important in patient monitoring (other tests may be warranted in some patients, depending on condition; » = major clinical significance):

Papanicolaou (Pap) test
(although a clear association has not been shown to date, patients with genital herpes may be at increased risk of developing cervical cancer; Pap tests should be done at least once a year to detect early cervical changes)

Side/Adverse Effects
The following side/adverse effects have been selected on the basis of their potential clinical significance (possible signs and symptoms in parentheses where appropriate)—not necessarily inclusive:

Those indicating need for medical attention only if they continue or are bothersome
Incidence more frequent—Approximately 28%
Mild pain, burning, or stinging

Incidence less frequent—Approximately 4%
Pruritus (itching)

Incidence rare—Approximately 0.3%
Skin rash; vulvitis (itching, stinging, or redness of the genital area)

Patient Consultation
As an aid to patient consultation, refer to *Advice for the Patient, Acyclovir (Topical).*

In providing consultation, consider emphasizing the following selected information (» = major clinical significance):

Proper use of this medication
Reading patient information about herpes simplex infections
» Avoiding contact with eyes
» Using medication as soon as possible after signs and symptoms of herpes begin to appear
» Proper administration technique

To use

Using a finger cot or rubber glove to prevent autoinoculation of other body sites and to prevent transmission of the infection to other persons

Applying sufficient medication to cover affected areas; a 1.25-cm (½-inch) strip of ointment per 25 cm ^{2} (4 inches ^{2}) of affected skin is usually sufficient

» Compliance with full course of therapy; not using more often or longer than prescribed

» Proper dosing
Missed dose: Applying as soon as possible; not applying if almost time for next dose

» Proper storage

Precautions while using this medication
» Women with herpes genitalis may be more likely to develop cervical cancer; annual or more frequent Pap tests may be required

Checking with physician if no improvement within 1 week or if the condition becomes worse

Possibility of resistance in recurrent HSV infections

Keeping affected areas as clean and dry as possible; wearing loose-fitting clothing to avoid irritation of lesions

» Herpes genitalis may be sexually transmitted, even if sexual partner is asymptomatic; avoiding sexual activity if either partner has symptoms of herpes genitalis; use of condom may help prevent transmission of herpes; however, topical acyclovir or the use of spermicidal jellies or diaphragms will not prevent transmission of herpes to others

General Dosing Information

Use of topical antivirals may lead to skin sensitization, resulting in hypersensitivity reactions with subsequent topical or systemic use of the medication.

Topical acyclovir is for cutaneous use only; it should not be used in the eyes.

Therapy should be initiated as soon as possible following the onset of signs and symptoms of herpes infection.

A 1.25-cm (½-inch) strip of ointment should be applied per 25 cm^2 (4 $inches^2$) of affected skin. A finger cot or rubber glove should be used to prevent autoinoculation of other body sites or to prevent transmission of the infection to other persons.

The recommended dose, frequency of application, and length of treatment should not be exceeded.

Acyclovir ointment and cream should not be used for the prevention of *recurrent* herpes simplex virus (HSV) infection.

Topical Dosage Forms

ACYCLOVIR CREAM

Usual adult and adolescent dose

Antiviral—

Topical, to the affected area, four to six times a day for up to ten days. Apply a sufficient quantity to cover all lesions adequately.

Usual adult and adolescent prescribing limits

Usual adult dose should not be exceeded. See *Usual adult dose*

Usual pediatric dose

Safety and efficacy have not been established.

Strength(s) usually available

U.S.—

Not commercially available.

Canada—

5% (50 mg per gram) (Rx) [*Zovirax* (cetostearyl alcohol; paraffin; poloxamer; propylene glycol; sodium lauryl sulfate)].

Packaging and storage

Store between 15 and 25 °C (59 and 77 °F) in a dry place, unless otherwise specified by manufacturer.

Auxiliary labeling

- For external use only.
- Do not use near the eyes or on mucous membranes.
- Continue medicine for full time of treatment.

ACYCLOVIR OINTMENT

Usual adult and adolescent dose

Antiviral—

In the U.S.—Topical, to the affected area, every three hours, six times a day, for seven days. Apply a sufficient quantity to cover all lesions adequately.

In Canada—Topical, to the affected area, four to six times a day for up to ten days. Apply a sufficient quantity to cover all lesions adequately.

Usual adult and adolescent prescribing limits

The usual adult dose should not be exceeded. See *Usual adult dose*

Usual pediatric dose

Safety and efficacy have not been established.

Strength(s) usually available

U.S.—

5% (50 mg per gram) (Rx) [*Zovirax* (in a polyethylene glycol (PEG) base)].

Canada—

5% (50 mg per gram) (Rx) [*Zovirax* (in a polyethylene glycol (PEG) base)].

Packaging and storage

Store between 15 and 25 °C (59 and 77 °F) in a dry place, unless otherwise specified by manufacturer.

Auxiliary labeling

- For external use only.
- Do not use in the eye.
- Continue medicine for full time of treatment.

Note

Acyclovir ointment has a polyethylene glycol base.

Although herpes virus may theoretically persist for up to 24 hours on any fomite, it is unlikely that herpes infections can be transmitted via contaminated ointment tubes.

Selected Bibliography

Pariser DM. Cutaneous viral infections: herpes simplex and varicella-zoster. Prim Care 1989 Sep;16(3): 577-89.

Revised: 08/30/2001
Developed: 09/02/1999

ADALIMUMAB Systemic

VA CLASSIFICATION (Primary): MS109

Commonly used brand name(s): *Humira.*

Note: For a listing of dosage forms and brand names by country availability, see *Dosage Forms* section(s).

Category

Antirheumatic; Biologic response modifier.

Indications

General Considerations

Treatment with adalimumab should not be initiated in patients with active infections including chronic or localized infections. Physicians should exercise caution when considering the use of adalimumab in patients with a history of recurring infections or with underlying conditions that may predispose patients to infections.

Accepted

Arthritis, psoriatic (treatment)—Adalimumab is indicated for reducing signs and symptoms of active arthritis in patients with psoriatic arthritis. Adalimumab can be used alone or in combination with DMARDs.

Arthritis, rheumatoid (treatment)—Adalimumab is indicated for reducing signs and symptoms, inducing major clinical response, inhibiting the progression of structural damage and improving physical function in adult patients with moderately to severely active arthritis. Adalimumab can be used alone or in combination with MTX or other DMARDs

Acceptance not established

Moderate to severely active Crohn's disease, in patients who have had an inadequate response to conventional therapy—Adalimumab has demonstrated efficacy compared to placebo for induction therapy in patients with moderate to severe Crohn's disease who experience inadequate response to concomitant therapy, while efficacy for adalimumab as maintenance therapy has been reported only in abstract form. Additional small, single-arm, open-label clinical trials report safety and activity of adalimumab in patients intolerant or refractory to infliximab. Injection-site reactions are the most common adverse events associated with adalimumab in the treatment of moderate to severe Crohn's disease. Tuberculosis and opportunistic infections have not been reported in clinical trials for this population of patients. Long-term safety concerns of adalimumab, including development of malignancies, have not been determined in this population.

Pharmacology/Pharmacokinetics

Physicochemical characteristics

Source—Adalimumab is produced by recombinant DNA technology in a mammalian cell expression system.

Chemical Group—Recombinant human IgG1 monoclonal antibody

Molecular weight—148 kilodaltons.

pH—Approximately 5.2

Mechanism of action/Effect

Adalimumab binds specifically to TNF-alpha and blocks its interaction with the p55 and p75 cell surface TNF receptors. Adalimumab lyses surface TNF expressing cells *in vitro* in the presence of complement. Adalimumab does not bind or inactivate lymphotoxin (TNF-beta).

Other actions/effects

Adalimumab also modulates biological responses that are induced or regulated by TNF, including changes in the levels of adhesion molecules responsible for leukocyte migration. Adalimumab decreases C-reactive protein, erythrocyte sedimentation rate, IL-6, and matrix metalloproteinases MMP-1 and MMP-3.

Absorption

Following a single 40 milligram subcutaneous dose the average bioavailability was 64%.

Canada—
80 mg per mL (OTC) [*Actimol Infants' Suspension*].
80 mg per 5 mL (OTC) [*Actimol Children's Suspension*].

Packaging and storage

Store below 40 °C (104 °F), preferably between 15 and 30 °C (59 and 86 °F), unless otherwise specified by manufacturer. Store in a tight container. Protect from freezing.

Auxiliary labeling

- Shake well.

ACETAMINOPHEN TABLETS USP

Usual adult and adolescent dose

See *Acetaminophen Capsules USP*.

Usual adult prescribing limits

See *Acetaminophen Capsules USP*.

Usual pediatric dose:

See *Acetaminophen Capsules USP*.

Strength(s) usually available

U.S.—
120 mg (OTC) [GENERIC].
160 mg (OTC) [*Panadol Junior Strength Caplets; Tylenol Junior Strength Caplets* (scored)].
325 mg (OTC) [*Aceta Tablets; Actamin; Aminofen; Apacet Regular Strength Tablets; Dapa; Genapap Regular Strength Tablets; Genebs Regular Strength Tablets; Phenaphen Caplets; Tylenol Arthritis Extended Relief* (hydroxyethyl cellulose; hydroxypropyl methylcellulose; magnesium stearate; microcrystalline cellulose; povidone; cellulose (powdered); pregelatinized starch; sodium starch glycolate; titanium dioxide; triacetin); *Tylenol Regular Strength Caplets; Tylenol Regular Strength Tablets* (scored); *Valorin;* GENERIC].

Note: In Canada, *Phenaphen* is available as capsules containing aspirin (ASA) and phenobarbital.

500 mg (OTC) [*Aceta Tablets; Actamin Extra; Aminofen Max; Apacet Extra Strength Caplets; Apacet Extra Strength Tablets; Aspirin Free Anacin Maximum Strength Caplets; Aspirin Free Anacin Maximum Strength Gel Caplets; Aspirin Free Anacin Maximum Strength Tablets; Banesin; Datril Extra-Strength; Genapap Extra Strength Caplets; Genapap Extra Strength Tablets; Genebs Extra Strength Caplets; Genebs X-Tra; Panadol Maximum Strength Caplets; Panadol Maximum Strength Tablets; Redutemp; Tapanol Extra Strength Caplets; Tapanol Extra Strength Tablets; Tylenol Extra Strength Caplets; Tylenol Extra Strength Gelcaps; Tylenol Extra Strength Tablets; Valorin Extra;* GENERIC].
650 mg (OTC) [GENERIC].

Canada—
160 mg (OTC) [*Actimol Junior Strength Caplets* (scored); *Tempra Caplets; Tylenol Junior Strength Caplets*].
325 mg (OTC) [*Anacin-3; Apo-Acetaminophen* (scored); *Atasol Caplets* (scored); *Atasol Tablets* (scored); *Exdol* (scored); *Panadol; Robigesic* (scored); *Rounox; Tylenol Caplets; Tylenol Tablets;* GENERIC].
500 mg (OTC) [*Anacin-3 Extra Strength; Apo-Acetaminophen* (scored); *Atasol Forte Caplets; Atasol Forte Tablets* (scored); *Exdol Strong* (scored); *Panadol Extra Strength; Tylenol Caplets; Tylenol Gelcaps; Tylenol Tablets;* GENERIC].

Packaging and storage

Store below 40 °C (104 °F), preferably between 15 and 30 °C (59 and 86 °F), unless otherwise specified by manufacturer. Store in a tight container.

Auxiliary labeling

- Avoid alcoholic beverages.

ACETAMINOPHEN TABLETS (CHEWABLE) USP

Usual adult and adolescent dose

See *Acetaminophen Capsules USP*.

Usual pediatric dose

See *Acetaminophen Capsules USP*.

Strength(s) usually available

U.S.—
80 mg (OTC) [*Genapap Children's Tablets; Panadol, Children's* (scored); *St. Joseph Aspirin-Free Fever Reducer for Children; Tempra; Tylenol Children's Chewable Tablets* (scored); GENERIC].
120 mg (OTC) [GENERIC].
160 mg (OTC) [*Tempra D.S* (scored); *Tylenol Junior Strength Chewable Tablets* (scored)].

Canada—
80 mg (OTC) [*Actimol Chewable Tablets; Panadol* (scored); *Tempra Chewable Tablets; Tylenol Children's Chewable Tablets* (scored); GENERIC].
160 mg (OTC) [*Tempra Chewable Tablets*].

Packaging and storage

Store below 40 °C (104 °F), preferably between 15 and 30 °C (59 and 86 °F), unless otherwise specified by manufacturer. Store in a tight container.

Auxiliary labeling

- Avoid alcoholic beverages.
- May be chewed.

ACETAMINOPHEN AND CAFFEINE TABLETS USP

Usual adult and adolescent dose

See *Acetaminophen Capsules USP*. Dosage is based on acetaminophen only.

Usual adult prescribing limits

See *Acetaminophen Capsules USP*. Dosage is based on acetaminophen only.

Usual pediatric dose

See *Acetaminophen Capsules USP*. Dosage is based on acetaminophen only.

Strength(s) usually available

U.S.—
500 mg of acetaminophen and 65 mg of caffeine (OTC) [*Aspirin-Free Excedrin Caplets; Bayer Select Maximum Strength Headache Pain Relief Formula*].
500 mg of acetaminophen and 65.4 mg of caffeine (OTC) [*Actamin Super*].

Canada—

Note: In the U.S., *Excedrin* contains aspirin, in addition to acetaminophen and caffeine. See *Acetaminophen and Salicylates (Systemic)*. The U.S. product corresponding to the Canadian *Excedrin* formulation is *Aspirin-Free Excedrin*.

325 mg of acetaminophen and 65 mg of caffeine (OTC) [*Excedrin Caplets*].
500 mg of acetaminophen and 65 mg of caffeine (OTC) [*Excedrin Extra Strength Caplets*].

Packaging and storage

Store below 40 °C (104 °F), preferably between 15 and 30 °C (59 and 86 °F), unless otherwise specified by manufacturer.

Auxiliary labeling

- Avoid alcoholic beverages.

Rectal Dosage Forms

ACETAMINOPHEN SUPPOSITORIES USP

Usual adult and adolescent dose

Analgesic and
Antipyretic—
Rectal, 325 to 500 mg every three hours, 325 to 650 mg every four hours, or 650 mg to 1 gram every six hours as needed, while symptoms persist.

Note: For patient self-medication, it is recommended that a physician be consulted if pain is not relieved within ten days, fever within three days, or sore throat within two days.

Usual adult prescribing limits

Up to 4 grams daily

Usual pediatric dose

Analgesic and
Antipyretic—
Rectal, 1.5 grams per square meter of body surface a day in divided doses; or for
Children up to 2 years of age—Dosage must be individualized by physician.
Children 2 to 4 years of age—Rectal, 160 mg every four hours as needed, while symptoms persist.
Children 4 to 6 years of age—Rectal, 240 mg every four hours as needed, while symptoms persist.
Children 6 to 9 years of age—Rectal, 320 mg every four hours as needed, while symptoms persist.
Children 9 to 11 years of age—Rectal, 320 to 400 mg every four hours as needed, while symptoms persist.
Children 11 to 12 years of age—Rectal, 320 to 480 mg every four hours as needed, while symptoms persist.

Distribution

Volume of distribution (Vol_D)—4.7 to 6.0 liters

Adalimumab concentration in the synovial fluid from five rheumatoid arthritis patients ranged from 31% to 96% of those in serum.

Terminal

Approximately 2 weeks; ranging from 10 to 20 days.

Time to peak concentration

131 ± 56 hours; following a single subcutaneous 40 milligram dose.

Peak serum concentration

4.7 ± 1.6 micrograms per milliliter

Pharmacokinetics of adalimumab were linear over a dose range of 0.5 to 10.0 milligram per kilogram.

Elimination

Systemic clearance of adalimumab is approximately 12 milliliters per hour.

Population pharmacokinetic analyses revealed that there was a trend toward higher apparent clearance of adalimumab in the presence of anti-adalimumab antibodies, and lower clearance with increasing age in patients aged 40 to >75 years.

Precautions to Consider

Carcinogenicity

Long term studies have not been done on adalimumab to evaluate its carcinogenic potential.

Mutagenicity

No clastogenic or mutagenic effects of adalimumab were observed in the *in vivo* mouse micronucleus test or the *Salmonella-Escherichia coli* (Ames) assay, respectively.

Pregnancy/Reproduction

Fertility—Long term studies have not been done on adalimumab to evaluate its effect on fertility.

Pregnancy—There are no adequate and well controlled studies in humans. Because animal reproductive studies and developmental studies are not always predictive of human response, adalimumab should be used during pregnancy only if clearly needed.

An embryo-fetal perinatal developmental toxicity study has been performed in cynomolgus monkeys at dosages up to 100 mg/kg (266 times human AUC when given 40 mg subcutaneous with MTX every week or 373 times human AUC when given 40 mg subcutaneous without MTX) and has revealed no evidence of harm to the fetuses due to adalimumab.

A pregnancy registry has been established to monitor outcomes of pregnant women exposed to adalimumab. Physicians are encouraged to register patients by calling 1-877-311-8972.

FDA Pregnancy Category B

Breast-feeding

It is not known if adalimumab is distributed in human milk or absorbed systemically after ingestion. Because many drugs and immunoglobulins are distributed in human milk, and because of the potential for serious adverse reactions in nursing infants from adalimumab, a decision should be made whether to continue nursing or to discontinue the drug, taking into account the importance of the drug to the mother.

Pediatrics

Safety and efficacy of adalimumab in pediatric patients have not been established.

Geriatrics

The frequency of serious infection and malignancy among adalimumab treated patients aged 65 and over were higher than for those under the age of 65. No overall difference in effectiveness was observed between these subjects and younger subjects. Because there is a higher incidence of infections and malignancies in the elderly population in general, caution should be used in treating the elderly.

Drug interactions and/or related problems

The following drug interactions and/or related problems have been selected on the basis of their potential clinical significance (possible mechanism in parentheses where appropriate)—not necessarily inclusive (» = major clinical significance):

Note: Combinations containing any of the following medications, depending on the amount present, may also interact with this medication.

» Anakinra
(concurrent use with another TNF-blocking agent showed serious infection in clinical studies with no added benefit; because of the nature of adverse events seen with this combination therapy, similar toxicities may also result in combination with other TNF-blocking agents; therefore, anakinra/adalimumab combination is not recommended)

» Immunosuppressive therapy, concomitant
(concomitant immunosuppressive therapy could predispose patients to serious infections)

» Live vaccines
(should not be given concomitantly with adalimumab)

Methotrexate (MTX)
(concomitant use reduced adalimumab clearance after single and multiple dosing by 29% and 44% respectively; no dosage adjustment of either agent is necessary)

Medical considerations/Contraindications

The medical considerations/contraindications included have been selected on the basis of their potential clinical significance (reasons given in parentheses where appropriate)—not necessarily inclusive (» = major clinical significance).

Except under special circumstances, this medication should not be used when the following medical problem exists:

» Hypersensitivity to adalimumab or any of its components

Hypersensitivity to rubber or latex

» Infections, active, including chronic or localized
(adalimumab treatment should not be initiated in these patients; adalimumab should be discontinued in patients who develop a serious infection; caution should be used in patients with a history of recurrent infection or underlying conditions which may predispose them to infections.)

» Tuberculosis
(cases of tuberculosis [frequently disseminated or extrapulmonary at clinical presentation] have been observed in patients receiving adalimumab therapy; before initiation of therapy patients should be evaluated for active or latent tuberculosis infection; treatment of latent tuberculosis infection should be initiated prior to starting adalimumab therapy; caution should be used in patients who have resided in regions where tuberculosis and histoplasmosis are endemic.)

Risk-benefit should be considered when the following medical problems exist:

» Central nervous system demyelinating disorders, pre-existing or recent onset
(use of TNF blocking agents, including adalimumab, has been associated with rare cases of exacerbation of clinical symptoms and/or radiographic evidence of demyelinating disease; caution is advised in considering use of adalimumab in these patients)

» Congestive heart failure (CHF)
(cases of worsening and new onset CHF have been reported with TNF blockers; worsening cases have also been observed with adalimumab; although adalimumab has not been formally studied in patients with CHF, a higher rate of CHF-related adverse events was observed in clinical studies with another TNF blocker; caution should be exercised and these patients should be carefully monitored)

Immunosuppression
(possibility exists for TNF blocking agents to affect host defenses against infections and malignancies; safety and efficacy of adalimumab in patients with immunosuppression have not been evaluated)

Rheumatoid arthritis
(patients with rheumatoid arthritis, particularly those with highly active disease, may be at a higher risk for the development of lymphoma; the role of TNF blockers in the development of malignancy is not known.)

Patient monitoring

The following may be especially important in patient monitoring (other tests may be warranted in some patients, depending on condition; » = major clinical significance):

» Infections
(Patients who develop a new infection while undergoing treatment with adalimumab should be monitored closely; serious infections and sepsis, including fatalities, have been reported with the use of TNF blocking agents, including adalimumab)

Invasive opportunistic fungal infections
(These have been observed in patients treated with TNF blocking agents)

Lupus-like syndrome
(Treatment with adalimumab may result in the formation of autoantibodies, and rarely in the development of a lupus-like syn-

drome. If a patient develops symptoms suggestive of a lupus-like syndrome following treatment, treatment should be discontinued.)

Tuberculosis

(Tuberculosis has been observed in patients treated with TNF blocking agents; patients should be evaluated for active or latent tuberculosis infection with a tuberculin skin test before starting adalimumab therapy; patients should be instructed to seek medical attention if they have symptoms suggestive of a tuberculosis infections)

Side/Adverse Effects

Serious infections and sepsis, including fatalities, have been reported with the use of TNF blocking agents including adalimumab. Many of the serious infections have occurred in patients on concomitant immunosuppressive therapy that, in addition to their rheumatoid arthritis, could predispose them to infections. Tuberculosis and invasive opportunistic fungal infections have been reported in patients treated with TNF blocking agents including adalimumab.

Lymphomas have been observed in patients treated with adalimumab. Patients treated with adalimumab had a higher incidence of lymphoma than the expected rate in the general population. During controlled portions of adalimumab trials in patients with moderately to severely active rheumatoid arthritis, 2 lymphomas were observed among 1922 treated patients versus one among 947 control patients (mean duration of controlled treatment approximately 5 months). In the controlled and open-label portions of these clinical trials of adalimumab in rheumatoid arthritis patients, the observed rate of lymphomas is approximately 0.15 per 100 patient-years in 2468 patients over 4870 patient-years of therapy.Other malignancies observed during use of adalimumab were breast, colon, prostate, lung and uterine.

The following side/adverse effects have been selected on the basis of their potential clinical significance (possible signs and symptoms in parentheses where appropriate)—not necessarily inclusive:

Those indicating need for medical attention

Incidence more frequent

Agranulocytosis (cough or hoarseness; fever with or without chills; general feeling of tiredness or weakness; lower back or side pain; painful or difficult urination; sore throat; sores, ulcers, or white spots on lips or in mouth; unusual bleeding or bruising)—<5%; ***cellulitis*** (itching, pain, redness, swelling, tenderness; warmth on skin)—<5%; ***cholecystitis*** (indigestion; stomach pain; severe nausea; vomiting)—<5%; ***cholelithiasis*** (abdominal fullness; gaseous abdominal pain; recurrent fever; yellow eyes or skin)—<5%; ***dehydration*** (confusion; decreased urination; dizziness; dry mouth; fainting; increase in heart rate; lightheadedness; rapid breathing; sunken eyes; thirst; unusual tiredness or weakness; wrinkled skin)—<5%; ***fever***—<5%; ***flu syndrome*** (chills; cough; diarrhea; fever; general feeling of discomfort or illness; headache; joint pain; loss of appetite; muscle aches and pains; nausea; runny nose; shivering; sore throat; sweating; trouble sleeping; unusual tiredness or weakness; vomiting); ***granulocytopenia*** (fever; chills; cough; sore throat; ulcers, sores, or white spots in mouth; shortness of breath; unusual tiredness or weakness)—<5%; ***infection*** (fever or chills; cough or hoarseness; lower back or side pain; painful or difficult urination)—<5%; ***lupus erythematosus syndrome*** (skin rash, hives, or itching; fever; sore throat; swollen or painful glands; bone or joint pain; unusual tiredness or weakness)—<5%; ***lymphoma like reaction*** (swollen glands; weight loss; general feeling of illness; black, tarry stools; yellow skin and eyes)—<5%; ***pyelonephritis*** (chills; fever; frequent or painful urination; headache; stomach pain)—<5%; ***sepsis*** (chills; confusion; dizziness; lightheadedness; fainting; fast heartbeat; fever; rapid, shallow breathing)—<5%; ***sinusitis*** (pain or tenderness around eyes and cheekbones; fever stuffy or runny nose; headache; cough; shortness of breath or troubled breathing; tightness of chest or wheezing); ***upper respiratory infection*** (ear congestion; nasal congestion; chills; cough, fever, sneezing, or sore throat; body aches or pain; headache; loss of voice; runny nose; unusual tiredness or weakness; difficulty in breathing); ***urinary tract infection*** (bladder pain; bloody or cloudy urine; difficult, burning, or painful urination; frequent urge to urinate; lower back or side pain)

Incidence less frequent

Adenoma—<5%; ***allergic reactions*** (cough; difficulty swallowing; dizziness; fast heartbeat; hives; itching, puffiness or swelling of the eyelids or around the eyes, face, lips or tongue; shortness of breath; skin rash; tightness in chest; unusual tiredness or weakness; wheezing)—including allergic rash, anaphylactoid reaction, fixed drug reaction, non-specified drug reaction, urticaria; ***arrhythmia; asthma*** (cough; difficulty breathing; noisy breathing; shortness of breath; tightness in chest; wheezing)—<5%; ***atrial fibrillation*** (dizziness; fainting; fast, slow, or irregular heartbeat)—<5%; ***bone fracture, non spontaneous*** (pain or swelling in arms or legs without any injury)—<5%; ***bone necrosis*** (pain in bones)—<5%; ***bronchospasm*** (cough; difficulty breathing; noisy breathing; shortness of breath; tightness in chest; wheezing)—<5%; ***carcinoma, breast*** (clear or bloody discharge from nipple; inverted nipple; dimpling of breast skin; lump in breast or under the arm; persistent crusting or scaling of nipple; redness or swelling of breast; sore on the skin of the breast that does not heal)—<5%; ***carcinoma, gastrointestinal*** (abdominal discomfort; blood in stool; change in bowel habits; difficulty swallowing or eating; lump or swelling in the abdomen; nausea; loss of appetite; unexplained weight loss; unusual tiredness or weakness; vomiting; yellow skin or eyes)—<5%; ***carcinoma, skin*** (persistent non-healing sore; reddish patch or irritated area; shiny bump; pink growth; white, yellow or waxy scar-like area)—<5%; ***carcinoma, urogenital*** (abdominal pain; abnormal vaginal bleeding or discharge; blood in urine; difficult or frequent urination; lump or swelling in abdomen)—<5%; ***cardiovascular disorder*** (fainting; fast or slow heartbeat; irregular pulse; troubled breathing [dyspnea] on exertion)—<5%; ***cataract*** (blindness; blurred vision; decreased vision)—<5%; ***chest pain***—<5%; ***congestive heart failure*** (chest pain; decreased urine output; dilated neck veins; extreme fatigue; irregular breathing; irregular heartbeat; shortness of breath; swelling of face, fingers, feet, or lower legs; tightness in chest; troubled breathing; weight gain; wheezing)—<5%; ***coronary artery disorder*** (arm, back or jaw pain; chest pain or discomfort; chest tightness or heaviness; fast or irregular heartbeat; shortness of breath; sweating; nausea)—<5%; ***cystitis*** (bloody or cloudy urine; difficult, burning, or painful urination; frequent urge to urinate)—<5%; ***dyspnea*** (shortness of breath; difficult or labored breathing; tightness in chest; wheezing)—<5%; ***erysipelas*** (raised, firm, bright red patches of skin on arm or leg)—<5%; ***fungal infection; gastrointestinal hemorrhage*** (black, tarry stools; bloody stools; vomiting of blood or material that looks like coffee grounds)—<5%; ***heart arrest*** (stopping of heart; no blood pressure or pulse; unconsciousness)—<5%; ***hematuria*** (blood in urine); ***hepatic necrosis*** (abdominal or stomach pain; black, tarry stools; chills; light-colored stools; dark urine; dizziness; fever; headache; itching; loss of appetite; nausea; rash; unpleasant breath odor; unusual tiredness or weakness; vomiting of blood; yellow eyes or skin)—<5%; ***herpes zoster*** (painful blisters on trunk of body)—<5%; ***hypertensive encephalopathy*** (agitation; back pain; blurred vision; coma; confusion; dizziness; drowsiness; fever; hallucinations; headache; irritability; mood or mental changes; seizures; stiff neck; unusual tiredness or weakness; vomiting)—<5%; ***ketosis*** (nausea; stomach pain; vomiting)—<5%; ***kidney calculus*** (blood in urine; nausea and vomiting; pain in groin or genitals; sharp back pain just below ribs)—<5%; ***leukopenia*** (black, tarry stools; chest pain; chills; cough; fever; painful or difficult urination; shortness of breath; sore throat; sores, ulcers, or white spots on lips or in mouth; swollen glands; unusual bleeding or bruising; unusual tiredness or weakness)—<5%; ***lung disorder*** (difficulty in breathing)—<5%; ***lung function, decreased*** (difficulty in breathing)—<5%; ***lymphoma*** (swollen glands; weight loss; general feeling of illness; black, tarry stools; yellow skin and eyes)—<5%; ***melanoma*** (new mole; change in size, shape or color of existing mole; mole that leaks fluid or bleeds)—<5%; ***multiple sclerosis*** (blurred vision; difficulty controlling your bladder or bowels; difficulty walking; feeling sad or depressed; forgetful; muscle cramps; numbness or tingling in your arms, legs, or face; slurred speech or problems swallowing; unusual tiredness or weakness)—<5%; ***myocardial infarct*** (chest pain or discomfort; pain or discomfort in arms, jaw, back or neck; shortness of breath; nausea; sweating; vomiting)—<5%; ***palpitations*** (fast, irregular, pounding, or racing heartbeat or pulse)—<5%; ***pancytopenia*** (high fever; chills; unexplained bleeding or bruising; bloody, black, or tarry stools; pale skin; unusual tiredness or weakness; cough; shortness of breath; sores, ulcers, or white spots on lips or in mouth; swollen glands)—<5%; ***paraproteinemia*** (bone pain or fracture; coma; confusion; decreased or increased urination; depression; dizziness; headache; nausea; pale skin; shortness of breath; unusual bleeding or bruising; unusual tiredness or weakness; visual disturbances; vomiting)—<5%; ***parathyroid disorder*** (bone fractures; confusion; constipation; dry skin; hair loss; headache; increased thirst; increased urination; loss of appetite; muscle cramps or spasms; nausea; seizures; trouble thinking; vomiting)—<5%; ***pericardial effusion*** (chest pain or discomfort; shortness of breath)—<5%; ***pericarditis*** (anxiety; blue or pale skin; chest pain, possibly moving to the left arm, neck, or shoulder; chills; shortness of breath; unusual tiredness or weakness)—<5%; ***peripheral edema*** (bloating or swelling of face, arms, hands, lower legs, or feet; rapid weight gain; tingling of hands or feet; unusual weight gain or loss)—<5%; ***pleural effusion*** (chest pain; shortness of breath)—<5%; ***pneumonia*** (chest pain; cough; fever or chills; sneezing; shortness of breath; sore throat; troubled breathing; tightness in chest; wheezing)—<5%; ***polycythe-***

mia (abdominal pain; bleeding from gums or nose; dizziness; eye pain; headache; ringing in the ears; tiredness; weakness)—<5%; ***subdural hematoma*** (blurred vision; irregular heartbeat; nausea and vomiting; severe headache)—<5%; ***syncope*** (fainting)—<5%; ***tachycardia*** (fast, pounding, or irregular heartbeat or pulse)—<5%; ***thrombosis, leg*** (pain in lower legs; redness or swelling to lower leg)—<5%; ***tuberculosis reactivated*** (chest pain; cough; coughing or spitting up blood; difficulty in breathing; sore throat; muscle aches; night sweats; sudden high fever or low-grade fever for months; unusual tiredness)—<5%; ***vascular disorder*** (changes in skin color; cold hands and feet; pain, redness, or swelling in arm or leg)—<5%

Incidence not determined—Observed during clinical practice, estimates of frequency can not be determined

Anaphylaxis (cough; difficulty swallowing; dizziness; fast heartbeat; hives; itching, puffiness or swelling of the eyelids or around the eyes, face, lips or tongue; shortness of breath; skin rash; tightness in chest; unusual tiredness or weakness; wheezing); ***blood dycrasias*** (fever and sore throat; unusual bruising or bleeding; unusual tiredness or weakness; pale skin); ***cutaneous vasculitis*** (blisters on skin); ***interstitial lung disease*** (cough; difficult breathing; fever; shortness of breath); ***pulmonary fibrosis*** (fever; cough; shortness of breath); ***thrombocytopenia*** (black, tarry stools; bleeding gums; blood in urine or stools; pinpoint red spots on skin; unusual bleeding or bruising)

Those indicating need for medical attention only if they continue or are bothersome

Incidence more frequent

Abdominal pain; back pain; headache; hypercholesterolemia (large amount of cholesterol in the blood); ***hyperlipidemia*** (large amount of fat in the blood); ***hypertension*** (blurred vision; dizziness; nervousness; headache; pounding in the ears; slow or fast heartbeat); ***injection site reaction*** (bleeding, blistering, burning, coldness, discoloration of skin; feeling of pressure; hives; infection; inflammation; itching; lumps; numbness; pain; rash; redness; scarring; soreness; stinging; swelling; tenderness; tingling; ulceration; warmth); ***liver function, decreased; nausea; rash***

Incidence less frequent

Arthritis (pain, swelling, or redness in joints; muscle pain or stiffness; difficulty in moving)—<5%; ***bone disorder*** (bone deformity; decrease in height; difficulty in moving or walking; headache; loss of hearing; pain in back, ribs, arms, or legs; redness or swelling in arms or legs)—<5%; ***confusion***—<5%; ***esophagitis*** (difficulty in swallowing; pain or burning in throat; chest pain; heartburn; vomiting; sores, ulcers, or white spots on lips or tongue or inside the mouth)—<5%; ***gastroenteritis*** (abdominal or stomach pain; diarrhea; loss of appetite; nausea; weakness)—<5%; ***gastrointestinal disorder*** (diarrhea; loss of appetite; nausea or vomiting; stomach pain, fullness, or discomfort; indigestion; passing of gas)—<5%; ***healing abnormal***—<5%; ***joint disorder*** (difficulty in moving; muscle pain or stiffness; pain, swelling, or redness in joints)—<5%; ***menstrual disorder*** (menstrual changes)—<5%; ***muscle cramps***—<5%; ***myasthenia*** (loss of strength or energy; muscle pain or weakness)—<5%; ***pain in extremities; paresthesia*** (burning, crawling, itching, numbness, prickling, "pins and needles", or tingling feelings)—<5%; ***pelvic pain***—<5%; ***pyogenic arthritis*** (muscle or joint stiffness, tightness, or rigidity)—<5%; ***synovitis*** (joint or muscle pain or stiffness)—<5%; ***tendon disorder*** (pain; swelling)—<5%; ***thorax pain***—<5%; ***tremor*** (trembling or shaking of hands or feet; shakiness in legs, arms, hands, feet)—<5%; ***vomiting***—<5%

Overdose

For more information on the management of overdose or unintentional ingestion, **contact a poison control center** (see *Poison Control Center Listing*).

The maximum tolerated dose of adalimumab has not been established. Multiple doses up to 10 mg/kg have been administered to patients in clinical trials without evidence of dose limiting toxicities.

Treatment of overdose

Monitoring—

In case of overdosage, it is recommended that the patient be monitored for any signs or symptoms of adverse reactions or effects and appropriate symptomatic treatment be instituted immediately.

Supportive care—

Patients in whom intentional overdose is confirmed or suspected should be referred for psychiatric consultation.

Patient Consultation

As an aid to patient consultation, refer to *Advice for the Patient, Adalimumab (Systemic)*.

In providing consultation, consider emphasizing the following selected information (» = major clinical significance):

Before using this medication

» Conditions affecting use, especially:

Hypersensitivity to adalimumab or any of its components

Pregnancy—Should be used during pregnancy only if clearly needed

Breast-feeding—Because many drugs are distributed in human milk and because of potential for serious adverse reactions in nursing infants from adalimumab, a risk-benefit decision should be made taking into account importance of drug to the mother

Other medications, especially anakinra, concomitant immunosuppressive therapy, or live vaccines

Other medical problems, especially active infections, including chronic or localized infections, central nervous system demyelinating disorders, congestive heart failure, or tuberculosis

Proper use of this medication

» Proper dosing

Missed dose: Taking as soon as possible; not taking if almost time for next scheduled dose; not doubling doses

» Importance of proper administration technique; especially for at home administration

Proper storage

Precautions while using this medication

» Regular visits to physician to check progress

» Patients should be instructed to seek medical attention immediately if they have symptoms suggestive of a tuberculosis infection

» Patients should be instructed to seek medical attention if they develop a new infection or anemia while being treated with adalimumab

Side/adverse effects

Signs of potential side effects, especially agranulocytosis, cellulitis, cholecystitis, cholelithiasis, dehydration, fever, flu syndrome, granulocytopenia, infection, lupus erythematosus syndrome, lymphoma like reaction, pyelonephritis, sepsis, sinusitis, upper respiratory infection, urinary tract infection, adenoma, allergic reactions, arrhythmia, asthma, atrial fibrillation, bone fracture, bone necrosis, bronchospasm, carcinomas such as breast, gastrointestinal, skin or urogenital, cardiovascular disorder, cataract, chest pain, congestive heart failure, coronary artery disorder, cystitis, dyspnea, erysipelas, fungal infection, gastrointestinal hemorrhage, heart arrest, hematuria, hepatic necrosis, herpes zoster, hypertensive encephalopathy, ketosis, kidney calculus, leg thrombosis, leukopenia, lung disorder, lung function decreased, lymphoma, melanoma, multiple sclerosis, myocardial infarction, palpitations, pancytopenia, paraproteinemia, parathyroid disorder, pericardial effusion, pericarditis, peripheral edema, pleural effusion, pneumonia, polycythemia, subdural hematoma, syncope, tachycardia, tuberculosis reactivated, vascular disorder

Signs of potential side effects observed during clinical practice, especially anaphylaxis, blood dycrasias, cutaneous vasculitis, interstitial lung disease, pulmonary fibrosis, and thrombocytopenia

General Dosing Information

For parenteral dosing forms:

The solution in the vial should be carefully inspected visually for particulate matter and discoloration prior to subcutaneous administration. If particulates and discolorations are noted then then product should not be used.

Injection sites should be rotated and injections should never be given in areas where the skin is tender, bruised, red, or hard.

The first injection should be performed under the supervision of a qualified health care professional. If a patient or caregiver is to administer adalimumab they should be instructed in injection techniques and their ability to inject subcutaneously should be assessed to ensure the proper administration of adalimumab. A puncture resistant container for disposal of needles should be used. Patients or caregivers should be instructed in the technique as well as proper syringe and needle disposal, and be cautioned against the reuse of these items.

Instructions for Activating the Needle Stick Device: Cartons for institutional use contain a syringe and needle with a needle protection device. To activate needle stick protection device after injection, hold the syringe in one hand, and, with the other hand, slide the outer protective shield over the exposed needle until it locks into place.

Parenteral Dosage Forms

ADALIMUMAB INJECTION

Usual adult dose

Arthritis, psoriatic

Arthritis, rheumatoid—

Subcutaneous, 40 mg every other week alone or in combination with methotrexate (MTX), glucocorticoids, salicylates, non-steroidal anti-inflammatories (NSAIDs), analgesics, or other disease modifying antirheumatic drugs (DMARDs).

For patients being treated for rheumatoid arthritis and not taking concomitant MTX: Subcutaneous, 40 mg every week (Patients may derive additional benefit from this increased dosing frequency.)

Usual geriatric dose

See *Usual adult dose.*

Strength(s) usually available

U.S.—

40 mg (0.8 mL) of adalimumab in 1-mL pre-filled syringe (Rx) [*Humira* (patient use syringe carton; sodium chloride; monobasic sodium phosphate dihydrate; dibasic sodium phosphate dihydrate; sodium citrate; citric acid monohydrate; mannitol; polysorbate 80; water for injection)].

40 mg (0.8 mL) of adalimumab per 1-mL pre-filled syringe (Rx) [*Humira* (institutional use syringe carton; sodium chloride; monobasic sodium phosphate dihydrate; dibasic sodium phosphate dihydrate; sodium citrate; citric acid monohydrate; mannitol; polysorbate 80; water for injection)].

Canada—

40 mg (0.8 mL) of adalimumab per 1-mL pre-filled syringe (Rx) [*Humira*].

Packaging and storage

Store between 2 and 8 °C (36 and 46 °F), in the original container. Store in the refrigerator and do not freeze.

Preparation of dosage form

Pre-filled syringes: Inject the full amount in the syringe (0.8 mL), which provides 40 mg of adalimumab.

Vials: 0.8 mL of solution providing 40 mL of adalimumab should be withdrawn from the vial.

Stability

Solution in the syringe should be carefully inspected visually for particulate matter and discoloration prior to subcutaneous administration. If particulates and discoloration are noted, the product should not be used.

Adalimumab does not contain preservatives and unused portions of drug remaining from syringe or vial should be discarded.

Auxiliary labeling

- Must be refrigerated.
- Do not freeze.
- Store in original carton until time of administration.
- Protect from light.

Caution

The needle cover of the syringe contains dry rubber (latex), which should not be handled by persons sensitive to this substance.

Note

Adalimumab is intended for use under the guidance and supervision of a physician. Patients may self-inject adalimumab if their physician determines it is appropriate and with medical follow-up if necessary, after proper training in injection technique.

Revised: 07/19/2006
Developed: 10/22/2003

ADAPALENE Topical

VA CLASSIFICATION (Primary): DE752

Commonly used brand name(s): *Differin.*

Note: For a listing of dosage forms and brand names by country availability, see *Dosage Forms* section(s).

Category

Antiacne agent (topical).

Indications

Accepted

Acne vulgaris (treatment)—Adapalene is indicated for the treatment of acne vulgaris. It is most effective for treating mild to moderate acne vulgaris.

Pharmacology/Pharmacokinetics

Physicochemical characteristics

Chemical Group—Synthetic retinoic acid analog; derivative of naphthoic acid.

Molecular weight—412.53.

Solubility—Slightly soluble in ethanol and insoluble in water.

Mechanism of action/Effect

The exact mechanism is not known. Adapalene exhibits some retinoic acid-like activity but it also has additional effects. It is thought that adapalene reduces important features of the pathology of acne vulgaris by normalizing the differentiation of follicular epithelial cells and keratinization to prevent microcomedone formation, similar to the mechanism of retinoic acid. Unlike retinoic acid, adapalene selectively binds to some nuclear retinoic acid receptors (RARs) and does not bind to cellular receptors called cytosolic retinoic acid binding proteins (CRABPs). It is hypothesized that by selectively binding to certain nuclear retinoic acid receptors and not others, adapalene enhances keratinocyte differentiation without inducing epidermal hyperplasia and severe irritation, such as is seen with retinoic acid. Also, adapalene may help reduce cell-mediated inflammation, an effect demonstrated by *in vitro* studies. Adapalene decreases formation of comedones and inflammatory and noninflammatory acne lesions.

Absorption

Low absorption through skin.

Onset of action

Although clinical response may be detected in 1 to 2 weeks, an optimal response is typically seen after 8 to 12 weeks.

Elimination

Fecal (biliary).

Precautions to Consider

Carcinogenicity/Tumorigenicity

Adapalene was not found to be carcinogenic in mice administered topical doses of 0.3, 0.9, and 2.6 mg per kg of body weight (mg/kg) per day. Oral doses of 0.15, 0.5, and 1.5 mg/kg given to rats increased the incidence of follicular cell adenomas and carcinomas of the thyroid in female rats, and benign and malignant pheochromocytomas in the adrenal medulla in male rats.

Although no photocarcinogenicity studies were conducted with adapalene, other topical retinoids have shown increased risk of tumorigenicity in animals when they were exposed to sunlight or ultraviolet irradiation in the laboratory under certain circumstances but not in all test systems. The significance of these animal studies to humans is not known.

Mutagenicity

Adapalene was not found to be mutagenic or genotoxic in a series of *in vivo* and *in vitro* studies.

Pregnancy/Reproduction

Pregnancy—Adequate and well-controlled studies in humans have not been done. Although problems have not been reported with topical adapalene in the dose used for acne, it is recommended that pregnant women not use adapalene, based on data for other topical retinoids. As a general precaution, women of reproductive age may want contraception counseling before initiating treatment.

Teratologic studies of topical adapalene use in rats and rabbits are inconclusive. An increased number of ribs was seen in studies done in rats given topical doses of 0.6, 2, and 6 mg/kg a day (doses up to 150 times greater than the usual topical human dose); fetotoxicity was not seen in rats or rabbits at these doses. In oral doses of 25 mg/kg a day, adapalene is teratogenic in rats and rabbits.

FDA Pregnancy Category C.

Breast-feeding

It is not known whether adapalene is distributed into breast milk.

Pediatrics

No information is available on the relationship of age to the effects of adapalene in pediatric patients. Safety and efficacy in children up to 12 years of age have not been established.

Geriatrics

No information is available on the relationship of age to the effects of adapalene in geriatric patients. Acne vulgaris is not likely to occur in this age group.

Drug interactions and/or related problems

The following drug interactions and/or related problems have been selected on the basis of their potential clinical significance (possible mechanism in parentheses where appropriate)—not necessarily inclusive (» = major clinical significance):

Note: Combinations containing any of the following medications, depending on the amount present, may also interact with this medication.

Acne products, topical, or topical products containing a peeling agent, such as
- Antibiotics, topical, such as
- Clindamycin, topical
- Erythromycin, topical
- Benzoyl peroxide
- Resorcinol
- Salicylic acid
- Sulfur or

Alcohol-containing products or products containing strong drying agents, such as
- After-shave lotions
- Astringents
- Cosmetics or soaps with a strong drying effect
- Shaving creams or lotions

Hair products, skin-irritating, such as hair permanents or hair removal products

Products containing lime or spices, topical

Soaps or skin cleansers, abrasive

(concurrent use with adapalene may cause a cumulative irritating or drying effect resulting in irritation of the skin and/or sensitivity to the sun; if these effects occur, adapalene should be discontinued or initiation of treatment delayed until skin irritation has subsided)

(use of benzoyl peroxide or topical antibiotics with adapalene on the same area of the skin at the same time is not recommended. A physical incompatibility between the medications or a change in pH may reduce adapalene's efficacy if used simultaneously. When used together for clinical effect, it is recommended that these medications be used at different times of the day, such as morning and night, to minimize possible skin irritation. If irritation results, the dose of adapalene may need to be reduced or temporarily discontinued until the skin is less sensitive)

Medical considerations/Contraindications

The medical considerations/contraindications included have been selected on the basis of their potential clinical significance (reasons given in parentheses where appropriate)—not necessarily inclusive (» = major clinical significance).

Risk-benefit should be considered when the following medical problems exist:

Dermatitis, seborrheic or
Eczema
(skin irritation may be increased)

Sensitivity to adapalene or other ingredients of the formulation

Side/Adverse Effects

The following side/adverse effects have been selected on the basis of their potential clinical significance (possible signs and symptoms in parentheses where appropriate)—not necessarily inclusive:

Those indicating need for medical attention

Incidence more frequent

Burning sensation or stinging of skin; erythema (redness of skin); ***pruritus*** (itching of skin); ***scaling*** (dryness and peeling of skin)

Note: A *burning sensation or stinging of skin, erythema*, or *scaling* is commonly seen within the first 4 weeks of use and usually lessens over time. If these effects are severe, dosage frequency of adapalene should be reduced or the medication discontinued until the severe skin irritation subsides. Twenty percent of patients report transient burning and itching of skin upon application of adapalene.

Those indicating need for medical attention only if they continue or are bothersome

Incidence rare

Acne flares (worsening of acne)—1%

Note: *Acne flares* are more commonly seen in the first month of treatment and decrease in frequency and severity thereafter.

Patient Consultation

In providing consultation, consider emphasizing the following selected information (» = major clinical significance):

Before using this medication

» Conditions affecting use, especially:
Sensitivity to adapalene or other ingredients of the formulation
Pregnancy—Problems not reported for topical doses used for acne; however, adapalene use is not recommended during pregnancy; alerting physician if pregnant or trying to become pregnant while using this medication

Proper use of this medication

» Importance of not using more medication than amount prescribed

» Not applying medication to windburned or sunburned skin or on open wounds

» Avoiding contact with the eyes, lips, and mucous membranes of inner nose

Proper administration

» Applying small amount to clean, dry skin; rubbing in gently and well; washing hands to remove medication afterwards

» Continuing to use for the full time of treatment

» Proper dosing
Missed dose: Applying next dose at regularly scheduled time; not doubling doses

» Proper storage

Precautions while using this medication

Possibility that acne may worsen during the first 3 weeks of therapy; not stopping medication unless irritation, dryness, or other symptoms become severe; checking with physician if improvement not seen by 8 to 12 weeks

Avoiding application of any other topical products at the same time as adapalene, especially alcohol-containing products; abrasive or drying agents; sun-sensitizing agents, such as those containing lime or spices; antiacne topical agents, such as antibiotics or peeling agents; abrasive soaps or skin cleansers; or irritating hair products (If using topical clindamycin, erythromycin, or benzoyl peroxide, applying at different times of the day (morning and evening).)

Alerting doctor if excessive skin irritation occurs or is bothersome; using moisturizers, creams, or lotions as necessary to reduce skin irritation or dryness

Avoiding or minimizing exposure of treated areas to direct and artificial sunlight, wind, or extremely cold temperatures; using sunscreens or sunblocking agents of at least SPF 15 and protective clothing over treated areas

Side/adverse effects

Signs of potential side effects, especially burning sensation or stinging of skin; erythema; pruritus; and scaling

General Dosing Information

Medication should not be applied to open wounds or windburned, sunburned, or otherwise irritated skin. If skin irritation occurs or is bothersome, adapalene should be discontinued until skin irritation subsides. Contact with the eyes, lips, and mucous membranes of inner nose should be avoided.

After applying a thin film of medication to skin, the medication should be rubbed in gently and well. Hands should be washed to remove any remaining medication.

Although temporary exacerbation of acne may occur during the first few weeks of use due to the action of adapalene on deep, previously unseen lesions, therapy should be continued.

Although clinical response may be detected in 1 to 2 weeks, treatment should be evaluated if no improvement is seen after 8 to 12 weeks.

Topical Dosage Forms

ADAPALENE GEL

Usual adult and adolescent dose

Acne vulgaris—
Topical, to the involved areas of the skin, once a day as a thin film applied to clean, dry skin at least one hour before bedtime.

Usual pediatric dose

Acne vulgaris—
Safety and efficacy have not been established.

Strength(s) usually available

U.S.—

0.1% (Rx) [*Differin* (edetate disodium; methylparaben; propylene glycol; sodium hydroxide)].

Canada—

0.1% (Rx) [*Differin* (edetate disodium; methylparaben; propylene glycol; sodium hydroxide)].

Packaging and storage

Store between 15 and 30 °C (59 and 86 °F).

Auxiliary labeling

- For external use only.

Note

Include patient instructions when dispensing.

Selected Bibliography

Shalita A, Weiss JS, Chalker DK, et al. A comparison of the efficacy and safety of adapalene gel 0.1% and tretinoin gel 0.025% in the treatment of acne vulgaris: a multicenter trial. J Am Acad Dermatol 1996; 34: 482-5.

Developed: 06/02/1997

ADEFOVIR Systemic†

VA CLASSIFICATION (Primary): AM810

Commonly used brand name(s): *Hepsera*.

Note: For a listing of dosage forms and brand names by country availability, see *Dosage Forms* section(s).

†Not commercially available in Canada.

Category

Antiviral (systemic).

Indications

Recombinant hepatitis B virus (HBV) variants containing lamivudine-resistance-associated mutations (L528M, M552I, M552V, L528M and M552V) in the HBV DNA polymerase gene were susceptible to adefovir *in vitro*. Adefovir has also demonstrated anti-HBV activity (median reduction in serum HBV DNA of 4.3 $\log_{10}$ copies/mL) against clinical isolates of HBV containing lamivudine-resistance-associated mutations. HBV variants with DNA polymerase mutations T476N and R or W501Q associated with resistance to hepatitis B immunoglobulin were susceptible to adefovir *in vitro*.

Accepted

Chronic Hepatitis B (treatment)—Adefovir is indicated for the treatment of chronic hepatitis B in adults with evidence of active viral replication and either evidence of persistent elevations in serum aminotransferases (ALT [SGPT] or AST [SGOT]) or histologically active disease.

Pharmacology/Pharmacokinetics

Physicochemical characteristics

Chemical Group—Adefovir is an acyclic nucleotide analog of adenosine monophosphate. Adefovir dipivoxil is a diester prodrug of the active moiety adefovir.

Molecular weight—Adefovir dipivoxil: 501.48.

Solubility—Aqueous solubility of 19 milligrams per milliliter at pH 2.0 and 0.4 milligrams per milliliter at pH 7.2.

Partition coefficient—

Octanol/aqueous phosphate buffer (log p)—1.91

Mechanism of action/Effect

Adefovir is an acyclic nucleotide analog of adenosine monophosphate. Adefovir is phosphorylated to the active metabolite, adefovir diphosphate, by cellular kinases. Adefovir diphosphate inhibits HBV DNA polymerase (reverse transcriptase) by competing with the natural substrate deoxyadenosine triphosphate and by causing DNA chain termination after its incorporation into viral DNA. The inhibition constant (K_i) for adefovir diphosphate for HBV DNA polymerase is 0.1 micromolar. Adefovir diphosphate is a weak inhibitor of human DNA polymerases alpha and gamma with K_i values of 1.18 micromolar and 0.97 micromolar, respectively.

The *in vitro* antiviral activity of adefovir was determined in HBV transfected human hepatoma cell lines. The concentration of adefovir that inhibited 50% of viral DNA synthesis (IC_{50}) varied from 0.2 to 2.5 micromolar.

Absorption

Oral bioavailability of adefovir from the administered prodrug, adefovir dipivoxil 10 mg, is approximately 59%; not affected when administered with food.

Distribution

Volume of distribution (Vol_D)—Steady state: 392 and 352 milliliters per kilogram following intravenous administration of 1 or 3 milligrams per kilogram per day, respectively.

Protein binding

Very low (≤ 4%)—*in vitro* binding to human plasma or human serum over a concentration range of 0.1 to 25 micrograms per milliliter.

Biotransformation

Following oral administration, adefovir dipivoxil is rapidly converted to adefovir.

Half-life

Elimination (terminal)—7.48 hours

Time to peak concentration

0.58 to 4 hours (median, 1.75 hours) following administration of a 10 milligram single-dose

Peak plasma concentration:

Approximately 18.4 nanograms per milliliter; following administration of a 10 milligram single-dose

Elimination

Renal—45% recovered as adefovir in urine over 24 hours at steady state following 10 milligram oral doses; eliminated by a combination of glomerular filtration and active tubular secretion

In subjects with moderately or severely impaired renal function or with end-stage renal disease (ESRD) requiring hemodialysis, C_{max}, AUC and half-life were increased compared to subjects with normal renal function.

In dialysis, a four hour period of hemodialysis removed approximately 35% of an adefovir dose. Adefovir removal by peritoneal dialysis has not been evaluated.

Precautions to Consider

Carcinogenicity

Carcinogenicity studies in mice and rats receiving adefovir have been conducted. In mice, at dose levels of 1, 3, 10 mg/kg/day, no treatment related increases in tumor incidence were found at 10 mg/kg/day (systemic exposure was 10 times that achieved in humans at a therapeutic dose of 10 mg/day). In rats dosed at levels of 0.5, 1.5, or 5 mg/kg/day, no drug related increase in tumour incidence was observed. The exposure at the high dose was four times that at the human therapeutic dose.

Mutagenicity

Adefovir dipivoxil was mutagenic in the *in vitro* mouse lymphoma cell assay (with or without metabolic activation). Adefovir induced chromosomal aberrations in the *in vitro* human peripheral blood lymphocyte assay without metabolic activation. Adefovir was not clastogenic in the *in vivo* mouse micronucleus assay at doses up to 2,000 mg/kg/day and it was not mutagenic in the Ames bacterial reverse mutation assay using *S. typhimurium* and *E. coli* strains in the presence and absence of metabolic activation.

Pregnancy/Reproduction

Fertility—In reproductive toxicology studies, no evidence of impaired fertility was seen in male or female rats at doses up to 30 mg/kg/day (systemic exposure 19 times that achieved in humans at the therapeutic doses).

Pregnancy—To monitor fetal outcomes of pregnant women exposed to adefovir, a pregnancy registry has been established. Healthcare providers are encouraged to register patients by calling 1–800–258–4263.

There are no adequate and well controlled studies in women. Adefovir should be used during pregnancy only if clearly needed and after careful consideration of the risks and benefits.

Reproduction studies conducted with adefovir dipivoxil administered orally have shown no embryotoxicity or teratogenicity in rats at doses up to 35 mg/kg/day (systemic exposure 23 times that achieved in humans at the therapeutic dose of 10 mg/day), or in rabbits at 20 mg/kg/day (systemic exposure 40 times human). When adefovir was administered intravenously to pregnant rats at doses associated with notable maternal toxicity (20 mg/kg/day, systemic exposure 38 times human), embryotoxicity and an increased incidence of fetal malformations (anasarca, depressed eye bulge, umbilical hernia and kinked tail) were observed. No adverse effects on development were seen with adefovir administered intravenously to pregnant rats at 2.5 mg/kg/day (systemic exposure 12 times human).

FDA Pregnancy Category C

Labor and delivery—There are no studies in pregnant women and no data on the effect of adefovir on transmission of HBV from mother to infant. Appropriate infant immunizations should be used to prevent neonatal acquisition of hepatitis B virus.

Breast-feeding

It is not known whether adefovir is distributed into breast milk. Mothers should be instructed not to breast-feed if they are taking adefovir.

Pediatrics

Appropriate studies on the relationship of age to the effects of adefovir have not been performed in the pediatric population. Safety and efficacy have not been established.

Geriatrics

Appropriate studies on the relationship of age to the effects of adefovir have not been performed in the geriatric population. Dose selection should be done with caution. Elderly patients are more likely to have age related problems such as decreased renal or cardiac function, and concomitant diseases or other drug therapy.

Drug interactions and/or related problems

The following drug interactions and/or related problems have been selected on the basis of their potential clinical significance (possible mechanism in parentheses where appropriate)—not necessarily inclusive (» = major clinical significance):

Adefovir does not inhibit common human CYP450 enzymes (CYP1A2, CYP2C9, CYP2C19, CYP2D6, CYP3A4) and is not a substrate for these enzymes.

Note: Combinations containing any of the following medications, depending on the amount present, may also interact with this medication.

Ibuprofen
(Ibuprofen 800 mg three times a day increased adefovir exposure 23%)

» Nephrotoxic agents, such as (See *Appendix II*)
» Aminoglycosides or
» Cyclosporine or
» Non-steroidal anti-inflammatory agents or
» Tacrolimus or
» Vancomycin
(Risk of nephrotoxicity in patients taking concomitant nephrotoxic agents)

» Nucleoside Analogs
(Lactic acidosis and severe hepatomegaly with steatosis, have been reported with the use of nucleoside analogs alone or in combination with other antiretrovirals; treatment should be suspended in any patient who develops clinical or laboratory findings suggestive of lactic acidosis or hepatotoxicity)

Note: This does not include lamivudine, trimethoprim/sulfamethoxazole, or acetaminophen.

» Renally excreted drugs or
» Renal function, drugs that affect
» Renal function, drugs that reduce
(Serum concentrations of either drug may be increased; patients should be monitored closely for adverse events when adefovir is coadministered with these drugs)

Laboratory value alterations

The following have been selected on the basis of their potential clinical significance (possible effect in parentheses where appropriate)—not necessarily inclusive (» = major clinical significance).

With physiology/laboratory test values
Amylase, serum or
Alanine aminotransferase (ALT [SGPT]) or
Aspartate aminotransferase (AST [SGOT]) or
(Serum values may be increased)

Medical considerations/Contraindications

The medical considerations/contraindications included have been selected on the basis of their potential clinical significance (reasons given in parentheses where appropriate)—not necessarily inclusive (» = major clinical significance).

Except under special circumstances, this medication should not be used when the following medical problem exists:

» Human immunodeficiency virus (HIV)
(HIV counseling and testing should be offered to patients with hepatitis B before they initiate adefovir. Treatment with anti-hepatitis B therapies, such as adefovir, that have an activity against HIV in a chronic Hepatitis B patient with unrecognized or untreated HIV infection may result in emergence of HIV resistance.)

» Hypersensitivity to adefovir or any components of the product

» Renal dysfunction
(Chronic administration of adefovir may result in nephrotoxicity; may require a dose adjustment)

Patient monitoring

The following may be especially important in patient monitoring (other tests may be warranted in some patients, depending on condition; » = major clinical significance):

» Hepatic function and
» Hepatitis exacerbations
(Hepatic function should be monitored periodically in patients who discontinue anti-hepatitis B therapy; severe acute exacerbations of hepatitis have been reported in patients who have discontinued anti-hepatitis B therapy; resumption of therapy may be warranted)

» Renal function
(Renal function should be monitored closely in all patients, especially those at risk of having underlying renal dysfunction; patients with renal insufficiency at baseline or during treatment may require an increase in the dosing interval; nephrotoxicity may occur)

Side/Adverse Effects

Severe acute exacerbations of hepatitis have been reported in patients who have discontinued adefovir anti-hepatitis B therapy.

Chronic use of adefovir may result in nephrotoxicity.

HIV resistance may may emerge in chronic hepatitis B patients with unrecognized or untreated human immunodeficiency virus (HIV) infection treated with anti-hepatitis B therapies that may have activity against HIV.

Lactic acidosis and severe hepatomegaly with steatosis, including fatal cases have been reported with the use of nucleoside analogs; a majority of these cases have been in women.

The most common treatment-related adverse reported in pre-liver and post-liver transplantation patients treated with adefovir with a 2% frequency or higher include: abnormal liver function, hepatic failure, increases in ALT and AST, increases in creatinine, increased cough, pharyngitis, pruritus, sinusitis, rash, renal failure and renal insufficiency.

The following side/adverse effects have been selected on the basis of their potential clinical significance (possible signs and symptoms in parentheses where appropriate)—not necessarily inclusive:

Those indicating need for medical attention

Incidence more frequent
Hematuria (blood in urine)

Incidence less frequent
Glycosuria (sugar in the urine)

Those indicating need for medical attention only if they continue or are bothersome

Incidence more frequent
Abdominal pain; asthenia (lack or loss of strength); ***headache***

Incidence less frequent
Diarrhea; dyspepsia (acid or sour stomach; belching; heartburn; indigestion; stomach discomfort, upset or pain); ***flatulence*** (bloated; full feeling; excess air or gas in stomach or intestines; passing gas); ***nausea***

Overdose

For more information on the management of overdose or unintentional ingestion, **contact a poison control center** (see *Poison Control Center Listing*).

Treatment of overdose

Doses of adefovir dipivoxil 500 mg daily for 2 weeks and 250 mg daily for 12 weeks have been associated with gastrointestinal side effects.

Supportive care—
Patients must be monitored for evidence of toxicity, and standard supportive treatment applied as necessary.
Following a 10 mg single dose of adefovir, a four hour hemodialysis session removed approximately 35% of the adefovir dose.
Patients in whom intentional overdose is confirmed or suspected should be referred for psychiatric consultation.

Patient Consultation

As an aid to patient consultation, refer to *Advice for the Patient, Adefovir (Systemic)*.

In providing consultation, consider emphasizing the following selected information (» = major clinical significance):

Before using this medication

» Conditions affecting use, especially:
Hypersensitivity to adefovir
Pregnancy—There are no adequate and well controlled studies in women. Adefovir should be used during pregnancy only if clearly needed and after careful consideration of the risks and benefits.
FDA Pregnancy Category C
Breast-feeding—Not recommended for use by nursing mothers.
Other medications, especially nephrotoxic agents, nucleoside analogs, renally excreted drugs, drugs that affect renal function, and drugs that reduce renal function
Other medical problems, especially HIV or renal dysfunction

Proper use of this medication

» Proper dosing
Missed dose: Taking as soon as possible; not taking more than one dose each day; not doubling doses
May take with or without food
Proper storage

Precautions while using this medication

» Regular visits to physician to check progress and monitor renal function
Notifying physician if pregnancy is suspected
Test for HIV before starting adefovir and during therapy if there is a chance your were exposed to HIV.
» Recognizing symptoms of lactic acidosis, such as abdominal discomfort; decreased appetite; diarrhea; fast, shallow breathing; general feeling of discomfort; muscle pain or cramping; or unusual sleepiness, tiredness, or weakness
» Getting immediate emergency medical help if symptoms of lactic acidosis occur
Monitoring hepatic function and hepatitis B levels after discontinuation of therapy

Side/adverse effects

Signs of potential side effects, especially hematuria and glycosuria

General Dosing Information

For oral dosing forms:

The optimal duration of adefovir treatment and the relationship between treatment response and long-term outcomes such as hepatocellular carcinoma or decompensated cirrhosis are not known.

Adefovir can be taken with or without food.

Oral Dosage Forms

ADEFOVIR DIPIVOXIL TABLETS

Usual adult dose

Hepatitis B, Chronic (treatment)—
Oral, 10 mg once a day, without regard to food

Note: The safety and effectiveness of the dosing interval adjustment guidelines below have not been clinically evaluated. These guidelines were derived from patients with pre-existing renal impairment at baseline. Creatinine clearance was calculated using the Cockcroft-Gault method using lean or ideal body weight. The guidelines may not be appropriate for patients in whom renal insufficiency evolves during treatment with adefovir. Clinical response to treatment and renal function should be closely monitored in these patients.

The dosing interval of adefovir should be adjusted in patients with baseline creatinine clearance < 50 mL/min using the following guidelines.

- Creatinine Clearance 20 to 49 mL/min: 10 mg every 48 hours
- Creatinine Clearance 10 to 19 mL/min: 10 mg every 72 hours
- Hemodialysis patients: 10 mg every 7 days following dialysis

Usual Pediatric Dose

Safety and efficacy have not been established.

Usual Geriatric Dose

Hepatitis B, Chronic (treatment)—
See *Usual adult prescribing limits.*

Note: Dose selection for elderly patients should be cautious due to the greater frequency of decreased renal or cardiac function due to concomitant disease or other drug therapy.

Strength(s) usually available

U.S.—
10 mg (Rx) [*Hepsera* (croscarmellose sodium; lactose monohydrate; magnesium stearate; pregelatinized starch; talc)].

Canada—
Not commercially available

Packaging and storage

Store in original container at 25 °C (77 °F), excursions permitted to 15 to 30°C (59 to 86 °F).

Auxiliary labeling

- This medication can be taken with or without food.
- Consult with your doctor or pharmacist about using this medication if you are pregnant, plan to become pregnant, or if you are breast-feeding.

Developed: 07/03/2003

ADENOSINE Systemic†

VA CLASSIFICATION (Primary/Secondary): CV300/DX900

Commonly used brand name(s): *Adenocard; Adenoscan.*

Note: For a listing of dosage forms and brand names by country availability, see *Dosage Forms* section(s).

†Not commercially available in Canada.

Category

Antiarrhythmic; diagnostic aid adjunct (ischemic heart disease).

Indications

Note: Bracketed information in the *Indications* section refers to uses that are not included in U.S. product labeling.

Accepted

Tachycardia, supraventricular, paroxysmal (treatment)—Adenosine is indicated for conversion to sinus rhythm of paroxysmal supraventricular tachycardia, including those due to atrioventricular (AV) node reentry and associated with accessory bypass tracts (Wolff-Parkinson-White syndrome), after appropriate vagal maneuvers (e.g., Valsalva maneuver) have been attempted.

Myocardial perfusion imaging, radionuclide (adjunct)[1]; or
[Stress echocardiography (adjunct)][1]—In patients unable to exercise adequately, adenosine is used to induce coronary artery vasodilation in conjunction with myocardial perfusion imaging (i.e., thallium-201 myocardial perfusion scintigraphy) or two-dimensional echocardiography for the detection of perfusion defects or regional contraction abnormalities associated with coronary artery disease.

Acceptance not established

Adenosine has been studied for the diagnosis and treatment of *tachyarrhythmias of ventricular origin* in neonates and for treatment of *pulmonary hypertension of the newborn.* More data are needed to assess the place in therapy for adenosine for these indications.

[1]Not included in Canadian product labeling.

Pharmacology/Pharmacokinetics

Mechanism of action/Effect

Antiarrhythmic—Slows impulse formation in the sinoatrial (SA) node, slows conduction time through the atrioventricular (AV) node, and can interrupt reentry pathways through the AV node. Adenosine depresses left ventricular function, but because of its short half-life, the effect is transient, allowing use in patients with existing poor left ventricular function.

Diagnostic aid—The precise mechanism of coronary vasodilation is not completely understood. However, it is speculated that adenosine may have a direct effect on smooth muscle receptors and may influence cellular calcium dynamics. Coronary vasodilation by adenosine contributes to the creation of heterogeneity of myocardial blood flow. The difference in coronary reserve in the vascular bed distal to a critical coronary stenosis versus that supplied by normal coronary arteries accounts for a significantly greater, 3- to 5-fold, increase in regional myocardial blood flow to normal epicardial vessels.

Other actions/effects

Administration of doses larger than 12 mg by intravenous infusion decreases blood pressure by reducing peripheral vascular resistance. Physiologically, naturally occurring adenosine functions as an intermediate metabolite in a number of processes including regulation of coronary and systemic vascular tone, platelet function, lipolysis in fat cells, and intracardiac conduction.

Biotransformation
Very rapid, by circulating enzymes in erythrocytes and vascular endothelial cells, by deamination, primarily to inactive inosine (further degraded to hypoxanthine and then to uric acid) and by phosphorylation to adenosine monophosphate (AMP).

Half-life
Less than 10 seconds.

Onset of action
Immediate.

Elimination
Principal elimination routes are cellular uptake, primarily by erythrocytes and vascular endothelial cells, and metabolism. Metabolites excreted renally. The predominant final excretory metabolite is uric acid.

Precautions to Consider

Carcinogenicity
Studies have not been done.

Mutagenicity
Mutagenicity tests in the Salmonella/mammalian microsome assay (Ames test) were negative. However, adenosine causes chromosomal alterations.

Pregnancy/Reproduction
Fertility—In rats and mice, intraperitoneal administration of 50, 100, and 150 mg per kg of body weight (mg/kg) per day for 5 days caused decreased spermatogenesis and increased numbers of abnormal sperm.

Pregnancy—Studies have not been done in humans. Because adenosine occurs naturally in the body, problems are not expected. Scant reports of adenosine use in pregnant women have not revealed fetal or maternal sequelae.

Studies have not been done in animals.

FDA Pregnancy Category C.

Breast-feeding
Because of rapid removal from circulation, adenosine is not expected to be distributed into breast milk.

Pediatrics
Studies performed to date on adenosine's use as an antiarrhythmic have not demonstrated pediatrics-specific problems that would limit the usefulness of this medication in the pediatric population.

The safety and effectiveness of adenosine, when used as an adjunct to myocardial perfusion imaging, have not been established in patients less than 18 years of age.

Geriatrics
Appropriate studies on the relationship of age to the effects of adenosine have not been performed in the geriatric population. However, geriatrics-specific problems that would limit the usefulness of this medication in the elderly are not expected.

Drug interactions and/or related problems
The following drug interactions and/or related problems have been selected on the basis of their potential clinical significance (possible mechanism in parentheses where appropriate)—not necessarily inclusive (» = major clinical significance):

Note: Combinations containing any of the following medications, depending on the amount present, may also interact with this medication.

Carbamazepine
(may increase heart block caused by adenosine)

Dipyridamole
(potentiates the effects of adenosine by inhibiting cellular uptake; dosage reduction is recommended)

Xanthines, especially caffeine and theophylline
(antagonize the effects of adenosine; larger doses of adenosine may be required or alternative therapy should be used)
(concurrent use with xanthines may invalidate test when adenosine is used as a diagnostic aid)

Medical considerations/Contraindications
The medical considerations/contraindications included have been selected on the basis of their potential clinical significance (reasons given in parentheses where appropriate)—not necessarily inclusive (» = major clinical significance).

Except under special circumstances, this medication should not be used when the following medical problem exists:

» Atrioventricular (AV) block, pre-existing second or third degree without pacemaker
(risk of complete heart block)

Risk-benefit should be considered when the following medical problems exist:

Angina pectoris, unstable
(may increase risk of developing fatal cardiac arrest, life threatening ventricular arrhythmias, and myocardial infarction)

Asthma
(although problems have not been reported with adenosine injection, inhaled adenosine has been reported to cause bronchoconstriction in asthmatic patients but not in normal individuals)

Hypotension
(patients with autonomic dysfunction, stenotic valvular heart disease, pericarditis or pericardial effusions, stenotic carotid artery disease with cerebrovascular insufficiency, or uncorrected hypovolemia are at a greater risk of hypotensive complications)

Sensitivity to adenosine

» Sick sinus syndrome
(sinus node recovery time prolonged; sinus bradycardia, sinus pause, or sinus arrest may occur)

Patient monitoring
The following may be especially important in patient monitoring (other tests may be warranted in some patients, depending on condition; » = major clinical significance):

» Blood pressure and
» Heart rate
(determinations recommended every 15 to 30 seconds for several minutes)

» Electrocardiogram (ECG)
(recommended to confirm efficacy of adenosine)

Side/Adverse Effects

Note: Side/adverse effects are usually transient, generally lasting less than one minute. However, loss of consciousness and prolonged hypotension have been reported rarely.

The following side/adverse effects have been selected on the basis of their potential clinical significance (possible signs and symptoms in parentheses where appropriate)—not necessarily inclusive:

Those indicating need for medical attention
Incidence more frequent
Arrhythmias, new, including premature ventricular contractions, atrial premature contractions, sinus bradycardia, sinus tachycardia, and skipped beats; chest, jaw, throat, or arm pain; dyspnea (shortness of breath)

Note: *New arrhythmias* usually last only a few seconds.

Incidence rare
Heart block, first-, second-, or third-degree

Note: *Heart block* is usually of short duration and may occur more frequently in patients who receive a rapid intravenous dose of adenosine. Episodes of transient asystole have been reported.

Those indicating need for medical attention only if they continue or are bothersome
Incidence more frequent
Flushing of face; gastrointestinal discomfort (abdominal or stomach pain; diarrhea; nausea; vomiting); ***headache***

Incidence less frequent
Cough; dizziness or lightheadedness; nausea; numbness or tingling in arms

General Dosing Information

If high-level heart block occurs after one dose of adenosine, it is recommended that additional doses not be given. The effect usually resolves quickly because of adenosine's short duration of action.

Rapid intravenous administration of adenosine is recommended for the treatment of paroxysmal supraventricular tachycardia in order to achieve the desired negative chronotropic and dromotropic activity. Slow administration may result in an increase in heart rate in response to vasodilation.

During myocardial perfusion imaging, adenosine should be given as a continuous peripheral intravenous infusion. Safety and efficacy of adenosine administered by the intracoronary route have not been established.

For treatment of adverse effects and/or overdose

Because of adenosine's extremely short duration of action, adverse effects are usually self-limiting. Treatment of prolonged adverse effects should be individualized. Xanthines (e.g., caffeine, theophylline) are competitive antagonists of adenosine.

Parenteral Dosage Forms

Note: Bracketed uses in the *Dosage Forms* section refer to categories of use and/or indications that are not included in U.S. product labeling.

ADENOSINE INJECTION

Usual adult dose

Antiarrhythmic—

Intravenous, rapid (over one to two seconds), 6 mg. If the first dose is not effective within one to two minutes, a rapid intravenous dose of 12 mg may be given, and repeated if necessary.

Diagnostic aid adjunct[1]—

Intravenous, 140 mcg (0.14 mg) per kg of body weight per minute given for six minutes.

Note: The following adenosine infusion nomogram may be used to determine the appropriate infusion rate corrected for total body weight:

Patient Weight kg	Patient Weight lbs	Infusion Rate mL/min
45	99	2.1
50	110	2.3
55	121	2.6
60	132	2.8
65	143	3.0
70	154	3.3
75	165	3.5
80	176	3.8
85	187	4.0
90	198	4.2

This nomogram was derived from the following general formula: 0.140 (mg/kg/min) × total body weight (kg) ÷ adenosine concentration (3 mg/mL) = infusion rate (mL/min).

In patients at increased risk for side/adverse effects, the dose may be titrated from 50 mcg (0.05 mg) per kg of body weight per minute up to 140 mcg (0.14 mg) per kg of body weight per minute at one-minute intervals. If side/adverse effects are severe, the infusion rate may be reduced to a more tolerable level. Doses of 75 and 100 mcg (0.075 and 0.1 mg) per kg of body weight per minute can adequately increase coronary blood flow.

Thallium is physically compatible with adenosine and may be injected directly into the adenosine infusion set; however, it has been suggested that thallium should be injected into a separate vein. Thallium is usually injected at the three- or four-minute mark (mid-point) of the adenosine infusion.

Note: To ensure that adenosine injection reaches the systemic circulation, it should be given directly into a vein or, if given into an intravenous line, be given as proximally as possible and followed by a rapid saline flush.

Usual adult prescribing limits

Up to 12 mg per dose.

Usual pediatric dose

Antiarrhythmic—

Intravenous, 50 mcg (0.05 mg) per kg of body weight. Dose may be increased in increments of 50 mcg (0.05 mg) per kg of body weight given every two minutes up to a maximum dose of 250 mcg (0.25 mg) per kg of body weight.

Diagnosis and treatment of supraventricular tachycardia in neonates—Intravenous, 100 mcg (0.1 mg) to 300 mcg (0.3 mg) per kg of body weight

Diagnostic aid adjunct—

Safety and effectiveness of adenosine in patients less than 18 years of age have not been established.

Strength(s) usually available

U.S.—

3 mg per mL (Rx) [*Adenocard*].

3 mg per mL (Rx) [*Adenoscan* (20 mL and 30 mL vials; sodium chloride (9 mg/mL); water for injection)].

Canada—

Not commercially available.

Packaging and storage

Store between 15 and 30 °C (59 and 86 °F), unless otherwise specified by manufacturer. Do not refrigerate. Protect from freezing.

Stability

Because adenosine injection contains no preservatives, any unused portion should be discarded.

Crystallization may occur if adenosine injection is refrigerated. If that occurs, the crystals may be dissolved by warming the injection to room temperature. The solution must be clear before use.

[1]Not included in Canadian product labeling.

Selected Bibliography

Parker RB, McCollam PL. Adenosine in the episodic treatment of paroxysmal supraventricular tachycardia. Clin Pharm 1990 Apr; 9: 261-71.

Gupta NC, Esterbrooks DJ, Hilleman DE, Mohiuddin SM. Comparison of adenosine and exercise thallium-201 single-photon emission computed tomography (SPECT) myocardial perfusion imaging. J Am Coll Cardiol 1992; 19: 248-57.

Rankin AC, Brooks R, Ruskin JN. Adenosine and the treatment of supraventricular tachycardia. Am J Med 1992; 92: 655-64.

Revised: 08/21/2000

AGALSIDASE BETA Systemic†

VA CLASSIFICATION (Primary): HS451

Commonly used brand name(s): *Fabrazyme*.

Note: For a listing of dosage forms and brand names by country availability, see *Dosage Forms* section(s).

†Not commercially available in Canada.

Category

Enzyme (alpha-galactosidase A) replenisher.

Indications

Accepted

Fabry disease (treatment)—Agalsidase beta is indicated for use in patients with Fabry disease for the purpose of providing an exogenous source of α-galactosidase A. A deficiency of α-galactosidase A leads to progressive accumulation of glycosphingolipids, mainly globotriasylceramide (GL-3), in many body tissues. Agalsidase beta will catalyze the hydrolysis of glycosphingolipids including GL-3.

Pharmacology/Pharmacokinetics

Physicochemical characteristics

Source—Agalsidase beta is produced by recombinant DNA technology in a Chinese Hamster Ovary mammalian cell expression system.

Molecular weight—Agalsidase beta: approximately 100 KD.

Specific activity—approximately 70 U/mg

Mechanism of action/Effect

Agalsidase catalyzes the hydrolysis of glycosphingolipids including GL-3, and provides an exogenous source of α-galactosidase A in Fabry disease patients.

Half-life

Terminal—45 to 102 minutes; dose independent

Precautions to Consider

Carcinogenicity/Mutagenicity

Studies in humans or animals have not been done.

Pregnancy/Reproduction

Fertility—Studies performed in rats given doses up to 30 times the human dose have revealed no evidence of impaired fertility.

Pregnancy—*Women of childbearing potential should be encouraged to enroll in the Fabry patient registry. For more information visit www.febryregistry.com or call (800) 745–4447.*

Adequate and well controlled studies in humans have not been done. Studies in animals have not shown that agalsidase beta causes adverse effects in the fetus. Because animals studies are not alway predictive of human response, agalsidase beta should only be used during pregnancy only if clearly needed.

FDA Pregnancy Category B

Breast-feeding

Nursing mothers should be encouraged to enroll in the Fabry patient registry. For more information visit www.fabryregistry.com or call (800) 745–4447.

It is not known whether agalsidase beta is distributed into breast milk. Because many drugs are distributed into breast milk caution is advised when administering agalsidase beta to a nursing woman.

Pediatrics

Safety and effectiveness of agalsidase beta in pediatric patients have not been established.

Geriatrics

No information is available on the relationship of age to the effects of agalsidase beta in geriatric patients.

Drug interactions and/or related problems

The following drug interactions and/or related problems have been selected on the basis of their potential clinical significance (possible mechanism in parentheses where appropriate)—not necessarily inclusive (» = major clinical significance):

No drug interaction studies were done.

Medical considerations/Contraindications

The medical considerations/contraindications included have been selected on the basis of their potential clinical significance (reasons given in parentheses where appropriate)—not necessarily inclusive (» = major clinical significance).

Except under special circumstances, this medication should not be used when the following medical problem exists:

» Hypersensitivity to agalsidase beta or any of its excipients.

Risk-benefit should be considered when the following medical problems exist:

» Cardiac function, compromised
(may be at a higher risk of severe complications from infusion reactions)

Patient monitoring

The following may be especially important in patient monitoring (other tests may be warranted in some patients, depending on condition; » = major clinical significance):

» Cardiac function, compromised
(should be monitored closely)

Side/Adverse Effects

The following side/adverse effects have been selected on the basis of their potential clinical significance (possible signs and symptoms in parentheses where appropriate)—not necessarily inclusive:

Those indicating need for medical attention

Incidence more frequent

Arthrosis (degenerative disease of the joint); ***bronchitis*** (cough producing mucus; difficulty breathing; shortness of breath; tightness in chest; wheezing); ***bronchospasm*** (cough; difficulty breathing; noisy breathing; shortness of breath; tightness in chest; wheezing); ***cardiomegaly*** (chest pain or discomfort; shortness of breath; irregular heartbeat; fatigue); ***chest pain; edema*** (swelling of ankles, feet, and lower legs); ***infusion reaction, including; abdominal pain; chills/rigors*** (feeling unusually cold shivering); ***chest tightness; dyspena*** (shortness of breath; difficult or labored breathing; tightness in chest, wheezing); ***headache; hypertension*** (blurred vision; dizziness; nervousness; headache; pounding in the ears; slow or fast heartbeat); ***hypotension*** (blurred vision; confusion; dizziness; faintness, or lightheadedness when getting up from a lying or sitting position suddenly; sweating; unusual tiredness or weakness); ***myalgia*** (joint pain; swollen joints, muscle aching or cramping; muscle pains or stiffness; difficulty in moving); ***pruritus*** (itching skin); ***urticaria*** (hives or welts; itching; redness of skin; skin rash); ***pain***

Incidence unknown

Ataxia (shakiness and unsteady walk; unsteadiness; trembling, or other problems with muscle control or coordination); ***bradycardia*** (chest pain or discomfort; lightheadedness; dizziness or fainting; shortness of breath, slow or irregular heartbeat; unusual tiredness); ***cardiac arrest*** (stopping of heart; no blood pressure or pulse; unconsciousness); ***cardiac arrhythmia*** (chest pain or discomfort; dizziness; fainting; fast, slow, or irregular heartbeat; lightheadedness; pounding or rapid pulse); ***decreased cardiac output; hypoacousia*** (partial loss of hearing); ***hypoacousia*** (swelling of the lip or ear); ***nephrotic syndrome*** (cloudy or bloody urine; high blood pressure; swelling of face, feet or lower legs); ***rash; stroke*** (confusion; difficulty in speaking; slow speech; inability to speak; inability to move arms, legs, or facial muscles; double vision, headache); ***tachycardia*** (fast, pounding, or irregular heartbeat or pulse); ***throat tightness; vertigo*** (dizziness or lightheadedness; feeling of constant movement of self or surroundings; sensation of spinning)

Those indicating need for medical attention only if they continue or are bothersome

Incidence more frequent

Anxiety (fear; nervousness); ***depression*** (discouragement; feeling sad or empty; irritability; lack of appetite; loss of interest or pleasure; tiredness; trouble concentrating; trouble sleeping); ***dizziness; dyspepsia*** (acid or sour stomach; belching; heartburn; indigestion; stomach discomfort upset or pain); ***fever, not related to infusion; immunogenicity*** (body produces substance that can bind to drug making it less effective or cause side effects); ***laryngitis*** (cough; dryness or soreness of throat; hoarseness; trouble in swallowing; voice changes); ***nausea; pallor*** (paleness of skin); ***paraesthesias*** (burning, crawling, itching, numbness, prickling, "pins and needles", or tingling feelings); ***pharyngitis*** (body aches or pain; congestion; cough; dryness or soreness of throat; fever; hoarseness; runny nose; tender, swollen glands in neck; trouble in swallowing; voice changes); ***rhinitis*** (stuffy nose; runny nose; sneezing); ***sensation of change in temperature; sinusitis*** (pain or tenderness around eyes and cheekbones; fever; stuffy or runny nose; headache; cough; shortness of breath or troubled breathing; tightness of chest or wheezing); ***skeletal pain; testicular pain*** (swelling of testes)

Overdose

For more information on the management of overdose or unintentional ingestion, **contact a poison control center** (see *Poison Control Center Listing*).

Treatment of overdose

There have been no reports of overdose with agalsidase beta. In clinical trials patients received doses up to 3 mg/kg of body weight.

Specific treatment—
Treatment should be symptomatic and supportive.

Supportive care—
Patients in whom intentional overdose is confirmed or suspected should be referred for psychiatric consultation.

Patient Consultation

As an aid to patient consultation, refer to *Advice for the Patient, Agalsidase beta (Systemic).*

In providing consultation, consider emphasizing the following selected information (» = major clinical significance):

Before using this medication

» Conditions affecting use, especially:
Hypersensitivity to agalsidase beta or any os its excipients
Pregnancy—Adequate and well controlled studies in humans have not been done; agalsidase beta should only be used during pregnancy only if clearly needed.
FDA Pregnancy Category B
Breast-feeding—It is not known whether agalsidase beta is distributed into breast milk. Because many drugs are distributed into breast milk caution is advised when administering agalsidase beta to a nursing woman.
Other medical problems, especially compromised cardiac function.

Proper use of this medication

» Proper dosing
Proper storage

Precautions while using this medication

» Importance of monitoring by the physician

» Infusion reactions have occurred in many patients. It is important to receive medication to treat the reaction before agalsidase beta is given.

» Importance of receiving agalsidase beta in healthcare facility with the appropriate medical support to treat severe infusion reactions.

Side/adverse effects

Signs of potential side effects, especially arthrosis, bronchitis, bronchospasm, cardiomegaly, chest pain, edema, infusion reaction, including, abdominal pain, chills/rigors, chest tightness, dyspena, headache, hypertension, hypotension, myalgia, pruritus, and urticaria, pain, Ataxia, bradycardia, cardiac arrest, cardiac arrhythmia, decreased cardiac output, hypoacousia, nephrotic syndrome, rash, stroke, tachycardia, throat tightness, vertigo

General Dosing Information

All patients should be pretreated with acetaminophen and an antihistamine prior to infusion.

If an infusion reaction occurs, decreasing the infusion rate, temporarily stopping the infusion and/or administering additional antipyretics, antihistamines, and/or steroids may ameliorate the symptoms.

Appropriate medical support should be readily available when agalsidase beta is administered, due to the potential for severe infusion reactions.

Some patients may develop IgE or skin test reactivity specific to agalsidase beta. Therefore, IgE testing should be considered in patients who experienced suspected allergic reactions to determine the risks and benefits of continued treatment with agalsidase beta.

There are no marketed test for antibodies against agalsidase beta. If testing is warranted, contact your local Genzyme Corporation at (800) 745–4777.

Patients should be informed and encouraged to participate in a voluntary Registry that has been established to better understand the variability and progression of Fabry disease in the population as a whole, in women, and the treatment effects of agalsidase beta. The Registry will also monitor the effect of agalsidase beta on pregnant women and their offspring, and determine if agalsidase beta is distributed into breast milk. For more information on the registry visit *www.fabryregistry.com or call (800) 745–4447.*

Parenteral Dosage Forms

AGALSIDASE BETA FOR INJECTION

Usual adult dose

Enzyme (alpha-galactosidase A) replenisher—

Intervenous infusion, 1 mg/kg of body weight infused every 2 weeks. The initial infusion rate should be no more than 0.25 mg/min (15 mg/hr). The rate may be slowed in the event of associated infusion reactions. When the patient has established tolerance to the infusion, the infusion rate may be increased in increments of 0.05 to 0.08 mg/min (3 to 5 mg/hr) each subsequent infusion. Patients have received infusions at rates ≥ 33 mg/hr.

Usual pediatric dose

Safety and efficacy have not been established

Usual geriatric dose

See *Usual adult dose.*

Strength(s) usually available

U.S.—

Note: Vial closure consists of a siliconized butyl stopper and an aluminum seal.

37 mg of agalsidase beta in 20-mL glass vial (Rx) [*Fabrazyme* (mannitol; sodium phosphate dibasic heptahydrate; sodium phosphate monobasic monohydrate; sterile water)].

Packaging and storage

Store between 2 and 8 °C (36 and 46 °F).

Preparation of dosage form

• Agalsidase beta vials and diluent should reach room temperature before reconstitution (approximately 30 minutes). The number of vials needed is based on body weight (kg) and the recommended dose of 1 mg/kg.

• Do not use filter needles during preparation of the infusion

• Reconstitute by slowly injecting 7.2 mL of Sterile Water for Injection, USP down the inside wall of each vial. Do not shake. Gently roll and tilt each vial to mix. Each vial will contain 5 mg/mL clear, colorless solution (35 mg, in 7 mL).

• Visually inspect the reconstituted solution for discoloration or particular matter. Do not use the reconstituted solution if there is particulate matter or if it is discolored.

• The reconstituted solution should be further diluted with 0.9% Sodium Chloride Injection, USP to a final volume of 500 mL. Before adding the volume of reconstituted agalsidase beta required for the patient dose, remove an equal volume of 0.9% Sodium Chloride for Injection, USP from the 500 mL infusion bag. Slowly withdraw the required dose volume from each reconstituted vial and then inject it directly into the Sodium Chloride solution. Do not inject into the air space within the infusion bag. Discard any unused reconstituted solution.

• To mix the solution gently invert the infusion bag, careful to avoid vigorous shaking and agitation.

• Agalsidase should not be infused in the same intervenous line with other products.

• An in line low protien-binding 0.2 μm filter may be used for filtration of the diluted solution during administration.

Stability

Since agalsidase contains no preservatives it should be used immediately upon reconstitution. If immediate use is not possible the reconstituted and diluted solution may be stored for up to 24 hours at 2 to 8°C (36 to 46°F).

DO NOT USE vials for reconstitution after the expiration date on the vial.

Auxiliary labeling

• Do not shake.
• For single use only. Discard unused drug.

Developed: 03/29/2004

ALATROFLOXACIN MESYLATE—See *Trovafloxacin (Systemic)*

ALBUMIN HUMAN Systemic

VA CLASSIFICATION (Primary): BL800

Commonly used brand name(s): *Albuminar-25; Albuminar-5; Albutein 25%; Albutein 5%; Buminate 25%; Buminate 5%; Plasbumin-25; Plasbumin-5.*

Note: For a listing of dosage forms and brand names by country availability, see *Dosage Forms* section(s).

Category

Blood volume expander; antihyperbilirubinemic.

Indications

General Considerations

The benefit of administration of albumin to seriously ill patients is currently controversial. A meta-analysis of randomized, controlled clinical studies of albumin use revealed excess mortality of approximately 6% (i.e., 1 excess death per 17 treated patients) for combined groups of patients with hypovolemia, burns, or hypoproteinemia who received albumin either instead of or in addition to crystalloid solutions. Also, for each of these patient subgroups, the risk of death in the albumin-treated group was higher than in the comparison group.

In response to this meta-analysis, the United States Food and Drug Administration suggested physicians exercise discretion in the use of albumin based on their own assessment of the above data until the results of further, well-focused studies are available. However, the recently published meta-analysis has received criticism from a number of clinicians. Some of the arguments against the validity of the conclusions drawn from the review involve the fact that the individual studies reviewed were heterogeneous, comparing different disease states, age groups, study designs and endpoints, and that the cause of death was ignored. Other concerns include the small number of patients included in the majority of the studies (17 out of 32 studies included 30 patients or less [range in all studies, 12–219]); the age of many of the studies; and the use of multiple methods of albumin administration, some of which may be outdated.

Current treatment guidelines such as those of the Subcommittee of the Victorian Drug Usage Advisory Committee and the University Hospital Consortium should be consulted until further information concerning albumin administration is available, while recognizing that these guidelines themselves may require change.

Accepted

Hypovolemia (treatment)—The 5 and 25% concentrations of albumin are indicated in the emergency treatment of hypovolemia with or without shock. Albumin restores intravascular volume and maintains cardiac output and colloid oncotic pressure. If blood loss is severe, a transfusion of whole blood or red blood cells may be indicated to restore the hemoglobin concentration and improve oxygen transport.

Hypoproteinemia (treatment)—The 25% concentration of albumin is indicated in the treatment of hypoproteinemia caused by loss of plasma proteins. Although the 5% concentration of albumin has been used, the 25% concentration is preferred.

Loss of plasma proteins may occur through decreased absorption in gastrointestinal disorders, inadequate synthesis in chronic liver disease, or excessive urinary loss and increased catabolism in chronic kidney disease. This loss of protein leads to edema secondary to a fluid shift from the intravascular space to the interstitium and a compensatory increase in salt and water retention. Albumin serves to restore colloid oncotic pressure and, in conjunction with a diuretic, promote diuresis.

The Subcommittee of the Victorian Drug Usage Advisory Committee (SVDUAC) states albumin use may be appropriate when the serum albumin is less than 25 grams per liter (g/L) and accompanied by edema and/or possibly clinically significant hypernatremia. Albumin also may be appropriate for use in extremely low hypoalbuminemia in critically ill patients.

Burns, severe (treatment adjunct)—The 5 and 25% concentrations of albumin are indicated, in conjunction with large volumes of crystalloid injection, to maintain plasma volume and protein concentration and to prevent the intravascular hemoconcentration accompanying severe burns.

Hyperbilirubinemia, neonatal (treatment)—The 25% albumin injection is indicated in the treatment of hyperbilirubinemia whether or not it is associated with hemolytic disease. It may be used prior to or during an exchange transfusion to bind free bilirubin and to enhance its removal.

Respiratory distress syndrome, adult (ARDS) (treatment adjunct)—The 25% albumin injection may be indicated, in conjunction with diuretics, to correct the fluid volume overload associated with ARDS.

Cardiopulmonary bypass (treatment adjunct)—The 5 and 25% concentrations of albumin may be indicated as adjuncts to provide hemodilution in cardiopulmonary bypass procedures.

Ascites (treatment adjunct)[1]—The 5 and 25% concentrations of albumin may be used to maintain cardiovascular function following the removal of large volumes of ascitic fluid.

Nephrosis, acute (treatment adjunct) or
Nephrotic syndrome, acute (treatment adjunct)—The 25% albumin injection may be indicated as an adjunct in the control of edema in patients refractory to cyclophosphamide and corticosteroid therapy.

Hemodialysis—The 25% albumin injection may be used as an adjunct in patients who are undergoing long-term hemodialysis and are susceptible to shock and hypotension, or in dialysis patients who are hypervolemic and may not tolerate large volumes of crystalloid injection as treatment for shock or hypotension.

Pancreatitis (treatment adjunct) or
Intra-abdominal infections (treatment adjunct)—The 5 and 25% concentrations of albumin may be indicated, along with crystalloids, as fluid replacement in the treatment of shock associated with acute hemorrhagic pancreatitis or peritonitis when there is loss of fluid into the third space.

Liver failure, acute (treatment adjunct)—The 5 and 25% concentrations of albumin may be indicated as adjuncts in the treatment of acute liver failure to stabilize the circulation, maintain plasma colloid oncotic pressure, and bind excess bilirubin.

Red blood cell resuspension—Albumin may be indicated to provide sufficient volume and to prevent excessive hypoproteinemia during certain types of exchange transfusions or during the administration of large volumes of previously frozen or washed red blood cells.

[Plasmapheresis[1]]—The 5% concentration of albumin is indicated as volume or fluid replacement in large-volume plasma exchange, which is defined as more than 20 mL per kg in one session, or more than 20 mL per kg per week in repeated sessions.

Unaccepted

Albumin has not been shown to be effective in the treatment of chronic cirrhosis or nephrosis.

Albumin does not contain all the essential amino acids and, therefore, is not an appropriate source of protein in the treatment of malnutrition. Given in excessive amounts, albumin may increase the catabolism of endogenous albumin.

[1]Not included in Canadian product labeling.

Pharmacology/Pharmacokinetics

Physicochemical characteristics

Source—

Obtained from source blood, plasma, serum, or placentas of healthy human donors by fractionation according to the Cohn cold ethanol process.

Albumin is heat pasteurized for 10 hours at 60 °C to inactivate human immunodeficiency virus (HIV) and hepatitis viruses; sodium caprylate and sodium acetyltryptophanate are added to prevent denaturation during this process.

Molecular weight—66,300 to 69,000.

pH—6.4 to 7.4.

Mechanism of action/Effect

Blood volume expander—Albumin is an important regulator of the volume of circulating blood. It accounts for 70 to 80% of the colloid oncotic pressure of plasma. An infusion of albumin 5% is oncotically equivalent to an equal volume of human plasma and increases blood volume by an amount approximately equal to the volume of albumin infused; albumin 25% is oncotically equivalent to approximately 5 times the volume of human plasma and draws into the circulation an amount of fluid approximately 3.5 times the volume of albumin infused. Albumin provides a temporary increase in blood volume, which reduces hemoconcentration and blood viscosity.

Antihyperbilirubinemic—Albumin is a transport protein that reversibly binds both endogenous and exogenous substances including bilirubin, fatty acids, hormones, enzymes, drugs, dyes, and trace metals.

Distribution

Albumin is distributed throughout the extracellular water; more than 60% is located in the extravascular fluid compartment.

Half-life

Elimination—15 to 20 days.

Other—Intravascular: 24 hours.

Onset of action

Blood volume expansion—With albumin 25% injection: 15 minutes, provided the patient is well hydrated.

Duration of action

Dependent upon the initial blood volume of the patient. If blood volume is reduced, volume expansion persists for many hours; however, if blood volume is normal, the effect lasts a shorter time.

Precautions to Consider

Pregnancy/Reproduction

Pregnancy—Studies have not been done in humans.

Studies have not been done in animals.

FDA Pregnancy Category C.

Breast-feeding

It is not known whether albumin is distributed into breast milk. However, problems in humans have not been documented.

Pediatrics

Appropriate studies performed to date have not demonstrated pediatrics-specific problems that would limit the usefulness of albumin in children.

Geriatrics

No information is available on the relationship of age to the effects of albumin in geriatric patients.

Medical considerations/Contraindications

The medical considerations/contraindications included have been selected on the basis of their potential clinical significance (reasons given in parentheses where appropriate)—not necessarily inclusive (» = major clinical significance).

Except under special circumstances, this medication should not be used when the following medical problems exist:

» Anemia, severe or
» Cardiac failure or
» Hypervolemia or
» Pulmonary edema
(these medical problems may increase the risk of and/or be exacerbated by circulatory overload)

Risk-benefit should be considered when the following medical problems exist:

Hypertension or
Normal serum albumin concentrations
(increased plasma volume may lead to circulatory overload; hypertension may be exacerbated)

Renal function impairment
(aluminum, sometimes present as a contaminant in albumin injections, may accumulate, leading to anemia, dialysis encephalopathy, hypercalcemia, or vitamin D-refractory osteomalacia)

Sensitivity to albumin

Patient monitoring

The following may be especially important in patient monitoring (other tests may be warranted in some patients, depending on condition; » = major clinical significance):

Aluminum concentrations, serum
(recommended in patients with renal function impairment, who are infused repeatedly with large volumes of albumin)

» Blood pressure measurements
(a rapid rise in blood pressure may reveal bleeding that was not apparent at the lower blood pressure)

Pulmonary wedge pressure determinations
(recommended to guard against circulatory overload)

Side/Adverse Effects

The following side/adverse effects have been selected on the basis of their potential clinical significance (possible signs and symptoms in parentheses where appropriate)—not necessarily inclusive:

Those indicating need for medical attention

Incidence less frequent

Congestive heart failure—especially in patients with compromised cardiovascular function; ***decreased myocardial contractility; pulmonary edema; salt and water retention***

Note: These side effects are more likely to occur in patients given large volumes of crystalloids prior to the administration of albumin.

Incidence rare

Changes in blood pressure, pulse, and respiration; chills; fever; increased salivation; nausea or vomiting; skin rash or hives; tachycardia

General Dosing Information

Albumin contains no blood group isoagglutinins and, therefore, may be given without regard to the blood group of the patient.

Albumin must be administered by intravenous infusion. It may be administered without dilution or diluted with 0.9% sodium chloride injection or 5% dextrose injection. **Sterile water for injection must not be used as a diluent for 25% albumin solutions as this results in a substantial reduction in osmolarity (tonicity), which increases the risks for potentially fatal hemolysis and acute renal failure, particularly when large volumes of the diluted solution are used in plasmapheresis.** It also may be administered with plasma, packed red blood cells, or whole blood; however, except when used as a red blood cell resuspension medium, albumin should not be added directly to any of these three components.

Note: Although 5% dextrose injection is considered an acceptable diluent, when it is used to dilute 25% albumin solutions and the resulting solution is used in the setting of plasma exchange or in conjunction with red blood cells, hemolysis might occur. Also, infusion of large volumes of the diluted solution can result in hyponatremia. Therefore, some clinicians recommend using only 0.9% sodium chloride injection as the diluting fluid except when there is concern about increasing the patient's sodium load and/or there is a need to maintain or restore the patient's blood glucose concentration.

Albumin may be administered at a rate of 1 to 2 mL per minute; however, the rate of infusion and the total volume of albumin administered ultimately must be guided by the hemodynamic response of the patient.

Patients with marked dehydration given 25% albumin injection require administration of additional fluids.

Transfusions of whole blood or packed red blood cells may be necessary following administration of large volumes of albumin to restore hemoglobin concentration and to prevent anemia.

Parenteral Dosage Forms

ALBUMIN HUMAN USP

Usual adult dose

Hypovolemia—

Intravenous infusion, 25 grams as a 5 or 25% injection, administered as rapidly as tolerated by the patient. If an adequate response is not achieved within fifteen to thirty minutes, an additional dose may be given.

Hypoproteinemia—

Intravenous infusion, 50 to 75 grams as a 25% injection, administered at a rate of 100 mL over thirty to forty minutes. For slow infusion, 50 grams in 300 mL of 10% dextrose injection, administered at a rate of 100 mL per hour.

Burns—

Therapy is usually begun with the administration of large volumes of crystalloid injection to maintain plasma volume. After 24 hours, albumin may be added at an initial dose of 25 grams, with the dose adjusted thereafter to maintain a plasma albumin concentration of 2.5 grams per 100 mL (25 grams/L), or a total serum protein concentration of 5.2 grams per 100 mL (52 grams/L).

Cardiopulmonary bypass—

Intravenous infusion, as a 5 or 25% injection, with crystalloid as a pump prime to achieve plasma albumin and hematocrit concentrations of 2.5 grams per 100 mL (25 grams/L) and 20%, respectively.

Nephrosis, acute or Nephrotic syndrome, acute—

Intravenous infusion, 25 grams as a 25% injection, administered with an appropriate diuretic once a day for seven to ten days.

Hemodialysis—

Intravenous infusion, 25 grams as a 25% injection.

Red blood cell resuspension—

20 to 25 grams as a 25% injection, per liter of red blood cells.

Usual adult prescribing limits

Up to 2 grams per kg of body weight within twenty-four hours.

Usual pediatric dose

Hypovolemia—

Intravenous infusion, 2.5 to 12.5 grams, or 0.5 to 1 gram per kg of body weight, administered as rapidly as tolerated by the patient. If an adequate response is not achieved within fifteen to thirty minutes, an additional dose may be given.

Burns—

Therapy is usually begun with the administration of large volumes of crystalloid injection to maintain plasma volume. After 24 hours, albumin may be added at an initial dose of 25 grams, with the dose adjusted thereafter to maintain a plasma albumin concentration of 2 to 2.5 grams per 100 mL (20 to 25 grams/L), or a total serum protein concentration of 5.2 grams per 100 mL (52 grams/L).

Hyperbilirubinemia, neonatal—

Intravenous infusion, 1 gram per kg of body weight as a 25% injection, administered during, or one to two hours prior to, exchange transfusion.

Strength(s) usually available

U.S.—

5% in 50 mL (Rx) [*Albuminar-5* (sodium ion 130–160 mEq per L; potassium ion ≤ 1 mEq per L); *Plasbumin-5;* GENERIC (sodium ion 130–160 mEq per L)].

5% in 250 mL (Rx) [*Albuminar-5* (sodium ion 130–160 mEq per L; potassium ion ≤ 1 mEq per L); *Albutein 5%* (sodium ion 130–160 mEq per L); *Buminate 5%* (sodium ion 130–160 mEq per L); *Plasbumin-5;* GENERIC (sodium ion 130–160 mEq per L)].

5% in 500 mL (Rx) [*Albuminar-5* (sodium ion 130–160 mEq per L; potassium ion ≤ 1 mEq per L); *Albutein 5%* (sodium ion 130–160 mEq per L); *Buminate 5%* (sodium ion 130–160 mEq per L); *Plasbumin-5;* GENERIC (sodium ion 130–160 mEq per L)].

5% in 1000 mL (Rx) [*Albuminar-5* (sodium ion 130–160 mEq per L; potassium ion ≤ 1 mEq per L)].

25% in 20 mL (Rx) [*Albuminar-25* (sodium ion 130–160 mEq per L; potassium ion ≤ 1 mEq per L); *Albutein 25%* (sodium ion 130–160 mEq per L); *Buminate 25%* (sodium ion 130–160 mEq per L); *Plasbumin-25;* GENERIC (sodium ion 130–160 mEq per L)].

25% in 50 mL (Rx) [*Albuminar-25* (sodium ion 130–160 mEq per L; potassium ion ≤ 1 mEq per L); *Albutein 25%* (sodium ion 130–160 mEq per L); *Buminate 25%* (sodium ion 130–160 mEq per L); *Plasbumin-25;* GENERIC (sodium ion 130–160 mEq per L)].

25% in 100 mL (Rx) [*Albuminar-25* (sodium ion 130–160 mEq per L; potassium ion ≤ 1 mEq per L); *Albutein 25%* (sodium ion 130–160 mEq per L); *Buminate 25%* (sodium ion 130–160 mEq per L); *Plasbumin-25;* GENERIC (sodium ion 130–160 mEq per L)].

Canada—

5% in 50 mL (Rx) [*Plasbumin-5*].

5% in 250 mL (Rx) [*Plasbumin-5*].

5% in 500 mL (Rx) [*Plasbumin-5*].

25% in 20 mL (Rx) [*Plasbumin-25*].

25% in 50 mL (Rx) [*Plasbumin-25*].

25% in 100 mL (Rx) [*Plasbumin-25*].

Packaging and storage

Store at 15 to 30 °C (59 to 86 °F), unless otherwise specified by manufacturer. Protect from freezing.

Preparation of dosage form

A 5% albumin solution may be prepared from the 25% solution by adding one volume of the 25% solution to four volumes of 0.9% sodium chloride injection or 5% dextrose injection. **Sterile water for injection must not be used as a diluent for 25% albumin solutions as this results in a substantial reduction in osmolarity (tonicity), which increases the risks for potentially fatal hemolysis and acute renal failure, particularly when large volumes of the diluted solution are used in plasmapheresis.**

Note: Although 5% dextrose injection is considered an acceptable diluent, when it is used to dilute 25% albumin solutions and the resulting solution is used in the setting of plasma exchange or in conjunction with red blood cells, hemolysis might occur. Also, infusion of large volumes of the diluted solution can result in hyponatremia. Therefore, some clinicians recommend using only 0.9%

sodium chloride injection as the diluting fluid except when there is concern about increasing the patient's sodium load and/or there is a need to maintain or restore the patient's blood glucose concentration.

Stability
Should not be used if solution is turbid or contains a precipitate. Albumin contains no preservative and should be used within 4 hours after the vial is opened. Partially used vials should be discarded.

Incompatibilities
Albumin is incompatible with verapamil hydrochloride, alcohol-containing solutions, amino acid solutions, fat emulsions, and protein hydrolysates.

Selected Bibliography

Tullis JL. Albumin 1. Background and use. JAMA 1977; 237: 355-60.

Tullis JL. Albumin 2. Guidelines for clinical use. JAMA 1977; 237: 460-3.

Subcommittee of the Victorian Drug Usage Advisory Committee. Human albumin solutions: consensus statements for use in selected clinical situations. Med J Aust 1992; 157: 340-3.

Vermeulen LC, Ratko TA, Erstad BL, et al. A paradigm for consensus. The University Hospital Consortium guidelines for the use of albumin, nonprotein colloid, and crystalloid solutions. Arch Intern Med 1995; 155: 373-9.

Revised: 08/17/1993

ALBUTEROL—See *Bronchodilators, Adrenergic (Inhalation-Local), Bronchodilators, Adrenergic (Systemic)*

ALCLOMETASONE—See *Corticosteroids (Topical)*

ALDESLEUKIN Systemic†

VA CLASSIFICATION (Primary): AN900

Commonly used brand name(s): *Proleukin*.

Other commonly used names are interleukin-2, recombinant, and rIL-2.

Note: For a listing of dosage forms and brand names by country availability, see *Dosage Forms* section(s).

†Not commercially available in Canada.

Category
Biological response modifier; antineoplastic.

Indications
Accepted
Carcinoma, renal (treatment)—Aldesleukin is indicated for treatment of metastatic renal carcinoma in patients 18 years of age and older.

Melanoma, metastatic (treatment)—Aldesleukin is indicated for treatment of metastatic melanoma in patients 18 years of age and older.

Note: *Because of its potential life-threatening toxicities, USP DI Advisory Panels recommend that this medication be used only after careful consideration of risk-benefit.* It is recommended that aldesleukin be used only by qualified specialists who are fully aware of and equipped to monitor and treat the potential toxicities of this medication.

Pharmacology/Pharmacokinetics
Note: Pharmacokinetics can be described by a 2-compartment model.

Physicochemical characteristics
Source—Synthetic. Produced by a recombinant DNA process involving genetically engineered *Escherichia coli* containing an analog of the human interleukin-2 gene. Genetic engineering techniques used to modify the human interleukin-2 gene result in an expression clone that encodes a modified human interleukin-2. Aldesleukin differs from naturally occurring interleukin-2 in that it is not glycosylated because it is derived from *Escherichia coli*, the molecule has no *N*-terminal alanine (the codon for this amino acid was deleted during the genetic engineering process), the molecule has serine substituted for cysteine at amino acid position 125 (this was accomplished by site-specific manipulation during the genetic engineering process), and the aggregation state of aldesleukin is likely to be different from that of native interleukin-2. The manufacturing process involves fermentation in a defined medium containing tetracycline hydrochloride; the presence of the antibiotic is not detectable in the final product.

Chemical Group—Related to naturally occurring interleukins, which are lymphokines, a subgroup of the hormone-like glycoprotein growth factors also known as cytokines.

Molecular weight—Approximately 15,600 daltons.

Mechanism of action/Effect
Aldesleukin has been shown to possess the biological activity of human native interleukin-2. *In vitro* studies performed on human cell lines demonstrate the immunoregulatory properties of aldesleukin, including:

- Enhancement of lymphocyte mitogenesis and stimulation of long-term growth of human interleukin-2 dependent cell lines;
- Enhancement of lymphocyte toxicity;
- Induction of killer cell (lymphokine-activated killer [LAK] cells and natural killer [NK] cells) activity; and
- Induction of interferon-gamma production.

The *in vivo* administration of aldesleukin in select murine tumor models and in the clinic produces multiple immunological effects in a dose-dependent manner. These effects include activation of cellular immunity with profound lymphocytosis, eosinophilia, and thrombocytopenia, and the production of cytokines, including tumor necrosis factor, interleukin-1 and gamma interferon. *In vivo* experiments in murine tumor models have shown inhibition of tumor growth. However, the exact mechanism by which aldesleukin mediates its antitumor activity in animals and humans is unknown.

Other actions/effects
Aldesleukin causes a capillary leak syndrome (CLS) as a result of increased capillary permeability, leading to extravasation of plasma proteins and fluid into the extravascular space and contributing to loss of vascular resistance. Interleukin-2 has been reported to reversibly decrease serum cholesterol concentrations. Interleukin-2 has been reported to transiently decrease serum testosterone and dihydroepiandrosterone concentrations and to transiently increase plasma estradiol concentrations. It has also been reported to transiently increase adrenal secretion of ACTH and cortisol.

Distribution
Studies of intravenous aldesleukin in humans and sheep indicate that approximately 30% of the administered dose is distributed to the plasma initially. This is consistent with studies in rats that demonstrate a rapid and preferential uptake of approximately 70% of an administered dose into the liver, kidneys, and lungs.

Biotransformation
Renal. Greater than 80% of the amount of aldesleukin distributed to plasma, cleared from the circulation, and presented to the kidney is metabolized to amino acids in the cells lining the proximal convoluted tubules.

Half-life
Distribution—13 minutes.

Elimination—85 minutes.

Duration of action
Tumor regression may continue for up to 12 months following initiation of therapy.

Elimination
Renal—. Cleared from the circulation by both glomerular filtration and peritubular extraction in the kidney. The dual mechanism for delivery of aldesleukin to the proximal tubule may account for the preservation of clearance in patients with rising serum creatinine values. The mean clearance rate in cancer patients is 268 mL per minute.

Precautions to Consider
Note: In general, risks associated with aldesleukin therapy are dose- and schedule-related; toxicity of the high-dose regimen currently recommended is high.

Cross-sensitivity and/or related problems
Patients sensitive to *Escherichia coli* –derived proteins may also be sensitive to aldesleukin.

Carcinogenicity/Mutagenicity
Studies have not been done.

Pregnancy/Reproduction
Fertility—Studies have not been done. However, aldesleukin should not be administered to fertile persons of either sex not practicing effective contraception.

Pregnancy—Studies have not been done in humans. It is also not known whether aldesleukin can cause fetal harm when administered to a pregnant woman or can affect reproduction capacity. However, in view of the known adverse effects of aldesleukin, it should be given to a pregnant woman only with extreme caution; the potential benefit should be weighed against the risks associated with therapy.

Studies have not been done in animals.

FDA Pregnancy Category C.

Breast-feeding

It is not known whether aldesleukin is distributed into breast milk. However, because of the potential for serious adverse reactions in nursing infants from aldesleukin, a decision should be made whether to discontinue nursing or to discontinue treatment with aldesleukin, taking into account the importance of aldesleukin therapy to the mother.

Pediatrics

Safety and efficacy have not been established in children up to 18 years of age. Use is not recommended.

Geriatrics

Although appropriate studies on the relationship of age to the effects of aldesleukin have not been performed in the geriatric population, clinical trials have included elderly patients. There is some evidence that elderly patients do not tolerate aldesleukin's toxicity as well as younger patients. Cardiac status is of particular concern. In addition, elderly patients are more likely to have age-related renal function impairment, which may require caution in patients receiving aldesleukin.

Dental

The impairment of neutrophil function caused by aldesleukin may result in an increased incidence of microbial infection, delayed healing, and gingival bleeding. Dental work, whenever possible, should be completed prior to initiation of therapy or deferred until blood counts have returned to normal. Patients should be instructed in proper oral hygiene during treatment, including caution in use of regular toothbrushes, dental floss, and toothpicks.

Aldesleukin also commonly causes stomatitis, and less commonly causes glossitis, which may be associated with considerable discomfort.

Drug interactions and/or related problems

The following drug interactions and/or related problems have been selected on the basis of their potential clinical significance (possible mechanism in parentheses where appropriate)—not necessarily inclusive (» = major clinical significance):

Note: Combinations containing any of the following medications, depending on the amount present, may also interact with this medication.

Blood dyscrasia-causing medications (see *Appendix II*)
(leukopenic and/or thrombocytopenic effects of aldesleukin may be increased with concurrent or recent therapy if these medications cause the same effects)

» Bone marrow depressants, other (see *Appendix II*) or
Radiation therapy
(additive bone marrow depression may occur)

» Cardiotoxic medications, other, including daunorubicin or doxorubicin
(concurrent use may result in increased cardiotoxicity)

Central nervous system (CNS) depressants
(concurrent use may result in increased CNS depression)

Contrast media, iodinated
(incidence of delayed [more than 1 hour after administration] reactions to intravenous iodinated contrast media [e.g., hypersensitivity, fever, skin rash, flu-like symptoms, joint pain, flushing, pruritus, emesis, hypotension, dizziness] may be increased in patients who have received interleukin-2; some symptoms may resemble a "recall" reaction to interleukin-2; supportive medical treatment may be necessary if symptoms are significant; there is some evidence that incidence of this reaction is reduced if contrast media administration is delayed until 6 weeks after interleukin-2 administration)

» Corticosteroids, glucocorticoid, systemic
(although glucocorticoids, especially dexamethasone, have been shown to reduce some adverse effects of aldesleukin, including fever, renal insufficiency, hyperbilirubinemia, confusion, and dyspnea, there is some evidence that concurrent use may reduce the antitumor efficacy of aldesleukin; therefore, it is generally recommended that dexamethasone be avoided, except in cases of life-threatening aldesleukin toxicity)

» Hepatotoxic medications, other (see *Appendix II*) or
» Nephrotoxic medications, other (see *Appendix II*)
(concurrent and/or sequential administration should be avoided since the potential for hepatotoxicity or nephrotoxicity may be increased, especially in the presence of hepatic or renal function impairment that may be caused by aldesleukin)

» Hypotension-producing medications, other (see *Appendix II*)
(concurrent use may result in increased hypotension)

Laboratory value alterations

The following have been selected on the basis of their potential clinical significance (possible effect in parentheses where appropriate)—not necessarily inclusive (» = major clinical significance).

With physiology/laboratory test values

Alanine aminotransferase (ALT [SGPT]) values, serum and
Alkaline phosphatase values, serum and
Aspartate aminotransferase (AST [SGOT]) values, serum and
Bilirubin concentrations, serum and
Lactate dehydrogenase (LDH) values, serum
(increased in most patients)

Albumin and
Protein
(plasma concentrations may be decreased and urinary concentrations increased as a sign of renal toxicity)

Bicarbonate and
Calcium and
Magnesium and
Phosphate and
Potassium and
Sodium
(serum concentrations may be decreased but return to normal shortly after withdrawal of interleukin-2)

Blood urea nitrogen (BUN) and
Creatinine concentrations, serum
(dose-related increases commonly occur, indicating renal toxicity)

Creatine kinase (CK)
(serum concentrations may be increased with or without symptoms of cardiotoxicity and may be associated with nonischemic myocardial injury or myocarditis rather than myocardial ischemia or infarction)

Electrocardiogram (ECG) changes, including:
QRS voltage reductions
ST segment changes
T-wave changes
(may occur as signs of cardiotoxicity)

Left ventricular ejection fraction and
Left ventricular stroke work index
(frequently decreased in cardiotoxicity; these effects resemble septic shock)

Prothrombin time
(may be prolonged)

Uric acid
(concentrations in blood and urine may be increased, possibly as a result of catabolism of lymphokine-activated killer [LAK] cells and natural killer [NK] cells)

Medical considerations/Contraindications

The medical considerations/contraindications included have been selected on the basis of their potential clinical significance (reasons given in parentheses where appropriate)—not necessarily inclusive (» = major clinical significance).

Except under special circumstances, high-dose regimens of this medication should not be used when the following medical problems exist:

» Cardiac function impairment, as determined by thallium stress test

» Organ allograft
(enhancement of cellular immune function by aldesleukin may increase the risk of allograft rejection)

» Pulmonary function impairment

» Because aldesleukin may exacerbate symptoms of clinically unrecognized or untreated central nervous system (CNS) metastases, generally treatment with aldesleukin should not begin until a patient has had thorough evaluation and treatment of CNS metastases, resulting in neurologic stability and a negative computed tomography (CT) scan.

Risk-benefit should be considered when the following medical problems exist:

Autoimmune disease, including autoimmune thyroiditis
(aldesleukin-associated hypothyroidism may be an autoimmune effect; autoimmune thyroiditis may be exacerbated)

» Bone marrow depression

» Cardiac function impairment, history of, even if function tests are normal
(may be exacerbated)

» Hepatic function impairment
(may be exacerbated)

Hypothyroidism, uncontrolled
(aldesleukin can cause hypothyroidism; no problems are anticipated in patients who are euthyroid as a result of thyroid hormone replacement therapy)

» Infection
(should be treated before initiation of aldesleukin therapy)

» Mental status impairment
(may be exacerbated)

Psoriasis
(may be exacerbated)

» Pulmonary function impairment, history of, even if function tests are normal
(may be exacerbated)

» Renal function impairment
(reduced elimination of aldesleukin, which may result in increased toxicity; impairment may be exacerbated by aldesleukin; patients with nephrectomy are eligible for high-dose aldesleukin therapy if their serum creatinine concentrations are less than or equal to 1.5 mg per deciliter)

» Seizure disorder, history of
(aldesleukin may cause seizures)

» Sensitivity to aldesleukin

» Caution should be used also in patients who have had previous cytotoxic drug therapy or radiation therapy.

Patient monitoring

The following are especially important in patient monitoring (other tests may be warranted in some patients, depending on condition; » = major clinical significance):

» Body weight and
» Electrolytes, serum and
» Vital signs, including temperature, pulse, blood pressure, and respiratory rate
(recommended daily; if blood pressure decreases to less than 90 millimeters of mercury [mm Hg], constant cardiac rhythm monitoring, hourly vital signs, and central venous pressure [CVP] checks are recommended; if an abnormal complex or rhythm is seen, performance of an ECG and determination of cardiac enzymes are recommended)

» Cardiac function, including thallium stress test
(determination recommended prior to initiation of therapy; ejection fraction should be normal and wall function unimpaired; in patients with minor wall motion abnormalities of questionable significance suggested by the thallium stress test, a stress echocardiogram to document normal wall motion and exclude significant coronary disease may be useful; during treatment, cardiac function should be assessed daily by clinical examination and assessment of vital signs, adding ECG examination and creatine kinase [CK] evaluation for patients exhibiting signs or symptoms of chest pain, murmurs, gallops, irregular rhythm, or palpitations; a repeat thallium stress test is recommended if there is evidence of cardiac ischemia or congestive heart failure; use of a cardiac monitor is recommended if patients require pressor support)

» Hematocrit or hemoglobin and
» Leukocyte count, total and, if appropriate, differential and
» Platelet count
(determinations recommended prior to initiation of therapy and at periodic intervals during therapy; frequency varies according to clinical state, agent, dose, and other agents being used concurrently)

» Hepatic function and
» Renal function
(determinations recommended prior to initiation of therapy and daily during therapy)

» Pulmonary function, including arterial blood gases
(determination recommended prior to initiation of therapy; adequate pulmonary function, as defined by FEV_1 of greater than 2 liters or 75% or more of that predicted for height and age, should be present; during treatment, pulmonary function should be routinely monitored by clinical examination, assessment of vital signs, and pulse oximetry, adding arterial blood gas determination for patients exhibiting dyspnea or clinical signs of respiratory impairment [tachypnea or rales])

Thyroid function
(determinations recommended at periodic intervals during therapy)

Side/Adverse Effects

Note: High-dose aldesleukin causes frequent, often serious, and sometimes fatal toxicity. Fatalities have occurred as a result of hepatic or renal failure, cardiac arrest, intestinal perforation, malignant hyperthermia, pulmonary edema, respiratory failure or arrest, pulmonary embolism, stroke, or severe depression leading to suicide.

Toxicity of aldesleukin is dose-related and schedule-dependent. Incidence of toxicity is probably increased in patients with a poor initial performance status.

Patient tolerance to interleukin-2 toxicity has been reported to decline with successive courses.

Most side/adverse effects are reversible within 2 or 3 days after aldesleukin is discontinued. However, permanent damage may result from myocardial infarction, bowel perforation or infarction, and gangrene.

Aldesleukin causes a dose-related capillary leak syndrome (CLS) as a result of increased capillary permeability, leading to extravasation of plasma proteins and fluid into the extravascular space and contributing to loss of vascular resistance. It is believed that hypotension and reduced organ perfusion that occur as a result of CLS are at least partially responsible for many of the toxicities of aldesleukin, including cardiac arrhythmias (supraventricular and ventricular), angina, myocardial infarction, respiratory insufficiency requiring intubation, gastrointestinal bleeding or infarction, renal insufficiency, and some mental status changes. The effects of CLS may be severe or fatal. CLS begins immediately after initiation of treatment, resulting initially, in most patients, in a decline in mean arterial blood pressure within 2 to 12 hours. Clinically significant hypotension (systolic blood pressure below 90 millimeters of mercury [mm Hg] or a 20 mm Hg decline from baseline systolic pressure) and hypoperfusion will occur with continued therapy. Protein and fluid extravasation will also cause edema and effusions; some patients may develop ascites or pleural effusions. Recovery from CLS begins soon after the end of aldesleukin therapy. Usually within a few hours, blood pressure rises, organ perfusion is restored, and resorption of extravasated fluid and protein begins.

In addition to CLS, other possible causes of interleukin-2 toxicity include growth of lymphocytes in visceral organs, which has been described in animal toxicology studies, and stimulation of secretion of other cytokines (e.g., tumor necrosis factor [TNF]) by cells of the immune system. For example, TNF and interleukin-1 secretion may be responsible for hemodynamic effects, which resemble septic shock.

Intravenous or subcutaneous aldesleukin administration frequently results in formation of low titers of non-neutralizing anti-interleukin-2 antibodies. Neutralizing antibodies have been detected in less than 1% of patients treated with aldesleukin. Evidence to date does not appear to indicate that antibody formation impairs response to aldesleukin.

It has been postulated that some toxicities (e.g., hypothyroidism, dermatologic effects) indicate a possible autoimmune effect of interleukin-2.

Hemodynamic and cardiac changes (e.g., peripheral vascular resistance, blood pressure, stroke index, left ventricular stroke volume, heart rate, ECG, creatine kinase) usually return to normal within a few days after interleukin-2 is discontinued.

The following side/adverse effects have been selected on the basis of their potential clinical significance (possible signs and symptoms in parentheses where appropriate)—not necessarily inclusive:

Those indicating need for medical attention

Incidence more frequent

Anemia—asymptomatic; ***arrhythmias, especially sinus tachycardia*** (fast or irregular heartbeat)—usually asymptomatic; ***diarrhea; dizziness; edema, including peripheral edema with symptomatic nerve or vessel compression*** (tingling of hands or feet); ***eosinophilia; fever and/or chills; hepatotoxicity*** (seen as changes on hepatic function tests that are attributable to severe cholestasis; yellow eyes and skin)—usually asymptomatic; ***hypotension*** (faintness)—usually asymptomatic; ***hypothyroidism*** (changes in menstrual periods; clumsiness; coldness; dry, puffy skin; headache; listlessness; muscle aches; sleepiness; tiredness; weakness; goiter [swelling in the front of the neck])—usually asymptomatic; ***infection*** (fever or chills); ***leukopenia*** (fever or chills; cough or hoarseness; lower back or side pain; painful or difficult urination)—usually asymptomatic; ***lymphocytosis; nausea and vomiting; neuropsychiatric effects, including mental status changes*** (agitation; confusion; mental depression; drowsiness; unusual tiredness); ***pulmonary toxicity, including pulmonary congestion, pulmonary edema, pleural effusion*** (shortness of breath); ***renal toxicity, including oliguria and anuria*** (unusual decrease in urination); ***stomatitis*** (sores in mouth and on lips); ***thrombocytopenia*** (unusual bleeding or bruising; black, tarry stools; blood in urine or stools; pinpoint red spots on skin)—usually asymptomatic; ***weight gain of 5 to 10 pounds or more***

Note: *Anemia* usually requires blood transfusions.

Supraventricular *arrhythmias* usually resolve after treatment has ended. Potentially fatal ventricular arrhythmias have been reported.

Diarrhea occurs in most patients. Severe diarrhea can lead to hypokalemia or acidosis.

Dizziness is a neurologic effect.

Eosinophilia, which can be pronounced, tends to occur near the end of therapy, during the first 5 days after treatment. Eosinophilic myocarditis has been reported.

Fever, chills, rigors, or *malaise* usually occurs within hours after administration.

Hepatic function tests usually return to normal within several days after treatment has ended.

Mean arterial pressure begins to decline within 2 to 12 hours after initiation of therapy, necessitating intravenous administration of fluids (to correct hypovolemia) and pressors (to maintain blood pressure and perfusion). *Hypotension* is accompanied by an increase in heart rate.

Hypothyroidism may require thyroid replacement therapy. A hyperthyroid phase may precede hypothyroidism. Thyroid function tests usually return to normal within a few days or weeks after therapy, although effects have been reported to persist for several months. In some patients, presence of antibodies to thyroglobulin suggests exacerbation or initiation of autoimmune thyroiditis.

Impaired neutrophil function (reduced chemotaxis) may also increase the risk of disseminated *infection.* Infection may include urinary tract, injection site, or central venous catheter tip infections, as well as bacterial endocarditis, phlebitis, or sepsis. Positive cultures may be found without symptomatic infection. Infections are usually gram-positive, although gram-negative infection has also been reported. Early signs and symptoms of sepsis (e.g., hypotension) may be masked by prophylactic medication for systemic effects.

Mental status changes, which appear after several days of treatment, may be signs of bacteremia or early bacterial sepsis, as well as cerebral edema or immune effects. Changes due solely to aldesleukin are usually reversible on withdrawal, although they may continue to progress for several days before recovery begins.

Nausea and vomiting occur in most patients.

Oliguria is accompanied by reversible prerenal azotemia (increased serum creatinine and BUN), hypoalbuminemia, and proteinuria. Fractional sodium excretion is also decreased. In a small percentage of patients, *renal toxicity* may require dialysis. Renal function tests usually return to normal within 7 to 30 days, although recovery may sometimes be prolonged or incomplete. Interstitial nephritis and glomerulonephritis have been reported.

Stomatitis may be severe enough to necessitate a liquid diet.

Weight gain may be 10% or more of pretreatment body weight. Reversal of weight gain may take up to 1 to 2 weeks after therapy, as patients diurese fluid.

Incidence less frequent

Aphasia (trouble in speaking); ***ascites*** (bloating and stomach pain); ***exfoliative dermatitis*** (blisters on skin); ***gastrointestinal bleeding*** (blood in stools; bloody vomit); ***glossitis*** (redness, swelling, and soreness of tongue); ***intestinal ischemic necrosis or perforation*** (bloody vomit; severe stomach pain); ***myocardial ischemia or myocardial infarction*** (chest pain); ***pulmonary toxicity, including respiratory failure, tachypnea, and wheezing*** (rapid breathing; severe shortness of breath); ***sensory neurologic effects*** (blurred or double vision; loss of taste)

Note: *Exfoliative dermatitis* can be fatal. Life-threatening bullous drug eruptions, resembling toxic epidermal necrolysis, have also been reported.

In a small percentage of patients, *gastrointestinal bleeding* may require surgery.

Frequency of *myocardial ischemia or infarction* can be reduced by careful patient screening before interleukin-2 treatment and monitoring during treatment.

Evidence of *pulmonary* infiltration may become apparent by the fourth day of therapy and usually resolves within a few weeks after therapy. Intubation may be required for *respiratory failure.*

Vision problems usually begin shortly after interleukin-2 administration and are reversible, although they may persist for several weeks.

Incidence rare

Cardiovascular effects, other, including congestive heart failure, endocarditis, myocarditis, cardiomyopathy, gangrene, stroke, and thrombosis (swelling of feet or lower legs; sudden weakness or inability to move); ***coma; injection site reaction*** (pain or redness at site of injection); ***pericardial effusion; seizures***

Those indicating need for medical attention only if they continue or are bothersome

Incidence more frequent

Dry skin; loss of appetite; macular erythema (skin rash or redness with burning or itching, followed by peeling); ***malaise*** (unusual feeling of discomfort or illness); ***weakness***

Note: *Macular erythema*, which seems to be an immunological effect, begins 2 to 3 days after initiation of treatment and usually begins to resolve, with desquamation, within 2 to 3 days after interleukin-2 is discontinued. Peeling of skin is most pronounced on palms and soles; skin appears normal within 2 to 3 weeks. It recurs with each cycle. Other dermatological effects, including angioedema, urticaria, and erythema nodosum, have also been reported.

Incidence less frequent

Arthralgia or myalgia (joint pain; muscle pain); ***constipation; headache***

Overdose

For more information on the management of overdose or unintentional ingestion, **contact a Poison Control Center** (see *Poison Control Center Listing*).

Treatment of overdose

Treatment consists of withdrawal of aldesleukin and supportive therapy.

Life-threatening toxicities have been ameliorated by the intravenous administration of dexamethasone; however, this may result in loss of aldesleukin's therapeutic effect.

Patient Consultation

As an aid to patient consultation, refer to *Advice for the Patient, Aldesleukin (Systemic).*

In providing consultation, consider emphasizing the following selected information (» = major clinical significance):

Before using this medication

» Conditions affecting use, especially:

Sensitivity to aldesleukin

Pregnancy—Use not recommended; advisability of using contraception; telling physician immediately if pregnancy is suspected

Breast-feeding—Not recommended because of risk of serious side effects

Other medications, especially other bone marrow depressants, other cardiotoxic medications, systemic glucocorticoids, other hepatotoxic medications, other hypotension-producing medications, other nephrotoxic medications, or other cytotoxic drug or radiation therapy

Other medical problems, especially cardiac function impairment, organ allograft, pulmonary function impairment, hepatic function impairment, infection, mental status impairment, renal function impairment, or history of seizure disorder

Proper use of this medication

» Proper dosing

Precautions while using this medication

Caution if impaired neutrophil function or thrombocytopenia occurs:

» Avoiding exposure to persons with infections, especially during periods of low blood counts; checking with physician immediately if fever or chills, cough or hoarseness, lower back or side pain, or painful or difficult urination occurs

» Checking with physician immediately if unusual bleeding or bruising; black, tarry stools; blood in urine or stools; or pinpoint red spots on skin occur

Caution in use of regular toothbrush, dental floss, or toothpick; physician, dentist, or nurse may suggest alternatives; checking with physician before having dental work done

Not touching eyes or inside of nose unless hands washed immediately before

Using caution to avoid accidental cuts with use of sharp objects such as safety razor or fingernail or toenail cutters
Avoiding contact sports or other situations where bruising or injury could occur

Side/adverse effects

Importance of discussing possible life-threatening toxicity with physician
Signs of potential side effects, especially anemia, arrhythmias, diarrhea, dizziness, edema, fever and/or chills, eosinophilia, hepatotoxicity, hypotension, hypothyroidism, infection, leukopenia, lymphocytosis, nausea and vomiting, mental status changes, pericardial effusion, pulmonary toxicity, renal toxicity, stomatitis, thrombocytopenia, weight gain, ascites, aphasia, exfoliative dermatitis, gastrointestinal bleeding, glossitis, intestinal ischemic necrosis or perforation, myocardial ischemia or myocardial infarction, sensory neurological effects, other cardiovascular effects, injection site reaction, and seizures
Asymptomatic side effects, including anemia, cardiotoxicity, hepatotoxicity, hypotension, hypothyroidism, eosinophilia, leukopenia, renal toxicity, and thrombocytopenia
Physician or nurse can help in dealing with side effects

General Dosing Information

Patients receiving aldesleukin should be under supervision of a physician experienced in cancer chemotherapy.

It is recommended that high-dose aldesleukin be administered in a tertiary care hospital setting, with an intensive care facility and specialists skilled in cardiopulmonary and intensive care medicine readily available.

Dosage of interleukin-2 is usually expressed in units of activity in promoting proliferation in a responsive cell line; conversion to Units from mg of protein varies somewhat, depending on the source of interleukin-2. In the literature, dosage of aldesleukin is expressed in terms of Cetus units; dosage of teceleukin, another form of recombinant interleukin-2, is expressed in Roche units or Nutley units. However, strength and dosage of commercially available aldesleukin are expressed in International Units (IU). Conversion to IU is as follows:
1 Cetus Unit = 6 International Units.
1 Roche Unit or Nutley Unit = 3 International Units.

In addition:
18 million IU = 1.1 mg protein.

It is recommended that acetaminophen and a nonsteroidal anti-inflammatory drug (NSAID) such as indomethacin be administered prior to initiation of aldesleukin therapy, to reduce fever. The increased risk of nephrotoxicity with concurrent use of indomethacin must be kept in mind. Meperidine may be added to control the rigors associated with fever.

Ranitidine or cimetidine may be given for prophylaxis of gastrointestinal irritation and bleeding.

Dosage adjustment of high-dose aldesleukin in response to toxicity is accomplished by withholding the medication rather than by decreasing the dosage. Toxicity usually reverses promptly (within several hours) on withdrawal of aldesleukin. It is recommended that aldesleukin be held and restarted according to the following guidelines:
• Atrial fibrillation, supraventricular tachycardia, or bradycardia that requires treatment or is recurrent or persistent—Hold dose. Obtain ECG and cardiac enzymes. Subsequent doses may be given if patient is asymptomatic with full recovery to normal sinus rhythm.
• Systolic blood pressure less than 90 mm Hg with increasing requirement for pressors—Hold dose. Subsequent doses may be given if systolic blood pressure becomes greater than or equal to 90 mm Hg and stable, or requirements for pressors are improving.
• Any ECG change consistent with myocardial infarction or ischemia with or without chest pain; suspicion of cardiac ischemia—Hold dose. Subsequent doses may be given if patient is asymptomatic, myocardial infarction has been ruled out, or clinical suspicion of angina and/or myocarditis is low.
• Oxygen saturation of less than 90% with 2 liters O_2 by nasal prongs—Hold dose. Subsequent doses may be given if O_2 saturation becomes greater than or equal to 90% with 2 liters O_2 by nasal prongs.
• Mental status changes, including moderate confusion or agitation—Hold dose. Subsequent doses may be given if mental status changes are completely resolved.
• Sepsis syndrome, where patient is clinically unstable—Hold dose. Subsequent doses may be given if sepsis syndrome has resolved, patient is clinically stable, and infection is under treatment.
• Serum creatinine greater than or equal to 5 mg per deciliter or serum creatinine of any level in the presence of severe volume overload, acidosis, or hyperkalemia—Hold dose. Subsequent doses may be given if serum creatinine is less than 4 mg per deciliter and fluid and electrolyte status is stable.
• Signs of hepatic failure including encephalopathy, increasing ascites, liver pain, hypoglycemia—Discontinue all treatment for that course. Consider starting a new course of treatment at least 7 weeks after cessation of adverse event and hospital discharge if all signs of hepatic failure have resolved.
• Stool guaiac repeatedly greater than 3-4+—Hold dose. Subsequent doses may be given if stool guaiac is negative.
• Bullous dermatitis or marked worsening of pre-existing skin condition—Hold dose. Subsequent doses may be given upon resolution of all signs of bullous dermatitis. Avoid topical steroid therapy.

High-dose aldesleukin therapy should also be withheld for oliguria unresponsive to fluid replacement or diuretics and for respiratory distress.

It is recommended that aldesleukin be permanently discontinued in patients who experienced the following toxicities in an earlier course of therapy:
• Sustained ventricular tachycardia (5 beats or more)
• Cardiac rhythm disturbances not controlled or unresponsive to management
• Recurrent chest pain with ECG changes consistent with angina or myocardial infarction
• Pericardial tamponade
• Intubation required for more than 72 hours
• Renal function impairment requiring dialysis for more than 72 hours
• Coma or toxic psychosis lasting more than 48 hours
• Repetitive or difficult to control seizures
• Bowel ischemia/perforation
• Gastrointestinal bleeding requiring surgery.

Special precautions are recommended in patients who develop thrombocytopenia as a result of administration of aldesleukin. These may include extreme care in performing invasive procedures; regular inspection of intravenous sites, skin (including perirectal area), and mucous membrane surfaces for signs of bleeding or bruising; limiting frequency of venipuncture and avoiding intramuscular injections; testing urine, emesis, stool, and secretions for occult blood; care in use of regular toothbrushes, dental floss, toothpicks, safety razors, and fingernail and toenail cutters; avoiding constipation; and using caution to prevent falls and other injuries. Such patients should avoid alcohol and aspirin intake because of the risk of gastrointestinal bleeding. Platelet transfusions may be required.

Patients should be observed carefully for signs of infection. Antibiotic support may be required. Because of the risk of infection, it is recommended that all patients with indwelling central lines receive antibiotic prophylaxis against *Staphylococcus aureus*, along with meticulous catheter care.

For treatment of adverse effects

Antiemetics and antidiarrheals may be given as needed to treat gastrointestinal effects. They usually are discontinued 12 hours after the last dose of aldesleukin.

Hydroxyzine or diphenhydramine and emollients may be used to prevent or control symptoms from pruritic rashes and are continued until resolution of pruritus. Some clinicians recommend that use of topical or systemic corticosteroids be avoided because of the risk of diminishing aldesleukin's therapeutic effect.

Supraventricular arrhythmias usually respond to conventional treatment (digoxin or verapamil).

Debilitating mental status changes may respond to low doses of haloperidol.

For capillary leak syndrome—
Capillary leak syndrome (CLS) is initially managed with careful monitoring of the patient's fluid and organ perfusion status by means of frequent determination of blood pressure and pulse and monitoring of organ function, including assessment of mental status and urine output. Hypovolemia is assessed by catheterization and central pressure monitoring. Because flexibility in fluid and pressor management is essential for maintaining organ perfusion and blood pressure, extreme caution is recommended in treating patients with fixed requirements for large volumes of fluid (e.g., patients with hypercalcemia).
Hypovolemia is managed by administration of intravenous fluids, either colloids or crystalloids, which are usually given when the central venous pressure (CVP) is below 3 to 4 mm Hg. Although correction of hypovolemia may require large volumes of fluids, caution is necessary because of the risk that unrestrained fluid administration may exacerbate problems associated with concomitant edema or effusions. A diuretic such as furosemide may be administered to reduce edema or pulmonary infiltration.
Management of edema, ascites, or pleural effusions depends on a careful balancing of the effects of fluid shifts so that neither the

consequences of hypovolemia (e.g., impaired organ perfusion) nor the consequences of fluid accumulation (e.g., pulmonary edema) exceed the patient's tolerance.

Early administration of dopamine (1 to 5 mcg per kg of body weight [mcg/kg] per minute), before the onset of hypotension, may help maintain organ perfusion, particularly to the kidney, and preserve urine output. Weight and urine output should be carefully monitored. If this dose of dopamine fails to sustain organ perfusion and blood pressure, some clinicians increase the dose of dopamine to 6 to 10 mcg/kg per minute or add phenylephrine (1 to 5 mcg/kg per minute) to the lower dose of dopamine. However, prolonged use of pressors, either individually or in combination, at relatively high doses may be associated with cardiac rhythm disturbances.

If organ perfusion cannot be maintained (demonstrated by altered mental status, reduced urine output, reduction in blood pressure below 90 mm Hg, or onset of cardiac arrhythmias), it is recommended that subsequent doses of aldesleukin be withheld until recovery of organ perfusion and return of systolic pressure to above 90 mm Hg.

Once recovery from CLS begins and blood pressure has normalized, use of diuretics may hasten recovery in patients in whom there has been excessive weight gain or edema formation, particularly if associated with shortness of breath from pulmonary congestion.

Oxygen is administered if pulmonary function monitoring confirms that P_aO_2 is decreased.

For relief of anemia and to ensure maximal oxygen carrying capacity, administration of packed red cells may be used.

To resolve absolute thrombocytopenia and reduce the risk of gastrointestinal bleeding, platelet transfusions may be given.

Parenteral Dosage Forms

ALDESLEUKIN FOR INJECTION

Usual adult dose

Carcinoma, renal or
Melanoma, metastatic—

High dose therapy: Intravenous infusion (over fifteen minutes), 600,000 International Units (IU) per kg of body weight (0.037 mg per kg of body weight) every eight hours for a total of fourteen doses. Following nine days of rest, the schedule is repeated for another fourteen doses, for a maximum of twenty-eight doses per course.

Note: Although aldesleukin has been given in lower doses and by other routes (e.g., continuous intravenous infusion, subcutaneous) by some investigators to reduce toxicity, relative efficacy of these regimens compared to the high-dose regimen has not been established.

Although glass bottles and plastic (polyvinyl chloride) bags have been used in clinical trials with comparable results, the manufacturer recommends that plastic bags be used as the dilution container since experimental studies suggest that use of plastic containers results in more consistent drug delivery.

Use of in-line filters is not recommended during aldesleukin administration because of the risk of adsorption of aldesleukin to the filter.

If the aldesleukin solution has been refrigerated, it should be brought to room temperature before administration.

Each treatment period should be separated by a rest period of at least seven weeks from the date of hospital discharge.

Dose modification in response to toxicity is accomplished by holding or interrupting a dose rather than reducing the dose. Some toxicities necessitate permanent withdrawal of aldesleukin. For recommendations concerning toxicities requiring either permanent withdrawal or holding of a dose, see *General Dosing Information*.

Usual pediatric dose

Safety and efficacy have not been established.

Strength(s) usually available

U.S.—

22 million IU (1.3 mg) (Rx) [*Proleukin* (mannitol; sodium dodecyl sulfate; monobasic sodium phosphate; dibasic sodium phosphate)].

Canada—

Not commercially available.

Packaging and storage

Store between 2 and 8 °C (36 and 46 °F), unless otherwise specified by the manufacturer. Protect from freezing.

Preparation of dosage form

Aldesleukin for injection is reconstituted for intravenous or subcutaneous administration by adding 1.2 mL of sterile water for injection to the vial (directing the diluent at the side of the vial and swirling the contents gently to avoid excess foaming), to produce a clear and colorless to slightly yellow solution containing 18 million Units (1.1 mg) per mL. The vial should not be shaken.

For administration by rapid intravenous infusion, the reconstituted solution is further diluted in 50 mL of 5% dextrose injection.

Stability

Reconstituted and diluted solutions should be stored in the refrigerator, since the product contains no preservative. Reconstituted solutions should be used within forty-eight hours. Any unused portion should be discarded.

Incompatibilities

Bacteriostatic water for injection or 0.9% sodium chloride injection should not be used for reconstitution because of increased aggregation.

Auxiliary labeling

- Do not shake.
- Do not freeze.

Revised: 09/30/1997
Developed: 09/15/1993

ALEFACEPT Systemic

VA CLASSIFICATION (Primary): DE801

Commonly used brand name(s): *Amevive*.

Note: For a listing of dosage forms and brand names by country availability, see *Dosage Forms* section(s).

Category

Antipsoriatic (systemic); Immunosuppressant.

Indications

Accepted

Psoriasis (treatment)—Alefacept is indicated for the treatment of moderate to severe chronic plaque psoriasis in adult patients who are candidates for systemic therapy or phototherapy.

Pharmacology/Pharmacokinetics

Physicochemical characteristics

Source—Recombinant DNA technology in a Chinese Hamster Ovary (CHO) mammalian cell expression system.

Molecular weight—91.4 kilodaltons.

pH—6.9, after reconstitution

Mechanism of action/Effect

Alefacept interferes with lymphocyte activation by specifically binding to the lymphocyte antigen, CD2, and inhibiting LFA-3/CD2 interaction. Activation of T lymphocytes involving the interaction between LFA-3 on antigen-presenting cells and CD2 on T lymphocytes plays a role in the pathophysiology of chronic plaque psoriasis. The majority of T lymphocytes in psoriatic lesions are of the memory effector phenotype characterized by the presence of the CD45RO marker, express activation markers (e.g., CD25, CD69) and release inflammatory cytokines, such as interferon γ.

Alefacept also causes a reduction in the subsets of CD2+ T lymphocytes (primarily CD45RO+), presumably by bridging between CD2 on target lymphocytes and immunoglobulin Fc receptors on cytotoxic cells, such as natural killer cells. Treatment with alefacept results in a reduction in circulating total CD4+ and CD8+ T lymphocyte counts. CD2 is also expressed at low levels on the surface of natural killer cells and certain bone marrow B-lymphocytes. Therefore, the potential exists for alefacept to affect the activation and numbers of cells other than T lymphocytes. In clinical studies of alefacept, minor changes in the numbers of circulating cells other than T lymphocytes have been observed.

Absorption

Bioavailability—63% after intramuscular injection

Distribution

Vol_D—94 mL per kg

Half-life

Elimination—270 hours

Elimination

Mean Clearance—0.25 mL per hr per kg

Precautions to Consider

Carcinogenicity

No carcinogenicity studies have been conducted with alefacept.

In a chronic toxicity study, cynomolgus monkeys were dosed weekly for 52 weeks with intravenous alefacept at 1 mg per kg per dose or 20 mg per kg per dose. One animal in the high dose group developed a B-cell lymphoma that was detected after 28 weeks of dosing. Additional animals in both dose groups developed B-cell hyperplasia of the spleen and lymph nodes. All animals in the study were positive for endemic primate gammaherpes virus also known as lymphocryptovirus (LCV). Latent LCV infection is generally asymptomatic, but can lead to B-cell lymphomas when animals are immune suppressed.

In a separate study, baboons given 3 doses of alefacept at 1 mg/kg every 8 weeks were found to have centroblast proliferation in B-cell dependent areas in the germinal centers of the spleen following a 116–day washout period.

The role of alefacept in the development of the lymphoid malignancy and the hyperplasia observed in non-human primates and the relevance to humans is unknown. Immunodeficiency-associated lymphocyte disorders (plasmacytic hyperplasia, polymorphic proliferation, and B-cell lymphomas) occur in patients who have congenital or acquired immunodeficiencies including those resulting from immunosuppressive therapy.

Mutagenicity

No evidence of mutagenicity was observed *in vitro* or *in vivo*.

Pregnancy/Reproduction

Fertility—No fertility studies have been conducted with alefacept.

Pregnancy—Adequate and well controlled studies in humans have not been done. Because the risk to the development of the fetal immune system and postnatal immune function in humans is unknown, alefacept should be used during pregnancy only if clearly needed. If pregnancy occurs while taking alefacept, continued use of the drug should be assessed.

Reproductive toxicology studies have been performed in cynomolgus monkeys at doses up to 5 mg per kg per week (about 62 times the human dose based on body weight) and have revealed no evidence of impaired fertility or harm to the fetus due to alefacept. No arbortifacient or teratogenic effects were observed in cynomolgus monkeys following intravenous bolus injections of alefacept administered weekly during the period of organogenesis to gestation. Alefacept underwent trans-placental passage and produced *in utero* exposure in developing monkeys. *In utero* serum levels of exposure in these monkeys were 23% of maternal serum levels. No evidence of fetal toxicity including adverse effects on immune system development were observed in any of these animals.

Women of childbearing potential make up a considerable segment of the patient population affected by psoriasis. Since the effect on pregnancy and fetal development, including immune system development, is not known, health care providers are encouraged to enroll patients currently taking alefacept who become pregnant into the Biogen Pregnancy Registry by calling 1–866–263–8483 (1–866–AMEVIVE).

FDA Pregnancy Category B

Breast-feeding

It is not known whether alefacept is distributed into human milk. Because many drugs are distributed into human milk, and because there exists the potential for serious adverse reactions in nursing infants from alefacept, a decision should be made whether to discontinue nursing while taking drug or to discontinue the use of the drug, taking into account the importance of the drug to the mother.

Pediatrics

No information is available on the relationship of age to the effects of alefacept in the pediatric population. Safety and efficacy have not been established. Alefacept is not indicated for use in pediatric patients.

Geriatrics

Although appropriate studies on the relationship of age to the effects of alefacept have not been performed in the geriatric population, no geriatrics-specific problems have been documented to date. However, elderly patients are more likely to have age related problems such as a higher incidence of infections and certain malignancies, which may require close monitoring for these adverse effects in patients receiving alefacept.

Drug interactions and/or related problems

The following drug interactions and/or related problems have been selected on the basis of their potential clinical significance (possible mechanism in parentheses where appropriate)—not necessarily inclusive (» = major clinical significance):

Note: Combinations containing any of the following medications, depending on the amount present, may also interact with this medication.

» Immunosuppressive agents, including methotrexate, or
» Phototherapy
(patients should not receive alefacept concurrently because of the possibility of excessive immunosuppression; the duration of the period following treatment with alefacept before one should consider starting other immunosuppressive therapy has not been evaluated)

Vaccines, live or live-attenuated
(safety and efficacy not studied in patients being treated with alefacept)

Laboratory value alterations

The following have been selected on the basis of their potential clinical significance (possible effect in parentheses where appropriate)—not necessarily inclusive (» = major clinical significance).

With physiology/laboratory test
» Alanine aminotransferase (ALT [SGPT]), serum and
» Aspartate aminotransferase (AST [SGOT]), serum
(post-marketing reports of elevated values)

Medical considerations/Contraindications

The medical considerations/contraindications included have been selected on the basis of their potential clinical significance (reasons given in parentheses where appropriate)—not necessarily inclusive (» = major clinical significance).

Except under special circumstances, this medication should not be used when the following medical problem exists:

» HIV infection
(alefacept should not be administered to HIV infected patients because it reduces CD4+ T lympocyte counts, which might accelerate disease progression or increase complications of disease in these patients)

» Hypersensitivity to alefacept or any of its components
(hypersensitivity reactions [urticaria, angioedema] are associated with the administration of alefacept; if anaphylactic or serious allergic reaction occurs, discontinue immediately and administer appropriate therapy; alefacept use is contraindicated in patients with a known hypersensitivity to alefacept or any of its components)

» Infection, clinically significant
(alefacept is an immunosuppressive agent and has the potential to increase the risk of infection and reactivate latent, chronic infections; alefacept should not be administered to patients with a clinically important infection; caution should be used in patients with chronic infections or history of recurrent infection; if patient develops a serious infection medicine should be discontinued)

» Lymphopenia
(alefacept induces dose-dependent reductions in circulating CD4+ and CD8+ lymphocyte counts; a course of therapy should not be started in patients with CD4+ below normal; dosing should be withheld if CD4+ lymphocyte counts are below 250 cells per μL; drug should be discontinued of the counts remain below 250 cells per μL for one month.)

» Malignancy, systemic, history of
(should not be administered to patients with a history of systemic malignancy; caution should be exercised in patients at high risk for malignancy; alefacept may increase the risk of malignancies; if a malignancy develops alefacept should be discontinued)

Patient monitoring

The following may be especially important in patient monitoring (other tests may be warranted in some patients, depending on condition; » = major clinical significance):

» CD4+ T lymphocyte counts
(patients should have normal counts prior to initial or subsequent course of alefacept; counts should be monitored weekly during the 12 week dosing period and used to guide dosing; dosing should be withheld if counts are below 250 micrograms/L and discontinued if counts remain below 250 micrograms per L for one month)

» Hepatic injury
(patients with signs or symptoms of liver injury should be fully evaluated and alefacept discontinued in those who develop significant clinical signs of liver injury)

» Infections, signs and symptoms
(patients should be monitored for signs and symptoms of an infection during and after a course of alefacept therapy; new infections

should be monitored closely; therapy should be discontinued if patient develops a serious infection)

Side/Adverse Effects

The following side/adverse effects have been selected on the basis of their potential clinical significance (possible signs and symptoms in parentheses where appropriate)—not necessarily inclusive:

Those indicating need for medical attention

Incidence more frequent

Lymphopenia (fever or chills; cough or hoarseness; lower back or side pain; painful or difficult urination)

Incidence less frequent

Pharyngitis (body aches or pain; congestion; cough; dryness or soreness of throat; fever; hoarseness; runny nose; tender, swollen glands in neck; trouble in swallowing; voice changes); ***serious infections***

Incidence rare

Cardiovascular events; coronary artery disorder (arm, back or jaw pain; chest pain or discomfort; chest tightness or heaviness; fast or irregular heartbeat; shortness of breath; sweating; nausea); ***hypersensitivity reactions*** (fainting or loss of consciousness; fast or irregular breathing; swelling of eyes or eyelids; trouble in breathing; tightness in chest,); ***malignancies; myocardial infarction*** (chest pain or discomfort; pain or discomfort in arms, jaw, back or neck; shortness of breath; nausea; sweating; vomiting)

Incidence not determined—Observed during clinical practice; estimates of frequency can not be determined

Fatty infiltration of the liver (abdominal pain; bloating of abdomen; dark urine; light-colored stools; nausea and vomiting; yellow eyes or skin); ***hepatitis*** (dark urine; general tiredness and weakness; light-colored stools; nausea and vomiting; upper right abdominal pain; yellow eyes and skin); ***hepatic injury*** (pruritus; dark urine; persistent anorexia; yellow eyes or skin; influenza (flu)-like symptoms; right upper quadrant tenderness); ***severe liver failure*** (headache; stomach pain; continuing vomiting; dark-colored urine; general feeling of tiredness or weakness; light-colored stools; yellow eyes or skin)

Those indicating need for medical attention only if they continue or are bothersome

Incidence more frequent

Chills; injection site reactions, including; pain; inflammation; bleeding; edema; mass; skin hypersensitivity

Incidence less frequent

Dizziness; cough, increased; myalgia (joint pain; swollen joints; muscle aching or cramping; muscle pains or stiffness; difficulty in moving); ***nausea; pruritus*** (itching skin)

Incidence Rare

Headache

Overdose

For more information on the management of overdose or unintentional ingestion, **contact a poison control center** (see *Poison Control Center Listing*).

Clinical effects of overdose

The following effects have been selected on the basis of their potential clinical significance (possible signs and symptoms in parentheses where appropriate)—not necessarily inclusive:

The highest dose tested in humans (0.75 mg/kg IV) was associated with the side effects below within one day of dosing.

Arthralgia (pain in joints; muscle pain or stiffness; difficulty in moving); ***chills; headache; sinusitis*** (pain or tenderness around eyes and cheekbones; fever; stuffy or runny nose; headache; cough; shortness of breath or troubled breathing; tightness of chest or wheezing)

Treatment of overdose

Monitoring—

Patients should be closely monitored for effects on total lymphocyte count and CD4+ T lymphocyte count

Supportive care—

Treatment should be symptomatic and supportive

Patients in whom intentional overdose is confirmed or suspected should be referred for psychiatric consultation.

Patient Consultation

As an aid to patient consultation, refer to *Advice for the Patient, Alefacept (Systemic)*.

In providing consultation, consider emphasizing the following selected information (» = major clinical significance):

Before using this medication

» Conditions affecting use, especially:

Hypersensitivity to alefacept or any of its components

Other medications, especially immunosuppressive agents (including methotrexate) and phototherapy

Other medical problems, especially history of systemic malignancy, HIV infection, lymphopenia, clinically significant infection

Proper use of this medication

» Proper dosing

Missed dose: Taking as soon as possible; not taking if almost time for next scheduled dose; not doubling doses

» Importance of proper reconstitution method

» Importance of proper administration

Proper storage

Precautions while using this medication

» Regular visits to physician weekly to check lymphocyte counts

» Patients should be instructed to contact physician immediately if they have symptoms suggestive of an infection or malignancy

» Importance of reporting signs or symptoms of liver injury including persistent nausea, anorexia, fatigue, vomiting, abdominal pain, jaundice, easy bruising, dark urine or pale stools

» Female patients should be instructed to contact physician if they become pregnant and should be instructed to enroll in the pregnancy registry

Side/adverse effects

Signs of potential side effects, especially cardiovascular events, coronary artery disorder, infection, myocardial infarction

Signs of potential side effects observed during clinical practice, especially fatty infiltration of the liver, hepatitis, hepatic injury, or severe liver failure

General Dosing Information

For parenteral dosing forms:

Alefacept should be reconstituted by a health care professional using aseptic technique. Each vial is intended for single patient use only. Do not use an alefacept dose tray beyond the date stamped on the carton, dose tray lid, vial label, or diluent container label.

Retreatment with an additional 12 week course may be initiated provided that the CD4+ lymphocyte counts are within the normal range, and a minimum of 12–week interval has passed since the previous course of treatment. Data on retreatment beyond 2 cycles are limited.

The reconstituted solution should be clear and colorless to slightly yellow. Visually inspect the solution for particulate matter and discoloration prior to administration. The solution should not be used if discolored or cloudy, or if undissolved material remains. Do not reconstitute with other diluents. Do not filter reconstituted solution during preparation or administration.

For intramuscular use: Inject the full 0.5 mL of solution. Rotate injection sites so that a different site is used for each new injection. New injections should be given at least 1 inch from an old site and never into areas where the skin is red, bruised, tender, or hard.

For intravenous use:

- Prepare 2 syringes with 3.0 mL of Normal Saline, USP for pre-and post-administration flush
- Prime the winged infusion set with 3.0 mL saline and insert the set into the vein.
- Attach the alefacept filled syringe to the infusion set and administer the solution over no more than 5 seconds.
- Flush the infusion set with 3.0 mL of saline, USP

Parenteral Dosage Forms

ALEFACEPT FOR INJECTION

Usual adult dose

Psoriasis—

Intramuscular, 15 mg given once a week for 12 weeks

Intravenous, 7.5 mg bolus given once a week for 12 weeks

Usual pediatric dose

Safety and efficacy have not been established

Usual geriatric dose

See *Usual adult dose*.

Strength(s) usually available

U.S.—

7.5 mg single-use vial (Rx) [*Amevive* (IM administration; sucrose; glycine; sodium citrate dihydrate; citric acid monohydrate)].

15 mg single-use vial (Rx) [*Amevive* (IV administration; glycine; sodium citrate dihydrate; citric acid monohydrate)].

Canada—

15 mg per 0.5 mL (Rx) [*Amevive*].

Packaging and storage

Store at controlled room temperature 15 to 30°C (59 to 86°F). Protect from light.

Preparation of dosage form

Alefacept should be reconstituted by a health care professional using aseptic technique. Using the supplied syringe and one of the supplied needles, withdraw only **0.6 mL** of the supplied diluent, (Sterile Water for Injection, USP). Keeping the needle pointed at the sidewall of the vial, slowly inject the diluent into the vial of alefacept. Some foaming will occur, which is normal. To avoid excessive foaming, do not shake or vigorously agitate. The contents should be swirled gently during dissolution. Dissolution generally takes less than 2 minutes. The solution should be used as soon as possible after reconstitution.

After reconstitution, remove the needle used for reconstitution and attach the other supplied needle. Withdraw 0.5 mL of the solution into the syringe. Some foam or bubbles may remain in the vial.

Note: 15 mg lyophilized powder for intramuscular (IM) administration should be reconstituted with 0.6 mL of the supplied diluent. 0.5 mL of the reconstituted solution contains 7.5 mg of alefacept.

7.5 mg lyophilized powder for intravenous (IV) administration should be reconstituted with 0.6 mL of the supplied diluent. 0.5 mL of the reconstituted solution contains 7.5 mg of alefacept.

Stability

Following reconstitution, the product should be used immediately or within 4 hours if stored in the vial at 2 to 8°C (36 to 46°F). **Alefacept not used within 4 hours of reconstitution should be discarded.**

Incompatibilities

Do not add other medications to solutions containing alefacept.

Auxiliary labeling

- Protect from light
- Store at controlled room temperature
- Do not use past expiration date

Revised: 11/16/2005
Developed: 12/04/2003

ALEMTUZUMAB Systemic

VA CLASSIFICATION (Primary): AN900

Commonly used brand name(s): *Campath.*

Note: For a listing of dosage forms and brand names by country availability, see *Dosage Forms* section(s).

Category

Antineoplastic; Monoclonal antibody.

Indications

Accepted

Leukemia, chronic lymphocytic (treatment)—Alemtuzumab is indicated for the treatment of patients with B-cell chronic lymphocytic leukemia (B-CLL) who have been treated with alkylating agents and who have failed fludarabine therapy.

Acceptance not established

Use of alemtuzumab for the first-line treatment of chronic lymphocytic leukemia has not been established, due to insufficient data supporting safety and/or efficacy. This consensus pertains to intravenous and subcutaneous administration. Comparative data to current first-line treatment standards are needed in order to qualify as a first-line treatment option, in a significant number of patients.

The subcutaneous route of administration has not been established in residual chronic lymphocytic leukemia, due to insufficient data supporting safety and/or efficacy. Comparison to intravenous administration, in a significant number of patients is needed. A fully published pharmacokinetics comparison to intravenous administration would be beneficial.

Pharmacology/Pharmacokinetics

Physicochemical characteristics

Source—Recombinant DNA-derived humanized monoclonal antibody that is directed against the 21–28 kD cell surface glycoprotein, CD52. The antibody is an IgG1 kappa with variable human framework and constant regions, and complementarity-determining regions from a murine (rat) monoclonal antibody. It is produced in mammalian cell (Chinese hamster ovary) suspension culture containing neomycin (neomycin is not detectable in the final product).

Molecular weight—150 kilodaltons.

pH—6.8 to 7.4

Mechanism of action/Effect

Alemtuzumab binds to CD52, a non-modulating antigen that is present on the surface of essentially all B and T lymphocytes, a majority of monocytes, macrophages, and NK cells, and a subpopulation of granulocytes.

The mechanism of action is expected to be antibody-dependent lysis of leukemic cells following cell surface binding. Alemtuzumab binding was seen in lymphocyte tissues and the mononuclear phagocyte system. A proportion of bone marrow cells, including some CD34+ cells, express variable levels of CD52.

Half-life

The overall average half-life over the dosing interval was about 288 hours.

Peak serum concentration

Steady state was approached by approximately week 6. Relative dose proportionality was demonstrated by both peak serum concentration and area under the curve (AUC)

Note: Peak and trough levels rose during the first few weeks of treatment, and there was marked inter-patient variability.

Precautions to Consider

Carcinogenicity

Long term studies in humans or animals have not been done.

Mutagenicity

Long term studies in humans or animals have not been done.

Pregnancy/Reproduction

Fertility—Studies in humans or animals have not been done. Women of childbearing potential and men of reproductive potential should use effective contraceptive methods during treatment and for a minimum of 6 months following alemtuzumab therapy.

Pregnancy—Immunoglobulin G (IgG) is known to cross the placenta, therefore alemtuzumab may cross the placental barrier. Alemtuzumab may cause fetal B and T lymphocyte depletion. Studies in humans or animals have not been done.

Use during pregnancy only if clearly needed.

It is recommended that women of childbearing potential and men of reproductive potential use effective contraception during treatment and for up to 6 months following treatment with alemtuzumab.

FDA Pregnancy Category C.

Breast-feeding

It is not known whether alemtuzumab is distributed into breast milk. However, human IgG is distributed into human milk. It is recommended that breast feeding be discontinued during treatment and for at least 3 months following the last dose of alemtuzumab.

Pediatrics

No information is available on the relationship of age to the effects of alemtuzumab in the pediatric population. Safety and efficacy have not been established.

Geriatrics

While studies using alemtuzumab did not include enough elderly patients to exclude important differences, no geriatrics-specific differences that would limit the usefulness of alemtuzumab in this population have been noted.

Dental

The bone marrow depressant, neutropenic, and thrombocytopenic effects of alemtuzumab may result in an increased incidence of microbial infection, delayed healing, or gingival bleeding. Dental work, whenever possible, should be completed prior to initiation of therapy or deferred until blood counts have returned to normal. Patients should be instructed in proper oral hygiene, including caution in use of regular toothbrushes, dental floss, and toothpicks.

Drug interactions and/or related problems

The following drug interactions and/or related problems have been selected on the basis of their potential clinical significance (possible

mechanism in parentheses where appropriate)—not necessarily inclusive (» = major clinical significance):

Note: Combinations containing any of the following medications, depending on the amount present, may also interact with this medication.

» Blood dyscrasia-causing medications (see *Appendix II*)
(leukopenic and/or thrombocytopenic effects of alemtuzumab may be increased with concurrent or recent therapy if alemtuzumab causes the same effects; dosage adjustment of alemtuzumab, if necessary, should be based on blood counts)

» Bone marrow depressants, other (see *Appendix II*) or
Radiation therapy
(additive bone marrow depression may occur; dosage reduction may be required when two or more bone marrow depressants, including radiation, are used concurrently or consecutively)

Antihypertensives
(careful monitoring of blood pressure and hypotensive symptoms with concomitant use with alemtuzumab)

Vaccines, killed virus
(because normal defense mechanisms may be suppressed by alemtuzumab therapy, the patient's antibody response to the vaccine may be decreased. The interval between discontinuation of medications that cause immunosuppression and restoration of the patient's ability to respond to the vaccine depends on the intensity and type of immunosuppression-causing medication used, the underlying disease, and other factors; estimates vary from 3 months to 1 year)

» Vaccines, live virus
(because normal defense mechanisms may be suppressed by alemtuzumab therapy, concurrent use with a live virus vaccine may potentiate the replication of the vaccine virus, may increase the side/adverse effects of the vaccine virus, and/or may decrease the patient's antibody response to the vaccine; immunization of these patients should be undertaken only with extreme caution after careful review of the patient's hematologic status and only with the knowledge and consent of the physician managing the alemtuzumab therapy. The interval between discontinuation of medications that cause immunosuppression and restoration of the patient's ability to respond to the vaccine depends on the intensity and type of immunosuppression-causing medication used, the underlying disease, and other factors; estimates vary from 3 months to 1 year. In addition, immunization with oral poliovirus vaccine should be postponed in persons in close contact with the patient, especially family members)

Diagnostic interference

The following drug interactions and/or related problems have been selected on the basis of their potential clinical significance (possible mechanism in parentheses where appropriate)—not necessarily inclusive (» = major clinical significance):

Alemtuzumab may interfere with subsequent diagnostic serum tests that utilize antibodies.

Medical considerations/Contraindications

The medical considerations/contraindications included have been selected on the basis of their potential clinical significance (reasons given in parentheses where appropriate)—not necessarily inclusive (» = major clinical significance).

Except under special circumstances, this medication should not be used when the following medical problems exist:

» Infections, systemic, active
(use of alemtuzumab is contraindicated until infection is resolved, then therapy may be reinstated)
(alemtuzumab induces profound lymphopenia, increasing risk of graft vs. host disease (GVHD); irradiation of any blood products administered prior to recovery from lymphopenia is recommended)
(rare instances of fatal myelosuppression; bone marrow aplasia and hypoplasia in clinical studies at recommended dose, increasing with higher doses; severe and fatal autoimmune anemia and thrombocytopenia have occurred and warrant discontinuation of therapy; no information on safety of use in the presence of autoimmune cytopenias or marrow aplasia; hematologic monitoring is required; all patients should receive prophylactic therapy)

» Immunodeficiency, underlying
(increased risk of infection for patients seropositive for HIV)

» Hypersensitivity (Type 1) or previous anaphylactic reactions to alemtuzumab, other monoclonal antibodies, or any of its components

Risk-benefit should be considered when the following medical problems exist:

» Bone marrow depression, existing or
(concurrent use of alemtuzumab increases risk of infection; hematologic monitoring is required and systemic infections should be treated; all patients should receive prophylactic therapy)

» Chickenpox, existing or recent (including recent exposure) or
» Herpes zoster
(risk of severe generalized disease)

Ischemic heart disease
(careful monitoring of blood pressure and hypotensive symptoms with concomitant use of alemtuzumab)

» Caution should be used also in patients who have had previous cytotoxic drug or radiation therapy

Patient monitoring

The following may be especially important in patient monitoring (other tests may be warranted in some patients, depending on condition; » = major clinical significance):

» Complete blood counts and
» Platelet counts
(recommended to monitor for anemia, neutropenia, and thrombocytopenia; obtain at weekly intervals during treatment and more frequently if worsening anemia, neutropenia, or thrombocytopenia is observed)

» CD4 counts
(assess after therapy until recovery to ≥ 200 cells/microLiter)

Blood pressure
(monitor during alemtuzumab therapy)

Infusion reactions
(monitor carefully during infusions)

Side/Adverse Effects

Note: Many "side effects" of antineoplastic therapy are unavoidable and represent the medication's pharmacologic action. Some of these (for example, leukopenia and thrombocytopenia) are actually used as parameters to aid in individual dosage titration.

Note: Serious and sometimes fatal bacterial, viral, fungal, and protozoal infections have been reported during alemtuzumab therapy.

The following side/adverse effects have been selected on the basis of their potential clinical significance (possible signs and symptoms in parentheses where appropriate)—not necessarily inclusive:

Those indicating need for medical attention

Incidence more frequent (greater than 50%)

Anemia (pale skin; troubled breathing, exertional; unusual bleeding or bruising; unusual tiredness or weakness); ***infusion-related reactions*** (chills; diarrhea; fever; headache; itching, hives, or rash; dizziness, faintness, or light-headedness when getting up from a lying or sitting position; sudden sweating; nausea and vomiting; shortness of breath; tightness in chest; unusual tiredness; wheezing); ***neutropenia*** (black, tarry stools; blood in urine; chills; cough; fever; painful or difficult urination; shortness of breath; sore throat; sores, ulcers, or white spots on lips or in mouth; swollen glands; unusual bleeding or bruising; unusual tiredness or weakness); ***thrombocytopenia*** (black, tarry stools; blood in urine; chills; cough; fever; painful or difficult urination; shortness of breath; sore throat; sores, ulcers, or white spots on lips or in mouth; swollen glands; unusual bleeding or bruising; unusual tiredness or weakness)

Note: Acute infusion-related events were most common during the first week of therapy. Incremental dosage escalation and premedication with antihistamines, acetaminophen, antiemetics, meperidine and corticosteroids can help lessen these effects.

Incidence less frequent (10 to 50%)

Bronchitis, pneumonitis, or pneumonia (chest pain or tightness; cough; troubled breathing); ***hypertension***—may be symptomless; ***hypotension*** (dizziness, faintness, or light-headedness when getting up from a lying or sitting position; sudden sweating); ***infection, viral or other*** (fever or chills; cough or hoarseness; lower back or side pain; painful or difficult urination); ***peripheral edema*** (decreased urination; rapid weight gain; bloating or swelling of face, hands, lower legs, and/or feet); ***sepsis*** (muscle weakness; rash; red or purple spots on the skin, varying in size and remain after pushing skin surface); ***tachycardia*** (fast, pounding, or irregular heartbeat or pulse; palpitations)

Incidence rare (less than 10%)

Allergic reaction, anaphylactic (flushing of the face or neck; swelling of eyelids, face, or lips; skin rash or itching; troubled breathing or wheezing); ***moniliasis*** (white patches on tongue, in mouth, or in folds of skin, including the genitals); ***pancytopenia*** (black, tarry stools; blood in urine; chills; cough; fever; painful or difficult urination; shortness of breath; sore throat; sores, ulcers, or white spots on lips or in mouth; swollen glands; unusual bleeding or bruising; unusual tiredness or weakness)

Those indicating need for medical attention only if they continue or are bothersome

Incidence more frequent (> 50%)

Nausea

Incidence less frequent (10 to 50%)

Abdominal pain; anorexia (loss of appetite; weight loss); ***asthenia*** (lack or loss of strength); ***back pain; diarrhea; dizziness; dysesthesias*** (burning, crawling, itching, numbness, prickling, "pins and needles", or tingling feelings); ***dyspepsia*** (acid or sour stomach; belching; heartburn; indigestion; stomach discomfort, upset or pain); ***herpes simplex*** (burning or stinging of skin; painful cold sores or blisters on lips, nose, eyes, or genitals); ***increased sweating; insomnia*** (sleeplessness); ***myalgia*** (muscle aches); ***pharyngitis*** (sore throat); ***skeletal pain*** (bone pain); ***stomatitis, ulcerative stomatitis, mucositis*** (swelling or inflammation of the mouth); ***vomiting***

Incidence rare (less than 10%)

Constipation; depression (mood or mental changes); ***epistaxis*** (bloody nose; unexplained nosebleeds); ***malaise*** (general feeling of discomfort or illness; unusual tiredness or weakness); ***rhinitis*** (stuffy nose); ***somnolence*** (sleepiness or unusual drowsiness); ***temperature change sensation; purpura*** (red or purple spots on skin, varying in size from pinpoint to large bruises); ***tremor***

Overdose

For more information on the management of overdose or unintentional ingestion, **contact a poison control center** (see *Poison Control Center Listing*).

Clinical effects of overdose

The following effects have been selected on the basis of their potential clinical significance (possible signs and symptoms in parentheses where appropriate)—not necessarily inclusive:

Initial doses of greater than 3 mg are not well-tolerated. Single doses of alemtuzumab of greater than 30 mg or cumulative weekly doses of greater than 90 mg should be avoided as higher doses have been associated with increased incidence of pancytopenia.

One patient given an initial 80 mg dose of alemtuzumab by intravenous infusion experienced the following, resulting in death. Tumor lysis syndrome was a suspected contributor.

Anuria (inability to urinate); ***bronchospasm, acute*** (troubled breathing, sudden; chest tightness); ***cough; shortness of breath***

Treatment of overdose

Supportive care—

There is no specific antidote for alemtuzumab.

Treatment consists of drug discontinuation and supportive therapy.

Patients in whom intentional overdose is confirmed or suspected should be referred for psychiatric consultation.

Patient Consultation

As an aid to patient consultation, refer to *Advice for the Patient, Alemtuzumab (Systemic)*.

In providing consultation, consider emphasizing the following selected information (» = major clinical significance):

Before using this medication

» Conditions affecting use, especially:

Hypersensitivity to alemtuzumab, other monoclonal antibodies, or any of its components

Pregnancy—Use is not recommended because of potential harm to fetus; advisability of using contraception for both males and females; informing physician immediately if pregnancy is suspected.

Breast-feeding—Not recommended because of potential serious adverse effects.

Other medications, especially blood dyscrasia-causing medications, other bone marrow depressants or previous cytotoxic drug or radiation therapy

Other medical problems, especially active and systemic infections, underlying immunodeficiency, bone marrow depression, active or systemic infection, chickenpox, and herpes zoster

Proper use of this medication

» Proper dosing

Precautions while using this medication

» Importance of close monitoring by physician

» Avoiding immunizations unless approved by physician; other persons in patient's household should avoid immunizations with oral poliovirus vaccine; avoiding other persons who have taken oral polio virus vaccine or wearing a protective mask that covers nose and mouth

» For women of childbearing potential and men of reproductive potential—Using effective contraceptive methods during treatment and for a minimum of 6 months following alemtuzumab therapy

Caution if bone marrow depression occurs:

» Avoiding exposure to persons with bacterial infections, especially during periods of low blood counts; checking with physician immediately if fever or chills, cough or hoarseness, lower back or side pain, or painful or difficult urination occur

» Checking with physician immediately if unusual bleeding or bruising; black, tarry stools; blood in urine or stools; or pinpoint red spots on skin occur

Caution in use of regular toothbrush, dental floss, or toothpick; physician, dentist, or nurse may suggest alternatives; checking with physician before having dental work done

Not touching eyes or inside of nose unless hands washed immediately before

Using caution to avoid accidental cuts with use of sharp objects such as safety razor or fingernail or toenail cutters

Avoiding contact sports or other situations where bruising or injury could occur

Side/adverse effects

Signs of potential side effects, especially anaphylactic, allergic reaction, anemia, bronchitis, pneumonitis, pneumonia, hypertension, hypotension, viral or other infection, infusion-related reactions, moniliasis, neutropenia, pancytopenia, peripheral edema, sepsis, tachycardia, or thrombocytopenia

General Dosing Information

Alemtuzumab should only be administered under the supervision of a physician experienced in the use of antineoplastic therapy.

Premedication should be given prior to the first dose of alemtuzumab, at dose escalations, and as clinically indicated to reduce infusion-related adverse effects. In clinical studies, patients received 650 mg of acetaminophen and 50 mg of diphenhydramine 30 minutes prior to the start of the alemtuzumab infusion. Hydrocortisone 200 mg may be given to alleviate severe infusion-related reactions. Gentle dose escalation is also helpful in reducing the incidence of reaction.

Alemtuzumab should be infused intravenously over 2 hours. Alemtuzumab should not be given as an intravenous bolus or push.

Alemtuzumab has been associated with infusion-related events including hypotension, rigors, fever, shortness of breath, bronchospasm, chills, and/or rash. Syncope, pulmonaryinfiltrates, ARDS, respiratory arrest, cardiac arrythmias, myocardial infarction and cardiac arrest have also been reported during infusions.

Patients should receive anti-infective prophylaxis to minimize risk of serious opportunistic infection. Patients in one study received oral trimethoprim/sulfamethoxazole DS twice daily three times per week and famciclovir 250 mg or equivalent twice a day during alemtuzumab therapy. Prophylactic therapy should continue for 2 months following completion of alemtuzumab therapy or until the CD4 cell count has risen above 200 cells per microliter, whichever is **later**.

Alemtuzumab therapy should not be continued during serious infection, serious hematologic toxicity, or other serious toxicity.Treatment should be permanently discontinued if there is evidence of autoimmune anemia or thrombocytopenia.

Antibodies to alemtuzumab have been discovered in patients who developed an immune response during treatment. Patients who develop hypersensitivity to alemtuzumab may have allergic or hypersensitivity reactions to other monoclonal antibodies.

Parenteral Dosage Forms

ALEMTUZUMAB FOR INJECTION

Note: Alemtuzumab should not be administered as an intravenous push or bolus. Alemtuzumab should be administered under the supervision of a physician who is experienced in the use of cancer chemotherapeutic agents.

Usual adult dose

Chronic lymphocytic leukemia—

- Initiation—
- Intravenous infusion, 3 mg administered over 2 hours, daily. When the daily dose of 3 mg is tolerated (e.g. infusion-related toxicities are ≤ Grade 2), the daily dose should be increased to 10 mg and continued until tolerated. When the 10 mg dose is tolerated, the maintenance dose may be initiated.
- Maintenance—
- Intravenous infusion, 30 mg per day, administered 3 times a week on alternate days for up to 12 weeks.

Note: In most patients dose escalation can be accomplished in 3 to 7 days.

Dose escalation to the recommended maintenance dose is required.

Recommended Concomitant Medications—

Premedication should be given prior to the first dose, at dose escalations and as clinically indicated.

Premedication

Diphenhydramine 50 mg and acetaminophen 650 mg; administered 30 minutes prior to alemtuzumab infusion.

In cases where severe infusion related events occur treatment with 200 mg hydrocortisone was used.

Concomitant Medications

Patients should receive anti-infective prophylaxis to minimize the risk of serious opportunistic infections.

The regimen used in one study was the following: trimethoprim/sulfamethoxazole DS twice daily (BID) three times a week and famciclovir or equivalent 250 mg twice a day (BID) upon initiation of alemtuzumab therapy.

Prophylaxis should be continued for two months after completion of alemtuzumab therapy or until the CD4+ count is ≥ 200 cells/microLiter whichever occurs later.

Dose Modification and Reinitiation of Therapy—

Alemtuzumab therapy should be discontinued during serious infection, serious hematologic toxicity, or other serious toxicity until the event resolves. Therapy should be permanently discontinued if evidence of an autoimmune anemia or thrombocytopenia appears.

See table below for dose modifications for severe neutropenia or thrombocytopenia.

Hematologic Toxicity	Dose Modification and Reinitiation of Therapy
For first occurrence of ANC < 250/microLiter and/or platelet count ≤ 25,000/microLiter	Withhold alemtuzumab therapy. When ANC ≥ 500/microLiter and platelet count ≥ 50,000/microLiter, resume alemtuzumab therapy at same dose. If delay between dosing is ≥7 days, initiate alemtuzumab therapy at 3 mg and escalate to 10 mg and then to 30 mg as tolerated.
For second occurrence of ANC < 250/microLiter and/or platelet count ≤ 25,000/microLiter	Withhold alemtuzumab therapy. When ANC ≥ 500/microLiter and platelet count ≥ 50,000/microLiter, resume alemtuzumab therapy at 10 mg. If delay between dosing is ≥ 7 days, initiate alemtuzumab therapy at 3 mg and escalate to 10 mg only.
For third occurrence of ANC < 250/microLiter and/or platelet count ≤ 25,000/microLiter.	Discontinue alemtuzumab therapy permanently.
For a decrease of ANC and/or platelet count to ≤ 50% of the baseline value in patients initiating therapy with a baseline ANC ≤ 500/microLiter and/or a baseline platelet count ≤ 25,000/microLiter	Withhold alemtuzumab therapy. When ANC ≥ 500/microLiter and platelet count return to baseline value(s), resume alemtuzumab therapy. If delay between dosing is ≥ 7 days, initiate alemtuzumab therapy at 3 mg and escalate to 10 mg and then to 30 mg as tolerated.

Usual adult prescribing limits

Initial doses of greater than 3 mg are not well-tolerated. Single doses greater than 30 mg or cumulative weekly doses of 90 mg should not be administered. Higher doses are associated with an increased incidence of pancytopenia.

Usual pediatric dose

Safety and efficacy have not been established.

Usual geriatric dose

See *Usual adult dose*.

Strength(s) usually available

U.S.—

30 mg per 1 mL of solution (Rx) [*Campath* (preservative-free; 8.0 mg sodium chloride; 1.44 mg dibasic sodium phosphate; 0.2 mg potassium chloride; 0.2 mg monobasic potassium phosphate; 0.1 mg polysorbate 80; 0.187 mg disodium edetate)].

Packaging and storage

Store between 2 and 8 °C (34 and 46°F). Do not freeze. Protect from direct sunlight. Discard if the vial has been frozen.

Preparation of dosage form

Do not shake the vial prior to use. Withdraw the necessary amount of drug into a syringe. Filter with a sterile, low-protein binding, non-fiber releasing 5 micrometer filter prior to dilution. Inject into 100 mL sterile 0.9% Sodium Chloride USP or 5% Dextrose in Water USP. Gently invert the bag to mix the solution. Discard syringe and any unused drug product.

Stability

Alemtuzumab should be used within 8 hours after dilution. It does not contain a preservative and should be protected from light. The solution may be stored at room temperature (15 to 30° C) or refrigerated.

Incompatibilities

Alemtuzumab has not shown any incompatibilities with polyvinylchloride (PVC) bags, PVC or any polyethylene-lined PVC administration sets, or low-protein binding filters. No data is available concerning the incompatibility with other drug substances. Other drug substances should not be added or simultaneously infused through the same intravenous line.

Auxiliary labeling

- For single dose only. Discard unused drug
- Do not shake
- Do not freeze

Revised: 02/04/2005
Developed: 06/13/2001

ALENDRONATE Systemic

VA CLASSIFICATION (Primary/Secondary): HS301/HS303
Commonly used brand name(s): *Fosamax*.

Note: For a listing of dosage forms and brand names by country availability, see *Dosage Forms* section(s).

Category

Bone resorption inhibitor.

Indications

Accepted

Osteoporosis, male (treatment)—Alendronate is indicated for the use in treatment of osteoporosis in men to increase bone mass.

Osteoporosis, glucocorticoid-induced (treatment adjunct)—Alendronate is indicated for the treatment of osteoporosis in men and women receiving glucocorticoids in a daily dosage equivalent to 7.5 milligrams or more of prednisone and who have a low bone mineral density. Alendronate should be used in conjunction with adequate amounts of vitamin D and calcium.

Osteoporosis, postmenopausal (treatment adjunct)—Alendronate is indicated for the treatment of osteoporosis in postmenopausal women, as confirmed by the finding of low bone mass (at least 2 standard deviations below the premenopausal mean) or by the presence or history of osteoporotic fracture. Alendronate should be used in conjunction with adequate intake of calcium (1 to 1.5 grams of elemental calcium a day) and vitamin D (400 to 800 Units a day) to aid in the prevention of progressive loss of bone mass.

Osteoporosis, postmenopausal (prophylaxis)—Alendronate is indicated for the prevention of osteoporosis in postmenopausal women who are at risk of developing osteoporosis and for whom the desired clinical outcome is to maintain bone mass and to reduce the risk of future fracture. Alendronate should be used in conjunction with adequate intake of calcium (1 to 1.5 grams of elemental calcium a day) and vitamin D (400 to 800 Units a day) to aid in the prevention of progressive loss of bone mass.

Paget's disease of bone (treatment)—Alendronate is indicated for the treatment of Paget's disease in patients with alkaline phosphatase concentrations at least two times the upper limit of normal, those who are symptomatic, or those at risk for future complications from the disease. Signs and symptoms of Paget's disease may include bone pain, deformity, and/or fractures; increased concentrations of *N*-telopeptide of type I collagen, serum alkaline phosphatase, and/or urinary hydroxyproline; neurologic disorders associated with skull lesions and spinal deformities; and elevated cardiac output and other vascular disorders associated with increased vascularity of bones.

Pharmacology/Pharmacokinetics

Physicochemical characteristics

Molecular weight—325.12.

Mechanism of action/Effect

Animal studies indicate that alendronate shows preferential localization to sites of bone resorption where it inhibits osteoclast activity, but does not interfere with osteoclast recruitment or attachment. Studies in rats and mice showed that normal bone mass was formed on top of alendronate, thereby incorporating alendronate in the bone matrix. Alendronate is not pharmacologically active when incorporated; therefore, it must be administered continuously to suppress osteoclasts on newly formed resorption surfaces. Studies in baboons and rats indicate that alendronate treatment reduces bone turnover (i.e., the number of sites at which bone is remodeled). In addition, bone formation exceeds bone resorption at these remodeling sites, leading to increased bone mass. Data from long-term animal studies indicate that the bone formed during alendronate therapy is of normal quality.

Absorption

Studies in humans showed that mean oral bioavailability in women was 0.7% for doses ranging from 5 to 40 mg when alendronate was administered after an overnight fast and 2 hours before a standardized breakfast. Oral bioavailability in men was 0.59% following administration of a 10-mg dose 2 hours before the first meal of the day. In postmenopausal women, bioavailability was decreased by approximately 40% when 10 mg of alendronate was given either 30 minutes or 1 hour before a standardized breakfast, when compared with dosing 2 hours before eating. Bioavailability was negligible when alendronate was administered with or up to 2 hours after a standardized breakfast. Concomitant administration with coffee or orange juice reduced bioavailability by approximately 60%.

Distribution

Studies in male rats given an intravenous dose of 1 mg per kilogram of body weight (mg/kg) showed that alendronate was transiently distributed to soft tissue, but was then rapidly redistributed to bone or excreted in the urine.

Vol_D—At least 28 L in humans.

Protein binding

High (approximately 78% in human plasma).

Biotransformation

There is no evidence that alendronate is metabolized in humans or animals.

Duration of action

In osteoporosis—Six weeks after a single 5-mg intravenous dose.

In Paget's disease of bone—Six months after a single 5-mg intravenous dose.

Elimination

Renal—approximately 50% of an intravenous dose was excreted in urine within 72 hours, with little or none of the dose recovered in the feces. Following a single 10-mg intravenous dose, the renal clearance of alendronate was 71 mL per minute (mL/min); the systemic clearance did not exceed 200 mL/min. Plasma concentrations fell by more than 95% within 6 hours following intravenous alendronate administration.

Precautions to Consider

Carcinogenicity/Tumorigenicity

In a 92-week carcinogenicity study in mice given alendronate at doses of 1, 3, and 10 mg per kilogram of body weight (mg/kg) per day (males) or 1, 2, and 5 mg/kg per day (females) (0.5 to 4 times the 10-mg human dose based on body surface area), harderian gland (a retro-orbital gland not present in humans) adenomas were increased in high-dose females. In a 2-year carcinogenicity study in rats, parafollicular cell (thyroid) adenomas were increased in high-dose males at doses of 1 and 3.75 mg/kg (1 and 3 times the 10-mg human dose, respectively, based on body surface area).

Mutagenicity

Alendronate was not genotoxic in the *in vitro* microbial mutagenesis assay with and without metabolic activation, in an *in vitro* mammalian cell mutagenesis assay, in an *in vitro* alkaline elution assay in rat hepatocytes, and in an *in vivo* chromosomal aberration assay in mice. However, in an *in vitro* chromosomal aberration assay in Chinese hamster ovary cells, alendronate was weakly positive at concentrations $\geq$ 5 mmol in the presence of cytotoxicity.

Pregnancy/Reproduction

Fertility—Studies in male and female rats given oral alendronate doses of up to 5 mg/kg per day (4 times the 10-mg human dose based on body surface area) found no effect on fertility.

Pregnancy—Adequate and well-controlled studies in humans have not been done.

Reproduction studies in rats given alendronate doses ranging from 1 to 10 mg/kg (1 to 9 times the 10-mg human dose based on body surface area) showed decreased postimplantation survival at 2 mg/kg per day and decreased body weight gain in normal pups at 1 mg/kg per day. Sites of incomplete fetal ossification of vertebrae (cervical, thoracic, and lumbar), skull, and sternebrae were statistically significantly increased in rats beginning at doses of 10 mg/kg per day. No similar fetal effects were seen when pregnant rabbits were treated at doses of up to 35 mg/kg per day (50 times the 10-mg human dose based on body surface area).

Both total and ionized calcium decreased in pregnant rats at doses of 15 mg/kg per day (13 times the 10-mg human dose based on body surface area), resulting in delays and failures of delivery. Protracted parturition due to maternal hypocalcemia occurred in rats at doses as low as 0.5 mg/kg per day (0.5 times the recommended human dose) when rats were treated from before mating through gestation. Maternotoxicity (late pregnancy deaths) occurred in the female rats treated with 15 mg/kg per day for varying periods of time, ranging from treatment only during premating to treatment only during early, middle, or late gestation; these deaths were decreased but not eliminated by cessation of treatment. Calcium supplementation, either in the drinking water or by minipump, did not ameliorate the hypocalcemia or prevent maternal and neonatal deaths due to delays in delivery; intravenous calcium supplementation prevented maternal, but not fetal, deaths.

FDA Pregnancy Category C.

Breast-feeding

It is not known whether alendronate is distributed into human breast milk. Alendronate was distributed into the milk of rats after an intravenous dose.

Pediatrics

No information is available on the relationship of age to the effects of alendronate in pediatric patients. Safety and efficacy have not been established.

Geriatrics

Appropriate studies performed to date have not demonstrated geriatrics-specific problems that would limit the usefulness of alendronate in the elderly.

Drug interactions and/or related problems

The following drug interactions and/or related problems have been selected on the basis of their potential clinical significance (possible mechanism in parentheses where appropriate)—not necessarily inclusive (» = major clinical significance):

Note: Combinations containing any of the following medications, depending on the amount present, may also interact with this medication.

Dietary supplements (including calcium) or
Food and beverages or
Medications, oral (including antacids)
(simultaneous use may interfere with the absorption of alendronate; patients should be advised to take alendronate at least 30 minutes before taking other medications, food, or beverages)

Ranitidine
(intravenous ranitidine was shown to double the bioavailability of oral alendronate; the clinical significance of this increased bioavailability is not known)

Salicylates or salicylate-containing compounds
(an increased incidence of upper gastrointestinal adverse events was reported in individuals taking more than 10 mg of alendronate a day concurrently with salicylates or salicylate-containing compounds)

Laboratory value alterations

The following have been selected on the basis of their potential clinical significance (possible effect in parentheses where appropriate)—not necessarily inclusive (» = major clinical significance).

With physiology/laboratory test values

Calcium, serum, and
Phosphate, serum
(alendronate has been reported to cause a 2% reduction in serum calcium concentrations and a 4 to 6% reduction in serum phosphate concentrations in the first month after initiation of therapy; no further decreases have been observed during the 3-year duration of therapy)

Medical considerations/Contraindications

The medical considerations/contraindications included have been selected on the basis of their potential clinical significance (reasons given in parentheses where appropriate)—not necessarily inclusive (» = major clinical significance).

Except under special circumstances, this medication should not be used when the following medical problems exist:

» Gastrointestinal diseases such as duodenitis, dysphagia, symptomatic esophageal diseases, frequent heartburn, gastritis, gastroesophageal reflux disease, hiatal hernia, or ulcers
(alendronate may exacerbate these conditions)

» Renal function impairment when creatinine clearance is < 35 mL per minute (0.58 mL/sec)
(use is not recommended because elimination of alendronate may be reduced; greater accumulation of alendronate in the bone may be expected)

» Sensitivity to alendronate

Risk-benefit should be considered when the following medical problems exist:

Hypocalcemia or
Vitamin D deficiency
(alendronate may exacerbate these conditions; hypocalcemia and vitamin D deficiency should be corrected before alendronate therapy is begun)

Patient monitoring

The following may be especially important in patient monitoring (other tests may be warranted in some patients, depending on condition; » = major clinical significance):

For Paget's disease

Alkaline phosphatase, serum or
Hydroxyproline, urinary
(serum alkaline phosphatase determinations recommended every 3 to 6 months; urinary hydroxyproline determinations recommended every 6 to 12 months; values should decrease with treatment)

Calcium, serum
(determinations recommended every 3 to 4 months; values should increase with treatment)

N-telopeptide of type I collagen, urinary
(determinations recommended every 3 to 6 months; values should decrease with treatment)

For postmenopausal osteoporosis

Bone mineral density
(determinations recommended every 1 to 2 years to assess effectiveness of therapy; clinicians recommend monitoring hip, femur, or spine; values should increase with treatment)

Calcium, serum or
Creatinine, serum
(determinations recommended every 6 to 12 months; serum calcium values should increase with treatment)

Side/Adverse Effects

The following side/adverse effects have been selected on the basis of their potential clinical significance (possible signs and symptoms in parentheses where appropriate)—not necessarily inclusive:

Those indicating need for medical attention

Incidence more frequent

Abdominal pain

Incidence less frequent

Dysphagia (difficulty swallowing); ***heartburn; irritation, pain, or ulceration of the esophagus***; ***muscle pain***

Note: There have been reports of severe *irritation, pain, or ulceration of the esophagus* in some patients. Presenting symptoms may include *dysphagia* and/or *heartburn*. Alendronate therapy should be discontinued if these symptoms develop.

Incidence rare

Skin rash

Those indicating need for medical attention only if they continue or are bothersome

Incidence less frequent

Abdominal distension (full or bloated feeling); ***constipation; diarrhea; flatulence*** (gas); ***headache; nausea***

Patient Consultation

As an aid to patient consultation, refer to *Advice for the Patient, Alendronate (Systemic)*.

In providing consultation, consider emphasizing the following selected information (» = major clinical significance):

Before using this medication

» Conditions affecting use, especially:
Sensitivity to alendronate
Pregnancy—Studies in animals showed decreased weight gain, incomplete fetal ossification, decreased survival of the fetus, and delays in delivery
Breast-feeding—Should not be given to nursing women because alendronate is distributed in milk of rats
Other medications, especially aspirin or compounds that contain aspirin
Other medical problems, especially gastrointestinal diseases or severe renal function impairment

Proper use of this medication

» Taking with 6 to 8 ounces of plain water on empty stomach, at least 30 minutes before first food, beverage, or medication of the day

» Not lying down for at least 30 minutes after taking alendronate

Possible need for calcium and vitamin D supplementation

» Proper dosing

Missed dose: Not taking later in the day; continuing usual schedule the next morning

» Proper storage

Side/adverse effects

Signs of potential adverse effects, especially abdominal pain; heartburn; dysphagia; irritation, pain, or ulceration of the esophagus; muscle pain; and skin rash

General Dosing Information

To facilitate delivery of alendronate to the stomach and reduce esophageal irritation, patients should not lie down for at least 30 minutes after taking alendronate and until after their first food of the day.

Safety of treatment for longer than 4 years has not been studied.

Diet/Nutrition

Alendronate should be taken with 6 to 8 ounces of plain water. Absorption of alendronate is best when taken in the morning, at least 30 minutes before the first food, beverage, or medication of the day. Food and beverages such as mineral water, coffee, tea, or juice will decrease the absorption of alendronate. Waiting longer than 30 minutes will improve the absorption of alendronate.

Alendronate should not be taken at bed time or before arising for the day.

Some patients may be instructed to take calcium or vitamin D supplements if their diet is inadequate. These supplements should be taken 30 minutes or longer after taking alendronate.

Oral Dosage Forms

ALENDRONATE TABLETS

Usual adult dose

Glucocorticoid-induced osteoporosis; men and women (treatment)—
Oral, 5 mg once a day in the morning, at least thirty minutes before the first food, beverage, or medication. In postmenopausal women not receiving estrogen, the dosage is 10 mg once a day in the morning, at least thirty minutes before the first food, beverage, or medication.The dose should be taken with six to eight ounces of plain water.

Osteoporosis, male (treatment)—
Oral, 10 mg once a day in the morning, at least thirty minutes before the first food, beverage, or medication.

Paget's disease of bone (treatment)—
Oral, 40 mg once a day in the morning, at least thirty minutes before the first food, beverage, or medication. Treatment should continue for six months. Re-treatment may be considered for certain patients following a six-month post-treatment evaluation period.

Postmenopausal osteoporosis (treatment)—
Oral, 10 mg once a day in the morning or 70 mg once a week in the morning, administered at least thirty minutes before the first food,

beverage, or medication. The dose should be taken with six to eight ounces of plain water.

Postmenopausal osteoporosis (prophylaxis)—
Oral, 5 mg once a day in the morning or 35 mg once a week in the morning, administered at least thirty minutes before the first food, beverage, or medication. The dose should be taken with six to eight ounces of plain water.

Usual pediatric dose
Safety and efficacy have not been established.

Strength(s) usually available
U.S.—
5 mg (Rx) [*Fosamax* (anhydrous lactose; croscarmellose sodium; magnesium stearate; microcrystalline cellulose)].
10 mg (Rx) [*Fosamax* (anhydrous lactose; croscarmellose sodium; carnauba wax; magnesium stearate; microcrystalline cellulose)].
35 mg (Rx) [*Fosamax* (anhydrous lactose; croscarmellose sodium; magnesium stearate; microcrystalline cellulose)].
40 mg (Rx) [*Fosamax* (anhydrous lactose; croscarmellose sodium; magnesium stearate; microcrystalline cellulose)].
70 mg (Rx) [*Fosamax* (anhydrous lactose; croscarmellose sodium; magnesium stearate; microcrystalline cellulose)].

Canada—
10 mg (Rx) [*Fosamax* (lactose)].
40 mg (Rx) [*Fosamax* (lactose)].

Packaging and storage
Store between 15 and 30 °C (59 and 86 °F), unless otherwise specified by manufacturer.

Auxiliary labeling
- Take on empty stomach.

Revised: 01/10/2001
Developed: 01/06/1997

ALFACALCIDOL—See *Vitamin D and Analogs (Systemic)*

ALFENTANIL—See *Fentanyl Derivatives (Systemic)*

ALFUZOSIN Systemic

VA CLASSIFICATION (Primary): GU900

Commonly used brand name(s): *Uroxatral; Xatral.*

Note: For a listing of dosage forms and brand names by country availability, see *Dosage Forms* section(s).

Category
Benign prostatic hyperplasia therapy agent.

Indications

Accepted
Benign prostatic hyperplasia (treatment)—Alfuzosin is indicated for the treatment of the signs and symptoms of benign prostatic hyperplasia.

Acceptance not established
Alfusozin is not indicated for the treatment of hypertension.

Pharmacology/Pharmacokinetics

Physicochemical characteristics
Molecular weight—425.9.
Solubility—Freely soluble in water, sparingly soluble in alcohol, practically insoluble in dichloromethane.

Mechanism of action/Effect
Alfuzosin is a selective antagonist of post-synaptic alpha$_1$-adrenoreceptors, which are located in the prostate, bladder base, bladder neck, prostatic capsule, and prostatic urethra. Blockade of these adrenoreceptors can cause smooth muscle in the bladder neck and prostate to relax, resulting in an improvement in urine flow and a reduction in symptoms of BPH.

Absorption
Absolute bioavailability—49%
AUC—194 ng per mL per hr
Effect of food—absorption is 50% lower under fasting conditions; should be taken immediately following a meal

Distribution
Vol_D—3.2 L per kg

Protein binding
Moderately bound (82 to 90%) to human plasma proteins

Biotransformation
Alfuzosin undergoes extensive metabolism by the liver, with only 11% of the administered dose excreted unchanged in the urine. Alfuzosin is metabolized by three metabolic pathways: oxidation, O-demethylations, and N-dealkylation. The metabolites are not pharmacologically active. CYP3A4 is the principal hepatic enzyme isoform involved in its metabolism.

Half-life
Elimination—10 hours

Time to peak concentration
T_{max}—8 hours
Steady-state plasma concentrations are reached with the second dose; steady-state alfuzosin plasma concentration are 1.2–to 1.6–fold higher than those observed after a single administration.

Peak plasma concentration
C_{max}—13.6 ng per mL

Elimination
Fecal—69%
Urine—24%

Special Populations
Elderly—Trough concentrations in subjects ≥ 75 years of age were approximately 35% greater than in those below 65 years of age. Peak concentrations were unaffected.

Renal Impairment—Relative to subjects with normal renal function, the mean C_{max} and AUC values were increased by approximately 50% in patients with mild, moderate, or severe renal impairment.

Hepatic Insufficiency—In patients with moderate or severe hepatic insufficiency (Child-Pugh categories B and C) the plasma apparent clearance (CL/F) was reduced to approximately one-third to one-fourth that observed in healthy subjects; this reduction in clearance results in three to four-fold higher plasma concentrations; has not been studied in patients with mild hepatic insufficiency

Precautions to Consider

Carcinogenicity/Tumorigenicity
There was no evidence of drug-related increase in the incidence of tumors in mice following dietary administration of alfuzosin for 98 weeks at 13 and 15 times the level of exposure in humans. The highest dose tested in female mice may not have constituted a maximally tolerated dose. There was no evidence of a drug-related increase in the incidence of tumors in rats following dietary administration of alfuzosin for 104 weeks at 53 and 37 times the level of exposure.

Mutagenicity
Alfuzosin showed no evidence of mutagenic effect in the Ames mouse and lymphoma assays, and was free of any clastogenic effects in the Chinese hamster ovary cell and in vivo mouse micronucleus assays. Alfuzosin treatment did not induce DNA repair in a human cell line.

Pregnancy/Reproduction
Fertility—There was no evidence of reproductive organ toxicity when male rats were given alfuzosin at daily oral (gavage) doses of up to 250 mg per kg per day for up to 26 weeks, which corresponds to levels of exposure several hundred times that in humans. No impairment of fertility was observed following oral (gavage) administration to male rats at doses of up to 125 mg per kg per day for 70 days. Estrous cycling was inhibited in rats and dogs at doses of 25 mg per kg and 20 mg per kg, respectively, corresponding to levels of systemic exposure (based on AUC of unbound drug) 12–and 18–fold higher, respectively, than in humans, although this did not result in impaired fertility in rats.

Pregnancy—Adequate and well controlled studies in humans have not been done. Alfuzosin is not indicated for use in women.

There was no evidence of teratogenicity or embryotoxicity in rats at maternal (oral gavage) doses up to 250 mg per kg per day, corresponding to systemic exposure levels 1,200–fold higher than in humans. In rabbits, up to the dose of 100 mg per kg per day (approximately 3 times the clinical dose by body surface area) given orally (via gavage), no evidence of fetal toxicity or teratogenicity was seen.

FDA Pregnancy Category B

Labor and delivery—Gestation was slightly prolonged in rats with a maternal dose >5 mg per kg per day (oral gavage), which corresponds to systemic exposure levels (based on AUC of unbound drug) 12 times higher than human exposure levels, but there were no difficulties with parturition.

Breast-feeding

It is not known whether alfuzosin is distributed into breast milk. Alfuzosin is not indicated for use in women.

Pediatrics

Appropriate studies on the relationship of age to the effects of alfuzosin have not been performed in the pediatric population. Alfuzosin is not indicated for use in children.

Geriatrics

No overall differences in safety and efficacy were observed between these subjects and younger subjects.

Drug interactions and/or related problems

The following drug interactions and/or related problems have been selected on the basis of their potential clinical significance (possible mechanism in parentheses where appropriate)—not necessarily inclusive (» = major clinical significance):

Note: Combinations containing any of the following medications, depending on the amount present, may also interact with this medication.

» Alpha blockers
(interactions have not been studied but may be expected; alfuzosin and other alpha blockers should not be used in combination)

» Atenolol
(C_{max} and AUC of both agents increased by approximately 20 to 30%; significant reductions in mean blood pressure and mean heart rate occurred)

Cimetidine
(repeated administration of cimetidine increased alfuzosin C_{max} and AUC values by 20%)

» Diltiazem
(C_{max} and AUC of both agents increased by 1.3- to 1.5-fold; no changes in blood pressure were observed in this study but the combination of these two medicines have the potential to cause hypotension in some patients)

» Potent CYP3A4 inhibitors such as
» Itraconazole or
» Ketoconazole or
» Ritonavir
(should not be co-administered since alfuzosin blood levels are increased)

(repeated administration of 400 mg of ketoconazole increased alfusozin C_{max} 2.3-fold and AUC_{last} 3.2-fold following a single 10 mg dose of alfuzosin)

Medications that prolong the QT interval
(care should be taken due to the potential for QT prolongation)

Medical considerations/Contraindications

The medical considerations/contraindications included have been selected on the basis of their potential clinical significance (reasons given in parentheses where appropriate)—not necessarily inclusive (» = major clinical significance).

Except under special circumstances, this medication should not be used when the following medical problem exists:

» Prostatic carcinoma
(carcinoma of the prostate and BPH cause many of the same symptoms and these two diseases frequently coexist; patients thought to have BPH should be examined prior to starting therapy with alfuzosin to rule out the presence of carcinoma of the prostate)

» Hypersensitivity to alfuzosin or any component of the tablets

» Hepatic Insufficiency, moderate or severe
(contraindicated in patients with Child-Pugh categories B and C as alfuzosin blood levels are increased in these patients)

Risk-benefit should be considered when the following medical problems exist:

Coronary insufficiency
(if symptoms of angina pectoris appear or worsen, alfuzosin should be discontinued)

QT prolongation, congenital or acquired
(there is no signal of Torsades de Pointes in post-marketing experience outside of the United States but care should be taken in prescribing alfuzosin in patients with a known history of QT prolongation)

Renal insufficiency
(systemic exposure was increased by 50% in patients with mild, moderate, and severe renal insufficiency; caution should be exercised in all patients, especially those with severe renal insufficiency)

» Symptomatic hypertension or
» Hypotensive response to other medications
(care should be used especially in these patients as postural hypotension can develop within a few hours of administration and there is the potential for syncope)

Patient monitoring

The following may be especially important in patient monitoring (other tests may be warranted in some patients, depending on condition; » = major clinical significance):

» Postural hypotension
(postural hypotension with or without symptoms (e.g., dizziness) may develop a few hours following administration of alfuzosin; as with other alpha-blockers there is a potential for syncope; patients should be warned)

Side/Adverse Effects

The following side/adverse effects have been selected on the basis of their potential clinical significance (possible signs and symptoms in parentheses where appropriate)—not necessarily inclusive:

Those indicating need for medical attention

Incidence not determined—Observed during clinical practice, estimates of frequency cannot be determined

Chest pain; priapism (painful or prolonged erection of the penis); ***tachycardia*** (fast, pounding, or irregular heartbeat or pulse)

Those indicating need for medical attention only if they continue or are bothersome

Incidence more frequent

Dizziness

Incidence less frequent

Abdominal pain; bronchitis (cough producing mucus; difficulty breathing; shortness of breath; tightness in chest; wheezing); ***constipation*** (difficulty having a bowel movement (stool)); ***dyspepsia*** (acid or sour stomach; belching; heartburn; indigestion; stomach discomfort, upset, or pain); ***fatigue*** (unusual tiredness or weakness); ***headache; impotence*** (loss in sexual ability, desire, drive, or performance; decreased interest in sexual intercourse; inability to have or keep an erection); ***nausea; pain; pharyngitis*** (body aches or pain; congestion; cough; dryness or soreness of throat; fever; hoarseness; runny nose; tender, swollen glands in neck; trouble in swallowing; voice changes); ***sinusitis*** (pain or tenderness around eyes and cheekbones; fever; stuffy or runny nose; headache; cough; shortness of breath or troubled breathing; tightness of chest or wheezing); ***upper respiratory tract infection*** (ear congestion; nasal congestion; chills; cough; fever; sneezing; sore throat; body aches or pain; headache; loss of voice; runny nose; unusual tiredness or weakness; difficulty in breathing)

Incidence not determined—Observed during clinical practice, estimates of frequency cannot be determined

Rash

Overdose

For more information on the management of overdose or unintentional ingestion, **contact a poison control center** (see *Poison Control Center Listing*).

Treatment of overdose

Specific treatment—

Should overdose of alfuzosin lead to hypotension, support of the cardiovascular system is of first importance. Restoration of blood pressure and normalization of the heart rate may be accomplished by keeping the patient in the supine position. If this measure is inadequate, then the administration of intravenous fluids should be considered. If necessary, vasopressors should then be used, and renal function should be monitored and supported as needed. Alfuzosin is 82% to 90% protein-bound; therefore, dialysis may not be of benefit.

Supportive care—

Patients in whom intentional overdose is confirmed or suspected should be referred for psychiatric consultation.

Patient Consultation

As an aid to patient consultation, refer to *Advice for the Patient, Alfuzosin (Systemic)*.

In providing consultation, consider emphasizing the following selected information (» = major clinical significance):

Before using this medication

» Conditions affecting use, especially:
Hypersensitivity to alfuzosin or any component of the tablets
Pregnancy—Not indicated for use in women

Breast-feeding—Not indicated for use in women
Other medications, especially alpha blockers, atenolol, cimetidine, diltiazem, potent CYP3A4 inhibitors such as itraconazole, ketoconazole, ritonavir
Other medical problems, especially hepatic insufficiency, moderate or severe, or prostatic carcinoma

Proper use of this medication

» Proper dosing
Missed dose: Taking as soon as possible; not taking if almost time for next scheduled dose; not doubling doses
Importance of taking tablets whole; not chewing or crushing tablets
Taking medicine with food and with the same meal each day
Proper storage

Precautions while using this medication

» Patients should be told about the possible occurrence of symptoms related to postural hypotension, such as dizziness when beginning alfuzosin. Caution if dizziness or drowsiness occurs; not driving machines, or doing anything else that may be hazardous during this period

Side/adverse effects

Signs of potential side effects, especially chest pain, priapism, tachycardia

General Dosing Information

For oral dosing forms:

Diet/Nutrition

The tablet should be taken with food and with the same meal each day. The tablets should not be chewed or crushed.

Oral Dosage Forms

ALFUZOSIN HYDROCHLORIDE EXTENDED RELEASE TABLETS

Usual adult dose

Benign prostatic hyperplasia—
Oral, 10 mg once a day, taken after the same meal each day.

Usual pediatric dose

Safety and efficacy have not been established.

Usual Geriatric Dose

See *Usual adult dose.*

Strength(s) usually available

U.S.—
10 mg (Rx) [*Uroxatral* (collodial silicon dioxide; ethylcellulose; hydrogenated castor oil; hydroxypropyl methylcellulose; magnesium stearate; mannitol; microcrystalline cellulose; povidone; yellow ferric oxide)].

Canada—
10 mg (Rx) [*Xatral* (hydroxypropylmethylcellulose; hydrogenated castor oil; ethylcellulose; yellow ferric oxide; colloidal hydrated silica; magnesium stearate; mannitol; povidone; microcrystalline cellulose)].

Packaging and storage

Store at 25 °C (77 °F), excursions permitted to 15 to 30°C (59 to 86°F). Protect from light and moisture.

Auxiliary labeling

- Keep out of the reach of children
- May cause dizziness or drowsiness
- Take with food

Revised: 03/05/2004
Developed: 01/20/2004

ALITRETINOIN Topical

VA CLASSIFICATION (Primary): DE600

Commonly used brand name(s): *Panretin.*

Note: For a listing of dosage forms and brand names by country availability, see *Dosage Forms* section(s).

Category

Antineoplastic (topical).

Indications

Accepted

Kaposi's sarcoma, cutaneous, AIDS-related (treatment)—Alitretinoin gel is indicated for the topical treatment of cutaneous lesions in patients with AIDS-related Kaposi's sarcoma.

Unaccepted

Alitretinoin gel is not indicated when systemic anti-Kaposi's sarcoma therapy is required.

Pharmacology/Pharmacokinetics

Physicochemical characteristics

Chemical Group—Alitretinoin (9-*cis*-retinoic acid) is chemically related to Vitamin A (retinol).
Molecular weight—300.44.
Solubility—Insoluble in water; slightly soluble in ethanol.

Mechanism of action/Effect

Alitretinoin is an endogenous retinoid that binds to and activates intracellular retinoid receptor subtypes (RARα, RARβ, RARγ, RXRα, RXRβ, and RXRγ), which modulates transcription and expression of genes that control the process of cellular differentiation and proliferation in both normal and cancerous cells. Alitretinoin inhibits the growth of Kaposi's sarcoma cells *in vitro.*

Absorption

There have been no studies examining plasma 9-*cis*-retinoic acid concentrations before and after treatment with alitretinoin gel. However, indirect evidence suggests that absorption is not extensive.

Biotransformation

In vitro studies indicate that alitretinoin is metabolized to 4-hydroxy-9-*cis*-retinoic acid and 4-oxo-9-*cis*-retinoic acid by CYP 2C9, 3A4, 1A1, and 1A2 enzymes. Following oral administration, 4-oxo-9-*cis*-retinoic acid is the major circulating metabolite.

Onset of action

Initial response may be seen after 2 weeks of application, but some patients may require up to 14 weeks of treatment.

Precautions to Consider

Cross-sensitivity and/or related problems

Patients sensitive to retinoids may also be sensitive to alitretinoin.

Carcinogenicity

Long-term studies in animals have not been done.

Mutagenicity

Alitretinoin was not found to be mutagenic in *in vitro* tests including the Chinese hamster ovary cell HGPRT mutation assay. It was not found to be clastogenic *in vitro* (chromosome aberration test in human lymphocytes) nor *in vivo* (mouse micronucleus test).

Pregnancy/Reproduction

Pregnancy—Adequate and well-controlled studies in women have not been done. It is recommended that women of childbearing potential be advised to avoid becoming pregnant during treatment because of the potential risks to the fetus. Also, if the medication is used during pregnancy, or the patient becomes pregnant during treatment, the patient should be informed of the potential risks.

Alitretinoin caused teratogenicity (fused sternebrae and limb and craniofacial defects) in rabbits given oral doses of 0.5 mg per kg of body weight (mg/kg) per day (approximately five times the estimated daily human topical dose on a mg per square meter basis). It also caused limb and craniofacial defects in mice given a single oral dose of 50 mg/kg on day eleven of gestation (approximately 127 times the estimated daily human topical dose on a mg per square meter basis). Oral alitretinoin was also embryocidal when given during the period of organogenesis to rabbits at doses of 1.5 mg/kg/day (about 15 times the estimated daily human topical dose on a mg per square meter basis) and rats at doses of 5 mg/kg/day (approximately 25 times the estimated daily human topical dose on a mg per square meter basis).

FDA Pregnancy Category D.

Breast-feeding

It is not known whether alitretinoin is distributed into breast milk. However, breast-feeding is not recommended during treatment because of the potential risks to the infant.

Pediatrics

The safety and efficacy of alitretinoin in pediatric patients have not been established.

Geriatrics

No information is available on the relationship of age to the effects of alitretinoin in geriatric patients.

Drug interactions and/or related problems

The following drug interactions and/or related problems have been selected on the basis of their potential clinical significance (possible mechanism in parentheses where appropriate)—not necessarily inclusive (» = major clinical significance):

Note: Combinations containing any of the following medications, depending on the amount present, may also interact with this medication.

» Insect repellents, DEET-containing
(concurrent use of topical alitretinoin and products containing DEET [*N,N-diethyl-m-toluamide*] such as insect repellents, may increase DEET toxicity)

Note: There is no clinical evidence in the vehicle-controlled studies of drug interactions with systemic antiretroviral agents, including protease inhibitors, macrolide antibiotics, and azole antifungals, although the effect of alitretinoin gel on the steady-state concentrations of these medications is not known. No drug interaction data are available on concomitant administration of alitretinoin gel and systemic anti-Kaposi's sarcoma agents.

Medical considerations/Contraindications

The medical considerations/contraindications included have been selected on the basis of their potential clinical significance (reasons given in parentheses where appropriate)—not necessarily inclusive (» = major clinical significance).

Except under special circumstances, this medication should not be used when the following medical problems exist:

» Hypersensitivity to retinoids

Risk-benefit should be considered when the following medical problems exist:

» Cutaneous T-cell lymphoma
(treatment-limiting toxicities may be more prevalent in patients with this condition)

Side/Adverse Effects

The following side/adverse effects have been selected on the basis of their potential clinical significance (possible signs and symptoms in parentheses where appropriate)—not necessarily inclusive:

Those indicating need for medical attention

Incidence more frequent

Burning or pain; edema (swelling at site of application); ***exfoliative dermatitis*** (peeling of skin; skin redness; blisters on skin); ***severe rash; skin disorders including cracking; crusting; drainage; eschar*** (sloughing of skin); ***excoriation*** (abrasion of the skin); ***fissure*** (groove in the skin); ***or oozing***

Incidence less frequent

Paresthesia (stinging or tingling of skin)

Those indicating need for medical attention only if they continue or are bothersome

Incidence more frequent

Pruritus (itching); ***rash***

Incidence less frequent

Photosensitivity (increased sensitivity of skin to the sun)

Overdose

For more information on the management of overdose or unintentional ingestion, **contact a Poison Control Center** (see *Poison Control Center Listing*).

Note: There has been no experience with acute overdose of alitretinoin gel in humans. Systemic toxicity following acute overdosage with topical application of alitretinoin gel is unlikely due to limited systemic plasma levels observed with normal therapeutic doses. There is no specific antidote for overdosage.

Patient Consultation

As an aid to patient consultation, refer to.

In providing information, consider emphasizing the following selected information (» = major clinical significance):

Before using this medication

» Conditions affecting use, especially:
Sensitivity to retinoids
Pregnancy—Avoiding pregnancy during treatment; telling physician immediately if pregnancy is suspected
Breast-feeding—Not recommended because of risk of serious side effects
Other medications, especially products containing DEET (insect repellents)
Other medical problems, especially cutaneous T-cell lymphoma

Proper use of this medication

» Avoiding the use of occlusive dressings
Reducing the frequency of application if local irritation occurs
» Proper dosing
Using as soon as possible; not using if almost time for next dose; not doubling doses
» Proper storage

Precautions while using this medication

» Checking with physician to assess effectiveness and side effects
» Avoiding exposure of treated areas to sunlight or sunlamps
» Avoiding application to normal skin surrounding the lesions due to possible irritation
» Avoiding application on or near mucosal surfaces of the body

Side/adverse effects

Signs of potential side effects especially burning or pain, edema, exfoliative dermatitis, paresthesia, severe rash, and skin disorders including excoriation, cracking, crusting, drainage, eschar, fissure, or oozing

General Dosing Information

Avoid application of the gel to normal skin surrounding the lesions. Allow the gel to dry for 3 to 5 minutes before covering with clothing. Do not apply the gel on or near mucosal surfaces.

Response to alitretinoin topical gel may not be apparent for 2 weeks or longer than 14 weeks after initiation of therapy.

Application should continue for as long as the patient continues to receive benefit.

Occlusive dressings should not be applied over areas treated with topical alitretinoin.

Topical Dosage Forms

ALITRETINOIN GEL

Usual adult dose

Kaposi's sarcoma, cutaneous, AIDS-related (treatment)—
Topical, initially apply gel to each lesion two times a day. Gradually increase the application frequency to three or four times a day according to individual lesion tolerance. Reduce the frequency of application if application site irritation occurs.
Enough gel should be applied to cover the lesion with a generous coating.

Usual pediatric dose

Safety and efficacy have not been established.

Strength(s) usually available

U.S.—
0.1% (Rx) [*Panretin* (dehydrated alcohol USP; polyethylene glycol 400 NF; hydroxypropyl cellulose NF; butylated hydroxytoluene NF)].

Packaging and storage

Store at 25° C (77° F). Excursions are permitted at controlled room temperature, 15 to 30° C (59 to 86° F).

Auxiliary labeling

- Avoid sunlight exposure
- For external use only

Revised: 12/02/1999

ALLOPURINOL Systemic

VA CLASSIFICATION (Primary/Secondary): MS400/GU900

Commonly used brand name(s): *Aloprim; Apo-Allopurinol; Purinol; Zyloprim.*

Note: For a listing of dosage forms and brand names by country availability, see *Dosage Forms* section(s).

Category

Antihyperuricemic; antigout agent; antiurolithic (uric acid calculi; calcium oxalate calculi).

Note: Antihyperuricemic is the basic category; the other categories are specific categories of use.

Indications

Note: Bracketed information in the *Indications* section refers to uses that are not included in U.S. product labeling.

Accepted

Gouty arthritis, chronic (treatment)—Allopurinol is indicated for the long-term management of hyperuricemia associated with primary or secondary gout. to reduce the number of acute gout attacks and decrease the risk of uric acid calculi and urate nephropathy in patients with chronic gout.

Allopurinol is recommended for patients in whom treatment with uricosuric antigout agents such as probenecid or sulfinpyrazone would be ineffective or inadvisable (e.g., patients who are hyperuricemic as a result of overproduction of urate, patients with extensive tophi or who are otherwise at risk for urate nephropathy, and patients with moderate to severe renal function impairment). Both allopurinol and the uricosuric antigout agents are effective in patients whose 24-hour renal excretion of uric acid is 800 mg (4.8 mmol) or less, i.e., individuals who are hyperuricemic as a result of underexcretion of uric acid. However, the uricosuric agents are less toxic than allopurinol and should be considered for use when appropriate.

Allopurinol has no anti-inflammatory activity and should not be used for the treatment of acute attacks of gouty arthritis. An anti-inflammatory agent, preferably a nonsteroidal anti-inflammatory drug (NSAID) or a corticosteroid (preferably via intrasynovial injection, when feasible), should be used to treat acute attacks. Also, initiation of antihyperuricemic therapy may lead to fluctuations in urate concentration that may result in prolongation of an acute attack or initiation of new attacks. The patient should be receiving appropriate anti-inflammatory therapy when allopurinol treatment is initiated.

Hyperuricemia (prophylaxis and treatment)—Allopurinol is indicated to control hyperuricemia secondary to blood dyscrasias(such as polycythemia vera or myeloid metaplasia), or their treatment. It is also indicated to prevent or treat hyperuricemia secondary to tumor lysis induced by cancer chemotherapy with cytotoxic antineoplastic agents or radiation therapy in patients with leukemias, lymphomas, or other neoplastic disease. [Allopurinol is also used to treat hyperuricemia secondary to the neoplastic disease itself.] Allopurinol prevents complications of hyperuricemia (e.g., acute uric acid nephropathy or renal calculi, tissue urate deposition, or gouty arthritis) in these patients. However, allopurinol may increase the toxicity of several antineoplastic agents, and some clinicians have questioned its routine administration during cancer chemotherapy.

[Allopurinol is also used to control hyperuricemia in patients with Lesch-Nyhan syndrome. However, it does not improve neurologic or behavioral abnormalities or affect the course of the disease in these patients.]

Nephropathy, uric acid (prophylaxis and treatment)—Allopurinol is indicated in the treatment of primary or secondary uric acid nephropathy (with or without accompanying symptoms of gouty arthritis) to prevent progression of the condition. However, this medicine will not reverse severe renal damage that has already occurred. Allopurinol is also indicated to prevent uric acid nephropathy in certain patients as described under *Hyperuricemia,* above.

Renal calculi, uric acid (prophylaxis)—Allopurinol is indicated to prevent recurrence of uric acid stone formation in patients. It is also indicated to prevent uric acid calculi in certain other patients as described under *Hyperuricemia,* above.

Renal calculi, calcium oxalate, (prophylaxis)—Allopurinol is indicated to prevent recurrence of calcium stone formation in patients with a history of recurrent calcium oxalate calculi associated with hyperuricosuria(i.e., uric acid excretion > 800 mg [4.8 mmol] per day in males or 750 mg [4.5mmol] per day in females).

Unaccepted

Allopurinol is not recommended for treatment of asymptomatic hyperuricemia associated with conditions or induced by medications other than those described above.

Pharmacology/Pharmacokinetics

Physicochemical characteristics

Chemical Group—A structural analog of hypoxanthine.

Molecular weight—

Allopurinol: 136.11.

Allopurinol sodium: 158.09.

pKa—

Allopurinol: 10.2.

Allopurinol sodium: 9.31.

Mechanism of action/Effect

Allopurinol and its metabolite, oxipurinol (alloxanthine), decrease the production of uric acid by inhibiting the action of xanthine oxidase, the enzyme that converts hypoxanthine to xanthine and xanthine to uric acid. Also, allopurinol increases reutilization of hypoxanthine and xanthine for nucleotide and nucleic acid synthesis via an action involving the enzyme hypoxanthine-guanine phosphoribosyltransferase (HGPRTase). The resultant increase in nucleotide concentration leads to feedback inhibition of de novo purine synthesis. Allopurinol thereby decreases uric acid concentrations in both serum and urine.

By lowering both serum and urine concentrations of uric acid below its solubility limits, allopurinol prevents or decreases urate deposition, thereby preventing the occurrence or progression of both gouty arthritis and urate nephropathy. In patients with chronic gout, allopurinol may prevent or decrease tophi formation and chronic joint changes, promote resolution of existing urate crystals and deposits, and, after several months of therapy, reduce the frequency of acute gout attacks.Also, reductions in urine urate concentration prevent or decrease the formation of uric acid or calcium oxalate calculi.

Other actions/effects

Allopurinol inhibits hepatic microsomal enzyme activity.

Allopurinol increases plasma and urine concentrations of xanthine and hypoxanthine. Although the concentrations of these oxypurines usually remain within their solubility limits, xanthine renal stones have been reported very rarely in patients with HGPRTase deficiency or very high pretreatment uric acid concentrations.

Absorption

About 80% to 90% of a single 300-mg dose is absorbed from the gastrointestinal tract.

Absolute bioavailability was approximately 50% when compared to IV dosing.

Protein binding

Neither allopurinol nor its metabolite, oxipurinol, is bound to plasma proteins.

Biotransformation

Primarily hepatic. About 70% to 76% of a dose is metabolized to the active metabolite, oxipurinol. One study indicates that allopurinol may also be taken up by, and metabolized in, red blood cells.

Half-life

Allopurinol—1 to 3 hours

Oxipurinol—12 to 30 hours (average about 15 hours); may be greatly prolonged in patients with renal function impairment.

Onset of action

A significant reduction of serum uric acid concentration usually occurs within 2 or 3 days.

Note: In some patients, especially those with severe tophaceous deposits or those who are underexcretors of uric acid, significant reduction of serum and urine uric acid concentrations may be substantially delayed, possibly because of mobilization of urate from existing tissue deposits.

Time to peak serum concentration

Allopurinol—0.5 to 2 hours following a single 300-mg dose.

Oxipurinol—4.5 to 5 hours

Peak serum concentration

Following a single 300-mg dose—

Allopurinol: About 2 to 3 mcg per mL (14.7 to 22.05 micromoles/L).

Oxipurinol: About 5 to 6.5 mcg per mL (32.85 to 42.7 micromoles/L); may be increased to 30 to 50 mcg per mL (197.1 to 328.5 micromoles/L) in patients with renal function impairment.

Time to peak effect

Reduction of serum uric acid concentration to normal range—1 to 3 weeks.

Reduction of frequency of acute gout attacks—Several months of therapy may be required, even though the serum uric acid concentration returns to normal values, possibly because of mobilization and recrystallization of urate as serum concentrations fluctuate.

Duration of action

The serum uric acid concentration usually returns to the pretreatment value 1 to 2 weeks after discontinuation of therapy.

Elimination

Renal—Up to 12% of a dose is excreted as unchanged allopurinol and about 70% to 76% as oxipurinol.

Fecal—About 20% of a dose.

In dialysis—Both allopurinol and oxipurinol are dialyzable.

Precautions to Consider

Carcinogenicity/Mutagenicity

Life-time dosing in mice and rats at doses equivalent to 1/6 to 1/3 recommended human doses (mg per square meter basis) showed no carcinogenic potential. Human lymphocytes harvested after a mean of 40 months treatment with allopurinol showed no evidence of clastogenicity during *in vitro* assays.

Pregnancy/Reproduction

Fertility—No impairment of fertility was observed in rats or rabbits given up to 20 times the usual human dose.

Pregnancy—Although adequate and well-controlled studies in humans have not been done, 3 reports indicate no evidence of birth defects in offspring of women receiving allopurinol during pregnancy.

In a study in mice, administration of 100 mg of allopurinol per kg of body weight (mg/kg) intraperitoneally on Day 10 or Day 13 of gestation caused an increased number of fetal deaths; no such effect was seen with a dose of 50 mg/kg. In the same study, 50 or 100 mg/kg caused external fetal malformations when administered intraperitoneally on Day 10 of gestation and skeletal malformations when administered intraperitoneally on Day 13 of gestation. Whether these effects were due to maternal toxicity or a direct effect on the fetus has not been determined. However, other studies in rats and rabbits given up to 20 times the usual human dose have not shown that allopurinol affects the fetus adversely.

FDA Pregnancy Category C.

Breast-feeding

Allopurinol and oxipurinol are distributed into breast milk. Whether this toxic medication may cause adverse effects in the nursing infant has not been determined. However, problems in humans have not been documented.

Pediatrics

Appropriate studies performed to date have not demonstrated pediatrics-specific problems that would limit the usefulness of allopurinol in children. However, use of allopurinol in pediatric patients has been limited to children with certain rare inborn errors of purine metabolism or hyperuricemia secondary to a malignancy or cancer therapy.

Geriatrics

No information is available on the relationship of age to the effects of allopurinol in geriatric patients. However, elderly patients are more likely to have age-related renal function impairment, which may require adjustment of the dose and/or dosing interval in patients receiving allopurinol.

Drug interactions and/or related problems

The following drug interactions and/or related problems have been selected on the basis of their potential clinical significance (possible mechanism in parentheses where appropriate)—not necessarily inclusive (» = major clinical significance):

Note: Combinations containing any of the following medications, depending on the amount present, may also interact with this medication.

Acidifiers, urinary, such as:
Ammonium chloride
Ascorbic acid
Potassium or sodium phosphate
(urinary acidification by these medications may increase the possibility of allopurinol-induced xanthine kidney stone formation)

Alcohol or
Diazoxide or
Mecamylamine or
Pyrazinamide
(these medications may increase serum uric acid concentrations; dosage adjustment of allopurinol may be necessary to control hyperuricemia and gout)

Amoxicillin or
Ampicillin or
Bacampicillin or
Hetacillin
(concurrent use with allopurinol may significantly increase the possibility of skin rash; however, it has not been established that allopurinol, rather than the presence of hyperuricemia, is responsible for this effect)

» Anticoagulants, coumarin- or indandione-derivative
(allopurinol may inhibit enzymatic metabolism of the anticoagulant, leading to potentiation of the anticoagulant effect; dosage adjustments based on increased monitoring of prothrombin time may be necessary during and after concurrent use)

Antineoplastics, such as:
Bleomycin or
Cyclophosphamide or
Doxorubicin or
Procarbazine or
Mechlorethamine
(rapidly cytolytic antineoplastic agents may increase serum uric acid concentrations; prophylactic administration of allopurinol may be indicated to prevent complications associated with antineoplastic agent-induced hyperuricemia; also, patients receiving allopurinol to treat pre-existing hyperuricemia or gout may require allopurinol dosage adjustment during and following concurrent therapy with one of these agents)
(concurrent use of allopurinol with cyclophosphamide and possibly other antineoplastic agents may increase the potential for bone marrow depression; although studies of this possibility have reported conflicting results, it is recommended that patients receiving allopurinol concurrently with antineoplastic agents, especially cyclophosphamide, be carefully monitored)

» Azathioprine or
» Mercaptopurine
(allopurinol-induced inhibition of xanthine oxidase decreases metabolism of these medications and may potentiate therapeutic and toxic effects, especially bone marrow depression; the effect on azathioprine metabolism is especially critical in renal transplant patients because of the high risk of oxipurinol accumulation and consequent azathioprine toxicity if the transplanted kidney is rejected; if concurrent use is essential, it is recommended that azathioprine or mercaptopurine dosage be reduced to one-third to one-fourth of the usual dosage, that the patient be carefully monitored, and that subsequent dosage adjustments be based on patient response and evidence of toxicity)
(mercaptopurine may increase serum uric acid concentration in some patients; patients receiving allopurinol to treat pre-existing hyperuricemia or gout may require allopurinol dosage adjustment when mercaptopurine therapy is initiated or discontinued)

Chlorpropamide
(allopurinol may inhibit renal tubular secretion of chlorpropamide; patients receiving the medications concurrently should be monitored for possible increased hypoglycemic effect)

Cyclosporine
(decreased cyclosporine metabolism; monitoring of cyclosporine levels is recommended and dosage adjustment may be necessary)

Dacarbazine
(dacarbazine inhibits xanthine oxidase and may cause additive hypouricemic effects when used concurrently with allopurinol)

Diuretics, thiazide
(caution and careful monitoring of the patient are advised when allopurinol and thiazide diuretics are used concurrently, especially in patients with known or possible renal function impairment, because severe hypersensitivity reactions to allopurinol may occur; although it has been suggested that compromised renal function, rather than the combination of medications, may be responsible for the adverse reactions, it has also been proposed that thiazide diuretics may increase serum oxipurinol concentrations by decreasing its renal excretion)

Probenecid
(probenecid increases urinary excretion of oxipurinol; however, the antihyperuricemic effects of the medications are additive, and increased therapeutic benefit has been reported with concurrent use)

Sulfinpyrazone
(the antihyperuricemic effects of allopurinol and sulfinpyrazone are additive; increased therapeutic benefit has been reported with concurrent use)

Vidarabine, systemic
(concurrent use with allopurinol may increase the risk of neurotoxicity and other side effects such as anemia, nausea, pain, and pruritus; caution is recommended if concurrent use is necessary)

Xanthines, such as:
Aminophylline
Oxtriphylline
Theophylline
(concurrent use of large doses [600 mg per day] of allopurinol with the xanthines [except dyphylline] may decrease theophylline clearance, resulting in increased serum theophylline concentrations; when steady-state theophylline concentration is 13 mcg per mL [72.15 micromoles/L] or higher and 600 mg of allopurinol per day is required, serum theophylline concentrations should be monitored and theophylline dosage adjusted if necessary)

Laboratory value alterations

The following have been selected on the basis of their potential clinical significance (possible effect in parentheses where appropriate)—not necessarily inclusive (» = major clinical significance).

With physiology/laboratory test values
Alkaline phosphatase activity, serum and
Bilirubin concentrations, serum and

Transaminase activity, serum
(may be increased, indicating hepatotoxicity, especially in patients with pre-existing hepatic or renal disease)

Blood urea nitrogen (BUN) and
Creatinine, serum
(concentrations may be increased, indicating nephrotoxicity, especially in patients with pre-existing renal disease)

Medical considerations/Contraindications

The medical considerations/contraindications included have been selected on the basis of their potential clinical significance (reasons given in parentheses where appropriate)—not necessarily inclusive (» = major clinical significance).

Risk-benefit should be considered when the following medical problems exist:

Renal function impairment or any illness that may predispose to a change in renal function, such as:
Congestive heart disease
Diabetes mellitus
Hypertension
(oxipurinol may accumulate; risk of severe allergic reactions and other adverse effects is increased; a reduction in dosage may be required)
(risk of renal failure may be increased, especially when allopurinol is being used for hyperuricemia secondary to neoplastic disease or urate nephropathy; monitoring of renal function may be especially important when these conditions exist)

Sensitivity to allopurinol, history of

Patient monitoring

The following may be especially important in patient monitoring (other tests may be warranted in some patients, depending on condition; » = major clinical significance):

Complete blood counts and
Hepatic function determinations and
Renal function determinations
(recommended at periodic intervals during therapy, especially during the first few months)

Prothrombin time
(recommended periodically in patients receiving dicumarol)

» Uric acid, serum
(monitoring may be required for proper dosing; the upper limit of normal is about 7 mg per 100 mL [416.36 micromoles/L] for males and postmenopausal females and about 6 mg per 100 mL [356.88 micromoles/L] for premenopausal females but may vary, depending on the patient and laboratory methodology)

Side/Adverse Effects

Note: Following initiation of allopurinol therapy for gouty arthritis, the most commonly encountered adverse effect is a temporary increase in the frequency of acute gout attacks. The occurrence of such reactions may be reduced by initiating therapy with a low dose that is gradually increased until the desired effect is obtained and by administration of prophylactic doses of colchicine or a nonsteroidal anti-inflammatory drug.

The following side/adverse effects have been selected on the basis of their potential clinical significance (possible signs and symptoms in parentheses where appropriate)—not necessarily inclusive:

Those indicating need for medical attention

Incidence more frequent

Dermatitis, allergic (skin rash, hives, or itching)

Note: *Maculopapular skin rash* occurs most often; however, *eczematoid, exfoliative, urticarial, vesicular bullous, or purpuric lesions* and *lichen planus* have also been reported rarely.

Very rarely, *skin rash* may be followed by more severe allergic reactions, usually in patients with renal function impairment and/or those receiving thiazide diuretics. *Generalized vasculitis, hepatotoxicity, and/or acute renal failure* may occur. Laboratory studies may indicate *eosinophilia* and *leukopenia* or *leukocytosis*. Several deaths have been attributed to these reactions.

Incidence rare

Agranulocytosis (fever with or without chills; sores, ulcers, or white spots on lips or in mouth; sore throat); ***anemia*** (unusual tiredness and/or weakness); ***angiitis [vasculitis], hypersensitivity*** (chills, fever, and sore throat; muscle aches, pains, or weakness; shortness of breath, troubled breathing, tightness in chest, or wheezing); ***aplastic anemia*** (shortness of breath, troubled breathing, tightness in chest, and/or wheezing; sores, ulcers, or white spots on lips or in mouth; swollen and/or painful glands; unusual bleeding or bruising; unusual tiredness or weakness); ***dermatitis, exfoliative*** (possible prodrome of chills, fever, sore throat, muscle aches or pains, and/or nausea with or without vomiting; red, thickened, scaly skin); ***erythema multiforme*** (possible prodrome of chills, fever, sore throat, muscle aches or pains, and/or nausea with or without vomiting; sores, ulcers, or white spots in mouth or on lips; skin rash or sores, hives, and/or itching); ***hepatotoxicity*** (swelling in upper abdominal area; yellow eyes or skin); ***hypersensitivity reaction, allopurinol-induced*** (initially skin rash immediately preceding or concurrent with chills, fever, and sore throat; muscle aches or pains; and/or nausea with or without vomiting; followed by signs and symptoms of angiitis [vasculitis], hepatotoxicity, and/or acute renal failure); ***loosening of fingernails; necrolysis, toxic epidermal*** (possible prodrome of chills, fever, sore throat, muscle aches or pains, and/or nausea with or without vomiting; redness, tenderness, itching, burning, or peeling of skin; red or irritated eyes); ***neuritis, peripheral*** (numbness, tingling, pain, or weakness in hands or feet); ***renal calculus, xanthine*** (blood in urine, difficult or painful urination, pain in lower back and/or side); ***renal failure, acute*** (sudden decrease in amount of urine; swelling of face, fingers, feet, and/or lower legs; weight gain, rapid); ***Stevens-Johnson syndrome*** (possible prodrome of chills, fever, sore throat, muscle aches and pains, and/or nausea with or without vomiting; sores, ulcers, or white spots in mouth or on lips; bleeding sores on lips); ***thrombocytopenia*** (usually asymptomatic; rarely, unusual bleeding or bruising; black, tarry stools; blood in urine or stools; pinpoint red spots on skin); ***unexplained nosebleeds***

Note: *Bone marrow depression* has been reported to occur 6 weeks to 6 years after initiation of allopurinol therapy. Most of the affected patients were also receiving other medications with the potential for causing this reaction. However, *bone marrow depression* affecting one or more cell lines has rarely occurred in patients receiving allopurinol alone.

Hepatotoxicity may be hypersensitivity-mediated; hepatic necrosis, granulomatous hepatitis, and cholestatic jaundice have been reported.

Renal failure associated with allopurinol therapy has been reported in patients being treated for hyperuricemia secondary to neoplastic diseases or gouty nephropathy as well as in patients experiencing *hypersensitivity reactions* to the medication.

Those indicating need for medical attention only if they continue or are bothersome

Incidence less frequent or rare

Diarrhea; drowsiness; headache; indigestion; nausea or vomiting without symptoms of skin rash, chills or fever, or muscle aches and pains; stomach pain; unusual hair loss

Overdose

For more information on the management of overdose or unintentional ingestion, **contact a Poison Control Center** (see *Poison Control Center Listing).*

Treatment of overdose

Immediate discontinuation of allopurinol.

To decrease absorption—Gastric lavage, if very large quantities have been ingested.

To enhance elimination—Although allopurinol and oxipurinol are dialyzable, the value of hemodialysis or peritoneal dialysis in the management of allopurinol overdose has not been established.

Monitoring—Renal function and urinalysis if chronic toxicity (stone formation) is suspected. Symptomatic treatment only for emergent adverse reactions; no specific antidotes are available.

Supportive care—Maintaining hydration. Patients in whom intentional overdose is known or suspected should be referred for psychiatric consultation.

Patient Consultation

As an aid to patient consultation, refer to *Advice for the Patient, Allopurinol (Systemic).*

In providing consultation, consider emphasizing the following selected information (» = major clinical significance):

Before using this medication

» Conditions affecting use, especially:
Other medications, especially coumarin- or indandione-derivative anticoagulants, azathioprine, and mercaptopurine

Proper use of this medication

Taking after meals, if necessary, to minimize gastrointestinal irritation
» Compliance with therapy

Importance of high fluid intake during therapy and compliance with therapy for alkalinization of urine, if prescribed, to help prevent kidney stones

Several months of continuous therapy may be required for maximum effectiveness in patients with chronic gout

» Medication helps prevent, but does not relieve, acute gout attacks; need to continue taking allopurinol with medication prescribed for gout attacks

» Proper dosing

Missed dose: Taking as soon as possible; not taking if almost time for next dose; not doubling doses

» Proper storage

Precautions while using this medication

Regular visits to physician to check progress during therapy; possible need for periodic blood tests to determine efficacy of therapy and/or occurrence of side effects

Avoiding large amounts of alcohol, which may increase uric acid concentrations and reduce effectiveness of medication

Possibility that vitamin C taken in large amounts may increase the potential for kidney stone formation

» Notifying physician immediately if skin rash occurs or if influenza-like symptoms (chills, fever, muscle aches and pains, or nausea or vomiting) occur concurrently with or shortly after skin rash; these symptoms may rarely indicate onset of severe hypersensitivity reaction

» Caution if drowsiness occurs

Side/adverse effects

Signs of potential adverse effects, especially allergic dermatitis, agranulocytosis, anemia, angiitis, aplastic anemia, exfoliative dermatitis, erythema multiforme, hepatotoxicity, hypersensitivity reaction, loosening of fingernails, toxic epidermal necrolysis, peripheral neuritis, renal caluli, renal failure, Stevens-Johnson syndrome, thrombocytopenia, and unexplained nosebleeds

General Dosing Information

For oral dosing forms:

Allopurinol may be administered after meals to lessen gastrointestinal irritation.

An increase in the frequency of acute attacks of gouty arthritis may occur during the early months of allopurinol therapy. The risk of precipitating acute gout attacks may be reduced by initiating allopurinol therapy with 100 to 200 milligrams, with weekly increases by 100–mg increments until the desired effect is obtained.Prophylactic doses of colchicine (or, if the patient cannot take colchicine, a nonsteroidal anti-inflammatory drug [NSAID]) are recommended concurrently during the first 3 to 6 months of allopurinol therapy.

Acute attacks of gout may occur during allopurinol therapy, even with colchicine or NSAID prophylactic therapy. During an attack, allopurinol therapy should be continued at the same dose while an appropriate anti-inflammatory agent (preferably an NSAID or a corticosteroid [preferably via intrasynovial injection, when feasible]) is administered to relieve the attack. Because of the toxicity associated with therapeutic doses of colchicine, its use for treatment of an acute attack of gout should be reserved for patients in whom the preferred medications are contraindicated or ineffective.

The total daily dose may be administered in divided doses or as a single dose. Each single dose should not exceed 300 mg. Daily dosage requirements exceeding 300 mg should be administered in divided doses.

Monitoring of serum uric acid concentrations may be necessary for proper dosing.

To reduce the risk of xanthine calculi formation, and to help prevent renal precipitation of urates in patients receiving concomitant uricosuric agents, a high fluid intake(no less than 2.5 to 3 liters daily) and maintenance of a neutral, or preferably slightly alkaline, urine are recommended.

When uricosuric therapy is being changed to allopurinol therapy, the dose of the uricosuric agent should be reduced gradually over a period of several weeks and the dose of allopurinol increased gradually to the dose required for maintenance of normal serum uric acid concentrations.

It is recommended that allopurinol therapy be discontinued at once if a skin rash or any other sign of adverse reaction occurs. Skin rash may be followed by more severe hypersensitivity reactions. After a severe reaction, therapy should be discontinued permanently. However, after a mild reaction, it may be possible to reinstate therapy at a lower dosage (50 mg per day initially and increased very gradually) after the reaction has subsided. If skin rash recurs, therapy should be discontinued permanently.

For parenteral dosing forms:

Initiate therapy 24 to 48 hours before chemotherapy regimens known to cause tumor cell lysis.

Maintain at least 2 liters daily of neutral to (preferably) slightly alkaline urinary output in adults.

Many parenteral drugs which might be used concurrently in cancer chemotherapy, including analgesics, anti-infectives, and antinauseants may be physically incompatible with allopurinol sodium for injection, and should not be mixed in the same container or administered through common intravenous access ports.

Daily doses may be given as a single daily infusion or divided into infusions given every 6-, 8-, or 12-hours for both adults and children.

The final concentration of the administered fluid should not exceed 6 milligrams per milliliter.

Monitoring of serum uric acid to maintain concentrations within the normal range is necessary for proper dosing.

For treatment of adverse effects

Hypersensitivity reactions—Administer glucocorticoids. Prolonged administration may be required after a severe reaction. If after recovery from mild episodes, allopurinol is reinstated and is followed by the recurrence of any rash, permanent withdrawal of allopurinol is recommended.

Oral Dosage Forms

ALLOPURINOL TABLETS USP

Usual adult and adolescent dose

Antigout agent—

Initial—Oral, 100 mg once a day, to be increased by 100 mg per day at one-week intervals until the desired serum uric acid concentration is attained, not to exceed the maximum recommended dosage of 800 mg per day.

Maintenance—Oral, 100 to 200 mg two or three times a day; or 300 mg as a single dose once a day. The usual maintenance dose is 200 to 300 mg per day in mild gout or 400 to 600 mg per day in moderately severe tophaceous gout.

Neoplastic disease therapy—

Initial—Oral, 600 to 800 mg per day starting twelve hours to three days (preferably two to three days) prior to initiation of chemotherapy or radiation therapy.

Maintenance—Dosage should be based on serum uric acid determinations performed approximately forty-eight hours after initiation of allopurinol therapy and periodically thereafter. Allopurinol should be discontinued following the period of tumor regression.

Antiurolithic (uric acid calculi)—

Oral, 100 to 200 mg one to four times a day; or 300 mg as a single dose once a day.

Antiurolithic (calcium oxalate calculi)—

Oral, 200 to 300 mg a day as a single dose or in divided doses.

Note: Because oxipurinol is excreted primarily by the kidneys, accumulation may occur in patients with renal failure. Patients receiving dialysis may require usual therapeutic doses of allopurinol; however, in patients not receiving dialysis, it is recommended that the dosage be reduced as follows:

Creatinine Clearance (mL/min)	Dose
10 to 20	200 mg daily
3 to 10	no more than 100 mg daily
< 3	100 mg at intervals of more than 24 hours may be necessary

Some patients with renal function impairment may require even lower doses or longer intervals between doses. In some cases, 300 mg twice a week, or even less, may suffice.

Usual adult prescribing limits

300 mg per dose; 800 mg per day.

Usual pediatric dose

Antihyperuricemic, in neoplastic disease therapy—

Children up to 6 years of age: Oral, 50 mg three times a day.

Children 6 to 10 years of age: Oral, 100 mg three times a day; or 300 mg as a single dose once a day.

Note: Dosage adjustment may be necessary after approximately forty-eight hours of therapy, depending on the patient's response.

Strength(s) usually available

U.S.—

100 mg (Rx) [*Zyloprim* (scored); GENERIC].

300 mg (Rx) [*Zyloprim* (scored); GENERIC].

Canada—

100 mg (Rx) [*Apo-Allopurinol* (scored); *Purinol* (scored); *Zyloprim* (scored)].

200 mg (Rx) [*Apo-Allopurinol* (scored); *Purinol* (scored); *Zyloprim* (scored); GENERIC].

300 mg (Rx) [*Apo-Allopurinol* (scored); *Purinol* (scored); *Zyloprim* (scored); GENERIC].

Packaging and storage

Store at 15 to 25 °C (59 and 77 °F) in a dry place and protect from light.

Auxiliary labeling

- Drink large amounts of fluids.

Parenteral Dosage Forms

ALLOPURINOL SODIUM INJECTION

Usual adult dose

Neoplastic disease therapy—

Initial—Intravenous, 200 to 400 milligrams per square meter per day starting 24 to 48 hours prior to initiation of chemotherapy therapy known to cause tumor cell lysis. The daily dose can be given as a single infusion or in equally divided infusions at 6-, 8-, or 12-hour intervals at the recommended final concentration of not greater than 6 mg per mL. The rate of infusion depends on the volume of infusate.

Maintenance—Dosage should be based on serum uric acid determinations performed approximately forty-eight hours after initiation of allopurinol therapy and periodically thereafter. The dosage of intravenous allopurinol to lower serum and urinary uric acid levels to normal or near-normal varies with the severity of the disease. Allopurinol should be discontinued following the period of tumor regression.

Note: Because oxipurinol is excreted primarily by the kidneys, accumulation may occur in patients with renal failure. Patients receiving dialysis may require usual therapeutic doses of allopurinol; however, in patients not receiving dialysis, it is recommended that the dosage be reduced as follows:

Creatinine Clearance (mL/min)	Dose
10 to 20	200 mg daily
3 to 10	100 mg daily
< 3	100 mg daily at extended intervals

Usual adult prescribing limits

Up to 600 mg daily

Usual pediatric dose

Neoplastic disease therapy:—

Initial—Intravenous, 200 milligrams per square meter per day starting 24 to 48 hours prior to initiation of chemotherapy therapy known to cause tumor cell lysis. The daily dose can be given as a single infusion or in equally divided infusions at 6-, 8-, or 12-hour intervals at the recommended final concentration of not greater than 6 mg per mL. The rate of infusion depends on the volume of infusate.

Maintenance—Dosage should be based on serum uric acid determinations performed approximately forty-eight hours after initiation of allopurinol therapy and periodically thereafter. The dosage of intravenous allopurinol to lower serum and urinary uric acid levels to normal or near-normal varies with the severity of the disease. Allopurinol should be discontinued following the period of tumor regression.

Note: See *Usual adult dose* for dose adjustment recommendations for renal impairment

Usual geriatric dose

See *Usual adult dose.*

Usual geriatric prescribing limits

See *Usual adult prescribing limits.*

Strength(s) usually available

U.S.—

Allopurinol sodium equivalent to 500 mg of allopurinol per 30-mL vial of lyophilized powder (Rx) [*Aloprim* (preservative free)].

Packaging and storage

Store unreconstituted powder at 25 °C (77 °F), with excursions permitted to 15°-30° C (59°-86° F).

Preparation of dosage form

Allopurinol for injection must be reconstituted and diluted. The 30-mL vials of allopurinol powder should be reconstituted with 25 mL of sterile water for injection. The reconstituted solution (pH of 11.1 to 11.8) should be diluted to the desired concentration with 0.9% sodium chloride injection or 5% dextrose for injection. Sodium bicarbonate-containing solutions should not be used. A final concentration of no greater than 6 mg per mL is recommended. The solution should not be used if particulate matter or discoloration is present. See the manufacturer's package insert for a detailed list of specific drugs which are physically incompatible in solution with allopurinol.

Stability

Following reconstitution and dilution, the final solution should be stored at 20° to 25° C (68° to 77° F) and administration should begin within 10 hours after reconstitution. The reconstituted and/or diluted solution should NOT be refrigerated.

Incompatibilities

See the manufacturer's package insert for a detailed list of specific drugs which are physically incompatible in solution with allopurinol.

Caution

During intravenous allopurinol therapy, a fluid intake sufficient to yield a daily urinary output of at least two liters and maintenance of a neutral or slightly alkaline urine are suggested.

Selected Bibliography

Ettinger B, Tang A, Citron JT et al: Randomized trial of allopurinol in the prevention of calcium oxalate calculi. N Engl J Med 1986; 315: 1386-1389.

Lupton GP & Odom RB: The allopurinol hypersensitivity syndrome. J Am Acad Dermatol 1979; 1: 365-374.

Revised: 03/30/2000

ALMOTRIPTAN Systemic

VA CLASSIFICATION (Primary): CN105

Commonly used brand name(s): *Axert.*

Note: For a listing of dosage forms and brand names by country availability, see *Dosage Forms* section(s).

Category

Antimigraine agent.

Indications

General Considerations

Almotriptan should only be prescribed for patients who have an established clear diagnosis of migraine. Almotriptan is not intended for the prophylactic therapy of migraine.

Accepted

Headache, migraine (treatment)—Almotriptan is indicated for the acute treatment of migraine headaches with or without aura in adult patients.

Unaccepted

Almotriptan is not indicated in the management of hemiplegic or basilar migraine. Efficacy and safety of almotriptan in these conditions have not been established.

Almotriptan is not indicated for use in cluster headaches. Efficacy and safety of almotriptan in this condition have not been established.

Pharmacology/Pharmacokinetics

Physicochemical characteristics

Source—Synthetic. Almotriptan is structurally related to serotonin (5-hydroxytryptamine, 5-HT).

Molecular weight—Almotriptan malate: 469.56.

Solubility—Almotriptan: Readily soluble in water.

Mechanism of action/Effect

Almotriptan selectively binds with high affinity to 5–hydroxytryptaminergic receptors (5–HT_{1D}, 5–HT_{1B} and 5–HT_{1F}). Almotriptan has weak affinity for 5–HT_{1A} and 5–HT_7 receptors, but has no significant affinity or pharmacological activity at 5–HT_2, 5–HT_3, 5–HT_4 or 5–HT_6 receptors. It has been proposed that migraine symptoms are due to local cranial vasodilatation and/or to the release of pro-inflammatory and vasoactive neuropeptides from the trigeminal nerve endings. Almotriptan most likely acts on the 5–$HT_{1B/1D}$ receptors on the extracerebral, intracranial dilated blood vessels during a migraine attack, and on nerve terminals in the trigeminal system resulting in cranial vessel constriction, inhibition of neuropeptide release, and reduced transmission in trigeminal pain pathways.

Absorption
Almotriptan is well absorbed after oral administration (absolute bioavailability about 70%). The rate and extent of absorption are not affected by administration with food.

Distribution
The mean apparent volume of distribution is 180 to 200 liters.

Protein binding
Low (approximately 35%).

Biotransformation
Almotriptan is metabolized by one minor and two major pathways. Monoamine oxidase (MAO)-mediated oxidative deamination (approximately 27% of the dose), and cytochrome P450–mediated oxidation (approximately 12% of the dose) are the major routes of metabolism, while flavin monooxygenase is the minor route.

Half-life
3 to 4 hours.

Time to peak concentration
Oral—1 to 3 hours after administration.

Elimination
Renal—almotriptan is eliminated primarily by renal excretion (about 75% of the oral dose). Approximately 40% of an administered dose is excreted unchanged in urine.

Fecal—approximately 13% of the administered dose is excreted via feces, both unchanged and metabolized.

Precautions to Consider

Carcinogenicity/Tumorigenicity
No evidence of tumorigenicity was found in studies up to 103 weeks in mice and 104 weeks in rats given almotriptan by oral gavage in quantities sufficient to achieve peak concentrations up to approximately 40 times and 78 times, in mice and rats respectively, the area under the plasma concentration-time curve [AUC] exposure in humans receiving a 25 mg dose, the maximum recommended daily dose [MRDD]. However, in both studies the mortality rates in female mice receiving high doses reached statistical significance. Therefore, studies were terminated between weeks 96 and 98 in all female rats, all male mice, and female mice receiving high doses.

Mutagenicity
No evidence of mutagenicity was found in a variety of *in vitro* studies including the Ames test and the thymidine locus mouse lymphoma assay. Almotriptan was not clastogenic in an *in vivo* mouse micronucleus assay but was weakly clastogenic in *in vitro* cytogenetic assays in human lymphocytes.

Pregnancy/Reproduction
Fertility—No adverse effects on fertility were found in reproduction studies in female rats given up to 25 mg per kg of body weight (mg/kg) per day orally (approximately 10 times the MRDD on a mg per square meter of body surface area [mg/m^2 basis]). Prolongation of the estrus cycle was observed at a dose of 100 mg/kg per day (approximately 40 times the MRDD on a mg/m^2 basis).

Pregnancy—Adequate and well-controlled studies have not been done in humans.

Studies in rats receiving daily oral gavage of almotriptan throughout the period of organogenesis at doses of 125, 250, 500, and 1000 mg/kg per day revealed an increase in embryolethality at the highest dose (maternal exposure, based on plasma AUC of the parent drug, was approximately 958 times the human exposure at the MRDD of 25 mg). Increased incidences of fetal skeletal variations (decreased ossification) were noted at doses greater than 125 mg/kg per day (maternal exposure 80 times the human exposure at the MRDD).

FDA Pregnancy Category C.

Breast-feeding
It is not known whether almotriptan is distributed into breast milk. However, almotriptan is distributed in the milk of rats at levels equivalent to maternal plasma levels at 0.5 hour and 7 times higher than plasma levels at 6 hours after dosing.

Pediatrics
No information is available on the relationship of age to the effects of almotriptan in patients up to 18 years of age. Safety and efficacy have not been established.

Geriatrics
Appropriate studies in the relationship of age to the effect of almotriptan have not been performed in the geriatric population.

Drug interactions and/or related problems
The following drug interactions and/or related problems have been selected on the basis of their potential clinical significance (possible mechanism in parentheses where appropriate)—not necessarily inclusive (» = major clinical significance):

All drug interaction studies were performed in healthy volunteers using a single 12.5-mg dose of almotriptan and multiple doses of the other drug.

Combinations containing any of the following medications, depending on the amount present, may also interact with this medication.

Dihydroergotamine or
Ergotamine or
Methysergide or
Other 5-hydroxytryptamine agonists such as:
Sumatriptan
Zolmitriptan
(a delay of 24 hours between administration of dihydroergotamine, ergotamine, or methysergide or other 5-hydroxytryptamine agonists and almotriptan is recommended because of the possibility of additive and/or prolonged vasoconstriction)

Ketoconazole or
Other potent cytochrome P450 CYP3A4 inhibitors, such as erythromycin, itraconazole, and ritonavir
(concurrent use with ketoconazole has resulted in a 60% increase in the area under the plasma concentration-time curve [AUC] and peak plasma concentration of almotriptan; though the interaction between almotriptan and other potent CYP3A4 inhibitors has not been studied, increased concentrations of almotriptan may be expected when almotriptan is used concurrently with these medications)

Monoamine oxidase (MAO) inhibitors
(concurrent use with moclobemide has resulted in a 27% decrease in the clearance of almotriptan; however, no adjustment in dosage is necessary)

Selective serotonin reuptake inhibitors, such as:
Fluoxetine
Fluvoxamine
Paroxetine
Sertraline
(concurrent use may result in weakness, hyperreflexia, and incoordination; careful monitoring is recommended)

Verapamil
(concurrent use has resulted in a 20% increase in the AUC and a 24% increase in the peak plasma concentration of almotriptan; however, these changes are not clinically significant, therefore, no adjustment in dosage is necessary)

Laboratory value alterations
The following have been selected on the basis of their potential clinical significance (possible effect in parentheses where appropriate)—not necessarily inclusive (» = major clinical significance).

With physiology/laboratory test values
Blood pressure
(may be increased, although increases are generally mild and transient)

Cholesterol and
Creatine phosphokinase, serum and
Gamma glutamyl transpeptidase (GGT) and
Glucose concentrations, blood and/or urine
(may be increased)

Medical considerations/Contraindications
The medical considerations/contraindications included have been selected on the basis of their potential clinical significance (reasons given in parentheses where appropriate)—not necessarily inclusive (» = major clinical significance).

Except under special circumstances, this medication should not be used when the following medical problems exist:

» Coronary artery disease, especially:
Angina pectoris or
Myocardial infarction, history of, or
Myocardial ischemia, silent, documented, or
Prinzmetal's angina, or

» Other conditions in which coronary vasoconstriction would be detrimental
(almotriptan may cause coronary vasospasms)

» Hypertension, uncontrolled
(may be exacerbated)

Risk-benefit should be considered when the following medical problems exist:

» Cerebrovascular accident, history of
(5-hydroxytryptamine [5-HT_1] agonists may cause cerebral hemorrhage, stroke, or subarachnoid hemorrhage; caution is recommended when administering almotriptan to patients at risk for cerebrovascular events)

» Coronary artery disease, predisposition to
(5-HT_1 agonists have caused serious coronary adverse effects; patients in whom coronary artery disease is a possibility on the basis of age or the presence of other risk factors, such as diabetes, hypercholesterolemia, obesity, a strong family history of coronary artery disease, female gender with physiological or surgical menopause, male gender over 40 years or age, or tobacco smoking should be evaluated for the presence of cardiovascular disease before almotriptan is prescribed; even after a satisfactory evaluation, the advisability of administering the patient's first dose under medical supervision should be considered)

» Hepatic function impairment
(caution is recommended because clearance of almotriptan may be impaired; a starting dose of 6.25 mg is recommended)

» Renal function impairment
(clearance of almotriptan was decreased by 65% in patients with creatinine clearances between 10 and 30 mL per minute and by 40% in patients with creatinine clearances between 31 and 71 mL per minute compared with healthy volunteers; in addition, peak plasma concentrations of almotriptan increased by approximately 80%; a starting dose of 6.25 mg is recommended)

Patient monitoring

The following may be especially important in patient monitoring (other tests may be warranted in some patients, depending on condition; » = major clinical significance):

Electrocardiogram (ECG)
(monitoring is recommended immediately following the first dose of almotriptan for patients with cardiovascular risk factors, and for long-term intermittent almotriptan users)

Side/Adverse Effects

Note: Most adverse events reported in clinical trials were mild in intensity and were transient, and did not lead to long-lasting effects. The incidence of adverse events in controlled clinical trials was not affected by gender, weight, age, presence of aura, or use of prophylactic medications or oral contraceptives.

Some of the adverse events reported after administration of almotriptan (e.g., nausea, vomiting, malaise, fatigue, dizziness, vertigo, weakness, drowsiness, sedation) often occur during and/or following a migraine headache; whether almotriptan contributes to their occurrence has not been established.

The following side/adverse effects have been selected on the basis of their potential clinical significance (possible signs and symptoms in parentheses where appropriate)—not necessarily inclusive:

Those indicating need for medical attention

Incidence less frequent

Chest pain; conjunctivitis (discharge from eye; redness of inner lining of eyelid); ***dermatitis*** (itching, redness, or swelling of skin); ***dyspnea*** (shortness of breath); ***erythema*** (redness of skin); ***eye irritation; laryngismus*** (tightness in the throat); ***neck pain or rigid neck; palpitations; pruritus*** (itching of skin); ***skin rash; tachycardia*** (fast heartbeat)

Incidence rare

Colitis (abdominal cramping or pain; anorexia; black, tarry stools; blood in stools; diarrhea, watery; weight loss); ***coronary artery vasospasm*** (chest pain; tightness in chest); ***esophageal reflux*** (chest pain; difficulty in swallowing; heartburn, repeated; regurgitation of food); ***eye pain; fever; gastritis or gastroenteritis*** (abdominal pain; anorexia; diarrhea; nausea; unusual tiredness or weakness; vomiting); ***hypertension; hyperventilation*** (rapid breathing); ***myocardial infarction*** (chest pain, severe; cool, pale skin; dizziness; increased sweating; nausea; shortness of breath); ***myocardial ischemia, transient*** (chest pain); ***otitis media*** (earache); ***scotoma*** (loss of vision); ***syncope*** (fainting); ***ventricular fibrillation; ventricular tachycardia*** (fast heartbeat)

Note: Most cases of *coronary artery vasospasm, myocardial infarction, transient myocardial ischemia, ventricular fibrillation,* and *ventricular tachycardia* have occurred in patients with risk factors predictive of coronary artery disease.

Those indicating need for medical attention only if they continue or are bothersome

Incidence more frequent

Dizziness; dry mouth; headache; nausea; paresthesia (burning, numbness, prickly, or tingling sensation); ***somnolence*** (sleepiness)

Incidence less frequent

Abdominal cramping or pain; anxiety; asthenia (lack or loss of strength); ***back pain; bronchitis*** (cough producing mucus; difficulty breathing; shortness of breath; tightness in chest; wheezing); ***chills; diaphoresis*** (profuse sweating); ***diarrhea; dysmenorrhea*** (painful menstural period); ***dyspepsia*** (belching; heartburn; indigestion; stomach discomfort, upset or pain); ***ear pain; epistaxis*** (nosebleed); ***fatigue; hyperacusis*** (increased sense of hearing); ***hypoesthesia*** (decreased sensitivity to touch); ***insomnia*** (trouble in sleeping); ***muscle weakness; myalgia*** (muscle aches); ***pharyngitis*** (sore throat); ***restlessness; rhinitis*** (runny or stuffy nose); ***sinusitis*** (aching, fullness, or tension in area of affected sinus); ***taste alteration; tremor*** (quivering or trembling); ***vasodilation*** (feeling of warmth or heat; flushing or redness of skin); ***vertigo*** (dizziness; feeling of constant movement of self or surroundings; sensation of spinning); ***vomiting***

Incidence rare

Abnormal coordination (clumsiness or unsteadiness); ***arthralgia*** (pain in joints); ***arthritis*** (pain, redness, swelling, or warmth in joints); ***change in dreams or nightmares; diplopia*** (double vision); ***dry eyes; euphoria*** (exaggerated feeling of mental and physical well-being); ***hyperreflexia*** (exaggeration of reflexes); ***hypertonia*** (muscle stiffness); ***impaired concentration; increased salivation; increased thirst; laryngitis*** (cough; dry or sore throat; difficulty in swallowing; hoarseness; loss of voice); ***mental depression; myopathy*** (muscle pain or weakness); ***nervousness; neuropathy*** (change in sense of touch; sensation of pins and needles; stabbing pain); ***nystagmus*** (continuous, uncontrolled, back-and-forth and/or rolling eye movements); ***parosmia*** (change in sense of smell); ***photosensitivity*** (increased sensitivity to sunlight); ***sneezing; tinnitus*** (buzzing or ringing in the ears)

Overdose

For more information on the management of overdose or unintentional ingestion, **contact a poison control center** (see *Poison Control Center Listing*).

No adverse effects were reported in patients and healthy volunteers who received single oral doses up to 200 mg.

Clinical effects of overdose

Signs and symptoms that might be anticipated are hypertension and other serious cardiovascular symptoms.

Treatment of overdose

Although there is no experience with overdose of almotriptan, treatment is essentially symptomatic and supportive.

To decrease absorption—Emptying the stomach with gastric lavage followed by activated charcoal.

Monitoring—Monitoring the clinical symptoms and electrocardiogram for at least 20 hours, even if clinical symptoms are not observed.

Supportive care—Maintaining an open airway and breathing, maintaining proper fluid and electrolyte balance, and/or correcting hypertension. Patients in whom intentional overdose is confirmed or suspected should be referred for psychiatric consultation.

Patient Consultation

As an aid to patient consultation, refer to *Advice for the Patient, Almotriptan (Systemic).*

In providing consultation, consider emphasizing the following selected information (» = major clinical significance):

Before using this medication

» Conditions affecting use, especially:
Sensitivity to almotriptan
Other medical problems, especially cerebrovascular accident (history of); coronary artery disease, predisposition to coronary artery disease, or other conditions that may be adversely affected by coronary artery constriction; hepatic function impairment; hypertension (uncontrolled); or renal function impairment

Proper use of this medication

» Not administering if atypical headache symptoms are present; checking with physician instead

Administering after onset of headache pain

Additional benefit may be obtained if the patient lies down in a quiet, dark room after administering medication

» Taking one additional dose, if needed, for return of migraine 2 hours or more after initial relief was obtained
» Compliance with prophylactic therapy, if prescribed
Proper dosing
Proper storage

Precautions while using this medication
Avoiding alcohol, which aggravates headaches
» Caution if drowsiness or dizziness occurs

Side/adverse effects
Signs of potential side effects, especially chest pain, conjunctivitis, dermatitis, dyspnea, erythema, eye irritation, laryngismus, neck pain or rigid neck, palpitations, pruritus, skin rash, tachycardia, colitis, coronary artery vasospasm, esophageal reflux, eye pain, fever, gastritis or gastroenteritis, hypertension, hyperventilation, myocardial infarction, transient myocardial ischemia, otitis media, scotoma, syncope, ventricular fibrillation, and ventricular tachycardia

General Dosing Information
The dose may be repeated after 2 hours if the headache returns, but no more than two doses should be given within a 24-hour period. Safety and efficacy of a second dose if the initial dose is ineffective have not been established.

Lying down and relaxing in a quiet, darkened room after administering a dose of antimigraine medication may contribute to relief of migraines.

Oral Dosage Forms
Note: Almotriptan tablets contain almotriptan malate. However, dosage and strength are expressed in terms of almotriptan base.

ALMOTRIPTAN TABLETS
Usual adult dose
Antimigraine agent—
Oral, 6.25 or 12.5 mg (base) as a single dose. If necessary, an additional dose may be taken after two hours.

Note: A starting dose of 6.25 mg is recommended in patients with hepatic or renal function impairment.

Controlled trials have not adequately established the efficacy of a second dose of almotriptan if the initial dose is ineffective.

Usual adult prescribing limits
Patients with normal hepatic and renal function—Two doses within twenty-four hours.

Patients with hepatic or renal function impairment—12.5 mg within twenty-four hours.

Usual pediatric dose
Safety and efficacy in patients up to 18 years of age have not been established.

Strength(s) usually available
U.S.—
6.25 mg (base) (Rx) [*Axert* (mannitol; cellulose; povidone; sodium starch glycolate; sodium stearyl fumarate; titanium dioxide; hydroxypropyl methylcellulose; polyethylene glycol; propylene glycol; iron oxide; carnauba wax)].

12.5 mg (base) (Rx) [*Axert* (mannitol; cellulose; povidone; sodium starch glycolate; sodium stearyl fumarate; titanium dioxide; hydroxypropyl methylcellulose; polyethylene glycol; propylene glycol; FD&C Blue No. 2; carnauba wax)].

Packaging and storage
Store at 25°C (77°F); excursions permitted between 15 and 30 °C (59 and 86 °F).

Revised: 09/17/2001
Developed: 07/24/2001

ALOSETRON Systemic†

Note: Products containing alosetron were withdrawn from the U.S. market by GlaxoWellcome on request of the Food and Drug Administration in November 2000. The Food and Drug Administration approved a restricted marketing program in September 2002.

USA: Alosetron hydrochloride
INN: Alosetron; BAN: Alosetron
VA CLASSIFICATION (Primary): GA900
Commonly used brand name(s): *Lotronex*.

Note: For a listing of dosage forms and brand names by country availability, see *Dosage Forms* section(s).

†Not commercially available in Canada.

Category
Serotonin antagonist; Irritable bowel syndrome therapy agent.

Indications
General Considerations
Efficacy of alosetron has not been observed in men at any dose.

Accepted
Bowel syndrome, irritable (treatment)—Alosetron is indicated for treatment of irritable bowel syndrome (IBS) in women with severe diarrhea-predominant irritable bowel syndrome (IBS) who have:
- chronic IBS symptoms (generally lasting 6 months or longer),
- had anatomic or biochemical abnormalities of the gastrointestinal tract excluded, and
- failed to respond to conventional therapy

Note: Diarrhea-predominant IBS is severe if it includes diarrhea and one or more of the following:frequent and severe abdominal pain/discomfortfrequent bowel urgency or fecal incontinencedisability or restriction of daily activities due to IBS

Less than 5% of IBS is considered severe.

Unaccepted
The safety and efficacy of alosetron in men with irritable bowel syndrome have not been established.

Pharmacology/Pharmacokinetics
Physicochemical characteristics
Molecular weight—330.8.

Solubility—The solubility of alosetron is 61 milligram per milliliter (mg/mL) in water, 42 mg/mL in 0.1M hydrochloric acid, 0.3 mg/mL in pH 6 phosphate buffer, and <0.1 mg/mL in pH 8 phosphate buffer.

Mechanism of action/Effect
Alosetron hydrochloride is a potent and selective antagonist of 5-hydroxytryptamine (serotonin) subtype 3 (5-HT_3) receptors. 5-HT_3 antagonists inhibit activation of non-selective cation channels, which results in the modulation of the enteric nervous system. The cause of irritable bowel syndrome (IBS) is not known; however, IBS is characterized by visceral hypersensitivity and hyperactivity of the gastrointestinal (GI) tract. This hyperactivity is responsible for abnormal sensations of pain and motor activity. 5-HT_3 receptors are extensively located on enteric neurons of the GI tract, as well as other peripheral and central neurons. Activation of these receptors ultimately affects the regulation of visceral pain, colonic transit, and GI secretions. By blocking these receptors, alosetron is able to effectively control IBS. When given to healthy volunteers, alosetron (2 milligrams (mg) twice daily for 8 days) increased colonic transit time without affecting orocecal transit time. A single 4-mg dose of alosetron increased basal jejunal water and sodium absorption. In IBS patients, alosetron (4 mg twice daily for 6.5 days) increases colonic compliance.

Absorption
Absorption is rapid and ranges from 30 to >90% after oral administration.

Co-administration of food with alosetron reduces absorption by 25% and resulted in a mean delay in time to peak concentration of 15 minutes.

Vol_D
65 to 95 liters (L)

Protein binding
High (82%) over a concentration range of 20 to 4000 ng per mL

Biotransformation
Alosetron is metabolized by human microsomal cytochrome P450.

In vitro enzymes shown to be involved include CYP2C9 (30%), CYP3A4 (18%), and CYP1A2 (10%). About 11% is by non-CYP mediated Phase I metabolic conversion. At least 13 metabolites have been detected in urine. It is not known if the metabolites have biological activity.

Half-life
Elimination—1.5 hours

Time to peak concentration
Approximately 1 hour

Peak plasma concentration:

In men, 5 nanograms per milliliter (ng/mL) and in women, 9 ng/mL, after an oral dose of 1 milligram.

Plasma concentrations increase proportionally with single oral doses up to 8 mg and more than proportionally at a single oral dose of 16 mg.

Elimination

Urine—73%; 7% as unchanged drug; 15% as 6-hydroxy metabolite and secondarily metabolized to a glucouronide (14%); 14% as bis-oxidized dicarbonyl and its monocarbonyl precursor (4%); renal clearance is approximately 94 mL per minute

Feces—24%; 1% as unchanged drug; 6% as monocarbonyl precursor

Precautions to Consider

Carcinogenesis/Tumorigenicity/Mutagenicity

Carcinogenic effects were not seen in 2-year studies in mice at doses up to 30 mg/kg/day and in rats at doses up to 40 mg/kg/day. Standard tests showed no mutagenic activity of alosetron.

Alosetron was not genotoxic in the Ames tests, the mouse lymphoma cell (L5178Y/TK) forward gene mutation test, the human lymphocyte chromosome aberration test, the *ex vivo* rat hepatocyte unscheduled DNA synthesis (UDS) test, or the *in vivo* rat micronucleus test for mutagenicity.

Pregnancy/Reproduction

Fertility—Oral alosetron had no effect on fertility or reproductive performance of male or female rats when given in doses up to 40 mg/kg/day (about 160 times the recommended daily human dose of 2 mg/day based on body surface area) or in rabbits at doses up to 30 mg/kg/day (about 240 times the recommended daily human dose based on body surface area).

Pregnancy—Adequate and well-controlled studies in humans have not been done.

Alosetron should be used during pregnancy only if clearly needed.

Studies in rats and in rabbits with oral doses up to 160 and 240 times the recommended human dose based on body surface area revealed no harm to the fetus.

FDA Pregnancy Category B

Breast-feeding

It is not known whether alosetron is distributed into human breast milk. However, alosetron is distributed in the milk of lactating rats. Caution should be exercised when alosetron is administered to a nursing woman.

Pediatrics

Appropriate studies have not been performed on the relationship of age to the effects of alosetron in the pediatric population. Safety and efficacy have not been established.

Geriatrics

Appropriate studies performed to date have not demonstrated geriatrics-specific problems that would limit the usefulness of alosetron in the elderly. However, elderly patients may be at greater risk for complications of constipation based on postmarketing experience.

Pharmacogenetics

Plasma concentrations of alosetron are 30 to 50% lower in men than in women given the same oral dose. In patients with irritable bowel syndrome, concentrations of alosetron are influenced by gender. Efficacy has not been established in men at any dose.

Drug interactions and/or related problems

The following drug interactions and/or related problems have been selected on the basis of their potential clinical significance (possible mechanism in parentheses where appropriate)—not necessarily inclusive (» = major clinical significance):

It is unlikely that alosetron will inhibit the hepatic metabolic clearance of drugs metabolized by CYP3A4, CYP2D6, CYP2C9, CYP2C19, CYP2E1, or CYP1A2 based on data from *in vitro* and *in vivo* studies.

Alosetron does not induce CYP3A, CYP2E1, or CYP2C19.

Alosetron is metabolized by a variety of hepatic CYP drug-metabolizing enzymes. Inducers or inhibitors of these enzymes may change the clearance of alosetron.

CYP1A2 inhibitors, moderate, including
Cimetidine or
Quinolone antibiotics
(concomitant use has not been evaluated; should be avoided unless clinically necessary because of potential drug interactions)

» Fluvoxamine
(concomitant use is **contraindicated;** fluvoxamine, a known strong inhibitor of CYP1A2, shown to increase alosetron AUC and half-life by approximately 6-fold and 3-fold, respectively)

Hydralazine or
Isoniazid or
Procainamide
(Although not studied with alosetron, inhibition of N-acetyltransferase may have clinically relevant consequences for these medications)

Ketoconazole or
Other potent CYP3A4 inhibitors including
Clarithromycin or
Itraconazole or
Protease inhibitors or
Telithromycin or
Voriconazole
(coadministration with ketoconazole increased alosetron AUC by 29%; caution should be used with concomitant use)

» Medications that decrease gastrointestinal motility,such as:
» Anticholinergics or other medications with anticholinergic activity, other (see *Appendix II*) or
» Antidiarrheals, antiperistaltic or
» Opioid (narcotic) analgesics
(concurrent use of medications that decrease gastrointestinal motility with alosetron may result in greater risk of serious complications of constipation)

Laboratory value alterations

The following have been selected on the basis of their potential clinical significance (possible effect in parentheses where appropriate)—not necessarily inclusive (» = major clinical significance).

Alanine aminotransferase (ALT [SGPT]), serum or
Alkaline phosphatase or
Aspartate aminotransferase (AST [SGOT]), serum or
Bilirubin
(abnormal or elevated concentrations were rare in clinical trials; causal association with alosetron has not been established)

Medical considerations/Contraindications

The medical considerations/contraindications included have been selected on the basis of their potential clinical significance (reasons given in parentheses where appropriate)—not necessarily inclusive (» = major clinical significance).

Except under special circumstances, this medication should not be used when the following medical problems exist:

» Constipation, active or history of or sequelae from or
» Crohn's disease, current or history of or
» Diverticulitis, active or history of or
» Hepatic impairment, severe or
» Hypercoagulable state, history of or
» Intestinal circulation, impaired, history of or
» Intestinal adhesions, obstructions, perforations, or strictures, history of or
» Ischemic colitis, history of or
» Thrombophlebitis, history of or
» Toxic megacolon, history of or
» Ulcerative colitis, current or history of
(alosetron is **contraindicated** in patients with these conditions)
» Compliance risk
(alosetron is **contraindicated** in patients who are unable to understand or comply with the Patient-Physician Agreement)
» Hypersensitivity to alosetron or to any component of the product

Risk-benefit should be considered when the following medical problem exists:

Hepatic insufficiency, mild or moderate
(reduced metabolism, resulting in increased exposure that may increase risk of serious adverse events; caution should be used in these patients)

Side/Adverse Effects

The following side/adverse effects have been selected on the basis of their potential clinical significance (possible signs and symptoms in parentheses where appropriate)—not necessarily inclusive:

Constipation: Serious complications of constipation, including obstruction, perforation, impaction, toxic megacolon, secondary colonic ischemia, and death have been reported with the use of alosetron. The incidence of serious complications of constipation in women during IBS clinical trials was approximately 1 per 1,000 patients and 10% of patients on alosetron withdrew prematurely because of constipation. Patients at greater risk for complications of constipation may include elderly patients, debilitated patients, or patients taking additional medications that decrease gastrointestinal motility.

Ischemic Colitis: The cumulative incidence of ischemic colitis in women receiving alosetron was 2 per 1,000 patients (95% confidence interval

1 to 3) over 3 months and was 3 per 1,000 patients (95% confidence interval 1 to 4) over 6 months. Estimates of incidence of ischemic colitis in patients taking alosetron for longer than 6 months are not available.

Those indicating need for medical attention

Incidence more frequent

Constipation (difficulty having a bowel movement (stool))

Note: Alosetron should be discontinued immediately in patients who develop constipation. Patients should immediately report constipation that does not resolve after discontinuation of alosetron to their physician. Patients with resolved constipation should resume alosetron only on the advice of their treating physician.

Incidence rare

Ischemic colitis (abdominal pain, new or worsening; bloody diarrhea; rectal bleeding)

Note: Alosetron should be discontinued immediately in patients with signs of ischemic colitis. Patients with symptoms of ischemic colitis should immediately report them to their physician. Because this condition can be life-threatening, patients with signs and symptoms of ischemic colitis should be evaluated promptly and have appropriate diagnostic testing performed. Treatment with alosetron should not be resumed in patients who develop ischemic colitis.

Incidence not determined—Observed during clinical practice; estimates of frequency cannot be determined

Ileus (abdominal pain; severe constipation; severe vomiting); ***impaction*** (constipation; nausea; severe stomach pain; vomiting); ***obstruction, bowel*** (diarrhea; pain or cramping in abdomen; nausea and vomiting); ***perforation, bowel*** (abdominal or stomach cramps or pain; black, tarry stools; diarrhea; fever; severe vomiting, sometimes with blood); ***small bowel mesenteric ischemia*** (abdominal pain, usually after eating a meal; constipation; diarrhea; nausea; vomiting); ***ulceration, bowel*** (abdominal or stomach pain, cramping, or burning; black, tarry stools; constipation; diarrhea; vomiting of blood or material that looks like coffee grounds; nausea; heartburn; indigestion)

Those indicating need for medical attention only if they continue or are bothersome

Incidence less frequent or rare

Abdominal discomfort and pain (stomach pain; stomach soreness or discomfort); ***abdominal distention*** (swelling of abdominal or stomach area; full or bloated feeling; pressure in the stomach); ***gastrointestinal discomfort or pain; hemorrhoids*** (bleeding after defecation; uncomfortable swelling around anus); ***regurgitation and reflux*** (heartburn; vomiting)

Incidence not determined—Observed during clinical practice; estimates of frequency cannot be determined

Headache; skin rash

Overdose

For more information on the management of overdose or unintentional ingestion, **contact a poison control center** (see *Poison Control Center Listing*).

Clinical effects of overdose

The following effects have been selected on the basis of their potential clinical significance (possible signs and symptoms in parentheses where appropriate)—not necessarily inclusive:

Acute

Ataxia (shakiness and unsteady walk; clumsiness, unsteadiness, trembling, or other problems with muscle control or coordination); ***convulsions*** (seizures); ***labored respiration*** (difficult breathing); ***subdued behavior*** (withdrawn or socially detached behavior); ***tremors*** (shakiness)

Note: Toxicity has not been observed in humans. The above effects were observed in female mice given single oral doses of 15 mg/kg and in female rats given 60 mg/kg (30 and 240 times, respectively, the recommended human dose based on body surface area).

Treatment of overdose

There is no known specific antidote to alosetron. Treatment should be appropriate supportive care

Patient Consultation

Note: Alosetron is available through a restricted marketing program because of serious bowel side effects, including some deaths, seen with the use of this medication. Only physicians enrolled in the prescribing program for alosetron can write a prescription. Each prescription order must be original with a special sticker attached. No telephone, facsimile, or computerized prescriptions are permitted with this program.

As an aid to patient consultation, refer to *Advice for the Patient, Alosetron (Systemic).*

In providing consultation, consider emphasizing the following selected information (» = major clinical significance):

Before using this medication

» Conditions affecting use, especially:

Hypersensitivity to alosetron or any components of the product

Pregnancy—Alosetron should be used during pregnancy only if clearly needed.

FDA Pregnancy Category B

Breast-feeding—It is not known whether alosetron is distributed into human breast milk. Caution should be exercised when alosetron is administered to a nursing woman.

Use in children—Safety and efficacy have not been established.

Use in the elderly—People who are older or weak from illness may be at greater risk for serious constipation problems.

Pharmacogenetics—Safety and efficacy have not been established in men at any dose.

Other medications, especially fluvoxamine and other constipating medications.

Other medical problems, especially constipation, Crohn's disease, diverticulitis, excessive blood clotting, impaired intestinal circulation, ischemic colitis, severe hepatic impairment, thrombophlebitis, toxic megacolon, ulcerative colitis or intestinal adhesions, obstructions, perforations, or strictures

Proper use of this medication

» Read the Medication Guide before starting alosetron for the first time and each time you refill your alosetron prescription.

» Your doctor will ask you to sign a Patient-Physician Agreement after you have read the Medication Guide for the first time. Signing the agreement means that you understand the risks and benefits of alosetron therapy and that you have read and understand the Medication Guide.

» Do not start taking alosetron if constipated.

May be taken with or without food

» Proper dosing

Missed dose: If you miss a dose of this medicine, skip the missed dose and go back to your regular dosing schedule. Do not double doses.

Proper storage

Precautions while using this medication

» Regular visits to physician to check progress

» Immediately stop taking alosetron and contact your doctor if you become constipated or have symptoms of ischemic colitis such as new or worsening abdominal pain, bloody diarrhea, or blood in the stool.

» Immediately contact your doctor again if the constipation does not resolve after stopping alosetron.

» Do not start taking alosetron again unless your doctor tells you to do so.

» Stop taking alosetron and contact your doctor if alosetron does not adequately control irritable bowel syndrome (IBS) symptoms after 4 weeks of taking one 1-mg tablet two times a day.

Side/adverse effects

Signs of potential side effects, especially constipation, ischemic colitis, ileus, impaction, bowel obstruction, bowel perforation, small bowel mesenteric ischemia, or bowel ulceration

General Dosing Information

Alosetron is approved with marketing restrictions for safety reasons.

Only physicians who attest to the following qualifications and accept the following responsibilities, and on that basis enroll in the GlaxoSmithKline Prescribing Program for *Lotronex*, should prescribe alosetron.

To enroll, physicians must attest that they are able and willing to:

- diagnose and treat irritable bowel syndrome (IBS)
- diagnose and manage ischemic colitis
- diagnose and manage constipation and complications of constipation
- refer patients to specialists as needed
- understand the risks and benefits of treatment with alosetron for severe diarrhea-predominant IBS, including the information in the package insert, Medication Guide, and Patient-Physician Agreement
- educate patients on the risks and benefits of treatment with alosetron and obtain the patient's signature on the Patient-Physician Agreement form, sign it, place the original signed form in the patient's medical record, and give a copy to the patient

- report serious adverse events to GlaxoSmithKline at 1-888-825-5249 or to the Food and Drug Administration's MedWatch Program at 1-800-FDA-1088
- affix program stickers to **all** prescriptions for *Lotronex* (i.e., the original and all subsequent refill prescriptions). Stickers will be provided as part of the GlaxoSmithKline Prescribing Program for *Lotronex.* No telephone, facsimile, or computerized prescriptions are permitted with this program.

To enroll in the prescribing Program for *Lotronex*, physicians should call 1-888-825-5249 or visit www.LOTRONEX.com

Diet/Nutrition
May be taken with or without food

For treatment of adverse effects
Alosetron should be discontinued immediately in patients who develop constipation or symptoms of ischemic colitis. The patient should immediately report constipation or symptoms of ischemic colitis to their physician.

Do not resume alosetron therapy in patients who develop ischemic colitis.

Patients with resolved constipation should resume alosetron only on the advice of their treating physician.

Oral Dosage Forms

ALOSETRON HYDROCHLORIDE TABLETS

Usual adult dose
Bowel syndrome, irritable (treatment)—

Oral, 0.5 mg (base) twice daily for 4 weeks. If, after 4 weeks, the 0.5 mg (base) twice daily dosage is well tolerated but does not adequately control irritable bowel syndrome (IBS) symptoms, then the dosage can be increased to 1 mg (base) twice daily, the dose used in controlled clinical trials.

Note: Alosetron should be discontinued in patients who have not had adequate control of IBS symptoms after 4 weeks of treatment with 1 mg (base) twice a day.

Alosetron should be discontinued immediately in patients who develop constipation or symptoms of ischemic colitis. Alosetron therapy should not be resumed in patients who develop ischemic colitis.

Clinical trial and postmarketing experience suggest that debilitated patients or patients taking additional medication that decrease gastrointestinal motility may be at greater risk of serious complications of constipation. If alosetron is prescribed for these patients, appropriate caution and follow-up is advised.

It is not known if dosage adjustment is needed in patients with renal impairment.

Alosetron is extensively metabolized by the liver and increased exposure to alosetron is likely to occur in patients with hepatic impairment. Caution should be used in patients with mild to moderate hepatic impairment. Alosetron use is contraindicated in patients with severe hepatic impairment.

Usual pediatric dose
Safety and efficacy have not been established

Usual geriatric dose
See *Usual adult dose.* Note: Postmarketing experience suggests that elderly patients may be at greater risk for complications of constipation. If alosetron is prescribed for elderly patients, appropriate caution and follow-up is advised.

Strength(s) usually available
U.S.—

Note: Products containing alosetron were withdrawn from the U.S. market by GlaxoWellcome on request of the Food and Drug Administration in November 2000. The Food and Drug Administration approved a restricted marketing program in September 2002.

0.5 mg (base) (Rx) [*Lotronex* (lactose, anhydrous; magnesium stearate; microcrystalline cellulose; pregelatinized starch; hypromellose; titanium dioxide; triacetin)].

1 mg (base) (Rx) [*Lotronex* (lactose, anhydrous; magnesium stearate; microcrystalline cellulose; pregelatinized starch; hypromellose; titanium dioxide; triacetin; indigo carmine)].

Canada—

Not commercially available.

Packaging and storage
Store at 25 °C (77 °F); excursions permitted between 15 and 30 °C (59 and 86 °F).

Auxiliary labeling
- You should take this medication exactly as prescribed. Do not skip or discontinue unless directed.
- Tell your doctor about all medications you are taking, prescription and nonprescription.

Revised: 04/20/2006
Developed: 04/18/2000

ALPRAZOLAM—See *Benzodiazepines (Systemic)*

ALPROSTADIL Local

VA CLASSIFICATION (Primary/Secondary): HS200/CV500; GU900; DX900

Note: For information pertaining to the use of alprostadil for other indications, see *Alprostadil (Systemic).* When using phentolamine or papaverine also, see *Phentolamine (Intracavernosal)* and *Papaverine (Intracavernosal)* monographs for additional information.

Commonly used brand name(s): *Caverject; Edex; Muse; Prostin VR; Prostin VR Pediatric.*

Other commonly used names are PGE, and prostaglandin E_1.

Note: For a listing of dosage forms and brand names by country availability, see *Dosage Forms* section(s).

Category
Impotence therapy agent; diagnostic aid, erectile dysfunction; diagnostic aid, penile vasculature imaging.

Indications
Note: Bracketed information in the *Indications* section refers to uses that are not included in U.S. product labeling.

Accepted
Erectile dysfunction (treatment)—Alprostadil for Injection and alprostadil intraurethral suppositories are indicated and [Alprostadil Injection USP][1] is used to facilitate erections in men with erectile dysfunction. [Low doses of a three-drug combination of alprostadil, papaverine, and phentolamine as an injection are sometimes used to achieve a synergistic action.][1] Erectile dysfunction that is medication-induced or caused by endocrine problems, such as hypogonadism or hyper- or hypothyroidism, should be evaluated and appropriately treated before alprostadil treatment is considered.

Erectile dysfunction (diagnosis) or
Penile vasculature imaging (diagnostic adjunct)—Alprostadil for Injection is indicated and [Alprostadil Injection USP][1] is used by intracavernosal injection as an aid in the evaluation of penile vasculature, alone or prior to angiography, cavernosography, or cavernosometry.

Unaccepted
Use of alprostadil to enhance erections in men who are not impotent is not recommended because of the risk of priapism and permanent damage to penile tissues.

[1]Not included in Canadian product labeling.

Pharmacology/Pharmacokinetics

Physicochemical characteristics
Description: Suppository—Measures 1.4 millimeters (mm) in diameter and 3 mm or 6 mm in length and is located within the stem of its delivery device. A depressable button on the body of the device initiates the suppository's release from the stem.

Molecular weight—354.49.

pKa—6.3.

Mechanism of action/Effect
Alprostadil is a prostaglandin, specifically prostaglandin E_1, that is produced endogenously to relax vascular smooth muscle and cause vasodilation. The total prostaglandin concentration occurring naturally in human seminal fluid is 100 to 200 mg per mL and includes prostaglandins E_1 and E_2.

Impotence therapy agent—When administered by intracavernosal injection or as an intraurethral suppository, alprostadil acts locally to relax the trabecular smooth muscle of the corpora cavernosa and the cavernosal arteries. Swelling, elongation, and rigidity of the penis result when arterial blood rapidly flows into the corpus cavernosum to expand the lacunar spaces. The entrapped blood reduces the venous blood outflow as sinusoids compress against the tunica albuginea.

Adding papaverine and phentolamine to the alprostadil regimen synergistically increases arterial blood flow via separate mechanisms. Papaverine relaxes the sinusoid and the smooth muscle of the helicine arteries, while phentolamine relaxes arterial smooth muscle and blocks the alpha-adrenergic receptors that inhibit an erection.

Absorption
Suppository—When inserted immediately after urination, residual urine in the urethra dissolves the urethral suppository. Within 10 minutes, alprostadil absorption occurs from the urethral lining, passing to the corpora cavernosa via the corpus spongiosum.

Biotransformation
Local, rapid within the urethra, prostate, and corpus cavernosum; if any alprostadil is systemically absorbed, it is metabolized by a single pass through the lungs.

Onset of action
5 to 10 minutes.

Time to peak effect
Within 20 minutes.

Duration of action
Injection—1 to 3 hours; dose-related.

Suppository—30 to 60 minutes.

Precautions to Consider

Carcinogenicity
Studies have not been done.

Mutagenicity
Alprostadil is not mutagenic, according to results of the Ames test and alkaline elution assay.

Pregnancy/Reproduction
Fertility—In an *in vitro* study of human sperm, an alprostadil concentration of 400 mcg/mL had no effect on sperm motility and viability.

Sperm number, motility, and morphology were not affected in a study of dogs given intraurethral doses greater than 3000 mcg a day for 13 weeks, a dose corresponding to 3.5 times the maximum recommended human dose (MRHD) when adjusted for body surface area.

Pregnancy—Adequate and well-controlled studies in humans have not been done. Despite lack of reported problems, males using the suppositories who have sexual intercourse with pregnant women should use condoms for barrier protection to prevent maternal and fetal exposure to alprostadil. Since alprostadil's effects in early pregnancy are unknown, couples should use adequate contraception if the female partner could become pregnant.

Studies of female animals indirectly exposed to the intraurethral suppository or intracavernosal injection by mating with male animals have not been done; however, direct intravaginal administration of 4000 mcg a day in pregnant rabbits (a dose corresponding to 12.5 times the MRHD) did not cause harmful effects in their fetuses. Other direct routes of administration to females using doses much larger than those used for erectile dysfunction have shown embryo and maternal toxicities in pregnant animals.

Suppository—FDA Pregnancy Category C.

Note: An FDA category has not been assigned for the injection dosage forms.

Geriatrics
Studies in healthy men 56 years of age and older have shown results similar to those seen in younger patients, although some older men required slightly higher maintenance doses when arterial occlusive disease was present. Older patients are likely to differ from younger patients in the course and etiology of their erectile dysfunction.

Drug interactions and/or related problems
The following drug interactions and/or related problems have been selected on the basis of their potential clinical significance (possible mechanism in parentheses where appropriate)—not necessarily inclusive (» = major clinical significance):

Note: Combinations containing any of the following medications, depending on the amount present, may also interact with this medication.

Sympathomimetic agents, alpha-adrenergic, especially epinephrine, metaraminol, and phenylephrine
(sympathomimetic agents reverse the vasodilating effect of alprostadil; phenylephrine and epinephrine may be used to treat priapism or overdose)

Medical considerations/Contraindications
The medical considerations/contraindications included have been selected on the basis of their potential clinical significance (reasons given in parentheses where appropriate)—not necessarily inclusive (» = major clinical significance).

Except under special circumstances, this medication should not be used when the following medical problems exist:

» Abnormalities of the penis, such as
Anatomical deformity
Angulation of the penis
Cavernosal fibrosis
Hypospadia, severe
Peyronie's disease
Urethral stricture
(patients who have an anatomical deformity, angulation of the penis, cavernosal fibrosis, or Peyronie's disease are at increased risk of developing problems when using parenteral or intraurethral dosage forms of alprostadil)
(use of urethral suppositories is not recommended in patients with urethral stricture or severe hypospadia)

» Balanitis or
» Urethritis
(use of urethral suppositories is not recommended because infection or inflammation may worsen, and abrasions or minor bleeding from penis may be more likely to occur)

Risk-benefit should be considered when the following medical problems exist:

» Coagulation defects, severe
(risk of bleeding may be increased because alprostadil inhibits platelet aggregation; may be especially problematic when an improperly administered suppository or injection causes either a urethral abrasion or a contusion)

» Leukemia or
» Myeloma, multiple or
» Polycythemia or
» Priapism, history of or
» Sickle cell disease or
» Thrombocythemia
(increased risk of priapism, especially if hyperviscosity of blood or venous thrombosis results from these predisposing conditions)

Sensitivity to alprostadil

Patient monitoring
The following may be especially important in patient monitoring (other tests may be warranted in some patients, depending on condition; » = major clinical significance):

Palpation of penis
(recommended at regular intervals by both the patient and the physician to check for developing fibrosis or curvature)

Side/Adverse Effects
The following side/adverse effects have been selected on the basis of their potential clinical significance (possible signs and symptoms in parentheses where appropriate)—not necessarily inclusive:

Those indicating need for medical attention
Incidence rare

Hypotension (faintness; lightheadedness)—incidence of 2%, more likely for injectable doses greater than 20 mcg; ***prolonged erection*** (erection continuing for 4 to 6 hours)—incidence of 0.3%; ***priapism*** (erection continuing for more than 6 hours with severe and continuing pain of the penis)—incidence of less than 0.1%; ***testicular pain or edema*** (swelling of testes)—incidence of less than 1% with use of injection and incidence of 5% with use of suppositories

Note: *Prolonged erection* can resolve spontaneously; at times it will require treatment, especially if *priapism* develops. Priapism usually is due to excessive dosage.

For injection only;
Fibrosis of penis (curving of penis with pain during erection)—incidence 5.2%

Signs and symptoms of systemic absorption—associated with excessive doses

Dizziness; faintness; hypertension, reflexive; prostatic disorders (pelvic pain); ***rapid pulse; respiratory infection*** (flu-like symptoms)

Those indicating need for medical attention only if they continue or are bothersome
Incidence more frequent

Pain at site of administration; penile pain during erection—incidences of 32% with use of suppository and 11% with use of injection

For injection only;
Bleeding at injection site, transient

For suppositories only;
Bleeding or spotting from urethra—incidence of 5%; ***stinging of urethra***—incidence of 12%

Note: When males used the suppository dosage form, 5.8% of female partners reported vaginal itching or stinging. These symptoms may partially result from an associated lack of recent sexual activity for these women.

Incidence rare
For injection only
Ecchymosis or hematoma at site of injection (bruising or localized blood clot in penis at site of injection)—incidence of 3%, usually due to incorrect injection technique

Patient Consultation

As an aid to patient consultation, refer to *Advice for the Patient, Alprostadil (Local)* and, when also using papaverine and phentolamine, *Advice for the Patient, Phentolamine and Papaverine (Intracavernosal).*

In providing consultation, consider emphasizing the following selected information (» = major clinical significance):

Before using this medication

» Conditions affecting use, especially:
Sensitivity to alprostadil
Other medical problems, especially abnormalities of the penis, balanitis, severe coagulation defects, leukemia, multiple myeloma, polycythemia, history of priapism, sickle cell disease, thrombocythemia, or urethritis

Proper use of this medication

» Reading patient package insert, although patient information may not be available for all products

For injection dosage forms
» Recognizing that different injection products have different mixing procedures

Proper preparation
Washing hands with soap and water; wiping tops of bottles but not needle with alcohol swab, then discarding the swab; attaching needle to the syringe if needed without taking the cap off needle

To mix
For *Caverject*—Adding plunger to the syringe; mixing alprostadil powder for injection with 1 mL of the diluent, Bacteriostatic Water for Injection USP, included in the packaging as a prefilled syringe or separate vial
For *Edex*—Adding plunger to the syringe; mixing alprostadil powder for injection with 1.2 mL of the diluent, Sodium Chloride Injection USP, included in the packaging as a prefilled syringe
For *Prostin VR* or *Prostin VR Pediatric*—Getting exact mixing instructions from the physician or pharmacist, and following them carefully if told to mix two solutions

Proper administration
» Checking that final solution is clear before measuring dose; not using if injection is cloudy, colored, or contains solids
» Drawing the correct dose into syringe; removing air bubbles; rechecking dose
» After cleansing injection site with alcohol swab, giving injection by keeping needle at a 90-degree angle to the penis while inserting and injecting slowly over 5 to 10 seconds and directly into corpus cavernosum at sides or midshaft of penis; avoiding subcutaneous administration and injection into arteries or veins or injection at top or head of penis or at base of penis near the scrotum; if inadvertently injected subcutaneously (as evidenced by pain at injection site), stopping injection and withdrawing and repositioning needle
» After removing and recapping needle, applying gentle pressure at the injection site for 5 minutes to prevent bruising; massaging penis as directed by physician to distribute medication
» Varying site of injection
» Throwing away any unused mixture remaining in syringe; not reusing needles

For suppository dosage forms
Proper administration
» Urinating just prior to insertion; residual urine in urethra helps to dissolve the suppository
» Removing delivery device and cap from applicator stem; inserting delivery stem into urethra after lengthening and stretching penis upward; withdrawing and reinserting delivery device if discomfort or pulling sensation is felt
After depressing button to release suppository, holding delivery device still for 5 seconds, then rocking delivery device gently from side to side; after removing delivery device, inspecting the device for complete suppository release and, if needed, repeating process to insert any remaining suppository
Rolling penis between hands for 10 seconds to distribute the suppository within the walls of the urethra; continuing motion for relief if stinging occurs
(Sitting, standing, or walking for 10 minutes while erection is developing to promote blood flow to the penis for a proper erection)

For injection and suppository dosage forms
Effect begins in about 5 to 10 minutes; attempting intercourse within 10 to 30 minutes after administration. Erection may continue after ejaculation

» *Proper disposal*
For suppository delivery device—Replacing cap on device; placing in foil pouch; throwing away
For syringes and needles from injection—Using plastic case with locking device that comes with some packaging, or using a heavy plastic container; cutting or breaking needle before disposing; alternatively, giving to a health care professional for disposal

» Proper dosing
» Proper storage

Precautions while using this medication

» Not using medication with a penile implant unless advised by physician
» Compliance with therapy; importance of not exceeding prescribed dosage and frequency of use; risk of priapism, tissue ischemia, and permanent damage with overdose
» Telling physician immediately if erection persists longer than 4 hours or becomes painful

For injection dosage forms:
If bleeding occurs at injection site, applying pressure; checking with physician if bleeding persists

For suppository dosage forms:
» Using a condom when having sexual intercourse with a pregnant female in order to protect the mother and fetus from exposure to alprostadil
» Using contraception when having sexual intercourse with a female of reproductive age

Side/adverse effects

Signs of potential side effects, especially hypotension; prolonged erection; priapism; testicular pain or edema; fibrosis of penis (injection only)
(Signs and symptoms of systemic absorption, usually resulting from excessive doses, including dizziness, faintness, reflexive hypertension, prostatic disorders, rapid pulse, or respiratory infection)

General Dosing Information

There is no information on administering alprostadil injections or suppositories to patients who also use a penile implant.

Patients receiving alprostadil should be under the supervision of a physician experienced in its use and familiar with proper management of prolonged erection and priapism. Medical personnel usually give the first dose(s) in a clinical setting, titrating the dose carefully according to guidelines. For all responses during the titration process, patient should remain under clinical supervision until complete detumescence occurs. Maintenance doses are usually self-administered.

Dosage adjustment should be made carefully, based on the degree and duration of tumescence achieved with the previous dose. In general, patients with neurogenic erectile dysfunction may be more sensitive to the effects of intracavernosal vasodilators, and may require lower doses.

For injection dosage forms

In one clinical study of 579 patients having erectile dysfunction due to various etiologies, the doses after titration ranged between 5 and 20 mcg for 56% of patients; the mean maintenance dose was 17.8 mcg. In an uncontrolled self-injection study, the mean maintenance dose used after 6 months was 20.7 mcg. Specific to the cause of erectile dysfunction, mean maintenance doses of 12.4 mcg for psychogenic, 15.8 mcg for neurogenic, and 18.5 mcg for vasculogenic erectile dysfunction have been reported by the manufacturer. Other studies have shown similar results.

For treatment of erectile dysfunction, alprostadil is slowly injected (over 5 to 10 seconds) directly into the corpus cavernosum at the sides or midshaft of the penis. A characteristic give should be noticed as the needle penetrates the tunica albuginea and enters the corpus cavernosum. Proper injection technique is necessary to avoid injury. Alprostadil should not be injected into the urethra, arteries, veins, scrotum, upper- or bottom-most part of the penis (top or head of penis or area on the penile shaft near the scrotum), or into the dorsal area of the penis.

Injection sites should be alternated. After completion of the injection, pressure is applied to the injection site to prevent bleeding. The entire length of the corpus cavernosum on the side receiving the injection should be squeezed firmly to distribute the medication. To uniformly distribute the medication within both corpora cavernosa, the other side also can be squeezed.

A low-dose three-drug combination injection (alprostadil, papaverine, and phentolamine) may be more effective and, in some cases, less painful than alprostadil injected alone. A thorough evaluation of comparative studies is still needed. While the doses used in studies vary, an accepted strength is 17.6 mg papaverine, 0.6 mg phentolamine, and 5.9 mcg alprostadil per mL. The amount prescribed for self-injection is titrated according to individual response.

For suppository dosage form

In two placebo-controlled, parallel group studies of 1511 patients with erectile dysfunction, 996 patients (66%) completed the titration process; some patients could not complete the titration process because of accompanying penile pain. Of the 874 patients completing 3 months of treatment, doses for about 10, 20, 30, and 40% of patients were titrated to 125, 250, 500, and 1000 mcg, respectively.

Prior to inserting the intraurethral suppository, the patient should urinate; the residual urine remaining in the urethra will help dissolve the suppository.

The delivery device is inserted into the urethra with ease after the penis is first stretched lengthwise and pressed at top and bottom. After depressing a button to release the suppository into the urethra, the device is held upright and immobile for 5 seconds to help dissolve the suppository. Moving the device and the penis as a unit gently side to side helps to dissolve the suppository and enhances its release from the device. Whenever the patient feels an uncomfortable or pulling sensation, the delivery system should be removed and the procedure repeated if needed. Also, the procedure can be repeated to insert a partial suppository not fully dislodged from the device.

After the delivery device is withdrawn, the patient should roll his penis between his hands for 10 seconds to further distribute the suppository within the walls of the urethra and to ease any stinging sensation. Sitting, standing, or walking for 10 minutes while erection is developing promotes blood flow.

Use of contraception is recommended by the manufacturer if the patient engages in sexual intercourse with a female of reproductive age because potential effects on early pregnancy are not known. Using a condom is recommended when having sexual intercourse with a pregnant female; it provides a barrier and protects the mother and fetus from the effects of alprostadil.

For treatment of prolonged erection or priapism

A prolonged erection should be treated if it persists longer than 4 hours; priapism should be treated promptly. If tumescence is not reversed, interruption of blood flow may result in penile tissue ischemia and permanent tissue damage.

Treatment of adverse effects should be initiated by a physician trained in treating drug-induced tumescence. Depending on the severity, treatment may include:
- Application of ice packs to inner thigh, alternating between thighs, for no more than 10 minutes to shorten the duration of a prolonged erection.
- Aspiration of intracavernosal blood.
- Intracavernosal administration of an alpha-adrenergic agonist; phenylephrine is preferred to epinephrine. While monitoring blood pressure, an injection of 0.5 mg/mL
- *Phenylephrine Hydrochloride Injection USP* is given, followed by a second dose, if needed, in 15 minutes.
- Irrigation of the corpus cavernosum with 0.9% Sodium Chloride Irrigation USP or 20 mL of dilute solutions of phenylephrine (20 mg
- *Phenylephrine Hydrochloride Injection USP* in 500 mL of 0.9% Sodium Chloride Irrigation USP) or epinephrine (1 mL 1:1000
- *Epinephrine Injection USP* in 1 liter of 0.9% Sodium Chloride Irrigation USP), using a 19-gauge needle to remove clotted blood.
- Surgery (rarely needed).

Intraurethral Dosage Forms

ALPROSTADIL SUPPOSITORIES

Usual adult dose

Impotence therapy agent—

Initial: Intraurethral, 125 or 250 mcg a day, followed by dose adjustments in stepwise fashion on separate occasions as instructed by a physician.

Maintenance: Intraurethral, an individual dose established by a physician is inserted by the patient between ten and thirty minutes before intercourse. Dosage adjustments require physician consultation. No more than two suppositories should be used within twenty-four hours.

Strength(s) usually available

U.S.—

125 mcg (Rx) [*Muse* (polyethylene glycol)].
250 mcg (Rx) [*Muse* (polyethylene glycol)].
500 mcg (Rx) [*Muse* (polyethylene glycol)].
1000 mcg (Rx) [*Muse* (polyethylene glycol)].

Canada—

Not commercially available.

Note: The unit-dose packaging includes a suppository and delivery device; six unit-dose packages are contained in one box.

Packaging and storage

Store between 2 and 8 °C (36 and 46 °F), unless otherwise specified by manufacturer. Protect from freezing. May be stored between 15 and 30 °C (59 and 86 °F) for up to fourteen days.

Auxiliary labeling

- Refrigerate.
- Do not freeze.

Note

Include patient package insert (PPI) when dispensing.

Parenteral Dosage Forms

Note: Bracketed information in the *Dosage Forms* section refers to uses that are not included in U.S. product labeling.

ALPROSTADIL INJECTION USP

Usual adult dose

[Impotence therapy agent][1]—

For patients with erectile dysfunction of penile vasculogenic or mixed etiology—

Initial—Intracavernosal, 2.5 mcg, followed by dosage adjustments as supervised by a physician according to patient response. The proper dose will produce a full erection that begins within five to twenty minutes, and lasts for no more than one hour. If an erection lasts longer than one hour, the dose should be reduced. Further dosing depends on whether the first dose produced a partial or no erectile response.

For patients partially responding to the first dose, 7.5 mcg can be injected twenty-four hours or longer following the first dose. Until the proper dose is established, further doses scheduled on no more than two consecutive days (twenty-four hours apart) or three times a week can be increased by 5- to 10-mcg increments thereafter until an erection suitable for intercourse is achieved.

For patients not responding to the first dose, 5 mcg more can be injected within the hour, resulting in a total daily dose of 7.5 mcg. Until proper dose is established, further doses scheduled on no more than two consecutive days (twenty-four hours apart) or three times a week can be increased by 5- to 10-mcg increments.

Maintenance—Intracavernosal, an individual dose established by a physician is injected by the patient ten to thirty minutes before intended intercourse. Alprostadil should not be used more often than three times a week or on more than two consecutive days; at least twenty-four hours should elapse between doses. Dosing adjustments require physician-patient consultation.

Note: For patients using a three-drug regimen, 0.25 mL (17.6 mg papaverine, 0.6 mg phentolamine, and 5.9 mcg alprostadil per mL) is the usual dose achieved after completing the titration process.

For patients with erectile dysfunction of psychogenic or neurogenic etiology—

Initial—Intracavernosal, 1.25 mcg, followed by dosage adjustments as supervised by the physician according to patient response. The proper dose will produce a full erection that begins within five to twenty minutes, and lasts for no more than one hour. If an erection lasts longer than one hour, the dose should be reduced. Further dosing depends on whether the first dose produced a partial or no erectile response.

For patients partially responding to the first dose, 2.5 mcg can be injected twenty-four hours or longer following the first dose. Until the proper dose is established, further doses scheduled on no more than two consecutive days (twenty-four hours apart) or three times a week can be increased by 5-mcg increments thereafter until an erection suitable for intercourse is achieved.

For patients not responding to the first dose, 1.25 mcg more can be injected within the hour, resulting in a total daily dose of 2.5 mcg. Until proper dose is established, further doses scheduled on no more than two consecutive days (twenty-four hours apart) or three times a week can be increased by 5-mcg increments.

Maintenance—Intracavernosal, an individual dose established by a physician is injected by the patient ten to thirty minutes before intended intercourse. Alprostadil should not be used more often than three times a week or on more than two consecutive days; at least twenty-four hours should elapse between doses. Dosing adjustments require physician-patient consultation.

Note: For patients using a three-drug regimen, 0.12 mL (17.6 mg papaverine, 0.6 mg phentolamine, and 5.9 mcg alprostadil per mL) is the usual dose achieved after completing the titration process.

Diagnostic aid adjunct (penile vasculature imaging)[1] or
Diagnostic aid (erectile dysfunction)[1]—

Intracavernosal, the lowest single dose to cause an erection of firm rigidity.

Note: These patients are more likely to develop priapism that may require penile aspiration.

Usual adult prescribing limits

Impotence therapy agent—

60 mcg (0.06 mg) of alprostadil per dose.

Strength(s) usually available

U.S.—

500 mcg (0.5 mg) per mL (Rx) [*Prostin VR Pediatric* (dehydrated alcohol)].

Canada—

500 mcg (0.5 mg) per mL (Rx) [*Prostin VR* (dehydrated alcohol)].

Note: Distribution of *Prostin VR Pediatric* in the U.S. and *Prostin VR* in Canada is limited to acute-care facilities. As an alternative, compounding from bulk products is being done to make a multidose vial, single-use vials, or prefilled syringes; use of filters and preservatives should be considered as needed.

Packaging and storage

Store between 2 and 8 °C (36 and 46 °F), unless otherwise specified by manufacturer. Protect from freezing.

Preparation of dosage form

To prepare a solution of 20 mcg/mL of alprostadil, inject 1 mL of 500 mcg/mL Alprostadil Injection USP and 4 mL of 0.9% Sodium Chloride Injection USP into an empty vial to make a 100 mcg/mL alprostadil intermediate solution. After mixing, inject a 1-mL aliquot of 100 mcg/mL Alprostadil Injection USP into five 5-mL multidose vials. To make a 20 mcg/mL alprostadil solution, add 4 mL of 0.9% Sodium Chloride Injection USP to each vial. This multidose vial may be dispensed or separated into five 1-mL single-use vials or five 1-mL prefilled syringes. Other concentrations may be appropriate.

Stability

Stability after dilution is unknown.

Auxiliary labeling

- Refrigerate.
- Do not freeze.

ALPROSTADIL FOR INJECTION

Usual adult dose

Impotence therapy agent or
Diagnostic aid adjunct (penile vasculature imaging) or
Diagnostic aid (erectile dysfunction)—

See *Alprostadil Injection USP*.

Usual adult prescribing limits

Impotence therapy agent—

See *Alprostadil Injection USP*.

Strength(s) usually available

U.S.—

5 mcg (0.005 mg) (Rx) [*Caverject* (benzyl alcohol 8.4 mg; lactose 172 mg; sodium citrate 47 mg)].

10 mcg (0.01 mg) (Rx) [*Caverject* (benzyl alcohol 8.4 mg; lactose 172 mg; sodium citrate 47 mg); *Edex* (alpha-cyclodextrin; lactose anhydrous 56.3 mg)].

20 mcg (0.02 mg) (Rx) [*Caverject* (benzyl alcohol 8.4 mg; lactose 172 mg; sodium citrate 47 mg); *Edex* (alpha-cyclodextrin; lactose anhydrous 56.3 mg)].

40 mcg (0.04 mg) (Rx) [*Edex* (alpha-cyclodextrin; lactose anhydrous 56.3 mg)].

Canada—

10 mcg (0.01 mg) (Rx) [*Caverject* (benzyl alcohol 8.4 mg; lactose 172 mg; sodium citrate 47 mg)].

20 mcg (0.02 mg) (Rx) [*Caverject* (benzyl alcohol 8.4 mg; lactose 172 mg; sodium citrate 47 mg)].

Note: For the prefilled syringe—The 5-, 10-, and 20-mcg strengths of *Caverject* and all strengths of *Edex* include in their packaging a single-use vial containing sterile alprostadil powder, prefilled diluent syringe and needle (22-gauge, 1½-inch needle; or 27- or 30-gauge, ½-inch needle), separate syringe plunger, and alcohol swabs. Needle may or may not be attached to the syringe.

For the single-use vials—The 10- and 20-mcg strengths of *Caverject* include in their packaging a single-use vial containing sterile alprostadil powder, a vial of diluent, and a preassembled 3-cc, 27-gauge, ½-inch syringe.

For each product—Six unit-dose packages are contained in one box.

Packaging and storage

Store between 15 and 25 °C (59 and 77 °F). Protect from freezing.

Preparation of dosage form

Alprostadil for Injection is prepared by adding diluent to a vial of sterile alprostadil powder. The diluent is packaged as a prefilled syringe or in a separate vial. Solution is mixed, then drawn using the same syringe.

For *Caverject*: Add 1 mL of diluent (Bacteriostatic Water for Injection USP containing benzyl alcohol) to a vial of sterile alprostadil powder.

For *Edex*: Add 1.2 mL of diluent (Sodium Chloride Injection USP) to a vial of sterile alprostadil powder.

Stability

Stability of the medication after dilution is unknown. The manufacturer recommends that the reconstituted solution be used immediately.

Auxiliary labeling

- Store in a cool, dry place.
- Do not freeze.

Note

Include patient package insert (PPI) for Alprostadil for Injection when dispensing.

---

[1]Not included in Canadian product labeling.

Selected Bibliography

Bernard F, Lue TF. Self-administration in the pharmacological treatment of impotence. Drugs 1990; 39(3): 394-8.

Bennett AH, Carpenter AJ, Barada JH. An improved vasoactive drug combination for a pharmacological erection program. J Urol 1991 Dec; 146: 1564-5.

Revised: 09/26/2000

ALTEPLASE, RECOMBINANT—See *Thrombolytic Agents (Systemic)*

ALUMINUM CARBONATE, BASIC—See *Antacids (Oral-Local)*

ALUMINUM HYDROXIDE—See *Antacids (Oral-Local)*

AMANTADINE Systemic

VA CLASSIFICATION (Primary/Secondary): AM890/AU305; CN900

Commonly used brand name(s): *Endantadine; Gen-Amantadine; Symmetrel.*

Note: For a listing of dosage forms and brand names by country availability, see *Dosage Forms* section(s).

Category

Antiviral (systemic); antidyskinetic; antifatigue, specifically in multiple sclerosis.

Indications

Note: Bracketed information in the *Indications* section refers to uses that are not included in U.S. product labeling.

Accepted

Influenza A (prophylaxis and treatment)—Amantadine is indicated as a primary agent in the prophylaxis and treatment of respiratory tract infections caused by influenza A virus strains in high-risk patients (including those with pulmonary or cardiovascular disease, the elderly, and residents of nursing homes and other long-term care facilities who have chronic medical conditions), hospital ward contacts of high-risk patients, immunocompromised patients, those in critical public service positions (e.g., police, firefighters, medical personnel), in high-risk patients for whom the influenza vaccine is contraindicated, and patients with severe influenza A viral infections. It is effective against all strains of influenza A virus that have been tested to date, including Russian, Brazilian, Texan, London, and others. It may be given as chemoprophylaxis concurrently with inactivated influenza A virus vaccine until protective antibodies develop. However, it should be emphasized that vaccination of high-risk persons each year is the single most important measure for reducing the impact of influenza. No well-controlled studies have examined whether amantadine prevents complications of influenza A in high-risk persons.

Resistant strains of influenza A have been reported in patients receiving rimantadine; these resistant strains were also apparently transmitted to household contacts. Rimantadine has a similar chemical structure, spectrum of activity, and mechanism of action to amantadine, and drug-resistant strains of virus have cross-resistance to amantadine and rimantadine.

Extrapyramidal reactions, drug-induced (treatment) or
Parkinsonism (treatment)—Amantadine is indicated in the treatment of idiopathic parkinsonism (paralysis agitans; shaking palsy), postencephalitic parkinsonism, drug-induced extrapyramidal reactions, including parkinsonism syndrome, dystonia, and akathisia, symptomatic parkinsonism following injury to the nervous system caused by carbon monoxide intoxication, and parkinsonism associated with cerebral arteriosclerosis in the elderly.

Amantadine has been used alone or in combination with anticholinergic antiparkinson drugs and with levodopa to treat parkinsonism. The final therapeutic benefit seen with amantadine is significantly less than that seen with levodopa.

[Fatigue, multiple sclerosis-associated (treatment)][1]—Amantadine is used in the management of certain aspects of fatigue associated with multiple sclerosis, including lowered energy level, decreased sense of well-being, decreased perceived attention and memory, and diminished problem solving ability.

Unaccepted

Amantadine is not effective against other respiratory viral infections, including influenza B and parainfluenza.

Amantadine is not effective in the management of drug-induced tardive dyskinesia.

[1]Not included in Canadian product labeling.

Pharmacology/Pharmacokinetics

Physicochemical characteristics

Molecular weight—187.71.

Mechanism of action/Effect

Antiviral (systemic)—Not completely understood; amantadine appears to block the uncoating of influenza A virus and the release of viral nucleic acid into respiratory epithelial cells. May also affect early replicative phase of viruses that have already penetrated cells.

Antidyskinetic—Unknown; amantadine causes an increase in dopamine release in the animal brain. Probably increases release of dopamine and norepinephrine from central nerve terminals; also inhibits the reuptake of dopamine and norepinephrine.

Absorption

Rapidly and almost completely absorbed from gastrointestinal tract.

Distribution

Distributed into saliva, tear film, and nasal secretions; in animals, tissue (especially lung) concentrations are higher than serum concentrations. Crosses the placenta and blood-brain barrier; distributed into breast milk. Cerebral spinal fluid concentrations were 52% of corresponding plasma concentrations in one patient.

Vol_D—
- 4.4 ± 0.2 liters per kg (normal renal function).
- 5.1 ± 0.2 liters per kg (renal failure).

Protein binding

Normal renal function—Approximately 67%.
Hemodialysis patients—Approximately 59%.

Biotransformation

No appreciable metabolism. Small amounts of an acetyl metabolite identified.

Half-life

Normal renal function—11 to 15 hours.
Elderly patients—24 to 29 hours.
Renal function impairment, severe—7 to 10 days.
Hemodialysis—24 hours.

Onset of action

Antidyskinetic—Usually within 48 hours.

Time to peak serum concentration

2 to 4 hours (range, 1 to 8 hours); steady-state concentrations achieved within 2 to 3 days of daily administration.

Peak serum concentration

Approximately 0.3 mcg per mL; steady-state trough concentrations after 50, 200, and 300 mg per day are approximately 0.1, 0.3, and 0.6 mcg per mL, respectively. Plasma concentrations exceeding 1.0 mcg per mL are considered to be in the toxic range.

Elimination

Renal; > 90% excreted unchanged in urine by glomerular filtration and renal tubular secretion. Rate of excretion rapidly increased in acid urine.

In dialysis—Only small amounts (approximately 4%) removed from the blood by hemodialysis.

Precautions to Consider

Carcinogenicity

Long-term studies have not been done in animals.

Mutagenicity

Amantadine was negative for mutagenesis in the Ames test and in a mammalian cell line assay using Chinese hamster ovary cells, both with and without metabolic activation. No evidence of chromosomal damage was observed in either an *in vitro* test using lymphocyes (with and without metabolic activation) or in an *in vivo* mouse bone marrow micronucleus test at doses of 140 to 550 mg per kg of body weight (mg/kg) (estimated human equivalent doses of 11.7 to 45.8 mg per kg of body weight, based on body surface area conversion).

Pregnancy/Reproduction

Fertility—Slightly impaired fertility was observed in a three-litter reproduction study performed in rats at a dose of 32 mg/kg per day (estimated human equivalent dose of 4.5 mg/kg per day, based on body surface area conversion). However, no effects on fertility were seen at a dose of 10 mg/kg per day (estimated human equivalent dose of 1.4 mg/kg per day, based on body surface area conversion). No tests were perfomed using intermediate doses.

Failed fertility has been reported during human *in vitro* fertilization (IVF) when the sperm donor ingested amantadine 2 weeks prior to and during the IVF cycle.

Pregnancy—Amantadine crosses the placenta. However, adequate and well-controlled studies in humans have not been done. Both tetralogy of Fallot and tibial hemimelia (normal karyotype) occurred in an infant whose mother was exposed to 100 mg amantadine orally for 7 days during the sixth and seventh weeks of gestation. Cardiovascular maldevelopment (single ventricle with pulmonary atresia) has been associated with maternal exposure to 100 mg of amantadine daily administered during the first 2 weeks of pregnancy. Amantadine should be used during pregnancy only if the potential benefit justifies the potential risk to the fetus.

Studies in animals have shown that amantadine is embryotoxic and teratogenic in rats at doses of 50 mg/kg per day. No adverse effects were seen in rats at doses of 37 mg/kg per day. No embryotoxic or teratogenic effects were seen in rabbits that received 32 mg/kg per day (estimated human equivalent dose of 9.6 mg/kg per day, based on body surface area conversion).

FDA Pregnancy Category C.

Breast-feeding

Amantadine is distributed into breast milk. However, the effects of amantadine in neonates and infants are not known. Use is not recommended in nursing mothers.

Pediatrics

Appropriate studies on the relationship of age to the effects of amantadine have not been performed in neonates and infants up to one year of age. However, use of amantadine in children older than l year of age has not been shown to cause any pediatrics-specific problems that would limit its usefulness in children.

Geriatrics

Geriatric patients may exhibit increased sensitivity to the anticholinergic-like side effects of amantadine, including confusion. A dosage reduction of 50% (≤ 100 mg per day) appears to reduce the frequency of side effects without compromising antiviral prophylactic effectiveness. In addition, elderly patients are more likely to have an age-related decline in renal function, which may require a dosage reduction of greater than 50% in patients receiving amantadine, depending on the extent of renal dysfunction.

Dental

Prolonged use of amantadine may decrease or inhibit salivary flow, thus contributing to the development of caries, periodontal disease, oral candidiasis, and discomfort.

Drug interactions and/or related problems

The following drug interactions and/or related problems have been selected on the basis of their potential clinical significance (possible mechanism in parentheses where appropriate)—not necessarily inclusive (» = major clinical significance):

Note: Combinations containing any of the following medications, depending on the amount present, may also interact with this medication.

» Alcohol
(concurrent use with amantadine is not recommended since this may increase the potential for central nervous system (CNS) effects such as dizziness, lightheadedness, orthostatic hypotension, or confusion)

» Anticholinergics (see *Appendix II*), or other medications with anticholinergic activity, or
Antidepressants, tricyclic or
Antidyskinetics, other or
Antihistamines or
Phenothiazines
(concurrent use with amantadine may potentiate the anticholinergic-like side effects, especially those of confusion, hallucinations, and nightmares; dosage adjustments of these medications or of amantadine may be necessary; also, patients should be advised to report the occurrence of gastrointestinal problems promptly since paralytic ileus may occur with concurrent therapy)

Antidiarrheals, opioid- and anticholinergic-containing
(concurrent use with amantadine may potentiate the anticholinergic-like side effects; although significant interaction is unlikely with usual doses of opioid- and anticholinergic-containing antidiarrheal agents, significant interaction may occur if these medications are abused)

Carbidopa and levodopa combination or
Levodopa
(concurrent use with amantadine may result in increased efficacy of carbidopa and levodopa combination, and levodopa; however, concurrent use is not recommended if there is a history of psychosis)

» CNS stimulation-producing medications, other (see *Appendix II*)
(concurrent use with amantadine may result in additive CNS stimulation to excessive levels, which may cause unwanted effects such as nervousness, irritability, or insomnia, and possibly seizures or cardiac arrhythmias; close observation is recommended)

Hydrochlorothiazide and
Triamterene
(one or both of these drugs may reduce the renal clearance of amantadine, resulting in increased plasma concentrations and possible amantadine toxicity)

» Quinidine or
» Quinine or
» Trimethoprim and sulfamethoxazole
(concurrent use may impair renal clearance of amantadine, resulting in higher plasma concentrations)

Medical considerations/Contraindications

The medical considerations/contraindications included have been selected on the basis of their potential clinical significance (reasons given in parentheses where appropriate)—not necessarily inclusive (» = major clinical significance).

Risk-benefit should be considered when the following medical problems exist:

Eczematoid rash, recurrent, history of

» Edema, peripheral or
» Heart failure, congestive
(amantadine may cause congestive heart failure and peripheral edema; presumed to be due to redistribution of fluid, not a gain of body water)

» Epilepsy, history of, or other seizure disorders
(amantadine may cause increased seizure activity; it may be necessary to reduce the dosage by 50% [≤ 100 mg per day]; this appears to reduce the frequency of side effects without compromising antiviral prophylactic effectiveness)

Hypersensitivity to amantadine

Psychiatric disorders, history of or
Substance abuse, history of
(amantadine can exacerbate mental problems in patients with a history of these conditions)

Psychosis or severe psychoneurosis
(anticholinergic-like side effects of amantadine may result in confusion, hallucinations, and nightmares; it may be necessary to reduce the dosage by 50% [≤ 100 mg per day]; this appears to reduce the frequency of side effects without compromising antiviral prophylactic effectiveness)

» Renal function impairment
(since amantadine is not metabolized and is excreted primarily in the urine, toxic concentrations may accumulate in patients with impaired renal function; it may be necessary to reduce the dosage by 50% [≤ 100 mg per day in such patients]; this appears to reduce the frequency of side effects without compromising antiviral prophylactic effectiveness)

Patient monitoring

The following may be especially important in patient monitoring (other tests may be warranted in some patients, depending on condition; » = major clinical significance):

Seizure activity
(patients with a history of epilepsy or other seizure disorders should be monitored for an increase in seizure activity)

Side/Adverse Effects

Note: In controlled studies, side effects, including nausea, dizziness, insomnia, nervousness, and impaired concentration, were reported in 5 to 10% of young healthy adults taking the standard adult dosage of 200 mg per day. Side effects may diminish or cease after the first week of use. Serious, less frequent CNS side effects, such as confusion or seizures, have affected usually only elderly patients, and patients with renal disease, seizure disorders, or altered mental/behavioral conditions. Reducing the dosage by 50% (≤ 100 mg per day) appears to reduce the frequency of side effects without compromising antiviral prophylactic effectiveness.

A small number of suicide attempts, some of which have been fatal, have been reported in patients treated with amantadine. The incidence of suicide attempts is not known, and the pathophysiologic mechanism is not understood. Suicidal ideation as well as suicide attempts have been reported in patients with and without a prior history of psychiatric illness. Amantadine can exacerbate mental problems in patients with a history of psychiatric disorders or substance abuse.

Sporadic cases of possible neuroleptic malignant syndrome (NMS) have been reported in association with dose reduction or withdrawal of amantadine therapy.

The following side/adverse effects have been selected on the basis of their potential clinical significance (possible signs and symptoms in parentheses where appropriate)—not necessarily inclusive:

Those indicating need for medical attention

Incidence less frequent

Anticholinergic-like effects (blurred vision; confusion; difficult urination; hallucinations); ***orthostatic hypotension*** (fainting); ***peripheral edema*** (swelling of hands, feet, or lower legs)

Incidence rare

Amnesia (loss of memory); ***CNS toxicity*** (difficulty in coordination; mental depression; seizures); ***congestive heart failure*** (swelling of feet or lower legs; unexplained shortness of breath)—usually only with chronic therapy; ***corneal deposits or other visual disturbances*** (irritation and swelling of the eye; decreased vision or any change in vision); ***dyspnea*** (shortness of breath); ***hyperkinesia*** (increase in body movements); ***hypertension*** (increased blood pressure); ***leukopenia or neutropenia*** (fever, chills, or sore throat); ***psychosis*** (severe mood or mental changes); ***skin rash; slurred speech; suicidal ideation or attempts*** (thoughts of suicide or attempts at suicide)

Those indicating need for medical attention only if they continue or are bothersome

Incidence more frequent

CNS toxicity (agitation, anxiety, or nervousness; difficulty concentrating; dizziness or lightheadedness; headache; insomnia; irritability; nightmares); ***gastrointestinal disturbances*** (loss of appetite; nausea); ***livedo reticularis*** (purplish red, net-like, blotchy spots on skin)—usually only with chronic therapy

Incidence less frequent

Anticholinergic-like effects (constipation; dry mouth, nose, and throat)—especially in elderly patients, patients receiving higher doses, and patients with renal dysfunction; ***diarrhea; fatigue*** (unusual tiredness or weakness); ***headache; somnolence*** (drowsiness)

Incidence rare

Decreased libido (decrease in sexual desire); ***euphoria*** (false sense of well-being); ***vomiting; weakness***

Overdose

Overdose with amantadine has resulted in death. One gram is the lowest reported amount of amantadine resulting in lethal overdose.

For specific information on the agents used in the management of amantadine overdose, see:

- *Charcoal, Activated (Oral-Local)* monograph; and/or
- *Physostigmine (Systemic)* monograph.

For more information on the management of overdose or unintentional ingestion, **contact a Poison Control Center** (see *Poison Control Center Listing*).

Clinical effects of overdose

The following effects have been selected on the basis of their potential clinical significance (possible signs and symptoms in parentheses where appropriate)—not necessarily inclusive:

Symptoms of overdose

Adult respiratory distress syndrome (cyanosis; quick, shallow breathing; shortness of breath); ***arrhythmias, including malignant tachyarrhythmias; central nervous system effects*** (aggressive behavior; agitation; anxiety; ataxia; coma; confusion; delirium; depersonalization; disorientation; fear; gait abnormality; hallucinations; hyperkinesia; hypertonia; insomnia; lethargy; psychotic reactions; somnolence); ***hypertension; hyperthermia; pulmonary edema; renal function impairment; seizures***—may be exacerbated in patients with existing seizure disorders; ***status epilepticus; tachycardia*** (fast heartbeat)

Treatment of overdose

There is no specific antidote for the treatment of amantadine overdose.

To decrease absorption—

Gastric decontamination with activated charcoal; gastric lavage may be performed if the ingestion was very recent.

Vomiting should not be induced due to the risk of seizures after the overdose.

To enhance elimination—

Because the excretion rate of amantadine increases rapidly when the urine is acidic, urinary acidifiers may be used to increase the elimination of amantadine from the body.

Hemodialysis is not effective in removing significant amounts of amantadine from the body.

Specific treatment—

Slow, intravenous administration of physostigmine may be used to treat central nervous system toxicity. See the manufacturer's prescribing information or *Physostigmine (Systemic)* for specific guidelines for use of this product.

If necessary, appropriate antiarrhythmic, anticonvulsant, and antihypotensive therapy should be given. However, care should be exercised when administering adrenergic agents such as isoproterenol because the dopaminergic activity of amantadine has been reported to induce malignant arrhythmias. A sedative may be administered if hyperactivity should occur.

Monitoring—

Blood electrolytes, blood pressure, pulse, respiration, temperature, urine pH, and urinary output should be monitored. Electrocardiographic monitoring also may be required. Patients should be observed for the possible development of arrhythmias, hyperactivity, hypotension, and seizures.

Supportive care—

General supportive measures should be employed. If there is no record of recent voiding, catheterization should be done. Adequate hydration of the patient should be maintained; if necessary, fluids should be given intravenously.

Patients in whom intentional overdose is confirmed or suspected should be referred for psychiatric consultation.

Patient Consultation

As an aid to patient consultation, refer to *Advice for the Patient, Amantadine (Systemic)*.

In providing consultation, consider emphasizing the following selected information (» = major clinical significance):

Before using this medication

» Conditions affecting use, especially:

Hypersensitivity to amantadine

Pregnancy—Amantadine crosses the placenta

Breast-feeding—Amantadine is distributed into breast milk

Use in the elderly—Geriatric patients may exhibit increased sensitivity to the anticholinergic-like side effects of amantadine

Other medications, especially alcohol, anticholinergics or other medications with anticholinergic activity, other CNS stimulation-producing medications, quinidine, quinine, or trimethoprim and sulfamethoxazole

Other medical problems, especially congestive heart failure, peripheral edema, renal function impairment, seizure disorders, or a history of epilepsy

Proper use of this medication

» Proper storage

» Proper dosing

Missed dose: Taking as soon as possible; not taking if almost time for next dose; not doubling doses

For use as an antiviral

Receiving a flu shot if have not already done so

» Taking before exposure or as soon as possible after exposure

» Compliance with full course of therapy

» Importance of not missing doses and taking at evenly spaced times

Proper administration technique for oral liquid

For use as an antidyskinetic

» Not taking more medication than the amount prescribed; not missing doses

May require up to 2 weeks for full benefit

Precautions while using this medication

» Avoiding alcoholic beverages

» Caution if mental acuity or eyesight is impaired

Caution when getting up suddenly from a lying or sitting position

» Checking with physician immediately if thoughts of suicide occur

Possible dryness of mouth, nose, and throat; using sugarless candy or gum, ice, or saliva substitute for relief of dry mouth; checking with physician or dentist if dry mouth continues for more than 2 weeks

Possible appearance of livedo reticularis; gradual disappearance within 2 to 12 weeks after stopping medication

For use as an antiviral:

Checking with physician if no improvement within a few days

For use as an antidyskinetic:

» Resuming physical activities gradually as condition improves

Checking with physician if medication gradually loses its effectiveness

» Checking with physician before discontinuing medication; gradual dosage reduction may be necessary

Side/adverse effects

Signs of potential side effects, especially anticholinergic-like effects, orthostatic hypotension, peripheral edema, amnesia, CNS toxicity, congestive heart failure, corneal deposits or other visual disturbances, dyspnea, hyperkinesia, hypertension, leukopenia or neutropenia, psychosis, skin rash, slurred speech, and suicidal ideation or attempts

General Dosing Information

In controlled studies, side effects, including nausea, dizziness, insomnia, nervousness, and impaired concentration, were reported in 5 to 10% of young healthy adults taking the standard adult dosage of 200 mg per day. Data suggest that comparable protection may be provided by a daily prophylactic dosage of 100 mg, but with fewer side effects. No studies have been done comparing 100-mg and 200-mg doses for the treatment of influenza A infection.

Amantadine does not prevent the potentially serious bacterial infections which may begin with influenza-like symptoms or which may co-exist with or occur as complications during the course of influenza.

Patients receiving doses exceeding 200 mg per day should be observed closely for signs of increased incidence of side effects or toxicity. Monitoring of such patients for blood pressure, pulse, respiration, and temperature should be considered, especially for a few days following the increase in dose. Patients with active seizure disorders may be at increased risk for seizures while receiving amantadine.

Changing from once-a-day to twice-a-day administration may eliminate or reduce the severity of side effects such as lightheadedness, insomnia, and nausea.

If possible, plasma concentrations should be monitored in patients with end-stage renal disease since a single dose may provide adequate concentrations for as long as 7 to 10 days.

Some patients have attempted suicide by overdosing with amantadine; therefore, prescriptions should be written for the smallest quantity consistent with good patient management.

Sporadic cases of possible neuroleptic malignant syndrome (NMS) have been reported in association with dose reduction or withdrawal of amantadine therapy. Therefore, patients should be observed carefully when the dosage of amantadine is reduced abruptly or discontinued, especially if the patient is receiving neuroleptics. The early diagnosis of NMS is important for the appropriate management of these patients.

For use in the prophylaxis and treatment of influenza type A virus infection

Chemoprophylactic administration should be started in anticipation of contact with, or as soon as possible after exposure to, persons having influenza A virus infections. Administration should be continued for at least 10 days following exposure. In influenza epidemics, amantadine should be given daily during the epidemic (usually 6 to 8 weeks in most communities) or until active immunity can be expected from administration of inactivated influenza A virus vaccine. However, rimantadine, chemically similar to amantadine, has been reported to be ineffective when used prophylactically in household members while concurrently treating index cases for influenza A. This was apparently due to transmission of drug-resistant strains of the virus.

If administered concurrently with inactivated influenza A virus vaccine until protective antibodies develop, amantadine should be continued chemoprophylactically for 2 to 3 weeks after the vaccine has been administered. Amantadine may then be discontinued. However, since the vaccine is only 70 to 80% effective, more prolonged administration of amantadine may be beneficial in elderly or high-risk patients. If the vaccine is unavailable or contraindicated, amantadine should be administered for up to 90 days in cases of possible repeated or unknown exposure.

Treatment of the symptoms of influenza A virus infections should be started within 24 to 48 hours after their onset and should be continued for 48 hours after their disappearance. Cough may persist for several weeks.

For use in the treatment of parkinsonism

Patients initially benefiting from the continuous administration of amantadine may experience a decline in effectiveness after a few months. Effectiveness may be restored by increasing the dose to 300 mg daily or temporarily discontinuing amantadine therapy for several weeks, and then resuming it.

Patients who have concurrent serious illnesses or are receiving high doses of other antiparkinsonian medications may be started on 100 mg of amantadine once a day. After one to several weeks, the dose may be increased to 100 mg two times a day, if necessary. If response is still not optimal, patients may benefit from a further increase to 400 mg daily in divided doses.

The maximal therapeutic benefit to be obtained with amantadine is usually seen within 1 week.

Concurrent administration of anticholinergic antiparkinsonian medications or levodopa with amantadine may provide additional benefit, including reduction in fluctuations in improvement occurring with levodopa alone. If dosage reductions of levodopa are required because of side effects, the benefit lost by the reduction may be restored by the concurrent administration of amantadine.

If carbidopa and levodopa combination or levodopa is initially being administered concurrently with amantadine, the dose of amantadine should be maintained at 100 mg one or two times a day while the dose of carbidopa and levodopa combination, or levodopa is gradually increased to provide optimal benefit.

Patients who have drug-induced extrapyramidal reactions may be started on 100 mg of amantadine two times a day. If response is not optimal, dose may be increased to 300 mg daily in divided doses.

When amantadine is to be discontinued, dosage should be reduced gradually in order to prevent a sudden increase in parkinsonian symptoms.

For treatment of adverse effects

Neuroleptic malignant syndrome (NMS)—Recommended treatment consists of the following:

- Providing intensive symptomatic treatment and medical monitoring.
- Treating any concomitant serious medical problems for which specific treatments are available; dopamine agonists, such as bromocriptine, and muscle relaxants, such as dantrolene, have been used often in treating NMS; however, their effectiveness has not been demonstrated in controlled clinical trials.

Oral Dosage Forms

Note: Bracketed uses in the *Dosage Forms* section refer to categories of use and/or indications that are not included in U.S. product labeling.

AMANTADINE HYDROCHLORIDE CAPSULES USP

Usual adult and adolescent dose

Antiviral (systemic)—

Oral, 200 mg once a day; or 100 mg every twelve hours.

Oral, 100 mg one or two times a day.

Antidyskinetic—

In patients who are taking amantadine alone: Oral, 100 mg two times a day.

In patients taking high doses of other antiparkinson medications or who have serious associated medical illnesses: Oral, 100 mg once a day. After one to several weeks, the dose may be increased to 100 mg two times a day, if necessary.

Note: If patients are not responding optimally at a dose of 200 mg daily, the dose may be increased up to 400 mg daily in divided doses. However, close physician supervision is necessary for these patients.

Drug-induced extrapyramidal reactions—

Oral, 100 mg two times a day. The dose may be increased to 300 mg daily in divided doses, if necessary.

[Antifatigue, multiple sclerosis-associated][1]—

Oral, 200 mg once a day; or 100 mg two times a day.

Note: Adults with impaired renal function may require a reduction in dose as noted below. Elderly patients, and patients with seizure disorders or altered mental/behavioral conditions may require even further dose reductions.

Creatinine clearance (mL/min)/(mL/sec)	Dose
> 50/0.83	See *Usual adult and adolescent dose*
30–50/0.5–0.83	200 mg the first day, then 100 mg once a day
15–29/0.25–0.48	200 mg the first day, then 100 mg every other day
< 15/0.25	200 mg once every 7 days
Hemodialysis patients	200 mg once every 7 days

Usual adult prescribing limits

Antiviral (systemic)—

200 mg daily.

Antidyskinetic—

400 mg daily.

Usual pediatric dose

Antiviral (systemic)—

Neonates and infants up to 1 year of age: Safety and efficacy have not been established.

Children 1 to 9 years of age: Oral, 1.5 to 3 mg per kg of body weight every eight hours; or 2.2 to 4.4 mg per kg of body weight every twelve hours. Maximum daily dose should not exceed 150 mg.

Children 9 to 12 years of age: Oral, 100 mg every twelve hours.

Children 12 years of age and over: See *Usual adult and adolescent dose.*

Note: For children 10 years of age or older weighing less than 45 kg of body weight, it may be advisable to use a dosage of 2.2 mg per kg of body weight every twelve hours.

Some references recommend doses as low as 1.5 mg per kg of body weight every twelve hours in children 1 to 9 years of age.

Usual pediatric prescribing limits

Children 1 to 9 years of age: 150 mg daily.

Children 9 to 12 years of age: 200 mg daily.

Usual geriatric dose

Antiviral (systemic)—

Oral, 100 mg once a day.

Antidyskinetic—

Oral, 100 mg once a day to start, titrating the dose to 100 mg two or three times a day.

Drug-induced extrapyramidal symptoms—
See *Usual adult and adolescent dose.*

Note: A daily dose of amantadine exceeding 100 mg should be used with caution in persons 65 years of age or older for influenza prophylaxis or treatment. If the patient has any renal function impairment, the dose should be reduced further.

Strength(s) usually available

U.S.—
100 mg (Rx) [; GENERIC].

Canada—
100 mg (Rx) [*Endantadine; Gen-Amantadine; Symmetrel;* GENERIC].

Packaging and storage

Store below 40 °C (104 °F), preferably between 15 and 30 °C (59 and 86 °F), unless otherwise specified by manufacturer. Store in a tight container.

Auxiliary labeling

- May cause dizziness or blurred vision.
- Avoid alcoholic beverages.
- Continue medicine for full time of treatment (antiviral).

AMANTADINE HYDROCHLORIDE SYRUP USP

Usual adult and adolescent dose

See *Amantadine Hydrochloride Capsules USP.*

Usual adult prescribing limits

See *Amantadine Hydrochloride Capsules USP.*

Usual pediatric dose

See *Amantadine Hydrochloride Capsules USP.*

Usual geriatric dose

See *Amantadine Hydrochloride Capsules USP.*

Strength(s) usually available

U.S.—
50 mg per 5 mL (Rx) [*Symmetrel;* GENERIC].

Canada—
50 mg per 5 mL (Rx) [*Symmetrel*].

Packaging and storage

Store below 40 °C (104 °F), preferably between 15 and 30 °C (59 and 86 °F), unless otherwise specified by manufacturer. Store in a tight container. Protect from freezing.

Auxiliary labeling

- May cause dizziness or blurred vision.
- Avoid alcoholic beverages.
- Continue medicine for full time of treatment (antiviral).

Note

When dispensing, include a calibrated liquid-measuring device for antiviral use.

AMANTADINE HYDROCHLORIDE TABLETS

Usual adult and adolescent dose

See *Amantadine Hydrochloride Capsules USP.*

Usual adult prescribing limits

See *Amantadine Hydrochloride Capsules USP.*

Usual pediatric dose

See *Amantadine Hydrochloride Capsules USP.*

Usual geriatric dose

See *Amantadine Hydrochloride Capsules USP.*

Strength(s) usually available

U.S.—
100 mg (Rx) [*Symmetrel*].

Canada—
Not commercially available.

Packaging and storage

Store below 40 °C (104 °F), preferably between 15 and 30 °C (59 and 86 °F), unless otherwise specified by manufacturer. Store in a tight container.

Auxiliary labeling

- May cause dizziness or blurred vision.
- Avoid alcoholic beverages.
- Continue medicine for full time of treatment (antiviral).

[1]Not included in Canadian product labeling.

Revised: 05/21/2001

AMBENONIUM—See *Antimyasthenics (Systemic)*

AMCINONIDE—See *Corticosteroids (Topical)*

AMIFOSTINE Systemic

VA CLASSIFICATION (Primary): AN700

Commonly used brand name(s): *Ethyol.*

Note: For a listing of dosage forms and brand names by country availability, see *Dosage Forms* section(s).

Category

Antineoplastic adjunct; cytoprotective agent.

Indications

Accepted

Note: Bracketed information in the *Indications* section refers to uses that are not included in U.S. product labeling.

Nephrotoxicity, cisplatin-induced (prophylaxis)—Amifostine is indicated to reduce the cumulative renal toxicity associated with repeated administration of cisplatin in patients with advanced ovarian cancer, or [advanced solid tumors of non-germ cell origin.]

Xerostomia, radiation-induced (prophylaxis)—Amifostine is indicated to reduce the incidence of moderate to severe xerostomia in patients undergoing post-operative radiation treatment for head and neck cancer, where the radiation port includes a substantial portion of the parotid glands.

[Bone marrow toxicity, antineoplastic agent-induced (prophylaxis)]—Amifostine is indicated to reduce acute and cumulative hematologic toxicities associated with a cisplatin and cyclophosphamide (CP) regimen in patients with advanced solid tumors of non-germ cell origin. [Amifostine is also indicated to decrease bone marrow toxicity during treatment with high-dose cisplatin alone for head and neck carcinoma (Evidence rating: IIIC), cyclophosphamide alone for malignant lymphoma (Evidence rating: IIIC), carboplatin for NSCLC (Evidence rating: IIIC), and carboplatin plus radiation therapy for head and neck carcinoma (Evidence rating: IIIC).][1]

[Neurotoxicity, cisplatin-induced (prophylaxis)][1]—Amifostine is also indicated to decrease the frequency or severity of cisplatin-induced peripheral neuropathy (Evidence rating: IC) and ototoxicity (Evidence rating: IC).

Note: Because some animal data indicate a possible interference with antitumorigenic efficacy, use of amifostine in patients with potentially curable malignancies is not recommended except in the context of a clinical study. However, amifostine did not interfere with the efficacy of a CP regimen for ovarian carcinoma, a cisplatin plus vinblastine regimen for non-small cell lung carcinoma, or any of the other treatments mentioned above.

[Mucositis following chemotherapy][1]

[Mucositis following radiation therapy][1]—Amifostine is indicated to reduce the incidence of mucositis in patients receiving radiation therapy or radiation combined with chemotherapy.

[Myelodysplastic syndrome (treatment)][1]—Amifostine may be used for salvage treatment, as part of a combination regimen (e.g., erythropoietin, topotecan, etoposide, cytarabine), for the treatment of myelodysplastic syndromes (MDS). There was not a clear consensus by the USP medical experts. Some of the experts are hesitant about the use of amifostine and suggest that individual case factors (e.g., International Prognostic Scoring System [IPSS] risk group, patient characteristics, etc.) be considered when choosing an appropriate treatment.

Unaccepted

Amifostine should not be administered in patients receiving definitive radiotherapy, except in the context of a clinical trial, since there are insufficient data to exclude a tumor-protective effect in this setting. Although studies have been done, they were only with standard fractionated radiotherapy and only when less than or equal to 75% of both parotid glands were exposed to radiation. The effects of amifostine on the incidence of xerostomia and on toxicity in the setting of combined chemotherapy and radiotherapy and in the setting of accelerated and hyperfractionated therapy have not been systematically studied.

[1]Not included in Canadian product labeling.

Pharmacology/Pharmacokinetics

Physicochemical characteristics

Molecular weight—214.23.

Solubility—Freely soluble in water.

Mechanism of action/Effect

Amifostine is a prodrug that is metabolized by alkaline phosphatase to an active free thiol metabolite. The active thiol metabolite reduces cytotoxicity by binding to and detoxifying reactive metabolites of cisplatin and alkylating agents and by acting as a scavenger of free radicals that may develop in tissues exposed to cisplatin or radiation. These actions occur more readily in normal tissue than in tumors because of the greater phosphatase activity, higher pH, and better vascularity in normal tissue, resulting in selective protection of normal tissues.

Distribution

Measurable concentrations of the active free thiol metabolite have been found in bone marrow cells 5 to 8 minutes after intravenous administration.

Biotransformation

Amifostine is dephosphorylated by alkaline phosphatase in tissues primarily to the active free thiol metabolite and, subsequently, to a less active disulfide metabolite.

Half-life

Distribution—Less than 1 minute.

Elimination—Approximately 8 minutes; less than 10% of amifostine remains in the plasma 6 minutes after drug administration.

Elimination

Primarily via rapid metabolism and uptake into tissues. Within 1 hour after infusion of 740 to 910 mg per square meter of body surface area (mg/m^2) over 15 minutes or rapid intravenous injection of 150 mg/m^2 over 10 seconds, urinary recovery of unchanged amifostine, the disulfide metabolite, and the thiol metabolite accounts for only 0.69%, 2.22%, and 2.64%, respectively, of the dose.

Precautions to Consider

Cross-sensitivity and/or related problems

Patients sensitive to other aminothiol compounds also may be sensitive to amifostine.

Carcinogenicity

Long-term animal studies to evaluate the carcinogenic potential of amifostine have not been done. However, data from *in vitro* and *in vivo* studies indicate that amifostine may protect against the genotoxic effects of antineoplastic agents and the carcinogenic effects of radiation.

Mutagenicity

Amifostine demonstrated no mutagenic effects in the Ames test and in the mouse micronucleus test. However, the free thiol metabolite demonstrated mutagenic effects in the Ames test and in *in vitro* mouse studies. This metabolite demonstrated no mutagenic effects in the mouse micronucleus test and did not demonstrate clastogenicity in human lymphocytes. Data from *in vitro* and *in vivo* studies indicate that amifostine may protect against the mutagenic effects of chemotherapeutic agents.

Pregnancy/Reproduction

Pregnancy—Adequate and well-controlled studies in humans have not been done. However, the potential risks associated with the antineoplastic agent(s) that the patient will also be receiving must be considered. It is usually recommended that use of antineoplastics, especially combination chemotherapy, be avoided whenever possible, especially during the first trimester.

Amifostine is embryotoxic in rabbits at 60% of the recommended human dose based on body surface area. Amifostine also produces dose-dependent embryotoxicity, but not teratogenicity, in rats given doses higher than 200 mg per kg of body weight.

FDA Pregnancy Category C.

Breast-feeding

It is not known whether amifostine or its metabolites are distributed into breast milk. Breast-feeding is not recommended during treatment.

Pediatrics

Although there is limited experience with amifostine in pediatric patients, appropriate studies on the relationship of age to the effects of amifostine have not been performed in the pediatric population. Safety, efficacy, and dosage have not been established.

Geriatrics

Although appropriate studies on the relationship of age to the effects of amifostine have not been performed in the geriatric population, no geriatrics-specific problems have been documented to date. However, elderly patients are more likely to have age-related decreased hepatic, renal, or cardiac function, concomitant disease, or other drug therapy, which may require cautious dose selection. Safety of amifostine has not been established in elderly patients.

Drug interactions and/or related problems

The following drug interactions and/or related problems have been selected on the basis of their potential clinical significance (possible mechanism in parentheses where appropriate)—not necessarily inclusive (» = major clinical significance):

Note: Combinations containing any of the following medications, depending on the amount present, may also interact with this medication.

» Antihypertensives or

» Hypotension-producing medications, other (see *Appendix II*)
(amifostine may temporarily produce hypotension; antihypertensive or other potentially hypotension-producing medications should be discontinued 24 hours prior to amifostine administration; patients receiving antihypertensive therapy that cannot be discontinued temporarily should not receive amifostine)

Radiotherapy
(there are at present insufficient data to exclude a tumorprotective effect in this setting; amifostine should not be administered in patients receiving radiotherapy)

Laboratory value alterations

The following have been selected on the basis of their potential clinical significance (possible effect in parentheses where appropriate)—not necessarily inclusive (» = major clinical significance).

With physiology/laboratory test values

Calcium, serum
(concentrations may be decreased; however, clinically significant hypocalcemia is rare)

Medical considerations/Contraindications

The medical considerations/contraindications included have been selected on the basis of their potential clinical significance (reasons given in parentheses where appropriate)—not necessarily inclusive (» = major clinical significance).

Except under special circumstances, this medication should not be used when the following medical problem exists:

» Known sensitivity to aminothiol compounds

Risk-benefit should be considered when the following medical problems exist:

Cardiovascular conditions, preexisting, such as:
Arrhythmias or
Congestive heart failure or
Ischemic heart disease
(safety of amifostine has not been evaluated in patients with preexisting cardiovascular conditions)

Cerebrovascular conditions, preexisting, such as:
Stroke, history of, or
Transient ischemic attacks, history of
(safety of amifostine has not been evaluated in patients with preexisting cerebrovascular conditions)

» Dehydration or

» Hypotension
(amifostine may produce a temporary reduction in blood pressure; use of amifostine prior to correction of these conditions is not recommended; use with caution in patients in whom hypotension may have serious consequences)

Hypocalcemia, predisposition to
(caution and careful monitoring of calcium concentrations are recommended in patients predisposed to hypocalcemia [e.g., patients with nephrotic syndrome])

Nausea or
Vomiting, predisposition to
(use with caution in patients in whom nausea and vomiting may have serious consequences; antiemetic medication should be administered prior to and in conjunction with amifostine, especially if therapy is in combination with highly emetogenic chemotherapy; carefully monitor fluid balance)

Patient monitoring

The following may be especially important in patient monitoring (other tests may be warranted in some patients, depending on condition; » = major clinical significance):

» Blood pressure determinations
(recommended every 5 minutes during amifostine infusionwhen administered for prophylaxis of chemotherapy-induced nephrotox-

icity and at least before and immediately after the infusion when administered for prophylaxis of radiation-induced xerostomia)

Calcium, serum
(recommended in patients at risk for developing hypocalcemia, e.g., those with nephrotic syndrome or those receiving multiple doses of amifostine)

Fluid balance
(monitoring recommended in patients receiving highly emetogenic chemotherapy)

» Hypersensitivity reaction
(patients should be monitored prior to, during, and after amifostine administration for allergic manifestations including anaphylaxis and severe cutaneous reactions)

Side/Adverse Effects

Allergic reactions characterized by one or more of the following manifestations have been observed during or after amifostine administration: hypotension, fever, chills/rigors, dyspnea, hypoxia, chest tightness, cutaneous eruptions, urticaria and laryngeal edema. Rare anaphylactoid reactions and cardiac arrest have been reported. In case of an acute allergic reaction, amifostine should be immediately and permanently discontinued.

Severe cutaneous reactions have been reported with amifostine, particularly when given as a radioprotectant. Severe cutaneous hypersensitivity reactions reported may include erythema multiforme, exfoliative dermatitis, Stevens-Johnson syndrome, toxic epidermal necrolysis, toxodermia. Some cases of cutaneous hypersensitivity reactions have been fatal or have required hospitalization and/or discontinuance of therapy. The patient should be evaluated from a cutaneous standpoint before each dose of amifostine is administered. Cutaneous reactions must be differentiated from radiation-induced dermatitis and cutaneous reactions of other etiology. Amifostine should be permanently discontinued for serious or severe cutaneous reactions or for cutaneous reactions associated with fever or other constitutional symptoms not known to be due to another etiology. A dermatologic consultation and biopsy should be considered for reactions or mucosal lesions of unknown etiology appearing outside of the injection site or radiation port and for erythematous, edematous, or bullous lesions on the palms of the hand or soles of the feet. Amifostine administration should only be resumed at the physician's discretion based on medical judgement and appropriate dermatologic evaluation.

The following side/adverse effects have been selected on the basis of their potential clinical significance (possible signs and symptoms in parentheses where appropriate)—not necessarily inclusive:

Those indicating need for medical attention

Incidence more frequent

Allergic reactions (fainting or loss of consciousness; fast or irregular breathing; swelling of eyes or eyelids; trouble in breathing; tightness in chest; wheezing; skin rash; itching); ***cutaneous eruptions*** (red, scaly, swollen, or peeling areas of skin); ***hypotension*** (blurred vision; confusion; dizziness, faintness, or lightheadedness when getting up from a lying or sitting position suddenly; sweating; unusual tiredness or weakness)

Note: *Hypotension* usually occurs 14 minutes after the start of the infusion and lasts 5 to 15 minutes (mean 6 minutes). Hypotension, usually brief systolic and diastolic, has been associated with one or more of the following: apnea, dyspnea, hypoxia, tachycardia, bradycardia, extrasystoles, chest pain, myocardial ischemia and convulsion. Rare cases of renal failure, myocardial infarction, respiratory and cardiac arrest have been observed during or after hypotension.

Nausea and vomiting

Note: *Nausea* and *vomiting* may be severe. Administration of amifostine in addition to cisplatin plus cyclophosphamide increases the occurrence of severe nausea and vomiting on the day of infusion; in one clinical trial, the incidences of severe nausea and vomiting in amifostine-treated patients were almost double those in patients receiving only cisplatin plus cyclophosphamide. However, amifostine did not increase the occurrence of delayed cisplatin-induced nausea and vomiting.

Incidence rare

Atrial fibrillation/flutter (fast or irregular heartbeat; dizziness; fainting)—may sometimes be associated with hypotension or allergic reactions; ***hypocalcemia*** (burning or tingling sensation; muscle cramps); ***loss of consciousness, short term and reversible; seizures*** (convulsions; muscle spasm or jerking of all extremities; sudden loss of consciousness; loss of bladder control); ***supraventricular tachycardia*** (fainting; fast, pounding, or irregular heartbeat or pulse; palpitations)—may sometimes be associated with hypotension or allergic reactions; ***syncope*** (fainting)

Those indicating need for medical attention only if they continue or are bothersome

Incidence less frequent or rare

Fever; hypertension, transient (blurred vision; dizziness; nervousness; headache; pounding in the ears; slow or fast heartbeat); ***somnolence*** (sleepiness, severe); ***sneezing***

Those not indicating need for medical attention

Incidence less frequent or rare

Dizziness; feeling unusually warm or cold; flushing or redness of face or neck; hiccups

Overdose

For more information on the management of overdose, **contact a Poison Control Center** (see *Poison Control Center Listing*)

Clinical effects of overdose

Although overdose has not been reported, the most likely symptom of amifostine overdose is hypotension.

At higher doses of amifostine, anxiety and reversible urinary retention have occurred.

Treatment of overdose

Treatment of hypotension includes infusion of 0.9% sodium chloride injection along with supportive treatment.

Patient Consultation

As an aid to patient consultation, refer to *Advice for the Patient, Amifostine (Systemic).*

In providing consultation, consider emphasizing the following selected information (» = major clinical significance):

Before using this medication

» Conditions affecting use, especially:
Hypersensitivity to aminothiol compounds
Pregnancy—Risk/benefit considerations
Breast-feeding—Discontinuation of breast-feeding is recommended
Use in the elderly—Cautious dose selection; safety not established
Other medications, especially antihypertensives or hypotension-producing medications
Other medical problems, especially dehydration or hypotension

Proper use of this medication

» Proper dosing

Side/adverse effects

Signs of potential side effects, especially allergic reaction, cutaneous eruptions, hypotension, severe nausea and vomiting, atrial fibrillation/flutter, hypocalcemia, loss of consciousness, seizures, supraventricular tachycardia, and syncope.

General Dosing Information

Amifostine should be administered as an intravenous infusion over a period of 15 minutes, beginning 30 minutes prior to chemotherapy. Longer infusion times are associated with a higher occurrence of side effects.

Amifostine should be administered as an intravenous infusion over a period of 3 minutes, beginning 15 to 20 minutes prior to radiation therapy of the head and neck.

Patients should be adequately hydrated prior to amifostine infusion.

Because amifostine may cause severe nausea and vomiting, patients should receive antiemetic therapy that includes intravenous dexamethasone (20 mg) and a serotonin receptor antagonist before amifostine is administered. Other antiemetics may also be required, depending on the antineoplastic agents being given.

Because amifostine may cause temporary hypotension, patients should be adequately hydrated before it is administered. Patients should remain in the supine position, and their blood pressure should be monitored every 5 minutes during the infusion.Despite adequate hydration and positioning of the patient, hypotension may occur during or shortly after amifostine administration.

During and after amifostine infusion, care should be taken to monitor the blood pressure of patients whose antihypertensive medication has been interrupted since hypertension may be exacerbated by discontinuation of antihypertensive medication and other causes such as intravenous hydration.

For treatment of adverse effects
If systolic blood pressure decreases significantly from baseline, it is recommended that the amifostine infusion be interrupted. A significant decrease is defined as:
- Baseline systolic blood pressure (mm Hg) < 100—A reduction of 20 mm Hg.
- Baseline systolic blood pressure (mm Hg) 100 to 119—A reduction of 25 mm Hg.
- Baseline systolic blood pressure (mm Hg) 120 to 139—A reduction of 30 mm Hg.
- Baseline systolic blood pressure (mm Hg) 140 to 179—A reduction of 40 mm Hg.
- Baseline systolic blood pressure (mm Hg) ≥ 180—A reduction of 50 mm Hg.

Patients who require an interruption in the amifostine infusion should be placed in the Trendelenburg position and given an intravenous infusion of 0.9% sodium chloride injection through a separate line. If blood pressure returns to normal within 5 minutes and the patient is asymptomatic, the infusion may be resumed and the full dose of amifostine administered. If the blood pressure does not return to normal, the amifostine dose for subsequent courses should be 740 mg per square meter of body surface area.

If clinically significant hypocalcemia occurs, administration of calcium supplements may be necessary.

In the event of a serious allergic reaction such as anaphylaxis, epinephrine and other appropriate measures should be available for treatment.

The patient should be evaluated from a cutaneous standpoint before each dose of amifostine is administered. The patient should be carefully monitored for cutaneous eruptions during and after amifostine administration.

Cutaneous reactions must be differentiated from radiation-induced dermatitis and cutaneous reactions of other etiology. If a cutaneous reaction appears at a distance from the injection site or the irradiated areas and has no other etiology, the administration of amifostine should be discontinued. Consultation with a dermatologist and a biopsy should be considered.

Cutaneous reactions should be treated symptomatically. The medical decision to resume amifostine should be based on medical judgement and dermatologic evaluations. Amifostine should be stopped permanently in the presence of any cutaneous reaction considered to be erythema multiforme, toxic epidermal necrolysis, Stevens-Johnson syndrome, or exfoliative dermatitis, as well as any cutaneous reaction associated with fever or other general signs which cannot be attributed to some other etiology.

Parenteral Dosage Forms

Note: Bracketed uses in the *Dosage Forms* section refer to indications that are not included in U.S. product labeling.

AMIFOSTINE FOR INJECTION

Usual adult dose
Cisplatin-induced nephrotoxicity prophylaxis
[Antineoplastic agent-induced bone marrow toxicity prophylaxis]
[Cisplatin-induced neurotoxicity prophylaxis][1]—
Intravenous infusion (over fifteen minutes), 910 mg per square meter of body surface area once a day, beginning thirty minutes prior to cisplatin chemotherapy.

Note: If systolic blood pressure decreases significantly from baseline, it is recommended that the amifostine infusion be interrupted. If blood pressure returns to normal within five minutes and the patient is asymptomatic, the infusion may be resumed and the full dose of amifostine administered. If blood pressure does not return to normal, the dose for subsequent courses should be reduced to 740 mg per square meter of body surface area.

Radiation-induced xerostomia prophylaxis—
Intravenous infusion (over three minutes), 200 mg per square meter of body surface area once a day, beginning fifteen to thirty minutes prior to radiation therapy of the head and neck
[Mucositis, radiation therapy or radiation combined with chemotherapy induced][1]
Intravenous infusion, 300 mg per square meter of body surface area once a day prior to radiation treatment.
[Myelodysplastic syndromes][1]—
Patients have benefited from an intravenous bolus dose of 200 mg per square meter of body surface area (over 15 minutes), 3 times a week for 3 weeks, followed by a 2–week rest, in combination with other agents.

Usual adult prescribing limits
Doses larger than 1300 mg per square meter of body surface area per day have not been studied.

Usual pediatric dose
Safety, efficacy, and dosage have not been established.

Strength(s) usually available
U.S.—
500 mg (anhydrous) single-dose vial (Rx) [*Ethyol*].
Canada—
500 mg (anhydrous) single-dose vial (Rx) [*Ethyol*].

Packaging and storage
Store between 20 and 25 °C (68 and 77 °F).

Preparation of dosage form
Amifostine for injection is reconstituted by adding 9.7 mL of 0.9% sodium chloride injection, producing a solution containing 50 mg per mL. The injection should be further diluted with additional 0.9% sodium chloride injection for administration by intravenous infusion.

Stability
After reconstitution, the amifostine injection is stable for up to 5 hours at room temperature (25 °C [77 °F]) and for up to 24 hours in the refrigerator (2 to 8 °C [36 to 46 °F]). After further dilution to a concentration of between 5 and 40 mg per mL, the amifostine injection, when stored in a polyvinyl chloride (PVC) bag, is stable for up to 5 hours at room temperature and for up to 24 hours in the refrigerator. The reconstituted solution should not be used if it is turbid or contains a precipitate.

Incompatibilities
Amifostine for injection should not be mixed in solutions other than 0.9% sodium chloride injection or in 0.9% sodium chloride injections that contain other additives.

[1]Not included in Canadian product labeling.

Revised: 11/28/2005
Developed: 06/29/1998

AMIKACIN—See *Aminoglycosides (Systemic)*

AMILORIDE—See *Diuretics, Potassium-sparing (Systemic)*

AMILORIDE AND HYDROCHLOROTHIAZIDE—See *Diuretics, Potassium-sparing and Hydrochlorothiazide (Systemic)*

AMINOCAPROIC ACID Systemic

JAN: Epsilon-aminocaproic acid
VA CLASSIFICATION (Primary): BL116
Commonly used brand name(s): *Amicar*.
Note: For a listing of dosage forms and brand names by country availability, see *Dosage Forms* section(s).

Category
Antifibrinolytic; antihemorrhagic.

Indications
Note: Bracketed information in the *Indications* section refers to uses that are not included in U.S. product labeling.

Accepted
Hemorrhage, hyperfibrinolysis-induced (treatment)
Hemorrhage, postsurgical (prophylaxis and treatment)
[Hemorrhage, oral, in patients with hemophilia (treatment)] or
[Hemorrhage, following dental and oral surgery, in patients with hemophilia (prophylaxis and treatment)]—Aminocaproic acid is indicated for treatment of severe bleeding that may occur following heart surgery (with or without cardiac bypass procedures) and portacaval shunt, prostatectomy, or nephrectomy, and in association with hematologic disorders (such as aplastic anemia), abruptio placentae (with laboratory confirmation of hyperfibrinolysis), hepatic cirrhosis, neoplastic disease, and polycystic or neoplastic diseases of the genitourinary system.

[Aminocaproic acid is used in the management of hemophilic patients (i.e., patients with Factor VIII or Factor IX deficiency) who have oral mucosal bleeding, or are undergoing oral surgery, including tooth extractions or other dental surgical procedures. The medication prevents or decreases hemorrhaging in these patients and reduces the need for administration of clotting factors, particularly when desmopressin is also used.]

[Aminocaproic acid is also used to prevent intra- and postoperative hemorrhaging in patients with clotting defects other than hemophilia (including von Willebrand disease or deficiencies of factors other than Factor VIII or Factor IX).][1]

[Aminocaproic acid is used to treat severe hemorrhaging caused by thrombolytic agents (alteplase [tissue-type plasminogen activator, recombinant], anistreplase [anisoylated plasminogen-streptokinase activator complex], streptokinase, or urokinase). However, controlled studies to demonstrate its efficacy for this use have not been done in humans.][1]

[Hemorrhage, subarachnoid, recurrence (prophylaxis)]—Aminocaproic acid is used to prevent recurrence of subarachnoid hemorrhage, especially when surgery is delayed.

Note: In some patients receiving treatment for hemorrhaging, other emergency measures including transfusion of whole blood, fresh frozen plasma, specific clotting factors, or fibrinogen may be needed.

Aminocaproic acid is ineffective in bleeding caused by loss of vascular integrity; a definite clinical diagnosis or laboratory findings indicative of hyperfibrinolysis (hyperplasminemia) is essential prior to initiation of aminocaproic acid therapy. However, some conditions and laboratory findings suggestive of hyperfibrinolysis are also present in disseminated intravascular coagulation; differentiation between the two conditions is essential because aminocaproic acid may promote thrombus formation in patients with disseminated intravascular coagulation and must *not* be used unless heparin is administered concurrently. The following criteria may be useful in differential diagnosis:

Test	Primary Hyperfibrinolysis Results	Disseminated Intravascular Coagulation Results
Platelet count*	Normal	Decreased
Protamine para-coagulation test	Negative	Positive
Euglobulin clot lysis time	Decreased	Normal

*Following extracorporeal circulation (during cardiovascular surgery), decreased platelet count may not be useful for differentiating between primary hyperfibrinolysis and disseminated intravascular coagulation; the other criteria may be more useful in differential diagnosis in these patients.

[1]Not included in Canadian product labeling.

Pharmacology/Pharmacokinetics

Physicochemical characteristics

Molecular weight—131.17.

Mechanism of action/Effect

Aminocaproic acid competitively inhibits activation of plasminogen, thereby reducing conversion of plasminogen to plasmin (fibrinolysin), an enzyme that degrades fibrin clots as well as fibrinogen and other plasma proteins including the procoagulant factors V and VIII. Aminocaproic acid also directly inhibits plasmin activity, but higher doses are required than are needed to reduce plasmin formation. *In vitro*, the antifibrinolytic potency of aminocaproic acid is approximately one-fifth to one-tenth that of tranexamic acid.

Absorption

Absorbed rapidly following oral administration.

Protein binding

Does not appear to bind to plasma protein.

Half-life

Elimination—

Terminal, 2 hours.

Time to peak concentration

Within 2 hours following a single oral dose.

Therapeutic plasma concentration

For inhibition of systemic hyperfibrinolysis—130 mcg per mL (991 micromoles/L).

For prevention of recurrent subarachnoid hemorrhage—150 to 300 mcg per mL (1143 to 2287 micromoles/L).

Elimination

Renal. Excreted rapidly, mostly as unchanged drug.

Precautions to Consider

Pregnancy/Reproduction

Fertility—Studies in rodents have suggested an adverse effect on fertility, consistent with aminocaproic acid's antifibrinolytic activity.

Pregnancy—Aminocaproic acid should be given to a pregnant woman only if clearly needed.

Studies have not been done in humans.

Studies have not been done in animals.

Note: When aminocaproic acid is used topically as an oral rinse to control gingival bleeding in hemophilic patients during the first and second trimesters of pregnancy, the patient should be instructed not to swallow the syrup.

FDA Pregnancy Category C.

Breast-feeding

It is not known whether aminocaproic acid is distributed into breast milk. However, problems in humans have not been documented. Because many drugs are distributed in human milk, caution should be exercised when aminocaproic acid is administered to a nursing woman.

Pediatrics

Although studies on the relationship of age to the effects of aminocaproic acid have not been performed in the pediatric population, no pediatrics-specific problems attributed to aminocaproic acid have been documented to date. Safety and efficacy in pediatric patients have not been established.

Note: Aminocaproic acid injection contains 0.9% benzyl alcohol as a preservative. Benzyl alcohol has been associated with a fatal "gasping syndrome" in neonates characterized by central nervous system depression, metabolic acidosis, gasping respirations when neonates and low-birth neonates are exposed to high levels of benzyl alcohol found in the blood and urine. Additional symptoms may include gradual neurological deterioration, seizures, intracranial hemorrhage, hematologic abnormalities, skin breakdown, hepatic and renal failure, hypotension, bradycardia, and cardiovascular collapse.

Geriatrics

Although studies on the relationship of age to the effects of aminocaproic acid have not been performed in the geriatric population, no geriatrics-specific problems have been documented to date. However, elderly patients are more likely to have age-related renal function impairment, which may require dosage reduction in patients receiving aminocaproic acid.

Drug interactions and/or related problems

The following drug interactions and/or related problems have been selected on the basis of their potential clinical significance (possible mechanism in parentheses where appropriate)—not necessarily inclusive (» = major clinical significance):

Note: Combinations containing any of the following medications, depending on the amount present, may also interact with this medication.

Anti-inhibitor coagulant complex or
Factor IX complex
(although aminocaproic acid is often used in conjunction with clotting factor replacement for the perisurgical management of hemophilic patients, concurrent use may increase the risk of thrombotic complications; using aminocaproic acid as an oral rinse for oral surgical procedures and tooth extractions may minimize this complication; some hematologists recommend that administration of aminocaproic acid be delayed for 8 hours following injection of either of the clotting factor complexes)

Contraceptives, estrogen-containing, oral or
Estrogens
(concurrent use with aminocaproic acid may increase the potential for thrombus formation)

Thrombolytic agents
(the actions of aminocaproic acid and of thrombolytic agents [e.g., alteplase (tissue-type plasminogen activator, recombinant; tPA), anistreplase (anisoylated plasminogen-streptokinase activator complex; APSAC), streptokinase, or urokinase] are mutually antagonistic; although controlled studies to demonstrate its efficacy for this use have not been done in humans, aminocaproic acid may be useful in treating severe hemorrhage caused by a thrombolytic agent)

Medical considerations/Contraindications

The medical considerations/contraindications included have been selected on the basis of their potential clinical significance (reasons given in parentheses where appropriate)—not necessarily inclusive (» = major clinical significance).

Except under special circumstances, this medication should not be used when the following medical problem exists:

» Disseminated intravascular coagulation [DIC] without concomitant heparin
(must not be used in the presence of DIC without concomitant heparin)

» Intravascular clotting, active
(risk of serious, even fatal, thrombus formation)

Risk-benefit should be considered when the following medical problems exist:

Cardiac disease
(aminocaproic acid may cause hypotension and bradycardia, especially with rapid intravenous administration or if the patient is hypovolemic; also, endocardial hemorrhages and myocardial fat degeneration have been demonstrated in animals)

Hematuria of upper urinary tract origin
(risk of intrarenal obstruction secondary to clot retention in the renal pelvis and ureters)

Hepatic disease
(cause of bleeding may be more difficult to diagnose)

Renal disease
(medication may accumulate; reduction in dosage may be required; also, aminocaproic acid has caused acute renal failure in a few patients and kidney concretions in animals)

Sensitivity to aminocaproic acid

Thrombosis, predisposition to, or history of
(medication inhibits clot dissolution and may interfere with mechanisms for maintaining blood vessel patency)

Patient monitoring

The following may be especially important in patient monitoring (other tests may be warranted in some patients, depending on condition; » = major clinical significance):

» Creatine phosphokinase (CPK) levels
(these muscle enzymes may be elevated due to rare skeletal muscle weakness with necrosis of muscle fibers reported following prolonged administration; CPK levels should be monitored in patients on long-term therapy; administration should be stopped if rise in CPK noted)

Side/Adverse Effects

Note: Patients receiving this medication must be monitored for signs of thromboembolic complications.

The following side/adverse effects have been selected on the basis of their potential clinical significance (possible signs and symptoms in parentheses where appropriate)—not necessarily inclusive:

Those indicating need for medical attention

Incidence less frequent

Bladder obstruction caused by blood clot formation (decreased urination); ***decrease in blood pressure***—may reach hypotensive levels; ***dizziness; headache; myopathy*** (muscular pain or weakness, severe and continuing)—may be associated with necrosis of muscle fibers; ***renal failure*** (sudden decrease in amount of urine; swelling of face, fingers, feet, or lower legs; rapid weight gain); ***ringing or buzzing in ears; skin rash; slow or irregular heartbeat***—after too-rapid intravenous administration; ***stomach cramps; stuffy nose; thrombosis or thromboembolism*** (pains in chest, groin, or legs [especially calves]; severe, sudden headache; sudden and unexplained shortness of breath, slurred speech, vision changes, and/or weakness or numbness in arm or leg; sudden loss of coordination)—signs and symptoms depend on site of thrombus formation or embolization; ***unusual tiredness or weakness***—after too-rapid intravenous administration

Incidence rare

Rhabdomyolysis with myoglobinuria and renal failure

Those indicating need for medical attention only if they continue or are bothersome

Incidence less frequent

Diarrhea; dry ejaculation—reported in hemophilia patients receiving the medication in conjunction with dental surgery; symptom has resolved within 24 to 48 hours after cessation of treatment in all cases reported to date; ***nausea or vomiting; unusual menstrual discomfort***—caused by clotting of menstrual fluid; ***unusual tiredness***—with long-term use; ***watery eyes***

Patient Consultation

As an aid to patient consultation, refer to *Advice for the Patient, Antifibrinolytic Agents (Systemic).*

In providing consultation, consider emphasizing the following selected information (» = major clinical significance):

Before using this medication

» Conditions affecting use, especially:
Sensitivity to aminocaproic acid
Pregnancy—Should be used during pregnancy only if clearly needed
Breast-feeding—Caution should be exercised when administered to a nursing woman
Use in children—Aminocaproic acid injection contains benzyl alcohol which has been associated with "gasping syndrome" in neonates
Other medical problems, especially active intravascular clotting or disseminated intravascular coagulation without concomitant heparin

Proper use of this medication

» Importance of not using more or less medication than the amount prescribed

» Proper dosing
Missed dose: Taking as soon as possible, then returning to regular dosing schedule or doubling next dose

» Proper storage

Side/adverse effects

Signs and symptoms of potential side effects, especially bladder obstruction caused by blood clot formation, decrease in blood pressure, dizziness, headache, myopathy, renal failure, ringing or buzzing in ears, skin rash, slow or irregular heartbeat, stomach cramps, stuffy nose, thrombosis or thromboembolism, unusual tiredness or weakness, and rhabdomyolysis with myoglobinuria and renal failure

General Dosing Information

When aminocaproic acid is used during surgery, the bladder must first be freed of clots. Aminocaproic acid may accumulate in the clots and inhibit their dissolution.

A reduction in dosage may be required in patients with renal function impairment.

Aminocaproic acid therapy may be discontinued when there is evidence of cessation of bleeding or when laboratory determinations of fibrinolysis indicate that the medication is no longer required.

Aminocaproic acid syrup may be given as an oral rinse for the control of bleeding during dental and oral surgery in hemophilic patients.

For parenteral dosage forms only

Intravenous injection of the undiluted aminocaproic acid solution is not recommended.

Rapid intravenous administration may induce hypotension, bradycardia and/or arrhythmia and should be avoided.

To help minimize the possibility of thrombophlebitis, careful attention to the proper insertion of the needle and the fixing of its position is necessary before administration of this medication.

Oral Dosage Forms

Note: Bracketed uses in the *Dosage Forms* section refer to categories of use and/or indications that are not included in U.S. product labeling.

AMINOCAPROIC ACID SYRUP USP

Usual adult dose

Acute bleeding syndromes—
Oral, 5 grams the first hour, followed by 1 or 1.25 grams per hour for approximately eight hours or until the desired response is obtained.

Note: Following prostatic surgery, a lower dose of 6 grams in the first twenty-four hours may be sufficient, since aminocaproic acid is concentrated in the urine. Also, the lower dosage may reduce the risk of clot formation and subsequent obstruction in the bladder.

[Prevention and treatment of oral hemorrhage, including hemorrhage following dental surgery, in hemophilic patients]—
Oral, 75 mg per kg of body weight (up to 6 grams) immediately following surgery, then every six hours for seven to ten days.
Oral rinse, 5 mL (1.25 grams) swished for thirty seconds four times a day for seven to ten days; small quantities may be swallowed, except when used during the first and second trimesters of pregnancy. In children or unconscious patients, the syrup may be applied with an applicator.

Note: When aminocaproic acid is used, a single factor VIII infusion of 40 International Units per kg of body weight, or coagulation factor IX infusion of 60 International Units per kg of body weight prior to surgery is often enough for normal hemostasis. However, because of an increased risk of thrombotic complications when aminocaproic acid and Factor IX or anti-inhibitor coagulant complex are administered concurrently, some hematologists recommend that aminocaproic acid not be administered within eight hours of these clotting factor concentrates.

[Hemorrhage, subarachnoid, recurrence]—

To be administered following initial intravenous therapy: Oral, 36 grams per day (3 grams every two hours) until surgery is performed. If surgery is not performed, continue therapy with 3 grams every two hours for twenty-one days after the last bleeding episode. Dosage should then be reduced to 24 grams per day (2 grams every two hours) for three days, then to 12 grams per day (1 gram every two hours) for three days, prior to discontinuation of the medication.

Usual adult prescribing limits

[Hemorrhage, subarachnoid, recurrence]—36 grams per twenty-four hours.

Other indications—Up to 24 grams per twenty-four hours.

Usual pediatric dose

Acute bleeding syndromes—

Oral, 100 mg per kg of body weight or 3 grams per square meter of body surface the first hour, followed by 33.3 mg per kg of body weight or 1 gram per square meter of body surface per hour, not to exceed 18 grams per square meter of body surface in twenty-four hours.

[Prevention and treatment of oral hemorrhage, including hemorrhage following dental surgery, in hemophilic patients]—

See *Usual adult dose*.

Strength(s) usually available

U.S.—

250 mg per mL (1.25 grams per 5 mL) (Rx) [*Amicar* (methylparaben, 0.2%; propylparaben, 0.05%; edetate disodium, 0.3%; citric acid; flavorings; sodium saccharin; sorbitol)].

Canada—

250 mg per mL (1.25 grams per 5 mL) (Rx) [*Amicar* (potassium sorbate 0.2%; sodium benzoate 0.1%)].

Packaging and storage

Store below 40 °C (104 °F), preferably between 15 and 30 °C (59 and 86 °F), unless otherwise specified by manufacturer. Store in a tight container. Protect from freezing.

AMINOCAPROIC ACID TABLETS USP

Usual adult dose

See *Aminocaproic Acid Syrup USP*.

Usual adult prescribing limits

See *Aminocaproic Acid Syrup USP*.

Usual pediatric dose

See *Aminocaproic Acid Syrup USP*.

Strength(s) usually available

U.S.—

500 mg (Rx) [*Amicar* (magnesium stearate; stearic acid; povidone)].

Canada—

500 mg (Rx) [*Amicar*].

Packaging and storage

Store below 40 °C (104 °F), preferably between 15 and 30 °C (59 and 86 °F), unless otherwise specified by manufacturer. Store in a tight container.

Parenteral Dosage Forms

Note: Bracketed uses in the *Dosage Forms* section refer to categories of use and/or indications that are not included in U.S. product labeling.

AMINOCAPROIC ACID INJECTION USP

Usual adult dose

Acute bleeding syndromes—

Intravenous infusion, initially 4 to 5 grams administered over a period of one hour, followed by continuous infusion at the rate of 1 gram per hour for approximately eight hours or until the desired response is obtained.

Note: Following prostatic surgery, a lower dose of 6 grams in the first twenty-four hours may be sufficient, since aminocaproic acid is concentrated in the urine. Also, the lower dosage may reduce the risk of clot formation and subsequent obstruction in the bladder.

[Prevention and treatment of oral hemorrhage, including hemorrhage following dental surgery, in hemophilic patients]—

Intravenous infusion, 75 mg per kg of body weight (up to 6 grams) immediately following surgery, then every six hours for seven to ten days.

Note: When aminocaproic acid is used, a single factor VIII infusion of 40 International Units per kg of body weight or coagulation factor IX infusion of 60 International Units per kg of body weight prior to surgery is often enough for normal hemostasis. However, because of an increased risk of thrombotic complications when aminocaproic acid and Factor IX or anti-inhibitor coagulant complex are administered concurrently, some hematologists recommend that aminocaproic acid not be administered within eight hours of these clotting factor concentrates.

[Hemorrhage, subarachnoid, recurrence]—

Intravenous infusion, 36 grams per day (18 grams in 400 mL of 5% dextrose injection infused over each twelve-hour period) for ten days. Therapy is continued using orally administered aminocaproic acid.

Usual adult prescribing limits

[Hemorrhage, subarachnoid, recurrence]—36 grams per twenty-four hours.

Other indications—Up to 24 grams per twenty-four hours.

Usual pediatric dose

Note: Aminocaproic acid injection contain benzyl alcohol, which is not recommended for use in neonates. A fatal syndrome called "gasping syndrome" consisting of metabolic acidosis, central nervous system depression, respiratory problems, renal failure, hypotension, and possibly seizures and intracranial hemorrhage has been associated with the administration of benzyl alcohol to neonates.

Acute bleeding syndromes—

Intravenous infusion, initially 100 mg per kg of body weight or 3 grams per square meter of body surface over a period of one hour, followed by continuous infusion at the rate of 33.3 mg per kg of body weight or 1 gram per square meter of body surface per hour, not to exceed 18 grams per square meter of body surface in twenty-four hours.

[Prevention and treatment of oral hemorrhage, including hemorrhage following dental surgery, in hemophilic patients]—

See *Usual adult dose*.

Strength(s) usually available

U.S.—

250 mg per mL (Rx) [*Amicar* (0.9% benzyl alcohol as a preservative; water for injection; may contain hydrochloric acid to adjust pH); GENERIC (may contain benzyl alcohol—see labeling for individual product)].

Canada—

250 mg per mL (Rx) [*Amicar* (benzyl alcohol)].

Packaging and storage

Store below 40 °C (104 °F), preferably between 15 and 30 °C (59 and 86 °F), unless otherwise specified by manufacturer. Protect from freezing.

Preparation of dosage form

For administration by slow intravenous infusion, the 250-mg-per-mL concentration must be diluted with a compatible intravenous vehicle such as sterile water for injection, 0.9% sodium chloride injection, 5% dextrose injection, or lactated Ringer's injection. Although sterile water for injection is compatible for intravenous injection, the resultant solution is hypo–osmolar. Dilution with sterile water for injection is not recommended when the medication is used in patients with subarachnoid hemorrhage.

Revised: 11/02/2004

AMINOGLYCOSIDES Systemic

This monograph includes information on the following: 1) Amikacin; 2) Gentamicin; 3) Kanamycin†; 4) Neomycin†; 5) Netilmicin; 6) Streptomycin; 7) Tobramycin.

VA CLASSIFICATION (Primary/Secondary):

Amikacin—AM300
Gentamicin—AM300
Kanamycin—AM300
Neomycin—AM300
Netilmicin—AM300
Streptomycin—AM300/AM500
Tobramycin—AM300

Commonly used brand name(s): *Amikin*[1]; *G-Mycin*[2]; *Garamycin*[2]; *Jenamicin*[2]; *Kantrex*[3]; *Nebcin*[7]; *Netromycin*[5].

Note: For a listing of dosage forms and brand names by country availability, see *Dosage Forms* section(s).

†Not commercially available in Canada.

Category

Antibacterial (systemic)—Amikacin; Gentamicin; Kanamycin; Netilmicin; Streptomycin; Tobramycin.

Antibacterial (antimycobacterial)—Streptomycin

Indications

General Considerations

Aminoglycosides are indicated in the treatment of serious systemic infections for which less toxic antibacterials are ineffective or contraindicated. The spectrum of aminoglycosides covers aerobic gram-negative bacilli, and some gram-positive organisms. They are not active against anaerobic organisms.

The antibacterial activity of aminoglycosides against different strains of organisms varies among institutions and regions. However, aminoglycosides are generally active against most Enterobacteriaceae, including *Escherichia coli*, *Proteus mirabilis*, indole-positive *Proteus*, *Citrobacter*, *Enterobacter*, *Klebsiella*, *Providencia*, and *Serratia* species. *Acinetobacter* and *Pseudomonas* species are also usually susceptible. Although tobramycin is more potent *in vitro* against *Pseudomonas aeruginosa*, and gentamicin is more potent *in vitro* against *Serratia* species, neither has been shown to be more clinically effective than other aminoglycosides if the organism is susceptible. Aminoglycosides are used concurrently with antipseudomonal penicillins or certain cephalosporins in the treatment of serious *Pseudomonas aeruginosa* infections.

Bacterial resistance to gentamicin and tobramycin is very similar, although a few organisms resistant to gentamicin remain susceptible to tobramycin. The antibacterial activity and resistance pattern of netilmicin is very similar to those of both gentamicin and tobramycin, although there are a few gentamicin- and tobramycin-resistant strains that remain susceptible to netilmicin.

Amikacin is similar to gentamicin, tobramycin, and netilmicin in its spectrum of activity; however, amikacin has the advantage of not being inactivated by the same enzymes that render other aminoglycosides inactive against resistant organisms. Therefore, amikacin may remain active against strains of *Pseudomonas aeruginosa* that are resistant to tobramycin and netilmicin. Kanamycin use has declined over the years due to the emergence of a large number of resistant organisms. However, because of its disuse, resistance has decreased in some areas.

Streptomycin is used primarily as an antitubercular and is active against *Mycobacterium tuberculosis* and *M. bovis*. It is also considered the drug of choice for the treatment of infections caused by *Francisella tularensis* and *Yersinia pestis*, and is often used to treat *Brucella* infections. Because many other gram-negative bacilli are resistant, streptomycin is rarely used to treat those organisms.

Aminoglycosides are also active against *Staphylococcus aureus*, but are rarely used as sole therapy since other, less toxic, antibiotics are available. Amikacin, gentamicin, netilmicin, or tobramycin, administered concurrently with a penicillin, is synergistic against certain susceptible strains of *Enterococcus faecalis*. Streptomycin has been used, in combination with penicillin or vancomycin, in the treatment of endocarditis caused by *Enterococcus faecalis* or *S. viridans*.

Aminoglycosides are indicated for the treatment of serious infections caused by, or strongly suspected to be caused by, susceptible gram-negative bacilli. Some aminoglycosides, such as amikacin, gentamicin, and tobramycin, may also be given as an aerosol nebulization. This is usually as an adjunct to parenteral therapy in patients with cystic fibrosis with acute exacerbations of pulmonary infections. Aminoglycosides are used to treat central nervous system (CNS) infections mainly in neonates due to better penetration across the blood-brain barrier in this age group; gentamicin may also be given intrathecally to treat CNS infections in adults. Aminoglycosides are also used in combination with other antibacterials for a possible synergistic effect.

Accepted

Biliary tract infections (treatment)—Amikacin, gentamicin, kanamycin, netilmicin, and tobramycin are indicated in the treatment of biliary tract infections caused by susceptible organisms.

Bone and joint infections (treatment)—Amikacin, gentamicin, kanamycin, netilmicin, and tobramycin are indicated in the treatment of bone and joint infections caused by susceptible organisms.

Brucellosis (treatment)—Streptomycin is indicated in the treatment of brucellosis caused by *Brucella* species.

Central nervous system infections (including meningitis and ventriculitis) (treatment)—Amikacin, gentamicin, kanamycin, netilmicin, and tobramycin are indicated in the treatment of central nervous system infections caused by susceptible organisms.

Granuloma inguinale (treatment)—Streptomycin is indicated in the treatment of granuloma inguinale.

Intra-abdominal infections (including peritonitis)(treatment)—Amikacin, gentamicin, kanamycin, netilmicin, and tobramycin are indicated in the treatment of intra-abdominal infections caused by susceptible organisms.

Plague (treatment)—Streptomycin is indicated in the treatment of plague.

Pneumonia, gram-negative, bacterial (treatment)—Amikacin, gentamicin, kanamycin, netilmicin, and tobramycin are indicated in the treatment of bacterial, gram-negative pneumonia caused by susceptible organisms.

Septicemia, bacterial (treatment)—Amikacin, gentamicin, kanamycin, netilmicin, and tobramycin are indicated in the treatment of bacterial septicemia caused by susceptible organisms.

Skin and soft tissue infections (including burn wound infections) (treatment)—Amikacin, gentamicin, kanamycin, netilmicin, and tobramycin are indicated in the treatment of skin and soft tissue infections caused by susceptible organisms.

Tuberculosis (treatment)—Streptomycin is indicated in the treatment of tuberculosis.

Tularemia (treatment)—Streptomycin is indicated in the treatment of tularemia.

Urinary tract infections (recurrent complicated)(treatment)—Amikacin, gentamicin, kanamycin, netilmicin, and tobramycin are indicated in the treatment of recurrent complicated urinary tract infections caused by susceptible organisms.

Not all species or strains of a particular organism may be susceptible to a specific aminoglycoside.

Unaccepted

Aminoglycosides are not indicated routinely in the treatment of staphylococcal infections since less toxic antibacterials are available.

Aminoglycosides are not routinely indicated in the initial treatment of uncomplicated urinary tract infections unless the organism is resistant to other less toxic antibacterials.

Parenteral neomycin has been replaced by safer and more effective agents. **Because of its potential toxicity, parenteral use of neomycin is not recommended for any indication.**

Pharmacology/Pharmacokinetics

Physicochemical characteristics

Molecular weight—
- Amikacin sulfate: 781.75.
- Kanamycin sulfate: 582.58.
- Netilmicin sulfate: 1441.54.
- Tobramycin sulfate: 1425.39.

Mechanism of action/Effect

Actively transported across the bacterial cell membrane, irreversibly binds to one or more specific receptor proteins on the 30 S subunit of bacterial ribosomes, and interferes with an initiation complex between messenger RNA (mRNA) and the 30 S subunit. DNA may be misread, thus producing nonfunctional proteins; polyribosomes are split apart and are unable to synthesize protein. This results in accelerated aminoglycoside transport, increasing the disruption of bacterial cytoplasmic membranes, and eventual cell death.

Note: Aminoglycosides are bactericidal, while most other antibiotics that interfere with protein synthesis are bacteriostatic.

Absorption

All aminoglycosides—
- Intramuscular: Rapidly and completely absorbed after intramuscular administration.
- Local; topical: May also be absorbed in significant amounts from body surfaces (except urinary bladder) following local irrigation or topical application. Intraperitoneal and intrapleural administration results in rapid absorption.
- Oral: Poorly absorbed from intact gastrointestinal tract after oral administration, but may accumulate in patients with renal failure.

Distribution
All aminoglycosides—
Distributed to extracellular fluid, including serum, abscesses, ascitic, pericardial, pleural, synovial, lymphatic, and peritoneal fluids.
High concentrations found in urine.
Low concentrations found in bile, breast milk, aqueous humor, bronchial secretions, sputum, and cerebral spinal fluid (CSF). In adults, does not cross the blood-brain barrier (BBB) in therapeutically adequate concentrations. Small improvement in penetration with inflamed meninges. Higher levels are achieved in the CSF of newborns than in adults.
Crosses the placenta.
Also distributed to all body tissues, where aminoglycosides accumulate intracellularly.
High concentrations found in highly perfused organs, such as the liver, lungs, and especially, the kidneys, where aminoglycosides accumulate in the renal cortex.
Lower concentrations are seen in muscle, fat, and bone.

Vol_D—
Adults—0.26 L per kg (range, 0.20 to 0.40 L per kg).
Children—0.2 to 0.4 L per kg.
Neonates—
$<$ 1 week old, $<$ 1500 grams: up to 0.68 L per kg.
$<$ 1 week old, $>$ 1500 grams: up to 0.58 L per kg.
Cystic fibrosis patients—0.30 to 0.39 L per kg.

Protein binding
All aminoglycosides—Low (0 to 10%).

Biotransformation
Not metabolized.

Half-life
All aminoglycosides—
Distribution half-life:
5 to 15 minutes.
Elimination half-life:
Adults—
Normal renal function: 2 to 4 hours.
Impaired renal function: Varies with degree of dysfunction; up to 100 hours.
Cystic fibrosis patients: 1 to 2 hours.
Burn patients and febrile patients: May have a shorter half-life than average due to increased clearance of the drug.
Pediatrics—
Neonates: 5 to 8 hours.
Children: 2.5 to 4 hours.
Terminal half-life:
$>$ 100 hours (release of intracellularly bound aminoglycoside).

Time to peak concentration
All aminoglycosides—
Intramuscular: 0.5 to 1.5 hours.
Intravenous (time to post-distributional peak level): 30 minutes after end of 30 minute infusion, or 15 minutes after end of 1 hour infusion.

Time to peak bile concentration
Kanamycin—Approximately 6 hours (intramuscular).

Peak serum concentrations
In adults with normal renal function—
Amikacin:
Intramuscular—7.5 mg per kg of body weight (mg/kg): 21 mcg per mL.
Intravenous over 30 minutes—7.5 mg/kg: 38 mcg per mL.
Gentamicin:
Intramuscular or intravenous—1.5 mg/kg: 6 mcg per mL.
Kanamycin:
Intramuscular or intravenous—7.5 mg/kg: 22 mcg per mL.
Netilmicin:
Intramuscular—2 mg/kg: 5.5 mcg per mL.
Intravenous over 30 minutes—2 mg/kg: 11.8 mcg per mL.
Streptomycin:
Intramuscular—1 gram: 25 to 50 mcg per mL.
Tobramycin:
Intramuscular or intravenous—1 mg/kg: 4 mcg per mL.

Bile concentration
Netilmicin—10% of serum concentrations; may vary up to 25% of serum concentrations with abnormal hepatic function.

Elimination
Renal; excreted unchanged by glomerular filtration. 70 to 95% of aminoglycoside dose recovered in urine over 24 hours. Small amount excreted in bile.

Hemodialysis—Each 4 to 6 hour hemodialysis period decreases plasma aminoglycoside concentrations by up to 50%.
Peritoneal dialysis—Less effective than hemodialysis. Removes approximately 25% of a dose in 48 to 72 hours.

Precautions to Consider

Cross-sensitivity and/or related problems
Patients hypersensitive to one aminoglycoside may be hypersensitive to other aminoglycosides also.

Carcinogenicity/Mutagenicity/Tumorigenicity
Amikacin and kanamycin—Studies on the carcinogenic or mutagenic effects in humans have not been done.
Netilmicin—Lifetime carcinogenicity studies in mice and rats have not shown any netilmicin-related tumors. Mutagenicity studies in mice and rats have shown negative results.

Pregnancy/Reproduction
Fertility—*Amikacin:* Reproduction studies in rats and mice have not shown that amikacin causes impaired fertility.
Gentamicin: Reproduction studies in rats and rabbits have not shown that gentamicin causes impaired fertility.
Kanamycin: Studies in rats and rabbits have not shown that kanamycin causes impaired fertility.
Netilmicin: Reproduction studies in rats and rabbits given intramuscular and subcutaneous doses of netilmicin approximately 13 to 15 times the highest adult human dose have not shown that netilmicin impairs fertility or causes adverse effects on the fetus.

Pregnancy—All aminoglycosides cross the placenta, sometimes resulting in significant concentrations in the cord blood and/or amniotic fluid. Aminoglycosides may be nephrotoxic in the human fetus. In addition, some aminoglycosides (e.g., streptomycin, tobramycin) have been reported to cause total irreversible, bilateral congenital deafness in children whose mothers received aminoglycosides during pregnancy.

Amikacin: Adequate and well-controlled studies in humans have not been done. Amikacin has not been shown to cause adverse effects on the fetus, even though peak fetal serum concentrations of amikacin average approximately 16% of peak maternal serum concentrations and amikacin may be concentrated in the fetal kidneys. However, since other aminoglycosides have been reported to cause deafness in the fetus, risk-benefit must be carefully considered when this medication is required in life-threatening situations or in serious diseases for which other medications cannot be used or are ineffective.

FDA Pregnancy Category D.

Gentamicin: Adequate and well-controlled studies in humans have not been done. Since other aminoglycosides have been reported to cause deafness in the fetus, risk-benefit must be carefully considered when this medication is required in life-threatening situations or in serious diseases for which other medications cannot be used or are ineffective.

Studies in rats and rabbits have not shown that gentamicin causes adverse effects on the fetus.

FDA Pregnancy Category C.

Kanamycin: Fetal serum concentrations average approximately 16 to 50% of maternal serum concentrations. Adequate and well-controlled studies in humans have not been done.

Studies in rats and rabbits have not shown that kanamycin is teratogenic. However, studies in rats and guinea pigs given doses of 200 mg/kg daily have shown that kanamycin causes hearing impairment in the fetus.

FDA Pregnancy Category D.

Netilmicin: Netilmicin has been detected in cord blood and in the human fetus. Therefore, risk-benefit must be carefully considered when this medication is required in life-threatening situations or in serious diseases for which other medications cannot be used or are ineffective.

Studies in rats given netilmicin subcutaneously during pregnancy have not shown that netilmicin causes ototoxicity in the fetus.

FDA Pregnancy Category D.

Streptomycin: Adequate and well-controlled studies in humans have not been done. Fetal serum concentrations are usually less than 50% of maternal serum concentrations. Streptomycin has been shown to cause deafness in infants whose mothers received streptomycin during pregnancy. Therefore, risk-benefit must be carefully considered when this medication is required in life-threatening situations or in serious diseases for which other medications cannot be used or are ineffective.

FDA Pregnancy Category D.

Tobramycin: Tobramycin concentrates in the fetal kidneys and has been shown to cause total irreversible bilateral congenital deafness in the human fetus. Therefore, risk-benefit must be carefully considered when this medication is required in life-threatening situations or in serious diseases for which other medications cannot be used or are ineffective.

FDA Pregnancy Category D.

Breast-feeding

Aminoglycosides are excreted in breast milk in small but variable amounts (e.g., up to 18 mcg per mL for kanamycin). However, aminoglycosides are poorly absorbed from the gastrointestinal tract and problems in nursing infants have not been documented.

Pediatrics

All aminoglycosides—CNS depression, characterized by stupor, flaccidity, coma, or deep respiratory depression, has been reported in very young infants receiving streptomycin at doses that exceeded the maximum recommended amount. However, all aminoglycosides have this potential to cause neuromuscular blockade.

Amikacin, gentamicin, kanamycin, netilmicin, and tobramycin—These aminoglycosides should be used with caution in premature infants and neonates because of these patients' immature renal capability, which may result in prolonged elimination half-life and aminoglycoside-induced toxicity. Dosage adjustments may be required in pediatric patients. See also *Patient monitoring* and *General Dosing Information.*

Geriatrics

Because of their toxicity, aminoglycosides should be used with caution in elderly patients, only after less toxic alternatives have been considered and/or found ineffective. Elderly patients are more likely to have an age-related decrease in renal function. Recommended doses should not be exceeded, and the patient's renal function should be carefully monitored during therapy. Geriatric patients may require smaller daily doses of aminoglycosides in accordance with their increased age, decreased renal function, and, possibly, decreased weight. In addition, loss of hearing may result even in patients with normal renal function.

Drug interactions and/or related problems

The following drug interactions and/or related problems have been selected on the basis of their potential clinical significance (possible mechanism in parentheses where appropriate)—not necessarily inclusive (» = major clinical significance):

Note: Combinations containing any of the following medications, depending on the amount present, may also interact with this medication.

» Aminoglycosides, 2 or more concurrently or
» Capreomycin
(concurrent and/or sequential use of 2 or more aminoglycosides by any route or concurrent use of capreomycin with aminoglycosides should be avoided since the potential for ototoxicity, nephrotoxicity, and neuromuscular blockade may be increased; hearing loss may occur and may progress to deafness even after discontinuation of the drug; loss of hearing may be reversible, but usually is permanent; neuromuscular blockade may result in skeletal muscle weakness and respiratory depression or paralysis [apnea]. Also, concurrent use of 2 or more aminoglycosides may result in reduced bacterial uptake of each one since the medications compete for the same uptake mechanism)

Antimyasthenics
(concurrent use of medications with neuromuscular blocking action may antagonize the effect of antimyasthenics on skeletal muscle; temporary dosage adjustments of antimyasthenics may be necessary to control symptoms of myasthenia gravis during and following use of medications with neuromuscular blocking action)

Beta-lactam antibiotics
(aminoglycosides can be inactivated by many beta-lactam antibiotics [cephalosporins, penicillins] *in vitro* and *in vivo* in patients with significant renal failure. Degradation depends on the concentration of the beta-lactam, storage time, and temperature)

Indomethacin, intravenous
(when aminoglycosides are administered concurrently with intravenous indomethacin in the premature neonate, renal clearance of aminoglycosides may be decreased, leading to increased plasma concentrations, elimination half-lives, and risk of aminoglycoside toxicity; dosage adjustment of aminoglycosides based on measurement of plasma concentrations and/or evidence of toxicity may also be required)

» Methoxyflurane or
» Polymyxins, parenteral
(concurrent and/or sequential use of these medications with aminoglycosides should be avoided since the potential for nephrotoxicity and/or neuromuscular blockade may be increased; neuromuscular blockade may result in skeletal muscle weakness and respiratory depression or paralysis [apnea]; caution is also recommended when methoxyflurane or polymyxins are used concurrently with aminoglycosides during surgery or in the postoperative period)

» Nephrotoxic medications, other (See *Appendix II*) or
» Ototoxic medications, other (See *Appendix II*)
(concurrent or sequential use of these medications with aminoglycosides may increase the potential for ototoxicity or nephrotoxicity; hearing loss may occur and may progress to deafness even after discontinuation of the drug and may be reversible, but usually is permanent; serial audiometric function determinations may be required with concurrent or sequential use of other ototoxic antibacterials; renal function determinations may be required)
(vancomycin and aminoglycosides must often be administered concurrently in the prophylaxis of bacterial endocarditis, in the treatment of endocarditis caused by streptococci and *Corynebacteria* species, in the treatment of resistant staphylococcal infections, or in penicillin-allergic patients; appropriate monitoring will help to reduce the risk of nephrotoxicity or ototoxicity; renal function determinations, serum aminoglycoside and vancomycin concentrations, dosage reductions, and/or dosage interval adjustments, or alternate antibacterials, may be required)

» Neuromuscular blocking agents or medications with neuromuscular blocking activity, other
(concurrent use of medications with neuromuscular blocking activity, including halogenated hydrocarbon inhalation anesthetics, opioid analgesics, and massive transfusions with citrate anticoagulated blood, with aminoglycosides should be carefully monitored since neuromuscular blockade may be enhanced, resulting in skeletal muscle weakness and respiratory depression or paralysis [apnea]; caution is recommended when these medications and aminoglycosides are used concurrently during surgery or in the postoperative period, especially if there is a possibility of incomplete reversal of neuromuscular blockade postoperatively; treatment with anticholinesterase agents or calcium salts may help reverse the blockade)

Laboratory value alterations

The following have been selected on the basis of their potential clinical significance (possible effect in parentheses where appropriate)—not necessarily inclusive (» = major clinical significance).

With physiology/laboratory test values
Alanine aminotransferase (ALT [SGPT]), serum and
Alkaline phosphatase, serum and
Aspartate aminotransferase (AST [SGOT]), serum and
Bilirubin, serum and
Lactate dehydrogenase (LDH), serum
(values may be increased)

Blood urea nitrogen (BUN) and
Creatinine, serum
(concentrations may be increased)

Calcium, serum and
Magnesium, serum and
Potassium, serum and
Sodium, serum
(concentrations may be decreased)

Medical considerations/Contraindications

The medical considerations/contraindications included have been selected on the basis of their potential clinical significance (reasons given in parentheses where appropriate)—not necessarily inclusive (» = major clinical significance).

Risk-benefit should be considered when the following medical problems exist:

» Botulism, infant or
» Myasthenia gravis or
» Parkinsonism
(aminoglycosides may cause neuromuscular blockade, resulting in further skeletal muscle weakness)

Dehydration or
» Renal function impairment
(possible increased risk of toxicity because of elevated serum concentrations; it is recommended that aminoglycosides be administered in a reduced dosage at a fixed interval, or in normal doses at prolonged intervals, to patients with impaired renal function)

» Eighth-cranial-nerve impairment
(aminoglycosides may cause auditory and vestibular toxicity)

» Previous allergic reaction to aminoglycosides
(hypersensitivity reaction to one aminoglycoside may contraindicate the use of other aminoglycosides due to known cross-sensitivity)

Patient monitoring

The following may be especially important in patient monitoring (other tests may be warranted in some patients, depending on condition; » = major clinical significance):

For all aminoglycosides

» Aminoglycoside concentrations, serum
(aminoglycoside levels should be monitored in all patients, especially neonates and the elderly, even without renal function impairment, to avoid potentially toxic concentrations from accumulation of the drug; peak levels should be drawn 30 minutes after a 30-minute aminoglycoside infusion, to allow for drug distribution, and trough levels, immediately prior to the next dose; see *General Dosing Information*)

» Audiograms and
» Renal function determinations and
» Vestibular function determinations
(may be required prior to, periodically during, and following treatment in patients with pre-existing renal or eighth-cranial-nerve impairment; twice-weekly or weekly audiometric testing to detect high-frequency hearing loss in patients old enough to be tested and daily renal function determinations may be required in patients on high-dose therapy or therapy continued for longer than 10 days, especially if renal function is changing; renal function determinations may be required to detect nephrotoxicity and to help prevent severe neurotoxic reactions; audiometric testing may also be required with concurrent or sequential administration of other ototoxic antibacterials; if renal, vestibular, or auditory function impairment occurs, reduction in dose or discontinuation of the aminoglycoside may be required)

» Urinalyses
(may be required prior to treatment and daily during treatment to detect albumin, casts, and cells in the urine, as well as decreased specific gravity)

For streptomycin

» Caloric stimulation tests
(may also be required prior to, periodically during, and following prolonged therapy to detect vestibular toxicity)

Side/Adverse Effects

Note: Leg cramps, skin rash, fever, and seizures have been reported when gentamicin was administered concurrently by the systemic and intrathecal routes.

Endotoxin-like reactions (shaking, chills, and fever) have been reported with once-daily dosing regimens of gentamicin, possibly due to elevated endotoxin levels in certain brands of the drug.

Neuromuscular blockade, respiratory paralysis, ototoxicity, and nephrotoxicity may occur following local irrigation and following topical application of aminoglycosides during surgery.

Because of its potential toxicity, use of parenteral neomycin is not recommended.

The following side/adverse effects have been selected on the basis of their potential clinical significance (possible signs and symptoms in parentheses where appropriate)—not necessarily inclusive:

Those indicating need for medical attention

Incidence more frequent

Nephrotoxicity (greatly increased or decreased frequency of urination or amount of urine; increased thirst; loss of appetite; nausea; vomiting); ***neurotoxicity*** (muscle twitching; numbness; seizures; tingling); ***ototoxicity, auditory*** (any loss of hearing; ringing or buzzing, or a feeling of fullness in the ears); ***ototoxicity, vestibular*** (clumsiness; dizziness; nausea; vomiting; unsteadiness); ***peripheral neuritis*** (burning of face or mouth; numbness; tingling)—streptomycin only

Incidence less frequent

Hypersensitivity (skin itching, redness, rash, or swelling); ***optic neuritis*** (any loss of vision)—streptomycin only

Incidence rare

Endotoxin-like reaction (shaking; chills; fever)—gentamicin only; ***neuromuscular blockade*** (difficulty in breathing; drowsiness; weakness)

Those indicating possible ototoxicity, vestibular toxicity, or nephrotoxicity and the need for medical attention if they occur and/or progress after medication is discontinued

Any loss of hearing; clumsiness or unsteadiness; dizziness; greatly increased or decreased frequency of urination or amount of urine; increased thirst; loss of appetite; nausea or vomiting; ringing or buzzing or a feeling of fullness in the ears

Overdose

For more informatin on the management of overdose or unintentional ingestion, **contact a Poison Control Center** (See *Poison Control Center Listing*).

Treatment of overdose

Specific treatment—

Hemodialysis or peritoneal dialysis to remove aminoglycosides from the blood of patients with impaired renal function.

Anticholinesterase agents, calcium salts, or mechanical respiratory assistance to treat neuromuscular blockade, resulting in prolonged skeletal muscle weakness and respiratory depression or paralysis (apnea), that may occur when two or more aminoglycosides are given concurrently.

Supportive care—Since there is no specific antidote, treatment of aminoglycoside overdose or toxic reactions should be symptomatic and supportive. Patients in whom intentional overdose is known or suspected should be referred for psychiatric consultation.

Patient Consultation

As an aid to patient consultation, refer to *Advice for the Patient, Aminoglycosides (Systemic)*.

In providing consultation, consider emphasizing the following selected information (» = major clinical significance):

Before using this medication

» Conditions affecting use, especially:
Hypersensitivity to aminoglycosides
Pregnancy—May be nephrotoxic in the fetus or cause irreversible deafness in children whose mothers received aminoglycosides during pregnancy
Use in children—Premature infants and neonates may be more susceptible to renal toxicity because of their immature renal capability
Use in the elderly—Geriatric patients may be at risk of renal toxicity because of an age-related decrease in renal function
Other medications, especially 2 or more aminoglycosides used together, capreomycin, other nephrotoxic or ototoxic medications, or other neuromuscular blocking agents
Other medical problems, especially eighth-cranial-nerve impairment, infant botulism, myasthenia gravis, parkinsonism, or renal function impairment

Proper use of this medication

» Importance of receiving medication for full course of therapy and on regular schedule
» Proper dosing

Side/adverse effects

Signs of potential side effects, especially hypersensitivity, endotoxin-like reaction, optic neuritis, neuromuscular blockade, nephrotoxicity, neurotoxicity, auditory and vestibular ototoxicity, and peripheral neuritis, which are more likely to occur in children and the elderly

General Dosing Information

Because of the low therapeutic index of aminoglycosides, it is best to base dosage calculations on ideal body weight (IBW) as follows:
IBW (males) = 50 kg + (2.3 kg × inches over 5 feet)
IBW (females) = 45 kg + (2.3 kg × inches over 5 feet)

Serum concentrations should be monitored, especially in neonates and the elderly, even without renal function impairment, and in patients with impaired renal function to ensure adequate concentrations and to avoid potentially toxic concentrations. Therapeutic concentrations are shown in the table below. Prolonged peak (post-distributional) concentrations(measured 15 to 30 minutes after injection) and trough concentrations (measured immediately prior to the next dose) greater than those shown below should be avoided.

Drug	Therapeutic Concentration (mcg/mL)	Maximum Peak Concentration (mcg/mL)	Maximum Trough Concentration (mcg/mL)
Amikacin	15–25	35	5
Gentamicin	4–10	10	2
Kanamycin	15–30	30–35	5
Netilmicin	6–12	16	2
Streptomycin		20–25*	—
Tobramycin	4–10	10	2

*In patients with renal damage. Peak concentrations greater than 50 mcg per mL are associated with increased risk of toxicity.

Because of their larger volume of distribution and reduced renal development, infants may require larger doses, given at less frequent intervals, for achievement of therapeutic serum concentrations. Cystic fibrosis patients and burn patients may also require larger doses, but because they eliminate the aminoglycoside faster than average, the dosing interval may need to be decreased too.

Serum concentrations should be used whenever possible to monitor aminoglycoside therapy. Creatinine clearance may be used to help monitor therapy, in conjunction with serum levels. Creatinine clearance (in mL per minute) may be calculated as follows:

Adult males: Creatinine clearance
= [(140 − age) × (ideal body weight in kg)]/[72 × serum creatinine (mg per dL)]

Adult females: Creatinine clearance
= [(140 − age) × (ideal body weight in kg)]/[72 × serum creatinine (mg per dL)] × 0.85

Creatinine clearance may also be calculated in SI units (as mL per second) as follows:

Adult males: Creatinine clearance
= [(140 − age) × (ideal body weight in kg)]/[50 × serum creatinine (micromoles per L)]

Adult females: Creatinine clearance
= [(140 − age) × (ideal body weight in kg)]/[50 × serum creatinine (micromoles per L)] × 0.85

The following dosing chart by Sarubbi and Hull (Ann Intern Med 1978; 89: 612-8) may be used to provide the clinician with an *initial* loading dose and maintenance dosage regimen in adult patients. *Further dosage adjustments should be individualized and based on peak and trough serum concentrations,* which should be drawn after the third maintenance dose.

1. Select loading dose based on the patient's ideal body weight (in mg per kg of body weight [mg/kg]) to provide peak serum concentration in the range listed below for the desired aminoglycoside.

Aminoglycoside	Usual Loading Dose (mg/kg)	Expected Peak Serum Concentrations (mcg/mL)
Gentamicin Tobramycin	1.5 to 2	4 to 10
Amikacin Kanamycin	5 to 7.5	15 to 30
Netilmicin	1.3 to 3.25	4 to 12

2. Select maintenance dose (as percentage of chosen loading dose) to maintain peak serum concentrations indicated above according to desired dosing interval and the patient's corrected creatinine clearance. This chart is not applicable to neonates and children.

CrCl (mL/min)/(mL/sec)	Half-life (hours)	Percentage of Loading Dose Required for Dosage Interval Selected		
		8 hours	12 hours	24 hours
90/1.50	3.1	84%	—	—
80/1.33	3.4	80	91%	—
70/1.17	3.9	76	88	—
60/1.00	4.5	71	84	—
50/0.83	5.3	65	79	—
40/0.67	6.5	57	72	92%
30/0.50	8.4	48	63	86
25/0.42	9.9	43	57	81
20/0.33	11.9	37	50	75
17/0.28	13.6	33	46	70
15/0.25	15.1	31	42	67
12/0.20	17.9	27	37	61
10*/0.17*	20.4	24	34	56
7/0.12	25.9	19	28	47
5/0.08	31.5	16	23	41
2/0.03	46.8	11	16	30
0/0	69.3	8	11	21

*Dosing for patients with CrCl <10 mL/min (<0.17 mL/sec) should be assisted by measured serum levels.

After an initial full therapeutic loading dose, neonates or patients with impaired renal, vestibular, or auditory function may require (1) a reduction in the maintenance dose administered either (a) by administration of the usual dose at prolonged intervals or (b) by administration of reduced dose at fixed intervals or (2) discontinuation of the aminoglycoside. Since aminoglycosides are not metabolized and are excreted primarily in the urine, toxic concentrations may accumulate in patients with impaired renal function.

Because of the high concentrations of aminoglycosides in the urine and excretory system, patients should be well hydrated to prevent or minimize chemical irritation of the renal tubules. Therapeutic serum aminoglycoside levels are usually not needed to effectively treat urinary tract infections.

If a dose of this medication is missed, give it as soon as possible. However, if it is almost time for the next dose, skip the missed dose and go back to the regular dosing schedule. Do not double doses.

AMIKACIN

Additional Dosing Information

For initial dosing guidelines for patients with renal function impairment, see the Sarubbi and Hull nomogram in *General Dosing Information.*

Burn and certain other patients may require a dose of 5 to 7.5 mg per kg of body weight (mg/kg) every four to six hours because of the shorter half-life (1 to 1.5 hours) in these patients.

Amikacin sulfate injection may also be administered as an aerosol nebulization.

Parenteral Dosage Forms

AMIKACIN SULFATE INJECTION USP

Usual adult and adolescent dose

Antibacterial (systemic)—

Intramuscular or intravenous infusion, 5 mg per kg of body weight every eight hours; or 7.5 mg per kg of body weight every twelve hours for seven to ten days.

Note: Urinary tract infections, bacterial (uncomplicated)—Intramuscular or intravenous infusion, 250 mg every twelve hours.

Following hemodialysis, a supplemental dose of 3 to 5 mg per kg of body weight may be administered.

Usual adult prescribing limits

Up to 15 mg per kg of body weight daily, but not to exceed 1.5 grams daily for more than ten days.

Usual pediatric dose

Antibacterial (systemic)—

Intramuscular or intravenous infusion—

Premature neonates:

—Initially, 10 mg per kg of body weight, then 7.5 mg per kg of body weight every eighteen to twenty-four hours for seven to ten days.

Neonates:

—Initially, 10 mg per kg of body weight, then 7.5 mg per kg of body weight every twelve hours for seven to ten days.

Older infants and children:

See *Usual adult and adolescent dose.*

Strength(s) usually available

U.S.—

50 mg per mL (Rx) [*Amikin* (sodium bisulfite 0.13%); GENERIC].

250 mg per mL (Rx) [*Amikin* (sodium bisulfite 0.66%); GENERIC].

Canada—

250 mg per mL (Rx) [*Amikin* (sodium bisulfite 0.66%)].

Packaging and storage

Store below 40 °C (104 °F), preferably between 15 and 30 °C (59 and 86 °F), unless otherwise specified by manufacturer. Protect from freezing.

Preparation of dosage form

To prepare initial dilution for intravenous use, add the contents of each 500-mg vial to 100 to 200 mL of 0.9% sodium chloride injection, 5% dextrose injection, or other suitable diluent. The resulting solution should be administered slowly over a 30- to 60-minute period to help avoid neuromuscular blockade. Pediatric patients may require a proportionately smaller volume of diluent.

Stability

Intravenous infusions of amikacin retain their potency for 24 hours at room temperature at concentrations of 0.25 and 5 mg per mL in dextrose injection, dextrose and sodium chloride injection, 0.9% sodium chloride injection, lactated Ringer's injection, and other electrolyte-containing solutions (see manufacturer's package insert).

Intravenous infusions of amikacin retain their potency for 60 days at 4 °C (39 °F) at concentrations of 0.25 and 5 mg per mL in the above-listed diluents. When these solutions are then stored at 25 °C (77 °F), they retain their potency for 24 hours.

Intravenous infusions of amikacin retain their potency for 30 days when frozen at −15 °C (5 °F) at concentrations of 0.25 and 5 mg per mL in the above-listed diluents. When these solutions are thawed and stored at 25 °C (77 °F), they retain their potency for 24 hours.

Solutions may vary in color from colorless to light straw or very pale yellow; this variation does not affect their potency. Discard dark-colored solutions.

Incompatibilities

Extemporaneous admixtures of beta-lactam antibacterials (penicillins and cephalosporins) and aminoglycosides may result in substantial mutual inactivation. If these groups of antibacterials are administered concurrently, they should be administered in separate sites. Do not mix them in the same intravenous bag or bottle.

Amikacin is incompatible with amphotericin B, cephalothin sodium, nitrofurantoin sodium, sulfadiazine sodium, and tetracyclines (in some solutions).

Since complexes form with a number of other drugs also, extemporaneous admixtures with Amikacin Sulfate Injection USP are not recommended.

Additional information

Commercially available amikacin sulfate injection contains sodium bisulfite, an antioxidant, but no preservatives.

GENTAMICIN

Additional Dosing Information

Surgical, obstetrical, gynecological, or burn patients receiving gentamicin doses adjusted on the basis of serum concentrations may require less than the minimum recommended dose or greater than the maximum recommended dose of gentamicin because of wide interpatient variability. In patients receiving gentamicin intrathecally, CSF concentrations should also be monitored.

For initial dosing guidelines for patients with renal function impairment, see the Sarrubi and Hull nomogram in *General Dosing Information.*

Subcutaneous administration is not recommended and may be painful.

Commercially available gentamicin piggyback injections should be administered by intravenous infusion only.

Preservative-free gentamicin may also be administered directly into the subdural space, directly into the ventricles, or by means of an implanted reservoir.

Gentamicin sulfate injection may also be administered as an aerosol nebulization.

Parenteral Dosage Forms

Note: The dosing and dosage forms available are expressed in terms of gentamicin base.

GENTAMICIN SULFATE INJECTION USP

Usual adult and adolescent dose

Antibacterial (systemic)—

Intramuscular or intravenous infusion, 1 to 1.7 mg (base) per kg of body weight every eight hours for seven to ten days or more.

Note: Urinary tract infections, bacterial (uncomplicated)—Intramuscular or intravenous infusion:

Adults less than 60 kg of body weight—3 mg (base) per kg of body weight once a day; or 1.5 mg per kg of body weight every twelve hours.

Adults 60 kg of body weight and over—160 mg (base) once a day; or 80 mg every twelve hours.

Following hemodialysis, a supplemental dose of 1 to 1.7 mg (base) per kg of body weight may be administered, depending on the severity of the infection.

Intralumbar or intraventricular, 4 to 8 mg (base) once a day.

Usual adult prescribing limits

Up to 8 mg (base) per kg of body weight daily in severe, life-threatening infections.

Note: Doses up to 15 mg (base) per kg of body weight daily have been used in the treatment of intraocular infections.

Usual pediatric dose

Antibacterial (systemic)—

Intramuscular or intravenous infusion—

Premature or full-term neonates up to 1 week of age:

2.5 mg (base) per kg of body weight every twelve to twenty-four hours for seven to ten days or more.

Older neonates and infants:

2.5 mg (base) per kg of body weight every eight to sixteen hours for seven to ten days or more.

Children:

2 to 2.5 mg (base) per kg of body weight every eight hours for seven to ten days or more.

Note: The dosing interval of gentamicin in pediatric patients may vary from every four hours to every twenty-four hours, depending on the medical condition of the patient (cystic fibrosis, burns, renal dysfunction); serum levels must be monitored.

Following hemodialysis, a supplemental dose of 2 to 2.5 mg (base) per kg of body weight may be administered, depending on the severity of the infection.

Intralumbar or intraventricular—

Infants up to 3 months of age:

Dosage has not been established.

Infants and children 3 months of age and over:

1 to 2 mg (base) once a day.

Note: Doses up to 8 mg (base) daily have been used in infants with functioning ventricular shunts.

Strength(s) usually available

U.S.—

Intramuscular and intravenous:

10 mg per mL (base) (Rx) [*Garamycin;* GENERIC (sodium bisulfite 3.2 mg)].

40 mg per mL (base) (Rx) [*Garamycin; G-Mycin; Jenamicin;* GENERIC (sodium bisulfite 3.2 mg)].

Intrathecal:

2 mg per mL (base) (Rx) [*Garamycin*].

Canada—

Intramuscular and intravenous:

10 mg per mL (base) (Rx) [*Garamycin* (sodium bisulfite)].

40 mg per mL (base) (Rx) [*Garamycin* (sodium bisulfite)].

Packaging and storage

Store below 40 °C (104 °F), preferably between 15 and 30 °C (59 and 86 °F), unless otherwise specified by manufacturer. Protect from freezing.

Preparation of dosage form

Intravenous—To prepare initial dilution for intravenous use, add each dose to 50 to 200 mL of 0.9% sodium chloride injection or 5% dextrose injection to provide a concentration not exceeding 1 mg (base) per mL (0.1%). The resulting solution should be administered slowly over a 30- to 60-minute period to help decrease the chance of neuromuscular blockade. Pediatric patients may require a proportionately smaller volume of diluent.

Intralumbar and/or intraventricular (2 mg per mL)—To prepare initial dilution for intralumbar use, each dose should be drawn up into a 5- or 10-mL sterile syringe. Following lumbar puncture and the removal of a specimen of cerebrospinal fluid (CSF) for laboratory analysis, the syringe containing gentamicin is inserted into the hub of the spinal needle. A quantity of CSF equal to approximately 10% of the total estimated CSF volume is allowed to flow into the syringe and mix with the gentamicin. The resulting solution should be administered over a 3- to 5-minute period with the bevel of the spinal needle directed upward. Gentamicin may also be diluted with sodium chloride injection (without preservatives) if the CSF is grossly purulent or unobtainable. Since the 2-mg-per-mL concentration contains no preservatives, it should be used promptly after being opened; unused portions should be discarded.

Stability

Do not use if injection is discolored or contains a precipitate.

Incompatibilities

Extemporaneous admixtures of beta-lactam antibacterials (penicillins and cephalosporins) and aminoglycosides may result in substantial mutual inactivation. If these groups of antibacterials are administered concurrently, they should be administered in separate sites. Do not mix them in the same intravenous bag or bottle.

Since complexes form with a number of other drugs also, extemporaneous admixtures with Gentamicin Sulfate Injection USP are not recommended.

Additional information

Intrathecal gentamicin is commercially available as a preservative-free injection.

GENTAMICIN SULFATE IN SODIUM CHLORIDE INJECTION

Usual adult and adolescent dose

Antibacterial (systemic)—

Intravenous infusion, 1 to 1.7 mg (base) per kg of body weight every eight hours for seven to ten days or more.

Note: Urinary tract infections, bacterial (uncomplicated)—Intravenous infusion:

Adults less than 60 kg of body weight—3 mg (base) per kg of body weight once a day; or 1.5 mg per kg of body weight every twelve hours.

Adults 60 kg of body weight and over—160 mg (base) once a day; or 80 mg every twelve hours.

Following hemodialysis, a supplemental dose of 1 to 1.7 mg (base) per kg of body weight may be administered, depending on the severity of the infection.

Usual adult prescribing limits

Up to 8 mg (base) per kg of body weight daily in severe, life-threatening infections.

Note: Doses up to 15 mg (base) per kg of body weight daily have been used in the treatment of intraocular infections.

Usual pediatric dose

Antibacterial (systemic)—

Intravenous infusion—

Premature or full-term neonates up to 1 week of age:

2.5 mg (base) per kg of body weight every twelve to twenty-four hours for seven to ten days or more.

Older neonates and infants:

2.5 mg (base) per kg of body weight every eight to sixteen hours for seven to ten days or more.

Children:

2 to 2.5 mg (base) per kg of body weight every eight hours for seven to ten days or more.

Note: The dosing interval of gentamicin in pediatric patients may vary from every four hours to every twenty-four hours, depending on the medical conditions of the patient (cystic fibrosis, burns, renal dysfunction); serum levels must be monitored.

Following hemodialysis, a supplemental dose of 2 to 2.5 mg (base) per kg of body weight may be administered, depending on the severity of the infection.

Strength(s) usually available

U.S.—

40 mg in 50 mL (base) (Rx) [GENERIC].
40 mg in 100 mL (base) (Rx) [GENERIC].
60 mg in 50 mL (base) (Rx) [GENERIC].
60 mg in 100 mL (base) (Rx) [GENERIC].
70 mg in 50 mL (base) (Rx) [GENERIC].
80 mg in 50 mL (base) (Rx) [GENERIC].
80 mg in 100 mL (base) (Rx) [GENERIC].
90 mg in 100 mL (base) (Rx) [GENERIC].
100 mg in 50 mL (base) (Rx) [GENERIC].
100 mg in 100 mL (base) (Rx) [GENERIC].
120 mg in 100 mL (base) (Rx) [GENERIC].
160 mg in 100 mL (base) (Rx) [GENERIC].
180 mg in 100 mL (base) (Rx) [GENERIC].

Canada—

60 mg in 50 mL (base) (Rx) [GENERIC].
70 mg in 50 mL (base) (Rx) [GENERIC].
80 mg in 100 mL (base) (Rx) [GENERIC].

Packaging and storage

Store between 2 and 30 °C (36 and 86 °F), unless otherwise specified by manufacturer. Protect from freezing.

Preparation of dosage form

Commercially available gentamicin piggyback injections require no further dilution prior to administration (see manufacturer's labeling for instructions). Since these injections contain no preservatives, they should be used promptly after being opened; unused portions should be discarded.

Stability

Do not use if injection is discolored or contains a precipitate.

Incompatibilities

Extemporaneous admixtures of beta-lactam antibacterials (penicillins and cephalosporins) and aminoglycosides may result in substantial mutual inactivation. If these groups of antibacterials are administered concurrently, they should be administered in separate sites. Do not mix them in the same intravenous bag or bottle.

Since complexes form with a number of other drugs also, extemporaneous admixtures with gentamicin in sodium chloride injection are not recommended.

Additional information

The sodium content is approximately 19.6 mEq (450 mg) per 50 mL. This must be considered in patients on a restricted sodium intake when calculating total daily sodium intake.

KANAMYCIN

Additional Dosing Information

For initial dosing guidelines for patients with renal function impairment, see the Sarubbi and Hull nomogram in *General Dosing Information.*

For intravenous use only:

- Direct intravenous administration of undiluted kanamycin sulfate injection is not recommended because of the possibility of neuromuscular blockade.

For intramuscular use only:

- Inject kanamycin sulfate injection deeply into the upper outer quadrant of the gluteal muscle.

For other routes:

- Kanamycin sulfate injection may also be administered as an irrigation in a concentration of 0.25%.
- Kanamycin sulfate injection may also be administered as an aerosol nebulization.
- Kanamycin sulfate injection may also be administered intraperitoneally in a concentration of 2.5%.

Parenteral Dosage Forms

KANAMYCIN SULFATE INJECTION USP

Usual adult and adolescent dose

Antibacterial (systemic)—

Inhalation treatment, 250 mg two to four times a day.

Intramuscular, 3.75 mg per kg of body weight every six hours; 5 mg per kg of body weight every eight hours; or 7.5 mg per kg of body weight every twelve hours for seven to ten days.

Intraperitoneal, 500 mg.

Intravenous infusion, 5 mg per kg of body weight every eight hours; or 7.5 mg per kg of body weight every twelve hours for seven to ten days.

Usual adult prescribing limits

Up to 15 mg per kg of body weight daily, but not to exceed 1.5 grams daily.

Note: The total daily dose should take into account the amounts given by all routes, including intraperitoneal, inhalation, and irrigation. In intraocular infections, initial intramuscular doses of 2 grams, followed by 1 gram every twelve hours, have been used.

Usual pediatric dose

Antibacterial (systemic)—Intramuscular or intravenous infusion: See *Usual adult and adolescent dose.*

Note: Doses up to 30 mg per kg of body weight daily have been used in children.

Strength(s) usually available

U.S.—

37.5 mg per mL (Rx) [*Kantrex;* GENERIC (sodium bisulfite 0.099%)].
250 mg per mL (Rx) [*Kantrex;* GENERIC (sodium bisulfite 0.66%)].
333.3 mg per mL (Rx) [*Kantrex;* GENERIC (sodium bisulfite 0.45%)].

Canada—

Not commercially available.

Packaging and storage

Store below 40 °C (104 °F), preferably between 15 and 30 °C (59 and 86 °F), unless otherwise specified by manufacturer. Protect from freezing.

Preparation of dosage form

Intraperitoneal—To prepare dilution for intraperitoneal use, add the contents of each 500-mg vial to 20 mL of sterile water for injection. The resulting solution may be instilled postoperatively through a polyethylene catheter sutured into the wound at closure. To help prevent or minimize neuromuscular blockade, instillation of kanamycin should be postponed until the patient has fully recovered from the effects of anesthesia or neuromuscular blocking agents.

Intravenous—To prepare initial dilution for intravenous use, add the contents of each 500-mg vial to 100 to 200 mL or the contents of each 1-gram vial to 200 to 400 mL of 0.9% sodium chloride injection, 5% dextrose injection, or other suitable diluent. The resulting solution should be administered over a 30- to 60-minute period. Pediatric patients may require a proportionately smaller volume of diluent.

Stability
Solutions may darken during storage; this darkening does not affect their potency.

Incompatibilities
Extemporaneous admixtures of beta-lactam antibacterials (penicillins and cephalosporins) and aminoglycosides may result in substantial mutual inactivation. If these groups of antibacterials are administered concurrently, they should be administered in separate sites. Do not mix them in the same intravenous bag or bottle.

Since complexes form with a number of other drugs also, extemporaneous admixtures with kanamycin sulfate injection are not recommended.

NEOMYCIN

NEOMYCIN SULFATE STERILE USP
Note: Parenteral neomycin has been replaced by safer and more effective agents. **Because of its potential toxicity, the parenteral use of neomycin is not recommended for any indication.**

Strength(s) usually available
U.S.—
500 mg (Rx) [GENERIC].

Canada—
Not commercially available.

NETILMICIN

Additional Dosing Information
Serum concentrations of netilmicin in febrile patients may be lower than in afebrile patients receiving the same dose because of shorter half-life. The half-life may also be shorter in anemic patients. However, when the body temperature returns to normal in febrile patients, serum concentrations may increase. Dosage adjustments are not usually necessary.

For initial dosing guidelines for patients with renal function impairment, see the Sarubbi and Hull nomogram in *General Dosing Information.*

In severely burned patients, serum concentrations of netilmicin may be lower than expected from a particular dose. Serum determinations are especially important in these patients for dosage adjustment.

Parenteral Dosage Forms
Note: The dosing and dosage forms available are expressed in terms of netilmicin base.

NETILMICIN SULFATE INJECTION USP
Usual adult and adolescent dose
Antibacterial (systemic)—
Intramuscular or intravenous—
Systemic infections (serious):
1.3 to 2.2 mg (base) per kg of body weight every eight hours; or 2 to 3.25 mg (base) per kg of body weight every twelve hours for seven to fourteen days.
Urinary tract infections, bacterial (complicated):
1.5 to 2 mg (base) per kg of body weight every twelve hours for seven to fourteen days.

Note: Following hemodialysis, a supplemental dose of 1 mg (base) per kg of body weight may be administered.

Usual adult prescribing limits
Up to 7.5 mg (base) per kg of body weight daily.

Note: Doses up to 12 mg (base) per kg of body weight daily have been used in cystic fibrosis patients.

Usual pediatric dose
Antibacterial (systemic)—
Intramuscular or intravenous—
Neonates up to 6 weeks of age:
2 to 3.25 mg (base) per kg of body weight every twelve hours for seven to fourteen days.
Infants and children 6 weeks to 12 years of age:
1.83 to 2.67 mg (base) per kg of body weight every eight hours; or 2.75 to 4 mg (base) per kg of body weight every twelve hours for seven to fourteen days.

Strength(s) usually available
U.S.—
100 mg per mL (base) (Rx) [*Netromycin* (benzyl alcohol 10 mg, sodium metabisulfite 2.4 mg, sodium sulfite 0.8 mg)].

Canada—
25 mg per mL (base) (Rx) [*Netromycin* (sodium metabisulfite 2.1 mg, sodium sulfite 1.2 mg)].
50 mg per mL (base) (Rx) [*Netromycin* (sodium metabisulfite 2.1 mg, sodium sulfite 1.2 mg)].
100 mg per mL (base) (Rx) [*Netromycin* (benzyl alcohol 10 mg, sodium metabisulfite 2.4 mg, sodium sulfite 0.8 mg)].

Packaging and storage
Store below 40 °C (104 °F), preferably between 15 and 30 °C (59 and 86 °F), unless otherwise specified by manufacturer. Protect from freezing.

Preparation of dosage form
To prepare initial dilution for intravenous use, each dose should be diluted in 50 to 200 mL of a suitable diluent (see manufacturer's package insert). The resulting solution should be administered slowly over a 30- to 60-minute period to help avoid neuromuscular blockade. Pediatric patients may require a proportionately smaller volume of diluent.

Stability
Intravenous infusions of netilmicin retain their potency for up to 72 hours at room temperature or when refrigerated and stored in glass containers at concentrations of 2.1 to 3 mg per mL in suitable diluents (see manufacturer's package insert).

Incompatibilities
Extemporaneous admixtures of beta-lactam antibacterials (penicillins and cephalosporins) and aminoglycosides may result in substantial mutual inactivation. If these groups of antibacterials are administered concurrently, they should be administered in separate sites. Do not mix them in the same intravenous bag or bottle.

STREPTOMYCIN

Summary of Differences
Indications: Used for the treatment of brucellosis, granuloma inguinale, plague, tuberculosis, and tularemia.

Pregnancy/Reproduction: Has been shown to cause deafness in humans.

Patient monitoring: Caloric stimulation tests may also be required.

Additional Dosing Information
Tuberculosis therapy may have to be continued for 1 to 2 years, and may even be required for up to several years or indefinitely, although in some patients shorter treatment regimens may also be effective. However, streptomycin should be discontinued when toxicity or toxic symptoms appear or are impending, when organisms have become resistant, or when the full therapeutic effect has been achieved.

Injection sites should be alternated and concentrations greater than 500 mg per mL are not recommended.

Parenteral Dosage Forms
Note: The dosing and dosage forms available are expressed in terms of streptomycin base.

STREPTOMYCIN INJECTION USP
Usual adult dose
Antibacterial (antimycobacterial)—
• **Daily dosing**—In combination with other antimycobacterials, 15 milligrams (base) per kilogram of body weight, up to a maximum dose of 1 gram, given by intramuscular injection once daily.
• **Twice weekly dosing**—In combination with other antimycobacterials, 25 to 30 milligrams (base) per kilogram of body weight, up to a maximum dose of 1.5 grams, given by intramuscular injection twice weekly.
• **Three times-a-week dosing**—In combination with other antimycobacterials, 25 to 30 milligrams (base) per kilogram of body weight, up to a maximum dose of 1.5 grams, given by intramuscular injection three times-a-week.
Tuberculosis—
Intramuscular:

Antibacterial (systemic)—
Other infections—
Intramuscular:
In combination with other antibacterials, 250 to 500 mg (base) every six hours; or 500 mg to 1 gram every twelve hours for moderate to severe infections. Do not exceed doses of 2 grams per day.

Note: Endocarditis (penicillin-sensitive alpha and non-hemolytic streptococcal endocarditis)—Intramuscular: 1 gram twice daily for first week, 500 milligrams twice daily for second week, given concomitantly with penicillin. Sensitivity: Penicillin MIC ≤ 0.1 microgram/milliliter.

Endocarditis (enterococcal)—Intramuscular: 1 gram twice daily for 2 weeks, then 500 milligrams twice daily for 4 weeks, given concomitantly with penicillin. Termination of streptomycin therapy prior to completion of the 6-week course of treatment may be necessary if ototoxicity occurs.

Plague—Intramuscular: 1 gram every twelve hours for a minimum of 10 days of therapy.

Tularemia—Intramuscular: 250 to 500 mg (base) every six hours; or 500 mg to 1 gram every twelve hours for seven to fourteen days until patient is afebrile for 5 to 7 days.

Usual adult prescribing limits

Tuberculosis—

1 gram daily or 1.5 grams two or three times weekly.The total dose over the course of therapy should not exceed 120 grams unless there are no other therapeutic options.

Other infections—

Intramuscular doses should not exceed 2 grams per day.

Usual pediatric and adolescent dose

Antibacterial (antimycobacterial)—

- **Daily dosing**—In combination with other antimycobacterials, 20 to 40 milligrams (base) per kilogram of body weight, up to a maximum dose of 1 gram, given by intramuscular injection once daily.
- **Twice weekly dosing**—In combination with other antimycobacterials, 25 to 30 milligrams (base) per kilogram of body weight, up to a maximum dose of 1.5 grams, given by intramuscular injection twice weekly.
- **Three times-a-week dosing**—In combination with other antimycobacterials, 25 to 30 milligrams (base) per kilogram of body weight, up to a maximum dose of 1.5 grams, given by intramuscular injection three times-a-week.

Tuberculosis—

Intramuscular:

Antibacterial (systemic)—

Other infections—

Intramuscular:

In combination with other antibacterials, 5 to 10 mg (base) per kg of body weight every six hours; or 10 to 20 mg per kg of body weight every twelve hours. Avoid excessive dosage in children.

Usual geriatric dose

Antibacterial (antimycobacterial)—

Tuberculosis—

Intramuscular:

In combination with other antimycobacterials, 500 to 750 mg (base) once a day.

Other bacterial infections—

Intramuscular:

Endocarditis (penicillin-sensitive alpha and non-hemolytic streptococcal endocarditis)—Intramuscular: 500 milligrams twice daily, given concomitantly with penicillin for two weeks in patients over 60 years of age. Sensitivity: Penicillin MIC ≤ 0.1 micrograms/milliliter.

Strength(s) usually available

U.S.—

1 gram per ampule (base) (Rx) [GENERIC (Pfizer—may contain sodium metabisulfite)].

Canada—

Not commercially available.

Packaging and storage

Store below 40 °C (104 °F), preferably between 15 and 30 °C (59 and 86 °F), unless otherwise specified by manufacturer. Protect from freezing.

Stability

Solutions may vary in color from colorless to yellow and may darken on exposure to light. This variation does not affect their potency.

Solutions should not be autoclaved since loss of potency may result.

STREPTOMYCIN FOR INJECTION USP

Usual adult dose

Antibacterial (antimycobacterial)—

- **Daily dosing**—In combination with other antimycobacterials, 15 milligrams (base) per kilogram of body weight, up to a maximum dose of 1 gram, given by intramuscular injection once daily.
- **Twice weekly dosing**—In combination with other antimycobacterials, 25 to 30 milligrams (base) per kilogram of body weight, up to a maximum dose of 1.5 grams, given by intramuscular injection twice weekly.
- **Three times-a-week dosing**—In combination with other antimycobacterials, 25 to 30 milligrams (base) per kilogram of body weight, up to a maximum dose of 1.5 grams, given by intramuscular injection three times-a-week.

Tuberculosis—

Intramuscular:

Antibacterial (systemic)—

Other infections—

Intramuscular:

In combination with other antibacterials, 250 to 500 mg (base) every six hours; or 500 mg to 1 gram every twelve hours for moderate to severe infections. Do not exceed doses of 2 grams per day.

Note: Endocarditis (penicillin-sensitive alpha and non-hemolytic streptococcal endocarditis)—Intramuscular: 1 gram twice daily for first week, 500 milligrams twice daily for second week, given concomitantly with penicillin. Sensitivity: Penicillin MIC ≤ 0.1 microgram/milliliter.

Endocarditis (enterococcal)—Intramuscular: 1 gram twice daily for 2 weeks, then 500 milligrams twice daily for 4 weeks, given concomitantly with penicillin. Termination of streptomycin therapy prior to completion of the 6-week course of treatment may be necessary if ototoxicity occurs.

Plague—Intramuscular: 1 gram every twelve hours for a minimum of 10 days of therapy.

Tularemia—Intramuscular: 250 to 500 mg (base) every six hours; or 500 mg to 1 gram every twelve hours for seven to fourteen days until patient is afebrile for 5 to 7 days.

Usual adult prescribing limits

Tuberculosis—

1 gram daily or 1.5 grams two or three times weekly. The total dose over the course of therapy should not exceed 120 grams unless there are no other therapeutic options.

Other infections—

Intramuscular doses should not exceed 2 grams per day.

Usual pediatric and adolescent dose

Antibacterial (antimycobacterial)—

- **Daily dosing**—In combination with other antimycobacterials, 20 to 40 milligrams (base) per kilogram of body weight, up to a maximum dose of 1 gram, given by intramuscular injection once daily.
- **Twice weekly dosing**—In combination with other antimycobacterials, 25 to 30 milligrams (base) per kilogram of body weight, up to a maximum dose of 1.5 grams, given by intramuscular injection twice weekly.
- **Three times-a-week dosing**—In combination with other antimycobacterials, 25 to 30 milligrams (base) per kilogram of body weight, up to a maximum dose of 1.5 grams, given by intramuscular injection three times-a-week.

Tuberculosis—

Intramuscular:

Antibacterial (systemic)—

Other infections—

Intramuscular:

In combination with other antibacterials, 5 to 10 mg (base) per kg of body weight every six hours; or 10 to 20 mg per kg of body weight every twelve hours. Avoid excessive dosage in children.

Usual geriatric dose

Antibacterial (antimycobacterial)—

Tuberculosis—

Intramuscular:

In combination with other antimycobacterials, 500 to 700 mg (base) once a day.

Other bacterial infections—

Intramuscular:

Endocarditis (penicillin-sensitive alpha and non-hemolytic streptococcal endocarditis)—Intramuscular: 500 milligrams twice daily, given concomitantly with penicillin for two weeks in patients over 60 years of age. Sensitivity: Penicillin MIC ≤ 0.1 micrograms/milliliter.

Strength(s) usually available
U.S.—
1 gram per vial (base) (Rx) [GENERIC].
Canada—
1 gram per vial (base) (Rx) [GENERIC].

Packaging and storage
Prior to reconstitution, store dry powder under controlled room temperature 15 and 30 °C (59 and 86 °F), unless otherwise specified by manufacturer. Protect from light.

Preparation of dosage form
To prepare initial dilution for intramuscular use, add 4.2 mL of sterile water for injection to each 1-gram vial, according to the manufacturer, to provide a concentration of 200 mg (base) per mL, 3.2 mL of diluent to provide a concentration of 250 mg per mL or 1.8 mL of diluent to provide a concentration of 400 mg per mL.

Stability
After reconstitution, sterile solutions should be protected from light and may be stored at room temperature for 1 week without significant loss of potency.

TOBRAMYCIN

Summary of Differences
Pregnancy/Reproduction: Has been shown to cause deafness in humans.

Additional Dosing Information
Commercially available tobramycin piggyback injections should be administered by intravenous infusion only.

Tobramycin sulfate injection may also be administered as an aerosol nebulization.

Parenteral Dosage Forms
Note: The dosing and dosage forms available are expressed in terms of tobramycin base.

TOBRAMYCIN SULFATE INJECTION USP

Usual adult and adolescent dose
Antibacterial (systemic)—
Intramuscular or intravenous infusion, 0.75 mg to 1.25 mg (base) per kg of body weight every six hours; or 1 to 1.7 mg per kg of body weight every eight hours for seven to ten days or more.

Usual adult prescribing limits
Up to 8 mg (base) per kg of body weight daily in severe, life-threatening infections.

Usual pediatric dose
Antibacterial (systemic)—
Intramuscular or intravenous infusion—
Premature or full-term neonates up to 1 week of age:
Up to 2 mg (base) per kg of body weight every twelve to twenty-four hours.
Older infants and children:
—1.5 to 1.9 mg (base) per kg of body weight every six hours; or 2 to 2.5 mg per kg of body weight every eight to sixteen hours.
Note: The dosing interval of tobramycin in pediatric patients may vary from every four hours to every twenty-four hours, depending on the medical condition of the patient (cystic fibrosis, burns, renal dysfunction); serum levels must be monitored.

Strength(s) usually available
U.S.—
10 mg per mL (base) (Rx) [*Nebcin* (sodium bisulfite 3.2 mg); GENERIC].
20 mg per mL (base) (Rx) [GENERIC].
40 mg per mL (base) (Rx) [*Nebcin* (sodium bisulfite 3.2 mg); GENERIC].
60 mg per mL (base) (Rx) [GENERIC].
80 mg per mL (base) (Rx) [GENERIC].
Canada—
10 mg per mL (base) (Rx) [*Nebcin* (sodium bisulfite)].
40 mg per mL (base) (Rx) [*Nebcin* (sodium bisulfite)].

Packaging and storage
Store below 40 °C (104 °F), preferably between 15 and 30 °C (59 and 86 °F), unless otherwise specified by manufacturer. Protect from freezing.

Preparation of dosage form
To prepare initial dilution for intravenous use, add each dose to 50 to 200 mL of 0.9% sodium chloride injection or 5% dextrose injection to provide a concentration not exceeding 1 mg (base) per mL (0.1%). The resulting solution should be administered slowly over a 30- to 60-minute period to avoid neuromuscular blockade. In addition, infusion periods of less than 20 minutes are not recommended since peak serum concentrations may exceed 12 mcg per mL. Pediatric patients may require a proportionately smaller volume of diluent.

Incompatibilities
Extemporaneous admixtures of beta-lactam antibacterials (penicillins and cephalosporins) and aminoglycosides may result in substantial mutual inactivation. If these groups of antibacterials are administered concurrently, they should be administered in separate sites. Do not mix them in the same intravenous bag or bottle.

Since complexes form with a number of other drugs also, extemporaneous admixtures with tobramycin sulfate injection are not recommended.

Additional information
Subcutaneous administration is not recommended and may be painful.

TOBRAMYCIN SULFATE STERILE USP

Usual adult and adolescent dose
Antibacterial (systemic)—
Intravenous infusion, 0.75 mg to 1.25 mg (base) per kg of body weight every six hours; or 1 to 1.7 mg per kg of body weight every eight hours for seven to ten days or more.

Usual adult prescribing limits
Up to 8 mg (base) per kg of body weight daily in severe, life-threatening infections.

Usual pediatric dose
Antibacterial (systemic)—
Intravenous infusion—
Premature or full-term neonates up to 1 week of age:
Up to 2 mg (base) per kg of body weight every twelve to twenty-four hours.
Older infants and children:
—1.5 to 1.9 mg (base) per kg of body weight every six hours; or 2 to 2.5 mg per kg of body weight every eight to sixteen hours.
Note: The dosing interval of tobramycin in pediatric patients may vary from every four hours to every twenty-four hours, depending on the medical condition of the patient (cystic fibrosis, burns, renal dysfunction); serum levels must be monitored.

Strength(s) usually available
U.S.—
1.2 grams (base) (Rx) [*Nebcin;* GENERIC].
Canada—
1.2 grams (base) (Rx) [*Nebcin*].

Packaging and storage
Prior to reconstitution, store below 40 °C (104 °F), preferably between 15 and 30 °C (59 and 86 °F), unless otherwise specified by manufacturer.

Preparation of dosage form
To prepare initial dilution for intravenous use, add 30 mL of sterile water for injection to each 1.2-gram vial to provide 40 mg (base) per mL. Withdraw each dose from the pharmacy bulk vial and add it to 50 to 200 mL of 0.9% sodium chloride injection or 5% dextrose injection to provide a final concentration not exceeding 1 mg per mL (0.1%). The resulting solution should be administered slowly over a 30- to 60-minute period to avoid neuromuscular blockade. In addition, infusion periods of less than 20 minutes are not recommended since peak serum concentrations may exceed 12 mcg per mL. Pediatric patients may require a proportionately smaller volume of diluent.

Stability
After reconstitution, solutions retain their potency for 24 hours at room temperature or for 96 hours if refrigerated.

Incompatibilities
Extemporaneous admixtures of beta-lactam antibacterials (penicillins and cephalosporins) and aminoglycosides may result in substantial mutual inactivation. If these groups of antibacterials are administered concurrently, they should be administered in separate sites. Do not mix them in the same intravenous bag or bottle.

Since complexes form with a number of other drugs also, extemporaneous admixtures with Sterile Tobramycin Sulfate USP are not recommended.

Additional information

Sterile Tobramycin Sulfate USP is available only in a pharmacy bulk vial (multiple-dose) and is intended for use in the extemporaneous preparation of intravenous admixtures.

TOBRAMYCIN SULFATE IN SODIUM CHLORIDE INJECTION

Usual adult and adolescent dose

See *Tobramycin Sulfate Injection USP*.

Usual adult prescribing limits

See *Tobramycin Sulfate Injection USP*.

Usual pediatric dose

See *Tobramycin Sulfate Injection USP*.

Strength(s) usually available

U.S.—

60 mg in 50 mL (base) (Rx) [GENERIC].
80 mg in 100 mL (base) (Rx) [GENERIC].

Canada—

Not commercially available.

Packaging and storage

Store between 2 and 30 °C (36 and 86 °F), unless otherwise specified by manufacturer. Protect from freezing.

Preparation of dosage form

Commercially available tobramycin piggyback injections require no further dilution prior to administration (see manufacturer's labeling for instructions).

Stability

Do not use if injection is discolored or contains a precipitate.

Incompatibilities

Extemporaneous admixtures of beta-lactam antibacterials (penicillins and cephalosporins) and aminoglycosides may result in substantial mutual inactivation. If these groups of antibacterials are administered concurrently, they should be administered in separate sites. Do not mix them in the same intravenous bag or bottle.

Since complexes form with a number of other drugs also, extemporaneous admixtures with tobramycin in sodium chloride injection are not recommended.

Additional information

The sodium content is approximately 19.6 mEq (450 mg) per 50 mL. This must be considered in patients on a restricted sodium intake when calculating total daily sodium intake.

Revised: 09/11/2002

AMINOPHYLLINE—See *Bronchodilators, Theophylline (Systemic)*

AMIODARONE Systemic

VA CLASSIFICATION (Primary): CV300

Commonly used brand name(s): *Cordarone; Cordarone Intravenous; Cordarone I've.; pms-Amiodarone.*

Note: For a listing of dosage forms and brand names by country availability, see *Dosage Forms* section(s).

Category

Antiarrhythmic.

Indications

Note: Bracketed information in the *Indications* section refers to uses that are not included in U.S. product labeling.

Accepted

Arrhythmias, ventricular (prophylaxis and treatment)—Amiodarone in the oral dosage form is indicated only for the treatment of documented, life-threatening recurrent hemodynamically unstable ventricular tachycardia and recurrent ventricular fibrillation unresponsive to documented adequate doses of other available antiarrhythmic medications or when alternative agents cannot be tolerated. In patients for whom the oral form of amiodarone is indicated, but who are unable to take oral medication, the intravenous form of amiodarone may be used.

Amiodarone in the intravenous dosage form is indicated for the initiation of treatment (acute treatment) and prophylaxis of frequently recurring ventricular fibrillation and hemodynamically unstable ventricular tachycardia in patients refractory to other therapy.

[Arrhythmias, supraventricular (prophylaxis and treatment)][1]—Amiodarone is used to suppress and prevent recurrence of supraventricular arrhythmias refractory to conventional treatment, especially when associated with Wolff-Parkinson-White (W-P-W) syndrome, including paroxysmal atrial fibrillation, atrial flutter, ectopic atrial tachycardia, and paroxysmal supraventricular tachycardia from both atrioventricular (AV) nodal re-entrant and AV re-entrant tachycardia in patients with W-P-W syndrome.

Note: Controlled clinical trials have not demonstrated that the use of amiodarone improves patient survival.

[1]Not included in Canadian product labeling.

Pharmacology/Pharmacokinetics

Physicochemical characteristics

Molecular weight—681.8.
pKa—5.6.
Other—Contains 37.3% iodine by weight; highly lipophilic.

Mechanism of action/Effect

Amiodarone prolongs the action potential duration and the refractory period in all cardiac tissues (including the sinus node, atrium, atrioventricular [AV] node, and ventricle) by a direct action on the tissues, without significantly affecting the membrane potential. Amiodarone also decreases sinus node automaticity and junctional automaticity, prolongs AV conduction, and slows automaticity of spontaneously firing fibers in the Purkinje system. Refractoriness is prolonged and conduction is slowed in accessory pathway tissue in patients with Wolff-Parkinson-White (W-P-W) syndrome. Noncompetitive alpha- and beta-adrenergic receptor antagonism and calcium channel inhibition also occur and thyroid hormone metabolism is affected, but the relationship of these effects to the antiarrhythmic action of amiodarone is unknown. In the Vaughan Williams classification of antiarrhythmics, amiodarone is considered to be a predominantly class III agent, with some class I properties.

Other actions/effects

Amiodarone has a mild negative inotropic effect that is more prominent with intravenous than with oral administration but that usually does not depress left ventricular function. Amiodarone causes coronary and peripheral vasodilation and, therefore, decreases peripheral vascular resistance (afterload) but only causes hypotension with large oral doses.

Absorption

Slow and variable; about 20 to 55% of an oral dose is absorbed.

Distribution

Volume of distribution is large and variable, a consequence of extensive accumulation in adipose tissue and highly perfused organs (liver, lung, spleen), and leads to slow achievement of steady-state and therapeutic plasma concentrations and prolonged elimination.

Protein binding

Very high (96%).

Biotransformation

Hepatic, extensive; one active metabolite (desethylamiodarone); possibly also by deiodination (a dose of 300 mg releases approximately 9 mg of elemental iodine).

Half-life

Elimination (biphasic)—

Initial:

Amiodarone—2.5 to 10 days.

Terminal:

Amiodarone—26 to 107 days (mean 53 days; 40 to 55 days in most patients).

Desethylamiodarone—Mean 61 days.

Onset of antiarrhythmic action

2 to 3 days to 2 to 3 months, even with loading doses.

Time to peak plasma concentration

3 to 7 hours.

Therapeutic plasma concentration

1 to 2.5 mcg (0.001 to 0.0025 mg) per mL at steady-state (after 2 months of therapy). However, antiarrhythmic effect is difficult to predict by means of plasma concentrations, and toxicity may occur even at therapeutic concentrations.

Elimination

Biliary.
In breast milk—About 25% of maternal dose is distributed into breast milk.
In dialysis—Not removable by hemodialysis.

Precautions to Consider

Carcinogenicity/Tumorigenicity

Studies in rats at doses one-half the maximum recommended human maintenance dose and greater found a dose-related increase in the incidence of thyroid follicular adenomas and/or carcinomas.

Mutagenicity

Mutagenicity studies (Ames, micronucleus, and lysogenic tests) with amiodarone were negative.

Pregnancy/Reproduction

Fertility—Studies in male and female rats at doses eight times the maximum recommended human maintenance dose found that amiodarone reduced fertility.

Pregnancy—Oral amiodarone should only be used during pregnancy if the potential benefit to the mother justifies the unknown risks to the fetus. The patient should be apprised of the potential hazard to the fetus if amiodarone is used during pregnancy or if the patient becomes pregnant while taking amiodarone.

Amiodarone crosses the placenta; neonatal plasma concentrations of amiodarone and desethylamiodarone are 10% and 25% of maternal plasma concentrations, respectively. Although studies in humans have not been done, some reports have indicated an absence of adverse effects when amiodarone was administered late in pregnancy. However, amiodarone can cause fetal harm when administered to pregnant women. Potential adverse effects include bradycardia and effects on thyroid status (iodine is known to cause fetal goiter, hypothyroidism, and mental retardation) in the neonate. There have been a small number of reports of congenital goiter/hypothyroidism and hyperthyroidism.

Note: An expert panel concluded that (based on animal studies) amiodarone I.V. administration may indirectly but adversely affect male reproductive tract development during fetal, infant, and toddler stages of development. The indirect effects may be linked to plasticizers that leach out from the I.V. tubing during certain administration conditions, such as higher amiodarone concentrations and lower flow rates.

Studies in rats and one strain of mice at doses 18 times and one half the maximum recommended human maintenance dose, respectively, have shown that amiodarone is embryotoxic. Amiodarone was not embryotoxic in a second strain of mice or in rabbits at doses up to nine times the maximum recommended human maintenance dose.

FDA Pregnancy Category D.

Labor and delivery—Although studies in humans have not been done, studies in rodents found no adverse effects of amiodarone on duration of gestation or on parturition.

Breast-feeding

The mother should be advised to discontinue nursing when amiodarone therapy is indicated.

Amiodarone and one of its major metabolites, desethylamiodarone (DEA), are distributed into human breast milk. The nursing infant could be exposed to a significant dose of amiodarone. Nursing offspring of lactating rats administered amiodarone were less viable and had reduced body-weight gains.

Pediatrics

Appropriate studies on the relationship of age to the effects of amiodarone have not been performed in the pediatric population. However, when amiodarone was used concurrently with digoxin, the interaction has been reported to be more acute in children than in adults. In addition, onset and duration of action of amiodarone may be shorter in pediatric patients.

Note: I.V. administration of amiodarone is not recommended for use in the pediatric population due to recent findings that show a potential for adverse male reproductive tract development during infant and toddler ages. In addition, amiodarone I.V. contains the preservative benzyl alcohol which has been associated with the potentially fatal "gasping syndrome" in neonates.

Geriatrics

Appropriate studies on the relationship of age to the effects of amiodarone have not been performed in the geriatric population. However, the elderly tend to be more sensitive to the effects of thyroid hormones and may also, therefore, be more sensitive to the effects of amiodarone on thyroid function. Thyroid function monitoring is particularly important in these patients. In addition, the elderly may experience an increased incidence of ataxia and other neurotoxic effects.

Surgical

Surgical—Close perioperative monitoring is recommended in patients undergoing general anesthesia who are on amiodarone therapy as they may be more sensitive to halogenated inhalational anesthetics' myocardial depressant and conduction effects.

Report of rare occurrences of hypotension upon discontinuation of cardiopulmonary bypass during open-heart surgery in patients receiving amiodarone; relationship of event to amiodarone is unknown.

Postoperative reports of adult respiratory distress syndrome (ARDS) in patients receiving amiodarone therapy who have undergone cardiac or noncardiac surgery. Although patients usually respond well to vigorous respiratory therapy, in rare instances the outcome has been fatal. Until further studies have been performed, recommended close monitoring of FiO_2 and determinants of oxygen delivery to the tissues (e.g., SaO_2, PaO_2) in amiodarone patients.

Drug interactions and/or related problems

The following drug interactions and/or related problems have been selected on the basis of their potential clinical significance (possible mechanism in parentheses where appropriate)—not necessarily inclusive (» = major clinical significance):

Note: Because of its slow elimination, amiodarone may interact with other medications for weeks to months after it is discontinued.

Combinations containing any of the following medications, depending on the amount present, may also interact with this medication.

Anesthetics, inhalation
(amiodarone may potentiate hypotension and atropine-resistant bradycardia)

» Antiarrhythmics, other
(amiodarone may produce additive cardiac effects with other antiarrhythmics and increase the risk of tachyarrhythmias; amiodarone increases plasma concentrations of quinidine, procainamide, flecainide, and phenytoin; concurrent use of amiodarone with quinidine, disopyramide, procainamide, or mexiletine has been reported to result in a more prolonged QT interval which could cause arrhythmiaand, rarely, *torsades de pointes*, and therefore, concurrent use with all class I antiarrhythmics requires great caution and should be reserved for patients with life-threatening ventricular arrhythmias who are incompletely responsive to a single agent or incompletely responsive to amiodarone; the doses of previously given antiarrhythmics should be reduced by 30 to 50% several days after initiation of amiodarone therapy and gradually withdrawn; if antiarrhythmic therapy is needed in addition to amiodarone, it should be initiated at one half the usual recommended dose)

» Anticoagulants, coumarin-derivative
(amiodarone inhibits metabolism and potentiates the anticoagulant effect, beginning as early as 4 to 6 days after initiation of amiodarone therapy and persisting as long as weeks or months after it is withdrawn; prothrombin times may double or triple, but effect is very erratic; it is recommended that the dose of anticoagulant be reduced by one third to one half and that prothrombin times be monitored closely)

» Azoles or
» Fluoroquinolones or
» Macrolide antibiotics
(known to cause QTc prolongation; reported QTc prolongation, with or without torsade de pointes, when these are administered concomitantly with amiodarone)

Beta-adrenergic blocking agents or
Calcium channel blocking agents
(amiodarone may cause potentiation of bradycardia, sinus arrest, and atrioventricular [AV] block, especially in patients with underlying sinus function impairment. If this occurs, dosage reduction of amiodarone or the beta-blocking agent or calcium channel blocking agent is recommended; in some cases, amiodarone therapy may be continued after insertion of a pacemaker)

Cholestyramine
(concomitant use increases amiodarone enterohepatic elimination and may reduce its serum levels and $t_{1/2}$)

Cyclosporine
(has been reported to produce persistently elevated cyclosporine plasma concentrations resulting in elevated creatinine, despite reduction in cyclosporine dose)

» CYP3A4 inducers, inhibitors or substrates (See *Appendix II*)
(potential for interactions exist and should be anticipated, especially for those associated with serious toxicity)

Dextromethorphan
(substrate for both CYP2D6 and CYP3A4 and amiodarone inhibits CYP2D6; additionally, chronic [greater than 2 weeks] *oral* amiodarone administration impairs dextromethorphan metabolism)

» Digitalis glycosides
(amiodarone increases serum concentrations of digoxin and probably other digitalis glycosides, possibly to toxic levels; when amiodarone therapy is initiated, the digitalis glycoside should be withdrawn or the dose reduced by 50%; if digitalis glycoside therapy is continued, serum concentrations should be carefully monitored; amiodarone and digitalis glycosides may also produce additive effects on sinoatrial [SA] and AV nodes)

Diltiazem or
Propranolol or
Verapamil
(observed hemodynamic and electrophysiologic interactions after concomitant administration)

Diuretics, loop or
Diuretics, thiazide or
Indapamide
(concurrent use of amiodarone with potassium-depleting diuretics may lead to an increased risk of arrhythmias associated with hypokalemia)

» Fentanyl
(concomitant use may cause hypotension, bradycardia, and decreased cardiac output)

» Grapefruit juice
(results in increased amiodarone plasma levels; grapefruit juice should not be taken during treatment with oral amiodarone)

Histamine H_2 antagonists including
Cimetidine
(cimetidine inhibits CYP3A4; can increase amiodarone levels)

Hypokalemia-causing medications, other (see *Appendix II*) or
Hypomagnesemia-causing medications, other
(caution is advised when coadministering amiodarone with drugs which may induce hypokalemia or hypomagnesemia since antiarrhythmic drugs may be ineffective or may be arrhythmogenic in patients with hypokalemia or hypomagnesemia; potassium or magnesium deficiency should be corrected before instituting and during amiodarone therapy)

Lidocaine
(reported sinus bradycardia with concomitant oral amiodarone and lidocaine given for local anesthesia; reported seizure, associated with increased lidocaine concentrations, when used concomitantly with intravenous amiodarone)

Methotrexate
(chronic [greater than 2 weeks] *oral* amiodarone administration impairs methotrexate metabolism)

» Phenytoin
(amiodarone may increase plasma concentrations of phenytoin, resulting in increased effects and/or toxicity; chronic [greater than 2 weeks] *oral* amiodarone administration impairs phenytoin metabolism)

Photosensitizing medications, other
(concurrent use with amiodarone may cause additive photosensitizing effects)

Protease inhibitors including
Indinavir
(case report of concomitant use with indinavir showed increase in amiodarone concentration with no evidence of toxicity; monitoring for amiodarone toxicity and amiodarone serum concentration measurement during concomitant therapy should be considered.)

Rifampin
(potent inducer of CYP3A4; concomitant administration has been shown to result in decreases in serum concentrations of amiodarone and desethylamiodarone)

» Simvastatin
(concomitant use has been associated with reports of myopathy/rhabdomyolysis)

Sodium iodide I 123 or
Sodium iodide I 131 or
Sodium pertechnetate Tc 99m
(thyroidal uptake may be inhibited by amiodarone)

St. John's Wort
(potential for reduced amiodarone levels with concomitant use because St. John's Wort induces CYP3A4 and amiodarone is a substrate for CYP3A4)

Laboratory value alterations

The following have been selected on the basis of their potential clinical significance (possible effect in parentheses where appropriate)—not necessarily inclusive (» = major clinical significance).

With physiology/laboratory test values
Alanine aminotransferase (ALT [SGPT]) and
Alkaline phosphatase and
Aspartate aminotransferase (AST [SGOT])
(serum values are commonly increased; hepatotoxicity is rare)

Antinuclear antibody (ANA) titer concentration
(may be increased but usually not symptomatic; elevated concentrations may be associated with pulmonary toxicity)

Electrocardiogram (ECG) changes, such as:
PR prolongation and
QRS widening, slight and
QT prolongation and
T-wave amplitude reduction with T-wave widening and bifurcation and
U-wave development
(occur in most patients; QT prolongation may in some cases be associated with worsening of arrhythmias)

Thyroid function changes, such as
Free and total serum thyroxine (T_4) concentrations
(may be increased)

Free and total serum triiodothyronine (T_3) concentrations
(may be decreased)

Serum reverse T_3 (rT_3) concentrations
(may be increased)

Serum thyroid-stimulating hormone (TSH) concentrations
(may be increased initially; increase in TSH with continued amiodarone treatment, along with a decrease in T_3, is the determining sign of hypothyroidism)

Note: Amiodarone inhibits peripheral conversion of T_4 to T_3, leading to increased serum T_4 and rT_3 and a slight decrease in serum T_3. Thyroid function abnormalities may persist for several weeks or months after withdrawal of amiodarone.

Medical considerations/Contraindications

The medical considerations/contraindications included have been selected on the basis of their potential clinical significance (reasons given in parentheses where appropriate)—not necessarily inclusive (» = major clinical significance).

Except under special circumstances, this medication should not be used when the following medical problems exist:

» Atrioventricular (AV) block, pre-existing 2nd or 3rd degree, without pacemaker
(risk of complete heart block)

» Bradycardic episodes resulting in syncope, unless controlled by pacemaker, or

» Cardiogenic shock or

» Sinus node function impairment, severe, causing marked sinus bradycardia, unless controlled by pacemaker
(amiodarone reduces sinus node automaticity and may cause atropine-resistant sinus bradycardia)

» Hepatitis, acute

» Hypersensitivity to amiodarone or any of the components of the product, including iodine

Risk-benefit should be considered when the following medical problems exist:

» Arrhythmia
(amiodarone may cause serious exacerbation of the presenting arrhythmia; concomitant antiarrhythmics may increase the risk)

Congestive heart failure
(mild negative inotropic effect of amiodarone usually does not cause problems; hemodynamic deterioration may occur secondary to sympatholytic blockage of augmented sympathetic drive)

Hepatic function impairment
(reduced metabolism; lower doses may be required)

Hypokalemia or
Hypomagnesia
(amiodarone may be ineffective or arrhythmogenic; should be corrected prior to initiation of amiodarone therapy)

» Pulmonary disease, pre-existing
(may be at greater risk for adverse effects if amiodarone-induced pulmonary toxicity develops)

» Thyroid abnormalities
(amiodarone may cause either hypothyroidism or hyperthyroidism; monitor thyroid function regularly; monitor patient for any new signs of arrhythmia, which may be associated with amiodarone-induced hyperthyroidism; abnormal thyroid function may persist for

several weeks or even months after amiodarone therapy is discontinued)

Caution is recommended also during open-heart surgery in patients receiving amiodarone because of the risk of hypotension upon discontinuation of cardiopulmonary bypass.

Patient monitoring

The following may be especially important in patient monitoring (other tests may be warranted in some patients, depending on condition; » = major clinical significance):

» Alanine aminotransferase (ALT [SGPT]) and
» Alkaline phosphatase and
» Aspartate aminotransferase (AST [SGOT])
(serum value determinations recommended at regular intervals, especially in patients receiving high maintenance doses; dosage reduction of amiodarone is recommended if concentrations increase to three times normal or double in patients with elevated baseline concentrations, or if hepatomegaly occurs)

Auscultation of the chest
(recommended at periodic intervals; presence of rales, decreased breath sounds, or pleuritic friction rub may indicate pulmonary toxicity)

Bronchoscopy with lung biopsy
(may be useful if symptoms of pulmonary toxicity occur that cannot be diagnosed from a chest x-ray)

Chest x-ray
(recommended prior to initiation of therapy and at 3- to 6-month intervals during therapy to detect diffuse interstitial changes or alveolar infiltrates associated with pulmonary toxicity)

» ECG
(continuous Holter monitoring may assist in assessing efficacy and adjusting dosage; usefulness of programmed electrical stimulation in clinical management is controversial, although it may be useful for predicting efficacy of amiodarone)

Gallium radionuclide scan
(may be useful if symptoms of pulmonary toxicity occur that cannot be diagnosed from a chest x-ray; may show marked uptake in the lung)

Ophthalmologic examinations
(slit-lamp examinations recommended prior to initiation of therapy and if symptoms of ocular toxicity occur)

Plasma amiodarone determinations
(may be useful in dosage adjustment or to assess lack of response or unexpectedly severe toxicity, although correlation does not always occur, especially within first 2 months of therapy)

Pulmonary function determinations, including diffusion capacity and total lung capacity
(recommended prior to initiation of amiodarone therapy and if symptoms of pulmonary toxicity occur that cannot be diagnosed from a chest x-ray)

» Thyroid function determinations
(because amiodarone can cause either hypothyroidism or hyperthyroidism, it is recommended that thyroid function be monitored prior to initiation of and at periodic intervals during amiodarone therapy, especially in patients with a history of thyroid nodules, goiter, or other thyroid dysfunction and in patients who are elderly; interpretation of thyroid function tests in patients receiving amiodarone can be difficult because its effects are complex; a flat TSH response to protirelin will help confirm the presence of hyperthyroidism)

Side/Adverse Effects

Note: Incidence of side/adverse effects is generally related to dose and duration of therapy. Side/adverse effects may occur even at therapeutic plasma amiodarone concentrations but are more common at concentrations over 2.5 mcg per mL and with continuous treatment for longer than 6 months.

Side/adverse effects may not appear until several days, weeks, or years after initiation of amiodarone therapy and may persist for several months after withdrawal.

Sinus bradycardia is symptomatic in only 2 to 4% of patients taking amiodarone. Sinus arrest and heart block occur rarely. Atrioventricular (AV) block occurs infrequently. New or exacerbated arrhythmias occur in 2 to 5% of patients and may include paroxysmal ventricular tachycardia, ventricular fibrillation, increased resistance to cardioversion, and *torsades de pointes*; they may be associated with marked QT prolongation. New or exacerbated arrhythmias may also be a sign of hyperthyroidism.

Amiodarone concentrations of > 3 mg per mL (mg/mL) in 5% Dextrose Injection USP (D_5W) have been associated with a high incidence of peripheral vein phlebitis; concentrations ≤ 2.5 mg/mL appear to be less irritating.

The following side/adverse effects have been selected on the basis of their potential clinical significance (possible signs and symptoms in parentheses where appropriate)—not necessarily inclusive:

Those indicating need for medical attention

Incidence more frequent

Hypotension (dizziness, lightheadedness, or fainting); ***neurotoxicity*** (trouble in walking; numbness or tingling in fingers or toes; trembling or shaking of hands; unusual and uncontrolled movements of body; weakness of arms or legs); ***photosensitivity, particularly to long-wave ultraviolet-A [UVA] light*** (sensitivity of skin to sunlight); ***pulmonary fibrosis or interstitial pneumonitis/alveolitis*** (cough; painful breathing; shortness of breath; slight fever)

Note: *Neurotoxicity* is the most common adverse effect occurring with oral amiodarone therapy; it occurs in 20 to 40% of patients, especially during administration of loading doses; neurotoxicity may occur within 1 week to several months after initiation of therapy and may persist for more than a year after withdrawal.

Hypotension is the most common adverse effect occurring with intravenous amiodarone therapy. In clinical trials, hypotension occurred in 16% of patients treated with intravenous amiodarone. Clinically significant hypotension during infusion of amiodarone was seen most often in the first several hours of treatment and appeared to be related to the rate of infusion, rather than the dose. However, mean daily doses of above 2100 mg are associated with an increased risk of hypotension. Alteration in amiodarone therapy to alleviate hypotension was required in 3% of patients. Permanent discontinuation of amiodarone therapy because of hypotension was necessary in fewer than 2% of patients.

Photosensitivity may occur even through window glass and thin cotton clothing and is not dose-related. Use of protective clothing and a topical product that prevents sunburn is recommended, especially for patients with fair skin or with excessive sun exposure.

Pulmonary fibrosis or interstitial pneumonitis/alveolitis is clinically significant in up to 10 to 15% of patients, but abnormal diffusion capacity occurs in a much higher percentage; it may occur more frequently with doses of 400 mg per day and after several months of treatment but may also occur with small doses; usually reversible after withdrawal of amiodarone, with or without steroid treatment, but is fatal in about 10% of cases, especially when not diagnosed promptly; recurrence has been reported after withdrawal of several months of steroid therapy; often mistaken for but rarely related to congestive heart failure or pneumonic infection.

Incidence less frequent

Arrhythmias, new or exacerbated (fast or irregular heartbeat); ***blue-gray coloring of skin on face, neck, and arms; congestive heart failure*** (swelling of feet or lower legs); ***hyperthyroidism*** (nervousness; sensitivity to heat; sweating; trouble in sleeping; weight loss); ***hypothyroidism*** (coldness; dry, puffy skin; unusual tiredness; weight gain); ***noninfectious epididymitis*** (pain and swelling in scrotum); ***ocular toxicity*** (blurred vision or blue-green halos seen around objects; dry eyes; sensitivity of eyes to light); ***including optic neuropathy and/or optic neuritis; sinus bradycardia*** (slow heartbeat)

Note: *Blue-gray skin coloring* occurs with prolonged use, usually longer than 1 year, especially in patients with fair skin or with excessive sun exposure; slowly, and occasionally incompletely, reversible after withdrawal.

Hyperthyroidism occurs in about 2% of patients, although thyroid hormone concentration changes are common and may persist for several months after withdrawal of amiodarone. If signs of a new *arrhythmia* appear, hyperthyroidism should be considered. Amiodarone-associated hyperthyroidism may be followed by a transient period of hypothyroidism.

Hypothyroidism occurs in less than 10% of patients, although thyroid hormone concentration changes are common and may persist for several months after withdrawal of amiodarone.

Optic neuropathy and/or optic neuritis, usually resulting in visual impairment and sometimes progressing to permanent blindness, have been reported and may occur at any time during treatment with amiodarone. If symptoms of visual impairment, such as changes in visual acuity and decreases in peripheral vision, occur, a prompt ophthalmologic examination is recommended and amiodarone treatment should be re-evaluated. Regular ophthalmologic examinations that include funduscopy and slit-lamp procedures are recommended during treatment with amiodarone. Bilateral and symmetric asymptomatic corneal deposits appearing as yellow-brown pigmentation on slit-lamp examination occur in all patients after 6 months of treatment, but may appear sooner; symptomatic corneal deposits occur in up to 10% of patients; macular degeneration and decreased visual acuity are rare; corneal deposits are reversible after withdrawal of amiodarone, although it may take up to 7 months.

Sinus bradycardia usually responds to dosage reduction but may require a pacemaker; atropine-resistant.

Incidence rare

Allergic reaction (skin rash); ***hepatitis*** (yellow eyes or skin)

Note: *Allergic reaction* usually occurs within the first 2 weeks of therapy.

In *hepatitis*, hepatic enzymes are commonly elevated to several times normal within 2 months after initiation of therapy; deaths as a result of hepatic failure resembling alcoholic cirrhosis have occurred rarely.

Incidence not determined—Observed during clinical practice, estimates of frequency can not be determined

Angioedema (large, hive-like swelling on face, eyelids, lips, tongue, throat, hands, legs, feet, sex organs); ***aplastic anemia*** (chest pain; chills; cough; fever; headache; shortness of breath; sores, ulcers, or white spots on lips or in mouth; swollen or painful glands; tightness in chest; unusual bleeding or bruising; unusual tiredness or weakness; wheezing); ***bronchiolitis obliterans organizing pneumonia*** (chest pain; cough; fever or chills; sneezing; shortness of breath; sore throat; troubled breathing; tightness in chest; wheezing); ***bronchospasm*** (cough; difficulty breathing; noisy breathing; shortness of breath; tightness in chest; wheezing); ***cholestatic hepatitis*** (abdominal or stomach pain; chills; clay-colored stools; dark urine; diarrhea; dizziness; fever; headache; itching; loss of appetite; nausea; rash; unpleasant breath odor; unusual tiredness or weakness; vomiting of blood; yellow eyes or skin); ***cirrhosis*** (yellow eyes or skin); ***confusional state*** (mood or mental change); ***delirium*** (unusual excitement, nervousness, or restlessness; hallucinations; confusion as to time, place, or person; holding false beliefs that cannot be changed by fact); ***disorientation*** (confusion about identity, place, and time); ***dyspnea*** (shortness of breath; difficult or labored breathing; tightness in chest; wheezing); ***epididymitis*** (chills; fever; pain in abdomen, groin, or scrotum; pain or burning with urination; swelling of scrotum); ***erythema multiforme*** (blistering, peeling, loosening of skin; chills; cough; diarrhea; fever; itching; joint or muscle pain; red irritated eyes; sore throat; sores, ulcers, or white spots in mouth or on lips; unusual tiredness or weakness); ***exfoliative dermatitis*** (cracks in the skin; loss of heat from the body; red, swollen skin; scaly skin); ***hallucinations*** (seeing, hearing, or feeling things that are not there); ***hemolytic anemia*** (back, leg, or stomach pains; bleeding gums; chills; dark urine; difficulty breathing; fatigue; fever; general body swelling; headache; loss of appetite; nausea or vomiting; nosebleeds; pale skin; sore throat; yellowing of the eyes or skin); ***hemoptysis*** (coughing or spitting up blood); ***hypoxia*** (confusion; dizziness; fast heartbeat; shortness of breath; weakness); ***impotence*** (loss in sexual ability, desire, drive, or performance; decreased interest in sexual intercourse; inability to have or keep an erection); ***neutropenia*** (black, tarry, stools; chills; cough; fever; lower back or side pain; painful or difficult urination; pale skin; shortness of breath; sore throat; ulcers, sores, or white spots in mouth; unusual bleeding or bruising; unusual tiredness or weakness); ***pancreatitis*** (bloating; chills; constipation; darkened urine; fast heartbeat; fever; indigestion; loss of appetite; nausea; pains in stomach, side, or abdomen, possibly radiating to the back; vomiting; yellow eyes or skin); ***pancytopenia*** (high fever; chills; unexplained bleeding or bruising; bloody, black, or tarry stools; pale skin; unusual tiredness or weakness; cough; shortness of breath; sores, ulcers, or white spots on lips or in mouth; swollen glands); ***pleuritis*** (chest pain; chills and fever; dry cough; troubled breathing); ***pruritus*** (itching skin); ***pseudotumor cerebri*** (blurred or double vision; dizziness; eye pain; severe headache; nausea, and vomiting); ***pulmonary infiltrates*** (cough; chest pain; unusual tiredness or weakness); ***respiratory disorders, including; respiratory distress*** (shortness of breath; troubled breathing; tightness in chest; wheezing); ***respiratory failure*** (blue lips, fingernails, or skin; difficult or troubled breathing; irregular, fast or slow, or shallow breathing; shortness of breath); ***respiratory arrest*** (no breathing); ***ARDS*** (shortness of breath; tightness in chest; troubled breathing; wheezing); ***rhabdomyolysis*** (dark-colored urine; fever; muscle cramps or spasms; muscle pain or stiffness; unusual tiredness or weakness); ***Stevens-Johnson syndrome*** (blistering, peeling, loosening of skin; chills; cough; diarrhea; itching; joint or muscle pain; red irritated eyes; red skin lesions, often with a purple center; sore throat; sores, ulcers, or white spots in mouth or on lips; unusual tiredness or weakness); ***syndrome of inappropriate antidiuretic hormone secretion (SIADH)*** (agitation; coma; confusion; decreased urine output; depression; dizziness; headache; hostility; irritability; lethargy; muscle twitching; nausea; rapid weight gain; seizures; stupor; swelling of face, ankles, or hands; unusual tiredness or weakness); ***thrombocytopenia*** (black, tarry stools; bleeding gums; blood in urine or stools; pinpoint red spots on skin; unusual bleeding or bruising); ***toxic epidermal necrolysis*** (blistering, peeling, loosening of skin; chills; cough; diarrhea; itching; joint or muscle pain; red irritated eyes; red skin lesions, often with a purple center; sore throat; sores, ulcers, or white spots in mouth or on lips; unusual tiredness or weakness); ***vasculitis*** (redness, soreness or itching skin; fever; sores, welting or blisters); ***wheezing*** (difficulty in breathing or troubled breathing)

Those indicating need for medical attention only if they continue or are bothersome

Incidence more frequent—approximately 25%, especially during administration of high doses, as during loading

Constipation; headache; loss of appetite—may lead to severe weight loss; ***nausea and vomiting***

Incidence less frequent

Bitter or metallic taste; decreased sexual ability in males; decrease in sexual interest; dizziness (central nervous system [CNS] effect; hypotension is rare); ***flushing of face***

Incidence not determined—Observed during clinical practice, estimates of frequency can not be determined

Muscle weakness; myopathy (muscular pain, tenderness, wasting or weakness)

Those indicating possible pulmonary toxicity and the need for medical attention if they occur after medication is discontinued

Cough; fever, slight; painful breathing; shortness of breath

Overdose

For more information on the management of overdose or unintentional ingestion, **contact a Poison Control Center** (see *Poison Control Center Listing*).

Treatment of overdose

Decrease absorption—Recent oral ingestion may benefit from emesis and/or lavage.

Specific treatment—

Primarily supportive and symptomatic.

Monitoring of cardiac rhythm and blood pressure is important.

For bradycardia, a beta-adrenergic agonist or pacemaker may be indicated.

Hypotension may respond to positive inotropic and/or vasopressor agents.

Patient Consultation

As an aid to patient consultation, refer to *Advice for the Patient, Amiodarone (Systemic)*.

In providing consultation, consider emphasizing the following selected information (» = major clinical significance):

Before using this medication

» Conditions affecting use, especially:

Hypersensitivity to amiodarone or any of the components of the product, including iodine

Pregnancy—Potential risk of bradycardia and iodine toxicity in fetus and hypo- and hyperthyroidism in neonates; patient should be apprised of potential hazard to the fetus if administered during pregnancy

Breast-feeding—Distributed into breast milk

Use in children—Shorter onset and duration of action; intravenous administration is not recommended

Use in the elderly—Increased sensitivity to effects on thyroid function and increased incidence of ataxia and other neurotoxic effects

Surgical—Postoperative monitoring for ARDS

Other medications, especially other antiarrhythmics, azoles, coumarin-derivative anticoagulants, CYP3A4 inducers, inhibitors, or substrates, digitalis glycosides, fentanyl, fluoroquinolones, grapefruit juice, macrolide antibiotics, phenytoin, or simvastatin

Other medical problems, especially pre-existing atrioventricular (AV) block without pacemaker, bradycardic episodes resulting in syncope (unless controlled by pacemaker), cardiogenic shock (unless controlled by pacemaker), severe sinus node function impairment causing marked bradycardia (unless controlled by pacemaker), acute hepatitis, arrhythmia, pulmonary disease (pre-existing), or thyroid abnormalities.

Proper use of this medication

» Compliance with therapy; taking as directed even if feeling well

» Taking amiodarone at the same time with regards to meals as directed by your doctor each time you take it.

» Proper dosing

Missed dose: Not taking at all; notifying physician if two or more doses in a row are missed; not doubling doses

» Proper storage

Precautions while using this medication

Regular visits to physician to check progress

Importance of reading the amiodarone tablets medication guide before treatment starts and each time a refill is obtained.

Carrying medical identification card or bracelet

» Caution if any kind of surgery (including dental surgery) or emergency treatment is required

» Importance of not taking grapefruit juice or any product containing grapefruit while taking oral amiodarone

» Importance of telling your doctor if you are taking any prescription or non-prescription medications including herbal supplements such as St. John's Wort or other nutritional supplements while taking oral amiodarone.

» Protecting skin from sunlight during and for several months following withdrawal of treatment; sunburns may occur even through window glass and thin cotton clothing; use of protective clothing and a topical product that prevents sunburn; checking with physician if severe sunburn occurs

Checking with physician if blue-gray discoloration of skin occurs

» Checking with physician if changes in vision, such as a decrease in peripheral vision or a decrease in clarity of vision, occur

Side/adverse effects

Signs and symptoms of potential side effects, especially hypotension; neurotoxicity; photosensitivity, particularly to long-wave ultraviolet-A (UVA) light; pulmonary fibrosis or interstitial pneumonitis/alveolitis; new or exacerbated arrhythmias; blue-gray coloring of skin on face, neck, and arms; congestive heart failure; hyperthyroidism; hypothyroidism; noninfectious epididymitis; ocular toxicity, including optic neuropathy and/or optic neuritis; sinus bradycardia; allergic reaction; and hepatitis

(Signs of potential side effects observed during clinical practice, especially angioedema, aplastic anemia, ARDS, bronchiolitis obliterans organizing pneumonia, bronchospasm, cholestatic hepatitis, cirrhosis, confusional state, delirium, disorientation, dyspnea, epididymitis, erythema multiforme, exfoliative dermatitis, hallucination, hemolytic anemia, hemoptysis, hypoxia, impotence, neutropenia, pancreatitis, pancytopenia, pleuritis, pruritus, pseudotumor cerebri, pulmonary infiltrates, respiratory arrest, respiratory distress, respiratory failure, rhabdomyolysis, Stevens-Johnson syndrome, syndrome of inappropriate antidiuretic hormone secretion, thrombocytopenia, toxic epidermal necrolysis, vasculitis, or wheezing)

General Dosing Information

Because of its delayed onset of action, difficulty in dosage adjustment, and potentially serious adverse effects, it is recommended that amiodarone administration be initiated in the hospital and that the patient remain in the hospital at least for the loading dose phase. Amiodarone should be administered only by physicians who are experienced in the treatment of life-threatening arrhythmias, are thoroughly familiar with the risks and benefits of amiodarone therapy, and have access to laboratory facilities equipped to adequately monitor the effectiveness and side effects of amiodarone therapy.

Dosage must be adjusted to meet the individual requirements of each patient, based on clinical response, appearance or severity of toxicity, and in some cases, plasma amiodarone concentrations.

Diet/Nutrition

Grapefruit juice and grapefruit products should not be taken during treatment with oral amiodarone to avoid significant increases in plasma drug concentrations and the area under the amiodarone plasma concentration-time curve (AUC). This information should be considered when changing from intravenous amiodarone to oral amiodarone.

Amiodarone tablets should be administered consistently with regard to meals because of the food effect on absorption.

For treatment of adverse effects

Recommended treatment consists of the following:

- Hypotension associated with intravenous amiodarone administration should be treated initially by slowing the infusion rate. Additional therapy, if needed, may include volume expansion and administration of vasopressor agents and/or positive inotropic agents.
- If hypothyroidism occurs, dosage reduction or withdrawal of amiodarone is recommended, along with addition of thyroid hormone supplementation.
- Hyperthyroidism, which may be associated with signs of new or breakthrough arrhythmias, should be treated by reducing the dose of or withdrawing amiodarone. Additional therapy may include the use of antithyroid drugs, beta adrenergic blocking agents, and/or temporary corticosteroid therapy. However, the effects of antithyroid drugs may be delayed due to substantial quantities of preformed thyroid hormones in the gland. Because amiodarone-induced hyperthyroidism is associated with low radioiodine uptake, radioactive iodine therapy is *contraindicated.* Thyroid surgery in this setting may be associated with a risk of inducing thyroid storm. Hyperthyroidism may be followed by a transient period of hypothyroidism.
- If signs or symptoms of pulmonary toxicity occur, it is recommended that amiodarone therapy be withdrawn until the cause has been determined. If pulmonary toxicity is related to amiodarone, withdrawal of amiodarone is recommended. Usefulness of steroid therapy is controversial, but such therapy may be useful for severe toxicity.
- Nausea and vomiting may be relieved by reduction of dose or administration of amiodarone in divided doses.
- If epididymitis occurs, dosage reduction or withdrawal of amiodarone is recommended.

Oral Dosage Forms

Note: Bracketed uses in the *Dosage Forms* section refer to categories of use and/or indications that are not included in U.S. product labeling.

AMIODARONE HYDROCHLORIDE TABLETS

Note: Because amiodarone has a long terminal plasma elimination half-life, the time to reach steady-state would take several months if the drug were administered at usual doses; therefore, loading doses are necessary in order to ensure that an antiarrhythmic effect occurs within a reasonable period of time. The patient should be closely monitored during the loading phase of therapy, especially until the risk of recurrent ventricular tachycardia or fibrillation has subsided. Elimination of ventricular fibrillation and tachycardia, along with a reduction in complex and total ventricular ectopic beats, usually occurs within 1 to 3 weeks.

Because of the potential for interactions with other antiarrhythmic drugs, it is recommended that an attempt be made to gradually discontinue the administration of prior antiarrhythmic drugs upon starting amiodarone therapy.

Usual adult dose

Ventricular arrhythmias (life-threatening ventricular fibrillation or hemodynamically unstable ventricular tachycardia)—

Loading: Oral, 800 mg to 1.6 grams per day for one to three weeks (or longer, if necessary) until an initial therapeutic response or side effects occur; may be given in divided doses with meals for doses greater than 1 gram per day or if gastrointestinal side effects occur. When adequate control is achieved or excessive side effects occur, the dose is reduced to 600 to 800 mg per day for one month and then decreased again to the lowest effective maintenance dose. The lowest effective maintenance dose should be used to prevent the occurrence of side effects.

Maintenance: Oral, approximately 400 mg per day, the dosage being increased or decreased as necessary. Higher maintenance doses (up to 600 mg per day) or lower maintenance doses may be required in some patients. The long-term maintenance dose should be determined according to the antiarrhythmic effect as assessed by symptoms, tolerance, and Holter recordings and/or programmed electrical stimulation. Amiodarone plasma concentration determinations may be helpful in evaluating nonresponsiveness or unexpectedly severe toxicity.

When dosage adjustments are necessary, patients should be closely monitored for an extended period of time because of the long and variable half-life of amiodarone and the difficulty of predicting the time required to attain a new steady-state amiodarone concentration.

[Supraventricular tachycardia][1]—

Loading: Oral, 600 to 800 mg per day for one week or until an initial therapeutic response or side effects occur. When adequate control is achieved or excessive side effects occur, the dose is reduced to 400 mg per day for three weeks.

Maintenance: Oral, 200 to 400 mg per day.

Usual pediatric dose

[Ventricular arrhythmias]

[Supraventricular arrhythmias][1]—

Loading: Oral, 10 mg per kg of body weight per day or 800 mg per 1.72 square meters of body surface area per day for ten days or until an initial therapeutic response or side effects occur. When adequate control is achieved or excessive side effects occur, the dose is reduced to 5 mg per kg of body weight or 400 mg per 1.72 square meters of body surface area per day for several weeks and then decreased gradually to the lowest effective maintenance dose.

Maintenance: Oral, 2.5 mg per kg of body weight per day or 200 mg per 1.72 square meters of body surface area per day.

Strength(s) usually available

U.S.—

200 mg (Rx) [*Cordarone* (scored; lactose)].

Canada—

200 mg (Rx) [*Cordarone* (scored; lactose); *pms-Amiodarone* (lactose; magnesium stearate; povidone; silicon dioxide; sodium starch glycolate; FD&C red #40 lake)].

Packaging and storage

Store below 40 °C (104 °F), preferably between 15 and 30 °C (59 and 86 °F), unless otherwise specified by the manufacturer. Protect from light.

Auxiliary labeling

- Grapefruit and grapefruit juice should not be taken with this medication.
- Tell your doctor about all medications you are taking, prescription and non-prescription.
- Please read patient information leaflet enclosed.

Parenteral Dosage Forms

Note: The surface properties of solutions containing injectable amiodarone are altered, reducing the solution drop size. This phenomenon may result in underdosing the patient by up to 30% if a drop counter infusion set is used; therefore, a volumetric infusion pump must be used to deliver amiodarone. Whenever possible, amiodarone should be administered through a central venous catheter dedicated to this purpose; an in-line filter should also be used during administration.

Note: An expert panel concluded that (based on animal studies) amiodarone I've. administration may indirectly but adversely affect male reproductive tract development during **fetal, infant, and toddler** stages of development. The indirect effects may be linked to plasticizers that leach out from the I've. tubing during certain administration conditions, such as higher amiodarone concentrations and lower flow rates.

AMIODARONE HYDROCHLORIDE INJECTION

Note: Amiodarone shows considerable interindividual variation in response; therefore, monitoring is necessary at dosage initiation, at dosage adjustments, and when switching to oral amiodarone therapy.

Usual adult dose

Ventricular arrhythmias (ventricular fibrillation or hemodynamically unstable ventricular tachycardia)—

Note: The recommended starting dose of intravenous amiodarone is about 1000 mg over the first twenty-four hours.

First twenty-four hours—

Loading infusions (may be individualized for each patient):

First, rapid intravenous infusion—

150 mg administered by rapid intravenous infusion over the first ten minutes (15 mg per minute).

Next, slow intravenous infusion—

360 mg administered by slow intravenous infusion over the next six hours (1 mg per minute).

Maintenance infusion (decreasing the rate of the slow intravenous infusion):

Intravenous infusion, 540 mg of amiodarone is delivered over the remaining eighteen hours (0.5 mg per minute).

After the first twenty-four hours—

The maintenance infusion rate of 0.5 mg per minute (720 mg per twenty-four hours) should be continued, using a concentration of 1 to 6 mg per mL (concentrations greater than 2 mg per mL should be administered via a central venous catheter). In the event of breakthrough episodes of ventricular fibrillation or hemodynamically unstable ventricular tachycardia, supplemental infusions of 150 mg may be administered. Such infusions should be administered over a period of ten minutes to minimize the potential for hypotension. The rate of the maintenance infusion may be increased to effectively achieve arrhythmia suppression.

Intravenous amiodarone should be used for acute treatment until the patient's ventricular arrhythmias have been stabilized. Most patients will require therapy for forty-eight to ninety-six hours, and intravenous amiodarone may be safely administered for longer periods of time if necessary, although intravenous amiodarone is not intended for maintenance treatment. There has been limited experience in patients receiving intravenous amiodarone for longer than three weeks. Patients whose arrhythmias have been suppressed by intravenous amiodarone may be switched to oral amiodarone.

Usual adult prescribing limits

The initial infusion rate should not exceed 30 mg per minute. Infusions lasting longer than one hour should not exceed a concentration of 2 mg per mL unless a central venous catheter is used. Amiodarone concentrations of > 3 mg/mL in 5% Dextrose Injection USP (D_5W), have been associated with a high incidence of peripheral vein phlebitis; concentrations ≤ 2.5 mg/mL appear to be less irritating. In clinical trials, mean daily doses of above 2100 mg were associated with an increased risk of hypotension.

A maintenance infusion of up to 0.5 mg per minute of amiodarone can be cautiously continued for two to three weeks, regardless of the patient's age, renal function, or left ventricular function, but experience is limited in patients receiving intravenous amiodarone for longer than three weeks.

Usual pediatric dose

Safety and efficacy have not been established in patients younger than 18 years of age; use is not recommended.

Strength(s) usually available

U.S.—

50 mg per mL (Rx) [*Cordarone I've.*].

Canada—

50 mg per mL (Rx) [*Cordarone Intravenous*].

Packaging and storage

Store at room temperature, between 15 and 25 °C (59 and 77 °F). Protect from light.

Note: Intravenous amiodarone does not need to be protected from light during administration.

Preparation of dosage form

To prepare the rapid intravenous infusion, add 3 mL of amiodarone (150 mg) to 100 mL of 5% Dextrose Injection USP (D_5W). The resulting concentration is 1.5 mg per mL.

To prepare the slow intravenous infusion, add 18 mL of amiodarone (900 mg) to 500 mL of 5% Dextrose Injection USP (D_5W). The resulting concentration is 1.8 mg per mL.

Stability

The dose administration schedule used in clinical trials was designed to take into consideration the adsorption of amiodarone to polyvinyl chloride (PVC) tubing. Because clinical trials were conducted using PVC tubing, its use is recommended for delivery of amiodarone. The recommended concentrations and infusion rates reflect those identified in clinical trials; it is important that these recommendations be followed closely. Amiodarone infusions exceeding 2 hours must be administered in glass or polyolefin bottles containing 5% Dextrose Injection USP (D_5W).

PVC container:

Amiodarone is physically compatible; amiodarone loss is less than 10% at 2 hours in 5% Dextrose Injection USP (D_5W) at a concentration of 1 to 6 mg of amiodarone per mL.

Polyolefin or glass container:

Amiodarone is physically compatible; no amiodarone loss occurs at 24 hours in 5% Dextrose Injection USP (D_5W) at a concentration of 1 to 6 mg of amiodarone per mL.

Incompatibilities

Amiodarone admixed with 5% Dextrose Injection USP (D_5W) to a concentration of 4 mg per mL is incompatible and forms a precipitate with aminophylline, cefamandole nafate, cefazolin sodium, and mezlocillin sodium. Amiodarone also forms a precipitate with sodium bicarbonate at a concentration of 3 mg per mL and with heparin sodium at an unknown concentration.

Additional information

Intravenous amiodarone is not intended for long-term (longer than 3 weeks) maintenance treatment; patients whose arrhythmias have been suppressed by intravenous amiodarone may be switched to oral amiodarone. The optimal dose to use when changing from intravenous to oral amiodarone will depend on the dose of intravenous amiodarone already administered, as well as the bioavailability of oral amiodarone. Clinical monitoring is recommended when patients, particularly the elderly, are changed to oral amiodarone therapy.

Recommendations for oral dosage after intravenous infusion*	
Duration of intravenous amiodarone infusion (assuming a 720 mg per day infusion [0.5 mg per minute])	Initial daily dose of oral amiodarone
< 1 week	800 to 1600 mg
1 to 3 weeks	600 to 800 mg
> 3 weeks	400 mg

*Based on a comparable total body amount of amiodarone delivered by the intravenous and oral routes, based on 50% bioavailability of oral amiodarone.

[1]Not included in Canadian product labeling.

Selected Bibliography

Product Information: Cordarone®, amiodarone HCl. Wyeth Laboratories, Philadelphia, PA, (PI revised 08/2003) reviewed 08/2004.

Revised: 01/31/2005

AMITRIPTYLINE—See *Antidepressants, Tricyclic (Systemic)*

AMLODIPINE Systemic

VA CLASSIFICATION (Primary/Secondary): CV200/CV250; CV409

Commonly used brand name(s): *Norvasc.*

Note: For a listing of dosage forms and brand names by country availability, see *Dosage Forms* section(s).

Category

Antianginal; antihypertensive.

Indications

Accepted

Angina, chronic stable (treatment)—Amlodipine is indicated for the treatment of chronic stable angina; it may be used alone or in combination with other antianginal agents.

Angina, vasospastic (treatment)[1]—Amlodipine is indicated for the treatment of confirmed or suspected vasospastic angina. It may be used alone or in combination with other antianginal agents.

Hypertension (treatment)—Amlodipine is indicated for the treatment of hypertension; it may be used alone or in combination with other antihypertensive agents.

For additional information on initial therapeutic guidelines related to the treatment of hypertension, see *Appendix III.*

[1]Not included in Canadian product labeling.

Pharmacology/Pharmacokinetics

Physicochemical characteristics

Molecular weight—567.05.

Mechanism of action/Effect

Amlodipine is a dihydropyridine calcium channel blocking agent. Like the other dihydropyridine agents, amlodipine selectively inhibits calcium influx across cell membranes in cardiac and vascular smooth muscle, with a greater effect on vascular smooth muscle. Amlodipine is a peripheral arteriolar vasodilator; thus it reduces afterload.

Other actions/effects

Amlodipine exhibits negative inotropic effects *in vivo*, but appears to have no significant effect on the sinoatrial (SA) or atrioventricular (AV) node in humans.

Absorption

Slowly and almost completely absorbed from the gastrointestinal tract; absorption not affected by food. Bioavailability is approximately 60 to 65%.

Distribution

Vol_D—21 L per kg.

Protein binding

Very high (95 to 98%).

Biotransformation

Undergoes minimal presystemic metabolism. Amlodipine undergoes slow but extensive hepatic metabolism, producing metabolites lacking significant pharmacological activity.

Half-life

Elimination—Mean, 35 hours in healthy volunteers; may be prolonged to a mean of 48 hours in hypertensive patients, 65 hours in the elderly, and 60 hours in patients with hepatic function impairment. Not affected by renal function impairment.

Time to peak concentration

Single-dose—6 to 9 hours.

Duration of action

24 hours.

Elimination

Renal—59 to 62% (about 5% as unchanged amlodipine).
Biliary/fecal—20 to 25%.
In dialysis—Amlodipine is not removed by hemodialysis.

Precautions to Consider

Carcinogenicity

No evidence of carcinogenicity was revealed in studies with rats and mice given amlodipine at dosages of 0.5, 1.25, and 2.5 mg per kg of body weight (mg/kg) per day for 2 years.

Mutagenicity

No evidence of mutagenicity was observed at the gene or chromosome level.

Pregnancy/Reproduction

Fertility—No impairment of fertility was observed in rats given amlodipine at doses 8 times the maximum recommended human dose prior to mating.

Pregnancy—Studies have not been done in humans.

No evidence of teratogenicity or other embryo/fetal toxicity was observed in rats or rabbits given up to 10 mg/kg during periods of major organogenesis. However, the number of intrauterine deaths increased about five-fold, and rat litter size was significantly decreased (by 50%).

FDA Pregnancy Category C.

Labor—Amlodipine has been shown to prolong the duration of labor in rats.

Breast-feeding

It is not known whether amlodipine is distributed into breast milk.

Pediatrics

No information is available on the relationship of age to the effects of amlodipine in pediatric patients. Safety and efficacy have not been established in children younger than 6 years of age.

Geriatrics

The half-life of amlodipine may be increased in the elderly. These patients may be more sensitive to the hypotensive effects of amlodipine and may require a lower initial dose.

Dental

Gingival hyperplasia is a rare side effect that has been reported with amlodipine. It also has been reported with other calcium channel blocking agents, such as diltiazem, felodipine, verapamil, and, most commonly, nifedipine. It usually starts as gingivitis or gum inflammation in the first 1 to 9 months of treatment. Resolution of the hyperplasia and improvement of the clinical symptoms usually occur one to four weeks after discontinuation of therapy. A strictly enforced program of professional teeth cleaning combined with plaque control by the patient will minimize growth rate and severity of gingival enlargement. Periodontal surgery may be indicated in some cases, and should be followed by careful plaque control to inhibit recurrence of gum enlargement.

Surgical

Recent evidence suggests that withdrawal of antihypertensive therapy prior to surgery may be undesirable. However, the anesthesiologist must be aware of such therapy.

Drug interactions and/or related problems

The following drug interactions and/or related problems have been selected on the basis of their potential clinical significance (possible mechanism in parentheses where appropriate)—not necessarily inclusive (» = major clinical significance):

Note: Combinations containing any of the following medications, depending on the amount present, may also interact with this medication.

Anesthetics, hydrocarbon inhalation
(concurrent use with amlodipine may produce additive hypotension; although calcium channel blocking agents may be useful to prevent supraventricular tachycardias, hypertension, or coronary spasm during surgery, caution is recommended during use)

Anti-inflammatory drugs, nonsteroidal (NSAIDs), especially indomethacin
(NSAIDs may reduce the antihypertensive effects of amlodipine by inhibiting renal prostaglandin synthesis and/or causing sodium and fluid retention)

Beta-adrenergic blocking agents
(although reports of adverse effects resulting from concurrent use of amlodipine with the beta-adrenergic blocking agents are lacking, caution is recommended given the similarity of amlodipine to nifedipine; concurrent use of nifedipine with the beta-adrenergic blocking agents, although usually well-tolerated, may produce excessive hypotension and, in rare cases, may increase the possibility of congestive heart failure)

Estrogens
(estrogen-induced fluid retention may tend to increase blood pressure; the patient should be carefully monitored to confirm that the desired effect is being obtained)

Highly protein-bound medications, such as: Anticonvulsants, hydantoin
Anticoagulants, coumarin- and indandione-derivative
Anti-inflammatory drugs, nonsteroidal
Quinine
Salicylates
Sulfinpyrazone
(caution is advised when these medications are used concurrently with amlodipine since amlodipine is highly protein bound; changes in serum concentrations of the free, unbound medications may occur)

Hypotension-producing medications, other (see *Appendix II*)
(antihypertensive effects may be potentiated when amlodipine is used concurrently with hypotension-producing medications; although some antihypertensive and/or diuretic combinations are frequently used for therapeutic advantage, when any of these medications are used concurrently, dosage adjustments may be necessary)

Lithium
(concurrent use with amlodipine potentially may result in neurotoxicity in the form of nausea, vomiting, diarrhea, ataxia, tremors, and/or tinnitus; caution is recommended)

Sympathomimetics
(concurrent use may reduce antihypertensive effects of amlodipine; the patient should be carefully monitored to confirm that the desired effect is being obtained)

Laboratory value alterations

The following have been selected on the basis of their potential clinical significance (possible effect in parentheses where appropriate)—not necessarily inclusive (» = major clinical significance).

» Hepatic enzyme values
(increases consistent with hepatitis or cholestasis have been reported; in some cases, the elevations have been severe enough to require hospitalization)

Medical considerations/Contraindications

The medical considerations/contraindications included have been selected on the basis of their potential clinical significance (reasons given in parentheses where appropriate)—not necessarily inclusive (» = major clinical significance).

Except under special circumstances, this medication should not be used when the following medical problem exists:

» Hypotension, severe
(amlodipine may aggravate this condition)

Risk-benefit should be considered when the following medical problems exist:

Aortic stenosis
(increased risk of heart failure because of fixed impedance to flow across aortic valve)

Congestive heart failure
(amlodipine should be used with caution in patients with congestive heart failure because of the slight risk for negative inotropic effect)

Hepatic function impairment
(clearance of amlodipine may be reduced since it undergoes extensive hepatic metabolism; elimination half-life may be prolonged to 60 hours)

Sensitivity to amlodipine

Patient monitoring

The following may be especially important in patient monitoring (other tests may be warranted in some patients, depending on condition; » = major clinical significance):

» Blood pressure determinations and
» ECG readings and
» Heart rate determinations and
Reduced frequency or severity of anginal attacks and
Decreased nitrate consumption and
Improved exercise tolerance without angina
(recommended primarily during dosage titration or when dosage is increased from established maintenance dosage level; also recommended when other medications are added that affect cardiac conduction or blood pressure)

(blood pressure determinations are recommended at periodic intervals to monitor efficacy and safety of amlodipine therapy; selected patients may be trained to perform blood pressure measurements at home and report the results at regular physician visits)

Side/Adverse Effects

The following side/adverse effects have been selected on the basis of their potential clinical significance (possible signs and symptoms in parentheses where appropriate)—not necessarily inclusive:

Those indicating need for medical attention

Incidence more frequent

Edema, peripheral (swelling of ankles and feet)—dose-related incidence of 1.8–10.8% between 2.5–10 mg daily; higher prevalence in women than men

Incidence less frequent

Dizziness—dose-related incidence of 1.1–3.4% between 2.5–10 mg daily; ***palpitations*** (pounding heartbeat)—dose-related incidence of 0.7–4.5% between 2.5–10 mg daily; higher prevalence in women than men

Incidence rare

Angina (chest pain); ***bradycardia*** (slow heartbeat); ***hypotension*** (dizziness); ***jaundice*** (dark yellow urine; yellow eyes or skin); ***orthostatic hypotension*** (dizziness or light-headedness when getting up from a lying or sitting position)

Those indicating need for medical attention only if they continue or are bothersome

Incidence more frequent

Abdominal pain; flushing—dose-related incidence of 0.7–2.6% between 2.5–10 mg daily; higher prevalence in women than men; ***headache; somnolence*** (sleepiness or unusual drowsiness)—higher prevalence in women than men

Incidence less frequent

Fatigue (unusual tiredness or weakness); ***nausea***

Overdose

For specific information on the agents used in the management of amlodipine or calcium channel blocking agent toxicity or overdose, see:
- *Atropine* in *Anticholinergics/Antispasmodics (Systemic)* monograph;
- *Calcium Chloride or Calcium Gluconate*in
- *Calcium Supplements (Systemic)* monograph;
- *Charcoal, Activated (Oral-Local)* monograph;
- *Dopamine, Dobutamine, Isoproterenol, Metaraminol, or Norepinephrine* in *Sympathomimetic Agents—Cardiovascular Use (Parenteral-Systemic)* monograph;
- *Lidocaine (Systemic)* monograph; and/or
- *Procainamide (Systemic)* monograph.

For more information on the management of overdose or unintentional ingestion, **contact a poison control center** (see *Poison Control Center Listing*).

Clinical effects of overdose

The following effects have been selected on the basis of their potential clinical significance (possible signs and symptoms in parentheses where appropriate)—not necessarily inclusive:

Hypotension, symptomatic; reflex tachycardia; bradycardia

Treatment of overdose

To decrease absorption—

Ipecac is not recommended since emesis may produce vagal stimulation and (theoretically) worsen an overdose with calcium antagonists. Furthermore, ipecac has not been demonstrated to improve patient outcome

Consider prehospital administration of activated charcoal as an aqueous slurry in patients who are awake and able to protect their airway. Activated charcoal is most effective when administered within one hour of ingestion.

To enhance elimination—

High protein binding of all calcium channel blocking agents would suggest hemodialysis or hemoperfusion would have limited usefulness.

Recommended treatment consists of the following:

• Hypotension, symptomatic—Intravenous fluids, intravenous dopamine or dobutamine, calcium gluconate, isoproterenol, metaraminol, or norepinephrine should be used as appropriate.

• Tachycardia, rapid ventricular rate in patients with antegrade conduction in atrial flutter fibrillation, and accessory pathway with Wolff-Parkinson-White or Lown-Ganong-Levine syndrome—Direct-current cardioversion, intravenous lidocaine, or intravenous procainamide. Intravenous fluids given by slow-drip.

• Bradycardia, rarely second or third degree atrioventricular (AV) block, with a few patients progressing to asystole—Intravenous atropine, isoproterenol, norepinephrine, or calcium chloride, or use of electronic cardiac pacemaker, as appropriate.

Specific treatment—

Supportive care—Patients in whom intentional overdose is confirmed or suspected should be referred for psychiatric consultation.

Monitoring—

Patients with suspected calcium channel blocker overdose should be placed on a cardiac monitor. Monitor hemodynamic status closely including heart rate blood pressure, EKG, and urinary output.

Monitor electrolytes, renal function tests and glucose. Swan Ganz monitoring may help guide fluid and hemodynamic management.

Monitor respiratory function and oxygenation; pulmonary edema may occur.

Calcium antagonist dosage forms are generally radiolucent. Sustained-release forms may be an exception.

Qualitative and/or quantitative serum levels for calcium antagonists are not readily available, predictive of toxicity, nor helpful in directing therapy.

Patient Consultation

As an aid to patient consultation, refer to *Advice for the Patient, Amlodipine (Systemic)*.

In providing consultation, consider emphasizing the following selected information (» = major clinical significance):

Before using this medication

» Conditions affecting use, especially:
  Sensitivity to amlodipine
  Use in children—Safety and efficacy not established in children younger than 6 years of age
  Use in the elderly—Half-life increased; increased sensitivity to hypotensive effects
  Dental—Risk of gingival hyperplasia
  Other medical problems, especially severe hypotension

Proper use of this medication

» Compliance with therapy; importance of not taking more medication than amount prescribed

» Proper dosing
  Missed dose: Taking as soon as possible; not taking if almost time for next scheduled dose; not doubling doses

» Proper storage

For use as an antihypertensive

Possible need for control of weight and diet, especially sodium intake

» Patient may not experience symptoms of hypertension; importance of taking medication even if feeling well

» Does not cure, but helps control hypertension; possible need for lifelong therapy; serious consequences of untreated hypertension

Precautions while using this medication

Regular visits to physician to check progress during therapy

Checking with physician before discontinuing medication; gradual dosage reduction may be necessary

» Discussing exercise or physical exertion limits with physician; reduced occurrence of chest pain may tempt patient to be overactive

Possible headache; checking with physician if continuing or severe

» Maintaining good dental hygiene and seeing dentist frequently for teeth cleaning to prevent tenderness, bleeding, and gum enlargement

For use as an antihypertensive:

» Not taking other medications, especially nonprescription sympathomimetics, unless discussed with physician

Side/adverse effects

Signs of potential side effects, especially peripheral edema, dizziness, palpitations, angina, bradycardia, hypotension, jaundice, or orthostatic hypotension

General Dosing Information

Concurrent administration of sublingual nitroglycerin, long-acting nitrates, beta-blockers, or other antianginal agents with amlodipine may produce additive antihypertensive and antianginal effects. Sublingual nitroglycerin may be used as needed to abort acute angina attacks during amlodipine therapy. Nitrate medication may be used during amlodipine therapy for angina prophylaxis. Amlodipine will not protect against the consequences of abrupt beta-blocker withdrawal; gradual beta-blocker dose reduction is recommended I.

Although no "rebound effect" has been reported upon discontinuation of amlodipine, a gradual decrease of dosage with physician supervision is recommended.

Oral Dosage Forms

AMLODIPINE BESYLATE TABLETS

Usual adult dose

Angina, chronic stable or
Angina, vasospastic[1] or
Hypertension—

Oral, 5 to 10 mg once a day.

Note: An initial antihypertensive dose of 2.5 mg is recommended for small, fragile, or elderly patients, patients with hepatic function impairment, or when adding amlodipine to other antihypertensive therapy. Because of amlodipine's prolonged elimination half-life, dosage increases should be accomplished slowly at five- to seven-day intervals. Rapid titration without complete assessment of the patient's response at each dosage level may result in hypotension.

An initial antianginal dose of 5 mg is recommended for the elderly and for patients with hepatic function impairment.

Usual pediatric dose

Antihypertensive—

Children younger than 6 years of age—Safety and efficacy have not been established.

Children 6 years of age and older—Oral, 2.5 to 5 mg once daily.

Strength(s) usually available

U.S.—
  2.5 mg (Rx) [*Norvasc*].
  5 mg (Rx) [*Norvasc*].
  10 mg (Rx) [*Norvasc*].

Canada—
  5 mg (Rx) [*Norvasc*].
  10 mg (Rx) [*Norvasc*].

Packaging and storage

Store at controlled room temperature between 15 and 30° C (59 and 86° F), in a tight, light-resistant container.

Auxiliary labeling

• Do not take other medicines without physician's advice.

[1]Not included in Canadian product labeling.

Selected Bibliography

Murdoch D, Heel RC. Amlodipine: a review of its pharmacodynamic and pharmacokinetic properties, and therapeutic use in cardiovascular disease. Drugs 1991; 41(3): 478-505.

Anon: The sixth report of the joint national committee on prevention, detection, evaluation, and treatment of high blood pressure. Arch Intern Med 1997; 157:2413-2446.

Revised: 11/17/2004

AMLODIPINE AND ATORVASTATIN Systemic†

VA CLASSIFICATION (Primary/Secondary): CV900/CV200; CV250; CV409; CV351

Commonly used brand name(s): *Caduet*.

Note: For a listing of dosage forms and brand names by country availability, see *Dosage Forms* section(s).

†Not commercially available in Canada.

Category

Antianginal—Amlodipine; antihyperlipidemic—Atorvastatin; antihypertensive—Amlodipine; HMG-CoA reductase inhibitor—Atorvastatin.

Indications

General Considerations

Amlodipine and atorvastatin is indicated in patients for whom treatment with both amlodipine and atorvastatin is appropriate.

Accepted

Angina, chronic stable (treatment)—Amlodipine is indicated for the treatment of chronic stable angina; it may be used alone or in combination with other antianginal agents.

Angina, vasospastic (treatment)—Amlodipine is indicated for the treatment of confirmed or suspected vasospastic angina. It may be used alone or in combination with other antianginal agents.

Hypertension (treatment)—Amlodipine is indicated for the treatment of hypertension. It may be used alone or in combination with other antihypertensive agents.

Hyperlipidemia (treatment)—Atorvastatin is indicated as an adjunct to diet to reduce elevated total cholesterol (total-C), low-density lipoprotein cholesterol (LDL-C), apolipoprotein B (apo B), and triglyceride (TG) concentrations and to increase HDL-C (high-density lipoprotein) in patients with primary hypercholesterolemia (heterozygous familial and nonfamilial) and mixed dyslipidemia (Fredrickson Types IIa and IIb). It is indicated as an adjunct to diet in the treatment of heterozygous familial hypercholesterolemia in boys and postmenarchal girls from 10 to 17 years of age if after an adequate trial of diet therapy the following findings are present:

- LDL-C remains greater than or equal to 190 mg/dL or
- LDL-C remains greater than or equal to 160 mg/dL and:
  —there is a positive family history of premature cardiovascular disease or
  —two or more other CVD risk factors are present in the pediatric patient

Atorvastatin is also indicated to reduce total-C and LDL-C in patients with homozygous familial hypercholesterolemia as an adjunct to other lipid-lowering treatments, such as low-density lipoprotein apheresis, or if such treatments are unavailable.

Atorvastatin is indicated for the treatment of patients with primary dysbetalipoproteinemia (Fredrickson Type III) who do not respond adequately to diet.

Atorvastatin is indicated as an adjunct to diet for the treatment of patients with elevated serum triglyceride levels (Fredrickson Type IV).

For additional information on initial therapeutic guidelines related to the treatment of hyperlipidemia or hypertension, see *Appendix III*.

Pharmacology/Pharmacokinetics

Physicochemical characteristics

Molecular weight—
Amlodipine besylate: 567.1.
Atorvastatin calcium: 1209.42.

Solubility—
Amlodipine besylate is slightly soluble in water and sparingly soluble in ethanol.
Atorvastatin calcium is very slightly soluble in distilled water, pH 7.4 phosphate buffer, and acetonitrile, slightly soluble in ethanol, and freely soluble in methanol. Atorvastatin is insoluble in aqueous solutions of pH 4 and below.

Mechanism of action/Effect

Amlodipine—
Amlodipine is a dihydropyridine calcium channel blocking agent that selectively inhibits calcium influx across cell membranes in cardiac and vascular smooth muscle, with a greater effect on vascular smooth muscle. Amlodipine is a peripheral arterial vasodilator that acts directly on vascular smooth muscle, thus it reduces afterload.

Atorvastatin—
3-hydroxy-3-methylglutaryl coenzyme A (HMG-CoA) reductase inhibitors competitively inhibit the enzyme that catalyzes the conversion of HMG-CoA to mevalonate, the rate-limiting step in cholesterol biosynthesis. The primary site of action of HMG-CoA reductase inhibitors is the liver, which is the principal site of cholesterol synthesis and low-density lipoprotein clearance. Cholesterol and triglycerides circulate in the bloodstream as part of lipoprotein complexes. These complexes are composed of high-density lipoprotein (HDL), intermediate-density lipoprotein (IDL), low-density lipoprotein (LDL), and very-low-density lipoprotein (VLDL). In the liver, triglycerides (TG) and cholesterol are incorporated into VLDL, which is released into the plasma for transport to the peripheral tissues. LDL is formed from VLDL and is catabolized primarily through the LDL receptor. Elevated plasma concentrations of total cholesterol (total-C), LDL-cholesterol (LDL-C), and apolipoprotein B (apo B) promote human atherosclerosis and are risk factors for developing cardiovascular disease. Increased plasma concentrations of HDL-C are associated with decreased cardiovascular risk. Atorvastatin lowers plasma cholesterol and lipoprotein concentrations by inhibiting HMG-CoA reductase and cholesterol synthesis in the liver and by increasing the number of hepatic LDL receptors on the cell surface to enhance uptake and catabolism of LDL. Atorvastatin also reduces LDL production and the number of LDL particles. Atorvastatin reduces total-C, LDL-C, and apo B in patients with homozygous and heterozygous familial hypercholesterolemia (FH), nonfamilial forms of hypercholesterolemia, and mixed dyslipidemia. Atorvastatin also reduces VLDL-C and TG and produces variable increases in HDL-C and apolipoprotein A-1.

Absorption

Amlodipine—64 to 90% absorbed. When administered alone, absorption is not altered by food.

Atorvastatin—Rapidly absorbed. The absolute bioavailability of atorvastatin is approximately 14%. Atorvastatin has a low systemic availability due to pre-systemic clearance in the gastrointestinal mucosa and/or hepatic first-pass metabolism. Food decreases the rate and extent of absorption by approximately 25% and 9%, respectively; although, LDL-C reduction is similar when atorvastatin is given with or without food. The concentration of atorvastatin in plasma (C_{max}) and the area under the plasma concentration-time curve (AUC) are lower by approximately 30% following evening administration when compared with morning administration. However, LDL-C reduction is the same, regardless of the time of day of administration.

Distribution

Volume of distribution (Vol_D)—
Amlodipine: 21 L per kg (L/kg).
Atorvastatin: approximately 381 liters (L).

Protein binding

Amlodipine—Very high (Approximately 93%).
Atorvastatin—Very high (≥ 98%).

Biotransformation

Amlodipine—extensively (about 90%) to inactive metabolites via hepatic metabolism.

Atorvastatin—extensive hepatic and/or extra-hepatic metabolism to form ortho- and parahydroxylated derivatives and various beta-oxidation products. It does not appear to undergo enterohepatic recirculation. Atorvastatin and its ortho- and parahydroxylated metabolites were found to have equal inhibitory effects on HMG-CoA reductase *in vitro*. The active metabolites are responsible for approximately 70% of the inhibition of HMG-CoA reductase. Studies *in vitro* suggest that atorvastatin is metabolized by the cytochrome P450 3A4 isozyme.

Half-life

Elimination—Amlodipine: 30 to 50 hours
Elimination—Atorvastatin: approximately 14 hours

Time to peak concentration

Amlodipine—6 to 12 hours, following an oral dose
Atorvastatin—1 to 2 hours, following an oral dose
Time to steady state concentrations—
Amlodipine—7 to 8 days of consecutive daily dosing

Elimination

Amlodipine—
Biliary/fecal—20 to 25%.
Renal: Approximately 70% (10% as amlodipine and 60% as metabolites).

Atorvastatin—
Biliary with less that 2% recovered in urine.
In dialysis—
Amlodipine: Not removable by hemodialysis.
Atorvastatin: Not removable by hemodialysis.

Precautions to Consider

Carcinogenicity

Amlodipine maleate—

No evidence of carcinogenicity was found in rats or mice given amlodipine maleate for 2 years at dietary doses of 0.5, 1.25, and 2.5 mg per kg (mg/kg) of body weight per day. For mice, the highest dose is approximately the maximum recommended human daily dose (MRHDD) on a mg per square meter of body surface area (mg/m^2) basis and is close to the maximum tolerated dose. For rats, this dose is approximately twice the MRHDD, on a mg/m^2 basis.

Atorvastatin calcium—

In a 2-year study in mice, doses of 100, 200, or 400 mg atorvastatin per kg (mg/kg) of body weight per day resulted in a marked increase in liver adenomas in male mice given high doses and liver carcinomas in female mice given high doses. These events occurred at area under the plasma concentration-time curve (AUC$_{[0-24]}$) values of approximately six times the mean human plasma drug exposure after an 80-mg oral dose.

In a 2-year study in rats, doses of 10, 30, and 100 mg/kg per day resulted in rare muscle tumors. Rhabdomyosarcoma occurred in one female rat given high doses and fibrosarcoma occurred in another female rat given high doses. The high dose represents an AUC$_{(0-24)}$ value of approximately 16 times the mean human plasma drug exposure after an 80-mg oral dose.

Mutagenicity

Amlodipine maleate—

Mutagenicity was not detected for amlodipine in studies at either the gene or chromosome level.

Atorvastatin calcium—

No evidence of mutagenicity or clastogenicity was found in *in vitro* tests, with and without metabolic activation, including the Ames test with *Salmonella typhimurium* and *Escherichia coli*, the HGPRT forward mutation assay in Chinese hamster lung cells, the chromosomal aberration assay in Chinese hamster lung cells, or in the *in vivo* mouse micronucleus test.

Pregnancy/Reproduction

Fertility—

Amlodipine—

No impairment of fertility was observed in rats given amlodipine at doses 8 times the maximum recommended human dose prior to mating.

Atorvastatin—

No changes in fertility were observed in studies in rats given doses of up to 175 mg/kg (15 times the human exposure) of atorvastatin. In 2 of 10 rats given 100 mg/kg per day for 3 months (16 times the human exposure at the 80-mg dose), aplasia and aspermia in the epididymis resulted. Testis weights were significantly decreased with 30 and 100 mg/kg doses and epididymal weight was lower at 100 mg/kg. Doses of 100 mg/kg per day given to male rats for 11 weeks prior to mating resulted in decreases in sperm motility and spermatid head concentration and increases in the number of abnormal sperm. No adverse effects were observed on semen parameters or in reproductive organ histopathology in dogs given doses of 10, 40, or 120 mg/kg for 2 years.

Pregnancy—Studies have not been done in humans.

No evidence of teratogenicity or other embryo/fetal toxicity was observed in rats or rabbits given up to 10 mg/kg during periods of major organogenesis. However, the number of intrauterine deaths increased about five-fold, and rat litter size was significantly decreased (by 50%).

Atorvastatin—

Atorvastatin therapy is *contraindicated* in pregnant women because it decreases cholesterol synthesis and possibly the synthesis of other biologically active substances, such as steroids and cell membranes, that are derived from cholesterol and are essential for fetal development.

There have been rare reports of congenital anomalies following intrauterine exposure to HMG-CoA reductase inhibitors. Severe congenital bony deformities, tracheo-esophageal fistula, and anal atresia (VATER association) were reported in a baby born to a woman who took the HMG-CoA reductase inhibitor lovastatin with dextroamphetamine sulfate during the first trimester of pregnancy.

In rats, atorvastatin crosses the placenta and reaches a concentration in fetal liver tissue equal to that in maternal plasma. No evidence of teratogenicity was found in rats given doses of up to 300 mg/kg per day or in rabbits given doses of up to 100 mg/kg per day. These doses represent 30 and 20 times, respectively, the human exposure based on body surface area (mg/m^2).

Studies in rats given 20, 100, or 225 mg/kg per day, from gestation day 7 through lactation day 21 (weaning), have shown decreased pup survival at birth, neonate, weaning, and maturity in pups of mothers given doses of 225 mg/kg per day. On days 4 and 21, body weight was decreased in pups of mothers given doses of 100 mg/kg per day; body weight was decreased at birth and at days 4, 21, and 91 in pups of mothers given 225 mg/kg per day. Pup development was delayed, as determined by rotorod performance (mothers given 100 mg/kg per day) and acoustic startle (mothers given 225 mg/kg per day). Development was also delayed in pinnae detachment and eye opening (mothers given 225 mg/kg per day). These doses represent 6 times (100 mg/kg) and 22 times (225 mg/kg) the human exposure at 80 mg per day.

FDA Pregnancy Category X

Labor and delivery—Studies on the effects of amlodipine and atorvastatin during labor and delivery have not been done. However, amlodipine has been shown to prolong the duration of labor in rats.

Breast-feeding

It is not known whether amlodipine is distributed into breast milk. However nursing rat pups taking atorvastatin had plasma and liver drug levels of 50% and 40% respectively, of that in there mother's milk. Because of the potential for adverse reactions in nursing infants, women should not breast-feed.

Pediatrics

Appropriate studies on the relationship of age to the effects of amlodipine and atorvastatin combination have not been performed in the pediatric population. Safety and efficacy have not been established.

Amlodipine—

The effect of amlodipine on blood pressure in patients less than 6 years of age is not known.

Atorvastatin—

Safety and effectiveness in patients 10 to 17 years of age with heterozygous familial hypercholesterolemia have been evaluated in controlled clinical trials. There was no detectable effect on growth or sexual maturation in boys or on menstrual cycle length in girls. Appropriate studies have not been performed on the relationship of the effect of atorvastatin with respect to age in prepubertal patients or patients younger than 10 years of age. Safety and efficacy of doses above 20 mg have not been studied in children.

Adolescents

Adolescent females taking atorvastatin therapy should be counseled on appropriate contraceptive methods.

Geriatrics

Appropriate studies on the relationship of age to the effects of amlodipine and atorvastatin combination have not been performed in the geriatric population. However, elderly patients are more likely to have age related decreased hepatic, renal, or cardiac function and concomitant disease or other drug therapy requiring caution in dose selection.

Amlodipine—

Elderly patients have a decreased clearance of amlodipine, resulting in a 40 to 60% increase in AUC. A lower initial dose may be required.

Drug interactions and/or related problems

The following drug interactions and/or related problems have been selected on the basis of their potential clinical significance (possible mechanism in parentheses where appropriate)—not necessarily inclusive (» = major clinical significance):

Note: Combinations containing any of the following medications, depending on the amount present, may also interact with this medication.

Note: No drug interaction studies have been conducted with the amlodipine and atorvastatin combination and other drugs, however studies have been done with the individual amlodipine and atorvastatin components.

» Alcohol, substantial use of
(caution when atorvastatin is used in patients with active liver disease or unexplained transaminase elevations.)

Antacids
(plasma concentrations of atorvastatin decreased by approximately 35%; however, reduction of LDL-C was not altered)

» Azole antifungals or
» Cyclosporine or
» Fibric acid derivatives or
» Niacin (nicotinic acid)
(increased risk of myopathy with concurrent administration of drugs in the HMG-CoA reductase inhibitor class and these drugs; potential benefits and risks should be weighed and patients closely monitored for signs of myopathy particularly during the initial months of therapy and periods of upward dosage titration of either drug.)

Cimetidine or
Ketoconazole or
Spironolactone
(caution if concomitant administration of HMG-CoA reductase inhibitors and drugs that may decrease the levels or activity of endogenous steroid hormones)

Colestipol
(concurrent use may decrease plasma concentrations of atorvastatin by approximately 25%; however, LDL-C reduction may be greater with combination therapy than with either medication given alone)

» Digoxin
(concurrent administration may increase steady-state digoxin plasma concentrations by approximately 20%; patients taking digoxin and atorvastatin should be followed closely for evidence of digoxin toxicity)

Erythromycin
(approximately 40% increase in atorvastatin plasma concentration when coadministered with erythromycin a known inhibitor of cytochrome P450 3A4; rare cases of rhabdomyolysis with acute renal failure secondary to myoglobinuria have been reported)

Oral contraceptives
(coadministration increased AUC values for norethindrone and ethinyl estradiol by approximately 30% and 20%; these increases should be considered when selecting an oral contraceptive for a woman taking atorvastatin)

Laboratory value alterations

The following have been selected on the basis of their potential clinical significance (possible effect in parentheses where appropriate)—not necessarily inclusive (» = major clinical significance).

With physiology/laboratory test values

Note: Amlodipine therapy has not been associated with clinically significant changes in routine laboratory tests. No clinically relevant changes were noted in serum potassium, serum glucose, total triglycerides, total cholesterol, HDL cholesterol, uric acid, blood urea nitrogen, or creatinine.

Transaminases, serum
(elevations in liver enzyme values usually occur within the first 3 months of treatment; persistent increases [> three times ULN, occurring on two or more occasions] in transaminase values occurred in 0.7% of patients in clinical trials; elevations in transaminase values are not usually associated with clinical signs or symptoms, although one patient in clinical trials developed jaundice; if elevations in aspartate aminotransferase [AST (SGOT)] or alanine aminotransferase [ALT (SGPT)] are > three times the ULN and persist, atorvastatin dosage should be reduced or discontinued; patients should be monitored until the abnormal values are resolved)

Medical considerations/Contraindications

The medical considerations/contraindications included have been selected on the basis of their potential clinical significance (reasons given in parentheses where appropriate)—not necessarily inclusive (» = major clinical significance).

Except under special circumstances, this medication should not be used when the following medical problem exists:

» Hypersensitivity to amlodipine or atorvastatin or any component of this medicine
» Hepatic disease, active or
» Elevations of transaminase values, unexplained, persistent
(use of atorvastatin contraindicated in patients with these conditions)

Risk-benefit should be considered when the following medical problems exist:

Aortic stenosis, severe
(increased risk of acute hypotension with amlodipine-induced vasodilation)

Congestive heart failure
(calcium channel blockers should be used with caution in patients with heart failure)

Coronary artery disease, severe, obstructive
(initiation or a dosage increase of calcium channel blocking agent therapy has resulted in an increase in the frequency, duration, and/or severity of angina or the development of acute myocardial infarction; the mechanism of this effect is not understood)

» Electrolyte, endocrine, or metabolic disorders, severe or
» Hypotension or
» Infection, severe acute or
» Myopathy or
» Seizures, uncontrolled or
» Surgery, major or
» Trauma
(these conditions may predispose a patient to the development of renal failure, secondary to rhabdomyolysis; atorvastatin should be discontinued or temporarily withheld)

Patient monitoring

The following may be especially important in patient monitoring (other tests may be warranted in some patients, depending on condition; » = major clinical significance):

Creatine phosphokinase (CPK), serum
(periodic determinations recommended in patients who develop muscle pain, tenderness, or weakness during therapy or if concurrently receiving azole antifungals, erythromycin, immunosuppressive drugs such as cyclosporine, or niacin; amlodipine and atorvastatin combination should be discontinued if elevated CPK levels occur or myopathy is diagnosed or suspected)

» Hepatic function determinations
(recommended prior to initiation of treatment and at 12 weeks of treatment or at a dosage increase, and periodically, such as every 6 months, thereafter.)

Side/Adverse Effects

The following side/adverse effects have been selected on the basis of their potential clinical significance (possible signs and symptoms in parentheses where appropriate)—not necessarily inclusive:

Those indicating need for medical attention

Incidence less frequent—Atorvastatin

Allergic reaction (cough; difficulty swallowing; dizziness; fast heartbeat; hives; itching; puffiness or swelling of the eyelids or around the eyes, face, lips or tongue; shortness of breath; skin rash; tightness in chest; unusual tiredness or weakness; wheezing)

Incidence rare—Amlodipine

Cardiac failure (chest pain or discomfort; dilated neck veins; extreme fatigue; irregular breathing; irregular heartbeat; shortness of breath; swelling of face, fingers, feet, or lower legs; weight gain; wheezing); ***extrasystoles*** (extra heartbeats); ***pulse irregularity***

Observed post—marketing incidence unknown-Atorvastatin

Erythema multiforme (blistering, peeling, loosening of skin; chills; cough; diarrhea; fever; itching; joint or muscle pain; red irritated eyes; sore throat; sores, ulcers, or white spots in mouth or on lips; unusual tiredness or weakness); ***rhabdomyolysis*** (dark-colored urine; fever; muscle cramps or spasms; muscle pain or stiffness; unusual tiredness or weakness); ***Stevens-Johnson syndrome*** (blistering, peeling, loosening of skin; chills; cough; diarrhea; itching; joint or muscle pain; red irritated eyes; red skin lesions, often with a purple center; sore throat; sores, ulcers, or white spots in mouth or on lip; unusual tiredness or weakness); ***toxic epidermal necrolysis*** (blistering, peeling, loosening of skin; chills; cough; diarrhea; itching; joint or muscle pain; red irritated eyes; red skin lesions, often with a purple center; sore throat; sores, ulcers, or white spots in mouth or on lips; unusual tiredness or weakness)

Those indicating need for medical attention only if they continue or are bothersome

Incidence more frequent—Amlodipine

Edema (swelling)—dose-related incidence of 1.8–10.8% between 2.5–10 mg daily; higher prevalence in women than men; ***headache***

Incidence more frequent—Atorvastatin

Arthralgia (pain in joints; muscle pain or stiffness; difficulty in moving); ***headache; myalgia*** (muscle or joint pain); ***pharyngitis*** (body aches or pain; congestion; cough; dryness or soreness of throat; fever hoarseness runny nose; tender, swollen glands in neck; trouble in swallowing voice changes); ***sinusitis*** (pain or tenderness around eyes and cheekbones; fever; stuffy or runny nose; headache; cough; shortness of breath or troubled breathing; tightness of chest or wheezing)

Incidence less frequent—Amlodipine

Abdominal pain (stomach pain); ***dizziness; fatigue*** (unusual tiredness or weakness); ***flushing*** (feeling of warmth; redness of the face, neck, arms and occasionally, upper chest); ***nausea; palpitations*** (fast, irregular, pounding, or racing heartbeat or pulse); ***somnolence*** (sleepiness or unusual drowsiness)

Incidence less frequent—Atorvastatin

Abdominal pain (stomach pain); ***accidental injury; asthenia*** (lack or loss of strength); ***back pain; constipation*** (difficulty having a bowel movement (stool)); ***diarrhea; dyspepsia*** (acid or sour stomach; belching; heartburn; indigestion; stomach discomfort upset or pain); ***flatulence*** (bloated full feeling; excess air or gas in stomach or intestines; passing gas); ***flu syndrome*** (chills; cough; diarrhea; fever; general feeling of discomfort or illness; headache; joint pain; loss of appetite; muscle aches and pains; nausea; runny nose; shivering; sore throat; sweating; trouble sleeping; unusual tiredness or weakness; vomiting); ***rash***

Incidence rare—Amlodipine

Abnormal visual accommodation (blurred vision; change in near or distance vision; difficulty in focusing eyes); ***agitation*** (anxiety; nervousness; restlessness; irritability; dry mouth; shortness of breath; hyperventilation; trouble sleeping; irregular heartbeats; shaking); ***alopecia*** (hair loss, thinning of hair); ***amnesia*** (loss of memory; problems with memory;); ***apathy*** (lack of feeling or emotion; uncaring); ***ataxia*** (shakiness and unsteady walk; unsteadiness; trembling, or other problems with muscle control or coordination); ***cold and clammy skin; coughing; dermatitis*** (blistering, crusting, irritation, itching, or reddening of skin; cracked, dry, scaly skin; swelling); ***dysuria*** (difficult or painful urination; burning while urinating); ***gastritis*** (burning feeling in chest or stomach; tenderness in stomach area; stomach upset; indigestion); ***hypertonia*** (excessive muscle tone; muscle tension or tightness; muscle stiffness); ***increased appetite; loose stools; migraine*** (headache, severe and throbbing); ***muscle weakness; parosmia*** (transient, mild, pleasant aromatic odor); ***polyuria*** (frequent urination; increased volume of pale, dilute urine); ***rhinitis*** (stuffy nose; runny nose; sneezing); ***skin discoloration*** (change in color of skin); ***skin dryness; taste perversion*** (change in taste bad unusual or unpleasant (after) taste); ***twitching; urticaria*** (hives or welts; itching; redness of skin; skin rash); ***xerophthalmia*** (dryness of eyes)

Overdose

For more information on the management of overdose or unintentional ingestion, **contact a poison control center** (see *Poison Control Center Listing*).

Clinical effects of overdose

The following effects have been selected on the basis of their potential clinical significance (possible signs and symptoms in parentheses where appropriate)—not necessarily inclusive:

Amlodipine

Hypotension (blurred vision; confusion; dizziness, faintness, or lightheadedness when getting up from a lying or sitting position suddenly; sweating; unusual tiredness or weakness); ***peripheral vasodilation*** (flushing); ***reflex tachycardia*** (fast or irregular heartbeat)

Treatment of overdose

There is no specific antidote to amlodipine and atorvastatin combination. Treatment is generally symptomatic and supportive.

To enhance elimination—

Hemodialysis is not expected to enhance clearance.

Specific treatment—

Administration of intravenous calcium gluconate may aide to reverse the effects of calcium entry blockade.

Monitoring—

Monitoring of cardiac and respiratory function should be instituted

Monitoring blood pressure measurements is essential.

Supportive care—

Elevation of the extremities and judicious administration of fluids, should hypotension occur.

Administration of vasopressors with attention or circulating volume and urine output if hypotension remains unresponsive to the above mentioned conservative measures.

Patients in whom intentional overdose is confirmed or suspected should be referred for psychiatric consultation.

Patient Consultation

As an aid to patient consultation, refer to *Advice for the Patient, Amlodipine and Atorvastatin (Systemic).*

In providing consultation, consider emphasizing the following selected information (» = major clinical significance):

Before using this medication

» Conditions affecting use, especially:

Hypersensitivity to amlodipine or atorvastatin or any component of this medicine.

Pregnancy—HMG-CoA reductase inhibitors are contraindicated during pregnancy or in women planning to become pregnant.

Breast-feeding—HMG-CoA reductase inhibitors are contraindicated in nursing mothers.

Use in children—Safety and effectiveness of amlodipine and atorvastatin combination have not been established.

Amlodipine—The effect of amlodipine on blood pressure in patients less than 6 years of age is not known.

Atorvastatin—Safety and effectiveness have been established in boys and postmenarchal girls 10 to 17 years of age for treating heterozygous familial hypercholesterolemia. Atorvastatin has not been studied in pre-pubertal patients, patients younger than 10 years of age, or doses above 20 mg in patients 10 to 17 years of age.

Use in adolescents—Careful counseling in females taking atorvastatin therapy on appropriate contraceptive methods

Use in the elderly—Elderly patients may require a lower dose.

Other medications, especially alcohol, azole antifungals, cyclosporine, digoxin, erythromycin, fibric acid derivatives, or niacin (nicotinic acid).

Other medical problems, especially active hepatic disease, elevations of transaminase values, hypotension, major surgery, myopathy, severe acute infection, severe electrolyte, endocrine, or metabolic disorders, uncontrolled seizures, or trauma.

Proper use of this medication

Compliance with therapy; taking medication at the same time each day to maintain the antihyperlipidemic effect

Compliance with prescribed diet during treatment

» Proper dosing

Missed dose: Taking as soon as possible; not taking if almost time for next scheduled dose; not doubling doses

Proper storage

Precautions while using this medication

» Regular visits to physician to check progress

» Notifying physician immediately if pregnancy is suspected because of possible harm to the fetus

» Caution if any kind of surgery (including dental surgery) or emergency treatment is required

» Not taking over-the-counter niacin preparations without consulting physician because of increased risk of rhabdomyolysis

» Not using alcohol excessively because elevations of liver enzymes may occur

» Notifying physician immediately if unexplained muscle pain, tenderness, or weakness occurs, especially if accompanied by unusual tiredness or fever

Checking with physician before discontinuing medication; gradual dosage reduction may be necessary

Side/adverse effects

Signs of potential side effects observed with the component amlodipine, especially cardiac failure, extrasystoles, or pulse irregularity

(Signs of potential side effects observed with the component atorvastatin, especially allergic reaction.)

(Signs of potential side effects observed post-marketing with the component atorvastatin, especially erythema multiforme, rhabdomyolysis, Stevens-Johnson syndrome or toxic epidermal necrolysis.)

General Dosing Information

Dosage must be adjusted to meet individual requirements on the basis of effectiveness and tolerance. In general, titration should proceed over 7 to 14 days so that the physician can fully assess the patient's response to each dose level. However, titration may proceed more rapidly if clinically warranted, provided the patient is assessed frequently.

Prior to treatment with atorvastatin, control of hypercholesterolemia with diet, exercise, weight reduction in obese patients, and treatment of underlying medical problems should be attempted. The patient should be placed on a standard cholesterol-lowering diet before receiving atorvastatin and should continue on this diet during treatment with atorvastatin.

Amlodipine and atorvastatin combination may be substituted for its individually titrated components, given to patients at equivalent doses or a dose with increased amounts of amlodipine, atorvastatin or both.

Amlodipine and atorvastatin combination may be used to provide additional therapy for patients already on one of its components. The starting dose should be based on the continuation of the component being used and the recommended starting dose for the added monotherapy.

Amlodipine and atorvastatin combination may be used to initiate treatment in patients with hyperlipidemia and either hypertension or angina. The recommended starting dose should be based on the recommendation for monotherapies.

Oral Dosage Forms

AMLODIPINE BESYLATE AND ATORVASTATIN CALCIUM TABLETS

Usual adult dose

Angina, chronic stable or
Angina, vasospastic or
Hypertension or
Hyperlipidemia—

Amlodipine: Oral, 1 tablet a day, as determined by individual dosage titration with the component agents.

Note: The recommended dose of amlodipine for chronic stable or vasospastic angina is 5 to 10 mg once daily, with the lower dose suggested in the elderly and in patients with hepatic insufficiency.

Heterozygous familial and nonfamilial hypercholesterolemia and mixed dyslipidemia (Fredrickson Types IIa and IIb)—

Atorvastatin: Oral, initially 10 to 20 mg once a day. The dosage range is 10 to 80 mg once a day, to be administered at any time of the day, with or without food. After initiation or titration of atorvastatin, lipid concentrations should be measured within 2 to 4 weeks and the dosage adjusted accordingly.

Note: The goal of therapy is to lower LDL-C. The National Cholesterol Education Program (NCEP) recommends that LDL-C concentrations be used to initiate and assess treatment response. Only if LDL-C concentrations are not available should total-C be used to monitor therapy.

Note: Dosage adjustment in patients with renal dysfunction is not necessary.

Homozygous familial hypercholesterolemia—

Atorvastatin: Oral, 10 to 80 mg a day.

Note: Atorvastatin should be used in these patients as an adjunct to other lipid-lowering treatments, such as LDL apheresis, or if such treatments are unavailable.

Usual adult prescribing limits

10 mg of amlodipine and 80 mg of atorvastatin per day

Usual pediatric dose

Antihypertensive—

Amlodipine: Oral, 2.5 to 5 mg per day in children ages 6 to 17 years of age

Heterozygous familial hypercholesterolemia—

Atorvastatin: Oral, 10 mg per day in boys and postmenarchal girls 10 to 17 years of age. Adjustments should be made at intervals of 4 weeks or more.

Note: Dosage adjustment in patients with renal dysfunction is not necessary.

Usual pediatric prescribing limits

Amlodipine—5 mg per day.
Atorvastatin—20 mg per day

Usual geriatric dose

See *Usual adult dose.*

Usual geriatric prescribing limits

See *Usual adult prescribing limits.*

Strength(s) usually available

U.S.—

2.5 mg amlodipine besylate and 10 mg atorvastatin calcium (Rx) [*Caduet* (white, CDT 251; calcium carbonate; colloidal silicon dioxide (anhydrous); croscarmellose sodium; hydroxypropyl cellulose; magnesium stearate; microcrystalline cellulose; PEG 3000; polysorbate 80; polyvinyl alcohol; pregelatinized starch; purified water; talc; titanium dioxide)].

2.5 mg amlodipine besylate and 20 mg atorvastatin calcium (Rx) [*Caduet* (white, CDT 252; calcium carbonate; colloidal silicon dioxide (anhydrous); croscarmellose sodium; hydroxypropyl cellulose; magnesium stearate; microcrystalline cellulose; PEG 3000; polysorbate 80; polyvinyl alcohol; pregelatinized starch; purified water; talc; titanium dioxide)].

2.5 mg amlodipine besylate and 40 mg atorvastatin calcium (Rx) [*Caduet* (white, CDT 254; calcium carbonate; colloidal silicon dioxide (anhydrous); croscarmellose sodium; hydroxypropyl cellulose; magnesium stearate; microcrystalline cellulose; PEG 3000; polysorbate 80; polyvinyl alcohol; pregelatinized starch; purified water; talc; titanium dioxide)].

5 mg amlodipine besylate and 10 mg atorvastatin calcium (Rx) [*Caduet* (white, CDT 051; calcium carbonate; colloidal silicon dioxide (anhydrous); croscarmellose sodium; hydroxypropyl cellulose; magnesium stearate; microcrystalline cellulose; PEG 3000; polysorbate 80; polyvinyl alcohol; pregelatinized starch; purified water; talc; titanium dioxide)].

5 mg amlodipine besylate and 20 mg atorvastatin calcium (Rx) [*Caduet* (white, CDT 052; calcium carbonate; colloidal silicon dioxide (anhydrous); croscarmellose sodium; hydroxypropyl cellulose; magnesium stearate; microcrystalline cellulose; PEG 3000; polysorbate 80; polyvinyl alcohol; pregelatinized starch; purified water; talc; titanium dioxide)].

5 mg amlodipine besylate and 40 mg atorvastatin calcium (Rx) [*Caduet* (white, CDT 054; calcium carbonate; croscarmellose sodium; microcrystalline cellulose; pregelatinized starch; polysorbate 80; hydroxypropyl cellulose; purified water; colloidal silicon dioxide (anhydrous); magnesium stearate; polyvinyl alcohol; titanium dioxide; PEG 3000; talc)].

5 mg amlodipine besylate and 80 mg atorvastatin calcium (Rx) [*Caduet* (white, CDT 058; calcium carbonate; colloidal silicon dioxide (anhydrous); croscarmellose sodium; hydroxypropyl cellulose; magnesium stearate; microcrystalline cellulose; PEG 3000; polysorbate 80; polyvinyl alcohol; pregelatinized starch; purified water; talc; titanium dioxide)].

10 mg amlodipine besylate and 10 mg atorvastatin calcium (Rx) [*Caduet* (blue, CDT 101; calcium carbonate; colloidal silicon dioxide (anhydrous); croscarmellose sodium; FD&C blue #2; hydroxypropyl cellulose; magnesium stearate; microcrystalline cellulose; PEG 3000; polysorbate 80; polyvinyl alcohol; pregelatinized starch; purified water; talc; titanium dioxide)].

10 mg amlodipine besylate and 20 mg atorvastatin calcium (Rx) [*Caduet* (blue, CDT 102; calcium carbonate; colloidal silicon dioxide (anhydrous); croscarmellose sodium; FD&C blue #2; hydroxypropyl cellulose; magnesium stearate; microcrystalline cellulose; PEG 3000; polysorbate 80; polyvinyl alcohol; pregelatinized starch; purified water; talc; titanium dioxide)].

10 mg amlodipine besylate and 40 mg atorvastatin calcium (Rx) [*Caduet* (blue, CDT 104; calcium carbonate; colloidal silicon dioxide (anhydrous); croscarmellose sodium; FD&C blue #2; hydroxypropyl cellulose; magnesium stearate; microcrystalline cellulose; PEG 3000; polysorbate 80; polyvinyl alcohol; pregelatinized starch; purified water; talc; titanium dioxide)].

10 mg amlodipine besylate and 80 mg atorvastatin calcium (Rx) [*Caduet* (blue, CDT 108; calcium carbonate; colloidal silicon dioxide (anhydrous); croscarmellose sodium; FD&C blue #2; hydroxypropyl cellulose; magnesium stearate; microcrystalline cellulose; PEG 3000; polysorbate 80; polyvinyl alcohol; pregelatinized starch; purified water; talc; titanium dioxide)].

Packaging and storage

Store at 25 °C (77 °F); excursions permitted to 15 to 30°C (59 to 86°F)

Auxiliary labeling

• This medication could be harmful if you are pregnant or breast-feeding. Consult your pharmacist or doctor about using this medication if you are pregnant, plan to become pregnant, or if you are breast-feeding.
• Do not take other medicines without physician's advice.

Developed: 11/08/2004

AMLODIPINE AND BENAZEPRIL Systemic†

VA CLASSIFICATION (Primary): CV408

Commonly used brand name(s): *Lotrel.*

Note: For a listing of dosage forms and brand names by country availability, see *Dosage Forms* section(s).

†Not commercially available in Canada.

Category

Antihypertensive.

Indications

Accepted

Hypertension (treatment)—The combination of amlodipine and benazepril is indicated for the treatment of hypertension. It is not indicated as initial treatment for hypertension.

For additional information on initial therapeutic guidelines related to the treatment of hypertension, see *Appendix III*.

Pharmacology/Pharmacokinetics

Mechanism of action/Effect

Amlodipine is a dihydropyridine calcium channel blocking agent. Like the other dihydropyridine agents, amlodipine selectively inhibits calcium influx across cell membranes in cardiac and vascular smooth muscle, with a greater effect on vascular smooth muscle. Amlodipine is a peripheral arteriolar vasodilator; thus it reduces afterload.

Benazepril is a nonsulfhydryl angiotensin-converting enzyme (ACE) inhibitor and a prodrug for benazeprilat, the active metabolite. Both benazepril and benazeprilat inhibit ACE. ACE catalyzes the conversion of angiotensin I to the vasoconstrictor angiotensin II. Angiotensin II normally stimulates secretion of aldosterone and inhibits the release of renin through a negative feedback mechanism. When ACE activity is inhibited, angiotensin II formation is decreased and the interruption of the negative feedback mechanism results in increased plasma renin concentrations. The reduction of angiotensin II formation also decreases aldosterone secretion and vasoconstriction. The decrease in aldosterone secretion causes a small increase in serum potassium concentrations. Suppression of the renin-angiotensin-aldosterone system is thought to be the primary mechanism through which ACE inhibitors lower blood pressure.

Other actions/effects

ACE is also known as kininase, an enzyme that degrades bradykinin. Benazepril may increase concentrations of bradykinin, a potent vasodepressor peptide, but its role in the therapeutic effects of this drug combination has not been determined.

Amlodipine exhibits negative inotropic effects *in vivo*, but appears to have no significant effect on the sinoatrial (SA) or atrioventricular (AV) node in humans.

Absorption

Amlodipine—64 to 90% absorbed.Slowly and almost completely absorbed from the gastrointestinal tract; absorption not affected by food.

Benazepril—Approximately 37% absorbed.

Distribution

Volume of distribution (Vol_D)—

Amlodipine: 21 L per kg (L/kg).

Benazeprilat: 0.7 L/kg, concentration-independent.

Protein binding

Amlodipine—Very high (Approximately 93%).

Benazeprilat—Very high (95.3%).

Biotransformation

Amlodipine—Undergoes minimal presystemic metabolism. Amlodipine undergoes slow but extensive hepatic metabolism, producing metabolites lacking significant pharmacological activity.

Benazepril—Almost completely converted, primarily in the liver, to its active metabolite, benazeprilat.

Half-life

Elimination—

Amlodipine: Mean, 35 hours in healthy volunteers; may be prolonged to a mean of 48 hours in hypertensive patients, 65 hours in the elderly, and 60 hours in patients with hepatic function impairment. Not significantly affected by renal function impairment.

Benazeprilat: 10 to 11 hours.

Time to peak concentration

Amlodipine—6 to 12 hours.

Benazepril—0.5 to 2 hours.

Benazeprilat—1.5 to 4 hours.

Duration of action

Amlodipine—24 hours.

Benazeprilat—24 hours.

Elimination

Amlodipine—

Biliary/fecal—20 to 25%.

Renal: Approximately 70% (10% as amlodipine and 60% as metabolites).

Benazepril—

Primarily renal, but also biliary.

In dialysis—

Amlodipine: Not reported to be removable by hemodialysis.

Benazeprilat: Slightly removable by hemodialysis.

Precautions to Consider

Cross-sensitivity and/or related problems

Patients hypersensitive to other angiotensin-converting enzyme (ACE) inhibitors also may be hypersensitive to benazepril.

Carcinogenicity

No evidence of carcinogenicity was found in rats or mice given amlodipine for 2 years at dietary doses of 0.5, 1.25, and 2.5 mg per kg of body weight (mg/kg) per day. For mice, the highest dose is approximately the maximum recommended human daily dose (MRHDD) on a mg per square meter of body surface area (mg/m^2) basis and is close to the maximum tolerated dose. For rats, this dose is approximately twice the MRHDD, on a mg/m^2 basis.

No evidence of carcinogenicity was found in rats or mice given benazepril for 104 weeks at doses of up to 150 mg/kg per day. This represents more than 100 times the MRHDD, based on body weight. Based on body surface area, this represents 18 and 9 times the MRHDD for rats and mice, respectively.

Mutagenicity

Mutagenicity was not detected for amlodipine in studies at either the gene or chromosome level.

Mutagenicity was not detected for benazepril in the Ames test in bacteria, in an *in vitro* test for forward mutations in cultured mammalian cells, or in a nucleus anomaly test.

Pregnancy/Reproduction

Fertility—No impairment of fertility was found in male or female rats treated with amlodipine 64 days and 14 days prior to mating, respectively, at doses of up to 10 mg/kg per day (eight times the MRHDD of 10 mg, on a mg/m^2 basis, assuming a 50-kg person).

Reproductive performance of male and female rats was not affected when given benazepril at doses of 50 to 500 mg/kg per day.This represents 38 to 375 times the MRHDD on a body weight basis and 6 to 61 times the MRHDD on a body surface area basis.

No impairment of fertility was found when amlodipine and benazepril combination was given to male and female rats.Amlodipine was administered at daily doses of up to 7.5 mg/kg and benazepril at daily doses of up to 15 mg/kg per day prior to mating and throughout gestation.

Pregnancy—ACE inhibitors can cause fetal and neonatal morbidity and mortality when administered to pregnant women during the second and third trimesters. Amlodipine and benazepril combination should be discontinued as soon as possible when pregnancy is detected unless no alternative therapy can be used. In the latter instance, serial ultrasound examinations should be performed to assess the intra-amniotic environment. If oligohydramnios is observed, amlodipine and benazepril combination should be discontinued unless it is considered lifesaving for the mother. Perinatal diagnostic tests, such as contraction-stress testing (CST), a nonstress test (NST), or biophysical profiling (BPP), also may be appropriate during the applicable week of pregnancy. Oligohydramnios may not be apparent until after the fetus has sustained irreversible damage.

Fetal exposure to ACE inhibitors during the second and third trimesters can cause hypotension, reversible or irreversible renal failure, anuria, neonatal skull hypoplasia, and death in the fetus or neonate. Maternal oligohydramnios, which may result from decreased fetal renal function, has been reported and is associated with fetal limb contractures, craniofacial deformation, and hypoplastic lung development. Other adverse effects that have been reported are prematurity, intrauterine growth retardation, and patent ductus arteriosus, although how these effects are related to exposure to ACE inhibitors is not clear. ACE inhibitor exposure, when limited to the first trimester, does not appear to be associated with these adverse effects.

Infants exposed *in utero* to ACE inhibitors should be observed closely for hypotension, oliguria, and hyperkalemia. Oliguria should be treated with support of blood pressure and renal perfusion. Dialysis or exchange transfusion may be necessary to reverse hypotension and/or substitute for disordered renal function.

Teratogenic effects were not observed in rabbits given daily combination doses of benazepril 1.5 mg/kg and amlodipine 0.75 mg/kg or in rats given daily combination doses of benazepril 50 mg/kg and amlodipine 25 mg/kg. These doses represent 0.97 and 24 times the maximum recommended human dose of the combination, respectively, on a mg/m^2 of body surface area basis, assuming a 50-kg woman.

FDA Pregnancy Category C (first trimester).

FDA Pregnancy Category D (second and third trimesters).

Labor—Dystocia was observed in rats given daily combination doses ranging from amlodipine 2.5 mg/kg and benazepril 5 mg/kg to amlodipine 25 mg/kg and benazepril 50 mg/kg. The 2.5 mg/kg per day dose of amlodipine is 3.6 times the amlodipine dose delivered, on a mg/m² basis, when the maximum recommended human dose of the combination is given to a 50-kg woman. The 5 mg/kg per day dose of benazepril represents approximately two times the benazepril dose delivered, on a mg/m² basis, when the maximum recommended dose of the combination is given to a 50-kg woman.

Breast-feeding
It is not known whether amlodipine is distributed into breast milk. Benazepril and benazeprilat are distributed into breast milk. Less than 0.1% of the maternal benazepril dose appears in breast milk. It is recommended that breast-feeding be discontinued during administration of amlodipine and benazepril combination.

Pediatrics
Appropriate studies on the relationship of age to the effects of amlodipine and benazepril combination have not been performed in the pediatric population. Safety and efficacy have not been established.

Geriatrics
Use of amlodipine and benazepril combination in a limited number of patients 65 years of age and older (19% of patients in clinical studies) has not demonstrated geriatrics-specific problems that would limit the usefulness of this combination in the elderly. However, amlodipine clearance may be decreased, resulting in 35 to 70% increases in amlodipine peak plasma concentrations, elimination half-life, and area under the plasma concentration-time curve. Elderly patients also may be more sensitive to the drug effects than younger individuals.

Pharmacogenetics
Black patients may benefit from a reduction in amlodipine-induced edema when benazepril is added to current amlodipine therapy, but an additional antihypertensive effect may not occur in these patients. Black patients have a higher incidence of ACE inhibitor-induced angioedema when compared with nonblack patients.

Dental
Gingival hyperplasia is a rare side effect that has been reported with amlodipine. It also has been reported with other calcium channel blocking agents, such as diltiazem, felodipine, verapamil, and, most commonly, nifedipine. It usually starts as gingivitis or gum inflammation in the first 1 to 9 months of treatment. Resolution of the hyperplasia and improvement of the clinical symptoms usually occur one to four weeks after discontinuation of therapy. A strictly enforced program of professional teeth cleaning combined with plaque control by the patient will minimize growth rate and severity of gingival enlargement. Periodontal surgery may be indicated in some cases, and should be followed by careful plaque control to inhibit recurrence of gum enlargement.

Surgical
Patients receiving amlodipine and benazepril combination may experience excessive hypotension when undergoing a major surgery or anesthesia with agents that produce hypotension. If hypotension in these patients is thought to be the result of ACE inhibition, it can be corrected by volume expansion.

Drug interactions and/or related problems
The following drug interactions and/or related problems have been selected on the basis of their potential clinical significance (possible mechanism in parentheses where appropriate)—not necessarily inclusive (» = major clinical significance):

Note: Combinations containing any of the following medications, depending on the amount present, may also interact with this medication.

» Diuretics
(concurrent use with ACE inhibitors may cause additive hypotension; the diuretic may need to be discontinued or salt intake cautiously increased prior to initiation of amlodipine and benazepril combination therapy)

» Diuretics, potassium-sparing or
» Potassium-containing salt substitutes or
» Potassium supplements
(concurrent use with ACE inhibitor therapy may increase the risk of hyperkalemia; serum potassium concentrations should be monitored appropriately)

Lithium
(concurrent use with an ACE inhibitor has resulted in increased serum lithium concentrations and symptoms of lithium toxicity; frequent monitoring of serum lithium concentrations is recommended)

Laboratory value alterations
The following have been selected on the basis of their potential clinical significance (possible effect in parentheses where appropriate)—not necessarily inclusive (» = major clinical significance).

With physiology/laboratory test values

Bilirubin concentrations, serum and
Hepatic enzyme values
(increases have been reported; significant elevations in hepatic enzymes may be associated with ACE inhibitor-related hepatotoxicity)

Blood urea nitrogen (BUN) and
Creatinine, serum
(minor and transient increases in concentrations may occur, especially in patients concurrently receiving a diuretic or in patients with renal function impairment)

Potassium, serum
(concentrations may be slightly increased as a result of reduced circulating aldosterone concentrations)

Uric acid, serum
(increases in concentrations have been reported)

Medical considerations/Contraindications
The medical considerations/contraindications included have been selected on the basis of their potential clinical significance (reasons given in parentheses where appropriate)—not necessarily inclusive (» = major clinical significance).

Except under special circumstances, this medication should not be used when the following medical problem exists:

» Hypersensitivity to benazepril, any other ACE inhibitor, or amlodipine

Risk-benefit should be considered when the following medical problems exist:

Aortic stenosis, severe
(increased risk of symptomatic hypotension with amlodipine-induced vasodilation)

Collagen-vascular disease, such as systemic lupus erythematosus (SLE) or scleroderma
(increased risk of developing neutropenia or agranulocytosis, especially if renal function is impaired)

» Congestive heart failure
(patients with or without renal function impairment may experience excessive hypotension as a result of ACE inhibitor therapy; excessive hypotension in these patients may be associated with oliguria, azotemia, acute renal failure, and/or death)

Coronary artery disease, severe, obstructive
(initiation or a dosage increase of calcium channel blocking agent therapy has resulted in an increase in the frequency, duration, and/or severity of angina or the development of acute myocardial infarction; the mechanism of this effect is not understood)

Dehydration (sodium or volume depletion due to excessive perspiration, vomiting, diarrhea, prolonged diuretic therapy, dialysis, or dietary salt restriction)
(increased risk of symptomatic hypotension with ACE inhibitor therapy)

Diabetes mellitus
(increased risk of hyperkalemia with ACE inhibitor therapy)

Dialysis with high-flux membranes or
Low-density lipoprotein apheresis with dextran sulfate absorption
(anaphylactoid reactions have been reported in patients undergoing these procedures while being treated with an ACE inhibitor)

Hepatic function impairment
(the plasma elimination half-life of amlodipine increases to 56 hours and the area under the plasma concentration-time curve for amlodipine may increase by 40 to 60% because of decreased hepatic clearance)

Hymenoptera venom desensitization treatment
(life-threatening anaphylactoid reactions have been reported in two patients undergoing desensitizing treatment with hymenoptera venom while receiving ACE inhibitors)

» Renal artery stenosis, bilateral or unilateral or
» Renal function impairment
(plasma concentration of benazeprilat may be increased due to decreased elimination; increased risk of developing neutropenia or agranulocytosis; increased risk of hyperkalemia; increases in blood urea nitrogen [BUN] and serum creatinine may occur, especially in patients who are pretreated with a diuretic; renal function should be monitored during the first few weeks of therapy; a

dosage adjustment and/or discontinuation of the diuretic or of amlodipine and benazepril combination may be necessary)

Patient monitoring

The following may be especially important in patient monitoring (other tests may be warranted in some patients, depending on condition; » = major clinical significance):

» Blood pressure measurements
(periodic monitoring is necessary for titration of dose according to the patient's response)

Renal function determinations
(monitoring may be necessary in renally impaired patients)

Leukocyte count determinations
(recommended for patients at risk of neutropenia or agranulocytosis, such as those with renal function impairment and/or a collagen-vascular disease)

Potassium, serum concentrations
(monitoring may be necessary in patients at risk of hyperkalemia, such as those with renal insufficiency, diabetes mellitus, or those concurrently taking potassium-sparing diuretics, potassium supplements, or potassium-containing salt substitutes)

Side/Adverse Effects

The following side/adverse effects have been selected on the basis of their potential clinical significance (possible signs and symptoms in parentheses where appropriate)—not necessarily inclusive:

Those indicating need for medical attention

Incidence less frequent

Edema, dependent (swelling of ankles, feet, and lower legs)—the incidence of amlodipine-associated edema is reduced when amlodipine is given in combination with benazepril; ***hyperkalemia*** (confusion; irregular heartbeat; nervousness; numbness or tingling in hands, feet, or lips; shortness of breath or difficulty breathing; weakness or heaviness of legs)—during clinical trials, hyperkalemia occurred in approximately 1.5% of patients; ***hypotension*** (dizziness, lightheadedness, or fainting)

Incidence rare

Anemia, hemolytic (bleeding gums; fatigue; nosebleeds; pale skin color); ***angioedema*** (sudden trouble in swallowing or breathing; swelling of face, mouth, hands, or feet; hoarseness); ***hepatotoxicity*** (yellow eyes or skin); ***neutropenia or agranulocytosis*** (chills; fever; sore throat)—occurs rarely in uncomplicated hypertension; occurs more frequently in patients with renal function impairment, especially if accompanied by a collagen-vascular disease; ***pancreatitis*** (abdominal pain and distention; fever; nausea; vomiting); ***pemphigus*** (blisters in the mouth followed by skin blisters on the trunk, scalp, or other areas); ***Stevens-Johnson syndrome*** (sudden onset of multiple skin lesions on the arms, feet, hands, legs, palms, mouth, and/or lips); ***thrombocytopenia*** (unusual bleeding or bruising)

Note: *Angioedema* is associated with ACE inhibitor therapy and may involve the face, extremities, lips, tongue, glottis, and larynx. Angioedema associated with laryngeal edema, resulting in airway obstruction, can be fatal. During clinical trials, angioedema occurred in 0.5% of patients taking benazepril alone. ACE inhibitor-associated angioedema occurs at a higher rate in black patients than in nonblack patients.

ACE inhibitor-associated *hepatotoxicity* occurs by a mechanism that is not understood, but is manifest as a syndrome of cholestatic jaundice, fulminant hepatic necrosis, and possibly death. Amlodipine and benazepril combination therapy should be discontinued in patients who develop jaundice or marked elevations of hepatic enzymes. Patients should receive appropriate medical follow-up.

Severe, life-threatening, anaphylactoid reactions have occurred in two patients using ACE inhibitors during desensitization protocols involving hymenoptera venom. Additionally, some patients treated with ACE inhibitors who have been exposed to either high-flux membrane dialysis or low-density lipoprotein apheresis with dextran sulfate absorption have also experienced anaphylactoid-like reactions.

Incidence not determined—Observed during clinical practice; estimates of frequency can not be determined

Esophagitis (difficulty in swallowing; pain or burning in throat; chest pain; heartburn; vomiting; sores, ulcers, or white spots on lips or tongue or inside the mouth); ***intestinal angioedema*** (stomach pain)

Note: Intestinal angioedema has been reported in patients treated with ACE inhibitors. These patients presented with abdominal pain (with or without nausea or vomiting); in some cases there was no prior history of facial angioedema and C-1 esterase levels were normal. Angioedema was diagnosed by procedures including abdominal CT scan or ultrasound, or at surgery. Symptoms resolved after stopping the ACE inhibitor. Intestinal angioedema should be included in differential diagnosis of patients on ACE inhibitors presenting with abdominal pain.

Those indicating need for medical attention only if they continue or are bothersome

Incidence less frequent

Cough, dry and persistent; dizziness; flushing (feeling of warmth; redness of the face, neck, arms and occasionally, upper chest); ***palpitations*** (heartbeat sensations); ***somnolence*** (sleepiness)

Note: *Cough* has been reported with ACE inhibitors and is thought to be due to increased plasma bradykinin concentrations as a result of kininase II inhibition. In clinical trials of benazepril, in combination with amlodipine and alone, the incidence of cough was 3.3% and 1.8%, respectively.

Incidence not determined—Observed during clinical practice; estimates of frequency can not be determined

Abdominal pain (stomach pain); ***anxiety*** (fear; nervousness); ***asthenia*** (lack or loss of strength); ***back pain; constipation*** (difficulty having a bowel movement [stool]); ***cramps; decreased libido or impotence*** (loss in sexual ability, desire, drive, or performance; decreased interest in sexual intercourse; inability to have or keep an erection); ***dermatitis*** (blistering, crusting, irritation, itching, or reddening of skin; cracked, dry, scaly skin; swelling); ***diarrhea; dry mouth; dyspepsia*** (acid or sour stomach; belching; heartburn; indigestion; stomach discomfort, upset or pain); ***fatigue*** (unusual tiredness or weakness); ***hot flashes*** (feeling of warmth; redness of the face, neck, arms and occasionally, upper chest; sudden sweating); ***insomnia*** (sleeplessness; trouble sleeping; unable to sleep); ***muscle cramps*** (stomach pain); ***musculoskeletal pain*** (muscle or bone pain); ***nausea; nervousness; pharyngitis*** (body aches or pain; congestion; cough; dryness or soreness of throat; fever; hoarseness; runny nose; tender, swollen glands in neck; trouble in swallowing; voice changes); ***polyuria*** (frequent urination; increased volume of pale, dilute urine); ***rash; skin nodule*** (small lump under the skin); ***tremor*** (trembling or shaking of hands or feet; shakiness in legs, arms, hands, feet)

Overdose

For specific information on the agents used in the management of amlodipine and benazepril combination overdose, see

- *Dopamine* and
- *Norepinephrine* in
- *Sympathomimetic Agents—Cardiovascular Use (Parenteral-Systemic)* monograph.

For more information on the management of overdose or unintentional ingestion, **contact a Poison Control Center** (see *Poison Control Center Listing*).

Clinical effects of overdose

The following effects have been selected on the basis of their potential clinical significance (possible signs and symptoms in parentheses where appropriate)—not necessarily inclusive:

Acute and chronic

Hypotension, severe (dizziness; fainting; lightheadedness); ***tachycardia*** (rapid heartbeat)

Treatment of overdose

Treatment is symptomatic and supportive. Calcium chloride and glucagon have been used to treat overdoses of other dihydropyridine calcium channel blocking agents, but their efficacy in the treatment of overdose is questionable.

For severe hypotension—Repletion of central fluid volume by placing the patient in a supine or Trendelenburg position and/or infusing normal saline. If necessary, vasopressors such as norepinephrine or high-dose dopamine may be used.

Monitoring—Patients should be monitored for possible pulmonary edema resulting from the return of peripheral vascular tone after dihydropyridine calcium channel blocking agent overdose.

Supportive care—Patients in whom intentional overdose is confirmed or suspected should be referred for psychiatric consultation.

Patient Consultation

As an aid to patient consultation, refer to *Advice for the Patient, Amlodipine and Benazepril (Systemic)*.

In providing consultation, consider emphasizing the following selected information (» = major clinical significance):

Before using this medication

» Conditions affecting use, especially:

Hypersensitivity to benazepril, other angiotensin-converting enzyme (ACE) inhibitors, or amlodipine

Pregnancy—ACE inhibitor-associated fetal and neonatal hypotension, skull hypoplasia, renal failure, and death reported in humans

Breast-feeding—Less than 0.1% of the maternal dose of benazepril is distributed into breast milk; breast-feeding should be discontinued

Use in the elderly—May be more sensitive to drug effects

Dental—Risk of gingival hyperplasia

Other medications, especially diuretics, potassium-containing salt substitutes, potassium-sparing diuretics, or potassium supplements

Other medical problems, especially congestive heart failure, renal artery stenosis, or renal function impairment

Proper use of this medication

» Compliance with therapy; taking medication at the same time each day to maintain the antihypertensive effect

» Proper dosing

Missed dose: Taking as soon as possible; not taking if almost time for next scheduled dose; not doubling doses

» Proper storage

Precautions while using this medication

Regular visits to physician to check progress

Notifying physician immediately if pregnancy is suspected because of possibility of fetal or neonatal injury and/or death

Not taking other medications, especially potassium supplements or salt substitutes that contain potassium, without consulting physician

Caution when driving or doing other things requiring alertness because of possible dizziness, lightheadedness, and fainting due to symptomatic hypotension

Reporting any signs of infection (fever, sore throat, chills) to physician because of risk of neutropenia

Reporting any signs of facial or extremity swelling and/or difficulty in swallowing or breathing because of risk of angioedema

Checking with physician if severe nausea, vomiting, or diarrhea occurs and continues because of risk of dehydration, which may result in hypotension

Caution when exercising or during exposure to hot weather because of the risk of dehydration, which may result in hypotension

» Maintaining good dental hygiene and seeing dentist frequently for teeth cleaning to prevent tenderness, bleeding, and gum enlargement

Telling physician you are taking this medication before undergoing any surgical procedure (including dental surgery) or emergency treatment

Side/adverse effects

Signs of potential side effects, especially dependent edema, hyperkalemia, hypotension, hemolytic anemia, angioedema, hepatotoxicity, neutropenia or agranulocytosis, pancreatitis, pemphigus, Stevens-Johnson syndrome, and thrombocytopenia

Signs of potential side effects observed during clinical practice, especially esophagitis or intestinal angioedema

General Dosing Information

Dosage must be adjusted to meet the individual requirements of each patient, on the basis of clinical response.

Combination amlodipine and benazepril therapy should be used only in patients who have failed to achieve the desired antihypertensive effect with one or the other medication as single-drug therapy, or have not been able to achieve the desired antihypertensive effect with amlodipine monotherapy without developing edema. For dosage ranges for the individual agents when given as single therapy, see

- *Amlodipine (Systemic)* monograph; and/or
- *Benazepril* in *Angiotensin-converting Enzyme (ACE) Inhibitors (Systemic)* monograph.

Black patients may benefit from a reduction in amlodipine-induced edema when benazepril is added to current amlodipine therapy, but additional antihypertensive effects may not occur in these patients.

Severe renal function impairment (creatinine clearance < 30 mL per minute) may increase the peak benazeprilat plasma concentrations and the time to steady state. Amlodipine and benazepril combination is not recommended in patients with a creatinine clearance of ≤ 30 mL per minute (serum creatinine > 3 mg per dL).

In patients with congestive heart failure, treatment should be initiated under close medical supervision. Patients who have heart failure should be followed closely for the first 2 weeks of treatment, at each increase in benazepril dosage, whenever a diuretic is added to the treatment, or when the dosage of a concurrently administered diuretic is increased.

For treatment of adverse effects

Recommended treatment consists of the following:

- Treatment of symptomatic hypotension involves placing the patient in a supine or Trendelenburg position and, if needed, administering normal saline intravenously.
- For treatment of ACE inhibitor-associated angioedema with swelling involving the tongue, glottis, or larynx, causing airway obstruction—Appropriate treatment, such as subcutaneous epinephrine, should be initiated immediately.

Oral Dosage Form

AMLODIPINE BESYLATE AND BENAZEPRIL HYDROCHLORIDE CAPSULES

Usual adult dose

Antihypertensive—

Oral, 1 to 2 capsules a day, as determined by individual dosage titration with the component agents.

Note: The elimination half-life of amlodipine in patients with hepatic function impairment increases to 56 hours. The recommended initial dose of amlodipine as a component of combination therapy in these patients is 2.5 mg.

The recommended initial dose of amlodipine as a component of combination therapy in small or frail patients is 2.5 mg.

Usual adult prescribing limits

5 mg of amlodipine and 20 mg of benazepril per day.

Usual pediatric dose

Safety and efficacy have not been established.

Usual geriatric dose

Antihypertensive—

Oral, initially, 2.5 mg of amlodipine as a component of combination therapy.

Strength(s) usually available

U.S.—

2.5 mg amlodipine base and 10 mg benazepril (Rx) [*Lotrel* (calcium phosphate; cellulose compounds; colloidal silicon dioxide; crospovidone; gelatin; hydrogenated castor oil; iron oxides; lactose; magnesium stearate; polysorbate 80; silicon dioxide; sodium lauryl sulfate; sodium starch (potato) glycolate; starch (corn); talc; titanium dioxide)].

5 mg amlodipine base and 10 mg benazepril (Rx) [*Lotrel* (calcium phosphate; cellulose compounds; colloidal silicon dioxide; crospovidone; gelatin; hydrogenated castor oil; iron oxides; lactose; magnesium stearate; polysorbate 80; silicon dioxide; sodium lauryl sulfate; sodium starch (potato) glycolate; starch (corn); talc; titanium dioxide)].

5 mg amlodipine base and 20 mg benazepril (Rx) [*Lotrel* (calcium phosphate; cellulose compounds; colloidal silicon dioxide; crospovidone; gelatin; hydrogenated castor oil; iron oxides; lactose; magnesium stearate; polysorbate 80; silicon dioxide; sodium lauryl sulfate; sodium starch (potato) glycolate; starch (corn); talc; titanium dioxide)].

10 mg amlodipine and 20 mg benazepril (Rx) [*Lotrel* (calcium phosphate; cellulose compounds; colloidal silicon dioxide; crospovidone; gelatin; hydrogenated castor oil; iron oxides; lactose; magnesium stearate; polysorbate 80; silicon dioxide; sodium lauryl sulfate; sodium starch (potato) glycolate; starch (corn); talc; titanium dioxide)].

Packaging and storage

Store below 30 °C (86 °F). Protect from moisture and light.

Auxiliary labeling

- Do not take other medicines without your doctor's advice.

Revised: 11/09/2004
Developed: 10/17/1997

AMMONIUM MOLYBDATE—See *Molybdenum Supplements (Systemic)*

AMOBARBITAL—See *Barbiturates (Systemic)*

AMOXAPINE—See *Antidepressants, Tricyclic (Systemic)*

AMOXICILLIN—See *Penicillins (Systemic)*

AMPHETAMINE—See *Amphetamines (Systemic)*

AMPHETAMINES Systemic

This monograph includes information on the following: 1) Amphetamine†; 2) Amphetamine and dextroamphetamine†; 3) Dextroamphetamine; 4) Methamphetamine†.

INN:
Amphetamine—Amfetamine
Dextroamphetamine—Dexamfetamine
Methamphetamine—Metamfetamine

VA CLASSIFICATION (Primary): CN801

Note: Controlled substances in the U.S. and Canada as follows:

Drug	U.S.	Canada
Amphetamine	II	†
Dextroamphetamine	II	C
Methamphetamine	II	†

Commonly used brand name(s): *Adderall*[2]; *Adderall XR*[2]; *Desoxyn*[4]; *Desoxyn Gradumet*[4]; *Dexedrine*[3]; *Dexedrine Spansule*[3]; *Dextrostat*[3].

Note: For a listing of dosage forms and brand names by country availability, see *Dosage Forms* section(s).

†Not commercially available in Canada.

Category

Central nervous system (CNS) stimulant.

Indications

Note: Bracketed information in the *Indications* section refers to uses that are not included in U.S. product labeling.

Accepted

Attention-deficit hyperactivity disorder (treatment)—Amphetamines are indicated as an integral part of a total treatment program that includes other remedial measures (psychological, educational, social) for a stabilizing effect in children [and adults][1] with attention-deficit hyperactivity disorder [ADHD], characterized by moderate to severe distractibility, short attention span, hyperactivity, emotional lability, and impulsivity. Nonlocalizing neurological signs, learning disability, and abnormal electroencephalogram (EEG) may be present also.

Narcolepsy (treatment)—Amphetamine and dextroamphetamine are indicated in the treatment of well-established and proven narcolepsy.

Unaccepted

Amphetamines are *not* recommended for use in patients who exhibit symptoms secondary to environmental factors and/or other primary psychiatric disorders, including psychosis, for the treatment of severe depression, or for the prevention or treatment of normal fatigue states.

Note: When remedial measures (i.e., appropriate educational placement and psychosocial intervention) are insufficient, the physician's assessment of the patient's symptoms must be taken into account in deciding to prescribe amphetamines for ADHD.

Due to their high potential for abuse, amphetamines are not recommended for use as appetite suppressants.

Amphetamines should not be used to combat fatigue or to replace rest in normal subjects.

[1]Not included in Canadian product labeling.

Pharmacology/Pharmacokinetics

Physicochemical characteristics

Molecular weight—
Amphetamine sulfate: 368.49.
Dextroamphetamine sulfate: 368.49.
Methamphetamine hydrochloride: 185.70.

Mechanism of action/Effect

Amphetamines are sympathomimetic amines that increase motor activity and mental alertness, and diminish drowsiness and a sense of fatigue.

In attention-deficit hyperactivity disorder, amphetamines decrease motor restlessness and enhance the ability to pay attention.

The exact mechanism of action has not been established. However, in animals, amphetamines facilitate the action of dopamine and norepinephrine by blocking reuptake from the synapse, inhibit the action of monoamine oxidase (MAO), and facilitate the release of catecholamines. Increase in locomotor activity at relatively low doses and increase in stereotypic behavior with a concomitant decrease in activity at higher doses appear to be due to stimulation of mesocorticolimbic and nigrostriatal dopaminergic pathways. Dextroamphetamine may also stimulate inhibitory autoreceptors in the substantia nigra and ventral tegmentum.

Some studies support the theory that amphetamine exerts a dual effect on the striatal dopaminergic nerve terminal, thus explaining the paradoxical effects of amphetamines. Amphetamines may selectively facilitate the dopaminergic transmission by promoting the release of recently synthesized dopamine from a reserpine-resistant pool and, in addition, may inhibit the classical dopaminergic neurotransmission involving the calcium-dependent depolarization-evoked release of dopamine from reserpine-sensitive storage sites.

Other actions/effects

Peripheral actions include elevation of both diastolic and systolic blood pressure, and weak bronchodilator and respiratory stimulant actions.

Biotransformation

Hepatic.

Half-life

Amphetamine—
10 to 30 hours; dependent on urinary pH.

Dextroamphetamine—
10 to 12 hours in adults; 6 to 8 hours in children.

Methamphetamine—
4 to 5 hours; dependent on urinary pH.

Time to peak concentration

For dextroamphetamine and amphetamine combination:

Immediate-release tablets—3 hours for both d-amphetamine and l-amphetamine

Extended-release capsules—7 hours

Food prolongs T_{max} by 2.5 hours: (5.2 hours at fasted state to 7.7 hours after a high-fat meal) for d-amphetamine; (5.6 hours at fasted state to 7.7 hours after a high-fat meal) for l-amphetamine

Elimination

Renal; dependent on urinary pH. Excretion is accelerated in acidic urine and slowed in alkaline urine.

Precautions to Consider

Cross-sensitivity and/or related problems

Patients sensitive to other sympathomimetics (for example, ephedrine, epinephrine, isoproterenol, metaproterenol, norepinephrine, phenylephrine, phenylpropanolamine, pseudoephedrine, terbutaline) may be sensitive to amphetamines also.

Carcinogenicity/Mutagenicity

No evidence of carcinogenicity was found in mice and rat studies in which d,l-amphetamine was administered at approximately 2.4, 1.5, and 0.8 times the maximum recommended human dose of 30 mg per day on a mg per m^2 basis in male mice, female mice, and in male and female rats, respectively.

Amphetamine was not clastogenic in the mouse bone marrow micronucleus test *in vivo* and was negative when tested in the E. coli component of the Ames test *in vitro*. Amphetamine has been reported to produce a positive response in the mouse bone marrow micronucleus test, an equivocal response in the Ames test, and negative responses in the *in vitro* sister chromatid exchange and chromosomal aberration assays.

Pregnancy/Reproduction

Fertility—Amphetamine did not adversely affect fertility or early embryonic development in rats at doses of up to 20 mg per kg of body weight per day (approximately 5 times the maximum recommended human dose of 30 mg per day on a mg per m^2 body surface area basis.

Pregnancy—Although adequate and well-controlled studies in humans have not been done, use of amphetamines during early pregnancy may be associated with an increased risk of congenital malformations, especially in the cardiovascular system and biliary tract.

Reproduction studies in animals have suggested both an embryotoxic and a teratogenic potential when amphetamines were administered at high multiples of the human dose. Several rodent studies indicate that prenatal or early postnatal exposure to amphetamine can result in long-term neurochemical and behavioral alterations including learning and memory deficits, altered locomotor activity, and changes in sexual function.

Amphetamines should be used during pregnancy only if potential benefit justifies potential risk to the fetus.

FDA Pregnancy Category C.

Delivery—Infants born to mothers dependent on amphetamines have an increased risk of premature delivery and low birth weight. These infants may experience symptoms of withdrawal, including agitation and significant drowsiness.

Breast-feeding

Amphetamines are distributed into breast milk. However, problems in nursing infants have not been documented. Mothers taking amphetamines should be advised to refrain from nursing.

Pediatrics

Long-term effects of amphetamines in children have not been well established. Data suggest that prolonged administration of amphetamines to children may inhibit growth. Careful monitoring during treatment is recommended.

Amphetamines are not recommended for use in children under 3 years of age.

Children who have psychotic disorders may experience exacerbation of symptoms of behavior disturbance and thought disorder.

Amphetamines may provoke or exacerbate motor and vocal tics and Tourette's syndrome, necessitating clinical evaluation before administration of amphetamines.

Geriatrics

No information is available on the relationship of age to the effects of the amphetamines in geriatric patients.

Drug interactions and/or related problems

The following drug interactions and/or related problems have been selected on the basis of their potential clinical significance (possible mechanism in parentheses where appropriate)—not necessarily inclusive (» = major clinical significance):

Note: Combinations containing any of the following medications, depending on the amount present, may also interact with this medication.

Acidifiers, gastrointestinal, such as:
- Ascorbic acid or
- Fruit juices
- Glutamic acid hydrochloride or
- Guanethidine or
- Reserpine or

Acidifiers, urinary, such as:
- Ammonium chloride or
- Sodium acid phosphate

(concurrent use may decrease the effects of amphetamines as a result of decreased absorption or increased elimination)

Alkalizers, gastrointestinal, such as:
- Antacids, calcium- and/or magnesium-containing or
- Citrates or
- Sodium bicarbonate or

Alkalizers, urinary such as:
- Carbonic anhydrase inhibitors including acetazolamide or
- Some thiazide drugs

(these drugs increase blood levels and potentiate actions of amphetamines)

Anesthetics, inhalation
(halothane and, to a much lesser extent, enflurane, isoflurane, and methoxyflurane, may sensitize the myocardium to the effects of sympathomimetics, including chronic use of amphetamines prior to anesthesia, so that the risk of severe ventricular arrhythmias is increased; sympathomimetics should be used with caution and in substantially reduced dosage in patients receiving these agents)

» Antidepressants, tricyclic
(although tricyclic antidepressants may be used concurrently with amphetamines for therapeutic effect, concurrent use may potentiate cardiovascular effects due to the release of norepinephrine, possibly resulting in arrhythmias, tachycardia, or severe hypertension or hyperpyrexia; close monitoring is recommended and dosage adjustments may be necessary)

Antihistamines
(concomitant use may counteract sedative effect of antihistamines)

Antihypertensives or
Diuretics used as antihypertensives
(hypotensive effects may be reduced when these medications are used concurrently with amphetamines; the patient should be carefully monitored to confirm that the desired effect is obtained)

» Beta-adrenergic blocking agents, including ophthalmics
(concurrent use with amphetamines may result in unopposed alpha-adrenergic activity with a risk of hypertension and excessive bradycardia and possible heart block; risk may be less with labetalol because of its alpha-blocking activity)

Chlorprozamine
(blocks dopamine and norepinephrine receptors inhibiting the central stimulant effect of amphetamines)

» CNS stimulation-producing medications, other (see *Appendix II*)
(additive CNS stimulation to excessive levels may result in nervousness, irritability, insomnia, or possibly seizures; close observation is recommended)
(also, concurrent use of amphetamines with other sympathomimetics may increase cardiovascular effects of either medication)
(in addition to possibly increasing CNS stimulation, concurrent use of norepinephrine with large doses of amphetamines may enhance the pressor response to norepinephrine; caution may also be warranted in patients receiving usual doses of amphetamines)

» Digitalis glycosides
(concurrent use with amphetamines may cause additive effects, resulting in cardiac arrhythmias)

Ethosuximide or
Phenobarbital or
Phenytoin
(concurrent use with amphetamines may cause a delay in the intestinal absorption of ethosuximide, phenobarbital, or phenytoin)

Haloperidol or
Loxapine or
Molindone or
Phenothiazines or
Pimozide or
Thioxanthenes
(central stimulant effects of amphetamines may be inhibited because of alpha-adrenergic blockade by these agents; also, concurrent use with amphetamines may reduce the antipsychotic effects of these agents)

Levodopa
(the risk of cardiac arrhythmias may be increased; dosage reduction of amphetamine is recommended)

Lithium
(central stimulant effects of amphetamines may be antagonized by lithium)

» Meperidine
(the analgesic effects of meperidine may be potentiated by amphetamines; however, concurrent use of meperidine is not recommended, as it may potentially result in hypotension, severe respiratory depression, coma, convulsions, hyperpyrexia, vascular collapse, and death in some patients due to the monoamine oxidase inhibition properties of amphetamines)

Metrizamide
(intrathecal administration of metrizamide may increase the risk of seizures because of lowered seizure threshold; it is recommended that amphetamines be discontinued for at least 48 hours before and 24 hours after myelography)

» Monoamine oxidase (MAO) inhibitors, including
- Furazolidine or
- Procarbazine or
- Selegiline

(concurrent use may prolong and intensify cardiac stimulant and vasopressor effects [including headache, cardiac arrhythmias, vomiting, sudden and severe hypertensive and hyperpyretic crises] of amphetamines because of the release of catecholamines that accumulate in intraneuronal storage sites during MAO inhibitor therapy; **amphetamines should not be administered during or within 14 days following the administration of an MAO inhibitor;** hypertensive crises may result)

Methenamine therapy
(increases urinary excretion of amphetamines and efficacy is reduced by acidifying agents used in methenamine therapy)

Norepinephrine
(amphetamines enhance adrenergic effect of norepinephrine)

Propoxyphene
(overdosage of propoxyphene may potentiate central stimulant effects of amphetamines; fatal convulsions can occur)

» Thyroid hormones
(the effects of either these medications or amphetamines may be increased; thyroid hormones enhance the risk of coronary insufficiency when amphetamines are administered to patients with coronary artery disease)

Veratrum alkaloids
(concomitant use inhibits hypotensive effect of veratrum alkaloids)

Laboratory value alterations

The following have been selected on the basis of their potential clinical significance (possible effect in parentheses where appropriate)—not necessarily inclusive (» = major clinical significance).

With diagnostic test results
Urinary steroid determinations
(may be altered, interfering with results of such tests as the metyrapone test)

With physiology/laboratory test values
Plasma corticosteroid concentrations
(may be increased, with greatest increase in evening)

Medical considerations/Contraindications

The medical considerations/contraindications included have been selected on the basis of their potential clinical significance (reasons given in parentheses where appropriate)—not necessarily inclusive (» = major clinical significance).

Except under special circumstances, this medication should not be used when the following medical problem exists:

» Agitated states or
» Arteriosclerosis, advanced or
» Cardiovascular disease, symptomatic or
» Drug abuse or dependence, history of or
» Glaucoma or
» Hypersensitivity or idiosyncrasy to the sympathomimetic amines or
» Hypertension, moderate to severe or
» Hyperthyroidism
» Structural cardiac abnormalities
(sudden death has been reported in association with amphetamine treatment in children with this condition; amphetamines generally should not be used in children or adults with structural cardiac abnormalities)

Risk-benefit should be considered when the following medical problems exist:

Hypertension, mild
(caution in prescribing amphetamines for these patients)

Psychoses, especially in children
(amphetamine administration may exacerbate symptoms of behavior disturbance and thought disorder)

» Tourette's syndrome or other motor and phonic tics
(clinical evaluation for these conditions in children and their families should precede use of amphetamines)

Patient monitoring

The following may be especially important in patient monitoring (other tests may be warranted in some patients, depending on condition; » = major clinical significance):

Assessment of potential tolerance, dependence, or drug-seeking behavior
(tolerance, extreme psychological dependence and severe social disability have occurred with extensive abuse; chronic intoxication manifestations may include severe dermatoses, marked insomnia, irritability, hyperactivity and personality changes; most severe manifestation is psychosis, often clinically indistinguishable from schizophrenia; prescribing the smallest amount of medication necessary for good patient management is recommended to minimize abuse and the possibility of overdosage)

Blood pressure and pulse determinations and
Cardiac rhythm determinations
(should be monitored at appropriate intervals during therapy, especially in patients with hypertension)

Monitoring of growth, both height and weight gain
(recommended during long-term therapy since data suggest that chronic administration of amphetamines may be associated with suppression of growth; treatment should be interrupted in patients who are not growing or gaining weight as expected)

Monitoring for motor and vocal tics
(recommended during therapy)

Reassessment of need for therapy and long-term usefulness of the drug
(interruption of therapy at periodic intervals is recommended to determine if a recurrence of behavioral symptoms is sufficient to continue therapy; effectiveness for long-term use [more than 3 weeks and 4 weeks in children and adults, respectively] has not been systematically evaluated)

Side/Adverse Effects

Note: Psychological dependence and tolerance may occur with amphetamines following prolonged use or high doses.

The following side/adverse effects have been selected on the basis of their potential clinical significance (possible signs and symptoms in parentheses where appropriate)—not necessarily inclusive:

Those indicating need for medical attention

Incidence more frequent
Agitation (anxiety; nervousness; restlessness; irritability; dry mouth; shortness of breath; hyperventilation; trouble sleeping; irregular heartbeats; shaking); ***emotional lability*** (crying; depersonalization; dysphoria; euphoria; mental depression; paranoia; quick to react or overreact emotionally; rapidly changing moods); ***irregular heartbeat; tachycardia*** (fast, pounding, or irregular heartbeat or pulse)

Incidence less frequent
Dyspnea (shortness of breath; difficult or labored breathing; tightness in chest wheezing); ***infection*** (fever or chills; cough or hoarseness; lower back or side pain; painful or difficult urination); ***viral infection*** (chills; cough or hoarseness; fever; cold flu-like symptoms)

Incidence rare
Allergic reaction (skin rash or hives); ***chest pain; CNS stimulation, severe, or Tourette's syndrome*** (uncontrolled movements of the head, neck, arms, and legs); ***hyperthermia*** (extremely high body temperature)

With prolonged use or high doses
Cardiomyopathy (chest discomfort or pain; difficulty in breathing; dizziness or feeling faint; irregular or pounding heartbeat; unusual tiredness or weakness); ***increase in blood pressure; psychotic reactions or toxic psychoses*** (mood or mental changes)

Those indicating need for medical attention only if they continue or are bothersome

Incidence more frequent
CNS stimulation (false sense of well-being; irritability; nervousness; restlessness; trouble in sleeping)—drowsiness, fatigue, trembling, or mental depression may follow the stimulant effects

Incidence less frequent
Accidental injury; asthenia (lack or loss of strength); ***blurred vision; changes in sexual desire or decreased sexual ability; constipation; diarrhea; fever; loss of appetite; nausea; stomach cramps or pain; weight loss; vomiting; dizziness; headache; lightheadedness; dryness of mouth or unpleasant taste; dysmenorrhea*** (pain; cramps; heavy bleeding); ***impotence*** (loss in sexual ability, desire, drive, or performance; decreased interest in sexual intercourse; inability to have or keep an erection); ***increased sweating; libido decreased*** (loss in sexual ability, desire, drive, or performance; decreased interest in sexual intercourse; inability to have or keep an erection); ***photosensitivity reaction*** (increased sensitivity of skin to sunlight; itching, redness or other discoloration of skin; severe sunburn; skin rash); ***somnolence*** (sleepiness or unusual drowsiness); ***speech disorder*** (difficulty in speaking); ***tooth disorder; twitching; urinary tract infection*** (bladder pain; bloody or cloudy urine; difficult, burning, or painful urination; frequent urge to urinate; lower back or side pain)

Those indicating possible withdrawal and the need for medical attention if they occur after medication is discontinued

Mental depression; nausea; stomach cramps or pain; vomiting; trembling; unusual tiredness or weakness

Overdose

For specific information on the agents used in the management of amphetamine overdose, see:
- *Barbiturates (Systemic)* monograph;
- *Chlorpromazine* in
- *Phenothiazines (Systemic)* monograph; and/or
- *Phentolamine (Systemic)* monograph.

For more information on the management of overdose or unintentional ingestion, **contact a Poison Control Center** (see *Poison Control Center Listing*).

Treatment of overdose

Since there is no specific antidote for overdosage with amphetamines, treatment is symptomatic and supportive.

To decrease absorption—
Induction of emesis and/or use of gastric lavage is primary.
Use of saline cathartics to hasten evacuation of sustained-release dosage forms.
To enhance elimination—
Acidification of urine to increase amphetamine excretion. Acidification is contraindicated in presence of rhabdomyolysis, myoglobinuria, or hemoglobinemia, as renal failure may result.
Forced diuresis if condition permits.
Specific treatment—
Barbiturate sedatives or chlorpromazine sometimes used to control excessive CNS stimulation.
Intravenous phentolamine to control hypertension.
Monitoring—
Cardiovascular and respiratory monitoring.
Supportive care—
Protection of patient from self-injury by use of restraints if necessary.
Intravenous fluids to control hypotension.
Patients in whom intentional overdose is confirmed or suspected should be referred for psychiatric consultation.

Patient Consultation

As an aid to patient consultation, refer to *Advice for the Patient, Amphetamines (Systemic)*.

In providing consultation, consider emphasizing the following selected information (» = major clinical significance):

Before using this medication

» Conditions affecting use, especially:
Hypersensitivity to amphetamines and other sympathomimetics or any component of the amphetamine product
Pregnancy—Increased risk of congenital malformations, especially in cardiovascular system and biliary tract; potential embryotoxic and teratogenic effects in animals given large doses; risk of premature delivery and low birth weight may be increased; newborn may experience withdrawal symptoms; should be used during pregnancy only if potential benefits to mother outweigh potential risk to fetus.
Breast-feeding—Not recommended since amphetamines are distributed into breast milk
Use in children—May inhibit growth; may provoke motor and vocal tics and Tourette's syndrome; may exacerbate behavior problems and thought disorder in psychotic children
Other medications, especially tricyclic antidepressants, beta-adrenergic blocking agents, digitalis glycosides, meperidine, monoamine oxidase inhibitors, other CNS stimulation-producing medications, or thyroid hormones
Other medical problems, especially agitated states, advanced arteriosclerosis, symptomatic cardiovascular disease, history of drug dependence, glaucoma, hypertension, hyperthyroidism, structural cardiac abnormalities, or Tourette's syndrome or other tics

Proper use of this medication

Taking the last dose of the day of the regular dosage form at least 6 hours before bedtime and the daily dose of the extended-release dosage form upon awakening to minimize the possibility of insomnia
Proper administration of extended-release dosage forms : Swallowing whole; not breaking, crushing, or chewing; For *Adderall XR* extended-release dosage form—Sprinkling capsule contents on small amount of food or swallowing whole
» Importance of not taking more medication than the amount prescribed because of habit-forming potential
» Not increasing dose if medication becomes less effective after a few weeks; checking with physician
» Proper dosing
Missed dose: If dosing schedule is—Once a day: Taking as soon as possible but not later than stated above; if remembered later, not taking until next day; not doubling doses Two or three times a day: Taking as soon as possible if remembered within an hour or so; not taking if remembered later; not doubling doses
» Proper storage

Precautions while using this medication

Regular visits to physician to check progress during therapy
» Checking with physician before discontinuing medication after prolonged high-dose therapy; gradual dosage reduction may be necessary to avoid possibility of withdrawal symptoms
» Caution if dizziness or euphoria occurs; not driving, using machinery, or doing other activities that are potentially hazardous
Avoiding extended exposure to sunlight or tanning beds due to possibility of photosensitivity reaction.
Caution if any laboratory tests required; possible interference with results of metyrapone test
» Suspected psychological or physical dependence; checking with physician

Side/adverse effects

Signs of potential side effects, especially agitation, emotional lability; irregular heartbeat; tachycardia; dyspnea, infection, viral infection, allergic reaction; chest pain; tics or other signs of severe CNS stimulation; hyperthermia; cardiomyopathy; increased blood pressure; psychotic reactions
Potential unwanted effects during long-term use in children
Possibility of withdrawal effects, especially mental depression, nausea, stomach cramps or pain, vomiting, trembling, or unusual tiredness or weakness

General Dosing Information

When the regular tablet dosage form of amphetamines is administered, the first dose should be taken on awakening, followed by 1 or 2 additional doses at intervals of 4 to 6 hours.

To reduce the possibility of insomnia, the last dose of the day of the regular dosage form should be administered at least 6 hours before bedtime, and the daily dose of the extended-release dosage form should be administered upon awakening.

The extended-release dosage form may be used for once-a-day dosing whenever it is feasible.

Note: *Adderall XR* extended-release dosage form **must be** used for once-daily dosing.

When symptoms of attention-deficit hyperactivity disorder are controlled in children, dosage reduction or interruption in therapy may be possible during the summer months and at other times when the child is under less stress; medication may be given on each of the 5 school days during the week, with medication-free weekends and school holidays.

Prolonged use of amphetamines may result in tolerance, extreme psychological dependence, or severe social disability.

When the medication is to be discontinued following prolonged high-dose administration, the dosage should be reduced gradually since abrupt withdrawal may result in extreme fatigue and mental depression.

Bioequivalence information

Patients taking divided doses of immediate-release *Adderall* may be switched to the extended-release formulation, *Adderall XR*at the same total daily dose taken once daily.

AMPHETAMINE

Oral Dosage Forms

Note: Bracketed uses in the *Dosage Forms* section refer to categories of use and/or indications that are not included in U.S. product labeling.

AMPHETAMINE SULFATE TABLETS USP

Usual adult dose

[Attention-deficit hyperactivity disorder] or
Narcolepsy—
Oral, 5 to 20 mg one to three times a day.

Usual pediatric dose

Attention-deficit hyperactivity disorder—
Children younger than 3 years of age: Use is not recommended.
Children 3 to 6 years of age: Oral, 2.5 mg once a day, the dosage being increased by 2.5 mg per day at one-week intervals until the desired response is obtained.
Children 6 years of age and older: Oral, 5 mg one or two times a day, the dosage being increased by 5 mg per day at one-week intervals until the desired response is obtained.
Narcolepsy—
Children younger than 6 years of age: Dosage has not been established.
Children 6 to 12 years of age: Oral, 2.5 mg two times a day, the dosage being increased by 5 mg per day at one-week intervals until the desired response is obtained or until the adult dose is reached.
Children 12 years of age and older: Oral, 5 mg two times a day, the dosage being increased by 10 mg per day at one-week intervals until the desired response is obtained or until the adult dose is reached.

Strength(s) usually available
U.S.—
5 mg (Rx) [GENERIC].
10 mg (Rx) [GENERIC].
Canada—
Not commercially available.

Packaging and storage
Store below 40 °C (104 °F), preferably between 15 and 30 °C (59 and 86 °F), unless otherwise specified by manufacturer. Store in a well-closed container.

Note
Controlled substance in the U.S.

AMPHETAMINE AND DEXTROAMPHETAMINE

Oral Dosage Forms

AMPHETAMINE ASPARTATE, AMPHETAMINE SULFATE, DEXTROAMPHETAMINE SACCHARATE, AND DEXTROAMPHETAMINE SULFATE EXTENDED-RELEASE CAPSULES

Usual adult dose
Attention-deficit hyperactivity disorder—
Oral, 20 mg once per day recommended in patients either starting treatment for the first time or switching from another medication. Patients switching from immediate-release tablets may be switched to the extended-release capsules at the same total daily dose taken once daily.

Usual pediatric dose
Attention-deficit hyperactivity disorder—
Children younger than 3 years of age: Use is not recommended.
Children 3 to 6 years of age: Use has not been studied in children under 6 years of age
Children 6 years of age and older: Oral, 10 mg once per day in the morning recommended in patients either starting treatment for the first time or switching from another medication. Daily dosage may be adjusted in 5 or 10 mg increments at weekly intervals. When a lower initial dose is appropriate, patients may begin treatment with 5 mg once daily.

Usual pediatric prescribing limits
Maximum recommended dose is 30 mg per day. Doses greater than 30 mg per day have not been studied in children.

Strength(s) usually available
U.S.—
5 mg (1.25 mg each: amphetamine aspartate, amphetamine sulfate, dextroamphetamine saccharate, dextroamphetamine sulfate) (Rx) [*Adderall XR* (gelatin capsules; hydroxypropyl methylcellulose; methacrylic acid copolymer; opadry beige; sugar spheres; talc; triethyl citrate; FD&C Blue #2)].
10 mg (2.5 mg each: amphetamine aspartate, amphetamine sulfate, dextroamphetamine saccharate, dextroamphetamine sulfate) (Rx) [*Adderall XR* (gelatin capsules; hydroxypropyl methylcellulose; methacrylic acid copolymer; opadry beige; sugar spheres; talc; triethyl citrate; FD&C Blue #2)].
15 mg (3.75 mg each: amphetamine aspartate, amphetamine sulfate, dextroamphetamine saccharate, dextroamphetamine sulfate) (Rx) [*Adderall XR* (gelatin capsules; hydroxypropyl methylcellulose; methacrylic acid copolymer; opadry beige; sugar spheres; talc; triethyl citrate; FD&C Blue #2)].
20 mg (5 mg each: amphetamine aspartate, amphetamine sulfate, dextroamphetamine saccharate, dextroamphetamine sulfate) (Rx) [*Adderall XR* (gelatin capsules; hydroxypropyl methylcellulose; methacrylic acid copolymer; opadry beige; sugar spheres; talc; triethyl citrate; red iron oxide; yellow iron oxide)].
25 mg (6.25 mg each: amphetamine aspartate, amphetamine sulfate, dextroamphetamine saccharate, dextroamphetamine sulfate) (Rx) [*Adderall XR* (gelatin capsules; hydroxypropyl methylcellulose; methacrylic acid copolymer; opadry beige; sugar spheres; talc; triethyl citrate; red iron oxide; yellow iron oxide)].
30 mg (7.5 mg each: amphetamine aspartate, amphetamine sulfate, dextroamphetamine saccharate, dextroamphetamine sulfate) (Rx) [*Adderall XR* (gelatin capsules; hydroxypropyl methylcellulose; methacrylic acid copolymer; opadry beige; sugar spheres; talc; triethyl citrate; red iron oxide; yellow iron oxide)].
Canada—
Not commercially available.

Packaging and storage
Store at 25 °C (77 °F) excursions permitted to 15 to 30 °C (59 to 86 °F), unless otherwise specified by manufacturer. Store in a tight, light-resistant container.

Auxiliary labeling
• Sprinkle capsule contents on small amount of food or swallow whole
• This medication may be taken with or without food.
• May cause drowsiness. Be careful while driving or operating machinery. Use caution until you become familiar with its effects.
• Avoid extended exposure to sunlight or tanning beds while taking this drug. Severe burns may result.
• This medication may be habit forming.
• Caution: Federal law prohibits the transfer of this drug to any person other than the patient for whom it was prescribed.

Note
Schedule II controlled substance in the U.S.

Additional information
The 5 mg, 10 mg, 15 mg, 20 mg, 25 mg, and 30 mg tablets are equivalent to 3.13 mg, 6.3 mg, 9.4 mg, 12.5 mg, 15.6 mg and 18.8 mg of amphetamine base, respectively.

AMPHETAMINE ASPARTATE, AMPHETAMINE SULFATE, DEXTROAMPHETAMINE SACCHARATE, AND DEXTROAMPHETAMINE SULFATE TABLETS

Usual adult dose
Narcolepsy—
Oral, 5 to 60 mg a day in divided doses.

Usual pediatric dose
Attention-deficit hyperactivity disorder—
Children younger than 3 years of age: Use is not recommended.
Children 3 to 6 years of age: Oral, initially 2.5 mg a day, the dosage being increased by 2.5 mg per day at one-week intervals until the desired response is obtained.
Children 6 years of age and older: Oral, initially 5 mg one or two times a day, the dosage being increased by 5 mg per day at one-week intervals until the desired response is obtained.
Narcolepsy—
Children younger than 6 years of age: Dosage has not been established.
Children 6 to 12 years of age: Oral, initially 5 mg a day, the dosage being increased by 5 mg per day at one-week intervals until the desired response is obtained.
Children 12 years of age and older: Oral, initially 10 mg a day, the dosage being increased by 10 mg per day at one-week intervals until the desired response is obtained.

Note: The usual pediatric dose rarely exceeds 40 mg a day.

Strength(s) usually available
U.S.—
5 mg (1.25 mg each: amphetamine aspartate, amphetamine sulfate, dextroamphetamine saccharate, dextroamphetamine sulfate) (Rx) [*Adderall* (double scored; acacia; corn starch; FD&C Blue #1; lactose; magnesium stearate; sucrose)].
10 mg (2.5 mg each: amphetamine aspartate, amphetamine sulfate, dextroamphetamine saccharate, dextroamphetamine sulfate) (Rx) [*Adderall* (double scored; acacia; corn starch; FD&C Blue #1; lactose; magnesium stearate; sucrose)].
20 mg (5 mg each: amphetamine aspartate, amphetamine sulfate, dextroamphetamine saccharate, dextroamphetamine sulfate) (Rx) [*Adderall* (double scored; acacia; corn starch; FD&C Yellow #6; lactose; magnesium stearate; sucrose)].
30 mg (7.5 mg each: amphetamine aspartate, amphetamine sulfate, dextroamphetamine saccharate, dextroamphetamine sulfate) (Rx) [*Adderall* (double scored; acacia; corn starch; FD&C Yellow #6; lactose; magnesium stearate; sucrose)].
Canada—
Not commercially available.

Packaging and storage
Store between 15 and 30 °C (59 and 86 °F), unless otherwise specified by manufacturer. Store in a tight, light-resistant container.

Auxiliary labeling
• May cause drowsiness. Be careful while driving or operating machinery. Use caution until you become familiar with its effects.
• Avoid extended exposure to sunlight or tanning beds while taking this drug. Severe burns may result.
• This medication may be habit forming.
• Caution: Federal law prohibits the transfer of this drug to any person other than the patient for whom it was prescribed.

Note
Controlled substance in the U.S.

Additional information
The 5 mg, 10 mg, 20 mg, and 30 mg tablets are equivalent to 3.13 mg, 6.3 mg, 12.5 mg, and 18.8 mg of amphetamine base, respectively.

DEXTROAMPHETAMINE

Oral Dosage Forms

Note: Bracketed uses in the *Dosage Forms* section refer to categories of use and/or indications that are not included in U.S. product labeling.

DEXTROAMPHETAMINE SULFATE EXTENDED-RELEASE CAPSULES

Note: The extended-release dosage form should not be used for initiation of dosage, nor should it be used until the conventional titrated daily dosage is equal to or greater than the dosage provided in the extended-release dosage form.

Usual adult dose
[Attention-deficit hyperactivity disorder][1] or
Narcolepsy—
Oral, 5 to 60 mg once a day, or in divided doses.

Usual pediatric dose
Attention-deficit hyperactivity disorder—
Children younger than 3 years of age: Use is not recommended.
Children 3 to 6 years of age: Oral, initially 2.5 mg once a day, the dosage being increased by 2.5 mg per day at one-week intervals until the desired response is obtained.
Children 6 years of age and older: Oral, 5 mg once or twice a day, the dosage being increased by 5 mg a day at one-week intervals until the desired response is obtained.

Narcolepsy—
Children younger than 3 years of age: Use is not recommended.
Children 3 to 6 years of age: Dosage has not been established.
Children 6 to 12 years of age: Oral, initially 5 mg once a day, the dosage being increased by 5 mg a day at one-week intervals until the desired response is obtained.
Children 12 years of age and older: Oral, initially 10 mg once a day, the dosage being increased by 10 mg a day at one-week intervals until the desired response is obtained.

Note: The usual pediatric dose rarely exceeds 40 mg a day.

Strength(s) usually available
U.S.—
5 mg (Rx) [*Dexedrine Spansule* (tartrazine)].
10 mg (Rx) [*Dexedrine Spansule* (tartrazine)].
15 mg (Rx) [*Dexedrine Spansule* (tartrazine)].
Canada—
10 mg (Rx) [*Dexedrine Spansule* (tartrazine)].
15 mg (Rx) [*Dexedrine Spansule* (tartrazine)].

Packaging and storage
Store between 15 and 30 °C (59 and 86 °F), in a tight, light-resistant container, unless otherwise specified by manufacturer.

Auxiliary labeling
- Swallow capsules whole.

Note
Controlled substance in both the U.S. and Canada.

DEXTROAMPHETAMINE SULFATE TABLETS USP

Usual adult dose
[Attention-deficit hyperactivity disorder][1] or
Narcolepsy—
Oral, 5 to 60 mg a day in divided doses as needed and tolerated.

Usual pediatric dose
Attention-deficit hyperactivity disorder—
Children younger than 3 years of age: Use is not recommended.
Children 3 to 6 years of age: Oral, 2.5 mg once a day, the dosage being increased by 2.5 mg a day at one-week intervals until the desired response is obtained.
Children 6 years of age and older: Oral, 5 mg one or two times a day, the dosage being increased by 5 mg a day at one-week intervals until the desired response is obtained.

Narcolepsy—
Children younger than 6 years of age: Dosage has not been established.
Children 6 to 12 years of age: Oral, 5 mg a day, the dosage being increased by 5 mg a day at one-week intervals until the desired response is obtained or until the adult dose is reached.
Children 12 years of age and older: Oral, 10 mg a day, the dosage being increased by 10 mg a day at one-week intervals until the desired response is obtained or until the adult dose is reached.

Note: The usual pediatric dose rarely exceeds 40 mg a day.

Strength(s) usually available
U.S.—
5 mg (Rx) [*Dexedrine* (tartrazine); *Dextrostat;* GENERIC].
10 mg (Rx) [GENERIC].
Canada—
5 mg (Rx) [*Dexedrine* (tartrazine)].

Packaging and storage
Store below 40 °C (104 °F), preferably between 15 and 30 °C (59 and 86 °F), unless otherwise specified by manufacturer. Store in a tight container.

Note
Controlled substance in both the U.S. and Canada.

[1]Not included in Canadian product labeling.

METHAMPHETAMINE

Oral Dosage Forms

METHAMPHETAMINE HYDROCHLORIDE TABLETS USP

Usual pediatric dose
Attention-deficit hyperactivity disorder—
Children younger than 6 years of age: Use is not recommended.
Children 6 years of age and older: Oral, 5 mg one or two times a day, the dosage being increased by 5 mg per day at one-week intervals until the desired response is obtained (usually 20 to 25 mg per day).

Strength(s) usually available
U.S.—
5 mg (Rx) [*Desoxyn* (lactose)].
Canada—
Not commercially available.

Packaging and storage
Store below 40 °C (104 °F), preferably between 15 and 30 °C (59 and 86 °F), in a well-closed container, unless otherwise specified by manufacturer.

Note
Controlled substance in the U.S.

METHAMPHETAMINE HYDROCHLORIDE EXTENDED-RELEASE TABLETS

Note: The extended-release dosage form should not be used for initiation of dosage or until the conventional titrated daily dosage is equal to or greater than the dosage provided in the extended-release dosage form.

Usual pediatric dose
Attention-deficit hyperactivity disorder—
Children younger than 6 years of age: Use is not recommended.
Children 6 years of age and older: Oral, 20 to 25 mg once a day.

Strength(s) usually available
U.S.—
5 mg (Rx) [*Desoxyn Gradumet*].
10 mg (Rx) [*Desoxyn Gradumet*].
15 mg (Rx) [*Desoxyn Gradumet* (tartrazine)].
Canada—
Not commercially available.

Packaging and storage
Store below 40 °C (104 °F), preferably between 15 and 30 °C (59 and 86 °F), in a well-closed container, unless otherwise specified by manufacturer.

Auxiliary labeling
- Swallow tablets whole.
- Keep container tightly closed.

Note
Controlled substance in the U.S.

Revised: 11/08/2004

AMPHOTERICIN B Systemic

VA CLASSIFICATION (Primary/Secondary): AM700/AP109

Commonly used brand name(s): *Amphocin; Fungizone Intravenous.*

Note: For a listing of dosage forms and brand names by country availability, see *Dosage Forms* section(s).

Category

Antifungal (systemic); antiprotozoal.

Indications

Note: Bracketed information in the *Indications* section refers to uses that are not included in U.S. product labeling.

General Considerations

General considerations for use in neonates

Although not approved for use in pediatric patients, amphotericin B deoxycholate is used frequently to treat disseminated candidiasis in neonates. Numerous studies on the use of amphotericin B deoxycholate in neonates have been conducted since the early-eighties. The studies do not establish the most appropriate dose of amphotericin B deoxycholate for this indication. Most of the studies are retrospective case series. Only one prospective, randomized trial using amphotericin to treat disseminated candidiasis has been conducted; this study compared amphotericin B deoxycholate to fluconazole to treat disseminated candidiasis in 24 neonates. There was no difference in survival rates between patients treated with amphotericin B and those treated with fluconazole. The death rate in studies of the use of amphotericin B in neonates ranged from 16 to 60%. Researchers have attempted to distinguish deaths directly attributable to candidiasis from deaths not directly attributable to candidiasis. Although making this distinction may be useful, it may not be possible in this extremely ill patient population.

It is difficult to examine the outcomes of treatment of central nervous system (CNS) infections. Several studies that included patients with CNS infections are available. However, in most of the studies, CNS involvement was present in three or fewer patients. In an additional study including eight patients with CNS involvement, the specifics of drug therapy were not included. One study showed that amphotericin B 0.5 to 1 mg per kg of body weight was not successful in treating CNS infection in many cases until flucytosine was added to the therapy. However, in this study 0.1 mg per kg of body weight amphotericin B was administered initially, and target doses were not reached until 5 days of therapy. Other researchers have reported that prompt therapy with rapid escalation of the dose to reach the target dose is important for favorable outcomes. One researcher reported that combined therapy with flucytosine and amphotericin B was successful in treating 14 of 17 patients. However, the patients in the study ranged in age from neonate to adult, and the manner in which the drugs were administered (concurrently or sequentially) varied.

In the published studies, amphotericin B was administered at doses of 0.25 to 1.5 mg per kg of body weight a day to treat disseminated candidiasis in neonates. The comparative efficacy of different doses of amphotericin B was not examined. The possibility that amphotericin B toxicity may have contributed to the deaths of some neonates was not examined fully. The high mortality rate in one series may have resulted, in part, from amphotericin B toxicity.

There are no studies comparing the use of amphotericin B deoxycholate with liposomal amphotericin B, intralipid amphotericin B, or amphotericin B cholesteryl complex. However, one researcher treated 44 neonates with disseminated fungal infections with liposomal amphotericin B. Thirty-two of the neonates survived (72.8%); all of the neonates who died were very low birth weight. Additionally, there are case reports in the literature of infants responding to a newer amphotericin B formulation after failing treatment with amphotericin B deoxycholate.

Accepted

Aspergillosis (treatment)—Parenteral amphotericin B is indicated in the treatment of aspergillosis caused by *Aspergillus fumigatus*. [Intracavitary amphotericin B has also been used in the treatment of pulmonary aspergilloma with hemoptysis.]

Blastomycosis (treatment)—Parenteral amphotericin B is indicated in the treatment of North American blastomycosis caused by *Blastomyces dermatitidis*.

Candidiasis, disseminated (treatment)—Parenteral amphotericin B is indicated in the treatment of disseminated candidiasis caused by *Candida* species.

Coccidioidomycosis (treatment)—Parenteral amphotericin B is indicated in the treatment of coccidioidomycosis caused by *Coccidioides immitis*.

Cryptococcosis (treatment)—Parenteral amphotericin B is indicated in the treatment of cryptococcosis caused by *Cryptococcus neoformans*.

Endocarditis, fungal (treatment)—Parenteral amphotericin B is indicated in the treatment of fungal endocarditis.

Endophthalmitis, candidal (treatment)—Parenteral and intraocular administration of amphotericin B are used in the treatment of candidal endophthalmitis.

Histoplasmosis (treatment)—Parenteral amphotericin B is indicated in the treatment of histoplasmosis caused by *Histoplasma capsulatum*.

Intra-abdominal infections (treatment)—Parenteral and intraperitoneal administration of amphotericin B, with or without concurrent administration of other antifungal medications, are used for the treatment of intra-abdominal infections, including dialysis-related and non-dialysis-related peritonitis.

Leishmaniasis, American mucocutaneous (treatment)—Parenteral amphotericin B is indicated as an alternative agent in the treatment of American mucocutaneous leishmaniasis caused by *Leishmania braziliensis* and *L. mexicana*.

Meningitis, cryptococcal (treatment) or
Meningitis, cryptococcal (suppression) or
Meningitis, fungal, other (treatment)—Parenteral amphotericin B is indicated, with or without concurrent administration of flucytosine, in the treatment and suppression of cryptococcal meningitis caused by *Cryptococcus neoformans*.

Parenteral amphotericin B is also indicated in the treatment of fungal meningitis caused by organisms such as *Coccidioides immitis*, *Candida* species, *Sporothrix schenckii*, and *Aspergillus* species.

Mucormycosis (treatment)—Parenteral amphotericin B is indicated in the treatment of mucormycosis (phycomycosis) caused by *Mucor*, *Rhizopus*, *Absidia*, *Entomophthora*, and *Basidiobolus* organisms.

Septicemia, fungal (treatment)—Parenteral amphotericin B is indicated in the treatment of fungal septicemia.

Sporotrichosis, disseminated (treatment)—Parenteral amphotericin B is indicated in the treatment of disseminated sporotrichosis caused by *Sporothrix schenckii*.

Urinary tract infections, fungal (treatment)—Parenteral administration [and continuous bladder irrigation] of amphotericin B are indicated in the treatment of fungal (particularly *Candida* species) urinary tract infections.

[Meningoencephalitis, primary amebic (treatment)][1]—Parenteral amphotericin B is used in the treatment of primary amebic meningoencephalitis caused by *Naegleria* species.

[Paracoccidioidomycosis (treatment)][1]—Parenteral amphotericin B is used as a secondary agent in the treatment of paracoccidioidomycosis caused by *Paracoccidioides brasiliensis*.

Not all species or strains of a particular organism may be susceptible to amphotericin B. Because of its toxicity, amphotericin B is indicated primarily in patients with progressive, potentially fatal infections in whom the diagnosis is firmly established, preferably by positive culture or histologic study.

Unaccepted

Amphotericin B is not effective against bacteria, rickettsiae, or viruses.

[1]Not included in Canadian product labeling.

Pharmacology/Pharmacokinetics

Physicochemical characteristics

Molecular weight—924.1.

Mechanism of action/Effect

Antifungal (systemic)—

Amphotericin B is fungistatic or fungicidal, depending on the concentration achieved and the susceptibility of the organism to amphotericin B. Amphotericin B acts by binding to sterols in the fungus cell membrane, producing a change in membrane permeability that allows leakage of intracellular components from the cell.

Distribution

Distributed to lungs, liver, spleen, kidneys, adrenal glands, muscle, and other tissues (potentially therapeutic concentrations); reaches approximately two-thirds the concurrent plasma concentration in the fluids of inflamed pleura, peritoneum, synovium and aqueous humor; concentrations in cerebrospinal fluid (CSF) usually undetectable.

Vol_D—
Neonates: Variable (range, 1.5 to 9.4 L per kg).
Children: Variable (range, 0.4 to 8.3 L per kg).
Adults: Approximately 4 L per kg.

Protein binding
Very high (90% or more).

Biotransformation
Metabolic pathways unknown.

Half-life
Elimination half-life—
Neonates: Variable (range, 18.8 to 62.5 hours).
Children: Variable (range, 5.5 to 40.3 hours).
Adults: Approximately 24 hours.
Terminal half-life—
Approximately 15 days.

Note: There is large interindividual variation among neonates in the elimination of amphotericin B. Amphotericin B may persist in the circulation of neonates for up to 17 days after it has been discontinued.

Peak plasma concentration
Approximately 0.5 to 2 mcg per mL, following repeated doses of approximately 0.5 mg per kg per day.

Elimination
Renal—Very slow; 2 to 5% of a dose eliminated in biologically active form in urine; approximately 40% excreted over a 7-day period. May be detected in urine for at least 7 weeks after medication is discontinued.
Biliary—Minimal excretion of active form.
In dialysis—Poorly dialyzable.

Precautions to Consider

Carcinogenicity/Mutagenicity
Long-term studies in animals have not been done to evaluate the carcinogenic or mutagenic potential of amphotericin B.

Pregnancy/Reproduction
Pregnancy—Amphotericin B crosses the placenta. Adequate and well-controlled studies in humans have not been done. However, no adverse fetal effects have been documented in numerous case reports where amphotericin B was used in all stages of pregnancy.
Studies in animals have not shown that amphotericin B causes adverse effects on the fetus.

FDA Pregnancy Category B.

Breast-feeding
It is not known whether amphotericin B is distributed into breast milk. However, problems in humans have not been documented.

Pediatrics
Appropriate studies on the relationship of age to the effects of amphotericin B have not been performed in the pediatric population. However, systemic fungal infections have been successfully treated in children and no pediatrics-specific problems have been documented to date.
See also *General considerations for use in neonates* in the *Indications* section.

Geriatrics
No information is available on the relationship of age to the effects of amphotericin B in geriatric patients.

Drug interactions and/or related problems
The following drug interactions and/or related problems have been selected on the basis of their potential clinical significance (possible mechanism in parentheses where appropriate)—not necessarily inclusive (» = major clinical significance):

Note: Combinations containing any of the following medications, depending on the amount present, may also interact with this medication.

Blood dyscrasia-causing medications (see *Appendix II*) or
» Bone marrow depressants (see *Appendix II*) or
» Radiation therapy
(concurrent use of these medications or radiation therapy with amphotericin B may increase the chance of anemia or other hematologic effects; dosage reduction may be required)

Carbonic anhydrase inhibitors or
» Corticotropin (ACTH), especially with chronic use or
» Corticosteroids, glucocorticoid, especially with significant mineralocorticoid activity or
» Corticosteroids, mineralocorticoid or
(concurrent use of these medications with parenteral amphotericin B may result in severe hypokalemia and should be undertaken with caution; patients should have serum potassium determinations at frequent intervals during concurrent therapy; cardiac function should also be monitored)
(concurrent use of corticotropin with parenteral amphotericin B may decrease adrenocortical responsiveness to corticotropin)

» Digitalis glycosides or
Neuromuscular blocking agents, nondepolarizing
(parenteral amphotericin B may induce hypokalemia, which may increase the potential for digitalis toxicity or enhance the blockade of nondepolarizing neuromuscular blocking agents)
(serum potassium determinations and correction of hypokalemia may be necessary prior to administration of nondepolarizing neuromuscular blocking agents or at frequent intervals during concurrent therapy with digitalis glycosides)

» Diuretics, potassium-depleting or
» Nephrotoxic medications, other (see *Appendix II*)
(concurrent use of diuretics and other nephrotoxic medications with amphotericin B may increase the potential for nephrotoxicity; dosage reduction or withdrawal of cyclosporine or amphotericin B may be necessary if renal impairment occurs. Concurrent use of diuretics with parenteral amphotericin B may also intensify electrolyte imbalance, particularly hypokalemia; frequent electrolyte determinations are necessary, and potassium supplementation may also be required)

Flucytosine
(concurrent use of amphotericin B and flucytosine may have additive or slightly synergistic effects; amphotericin B–induced renal dysfunction may decrease the clearance of flucytosine, which may result in increased flucytosine adverse effects, such as bone marrow toxicity. However, two-drug therapy may allow the total daily dose of amphotericin B to be lowered, decreasing the risk of nephrotoxicity)

Laboratory value alterations
The following have been selected on the basis of their potential clinical significance (possible effect in parentheses where appropriate)—not necessarily inclusive (» = major clinical significance).

With physiology/laboratory test values
Alanine aminotransferase (ALT [SGPT]) and
Alkaline phosphatase and
Aspartate aminotransferase (AST [SGOT]) and
Bilirubin, serum and
Gamma-glutamyltransferase (GGT)
(values may be increased)

Blood urea nitrogen (BUN) and
Creatinine, serum
(concentration may be increased)

Electrolytes, serum
(concentrations may be increased or decreased)

Hematocrit and
Hemoglobin concentration and
Neutrophil count
(values may be decreased)

Medical considerations/Contraindications
The medical considerations/contraindications included have been selected on the basis of their potential clinical significance (reasons given in parentheses where appropriate)—not necessarily inclusive (» = major clinical significance).

Risk-benefit should be considered when the following medical problems exist:
Hypersensitivity to amphotericin B
» Renal function impairment
(although amphotericin B is not renally excreted, it can be nephrotoxic and worsen any pre-existing renal function impairment)

Patient monitoring
The following may be especially important in patient monitoring (other tests may be warranted in some patients, depending on condition; » = major clinical significance):

» Blood urea nitrogen (BUN) and
» Creatinine, serum
(concentrations recommended every other day while dosage is being increased and then at least twice weekly thereafter during therapy; if the BUN and/or the serum creatinine increase to clinically significant concentrations, discontinuation of the medication may be necessary until renal function is improved)

Complete blood count (CBC) and
Platelet count
(recommended at weekly intervals during therapy)

Magnesium, serum and
» Potassium, serum
(concentrations recommended twice weekly during therapy)

Side/Adverse Effects

Note: Since amphotericin B is frequently the only effective treatment for certain potentially fatal fungal infections, its life-saving benefits must be balanced against its potential for dangerous side/adverse effects.

Administration of an antipyretic, antihistamine, meperidine, and/or corticosteroid just prior to the amphotericin B infusion may decrease the fever and shaking chills that can be associated with amphotericin B administration.

The following side/adverse effects have been selected on the basis of their potential clinical significance (possible signs and symptoms in parentheses where appropriate)—not necessarily inclusive:

Those indicating need for medical attention

Incidence more frequent

With intravenous infusion

Anemia (unusual tiredness or weakness)—normocytic, normochromic; ***hypokalemia*** (irregular heartbeat; muscle cramps or pain; unusual tiredness or weakness); ***infusion-related reaction*** (fever and chills; nausea and vomiting; hypotension); ***renal function impairment*** (increased or decreased urination)—renal tubular toxicity may cause decreased concentrating ability and result in renal loss of potassium; ***thrombophlebitis*** (pain at infusion site)

Incidence less frequent or rare

With intravenous infusion

Blurred or double vision; cardiac arrhythmias (irregular heartbeat)—usually with rapid infusion; ***hypersensitivity*** (skin rash; itching; shortness of breath; trouble in breathing; wheezing; tightness in chest); ***leukopenia*** (sore throat and fever); ***polyneuropathy*** (numbness, tingling, pain, or weakness in hands or feet); ***seizures; thrombocytopenia*** (unusual bleeding or bruising)

With intrathecal injection

Blurred vision or any change in vision; difficult urination; polyneuropathy (numbness, tingling, pain, or weakness)

Those indicating need for medical attention only if they continue or are bothersome

Incidence more frequent

With intravenous infusion

Gastrointestinal disturbance (indigestion; loss of appetite; nausea; vomiting; diarrhea; stomach pain); ***headache***

Incidence less frequent

With intrathecal injection

Back, leg, or neck pain; dizziness or lightheadedness; headache; nausea or vomiting

Overdose

For more information on the management of overdose or unintentional ingestion, **contact a Poison Control Center** (see *Poison Control Center Listing*).

Treatment of overdose

Treatment of amphotericin overdose is supportive.

To enhance elimination—Amphotericin B is not hemodialyzable.

Monitoring—The patient's clinical status, including cardio-respiratory and hematologic status, liver and renal function, and serum electrolytes should be monitored.

Patient Consultation

As an aid to patient consultation, refer to *Advice for the Patient, Amphotericin B (Systemic)*.

In providing consultation, consider emphasizing the following selected information (» = major clinical significance):

Before using this medication

» Conditions affecting use, especially:

Hypersensitivity to amphotericin B

Other medications, especially bone marrow depressants, corticosteroids, corticotropin, digitalis glycosides, other nephrotoxic medications, potassium-depleting diuretics, or radiation therapy

Other medical problems, especially renal function impairment

Side/adverse effects

Signs of potential side effects, especially anemia, hypokalemia, infusion-related reaction, renal function impairment, thrombophlebitis, blurred or double vision, cardiac arrhythmias, leukopenia, polyneuropathy, seizures, thrombocytopenia, or difficult urination

General Dosing Information

Therapy interrupted for more than 7 days should be resumed by starting with the lowest dosage and gradually increasing to the desired dosage.

Therapy should be continued for a sufficient period of time to minimize the possibility of a relapse.

The intravenous administration of small doses of corticosteroids (i.e., ≤ 25 mg of hydrocortisone) just prior to or during intravenous infusion of amphotericin B may reduce the incidence of febrile reactions. Dosage and duration of concurrent corticosteroid therapy should be kept to a minimum. Also, acetaminophen, antihistamines, meperidine, and/or phenothiazines have been given empirically, just prior to the infusion, to decrease the nausea, fever, and chills associated with amphotericin B administration.

Amphotericin B should be infused over a period of 2 to 6 hours. In patients with normal renal function, rapid infusions of 1 to 2 hours have been used with infusion-related reactions similar to those associated with 4 to 6 hour infusions. However, rapid infusions have been associated with earlier infusion-related toxicity and more complaints of nausea and vomiting.

Full dosage of amphotericin B is required even in patients with impaired renal function since the primary route of excretion is not renal. Patients should be observed closely if there is further loss of renal function. Nephrotoxicity may be decreased in sodium-depleted patients by salt loading prior to administration; however, routine prophylactic sodium loading is not recommended, especially in patients with underlying renal or cardiac disease.

Extravasation of the drug may cause severe local irritation.

To minimize local thrombophlebitis, which may occur with intravenous administration, heparin may be added to the amphotericin B infusion or the medication may be administered on alternate days. Administration on alternate days may also reduce the incidence of anorexia.

Alternate-day dosage should not exceed 1.5 mg per kg of body weight (mg/kg).

Parenteral Dosage Forms

Note: The dosing and dosage forms available are expressed in terms of amphotericin B base.

AMPHOTERICIN B FOR INJECTION USP

Usual adult and adolescent dose

Antifungal (systemic)—

Intracavitary instillation, initially 5 mg (base) in 10 to 20 mL of 5% dextrose injection administered over three to five minutes; then, 50 mg (base) of amphotericin B in 10 to 20 mL of 5% dextrose injection administered over three to five minutes each day. This is usually followed eight to twelve hours later by 20 mL of 5% N-acetylcysteine and overnight low-continuous wall suction.

Intrathecal, initially 0.01 to 0.1 mg (base) every forty-eight to seventy-two hours, the dosage being increased gradually to 0.5 mg as tolerated.

Note: Intrathecal administration is not included in the product labeling in the U.S. or Canada. The death rate was high in one case series in which intrathecal administration of amphotericin B was used as the sole therapy in some infants and neonates for *Candida* meningitis.

Intravenous infusion, initially 1 mg (base) as a test dose, administered in 20 to 50 mL of 5% dextrose injection over a period of ten to thirty minutes; the dosage may then be increased in 5- to 10-mg increments or more according to patient tolerance and severity of infection, up to a maximum of 50 mg per day, and administered over a period of two to six hours.

Note: In severely ill patients, some clinicians prefer to initiate therapy utilizing full dosage of amphotericin B.

Continuous bladder irrigation, 5 mg (base) of amphotericin B in 1000 mL of sterile water per day, administered at a rate of 40 mL per hour via a three-way catheter for five to ten days.

Note: Administration by continuous bladder irrigation is not included in the product labeling in the U.S. or Canada.

Usual pediatric dose

[Candidiasis, disseminated][1]—

Intravenous infusion, 0.5 to 1 mg (base) per kg of body weight a day, administered in 5% dextrose injection over a period of six hours.

Note: Studies reported in the literature do not establish the best dosing regimen to treat disseminated candidiasis. In the studies, amphotericin B was administered 0.25 to 1.5 mg per kg of body weight a day. The comparative efficacy of different doses of amphotericin B was not examined. The possibility that amphotericin B toxicity contributed to the deaths of some patients was not examined fully.

USP experts recommend a range for the duration of therapy with amphotericin B depending on the severity of the infection. *Candida* blood infection resulting from isolated catheter colonization may require treatment for only seven to ten days if the catheter is removed promptly. Candidal meningitis or osteomylitis may require four to six weeks of therapy. Some clinicians administer amphotericin B until a total cumulative dose of 15 to 25 mg per kg of body weight is reached.

[Antifungal (systemic)][1]—

Intravenous infusion, initially 0.25 mg (base) per kg of body weight a day, administered in 5% dextrose injection over a period of six hours, the dosage being increased gradually (usually by 0.125 to 0.25 mg per kg of body weight increments every day or every other day) as tolerated, up to a maximum of 1 mg per kg of body weight or 30 mg per square meter of body surface per day.

Note: In severely ill patients, some clinicians prefer to initiate therapy utilizing full dosage of amphotericin B or by escalating the dose rapidly to reach full dosage. Rapid escalation of the dose to reach the target dose may be important for favorable outcomes.

Strength(s) usually available

U.S.—

50 mg (base) (Rx) [*Amphocin; Fungizone Intravenous* (lyophilized; 41 mg sodium desoxycholate; 20.1 mg sodium phosphate); GENERIC].

Canada—

50 mg (base) (Rx) [*Fungizone Intravenous*].

Packaging and storage

Prior to reconstitution, store between 2 and 8 °C (36 and 46 °F). Protect from light.

Preparation of dosage form

To prepare initial dilution for intrathecal use or intravenous infusion, add 10 mL of sterile water for injection, without a bacteriostatic agent, to the vial containing 50 mg (base) of amphotericin B. For intrathecal use, the resulting solution containing 5 mg of amphotericin B per mL may be further diluted to a final concentration of 0.25 mg per mL by adding 1 mL (5 mg) of the solution to 19 mL of 5% dextrose injection with a pH above 4.2. Before injection, the dose is diluted with 5 to 30 mL of cerebrospinal fluid in the syringe. For intravenous infusion, the resulting solution containing 5 mg of amphotericin B per mL may be diluted to a final concentration of 0.1 mg per mL by adding 1 mL (5 mg) of the solution to 49 mL of 5% dextrose injection with a pH above 4.2.

The pH of the dextrose injection should be determined aseptically before the injection is used to dilute the 5-mg-per-mL concentration of the amphotericin B solution. If the pH is below 4.2, it should be adjusted. See the manufacturer's package insert for buffering procedure.

Amphotericin B should be reconstituted only with the diluents recommended, since solutions containing sodium chloride or a bacteriostatic agent (for example, benzyl alcohol) may cause precipitation of the medication.

Stability

After reconstitution, concentrated solutions (5 mg per mL) in sterile water for injection retain their potency for 24 hours at room temperature, protected from light, or for 1 week if refrigerated. Diluted solutions for intravenous infusion (0.1 mg per mL or less) in 5% dextrose injection should be used promptly after dilution.

The manufacturer recommends that the intravenous infusion be protected from light during administration. However, this is probably not necessary, since it has been reported that the loss of drug potency is negligible when amphotericin B infusions are exposed to normal lighting conditions in a hospital.

Do not use if the initial concentrate or the infusion is cloudy or contains a precipitate or foreign matter.

Incompatibilities

May be incompatible with sodium chloride or bacteriostatic agents such as benzyl alcohol.

Additional information

Since the reconstituted preparation is a colloidal suspension, membrane filters in intravenous infusion lines may remove clinically significant amounts of the medication. If an in-line membrane filter is used, the mean pore diameter should be no less than 1 micron.

[1]Not included in Canadian product labeling.

Revised: 06/08/1999

AMPHOTERICIN B Topical*†

VA CLASSIFICATION (Primary): DE102

Commonly used brand name(s):

Note: For a listing of dosage forms and brand names by country availability, see *Dosage Forms* section(s).

*Not commercially available in U.S.

†Not commercially available in Canada.

Category

Antifungal (topical).

Indications

Unaccepted

Topical amphotericin B has been used for the topical treatment of cutaneous and mucocutaneous candidiasis caused by *Candida (Monilia)* species. However, in the opinion of most USP medical experts, it has been superseded by newer and more effective topical antifungal agents such as ciclopirox and the imidazoles (e.g., clotrimazole, econazole, miconazole).

Although topical amphotericin B exhibits some *in vitro* activity against ringworm, it has not demonstrated an effectiveness *in vivo*.

Topical amphotericin B has no significant effect either *in vitro* or clinically against viruses or gram-positive or gram-negative bacteria.

Pharmacology/Pharmacokinetics

Physicochemical characteristics

Chemical Group—Polyene.

Molecular weight—924.09.

Mechanism of action/Effect

Fungistatic and fungicidal *in vitro* against yeast and yeast-like fungi; amphotericin B probably exerts its antifungal effects by binding to sterols in the fungus cell membrane, producing a change in membrane permeability that allows loss of potassium and small molecules from the cell.

Precautions to Consider

Carcinogenicity

Long-term studies in animals have not been done.

Mutagenicity

Studies have not been done to determine the mutagenic potential.

Pregnancy/Reproduction

Fertility—Studies have not been done to determine if amphotericin B affects fertility in males or females.

Pregnancy—Adequate and well-controlled studies have not been conducted in humans. Problems in humans have not been documented.

Reproduction studies in animals have not shown whether amphotericin B causes harm to the fetus.

FDA Pregnancy Category B.

Breast-feeding

It is not known if amphotericin B is distributed into human milk. Problems in humans have not been documented.

Pediatrics

Appropriate studies on the relationship of age to the effects of amphotericin B topical preparations have not been performed in the pediatric population. However, pediatrics-specific problems that would limit the usefulness of this medication in children are not expected.

Geriatrics

Appropriate studies on the relationship of age to the effects of amphotericin B topical preparations have not been performed in the geriatric population. However, geriatrics-specific problems that would limit the usefulness of this medication in older persons are not expected.

Medical considerations/Contraindications

The medical considerations/contraindications included have been selected on the basis of their potential clinical significance (reasons given in parentheses where appropriate)—not necessarily inclusive (» = major clinical significance).

Risk-benefit should be considered when the following medical problem exists:

Sensitivity to topical amphotericin B preparations

Side/Adverse Effects

The following side/adverse effects have been selected on the basis of their potential clinical significance (possible signs and symptoms in parentheses where appropriate)—not necessarily inclusive:

Those indicating need for medical attention

Incidence less frequent

Hypersensitivity or local irritation, especially in intertriginous areas (burning, itching, redness or other signs of irritation not present before therapy)

Incidence rare

Allergic contact dermatitis (skin rash)

Those indicating need for medical attention only if they continue or are bothersome

Incidence less frequent

Dryness of skin—for cream dosage form

Patient Consultation

As an aid to patient consultation, refer to *Advice for the Patient, Amphotericin B (Topical).*

In providing consultation, consider emphasizing the following selected information (» = major clinical significance):

Before using this medication

» Conditions affecting use, especially:
Sensitivity to amphotericin B

Proper use of this medication

Applying sufficient medication to cover affected areas, and rubbing in gently

» Not applying an occlusive dressing or airtight covering over medication

» Compliance with full course of therapy, which may take several months or longer

» Not for ophthalmic use

» Proper dosing
Missed dose: Applying as soon as possible

» Proper storage

Precautions while using this medication

Checking with physician if no improvement within 1 to 2 weeks

May stain skin or nails

Cream or lotion form may stain clothing; removal of stain by hand-washing clothing with soap and warm water

Ointment form may stain clothing; removal of stain with standard cleaning fluid

Side/adverse effects

Signs of potential side effects, especially hypersensitivity; local irritation, especially in intertriginous areas; and allergic contact dermatitis

General Dosing Information

Use of topical antifungals may lead to skin sensitization, resulting in hypersensitivity reactions with subsequent topical or systemic use of the medication.

Therapy is usually necessary for a period of 1 to 3 weeks for intertriginous lesions; 1 to 2 weeks for candidiasis of the diaper area, perlèche, or glabrous skin lesions; 2 to 4 weeks for interdigital lesions or paronychia; and several months for onychomycoses that respond to treatment.

A single course of therapy may be sufficient, but additional courses may be necessary, especially in the treatment of interdigital lesions, paronychia, and onychomycoses.

Occlusive dressings should be avoided in the treatment of candidiasis since they provide conditions that favor the growth of yeast and the release of its irritating endotoxin.

Topical Dosage Forms

AMPHOTERICIN B CREAM USP

Usual adult and adolescent dose

Candidiasis—
Topical, to the skin, two to four times a day.

Usual pediatric dose

See *Usual adult and adolescent dose.*

Usual geriatric dose

See *Usual adult and adolescent dose.*

Strength(s) usually available

U.S.—

Note: Not commercially available

Canada—
Not commercially available.

Packaging and storage

Store below 40 °C (104 °F), preferably between 15 and 30 °C (59 and 86 °F), unless otherwise specified by manufacturer. Store in a collapsible tube or other well-closed container. Protect from freezing.

Auxiliary labeling

- For external use only.
- Continue medication for full time of treatment.

Note

Fabric stains caused by the cream may be removed with soap and warm water.

AMPHOTERICIN B LOTION USP

Usual adult and adolescent dose

See *Amphotericin B Cream USP.*

Usual pediatric dose

See *Amphotericin B Cream USP.*

Usual geriatric dose

See *Amphotericin B Cream USP.*

Strength(s) usually available

U.S.—

Note: Not commercially available

Canada—
Not commercially available.

Packaging and storage

Store below 40 °C (104 °F), preferably between 15 and 30 °C (59 and 86 °F), unless otherwise specified by manufacturer. Store in a well-closed container. Protect from freezing.

Auxiliary labeling

- Shake gently.
- For external use only.
- Continue medication for full time of treatment.

Note

Fabric stains caused by the lotion may be removed with soap and warm water.

AMPHOTERICIN B OINTMENT USP

Usual adult and adolescent dose

See *Amphotericin B Cream USP.*

Usual pediatric dose

See *Amphotericin B Cream USP.*

Usual geriatric dose

See *Amphotericin B Cream USP.*

Strength(s) usually available

U.S.—

Note: Not commercially available

Canada—
Not commercially available.

Packaging and storage

Store below 40 °C (104 °F), preferably between 15 and 30 °C (59 and 86 °F), unless otherwise specified by manufacturer. Store in a collapsible tube or other well-closed container. Protect from freezing.

Auxiliary labeling

- For external use only.
- Continue medication for full time of treatment.

Note

Standard cleaning fluid may be used to remove fabric stains caused by the ointment.

Revised: 05/07/2003

AMPHOTERICIN B CHOLESTERYL COMPLEX Systemic

VA CLASSIFICATION (Primary): AM700

Commonly used brand name(s): *Amphotec*.

Note: For a listing of dosage forms and brand names by country availability, see *Dosage Forms* section(s).

Category

Antifungal (systemic).

Indications

General Considerations

Amphotericin B cholesteryl complex is active *in vitro* against *Aspergillus* and *Candida* species, as well as against other fungi.

Fungal type variants with reduced susceptibility to amphotericin B have been isolated from several fungal species after serial passage in cell culture media containing amphotericin B, and from some patients receiving prolonged therapy with amphotericin B. Although the relevance of drug resistance to clinical outcome has not been established, fungal organisms that are resistant to amphotericin B may also be resistant to amphotericin B cholesteryl complex.

Accepted

Aspergillosis (treatment)—Amphotericin B cholesteryl complex is indicated in the treatment of invasive aspergillosis in patients who are refractory to or intolerant of amphotericin B deoxycholate therapy.

Pharmacology/Pharmacokinetics

Physicochemical characteristics

Chemical Group—Amphotericin B complexed with cholesteryl sulfate in a 1:1 molar ratio.

Molecular weight—Amphotericin B: 924.1.

Mechanism of action/Effect

Amphotericin B binds primarily to ergosterol in cell membranes of sensitive fungi, causing leakage of intracellular contents and cell death due to changes in membrane permeability. Amphotericin B also binds to cholesterol in mammalian cell membranes; this action is believed to account for its toxicity in animals and humans.

Distribution

Vol_D (at steady state) of amphotericin B following administration of four doses of amphotericin B cholesteryl complex at a dose of—

3 mg per kg of body weight (mg/kg): 3.8 L per kg.

4 mg/kg: 4.1 L per kg.

Half-life

Distribution of amphotericin B following administration of four doses of amphotericin B cholesteryl complex at a dose of—

3 mg/kg: 3.5 minutes.

4 mg/kg: 3.5 minutes.

Elimination of amphotericin B following administration of four doses of amphotericin B cholesteryl complex at a dose of—

3 mg/kg: 27.5 hours.

4 mg/kg: 28.2 hours.

Peak plasma concentration

2.6 to 2.9 mcg per mL, following administration of 1 to 4 mg/kg per day for four days.

Elimination

Amphotericin B cholesteryl complex is not dialyzable.

Precautions to Consider

Carcinogenicity

Long-term studies in animals have not been done to evaluate the carcinogenic potential of amphotericin B cholesteryl complex.

Mutagenicity

No mutagenic effects were found *in vitro* in the *Salmonella* reverse mutation assay, the CHO cell chromosomal aberration assay, or the mouse lymphoma forward mutation assay, or *in vivo* in the mouse bone marrow micronucleus assay.

Pregnancy/Reproduction

Fertility—Studies have not been done to evaluate the effects of amphotericin B cholesteryl complex on fertility. However, doses of up to 0.4 and 0.5 times the recommended human dose given to dogs and rats, respectively, for up to 13 weeks did not affect ovarian or testicular histology.

Pregnancy—Adequate and well-controlled studies in humans have not been done.

Studies at doses of up to 0.4 and 1.1 times the recommended human dose given to rats and rabbits, respectively, showed no evidence of fetal harm.

FDA Pregnancy Category B.

Breast-feeding

It is not known whether amphotericin B cholesteryl complex is distributed into breast milk. Because of the potential for serious adverse effects in nursing infants, a decision should be made to either stop breast-feeding or discontinue taking amphotericin B cholesteryl complex.

Pediatrics

Ninety-seven pediatric patients have been treated with amphotericin B cholesteryl complex at daily doses similar to those in adults (on a mg per kg of body weight basis), and no unexpected adverse events have been reported.

Geriatrics

Sixty-eight patients 65 years of age and older have been treated with amphotericin B cholesteryl complex, and no unexpected events have been reported.

Drug interactions and/or related problems

The following drug interactions and/or related problems have been selected on the basis of their potential clinical significance (possible mechanism in parentheses where appropriate)—not necessarily inclusive (» = major clinical significance):

Note: Combinations containing any of the following medications, depending on the amount present, may also interact with this medication.

» Antineoplastic agents
(concurrent use with amphotericin B cholesteryl complex may enhance the potential for bronchospasm, hypotension, and renal toxicity; caution is required if these medications are to be used concurrently)

Clotrimazole or
Fluconazole or
Ketoconazole or
Miconazole or
Other imidazoles
(*in vitro* and *in vivo* animal studies have reported antagonism between amphotericin B and imidazole derivatives, such as ketoconazole and miconazole, that inhibit ergosterol synthesis; the clinical significance of these findings has not been determined)

» Corticosteroids or
» Corticotropin (ACTH)
(concurrent use with amphotericin B cholesteryl complex may potentiate hypokalemia, which may predispose the patient to cardiac dysfunction; cardiac function and serum electrolytes should be monitored)

Cyclosporine or
Tacrolimus
(adult and pediatric patients receiving amphotericin B cholesteryl complex with cyclosporine or tacrolimus had a 31% incidence of renal toxicity [a doubling or an increase of 1 mg per dL or more from baseline serum creatinine, or ≥ 50% decrease from baseline calculated creatinine clearance], compared with a 68% incidence of renal toxicity for patients receiving amphotericin B deoxycholate with cyclosporine or tacrolimus)

» Digitalis glycosides
(concurrent use with amphotericin B cholesteryl complex may induce hypokalemia and may potentiate digitalis toxicity; serum potassium concentrations should be monitored closely)

Flucytosine
(concurrent use with amphotericin B cholesteryl complex may increase the toxicity of flucytosine by possibly increasing its cellular uptake and/or impairing its renal excretion; caution should be used if flucytosine is to be used concurrently)

» Nephrotoxic medications (see *Appendix II*)
(concurrent use of amphotericin B cholesteryl complex with nephrotoxic medications, such as aminoglycosides or pentamidine, may potentiate medication-induced renal toxicity; caution is required if nephrotoxic medications are to be used concurrently, and renal function should be monitored frequently)

» Neuromuscular blocking agents, nondepolarizing
(amphotericin B may induce hypokalemia, which may enhance the activity of nondepolarizing neuromuscular blocking agents; serum potassium concentrations should be monitored closely)

Laboratory value alterations

The following have been selected on the basis of their potential clinical significance (possible effect in parentheses where appropriate)—not necessarily inclusive (» = major clinical significance).

With diagnostic test results
- Hepatic function tests
  (values may be increased or decreased)

With physiology/laboratory test values
- Alkaline phosphatase and
- » Creatine kinase
  (serum values may be increased)
- Bilirubin and
- Glucose, plasma
  (concentrations may be increased)
- Calcium and
- Magnesium and
- Potassium
  (serum concentrations may be decreased)

Medical considerations/Contraindications

The medical considerations/contraindications included have been selected on the basis of their potential clinical significance (reasons given in parentheses where appropriate)—not necessarily inclusive (» = major clinical significance).

Risk-benefit should be considered when the following medical problem exists:

» Hypersensitivity to amphotericin B cholesteryl complex

Patient monitoring

The following may be especially important in patient monitoring (other tests may be warranted in some patients, depending on condition; » = major clinical significance):

Complete blood count (CBC)
(counts should be monitored as medically indicated)

Electrolytes, serum
(concentrations should be monitored as medically indicated)

Hepatic function tests and
Prothrombin time (PT) and
Renal function tests
(values should be monitored as medically indicated)

Side/Adverse Effects

Note: Anaphylaxis has been reported with amphotericin B–containing medications.

Acute infusion-related reactions, including chills, fever, headache, hypotension, hypoxia, nausea, and tachypnea, usually occur 1 to 3 hours after intravenous infusion has been initiated. These reactions are usually more severe or more frequent with initial doses of amphotericin B cholesteryl complex and usually diminish with subsequent doses.

The following side/adverse effects have been selected on the basis of their potential clinical significance (possible signs and symptoms in parentheses where appropriate)—not necessarily inclusive:

Those indicating need for medical attention

Incidence more frequent

Infusion-related reaction (chills; fever; headache; hypoxia; nausea)

Incidence less frequent

Dyspnea (difficulty in breathing); ***hypertension; hypotension*** (dizziness or fainting); ***tachycardia*** (increased heartbeat); ***thrombocytopenia*** (unusual bleeding or bruising)

Incidence rare

Anaphylactic reaction (difficulty in breathing or swallowing; hives; itching, especially of feet or hands; reddening of skin, especially around ears; swelling of eyes, face, or inside of nose; unusual tiredness or weakness, sudden and severe)

Those indicating need for medical attention only if they continue or are bothersome

Incidence less frequent

Nausea; vomiting

Overdose

Amphotericin B deoxycholate overdose has been reported to result in cardiopulmonary arrest.

Amphotericin B cholesteryl complex is not dialyzable.

For more information on the management of overdose or unintentional ingestion, **contact a Poison Control Center** (see *Poison Control Center Listing*).

Treatment of overdose

Supportive care—Patients in whom intentional overdose is confirmed or suspected should be referred for psychiatric consultation.

Patient Consultation

As an aid to patient consultation, refer to *Advice for the Patient, Amphotericin B Cholesteryl Complex (Systemic)*.

In providing consultation, consider emphasizing the following selected information (» = major clinical significance):

Before using this medication

» Conditions affecting use, especially:
Sensitivity to amphotericin B cholesteryl complex
Other medications, especially antineoplastic agents, corticosteroids, corticotropin (ACTH), digitalis glycosides, nephrotoxic medications, or nondepolarizing neuromuscular blocking agents

Side/adverse effects

Signs of potential side effects, especially infusion-related reaction, dyspnea, hypertension, hypotension, tachycardia, thrombocytopenia, or anaphylactic reaction

General Dosing Information

Intravenous infusion should be administered at a rate of 1 mg per kg of body weight per hour. A test dose immediately preceding the first dose is advisable when beginning all new courses of treatment. A small amount of the medication (e.g., 10 mL of the final preparation containing 1.6 to 8.3 mg) should be infused over 15 to 30 minutes, and the patient carefully observed for the next 30 minutes.

The infusion time may be shortened to a minimum of 2 hours for patients who show no evidence of intolerance or infusion-related reactions. If the patient experiences acute reactions or cannot tolerate the infusion volume, the infusion time may be extended.

For treatment of adverse effects

Recommended treatment consists of the following:
- For anaphylactic reaction
  —Immediately administer airway management, epinephrine, intravenous steroids, and oxygen as indicated.
  —For severe respiratory distress, immediately discontinue the infusion; the patient should not receive further infusions of amphotericin B cholesteryl complex.
- For infusion-related reaction
  —Reduce the rate of infusion and promptly administer antihistamines and corticosteroids.
  —In patients with a history of infusion-related reaction, pretreat the patients with antihistamines and corticosteroids.

Parenteral Dosage Forms

AMPHOTERICIN B CHOLESTERYL SULFATE COMPLEX FOR INJECTION

Note: Rapid intravenous infusion should be avoided.

Usual adult and adolescent dose

Aspergillosis—
Intravenous infusion, 3 to 4 mg per kg of body weight, once a day.

Usual pediatric dose

See *Usual adult and adolescent dose.*

Usual geriatric dose

See *Usual adult and adolescent dose.*

Strength(s) usually available

U.S.—
50 mg (Rx) [*Amphotec* (lactose [950 mg])].
100 mg (Rx) [*Amphotec* (lactose [1900 mg])].

Packaging and storage

Prior to reconstitution, store between 15 and 30 °C (59 and 86 °F), unless otherwise specified by manufacturer.

After reconstitution with sterile water for injection, store between 2 and 8 °C (36 and 46 °F). Do not freeze. Use within 24 hours.

After further dilution with 5% dextrose for injection, store between 2 and 8 °C (36 and 46 °F). Do not freeze. Use within 24 hours. Discard any partially used vials.

Preparation of dosage form

Amphotericin B cholesteryl complex for injection should be reconstituted by the addition of sterile water for injection. Using a sterile syringe and a 20-gauge needle, rapidly add 10 or 20 mL of sterile water for injection to a 50-mg or 100-mg vial, respectively, to obtain a solution containing 5 mg of amphotericin B per mL. Shake gently by hand, rotating the vial until all solids have dissolved. The fluid may be clear or opalescent.

For infusion, further dilute the reconstituted solution to a final concentration of approximately 0.6 mg per mL (mg/mL) (range, 0.16 to 0.83 mg/mL) according to the following recommendations:

Dose (mg)	Volume of reconstituted solution (mL)	Infusion bag size for 5% dextrose for injection (mL)
10–35	2–7	50
35–70	7–14	100
70–175	14–35	250
175–350	35–70	500
350–1000	70–200	1000

Stability

After reconstitution in sterile water for injection, use within 24 hours.

Incompatibilities

The lyophilized powder should not be reconstituted with saline or dextrose solution, and the reconstituted liquid should not be admixed with saline or electrolytes. The use of any solution other than those recommended, or the presence of a bacteriostatic agent (e.g., benzyl alcohol) in the solution, may induce precipitation of amphotericin B cholesteryl complex.

The infusion admixture should not be mixed with other medications. If administered through an existing intravenous line, the line should be flushed with 5% dextrose for injection prior to infusion of amphotericin B cholesteryl complex. Alternatively, the admixture should be administered via a separate line.

The solution should not be filtered or used with an in-line filter.

Additional information

The solution should be visually inspected for particulate matter and discoloration prior to administration. The solution should not be used if a precipitate or foreign matter is present, or if the seal is not intact. Strict aseptic technique should always be observed since no preservatives are present in the lyophilized medication or in the solutions used for reconstitution and dilution.

Revised: 04/28/1998
Developed: 11/04/1997

AMPHOTERICIN B LIPID COMPLEX Systemic

VA CLASSIFICATION (Primary): AM700

Commonly used brand name(s): *ABELCET*.

Note: For a listing of dosage forms and brand names by country availability, see *Dosage Forms* section(s).

Category

Antifungal (systemic).

Indications

Accepted

Fungal infections, invasive (treatment)—Amphotericin B lipid complex is indicated in the treatment of invasive fungal infections in patients who are refractory to or intolerant of conventional amphotericin B therapy.

Pharmacology/Pharmacokinetics

Physicochemical characteristics

Chemistry—

A suspension of amphotericin B complexed with two phospholipids, L-alpha-dimyristoylphosphatidylcholine (DMPC) and L-alpha-dimyristoylphosphatidylglycerol (DMPG), in a 1:1 drug-to-lipid molar ratio.

Molecular weight—Amphotericin B: 924.1.

Mechanism of action/Effect

Amphotericin B acts by binding to sterols in the cell membrane of susceptible fungi, with a resultant change in the permeability of the membrane.

Distribution

High concentrations are found in the spleen, lung, and liver; also found in lymph node, kidney, heart, and brain tissues.

Apparent Vol_D—Approximately 131 L per kg.

Biotransformation

Metabolic pathways unknown.

Half-life

Terminal—Approximately 7.2 days.

Peak plasma concentration

After 5 mg per kg of body weight per day for 5 to 7 days—Approximately 1.7 micrograms per mL (1.8 micromoles per liter).

Elimination

Renal; approximately 0.9% is excreted in the urine over 24 hours after administration of the last dose.

In dialysis—Amphotericin B lipid complex is not hemodialyzable.

Precautions to Consider

Carcinogenicity

Long-term studies in animals to evaluate the carcinogenic potential of amphotericin B lipid complex have not been done.

Mutagenicity

No mutagenic effects were found in the bacterial reverse mutation assay, mouse lymphoma forward mutation assay, chromosomal aberration assay in CHO cells, or the *in vivo* mouse micronucleus assay.

Pregnancy/Reproduction

Fertility—No impact on fertility was found in studies done in male and female rats at doses of up to 0.32 times the recommended human dose, based on body surface area.

Pregnancy—Adequate and well-controlled studies in humans have not been done.

Studies in rats and rabbits at doses of up to 0.64 times the recommended human dose, based on body surface area, revealed no harm to the fetus.

FDA Pregnancy Category B.

Breast-feeding

It is not known whether amphotericin B lipid complex is distributed into breast milk. Because of the potential for serious side effects in nursing infants, a decision should be made to either stop breast-feeding or discontinue taking amphotericin B lipid complex.

Pediatrics

One hundred eleven children 16 years of age and younger have been treated with amphotericin B lipid complex. No serious or unexpected adverse events have been reported.

Geriatrics

Forty-nine patients 65 years of age and older have been treated with amphotericin B lipid complex. No serious or unexpected adverse events have been reported.

Drug interactions and/or related problems

The following drug interactions and/or related problems have been selected on the basis of their potential clinical significance (possible mechanism in parentheses where appropriate)—not necessarily inclusive (» = major clinical significance):

Note: Combinations containing any of the following medications, depending on the amount present, may also interact with this medication.

Antifungals, azole
(azole antifungals have been reported to be antagonistic with amphotericin B in *in vitro* and *in vivo* animal studies)

Blood dyscrasia-causing medications (See *Appendix II*) or
» Bone marrow depressants (See *Appendix II*) or
» Radiation therapy
(concurrent use of these medications or radiation therapy with amphotericin B may increase the chance of renal toxicity, bronchospasm, and hypotension; these medications should be used with amphotericin B lipid complex with caution)

» Corticosteroids, glucocorticoid, especially with significant mineralocorticoid activity or
» Corticosteroids, mineralocorticoid or
» Corticotropin (ACTH), especially with long-term use
(concurrent use of these medications with amphotericin B lipid complex may result in hypokalemia, which could predispose the

patient to cardiac arrhythmias; serum electrolytes and cardiac function should be monitored)

» Cyclosporin A or
» Nephrotoxic medications, other (See *Appendix II*)
(concurrent use of these medications may increase the chance for medication-induced renal toxicity; these medications should be used with amphotericin B lipid complex with caution)

» Digitalis glycosides or
Neuromuscular blocking agents, nondepolarizing
(amphotericin B may induce hypokalemia, which may increase the potential for digitalis toxicity or enhance the blockade of nondepolarizing neuromuscular blocking agents; serum potassium determinations and correction of hypokalemia may be necessary prior to administration of nondepolarizing neuromuscular blocking agents or at frequent intervals during concurrent therapy with digitalis glycosides)

Flucytosine
(concurrent use may increase flucytosine toxicity, possibly by increasing its cellular intake and/or impairing its renal excretion)

Zidovudine
(increased myelotoxicity and nephrotoxicity were seen in dogs that were administered either amphotericin B lipid complex at doses 0.16 or 0.5 times the recommended human dose or amphotericin B desoxycholate concurrently with zidovudine for 30 days; renal and hematologic functions should be monitored closely)

Laboratory value alterations

The following have been selected on the basis of their potential clinical significance (possible effect in parentheses where appropriate)—not necessarily inclusive (» = major clinical significance).

With physiology/laboratory test values
Alanine aminotransferase (ALT [SGPT]) and
Alkaline phosphatase and
Amylase and
Aspartate aminotransferase (AST [SGOT])
(serum values may be increased)

Blood urea nitrogen (BUN) and
Creatinine, serum and
Potassium, serum
(concentrations may be increased)

Calcium, serum and
Magnesium, serum
(concentrations may be decreased)

Medical considerations/Contraindications

The medical considerations/contraindications included have been selected on the basis of their potential clinical significance (reasons given in parentheses where appropriate)—not necessarily inclusive (» = major clinical significance).

Except under special circumstances, this medication should not be used when the following medical problem exists:

» Leukocyte transfusions
(acute pulmonary toxicity has been reported in patients receiving amphotericin B lipid complex and leukocyte transfusions; leukocyte transfusions and amphotericin B lipid complex should not be given concurrently)

Risk-benefit should be considered when the following medical problems exist:

Hypersensitivity to amphotericin B

» Renal function impairment
(amphotericin B lipid complex can produce dose-dependent nephrotoxicity; however, some patients with a serum creatinine above 2.5 mg per deciliter being treated for aspergillosis with amphotericin B lipid complex experienced a decline in serum creatinine during treatment)

Patient monitoring

The following may be especially important in patient monitoring (other tests may be warranted in some patients, depending on condition; » = major clinical significance):

Complete blood count (CBC)
(counts should be monitored frequently)

Creatinine, serum and
Magnesium, serum and
Potassium, serum
(concentrations should be monitored frequently)

Liver function tests
(values should be monitored frequently)

Side/Adverse Effects

Note: One case of anaphylaxis has been reported.

Acute reactions, including fever and chills, may occur 1 to 2 hours after initiation of an infusion of amphotericin B lipid complex. These reactions are more likely to occur with the first few doses and generally diminish with subsequent doses. Amphotericin B lipid complex has rarely been associated with hypotension, bronchospasm, arrhythmias, and shock.

The following side/adverse effects have been selected on the basis of their potential clinical significance (possible signs and symptoms in parentheses where appropriate)—not necessarily inclusive:

Those indicating need for medical attention

Incidence more frequent
Infusion-related reaction (fever and chills; headache; nausea and vomiting)

Incidence less frequent
Anemia (unusual tiredness and weakness); ***leukopenia*** (sore throat and fever); ***respiratory distress*** (difficulty in breathing); ***thrombocytopenia*** (unusual bleeding or bruising)

Incidence rare
Renal function impairment (increased or decreased urination)

Those indicating need for medical attention only if they continue or are bothersome

Incidence more frequent
Gastrointestinal disturbance (diarrhea; loss of appetite; nausea; stomach pain; vomiting)

Overdose

For more information on the management of overdose or unintentional ingestion, **contact a Poison Control Center** (see *Poison Control Center Listing*).

Clinical effects of overdose

Amphotericin B desoxycholate overdose has resulted in cardiopulmonary arrest. Fifteen patients have been reported to have received one or more doses of 7 to 13 mg per kg of body weight of amphotericin B lipid complex. None of these patients had a serious acute reaction. Amphotericin B lipid complex is not hemodialyzable.

Treatment of overdose

Supportive care—Patients in whom intentional overdose is confirmed or suspected should be referred for psychiatric consultation.

Patient Consultation

As an aid to patient consultation, refer to *Advice for the Patient, Amphotericin B Lipid Complex (Systemic)*.

In providing consultation, consider emphasizing the following selected information (» = major clinical significance):

Before using this medication

» Conditions affecting use, especially:
Hypersensitivity to amphotericin B
Breast-feeding—Not recommended, due to potential serious side effects in the nursing infant
Other medications, especially bone marrow depressants, corticosteroids, corticotropin, cyclosporin A, digitalis glycosides, other nephrotoxic medications, or radiation therapy
Other medical problems, especially leukocyte transfusions or renal function impairment

Side/adverse effects

Signs of potential side effects, especially infusion-related reactions, anemia, leukopenia, respiratory distress, thrombocytopenia, or renal function impairment

General Dosing Information

Renal toxicity has been shown to be dose-dependent. There are no firm guidelines for adjusting the dose based on laboratory test results.

The infusion should be administered at a rate of 2.5 mg per kg of body weight per hour. If the infusion time exceeds 2 hours, the contents of the infusion bag should be shaken every 2 hours.

Parenteral Dosage Forms

AMPHOTERICIN B LIPID COMPLEX INJECTION

Usual adult and adolescent dose

Fungal infections, invasive—Intravenous infusion, 5 mg per kg of body weight per day, administered at a rate of 2.5 mg per kg of body weight per hour.

Usual pediatric dose
See *Usual adult and adolescent dose.*

Usual geriatric dose
See *Usual adult and adolescent dose.*

Strength(s) usually available
U.S.—
100 mg in 20 mL (Rx) [*ABELCET* (L-alpha-dimyristoylphosphatidylcholine [DMPC]; L-alpha-dimyristoylphosphatidylglycerol [DMPG])].

Packaging and storage
Prior to admixing, store between 2 and 8 °C (36 and 46 °F). Protect from light. Do not freeze.
After dilution with 5% dextrose injection, the admixture may be stored for up to 48 hours at 2 to 8 °C (36 to 46 °F) and an additional 6 hours at room temperature. Do not freeze.

Preparation of dosage form
The vial should be shaken gently until there is no evidence of any yellow sediment at the bottom. The appropriate dose of amphotericin B lipid complex should be withdrawn from the required number of vials into one or more 20-mL syringes using an 18-gauge needle. The needle is then replaced with the 5-micron filter needle supplied with each vial. Empty the contents of the syringe into a bag of 5% dextrose injection so that the final concentration is 1 mg per mL. For pediatric patients and patients with cardiovascular disease, the final infusion concentration may be 2 mg per mL. Before infusion, the bag should be shaken until the contents are thoroughly mixed.

Incompatibilities
Compatibility has not been established with sodium chloride injection or with other medications or electrolytes. An existing intravenous line should be flushed with 5% dextrose injection before infusion of amphotericin B lipid complex, or a separate infusion line should be used. **In-line filters should not be used.**

Developed: 05/28/1996

AMPHOTERICIN B LIPOSOMAL COMPLEX Systemic

VA CLASSIFICATION (Primary/Secondary): AM700/AP109
Commonly used brand name(s): *AmBisome.*
Note: For a listing of dosage forms and brand names by country availability, see *Dosage Forms* section(s).

Category
Antifungal (systemic); antiprotozoal.

Indications

General Considerations
Amphotericin B liposomal complex is active *in vitro* and *in vivo* against *Aspergillus* and *Candida* species, *Blastomyces dermatitidis*, and *Cryptococcus neoformans*. *In vivo* activity has also been demonstrated against *Coccidioides immitis*, *Histoplasma capsulatum*, *Paracoccidioides brasiliensis*, *Leishmania donovani*, and *Leishmania infantum*.
Fungal variants with reduced susceptibility to amphotericin B have been isolated from several fungal species after serial passage in cell culture media containing amphotericin B, and from some patients receiving prolonged therapy with amphotericin B. Drug combination studies *in vitro* and *in vivo* suggest that imidazoles may induce resistance to amphotericin B. However, the clinical relevance of drug resistance has not been established.

Accepted
Aspergillosis (treatment)
Candidiasis (treatment) or
Cryptococcosis (treatment)—Amphotericin B liposomal complex is indicated in the treatment of systemic fungal infections caused by *Aspergillus, Candida*, or *Cryptococcus* in patients refractory to or intolerant of amphotericin B deoxycholate.
Cryptococcal meningitis (treatment)—Amphotericin B liposomal complex is indicated as therapy for cryptococcal meningitis in HIV-infected patients.
Fungal infection, presumed, in febrile neutropenia (treatment)—Amphotericin B liposomal complex is indicated as empiric therapy for presumed fungal infection in patients with febrile neutropenia.
Leishmaniasis, visceral (treatment)—Amphotericin B liposomal complex is indicated in the treatment of visceral leishmaniasis.

Pharmacology/Pharmacokinetics
Note: The pharmacokinetic profile of amphotericin B liposomal complex was determined in febrile neutropenic cancer and bone marrow transplant patients receiving 1- to 2-hour infusions of amphotericin B liposomal complex for 3 to 20 days.

Physicochemical characteristics
Chemical Group—Macrocyclic, polyene, antifungal antibiotic; amphotericin B liposomal complex drug delivery system contains amphotericin B intercalated into a single bilayer liposome consisting of alpha-tocopherol, distearoylphosphatidylglycerol, and hydrogenated soy phosphatidylcholine.
Molecular weight—Amphotericin B: 924.09.

Mechanism of action/Effect
Amphotericin B binds primarily to ergosterol in cell membranes of sensitive fungi, causing changes in membrane permeability, which result in leakage of intracellular contents and cell death. Amphotericin B also binds to cholesterol in mammalian cell membranes, leading to cytotoxicity. Amphotericin B liposomal complex penetrates the cell wall of both extracellular and intracellular forms of susceptible fungi.

Distribution
Vol_D (steady-state) with a dose of—
1 mg per kg of body weight (mg/kg) per day: 0.14 ± 0.05 L per kg;
2.5 mg/kg per day: 0.16 ± 0.09 L per kg;
5 mg/kg per day: 0.1 ± 0.07 L per kg.
Steady-state concentrations are generally achieved within 4 days of dosing.

Half-life
Distribution—
7 to 10 hours (mean) following a 24-hour period dosing interval.
Terminal elimination—
100 to 153 hours (mean) following up to 49 days after dosing; the long terminal elimination half-life is probably due to slow redistribution from tissues.

Peak serum concentration
With a dose of—
1 mg/kg per day: 12.2 ± 4.9 mcg/mL.
2.5 mg/kg per day: 31.4 ± 17.8 mcg/mL.
5 mg/kg per day: 83 ± 35.2 mcg/mL.

Elimination
Excretion of amphotericin B liposomal complex has not been studied. The mean clearance at steady state is independent of dose.

Precautions to Consider

Carcinogenicity
Long-term studies in animals have not been done to evaluate the carcinogenic potential of amphotericin B liposomal complex.

Mutagenicity
Amphotericin B liposomal complex has not been tested to determine its mutagenic potential.

Pregnancy/Reproduction
Fertility—Amphotericin B liposomal complex does not affect fertility in rats.
Pregnancy—Adequate and well-controlled studies in humans have not been done. However, a small number of pregnant women have been successfully treated for systemic fungal infections with amphotericin B deoxycholate.
Female rats given doses of 10 and 15 mg per kg of body weight (mg/kg), equivalent to 1.6 and 2.4 mg/kg in humans based on body surface area considerations, exhibited an abnormal estrous cycle (prolonged diestrus) and decreased number of corpora lutea. There were no effects on male reproductive function. Amphotericin B liposomal complex is not teratogenic in rats or in rabbits. In rats, the maternal nontoxic dose was estimated to be 5 mg/kg (0.16 to 0.8 times the recommended human clinical dose range [1 to 5 mg/kg]), and in rabbits, 3 mg/kg (0.2 to 1 time the recommended human clinical dose range). Rabbits receiving doses equivalent to 0.5 to 2 times the recommended human dose of amphotericin B liposomal complex experienced a higher rate of spontaneous abortions than did control animals.
FDA Pregnancy Category B.

Breast-feeding
It is not known whether amphotericin B liposomal complex is distributed into breast milk. Because of the potential for serious adverse effects

in nursing infants, a decision should be made to either stop breast-feeding or discontinue taking amphotericin B liposomal complex.

Pediatrics

The pharmacokinetics of amphotericin B liposomal complex have not been studied in pediatric patients. However, infants and children 1 month to 16 years of age have been successfully treated with amphotericin B liposomal complex. Studies in which pediatric patients were treated with amphotericin B or amphotericin B liposomal complex demonstrated no differences in safety or efficacy of amphotericin B liposomal complex compared with those in adults.

Safety and efficacy have not been established for infants up to 1 month of age.

Geriatrics

The pharmacokinetics of amphotericin B liposomal complex have not been studied in geriatric patients. However, 71 patients, 65 years of age and older, have been treated with amphotericin B liposomal complex, and no adjustment in dose was necessary.

Drug interactions and/or related problems

The following drug interactions and/or related problems have been selected on the basis of their potential clinical significance (possible mechanism in parentheses where appropriate)—not necessarily inclusive (» = major clinical significance):

Note: Combinations containing any of the following medications, depending on the amount present, may also interact with this medication.

» Antineoplastic agents
(concurrent use with amphotericin B liposomal complex may enhance the potential for bronchospasm, hypotension, and renal toxicity of these agents; caution should be used when these medications are administered concurrently with amphotericin B liposomal complex)

» Corticosteroids or
» Corticotropin (ACTH)
(concurrent use may potentiate hypokalemia, which may predispose the patient to cardiac dysfunction; cardiac function and serum electrolytes should be monitored)

» Digitalis glycosides
(amphotericin B may induce hypokalemia, which may potentiate digitalis toxicity when this medication is used concurrently with digitalis glycosides; serum potassium concentrations should be monitored closely)

Flucytosine
(concurrent use may increase the toxicity of flucytosine possibly by increasing its cellular uptake and/or impairing its renal excretion)

Imidazoles
(animal studies have suggested that imidazoles may induce fungal resistance to amphotericin B; caution should be used when administering these medications concurrently, especially in immunocompromised patients)

» Nephrotoxic medications, other (see *Appendix II*)
(concurrent use with nephrotoxic medications may potentiate medication-induced renal toxicity; caution should be exercised when these medications are used concurrently with amphotericin B liposomal complex, and renal function should be monitored frequently)

» Neuromuscular blocking agents, nondepolarizing
(amphotericin B may induce hypokalemia, which may enhance the activity of nondepolarizing neuromuscular blocking agents; serum potassium concentrations should be monitored closely)

Laboratory value alterations

The following have been selected on the basis of their potential clinical significance (possible effect in parentheses where appropriate)—not necessarily inclusive (» = major clinical significance).

With physiology/laboratory test values

Alkaline phosphatase and
Creatine kinase (CK)
(serum values may be increased)

Calcium and
Magnesium and
» Potassium
(serum concentrations may be decreased)

Bilirubin, blood and
Blood urea nitrogen (BUN) and
Glucose, plasma
(concentrations may be increased)

Medical considerations/Contraindications

The medical considerations/contraindications included have been selected on the basis of their potential clinical significance (reasons given in parentheses where appropriate)—not necessarily inclusive (» = major clinical significance).

Except under special circumstances, this medication should not be used when the following medical problems exist:

» Hypersensitivity to amphotericin B liposomal complex

» Leukocyte transfusions
(acute pulmonary toxicity has been reported in patients concurrently receiving intravenous amphotericin B and leukocyte transfusions)

Risk-benefit should be considered when the following medical problem exists:

Renal function impairment
(amphotericin B may produce nephrotoxicity)

Patient monitoring

The following may be especially important in patient monitoring (other tests may be warranted in some patients, depending on condition; » = major clinical significance):

» Electrolytes, serum
(concentrations should be monitored)

Hematopoietic function tests and
Hepatic function tests and
Renal function tests
(values should be monitored)

Side/Adverse Effects

Note: There have been a few reports of back pain with or without chest tightness, chest pain, and flushing associated with administration of amphotericin B liposomal complex; on occasion these effects have been severe. These reactions developed within a few minutes after the start of infusion and disappeared rapidly when the infusion was stopped.

The following side/adverse effects have been selected on the basis of their potential clinical significance (possible signs and symptoms in parentheses where appropriate)—not necessarily inclusive:

Those indicating need for medical attention

Incidence more frequent

Chills; fever; hypokalemia (irregular heartbeat; muscle cramps or pain; unusual tiredness or weakness)

Incidence less frequent

Back pain; chest pain; dark urine; dyspnea (difficulty in breathing); ***infusion-related reaction*** (chills; fever; headache); ***yellowing of eyes or skin***

Incidence rare

Anaphylactic reaction (difficulty in swallowing; hives; itching, especially of feet or hands; reddening of skin, especially around ears; swelling of eyes, face, or inside of nose; unusual tiredness or weakness, sudden and severe)

Those indicating need for medical attention only if they continue or are bothersome

Incidence more frequent

Abdominal pain; cough; diarrhea; dizziness; headache; nausea; vomiting

Incidence less frequent

Skin rash

Overdose

Repeated daily doses of up to 7.5 mg per kg of body weight have been administered in clinical trials with no reported dose-related toxicity.

For more information on the management of overdose or unintentional ingestion, **contact a Poison Control Center** (see *Poison Control Center Listing*).

Treatment of overdose

In the case of overdose, administration should cease immediately.

Monitoring—Renal function should be monitored.

Supportive care—Treatment should be supportive and symptomatic. Patients in whom intentional overdose is confirmed or suspected should be referred for psychiatric consultation.

Patient Consultation

As an aid to patient consultation, refer to *Advice for the Patient, Amphotericin B Liposomal Complex (Systemic).*

In providing consultation, consider emphasizing the following selected information (» = major clinical significance):

Before using this medication

» Conditions affecting use, especially:

Hypersensitivity to amphotericin B liposomal complex

Breast-feeding—It is recommended either to stop breast-feeding or to discontinue taking amphotericin B liposomal complex

Other medications, especially antineoplastic agents, corticosteroids, corticotropin (ACTH), digitalis glycosides, other nephrotoxic medications, or nondepolarizing neuromuscular blocking agents

Other medical problems, especially leukocyte transfusions

Side/adverse effects

Signs of potential side effects, especially chills, fever, hypokalemia, back pain, chest pain, dark urine, dyspnea, infusion-related reaction, yellowing of eyes or skin, or anaphylactic reaction

General Dosing Information

Intravenous infusion should be administered over a period of approximately 120 minutes. The infusion time may be reduced to approximately 60 minutes in patients in whom the treatment is well-tolerated. If the patient experiences discomfort during infusion, the duration of infusion may be increased.

Parenteral Dosage Forms

AMPHOTERICIN B LIPOSOME INJECTION

Usual adult and adolescent dose

Aspergillosis or
Candidiasis or
Cryptococcosis—
Intravenous infusion, 3 to 5 mg per kg of body weight per day.

Cryptococcal meningitis in HIV-infected patients—
Intravenous infusion, 6 mg per kg of body weight per day

Leishmaniasis, immunocompetent patients—
Intravenous infusion, a three-week course of therapy consisting of 3 mg per kg of body weight per day for days one through five, on day fourteen and day twenty-one.

Note: Patients who do not achieve parasitic clearance may require a repeat course of therapy.

Leishmaniasis, immunocompromised patients—
Intravenous, a thirty-eight-day course of therapy consisting of 4 mg per kg of body weight per day for days one through five, on day ten, day seventeen, day twenty-four, day thirty-one, and day thirty-eight.

Note: Patients who do not achieve parasitic clearance or who experience relapses should seek expert advice regarding further treatment.

Presumed fungal infections in patients with febrile neutropenia—
Intravenous infusion, 3 mg per kg of body weight per day.

Usual pediatric dose

Infants and children 1 month to 12 years of age—See *Usual adult and adolescent dose*.

Infants up to 1 month of age—Safety and efficacy have not been established.

Usual geriatric dose

See *Usual adult and adolescent dose*.

Strength(s) usually available

U.S.—
50 mg (Rx) [*AmBisome* (sucrose [900 mg])].

Packaging and storage

Prior to reconstitution, store between 2 and 8 °C (36 and 46 °F), unless otherwise specified by the manufacturer. Protect from freezing.

Preparation of dosage form

Add 12 mL of sterile water for injection (without a bacteriostatic agent) to each 50-mg vial to provide a concentration of 4 mg amphotericin B per mL. Immediately shake the vial vigorously for at least 30 seconds until all particulate matter is completely dispersed. Withdraw the appropriate volume of amphotericin B liposomal complex suspension and, using a 5-micron filter, dilute into 5% dextrose injection to provide a concentration of 1 to 2 mg per mL. Lower concentrations (0.2 to 0.5 mg per mL) may be appropriate for infants and small children to provide sufficient volume for infusion.

Stability

Once reconstituted with sterile water for injection, the suspension is stable for up to 24 hours at 2 to 8 °C (36 to 46 °F). Do not freeze.

Once diluted with 5% dextrose injection, infusion should begin within 6 hours.

Incompatibilities

To avoid possible precipitation, amphotericin B liposomal complex should not be reconstituted or admixed with saline or any solution containing a bacteriostatic agent.

The infusion admixture should not be mixed with other medications. If administered through an existing intravenous line, the line should be flushed with 5% dextrose injection prior to infusion of amphotericin B liposomal complex. Alternatively, the medications should be administered through separate lines.

An in-line membrane filter may be used for the intravenous infusion of amphotericin B liposomal complex provided the filter has a mean pore diameter of at least 1 micron.

Revised: 03/26/1998
Developed: 11/13/1997

AMPICILLIN—See *Penicillins (Systemic)*

ANABOLIC STEROIDS Systemic

This monograph includes information on the following: 1) Nandrolone; 2) Oxandrolone†; 3) Oxymetholone; 4) Stanozolol†.

VA CLASSIFICATION (Primary/Secondary):
Nandrolone—HS101/AN900; BL400
Oxandrolone—HS101
Oxymetholone—HS101/BL400; IM900
Stanozolol—HS101/BL400; IM900

Note: Controlled substance classification

U.S.: Schedule III

Canada: C

Commonly used brand name(s): *Anadrol-50*[3]; *Anapolon 50*[3]; *Deca-Durabolin*[1]; *Durabolin*[1]; *Durabolin-50*[1]; *Hybolin Decanoate*[1]; *Hybolin-Improved*[1]; *Kabolin*[1]; *Oxandrin*[2]; *Winstrol*[4].

Note: For a listing of dosage forms and brand names by country availability, see *Dosage Forms* section(s).

†Not commercially available in Canada.

Category

Note: All anabolic steroids are approximately equal in efficacy. Selection of a particular generic substance or dosage form is dependent upon the incidence of side effects, preferred route of administration, or the duration of action desired. Indications listed for individual generic products included are based on currently marketed product labeling.

Anabolic steroid—Nandrolone; Oxandrolone; Oxymetholone; Stanozolol.
Antianemic—Nandrolone; Oxymetholone; Stanozolol.
Antineoplastic—Nandrolone.
Antiangioedema (hereditary) agent—Oxymetholone; Stanozolol

Indications

Note: Bracketed information in the *Indications* section refers to uses that are not included in U.S. product labeling.

Accepted

Catabolic or tissue-depleting processes (treatment)—[Nandrolone decanoate, stanozolol], and oxandrolone are indicated in conditions such as chronic infections, extensive surgery, [corticosteroid-induced myopathy, decubitus ulcers, burns], or severe trauma, which require reversal of catabolic processes or protein-sparing effects. These agents are adjuncts to, and not replacements for, conventional treatment of these disorders.

Anemia (treatment)—Nandrolone decanoate[1] is indicated for the treatment of anemia associated with renal insufficiency [and as adjuvant therapy for aplastic and sickle cell anemias]. Adequate iron intake is necessary for maximum therapeutic response.

[Nandrolone phenpropionate is indicated in the treatment of refractory deficient red cell production anemias. These may include aplastic anemia, myelofibrosis, myelosclerosis, agnogenic myeloid metaplasia, and hypoplastic anemias caused by malignancy or myelotoxic drugs.

Anabolic steroid therapy should not replace other supportive measures.]

Oxymetholone is indicated in the treatment of bone marrow failure anemias and deficient red cell production anemias. Acquired and congenital aplastic anemias, myelofibrosis, and hypoplastic anemias due to myelotoxic medication often respond to oxymetholone. Oxymetholone should not replace other supportive measures such as transfusions; correction of iron, folic acid, vitamin B_{12}, or pyridoxine deficiency; antibacterial therapy; or the use of corticosteroids.

[Stanozolol is effective in raising hemoglobin concentrations in some cases of aplastic anemia (congenital or idiopathic).]

Carcinoma, breast (treatment)—Anabolic steroids such as [nandrolone decanoate][1] and nandrolone phenpropionate are indicated as treatment for palliation of inoperable metastatic breast cancer in postmenopausal women. However, anabolic steroids should be considered for use only after inadequate response to newer, less toxic medications such as tamoxifen in hormonally responsive breast cancer. Anabolic steroids have also been used to treat breast cancer in premenopausal women who have undergone oophorectomy and are considered to have a hormone-responsive tumor.

Angioedema, hereditary (prophylaxis)—Stanozolol and oxymetholone[1] are indicated in the prophylaxis of hereditary angioedema to decrease the frequency and severity of attacks.

Angioedema, hereditary (treatment)—[Stanozolol] and oxymetholone[1] are used in the treatment of hereditary angioedema.

[Antithrombin III deficiency (treatment)] or
[Fibrinogen excess (treatment)]—Stanozolol is indicated in the treatment of conditions associated with decreased fibrinolytic activity due to antithrombin III deficiency or excess fibrinogen. These conditions may include cutaneous vasculitis, scleroderma of Raynaud's disease, vasculitis of Behcet's disease, and complications of deep vein thrombosis such as venous lipodermatosclerosis. Stanozolol is indicated in the prevention of recurrent venous thrombosis associated with antithrombin III deficiency. Stanozolol may be of benefit in patients susceptible to or with a history of thromboembolism for the treatment of vascular disorders associated with these forms of reduced fibrinolytic activity.

[Growth failure (treatment adjunct)]—Anabolic steroids may be used in children as an adjunct in the treatment of growth failure caused by pituitary growth hormone (GH) deficiency (pituitary dwarfism) or if the response to human growth hormone administration is inadequate.

[Turner's syndrome (treatment)]—Oxandrolone is used in the treatment of the short stature that accompanies Turner's syndrome (gonadal dysgenesis in females). Although the therapy is controversial, recent experimental reports seem to indicate that oxandrolone may be as effective as growth hormone and that oxandrolone may increase the efficacy of growth hormone therapy.

Unaccepted

Anabolic steroids have been used for the treatment of symptoms associated with osteoporosis. However, this use has largely been discontinued because the questionable efficacy of these agents for this indication does not justify the risk of serious adverse effects.

Oxandrolone and oxymetholone have been used for the treatment of alcoholic hepatitis with encephalopathy. However, there is currently insufficient evidence to establish the efficacy of these agents for this indication.

Use of anabolic steroids by athletes is not recommended. Objective evidence is conflicting and inconclusive as to whether these medications significantly increase athletic performance by increasing muscle strength. Weight gains reported by athletes are due in part to fluid retention, which is a potentially hazardous side effect of anabolic steroid therapy. The risk of other unwanted effects, such as testicular atrophy and suppression of spermatogenesis in males; menstrual disturbances and virilization, such as deepening of voice, development of acne, and unnatural growth of body hair in females; peliosis hepatis or other hepatotoxicity; and hepatic cancer outweigh any possible benefit received from anabolic steroids and make their use in athletes inappropriate.

[1]Not included in Canadian product labeling.

Pharmacology/Pharmacokinetics

Physicochemical characteristics

Chemical Group—Anabolic steroids are synthetic derivatives of testosterone, and as such have androgenic properties. The deletion of the CH_3 group from the C-19 position results in reduction of its androgenic properties and retention of its anabolic, tissue-building properties. Since complete dissociation of anabolic and androgenic effects is not possible, many of the actions of anabolic steroids are similar to those of androgens. The 17-alpha alkylated (oral methylated) anabolic steroids are oxandrolone, oxymetholone, and stanozolol.

Molecular weight—
- Nandrolone decanoate: 428.66.
- Nandrolone phenpropionate: 406.57.
- Oxandrolone: 306.45.
- Oxymetholone: 332.49.
- Stanozolol: 328.50.

Mechanism of action/Effect

Anabolic steroid—
- Reverses catabolic processes and negative nitrogen balance by promoting protein anabolism and stimulating appetite if there is concurrently a proper intake of calories and proteins.

Antianemic—
- Anemias due to bone marrow failure: Increases production and urinary excretion of erythropoietin.
- Anemias due to deficient red cell production: Stimulates erythropoietin production and may have a direct action on bone marrow.
- Anemias associated with renal disease: Increases hemoglobin and red blood cell volume.

Angioedema (hereditary) prophylactic—
- Increases serum concentration of C1 esterase inhibitor and, as a result, C2 and C4 concentrations.

Half-life

Oxandrolone—
- Biphasic:
  - 1st phase—0.55 hours.
  - 2nd phase—9 hours.

Time to peak serum concentration

Nandrolone decanoate intramuscular—100-mg dose: 3 to 6 days.
Nandrolone phenpropionate intramuscular—100-mg dose: 1 to 2 days.

Elimination

Oxandrolone—Renal; small amount fecal.

Precautions to Consider

Carcinogenicity

Hepatocellular carcinoma has been associated rarely with long-term, high-dose anabolic steroid therapy.

Tumorigenicity

Hepatic neoplasms have been associated rarely with long-term, high-dose anabolic steroid therapy.

Mutagenicity

For oxandrolone—Animal or *in vitro* mutagenicity studies have not been done.
For oxymetholone—Studies have not been done.
For stanozolol—Animal studies have not been done.

Pregnancy/Reproduction

Pregnancy—Anabolic steroids are contraindicated for use during pregnancy, since studies in animals have shown that anabolic steroids cause masculinization of the fetus.

For oxandrolone: Animal studies have also shown oxandrolone to cause embryotoxicity, fetotoxicity, and infertility, in addition to masculinization in offspring of animals receiving 9 times the human dose.

FDA Pregnancy Category X.

Breast-feeding

It is not known whether anabolic steroids are distributed into breast milk. Problems in humans have not been documented. Women who take anabolic steroids should not breast feed.

Pediatrics

Anabolic steroids should be used with caution in children and adolescents and only by specialists who are aware of their effects on bone maturation because of possible premature epiphyseal closure, precocious sexual development in males, and virilization in females. The epiphyseal maturation may be accelerated more rapidly than linear growth in children, and the effect may continue for 6 months after the medication has been discontinued.

For stanozolol—The safety and efficacy of stanozolol in children with hereditary angioedema have not been established. Attacks of hereditary angioedema may include symptoms such as life-threatening upper respiratory obstruction with or without severe gastrointestinal colic, but are generally infrequent in childhood. The risks from stanozolol therapy are substantially increased with long-term use. Therefore, long-term administration of stanozolol is generally not recommended in children, and should not be undertaken without consideration of risk-benefit involved and close follow-up for endocrine effects.

Geriatrics
Treatment of geriatric male patients with anabolic steroids may cause increased risk of prostatic hyperplasia or prostatic carcinoma. In general, dose selection of an elderly patient should be cautious, usually starting at the low end of the dosing range, reflecting the greater frequency of decreased hepatic, renal, or cardiac function, and of concomitant disease or other drug therapy.

Drug interactions and/or related problems
The following drug interactions and/or related problems have been selected on the basis of their potential clinical significance (possible mechanism in parentheses where appropriate)—not necessarily inclusive (» = major clinical significance):

Note: Combinations containing any of the following medications, depending on the amount present, may also interact with this medication.

» Anticoagulants, coumarin- or indandione-derivative or
Anti-inflammatory analgesics, nonsteroidal or
Salicylates, in therapeutic doses
(anticoagulant effect may be increased during concurrent use with anabolic steroids, especially 17-alpha-alkylated compounds, because of decreased procoagulant factor concentration caused by alteration of procoagulant factor synthesis or catabolism and increased receptor affinity for the anticoagulant; anticoagulant dosage adjustment based on prothrombin time determinations may be required during and following concurrent use)
(warfarin dose may need to be adjusted until a stable target international normalized ratio (INR) or prothrombin time (PT) has been achieved)

Antidiabetic agents, sulfonylurea or
Insulin
(anabolic steroids may decrease blood glucose concentration; diabetic patients should be closely monitored for signs of hypoglycemia and dosage of hypoglycemic agent adjusted if necessary)

Corticosteroids, glucocorticoid, especially with significant mineralocorticoid activity or
Corticosteroids, mineralocorticoid or
Corticotropin, especially prolonged therapeutic use or
Sodium-containing medications or foods
(concurrent use with anabolic steroids may increase the possibility of edema; in addition, concurrent use of glucocorticoids or corticotropin with anabolic steroids may promote development of severe acne)

» Hepatotoxic medications, other (see *Appendix II*)
(concurrent use with anabolic steroids may result in an increased incidence of hepatotoxicity; patients, especially those on prolonged administration or those with a history of liver disease, should be carefully monitored)

Somatrem or
Somatropin
(concurrent use of anabolic steroids with somatrem or somatropin may accelerate epiphyseal maturation)

Laboratory value alterations
The following have been selected on the basis of their potential clinical significance (possible effect in parentheses where appropriate)—not necessarily inclusive (» = major clinical significance).

With diagnostic test results

Fasting blood sugar and
Glucose tolerance test and
Metyrapone test
(may be altered)

Thyroid function tests
(radioactive iodine uptake and thyroxine-binding capacity [TBC] may be decreased; the decreased concentrations of thyroxine-binding globulin result in decreased total T_3 and T_4 serum concentrations and increased resin uptake of T_3 and T_4; altered tests usually persist for 2 to 3 weeks after stopping therapy)

With physiology/laboratory test values

Alanine aminotransferase (ALT [SGPT]) and
Alkaline phosphatase and
Aspartate aminotransferase (AST [SGOT]) and
Creatine kinase (CK)
(values may be increased)

Bilirubin, serum and
Calcium, chloride, inorganic phosphates, potassium, and sodium, serum
(concentrations may be increased)

Clotting factors II, V, VII, and X
(concentrations may be decreased)

Creatine and creatinine excretion
(may be increased; effect usually lasts up to 2 weeks after therapy is discontinued)

Lipoproteins, high-density and
Lipoproteins, low-density
(high-density lipoprotein concentration may be lowered; low-density lipoprotein concentration may be elevated)

Prothrombin time
(may be increased)

Serum lipid, especially triglyceride, concentrations and
Urinary 17-ketosteroid (17-KS) excretion
(may be decreased)

Medical considerations/Contraindications
The medical considerations/contraindications included have been selected on the basis of their potential clinical significance (reasons given in parentheses where appropriate)—not necessarily inclusive (» = major clinical significance).

Except under special circumstances, these medications should not be used when the following medical problems exist:

» Breast cancer, disseminated, in females with active hypercalcemia
» Breast cancer in males
» Hepatic function impairment, severe
» Hypercalcemia, active or history of
(may be exacerbated or recurrence may result)
» Nephrosis or nephrotic phase of nephritis
» Prostate cancer
(tumor growth may be promoted)

Risk-benefit should be considered when the following medical problems exist:

Cardiac function impairment or
Hepatic function impairment or
Renal function impairment
(use of these medications may cause retention of sodium and water, resulting in edema, with or without congestive heart failure)

» Coronary artery disease, history of or
» Myocardial infarction, history of
(because of hypercholesterolemic effects of anabolic steroids)

Diabetes mellitus
(anabolic steroids may decrease blood sugar concentrations; insulin or oral hypoglycemic dosage may need to be adjusted)

Intolerance to anabolic steroids or androgens

Prostatic hyperplasia, benign
(further enlargement may occur)

Patient monitoring
The following may be especially important in patient monitoring (other tests may be warranted in some patients, depending on condition; » = major clinical significance):

Bone age determinations
(x-ray studies recommended at 6-month intervals in children to monitor bone age in order to prevent the risk of compromising adult height)

Calcium
(measurement of serum concentrations recommended at regular intervals during anabolic steroid therapy in females with breast cancer)

» Cholesterol
(measurement of serum concentrations recommended at regular intervals during therapy because of possible decreased high-density lipoprotein and increased low-density lipoprotein, which may increase the risk of atherosclerosis)

Hematocrit value and
Hemoglobin concentration
(recommended periodically to detect polycythemia in patients taking high doses of anabolic steroids)

» Hepatic function determinations
(recommended at regular intervals during therapy because of possibility of hepatic dysfunction, peliosis hepatis, and liver cell tumors, especially with 17-alpha-alkylated compounds, which are more likely to cause hepatic dysfunction)

International normalized ratio or
Occult bleeding or
Prothrombin time
(close monitoring is recommended when anabolic steroids are administered concomitantly with warfarin; warfarin dose should be adjusted to achieve stable target INR and PT)

Iron concentrations, serum and
Total iron-binding capacity (TIBC) determinations
(recommended at regular intervals during therapy because of possible iron deficiency anemia manifested by low serum iron and decrease in percentage of transferrin saturation)

Side/Adverse Effects

Note: Peliosis hepatis and hepatic neoplasms, including hepatocellular carcinoma, have been associated with long-term, high-dose anabolic steroid therapy. These adverse reactions can be life-threatening or fatal.

The following side/adverse effects have been selected on the basis of their potential clinical significance (possible signs and symptoms in parentheses where appropriate)—not necessarily inclusive:

Those indicating need for medical attention

Incidence more frequent

In females only

Virilism (acne or oily skin; enlarging clitoris; hoarseness or deepening of voice; menstrual irregularities; unnatural hair growth or loss)

Note: *Enlarging clitoris, hoarseness or deepening of voice,* and *unnatural hair growth or loss* usually are not reversible even after prompt discontinuance of therapy. The concurrent use of estrogens will not prevent virilization in females.

In prepubertal males only

Virilism (acne; enlarging penis; increased frequency of erections; unnatural hair growth)

In postpubertal males only

Bladder irritability (frequent urge to urinate); ***breast soreness; gynecomastia*** (enlargement of breasts); ***priapism*** (frequent or continuing erections)

Incidence less frequent

In both females and males

Anemia, iron deficiency (loss of appetite; sore tongue); ***edema*** (swelling of feet or lower legs; rapid weight gain); ***gastric irritation*** (nausea; vomiting); ***hepatic dysfunction*** (yellow eyes or skin); ***leukemia*** (bone pain); ***suppression of clotting factors*** (unusual bleeding)

In females only

Hypercalcemia (mental depression; nausea; vomiting; unusual tiredness)

In prepubertal males only

Unexplained darkening of skin

In geriatric males only

Prostatic carcinoma or prostatic hyperplasia (difficult or frequent urination)

Incidence rare—with prolonged therapy

In both females and males

Hepatic necrosis (black, tarry stools; continuing feeling of discomfort; continuing headache; continuing unpleasant breath odor; vomiting of blood); ***hepatocellular carcinoma*** (abdominal or stomach pain; unexplained weight loss); ***peliosis hepatis*** (continuing loss of appetite; dark-colored urine; fever; hives; light-colored stools; nausea and vomiting; purple- or red-colored spots on body or inside the mouth or nose; sore throat)

Incidence not known

Epiphyseal closure, premature (lack or slowing of normal growth in children)

Those indicating need for medical attention only if they continue or are bothersome

Incidence more frequent

In males only

Acne

Incidence less frequent

In both females and males

Chills; decrease or increase in libido; diarrhea; feeling of abdominal or stomach fullness; muscle cramps; trouble in sleeping

In males only

Decreased sexual ability

Overdose

For more information on the management of overdose or unintentional ingestion, **contact a Poison Control Center** (see *Poison Control Center Listing*).

Clinical effects of overdose

The following effects have been selected on the basis of their potential clinical significance (possible signs and symptoms in parentheses where appropriate)—not necessarily inclusive:

Hepatotoxicity

Treatment of overdose

Treatment of overdose is symptomatic and supportive.

To decrease absorption—In acute oral overdose, decontamination includes induced emesis and/or gastric lavage.

Monitoring—Hepatic function.

Supportive care—Patients in whom intentional overdose is confirmed or suspected should be referred for psychiatric consultation.

Patient Consultation

As an aid to patient consultation, refer to *Advice for the Patient, Anabolic Steroids (Systemic).*

In providing consultation, consider emphasizing the following selected information (» = major clinical significance):

Before using this medication

» Conditions affecting use, especially:
Hepatocellular carcinoma associated with long-term, high-dose therapy
Hepatic neoplasms associated with long-term, high-dose therapy
Pregnancy—Not recommended during pregnancy because of possible masculinization of fetus
Use in children—Cautious use because of effects on bone growth and possible premature ephiphyseal closure and sexual development (precocious sexual development in males, virilization in females)
Use in the elderly—Increased risk of prostatic hyperplasia or prostatic carcinoma
Other medications, especially anticoagulants (coumarin- or indandione-derivatives), or hepatotoxic medications
Other medical problems, especially breast cancer, coronary artery disease, hepatic function impairment, hypercalcemia, myocardial infarction, nephrosis, nephrotic phase of nephritis, or prostatic cancer

Proper use of this medication

» Importance of not taking more medication than the amount prescribed; to do so may increase chance of side effects
» Importance of diet high in proteins and calories while taking this medication to achieve maximum therapeutic effect
» Proper dosing
Missed dose: If dosing schedule is—
Once daily: Taking as soon as possible; if not remembered until next day, not taking at all; not doubling doses
More than once daily: Taking as soon as possible; not taking if almost time for next dose; not doubling doses
» Proper storage

Precautions while using this medication

Regular visits to physician to check progress during therapy
Pediatric and adolescent patients: Importance of monitoring bone growth by x-ray studies at 6-month intervals
Diabetics: May decrease blood sugar concentrations

Side/adverse effects

Signs of potential side effects, especially
In females only—Virilism or hypercalcemia
In prepubertal males only—Virilism or unexplained darkening of skin
In postpubertal males only—Bladder irritability, breast soreness, gynecomastia, or priapism
In geriatric males only—Prostatic carcinoma or prostatic hyperplasia
In all patients, in addition to those side effects listed above—Anemia, iron deficiency; edema; gastric irritation; hepatic dysfunction, necrosis, or carcinoma; leukemia; premature epiphyseal closure in children, suppression of clotting factors; or peliosis hepatis

General Dosing Information

Many of the side/adverse effects of anabolic steroids are dose-related; therefore, patients should be placed on the lowest possible effective dose.

Anabolic steroids should be administered cautiously to pediatric patients by specialists who are aware of their effects on bone maturation.

Diet/Nutrition

A well-balanced diet that provides adequate proteins and calories should accompany all anabolic steroid therapy to achieve a maximum therapeutic effect.

NANDROLONE

Summary of Differences

Category:
Nandrolone decanoate—Antianemic.
Nandrolone phenpropionate—Antineoplastic.

Indications:
Nandrolone decanoate is indicated in the treatment of anemia associated with renal insufficiency.
Nandrolone phenpropionate is indicated in the treatment of metastatic breast cancer in women.

Additional Dosing Information

See also *General Dosing Information.*

Nandrolone injections should be administered intramuscularly, preferably deep into the gluteal muscle.

When using nandrolone decanoate injection, an adequate iron intake is required for maximum response.

Parenteral Dosage Forms

NANDROLONE DECANOATE INJECTION USP

Usual adult and adolescent dose

Females—Intramuscular, 50 to 100 mg given at one- to four-week intervals.

Males—Intramuscular, 50 to 200 mg given at one- to four-week intervals.

Note: When given at three- to four-week intervals, therapy may be continued for up to 12 weeks. If necessary, cycle may be repeated if second course is preceded by a four-week rest period.

In the treatment of severe disease states, such as metastatic breast cancer and refractory anemias, a higher dose, based on therapeutic response and the benefit-to-risk ratio, may be required.

Usual pediatric dose

Children up to 2 years of age—Dosage has not been established.

Children 2 to 13 years of age—Intramuscular, 25 to 50 mg every three to four weeks.

Children 14 years of age and over—See *Usual adult and adolescent dose.*

Strength(s) usually available

U.S.—
50 mg per mL (Rx) [*Deca-Durabolin; Hybolin Decanoate; Kabolin;* GENERIC].
100 mg per mL (Rx) [*Deca-Durabolin; Hybolin Decanoate;* GENERIC].
200 mg per mL (Rx) [*Deca-Durabolin;* GENERIC].

Canada—
50 mg per mL (Rx) [*Deca-Durabolin* (benzyl alcohol 10%; sesame oil)].
100 mg per mL (Rx) [*Deca-Durabolin* (benzyl alcohol 10%; sesame oil)].

Packaging and storage

Store below 40 °C (104 °F), preferably between 15 and 30 °C (59 and 86 °F), unless otherwise specified by the manufacturer. Protect from light. Protect from freezing.

NANDROLONE PHENPROPIONATE INJECTION USP

Usual adult dose

Intramuscular, 25 to 100 mg per week.

Note: Therapy may be continued for up to 12 weeks. If necessary, cycle may be repeated if second course is preceded by a four-week rest period.

Usual pediatric dose

Dosage has not been established.

Strength(s) usually available

U.S.—
25 mg per mL (Rx) [*Durabolin;* GENERIC].
50 mg per mL (Rx) [*Durabolin-50; Hybolin-Improved;* GENERIC].

Canada—
Not commercially available.

Packaging and storage

Store below 40 °C (104 °F), preferably between 15 and 30 °C (59 and 86 °F), unless otherwise specified by the manufacturer. Protect from light. Protect from freezing.

OXANDROLONE

Summary of Differences

Indications: Indicated in the treatment of catabolic or tissue-depleting processes.

Additional Dosing Information

See also *General Dosing Information.*

In adults, 2 to 4 weeks of therapy are usually adequate. In both adults and children, therapy may be repeated intermittently as needed.

Oral Dosage Forms

Note: Bracketed uses in the *Dosage Forms* section refer to categories of use and/or indications that are not included in U.S. product labeling.

OXANDROLONE TABLETS USP

Usual adult and adolescent dose

Oral, 2.5 mg two to four times a day.

Note: The dosage may range from 2.5 to 20 mg per day.

Usual pediatric dose

Children—Oral, 250 mcg (0.25 mg) per kg of body weight per day.

[Turner's syndrome]—
Oral, 50 mcg to 125 mcg (0.05 to 0.125 mg) per kg of body weight per day. Generally, the patient should be started and maintained on the lowest effective dose to minimize the potential for adverse effects.

Strength(s) usually available

U.S.—
2.5 mg (Rx) [*Oxandrin* (scored; lactose)].

Canada—
Not commercially available.

Packaging and storage

Store below 40 °C (104 °F), preferably between 15 and 30 °C (59 and 86 °F), unless otherwise specified by the manufacturer. Store in a tight, light-resistant container.

OXYMETHOLONE

Summary of Differences

Category: Antianemic; angioedema (hereditary) agent.

Indications: Indicated in treatment of bone marrow failure anemias and in deficient red cell production anemias; also used in prophylaxis and treatment of hereditary angioedema.

Additional Dosing Information

See also *General Dosing Information.*

Oxymetholone should be used for a minimum of 3 to 6 months, since a response is not always immediately observed.

Following remission of the anemia, some patients may be maintained without oxymetholone while others may be maintained on a low daily dose. Patients with congenital aplastic anemia usually require continued therapy with an appropriate maintenance dose.

Oral Dosage Forms

OXYMETHOLONE TABLETS USP

Usual adult and adolescent dose

Oral, 1 to 5 mg per kg of body weight per day.

Note: The usual effective dose is 1 to 2 mg per kg of body weight a day, but higher doses may be required in some patients. Treatment of refractory anemias may require 3 to 6 months.

Usual pediatric dose

Premature infants and neonates—Oral, 175 mcg (0.175 mg) per kg of body weight or 5 mg per square meter of body surface area per day as a single dose.

Infants and children—See *Usual adult and adolescent dose.*

Strength(s) usually available

U.S.—
50 mg (Rx) [*Anadrol-50* (scored)].

Canada—
50 mg (Rx) [*Anapolon 50* (scored; lactose)].

Packaging and storage

Store at controlled room temperature 20° to 25°C (68° to 77°F), excursions permitted to 15 and 30 °C (59 and 86 °F), unless otherwise specified by the manufacturer. Store in a well-closed container.

STANOZOLOL

Summary of Differences

Category: Angioedema (hereditary) prophylactic.

Indications: Stanozolol is indicated in the prophylaxis of hereditary angioedema to decrease the frequency and severity of attacks and used in treatment of hereditary angioedema.

Oral Dosage Forms

STANOZOLOL TABLETS USP

Usual adult and adolescent dose

Oral, 2 mg three times a day to 4 mg four times a day for 5 days, initially.

Note: A dose of 2 mg two times a day may be used in young women, who are particularly susceptible to the androgenic effects of stanozolol.

The dosage for continuous treatment of hereditary angioedema should be individualized according to patient response. After a favorable response is obtained, the dose should be decreased at intervals of 1 to 3 months to a maintenance dose of 2 mg a day; some patients may respond to a maintenance dose of 2 mg every other day. During the dose-reduction phase, close monitoring of patient response is indicated, especially if the patient has a history of upper respiratory tract involvement.

Usual pediatric dose

Children up to 6 years of age—Oral, 1 mg a day, to be administered only during an attack.

Children 6 to 12 years of age—Oral, up to 2 mg a day, to be administered only during an attack.

Strength(s) usually available

U.S.—

2 mg (Rx) [*Winstrol* (scored; lactose)].

Canada—

Not commercially available.

Packaging and storage

Store below 40 °C (104 °F), preferably between 15 and 30 °C (59 and 86 °F), unless otherwise specified by the manufacturer. Store in a tight, light-resistant container.

Revised: 10/28/2004

ANAGRELIDE Systemic

VA CLASSIFICATION (Primary): BL400

Commonly used brand name(s): *Agrylin*.

Note: For a listing of dosage forms and brand names by country availability, see *Dosage Forms* section(s).

Category

Platelet count–reducing agent.

Indications

Accepted

Thrombocythemia (treatment)—Anagrelide is indicated for the treatment of patients with thrombocythemia, secondary to myeloproliferation disorders, to reduce the elevated platelet count and the risk of thrombosis and to ameliorate associated symptoms including thrombo-hemorrhagic events..

Note: Decisions about whether or not to treat asymptomatic young adults with thrombocythemia secondary to myeloproliferative disorders should be made on an individual patient basis.

Pharmacology/Pharmacokinetics

Physicochemical characteristics

Molecular weight—Anagrelide hydrochloride: 310.55.

Solubility—Very slightly soluble in water; sparingly soluble in dimethyl sulfoxide and in dimethylformamide.

Mechanism of action/Effect

The exact mechanism of action has not been established but it is thought to involve a dose-related reduction of platelet production through a decrease in megakaryocyte hypermaturation.

Other actions/effects

Anagrelide does not affect white cell counts or coagulation parameters at therapeutic doses and may have a small but clinically insignificant effect on red cell parameters. It inhibits platelet aggregation at doses higher than those necessary to reduce platelet counts. It inhibits cyclic adenosine monophosphate (cAMP)-phosphodiesterase, as well as adenosine diphosphate (ADP)-induced and collagen-induced platelet aggregation.

Absorption

Limited data indicate probable dose linearity between doses of 500 mcg (0.5 mg) and 2 mg. Bioavailability was found to be modestly reduced by an average of 13.8% when anagrelide was administered after food. However, this is considered not clinically significant.

Distribution

The volume of distribution (Vol_D) is 12 liters per kilogram of body weight (L/kg).

Biotransformation

Extensive; less than 1% is recovered in the urine unchanged.

Half-life

Elimination—

Plasma: 1.3 hours (at a dose of 0.5 mg while fasting).

Note: Plasma half-life was found to be increased (to 1.8 hours) when anagrelide was taken after food.

Steady-state plasma concentration measurements show no accumulation of anagrelide in plasma with repeated administration.

Onset of action

Platelet count response—Within 7 to 14 days at the proper dosage, which is usually between 1.5 and 3 mg per day.

Time to peak concentration

Plasma—Delayed by 2 hours when anagrelide is taken after food.

Serum—Occurs approximately 1 hour after dosing.

Peak plasma concentration

Reduced by an average of 45% when anagrelide is taken after food.

Duration of action

Increases in platelet counts are observed within 4 days following sudden withdrawal of anagrelide.

Elimination

Renal—More than 70% (less than 1% unchanged).

Fecal—Approximately 10%.

Precautions to Consider

Carcinogenicity

Long-term studies in animals have not been done.

Mutagenicity

Anagrelide was not found to be mutagenic in the Ames test, the mouse lymphoma cell (L5178Y, $TK^{+/-}$) forward mutation test, the human lymphocyte chromosome aberration test, and the mouse micronucleus test.

Pregnancy/Reproduction

Fertility—Studies in male rats given oral doses of up to 240 mg per kg of body weight (mg/kg) per day (1440 mg per square meter of body surface area [mg/m^2] per day, which is 195 times the maximum recommended human dose [MRHD] based on body surface area), found no effect on fertility and reproduction. However, studies in female rats given oral doses of 60 mg/kg per day (360 mg/m^2 per day, which is 49 times the MRHD based on body surface area), or higher found disruption of implantation when anagrelide was administered during early pregnancy, and retarded or blocked parturition when anagrelide was administered in late pregnancy.

Pregnancy—Adequate and well-controlled studies in humans have not been done. However, five women became pregnant during treatment with 1 to 4 mg per day of anagrelide; the medication was stopped immediately when the pregnancy was discovered and the women delivered normal healthy babies.

Studies in pregnant rats given oral doses of up to 900 mg/kg per day (5400 mg/m^2 per day, which is 730 times the MRHD based on body surface area), and in pregnant rabbits given oral doses of up to 20 mg/kg per day (240 mg/m^2 per day, which is 32 times the MRHD based on body surface area), found no evidence of teratogenicity. Reproductive studies in female rats given oral doses of 60 mg/kg per day (360 mg/m^2 per day, which is 49 times the MRHD based on body surface area) or higher showed adverse effects on embryo/fetal survival; a perinatal and postnatal study at the same dose found deaths of nondelivering pregnant dams and their fully developed fetuses, and increased mortality in the pups born.

Because of the risks to the fetus, use of anagrelide is not recommended in women who are or who may become pregnant. Use of birth control is recommended during treatment with anagrelide. Patients who take the medication during pregnancy or who become pregnant during treatment with anagrelide should be advised of the risks to the fetus.

FDA Pregnancy Category C.

Breast-feeding

It is not known whether anagrelide is distributed into breast milk. However, because of the risk of serious adverse effects in the infant, a decision as to whether the medication should be discontinued or nursing should be discontinued should take into account the importance of the medication to the mother.

Pediatrics
Appropriate studies performed to date have not demonstrated pediatrics-specific problems that would limit the usefulness of anagrelide in children. However, the medication has been administered successfully to 12 patients ages 6.8 to 17.4 years (including eight with essential thrombocythemia, two with chronic myelogenous leukemia, one with polycythemia vera, and one with another type of myeloproliferative disorder) at doses of 2 to 10 mg per day.

Geriatrics
Appropriate studies performed to date have not demonstrated geriatrics-specific problems that would limit the usefulness of anagrelide in the elderly. However, a greater sensitivity to anagrelide in the elderly cannot be ruled out.

Drug interactions and/or related problems
The following drug interactions and/or related problems have been selected on the basis of their potential clinical significance (possible mechanism in parentheses where appropriate)—not necessarily inclusive (» = major clinical significance):

Amrinone or
Cilostazol or
Enoximone or
Milrinone or
Olprinone
(the effect of these drugs may be exacerbated by anagrelide when given concomitantly)

CYP1A2 inhibitors including:
Fluvoxamine
(could theoretically adversely influence anagrelide clearance if given concomitantly)

Sucralfate
(a case report has suggested that sucralfate may interfere with anagrelide absorption)

Theophylline
(may present a theoretical potential for interaction with concomitant use due to anagrelide's demonstrated limited inhibitory activity towards CYP1A2)

Laboratory value alterations
The following have been selected on the basis of their potential clinical significance (possible effect in parentheses where appropriate)—not necessarily inclusive (» = major clinical significance).

With physiology/laboratory test values
Blood pressure
(standing blood pressure is reduced by an average of 22/15 mm Hg after a single 5-mg dose, usually causing dizziness; however, blood pressure changes are minimal following a 2-mg dose)

Hepatic enzymes
(may rarely be increased during therapy)

Medical considerations/Contraindications
The medical considerations/contraindications included have been selected on the basis of their potential clinical significance (reasons given in parentheses where appropriate)—not necessarily inclusive (» = major clinical significance).

Except under special circumstances, this medication should not be used when the following medical problem exists:

» Hepatic function impairment, severe
(use is contraindicated; studies have not been done)

Risk-benefit should be considered when the following medical problems exist:

» Cardiac disease, known or suspected
(because of its positive inotropic effects and cardiac side effects [vasodilation, tachycardia, palpitations, congestive heart failure], anagrelide should be used only after consideration of risk-benefit; a cardiovascular examination prior to initiation of therapy, as well as careful monitoring during therapy, is recommended)

» Hepatic function impairment, mild or moderate
(risk-benefit should be considered before administering anagrelide to patients with hepatic function values [bilirubin, SGOT, or other hepatic function tests] more than 1.5 times the upper limit of normal; close monitoring for signs of hepatotoxicity is recommended during therapy; anagrelide exposure increased 8-fold in patients with moderate hepatic impairment)

» Renal function impairment
(risk-benefit should be considered before administering anagrelide to patients with renal insufficiency [serum creatinine of 2 mg per deciliter or more]; no dosage adjustment is required; close monitoring for signs of renal toxicity is recommended during therapy)

Patient monitoring
The following may be especially important in patient monitoring (other tests may be warranted in some patients, depending on condition; » = major clinical significance):

Alanine aminotransferase (ALT [SGPT]) values, serum and
Aspartate aminotransferase (AST [SGOT]) values, serum and
Blood urea nitrogen (BUN) concentrations and
Creatinine concentrations, serum and
Hemoglobin and
White blood cell counts
(monitoring is recommended while the platelet count is being lowered, which usually occurs during the first 2 weeks of therapy)

» Platelet counts
(determinations are recommended every 2 days during the first week of treatment and at least weekly after that until the maintenance dose is reached, in order to monitor the effect of anagrelide and prevent thrombocytopenia)

Signs and symptoms of cardiovascular effects
(therapeutic doses of anagrelide may cause cardiovascular effects, including vasodilation, tachycardia, palpitations, and congestive heart failure; close clinical supervision is recommended)

Side/Adverse Effects
Note: Although most side/adverse effects reported have been mild and have decreased in frequency with continued therapy, serious cardiac, central nervous system (CNS), gastric, and pulmonary effects have occurred.

The following side/adverse effects have been selected on the basis of their potential clinical significance (possible signs and symptoms in parentheses where appropriate)—not necessarily inclusive:

Those indicating need for medical attention
Incidence more frequent (≥ 10%)

Abdominal or stomach pain; asthenia (weakness); ***dizziness; palpitations; pulmonary infiltrates or pulmonary fibrosis*** (shortness of breath)

Note: *Abdominal or stomach pain* may be a symptom of a gastric or duodenal ulcer or of pancreatitis.

Dizziness may be a symptom of hypotension.

Incidence less frequent (< 10%)

Asthma, bronchitis, or pneumonia (difficulty in breathing; shortness of breath); ***cardiac toxicity, including congestive heart failure*** (shortness of breath; swelling of feet or lower legs; unusual tiredness or weakness); ***cardiomyopathy; cardiomegaly; complete heart block; atrial fibrillation*** (rapid or irregular heartbeat); ***myocardial infarction*** (anxiety; cold sweating; increased heart rate; nausea or vomiting; severe pain or pressure in the chest and/or the jaw, neck, back, or arms; shortness of breath); ***or pericarditis; cerebrovascular accident*** (sudden severe headache or weakness); ***blurred or double vision; dysuria*** (painful or difficult urination); ***hematuria*** (blood in urine); ***paresthesias*** (numbness or tingling in hands or feet); ***thrombocytopenia*** (unusual bleeding or bruising); ***vasodilation*** (flushing; faintness)

Note: Renal abnormalities (including *dysuria* and *hematuria* occurred in approximately 1.6% of patients (15 of 942) in clinical trials. Of those, four experienced renal failure presumed to be drug-related. The other 11were found to have pre-existing renal function impairment; no dosage adjustment was necessary.

Thrombocytopenia (platelet counts less than 100,000 per microliter) occurred in 84 of 942 patients in clinical trials; reductions below 50,000 per microliter occurred in 44 of 942 patients. Platelet counts recovered promptly after withdrawal of anagrelide.

Those indicating need for medical attention only if they continue or are bothersome
Incidence more frequent (≥ 10%)

Diarrhea; dyspepsia (heartburn); ***flatulence*** (gas or bloating of stomach); ***headache; nausea; pain***

Incidence less frequent (< 10%)

Aphthous stomatitis (canker sore); ***arthralgia*** (joint pain); ***back pain; confusion; constipation; fever or chills; insomnia*** (trouble in sleeping); ***leg cramps; loss of appetite; malaise*** (general feeling of discomfort or illness); ***mental depression; myalgia*** (muscle pain); ***nervousness; rhinitis*** (stuffy or runny nose); ***ringing in the ears; skin rash or itching; somnolence*** (sleepiness); ***unusual sensitivity to light; vomiting***

Those not indicating need for medical attention

Incidence less frequent or rare

Alopecia (loss of hair)

Overdose

For more information on the management of overdose or unintentional ingestion, **contact a Poison Control Center** (see *Poison Control Center Listing*).

Clinical effects of overdose

The following effects have been selected on the basis of their potential clinical significance (possible signs and symptoms in parentheses where appropriate)—not necessarily inclusive:

Acute

Cardiac toxicity; CNS toxicity; thrombocytopenia, which potentially can cause bleeding

Note: There are no reports of overdosage with anagrelide in humans. In mice, rats, and monkeys, single oral doses of anagrelide hydrochloride of 2500, 1500, and 200 mg per kg of body weight, respectively, were not lethal.

Treatment of overdose

Close clinical supervision of the patient.

Monitoring—Platelet count, for thrombocytopenia.

Dosage should be decreased or anagrelide withdrawn, as appropriate, until the platelet count returns to normal.

Patient Consultation

As an aid to patient consultation, refer to *Advice for the Patient, Anagrelide (Systemic)*.

In providing consultation, consider emphasizing the following selected information (» = major clinical significance):

Before using this medication

» Conditions affecting use, especially:

Pregnancy—Use is not recommended; advisability of using contraception; telling physician immediately if pregnancy is suspected

Breast-feeding—Risk-benefit should be considered

Use in children—Limited data but no overall difference in dosing and safety observed between pediatric and adult patients

Other medical problems, especially cardiac disease (known or suspected), renal function impairment or severe hepatic function impairment

Proper use of this medication

» Proper dosing

» Proper storage

Precautions while using this medication

» Importance of close monitoring by the physician

» Notifying physician and/or getting emergency help immediately if signs and symptoms of a heart attack occur

Side/adverse effects

Signs of potential side effects, especially abdominal or stomach pain, asthenia, dizziness, palpitations, pulmonary infiltrates or pulmonary fibrosis, asthma, bronchitis, pneumonia, cardiac toxicity, cerebrovascular accident, blurred or double vision, dysuria, hematuria, paresthesias, thrombocytopenia, and vasodilation

General Dosing Information

It is recommended that anagrelide therapy be initiated under close medical supervision.

Dosage reduction or withdrawal of anagrelide is recommended if thrombocytopenia occurs. Platelet counts usually recover promptly after withdrawal.

Diet/Nutrition

Food has no significant effect on anagrelide bioavailability.

Oral Dosage Forms

ANAGRELIDE HYDROCHLORIDE CAPSULES

Note: Dose and strength are expressed in terms of anagrelide base.

Usual adult and geriatric dose

Thrombocythemia—

Initial: Oral, 0.5 mg four times per day or 1 mg two times per day for at least one week. Dosage is then adjusted to the lowest effective dose that reduces and maintains platelet counts below 600,000 per microliter and ideally within the normal range.

Note: Dosage increases should not exceed 0.5 mg per day in any one week.

Single dosages should not exceed 2.5 mg per dose.

For patients with moderate hepatic impairment it is recommended that they start anagrelide therapy at a dose of 0.5 mg per day and be maintained for a minimum of one week with careful monitoring of cardiovascular effects. Dosage increases should not exceed 0.5 mg per day in any one week. Patients with mild and moderate hepatic impairment should then be assessed before treatment is commenced. Anagrelide is contraindicated in patients with severe hepatic impairment.

Usual adult and geriatric prescribing limits

10 mg per day or 2.5 mg in a single dose.

Usual pediatric dose

Thrombocythemia—

Initial: Oral, 0.5 mg once daily recommended as there are limited data on the appropriate starting dose for pediatric patients. Starting doses have ranged from 0.5 mg once daily to 0.5 mg 4 times per day. Dosage is then adjusted to the lowest effective dose that reduces and maintains platelet counts below 600,000 per microliter and ideally within the normal range. Dosage increases should not exceed 0.5 mg per day in any one week.

Usual pediatric prescribing limits

See *Usual adult prescribing limits.*

Strength(s) usually available

U.S.—

0.5 mg (base) (Rx) [*Agrylin* (lactose)].

1 mg (base) (Rx) [*Agrylin* (lactose)].

Canada—

0.5 mg (base) (Rx) [*Agrylin* (crospovidone; black iron oxide; gelatin; lactose monohydrate; magnesium stearate; microcrystalline celluloses; povidone; silicone dioxide; sodium lauryl sulfate; titanium dioxide)].

Packaging and storage

Store at 25 °C (77°F), excursions permitted to 15 to 30 °C (59 and 86 °F). Protect from light.

Revised: 02/14/2005
Developed: 11/17/1997

ANAKINRA Systemic

VA CLASSIFICATION (Primary): MS109

Commonly used brand name(s): *Kineret.*

Note: For a listing of dosage forms and brand names by country availability, see *Dosage Forms* section(s).

Category

Antirheumatic; Biological response modifier.

Indications

Accepted

Arthritis, rheumatoid (treatment)—Anakinra is indicated for the reduction in signs and symptoms of moderately to severely active rheumatoid arthritis, in patients 18 years of age or older who have failed one or more disease modifying antirheumatic drugs (DMARDs). Anakinra can be used alone or in combination with DMARDs such as azothiaprine, gold, hydrochloroquine, leflunomide, methotrexate, and sulfasalazine. It should not be used with other tumor necrosis factor (TNF) blocking agents.

Acceptance not established

There is insufficient data to establish the safety and efficacy of anakinra for the treatment of *reactive arthritis, inflammatory bowel disease and ankylosing spondylitis.*

Pharmacology/Pharmacokinetics

Physicochemical characteristics

Source—Anakinra is produced by recombinant DNA technology using an *E. coli* bacterial expression system.

Molecular weight—17.3 kilodaltons.

pH—pH of prepared solution is 6.5

Mechanism of action/Effect

Anakinra blocks the biologic activity of IL-1 by competitively inhibiting IL-1 binding to the interleukin-1 type I receptor (IL-1RI), which is expressed in a wide variety of tissues and organs.

IL-1 production is induced in response to inflammatory stimuli and mediates various physiologic responses including inflammatory and immunological responses. IL-1 has a broad range of activities including cartilage degradation by its induction of the rapid loss of proteoglycans, as well as stimulation of bone resorption. The levels of the naturally occurring interleukin-1 receptor antagonist (IL-1Ra) in synovium and synovial fluid from rheumatoid arthritis patients are not sufficient to compete with the elevated amount of locally produced IL-1.

Absorption
Absolute bioavailability 95%

Half-life
Terminal—
- Subcutaneous administration—4 to 6 hours

Time to peak concentration
Subcutaneous administration—3 to 7 hours

Renal impairment
The mean plasma clearance of anakinra decreased 70 to 75% in normal subjects with severe or end stage renal disease.

Precautions to Consider

Carcinogenicity
Studies in animals have not been done to evaluate the carcinogenic potential of anakinra.

Mutagenicity
In studies using a standard *in vivo* and *in vitro* battery of mutagenesis assays, anakinra did not induce gene mutations in either bacteria or mammalian cells.

Pregnancy/Reproduction
Fertility—Anakinra had no adverse effects on male or female fertility in rats and rabbits at doses of up to 100-fold greater than the human dose.

Pregnancy—Adequate and well-controlled studies have not been done in humans.

Reproductive studies conducted with anakinra on rats and rabbits at doses up to 100 times the human dose have revealed no evidence of harm to the fetus. Because animal reproduction studies are not always predictive of human response, anakinra should be used during pregnancy only if clearly needed.

FDA Pregnancy Category B

Breast-feeding
It is not known whether anakinra is distributed into human breast milk. Because many drugs are distributed into human breast milk, caution should be exercised if anakinra is administered to a nursing woman.

Pediatrics
Safety and efficacy of anakinra in patients with juvenile rheumatoid arthritis [JRA] have not been established.

Geriatrics
Appropriate studies performed to date do not identify differences in safety or efficacy between the elderly and younger patients.However, greater sensitivity of some older individuals cannot be ruled out. Therefore, dose selection for elderly patients should be cautious reflecting the greater frequency of infections and impaired renal function.

Drug interactions and/or related problems
The following drug interactions and/or related problems have been selected on the basis of their potential clinical significance (possible mechanism in parentheses where appropriate)—not necessarily inclusive (» = major clinical significance):

» Vaccines, live virus
(no data are available on the effects of vaccination with live virusesor secondary transmission of infection by live vaccines in patients receiving anakinra therapy; concurrent use of live-virus vaccinesis not recommended; vaccination may not be effective in patients receiving anakinra)

» Vaccines, inactivated virus or bacterial antigens
(no data are available on the effects of vaccination with inactivated virus or bacterial antigens; vaccinations may not be effective if patient is taking anakinra)

» Etanercept
(when used concurrently, there is a higher incidence of serious infections; risk benefit assessment should be performed and patients monitored carefully when considering initiation of concurrent therapy)

» Tumor necrosis factor (TNF) blocking agents
(other TNF blocking agents should only be used with extreme caution when no satisfactory alternatives exist)

Laboratory value alterations
The following have been selected on the basis of their potential clinical significance (possible effect in parentheses where appropriate)—not necessarily inclusive (» = major clinical significance).

With physiology/laboratory test values
Neutrophil count
(may be decreased; should be assessed prior to initiating and while receiving anakinra treatment monthly for three months, then quarterly for up to one year)

Medical considerations/Contraindications
The medical considerations/contraindications included have been selected on the basis of their potential clinical significance (reasons given in parentheses where appropriate)—not necessarily inclusive (» = major clinical significance).

Except under special circumstances, this medication should not be used when the following medical problem exists:

» Hypersensitivity to anakinra or any of its components or
» Hypersensitivity to *E. coli*-derived proteins
(anakinra use contraindicated in these patients)

» Infections, active
(anakinra may potentially suppress normal defense mechanisms against infections)
(anakinra therapy should not be initiated in patients with active infections; if a patient develops a serious infection while receiving anakinra, continueduse of anakinra should be evaluated by the physician; the safety and efficacy of anakinra in patients with a history of certain chronic infections have not been evaluated)

Risk-benefit should be considered when the following medical problems exist:

» Asthma
(patients with asthma appeared to be at higher risk of developing serious infections in clinical trials)

» Immunosuppression
(safety and efficacy of anakinra in immunosuppressed patients have not been evaluated)

» Severe or end stage renal disease
(mean plasma clearance of anakinra decreased 70 to 75% in normal subjects with severe or end stage renal disease; renal status should be assessed periodically throughout therapy)

Patient monitoring
The following may be especially important in patient monitoring (other tests may be warranted in some patients, depending on condition; » = major clinical significance):

» Neutrophil count
(should be assessed prior to initiating anakinra treatment, and monthly for the firstthree months while receiving anakinra, and quarterly thereafter for a period up to one year)

Side/Adverse Effects
The following side/adverse effects have been selected on the basis of their potential clinical significance (possible signs and symptoms in parentheses where appropriate)—not necessarily inclusive:

Those indicating need for medical attention
Incidence more frequent

Infections such as bone and joint infection (pain in the bone or joint; swelling; tenderness or warmth on skin; fever); ***cellulitis*** (itching; pain; redness; swelling; tenderness or warmth on skin); ***and pneumonia*** (chest pain; cough; fever or chills; sneezing; shortness of breath; sore throat; troubled breathing; tightness in chest; wheezing); ***influenza-like symptoms*** (chills; cough; diarrhea; fever; general feeling of discomfort or illness; headache; joint pain; loss of appetite; muscle aches and pains; nausea; runny nose; shivering; sore throat; sweating; trouble sleeping; unusual tiredness or weakness; vomiting); ***injection site reaction*** (redness or purple discoloration of skin; inflammation; pain); ***sinusitis*** (pain or tenderness around eyes and cheekbones; fever; stuffy or runny nose; headache; cough; shortness of breath or troubled breathing; tightness of chest or wheezing); ***upper respiratory tract infection*** (cough; fever; sneezing or sore throat)

Note: Note: Patients with asthma may have a higher risk of developing serious *infections.*

Incidence rare

Hypersensitivity reactions (itching; rash; hives; swelling of face or lips; tightness in chest; wheezing or troubled breathing); ***neutropenia*** (black, sticky stools; chills; cough; fever; lower back or side pain; painful or difficult urination; pale skin; shortness of breath; sore throat; ulcers, sores, or white spots in mouth; unusual bleeding or bruising; unusual tiredness or weakness)

Those indicating need for medical attention only if they continue or are bothersome

Incidence more frequent

Abdominal pain; diarrhea; headache; nausea

Overdose

For more information on the management of overdose or unintentional ingestion, **contact a poison control center** (see *Poison Control Center Listing).*

Note: No serious toxicities attributed to anakinra were seen in sepsis trials when administered at doses up to 35 times those given to patients with rheumatoid arthritis over a 72-hour treatment period.

Treatment of overdose

Supportive care—

Patients in whom intentional overdose is confirmed or suspected should be referred for psychiatric consultation.

Patient Consultation

As an aid to patient consultation, refer to *Advice for the Patient, Anakinra (Systemic).*

In providing consultation, consider emphasizing the following selected information (» = major clinical significance):

Before using this medication

» Conditions affecting use, especially:

Other medications, especially vaccines (live virus), vaccines (inactivated virus or bacterial antigen), etanercept, or tumor necrosis factor blocking agents (TNF).

Other medical problems, especially asthma, hypersensitivity to anakinra or any of its components, hypersensitivity to *E. coli*-derived products, infections (active), immunosuppression, and severe or end stage renal disease.

Proper use of this medication

» Reading patient directions carefully with regard to:

- Safe handling and disposal of needles and syringes
- Proper injection technique
- Stability of the injection

» Proper dosing

Missed dose: Taking as soon as possible; not taking if almost time for next scheduled dose; not doubling doses.

Proper storage

Precautions while using this medication

» Importance of close monitoring by physician, especially for infections

» Telling physician right away if signs or symptoms of infections such as bone and joint infection (pain in the bone or joint, swelling, fever), cellulitis (itching, pain, redness, swelling or tenderness on skin), and pneumonia (chest pain, fever or chills, cough or hoarseness) occur

» Avoiding immunizations unless approved by physician

Side/adverse effects

Signs of potential side effects, especially infections, influenza-like symptoms, injection site reaction, sinusitis, upper respiratory infection, hypersensitivity reactions, or neutropenia.

Parenteral Dosage Forms

ANAKINRA INJECTION

Usual adult dose

Arthritis, rheumatoid—

Subcutaneous, 100 mg per day

Usual adult prescribing limits

100 mg per day

Usual pediatric dose

Safety and efficacy have not been established.

Usual geriatric dose

See *Usual adult dose*

Usual geriatric prescribing limits

See *Usual adult prescribing limits*

Strength(s) usually available

U.S.—

100 mg (Rx) [*Kineret* (sodium citrate 1.29 mg; sodium chloride 5.48 mg; disodium EDTA 0.12 mg; polysorbate 80 (0.70 mg); water for injection, USP)].

Canada—

100 mg (Rx) [*Kineret*].

Note: Anakinra is supplied in single-use, preservative free, prefilled, glass syringes with 27 gauge needles. Anakinra is dispensed in packs containing 7 or 28 syringes.

Packaging and storage

Store between 2 and 8 °C (36 and 46 °F).Protect from freezing. Protect from light.

Stability

Because the single-dose injection contains no preservative, each syringe should be used to administer one dose only. Any unused portion of the solution must be discarded. Do not save unused drug for later administration.

Auxiliary labeling

- Do not shake.
- Do not freeze.
- Visually inspect prefilled syringe for particulate matter and discoloration before administration. If particulates or discoloration are observed, do not use.

Revised: 12/18/2003
Developed: 04/08/2002

ANASTROZOLE Systemic

VA CLASSIFICATION (Primary): AN500

Commonly used brand name(s): *Arimidex.*

Note: For a listing of dosage forms and brand names by country availability, see *Dosage Forms* section(s).

Category

Antineoplastic.

Indications

Accepted

Carcinoma, breast (treatment)—Anastrozole is indicated for the first-line treatment of postmenopausal woman with hormone receptor positive or hormone receptor unknown locally advanced or metastatic breast cancer. It is also indicated for treatment of advanced breast cancer in postmenopausal women with disease progression following tamoxifen therapy.

Note: Patients with E-R negative disease and patients who have had no response to previous tamoxifen therapy rarely respond to anastrozole.

[Breast cancer, neoadjuvant treatment for hormone receptor-positive, operable or potentially operable, locally advanced disease in postmenopausal women]—Anastrozole is an option for the neoadjuvant treatment of hormone receptor-positive, locally advanced breast cancer in postmenopausal women. Two phase 2, randomized, double-blind clinical trials found anastrozole to be at least as effective as tamoxifen in response rates and rates of improved surgery. A phase 2, unpublished abstract reported no differences between neoadjuvant anastrozole and chemotherapy (doxorubicin and paclitaxel) in response rates, number of patients qualifying for breast-conserving surgery, and 3-year disease-free survival. An international expert panel recommends neoadjuvant endocrine therapy in postmenopausal women who would benefit from preoperative chemotherapy but are ineligible to receive it. Anastrozole was well-tolerated.

Unaccepted

Anastrozole is not recommended for use in premenopausal women. Safety and efficacy have not been established.

Pharmacology/Pharmacokinetics

Physicochemical characteristics

Molecular weight—293.4.

Mechanism of action/Effect

Anastrozole is a nonsteroidal aromatase inhibitor that interferes with estradiol production in peripheral tissues. Adrenally generated androstenedione, the chief source of circulating estrogen in postmenopausal women, is converted by aromatase to estrone, which is further converted to estradiol. Growth of many breast cancer tumors containing estrogen receptors and aromatase can be promoted by estrogen.

Absorption

Well absorbed; the extent of absorption of anastrozole may be altered in the presence of food.

Protein binding
Moderate (40%).

Biotransformation
Hepatic; metabolized primarily by *N*-dealkylation, hydroxylation, and glucuronidation to inactive metabolites. Primary metabolite is an inactive triazole.

Half-life
Elimination—Approximately 50 hours.

Onset of action
A 70% reduction of serum estradiol usually occurs within 24 hours, with an 80% reduction in serum estradiol occurring after 14 days.

Time to peak concentration
Steady state concentrations are achieved after approximately 7 days.

Duration of action
Estrogen antagonism may persist for up to 6 days following the discontinuation of anastrozole.

Elimination
Primary route—Biliary: Approximately 85%.
Secondary route—Renal: Approximately 11% (about 10% unchanged and 60% as metabolites).

Precautions to Consider

Carcinogenicity
Studies with anastrozole have not been done.

Mutagenicity
Anastrozole demonstrated no mutagenic effects in the Ames test, *Escherichia coli* bacterial test, Chinese hamster ovary-K1 mutation assay. It was not clastogenic in a *in vitro* chromosomal aberration human lymphocyte assay or in an *in vivo* micronucleus test in rats.

Pregnancy/Reproduction
Fertility—Adequate and well-controlled studies in humans have not been done.
Long-term studies in rats, at doses equal or greater than 1mg/kg/day (this dose produced plasma levels that were 9 to 19 times higher than the respective values found in healthy post-menopausal humans at the recommended dose.), have shown that anastrozole produces ovarian hypertrophy and follicular cysts. Studies in dogs have shown that anastrozole causes hyperplastic uteri at doses equal to or greater than 1 mg/kg/day (this dose produced plasma levels that were 22 and 16 times higher than the respective values found in healthy post-menopausal humans at the recommended dose.) It is unknown if these effects on the reproductive organs of animals are associated with impairment of fertility in premenopausal women..
Pregnancy—Adequate and well-controlled studies in humans have not been done. Before starting treatment with anastrozole, pregnancy must be excluded. If anastrozole is used during pregnancy, or if the patient becomes pregnant while receiving this drug, the patient should be apprised of the potential hazard to the fetus or potential risk for loss of pregnancy.
Studies in rats and rabbits, at 75% and 150% of the recommended human dose, respectively, have shown that anastrozole crosses the placenta. Rats and rabbits given doses of anastrozole during organogenesis that were equal to or greater than 0.1 and 0.02 mg/kg/day (about 75% and 33%, respectively, of the recommended human dose) showed increased pregnancy losses (increased pre- and/or post-implantation loss, increased resorption, and decreased numbers of live fetuses) and dose related effects in rats. Placental weights were significantly increased in rats at doses of 0.1 mg/kg/day or more.
Anastrozole is fetotoxic in rats, causing decreased fetal body weights, delayed fetal development and incomplete ossification, at doses that produce a plasma concentration 19 times and 9 times greater than the plasma concentration associated with the recommended human dose. Anastrozole is not teratogenic in rats given doses up to 1.0 mg/kg per day. In rabbits at doses that produce plasma concentrations that are 19 and 3 times, respectively, greater than the plasma concentration associated with the recommended human dose. Studies in rabbits, at doses that produce a plasma concentration 16 times greater than the plasma concentration associated with the recommended human dose, have shown that anastrozole may cause pregnancy failure. Studies in rats, given 75% of the recommended human dose, have shown that anastrozole may cause an increase in placental weight.
FDA Pregnancy Category D.

Breast-feeding
It is not known whether anastrozole is distributed into breast milk. Because many drugs are distributed in human milk, caution should be exercised when anastrozole is administered to a nursing woman.

Pediatrics
No information is available on the relationship of age to the effects of anastrozole in pediatric patients. Safety and efficacy have not been established.

Geriatrics
Appropriate studies performed to date have not demonstrated geriatrics-specific problems that would limit the usefulness of anastrozole in the elderly.

Drug interactions and/or related problems
The following drug interactions and/or related problems have been selected on the basis of their potential clinical significance (possible mechanism in parentheses where appropriate)—not necessarily inclusive (» = major clinical significance):

» Estrogen-containing therapies
(should not be used with anastrozole; concomitant use may diminish anastrozole pharmacologic action)

» Tamoxifen
(should not be co-administered; concomitant use resulted in 27% reduction of anastrozole plasma levels compared to anastrozole alone)

Laboratory value alterations
The following have been selected on the basis of their potential clinical significance (possible effect in parentheses where appropriate)—not necessarily inclusive (» = major clinical significance).

With physiology/laboratory test values
Alanine aminotransferase (ALT [SGPT]), serum and
Alkaline phosphatase, serum and
Aspartate aminotransferase (AST [SGOT]), serum and
Gamma glutamyl transferase, serum
(values may be increased up to three times, especially in patients with liver metastases)

Bone mineral density [BMD]
(anastrozole may cause a reduction in BMD because it lowers circulating estrogen levels; ATAC trial bone study demonstrated that patients receiving anastrozole had a mean decrease in both lumbar spine and total hip BMD compared to baseline)

Cholesterol, serum, total and
Low-density lipoprotein (LDL), serum
(concentrations may be increased)

Medical considerations/Contraindications
The medical considerations/contraindications included have been selected on the basis of their potential clinical significance (reasons given in parentheses where appropriate)—not necessarily inclusive (» = major clinical significance).

Except under special circumstances, this medication should not be used when the following medical problem exists:
» Hypersensitivity to anastrozole or any of the excipients

Side/Adverse Effects

The following side/adverse effects have been selected on the basis of their potential clinical significance (possible signs and symptoms in parentheses where appropriate)—not necessarily inclusive:

Those indicating need for medical attention
Incidence more frequent
Chest pain; dyspnea (shortness of breath); ***edema, peripheral*** (swelling of feet or lower legs)

Incidence less frequent
Anemia (unusual tiredness or weakness); ***hypertension*** (dizziness, severe; continuing headache)—usually asymptomatic; ***leukopenia, with or without infection*** (fever or chills; cough or hoarseness; lower back or side pain; painful or difficult urination; sore throat)—usually asymptomatic; ***thromboembolism*** (sudden shortness of breath); ***thrombophlebitis*** (pain or tenderness in leg or foot; blue color in leg or foot; swelling of leg or foot); ***vaginal hemorrhage*** (heavy vaginal bleeding)

Incidence not determined—Observed during clinical practice; estimates of frequency can not be determined
Anaphylaxis (cough; difficulty swallowing; dizziness; fast heartbeat; hives; itching, puffiness or swelling of the eyelids or around the eyes, face, lips or tongue; shortness of breath; skin rash; tightness in chest; unusual tiredness or weakness; wheezing); ***angioedema*** (large, hive-like swelling on face, eyelids, lips, tongue, throat, hands, legs, feet, sex organs); ***erythema multiforme*** (blistering, peeling, loosening of skin; chills; cough; diarrhea; fever; itching; joint or muscle pain; red irritated eyes; sore throat; sores, ulcers, or white spots in mouth or on lips; unusual tiredness or weakness); ***Stevens-Johnson syndrome***

(blistering, peeling, loosening of skin; chills; cough; diarrhea; itching; joint or muscle pain; red irritated eyes; red skin lesions, often with a purple center; sore throat; sores, ulcers, or white spots in mouth or on lips; unusual tiredness or weakness); ***urticaria*** (hives or welts; itching; redness of skin; skin rash)

Those indicating need for medical attention only if they continue or are bothersome

Incidence more frequent

Asthenia (weakness); ***anorexia*** (loss of appetite; weight loss); ***back pain; bone pain; cough; constipation; depression*** (mood or mental changes); ***dizziness; dry mouth; flushing*** (feeling of warmth; redness of face and neck); ***gastrointestinal disturbances, including abdominal pain, diarrhea, nausea, or vomiting; headache; hot flashes; increased appetite; pain; pelvic pain; pharyngitis*** (body aches or pain; congestion; cough; dryness or soreness of throat; fever; hoarseness; runny nose; tender, swollen glands in neck; trouble in swallowing; voice changes); ***skin rash; sweating***

Incidence less frequent

Anxiety and confusion; arthralgia (joint pain); ***breast pain; bronchitis*** (cough producing mucus; difficulty breathing; shortness of breath; tightness in chest; wheezing); ***flu syndrome*** (chills; cough; diarrhea; fever; general feeling of discomfort or illness; headache; joint pain; loss of appetite; muscle aches and pains; nausea; runny nose; shivering; sore throat; sweating; trouble sleeping; unusual tiredness or weakness; vomiting); ***insomnia*** (sleeplessness; trouble sleeping; unable to sleep); ***myalgia*** (muscle pain); ***nervousness; paresthesia*** (numbness or tingling sensation of hands and feet); ***pruritus*** (itchy skin); ***sinusitis or rhinitis*** (stuffy nose); ***somnolence*** (sleepiness or unusual drowsiness); ***vaginal dryness; weight gain***

Incidence not determined—Observed during clinical practice; estimates of frequency can not be determined

Joint pain and stiffness

Those not indicating need for medical attention

Incidence less frequent

Alopecia (loss of hair)

Overdose

For more information on the management of overdose or unintentional ingestion, **contact a Poison Control Center** (see *Poison Control Center Listing*).

Note: Clinical trials have shown doses of 60 mg given in a single dose to male participants and doses up to 10 mg have been given to postmenopausal women with breast cancer and have been well tolerated. A single dose that results in life-threatening symptoms has not been established.

Treatment of overdose

Treatment is essentially symptomatic and supportive and may consist of the following:

Note: In the treatment of the overdose it is important to note that multiple agents may have been taken by the patient.

- Emptying the stomach via induction of emesis if patient is alert.
- Hemodialysis may be beneficial.

Supportive care—

General supportive care such as monitoring vital signs and careful patient observation is suggested.

Patients in whom intentional overdose is confirmed or suspected should be referred for psychiatric consultation.

Patient Consultation

As an aid to patient consultation, refer to *Advice for the Patient, Anastrozole (Systemic)*.

In providing consultation, consider emphasizing the following selected information (» = major clinical significance):

Before using taking this medication

» Conditions affecting use, especially:

Hypersensitivity to anastrozole or any of its excipients

Pregnancy—Before starting treatment with anastrozole, pregnancy must be excluded. If anastrozole is used during pregnancy, or if the patient becomes pregnant while receiving this drug, the patient should be apprised of the potential hazard to the fetus or potential risk for loss of pregnancy.

Breast-feeding—Caution should be exercised when administering anastrazole to a nursing woman

Proper use of this medication

Importance of taking medication only as directed by physician; not taking more medication or more frequently than as ordered by physician

Importance of continuing medication even if nausea, vomiting, or diarrhea occurs

» Proper dosing

» Proper storage

Precautions while using this medication

Importance of close monitoring by physician

Side/adverse effects

Signs of potential side effects, especially chest pain; dyspnea; peripheral edema; anemia; hypertension; leukopenia, with or without infection; thromboembolism; thrombophlebitis; or vaginal hemorrhage

Signs of potential side effects observed during clinical practice, especially anaphylaxis, angioedema, erythema multiforme, Stevens-Johnson syndrome, or urticaria

Possibility of hair loss

General Dosing Information

Patients receiving anastrozole should be under supervision of a physician experienced in cancer chemotherapy.

Dosing adjustments are not necessary for patients with mild-to-moderate hepatic impairment because plasma concentrations of anastrozole in these patients remain within the limit found in patients with normal hepatic function. It is recommended, however, that these patients be monitored for adverse effects.

Anastrozole has no effect on cortisol or aldosterone secretion; therefore, glucocorticoid or mineralocorticoid replacement therapy is not required.

Oral Dosage Forms

ANASTROZOLE TABLETS

Usual adult dose

Carcinoma, breast—

Oral, 1 mg once a day.

For patients with advanced breast cancer, anastrozole should be continued until tumor progression.

For adjuvant treatment of early breast cancer in postmenopausal women, the optimal duration of therapy is unknown. Median duration of therapy at time of data analysis was 31 months; ongoing ATAC trial is planned for five years of treatment.

Note: In patients with mild to moderate hepatic impairment, no changes in dose are recommended. However, patients should be monitored for side effects.

Anastrozole has not been studied in patients with severe hepatic impairment.

In patients with renal impairment, no changes in dose are necessary.

Usual geriatric dose

See *Usual adult dose*.

Strength(s) usually available

U.S.—

1 mg (Rx) [*Arimidex* (lactose; magnesium stearate; hydroxypropylmethylcellulose; polyethylene glycol; povidone; sodium starch glycolate; titanium dioxide)].

Canada—

1 mg (Rx) [*Arimidex* (lactose monohydrate; macrogol 300; magnesium stearate; hypromellose; povidone; sodium starch glycolate; titanium dioxide)].

Packaging and storage

Store between 20 and 25 °C (68 and 77 °F).

Revised: 07/19/2006
Developed: 08/13/1998

ANDROGENS Systemic

This monograph includes information on the following: 1) Fluoxymesterone; 2) Methyltestosterone; 3) Testosterone.

VA CLASSIFICATION (Primary/Secondary):

Fluoxymesterone—HS101/AN900; BL400
Methyltestosterone—HS101/AN900
Testosterone—HS101/AN900
Testosterone cypionate—HS101/AN900; BL400
Testosterone enanthate—HS101/AN900; BL400

Testosterone propionate—HS101/AN900
Testosterone undecanoate—HS101

Note: Controlled substance classification

U.S.: Schedule III

Commonly used brand name(s): *Andriol*[3]*; Andro L.A. 200*[3]*; AndroGel*[3]*; Androderm*[3]*; Android*[2]*; Android-F*[1]*; Andronate 100*[3]*; Andronate 200*[3]*; Andropository 200*[3]*; Andryl 200*[3]*; Delatest*[3]*; Delatestryl*[3]*; Depo-Testosterone*[3]*; Depo-Testosterone Cypionate*[3]*; Depotest*[3]*; Everone 200*[3]*; Halotestin*[1]*; Malogen in Oil*[3]*; Metandren*[2]*; ORETON Methyl*[2]*; Scheinpharm Testone-Cyp*[3]*; T-Cypionate*[3]*; Testamone 100*[3]*; Testaqua*[3]*; Testex*[3]*; Testoderm*[3]*; Testoderm TTS*[3]*; Testoderm with Adhesives*[3]*; Testopel Pellets*[3]*; Testred*[2]*; Testred Cypionate 200*[3]*; Testrin-P.A*[3]*; Virilon*[2]*; Virilon IM*[3].

Note: For a listing of dosage forms and brand names by country availability, see *Dosage Forms* section(s).

Category

Androgen—Fluoxymesterone; Methyltestosterone; Testosterone; Testosterone Undecanoate.

Antineoplastic—Fluoxymesterone; Methyltestosterone; Testosterone.

Antianemic—Fluoxymesterone; Testosterone Cypionate; Testosterone Enanthate

Indications

Note: Bracketed information in the *Indications* section refers to uses that are not included in U.S. product labeling.

General Considerations

Whenever long-term therapy is needed in men, testosterone or a testosterone ester is preferred over the oral methylated androgens (fluoxymesterone and methyltestosterone) because hepatotoxicity is less likely to occur.

Accepted

Androgen deficiency, due to primary or secondary hypogonadism (treatment)—Androgens are primarily indicated in males as replacement therapy when congenital or acquired endogenous androgen absence or deficiency is associated with primary or secondary hypogonadism. Primary hypogonadism includes conditions such as: testicular failure due to cryptorchidism, bilateral torsion, orchitis, or vanishing testis syndrome; inborn errors in testosterone biosynthesis; or bilateral orchidectomy. Hypogonadotropic hypogonadism (secondary hypogonadism) conditions include gonadotropin-releasing hormone (GnRH) deficiency or pituitary-hypothalamic injury as a result of surgery, tumors, trauma, or radiation and are the most common forms of hypogonadism seen in older adults. Dosage adjustment is needed to accommodate individual clinical requirements for such life changes as induction of puberty, development of secondary sexual characteristics, impotence due to testicular failure, or infertility due to oligospermia.

Puberty, delayed male (treatment)—A 6-month-or-shorter course of an androgen is indicated for induction of puberty in patients with familial delayed puberty, a condition characterized by spontaneous, nonpathologic, late-onset puberty, if the patient does not respond to psychological treatment. Testosterone transdermal products are not presently indicated for treatment of delayed male puberty.

Carcinoma, breast (treatment)—Androgens are indicated as secondary or tertiary hormonal treatment for palliation of metastatic breast cancer in women who have been postmenopausal for 1 to 5 years or who are surgically menopausal, who have hormone receptor–positive tumors, or who have previously demonstrated a response to hormone therapy. Androgens have also been used in the treatment of metastatic breast cancer as a supplement to chemotherapy. Transdermal testosterone systems and subcutaneous implants are not indicated for these uses and should not be used by females.

[Anemia (treatment)][1]—Fluoxymesterone and testosterone cypionate or enanthate have been used to treat certain types of anemia, such as aplastic anemia, myelofibrosis, myelosclerosis, agnogenic myeloid metaplasia, and hypoplastic anemias caused by malignancy or myelotoxic drugs.

[Constitutional delay in growth (treatment)][1]—Androgens are used in the treatment of constitutional delay in growth. However, they are no longer considered the treatment of choice for most patients.

[Gender change, female-to-male][1]—Testosterone is used for the development and maintenance of secondary sexual characteristics in female-to-male transsexuals.

[Lichen sclerosus (treatment adjunct)][1]—Extemporaneously compounded topical testosterone is used for the treatment of itching resulting from lichen sclerosus.

[Microphallus (treatment)][1]—Intramuscular preparations of testosterone and testosterone esters, and extemporaneously compounded topical testosterone are used in the treatment of microphallus.

Acceptance not established

Although testosterone cypionate and testosterone undecanoate are indicated in Canada for the following conditions if they are not due to primary or secondary hypogonadism, further studies are needed to define the role, safety, and efficacy of androgens to treat *male climacteric symptoms* and *male infertility due to oligospermia*. Further studies are also needed to assess androgens as adjunctive treatment for *male or female osteoporosis*.

Unaccepted

Use of androgens to enhance athletic performance is illegal. Increases in muscle mass and muscle strength can be sufficient to enhance athletic performance. However, the risk of unwanted effects, such as suppression of spermatogenesis, testicular atrophy, menstrual disturbances, virilization in females, peliosis hepatis (hepatic parenchymal injury), hepatotoxicity, potential adverse effects on cardiovascular health, and development of hepatic cancer, counter athletic benefits received from androgens and make their use in athletes inappropriate. Furthermore, behavioral disturbances, including aggressive or violent behavior, have been reported with supraphysiological self-administered doses in athletes.

Androgens are not recommended for accelerating the healing of fractures or shortening the duration of postsurgical convalescence.

The use of androgens for the prevention of postpartum breast engorgement is not recommended. In most patients, postpartum breast engorgement is a benign, self-limiting condition that may respond to breast support and mild analgesics, such as acetaminophen and ibuprofen. Evidence supporting the efficacy of androgens for this indication is lacking.

---

[1]Not included in Canadian product labeling.

Pharmacology/Pharmacokinetics

Physicochemical characteristics

Description—

Testosterone implants are compressed crystalline testosterone, cylindrically shaped, measuring 3.2 millimeters (mm) in diameter and 8 to 9 mm in length.

Two types of testosterone transdermal systems are available:

Drug-in-adhesive matrix on film (matrix-type)—*Testoderm* contains three layers: a polyester liner that must be removed before using; an adhesive matrix containing testosterone; and the back outermost layer, a flexible polyurethane protective film with epoxy resin. *Testoderm with Adhesives* incorporates five additional adhesive strips onto the adhesive matrix of the drug film.

Membrane-controlled drug reservoir (reservoir-type)—*Androderm* contains: a protective liner that must be removed before using; a disc, matted between adhesive layers, that protects the central drug reservoir and is removed before using; an adhesive layer; a membrane providing extended release of testosterone; a drug reservoir holding the testosterone, glycerin, glycerol monooleate, methyl laurate, purified water and alcohol gelled with an acrylic acid copolymer; and the back outermost layer, a polyester protective film. *Testoderm TTS* is similar but does not contain the protective disc.

The matrix-type transdermal system is thinner than the reservoir-type.

Transdermal testosterone gel is a clear, colorless hydroalcoholic gel containing 1% testosterone. The gel provides continuous transdermal delivery of testosterone for 24 hours following a single application.

Chemical Group—

Naturally occurring androgens include testosterone.

Semi-synthetic androgens are testosterone cypionate, testosterone enanthate, and testosterone propionate.

Synthetic androgens include fluoxymesterone and methyltestosterone.

Oral methylated androgens (17-alpha-alkylated androgens) include fluoxymesterone and methyltestosterone.

Molecular weight—

Fluoxymesterone: 336.45.
Methyltestosterone: 302.46.
Testosterone: 288.43.
Testosterone cypionate: 412.62.
Testosterone enanthate: 400.6.
Testosterone propionate: 344.5.
Testosterone undecanoate: 456.7.

Mechanism of action/Effect

Endogenous plasma testosterone is maintained and regulated by gonadotropins within a normal range by a negative feedback system involving the hypothalamus and pituitary. Supraphysiologic doses of testosterone can effectively suppress the gonadotropins and spermatogenesis in eugonadal men.

Androgens are highly lipid-soluble and enter cells of target tissues by passive diffusion. Testosterone or 5-alpha-dihydrotestosterone (DHT), a metabolite produced from testosterone by the enzyme 5-alpha-reductase, binds to an intracellular androgen receptor. The hormone receptor complex translocates into the nucleus and attaches to specific hormone receptor elements on the chromosome to initiate or suppress transcription and protein synthesis. Testosterone can produce estrogenic effects as a result of its conversion to estrogen.

Androgen deficiency—

Physiologic concentrations of androgens stimulate spermatogenesis and male sexual maturity at puberty, and develop and maintain male secondary sexual characteristics. These effects include growth and maturation of the prostate, seminal vesicles, penis, and scrotum; male hair and muscle-to-fat body mass distribution; enlargement of the larynx; and thickening of vocal cords. In children, exogenous androgens increase linear bone growth rates and help fuse the epiphyseal growth centers. An increase in bone growth rate can also correspond to a disproportionate advancement of bone maturation.

Microphallus—

Intramuscular administration of testosterone or testosterone esters or local application of testosterone propionate ointment may result in an increase in circulating serum concentrations of DHT, which is principally responsible for phallic growth.

Lichen sclerosus—

The signs and symptoms of lichen sclerosus (vulvar itching, abnormal vulvar skin histology) may be the result of a deficiency of 5-alpha-reductase activity and subsequently reduced local DHT concentrations. Local application of testosterone propionate ointment may correct this deficiency in 5-alpha-reductase activity. Testosterone may cause a slight increase in local DHT concentrations, which may induce 5-alpha-reductase activity, and further increase local DHT concentrations.

Antianemic—

Androgens stimulate the production of red blood cells by enhancing production of erythropoietic stimulating factors.

Absorption

Methyltestosterone—

Absorbed from oral mucosa and gastrointestinal tract.

Matrix-type transdermal system: The patch must be applied to scrotal skin (5 to 30 times more permeable to testosterone than other skin sites) to produce an adequate testosterone serum concentration. A matrix transdermal system will not produce adequate serum testosterone concentrations if applied to nonscrotal skin. Serum testosterone concentrations reach a plateau at 3 to 4 weeks and, although testosterone is absorbed throughout a 24-hour period, concentrations do not simulate the circadian rhythm of endogenous testosterone in normal males. Interpatient variation in total plasma testosterone concentrations is high, approximately 35 to 49%; the average variation of concentration in a patient is approximately 30 to 41%.

Reservoir-type transdermal system: Patients should avoid applying the reservoir-type patch to scrotal skin. The reservoir transdermal systems have similar sites of application, but manufacturers, depending on their clinical studies, recommend different sites and times for patch application. Since the reservoir patches show differences in time to peak effect, applying them either in the morning or at night, depending on the reservoir transdermal system and manufacturer instructions, achieves normal serum testosterone concentrations of circadian rhythm, peaking in the morning and decreasing throughout the rest of the day to plateau at night. Normal serum testosterone concentrations are reached during the first day of dosing, and drug accumulation does not occur with repeated applications.

For *Androderm*—Using two transdermal systems that deliver 2.5 mg of testosterone per day each, hypogonadal men absorb 4 to 5 mg of testosterone in 24 hours, and, if the patches are applied at 10 p.m. to the abdomen, back, thighs, or upper arms, concentrations simulate the circadian rhythm of endogenous testosterone in normal males. Similar results are expected with use of a single 5-mg patch. Hypogonadal men applying the patch to the chest or shin absorb 3 to 4 mg of testosterone in 24 hours.

For *Testoderm TTS*—Studies of the three application sites (upper buttocks, arm, and back) showed that when a 5-mg patch was applied at 8 a.m., testosterone concentrations simulated the circadian rhythm of endogenous testosterone in normal males.

Subcutaneous implant: Approximately one third of the testosterone dose is absorbed in the first month, one fourth in the second month, and one sixth in the third month. Absorption continues until the implant completely dissolves, which may take up to 6 months.

Testosterone gel: In a study with the 10-gram dose (to deliver 100 mg testosterone), all patients showed an increase in serum testosterone within 30 minutes, and 8 of 9 patients had a serum testosterone concentration within the normal range by 4 hours after the initial application. Absorption of testosterone into the blood continues for the entire 24-hour dosing interval. Serum concentrations approximate the steady state level by the end of the first 24 hours and are at steady state by the second or third day of dosing.

Testosterone—

Protein binding

Testosterone—Very high (approximately 99%; 80% to sex hormone-binding globulin [SHBG], 19% to albumin, and 1% free). The metabolite DHT has greater affinity for SHBG than does testosterone.

Biotransformation

Hepatic.

Fluoxymesterone; methyltestosterone—Presence of 17-alpha alkyl group reduces susceptibility to hepatic enzyme degradation, which slows metabolism and allows oral administration.

Testosterone—Free testosterone is further converted into two of the major active metabolites, DHT and estradiol. Orally administered testosterone, but not testosterone undecanoate, undergoes nearly complete first-pass metabolism; both intramuscular and transdermal administration avoid first-pass metabolism.

Oral: In first-pass metabolism, 90% of the oral testosterone dose is metabolized primarily to etiocholanolone, androsterone, and androstanediol, which are then conjugated. Unlike oral testosterone, oral testosterone undecanoate does not undergo hepatic first-pass metabolism.

Injection: Testosterone esters (cypionate, enanthate, propionate) first undergo hydrolysis of the ester to the active form, free testosterone.

Matrix-type transdermal systems: A threefold increase in DHT serum concentrations has been reported with the matrix-type testosterone transdermal system applied to scrotal skin due to high conversion to DHT by 5-alpha-reductase in the scrotal tissue. Normal ranges of estradiol concentrations are produced; however, 3 of 72 male patients using the matrix patch experienced sporadic elevations of serum estradiol concentrations that were not associated with feminizing adverse effects.

Reservoir-type transdermal systems: The reservoir-type patch applied to nonscrotal skin produced normal DHT and estradiol serum concentrations.

Testosterone gel: DHT concentrations increased in parallel with testosterone concentrations during testosterone gel treatment. After 180 days of treatment, mean DHT concentrations were within the normal range with a 5–gram dose of *Androgel* and were about 7% above the normal range after a 10–gram dose. The mean steady state DHT/T ratio during 180 days of treatment remained within normal limits and ranged from 0.23 to 0.29 (5 grams/day) and from 0.27 to 0.33 (10 grams/day).

Half-life

The activity of testosterone in many tissues appears to be dependent on its reduction to DHT and the binding capacity of sex hormone-binding globulin (high in prepubertal children, declining through puberty and adulthood, and increasing again later in life).

Fluoxymesterone—Approximately 9.2 hours.

Methyltestosterone—2.5 to 3.5 hours.

Testosterone (intramuscular injection and matrix-type and reservoir-type transdermal systems and transdermal gel)—10 to 100 minutes (plasma).

Testosterone cypionate (intramuscular)—Approximately 8 days.

Time to peak concentration

Methyltestosterone—

Tablets: 2 hours.

Testosterone undecanoate—

Capsules: 4 to 5 hours.

Testosterone—

Matrix-type transdermal systems: At steady state, approximately 2 to 4 hours after application.

Reservoir-type transdermal systems:

For *Androderm*: Approximately 6 to 10 hours after application.When the reservoir-type transdermal system was applied to the back, peak serum testosterone concentrations were achieved 6 to 12 hours after the application.

For *Testoderm TTS*: At steady state, approximately 4 hours after application.

For *AndroGel*: Approximately 2 hours after application.

Peak serum concentration

For testosterone transdermal systems—

For matrix-type:

Testosterone, serum concentration—593 nanograms of testosterone per deciliter (nanograms/dL) (20.6 nanomoles per liter [nanomoles/L]), mean serum concentration. At steady state (up to 3 weeks), approximately 60% of 30 hypogonadal males in a study had maximum testosterone serum concentrations reaching higher than 500 nanograms/dL (17.3 nanomoles/L, ranging from 11.5 to 44.9 nanomoles/L).

DHT, serum concentration—Mean serum concentrations were elevated for the matrix-type transdermal system (range, 134 to 162 nanograms/dL [5.2 to 6.3 nanomoles/L] compared with the normal range of 30 to 85 nanograms/dL [1.2 to 3.3 nanomoles/L]). One 6-year study of hypogonadal men using scrotal transdermal systems reported normal serum testosterone concentrations from 306 to 1031 nanograms/dL (10.6 and 35.8 nanomoles/L) with the elevated DHT serum concentrations remaining stable.

Estrogen, serum concentration—Serum concentrations of estrogen in patch users were normal. However, sporadic elevations above the normal range occurred in 3 of 72 patients using the matrix patch, but were not associated with feminizing side effects.

For reservoir-type:

Unlike the matrix-type system, which is placed on the scrotum, the reservoir-type system showed an average DHT and estrogen serum concentrations comparable to that of normal men.

Testosterone, serum concentrations—

For *Androderm*, beginning with a mean serum testosterone baseline of 76 nanograms/dL (2.6 nanomoles/L):

2.5 mg patch—424 nanograms/dL (14.7 nanomoles/L), average peak serum concentration (C_{avg}).

5 mg patch—584 nanograms/dL (20.2 nanomoles/L), C_{avg}; in another study of hypogonadal men (unknown baseline), 753 ± 276 nanograms/dL (26.1 nanomoles/L), mean peak serum concentration (C_{max}).

7.5 mg patch—766 nanograms/dL (26.6 nanomoles/L), C_{avg}.

For *Testoderm TTS*, beginning with a mean serum testosterone baseline of 150 nanograms/dL (5.2 nanomoles/L):

5 mg patch—366 nanograms/dL (12.7 nanomoles/L), C_{avg}; 462 to 499 nanograms/dL (16 to 17.3 nanomoles/L), mean C_{max}.

For transdermal gel:

Mean peak concentrations at steady state: 5 grams—830 ± 347 ng/dL; 7.5 grams—901 ± 471 ng/dL; and 10 grams—1083 ± 434 ng/dL.

Duration of action

Testosterone—Dependent upon the ester, dosage form, and route of administration.

Injection: Enanthate and cypionate esters are longer acting than propionate ester and base.

Oral: Undecanoate ester action continues for about 10 hours.

Subcutaneous implants: Three to 4 months, but may continue for 6 months.

Transdermal systems (matrix-type and reservoir-type): At 22 hours after application, serum testosterone concentration gradually falls to 60 to 80% of the peak serum concentration. On removal of the systems, testosterone serum concentration declines to baseline within 2 hours.

Transdermal gel: When treatment is discontinued after achieving steady state, serum testosterone levels remain in the normal range for 24 to 48 hours but return to their pretreatment levels by the fifth day after the last application.

Elimination

Generally renal excretion of metabolites. Approximately 90% of the administered dose is excreted in the urine, primarily as glucuronide or sulfated conjugates of the metabolites. Some fecal excretion due to enterohepatic circulation.

Fluoxymesterone—Less than 5% is excreted in urine as free steroid and glucuronide conjugate over a 24-hour period after oral doses of 20 to 200 mg.

Testosterone—Approximately 6% of dose is excreted in the feces, primarily in unconjugated form.

Testosterone undecanoate—Approximately 77 to 93% of an orally administered dose is excreted in the urine and feces within 3 to 4 days.

Precautions to Consider

Cross-sensitivity and/or related problems

Patients allergic to testosterone that is chemically synthesized from soy may also be allergic to some testosterone-containing products.

Carcinogenicity/Tumorigenicity

Hepatic neoplasms have been associated with long-term, high-dose androgen therapy in humans; some cases were irreversible after androgen withdrawal. This effect is more likely with oral methylated androgens.

It has been suggested that some strains of female mice injected with testosterone are at greater risk of hepatoma. When liver tumors were chemically induced in rats, testosterone increased the number of tumors and decreased tumor cell differentiation.

For testosterone—Studies in female mice given subcutaneous implants of testosterone showed an increase in cervical-uterine tumors. Some of these tumors metastasized. This effect was not seen in mice and rats given subcutaneous injections of testosterone or in rats given subcutaneous implants.

Pregnancy/Reproduction

Fertility—In males, oligospermia, azoospermia, or reduced sperm function or ejaculatory volume resulting in possible infertility may occur during high-dose therapy with androgens if spermatogenesis is suppressed by a negative feedback mechanism. In females treated with androgens, amenorrhea may result, impairing fertility. In both females and males, fertility usually returns following cessation of therapy in females and dosage reduction or discontinuation in males.

Pregnancy—Androgens are contraindicated during pregnancy. Studies in humans have shown that androgens cause masculinization of the external genitalia of the female fetus, including clitoromegaly, abnormal vaginal development, and fusion of genital folds to form a scrotal-like structure. The degree of masculinization is dose-related.

FDA Pregnancy Category X.

Breast-feeding

It is not known whether androgens are distributed into breast milk. Problems in humans have not been documented. However, androgens are rarely used by breast-feeding women and are not recommended. Potential adverse effects in infants include precocious sexual development in males and virilization of external genitalia in females.

Pediatrics

Androgens should be used with caution in children and adolescents who are still growing because of possible premature epiphyseal closure in males and females, precocious sexual development in prepubertal males, or virilization in females. Skeletal maturation should be monitored at 6-month intervals by an x-ray of the hand and wrist. *AndroGel* or *Testoderm* have not been evaluated in male children up to 18 years of age. *Androderm* has not been evaluated in children up to 15 years of age.

Geriatrics

Treatment of male patients 50 years of age and older with androgens should be preceded by a thorough examination of the prostate and baseline measurement of prostate-specific antigen serum concentration, since androgens may increase the risk of hyperplasia or may stimulate the growth of occult prostatic carcinoma. Periodic evaluation of prostate function also should be performed during the course of therapy.

For the testosterone transdermal system (reservoir-type)—No age-related differences in men up to 65 years of age were seen in clinical trials; however, absorption was 20% lower when the *Androderm* transdermal system was applied to the backs of men between 65 and 79 years of age.

Drug interactions and/or related problems

The following drug interactions and/or related problems have been selected on the basis of their potential clinical significance (possible mechanism in parentheses where appropriate)—not necessarily inclusive (» = major clinical significance):

Note: Combinations containing any of the following medications, depending on the amount present, may also interact with this medication.

» Anticoagulants, coumarin- or indandione-derivative
(anticoagulant effect may be increased because of decreased procoagulant factor concentration caused by alteration of procoagulant factor synthesis or catabolism and increased receptor affinity for the anticoagulant; anticoagulant dosage adjustment may be required during and following concurrent use)

Antidiabetic agents, sulfonylurea or
Insulin
(androgens may increase or decrease blood glucose; doses of insulin or antidiabetic sulfonylurea medications may need to be adjusted, especially if hypoglycemia occurs)

Corticosteroids or
Corticotropin
(testosterone may contribute to the edema that can occur with administration of corticotropin or corticosteroids; caution is recommended during concomitant administration in patients who have special risks, such as patients who have cardiac or hepatic disease)

Cyclosporine
(methyltestosterone has been reported to increase plasma concentrations of cyclosporine and may increase the risk of nephrotoxicity; other androgens may have the same effect)

» Hepatotoxic medications, other (see *Appendix II*)
(may result in an increased incidence of hepatotoxicity; patients should be carefully monitored, especially those undergoing long-term therapy or those with a history of liver disease)

Human growth hormone (somatrem or somatropin)
(use of excessive doses of androgens in prepubertal males may accelerate epiphyseal maturation, although supplemental use of androgens may be necessary in patients with androgen deficiency to continue the growth response to human growth hormone)

Oxyphenbutazone
(concurrent administration of oxyphenbutazone and androgens may result in elevated serum levels of oxyphenbutazone)

Propranolol
(testosterone cypionate increases the clearance of propranolol; appropriate patient monitoring may be needed)

Laboratory value alterations

The following have been selected on the basis of their potential clinical significance (possible effect in parentheses where appropriate)—not necessarily inclusive (» = major clinical significance).

With diagnostic test results

Fasting blood sugar (FBS) and
Glucose tolerance test
(may be altered)

With physiology/laboratory test values

Alkaline phosphatase
(value may be increased)

Aspartate aminotransferase (AST [SGOT]), serum and
Calcium, chloride, inorganic phosphates, potassium, and sodium, serum and
17-Ketosteroid (17-KS), urine
(concentrations may be increased)

Bilirubin
(serum concentrations may be increased)

Clotting factors II, V, VII, and X
(may be suppressed)

Corticosteroid-binding globulin
(concentration may be decreased; free hormone concentration remains unchanged)

Creatinine
(serum concentrations may be increased; effect usually lasts up to 2 weeks after discontinuation of therapy)

Follicle-stimulating hormone (FSH) and
Luteinizing hormone (LH)
(serum concentrations may decrease)
(in one small study that used the testosterone transdermal system [reservoir-type], the LH serum concentrations decreased to normal within 6 to 12 months for 48% of the males with hypergonadotropic hypogonadism. For some men, the LH concentration may continue to be high despite normal testosterone concentrations)

Glucose
(blood concentrations may be increased or decreased, especially with pharmacologic doses or oral formulations; physiologic doses of androgens rarely cause hypoglycemia or hyperglycemia)

Hamster ova penetration test (HOPT) and
Spermatozoa count
(may be severely reduced at high doses)

Hematocrit and
Hemoglobin
(values may be increased with high-dose or long-term therapy)

High density lipoproteins (HDL)
(serum concentrations may be decreased, especially with pharmacologic doses and oral formulations)

Low density lipoproteins (LDL)
(serum concentrations may be increased, especially with pharmacologic doses and oral formulations; one study showed a slight reduction with testosterone)

Sex steroid–binding globulin
(concentration may be decreased; free hormone concentration remains unchanged)

Thyroxine-binding globulin
(may be decreased, resulting in decreased total T_4 serum concentrations and increased resin uptake of T_3 and T_4; free thyroid hormone levels remain unchanged, showing no clinical evidence of thyroid impairment)

Medical considerations/Contraindications

The medical considerations/contraindications included have been selected on the basis of their potential clinical significance (reasons given in parentheses where appropriate)—not necessarily inclusive (» = major clinical significance).

Except under special circumstances, these medications should not be used when the following medical problems exist:

» Breast cancer in males or
» Prostate cancer, known or suspected
(tumor growth may be promoted)

» Hypersensitivity to anabolic steroids, androgens, or any of its ingredients of this medicine

Risk-benefit should be considered when the following medical problems exist:

» Cardiac failure or
Cardiac function impairment or
» Cardiorenal disease, severe or
Edema or
Hepatic function impairment or
» Nephritis or
» Nephrosis or
Renal function impairment
(may cause fluid retention, resulting in edema with or without congestive heart failure; diuretics may be required before and during therapy)

Coronary artery disease or
» Myocardial infarction, history of
(may be worsened, due to hypercholesterolemic effects of androgens)

Diabetes mellitus
(use of androgens may increase or decrease blood glucose and produce an unfavorable profile of lipoprotein metabolism in patients without diabetes mellitus; a more exaggerated response can be expected in patients with diabetes mellitus, especially in obese patients. Effects may be greater for oral formulations or when pharmacologic doses of androgens are used. Doses of insulin or antidiabetic sulfonylurea medications may need to be adjusted, especially if hypoglycemia occurs. Physiologic doses of androgens rarely cause hypoglycemia or hyperglycemia)

» Hepatic function impairment
(biotransformation of androgens may be impaired, resulting in increased elimination half-life and increase in the incidence of gynecomastia)

» Hypercalcemia, due to metastatic breast cancer
(may be exacerbated)

» Prostatic hyperplasia, benign with urethral obstructive symptoms
(further enlargement may occur)

Patient monitoring

The following may be especially important in patient monitoring (other tests may be warranted in some patients, depending on condition; » = major clinical significance):

Bone age determinations
(x-rays of hand and wrist are recommended every 6 months for children and growing adolescents to determine rate of bone maturation and effects on epiphyseal centers)

Cholesterol and/or
High density lipoproteins and
Low density lipoproteins
(serum profile determinations are recommended prior to initiation of therapy and, in some patients, at regular intervals during therapy)

Dihydrotestosterone, serum or
Testosterone, total, serum
(concentrations may be determined to ensure proper dosing; when done for *Testoderm* products, measurements are recommended after the patch has been used for 3 to 4 weeks and should be performed 2 to 4 hours after patch application)

Hematocrit determinations and
Hemoglobin
(recommended at regular intervals in patients receiving prolonged therapy or high doses of androgens to check for possible erythrocytosis)

Hepatic function determinations
(recommended at regular intervals during therapy, especially with oral methylated androgens)

Prostate-specific antigen and
Prostatic acid phosphatase
(recommended at regular intervals during therapy)

For treatment of breast carcinoma

Alkaline phosphatase, serum values and
Physical examination and
X-rays of known or suspected metastases
(recommended at regular intervals during therapy to monitor objective evidence of tumor response)

Calcium
(measurement of serum concentrations recommended at regular intervals in women with disseminated breast carcinoma)

For gender change androgen therapy

» Luteinizing hormone
(measurement of serum concentrations is recommended every 6 months to monitor success of therapy)

» Alanine aminotransferase (ALT [SGPT])
(measurement of serum values is recommended every 6 months to monitor for adverse effects)

Side/Adverse Effects

Note: The side effects of testosterone enanthate and testosterone cypionate cannot be quickly reversed by discontinuing medication due to the long durations of action of these medications.

Replacement doses of androgens return the prostate to normal size and function for hypogonadal males. Although there is no evidence that exogenous androgens can induce development of prostate carcinoma, long-term androgen therapy or normal prostate activity carries a theoretical risk of prostatic hyperplasia or growth of occult prostatic carcinoma.

Behavioral disturbances, including aggressive or violent behavior, have been reported with self-administered supraphysiologic doses in athletes.

The following side/adverse effects have been selected on the basis of their potential clinical significance (possible signs and symptoms in parentheses where appropriate)—not necessarily inclusive:

Those indicating need for medical attention

Incidence more frequent

In females only

Amenorrhea or oligomenorrhea (absence of or unusual menstrual periods); ***virilism*** (acne; decreased breast size; enlarged clitoris; hoarseness or deepening of voice; male pattern baldness; oily skin; unnatural and excessive hair growth)

Note: *Virilism* may occur with usual systemic doses, as well as with excessive doses of topical testosterone. Hoarseness or deepening of voice and enlarged clitoris may not be reversible even after the medication has been discontinued. Virilism has also been reported in the female sexual partner of a male patient during his treatment with topical testosterone. The reservoir-type of testosterone transdermal system has a protective film that makes testosterone transfer between sexual partners unlikely.

In males only

Bladder irritability or urinary tract infection (frequent urge to urinate)—may be asymptomatic; ***blistering of skin, local; breast soreness; erythema or pruritus, local*** (itching of skin under skin patch, mild to severe; redness of skin under patch or at implant insertion site, mild to severe); ***gynecomastia*** (enlargement of breasts); ***penile erections, frequent or continuing*** (penile erections lasting up to 4 hours); ***priapism*** (painful erections lasting longer than 4 hours)—sign of excessive dosage

Note: *Blistering of skin* occurred as a single incident on one skin site in many patients; in most cases, it occurred when the reservoir-type of testosterone transdermal system was applied to skin over a bony prominence. This effect is less likely if such areas are avoided. It should be treated like a burn.

Medication should be discontinued and the patient given immediate medical attention if *priapism* occurs. If tumescence is not reversed, interruption of blood flow may result in penile tissue ischemia and permanent tissue damage.

In prepubertal males only

Virilism (acne; enlargement of penis; frequent or continuing erections; early growth of pubic hair)

Incidence less frequent

In females and males

Asthenia (lack or loss of strength); ***edema*** (rapid weight gain; swelling of feet or lower legs); ***breast pain; emotional lability*** (crying; depersonalization; dysphoria; euphoria; mental depression; paranoia; quick to react or overreact emotionally; rapidly changing moods); ***erythrocytosis or secondary polycythemia*** (dizziness; flushing or redness of skin; headache, frequent or continuing; unusual bleeding; unusual tiredness)—in severe cases using oral or injection dosage forms; ***gastrointestinal irritation*** (nausea; vomiting); ***headache; hepatic dysfunction, including cholestatic jaundice*** (yellow eyes or skin; itching of skin)—more likely with the oral methylated androgens; ***hypercalcemia*** (confusion; constipation; increased thirst; mental depression; nausea; increased frequency of urination and quantity of urine; unusual tiredness; vomiting)—in females with breast cancer or immobilized patients; ***hypertension*** (high blood pressure)

In males only

Benign prostatic hyperplasia (difficulty urinating); ***burning sensation at transdermal application site***—incidence of 3%; ***contact dermatitis, allergic*** (itching and redness of skin, severe; skin rash, severe)—incidence of 4% with use of testosterone transdermal system (reservoir-type); ***epididymitis, acute, nonspecific*** (chills; pain in scrotum or groin); ***gastrointestinal bleeding*** (black, tarry stools; vomiting of blood or material that looks like coffee grounds); ***induration, local*** (hardening or thickening of skin under patch)—with use of testosterone transdermal system (reservoir-type); ***pain at implant insertion site, continuing***—for subcutaneous implants; ***testis disorder***

Incidence rare

In females and males—more likely with oral or injection dosage forms, usually associated with long-term use or high doses

Depression (mood or mental changes); ***hepatic necrosis*** (abdominal or stomach pain, continuing; black, tarry stools; headache, continuing; malaise, continuing; unpleasant breath odor, continuing; vomiting of blood); ***hepatocellular tumor*** (pain or tenderness in upper abdomen; swelling of abdomen); ***leukopenia*** (fever; sore throat); ***peliosis hepatis*** (continuing loss of appetite; darkened urine; fever; hives; light-colored stools; nausea; purple or red spots on body or inside the mouth or nose; sore throat; vomiting)

Those indicating need for medical attention only if they continue or are bothersome

Incidence less frequent

In females and males

Acne, mild; alopecia (hair loss; thinning of hair); ***decrease or increase in libido; diarrhea; increase in pubic hair growth; infection, pain, redness or other irritation at site of injection***—for intramuscular injection only; ***nervousness; stomach pain; trouble in sleeping***

In males only

Infection, pain, redness, swelling, sores or other skin irritation, local—for transdermal systems; ***testicular atrophy*** (decrease in testicle size)—usually associated with high doses for oral or injection dosage forms

Overdose

For more information on the management of overdose or unintentional ingestion, **contact a poison control center** (see *Poison Control Center Listing*).

Clinical effects of overdose

The following effects have been selected on the basis of their potential clinical significance (possible signs and symptoms in parentheses where appropriate)—not necessarily inclusive:

For testosterone enanthate

Cerebrovascular accident (blurred vision; headache; sudden and severe inability to speak; seizures; slurred speech; temporary blindness; weakness in arm and/or leg on one side of the body, sudden and severe)

Note: One report has described acute overdosage with testosterone enanthate. Testosterone concentrations of up to 11,400 ng/dL were implicated in a cerebrovascular accident.

Treatment of overdose

Patients in whom intentional overdose is confirmed or suspected should be referred for psychiatric consultation.

Patient Consultation

As an aid to patient consultation, refer to *Advice for the Patient, Androgens (Systemic).*

In providing consultation, consider emphasizing the following selected information (» = major clinical significance):

Before using this medication

» Conditions affecting use, especially:

Hypersensitivity to androgens, anabolic steroids, or testosterone chemically synthesized from soy

Carcinogenicity—Hepatocellular carcinoma is associated with long-term, high-dose therapy

Tumorigenicity—Hepatic neoplasms are associated with long-term, high-dose therapy

Fertility—May be severely impaired in males

Pregnancy—Contraindicated for use during pregnancy because of possible masculinization of female fetus

Breast-feeding—Not recommended

Use in children—Cautious use due to effects on growth and sexual development (precocious sexual development in males, virilization in females)

Use in the elderly—Increased risk of prostatic hyperplasia or occult prostatic carcinoma

Other medications, especially anticoagulants (coumarin- or indandione-derivative) or hepatotoxic medications

Other medical problems, especially breast cancer (male), cardiac failure, cardiorenal disease (severe), hepatic function impairment, hypercalcemia due to breast cancer, myocardial infarction (history of), nephritis, nephrosis, prostate cancer (known or suspected), or prostatic hyperplasia

Proper use of this medication

» Importance of not taking or using more medication than the amount prescribed

Understanding difference between the two types of testosterone patches; reading patient directions carefully before using the patch

Taking fluoxymesterone and methyltestosterone with food to minimize possible stomach upset

Proper administration of testosterone transdermal systems

For the matrix-type transdermal system—Applying to dry, clean, and hairless skin of scrotum; may be removed and reapplied after bathing, swimming, showering, or sexual activity

For the reservoir-type transdermal system—Applying *Androderm* to abdomen, back, thighs, or upper arms; rotating site. Applying *Testoderm TTS* to back, arms, or upper buttocks. Not applying the patches to the scrotum, chest, shin, bony prominences, or areas subject to prolonged pressure when sleeping or sitting. Not removing for showering, bathing, swimming, or sexual activity

» Proper dosing

Missed dose: For injection or oral dosage forms—Taking or using as soon as possible; not taking or using if almost time for next dose; not doubling doses

For transdermal patches—If dose is missed or patch falls off after being worn for 12 hours and cannot be reapplied, not using a new patch, returning to regular dosing schedule; not doubling doses

» Proper storage

Precautions while using this medication

Regular visits to physician to check progress during therapy

Diabetics: May alter blood sugar concentrations at high doses; minimal effect at physiologic doses

For testosterone transdermal system (matrix-type)—Checking with doctor if female sexual partner develops mild virilization when male partner uses the scrotal patch

For alcohol based gels, avoid fire, flame, or smoking until the gel is dried. Wait 5 or 6 hours after application to shower or swim.

Side/adverse effects

Signs of potential side effects, especially:

In females only—Amenorrhea, oligomenorrhea, or virilism

In males only—Bladder irritability or urinary tract infection; blistering of skin, local; breast soreness; erythema or pruritus of skin, mild to moderate, local; gynecomastia; penile erections, frequent or continuing; priapism; benign prostatic hyperplasia; burning sensation at transdermal application site; contact dermatitis, allergic; epididymitis, acute, nonspecific; gastrointestinal bleeding; induration, local; pain at implant insertion site, continuing, testis disorder

In prepubertal males only—Virilism

In all patients—Asthenia, breast pain, edema, emotional lability, erythrocytosis or secondary polycythemia, gastrointestinal irritation, headache, hepatic dysfunction, hepatic necrosis, hepatocellular tumor, hypercalcemia (in patients with breast cancer or immobilized patients), hypertension, leukopenia, or peliosis hepatis

General Dosing Information

The dosage and duration of therapy depend on the patient's age, sex, diagnosis, and response to therapy, and the appearance of adverse effects.

It is usually preferable to begin treatment for anemia and carcinoma with full therapeutic doses and to adjust later to individual requirements.

For treatment of delayed puberty

The dosage used in delayed puberty generally is in the lower range of the usual adult dose for androgen replacement therapy and is given for a limited duration, usually 3 to 6 months. The chronologic and skeletal ages should be considered, both in determining the initial dose and in adjusting the dose. After 3 to 6 months of therapy, the medication should be discontinued for 1 to 3 months and x-rays taken to determine the effect on bone growth or maturation.

Various dosage regimens have been used to induce pubertal changes in hypogonadal males. Some physicians prescribe a lower dose initially, gradually increase the dose as puberty progresses, and follow with a maintenance dose, which may be decreased. Other physicians use high initial doses to induce puberty, then decrease to an adjusting maintenance dose as puberty progresses.

Transdermal systems have not been investigated for this use.

For treatment of breast cancer

To determine whether there will be an objective response to antineoplastic therapy, treatment should be continued for at least 3 months, during which time a response to therapy is usually apparent. Therapy should be discontinued if the disease becomes progressive again. If clinical circumstances allow for an observation period, the patient should be observed for a period of improvement known as rebound regression.

Women should be checked for signs of virilization during androgen therapy. Some effects, such as voice changes or clitoromegaly, may not be reversible. A decision should be made by the patient and physician as to how much virilization will be tolerated as a result of androgen therapy. Alternatively, the drug should be discontinued or the dosage reduced. If virilization is to be prevented, medication must be discontinued when signs of mild virilization appear and before the process becomes irreversible.

Women with metastatic breast cancer should be followed closely because androgen therapy occasionally accelerates the disease. A shorter-acting androgen is preferred over one with prolonged activity, especially during the early stages of androgen therapy.

For testosterone injection dosage form

The suspension dosage form is absorbed relatively slowly; therefore, frequent injections may cause overdosage.

Testosterone cypionate or testosterone enanthate should not be used interchangeably with testosterone propionate or testosterone base because of different durations of action.

The intramuscular injections should be administered deeply into the gluteal muscle or the deltoid muscle in larger men. Injections should not be administered intravenously.

For testosterone implant dosage form

Insertion of testosterone implants requires a 15-minute procedure using local anesthesia. The number of implants inserted can vary according to patient need, diagnosis, and tolerance of testosterone. A good way to establish a proper testosterone dose for the implant is to assess patient response to a short-acting injectable form of testosterone. A 25-mg dose of testosterone propionate per week is equivalent to two 75-mg implants that last for 3 months.

The preferred application site is the lower abdomen, 5 cm away from the umbilicus; other sites used include the deltoid and gluteal muscles, and upper thigh. The clinician inserts and releases each implant into separate fan-like tracks using a trocar that is inserted into the 1-cm incision.

Afterwards, the patient should feel only minor discomfort and can apply pressure to stop minor bleeding at the incision site. Use of steri-strips covered by a water-resistant dressing for one week adequately closes and protects the incision without sutures. Postsurgical use of antibiotics is not needed.

The crystallized testosterone implants dissolve subcutaneously and rarely require removal. If needed, minor surgery to remove implants can rapidly terminate the effect of the medication.

For testosterone transdermal system dosage forms

There is a potential for transfer of testosterone from the matrix-type, scrotal transdermal system, or testosterone gel to the female sexual partner, resulting in mild virilization, such as changes in body hair distribution and increase in acne. The reservoir-type transdermal system includes a protective liner that makes transfer to a sexual partner unlikely. To avoid transfer while using testosterone gel, patients should wash their hands immediately with soap and water after application; the application site should be covered with clothing after the gel has dried; if contact with another person does occur, the area of contact should be washed with soap and water as soon as possible.

The matrix-type transdermal system should be applied to clean, dry, and dry-shaved scrotal skin for optimal skin contact. Chemical depilatories should not be used.

The reservoir-type transdermal system should not be applied to scrotal skin. Instead, the abdomen, back, thighs, and upper arms are the optimal areas for application for *Androderm* and the arm, back, or upper buttocks for *Testoderm TTS*. Application areas for *Androderm* should be rotated, and a site should not be reused for 7 days. A patch added to or removed from the treatment regimen can change the testosterone concentrations by 27 to 37%. In addition, a 20% decrease in serum testosterone concentration was demonstrated in men over 65 years of age who applied *Androderm* to their backs.

For treatment of adverse effects

For all androgens—

For prolonged erection or priapism:

A prolonged erection should be treated if it persists for longer than 4 hours; priapism should be treated promptly. If tumescence is not reversed, interruption of blood flow may result in penile tissue ischemia and permanent tissue damage.

Treatment of adverse effects should be initiated by a physician trained in treating drug-induced tumescence. Depending on the severity, treatment may include:

- Application of ice packs to inner thigh, alternating between thighs, for no more than 10 minutes to shorten the time of a prolonged erection.
- Aspiration of intracavernosal blood.
- Intracavernosal administration of an alpha-adrenergic agonist; phenylephrine is preferred over epinephrine. While monitoring blood pressure, an injection of 0.5 mg/mL Phenylephrine Hydrochloride Injection USP is given, followed by a second dose, if needed, in 15 minutes.
- Irrigation of the corpus cavernosum with 0.9% Sodium Chloride Irrigation USP or 20 mL of dilute solutions of phenylephrine (20 mg Phenylephrine Hydrochloride Injection USP in 500 mL of 0.9% Sodium Chloride Irrigation USP) or epinephrine (1 mL 1:1000 Epinephrine Injection USP in 1 liter of 0.9% Sodium Chloride Irrigation USP) using a 19-gauge needle to remove clotted blood.
- Surgery (rarely needed).

For testosterone transdermal system (reservoir-type)—

For chemical-induced blistering—Symptomatic relief can be provided by administering a corticosteroid cream (not an ointment because ointments significantly reduce testosterone absorption) to relieve mild skin irritation underneath the patch. If burn-like blisters appear under the patch, use of patch should be discontinued and treatment of skin area should follow standard guidelines for treatment of burns.

FLUOXYMESTERONE

Summary of Differences

Indications: Also used as an antianemic.

Side/adverse effects: Methylated androgens are more likely to cause jaundice.

Oral Dosage Forms

Note: Bracketed uses in the *Dosage Forms* section refer to categories of use and/or indications that are not included in U.S. product labeling.

FLUOXYMESTERONE TABLETS USP

Usual adult dose

Androgen deficiency, due to primary or secondary hypogonadism—

Oral, 5 mg one to four times a day. Replacement therapy is usually started at 10 mg per day, with subsequent adjustments as necessary.

Breast cancer in females—

Oral, 10 to 40 mg per day in divided doses.

[Antianemic][1]—

Oral, 20 to 50 mg per day, for minimum trial of two to six months.

Usual pediatric dose

Delayed puberty in males—

Oral, 2.5 to 10 mg per day titrated to the lowest dose and to skeletal monitoring for a limited duration, usually four to six months.

Strength(s) usually available

U.S.—

2 mg (Rx) [*Halotestin* (scored; lactose; sucrose; tartrazine)].

5 mg (Rx) [*Halotestin* (scored; lactose; sucrose; tartrazine)].

10 mg (Rx) [*Android-F* (scored); *Halotestin* (scored; lactose; sucrose; tartrazine); GENERIC (scored; may contain lactose and tartrazine)].

Canada—

5 mg (Rx) [*Halotestin* (scored; tartrazine)].

Packaging and storage

Store below 40 °C (104 °F), preferably between 15 and 30 °C (59 and 86 °F), unless otherwise specified by manufacturer. Store in a well-closed container. Protect from light.

Auxiliary labeling

- Take with food.

[1]Not included in Canadian product labeling.

METHYLTESTOSTERONE

Summary of Differences

Side/adverse effects: Methylated androgens are more likely to cause jaundice.

Oral Dosage Forms

METHYLTESTOSTERONE CAPSULES USP

Usual adult dose

Androgen deficiency, due to primary or secondary hypogonadism—

Oral, 10 to 50 mg per day.

Breast cancer in females—

Oral, 50 mg one to four times a day. After two to four weeks, dose may be decreased to 50 mg two times a day if response occurs.

Usual pediatric dose

Delayed puberty in males—

Oral, 5 to 25 mg per day for a limited duration, usually four to six months.

Strength(s) usually available

U.S.—

10 mg (Rx) [*Android; Testred; Virilon*].

Canada—

Not commercially available.

Packaging and storage

Store below 40 °C (104 °F), preferably between 15 and 30 °C (59 and 86 °F), unless otherwise specified by manufacturer. Store in a well-closed container.

Auxiliary labeling

- Take with food.

METHYLTESTOSTERONE TABLETS (Oral) USP

Usual adult dose

Androgen deficiency, due to primary or secondary hypogonadism or

Breast cancer in females—

See *Methyltestosterone Capsules USP*.

Usual pediatric dose

Delayed puberty in males—

See *Methyltestosterone Capsules USP*.

Strength(s) usually available

U.S.—

10 mg (Rx) [*Android; ORETON Methyl* (lactose); GENERIC].

25 mg (Rx) [*Android;* GENERIC].

Canada—

10 mg (Rx) [*Metandren* (scored; lactose)].

25 mg (Rx) [*Metandren* (scored; lactose)].

Packaging and storage

Store below 40 °C (104 °F), preferably between 15 and 30 °C (59 and 86 °F), unless otherwise specified by manufacturer. Store in a well-closed container.

Auxiliary labeling

- Take with food.

TESTOSTERONE

Summary of Differences

Indications: Testosterone cypionate and testosterone enanthate are used as antianemics and in androgen replacement in impotence or for male climacteric symptoms. Testosterone cypionate and testosterone enanthate are also used for female-to-male gender change. Intramuscular testosterone and testosterone esters, and extemporaneously compounded testosterone propionate ointments are used in the treatment of microphallus. Extemporaneously compounded testosterone propionate ointments are used in the treatment of lichen sclerosus.

Side/adverse effects: Side effects of the enanthate and cypionate forms cannot be quickly reversed because of the long duration of action of medication form and can include hives, infection, pain, redness, or irritation at site of injection.

Oral Dosage Forms

TESTOSTERONE UNDECANOATE CAPSULES

Usual adult dose

Androgen deficiency, due to primary or secondary hypogonadism—
Oral, 120 to 160 mg divided into two doses a day with meals for two to three weeks. The dose may be decreased to 40 to 120 mg a day in divided doses, as appropriate, with meals.

Usual pediatric dose

Androgen deficiency, due to primary or secondary hypogonadism—
Use and dose have not been established.

Strength(s) usually available

U.S.—
Not commercially available.

Canada—
40 mg (Rx) [*Andriol*].

Packaging and storage

Before dispensing, store between 2 and 8 °C (36 and 46 °F). Protect from freezing. Store in a well-closed container. Protect from light.

After dispensing, store between 15 and 25 °C (59 and 77 °F). Protect from light.

Stability

After the bottle is opened, capsules retain their potency for 90 days.

Auxiliary labeling

- Take with food.
- Beyond use date.

Parenteral Dosage Forms

Note: Bracketed uses in the *Dosage Forms* section refer to categories of use and/or indications that are not included in U.S. product labeling.

TESTOSTERONE INJECTABLE SUSPENSION USP

Note: Formerly known as Sterile Testosterone Suspension USP.

Usual adult dose

Androgen deficiency, due to primary or secondary hypogonadism—
Intramuscular, 25 to 50 mg two or three times a week.

Breast cancer in females—
Intramuscular, 50 to 100 mg three times a week.

Usual pediatric dose

Delayed puberty in males—
Intramuscular, 100 mg (maximum) per month for a limited duration, usually four to six months.

Strength(s) usually available

U.S.—
25 mg per mL (Rx) [GENERIC (may contain thimerosal)].
50 mg per mL (Rx) [*Testaqua* (thimerosal); GENERIC (may contain thimerosal)].
100 mg per mL (Rx) [*Testamone 100* (thimerosal); *Testaqua* (thimerosal); GENERIC (may contain thimerosal)].

Canada—
Not commercially available.

Packaging and storage

Store below 40 °C (104 °F), preferably between 15 and 30 °C (59 and 86 °F), unless otherwise specified by manufacturer. Protect from freezing.

Auxiliary labeling

- Shake well.

TESTOSTERONE CYPIONATE INJECTION USP

Usual adult dose

Androgen deficiency, due to primary or secondary hypogonadism—
Intramuscular, 50 to 400 mg every two to four weeks.

Breast cancer in females—
Intramuscular, 200 to 400 mg every two to four weeks.

[Gender change][1]—
Intramuscular, 200 mg every two weeks. Occasional patients may require a higher dose to cause cessation of menses.

Usual pediatric dose

Delayed puberty in males—
Intramuscular, 100 mg (maximum) per month for a limited duration, usually four to six months.

Strength(s) usually available

U.S.—
100 mg per mL (Rx) [*Andronate 100* (benzyl alcohol); *Depotest* (benzyl alcohol); *Depo-Testosterone* (benzyl alcohol 9.45 mg per mL; benzyl benzoate 0.1 mL per mL; cottonseed oil); GENERIC (may contain benzyl alcohol and benzyl benzoate)].
200 mg per mL (Rx) [*Andronate 200* (benzyl alcohol; benzyl benzoate); *Depotest* (benzyl alcohol; benzyl benzoate); *Depo-Testosterone* (benzyl alcohol 9.45 mg per mL; benzyl benzoate 0.2 mL per mL; cottonseed oil); *T-Cypionate; Testred Cypionate 200* (benzyl alcohol 0.9%; benzyl benzoate 20%); *Virilon IM;* GENERIC (may contain benzyl alcohol and benzyl benzoate)].

Canada—
100 mg per mL (Rx) [*Depo-Testosterone Cypionate* (benzyl alcohol; benzyl benzoate; cottonseed oil); *Scheinpharm Testone-Cyp* (benzyl alcohol; cottonseed oil)].

Packaging and storage

Store below 40 °C (104 °F), preferably between 15 and 30 °C (59 and 86 °F), unless otherwise specified by manufacturer. Protect from light. Protect from freezing.

Stability

Crystals may form at low temperatures; warming and shaking the vial will redissolve any crystals.

Use of a wet needle or wet syringe may cause solution to cloud; however, potency of the medication will not be affected.

TESTOSTERONE ENANTHATE INJECTION USP

Usual adult dose

Androgen deficiency, due to primary or secondary hypogonadism or
Breast cancer in females or
[Gender change][1]—
See *Testosterone Cypionate Injection USP*.

[Antianemic][1]—
Intramuscular, 400 mg a day for one week, then 400 mg one or two times a week. The maintenance dose is 200 to 400 mg every four weeks.

Usual pediatric dose

Delayed puberty in males—
See *Testosterone Cypionate Injection USP*.

[Microphallus][1]—
Intramuscular, 25 to 50 mg every month for 3 to 6 months.

Strength(s) usually available

U.S.—
100 mg per mL (Rx) [*Delatest* (chlorobutanol); GENERIC (may contain benzyl alcohol)].
200 mg per mL (Rx) [*Andro L.A. 200* (chlorobutanol 0.5%); *Andropository 200; Andryl 200* (chlorobutanol); *Delatestryl* (chlorobutanol 5 mg per mL); *Everone 200* (chlorobutanol); *Testrin-P.A* (chlorobutanol); GENERIC (may contain benzyl alcohol)].

Canada—
200 mg per mL (Rx) [*Delatestryl* (chlorobutanol 0.5%)].

Packaging and storage

Store below 40 °C (104 °F), preferably between 15 and 30 °C (59 and 86 °F), unless otherwise specified by manufacturer. Protect from freezing.

Stability

Crystals may form at low temperatures; warming and shaking the vial will redissolve any crystals.

Use of a wet needle or wet syringe may cause solution to cloud; however, potency of the medication will not be affected.

TESTOSTERONE PROPIONATE INJECTION USP

Usual adult dose

Androgen deficiency, due to primary or secondary hypogonadism or
Breast cancer in females—
See *Testosterone Injectable Suspension USP*.

Usual pediatric dose
Delayed puberty in males—
See *Testosterone Injectable Suspension USP*.

Strength(s) usually available
U.S.—
100 mg per mL (Rx) [*Testex* (benzyl alcohol); GENERIC].

Canada—
100 mg per mL (Rx) [*Malogen in Oil*].

Packaging and storage
Store below 40 °C (104 °F), preferably between 15 and 30 °C (59 and 86 °F), unless otherwise specified by manufacturer. Protect from freezing.

Stability
Crystals may form at low temperatures; warming and shaking the vial will redissolve any crystals.

Use of a wet needle or wet syringe may cause solution to cloud; however, potency of the medication will not be affected.

Subcutaneous Dosage Forms

TESTOSTERONE IMPLANTS

Usual adult dose
Androgen deficiency, due to primary or secondary hypogonadism—
Subcutaneous, 150 to 450 mg every three to four months or, in some cases, as long as six months.

Usual pediatric dose
Puberty, delayed, male—
Subcutaneous, dose to be determined by the physician. Low doses are used initially and increased gradually as puberty progresses.

Strength(s) usually available
U.S.—
75 mg (Rx) [*Testopel Pellets*].

Canada—
Not commercially available.

Packaging and storage
Store below 40 °C (104 °F), preferably between 15 and 30 °C (59 and 86 °F), unless otherwise specified by manufacturer.

Topical Dosage Forms

Note: Bracketed uses in the *Dosage Forms* section refer to categories of use and/or indications that are not included in U.S. product labeling.

TESTOSTERONE GEL

Usual adult dose
Androgen deficiency, due to primary or secondary hypogonadism (congenital or acquired)—
Topical, recommended starting dose is 5 grams (to deliver 50 mg of testosterone) applied once daily in the morning to clean, dry, intact skin of the shoulders and upper arms and/or abdomen

Note: If the serum testosterone concentration is below the normal range, or the clinical response is not achieved, the daily dose of testosterone 1% may be increased from 5 grams to 7.5 grams and from 7.5 grams to 10 grams as guided by the physician.

Usual pediatric dose
Androgen deficiency, due to primary or secondary hypogonadism (congenital or acquired)—
Use and dose have not been established.

Strength(s) usually available
U.S.—
2.5 grams per packet to deliver 25 mg of testosterone (Rx) [*AndroGel*].
5 grams per packet to deliver 50 mg of testosterone (Rx) [*AndroGel*].
1.25 grams per pump to deliver 5 mg of testosterone systemically (Rx) [*AndroGel*].

Canada—
Not commercially available.

Packaging and storage
Store at controlled room temperature 20 to 25 °C (68 to 77 °F)

Auxiliary labeling
- Please read patient information leaflet enclosed
- External use only.
- Keep out of reach of children
- Flammable- keep away from heat and flame

Note
AndroGel should not be applied to the genitals. Application sites should be allowed to dry prior to dressing. Hands should be washed with soap and water after Androgel has been applied.

TESTOSTERONE PROPIONATE OINTMENT

Usual adult dose
[Lichen sclerosus][1]—
Initial, topical, to the vulva, as a 1 or 2% ointment, two times a day for six weeks or until relief of itching occurs. Dosage should be decreased to the minimum effective dose.

Usual pediatric dose
[Microphallus][1]—
Topical, to the penis, as a 5% ointment, two times a day for three months.

Strength(s) usually available
U.S.—
Not commercially available. Compounding required for prescription.

Canada—
Not commercially available. Compounding required for prescription.

Preparation of dosage form
Formulations that have been used for the extemporaneous compounding of testosterone propionate ointments are as follows:

For 15 grams of 2% testosterone propionate ointment
- 3 mL of 100-mg-per-mL testosterone propionate injection
- 12 grams of white petrolatum.

For 15 grams of 5% testosterone propionate ointment
- 7.5 mL of 100-mg-per-mL testosterone propionate injection
- 7.5 grams of white petrolatum.

TESTOSTERONE TRANSDERMAL SYSTEMS (Matrix-type)

Usual adult dose
Androgen deficiency, due to primary or secondary hypogonadism—
Topical, one 6-mg transdermal dosage system (15 mg per sixty-centimeters-squared patch) applied to clean, dry and hairless skin of scrotum at approximately 8 a.m., every twenty-two to twenty-four hours. If scrotal area is inadequate, the smaller-sized 4-mg transdermal dosage system (10 mg per forty-centimeters-squared patch) should be used every twenty-two to twenty-four hours.

Note: Discontinue if desired response is not reached by six to eight weeks.

Usual pediatric dose
Children up to 18 years of age—Dosage has not been established.

Strength(s) usually available
U.S.—
4 mg delivered per system per day (Rx) [*Testoderm*].
6 mg delivered per system per day (Rx) [*Testoderm; Testoderm with Adhesives*].

Canada—
Not commercially available.

Packaging and storage
Store between 15 and 30 °C (59 and 86 °F).

Auxiliary labeling
- For external use only.
- Apply patch to a clean, dry, hair-free area of the skin.

Note
The manufacturer's directions for the patient should be dispensed with the product.

Patients should be instructed to apply the patches to the scrotum.

TESTOSTERONE TRANSDERMAL SYSTEMS (Reservoir-type)

Usual adult dose
Androgen deficiency, due to primary or secondary hypogonadism—
Topical, 5 mg applied to clean, dry skin of the back, abdomen, upper arms, or thighs for *Androderm* at 10 p.m. every twenty-four hoursand to the back, arms, or upper buttocks for *Testoderm TTS* at 8 a.m. every twenty-two to twenty-four hours. 2.5 mg may be used for nonvirilized patients or dose may be increased to 7.5 mg as appropriate.

Note: Patients should not apply the patches to the scrotum, bony prominences (deltoid region of the upper arm, the greater trochanter of the femur, and the ischial tuberosity), chest, or shin, or areas subject to prolonged pressure while sleeping or sitting.

Usual pediatric dose

Androgen deficiency, due to primary or secondary hypogonadism—
For Androderm—
Children up to 15 years of age—Use and dose have not been established.
Children 15 years of age and older—See *Usual adult dose*.
For Testoderm TTS—
Children up to 18 years of age—Use and dose have not been established.

Usual geriatric dose

Androgen deficiency, due to primary or secondary hypogonadism—
See *Usual adult dose*.

Strength(s) usually available

U.S.—
2.5 mg delivered per system per day (Rx) [*Androderm*].
5 mg delivered per system per day (Rx) [*Androderm; Testoderm TTS*].
Canada—
Not commercially available.

Packaging and storage

For *Androderm*, store between 15 and 30 °C (59 and 86 °F). For *Testoderm TTS*, store below 25 °C (77 °F).

Auxiliary labeling

- For external use only.
- Apply patch to a clean, dry, hair-free area of the skin.

Note

The manufacturer's directions for the patient should be dispensed with the product.

[1]Not included in Canadian product labeling.

Revised: 02/15/2005

ANDROGENS AND ESTROGENS Systemic

This monograph includes information on the following: 1) Estrogens, Esterified, and Methyltestosterone; 2) Testosterone and Estradiol.

VA CLASSIFICATION (Primary/Secondary): HS900/GU900

Commonly used brand name(s): *Climacteron[2]; Depo-Testadiol[2]; Estratest[1]; Estratest H.S[1]; Valertest No. 1[2]*.

NOTE: The *Androgens and Estrogens (Systemic)* monograph is maintained on the *USP DI* electronic data base. A copy of the most recent revision of the complete monograph can be accessed on the *USP DI* Updates Online website. See the front cover of book for details on accessing the site.

For information on the specific components of this combination, see the *USP DI* monographs for *Androgens (Systemic)* and *Estrogens (Systemic)*.

The information that follows is selectively abstracted from the complete monograph and is provided to facilitate drug use review and patient counseling.

Note: For a listing of dosage forms and brand names by country availability, see *Dosage Forms* section(s).

Category

Androgen-estrogen.

Indications

Note: Bracketed information in the *Indications* section refers to uses that are not included in U.S. product labeling.

Accepted

Menopause, vasomotor symptoms of (treatment)—The following are indicated in the treatment of the vasomotor symptoms of menopause: diethylstilbestrol and methyltestosterone, conjugated estrogens and methyltestosterone, esterified estrogens and methyltestosterone, fluoxymesterone and ethinyl estradiol, testosterone cypionate and estradiol cypionate, testosterone enanthate and estradiol valerate and testosterone enanthate benzilic acid hydrazone, estradiol dienanthate, and estradiol benzoate

[Osteoporosis, estrogen deficiency–induced (treatment)]—testosterone enanthate benzilic acid hydrazone, estradiol dienanthate, and estradiol benzoate is indicated in the treatment of estrogen deficiency induced osteoporosis.

Unaccepted

There is conflicting evidence and opinion as to whether the possible benefits of postmenopausal androgen pharmacologic or replacement therapy outweigh the risks of the frequently occurring virilizing side effects, adverse effects on serum cholesterol profile, or hepatotoxicity. Virilization may be somewhat reduced with the concomitant use of estrogens. However, because further data are needed regarding the efficacy of androgens in combination with estrogen and because side effects are frequent, the routine use of these products for any indication is not recommended.

Patient Consultation

As an aid to patient consultation, refer to *Advice for the Patient, Androgens and Estrogens (Systemic)*.

In providing consultation, consider emphasizing the following selected information (» = major clinical significance):

Before using this medication

» Conditions affecting use, especially:
Sensitivity to anabolic steroids, androgens, or estrogens
Carcinogenicity/tumorigenicity—Hepatocellular carcinoma and neoplasms associated with long-term, high-dose androgen therapy; increased risk of endometrial cancer for patients with intact uteri when progestin is not used with estrogen; risk is decreased when a progestin is used with estrogen; continuous, long-term estrogen use in animal studies increased frequency of cancers of the breast, cervix, and liver
Pregnancy—Androgens are not recommended for use during pregnancy, because of possible masculinization of female fetus; suggestion that use of some estrogens may be associated with congenital abnormalities
Breast-feeding—Use is not recommended, because estrogens are distributed into breast milk and may have unpredictable effects; not known if androgens are distributed into breast milk; androgens could have adverse effects on the infant such as slowing or cessation of growth, precocious sexual development in males, or virilization in females
Other medications, especially anticoagulants (coumarin- or indandione-derivatives), cyclosporine, or hepatotoxic medications
Other medical problems, especially abnormal and undiagnosed vaginal bleeding; breast cancer; cardio-renal disease; cardiac failure; hepatic dysfunction or failure; history of myocardial infarction; nephrosis; nephritis; active thrombophlebitis or thromboembolic disorders

Proper use of this medication

Reading patient package insert carefully
» Compliance with therapy
» Importance of not taking more medication than the amount prescribed
Taking with or immediately after food to reduce nausea
» Proper dosing
Missed dose: Taking as soon as possible; not taking if almost time for next dose; not doubling doses
» Proper storage

Precautions while using this medication

» Regular visits to physician at least every 6 to 12 months, or more often if so directed, to check progress

Importance of mammography and regular self-breast examinations

Possibility of dental problems, such as tenderness, swelling, or bleeding of gums; brushing and flossing teeth, massaging gums, and having dentist clean teeth regularly; checking with dentist if there are questions about care of teeth or gums or if tenderness, swelling, or bleeding of gums is noticed

Diabetics: May alter blood glucose concentrations

» Stopping medication immediately and checking with physician if pregnancy is suspected

Smoking while taking oral contraceptives containing estrogens can increase risk of cardiovascular side effects; not known whether elevated risk occurs with estrogen therapy

Importance of not giving medication to anyone else

Side/adverse effects

Withdrawal bleeding will occur in many postmenopausal patients placed on cyclic androgen and estrogen therapy with a progestin
Signs of potential side effects, especially anaphylaxis, breast tumors, chorea, peripheral edema, erythrocytosis, gallbladder obstruction, hepatic necrosis, hepatitis, hepatocellular tumor, hepatic dysfunction, leukopenia, menstrual irregularities, peliosis hepatis, polycythemia, virilism

ESTROGENS, ESTERIFIED, AND METHYLTESTOSTERONE

Oral Dosage Forms

ESTERIFIED ESTROGENS AND METHYLTESTOSTERONE TABLETS

Usual adult dose

Menopause, vasomotor symptoms of (treatment)—

Oral, 625 mcg (0.625 mg) to 2.5 mg of esterified estrogens and 1.25 to 5 mg of methyltestosterone a day for twenty-one days, the dosage being repeated cyclically following seven days of no medication.

Strength(s) usually available

U.S.—

625 mcg (0.625 mg) of esterified estrogens and 1.25 mg of methyltestosterone (Rx) [*Estratest H.S* (lactose; methylparaben; propylparaben; sodium benzoate; sucrose)].

1.25 mg of esterified estrogens and 2.5 mg of methyltestosterone (Rx) [*Estratest* (lactose; methylparaben; propylparaben; sodium benzoate; sucrose)].

TESTOSTERONE AND ESTRADIOL

Parenteral Dosage Forms

TESTOSTERONE CYPIONATE AND ESTRADIOL CYPIONATE INJECTION

Usual adult dose

Menopause, vasomotor symptoms of (treatment)—

Intramuscular, 50 mg of testosterone cypionate and 2 mg of estradiol cypionate every four weeks.

Strength(s) usually available

U.S.—

50 mg of testosterone cypionate and 2 mg of estradiol cypionate per mL (Rx) [*Depo-Testadiol* (chlorobutanol anhydrous 5.4 mg per mL; cottonseed oil 874 mg per mL)].

TESTOSTERONE ENANTHATE AND ESTRADIOL VALERATE INJECTION

Usual adult dose

Menopause, vasomotor symptoms of (treatment)—

Intramuscular, 90 mg of testosterone enanthate and 4 mg of estradiol valerate every four weeks.

Strength(s) usually available

U.S.—

90 mg of testosterone enanthate and 4 mg of estradiol valerate per mL (Rx) [*Valertest No. 1* (chlorobutanol; sesame oil)].

TESTOSTERONE ENANTHATE BENZILIC ACID HYDRAZONE, ESTRADIOL DIENANTHATE, AND ESTRADIOL BENZOATE INJECTION

Usual adult dose

Menopause, vasomotor symptoms of (treatment) or

Osteoporosis, estrogen deficiency–induced (treatment)—

Intramuscular, 150 mg of testosterone enanthate benzilic acid hydrazone, 7.5 mg of estradiol dienanthate, and 1 mg of estradiol benzoate every four to eight weeks or less frequently.

Usual adult prescribing limits

Intramuscular, 150 mg testosterone enanthate benzilic acid hydrazone, 7.5 mg of estradiol dienanthate, and 1 mg of estradiol benzoate every four weeks

Strength(s) usually available

U.S.—

Not commercially available.

Canada—

150 mg of testosterone enanthate benzilic acid hydrazone (69 mg base), 7.5 mg of estradiol dienanthate, and 1 mg of estradiol benzoate per mL (Rx) [*Climacteron* (benzoate alcohol 7.5%; benzyl benzoate)].

Revised: 01/14/2003

ANESTHETICS Mucosal-Local

This monograph includes information on the following: 1) Benzocaine; 2) Benzocaine, Butamben, and Tetracaine; 3) Dibucaine; 4) Dyclonine; 5) Lidocaine; 6) Pramoxine; 7) Tetracaine.

Note: See also individual *Cocaine (Mucosal-Local)* monograph.

INN:
Dibucaine—Cinchocaine
Pramoxine—Pramocaine

BAN:
Dibucaine—Cinchocaine
Dyclonine—Dyclocaine
Lidocaine—Lignocaine
Tetracaine—Amethocaine

JAN: Benzocaine—Ethyl aminobenzoate

VA CLASSIFICATION (Primary/Secondary):

Note: Several of the dosage forms listed below are commercially available in more than one formulation. Because the vehicle into which a local anesthetic is incorporated may determine the appropriate usage and/or site(s) of application for a product, some of the VA classifications listed for a dosage form may apply only to specific formulations.

Benzocaine Dental paste—OR600
Benzocaine Gel—NT300/GU900; OR600; RS900
Benzocaine Lozenges—OR600
Benzocaine Ointment—RS201/DE700; OR600; RS900
Benzocaine Topical aerosol—DE700/NT300; OR600
Benzocaine Topical solution—NT300/OR600
Benzocaine and Menthol Lozenges—OR600
Benzocaine and Phenol Gel—OR600
Benzocaine and Phenol Topical solution—OR600
Benzocaine, Butamben, and Tetracaine Gel—NT300/GU900; OR600; RS900
Benzocaine, Butamben, and Tetracaine Ointment—NT300/OR600
Benzocaine, Butamben, and Tetracaine Topical aerosol—NT300/OR600
Benzocaine, Butamben, and Tetracaine Topical solution—NT300/OR600
Dibucaine Ointment—RS201/DE700; RS900
Dyclonine Lozenges—OR600
Dyclonine Topical solution—NT300/GU900; OR600; RS900
Lidocaine Ointment—NT300/DE700; OR600
Lidocaine Oral topical solution—OR600
Lidocaine Topical aerosol—NT300/OR600
Lidocaine Hydrochloride Jelly—NT300/GU900
Lidocaine Hydrochloride Oral topical solution—NT300/OR600
Lidocaine Hydrochloride Topical solution—NT300/OR600
Lidocaine Hydrochloride Topical spray solution—NT300
Pramoxine Aerosol foam—RS201/RS900
Pramoxine Cream—RS201/DE700; RS900
Pramoxine Ointment—RS201
Tetracaine Cream—RS201/DE700; RS900
Tetracaine Hydrochloride Topical Solution—NT300
Tetracaine and Menthol Ointment—RS201/DE700; RS900

Note: For information on local anesthetics applied topically to the skin to relieve minor dermatological conditions, see *Anesthetics (Topical)*.

For information on use of lidocaine hydrochloride by transtracheal injection to anesthetize the larynx and trachea, see *Anesthetics (Parenteral-Local)*.

Commonly used brand name(s): *Americaine[1]; Americaine Anesthetic Lubricant[1]; Americaine Hemorrhoidal[1]; Anbesol, Baby[1]; Anbesol Baby Jel[1]; Anbesol Gel[1]; Anbesol Liquid[1]; Anbesol Maximum Strength Gel[1]; Anbesol Maximum Strength Liquid[1]; Anbesol Regular Strength Gel[1]; Anbesol Regular Strength Liquid[1]; Anestacon Jelly[5]; Benzodent[1]; Cetacaine Topical Anesthetic[2]; Chloraseptic Lozenges[1]; Chloraseptic Lozenges Cherry Flavor[1]; Chloraseptic Lozenges, Children's[1]; Dent-Zel-Ite[1]; Dentapaine[1]; Dentocaine[1]; Dyclone[4]; Fleet Relief[6]; Hurricaine[1]; Num-Zit Gel[1]; Num-Zit Lotion[1]; Numzident[1]; Nupercainal[3]; Orabase, Baby[1]; Orabase-B with Benzocaine[1]; Orajel[1]; Orajel, Baby[1]; Orajel Extra Strength[1]; Orajel Liquid[1]; Orajel Maximum Strength[1]; Orajel Nighttime Formula, Baby[1]; Oratect Gel[1]; Pontocaine[7]; Pontocaine Cream[7]; Pontocaine Ointment[7]; ProctoFoam/non-steroid[6]; Rid-A-Pain[1]; SensoGARD Canker Sore Relief[1]; Spec-T Sore Throat Anesthetic[1]; Sucrets, Children's[4]; Sucrets Maximum Strength[4]; Sucrets*

Regular Strength[4]; Topicaine[1]; Tronolane[6]; Tronothane[6]; Xylocaine[5]; Xylocaine Dental Ointment[5]; Xylocaine Endotracheal[5]; Xylocaine Viscous[5]; Zilactin-L[5].

Some other commonly used names are:
Amethocaine [Tetracaine]
Butyl aminobenzoate [Butamben]
Cinchocaine [Dibucaine]
Dyclocaine [Dyclonine]
Ethyl aminobenzoate [Benzocaine]
Lignocaine [Lidocaine]
Pramocaine [Pramoxine]

Note: For a listing of dosage forms and brand names by country availability, see *Dosage Forms* section(s).

Category

Anesthetic (mucosal-local).

Indications

Note: Bracketed information in the *Indications* section refers to uses that are not included in U.S. product labeling.

Gel, ointment, and topical solution dosage forms of benzocaine, ointment and topical solution dosage forms of lidocaine, and topical solution dosage forms of lidocaine hydrochloride are available in more than one formulation. The vehicles present in different formulations may determine the indication(s) for which the formulations are used. Therefore, some gel, ointment, or topical solution formulations that contain the same local anesthetic cannot be used interchangeably. For additional information regarding formulations and brand name products that may be used for specific indications, see the *Dosage Forms* section.

Accepted

Anesthesia, local—Indicated to provide topical anesthesia of accessible mucous membranes prior to examination, endoscopy or instrumentation, or other procedures involving the:

Esophagus
(Benzocaine (gel and topical solution); benzocaine, butamben, and tetracaine; dyclonine (topical solution); lidocaine hydrochloride (4% topical solution, topical spray solution, and [oral topical solution]); and tetracaine hydrochloride (topical solution).)

Larynx
(Benzocaine (gel and topical solution); benzocaine, butamben, and tetracaine; dyclonine (topical solution); lidocaine hydrochloride (4% topical solution and topical spray solution); and tetracaine hydrochloride (topical solution).)

Mouth (in dental procedures and oral surgery)
(Benzocaine (gel, topical aerosol, and topical solution); benzocaine, butamben, and tetracaine; dyclonine (topical solution); lidocaine (ointment, topical aerosol, and oral topical solution); and lidocaine hydrochloride (oral topical solution and 4% topical solution).)

Nasal cavity
(Benzocaine (gel); benzocaine, butamben, and tetracaine; lidocaine hydrochloride (jelly and 4% topical solution); and tetracaine (topical solution).)

Pharynx or throat
(Benzocaine (gel, topical aerosol, and topical solution); benzocaine, butamben, and tetracaine; dyclonine (topical solution); lidocaine (ointment and topical aerosol); lidocaine hydrochloride (jelly, oral topical solution, and topical spray solution); and tetracaine (topical solution).)

Rectum
(Benzocaine (gel); benzocaine, butamben, and tetracaine (gel); and lidocaine hydrochloride (jelly).)

Respiratory tract or trachea
(Benzocaine (gel, topical aerosol, and topical solution); benzocaine, butamben, and tetracaine; dyclonine (topical solution); lidocaine (ointment); lidocaine hydrochloride (jelly, [oral topical solution], and 4% and 10% topical solution); and tetracaine (topical solution).)

Urinary tract
(Benzocaine (gel); dyclonine (topical solution); and lidocaine hydrochloride (jelly).)

Vagina
(Benzocaine (gel); benzocaine, butamben, and tetracaine (gel); and dyclonine (topical solution).)

Gag reflex suppression:
Indicated to suppress the gag reflex and/or other laryngeal and esophageal reflexes to facilitate dental examination or procedures (including oral surgery), endoscopy, or intubation: Benzocaine (gel, topical aerosol, and topical solution); benzocaine, butamben, and tetracaine (topical aerosol); dyclonine (0.5% topical solution); [lidocaine (topical aerosol)]; lidocaine hydrochloride (oral topical solution and 10% topical solution); and tetracaine hydrochloride (topical solution).

Anorectal disorders (treatment)—Indicated for the symptomatic relief of:
Hemorrhoids
Inflammation, anorectal and
Pain, anorectal
(Benzocaine (ointment); dibucaine; pramoxine; tetracaine hydrochloride (cream); and tetracaine and menthol. These medications are effective when applied to the anal, perianal, or anorectal areas. However, they are not likely to relieve symptoms associated with conditions confined to the rectum, which lacks sensory nerve fibers.)
Pain, anogenital lesion-associated
(Dyclonine (0.5% solution).)
Pain, anogenital, external and
Pruritus, anogenital
(Benzocaine (ointment); dibucaine; pramoxine (aerosol foam and cream); tetracaine hydrochloride (cream); tetracaine and menthol.)

Oral cavity disorders (treatment); and Perioral lesions (treatment)—Indicated for relief of:
Canker sores or
Cold sores or
Fever blisters
(Benzocaine (gel and topical solution); benzocaine and phenol (gel and topical solution); and lidocaine (2.5% topical solution).)
Pain, gingival or oral mucosal (i.e., pain caused by mouth or gum irritation, inflammation, lesions, or minor dental procedures)
(Benzocaine (gel, dental paste, lozenges, and topical solution); dyclonine (lozenges and 0.5% topical solution); benzocaine and phenol (gel and topical solution); lidocaine (oral topical solution); and lidocaine hydrochloride (oral topical solution).)
Pain, dental prosthetic (i.e., pain or irritation caused by dentures or other dental or orthodontic appliances)
(Benzocaine (dental paste, gel, ointment, and topical solution); benzocaine and phenol (gel and topical solution); and lidocaine (ointment).)
Pain, teething
(Benzocaine (7.5% and 10% gel).)
Toothache
(Benzocaine (10% and 20% gel and topical solution); and benzocaine and phenol (gel and topical solution).)

Pain, esophageal (treatment):
Dyclonine (topical solution)ð [lidocaine hydrochloride (oral topical solution)].

Pain, pharyngeal (treatment):
Benzocaine (lozenges); benzocaine and menthol (lozenges); dyclonine (lozenges); and lidocaine hydrochloride (oral topical solution).

Pain, vaginal (treatment):
Indicated to relieve pain following procedures such as episiotomy or perineorraphy: Benzocaine (topical aerosol and topical solution); and dyclonine (topical solution).

Urethritis (treatment):
Indicated to relieve or control pain: Lidocaine hydrochloride (jelly).

Pharmacology/Pharmacokinetics

Physicochemical characteristics

Chemical Group—
Amides: Dibucaine, lidocaine
Esters, aminobenzoic acid (para-aminobenzoic acid, PABA)–derivative: Benzocaine, butamben, tetracaine
Unclassified: Dyclonine, pramoxine

Molecular weight—
Benzocaine: 165.19.
Butamben: 193.25.
Dibucaine: 343.47.
Dyclonine hydrochloride: 325.88.
Lidocaine: 234.34.
Lidocaine hydrochloride: 288.82.
Pramoxine hydrochloride: 329.87.
Tetracaine: 264.37.
Tetracaine hydrochloride: 300.83.

pKa—
Dibucaine: 8.8.
Lidocaine: 7.9.
Tetracaine: 8.2.

Mechanism of action/Effect
Local anesthetics block both the initiation and conduction of nerve impulses by decreasing the neuronal membrane's permeability to sodium ions. This reversibly stabilizes the membrane and inhibits depolarization, resulting in the failure of a propagated action potential and subsequent conduction blockade.

Other actions/effects
If substantial quantities of local anesthetics are absorbed through the mucosa, actions on the central nervous system (CNS) may cause CNS stimulation and/or CNS depression. Actions on the cardiovascular system may cause depression of cardiac conduction and excitability and, with some of these agents, peripheral vasodilation.

Absorption
Except for benzocaine, which is minimally absorbed, these agents are readily absorbed through mucous membranes into the systemic circulation. The rate of absorption is influenced by the vascularity or rate of blood flow at the site of application, the total dosage (concentration and volume) administered, and the duration of exposure. Absorption from mucous membranes of the throat or respiratory tract may be especially rapid. Addition of a vasoconstrictor to the anesthetic may not reduce or slow absorption sufficiently to protect against systemic effects.

Protein binding
Lidocaine—Concentration-dependent, to alpha 1-acid glycoprotein; usually about 60 to 80% at concentrations of 1 to 4 mcg per mL (4.3 to 17.2 micromoles per L).

Biotransformation
Amides—
Hepatic and some renal.
Lidocaine: Xylidide metabolites are active and toxic, but less so than the parent compound.
Esters (PABA-derivative)—
Hydrolyzed by plasma cholinesterases and, to a much lesser extent, by hepatic cholinesterases to PABA-containing metabolites.

Onset of action
Benzocaine—About 1 minute.
Benzocaine, butamben, and tetracaine—About 30 seconds.
Dibucaine—Up to 15 minutes.
Dyclonine—Up to 10 minutes.
Lidocaine—Within 1 to 5 minutes, depending on formulation.
Pramoxine—3 to 5 minutes.
Tetracaine—3 to 10 minutes.

Duration of action
Benzocaine—
15 to 20 minutes.
Dibucaine—
2 to 4 hours.
Dyclonine—
Approximately 30 to 60 minutes.
Lidocaine—
Approximately 30 to 60 minutes.
Lidocaine oral topical solution: 15 to 20 minutes.
Lidocaine topical aerosol: 10 to 15 minutes.
Tetracaine—
Approximately 30 to 60 minutes.

Elimination
Amides—
Renal, primarily as metabolites.
Lidocaine: Up to 10% of a dose may be excreted unchanged.
Esters—
Renal, primarily as metabolites.

Precautions to Consider

Cross-sensitivity and/or related problems
Patients sensitive to one ester derivative (especially an aminobenzoic acid [para-aminobenzoic acid; PABA] derivative) may be sensitive to other ester derivatives also.

Patients sensitive to PABA, parabens, or paraphenylenediamine (a hair dye) may be sensitive to PABA-derivative local anesthetics also.

Patients sensitive to one amide derivative may rarely be sensitive to other amide derivatives also.

Cross-sensitivity between amide derivatives and ester derivatives, or between amides or esters and chemically unrelated local anesthetics (i.e., dyclonine or pramoxine), has not been reported. However, some lidocaine formulations and pramoxine cream contain parabens, to which cross-sensitivity with PABA-derivative local anesthetics may exist.

Pregnancy/Reproduction
Fertility—
Dyclonine—
Studies have not been done.
Lidocaine—
Studies have not been done.

Pregnancy—
Benzocaine—
Studies in humans have not been done.
Studies in animals have not been done.
Benzocaine gel: FDA Pregnancy Category C.
Dyclonine—
Studies in humans have not been done.
Studies in animals have not been done.
Dyclonine topical solution: FDA Pregnancy Category C.
Lidocaine—
Adequate and well-controlled studies in humans have not been done.
Studies in rats given up to 6.6 times the human dose have not shown evidence of teratogenicity or harm to the fetus.
FDA Pregnancy Category B.
Other mucosal-local anesthetics—
Problems in humans have not been documented.

Breast-feeding
Lidocaine—
Distributed into breast milk in very small quantities that pose no risk to the infant.
Other mucosal-local anesthetics—
Problems in humans have not been documented.

Pediatrics
Benzocaine—
Benzocaine should be used with caution in infants and young children because increased absorption may result in methemoglobinemia. Nonprescription teething products (i.e., 7.5% or 10% benzocaine gel) should not be used in infants younger than 4 months of age unless prescribed by a physician or dentist. Other nonprescription products that contain benzocaine for relief of dental pain, perioral lesions, or sore throat (e.g., gel, lozenges, ointment, or topical solution and combinations containing benzocaine with menthol or phenol) should not be used in children younger than 2 years of age unless prescribed by a physician or dentist.
Other mucosal-local anesthetics—
Pediatric patients may be more susceptible to systemic toxicity with these medications. Nonprescription products that contain dyclonine or lidocaine for relief of sore throat or perioral lesions should not be used in children younger than 2 years of age unless prescribed by a physician or dentist. Dosage of other mucosal-local anesthetic formulations should be individualized, based on the child's age, weight, and physical condition.

Geriatrics
Systemic toxicity may be more likely to occur in geriatric patients, who may require lower concentrations and/or lower total dosages of mucosal-local anesthetics, especially for endoscopic procedures.

Drug interactions and/or related problems
See also *Laboratory value alterations.*

The following drug interactions and/or related problems have been selected on the basis of their potential clinical significance (possible mechanism in parentheses where appropriate)—not necessarily inclusive (» = major clinical significance):

Note: Combinations containing any of the following medications, depending on the amount present, may also interact with this medication.

For ester derivatives only
Cholinesterase inhibitors
(metabolism of an ester-derivative local anesthetic may be inhibited, leading to increased risk of systemic toxicity, when it is administered to a patient receiving a cholinesterase inhibitor)
Sulfonamides
(metabolites of PABA-derivative local anesthetics may antagonize antibacterial activity of sulfonamides)

For lidocaine only
Antiarrhythmic agents, amide local anesthetic–derivative, other, such as:
Mexiletine
Tocainide or
Lidocaine, systemic or parenteral-local
(risk of cardiotoxicity associated with additive cardiac effects, and, with systemic or parenteral-local lidocaine, the risk of overdose,

may be increased in patients receiving these medications when lidocaine is applied to the mucosa, especially if it is applied in large quantities, used repeatedly, used in the oral or pharyngeal area, or swallowed)

Beta-adrenergic blocking agents
(concurrent use may slow metabolism of lidocaine because of decreased hepatic blood flow, leading to increased risk of lidocaine toxicity, especially if lidocaine is applied to the mucosa in large quantities, used repeatedly, used in the oral or pharyngeal area, or swallowed)

Cimetidine
(cimetidine may inhibit hepatic metabolism of lidocaine, leading to increased risk of lidocaine toxicity, especially if lidocaine is applied to the mucosa in large quantities, used repeatedly, used in the oral or pharyngeal area, or swallowed)

Laboratory value alterations

The following have been selected on the basis of their potential clinical significance (possible effect in parentheses where appropriate)—not necessarily inclusive (» = major clinical significance).

With diagnostic test results

Cystoscopic procedures following pyelography
(dyclonine interferes with visualization by reacting with iodine-containing contrast agents, resulting in precipitation of iodine)

Pancreatic function determination using bentiromide
(administration of PABA-derivative anesthetics or lidocaine prior to the bentiromide test will invalidate test results [if the anesthetics are absorbed in sufficient quantity] since they are also metabolized to arylamines and will thus increase the apparent quantity of PABA recovered; discontinuation of these medications at least 3 days prior to the test is recommended)

Medical considerations/Contraindications

The medical considerations/contraindications included have been selected on the basis of their potential clinical significance (reasons given in parentheses where appropriate)—not necessarily inclusive (» = major clinical significance).

Risk-benefit should be considered when the following medical problems exist:

Hemorrhoids, bleeding—for rectal use

Local infection at area of treatment
(may alter pH at site of application, leading to decrease or loss of local anesthetic effect)

Sensitivity to the local anesthetic being considered for use and/or chemically related anesthetics or other compounds, history of

Traumatized mucosa, severe
(increased absorption of anesthetic, leading to increased risk of systemic toxicity)

Caution is also advised in pediatric, geriatric, acutely ill, or debilitated patients, who may be more susceptible to systemic toxicity with these medications.

Side/Adverse Effects

Note: Adverse reactions are due to excessive dosage or rapid absorption, which produces high plasma concentrations, as well as to idiosyncrasy, hypersensitivity, or decreased patient tolerance.

Benzocaine and tetracaine are more likely to cause contact sensitization than are the other mucosal-local anesthetics. Also, tetracaine is more toxic than other mucosal-local anesthetics.

The following side/adverse effects have been selected on the basis of their potential clinical significance (possible signs and symptoms in parentheses where appropriate)—not necessarily inclusive:

Those indicating need for medical attention

Incidence less frequent

Allergic contact dermatitis (skin rash, redness, itching, or hives); ***angioedema*** (large, hive-like swellings on skin or in mouth or throat); ***burning, stinging, swelling, or tenderness not present before therapy***

Incidence rare

Urethritis (blood in urine, increased frequency of urination, pain or burning during urination)—with urethral application

Overdose

For specific information on the agents used in the management of an overdose, see:

- *Ascorbic Acid (Systemic)* monograph;
- *Benzodiazepines (Systemic)* monograph;
- *Methylene Blue (Systemic)* monograph; and/or
- *Sympathomimetic Agents—Cardiovascular Use (Parenteral-Systemic)* monograph.

For more information on the management of overdose or unintentional ingestion, **contact a Poison Control Center** (see *Poison Control Center Listing*).

Clinical effects of overdose

The following effects have been selected on the basis of their potential clinical significance (possible signs and symptoms in parentheses where appropriate)—not necessarily inclusive:

Acute and chronic effects

Cardiovascular system depression (increased sweating, low blood pressure, pale skin, slow or irregular heartbeat)—may lead to cardiac arrest; ***CNS toxicity*** (blurred or double vision; confusion; convulsions; dizziness or lightheadedness; drowsiness; feeling hot, cold, or numb; ringing or buzzing in ears; shivering or trembling; unusual anxiety, excitement, nervousness, or restlessness); ***methemoglobinemia*** (difficulty in breathing on exertion, dizziness, headache, tiredness, weakness)

Note: Stimulant and/or depressant manifestations of *CNS toxicity* may occur. CNS stimulation usually occurs first, followed by CNS depression. However, CNS stimulation may be transient or absent so that drowsiness may be the first symptom of toxicity in some patients. CNS depression may lead to unconsciousness and respiratory arrest.

Treatment of overdose

Specific treatment—

For circulatory depression—Administering a vasopressor and intravenous fluids.

For convulsions—Administering a benzodiazepine anticonvulsant, keeping in mind that intravenously administered benzodiazepines may cause respiratory and circulatory depression, especially when administered rapidly. Medications and equipment needed for support of respiration and for resuscitation must be immediately available.

For methemoglobinemia—Administering methylene blue (1 to 2 mg per kg of body weight, intravenously) and/or ascorbic acid (100 to 200 mg orally).

Supportive care—

Securing and maintaining a patent airway, administering 100% oxygen, and instituting assisted or controlled respiration as required. In some patients, endotracheal intubation may be required.

Patient Consultation

As an aid to patient consultation, refer to *Advice for the Patient, Anesthetics (Dental)* and *Anesthetics (Rectal)*.

In providing consultation, consider emphasizing the following selected information (» = major clinical significance):

Before using this medication

» Conditions affecting use, especially:

Allergies to local anesthetics of the same chemical class, and, for ester derivatives only, aminobenzoic acid, parabens, or hair dye

Use in children—Caution recommended, especially with use of benzocaine or lidocaine in infants and young children

Use in the elderly—Increased risk of side effects

Proper use of this medication

Following physician's or dentist's instructions if prescribed

Following manufacturer's instructions if self-medicating

» Not using more, more often, or for a longer period of time than prescribed by physician or dentist or recommended on package label

» Checking with physician or dentist before using for problems other than those for which medication was prescribed or those stated on package label

Proper administration technique

For lidocaine hydrochloride oral topical solution

» Measuring dose accurately

Applying with cotton swab or swishing around in mouth (for mouth or gum conditions) or gargling (for throat conditions)

» Not swallowing unless specifically directed by physician or dentist

For benzocaine film-forming gel

Drying affected area with one of the swabs provided before applying

Applying gel to a second swab, then rolling the swab over the affected area

Keeping mouth open and dry for 30 to 60 seconds after applying, while film forms

Not removing film, which will slowly disintegrate over 6 hours

For other nonprescription gel and solution dosage forms
Applying to affected area(s) with a clean finger, a cotton-tipped applicator, or gauze
If using for pain caused by dental appliances, applying to sore area and, after relief is obtained, rinsing mouth before reinserting appliance; not applying directly to or using under appliance unless directed to do so by dentist
For benzocaine dental paste
Dabbing small amounts onto affected areas with cotton-tipped applicator; not rubbing or spreading, to prevent crumbling or grittiness
For topical aerosol or spray dosage forms
Using care not to inhale medication
Avoiding spraying back of throat or mouth unless specifically directed by physician or dentist
For lozenges
Dissolving slowly in mouth; not biting or chewing lozenges or swallowing them whole
For rectal cream or ointment
Reading patient directions
If applying externally: Cleansing area with mild soap and water or a cleansing wipe, rinsing thoroughly, and drying gently before applying
If inserting into anal canal: Using special applicator provided; lubricating applicator with a small amount of cream or ointment before inserting; washing reusable applicator after each use; discarding pre-filled disposable applicator
For rectal aerosol foam
Reading patient directions before use
Not inserting container into rectum; shaking container, attaching and filling the applicator provided, then detaching applicator from container prior to use
Applying a small amount of foam to lubricate the applicator before inserting
Taking applicator apart and washing thoroughly after each use

» Proper dosing
Missed dose (if prescribed for scheduled dosing)—Using as soon as possible; not using if almost time for next dose; not doubling doses of dental-local anesthetics

» Proper storage

Precautions while using this medication

» Contacting physician:
if using for sore throat and sore throat is severe, persists for more than 2 days, or is accompanied or followed by other symptoms such as fever, headache, rash, swelling, nausea, or vomiting
if using for hemorrhoids or other perianal conditions and condition does not improve within 7 days, bleeding occurs, or symptoms such as redness, irritation, swelling, or pain develop or worsen during treatment

» Contacting physician or dentist if using for perioral lesions and symptoms do not improve within 7 days, irritation or pain persists or worsens, or swelling, rash, or fever develops

» Contacting dentist:
as soon as possible to arrange an appointment if using to relieve toothache; medication is a temporary measure only
at regular intervals when medication used to relieve pain during adjustment of new dentures or other dental appliances

Not using benzocaine, lidocaine, or tetracaine for 72 hours prior to having pancreatic function test using bentiromide because of potential interference with test results

For use in mouth or throat area:

» Not eating for one hour following use of medication because may impair swallowing, leading to risk of aspiration

» Not chewing gum or food while numbness persists because of risk of biting tongue or buccal mucosa

Side/adverse effects

Signs and symptoms of potential side effects, especially allergic contact dermatitis; angioedema; and burning, stinging, swelling, or tenderness not present before therapy

General Dosing Information

The safety and effectiveness of local anesthetics, when they are used for examination or instrumentation procedures (especially those involving the esophagus, larynx, pharynx, respiratory tract, or urinary tract) depend upon proper dosage, correct administration technique, adequate precautions, and readiness for emergencies. *Resuscitative equipment, oxygen, and other required medications should be immediately available.*

The dosage of mucosal-local anesthetics, when they are used for examination or instrumentation procedures, depends on the technique of anesthesia, the area to be anesthetized, the vascularity of the tissues at the application site, and the patient's tolerance.

For use in examination or instrumentation procedures, the recommended adult doses are given as a guideline for use in the average adult. *The actual dosage and maximum dosage must be individualized,* based on the age, size, and physical status of the patient and the expected rate of systemic absorption from the administration site.

Depending on the area to be anesthetized, lower concentrations and/or lower total dosage may be required for pediatric, geriatric, acutely ill, or debilitated patients.

A standard textbook should be consulted for specific techniques and procedures applicable to the use of mucosal-local anesthetics for individual diagnostic and treatment procedures.

BENZOCAINE

Summary of Differences

Pharmacology/pharmacokinetics:
Physicochemical characteristics—
Benzocaine is a PABA derivative ester-type local anesthetic.
Absorption—
Minimally absorbed.
Precautions:
Cross-sensitivity and/or related problems—
May occur with other ester-type local anesthetics, especially other PABA derivatives, parabens, and paraphenylenediamine.
Pediatrics—
May cause methemoglobinemia in infants.
Drug interactions and/or related problems—
Cholinesterase inhibitors inhibit metabolism of benzocaine.
May antagonize antibacterial activity of sulfonamides.
Side/adverse effects:
More likely to cause contact sensitization than most other local anesthetics.
See also *Side/Adverse Effects.*

Dental Dosage Forms

Note: The gel, ointment, and topical solution dosage forms included in this section are specifically formulated for application only to the gingival or buccal mucosa or to perioral tissues. Gel and topical solution formulations that may be applied to other mucosal tissues (in addition to the gingival or buccal mucosa) are included in the *Topical Dosage Forms* section.

BENZOCAINE GEL (DENTAL)

Usual adult and adolescent dose

Anesthetic, mucosal-local—Topical, as a 10 or 20% gel, applied to affected area(s) up to four times a day or as directed by a physician or dentist.

Note: The medication may be applied with cotton, a cotton swab, or a fingertip.
The gel should not be applied directly to, or used beneath, a dental appliance unless the patient is under the supervision of a dentist. Patients using this medication without the supervision of a dentist for relief of dental appliance pain should apply the medication directly to the affected gum area, wait until relief is obtained, and rinse the mouth before reinserting the appliance.

Usual pediatric dose

Anesthetic, mucosal-local—
For teething pain—
Infants up to 4 months of age—Dosage must be individualized by a physician or dentist.
Infants and children 4 months to 2 years of age—Topical, as a 7.5 or 10% gel, applied to affected area(s) up to four times a day as needed or as directed by a physician or dentist.
Children 2 years of age and older—Topical, as a 7.5% or stronger gel, applied to affected area(s) up to four times a day or as directed by a physician or dentist.
For toothache—
Children 2 years of age and older—See *Usual adult and adolescent dose.*

Note: Product may be applied with cotton, a cotton swab, or a fingertip.

Strength(s) usually available

U.S.—
7.5% (OTC) [*Anbesol, Baby; Num-Zit Gel; Orabase, Baby; Orajel, Baby*].
10% (OTC) [*Numzident; Orajel; Orajel Nighttime Formula, Baby; Rid-A-Pain*].

20% (OTC) [*Anbesol Maximum Strength Gel* (alcohol 60%); *Orajel Maximum Strength; SensoGARD Canker Sore Relief*].

Canada—

7.5% (OTC) [*Anbesol Baby Jel*].

20% (OTC) [*Orajel Extra Strength; Topicaine*].

Packaging and storage
Store below 40 °C (104 °F), preferably between 15 and 30 °C (59 and 86 °F), unless otherwise specified by manufacturer. Protect from freezing.

BENZOCAINE FILM-FORMING GEL

Usual adult and adolescent dose
Anesthetic, mucosal-local—Topical, as a 15% gel, applied with a cotton swab to affected area(s) up to four times a day or as directed by a physician or dentist. The area should be dried with a cotton swab prior to application.

Usual pediatric dose
Anesthetic, mucosal-local—

Infants and children up to 2 years of age: Dosage must be individualized by a physician or dentist.

Children 2 years of age and older: See *Usual adult and adolescent dose.*

Note: To ensure that this medication is applied correctly, children up to 12 years of age should apply it under the supervision of an adult.

Strength(s) usually available
U.S.—

15% (OTC) [*Oratect Gel*].

Packaging and storage
Store below 40 °C (104 °F), preferably between 15 and 30 °C (59 and 86 °F), unless otherwise specified by manufacturer. Protect from freezing.

BENZOCAINE LOZENGES

Usual adult and adolescent dose
Anesthetic, mucosal-local—Oral, one 10-mg lozenge to be dissolved slowly in the mouth. May be repeated at two-hour intervals as needed.

Usual pediatric dose
Anesthetic, mucosal-local—

Children up to 2 years of age: Dosage must be individualized by a physician.

Children 2 years of age and older: Oral, one 5-mg lozenge to be dissolved slowly in the mouth. May be repeated at two-hour intervals, if needed.

Usual pediatric prescribing limits
Not to exceed twelve 5-mg lozenges per day.

Strength(s) usually available
U.S.—

5 mg (OTC) [*Chloraseptic Lozenges, Children's*].

10 mg (OTC) [*Spec-T Sore Throat Anesthetic*].

Packaging and storage
Store below 40 °C (104 °F), preferably between 15 and 30 °C (59 and 86 °F), unless otherwise specified by manufacturer.

BENZOCAINE OINTMENT (DENTAL) USP

Usual adult and adolescent dose
Anesthetic, mucosal-local—Topical, applied to cleaned and dried dentures up to four times a day.

Usual pediatric dose
Dosage has not been established.

Strength(s) usually available
U.S.—

20% (OTC) [*Benzodent; Dentapaine*].

Packaging and storage
Store below 30 °C (86 °F). Store in a tight container. Protect from light. Protect from freezing.

BENZOCAINE DENTAL PASTE

Usual adult and adolescent dose
Anesthetic, mucosal-local—Topical, applied to the affected area as needed.

Usual pediatric dose
Anesthetic, mucosal-local—

Children up to 6 years of age: Dosage must be individualized by physician or dentist.

Children 6 years of age and older: See *Usual adult and adolescent dose.*

Strength(s) usually available
U.S.—

20% (OTC) [*Orabase-B with Benzocaine*].

Packaging and storage
Store below 40 °C (104 °F), preferably between 15 and 30 °C (59 and 86 °F), unless otherwise specified by manufacturer. Protect from freezing.

BENZOCAINE TOPICAL SOLUTION (DENTAL) USP

Usual adult and adolescent dose
Anesthetic, mucosal-local—Topical, as a 20% solution, applied to affected area(s) up to four times a day or as directed by a physician or dentist.

Note: The medication may be applied with cotton, a cotton swab, or a fingertip.

Usual pediatric dose
Anesthetic, mucosal-local—

Infants and children up to 2 years of age: Dosage must be individualized by a physician or dentist.

Children 2 years of age and older: See *Usual adult and adolescent dose.*

Strength(s) usually available
U.S.—

Note: In Canada, *Anbesol Maximum Strength Liquid* also contains 0.45% of phenol. See *Benzocaine and Phenol Topical Solution.*

0.2% (OTC) [*Num-Zit Lotion* (alcohol 12.6%)].

5% (OTC) [*Dent-Zel-Ite* (alcohol 81%)].

20% (OTC) [*Anbesol Maximum Strength Liquid* (alcohol 60%)].

Canada—

6.5% (OTC) [*Dentocaine*].

7.5% (OTC) [*Orajel, Baby*].

20% (OTC) [*Orajel Liquid*].

Packaging and storage
Store below 30 °C (86 °F). Store in a tight container. Protect from light. Protect from freezing.

BENZOCAINE AND MENTHOL LOZENGES

Usual adult and adolescent dose
Anesthetic, mucosal-local—Oral, one lozenge dissolved slowly in the mouth every two hours as needed or as directed by a physician or dentist.

Usual pediatric dose
Anesthetic, mucosal-local—

Children up to 2 years of age: Dosage must be individualized by a physician or dentist.

Children 2 years of age and older: See *Usual adult and adolescent dose.*

Strength(s) usually available
U.S.—

6 mg of benzocaine and 10 mg of menthol (OTC) [*Chloraseptic Lozenges*].

Canada—

6 mg of benzocaine and 10 mg of menthol (OTC) [*Chloraseptic Lozenges Cherry Flavor*].

Packaging and storage
Store below 40 °C (104 °F), preferably between 15 and 30 °C (59 and 86 °F), unless otherwise specified by manufacturer.

BENZOCAINE AND PHENOL GEL

Usual adult and adolescent dose
Anesthetic, mucosal-local—Topical, applied to affected area(s) up to four times a day or as directed by a physician or dentist.

Note: The medication may be applied with cotton, a cotton swab, or a fingertip.

The gel should not be applied directly to, or used beneath, a dental appliance unless the patient is under the supervision of a dentist. Patients using this medication without the supervision of a dentist for relief of dental appliance pain should apply the medication directly to the affected gum area, wait until relief is obtained, and rinse the mouth before reinserting the appliance.

Usual pediatric dose
Anesthetic, mucosal-local—

Infants and children up to 2 years of age: Dosage must be individualized by a physician or dentist.

Children 2 years of age and older: See *Usual adult and adolescent dose.*

Strength(s) usually available

U.S.—

6.3% of benzocaine and 0.5% of phenol (OTC) [*Anbesol Regular Strength Gel* (alcohol 70%)].

Canada—

6.4% of benzocaine and 0.5% of phenol (OTC) [*Anbesol Gel* (alcohol)].

Packaging and storage

Store below 40 °C (104 °F), preferably between 15 and 30 °C (59 and 86 °F), unless otherwise specified by manufacturer. Protect from freezing.

BENZOCAINE AND PHENOL TOPICAL SOLUTION

Usual adult and adolescent dose

Anesthetic, mucosal-local—Topical, applied to affected area(s) up to four times a day or as directed by a physician or dentist.

Note: The medication may be applied with cotton, a cotton swab, or a fingertip.

Usual pediatric dose

Anesthetic, mucosal-local—

Infants and children up to 2 years of age: Dosage must be individualized by a physician or dentist.

Children 2 years of age and older: See *Usual adult and adolescent dose*.

Strength(s) usually available

U.S.—

6.3% of benzocaine and 0.5% of phenol (OTC) [*Anbesol Regular Strength Liquid* (alcohol 70%)].

Canada—

Note: In the U.S., *Anbesol Maximum Strength Liquid* does not contain phenol. See *Benzocaine Topical Solution USP (Dental)*.

6.5% of benzocaine and 0.45% of phenol (OTC) [*Anbesol Liquid* (alcohol)].

20% of benzocaine and 0.45% of phenol (OTC) [*Anbesol Maximum Strength Liquid* (alcohol)].

Packaging and storage

Store below 40 °C (104 °F), preferably between 15 and 30 °C (59 and 86 °F), unless otherwise specified by manufacturer. Protect from freezing.

Rectal Dosage Forms

BENZOCAINE OINTMENT (RECTAL) USP

Usual adult and adolescent dose

Anesthetic, mucosal-local—Topical, applied to the perianal area up to six times a day after the area has been cleansed and dried. Medication should not be inserted into the rectum.

Usual pediatric dose

Dosage has not been established.

Strength(s) usually available

U.S.—

20% (OTC) [*Americaine Hemorrhoidal*].

Packaging and storage

Store below 30 °C (86 °F). Store in a tight container. Protect from light. Protect from freezing.

Topical Dosage Forms

BENZOCAINE GEL

Usual adult and adolescent dose

Anesthetic, mucosal-local—

Dental procedures: Topical, as a 20% gel, applied to area with a cotton applicator as needed.

Other examination or instrumentation procedures: Topical, as a 20% gel, applied to area with a cotton applicator, or to instrument prior to insertion.

Usual pediatric dose

Dosage has not been established.

Strength(s) usually available

U.S.—

20% (OTC) [*Americaine Anesthetic Lubricant; Hurricaine*].

Packaging and storage

Store below 40 °C (104 °F), preferably between 15 and 30 °C (59 and 86 °F), unless otherwise specified by manufacturer. Protect from freezing.

BENZOCAINE TOPICAL AEROSOL USP

Usual adult and adolescent dose

Anesthetic, mucosal-local—Topical, as a 20% solution, sprayed on area for one second. May be repeated if necessary.

Usual pediatric dose

Dosage has not been established.

Strength(s) usually available

U.S.—

20% (OTC) [*Americaine; Hurricaine*].

Packaging and storage

Store below 40 °C (104 °F), unless otherwise specified by manufacturer.

BENZOCAINE TOPICAL SOLUTION USP

Usual adult and adolescent dose

Anesthetic, mucosal-local—Topical, as a 20% solution, applied to area with a cotton applicator as needed.

Usual pediatric dose

Dosage has not been established.

Strength(s) usually available

U.S.—

20% (OTC) [*Hurricaine*].

Packaging and storage

Store below 30 °C (86 °F). Store in a tight container. Protect from light. Protect from freezing.

BENZOCAINE, BUTAMBEN, AND TETRACAINE

Summary of Differences

Pharmacology/pharmacokinetics:

Physicochemical characteristics—

Benzocaine, butamben, and tetracaine are all PABA-derivative ester-type local anesthetics.

Precautions:

Cross-sensitivity and/or related problems—

May occur with other ester-type local anesthetics, especially other PABA derivatives, parabens, and paraphenylenediamine.

Drug interactions and/or related problems—

Cholinesterase inhibitors inhibit metabolism of these local anesthetics.

May antagonize antibacterial activity of sulfonamides.

Side/adverse effects:

Benzocaine and tetracaine are more likely to cause contact sensitization than other local anesthetics.

Tetracaine is more toxic than other mucosal-local anesthetics.

See also *Side/Adverse Effects*.

Additional Dosing Information

See also *General Dosing Information*.

In dentistry, this medication should not be used under dentures or cotton rolls, because retention under these materials may result in sloughing of tissue.

Topical Dosage Forms

BENZOCAINE, BUTAMBEN, AND TETRACAINE HYDROCHLORIDE GEL USP

Usual adult and adolescent dose

Anesthetic, mucosal-local—Topical, applied directly to desired area, or to instrument prior to insertion.

Usual adult prescribing limits

For the tetracaine component—20 mg.

Usual pediatric dose

Dosage has not been established.

Strength(s) usually available

U.S.—

14% of benzocaine, 2% of butamben, and 2% of tetracaine hydrochloride (Rx) [*Cetacaine Topical Anesthetic*].

Packaging and storage

Store below 40 °C (104 °F), preferably between 15 and 30 °C (59 and 86 °F), unless otherwise specified by manufacturer. Protect from freezing.

BENZOCAINE, BUTAMBEN, AND TETRACAINE HYDROCHLORIDE OINTMENT USP

Usual adult and adolescent dose

Anesthetic, mucosal-local—Topical, applied with a cotton pledget or directly to tissue.

Note: Cotton pledget should not be held in position for extended periods of time, because of increased risk of local reactions to the anesthetics.

Usual adult prescribing limits

For the tetracaine component—20 mg.

Usual pediatric dose

Dosage has not been established.

Strength(s) usually available

U.S.—

14% of benzocaine, 2% of butamben, and 2% of tetracaine hydrochloride (Rx) [*Cetacaine Topical Anesthetic*].

Packaging and storage

Store below 40 °C (104 °F), preferably between 15 and 30 °C (59 and 86 °F), unless otherwise specified by manufacturer. Protect from freezing.

BENZOCAINE, BUTAMBEN, AND TETRACAINE HYDROCHLORIDE TOPICAL AEROSOL USP

Usual adult and adolescent dose

Anesthetic, mucosal-local—Topical, sprayed on desired area for approximately one second or less.

Usual adult prescribing limits

Duration of spray should not exceed two seconds.

Usual pediatric dose

Dosage has not been established.

Strength(s) usually available

U.S.—

14% of benzocaine, 2% of butamben, and 2% of tetracaine hydrochloride (Rx) [*Cetacaine Topical Anesthetic*].

Packaging and storage

Store below 40 °C (104 °F), preferably between 15 and 30 °C (59 and 86 °F), unless otherwise specified by manufacturer.

Auxiliary labeling

- Shake well.

BENZOCAINE, BUTAMBEN, AND TETRACAINE HYDROCHLORIDE TOPICAL SOLUTION USP

Usual adult and adolescent dose

Anesthetic, mucosal-local—Topical, applied with a cotton pledget or directly to tissue.

Note: Cotton pledget should not be held in position for extended periods of time, because of increased risk of local reactions to the anesthetics.

Usual adult prescribing limits

For the tetracaine component—20 mg.

Usual pediatric dose

Dosage has not been established.

Strength(s) usually available

U.S.—

14% of benzocaine, 2% of butamben, and 2% of tetracaine hydrochloride (Rx) [*Cetacaine Topical Anesthetic*].

Packaging and storage

Store below 40 °C (104 °F), preferably between 15 and 30 °C (59 and 86 °F), unless otherwise specified by manufacturer. Protect from freezing.

DIBUCAINE

Summary of Differences

Indications:

Indicated for treatment of hemorrhoids and other anorectal disorders.

Pharmacology/pharmacokinetics:

Physicochemical characteristics—

Dibucaine is an amide-type local anesthetic.

Precautions:

Cross-sensitivity and/or related problems—Rarely, may occur with other amide-type local anesthetics.

Laboratory value alterations—No interference with pancreatic function test using bentiromide.

Rectal Dosage Forms

DIBUCAINE OINTMENT USP

Usual adult and adolescent dose

Anesthetic, mucosal-local—

Rectal, a comfortable quantity, inserted three or four times a day, in the morning, in the evening, and after bowel movements; and/or

Topical, to the perianal area three or four times a day, in the morning, in the evening, and after bowel movements.

Usual pediatric dose

Dosage has not been established.

Strength(s) usually available

U.S.—

1% (OTC) [*Nupercainal* (acetone sodium bisulfite); GENERIC].

Canada—

1% (OTC) [*Nupercainal* (bisulfite)].

Packaging and storage

Store below 40 °C (104 °F), preferably between 15 and 30 °C (59 and 86 °F), unless otherwise specified by manufacturer. Store in a collapsible tube or in a tight, light-resistant container. Protect from freezing.

DYCLONINE

Summary of Differences

Pharmacology/pharmacokinetics:

Physicochemical characteristics—

Dyclonine is neither an ester-type nor an amide-type local anesthetic.

Precautions:

Cross-sensitivity and/or related problems—

Does not occur with either ester-type or amide-type local anesthetics.

Laboratory value alterations—

May cause precipitation of iodine from contrast agents used in cystoscopic procedures following pyelography.

No interference with pancreatic function test using bentiromide.

Dental Dosage Forms

DYCLONINE HYDROCHLORIDE LOZENGES

Usual adult and adolescent dose

Anesthetic, mucosal-local—Oral, one 2-mg or 3-mg lozenge to be dissolved slowly in the mouth. May be repeated at two-hour intervals, if needed.

Usual pediatric dose

Anesthetic, mucosal-local—

Children up to 2 years of age: Dosage has not been established.

Children 2 years of age and older: Oral, one 1.2-mg lozenge to be dissolved slowly in the mouth. May be repeated at two-hour intervals, if needed.

Strength(s) usually available

U.S.—

1.2 mg (OTC) [*Sucrets, Children's*].

2 mg (OTC) [*Sucrets Regular Strength*].

3 mg (OTC) [*Sucrets Maximum Strength*].

Packaging and storage

Store below 40 °C (104 °F), preferably between 15 and 30 °C (59 and 86 °F), unless otherwise specified by manufacturer.

Topical Dosage Forms

DYCLONINE HYDROCHLORIDE TOPICAL SOLUTION USP

Usual adult and adolescent dose

Anesthetic, mucosal-local—

Topical, 40 to 200 mg as a 0.5 or 1% solution; specifically:—

For anogenital pain—

Topical, as a 0.5% solution, applied with sponges or cotton pledgets.

For dental procedures—

Topical, as a 0.5% solution, used as a mouthwash or gargle and the excess expelled.

For otorhinolaryngologic examinations—

Topical, as a 0.5% solution, used as a spray or gargle.

For perioral lesion pain—
Topical, to the affected area(s), as a 0.5% solution, used as a rinse or swab.
For vaginal pain—
Topical, a 0.5 or 1% solution, applied as a wet compress or spray.
For esophageal lesion pain—
Oral, 25 to 150 mg (5 to 15 mL of a 0.5 or 1% solution).

Usual adult prescribing limits
Up to 300 mg (30 mL of a 1% solution) per examination, although this dose is rarely required. Adequate anesthesia is usually achieved with smaller quantities.

Usual pediatric dose
Dosage has not been established.

Strength(s) usually available
U.S.—
0.5% (Rx) [*Dyclone*].
1% (Rx) [*Dyclone*].

Packaging and storage
Store below 40 °C (104 °F), preferably between 15 and 30 °C (59 and 86 °F), unless otherwise specified by manufacturer. Store in a tight, light-resistant container. Protect from freezing.

LIDOCAINE

Summary of Differences

Pharmacology/pharmacokinetics:
Physicochemical characteristics—Lidocaine is an amide-type local anesthetic.
Protein binding—Concentration-dependent; 60 to 80% at nontoxic plasma concentrations.
Precautions:
Cross-sensitivity and/or related problems—Rarely, may occur with other amide-type local anesthetics.
Breast-feeding—Distributed into breast milk in very small quantities.
Drug interactions and/or related problems—Also interacts with beta-adrenergic blocking agents, cimetidine, and amide local anesthetic–derivative antiarrhythmic agents.

Dental Dosage Forms

Note: The topical solution formulations included in this section are specifically formulated for application only to gingival or buccal mucosa or to perioral tissues. Topical solution formulations that are applied to other mucosal tissues (in addition to the gingival or buccal mucosa) are included in the *Topical Dosage Forms* section.

LIDOCAINE TOPICAL AEROSOL USP

Usual adult and adolescent dose
Anesthetic, mucosal-local—Topical, to gingival and oral mucous membranes, 20 mg (two metered sprays) per quadrant of gingiva and oral mucosa.

Usual adult prescribing limits
Not to exceed 30 mg of lidocaine (three metered sprays) per quadrant of gingiva and oral mucosa over a one-half-hour period or 200 mg (twenty metered sprays) in twenty-four hours.

Usual pediatric dose
Anesthetic, mucosal-local—Topical, to gingival and oral mucous membranes, up to a total of 3 mg per kg of body weight.

Strength(s) usually available
U.S.—
10% (10 mg per metered spray) (Rx) [*Xylocaine*].
Canada—
10% (10 mg per metered spray) (OTC) [*Xylocaine*].

Packaging and storage
Store below 40 °C (104 °F), preferably between 15 and 30 °C (59 and 86 °F), unless otherwise specified by manufacturer. Protect from freezing.

Auxiliary labeling
• Shake well.

LIDOCAINE ORAL TOPICAL SOLUTION USP

Usual adult and adolescent dose
Anesthesia, mucosal-local—
Dental procedures: Topical, 50 to 200 mg as a 5% solution, applied to the oral mucosa with a cotton applicator.
Perioral lesions: Topical, as a 2.5% solution, applied to affected area(s) with a cotton swab every one or two hours for the first three days, then as needed.

Usual adult prescribing limits
Dental procedures—Not to exceed a total of 250 mg (5 mL of a 5% solution) for all quadrants in a three-hour period.

Usual pediatric dose
Anesthesia, mucosal-local—Dental procedures: Topical, the dosage being individualized, based on the child's age, weight, and physical condition up to a maximum of 4.5 mg per kg of body weight as 5% solution.

Strength(s) usually available
U.S.—
2.5% (OTC) [*Zilactin-L*].
5% (Rx) [*Xylocaine;* GENERIC].
Canada—
5% (OTC) [*Xylocaine*].

Packaging and storage
Store below 40 °C (104 °F), preferably between 15 and 30 °C (59 and 86 °F), unless otherwise specified by manufacturer. Store in a tight container. Protect from freezing.

Topical Dosage Forms

LIDOCAINE OINTMENT USP

Usual adult and adolescent dose
Anesthetic, mucosal-local—
Oral mucosa—
Topical, as a 5% ointment, to previously dried oral mucosa.
For use during fitting of new dentures—Apply to all denture surfaces that contact the mucosa, up to a maximum of 5 grams of ointment (250 mg of lidocaine) per single dose or 20 grams of ointment (1000 mg of lidocaine) per day.
Note: The patient should be advised to consult the prescribing dentist at intervals not exceeding 48 hours throughout the fitting period.

Oropharynx—
Topical, as a 5% ointment, applied to desired area, or to instrument prior to insertion.

Usual pediatric dose
Anesthetic, mucosal-local—Topical, the dosage being individualized, based on the child's age, weight, and physical condition, up to a maximum of 4.5 mg per kg of body weight or 2.5 grams of ointment in a six-hour period.

Strength(s) usually available
U.S.—
5% (Rx) [*Xylocaine;* GENERIC].
Canada—
5% (OTC) [*Xylocaine Dental Ointment*].

Packaging and storage
Store below 40 °C (104 °F), preferably between 15 and 30 °C (59 and 86 °F), unless otherwise specified by manufacturer. Store in a tight container. Protect from freezing.

LIDOCAINE HYDROCHLORIDE JELLY USP

Usual adult and adolescent dose
Anesthetic, mucosal-local—
Esophagus, larynx, trachea—
Topical, as a 2% jelly, applied to the outer surface of the instrument prior to insertion.
Note: Care should be taken to avoid depositing any of the medication on the inner surface of an endoscope or other instrument. It may dry on the inner surface and leave a residue that may cause narrowing or, rarely, occlusion of the lumen.

Urinary tract—
Female:
Urethral, 3 to 5 mL, as a 2% jelly, several minutes prior to examination.
Note: Jelly may be deposited on a cotton swab and introduced into urethra.
Male:
Prior to catheterization: Urethral, 100 to 200 mg (5 to 10 mL) as a 2% jelly.
Prior to sounding or cystoscopy: Urethral, 600 mg (30 mL) to fill and dilate urethra. The medication is usually administered in two divided doses, with a penile clamp applied for several minutes between doses.

Usual adult prescribing limits
Not more than 600 mg (30 mL) in a twelve-hour period.

Usual pediatric dose
Anesthetic, mucosal-local—Topical, as a 2% jelly, dosage to be individualized, based on the child's age, weight, and physical condition, up to a maximum of 4.5 mg per kg of body weight.

Strength(s) usually available
U.S.—
2% (Rx) [*Anestacon Jelly; Xylocaine;* GENERIC].
Canada—
2% (OTC) [*Xylocaine*].

Packaging and storage
Store below 40 °C (104 °F), preferably between 15 and 30 °C (59 and 86 °F), unless otherwise specified by manufacturer. Store in a tight container. Protect from freezing.

LIDOCAINE HYDROCHLORIDE ORAL TOPICAL SOLUTION USP

Note: Previous name—Lidocaine Hydrochloride Viscous Solution.

Usual adult and adolescent dose
Anesthetic, mucosal-local—
Oral cavity disorders: Topical, 300 mg (15 mL) swished around in the mouth, then expelled, or applied with a cotton-tipped applicator, every three hours as needed.
Pharyngeal pain: Topical, 300 mg (15 mL) used as a gargle every three hours as needed. May be swallowed if necessary.

Usual adult prescribing limits
Single dose—Not to exceed 4.5 mg per kg of body weight or 300 mg (15 mL). This dose should not be repeated more often than every three hours.
Multiple doses—Not to exceed 8 doses (2.4 grams or 120 mL) in twenty-four hours.

Usual pediatric dose
Anesthetic, mucosal-local—
Infants and children up to 3 years of age—
Topical, up to 1.25 mL of a 2% solution, applied to affected area(s) with a cotton-tipped applicator every three hours.
Note: It is recommended that the dosage be accurately measured and applied to the immediate area or specific lesion with a cotton-tipped applicator. The risk of systemic toxicity, especially convulsions, is increased if dosage is not carefully controlled and/or if the patient swallows significant quantities of the medication.
Children 3 years of age and older—
Topical, the dosage being individualized, based on the child's age, weight, and physical condition, up to a maximum of 4.5 mg per kg of body weight as 2% solution in a three-hour period.

Strength(s) usually available
U.S.—
2% (Rx) [*Xylocaine Viscous;* GENERIC].
Canada—
2% (OTC) [*Xylocaine Viscous*].

Packaging and storage
Store below 40 °C (104 °F), preferably between 15 and 30 °C (59 and 86 °F), unless otherwise specified by manufacturer. Store in a tight container. Protect from freezing.

LIDOCAINE HYDROCHLORIDE TOPICAL SOLUTION USP

Usual adult and adolescent dose
Anesthetic, mucosal-local—Oral or nasal cavity or esophagus: Topical, as a 4% solution, 600 mcg (0.6 mg) to 3 mg per kg of body weight; or 40 to 200 mg (1 to 5 mL).
Note: May be applied as a spray, with cotton applicators or packs, or instilled directly into cavity.

Usual adult prescribing limits
For use in oral or nasal cavities or upper gastrointestinal tract—Not to exceed 4.5 mg per kg of body weight or 300 mg (7.5 mL of a 4% solution).

Usual pediatric dose
Dosage must be individualized by physician.

Strength(s) usually available
U.S.—
4% (Rx) [*Xylocaine;* GENERIC].
Canada—
4% (OTC) [*Xylocaine*].

Packaging and storage
Store below 40 °C (104 °F), preferably between 15 and 30 °C (59 and 86 °F), unless otherwise specified by manufacturer. Store in a tight container. Protect from freezing.

LIDOCAINE HYDROCHLORIDE TOPICAL SPRAY SOLUTION

Note: The dosing and strength of this dosage form are expressed in terms of lidocaine base.

Usual adult and adolescent dose
Anesthetic, mucosal-local—Endoscopic procedures: Topical, up to 20 metered sprays (200 mg [base]) as a 10% (base) solution, sprayed onto the oropharyngeal or tracheal mucosa.

Usual pediatric dose
Anesthetic, mucosal-local—
Infants and children up to 3 years of age—
Use is not recommended; a less concentrated solution should be used instead.
Children 3 to 12 years of age—
Larynx or trachea—Topical, up to 1.5 mg (base) per kg of body weight.
Other mucosa—Topical, up to 3 mg (base) per kg of body weight.

Strength(s) usually available
U.S.—
Not commercially available.
Canada—
10% (base; 12 mg of lidocaine hydrochloride equivalent to 10 mg of lidocaine base per metered spray) (OTC) [*Xylocaine Endotracheal*].

Packaging and storage
Store below 40 °C (104 °F), preferably between 15 and 30 °C (59 and 86 °F), unless otherwise specified by manufacturer. Store in a tight container. Protect from freezing.

PRAMOXINE

Summary of Differences

Indications:
Indicated for the treatment of hemorrhoids and other anorectal disorders.
Pharmacology/pharmacokinetics:
Physicochemical characteristics—
Pramoxine is neither an amide-type nor an ester-type local anesthetic.
Precautions:
Cross-sensitivity and/or related problems—Does not occur with either ester-type or amide-type local anesthetics.
Laboratory value alterations—No interference with pancreatic function test using bentiromide.

Rectal Dosage Forms

PRAMOXINE HYDROCHLORIDE AEROSOL FOAM

Usual adult and adolescent dose
Anesthetic, mucosal-local—
Rectal, one applicatorful two to three times a day; or
Topical, to the external anorectal area two to three times a day.

Usual pediatric dose
Dosage has not been established.

Strength(s) usually available
U.S.—
1% (OTC) [*ProctoFoam/non-steroid* (propylparaben)].

Packaging and storage
Store below 40 °C (104 °F), preferably between 15 and 30 °C (59 and 86 °F), unless otherwise specified by manufacturer. Protect from freezing.

Auxiliary labeling
- Shake well.
- For anorectal use only.

PRAMOXINE HYDROCHLORIDE CREAM USP

Usual adult and adolescent dose
Anesthetic, mucosal-local—Topical, to the anorectal area, up to five times a day, after the area has been cleansed and dried.

Usual pediatric dose
Children up to 12 years of age—Dosage must be individualized by physician.

Strength(s) usually available
U.S.—
1% (OTC) [*Tronolane; Tronothane*].
Canada—
1% (OTC) [*Tronothane*].

Packaging and storage
Store below 40 °C (104 °F), preferably between 15 and 30 °C (59 and 86 °F), unless otherwise specified by manufacturer. Store in tight container. Protect from freezing.

PRAMOXINE HYDROCHLORIDE OINTMENT

Usual adult and adolescent dose
Anesthetic, mucosal-local—
Rectal, introduced into the rectum as a 1% ointment up to five times per day, in the morning, at night, and after bowel movements; or
Topical, to the anorectal area as a 1% ointment up to five times a day.

Usual pediatric dose
Children up to 12 years of age—Dosage must be individualized by physician.

Strength(s) usually available
U.S.—
1% (OTC) [*Fleet Relief*].

Note: Available in tubes and in pre-filled 4-mL disposable applicators.

Packaging and storage
Store below 40 °C (104 °F), preferably between 15 and 30 °C (59 and 86 °F), unless otherwise specified by manufacturer. Protect from freezing.

TETRACAINE

Summary of Differences

Pharmacology/pharmacokinetics:
Physicochemical characteristics—
Tetracaine is a PABA-derivative ester-type local anesthetic.
Precautions:
Cross-sensitivity and/or related problems—
May occur with other ester-type local anesthetics, especially other PABA derivatives, parabens, and paraphenylenediamine.
Drug interactions and/or related problems—
Cholinesterase inhibitors inhibit metabolism of tetracaine.
May antagonize antibacterial activity of sulfonamides.
Side/adverse effects:
More likely to cause contact sensitization than most other local anesthetics.
More toxic than other mucosal-local anesthetics.
See also *Side/Adverse Effects*.

Rectal Dosage Forms

TETRACAINE HYDROCHLORIDE CREAM USP

Note: The dosing and strength of this dosage form are expressed in terms of tetracaine base.

Usual adult and adolescent dose
Anesthetic, mucosal-local—Rectal, introduced into rectum as a 1% (base) cream up to six times a day.

Usual adult prescribing limits
Not more than 28.35 grams in a twenty-four-hour period.

Usual pediatric dose
Dosage has not been established.

Strength(s) usually available
U.S.—
1% (base) (OTC) [*Pontocaine Cream*].
Canada—
Not commercially available.

Packaging and storage
Store below 40 °C (104 °F), preferably between 15 and 30 °C (59 and 86 °F), unless otherwise specified by manufacturer. Protect from freezing.

TETRACAINE AND MENTHOL OINTMENT USP

Usual adult and adolescent dose
Anesthetic, mucosal-local—
Rectal, introduced into rectum as a 0.5% ointment up to six times a day.
Topical, applied as a 0.5% ointment spread with gauze or cotton, to anorectal area up to six times a day.

Usual adult prescribing limits
Not more than 28.35 grams in a twenty-four-hour period.

Usual pediatric dose
Dosage has not been established.

Strength(s) usually available
U.S.—
0.5% of tetracaine and 0.5% of menthol (OTC) [*Pontocaine Ointment*].
Canada—
Not commercially available.

Packaging and storage
Store below 40 °C (104 °F), preferably between 15 and 30 °C (59 and 86 °F), unless otherwise specified by manufacturer. Protect from freezing.

Topical Dosage Forms

TETRACAINE HYDROCHLORIDE TOPICAL SOLUTION USP

Usual adult and adolescent dose
Anesthetic, mucosal-local—Larynx, trachea, or esophagus—
Topical, as a 0.25 or 0.5% solution prior to procedure; or
Oral inhalation, as a nebulized 0.5% solution.

Note: 0.06 mL of 0.1% (1:1000) epinephrine may be added to each mL of tetracaine solution, to reduce absorption.

Usual adult prescribing limits
Not to exceed 20 mg.

Usual pediatric dose
Dosage has not been established.

Strength(s) usually available
U.S.—
2% (Rx) [*Pontocaine*].
Canada—
Not commercially available.

Packaging and storage
Store between 2 and 8 °C (36 and 46 °F), unless otherwise specified by manufacturer. Store in a tight, light-resistant container. Protect from freezing.

Stability
Do not use if solution is cloudy or discolored or contains crystals.

Revised: 06/13/2000

ANESTHETICS Parenteral-Local

This monograph includes information on the following: 1) Articaine; 2) Bupivacaine; 3) Chloroprocaine; 4) Etidocaine; 5) Levobupivacaine; 6) Lidocaine; 7) Mepivacaine; 8) Prilocaine; 9) Procaine; 10) Tetracaine.

INN: Lidocaine—Lignocaine

BAN: Articaine—Carticaine

VA CLASSIFICATION (Primary): CN204

Commonly used brand name(s): *Astracaine 4%*[1]; *Astracaine 4% Forte*[1]; *Carbocaine*[7]; *Carbocaine with Neo-Cobefrin*[7]; *Chirocaine*[5]; *Citanest Forte*[8]; *Citanest Plain*[8]; *Dalcaine*[6]; *Dilocaine*[6]; *Duranest*[4]; *Duranest-MPF*[4]; *Isocaine*[7]; *Isocaine 2%*[7]; *Isocaine 3%*[7]; *L-Caine*[6]; *Lidoject-1*[6]; *Lidoject-2*[6]; *Marcaine*[2]; *Marcaine Spinal*[2]; *Nesacaine*[3]; *Nesacaine-CE*[3]; *Nesacaine-MPF*[3]; *Novocain*[9]; *Octocaine*[6]; *Octocaine-100*[6]; *Octocaine-50*[6]; *Polocaine*[7]; *Polocaine-MPF*[7]; *Pontocaine*[10]; *Sensorcaine*[2]; *Sensorcaine Forte*[2]; *Sensorcaine-MPF*[2]; *Sensorcaine-MPF Spinal*[2]; *Septocaine*™[1]; *Ultracaine D-S*[1]; *Ultracaine D-S Forte*[1]; *Xylocaine*[6]; *Xylocaine 5% Spinal*[6]; *Xylocaine Test Dose*[6]; *Xylocaine-MPF*[6]; *Xylocaine-MPF with Glucose*[6].

A commonly used name for lidocaine is lignocaine.

Note: For a listing of dosage forms and brand names by country availability, see *Dosage Forms* section(s).

Category

Anesthetic (local).

Indications

Note: Bracketed information in the *Indications* section refers to uses that are not included in U.S. product labeling.

General Considerations

Parenteral-local anesthetics are generally used to provide local or regional anesthesia, analgesia, and varying degrees of motor blockade prior to surgical procedures, dental procedures, and obstetric delivery. They also may be used for other diagnostic or therapeutic purposes via routes of administration that are stated in product labeling.

Mixtures or combinations of local anesthetics are sometimes used to provide a rapid onset of action and a prolonged duration of action. However, the possibility of additive toxicity must be considered when such combinations are used.

Vasoconstrictors are added to local anesthetic injections to decrease the rate of local clearance of the local anesthetic. Local anesthetic injections containing a vasoconstrictor generally have the same indications as the corresponding local anesthetic injection without a vasoconstrictor. However, additional precautions pertinent to the use of a vasoconstrictor must be considered.

Dextrose is added to anesthetic solutions for subarachnoid administration to render the solution hyperbaric (heavier than cerebrospinal fluid [CSF]); the local anesthetic will exert its effect above or below the site of injection, depending upon the position of the patient during and immediately following the injection.

Local anesthetics may be combined with opioid analgesics for epidural administration for inducing postoperative analgesia. This combination may allow lower doses of both the local anesthetic and the opioid to be used as compared with either agent used alone, and may reduce the incidence of motor block, nausea, and urinary retention.

Accepted

Central neural blocks—Caudal or lumbar epidural: Bupivacaine (with or without epinephrine), chloroprocaine, etidocaine (with or without epinephrine), lidocaine (with or without epinephrine), levobupivacaine, and mepivacaine are indicated. Only single-dose vials that do not contain an antimicrobial preservative should be used.

Subarachnoid: Bupivacaine and dextrose, lidocaine and dextrose, procaine[1], and tetracaine (with or without dextrose) are indicated. Commercially available products intended specifically for subarachnoid administration contain no antimicrobial preservatives. Solutions and diluents containing antimicrobial preservatives are not to be injected into the subarachnoid space and should not be used when preparing injections for administration via this route.

Dental infiltration or nerve block—Articaine with epinephrine; bupivacaine and epinephrine; chloroprocaine (with or without added epinephrine); etidocaine and epinephrine; lidocaine (with or without epinephrine); mepivacaine (with or without levonordefrin); prilocaine (with or without epinephrine) are indicated. Unless specifically contraindicated, a vasoconstrictor-containing solution is preferred.

Intravenous regional anesthesia (Bier block)[1]—[Chloroprocaine], lidocaine, and [mepivacaine] are indicated.

Local infiltration—Bupivacaine (with or without epinephrine), chloroprocaine, etidocaine (with or without epinephrine), levobupivacaine, lidocaine (with or without epinephrine), mepivacaine, and procaine are indicated.

Peripheral nerve block—Bupivacaine (with or without epinephrine), chloroprocaine, etidocaine (with or without epinephrine), levobupivacainelidocaine (with or without epinephrine), mepivacaine, and procaine are indicated.

Retrobulbar block: Bupivacaine, etidocaine, lidocaine, and [procaine][1] are indicated.

Sympathetic block—Bupivacaine (with or without epinephrine) and lidocaine (with or without epinephrine) are indicated.

Transtracheal—Lidocaine, [mepivacaine][1], and [tetracaine][1] are indicated.

Unaccepted

For paracervical administration—Use of bupivacaine is not recommended for nonobstetrical procedures because of insufficient data concerning safety and dosage. Use of bupivacaine is not recommended in obstetrical procedures because such use has resulted in fetal bradycardia and death.

Solutions containing a vasoconstrictor should not be used for intravenous regional anesthesia (Bier block). Also, bupivacaine and levobupivacaine are not recommended for intravenous regional anesthesia.

For central neural block (peridural [lumbar or caudal epidural] or subarachnoid [spinal] administration)—Do not use solutions containing an antimicrobial preservative such as chlorobutanol or methylparaben.

Chloroprocaine and mepivacaine are not recommended for subarachnoid (spinal) administration.

[1]Not included in Canadian product labeling.

Pharmacology/Pharmacokinetics

See *Table 1*, page 191.

Physicochemical characteristics

Chemical Group—Amides: Articaine, bupivacaine, etidocaine, levobupivacaine, lidocaine, mepivacaine, prilocaineEsters, aminobenzoic acid (PABA)-derivative: Chloroprocaine, procaine, tetracaine

Molecular weight—
- Articaine: 284.38.
- Bupivacaine hydrochloride: 342.91.
- Chloroprocaine hydrochloride: 307.22.
- Etidocaine: 276.42.
- levobupivacaine: 324.9.
- Lidocaine hydrochloride: 288.82.
- Mepivacaine hydrochloride: 282.81.
- Prilocaine hydrochloride: 256.78.
- Procaine hydrochloride: 272.78.
- Tetracaine hydrochloride: 300.83.

pKa—
- See *Table 1*

Lipid solubility—
- See *Table 1.*

Mechanism of action/Effect

Local anesthetics—

Local anesthetics block both the initiation and conduction of nerve impulses by decreasing the neuronal membrane's permeability to sodium ions, perhaps by attaching to a site on the sodium channel. This reversibly stabilizes the membrane and inhibits depolarization, resulting in the failure of a propagated action potential and subsequent conduction blockade.

The concentration of drug needed to block large nerve trunks is greater than that needed for smaller peripheral nerves.

Vasoconstrictors—

Act on alpha-adrenergic receptors in the vasculature of the skin, mucous membranes, conjunctiva, and viscera to produce vasoconstriction, thereby decreasing blood flow in the area of injection. The resultant reduction in the rate of local clearance of the local anesthetic prolongs the duration of action, lowers the peak serum concentration, decreases the risk of systemic toxicity, and increases the frequency of complete conduction blocks with low concentrations of the local anesthetic. Vasoconstrictors may also reduce bleeding when injected at the site of surgery.

Other actions/effects

Local anesthetics—Actions on the central nervous system (CNS) may cause CNS stimulation and/or CNS depression. Actions on the cardiovascular system may cause depression of cardiac conduction and excitability and, with most of these agents, peripheral vasodilation.

Vasoconstrictors—Vasoconstrictors having beta-adrenergic activity (epinephrine, levonordefrin, and norepinephrine) may cause cardiac stimulation resulting in increased heart rate, contractility, conduction velocity, and irritability. Also, when used for obstetrical anesthesia, vasoconstrictors having beta-adrenergic activity may decrease the intensity of uterine contractions and prolong labor. Phenylephrine is also rarely used as a vasoconstrictor in conjunction with local anesthesia; it has only alpha-adrenergic activity and does not have these additional effects.

Absorption

Complete systemic absorption. The rate of absorption is influenced by the site and route of administration (especially the vascularity or rate of blood flow at the injection site), total dosage (volume and concentration) administered, physical characteristics (such as degree of protein binding and lipid solubility) of the individual agent, and whether or not a vasoconstrictor is used concurrently.

Biotransformation

Amides—

Hepatic.

Articaine: Inactivated by ester hydrolysis via plasma carboxyesterase to articainic acid. Approximately 5% to 10% of articaine is metabolized by liver microsome P450 isoenzymes to articainic acid.

Levobupivacaine: Metabolized by cytochrome P450 (CYP) 3A4 and CYP1A2 isoforms to desbutyl levobupivacaine and 3–hydroxy levobupivacaine, respectively.

Lidocaine: Xylidide metabolites are active and toxic, but less so than the parent compound.

Prilocaine: May also be metabolized renally to some extent.

Esters—

PABA derivatives: Hydrolyzed primarily in the plasma and, to a much lesser extent, in the liver, by cholinesterases. Procaine is hydrolyzed to PABA. Chloroprocaine and tetracaine are hydrolyzed to PABA-containing compounds.

Time to peak concentration
Usually 10 to 30 minutes. May occur 1 to 3 minutes after intravascular or transtracheal injection.

Elimination
Renal, primarily as metabolites. For some of these agents, including lidocaine, mepivacaine, and tetracaine, renal excretion may follow biliary excretion into, and reabsorption from, the gastrointestinal tract.
Quantity of dose excreted unchanged—
Articaine: 2% to 5%.
Bupivacaine: 5%.
Etidocaine: Less than 10%.
Lidocaine: 10%.
Levobupivacaine: 0%
Mepivacaine: 5 to 10%.
Procaine: Less than 2%.

Precautions to Consider

Cross-sensitivity and/or related problems
Patients sensitive to para-aminobenzoic acid (PABA) or parabens may be sensitive to procaine, chloroprocaine, or tetracaine also. They may also be sensitive to other local anesthetic solutions containing parabens as preservatives.
Patients sensitive to one ester-type local anesthetic may be sensitive to other ester-type local anesthetics also.
Patients sensitive to one amide-type local anesthetic rarely may be sensitive to other amide-type local anesthetics also.
Cross-sensitivity between ester-type local anesthetics and amide-type local anesthetics has not been reported.

Carcinogenicity
Articaine—Studies evaluating the carcinogenic potential of articaine in animals have not been conducted.

Mutagenicity
Articaine—*In vitro* (nonmammalian Ames test, mammalian Chinese hamster ovary chromosomal aberration test, mammalian gene mutation test) and *in vivo* (mouse micronucleous tests) mutagenicity tests showed no mutagenic effects.

Pregnancy/Reproduction
Fertility—*Articaine*—In rats, doses approximately 2 times the maximum recommended human dose (MRHD) had no effect on male or female fertility.

Pregnancy—Local anesthetics cross the placenta by diffusion. The rate and degree of diffusion vary considerably among the various agents as determined by their rate of metabolism and physical characteristics such as plasma protein binding (reduced placental transfer with highly protein-bound agents), lipid solubility (greater placental transfer with highly lipid soluble agents), and degree of ionization (greater placental transfer with nonionized form of agent).

All parenteral-local anesthetics—Adequate and well-controlled prospective studies in humans have not been done. Retrospective studies of pregnant women receiving local anesthetics for emergency surgery early in pregnancy have not shown that local anesthetics cause birth defects.

Articaine—Adequate and well-controlled studies in humans have not been done. Studies of articaine in rats and rabbits using doses of up to 2.9 times the maximum recommended human dose (MRHD) have not shown adverse effects on the fetus. In rabbits, doses approximately 4 times the MRHD did cause fetal death and increase fetal skeletal variations, but these effects may be attributable to severe maternal toxicity. In rats, doses approximately 2 times the MRHD increased the number of stillbirths and adversely affected passive avoidance (a measure of learning).

FDA Pregnancy Category C

Bupivacaine—Studies in rats and rabbits using doses 9 and 5 times the MRHD, respectively, have shown decreased survival in newborn rats and embryocidal effects in rabbits.

FDA Pregnancy Category C.

Chloroprocaine, mepivacaine, and tetracaine—Studies in animals have not been done.

FDA Pregnancy Category C.

Etidocaine, levobupivacaine, lidocaine, and prilocaine—Studies in rats or rabbits with etidocaine (using up to 1.7 times the MRHD), levobupivacaine (using 0.5 times the MRHD), lidocaine (using up to 6.6 times the MRHD), or prilocaine (using 30 times the MRHD) have not shown adverse effects on the fetus.

FDA Pregnancy Category B.

Procaine—Studies in animals have not been done.

FDA Pregnancy Category C.

Labor and delivery—Epidural, subarachnoid, paracervical, or pudendal administration of a local anesthetic may produce changes in uterine contractility and/or maternal expulsive efforts. Paracervical block may shorten the first stage of labor and facilitate cervical dilation. However, epidural or subarachnoid administration of local anesthetics may prolong the second stage of labor by interfering with motor function or removing the patient's reflex urge to bear down. Use of a local anesthetic during delivery may increase the need for forceps-assisted delivery. Bupivacaine and etidocaine are not recommended for paracervical administration. Also, etidocaine may cause profound motor block; epidural administration of this agent is not recommended for normal vaginal delivery (although it may be used for cesarean section).

Labor and delivery—Maternal hypotension, caused by sympathetic nerve blockade resulting in vasodilation, may occur during regional anesthesia.

Labor and delivery—Maternal convulsions and cardiovascular collapse have been reported following paracervical administration of local anesthetics early in pregnancy (for elective abortion), suggesting rapid systemic absorption under these circumstances.

Labor and delivery—Maternal fatalities due to cardiac arrest have been reported following inadvertent intravascular injection of 0.75% bupivacaine during intended placement of an epidural block. Although the 0.75% strength is not recommended for epidural administration in obstetrics, lower concentrations of bupivacaine may be used.

Labor and delivery—Fetal bradycardia, possibly associated with fetal acidosis, has been reported in 20 to 30% of patients receiving amide-type local anesthetics via paracervical block. Fetal bradycardia without fetal acidosis also has been reported in 5 to 10% of patients receiving chloroprocaine via paracervical block. The risk of this complication may be increased if prematurity, postmaturity, toxemia of pregnancy, pre-existing fetal distress, or uteroplacental insufficiency is present. Risk-benefit must be considered when amide-type local anesthetics are considered for paracervical block in these conditions. Paracervical block with chloroprocaine is not recommended if prematurity, pre-existing fetal distress, or toxemia of pregnancy is present because its safety in these conditions has not been established. Monitoring of fetal heart rate is recommended during paracervical block.

Postpartum—

Neonatal neurological disturbances such as diminished muscle strength and tone may occur for 1 to 2 days postpartum. Marked neonatal CNS depression has been reported following paracervical block. Also, inadvertent fetal intracranial injection during intended caudal, paracervical, or pudendal administration may cause neonatal depression and convulsions.

Breast-feeding
It is not known whether most local anesthetics are distributed into breast milk. Bupivacaine is distributed into breast milk in small quantities. Lidocaine is distributed into breast milk. However, problems in humans have not been documented.

Pediatrics
Although there is some evidence that systemic toxicity may be more likely to occur in pediatric patients, appropriate studies performed to date with mepivacaine have not demonstrated pediatrics-specific problems that would limit the use of the medication in children. Also, no information is available on the relationship of age to the effects of procaineand levobupivacaine in pediatric patients. Although articaine is not approved for use in children younger than 4 years of age, a retrospective study of its use in patients younger than 4 years of age did not reveal any pediatrics-specific problems that would limit its use in children.

Infants up to 9 months of age have low plasma concentrations of alpha$_1$-acid glycoprotein (AAG). This results in an increased unbound fraction of bupivacaine and etidocaine, and may lead to systemic toxicity.

Reduced clearance of bupivacaine in pediatric patients may be more important than AAG concentrations in causing toxicity. Neonates may have total body clearance of bupivacaine only one third to one half the clearance of adults.

Appropriate studies performed to date have not demonstrated pediatrics-specific problems that would limit the usefulness of lidocaine in children.

Geriatrics
Systemic toxicity may be more likely to occur in geriatric patients.

Drug interactions and/or related problems
The following drug interactions and/or related problems have been selected on the basis of their potential clinical significance (possible mechanism in parentheses where appropriate)—not necessarily inclusive (» = major clinical significance):

Note: Combinations containing any of the following medications, depending on the amount present, may also interact with this medication.

For all local anesthetics

Anticoagulants, such as:
- Ardeparin or
- Dalteparin or
- Danaparoid or
- Enoxaparin or
- Heparin or
- Warfarin

(trauma to a blood vessel during peridural or subarachnoid administration of the local anesthetic may result in CNS or soft tissue hemorrhage in patients receiving anticoagulant therapy)

Antimyasthenics
(inhibition of neuronal transmission by local anesthetics may antagonize the effects of antimyasthenics on skeletal muscle, especially if large quantities of the anesthetic are rapidly absorbed; temporary dosage adjustment of antimyasthenics may be necessary to control symptoms of myasthenia gravis)

Beta-adrenergic blocking agents
(may slow metabolism of lidocaine by reducing hepatic blood flow, leading to increased risk of lidocaine toxicity)

Cimetidine
(cimetidine may inhibit hepatic metabolism of bupivacaine and lidocaine, leading to increased risk of toxicity)

» CNS depression-producing medications, including those commonly used as preanesthetic medication or for supplementation of local anesthesia (see *Appendix II*)
(concurrent use with a local anesthetic may result in additive depressant effects)

Disinfectant solutions containing heavy metals
(local anesthetics may cause release of heavy metal ions from these solutions, which, if injected along with the anesthetic, may cause severe local irritation, swelling, and edema; such solutions are not recommended for chemical disinfection of the container, and preventive measures are recommended if they are used for skin or mucous membrane disinfection prior to anesthetic administration)

Guanadrel or
Guanethidine or
Mecamylamine or
Trimethaphan
(the risk of severe hypotension and/or bradycardia may be increased if high levels of spinal or epidural anesthesia [i.e., sufficient to produce sympathetic blockade] are induced in patients receiving these ganglionic-blocking antihypertensive agents)

Halothane
(may increase the cardiotoxicity of bupivacaine)

Monoamine oxidase (MAO) inhibitors, including furazolidone, procarbazine, and selegiline
(concurrent use in patients receiving local anesthetics may increase the risk of hypotension; discontinuation of MAO inhibitors 10 days before elective surgery may be advisable if subarachnoid block anesthesia is planned)

Neuromuscular blocking agents
(inhibition of neuronal transmission by local anesthetics may enhance or prolong the action of neuromuscular blocking agents if large quantities of the anesthetic are rapidly absorbed)

Opioid (narcotic) analgesic anesthesia adjuncts
(alterations in respiration caused by high levels of spinal or peridural blockade may be additive to opioid analgesic-induced alterations in respiratory rate and alveolar ventilation)
(the vagal effects of alfentanil, fentanyl, or sufentanil may also be more pronounced in patients with high levels of spinal or epidural anesthesia, and may lead to bradycardia and/or hypotension)

» Vasoconstrictors such as epinephrine, methoxamine, or phenylephrine
(use of methoxamine in combination with local anesthetics to prolong their action at local sites is not recommended, since methoxamine's extended effect may cause excessive restriction of circulation and lead to sloughing of tissue)
(other vasoconstrictors should be used cautiously and in carefully circumscribed quantities, if at all, with local anesthetics when anesthetizing areas with end arteries [such as the fingers, nose, toes, or penis] or with otherwise compromised blood supply; ischemia leading to gangrene may result)

For ester-type local anesthetics (in addition to those interactions listed above as applying to all local anesthetics)

Cholinesterase inhibitors such as:
- Antimyasthenics
- Cyclophosphamide
- Demecarium
- Echothiophate
- Insecticides, neurotoxic, possibly including large quantities of topical malathion
- Isoflurophate
- Thiotepa

(concurrent use with an ester-type local anesthetic may inhibit the metabolism of the anesthetic, leading to increased risk of toxicity)

Sulfonamides
(antibacterial activity may be antagonized by ester-type local anesthetics, which are metabolized to PABA or PABA derivatives)

Note: The risk of a significant systemic effect resulting from an interaction between any of the following and a vasoconstrictor-containing local anesthetic solution depends on the total dose (volume and concentration) of vasoconstrictor administered and on factors affecting the rate of absorption of the vasoconstrictor (site and route of administration and potential for inadvertent intravascular administration).

For concurrent use of sympathomimetic vasoconstrictors such as epinephrine, levonordefrin, norepinephrine, or phenylephrine (in addition to those interactions listed above and applicable to the specific local anesthetic)

Alpha-adrenergic blocking agents, such as
- Labetalol
- Phenoxybenzamine
- Phentolamine
- Prazosin
- Tolazoline or

Other medications with alpha-adrenergic blocking action, such as
- » Droperidol
- » Haloperidol
- Loxapine
- » Phenothiazines
- Thioxanthenes or
- Vasodilators, rapidly acting, such as nitrates

(these medications may reduce the efficacy of the vasoconstrictor)
(in patients receiving epinephrine alpha-adrenergic blockade may result in unopposed beta-adrenergic activity with a risk of severe hypotension and tachycardia)
(vasoconstrictors may also decrease the therapeutic effects of vasodilators, including the antianginal effects of nitrates)

» Anesthetics, hydrocarbon inhalation
(halothane and, to a much lesser extent, enflurane, isoflurane, or methoxyflurane may sensitize the heart to the effects of a sympathomimetic vasoconstrictor; concurrent use with a vasoconstrictor may cause dose-related cardiac arrhythmias)

» Antidepressants, tricyclic or
» Maprotiline
(concurrent use may potentiate the cardiovascular effects of the vasoconstrictor, possibly resulting in arrhythmias, tachycardia, or severe hypertension or hyperpyrexia)

Antihypertensives
(antihypertensive effects may be decreased by vasoconstrictors; monitoring of blood pressure is recommended)

» Beta-adrenergic blocking agents, including ophthalmic agents
(concurrent use of nonselective beta-adrenergic blocking agents with a vasoconstrictor may result in unopposed alpha-adrenergic activity with a dose-dependent risk of hypertension and bradycardia with possible heart block)

CNS stimulation-producing medications, other, (see *Appendix II*), especially

» Cocaine, mucosal-local
(concurrent use with a vasoconstrictor may result in excessive CNS stimulation, leading to nervousness, irritability, insomnia, and possibly convulsions or cardiac arrhythmias; close observation of the patient is recommended)
(concurrent use of other sympathomimetics with vasoconstrictors also increases the risk of adverse cardiovascular effects; although vasoconstrictor-containing local anesthetic solutions are sometimes used in conjunction with low doses of cocaine for mucous membrane anesthesia, caution is recommended)
(concurrent use of doxapram, mazindol, or methylphenidate with a vasoconstrictor may also increase the pressor effects of the vasoconstrictor; concurrent use may also increase the pressor effect of doxapram)

» Digitalis glycosides or
Levodopa
(concurrent use with a vasoconstrictor may increase the risk of cardiac arrhythmias)

Ergot derivatives, including antimigraine agents and oxytocics
(the vasoconstrictive effects of ergot derivatives may be additive to those of sympathomimetic vasoconstrictors; concurrent or se-

quential administration may cause severe, persistent hypertension; rarely, rupture of a cerebral blood vessel has occurred postpartum after an ergot-type oxytocic was administered within 3 to 4 hours following caudal block anesthesia with a vasoconstrictor)

Monoamine oxidase (MAO) inhibitors, including furazolidone, procarbazine, and selegiline
(concurrent use may prolong and intensify cardiac stimulant and vasopressor effects of phenylephrine, possibly leading to headache, cardiac arrhythmias, and/or severe, sustained hypertension)

Rauwolfia alkaloids
(in addition to possibly decreasing the antihypertensive effect of rauwolfia alkaloids, a "denervation supersensitivity" response is possible; although problems with systemic vasoconstrictors have not been reported, a significant increase in blood pressure has been documented with administration of phenylephrine ophthalmic drops to patients taking reserpine; caution and close observation are recommended)

Ritodrine
(concurrent use with epinephrine, levonordefrin, or norepinephrine may increase the effect of either medication and the risk of side effects)

Thyroid hormones
(concurrent use with a sympathomimetic agent may increase the risk of coronary insufficiency in patients with coronary artery disease; dosage adjustment of the sympathomimetic is recommended, although the risk is reduced in euthyroid patients)

Laboratory value alterations

The following have been selected on the basis of their potential clinical significance (possible effect in parentheses where appropriate)—not necessarily inclusive (» = major clinical significance).

With diagnostic test results
Pancreatic function determinations using bentiromide
(administration of PABA-derivative local anesthetics or of lidocaine within 3 days before the bentiromide test may invalidate the test results because these anesthetics are metabolized to PABA or other arylamines and will therefore increase the true or apparent quantity of PABA recovered)

Medical considerations/Contraindications

The medical considerations/contraindications included have been selected on the basis of their potential clinical significance (reasons given in parentheses where appropriate)—not necessarily inclusive (» = major clinical significance).

Note: A standard reference source should be consulted for more specific information concerning medical problems that may apply to specific local anesthetic procedures.

Except under special circumstances, this medication should not be used when the following medical problems exist:

For levobupivacaine and bupivacaine
For paracervical administration in obstetrics
(increased risk of fetal bradycardia and death)

For prilocaine only
» Methemoglobinemia
(may be induced or exacerbated)

For subarachnoid block
» Complete heart block or
» Hemorrhage, severe or
» Hypotension, severe or
» Shock
(may be exacerbated by cardiac depressant effects and vasodilation; also, metabolism of amides may be decreased because of reduced hepatic blood flow)
» Local infection at site of proposed lumbar puncture
(lumbar puncture may spread infection into the arachnoid space; also, infection may alter pH at site of injection, resulting in decrease or loss of local anesthetic effect)
» Septicemia
(decreased patient tolerance to CNS stimulant effects)

Risk-benefit should be considered when the following medical problems exist:

For all local anesthetic usage
Any condition in which hepatic blood flow may be decreased, such as:
Congestive heart failure or
Hepatic disease or impairment
(increased risk of toxicity because of reduced clearance, especially with amides; a decrease in dosage and/or an increase in the interval between doses may be necessary, especially with lidocaine)
» Cardiovascular function impairment, especially heart block or shock or
Hypotension or
Hypovolemia
(cardiovascular function impairment may be exacerbated by cardiac depressant effects)
» Drug sensitivity, history of, especially to the anesthetic being considered for use and chemically related anesthetics or other compounds
(increased risk of hypersensitivity reactions)
» Inflammation and/or infection in region of injection
(may alter pH at site of injection resulting in decrease or loss of anesthetic effect)
Plasma cholinesterase deficiency—for esters
(increased risk of toxicity because of decreased metabolism)
Renal disease
(anesthetic or metabolites may accumulate)
Caution is also recommended in very young, elderly, acutely ill, or debilitated patients, who may be more susceptible to systemic toxicity induced by local anesthetics.

For paracervical administration in obstetrics
Fetal distress, pre-existing or
Prematurity or
Postmaturity or
Toxemia of pregnancy or
Uteroplacental insufficiency, pre-existing
(increased risk of fetal bradycardia and acidosis)
Note: Use of chloroprocaine is not recommended if prematurity, pre-existing fetal distress, or toxemia of pregnancy is present because its safety in these conditions has not been established.

For peridural (caudal or lumbar epidural) anesthesia
Neurological disease, pre-existing
Septicemia
(decreased patient tolerance to CNS stimulant effects)
Spinal deformity that may interfere with administration and/or effectiveness of local anesthetic

For subarachnoid anesthesia
Backache, chronic
(may be exacerbated)
» CNS disease, pre-existing, attributable to infection, tumor or other causes
» Coagulation defects induced by anticoagulant therapy or hematologic disorders
(trauma to a blood vessel during administration may result in uncontrollable CNS or soft tissue hemorrhage)
Headache, pre-existing, especially history of migraine
(may be induced or exacerbated)
Hemorrhagic spinal fluid
(risk of inadvertent intravascular administration)
Hypertension
Hypotension
(may be exacerbated by cardiac depressant and vasodilating effects)
Paresthesias, persistent
Psychosis, hysteria or uncooperative patient
Spinal conditions or deformities that may interfere with administration and/or effectiveness of anesthetic

For vasoconstrictor-containing preparations
Asthma
(increased risk of anaphylactic or bronchospastic allergic-like reactions induced by the sulfites in commercially available solutions)
» Cardiac disease or arrhythmias or
Diabetes mellitus or
» Hyperthyroidism
(cardiac stimulant effects may be detrimental to patients with these conditions)
» Hypertension or
» Vascular disease, peripheral
(exaggerated vasoconstrictor response may occur, leading to increased risk of severe hypertension or ischemic injury or necrosis)

Patient monitoring

The following may be especially important in patient monitoring (other tests may be warranted in some patients, depending on condition; » = major clinical significance):

Cardiovascular status and
Respiratory status and
State of consciousness
(should be monitored after each local anesthetic injection to detect impending CNS and/or cardiovascular toxicity.Early signs of CNS toxicity include restlessness, anxiety, incoherent speech, lightheadedness, numbness and tingling of the mouth and lips,

metallic taste, tinnitus, dizziness, blurred vision, tremors, twitching, depression, or drowsiness.)

Fetal heart rate
(should be monitored during paracervical administration in obstetrics to detect fetal bradycardia)

Side/Adverse Effects

Note: Adverse reactions are generally dose-related and may result from high plasma concentrations of anesthetic caused by inadvertent intravascular administration, excessive dosage, or rapid absorption from the injection site as well as reduced patient tolerance, idiosyncrasy, or hypersensitivity.

Adverse effects are also related to the specific local anesthetic used and the route and site of administration. Small doses of local anesthetics injected into the head and neck area (including retrobulbar, dental, and stellate ganglion blocks) or in the tracheobronchial area may produce adverse reactions similar to those caused by inadvertent intravascular injection of larger doses. Also, unintentional subarachnoid administration during intended performance of a peridural block or a nerve block near the vertebral column (especially in the head and neck area) may result in adverse effects that depend at least partially on the quantity of anesthetic administered subdurally.

Systemic reactions may occur rapidly or may be delayed for up to 30 minutes following administration.

The following side/adverse effects have been selected on the basis of their potential clinical significance (possible signs and symptoms in parentheses where appropriate)—not necessarily inclusive:

Those indicating need for medical attention

Incidence less frequent or rare

Anemia (pale skin; troubled breathing, exertional; unusual bleeding or bruising; unusual tiredness or weakness); ***back pain; bradycardia*** (dizziness); ***cardiac arrhythmias*** (irregular heartbeat); ***chest pain***—may be sympathomimetic effect caused by vasoconstrictor added to local anesthetic, or may be caused by decreased perfusion resulting from hypotension; ***constipation; dizziness; drowsiness; headache; hives*** (raised red swellings on the skin, lips, tongue, or in the throat); ***hypertension***—may be sympathomimetic effect caused by vasoconstrictor added to local anesthetic; ***hypotension*** (dizziness); ***fever; hypothermia*** (shivering); ***impotence*** (loss of sexual function); ***incontinence, fecal and/or urinary*** (inability to hold bowel movement and/or urine)—may indicate *cauda equina syndrome; **methemoglobinemia*** (bluish lips and fingernails; breathing problems; dizziness; fatigue; headache; rapid heart rate; weakness); ***nausea and/or vomiting; numbness or tingling of lips and mouth, prolonged***—may occur when an anesthetic is used for dental anesthesia; ***paralysis of legs***—may indicate *cauda equina syndrome; **paresthesias*** (tingling or "pins and needles" sensation)—may indicate *cauda equina syndrome; **persistent anesthesia*** (numbness); ***pruritus*** (itching); ***respiratory paralysis*** (inability to breath without assistance); ***restlessness***—may be caused by vasoconstrictor added to local anesthetic; ***seizures*** (convulsions); ***skin rash; tachycardia*** (rapid heart rate)—may be caused by vasoconstrictor added to local anesthetic; ***trismus of facial muscles*** (difficulty in opening the mouth)—may occur when an anesthetic is used for dental anesthesia; ***unconsciousness; vasodilation, peripheral*** (dizziness)

Note: Anaphylactoid reactions, including shock, have been reported rarely. The effectiveness of a small test dose in predicting the risk of allergic reactions has not been determined.

Motor and sensory block extending higher on the trunk of the body than intended may occur following subarachnoid administration of local anesthetics. This may also occur following inadvertent subarachnoid administration during intended performance of a peridural block. Occasionally paralysis of chest wall muscles may result in *respiratory paralysis*.

Some patients receiving lidocaine for spinal anesthesia have developed neurologic complications following anesthesia. The neurologic complications usually are temporary *paresthesias* and *back pain (transient radicular irritation)*. However, persistent *paresthesia, paralysis of legs*, or impairment of bodily functions (e.g., *incontinence*) may indicate a serious neurologic complication, *cauda equina syndrome*. Uneven distribution of hyperbaric lidocaine following spinal administration may contribute to *cauda equina syndrome*. In cases of *transient radicular irritation*, symptoms resolve within a few days to a few weeks. However, neurotoxic effects may not resolve in cases of *cauda equina syndrome*. Other anesthetics may cause *cauda equina syndrome* also.

Overdose

For specific information on the agents used in the management of a local anesthetic overdose, see:
- *Benzodiazepines (Systemic)* monograph;
- Ephedrine in
- *Sympathomimetic Agents—Cardiovascular Use (Parenteral-Systemic);*
- Mephentermine in
- *Sympathomimetic Agents—Cardiovascular Use (Parenteral-Systemic);*
- Metaraminol in
- *Sympathomimetic Agents—Cardiovascular Use (Parenteral-Systemic);*
- *Methylene Blue (Systemic)* monograph;
- *Neuromuscular Blocking Agents (Systemic)* monograph; and/or
- Thiopental in
- *Anesthetics, Barbiturate (Systemic)* monograph.

For more information on the management of overdose or unintentional ingestion, **contact a Poison Control Center** (see *Poison Control Center Listing*).

Clinical effects of overdose

The following effects have been selected on the basis of their potential clinical significance (possible signs and symptoms in parentheses where appropriate)—not necessarily inclusive:

Acute
Apnea; circulatory depression; methemoglobinemia; seizures

Treatment of overdose

Specific treatment—

For circulatory depression: Administering a vasopressor and intravenous fluids is recommended. For maternal hypotension during obstetrical anesthesia, it is recommended that the patient be placed on her left side, if possible, to correct aortocaval compression by the gravid uterus. Delivery of the fetus may improve the response of the obstetric patient to cardiopulmonary resuscitation.

For seizures: Protect the patient and administer oxygen immediately. If seizures do not respond to respiratory support, administering a benzodiazepine such as diazepam or an ultrashort-acting barbiturate such as thiopental or thiamylal intravenously is recommended. The fact that these agents, especially the barbiturates, may cause circulatory depression when administered intravenously must be kept in mind. A neuromuscular blocking agent may also be used to decrease the muscular manifestations of persistent seizures if positive-pressure ventilation can be immediately provided. Hypoxia, hypercapnea, and acidosis can develop quickly following the onset of seizures.

For methemoglobinemia: If methemoglobinemia does not respond to administration of oxygen, administration of methylene blue is recommended.

Monitoring—Blood pressure, heart rate, neurologic status, and respiratory status should be monitored continuously.

Supportive care—Securing and maintaining a patent airway, administering oxygen, and instituting assisted or controlled respiration as required. In some patients, endotracheal intubation may be required.

Patient Consultation

As an aid to patient consultation, refer to *Advice for the Patient, Anesthetics (Parenteral-Local)*.

In providing consultation, consider emphasizing the following selected information (» = major clinical significance):

Before receiving this medication

» Conditions affecting use, especially:

Allergies to the anesthetic considered for use, related anesthetics, other related compounds, and additives (methylparaben, sulfites)

Pregnancy—Potential rare unwanted effects with obstetrical use

Use in children—Increased risk of systemic toxicity

Use in the elderly—Increased risk of systemic toxicity

Other medications, especially nonselective beta-adrenergic blocking agents, CNS depression-producing medications, cocaine, digitalis glycosides, droperidol, haloperidol, hydrocarbon inhalation anesthetics, maprotiline, phenothiazines, tricyclic antidepressants, or vasoconstrictors such as epinephrine, methoxamine or phenylephrine

Other medical problems, especially cardiac disease or arrhythmias, cardiovascular function impairment, coagulation defects, hypertension, hyperthyroidism, local infection at the site of injection or proposed lumbar puncture, methemoglobinemia, peripheral vascular disease, pre-existing CNS disease

Proper use of this medication
Proper dosing

Precautions after receiving this medication
Caution that injury may occur undetected while numbness persists in the affected area; using care to prevent injury, including not eating or chewing gum following dental anesthesia (to prevent biting trauma)

Side/adverse effects
Signs and/or symptoms of potential side effects, especially anemia, back pain, bradycardia, constipation, cardiac arrhythmias, chest pain, dizziness, drowsiness, fever, headache, hives, hypertension, hypotension, hypothermia, impotence, incontinence (fecal and/or urinary), methemoglobinemia, nausea and/or vomiting, numbness or tingling of lips and mouth (prolonged), paralysis of legs, paresthesias, persistent anesthesia, pruritus, respiratory paralysis, restlessness, seizures, skin rash, tachycardia, trismus of facial muscles, vasodilation (peripheral)

General Dosing Information

The safety and effectiveness of local anesthetics depend upon proper dosage, correct technique, adequate precautions, and readiness for emergencies. *Local anesthetics should only be administered by clinicians who are well versed in the diagnosis and management of drug-related toxicity and other acute emergencies which might arise from the block being administered. Resuscitative equipment, oxygen, and other resuscitative drugs should be immediately available when any local anesthetic is used.*

A standard text should be consulted for specific techniques and procedures for administering local anesthetics.

The dosage of local anesthetics depends on the specific anesthetic procedure; vascularity of the tissues at or near the site of injection; specific nerve, plexus, or fiber to be blocked; type of surgery being performed (number of neuronal segments to be blocked, depth of anesthesia and degree of muscle relaxation required, and duration of anesthesia desired); and patient variables such as age and weight.

The recommended adult doses are given as a guideline for use in the average adult. *The actual dosage and maximum dosage must be individualized,* based on the age, size, and physical status of the patient and the expected rate of systemic absorption from the injection site. The lowest dosage (volume and concentration) that produces the desired results should be used.

Lower doses should be used for pediatric, geriatric, acutely ill, or debilitated patients and patients with cardiac or hepatic disease. Lower doses are also required for repeated injections (as for multiple nerve blocks or continuous catheter [intermittent] administration techniques), and for nerve blocks in highly vascular areas, in order to prevent excessively high plasma concentrations.

Dilutions of anesthetics for epidural injections should be made with preservative free 0.9% saline according to standard hospital procedures for sterility.

Local anesthetics may be administered as single injections or continuously or intermittently through an indwelling catheter. Fractional doses are especially recommended for peridural blocks.

Local anesthetics should be injected slowly, with frequent aspirations before and during the injection, to reduce the risk of inadvertent intravascular administration. Additional aspirations should be performed before and during each supplemental injection via an indwelling catheter. However, intravascular administration is possible even when aspiration for blood is negative. Consider including epinephrine with a test dose because circulatory changes compatible with epinephrine may also serve as a warning sign of unintended intravascular injection. In one study, intravascular administration occurred despite negative results on aspiration in 20% of patients undergoing dental treatment.

For epidural anesthesia it is recommended that a test dose of a local anesthetic with a fast onset be administered initially and that the patient be monitored for central nervous system and cardiovascular toxicity, as well as for signs of unintended intrathecal administration before proceeding.

For central neural blocks in obstetrical anesthesia, the anesthetic should not be injected during a strong uterine contraction or while the patient is bearing down because excessively high levels of anesthesia may result.

For peridural blocks, injection of a small test dose (usually 2 to 5 mL of solution, consult manufacturers" product information for details) is recommended so that the patient can be monitored for signs of inadvertent subarachnoid or intravascular administration. If clinical conditions permit, the use of a vasoconstrictor-containing solution is recommended because circulatory changes produced by a vasoconstrictor may indicate intravascular administration. The test dose should be repeated if a patient is moved in any manner that may cause displacement of the catheter.

For retrobulbar block, lack of corneal sensation should not be relied upon to determine readiness for surgery because lack of corneal sensation usually precedes clinically acceptable external ocular muscle akinesia.

The extent and degree of subarachnoid block depend on the position of the patient during and immediately after injection, dosage, specific gravity of the solution, volume of solution used, force of injection, and the level of puncture. Hyperbaric solutions (with dextrose added to render the solution heavier than cerebrospinal fluid [CSF]) are usually used for low spinal anesthesia. Isobaric solutions (having the same specific gravity as CSF) produce anesthesia at the level of intrathecal injection. Hypobaric solutions (diluted to have a lower specific gravity than CSF) are used to produce anesthesia of thoracic structures and for low spinal anesthesia. A standard text and/or manufacturers" product information may be consulted for details concerning dilution and positioning of patient during and following administration.

Vasoconstrictors decrease the rate of local clearance of the local anesthetic, thereby reducing the risk of systemic toxic reactions, prolonging the anesthetic effect, increasing the frequency of complete conduction blocks at low anesthetic concentrations, and permitting larger maximum single doses of anesthetic to be administered. Epinephrine 1:200,000 is the most commonly used vasoconstrictor for most purposes; levonordefrin, norepinephrine, and phenylephrine may also be used. In dentistry, epinephrine 1:50,000 to 1:200,000 and levonordefrin 1:20,000 are the most commonly used vasoconstrictors.

Solutions containing a vasoconstrictor should be used cautiously and in carefully circumscribed quantities, if at all, in tissues supplied by end arteries (such as the fingers, nose, toes, or penis) or having otherwise compromised blood supply; ischemia leading to gangrene may result. Also, a vasoconstrictor should not be injected repeatedly at the same site for dental procedures because reduced blood flow and increased oxygen consumption in the affected tissues may cause tissue anoxia, delayed healing, edema, or necrosis at the injection site.

Intravenous access should be obtained prior to the placement of major nerve blocks to permit the administration of emergency drugs during resuscitation if a serious adverse reaction occurs.

For treatment of adverse effects

Recommended treatment consists of the following:

- For seizures—If seizures do not respond to respiratory support, administering a benzodiazepine such as diazepam (in 2.5-mg increments) or an ultrashort-acting barbiturate such as thiopental or thiamylal (in 50- to 100-mg increments) intravenously every 2 to 3 minutes is recommended. The fact that these agents, especially the barbiturates, may cause circulatory depression when administered intravenously must be kept in mind. A neuromuscular blocking agent may also be used to decrease the muscular manifestations of persistent seizures; artificial respiration is mandatory if such an agent is used.
- For methemoglobinemia—If methemoglobinemia does not respond to administration of oxygen, administration of methylene blue (intravenous, 1 to 2 mg per kg of body weight (mg/kg) as a 1% solution, over a 5-minute period) is recommended.

ARTICAINE

Summary of Differences

Indications:
Indicated for dental infiltration or nerve block.

Note: Anesthesia of mandibular pulpal and lingual soft tissue and of maxillary palatal soft tissue with buccal infiltration of articaine is not effective in all patients who require the administration of articaine by nerve block technique. In a study in adults, there was no difference between prilocaine and articaine in providing successful anesthesia of mandibular pulpal and lingual soft tissue and of maxillary palatal soft tissue with buccal infiltration. After buccal infiltration of articaine, anesthesia was successful in 63% of cases for the mandibular pulp, 50% for mandibular lingual tissue, and 20% for palatal tissue. The use of mandibular infiltration in pediatric patients for procedures in primary mandibular teeth has had mixed success, with one study showing results similar to those seen in adults.

Pharmacology/pharmacokinetics:
Physicochemical characteristics—
Chemical group: Amide-type local anesthetic with an ester linkage and a thiophene ring
Molecular weight: 284.38

Half-life—
1.2 hours
Onset of action—
Rapid (within 1 to 6 minutes)
Duration of action—
Intermediate (1 to 3 hours)

Precautions:
Cross-sensitivity and/or related problems—
May occur with other amide-type local anestheticsand additives (sulfites).
Pediatrics—
Although articaine is not approved for use in children younger than 4 years of age, a retrospective study of its use in 211 pediatric patients younger than 4 years of age did not reveal any pediatrics-specific problems that would limit its use in children.

Additional Dosing Information

See *General Dosing Information.*

Parenteral Dosage Forms

ARTICAINE HYDROCHLORIDE WITH EPINEPHRINE INJECTION

Usual adult and adolescent dose

Dental infiltration anesthesia—
20 to 100 mg (0.5 to 2.5 mL) as a 4% solution.
Dental nerve block anesthesia—
20 to 136 mg (0.5 to 3.4 mL) as a 4% solution.
Oral surgery anesthesia—
40 to 204 mg (1 to 5.1 mL) as a 4% solution.

Usual adult prescribing limits

7 mg per kg of body weight (0.175 mL/kg).

Usual pediatric dose

Children younger than 4 years of age—Safety and efficacy have not been established.
Children 4 to 12 years of age—Dosage must be individualized, based on the age and weight of the patient.

Usual pediatric prescribing limits

Children 4 to 12 years of age—5 mg per kg of body weight.

Strength(s) usually available

U.S.—
4% (40 mg per mL), with epinephrine 1:100,000 (Rx) [*Septocaine*™ (sodium chloride 1.8 mg per mL; sodium metabisulfite 0.5 mg per mL)].
Canada—
4% (40 mg per mL), with epinephrine 1:100,000 (Rx) [*Ultracaine D-S Forte* (sodium metabisulfite 0.5 mg per mL; methylparaben 1 mg per mL); *Astracaine 4% Forte* (sodium metabisulfite)].
4% (40 mg per mL), with epinephrine 1:200,000 (Rx) [*Ultracaine D-S* (sodium metabisulfite 0.5 mg per mL; methylparaben 1 mg per mL); *Astracaine 4%* (sodium metabisulfite)].

Packaging and storage

Store below 25 °C (77 °F), unless otherwise specified by manufacturer. Protect from freezing. Protect from light.

BUPIVACAINE

Summary of Differences

Indications:
Except as noted below, indicated (without epinephrine) for retrobulbar block; indicated (with or without epinephrine) for caudal or lumbar epidural block, local infiltration, peripheral nerve block, and sympathetic block; indicated (with epinephrine) for dental infiltration or nerve block; and indicated (with dextrose) for subarachnoid block.
Paracervical administration not recommended.
Not recommended for intravenous regional anesthesia (Bier block).

Pharmacology/pharmacokinetics:
Physicochemical characteristics—
Chemical group: Amide-type local anesthetic
Molecular weight: bupivacaine hydrochloride—342.91
pKa: 8.1
Lipid solubility: High
Protein binding—
Very high
Half-life—
3.5 hours (adults); 8.1 to 14 hours (neonates)
Onset of action—
Intermediate
Duration of action—
Long (3 to 10 hours)
Elimination—
5% of a dose may be excreted unchanged

Precautions:
Cross-sensitivity and/or related problems—
May occur rarely with other amide-type local anesthetics
Pregnancy—
Embryocidal effects have been demonstrated in rats and rabbits
Breast-feeding—
Distributed into breast milk
Pediatrics—
Infants up to 9 months of age may have low plasma concentrations of alpha$_1$-acid glycoprotein (AAG). This results in an increased unbound fraction of bupivacaine, and may lead to systemic toxicity.
Reduced clearance of bupivacaine in pediatric patients may be more important than AAG concentrations in causing toxicity. Neonates may have total body clearance of bupivacaine only one third to one half the clearance of adults.

Drug interactions and/or related problems:
Interaction with cimetidine.
Interaction with halothane.

Side/adverse effects:
Prolonged cardiovascular depression and arrhythmias have been reported. The cardiotoxicity of bupivacaine may be increased if the patient experiences hypothermia, hyponatremia, hyperkalemia or myocardial ischemia. Concomitant use of halothane may cause increased cardiotoxicity of bupivacaine.

Additional Dosing Information

See also *General Dosing Information.*

Bupivacaine 0.25% generally produces incomplete motor block and is used when muscle relaxation is not important. However, intercostal nerve block with this strength of bupivacaine may produce complete motor block for intra-abdominal surgery in some patients.

Bupivacaine 0.5% produces motor block and some muscle relaxation when used for caudal, epidural, or nerve block. With continuous catheter (intermittent) administration techniques, repeat doses increase the degree of motor block. The first repeat dose of 0.5% bupivacaine may produce complete motor block.

Bupivacaine 0.75% produces complete motor block and complete muscle relaxation. When used for epidural block, the 0.75% solution is intended for single-dose administration only; it should not be used for intermittent administration techniques.

Bupivacaine 0.75% is not recommended for epidural block in obstetrics because inadvertent intravascular injection has caused maternal cardiac arrest. However, lower concentrations may be used. When bupivacaine is used for epidural block in obstetrics, the dose of bupivacaine should be chosen to provide safe and adequate relief of pain without causing toxicity, prolonged hypotension, or loss of motor strength. The majority of obstetric patients will achieve analgesia with continuous epidural infusions of 0.0625 to 0.125% bupivacaine at 10 to 15 mL per hour. The addition of subarachnoid narcotics or epidural fentanyl (1 to 2 mcg per mL) or sufentanil (0.1 to 0.2 mcg per mL) usually will allow the use of a lower concentration or a lower infusion rate of bupivacaine. The use of the lowest possible concentration usually will reduce the risk of fetal or maternal toxicity while providing appropriate analgesia. However, in some patients where the goals are different, e.g., blood pressure control or the obliteration of any contraction sensation, higher concentrations may be required.

Parenteral Dosage Forms

Note: Bracketed uses in the *Dosage Forms* section refer to categories of use and/or indications that are not included in U.S. product labeling.

BUPIVACAINE HYDROCHLORIDE INJECTION USP

Usual adult and adolescent dose

Caudal anesthesia—
Moderate motor block: 37.5 to 75 mg (15 to 30 mL) as a 0.25% solution, repeated once every three hours as needed.
Moderate to complete motor block: 75 to 150 mg (15 to 30 mL) as a 0.5% solution, repeated once every three hours as needed.
Epidural anesthesia—
Partial to moderate motor block: 25 to 50 mg (10 to 20 mL) as a 0.25% solution, repeated once every three hours as needed.
Moderate to complete motor block: 50 to 100 mg (10 to 20 mL) as a 0.5% solution, repeated once every three hours as needed.
Complete motor block: 75 to 150 mg (10 to 20 mL) as a 0.75% solution.

Epidural obstetric analgesia—
Continuous infusion, 6.25 to 18.75 mg per hour as a 0.0625 to 0.125% solution.

Local infiltration—
Single dose: 175 mg (70 mL) as a 0.25% solution.

Peripheral nerve block—
Moderate to complete motor block: 12.5 to 175 mg (5 to 70 mL) as a 0.25% solution; or 25 to 175 mg (5 to 37.5 mL) as a 0.5% solution. Dosage may be repeated every three hours if necessary.

Retrobulbar block—
15 to 30 mg (2 to 4 mL) as a 0.75% solution.

Sympathetic block—
50 to 125 mg (20 to 50 mL) as a 0.25% solution, repeated once every three hours as needed.

Usual adult prescribing limits

175 mg as a single dose or 400 mg per day.

Usual pediatric dose

Children weighing over 10 kg—

[Caudal analgesia, single dose]—
1 to 2.5 mg per kg of body weight as a 0.125 or 0.25% solution.

[Caudal analgesia, continuous infusion]—
0.2 to 0.4 mg per kg of body weight per hour as a 0.1, 0.125, or 0.25% solution, not to exceed 0.4 mg per kg of body weight per hour.

[Caudal or epidural anesthesia, single dose]—
1 to 2.5 mg per kg of body weight as a 0.125 or 0.25% solution.

[Caudal or epidural anesthesia, continuous infusion]—
0.2 to 0.4 mg per kg of body weight per hour as a 0.1, 0.125, or 0.25% solution, not to exceed 0.4 mg per kg of body weight per hour.

[Local infiltration]—
0.5 to 2.5 mg per kg of body weight as a 0.25 or 0.5% solution.

[Peripheral nerve block]—
0.3 to 2.5 mg per kg of body weight as a 0.25 or 0.5% solution.

Infants and children weighing up to 10 kg—

[Caudal analgesia, single dose]—
1 to 1.25 mg per kg of body weight as a 0.125 or 0.25% solution.

[Caudal analgesia, continuous infusion]—
0.1 to 0.2 mg per kg of body weight per hour as a 0.1, 0.125, or 0.25% solution, not to exceed 0.2 mg per kg of body weight per hour.

[Caudal or epidural anesthesia, single dose]—
1 to 1.25 mg per kg of body weight as a 0.125 or 0.25% solution.

[Caudal or epidural anesthesia, continuous infusion]—
0.1 to 0.2 mg per kg of body weight per hour as a 0.1, 0.125, or 0.25% solution, not to exceed 0.2 mg per kg of body weight per hour.

[Local infiltration]—
0.5 to 2.5 mg per kg of body weight as a 0.25 or 0.5% solution.

[Peripheral nerve block]—
0.3 to 2.5 mg per kg of body weight as a 0.25 or 0.5% solution.

Note: Bupivacaine is approved in the U.S. for use in patients older than 12 years of age. Bupivacaine is approved in Canada for use in patients older than 2 years of age.

Usual pediatric prescribing limits

[Local infiltration or]
[Peripheral nerve block]—
The usual maximum dose is 1 mL per kg of body weight of 0.25% bupivacaine. If bupivacaine 0.5% is used, the usual maximum is 0.5 mL per kg of body weight. The maximum dose to be used depends on the site of administration.

Strength(s) usually available

U.S.—

With preservative (methylparaben 1 mg per mL):
0.25% (2.5 mg per mL) (Rx) [*Marcaine; Sensorcaine;* GENERIC].
0.5% (5 mg per mL) (Rx) [*Marcaine; Sensorcaine;* GENERIC].

Without preservative:
0.25% (2.5 mg per mL) (Rx) [*Marcaine; Sensorcaine-MPF;* GENERIC].
0.5% (5 mg per mL) (Rx) [*Marcaine; Sensorcaine-MPF;* GENERIC].
0.75% (7.5 mg per mL) (Rx) [*Marcaine; Sensorcaine-MPF;* GENERIC].

Canada—

With preservative (methylparaben 1 mg per mL):
0.25% (2.5 mg per mL) (Rx) [*Marcaine*].
0.5% (5 mg per mL) (Rx) [*Marcaine*].

Without preservative:
0.25% (2.5 mg per mL) (Rx) [*Marcaine; Sensorcaine*].
0.5% (5 mg per mL) (Rx) [*Marcaine; Sensorcaine*].
0.75% (7.5 mg per mL) (Rx) [*Marcaine*].

Packaging and storage

Store below 40 °C (104 °F), preferably between 15 and 30 °C (59 and 86 °F), unless otherwise specified by manufacturer. Protect from freezing.

Stability

May be autoclaved.

For chemical disinfection of container surface, 91% isopropyl alcohol or 70% ethyl alcohol without denaturants is recommended; solutions containing heavy metals should not be used.

Unused portions of solutions without a preservative must be discarded.

BUPIVACAINE HYDROCHLORIDE AND EPINEPHRINE INJECTION USP

Usual adult and adolescent dose

Dental—
For infiltration and nerve block in maxillary and mandibular area: 9 mg (1.8 mL) of bupivacaine hydrochloride as a 0.5% solution with epinephrine 1:200,000 per injection site. A second dose may be administered if necessary to produce adequate anesthesia after allowing up to 10 minutes for onset.

Other indications—
See *Bupivacaine Hydrochloride Injection USP*. Administration of epinephrine concurrently with the local anesthetic may permit use of doses somewhat larger than those listed.

Usual adult prescribing limits

In dentistry—
90 mg of bupivacaine hydrochloride per dental visit.

Other indications—
225 mg as a single dose or 400 mg per day of bupivacaine hydrochloride.

Usual pediatric dose

See *Bupivacaine Hydrochloride Injection USP*.

Strength(s) usually available

U.S.—

With preservative (methylparaben 1 mg per mL):
0.25% (2.5 mg per mL), with epinephrine 1:200,000 (Rx) [*Marcaine* (sodium metabisulfite 0.5 mg per mL; edetate calcium disodium); *Sensorcaine* (sodium metabisulfite 0.5 mg per mL); GENERIC].
0.5% (5 mg per mL), with epinephrine 1:200,000 (Rx) [*Marcaine* (sodium metabisulfite 0.5 mg per mL; edetate calcium disodium); *Sensorcaine* (sodium metabisulfite 0.5 mg per mL); GENERIC].

Without preservative:
0.25% (2.5 mg per mL), with epinephrine 1:200,000 (Rx) [*Marcaine* (sodium metabisulfite 0.5 mg per mL; edetate calcium disodium); *Sensorcaine-MPF* (sodium metabisulfite 0.5 mg per mL; citric acid, anhydrous 0.2 mg per mL); GENERIC].
0.5% (5 mg per mL), with epinephrine 1:200,000 (Rx) [*Marcaine* (sodium metabisulfite 0.5 mg per mL; edetate calcium disodium); *Sensorcaine-MPF* (sodium metabisulfite 0.5 mg per mL; citric acid, anhydrous 0.2 mg per mL); GENERIC].
0.75% (7.5 mg per mL), with epinephrine 1:200,000 (Rx) [*Marcaine* (sodium metabisulfite 0.5 mg per mL; edetate calcium disodium); *Sensorcaine-MPF* (sodium metabisulfite 0.5 mg per mL; citric acid, anhydrous 0.2 mg per mL); GENERIC].

For dental use:
0.5% (5 mg per mL; 9 mg per 1.8-mL dental cartridge), with epinephrine 1:200,000 (Rx) [*Marcaine* (sodium metabisulfite 0.5 mg per mL; edetate calcium disodium)].

Canada—

Without preservative:
0.25% (2.5 mg per mL), with epinephrine 1:200,000 (Rx) [*Marcaine* (sodium bisulfite 0.5 mg per mL; edetate calcium disodium); *Sensorcaine* (sodium bisulfite 0.55 mg per mL; citric acid 0.2 mg per mL)].
0.5% (5 mg per mL), with epinephrine 1:200,000 (Rx) [*Marcaine* (sodium bisulfite 0.5 mg per mL; edetate calcium disodium); *Sensorcaine* (sodium bisulfite 0.55 mg per mL; citric acid 0.2 mg per mL)].

For dental use:
0.5% (5 mg per mL; 9 mg per 1.8-mL dental cartridge), with epinephrine 1:200,000 (Rx) [*Sensorcaine Forte* (sodium metabisulfite 0.55 mg per mL; citric acid 0.2 mg per mL)].

Packaging and storage

Store below 40 °C (104 °F), preferably between 15 and 30 °C (59 and 86 °F), unless otherwise specified by manufacturer. Protect from light. Protect from freezing.

Stability

On removal of doses from the vial, air is introduced, which slowly oxidizes the epinephrine causing discoloration of the solution and possible loss of potency. Do not use if solution is discolored or contains a precipitate.

Should not be autoclaved. For chemical disinfection of the container surface, 91% isopropyl alcohol or 70% ethyl alcohol without denaturants is recommended; solutions containing heavy metals are not recommended.

Unused portions of solutions without a preservative must be discarded.

BUPIVACAINE HYDROCHLORIDE IN DEXTROSE INJECTION USP

Usual adult dose

Hyperbaric spinal anesthesia—
- Obstetrical anesthesia—
  - Normal vaginal delivery—6 mg (0.8 mL) of bupivacaine hydrochloride as a 0.75% solution.
  - Cesarean section—7.5 to 10.5 mg (1 to 1.4 mL) of bupivacaine hydrochloride as a 0.75% solution.
- Surgical anesthesia—
  - Lower extremity and perineal procedures—7.5 mg (1 mL) of bupivacaine hydrochloride as a 0.75% solution.
  - Lower abdominal procedures—12 mg (1.6 mL) of bupivacaine hydrochloride as a 0.75% solution.
  - Upper abdominal surgery—15 mg (2 mL) in the horizontal position.

Usual pediatric dose

[Hyperbaric spinal anesthesia]—
0.3 to 0.6 mg per kg of body weight as a 0.75% solution.

Strength(s) usually available

U.S.—
- Without preservative:
  - 0.75% (7.5 mg per mL), with dextrose 8.25% (82.5 mg per mL) (Rx) [*Marcaine Spinal; Sensorcaine-MPF Spinal;* GENERIC].

Canada—
- Without preservative:
  - 0.75% (7.5 mg per mL), with dextrose 8.25% (82.5 mg per mL) (Rx) [*Marcaine*].

Packaging and storage

Store below 40 °C (104 °F), preferably between 15 and 30 °C (59 and 86 °F), unless otherwise specified by manufacturer. Protect from freezing.

Stability

May be autoclaved once; with repeated autoclaving or prolonged storage, caramelization of the dextrose may occur, leading to discoloration. Discolored solutions should not be used.

Do not use if solution contains a precipitate.

CHLOROPROCAINE

Summary of Differences

Indications:
- Indicated for caudal or lumbar epidural block, dental infiltration or nerve block, local infiltration, peripheral nerve block, and intravenous regional anesthesia (Bier block).
- Not recommended for subarachnoid administration.

Pharmacology/pharmacokinetics:
- Physicochemical characteristics—
  - Chemical group: Ester-type local anesthetic
  - Molecular weight: chloroprocaine hydrochloride—307.22
  - pKa: 9
- Biotransformation—
  - Metabolized to a PABA derivative
- Half-life—
  - 19 to 26 seconds (adults); 41 to 45 seconds (neonates)
- Onset of action—
  - Rapid
- Duration of action—
  - Short (30 to 60 minutes)

Precautions:
- Cross-sensitivity and/or related problems—
  - May occur with PABA, parabens, or other ester-type local anesthetics.
- Pregnancy—
  - Paracervical administration not recommended if prematurity, preexisting fetal distress, or toxemia of pregnancy present, because safety in these conditions has not been established.
  - May cause uterine artery constriction.
- Drug interactions and/or related problems—
  - Interaction with cholinesterase inhibitors
  - Interaction with sulfonamides

Side/adverse effects:
- May be especially likely to cause neuropathies.
- More likely than amide-type local anesthetics to cause hypersensitivity reactions.

Additional Dosing Information

See also *General Dosing Information*.

Epinephrine 1:200,000 may be added to chloroprocaine *without* preservatives to prolong the duration of anesthetic effect.

Parenteral Dosage Forms

CHLOROPROCAINE HYDROCHLORIDE INJECTION USP

Usual adult and adolescent dose

Caudal anesthesia—
- 300 to 500 mg (15 to 25 mL) as a 2% solution; or 450 to 750 mg (15 to 25 mL) as a 3% solution, repeated at forty- to sixty-minute intervals as needed.

Epidural anesthesia (lumbar and sacral regions)—
- 40 to 50 mg (2 to 2.5 mL) as a 2% solution per segment; or 60 to 75 mg (2 to 2.5 mL) as a 3% solution per segment. The usual total dose is 300 to 750 mg (15 to 25 mL as a 2 or 3% solution). May be repeated at forty- to sixty-minute intervals using 40 to 120 mg (2 to 6 mL) less than original total dose as a 2% solution or 60 to 180 mg (2 to 6 mL) less than original total dose as a 3% solution.

Local infiltration—
- Depends on site to be infiltrated and extent of surgical procedure.

Nerve block—
- Brachial plexus—
  - 600 to 800 mg (30 to 40 mL) as a 2% solution.
- Digital—
  - 30 to 40 mg (3 to 4 mL) as a 1% solution.
- Infraorbital—
  - 10 to 20 mg (0.5 to 1 mL) as a 2% solution.
- Mandibular—
  - 40 to 60 mg (2 to 3 mL) as a 2% solution.
- Obstetrics—
  - Paracervical block—30 mg (3 mL) as a 1% solution per each of four sites.
  - Pudendal block—200 mg (10 mL) as a 2% solution per side.

Usual adult prescribing limits

Without epinephrine—
800 mg per total dose.

With added epinephrine 1:200,000—
1 gram per total dose.

Usual pediatric dose

Local infiltration—
11 mg per kg of body weight as a 0.5 to 1% solution.

Nerve block—
11 mg per kg of body weight as a 1 to 1.5% solution.

Note: Dosage must be individualized, based on the age and weight of the patient.

Strength(s) usually available

U.S.—
- With preservative (methylparaben 1 mg per mL):
  - 1% (10 mg per mL) (Rx) [*Nesacaine* (edetate disodium 0.11 mg per mL)].
  - 2% (20 mg per mL) (Rx) [*Nesacaine* (edetate disodium 0.11 mg per mL)].
- Without preservative:
  - 2% (20 mg per mL) (Rx) [*Nesacaine-MPF;* GENERIC].
  - 3% (30 mg per mL) (Rx) [*Nesacaine-MPF;* GENERIC].

Canada—
- Without preservative:
  - 2% (20 mg per mL) (Rx) [*Nesacaine-CE* (edetate calcium disodium; sodium bisulfite 0.7 mg per mL)].
  - 3% (30 mg per mL) (Rx) [*Nesacaine-CE* (edetate calcium disodium; sodium bisulfite 0.7 mg per mL)].

Packaging and storage

Store below 40 °C (104 °F), preferably between 15 and 30 °C (59 and 86 °F), unless otherwise specified by manufacturer. Protect from freezing. Protect from light.

Preparation of dosage form

For administration to pediatric patients in concentrations lower than those commercially available—Dilute available concentrations with the quantity of 0.9% sodium chloride injection needed to obtain the required final concentration of local anesthetic solution.

Stability

May be autoclaved (prior to addition of epinephrine, if added).

Sterilization of vials with ethylene oxide is not recommended because absorption through the closure may occur.

Solutions may become discolored after prolonged exposure to light. Protection from direct sunlight is recommended. The solution should not be used if discoloration occurs.

Exposure to low temperatures may cause precipitation of chloroprocaine hydrochloride crystals. These crystals usually redissolve when the solution is returned to room temperature. Solutions containing undissolved material should not be used.

Unused portions of solutions without a preservative must be discarded.

ETIDOCAINE

Summary of Differences

Indications:

Indicated (without epinephrine) for retrobulbar block; indicated (with or without epinephrine) for caudal or lumbar epidural block, local infiltration, and peripheral nerve block; and indicated (with epinephrine) for dental infiltration or nerve block.

Pharmacology/pharmacokinetics:

Physicochemical characteristics—

Chemical group: Amide-type local anesthetic

Molecular weight: 276.42

pKa: 7.74

Lipid solubility: High

Protein-binding—

Very high

Half-life—

2.5 hours (adults); 4 to 8 hours (neonates)

Onset of action—

Rapid

Duration of action—

Long (3 to 10 hours)

Note: The addition of epinephrine does not prolong the duration of analgesia but allows maintenance of lower plasma concentrations of the anesthetic.

Elimination—

Less than 10% of a dose may be excreted unchanged.

Precautions:

Cross-sensitivity and/or related problems—

May occur rarely with other amide-type local anesthetics.

Pregnancy—

Studies in animals have not shown adverse effects on the fetus.

Epidural administration not recommended for normal vaginal delivery.

Not recommended for paracervical administration.

Pediatrics—

Infants up to 9 months of age may have low plasma concentrations of alpha$_1$-acid glycoprotein (AAG). This results in an increased unbound fraction of etidocaine, and may lead to systemic toxicity.

Additional Dosing Information

Etidocaine produces a profound motor block after epidural administration. This may be useful for abdominal surgery, but profound motor block is usually not desirable for normal obstetric delivery.

Parenteral Dosage Forms

ETIDOCAINE HYDROCHLORIDE INJECTION

Usual adult and adolescent dose

See *Etidocaine Hydrochloride and Epinephrine Injection.* Doses somewhat smaller than those listed may be required when epinephrine is not used concurrently with the local anesthetic.

Usual adult prescribing limits

4 mg per kg of body weight or 300 mg per injection.

Usual pediatric dose

Dosage has not been established.

Strength(s) usually available

U.S.—

Without preservative:

1% (10 mg per mL) (Rx) [*Duranest-MPF*].

Canada—

Not commercially available.

Packaging and storage

Store below 40 °C (104 °F), preferably between 15 and 30 °C (59 and 86 °F), unless otherwise specified by manufacturer. Protect from freezing.

Stability

May be autoclaved.

Unused portions of solutions must be discarded because they contain no preservative.

ETIDOCAINE HYDROCHLORIDE AND EPINEPHRINE INJECTION

Usual adult and adolescent dose

Caudal anesthesia—

50 to 150 mg (10 to 30 mL) of etidocaine hydrochloride as a 0.5% solution; or 100 to 300 mg (10 to 30 mL) of etidocaine hydrochloride as a 1% solution. Additional incremental doses may be administered at two- to three-hour intervals as needed.

Lumbar peridural anesthesia—

Cesarean section or

Intra-abdominal or pelvic surgery or

Lower-limb surgery: 100 to 300 mg (10 to 30 mL) of etidocaine hydrochloride as a 1% solution; or 150 to 300 mg (10 to 20 mL) of etidocaine hydrochloride as a 1.5% solution. Additional incremental doses may be administered at two- to three-hour intervals as needed.

Gynecological procedures: 50 to 150 mg (10 to 30 mL) of etidocaine hydrochloride as a 0.5% solution; or 50 to 200 mg (5 to 20 mL) of etidocaine hydrochloride as a 1% solution. Additional incremental doses may be administered at two- to three-hour intervals as needed.

Dental infiltration or nerve block—

15 to 75 mg (1 to 5 mL) as a 1.5% solution.

Percutaneous infiltration—

5 to 400 mg (1 to 80 mL) of etidocaine hydrochloride as a 0.5% solution.

Peripheral nerve block—

25 to 400 mg (5 to 80 mL) of etidocaine hydrochloride as a 0.5% solution; or 50 to 400 mg (5 to 40 mL) of etidocaine hydrochloride as a 1% solution. Additional incremental doses may be administered at two- to three-hour intervals as needed.

Usual adult prescribing limits

5.5 mg per kg of body weight or 400 mg per injection of etidocaine hydrochloride with epinephrine 1:200,000.

Usual pediatric dose

Dosage has not been established.

Strength(s) usually available

U.S.—

Without preservative:

1% (10 mg per mL), with epinephrine 1:200,000 (Rx) [*Duranest-MPF* (sodium metabisulfite 0.5 mg per mL)].

1.5% (15 mg per mL), with epinephrine 1:200,000 (Rx) [*Duranest-MPF* (sodium metabisulfite 0.5 mg per mL)].

For dental use:

1.5% (15 mg per mL; 27 mg per 1.8-mL dental cartridge), with epinephrine 1:200,000 (Rx) [*Duranest* (sodium metabisulfite 0.5 mg per mL)].

Canada—

Not commercially available.

Packaging and storage

Store below 40 °C (104 °F), preferably between 15 and 30 °C (59 and 86 °F), unless otherwise specified by manufacturer. Protect from freezing. Protect from light.

Stability

Do not autoclave.

Do not use if solution is discolored.

Unused portions of solutions not containing a preservative must be discarded.

LEVOBUPIVACAINE

Summary of Differences

Indications:

Indicated for

Surgical anesthesia including obstetrics

Epidural, peripheral neural blockade, local infiltration.

Post-operative pain management

Continuous epidural infusion or intermittent epidural neural blockade; continuous or intermittent peripheral neural blockade or local infiltration.

For continuous epidural analgesia, levobupivacaine may be administered in combination with epidural fentanyl or clonidine.

Paracervical administration not recommended.

Not recommended for intravenous regional anesthesia (Bier block).

Pharmacology/pharmacokinetics:

Physicochemical characteristics—

Chemical group: Amide-type local anesthetic

Molecular weight: 324.9

pKa:8.1

Lipid solubility: High

Protein binding—

Very high

Half-life—

1.3 hours

Onset of action—

Immediate to slow

Duration of action—

Short to long

Elimination—

0% of a dose may be excreted unchanged.

Precautions:

Cross-sensitivity and/or related problems—

May occur rarely with other amide–type local anesthetics.

Drug interactions and/or related problems—

Interactions may occur with cytochrome P450 (CYP) 3A4 inducers (such as phenytoin, phenobarbital, rifampin), CYP3A4 inhibitors (azole antifungals, protease inhibitors, macrolide antibiotics), CYP1A2 inducers (omeprazole), and CYP1A2 inhibitors (clarithromycin).

Additional Dosing Information

See also *General Dosing Information.*

Central nervous system and cardiac toxicity is dose related, therefore, when performing a peripheral nerve block, where large volumes of local anesthetic are needed, use caution when using the higher milligrams per milliliter concentrations.

Levobupivacaine 0.75% is not recommended in obstetrical patients. Historically inadvertent and rapid intravascular injection of bupivacaine has caused maternal cardiac arrhythmias, cardiac/circulatory arrest and death. However, concentrations of 0.5% (up to 150 milligrams) of levobupivacaine may be used for cesarean sections.

Parenteral Dosage Forms

LEVOBUPIVACAINE INJECTION

Usual adult and adolescent dose

Note: The smallest dose and concentration required to produce the desired result should be administered.

Epidural for surgery—

Moderate to complete block: 50 to 150 mg (10 to 20 mL) as a 0.5% and 0.75% solution.

Epidural for cesarean section—

Moderate to complete block: 100 to 150 mg (20 to 30 mL) as a 0.5% solution. Concentrations of 0.75% is not recommended.

Epidural during labor—

Minimal to moderate block: 25 to 50 mg (10 to 20 mL) as a 0.25% solution.

Epidural for post-operative pain—

Minimal to moderate block: 5 to 25 mg per hour (4 to 10 mL per hour) as a 0.125% and 0.25% solution.The 0.125% is to be used ONLY as adjunct therapy in combination with fentanyl or clonidine.

Peripheral nerve—

Moderate to complete block: 75 to 150 mg or 1 to 2 mg per kilogram (30 mL or 0.4 mL per kilogram) as a 0.25% and 0.5% solution.

Local infiltration—

150 mg (60 mL) as a 0.25% solution.

Peribulbar Block—

Moderate to complete block: 37.5 to 112.5 mg (5 to 15 mL) as a 0.75% solution.

Usual adult prescribing limits

During surgical procedure—

Up to 375 mg administered incrementally as epidural doses.

Intraoperative block

Postoperative pain management—

695 mg in 24 hours.

Post-operative epidural infusion—

570 mg over 24 hours.

Brachial plexus block—

300 mg as a single fractionated injection.

Strength(s) usually available

U.S.—

Without preservative:

0.25% (2.5 mg per mL) [*Chirocaine* (preservative free)].

0.5% (5 mg per mL) [*Chirocaine* (preservative free)].

0.75% (7.5 mg per mL) [*Chirocaine* (preservative free)].

Packaging and storage

Store at controlled room temperature, 20 to 25° C (68 to 77°F), excursions permitted to 15 to 30° C (59 to 86°F).

Preparation of dosage form

Use preservative-free 0.9% saline to dilute levobupivacaine for solutions.

For chemical disinfection of the container surface, 91% isopropyl alcohol or 70% ethyl alcohol is recommended.

Stability

Levobupivacaine is physically and chemically stable at ambient room temperature for up to 24 hours when diluted to 0.625 to 2.5 mg per mL in 0.9% sodium chloride injection and stored in polyvinyl chloride bags.

May be autoclaved once; stable following autoclave cycle at 121 °C for 15 minutes. Discard solutions if it contains precipitate or if discolored.

Unused portions of solutions must be discarded because they contain no preservative.

LIDOCAINE

Summary of Differences

Indications:

Indicated (without epinephrine) for retrobulbar block, transtracheal anesthesia, and intravenous regional anesthesia (Bier block); indicated (with or without epinephrine) for caudal or lumbar epidural block, dental infiltration or nerve block, local infiltration, peripheral nerve block, and sympathetic block; and indicated (with dextrose) for subarachnoid block.

Pharmacology/pharmacokinetics:

Physicochemical characteristics—

Chemical group: Amide-type local anesthetic.

Molecular weight: lidocaine hydrochloride—288.82

pKa: 7.9

Lipid solubility: Medium

Protein-binding—

Moderate to high (60 to 90%), primarily to alpha$_1$-acid glycoprotein

Biotransformation—

Xylidide metabolites are active and toxic, but less so than the parent compound

Half-life—

1.5 to 2 hours (adults); 3.2 hours (neonates)

Onset of action—

Rapid

Duration of action—

Intermediate (1 to 3 hours)

Relative toxicity (compared to procaine)—

2

Elimination—

10% of a dose may be excreted unchanged.

Precautions:

Cross-sensitivity and/or related problems—

May occur rarely with other amide-type local anesthetics.

Lidocaine and epinephrine injection contains sodium metabisulfite. Sodium metabisulfite can cause an anaphylactic reaction in some persons.

Pregnancy—

Studies in animals have not shown adverse effects on the fetus.

May cause uterine artery constriction.

Breast-feeding:

Distributed into breast milk.

Drug interactions and/or related problems—

Interaction with beta-adrenergic blocking agents.

Interaction with cimetidine.

Side/adverse effects:

May be more likely than other local anesthetics to cause lumbosacral nerve root damage when used for spinal anesthesia.

Additional Dosing Information

See also *General Dosing Information.*

Solutions containing epinephrine should be used when large doses are required.

A reduction in the dose of lidocaine, or an increase in the interval between doses, may be necessary in patients with decreased hepatic blood flow or hepatic function impairment.

For intravenous regional anesthesia, proper tourniquet technique is essential. Only the single-dose containers designated for intravenous regional anesthesia should be used. A vasoconstrictor should not be used.

Solutions containing dextrose are hyperbaric and are indicated for subarachnoid (spinal) anesthesia.

Some patients receiving lidocaine for spinal anesthesia have developed neurologic complications following anesthesia. The neurologic complications usually are temporary *paresthesias* and *back pain (transient radicular irritation)*. However, persistent *paresthesia, paralysis of legs*, or impairment of bodily functions (e.g., *incontinence*) may indicate a serious neurologic complication, *cauda equina syndrome*. Uneven distribution of hyperbaric lidocaine following spinal administration may contribute to *cauda equina syndrome*. In cases of *transient radicular irritation*, symptoms resolve within a few days to a few weeks. However, neurotoxic effects may not resolve in cases of *cauda equina syndrome*. Other anesthetics may cause *cauda equina syndrome* also. Diabetic patients and patients in lithotomy position may be at increased risk for cauda equina syndrome. Although not yet proven in clinical trials to decrease the incidence of cauda equina syndrome, it is recommended that hyperbaric 5% lidocaine be diluted with an equal volume of cerebrospinal fluid or preservative-free saline when it is used for spinal anesthesia. Alternatively, hyperbaric 2% lidocaine may be used for spinal anesthesia. The smallest dose necessary should be used. Spinal anesthesia should not be attempted again after failure of the first attempt. Lidocaine 5% with 7.5% glucose is not recommended for continuous spinal anesthesia.

Parenteral Dosage Forms

Note: Bracketed uses in the *Dosage Forms* section refer to categories of use and/or indications that are not included in U.S. product labeling.

LIDOCAINE HYDROCHLORIDE INJECTION USP

Usual adult and adolescent dose

Caudal anesthesia—
- Obstetrical analgesia: 100 to 300 mg as a 0.5 to 1% solution.
- Surgical analgesia: 225 to 300 mg (15 to 20 mL) as a 1.5% solution.

Note: For continuous catheter (intermittent administration) techniques, the maximum dose should not be administered at intervals of less than 90 minutes.

Epidural anesthesia—
- Lumbar—
  - Analgesia—250 to 300 mg (25 to 30 mL) as a 1% solution.
  - Anesthesia—225 to 300 mg (15 to 20 mL) as a 1.5% solution; or 200 to 300 mg (10 to 15 mL) as a 2% solution.
- Thoracic: 200 to 300 mg (20 to 30 mL) as a 1% solution.

Note: Dosages given for epidural anesthesia are usual total doses; actual dosage must be based on the number of dermatomes to be anesthetized (2 to 3 mL of the indicated concentration per dermatome).

For continuous catheter (intermittent administration) techniques, the maximum dose should not be administered at intervals of less than 90 minutes.

Infiltration—
- Intravenous regional: 50 to 300 mg (10 to 60 mL) as a 0.5% solution.
- Percutaneous: 5 to 300 mg (up to 60 mL as a 0.5% solution; up to 30 mL as a 1% solution).

Peripheral nerve block—
- Brachial: 225 to 300 mg (15 to 20 mL) as a 1.5% solution.
- Dental: 20 to 100 mg (1 to 5 mL) as a 2% solution.
- Intercostal: 30 mg (3 mL) as a 1% solution.
- Paracervical: 100 mg (10 mL) per side as a 1% solution; may be repeated if necessary at intervals of not less than 90 minutes.
- Paravertebral: 30 to 50 mg (3 to 5 mL) as a 1% solution.
- Pudendal: 100 mg (10 mL) per side as a 1% solution.

Retrobulbar—
- 120 to 200 mg (3 to 5 mL) as a 4% solution.

Sympathetic nerve block—
- Cervical (stellate ganglion): 50 mg (5 mL) as a 1% solution.
- Lumbar: 50 to 100 mg (5 to 10 mL) as a 1% solution.

Transtracheal—
- 80 to 120 mg (2 to 3 mL) as a 4% solution. In addition, topical administration of the 4% solution to the pharynx (as a spray) may be required to achieve complete analgesia. For combined use of injection and spray, it should rarely be necessary to administer more than 200 mg (5 mL) or 3 mg per kg of body weight.

Usual adult prescribing limits

Not to exceed 4.5 mg per kg of body weight or 300 mg per dose, except as noted below—
- Intravenous regional anesthesia: Do not exceed 4 mg per kg of body weight.

Usual pediatric dose

Local infiltration or
Nerve block—
- Up to 5 mg per kg of body weight as a 0.25 to 1% solution.

Intravenous regional anesthesia—
- Up to 3 mg per kg of body weight as a 0.25 to 0.5% solution.

Usual pediatric prescribing limits

5 mg per kg of body weight.

Strength(s) usually available

U.S.—
- With preservative (methylparaben 1 mg per mL):
  - 0.5% (5 mg per mL) (Rx) [*Xylocaine;* GENERIC].
  - 1% (10 mg per mL) (Rx) [*Dilocaine; L-Caine; Lidoject-1; Xylocaine;* GENERIC].
  - 2% (20 mg per mL) (Rx) [*Dilocaine; L-Caine; Lidoject-2; Xylocaine;* GENERIC].
- Without preservative:
  - 0.5% (5 mg per mL) (Rx) [*Xylocaine-MPF*].
  - 1% (10 mg per mL) (Rx) [*Xylocaine-MPF;* GENERIC].
  - 1.5% (15 mg per mL) (Rx) [*Xylocaine-MPF;* GENERIC].
  - 2% (20 mg per mL) (Rx) [*Dalcaine; Xylocaine-MPF;* GENERIC].
  - 4% (40 mg per mL) (Rx) [*Xylocaine-MPF;* GENERIC].
- For dental use:
  - 2% (20 mg per mL; 36 mg per 1.8-mL dental cartridge) (Rx) [*Xylocaine*].

Canada—
- With preservative (methylparaben 1 mg per mL):
  - 0.5% (5 mg per mL) (Rx) [*Xylocaine;* GENERIC].
  - 1% (10 mg per mL) (Rx) [*Xylocaine;* GENERIC].
  - 2% (20 mg per mL) (Rx) [*Xylocaine;* GENERIC].
- Without preservative:
  - 1% (10 mg per mL) (Rx) [*Xylocaine*].
  - 1.5% (15 mg per mL) (Rx) [*Xylocaine;* GENERIC].
  - 2% (20 mg per mL) (Rx) [*Xylocaine;* GENERIC].

Packaging and storage

Store below 40 °C (104 °F), preferably between 15 and 30 °C (59 and 86 °F), unless otherwise specified by manufacturer. Protect from freezing.

Preparation of dosage form

For administration to pediatric patients in concentrations lower than those commercially available—Dilute available concentrations with the quantity of 0.9% sodium chloride injection needed to obtain the required final concentration of local anesthetic solution.

Stability

May be autoclaved.

For chemical disinfection of the container surface, 91% isopropyl alcohol or 70% ethyl alcohol without denaturants is recommended; solutions containing heavy metals are not recommended.

Dental cartridges sealed with aluminum caps should not be kept in solutions made from antirust tablets or solutions containing quaternary ammonium salts such as benzalkonium chloride.

Unused portions of solutions without a preservative must be discarded.

LIDOCAINE HYDROCHLORIDE AND DEXTROSE INJECTION USP

Usual adult dose

Obstetrical low spinal (saddle block) anesthesia—
- Normal vaginal delivery: 9 to 15 mg (0.6 to 1 mL) of lidocaine hydrochloride as a 1.5% solution; or 50 mg (1 mL) of lidocaine hydrochloride as a 5% solution to provide perineal anesthesia for about one hundred minutes and analgesia for about another forty minutes.
- Cesarean section and deliveries requiring intrauterine manipulation: 75 mg (1.5 mL) of lidocaine hydrochloride as a 5% solution.

Surgical anesthesia
Abdominal—
- 75 to 100 mg (1.5 to 2 mL) of lidocaine hydrochloride as a 5% solution.

Usual pediatric dose
Spinal anesthesia—
Infants and children weighing up to 5 kg—
2.5 mg per kg of body weight.
Infants and children weighing 5 to 15 kg—
2 mg per kg of body weight.
Children weighing more than 15 kg—
1.5 mg per kg of body weight.

Strength(s) usually available
U.S.—
Without preservative:
1.5% (15 mg per mL), with dextrose 7.5% (75 mg per mL) (Rx) [*Xylocaine-MPF*].
5% (50 mg per mL), with dextrose 7.5% (75 mg per mL) (Rx) [*Xylocaine-MPF with Glucose;* GENERIC].
Canada—
Without preservative:
5% (50 mg per mL), with dextrose 7.5 % (75 mg per mL) (Rx) [*Xylocaine 5% Spinal*].

Packaging and storage
Store below 40 °C (104 °F), preferably between 15 and 30 °C (59 and 86 °F), unless otherwise specified by manufacturer. Protect from freezing.

Stability
May be autoclaved once; with repeated autoclaving or prolonged storage, caramelization of the dextrose may occur, leading to discoloration. Discolored solutions should not be used.
Do not use if solution contains a precipitate.
For chemical disinfection of the container surface, 91% isopropyl alcohol or 70% ethyl alcohol without a denaturant is recommended; solutions containing heavy metals are not recommended.
Unused portions of solutions must be discarded because they contain no preservative.

LIDOCAINE HYDROCHLORIDE AND EPINEPHRINE INJECTION USP

Usual adult and adolescent dose
Dental anesthesia (for infiltration or nerve block)—
20 to 100 mg (1 to 5 mL) of lidocaine hydrochloride as a 2% solution with epinephrine 1:100,000 or 1:50,000.
Other indications—
See *Lidocaine Hydrochloride Injection USP*. Administration of epinephrine concurrently with the local anesthetic may permit use of doses somewhat larger than those listed.

Usual adult prescribing limits
Dental anesthesia—
7 mg per kg of body weight or 500 mg of lidocaine hydrochloride.
Note: A lower limit may apply for poor patient condition, or for some sites of administration. A higher limit may sometimes apply with the use of adjunct drugs. The utility of adjunct drugs to protect the patient from side effects varies depending on the drug and the side effect. For example, the use of benzodiazepines may help prevent seizures during the period of peak absorption of the anesthetic, but will not protect the patient from its cardiovascular toxicity.

Other indications—
7 mg of lidocaine hydrochloride per kg of body weight but not exceeding 500 mg as a single dose.

Usual pediatric dose
Dental anesthesia—
20 to 30 mg (1 to 1.5 mL) of lidocaine hydrochloride as a 2% solution with epinephrine 1:100,000.
Local infiltration or
Nerve block—
Up to 7 mg per kg of body weight, as a 0.25 to 1% solution.
Caudal epidural anesthesia—
Up to 7 mg per kg of body weight, as a 0.5 to 1% solution.

Usual pediatric prescribing limits
Dental anesthesia—
4 to 5 mg of lidocaine hydrochloride per kg of body weight or 100 to 150 mg as a single dose.
Local infiltration or
Nerve block or local infiltration—
7 mg of lidocaine hydrochloride per kg of body weight as a 0.25 to 1% solution with epinephrine 1:200,000.

Strength(s) usually available
U.S.—
With preservative (methylparaben 1 mg per mL):
0.5% (5 mg per mL), with epinephrine 1:200,000 (Rx) [*Xylocaine* (sodium metabisulfite 0.5 mg per mL)].
1% (10 mg per mL), with epinephrine 1:100,000 (Rx) [*Xylocaine* (sodium metabisulfite 0.5 mg per mL); GENERIC].
2% (20 mg per mL), with epinephrine 1:100,000 (Rx) [*Xylocaine* (sodium metabisulfite 0.5 mg per mL); GENERIC].
Without preservative:
1% (10 mg per mL), with epinephrine 1:100,000 (Rx) [GENERIC].
1% (10 mg per mL), with epinephrine 1:200,000 (Rx) [*Xylocaine-MPF* (sodium metabisulfite 0.5 mg per mL)].
1.5% (15 mg per mL), with epinephrine 1:200,000 (Rx) [*Xylocaine-MPF* (sodium metabisulfite 0.5 mg per mL)].
2% (20 mg per mL), with epinephrine 1:200,000 (Rx) [*Xylocaine-MPF* (sodium metabisulfite 0.5 mg per mL)].
For dental use:
2% (20 mg per mL; 36 mg per 1.8-mL dental cartridge), with epinephrine 1:100,000 (Rx) [*Octocaine* (sodium metabisulfite); *Xylocaine* (sodium metabisulfite 0.5 mg per mL)].
2% (20 mg per mL; 36 mg per 1.8-mL dental cartridge), with epinephrine 1:50,000 (Rx) [*Octocaine* (sodium metabisulfite); *Xylocaine* (sodium metabisulfite 0.5 mg per mL)].
Canada—
With preservative (methylparaben):
0.5% (5 mg per mL), with epinephrine 1:100,000 (Rx) [*Xylocaine* (sodium metabisulfite)].
1% (10 mg per mL), with epinephrine 1:200,000 (Rx) [*Xylocaine* (sodium metabisulfite)].
1% (10 mg per mL), with epinephrine 1:100,000 (Rx) [*Xylocaine* (sodium metabisulfite)].
2% (20 mg per mL), with epinephrine 1:100,000 (Rx) [*Xylocaine* (sodium metabisulfite)].
Without preservative:
0.5% (5 mg per mL), with epinephrine 1:200,000 (Rx) [*Xylocaine* (sodium metabisulfite)].
1.5% (15 mg per mL), with epinephrine 1:200,000 (Rx) [*Xylocaine* (sodium metabisulfite); *Xylocaine Test Dose* (sodium metabisulfite)].
2% (20 mg per mL), with epinephrine 1:200,000 (Rx) [*Xylocaine* (sodium metabisulfite)].
2% (20 mg per mL), with epinephrine 1:100,000 (Rx) [*Xylocaine* (sodium metabisulfite)].
For dental use:
2% (20 mg per mL; 36 mg per 1.8-mL dental cartridge), with epinephrine 1:100,000 (Rx) [*Octocaine-100* (sodium metabisulfite); *Xylocaine* (sodium metabisulfite)].
2% (20 mg per mL; 36 mg per 1.8-mL dental cartridge), with epinephrine 1:50,000 (Rx) [*Octocaine-50* (sodium metabisulfite); *Xylocaine* (sodium metabisulfite)].

Packaging and storage
Store below 40 °C (104 °F), preferably between 15 and 30 °C (59 and 86 °F), unless otherwise specified by manufacturer. Protect from freezing. Protect from light.

Preparation of dosage form
For administration to pediatric patients in concentrations lower than those commercially available—Dilute available concentrations with the quantity of 0.9% sodium chloride injection needed to obtain the required final concentration of local anesthetic solution.

Stability
Should not be autoclaved.
Do not use if solution is discolored or contains a precipitate.
For chemical disinfection of the container surface, 91% isopropyl alcohol or 70% ethyl alcohol without denaturants is recommended; solutions containing heavy metals are not recommended.
Dental cartridges sealed with aluminum caps should not be kept in solutions made from antirust tablets or solutions containing quaternary ammonium salts such as benzalkonium chloride.
Unused portions of solutions without a preservative must be discarded.

MEPIVACAINE

Summary of Differences

Indications:
Indicated for caudal or lumbar epidural block, local infiltration, intravenous regional anesthesia (Bier block), peripheral nerve block,

and transtracheal anesthesia; and indicated (with or without levonordefrin) for dental infiltration or nerve block.

Not recommended for subarachnoid administration

Pharmacology/pharmacokinetics:

Physicochemical characteristics—

Chemical group: Amide-type local anesthetic

Molecular weight: mepivacaine hydrochloride—282.81

pKa: 7.6

Lipid solubility: Medium

Protein-binding—

High

Half-life—

1.9 to 3.2 hours (adults); 9 hours (neonates)

Onset of action—

Rapid to intermediate

Duration of action—

Intermediate (1 to 3 hours)

Relative toxicity (compared to procaine)—

2

Elimination—

5 to 10% of a dose may be excreted unchanged.

Precautions:

Cross-sensitivity and/or related problems—

May occur rarely with other amide-type local anesthetics

Pediatrics—

Appropriate studies have not shown pediatrics-specific problems.

Additional Dosing Information

See also *General Dosing Information.*

Mepivacaine 1, 1.5, and 2% are not intended for dental use.

Parenteral Dosage Forms

MEPIVACAINE HYDROCHLORIDE INJECTION USP

Usual adult and adolescent dose

Peripheral nerve block—

Brachial, cervical, intercostal, or pudendal: 50 to 400 mg (5 to 40 mL) as a 1% solution; or 100 to 400 mg (5 to 20 mL) as a 2% solution

Caudal and lumbar epidural block—

150 to 300 mg (15 to 30 mL) as a 1% solution; or 150 to 375 mg (10 to 25 mL) as a 1.5% solution; or 200 to 400 mg (10 to 20 mL) as a 2% solution.

Dental—

Single site in upper or lower jaw: 54 mg (1.8 mL) as a 3% solution.

Infiltration and nerve block of entire oral cavity—270 mg (9 mL) as a 3% solution.

Larger doses required for an extensive procedure should be calculated according to the patient's weight. Up to 6.6 mg per kg of body weight may be administered.

Local infiltration (other than in dentistry)—

Up to 400 mg (up to 40 mL) as a 0.5% or 1% solution.

Paracervical block—

Up to 100 mg (up to 10 mL) as a 1% solution per side; may be repeated if necessary in not less than 90 minutes.

Therapeutic block (management of pain)—

10 to 50 mg (1 to 5 mL) as a 1% solution; or 20 to 100 mg (1 to 5 mL) as a 2% solution.

Transvaginal (paracervical plus pudendal) block—

Up to 150 mg (up to 15 mL) as a 1% solution per side.

Usual adult prescribing limits

Dental—

6.6 mg per kg of body weight but not to exceed 400 mg per visit.

Other indications—

7 mg per kg of body weight or 400 mg per procedure.

Note: Although doses of 550 mg have been administered without adverse effects, they are not recommended. If doses of 550 mg are needed, they should not be given at intervals of less than 1½ hours nor should more than 1 gram be given in 24 hours.

Usual pediatric dose

Up to 5 to 6 mg per kg of body weight.

Note: Dosage must be individualized based on the patient's age and weight. For local infiltration, concentrations of 0.2 to 0.5% are recommended for infants and children up to 3 years of age; concentrations of 0.5 to 1% are recommended for children over 3 years of age and weighing more than 13.65 kg. For nerve block in children, concentrations of 0.5 to 1% are recommended.

Maximum pediatric dosage in dentistry must be carefully calculated on the basis of the patient's weight but must not exceed 270 mg (9 mL) of the 3% solution.

Strength(s) usually available

U.S.—

With preservative (methylparaben 1 mg per mL):

1% (10 mg per mL) (Rx) [*Carbocaine; Polocaine;* GENERIC].

2% (20 mg per mL) (Rx) [*Carbocaine; Polocaine;* GENERIC].

Without preservative:

1% (10 mg per mL) (Rx) [*Carbocaine; Polocaine-MPF*].

1.5% (15 mg per mL) (Rx) [*Carbocaine; Polocaine-MPF*].

2% (20 mg per mL) (Rx) [*Carbocaine; Polocaine-MPF*].

For dental use:

3% (30 mg per mL; 54 mg per 1.8-mL dental cartridge) (Rx) [*Carbocaine; Isocaine; Polocaine;* GENERIC].

Canada—

With preservative (methylparaben 1 mg per mL):

1% (10 mg per mL) [*Carbocaine*].

Without preservative:

1% (10 mg per mL) [*Carbocaine*].

2% (20 mg per mL) [*Carbocaine*].

For dental use:

3% (30 mg per mL; 54 mg per 1.8-mL dental cartridge) [*Isocaine 3%; Polocaine*].

Packaging and storage

Store below 40 °C (104 °F), preferably between 15 and 30 °C (59 and 86 °F), unless otherwise specified by manufacturer. Protect from freezing.

Preparation of dosage form

For administration to pediatric patients in concentrations lower than those commercially available—Dilute available concentrations with the quantity of 0.9% sodium chloride injection needed to obtain the required final concentration of local anesthetic solution.

Stability

May be autoclaved (except for dental cartridges).

Dental cartridges sealed with aluminum caps should not be kept in solutions made from antirust tablets or solutions containing quaternary ammonium salts such as benzalkonium chloride.

Unused portions of solutions not containing a preservative must be discarded.

MEPIVACAINE HYDROCHLORIDE AND LEVONORDEFRIN INJECTION USP

Usual adult and adolescent dose

Dental infiltration and nerve block—

Single site: 36 mg (1.8 mL) of mepivacaine hydrochloride as a 2% solution with levonordefrin 1:20,000.

Entire oral cavity: 180 mg (9 mL) of mepivacaine hydrochloride as a 2% solution with levonordefrin 1:20,000.

Note: Larger doses required for an extensive procedure should be calculated according to the patient's weight, and the injections spread out over time as required.

Usual adult prescribing limits

6.6 mg per kg of body weight but not to exceed 400 mg of mepivacaine hydrochloride per visit.

Usual pediatric dose

Dental infiltration and nerve block—

Must be individualized according to patient's weight.

Usual pediatric prescribing limits

Maximum dosage should be calculated on the basis of the patient's body weight, but should not exceed 6.6 mg per kg of body weight or 180 mg of mepivacaine hydrochloride as a 2% solution with levonordefrin 1:20,000.

Strength(s) usually available

U.S.—

For dental use:

2% (20 mg per mL; 36 mg per 1.8-mL dental cartridge), with levonordefrin 1:20,000 (Rx) [*Carbocaine with Neo-Cobefrin* (acetone sodium bisulfite 2 mg per mL); *Isocaine* (sodium bisulfite); *Polocaine* (sodium metabisulfite 0.5 mg per mL); GENERIC].

Canada—

For dental use:

2% (20 mg per mL; 36 mg per 1.8-mL dental cartridge), with levonordefrin 1:20,000 [*Isocaine 2%* (sodium bisulfite 1 mg per mL); *Polocaine* (sodium metabisulfite 0.5 mg per mL)].

Packaging and storage

Store below 40 °C (104 °F), preferably between 15 and 30 °C (59 and 86 °F), unless otherwise specified by manufacturer. Protect from freezing.

Stability

Do not autoclave dental cartridges.

Dental cartridges sealed with aluminum caps should not be kept in solutions made from antirust tablets or solutions containing quaternary ammonium salts such as benzalkonium chloride.

Unused portion of solution must be discarded.

PRILOCAINE

Summary of Differences

Indications:
  Indicated only for dental use.
Pharmacology/pharmacokinetics:
  Physicochemical characteristics—
    Chemical group: Amide-type local anesthetic.
    Molecular weight: prilocaine hydrochloride—256.78.
    pKa: 7.9.
    Lipid solubility: Medium.
  Protein-binding—
    Moderate.
  Biotransformation—
    Also metabolized by kidney and lung tissue.
  Half-life—
    1.6 hours.
  Onset of action—
    Rapid.
  Duration of action—
    Intermediate (1 to 3 hours).
  Relative toxicity (compared to procaine)—
    1.7.
Precautions:
  Cross-sensitivity and/or related problems—
    May occur rarely with other amide-type local anesthetics.
  Pregnancy—
    Studies in animals have not shown adverse effects on the fetus with doses of up to 30 times the maximum human dose.
Side/adverse effects:
  More likely than other local anesthetics to cause methemoglobinemia.

Parenteral Dosage Forms

PRILOCAINE HYDROCHLORIDE INJECTION USP

Usual adult and adolescent dose

Dental anesthesia—
  For local infiltration or nerve block: 40 to 80 mg (1 to 2 mL) as a 4% solution initially.

Usual adult prescribing limits

Dental—
  8 mg per kg of body weight, not to exceed 600 mg (15 mL) as a 4% solution within a two-hour period.

Usual pediatric dose

Dental—
  Children up to 10 years of age: Doses greater than 40 mg (1 mL) as a 4% solution per procedure are rarely needed.

Strength(s) usually available

U.S.—
  For dental use:
    4% (40 mg per mL; 72 mg per 1.8-mL dental cartridge) (Rx) [*Citanest Plain*].
Canada—
  For dental use:
    4% (40 mg per mL; 72 mg per 1.8-mL dental cartridge) [*Citanest Plain*].

Packaging and storage

Store below 40 °C (104 °F), preferably between 15 and 30 °C (59 and 86 °F), unless otherwise specified by manufacturer. Protect from freezing.

Stability

Dental cartridges should not be autoclaved.

For chemical disinfection of the container surface, 91% isopropyl alcohol or 70% ethyl alcohol without denaturants is recommended; solutions containing heavy metals are not recommended.

Dental cartridges are sealed with aluminum caps and therefore should not be kept in solutions made from antirust tablets or solutions containing quaternary ammonium salts such as benzalkonium chloride.

PRILOCAINE AND EPINEPHRINE INJECTION USP

Usual adult and adolescent dose

Dental infiltration and nerve block—
  40 to 80 mg (1 to 2 mL) of prilocaine hydrochloride as a 4% solution with epinephrine 1:200,000 initially.

Usual adult prescribing limits

8 mg per kg of body weight, not to exceed 600 mg (15 mL) of prilocaine hydrochloride within a two-hour period.

Usual pediatric dose

Dental infiltration and nerve block in children up to 10 years of age—
  Doses greater than 40 mg (1 mL) of prilocaine hydrochloride as a 4% solution with epinephrine 1:200,000 are rarely needed.

Strength(s) usually available

U.S.—
  For dental use:
    4% (40 mg per mL; 72 mg per 1.8-mL dental cartridge), with epinephrine 1:200,000 (Rx) [*Citanest Forte* (sodium metabisulfite 0.5 mg per mL)].
Canada—
  For dental use:
    4% (40 mg per mL; 72 mg per 1.8-mL dental cartridge), with epinephrine 1:200,000 [*Citanest Forte* (sodium metabisulfite 0.5 mg per mL); GENERIC].

Packaging and storage

Store below 40 °C (104 °F), preferably between 15 and 30 °C (59 and 86 °F), unless otherwise specified by manufacturer. Protect from freezing. Protect from light.

Stability

Do not autoclave.

Do not use if solution is discolored.

For chemical disinfection of the container surface, 91% isopropyl alcohol or 70% ethyl alcohol without denaturants is recommended; solutions containing heavy metals are not recommended.

Dental cartridges are sealed with aluminum caps and therefore should not be kept in solutions made from antirust tablets or solutions containing quaternary ammonium salts such as benzalkonium chloride.

Unused portion of solution must be discarded.

PROCAINE

Summary of Differences

Indications:
  Indicated for subarachnoid block, local infiltration, peripheral nerve block, and retrobulbar block.
Pharmacology/pharmacokinetics:
  Physicochemical characteristics—
    Chemical group: An ester-type local anesthetic.
    Molecular weight: procaine hydrochloride—272.78.
    pKa: 8.9.
    Lipid solubility: Low.
  Protein-binding—
    Very low.
  Biotransformation—
    Metabolized to PABA. Hydrolyzed primarily in the plasma and, to a much lesser extent, in the liver, by cholinesterases.
  Half-life—
    30 to 50 seconds (adults); 54 to 114 seconds (neonates).
  Onset of action—
    Intermediate.
  Duration of action—
    Short (30 to 60 minutes).
  Relative toxicity—
    1. Procaine is the standard against which other local anesthetics are compared.
  Elimination—
    Less than 2% of a dose may be excreted unchanged.
Precautions:
  Cross-sensitivity and/or related problems—
    May occur with PABA, parabens, or other ester-type local anesthetics.
  Drug interactions and/or related problems—
    Interaction with cholinesterase inhibitors.
    Interaction with sulfonamides.
Side/adverse effects:
  More likely than amide-type local anesthetics to cause hypersensitivity reactions.

Additional Dosing Information

See also *General Dosing Information.*

For peripheral nerve block, the 2% solution of procaine should be reserved for cases requiring a small volume of solution (up to 25 mL).

Epinephrine 1:200,000 or epinephrine 1:100,000 (0.5 to 1 mL of epinephrine 1:1000 per 100 mL of anesthetic solution) may be added to solutions of procaine hydrochloride for vasoconstrictive effect.

Procaine 10% is indicated for subarachnoid administration. The solution is to be diluted with 0.9% sodium chloride injection, sterile water for injection, CSF, or, for hyperbaric techniques, 10% dextrose injection. Consult a standard text or manufacturer's product information for details concerning dilution and injection sites.

Parenteral Dosage Forms

Note: Bracketed uses in the *Dosage Forms* section refer to categories of use and/or indications that are not included in U.S. product labeling.

PROCAINE HYDROCHLORIDE INJECTION USP

Usual adult and adolescent dose

Infiltration—
350 to 600 mg as a 0.25 or 0.5% solution.

Peripheral nerve block—
500 mg as a 0.5, 1, or 2% solution.

Subarachnoid—
Perineum: 50 mg (0.5 mL) as a 10% solution diluted with an equal volume of diluent.
Perineum and lower extremities: 100 mg (1 mL) as a 10% solution diluted with an equal volume of diluent.
Up to costal margin: 200 mg (2 mL) as a 10% solution diluted with 1 mL of diluent.

Usual adult prescribing limits

Not to exceed 1 gram initially.

Usual pediatric dose

Up to 15 mg per kg of body weight of a 0.5% solution.

Strength(s) usually available

U.S.—
With preservative (chlorobutanol 2.5 mg per mL):
1% (Rx) [*Novocain* (acetone sodium bisulfite 2 mg per mL); GENERIC].
2% (Rx) [*Novocain* (acetone sodium bisulfite 2 mg per mL); GENERIC].
Without preservative:
1% (Rx) [*Novocain* (acetone sodium bisulfite 2 mg per mL); GENERIC].
10% (Rx) [*Novocain* (acetone sodium bisulfite 2 mg per mL)].

Canada—
With preservative (chlorobutanol 2.5 mg per mL):
2% [*Novocain* (acetone sodium bisulfite 2 mg per mL)].

Packaging and storage

Store below 40 °C (104 °F), preferably between 15 and 30 °C (59 and 86 °F), protected from light, unless otherwise specified by manufacturer. Protect from freezing.

Preparation of dosage form

For 0.25 or 0.5% concentrations for infiltration or nerve block—Dilute available concentration with enough sterile water for injection to provide the desired quantity and concentration of solution.

Stability

May be autoclaved (prior to addition of epinephrine, if added); however, repeated autoclaving is not recommended because of the increased likelihood of crystal formation. Autoclaving of the solution following dilution with dextrose injection may result in discoloration of the solution caused by caramelization of the dextrose.

Do not use if solution is cloudy or discolored or contains a precipitate.

For chemical disinfection of the container surface, 91% isopropyl alcohol or 70% ethyl alcohol without denaturants is recommended; solutions containing heavy metals are not recommended. Immersion of the container in antiseptic solution is not recommended.

Unused portions of solutions not containing a preservative must be discarded.

TETRACAINE

Summary of Differences

Indications:
Indicated (with or without dextrose) for subarachnoid block; and indicated (without dextrose) for transtracheal anesthesia.

Pharmacology/pharmacokinetics:
Physicochemical characteristics—
Chemical group: Ester-type local anesthetic.
Molecular weight: tetracaine hydrochloride—300.83.
pKa: 8.2.
Lipid solubility: High.
Protein-binding—
High.
Biotransformation—
Metabolized to a PABA derivative.
Onset of action—
Rapid.
Duration of action—
Intermediate to long (1 to > 3 hours).
Relative toxicity (compared to procaine)—
10.

Precautions:
Cross-sensitivity and/or related problems—
May occur with PABA, parabens, or other ester-type local anesthetics.
Drug interactions and/or related problems—
Interaction with cholinesterase inhibitors.
Interaction with sulfonamides.

Side/adverse effects:
More likely than amide-type local anesthetics to cause hypersensitivity reactions.

Additional Dosing Information

See also *General Dosing Information.*

Tetracaine hydrochloride injection 1% is isobaric. When used for isobaric spinal anesthesia, the solution is to be diluted with CSF prior to administration. Also, it may be diluted with 10% dextrose injection to provide a hyperbaric solution.

Isobaric or hyperbaric solutions prepared using sterile tetracaine hydrochloride are to be diluted with CSF prior to administration. A hypobaric solution may also be prepared using sterile tetracaine hydrochloride.

Consult a standard text and/or manufacturer's product information for preparation and administration techniques and for proper injection sites.

Parenteral Dosage Forms

Note: Bracketed uses in the *Dosage Forms* section refer to categories of use and/or indications that are not included in U.S. product labeling.

TETRACAINE HYDROCHLORIDE INJECTION USP

Usual adult and adolescent dose

Spinal anesthesia—
Low spinal (saddle block) anesthesia for vaginal delivery: 2 to 5 mg (0.2 to 0.5 mL) as a 1% solution, to be diluted with 10% dextrose injection.
Perineum: 5 mg (0.5 mL) as a 1% solution, to be diluted with CSF or 10% dextrose injection, depending upon technique used.
Perineum and lower extremities: 10 mg (1 mL) as a 1% solution, to be diluted with CSF or 10% dextrose injection, depending upon technique used.
Up to costal margin: 15 to 20 mg (1.5 to 2 mL) as a 1% solution diluted with CSF.
Doses greater than 15 mg are rarely required.

Usual pediatric dose

[Spinal anesthesia][1]—
Neonates and infants up to 3 months of age: 0.4 to 0.5 mg per kg of body weight.
Infants and children 3 months to 2 years of age: 0.3 to 0.4 mg per kg of body weight.
Children 2 years of age and older: 0.2 to 0.3 mg per kg of body weight.

Strength(s) usually available

U.S.—
Without preservative:
1% (10 mg per mL) (Rx) [*Pontocaine* (acetone sodium bisulfite 2 mg per mL)].

Canada—
Not commercially available.

Packaging and storage

Store between 2 and 8 °C (36 and 46 °F). (Exception: Injections supplied as a component of spinal anesthesia trays may be stored at room temperature for 12 months.) Protect from light. Protect from freezing.

Preparation of dosage form

For isobaric techniques—Dilute with an equal volume of CSF.

For hyperbaric techniques—Dilute with an equal volume of 10% dextrose injection.

Stability

May be autoclaved once; repeated autoclaving is not recommended because of the increased likelihood of crystal formation. Unused autoclaved ampuls should be discarded.

Do not use if solution is cloudy or discolored or contains crystals prior to diluting with CSF.

Immersion of the container in an antiseptic solution is not recommended.

Unused portion of the solution must be discarded because it contains no preservative.

STERILE TETRACAINE HYDROCHLORIDE USP

Usual adult and adolescent dose

Spinal anesthesia—
- Low spinal (saddle block) anesthesia for vaginal delivery: 2 to 5 mg.
- Perineum: 5 mg.
- Perineum and lower extremities: 10 mg.
- Up to costal margin: 15 to 20 mg.
- Doses exceeding 15 mg are rarely required.

Usual pediatric dose

[Spinal anesthesia][1]—
- *See Tetracaine Hydrochloride Injection USP*

Strength(s) usually available

U.S.—
- Without preservative:
  - 20 mg (Rx) [*Pontocaine*].

Canada—
- Without preservative:
  - 20 mg [*Pontocaine*].

Packaging and storage

Prior to reconstitution, store below 40 °C (104 °F), preferably between 15 and 30 °C (59 and 86 °F), unless otherwise specified by manufacturer.

Preparation of dosage form

For isobaric techniques—Dissolve in CSF to give a concentration of 5 mg per mL.

For hyperbaric techniques—Dissolve 10 mg of sterile tetracaine hydrochloride in 1 mL of 10% dextrose injection. Dilute further with 1 mL of CSF to give a final concentration of 5 mg of tetracaine hydrochloride per mL and 5% of dextrose.

For hypobaric techniques—Dissolve the sterile tetracaine hydrochloride in enough sterile water for injection to provide a concentration of 1 mg per mL.

Stability

May be autoclaved. Autoclaving may cause the powder to undergo a change in appearance and to adhere to the sides of the ampul. This may slightly decrease the rate of dissolution of the powder but does not affect anesthetic potency.

TETRACAINE HYDROCHLORIDE IN DEXTROSE INJECTION USP

Usual adult and adolescent dose

Obstetrical low spinal (saddle block) anesthesia—
- 2 to 4 mg (1 to 2 mL) of tetracaine hydrochloride as a 0.2% solution.

Spinal anesthesia—
- Lower abdomen: 9 to 12 mg (3 to 4 mL) of tetracaine hydrochloride as a 0.3% solution.
- Perineal: 3 to 6 mg (1 to 2 mL) of tetracaine hydrochloride as a 0.3% solution.
- Upper abdomen: 15 mg (5 mL) of tetracaine hydrochloride as a 0.3% solution.

Usual pediatric dose

[Spinal anesthesia][1]—
- *See Tetracaine Hydrochloride Injection USP*

Strength(s) usually available

U.S.—
- Without preservative:
  - 0.2% of tetracaine hydrochloride (2 mg per mL) and 6% of dextrose (60 mg per mL) (Rx) [*Pontocaine*].
  - 0.3% of tetracaine hydrochloride (3 mg per mL) and 6% of dextrose (60 mg per mL) (Rx) [*Pontocaine*].

Canada—
- Not commercially available.

Packaging and storage

Store below 40 °C (104 °F), preferably between 15 and 30 °C (59 and 86 °F), protected from light. Protect from freezing.

Stability

May be autoclaved once; repeated autoclaving is not recommended because of the increased likelihood of crystal formation. Also, with repeated autoclaving, caramelization of the dextrose may occur, leading to discoloration. Unused autoclaved ampuls should be discarded.

Do not use if solution is cloudy or discolored or contains crystals.

Unused portions of solutions must be discarded because they contain no preservative.

---

[1]Not included in Canadian product labeling.

Revised: 10/09/2000

Table 1. Pharmacology/Pharmacokinetics—Anesthetics (Parenteral-Local)

Drug	pKa	Lipid solubility (pH 7.4)	Protein binding	Half-life adult/neonate	Onset of action*	Duration of action†	Relative toxicity‡
Articaine	7.8	High	Medium (60% to 80%)	1.2 hr	Rapid (1 to 6 minutes)	Intermediate (1 hour)	
Bupivacaine	8.1	High	Very high	3.5 hr/8.1–14 hr	Intermediate to Slow	Long§	
Chloroprocaine	9			19–26 sec/41–45 sec	Rapid	Short	
Etidocaine	7.74	High	Very high	2.5 hr/4–8 hr	Rapid	Long	
Levobupivacaine	8.1	High	Very high	1.3 hours	Immediate to slow	Short to long	
Lidocaine	7.9	Medium	Moderate to high	1.5–2 hr/3.2 hr	Rapid#	Intermediate	2
Mepivacaine	7.6	Medium	High	1.9–3.2 hr/9 hr	Rapid to intermediate#	Intermediate	2
Prilocaine	7.9	Medium	Moderate	1.6 hr	Rapid	Intermediate	1.7
Procaine	8.9	Low	Very low	30–50 sec/54–114 sec	Intermediate	Short	1
Tetracaine	8.2	High	High		Rapid	Intermediate to long	10

*Influenced by the site, route, and technique of administration; dosage (volume and concentration) administered; pH at injection site; physical characteristics, such as lipid solubility, molecular size, and pKa of the individual anesthetic; and individual patient.

†Short = 30 to 60 minutes; Intermediate = 1 to 3 hours; Long = 3 to 10 hours. Influenced by factors affecting rate of clearance from the injection site and individual patient.

‡As compared with procaine (the least toxic of these agents).

§Via nerve block, may produce analgesia for considerably longer than 10 hours.

#Adjustment of pH with 1 mEq (1 mmol) of sodium bicarbonate per 10 mL may increase the onset of conduction blocks (lidocaine hydrochloride injection, lidocaine and epinephrine injection, or mepivacaine hydrochloride injection).

ANESTHETICS Topical

This monograph includes information on the following: 1) Benzocaine; 2) Benzocaine and Menthol; 3) Butamben; 4) Dibucaine; 5) Lidocaine; 6) Pramoxine; 7) Pramoxine and Menthol; 8) Tetracaine†; 9) Tetracaine and Menthol†.

Note: See also individual *Lidocaine and Prilocaine (Topical)* monograph.

INN:
Dibucaine—Cinchocaine
Pramoxine—Pramocaine

BAN:
Dibucaine—Cinchocaine
Lidocaine—Lignocaine
Tetracaine—Amethocaine

JAN: Benzocaine—Ethyl aminobenzoate

VA CLASSIFICATION (Primary/Secondary):

Note: Several of the dosage forms listed below are commercially available in more than one formulation. Because the vehicle into which a local anesthetic is incorporated may determine the appropriate usage and/or site(s) of application of a product, some of the VA classifications listed for a dosage form may apply only to specific formulations.

- Benzocaine
  - Cream—DE700
  - Ointment—RS201/DE700; RS900
  - Topical Aerosol—DE700/NT300; OR600
  - Topical Spray Solution—DE700
- Benzocaine and Menthol—DE700
- Butamben—DE700
- Dibucaine
  - Cream—DE700
  - Ointment—RS201/DE700; RS900
- Lidocaine
  - Ointment 2.5%—DE700
  - Ointment 5%—NT300/DE700; OR600
  - Topical Spray Solution—DE700
- Lidocaine Hydrochloride
  - Topical Aerosol—DE700
  - Film-forming Gel—DE700
  - Jelly—NT300/GU900; DE700
  - Ointment—DE700
- Pramoxine
  - Cream—RS201/DE700; RS900
  - Lotion—DE700
- Pramoxine and Menthol
  - Gel—DE700
  - Lotion—DE700
- Tetracaine
  - Cream—RS201/DE700; RE900
- Tetracaine and Menthol
  - Ointment—RS201/DE700; RE900

Note: For information on local anesthetics applied topically to the oral, rectal, or other mucosa, see *Anesthetics (Mucosal-Local)*.

In Canada, *Nupercainal Cream* contains domiphen bromide in addition to dibucaine.

Commonly used brand name(s): *After Burn Double Strength Gel*[5]; *After Burn Double Strength Spray*[5]; *After Burn Gel*[5]; *After Burn Spray*[5]; *Almay Anti-itch Lotion*[7]; *Alphacaine*[5]; *Americaine Topical Anesthetic First Aid Ointment*[1]; *Americaine Topical Anesthetic Spray*[1]; *Butesin Picrate*[3]; *DermaFlex*[5]; *Dermoplast*[2]; *Endocaine*[1]; *Lagol*[1]; *Norwood Sunburn Spray*[5]; *Nupercainal Cream*[4]; *Nupercainal Ointment*[4]; *Pontocaine Cream*[8]; *Pontocaine Ointment*[9]; *Pramegel*[7]; *Prax*[6]; *Shield Burnasept Spray*[1]; *Tronothane*[6]; *Xylocaine*[5].

Other commonly used names are: Amethocaine [Tetracaine] Butyl aminobenzoate [Butamben] Cinchocaine [Dibucaine] Ethyl aminobenzoate [Benzocaine] Lignocaine [Lidocaine] Pramocaine [Pramoxine]

Note: For a listing of dosage forms and brand names by country availability, see *Dosage Forms* section(s).

†Not commercially available in Canada.

Category

Anesthetic, local.

Indications

Accepted

Skin disorders, minor (treatment)—Topical anesthetics are indicated to relieve pain, pruritus, and inflammation associated with minor skin disorders, including:
- Burns, minor, including sunburn.
- Bites (or stings), insect.
- Dermatitis, contact, including poison ivy, poison oak, or poison sumac.
- Wounds, minor, such as cuts and scratches.

Pharmacology/Pharmacokinetics

Physicochemical characteristics

Chemical Group—Amides:
- Dibucaine, lidocaine.
- Esters, aminobenzoic acid (para-aminobenzoic acid, PABA)–derivative: Benzocaine, butamben, tetracaine.
- Unclassified: Pramoxine.

Molecular weight—
- Benzocaine: 165.19.
- Butamben picrate: 615.60.
- Dibucaine: 343.47.
- Lidocaine: 234.34.
- Lidocaine hydrochloride: 288.82.
- Pramoxine hydrochloride: 329.87.
- Tetracaine: 264.37.
- Tetracaine hydrochloride: 300.83.

pKa—
- Dibucaine: 8.8.
- Lidocaine: 7.9.
- Tetracaine: 8.2.

Mechanism of action/Effect

Local anesthetics block both the initiation and conduction of nerve impulses by decreasing the neuronal membrane's permeability to sodium ions. This reversibly stabilizes the membrane and inhibits depolarization, resulting in the failure of a propagated action potential and subsequent conduction blockade.

Other actions/effects

If significant quantities of topical anesthetics are absorbed, actions on the central nervous system (CNS) may lead to CNS stimulation and/or CNS depression. Actions on the cardiovascular system may cause depression of cardiac conduction and excitability, and possibly peripheral vasodilation.

Absorption

Absorption is variable; dependent on specific drug and/or its specific salt. Benzocaine is minimally absorbed. In general, ionized forms(salts) of local anesthetics are not readily absorbed through intact skin. However, both nonionized (bases) and ionized forms of local anesthetics are readily absorbed through traumatized or abraded skin into the systemic circulation.

Biotransformation

Amides—
- Hepatic and some renal.
- Lidocaine: Xylidide metabolites are active and toxic, but less so than the parent compound.

Esters, PABA-derivative—
- Hydrolyzed by plasma cholinesterases, and to a much lesser extent by hepatic cholinesterases, to PABA-containing metabolites.

Onset of action

Dibucaine—Up to 15 minutes.
Pramoxine—3 to 5 minutes.
Tetracaine—Slow.

Duration of action

Lidocaine—Approximately 45 minutes.

Tetracaine—Approximately 30 to 45 minutes.

Elimination

Amides—
- Renal, primarily as metabolites.
- Lidocaine: Up to 10% of an absorbed dose may be excreted unchanged.

Esters—
- Renal, as metabolites.

Precautions to Consider

Cross-sensitivity and/or related problems

Patients sensitive to one ester-derivative (especially a PABA-derivative) local anesthetic may be sensitive to other ester derivatives also.

Patients sensitive to PABA, parabens, or paraphenylenediamine (a hair dye) may be sensitive to PABA-derivative topical anesthetics also.
Patients sensitive to one amide derivative may rarely be sensitive to other amide derivatives also.
Cross-sensitivity between amide derivatives and ester derivatives, or between amides or esters and the chemically unrelated pramoxine, has not been reported.

Pregnancy/Reproduction

Pregnancy—Problems in humans with topical anesthetics have not been documented.

Benzocaine, butamben, dibucaine, and pramoxine—
Studies in humans have not been done.
Studies in animals have not been done.

Lidocaine—
Adequate and well-controlled studies in humans have not been done.
Studies in animals given up to 6.6 times the human dose have shown no adverse effects on the fetus.
Lidocaine ointment 5%—FDA Pregnancy Category B.

Tetracaine—
Studies in humans have not been done.
Studies in animals have not been done.
FDA Pregnancy Category C.

Breast-feeding

Problems in humans have not been documented.

Pediatrics

Benzocaine—Benzocaine should be used with caution in infants and young children because increased absorption through the skin (with excessive use) may result in methemoglobinemia. Benzocaine-containing topical formulations should not be used in children younger than 2 years of age unless prescribed by a physician.
Other topical anesthetics—No information is available on the relationship of age to the effects of these medications in pediatric patients following application to the skin. However, it is recommended that a physician be consulted before any topical local anesthetic is used in children younger than 2 years of age.

Geriatrics

No information is available on the relationship of age to the effects of topical anesthetics in geriatric patients following application to the skin.

Drug interactions and/or related problems

The following drug interactions and/or related problems have been selected on the basis of their potential clinical significance (possible mechanism in parentheses where appropriate)—not necessarily inclusive (» = major clinical significance):

Note: Combinations containing any of the following medications, depending on the amount present, may also interact with this medication.

For ester derivatives
Cholinesterase inhibitors such as
Antimyasthenics
Cyclophosphamide
Demecarium
Echothiophate
Insecticides, neurotoxic, possibly including large quantities of topical malathion
Isoflurophate
Thiotepa
(these agents may inhibit metabolism of ester derivatives; absorption of significant quantities of ester derivatives in patients receiving a cholinesterase inhibitor may lead to increased risk of toxicity)
Sulfonamides
(metabolites of PABA-derivative topical anesthetics may antagonize antibacterial activity of sulfonamides, especially if the anesthetics are absorbed in significant quantities over prolonged periods of time)

For lidocaine
Antiarrhythmic agents, amide local anesthetic–derivative, other, such as
Mexiletine
Tocainide or
Lidocaine, systemic or parenteral-local
(risk of cardiotoxicity associated with additive cardiac effects, and, with systemic or parenteral-local lidocaine, the risk of overdose, may be increased in patients receiving these medications if large quantities of topically applied lidocaine are absorbed)
Beta-adrenergic blocking agents
(concurrent use may slow metabolism of lidocaine because of decreased hepatic blood flow, leading to increased risk of lidocaine toxicity if large quantities are absorbed)
Cimetidine
(cimetidine inhibits hepatic metabolism of lidocaine; concurrent use may lead to lidocaine toxicity if large quantities are absorbed)

Laboratory value alterations

The following have been selected on the basis of their potential clinical significance (possible effect in parentheses where appropriate)—not necessarily inclusive (» = major clinical significance).

With diagnostic test results
Pancreatic function determinations using bentiromide
(use of PABA-derivative topical anesthetics or lidocaine prior to the bentiromide test may invalidate test results since these medications are also metabolized to PABA or other arylamines and will thus increase the real or apparent quantity of PABA recovered; patients should be advised to discontinue use of these anesthetics 3 days prior to bentiromide administration)

Medical considerations/Contraindications

The medical considerations/contraindications included have been selected on the basis of their potential clinical significance (reasons given in parentheses where appropriate)—not necessarily inclusive (» = major clinical significance).

Risk-benefit should be considered when the following medical problems exist:
Local infection at site of application
(infection may alter the pH at the treatment site, leading to decrease or loss of local anesthetic effect)
Sensitivity to the topical anesthetic being considered for use or to chemically related anesthetics and, for the ester derivatives, to PABA, parabens, or paraphenylenediamine, or
Sensitivity to other ingredients in the formulation
Skin disorders, severe or extensive, especially if skin is abraded or broken
(increased absorption of anesthetic)

Side/Adverse Effects

Note: Adverse reactions are due to excessive dosage or rapid absorption, which produces high plasma concentrations, as well as to idiosyncrasy, hypersensitivity, or decreased patient tolerance.
Benzocaine and tetracaine are more likely to cause contact sensitization than are the other local anesthetics.

The following side/adverse effects have been selected on the basis of their potential clinical significance (possible signs and symptoms in parentheses where appropriate)—not necessarily inclusive:

Those indicating need for medical attention

Incidence less frequent
Angioedema (large, hive-like swellings on skin, mouth, or throat); ***dermatitis, contact*** (skin rash, redness, itching, or hives; burning, stinging, swelling, or tenderness not present before therapy)

Overdose

For specific information on the agents used in the management of topical anesthetics overdose, see:
- *Ascorbic Acid (Systemic)* monograph;
- *Benzodiazepines (Systemic)* monograph;
- *Sympathomimetic Agents—Cardiovascular Use (Parenteral-Systemic)* monograph; and/or
- *Methylene Blue (Systemic)* monograph.

For more information on the management of overdose or unintentional ingestion, **contact a Poison Control Center** (see *Poison Control Center Listing*).

Clinical effects of overdose

The following effects have been selected on the basis of their potential clinical significance if excessive systemic absorption occurs (possible signs and symptoms in parentheses where appropriate)—not necessarily inclusive:

Cardiovascular system depression (low blood pressure; slow or irregular heartbeat; unusual paleness; increased sweating)—may lead to cardiac arrest; ***CNS toxicity*** (blurred or double vision; confusion; convulsions; dizziness or lightheadedness; drowsiness; feeling hot, cold, or numb; ringing or buzzing in the ears; shivering or trembling; unusual anxiety, excitement, nervousness, or restlessness); ***methemoglobinemia*** (difficulty in breathing on exertion; dizziness; headache; unusual tiredness or weakness)

Note: Stimulant and/or depressant manifestations of *CNS toxicity* may occur. CNS stimulation usually occurs first, followed by CNS depression. However, CNS stimulation may be transient or absent, so that drowsiness may be the first symptom of toxicity in some patients. CNS depression may lead to unconsciousness and respiratory arrest.

Treatment of overdose

Recommended treatment includes:

Specific treatment—

For methemoglobinemia—Administering methylene blue (1 to 2 mg per kg of body weight, intravenously) and/or ascorbic acid (100 to 200 mg orally).

For circulatory depression—Administration of a vasopressor and intravenous fluids is recommended.

For convulsions—Administering an anticonvulsant, usually a benzodiazepine, keeping in mind that benzodiazepines may cause respiratory and circulatory depression, especially when administered rapidly. Medications and equipment needed for support of respiration and for resuscitation must be immediately available.

Supportive Care—

For systemic reactions caused by excessive absorption—Securing and maintaining a patent airway, administering oxygen, and instituting assisted or controlled respiration as required. In some patients, endotracheal intubation may be required.

Patient Consultation

As an aid to patient consultation, refer to *Advice for the Patient, Anesthetics (Topical)*.

In providing consultation, consider emphasizing the following selected information (» = major clinical significance):

Before using this medication

» Conditions affecting use, especially:

Sensitivity to local anesthetics of the same chemical class, and, for ester derivatives only, aminobenzoic acid, parabens, or hair dye

Use in children—Caution that excessive quantities of benzocaine may cause methemoglobinemia in children younger than 2 years of age; consulting physician before using any topical local anesthetic in children younger than 2 years of age

Proper use of this medication

Following physician's instructions if prescribed

Following manufacturer's instructions if self-medicating

» Not using on large areas, especially if skin broken or abraded, or for prolonged periods of time, without physician's advice

» Checking with physician before using for problems other than prescribed or recommended on package label, or if any suspicion of infection

» Not using products containing alcohol, which is flammable, near fire or open flame or while smoking; not smoking until area completely dry

» Using care not to get in eyes, mouth, or nose; if using topical aerosol or spray dosage forms, applying to face with hand or other suitable applicator

» Proper dosing

Missed dose (if on scheduled dosing): Applying as soon as possible; not applying if almost time for next dose

» Proper storage

For butamben

Butamben may permanently stain clothing and hair; covering area with a loose bandage after application to protect clothing and not allowing hair to come into contact with the medication

For lidocaine film-forming gel

Proper application technique: Drying area before applying; applying medication, then waiting 60 seconds until transparent film forms

Precautions while using this medication

» Taking precautions to prevent children from transferring medication to their mouths after application

» *Discontinuing use and checking with physician:*

If condition does not improve within 7 days or worsens

(If problem area becomes infected)

(If rash, irritation, or other symptoms not present before use occur)

(If medication is swallowed)

Side/adverse effects

Signs and symptoms of potential side effects, especially angioedema, contact dermatitis, and overdose

General Dosing Information

These medications should not be applied over large areas, or for prolonged periods of time, especially to broken or abraded skin, because of the increased risk of systemic absorption and toxicity.

Topical anesthetic-containing medications may be sprayed or applied directly to the affected area, or applied with a suitable applicator (for example, a sterile gauze pad or cotton swab).

BENZOCAINE

Summary of Differences

Physicochemical characteristics:

An ester-type (PABA-derivative) local anesthetic.

Precautions:

Cross-sensitivity and/or related problems—

May occur with other ester-type anesthetics, especially other PABA derivatives, with PABA or parabens, and with paraphenylenediamine.

Pediatrics—

Excessive use may cause methemoglobinemia in infants and young children.

Drug interactions and/or related problems—

Cholinesterase inhibitors may inhibit metabolism of benzocaine.

Benzocaine may antagonize antibacterial activity of sulfonamides.

Side/adverse effects:

More likely to cause contact sensitization than most other topical anesthetics.

See also *Side/Adverse Effects.*

Topical Dosage Forms

BENZOCAINE CREAM USP

Usual adult and adolescent dose

Anesthetic, local—

Topical, to the affected area three or four times a day as needed.

Usual pediatric dose

Anesthetic, local—

Children up to 2 years of age: Dosage must be individualized by a physician.

Children 2 years of age and older: See *Usual adult and adolescent dose.*

Strength(s) usually available

U.S.—

5% (OTC) [GENERIC].

Packaging and storage

Store below 30 °C (86 °F). Store in a tight container. Protect from light. Protect from freezing.

Auxiliary labeling

• For external use only.

BENZOCAINE OINTMENT USP

Usual adult and adolescent dose

Anesthetic, local—

Topical, to the affected area three or four times a day as needed.

Usual pediatric dose

Anesthetic, local—

Children up to 2 years of age: Dosage must be individualized by a physician.

Children 2 years of age and older: See *Usual adult and adolescent dose.*

Strength(s) usually available

U.S.—

5% (OTC) [*Lagol*].

20% (OTC) [*Americaine Topical Anesthetic First Aid Ointment*].

Packaging and storage

Store below 30 °C (86 °F). Store in a tight container. Protect from light. Protect from freezing.

Auxiliary labeling

• For external use only.

BENZOCAINE TOPICAL AEROSOL USP

Usual adult and adolescent dose

Anesthetic, local—

Topical, sprayed on or applied to affected area three or four times a day as needed.

Usual pediatric dose

Anesthetic, local—

Children up to 2 years of age: Dosage must be individualized by a physician.

Children 2 years of age and older: See *Usual adult and adolescent dose.*

Strength(s) usually available

U.S.—

20% (OTC) [*Americaine Topical Anesthetic Spray*].

Packaging and storage
Store below 40 °C (104 °F), preferably between 15 and 30 °C (59 and 86 °F), unless otherwise specified by manufacturer.

Auxiliary labeling
- Shake well.
- For external use only.

BENZOCAINE TOPICAL SPRAY SOLUTION

Usual adult and adolescent dose
Anesthetic, local—

Topical, sprayed on or applied to affected area three or four times a day as needed.

Usual pediatric dose
Anesthetic, local—

Children up to 2 years of age: Dosage must be individualized by a physician.

Children 2 years of age and older: See *Usual adult and adolescent dose.*

Strength(s) usually available
U.S.—

Canada—

2% (OTC) [*Shield Burnasept Spray*].

20% (OTC) [*Endocaine*].

Packaging and storage
Store below 40 °C (104 °F), preferably between 15 and 30 °C (59 and 86 °F), unless otherwise specified by manufacturer.

Auxiliary labeling
- For external use only.

BENZOCAINE AND MENTHOL

Summary of Differences
Physicochemical characteristics:

An ester-type (PABA-derivative) local anesthetic.

Precautions:

Cross-sensitivity and/or related problems—

May occur with other ester-type anesthetics, especially other PABA derivatives, with PABA or parabens, and with para-phenylenediamine.

Pediatrics—

Excessive use may cause methemoglobinemia in infants and young children.

Drug interactions and/or related problems—

Cholinesterase inhibitors may inhibit metabolism of benzocaine.

Benzocaine may antagonize antibacterial activity of sulfonamides.

Side/adverse effects:

More likely to cause contact sensitization than most other topical anesthetics.

See also *Side/Adverse Effects.*

Topical Dosage Forms

BENZOCAINE AND MENTHOL LOTION

Usual adult and adolescent dose
Anesthetic, local—

Topical, to the affected area three or four times a day as needed.

Usual pediatric dose
Anesthetic, local—

Children up to 2 years of age: Dosage must be individualized by a physician.

Children 2 years of age and older: See *Usual adult and adolescent dose.*

Strength(s) usually available
U.S.—

8% of benzocaine and 0.5% of menthol (OTC) [*Dermoplast* (methylparaben)].

Packaging and storage
Store below 30 °C (86 °F). Protect from freezing.

Auxiliary labeling
- For external use only.

BENZOCAINE AND MENTHOL TOPICAL AEROSOL

Usual adult and adolescent dose
Anesthetic, local—

Topical, sprayed on or applied to affected area three or four times a day as needed.

Usual pediatric dose
Anesthetic, local—

Children up to 2 years of age: Dosage must be individualized by a physician.

Children 2 years of age and older: See *Usual adult and adolescent dose.*

Strength(s) usually available
U.S.—

8% of benzocaine and 0.5% of menthol (OTC) [*Dermoplast* (methylparaben)].

Canada—

4.5% of benzocaine and 0.5% of menthol (OTC) [*Dermoplast* (methylparaben; isopropyl alcohol)].

Packaging and storage
Store below 40 °C (104 °F), preferably between 15 and 30 °C (59 and 86 °F), unless otherwise specified by manufacturer.

Auxiliary labeling
- Shake well.
- For external use only.

BUTAMBEN

Summary of Differences
Physicochemical characteristics:

Butamben is an ester-type (PABA derivative) local anesthetic.

Precautions:

Cross-sensitivity and/or related problems—

May occur with other ester-type anesthetics, especially other PABA derivatives, with PABA or parabens, and with para-phenylenediamine.

Drug interactions and/or related problems—

Cholinesterase inhibitors may inhibit metabolism of butamben.

Butamben may antagonize antibacterial activity of sulfonamides.

Topical Dosage Forms

BUTAMBEN PICRATE OINTMENT

Usual adult and adolescent dose
Anesthetic, local—

Topical, to the skin, as a 1% ointment three or four times a day as needed.

Note: Area should be loosely bandaged to protect clothing from staining.

Usual pediatric dose
Dosage has not been established.

Strength(s) usually available
U.S.—

1% (OTC) [*Butesin Picrate*].

Packaging and storage
Store below 25 °C (77 °F), unless otherwise specified by manufacturer. Protect from freezing.

Auxiliary labeling
- For external use only.

DIBUCAINE

Summary of Differences
Physicochemical characteristics:

Dibucaine is an amide-type local anesthetic.

Precautions:

Cross-sensitivity and/or related problems—Rarely, may occur with other amide-type local anesthetics.

Laboratory value alterations—No interference with bentiromide test for pancreatic function.

Topical Dosage Forms

DIBUCAINE CREAM USP

Usual adult and adolescent dose
Anesthetic, local—

Topical, to the skin, as a 0.5% cream three or four times a day as needed.

Usual pediatric dose
Anesthetic, local—

Children up to 2 years of age: Dosage must be individualized by a physician.

Children 2 years of age and older: See *Usual adult and adolescent dose.*

Strength(s) usually available

U.S.—

Note: In Canada, *Nupercainal Cream* also contains domiphen bromide.

0.5% (OTC) [*Nupercainal Cream* (acetone sodium bisulfite); GENERIC].

Packaging and storage

Store below 40 °C (104 °F), preferably between 15 and 30 °C (59 and 86 °F), unless otherwise specified by manufacturer. Store in a collapsible tube or a tight, light-resistant container. Protect from freezing.

Auxiliary labeling

- For external use only.

DIBUCAINE OINTMENT USP

Usual adult and adolescent dose

Anesthetic, local—

Topical, to the skin, as a 1% ointment three or four times a day as needed.

Note: Area may be lightly covered for protection.

Usual adult prescribing limits

Not more than 30 grams in a twenty-four-hour period.

Usual pediatric dose

Anesthetic, local—

Children up to 2 years of age: Dosage must be individualized by a physician.

Children 2 years of age and older: See *Usual adult and adolescent dose.*

Usual pediatric prescribing limits

Not more than 7.5 grams in a twenty-four-hour period.

Strength(s) usually available

U.S.—

1% (OTC) [*Nupercainal Ointment;* GENERIC].

Canada—

1% (OTC) [*Nupercainal Ointment*].

Packaging and storage

Store below 40 °C (104 °F), preferably between 15 and 30 °C (59 and 86 °F), unless otherwise specified by manufacturer. Store in a collapsible tube or in a tight, light-resistant container. Protect from freezing.

Auxiliary labeling

- For external use only.

LIDOCAINE

Summary of Differences

Physicochemical characteristics:

Lidocaine is an amide-type local anesthetic.

Precautions:

Cross-sensitivity and/or related problems—Rarely, may occur with other amide-type local anesthetics.

Drug interactions—Possibility of toxicity in patients receiving local anesthetic–derivative antiarrhythmic agents, lidocaine via other routes of administration, beta-adrenergic blocking agents, or cimetidine if large quantities of topically administered lidocaine are absorbed.

Topical Dosage Forms

LIDOCAINE OINTMENT USP

Usual adult and adolescent dose

Anesthetic, local—

Topical, as a 2.5% or 5% ointment, to the affected area three or four times a day as needed.

Usual adult prescribing limits

For the 5% ointment—Not more than 5 grams per single application or 20 grams per day.

Usual pediatric dose

Anesthetic, local—

Dosage must be individualized, depending on the child's age, weight, and physical condition, up to a maximum of 4.5 mg per kg of body weight.

Strength(s) usually available

U.S.—

2.5% (OTC) [*Xylocaine*].

5% (Rx) [*Xylocaine;* GENERIC].

Canada—

5% (OTC) [*Alphacaine; Xylocaine*].

Packaging and storage

Store below 40 °C (104 °F), preferably between 15 and 30 °C (59 and 86 °F), unless otherwise specified by manufacturer. Store in a tight container. Protect from freezing.

Auxiliary labeling

- For external use only.

LIDOCAINE TOPICAL SPRAY SOLUTION

Usual adult and adolescent dose

Anesthetic, local—

Topical, sprayed on or applied to affected area three or four times a day as needed.

Usual pediatric dose

Dosage has not been established.

Strength(s) usually available

U.S.—

Canada—

2% (OTC) [*Norwood Sunburn Spray*].

Packaging and storage

Store below 40 °C (104 °F), preferably between 15 and 30 °C (59 and 86 °F), unless otherwise specified by manufacturer. Protect from freezing.

Auxiliary labeling

- For external use only.

LIDOCAINE HYDROCHLORIDE TOPICAL AEROSOL

Usual adult and adolescent dose

Anesthetic, local—

Topical, sprayed on or applied to the affected area three or four times a day as needed.

Usual pediatric dose

Dosage has not been established.

Strength(s) usually available

U.S.—

Canada—

0.5% (OTC) [*After Burn Spray*].

1% (OTC) [*After Burn Double Strength Spray*].

Packaging and storage

Store below 40 °C (104 °F), preferably between 15 and 30 °C (59 and 86 °F), unless otherwise specified by manufacturer. Protect from freezing.

Auxiliary labeling

- Shake well.
- For external use only.

LIDOCAINE HYDROCHLORIDE FILM-FORMING GEL

Usual adult and adolescent dose

Anesthetic, local—

Topical, applied to affected area three or four times a day as needed.

Usual pediatric dose

Dosage has not been established.

Strength(s) usually available

U.S.—

2.5% (OTC) [*DermaFlex*].

Packaging and storage

Store below 40 °C (104 °F), preferably between 15 and 30 °C (59 and 86 °F), unless otherwise specified by manufacturer. Protect from freezing.

Auxiliary labeling

- For external use only.

LIDOCAINE HYDROCHLORIDE JELLY USP

Usual adult and adolescent dose

Anesthetic, local—

Topical, to the affected area three or four times a day as needed.

Usual pediatric dose

Dosage has not been established.

Strength(s) usually available

U.S.—

Canada—

0.5% (OTC) [*After Burn Gel*].

1% (OTC) [*After Burn Double Strength Gel*].

Packaging and storage
Store below 40 °C (104 °F), preferably between 15 and 30 °C (59 and 86 °F), unless otherwise specified by manufacturer. Protect from freezing.

Auxiliary labeling
• For external use only.

LIDOCAINE HYDROCHLORIDE OINTMENT

Usual adult and adolescent dose
Anesthetic, local—
Topical, as a 5% ointment, to the affected area three or four times a day as needed.

Usual pediatric dose
Anesthetic, local—
Children up to 2 years of age: Dosage has not been established.
Children 2 years of age and older: See *Usual adult and adolescent dose.*

Strength(s) usually available
U.S.—
5% (Rx) [GENERIC].

Packaging and storage
Store below 40 °C (104 °F), preferably between 15 and 30 °C (59 and 86 °F), unless otherwise specified by manufacturer. Protect from freezing.

Auxiliary labeling
• For external use only.

PRAMOXINE

Summary of Differences

Physicochemical characteristics: Pramoxine is an unclassified (neither an amide-type nor an ester-type) local anesthetic.
Precautions: Diagnostic interference—No interference with bentiromide test for pancreatic function.

Topical Dosage Forms

PRAMOXINE HYDROCHLORIDE CREAM USP

Usual adult and adolescent dose
Anesthetic, local—
Topical, as a 1% cream, every three to four hours as needed.

Usual pediatric dose
Anesthetic, local—
Children up to 2 years of age: Dosage has not been established.
Children 2 years of age and older: See *Usual adult and adolescent dose.*

Strength(s) usually available
U.S.—
1% (OTC) [*Prax; Tronothane*].
Canada—
1% (OTC) [*Tronothane*].

Packaging and storage
Store below 40 °C (104 °F), preferably between 15 and 30 °C (59 and 86 °F), unless otherwise specified by manufacturer. Store in tight container. Protect from freezing.

Auxiliary labeling
• For external use only.

PRAMOXINE HYDROCHLORIDE LOTION

Usual adult and adolescent dose
Anesthetic, local—
Topical, as a 1% lotion, every three or four hours as needed.

Usual pediatric dose
Anesthetic, local—
Children up to 2 years of age: Dosage has not been established.
Children 2 years of age and older: See *Usual adult and adolescent dose.*

Strength(s) usually available
U.S.—
1% (OTC) [*Prax*].

Packaging and storage
Store below 40 °C (104 °F), preferably between 15 and 30 °C (59 and 86 °F), unless otherwise specified by manufacturer. Protect from freezing.

Auxiliary labeling
• For external use only.

PRAMOXINE HYDROCHLORIDE AND MENTHOL

Summary of Differences

Physicochemical characteristics: Pramoxine is an unclassified (neither an amide-type nor an ester-type) local anesthetic.
Precautions: Diagnostic interference—No interference with bentiromide test for pancreatic function.

Topical Dosage Forms

PRAMOXINE HYDROCHLORIDE AND MENTHOL GEL

Usual adult and adolescent dose
Anesthetic, local—
—Topical, applied to affected areas three or four times a day as needed.

Usual pediatric dose
Anesthetic, local—
Children up to 2 years of age: Dosage has not been established.
Children 2 years of age and older: See *Usual adult and adolescent dose.*

Strength(s) usually available
U.S.—
1% of pramoxine hydrochloride and 0.5% of menthol (OTC) [*Pramegel*].
Canada—
1% of pramoxine hydrochloride and 0.5% of menthol (OTC) [*Pramegel*].

Packaging and storage
Store below 40 °C (104 °F), preferably between 15 and 30 °C (59 and 86 °F), unless otherwise specified by manufacturer. Protect from freezing.

Auxiliary labeling
• For external use only.

PRAMOXINE HYDROCHLORIDE AND MENTHOL LOTION

Usual adult and adolescent dose
Anesthetic, local—
Topical, applied to affected areas three or four times a day as needed.

Usual pediatric dose
Anesthetic, local—
Children up to 2 years of age: Dosage has not been established.
Children 2 years of age and older: See *Usual adult and adolescent dose.*

Strength(s) usually available
U.S.—
1% of pramoxine hydrochloride and 0.2% of menthol (OTC) [*Almay Anti-itch Lotion*].

Packaging and storage
Store below 40 °C (104 °F), preferably between 15 and 30 °C (59 and 86 °F), unless otherwise specified by manufacturer. Protect from freezing.

Auxiliary labeling
• For external use only.

TETRACAINE

Summary of Differences

Physicochemical characteristics:
An ester-type (PABA-derivative) local anesthetic.
Precautions:
Cross-sensitivity and/or related problems—May occur with other ester-type anesthetics, especially other PABA derivatives, with PABA or parabens, and with paraphenylenediamine.
Drug interactions and/or related problems:
Cholinesterase inhibitors may inhibit metabolism of tetracaine.
Tetracaine may antagonize antibacterial activity of sulfonamides.
Side/adverse effects:
More likely to cause contact sensitization than most other topical anesthetics.
See also *Side/Adverse Effects.*

Topical Dosage Forms

TETRACAINE HYDROCHLORIDE CREAM USP

Usual adult and adolescent dose

Anesthetic, local—

Topical, applied as a 1% cream to affected areas three or four times a day as needed.

Usual adult prescribing limits

Not more than 28.35 grams in a twenty-four-hour period.

Usual pediatric dose

Anesthetic, local—

Children up to 2 years of age: Dosage must be individualized by a physician.

Children 2 years of age and older: See *Usual adult and adolescent dose.*

Usual pediatric prescribing limits

Not more than 7 grams in a twenty-four-hour period.

Strength(s) usually available

U.S.—

1% (OTC) [*Pontocaine Cream*].

Canada—

Not commercially available.

Packaging and storage

Store below 40 °C (104 °F), preferably between 15 and 30 °C (59 and 86 °F), unless otherwise specified by manufacturer. Protect from freezing.

Auxiliary labeling

• For external use only.

TETRACAINE AND MENTHOL

Summary of Differences

Physicochemical characteristics:

An ester-type (PABA-derivative) local anesthetic.

Precautions:

Cross-sensitivity and/or related problems—May occur with other ester-type anesthetics, especially other PABA derivatives, with PABA or parabens, and with paraphenylenediamine.

Drug interactions and/or related problems:

Cholinesterase inhibitors may inhibit metabolism of tetracaine.

Tetracaine may antagonize antibacterial activity of sulfonamides.

Side/adverse effects:

More likely to cause contact sensitization than most other topical anesthetics.

See also *Side/Adverse Effects.*

Topical Dosage Forms

TETRACAINE AND MENTHOL OINTMENT USP

Usual adult and adolescent dose

Anesthetic, local—

Topical, applied to affected area as a 0.5% ointment three or four times a day as needed.

Usual adult prescribing limits

Not more than 28.35 grams in a twenty-four-hour period.

Usual pediatric dose

Anesthetic, local—

Children up to 2 years of age: Dosage must be individualized by a physician.

Children 2 years of age and older: See *Usual adult and adolescent dose.*

Usual pediatric prescribing limits

Not more than 7 grams in a twenty-four-hour period.

Strength(s) usually available

U.S.—

0.5% of tetracaine and 0.5% of menthol (OTC) [*Pontocaine Ointment*].

Canada—

Not commercially available.

Packaging and storage

Store below 40 °C (104 °F), preferably between 15 and 30 °C (59 and 86 °F), unless otherwise specified by manufacturer. Protect from freezing.

Auxiliary labeling

• For external use only.

Revised: 08/29/1994

ANGIOTENSIN-CONVERTING ENZYME (ACE) INHIBITORS Systemic

This monograph includes information on the following: 1) Benazepril; 2) Captopril; 3) Cilazapril*; 4) Enalapril; 5) Fosinopril; 6) Lisinopril; 7) Moexipril†; 8) Perindopril; 9) Quinapril; 10) Ramipril; 11) Trandolapril.

VA CLASSIFICATION (Primary/Secondary):

Benazepril—CV800/CV409; CV900
Captopril—CV800/CV409; CV900
Cilazapril—CV800/CV409; CV900
Enalapril—CV800/CV409; CV900
Enalaprilat—CV800/CV409; CV900
Fosinopril—CV800/CV409; CV900
Lisinopril—CV800/CV409; CV900
Moexipril—CV800/CV409; CV900
Perindopril—CV800/CV409; CV900
Quinapril—CV800/CV409; CV900
Ramipril—CV800/CV409; CV900
Trandolapril—CV800/CV409; CV900

Commonly used brand name(s): *Accupril*[9]; *Aceon*[8]; *Altace*[10]; *Capoten*[2]; *Coversyl*[8]; *Inhibace*[3]; *Lotensin*[1]; *Mavik*[11]; *Monopril*[5]; *Prinivil*[6]; *Univasc*[7]; *Vasotec*[4]; *Zestril*[6].

Note: For a listing of dosage forms and brand names by country availability, see *Dosage Forms* section(s).

*Not commercially available in U.S.
†Not commercially available in Canada.

Category

Antihypertensive—Benazepril; Captopril; Cilazapril; Enalapril; Enalaprilat; Fosinopril; Lisinopril; Moexipril; Perindopril; Quinapril; Ramipril; Trandolapril.

Vasodilator, congestive heart failure—Benazepril; Captopril; Cilazapril; Enalapril; Fosinopril; Lisinopril; Quinapril; Ramipril; Trandolapril

Indications

Note: Bracketed information in the *Indications* section refers to uses that are not included in U.S. product labeling.

Accepted

Hypertension (treatment)—Angiotensin-converting enzyme (ACE) inhibitors are indicated, alone or in combination with a thiazide diuretic, in the treatment of hypertension.

ACE inhibitors are also used for [treatment of malignant, refractory, or accelerated hypertension][1], and for treatment of renovascular hypertension (except in patients with bilateral renal artery stenoses or renal artery stenosis in a solitary kidney—See *Medical considerations/contraindications*).

Enalaprilat intravenous injection is for the treatment of hypertension when oral therapy is not practical.

For additional information on initial therapeutic guidelines related to the treatment of hypertension, see *Appendix III.*

Congestive heart failure (treatment)—[Benazepril][1] captopril, [cilazapril], enalapril, fosinopril, lisinopril, quinapril, and [ramipril][1] are also indicated, in combination with diuretics and digitalis therapy, for treatment of congestive heart failure not responding to other measures.

Congestive heart failure, post-myocardial infarction (treatment)—Ramipril, and trandolapril are indicated in stable patients with clinical signs of congestive heart failure within the first few days after sustaining an acute myocardial infarction. Ramipril and trandolapril have been shown to decrease the risk of cardiovascular death and also the risk of heart failure-related hospitalization

Left ventricular dysfunction, asymptomatic (treatment)[1]—Enalapril is indicated for the treatment of left ventricular dysfunction (ejection fraction $\leq$ 35%) in clinically stable patients who are asymptomatic. Enalapril has been shown to decrease the rate of development of overt heart failure and decrease the frequency of hospitalization secondary to heart failure.

—Captopril and trandolapril are indicated following myocardial infarction in clinically stable patients with left ventricular dysfunction to improve survival and decrease the incidence of overt heart failure and subsequent hospitalization for congestive heart failure. Left ventricular dysfunction was determined by ejection fraction $\leq$ 40% for the captopril study, and by identification of wall motion abnormalities for the trandolapril study.

Myocardial infarction, acute—Lisinopril is indicated for the treatment of hemodynamically stable patients within 24 hours of an acute myocardial infarction to improve survival

Diabetic nephropathy (treatment)—Captopril may be used in the treatment of nephropathy in patients with Type 1 insulin-dependent diabetes mellitus (IDDM). Captopril has been shown to slow the progression of diabetic nephropathy in normotensive and hypertensive IDDM patients with documented diabetic retinopathy, a serum creatinine concentration of $\leq$ 2.5 mg per deciliter, and urinary protein excretion of $\geq$ 500 mg in 24 hours. The greatest effect has been seen in those patients with poorer renal function at baseline (mean serum creatinine concentration $\geq$ 1.5 mg per deciliter).

Risk reduction for myocardial infarction, stroke and death from cardiovascular causes[1]—Ramipril is indicated in patients 55 years of age and older who are at high risk of developing a major cardiovascular event with a history of coronary artery disease, stroke, peripheral vascular disease or diabetes that is accompanied by at least one other cardiovascular risk factor (hypertension, elevated total cholesterol levels, low HDL levels, cigarette smoking, or documented microalbuminuria). Ramipril can be used in addition to other needed treatment such as antihypertensive, antiplatelet or lipid-lowering therapy.

[Scleroderma, hypertension in (treatment)][1] or
[Scleroderma, renal crisis in (treatment)][1]—ACE inhibitors are also used for treatment of hypertension or renal crisis in scleroderma.

Acceptance not established

Captopril has been studied for the treatment of congestive heart failure and hypertension in neonates. However, there are insufficient data to establish its efficacy for these indications; therefore, further studies, especially randomized controlled studies, are warranted.

[1]Not included in Canadian product labeling.

Pharmacology/Pharmacokinetics

Physicochemical characteristics

Molecular weight—
- Benazepril hydrochloride: 460.96.
- Captopril: 217.29.
- Cilazapril: 435.52.
- Enalapril: 492.52.
- Enalaprilat (active metabolite): 384.43.
- Fosinopril sodium: 585.65.
- Lisinopril: 441.52.
- Moexipril hydrochloride: 535.04.
- Perindopril erbumine: 441.61.
- Quinapril hydrochloride: 474.98.
- Ramipril: 416.52.
- Trandolapril: 430.54.

pKa—Captopril: 3.7 and 9.8 (apparent).

Mechanism of action/Effect

Benazepril—Benazeprilat (active metabolite)
Captopril—Not a prodrug
Cilazapril—Cilazaprilat (active metabolite)
Enalapril—Enalaprilat (active metabolite)
Fosinopril—Fosinoprilat (active metabolite)
Lisinopril—Not a prodrug
Moexipril—Moexiprilat (active metabolite)
Perindopril—Perindoprilat (active metabolite)
Quinapril—Quinaprilat (active metabolite)
Ramipril—Ramiprilat (active metabolite)
Trandolapril—Trandolaprilat (active metabolite)

Antihypertensive—Exact mechanism of antihypertensive action is unknown but is thought to be related to competitive inhibition of angiotensin I–converting enzyme (ACE) activity, resulting in a decreased rate of conversion of angiotensin I to angiotensin II, which is a potent vasoconstrictor. Decreased angiotensin II concentrations result in a secondary increase in plasma renin activity (PRA), through removal of the negative feedback of renin release, and a direct reduction in aldosterone secretion resulting in small increases in serum potassium, sodium, and fluid loss. ACE inhibitors may be less effective in control of blood pressures among low renin hypertensives, predominantly the black patient population, as compared to normal or high renin hypertensive patients. ACE inhibitors reduce peripheral arterial resistance. In addition, a possible effect on the kallikrein-kinin system (interference with degradation and resulting increased concentrations of bradykinin) and an increase in prostaglandin synthesis have been suggested but not proven.

Vasodilator, congestive heart failure—Decrease in peripheral vascular (afterload) resistance, pulmonary capillary wedge pressure (preload), and pulmonary vascular resistance; and improved cardiac output and exercise tolerance.

Other actions/effects

Captopril may reduce proteinuria in hypertensive patients with diabetic nephropathy.This effect may be due to the beneficial change in intrarenal hemodynamics (renal vasodilatation and reduced filtration pressure) produced by captopril resulting in decreased urinary protein excretion.

Absorption

Benazepril—At least 37% absorbed from the gastrointestinal tract; presence of food does not affect the extent of absorption but may increase the time to peak concentration.

Captopril—Rapidly and at least 75% absorbed from the gastrointestinal tract. Absorption is reduced by 30 to 55% in the presence of food.

Cilazapril—Rapidly; about 57% absorbed from the gastrointestinal tract. Absorption is reduced by 14% and peak is delayed by 1 hour in the presence of food; however, this has little influence on plasma ACE inhibition.

Enalapril—Approximately 60%; not affected by the presence of food.

Fosinopril—Slowly; about 36% absorbed from the gastrointestinal tract. Absorption rate may be decreased in presence of food, but extent of absorption is not affected.

Lisinopril—Approximately 25%, but widely variable between individuals (6 to 60%); not affected by the presence of food.

Moexipril—Approximately 13% absorbed from the gastrointestinal tract; presence of food reduces the extent of absorption by 40%, and approximately 10% more is reduced with high fat content foods.

Perindopril—Rapidly, at least 65% to 75% from the gastrointestinal tract; presence of food does not affect the rate or extent of absorption of perindopril, but absolute bioavailability of perindoprilat is reduced 35%.

Quinapril—Approximately 60%; presence of food does not affect extent of absorption, but may increase the time to peak drug concentration. High-fat meals may moderately decrease, 25–30%, the rate and extent of absorption.

Ramipril—Rapidly and at least 50 to 60% absorbed from the gastrointestinal tract. Extent of absorption is not affected by the presence of food; however, the rate of absorption is reduced.

Trandolapril—Approximately 10%; presence of food slows the rate but not the extent of absorption.

Protein binding

Benazepril—Very high (96.7%).
Benazeprilat (active metabolite)—Very high (95.3%).
Captopril—Low (25 to 30%), primarily to albumin.
Enalaprilat—Moderate (50 to 60%).
Fosinoprilat (active metabolite)—Very high (97 to 98%).
Lisinopril—None.
Moexiprilat—Moderate (50%).
Perindopril—Moderate (60%).
Perindoprilat (active metabolite)—Low (10% to 20%).
Quinaprilat (active metabolite)—Very high (97%).
Ramipril—High (73%).
Ramiprilat (active metabolite)—High (56%).
Trandolapril—High (80%), concentration independent.
Trandolaprilat (active metabolite)—Moderate to high (65 to 94%), concentration dependent.

Biotransformation

Benazepril—Hepatic, to benazeprilat, the active metabolite.
Captopril—Hepatic.
Enalapril—Hepatic, by hydrolysis, to enalaprilat, the active metabolite.
Enalaprilat—None.
Fosinopril—Hepatic, gastrointestinal mucosa; by hydrolysis to fosinoprilat, the active metabolite.
Lisinopril—None.
Moexipril—Converted in various organs and hepatically to moexiprilat, the active metabolite.
Perindopril—Hepatic, by hydrolysis, to perindoprilat, the active metabolite, and to other metabolites by glucuronidation and cyclization via dehydration.
Quinapril—Hepatic, gastrointestinal tract, extravascular tissue; by hydrolysis to quinaprilat, the active metabolite.
Ramipril—Hepatic.

Trandolapril—Hepatic, by hydrolysis to trandolaprilat, the active metabolite.

Half-life

Benazepril—0.6 hours.
Benazeprilat (active metabolite)—Effective accumulation half-life is 10 to 11 hours.
Captopril—Less than 3 hours; increased in renal failure (3.5 to 32 hours).
Enalaprilat (active metabolite)—11 hours; increased in renal failure.
Fosinoprilat (active metabolite)—Effective accumulation half-life is approximately 11.5 hours.
Lisinopril—12 hours; increased in renal failure.
Moexipril—1.3 hours
Moexiprilat (active metabolite)—Functional elimination half-life of approximately 12 hours.
Quinapril—Approximately 1 to 2 hours.
Quinaprilat (active metabolite)—Effective accumulation half-life is approximately 3 hours.
Perindopril—Approximately 0.8 to 1 hour.
Perindoprilat (active metabolite)—Apparent mean half-life of 3 to 10 hours; terminal elimination half-life of 30 to 120 hours.
Ramipril—5.1 hours.
Ramiprilat (active metabolite)—Effective accumulation half-life is 13 to 17 hours; increased in renal failure.
Trandolapril—6 hours
Trandolaprilat (active metabolite)—10 hours

Onset of action

Single dose—
- Benazepril: Within 1 hour.
- Captopril: 15 to 60 minutes.
- Enalapril: 1 hour.
- Enalaprilat (intravenous): 15 minutes.
- Fosinopril: Within 1 hour.
- Lisinopril: 1 hour.
- Moexipril: 1 hour.
- Perindopril: Within 1 to 2 hours.
- Quinapril: Within 1 hour.
- Ramipril: Within 1 to 2 hours.
- Trandolapril: 2 hours.

Time to peak serum concentration

Benazepril—0.5 to 1 hour.
Benazeprilat (active metabolite)—1 to 1.5 hours.
Captopril—30 to 90 minutes.
Enalapril—1 hour (3 to 4 hours for enalaprilat).
Enalaprilat (intravenous)—15 minutes.
Fosinoprilat (active metabolite)—2 to 4 hours.
Lisinopril—7 hours.
Moexiprilat (active metabolite)—1.5 hours.
Perindoprilat (active metabolite)—3 to 7 hours.
Quinapril—Within 1 hour.
Quinaprilat (active metabolite)—Within 2 hours.
Ramipril—Within 1 hour.
Ramiprilat (active metabolite)—3 hours.
Trandolapril—1 hour.
Trandolaprilat (active metabolite)—4 to 10 hours.

Time to peak effect

Single dose—
- Benazepril: 2 to 4 hours.
- Captopril: 60 to 90 minutes.
- Enalapril: 4 to 6 hours.
- Enalaprilat (intravenous): 1 to 4 hours.
- Fosinopril: 2 to 6 hours.
- Moexipril: 3 to 6 hours.
- Lisinopril: 6 hours.
- Perindopril: 3 to 7 hours.
- Quinapril: 2 to 4 hours.
- Ramipril: 4 to 6.5 hours.
- Trandolapril: Approximately 8 hours.

Multiple doses—
- The full therapeutic effect may not be noticed until several weeks after initiation of oral therapy.

Duration of action

Single dose—
- Benazepril: Approximately 24 hours.
- Captopril: Approximately 6 to 12 hours; dose related.
- Enalapril: Approximately 24 hours.
- Enalaprilat (intravenous): Approximately 6 hours.
- Fosinopril: Approximately 24 hours.
- Lisinopril: Approximately 24 hours.
- Perindopril: Approximately 24 hours.
- Moexipril: Approximately 24 hours.
- Quinapril: Up to 24 hours; dose related.
- Ramipril: Approximately 24 hours.
- Trandolapril: Approximately 24 hours.

Elimination

Benazepril—
- Predominantly renal.
- Nonrenal (biliary): 11 to 12%.
- In dialysis: Benazeprilat is slightly removable by hemodialysis.

Captopril—
- Renal: More than 95%; 40 to 50% unchanged (may be less in patients with congestive heart failure); remainder as metabolites.
- In dialysis: Captopril is removable by hemodialysis.

Enalapril—
- Renal: 60% (20% as enalapril and 40% as enalaprilat).
- Fecal: 33% (6% as enalapril and 27% as enalaprilat).
- In dialysis: Enalaprilat is removable by hemodialysis, at the rate of 62 mL per minute, and by peritoneal dialysis.

Enalaprilat—
- Renal: 100% unchanged.
- In dialysis: Enalaprilat is removable by hemodialysis at the rate of 62 mL per minute.

Fosinopril—
- Renal: 44 to 50%.
- Fecal: 46 to 50%.
- In dialysis: Fosinopril is not well dialyzed. Fosinoprilat clearance by hemodialysis and peritoneal dialysis is approximately 2% and 7%, respectively, of urea clearance.

Lisinopril—
- Renal: 100% unchanged.
- In dialysis: Lisinopril is removable by hemodialysis.

Moexipril—
- Renal: 13% (1% as moexipril, 7% as moexiprilat, and 5% as other metabolites).
- Fecal: 53% (52% as moexiprilat and 1% as moexipril).
- In dialysis: It is not known whether moexipril or moexiprilat is removable by hemodialysis.

Perindopril—
- Renal: 75% (4% to 12% as perindopril, 4.5% to 22% as perindoprilat).
- Fecal: 25%
- In dialysis: Mean dialysis clearance of perindopril is 52 mL per minute; perindoprilat mean dialysis clearance is 67.2 mL per minute.

Quinapril—
- Renal: 61% (56% as quinapril and quinaprilat).
- Fecal: 37%.
- In dialysis: Minimal effect on the elimination of quinapril and quinaprilat.

Ramipril—
- Renal: Approximately 60%.
- Fecal: Approximately 40%.
- In dialysis: It is not known whether ramipril or ramiprilat is removable by hemodialysis.

Trandolapril—
- Renal: 33% (15% as trandolaprilat).
- Fecal: 66% (38% as trandolaprilat).
- In dialysis: Minimal effect on the elimination of trandolapril and trandolaprilat.

Precautions to Consider

Cross-sensitivity and/or related problems

Patients sensitive to one ACE inhibitor also may be sensitive to another.

Carcinogenicity

Benazepril—Studies in mice and rats given doses of 150 mg per kg of body weight (mg/kg) per day (110 times the maximum recommended human dose by weight) for up to 2 years revealed no evidence of carcinogenicity.

Captopril—Two-year studies in mice and rats at doses of 50 to 1350 mg/kg per day showed no evidence of carcinogenicity.

Enalapril—Studies in rats for 106 weeks and in mice for 94 weeks at doses up to 150 and 300 times the maximum daily human dose (based on a patient weight of 50 kg), respectively, found no evidence of tumorigenicity or carcinogenicity.

Enalaprilat (intravenous)—Studies have not been done. However, since actions of enalapril maleate are caused by enalaprilat, the active metabolite, the same information would be expected to apply.

Fosinopril—Studies in mice and rats given doses up to 400 mg/kg per day for up to 24 months revealed no evidence of carcinogenicity. However, a slightly higher incidence of mesentery/omentum lipomas was found in male rats given the highest dose level (about 250 times the maximum human dose by weight).

Lisinopril—Studies in male and female rats for 105 weeks at doses up to 56 times the maximum recommended human daily dose (based on a patient weight of 50 kg) and in male and female mice for 92 weeks at doses up to 84 times the maximum recommended human daily dose (based on a patient weight of 50 kg) found no evidence of tumorigenicity.

Moexipril—Long-term studies in mice and rats given doses up to 14 or 27.3 times the maximum recommended human daily dose (based on a milligrams per square meter of body surface area) found no evidence of carcinogenicity.

Perindopril—Long-term studies in mice and rats given doses up to 20 times (based on milligrams per kilogram) or 2 to 4 times (based on a milligrams per square meter of body surface area) the proposed clinical dose of 16 milligrams per day found no evidence of carcinogenicity.

Quinapril—Studies in mice and rats given doses up to 75 or 100 mg/kg per day (50 to 60 times the maximum recommended human daily dose by weight) for 104 weeks revealed no evidence of carcinogenicity. However, female rats given the highest dose level had an increased incidence of mesenteric lymph node hemangiomas and skin/subcutaneous lipomas.

Ramipril—Studies in rats and mice given doses up to 500 mg/kg per day for 24 months and up to 1000 mg/kg per day for 18 months, respectively, revealed no evidence of tumorigenicity. Renal juxtaglomerular apparatus hypertrophy was found in mice, rats, dogs, and monkeys given doses greatly in excess of recommended human doses.

Trandolapril—Long-term studies in mice at doses up to 25 mg/kg per day and in rats at doses up to 8 mg/kg per day, showed no evidence of carcinogenicity.

Mutagenicity

Benazepril—No evidence of mutagenicity was found in tests including the Ames bacterial assay (with or without metabolic activation), an *in vitro* test for forward mutations in cultured mammalian cells, and a nucleus anomaly test.

Enalapril and *enalaprilat*—No evidence of mutagenicity was found in tests including the Ames bacterial assay with or without metabolic activation, rec-assay, reverse mutation assay with *E. coli*, sister chromatid exchange with cultured mammalian cells, the micronucleus test with mice, and in an *in vivo* cytogenic study using mouse bone marrow.

Fosinopril—No evidence of mutagenicity was found in tests including the Ames bacterial assay, the mouse lymphoma forward mutation assay, and a mitotic gene conversion assay. No evidence of genotoxicity was found in a mouse micronucleus test *in vivo* and a mouse bone marrow cytogenetic assay *in vivo*. An increased frequency of chromosomal aberrations was found in the Chinese hamster ovary cell cytogenetic assay at toxic cell concentrations tested without metabolic activation. However, this increase was not found at lower drug concentrations without metabolic activation or at any other concentration with metabolic activation.

Lisinopril—No evidence of mutagenicity was found in tests including the Ames bacterial assay with or without metabolic activation, forward mutation assay using Chinese hamster lung cells, *in vitro* alkaline elution rat hepatocyte assay, and chromosomal aberration studies *in vitro* in Chinese hamster ovary cells and *in vivo* in mouse bone marrow.

Moexipril—No evidence of mutagenicity was found in the Ames test and microbial reverse mutation assay, with and without activation, or in an *in vivo* nucleus anomaly test. However, at 20 hours harvest time, increased chromosomal aberration frequency in Chinese hamster ovary cells was detected under metabolic activation conditions.

Perindopril—No evidence of mutagenicity was found in the Ames bacterial assay, the *Saccharomyces cerevisiae* D4 test, cultured human lymphocytes, TK ± mouse lymphoma assay, mouse and rat micronucleus tests, and Chinese hamster bone marrow assay.

Quinapril—No evidence of mutagenicity was found in the Ames bacterial assay with or without metabolic activation.

Ramipril—No evidence of mutagenicity was found in tests including the Ames bacterial assay, the micronucleus test in mice, unscheduled DNA synthesis in a human cell line, and a forward gene-mutation assay in a Chinese hamster ovary cell line.

Trandolapril—No evidence of mutagenicity was found in the Ames test, the point mutation and chromosome aberration assays in Chinese hamster V79 cells, and the micronucleus test in mice.

Pregnancy/Reproduction

Fertility—*Benazepril:* No adverse effect on the reproductive performance of male and female rats was found.

Captopril: No impairment of fertility was found in rats.

Enalapril: No adverse effects on reproductive performance were found in male and female rats given 10 to 90 mg/kg of enalapril per day.

Fosinopril: No adverse reproductive effects were found in male and female rats given doses up to 60 mg/kg per day (about 38 times the maximum recommended human dose by weight). However, a slight increase in pairing time was observed in rats given a toxic dose of 240 mg/kg per day (150 times the maximum recommended human dose by weight).

Lisinopril: No adverse effects on reproductive performance were found in male and female rats given doses up to 300 mg/kg per day of lisinopril.

Moexipril: No evidence of impaired fertility, reproductive toxicity, or teratogenicity was detected in reproduction studies performed in rabbits and rats at doses up to 0.7 and 90.9 times the maximum recommended human dose, respectively, on a mg per square meter basis.

Perindopril: No adverse effects on reproductive performance or fertility were found in male and female rats given doses 30 times (based on milligrams per kilogram) or 6 times (milligrams per square meter) the proposed maximum clinical dose of perindopril.

Quinapril: No adverse effects on fertility or reproduction were found in rats given doses up to 100 mg/kg per day (60 times the maximum daily human dose based on weight).

Ramipril: No impairment of fertility was found in rats given doses up to 500 mg/kg per day.

Trandolapril: No impairment of fertility was found in rats administered doses of up to 100 mg/kg per day, which is 1250 times the maximum recommended human dose based on weight.

Pregnancy—In humans, ACE inhibitors can cause fetal and neonatal morbidity and mortality when administered to pregnant women. ACE inhibitors should be discontinued as soon as possible when pregnancy is detected.

ACE inhibitors cross the placenta. Fetal exposure to ACE inhibitors during the second and third trimesters can cause hypotension, renal failure, anuria, skull hypoplasia, and even death in the newborn. Maternal oligohydramnios has also been reported, probably reflecting decreasing fetal renal function.

Enalapril and lisinopril have been removed from neonatal circulation by peritoneal dialysis. Captopril is not removable by peritoneal dialysis. There are inadequate data concerning the effectiveness of hemodialysis and there is no information concerning use of exchange transfusion for removing captopril from general circulation. There has been no experience with hemodialysis, peritoneal dialysis, or exchange transfusion for removing benazepril, fosinopril, perindopril, quinapril, or ramipril from neonatal circulation.

It is recommended that infants exposed in utero to ACE inhibitors be closely observed for hypotension, oliguria, and hyperkalemia. Oliguria should be treated with support of blood pressure and renal perfusion by administration of fluids and pressors as appropriate.

Benazepril: Studies in pregnant rats, mice, and rabbits at doses 300, 90, and more than 3 times, respectively, the maximum recommended human dose by weight, revealed no embryotoxic, fetotoxic, or teratogenic effects.

Captopril: Several cases of intrauterine growth retardation, fetal distress and hypotension, and one case of cranial malformation have been reported. Neonatal deaths have occurred in rats at up to 400 times the recommended human dose. Fetal deaths have occurred when rabbits were given 2 to 70 times the maximum recommended human dose, and a low incidence of cranial malformations occurred in offspring. No teratogenicity has been noted in hamsters or rats.

Enalapril: Fetal toxicity (decrease in average fetal weight) has occurred in rats at doses of enalapril 2000 times the maximum daily human dose, and maternal and fetal toxicity has occurred in rabbits at doses almost double the maximum daily human dose. In some cases, saline supplementation prevented maternal and fetal toxicity. No teratogenicity has been noted in rabbits and neither fetal toxicity nor teratogenicity occurred in rats at doses up to 333 times the maximum daily human dose.

Fosinopril: Maternal toxicity was evident in pregnant rabbits given doses up to 40 mg/kg per day (about 50 times the maximum recommended human dose). Fosinopril at doses up to 40 mg/kg per day (about 50 times the maximum recommended human dose) was embryocidal in rabbits, probably due to marked decreases in blood pressure secondary to ACE inhibition in this species. There was no evidence of teratogenicity in rabbits at any dosage level. Maternal toxicity was evident in pregnant rats at all dose levels tested up to 400 mg/kg per day (about 500 times the maximum recommended human dose). Furthermore, all dose levels produced slight reductions in placental weights and some degree of skeletal ossification. High doses resulted in reduced fetal body weight. Three similar orofacial malformations and one fetus with situs inversus occurred in animals given fosinopril. It is uncertain whether these anomalies were associated with drug treatment.

Lisinopril: Lisinopril was not teratogenic in mice given doses up to 625 times the maximum recommended human dose on days 6 to 15 of gestation; an increase in fetal resorptions occurred at doses of 62.5 times the maximum recommended human dose, but was prevented at doses of 625 times the maximum recommended human dose by saline supplementation. No fetotoxicity or teratogenicity occurred in rats given doses up to 188 times the maximum recommended human dose on days 6 to 17 of gestation, but an increased incidence of pup deaths and a lower average birth weight (both preventable by saline supplementation) occurred postpartum in rats given lisinopril on day 15 of gestation through day 21 postpartum. Lisinopril crosses the placenta in rats but has not been found in the fetus. Lisinopril did not cause teratogenicity in saline-supplemented rabbits given doses up to 1 mg/kg per day but did cause fetotoxicity (increased fetal resorptions, increased incidence of incomplete ossification).

Moexipril: No teratogenicity was observed in rats or rabbits given up to 90.9 and 0.7 times the maximum recommended human dose, respectively, on a mg per square meter basis.

*Perindopril:*No teratogenicity was observed after exposure to doses 6 times, 670 times, 50 times, and 17 times the maximum recommended human dose (MRHD) in mice, rats, rabbits, or monkeys, based on a mg per square meter basis, respectively. On a mg/kg basis, the values are 60 times, 3750 times, 150 times, and 50 times the MRHD, respectively

Quinapril: Quinapril at doses as high as 300 mg/kg per day (180 times the maximum daily human dose by weight) did not produce fetotoxic or teratogenic effects in rats, despite maternal toxicity at 150 mg/kg per day. However, reduced offspring body weight was observed at doses greater than 25 mg/kg per day, and changes in renal histology (juxtaglomerular cell hypertrophy, tubular/pelvic dilation, glomerulosclerosis) were seen in dams and offspring given 150 mg/kg per day when tested later in gestation and during lactation. Quinapril did not produce teratogenic effects in rabbits. However, in some rabbits maternal toxicity and embryotoxicity were observed at doses as low as 0.5 mg/kg per day (one time the recommended human dose) and 1.0 mg/kg per day.

Ramipril: Studies of pregnant rats, rabbits and cynomolgus monkeys showed no teratogenic effects when doses up ot approximately 400 times (in rats and monkeys) and 2 times (in rabbits) the recommended human dose were given.

Trandolapril: Teratogenic effects were not observed in rabbits given doses of 0.8 mg/kg per day, in rats given doses of 1000 mg/kg per day, or in monkeys given doses of 25 mg/kg per day. These doses represent 10, 1250, and 312 times the maximum recommended human dose by weight, respectively.

For all ACE inhibitors: **When used during the second and third trimesters, ACE inhibitors can cause injury, including hypotension, neonatal skull hypoplasia, anuria, reversible or irreversible renal failure, and even death to the developing fetus. Oligohydramnios has also been reported. When pregnancy is detected, the ACE inhibitor should be discontinued as soon as possible.**

FDA Pregnancy Category C—First trimester.

FDA Pregnancy Category D—Second and third trimesters.

Breast-feeding

Benazepril—Benazepril and benazeprilat are distributed into breast milk. A nursing infant would receive less than 0.1% of the mg/kg maternal dose of benazepril and benazeprilat.

Cilazapril—It is not known whether cilazapril is distributed into human breast milk; cilazaprilat appears to distribute into the milk of lactating rats. However, problems in humans have not been documented.

Captopril—Captopril is distributed into breast milk; concentrations in breast milk are approximately 1% of maternal blood concentrations. However, problems in humans have not been documented.

Enalapril— Enalapril and enalaprilat are distributed into breast milk. However, problems in humans have not been documented.

Fosinopril—Fosinoprilat (active metabolite) is distributed into breast milk. Detectable levels of fosinoprilat in breast milk were found following ingestion of 20 mg per day for 3 days.

Lisinopril—It is not known whether lisinopril is distributed into human breast milk; it appears to distribute into the milk of lactating rats. However, problems in humans have not been documented.

Moexipril—It is not known whether moexipril is distributed into breast milk. However, problems in humans have not been documented.

Perindopril—It is not known whether perindopril is distributed into human breast milk; it appears to distribute into the milk of lactating rats. However, problems in humans have not been documented.

Quinapril—It is not known whether quinapril or its metabolites are distributed into human breast milk; quinapril appears to distribute into the milk of lactating rats. However, problems in humans have not been documented.

Ramipril—A 10-mg dose of ramipril resulted in undetectable amounts of ramipril and its metabolites in breast milk. However, multiple doses may produce low milk concentrations.

Trandolapril—It is not known whether trandolapril is distributed into breast milk. Trandolapril and/or its metabolites are distributed into the milk of lactating rats. However, problems in humans have not been documented.

Pediatrics

Appropriate studies on the relationship of age to the effects of ACE inhibitors have not been done in the pediatric population. However, the use of ACE inhibitors in a limited number of neonates and infants has identified some potential pediatrics-specific problems. In neonates and infants, there is a risk of oliguria and neurologic abnormalities, possibly as a result of decreased renal and cerebral blood flow secondary to marked and prolonged reductions in blood pressure caused by ACE inhibitors; a lower initial dose and close monitoring are recommended.

Benazepril—

Children 6 years of age and older: Appropriate studies performed to date have not demonstrated pediatrics-specifics problems that would limit the usefulness of benazepril.

Children younger than 6 years of age: Treatment with benazepril not recommended; insufficient data available to support a dosing recommendation.

Enalapril—

Children 1 month to 16 years of age: Appropriate studies performed to date have not demonstrated pediatrics-specifics problems that would limit the usefulness of enalapril.

Neonates: Treatment with enalapril not recommended.

Fosinopril—

Children weighing greater than 50 kg: Appropriate studies performed to date have not demonstrated pediatrics-specifics problems that would limit the usefulness of fosinopril.

Children weighing less than 50 kg: Appropriate dosage strength is not available.

Lisinopril—

Children 6 to 16 years of age: Appropriate studies performed to date have not demonstrated pediatrics-specifics problems that would limit the usefulness of lisinopril.

Children younger than 6 years of age: Safety and efficacy have not been established.

Geriatrics

ACE inhibitors are thought to be most effective in reducing blood pressure in patients with normal or high plasma renin activity. Since plasma renin activity appears to decline with increasing age, elderly individuals may be less sensitive to the hypotensive effects of ACE inhibitors. However, elevated serum ACE inhibitor concentrations resulting from age-related decline in renal function may compensate for the lower renin dependence. Pharmacokinetic studies with lisinopril, perindopril, quinapril, and ramipril have revealed higher peak serum concentrations and area under the curve (AUC) in elderly patients given doses similar to those given to younger adults. The net result is that no significant differences in blood pressure response or side/adverse effects have been noted in elderly patients receiving ACE inhibitors. Nevertheless, some elderly patients may be more sensitive to the hypotensive effects of these medications and may require caution when receiving an ACE inhibitor.

Drug interactions and/or related problems

The following drug interactions and/or related problems have been selected on the basis of their potential clinical significance (possible mechanism in parentheses where appropriate)—not necessarily inclusive (» = major clinical significance):

Note: Combinations containing any of the following medications, depending on the amount present, may also interact with this medication.

For all ACE inhibitors

» Alcohol or

» Diuretics or

Hypotension-producing medications, other (see *Appendix II*)

(concurrent use with ACE inhibitors may produce additive hypotensive effects)

(antihypertensive agents that cause renin release or affect sympathetic activity have the greatest additive effect; concurrent use of captopril with beta-adrenergic blocking agents produces an increased but less than fully additive effect; although some antihypertensive and/or diuretic combinations may be used for therapeutic advantage, dosage adjustments may be necessary during concurrent use or when one drug is discontinued)

(if significant systemic absorption of ophthalmic beta-blockers occurs, hypotensive effects of ACE inhibitors may be potentiated)

(sudden and severe hypotension may occur within the first 1 to 5 hours after the initial dose of an ACE inhibitor, particularly in patients who are sodium- and volume-depleted as a result of diuretic therapy. Withdrawal of the diuretic or increase of salt intake approximately 1 week before start of captopril therapy or 2 to 3 days before start of benazepril, enalapril, fosinopril, lisinopril, quinapril, perindopril, or ramipril therapy, or initiating ACE inhibitor therapy in lower doses, will minimize the reaction; this reaction does not usually recur with sub-

sequent doses, although caution in increasing doses is recommended; diuretics may be reinstituted as necessary)
(risk of renal failure may be increased in patients who are sodium- and volume-depleted as a result of diuretic therapy)
(ACE inhibitors may reduce the secondary aldosteronism and hypokalemia caused by diuretics)

Antacids
(concurrent use with fosinopril and trandolapril reduced serum levels and urinary excretion of fosinopril and trandolapril as compared with the ACE inhibitors administered alone, which suggests antacids may impair the absorption of ACE inhibitors; if concurrent use is indicated, dosing should be separated by 2 hours.)

Anti-inflammatory drugs, nonsteroidal (NSAIDs), especially indomethacin
(concurrent use of these agents may reduce the antihypertensive effects of ACE inhibitors; indomethacin, and possibly other NSAIDs, may antagonize the antihypertensive effect by inhibiting renal prostaglandin synthesis and/or causing sodium and fluid retention; the patient should be carefully monitored to confirm that the desired effect is being obtained)

Blood from blood bank (may contain up to 30 mEq [mmol] of potassium per liter of plasma or up to 65 mEq [mmol] per liter of whole blood when stored for more than 10 days) or
Cyclosporine or
» Diuretics, potassium-sparing or
» Low-salt milk (may contain up to 60 mEq [mmol] of potassium per liter) or
» Potassium-containing medications or
» Potassium supplements or substances containing high concentrations of potassium or
» Salt substitutes (most contain substantial amounts of potassium)
(concurrent administration with ACE inhibitors may result in hyperkalemia since reduction of aldosterone production induced by ACE inhibitors may lead to elevation of serum potassium; frequent determination of serum potassium concentrations is recommended if concurrent use of these agents is necessary; concurrent use is not recommended in patients with congestive heart failure)

Allopurinol or
Cytostatic agents or
Procainamide or
Systemic corticosteroids or
Bone marrow depressants (see *Appendix II*)
(concurrent administration with an ACE inhibitor may result in an increased risk of development of potentially fatal neutropenia and/or agranulocytosis)

Lithium
(reversible increases in serum lithium concentrations and toxicity have been reported during concurrent use with ACE inhibitors; frequent monitoring of serum lithium concentrations is recommended during concurrent use)

Sympathomimetics
(concurrent use of these agents may reduce the antihypertensive effects of ACE inhibitors; the patient should be carefully monitored to confirm that the desired effect is being obtained)

For quinapril only
Tetracyclines or
Other drugs that interact with magnesium
(concurrent use of these agents with quinapril may reduce their absorption; absorption of tetracycline is reduced by approximately 28 to 37%, possibly due to the high magnesium content in Accupril brand of quinapril tablets)

For ramipril only
Hypoglycemic agents, oral or
Insulin
(rare post-marketing reports of hypoglycemia with concomitant use)

Laboratory value alterations

The following have been selected on the basis of their potential clinical significance (possible effect in parentheses where appropriate)—not necessarily inclusive (» = major clinical significance).

With diagnostic test results

For all ACE inhibitors
Iodohippurate sodium I 123/I 131 renal imaging or
Technetium Tc 99m pentetate renal imaging
(in patients with renal artery stenosis, captopril [and probably all ACE inhibitors] may cause a reversible decrease in localization and excretion of iodohippurate I 123/I 131 or technetium Tc 99m pentetate in the affected kidney; may cause confusion as to whether decreased renal function is drug-related)

For captopril only
Urinary acetone test
(captopril may produce false-positive results)

For fosinopril only
Digoxin levels
(fosinopril may cause a false low serum digoxin level with the Digi-Tab RIA Kit)

With physiology/laboratory test values

For benazepril only
ECG changes

For quinapril only
Hematuria

For all ACE inhibitors
Alkaline phosphatase, serum and
Bilirubin, serum and
Transaminases, serum
(concentration increases have been reported)

Antinuclear antibody (ANA) titer
(positive ANA has been reported)

Blood urea nitrogen (BUN) and
Creatinine, serum
(concentrations may be transiently increased, especially in patients with renal parenchymal and renovascular disease in patients who are volume- or sodium-depleted, in patients with renal artery stenosis, or after rapid reduction of long-standing or severe high blood pressure)

Glucose, serum
(may be elevated)

Hematocrit or
Hemoglobin
(may rarely be slightly decreased)

Lymphocytes or
Neutrophiles
(may be lowered)

Protein, urinary
(concentration may be transiently increased in patients with preexisting proteinuria or diabetes mellitus)

Potassium, serum
(concentrations may be slightly increased as a result of reduced circulating aldosterone concentrations and concomitant reduction in glomerular filtration rate [GFR], especially in patients with renal function impairment)

Sodium, serum
(concentrations may be slightly decreased, especially during initial therapy)

Medical considerations/Contraindications

The medical considerations/contraindications included have been selected on the basis of their potential clinical significance (reasons given in parentheses where appropriate)—not necessarily inclusive (» = major clinical significance).

Except under special circumstances, this medication should not be used when the following medical problem exists:

» Hypersensitivity to the ACE inhibitor prescribed or any of its components or any other ACE inhibitor

Risk-benefit should be considered when the following medical problems exist:

For all ACE inhibitors
» Angioedema, history of, related to previous ACE inhibitor therapy or
» Hereditary angioedema or
» Idiopathic angioedema
(increased risk for development of ACE inhibitor-related angioedema)

Aortic stenosis or
Cerebrovascular disease or
Ischemic heart disease
(reduction in blood pressure from ACE inhibitor therapy could aggravate these conditions)

Autoimmune disease, severe, especially systemic lupus erythematosus (SLE), other collagen vascular diseases, or scleroderma
(increased risk for development of neutropenia or agranulocytosis)

Bone marrow depression
(increased risk for agranulocytosis and neutropenia)

Diabetes mellitus
(increased risk of hyperkalemia, insulin sensitivity and/or increased glucose tolerance has been reported in diabetic patients receiving ACE inhibitors)

» Hyperkalemia
» Renal artery stenosis, bilateral or in a solitary kidney or
» Renal transplant
(increased risk of renal function impairment; increased risk of agranulocytosis and neutropenia when immunosuppressants are also administered to the patient)

» Renal function impairment
(decreased elimination of active ACE inhibitor [except fosinopril], resulting in higher plasma concentrations; increased risk of hyperkalemiaor, for captopril, proteinuria, neutropenia, and agranulocytosis. Patients with impaired renal function may require lower or less frequent doses and smaller increments in dose. However, dosage adjustment may not be necessary with fosinopril since total body drug clearance even in severe renal function impairment is not decreased significantly, possibly due to compensatory hepatobiliary elimination. If a diuretic is also required, a loop diuretic is recommended instead of a thiazide diuretic in patients with severe renal function impairment)

» Caution is required also in patients on severe dietary sodium restriction or dialysis; these patients may be volume-depleted, and sudden reduction by the initial dose of ACE inhibitor in the angiotensin II levels that have been maintaining them at a near-normotensive state may result in sudden and severe hypotension. In addition, the risk of ACE inhibitor-induced renal failure may be increased in patients who are sodium- and volume-depleted, especially those with congestive heart failure.

For benazepril, captopril, enalapril, fosinopril, moexipril, perindopril, quinapril, ramipril, and trandolapril (in addition to the above)

» Hepatic function impairment
(may reduce metabolism of captopril and may reduce conversion of prodrug to active moiety with benazepril, enalapril, fosinopril, moexipril, perindopril, quinapril, ramipril, and trandolapril)

Patient monitoring

The following may be especially important in patient monitoring (other tests may be warranted in some patients, depending on condition; » = major clinical significance):

» Blood pressure measurements
(recommended at periodic intervals in patients being treated for hypertension; selected patients may be trained to perform blood pressure measurements at home and report the results at regular physician visits)

Leukocyte count determinations, total and differential
(recommended prior to initiation of ACE inhibitor therapy and periodically thereafter; recommended every month for the first 3 to 6 months of therapy, and at periodic intervals thereafter for a period of up to 1 year in patients at increased risk for neutropenia [i.e., those with renal function impairment or collagen vascular disease] or receiving high doses; also recommended at the first sign of infection. It is recommended that ACE inhibitor therapy be withdrawn if neutropenia [neutrophil count less than 1000 per cubic millimeter (1×10^9/L)] is confirmed)

» Liver function tests
(recommended baseline for patients with pre-existing liver abnormalities and for patients on captopril; also for patients taking ACE inhibitors when experiencing any unexplained symptoms during the first weeks or months of treatment; rarely, ACE inhibitors have been associated with a syndrome that starts with cholestatic jaundice and progresses to fulminant hepatic necrosis and [sometimes] death; patients receiving ACE inhibitors who develop jaundice or marked hepatic enzyme elevations should discontinue the drug and receive appropriate medical follow-up)

Potassium, serum
(recommended periodically in patients at risk for hyperkalemia, such as those with renal insufficiency, or diabetes mellitus, or for patients on concurrent potassium-sparing diuretic therapy, potassium supplements, and/or potassium containing salt substitutes)

Renal function determinations
(recommended at periodic intervals, especially in patients who are sodium- and volume-depleted as a result of diuretic therapy or who have severe congestive heart failure)

Urinary protein estimates by means of dipstick on first morning urine
(recommended prior to initiation of therapy and at periodic intervals thereafter for up to 1 year in patients with renal function impairment or those receiving doses of captopril greater than 150 mg per day; if excessive or increasing proteinuria occurs, it is recommended that ACE inhibitor therapy be re-evaluated)

Side/Adverse Effects

Note: Proteinuria has occurred in about 1% of patients receiving greater than 150 mg of captopril per day. This adverse effect is thought to be due to the sulfhydryl moiety of captopril. However, whether this is a true causal relationship is unknown. Proteinuria usually occurs in patients with existing renal function impairment within 8 months of initiation of captopril therapy and usually reverses within 6 months even with continuation of therapy. Membranous glomerulopathy has been reported in some of these patients, especially with doses of captopril greater than 150 mg per day. Proteinuria has also been reported in patients receiving enalapril and lisinopril. Reported incidences range from 0% to 1.4% for enalapril and 0.7% for lisinopril.

There have been reports of reversible renal failure during ACE inhibitor therapy, especially in patients with bilateral renal artery stenoses or renal artery stenosis in a solitary kidney. There is also evidence that renal failure may be related to sodium and volume depletion from previous diuretic therapy or severe sodium restriction, especially in patients with congestive heart failure.

Hepatotoxicity has been reported rarely in patients receiving captopril, enalapril, and lisinopril. Cholestasis has been reported most frequently, although hepatic necrosis and hepatocellular injury have also been reported. The most common presenting symptoms are jaundice, pruritus, and abdominal tenderness. ACE inhibitor-associated hepatotoxicity is usually reversible upon discontinuation of therapy. Apparent cross-reactivity has been reported between captopril and enalapril and between lisinopril and enalapril.

Angioedema involving the extremities, face, lips, mucous membranes, tongue, glottis or larynx has been seen in patients treated with ACE inhibitors, including captopril. If angioedema involves the tongue, glottis or larynx, airway obstruction may occur and be fatal. Emergency therapy, including but not necessarily limited to, subcutaneous administration of a 1:1000 solution of epinephrine should be promptly instituted.

Intestinal angioedema has been reported in patients treated with ACE inhibitors. These patients presented with abdominal pain. The angioedema was diagnosed by procedures including abdominal CT scan or ultrasound, or at surgery. Intestinal angioedema should be included in the differential diagnosis of patients on ACE inhibitors presenting with abdominal pain.

Severe, life-threatening, anaphylactoid reactions have occurred in two patients using ACE inhibitors during desensitization protocols involving hymenoptera venom. Additionally, some patients treated with ACE inhibitors who have been exposed to either high-flux membrane dialysis or low-density lipoprotein apheresis with dextran sulfate absorption have also experienced anaphylactoid-like reactions

Rarely, ACE inhibitors, including ramipril, have been associated with a syndrome that starts with cholestatic jaundice and progresses to fulminant hepatic necrosis and (sometimes) death. The mechanism of this syndrome is not understood. Patients receiving ACE inhibitors who develop jaundice or marked elevations of hepatic enzymes should discontinue the ACE inhibitor and receive appropriate medical follow-up.

The following side/adverse effects have been selected on the basis of their potential clinical significance (possible signs and symptoms in parentheses where appropriate)—not necessarily inclusive:

Those indicating need for medical attention

Incidence less frequent

Hypotension (dizziness, light-headedness, or fainting)—especially following the initial dose in sodium- or volume-depleted patients or in patients receiving an ACE inhibitor for congestive heart failure; ***skin rash, with or without itching, fever, or joint pain***

Note: Maculopapular or, rarely, urticarial rash usually occurs during the first 4 weeks of the therapy with captopril and usually disappears with dosage reduction or withdrawal, or administration of an antihistamine; between 7 and 10% of these patients may show eosinophilia and/or positive antinuclear antibody (ANA) titers. The reaction may also occur, less frequently, with the other ACE inhibitors.

Rarely, a persistent lichenoid or pemphigoid reaction, possibly with a photosensitive factor, has been reported with captopril.

Incidence rare

Angioedema of the extremities, face, lips, mucous membranes, tongue, glottis, and/or larynx (sudden trouble in swallowing or breathing; swelling of face, mouth, hands, or feet; hoarseness)—especially following the initial dose; ***chest pain; hyperkalemia*** (confusion; irregular heartbeat; nervousness; numbness or tingling in hands, feet, or lips; shortness of breath or difficult breathing; weakness or heaviness of legs); ***intestinal angioedema*** (stomach pain); ***neutropenia or agranulocytosis*** (fever and chills); ***pancreatitis*** (abdominal pain; nausea; vomiting; abdominal distention; fever)

Note: *Angioedema* involving the tongue, glottis, or larynx may cause airway obstruction, which could be fatal.

Chest pain is usually associated with severe hypotension.

Incidence of *neutropenia or agranulocytosis* is much higher in patients with renal function impairment (0.2% for captopril) or collagen vascular disease (e.g., SLE or scleroderma) (3.7% for captopril). Neutropenia appears to be dose-related and may begin within 3 months after initiation of therapy, with the nadir of the leukocyte count occurring after 10 to 30 days and persisting about 2 weeks after withdrawal. Deaths from pancytopenia and sepsis have been reported with captopril in patients with and without autoimmune disease.

Those indicating need for medical attention only if they continue or are bothersome

Incidence more frequent

Cough, dry, persistent; headache

Note: *Cough* usually occurs within the first week of therapy (onset varies from 24 hours to several weeks after initiation), persists throughout therapy, and disappears within a few days after withdrawal of the ACE inhibitor. Characteristically the cough begins as a tickling sensation in the back of the throat leading to a dry, nonproductive, persistent cough; may be worse at night or in the supine position; onset can be paroxysmal and course may be episodic or intermittent; may occasionally lead to hoarseness or vomiting.

Incidence less frequent

Diarrhea; dysgeusia (loss of taste); ***fatigue*** (unusual tiredness); ***nausea***

Note: *Loss of taste* is usually reversible after 2 to 3 months even with continued treatment, and may be associated with weight loss.

Overdose

For more information on the management of overdose or unintentional ingestion, **contact a Poison Control Center** (see *Poison Control Center Listing*).

Treatment of overdose

Treatment of overdose consists of volume expansion for correction of hypotension and established procedures for treating dehydration and electrolyte imbalance. Captopril, enalaprilat, lisinopril, trandolaprilat, and perindoprilat are removable by hemodialysis. Benazeprilat is slightly removable by hemodialysis.

Patient Consultation

As an aid to patient consultation, refer to *Advice for the Patient, Angiotensin-converting Enzyme (ACE) Inhibitors*.

In providing consultation, consider emphasizing the following selected information (» = major clinical significance):

Before using this medication

» Conditions affecting use, especially:

Hypersensitivity to the ACE inhibitor prescribed or any of its components or any other ACE inhibitor

Pregnancy—ACE inhibitors cross the placenta; ACE inhibitor-associated fetal hypotension, oliguria, and death reported in humans; fetotoxicity found in animals; **when pregnancy is detected, ACE inhibitor should be discontinued as soon as possible**

Breast-feeding—Benazepril, captopril, and fosinopril are distributed into breast milk

Other medications, especially alcohol, diuretics (particularly potassium-sparing), potassium-containing medications, or potassium supplements

Use of low-salt milk or salt substitutes

Other medical problems, especially angioedema related to previous ACE inhibitor therapy, hepatic function impairment, hyperkalemia, renal artery stenosis, renal transplant, renal function impairment, or sodium and volume depletion

Proper use of this medication

Compliance with therapy; taking medication at the same time each day to maintain the therapeutic effect

» Proper dosing

Missed dose: Taking as soon as possible; not taking if almost time for next dose; not doubling doses

For captopril and moexipril

For best results, taking on an empty stomach 1 hour before meals

For use as an antihypertensive

Possible need for control of weight and diet, especially sodium intake; risks associated with sodium depletion; not taking salt substitutes or using low-salt milk unless approved by physician

» Patient may not experience symptoms of hypertension; importance of taking medication even if feeling well

» Does not cure, but helps control hypertension; possible need for lifelong therapy; checking with physician before discontinuing medication; serious consequences of untreated hypertension

» Proper storage

Precautions while using this medication

Making regular visits to physician to check progress

Receiving immediate medical attention for any signs of facial or extremity swelling and/or difficulty in swallowing or breathing, because of the risk of angioedema

» Notifying physician immediately if pregnancy is suspected

Caution when driving or doing other things requiring alertness, because of possible dizziness, especially after initial dose of ACE inhibitor in patients taking diuretics

Checking with physician if severe nausea, vomiting, or diarrhea occurs and continues, because of the risk of dehydration, which may result in hypotension

Contacting physician if signs and symptoms of jaundice (yellow skin or eyes) or hepatitis occur

Caution when exercising or during exposure to hot weather because of the risk of dehydration (due to excessive perspiration), which may result in hypotension

Caution if any kind of surgery (including dental surgery) or emergency treatment is required

Reporting any signs of infection (chills, fever, or sore throat) to physician, because of the risk of neutropenia

For use as an antihypertensive:

» Not taking other medications, especially nonprescription sympathomimetics, unless discussed with physician

For captopril and fosinopril:

Caution if any laboratory tests required; possible interference with test results

Side/adverse effects

Signs of potential side effects, especially hypotension, skin rash (with or without itching, fever, or joint pain), angioedema, chest pain, hyperkalemia, neutropenia or agranulocytosis, and pancreatitis.

General Dosing Information

Dosage must be adjusted to meet the individual requirements of each patient, on the basis of clinical response.

The hypotensive effect of ACE inhibitors is about the same in both standing and supine positions.

Recent evidence suggests that withdrawal of antihypertensive therapy prior to surgery may be undesirable. However, the anesthesiologist must be aware of such therapy.

If increased blood urea nitrogen (BUN) and creatinine concentrations occur, reduction in dosage of the ACE inhibitor and/or withdrawal of the diuretic may be required. The possibility of renovascular hypertension should also be considered, especially in the presence of a solitary kidney, transplanted kidney, or bilateral renal artery stenosis.

Caution is recommended in initiating ACE inhibitor therapy for congestive heart failure in patients who have been receiving digitalis glycosides and/or diuretics. If the patient is sodium- and water-depleted, a lower initial dosage should be used.

If symptomatic hypotension occurs, dosage reduction of the ACE inhibitor or withdrawal of the ACE inhibitor or diuretic may be necessary.

For treatment of adverse effects

For angioedema with swelling confined to the face, mucous membranes of the mouth, lips, and extremities, treatment other than withdrawal of the medication is usually not necessary, although antihistamines may relieve the symptoms.

Treatment of angioedema involving the tongue, glottis, or larynx may include the following:

- Withdrawal of the ACE inhibitor and hospitalization of the patient.
- Subcutaneous (or, rarely, intravenous) epinephrine.
- Intravenous diphenhydramine hydrochloride.
- Intravenous hydrocortisone.

BENAZEPRIL

Summary of Differences

Precautions:

Breast-feeding—Benazepril and benazeprilat are distributed into breast milk.

Additional Dosing Information

See also *General Dosing Information*.

It is recommended that previous diuretic therapy be withdrawn 2 to 3 days before benazepril therapy is initiated, except in patients with accelerated or malignant hypertension or hypertension that is difficult to control. In these patients, benazepril therapy may be initiated immediately at a lower dose under careful medical supervision, and doses increased cautiously.

Benazepril is usually effective in once-daily dosing. However, if the antihypertensive effect is diminished before 24 hours, the total daily dose may be given as 2 divided doses.

Oral Dosage Forms

Note: Bracketed uses in the *Dosage Forms* section refer to categories of use and/or indications that are not included in U.S. product labeling.

The dosing and strengths of the dosage forms available are expressed in terms of benazepril base (not the hydrochloride salt).

BENAZEPRIL HYDROCHLORIDE TABLETS

Usual adult dose

Antihypertensive—

Initial: Oral, 10 mg (base) once a day.

Maintenance: Oral, 20 to 40 mg (base) once a day as a single dose or in two divided doses.

Note: An initial dose of 5 mg (base) should be used in patients who are sodium- and water-depleted as a result of prior diuretic therapy, in patients continuing to receive diuretic therapy, and patients with renal failure (creatinine clearance less than 30 mL per minute per 1.73m ^{2}). Such patients should be kept under medical supervision for at least two hours after this initial dose (and for an additional hour after blood pressure has stabilized), to watch for excessive hypotension.

[Vasodilator, congestive heart failure][1]—

Initial: Oral, 5 mg (base) once a day.

Maintenance: Oral, 5 to 10 mg (base) once a day.

Usual adult prescribing limits

Doses above 80 mg per day have not been evaluated.

Usual pediatric dose

Antihypertensive—

Children 6 years of age and older—Oral, initially 0.2 mg per kg of body weight per day up to 10 mg per day.

Children younger than 6 years of age—Safety and efficacy have not been established.

Note: Benazepril should not be administered to pediatric patients with creatinine clearance less than 30 mL per minute per 1.73 m^2.

Usual pediatric prescribing limits

0.6 mg per kg of body weight per day up to 40 mg per day.

Strength(s) usually available

U.S.—

5 mg (base) (Rx) [*Lotensin*].
10 mg (base) (Rx) [*Lotensin*].
20 mg (base) (Rx) [*Lotensin*].
40 mg (base) (Rx) [*Lotensin*].

Canada—

5mg (Rx) [*Lotensin*].
10mg (Rx) [*Lotensin*].
20mg (Rx) [*Lotensin*].
40 mg (Rx) [*Lotensin*].

Packaging and storage

Store below 30 °C (86 °F), preferably between 15 and 30 °C (59 and 86 °F), unless otherwise specified by manufacturer. Store in a tight container.

Auxiliary labeling

• Do not take other medicines without your doctor's advice.

Note

Check refill frequency to determine compliance in hypertensive patients.

[1]Not included in Canadian product labeling.

CAPTOPRIL

Summary of Differences

Pharmacology/pharmacokinetics:

Mechanism of action/Effect—Captopril is not a prodrug.

Duration of action—Single dose: 6 to 12 hours.

Precautions:

Breast-feeding—Captopril is distributed into breast milk.

Laboratory value alterations—May produce false-positive results in urinary acetone test.

Side/adverse effects:

Causes maculopapular or urticarial skin rash, sometimes with fever, joint pain, or elevated antinuclear antibody (ANA) titers.

Additional Dosing Information

See also *General Dosing Information*.

It is recommended that previous antihypertensive therapy be withdrawn 1 week before captopril therapy is initiated, except in patients with accelerated or malignant hypertension or hypertension that is difficult to control. In these patients, captopril therapy may be initiated at the lowest dose immediately after previous therapy (except diuretics) is discontinued, under careful medical supervision, and the dosage increased every 24 hours or less until the medication is effective or the maximum dose is reached.

Oral Dosage Forms

CAPTOPRIL TABLETS USP

Usual adult and adolescent dose

Antihypertensive—

Initial: Oral, 25 mg two or three times a day, the dosage being increased if necessary after one or two weeks to 50 mg two or three times a day.

Left ventricular dysfunction following myocardial infarction—

Initial: Oral, a single dose of 6.25 mg. Then 12.5 mg three times a day, gradually increased to 25 mg three times a day over several days.

Maintenance: Oral, 50 mg three times a day.

Note: Captopril therapy may be initiated as early as three days following a myocardial infarction.

Diabetic nephropathy—

Oral, 25 mg three times a day.

Vasodilator, congestive heart failure—

Initial: Oral, 25 mg two or three times a day, the dosage being increased gradually as necessary on a daily basis up to 50 mg two or three times a day. If further increases in dosage are needed, it is recommended that they be made after an interval of two weeks so that the full effects of captopril will be apparent.

Maintenance: Oral, 50 to 100 mg two or three times a day.

Note: An initial dose of 6.25 to 12.5 mg two or three times a day should be used in patients who are sodium- and water-depleted as a result of diuretic therapy, in patients continuing to receive diuretic therapy, or in patients with renal function impairment. Such patients should be kept under medical supervision for one hour after this initial dose, to watch for excessive hypotension.

Dosage increases in patients with significant renal function impairment should proceed slowly (one- to two-week intervals), and smaller increments should be used.

Usual adult prescribing limits

150 mg per day for hypertension and left ventricular dysfunction, post-myocardial infarction.

450 mg per day for congestive heart failure.

Usual pediatric dose

Newborns—

Initial: Oral, 10 mcg (0.01 mg) per kg of body weight two or three times a day, the dosage being adjusted as needed and tolerated.

Children—

Initial: Oral, 300 mcg (0.3 mg) per kg of body weight three times a day, the dosage being increased if necessary in increments of 300 mcg (0.3 mg) per kg of body weight, at intervals of eight to twenty-four hours to the minimum effective dose.

Note: An initial dose of 150 mcg (0.15 mg) per kg of body weight three times a day should be used in patients who are sodium- and water-depleted as a result of diuretic therapy, in patients continuing to receive diuretic therapy, and in patients with renal function impairment.

Strength(s) usually available

U.S.—

12.5 mg (Rx) [*Capoten* (scored)].
25 mg (Rx) [*Capoten* (scored)].
50 mg (Rx) [*Capoten* (scored)].
100 mg (Rx) [*Capoten* (scored)].

Canada—

12.5 mg (Rx) [*Capoten*].
25 mg (Rx) [*Capoten* (scored)].

50 mg (Rx) [*Capoten* (scored)].
100 mg (Rx) [*Capoten* (scored)].

Packaging and storage

Store below 40 °C (104 °F), preferably between 15 and 30 °C (59 and 86 °F), in a tight container, unless otherwise specified by manufacturer.

Preparation of dosage form

For patients who cannot take oral solids—Captopril oral solution may be prepared by crushing a 25-mg tablet, dissolving it in 25 or 100 mL of water, and shaking the solution well for at least 5 minutes. After the tablet has dissolved, the clear solution is poured off for administration and the remaining filler, which does not dissolve, is discarded. Because captopril is very unstable when dissolved in water, the solution should be used within one-half hour after preparation.

Auxiliary labeling

- Take on an empty stomach, one hour before meals.
- Do not take other medicines without your doctor's advice.

Note

Tablets may have a slight sulfurous odor.

Check refill frequency to determine compliance in hypertensive patients.

CILAZAPRIL

Additional Dosing Information

See also *General Dosing Information.*

It is recommended that previous diuretic therapy be withdrawn 2 to 3 days before cilazapril therapy is initiated, except in patients with hypertension that is difficult to control. In these patients, cilazapril therapy may be initiated immediately at a lower dose under careful medical supervision, and increased cautiously.

Cilazapril is usually effective in once-daily dosing. However, if the antihypertensive effect is diminished before 24 hours, the total daily dose may be given as 2 divided doses, or the dosage may be increased.

Oral Dosage Forms

CILAZAPRIL TABLETS

Usual adult and adolescent dose

Antihypertensive—

Initial: Oral, 2.5 mg once a day. Dosage may be increased if necessary after two weeks.

Maintenance: Oral, 2.5 to 10 mg once daily or in divided doses.

Note: An initial dose of 1 mg should be used in renal-compromised patients with a creatinine clearance greater than 40 mL per minute. An initial dose of 0.5 mg should be used in patients continuing to receive diuretic therapy, patients with liver cirrhosis, or patients with renal failure (creatinine clearance of 10 to 40 mL per minute). An initial dose of 1.25 mg or less should be used in geriatric patients over 65 years of age. Such patients should be kept under medical supervision after the first dose until stabilized.

Vasodilator, congestive heart failure—

Initial: Oral, 0.5 mg once daily.

Maintenance: Oral, 1 to 5 mg per day.

Note: An initial dose of 0.25 mg should be used in patients with renal failure (creatinine clearance of 10 to 40 mL per minute).

Usual adult prescribing limits

10 mg per day

Strength(s) usually available

U.S.—

Not commercially available.

Canada—

1 mg (Rx) [*Inhibace*].
2.5 mg (Rx) [*Inhibace*].
5 mg (Rx) [*Inhibace*].

Packaging and storage

Store between 15 and 30 °C (59 and 86 °F), in a well-closed container.

Auxiliary labeling

- Do not take other medicines without your doctor's advice.

Note

Check refill frequency to determine compliance in hypertensive patients.

ENALAPRIL

Summary of Differences

Pharmacology/pharmacokinetics:

Onset of action—

Enalapril maleate: Oral—Single dose: 1 hour.
Enalaprilat: Intravenous—Single dose: 15 minutes.

Additional Dosing Information

See also *General Dosing Information.*

It is recommended that previous diuretic therapy be withdrawn 2 to 3 days before enalapril therapy is initiated, except in patients with accelerated or malignant hypertension or hypertension that is difficult to control. In these patients, enalapril therapy may be initiated immediately at a lower dose under careful medical supervision, and increased cautiously.

Enalapril is usually effective in once-daily dosing. However, if the antihypertensive effect is diminished before 24 hours, the total daily dose may be given as 2 divided doses.

Hemodialysis reduces serum enalaprilat concentrations by approximately 35%.

Oral Dosage Forms

ENALAPRIL MALEATE TABLETS USP

Usual adult and adolescent dose

Antihypertensive—

Initial: Oral, 5 mg once a day, the dosage being adjusted after one or two weeks according to clinical response.

Maintenance: Oral, 10 to 40 mg per day, as a single dose or in two divided doses.

Note: An initial dose of 2.5 mg should be used in patients who are sodium- and water-depleted as a result of prior diuretic therapy, patients continuing to receive diuretic therapy, or patients with renal failure (creatinine clearance less than 30 mL per minute). Such patients should be kept under medical supervision for at least two hours after this initial dose (and for an additional hour after blood pressure has stabilized), to watch for excessive hypotension.

Vasodilator, congestive heart failure—

Initial: Oral, 2.5 mg once or twice a day, the dosage being adjusted after a few days or weeks according to clinical response.

Maintenance: Oral, 5 to 40 mg per day, as a single dose or in two divided doses.

Left ventricular dysfunction, asymptomatic—

Oral, 2.5 mg two times a day titrated as tolerated up to a target dose of 20 mg a day in divided doses.

Note: Patients should be kept under medical supervision for at least two hours and until blood pressure has stabilized for an additional hour after the initial dose.

In patients with hyponatremia (serum sodium concentration less than 130 mEq per liter) or serum creatinine greater than 1.6 mg per deciliter, an initial dose of 2.5 mg once a day is recommended.

If possible, the dose of the diuretic should be reduced to decrease the likelihood of hypotension.

Usual adult prescribing limits

40 mg per day.

Usual pediatric dose

Antihypertensive—

Children 1 month to 16 years of age—Oral, initially 0.08 mg per kg of body weight per day up to 5 mg per day.

Neonates—Safety and efficacy have not been established.

Note: Enalapril should not be administered to pediatric patients with creatinine clearance less than 30 mL per minute per 1.73 m^2.

Usual pediatric prescribing limits

0.6 mg per kg of body weight per day up to 40 mg per day.

Strength(s) usually available

U.S.—

2.5 mg (Rx) [*Vasotec* (scored)].
5 mg (Rx) [*Vasotec* (scored)].
10 mg (Rx) [*Vasotec*].
20 mg (Rx) [*Vasotec*].

Canada—

2.5 mg (Rx) [*Vasotec* (scored)].
5 mg (Rx) [*Vasotec* (scored)].

10 mg (Rx) [*Vasotec*].
20 mg (Rx) [*Vasotec*].

Packaging and storage
Store below 50 °C (122 °F), preferably between 15 and 30 °C (59 and 86 °F), in a well-closed container, unless otherwise specified by manufacturer.

Auxiliary labeling
• Do not take other medicines without your doctor's advice.

Note
Check refill frequency to determine compliance in hypertensive patients.

Parenteral Dosage Forms

ENALAPRILAT INJECTION

Usual adult and adolescent dose
Antihypertensive—
Intravenous (over at least five minutes), 1.25 mg every six hours.
Note: An initial dose of 625 mcg (0.625 mg) should be used in patients who are sodium- and water-depleted as a result of prior diuretic therapy, patients continuing to receive diuretic therapy, or patients with renal failure (creatinine clearance less than or equal to 30 mL per minute). Such patients should be observed for one hour after this initial dose, to watch for excessive hypotension. If the clinical response is inadequate after one hour, the 625 mcg (0.625 mg) dose may be repeated, and therapy continued at a dose of 1.25 mg every six hours.

Usual pediatric dose
For severe hypertension—
Intravenous, 0.05 to 0.1 mg per kg of body weight per dose up to 1.25 mg per dose
Neonates—Safety and efficacy have not been established.
Note: Enalapril should not be administered to pediatric patients with creatinine clearance less than 30 mL per minute per 1.73 m^2.
Note: Use of products containing benzyl alcohol is not recommended in neonates. A fatal toxic syndrome consisting of metabolic acidosis, CNS depression, respiratory problems, renal failure, hypotension, and possibly seizures and intracranial hemorrhages has been associated with this use.

Strength(s) usually available
U.S.—
1.25 mg per mL (Rx) [*Vasotec* (benzyl alcohol)].
Canada—
1.25 mg per mL (Rx) [*Vasotec* (benzyl alcohol)].

Packaging and storage
Store below 40 °C (104 °F), preferably between 15 and 30 °C (59 and 86 °F), unless otherwise specified by manufacturer.

Preparation of dosage form
Enalaprilat injection may be administered undiluted, or may be diluted with up to 50 mL of a compatible diluent.

Stability
Stable in compatible diluents (5% dextrose injection, 0.9% sodium chloride injection, 0.9% sodium chloride in 5% dextrose injection, 5% dextrose in lactated Ringers injection) for 24 hours.

FOSINOPRIL

Summary of Differences

Precautions:
Breast-feeding—Fosinoprilat (active metabolite) is distributed into breast milk.
Medical considerations/contraindications—Dosage adjustment is not necessary in renal function impairment.
Laboratory value alterations—May cause a false low serum digoxin level with the Digi-Tab RIA Kit.

Additional Dosing Information

See also *General Dosing Information.*

It is recommended that previous diuretic therapy be withdrawn 2 to 3 days before fosinopril therapy is initiated, except in patients with accelerated or malignant hypertension or hypertension that is difficult to control. In these patients, fosinopril therapy may be initiated immediately at a lower dose under careful medical supervision (for at least 2 hours and until blood pressure has stabilized for at least an additional hour), and doses increased cautiously.

Fosinopril is usually effective in once-daily dosing. However, if the antihypertensive effect is diminished before 24 hours, the total daily dose may be given as 2 divided doses.

Oral Dosage Forms

FOSINOPRIL SODIUM TABLETS

Usual adult dose
Antihypertensive—
Initial: Oral, 10 mg once a day, the dosage being adjusted according to clinical response.
Maintenance: Oral, 20 to 40 mg once a day.
Note: In patients continuing to receive diuretic therapy, an initial fosinopril dose of 10 mg may be given with careful medical supervision for several hours and until blood pressure is stabilized.

Vasodilator, congestive heart failure—
Initial: Oral, 10mg once a day, the dosage being increased over a several week period.
Maintenance: Oral, 20 to 40 mg once a day.
Note: An initial dose of 5 mg should be used in patients who are sodium and water depleted as a result of diuretic therapy, and also for patients who have moderate to severe renal failure.

Usual adult prescribing limits
80 mg per day.

Usual pediatric dose
Antihypertensive—
Children weighing greater than 50 kg—Oral, initially 5 to 10 mg per day.
Children weighing less than 50 kg—Safety and efficacy have not been established.
Note: Fosinopril should not be administered to pediatric patients with creatinine clearance less than 30 mL per minute per 1.73 m^2.

Usual pediatric prescribing limits
40 mg per day.

Strength(s) usually available
U.S.—
10 mg (Rx) [*Monopril*].
20 mg (Rx) [*Monopril*].
40 mg (Rx) [*Monopril*].
Canada—
10 mg (Rx) [*Monopril*].
20 mg [*Monopril*].

Packaging and storage
Store below 30 °C (86 °F), preferably between 15 and 30 °C (59 and 86 °F), unless otherwise specified by manufacturer. Store in a tight container.

Auxiliary labeling
• Do not take other medicines without your doctor's advice.

Note
Check refill frequency to determine compliance in hypertensive patients.

LISINOPRIL

Summary of Differences

Pharmacology/pharmacokinetics:
Mechanism of action/Effect—Lisinopril is not a prodrug.
Protein binding—None.
Biotransformation—None.

Additional Dosing Information

See also *General Dosing Information.*

It is recommended that previous diuretic therapy be withdrawn 2 to 3 days before lisinopril therapy is initiated, except in patients with accelerated or malignant hypertension or hypertension that is difficult to control. In these patients, lisinopril therapy may be initiated immediately at a lower dose under careful medical supervision (for at least 2 hours and until blood pressure has stabilized for at least an additional hour), and increased cautiously.

Lisinopril is usually effective in once-daily dosing. However, if the antihypertensive effect is diminished before 24 hours, an increase in dosage may be necessary.

Oral Dosage Forms

LISINOPRIL TABLETS

Usual adult and adolescent dose

Antihypertensive—

Initial: Oral, 10 mg once a day, the dosage being adjusted according to clinical response.

Maintenance: Oral, 20 to 40 mg once a day.

Note: An initial dose of 5 mg should be used in patients who are sodium- and water-depleted as a result of prior diuretic therapy, patients continuing to receive diuretic therapy, or patients with renal failure (creatinine clearance less than or equal to 30 mL per minute). An initial dose of 2.5 mg should be used in patients with a creatinine clearance less than 10 mL per minute. Such patients should be kept under medical supervision for at least two hours after this initial dose (and for an additional hour after blood pressure has stabilized), to watch for excessive hypotension.

Vasodilator, congestive heart failure—

Initial: Oral, 5 mg per day, the dosage being adjusted according to clinical response.

Maintenance: Oral, 5 to 20 mg per day.

Note: An initial dose of 2.5 mg per day should be used in patients with hyponatremia or who have moderate to severe renal impairment (creatinine clearance less than or equal to 30 mL per minute).

Acute myocardial infarction—

Initial: Oral, 5 mg within 24 hours of onset of an acute myocardial infarction, followed by 5 mg after 24 hours, 10 mg after 48 hours, then 10 mg per day.

Maintenance: Oral, 10 mg per day for six weeks.

Note: In patients with low systolic blood pressure (≤ 120 mmHg), an initial dose of 2.5 mg should be used when treatment begins, or during the first three days after the infarction. If hypotension occurs (systolic blood pressure is less than or equal to 100 mmHg), a daily maintenance dose of 5 mg may be given with temporary reduction to 2.5 mg if needed. If prolonged hypotension occurs (systolic blood pressure ≤ 90 mmHg for more than 1 hour), lisinopril should be withdrawn.

Usual adult prescribing limits

Doses up to 80 mg per day have been used.

Usual pediatric dose

Antihypertensive—

Children 6 to 16 years of age—Oral, initially 0.07 mg per kg of body weight per day adjusted according to blood pressure response up to 5 mg per day.

Children younger than 6 years of age—Safety and efficacy have not been established.

Note: Lisinopril should not be administered to pediatric patients with creatinine clearance less than 30 mL per minute per 1.73 m^2.

Usual pediatric prescribing limits

0.61 mg per kg of body weight per day or 40 mg per day.

Strength(s) usually available

U.S.—

2.5 mg (Rx) [*Prinivil; Zestril*].
5 mg (Rx) [*Prinivil* (scored); *Zestril* (scored)].
10 mg (Rx) [*Prinivil; Zestril*].
20 mg (Rx) [*Prinivil; Zestril*].
40 mg (Rx) [*Prinivil; Zestril*].

Canada—

5 mg (Rx) [*Prinivil* (scored); *Zestril* (scored)].
10 mg (Rx) [*Prinivil; Zestril*].
20 mg (Rx) [*Prinivil; Zestril*].

Packaging and storage

Store below 40 °C (104 °F), preferably between 20 and 25 °C (68 and 77 °F), in a well-closed container, unless otherwise specified by manufacturer.

Auxiliary labeling

- Do not take other medicines without your doctor's advice.

Note

Check refill frequency to determine compliance in hypertensive patients.

MOEXIPRIL

Additional Dosing Information

See also *General Dosing Information.*

It is recommended that previous diuretic therapy be withdrawn 2 to 3 days before moexipril therapy is initiated, except in patients with hypertension that is difficult to control. In these patients, moexipril can be initiated at a lower dose under close medical supervision (for at least 2 hours and until blood pressure has stabilized for at least an additional hour), and doses increased cautiously.

Moexipril is usually effective as once-daily dosing. However, if antihypertensive effect is diminished before 24 hours, the total daily dose may be given as 2 divided doses, or the dosage may be increased, as appropriate.

Oral Dosage Forms

MOEXIPRIL HYDROCHLORIDE TABLETS

Usual adult dose

Antihypertensive—

Initial: Oral, 7.5 mg once a day 1 hour prior to meals, the dosage being adjusted according to clinical response.

Maintenance: Oral, 7.5 to 30 mg daily, in one or two divided doses 1 hour prior to meals.

Note: An initial dose of 3.75 mg, given under medical supervision, is recommended for patients with a creatinine clearance ≤ 40 mL/min, or for patients on diuretic therapy that cannot be discontinued. Dosage may be cautiously titrated upward to a maximum daily dose of 15 mg for renally compromised patients.

Usual adult prescribing limits

30 mg per day; 15 mg per day for patients with a creatinine clearance ≤ 40 mL/min. Doses above 60 mg per day have not been studied.

Usual pediatric dose

Safety and efficacy have not been established.

Strength(s) usually available

U.S.—

7.5 mg (Rx) [*Univasc* (scored)].
15 mg (Rx) [*Univasc* (scored)].

Canada—

Not commercially available.

Packaging and storage

Store at controlled room temperature, preferably between 20 and 25 °C (68 and 77 °F), in a well-closed container, unless otherwise specified by manufacturer.

Auxiliary labeling

- Do not take other medicines without your doctor's advice.
- Take on an empty stomach, one hour before a meal.

Note

Check refill frequency to determine compliance in hypertensive patients.

PERINDOPRIL

Additional Dosing Information

See also *General Dosing Information.*

It is recommended that previous diuretic therapy be withdrawn two to three days before perindopril therapy is initiated, except in patients with hypertension that is difficult to control. In these patients, perindopril therapy may be initiated immediately at a lower dose under careful medical supervision (for several hours and until blood pressure has stabilized for at least an additional hour), and doses increased cautiously.

Perindopril is usually effective in once-daily dosing. However, if the antihypertensive effect is diminished before 24 hours, an increase in dosage may be necessary or the total daily dose may be given in 2 divided doses.

Oral Dosage Forms

PERINDOPRIL ERBUMINE TABLETS

Usual adult dose

Antihypertensive—

Initial: Oral, 4 mg once daily, the dosage being adjusted slowly (at 2-week intervals) and according to clinical response.

Maintenance: Oral, 4 to 8 mg once daily.

Note: An initial dose of 2 mg to 4 mg should be used in geriatric patients and patients continuing to receive diuretic therapy. An initial dose of 2 mg is recommended in renally impaired patients with a creatinine clearance > 30 mL per minute (mL/min). Such patients should be kept under medical supervision for at least two hours after the initial dose (and for an additional hour after blood pressure has stabilized), to watch for excessive hypotension.Safety and efficacy in patients with creatinine clearance < 30 mL/min are not clearly established.

Usual adult prescribing limits

16 mg per day.

Strength(s) usually available

U.S.—

2 mg (Rx) [*Aceon* (colloidal silica; lactose; magnesium stearate; microcrystalline cellulose)].

4 mg (Rx) [*Aceon* (colloidal silica; lactose; magnesium stearate; microcrystalline cellulose)].

8 mg (Rx) [*Aceon* (colloidal silica; lactose; magnesium stearate; microcrystalline cellulose)].

Canada—

2 mg (Rx) [*Coversyl*].

4 mg (Rx) [*Coversyl*].

Packaging and storage

Store at controlled room temperature, preferably between 20 and 25 °C (68 and 77 °F), in a well-closed container.

Auxiliary labeling

- Do not take other medicines without your doctor's advice.

Note

Check refill frequency to determine compliance in hypertensive patients.

QUINAPRIL

Summary of Differences

Precautions:

Drug interactions and/or related problems—Quinapril may reduce absorption of tetracycline or other drugs that interact with magnesium, since quinapril has a high magnesium content.

Additional Dosing Information

See also *General Dosing Information*.

It is recommended that previous diuretic therapy be withdrawn 2 to 3 days before quinapril therapy is initiated, except in patients with accelerated or malignant hypertension or hypertension that is difficult to control. In these patients, quinapril therapy may be initiated immediately at a lower dose under careful medical supervision (for at least 2 hours and until blood pressure has stabilized for at least an additional hour), and doses increased cautiously.

Quinapril is usually effective in once-daily dosing. However, if the antihypertensive effect is diminished before 24 hours, an increase in dosage may be necessary or the total daily dose may be given as 2 divided doses.

Oral Dosage Forms

Note: The dosing and strengths of the dosage forms available are expressed in terms of quinapril base (not the hydrochloride salt).

QUINAPRIL HYDROCHLORIDE TABLETS

Usual adult dose

Antihypertensive—

Initial: Oral, 10 or 20 mg (base) once a day, the dosage being adjusted slowly (at 2-week intervals) and according to clinical response.

Maintenance: Oral, 20 to 80 mg (base) once a day or divided into two equal doses.

Note: An initial dose of 5 mg should be used in patients who are sodium- and water-depleted as a result of prior diuretic therapy, patients continuing to receive diuretic therapy, or in patients with a creatinine clearance of 30 to 60 mL per minute. An initial dose of 2.5 mg should be used in patients with a creatinine clearance of 10 to 30 mL per minute. Such patients should be kept under medical supervision for at least two hours after this initial dose (and for an additional hour after blood pressure has stabilized), to watch for excessive hypotension.

There are insufficient data for a dosage recommendation in patients with a creatinine clearance less than 10 mL per minute.

Vasodilator, congestive heart failure—

Initial: Oral, 5 mg (base) twice a day, dosage adjusted weekly until effective clinical response is achieved.

Maintenance: Oral, 20 to 40 mg daily divided into two equal doses.

Usual pediatric dose

Safety and efficacy have not been established.

Strength(s) usually available

U.S.—

5 mg (Rx) [*Accupril* (scored)].

10 mg (Rx) [*Accupril*].

20 mg (Rx) [*Accupril*].

40 mg (Rx) [*Accupril*].

Canada—

5 mg (Rx) [*Accupril*].

10 mg (Rx) [*Accupril*].

20 mg (Rx) [*Accupril*].

40 mg (Rx) [*Accupril*].

Packaging and storage

Store below 40 °C (104 °F), preferably between 15 and 30 °C (59 and 86 °F), in a well-closed container. Protect from light.

Auxiliary labeling

- Do not take other medicines without your doctor's advice.

Note

Check refill frequency to determine compliance in hypertensive patients.

RAMIPRIL

Additional Dosing Information

See also *General Dosing Information*.

It is recommended that previous diuretic therapy be withdrawn 2 to 3 days before ramipril therapy is initiated, except in patients with accelerated or malignant hypertension or hypertension that is difficult to control. In these patients, ramipril therapy may be initiated immediately at a lower dose under careful medical supervision (for at least 2 hours and until blood pressure has stabilized for at least an additional hour), and doses increased cautiously.

Ramipril is usually effective in once-daily dosing. However, if the antihypertensive effect is diminished before 24 hours, an increase in dosage may be necessary or the total daily dose may be given as 2 divided doses.

Oral Dosage Forms

RAMIPRIL CAPSULES

Usual adult dose

Antihypertensive—

Initial: Oral, 2.5 mg once a day, the dosage being adjusted according to clinical response.

Maintenance: Oral, 2.5 to 20 mg once a day or divided into two equal doses.

Note: An initial dose of 1.25 mg should be used in patients who are sodium- and water-depleted as a result of prior diuretic therapy, patients continuing to receive diuretic therapy, or in patients with a creatinine clearance less than 40 mL per minute per 1.73 m^2. Such patients should be kept under medical supervision for at least two hours after this initial dose (and for an additional hour after blood pressure has stabilized), to watch for excessive hypotension.

Dosage may be slowly titrated upward until adequate blood pressure control is achieved or to a maximum total daily dose of 5 mg.

Congestive heart failure, post-myocardial infarction—

Initial: Oral, 2.5 mg twice daily, the dosage being adjusted slowly according to clinical response.

Maintenance: Oral, 5 mg twice daily.

Note: A patient who becomes hypotensive at the initial dose may be switched to 1.25 mg twice daily, then titrated to the target dose of 5 mg twice daily. Such patients should be kept under supervision for at least an hour and for an additional hour after blood pressure has been stabilized. For patients with heart failure and renal compromise, the recommended initial dose is 1.25 mg ramipril once daily.The dose may then be increased to 1.25 mg twice daily and up to a maximum dose of 2.5 mg twice a day, depending upon clinical response.

Risk reduction for myocardial infarction, stroke and death from cardiovascular causes[1]—

Initial: Oral, 2.5 mg once a day for 1 week then increase to 5 mg once a day for the next three weeks, and then increased as tolerated, to a maintenance dose of 10 mg a day.

Note: Indicated for use in patients aged 55 and older.

Note: If the patient is hypertensive or recently post myocardial infarction, it can be given as a divided dose.

Usual pediatric dose

Safety and efficacy have not been established.

Strength(s) usually available

U.S.—

1.25 mg (Rx) [*Altace* (pregelatinized starch; gelatin; titanium dioxide)].
2.5 mg (Rx) [*Altace* (pregelatinized starch; gelatin; titanium dioxide)].
5 mg (Rx) [*Altace* (pregelatinized starch; gelatin; titanium dioxide)].
10 mg (Rx) [*Altace* (pregelatinized starch; gelatin; titanium dioxide)].

Canada—

1.25 mg (Rx) [*Altace*].
2.5 mg (Rx) [*Altace*].
5 mg (Rx) [*Altace*].
10 mg (Rx) [*Altace*].

Packaging and storage

Store below 40 °C (104 °F), preferably between 15 and 30 °C (59 and 86 °F), in a well-closed container, unless otherwise specified by manufacturer.

Preparation of dosage form

For patients who cannot take oral solids—The contents of the capsule may be opened and dissolved in 4 ounces of water or apple juice or sprinkled over 4 ounces of applesauce, To insure that ramipril is not lost when such a mixture is used, the mixture should be consumed in its entirety. The mixture may be stored up to 24 hours at room temperature or 18 hours in the refrigerator, if necessary.

Auxiliary labeling

- Do not take other medicines without your doctor's advice.

Note

Check refill frequency to determine compliance in hypertensive patients.

[1]Not included in Canadian product labeling.

TRANDOLAPRIL

Summary of Differences

Initial doses for treatment of hypertension for black and nonblack patients are different.

Additional Dosing Information

See also *General Dosing Information.*

It is recommended that previous diuretic therapy be withdrawn 2 to 3 days before trandolapril therapy is initiated, except in patients with hypertension that is difficult to control. In these patients, trandolapril therapy may be initiated immediately at a lower dose under careful medical supervision (for at least 2 hours and until blood pressure has stabilized for at least an additional hour), and doses increased cautiously.

Trandolapril is usually effective in once-daily dosing. However, if the antihypertensive effect is diminished before 24 hours, an increase in dosage may be necessary or the total daily dose may be given in 2 divided doses.

Oral Dosage Forms

TRANDOLAPRIL TABLETS

Usual adult dose

Antihypertensive—

Initial: Oral, 1 mg once daily in nonblack patients, and 2 mg once daily in black patients, the dosage being adjusted at intervals of at least one week, according to clinical response.

Maintenance: Oral, 2 to 4 mg daily, in single or divided doses. If blood pressure is not controlled with trandolapril alone, a diuretic may be added.

Note: An initial dose of 0.5 mg trandolapril should be used in patients who are also treated with a diuretic, patients who have a creatinine clearance less than or equal to 30 mL per minute, or patients who have hepatic cirrhosis. Such patients should be kept under medical supervision for at least two hours after this initial dose (and for an additional hour after blood pressure has stabilized), to watch for excessive hypotension. Dosage may be cautiously titrated upward to achieve the clinically optimal response.

Congestive heart failure, post-myocardial infarction—

Initial: Oral, 1 mg once a day.

Maintenance: 4 mg daily, or up to the highest tolerated dose.

Usual adult prescribing limits

8 mg per day

Usual pediatric dose

Safety and efficacy have not been established.

Strength(s) usually available

U.S.—

1 mg (Rx) [*Mavik* (scored; lactose)].
2 mg (Rx) [*Mavik* (lactose)].
4 mg (Rx) [*Mavik* (lactose)].

Canada—

0.5 mg [*Mavik*].
1 mg [*Mavik*].
2 mg [*Mavik*].

Packaging and storage

Store between 20 and 25 °C (68 and 77 °F), in a well-closed container, unless otherwise specified by manufacturer.

Auxiliary labeling

- Do not take other medicines without your doctor's advice.

Note

Check refill frequency to determine compliance in hypertensive patients.

Selected Bibliography

For benazepril

Balfour JA, Goa KL. Benazepril. A review of its pharmacodynamic and pharmacokinetic properties, and therapeutic efficacy in hypertension and congestive heart failure. Drugs 1991; 42(3): 511-39.

For captopril

Vidt DG, Bravo EL, Fouad FM. Captopril. N Engl J Med 1982 Jan 28; 306: 214-9.

Ram CVS. Captopril. Arch Intern Med 1982 May; 142: 914-6.

For enalapril

Cleary JD, Taylor JW. Enalapril: a new angiotensin converting enzyme inhibitor. Drug Intell Clin Pharm 1986 Mar; 20: 177-86.

Vlasses PH, Larijani GE, Conner DP, Ferguson RK. Enalapril, a nonsulfhydryl angiotensin-converting enzyme inhibitor. Clin Pharm 1985; 4: 27-40.

For fosinopril

Sica DA, Cutler RE, Parmer RJ, Ford NF. Comparison of the steady-state pharmacokinetics of fosinopril, lisinopril and enalapril in patients with chronic renal insufficiency. Clin Pharmacokinet 1991; 20(5): 420-7.

Oren S, Messerli FH, Grossman E, Garavaglia GE, Frohlich ED. Immediate and short-term cardiovascular effects of fosinopril, a new angiotensin-converting enzyme inhibitor, in patients with essential hypertension. J Am Coll Cardiol 1991; 17: 1183-7.

For lisinopril

Armayor GM, Lopez LM. Lisinopril: A new angiotensin-converting enzyme inhibitor. Drug Intell Clin Pharm 1988 May; 22: 365-72.

Lisinopril for hypertension. Med Lett Drugs Ther 1988 Apr 8; 30: 41-2.

Chase SL, Sutton JD. Lisinopril: A new angiotensin-converting enzyme inhibitor. Pharmacother 1989; 9(3): 120-30.

For quinapril

Cropp AB. Quinapril: A new second-generation ACE inhibitor. DICP 1991; 25: 499-504.

Wadworth AN, Brogden RN. Quinapril. A review of its pharmacologic properties, and therapeutic efficacy in cardiovascular disorders. Drugs 41(3): 378-99.

For ramipril

Todd PA, Benfield P. Ramipril. A review of its pharmacological properties and therapeutic efficacy in cardiovascular disorders. Drugs 1990; 39(1): 110-35.

General

Weber MA. Safety issues during antihypertensive treatment with angiotensin converting enzyme inhibitors. Am J Med 1988; 84(suppl 4A): 16-23.

Williams GH. Converting-enzyme inhibitors in the treatment of hypertension. N Engl J Med 1988 Dec 8; 1517-25.

Massie BM. New trends in the use of angiotensin converting enzyme inhibitors in chronic heart failure. Am J Med 1988 Apr 15; 84(Suppl 4A): 36-46.

Revised: 02/03/2005

ANGIOTENSIN-CONVERTING ENZYME (ACE) INHIBITORS AND HYDROCHLOROTHIAZIDE Systemic

This monograph includes information on the following: 1) Benazepril and Hydrochlorothiazide†; 2) Captopril and Hydrochlorothiazide†; 3) Enalapril and Hydrochlorothiazide; 4) Lisinopril and Hydrochlorothiazide; 5) Moexipril and Hydrochlorothiazide†; 6) Quinapril and Hydrochlorothiazide.

VA CLASSIFICATION (Primary/Secondary): CV408/CV800; CV701

Commonly used brand name(s): *Accuretic*[6]*; Capozide*[2]*; Lotensin HCT*[1]*; Prinzide*[4]*; Uniretic*[5]*; Vaseretic*[3]*; Zestoretic*[4].

Note: For a listing of dosage forms and brand names by country availability, see *Dosage Forms* section(s).

†Not commercially available in Canada.

Category

Antihypertensive; vasodilator, congestive heart failure.

Indications

Note: Bracketed information in the *Indications* section refers to uses that are not included in U.S. product labeling.

Accepted

Hypertension (treatment)—The combination of benazepril, captopril, enalapril, lisinopril, moexipril, or quinapril and hydrochlorothiazide is indicated in the treatment of hypertension.

Fixed-dosage combinations generally are not recommended for initial therapy, but are utilized in maintenance therapy after the required dose is established in order to increase convenience, economy, and patient compliance.

For additional information on initial therapeutic guidelines related to the treatment of hypertension, see *Appendix III*.

[Congestive heart failure (treatment)[1]]—Captopril, enalapril, or lisinopril plus a diuretic, such as hydrochlorothiazide, and a digitalis glycoside are also used for treatment of severe congestive heart failure not responding to other measures.

[1]Not included in Canadian product labeling.

Pharmacology/Pharmacokinetics

Physicochemical characteristics

Molecular weight—
- Benazepril: 460.96.
- Captopril: 217.28.
- Chlorothiazide: 295.72.
- Enalapril: 492.52.
- Enalaprilat (active metabolite): 384.43.
- Hydrochlorothiazide: 297.73.
- Lisinopril: 441.52.
- Moexipril: 535.04.
- Quinapril: 474.98.

pKa—
- Captopril: 3.7 and 9.8 (apparent).
- Chlorothiazide: 6.7 and 9.5.
- Hydrochlorothiazide: 7.9 and 9.2.

Mechanism of action/Effect

ACE inhibitors—

Activity of benazepril, enalapril, moexipril, and quinapril is due to the active metabolites benazeprilat, enalaprilat, moexiprilat, and quinaprilat respectively.

Antihypertensive: Exact mechanism of antihypertensive action is unknown but is thought to be related to competitive inhibition of angiotensin I–converting enzyme (ACE) activity, resulting in a decreased rate of conversion of angiotensin I to angiotensin II, which is a potent vasoconstrictor. Decreased angiotensin II concentrations result in a secondary increase in plasma renin activity (PRA), through removal of the negative feedback of renin release, and a direct reduction in aldosterone secretion. ACE inhibitors may be less effective in controlling blood pressure among low-renin hypertensive patients, predominantly among the black patient population, as compared to normal- or high- renin hypertensive patients. ACE inhibitors reduce peripheral arterial resistance. In addition, a possible effect on the kallikrein-kinin system (interference with degradation and resulting increased concentrations of bradykinin) and an increase in prostaglandin synthesis have been suggested but not proven.

Vasodilator, congestive heart failure: Decrease in peripheral vascular (afterload) resistance, pulmonary capillary wedge pressure (preload), and pulmonary vascular resistance; and improved cardiac output and exercise tolerance.

Thiazide diuretics—

Diuretic: Thiazide diuretics increase urinary excretion of sodium and water by inhibiting sodium reabsorption in the early distal tubules. They increase the rate of delivery of tubular fluid and electrolytes to the distal sites of hydrogen and potassium ion secretion, while plasma volume contraction increases aldosterone production. The increased delivery and increase in aldosterone levels promote sodium reabsorption at the distal tubules, thus increasing the loss of potassium and hydrogen ions.

Antihypertensive: Diuretics lower blood pressure initially by reducing plasma and extracellular fluid volume; cardiac output also decreases. Eventually, cardiac output returns to normal. Thiazide diuretics decrease peripheral resistance by a direct peripheral effect on blood vessels.

Absorption

Benazepril—Approximately 37%; not affected by the presence of food.

Captopril—Rapidly and at least 75% absorbed from the gastrointestinal tract. Absorption is reduced by 30 to 40% in the presence of food.

Enalapril—Approximately 60%; not affected by the presence of food.

Hydrochlorothiazide—Absorbed relatively rapidly after oral administration.

Lisinopril—Approximately 25%, but widely variable between individuals (6 to 60%); not affected by the presence of food.

Moexipril—Approximately 13%. Absorption is reduced by 40 to 50% in the presence of food.

Quinapril—Approximately 60%. Absorption rate is reduced by 14% when administered during a high fat meal, but extent of absorption is unchanged.

Protein binding

Benazeprilat (active metabolite)—Very high (95.3%).

Captopril—Low (25 to 30%), primarily to albumin.

Enalaprilat (active metabolite)—Moderate (50 to 60%).

Lisinopril—None.

Moexiprilat—Moderate (50%).

Quinaprilat—Very high (97%).

Biotransformation

Benazepril—Hepatic, by de-esterification, to benazeprilat, the active metabolite.

Captopril—Hepatic.

Enalapril—Hepatic, by hydrolysis, to enalaprilat, the active metabolite.

Lisinopril—None.

Moexipril—Rapidly converted to moexiprilat, the active metabolite in organs or tissues other than the gastrointestinal tract, in which carboxyesterases occur.

Quinaprilat—De-esterified to quinalaprilat.

Half-life

Benazepril—10 to 11 hours.

Captopril—Less than 3 hours; increased in renal failure (3.5 to 32 hours).

Enalaprilat (active metabolite)—11 hours; increased in renal failure.

Hydrochlorothiazide—5.6 to 14.8 hours.

Lisinopril—12 hours; increased in renal failure.

Moexipril—Approximately 12 hours; increased in renal failure by a factor of 3 or 4.

Quinaprilat—25 hours; increased in renal failure.

Onset of action

Single dose—
- Benazepril: Less than 1 hour.
- Captopril: 15 to 60 minutes.
- Enalapril: 1 hour.
- Lisinopril: 1 hour.
- Moexipril: 1 hour.
- Quinapril: 1 hour.

Time to peak serum concentration

Benazepril—30 to 60 minutes (1 to 2 hours for benazeprilat in a fasting state and 2 to 4 hours in a nonfasting state).

Captopril—30 to 90 minutes.

Enalapril—1 hour (3 to 4 hours for enalaprilat).

Lisinopril—7 hours.

Moexipril—0.8 hour (1.6 hours for moexiprilat).

Quinapril—2 hours.

Time to peak effect

Single dose—
- Benazepril: 2 to 4 hours.
- Captopril: 60 to 90 minutes.
- Enalapril: 4 to 6 hours.
- Lisinopril: 6 hours.
- Moexipril—3 to 6 hours.
- Quinapril—2 to 4 hours.

Multiple doses—
- The full therapeutic effect of ACE inhibitors may not be noticed until several weeks after initiation of oral therapy. The antihypertensive effects of hydrochlorothiazide may be noted after 3 to 4 days of therapy, although up to 3 to 4 weeks may be required for optimal effect.

Duration of action

Single-dose—
- Benazepril: Approximately 24 hours.
- Captopril: Approximately 6 to 12 hours; dose related.
- Enalapril: Approximately 24 hours.
- Hydrochlorothiazide: Antihypertensive effects persist for up to 1 week after withdrawal of therapy.
- Lisinopril: Approximately 24 hours.
- Moexipril: Approximately 24 hours.
- Quinapril: Approximately 24 hours.

Elimination

Benazepril—
- Renal: Approximately 90%.
- Fecal: 11–12% az benazeprilat.
- In dialysis: Only 6% is removed as benazeprilat.

Captopril—
- Renal: More than 95%; 40 to 50% unchanged (may be less in patients with congestive heart failure); with the remainder as metabolites.
- In dialysis: Captopril is removable by hemodialysis.

Enalapril—
- Renal: 60% (20% as enalapril and 40% as enalaprilat).
- Fecal: 33% (6% as enalapril and 27% as enalaprilat).
- In dialysis: Enalaprilat is removable by hemodialysis, at the rate of 62 mL per minute, and by peritoneal dialysis.

Hydrochlorothiazide—
- Unchanged; almost totally via the kidneys, with minute quantities in the bile.

Lisinopril—
- Renal, 100% unchanged.
- In dialysis: Lisinopril is removable by hemodialysis.

Moexipril—
- Renal: 13% (1% as moexipril, 7% as moexiprilat, and 5% as other metabolites).
- Fecal: 53% (52% as moexiprilat and 1% as moexipril).
- In dialysis: It is not known whether moexipril is dialyzable.

Quinapril—
- Renal, 96% as quinaprilat.
- In dialysis: Hemodialysis has little effect on the elimination of quinapril and quinaprilat.

Precautions to Consider

Cross-sensitivity and/or related problems

Patients sensitive to one ACE inhibitor may also be sensitive to another.

Patients sensitive to other sulfonamide-type medications, bumetanide, furosemide, or carbonic anhydrase inhibitors may be sensitive to hydrochlorothiazide also.

Carcinogenicity

Benazepril—Two-year study in rats and mice at doses of up to 150 mg per kg of body weight per day showed no evidence of carcinogenicity.

Captopril—Two-year studies in mice and rats at doses of 50 to 1350 mg per kg of body weight (mg/kg) per day showed no evidence of carcinogenicity.

Enalapril—Studies in rats for 106 weeks and in mice for 94 weeks at doses up to 150 and 300 times the maximum daily human dose (based on a patient weight of 50 kg), respectively, found no evidence of tumorigenicity or carcinogenicity.

Hydrochlorothiazide—No evidence of carcinogenicity was found in female mice given daily dietary doses of up to 600 mg per kg of body weight (mg/kg) for 2 years, or in rats given daily dietary doses of up to 100 mg/kg of hydrochlorothiazide for 2 years. However, evidence of hepatocarcinogenicity occurred in male mice given the same dose as that given to the female mice.

Lisinopril—Studies in male and female rats for 105 weeks at doses up to 56 times the maximum recommended human daily dose (based on a patient weight of 50 kg) and in male and female mice for 92 weeks at doses up to 84 times the maximum recommended human daily dose (based on a patient weight of 50 kg) found no evidence of tumorigenicity.

Moexipril—No evidence of carcinogenicity was found in long-term studies in mice and rats given doses of up to 14 or 27.3 times the maximum recommended human dose (MRHD) on a mg per square meter of body surface area (mg/m^2) basis.

Mutagenicity

Benazepril—No evidence of mutagenicity was found in tests including the Ames test in bacteria with or without metabolic activation, in an *in vitro* test for forward mutations in cultured mammalian cells, or in a nucleus anomaly test.

Captopril—No evidence of mutagenicity was found in tests including the Ames bacterial reverse-mutation assay with or without metabolic activation, in a forward mutation study in bacteria, and in a sister-chromatid exchange study in human lymphocytes.

Enalapril—No evidence of mutagenicity was found in tests including the Ames bacterial assay with or without metabolic activation, rec-assay, reverse mutation assay with *E. coli*, sister chromatid exchange with cultured mammalian cells, the micronucleus test with mice, and in an *in vivo* cytogenic study using mouse bone marrow.

Hydrochlorothiazide—No evidence of genotoxicity of hydrochlorothiazide was found in *in vitro* assays using multiple strains of *Salmonella typhimurium* (the Ames test); in the CHO test for chromosomal aberrations; or in *in vivo* assays using mouse germinal cell chromosomes, Chinese hamster bone marrow chromosomes, and the *Drosophila* sex-linked recessive lethal trait gene. Hydrochlorothiazide was found to be clastogenic in the *in vitro* CHO sister chromatid exchange test and mutagenic in the mouse lymphoma cell assays, using concentrations of hydrochlorothiazide of 43 to 1300 micrograms per mL (mcg/mL). Positive test results were also obtained in the *Aspergillus nidulans* nondisjunction assay, using hydrochlorothiazide at an unspecified concentration.

Lisinopril—No evidence of mutagenicity was found in tests including the Ames bacterial assay with or without metabolic activation, forward mutation assay using Chinese hamster lung cells, *in vitro* alkaline elution rat hepatocyte assay, and chromosomal aberration studies *in vitro* in Chinese hamster ovary cells and *in vivo* in mouse bone marrow.

Moexipril—No evidence of mutagenicity was found in the Ames test and microbial reverse mutation assay, with and without activation, or in an *in vivo* nucleus anomaly test. However, under metabolic activation conditions at a 20-hour harvest time, increased frequency of chromosomal aberration was detected in Chinese hamster ovary cells.

Pregnancy/Reproduction

Fertility—*Benazepril:* No adverse effects were found in the reproductive performance of male and female rats.

Captopril: No impairment of fertility was found in rats.

Enalapril: No adverse effects on reproductive performance were found in male and female rats given enalapril in doses of 10 to 90 mg/kg per day.

Hydrochlorothiazide: No evidence of impaired fertility was found in studies in mice and rats given daily dietary doses prior to mating and throughout gestation of up to 100 and 4 mg/kg of hydrochlorothiazide, respectively.

Lisinopril: No adverse effects on reproductive performance were found in male and female rats given lisinopril in doses up to 300 mg/kg per day.

Moexipril: No evidence of impaired fertility, reproductive toxicity, or teratogenicity was detected in studies performed in rabbits and rats given oral doses of moexipril of up to 0.7 and 90.9 times the MRHD, respectively, on a mg/m^2 basis

Quinapril: No impairment of fertility were found in rats given doses up to 100 mg/kg per day.

Pregnancy—Adequate and well-controlled studies have not been done with ACE inhibitors in humans. However, ACE inhibitors can cause fetal and neonatal morbidity and mortality when administered to pregnant women. ACE inhibitors should be discontinued as soon as possible when pregnancy is detected.

Fetal exposure to ACE inhibitors during the second and third trimesters can cause hypotension, renal failure, anuria, skull hypoplasia, and even death in the newborn. Maternal oligohydramnios has also been reported, probably reflecting decreasing fetal renal function. Enalapril and lisinopril have been removed from neonatal circulation by peritoneal dialysis. Captopril is not removable by peritoneal dialysis. There is inadequate data concerning the effectiveness of hemodialysis and there is no information concerning use of exchange transfusion for removing captopril from general circulation. It is recommended that infants exposed in utero to ACE inhibitors be closely observed for hypotension, oliguria, and hyperkalemia. Oliguria should be treated with support of blood pressure and renal perfusion by administration of fluids and pressors as appropriate.

Benazepril—

Benazepril crosses the placenta.

No teratogenic effects were seen when benazepril and hydrochlorothiazide were administered to pregnant rats, mice, and rabbits administered 300 times, 90 times, and 3 times, respectively, the maximum recommended human dose on a mg per kg basis.

Captopril—

Captopril crosses the placenta. Several cases of intrauterine growth retardation, fetal distress and hypotension, and one case of cranial malformation have been reported in humans.

Fetal deaths have occurred when rabbits were given 2 to 70 times the maximum recommended human dose and a low incidence of cranial malformations occurred in offspring. Neonatal deaths have occurred in rats at up to 400 times the recommended human dose. No teratogenicity has been noted in hamsters or rats.

Enalapril—

Enalapril crosses the placenta.

Fetal toxicity (decrease in average fetal weight) has occurred in rats at doses of enalapril 2000 times the maximum daily human dose, and maternal and fetal toxicity has occurred in rabbits at doses almost double the maximum daily human dose. In some cases, saline supplementation prevented maternal and fetal toxicity. No teratogenicity has been noted in rabbits and neither fetal toxicity nor teratogenicity occurred in rats at doses up to 333 times the maximum daily human dose.

Hydrochlorothiazide—

Thiazide diuretics cross the placenta and appear in cord blood. Although studies in humans have not been done, thiazide diuretics can cause fetal harm when given to pregnant women. Fetal or neonatal jaundice has been reported.

Studies in rabbits, mice, and rats at doses up to 100 mg/kg per day (50 times the maximum recommended human dose) have not shown that hydrochlorothiazide causes adverse effects on the fetus.

Lisinopril—

Lisinopril was not teratogenic in mice given doses up to 625 times the maximum recommended human dose on days 6 to 15 of gestation; an increase in fetal resorptions occurred at doses of 62.5 times the maximum recommended human dose, but was prevented at doses of 625 times the maximum recommended human dose by saline supplementation. No fetotoxicity or teratogenicity occurred in rats given doses up to 188 times the maximum recommended human dose on days 6 to 17 of gestation, but an increased incidence of pup deaths and a lower average birth weight (both preventable by saline supplementation) occurred postpartum in rats given lisinopril on day 15 of gestation through day 21 postpartum. Lisinopril crosses the placenta in rats but has not been found in the fetus. Lisinopril did not cause teratogenicity in saline-supplemented rabbits given doses up to 1 mg/kg per day, but did cause fetotoxicity (increased fetal resorptions, increased incidence of incomplete ossification).

Moexipril—

No embryotoxic, fetotoxic, or teratogenic effects were seen in rats or in rabbits treated with up to 90.9 and 0.7 times, respectively, the MRHD on a mg/m^2 basis.

The moexipril and hydrochlorothiazide combination was not teratogenic in rats given up to the lethal dose of 800 mg/kg per day, or in rabbits given up to the maternotoxic dose of 160 mg/kg per day.

Quinapril—

Quinapril was not teratogenic in rats given doses up to 180 times the maximum daily human dose. However, offspring body weights were reduced in rats treated late in gestation and during lactation with doses of 25 mg/kg per day. No teratogenicity was found in rabbits. However, maternal and embryo toxicity were seen in some rabbits at doses of 0.5 to 1 mg/kg per day.

Angiotensin-converting enzyme (ACE) inhibitors and hydrochlorothiazide combinations:—

FDA Pregnancy Category C: First trimester.

FDA Pregnancy Category D: Second and third trimesters.

Breast-feeding

*Benazepril—*Benazepril is distributed into breast milk in concentrations of approximately 0.1% of the maternal dose. However, problems in humans have not been documented.

*Captopril—*Captopril is distributed into breast milk; concentrations in breast milk are approximately 1% of maternal blood concentrations. However, problems in humans have not been documented.

*Enalapril—*Enalapril is distributed into breast milk. However, problems in humans have not been documented.

*Hydrochlorothiazide—*Thiazide diuretics are distributed into breast milk. However, problems in humans have not been documented.

*Lisinopril—*It is not known whether lisinopril is distributed into human breast milk. However, problems in humans have not been documented. Lisinopril appears to be distributed into the milk of rats.

*Moexipril—*It is not known whether moexipril or moexiprilat is distributed into breast milk. However, problems in humans have not been documented.

*Quinapril—*Quinapril is distributed into breast milk. However, problems in humans have not been documented.

Pediatrics

*Benazepril—*Safety and efficacy in pediatric patients have not been established.

*Captopril, enalapril, and lisinopril—*Appropriate studies on the relationship of age to the effects of ACE inhibitors have not been done in the pediatric population. However, the use of ACE inhibitors in a limited number of neonates and infants has identified some potential pediatrics-specific problems. In neonates and infants, there is a risk of oliguria and neurologic abnormalities, possibly as a result of decreased renal and cerebral blood flow secondary to marked and prolonged reductions in blood pressure caused by ACE inhibitors; a lower initial dose and close monitoring are recommended.

*Hydrochlorothiazide—*Although appropriate studies on the relationship of age to the effects of hydrochlorothiazide have not been performed in the pediatric population, pediatrics-specific problems that would limit the usefulness of this medication in children are not expected. However, caution is required in jaundiced infants because of the risk of hyperbilirubinemia.

*Moexipril—*Safety and efficacy in pediatric patients have not been established.

*Quinapril—*Safety and efficacy in pediatric patients have not been established.

Geriatrics

*Benazepril, captopril, enalapril, lisinopril, moexipril, and quinapril—*ACE inhibitors are thought to be most effective in reducing blood pressure in patients with normal or high plasma renin activity. Since plasma renin activity appears to decline with increasing age, elderly individuals may be less sensitive to the hypotensive effects of ACE inhibitors. However, elevated serum ACE inhibitor concentrations resulting from age-related decline in renal function may compensate for the lower renin dependence. Pharmacokinetic studies with lisinopril and moexipril have revealed higher peak serum concentrations and area under the curve (AUC) in elderly patients given doses similar to those given to younger adults. The net result is that no significant differences in blood pressure response or side/adverse effects have been noted in elderly patients receiving ACE inhibitors. Nevertheless, some elderly patients may be more sensitive to the hypotensive effects of these medications and may require caution when receiving an ACE inhibitor.

*Hydrochlorothiazide—*Although appropriate studies on the relationship of age to the effects of hydrochlorothiazide have not been performed in the geriatric population, the elderly may be more sensitive to the hypotensive and electrolyte effects. In addition, elderly patients are more likely to have age-related renal function impairment, which may require caution in patients receiving hydrochlorothiazide.

Drug interactions and/or related problems

The following drug interactions and/or related problems have been selected on the basis of their potential clinical significance (possible mechanism in parentheses where appropriate)—not necessarily inclusive (» = major clinical significance):

Note: Combinations containing any of the following medications, depending on the amount present, may also interact with this medication.

» Alcohol or

» Diuretics or

Hypotension-producing medications, other (see *Appendix II*)

(hypotensive effects may be potentiated when these medications are used concurrently with ACE inhibitors and hydrochlorothiazide; although some antihypertensive and/or diuretic combinations are frequently used for therapeutic advantage, dosage adjustments may be necessary during concurrent use)

(antihypertensive agents that cause renin release or affect sympathetic activity have the greatest additive effect; concurrent use of captopril with beta-adrenergic blocking agents produces an increased but less than fully additive effect; although some antihypertensive and/or diuretic combinations may be used for therapeutic advantage, dosage adjustments may be necessary during concurrent use or when one drug is discontinued)

(if significant systemic absorption of ophthalmic beta-blockers occurs, hypotensive effects of ACE inhibitors may be potentiated)

(sudden and severe hypotension may occur within the first 1 to 5 hours after the initial dose of an ACE inhibitor, particularly in patients who are sodium- and volume-depleted as a result of diuretic therapy. Withdrawal of the diuretic or increase of salt intake approximately 1 week before start of captopril therapy or 2 to 3 days before start of benazepril, enalapril, lisinopril, moexipril, or quinapril therapy, or initiating ACE inhibitor therapy in lower doses, will minimize the reaction; this reaction does not usually recur with subsequent doses, although caution in increasing doses is recommended; diuretics may be reinstituted as necessary)

(risk of renal failure may be increased in patients who are sodium- and volume-depleted as a result of diuretic therapy)

(ACE inhibitors may reduce the secondary aldosteronism and hypokalemia caused by diuretics)

Amantadine
(hydrochlorothiazide may reduce the renal clearance of amantadine, resulting in increased plasma concentrations and possible amantadine toxicity)

Amiodarone
(concurrent use of thiazide diuretics with amiodarone may lead to an increased risk of arrhythmias associated with hypokalemia)

Anticoagulants, coumarin- or indandione-derivative
(anticoagulant effects may be decreased when used concurrently with thiazide diuretics as a result of reduction of plasma volume leading to concentration of procoagulant factors in the blood; in addition, diuretic-induced improvement of hepatic congestion may lead to improved hepatic function resulting in increased procoagulant factor synthesis; dosage adjustments may be necessary)

Antidiabetic agents, oral or
Insulin
(thiazide diuretics may raise blood glucose concentrations; for adult-onset diabetics, dosage adjustment of hypoglycemic medications may be necessary during and after thiazide diuretic therapy; insulin requirements may be increased, decreased, or unchanged)

Anti-inflammatory drugs, nonsteroidal (NSAIDs), especially indomethacin
(concurrent use of these agents may reduce the antihypertensive effects of ACE inhibitors and hydrochlorothiazide; indomethacin, and possibly other NSAIDs, may antagonize the antihypertensive effect by inhibiting renal prostaglandin synthesis and/or causing sodium and fluid retention; the patient should be carefully monitored to confirm that the desired effect is being obtained)

(in addition, concurrent use of NSAIDs with a diuretic may increase the risk of renal failure secondary to a decrease in renal blood flow caused by inhibition of renal prostaglandin synthesis)

Blood from blood bank (may contain up to 30 mEq [mmol] of potassium per liter of plasma or up to 65 mEq [mmol] per liter of whole blood when stored for more than 10 days) or
Cyclosporine or
» Diuretics, potassium-sparing or
» Low-salt milk (may contain up to 60 mEq [mmol] of potassium per liter) or
» Potassium-containing medications or
» Potassium supplements or substances containing high concentrations of potassium or
» Salt substitutes (most contain substantial amounts of potassium)
(concurrent administration with ACE inhibitors may result in hyperkalemia since reduction of aldosterone production induced by ACE inhibitors may lead to elevation of serum potassium; frequent determination of serum potassium concentrations is recommended if concurrent use of these agents is necessary; concurrent use is not recommended in patients with congestive heart failure)

Bone marrow depressants (See *Appendix II*)
(concurrent administration with an ACE inhibitor may result in an increased risk of development of potentially fatal neutropenia and/or agranulocytosis)

Calcium-containing medications
(concurrent use of hydrochlorothiazide with large doses of calcium may result in hypercalcemia because of reduced calcium excretion)

» Cholestyramine or
» Colestipol
(may inhibit gastrointestinal absorption of hydrochlorothiazide; administration of hydrochlorothiazide 1 hour before or 4 hours after cholestyramine or colestipol is recommended)

Corticosteroids or
Adrenocorticotropic hormone (ACTH)
(concurrent use with hydrochlorothiazide may intensify electrolyte depletion, particularly hypokalemia)

Diazoxide
(concurrent use with thiazide diuretics may enhance hyperglycemic effects; monitoring of blood glucose levels and/or dosage adjustment of one or both agents may be necessary)

Diflunisal
(concurrent use of hydrochlorothiazide with diflunisal produces significantly increased plasma concentrations of hydrochlorothiazide; in addition, the hyperuricemic effect of hydrochlorothiazide is decreased)

» Digitalis glycosides
(concurrent use with hydrochlorothiazide may enhance the possibility of digitalis toxicity associated with hypokalemia)

Dopamine
(concurrent use may increase the diuretic effect of either hydrochlorothiazide or dopamine, as a result of dopamine's direct effect on dopaminergic receptors to produce vasodilation of renal vasculature and increase renal blood flow; dopamine also has a direct natriuretic effect)

» Lithium
(concurrent use with hydrochlorothiazide is not recommended, as it may provoke lithium toxicity because of reduced renal clearance caused by thiazides; in addition, lithium has nephrotoxic effects)

(reversible increases in serum lithium concentrations and toxicity have been reported during concurrent use with ACE inhibitors; caution and frequent monitoring of serum lithium concentrations are recommended during concurrent use)

Neuromuscular blocking agents, nondepolarizing
(hydrochlorothiazide may induce hypokalemia, which may enhance the blockade of nondepolarizing neuromuscular blocking agents; serum potassium determinations may be necessary prior to administration of nondepolarizing neuromuscular blocking agents; careful postoperative monitoring of the patient may be necessary following concurrent or sequential use, especially if there is a possibility of incomplete reversal of neuromuscular blockade)

Sympathomimetics, such as:
» Cocaine
Dobutamine
Dopamine
Ephedrine
Epinephrine
Mephentermine
Metaraminol
Methoxamine
» Norepinephrine
» Phenylephrine
Phenylpropanolamine
(may antagonize the antihypertensive effect of ACE inhibitors and hydrochlorothiazide; the patient should be carefully monitored to confirm that the desired effect is being obtained; if concurrent use of cocaine, norepinephrine, or phenylephrine is indicated, caution is required, and only very small initial doses should be administered)

» Tetracycline
(concurrent use with quinapril reduces the absorption of tetracycline in healthy volunteers by 28 to 37% due to the presence of magnesium carbonate as an excipient in the formulation)

Laboratory value alterations

The following have been selected on the basis of their potential clinical significance (possible effect in parentheses where appropriate)—not necessarily inclusive (» = major clinical significance).

With diagnostic test results
Bentiromide
(administration of hydrochlorothiazide during a bentiromide test period will invalidate test results since thiazide diuretics are also metabolized to arylamines and will thus increase the percent of para-aminobenzoic acid [PABA] recovered; discontinuation of hydrochlorothiazide at least 3 days prior to the administration of bentiromide is recommended)

Iodohippurate sodium I 123/I 131 renal imaging or

Technetium Tc 99m pentetate renal imaging
(in patients with renal artery stenosis, captopril [and probably enalapril and lisinopril also] may cause a reversible decrease in localization and excretion of iodohippurate I 123/I 131 or technetium Tc 99m pentetate in the affected kidney; may cause confusion as to whether decreased renal function is drug-related)

Urinary acetone test
(captopril may produce false-positive results)

With physiology/laboratory test values

Alkaline phosphatase, serum and
Bilirubin, serum and
Transaminase, serum
(concentration increases have been reported with ACE inhibitors)
(serum bilirubin concentrations may be increased by displacement from albumin binding by hydrochlorothiazide)

Antinuclear antibody (ANA) titer
(positive ANA has been reported)

Blood urea nitrogen (BUN) and
Creatinine, serum
(concentrations may be transiently increased by ACE inhibitors, especially in patients with renal parenchymal and renovascular disease in patients who are volume- or sodium-depleted, or after rapid reduction of long-standing or severe high blood pressure)

Calcium, serum
(concentrations may be increased by hydrochlorothiazide; hydrochlorothiazide should be discontinued before parathyroid function tests are carried out)

Calcium, urinary
(concentrations may be decreased by hydrochlorothiazide)

Cholesterol, low-density lipoprotein, and triglyceride
(serum concentrations may be increased by hydrochlorothiazide)

Glucose, blood and urine
(concentrations may be increased by hydrochlorothiazide, usually only in patients with a predisposition to glucose intolerance)

Hematocrit or
Hemoglobin
(may rarely be slightly decreased by ACE inhibitors)

Magnesium
(serum concentrations may be decreased by hydrochlorothiazide; serum magnesium concentrations may increase in uremic patients)

Potassium
(although the effects by ACE inhibitors and hydrochlorothiazide on serum potassium may counterbalance each other, serum potassium concentrations should be monitored initially and periodically to detect imbalances; serum concentrations may be slightly increased by ACE inhibitors as a result of reduced circulating aldosterone concentrations and concomitant reduction in glomerular filtration rate [GFR], especially in patients with renal function impairment; may be decreased by hydrochlorothiazide)

Protein-bound iodine (PBI)
(serum concentrations may be decreased by the ACE inhibitor and hydrochlorothiazide combination without signs of thyroid disturbances; hydrochlorothiazide should be discontinued before parathyroid function tests are carried out)

Sodium
(serum concentrations may be slightly decreased by ACE inhibitors, especially during initial therapy, and by hydrochlorothiazide)

Uric acid
(serum concentrations may be increased by hydrochlorothiazide)

Medical considerations/Contraindications

The medical considerations/contraindications included have been selected on the basis of their potential clinical significance (reasons given in parentheses where appropriate)—not necessarily inclusive (» = major clinical significance).

Except under special circumstances, this medication should not be used when the following medical problems exist:

» Angioedema, history of, related to previous ACE inhibitor therapy or
» Hereditary angioedema or
» Idiopathic angioedema
(increased risk of development of ACE inhibitor-related angioedema)

» Anuria or severe renal function impairment
(hydrochlorothiazide may aggravate this condition)

» Hypersensitivity to any ACE inhibitors, hydrochlorothiazide, or other sulfonamide-derived medications like hydrochlorothiazide

Risk-benefit should be considered when the following medical problems exist:

Autoimmune disease, severe, especially systemic lupus erythematosus (SLE) or scleroderma
(increased risk of development of neutropenia or agranulocytosis)

Bone marrow depression—for ACE inhibitors

Cerebrovascular insufficiency or
Coronary insufficiency
(ischemia may be aggravated as a result of reduced blood pressure; cerebrovascular accident or myocardial infarction could be precipitated)

Diabetes mellitus
(increased risk of hyperkalemia with ACE inhibitors; hypoglycemic medication requirements may be altered by hydrochlorothiazide)

Gout, history of or
Hyperuricemia
(serum uric acid concentrations may be elevated by hydrochlorothiazide)

Hepatic function impairment
(reduced breakdown of captopril and reduced conversion of enalapril to enalaprilat)
(risk of dehydration with hydrochlorothiazide, which may precipitate hepatic coma and death; plasma half-life is unaltered)

Hypercalcemia—for hydrochlorothiazide

» Hyperkalemia—for ACE inhibitors

Hyponatremia—for hydrochlorothiazide

Lupus erythematosus, history of
(exacerbation or activation by thiazide diuretics has been reported)

Pancreatitis—for hydrochlorothiazide

» Renal artery stenosis, bilateral or in a solitary kidney or
» Renal transplant
(increased risk of renal function impairment caused by captopril or enalaprilat)

» Renal function impairment
(retention of captopril, enalaprilat, or lisinopril occurs; increased risk of hyperkalemia or, for captopril, proteinuria, neutropenia, and agranulocytosis. Patients with impaired renal function may require lower or less frequent doses and smaller increments in dose. If a diuretic is also required, a loop diuretic is recommended instead of a thiazide diuretic in patients with severe renal function impairment)

Sensitivity to the ACE inhibitor prescribed or to hydrochlorothiazide

Sympathectomy
(antihypertensive effects of hydrochlorothiazide may be enhanced)

» Caution is required also in patients on severe dietary sodium restriction or dialysis; these patients may be volume-depleted, and sudden reduction by the initial dose of ACE inhibitor in the angiotensin II levels that have been maintaining them at a near-normotensive state may result in sudden and severe hypotension. In addition, the risk of ACE inhibitor-induced renal failure may be increased in patients who are sodium- and volume-depleted, especially those with congestive heart failure.

» Caution is required also in jaundiced infants because of the risk of hyperbilirubinemia caused by thiazide diuretics.

Patient monitoring

The following may be especially important in patient monitoring (other tests may be warranted in some patients, depending on condition; » = major clinical significance):

Blood glucose concentrations and
Blood urea nitrogen (BUN) concentrations and
Uric acid concentrations, serum
(recommended prior to initiation of hydrochlorothiazide therapy and if clinical signs of a significant increase occur)

» Blood pressure measurements
(recommended at periodic intervals in patients being treated for hypertension; selected patients may be trained to perform blood pressure measurements at home and report the results at regular physician visits)

Cholesterol, serum and
Triglycerides, serum
(determinations recommended after 6 months of therapy and annually thereafter)

Electrolyte concentrations, serum
(may be required for patients on long-term hydrochlorothiazide therapy, especially if they are also taking cardiac glycosides or systemic steroids, or when severe cirrhosis is present)

Leukocyte count determinations, total and differential
(recommended prior to initiation of ACE inhibitor therapy and periodically thereafter; recommended every month for the first 3 to 6 months of therapy, and at periodic intervals thereafter for a period of up to 1 year in patients at increased risk for neutropenia [i.e., those with renal function impairment or collagen vascular disease] or receiving high doses; also recommended at the first sign of infection. It is recommended that ACE inhibitor therapy be withdrawn if neutropenia [neutrophil count less than 1000 per cubic millimeter (1×10^9/L)] is confirmed)

Renal function determinations
(recommended at periodic intervals in patients receiving ACE inhibitors, especially in patients who are sodium- and volume-depleted as a result of diuretic therapy or who have severe congestive heart failure)

Urinary protein estimates by means of dip-stick on first morning urine
(recommended prior to initiation of ACE inhibitor therapy and at periodic intervals thereafter for up to 1 year in patients with renal function impairment or those receiving doses of captopril greater than 150 mg per day [data with high doses of enalapril or lisinopril are not available]; if excessive or increasing proteinuria occurs, it is recommended that ACE inhibitor therapy be re-evaluated)

Side/Adverse Effects

Note: Proteinuria has occurred in about 1% of patients receiving greater than 150 mg of captopril per day. This adverse effect is thought to be due to the sulfhydryl moiety of captopril. However, whether this is a true causal relationship is unknown. Proteinuria usually occurs in patients with existing renal function impairment within 8 months of initiation of captopril therapy and usually reverses within 6 months even with continuation of therapy. Membranous glomerulopathy has been reported in some of these patients, especially with doses of captopril greater than 150 mg per day. Proteinuria has also been reported in patients receiving enalapril and lisinopril. Reported incidences range from 0% to 1.4% for enalapril and 0.7% for lisinopril.

There have been reports of reversible renal failure during ACE inhibitor therapy, especially in patients with bilateral renal artery stenoses or renal artery stenosis in a solitary kidney. There is also evidence that renal failure may be related to sodium and volume depletion from previous diuretic therapy or severe sodium restriction, especially in patients with congestive heart failure.

The following side/adverse effects have been selected on the basis of their potential clinical significance (possible signs and symptoms in parentheses where appropriate)—not necessarily inclusive:

Those indicating need for medical attention

Incidence less frequent

Edema, peripheral (swelling of ankles, feet, or legs); ***hypotension*** (dizziness, lightheadedness, or fainting)—especially following the initial dose in sodium- or volume-depleted patients or in patients receiving an ACE inhibitor for congestive heart failure; ***skin rash, with or without itching, fever, or joint pain***

Note: Maculopapular or, rarely, urticarial rash usually occurs during the first 4 weeks of the therapy with captopril and usually disappears with dosage reduction or withdrawal, or administration of an antihistamine; between 7 and 10% of these patients may show eosinophilia and/or positive antinuclear antibody (ANA) titers. The reaction may also occur, less frequently, with enalapril and lisinopril.

Rarely, a persistent lichenoid or pemphigoid reaction, possibly with a photosensitive factor, has been reported with captopril.

Skin rash or hives may also be a symptom of an allergic reaction to hydrochlorothiazide.

Incidence rare

Anaphylactoid reactions (abnormal, high-pitched, breathing sounds; anxiety; blueness of the skin, including the lips or nail beds; confusion; generalized itching; heartbeat sensations; hives; wheezing or difficulty breathing); ***Angioedema of the extremities, face, lips, mucous membranes, tongue, glottis, and/or larynx*** (sudden trouble in swallowing or breathing; swelling of face, mouth, hands, or feet; hoarseness)—especially following the initial dose; ***chest pain; cholecystitis or pancreatitis*** (severe stomach pain with nausea and vomiting); ***hepatic function impairment*** (yellow eyes or skin); ***hyperuricemia or gout*** (joint pain; lower back or side pain); ***neutropenia or agranulocytosis*** (fever and chills); ***thrombocytopenia*** (unusual bleeding or bruising)

Note: *Angioedema involving the tongue, glottis, or larynx* may cause airway obstruction, which could be fatal.

Chest pain is usually associated with severe hypotension.

Incidence of *neutropenia or agranulocytosis* is much higher in patients with renal function impairment (0.2% for captopril) or collagen vascular disease (e.g., SLE or scleroderma) (3.7% for captopril). Neutropenia appears to be dose-related and may begin within 3 months after initiation of therapy, with the nadir of the leukocyte count occurring after 10 to 30 days and persisting about 2 weeks after withdrawal. Deaths from pancytopenia and sepsis have been reported with captopril in patients with and without autoimmune disease.

Incidence not determined—Observed during clinical practice; estimates of frequency can not be determined

Intestinal angioedema (stomach pain)

Note: Intestinal angioedema has been reported in patients treated with ACE inhibitors. These patients presented with abdominal pain (with or without nausea or vomiting); in some cases there was no prior history of facial angioedema and C-1 esterase levels were normal. Angioedema was diagnosed by procedures including abdominal CT scan or ultrasound, or at surgery. Symptoms resolved after stopping the ACE inhibitor. Intestinal angioedema should be included in differential diagnosis of patients on ACE inhibitors presenting with abdominal pain.

Signs and/or symptoms of electrolyte imbalance

Dryness of mouth; increased thirst; irregular heartbeat; mood or mental changes; muscle cramps or pain; numbness or tingling in hands, feet, or lips; weakness or heaviness of legs; weak pulse

Those indicating need for medical attention only if they continue or are bothersome

Incidence more frequent

Cough, dry, persistent

Note: *Persistent dry cough* usually occurs within the first week of therapy (onset varies from 24 hours to several weeks after initiation), persists throughout therapy, and disappears within a few days after withdrawal of the ACE inhibitor. Characteristically, the cough begins as a tickling sensation in the back of the throat leading to a dry, nonproductive, persistent cough; may be worse at night or in the supine position; onset can be paroxysmal and course may be episodic or intermittent; may occasionally lead to hoarseness or vomiting.

Incidence less frequent

Anorexia (loss of appetite); ***diarrhea; headache; photosensitivity*** (increased sensitivity of skin to sunlight); ***loss of taste; stomach upset; unusual tiredness***

Note: *Loss of taste* is usually reversible after 2 to 3 months, even with continued ACE inhibitor treatment; may be associated with weight loss.

Overdose

For more information on the management of overdose or unintentional ingestion, **contact a Poison Control Center** (see *Poison Control Center Listing*).

Treatment of overdose

Treatment of ACE inhibitor overdose consists of volume expansion for correction of hypotension with infusion of normal saline solution. Captopril, enalaprilat (enalapril active metabolite), and lisinopril are removable by hemodialysis.

Thiazide diuretic overdose should be treated by immediate evacuation of the stomach with emesis and/or gastric lavage, followed by supportive, symptomatic treatment and monitoring of serum electrolyte concentrations and renal function.

Monitoring renal function and serum electrolytes, including serum potassium, should be included in observing the patient.

Patient Consultation

As an aid to patient consultation, refer to *Advice for the Patient, Angiotensin-converting Enzyme (ACE) Inhibitors and Hydrochlorothiazide (Systemic)*.

In providing consultation, consider emphasizing the following selected information (» = major clinical significance):

Before using this medication

» Conditions affecting use, especially:

Sensitivity to any ACE inhibitor, thiazide diuretic, carbonic anhydrase inhibitor, or other sulfonamide-type medications

Pregnancy—ACE inhibitor-associated fetal hypotension, oliguria, and death reported in humans; and fetotoxicity found in animals; hydrochlorothiazide may cause jaundice, thrombocytopenia, hypokalemia in infant

Breast-feeding—Captopril, enalapril, quinapril, and hydrochlorothiazide are distributed into breast milk

Use in children—Caution if giving to infants with jaundice

Use in the elderly—May be more sensitive to hypotensive and electrolyte effects

Other medications, especially alcohol, cholestyramine, colestipol, diuretics (particularly potassium-sparing), potassium-containing medications, potassium supplements, low salt milk, salt substitutes, digitalis glycosides, lithium, cocaine, norepinephrine, phenylephrine, or tetracycline when quinapril is prescribed

Other medical problems, especially angioedema related to previous ACE inhibitor therapy, hereditary angioedema, idiopathic angioedema, hyperkalemia, renal artery stenosis, renal transplant, renal function impairment, or sodium and volume depletion

Proper use of this medication

Compliance with therapy; taking medication at the same time each day to maintain the therapeutic effect

Diuretic effects of the medication and timing of doses to minimize inconvenience of diuresis

» Proper dosing

Missed dose: Taking as soon as possible; not taking if almost time for next dose; not doubling doses

» Proper storage

For captopril and hydrochlorothiazide or moexipril and hydrochlorothiazide

For best results, taking on an empty stomach 1 hour before meals

For use as an antihypertensive

Possible need for control of weight and diet, especially sodium intake; risks associated with sodium depletion; not taking salt substitutes or using low-salt milk unless approved by physician

» Patient may not experience symptoms of hypertension; importance of taking medication even if feeling well

» Does not cure, but helps control hypertension; possible need for life-long therapy; checking with physician before discontinuing medication; serious consequences of untreated hypertension

Precautions while using this medication

Making regular visits to physician to check progress

Caution when driving or doing other things requiring alertness, because of possible dizziness, especially with initial dose

To prevent dehydration and hypotension, checking with physician if severe nausea, vomiting, or diarrhea occurs and continues

Caution when exercising or during hot weather because of the risk of dehydration and hypotension due to reduced fluid volume

Caution if any kind of surgery (including dental surgery) or emergency treatment is required

Caution in using alcohol

Diabetics: May increase blood sugar levels

Possible photosensitivity; avoiding unprotected exposure to sun; using protective clothing and sun block product; avoiding use of sunlamp

Caution if any laboratory tests required; possible interference with test results

Notifying physician if there is any indication of infections, such as sore throat, fever, and/or chills, which could be a sign of neutropenia

For use as an antihypertensive:

» Not taking other medications, especially nonprescription sympathomimetics, unless discussed with physician

Side/adverse effects

Signs of potential side effects, especially peripheral edema, hypotension, skin rash (with or without itching, fever, or joint pain), anaphylactic reactions, angioedema, chest pain, cholecystitis or pancreatitis, hepatic function impairment, hyperuricemia or gout, neutropenia or agranulocytosis, thrombocytopenia, and electrolyte imbalance.

(Signs of potential side effects observed during clinical practice, especially intestinal angioedema)

General Dosing Information

Dosage must be adjusted to meet the individual requirements of each patient, on the basis of clinical response.

Black hypertensive patients may be less responsive to ACE inhibitors due to having lower renin activity, and they have a greater risk of developing ACE inhibitor-induced angioedema.

Fixed-dosage combinations generally are not recommended for initial therapy, but are utilized in maintenance therapy after the required dose is established in order to increase convenience, economy, and patient compliance.

The hypotensive effect of ACE inhibitors is the same in both standing and supine positions.

The lowest effective dosage of thiazide diuretics should be utilized to minimize potential electrolyte imbalance and the reflex increase in renin and aldosterone levels.

If increased blood urea nitrogen (BUN) and creatinine concentrations occur, reduction in dosage of the ACE inhibitor and/or withdrawal of the diuretic may be required. The possibility of renovascular hypertension should also be considered, especially in the presence of a solitary kidney, transplanted kidney, or bilateral renal artery stenosis.

Caution is recommended in initiating ACE inhibitor therapy for congestive heart failure in patients who have been receiving digitalis glycosides and/or diuretics. If the patient is sodium- and water-depleted, a lower initial dosage should be used.

Concurrent administration of potassium supplements or potassium-sparing diuretics may be indicated in patients considered to be at higher risk for developing hypokalemia. Caution in administering potassium supplements is recommended, however, since loss of potassium caused by thiazide diuretics is not clinically significant in most patients and ACE inhibitors reduce diuretic-induced hypokalemia; supplementation leads to a risk of development of hyperkalemia.

Recent evidence suggests that withdrawal of antihypertensive therapy prior to surgery is not necessary, but that the anesthesiologist must be aware of such therapy. If hypotension occurs during surgery, it may be corrected with volume expansion.

If symptomatic hypotension occurs, dosage reduction or withdrawal of the ACE inhibitor or diuretic may be necessary.

For treatment of adverse effects

For angioedema with swelling confined to the face, mucous membranes of the mouth, lips, and extremities, treatment other than withdrawal of the medication is usually not necessary, although antihistamines may relieve the symptoms.

Treatment of angioedema involving the tongue, glottis, or larynx may include the following:

- Withdrawal of the ACE inhibitor and hospitalization of the patient.
- Subcutaneous (or, rarely, intravenous) epinephrine.
- Intravenous diphenhydramine hydrochloride.
- Intravenous hydrocortisone.

BENAZEPRIL AND HYDROCHLOROTHIAZIDE

Summary of Differences

For benazepril:

Pharmacology/pharmacokinetics—

Absorption—Not affected by the presence of food.

Protein-binding—Very high (95.3%).

Elimination—Only slightly dialyzable, and dialysis is useful only in overdosed patients with severe renal impairment.

Oral Dosage Forms

BENAZEPRIL HYDROCHLORIDE AND HYDROCHLOROTHIAZIDE TABLETS

Usual adult and adolescent dose

Antihypertensive—

Oral, 1 tablet once daily as determined by titration of the individual agents.

Usual pediatric dose

Dosage has not been established

Strength(s) usually available

U.S.—

5 mg of benazepril and 6.25 mg of hydrochlorothiazide (Rx) [*Lotensin HCT* (scored; lactose)].

10 mg of benazepril and 12.5 mg of hydrochlorothiazide (Rx) [*Lotensin HCT* (scored; lactose)].

20 mg of benazepril and 12.5 mg of hydrochlorothiazide (Rx) [*Lotensin HCT* (scored; lactose)].

20 mg of benazepril and 25 mg of hydrochlorothiazide (Rx) [*Lotensin HCT* (scored; lactose)].

Canada—

Not commercially available.

Packaging and storage

Store below 30 °C (86 °F) in a tight container, unless otherwise specified by manufacturer.

Auxiliary labeling
- Avoid too much sun or use of sunlamp.
- Do not take other medicines without your doctor's advice.

Note
Check refill frequency to determine compliance in hypertensive patients.

CAPTOPRIL AND HYDROCHLOROTHIAZIDE

Summary of Differences

For captopril:
Pharmacology/pharmacokinetics—
Absorption—Reduced by 30 to 40% in presence of food.
Half-life—Less than 3 hours (3.5–32 hours in renal failure).
Duration of action—Single dose: 6 to 12 hours.
Precautions—
Laboratory value alterations—May produce false-positive results in urinary acetone test.
Side/adverse effects—
Causes maculopapular or urticarial skin rash, sometimes with fever, joint pain, or elevated antinuclear antibody (ANA) titers.

Oral Dosage Forms

Note: Bracketed uses in the *Dosage Forms* section refer to categories of use and/or indications that are not included in U.S. product labeling.

CAPTOPRIL AND HYDROCHLOROTHIAZIDE TABLETS

Usual adult and adolescent dose
Antihypertensive or
[Vasodilator, congestive heart failure]—
Oral, 1 tablet two or three times a day, as determined by individual titration with the component agents, for a maximum of 150 mg captopril and 50 mg hydrochlorothiazide.

Note: Geriatric patients may be more sensitive to the effects of the usual adult dose.

Usual pediatric dose
Oral, as determined by individual titration with the component agents
Captopril: Oral, 300 mcg (0.3 mg) per kg of body weight three times a day, the dosage being increased if necessary in increments of 300 mcg (0.3 mg) per kg of body weight at intervals of eight to twenty-four hours to the minimum effective dose.
Hydrochlorothiazide: Oral, 1 to 2 mg per kg of body weight or 30 to 60 mg per square meter of body surface per day, as a single dose or in two divided daily doses, the dosage being adjusted according to response.

Strength(s) usually available
U.S.—
25 mg of captopril and 15 mg of hydrochlorothiazide (Rx) [*Capozide* (scored; lactose); GENERIC].
25 mg of captopril and 25 mg of hydrochlorothiazide (Rx) [*Capozide* (scored; lactose); GENERIC].
50 mg of captopril and 15 mg of hydrochlorothiazide (Rx) [*Capozide* (scored; lactose); GENERIC].
50 mg of captopril and 25 mg of hydrochlorothiazide (Rx) [*Capozide* (scored; lactose); GENERIC].
Canada—
Not commercially available.

Packaging and storage
Store below 30 °C (86 °F), in a tight container, unless otherwise specified by manufacturer.

Auxiliary labeling
- Take on an empty stomach, 1 hour before meals.
- Avoid too much sun or use of sunlamp.
- Do not take other medicines without your doctor's advice.

Note
Check refill frequency to determine compliance in hypertensive patients.

ENALAPRIL AND HYDROCHLOROTHIAZIDE

Summary of Differences

For enalapril:
Pharmacology/pharmacokinetics—
Mechanism of action/effect—Activity due to active metabolite, enalaprilat.
Absorption—Not affected by presence of food.
Half-life—11 hours (increased in renal failure).
Duration of action—Single dose: Approximately 24 hours.

Oral Dosage Forms

Note: Bracketed uses in the *Dosage Forms* section refer to categories of use and/or indications that are not included in U.S. product labeling.

ENALAPRIL MALEATE AND HYDROCHLOROTHIAZIDE TABLETS

Usual adult and adolescent dose
Antihypertensive or
[Vasodilator, congestive heart failure]—
Oral, 1 tablet once or twice per day, as determined by individual titration with the component agents, for a maximum of 20 mg of enalapril and 50 mg of hydrochlorothiazide.

Note: Geriatric patients may be more sensitive to the effects of the usual adult dose.

Usual pediatric dose
Oral, as determined by individual titration with the component agents
Enalapril: Oral, initially 100 mcg (0.1 mg) per kg of body weight per day, the dosage being adjusted as needed and tolerated, up to a maximum of 500 mcg (0.5 mg) per kg of body weight per day.
Hydrochlorothiazide: Oral, 1 to 2 mg per kg of body weight or 30 to 60 mg per square meter of body surface per day, as a single dose or in two divided doses, the dosage being adjusted according to response.

Strength(s) usually available
U.S.—
5 mg of enalapril maleate and 12.5 mg of hydrochlorothiazide (Rx) [*Vaseretic* (lactose)].
10 mg of enalapril maleate and 25 mg of hydrochlorothiazide (Rx) [*Vaseretic* (lactose)].
Canada—
10 mg of enalapril maleate and 25 mg of hydrochlorothiazide (Rx) [*Vaseretic*].

Packaging and storage
Store below 40 °C (104 °F), preferably between 15 and 30 °C (59 and 86 °F), in a tight container, unless otherwise specified by manufacturer.

Auxiliary labeling
- Avoid too much sun or use of sunlamp.
- Do not take other medicines without your doctor's advice.

Note
Check refill frequency to determine compliance in hypertensive patients.

LISINOPRIL AND HYDROCHLOROTHIAZIDE

Summary of Differences

For lisinopril:
Pharmacology/pharmacokinetics—
Absorption—Not affected by presence of food.
Protein-binding—None.
Half-life—12 hours.
Duration of action—Approximately 24 hours.

Oral Dosage Forms

Note: Bracketed uses in the *Dosage Forms* section refer to categories of use and/or indications that are not included in U.S. product labeling.

LISINOPRIL AND HYDROCHLOROTHIAZIDE TABLETS

Usual adult and adolescent dose
Antihypertensive or
[Vasodilator, congestive heart failure]—
Oral, 1 or 2 tablets once a day, as determined by individual titration with the component agents, up to a maximum of 40 mg lisinopril and 50 mg hydrochlorothiazide.

Note: Geriatric patients may be more sensitive to the effects of the usual adult dose.

Usual pediatric dose
Dosage has not been established.

Strength(s) usually available
U.S.—
10 mg of lisinopril and 12.5 mg of hydrochlorothiazide (Rx) [*Prinzide; Zestoretic*].
20 mg of lisinopril and 12.5 mg of hydrochlorothiazide (Rx) [*Prinzide; Zestoretic*].

20 mg of lisinopril and 25 mg of hydrochlorothiazide (Rx) [*Prinzide*; *Zestoretic*].

Canada—

10 mg of lisinopril and 12.5 mg of hydrochlorothiazide (Rx) [*Prinzide*; *Zestoretic*].

20 mg of lisinopril and 12.5 mg of hydrochlorothiazide (Rx) [*Prinzide*; *Zestoretic*].

20 mg of lisinopril and 25 mg of hydrochlorothiazide (Rx) [*Prinzide*; *Zestoretic*].

Packaging and storage

Store below 40 °C (104 °F), preferably between 15 and 30 °C (59 and 86 °F), in a well-closed container, unless otherwise specified by manufacturer.

Auxiliary labeling

- Avoid too much sun or use of sunlamp.
- Do not take other medicines without your doctor's advice.

Note

Check refill frequency to determine compliance in hypertensive patients.

MOEXIPRIL AND HYDROCHLOROTHIAZIDE

Summary of Differences

For moexipril:

Pharmacology/pharmacokinetics—

Mechanism of action/effect—Activity due to active metabolite, moexiprilat.

Absorption—Affected significantly by the presence of food.

Half-life—12 hours (increased in renal failure).

Duration of action—Single dose: approximately 24 hours.

Oral Dosage Forms

MOEXIPRIL HYDROCHLORIDE AND HYDROCHLOROTHIAZIDE TABLETS

Usual adult dose

Antihypertensive—

Oral, 1 to 2 tablets daily, one hour before a meal, as determined by individual titration with the component agents and according to clinical response, usually not to exceed 30 mg moexipril and 50 mg hydrochlorothiazide. The hydrochlorothiazide dose should not be increased until two or three weeks after initiation of treatment.

One-half tablet may be used in patients who experience excessive reduction in blood pressure with the 7.5/12.5 mg tablet.

Usual pediatric dose

Safety and efficacy have not been established.

Strength(s) usually available

U.S.—

7.5 mg of moexipril hydrochloride and 12.5 mg of hydrochlorothiazide (Rx) [*Uniretic* (scored; lactose)].

15 mg of moexipril hydrochloride and 25 mg of hydrochlorothiazide (Rx) [*Uniretic* (scored; lactose)].

Canada—

Not commercially available.

Packaging and storage

Store at controlled room temperature, between 20 and 25 °C (68 and 77 °F) in a tightly-closed container. Protect from excessive moisture.

Auxiliary labeling

- Take on an empty stomach, one hour before meals.
- Avoid too much sun or use of sunlamp.
- Do not take other medicines without your doctor's advice.

Note

Check refill frequency to determine compliance in hypertensive patients.

QUINAPRIL AND HYDROCHLOROTHIAZIDE

Summary of Differences

For quinapril:

Pharmacology/pharmacokinetics—

Mechanism of action/effect—Activity due to active metabolite, quinaprilat.

Absorption—Affected by the presence of high-fat foods.

Protein-binding—97% protein bound.

Half-life—25 hours.

Duration of action—Approximately 24 hours.

Precautions—

Drug interaction—Reduced absorption of tetracycline.

Oral Dosage Forms

Note: Bracketed uses in the *Dosage Forms* section refer to categories of use and/or indications that are not included in U.S. product labeling.

QUINAPRIL HYDROCHLORIDE AND HYDROCHLOROTHIAZIDE TABLETS

Usual adult and adolescent dose

Antihypertensive—

Oral, 1 tablet once or twice a day, as determined by individual titration with the component agents for a maximum of 40 mg quinapril and 25 mg hydrochlorothiazide daily.

Note: Geriatric patients may be more sensitive to the effects of the usual adult dose.

Usual pediatric dose

Safety and efficacy have not been established.

Strength(s) usually available

U.S.—

10 mg of quinapril and 12.5 mg of hydrochlorothiazide (Rx) [*Accuretic*].

20 mg of quinapril and 12.5 mg of hydrochlorothiazide (Rx) [*Accuretic*].

20 mg of quinapril and 25 mg of hydrochlorothiazide (Rx) [*Accuretic*].

Canada—

10 mg of quinapril and 12.5 mg of hydrochlorothiazide (Rx) [*Accuretic*].

20 mg of quinapril and 12.5 mg of hydrochlorothiazide (Rx) [*Accuretic*].

Packaging and storage

Store between 20 and 25 °C (68 and 77 °F), in a well-closed container.

Auxiliary labeling

- Avoid too much sun or use of sunlamp.
- Do not take other medicines without your doctor's advice.

Note

Check refill frequency to determine compliance in hypertensive patients.

Selected Bibliography

The fifth report of the Joint National Committee on Detection, Evaluation, and Treatment of High Blood Pressure (JNC V). Arch Intern Med 1993; 153(2): 154-83.

Revised: 11/09/2004

ANIDULAFUNGIN Systemic†

VA CLASSIFICATION (Primary): AM700

Commonly used brand name(s): *Eraxis*.

Note: For a listing of dosage forms and brand names by country availability, see *Dosage Forms* section(s).

†Not commercially available in Canada.

Category

Antifungal, systemic.

Indications

General Considerations

Anidulafungin is active *in vitro* against *Candida albicans*, *C. glabrata*, *C. parapsilosis*, and *C. tropicalis*.

Emergence of resistance to anidulafungin has not been studied. Anidulafungin was active against *Candida albicans* resistant to fluconazole. Cross resistance with other echinocandins has not been studied.

Accepted

Candidemia (treatment) or

Candidiasis, esophageal (treatment) or

Candidiasis, intra-abdominal abscesses (treatment) or

Candidiasis, peritonitis (treatment)—Anidulafungin is indicated for use in the treatment of the following fungal infections: Candidemia and other forms of *Candida* infections (intra-abdominal abscess, and peritonitis) and esophageal candidiasis.

Acceptance not established
Anidulafungin has not been studied in endocarditis, osteomyelitis, and meningitis due to *Candida* and has not been studied in sufficient numbers of neutropenic patients to determine efficacy in these groups.

Pharmacology/Pharmacokinetics

Physicochemical characteristics
Molecular weight—1140.3.
Solubility—Slightly soluble in ethanol, practically insoluble in water.

Mechanism of action/Effect
Anidulafungin inhibits glucan synthase, an enzyme present in fungal, but not mammalian cells. This results in inhibition of the formation of 1,3-beta-D-glucan, an essential component of fungal cell walls.

Distribution
Volume of distribution (Vol_D)—30 to 50 L, similar to total body fluid volume

Protein binding
High (84%)

Biotransformation
Slow chemical degradation at physiologic temperature and pH to a ring-opened peptide lacking antifungal activity; *in vitro* degradation half-life of anidulafungin under physiologic conditions is about 24 hours; *in vivo*, ring-opened product subsequently converted to peptidic degradants and eliminated

Half-life
Terminal—40 to 50 hours

Elimination
Fecal—Approximately 30% (less than 10% intact drug)
Urine—Less than 1%

Precautions to Consider

Cross-sensitivity and/or related problems

Carcinogenicity
Long-term animal carcinogenicity studies of anidulafungin have not been conducted.

Mutagenicity
Anidulafungin was not genotoxic in the following *in vitro* studies: bacterial reverse mutation assays, a chromosome aberration assay with Chinese hamster ovary cells, and a forward gene mutation assay with mouse lymphoma cells. It was not genotoxic in mice using the *in vivo* micronucleus assay.

Pregnancy/Reproduction
Fertility—Fertility in male or female rats given intravenous doses of anidulafungin of 20 mg per kg per day (equal to 2 times the 100 mg per day proposed maintenance dose on the basis of relative body surface area) was not affected.

Pregnancy—There are no adequate and well-controlled studies in pregnant women. Because animal reproduction studies are not always predictive of human response, anidulafungin should be used during pregnancy only if the potential benefit justifies the risk to the fetus.

Embryo-fetal development studies were conducted in rats and rabbits with doses up to 20 mg per kg per day (equal to 2 and 4 times, respectively, the 100 mg per day proposed maintenance dose on the basis of relative body surface area). Results showed skeletal changes in rat fetuses including incomplete ossification of various bones and wavy, misaligned or misshapen ribs. These changes were not dose-related and were within the laboratory's historical control database range. Anidulafungin crossed the placental barrier in rats and was detected in fetal plasma. Results for rabbits revealed developmental effects (slightly reduced fetal weights) in the high dose group, a dose that also produced maternal toxicity.

FDA Pregnancy Category C

Breast-feeding
It is not known if anidulafungin is distributed into breast milk. However, anidulafungin has been found in the milk of lactating rats. Anidulafungin should be administered to nursing mothers only if the potential benefit justifies the risk.

Pediatrics
Safety and efficacy of anidulafungin in pediatric patients have not been established.

Geriatrics
Appropriate studies performed to date have not demonstrated geriatrics-specific problems that would limit the usefulness of anidulafungin in the elderly.

Pharmacogenetics
In multiple-dose patient studies, drug clearance was slightly faster (approximately 22%) in men compared with women. However, no dosage adjustments were required based on gender.

Anidulafungin pharmacokinetics were similar among Whites, Black, Asians, and Hispanics. Therefore, no dosage adjustments are required based on race.

Drug interactions and/or related problems
The following drug interactions and/or related problems have been selected on the basis of their potential clinical significance (possible mechanism in parentheses where appropriate)—not necessarily inclusive (» = major clinical significance):

Note: Combinations containing any of the following medications, depending on the amount present, may also interact with this medication.

Cyclosporine
(concomitant use slightly increased steady state AUC of anidulafungin by 22%; *in vitro* study showed no effect by anidulafungin on cyclosporine metabolism; no dosage adjustment of either drug is necessary with coadministration)

Laboratory value alterations
The following have been selected on the basis of their potential clinical significance (possible effect in parentheses where appropriate)—not necessarily inclusive (» = major clinical significance).

With physiology/laboratory test values
Alanine aminotransferase (ALT [SGPT]) and
Alkaline phosphatase, serum and
Aspartate aminotransferase (AST [SGOT]) and
Bilirubin, serum and
Gamma-glutamyl transferase (GGT) and
Hepatic enzymes
(values may be increased)

Amylase and
Lipase
(values may be increased)

Blood urea and
Creatine phosphokinase (CPK) and
Creatinine
(concentrations may be increased)

Magnesium, serum and
Potassium, serum
(concentrations may be decreased)

Platelet count
(value may be increased or decreased)

Prothrombin time
(may be prolonged)

Medical considerations/Contraindications
The medical considerations/contraindications included have been selected on the basis of their potential clinical significance (reasons given in parentheses where appropriate)—not necessarily inclusive (» = major clinical significance).

Except under special circumstances, this medication should not be used when the following medical problem exists:

» Hypersensitivity to anidulafungin or any component of the product or to other echinocandins

Risk-benefit should be considered when the following medical problems exist:

Hepatic function
(lab abnormalities in liver function tests observed with anidulafungin use; isolated cases of significant hepatic dysfunction, hepatitis, or worsening hepatic failure reported but causal relationship to anidulafungin not established)

Patient monitoring
The following may be especially important in patient monitoring (other tests may be warranted in some patients, depending on condition; » = major clinical significance):

Hepatic effects
(patients who develop abnormal liver function tests during anidulafungin therapy should be monitored for worsening hepatic function and evaluated for risk/benefit of continued anidulafungin therapy)

Side/Adverse Effects
Possible histamine-mediated symptoms have been reported with anidulafungin, including rash, urticaria, flushing, pruritus, dyspnea, and hypotension. These events are infrequent when the rate of infusion does not exceed 1.1 mg per minute.

The following side/adverse effects have been selected on the basis of their potential clinical significance (possible signs and symptoms in parentheses where appropriate)—not necessarily inclusive:

Those indicating need for medical attention

Incidence less frequent

Hypokalemia (convulsions; decreased urine; dry mouth; irregular heartbeat; increased thirst; loss of appetite; mood changes; muscle pain or cramps; nausea or vomiting; numbness or tingling in hands, feet, or lips; shortness of breath; unusual tiredness or weakness); ***neutropenia*** (black, tarry stools; chills; cough; fever; lower back or side pain; painful or difficult urination; pale skin; shortness of breath; sore throat; ulcers, sores, or white spots in mouth; unusual bleeding or bruising; unusual tiredness or weakness)

Incidence rare

Angioneurotic edema (large, hive-like swelling on face, eyelids, lips, tongue, throat, hands, legs, feet, sex organs); ***atrial fibrillation*** (fast or irregular heartbeat; dizziness; fainting); ***bundle branch block (right)*** (shortness of breath, palpitations, fatigue, irregular fast heartbeat); ***candidiasis*** (white patches in the mouth or throat or on the tongue; white patches with diaper rash); ***cholestasis*** (abdominal or stomach pain; chills; clay-colored stools; dark urine; dizziness; fever; headache; itching; loss of appetite; nausea; rash; unpleasant breath odor; unusual tiredness or weakness; vomiting of blood; yellow eyes or skin); ***clostridial infection*** (diarrhea, nausea and vomiting, abdominal pain, bloody stools); ***coagulopathy*** (unusual bleeding or bruising); ***convulsions*** (seizures); ***deep vein thrombosis*** (pain, redness, or swelling in arm or leg); ***electrocardiogram (ECG) changes; erythema*** (flushing, redness of skin; unusually warm skin); ***fungemia*** (infection of blood); ***hepatic necrosis*** (abdominal or stomach pain; black, tarry stools; chills; light-colored stools; dark urine; dizziness; fever; headache; itching; loss of appetite; nausea; rash; unpleasant breath odor; unusual tiredness or weakness; vomiting of blood; yellow eyes or skin); ***hypercalcemia*** (abdominal pain; confusion; constipation; depression; dry mouth; headache; incoherent speech; increased urination; loss of appetite; metallic taste; muscle weakness; nausea; thirst; unusual tiredness; vomiting; weight loss); ***hyperglycemia*** (abdominal pain; blurred vision; dry mouth; fatigue; flushed, dry skin; fruit-like breath odor; increased hunger; increased thirst; increased urination; nausea; sweating; troubled breathing; unexplained weight loss; vomiting); ***hypernatremia*** (dizziness; fast heartbeat; high blood pressure; irritability; muscle twitching; restlessness; seizures; swelling of feet or lower legs; weakness); ***hypertension*** (blurred vision; dizziness; nervousness; headache; pounding in the ears; slow or fast heartbeat); ***hypomagnesia*** (drowsiness; loss of appetite; mood or mental changes; muscle spasms [tetany] or twitching; seizures; nausea or vomiting; trembling; unusual tiredness or weakness); ***hypotension*** (blurred vision; confusion; dizziness, faintness, or lightheadedness when getting up from a lying or sitting position suddenly; sweating; unusual tiredness or weakness); ***infusion related reaction*** (back pain; chest tightness; chills; fever; flushing; headache; nausea and vomiting; weakness; trouble breathing); ***leukopenia*** (black, tarry stools; chest pain; chills; cough; fever; painful or difficult urination; shortness of breath; sore throat; sores, ulcers, or white spots on lips or in mouth; swollen glands; unusual bleeding or bruising; unusual tiredness or weakness); ***oral candidiasis*** (sore mouth or tongue; white patches in mouth and/or on tongue); ***phlebitis*** (bluish color; changes in skin color; pain, tenderness, and swelling of foot or leg); ***pruritis*** (itching skin); ***rash; sinus arrhythmia*** (fainting, dizziness, chest pain, shortness of breath); ***thrombocytopenia*** (black, tarry stools; bleeding gums; blood in urine or stools; pinpoint red spots on skin; unusual bleeding or bruising); ***thrombophlebitis, superficial*** (changes in skin color; pain, tenderness, and swelling of foot or leg); ***urticaria*** (hives or welts; itching; redness of skin; skin rash); ***ventricular extrasystoles*** (extra heartbeats)

Those indicating need for medical attention only if they continue or are bothersome

Incidence less frequent

Diarrhea; headache; nausea

Incidence rare

Back pain; constipation (difficulty having a bowel movement [stool]); ***cough; dizziness; dyspepsia aggravated*** (acid or sour stomach; belching; heartburn; indigestion; stomach discomfort, upset, or pain); ***eye pain; fecal incontinence*** (loss of bowel control); ***flushing*** (feeling of warmth; redness of the face, neck, arms and occasionally, upper chest); ***hot flushes; peripheral edema*** (bloating or swelling of face, arms, hands, lower legs, or feet; rapid weight gain; tingling of hands or feet; unusual weight gain or loss); ***pyrexia*** (fever); ***rigors*** (feeling unusually cold; shivering); ***sweating increased; upper abdominal pain*** (stomach pain); ***vision blurred; visual disturbance*** (blurred or loss of vision; disturbed color perception; night blindness; double vision; tunnel vision; halos around lights; overbright appearance of lights); ***vomiting***

Overdose

For more information on the management of overdose or unintentional ingestion, **contact a poison control center** (see *Poison Control Center Listing*).

Clinical effects of overdose

During clinical trials, a 400-mg anidulafungin dose was inadvertently administered as a loading dose. No adverse events were reported.

In a study of 10 healthy subjects, anidulafungin was generally well tolerated when administered at a loading dose of 260 mg and a maintenance dose of 130 mg per day. Three of the ten subjects experienced transient, asymptomatic transaminase elevations ($\leq$3 x ULN).

Treatment of overdose

Anidulafungin is not dialyzable.

Supportive care—

Treatment should be symptomatic and supportive.

Patients in whom intentional overdose is confirmed or suspected should be referred for psychiatric consultation.

Patient Consultation

As an aid to patient consultation, refer to *Advice for the Patient, Anidulafungin (Systemic)*.

In providing consultation, consider emphasizing the following selected information (» = major clinical significance):

Before using this medication

» Conditions affecting use, especially:

Hypersensitivity to anidulafungin or any component of the product or to other echinocandins

Pregnancy—Risk/benefit considerations in administering to a pregnant woman

Breast-feeding—Risk/benefit considerations in administering to a nursing woman

Use in children—Safety and efficacy not established

Proper use of this medication

» Proper dosing

Proper storage

Precautions while using this medication

» Importance of adhering to the doctor's course of treatment

Side/adverse effects

Signs of potential side effects, especially hypokalemia, neutropenia, angioneurotic edema, atrial fibrillation, bundle branch block (right), candidiasis, cholestasis, clostridial infection, coagulopathy, convulsions, deep vein thrombosis, electrocardiogram (ECG) changes, erythema, fungemia, hepatic necrosis, hypercalcemia, hyperglycemia, hypernatremia, hypertension, hypomagnesia, hypotension, infusion related reaction, leukopenia, oral candidiasis, phlebitis, pruritis, rash, sinus arrhythmia, thrombocytopenia, thrombophlebitis (superficial), urticaria, or ventricular extrasystoles.

General Dosing Information

Anidulafungin is NOT for direct intravenous injection.

The rate of infusion should not exceed 1.1 mg per minute.

Specimens for fungal culture and other relevant laboratory studies (including histopathology) should be obtained prior to therapy to isolate and identify causative organism(s). Therapy may be instituted prior to these lab results becoming available. However, once these results become available, antifungal therapy should be adjusted accordingly.

Parenteral Dosage Forms

ANIDULAFUNGIN FOR INJECTION

Usual adult dose

Candidemia (treatment) or

Candidiasis, intra-abdominal abscesses (treatment) or

Candidiasis, peritonitis (treatment)—

Intravenous infusion, Initial single 200 mg loading dose on day 1, followed by 100 mg daily maintenance dose, thereafter. Duration of treatment should be based on the patient's clinical response. In general, antifungal therapy should continue for at least 14 days after the last positive culture.

Candidiasis, esophageal (treatment)—

Intravenous infusion, Initial single 100 mg loading dose on day 1, followed by 50 mg daily maintenance dose, thereafter. Patients should be treated for a minimum of 14 days and for at least 7 days following resolution of symptoms. Duration of treatment should be based on the patient's clinical response. Because of risk of relapse of esophageal candidiasis in HIV patients, suppressive antifungal therapy may be considered after a course of treatment.

Note: No dosage adjustments are required for patients with renal or hepatic impairment, patients using concomitant medications or those in other special populations.

Usual pediatric dose
Safety and efficacy have not been established.

Usual geriatric dose
See *Usual adult dose.*

Strength(s) usually available
U.S.—

50 mg (Rx) [*Eraxis* (single-use; 50 mg fructose; 250 mg mannitol; 125 mg polysorbate 80; 5.6 mg tartaric acid; sodium hydroxide and/or hydrochloric acid for pH adjustment)].

Packaging and storage
Store unreconstituted vials and companion diluent vials at 25 °C (77 °F); excursions permitted to 15 to 30 °C (59 and 86 °F). Do not freeze.
Store reconstituted vials for injection at 25 °C (77 °F); excursions permitted to 15 to 30 °C (59 and 86 °F). Do not freeze. The reconstituted vials must be further diluted and administered within 24 hours.
Store diluted anidulafungin for injection at 25 °C (77 °F); excursions permitted to 15 to 30 °C (59 and 86 °F). Do not freeze.

Preparation of dosage form
The reconstitution of anidulafungin for injection is a two step process in which the lyophilized product is reconstituted with the companion diluent (20% [w/w] Dehydrated Alcohol in Water for Injection) and subsequently diluted with only 5% Dextrose Injection, USP or 0.9% Sodium Chloride Injection, USP (normal saline) as follows:

Reconstitution
- Aseptically reconstitute each 50 mg vial with 15 mL of the companion diluent (20% dehydrated alcohol in water for injection) to provide a concentration of 3.33 mg per mL.
- The reconstituted solution must be further diluted and administered within 24 hours.

Dilution
- Aseptically transfer the contents of the reconstituted vial(s) into an IV bag (or bottle) containing either 5% dextrose injection or 0.9% sodium chloride injection.
- The following table provides the number of vials and volumes required for each dose:

Dose	Number of 50 mg vials	Total reconstituted volume	Diluent volume required	Total infusion volume
50 mg	1	15 mL	85 mL	100 mL
100 mg	2	30 mL	170 mL	200 mL
200 mg	4	60 mL	340 mL	400 mL

Stability
Anidulafungin vials that have been reconstituted with 20% dehydrated alcohol must be further diluted and administered within 24 hours.

Incompatibilities
The compatibility of reconstituted anidulafungin with intravenous substances, additives, or medications other than 5% Dextrose Injection, USP or 0.9% Sodium Chloride Injection, USP (normal saline) has not been established.

Auxiliary labeling
- For single dose only. Discard unused drug

Caution
Parenteral drug should be inspected visually for particulate matter and discoloration prior to administration. If particulate matter or discoloration are identified, discard the solution.

Developed: 03/17/2006

ANILERIDINE—See *Opioid (Narcotic) Analgesics (Systemic)*

ANISINDIONE—See *Anticoagulants (Systemic)*

ANISOTROPINE—See *Anticholinergics/Antispasmodics (Systemic)*

ANISTREPLASE—See *Thrombolytic Agents (Systemic)*

ANTIANDROGENS, NONSTEROIDAL Systemic

This monograph includes information on the following: 1) Bicalutamide; 2) Flutamide; 3) Nilutamide.
VA CLASSIFICATION (Primary): AN900
Commonly used brand name(s): *Anandron*[3]; *Casodex*[1]; *Euflex*[2]; *Eulexin*[2]; *Nilandron*[3].

Note: For a listing of dosage forms and brand names by country availability, see *Dosage Forms* section(s).

Category
Antineoplastic.

Indications
Note: Bracketed information in the *Indications* section refers to uses that are not included in U.S. product labeling.

All of the nonsteroidal antiandrogens have similar pharmacologic actions; however, clinical uses among specific agents may vary because of availability of specific testing, differences in side effects, and/or availability of clinical-use data.

Accepted
Carcinoma, prostatic (treatment)—Nonsteroidal antiandrogens are indicated, in conjunction with testosterone-lowering measures, such as administration of a luteinizing hormone-releasing hormone (LHRH) analog (e.g., goserelin or leuprolide) or surgical castration (bilateral orchiectomy), for the treatment of prostatic carcinoma. Specifically:

Bicalutamide is indicated, in combination with an LHRH analog or [bilateral orchiectomy], for the treatment of locally advanced (stage B_2 or C) or metastatic (stage D_2) prostatic carcinoma.

Flutamide is indicated, in combination with an LHRH analog or [bilateral orchiectomy], for the treatment of locally advanced (stage B_2 or C) or metastatic (stage D_2) prostatic carcinoma.

Nilutamide is indicated, in conjunction with bilateral orchiectomy [or an LHRH analog][1] (Evidence rating: IIID), for the treatment of metastatic (stage D_2) prostatic carcinoma.

Acceptance not established
Flutamide is being studied, alone and in combination with other medications with antiandrogenic activity, for the treatment of hirsutism. Flutamide seems to be effective for treating idiopathic hirsutism (Evidence rating: III) as well as hirsutism due to polycystic ovary syndrome (PCOS) (Evidence rating: III), and data from a limited number of patients indicate that flutamide also relieves associated skin conditions (i.e., acne and seborrhea) (Evidence rating: III). However, its place in the treatment of hirsutism has not been established because of concerns about safety; severe hepatotoxicity has occurred during treatment. At least three comparative studies have found other antiandrogenic medications to be equally effective, and other studies have shown that reversal of flutamide's beneficial effects begins within a few months after treatment is discontinued. Until the benefits and risks of treatment have been better defined, especially with long-term or repeated use, flutamide should be considered only for severe cases unresponsive to other therapy and used in the lowest effective dosage. Also, flutamide must be used in conjunction with adequate contraception and should not be used during breast-feeding because of the potential risks (feminization of a male fetus and adverse developmental or toxic effects in nursing infants).

Unaccepted
Use of flutamide for benign prostatic hyperplasia (BPH) is not recommended because of limited efficacy and the risk of adverse effects, including severe, potentially fatal, hepatotoxicity.
Flutamide has been studied, and found ineffective, for treatment of hepatocellular carcinoma (Evidence rating: IA) or ovarian carcinoma (Evidence rating: IIID).

[1]Not included in Canadian product labeling.

Pharmacology/Pharmacokinetics

Physicochemical characteristics
Molecular weight—
Bicalutamide: 430.38.
Flutamide: 276.22.
Nilutamide: 317.23.

pKa—Bicalutamide: Approximately 12.

Other characteristics—

Bicalutamide is a racemate. The *R*-enantiomer is responsible for almost all of the medication's activity. The *S*-enantiomer is virtually inactive.

Mechanism of action/Effect

Nonsteroidal antiandrogens bind to cytosol androgen receptors and competitively inhibit the uptake and/or binding of androgens in target tissues, thereby interfering with the actions of androgens at the cellular level. Prostatic carcinoma is androgen-sensitive; ablation of endogenous androgen activity inhibits tumor growth and causes tumor regression. The antiandrogenic effect of these medications complements medical or surgical treatments (luteinizing hormone-releasing hormone [LHRH] analog therapy or bilateral orchiectomy) that result in inhibition or cessation of testicular (but not adrenal) androgen production.

When administered in conjunction with an LHRH analog, nonsteroidal antiandrogens inhibit the temporary surge in plasma testosterone concentration and the resultant "flare" reaction that may occur, prior to the sustained decrease in testosterone production, when monotherapy with an LHRH analog is initiated.

Other actions/effects

When administered alone, nonsteroidal antiandrogens inhibit the negative feedback response to testosterone by the hypothalamus. In patients who have not undergone surgical castration, this effect results in increased serum concentrations of testosterone and, consequently, of estrogen. Concurrent administration of an LHRH analog inhibits the stimulant effect of the nonsteroidal antiandrogen (but not the suppressant effect of the LHRH analog) on the serum testosterone concentration.

Nilutamide inhibits hepatic cytochrome P450 enzymes.

Bicalutamide has been shown to induce hepatic enzymes in animal studies, but enzyme induction has not been detected in humans receiving up to 150 mg per day (three times the recommended daily dose).

Absorption

Bicalutamide—Extensive; the rate and extent of absorption are not affected by concurrent administration with food.

Flutamide—Rapid and complete.

Nilutamide—Rapid and complete; not affected by concurrent administration with food.

Protein binding

Bicalutamide—Very high (96%).

Flutamide—Very high (94 to 96% for flutamide; 92 to 94% for the active alpha-hydroxylated metabolite hydroxyflutamide at steady-state).

Nilutamide—Moderate (84%), to plasma proteins; low, to erythrocytes. Binding studies confirm linear pharmacokinetics.

Biotransformation

Bicalutamide—Hepatic; extensive. Metabolism is stereospecific. The active *R*-enantiomer is metabolized primarily by oxidation to an inactive metabolite, which, in turn, undergoes glucuronidation. The inactive *S*-enantiomer is metabolized primarily by glucuronidation. The *S*-enantiomer is cleared more rapidly than the *R*-enantiomer.

Flutamide—Hepatic; rapid and extensive. At least six metabolites have been identified. The major metabolite found in plasma is a biologically active alpha-hydroxy derivative, hydroxyflutamide. Another metabolite is 4-nitro-3-fluoro-methylaniline, which may cause aniline toxicity (e.g., cholestatic jaundice, hemolytic anemia, methemoglobinemia) in susceptible individuals.

Nilutamide—Hepatic; extensive. Five metabolites have been identified. *In vitro*, one of the metabolites showed 25 to 50% of the activity of the parent compound; the activity of the D-isomer of this metabolite was equal to or greater than that of the L-isomer.

Half-life

Elimination—

Bicalutamide: 5.8 days to 1 week (for the active *R*-enantiomer). Values are significantly prolonged in patients with severe hepatic function impairment, but not in patients with mild to moderate hepatic disease.

Flutamide: The half-life of the active metabolite hydroxyflutamide is approximately 6 hours. Values are prolonged in geriatric patients to approximately 8 hours following administration of a single dose and approximately 9.6 hours at steady-state, and are slightly prolonged in patients with chronic renal function impairment (creatinine clearance < 29 mL/min). In geriatric patients, the half-life of the parent compound, flutamide, is approximately 7.8 hours at steady-state.

Nilutamide: Mean, 39 to 59.1 hours (most values between 41 and 49 hours) after a single dose of 100 to 300 mg. Although the pharmacokinetics of nilutamide's metabolites have not been investigated fully, the half-life of at least one metabolite is known to be longer than that of the parent compound (59 to 126 hours).

Time to peak concentration

Bicalutamide—For the active *R*-enantiomer: Mean, 31.3 hours.

Flutamide—In geriatric volunteers: 1.9 and 2.7 hours for flutamide and hydroxyflutamide, respectively, after administration of a single dose; 1.3 and 1.9 hours for flutamide and hydroxyflutamide, respectively, at steady-state.

Peak serum concentration

Bicalutamide—For the active *R*-enantiomer: 0.768 mcg per mL (mcg/mL).

Flutamide—In geriatric volunteers, following a single dose: 25 nanograms per mL (nanograms/mL) for flutamide and 894 nanograms/mL for hydroxyflutamide. Maximum concentrations and the area under the flutamide plasma concentration-time curve (AUC) are not altered in patients with chronic renal function impairment, but the effect of hepatic function impairment is unknown.

Time to steady-state concentration

Flutamide—In geriatric patients receiving 250 mg three times a day, steady-state concentrations of flutamide and hydroxyflutamide are approached after the fourth dose.

Nilutamide—In patients receiving 150 mg twice a day, steady-state conditions are reached in 2 to 4 weeks.

Steady-state plasma concentration

Bicalutamide—Mean, approximately 9 mcg/mL (approximately 99% of which is the active *R*-enantiomer) following administration of 50 mg per day.

Flutamide—For the active metabolite hydroxyflutamide: Mean minimum and maximum concentrations are approximately 673 and 1629 nanograms/mL, respectively.

Nilutamide—Steady-state values for the area under the nilutamide plasma concentration-time curve for 12 hours after dosing (AUC_{0-12}) are approximately 110% higher than single-dose values, which, together with *in vitro* metabolism data, suggests metabolic enzyme inhibition.

Elimination

Bicalutamide—Renal and fecal (34% and 43% of a dose, respectively, within 9 days), as glucuronide derivatives. The rate of elimination is not significantly affected by renal function impairment.

Flutamide—Primarily renal; only 4.2% of a dose is eliminated in the feces within 72 hours.

Nilutamide—Renal, 62% of a dose (< 2% as unchanged nilutamide) within 120 hours after administration of a single dose. Small quantities (1.4 to 7% of a dose) are eliminated in the feces.

In dialysis—

Because all of the nonsteroidal antiandrogens are extensively bound to plasma proteins, significant quantities are not likely to be removed from the circulation by dialysis.

Precautions to Consider

Carcinogenicity/Tumorigenicity

Bicalutamide—Oral carcinogenicity studies in male and female rats and mice given 5, 15, or 75 mg per kg of body weight (mg/kg) per day for 2 years showed target organ effects attributable to bicalutamide's antiandrogenic activity. Testicular benign interstitial (Leydig) cell tumors occurred in male rats at all dose levels, which provided concentrations equivalent to or higher than two thirds of the human therapeutic concentration (the concentration achieved by administering 50 mg per day to a 70-kg patient). Uterine adenocarcinomas occurred in female rats given 75 mg/kg per day (which produced concentrations equivalent to 1.5 times the human therapeutic concentration). Also, a small increase in the incidence of hepatocellular carcinoma occurred in male mice given 75 mg/kg per day (which produced concentrations equivalent to four times the human therapeutic concentration), and an increased incidence of benign thyroid follicular cell adenomas occurred in rats given 5 mg/kg per day (which produced concentrations equivalent to two thirds of the human therapeutic concentration) or more. These neoplastic changes were progressions of nonneoplastic changes related to hepatic enzyme induction (which has been observed in animal toxicity studies, but not in humans receiving up to 150 mg per day). There were no tumorigenic effects suggestive of genotoxic carcinogenesis. Leydig cell hyperplasia has not been observed in humans receiving bicalutamide.

Flutamide—Although a causal relationship has not been established, malignant breast tumors have been reported in two men receiving flutamide therapy. In animal carcinogenicity studies, testicular interstitial cell adenomas and mammary adenomas, adenocarcinomas, and fibroadenomas developed in male rats given daily oral doses of 10, 30, and 50 mg/kg per day (which produced maximum concentrations equivalent to one, two to three, and four times, respectively, the concentration produced in humans by therapeutic doses).

Nilutamide—In an 18-month study, benign Leydig cell tumors occurred in 35% of male rats given 45 mg/kg per day (which produced area under the nilutamide plasma concentration-time curve [AUC] values equivalent to one or two times the values achieved in humans receiving therapeutic doses). This effect is attributable to elevated luteinizing hormone (LH) concentrations resulting from loss of feedback inhibition, which does not occur in castrated men receiving the medication. Nilutamide had no other effect on the incidence, size, or time of onset of spontaneous tumor development in animals.

Mutagenicity

Bicalutamide—No evidence of genotoxic activity was found in several *in vitro* and *in vivo* tests (including yeast gene conversion, Ames, *E. coli*, CHO/HGPRT, human lymphocyte cytogenetic, mouse micronucleus, and rat bone marrow cytogenetic tests).

Flutamide—No evidence of mutagenicity was found in the Ames *Salmonella* /microsome mutagenesis assay or in the dominant lethal test in rats.

Nilutamide—No evidence of mutagenicity was found in a variety of *in vitro* and *in vivo* tests, including the Ames test, mouse micronucleus test, and two chromosomal aberration studies.

Pregnancy/Reproduction

Note: The effect on fertility and reproduction of other treatments used concurrently with the nonsteroidal antiandrogen, i.e., luteinizing hormone-releasing hormone (LHRH) analog therapy or bilateral orchiectomy, must be considered.

Fertility—*Bicalutamide*: May inhibit spermatogenesis. Long-term effects on male fertility have not been studied in humans. In male rats given 250 mg/kg per day (which produced concentrations equivalent to two times the human therapeutic concentration), the precoital interval and time to successful mating were increased in the first pairing, but no effects on fertility after successful mating were seen. Observed effects were reversed by 7 weeks after the end of an 11-week treatment period. There were no effects on female rats given 10, 50, or 250 mg/kg per day (which produced concentrations equivalent to two thirds, one, and two times the human therapeutic concentration, respectively).

Flutamide: Flutamide monotherapy caused decreased sperm counts in a 6-week study in humans. In animal studies, flutamide had no effect on the estrous cycle and caused no interference with the mating behavior of female and male rats given 25 or 75 mg/kg per day prior to mating. Although males treated with 150 mg/kg per day (30 times the minimum effective antiandrogenic dose) failed to mate, mating behavior returned to normal after the medication was discontinued. Conception rates were decreased at all dosage levels. Also, suppression of spermatogenesis occurred in rats given approximately 3, 8, or 17 times the human dose for 52 weeks and in dogs given 1.4, 2.3, and 3.7 times the human dose for 78 weeks.

Nilutamide: Studies in male and female rats showed no effect on reproductive function with doses as high as 45 mg/kg per day (which produced AUC values one to two times those achieved in humans receiving therapeutic doses).

Pregnancy—There are currently no indications in U.S. or Canadian product labeling for use of any of the nonsteroidal antiandrogens in female patients. However, if a nonsteroidal antiandrogen is given to a female of child-bearing potential (e.g., administration of flutamide for hirsutism), it must be used in conjunction with adequate contraception because of the risk of causing feminization of a male fetus.

Bicalutamide—

Animal studies revealed no adverse effects on the female offspring of rats given 10, 50, or 250 mg/kg per day (which produced concentrations equivalent to two thirds, one, and two times the human therapeutic concentration, respectively). However, reduced anogenital distance and feminization leading to hypospadias and impotence occurred in the male offspring. No other teratogenic effects were found in rabbits receiving up to 200 mg/kg per day or in rats receiving up to 250 mg/kg per day (which produced concentrations equivalent to approximately one third and two times the human therapeutic concentration, respectively).

FDA Pregnancy Category X.

Flutamide—

Studies in rats given 30, 100, or 200 mg/kg per day (3, 9, and 19 times the human dose, respectively) found a decrease in 24-hour survival of offspring. In addition, at the two higher doses, feminization of male offspring and a slight increase in minor variations in the development of the sternebrae and vertebrae occurred. Studies in rabbits at a dose of 15 mg/kg per day (1.4 times the human dose) found a decreased survival rate in offspring.

FDA Pregnancy Category D.

Nilutamide—

Studies in humans have not been done. Studies in rats given up to 45 mg/kg per day (which produced AUC values one to two times the values produced in humans by therapeutic doses) showed no lethal, teratogenic, or growth-suppressive effects.

FDA Pregnancy Category C.

Breast-feeding

There are currently no indications in U.S. or Canadian product labeling for use of any of the nonsteroidal antiandrogens in female patients. It is not known whether any of these medications is distributed into breast milk. However, it is recommended that breast-feeding be avoided by any woman who might be receiving a nonsteroidal antiandrogen (e.g., flutamide therapy for hirsutism) because of the potential risks to the infant (adverse developmental and toxic effects).

Pediatrics

Studies with the nonsteroidal antiandrogens have not been done in pediatric patients. Safety and efficacy have not been established. Possible adverse effects on the sexual development of young males must be considered.

Geriatrics

Appropriate studies performed to date have not demonstrated geriatrics-specific problems that would limit the use of any of the nonsteroidal antiandrogens in geriatric patients.

Bicalutamide: Pharmacokinetic studies in patients receiving up to 150 mg of bicalutamide per day have shown that steady-state concentrations of total bicalutamide and its active enantiomer are not significantly different in geriatric patients than in younger adults.

Flutamide: Although the elimination half-life of flutamide and its active metabolite hydroxyflutamide are increased in the elderly, no adjustment of dosage on the basis of age is needed.

Pharmacogenetics

Nilutamide: A significantly higher incidence of interstitial pneumonitis (17% versus 2% in the overall patient population) and a higher frequency of increased transaminase values occurred in a small study performed in Japan. There were no significant differences in the pharmacokinetics of nilutamide in these patients, compared with Caucasian patients, that might account for this finding. Caution in the treatment of Asian patients is recommended.

Drug interactions and/or related problems

The following drug interactions and/or related problems have been selected on the basis of their potential clinical significance (possible mechanism in parentheses where appropriate)—not necessarily inclusive (» = major clinical significance):

Note: Combinations containing any of the following medications, depending on the amount present, may also interact with this medication.

For bicalutamide, flutamide, and nilutamide only

» Anticoagulants, coumarin-derivative

(caution and increased monitoring of prothrombin time [PT] or International Normalized Ratio [INR] are recommended if treatment with bicalutamide, flutamide, or nilutamide is initiated in a patient stabilized on a coumarin-derivative anticoagulant. Bicalutamide may displace coumarin anticoagulants, such as warfarin, from their protein-binding sites. Increases in PT have occurred after flutamide therapy was started in patients receiving long-term warfarin treatment. Also, inhibition of hepatic cytochrome P450 [CYP 450] isoenzymes by nilutamide, which may interfere with anticoagulant metabolism, may result in increased anticoagulant activity during concurrent use. Adjustment of anticoagulant dosage may be necessary)

For nilutamide only (in addition to the interaction listed above)

» Alcohol

(alcohol intolerance, characterized by symptoms of facial flushing, malaise, and hypotension, has been reported in approximately 5% of patients treated with nilutamide; patients who experience such reactions should be advised to avoid further alcohol consumption during nilutamide therapy)

» Medications with narrow therapeutic margins that are metabolized by hepatic CYP 450 isoenzymes, such as:
Phenytoin
Theophylline
(inhibition of hepatic CYP 450 isoenzymes by nilutamide may result in delayed elimination, increased elimination half-life, and increased risk of toxicity of medications that are metabolized by these enzymes; dosage reduction, especially of medications with narrow therapeutic margins, may be necessary during concurrent use)

Laboratory value alterations

The following have been selected on the basis of their potential clinical significance (possible effect in parentheses where appropriate)—not necessarily inclusive (» = major clinical significance).

With physiology/laboratory test values
» Alanine aminotransferase (ALT [SGPT]), serum, and
» Aspartate aminotransferase (AST [SGOT]), serum
(may be increased; rarely, may indicate hepatitis or jaundice)

Alkaline phosphatase, serum
(may be increased)

Bilirubin, serum or
Blood urea nitrogen (BUN) or
Creatinine, serum
(concentrations may be increased)

Estradiol, plasma or
Testosterone, plasma
(concentrations may be increased if a nonsteroidal antiandrogen is administered without an LHRH analog to a patient who has not undergone bilateral orchiectomy)

Glucose, blood
(concentrations may be increased, possibly to hyperglycemic levels, with bicalutamide or nilutamide)

Hemoglobin values or
White blood cell count
(may be decreased)

Medical considerations/Contraindications

The medical considerations/contraindications included have been selected on the basis of their potential clinical significance (reasons given in parentheses where appropriate)—not necessarily inclusive (» = major clinical significance).

Except under special circumstances, this medication should not be used when the following medical problems exist:

For nilutamide only
» Hepatic function impairment
(use of nilutamide not recommended because the medication has been reported to cause substantial hepatotoxicity, which may have particularly serious consequences in patients with pre-existing hepatic function impairment)
» Respiratory impairment, severe
(use of nilutamide is not recommended because the medication has caused interstitial pneumonitis in clinical trials; the frequency of occurrence was substantially higher in Japanese patients than in the overall patient population)

For flutamide only
» Hepatic function impairment
(use of flutamide is not recommended because the medication has been reported to cause substantial hepatotoxicity, which may have particularly serious consequences in patients with pre-existing hepatic function impairment)

Risk-benefit should be considered when the following medical problems exist:

For all nonsteroidal antiandrogens
» Hypersensitivity to the nonsteroidal antiandrogen considered for use, history of

For bicalutamide only (in addition to the medical problem listed above for all nonsteroidal antiandrogens)
» Hepatic function impairment, moderate to severe
(metabolism of bicalutamide may be delayed, resulting in prolonged elimination half-life and increased risk of toxicity)

For flutamide only (in addition to the medical problem listed above for all nonsteroidal antiandrogens)
» Conditions predisposing to aniline toxicity, such as:
» Glucose-6-phosphate dehydrogenase (G6PD) deficiency or
» Hemoglobin M disease or
» Tobacco smoking
(increased risk of toxicity associated with aniline exposure, such as methemoglobinemia, hemolytic anemia, and cholestatic jaundice [one metabolite of flutamide is a methylaniline derivative])

Patient monitoring

The following may be especially important in patient monitoring (other tests may be warranted in some patients, depending on condition; » = major clinical significance):

For all nonsteroidal antiandrogens
» Hepatic function tests
(determinations recommended prior to nilutamide or flutamide therapy because nilutamide or flutamide should not be used in patients with pre-existing hepatic function abnormalities)

(recommended prior to starting treatment with bicalutamide, monthly for the first 4 months and periodically during therapy with flutamide and bicalutamide, recommended every 3 months during treatment with nilutamide., because of the possibility of transaminase elevations and hepatotoxicity during treatment. Treatment should be discontinued immediately if there is laboratory evidence of hepatic injury [e.g., transaminase values higher than two or three times the upper limit of normal] in the absence of hepatic metastases, or if clinical signs and symptoms of hepatotoxicity [e.g., jaundice, pruritus, dark urine, fatigue, persistent anorexia, abdominal pain or upper right quadrant tenderness, unexplained "flu-like" symptoms, unexplained gastrointestinal symptoms, and nausea or vomiting] occur. Hepatotoxicity is usually reversible after discontinuation of therapy, but hepatotoxicity-related deaths have been reported, rarely, in patients receiving flutamide or nilutamide)

Prostate specific antigen (PSA), serum
(may be helpful in assessing response to treatment; the patient should be re-evaluated for disease progression if values rise during therapy)

For flutamide only (in addition to the tests listed above for all nonsteroidal antiandrogens)
Methemoglobin concentrations
(monitoring recommended in patients susceptible to aniline toxicity)

For nilutamide only (in addition to the tests listed above for all nonsteroidal antiandrogens)
Chest radiograph
(recommended prior to initiation of therapy and at the first sign of new or increasing dyspnea or other indication of possible pneumonitis; if there are findings suggestive of interstitial pneumonitis, nilutamide should be discontinued)

Pulmonary function studies, including diffusing capacity of the lung for carbon monoxide (DL_{CO})
(recommended if a chest radiograph performed to evaluate onset or worsening of dyspnea is normal; if DL_{CO} is significantly decreased and/or a restrictive pattern is observed, nilutamide should be discontinued)

Side/Adverse Effects

Note: The side/adverse effects listed below for bicalutamide and for flutamide were reported during concurrent use of the antiandrogen with a luteinizing hormone-releasing hormone (LHRH) analog. For flutamide, the reported effects occurred in long-term studies in patients with Stage D_2 prostatic carcinoma. In a relatively short-term study in which the medications were given in conjunction with radiation therapy for Stage B_2 or Stage C disease, the reported adverse effects (i.e., diarrhea, cystitis, rectal bleeding, proctitis, hematuria) were not significantly different or more frequent than with radiation therapy alone. The side/adverse effects listed below for nilutamide were reported in two separate studies in which the medication was used in conjunction with bilateral orchiectomy or with an LHRH analog. Many adverse effects occurred exclusively or significantly more often with the nilutamide plus LHRH analog regimen; only the higher frequency of occurrence is reported below. Placebo-controlled clinical trials with flutamide or nilutamide showed that many of the adverse effects, especially those related to low androgen activity (i.e., hot flashes, impotence, loss of libido, gynecomastia) may occur with an LHRH analog or bilateral orchiectomy alone.

In addition to the side/adverse effects listed below, urogenital effects including hematuria, urinary tract infections, and dysuria or urinary retention have been reported during treatment with these medications. Such symptoms commonly occur in men with prostatic tumors and may improve, as a result of tumor regression, during successful antiandrogen therapy.

The following side/adverse effects have been selected on the basis of their potential clinical significance (possible signs and symptoms in parentheses where appropriate)—not necessarily inclusive:*	Legend: I=Bicalutamide II=Flutamide III=Nilutamide		
	I	II	III
Medical attention needed			
Anemia† (unusual tiredness or weakness)—usually asymptomatic	L	L	L
Dyspnea (shortness of breath or difficult breathing)	L	U	L
Edema (swelling of face, fingers, feet, or lower legs)	L	L	M
Fever	L	U	L
Gastrointestinal or rectal bleeding (bloody or black, tarry stools)	L	U	R
Hepatitis or jaundice, including cholestatic jaundice‡ (dark urine; "flu-like" symptoms; gastrointestinal upset; loss of appetite; nausea or vomiting; pain or tenderness in upper right area of abdomen; unusual tiredness; yellow eyes or skin)	R	R	R
Hypertension—usually asymptomatic	L	R	L
Infection, including pulmonary or upper respiratory tract infection§ (cough or hoarseness; fever; runny nose; shortness of breath, troubled breathing, tightness in chest, or wheezing; sneezing; sore throat)	M	U	M
Itching of skin	L	R	L
Leukopenia (cough or hoarseness; fever or chills; lower back or side pain; painful or difficult urination)—usually asymptomatic	U	L	U
Mental depression	L	R	L
Methemoglobinemia (bluish-colored lips, fingernails, or palms of hands; dizziness, severe, or fainting; feeling of severe pressure in head; shortness of breath; weak and fast heartbeat)—usually asymptomatic	U	U#	U
Neuromuscular symptoms or neuropathy (numbness, tingling, pain, or muscle weakness in hands, arms, feet, or legs)	L	L	U
Pulmonary disorder** (chest pain; cough; shortness of breath or troubled breathing)	L	R	L
Skin rash	L	L††	L
Thrombocytopenia (black, tarry stools; blood in urine or stools; pinpoint red spots on skin; unusual bleeding or bruising)	U	R	U
Medical attention needed only if continuing or bothersome			
Alcohol intolerance (dizziness or lightheadedness; feeling faint; flushing of face; general feeling of illness)	U	U	L
Bloated feeling, gas, or indigestion	L	U#	L
Chills	L	U	U
Confusion	L	R	U
Constipation	M	U#	M
Decrease in or loss of appetite	L	L	M
Diarrhea‡‡	M	M	L
Dizziness	L	R	M
Drowsiness	L	R	R
Dryness of mouth	L	U	L
Flu-like syndrome (fever; headache; muscle or joint pain; tiredness)	L	U	L
Gynecomastia (pain or tenderness in breasts; swelling of breasts)	L	L	M
Headache	L	R	M
Impaired adaptation of eyes to dark (delay in seeing clearly when going from light to dark areas)—effect may last from seconds to minutes	U	U	M
Impotence or decrease in sexual desire	L	M	M
Nausea	M	M	M
Nervousness	L	R	L
Trouble in sleeping	L	R	M
Visual disturbances, including chromatopsia (change in color vision) ***and impaired adaptation or increased sensitivity to light***	U	U	L
Vomiting	L	L	L
Weakness	M	R	M
Medical attention not needed			
Hot flashes (feeling of warmth; flushing; sudden sweating)	M	M	M
Urine discoloration (amber or yellow-green urine coloration)—attributed to presence of flutamide or its metabolites	U	U#	U

*Differences in frequency of occurrence may reflect either lack of clinical-use data or actual pharmacologic distinctions among agents. M = more frequent (10% or higher); L = less frequent (> 1% to < 10%); R = rare (1% or lower); U = unknown.

†Hypochromic anemia and iron deficiency anemia have been reported with bicalutamide. In addition to unspecified anemia(s), there have been postmarketing reports of hemolytic anemia and macrocytic anemia with flutamide, and, although a causal relationship has not been established, of aplastic anemia with nilutamide.

‡Hepatotoxicity, especially when detected by hepatic function test abnormalities before symptoms occur, usually resolves when therapy is withdrawn. However, progression to hepatic encephalopathy and hepatic necrosis has been reported with flutamide, and fatalities have been reported with flutamide and nilutamide.

§Bronchitis, pneumonia, sepsis, and other unspecified infections have been reported during bicalutamide therapy, and upper respiratory tract infections and pneumonia have been reported during nilutamide therapy.

#Has been reported, generally postmarketing; actual frequency of occurrence unknown.

**Interstitial pneumonitis has been reported with nilutamide, unspecified pulmonary symptoms have been reported with flutamide, and other unspecified lung disorder(s) have been reported with bicalutamide and nilutamide. Signs of nilutamide-associated interstitial pneumonitis, including interstitial or alveolo-interstitial changes in the chest radiograph, usually occur within the first 3 months of nilutamide therapy and are usually reversible upon discontinuation of therapy.

††There also have been reports of photosensitivity-associated erythema, ulceration, bullous eruptions, and epidermal necrolysis during flutamide therapy.

‡‡In a clinical trial comparing the efficacy and toxicity of bicalutamide and flutamide, each in conjunction with an LHRH agonist, severe diarrhea resulting in discontinuation of therapy occurred substantially more often with flutamide than with bicalutamide.

Overdose

For more information on the management of overdose or unintentional ingestion, **contact a Poison Control Center** (see *Poison Control Center Listing*).

Bicalutamide: A single dose that would result in potentially life-threatening symptoms has not been established. Doses as high as 200 mg per day (four times the usual daily dose) were well tolerated in clinical trials. Also, bicalutamide showed low acute toxicity in animal studies. It has been estimated that doses in excess of 2000 mg per kg of body weight (mg/kg) would be required to produce significant mortality in mice and rats.

Flutamide: A single dose that would result in potentially life-threatening symptoms has not been established. Doses as high as 1500 mg per day (two times the usual daily dose), given for up to 36 weeks in clinical trials, caused gynecomastia, breast tenderness, and increased hepatic enzyme concentrations, all of which have been reported with usual adult doses. Signs of acute overdosage in animal studies included hypoactivity, piloerection, ataxia, lacrimation, anorexia, emesis, methemoglobinemia, tranquilization, and slow respiration. In chronic toxicity studies in beagle dogs, flutamide caused cardiac lesions, including chronic myxomatous degeneration, intra-atrial fibrosis, myocardial acidophilic degeneration, vasculitis, and perivasculitis, in 2 of 10 animals given 25 mg/kg per day for 78 weeks and in 3 of 16 animals given 40 mg/kg per day for 2 to 4 years. These doses produced hydroxyflutamide concentrations 1- to 12-fold higher than those present in humans receiving therapeutic doses.

Nilutamide: There has been one report of massive overdosage, in which a 79-year-old man ingested 13 grams of nilutamide (43 times the maximum recommended dose). Although gastric lavage was performed and active charcoal was given orally, plasma nilutamide concentrations peaked at six times the usual therapeutic range, and concentrations 3.5 times the usual therapeutic range were present 72 hours after ingestion. Symptoms were limited to moderate vomiting and diarrhea during the first 12 hours, and the patient recovered. In repeated-dose tolerance studies, doses of 600 and 900 mg per day (up to three to six times the usual daily dose), administered to nine and four patients, respectively, caused nausea, vomiting, malaise, headache, and dizziness, but no major toxicity, although hepatic enzyme concentrations were increased transiently in one patient. In chronic toxicity studies in beagle dogs, fatalities related to hepatotoxicity occurred in 100% of the animals given 60 mg/kg per day for 1 month; 70% and 20% of the animals given 30 or 20 mg/kg per day, respectively, for 6 months; and 50%, 33%, and 8% of the animals given 12, 6, or 3 mg/kg per day, respectively, for 1 year. Hepatocellular swelling and vacuolization were found in the affected animals. However, hepatotoxicity was not consistently associated with elevated hepatic enzyme concentrations. In chronic toxicity studies in rats, administration of 45 mg/kg per day of nilutamide for 18 months caused lung pathology (granulomatous inflammation and chronic alveolitis).

Treatment of overdose

There is no specific antidote to overdose with these agents. Vomiting may be induced if the patient is alert and does not vomit spontaneously. Dialysis is not likely to remove significant quantities of these medications from the body because of extensive protein binding. General supportive care, including frequent monitoring of vital signs and close observation of the patient, is recommended, with treatment of observed symptoms as warranted.

Patients in whom intentional overdose is confirmed or suspected should be referred for psychiatric consultation.

Patient Consultation

As an aid to patient consultation, refer to *Advice for the Patient, Antiandrogens, Nonsteroidal (Systemic)*.

In providing consultation, consider emphasizing the following selected information (» = major clinical significance):

Before using this medication

» Conditions affecting use, especially:
- Sensitivity to the nonsteroidal antiandrogen considered for use
- Fertility—Nonsteroidal antiandrogens, and other treatments used concurrently for prostatic carcinoma, may decrease sperm count and impair fertility
- Pregnancy—Adequate contraception essential if being given to a woman of child-bearing potential because of the risk of causing feminization of a male fetus
- Breast-feeding—Not recommended because of the potential for causing adverse developmental and toxic effects in the infant
- Pharmacogenetics—For nilutamide only: Caution in Asian patients because of increased risk of interstitial pneumonitis
- Other medications, especially coumarin-derivative anticoagulants (for flutamide and nilutamide), and, for nilutamide only, alcohol and medications with narrow therapeutic margins metabolized by hepatic cytochrome P450 isoenzymes (e.g., phenytoin, theophylline)
- Other medical problems, especially hepatic function impairment and, for flutamide only, conditions predisposing to aniline toxicity, such as glucose 6–phosphate dehydrogenase (G6PD) deficiency, hemoglobin M disease, and tobacco smoking, for nilutamide only, respiratory impairment

Proper use of this medication

» Importance of not using more or less medication than the amount prescribed

» Taking medication at the same time each day

Bicalutamide and nilutamide may be taken with or without food

» Importance of following physicians instructions for concurrent use of LHRH analog (if patient has not undergone bilateral orchiectomy)

» Importance of continuing medication despite side effects

Checking with physician if vomiting occurs shortly after dose is taken

» Proper dosing

Missed dose: Taking as soon as possible; not taking if not remembered until next day (bicalutamide or nilutamide) or almost time for next dose (flutamide); not doubling doses

» Proper storage

Precautions while using this medication

» Importance of regular visits to physician to monitor progress

» Checking with physician immediately if symptoms of hepatotoxicity occur

For nilutamide only:

» Checking with physician immediately if shortness of breath occurs or worsens

» Possible ocular effects, including delay in visual adaptation from light to dark (which may persist for several seconds to several minutes), delayed adaptation from dark to light, and increased sensitivity of eyes to light; using caution when driving, especially after entering or emerging from tunnels; tinted glasses may alleviate these effects

» Avoiding further alcohol ingestion if symptoms of alcohol intolerance (facial flushing, malaise, hypotension) occur

Side/adverse effects

Signs of potential side effects, especially anemia, dyspnea or other symptoms of a pulmonary disorder, edema, fever or other sign of infection (bicalutamide, nilutamide), gastrointestinal or rectal bleeding (bicalutamide, nilutamide), hepatitis or jaundice, hypertension, itching of skin, leukopenia (flutamide), mental depression, methemoglobinemia (flutamide), neuromuscular symptoms or neuropathy (bicalutamide, flutamide), skin rash, and thrombocytopenia (flutamide)

General Dosing Information

Patients taking a nonsteroidal antiandrogen should be under supervision of a physician experienced in cancer chemotherapy.

BICALUTAMIDE

Summary of Differences

Indications:
- Indicated, in conjunction with medical or surgical castration, for treatment of advanced or metastatic prostatic carcinoma.

Pharmacology/pharmacokinetics:
- Physicochemical characteristics—A racemate; only the *R*-enantiomer is active.
- Other actions/effects—Induction of hepatic enzymes has been demonstrated in animal studies, but not in humans receiving up to 150 mg per day (three times the recommended daily dose).
- Protein binding—Very high (96%).
- Biotransformation—Stereospecific; the inactive *S*-enantiomer is cleared more rapidly than the active *R*-enantiomer.
- Half-life (elimination)—5.8 days to 1 week for the active *R*-enantiomer.
- Time to peak concentration—31.3 hours for the active *R*-enantiomer.
- Peak serum concentration—0.768 mcg per mL for the active *R*-enantiomer.
- Steady-state plasma concentration (dose of 50 mg per day)—9 mcg per mL, approximately 99% of which is the active *R*-enantiomer.
- Elimination—Renal and fecal, as glucuronide derivatives. The rate of elimination is not significantly affected by renal function impairment.

Precautions to consider:
- Medical considerations/contraindications—Risk-benefit should be considered in patients with moderate to severe hepatic function impairment.
- Patient monitoring—Periodic assessment of hepatic function should be considered during long-term use.

Side/adverse effects:
- Hypochromic and iron deficiency anemia have been reported.
- Bronchitis, pneumonia, sepsis, other unspecified infections, and other unspecified lung disorders have been reported.

Additional Dosing Information

Treatment with bicalutamide should be initiated at the same time as treatment with a luteinizing hormone-releasing hormone (LHRH) analog or surgical castration.

Bicalutamide should be taken at the same time every day (usually in the morning or evening).

No dosage adjustment is needed in patients with renal function impairment or mild hepatic function impairment.

Bicalutamide may be taken with food or on an empty stomach.

Oral Dosage Forms

BICALUTAMIDE TABLETS

Usual adult dose

Carcinoma, prostatic—

Oral, 50 mg once a day, in the morning or evening. The medication is to be used concurrently with an LHRH analog or after surgical castration.

Usual pediatric dose

Safety, efficacy, and dosage have not been established.

Usual geriatric dose
See *Usual adult dose.*

Strength(s) usually available
U.S.—
50 mg (Rx) [*Casodex* (lactose)].
Canada—
50 mg (Rx) [*Casodex* (lactose)].

Packaging and storage
Store between 15 and 30 °C (59 and 86 °F).

FLUTAMIDE

Summary of Differences
Indications:
Indicated, in conjunction with medical or surgical castration, for treatment of advanced or metastatic prostatic carcinoma.
Pharmacology/pharmacokinetics:
Protein binding—Very high (94 to 96% for flutamide, 92 to 94% for the active metabolite).
Biotransformation—Major metabolite hydroxyflutamide is active antiandrogenic substance; another metabolite is an aniline derivative that may cause aniline toxicity.
Half-life (elimination)—For hydroxyflutamide, approximately 6 hours; may be prolonged in geriatric patients and in patients with chronic renal function impairment.
Time to peak concentration (in geriatric volunteers)—For hydroxyflutamide, 2.7 and 1.9 hours after administration of a single dose and at steady-state, respectively. For flutamide, 1.9 and 1.3 hours after administration of a single dose and at steady-state, respectively.
Peak serum concentration (geriatric volunteers, following a single dose)—25 and 894 nanograms per mL for flutamide and hydroxyflutamide, respectively; not affected by chronic renal function impairment.
Time to steady-state concentration (administration three times a day)—Steady-state conditions approached after the fourth dose.
Steady-state concentration (hydroxyflutamide)—Mean minimum and maximum concentrations are approximately 673 and 1629 nanograms per mL, respectively.
Elimination—Primarily renal; small quantities eliminated in the feces.
Precautions to consider:
Pregnancy—Decreased survival rates and minor variations in development of sternebrae and vertebrae demonstrated in animal studies. Flutamide had not been studied in pregnant women and there are no indications for use of flutamide in women.
Drug interactions and/or related problems—Increase in prothrombin time reported in patients receiving concurrent therapy with coumarin-derivative anticoagulant.
Medical considerations/contraindications—Caution also recommended in conditions predisposing to aniline toxicity.
Contraindicated in severe hepatic impairment.
Patient monitoring—Periodic assessment of hepatic function (all patients) and methemoglobin concentrations (patients at risk for aniline toxicity) recommended.
Side/adverse effects:
Hepatotoxicity progressing to hepatic encephalopathy, hepatic necrosis, and fatalities has been reported.
Hemolytic anemia, macrocytic anemia, leukopenia, methemoglobinemia, and thrombocytopenia have been reported.
Unspecified pulmonary symptoms and photosensitivity-associated erythema, ulcerations, bullous eruptions, and epidermal necrolysis have also been reported.
More likely than bicalutamide to cause severe diarrhea requiring discontinuation of treatment.
More likely than other antiandrogens to cause hot flashes, nausea, skin rash, and vomiting.

Additional Dosing Information
When flutamide is used for the treatment of Stage B_2 or Stage C carcinoma, treatment should begin simultaneously with, or 24 hours prior to, initiation of LHRH analog therapy. Treatment with both agents should commence 8 weeks prior to, and continue throughout, radiation therapy. When flutamide is used in conjunction with an LHRH analog for treatment of metastatic (Stage D_2) carcinoma, therapy should begin simultaneously with, or 24 hours prior to, initiation of LHRH analog therapy. Treatment should continue until disease progression is documented.

Oral Dosage Forms

FLUTAMIDE CAPSULES USP

Usual adult dose
Carcinoma, prostatic—
Oral, 250 mg every eight hours.

Usual pediatric dose
Dosage has not been established.

Usual geriatric dose
See *Usual adult dose.*

Strength(s) usually available
U.S.—
125 mg (Rx) [*Eulexin* (lactose)].
Canada—
Not commercially available.

Packaging and storage
Store below 40 °C (104 °F), preferably between 15 and 30 °C (59 and 86 °F). Store in a well-closed, light-resistant container.

FLUTAMIDE TABLETS

Usual adult dose
See *Flutamide Capsules USP.*

Usual pediatric dose
Dosage has not been established.

Usual geriatric dose
See *Flutamide Capsules USP.*

Strength(s) usually available
U.S.—
Not commercially available.
Canada—
250 mg (Rx) [*Euflex* (scored; lactose)].

Packaging and storage
Store below 40 °C (104 °F), preferably between 15 and 30 °C (59 and 86 °F), in a well-closed container, unless otherwise specified by the manufacturer.

NILUTAMIDE

Summary of Differences
Indications:
Indicated, in conjunction with surgical or medical castration, for treatment of metastatic prostatic carcinoma. Should be used only in patients with normal hepatic function.
Pharmacology/pharmacokinetics:
Other actions/effects—Inhibits hepatic cytochrome P450 (CYP 450) isoenzymes.
Protein binding—Moderate (84%), to plasma proteins; low, to erythrocytes.
Biotransformation—One metabolite has 25 to 50% of the antiandrogenic activity of the parent compound.
Half-life (elimination)—Mean, 39 to 59.1 hours (mostly between 41 and 49 hours).
Time to steady-state concentration (doses of 150 mg twice a day)—2 to 4 weeks.
Elimination—Primarily renal; small quantities eliminated in the feces.
Precautions to consider:
Pharmacogenetics—Caution in administration to Asian patients recommended; increased risk of interstitial pneumonitis has been demonstrated in Japanese patients.
Drug interactions and/or related problems—Caution also required with medications with narrow therapeutic margins that are metabolized by hepatic CYP 450 isoenzymes (e.g., coumarin-derivative anticoagulants, phenytoin, theophylline); also, has caused alcohol intolerance in some patients.
Medical considerations/contraindications—Use in patients with hepatic function impairment or severe respiratory impairment not recommended.
Patient monitoring—Hepatic function should be assessed prior to initiation of treatment and every 3 months during therapy.
Side/adverse effects:
Fatality associated with hepatotoxicity has been reported.
Pneumonia, upper respiratory tract infections, and interstitial pneumonitis and other unspecified lung disorders have been reported.
Visual disturbances, including impaired adaptation of eyes to dark or light, chromatopsia, and ocular photosensitivity have been reported.

Additional Dosing Information

For maximum benefit, it is recommended that nilutamide therapy be initiated on the same day as or the day after surgical castration.

Nilutamide may be taken with food or on an empty stomach.

At the first sign of dyspnea or worsening of pre-existing dyspnea, it is recommended that nilutamide be withheld and a chest radiograph obtained. If signs of interstitial pneumonitis are seen, it is recommended that nilutamide therapy be discontinued. If the chest radiograph is normal, pulmonary function tests including DL_{CO} (diffusing capacity of the lung for carbon monoxide) are recommended. A significant decrease in DL_{CO} and/or a restrictive pattern observed on pulmonary function testing is cause for discontinuing nilutamide therapy. If neither chest radiograph nor pulmonary function test findings confirm interstitial pneumonitis, nilutamide treatment may be reinstituted with close monitoring of pulmonary symptoms.

At the first sign or symptom of hepatotoxicity, nilutamide should be withheld and appropriate laboratory testing performed. If serum transaminases exceed three times the upper limit of normal, nilutamide therapy should be discontinued immediately.

Oral Dosage Forms

NILUTAMIDE TABLETS

Usual adult dose

Carcinoma, prostatic—
  Oral, 300 mg once a day for thirty days, then 150 mg once a day thereafter.
  Note: If the patient is unable to tolerate the 300-mg dose, the lower dose may be instituted earlier.

Usual pediatric dose

Safety and efficacy have not been established.

Usual geriatric dose

See *Usual adult dose.*

Strength(s) usually available

U.S.—
  50 mg (Rx) [*Nilandron* (lactose)].

Canada—
  50 mg (Rx) [*Anandron* (lactose)].

Packaging and storage

Store between 15 and 30 °C (59 and 86 °F), protected from light.

Auxiliary labeling

- Protect from light.

Selected Bibliography

Smith JA Jr, Janknegt RA, Abbou CC, et al. Effect of androgen deprivation therapy on local symptoms and tumour progression in men with metastatic carcinoma of the prostate. Eur Urol 1997; 31 Suppl 3: 25-9.

Schellhammer PF, Sharifi R, Block NL, et al. Clinical benefits of bicalutamide compared with flutamide in combined androgen blockade for patients with advanced prostatic carcinoma: final report of a double-blind, randomized, multicenter trial. Urology 1997; 50: 330-6.

Revised: 08/22/2001

ANTICHOLINERGICS/ ANTISPASMODICS Systemic

This monograph includes information on the following: 1) Anisotropine†; 2) Atropine; 3) Belladonna†; 4) Clidinium†; 5) Dicyclomine; 6) Glycopyrrolate; 7) Homatropine†; 8) Hyoscyamine; 9) Mepenzolate†; 10) Methantheline†; 11) Methscopolamine†; 12) Pirenzepine*; 13) Propantheline; 14) Scopolamine.

INN:
  Anisotropine—Octatropine
  Dicyclomine—Dicycloverine
  Glycopyrrolate—Glycopyrronium Bromide
  Methantheline—Methanthelinium
  Methscopolamine—Hyoscine Methobromide

VA CLASSIFICATION (Primary/Secondary):
  Anisotropine—AU305/GA801
  Atropine Oral—AU305/GA801; GU201; AD900
  Atropine Parenteral—AU305/GA801; CV300; GU201; AD900
  Belladonna—AU305/GA801
  Clidinium—AU305/GA801
  Dicyclomine—AU305/GA801
  Glycopyrrolate Oral—AU305/GA801; GA208
  Glycopyrrolate Parenteral—AU305/GA801; CV300; GA208; AD900
  Homatropine—AU305/GA801
  Hyoscyamine Oral—AU305/GA801; GU201
  Hyoscyamine Parenteral—AU305/GA801; GU201; CV300; AD900
  Mepenzolate—AU305/GA801
  Methantheline—AU305/GA801; GU201
  Methscopolamine—AU305/GA801
  Pirenzepine—AU305/GA801
  Propantheline—AU305
  Scopolamine Oral—AU305/GA801; CN550; GA609; GU201
  Scopolamine Parenteral—AU305/GA801; CV300; CN206; CN550; GA609
  Scopolamine Rectal—AU305
  Scopolamine Transdermal—CN550

Commonly used brand name(s): *A-Spas S/L*[8]; *Anaspaz*[8]; *Banthine*[10]; *Bentyl*[5]; *Bentylol*[5]; *Buscopan*[14]; *Cantil*[9]; *Cystospaz*[8]; *Cystospaz-M*[8]; *Donnamar*[8]; *ED-SPAZ*[8]; *Formulex*[5]; *Gastrosed*[8]; *Gastrozepin*[12]; *Homapin*[7]; *Levbid*[8]; *Levsin*[8]; *Levsin/SL*[8]; *Levsinex Timecaps*[8]; *Pro-Banthine*[13]; *Propanthel*[13]; *Quarzan*[4]; *Robinul*[6]; *Robinul Forte*[6]; *Spasmoban*[5]; *Symax SL*[8]; *Symax SR*[8]; *Transderm-Scop*[14]; *Transderm-V*[14].

Other commonly used names are: Dicycloverine [Dicyclomine] Glycopyrronium bromide [Glycopyrrolate] Hyoscine hydrobromide [Scopolamine] Hyoscine methobromide [Methscopolamine] Methanthelinium [Methantheline] Octatropine [Anisotropine]

Note: For a listing of dosage forms and brand names by country availability, see *Dosage Forms* section(s).

*Not commercially available in U.S.
†Not commercially available in Canada.

Category

Note: All of these medications have anticholinergic and, to some extent, antispasmodic actions; however, the labeled indications for specific agents may vary because of minor differences in potency and/or receptor selectivity. **In general, there is a lack of specific testing and/or clinical-use data to support the indication of anticholinergics/antispasmodics in most conditions.**

Anticholinergic—Anisotropine; Atropine; Belladonna; Clidinium; Dicyclomine; Glycopyrrolate; Homatropine; Hyoscyamine; Mepenzolate; Methantheline; Methscopolamine; Pirenzepine; Propantheline; Scopolamine.

Antispasmodic, gastrointestinal—Dicyclomine; Scopolamine Butylbromide.

Antidysmenorrheal—Belladonna; Scopolamine Butylbromide.

Antiarrhythmic—Atropine (parenteral only); Glycopyrrolate (parenteral only); Hyoscyamine (parenteral only); Scopolamine (parenteral only).

Antidote (to cholinesterase inhibitors)—Atropine; Hyoscyamine (parenteral only).

Antidote (to muscarine)—Atropine; Hyoscyamine (parenteral only).

Antidote (to organophosphate pesticides)—Atropine.

Antispasmodic, urinary—Atropine; Scopolamine.

Cholinergic adjunct (curariform block)—Atropine (parenteral only); Glycopyrrolate (parenteral only); Hyoscyamine (parenteral only).

Anesthesia adjunct—Scopolamine (parenteral only).

Antiemetic—Scopolamine.

Antivertigo agent—Belladonna; Scopolamine.

Antidiarrheal—Glycopyrrolate

Indications

Note: Bracketed information in the *Indications* section refers to uses that are not included in U.S. product labeling.

Accepted

Ulcer, peptic (treatment adjunct)—All anticholinergics included in this monograph, except dicyclomine and scopolamine hydrobromide, are FDA approved in conjunction with antacids or histamine H_2-receptor antagonists in the treatment of peptic ulcer, to reduce further gastric acid secretion and delay gastric emptying. However, the use of most anticholinergics as treatment adjunct in peptic ulcer has been replaced by the use of more effective agents. Results with anticholinergics usually are inconsistent and transient and require high doses, which result in significant side effects. Atropine, belladonna, clidinium, hyoscyamine, pirenzepine, and propantheline taken orally may be used rarely. Intravenous use of hyoscyamine may be indicated for prompt relief of pain in the treatment of both the moderately severe and the severe peptic ulcer. Anisotropine, homatropine, mepenzolate, methantheline, and methscopolamine are generally no longer used for this indication.

Bowel syndrome, irritable (treatment)—Atropine, belladonna, [clidinium], dicyclomine, [glycopyrrolate], hyoscyamine, [propantheline], and [scopolamine] are indicated in the treatment of irritable bowel syndrome, mainly in patients in whom other therapy, such as sedation and/or change in diet, has failed. However, results usually are inconsistent and transient and require high doses, which result in significant side effects. Anisotropine, mepenzolate, methantheline, methscopolamine, and pirenzepine are generally no longer used for this indication.

Urologic disorders, symptoms of (treatment)—Oral hyoscyamine is indicated to control hypermotility in cystitis. However, results of anticholinergic treatment usually are inconsistent and transient and require high doses, which result in significant side effects. Atropine and scopolamine butylbromide are generally no longer used for this indication.

Urinary incontinence (treatment)—[Propantheline][1] is used in the treatment of uninhibited hypertonic neurogenic bladder to increase bladder capacity by reducing amplitude and frequency of bladder contractions. Atropine and methantheline are generally no longer used for this indication.

Hypersecretory conditions, gastric, in anesthesia (prophylaxis)—Parenteral glycopyrrolate is indicated as preanesthetic medication to reduce gastric acid secretion.

Salivation and respiratory tract secretions, excessive, in anesthesia (prophylaxis)—Oral and parenteral atropine and the parenteral forms of glycopyrrolate and scopolamine[1] are indicated as antisialagogue preanesthetic medications to prevent or reduce salivation and respiratory tract secretions. Parenteral hyoscyamine is no longer used for these indications.

Arrhythmias, succinylcholine-induced (prophylaxis) or
Arrhythmias, surgical procedure-induced (prophylaxis)—The parenteral form of atropine is indicated as adjunct to anesthesia to prevent reflex bradycardia, sinus arrest, and hypotension induced by succinylcholine during intubation of the trachea or produced by certain surgical manipulations. Parenteral scopolamine is generally no longer used for these indications.

Arrhythmias, cardiac (treatment) or
Bradycardia, sinus (treatment)—Parenteral atropine is indicated to reduce severe sinus bradycardia and syncope associated with hyperactive carotid sinus reflex; and to lessen the degree of atrioventricular heart block in Type I atrioventricular (AV) conduction deficits. It is also used to treat ventricular asystole. Parenteral atropine also is indicated as an antidote for sinus bradycardia resulting from the improper administration of a choline ester medication. Parenteral hyoscyamine is generally no longer used for these indications.

Arrhythmias, in anesthesia (treatment) or
Arrhythmias, in surgery (treatment)—The parenteral form of atropine is indicated to restore cardiac rate and arterial pressure when increased vagal activity has reduced pulse rate and cardiac action. Parenteral glycopyrrolate is indicated to block cardiac vagal inhibitory reflexes during induction of anesthesia and intubation. Parenteral glycopyrrolate is also indicated intraoperatively to counteract drug-induced or vagal traction reflexes with the associated arrhythmias. Parenteral hyoscyamine and parenteral scopolamine are generally no longer used for these indications.

Toxicity, cholinesterase inhibitor (prophylaxis)—The parenteral forms of atropine and glycopyrrolate are indicated for administration prior to or concurrently with neostigmine or pyridostigmine during reversal of nondepolarizing neuromuscular blockade to protect against the muscarinic effects of these drugs, such as bradycardia and excessive secretions. Parenteral hyoscyamine is generally no longer used for this indication.

Toxicity, cholinesterase inhibitor (treatment)
Toxicity, muscarine (treatment) or
Toxicity, organophosphate pesticide (treatment)—Oral and parenteral atropine are indicated in the treatment of poisoning from cholinesterase inhibitors such as neostigmine, pilocarpine, physostigmine, and methacholine, and in the treatment of the rapid type of mushroom (muscarine) poisoning. Atropine is also indicated in the treatment of poisoning caused by pesticides that are organophosphate cholinesterase inhibitors, chemical warfare, and "nerve" gases. Parenteral hyoscyamine is generally no longer used for these indications.

Anesthesia, general, adjunct—Parenteral administration of scopolamine[1], in combination with morphine or meperidine, is indicated in preanesthesia to reduce excitement and produce amnesia. Scopolamine may also be used for opioid-induced respiratory depression. Parenteral scopolamine[1] is also indicated in conjunction with analgesics in cardiopulmonary bypass patients who cannot be deeply anesthetized because of the risk of severe hypotension or circulatory collapse.

Motion sickness (prophylaxis and treatment)—Transdermal scopolamine is indicated for prophylaxis of nausea and vomiting associated with motion sickness.

Nausea and vomiting, post operative (prophylaxis)[1]—Transdermal scopolamine is indicated for the prevention of nausea and vomiting associated with recovery from anesthesia and surgery, post operative nausea and vomiting (PONV).

Pneumonitis, aspiration (prophylaxis)—Parenteral glycopyrrolate may provide some protection against aspiration of gastric contents during anesthesia.

[Asthma (treatment adjunct)][1]—Inhaled atropine is indicated for the treatment of asthma in adult and pediatric patients, as part of a combination regimen. Atropine is to be used for its acute bronchodilatory effects, when ipratropium is not a feasible alternative.

[Salivation, excessive, postsurgical (prophylaxis)][1] or
[Salivation, excessive, medical condition-related (prophylaxis)][1]—Transdermal scopolamine is used for short-term control of drooling in postsurgical patients and in patients with goiter or other medical conditions in whom excessive salivation becomes a social problem.

[Salivation, excessive, in dental procedures (prophylaxis)][1]—The oral forms of atropine, glycopyrrolate, methantheline, and propantheline are used to control excessive salivation that interferes with dental procedures. Belladonna is generally no longer used for this indication.

Anticholinergics/antispasmodics listed below are FDA (U.S.) and HPB (Canada) approved for the following indications; however, they generally have been replaced by more effective agents—

- Biliary tract disorders (treatment adjunct)—Atropine, hyoscyamine, and scopolamine butylbromide.
- Radiography, gastrointestinal, adjunct—Parenteral atropine and parenteral hyoscyamine.
- Dysmenorrhea (treatment)—Belladonna and scopolamine butylbromide.
- Enuresis, nocturnal (treatment)—Belladonna and scopolamine butylbromide.
- Rhinitis, allergic, severe (treatment)—Oral hyoscyamine.

Anticholinergics/antispasmodics listed below have been used for the following indications; however, they generally have been replaced by more effective agents—

- [Diarrhea (treatment)][1]—Glycopyrrolate.
- [Parkinsonism (treatment)][1]—Oral atropine, belladonna, parenteral hyoscyamine, oral hyoscyamine and scopolamine combination, and oral scopolamine.

Unaccepted

Hyoscyamine elixir and oral solution have been used in the treatment of infant colic. However, there is no conclusive evidence of effectiveness for this use.

---

[1]Not included in Canadian product labeling.

Pharmacology/Pharmacokinetics

Physicochemical characteristics

Chemical Group—
Tertiary amines: Atropine, belladonna, hyoscyamine, and scopolamine.
Quaternary ammonium compounds: Anisotropine, clidinium, glycopyrrolate, homatropine, mepenzolate, methantheline, methscopolamine, and propantheline.

Molecular weight—
Anisotropine methylbromide: 362.35.
Atropine: 289.37.
Clidinium bromide: 432.36.
Dicyclomine hydrochloride: 345.95.
Glycopyrrolate: 398.34.
Homatropine methylbromide: 370.29.
Hyoscyamine: 289.37.
Hyoscyamine sulfate: 712.85.
Mepenzolate bromide: 420.35.
Methantheline bromide: 420.35.
Methscopolamine bromide: 398.30.
Pirenzepine: 351.41.
Propantheline bromide: 448.40.
Scopolamine hydrobromide: 438.31.

pKa—
Atropine: 9.8.
Dicyclomine: 9.0.
Scopolamine: 7.55–7.81.

Mechanism of action/Effect

Anticholinergic—The naturally occurring belladonna alkaloids, semisynthetic derivatives, quaternary ammonium compounds, and, to a lesser extent, the synthetic tertiary amines inhibit the muscarinic actions of acetylcholine on structures innervated by postganglionic cholinergic nerves as well as on smooth muscles that respond to acetylcholine but lack cholinergic innervation. These postganglionic receptor sites are present in the autonomic effector cells of the smooth muscle, cardiac muscle, sinoatrial and atrioventricular nodes, and exocrine glands. Depending on the dose, anticholinergics may reduce the motility and secretory activity of the gastrointestinal system, and the tone of the ureter and urinary bladder and may have a slight relaxant action on the bile ducts and gallbladder. In general, the smaller doses of anticholinergics inhibit salivary and bronchial secretions, sweating, and accommodation; cause dilatation of the pupil; and increase the heart rate. Larger doses are required to decrease motility of the gastrointestinal and urinary tracts and to inhibit gastric acid secretion.

Antispasmodic, gastrointestinal—Unproven. A local and direct action on smooth muscle, to reduce tone and motility of the gastrointestinal tract, has been suggested to explain the apparent gastrointestinal antispasmodic effect of the synthetic tertiary amine compounds.

Antidysmenorrheal—Effectiveness in relieving dysmenorrhea is due to spasmolytic action.

Antiarrhythmic—Inhibition of muscarinic actions of acetylcholine at postganglionic receptor sites present in the autonomic effector cells of the cardiac muscle, and sinoatrial and atrioventricular nodes.

Antidote (to cholinesterase inhibitors; to muscarine; to organophosphate pesticides)—Atropine and hyoscyamine antagonize the actions of cholinesterase inhibitors at muscarinic receptor sites, including increased tracheobronchial and salivary secretion, bronchoconstriction, autonomic ganglionic stimulation, and, to a moderate extent, central actions.

Cholinergic adjunct (curariform block)—Atropine and hyoscyamine antagonize the actions, such as vagal and secretory enhancing effects, of cholinesterase inhibitors used in the treatment of nondepolarizing neuromuscular blockade.

Anesthesia adjunct—Scopolamine depresses the cerebral cortex; in large doses and in conjunction with analgesics, produces loss of memory.

Antiemetic—Belladonna and scopolamine act primarily by reducing the excitability of the labyrinthine receptors and by depressing conduction in the vestibular cerebellar pathway.

Antivertigo—The exact mechanism by which belladonna and scopolamine exert their antimotion sickness and antivertigo effects is unknown; however, they probably act either on the cortex or more peripherally on the maculae of the utricle and saccule.

Antidiarrheal—Glycopyrrolate may reduce the activity of the gastrocolic reflex and the excessive peristaltic activity of both the small and large bowels.

Other actions/effects

Natural tertiary amines—

Atropine: Stimulates or depresses the central nervous system (CNS), depending on the dose; and has a more prolonged and potent action than the other belladonna alkaloids on the heart, intestine, and bronchial muscle.

Belladonna alkaloids: In parkinsonism, selectively depress certain central motor mechanisms in the CNS, controlling muscle tone and movement.

Hyoscyamine: Has actions similar to those of atropine, but is more potent in both its central and peripheral effects.

Scopolamine: Has peripheral action similar to that of atropine but, in contrast to atropine, is depressant to the CNS at therapeutic doses; it does not stimulate the medullary centers and therefore does not increase respiration or elevate blood pressure. Scopolamine has a more potent action than atropine on the sphincter muscle of the iris and the ciliary muscle of the lens, and on the secretory glands such as salivary, bronchial, and sweat glands.

Quaternary ammonium compounds, semisynthetic and synthetic—

In contrast to atropine and scopolamine, effects of these medications on the CNS are negligible. These medications are also less likely to affect the pupil or ciliary muscle of the eye. Ganglionic blockade is attributed to some increased effects of the high dosage range, and toxic doses produce neuromuscular blockade.

Synthetic tertiary amines—

These medications produce less prominent CNS effects than do the natural tertiary amines.

Absorption

Tertiary amines—Rapidly absorbed from gastrointestinal tract; also enter the circulation through the mucosal surfaces of the body.

Quaternary ammonium compounds—Gastrointestinal absorption is poor and irregular. Total absorption after an oral dose is about 10 to 25%.

Distribution

Exact distribution of anticholinergics has not been fully determined. However, tertiary amines appear to be distributed throughout the entire body and readily cross the blood-brain barrier, while quaternary ammonium compounds exhibit minimal passage across the blood-brain barrier and into the eye.

Atropine, belladonna, and hyoscyamine are distributed into breast milk.

Protein binding

Atropine—Moderate.
Hyoscyamine—Moderate.
Scopolamine hydrobromide—Low.

Biotransformation

Most anticholinergics—Hepatic, by enzymatic hydrolysis.

Half-life

Elimination—

Atropine: 2.5 hours.
Dicyclomine hydrochloride: 1.8 hours (initial phase) and 9 to 10 hours (secondary phase).
Glycopyrrolate: 1.7 hours (range 0.6–4.6 hours).
Hyoscyamine: 3.5 hours.
Pirenzepine—10 to 12 hours.
Propantheline bromide—1.6 (mean) hours.
Scopolamine—8 hours.

Time to peak effect

Glycopyrrolate—Intramuscular: 30 to 45 minutes.

Drug	Onset of Action	Duration of Action	Elimination (% excreted unchanged)
Anisotropine methylbromide			*
Atropine		Oral: 4–6 hr Parenteral: Brief	Renal (30–50)
Belladonna	1–2 hr	4 hr	Renal (30–50 of atropine and 1 of scopolamine)
Clidinium bromide	1 hr	Up to 3 hr	*
Dicyclomine hydrochloride			*
Glycopyrrolate	IM or SC: 15–30 min IV: 1 min	Antisialagogue: Up to 7 hr Vagal blocking effect: 2–3 hr	Renal
Homatropine			*
Hyoscyamine sulfate	Oral: 20–30 min Parenteral: 2–3 min	4–6 hr	Renal (majority)
Mepenzolate bromide			Renal (3–22)
Methantheline bromide			*
Methscopolamine bromide	1 hr	6–8 hr	*
Pirenzepine hydrochloride			Renal/hepatic (80–90)
Propantheline bromide		6 hr	Renal (<6)
Scopolamine		Transdermal: Up to 72 hr	Renal
Scopolamine hydrobromide	Antisialagogue—Oral: 30–60 min Parenteral: 30 min	Oral: 4–6 hr Parenteral: 4 hr	Renal (1 of oral dose) (3.4 of SC dose)

*Assumed to be renal/fecal.

Precautions to Consider

Cross-sensitivity and/or related problems

For all anticholinergics—Patients sensitive to one belladonna alkaloid or derivative may be sensitive to the other belladonna alkaloids or derivatives also.

Pregnancy/Reproduction

Pregnancy—

For anistropine methylbromide—

Problems in humans have not been documented.

FDA pregnancy category not currently included in product labeling.

For atropine—

Atropine crosses the placenta. Well-controlled studies in humans have not been done. Intravenous administration of atropine during pregnancy or near term may produce tachycardia in the fetus.

Studies in mice have not shown that atropine given in doses of 50 mg per kg of body weight (mg/kg) has adverse effects on the fetus.

FDA Pregnancy Category C.

For belladonna—

Belladonna crosses the placenta. Studies with belladonna have not been done in either animals or humans.

FDA Pregnancy Category C.

For clidinium—

Adequate and well-controlled studies in humans have not been done.

Reproduction studies in rats have not shown that clidinium has adverse effects on the fetus.

FDA pregnancy category not currently included in product labeling.

For dicyclomine—

Dicyclomine has been associated in several isolated cases with human malformations; however, in retrospective studies there has been no evidence of dicyclomine having any untoward effect on the embryo.

FDA pregnancy category not currently included in product labeling.

For glycopyrrolate—

Controlled studies in humans have not been done. However, single-dose studies in humans found that very small amounts of glycopyrrolate passed the placental barrier.

Studies in rats and rabbits have not shown that glycopyrrolate causes teratogenic effects. However, studies in rats have shown that rates of conception and of survival at weaning decreased in a dose-related manner with glycopyrrolate. Studies in dogs with high doses of glycopyrrolate suggest that this may be caused by a decrease in seminal secretion. Because animal reproduction studies are not always predictive of human response, this drug should be used during pregnancy only if clearly needed.

Nonteratogenic effects—Glycopyrrolate in normal doses (0.004 mg per kg of body weight) does not appear to affect fetal heart rate or fetal heart rate variability to a significant degree. Concentrations in umbilical venous and arterial blood and in amniotic fluid are low after intramuscular administration to parturients. In rat reproduction studies, dietary administration of glycopyrrolate resulted in diminished rates of pup survival in a dose-related manner.

FDA Pregnancy Category B.

For hyoscyamine—

Hyoscyamine crosses the placenta. Studies with hyoscyamine have not been done in either animals or humans. Intravenous administration of hyoscyamine during pregnancy, especially near term, may produce tachycardia in the fetus.

FDA Pregnancy Category C.

For mepenzolate—

Adequate and well-controlled studies in humans have not been done.

Reproduction studies in rats and rabbits have not shown that mepenzolate has adverse effects on the fetus.

FDA pregnancy category not currently included in product labeling.

For propantheline—

Studies have not been done in either animals or humans.

FDA Pregnancy Category C.

For scopolamine—

Scopolamine crosses the placenta. Studies with scopolamine have not been done in either animals or humans.

FDA Pregnancy Category C.

Labor—For scopolamine: Parenteral administration of scopolamine before the onset of labor may cause CNS depression in the neonate and may contribute to neonatal hemorrhage due to reduction in vitamin K-dependent clotting factors in the neonate.

Breast-feeding

For all anticholinergics—Anticholinergics may inhibit lactation.

For atropine, belladonna, and hyoscyamine—These drugs are distributed into breast milk. Although amounts have not been quantified, the chronic use of these medications should be avoided during nursing since infants are usually very sensitive to the effects of anticholinergics.

For dicyclomine—Although a causal relationship has not been established, the use of dicyclomine in nursing mothers is not recommended, since respiratory distress has been reported in infants less than 3 months of age who ingested dicyclomine directly (not through breast milk).

For glycopyrrolate—It is not known whether this drug is distributed into human breast milk. Because many drugs are distributed in human milk, caution should be exercised when administering glycopyrrolate to a nursing woman.

For quaternary ammonium compounds—It is unlikely that these drugs are excreted in breast milk since they are incompletely absorbed from the gastrointestinal tract and have poor lipid solubility.

Pediatrics

For all anticholinergics—

Infants and young children are especially susceptible to the toxic effects of anticholinergics.

Close supervision is recommended for infants and children with spastic paralysis or brain damage since an increased response to anticholinergics has been reported in these patients and dosage adjustments are often required.

When anticholinergics are given to children where the environmental temperature is high, there is risk of a rapid increase in body temperature because of these medications' suppression of sweat gland activity.

A paradoxical reaction characterized by hyperexcitability may occur in children taking large doses of anticholinergics.

For dicyclomine—

Respiratory symptoms, such as difficulty in breathing, shortness of breath, respiratory collapse and apnea; as well as seizures, syncope, asphyxia, pulse rate fluctuations, muscular hypotonia, and coma have been reported in some infants, 3 months old and under, with the use of dicyclomine syrup. These side effects occurred within minutes of ingestion and lasted 20 to 30 minutes. They are believed to have been caused by local irritation and/or aspiration rather than by a direct pharmacologic action.

For glycopyrrolate—

Safety and efficacy in pediatric patients below the age of 16 years have not been established. Dysrhythmias associated with the use of glycopyrrolate intravenously as a premedicant or during anesthesia have been observed in pediatric patients.

Peptic ulcer treatment—Safety and efficacy in pediatric patients have not been established.

Robinul Injection contains benzyl alcohol and should not be administered to neonates (less than 1 month of age) because the preservative has been associated with a fatal "gasping syndrome" in these patients.

Geriatrics

Geriatric patients may respond to usual doses of anticholinergics with excitement, agitation, drowsiness, or confusion. In general dose selection should be cautious, usually starting at the low end of the dosing range, reflecting the greater frequency of decreased hepatic, renal, or cardiac function, and of concomitant disease or other therapy.

Geriatric patients are especially susceptible to the anticholinergic side effects, such as constipation, dryness of mouth, and urinary retention (especially in males). If these side effects occur and continue or are severe, medication should probably be discontinued.

Caution is also recommended when anticholinergics are given to geriatric patients, because of the danger of precipitating undiagnosed glaucoma.

Memory may become severely impaired in geriatric patients, especially those who already have memory problems, with the continued use of anticholinergics since these drugs block the actions of acetylcholine, which is responsible for many functions of the brain, including memory functions.

Dental

Prolonged use of anticholinergics may decrease or inhibit salivary flow, thus contributing to the development of caries, periodontal disease, oral candidiasis, and discomfort.

Drug interactions and/or related problems

The following drug interactions and/or related problems have been selected on the basis of their potential clinical significance (possible mechanism in parentheses where appropriate)—not necessarily inclusive (» = major clinical significance):

Note: Combinations containing any of the following medications, depending on the amount present, may also interact with this medication.

Only specific interactions between anticholinergics and other oral medications have been identified in this monograph. However, because of decreased gastrointestinal motility and delayed gastric emptying, absorption of other oral medications may be decreased during concurrent use with anticholinergics.

For all anticholinergics

Alkalizers, urinary, such as:
Antacids, calcium- and/or magnesium-containing
Carbonic anhydrase inhibitors
Citrates
Sodium bicarbonate
(urinary excretion of anticholinergics may be delayed by alkalinization of the urine, thus potentiating the anticholinergics" therapeutic and/or side effects)

» Antacids or
» Antidiarrheals, adsorbent
(simultaneous use of these medications may reduce absorption of anticholinergics, resulting in decreased therapeutic effectiveness; doses of these medications should be spaced 2 or 3 hours apart from doses of anticholinergics)

» Anticholinergics or other medications with anticholinergic activity, other (see *Appendix II*)
(concurrent use with anticholinergics may intensify anticholinergic effects; patients should be advised to report occurrence of gastrointestinal problems promptly since paralytic ileus may occur with concurrent therapy)

Antimyasthenics
(concurrent use with anticholinergics may further reduce intestinal motility; therefore, caution is recommended; although atropine may be used to reduce or prevent the muscarinic effects of antimyasthenics, routine concurrent use is not recommended since the muscarinic effects may be the first signs of antimyasthenic overdose, and masking such effects with atropine may prevent early recognition of cholinergic crisis)

» Cyclopropane
(concurrent intravenous administration of anticholinergics with cyclopropane anesthesia may result in ventricular arrhythmias; however, if the anticholinergic used is glycopyrrolate, the risk is reduced if glycopyrrolate is given in increments of 100 mcg [0.1 mg] or less)

Haloperidol
(antipsychotic effectiveness of haloperidol may be decreased in schizophrenic patients)

» Ketoconazole
(anticholinergics may increase gastrointestinal pH, possibly resulting in a marked reduction in ketoconazole absorption during concurrent use with anticholinergics; patients should be advised to take these medications at least 2 hours after ketoconazole)

Metoclopramide
(concurrent use with anticholinergics may antagonize metoclopramide's effects on gastrointestinal motility)

Opioid (narcotic) analgesics
(concurrent use with anticholinergics may result in increased risk of severe constipation, which may lead to paralytic ileus, and/or urinary retention)

» Potassium chloride, especially wax-matrix preparations
(concurrent use with anticholinergics may increase severity of potassium chloride–induced gastrointestinal lesions)

For scopolamine (in addition to interactions listed above)

» CNS depression-producing medications, other (see *Appendix II*)
(concurrent use may potentiate the effects of either these medications or scopolamine, resulting in additive sedation)

Lorazepam, parenteral
(concurrent use of scopolamine and parenteral lorazepam is reported to have no added beneficial effect and their combined effect may increase the incidence of sedation, hallucination, and irrational behavior)

Laboratory value alterations

The following have been selected on the basis of their potential clinical significance (possible effect in parentheses where appropriate)—not necessarily inclusive (» = major clinical significance).

With diagnostic test results

For all anticholinergics

» Gastric acid secretion test
(concurrent use of anticholinergics may antagonize the effect of pentagastrin and histamine in the evaluation of gastric acid secretory function; administration of anticholinergics is not recommended during the 24 hours preceding the test)

Radionuclide gastric emptying studies
(use of anticholinergics may result in delayed gastric emptying)

For atropine (in addition to those listed for all anticholinergics)

» Phenolsulfonphthalein (PSP) excretion test
(atropine utilizes the same tubular mechanism of excretion as PSP resulting in decreased urinary excretion of PSP; concurrent use of atropine is not recommended in patients receiving PSP excretion test)

For scopolamine (in addition to those listed for all anticholinergics)

Neuroradiological tests
(residual cycloplegia and mydriasis following use of transdermal disk of scopolamine may affect results of neuroradiological tests for intracranial neoplasm, subdural hematoma, or aneurysm)

With physiology/laboratory test values

For glycopyrrolate

Serum uric acid
(may be decreased in patients with hyperuricemia or gout)

Medical considerations/Contraindications

The medical considerations/contraindications included have been selected on the basis of their potential clinical significance (reasons given in parentheses where appropriate)—not necessarily inclusive (» = major clinical significance).

Except under special circumstances, this medication should not be used when the following medical problem exists:

» Hypersensitivity to any belladonna alkaloids or derivatives or any component of the product

Note: For glycopyrrolate—The following concurrent conditions may be contraindicated in the management of peptic ulcer patients because of the longer duration of therapy: glaucoma, intestinal atony of the elderly or debilitate patient, myasthenia gravis, obstructive disease of the gastrointestinal tract (i.e., achalasia or pyloroduodenal stenosis), obstructive uropathy (i.e., bladder neck obstruction due to prostatic hypertrophy), paralytic ileus, toxic megacolon complicating ulcerative colitis, severe ulcerative colitis, or unstable cardiovascular status in acute hemorrhage. Glycopyrrolate should be used with caution, if at all, in patients with glaucoma.

Risk-benefit should be considered when the following medical problems exist:

Brain damage, in children
(CNS effects may be exacerbated)

» Cardiac disease, especially cardiac arrhythmias, congestive heart failure, coronary artery disease, and mitral stenosis
(increase in heart rate may be undesirable)

Down's syndrome
(abnormal increase in pupillary dilation and acceleration of heart rate may occur)

» Esophagitis, reflux
(decrease in esophageal and gastric motility and relaxation of lower esophageal sphincter may promote gastric retention by delaying gastric emptying and may increase gastroesophageal reflux through an incompetent sphincter)

Fever
(may be increased through suppression of sweat gland activity)

» Gastrointestinal tract obstructive disease as in achalasia and pyloroduodenal stenosis
(decrease in motility and tone may occur, resulting in obstruction and gastric retention)

» Glaucoma, angle-closure, or predisposition to
(mydriatic effect resulting in increased intraocular pressure may precipitate an acute attack of angle-closure glaucoma)

» Glaucoma, open-angle
(mydriatic effect may cause a slight increase in intraocular pressure; glaucoma therapy may need to be adjusted)

Heat prostration conditions including
Fever or
High environmental temperature or
Physical exercise
(heat prostration can occur due to decreased sweating with anticholinergic agent use, particularly in children and elderly)

» Hemorrhage, acute, with unstable cardiovascular status
(increase in heart rate may be undesirable)

Hepatic function impairment
(decreased metabolism of anticholinergic)

» Hernia, hiatal, associated with reflux esophagitis
(anticholinergics may aggravate condition)

Hypertension
(may be aggravated)

Hyperthyroidism
(characterized by tachycardia, which may be increased)

» Intestinal atony in the elderly or debilitated patient or
» Paralytic ileus
(anticholinergic use may result in obstruction)

Lung disease, chronic, especially in infants, small children, and debilitated patients
(reduction in bronchial secretion can lead to inspissation and formation of bronchial plugs)

» Myasthenia gravis
(condition may be aggravated because of inhibition of acetylcholine action)

Neuropathy, autonomic
(urinary retention and cycloplegia may be aggravated)

» Prostatic hypertrophy, nonobstructive or
» Urinary retention, or predisposition to or
» Uropathy, obstructive, such as bladder neck obstruction due to prostatic hypertrophy
(urinary retention may be precipitated or aggravated)

» Pyloric obstruction
(may be aggravated)

» Renal function impairment
(decreased excretion may increase the risk of side effects; dosage adjustments may be necessary)

Spastic paralysis, in children
(response to anticholinergics may be increased)

» Tachycardia
(may be increased)

Toxemia of pregnancy
(hypertension may be aggravated)

» Ulcerative colitis
(large anticholinergic doses may suppress intestinal motility, possibly causing paralytic ileus; also, use may precipitate or aggravate the serious complication, toxic megacolon)

Xerostomia
(prolonged use may further reduce limited salivary flow)

Caution in use is also recommended in patients over 40 years of age because of the danger of precipitating undiagnosed glaucoma.

Patient monitoring

The following may be especially important in patient monitoring (other tests may be warranted in some patients, depending on condition; » = major clinical significance):

Intraocular pressure determinations
(recommended at periodic intervals, as these medications may increase the intraocular pressure by producing mydriasis)

Side/Adverse Effects

Note: When anticholinergics are given to patients, especially children, where the environmental temperature is high, there is risk of a rapid increase in body temperature because of suppression of sweat gland activity.

Infants, patients with Down's syndrome, and children with spastic paralysis or brain damage may show an increased response to anticholinergics, thus increasing the potential for side effects.

Geriatric or debilitated patients may respond to usual doses of anticholinergics with excitement, agitation, drowsiness, or confusion.

Following use of the transdermal disk of scopolamine, a dilated and fixed pupil has been reported on the side where the disk was worn. This condition usually resolves spontaneously within a few days, but may persist for up to 2 weeks after the disk has been removed and thus may be mistaken for a sign of intracranial neoplasm, subdural hematoma, or aneurysm. To avoid extensive neuroradiological tests, instillation of 1% pilocarpine solution is recommended as an aid in the diagnosis of non-neurogenic dilation of the pupil.

Post-marketing side effects the have been reported with glycopyrrolate include: malignant hyperthermia, cardiac arrhythmias (including bradycardia, ventricular tachycardia, ventricular fibrillation), cardiac arrest, hypertension, hypotension, seizures, and respiratory arrest. Injection site reactions including pruritus, edema, erythema, and pain have also been reported. Additionally, post-marketing reports have included cases of heart block and QTc interval prolongation associated with the combined use of glycopyrrolate and an anticholinesterase.

See *Table 1,* page 245.

Overdose

For specific information on the agents used in the management of overdose with anticholinergics/antispasmodics, see:

- *Benzodiazepines (Systemic)* monograph;
- *Charcoal, Activated (Oral-Local)* monograph;
- *Chloral Hydrate (Systemic)* monograph;
- *Neostigmine Methylsulfate* in *Antimyasthenics (Systemic)* monograph;
- *Norepinephrine Bitartrate* or *Metaraminol Bitartrate* in *Sympathomimetic Agents—Cardiovascular Use (Parenteral-Systemic)* monograph;
- *Physostigmine Salicylate (Systemic)* monograph; and/or
- *Thiopental* in *Anesthetics, Barbiturate (Systemic)* monograph.

For more information on the management of overdose or unintentional ingestion, **contact a Poison Control Center** (see *Poison Control Center Listing*).

Clinical effects of overdose

The following effects have been selected on the basis of their potential clinical significance (possible signs and symptoms in parentheses where appropriate)—not necessarily inclusive:

Blurred vision, continuing, or changes in near vision; clumsiness or unsteadiness; confusion; difficulty in breathing—may lead to respiratory paralysis with quaternary ammonium compounds because of curare-like effects; ***dizziness; drowsiness, severe; dryness of mouth, nose, or throat, severe; fast heartbeat; fever; hallucinations; muscle weakness, severe***—may lead to respiratory paralysis with quaternary ammonium compounds because of curare-like effects; ***seizures; slurred speech; tiredness, severe***—may lead to respiratory paralysis with quaternary ammonium compounds because of curare-like effects; ***unusual excitement, nervousness, restlessness, or irritability; unusual warmth, dryness, and flushing of skin***

Treatment of overdose

Recommended treatment for anticholinergic overdose includes the following:

To decrease absorption—
Emesis or gastric lavage with 4% tannic acid solution.
Administration of an aqueous slurry of activated charcoal.

Specific treatment—
To reverse severe anticholinergic symptoms, slow, intravenous administration of physostigmine in doses of 0.5 to 2 mg (0.5 to 1 mg in children, up to a total dose of 2 mg), at a rate not to exceed l mg per minute; may be given in repeated doses of 1 to 4 mg as needed, up to a total dose of 5 mg in adults.
Or, neostigmine methylsulfate administered intramuscularly in doses of 0.5 to 1 mg, repeated every 2 to 3 hours; or intravenously in doses of 0.5 to 2 mg, repeated as needed.
To control excitement or delirium, administration of small doses of a short-acting barbiturate (100 mg thiopental sodium) or benzodiazepines, or rectal infusion of 2% solution of chloral hydrate.
To restore blood pressure, infusion of norepinephrine bitartrate or metaraminol.

Supportive care—
Artificial respiration with oxygen if needed for respiratory depression.
Adequate hydration.
Symptomatic treatment as necessary.
Patients in whom intentional overdose is confirmed or suspected should be referred for psychiatric consultation.

Patient Consultation

As an aid to patient consultation, refer to *Advice for the Patient, Anticholinergics/Antispasmodics (Systemic).*

In providing consultation, consider emphasizing the following selected information (» = major clinical significance):

Before using this medication

» Conditions affecting use, especially:
- Hypersensitivity to any of the belladonna alkaloids or derivatives or any component of the product
- Pregnancy—Should be used during pregnancy if clearly needed
- Breast-feeding—Distributed in breast milk (except for quaternary ammonium compounds); possible inhibition of lactation; Caution should be used
- Use in children—Increased susceptibility to toxic effects of anticholinergics; increased response in infants and children with spastic paralysis or brain damage; risk of increased body temperature in hot weather; hyperexcitability (paradoxical reaction) with large doses; increased risk of respiratory depression and collapse (with dicyclomine)
- Use in the elderly—Increased susceptibility to mental and other toxic effects of anticholinergics; danger of precipitating undiagnosed glaucoma; possible impairment of memory
- Dental—Possible development of dental problems because of decreased salivary flow
- Other medications, especially other anticholinergics, antacids, antidiarrheals, cyclopropane, ketoconazole, CNS depressants (with scopolamine), and potassium chloride
- Other medical problems, especially cardiac disease, glaucoma, hemorrhage, hiatal hernia, intestinal atony or paralytic ileus, myasthenia gravis, obstruction in gastrointestinal or urinary tract, prostatic hypertrophy, renal function impairment, reflux esophagitis, tachycardia, and ulcerative colitis

Proper use of this medication

For oral dosage forms
- Taking medication 30 minutes to 1 hour before meals

For rectal dosage forms
- Proper administration technique

For transdermal scopolamine
- Reading patient directions
- Washing and drying hands thoroughly before and after application
- Applying to hairless, intact area of skin behind ear; not applying over cuts or irritations

» Importance of not taking more medication than the amount prescribed
- Taking as soon as possible; not taking if almost time for next dose; not doubling doses

» Proper dosing
» Proper storage

Precautions while using this medication

» Suspected overdose: Getting emergency help at once
» Caution during exercise or hot weather; overheating may result in heat stroke
» Possible increased sensitivity of eyes to light
- Caution about abrupt withdrawal

» Caution if blurred vision occurs
» Possible dizziness or drowsiness; caution when driving or doing things requiring alertness
- Possible dizziness or lightheadedness; caution when getting up suddenly from a lying or sitting position
- Possible dryness of mouth; using sugarless candy or gum, ice or saliva substitute for relief; checking with physician or dentist if dry mouth continues for more than 2 weeks

For scopolamine:
» Avoiding use of alcohol or other CNS depressants

For oral dosage forms:
- Avoiding use of antacids and antidiarrheal medications within 2 or 3 hours of taking this medication

Side/adverse effects

Signs of potential side effects, especially allergic reaction, anaphylactic/anaphylactoid reactions, confusion, hypersensitivity, increased intraocular pressure, orthostatic hypotension (especially with high doses of quaternary ammonium compounds), palpitation, pruritus, or tachycardia

General Dosing Information

Tolerance to some of the adverse reactions may develop following continued use and/or smaller doses of anticholinergics, but effectiveness may also be reduced.

Dosage adjustments are often required for infants, patients with Down's syndrome, children with brain damage or spasticity, since an increased responsiveness to anticholinergics has been reported in these patients.

Geriatric and debilitated patients may respond to usual doses with excitement, agitation, drowsiness, or confusion; lower doses may be required in these patients.

Anticholinergics should not be withdrawn abruptly since withdrawal-like symptoms may occur. Vomiting, malaise, sweating, transient dizziness, and salivation have been reported after sudden withdrawal of large doses of scopolamine.

If scopolamine is used as antisialagogue preanesthetic medication in minor surgical procedures that do not require more than a few hours' stay in the hospital, the patient should be alerted at time of discharge about scopolamine's lingering detrimental effects on memory and motor tasks.

High dosage of quaternary ammonium compounds should not be given continuously for prolonged periods, since ganglionic and skeletal neuromuscular transmission may be blocked. Stimulation of the CNS and a curare-like action may result.

For oral dosage forms only

Administration of anticholinergics 30 minutes to 1 hour before meals is recommended to maximize absorption.

For parenteral dosage forms only

Atropine, hyoscyamine, and scopolamine may be administered by intramuscular, subcutaneous, or intravenous injection.

Glycopyrrolate may be administered by intramuscular or intravenous injection.

After parenteral administration a temporary feeling of lightheadedness and local irritation may occur.

For transdermal dosage forms only

Transdermal application delivers reduced doses of scopolamine, which are large enough to be effective but small enough to eliminate most of the adverse effects, except drowsiness and cycloplegia.

ANISOTROPINE

Oral Dosage Forms

ANISOTROPINE METHYLBROMIDE TABLETS

Usual adult and adolescent dose

Anticholinergic—
- Oral, 50 mg three times a day, the dosage being adjusted as needed and tolerated.

Note: Geriatric patients may be more sensitive to the effects of the usual adult dose.

Usual pediatric dose

Dosage has not been established.

Strength(s) usually available

U.S.—
- 50 mg (Rx) [GENERIC].

Canada—
- Not commercially available.

Packaging and storage

Store between 15 and 30 °C (59 and 86 °F), unless otherwise specified by manufacturer.

Auxiliary labeling

- May cause blurred vision.

ATROPINE

Summary of Differences

Category:
- Also an antidote (to cholinesterase inhibitors; to organophosphate pesticides; to muscarine) and a urinary antispasmodic. Parenteral atropine is used as an antiarrhythmic and cholinergic adjunct (curariform block).

Indications:
- Also indicated for biliary tract disorders and duodenography. In preanesthesia and dental anesthesia, indicated as antisialagogue.

Pharmacology/pharmacokinetics:
- Protein binding—Moderate.
- Half-life (elimination)—2.5 hours.
- Duration of action—Oral, 4 to 6 hours; parenteral, brief.
- Elimination—Renal; 30 to 50% excreted unchanged.

Precautions:
Pregnancy—Intravenous administration may produce tachycardia in fetus.
Laboratory value alterations—May decrease excretion of phenolsulfonphthalein (PSP) during PSP excretion test.

Additional Dosing Information

See also *General Dosing Information.*

Doses of 0.5 to 1 mg of atropine are mildly stimulating to the CNS. Larger doses may produce mental disturbances; very large doses have depressant effect.

The fatal dose of atropine in children may be as low as 10 mg.

Oral Dosage Forms

ATROPINE SULFATE TABLETS USP

Usual adult and adolescent dose

Anticholinergic—
Oral, 300 mcg (0.3 mg) to 1.2 mg every four to six hours.
Prophylaxis of excessive salivation and respiratory tract secretions, in anesthesia—
Oral, 2 mg.

Note: Geriatric patients may be more sensitive to the effects of the usual adult dose.

Usual pediatric dose

Anticholinergic—
Oral, 10 mcg (0.01 mg) per kg of body weight, not to exceed 400 mcg (0.4 mg), or 300 mcg (0.3 mg) per square meter of body surface, every four to six hours.

Strength(s) usually available

U.S.—
400 mcg (0.4 mg) (Rx) [GENERIC].
Canada—
Not commercially available.

Packaging and storage

Store below 40 °C (104 °F), preferably between 15 and 30 °C (59 and 86 °F), in a well-closed container, unless otherwise specified by manufacturer.

Auxiliary labeling

- May cause blurred vision.

ATROPINE SULFATE SOLUBLE TABLETS

Usual adult and adolescent dose

Anticholinergic—
Oral, 300 mcg (0.3 mg) to 1.2 mg every four to six hours.
Prophylaxis of excessive salivation and respiratory tract secretions, in anesthesia—
Oral, 2 mg.

Note: Geriatric patients may be more sensitive to the effects of the usual adult dose.

Usual pediatric dose

Anticholinergic—
Oral, 10 mcg (0.01 mg) per kg of body weight, not to exceed 400 mcg (0.4 mg), or 300 mcg (0.3 mg) per square meter of body surface, every four to six hours.

Strength(s) usually available

U.S.—
400 mcg (0.4 mg) (Rx) [GENERIC].
600 mcg (0.6 mg) (Rx) [GENERIC].
Canada—
Not commercially available.

Packaging and storage

Store below 40 °C (104 °F), preferably between 15 and 30 °C (59 and 86 °F), in a well-closed container, unless otherwise specified by manufacturer.

Auxiliary labeling

- May cause blurred vision.

Parenteral Dosage Forms

Note: Bracketed information in the *Dosage Forms* section refer to categories of use and/or indications that are not included in U.S. product labeling.

ATROPINE SULFATE INJECTION USP

Usual adult and adolescent dose

Anticholinergic—
Intramuscular, intravenous, or subcutaneous, 400 to 600 mcg (0.4 to 0.6 mg) every four to six hours.
Gastrointestinal radiography—
Intramuscular, 1 mg.
Prophylaxis of excessive salivation and respiratory tract secretions, in anesthesia—
Intramuscular, 200 to 600 mcg (0.2 to 0.6 mg) one-half to one hour before surgery.
Antiarrhythmic—
Intravenous, 400 mcg (0.4 mg) to 1 mg every one to two hours as needed, up to a maximum of 2 mg.
Cholinergic adjunct (curariform block)—
Intravenous, 600 mcg (0.6 mg) to 1.2 mg administered a few minutes before or concurrently with 500 mcg (0.5 mg) to 2 mg of neostigmine methylsulfate, using separate syringes.
Antidote (to cholinesterase inhibitors)—
Intravenous, 2 to 4 mg initially, then 2 mg repeated every five to ten minutes until muscarinic symptoms disappear or signs of atropine toxicity appear.
Antidote (to muscarine in mushroom poisoning)—
Intramuscular or intravenous, 1 to 2 mg every hour until respiratory effects subside.
Antidote (to organophosphate pesticides)—
Intramuscular or intravenous, 1 to 2 mg, repeated in twenty to thirty minutes as soon as cyanosis has cleared. Continue dosage until definite improvement occurs and is maintained, sometimes for two days or more.
[Antiasthmatic][1]—
Administered as an inhalation solution, diluted with saline, patients have benefited from a dose of 0.05 to 0.1 mg/kg, nebulized three to four times daily. Total dose should not exceed 2.5 mg.

Note: Geriatric patients may be more sensitive to the effects of the usual adult dose.

Usual pediatric dose

Anticholinergic—
Subcutaneous, 10 mcg (0.01 mg) per kg of body weight, not to exceed 400 mcg (0.4 mg), or 300 mcg (0.3 mg) per square meter of body surface, every four to six hours.
Prophylaxis of excessive salivation and respiratory tract secretions, in anesthesia or
Prophylaxis of succinylcholine- or surgical procedure-induced arrhythmias—
Subcutaneous:
Children weighing up to 3 kg: 100 mcg (0.1 mg).
Children weighing 7 to 9 kg: 200 mcg (0.2 mg).
Children weighing 12 to 16 kg: 300 mcg (0.3 mg).
Children weighing 20 to 27 kg: 400 mcg (0.4 mg).
Children weighing 32 kg: 500 mcg (0.5 mg).
Children weighing 41 kg: 600 mcg (0.6 mg).
Antiarrhythmic—
Intravenous, 10 to 30 mcg (0.01 to 0.03 mg) per kg of body weight.
Antidote (to cholinesterase inhibitors)—
Intravenous or intramuscular, 1 mg initially, then 0.5 to 1 mg every five to ten minutes until muscarinic symptoms disappear or signs of atropine toxicity appear.
[Antiasthmatic][1]—
Administered as an inhalation solution, diluted with saline, pediatric patients have benefited from a dose of 0.025 to 0.05 mg/kg, nebulized three to four times daily. Total dose should not exceed 2.5 mg.

Strength(s) usually available

U.S.—
50 mcg (0.05 mg) per mL (Rx) [GENERIC].
100 mcg (0.1 mg) per mL (Rx) [GENERIC].
300 mcg (0.3 mg) per mL (Rx) [GENERIC].
400 mcg (0.4 mg) per mL (Rx) [GENERIC].
500 mcg (0.5 mg) per mL (Rx) [GENERIC].
800 mcg (0.8 mg) per mL (Rx) [GENERIC].
1 mg per mL (Rx) [GENERIC].
Canada—
400 mcg (0.4 mg) per mL (Rx) [GENERIC].
600 mcg (0.6 mg) per mL (Rx) [GENERIC].

Packaging and storage

Store below 40 °C (104 °F), preferably between 15 and 30 °C (59 and 86 °F), unless otherwise specified by manufacturer. Protect from freezing.

Additional information
The intravenous injection of atropine should be administered *slowly*.

[1]Not included in Canadian product labeling.

BELLADONNA

Summary of Differences

Category:
Also an antidysmenorrheal and antivertigo agent.
Indications:
Also indicated in nocturnal enuresis. In dental procedures, may be used as antisialagogue.
Pharmacology/pharmacokinetics:
Onset of action—1 to 2 hours.
Duration of action—4 hours.
Elimination—Renal; 30 to 50% of atropine and 1% of scopolamine excreted unchanged.

Oral Dosage Forms

BELLADONNA TINCTURE USP

Usual adult and adolescent dose
Anticholinergic—
Oral, 180 to 300 mcg (0.18 to 0.3 mg) three or four times a day, thirty minutes to one hour before meals and at bedtime, the dosage being adjusted as needed and tolerated.
Note: Geriatric patients may be more sensitive to the effects of the usual adult dose.

Usual pediatric dose
Anticholinergic—
Oral, 9 mcg (0.009 mg) per kg of body weight or 240 mcg (0.24 mg) per square meter of body surface a day, in three or four divided doses.

Strength(s) usually available
U.S.—
300 mcg (0.3 mg) per mL (Rx) [GENERIC].
Note: Belladonna tincture contains 300 mcg (0.3 mg) of belladonna alkaloids (principally hyoscyamine and atropine) per mL.
Canada—
Not commercially available.

Packaging and storage
Store below 40 °C (104 °F), preferably between 15 and 30 °C (59 and 86 °F), unless otherwise specified by manufacturer. Store in a tight, light-resistant container. Protect from freezing.

Auxiliary labeling
- May cause blurred vision.
- Keep container tightly closed.

CLIDINIUM

Summary of Differences

Pharmacology/pharmacokinetics:
Onset of action—1 hour.
Duration of action—Up to 3 hours.

Oral Dosage Forms

CLIDINIUM BROMIDE CAPSULES USP

Usual adult and adolescent dose
Anticholinergic—
Oral, 2.5 to 5 mg three or four times a day, before meals and at bedtime, the dosage being adjusted as needed and tolerated.
Note: Geriatric or debilitated patients—Oral, 2.5 mg three times a day before meals.

Usual pediatric dose
Dosage has not been established.

Strength(s) usually available
U.S.—
2.5 mg (Rx) [*Quarzan*].
5 mg (Rx) [*Quarzan*].
Canada—
Not commercially available.

Packaging and storage
Store below 40 °C (104 °F), preferably between 15 and 30 °C (59 and 86 °F), unless otherwise specified by manufacturer. Store in a tight, light-resistant container.

Auxiliary labeling
- May cause blurred vision.

DICYCLOMINE

Summary of Differences

Category:
Also gastrointestinal antispasmodic.
Indications:
Not indicated for peptic ulcer.
Pharmacology/pharmacokinetics:
Half-life (elimination)—1.8 hours (initial phase) and 9 to 10 hours (secondary phase).
Precautions:
Pediatrics—Respiratory symptoms, seizures, syncope, asphyxia, pulse rate fluctuations, muscular hypotonia, and coma reported with the use of the syrup in some infants 3 months old and under.

Oral Dosage Forms

DICYCLOMINE HYDROCHLORIDE CAPSULES USP

Usual adult and adolescent dose
Antispasmodic, gastrointestinal: Irritable bowel syndrome—
Oral, 10 to 20 mg three or four times a day, the dosage being adjusted as needed and tolerated.
Note: Geriatric patients may be more sensitive to the effects of the usual adult dose.

Usual adult prescribing limits
Up to 160 mg daily.

Usual pediatric dose
Antispasmodic, gastrointestinal—
Children up to 6 years of age: Product not suitable for pediatric administration. See *Dicyclomine Hydrochloride Syrup USP*.
Children 6 years of age and over: Oral, 10 mg three or four times a day, the dosage being adjusted as needed and tolerated.

Strength(s) usually available
U.S.—
10 mg (Rx) [*Bentyl;* GENERIC].
20 mg (Rx) [GENERIC].
Canada—
10 mg (Rx) [*Formulex*].

Packaging and storage
Store below 40 °C (104 °F), preferably between 15 and 30 °C (59 and 86 °F), unless otherwise specified by manufacturer. Store in a well-closed container.

Auxiliary labeling
- May cause blurred vision.

DICYCLOMINE HYDROCHLORIDE SYRUP USP

Usual adult and adolescent dose
Antispasmodic, gastrointestinal: Irritable bowel syndrome—
Oral, 10 to 20 mg three or four times a day, the dosage being adjusted as needed and tolerated.
Note: Geriatric patients may be more sensitive to the effects of the usual adult dose.

Usual adult prescribing limits
Up to 160 mg daily.

Usual pediatric dose
Antispasmodic, gastrointestinal—
Children up to 6 months of age: Use is not recommended.
Children 6 months to 2 years of age: Oral, 5 to 10 mg three or four times a day, the dosage being adjusted as needed and tolerated.
Children 2 years of age and over: Oral, 10 mg three or four times a day, the dosage being adjusted as needed and tolerated.

Strength(s) usually available
U.S.—
10 mg per 5 mL (Rx) [*Bentyl;* GENERIC].
Canada—
10 mg per 5 mL (Rx) [*Bentylol*].

Packaging and storage
Store below 40 °C (104 °F), preferably between 15 and 30 °C (59 and 86 °F), unless otherwise specified by manufacturer. Store in a tight container. Protect from freezing.

Auxiliary labeling
• May cause blurred vision.

DICYCLOMINE HYDROCHLORIDE TABLETS USP

Usual adult and adolescent dose
Antispasmodic, gastrointestinal: Irritable bowel syndrome—

Oral, 10 to 20 mg three or four times a day, the dosage being adjusted as needed and tolerated.

Note: Geriatric patients may be more sensitive to the effects of the usual adult dose.

Usual adult prescribing limits
Up to 160 mg daily.

Usual pediatric dose
Antispasmodic, gastrointestinal—

Children up to 6 years of age: Product not suitable for pediatric administration. See *Dicyclomine Hydrochloride Syrup USP*.

Children 6 years of age and over: Oral, 10 mg three or four times a day, the dosage being adjusted as needed and tolerated.

Strength(s) usually available
U.S.—

20 mg (Rx) [*Bentyl;* GENERIC].

Canada—

10 mg (Rx) [*Bentylol*].

20 mg (Rx) [*Bentylol; Spasmoban*].

Packaging and storage
Store below 40 °C (104 °F), preferably between 15 and 30 °C (59 and 86 °F), unless otherwise specified by manufacturer. Store in a well-closed container.

Auxiliary labeling
• May cause blurred vision.

DICYCLOMINE HYDROCHLORIDE EXTENDED-RELEASE TABLETS

Usual adult and adolescent dose
Antispasmodic, gastrointestinal—

Oral, 30 mg two times a day.

Note: Geriatric patients may be more sensitive to the effects of the usual adult dose.

Usual pediatric dose
Antispasmodic, gastrointestinal—

Product not suitable for pediatric administration. See *Dicyclomine Hydrochloride Syrup USP*.

Strength(s) usually available
U.S.—

Not commercially available.

Canada—

Not commercially available.

Packaging and storage
Store below 40 °C (104 °F), preferably between 15 and 30 °C (59 and 86 °F), unless otherwise specified by manufacturer. Store in a tight container.

Auxiliary labeling
• May cause blurred vision.

Parenteral Dosage Forms

DICYCLOMINE HYDROCHLORIDE INJECTION USP

Usual adult and adolescent dose
Antispasmodic, gastrointestinal: Irritable bowel syndrome—

Intramuscular, 20 mg every four to six hours, the dosage being adjusted as needed and tolerated.

Note: Not for intravenous use.

Geriatric patients may be more sensitive to the effects of the usual adult dose.

Usual pediatric dose
Dosage has not been established.

Strength(s) usually available
U.S.—

10 mg per mL (Rx) [*Bentyl;* GENERIC].

Canada—

Not commercially available.

Packaging and storage
Store below 40 °C (104 °F), preferably between 15 and 30 °C (59 and 86 °F), unless otherwise specified by manufacturer. Protect from freezing.

GLYCOPYRROLATE

Summary of Differences
Category:

Also, an [antidiarrheal]. Parenteral glycopyrrolate is used as an antiarrhythmic and cholinergic adjunct (curariform block).

Indications:

Indicated as antisialagogue in preanesthesia. Also, indicated as antiarrhythmic in preanesthesia, anesthesia, and surgery. In addition, indicated to prevent aspiration pneumonitis during anesthesia. May be used as antidiarrheal and for cholinesterase inhibitor toxicity.

Pharmacology/pharmacokinetics:

Half-life (elimination)—1.7 hours (range 0.6–4.6 hours).

Onset of action—15 to 30 minutes with intramuscular or subcutaneous administration; 1 minute with intravenous administration.

Duration of action—Antisialagogue effect up to 7 hours; vagal blocking effect 2 to 3 hours.

Precautions:

Pregnancy—Rates of conception and survival at weaning decreased in studies with rats.

Laboratory value alterations—Serum uric acid may be decreased in patients with hyperuricemia or gout.

Oral Dosage Forms

GLYCOPYRROLATE TABLETS USP

Usual adult and adolescent dose
Anticholinergic: Peptic ulcer—

Oral, initially 1 to 2 mg two or three times a day and occasionally 2 mg at bedtime, then 1 mg two times a day, the dosage being adjusted as needed and tolerated.

Note: Geriatric patients may be more sensitive to the effects of the usual adult dose.

Usual adult prescribing limits
Up to 8 mg daily.

Usual pediatric dose
Dosage has not been established.

Strength(s) usually available
U.S.—

1 mg (Rx) [*Robinul;* GENERIC].

2 mg (Rx) [*Robinul Forte;* GENERIC].

Canada—

1 mg (Rx) [*Robinul*].

2 mg (Rx) [*Robinul Forte*].

Packaging and storage
Store below 40 °C (104 °F), preferably between 15 and 30 °C (59 and 86 °F), unless otherwise specified by manufacturer. Store in a tight container.

Auxiliary labeling
• May cause blurred vision.

Parenteral Dosage Forms

GLYCOPYRROLATE INJECTION USP

Usual adult and adolescent dose
Anticholinergic—

Peptic ulcer—

Intramuscular or intravenous, 100 to 200 mcg (0.1 to 0.2 mg), the dosage being repeated, if necessary, at four-hour intervals up to a maximum of four times a day.

Prophylaxis of excessive salivation and respiratory tract secretions, in anesthesia and—

Prophylaxis of gastric hypersecretory conditions, in anesthesia—

Intramuscular, 4 mcg (0.004 mg) per kg of body weight one-half to one hour before induction of anesthesia or at the time the preanesthetic narcotic and/or sedative are administered.

Antiarrhythmic, in anesthesia or

Antiarrhythmic, in surgery—

Intravenous, 100 mcg (0.1 mg), the dosage being repeated if necessary at two- to three-minute intervals.

Cholinergic adjunct (curariform block)—
Intravenous, 200 mcg (0.2 mg) for each 1 mg of neostigmine or 5 mg of pyridostigmine given simultaneously; may be mixed in the same syringe.

Note: Geriatric patients may be more sensitive to the effects of the usual adult dose.

Usual pediatric dose

Anticholinergic—
Peptic ulcer—
Glycopyrrolate is not recommended for the treatment of peptic ulcer in pediatric patients. Safety and efficacy have not been established.

Prophylaxis of excessive salivation and respiratory tract secretions, in anesthesia and—
Prophylaxis of gastric hypersecretory conditions, in anesthesia—
Intramuscular, 4 mcg (0.004) per kg of body weight one-half to one hour before induction of anesthesia or at the time the preanesthetic narcotic and/or sedative are administered. Infants (1 month to 2 years of age) may require up to 9 mcg (0.009 mg) per kg of body weight.

Antiarrhythmics, in anesthesia or
Antiarrhythmic, in surgery—
Intravenous, 4 mcg (0.004 mg) per kg of body weight up to a maximum of 100 mcg (0.1 mg), the dosage being repeated, if necessary, at two- to three-minute intervals.

Cholinergic adjunct (curariform block)—
Intravenous, 400 mcg (0.4 mg) for each 1 mg of neostigmine or 5 mg of pyridostigmine given simultaneously; may be mixed in the same syringe.

Strength(s) usually available

U.S.—
200 mcg (0.2 mg) per mL (Rx) [*Robinul* (water for injection; benzyl alcohol 0.9% as a preservative; sodium hydroxide, if necessary, for pH adjustment; hydrochloric acid, if necessary, for pH adjustment); GENERIC].

Canada—
200 mcg (0.2 mg) per mL (Rx) [*Robinul*].

Packaging and storage

Store between 20 and 25 °C (68 and 77 °F), unless otherwise specified by manufacturer.

Preparation of dosage form

Glycopyrrolate may be mixed and administered with glucose 5 or 10% in water or saline, meperidine injection, morphine sulfate, fentanyl plus droperidol injection, hydroxyzine injection, neostigmine injection, or pyridostigmine injection.

Stability

Stability of glycopyrrolate may be affected at a pH higher than 6. A pH above 6 will result when glycopyrrolate is mixed with dexamethasone sodium phosphate or a buffered solution of lactated Ringer's solution.

Incompatibilities

Chloramphenicol, dexamethasone, diazepam, dimenhydrinate, methohexital sodium, pentazocine, pentobarbital sodium, secobarbital sodium, thiopental sodium, and sodium bicarbonate are *not* suitable for mixing in the same syringe with glycopyrrolate since a gas or a precipitate may result.

Caution

Glycopyrrolate injections that contain benzyl alcohol should not be administered to premature neonates because the preservative has been associated with a fatal "gasping syndrome" in these patients.

Caution if patient has latex allergy. *Robinul* vial stopper contains dry natural rubber (latex).

HOMATROPINE

Oral Dosage Forms

HOMATROPINE METHYLBROMIDE TABLETS USP

Usual adult and adolescent dose

Anticholinergic—
Oral, 5 to 10 mg three or four times a day, the dosage being adjusted as needed and tolerated.

Note: Geriatric patients may be more sensitive to the effects of the usual adult dose.

Usual pediatric dose

Dosage has not been established.

Strength(s) usually available

U.S.—
5 mg (Rx) [*Homapin*].
10 mg (Rx) [*Homapin*].

Canada—
Not commercially available.

Packaging and storage

Store below 40 °C (104 °F), preferably between 15 and 30 °C (59 and 86 °F), unless otherwise specified by manufacturer. Store in a tight, light-resistant container.

Auxiliary labeling

• May cause blurred vision.

HYOSCYAMINE

Summary of Differences

Category:
Parenteral hyoscyamine is also an antiarrhythmic, antidote (to cholinesterase inhibitors and to muscarine), and a cholinergic adjunct (curariform block).

Indications:
Also indicated for biliary disorders, cystitis, duodenography, and acute rhinitis. In preanesthesia, indicated as antisialagogue and also as antiarrhythmic during anesthesia and surgery.

Pharmacology/pharmacokinetics:
Protein binding—Moderate.
Half-life (elimination)—3.5 hours.
Onset of action—20 to 30 minutes with oral administration of hyoscyamine sulfate; 2 to 3 minutes with parenteral administration.
Duration of action—4 to 6 hours.
Elimination—Renal; majority of drug excreted unchanged.

Precautions:
Pregnancy—Intravenous administration may produce tachycardia in fetus.

Side/adverse effects:
Constipation has been reported less often with hyoscyamine.

Additional Dosing Information

See also *General Dosing Information*.

Hyoscyamine is effective at half the dosage of atropine.

In dehydrated patients, such as those with diarrhea and vomiting, treatment with hyoscyamine should be initiated at a lower dosage.

Oral Dosage Forms

HYOSCYAMINE TABLETS USP

Usual adult and adolescent dose

Anticholinergic—
Oral, 125 to 500 mcg (0.125 to 0.5 mg) three or four times a day, thirty minutes to one hour before meals and at bedtime, the dosage being adjusted as needed and tolerated.

Note: Geriatric patients may be more sensitive to the effects of the usual adult dose.

Usual pediatric dose

Dosage must be individualized by physician.

Strength(s) usually available

U.S.—
150 mcg (0.15 mg) (Rx) [*Cystospaz*].

Canada—
Not commercially available.

Packaging and storage

Store below 40 °C (104 °F), preferably between 15 and 30 °C (59 and 86 °F), unless otherwise specified by manufacturer. Store in a well-closed, light-resistant container.

Auxiliary labeling

• May cause blurred vision.

HYOSCYAMINE SULFATE EXTENDED-RELEASE CAPSULES

Usual adult and adolescent dose

Anticholinergic—
Oral, 375 mcg (0.375 mg) two times a day, in the morning and at bedtime, the dosage being increased, if necessary, to obtain the desired response.

Note: Geriatric patients may be more sensitive to the effects of the usual adult dose.

Usual pediatric dose
Anticholinergic—
Children up to 12 years of age: Use is not recommended.
Children 12 years of age and over: See *Usual adult and adolescent dose.*

Strength(s) usually available
U.S.—
375 mcg (0.375 mg) (Rx) [*Cystospaz-M; Levsinex Timecaps; Symax SR;* GENERIC].
Canada—
Not commercially available.

Packaging and storage
Store below 40 °C (104 °F), preferably between 15 and 30 °C (59 and 86 °F), in a tight, light-resistant container, unless otherwise specified by manufacturer.

Auxiliary labeling
- Swallow capsules whole.
- May cause blurred vision.

HYOSCYAMINE SULFATE EXTENDED-RELEASE TABLETS

Usual adult and adolescent dose
Anticholinergic—
Oral, 375 mcg (0.375 mg) to 750 mcg (0.75 mg) every twelve hours, not to exceed four tablets in twenty-four hours. Tablets may be broken for dosage titration.

Usual pediatric dose
Anticholinergic—
Children up to 12 years of age: Use is not recommended.
Children 12 years of age and over: See *Usual adult and adolescent dose.*

Strength(s) usually available
U.S.—
375 mcg (0.375 mg) (Rx) [*Levbid* (scored)].
Canada—
Not commercially available.

Packaging and storage
Store below 40 °C (104 °F), preferably between 15 and 30 °C (59 and 86 °F), in a tight, light-resistant container, unless otherwise specified by manufacturer.

Auxiliary labeling
- May cause blurred vision.

HYOSCYAMINE SULFATE ELIXIR USP

Usual adult and adolescent dose
Anticholinergic—
Oral, 125 to 250 mcg (0.125 to 0.25 mg) every four to six hours, the dosage being adjusted as needed and tolerated.
Note: Geriatric patients may be more sensitive to the effects of the usual adult dose.

Usual pediatric dose
Anticholinergic—
Oral, the following doses every four hours as needed:
Children weighing 2.3 to 3.3 kg—12.5 mcg (0.0125 mg).
Children weighing 3.4 to 4.4 kg—15.6 mcg (0.0156 mg).
Children weighing 4.5 to 6.7 kg—18.8 mcg (0.0188 mg).
Children weighing 6.8 to 9 kg—25 mcg (0.025 mg).
Children weighing 9.1 to 13.5 kg—31.3 mcg (0.0313 mg).
Children weighing 13.6 to 22.6 kg—63 mcg (0.063 mg).
Children weighing 22.7 to 33 kg—94 to 125 mcg (0.094 to 0.125 mg).
Children weighing 34 to 36 kg—125 to 187 mcg (0.125 to 0.187 mg).

Strength(s) usually available
U.S.—
125 mcg (0.125 mg) per 5 mL (Rx) [*Levsin*].
Canada—
Not commercially available.

Packaging and storage
Store between 15 and 30 °C (59 and 86 °F), unless otherwise specified by manufacturer. Store in a tight, light-resistant container. Protect from freezing.

Auxiliary labeling
- May cause blurred vision.
- Keep container tightly closed.

HYOSCYAMINE SULFATE ORAL SOLUTION USP

Usual adult and adolescent dose
Anticholinergic—
Oral, 125 to 250 mcg (0.125 to 0.25 mg) every four to six hours, the dosage being adjusted as needed and tolerated.
Note: Geriatric patients may be more sensitive to the effects of the usual adult dose.

Usual pediatric dose
Anticholinergic—
Oral, the following doses every four hours as needed:
Children weighing 2.3 to 3.3 kg—12.5 mcg (0.0125 mg).
Children weighing 3.4 to 4.4 kg—15.6 mcg (0.0156 mg).
Children weighing 4.5 to 6.7 kg—18.8 mcg (0.0188 mg).
Children weighing 6.8 to 9 kg—25 mcg (0.025 mg).
Children weighing 9.1 to 13.5 kg—31.3 mcg (0.0313 mg).
Children weighing 13.6 to 22.6 kg—63 mcg (0.063 mg).
Children weighing 22.7 to 33 kg—94 to 125 mcg (0.094 to 0.125 mg).
Children weighing 34 to 36 kg—125 to 187 mcg (0.125 to 0.187 mg).

Strength(s) usually available
U.S.—
125 mcg (0.125 mg) per mL (Rx) [*Gastrosed; Levsin* (alcohol 5%)].
Canada—
125 mcg (0.125 mg) per mL (Rx) [*Levsin* (alcohol 5%)].
Note: 1 mL = approximately 28 drops (may vary with dropper).

Packaging and storage
Store below 40 °C (104 °F), preferably between 15 and 30 °C (59 and 86 °F), unless otherwise specified by manufacturer. Store in a tight, light-resistant container. Protect from freezing.

Auxiliary labeling
- May cause blurred vision.
- Keep container tightly closed.

Note
Dispense in dropper bottle.

HYOSCYAMINE SULFATE TABLETS USP

Usual adult and adolescent dose
Anticholinergic—
Oral or sublingual, 125 to 500 mcg (0.125 to 0.5 mg) three or four times a day, thirty minutes to one hour before meals and at bedtime, the dosage being adjusted as needed and tolerated.
Note: Geriatric patients may be more sensitive to the effects of the usual adult dose.

Usual pediatric dose
Anticholinergic—
Children weighing up to 22.7 kg—Product not suitable for pediatric administration. See *Hyoscyamine Sulfate Oral Solution USP.*
Children weighing 22.7 to 33 kg—Oral, 94 to 125 mcg (0.094 to 0.125 mg).
Children weighing 34 to 36 kg—Oral, 125 to 187 mcg (0.125 to 0.187 mg).

Strength(s) usually available
U.S.—
125 mcg (0.125 mg) (Rx) [*Anaspaz; A-Spas S/L; Donnamar; ED-SPAZ; Gastrosed; Levsin; Levsin/SL; Symax SL;* GENERIC].
Canada—
125 mcg (0.125 mg) (Rx) [*Levsin*].

Packaging and storage
Store below 40 °C (104 °F), preferably between 15 and 30 °C (59 and 86 °F), unless otherwise specified by manufacturer. Store in a tight, light-resistant container.

Auxiliary labeling
- May be chewed, swallowed whole, or allowed to dissolve under the tongue.
- May cause blurred vision.

Parenteral Dosage Forms

HYOSCYAMINE SULFATE INJECTION USP

Usual adult and adolescent dose
Anticholinergic—
Intramuscular, intravenous, or subcutaneous, 250 to 500 mcg (0.25 to 0.5 mg) every four to six hours.
Gastrointestinal radiography—
Intramuscular, intravenous, or subcutaneous, 250 to 500 mcg (0.25 to 0.5 mg) five to ten minutes prior to the diagnostic procedure.

Peptic ulcer—
Initial: Intravenous, 250 to 500 mcg (0.25 to 0.5 mg).
Maintenance: Intramuscular or subcutaneous, 250 to 500 mcg (0.25 to 0.5 mg) every six hours until all pain has ceased.
Prophylaxis of excessive salivation and respiratory tract secretions, in anesthesia—
Intramuscular, intravenous, or subcutaneous, 500 mcg (0.5 mg); or 5 mcg (0.005 mg) per kg of body weight thirty to sixty minutes before induction of anesthesia.
Antiarrhythmic—
Intravenous, 125 mcg (0.125 mg), repeated as needed.
Cholinergic adjunct (curariform block)—
Intravenous, 200 mcg (0.2 mg) for each 1 mg of neostigmine or the equivalent dose of physostigmine or pyridostigmine.

Note: Geriatric patients may be more sensitive to the effects of the usual adult dose.

Usual pediatric dose
Anticholinergic—
Prophylaxis of excessive salivation and respiratory tract secretions, in anesthesia:
Children up to 2 years of age—Use is not recommended.
Children 2 years of age and over—Intramuscular, intravenous, or subcutaneous, 5 mcg (0.005 mg) per kg of body weight thirty to sixty minutes before induction of anesthesia.

Strength(s) usually available
U.S.—
500 mcg (0.5 mg) per mL (Rx) [*Levsin*].
Canada—
Not commercially available.

Packaging and storage
Store below 40 °C (104 °F), preferably between 15 and 30 °C (59 and 86 °F), unless otherwise specified by manufacturer. Protect from freezing.

MEPENZOLATE

Summary of Differences
Pharmacology/pharmacokinetics:
Elimination—Renal; 3 to 22% excreted unchanged.
Precautions:
Pregnancy—Reproduction studies in rats and rabbits have not shown adverse effects on fetus.

Oral Dosage Forms
MEPENZOLATE BROMIDE TABLETS
Usual adult and adolescent dose
Anticholinergic—
Oral, 25 to 50 mg four times a day with meals and at bedtime, the dosage being adjusted as needed and tolerated.

Note: Geriatric patients may be more sensitive to the effects of the usual adult dose.

Usual pediatric dose
Dosage has not been established.

Strength(s) usually available
U.S.—
25 mg (Rx) [*Cantil*].
Canada—
Not commercially available.

Packaging and storage
Store below 40 °C (104 °F), preferably between 15 and 30 °C (59 and 86 °F), unless otherwise specified by manufacturer. Store in a well-closed container.

Auxiliary labeling
- May cause blurred vision.

METHANTHELINE

Summary of Differences
Indications:
Also indicated for urinary incontinence.

Oral Dosage Forms
METHANTHELINE BROMIDE TABLETS
Usual adult and adolescent dose
Anticholinergic—
Oral, 50 to 100 mg every six hours, the dosage being adjusted as needed and tolerated.

Note: Geriatric patients may be more sensitive to the effects of the usual adult dose.

Usual pediatric dose
Anticholinergic—
Children up to 1 month of age: Oral, 12.5 mg two times a day, the dosage being increased to three times a day if needed and tolerated.
Children 1 month to 1 year of age: Oral, 12.5 mg four times a day, the dosage being increased to 25 mg four times a day if needed and tolerated.
Children 1 year of age and over: Oral, 12.5 to 50 mg four times a day, the dosage being adjusted as needed and tolerated.

Strength(s) usually available
U.S.—
50 mg (Rx) [*Banthine* (scored)].
Canada—
Not commercially available.

Packaging and storage
Store below 40 °C (104 °F), preferably between 15 and 30 °C (59 and 86 °F), unless otherwise specified by manufacturer. Store in a well-closed container.

Auxiliary labeling
- May cause blurred vision.

METHSCOPOLAMINE

Summary of Differences
Pharmacology/pharmacokinetics:
Onset of action—1 hour.
Duration of action—6 to 8 hours.

Oral Dosage Forms
METHSCOPOLAMINE BROMIDE TABLETS
Usual adult and adolescent dose
Anticholinergic—
Oral, 2.5 mg four times a day, one-half hour before meals and 2.5 to 5 mg at bedtime.
For severe symptoms: Oral, initially 5 mg four times a day, one-half hour before meals and at bedtime, the dosage being increased, if necessary, to obtain the desired response.

Note: Geriatric patients may be more sensitive to the effects of the usual adult dose.

Usual pediatric dose
Anticholinergic—
Oral, 200 mcg (0.2 mg) per kg of body weight or 6 mg per square meter of body surface a day (in four divided doses, before meals and at bedtime).

Strength(s) usually available
U.S.—
Not commercially available.
Canada—
Not commercially available.

Packaging and storage
Store between 15 and 30 °C (59 and 86 °F), unless otherwise specified by manufacturer. Store in a tight container.

Auxiliary labeling
- May cause blurred vision.

PIRENZEPINE

Summary of Differences
Pharmacology/pharmacokinetics:
Half-life (elimination)—10 to 12 hours.
Elimination—Renal and hepatic; 80 to 90% of drug excreted unchanged.

Oral Dosage Forms

PIRENZEPINE HYDROCHLORIDE TABLETS

Usual adult and adolescent dose

Anticholinergic—

Oral, 50 mg two times a day, in the morning and at bedtime, the dosage being increased to three times a day, if needed and tolerated.

Note: Geriatric patients may be more sensitive to the effects of the usual adult dose.

Usual pediatric dose

Dosage has not been established.

Strength(s) usually available

U.S.—

Not commercially available.

Canada—

50 mg (Rx) [*Gastrozepin*].

Packaging and storage

Store below 40 °C (104 °F), preferably between 15 and 30 °C (59 and 86 °F), unless otherwise specified by manufacturer.

Auxiliary labeling

- May cause blurred vision.

PROPANTHELINE

Summary of Differences

Indications:

Also used for duodenography and urinary incontinence.

Pharmacology/pharmacokinetics:

Half-life (elimination)—1.6 (mean) hours.

Duration of action—6 hours.

Elimination—Renal; less than 6% of drug excreted unchanged.

Oral Dosage Forms

PROPANTHELINE BROMIDE TABLETS USP

Usual adult and adolescent dose

Anticholinergic—

Oral, 15 mg three times a day, one-half hour before meals, and 30 mg at bedtime, the dosage being adjusted as needed and tolerated.

Note: Patients of less than average body weight may require only 7.5 mg three or four times a day.

Usual adult prescribing limits

Up to 120 mg daily.

Usual pediatric dose

Anticholinergic—

Oral, 375 mcg (0.375 mg) per kg of body weight or 10 mg per square meter of body surface four times a day, the dosage being adjusted as needed and tolerated.

Note: Pediatric administration is limited by the available dosage form. The tablets are not suitable for subdivision.

Usual geriatric dose

Oral, 7.5 mg three or four times a day.

Strength(s) usually available

U.S.—

7.5 mg (Rx) [*Pro-Banthine*].

15 mg (Rx) [*Pro-Banthine;* GENERIC].

Canada—

7.5 mg (Rx) [*Pro-Banthine*].

15 mg (Rx) [*Pro-Banthine; Propanthel*].

Packaging and storage

Store below 40 °C (104 °F), preferably between 15 and 30 °C (59 and 86 °F), unless otherwise specified by manufacturer. Store in a well-closed container.

Auxiliary labeling

- May cause blurred vision.

SCOPOLAMINE

Summary of Differences

Category:

Also a gastrointestinal antispasmodic, antidysmenorrheal, urinary antispasmodic, antiemetic, and antivertigo agent. Parenteral scopolamine is used as an antiarrhythmic and anesthesia adjunct.

Indications—

Indicated in preanesthesia as antisialagogue. Also indicated for biliary tract disorders, nocturnal enuresis, and excessive salivation. Not indicated for peptic ulcer.

Pharmacology/pharmacokinetics:

Protein binding—

Scopolamine hydrobromide: Low.

Half-life (elimination)—

8 hours.

Onset of action—

Oral scopolamine hydrobromide:

30 to 60 minutes (antisialagogue effect).

Parenteral scopolamine hydrobromide:

30 minutes (antisialagogue effect).

Duration of action—

Scopolamine hydrobromide:

Oral—4 to 6 hours.

Parenteral—4 hours.

Scopolamine Transdermal:

Up to 72 hours.

Elimination—

Renal; 1% of oral dose excreted unchanged, and 3.4% of subcutaneous dose excreted unchanged.

Precautions:

Pregnancy—

Parenteral administration before onset of labor may cause CNS depression and hemorrhage in neonate.

Drug interactions and/or related problems—

Additive sedation with other CNS depressants.

Laboratory value alterations—

Residual cycloplegia and mydriasis with transdermal dosage form may affect results of neuroradiological tests for intracranial neoplasm, subdural hematoma, or cerebral aneurysm.

Side/adverse effects:

Scopolamine has been reported to cause paradoxical reaction (trouble in sleeping). Anxiety, irritability, nightmares, and trouble in sleeping may indicate rebound reduction in rapid eye movement (REM) time. Drowsiness and a false sense of well being are more common also.

Additional Dosing Information

See also *General Dosing Information.*

In the presence of pain, scopolamine may act as a stimulant, often producing delirium, if used without morphine or meperidine.

Cardiac rate is much slower with low doses of scopolamine (0.1 to 0.2 mg) than with average clinical doses of atropine. With higher doses, a short-lived cardioacceleration occurs followed within 30 minutes by a return to the normal rate.

Oral Dosage Forms

SCOPOLAMINE BUTYLBROMIDE TABLETS

Usual adult and adolescent dose

Anticholinergic or
Antispasmodic, gastrointestinal or
Antidysmenorrheal—

Oral, 10 to 20 mg three or four times a day, the dosage being adjusted as needed and tolerated.

Note: Geriatric patients may be more sensitive to the effects of the usual adult dose.

Usual pediatric dose

Dosage has not been established.

Strength(s) usually available

U.S.—

Not commercially available.

Canada—

10 mg (Rx) [*Buscopan*].

Packaging and storage

Store below 40 °C (104 °F), preferably between 15 and 30 °C (59 and 86 °F), in a well-closed container, unless otherwise specified by manufacturer.

Auxiliary labeling

- May cause drowsiness or blurred vision.
- Avoid alcoholic beverages.

Parenteral Dosage Forms

SCOPOLAMINE BUTYLBROMIDE INJECTION

Usual adult and adolescent dose

Anticholinergic or
Antispasmodic, gastrointestinal—
Intramuscular, intravenous, or subcutaneous, 10 to 20 mg three or four times a day, the dosage being adjusted as needed and tolerated.

Usual pediatric dose

Dosage has not been established.

Strength(s) usually available

U.S.—
Not commercially available.
Canada—
20 mg per mL (Rx) [*Buscopan*].

Packaging and storage

Store below 40 °C (104 °F), preferably between 15 and 30 °C (59 and 86 °F), unless otherwise specified by manufacturer. Protect from freezing.

SCOPOLAMINE HYDROBROMIDE INJECTION USP

Usual adult and adolescent dose

Anticholinergic—
Intramuscular, intravenous, or subcutaneous, 300 to 600 mcg (0.3 to 0.6 mg) as a single dose.
Prophylaxis of excessive salivation and respiratory tract secretions, in anesthesia—
Intramuscular, 200 to 600 mcg (0.2 to 0.6 mg) one-half to one hour before induction of anesthesia.
Antiemetic—
Intramuscular, intravenous, or subcutaneous, 300 to 600 mcg (0.3 to 0.6 mg) as a single dose.
Anesthesia adjunct—
Sedation-hypnosis—
Intramuscular, intravenous, or subcutaneous, 600 mcg (0.6 mg) three or four times a day.
Amnesia—
Intramuscular, intravenous, or subcutaneous, 320 to 650 mcg (0.32 to 0.65 mg).

Note: Geriatric patients may be more sensitive to the effects of the usual adult dose.

Usual pediatric dose

Anticholinergic or
Antiemetic—
Intramuscular, intravenous, or subcutaneous, 6 mcg (0.006 mg) per kg of body weight or 200 mcg (0.2 mg) per square meter of body surface, as a single dose.
Prophylaxis of excessive salivation and respiratory tract secretions, in anesthesia—
Intramuscular, administered forty-five minutes to one hour before induction of anesthesia for:
Children up to 4 months of age—Use is not recommended.
Children 4 to 7 months of age—100 mcg (0.1 mg).
Children 7 months to 3 years of age—150 mcg (0.15 mg).
Children 3 to 8 years of age—200 mcg (0.2 mg).
Children 8 to 12 years of age—300 mcg (0.3 mg).

Strength(s) usually available

U.S.—
300 mcg (0.3 mg) per mL (Rx) [GENERIC].
400 mcg (0.4 mg) per mL (Rx) [GENERIC].
500 mcg (0.5 mg) per mL (Rx) [GENERIC].
600 mcg (0.6 mg) per mL (Rx) [GENERIC].
860 mcg (0.86 mg) per mL (Rx) [GENERIC].
1 mg per mL (Rx) [GENERIC].
Canada—
Not commercially available.

Packaging and storage

Store below 40 °C (104 °F), preferably between 15 and 30 °C (59 and 86 °F), unless otherwise specified by manufacturer. Store in a light-resistant container. Protect from freezing.

Preparation of dosage form

When given intravenously, scopolamine should be diluted with sterile water for injection before administration.

Rectal Dosage Forms

SCOPOLAMINE BUTYLBROMIDE SUPPOSITORIES

Usual adult and adolescent dose

Anticholinergic or
Antispasmodic, gastrointestinal or
Antidysmenorrheal—
Rectal, 10 mg three or four times a day, the dosage being adjusted as needed and tolerated.

Note: Geriatric patients may be more sensitive to the effects of the usual adult dose.

Usual pediatric dose

Dosage has not been established.

Strength(s) usually available

U.S.—
Not commercially available.
Canada—
10 mg (Rx) [*Buscopan*].

Packaging and storage

Store below 40 °C (104 °F), preferably between 15 and 30 °C (59 and 86 °F), unless otherwise specified by manufacturer.

Auxiliary labeling

- May cause drowsiness or blurred vision.

Note

Include patient instructions when dispensing.

Transdermal Dosage Forms

SCOPOLAMINE TRANSDERMAL SYSTEM

Usual adult and adolescent dose

Note: Geriatric patients may be more sensitive to the effects of the usual adult dose.

Antiemetic or
Antivertigo agent—
Topical, to the postauricular skin, 1 transdermal system delivering 1.0 mg over a period of three days, applied at least four hours before antiemetic effect is needed to prevent motion sickness.

Note: Canadian brand product delivers 1 mg over a period of three days and should be applied approximately twelve hours before the antiemetic effect is required.

Antiemetic, post operative[1]—
Topical to the postauricular skin, 1 transdermal system applied the evening before a scheduled surgery, to prevent post operative nausea and vomiting. For the perioperative period, the patch should be kept in place for 24 hours following surgery.

Note: To minimize exposure to a newborn baby, the patch should be applied one hour prior to cesarean section

Usual pediatric dose

Use is not recommended.

Strength(s) usually available

U.S.—
1.5 mg (Rx) [*Transderm-Scop*].
Canada—
1.5 mg (Rx) [*Transderm-V*].

Packaging and storage

Store below 40 °C (104 °F), preferably between 15 and 30 °C (59 and 86 °F), unless otherwise specified by manufacturer.

Auxiliary labeling

- May cause drowsiness or blurred vision.

Note

Include patient instructions when dispensing.

---

[1]Not included in Canadian product labeling.

Revised: 01/31/2005

Table 1. Side/Adverse Effects*

The following side/adverse effects have been selected on the basis of their potential clinical significance (possible signs and symptoms in parentheses where appropriate)—not necessarily inclusive:

Legend:
I=Anisotropine
II=Atropine
III=Belladonna
IV=Clidinium
V=Dicyclomine
VI=Glycopyrrolate
VII=Homatropine
VIII=Hyoscyamine
IX=Mepenzolate
X=Methantheline
XI=Methscopolamine
XII=Pirenzepine
XIII=Propantheline
XIV=Scopolamine

	I	*II*	*III*	*IV*	*V*	*VI*	*VII*	*VIII*	*IX*	*X*	*XI*	*XII*	*XIII*	*XIV*
Medical attention needed														
Allergic reaction (skin rash or hives)	R	R	R	R	R	R	R	R	R	R	R	R	R	R
Anaphylactic/anaphylactoid reactions						U								
Confusion#	R	R	R	R	R	R	R	R	R	R	R	R	R	R
Hypersensitivity						U								
Increased intraocular pressure (eye pain)†	R	R	R	R	R	R	R	R	R	R	R	R	R	R
Orthostatic hypotension (dizziness, feeling faint, or continuing lightheadedness)	§	R	R	§	R	§	§	R	§	§	§	R	§	R
Palpitation						U								
Pruritus						U								
Tachycardia						U								
Urticaria						U								
Medical attention needed only if continuing or bothersome														
Bloated feeling	R	R	R	R	R	R	R	R	R	R	R	R	R	R
Constipation	M	M	M	M	M	M	M	L	M	M	M	M	M	M
Decreased flow of breast milk	L	L	L	L	L	L	L	L	L	L	L	L	L	L
Decreased salivary secretion (difficulty in swallowing)	L	L	L	L	L	L	L	L	L	L	L	L	L	L
Decreased sweating	M	M	M	M	M	M	M	M	M	M	M	M	M	M
Difficult urination**	R	R	R	R	R	R	R	R	R	R	R	R	R	R
Difficulty in accommodation of the eye (blurred vision)†	R	L	L	R	L	R	R	L	R	R	R	L	R	L
Dizziness						U								
Drowsiness††	R	R	R	R	R	R	R	R	R	R	R	R	R	M
Dryness of mouth, nose, throat, or skin	M	M	M	M	M	M	M	M	M	M	M	M	M	M
False sense of well-being	U	U	U	U	U	U	U	U	U	U	U	U	U	R
Headache	R	R	R	R	R	R	R	R	R	R	R	R	R	R

Table 1. Side/Adverse Effects* *(continued)*

The following side/adverse effects have been selected on the basis of their potential clinical significance (possible signs and symptoms in parentheses where appropriate)—not necessarily inclusive:	Legend: I=Anisotropine II=Atropine III=Belladonna IV=Clidinium				V=Dicyclomine VI=Glycopyrrolate VII=Homatropine VIII=Hyoscyamine				IX=Mepenzolate X=Methantheline XI=Methscopolamine			XII=Pirenzepine XIII=Propantheline XIV=Scopolamine		
	I	II	III	IV	V	VI	VII	VIII	IX	X	XI	XII	XIII	XIV
Impotence						U								
Lightheadedness, temporary—with parenteral administration	U	U	U	U	R	R	U	R	U	U	U	U	U	R
***Loss of memory*‡‡**	R	R	R	R	R	R	R	R	R	R	R	R	R	M
Loss of taste						U								
Mydriatic effect (increased sensitivity of eyes to light)†	R	L	L	R	L	R	R	L	R	R	R	L	R	L
Nausea or vomiting	R	R	R	R	R	R	R	R	R	R	R	R	R	R
Nervousness						U								
Paradoxical reaction (trouble in sleeping)	U	U	U	U	U	U	U	U	U	U	U	U	U	R
Redness or other signs of irritation at injection site	U	M	U	U	M	M	U	M	U	U	U	U	U	M
Unusual tiredness or weakness	R	R	R	R	R	R	R	R	R	R	R	R	R	R
Medical attention needed if they occur after scopolamine is discontinued														
Anxiety	U	U	U	U	U	U	U	U	U	U	U	U	U	§§
Irritability	U	U	U	U	U	U	U	U	U	U	U	U	U	§§
Nightmares	U	U	U	U	U	U	U	U	U	U	U	U	U	§§
Trouble in sleeping	U	U	U	U	U	U	U	U	U	U	U	U	U	§§

*Differences in frequency of occurrence may reflect either lack of clinical-use data or actual pharmacologic distinctions among agents (although their pharmacologic similarity suggests that side effects occurring with one may occur with the others). M=more frequent; L=less frequent; R=rare; U=unknown.

†Quaternary ammonium compounds are fully ionized in the pH range of body fluids and possess reduced lipid solubility. Therefore, they penetrate cellular barriers less effectively and only pass across the blood-brain barrier or into the eye with difficulty. Central and ocular effects are negligible and/or less likely to occur with quaternary ammonium compounds.

‡With quaternary ammonium compounds, difficulty in breathing, severe muscle weakness, and severe tiredness may occur because of the compounds" curare-like effects; these effects may lead to respiratory paralysis.

§Orthostatic hypotension, due to ganglion-blocking activity, is more likely to occur with high doses of quaternary ammonium compounds.

#Confusion may occur more frequently in geriatric patients.

**Difficult urination is more likely to occur in older men and may require medical attention in patients with symptoms of prostatism.

††More frequent with high doses of anticholinergics, but a common side effect with therapeutic doses of oral or parenteral scopolamine.

‡‡Scopolamine, administered parenterally as preanesthetic medication and/or given in large doses, may have a temporary but detrimental effect on memory. In geriatric patients, especially those who already have memory problems, the continued use of any anticholinergic may severely impair memory.

§§May indicate rebound reduction in rapid eye movement (REM) time.

ANTICOAGULANTS Systemic

This monograph includes information on the following: 1) Acenocoumarol*; 2) Anisindione†; 3) Dicumarol†; 4) Warfarin.

Note: See also individual *Antithrombin III (Systemic)*, *Ardeparin (Systemic)*, *Dalteparin (Systemic)*, *Danaparoid (Systemic)*, *Enoxaparin (Systemic)*, and *Heparin (Systemic)* monographs.

INN: Dicumarol—Dicoumarol

BAN: Acenocoumarol—Nicoumalone

VA CLASSIFICATION (Primary): BL114

Commonly used brand name(s): *Coumadin*[4]; *Miradon*[2]; *Sintrom*[1]; *Warfilone*[4].

Other commonly used names are nicoumalone [acenocoumarol] and dicoumarol [dicumarol]

Note: For a listing of dosage forms and brand names by country availability, see *Dosage Forms* section(s).

*Not commercially available in U.S.
†Not commercially available in Canada.

Category

Anticoagulant.

Indications

Note: Bracketed information in the *Indications* section refers to uses that are not included in U.S. product labeling.

General Considerations

This monograph includes information on two types of anticoagulants—coumarin derivatives (acenocoumarol, dicumarol, warfarin) and indanedione derivatives (anisindione). Warfarin is usually the oral anticoagulant of choice. In general, because of their higher risk of hemorrhage, indanedione derivatives are used only when an oral anticoagulant is indicated but use of coumarin derivatives is not possible. Dicumarol is seldom used because of its unpredictable response and high incidence of gastrointestinal side effects.

Decisions about whether to use anticoagulants should take into account the balance between potential benefits (prevention of thromboembolism, reduced mortality) and risks (hemorrhage, possible increased mortality). The presence or absence of risk factors (e.g., advanced age, history of bleeding or stroke, diabetes, hypertension) strongly influences both the decision about whether to initiate anticoagulant therapy and the choice of anticoagulant. Multiple indications also may be present (e.g., atrial fibrillation in patients with prosthetic heart valves) and may affect treatment decisions.

Several of the indications for the oral anticoagulants are identical to those for aspirin, heparin, other antithrombotic agents, other platelet aggregation inhibitors, and thrombolytic agents. Choice of agent may depend on the specific condition, associated risk factors, and desired effect. In some cases, oral anticoagulants may be used in combination with, or sequentially with, one or more of these agents.

Since the full therapeutic effects of oral anticoagulants is delayed for several days, heparin is the agent of choice when an immediate anticoagulant effect is required. Oral anticoagulants are used when treatment is not urgent or for long-term anticoagulant therapy following initial heparin or thrombolytic therapy.

Warfarin injection is used when coumarin anticoagulant therapy is desired in patients who cannot take oral warfarin.

Accepted

Thrombosis (prophylaxis and/or treatment) or

Thromboembolism (prophylaxis and/or treatment)—Anticoagulants are indicated for prophylaxis and/or treatment of venous [or arterial] thrombosis (and its extension) and pulmonary embolism.

Deep vein thrombosis (DVT) or pulmonary embolism (treatment)

Oral anticoagulants are used during and following initial heparin therapy to decrease the risk of extension, recurrence, or death.

Note: Oral anticoagulant therapy is usually initiated at the same time as heparin therapy, or at least overlapped with heparin therapy; heparin therapy is withdrawn when a therapeutic prothrombin time has been maintained for an appropriate period.

DVT or pulmonary embolism (prophylaxis)

Oral anticoagulants are used to prevent thromboembolic complications after surgery, although low-dose subcutaneous heparin is used more commonly.

Note: Perioperative warfarin is recommended in selected very-high-risk general surgery patients.

Warfarin may be started preoperatively in patients undergoing elective total hip replacement or total knee replacement surgery, and continued postoperatively.

Warfarin may be started preoperatively or immediately postoperatively in patients undergoing hip fracture surgery.

Low-dose warfarin is recommended in patients with long-term indwelling central vein catheters to prevent axillary-subclavian venous thrombosis.

Atrial fibrillation

Anticoagulants are indicated for prophylaxis and/or treatment of thromboembolic complications (ischemic stroke) associated with atrial fibrillation. They are strongly recommended in patients at high risk of stroke (including patients with recent stroke, transient ischemic attack, or systemic embolism; poor left ventricular function; age over 75 years; hypertension; rheumatic mitral valve disease; mechanical or tissue prosthetic heart valves).

Note: In patients with one or more lower-risk factors (diabetes mellitus, coronary artery disease, age 65 to 75 years, thyrotoxicosis), the decision about whether to use oral anticoagulants should balance the relative efficacy (compared to aspirin) against the risk of hemorrhage.

Oral anticoagulant therapy is strongly recommended for 3 weeks before elective cardioversion of chronic atrial fibrillation, and should be continued until normal sinus rhythm has been maintained for 4 weeks, to reduce the risk of postconversion emboli. Similar antithrombotic therapy may also be considered at the time of cardioversion in atrial flutter, but antithrombotic therapy is not recommended for cardioversion of chronic supraventricular tachycardia.

Myocardial infarction

Anticoagulants are indicated after myocardial infarction to reduce the risk of death, recurrent myocardial infarction, and thromboembolic events such as stroke or systemic embolization.

Note: Anticoagulants are used after initial heparin therapy, primarily in high-risk patients such as those with shock, congestive heart failure, prolonged arrhythmias (especially atrial fibrillation), previous myocardial infarction, or history of systemic or pulmonary thromboembolism.

The risk of cardioembolic stroke may be decreased by oral anticoagulants, but the risk of hemorrhagic stroke may be increased. Additional studies are needed to help identify subgroups of patients most likely to benefit from anticoagulant therapy.

Ischemia, myocardial

Oral anticoagulants are indicated, alone or in combination with aspirin, for primary prevention of thrombotic complications of coronary artery disease in patients without history of myocardial infarction, stroke, or transient ischemic attacks but with increasing levels of risk.

Note: Because of the risk of cerebral hemorrhage with combined use of aspirin and anticoagulants, as well as the costs and complexity of warfarin therapy, aspirin monotherapy is usually recommended. Low-dose warfarin therapy is recommended as an alternative to aspirin for men at high risk of cardiovascular events, to prevent those events and reduce all-cause mortality. Combination therapy with aspirin and low-dose warfarin may be considered in men at very high risk.

Prosthetic heart valves

Anticoagulants are indicated for prophylaxis and/or treatment of thromboembolic complications associated with tissue and mechanical cardiac valve replacement.

Note: Concurrent use of aspirin may increase effectiveness in patients who experience embolism in spite of adequate anticoagulant therapy but is associated with an increased risk of hemorrhage if the international normalized ratio (INR) is not kept at a low level.

[Valvular heart disease]

Anticoagulants are used in certain patients with valvular heart disease to prevent systemic embolization.

Note: Warfarin is strongly recommended in rheumatic mitral valve disease in patients who have either a history of systemic embolism or who have paroxysmal or chronic atrial fibrillation. Long-term warfarin therapy should be considered in rheumatic mitral valve disease in patients with normal sinus rhythm if the left atrial diameter exceeds 5 centimeters.

Long-term warfarin therapy is not recommended in aortic valve disease unless there is concomitant mitral valve disease, atrial fibrillation, or a history of systemic embolism.

Long-term warfarin therapy is strongly recommended in mitral valve prolapse, but only in patients who have documented systemic embolism, chronic or paroxysmal atrial fibrillation, or recurrent transient ischemic attacks despite aspirin therapy.

Long-term warfarin therapy is recommended in mitral annular calcification, but only in patients with systemic embolism not documented to be calcific embolism or in patients with associated atrial fibrillation.

Long-term warfarin therapy is strongly recommended in patent foramen ovale (PFO) and atrial septal aneurysm in patients with unexplained systemic embolism or transient ischemic attacks and demonstrable venous thrombosis or pulmonary embolism, unless venous interruption or surgical closure of the PFO is preferable.

Long-term warfarin therapy may be continued if infective endocarditis occurs in patients with mechanical prosthetic valves, unless there are specific contraindications, because of the high incidence of systemic thromboembolism in these patients; however, the risk of intracranial hemorrhage is significant with this therapy. The therapeutic decision regarding use of anticoagulant therapy when systemic embolism occurs during the course of infective endocarditis involving a native or bioprosthetic heart valve should involve consideration of comorbid factors (atrial fibrillation, evidence of left atrial thrombus, evidence and size of valvular vegetations) as well as the success of antibiotic therapy.

[Vascular disease, peripheral]

Oral anticoagulants are used, following initial heparinization, to prevent recurrent thromboembolism in peripheral arterial occlusive disease. They are not indicated for routine prophylaxis after intrainguinal bypass and other vascular reconstructions but are indicated, usually in combination with aspirin, in patients at high risk of graft thrombosis.

Acceptance not established

There are insufficient data to evaluate safety and efficacy of oral anticoagulants for prevention of worsening or recurrence of *acute ischemic (atherothrombotic) stroke* (i.e., noncardioembolic stroke). At effective INRs, the risk of hemorrhage appears to outweigh the potential benefit.

There are insufficient data to determine efficacy of oral anticoagulants for prevention of occlusion of saphenous veins used in *coronary artery bypass grafts;* aspirin therapy, however, is well-established.

Although there is a good theoretical basis for use of anticoagulants in the *primary treatment of cancer*, efficacy has not been established in clinical trials.

Unaccepted

Warfarin is no longer recommended for use in the prevention of subacute thrombosis after *intracoronary stent placement*, because studies have shown that the combination of aspirin and ticlopidine is more effective.

Pharmacology/Pharmacokinetics

Physicochemical characteristics

Chemical Group—

Coumarin derivatives: Acenocoumarol, dicumarol, warfarin.

Indanedione derivative: Anisindione.

Molecular weight—

Acenocoumarol: 353.33.

Anisindione: 252.27.

Dicumarol: 336.3.

Warfarin sodium: 330.32.

Mechanism of action/Effect

Both coumarin and indanedione derivatives are indirect-acting anticoagulants. They prevent the formation of active procoagulation factors II, VII, IX, and X, as well as the anticoagulant proteins C and S, in the liver by inhibiting the vitamin K-mediated gamma-carboxylation of precursor proteins. These agents have no direct thrombolytic effect and do not reverse ischemic tissue damage, although they may limit extension of existing thrombi and prevent secondary thromboembolic complications.

Commercially available warfarin is a racemic mixture of R- and S-enantiomers. The S-enantiomer has 2 to 5 times the anticoagulant activity of the R-enantiomer but also has more rapid clearance.

Absorption

Acenocoumarol—Rapid; bioavailability is at least 60%.

Anisindione—Accumulation does not occur with repeated dosing.

Dicumarol—Irregular.

Warfarin—Rapidly and completely absorbed from the gastrointestinal tract. The rate, but not the extent, of warfarin absorption is decreased by food.

Protein binding

Acenocoumarol—Very high (98.7%), primarily to albumin.

Dicumarol—Very high (approximately 97%), to albumin.

Warfarin—Very high (approximately 99%), primarily to albumin. Affinity of the R-isomer is higher than than of the S-isomer, which could result in stereospecific displacement from binding by other medications.

Biotransformation

Hepatic. Enterohepatic recirculation of warfarin occurs.

Acenocoumarol—At least two metabolic pathways are involved, oxidation and reduction to pharmacologically inactive metabolites. Oxidation produces two hydroxylated metabolites. Reduction of the ketone produces two different alcohol metabolites; reduction of the nitrite produces an amine metabolite, a major portion of which is further transformed to the corresponding acetamide metabolite. An additional unidentified strongly polar metabolite fraction has also been detected.

Warfarin—Stereoselective metabolism by hepatic microsomal enzymes to inactive hydroxylated metabolites and by reductases to reduced metabolites (warfarin alcohols), which have minimal anticoagulant activity. The major hepatic isoenzyme involved appears to be CYP 2C9.

Half-life

Acenocoumarol—

8 to 11 hours.

Dicumarol—

1 to 2 days.

Warfarin—

Distribution: 6 to 12 hours.

Elimination: Approximately 1 week after a single dose; however, the effective half-life is 20 to 60 hours (mean, about 40 hours). The half-life is 37 to 89 hours for the R-enantiomer and 21 to 43 hours for the S-enantiomer.

Onset of action

Anisindione—

Effect on prothrombin time (PT): Prolonged, within 6 hours, to 50% of baseline prothrombin activity; prothrombin activity decreases slowly thereafter.

Dicumarol—

Induction of hypoprothrombinemia: 36 to 48 hours.

Effect on PT: 1 to 5 days.

Warfarin (oral)—

Effect on PT: Within 24 hours.

Note: Full therapeutic action is delayed until circulating coagulation factors are removed by normal catabolism, which occurs at different rates for each factor. Although PT may be prolonged when factor VII (which has the shortest half-life) is depleted, it is believed that peak antithrombotic effects are not achieved until all four factors are removed.

Prolonged PT may reflect early depletion of factor VII rather than peak antithrombotic effects. Use of an initial loading dose might also produce this effect; however, loading doses currently are not recommended.

Time to peak plasma concentration

Acenocoumarol—Within 1 to 3 hours.

Dicumarol—1 to 9 hours.

Warfarin—Oral: Within 4 hours.

Peak plasma concentration

Acenocoumarol—Following a single dose of 10 mg: 0.3 mcg per mL. Both peak plasma concentrations and areas under the concentration-time curve (AUCs) are proportional to the size of the dose over a range of 8 to 16 mg.

Note: Because plasma concentrations achieved are variable among patients, there is no direct correlation between plasma concentration and effect on PT.

Time to peak effect

Effect on PT—

Acenocoumarol: 36 to 48 hours.

Anisindione: 48 to 72 hours, to 15 to 30% of baseline.

Warfarin: Oral or intravenous—72 to 96 hours.

Duration of action

Acenocoumarol: Within 48 hours.

Anisindione: 1 to 3 days.

Dicumarol: 5 to 6 days.

Warfarin: Single dose—2 to 5 days.

Elimination

Primarily renal, almost entirely as metabolites, and to a lesser extent biliary.

Acenocoumarol—
- Renal, 60%.
- Fecal, 29%.

Warfarin—
- Renal, up to 92%.
- In dialysis—
  Half-life of warfarin is significantly decreased in hemodialysis.

Precautions to Consider

Carcinogenicity

Anisindione: Long-term studies have not been done.

Warfarin: Studies have not been done.

Mutagenicity

Anisindione: No information is available.

Warfarin: Studies have not been done.

Pregnancy/Reproduction

Pregnancy—Coumarin- and indanedione-derivative anticoagulants cross the placenta. Concentrations of warfarin in fetal plasma are nearly as high as maternal concentrations.

Congenital malformations have been reported in infants of mothers who took warfarin during the first trimester, including a syndrome characterized by severe nasal hypoplasia and stippled epiphyseal calcifications that resemble chondrodysplasia punctata, as well as central nervous system (CNS) abnormalities, including dorsal midline dysplasia (characterized by agenesis of the corpus callosum, Dandy-Walker malformation, and midline cerebellar atrophy), and ventral midline dysplasia (characterized by optic atrophy). Mental retardation, blindness, and other CNS abnormalities have been reported in infants born to mothers taking these agents during the second and third trimesters. Other rare teratogenic effects include urinary tract anomalies, such as single kidney, asplenia, anencephaly, spina bifida, cranial nerve palsy, hydrocephalus, cardiac defects and congenital heart disease, polydactyly, deformities of toes, diaphragmatic hernia, corneal leukoma, cleft palate, cleft lip, schizencephaly, and microcephaly.

Spontaneous abortion and stillbirth have occurred, as well as low birth weight and growth retardation. In addition, fetal or neonatal hemorrhage, fetal death from hemorrhage *in utero*, and increased risk of maternal hemorrhage during the second and third trimesters have been reported. There is some evidence that embryopathy occurs only with oral anticoagulant administration between the 6th and 12th weeks of gestation.

The polymorphism in the factor V gene, known as factor V Leiden, that causes activated protein C resistance to anticoagulant therapy is associated with an increased incidence of venous thrombosis cases during pregnancy. Pregnancy is considered a high-risk state, and anticoagulant treatment should be adjusted accordingly, when these genetic factors are present.

In general, clinicians recommend that coumarin- or indanedione-derivative anticoagulants not be used at any time during pregnancy. Women of childbearing potential should be informed of the risks of becoming pregnant while receiving a coumarin or indanedione derivative. If the patient becomes pregnant during anticoagulant therapy, the possibility of termination of the pregnancy may be considered.

If an anticoagulant is required during pregnancy, heparin may be preferred because it does not cross the placenta. For patients receiving a coumarin or indanedione derivative who wish to become pregnant, some clinicians recommend conversion to heparin therapy prior to conception, while others recommend careful monitoring of the patient and conversion to heparin as soon as pregnancy is confirmed.

Anisindione: FDA Pregnancy Category X.

Warfarin: FDA Pregnancy Category X.

Labor and delivery—If a coumarin or indanedione derivative is used during the third trimester, it should be discontinued after the 37th week of gestation, and heparin substituted if maternal anticoagulation is required, to reduce the risk of fetal hemorrhage during labor and of neonatal hemorrhage following delivery. Anticoagulants also increase the risk of maternal hemorrhage during or following delivery. Anticoagulant therapy may be reinstated 5 to 7 days postpartum.

Postpartum—

Administration of anticoagulants in the immediate postpartum period may increase the risk of maternal hemorrhage.

Breast-feeding

Acenocoumarol is distributed into breast milk, but in quantities that are too small for detection.

Warfarin is distributed into breast milk only in its inactive form; studies in infants who were breast-fed while their mothers were taking warfarin did not find any effect on prothrombin time (PT).

Pediatrics

Safety and efficacy of warfarin in children younger than 18 years of age have not been established in randomized, controlled clinical trials, although such trials are currently being conducted. However, use of warfarin in children is well documented for prophylaxis and treatment of thromboembolism.

Infants, especially neonates, may be more susceptible to the effects of anticoagulants because of vitamin K deficiency. Levels of vitamin K-dependent coagulant factors and inhibitors at birth are approximately 50% of those in adults, similar to the level in adults receiving oral anticoagulant therapy. Levels of vitamin K-dependent proteins increase rapidly after the neonatal period, to within the adult range by the age of 6 months, but average values are approximatley 20% below adult values until the late teenage years. As a result, there is a possibility that the optimal goal of the international normalized ratio (INR) for anticoagulant therapy will be lower in children than in adults.

Breast-fed infants are very sensitive to oral anticoagulants because of the low concentrations of vitamin K in breast milk. Some children are resistant to oral anticoagulant effects because of impaired absorption, use of total parenteral nutrition, or use of nutrient formulas supplemented with vitamin K.

Because there have been reports of difficulty in achieving and maintaining therapeutic PT/INR ranges in pediatric patients, more frequent monitoring is recommended.

Studies in animals suggest that anticoagulants given during periods of rapid bone growth (i.e., mainly in children) might cause bone abnormalities similar to those that occur in infants whose mothers received anticoagulants during pregnancy (hypoplasia of the nasal bridge and distal phalanges and excessive irregular calcifications in epiphyses and vertebrae). Studies in humans have not been done.

Geriatrics

Geriatric patients may be more susceptible to the effects of anticoagulants, increasing the risk of hemorrhage. Geriatric patients may have advanced vascular disease that alters hemostatic mechanisms, hepatic function impairment that decreases procoagulant factor synthesis or anticoagulant metabolism, or they may have renal function impairment. Lower maintenance doses than those usually recommended for adults may be required for these patients.

Warfarin—Although there are no age-related differences in pharmacokinetics of racemic warfarin, there is some evidence of a slight decrease in clearance of the R-enantiomer in elderly patients. In addition, elderly patients (60 years of age and over) appear to be more sensitive to the PT/INR effects of warfarin.

Pharmacogenetics

Certain hereditary or familial conditions that predispose an individual to thrombosis may affect indications for, as well as dose and duration of, anticoagulant therapy. These may include factor V Leiden (a polymorphism in the factor V gene) or a prothrombin gene mutation, which causes activated protein C resistance, deficiency of protein C or S, deficiency of antithrombin III, hyperhomocysteinemia, and dysfibrinogenemia. A study has confirmed a strong association between multiple genetic defects and the risk of venous thrombosis. In addition, patients with hereditary or familial protein C deficiency may be at increased risk of development of skin or tissue necrosis.

Heterozygosity for the factor V Leiden mutation is between 1 and 8.5% in Causasians (including European), Jewish, Israeli Arab, and Indian populations, but does not appear to occur in African Blacks, Chinese, Japanese, or Native American populations. Incidence of the prothrombin gene mutations (G to A transversion of position 20210 in the 3′-untranslated region) has been reported to be 2% in the Netherlands.

Some patients exhibit resistance to anticoagulant therapy because of genetic variations in the vitamin K receptor site. Doses much higher than those usually recommended may be required to achieve successful anticoagulation in these patients.

Dental

Bleeding from gingival tissue may occur in anticoagulated patients.

Anticoagulant therapy increases the risk of localized hemorrhage during and following oral surgical procedures. Consultation with the prescribing physician may be advisable prior to oral surgery, to determine whether a temporary dosage reduction or withdrawal of anticoagulant therapy is feasible. Also, local measures to minimize bleeding should be used at the time of surgery.

Surgical

Careful monitoring and dosage adjustment are required because interruption of anticoagulant therapy may precipitate thromboembolism, while continuation of full-dose therapy is associated with a risk of hemorrhage. It is recommended that the operative site be sufficiently limited to permit effective use of local procedures for hemostasis (including absorbable hemostatic agents, sutures, and pressure dressings) if necessary.

A severe elevation (more than 50 seconds) in activated partial thromboplastin time (aPTT), with PT/INR in the desired range, may be an indication of increased risk of postoperative hemorrhage.

Drug interactions and/or related problems

The interactions between anticoagulants and other specific medications are complex and sometimes multiple or conflicting, and may vary depending on dose, duration, intermittent versus chronic use, and other factors. The use of multiple medications with additive or conflicting effects further complicates prediction of the effect. Therefore, the net effect may be unpredictable. Decisions regarding dosage adjustment of the anticoagulant should be based on prothrombin time (PT) and/or international normalized ratio (INR) determinations whenever possible. However, it is important to keep in mind that some medications may increase the risk of bleeding without affecting the PT.

Some medication effects that may increase the risk of bleeding during anticoagulant therapy but that are not associated with an increase in PT include inhibition of platelet aggregation, inhibition of platelet formation, hypoprothrombinemia, effects on vascular integrity, gastrointestinal ulceration or hemorrhage, thrombocytopenia, and direct anticoagulant effects.

Clinical effects from an interaction may be apparent immediately or may take several days or weeks to appear. The strength of the effect of interacting medications may be related to a number of factors, including dose, duration of therapy, and even relative effect on the S- or R-isomer of warfarin. The significance and duration of effect also depend on the type of interaction; for example, displacement from plasma protein binding will produce an initial increase in anticoagulant concentration, but a new equilibrium is established within a few days, so the effect is of limited significance.

Only brief information about documented interactions between anticoagulants and other medications has been provided in this monograph. In addition, information regarding the potential mechanism of the interactions is frequently conflicting and incomplete. For additional information about the interactions listed below, please refer to the corresponding *USP DI* monograph and/or the medical literature.

In addition to the listed interactions, there is a possibility that the risk of hemorrhage may be increased by concurrent use of any medication that may inhibit platelet aggregation or cause hypoprothrombinemia, thrombocytopenia, or gastrointestinal ulceration. Conversely, there is a possibility that medications that promote blood clotting may interfere with the anticoagulant effect.

Because of the possible serious consequences of interference with anticoagulant therapy, increased monitoring of the PT/INR is recommended on addition, dosage change, or withdrawal of *any* medication from the regimen of a patient stabilized on a coumarin or indanedione derivative, or if the dosage of a concurrently used medication is changed. Anticoagulant dosage must be adjusted as necessary to prevent hemorrhage or loss of effect. Also, substantial alteration of initial anticoagulant dosage may be necessary when anticoagulant therapy is initiated in a patient receiving a medication known to cause significant alteration of anticoagulant effect.

The following drug interactions and/or related problems have been selected on the basis of their potential clinical significance (possible mechanism in parentheses where appropriate)—not necessarily inclusive (» = major clinical significance).

Note: Combinations containing any of the following medications, depending on the amount present, may also interact with this medication.

Acetaminophen, chronic high-dose usage
(effects of anticoagulants may be **increased**; this effect is unlikely to occur with occasional use or chronic use of less than 2 grams of acetaminophen per day)

Alcohol, acute intoxication
(effects of anticoagulants may be **increased** because of inhibition of hepatic metabolism; other acute effects of alcohol on the liver may also be involved)

Alcohol, chronic abuse
(effects of anticoagulants may be **decreased** because of accelerated metabolism of anticoagulant secondary to stimulation of hepatic microsomal enzyme activity; however, **increased** activity is also possible in advance hepatic cirrhosis)

Allopurinol
(effects of anticoagulants may be **increased** because of inhibition of hepatic metabolism)

» Amiodarone
(effects of anticoagulants may be **increased**, possibly because of inhibition of hepatic metabolism; potentiation is reported to occur within 3 to 4 weeks after initiation of amiodarone therapy and persists up to 4 months following withdrawal of amiodarone)

» Anabolic steroids, especially 17-alpha-alkylated compounds, or
» Androgens or
» Danazol
(effects of anticoagulants are **increased** within 2 to 3 days; dosage reduction of the anticoagulant may be necessary)

Anesthetics, inhalation
(effects of anticoagulants may be **increased**)

Antibiotics (see also individual antibiotic entries)
(theoretically, effects of anticoagulants may be **increased** because of decreased vitamin K synthesis secondary to alterations in intestinal flora; however, significant potentiation is very rare if dietary intake of vitamin K is adequate)

Anticonvulsants, hydantoin
(effects of anticoagulants may be **increased** because of displacement of anticoagulant from protein binding sites)
(effects of anticoagulants may be **decreased** with continued concurrent use because of accelerated metabolism of anticoagulant secondary to stimulation of hepatic microsomal enzyme activity)
(hepatic metabolism of hydantoin anticonvulsants, especially phenytoin, may be decreased, leading to increased anticonvulsant plasma concentrations, half-life, and risk of toxicity)

Antidiabetic agents, sulfonylurea, including glimepiride
(effects of anticoagulants may be **increased** initially because of displacement of anticoagulant from protein binding sites)
(hepatic metabolism of the antidiabetic agent may be decreased, especially by dicumarol, leading to increased plasma concentration and half-life, hypoglycemic effect, and risk of toxicity of the antidiabetic agent)

» Antifungals, azole
(effects of anticoagulants may be **increased**)

» Anti-inflammatory drugs, nonsteroidal (NSAIDs)
(effects of anticoagulants may be **increased** because of displacement of anticoagulant from protein binding sites by fenoprofen, indomethacin, meclofenamate, mefenamic acid, phenylbutazone, or sulindac, and possibly other NSAIDs; in addition, phenylbutazone may inhibit hepatic metabolism of the anticoagulant)
(inhibition of platelet aggregation by NSAIDs [except meclofenamate and mefenamic acid] may result in increased risk of hemorrhage; risk of gastrointestinal ulceration and hemorrhage caused by NSAIDs may be increased; these effects cannot be shown by measurement of PT)

Antineoplastics or
Radiation therapy, recent
(the effect of individual agents is difficult to predict because of the common use of combination therapy; mechanisms for the observed effects generally have not been determined)
(effects of anticoagulants may be **increased** or **decreased** by cyclophosphamide or mercaptopurine)
(effects of anticoagulants may be **increased** by bicalutamide, etoposide, flutamide, fluorouracil, ifosfamide, methotrexate, nilutamide, tamoxifen, and vindesine)
(effects of anticoagulants may be **decreased** by aminoglutethimide, which may induce hepatic enzymes)
(antineoplastics that cause thrombocytopenia may also **increase** the risk of bleeding [see also *Thrombocytopenia-causing medications*])
(imbalances in coagulation factors have been noted with the use of pegaspargase, predisposing the patient to bleeding and/or thrombosis; caution should be used when administering any concurrent anticoagulant therapy; it has also been suggested that blood coagulation factor XIII participates in the cross-linking between fibrins and between fibrin and asparaginase)

» Antithyroid agents
(effects of anticoagulants may be **increased** paradoxically because of decreased hepatic synthesis of procoagulant factors; this effect may depend on antithyroid dosage and subsequent thyroid status of the patient)

» Cephalosporins, second- and third-generation
(effects of anticoagulants may be **increased** because of decreased vitamin K synthesis)
(concurrent use of anticoagulants with cefamandole, cefmetazole, cefoperazone, or cefotetan may **increase** the risk of bleeding because the *N*-methylthiotetrazole [NMTT] side chain on these medications may inhibit the metabolism of anticoagulants; however, critical illness, poor nutritional status, and the presence of liver disease may be more important risk factors for hypoprothrombinemia and bleeding)

Chloral hydrate
(initially, effects of anticoagulants may be **increased** because of displacement of anticoagulant from protein binding sites; however, with continued use, anticoagulant activity may return to baseline level or be **decreased** as a new equilibrium warfarin concentration is established)

Chloramphenicol
(effects of anticoagulants may be **increased** because of inhibition of hepatic metabolism)

Cholestyramine
(effects of anticoagulants may be **decreased** because of decreased absorption from the gastrointestinal tract and interference with enterohepatic circulation)
(effects of anticoagulants may be **increased** because of decreased vitamin K absorption or synthesis)

» Cimetidine
(effects of anticoagulants may be **increased** because of inhibition of hepatic metabolism)

» Cinchophen
(effects of anticoagulants may be **increased**)

Cisapride
(effects of acenocoumarol may be **increased** because of increased absorption from the gastrointestinal tract)

» Clofibrate
(effects of anticoagulants may be **increased**, possibly because of alteration of procoagulant factor synthesis or catabolism or displacement of anticoagulant from protein binding sites)

Corticosteroids, glucocorticoid, or
Corticotropin
(effects of anticoagulants may be **increased** or **decreased** by an unknown mechanism)

» Dextrothyroxine
(effects of anticoagulants may be **increased** because of alteration of procoagulant factor synthesis or catabolism and increased receptor affinity for the anticoagulant; this effect may depend on the thyroid status of the patient)

» Diflunisal
(effects of anticoagulants may be **increased**, possibly in part because of displacement of anticoagulant from protein binding sites)

Disopyramide
(effects of anticoagulants may be **increased** or **decreased** by an unknown mechanism)

» Disulfiram
(effects of anticoagulants may be **increased**; disulfiram may act in the liver to directly increase the hypoprothrombinemia-inducing activity of coumarin derivatives)

Diuretics
(effects of anticoagulants may be **decreased** because of reduction of plasma volume leading to concentration of procoagulant factors in the blood)
(effects of anticoagulants may be **increased** by ethacrynic acid, possibly in part because of displacement of anticoagulant from protein binding sites; clinical significance has not been determined)

Erythromycins
(effects of anticoagulants may be **increased** because of inhibition of enzymatic metabolism)

Estrogens
(effects of anticoagulants may be **decreased** because of increased hepatic synthesis of procoagulant factors)
(use of estrogens in patients with thrombophilic disorders tends to increase the risk of thrombosis, especially in patients with activated protein C resistance due to factor V Leiden mutation)

Estrogens and progestins (oral contraceptives)
(effects of anticoagulants may be **decreased** because of increased hepatic synthesis of procoagulant factors by estrogens; however, **increased** effects have also been reported)
(use of estrogen-containing oral contraceptives in patients with thrombophilic disorders tends to increase the risk of thrombosis, especially in patients with activated protein C resistance due to factor V Leiden mutation)

Ethchlorvynol
(effects of anticoagulants may be **decreased** because of accelerated metabolism of anticoagulant secondary to stimulation of hepatic microsomal enzyme activity)

Fluoroquinolones
(effects of anticoagulants may be **increased**)

Fluoxetine
(effects of anticoagulants may be **increased**, possibly in part because of displacement of anticoagulant from protein binding sites)

» Fluvoxamine
(concurrent use with warfarin for 2 weeks resulted in warfarin plasma concentration **increases** of up to 98% and prolonged prothrombin time)

Gemfibrozil
(effects of anticoagulants may be **increased** because of inhibition of hepatic metabolism)

Glucagon
(effects of anticoagulants may be **increased**; however, dosage reduction of warfarin is recommended only with glucagon doses above 25 mg per day for 2 or more days, which are rarely, if ever, used)

» Glutethimide
(effects of anticoagulants may be **decreased** because of accelerated metabolism of anticoagulant secondary to stimulation of hepatic microsomal enzyme activity)

» Griseofulvin
(effects of anticoagulants may be **decreased** because of accelerated metabolism of anticoagulant secondary to stimulation of hepatic microsomal enzyme activity)

Heparin or
Heparin, low-density, including:
Ardeparin
Dalteparin
Danaparoid
Enoxaparin
(the anticoagulant activity of heparin or low-density heparins may result in an **increased** risk of hemorrhage; low-density heparins and low doses of heparin do not prolong PT)
(heparin may prolong PT when it is given as an intravenous bolus or if full therapeutic doses are given subcutaneously; to minimize problems, it is recommended that blood for the PT test be drawn just prior to, or 5 hours after, the intravenous bolus dose or 24 hours of subcutaneous injection of a full therapeutic dose of heparin)

» Hepatic enzyme inducers (see *Appendix II*)
(effects of anticoagulants may be **decreased** because of induction of hepatic microsomal enzymes; the effect of primidone may be caused by a barbiturate metabolite)

Hepatotoxic medications
(effects of anticoagulants may be **increased** because of slow metabolism and impaired synthesis of clotting factors)

HMG-CoA reductase inhibitors
(concurrent use has been reported to **increase** bleeding and/or PT)

Influenza virus vaccine
(effects of anticoagulants have been reported to be **increased**; however, recent studies have failed to show a significant impact of influenza virus vaccine on the laboratory or clinical effect of warfarin, and patients taking these medications can be vaccinated safely without special precautions or monitoring)

Intrauterine devices (IUDs), copper or progesterone
(administration of anticoagulants during IUD use may **increase** the risk of abnormal uterine bleeding and anemia secondary to menorrhagia and/or hypermenorrhea; the risk of abnormal uterine

bleeding increases around the time of IUD insertion and lessens with continued use, although spotting may persist)

Isoniazid
(effects of anticoagulants may be **increased** because of inhibition of hepatic metabolism)

» Lepirudin
(effects of anticoagulants may be **increased;** gradual reduction in dose and/or infusion rate of lepirudin is recommended prior to switching to an oral anticoagulant)

» Metronidazole
(effects of anticoagulants may be **increased** because of inhibition of hepatic metabolism)

Nalidixic acid
(effects of anticoagulants may be **increased**, possibly in part because of displacement of anticoagulant from protein binding sites)

Olsalazine
(may **increase** the PT)

» Omeprazole
(inhibition of the cytochrome P450 enzyme system by omeprazole, especially in high doses, may cause a decrease in hepatic metabolism of anticoagulants, which may result in delayed elimination and **increased** blood concentrations)

Opioid (narcotic) analgesics
(effects of anticoagulants may be **increased** with prolonged use)

» Paroxetine
(a pharmacodynamic interaction may occur that causes an **increased** bleeding diathesis despite unaltered PT; since there is little clinical experience, caution is advised when these agents are used concomitantly)

Penicillins
(inhibition of platelet aggregation by high-dose parenteral penicillins may result in **increased** risk of hemorrhage; this effect cannot be shown by measurement of PT)
(dicloxacillin and nafcillin may **decrease** the effects of anticoagulants by inducing hepatic enzymes)

Pentosan
(because pentosan has weak anticoagulant activity, the risk of hemorrhage may be **increased**)

Pentoxifylline
(pentoxifylline inhibits platelet aggregation and has also caused prolongation of PT and bleeding; concurrent use with any of these medications may **increase** the risk of bleeding because of additive interference with blood clotting)

» Platelet aggregation inhibitors
(effects of anticoagulants may be **increased**; the effect will not be reflected in PT)

» Plicamycin
(effects of anticoagulants may be **increased** because of plicamycin's hypoprothrombinemic effect)
(interference with platelet formation by plicamycin may result in increased risk of hemorrhage; this effect cannot be shown by measurement of PT)

» Propafenone
(concurrent use results in a significant increase [approximately 39%] in mean steady-state warfarin plasma concentrations, with a corresponding **increase** in PT of approximately 25%)

Propranolol
(effects of anticoagulants may be **increased**)

» Quinidine
(effects of anticoagulants may be **increased** because of alteration of procoagulant factor synthesis; however, **decreased** anticoagulant effect has also been reported)

Quinine
(effects of anticoagulants may be **increased** because of decreased hepatic synthesis of procoagulant factors)

Repaglinide
(effects of anticoagulants may be **increased** because of displacement from plasma protein-binding sites)

Rifabutin
(rifampin is structurally related to rifabutin; rifampin is know to **decrease** the activity of many drugs due to its hepatic enzyme-inducing properties; rifabutin appears to be a less potent enzyme inducer of the hepatic cytochrome P450 system than rifampin; drug interactions data are unavailable for rifabutin itself; therefore, it is recommended that patients taking rifabutin concurrently with anticoagulants be monitored since the significance of possible drug interactions is not known)

» Salicylates, including bismuth subsalicylate
(effects of anticoagulants may be **increased** because of the hypoprothrombinemic effect [with large doses])
(inhibition of platelet aggregation by aspirin may result in increased risk of hemorrhage; risk of gastrointestinal ulceration or hemorrhage caused by salicylates may be increased; these effects cannot be shown by measurement of PT)

» Sertraline
(caution in concurrent use with anticoagulants is recommended because of possible displacement of either medication from protein-binding sites, leading to increased plasma concentrations of the free [unbound] medications and **increased** risk of adverse effects)

Smoking, tobacco
(effects of anticoagulants may be **decreased** because of accelerated metabolism of the anticoagulant secondary to stimulation of hepatic microsomal enzyme activity)

Sucralfate
(effects of anticoagulants may be **decreased**)

» Sulfapyridine or
» Sulfasalazine
(anticoagulants may be displaced from protein-binding sites and/or metabolism may be inhibited by sulfonamides, resulting in **increased** or prolonged effects and/or toxicity; dosage adjustments may be necessary during and after sulfonamide therapy)

» Sulfinpyrazone
(effects of anticoagulants may be **increased** because of inhibition of hepatic metabolism and displacement of the anticoagulant from protein-binding sites; a biphasic response, with decreased anticoagulation occurring following initial potentiation, has been reported; the reason for the effect is unclear since other reports indicate only potentiation of the anticoagulant effect)
(inhibition of platelet aggregation by sulfinpyrazone may result in increased risk of hemorrhage; risk of gastrointestinal ulceration or hemorrhage caused by sulfinpyrazone may be increased; these effects cannot be shown by measurement of PT)

Sulfonamides, long-acting, including co-trimoxazole
(effects of anticoagulants may be **increased**, possibly in part because of displacement of anticoagulant from protein-binding sites)

Tamsulosin
(caution is recommended when used with warfarin because of inconclusive results from *in vitro* and *in vivo* studies)

» Thrombocytopenia-causing medications
(effects of anticoagulants may be **increased**)

» Thrombolytic agents
(thrombolytic effect may lead to hemorrhage; concurrent use is not recommended, although sequential use may be indicated)
(anticoagulants are recommended to prevent additional thrombus formation following thrombolytic therapy for most indications; however, following intravenous thrombolytic therapy for acute coronary arterial occlusion, the need for anticoagulant administration should be determined on an individual basis; if an anticoagulant is administered under these circumstances, careful monitoring of the patient is recommended because of the risk of hemorrhage)

» Thyroid hormones
(effects of anticoagulants may be **increased** because of alteration of procoagulant factor synthesis or catabolism and increased receptor affinity for anticoagulant; this effect may depend upon dosage and subsequent thyroid status of the patient)

» Ticlopidine
(the possibility of additive effects on blood clotting mechanism leading to an **increased** risk of bleeding cannot be discounted; particularly careful clinical monitoring of the patient is recommended if concurrent use is necessary)
(in one study, concurrent administration of warfarin and ticlopidine was associated with an increased risk of medication-induced cholestatic hepatitis)

Valproic acid or
Divalproex
(effects of anticoagulants may be **increased** by valproic acid because of decreased hepatic synthesis of procoagulant factors)
(inhibition of platelet aggregation by divalproex or valproic acid may result in increased risk of hemorrhage; this effect cannot be shown by measurement of PT)

Vitamin E
(effects of anticoagulants may be **increased** with concurrent use of high doses of vitamin E)

» Vitamin K
(effects of anticoagulants may be **decreased** because of increased hepatic synthesis of procoagulant factors; increased vitamin K intake can occur during weight-reduction diets high in green vegetables, certain vegetable oils, or vitamin K-containing supplements)

» Zafirlukast
(the concurrent use of a single 25-mg warfarin dose with multiple doses of zafirlukast resulted in an **increase** of approximately 35% in the mean PT, due to an inhibition of the cytochrome P450 2C9 isoenzyme)

» Zileuton
(concurrent administration of zileuton and warfarin results in a clinically significant **increase** in the PT)

Laboratory value alterations

The following have been selected on the basis of their potential clinical significance (possible effect in parentheses where appropriate)—not necessarily inclusive (» = major clinical significance).

With diagnostic test results

Urinalysis, spectrophotometric
(tests based on color changes may be interfered with because alkaline urine may turn red-orange following administration of anisindione; acidification of the urine to pH 4 eliminates this color)

Activated partial thromboplastin time (aPTT)
(may be increased by warfarin, even in the absence of heparin, but interference with heparin anticoagulation during initial combined therapy is of minimal clinical significance)

Hepatic enzyme values
(may rarely be increased)

Medical considerations/Contraindications

The medical considerations/contraindications included have been selected on the basis of their potential clinical significance (reasons given in parentheses where appropriate)—not necessarily inclusive (» = major clinical significance).

Note: Many of the conditions listed below are common risk factors that underlie the condition for which the anticoagulant therapy is indicated. The relative effect on the decision to prescribe anticoagulants depends on the specific condition for which anticoagulant therapy is being contemplated. Decisions about whether to use anticoagulants should balance the risk of hemorrhage associated with the condition against the potential clinical benefit of anticoagulant therapy.

For conditions that alter the PT, careful monitoring of PT and/or international normalized ratio (INR) and appropriate adjustment of anticoagulant dose are recommended. For conditions in which the effect on bleeding may not be reflected in the PT/INR, careful monitoring of the patient for indications of bleeding is recommended.

The presence of multiple underlying conditions with additive or conflicting effects may complicate prediction of the effect on response to the anticoagulant. The net effect may be unpredictable. Decisions regarding dosage adjustment of the anticoagulant should be based on PT/INR determinations and observation for possible bleeding.

A strong association has been found between single or multiple genetic defects (e.g., factor V Leiden, prothrombin mutation, antithrombin III deficiency) and risk of thrombosis, which indicates that one or more of these defects may be present in individuals with thrombophilic conditions. However, these effects may also be subclinical and patients may be asymptomatic until their first thrombotic event.

In addition to the specific conditions listed below, caution is recommended with use of anticoagulants in any condition associated with a risk of hemorrhage, necrosis, and/or gangrene.

Except under special circumstances, these medications should not be used when the following medical problems exist:

» Abortion, threatened or incomplete
(increased risk of uncontrollable hemorrhage)

» Aneurysm, cerebral or dissecting aorta
(increased risk of uncontrollable hemorrhage)

» Bleeding, active
(increased risk of uncontrollable hemorrhage)

» Blood dyscrasias, hemorrhagic, such as:
Thrombocytopenia or
» Hemophilia or
» Hemorrhagic tendency, other, including:
Leukemia
Polycythemia vera or
Purpura
(increased risk of hemorrhage)
(in patients with heparin-induced thrombocytopenia, cases of venous limb ischemia, necrosis, and gangrene have occurred when heparin therapy was discontinued and warfarin therapy initiated; sequelae have included amputation of the involved area and/or death)

» Cerebrovascular hemorrhage, confirmed or suspected
(increased risk of uncontrollable hemorrhage)

» Eclampsia or pre-eclampsia
(increased risk of hemorrhage)

» Hypertension, severe uncontrolled and/or malignant
(increased risk of cerebral hemorrhage)

» Neurosurgery, recent or contemplated or
» Ophthalmic surgery, recent or contemplated or
» Surgery, major, other, especially if resulting in large open surfaces
(increased risk of uncontrollable hemorrhage)
(although anticoagulants are generally contraindicated following major surgery, they may be required following orthopedic (hip) surgery to reduce the risk of thromboembolism)

» Pericardial effusion or
» Pericarditis
(increased risk of severe hemorrhagic pericardial effusions and pericardial tamponade)

Risk-benefit should be considered when the following medical problems exist:

Allergic or anaphylactic disorders, severe

Antiphospholipid syndrome or
Antithrombin III deficiency
(may reduce the effectiveness of the anticoagulant)

Biliary fistula
(may increase the patient's response to the anticoagulant, leading to an increased risk of bleeding)

Cancer, especially gastrointestinal
(venous thrombosis associated with cancer may be resistant to anticoagulant therapy)

» Carcinoma, visceral
(may increase the patient's response to the anticoagulant, leading to an increased risk of bleeding)

» Childbirth, recent
(increased risk of hemorrhage)

Collagen vascular disease
(may increase the patient's response to the anticoagulant, leading to an increased risk of bleeding)

Conditions that may result in less compliance by unsupervised outpatients, such as:
Alcoholism, active
Emotional instability
Psychosis, unsupervised
Senility, unsupervised
Uncooperative patient

Congestive heart failure
(may increase the patient's response to the anticoagulant, leading to an increased risk of bleeding)

Coumarin resistance, hereditary
(response to coumarin anticoagulants may be decreased)

» Diabetes mellitus, severe
(increased risk of hemorrhage)

Diarrhea, prolonged
(may increase the patient's response to the anticoagulant, leading to an increased risk of bleeding)

Dietary insufficiency, prolonged, especially:
Steatorrhea or low-fat diet
» Vitamin K deficiency or malabsorption
(may increase the patient's response to the anticoagulant, leading to an increased risk of bleeding)

Diets high in phylloquinone (e.g., green leafy vegetables, certain vegetable oils, supplements)
(may decrease the anticoagulant effect)

» Diverticulitis
Edema
(may reduce the effectiveness of the anticoagulant)
» Endocarditis, subacute bacterial
(increased risk of hemorrhage into infarcted area)
Fever
(may increase the patient's response to the anticoagulant, leading to an increased risk of bleeding)
» Hepatic function impairment
(may increase the patient's response to the anticoagulant, both through impaired synthesis of clotting factors and decreased metabolism, leading to an increased risk of bleeding)
Hepatitis, infectious
(may increase the patient's response to the anticoagulant, leading to an increased risk of bleeding)
Hyperhomocystinemia
(may reduce the effectiveness of the anticoagulant)
Hyperlipidemia, including hypercholesterolemia
(may reduce the effectiveness of the anticoagulant)
Hypertension, moderate
Hyperthyroidism
(may increase the patient's response to the anticoagulant, leading to an increased risk of bleeding)
Hypoprothrombinemia
(may increase the patient's response to the anticoagulant)
Hypothyroidism
(may reduce the effectiveness of the anticoagulant)
Infection or
Disturbances of intestinal flora, such as sprue
(may increase the patient's response to the anticoagulant)
Procedures (medical or dental) in which the risk of bleeding or hemorrhage is present, such as:
» Anesthetics, regional or lumbar block
Catheters, indwelling
Drainage tubes in any orifice or wound
» Spinal puncture
(increased risk of uncontrollable hemorrhage)
Protein C deficiency, hereditary, familial, or clinical, known or suspected or
Protein S deficiency, hereditary or acquired or
Other conditions predisposing to tissue necrosis
(increased risk of anticoagulant-induced tissue necrosis, although patients with protein C deficiency may require long-term anticoagulant therapy to prevent recurrent thrombus formation; administration of heparin, protein C concentrate, or fresh frozen plasma during the first few days of oral anticoagulant therapy may reduce the risk of tissue necrosis caused by protein C deficiency)
(protein C deficiency should be suspected if there is a history of recurrent episodes of thromboembolic disorders in the patient or the family)
Renal function impairment
(possible increased risk of hemorrhage; however, dosage adjustment is usually not required)
(in nephrotic syndrome, decreased half-life and decreased effect may occur as a result of hypoproteinemia)
Sensitivity to the anticoagulant prescribed
» Trauma, especially to the central nervous system (CNS)
(increased risk of internal hemorrhage)
Tuberculosis, active
(increased risk of hemorrhage)
» Ulceration or other lesions, active, of:
Gastrointestinal tract, including ulcerative colitis
Respiratory tract
Urinary tract
(increased risk of hemorrhage)
Ulceration or other lesions of gastrointestinal tract, history of
(increased risk of hemorrhage)
» Vasculitis
(increased risk of hemorrhage)
» Wounds, open ulcerative, traumatic, or surgical
(increased risk of hemorrhage)

Caution is also recommended in severely debilitated patients, who may be more sensitive to the effects of anticoagulants.

Caution is also recommended during prolonged hot weather, during which the risk of bleeding may be increased.

Patient monitoring

The following may be especially important in patient monitoring (other tests may be warranted in some patients, depending on condition; » = major clinical significance):

For all anticoagulants
Blood in urine
Occult blood in stool
(determinations recommended at periodic intervals during therapy)
» Prothrombin time (PT) and/or
International normalized ratio (INR)
(determination of PT/INR is the primary means of establishing correct dose; determinations are recommended prior to initiation of therapy, at 24-hour intervals while maintenance dosage is being established, then gradually less frequently for the duration of therapy; additional PT/INR determinations are recommended when patients are switched to different brands or formulations, and whenever other medications are initiated, changed, taken irregularly, or discontinued)
(PT/INR monitoring generally is not done during fixed low-dose warfarin therapy)
(the availability of portable PT monitors has made point-of-care self-monitoring by the patient feasible in selected circumstances, following initial dosage stabilization, as an adjunct to regular monitoring by medical professionals)
(PT reflects depression of vitamin K-dependent factors II, VII, and X; PT is often reported by listing the value in seconds along with the control value in seconds; alternately, PT may be reported as the ratio of the prolonged [therapeutic] value to the control value)
(the one-stage PT test is the usual test used; there is inter-laboratory variability in types [sensitivity] of rabbit brain thromboplastins, as well as one-stage methods, used to determine PT; the appropriate therapeutic PT range used to determine and adjust anticoagulant dosage should be based on the experience of the specific laboratory; a clear understanding of the particular method [e.g., Quick one-stage PT] is important in order to facilitate appropriate anticoagulant dosage adjustment)
(the INR provides a common basis for communication of PT results and interpretation of therapeutic ranges; the INR system is based on a logarithmic relationship between the PT ratios of the test and reference preparation; the International Reference Preparation [IRP] is a sensitive thromboplastin reagent prepared from human brain tissue; the INR is the PT ratio that would be obtained if the IRP, which has an International Sensitivity Index [ISI] of 1.0, were used to perform the test; the INR is calculated as: INR = (observed PT ratio)^{ISI}, where the ISI is the correction factor in the equation that relates the PT ratio of the local reagent to the reference preparation and is a measure of the sensitivity of a given thromboplastin to reduction of vitamin K-dependent coagulation factors; the lower the ISI, the more "sensitive" the reagent and the closer the derived INR will be to the observed PT ratio)
(with the rabbit brain thromboplastins currently commercially available in North America, PT values of 1.2 to 1.5 times the control value are equivalent to INR values of 2 to 3 times the control value, and PT values of 1.5 to 2 times the control value are equivalent to INR values of 3 to 4.5 times the control value; thromboplastins with recombinant tissue factor, which have an IS of approximately 1 [and thus a PT ratio essentially equivalent to the ISR] have recently been introduced; for other thromboplastins, the INR can be calculated using the ISI [available from the manufacturer] as a calibration factor)

For anisindione (in addition to the above)
Hematopoietic function and
Hepatic function and
Protein, urinary and
Renal function
(determinations may be advisable at periodic intervals during anisindione therapy because of the risk of blood dyscrasias, hepatotoxicity, and nephrotoxicity associated with phenindione [an anticoagulant chemically related to anisindione that is no longer available])

Side/Adverse Effects

Note: Differences in frequency of side/adverse effects between anticoagulants may reflect either lack of clinical use data or actual pharmacologic distinctions among agents.

Studies in animals suggest that anticoagulants given during periods of rapid bone growth (i.e., mainly in children) might cause bone abnormalities similar to those that occur in infants whose mothers received anticoagulants during pregnancy (hypoplasia of the nasal bridge and distal phalanges and excessive irregular calcifications in epiphyses and vertebrae). Studies in humans have not been done.

Although not all of the side/adverse effects listed below have been documented with anisindione, they have been reported with phenindione, an indanedione derivative that is no longer commercially available. Other adverse effects or abnormalities reported with phenindione include accommodation paralysis (blurred vision or other problems), aplastic anemia, eosinophilia, leukocytosis, thrombocytopenia, atypical mononuclear cells, red cell aplasia, presence of leukocyte agglutinins, and exfoliative dermatitis. Because anisindione is chemically related to phenindione, these side/adverse effects should be considered potential side/adverse effects of anisindione also.

The following side/adverse effects have been selected on the basis of their potential clinical significance (possible signs and symptoms in parentheses where appropriate)–not necessarily inclusive:

Those indicating need for medical attention

Incidence dose-related

Symptoms of minor bleeding

Blood in urine; epistaxis (nosebleeds); ***gingival bleeding*** (bleeding from gums when brushing teeth); ***petechiae*** (pinpoint red spots on skin); ***unusual bleeding or bruising; unusually heavy bleeding or oozing from cuts or wounds; uterine bleeding, excessive*** (unusually heavy or unexpected menstrual bleeding)

Symptoms of major or internal bleeding or hemorrhage

Adrenal hemorrhage (abdominal or stomach pain; diarrhea; dizziness or fainting; headache; loss of appetite; nausea with or without vomiting; nervousness; weakness); ***bleeding into joints*** (joint pain, stiffness, or swelling); ***gastrointestinal bleeding*** (black, tarry stools; blood in stools; bloody vomit or vomit that looks like coffee grounds; constipation); ***hepatic hemorrhage*** (asymptomatic); ***hypotension or shock*** (dizziness or fainting); ***intracranial hemorrhage; including spinal hemorrhage*** (confusion; dizziness; headache, continuing or severe; nausea and vomiting; paralysis; paresthesias; weakness); ***ophthalmic hemorrhage*** (bleeding in eye; blurred vision); ***ovarian hemorrhage at time of ovulation*** (abdominal or stomach pain); ***pericardial hemorrhage*** (chest pain); ***pulmonary bleeding*** (coughing up blood; shortness of breath); ***retroperitoneal bleeding*** (abdominal pain or swelling; back pain or backaches)

Note: *Fatal or nonfatal bleeding or hemorrhage* can occur from any tissue or organ. Signs, symptoms, and severity vary depending on the site and extent of bleeding. Therefore, bleeding should be considered as a potential cause of any sign or symptom not otherwise explainable.

Incidence of *bleeding or hemorrhage* depends on dose and duration of anticoagulant therapy, as well as age and other medications and underlying conditions. Incidence is increased at an INR over 3, although bleeding may not always correlate with PT. Incidence of hemorrhage is not increased with use of fixed low-dose warfarin (1 mg per day), which produces an INR of 1.3 to 1.9.

Adrenal hemorrhage may result in acute adrenal insufficiency. Diagnosis may be difficult because the initial symptoms (abdominal pain, apprehension, diarrhea, dizziness or fainting, headache, loss of appetite, nausea or vomiting, and weakness) are nonspecific and variable.

The occurrence of *gastrointestinal or genitourinary hemorrhage* during anticoagulant therapy, especially if the prothrombin time (PT) is within the therapeutic range, may indicate the presence of an underlying occult lesion such as a tumor or ulcer.

Gastrointestinal bleeding may also be a symptom of ulceration.

Constipation may be a symptom of hemorrhage-induced paralytic ileus or intestinal obstruction caused by submucosal or intramural hemorrhage.

Intracranial hemorrhage (ICH) includes intracerebral, subdural/epidural, and subarachnoid hemorrhage and commonly results in fatalities. Incidence of ICH appears to be dose-related; however, it has been reported at INRs well within the therapeutic range. Neurologic deficits may evolve rapidly or slowly (over 6 to 24 hours) as the bleeding evolves and expands slowly.

With anisindione, the possibility exists that *unusual bleeding or bruising* may also indicate thrombocytopenia.

Incidence less frequent

Dermatitis, allergic (skin rash, hives, and/or itching)—rare with dicumarol and warfarin; ***fever; leukopenia*** (fever or chills; cough or hoarseness; lower back or side pain; painful or difficult urination)

Incidence rare

Agranulocytosis (fever or chills; cough or hoarseness; lower back or side pain; painful or difficult urination)—with anisindione; ***calcification, tracheal or tracheobronchial*** (trouble in breathing)—with long-term warfarin; ***hepatotoxicity*** (usually asymptomatic and seen on laboratory tests; dark urine; yellow eyes or skin); ***lipid emboli; including systemic atheroemboli and cholesterol microemboli; necrosis and/or gangrene, hemorrhagic, of skin and other tissues*** (sores on skin, especially on thighs, breasts, penis, or buttocks); ***purple toes syndrome*** (blue or purple toes; pain in toes); ***renal damage, with resultant edema and proteinuria*** (bloody or cloudy urine; difficult or painful urination; sudden increase or decrease in amount of urine; swelling of face, feet, and/or lower legs); ***sores, ulcers, or white spots in mouth or throat; vasculitis*** (fever; itching; skin sores or blisters)

Note: *Systemic atheroemboli and cholesterol microemboli* can present with a variety of signs and symptoms, including purple toes syndrome; livedo reticularis; rash; gangrene; abrupt and intense pain in the leg, foot, or toes; foot ulcers; myalgia; penile gangrene; abdominal pain, flank pain, or back pain; hematuria; renal insufficiency; hypertension; cerebral ischemia; spinal cord infarction; pancreatitis; symptoms simulating polyarteritis; or any other sequelae of vascular compromise due to embolic occlusion. The most commonly involved visceral organs are the kidneys, followed by the pancreas, spleen, and liver. Some cases have progressed to necrosis or death.

Necrosis is caused by thrombosis of the venules and capillaries within the subcutaneous fat. It usually occurs on the 3rd to 8th day of therapy and may be more frequent in patients with protein C deficiency. Initial lesions, which are painful, are erythematous or ecchymotic with a sharply demarcated border, subsequently developing bullae with full-thickness skin necrosis. It is important to determine whether necrosis is caused by the anticoagulant or by an underlying disease. In severe cases, debridement or even amputation of affected tissue, limb, breast, or penis may be necessary. Fatalities have occurred.

Purple toes syndrome may develop 3 to 10 weeks after initiation of anticoagulant therapy; it results from systemic cholesterol microembolization. Anticoagulant therapy may enhance the release of atheromatous plaque emboli, which may increase the risk of purple toes syndrome and other complications of systemic cholesterol embolization. Purple spots may blanch with pressure or elevation of the leg. The syndrome is usually reversible but in some cases may progress to gangrene or necrosis.

Those indicating need for medical attention only if they continue or are bothersome

Incidence less frequent or rare

Bloated stomach or gas; cold intolerance; diarrhea—more frequent with dicumarol; ***loss of appetite; nausea or vomiting***—more frequent with dicumarol; ***stomach cramps or pain***

Those not indicating need for medical attention

Incidence less frequent or rare

Alopecia of scalp (loss of hair on scalp)—with long-term use; ***orange-red color in alkaline urine***—with anisindione

Overdose

For specific information on the agents used in the management of anticoagulant overdose, see the

Vitamin K (Systemic) and *Factor IX (Systemic)* monographs. For more information on the management of overdose or unintentional ingestion, **contact a Poison Control Center** (see *Poison Control Center Listing*).

Clinical effects of overdose

The following effects have been selected on the basis of their potential clinical significance (possible signs and symptoms in parentheses where appropriate)—not necessarily inclusive:

Early signs of overdose

Overt or suspected bleeding; including petechiae (pinpoint red spots on skin); ***unusual bleeding or bruising; unusually heavy bleeding or oozing from cuts or wounds; uterine bleeding, excessive*** (unusually heavy or unexpected menstrual bleeding)

Possible symptoms of internal bleeding
Adrenal hemorrhage (abdominal or stomach pain; diarrhea; dizziness or fainting; headache; loss of appetite; nausea with or without vomiting; nervousness; weakness); ***bleeding into joints*** (joint pain, stiffness, or swelling); ***gastrointestinal bleeding*** (black, tarry stools; blood in stools; bloody vomit or vomit that looks like coffee grounds; constipation); ***genitourinary bleeding; including urinary bleeding*** (blood in urine); ***or ovarian hemorrhage at time of ovulation*** (abdominal or stomach pain); ***hepatic hemorrhage*** (asymptomatic); ***hypotension or shock*** (dizziness or fainting); ***intracranial hemorrhage; including spinal hemorrhage*** (confusion; dizziness; headache, continuing or severe; nausea and vomiting; paralysis; paresthesias; weakness); ***ophthalmic hemorrhage*** (bleeding in eye; blurred vision); ***pericardial hemorrhage*** (chest pain); ***pulmonary bleeding*** (coughing up blood; shortness of breath); ***retroperitoneal bleeding*** (abdominal pain or swelling; back pain or backaches)

Treatment of overdose

If excessive increases in prothrombin time (PT) and/or international normalized ratio (INR), without bleeding or prospective surgery, occur, the INR should be reduced to a safe level (e.g., less than 5). If serious bleeding is present, the INR should be reduced to 1 as soon as possible. If elective surgery or urgent surgery is required, the INR can be reduced to 1 to 1.5 at the time of surgery.

Reduction of INR can usually be accomplished by temporarily withdrawing anticoagulant therapy and, if necessary, administering oral or parenteral vitamin K_1. Reversal of anticoagulation is not maximal for 24 to 48 hours after withholding the anticoagulant, until synthesis of fully carboxylated coagulation proteins is complete. For serious overdose or life-threatening bleeding, when immediate restoration of clotting factors is necessary, transfusion of fresh plasma or prothrombin (factor IX) complex concentrate along with vitamin K_1 may be necessary. Use of these blood products is associated with an increased risk of hepatitis and other viral diseases; use of prothrombin complex is also associated with an increased risk of thrombosis. Use of purified factor IX complex preparations (Coagulation Factor IX [Human or Recombinant]) is not recommended because they will not increase concurrently depressed levels of factor II, factor VII, and factor X. Packed red blood cells may be administered for significant blood loss. Although whole blood may be given if blood loss has been extensive, transfusion of whole blood will not elevate procoagulant factor concentrations sufficiently to eliminate the need for administration of plasma or prothrombin complex concentrate. Caution and careful monitoring are recommended during infusion of blood or plasma to avoid precipitating pulmonary edema in elderly patients or patients with cardiac disease.

Vitamin K_1—Overcomes the anticoagulant effect because it is reduced through a different warfarin-resistant enzyme system. Repeated doses may be necessary. The fact that large doses of vitamin K_1 (5 mg or more) will reduce the response to subsequent anticoagulant therapy for up to a week or longer must be kept in mind. Although resumption of anticoagulant therapy can produce therapeutic PT/INR with careful dosage adjustment, heparin may be preferable for initial therapy and/or if rapid anticoagulation is desired.

Fresh whole blood or plasma—200 to 500 mL may be required.

Prothrombin complex concentrate—A factor IX product (Factor IX Complex USP) that may also contain clinically useful quantities of factors II, VII, and X. May also contain other proteins, including proteins C and S; high molecular weight kininogen; and small quantities of activated clotting factors II, VII, IX, or X. The usual dose is 1500 Units.

Patient Consultation

As an aid to patient consultation, refer to *Advice for the Patient, Anticoagulants (Systemic)*.

In providing consultation, consider emphasizing the following selected information (» = major clinical significance):

Before using this medication

» Conditions affecting use, especially:
- Sensitivity to the anticoagulant prescribed
- Pregnancy—Possibility of birth defects or bleeding in the fetus or bleeding in the mother; not becoming pregnant during therapy without first discussing with physician; telling physician immediately if pregnancy is suspected
- Infants may be more sensitive to the effects of anticoagulants
- Elderly patients (60 years of age and older) may be more sensitive to the effects of anticoagulants
- Other medications of any kind
- Other medical problems

Proper use of this medication

» Compliance with therapy; taking at same time each day

» Regular visits to physician or clinic to check progress; possibility of monitoring PT/INR and adjusting dosage at home for some patients

» Proper dosing

Missed dose: Taking as soon as possible; not taking if not remembered until next day; not doubling doses; keeping a record of doses taken to avoid mistakes; keeping record of missed doses to give physician

» Proper storage

Precautions while using this medication

» Informing all physicians, dentists, and/or pharmacists that anticoagulant is being used

» Checking with physician immediately if any signs or symptoms of bleeding occur

» Not taking, stopping, or changing other medications, including over-the-counter (OTC) medications, without first discussing with physician

» Carrying or wearing identification indicating use of anticoagulant

Not engaging in activities that may lead to injury

Caution in activities with risk of cutting or bleeding (e.g., shaving)

Minimizing alcohol consumption

» Eating a normal, balanced diet; caution with weight-loss diets; not changing diet, taking vitamins, or using nutritional supplements without first discussing with physician because of possible alteration of anticoagulant effect by substantial changes in intake of vitamin K

Checking with physician if unable to eat for several days or if continuing gastric upset, diarrhea, or fever occurs

Caution in prolonged hot weather

» Caution when anticoagulant therapy is discontinued, and for several days after withdrawal of therapy, as blood clotting returns to normal

Side/adverse effects

Signs and symptoms of potential side effects, especially bleeding or hemorrhage, allergic dermatitis, fever, leukopenia, agranulocytosis (for anisindione), tracheal or tracheobronchial calcification, hepatotoxicity, lipid emboli including systemic atheroemboli and cholesterol microemboli, necrosis and/or gangrene, purple toes syndrome, renal damage, sores in mouth or throat, and vasculitis

Checking with physician if red-orange color of urine occurs with anisindione; not harmful but may interfere with certain urine tests

General Dosing Information

Dosage should be adjusted to achieve the goal of impeding the coagulation or clotting mechanism to the point that thrombosis will not occur but spontaneous bleeding will be avoided.

Patient compliance is essential to the safe use of these medications. The patient must be responsible and willing to deal with the demands of therapy with these medications.

Determination of dose is complicated by the narrow therapeutic window and wide variability in dose response to warfarin. It has been estimated that 20 to 25% of patients never achieve a stable therapeutic dose. Dosage of anticoagulants must be individualized and should be adjusted according to prothrombin time (PT) and/or international normalized ratio (INR) determinations. Determinations of clotting time, bleeding time, or anticoagulant plasma concentration are not effective measures for monitoring anticoagulant therapy. However, it is important to keep in mind that certain medications or medical conditions may increase risk of hemorrhage without increasing PT (e.g., by causing inhibition of platelet aggregation or thrombolysis). Monitoring of PT/INR must be accompanied by careful monitoring for possible bleeding or hemorrhage, and anticoagulant dosage adjusted accordingly.

Some patients may exhibit resistance to anticoagulant therapy because of genetic predisposition, acquired resistance (e.g., antiphospholipid antibodies), or an increased rate of anticoagulant metabolism and excretion. Doses much higher than those usually recommended may be required to achieve successful anticoagulation in these patients. The presence of acquired or hereditary coumarin resistance should be considered if large daily doses are required to maintain the patient's PT/INR within a normal therapeutic range.

Some patients may exhibit unusual sensitivity to the effects of warfarin. The cause has been postulated to be vitamin K depletion but this has not been studied.

Manufacturers" dosage recommendations may include administration of an initial large loading dose, which is gradually reduced to the maintenance level according to PT/INR determinations. However, many clinicians do not recommend use of large loading doses because of the increased risk of hemorrhage, and because a more rapid anticoagulant effect can be achieved by initiating therapy with heparin.

The therapeutic value of the PT was previously considered to be 1.5 to 2.5 times the control value. Because the rabbit brain thromboplastins currently used in the U.S. for PT determinations are less sensitive than the human brain thromboplastins used previously, the optimal therapeutic value of the PT is now considered to be 1.3 to 1.5 times the control value. However, in the presence of a very high risk of thromboembolism (e.g., in patients with a history of recurrent systemic embolism or patients with mechanical heart valves), maintaining the PT at 1.5 to 2 times the control value may be necessary.

The target INR for any given indication can be defined in general, but may vary depending on severity of the condition, associated risk factors for thrombosis, risk factors for major hemorrhage, combination therapy with other agents, and other relevant conditions. For specific guidelines concerning INR values in determining the appropriate dose of anticoagulant therapy, the prescriber should refer to the literature or to published guidelines, such as those developed in 1998 by the Fifth American College of Chest Physicians (ACCP) Consensus Conference on Antithrombotic Therapy.

In general, an INR of 2 to 3 is recommended for prevention or treatment of venous thromboembolism, including pulmonary embolism, atrial fibrillation, valvular heart disease, or with bioprosthetic heart valves. An INR of 2.5 to 3.5 is recommended after myocardial infarction, in patients with mechanical prosthetic heart valves, or in certain patients with thrombosis and the antiphospholipid syndrome. Higher INR may be recommended for recurrent systemic embolism. Effectiveness of warfarin is reduced at INRs of less than 2, although some benefit can be obtained in some conditions (e.g., prevention of deep vein thrombosis in patients with indwelling central vein catheters) with fixed low-dose warfarin (1 mg per day) at an INR of 1.3 to 2.

Increased monitoring of PT/INR is recommended when *any* new medication, including nonprescription (over-the-counter [OTC]), is added to or withdrawn from the regimen of a patient stabilized on a coumarin or indanedione anticoagulant, or when the dosage of a concurrently used medication is changed. Anticoagulant dosage must be adjusted as necessary to prevent hemorrhage or loss of effect. Also, substantial alteration of initial anticoagulant dosage may be necessary when anticoagulant therapy is initiated in a patient receiving a medication known to cause significant alteration of anticoagulant effect.

When anticoagulant therapy is initiated with heparin and continued with a coumarin or indanedione anticoagulant, it is recommended that both agents be given concurrently until PT/INR determinations indicate an adequate response to the coumarin or indanedione anticoagulant. However, the fact that heparin may prolong the PT must be kept in mind. Subcutaneous or bolus intravenous administration of full therapeutic doses of heparin may prolong the PT considerably because of the high concentrations of heparin achieved in the blood. On the other hand, continuous intravenous infusion of full therapeutic doses or subcutaneous administration of low (prophylactic) doses usually do not increase the PT by more than a few seconds. To minimize problems in interpreting PT test results, it is recommended that blood for the PT test be drawn just prior to, or at least 5 hours after, a bolus intravenous dose or 24 hours after subcutaneous administration of a full therapeutic dose of heparin. Also, the fact that reduction in PT may reflect early depletion of factor VII rather than peak antithrombotic effects of coumarin or indanedione derivatives must be kept in mind. Some clinicians recommend continuation of heparin therapy for up to 4 to 5 days after initiation of therapy with a coumarin or indanedione anticoagulant to ensure that peak antithrombogenic activity has been reached.

Duration of anticoagulant therapy that is appropriate for any given indication can be defined in general, but may vary widely depending on the severity of the condition, associated risk factors for thrombosis, risk factors for major hemorrhage, combination therapy with other agents, and other relevant conditions. For specific guidelines concerning INR values as an aid in determining the appropriate duration of anticoagulant therapy, the prescriber should refer to the literature or to published guidelines, such as those developed in 1998 by the Fifth American College of Chest Physicians (ACCP) Consensus Conference on Antithrombotic Therapy.

Because of the risk of rebound hypercoagulability (which may not be detected by clotting tests) when anticoagulant therapy is discontinued, gradual withdrawal over 3 to 4 weeks is recommended.

Diet/Nutrition

Dietary vitamin K fluctuations are especially important in patients taking low-dose warfarin.

Loss of anticoagulant effect may occur in a previously stabilized patient following increased intake of vitamin K from dietary sources (green leafy vegetables such as broccoli, cabbage, collard greens, kale, lettuce, or spinach and certain vegetable oils) or vitamin K-containing multiple vitamins or nutritional supplements.

Increased anticoagulant effect may occur in a previously stabilized patient if prolonged malnutrition or vitamin C deficiency develops, or if diarrhea, other illness, or changes in diet resulting in decreased intake or absorption of vitamin K occur during therapy.

For parenteral dosage form of warfarin only

It is recommended that parenteral warfarin be administered by slow intravenous injection (over 1 to 2 minutes) into a peripheral vein.

Intramuscular administration of warfarin is not recommended.

For prevention or treatment of adverse effects

If excessive increases in PT/INR, without bleeding or prospective surgery, occur, the INR should be reduced to a safe level (e.g., less than 5). If serious bleeding is present, the INR should be reduced to 1 as soon as possible. Reduction of INR may be accomplished by temporarily withdrawing anticoagulant therapy, administering vitamin K_1, and, in life-threatening situations, by transfusing fresh plasma or prothrombin complex concentrate. (See *Treatment of overdose* for more information.) If elective or urgent surgery is required, the INR can be reduced to 1 to 1.5 at the time of surgery.

It is recommended that intramuscular injections of concomitant medications be avoided whenever possible, because of the risk of hematoma, or be administered in the upper extremities to ensure easy access for manual compression, inspections for bleeding, and use of pressure bandages.

If acute adrenal hemorrhage or insufficiency is suspected, anticoagulant therapy should be discontinued, plasma cortisol concentrations measured, and high-dose intravenous corticosteroid therapy (preferably with hydrocortisone, since other glucocorticoids may not provide sufficient sodium retention) instituted immediately. Delay of treatment while laboratory confirmation of the diagnosis is awaited may prove fatal for the patient. It has been proposed that abdominal computerized axial tomographic (CAT) scanning may be useful in diagnosing this condition more rapidly.

It is recommended that coumarin or indanedione anticoagulant therapy be discontinued at the first sign of anticoagulant-induced tissue necrosis. If necessary, anticoagulant therapy can be continued with heparin monotherapy. No uniformly effective treatment for anticoagulant-induced tissue necrosis has been established, although some success has been achieved with reintroduction of warfarin at low doses in combination with therapeutic doses of heparin, with gradual increases in warfarin dose over several weeks, or with use of protein C concentrate or fresh frozen plasma until stable anticoagulation is achieved. This approach may prevent an abrupt fall in protein C concentrations before factors II, IX, and X concentrations can fall.

It is recommended that anticoagulant therapy be withdrawn (and replaced by heparin if necessary) at the first sign of:
- Agranulocytosis
- Hypersensitivity
- Intracranial hemorrhage
  (aggressive treatment is necessary because of the slow evolution and growth of the bleeding area in about half of the cases)
- Purple toes syndrome
- Systemic atheroemboli or cholesterol microemboli.

ACENOCOUMAROL

Summary of Differences

Another commonly used name is nicoumalone.
Physicochemical characteristics:
Coumarin derivative.
Pharmacology/pharmacokinetics:
See *Pharmacology/Pharmacokinetics*.

Oral Dosage Forms

ACENOCOUMAROL TABLETS

Usual adult dose

Oral, 1 to 10 mg per day, as indicated by PT/INR determinations.

Usual pediatric dose

Dosage has not been established.

Strength(s) usually available

U.S.—
Not commercially available.
Canada—
1 mg (Rx) [*Sintrom*].
4 mg (Rx) [*Sintrom* (scored)].

Packaging and storage
Store below 40 °C (104 °F), preferably between 15 and 30 °C (59 and 86 °F), unless otherwise specified by manufacturer.

Auxiliary labeling
• Do not take other medicines without advice from your doctor.

ANISINDIONE

Summary of Differences
Physicochemical characteristics:
Indanedione derivative.
Pharmacology/pharmacokinetics:
See *Pharmacology/Pharmacokinetics.*
Precautions:
Laboratory value alterations—Alkaline urine may turn red-orange.
Side/adverse effects:
See *Side/Adverse Effects.*

Oral Dosage Forms
ANISINDIONE TABLETS
Usual adult dose
Oral, 25 to 250 mg a day, as indicated by PT/INR determinations.

Usual pediatric dose
Dosage has not been established.

Strength(s) usually available
U.S.—
50 mg (Rx) [*Miradon* (scored; lactose)].
Canada—
Not commercially available.

Packaging and storage
Store below 40 °C (104 °F), preferably between 15 and 30 °C (59 and 86 °F), unless otherwise specified by manufacturer.

Auxiliary labeling
• Do not take other medicines without advice from your doctor.

DICUMAROL

Summary of Differences
Physicochemical characteristics:
Coumarin derivative.
Pharmacology/pharmacokinetics:
See *Pharmacology/Pharmacokinetics.*
Side/adverse effects:
See *Side/Adverse Effects.*
Incidence of gastrointestinal side/adverse effects may be higher.

Oral Dosage Forms
DICUMAROL TABLETS USP
Usual adult dose
Oral, 25 to 200 mg a day, as indicated by PT/INR determinations.

Usual pediatric dose
Dosage has not been established.

Strength(s) usually available
U.S.—
25 mg (Rx) [GENERIC (lactose)].
Canada—
Not commercially available.

Packaging and storage
Store below 25 °C (77 °F).

Auxiliary labeling
• Do not take other medicines without advice from your doctor.

WARFARIN

Summary of Differences
Physicochemical characteristics:
Coumarin derivative.
Pharmacology/pharmacokinetics:
See *Pharmacology/Pharmacokinetics.*
Side/adverse effects:
See *Side/Adverse Effects.*

Oral Dosage Forms
WARFARIN SODIUM TABLETS USP
Usual adult dose
Regular-dose (adjusted) therapy—
Initial: Oral, 2 to 5 mg per day, the dosage being adjusted according to PT/INR determinations.
Maintenance: Oral 2 to 10 mg per day, as indicated by PT/INR determinations.
Low-dose (fixed) therapy—
Oral, 1 mg per day.
Note: There have been a number of reports of use of fixed low-dose warfarin (1 mg per day) for prophylaxis of deep vein thrombosis (e.g., in patients with indwelling central vein catheters). However, results of studies do not support use of fixed low-dose warfarin for treatment of patients with acute myocardial infarction or atrial fibrillation.

Usual pediatric dose
Dosage has not been established.

Strength(s) usually available
U.S.—
1 mg (Rx) [*Coumadin* (scored; lactose); GENERIC (may contain lactose)].
2 mg (Rx) [*Coumadin* (scored; lactose); GENERIC (may contain lactose)].
2.5 mg (Rx) [*Coumadin* (scored; lactose); GENERIC (may contain lactose)].
3 mg (Rx) [*Coumadin* (scored; lactose)].
4 mg (Rx) [*Coumadin* (scored; lactose); GENERIC (may contain lactose)].
5 mg (Rx) [*Coumadin* (scored; lactose); GENERIC (may contain lactose)].
6 mg (Rx) [*Coumadin* (scored; lactose)].
7.5 mg (Rx) [*Coumadin* (scored; lactose); GENERIC (may contain lactose)].
10 mg (Rx) [*Coumadin* (scored; lactose); GENERIC (may contain lactose)].
Canada—
1 mg (Rx) [*Coumadin* (scored; lactose)].
2 mg (Rx) [*Coumadin* (scored; lactose)].
2.5 mg (Rx) [*Coumadin* (scored; lactose)].
4 mg (Rx) [*Coumadin* (scored; lactose)].
5 mg (Rx) [*Coumadin* (scored; lactose); *Warfilone* (scored; tartrazine)].
10 mg (Rx) [*Coumadin* (scored; lactose)].

Packaging and storage
Store between 15 and 30 °C (59 and 86 °F), unless otherwise specified by manufacturer. Protect from light.

Auxiliary labeling
• Do not take other medicines without advice from your doctor.

Parenteral Dosage Forms
WARFARIN SODIUM FOR INJECTION USP
Usual adult dose
Initial—
Intravenous (over one to two minutes into a peripheral vein), 2 to 5 mg per day, the dosage being adjusted according to PT/INR determinations.
Maintenance—
Intravenous (over one to two minutes into a peripheral vein), 2 to 10 mg per day, as indicated by PT/INR determinations.

Usual pediatric dose
Dosage has not been established.

Strength(s) usually available
U.S.—
5 mg (Rx) [*Coumadin* (sodium phosphate, dibasic, heptahydrate; sodium phosphate, monobasic, monohydrate; sodium chloride; mannitol; sodium hydroxide)].
Canada—
5 mg (Rx) [*Coumadin* (sodium phosphate, dibasic, heptahydrate; sodium phosphate, monobasic, monohydrate; sodium chloride; mannitol; sodium hydroxide)].

Packaging and storage
Store between 15 and 30 °C (59 and 86 °F), unless otherwise specified by manufacturer. Do not refrigerate. Protect from light.

Preparation of dosage form

Warfarin sodium for injection is prepared for administration by adding 2.7 mL of sterile water for injection to the 5-mg vial, producing a solution containing 2 mg of warfarin sodium per mL.

Stability

It is recommended that the reconstituted solution be used within 4 hours. Any unused portion should be discarded.

Incompatibilities

Warfarin sodium solutions are incompatible with amikacin sulfate, epinephrine hydrochloride, metaraminol tartrate, oxytocin, promazine hydrochloride, tetracycline hydrochloride, and vancomycin hydrochloride.

Some adsorption of warfarin sodium by polyvinyl chloride has been demonstrated when the warfarin was dissolved in 0.9% sodium chloride injection or 5% glucose injection.

Selected Bibliography

Dalen JE, Hirsh J, editors. Fifth ACCP Consensus Conference on Antithrombotic Therapy. Chest 1998 Nov; 114(5 Suppl): entire issue.

Poller L, Hirsh J, editors. Oral anticoagulants. London: Arnold; 1996.

Revised: 05/18/1999

ANTICONVULSANTS, HYDANTOIN Systemic

This monograph includes information on the following: 1) Ethotoin†; 2) Fosphenytoin; 3) Mephenytoin†; 4) Phenytoin.

BAN: Mephenytoin—Methoin

VA CLASSIFICATION (Primary/Secondary):

Ethotoin—CN400
Fosphenytoin—CN400
Mephenytoin—CN400
Phenytoin—CN400/CV300; MS200

Commonly used brand name(s): *Cerebyx[2]; Dilantin[4]; Dilantin Infatabs[4]; Dilantin Kapseals[4]; Dilantin-125[4]; Dilantin-30[4]; Mesantoin[3]; Peganone[1]; Phenytek[4].*

Another commonly used name for phenytoin is diphenylhydantoin.

Note: For a listing of dosage forms and brand names by country availability, see *Dosage Forms* section(s).

†Not commercially available in Canada.

Category

Anticonvulsant—Ethotoin; Fosphenytoin; Mephenytoin; Phenytoin.
Antiarrhythmic—Phenytoin.
Antineuralgic (trigeminal neuralgia)—Phenytoin.
Skeletal muscle relaxant—Phenytoin

Indications

Note: Bracketed information in the *Indications* section refers to uses that are not included in U.S. product labeling.

Accepted

Epilepsy (treatment)—Hydantoin anticonvulsants are indicated in the suppression and control of tonic-clonic (grand mal) and simple or complex partial (psychomotor or temporal lobe) seizures.

Ethotoin may be administered as a second-line agent when seizures have not been adequately controlled by the primary anticonvulsants and before proceeding to more toxic anticonvulsants.

Mephenytoin also is used in the treatment of simple partial (focal and Jacksonian) seizures in patients who have not responded to less toxic anticonvulsants.

Status epilepticus (treatment)—Parenteral fosphenytoin and phenytoin are both indicated for the control of tonic-clonic type status epilepticus. Although parenteral benzodiazepines are often used initially for rapid control of status epilepticus, both fosphenytoin and phenytoin are indicated for sustained control of seizure activity.

Seizures in neurosurgery (prophylaxis and treatment)—Fosphenytoin and phenytoin are both indicated for the prevention and treatment of seizures during and following neurosurgery.

[Arrhythmias, digitalis-induced (treatment)][1]—Phenytoin is used in the correction of atrial and ventricular arrhythmias, especially those caused by digitalis glycoside toxicity.

[Choreoathetosis, paroxysmal (treatment)][1]—Phenytoin may be effective in treating paroxysmal choreoathetosis, especially the kinesigenic type. This condition, which is considered a form of reflex epilepsy, is characterized by tonic, dystonic, or choreoathetoid contortions of the extremities, trunk, or face, which are usually precipitated by the patient's initiation of sudden voluntary movement.

[Neuralgia, trigeminal (treatment)][1]—Phenytoin is used alone or with other anticonvulsants to control paroxysmal pain in some patients with trigeminal neuralgia (tic douloureux). Carbamazepine is considered the first-line agent, effectively relieving pain in about 66% of patients. However, since phenytoin relieves pain during long-term use in approximately 20% of patients, it may be used alone in some patients or added to carbamazepine therapy when symptoms persist.

[Neuromyotonia (treatment)][1]
[Myotonia congenita (treatment)][1] or
[Myotonic muscular dystrophy (treatment)][1]—Phenytoin is effective in some patients as a muscle relaxant in the treatment of muscle hyperirritability, characterized by delayed relaxation of muscle after voluntary or mechanically induced contraction and by a state of continuous muscle contraction at rest. Neuromyotonia includes continuous muscle fiber activity syndrome, Isaac's syndrome, and "stiff man" syndrome.

[Toxicity, tricyclic antidepressant (treatment adjunct)][1]—Intravenous phenytoin loading has been used to treat quinidine-like conduction defects, bradyarrhythmias, or heart block, in tricyclic antidepressant overdose. Although its use has been supplanted by other agents, in some instances it remains a therapeutic option.

Unaccepted

Hydantoin anticonvulsants are *not* indicated in the treatment of absence (petit mal) seizures, or as first-line treatment of febrile, hypoglycemic, or other metabolic seizures. When tonic-clonic (grand mal) seizures coexist with absence seizures, combined therapy may be necessary.

Although phenytoin has been used in patients with recessive dystrophic epidermolysis bullosa for the treatment of blistering and erosions of the skin that may result from even minor trauma or injury, it is no longer considered preferred therapy.

[1]Not included in Canadian product labeling.

Pharmacology/Pharmacokinetics

Physicochemical characteristics

Molecular weight—
Ethotoin: 204.23.
Fosphenytoin sodium: 406.24.
Mephenytoin: 218.26.
Phenytoin: 252.27.
Phenytoin sodium: 274.26.

pKa—Phenytoin: 8.06 to 8.33.

pH—
Fosphenytoin sodium injection: 8.6 to 9.
Phenytoin sodium injection: 12.

Note: Fosphenytoin is a water-soluble prodrug that is rapidly converted to phenytoin following parenteral administration.

Mechanism of action/Effect

Anticonvulsant—The mechanism of action is not completely known, but is thought to involve stabilization of neuronal membranes at the cell body, axon, and synapse and limitation of the spread of neuronal or seizure activity. In neurons, phenytoin decreases sodium and calcium ion influx by prolonging voltage-dependent channel inactivation time during generation of nerve impulses. Phenytoin blocks the voltage-dependent sodium channels of neurons and inhibits the calcium flux across neuronal membranes, thus helping to stabilize neurons. It also decreases synaptic transmission, and decreases post-tetanic potentiation at the synapse. Phenytoin enhances the sodium-potassium ATPase activity of neurons and/or glial cells. It also influences second messenger systems by inhibiting calcium-calmodulin protein phosphorylation and possibly altering cyclic nucleotide production or metabolism.

Antiarrhythmic—Phenytoin may act to normalize influx of sodium and calcium to cardiac Purkinje fibers. Abnormal ventricular automaticity and membrane responsiveness are decreased. Also, phenytoin shortens the refractory period, and therefore shortens the QT interval and the duration of the action potential.

Antineuralgic—Exact mechanism is unknown. Phenytoin may act in the central nervous system (CNS) to decrease synaptic transmission or to decrease summation of temporal stimulation leading to neuronal discharge (antikindling). Phenytoin raises the threshold of facial pain and shortens the duration of attacks by diminishing self-maintenance of excitation and repetitive firing.

Skeletal muscle relaxant—Phenytoin's mechanism of action as a muscle relaxant is thought to be similar to its anticonvulsant action. In movement disorders, the membrane-stabilizing effect reduces abnormal sustained repetitive firing and potentiation of nerve and muscle cells.

Other actions/effects

Therapy with phenytoin significantly increases the amounts and activities of some CYP P450 isoenzymes, the uridine diphosphate glucuronosyltransferase (UDPGT) system, and epoxide hydrolase enzymes, thus enhancing the metabolism of many other drugs. Also, phenytoin may compete with drugs metabolized by the same CYP isoenzymes (CYP2C9 and CYP2C19), thus decreasing the metabolic clearance of those agents.

Absorption

Ethotoin—
- Rapid.

Fosphenytoin—
- Intravenous: Immediate.
- Intramuscular: Rapid and complete.
- Note: Bioavailability from either the intravenous or intramuscular route is essentially 100%.

Mephenytoin—
- Rapid.

Phenytoin—
- Oral: Slow and variable among products; poor in neonates.
- Intravenous: Immediate.
- Intramuscular: Very slow, but complete (92%).

Distribution

Fosphenytoin—Most likely distributed in humans to heart, kidneys, small intestine, liver, lungs, and spleen, where it is hydrolyzed by phosphatases to phenytoin. Predominately distributed in the central (plasma) compartment. The volume of distribution (Vol_D) ranges from 4.3 to 10.8 liters, and increases with increasing dose and administration rate of fosphenytoin.

Phenytoin—Distributed into cerebrospinal fluid, saliva, semen, gastrointestinal fluids, bile, and breast milk; also crosses the placenta, with fetal serum concentrations equal to those of the mother.

Protein binding

Fosphenytoin—Very high (95 to 99%); degree of binding is saturable, with the result that the percent bound decreases as the total plasma fosphenytoin concentration increases.

Phenytoin—Very high (90% or more); may be lower in neonates (84%) and in hyperbilirubinemic infants (80%); also altered in patients with hypoalbuminemia ($<$ 37 mg per dL), uremia, or acute trauma, and in pregnant patients.

Note: Fosphenytoin has a high affinity for phenytoin protein binding sites; before its conversion to phenytoin, it binds to these sites, retarding the binding of newly formed phenytoin, thus increasing free (unbound) phenytoin concentrations. In the absence of fosphenytoin, approximately 12% of total plasma phenytoin exists in the free (unbound) state over the clinically relevant concentration range. With the administration of fosphenytoin, total free (unbound) phenytoin plasma concentrations may increase up to 30% during the period required for the conversion of fosphenytoin to phenytoin (approximately 30 to 60 minutes postinfusion).

In patients with renal or hepatic function impairment or hypoalbuminemia, fosphenytoin conversion to phenytoin may be increased without a similar increase in the clearance of phenytoin, potentially leading to an increased incidence of adverse effects.

Biotransformation

Hepatic via microsomal oxidative enzymes of the P450 system, specifically the CYP2 family of isozymes; rate increased in younger children, in pregnant women, in women during menses, and in patients with acute trauma; rate decreases with advancing age.

Mephenytoin has an active metabolite, nirvanol (5-ethyl-5-phenylhydantoin). The metabolism of mephenytoin is genetically determined. Patients who are slow metabolizers of mephenytoin are at risk of increased adverse effects; Oriental and black populations are more likely than white populations to be slow metabolizers of mephenytoin.

The major inactive metabolite of phenytoin is 5-(*p*-hydroxyphenyl)-5-phenylhydantoin (HPPH). Phenytoin also may be metabolized slowly in a small number of individuals due to genetic predisposition, which may cause limited enzyme availability and lack of induction.

Fosphenytoin undergoes rapid hydrolysis to phenytoin. *In vivo*, 1.5 mg of fosphenytoin sodium injection liberates 1 mg of phenytoin sodium; thus, 75 mg of fosphenytoin sodium is essentially equivalent to 50 mg of phenytoin sodium. Conversion of fosphenytoin also yields two additional metabolites, phosphate and formaldehyde. Formaldehyde is subsequently converted to formate, which in turn is metabolized via a folate-dependent mechanism. Biological effects from the production of phosphate and formaldehyde generally occur only at doses exceeding usual clinical doses of fosphenytoin. Phosphatase enzymes probably play a major role in the conversion of fosphenytoin to phenytoin.

Half-life

Ethotoin—3 to 9 hours.

Fosphenytoin—The conversion half-life to phenytoin ranges from 8 to 15 minutes. This value is independent of dose, infusion rate, or plasma concentrations of either fosphenytoin or phenytoin. The elimination half-life of fosphenytoin after intravenous or intramuscular injection also is independent of dose.

Mephenytoin—About 7 hours, but for active metabolite, nirvanol, about 95 to 144 hours.

Phenytoin—Because phenytoin exhibits saturable, zero-order, or dose-dependent pharmacokinetics, the apparent half-life of phenytoin changes with dose and serum concentration. This is due to the saturation of the enzyme system responsible for metabolizing phenytoin, which occurs at therapeutic concentrations of the drug. Thus, a constant amount of drug is metabolized (capacity-limited metabolism), and small increases in dose may cause disproportionately large increases in serum concentrations and apparent half-life, possibly causing unexpected toxicity.

Time to peak concentration

Fosphenytoin—
- Intravenous: 6 minutes (average) after administration.
- Intramuscular: 36 minutes (average) after administration; one dose administered in more than one injection resulted in an increase in time to peak concentration.

Mephenytoin—
- 45 minutes to 4 hours.
- Nirvanol: 16 to 36 hours.

Phenytoin (tablets or oral suspension)—
- 1½ to 3 hours.

Phenytoin sodium—
- Extended capsules: 4 to 12 hours.
- Prompt capsules: 1½ to 3 hours.

Therapeutic serum concentration

Ethotoin—
- 15 to 50 mcg per mL (74 to 245 micromoles per L).

Mephenytoin—
- 25 to 40 mcg per mL (115 to 183 micromoles per L) (in combination with nirvanol).

Phenytoin—
- 10 to 20 mcg per mL (40 to 80 micromoles per L). Steady-state serum concentration is usually achieved in 5 to 10 days with daily oral dosage of 300 mg. Serum concentrations of 20 to 40 mcg per mL (80 to 159 micromoles per L) usually produce symptoms of toxicity; $>$ 40 mcg per mL (159 micromoles per L) usually produce severe toxicity. The serum concentrations of phenytoin needed for efficacy may be influenced by seizure type. Higher concentrations (23 mcg per mL [91 micromoles per L] or greater) may be needed to control simple or complex partial seizures, with or without tonic-clonic seizures, or status epilepticus than are necessary for control of tonic-clonic seizures alone (10 to 20 mcg per mL [40 to 80 micromoles per L]). Occasionally, a patient may have seizure control with serum phenytoin concentrations of 6 to 9 mcg per mL (24 to 36 micromoles per L). Effective treatment, therefore, should be guided by clinical response, not drug serum concentrations. In patients who have hypoalbuminemia and/or renal failure, or who are taking other medications that displace phenytoin from binding sites, hydantoin serum concentrations of 5 to 10 mcg per mL (20 to 40 micromoles per L) may be adequate. For cardiac arrhythmias, plasma concentrations of 10 to 18 mcg per mL (40 to 71 micromoles per L) have been reported to be effective.

Therapeutic concentrations of free (unbound) phenytoin, which are frequently monitored in patients with altered protein binding (e.g., in neonates and in patients with renal failure, hypoalbuminemia, or acute trauma), usually fall in the range of 0.8 to 2 mcg per mL (3 to 8 micromoles per L).

Note: The pharmacokinetic parameters of phenytoin derived from fosphenytoin administered by intravenous or intramuscular injection do not differ from those values for trough concentrations or area under the plasma concentration-time curve (AUC) of orally administered equivalent doses of phenytoin.

Elimination

Ethotoin, mephenytoin, and phenytoin—Primarily renal as metabolites; also in feces. Very little phenytoin is excreted in the feces; most is excreted in the bile as metabolites that are reabsorbed in the intestine and excreted in the urine. Phenytoin excretion is enhanced by alkaline urine.

Fosphenytoin—Not excreted in urine. Phenytoin derived from fosphenytoin is excreted in the urine, primarily as metabolites; little unchanged phenytoin (about 1 to 5% of the fosphenytoin dose) is recovered in the urine.

Precautions to Consider

Cross-sensitivity and/or related problems

Patients sensitive to one hydantoin anticonvulsant may be sensitive to other hydantoin anticonvulsants also. In addition, cross-sensitivity to structurally similar compounds, such as barbiturates, succinimides, and oxazolidinediones, may occur.

Tumorigenicity

Phenytoin: There have been isolated reports of malignancies, including neuroblastoma, in children whose mothers received phenytoin during pregnancy.

Mutagenicity

Fosphenytoin: Structural chromosome aberration frequency in cultured V79 Chinese hamster lung cells was increased by exposure to fosphenytoin in the presence of metabolic activation. No evidence of mutagenicity of fosphenytoin was observed in bacteria (Ames test) or Chinese hamster lung cells *in vitro*. No evidence of clastogenic activity of fosphenytoin was observed in the *in vivo* mouse bone marrow micronucleus test.

Pregnancy/Reproduction

Pregnancy—Hydantoin anticonvulsants cross the placenta; risk-benefit must be considered, although a definite cause and effect relationship has not been established between the hydantoins and teratogenic effects. Reports in recent years indicate a higher incidence of congenital abnormalities in children whose mothers used anticonvulsant medication during pregnancy, although most epileptic mothers have delivered normal infants. Reported abnormalities include cleft lip, cleft palate, heart malformations, and the "fetal hydantoin syndrome" (also known as the "fetal anticonvulsant syndrome" and characterized by prenatal growth deficiency, microcephaly, craniofacial abnormalities, hypoplasia of the fingernails, and mental deficiency associated with intrauterine development during therapy). Medication has not been definitively proven to be the cause of "fetal hydantoin syndrome". The reports, to date, relate primarily to the more widely used anticonvulsants, phenytoin and phenobarbital. Pending availability of more precise information, this risk-benefit consideration of anticonvulsant use during pregnancy is extended to the entire family of anticonvulsant medications.

Ethotoin, phenytoin—FDA Pregnancy Category C.

Fosphenytoin—FDA Pregnancy Category D.

Mephenytoin—FDA pregnancy category not included in product labeling.

Because of altered absorption and protein binding and/or increased metabolic clearance of hydantoin anticonvulsants during pregnancy, pregnant women receiving these medications may experience an increased incidence of seizures. Serum hydantoin concentrations must be monitored and doses increased accordingly. A gradual resumption of the patient's usual dosage may be necessary after delivery. However, some patients may experience a rapid reduction in maternal hepatic phenytoin metabolism at time of delivery, requiring the dosage to be reduced within 12 hours postpartum.

Delivery—Exposure to hydantoins prior to delivery may lead to an increased risk of life-threatening hemorrhage (related to decreased concentrations of vitamin K-dependent clotting factors) in the neonate, usually within 24 hours of birth. Hydantoins may also produce a deficiency of vitamin K in the mother, causing increased maternal bleeding during delivery. Risk of maternal and infant bleeding may be reduced by administering vitamin K to the mother during delivery and to the neonate, intramuscularly or subcutaneously, immediately after birth.

Breast-feeding

Ethotoin and phenytoin are distributed into breast milk; significant amounts may be ingested by the infant. Information is not available for mephenytoin.

Pediatrics

Children and young adults are more susceptible to gingival hyperplasia than older adults. See *Dental* section.

Some reports suggest that children may experience decreased school performance during long-term treatment with hydantoin anticonvulsants, especially at high therapeutic or toxic concentrations.

Coarsening of facial features and excessive body hair growth may be more pronounced in young patients.

Other anticonvulsants less likely to cause problems should be considered first.

Fosphenytoin: Limited pharmacokinetic data in children older than 5 years of age suggest that the conversion of fosphenytoin to phenytoin occurs in a manner similar to that in adults. However, the safety of fosphenytoin in children has not been established.

Geriatrics

Geriatric patients tend to metabolize hydantoins slowly, thereby increasing the possibility of the medication reaching toxic serum concentrations. Also, serum albumin may be low in older patients, causing a decrease in protein binding of phenytoin. Lower dosage and subsequent adjustments may be required. The rate of administration of intravenous dosage should be no more than 25 mg per minute, and possibly as low as 5 to 10 mg per minute.

Pharmacogenetics

The metabolism of mephenytoin is genetically determined. Patients who are slow metabolizers of mephenytoin are at risk of increased adverse effects; Oriental and black populations are more likely than white populations to be slow metabolizers of mephenytoin.

Phenytoin also may be metabolized slowly in a small number of individuals due to genetic predisposition, which may cause limited enzyme availability and lack of induction.

Dental

Gingival hyperplasia, a common complication of phenytoin or mephenytoin therapy, usually starts during the first 6 months of treatment as gingivitis or gum inflammation. The incidence is higher in patients up to 23 years of age than in older patients, and severe gingival hyperplasia is less likely to occur with dosage under 500 mg per day. Anterior tissue overgrowth may be greater than posterior overgrowth, creating esthetic and psychological problems for the young patient. A strictly enforced program of teeth cleaning by a professional, combined with plaque control by the patient, if begun within 10 days of initiation of hydantoin anticonvulsant therapy, will minimize growth rate and severity of gingival enlargement. Periodontal surgery may be indicated, and should be followed by careful plaque control to inhibit recurrence of gum enlargement. If gingival hyperplasia cannot be controlled by standard dental procedures, ethotoin may be substituted for phenytoin, without loss of seizure control, usually at doses four to six times greater than those of phenytoin.

In addition, the leukopenic effects of hydantoin anticonvulsants may result in an increased incidence of microbial infection, delayed healing, and gingival bleeding. If leukopenia occurs, dental work should be deferred until blood counts have returned to normal. Patient instruction in proper oral hygiene should include caution in use of regular toothbrushes, dental floss, and toothpicks.

Drug interactions and/or related problems

The following drug interactions and/or related problems have been selected on the basis of their potential clinical significance (possible mechanism in parentheses where appropriate)—not necessarily inclusive (» = major clinical significance):

Note: Possible interactions of hydantoin anticonvulsants, particularly phenytoin, with medications known to be metabolized by the hepatic cytochrome P450 enzyme system should be considered. Phenytoin therapy significantly increases the amounts and activities of some CYP isoenzymes, the uridine diphosphate glucuronosyltransferase (UDPGT) system, and epoxide hydrolase enzymes, thus enhancing the metabolism of many other drugs. Also, phenytoin may compete with drugs metabolized by the same CYP isoenzymes (CYP2C9 and CYP2C19), thus decreasing the metabolic clearance of those agents. Metabolism of phenytoin is particularly susceptible to inhibition by other medications using the P450 enzyme system, due to phenytoin's potentially saturable metabolism.

In addition, other highly protein-bound medications may displace phenytoin from its serum protein binding sites, increasing serum concentrations of free (unbound) phenytoin and increasing the risk of toxicity.

The possibility of significant interactions with hepatic enzyme inducers, hepatic enzyme inhibitors, and medications metabolized by the hepatic P450 isoenzyme system, other than those listed below, should be considered and the patient should be carefully monitored during and following concurrent use.

Combinations containing any of the following medications, depending on the amount present, may also interact with this medication.

Acetaminophen
(risk of hepatotoxicity from a single toxic dose or prolonged use of acetaminophen may be increased and therapeutic efficacy may be decreased in patients regularly taking other hepatic enzyme-inducing agents such as phenytoin)

» Alcohol or
» CNS depression-producing medications (see *Appendix II*)
(CNS depression may be enhanced)
(chronic use of alcohol may decrease the serum concentrations and effectiveness of hydantoins; concurrent use of hydantoin anticonvulsants with acute alcohol intake may increase serum hydantoin concentrations)

» Amiodarone
(concurrent use with phenytoin and possibly with other hydantoin anticonvulsants may increase plasma concentrations of the hydantoin, resulting in increased effects and/or toxicity)

» Antacids, aluminum and/or magnesium-containing and calcium carbonate-containing
(concurrent use may decrease the bioavailability of phenytoin; doses of antacids and phenytoin should be separated by about 2 to 3 hours)

» Anticoagulants, coumarin- or indandione-derivative or
» Chloramphenicol or
» Cimetidine or
» Disulfiram or
Influenza virus vaccine or
» Isoniazid or
Methylphenidate or
Metronidazole or
» Phenylbutazone or
Ranitidine or
Salicylates or
» Sulfonamides or
Trazodone or
Trimethoprim
(serum phenytoin concentrations may be increased because of inhibition of its metabolism by these agents, resulting in increased effects and/or toxicity of phenytoin; dosage adjustments may be necessary)
(in addition, the anticoagulant effect of coumarin- or indandione-derivative anticoagulants may be increased initially, but decreased with continued concurrent use)
(phenylbutazone and salicylates also may displace phenytoin from protein binding sites, resulting in increased free [unbound] phenytoin concentrations)
(trimethoprim may increase the half-life of phenytoin by up to 50%, and decrease its clearance by 30% through inhibition of metabolism of phenytoin)

Anticonvulsants, succinimide
(induction of hepatic microsomal enzyme activity may result in decreased serum concentrations of either succinimide or hydantoin anticonvulsants; careful monitoring is suggested, especially when any anticonvulsant is added to or withdrawn from an existing regimen)

» Corticosteroids, glucocorticoid or
Cyclosporine or
Digitalis glycosides or
Disopyramide or
Doxycycline or
Furosemide or
Levodopa or
Mexiletine or
Quinidine
(therapeutic effects of these medications may be decreased because of increased metabolism and decreased plasma concentrations, which may result from hydantoin anticonvulsants' induction of hepatic microsomal enzymes; dosage adjustments of these medications may be necessary)

Antidepressants, tricyclic or
Bupropion or
Clozapine or
Haloperidol or
Loxapine or
Maprotiline or
Molindone or
Monoamine oxidase (MAO) inhibitors, including furazolidone, procarbazine, and selegiline or
Phenothiazines or
Pimozide or
Thioxanthenes
(these medications may lower the seizure threshold and decrease the anticonvulsant effects of hydantoin anticonvulsants; CNS depression may be enhanced; dosage adjustment of the hydantoin anticonvulsant may be necessary)
(concurrent use of phenytoin with tricyclic antidepressants may lower serum concentrations of the antidepressant; dosage increases of the tricyclic antidepressant may be required to produce improvement of the depressed state)
(concurrent use of phenytoin with haloperidol may result in significant reductions in haloperidol serum concentrations)
(molindone contains calcium ions, which interfere with the absorption of phenytoin; patients should be advised to take phenytoin and molindone one to three hours apart)
(concurrent use of phenothiazines may inhibit phenytoin metabolism, leading to phenytoin intoxication)

Antidiabetic agents, oral or
Insulin
(hydantoin anticonvulsants may increase serum glucose concentrations and the possibility of hyperglycemia; dosage adjustment of either or both medications may be necessary)
(tolbutamide may displace phenytoin from protein binding sites, resulting in increased plasma phenytoin concentrations)

» Antifungals, azole, including:
» Fluconazole or
» Itraconazole or
» Ketoconazole or
» Miconazole
(concurrent use of any azole antifungal with phenytoin may decrease the metabolism of phenytoin, resulting in increased plasma phenytoin concentrations; a 75% increase in the area under the plasma concentration-time curve [AUC] of phenytoin was found in volunteers given 200 mg of fluconazole per day; concurrent use has also been reported to decrease the plasma concentration of azole antifungals, which may lead to clinical failure or relapse of the fungal infection; response to both medications should be closely monitored)

Antineoplastic agents, such as:
Bleomycin
Carmustine (BCNU)
Cisplatin
Dacarbazine
Doxorubicin
Ifosfamide
Methotrexate
Vinblastine
(increased metabolism of phenytoin may occur, although other factors such as reduced absorption secondary to chemotherapy-induced gastrointestinal toxicity and concomitant administration of steroids and antacids may contribute to this effect)
(phenytoin may induce the metabolism of ifosfamide to its alkylating metabolites, resulting in increased toxicity)

Barbiturates or
Primidone
(phenytoin and phenobarbital interact reciprocally through multiple mechanisms; concurrent use may produce variable and unpredictable effects; close monitoring of the patient is advised)
(metabolism of primidone to phenobarbital may be increased by phenytoin)

» Calcium
(when used as an excipient in phenytoin capsules, calcium sulfate can decrease phenytoin absorption by as much as 20%)
(concurrent use of phenytoin with calcium supplements or any tablets or capsules that contain calcium sulfate as an excipient may result in formation of nonabsorbable complexes, thereby decreasing the bioavailability of both calcium and phenytoin; patients should be advised to take these medications 1 to 3 hours apart)

Calcium channel blocking agents, including:
Diltiazam or
Nifedipine or
Verapamil
(caution is advised when these medications are used concurrently with phenytoin because of their ability to displace phenytoin from its protein binding sites, increasing serum free [unbound] phenytoin concentrations)
(phenytoin also may induce the metabolism of these medications, causing decreased efficacy)

Carbamazepine
(carbamazepine has complex and variable effects on phenytoin; it may increase or decrease the clearance of phenytoin; in most patients, phenytoin metabolism is inhibited and plasma concentrations may increase significantly, resulting in phenytoin toxicity, which can be mistaken for carbamazepine toxicity. In addition, phenytoin may reduce plasma carbamazepine concentrations, mainly by increasing CYP enzymes; in many cases, plasma concentrations of carbamazepine's active metabolite do not change, but the ratio of metabolite to parent drug concentration increases, with a higher contribution of carbamazepine-10,11-epoxide to the overall clinical effects. Monitoring of plasma concentrations is recommended as a guide to dosage, especially when either medication is added to or withdrawn from an existing regimen)

Carbonic anhydrase inhibitors
(osteopenia induced by hydantoin anticonvulsants may be enhanced; it is recommended that patients receiving concurrent therapy be monitored for early signs of osteopenia and that the carbonic anhydrase inhibitor be discontinued and appropriate treatment initiated if necessary)

Chlordiazepoxide or
Clonazepam or
Diazepam
(chlordiazepoxide and diazepam may cause increased plasma concentrations of phenytoin due to inhibition of its metabolism; phenytoin may increase the clearance of clonazepam and diazepam, decreasing their efficacy; careful monitoring is recommended, since the clinical significance of this interaction is controversial)

» Contraceptives, estrogen-containing, oral or
» Contraceptives, progestin-containing, oral, injection, or subdermal implants
(concurrent use of hydantoin anticonvulsants with estrogen- or progestin-containing contraceptives may result in breakthrough bleeding and contraceptive failure due to the increased rate of hepatic enzyme metabolism of steroids induced by hydantoins; phenytoin has also been shown to increase sex hormone-binding globulin [SHBG], which may lower the amount of free progestin available for biological action and contribute to the lowered effectiveness of the oral contraceptive)

» Diazoxide, oral
(concurrent use with hydantoin anticonvulsants may decrease the efficacy of phenytoin and the hyperglycemic effect of diazoxide and is not recommended)

Dopamine
(use of intravenous phenytoin in patients maintained on dopamine may produce sudden hypotension and bradycardia; this reaction is considered to be dose-rate dependent; if anticonvulsant therapy is necessary during administration of dopamine, an alternative to phenytoin should be considered)

Enteral feeding solutions
(concurrent use with phenytoin may decrease absorption of phenytoin, possibly necessitating an increase in dosage; some clinicians recommend that at least 2 hours should elapse between feeding and phenytoin administration; if phenytoin suspension or capsule contents are administered via nasogastric tubing, flushing the tube with 2 to 4 ounces of water before and after administration has been suggested; phenytoin serum concentrations should be carefully monitored during concurrent therapy)

» Estrogens or
» Progestins
(therapeutic effects of these medications may be decreased because of increased metabolism and decreased plasma concentrations, which may result from induction of hepatic microsomal enzymes by hydantoin anticonvulsants; phenytoin plasma concentrations may also be increased; dosage adjustments of these medications may be necessary)

» Felbamate
(felbamate is a competitive inhibitor of phenytoin metabolism; when felbamate is added to a phenytoin regimen, a decrease of approximately 20 to 33% of the phenytoin dose is necessary; phenytoin also induces the metabolism of felbamate)

» Fluoxetine
(concurrent use of fluoxetine with phenytoin has been reported to cause elevated plasma phenytoin concentrations, resulting in symptoms of toxicity; caution and close monitoring are suggested)

Folic acid or
Leucovorin
(although hydantoin anticonvulsants deplete the body of folate stores, supplementation with folic acid may result in lowered serum hydantoin concentrations and possible loss of seizure control; therefore, an increase in hydantoin dosage may be necessary in patients who receive folate supplementation)
(because leucovorin is a reduced form of folic acid, large doses may counteract the anticonvulsant effects of hydantoin anticonvulsants)

Halothane (and possibly enflurane or methoxyflurane)
(chronic use of hydantoin anticonvulsants prior to anesthesia may increase metabolism of anesthetic, leading to increased risk of hepatotoxicity, and may result in increased phenytoin concentrations, leading to increased risk of hydantoin toxicity)

Lamotrigine
(effects of lamotrigine may be reduced because of phenytoin's ability to induce the metabolism [specifically, the UDPGT-dependent glucuronidation] of lamotrigine)

Levothyroxine
(concurrent use with phenytoin may reduce serum protein binding of levothyroxine and reduce total serum thyroxine [T_4] by 15 to 25%; however, most patients remain euthyroid, and dosage of thyroid hormone does not need to be altered)

» Lidocaine or
Propranolol and probably other beta-adrenergic blocking agents
(concurrent use with intravenous phenytoin may produce additive cardiac depressant effects; hydantoin anticonvulsants may also increase hepatic enzyme metabolism of lidocaine, reducing its concentration)
(in addition, propranolol may inhibit the metabolism of phenytoin, increasing the risk of adverse effects)

» Methadone
(long-term use of phenytoin may increase metabolism of methadone, probably by induction of hepatic microsomal enzyme activity, and may precipitate withdrawal symptoms in patients being treated for opioid dependence; methadone dosage adjustments may be necessary when phenytoin therapy is initiated or discontinued)

Omeprazole
(inhibition of the cytochrome P450 enzyme system by omeprazole, especially at higher doses, may cause a decrease in the hepatic metabolism of phenytoin; delayed elimination and increased serum concentrations may result, with considerable interpatient variability)

Paroxetine
(concomitant administration with phenytoin may decrease the systemic availability of either agent; also, both medications may exhibit nonlinear pharmacokinetic properties; no initial dosage adjustments are recommended, but subsequent titration should be based on clinical effects)

» Phenacemide
(risk of additive toxicity when phenacemide is used concurrently with hydantoin anticonvulsants; concurrent use of phenacemide with ethotoin has been reported to cause paranoid symptoms; extreme caution is recommended during concurrent use of these medications)

Praziquantel
(one small, single-dose, controlled study found that epileptic patients taking phenytoin had significantly lower plasma concentrations of praziquantel [24% of the control group]; this effect is thought to be due to induction of the cytochrome P450 microsomal enzyme system by phenytoin; patients on phenytoin may require a larger dose of praziquantel)

» Rifampin
(concurrent use with phenytoin may stimulate the hepatic metabolism of phenytoin, increasing its elimination and thus counteracting its anticonvulsant effect; careful monitoring of serum hydantoin concentrations and dosage adjustments may be necessary)

» Streptozocin
(phenytoin may protect pancreatic beta cells from the toxic effects of streptozocin, thus reducing streptozocin's therapeutic effects; concurrent use is not recommended)

» Sucralfate
(concurrent use of sucralfate may decrease the absorption of hydantoin anticonvulsants)

Ticlopidine
(several cases of elevated phenytoin plasma concentrations with associated somnolence and lethargy have been reported following ticlopidine administration)

» Valproic acid
(valproic acid may displace phenytoin from protein-binding sites and may inhibit the metabolism of phenytoin; phenytoin, through enzyme induction, may lower valproate concentrations; there may be an increased risk of liver toxicity, especially in infants; close monitoring of the patient is required since variable serum phenytoin concentrations have resulted; monitoring of free [unbound] phenytoin concentrations as well as total plasma phenytoin concentrations is advised by some clinicians; dosage of phenytoin should be adjusted as required by clinical situation; caution is advised also for use with other hydantoin anticonvulsants)

Vitamin D
(hydantoin anticonvulsants may reduce effect of vitamin D by accelerating metabolism through hepatic microsomal enzyme induction; patients on long-term anticonvulsant therapy may require vitamin D supplementation to prevent osteomalacia, although rickets is rare)

Xanthines, such as:
Aminophylline
Caffeine
Oxtriphylline
» Theophylline
(concurrent use may stimulate hepatic metabolism of theophylline [and possibly other xanthines except dyphylline], resulting in increased theophylline clearance, especially if plasma phenytoin concentrations are in the usual therapeutic range for at least 5 days; also, simultaneous use with theophylline may inhibit phenytoin absorption, resulting in decreased serum phenytoin concentrations; serum concentrations of phenytoin and theophylline should be monitored during concurrent therapy; dosage adjustments of both phenytoin and theophylline may be necessary)

Laboratory value alterations

The following have been selected on the basis of their potential clinical significance (possible effect in parentheses where appropriate)—not necessarily inclusive (» = major clinical significance).

With diagnostic test results

Dexamethasone test or
Metyrapone test
(results may be inaccurate because of increased dexamethasone or metyrapone metabolism resulting from enzyme induction; dexamethasone or metyrapone doses may need to be increased)

Gallium citrate Ga 67 imaging
(phenytoin may stimulate a benign alteration in lymphoid tissue, which may result in a Ga 67 scintigram similar to that seen in patients with malignant melanoma)

Schilling test
(phenytoin in combination with other anticonvulsant medications may cause a reversible malabsorption of vitamin B_{12})

Thyroid function tests
(free, circulating thyroxine [FT_4] and total thyroxine [T_4] concentrations are decreased by phenytoin therapy, mainly due to enhanced conversion to triiodothyronine [T_3]; however, T_3 and thyroid stimulating hormone [TSH] concentrations generally remain unchanged, and most patients remain euthyroid)

With physiology/laboratory test values

Alkaline phosphatase and
Gamma-glutamyl transpeptidase (GGT)
(values may be increased)

Glucose, serum
(concentrations may be increased)

Medical considerations/Contraindications

The medical considerations/contraindications included have been selected on the basis of their potential clinical significance (reasons given in parentheses where appropriate)—not necessarily inclusive (» = major clinical significance).

Except under special circumstances, this medication should not be used when the following medical problem exists:

» Cardiac function impairment, such as Adams-Stokes syndrome, second- and third-degree AV block, sino-atrial block, and sinus bradycardia
(parenteral phenytoin administration may affect ventricular automaticity and result in ventricular arrhythmias)

Risk-benefit should be considered when the following medical problems exist:

Alcoholism, active
(serum phenytoin concentrations may be decreased)

» Blood dyscrasias
(risk of serious infections may be increased)

Cardiovascular disease
(intravenous phenytoin administration may result in atrial and ventricular conduction depression, ventricular fibrillation, or reduced cardiac output, especially in the elderly or seriously ill patients; phenytoin should be administered at a rate of no more than 25 mg per minute, and if necessary, at a slow rate of 5 to 10 mg per minute)

Diabetes mellitus
(hyperglycemia may be potentiated)

Fever or febrile illness—temperature > 38.2 °C (101 °F) for more than 24 hours
(serum concentrations of hydantoin anticonvulsants may be decreased because of induction of hepatic oxidative enzymes during fever)

» Hepatic function impairment
(metabolism of hydantoin anticonvulsants may be reduced, thereby increasing the possibility of toxic serum concentrations; alterations in protein binding are also likely, due to a secondary decrease in albumin concentrations)

» Porphyria
(risk of exacerbation)

» Renal function impairment
(excretion and protein binding may be altered)

» Sensitivity to hydantoin anticonvulsants, or to structurally similar compounds such as barbiturates, succinimides, and oxazolidinediones

Systemic lupus erythematosus
(risk of exacerbation)

Thyroid function impairment
(free, circulating thyroxine [FT_4] and total thyroxine [T_4] concentrations are decreased by phenytoin therapy; patients usually remain euthyroid)

Patient monitoring

The following may be especially important in patient monitoring (other tests may be warranted in some patients, depending on condition; » = major clinical significance):

Albumin concentrations, serum and
Calcium concentrations, serum and
» Complete blood cell and platelet counts and
» Hepatic function determinations
(some or all may be required at periodic intervals during therapy depending on individual needs of the patient; however, these determinations may be necessary only during early weeks or months of treatment)

» Blood pressure determinations and
» Cardiac function and
» Respiratory function
(patients receiving fosphenytoin or phenytoin intravenously should be carefully monitored; hypotension may occur; severe cardiovascular reactions [including atrial and ventricular conduction depression and ventricular fibrillation] and fatalities have occurred following intravenous administration of phenytoin; severe complications occur most commonly in elderly or seriously ill patients)

» Dental examinations
(recommended at 3-month intervals for teeth cleaning and reinforcement of patient's plaque control for inhibition of gingival hyperplasia)

» Electroencephalograms (EEGs) and
» Hydantoin concentrations, serum
(in patients maintained at steady-state hydantoin concentrations with well-controlled seizures, routine screening usually is not needed; however, in newly diagnosed patients or in those with poorly controlled seizures, periodic monitoring, possibly with video recording of seizures, and medical and physical reassessment may prevent neurotoxicity and facilitate dosage titration)

(when monitoring hydantoin serum concentrations, all blood samples should be drawn at standardized times within the dosing schedule, preferably just before a dose is administered [except for fosphenytoin]; since the hepatic metabolism of phenytoin is saturable, a small increment in dose, at higher doses, will produce a disproportionate and unpredictable increase in serum concentrations to the upper therapeutic ranges, and can lead to clinical toxicity. After administration of fosphenytoin, phenytoin concentrations should not be measured until conversion to phenytoin is essentially complete [i.e., 2 hours after the end of an intravenous infusion or 4 hours after an intramuscular injection]. Prior to complete conversion of fosphenytoin to phenytoin, commonly used immunoanalytical techniques [such as TDx®/TDxFLx™ (fluorescence polarization) and Emit® 2000 (enzyme multiplied)] may significantly overestimate plasma phenytoin concentrations because of cross-reactivity with fosphenytoin. The error is dependent on plasma concentrations of phenytoin and fosphenytoin, which are influenced by the dose, route, and rate of administration of fosphenytoin, the time of sampling relative to dosing, and the analytical method. Chromatographic assay methods accurately quantitate phenytoin concentrations in biological fluids in the presence of fosphenytoin. Prior to complete conversion, blood samples for phenytoin monitoring should be collected in tubes containing EDTA as an anticoagulant to minimize *ex vivo* conversion of fosphenytoin to phenytoin. However, even with specific assay methods, phenytoin concentrations measured before conversion of fosphenytoin is complete will not accurately reflect phenytoin concentrations ultimately achieved)

(free [unbound] hydantoin serum concentrations should be monitored in patients with altered protein binding of phenytoin [e.g., neonates, and patients with renal failure, hypoalbuminemia, or acute trauma] and in patients experiencing adverse reactions who have phenytoin concentrations within the therapeutic or target range)

(because of altered metabolism and protein binding, and/or increased metabolic clearance of hydantoin anticonvulsants during pregnancy, monthly measurements of serum hydantoin concentrations are recommended to assess the need for an increase in dosage; weekly measurements are recommended during the postpartum period to ascertain adequate reduction of dosage; some patients may have a significant decrease in hydantoin metabolism at time of delivery; therefore, serum hydantoin concentrations should be followed closely during the immediate postpartum period [within 12 hours])

Folate concentrations, serum
(recommended periodically because of increased folate requirements of patients on long-term phenytoin therapy)

Phosphate concentrations in patients with renal insufficiency receiving fosphenytoin
(these patients may be prone to phosphate intoxication; the phosphate load from administration of fosphenytoin is 0.0037 millimoles of phosphate per mg of phenytoin sodium equivalents [PE])

Physical examination, with special attention to lymph glands and skin
(all cases of lymphadenopathy or skin rash should be monitored for an extended period because of possible phenytoin hypersensitivity syndrome with lymphadenopathy or pseudolymphoma; should these problems occur, every effort should be made to achieve seizure control using alternative anticonvulsants)

Thyroid function determinations
(recommended during the first few months of therapy to detect symptoms of hypothyroidism, which may be unmasked by hydantoins; when a patient receiving phenytoin is suspected of having hypothyroidism, T_3 and thyroid-stimulating hormone [TSH] concentrations should be measured rather than T_4 and free T_4 index [FTI], since the latter are both typically depressed in patients receiving phenytoin)

Note: Even after patients have been stabilized on a maintenance dose, it is important that they have periodic examinations during therapy since phenytoin (and possibly other hydantoins) may deplete body stores of folic acid and vitamin D, possibly resulting in megaloblastic anemia or osteomalacia.

Side/Adverse Effects

Note: Although not all of these side effects have been attributed specifically to each hydantoin anticonvulsant, a potential exists for their occurrence during the use of any hydantoin.

The following side/adverse effects have been selected on the basis of their potential clinical significance (possible signs and symptoms in parentheses where appropriate)—not necessarily inclusive:

Those indicating need for medical attention

Incidence more frequent

CNS toxicity, including ataxia (clumsiness or unsteadiness); ***confusion; nystagmus*** (uncontrolled back-and-forth and/or rolling eye movements); ***slurred speech or stuttering; trembling of hands; and unusual excitement, nervousness, or irritability; gingival hyperplasia*** (bleeding, tender, or enlarged gums)—higher incidence in children and young adults; incidence in all age groups rare with ethotoin; ***lupus erythematosus, phenytoin hypersensitivity syndrome, Stevens-Johnson syndrome, or toxic epidermal necrolysis*** (fever; muscle pain; skin rash; sore throat)

Note: *CNS toxicity* usually occurs with long-term use, but may be dose-related.

Phenytoin hypersensitivity syndrome may be manifested in many ways. Fever, rash, and lymphadenopathy frequently occur together, and may be part of more than one hypersensitivity syndrome. Skin rash is the most frequent hypersensitivity reaction; licheniform or maculopapular or morbilliform rash, often pruritic, may present simply or may be prodromal of more serious dermatological reactions such as *Stevens-Johnson syndrome* or *toxic epidermal necrolysis*. Lymphoid syndromes (including lymphoid hyperplasia, pseudolymphomas, and pseudo-pseudolymphomas) occur less commonly and are generally reversible upon discontinuation of phenytoin. Phenytoin-induced hepatitis and hepatic necrosis are other major hypersensitivity reactions, as is eosinophilia, which occurs commonly. Less commonly occurring syndromes include polyarteritis, polymyositis, or systemic *lupus erythematosus;* disseminated intravascular coagulopathy, serum sickness, and renal failure may also occur.

Rash usually appears in the first 2 weeks of treatment; *hypersensitivity syndrome* usually occurs 3 to 8 weeks after, but may occur as long as 12 weeks after initiation of phenytoin therapy. The syndrome may be life-threatening, but early intervention may prevent renal failure, severe rhabdomyolysis, or hepatic necrosis. Other factors, such as a positive family history for phenytoin hypersensitivity reactions or concomitant administration of cranial radiation therapy, may increase the risk of hypersensitivity syndrome occurring.

Incidence rare

Blood dyscrasias, including agranulocytosis (chills; fever; sore throat; unusual tiredness or weakness); ***leukopenia*** (fever; chills; sore throat); ***pancytopenia*** (nosebleeds or other unusual bleeding or bruising); ***and thrombocytopenia*** (fever; sore throat; unusual bleeding or bruising); ***cholestatic jaundice or hepatitis*** (dark urine; light gray–colored stools; loss of appetite and weight; severe stomach pain; yellow eyes or skin; skin rash or itching; dizziness; nausea or vomiting; joint pain; unusual tiredness or weakness); ***choreoathetoid movements, transient*** (restlessness or agitation; uncontrolled jerking or twisting movements of hands, arms, or legs; uncontrolled movements of lips, tongue, or cheeks); ***cognitive impairment*** (defects in intelligence, short-term memory, learning ability, and attention); ***periarteritis nodosa*** (abdominal pain; soreness of muscles; unusual tiredness or weakness; fever with or without chills; headache; loss of appetite and weight); ***Peyronie's disease*** (pain of penis on erection); ***pulmonary infiltrates or fibrosis*** (fever; troubled or quick, shallow breathing; unusual tiredness or weakness; loss of appetite and weight; chest discomfort); ***vitamin D and/or calcium imbalance*** (frequent bone fractures; bone malformations; slowed growth)

Note: Many cases of mephenytoin-induced *blood dyscrasias* occur in patients given mephenytoin for a second time after a period of abstinence.

Choreoathetoid movements may be due to rapid administration of intravenous phenytoin for status epilepticus; the effect usually lasts 24 to 48 hours after discontinuation of phenytoin and may resolve spontaneously; it is unrelated to serum hydantoin toxicity or duration of use.

With chronic use

Peripheral polyneuropathy, predominantly sensory (numbness, tingling, or pain in hands or feet)—with phenytoin

With parenteral use only

Note: Both phenytoin and fosphenytoin may cause hypotension and cardiovascular collapse and/or CNS depression when administered rapidly by the intravenous route, although hypotension and cardiac sequelae are less likely with fosphenytoin. Cardiovascular collapse following rapid intravenous infusion of phenytoin may be primarily attributable to its propylene glycol vehicle. The rate of intravenous infusion of phenytoin should not exceed 50 mg per minute; the rate of fosphenytoin infusions should not exceed 150 mg phenytoin sodium equivalents (PE) per minute. The incidence of cardiovascular effects may be higher in patients who are hypoxic or who have ischemic heart disease.

Phenytoin

Burning pain or irritation at injection site—rarely with necrosis and sloughing

Note: Fosphenytoin also may be associated with *irritation at injection site*, but usually to a lesser degree, due to its water-solubility and its more favorable pH.

Fosphenytoin;

Paresthesias and pruritus (burning; tingling; pain; or itching)—occurring most commonly in groin areas, but also in face, scalp, head, and neck areas, in lower back, buttocks, and abdominal areas

Note: *Paresthesias and pruritus* may be severe; occurrence and intensity can often be lessened by slowing or temporarily stopping the intravenous infusion. Most alert patients who received intravenous fosphenytoin doses of 15 mg PE per kg or greater at a rate of 150 mg PE per minute experienced some degree of discomfort. Most effects resolved within 10 minutes following completion of the infusion; however, some patients experienced sensory disturbances for hours. The pharmacologic basis for these effects is not known, but similar symptoms have been reported with other phosphate ester drugs that deliver phosphate loads. These sensory disturbances are seen more frequently following intravenous than intramuscular injections of fosphenytoin.

Those indicating need for medical attention only if they continue or are bothersome

Incidence more frequent

Constipation; mild dizziness; mild drowsiness; nausea and vomiting

Incidence less frequent

Diarrhea—with ethotoin; ***enlargement of facial features, including thickening of lips, widening of nasal tip, and protrusion of jaw; gynecomastia*** (swelling of breasts)—in males; ***headache; hypertrichosis*** (unusual and excessive hair growth on body and face)—primarily with phenytoin; ***insomnia*** (trouble in sleeping); ***muscle twitching***

Overdose

For specific information on the agents used in the management of hydantoin anticonvulsant overdose, see the *Charcoal, Activated (Oral-Local)* monograph.

For more information on the management of overdose or unintentional ingestion, **contact a Poison Control Center** (see *Poison Control Center Listing*).

Clinical effects of overdose

The following effects have been selected on the basis of their potential clinical significance (possible signs and symptoms in parentheses where appropriate)—not necessarily inclusive:

Ataxia (clumsiness or unsteadiness); ***or staggering walk; blurred or double vision; severe confusion; severe dizziness or drowsiness; dysarthria*** (stuttering); ***or slurred speech; hyperreflexia; nausea and vomiting; nystagmus*** (continuous, uncontrolled back-and-forth and/or rolling eye movements); ***seizures; tremor; unusual tiredness or weakness***

Note: The lethal dose of phenytoin in adults is estimated to be 2 to 5 grams. The lethal dose in children is unknown.

The formate and phosphate metabolites of fosphenytoin may contribute to toxicity. Formate toxicity is associated with severe anion-gap metabolic acidosis. Large increases in phosphate concentrations may cause hypocalcemia with paresthesias, muscle spasms, and seizures.

Treatment of overdose

Since there is no specific antidote for overdose with hydantoin anticonvulsants, treatment is symptomatic and supportive.

To decrease absorption—Induction of emesis or gastric lavage. Multiple oral doses of activated charcoal and cathartic may shorten the duration of symptoms.

To enhance elimination—Forced fluid diuresis, peritoneal dialysis, exchange transfusions, hemodialysis, and plasmapheresis are ineffective; there is little renal elimination and a danger of fluid overload.

Monitoring—If an overdose of fosphenytoin is suspected, ionized free calcium concentrations should be monitored as a sign of phosphate toxicity.

Supportive care—Oxygen, vasopressors, and assisted ventilation may be necessary for CNS, respiratory, or cardiovascular depression. Patients in whom intentional overdose is confirmed or suspected should be referred for psychiatric consultation.

Following recovery, careful evaluation of blood-forming organs is advisable.

Patient Consultation

As an aid to patient consultation, refer to *Advice for the Patient, Anticonvulsants, Hydantoin (Systemic)*.

In providing consultation, consider emphasizing the following selected information (» = major clinical significance):

Before using this medication

» Conditions affecting use, especially:

Sensitivity to hydantoin anticonvulsants or to structurally similar compounds, such as barbiturates, succinimides, and oxazolidinediones

Pregnancy—Hydantoin anticonvulsants cross the placenta; risk-benefit should be considered because of possibility of increased birth defects; seizures may increase during pregnancy with need for dose increase; bleeding problems may occur in mother during delivery and in baby immediately after delivery

Breast-feeding—Ethotoin and phenytoin distributed into breast milk

Use in children—Bleeding, tender, and enlarged gums more common in children; unusual and excessive hair growth, more noticeable in young girls; decreased performance in school (cognitive impairment) may occur with long-term use of high doses

Use in the elderly—Side effects more likely to occur in the elderly; hydantoin anticonvulsants metabolized more slowly in elderly, possibly leading to toxicity

Dental—Gingival hyperplasia may appear; good dental hygiene and visits to dentist every 3 months for cleaning recommended; agranulocytosis or thrombocytopenia may cause gingival bleeding, slowed healing, and infections

Other medications, especially alcohol, amiodarone, antacids, anticoagulants, azole antifungals, calcium-containing medicine, chloramphenicol, cimetidine, CNS depressants, corticosteroids, diazoxide, disulfiram, estrogen- or progestin-containing contraceptives, estrogens, felbamate, fluoxetine, isoniazid, lidocaine, methadone, phenacemide, phenylbutazone, progestins, rifampin, streptozocin, sucralfate, sulfonamides, theophylline, or valproic acid

Other medical problems, especially blood dyscrasias, cardiac function impairment, hepatic function impairment, history of hydantoin hypersensitivity, porphyria, or renal function impairment

Proper use of this medication

Proper administration

For liquid dosage forms—Shaking well; using an accurate measuring device, such as a specially marked measuring spoon, a plastic syringe, or a small graduated cup

For chewable tablet dosage form—Chewing or crushing tablets or swallowing them whole

For capsule dosage form—Swallowing capsule whole

Taking with food to reduce gastrointestinal irritation

» Compliance with therapy; taking every day exactly as directed

» Proper dosing

Missed dose: If dosing schedule is—

One dose a day: Taking as soon as possible unless next day, then continuing on schedule; not doubling doses

Several doses a day: Taking as soon as possible unless within 4 hours of next scheduled dose, then continuing on regular schedule; not doubling doses

Checking with doctor if doses are missed for 2 or more days in a row

» Proper storage

Precautions while using this medication

» Regular visits to physician to check progress of therapy

» Not taking other medication without physician's advice

» Avoiding the use of alcoholic beverages and other CNS depressants while taking this medicine

Not taking within 2 to 3 hours of taking antacids or medication for diarrhea

Not changing brands or dosage forms of phenytoin without checking with physician or pharmacist

» Checking with physician before discontinuing medication; gradual dosage reduction is usually needed to maintain seizure control

Carrying medical identification card or bracelet during therapy

Diabetic patients: Checking blood or urine sugar concentrations

Caution if any laboratory tests required; possible interference with test results of dexamethasone, metyrapone, or Schilling tests, thyroid function tests, or gallium citrate Ga 67 imaging

» Caution if any kind of surgery, dental treatment, or emergency treatment is required

» Caution when driving, using machines, or doing other jobs requiring alertness

» Using different or additional means of birth control than estrogen- or progestin-containing contraceptives

For phenytoin or mephenytoin only:

» Maintaining good dental hygiene and seeing dentist every 3 months for teeth cleaning, to prevent tenderness, bleeding, and enlargement of gums

Side/adverse effects

Increased incidence of gingival hyperplasia in children and young adults taking phenytoin or mephenytoin

Unusual and excessive hair growth more noticeable in young girls

Signs of potential side effects, especially CNS toxicity, lupus erythematosus, phenytoin hypersensitivity syndrome, Stevens-Johnson syndrome, toxic epidermal necrolysis, blood dyscrasias, cholestatic jaundice, hepatitis, transient choreoathetoid movements, cognitive impairment, periarteritis nodosa, Peyronie's disease, pulmonary infiltrates or fibrosis, or vitamin D and/or calcium imbalance

General Dosing Information

Dosage must be individualized. Monitoring of serum phenytoin concentrations is recommended because of the great variation of response among patients to the hydantoin anticonvulsants and because of the relatively narrow therapeutic serum concentration range.

Geriatric patients, seriously ill patients, or patients with impaired hepatic function may require lower initial dosage with subsequent adjustments, because of slow hydantoin metabolism or decreased protein binding. If phenytoin is administered intravenously, the rate must be slowed to not more than 25 mg a minute, and possibly to as low as 5 to 10 mg a minute.

When patients are transferred from hydantoins to other anticonvulsant medication or vice versa, there should be a gradual (over a period of a few weeks) increase in the dosage of the added medication and a gradual decrease in the dosage of the medication to be discontinued. When an enzyme-inducing medication is added to or removed from a regimen, the metabolism of the other medications will be altered. In most patients, changes in enzyme induction may occur over a period of weeks.

When single-drug anticonvulsant therapy is to be discontinued in patients with seizure disorders, dosage should be reduced gradually over a period of 6 to 12 months to prevent possible recurrence of seizures. Abrupt withdrawal may lead to status epilepticus.

Diet/Nutrition

Oral hydantoin anticonvulsants may be taken with or immediately after meals to lessen gastric irritation. However, the medication should always be taken at the same time in relation to meals to ensure consistent absorption.

Patients on long-term hydantoin therapy may have increased folic acid requirements. However, increased hydantoin dosages may be necessary in patients who receive folate supplementation because such supplementation may result in decreased serum hydantoin concentrations and possible loss of seizure control.

Patients on long-term hydantoin therapy may also require vitamin D supplementation, especially those patients taking high doses of phenytoin, those with low dietary intake of vitamin D, those with limited sun exposure, and those with reduced levels of physical activity.

For treatment of adverse effects

Intolerance or allergic reactions—Hydantoin anticonvulsants should be discontinued immediately. Effects are usually observed within 9 to 14 days after start of therapy. If rash is morbilliform (measles-like) or scarlatiniform (scarlet fever–like), therapy may be restarted after the rash has completely disappeared, but should be discontinued if the rash reappears. If rash is exfoliative, purpuric, bullous, or if lupus erythematosus or Stevens-Johnson syndrome is suspected, hydantoin therapy should not be resumed. Attempts should be made to differentiate lymph gland enlargement from other lymph node pathology. The patient should be monitored closely for an extended length of time, and alternative (nonhydantoin) anticonvulsant therapy initiated.

CNS or cerebellar toxicity—Dosage reduction or discontinuation of hydantoin anticonvulsant may improve or reverse effects. Cerebellar toxicity may occur after long-term administration, usually at serum concentrations above 30 mcg. However, CNS toxicity has also been reported at lower serum concentrations, due to free fraction variability.

Gingival or gum enlargement—Consultation with dentist; following recommendations for care to reduce effects.

ETHOTOIN

Summary of Differences

Pharmacology/pharmacokinetics:

Half-life—

3 to 9 hours.

Side/adverse effects:

Diarrhea has been reported.

Drowsiness and sedation are dose related and quite common.

Gum hyperplasia is rare; ethotoin is sometimes substituted for phenytoin therapy when gingival hyperplasia is a problem.

Incidence of ataxia is rare.

Incidence of hypertrichosis is lower than with other hydantoin anticonvulsants.

Additional Dosing Information

See also *General Dosing Information.*

Ethotoin may be substituted for phenytoin without loss of seizure control for improvement of gum hyperplasia, or other side effects, during anticonvulsant therapy. Ethotoin doses are usually four to six times greater than those of phenytoin.

Oral Dosage Forms

ETHOTOIN TABLETS USP

Usual adult and adolescent dose

Anticonvulsant—

Oral, 500 mg to 1 gram the first day, usually divided into four to six doses, the dosage being gradually increased over several days until seizure control is obtained.

Note: Maintenance dosage of less than 2 grams a day has been found to be ineffective in most adults.

Debilitated patients may require a lower initial dosage.

Usual adult prescribing limits

Up to 3 grams a day.

Usual pediatric dose

Anticonvulsant—

Oral, up to 750 mg a day initially, on the basis of age and weight, the dosage being adjusted as needed and tolerated until seizure control is obtained.

Note: A total daily dose of 3 grams may be required for some patients.

Usual geriatric dose

See *Usual adult and adolescent dose.* However, geriatric patients may require a lower initial dosage.

Strength(s) usually available

U.S.—

250 mg (Rx) [*Peganone* (scored; lactose)].

500 mg (Rx) [*Peganone* (scored; lactose)].

Canada—

Not commercially available.

Packaging and storage

Store below 40 °C (104 °F), preferably between 15 and 30 °C (59 and 86 °F), unless otherwise specified by manufacturer. Store in a tight container.

Auxiliary labeling

- May cause drowsiness.
- Avoid alcoholic beverages.

FOSPHENYTOIN

Summary of Differences

Physicochemical characteristics: Fosphenytoin is a water-soluble prodrug that is rapidly converted to phenytoin following parenteral administration.

Pharmacology/pharmacokinetics: Fosphenytoin has no intrinsic pharmacologic activity before its conversion to phenytoin. After conversion, the pharmacologic and toxicologic effects are essentially the same as those of phenytoin. For each millimole of fosphenytoin administered, one millimole of phenytoin is produced. This means that 1.5 mg of fosphenytoin liberates 1 mg of phenytoin, or that 75 mg of fosphenytoin sodium is essentially equivalent to 50 mg of phenytoin sodium. To avoid performing molecular weight–based adjustments when converting between fosphenytoin sodium and phenytoin sodium, the amount and concentration of fosphenytoin is expressed in terms of phenytoin sodium equivalents (PE). Fosphenytoin should always be prescribed and dispensed in phenytoin sodium equivalents (PE).

Pharmacokinetics of fosphenytoin following intravenous administration are complex; when used in an emergent setting, such as status epilepticus, differences in the rate of availability of phenytoin could be critical. Therefore, studies have empirically determined infusion rates for fosphenytoin that produce the rate and extent of systemic phenytoin availability similar to that obtained from a phenytoin sodium infusion of 50 mg per minute.

Side/adverse effects: The incidence of adverse reactions following intravenous administration of fosphenytoin tends to increase with dose and infusion rate. Doses of 15 mg PE per kg of body weight administered at 150 mg PE per minute may cause transient pruritus, tinnitus, nystagmus, somnolence, and ataxia to occur two to three times more often than do lower doses or slower administration rates.

Additional Dosing Information

See also *General Dosing Information.*

Dosing of fosphenytoin sodium injection is always expressed in terms of phenytoin sodium equivalents (PE).

Bioequivalence information

In vivo, 1.5 mg of fosphenytoin sodium injection liberates 1 mg of phenytoin sodium; thus, 75 mg of fosphenytoin sodium is essentially equivalent to 50 mg of phenytoin sodium.

Parenteral Dosing Forms

FOSPHENYTOIN SODIUM INJECTION

Note: Dosing for fosphenytoin sodium injection is expressed in terms of phenytoin sodium equivalents (PE).

During intravenous infusion of fosphenytoin, continuous monitoring of the patient's electrocardiogram (ECG), blood pressure, and respiration is essential.

Intramuscular fosphenytoin doses of 20 to 30 mL have been safely administered as a single intramuscular injection, with little or no local irritation reported.

Usual adult and adolescent dose

Anticonvulsant in status epilepticus—

Loading: Intravenous, 15 to 20 mg phenytoin sodium equivalents (PE) per kg of body weight, administered at a rate of 100 to 150 mg PE per minute. The infusion rate should not exceed 150 mg PE per minute.

Maintenance: Intravenous or intramuscular, initially 4 to 6 mg PE per kg of body weight per day.

Note: Because the effect of fosphenytoin is not immediate, other measures including concomitant administration of a benzodiazepine will usually be necessary in status epilepticus.

Anticonvulsant for nonemergent conditions—

Loading: Intravenous or intramuscular, 10 to 20 mg phenytoin sodium equivalents (PE) per kg of body weight.

Maintenance: Initially 4 to 6 mg PE per kg of body weight per day.

As substitute for oral phenytoin therapy—

The same total daily dose and frequency as phenytoin sodium has been administered. Since fosphenytoin is 100% bioavailable by both intravenous and intramuscular routes, either route may be used. However, the intramuscular route obviates the need for monitoring and the equipment necessary for intravenous infusion. Since phenytoin sodium delayed-release capsules are approximately 90% bioavailable, plasma concentrations of phenytoin may increase modestly when parenteral fosphenytoin is substituted. Clinical response and therapeutic plasma phenytoin concentrations should be used to guide fosphenytoin therapy after 3 to 5 days.

Usual pediatric dose

Anticonvulsant in status epilepticus[1]—

Loading: Intravenous, 15 to 20 mg phenytoin sodium equivalents (PE) per kg of body weight, administered at up to 3 mg PE per kg of body weight per minute.

Maintenance: Intravenous or intramuscular, initially 4 to 6 mg PE per kg of body weight.

Usual geriatric dose

Anticonvulsant in status epilepticus—

Loading: Intravenous, 14 mg phenytoin sodium equivalents (PE) per kg of body weight.

Note: In patients who require phosphate restriction, such as those with severe renal function impairment, the contribution of fosphenytoin of 0.0037 millimole of phosphate per mg phenytoin sodium equivalent (PE) must be considered.

Strength(s) usually available

U.S.—

75 mg per mL, equivalent to 50 mg of phenytoin sodium per mL (Rx) [*Cerebyx* (Tromethamine USP (TRIS); Hydrochloric acid NF; Sodium hydroxide NF; Water for injection USP)].

Canada—

75 mg per mL, equivalent to 50 mg of phenytoin sodium per mL (Rx) [*Cerebyx* (Tromethamine buffer 12 mg/mL; Hydrochloric acid NF; Sodium hydroxide NF; Water for injection USP)].

Packaging and storage

Store between 2 and 8 °C (36 to 46 °F), unless otherwise specified by manufacturer. Do not store at room temperature for more than 48 hours.

Preparation of dosage form

Prior to intravenous administration, fosphenytoin sodium must be diluted in 5% dextrose injection or 0.9% sodium chloride injection to a concentration of 1.5 to 25 mg phenytoin sodium equivalents (PE) per mL.

Stability

Unopened vials should be refrigerated; however, unopened vials will remain stable for 48 hours at room temperature. Vials that develop particulate matter should not be used.

Once diluted for intravenous administration, fosphenytoin sodium solutions are stable for 8 hours at room temperature and 24 hours under refrigeration.

Additional information

Fosphenytoin sodium injection is buffered to a pH of 8.6 to 9.

[1]Not included in Canadian product labeling.

MEPHENYTOIN

Summary of Differences

Pharmacology/pharmacokinetics: Half-life is approximately 7 hours but averages 95 to 144 hours for the active metabolite, nirvanol.

Side/adverse effects: Drowsiness and sedation are dose related and quite common.

Additional Dosing Information

See also *General Dosing Information.*

Mephenytoin usually is used only after safer anticonvulsants have been tried and have proven unsatisfactory.

Oral Dosage Forms

MEPHENYTOIN TABLETS USP

Usual adult and adolescent dose

Anticonvulsant—

Oral, 50 to 100 mg once a day, the dosage being increased by an additional 50 to 100 mg a day at one-week intervals until seizure control is obtained.

Note: Debilitated patients may require a lower initial dosage.

Usual adult prescribing limits

1.2 grams a day.

Usual pediatric dose

Anticonvulsant—

Oral, 25 to 50 mg a day, the dosage being increased by an additional 25 to 50 mg a day at one-week intervals until seizure control is obtained.

Usual pediatric prescribing limits

400 mg a day.

Note: Dose may be divided and should be based on severity of seizures, age, and serum concentrations.

Usual geriatric dose

See *Usual adult and adolescent dose.* However, geriatric patients may require a lower initial dosage.

Strength(s) usually available

U.S.—

100 mg (Rx) [*Mesantoin* (scored; lactose; sucrose)].

Canada—

Not commercially available.

Packaging and storage

Store below 40 °C (104 °F), preferably between 15 and 30 °C (59 and 86 °F), unless otherwise specified by manufacturer. Store in a well-closed container.

Auxiliary labeling
- May cause drowsiness.
- Avoid alcoholic beverages.

PHENYTOIN

Summary of Differences
Category: Also used as an antiarrhythmic, for ventricular arrhythmias, especially when arrhythmia is digitalis-induced or caused by tricyclic antidepressant toxicity; as an antineuralgic in trigeminal neuralgia; and as a muscle relaxant in certain movement disorders.

Pharmacology/pharmacokinetics: Because phenytoin exhibits saturable, zero-order, or dose-dependent pharmacokinetics, the apparent half-life of phenytoin changes with dose and serum concentration.

Side/adverse effects: Incidence of hypertrichosis is more frequent than with other hydantoin anticonvulsants.

Additional Dosing Information
See also *General Dosing Information.*

For oral dosage forms
Extended Phenytoin Sodium Capsules USP is the only dosage form used for once-a-day dosing, and then, only after patients have been stabilized on a divided dosage, generally 300 to 400 mg a day.

Phenytoin oral suspension is generally not recommended for once-a-day dosing because it is not an extended-release dosage form. The suspension may be adequate for more frequent dosing, if vigorously shaken to avoid inadequate dispersal of phenytoin throughout the vehicle.

For parenteral dosage forms
Intravenous phenytoin sodium should be administered by direct intravenous injection into a large vein through a large-gauge needle or intravenous catheter at a rate not to exceed 50 mg a minute. Faster rates of administration may result in hypotension, cardiovascular collapse, or CNS depression, related to the propylene glycol diluent.

Intravenous administration should be monitored by cardiac function and blood pressure readings.

To minimize local venous irritation from intravenous injection of phenytoin, each dose must be followed by 0.9% sodium chloride injection through the same in-place needle or catheter. Extravasation should be avoided, as phenytoin injection is caustic to tissues because of its high alkalinity (pH = 12), and possibly also because of the propylene glycol in the vehicle. Soft tissue injury ranging from irritation to extensive necrosis and sloughing has been reported even when extravasation has not occurred.

Some clinicians suggest that, to prevent serious local inflammatory reactions, intermittent phenytoin infusion may be desirable and that such an infusion can be made feasible if all of the following criteria are met:
- Phenytoin injection is admixed only with no more than 50 mL of 0.9% sodium chloride injection.
- The final concentration of phenytoin is between 1 and 10 mg per mL.
- Admixture is done *immediately* before beginning the infusion.
- Infusion is completed within 1 hour.
- All tubing is flushed with 0.9% sodium chloride injection before and after infusion.
- A 0.45- to 0.22-micron filter is placed on the line.

When phenytoin injection is administered by infusion, the maximum rate of infusion is 50 mg a minute. However, for patients who may develop hypotension, who are on a sympathomimetic medication, who have cardiovascular disease, or who are older than 65 years of age, the maximum rate of infusion should be 25 mg a minute and possibly as low as 5 to 10 mg a minute. Vigilant ECG monitoring of cardiovascular status throughout the duration of infusion is required. For rapid control of seizures, concomitant administration of an intravenous benzodiazepine or a short-acting barbiturate may be necessary because of the slow rate of administration necessary for phenytoin injection.

Because of the delayed absorption of intramuscularly administered phenytoin and the high degree of local irritation from the alkaline solution, the intramuscular route of administration is not recommended when the intravenous or oral route is available.

Intramuscular administration is not recommended for treatment of status epilepticus since serum concentrations in the therapeutic range cannot be readily achieved for up to 24 hours. Erratic absorption is partly caused by tissue precipitation of phenytoin. Muscle necrosis has also been reported.

Intramuscular administration during neurosurgery, for patients stabilized on oral phenytoin, requires a dose 50% greater than the oral dosage used to maintain serum concentrations. When a patient is returned to the oral route, dosage should be reduced by 50% of the original oral dosage for 1 week to compensate for the sustained release of medication from prior intramuscular injections.

If the need for intramuscular administration continues for more than 1 week, alternative routes such as gastric intubation should be considered.

Bioequivalence information
For oral dosage forms only—

The prescribing physician should be consulted before a prescription is changed from one phenytoin dosage form to another because of possible differences in bioavailability, due to varying amounts of calcium sulfate excipient or amount of phenytoin acid contained in the product. Phenytoin dosage forms based on phenytoin acid (oral suspension and chewable tablets) contain 8% more drug on a mg-per-mg basis than those based on phenytoin sodium. Phenytoin intoxication has been reported following weight-for-weight substitution of phenytoin acid for phenytoin sodium.

Oral Dosage Forms
Note: Bracketed uses in the *Dosage Forms* section refer to categories of use and/or indications that are not included in U.S. product labeling.

PHENYTOIN ORAL SUSPENSION USP
Note: Phenytoin Oral Suspension USP is not an extended phenytoin product and is not intended for once-a-day dosage.

Usual adult and adolescent dose
Anticonvulsant—

Oral, initially 125 mg three times a day, the dosage being adjusted at seven- to ten-day intervals as needed and tolerated.

Note: For seriously ill or debilitated patients, or patients with impaired hepatic function, the total dose is often reduced.

Usual pediatric dose
Anticonvulsant—

Initial: Oral, 5 mg per kg of body weight a day, divided into two or three doses, the dosage being adjusted as needed and tolerated.

Maintenance: Oral, 4 to 8 mg per kg of body weight or 250 mg per square meter of body surface area a day, divided into two or three doses.

Usual geriatric dose
Anticonvulsant—

Oral, initially 3 mg per kg of body weight a day, in divided doses, the dosage being adjusted according to serum hydantoin concentrations and the patient's response.

Strength(s) usually available
U.S.—

125 mg per 5 mL (Rx) [*Dilantin-125* (sucrose); GENERIC].

Canada—

30 mg per 5 mL (Rx) [*Dilantin-30*].

125 mg per 5 mL (Rx) [*Dilantin-125*].

Packaging and storage
Store below 40 °C (104 °F), preferably between 15 and 30 °C (59 and 86 °F), unless otherwise specified by manufacturer. Store in a tight container. Protect from freezing.

Auxiliary labeling
- Shake well.
- Protect from freezing.
- Avoid alcoholic beverages.

Note
Remind patient to shake bottle well before removing each dose.

Advise patient to use an accurate measuring spoon, plastic syringe, or graduated measuring cup.

Additional information
May contain 0.6% alcohol.

PHENYTOIN TABLETS (CHEWABLE) USP
Note: Phenytoin chewable tablets are not intended for once-a-day dosage as they may be too promptly bioavailable. Once-a-day use of phenytoin chewable tablets may result in toxic serum concentrations of phenytoin.

Usual adult and adolescent dose

Anticonvulsant—

Oral, initially 100 to 125 mg three times a day, the dosage being adjusted at seven- to ten-day intervals as needed and tolerated.

Note: For seriously ill or debilitated patients, or patients with impaired hepatic function, the total dose is often reduced.

Usual pediatric dose

Anticonvulsant—

Initial: Oral, 5 mg per kg of body weight a day, divided into two or three doses, the dosage being adjusted as needed and tolerated.

Maintenance: Oral, 4 to 8 mg per kg of body weight or 250 mg per square meter of body surface area a day, divided into two or three doses.

Usual geriatric dose

Anticonvulsant—

Oral, initially 3 mg per kg of body weight a day, in divided doses, the dosage being adjusted according to serum hydantoin concentrations and the patient's response.

Strength(s) usually available

U.S.—

50 mg (Rx) [*Dilantin Infatabs* (saccharin; sucrose)].

Canada—

50 mg (Rx) [*Dilantin Infatabs*].

Note: One 100-mg capsule of phenytoin sodium contains 92% phenytoin and is therefore not equivalent to two 50-mg phenytoin chewable tablets containing 100% phenytoin.

Packaging and storage

Store below 40 °C (104 °F), preferably between 15 and 30 °C (59 and 86 °F), unless otherwise specified by manufacturer. Store in a well-closed container.

Auxiliary labeling

- May be chewed or crushed.
- Avoid alcoholic beverages.

EXTENDED PHENYTOIN SODIUM CAPSULES USP

Note: Only phenytoin sodium capsules labeled "Extended" are to be used for once-a-day dosage. Once-a-day use of capsules labeled "Prompt" may result in toxic serum phenytoin concentrations.

Usual adult and adolescent dose

Anticonvulsant—

Oral, initially 100 mg three times a day, the dosage being adjusted at seven- to ten-day intervals as needed and tolerated. When established, the daily maintenance dosage may be given on a once-a-day basis in accordance with patient tolerance.

Note: An oral loading dose of 1 gram may be given, the dose being divided as follows: Initially 400 mg, then 300 mg after two hours, followed by an additional 300 mg in two hours; normal maintenance dosing is started twenty-four hours after the loading dose. Alternatively, some clinicians recommend an oral loading dose of 20 mg per kg of body weight, divided into three to four doses and administered at two-hour intervals.

Patients with a history of renal or liver disease should not receive a loading dose. Use of this regimen should be limited to patients in a clinic or hospital setting where phenytoin serum concentrations can be closely monitored.

Once-a-day dosage should be considered only for adult patients whose condition has been stabilized by divided doses of extended phenytoin sodium capsules given as 100 mg three times a day. This single 300-mg daily dosage has the advantage of convenience and improved compliance.

For seriously ill patients or for debilitated patients or patients with impaired hepatic function, the total dose is often reduced.

[Antineuralgic][1]—

Oral, 200 to 600 mg a day, in divided doses, the dose being adjusted as needed and tolerated.

[Skeletal muscle relaxant][1]—

Oral, up to 300 to 600 mg a day, as needed and tolerated.

Usual pediatric dose

Anticonvulsant—

Initial: Oral, 5 mg per kg of body weight a day, divided into two or three doses, the dosage then being adjusted as needed and tolerated.

Maintenance: Oral, 4 to 8 mg per kg of body weight or 250 mg per square meter of body surface area a day, divided into two or three doses.

Usual geriatric dose

Anticonvulsant—

Oral, initially 3 mg per kg of body weight a day, in divided doses, the dosage being adjusted according to serum hydantoin concentrations and the patient's response.

Note: For geriatric patients, the total dose is often reduced.

Strength(s) usually available

U.S.—

30 mg (Rx) [*Dilantin Kapseals* (lactose; sucrose); GENERIC].

100 mg (Rx) [*Dilantin Kapseals* (lactose; sucrose); *Phenytek;* GENERIC].

Canada—

30 mg (Rx) [*Dilantin* (lactose)].

100 mg (Rx) [*Dilantin* (lactose)].

Note: One 100-mg capsule of phenytoin sodium contains 92% phenytoin and is therefore not equivalent to two 50-mg phenytoin chewable tablets containing 100% phenytoin.

Packaging and storage

Store below 40 °C (104 °F), preferably between 15 and 30 °C (59 and 86 °F), unless otherwise specified by manufacturer. Store in a tight container.

Auxiliary labeling

- Avoid alcoholic beverages.

Additional information

The sodium content of phenytoin sodium is 0.35 mEq (8 mg) per 100-mg capsule.

PROMPT PHENYTOIN SODIUM CAPSULES USP

Note: Phenytoin sodium capsules labeled "Prompt" are not intended for once-a-day dosage because the phenytoin may be too promptly bioavailable and may cause toxic serum concentrations of phenytoin.

Usual adult and adolescent dose

Anticonvulsant—

Oral, 100 mg three times a day, the dosage being adjusted at seven- to ten-day intervals as needed and tolerated.

Note: For seriously ill patients, debilitated patients, or patients with impaired hepatic function, the total dose is often reduced.

Usual pediatric dose

Anticonvulsant—

Initial: Oral, 5 mg per kg of body weight a day, divided into two or three doses, the dosage then being adjusted as needed and tolerated.

Maintenance: Oral, 4 to 8 mg per kg of body weight or 250 mg per square meter of body surface area a day, divided into two or three doses in accordance with patient tolerance.

Usual geriatric dose

Anticonvulsant—

Oral, initially 3 mg per kg of body weight a day, in divided doses, the dosage being adjusted according to serum hydantoin concentrations and the patient's response.

Note: For geriatric patients, the total dose is often reduced.

Strength(s) usually available

U.S.—

30 mg (Rx) [GENERIC].

100 mg (Rx) [GENERIC].

Canada—

Not commercially available.

Note: One 100-mg capsule of phenytoin sodium contains 92% phenytoin and is therefore not equivalent to two 50-mg phenytoin chewable tablets containing 100% phenytoin.

Packaging and storage

Store below 40 °C (104 °F), preferably between 15 and 30 °C (59 and 86 °F), unless otherwise specified by manufacturer. Store in a tight container.

Auxiliary labeling

- Avoid alcoholic beverages.

Additional information

The sodium content of phenytoin sodium is 0.35 mEq (8 mg) per 100-mg capsule.

Parenteral Dosage Forms

Note: Bracketed uses in the *Dosage Forms* section refer to categories of use and/or indictions that are not included in U.S. product labeling.

PHENYTOIN SODIUM INJECTION USP

Usual adult and adolescent dose

Anticonvulsant in status epilepticus—

Initial—

Intravenous, direct, 15 to 20 mg per kg of body weight, administered at a rate not to exceed 50 mg a minute.

Note: For obese patients, the loading dose should be calculated on the basis of ideal body weight plus 1.33 times the excess weight over ideal weight, since phenytoin preferentially distributes into fat.

Maintenance—

Intravenous, direct, 100 mg every six to eight hours, at a rate not to exceed 50 mg a minute.

Note: Maintenance therapy, intravenously, 100 mg every six to eight hours, or orally, 5 mg per kg of body weight a day, divided into two to four doses, should begin about twelve to twenty-four hours after a loading dose is given.

[Antiarrhythmic][1]—

Intravenous, direct, 50 to 100 mg every ten to fifteen minutes as needed and tolerated to stop arrhythmia, but not to exceed a total dose of 15 mg per kg of body weight, administered slowly at a rate no greater than 50 mg a minute.

Note: For geriatric or seriously ill patients or for debilitated patients or patients with impaired hepatic function, the total dose is often reduced and the rate of intravenous administration slowed to 25 mg a minute, possibly as low as 5 to 10 mg a minute, to lessen the possibility of side effects.

During intravenous infusion of phenytoin, continuous monitoring of the patient's electrocardiogram (ECG), blood pressure, and respiration is essential.

Although the manufacturers recommend that phenytoin not be added to intravenous infusions, some clinicians routinely use such infusions. If phenytoin is administered by infusion, the rate of administration should not exceed 50 mg per minute; some investigators have suggested rates of 20 to 40 mg per minute.

Usual pediatric dose

Anticonvulsant in status epilepticus—

Intravenous, direct, 15 to 20 mg per kg of body weight, or 250 mg per square meter of body surface area, administered at a rate of 1 mg per kg of body weight per minute, not to exceed 50 mg a minute.

Usual geriatric dose

See *Usual adult and adolescent dose*.

Strength(s) usually available

U.S.—

50 mg per mL (Rx) [*Dilantin* (alcohol 10%); GENERIC].

Canada—

50 mg per mL (Rx) [*Dilantin* (alcohol 10%); GENERIC].

Packaging and storage

Store between 15 and 30 °C (59 and 86 °F). Protect from freezing.

Stability

A slight yellowing of the solution will not affect its potency. After being refrigerated, solution may form a precipitate that usually dissolves after being warmed to room temperature; however, do not use if the solution is not clear.

Incompatibilities

The manufacturers recommend that parenteral phenytoin sodium not be added to intravenous infusions or mixed with other medication because precipitation of phenytoin may occur. However, some clinicians routinely use infusion solutions of phenytoin in 0.9% sodium chloride in concentrations of 1 to 10 mg of phenytoin per mL, provided the infusion is started immediately after preparation and is completed within 1 hour; the admixture must be carefully observed for signs of precipitation, and use of a 0.45- to 0.22-micron in-line filter is recommended; in addition, flushing of all tubing with 0.9% sodium chloride injection before and after infusion of phenytoin is recommended.

Additional information

The sodium content of phenytoin sodium injection is approximately 0.2 mEq (4.5 mg) per mL.

[1]Not included in Canadian product labeling.

Selected Bibliography

Levy RH, Mattson RH, Meldrum BS, editors. Antiepileptic drugs. 4th ed. New York: Raven Press; 1995. p. 45-6, 64-77, 315-57, 711, 813-4.

Boucher BA. Fosphenytoin: a novel phenytoin prodrug. Pharmacotherapy 1996; 16(5): 777-91.

Revised: 05/01/2000

ANTICONVULSANTS, SUCCINIMIDE Systemic

This monograph includes information on the following: 1) Ethosuximide; 2) Methsuximide.

INN: Methsuximide—Mesuximide

VA CLASSIFICATION (Primary): CN400

Commonly used brand name(s): *Celontin*[2]; *Zarontin*[1].

Note: For a listing of dosage forms and brand names by country availability, see *Dosage Forms* section(s).

Category

Anticonvulsant.

Indications

Note: Bracketed information in the *Indications* section refers to uses that are not included in U.S. product labeling.

Accepted

Epilepsy, absence seizure pattern (treatment)—Ethosuximide, the drug of choice, is indicated for the control of seizures in absence (petit mal) epilepsy. Methsuximide is indicated for the management of absence seizures refractory to other medication.

[Epilepsy, complex partial seizure pattern (treatment)][1]—Methsuximide may be used in the treatment of complex partial seizures.

[1]Not included in Canadian product labeling.

Pharmacology/Pharmacokinetics

Physicochemical characteristics

Molecular weight—

Ethosuximide: 141.17.

Methsuximide: 203.24.

Mechanism of action/Effect

Poorly defined; succinimide anticonvulsants are thought to increase the seizure threshold and suppress the paroxysmal three-cycle-per-second spike-and-wave pattern seen with absence (petit mal) seizures. The frequency of attacks is reduced by depression of nerve transmission in the motor cortex. These effects may be due to direct modification of membrane function in excitable cells and/or alteration of chemically mediated neurotransmission. The specific effect of ethosuximide against absence seizures appears to be due to its ability to block T-type calcium channels at concentrations that do not affect other ion channels.

Absorption

Generally rapid and complete.

Distribution

Freely distributed to all body tissues, except fat. Concentrations of ethosuximide in saliva and tears are equivalent to plasma concentrations. Concentrations of ethosuximide in breast milk may approach 94% of plasma concentrations.

Protein binding

Not significant.

Biotransformation

Hepatic. Methsuximide metabolized to the active metabolite *N*-desmethylmethsuximide.

Half-life

Ethosuximide—

Adults: 56 to 60 hours.

Children: 30 to 36 hours.

Methsuximide—

1 to 3 hours.

N-desmethylmethsuximide—

34 to 80 hours.

Time to peak concentration

Ethosuximide—

Adults: 2 to 4 hours.

Children: 3 to 7 hours.

Methsuximide—

1 to 4 hours.

Therapeutic serum concentration

Ethosuximide—40 to 100 mcg/mL (283.4 to 708.4 micromoles per L).

N-desmethylmethsuximide—10 to 40 mcg/mL (49.2 to 196.8 micromoles per L).

Elimination
Renal (ethosuximide, up to 20% unchanged).

Precautions to Consider

Cross-sensitivity and/or related problems
Patients sensitive to one succinimide anticonvulsant may be sensitive to the other also.

Pregnancy/Reproduction
Pregnancy—Problems in humans have not been documented; however, teratogenic effects have been associated with other anticonvulsant medications.

Breast-feeding
Ethosuximide is distributed into breast milk. It is not known whether methsuximide is distributed into breast milk. Problems in humans have not been documented.

Pediatrics
Appropriate studies performed to date have not demonstrated pediatrics-specific problems that would limit the usefulness of succinimide anticonvulsants in children.

Geriatrics
Appropriate studies on the relationship of age to the effects of succinimide anticonvulsants have not been performed in the geriatric population. However, no geriatrics-specific problems have been documented to date.

Dental
The blood dyscrasia-causing effects of succinimide anticonvulsants may result in an increased incidence of microbial infection, delayed healing, and gingival bleeding. If leukopenia or thrombocytopenia occurs, dental work should be deferred until blood counts have returned to normal. Patients should be instructed in proper oral hygiene during treatment, including caution in use of regular toothbrushes, dental floss, and toothpicks.

Drug interactions and/or related problems
The following drug interactions and/or related problems have been selected on the basis of their potential clinical significance (possible mechanism in parentheses where appropriate)—not necessarily inclusive (» = major clinical significance):

Note: Combinations containing any of the following medications, depending on the amount present, may also interact with this medication.

Alcohol or
» Central nervous system (CNS) depression-producing medications, other (see *Appendix II*)
(CNS depression may be enhanced)

Antidepressants, tricyclic, or
Loxapine or
Maprotiline or
Molindone or
Monoamine oxidase (MAO) inhibitors or
Phenothiazines or
Pimozide or
Thioxanthenes
(concurrent use may lower the convulsive threshold, enhance CNS depression, and decrease the effects of the anticonvulsant medication)

Carbamazepine or
Phenobarbital or
Phenytoin or
Primidone
(induction of hepatic microsomal enzyme activity resulting in increased metabolism and decreased serum concentrations and elimination half-lives of succinimide anticonvulsants and/or these medications may occur during concurrent therapy; monitoring of serum concentrations as a guide to dosage is recommended, especially when any anticonvulsant is added to or withdrawn from an existing regimen)

Folic acid
(requirements for folic acid may be increased in patients receiving anticonvulsant therapy)

» Haloperidol
(concurrent use may cause a change in the pattern and/or the frequency of epileptiform seizures; dosage adjustments of the anticonvulsant may be necessary; serum concentrations of haloperidol may be significantly reduced)

Phenacemide
(concurrent use may result in additive toxicity)

Valproic acid
(concurrent use of valproic acid has been reported to both increase and decrease ethosuximide concentrations due to changes in metabolism; monitoring of serum concentrations as a guide to dosage is recommended)

Medical considerations/Contraindications
The medical considerations/contraindications included have been selected on the basis of their potential clinical significance (reasons given in parentheses where appropriate)—not necessarily inclusive (» = major clinical significance).

Risk-benefit should be considered when the following medical problems exist:

Blood dyscrasias
(condition may be exacerbated)

Hepatic function impairment or
Renal function impairment, severe
(morphological and functional changes may occur in liver or kidneys)

Intermittent porphyria
(condition may be exacerbated)

Sensitivity to succinimide anticonvulsants

Patient monitoring
The following may be especially important in patient monitoring (other tests may be warranted in some patients, depending on condition; » = major clinical significance):

» Blood cell counts, including platelets, and
Hepatic function determinations and
Renal function determinations and
Urinalysis
(recommended at periodic intervals for patients on prolonged therapy)

Side/Adverse Effects
The following side/adverse effects have been selected on the basis of their potential clinical significance (possible signs and symptoms in parentheses where appropriate)—not necessarily inclusive:

Those indicating need for medical attention
Incidence more frequent

Stevens-Johnson syndrome or systemic lupus erythematosus (skin rash and itching; swollen glands; sore throat and fever; muscle pain)

Incidence less frequent

Aggressiveness; difficulty in concentrating; mental depression; nightmares

Incidence rare

Blood dyscrasias, including agranulocytosis (chills; fever; sore throat; unusual tiredness or weakness); ***aplastic anemia*** (shortness of breath, troubled breathing, wheezing, or tightness in chest; sores, ulcers, or white spots on lips or in mouth; swollen or painful glands; unusual bleeding or bruising); ***eosinophilia*** (fever); ***leukopenia*** (fever; chills; sore throat); ***pancytopenia*** (nosebleeds or other unusual bleeding or bruising); ***precipitation of tonic-clonic convulsions; paranoid psychosis*** (mood or mental changes); ***pruritic erythematous rash*** (skin rash and itching)

Those indicating need for medical attention only if they continue or are bothersome
Incidence more frequent

Anorexia (loss of appetite); ***ataxia*** (clumsiness or unsteadiness); ***dizziness; drowsiness; headache; hiccups; nausea or vomiting; stomach cramps***

Incidence less frequent

Irritability; unusual tiredness or weakness

Overdose
For specific information on the agents used in the management of succinimide anticonvulsants, see: *Charcoal, Activated (Oral-Local)* monograph.

For more information on the management of overdose or unintentional ingestion, **contact a Poison Control Center** (see *Poison Control Center Listing*).

Clinical effects of overdose
The following effects have been selected on the basis of their potential clinical significance (possible signs and symptoms in parentheses where appropriate)—not necessarily inclusive:

Central nervous system (CNS) depression (severe drowsiness); ***severe nausea and vomiting; respiratory depression*** (shortness of breath; slow or irregular breathing; troubled breathing)

Note: Methsuximide poisoning may have a biphasic profile due to the *N*-desmethyl metabolite; therefore it is important to monitor serum concentrations of *N*-desmethylmethsuximide.

Treatment of overdose

Because no specific antidote is available, treatment is essentially symptomatic and supportive.

To decrease absorption—
- Induction of emesis (unless the patient is or could rapidly become obtunded, comatose, or convulsing) or gastric lavage.
- Instillation of activated charcoal.
- Use of cathartics.

To enhance elimination—
- Hemodialysis may be useful in treating ethosuximide overdoses.
- Charcoal hemoperfusion may be useful to remove the *N*-desmethyl metabolite of methsuximide.
- Forced diuresis and exchange transfusions are ineffective in the treatment of succinimide anticonvulsant overdoses.

Supportive care—
- Patients in whom intentional overdose is confirmed or suspected should be referred for psychiatric consultation.

Patient Consultation

As an aid to patient consultation, refer to *Advice for the Patient, Anticonvulsants, Succinimide (Systemic).*

In providing consultation, consider emphasizing the following selected information (» = major clinical significance):

Before using this medication

» Conditions affecting use, especially:
- Sensitivity to succinimide anticonvulsants
- Pregnancy—Possible birth defects
- Other medications, especially CNS depressants or haloperidol
- Other medical problems, especially blood dyscrasias, hepatic function impairment, severe renal function impairment, or intermittent porphyria

Proper use of this medication

» Compliance with therapy; taking daily in regularly spaced doses as ordered

Taking with food or milk to reduce gastric irritation

» Proper dosing

Missed dose: Taking as soon as possible; if remembered within 4 hours of next dose, skipping missed dose and continuing on regular dosing schedule; not doubling doses

» Proper storage

Precautions while using this medication

» Regular visits to physician to check progress of therapy

» Checking with physician before discontinuing this medication; gradual dosage reduction may be necessary

» Not starting or stopping other medication without physician's advice

» Avoiding the use of alcoholic beverages and other CNS depressants while taking this medication

» Possibility of drowsiness; caution if driving or doing jobs requiring alertness

» Caution if any kind of surgery, dental treatment, or emergency treatment is required

Carrying medical identification card or bracelet

For methsuximide:

Not taking capsules that are melted or not full; effectiveness may be reduced

Side/adverse effects

Signs of potential side effects, especially Stevens-Johnson syndrome, systemic lupus erythematosus, aggressiveness, difficulty in concentration, mental depression, nightmares, blood dyscrasias, tonic-clonic convulsions, paranoid psychosis, or pruritic erythematous rash

General Dosing Information

When succinimide anticonvulsants are to be discontinued, dosage should be reduced gradually to prevent possible occurrence of petit mal status.

When used to replace other anticonvulsant therapy, the dosage of the succinimide anticonvulsant should be increased gradually while that of the other medication is gradually decreased, to maintain seizure control.

If succinimide anticonvulsants are used to supplement an existing anticonvulsant regimen, their dosage should be gradually increased to the required level.

When succinimide anticonvulsants are used alone in mixed types of epilepsy, the frequency of primary generalized tonic-clonic seizures may be increased in some patients.

ETHOSUXIMIDE

Summary of Differences

Pharmacology/pharmacokinetics:
- Half-life—56 to 60 hours in adults; 30 to 36 hours in children.
- Peak effect—3 to 7 hours.
- Serum concentrations, therapeutic—40 to 100 mcg/mL.

Additional Dosing Information

See also *General Dosing Information.*

Strict supervision by the physician is required if total daily dosage of ethosuximide exceeds 1.5 grams for adults or 1 gram for children up to 6 years of age.

Ethosuximide dosage may be initiated at maintenance level. When this medication is used concurrently with intravenous diazepam in management of absence status epilepticus (petit mal status), higher-than-usual starting doses may be required to rapidly achieve a therapeutic serum level.

Oral Dosage Forms

ETHOSUXIMIDE CAPSULES USP

Usual adult and adolescent dose

Anticonvulsant—
- Oral, 15 to 30 mg per kg of body weight a day; or initially 250 mg two times a day, the dosage being increased by an additional 250 mg a day at four- to seven-day intervals until seizure control is obtained or until the total daily dose reaches 1.5 grams.

Usual pediatric dose

Anticonvulsant—
- Children up to 6 years of age: Oral, 15 to 40 mg per kg of body weight a day; or initially 250 mg once a day, the dosage being increased by an additional 250 mg a day at four- to seven-day intervals until seizure control is obtained or until the total daily dose reaches 1 gram.
- Children 6 years of age and over: See *Usual adult and adolescent dose.*

Note: The optimal dosage for most children is 20 mg per kg of body weight a day.

Strength(s) usually available

U.S.—
- 250 mg (Rx) [*Zarontin*].

Canada—
- 250 mg (Rx) [*Zarontin*].

Packaging and storage

Store below 30 °C (86 °F), preferably between 15 and 30 °C (59 and 86 °F), unless otherwise specified by manufacturer. Store in a tight container.

Auxiliary labeling

- May cause drowsiness.
- Keep container tightly closed.

ETHOSUXIMIDE SYRUP

Usual adult and adolescent dose

See *Ethosuximide Capsules USP.*

Usual pediatric dose

See *Ethosuximide Capsules USP.*

Strength(s) usually available

U.S.—
- 250 mg per 5 mL (Rx) [*Zarontin* (sucrose); GENERIC].

Canada—
- 250 mg per 5 mL (Rx) [*Zarontin*].

Packaging and storage

Store between 15 and 30 °C (59 and 86 °F), in a tight, light-resistant container, unless otherwise specified by manufacturer. Protect from freezing.

Auxiliary labeling

- May cause drowsiness.

METHSUXIMIDE

Summary of Differences

Category:
Indicated in absence seizures refractory to other medication.
Pharmacology/pharmacokinetics:
Half-life—1 to 3 hours (36 to 45 hours for active metabolites).
Serum concentration, therapeutic—10 to 40 mcg/mL.

Oral Dosage Forms

METHSUXIMIDE CAPSULES USP

Usual adult and adolescent dose

Anticonvulsant—
Oral, initially 300 mg once a day, the dosage being increased by 300 mg a day at one-week intervals until seizure control is obtained or until the total daily dose reaches 1.2 grams. Alternatively, some clinicians advocate making dosage increases of 150 to 300 mg at intervals of no less than 14 days to allow plasma concentrations to reach steady-state levels.

Usual pediatric dose

See *Usual adult and adolescent dose.* (Small children may require dosage adjustments utilizing the 150-mg capsules.)

Strength(s) usually available

U.S.—
150 mg (Rx) [*Celontin*].
300 mg (Rx) [*Celontin*].
Canada—
300 mg (Rx) [*Celontin*].

Packaging and storage

Store below 30 °C (86 °F), preferably between 15 and 30 °C (59 and 86 °F), unless otherwise specified by manufacturer. Store in a tight container. Avoid exposure to excessive heat.

Stability

Methsuximide has a relatively low melting range (50 to 56 °C [122 to 133 °F]). Improper storage may result in melting and subsequent impaired absorption of the capsule contents.

Auxiliary labeling

- May cause drowsiness.

Note

Do not dispense or use capsules that are not full or in which contents have melted. Protect from excessive heat (40 °C [104 °F]).

Revised: 02/05/2001

ANTIDEPRESSANTS, MONOAMINE OXIDASE (MAO) INHIBITOR Systemic

This monograph includes information on the following: 1) Isocarboxazid†; 2) Phenelzine; 3) Tranylcypromine.

VA CLASSIFICATION (Primary/Secondary): CN602/CN900

Commonly used brand name(s): *Marplan*[1]; *Nardil*[2]; *Parnate*[3].

Note: This monograph does not cover other MAO inhibitors, such as furazolidone and procarbazine, which are not used as antidepressants, and selegiline, which has its own monograph.

Note: For a listing of dosage forms and brand names by country availability, see *Dosage Forms* section(s).

†Not commercially available in Canada.

Category

Antidepressant; antipanic agent; headache (vascular; tension) prophylactic.

Indications

Note: Bracketed information in the *Indications* section refers to uses that are not included in U.S. product labeling.

Accepted

Depression, major (treatment)—Isocarboxazid is indicated for the treatment of major depression. Because of its potentially serious side effects, it is not recommended as a first choice treatment of newly diagnosed depressed patients.

Phenelzine is effective in the treatment of patients with major depression with or without melancholia, or with atypical, nonendogenous depression, or depressive neurosis. These patients often have mixed anxiety and depression with phobic or hypochondriacal features. Phenelzine is more often used as a second-line antidepressant in patients who have failed to respond to other antidepressants. Nevertheless, many clinicians may consider phenelzine the first choice for treatment of certain dysphorias and minor periodic or chronic depressions (dysthymic disorders).

Tranylcypromine is indicated for treatment of major depression [with or] without melancholia in closely supervised adult patients not responding to or unable to tolerate other antidepressants. [It is also used to treat the depressed phase of bipolar disorder and depressive neurosis of moderate to severe intensity.]

[Panic disorder (treatment)][1]—Phenelzine and, to a lesser extent, tranylcypromine are used in conjunction with psychotherapy and behavioral therapy in the treatment of panic disorder, with or without agoraphobia.

[Headache, vascular (prophylaxis)][1] or
[Headache, tension (prophylaxis)][1]—Monoamine oxidase inhibitors are used in the prophylaxis of vascular headaches (including migraine), tension-type headaches, and mixed headache syndrome. However, due to potentially severe side effects, these agents are not considered first-line therapy.

[1]Not included in Canadian product labeling.

Pharmacology/Pharmacokinetics

Physicochemical characteristics

Molecular weight—
Isocarboxazid: 231.26.
Phenelzine sulfate: 234.27.
Tranylcypromine sulfate: 364.46.

Mechanism of action/Effect

The exact mechanism of antidepressant effect is unknown; however, it is established that the activity of the enzyme monoamine oxidase (MAO) is inhibited. MAO subtypes A and B are involved in the metabolism of serotonin and catecholamine neurotransmitters such as epinephrine, norepinephrine, and dopamine. Phenelzine, isocarboxazid, and tranylcypromine, as nonselective MAO inhibitors, bind irreversibly to monoamine oxidase–A (MAO-A) and monoamine oxidase–B (MAO-B). The reduced MAO activity results in an increased concentration of these neurotransmitters in storage sites throughout the central nervous system (CNS) and sympathetic nervous system. This increased availability of one or more monoamines has been thought to be the basis for the antidepressant activity of MAO inhibitors. The effects of the nonselective MAO inhibitors isocarboxazid, phenelzine, and tranylcypromine lead to downregulation (desensitization) of alpha$_2$- or beta-adrenergic and serotonin receptors. It is thought that changes in receptor characteristics produced by chronic administration of MAO inhibitors correlate better with antidepressant action than does the increased activity of the neuron secondary to increased neurotransmitter concentrations, and may also account for the delay of 2 to 4 weeks in therapeutic response.

Other actions/effects

MAO inhibitors exhibit a hypotensive effect, which varies with the specific agent; the hypotensive mechanism of action is probably mediated through central inhibition of vasomotor centers, or it may be due to chronic accumulation of the false neurotransmitter octopamine in adrenergic terminals.

MAO inhibitors prevent the inactivation of tyramine by hepatic and gastrointestinal monoamine oxidase. Circulating tyramine releases norepinephrine from the sympathetic nerve terminals and produces a sudden increase in blood pressure.

Absorption

Well absorbed from the gastrointestinal tract.

Biotransformation

Hepatic; rapid; by oxidation; possible active metabolites.

Onset of action

As early as 7 to 10 days with appropriate dosage in some patients, but may take up to 4 to 8 weeks to achieve full therapeutic effect.

Time to peak plasma concentration

Phenelzine—2 to 4 hours after oral dose.
Tranylcypromine—1 to 3.5 hours.

Duration of action

At least 10 days for MAO activity to be recovered because of irreversible binding.

Elimination
Renal, as metabolites.

Precautions to Consider

Tumorigenicity
Phenelzine, like other hydrazine derivatives, has been reported in an uncontrolled lifetime study to induce pulmonary and vascular tumors in mice.

Pregnancy/Reproduction
Pregnancy—Tranylcypromine (and probably phenelzine) crosses the placenta. A limited study in humans reported an increased risk of fetal malformations when these medications were administered in the first trimester.

Animal studies have shown that MAO inhibitors, in doses much higher than the maximum recommended human dose (MRHD), cause hyperexcitability and a reduced rate of growth in the neonate.

For isocarboxazid: FDA Pregnancy Category C

For phenelzine: FDA Pregnancy Category C.

For tranylcypromine: FDA pregnancy category not currently included in product labeling.

Breast-feeding
Tranylcypromine is distributed into human breast milk; it is not known whether phenelzine or isocarboxazid is distributed into human breast milk. Problems in humans have not been documented.

Pediatrics
Antidepressants increase the risk of suicidal thinking and behavior (suicidality) in children and adolescents with major depressive disorder (MDD) and other psychiatric disorders. Anyone considering the use of any antidepressant in a child or adolescent must balance this risk with the clinical need.

Pooled analyses of short-term placebo controlled trials of nine antidepressant drugs in children and adolescents with MDD, obsessive compulsive disorder, or other psychiatric disorders have revealed a greater risk of adverse events representing suicidality during the first few months of treatment in those receiving antidepressants.

Animal studies have shown that these medications may cause growth retardation in the young.

Geriatrics
Experience with the use of MAO inhibitors in the elderly is relatively limited. However, there have been reports that phenelzine is safe and effective in the treatment of elderly depressed patients with a history of atypical depression or depressive neurosis. MAO inhibitors may also be useful for anergic or apathetic retarded depressions. The potential for increased vascular accidents (especially in the event of sudden hypertensive episodes), increased sensitivity to hypotensive effects, and reduced metabolic capacity discourages the first-time use of MAO inhibitors in patients over 60 years of age. When an MAO inhibitor is prescribed for an elderly patient, the patient's history of depression, ability to comply with prescribing instructions, and any potential drug interactions must also be considered.

Drug interactions and/or related problems
The following drug interactions and/or related problems have been selected on the basis of their potential clinical significance (possible mechanism in parentheses where appropriate)—not necessarily inclusive (» = major clinical significance):

Note: Combinations containing any of the following medications, depending on the amount present, may also interact with this medication.

» Alcohol or
» CNS depression-producing medications, other, (see *Appendix II*)
(concurrent use with MAO inhibitors may increase CNS depressant effects)
(also, possible tyramine content in some alcoholic beverages, especially beer, wine, or ale, may induce hypertensive reactions)
(in addition to additive CNS depressant effects caused by some antihypertensives such as clonidine, guanabenz, methyldopa, metyrosine, and pargyline, postural hypotension may be aggravated)

» Anesthetics, local, with epinephrine or levonordefrin or
» Cocaine
(concurrent use with MAO inhibitors may cause severe hypertension due to sympathomimetic effects)
(cocaine should not be administered during or within 14 days following administration of an MAO inhibitor; phenelzine also inhibits cholinesterase activity and may reduce or slow cocaine metabolism, thereby increasing the risk of cocaine toxicity)

Anesthetics, spinal
(use of MAO inhibitors in patients receiving local anesthetics via subarachnoid block may increase the risk of hypotension; discontinuation of MAO inhibitors 10 days before elective surgery may be advisable; however, to avoid interruption of antidepressant therapy, patients receiving long-term MAO inhibition may undergo surgery without discontinuation of the MAO inhibitor; dosages of the anesthetic must be adjusted carefully)

Anticholinergics or other medications with anticholinergic activity (see *Appendix II*) or
Antidyskinetic agents or
Antihistamines
(concurrent use with MAO inhibitors may intensify the anticholinergic effects of these medications because of secondary anticholinergic activities of MAO inhibitors)
(also, concurrent use with MAO inhibitors may block detoxification of anticholinergics, thus potentiating their action; patients should be advised to report occurrence of gastrointestinal problems promptly since paralytic ileus may occur with concurrent therapy)
(concurrent use with MAO inhibitors may also prolong and intensify the CNS depressant and anticholinergic effects of antihistamines; concurrent use is not recommended)

Anticoagulants, coumarin- or indandione-derivative
(concurrent use may increase anticoagulant activity; although the mechanism of action and clinical significance are unknown, caution is recommended)

Anticonvulsants
(in addition to increasing CNS depressant effects, concurrent use with MAO inhibitors may cause a change in the pattern of epileptiform seizures; dosage adjustment of anticonvulsant may be necessary)

» Antidepressants, tricyclic or
» Fluoxetine or
» Paroxetine or
» Sertraline or
» Trazodone
(a potentially lethal hyperserotonergic state known as the serotonin syndrome may occur as the result of combining serotonergic agents [such as amitriptyline, clomipramine, doxepin, or imipramine; fluoxetine, paroxetine, or sertraline; or trazodone] with MAO inhibitors. The syndrome may be manifested by mental status changes [confusion, hypomania], restlessness, myoclonus, hyperreflexia, diaphoresis, shivering, tremor, diarrhea, incoordination, and/or fever. If recognized early, the syndrome usually resolves quickly upon withdrawal of the offending agents)
(in addition to increased anticholinergic effects, concurrent use of tricyclic antidepressants with MAO inhibitors has resulted in an increased risk of hyperpyretic episodes, hypertensive crises, severe convulsions, and death; however, recent studies have shown that some tricyclic antidepressants can be used concurrently with MAO inhibitors for refractory depression with no adverse effects if both medications are initiated simultaneously at lower than usual doses and the doses raised gradually, or if the MAO inhibitor is gradually added to the tricyclic, also at low doses; tricyclics should not be added to an established MAO inhibitor regimen; clomipramine, desipramine, imipramine, nortriptyline, and protriptyline are not recommended for use in such a regimen; careful monitoring for side effects of either medication is necessary)
(concurrent use of fluoxetine with MAO inhibitors may result in confusion, agitation, restlessness, and gastrointestinal symptoms, or possibly hyperpyretic episodes, severe convulsions, and hypertensive crises. Based on experience with tricyclic antidepressants, at least 14 days should elapse between discontinuation of an MAO inhibitor and initiation of fluoxetine. However, because of the long half-lives of fluoxetine and its active metabolite, at least 5 weeks [approximately 5 half-lives of norfluoxetine] should elapse between discontinuation of fluoxetine and initiation of therapy with an MAO inhibitor. Administration of an MAO inhibitor within 5 weeks of discontinuation of fluoxetine may increase the risk of serious events. While a causal relationship to fluoxetine has not been established, death has been reported following the initiation of an MAO inhibitor shortly after fluoxetine administration was stopped)

» Antidiabetic agents, oral or
» Insulin
(hypoglycemic effects may be enhanced by MAO inhibitors; reduction in dosage of hypoglycemic medication may be necessary during and after concurrent therapy)

Antihypertensive medications
(isocarboxazid may have a marked potentiating effect on antihypertensive drugs, resulting in hypotension)

Beta-adrenergic blocking agents
(a few cases of significant bradycardia have been reported in elderly patients receiving a beta-adrenergic blocking agent concurrently with phenelzine; monitoring of pulse rate during concurrent administration has been recommended)

Bromocriptine
(concurrent use may increase serum prolactin concentrations and interfere with effects of bromocriptine; dosage adjustment of bromocriptine may be necessary)

» Bupropion
(concurrent use of MAO inhibitors with bupropion may increase the risk of acute bupropion toxicity and is contraindicated; a medication-free interval of at least 2 weeks should elapse between discontinuation of the MAO inhibitor and initiation of bupropion therapy)

» Buspirone
(concurrent use with MAO inhibitors is not recommended because elevation of blood pressure may occur; at least 10 days should elapse between discontinuation of one medication and initiation of the other)

» Caffeine-containing medications
(concurrent use of excessive amounts of caffeine, consumed in coffee, tea, cola, chocolate, or "stay awake" products, with MAO inhibitors may produce dangerous cardiac arrhythmias or severe hypertension because of sympathomimetic side effects of caffeine)

» Carbamazepine or
» Cyclobenzaprine or
» Maprotiline or
» Monoamine oxidase (MAO) inhibitors, other, including furazolidone, procarbazine, or selegiline
(concurrent use with MAO inhibitors has resulted in hyperpyretic crises, hypertensive crises, severe convulsions, and death; a medication-free interval of at least 2 weeks should elapse between discontinuation of one medication and initiation of another; for patients switching from one MAO inhibitor to another, an interval of 2 weeks is recommended)
(in addition, MAO inhibitors cause a change in the pattern of epileptiform seizures in patients receiving carbamazepine as an anticonvulsant)

» Dextromethorphan
(concurrent use with MAO inhibitors may cause excitation, hypertension, and hyperpyrexia)

Diuretics
(concurrent use with MAO inhibitors may result in an increased hypotensive effect)

» Doxapram
(concurrent use may increase the pressor effects of either doxapram or the MAO inhibitor)

» Guanadrel or
» Guanethidine or
» Rauwolfia alkaloids
(concurrent use with these agents may result in moderate to severe hypertension due to release of catecholamines; withdrawal of MAO inhibitor at least 1 week prior to initiation of therapy with these agents is recommended)
(when an MAO inhibitor is added to existing therapy with a rauwolfia alkaloid, serious potentiation of CNS depressant effects may result; however, if a rauwolfia alkaloid is added to an MAO inhibitor regimen, CNS excitation and hypertension may result from release of excessive amounts of accumulated norepinephrine and serotonin)

Haloperidol or
Loxapine or
Molindone or
Phenothiazines or
Pimozide or
Thioxanthenes
(concurrent use may prolong and intensify the sedative, hypotensive, and anticholinergic effects of either these medications or MAO inhibitors)

» Levodopa
(concurrent use with MAO inhibitors is not recommended, as the combination may result in sudden moderate to severe hypertensive crisis; it is recommended that MAO inhibitors be discontinued for 2 to 4 weeks prior to initiation of levodopa therapy)

» Meperidine, and possibly other opioid (narcotic) analgesics
(concurrent use with MAO inhibitors may produce immediate excitation, sweating, rigidity, and severe hypertension; in some patients, hypotension, severe respiratory depression, coma, convulsions, hyperpyrexia, vascular collapse, and death may occur; reactions may be due to accumulation of serotonin resulting from MAO inhibition; avoidance of meperidine use within 2 to 3 weeks following MAO inhibition is recommended; other opioid analgesics such as morphine are not likely to cause such severe reactions and may be used cautiously in reduced dosage in patients receiving MAO inhibitors; however, it is recommended that a small test dose [¼ of the usual dose] or several small incremental test doses over a period of several hours should first be administered to permit observation of any adverse effects; caution is also recommended in the use of alfentanil, fentanyl, or sufentanil as an adjunct to anesthesia if the patient has received an MAO inhibitor within 14 days; although the risk of a significant interaction has been questioned, the use of a small test dose is advised to detect any possible interaction)

» Methyldopa
(may cause hyperexcitability in patients receiving an MAO inhibitor; also headache, severe hypertension, and hallucinations have been reported with concurrent use)

» Methylphenidate
(concurrent use with MAO inhibitors may potentiate the CNS stimulant effects of methylphenidate, possibly resulting in a hypertensive crisis; methylphenidate should not be administered during or within 14 days following the administration of MAO inhibitors)

Metrizamide
(concurrent use with MAO inhibitors may lower the seizure threshold and increase the risk of seizures; MAO inhibitors should be discontinued at least 48 hours before myelography and should not be resumed for at least 24 hours after procedure)

Phenylephrine, nasal or ophthalmic
(if significant systemic absorption of nasal or ophthalmic phenylephrine occurs, concurrent use with MAO inhibitors may potentiate the pressor effect of phenylephrine; nasal or ophthalmic phenylephrine should not be administered during or within 14 days following the administration of an MAO inhibitor)

Succinylcholine
(concurrent use with phenelzine may decrease plasma concentrations or activity of pseudocholinesterase, the enzyme that metabolizes succinylcholine, thereby enhancing the neuromuscular blockade of succinylcholine and possibly resulting in prolonged respiratory depression or apnea)

» Sympathomimetics
(concurrent use with MAO inhibitors may prolong and intensify cardiac stimulant and vasopressor effects [including headache, cardiac arrhythmias, vomiting, sudden and severe hypertensive and hyperpyretic crises] of these medications because of release of catecholamines that accumulate in intraneuronal storage sites during MAO inhibitor therapy; these medications should not be administered during or within 14 days following the administration of an MAO inhibitor)

» Tryptophan
(concurrent use with MAO inhibitors may cause hyperreflexia, shivering, hyperventilation, hyperthermia, mania or hypomania, and disorientation or confusion; if tryptophan is added to an MAO inhibitor regimen, especially tranylcypromine, it should be started in low dosages and the dose titrated upwards gradually with close monitoring of mental status and blood pressure)

» Tyramine- or other high pressor amine-containing foods and beverages, such as aged cheese; fava or broad bean pods; yeast/protein extracts; smoked or pickled meats, poultry, or fish; fermented sausage (bologna, pepperoni, salami, summer sausage) or other fermented meat; sauerkraut; any overripe fruit; beer; reduced-alcohol and alcohol-free beer and wine; red and white wines; sherry; and liqueurs
(concurrent use with MAO inhibitors may cause sudden and severe hypertensive reactions; reactions are usually limited to a few hours and easily treated with rapidly acting hypotensive agents [such as labetolol, nifedipine, or if necessary in severe cases refractory to other agents, phentolamine]; severity depends on amount of tyramine ingested, rate of gastric emptying, and length of interval between dose of MAO inhibitor and ingestion of tyramine; when MAO inhibitors are discontinued, dietary restrictions must continue for at least 2 weeks; other tyramine- or high pressor amine-containing foods, such as yogurt, sour cream, cream cheese, cottage cheese, chocolate, and soy sauce, if eaten when

fresh and in moderation, are considered unlikely to cause serious problems)

Medical considerations/Contraindications

The medical considerations/contraindications included have been selected on the basis of their potential clinical significance (reasons given in parentheses where appropriate)—not necessarily inclusive (» = major clinical significance).

Except under special circumstances, this medication should not be used when the following medical problems exist:

» Alcoholism, active

» Congestive heart failure

» Hepatic function impairment, severe
(hepatic precoma may be precipitated in patients with cirrhosis, who are extremely sensitive to effects of MAO inhibitors)

» Pheochromocytoma
(pressor substances secreted by such tumors may alter blood pressure during therapy with MAO inhibitors)

» Renal function impairment, severe
(cumulative effects of MAO inhibitors may occur because of reduced renal excretion)

Sensitivity to any MAO inhibitor, including furazolidone, procarbazine, or selegiline

Risk-benefit should be considered when the following medical problems exist:

Asthma or bronchitis
(medications used in the treatment of these conditions may interact with MAO inhibitors)

Bipolar disorder
(switch from depressive to manic phase may occur)

» Cardiac arrhythmias

» Cardiovascular disease or coronary insufficiency or Cerebrovascular disease
(ischemia may be aggravated as a result of reduced blood pressure; however, in patients with serious heart block or a conduction disturbance, an MAO inhibitor may be preferred to a tricyclic antidepressant because of significant slowing of resting pulse [heart rate] or shortening of the PR and QT intervals, and a significant decrease in blood pressure)

Diabetes mellitus
(insulin or oral hypoglycemic requirements may be altered)

Epilepsy
(pattern of epileptiform seizures may be changed)

» Headaches, severe or frequent
(headache as a first sign of hypertensive reaction during therapy may be masked)

» Hepatic function impairment
(hepatic precoma may be precipitated in patients with cirrhosis, who are extremely sensitive to effects of MAO inhibitors)

» Hypertension
(use of MAO inhibitors is not recommended in patients on multiple-drug therapy since hypotensive effects may be potentiated; hypertensive crises resulting from dietary lapses may be more severe in hypertensive patients)

Hyperthyroidism
(sensitivity to pressor amines may be increased)

Parkinson's disease
(may be aggravated)

» Renal function impairment
(cumulative effects may occur)

» Schizophrenia
(MAO inhibitors may aggravate psychosis and/or cause excessive stimulation in schizophrenic patients)

» Suicidal tendencies
(patients may continue to exhibit suicidal tendencies because significant improvement may not occur for several weeks after initiation of therapy with MAO inhibitors)

» Caution is required also in patients who have undergone sympathectomy; these patients may be more sensitive to the hypotensive effects of MAO inhibitors.

Patient monitoring

The following may be especially important in patient monitoring (other tests may be warranted in some patients, depending on condition; » = major clinical significance):

» Blood pressure measurements
(careful and frequent monitoring is recommended because of the variety of factors that may produce dangerous alterations in pressure during therapy)

Careful supervision of depressed patients including those with:
Abnormal behaviors (i.e., agitation, panic attacks, hostility) or
Clinical worsening of their depression or
Suicidal ideation and behavior (suicidality)
(recommended especially during early treatment phase before peak effectiveness of antidepressant is achieved or at the time of increases or decreases in dose; prescribing the smallest number of tablets necessary for good patient management is recommended to decrease the risk of overdose; consideration should be given to changing the therapeutic regimen, including possibly discontinuing the medicine, in patients whose depression is persistently worse or whose emergent suicidality or other symptoms are severe, abrupt in onset, or were not part of the patient's presenting symptoms)

Hepatic function determinations
(although rare, drug-induced hepatitis has occurred with MAO inhibitor therapy)

Side/Adverse Effects

The following side/adverse effects have been selected on the basis of their potential clinical significance (possible signs and symptoms in parentheses where appropriate)—not necessarily inclusive:

Those indicating need for medical attention

Incidence more frequent

Orthostatic hypotension, severe (dizziness or lightheadedness, especially when getting up from a lying or sitting position)

Note: Falling or fainting may result. *Orthostatic hypotension* occurs in hypertensive as well as normal and hypotensive patients. Reduction in the dosage of MAO inhibitor may be required to bring blood pressure up to pretreatment levels.

Incidence less frequent

Diarrhea; peripheral edema (swelling of feet and lower legs); ***sympathetic stimulation*** (fast or pounding heartbeat; unusual excitement or nervousness)

Note: *Edema* may subside spontaneously within a week. However, if edema persists, electrolytes should be monitored to rule out syndrome of inappropriate antidiuretic hormone secretion (SIADH).

Incidence rare

Hepatitis (dark urine; skin rash; yellow eyes or skin); ***leukopenia*** (fever; sore throat); ***parkinsonian syndrome*** (slurred speech; staggering gait)

Note: A potentially lethal hyperserotonergic state known as the serotonin syndrome may occur, typically as the result of combining serotonergic agents (such as amitriptyline, clomipramine, doxepin, or imipramine; fluoxetine, paroxetine, or sertraline; or trazodone) with MAO inhibitors. The syndrome may be manifested by mental status changes (confusion, hypomania), restlessness, myoclonus, hyperreflexia, diaphoresis, shivering, tremor, diarrhea, incoordination, and fever. If recognized early, the syndrome usually resolves quickly upon withdrawal of the offending agents.

Symptoms of hypertensive crisis

Severe chest pain; enlarged pupils; fast or slow heartbeat; severe headache; increased sensitivity of eyes to light; increased sweating, possibly with fever or cold, clammy skin; nausea or vomiting; stiff or sore neck

Note: Intracranial bleeding (sometimes fatal in outcome) has occurred in association with *hypertensive crisis.*

Palpitation or frequent headaches may be prodromal signs of a hypertensive reaction.

Those indicating need for medical attention only if they continue or are bothersome

Incidence more frequent

Anticholinergic effect or syndrome of inappropriate antidiuretic hormone secretion [SIADH] (decreased urine output); ***blurred vision; CNS stimulation*** (muscle twitching during sleep; restlessness or agitation; trouble in sleeping)—more likely with tranylcypromine; ***decreased sexual ability; drowsiness***—more likely with isocarboxazid and phenelzine; ***mild headache without increase in blood pressure; increased appetite and weight gain, related to carbohydrate craving; increased sweating; nausea; orthostatic hypo-***

tension, mild (dizziness or lightheadedness; tiredness and weakness); ***shakiness or trembling; weakness***

Note: *Decreased sexual ability* may include anorgasmia in males and females; ejaculatory disorders; and, less commonly, impotence in males.

Incidence less frequent or rare

Anorexia (decreased appetite); ***chills; constipation; dryness of mouth***—more frequent with isocarboxazid

Overdose

For specific information on the agents used in the management of monoamine oxidase (MAO) inhibitor antidepressant overdose, see:
- *Charcoal, Activated (Oral-Local)* monograph;
- *Dantrolene (Systemic)* monograph; and/or
- *Diazepam* in *Benzodiazepines (Systemic)* monograph.

For more information on the management of overdose or unintentional ingestion, **contact a Poison Control Center** (see *Poison Control Center Listing*).

Clinical effects of overdose

The following effects have been selected on the basis of their potential clinical significance (possible signs and symptoms in parentheses where appropriate)—not necessarily inclusive:

Severe anxiety; confusion; convulsions; cool, clammy skin; severe dizziness; severe drowsiness; fast and irregular pulse; fever; hallucinations; severe headache; high or low blood pressure; hyperactive reflexes; muscle stiffness; respiratory depression or failure (troubled breathing); ***slowed reflexes; sweating; severe trouble in sleeping; unusual irritability***

Treatment of overdose

Note: *Symptoms of overdose* may be absent or minimal for nearly 12 hours after ingestion, and develop slowly thereafter, reaching a maximum in 24 to 48 hours. Immediate hospitalization with close monitoring of patient is essential during this period. Death has resulted.

To decrease absorption—

Induction of vomiting or gastric lavage with protected airway followed by instillation of charcoal slurry in early overdose.

To enhance elimination—

In tranylcypromine overdose, acidification of urine to pH of 5.

Hemodialysis may be beneficial but is of unproven value.

Specific treatment—

Treatment of signs and symptoms of CNS stimulation with diazepam, administered intravenously and slowly. Phenothiazines should not be used because of additive hypotensive effects.

Treatment of hypotension and vascular collapse with intravenous fluids and a dilute pressor agent.

Close monitoring of body temperature, and vigorous treatment of hyperpyrexia with antipyretics and a cooling blanket. Maintenance of fluid and electrolyte balance is essential.

Reduction of symptoms of hypermetabolic state (coma, respiratory failure, hyperpyrexia, tachycardia, muscular rigidity, tremor, and hyperreflexia) with intravenous dantrolene sodium at 2.5 mg per kg of body weight (mg/kg) a day in divided doses, with careful monitoring for signs of hepatotoxicity and pleural or pericardial effusions.

Monitoring—

Close monitoring of body temperature.

Monitoring of liver function at the time of overdosage and during the 4 to 6 weeks after recovery.

Supportive care—

Support of respiration by management of the airway, and mechanical ventilation with the use of supplemental oxygen, as required.

Patients in whom intentional overdose is known or suspected should be referred for psychiatric consultation.

Note: Pathophysiologic effects of massive overdose may persist for several days; recovery from mild overdose may take 3 to 4 days.

Patient Consultation

As an aid to patient consultation, refer to *Advice for the Patient, Antidepressants, Monoamine Oxidase (MAO) Inhibitor (Systemic)*.

In providing consultation, consider emphasizing the following selected information (» = major clinical significance):

Before using this medication

» Conditions affecting use, especially:

Sensitivity to any MAO inhibitor, including furazolidone or procarbazine

Pregnancy—MAO inhibitors cross placenta; no appropriate human studies done; animal studies have shown hyperexcitability and reduced growth rate in neonates

Breast-feeding—Not known if distributed into human breast milk; animal studies have shown distribution into milk

Use in the elderly—Increased sensitivity to hypotensive effects

Other medications, especially CNS depressants, tricyclic antidepressants, oral antidiabetic agents, insulin, bupropion, buspirone, caffeine in high doses, carbamazepine, cyclobenzaprine, cocaine, maprotiline, dextromethorphan, fluoxetine, paroxetine, or sertraline, trazodone, guanadrel, guanethidine, rauwolfia alkaloids, levodopa, meperidine, methyldopa, methylphenidate, sympathomimetics, tryptophan, or foods and beverages containing tyramine

Other medical problems, especially alcoholism (active), congestive heart failure, hepatic function impairment, pheochromocytoma, renal function impairment, cardiac arrhythmias, cardiovascular disease, coronary insufficiency, severe or frequent headaches, hypertension, schizophrenia, or suicidal tendencies

Proper use of this medication

» May require up to 3 or 4 weeks of therapy to obtain signs of improvement; regular visits to physician, especially during first few months of therapy, to check progress of therapy and to check for unwanted effects

» Taking exactly as directed by physician

» Importance of not taking more medication than the amount prescribed

» Proper dosing

Missed dose: Taking as soon as possible within 2 hours of next dose; going back to regular dosing schedule; not doubling doses

» Proper storage

Precautions while using this medication

» Avoiding tyramine-containing foods, alcoholic beverages, and large quantities of caffeine-containing beverages, over-the-counter cold and cough medicines, and other medications, unless prescribed; having list of such for reference

» Checking with hospital emergency room or physician if symptoms of hypertensive crisis develop

» Checking with physician before discontinuing medication; gradual reduction may be needed to prevent withdrawal effects

» Importance of patient or caregiver notifying physician immediately if any signs of abnormal behavior, worsening depression or suicidality occur.

» Dizziness may occur; caution when getting up suddenly from a lying or sitting position

» Drowsiness and blurred vision may occur; caution when driving or doing things requiring alertness or clear vision

» Caution if any kind of surgery, dental treatment, or emergency treatment is required

Carrying medical identification card

» Patients with angina: Not increasing physical activities without consulting physician

Diabetic patients: Carefully checking urine or blood sugar; results may be lowered by this medication

» Obeying rules of caution for 14 days after discontinuing medication

Side/adverse effects

» Signs of potential side effects, especially symptoms of hypertensive crisis, severe orthostatic hypotension, diarrhea, peripheral edema, sympathetic stimulation, hepatitis, leukopenia, or parkinsonian syndrome

General Dosing Information

This medication is usually used for closely supervised patients who have not responded to other antidepressant therapy.

Patient response to these agents is variable, and patients not responsive to one MAO inhibitor may be treated successfully with another.

Potentially suicidal patients should not have access to large quantities of this medication since depressed patients, particularly those who use alcohol excessively, may continue to exhibit suicidal tendencies until significant improvement occurs.

It has been recommended that therapy with an MAO inhibitor be withdrawn gradually at least 10 to 14 days prior to surgery; however, to avoid interruption of antidepressant therapy, patients receiving long-term MAO inhibition may undergo surgery without discontinuation of the MAO inhibitor. Reduction of opioid (narcotic) analgesic or other premedication dosage to ¼ of the usual dose is recommended, along with careful adjustment of anesthetic dosage. Avoidance of meperidine or cocaine use within 2 to 3 weeks following MAO inhibition is recommended.

Because insomnia or other sleep disturbances may be produced by their psychomotor-stimulating effect, these medications are usually not given in the evening.

After dosage is stopped, the effects of these medications may persist for up to 2 weeks (time required for regeneration of monoamine oxidase). During this period, food and drug contraindications must be observed.

Diet/Nutrition

Foods and beverages containing tyramine or other high pressor amines, such as aged cheese; fava or broad bean pods; yeast/protein extracts; smoked or pickled meats, poultry, or fish; fermented sausage (bologna, pepperoni, salami, summer sausage) or other fermented meat; sauerkraut; any overripe fruit; beer; reduced-alcohol and alcohol-free beer and wine; red and white wines; sherry; and liqueurs, when used concurrently with MAO inhibitors, may cause sudden and severe hypertensive reactions. The reactions are usually limited to a few hours and are easily treated with rapidly acting hypotensive agents (such as labetalol, nifedipine, or if necessary in severe cases refractory to other agents, phentolamine). The severity depends on the amount of tyramine ingested, rate of gastric emptying, and length of the interval between the dose of MAO inhibitor and ingestion of tyramine. When MAO inhibitors are discontinued, dietary restrictions must continue for at least 2 weeks. Other foods, such as yogurt, sour cream, cream cheese, cottage cheese, chocolate, and soy sauce, if eaten when fresh and in moderation, are considered unlikely to cause serious problems.

For treatment of hypertensive crisis

Recommended treatment includes:

- Discontinuing MAO inhibitor.
- Lowering blood pressure immediately with intravenous administration of 5 mg of phentolamine, with care being taken to inject slowly, to prevent excessive hypotensive effect. Alternatively, some clinicians prefer to use labetalol (intravenously or orally), reserving phentolamine for severe or non-responding cases.
- Reducing fever by external cooling.

ISOCARBOXAZID

Oral dosage form

ISOCARBOXAZID TABLETS USP

Usual adult dose

Antidepressant—

Initial: Oral, 10 milligrams (mg) twice daily. If tolerated, dose may be increased by 10 mg every 2 to 4 days to achieve a dose of 40 mg daily by the end of the first week of treatment. If needed and tolerated, dose may be increased to 60 mg daily.

Maintenance: Oral, the lowest effective dose should be used. After maximum clinical effect is achieved, an attempt should be made to reduce the dose over several weeks without jeopardizing the therapeutic response.

Usual adult prescribing limits

60 mg per day.

Usual pediatric dose

Children younger than 16 years of age—Safety and efficacy have not been established.

Usual geriatric dose

See *Usual adult dose*

Strength(s) usually available

U.S.—

10 mg (Rx) [*Marplan* (scored; corn starch; gelatin; lactose; magnesium stearate; talc; FD&C Red No. 3; FD&C Yellow No. 6)].

Canada—

Not commercially available.

Packaging and storage

Store between 15 and 30 °C (59 and 86 °F). Store in a tight container. Protect from heat and light.

Auxiliary labeling

- Avoid alcoholic beverages.
- May cause drowsiness.

Note

Depressed patients with suicidal tendencies, particularly those who use alcohol excessively, should not have access to large quantities of MAO inhibitors.

PHENELZINE

Additional Dosing Information

See also *General Dosing Information.*

The initial dosage should be increased gradually, depending on patient tolerance. Rapid dosage increases can cause early hypotensive effects and may result in patient noncompliance. A more conservative increase usually avoids this. At least 4 weeks at a given dosage may be necessary for some patients to achieve improvement and significant MAO inhibition.

Oral Dosage Forms

Note: Bracketed uses in the *Dosage Forms* section refer to categories of use and/or indications that are not included in U.S. product labeling.

PHENELZINE SULFATE TABLETS USP

Usual adult dose

Antidepressant—

Initial: Oral, 1 mg per kg of body weight a day.

Maintenance: Oral, 45 mg a day.

[Antipanic agent][1]—

Oral, initially 15 mg every morning for the first four days, the dosage being increased gradually over two weeks as needed and tolerated, up to 15 mg three or four times a day.

Usual adult prescribing limits

90 mg per day.

Usual pediatric dose

Children younger than 16 years of age—Safety and efficacy have not been established.

Usual geriatric dose

Antidepressant—

Oral, initially 0.8 to 1 mg per kg of body weight a day in divided doses, the dosage being gradually increased as needed and tolerated, up to a maximum of 60 mg a day.

Note: Elderly patients are often started on 15 mg in the morning and require a more gradual titration of dose than other adults, to minimize the adverse effects, especially hypotension.

Strength(s) usually available

U.S.—

15 mg (Rx) [*Nardil* (acacia; calcium carbonate; carnauba wax; corn starch; FD&C Yellow No. 6; gelatin; kaolin; magnesium stearate; mannitol; pharmaceutical glaze; povidone; sucrose; talc; white wax; white wheat flour)].

Canada—

15 mg (Rx) [*Nardil*].

Packaging and storage

Store between 15 and 30 °C (59 and 86 °F). Store in a tight container. Protect from heat and light.

Auxiliary labeling

- Avoid alcoholic beverages.
- May cause drowsiness.

Note

Depressed patients with suicidal tendencies, particularly those who use alcohol excessively, should not have access to large quantities of MAO inhibitors.

[1]Not included in Canadian product labeling.

TRANYLCYPROMINE

Summary of Differences

Side/adverse effects: May produce more CNS stimulation than other MAO inhibitors.

Additional Dosing Information

See also *General Dosing Information.*

Dosage should be individualized. If there are no signs of improvement after up to 2 weeks on the usual effective dosage of 30 mg a day, the dosage may be increased by 10 mg a day at intervals of 1 to 3 weeks, up to a maximum of 60 mg a day.

When electroconvulsive therapy is being administered concurrently, 10 mg twice a day can usually be given during the series, the dose being reduced to 10 mg a day for maintenance therapy.

Gradual withdrawal from tranylcypromine is recommended, to avoid recurrence of original symptoms, which may reappear if medication is withdrawn prematurely.

Oral Dosage Forms

Note: Bracketed uses in the *Dosage Forms* section refer to categories of use and/or indications that are not included in U.S. product labeling.

TRANYLCYPROMINE SULFATE TABLETS

Usual adult dose

Antidepressant—

Initial: Oral, 30 mg a day in divided doses. If there are no signs of improvement after two weeks, the dosage may be increased by 10 mg a day at intervals of one to three weeks, up to a maximum of 60 mg a day.

Maintenance: Oral, 10 to 40 mg a day.

[Antipanic agent][1]—

Oral, initially 10 mg in the morning for the first four days, the dosage being increased gradually over two weeks as needed and tolerated, up to 20 to 30 mg a day.

Usual adult prescribing limits

60 mg per day.

Usual pediatric dose

Children younger than 16 years of age—Safety and efficacy have not been established.

Usual geriatric dose

Antidepressant—

Oral, initially 2.5 to 5 mg a day, the dosage being increased gradually in increments of 2.5 to 5 mg every three to four days, up to a maximum of 45 mg a day.

Strength(s) usually available

U.S.—

10 mg (Rx) [*Parnate* (acacia; calcium sulfate; cellulose; ethylcellulose; FD&C Red No. 3; FD&C Yellow No. 6; gelatin; iron oxide; magnesium stearate; starch; sucrose)].

Canada—

10 mg (Rx) [*Parnate* (gluten; sodium <1 mmol [0.003 mg]; sucrose)].

Packaging and storage

Store below 40 °C (104 °F), preferably between 15 and 30 °C (59 and 86 °F), unless otherwise specified by manufacturer. Store in a well-closed, light-resistant container.

Auxiliary labeling

- Avoid alcoholic beverages.
- May cause drowsiness.

Note

Depressed patients with suicidal tendencies, particularly those who use alcohol excessively, should not have access to large quantities of MAO inhibitors.

[1]Not included in Canadian product labeling.

Revised: 02/02/2005

ANTIDEPRESSANTS, TRICYCLIC Systemic

This monograph includes information on the following: 1) Amitriptyline; 2) Amoxapine; 3) Clomipramine; 4) Desipramine; 5) Doxepin; 6) Imipramine; 7) Nortriptyline; 8) Protriptyline; 9) Trimipramine.

VA CLASSIFICATION (Primary/Secondary):

Amitriptyline—CN601/GU900; CN103; GA309; CN900
Amoxapine—CN601
Clomipramine—CN601/CN900; CN103
Desipramine—CN601/CN103; CN900
Doxepin—CN601/CN900; DE890; CN103; GA309
Imipramine—CN601/GU900; CN900; CN103
Nortriptyline—CN601/CN103; CN900
Protriptyline—CN601/CN900
Trimipramine—CN601/GA309; CN103

Commonly used brand name(s): *Anafranil*[3]; *Apo-Amitriptyline*[1]; *Apo-Imipramine*[6]; *Apo-Trimip*[9]; *Asendin*[2]; *Aventyl*[7]; *Elavil*[1]; *Endep*[1]; *Impril*[6]; *Levate*[1]; *Norfranil*[6]; *Norpramin*[4]; *Novo-Doxepin*[5]; *Novo-Tripramine*[9]; *Novopramine*[6]; *Novotriptyn*[1]; *Pamelor*[7]; *Pertofrane*[4]; *Rhotrimine*[9]; *Sinequan*[5]; *Surmontil*[9]; *Tipramine*[6]; *Tofranil*[6]; *Tofranil-PM*[6]; *Triadapin*[5]; *Triptil*[8]; *Vivactil*[8].

Note: For a listing of dosage forms and brand names by country availability, see *Dosage Forms* section(s).

Category

Note: All of the tricyclic antidepressants have similar pharmacologic actions; however, clinical uses among specific agents may vary because of actual pharmacokinetic differences, availability of specific testing, differences in side effects, and/or availability of clinical-use data.

Antidepressant—Amitriptyline; Amoxapine; Clomipramine; Desipramine; Doxepin; Imipramine; Nortriptyline; Protriptyline; Trimipramine.

Antienuretic—Amitriptyline; Imipramine Hydrochloride.

Antiobsessive-compulsive agent—Clomipramine.

Antipanic agent—Clomipramine; Desipramine; Doxepin; Imipramine; Nortriptyline.

Antineuralgic—Amitriptyline; Clomipramine; Desipramine; Doxepin; Imipramine; Nortriptyline; Trimipramine.

Antiulcer agent—Amitriptyline; Doxepin; Trimipramine.

Antinarcolepsy adjunct—Imipramine; Protriptyline.

Anticataplectic—Clomipramine; Desipramine; Imipramine; Protriptyline.

Antibulimic—Amitriptyline; Clomipramine; Desipramine; Imipramine.

Antipruritic—Doxepin

Indications

Note: Bracketed information in the *Indications* section refers to uses that are not included in U.S. product labeling.

Accepted

Depression, mental (treatment)—Amitriptyline, amoxapine, [clomipramine], desipramine, doxepin, imipramine, nortriptyline, protriptyline, and trimipramine are indicated for the relief of symptoms of major depressive episodes; bipolar disorder, depressed type; dysthymia; and atypical depressions. Some conditions associated with or accompanied by depression that are treated with tricyclic antidepressants include alcoholism, organic disease such as stroke or Parkinson's disease, and agitation or anxiety.

Enuresis (treatment adjunct)—Imipramine hydrochloride, but not pamoate, and [amitriptyline] are indicated as aids in the temporary treatment of nocturnal enuresis in children 6 years of age or older, after possible organic causes have been excluded by appropriate tests.

Obsessive-compulsive disorder (treatment)—Clomipramine is used to relieve symptoms of obsessive-compulsive disorders, independent of concomitant depression.

[Panic disorder (treatment)][1]—Tricyclic antidepressants, especially clomipramine, desipramine, doxepin, imipramine, and nortriptyline are used in conjunction with psychotherapy and behavior therapy to block the recurrence of panic attacks, with or without phobias. Imipramine's antipanic effect does not appear to be correlated with presence of depressive symptoms.

[Pain, neurogenic (treatment)][1]—Tricyclic antidepressants, especially amitriptyline, clomipramine, desipramine, doxepin, imipramine, nortriptyline, and trimipramine are used in patients with normal or depressed mood for the management of chronic, severe pain as in cancer; migraine and chronic, daily muscle-contraction headaches; rheumatic disorders; atypical facial pain; post-herpetic neuralgia; post-traumatic neuropathy; and diabetic or other peripheral neuropathy.

[Attention deficit hyperactivity disorder (treatment)][1]—Desipramine, imipramine, and protriptyline are used to relieve the symptoms of attention deficit hyperactivity disorder in some children over 6 years of age and in young adults. Tricyclic antidepressants may be more useful than stimulants when the patient has become withdrawn and depressed.

[Headache (prophylaxis)][1]—Tricyclic antidepressants are used in the prophylaxis of vascular headache (including migraine) and mixed headache syndrome.

[Ulcer, peptic (treatment)][1]—Although amitriptyline, doxepin, and trimipramine are effective in the treatment of peptic ulcer disease and in relieving nocturnal ulcer pain, their use has been largely supplanted by histamine H_2-receptor antagonists, omeprazole, and sucralfate.

[Narcolepsy/cataplexy syndrome (treatment)][1] or
[Narcolepsy/cataplexy syndrome (treatment adjunct)][1]—Tricyclic antidepressants, especially clomipramine, desipramine, imipramine, and protriptyline, are used to treat cataplexy associated with narcolepsy, with little or no effect on narcoleptic sleep attacks. Imipramine may be used in combination with amphetamines or methylphenidate when a patient requires treatment for both cataplexy and sleep attacks. Pa-

tients with sleep disorders such as hypersomnia or impaired morning arousal may benefit by the use of protriptyline.

[Bulimia nervosa (treatment)][1]—Amitriptyline, clomipramine, desipramine, and imipramine have been shown to be effective in controlling the binge eating and subsequent purging of bulimia nervosa.

[Cocaine withdrawal (treatment)][1]—Desipramine and imipramine are used to reduce craving and/or prevent depression upon withdrawal of cocaine.

[Urinary incontinence (treatment)][1]—Imipramine is used for the treatment of stress and urge incontinence.

[Pruritus (treatment)][1]—Doxepin is used in treatment of pruritus in idiopathic cold urticaria.

[Nicotine dependence (treatment adjunct)][1]—Nortriptyline is indicated as an aid to smoking cessation treatment.

---

[1]Not included in Canadian product labeling.

Pharmacology/Pharmacokinetics

See *Table 1*, page 292.

Physicochemical characteristics

Molecular weight—
- Amitriptyline hydrochloride: 313.87.
- Amoxapine: 313.79.
- Clomipramine hydrochloride: 351.32.
- Desipramine hydrochloride: 302.85.
- Doxepin hydrochloride: 315.84.
- Imipramine hydrochloride: 316.87.
- Imipramine pamoate: 949.2.
- Nortriptyline hydrochloride: 299.84.
- Protriptyline hydrochloride: 299.84.
- Trimipramine maleate: 410.51.

pKa—
- Amitriptyline: 9.4.
- Amoxapine: 7.6.
- Clomipramine: 9.5.
- Desipramine: 1.5 and 10.2.
- Doxepin: 9.0.
- Imipramine: 9.5.
- Nortriptyline: 9.7.
- Trimipramine: 8.0.

Mechanism of action/Effect

Antidepressant—

Although the exact mechanism of action in the treatment of depression is unclear, tricyclic antidepressants have been thought to increase the synaptic concentration of norepinephrine (levarterenol; NE) and/or serotonin (5-hydroxytryptamine; 5-HT) in the central nervous system (CNS). One theory suggests that these neurotransmitters are increased through inhibition of their reuptake by the presynaptic neuronal membrane.

Amoxapine, desipramine, trimipramine, nortriptyline, and probably protriptyline mainly inhibit the reuptake of norepinephrine. Amitriptyline and clomipramine appear to be more potent than other tricyclics in blocking serotonin, although, through their metabolites, they become powerful inhibitors of norepinephrine reuptake also. Clomipramine's effectiveness in the treatment of obsessive-compulsive disorder may be related to the inhibition of serotonin reuptake. Imipramine inhibits reuptake of norepinephrine and serotonin equally. Doxepin is a moderate inhibitor of norepinephrine and a weak inhibitor of serotonin.

Recent research has shown that after long-term treatment with antidepressants, changes in postsynaptic beta-adrenergic receptor sensitivity and increased responsiveness of the adrenergic and serotonergic systems to physiologic and environmental stimuli contribute to the mechanism of action. Antidepressants may produce a downregulation (desensitization) of alpha$_2$- or beta-adrenergic and serotonin receptors, equilibrating the noradrenergic system, and thus correcting the dysregulated monoamine output of depressed patients. Receptor changes resulting from chronic administration of tricyclic antidepressants appear to correlate better with antidepressant action than does the synaptic reuptake blockade of neurotransmitters, and may also account for the delay of 2 to 4 weeks in therapeutic response.

Amoxapine, as a metabolite of the neuroleptic, loxapine, also has a potent postsynaptic dopamine-blocking effect. This may account for the extrapyramidal side effects and increases in serum prolactin concentrations seen with amoxapine. Amoxapine is metabolized to 7-hydroxyamoxapine, also a potent dopamine-blocking agent.

Antienuretic—

The exact antienuretic action of imipramine hydrochloride has not been established. It is thought to be associated with the anticholinergic effects of imipramine.

Antiobsessional agent—

The exact antiobsessional action of clomipramine has not been established. It is thought to be associated with clomipramine's inhibition of serotonin reuptake and compensatory down regulation of serotonin receptor subtypes.

Antianxiety agent—

In panic disorders, studies suggest an impaired function of the autonomic nervous system that causes an excessive release of norepinephrine from the locus ceruleus. Tricyclic antidepressants are thought to decrease the firing rate of the locus ceruleus by regulating the alpha$_2$- and beta-adrenergic receptor functions and norepinephrine turnover.

Antineuralgic—

The exact mechanism by which tricyclic antidepressants relieve chronic pain is also unknown. Some studies support the theory that pain relief results when depression is relieved. However, other studies have found that pain may be ameliorated without a significant change in depression. Analgesic activity may be effected by the changing concentrations of central monoamines, especially serotonin, and by the direct or indirect effect of tricyclic antidepressants on the endogenous opioid systems.

Antiulcer agent—

In peptic ulcer disease, tricyclic antidepressants are effective in relieving pain and aid in complete healing because of their histamine$_2$-receptor blocking property on the parietal cells, and their sedative and anticholinergic effects.

Antibulimic—

In bulimia nervosa, the mechanism of action is unclear, although it may be similar to that in depression. Evidence shows there is a distinct antibulimic effect in patients without depression and in depressed patients whose bulimia was relieved without a concomitant relief of depression.

Urinary incontinence—

The exact mechanism by which imipramine enhances urinary continence has not been established but may include anticholinergic activity, resulting in increased bladder capacity; direct beta-adrenergic stimulation; alpha-adrenergic agonist activity, resulting in increased sphincter tone; and central blockade of serotonin uptake.

Other actions/effects

Tricyclic antidepressants also produce prominent peripheral and central anticholinergic effects due to their potent and high binding affinity for muscarinic receptors; sedative effects due to strong binding affinity for histamine H$_1$-receptors (although the central actions of histamine are poorly understood, increased cholinoceptive activity in the brain has been associated with clinical depression); and orthostatic hypotension due to alpha blockade. In addition, tricyclic antidepressants are Class 1A antiarrhythmic agents which, like quinidine, moderately slow ventricular conduction in therapeutic doses, and in overdose may cause severe conduction block and occasional ventricular arrhythmia.

Absorption

Rapidly and well absorbed after oral administration.

Protein binding

Very highly protein bound (90% or more) in plasma and tissues.

Biotransformation

Exclusively hepatic, with first-pass effect.

Onset of action

Antidepressant—2 to 3 weeks.

Elimination

As metabolites, primarily renal, over several days; poorly dialyzable because of high protein binding.

Precautions to Consider

Cross-sensitivity and/or related problems

Patients sensitive to one tricyclic antidepressant may be sensitive to other tricyclic antidepressants, and possibly to carbamazepine, maprotiline, and trazodone, also.

Carcinogenicity/Mutagenicity

Amitriptyline—In one study with rats, no evidence of increase in incidence of any tumor was found. However, amitriptyline has not been adequately studied in animals to permit an evaluation of its carcinogenic potential. No evidence of mutagenicity was found in rats tested with the Ames salmonella test.

Amoxapine—Pancreatic islet cell hyperplasia occurred in rats, with slightly increased incidence at doses 5 to 10 times the human dose.

Pregnancy/Reproduction

Pregnancy—

For amitriptyline—

Adequate and well-controlled studies in pregnant women have not been done.

Animal studies have shown amitriptyline to cause teratogenic effects when used in doses many times the human dose.

FDA Pregnancy Category C.

For amoxapine—

Adequate and well-controlled studies in pregnant women have not been done.

Animal studies have shown amoxapine to cause embryotoxic effects in doses approximating the human dose and fetotoxic effects such as intrauterine death, stillbirth, decreased birth weight, and decreased postnatal (0 to 4 days) survival at doses many times the human dose.

FDA Pregnancy Category C.

For clomipramine, desipramine, and nortriptyline—

Adequate and well-controlled studies in pregnant women have not been done.

Animal reproduction studies have been inconclusive.

FDA Pregnancy Category C.

For doxepin—

Adequate and well-controlled studies in pregnant women have not been done.

Animal studies have shown no evidence of teratogenic effects at doses up to 25 mg per kg of body weight (mg/kg) per day for 8 to 9 months and no changes in litter size, number of live births, or lactation. However, a decreased rate of conception was observed when male rats were given 25 mg/kg per day for prolonged periods.

For imipramine—

Adequate and well-controlled studies in pregnant women have not been done. However, there have been clinical reports of congenital malformations associated with the use of imipramine.

Animal reproduction studies have been inconclusive.

For protriptyline—

Adequate and well-controlled studies in pregnant women have not been done.

Animal reproduction studies have shown that protriptyline causes no apparent adverse effects at doses 10 times greater than recommended human doses.

For trimipramine—

Adequate and well-controlled studies in pregnant women have not been done.

Animal studies have shown trimipramine to cause embryotoxicity and major anomalies at 20 times the human dose.

FDA Pregnancy Category C.

Delivery—For all tricyclic antidepressants: There have been reports of cardiac problems, irritability, respiratory distress, muscle spasms, seizures, and urinary retention in infants whose mothers received tricyclic antidepressants immediately prior to delivery.

Breast-feeding

Tricyclic antidepressants have been found in small amounts in breast milk in an approximate milk to plasma ratio of 0.4:1.5. Doxepin has been reported to cause sedation and respiratory depression in the nursing infant.

Pediatrics

Although tricyclic antidepressants are generally not recommended for depression in children under 12 years of age, some, especially amitriptyline, desipramine, imipramine, and nortriptyline, are used in children over the age of 6 years for recognized major depressive illness. However, the effectiveness of tricyclic antidepressants in the treatment of depression in children and adolescents has not been definitively established. Amitriptyline and imipramine are also used for treatment of enuresis in children 6 years of age or older. Clomipramine is used for the treatment of obsessive-compulsive disorder in children 10 years of age or older. Imipramine, desipramine, and protriptyline are being used in the treatment of attention deficit hyperactivity disorder in children over 6 years of age and adolescents. However, deaths have been reported in children treated with desipramine for hyperactivity.

Antidepressants increase the risk of suicidal thinking and behavior (suicidality) in children and adolescents with major depressive disorder (MDD) and other psychiatric disorders. Anyone considering the use of any antidepressant in a child or adolescent must balance this risk with the clinical need.

Pooled analyses of short-term placebo controlled trials of nine antidepressant drugs in children and adolescents with MDD, obsessive compulsive disorder, or other psychiatric disorders have revealed a greater risk of adverse events representing suicidality during the first few months of treatment in those receiving antidepressants.

Children are more sensitive than adults to acute overdosage, which should be considered serious and potentially fatal. Increasing the dose in children increases the risk of adverse effects, such as alterations in electrocardiogram (ECG) patterns, nervousness, sleep disorders, tiredness, hypertension in some children, or mild gastrointestinal problems, without necessarily enhancing the therapeutic effect. Adolescent patients may require reduced dosage because they are also prone to exhibit increased dose sensitivity.

Geriatrics

Elderly patients often require lower dosage and more gradual dose increases to avoid toxicity, because of slower metabolic rates and/or excretion and an increased ratio of fat to lean tissue. The elderly also exhibit increased sensitivity to anticholinergic effects, such as urinary retention (especially in older men with prostatic hypertrophy), anticholinergic delirium, and increased sedative and hypotensive effects. Increased anxiety may result from these adverse effects, possibly leading to unnecessary dose increases. If cardiovascular disease is present, the risk of conduction defects, arrhythmias, tachycardia, stroke, congestive heart failure, or myocardial infarction is increased.

Dental

The peripheral anticholinergic effects of tricyclic antidepressants may decrease or inhibit salivary flow, especially in middle-aged or elderly patients, thus contributing to the development of caries, periodontal disease, oral candidiasis, and discomfort.

The blood dyscrasia-causing effects of tricyclic antidepressants, although rare, may be life-threatening. The result may be an increased incidence of microbial infection, delayed healing, and gingival bleeding. If agranulocytosis, leukopenia, or thrombocytopenia occurs, dental work should be deferred until blood counts have returned to normal. Patient instruction in proper oral hygiene should include caution in use of regular toothbrushes, dental floss, and toothpicks.

Extrapyramidal reactions that may be induced by amoxapine will result in increased motor activity of the head, face, and neck. Occlusal adjustments, bite registrations, and treatment for bruxism may be made less reliable.

Drug interactions and/or related problems

The following drug interactions and/or related problems have been selected on the basis of their potential clinical significance (possible mechanism in parentheses where appropriate)—not necessarily inclusive (» = major clinical significance):

Note: Combinations containing any of the following medications, depending on the amount present, may also interact with this medication.

Although not all of the following interactions have been reported for every tricyclic antidepressant, the potential for their occurrence exists and should be considered.

» Alcohol or

» CNS depression-producing medications, other (See *Appendix II*)

(concurrent use with tricyclic antidepressants may result in serious potentiation of CNS depression, respiratory depression, and hypotensive effects; caution is recommended, and dosage of one or both agents should be reduced)

(in addition, tricyclics may increase the effects of alcohol, especially during first few days of tricyclic antidepressant treatment; in patients who use alcohol excessively, tricyclics may increase the danger inherent in any suicide attempt)

Amantadine or

Anticholinergics or other medications with anticholinergic activity (See *Appendix II*) or

Antidyskinetics or

Antihistamines

(concurrent use with tricyclic antidepressants may intensify anticholinergic effects, especially mental confusion, hallucinations, and nightmares, because of secondary anticholinergic activities of tricyclic antidepressants)

(concurrent use may potentiate the CNS depressant effects of either antihistamines or tricyclic antidepressants)

(concurrent use with tricyclic antidepressants may block detoxification of atropine and related compounds; patients should be advised to report occurrence of gastrointestinal problems promptly since paralytic ileus may occur with concurrent therapy)

Anticoagulants, coumarin- or indandione-derivative
(concurrent use with tricyclic antidepressants, especially amitriptyline or nortriptyline, may increase anticoagulant activity, possibly by inhibiting enzymatic metabolism of the anticoagulant)

Anticonvulsants
(tricyclic antidepressants may enhance CNS depression, lower the seizure threshold when taken in high doses, and decrease the effects of the anticonvulsant medication; dosage adjustment of the anticonvulsant may be necessary to control seizures; monitoring of serum concentrations of both medications may be necessary to detect possible interaction; concurrent use of phenytoin with desipramine may lower serum concentrations of desipramine; dosage increases of desipramine above maximum recommended doses may be required to produce clinical improvement in depression)

» Antithyroid agents
(concurrent use with tricyclic antidepressants may increase the risk of agranulocytosis)

Barbiturates or
Carbamazepine
(plasma concentrations and therapeutic effects of tricyclic antidepressants may be decreased during concurrent use with barbiturates, especially phenobarbital, or carbamazepine because of increased metabolism resulting from induction of hepatic microsomal enzymes)

Bupropion or
Clozapine or
Cyclobenzaprine or
Haloperidol or
Loxapine or
Maprotiline or
Molindone or
» Phenothiazines or
Thioxanthenes
(the sedative and anticholinergic effects of either these medications or tricyclic antidepressants may be prolonged and intensified; these medications may increase the risk of seizures by lowering the seizure threshold and should be added or withdrawn with caution; psychotic depressions respond well to a combination of tricyclic antidepressant and antipsychotic agent, but both medications must be initially administered at lower doses and are increased only as clinically indicated)
(concurrent use of phenothiazines may increase serum concentrations of tricyclic antidepressants, especially desipramine and imipramine, due to inhibition of metabolism; conversely, tricyclics may inhibit phenothiazine metabolism; also, the risk of neuroleptic malignant syndrome [NMS] may be increased)

» Cimetidine
(cimetidine may inhibit tricyclic metabolism and increase plasma concentrations, leading to toxicity; lowering the dose of the tricyclic antidepressant by 20 to 30% may be necessary when cimetidine is given concurrently; patient should be closely observed for sedation, anticholinergic effects, and orthostatic hypotension)

» Clonidine or
» Guanadrel or
» Guanethidine
(concurrent use may decrease the hypotensive effects of these medications)
(concurrent use of clonidine with tricyclic antidepressants may result in potentiation of CNS depressant effects)

Cocaine
(concurrent use with tricyclic antidepressants may increase the risk of cardiac arrhythmias; if use of cocaine is necessary in patients receiving tricyclics, it is recommended that the cocaine be administered with caution, in reduced dosage, and in conjunction with electrocardiographic monitoring)

Contraceptives, oral, estrogen-containing or
Estramustine or
Estrogens
(concurrent use of imipramine and possibly other tricyclic antidepressants by chronic long-term users of oral contraceptives or estrogens may increase the bioavailability of imipramine because of inhibition of hepatic enzyme metabolism; this may result in toxicity, obscuring therapeutic effects and worsening depression; may be dose-related, with lower doses of estrogens having less effect on enzyme inhibition than larger doses; dosage adjustments of the tricyclic may be necessary)

Corticosteroids, glucocorticoid
(tricyclic antidepressants do not relieve, and may exacerbate, corticosteroid-induced mental depression)

Disulfiram or
Ethchlorvynol
(concurrent use with tricyclics, especially amitriptyline, may result in transient delirium)
(also, CNS depressant effects may be increased when ethchlorvynol is used concurrently with tricyclic antidepressants)

Electroconvulsive therapy
(although electroconvulsive therapy may be used in conjunction with tricyclic antidepressants, caution should be used as hazards may be increased)

» Extrapyramidal reaction-causing medications, other (See *Appendix II*)
(concurrent use with amoxapine and possibly other tricyclic antidepressants may increase the severity and frequency of extrapyramidal effects)

Fluoxetine
(concurrent use with tricyclic antidepressants has produced increased plasma concentrations of the tricyclic antidepressant, possibly due to inhibition of tricyclic antidepressant metabolism; some clinicians recommend dosage reductions for tricyclic antidepressants of about 50% if used concurrently with fluoxetine)

Methylphenidate
(serum concentrations of tricyclic antidepressants, especially desipramine and imipramine, may be increased due to inhibition of metabolism when methylphenidate is used concurrently; also, concurrent use may antagonize the effects of methylphenidate)

» Metrizamide
(administration of intrathecal metrizamide may lower the seizure threshold and increase the risk of seizures in patients taking tricyclic antidepressants; it is recommended that tricyclic antidepressants be discontinued for at least 48 hours before and at least 24 hours after myelography)

» Monoamine oxidase (MAO) inhibitors, including furazolidone, procarbazine, and selegiline
(concurrent use with tricyclic antidepressants has resulted in an increased incidence of hyperpyretic episodes, severe convulsions, hypertensive crises, and death; however, recent studies have shown that concurrent use of some tricyclic antidepressants with MAO inhibitors can be used for refractory depression with no adverse effects if both medications are initiated simultaneously at lower than usual doses, with doses being raised gradually thereafter, or if the MAO inhibitor is gradually added to the tricyclic, also at low doses; a tricyclic should not be added to an existing MAO inhibitor regimen; the tricyclic antidepressants most commonly used in this combined therapy are amitriptyline, doxepin, and trimipramine; imipramine, desipramine, nortriptyline, protriptyline, and clomipramine are not recommended for use in such a regimen because of potential excessive stimulation)

Naphazoline, ophthalmic or
Oxymetazoline, nasal or ophthalmic or
Phenylephrine, nasal or ophthalmic or
Xylometazoline, nasal
(if significant systemic absorption occurs, concurrent use with tricyclic antidepressants may potentiate pressor effects of these medications)

Pimozide
(concurrent use with tricyclic antidepressants may potentiate cardiac arrhythmias, which are seen on ECG as prolongation of the QT interval)

Probucol
(additive QT interval prolongation may increase risk of ventricular tachycardia)

» Sympathomimetics
(concurrent use with tricyclic antidepressants may potentiate cardiovascular effects possibly resulting in arrhythmias, tachycardia, or severe hypertension or hyperpyrexia; phentolamine can control the adverse reaction)
(significant systemic absorption of ophthalmic epinephrine may also potentiate cardiovascular effects; also, local anesthetics with vasoconstrictors should be avoided or a minimal amount of the vasoconstrictor should be used with the local anesthetic)
(concurrent use with tricyclic antidepressants may decrease the pressor effect of ephedrine and mephentermine)

Thyroid hormones
(concurrent use with tricyclic antidepressants may increase the therapeutic and toxic effects of both medications, possibly due to increased receptor sensitivity to catecholamines; toxic effects include cardiac arrhythmias and CNS stimulation)

Laboratory value alterations

The following have been selected on the basis of their potential clinical significance (possible effect in parentheses where appropriate)—not necessarily inclusive (» = major clinical significance).

With diagnostic test results
ECG
(changes include prolonged PR intervals, widened QRS complexes, and inverted or flattened T-waves)
Metyrapone test
(amitriptyline may decrease the response to metyrapone)

With physiology/laboratory test values
Blood sugar concentrations
(may be increased or decreased)

Medical considerations/Contraindications

The medical considerations/contraindications included have been selected on the basis of their potential clinical significance (reasons given in parentheses where appropriate)—not necessarily inclusive (» = major clinical significance).

Note: This medication should *not* be used during the acute recovery period following a myocardial infarction.

Risk-benefit should be considered when the following medical problems exist:

» Alcoholism, active
(CNS depression may be potentiated)

» Asthma
(may be aggravated)

» Bipolar disorder
(swing to hypomanic or manic phase may be accelerated and reversible rapid cycling between mania and depression may be induced by antidepressants in some patients; tricyclic antidepressant may have to be discontinued and lithium considered for a sustained remission)

» Blood disorders
(may be potentiated)

» Cardiovascular disorders, especially in children and the elderly
(increased risk of arrhythmias, heart block, congestive heart failure, myocardial infarction, or stroke)

» Gastrointestinal disorders
(risk of paralytic ileus)

Genitourinary disease
(may be masked by the use of imipramine for enuresis in children)

» Glaucoma, narrow-angle, predisposition to or
» Increased intraocular pressure
(may be aggravated)

» Hepatic function impairment
(metabolism of tricyclic may be altered)

» Hyperthyroidism
(risk of cardiovascular toxicity)

» Prostatic hypertrophy
(risk of urinary retention)

» Renal function impairment
(excretion of tricyclic may be altered)

» Schizophrenia
(psychosis may be activated)

» Seizure disorders
(seizure threshold may be lowered)

» Sensitivity to tricyclic antidepressants, carbamazepine, maprotiline, or trazodone

» Urinary retention
(may be aggravated)

Patient monitoring

The following may be especially important in patient monitoring (other tests may be warranted in some patients, depending on condition; » = major clinical significance):

Blood cell counts (usually during extended therapy and in patients with sore throat or fever) and
Blood pressure and pulse measurements and
Glaucoma tests and
Hepatic function determinations and
Renal function determinations
(may be required at periodic intervals during therapy to detect development of adverse effects that may not be evident to the patient)

Cardiac function monitoring
(ECG may be required in the elderly, in children, and in patients with existing cardiac disease, or in patients receiving antiarrhythmics such as quinidine, procainamide, or disopyramide, before initiation of therapy as a baseline and at periodic intervals thereafter)
(for children taking imipramine for enuresis who are not responding to standard doses, ECG may be required before dosage is increased)

Careful supervision of depressed patients including those with:
Abnormal behaviors (i.e., agitation, panic attacks, hostility) or
Clinical worsening of their depression or
Suicidal ideation and behavior (suicidality)
(recommended especially during early treatment phase before peak effectiveness of antidepressant is achieved or at the time of increases or decreases in dose; prescribing the smallest number of capsules or tablets necessary for good patient management is recommended to decrease the risk of overdose; consideration should be given to changing the therapeutic regimen, including possibly discontinuing the medicine, in patients whose depression is persistently worse or whose emergent suicidality or other symptoms are severe, abrupt in onset, or were not part of the patient's presenting symptoms)

Dental examination
(recommended at least twice yearly)

Plasma tricyclic determinations
(recommended for patients who fail to respond to treatment, when there are increased side effects, when patient is at high risk, when there is doubt about patient compliance, or as a means of maximizing the response; optimum sampling time is immediately before the first morning dose or a minimum of 8 hours after a dose; See *Table 1* for therapeutic plasma concentration ranges)

For amoxapine (in addition to the above)
Careful observation for early signs of tardive dyskinesia
(recommended at periodic intervals, especially in the elderly; if early symptoms of tardive dyskinesia appear, amoxapine should be discontinued)

Side/Adverse Effects

Note: Although not all of these side effects have been attributed specifically to each tricyclic antidepressant, a potential exists for their occurrence during the use of any tricyclic antidepressant.

The following side/adverse effects have been selected on the basis of their potential clinical significance (possible signs and symptoms in parentheses where appropriate)—not necessarily inclusive:

Those indicating need for medical attention

Incidence less frequent

For all tricyclic antidepressants

Anticholinergic effects (blurred vision; confusion; delirium or hallucinations; constipation, especially in the elderly, possibly resulting in paralytic ileus; difficult urination; eye pain due to aggravation of glaucoma); ***fast, slow, or irregular heartbeat; fine-muscle tremors, especially in arms, hands, head, and tongue*** (shakiness); ***hypotension*** (fainting); ***nervousness or restlessness; Parkinsonian syndrome*** (difficulty in speaking or swallowing; loss of balance control; mask-like face; shuffling walk; slowed movements; stiffness of arms and legs; trembling and shaking of fingers and hands); ***sexual function impairment***—more common with amoxapine and clomipramine

For amoxapine only (in addition to the above)

Tardive dyskinesia (lip smacking or puckering; puffing of cheeks; rapid or worm-like movements of tongue; uncontrolled chewing movements; uncontrolled movements of the arms or legs)

Incidence rare

For all tricyclic antidepressants

Agranulocytosis or other blood dyscrasias (red or brownish spots on skin; sore throat and fever; unusual bleeding or bruising); ***allergic reaction*** (increased sensitivity to sunlight; skin rash and itching; swelling of face and tongue); ***alopecia*** (hair loss); ***anxiety; breast enlargement in both males and females***—more common with amoxapine; ***cholestatic jaundice*** (yellow eyes or skin); ***galactorrhea*** (inappropriate secretion of milk)—in females; ***seizures***—more common with clomipramine; ***syndrome of inappropriate secretion of antidiuretic hormone [SIADH]*** (irritability; muscle twitching; weakness); ***testicular swelling***—more common with amoxapine; ***tinnitus*** (ringing, buzzing, or other unexplained noises in the ears); ***trouble with teeth or gums***—more common with clomipramine

For amoxapine only (in addition to the above)

Neuroleptic malignant syndrome (NMS) (convulsions; difficult or fast breathing; fast heartbeat or irregular pulse; fever; high or low [irregular] blood pressure; increased sweating; loss of bladder control; severe muscle stiffness; unusually pale skin; unusual tiredness or weakness)

Note: May occur after prolonged treatment or after combined treatment with *tricyclic antidepressants* and *neuroleptics*.

Those indicating need for medical attention only if they continue or are bothersome

Incidence more frequent

Drowsiness; dryness of mouth; headache; increased appetite—may include craving for sweets; ***nausea; orthostatic hypotension*** (dizziness); ***tiredness or weakness, mild; unpleasant taste; weight gain***

Incidence less frequent

Diarrhea; excessive sweating; heartburn; trouble in sleeping—more common with protriptyline, especially when taken late in the day; ***vomiting***

Those indicating possible withdrawal and the need for medical attention if they occur after medication is discontinued

Occurring upon abrupt withdrawal, due to cholinergic rebound

For all tricyclic antidepressants

Headache; nausea, vomiting, or diarrhea; trouble in sleeping, with vivid dreams; unusual excitement

Occurring with gradual withdrawal after long-term treatment

For all tricyclic antidepressants

Irritability; restlessness; trouble in sleeping, with vivid dreams

For amoxapine only (in addition to the above)

Tardive dyskinesia, withdrawal-emergent (lip smacking or puckering; puffing of cheeks; rapid or worm-like movements of tongue; uncontrolled chewing movements; uncontrolled movements of the arms and legs)

Overdose

For specific information on the agents used in the management of tricyclic antidepressant overdose, see:

- *Anesthetics, Inhalation (Systemic)* monograph;
- *Charcoal, Activated (Oral-Local)* monograph;
- *Diazepam* in *Benzodiazepines (Systemic)* monograph;
- *Digitalis Glycosides (Systemic)* monograph;
- *Lidocaine (Systemic)* monograph;
- *Paraldehyde (Systemic)* monograph;
- *Phenytoin* in *Anticonvulsants, Hydantoin (Systemic)* monograph;
- *Physostigmine (Systemic)* monograph;
- *Propranolol* in *Beta-adrenergic Blocking Agents (Systemic)* monograph; and/or
- *Sodium Bicarbonate (Systemic)* monograph.

For more information on the management of overdose or unintentional ingestion, **contact a Poison Control Center** (see *Poison Control Center Listing*).

Clinical effects of overdose

The following effects have been selected on the basis of their potential clinical significance (possible signs and symptoms in parentheses where appropriate)—not necessarily inclusive:

Acute

Confusion; convulsions—more severe and refractory with amoxapine; ***disturbed concentration; drowsiness, severe; enlarged pupils; fast, slow, or irregular heartbeat; fever; hallucinations; restlessness and agitation; shortness of breath or troubled breathing; unusual tiredness or weakness, severe; vomiting***

Treatment of overdose

Treatment is essentially symptomatic and supportive, possibly including:

To decrease absorption—

Emptying stomach with gastric lavage.

To enhance elimination—

Administering activated charcoal slurry repeatedly, followed by a stimulant cathartic.

Specific treatment—

Digitalizing cautiously for congestive heart failure.

Controlling cardiac arrhythmias with lidocaine or by alkalinizing blood to pH 7.4 to 7.5 with intravenous sodium bicarbonate. Arrhythmias refractory to lidocaine and sodium bicarbonate may be managed with slow intravenous infusion of phenytoin while monitoring ECG. Propranolol is also effective but should be used with caution because of its negative inotropic and hypotensive effects. Quinidine and procainamide should be avoided.

For all tricyclics except amoxapine: Although routine use is not recommended, administering physostigmine salicylate, 1 to 3 mg (adults) by slow intravenous infusion over 2 to 3 minutes, may help reverse severe anticholinergic effects (myoclonic seizures, severe hallucinations, hypertension, and ventricular arrhythmias). For children, start with 0.5 mg and repeat dosage at 5 minute intervals to determine the minimum effective dose, not exceeding 2 mg per dose. Because of the short duration of action of physostigmine, dosage may need to be repeated at 30- to 60-minute intervals, especially if life-threatening symptoms occur. Routine administration of physostigmine is not recommended because of its toxicity. When used in tricyclic antidepressant overdose, it may cause bronchospasm, increased respiratory secretions, muscle weakness, bradycardia, hypotension, and may itself cause seizures. Physostigmine should be reserved for patients in coma with respiratory depression, uncontrollable seizures, severe hypertension, or serious cardiac arrhythmias. Physostigmine is contraindicated in amoxapine overdose because it may increase seizure activity.

Administering anticonvulsants such as diazepam, paraldehyde, phenytoin, or an inhalation anesthetic to control convulsions. Seizures may be especially severe and refractory with amoxapine overdose and may lead to acute tubular necrosis and rhabdomyolysis.

Monitoring—

Monitoring cardiovascular function (ECG) for not less than 5 days.

Supportive care—

Maintaining respiratory and cardiac function.

Maintaining body temperature.

Using standard measures to manage circulatory shock and metabolic acidosis.

Patients in whom intentional overdose is known or suspected should be referred for psychiatric consultation.

Note: Hemodialysis, peritoneal dialysis, exchange transfusions, and forced diuresis of tricyclic antidepressants have not been successful because of their high protein binding and rapid fixation in tissues.

Patient Consultation

As an aid to patient consultation, refer to *Advice for the Patient: Antidepressants, Tricyclic (Systemic)*

In providing consultation, consider emphasizing the following selected information (» = major clinical significance):

Before using this medication

» Conditions affecting use, especially:

Sensitivity to tricyclic antidepressants, maprotiline, or trazodone

Pregnancy—Clinical reports of fetal malformations with imipramine; animal studies have shown some tricyclics to cause embryotoxic or fetotoxic effects, and decreased rate of conception; when tricyclics taken by mother immediately before delivery, clinical reports of newborns suffering from muscle spasms, and heart, breathing, and urinary problems

Breast-feeding—Pass into breast milk and may cause drowsiness in nursing baby

Use in children—Children and adolescents more sensitive to effects, requiring lower doses; may cause nervousness, sleeping problems, tiredness, mild stomach upset; generally not recommended for depression in children

Use in the elderly—Elderly more sensitive to effects; lower doses and more gradual increases required

Dental—Decreased salivary flow contributes to caries, periodontal disease, candidiasis, and discomfort; blood dyscrasias may cause increased infections, delayed healing, and gingival bleeding; increased extrapyramidal motor activity of head, face, and neck with amoxapine may cause difficulty with occlusal and other procedures

Other medications, especially CNS depressants, antithyroid agents, cimetidine, clonidine, guanadrel, guanethidine, phenothiazines, extrapyramidal reaction-causing medications, MAO inhibitors, metrizamide, or sympathomimetics

Other medical problems, especially alcoholism (active), asthma, bipolar disorder, blood disorders, cardiovascular disorders, gastrointestinal disorders, glaucoma or increased intraocular pressure, hepatic function impairment, hyperthyroidism, prostatic hypertrophy, renal function impairment, schizophrenia, seizure disorders, or urinary retention

Proper use of this medication

Taking with food to reduce gastrointestinal irritation

» Compliance with therapy; not taking more or less medicine than prescribed

» May require from 1 to 6 weeks of therapy to obtain antidepressant effects

Proper administration of doxepin oral solution

Using dropper provided by manufacturer for accurate measurement

Diluting medication in one-half glass of recommended beverage (water, milk, or fruit juice, but not grape juice or carbonated beverages) immediately before use

Not preparing or storing bulk solutions

» Proper dosing

Missed dose: If dosing schedule is—More than one dose a day: Taking as soon as possible unless almost time for next dose; not doubling doses One dose at bedtime: Not taking in morning because of side effects; checking with physician

» Proper storage

Precautions while using this medication

Regular visits to physician to check progress of therapy

» Avoiding the use of alcoholic beverages; not taking other medication unless prescribed by physician

» Possible drowsiness; caution when driving or doing things requiring alertness

» Possible dizziness or lightheadedness; caution when getting up suddenly from a lying or sitting position

» Possible dryness of mouth; using sugarless gum or candy, ice, or saliva substitute for relief; checking with physician or dentist if dry mouth continues for more than 2 weeks

» Possible skin photosensitivity; avoiding unprotected exposure to sun; using protective clothing; using a sun block product that includes protection against both UVA-caused photosensitivity reactions and UVB-caused sunburn reactions; avoiding use of sunlamp, tanning bed, or tanning booth

Caution if any laboratory tests required; possible interference with results of metyrapone test.

» Caution if any kind of surgery, dental treatment, or emergency treatment is required

» Checking with physician before discontinuing medicine; gradual dosage reduction may be needed to avoid worsening of condition or withdrawal symptoms

» Observing precautions for 3 to 7 days after stopping medication

For protriptyline:

Possibility of sleep interference if taken late in the day

Side/adverse effects

Signs of potential side effects, especially anticholinergic effects; hypotension; fast, slow, or irregular heartbeat; Parkinsonian syndrome; nervousness or restlessness; sexual function impairment; shakiness or tremors; neuroleptic malignant syndrome (NMS) or tardive dyskinesia (with amoxapine only); anxiety; breast enlargement in males and females; galactorrhea; testicular swelling; alopecia; allergic reactions; blood dyscrasias; cholestatic jaundice; seizures; SIADH; tinnitus; or trouble with teeth or gums

General Dosing Information

Dosage of tricyclic antidepressants must be individualized for each patient by titration.

Plasma concentrations of tricyclic antidepressants, in general, vary greatly among patients. However, nortriptyline appears to have a well-defined "therapeutic window" at 50 to 150 nanograms per mL of plasma. Other therapeutic plasma concentration ranges that are generally accepted include desipramine, 150 to 250 nanograms per mL, and imipramine, 200 to 250 nanograms per mL. See *Table 1*.

Although a sedative action may occur following the initial dose (with the possible exception of protriptyline), 1 to 6 weeks of therapy may be required before the desired antidepressant response is obtained.

Maintenance therapy of the sedating tricyclic antidepressants is usually given as a single dose at bedtime. A divided dose may be preferred, however, for protriptyline, and for all tricyclic antidepressants in geriatric or cardiovascular patients, or in adolescents or children. Maintenance is often continued for 6 months to 1 year. Recent data suggest that some patients with recurrent depression may benefit from prolonged maintenance treatment at the full (acute treatment) daily dose.

A trial of four to six weeks at the upper therapeutic dose range may be considered an adequate antidepressant trial, after which alternate therapy should be considered.

The single daily dose at bedtime is useful when side effects such as excessive drowsiness or dizziness might be bothersome or dangerous during working hours. An exception to bedtime dosage is protriptyline, which if taken late in the day may cause insomnia or nightmares in some patients. Therefore, protriptyline is often given in divided doses with the last daily dose in the afternoon.

Withdrawal symptoms, such as headache, malaise, nausea or vomiting, and vivid dreams, may occur if high or prolonged dosage is abruptly discontinued. Also, patients with a history of only unipolar depression may experience a fast-cycling bipolar disorder (manic-depressive illness) with mania or hypomania. Although this has not been reported with all of the tricyclics, a gradual reduction in dosage over a 1- to 2-month period is recommended when any of these medications is to be discontinued.

Potentially suicidal patients should not have access to large quantities of these medications since depressed patients, particularly those who may use alcohol excessively, may continue to exhibit suicidal tendencies until significant improvement occurs. Some clinicians recommend that not more than the equivalent of 1 gram of amitriptyline be dispensed to such patients at any one time. However, most clinicians agree that the judgment must be made according to each patient's individual condition.

The condition of depressed patients with bipolar disorder may sometimes change to the manic phase during tricyclic antidepressant therapy, although such change has not been reported with every tricyclic antidepressant.

Diet/Nutrition

Oral doses may be taken with or immediately after food to lessen gastric irritation.

The requirements for riboflavin may be increased in patients receiving amitriptyline or imipramine.

For treatment of adverse effects

Treatment is essentially symptomatic and supportive and includes

- *Discontinuing amoxapine immediately.*
- Hyperthermia: Administering antipyretics (aspirin or acetaminophen); using cooling blanket.
- Dehydration: Restoring fluids and electrolytes.
- Cardiovascular instability: Monitoring blood pressure and cardiac rhythm closely.
- Hypoxia: Administering oxygen; considering airway insertion and assisted ventilation.
- Muscle rigidity: Dantrolene sodium may be administered (100 to 300 mg a day in divided doses; 0.75 to 1 mg per kg, intravenously, every 6 hours, increased up to 3 mg per kg every 6 hours as needed).

Neuroleptic malignant syndrome (NMS) (for amoxapine only)—

Parkinsonism—

In most cases, mild effects may be reversed by dosage reduction. Administration of antiparkinsonism drugs such as benztropine, diphenhydramine, or trihexyphenidyl may reverse severe reactions.

Recommended treatment includes

- *Discontinuing tricyclic antidepressant.*
- If urgent treatment is required, administering several hundred milliliters of 5% sodium chloride intravenously over several hours while monitoring serum sodium concentration and the symptoms, and watching for fluid overload.
- After initial phase, or for less urgent treatment, restricting water intake to 1000 mL a day.
- Monitoring serum electrolytes for several days.

Secretion of inappropriate antidiuretic hormone syndrome (SIADH)—

Tardive dyskinesia (for amoxapine only)—

No known effective treatment. Dosage of the tricyclic should be lowered or medication gradually discontinued at earliest signs of tardive dyskinesia, to prevent irreversible effects.

AMITRIPTYLINE

Summary of Differences

Indications:

Also used to manage some types of chronic, severe, neurogenic pain, and to treat bulimia and peptic ulcer disease.

Pharmacology/pharmacokinetics:

Effects—

Anticholinergic: High.

Sedative: High.

Orthostatic hypotension: Moderate to high.

Oral Dosage Forms

Note: Bracketed uses in the *Dosage Forms* section refer to categories of use and/or indications that are not included in U.S. product labeling.

AMITRIPTYLINE HYDROCHLORIDE TABLETS USP

Usual adult dose

Antidepressant—
Oral, initially 25 mg two to four times a day, the dosage being adjusted gradually as needed and tolerated.

Usual adult prescribing limits

Outpatients—Up to 150 mg a day.
Hospitalized patients—Up to 300 mg a day.
Geriatric patients—Up to 100 mg a day.

Usual pediatric dose

Antidepressant—
Children 6 to 12 years of age: Oral, 10 to 30 mg, or 1 to 5 mg per kg of body weight, a day in two divided doses.
Adolescents: Oral, initially 10 mg three times a day and 20 mg at bedtime, the dosage being adjusted as needed and tolerated, up to a maximum of 100 mg a day in divided doses or as a single dose at bedtime.

[Enuresis]—
Children up to 6 years of age: Oral, 10 mg a day as a single dose at bedtime.
Children over 6 years of age: Oral, initially 10 mg a day as a single dose at bedtime, the dose being increased as needed and tolerated up to a maximum of 25 mg.

Usual geriatric dose

Antidepressant—
Oral, initially 25 mg at bedtime, the dosage being adjusted as needed and tolerated, up to 10 mg three times a day and 20 mg at bedtime.

Strength(s) usually available

U.S.—
10 mg (Rx) [*Elavil; Endep* (scored); GENERIC].
25 mg (Rx) [*Elavil; Endep* (scored); GENERIC].
50 mg (Rx) [*Elavil; Endep* (scored); GENERIC].
75 mg (Rx) [*Elavil; Endep* (scored); GENERIC].
100 mg (Rx) [*Elavil; Endep* (scored); GENERIC].
150 mg (Rx) [*Elavil; Endep* (scored); GENERIC].

Canada—
10 mg (Rx) [*Apo-Amitriptyline; Elavil; Novotriptyn*].
25 mg (Rx) [*Apo-Amitriptyline; Elavil; Novotriptyn*; GENERIC].
50 mg (Rx) [*Apo-Amitriptyline; Elavil; Novotriptyn*].
75 mg (Rx) [*Apo-Amitriptyline; Elavil; Levate*].

Packaging and storage

Store below 40 °C (104 °F), preferably between 15 and 30 °C (59 and 86 °F), unless otherwise specified by manufacturer. Store in a well-closed container.

Auxiliary labeling

- May cause drowsiness.
- Avoid alcoholic beverages.

AMITRIPTYLINE PAMOATE SYRUP

Usual adult dose

Antidepressant—
Oral, initially 25 mg (base) two to four times a day, the dosage being adjusted gradually as needed and tolerated.

Usual pediatric dose

Antidepressant—
Children 6 to 12 years of age: Oral, 10 to 30 mg (base), or 1 to 5 mg per kg of body weight, a day in two divided doses.
Adolescents: Oral, initially 10 mg (base) three times a day and 20 mg at bedtime, the dosage being adjusted as needed and tolerated, up to a maximum of 100 mg a day, in divided doses or as a single dose at bedtime.

[Enuresis]—
Children up to 6 years of age: Oral, 10 mg (base) a day as a single dose at bedtime.
Children over 6 years of age: Oral, initially 10 mg (base) a day as a single dose at bedtime, the dose being increased as needed and tolerated up to a maximum of 25 mg.

Usual geriatric dose

Antidepressant—
Oral, initially 10 mg (base) three times a day and 20 mg at bedtime, the dosage being adjusted as needed and tolerated, up to a maximum of 100 mg a day, in divided doses or as a single dose at bedtime.

Strength(s) usually available

U.S.—
Not commercially available.

Canada—
10 mg (base) per 5 mL (Rx) [*Elavil* (methyl- and propylparaben)].

Packaging and storage

Store below 40 °C (104 °F), preferably between 15 and 30 °C (59 and 86 °F), in a well-closed container, unless otherwise specified by manufacturer.

Auxiliary labeling

- May cause drowsiness.
- Avoid alcoholic beverages.

Parenteral Dosage Forms

AMITRIPTYLINE HYDROCHLORIDE INJECTION USP

Usual adult dose

Antidepressant—
Intramuscular, 20 to 30 mg four times a day.

Usual pediatric dose

Antidepressant—
Children up to 12 years of age: Dosage has not been established.

Strength(s) usually available

U.S.—
10 mg per mL (Rx) [*Elavil* (dextrose; methylparaben; propylparaben); GENERIC].

Canada—
Not commercially available.

Packaging and storage

Store below 40 °C (104 °F), preferably between 15 and 30 °C (59 and 86 °F), unless otherwise specified by manufacturer. Protect from freezing.

AMOXAPINE

Summary of Differences

Pharmacology/pharmacokinetics:
Effects—
Anticholinergic: Moderate.
Sedative: Low to moderate.
Orthostatic hypotension: Low.
Onset of action—
Antidepressant: Within 1 to 2 weeks.

Side/adverse effects:
Neuroleptic malignant syndrome, parkinsonian reactions and tardive dyskinesia may occur. Sexual function impairment, breast enlargement in both males and females, testicular swelling, and severe, refractory seizures on acute overdose are all more frequent with amoxapine than with other tricyclic antidepressants.

Oral Dosage Forms

AMOXAPINE TABLETS USP

Usual adult dose

Antidepressant—
Oral, initially 50 mg two or three times a day, the dosage being increased to 100 mg two or three times a day within the first week of treatment as needed and tolerated.

Note: Increases above 300 mg a day should be made with caution and only if 300 mg a day has been ineffective during a trial period of at least two weeks.

Usual adult prescribing limits

Hospitalized patients—Up to 600 mg a day in divided doses.

Usual pediatric dose

Children up to 16 years of age—Dosage has not been established.

Usual geriatric dose

Antidepressant—
Oral, initially 25 mg two or three times a day, the dosage being increased, if tolerated, to 50 mg two or three times a day within the first week.

Strength(s) usually available

U.S.—
25 mg (Rx) [*Asendin* (scored); GENERIC].
50 mg (Rx) [*Asendin* (scored); GENERIC].
100 mg (Rx) [*Asendin* (scored); GENERIC].
150 mg (Rx) [*Asendin* (scored); GENERIC].

Canada—
25 mg (Rx) [*Asendin* (scored)].
50 mg (Rx) [*Asendin* (scored)].
100 mg (Rx) [*Asendin* (scored)].
150 mg (Rx) [*Asendin* (scored)].

Packaging and storage

Store below 40 °C (104 °F), preferably between 15 and 30 °C (59 and 86 °F), in a well-closed container, unless otherwise specified by manufacturer.

Auxiliary labeling

- May cause drowsiness.
- Avoid alcoholic beverages.

CLOMIPRAMINE

Summary of Differences

Indications:
Also used to treat obsessive-compulsive disorder, panic disorder, bulimia nervosa, cataplexy associated with narcolepsy, and to manage some types of chronic, severe, neurogenic pain.

Pharmacology/pharmacokinetics:
Effects—
Anticholinergic: High.
Sedative: Moderate.
Orthostatic hypotension: Moderate.

Precautions:
Drug interactions and/or related problems—
Not recommended for concurrent use with monoamine oxidase inhibitors.

Side/adverse effects:
Sexual function impairment, seizures, and nausea and vomiting may occur more frequently with clomipramine than with other tricyclic antidepressants.

Additional Dosing Information

See also *General Dosing Information.*

Clomipramine should be given in divided doses with meals during initial titration to minimize gastrointestinal side effects; after titration, the total daily dose may be given at bedtime to minimize daytime sedation.

Oral Dosage Forms

Note: Bracketed uses in the *Dosage Forms* section refer to categories of use and/or indications that are not included in U.S. product labeling.

CLOMIPRAMINE HYDROCHLORIDE CAPSULES

Usual adult dose

[Antidepressant]—
Oral, initially 25 mg three times a day, the dosage being adjusted as needed and tolerated.

Antiobsessional agent—
Oral, initially 25 mg once a day, the dosage being gradually increased to 100 mg during the first two weeks. The dosage may be further increased over the next several weeks, up to a maximum of 250 mg a day.

Usual adult prescribing limits

Outpatients: Up to 250 mg a day.
Hospitalized patients: Up to 300 mg a day.

Usual pediatric dose

[Antidepressant]—
Children up to 12 years of age: Dosage has not been established.
Adolescents: Oral, 20 to 30 mg a day, the dosage being increased by 10 mg at 4 or 5 day intervals as needed and tolerated.

Antiobsessional agent—
Children up to 10 years of age: Dosage has not been established.
Children 10 years of age and over, and adolescents: Oral, initially 25 mg once a day, the dose being increased as needed and tolerated up to 100 mg a day or 3 mg per kg of body weight, whichever is less. The dosage may be further increased up to a maximum of 200 mg a day or 3 mg per kg of body weight, whichever is less.

Note: The strengths of the specific products may not conform to the recommended pediatric doses.

Usual geriatric dose

Oral, 20 to 30 mg a day, the dosage being increased as needed and tolerated.

Note: The strengths of the specific products may not conform to the recommended geriatric doses.

Strength(s) usually available

U.S.—
25 mg (Rx) [*Anafranil* (methylparaben; propylparaben); GENERIC].
50 mg (Rx) [*Anafranil* (methylparaben; propylparaben); GENERIC].
75 mg (Rx) [*Anafranil* (methylparaben; propylparaben); GENERIC].

Canada—
Not commercially available.

Packaging and storage

Store below 40 °C (104 °F), preferably between 15 and 30 °C (59 and 86 °F), in a tight, light-resistant container, unless otherwise specified by manufacturer.

Auxiliary labeling

- May cause drowsiness.
- Avoid alcoholic beverages.

CLOMIPRAMINE HYDROCHLORIDE TABLETS

Usual adult dose

See *Clomipramine Hydrochloride Capsules.*

Usual adult prescribing limits

See *Clomipramine Hydrochloride Capsules.*

Usual pediatric dose

See *Clomipramine Hydrochloride Capsules.*

Usual geriatric dose

See *Clomipramine Hydrochloride Capsules.*

Strength(s) usually available

U.S.—
Not commercially available.

Canada—
10 mg (Rx) [*Anafranil* (lactose)].
25 mg (Rx) [*Anafranil* (lactose)].
50 mg (Rx) [*Anafranil* (lactose)].

Packaging and storage

Store below 40 °C (104 °F), preferably between 15 and 30 °C (59 and 86 °F), in a tight, light-resistant container, unless otherwise specified by manufacturer.

Auxiliary labeling

- May cause drowsiness.
- Avoid alcoholic beverages.

DESIPRAMINE

Summary of Differences

Indications:
Also used to manage some types of chronic, severe, neurogenic pain; to reduce craving and/or prevent depression upon withdrawal of cocaine; to control binge eating and purging in bulimia; and to treat cataplexy associated with narcolepsy; and is being used to relieve the symptoms of attention deficit hyperactivity disorder in children over 6 years of age and in adolescents.

Pharmacology/pharmacokinetics:
Effects—
Anticholinergic: Low.
Sedative: Low.
Orthostatic hypotension: Moderate.

Precautions:
Drug interactions and/or related problems—
Not recommended for concurrent use with monoamine oxidase inhibitors.
Concurrent use of phenytoin with desipramine may lower serum concentrations of desipramine; dosage increases above maximum recommended doses of desipramine may be necessary for clinical improvement of depression.

Oral Dosage Forms

DESIPRAMINE HYDROCHLORIDE TABLETS USP

Usual adult dose

Antidepressant—
Oral, 100 to 200 mg a day in divided doses or as a single dose, the dosage being adjusted as needed and tolerated.

Usual adult prescribing limits

Up to 300 mg a day.

Note: Geriatric patients—Up to 150 mg a day.

Usual pediatric dose
Antidepressant—
Children 6 to 12 years of age: Oral, 10 to 30 mg, or 1 to 5 mg per kg of body weight, a day in divided doses.
Adolescents: Oral, 25 to 50 mg a day in divided doses, the dosage being adjusted as needed and tolerated, up to a maximum of 100 mg a day.

Usual geriatric dose
Antidepressant—
Oral, 25 to 50 mg a day in divided doses, the dosage being adjusted as needed and tolerated, up to a maximum of 150 mg a day.

Strength(s) usually available
U.S.—
10 mg (Rx) [*Norpramin;* GENERIC].
25 mg (Rx) [*Norpramin;* GENERIC].
50 mg (Rx) [*Norpramin;* GENERIC].
75 mg (Rx) [*Norpramin;* GENERIC].
100 mg (Rx) [*Norpramin;* GENERIC].
150 mg (Rx) [*Norpramin;* GENERIC].
Canada—
10 mg (Rx) [*Norpramin* (sucrose; mannitol; corn starch)].
25 mg (Rx) [*Norpramin; Pertofrane;* GENERIC].
50 mg (Rx) [*Norpramin; Pertofrane;* GENERIC].
75 mg (Rx) [*Norpramin;* GENERIC].
100 mg (Rx) [*Norpramin*].

Packaging and storage
Store below 40 °C (104 °F), preferably between 15 and 30 °C (59 and 86 °F), unless otherwise specified by manufacturer. Store in a tight container.

Auxiliary labeling
- May cause drowsiness.
- Avoid alcoholic beverages.

DOXEPIN

Summary of Differences

Indications:
Also used in treatment of some types of chronic, severe neurogenic pain; peptic ulcer disease; and pruritus in idiopathic cold urticaria.
Pharmacology/pharmacokinetics:
Effects—
Anticholinergic: High.
Sedative: High.
Orthostatic hypotension: High.

Additional Dosing Information

See also *General Dosing Information.*

Patients with mild symptomology or emotional symptoms accompanying organic disease may be controlled on doses as low as 25 to 50 mg a day.

The once-a-day dosage maximum is 150 mg, which may be given at bedtime.

Oral Dosage Forms

Note: Bracketed uses in the *Dosage Forms* section refer to categories of use and/or indications that are not included in U.S. product labeling.

DOXEPIN HYDROCHLORIDE CAPSULES USP

Usual adult dose
Antidepressant—
Oral, initially 25 mg (base) three times a day, the dosage being adjusted gradually as needed and tolerated.
[Antipruritic][1]—
Oral, initially 10 mg (base) at bedtime, the dosage being increased gradually up to 25 mg, as needed and tolerated.

Usual adult prescribing limits
Outpatients: Up to 150 mg (base) a day.
Hospitalized patients: Up to 300 mg (base) a day.

Usual pediatric dose
Antidepressant—
Children up to 12 years of age: Dosage has not been established.

Usual geriatric dose
Antidepressant—
Oral, initially 25 to 50 mg (base) a day, the dosage being adjusted gradually as needed and tolerated.

Strength(s) usually available
U.S.—
10 mg (base) (Rx) [*Sinequan;* GENERIC].
25 mg (base) (Rx) [*Sinequan;* GENERIC].
50 mg (base) (Rx) [*Sinequan;* GENERIC].
75 mg (base) (Rx) [*Sinequan;* GENERIC].
100 mg (base) (Rx) [*Sinequan;* GENERIC].
150 mg (base) (Rx) [*Sinequan;* GENERIC].
Canada—
10 mg (base) (Rx) [*Sinequan; Triadapin*].
25 mg (base) (Rx) [*Novo-Doxepin; Sinequan; Triadapin*].
50 mg (base) (Rx) [*Novo-Doxepin; Sinequan; Triadapin*].
75 mg (base) (Rx) [*Novo-Doxepin; Sinequan; Triadapin*].
100 mg (base) (Rx) [*Novo-Doxepin; Sinequan; Triadapin*].
150 mg (base) (Rx) [*Novo-Doxepin; Sinequan*].

Packaging and storage
Store between 15 and 30 °C (59 and 86 °F), unless otherwise specified by manufacturer. Store in a well-closed container.

Auxiliary labeling
- May cause drowsiness.
- Avoid alcoholic beverages.

Note
The 150-mg capsule is intended for maintenance therapy only, and not for initiation of therapy.

DOXEPIN HYDROCHLORIDE ORAL SOLUTION USP

Usual adult dose
See *Doxepin Hydrochloride Capsules USP.*

Usual adult prescribing limits
See *Doxepin Hydrochloride Capsules USP.*

Usual pediatric dose
See *Doxepin Hydrochloride Capsules USP.*

Strength(s) usually available
U.S.—
10 mg (base) per mL (Rx) [*Sinequan;* GENERIC].
Canada—
Not commercially available.

Packaging and storage
Store between 15 and 30 °C (59 and 86 °F), unless otherwise specified by manufacturer. Store in a tight, light-resistant container.

Incompatibilities
Oral solution may be incompatible with many carbonated beverages and with grape juice.

Auxiliary labeling
- May cause drowsiness.
- Avoid alcoholic beverages.
- Must be diluted before taking.

Note
When dispensing, include the manufacturer-provided graduated dropper.

[1]Not included in Canadian product labeling.

IMIPRAMINE

Summary of Differences

Indications:
Imipramine hydrochloride (but not pamoate) is indicated in treatment of childhood enuresis.
Imipramine is also used to manage some types of chronic, severe, neurogenic pain; to reduce craving and/or prevent depression upon cocaine withdrawal; to relieve symptoms of attention deficit hyperactivity disorder in children over 6 years of age and in adolescents; as a treatment adjunct with amphetamines or methylphenidate in cataplexy associated with narcolepsy; to block the recurrence of panic attacks, with or without phobias; in the treatment of stress and urge incontinence; and to control binge eating and purging in bulimia.
Pharmacology/pharmacokinetics:
Effects—
Anticholinergic: Moderate.
Sedative: Moderate.
Orthostatic hypotension: High.
Precautions:
Drug interactions and/or related problems—
Not recommended for concurrent use with monoamine oxidase inhibitors.

Additional Dosing Information

See also *General Dosing Information.*

For oral dosage forms only

In enuretic children, a daily dose exceeding 75 mg does not normally increase results. The usual pediatric prescribing limits are 2.5 mg per kg of body weight (mg/kg) a day.

For early-night bedwetters, the dosage may be more effective when one-half of the dose is given at mid-afternoon and one-half at bedtime.

A gradual decrease in dosage is less likely to cause relapse than an abrupt discontinuation.

Younger children should not be allowed to self-administer imipramine because of their increased sensitivity to side effects, especially cardiovascular effects and acute overdosage (plasma concentrations over 225 nanograms per mL), which are potentially fatal.

A medication-free interval after adequate therapeutic trial should be considered for children. However, dosage should be decreased gradually to prevent relapse. Children who have relapsed may not respond when treatment is reinitiated.

For parenteral dosage forms only

Used only for initiating therapy in patients who are not able or are unwilling to take oral medication. Oral dosage forms should replace the parenteral as soon as possible.

Oral Dosage Forms

Note: Bracketed uses in the *Dosage Forms* section refer to categories of use and/or indications that are not included in U.S. product labeling.

IMIPRAMINE HYDROCHLORIDE TABLETS USP

Usual adult dose

Antidepressant—

Oral, 25 to 50 mg three or four times a day, the dosage being adjusted as needed and tolerated.

[Urinary incontinence][1]—

Oral, 10 to 50 mg a day, the dosage being adjusted as needed and tolerated, to a maximum of 150 mg a day.

Usual adult prescribing limits

Outpatients: Up to 200 mg a day.
Hospitalized patients: Up to 300 mg a day.
Geriatric patients: Up to 100 mg a day.

Usual pediatric dose

Antidepressant—

Children up to 6 years of age: Use is not recommended.

Children 6 to 12 years of age: Oral, 10 to 30 mg a day in two divided doses.

Adolescents: Oral, 25 to 50 mg a day in divided doses, the dosage being adjusted as needed and tolerated, up to 100 mg a day.

Antienuretic—

Oral, 25 mg once a day, one hour before bedtime. If a satisfactory response is not obtained within one week, the dosage may be increased to 50 mg nightly in children under 12 years of age and to 75 mg nightly in children 12 or over.

Usual geriatric dose

Antidepressant—

Oral, initially 25 mg at bedtime, the dosage being adjusted as needed and tolerated, up to 100 mg a day in divided doses.

Strength(s) usually available

U.S.—

10 mg (Rx) [*Tipramine; Tofranil;* GENERIC].
25 mg (Rx) [*Norfranil; Tipramine; Tofranil;* GENERIC].
50 mg (Rx) [*Norfranil; Tipramine; Tofranil;* GENERIC].

Canada—

10 mg (Rx) [*Apo-Imipramine; Novopramine; Tofranil*].
25 mg (Rx) [*Apo-Imipramine; Novopramine; Tofranil*].
50 mg (Rx) [*Apo-Imipramine; Novopramine; Tofranil*].
75 mg (Rx) [*Apo-Imipramine* (scored); *Impril; Tofranil*].

Packaging and storage

Store between 15 and 30 °C (59 and 86 °F), unless otherwise specified by manufacturer. Store in a tight container.

Auxiliary labeling

- May cause drowsiness.
- Avoid alcoholic beverages.

IMIPRAMINE PAMOATE CAPSULES

Usual adult dose

Antidepressant—

Oral, initially 75 mg a day, usually given at bedtime, the dosage being adjusted as needed and tolerated.

Note: The dose level at which optimum response is usually obtained is 150 mg a day, usually given at bedtime.

Usual adult prescribing limits

Outpatients: Up to 200 mg a day.
Hospitalized patients: Up to 300 mg a day.

Usual pediatric dose

Antidepressant—

Children up to 12 years of age: Use is not recommended.

Strength(s) usually available

U.S.—

Note: The above strengths of imipramine pamoate are equivalent to the same strengths of imipramine hydrochloride.

75 mg (Rx) [*Tofranil-PM*].
100 mg (Rx) [*Tofranil-PM*].
125 mg (Rx) [*Tofranil-PM*].
150 mg (Rx) [*Tofranil-PM*].

Canada—

Not commercially available.

Packaging and storage

Store between 15 and 30 °C (59 and 86 °F), in a tight container, unless otherwise specified by manufacturer.

Auxiliary labeling

- May cause drowsiness.
- Avoid alcoholic beverages.

Parenteral Dosage Forms

IMIPRAMINE HYDROCHLORIDE INJECTION USP

Usual adult dose

Antidepressant—

Intramuscular, up to 100 mg a day in divided doses.

Usual adult prescribing limits

Up to 300 mg a day.

Usual pediatric dose

Antidepressant—

Children up to 12 years of age: Use is not recommended.

Strength(s) usually available

U.S.—

12.5 mg per mL (Rx) [*Tofranil* (ascorbic acid 1 mg; sodium bisulfite 0.5 mg; anhydrous sodium sulfite 0.5 mg)].

Canada—

Not commercially available.

Packaging and storage

Store below 40 °C (104 °F), preferably between 15 and 30 °C (59 and 86 °F), unless otherwise specified by manufacturer. Protect from freezing.

Auxiliary labeling

- For intramuscular use only.

---

[1]Not included in Canadian product labeling.

NORTRIPTYLINE

Summary of Differences

Indications:

Also used to manage some types of chronic, severe, neurogenic pain and in the treatment of panic disorder.

Pharmacology/pharmacokinetics:

Effects—

Anticholinergic: Low.
Sedative: Moderate.
Orthostatic hypotension: Low.

Oral Dosage Forms

NORTRIPTYLINE HYDROCHLORIDE CAPSULES USP

Usual adult dose

Antidepressant—

Oral, 25 mg (base) three or four times a day, the dosage being adjusted as needed and tolerated.

Nicotine dependence—

Oral, 25 to 100 mg per day.

Usual adult prescribing limits

Up to 150 mg (base) a day.

Usual pediatric dose

Antidepressant—

Children 6 to 12 years of age: Oral, 10 to 20 mg (base), or 1 to 3 mg per kg of body weight, a day in divided doses.

Adolescents: Oral, 25 to 50 mg, or 1 to 3 mg per kg of body weight, a day in divided doses, the dosage being adjusted as needed and tolerated.

Usual geriatric dose

Oral, 30 to 50 mg a day in divided doses, the dosage being adjusted as needed and tolerated.

Strength(s) usually available

U.S.—

10 mg (base) (Rx) [*Aventyl; Pamelor;* GENERIC].
25 mg (base) (Rx) [*Aventyl; Pamelor;* GENERIC].
50 mg (base) (Rx) [*Pamelor;* GENERIC].
75 mg (base) (Rx) [*Pamelor;* GENERIC].

Canada—

10 mg (base) (Rx) [*Aventyl*].
25 mg (base) (Rx) [*Aventyl*].

Packaging and storage

Store between 15 and 30 °C (59 and 86 °F), unless otherwise specified by manufacturer. Store in a tight container.

Auxiliary labeling

- May cause drowsiness.
- Avoid alcoholic beverages.

NORTRIPTYLINE HYDROCHLORIDE ORAL SOLUTION USP

Usual adult dose

See *Nortriptyline Hydrochloride Capsules USP*.

Usual pediatric dose

See *Nortriptyline Hydrochloride Capsules USP*.

Strength(s) usually available

U.S.—

10 mg (base) per 5 mL (Rx) [*Aventyl* (alcohol 4%); *Pamelor* (alcohol 4%)].

Canada—

Not commercially available.

Packaging and storage

Store below 40 °C (104 °F), preferably between 15 and 30 °C (59 and 86 °F), unless otherwise specified by manufacturer. Store in a tight, light-resistant container. Protect from freezing.

Auxiliary labeling

- May cause drowsiness.
- Avoid alcoholic beverages.

PROTRIPTYLINE

Summary of Differences

Indications:

Also used in the treatment of narcolepsy, as an adjunct with amphetamines or methylphenidate in the treatment of cataplexy associated with narcolepsy, in sleep disorders such as hypersomnia or impaired morning arousal, and may be used to relieve symptoms of attention deficit hyperactivity disorder in some children over 6 years of age and in adolescents.

Pharmacology/pharmacokinetics:

Effects—

Anticholinergic: Moderate.
Sedative: Very low.
Orthostatic hypotension: Low.

Additional Dosing Information

See also *General Dosing Information.*

When dosage increases of protriptyline are indicated, the increase should be made in the morning. This drug often has a psychic-energizing action and usually not the sedative action exhibited by other tricyclics, although it may intensify the sedative effect of other medications.

Protriptyline is often given in divided doses with the last daily dose in the afternoon to avoid insomnia or nightmares when given to some patients before bedtime.

When protriptyline is used in narcolepsy, 15 to 20 mg given in a single daily dose at bedtime may relieve symptoms of arousal difficulty and daytime sleepiness.

Oral Dosage Forms

Note: Bracketed uses in the *Dosage Forms* section refer to categories of use and/or indications that are not included in U.S. product labeling.

PROTRIPTYLINE HYDROCHLORIDE TABLETS USP

Usual adult dose

Antidepressant—

Oral, initially 5 to 10 mg three or four times a day, the dosage being adjusted as needed and tolerated.

[Anticataplectic][1]—

Oral, 15 to 20 mg a day at bedtime.

Usual adult prescribing limits

Up to 60 mg a day.

Usual pediatric dose

Antidepressant—

Children up to 12 years of age: Dosage has not been established.

Adolescents: Oral, initially 5 mg three times a day, the dosage being adjusted as needed and tolerated.

Usual geriatric dose

Antidepressant—

Oral, initially 5 mg three times a day, the dosage being adjusted as needed and tolerated.

Note: When the daily dose for geriatric patients exceeds 20 mg, the cardiovascular response should be closely monitored.

Strength(s) usually available

U.S.—

5 mg (Rx) [*Vivactil* (lactose); GENERIC].
10 mg (Rx) [*Vivactil* (lactose); GENERIC].

Canada—

10 mg (Rx) [*Triptil*].

Packaging and storage

Store between 15 and 30 °C (59 and 86 °F), unless otherwise specified by manufacturer. Store in a tight container.

Auxiliary labeling

- May cause drowsiness.
- Avoid alcoholic beverages.

---

[1]Not included in Canadian product labeling.

TRIMIPRAMINE

Summary of Differences

Indications:

Also used in treatment of peptic ulcer disease and in the management of some types of chronic, severe, neurogenic pain.

Pharmacology/pharmacokinetics:

Effects—

Anticholinergic: High.
Sedative: High.
Orthostatic hypotension: Moderate.

Additional Dosing Information

See also *General Dosing Information.*

For patient compliance and convenience of therapy for outpatients, the total daily dosage may be given at bedtime.

Following remission, maintenance therapy should continue for about 3 months at the lowest dose necessary to maintain remission.

In resistant cases of depression in adults in which dosage exceeds 2.5 mg per kg of body weight (mg/kg) a day, the ECG should be monitored during initiation of therapy and at appropriate intervals during stabilization of dose.

Oral Dosage Forms

Note: The dosing and strengths of the dosage forms available are expressed in terms of trimipramine base (not the maleate).

TRIMIPRAMINE MALEATE CAPSULES

Usual adult dose

Antidepressant—
- Outpatients—
  - Initial—Oral, 75 mg (base) a day in divided doses, the dosage being adjusted gradually to 150 mg a day as needed and tolerated, up to a maximum of 200 mg a day.
  - Maintenance—Oral, 50 to 150 mg (base) a day.
- Hospitalized patients—
  - Oral, initially 100 mg (base) a day in divided doses, the dosage being increased gradually in a few days to 200 mg a day, up to 250 to 300 mg a day in two to three weeks.

Usual pediatric dose

Antidepressant—
- Children up to 12 years of age: Dosage has not been established.
- Adolescents: Oral, initially 50 mg (base) a day in divided doses, the dosage being adjusted as needed and tolerated, up to a maximum of 100 mg a day.

Usual geriatric dose

Oral, initially 50 mg (base) a day in divided doses, the dosage being adjusted as needed and tolerated, up to a maximum of 100 mg a day.

Strength(s) usually available

U.S.—
- 25 mg (base) (Rx) [*Surmontil;* GENERIC].
- 50 mg (base) (Rx) [*Surmontil;* GENERIC].
- 100 mg (base) (Rx) [*Surmontil;* GENERIC].

Canada—
- 75 mg (base) (Rx) [*Apo-Trimip; Rhotrimine; Surmontil*].

Packaging and storage

Store between 15 and 30 °C (59 and 86 °F), in a tight container, unless otherwise specified by manufacturer.

Auxiliary labeling
- May cause drowsiness.
- Avoid alcoholic beverages.

TRIMIPRAMINE MALEATE TABLETS

Usual adult dose

See *Trimipramine Maleate Capsules.*

Usual pediatric dose

See *Trimipramine Maleate Capsules.*

Usual geriatric dose

Antidepressant—
- Oral, initially 25 to 50 mg (base) a day in divided doses, the dosage being increased by 25 mg a week, up to a maximum of 150 mg a day.

Strength(s) usually available

U.S.—
- Not commercially available.

Canada—
- 12.5 mg (base) (Rx) [*Apo-Trimip; Rhotrimine; Surmontil*].
- 25 mg (base) (Rx) [*Apo-Trimip; Novo-Tripramine; Rhotrimine; Surmontil*].
- 50 mg (base) (Rx) [*Apo-Trimip; Novo-Tripramine; Rhotrimine; Surmontil*].
- 100 mg (base) (Rx) [*Apo-Trimip; Novo-Tripramine; Rhotrimine; Surmontil*].

Packaging and storage

Store between 15 and 30 °C (59 and 86 °F), in a tight container, unless otherwise specified by manufacturer.

Auxiliary labeling
- May cause drowsiness.
- Avoid alcoholic beverages.

Revised: 02/01/2005

Table 1. Pharmacology/Pharmacokinetics

Drug	Anticholinergic Effects*	Sedation*	Orthostatic Hypotension*	Active Metabolites	Protein Binding (%)	Volume of Distribution (L/Kg)	Half-life (hours)	Therapeutic Plasma Concentration (ng/mL)†
Amitriptyline	High	High	Moderate to high	Nortriptyline 10-Hydroxyamitriptyline	95	12–18	10–26	
Amoxapine	Moderate	Low to moderate	Low	7- and 8-Hydroxyamoxapine	92	N.A.‡	8–30	
Clomipramine	High	Moderate	Moderate	Desmethylclomipramine	96–97	12	21–31	
Desipramine	Low	Low	Moderate	2-Hydroxydesipramine	90–92	17–42	12–27	125–300
Doxepin	High	High	High	Desmethyldoxepin	N.A.‡	12–28	11–23	
Imipramine	Moderate	Moderate	High	Desipramine 2-Hydroxydesipramine	89–95	15–31	11–25	150–300§
Nortriptyline	Low	Moderate	Low	10-Hydroxynortriptyline	92	14–22	18–44	50–150**
Protriptyline	Moderate	Very low	Low	N.A.‡	92	22	67–89	
Trimipramine	High	High	Moderate	N.A.‡	N.A.‡	N.A.‡	9–11	

*Relative effects among tricyclic antidepressants only.

†Although various values have been reported, there is little consensus about therapeutic plasma concentrations, except for desipramine, imipramine, and nortriptyline. Steady-state plasma levels exhibit marked interindividual variations due to genetic factors (e.g., hepatic metabolism) and physiochemical properties of the medication (e.g., lipid solubility).

‡Not available.

§Includes metabolites.

**Denotes therapeutic window, outside of which effects are lessened.

ANTIDIABETIC AGENTS, SULFONYLUREA Systemic

This monograph includes information on the following: 1) Acetohexamide; 2) Chlorpropamide; 3) Gliclazide*; 4) Glimepiride†; 5) Glipizide†; 6) Glyburide; 7) Tolazamide†; 8) Tolbutamide.

INN: Glyburide—Glibenclamide

BAN: Glyburide—Glibenclamide

JAN: Glyburide—Glibenclamide

VA CLASSIFICATION (Primary/Secondary):

Acetohexamide—HS502
Chlorpropamide—HS502/CV900
Gliclazide—HS502
Glimepiride—HS502
Glipizide—HS502
Glyburide—HS502
Tolazamide—HS502
Tolbutamide—HS502

Commonly used brand name(s): *Albert Glyburide*[6]; *Amaryl*[4]; *Apo-Chlorpropamide*[2]; *Apo-Glyburide*[6]; *Apo-Tolbutamide*[8]; *DiaBeta*[6]; *Diabinese*[2]; *Diamicron*[3]; *Dimelor*[1]; *Dymelor*[1]; *Euglucon*[6]; *Gen-Glybe*[6]; *Glucotrol*[5]; *Glucotrol XL*[5]; *Glynase PresTab*[6]; *Med Glybe*[6]; *Micronase*[6]; *Novo-Butamide*[8]; *Novo-Glyburide*[6]; *Novo-Propamide*[2]; *Nu-Glyburide*[6]; *Orinase*[8]; *Tolinase*[7].

Note: For a listing of dosage forms and brand names by country availability, see *Dosage Forms* section(s).

*Not commercially available in U.S.
†Not commercially available in Canada.

Category

Antidiabetic—Acetohexamide; Chlorpropamide; Gliclazide; Glimepiride; Glipizide; Glyburide; Tolazamide; Tolbutamide.

Antidiuretic—Chlorpropamide

Indications

Note: Bracketed information in the *Indications* section refers to uses that are not included in U.S. product labeling.

Accepted

Diabetes, type 2 (treatment)—Sulfonylureas are indicated as adjunctive therapy to diet and exercise in the treatment and control of certain patients with type 2 diabetes (previously known as non-insulin-dependent diabetes mellitus [NIDDM], adult-onset diabetes, maturity-onset diabetes, ketosis-resistant diabetes, or stable diabetes), which occurs in individuals who produce or secrete insufficient quantities of endogenous insulin or who have developed resistance to endogenous insulin. An attempt to control diabetes through changes in diet and level of physical activity is usually first-line management before beginning pharmacologic treatment. Patients not responding adequately to diet alone or patients who require diet plus insulin, especially if they require 40 USP Units or less of insulin a day, may be candidates for therapy with a sulfonylurea as monotherapy or combination therapy.

Diabetes mellitus, other, associated with certain conditions or syndromes, such as:

- Endocrine disease, including endocrine overactivity due to Cushing's syndrome, hyperthyroidism, pheochromocytoma, somatostatinoma, or aldosteronoma; or endocrine underactivity due to hypoparathyroidism-hypocalcemia, type I isolated growth hormone deficiency, or multitropic pituitary deficiency or
- Genetic syndromes, including inborn errors of metabolism, such as glycogen-storage disease type I, or insulin-resistant syndromes, such as muscular dystrophies, late onset proximal myopathy, or Huntington's chorea.
- Sulfonylureas may be used in conditions causing diabetes mellitus induced by hormones, medications, or chemicals in patients who have functioning pancreatic beta cells when the diabetes cannot be controlled by diet or exercise.

Combination use of insulin and sulfonylurea agents in patients with type 1 diabetes is controversial because many studies have indicated that sulfonylureas are not effective in the treatment of these patients.

Short-term administration of a sulfonylurea or insulin for transient loss of blood glucose control may be sufficient for patients with type 2 diabetes whose blood glucose levels are normally well-controlled with diet. Switching to another sulfonylurea agent may be beneficial if one particular sulfonylurea does not optimally control the diabetes mellitus; however, use of a sulfonylurea should be discontinued if satisfactory reduction of blood glucose concentration is not achieved.

The effectiveness of sulfonylureas in controlling blood glucose can decrease over time. If maximum doses of a sulfonylurea fail to control blood glucose, switching to another sulfonylurea or adding metformin to a sulfonylurea treatment regimen may be beneficial in increasing glycemic control and lipoprotein metabolism and may help avoid initiation of insulin therapy. This is especially successful in patients with type 2 diabetes whose blood sugar levels are poorly controlled by insulin alone, in short-term diabetics, or in patients who are 120 to 160% over ideal baseline body weight but who are not excessively insulin-resistant. Glimepiride and metformin may be used concomitantly when diet, exercise and glimepiride or metformin alone do not adequately control blood glucose levels. Combined use of glimepiride and metformin may increase the potential for hypoglycemia. Alternatively, low-dose insulin in conjunction with sulfonylureas can help to avoid using large doses of insulin, especially for patients with type 2 diabetes who are obese. However, complications, such as weight gain, the effects of hyperinsulinemia, and an increased risk of hypoglycemia need to be considered. Some patients with type 2 diabetes who are nonobese and who are experiencing secondary sulfonylurea failure may be best treated with insulin. A sulfonylurea should be discontinued any time it fails to contribute to the lowering of plasma glucose in a patient for whom compliance with proper diet and sulfonylurea dosing has been determined to be adequate.

[Diabetes insipidus, central, partial (treatment)][1]—Chlorpropamide is also indicated as secondary therapy in selected patients to treat partial central diabetes insipidus. Used as an antidiuretic, chlorpropamide has successfully reduced polyuria in about 50% of such treated patients. Chlorpropamide may be used alone or in combination with another agent such as carbamazepine or clofibrate so that the dose of both can be reduced and side effects minimized. Desmopressin is considered the primary treatment for diabetes insipidus.

Unaccepted

Sulfonylureas are not effective in the treatment of type 1 diabetes (previously known as insulin-dependent diabetes mellitus [IDDM]).

Chlorpropamide is not effective in the treatment of nephrogenic diabetes insipidus.

[1]Not included in Canadian product labeling.

Pharmacology/Pharmacokinetics

See *Table 1*, page 306.

Physicochemical characteristics

Chemical Group—Sulfonylurea.

First generation: Acetohexamide, chlorpropamide, tolazamide, tolbutamide.

Second generation: Gliclazide, glimepiride, glipizide, glyburide.

Molecular weight—

Acetohexamide: 324.4.
Chlorpropamide: 276.75.
Gliclazide: 323.42.
Glimepiride: 490.63.
Glipizide: 445.55.
Glyburide: 494.01.
Tolazamide: 311.41.
Tolbutamide: 270.35.

pKa—

Chlorpropamide: 4.8.
Gliclazide: 5.98.
Glipizide: 5.9.
Glyburide: 5.3.
Tolazamide: 3.5, 5.7.
Tolbutamide: 5.3.

Mechanism of action/Effect

Antidiabetic—

Sulfonylureas lower blood glucose in patients with type 2 diabetes by directly stimulating the acute release of insulin from functioning beta cells of pancreatic islet tissue by an unknown process that involves a sulfonylurea receptor on the beta cell. Sulfonylureas inhibit the ATP-potassium channels on the beta cell membrane and potassium efflux, which results in depolarization and calcium influx, calcium-calmodulin binding, kinase activation, and release of insulin-containing granules by exocytosis, an effect similar to that of glucose. Insulin is a hormone that lowers blood glucose and controls the storage and metabolism of carbohydrates, proteins, and fats. Sulfonylureas are effective only in patients whose pancreata are capable of producing insulin.

With chronic sulfonylurea treatment, insulin production is not increased and may return to pretreatment values, but insulin efficacy continues and is thought to involve extrapancreatic mechanisms to increase insulin sensitivity in target tissues, such as liver, muscle, and fat as well as in other cells, such as monocytes and erythrocytes. This can result in a decrease in hepatic glycogenolysis and gluconeogenesis. It is unclear if the sulfonylurea's extrapancreatic actions that increase insulin's efficacy are direct or indirect effects, but it is clear that the mechanism of action is not due to a direct sulfonylurea action on the insulin receptor. Because this peripheral effect is not apparent in patients with type 1 diabetes, the evidence suggests that this may not be the clinically significant mechanism of sulfonylurea action in patients with type 2 diabetes either. However, it is clear that tissues of sulfonylurea-treated patients with type 2 diabetes become more responsive to lower concentrations of endogenous insulin. Primary failure of sulfonylurea therapy may occur if beta-cell function is severely impaired. In addition to stimulating insulin secretion through the beta cell–sulfonylurea receptor, gliclazide may have a direct effect on intracellular calcium transport that specifically improves the biphasic response of the beta cell to a meal, that is, the immediate first phase of insulin release as well as the normally delayed second phase.

Antidiuretic—

Chlorpropamide seems to potentiate the effect of minimal concentrations of antidiuretic hormone present in patients with partial central diabetes insipidus.

Other actions/effects

Acetohexamide and its more potent major metabolite, hydroxyhexamide, have uricosuric properties. Gliclazide, at therapeutic doses, reduces platelet adhesiveness and aggregation by inhibiting arachidonic acid release and thromboxane synthesis, and increasing production of prostacyclin (PGI_2) and release of plasminogen activator, which increases fibrinolysis. It is also thought that gliclazide and glyburide have protective activity against cardiac arrhythmias because they can stabilize potassium and calcium concentrations by inhibition of the sodium-potassium-ATPase pump transport system. Tolbutamide and chlorpropamide decrease free water clearance while glyburide, glipizide, and tolazamide produce a mild diuresis effect by enhancement of renal free water clearance. In contrast to glyburide, tolazamide and tolbutamide increase hexose uptake in adipocytes and myocytes. Sulfonylureas directly increase the secretion of pancreatic and gastric somatostatin and do not seem to have a direct effect on glucagon.

Absorption

Rapidly and well absorbed but may have wide inter- and intra-individual variability. By impairing gastric motility and gastric emptying, hyperglycemia may significantly delay sulfonylurea absorption; glipizide plasma concentration has been shown to be reduced by 50% with plasma glucose concentrations over 198 mg/dL (11 millimoles/L).

Chlorpropamide—Food delays absorption of chlorpropamide.

Gliclazide—Food delays absorption of gliclazide up to 187 minutes; may be best taken 30 minutes before or with a meal.

Glimepiride—Food decreases mean peak drug concentrations (C_{max}) and the area under the plasma concentration-time curve (AUC) (by 8% and 9%, respectively) and increases the mean time to reach C_{max} (T_{max}) (by 12%) in healthy volunteers. It is recommended that glimepiride be taken with breakfast or the first main meal.

Glipizide—Food delays absorption of immediate-release glipizide by 40 minutes; therefore, it is recommended that glipizide be taken 30 minutes before a meal. While food had no effect on the lag time of absorption (3 to 4 hours) for extended-release glipizide, administration of glipizide to normal males before a meal high in fat showed a 40% increase in the time to peak serum concentrations; AUC was not affected.

Glyburide—Bioavailability of nonmicronized glyburide is lowest when given with a high-fat diet compared to fasting or a high-carbohydrate diet. Micronized glyburide is more consistent in its bioavailability and in its T_{max} with regard to all meal types than is the nonmicronized formulation. Also, micronized glyburide is better absorbed and is effective at a lower dose than is nonmicronized glyburide.

Tolbutamide—Absorption is unaltered if taken with food but is increased with high pH.

Precautions to Consider

Cross-sensitivity and/or related problems

Patients sensitive to one of the sulfonylureas may be sensitive to the others also; cross-sensitivity to other sulfonamide- or thiazide-type medications may also occur.

Carcinogenicity

Acetohexamide—Long-term studies in rats and mice showed no evidence of carcinogenicity.

Chlorpropamide—Chronic toxicity studies in dogs treated for 6, 13, and 20 months with doses of chlorpropamide greater than 20 times the human dose showed no histological or pathological abnormalities.

Gliclazide—Specific carcinogenicity studies have not been done in animals; however, long-term toxicity studies have not shown any evidence of drug-related carcinogenicity.

Glimepiride—A 24-month study in rats given doses approximately 340 times the maximum recommended human dose based on body surface area showed no evidence of carcinogenicity.

Glipizide—Large-dose studies using up to 75 times the maximum human dose in rats and in mice for 20 and 18 months, respectively, showed no evidence of drug-related carcinogenicity.

Glyburide—An 18-month study in rats given doses of up to 300 mg per kg of body weight (mg/kg) a day and a 2-year oncogenicity study in mice showed no evidence of drug-related carcinogenicity.

Tolazamide—A 103-week study in rats and mice at both low and high doses showed no evidence of carcinogenicity.

Tolbutamide—A 78-week study in male and female rats and mice showed no evidence of carcinogenicity.

Mutagenicity

Acetohexamide—Sister chromatid exchange testing showed no evidence of mutagenicity.

Chlorpropamide—The micronucleus test in one strain of Swiss mice given chlorpropamide doses of 200, 400, 800, and 1600 mg/kg (32 times greater than the therapeutic adult dose) showed no evidence of mutagenicity. However, three strains of mice showed positive results when evaluated using the *Salmonella*/microsome test. The results are questionable because negative results were also shown in rats and Chinese hamsters. Although an increase in chromosomal breakage has not been observed in treated mammals, Chinese hamsters, rats, or mice, the sister chromatin exchange showed a positive reaction with Chinese hamster cells *in vivo* and *in vitro;* however, spontaneous breakage in this study was not even doubled in extremely high doses. It is difficult to assign a cause-and-effect explanation to the slightly positive results in these animal studies.

Gliclazide—The Ames test, human lymphocyte test, and micronucleus test did not reveal mutagenicity.

Glimepiride—A series of *in vitro* and *in vivo* studies, including the Ames test, somatic cell mutation, chromosomal aberration, unscheduled DNA synthesis, and mouse micronucleus test, showed no evidence of mutagenicity.

Glipizide—Bacterial and *in vivo* mutagenicity testing showed no evidence of mutagenicity.

Glyburide—Testing with the Ames test, DNA damage/alkaline elution assay, and the micronucleus test (at doses 60 to 240 times the average human therapeutic dose) showed no evidence of mutagenicity.

Tolbutamide—The Ames test and the micronucleus test in mice (at doses of 500 mg/kg) showed no evidence of mutagenicity.

Pregnancy/Reproduction

Fertility—

Acetohexamide, tolazamide, tolbutamide—

Studies in humans have not been done.

Studies in animals have not been done.

Chlorpropamide—

Studies in humans have not been done.

Studies in rats treated with high doses of chlorpropamide (125 mg/kg) for 6 to 12 months showed varying degrees of spermatogenesis suppression.

Gliclazide—

Studies in humans have not been done.

Studies in female rats and the first generation offspring of treated male and female rats showed no evidence of impaired fertility.

Glimepiride—

Studies in humans have not been done.

Studies in male mice and male and female rats given more than 1700 times and approximately 4000 times, respectively, the maximum recommended human dose based on body surface area showed no evidence of impaired fertility.

Glipizide—

Studies in humans have not been done.

Studies in male and female rats given 75 times the maximum human dose showed no evidence of impaired fertility.

Glyburide—

Studies in humans have not been done.

Studies in rats and rabbits given 500 times the human dose have not shown evidence of impaired fertility.

Pregnancy—Chlorpropamide crosses the placenta; glyburide does not significantly cross the placenta, and it is not known whether other sulfonylureas cross the placenta. Use of insulin rather than sulfonylurea antidiabetic agents during pregnancy allows for the maintenance of blood glucose concentrations that are as close to normal as possible.

Abnormal blood glucose concentrations in the mother have been associated with a higher incidence of congenital abnormalities during early pregnancy, and with increased perinatal morbidity and mortality later in pregnancy. Adequate and well-controlled studies in humans have not been done to determine whether sulfonylureas are teratogenic. It remains possible that sulfonylureas cause congenital malformations if they cross the placenta, but current data leave unresolved the issue of whether the abnormalities are due to poor glucose control or to sulfonylurea treatment. Generally, sulfonylureas are not recommended during pregnancy. In the rare case that sulfonylureas are used during pregnancy, they should be discontinued to allow an interval before delivery appropriate for the particular sulfonylurea being used because of the risk that they will cause insulin release and hypoglycemia in the neonate at delivery.

Acetohexamide—

Adequate and well-controlled studies in humans have not been done.

Acetohexamide has been shown to be teratogenic in animal studies when large doses were administered.

FDA Pregnancy Category C.

Chlorpropamide—

Chlorpropamide crosses the placenta. Adequate and well-controlled studies have not been done in humans. Low doses (250 mg a day or less) of chlorpropamide have been used in pregnant women without adverse effects. The manufacturer recommends discontinuing chlorpropamide at least 1 month before the expected delivery date.

Using an *in vitro* method and whole embryo mouse culture, one study compared growth differences between untreated embryos and those bathed in hypoglycemic and euglycemic chlorpropamide-treated rat serums. The teratologic evaluation of the treated early somite mouse embryos showed malformations and growth retardation at doses similar to human therapeutic concentrations, which suggested that the teratogenicity was due to chlorpropamide and not to hypoglycemia; untreated mouse embryos showed normal development.

FDA Pregnancy Category C.

Gliclazide—

Studies in humans have not been done. Gliclazide is not recommended for use during pregnancy.

No teratogenic effects were found in studies of mice and rabbits. Embryotoxicity was not seen in studies of rats. However, a significant decrease in offspring viability at 48 hours was seen when pregnant females were treated up to delivery. It is unclear how this relates to the use of gliclazide or if it applies to humans.

Glimepiride—

Studies in humans have not been done.

Based on the results of animal studies, glimepiride should not be used during pregnancy. Use of insulin during pregnancy allows for the maintenance of blood glucose concentrations that are as close to normal as possible. Abnormal blood glucose concentrations have been associated with a higher incidence of congenital abnormalities.

No evidence of teratogenicity was found in rats following oral administration of glimepiride at doses approximately 4000 times the maximum recommended human dose based on body surface area, or in rabbits following administration of glimepiride at doses approximately 60 times the maximum recommended human dose based on body surface area. However, glimepiride use has been associated with intrauterine death in rats administered doses 50 times the human dose based on body surface area, and in rabbits administered doses 0.1 time the human dose based on body surface area. This fetotoxicity, observed only at doses inducing maternal hypoglycemia, has been similarly noted with other sulfonylureas and is believed to be directly related to the hypoglycemic action of glimepiride.

FDA Pregnancy Category C.

Glipizide—

Studies in humans have not been done. Glipizide should be discontinued at least 1 month before the expected delivery date.

Studies in rats have shown glipizide to be fetotoxic at all doses from 5 to 50 mg/kg; the fetotoxicity is thought to be due to the pharmacologic hypoglycemic effect during the perinatal period. No teratogenic effects were found in studies in rats and rabbits.

FDA Pregnancy Category C.

Glyburide—

Glyburide does not significantly cross the placenta according to an *in vitro* study using human placentas. Studies in humans have not been done. Use should be discontinued at least 2 weeks before the expected delivery date.

Studies in rats and rabbits given up to 500 times the human dose have produced no evidence of teratogenicity.

FDA Pregnancy Category B (*Micronase, Glynase PresTab*).

FDA Pregnancy Category C (*DiaBeta*).

Tolazamide—

Studies in humans have not been done. Use should be discontinued at least 2 weeks before the expected delivery date.

Studies in rats given 10 times the human dose have shown tolazamide to cause reduced litter sizes. No teratogenic effects were found. High doses of 100 mg/kg a day also produced reduced litter sizes and increased perinatal mortality in pups.

FDA Pregnancy Category C.

Tolbutamide—

Studies in humans have not been done. Use should be discontinued at least 2 weeks before the expected delivery date.

Studies in rats given doses of tolbutamide that were 25 to 100 times greater than the human dose have shown teratogenic effects, such as ocular and bone abnormalities, and increased mortality in the offspring. Repeat studies in rabbits showed no teratogenic effects.

FDA Pregnancy Category C.

Delivery—Prolonged severe hypoglycemia lasting for 4 to 10 days has been reported in neonates born to mothers who were receiving a sulfonylurea antidiabetic agent at the time of delivery. This effect has been reported more frequently with those agents with longer half-lives, such as chlorpropamide. If sulfonylureas are used during pregnancy, they should be discontinued according to the manufacturer's labeling.

Breast-feeding

Chlorpropamide and tolbutamide are distributed into human breast milk and potentially may cause hypoglycemia in the infant. Glimepiride is distributed into the milk of rats. It is not known whether acetohexamide, gliclazide, glipizide, glyburide, or tolazamide is distributed into breast milk.

Chlorpropamide: Chlorpropamide has been found to be distributed into breast milk at a concentration of 5 mcg per mL after 5 hours for a single 500-mg dose (after 5 hours, blood concentration for a single dose of 250 mg chlorpropamide is 30 mcg per mL); therefore, its use during breast-feeding is not recommended. Its effect on the nursing infant is not known.

Glimepiride: Glimepiride is distributed into the milk of rats in significant concentrations. The offspring of rats exposed to high concentrations during pregnancy developed skeletal abnormalities after nursing. Glimepiride should be discontinued in nursing mothers.

Tolbutamide: Tolbutamide was distributed into breast milk at a concentration averaging 3 and 18 mcg per mL in two patients taking 500 mg twice a day (milk:plasma ratio of 0.09 and 0.4, respectively). The effect on the nursing infants is not known. The American Academy of Pediatrics considers tolbutamide to be compatible with breast-feeding.

Pediatrics

Oral antidiabetic agents are not effective in type 1 (juvenile-onset) diabetes. Because type 2 diabetes occurs rarely in this age group, very little or no published pediatrics-specific information is available. Safety and efficacy have not been established.

Geriatrics

In general, no overall difference in safety or efficacy was apparent in persons over 65 years of age when compared to persons younger than 65 years of age taking sulfonylureas for type 2 diabetes. Lower doses are used initially because of possible increased sensitivity to these agents due to age-related metabolism and excretion changes; the steady state concentration of extended-release glipizide has been delayed for 1 or 2 days in elderly patients. The risk of adverse reactions is relatively low when other factors for toxicity, including liver and kidney disease and known drug interactions, are considered. Special counseling with emphasis on hydration, diet, and exercise may be necessary because of the greater risk of hypoglycemia in this age group. Special instruction to recognize hypoglycemia may be needed because early warning adrenergic symptoms of hypoglycemia (such as sweating, weakness, tachycardia, and nervousness) are absent in many patients. Hypoglycemia manifests as neurological symptoms (such as headache, irritability, mental confusion, unusual tiredness, and drowsiness) and may be more prolonged and severe in the elderly. Combining antidiabetic agents (sulfonylureas with metformin or insulin) or using long-acting sulfonylureas, such as chlorpropamide and glyburide, is most often associated with hypoglycemia in elderly patients and is not generally recommended; shorter-acting sulfonylureas cause fewer problems. Also, instructions may be needed to help the patient monitor urine or blood glucose if visual problems are present.

Geriatric patients may be more likely to develop a reversible syndrome of inappropriate antidiuretic hormone (SIADH) from the use of chlorpropamide. The incidence of SIADH is rare and occurs with greater incidence when thiazides are taken concurrently with chlorpropamide than when chlorpropamide is taken alone (10% versus 3%, respectively). In one study, women over 70 years of age were affected 10 times more often than women under 60 years of age when thiazides were used concurrently with chlorpropamide. It is not thought to be a gender-oriented effect. SIADH has been rarely reported with tolbutamide.

Drug interactions and/or related problems

The following drug interactions and/or related problems have been selected on the basis of their potential clinical significance (possible mechanism in parentheses where appropriate)—not necessarily inclusive (» = major clinical significance):

Note: Combinations containing any of the following medications, depending on the amount present, may also interact with this medication.

There is an increased chance of hypoglycemia occurring if more than one hypoglycemia-causing agent is used concurrently with sulfonylureas. If the need exists to administer any medications that may affect metabolic or glycemic control of type 2 diabetes, blood glucose concentrations should be monitored by the patient or health care professional. This is particularly important when any medication is added to or removed from an established drug regimen. Subsequent adjustments in diet or antidiabetic agent dosage or both may be necessary; these adjustments may differ depending on the severity of the diabetes.

» Alcohol
(a disulfiram-like reaction, which is characterized primarily by flushing of the face, neck, and arms, may occur with any of the sulfonylureas when alcohol is ingested concurrently but has not been reported with glipizide; risk is lowest with tolbutamide and glyburide and highest with chlorpropamide; it has occurred 12 hours after a single 250-mg dose of chlorpropamide and 40 mL of 18% alcohol)

(the risk of hypoglycemia may be increased or prolonged when moderate or large amounts of alcohol have been consumed concurrently with sulfonylurea antidiabetic agents; small amounts of alcohol taken with meals do not usually result in hypoglycemia)

Allopurinol
(increased risk of hypoglycemia due to inhibition of renal tubular secretion of chlorpropamide; closer monitoring required)

Angiotensin-converting enzyme inhibitors, such as:
Captopril or
Enalapril
(the mechanism of enhanced hypoglycemia that occurs rarely is unknown; concurrent use need not be avoided and may be advantageous in the treatment of type 2 diabetes; however, the dosage of the sulfonylurea may need to be modified in some patients)

» Anticoagulants, coumarin- or indandione-derivative
(the mechanism is not completely known; however, mutual interactions of both agents have increased their anticoagulant and hypoglycemic effects. A hypoglycemic effect may be partially due to the decrease in hepatic metabolism of sulfonylureas caused by anticoagulants, which can prolong the half-life of the sulfonylureas twofold to threefold. An increased protein binding displacement of anticoagulants by sulfonylureas has been found to prolong prothrombin times; however, because of the increase in the metabolism of dicumarol that can shorten its half-life by as much as 50%, an increase, decrease, or no effect on coagulation may result. Although these effects have been reported specifically for chlorpropamide, tolbutamide, and dicumarol, concurrent use of all sulfonylurea antidiabetic agents with anticoagulants should be well-monitored and dosage adjustments of both agents may be required)

(glipizide and glyburide have lower plasma concentrations than other sulfonylureas and exhibit only nonionic plasma protein binding; therefore, they may be less susceptible to displacement from plasma proteins by other medications that exhibit ionic binding to plasma proteins; studies have not been done and caution is still warranted)

» Antifungals, azole, systemic, such as:
Miconazole
Fluconazole
(severe hypoglycemia has been reported shortly after concurrent use of tolbutamide, glyburide, and glipizide with these oral azole antifungal agents. In one study, glipizide and fluconazole increased the area under the plasma concentration-time curve [AUC] of glipizide 56.9% [range, 35–81%]. Also, hypoglycemia has been reported for gliclazide taken concurrently with miconazole, but not with fluconazole)

Appetite suppressants
(when appetite suppressants and a concurrent dietary regimen are used, blood glucose concentrations may be altered in patients with diabetes; dosage adjustment of the antidiabetic agent may be necessary during and after therapy)

» Asparaginase or
» Corticosteroids or
» Diuretics, thiazide or
» Lithium
(these medications have intrinsic hyperglycemic activity in both diabetic and nondiabetic patients; dosage of the sulfonylurea may need to be modified during and after treatment. Some studies of lithium have reported hypoglycemia)

(concurrent treatment using thiazides with chlorpropamide, and more rarely with tolbutamide, may increase the chance of hyponatremia and hypo-osmolality, especially in patients over 70 years of age)

Barbiturates
(chlorpropamide may prolong the effect of barbiturates and barbiturates may prolong the effect of gliclazide; other sulfonylureas may also exhibit these effects; dosage adjustment of the sulfonylurea or the barbiturate may be necessary)

» Beta-adrenergic blocking agents, including ophthalmics, if significant absorption occurs
(beta-adrenergic blocking agents may decrease the hypoglycemic effects of sulfonylureas to some extent by inhibition of insulin secretion, modification of carbohydrate metabolism, and increased peripheral insulin resistance, leading to hyperglycemia; an adjustment in dose may be required. Other mechanisms that control the normal physiological response to a fall in blood glucose may be affected also, such as a blocked catecholamine-mediated response to hypoglycemia [glycogenolysis and mobilization of glucose], thereby prolonging the time it takes to achieve euglycemia and increasing the risk of a severe hypoglycemic reaction. Selective beta$_1$-adrenergic blocking agents [such as acebutolol, atenolol, betaxolol, bisoprolol, and metoprolol] exhibit the above actions to a lesser extent; however, any of the agents can blunt some of the symptoms of developing hypoglycemia, such as increased heart rate or tremors [increased sweating and blood pressure may not be altered], making detection of this complication more difficult)

» Cimetidine or
» Ranitidine
(these agents, in therapeutic doses, can significantly decrease the postprandial rise in blood glucose and increase the hypoglycemic effects of glipizide, gliclazide, and glyburide in patients with diabetes; also, cimetidine has decreased tolbutamide's elimination and increased absorption of tolbutamide and glyburide; ranitidine did not affect glyburide's AUC; close monitoring for dose adjustments of sulfonylureas may be needed when these agents are added or withdrawn)

» Cyclosporine
(glipizide may significantly increase the plasma concentration of cyclosporine by reducing its metabolism; dose reduction of cyclosporine may be necessary; similar effects may be possible with other sulfonylureas)

CYP2C9 inhibitors such as
Fluconazole or
CYP2C9 inducers such as
Rifampicin
(potential interaction of glimepiride with inhibitors and inducers of cytochrome P450 2C9)

» Fluoroquinolones, such as ciprofloxacin
(use of glyburide with ciprofloxacin has caused hypoglycemia; since the mechanism is not understood, similar effects with other sulfonylurea antidiabetic agents should be considered when these medications are used together)

» Guanethidine or
» Monoamine oxidase (MAO) inhibitors, including furazolidone, procarbazine, and selegiline or
» Quinidine or
» Quinine or
» Salicylates, in large doses
(these medications have intrinsic hypoglycemic activity in both diabetic and nondiabetic patients, possibly severe with quinine, quinidine, or salicylates in high doses but unlikely with low doses of salicylates. Also, salicylates may interfere with chlorpropamide's renal excretion. Salicylate dose may need to be reduced)

Hemolytics, other (see *Appendix II*)
(concurrent use may increase the incidence of sulfonylurea-induced hemolysis through a possible additive effect; reported cases of hemolysis effects have rarely occurred with chlorpropamide or tolbutamide and have not been reported with other sulfonylureas)

Hepatic enzyme inducers, such as:
Rifabutin
Rifampin
(metabolism of sulfonylureas may be increased due to stimulation of hepatic microsomal enzymes; dosage adjustments may be necessary during and after concurrent treatment)
(drug interaction data for rifabutin are not available; it is structurally related to rifampin but appears to be a less potent enzyme inducer of the hepatic cytochrome P450 system than is rifampin. It is recommended that patients taking rifabutin concurrently with sulfonylurea antidiabetic agents be monitored since the significance of possible drug interactions is not known)

Hepatic enzyme inhibitors, such as:
» Chloramphenicol
(metabolism of sulfonylureas may be decreased due to inhibition of hepatic microsomal enzymes; dosage adjustments may be necessary during and after concurrent use)
(also, with concurrent use, chlorpropamide's half-life has increased up to 146 hours; this may be partially due to interference with renal excretion of chlorpropamide by chloramphenicol)

Highly protein-bound medications such as:
Anti-inflammatory drugs, nonsteroidal (NSAIDs), such as phenylbutazone
Clofibrate
Probenecid
Sulfinpyrazone
Sulfonamides
(these medications enhance the hypoglycemic effects of sulfonylureas when given concurrently; the mechanism is unknown but may be due to displacement of sulfonylureas from protein binding sites and alterations in their renal excretion; concurrent use need not be avoided; however, the dosage of the sulfonylurea may need to be modified in some patients)
(clofibrate also shows intrinsic hypoglycemic effects by causing increased insulin sensitivity and has been used advantageously in the treatment of diabetes mellitus; also, clofibrate has intrinsic antidiuretic effects that have been used to treat diabetes insipidus; this effect may be lessened with concurrent use of glyburide or increased with concurrent use of chlorpropamide or tolbutamide)
(sulfinpyrazone and phenylbutazone have been shown to inhibit the hepatic metabolism of tolbutamide; they also inhibit the renal excretion of acetohexamide but not of glyburide; the effect on other sulfonylureas by NSAIDs [other than ibuprofen, naproxen, sulindac, and tolmetin, which do not affect sulfonylureas] is not known)
(NSAIDs inhibit synthesis of prostaglandin E, which inhibits endogenous insulin secretion; this increases basal insulin secretion, the response to a glucose load, and the hypoglycemic effect of insulin secretion; dosage adjustment of each medication used may be necessary following chronic use of NSAIDs)
(glipizide and glyburide have lower plasma concentrations than other sulfonylureas and exhibit nonionic plasma protein binding only; therefore, these sulfonylureas may be less susceptible to displacement from plasma proteins by other medications that exhibit ionic binding to plasma proteins)

Hyperglycemia-causing agents, such as:
Anticonvulsants, hydantoin
Calcium channel blocking agents
Clonidine
Danazol
Dextrothyroxine
Diazoxide, parenteral
Estrogens
Estrogen-progestin-containing oral contraceptives
Furosemide
Glucagon
Growth hormone
Isoniazid
Morphine
Niacin
Phenothiazines, such as chlorpromazine
Sympathomimetic agents, such as beta-adrenergic agonists
Thyroid hormones
(these medications may change many factors that affect the metabolic control of glucose concentrations and, unless the changes can be controlled with diet, may necessitate an increased sulfonylurea dose and regular monitoring)
(hyperglycemic effects have resulted with doses greater than 100 mg of chlorpromazine; other phenothiazines or lower doses of chlorpromazine have not had this effect. However, caution may be warranted for concurrent use of phenothiazines with sulfonylureas)
(isoniazid usually causes hyperglycemia, but hypoglycemia has occurred in some patients with diabetes who are taking tolbutamide; a decrease in the dose of tolbutamide is then warranted)
(beta-adrenergic agonists increase risk of hyperglycemia by increasing glycogenolysis. If given during pregnancy, these agents may cause hypoglycemia in the fetus, independent of maternal blood glucose concentrations, by causing a depletion of fetal glycogen stores; sulfonylurea dose adjustment may be necessary if these agents are given together during pregnancy)

Hypoglycemia-causing agents, such as:
Anabolic steroids
Androgens
Bromocriptine
Disopyramide
Pyridoxine
Tetracycline
Theophylline
(these medications may change metabolic control of glucose concentrations and, unless the changes can be controlled with diet, may necessitate a decreased sulfonylurea dose; patients susceptible to hypoglycemia should be monitored closely)

Insulin
(sulfonylurea agents chronically stimulate the pancreatic beta cell to release insulin and increase receptor and tissue sensitivity to insulin; although concurrent use of the medications with insulin may increase the hypoglycemic response, the effect may be unpredictable)
(although the combination has been used to treat a select group of patients with diabetes whose condition is not well-controlled with either agent alone, many studies have shown there is generally no additional benefit from using oral agents for the treatment of type 1 diabetes)

» Octreotide
(octreotide suppresses pancreatic insulin and counterregulatory hormones, such as glucagon and growth hormone, and delays or lowers glucose absorption from the gastrointestinal tract; depending on the dose, concurrent use with sulfonylureas may cause hypoglycemia or hyperglycemia so that dose adjustment of the sulfonylurea may be needed; octreotide has been used beneficially for sulfonylurea overdose or insulinomas)

» Pentamidine
(pentamidine has a toxic effect on pancreatic beta cells resulting in a biphasic effect on glucose concentration, i.e., initial insulin release and hypoglycemia followed by hypoinsulinemia and hyperglycemia with continued use of pentamidine; dose alterations and continued use of sulfonylureas should be considered)

Laboratory value alterations

The following have been selected on the basis of their potential clinical significance (possible effect in parentheses where appropriate)—not necessarily inclusive (» = major clinical significance).

With diagnostic test results

Blood urea nitrogen (BUN)
(acetohexamide produces a reaction with diacetyl and falsely elevates results of this test)

Creatinine, serum
(acetohexamide has significantly increased the creatinine concentration for some laboratory tests by as much as 2.2 or 3.3 mg/dL and as little as 0.3 mg/dL for others)

Protein, total, serum
(tolbutamide interferes with sulfosalicylic acid test by causing turbidity)

» Sodium iodide I 123 or
» Sodium iodide I 131
(tolbutamide may decrease thyroidal uptake of I 123 or I 131; withdrawal of tolbutamide 1 week or longer before reactive iodine uptake test is necessary to prevent interference)

With physiology/laboratory test values

Alanine aminotransferase (ALT [SGPT]) or
Alkaline phosphatase or
Aspartate aminotransferase (AST [SGOT]) or

Lactate dehydrogenase (LDH)
(values may be mildly increased, usually are not associated with clinical symptoms, and may be due to the sulfonylurea or to the underlying diabetes; however, hepatitis or cholestatic jaundice is caused rarely by sulfonylureas and should be considered with high values)

Bile, urine or
Bilirubin, urine
(concentrations may be mildly increased and usually do not present with clinical symptoms; however, hepatitis or cholestatic jaundice is caused rarely by sulfonylureas and should be considered with high values)

C-peptide, serum
(increased concentration for the first three months of sulfonylurea treatment; can return to pretreatment values long-term [18 months in one study])

Osmolality, urine or
Sodium, serum
(may be decreased with acetohexamide, gliclazide, glipizide, glyburide, or tolazamide because of their slight diuretic effect)

(chlorpropamide increases osmolality because of its antidiuretic effect and has caused dilutional hyponatremia)

(sodium may also decrease in response to hyperglycemia; each 100 mg/dL [5.51 mmol/L] increase in blood glucose decreases serum sodium by 1.6 mEq/L)

Uric acid, serum
(concentrations are considerably reduced by use of acetohexamide due to its mild uricosuric effect)

Urine collection, 24-hour
(quantity is mildly increased due to normal slight diuretic response by acetohexamide, gliclazide, glipizide, glyburide, or tolazamide)

(quantity is decreased with chlorpropamide due to its antidiuretic effect)

For gliclazide

Factors VIII, XI
(concentrations may be decreased)

Tissue plasminogen activator
(concentrations may be increased)

Medical considerations/Contraindications

The medical considerations/contraindications included have been selected on the basis of their potential clinical significance (reasons given in parentheses where appropriate)—not necessarily inclusive (» = major clinical significance).

Except under special circumstances, this medication should not be used when the following medical problems exist:

For all oral sulfonylurea antidiabetic agents

» Acidosis, significant or
» Burns, severe or
» Diabetic coma or
» Diabetic ketoacidosis, with or without coma or
» Hyperosmolar nonketotic coma or
» Surgery, major or
» Trauma, severe or
» Any other condition that causes severe blood glucose fluctuations or
» Any other condition in which insulin needs change rapidly
(fluctuations in blood glucose concentrations associated with certain disease states are more closely controlled by titration of insulin dosing, possibly on a short-term basis, rather than with oral antidiabetic agents, such as sulfonylureas)

» Hypersensitivity to sulfonylurea antidiabetic agents, sulfonamides, or thiazide-type diuretics

Risk-benefit should be considered when the following medical problems exist:

For all oral sulfonylurea antidiabetic agents

» Diarrhea, severe or
» Gastroparesis or
» Intestinal obstruction or
» Vomiting, prolonged or
» Other conditions causing delayed food absorption
(delayed stomach emptying or intestinal movement or vomiting may require modification of a sulfonylurea dose or a change to insulin therapy)

» Hepatic disease
(sulfonylureas that are extensively metabolized in the liver should not be used when there is hepatic impairment; hypoglycemia that develops may be more severe when these sulfonylureas are being used)

» Hyperglycemia-causing conditions, such as:
Female hormone changes or
Fever, high or
Hyperadrenalism, not optimally controlled or
Infection, severe or
Psychological stress
(these conditions, by increasing blood glucose, may increase the need for more frequent glucose monitoring and for a permanent or temporary dose increase for sulfonylureas or a change to insulin if blood glucose is uncontrolled)

» Hyperthyroidism, not optimally controlled
(hyperthyroidism aggravates diabetes mellitus by increasing plasma glycogen concentrations and glucose absorption and by impairing glucose tolerance; thyroid hormone has dose-dependent biphasic effects on glycogenolysis and gluconeogenesis; hyperthyroidism can make glycemic control difficult until the patient is euthyroid; patients with this condition may require an increased dose of the sulfonylurea until euthyroidism is achieved)

» Hypoglycemia-causing conditions, such as:
Adrenal insufficiency, not optimally controlled or
Debilitated physical condition or
Malnutrition or
Pituitary insufficiency, not optimally controlled
(these conditions, which inherently predispose patients to the risk of developing hypoglycemia, increase the patient's risk of developing severe hypoglycemia with concurrent treatment of sulfonylurea antidiabetic agents; reduced sulfonylurea dose or more frequent monitoring may be required for patients with these conditions)

Hypothyroidism, not optimally controlled
(sulfonylurea metabolism may be reduced with hypothyroidism and may mildly aggravate this underlying condition, which already exhibits reduced glucose absorption and altered glucose and lipoprotein metabolism [tolbutamide has goitrogenic properties]; low doses of a sulfonylurea may be needed when hypothyroid conditions exist, and an increase in sulfonylurea dosing may be required when initiating thyroid treatment; euglycemic control may be difficult until the patient is euthyroid)

» Renal function impairment
(use of sulfonylureas increases the risk of possibly prolonged hypoglycemia with renal function impairment)
(the elimination half-lives of all the sulfonylureas are increased with renal function impairment, especially where tubular involvement predominates or if azotemia is present, but less so if the glomerular filtration rate is mildly reduced; sulfonylureas with longer half-lives, such as acetohexamide and chlorpropamide, are not recommended since renal excretion is important in the elimination of chlorpropamide and the active metabolite of acetohexamide [hydroxyhexamide]; weakly active metabolites of tolazamide and glyburide may also accumulate, particularly in those patients with a creatinine clearance of less than 30 mL/min [0.5 mL/sec]; sulfonylureas with shorter half-lives, such as gliclazide, glipizide, or tolbutamide, should present fewer problems but should be used cautiously in renal impairment)

For chlorpropamide or tolbutamide

» Congestive heart failure
(fluid retention, caused rarely by chlorpropamide and even less often by tolbutamide, may result in hyponatremia and precipitate congestive heart failure in the elderly when other risk factors for congestive heart failure are present)

Patient monitoring

The following may be especially important in patient monitoring (other tests may be warranted in some patients, depending on condition; » = major clinical significance):

» Blood glucose determinations
(blood or plasma glucose reflects the current degree of metabolic control and should be routinely self-monitored by the patient at home and by the physician [every 3 months, or more often when patient is not stabilized] to confirm that blood glucose concentration is maintained within agreed-upon targets by the selected diet and dosing regimen; this is particularly important during dosage adjustments. Self-monitoring of blood glucose by the patient may require testing multiple times during the day or once to several times a week)

(caution in interpreting blood glucose concentrations is needed because normal whole blood glucose values are approximately 15% lower than plasma glucose values; glucose values are also laboratory- and method-specific. Normal fasting whole blood glucose for adults of all ages is 65 to 95 mg/dL [3.6 to 5.3 mmol/L]. Normal fasting serum glucose is 70 to 105 mg/dL [3.9 to 5.8 mmol/L] for adults younger than 60 years of age and 80 to 115 mg/dL [4.4 to 6.4 mmol/L] for adults 60 years of age or older. For pregnant women with diabetes, a normal fasting serum glucose is less than 105 mg/dL [5.8 mmol/L] and a fasting whole blood glucose is less than 120 mg/dL [6.7 mmol/L]. Goals of conventional sulfonylurea antidiabetic therapy are based on the absence of symptoms of hyperglycemia and hypoglycemia)

(capillary blood glucose measurement provides important information when done properly, but caution is warranted because of potential errors in technique and readings; it has been suggested that the values be relied upon only if the reported glucose concentration for patients in whom diabetes is stable is between 75 mg/dL and 325 mg/dL [4.12 mmol/L and 17.88 mmol/L, respectively])

» Complete blood count (CBC)
(leukopenia, agranulocytosis, thrombocytopenia, and hemolytic and aplastic anemias have occurred rarely with sulfonylureas)

Glucose, urine or
Ketones, urine
(if blood glucose concentrations exceed 200 mg/dL [11.1 mmol/L], monitoring of urine for the presence of glucose and ketones may be necessary; normalization of glucose in the urine generally lags quantitatively behind serum glucose concentrations; test methods are generally capable of detecting serum glucose concentrations greater than 180 mg/dL [10 mmol/L])

» Glycosylated hemoglobin (hemoglobin A_{1c}) determinations
(hemoglobin A_{1c} values [normal whole blood hemoglobin A_{1c} is approximately 4 to 6% of total hemoglobin; specific values are laboratory-dependent] reflect the metabolic control over the preceding 3 months, but assessment of this parameter does not eliminate the need for daily blood glucose monitoring. Hemoglobin A_{1c} may be falsely elevated in patients whose diabetes is unstable when the intermediate precursor is elevated [e.g., in alcoholism] and falsely lowered in conditions of shortened red blood cell lifespan [e.g., in anemia and acute or chronic blood loss] or in patients with hemoglobinopathies [e.g., sickle cell disease])

Osmolarity determinations, plasma or
Sodium concentrations, serum
(may be necessary with use of chlorpropamide or tolbutamide, especially for the elderly or when thiazide diuretics are being taken concurrently)

pH measurements, serum or
Potassium concentrations, serum
(determinations may be important if patient is hypoglycemic and ketoacidotic)

Side/Adverse Effects

Note: It has been suggested by some studies, including the University Group Diabetes Program (UGDP), that certain sulfonylurea antidiabetic agents increase cardiovascular mortality in diabetic patients, a population that already has a greater risk of cardiovascular disease and mortality when blood glucose is not controlled. Other studies have not reached a similar conclusion and have in fact suggested that control of elevated blood glucose with sulfonylurea antidiabetic agents may lessen the danger of cardiovascular disease and mortality. Despite questions regarding the interpretation of the results and the adequacy of the experimental design, the findings of the UGDP study provide an adequate basis for caution, especially for certain high risk patients with coronary artery disease, congestive heart failure, or angina pectoris. If sulfonylurea treatment is necessary, glyburide or gliclazide may be the preferred sulfonylureas for use in patients at risk for conditions causing cardiac hypoxia. The patient should be informed of the potential risks and advantages of sulfonylurea antidiabetic agents and of alternative modes of therapy.

The following side/adverse effects have been selected on the basis of their potential clinical significance (possible signs and symptoms in parentheses where appropriate)—not necessarily inclusive:

Those indicating need for medical attention

Incidence more frequent

Hypoglycemia—mild, including nocturnal hypoglycemia (anxiety; behavior change similar to drunkenness; blurred vision; cold sweats; confusion; cool pale skin; difficulty in concentrating; drowsiness; excessive hunger; fast heartbeat; headache; nausea; nervousness; nightmares; restless sleep; shakiness; slurred speech; unusual tiredness or weakness); ***weight gain***

Note: Predisposing factors related to diet, exercise, age, or concurrent use of other hypoglycemia-causing drugs (including insulin) increase the chances of hypoglycemic episodes occurring. The occurrence of a recent episode of *hypoglycemia* may lessen the symptoms of a second episode. In the elderly, *hypoglycemia* symptoms are variable and harder to identify. Furthermore, *nocturnal hypoglycemia* may be asymptomatic in 33% or more of affected patients. Hypoglycemic episodes are experienced by 20% of the patients taking sulfonylureas every 6 months (6% experiencing monthly episodes).

Weight gain is greater with combination use of insulin and sulfonylureas than with sulfonylurea therapy alone. Gliclazide alone, or metformin in combination with sulfonylureas, usually results in less weight gain than other sulfonylureas and has exhibited a weight loss effect.

Incidence less frequent

Erythema multiforme or exfoliative dermatitis (peeling of skin; skin redness, itching, or rash); ***hypoglycemia—severe*** (coma; seizures)

For chlorpropamide or, rarely, tolbutamide

Dilutional hyponatremia, hypo-osmolality, or syndrome of inappropriate antidiuretic hormone (SIADH) (depression; dizziness; headache; lethargy; nausea; swelling or puffiness of face, ankles, or hands with occasional progression to seizures, coma, or stupor)

Note: The incidence of *severe hypoglycemia* episodes is 0.22 episodes per 1000 patient-years. It occurs more often with long-acting sulfonylureas, such as chlorpropamide or glyburide, when other predisposing factors or conditions are present, and can be relapsing and prolonged; glyburide results in a higher fatality rate than does chlorpropamide.

Incidence rare

Anemia, aplastic or hemolytic (continuing and unexplained tiredness or weakness, headache, shortness of breath brought on by exercise); ***blood dyscrasias, specifically, agranulocytosis, leukopenia, pancytopenia*** (fever and sore throat; pale skin; unusual bleeding or bruising; unusual tiredness or weakness); ***cholestasis, cholestatic jaundice, hepatic function impairment, hepatic porphyria, hepatitis, or porphyria cutanea tarda*** (dark urine; fluid-filled skin blisters; itching of the skin; light-colored stools; sensitivity to the sun; skin thinness; yellow eyes or skin); ***eosinophilia*** (blood in sputum; chest pain; chills; general feeling of ill health; increased production of sputum; increased sweating; shortness of breath); ***thrombocytopenia*** (unusual bleeding or bruising)

Note: Sulfonylurea-induced *blood dyscrasias* and dermatologic conditions generally occur within the initial six weeks of therapy and are thought to be hypersensitivity reactions.

Those indicating need for medical attention only if they continue or are bothersome

Incidence more frequent

Changes in sense of taste; dizziness; drowsiness; gastrointestinal disturbances (constipation; diarrhea; flatulence; heartburn; loss of or increase in appetite; nausea; stomach pain, fullness, or discomfort; vomiting); ***headache***; ***polyuria*** (increased volume of urine and frequency of urination)

Incidence less frequent or rare

Blurred vision and/or changes in accommodation (difficulty in focusing the eyes); ***photosensitivity*** (increased sensitivity of skin to sunlight)

Note: *Blurred vision and/or changes in accommodation* may be more pronounced when therapy is initiated and are thought to be caused by changes in blood glucose concentration.

Patient Consultation

As an aid to patient consultation, refer to *Advice for the Patient, Antidiabetic Agents, Sulfonylurea (Systemic)*.

In providing consultation, consider emphasizing the following selected information (» = major clinical significance):

Before using this medication

» Conditions affecting use, especially:

Hypersensitivity to sulfonylurea antidiabetic agents, sulfonamides, or thiazide diuretics

Pregnancy—Chlorpropamide crosses the placenta. Sulfonylureas should not be used during pregnancy, especially when insulin is available. In the rare cases that a sulfonylurea is used, chlorpropamide and glipizide should be discontinued at least 1 month before delivery date and other sulfonylureas stopped at least 2 weeks before delivery date. Glimepiride should not be used during pregnancy. Importance of controlling and monitoring blood glucose concentrations before, during, and after pregnancy by adjusting antidiabetic agent dosing in order to help prevent maternal and fetal problems, including fetal macrosomnia, anomalies, and hyperglycemia

Breast-feeding—Chlorpropamide and tolbutamide are distributed into human breast milk, and their effect on breast-fed infants is not known; some physicians believe that tolbutamide is compatible with breast-feeding; it is not known whether other sulfonylureas are distributed into human breast milk. Glimepiride should be discontinued in nursing mothers.

Use in the elderly—The elderly may be more susceptible to hypoglycemia, especially when treated with glyburide and chlorpropamide or when other hypoglycemia-causing agents are concurrently being prescribed along with sulfonylureas; also, the elderly have a higher risk of developing hyponatremia or a reversible syndrome of inappropriate antidiuretic hormone when treated with chlorpropamide

Other medications, especially alcohol; asparaginase; azole antifungals; beta-adrenergic blocking agents; chloramphenicol; cimetidine; corticosteroids; coumarin- or indandione-derivative anticoagulants; cyclosporine; fluoroquinolones; guanethidine; lithium; MAO inhibitors including furazolidone, procarbazine, and selegiline; octreotide; pentamidine; quinidine; quinine; ranitidine; salicylates, large doses; or thiazide diuretics

Other medical problems, especially conditions causing delayed food absorption including gastroparesis, intestinal obstruction, prolonged vomiting, or severe diarrhea; conditions that cause severe blood glucose fluctuations or rapidly change insulin needs including diabetic coma, diabetic ketoacidosis, hyperosmolar nonketotic coma, major surgery, severe burns, severe trauma, or significant acidosis; hyperglycemia-causing conditions including female hormone changes, high fever, hyperadrenalism that is not optimally controlled, psychological stress, or severe infection; hypoglycemia-causing conditions including adrenal or pituitary insufficiency that is not optimally controlled, debilitated physical condition, hepatic disease, hyperthyroidism that is not optimally controlled, malnutrition; or renal function impairment; in addition, for chlorpropamide or tolbutamide, congestive heart failure

Proper use of this medication

» Compliance with therapy, including not taking more or less medication than directed

» Importance of adherence to recommended regimens for diet, exercise, glucose monitoring, and sick-day management

For extended-release glipizide tablets

Swallowing tablets whole without breaking, crushing, or chewing (Patient may notice empty shell in stool left over after medication is absorbed)

» Proper dosing

Missed dose: Taking as soon as possible; not taking if almost time for next dose; not doubling doses

» Proper storage

Precautions while using this medication

» Regular visits to physician to check progress

» *Carefully following special instructions of health care team:*

Discussing use of alcohol and tobacco

Not taking other medications unless discussed with physician

Getting counseling for family members to help them assist the patient with diabetes; also, special counseling for pregnancy planning and contraception

Making travel plans to include preparedness for diabetic emergencies and keeping meal times near the usual times with changing time zones

Wearing sunscreen and protective clothing to protect against sunburn and photosensitivity

» Preparing for and understanding what to do in case of an emergency by carrying medical history and current medication list, wearing medical identification, keeping quick-acting sugar and nonexpired glucagon kit and needles close by

» Recognizing symptoms of hypoglycemia: anxiety; behavior change similar to drunkenness; blurred vision; cold sweats; confusion; cool, pale skin; difficulty in concentrating; drowsiness; excessive hunger; fast heartbeat; headache; nausea; nervousness; nightmares; restless sleep; shakiness; slurred speech; and unusual tiredness and weakness

» Recognizing what brings on symptoms of hypoglycemia, such as delaying or missing a meal or snack, exercising more than usual, drinking significant amounts of alcohol, taking certain medications, using too much antidiabetic medication, such as insulin or sulfonylurea, or illness, including vomiting or diarrhea

» Knowing what to do if symptoms of hypoglycemia occur, such as eating glucose tablets or gel, corn syrup, honey, or sugar cubes; or drinking fruit juice, nondiet soft drink, or sugar dissolved in water; also, eating small snack, such as crackers or half sandwich, when scheduled meal is longer than 1 hour away; not eating foods high in fat, such as chocolate, since fat slows gastric emptying; or using glucagon injection if the patient becomes unconscious

» Recognizing symptoms of hyperglycemia and ketoacidosis: blurred vision; drowsiness; dry mouth; flushed, dry skin; fruit-like breath odor; increased urination (frequency and volume); ketones in urine; loss of appetite; stomachache, nausea, or vomiting; tiredness; troubled breathing (rapid and deep); unconsciousness; and unusual thirst

» Recognizing what brings on symptoms of hyperglycemia, such as diarrhea, fever, or infection; not taking enough or skipping a dose of insulin; exercising less than usual; or overeating or not following meal plan

» Knowing what to do if symptoms of hyperglycemia occur, such as checking blood glucose and contacting a member of the health care team

Side/adverse effects

Signs of potential side effects, especially mild or severe hypoglycemia; weight gain; erythema multiforme or exfoliative dermatitis; aplastic or hemolytic anemia; blood dyscrasias; cholestasis, cholestatic jaundice, hepatic function impairment, hepatic porphyria, hepatitis, or porphyria cutanea tarda; eosinophilia; and thrombocytopenia; in addition, for chlorpropamide or, rarely, tolbutamide—dilutional hyponatremia, hypo-osmolality, or syndrome of inappropriate antidiuretic hormone (SIADH)

General Dosing Information

There is little evidence that one sulfonylurea is more effective in lowering blood glucose than another, especially between first and second generation sulfonylureas. Some pharmacokinetic differences between sulfonylureas may result in small qualitative and temporal differences that may make one medication more suitable in a certain situation. For instance, glyburide (possibly due to its longer duration of action and effect on hepatic glucose suppression) and gliclazide exert a better effect on fasting blood glucose than does glipizide, which results in lowered nocturnal and morning blood glucose; glipizide has greater postprandial insulin release and lower postprandial blood glucose concentrations. Overall, the resulting reduction in blood glucose concentration is similar between sulfonylureas.

Conservative initial and maintenance doses may be required in patients with medical problems that make them more sensitive to effects of sulfonylureas.

Secondary failure of oral antidiabetic therapy may occur in certain patients. This may be due to increasing severity of diabetes or to diminished responsiveness to the medication.

When adding a sulfonylurea to an insulin regimen that is poorly controlled with insulin alone, the insulin dose at times may be reduced by 25 to 50%.

When adding a sulfonylurea to maximum doses of metformin or metformin to maximum doses of a sulfonylurea, even if primary or secondary failure of a sulfonylurea has occurred, the new medication should be added gradually and titrated to the lowest effective dose. Both agents should be discontinued and insulin should be initiated if the patient does not respond to maximum doses within 3 months (or less, depending on clinician's decision). No transition time is needed when transferring between sulfonylureas, metformin, or insulin, except with chlorpropamide, which may require a 2-week transition because of chlorpropamide's prolonged duration of action.

Diet/Nutrition

Absorption of chlorpropamide or glipizide may be delayed if the medication is ingested with food; glipizide should be taken 30 minutes before a meal. Gliclazide may be taken 30 minutes before a meal or with a meal but not after a meal. Glimepiride should be taken with breakfast or the first main meal. Nonmicronized glyburide should not be taken with a diet high in fat; nonmicronized glyburide does not have any other dietary restrictions.

For treatment of adverse effects and/or overdose

Recommended treatment consists of the following:

For mild to moderate hypoglycemia—

• Treating with immediate ingestion of a source of sugar, such as glucose gel, glucose tablets, fruit juice, corn syrup, nondiet soft drinks, honey, sugar cubes, or table sugar dissolved in water. A frequently used source of sugar is a glassful of orange juice.

• Documenting blood glucose and rechecking in 15 minutes.
• Counseling patient to seek medical assistance promptly.
• Closely monitoring for at least 3 to 5 days patients who develop hypoglycemia during use of chlorpropamide.

Note: Glucose administration is the basis for treatment of hypoglycemia; however, an exposure to sudden or excessive hyperglycemia caused by an injection of hypertonic glucose solution may further stimulate the sulfonylurea-primed pancreas to release more insulin, worsening the hypoglycemia.

For severe hypoglycemia or acute overdose, including coma—
• Counseling patient to obtain emergency medical assistance immediately
• Immediately treating with 50 mL of 50% dextrose injection given intravenously to stabilize the patient. Then, administering a continuous infusion of 5 to 10% dextrose injection to maintain slight hyperglycemia (approximately 100 mg/dL blood glucose concentration) for up to 12 days. The intravenous glucose therapy should not be terminated suddenly. A central venous line for long-term use (24 to 48 hours) in cases of chlorpropamide overdose may be required. (Oral glucose cannot be relied upon to maintain euglycemia because 60% of an oral glucose dose is stored as hepatic glycogen with only 15% left for brain utilization and 15% for insulin-dependent tissues even though 75% of oral glucose is absorbed after 150 to 180 minutes.)
• Glucagon, 1 to 2 mg administered intramuscularly, is useful for fast onset of action to mobilize hepatic glucose stores but may be ineffective or variable in its effect if glycogen stores are depleted and must follow the use of glucose.
• Diazoxide therapy (200 mg orally every 4 hours or 300 mg intravenously over a 30-minute period every 4 hours) can be used for patients who do not respond to glucose therapy or for patients in a coma as an aid to glucose infusion to reduce hypoglycemia; the patient should be monitored for sodium concentration and for hypotension.
• Emesis can be induced with ipecac syrup if sulfonylurea overdose is recent (within the past 30 minutes) and the patient is alert, has an intact gag reflex, and is not obtunded or convulsing. Otherwise, gastric lavage after endotracheal tube placement is required.
• Gastric removal by administration of repeated doses of oral activated charcoal with appropriate cathartic, although the usefulness of this has not been established.
• Alkalinization of urine with sodium bicarbonate to pH of 8 can eliminate 80% of chlorpropamide over 24 hours, but is not useful with other sulfonylureas. Caution with concurrent use with diazoxide treatment because of possible significant sodium retention.
• Monitoring vital signs, arterial blood gases, blood glucose, and serum electrolytes (especially calcium, potassium, and sodium) as required. Initially, blood glucose concentrations should be monitored as frequently as every 1 to 3 hours. Blood urea nitrogen and serum creatinine concentrations should also be obtained.
• Cerebral edema—Managing with mannitol and dexamethasone.
• Hypokalemia—Managing with potassium supplements.
• Hospitalization for 6 to 91 hours (mean, 24 hours) because the hypoglycemia may be recurrent and prolonged; for chlorpropamide this period may be extended to 3 to 5 days or longer.
• Other supportive measures should also be employed as needed.

ACETOHEXAMIDE

Summary of Differences

Pharmacology/pharmacokinetics:
Protein binding—Very high, ionic.
Serum half-life—Parent 1.3 hours; metabolite 6 hours.
Duration of action—8 to 24 hours.
Active metabolite.

Precautions:
Laboratory value alterations—Reduces serum uric acid concentration.
Medical considerations/contraindications—Not recommended for use in patients with renal function impairment.

Additional Dosing Information

See also *General Dosing Information.*

When patients are transferred to acetohexamide from another sulfonylurea antidiabetic medication (with the exception of chlorpropamide), no transition period is required. When transferring patients from chlorpropamide, caution should be exercised during the first 1 to 2 weeks because of the prolonged retention of chlorpropamide in the body.

During conversion from insulin therapy to acetohexamide therapy, no gradual dosage adjustment usually is required for patients using less than 20 USP Units of insulin daily. For patients using 20 or more USP Units daily, a 25 to 30% reduction in insulin every day or every second day with gradual dosage adjustment is advisable. Hospitalization for some patients on a higher insulin dosage may be required for uneventful conversion.

Oral Dosage Forms

ACETOHEXAMIDE TABLETS USP

Usual adult dose

Antidiabetic—
Initial: Oral, 250 mg once a day, the dosage being increased by 250 or 500 mg every five to seven days as needed.
Maintenance: Oral, 250 to 1000 mg once a day before breakfast or 1000 to 1500 mg divided into two doses taken before breakfast and evening meals.

Usual adult prescribing limits

1.5 grams daily.

Usual pediatric dose

Safety and efficacy have not been established.

Usual geriatric dose

See *Usual adult dose.*

Note: If an elderly patient tends toward hypoglycemia during the first twenty-four hours after an initial dose of 250 mg at breakfast, the dose should be reduced or the medication discontinued.

Strength(s) usually available

U.S.—
250 mg (Rx) [*Dymelor* (scored); GENERIC].
500 mg (Rx) [*Dymelor* (scored); GENERIC].

Canada—
500 mg (Rx) [*Dimelor* (scored)].

Packaging and storage

Store below 40 °C (104 °F), preferably between 15 and 30 °C (59 and 86 °F), unless otherwise specified by manufacturer. Store in a well-closed container.

Auxiliary labeling

• Avoid alcoholic beverages.
• Do not take other medicines without advice from your doctor.
• Avoid too much sun.

CHLORPROPAMIDE

Summary of Differences

Indications:
Also indicated in the treatment of central diabetes insipidus.

Pharmacology/pharmacokinetics:
Other actions/effects—Antidiuretic effect.
Protein binding—Very high, ionic.
Half-life, serum—36 hours.

Precautions:
Pregnancy—Crosses the placenta.
Breast-feeding—Distributed into breast milk.
Geriatrics—Use is generally avoided.
Drug interactions and/or related problems—Risk of disulfiram-like reaction with alcohol is higher with chlorpropamide than with other sulfonylureas.
Medical considerations/contraindications—Not recommended for use in patients with renal function impairment or congestive heart failure.

Side/adverse effects:
Potential for serious adverse effects (e.g., prolonged hypoglycemia and severe hyponatremia) because of prolonged action of chlorpropamide, especially with predisposed individuals.

Additional Dosing Information

See also *General Dosing Information.*

When patients are transferred to chlorpropamide from another sulfonylurea, no transition period is required. When transferring patients from chlorpropamide, caution should be exercised during the first 1 to 2 weeks because of the prolonged retention of chlorpropamide in the body.

During conversion from insulin therapy to chlorpropamide therapy, no gradual dosage adjustment usually is required for patients using less than 40 USP Units of insulin daily. For patients using 40 USP Units or more daily, a 50% reduction in insulin the first few days is advisable. Hospitalization for some patients on a higher insulin dosage may be required for uneventful conversion.

Oral Dosage Forms

Note: Bracketed uses in the *Dosage Forms* section refer to categories of use and/or indications that are not included in U.S. product labeling.

CHLORPROPAMIDE TABLETS USP

Usual adult dose

Antidiabetic—

Initial: Oral, 250 mg once a day, the dosage being changed by 50 to 125 mg every three to five days if needed.

Maintenance: Oral, 100 to 500 mg a day as a single dose.

[Antidiuretic][1]—

Oral, 100 to 250 mg as a single dose daily, the dosage being adjusted at two- or three-day intervals as needed and tolerated.

Note: Occasionally, divided doses are administered, usually twice a day before the morning and evening meals, to improve gastrointestinal tolerance.

Usual adult prescribing limits

Antidiabetic—

750 mg per day.

[Antidiuretic][1]—

500 mg per day.

Usual pediatric dose

Safety and efficacy have not been established.

Usual geriatric dose

Antidiabetic—

Oral, initially 100 to 125 mg once a day, the dosage being increased by 50 to 125 mg at three- to five-day intervals as needed.

Strength(s) usually available

U.S.—

100 mg (Rx) [*Diabinese* (scored); GENERIC (may be scored)].

250 mg (Rx) [*Diabinese* (scored); GENERIC (may be scored)].

Canada—

100 mg (Rx) [*Apo-Chlorpropamide* (scored); *Diabinese* (scored); GENERIC].

250 mg (Rx) [*Apo-Chlorpropamide* (scored); *Diabinese* (scored); *Novo-Propamide* (scored); GENERIC].

Packaging and storage

Store below 40 °C (104 °F), preferably between 15 and 30 °C (59 and 86 °F), unless otherwise specified by manufacturer. Store in a well-closed container.

Auxiliary labeling

- Avoid alcoholic beverages.
- Do not take other medicines without advice from your doctor.
- Avoid too much sun.

[1]Not included in Canadian product labeling.

GLICLAZIDE

Summary of Differences

Pharmacology/pharmacokinetics:

Other actions/effects—Protective activity for some cardiac arrhythmias; also, reduces platelet adhesiveness and aggregation and has fibrinolytic activity.

Protein binding—Very high, nonionic.

Serum half-life—Approximately 10.4 hours.

Duration of action—Approximately 24 hours.

Precautions:

Drug interactions and/or related problems—Displacement from plasma proteins by other medications is less likely.

Medical considerations/contraindications—May be preferred for those patients with moderate renal function impairment; should not be used with severe renal failure.

Side/adverse effects:

Less weight gain when compared to other sulfonylureas.

Additional Dosing Information

See also *General Dosing Information.*

When patients are transferred to gliclazide from another sulfonylurea antidiabetic medication (with the exception of chlorpropamide), no transition period is required. When transferring patients from chlorpropamide, caution should be exercised during the first 1 to 2 weeks because of the prolonged retention of chlorpropamide in the body.

During conversion from insulin therapy to gliclazide therapy, no gradual dosage adjustment usually is required for patients using less than 20 USP Units of insulin daily. For patients using 20 or more USP Units daily, a 25 to 30% reduction in insulin every day or every second day with gradual dosage adjustment is advisable. Hospitalization for some patients on a higher insulin dosage may be required for uneventful conversion.

Oral Dosage Forms

GLICLAZIDE TABLETS

Usual adult dose

Antidiabetic—

Initial: Oral, 160 mg two times a day with meals.

Maintenance: Oral, 80 to 320 mg a day with meals.

Usual adult prescribing limits

320 mg daily.

Usual pediatric dose

Safety and efficacy have not been established.

Usual geriatric dose

See *Usual adult dose.*

Strength(s) usually available

U.S.—

Not commercially available.

Canada—

80 mg (Rx) [*Diamicron* (quad-scored)].

Packaging and storage

Store below 40 °C (104 °F), preferably between 15 and 30 °C (59 and 86 °F), in a well-closed container, unless otherwise specified by manufacturer.

Auxiliary labeling

- Avoid alcoholic beverages.
- Do not take other medicines without advice from your doctor.
- Avoid too much sun.

GLIMEPIRIDE

Summary of Differences

Pharmacology/pharmacokinetics:

Protein binding—Very high.

Serum half-life—5 and 9.2 hours following single and multiple doses, respectively.

Precautions:

Breast-feeding—Distributed into the milk of rats in significant concentrations. Offspring of rats exposed to high concentrations during pregnancy developed skeletal abnormalities after nursing. Not recommended for use by nursing mothers.

Additional Dosing Information

See also *General Dosing Information.*

Secondary failure may be treated by using insulin in combination with glimepiride. The fasting glucose concentration for instituting combination therapy is > 150 mg per dL in plasma or serum. Periodic adjustments in insulin dosage may be necessary as guided by glucose and glycosylated hemoglobin concentrations. Combination insulin-glimepiride therapy may increase the potential for development of hypoglycemia.

When patients are transferred to glimepiride from another sulfonylurea antidiabetic medication (with the exception of chlorpropamide), no transition period is required. When transferring patients from chlorpropamide, caution should be exercised during the first 1 to 2 weeks because of the prolonged retention of chlorpropamide in the body.

Oral Dosage Forms

GLIMEPIRIDE TABLETS

Usual adult dose

Antidiabetic—

Monotherapy—

Initial: Oral, 1 to 2 mg once a day with breakfast or the first main meal.

Note: Patients with renal function impairment should receive an initial dose of 1 mg once a day.

Maintenance: Oral, 1 to 4 mg once a day. After reaching a dose of 2 mg, increases in dosage should be made in increments of up to 2 mg every one to two weeks based on blood glucose response.

Combination therapy with insulin—
Oral, 8 mg once a day with breakfast or the first main meal.

Combination therapy with metformin—
Oral, 8 mg once a day with breakfast or the first main meal.

Note: Attempts should be made to identify the minimum effective dose of each drug.

Usual adult prescribing limits
8 mg once a day.

Usual pediatric dose
Safety and efficacy have not been established.

Usual geriatric dose
See *Usual adult dose.*

Note: Geriatric patients should receive an initial dose of 1 mg once a day.

Strength(s) usually available
U.S.—
1 mg (Rx) [*Amaryl* (scored)].
2 mg (Rx) [*Amaryl* (scored)].
4 mg (Rx) [*Amaryl* (scored)].
Canada—
Not commercially available.

Packaging and storage
Store between 15 and 30 °C (59 and 86 °F) in a well-closed container, unless otherwise specified by manufacturer.

Auxiliary labeling
- Avoid alcoholic beverages.
- Do not take other medicines without advice from your doctor.

GLIPIZIDE

Summary of Differences

Pharmacology/pharmacokinetics:
Other actions/effects—Has mild diuretic effect.
Protein binding—Very high, nonionic.
Serum half-life—2 to 4 hours.
Duration of action—12 to 24 hours.
Precautions:
Drug interactions and/or related problems—
Displacement from plasma proteins by other medications is less likely than with ionic sulfonylureas.

Additional Dosing Information

See also *General Dosing Information.*

When patients are transferred to glipizide from another sulfonylurea antidiabetic medication (with the exception of chlorpropamide), no transition period is required. When transferring patients from chlorpropamide, caution should be exercised during the first 1 to 2 weeks because of the prolonged retention of chlorpropamide in the body.

During conversion from insulin therapy to glipizide therapy, no gradual dosage adjustment usually is required for patients using less than 20 USP Units of insulin daily. For patients using 20 or more USP Units daily, a 50% reduction of insulin the first day, with gradual dosage adjustments of glipizide as needed, is desirable. Hospitalization for some patients on a higher insulin dosage may be required for uneventful conversion.

Oral Dosage Forms

GLIPIZIDE TABLETS USP

Usual adult dose
Antidiabetic—
Initial: Oral, 5 mg once a day thirty minutes before breakfast, with dosage being changed by 2.5 to 5 mg every several days as needed.
Maintenance: Oral, up to 40 mg a day thirty minutes before meals. Single daily doses are adequate with 15 mg or less but may be divided when necessary, while larger doses should be divided into two doses a day and taken thirty minutes before meals.

Usual adult prescribing limits
40 mg daily.

Usual pediatric dose
Safety and efficacy have not been established.

Usual geriatric dose
Antidiabetic—
Initial: Oral, 2.5 mg per day thirty minutes before breakfast, with dosage being changed by 2.5 to 5 mg every several days as needed.
Maintenance: See *Usual adult dose.*

Strength(s) usually available
U.S.—
5 mg (Rx) [*Glucotrol* (scored); GENERIC (may be scored)].
10 mg (Rx) [*Glucotrol* (scored); GENERIC (may be scored)].
Canada—
Not commercially available.

Packaging and storage
Store below 40 °C (104 °F), preferably between 15 and 30 °C (59 and 86 °F), unless otherwise specified by manufacturer. Store in a tight container.

Auxiliary labeling
- Avoid alcoholic beverages.
- Do not take other medicines without advice from your doctor.
- Avoid too much sun.
- Take this medication on an empty stomach, 30 minutes before meals.

GLIPIZIDE EXTENDED-RELEASE TABLETS

Usual adult dose
Antidiabetic—
Initial: Oral, 5 mg once daily with breakfast; dosage is increased by 5 mg based on resulting hemoglobin A_{1c} measurements taken three months later or, less commonly, based on two or more consecutive fasting blood glucose measurements taken seven days apart.
Maintenance: Oral, 5 to 10 mg once a day with breakfast.

Note: In most cases, if no improvement of hemoglobin A_{1c} is noted after three months of use of a higher dose, the previous dose should be resumed.

Usual adult prescribing limits
20 mg once a day.

Usual pediatric dose
Safety and efficacy have not been established.

Usual geriatric dose
See *Usual adult dose.*

Note: When adjusting the dose in the elderly, consider that steady-state concentrations for glipizide extended-release tablets may be delayed by approximately one or two days as compared to other age groups.

Strength(s) usually available
U.S.—
Note: Although similar in appearance to a conventional tablet, *Glucotrol XL* actually is a specially formulated gastrointestinal system (GITS) consisting of a semipermeable membrane surrounding an osmotically active drug core, which is designed to release glipizide at a constant rate over twenty-four hours; following drug release, the system is eliminated in the feces as an insoluble shell.
5 mg (Rx) [*Glucotrol XL*].
10 mg (Rx) [*Glucotrol XL*].
Canada—
Not commercially available.

Packaging and storage
Store below 40 °C (104 °F), preferably between 15 and 30 °C (59 and 86 °F), in a tight container, unless otherwise specified by manufacturer.

Auxiliary labeling
- Swallow tablet whole. Do not break, crush, or chew.
- Avoid alcoholic beverages.
- Do not take other medicines without advice from your doctor.
- Avoid too much sun.

GLYBURIDE

Summary of Differences

Pharmacology/pharmacokinetics:
Other actions/effects—Protective activity for some cardiac arrhythmias; also, has mild diuretic activity.
Protein binding—Very high, nonionic.
Half-life—10 hours.
Duration of action—24 hours.
Elimination—
Biliary: 50%.
Renal: 50%.
Precautions:
Geriatrics—
Use is generally avoided.
Drug interactions and/or related problems—
Disulfiram-type reaction with concurrent alcohol use less likely with glyburide than with other antidiabetics. Also, displacement from plasma proteins by other medications is less likely.

Side/adverse effects:
Fatal hypoglycemia occurs more often with glyburide than with chlorpropamide; potential for serious adverse effect because of prolonged action of glyburide, especially with predisposed individuals.

Additional Dosing Information

See also *General Dosing Information.*

When patients are transferred to glyburide from another sulfonylurea antidiabetic medication (with the exception of chlorpropamide), no transition period is required. When transferring patients from chlorpropamide, caution should be exercised during the first 1 to 2 weeks because of the prolonged retention of chlorpropamide in the body and subsequent overlapping of drug effects that could cause hypoglycemia.

During conversion from insulin therapy to glyburide therapy, no gradual dosage adjustment usually is required for patients using less than 40 USP Units of insulin daily. Patients requiring more than 40 USP Units should receive a 50% reduction of insulin the first day with initiation of 3 mg of micronized glyburide or 5 mg of nonmicronized glyburide as a single dose and gradual dosage adjustments of glyburide as needed. Hospitalization for some patients on a higher insulin dosage may be required for uneventful conversion.

Bioequivalence information

Micronized glyburide cannot be substituted for nonmicronized glyburide. Bioavailability studies have demonstrated that micronized glyburide is not bioequivalent to glyburide (nonmicronized); retitration is necessary if patients are transferred.

Micronized glyburide has an AB rating but may not be deemed bioequivalent according to some state formularies when the scored tablet is divided.

Glyburide (nonmicronized) has a BX rating and is not substitutable. However, some specific products are manufactured under the same new drug application (NDA) and may be deemed bioequivalent by some state formularies:

• Pharmacia & Upjohn's product, *Micronase*, and Greenstone's generic glyburide (nonmicronized) are manufactured at Pharmacia & Upjohn under the same NDA; Greenstone's generic product is distributed by Geneva and Greenstone.

• Aventis Pharmaceuticals produces *DiaBeta* and its own generic, which is distributed by Copley, under the same NDA.

• The products manufactured under one NDA cannot be substituted for those products produced under the other NDA; the products are not bioequivalent nor substitutable. The FDA Orange Book will list an NDA only once with the original manufacturer that applied for the product; hence, the Orange Book does not address multiple manufacturers under one NDA. Pharmacists should verify the regulations and formularies of their state or verify with the physician before substituting a BX-rated product under one NDA for a similar product under another.

Oral Dosage Forms

GLYBURIDE TABLETS USP

Note: Glyburide (nonmicronized) has an FDA BX rating denoting that data are insufficient to determine therapeutic equivalence. However, glyburide produced and distributed by the U.S. manufacturer Hoescht Marion Roussel and also distributed by Copley may be substitutable by some state pharmacy formularies because they use the same NDA. Similarly, glyburide distributed by the U.S. manufacturers Greenstone and Pharmacia & Upjohn share the same NDA. As long as glyburide holds a BX rating, substitution of products of different NDAs is not permissible without the physician's permission.

In contrast, glyburide (micronized) has an AB rating, denoting that bioequivalence for many state formularies has been resolved; however, some state formularies have deemed the AB-rated generic nonsubstitutable if a scored tablet is divided. State formularies should be checked before substitution is made with this type of product.

Usual adult dose

Antidiabetic—
Initial: Oral, 2.5 to 5 mg once a day with breakfast or the first main meal, with dosage changes being made by no more than 2.5 mg at weekly intervals if needed. Patients more sensitive to hypoglycemia may need 1.25 mg a day.
Maintenance: Oral, 1.25 to 20 mg a day, of which doses up to 10 mg are usually taken as a single dose with breakfast or the first main meal, while doses over 10 mg are usually divided into two daily doses with meals.

Usual adult prescribing limits

20 mg daily.

Usual pediatric dose

Safety and efficacy have not been established.

Usual geriatric dose

Antidiabetic—
Initial: Oral, 1.25 to 2.5 mg a day with breakfast, with dosage changes being made by no more than 2.5 mg at weekly intervals if needed.
Maintenance: See *Usual adult dose.*
Note: This dose should also be used in patients with medical problems that make them more sensitive to the effects of glyburide.

Strength(s) usually available

U.S.—
1.25 mg (Rx) [*DiaBeta* (scored); *Micronase* (scored); GENERIC (may be scored)].
2.5 mg (Rx) [*DiaBeta* (scored); *Micronase* (scored); GENERIC (may be scored)].
5 mg (Rx) [*DiaBeta* (scored); *Micronase* (scored); GENERIC (may be scored)].

Canada—
2.5 mg (Rx) [*Albert Glyburide* (scored); *Apo-Glyburide* (scored); *DiaBeta* (scored); *Euglucon* (scored); *Gen-Glybe* (scored); *Med Glybe; Novo-Glyburide* (scored); *Nu-Glyburide* (scored)].
5 mg (Rx) [*Albert Glyburide* (scored); *Apo-Glyburide* (scored); *DiaBeta* (scored); *Euglucon* (scored); *Gen-Glybe* (scored); *Med Glybe; Novo-Glyburide* (scored); *Nu-Glyburide* (scored)].

Packaging and storage

Store below 40 °C (104 °F), preferably between 15 and 30 °C (59 and 86 °F), unless otherwise specified by manufacturer. Store in a well-closed container.

Auxiliary labeling

• Avoid alcoholic beverages.
• Do not take other medicines without advice from your doctor.
• Avoid too much sun.

GLYBURIDE TABLETS (MICRONIZED)

Note: Micronized glyburide has an AB rating. However, some state formularies may not consider certain generic products bioequivalent when scored tablets are divided; state formularies should be checked before substituting one product for another.

Micronized glyburide cannot be substituted for nonmicronized glyburide. Bioavailability studies have demonstrated that micronized glyburide is not bioequivalent to glyburide (nonmicronized); retitration is necessary if patients are transferred.

Usual adult dose

Antidiabetic—
Initial: Oral, 1.5 to 3 mg once a day with breakfast or the first main meal. Some patients sensitive to glyburide's effects may need to be started on 0.75 mg a day. Dose titration should be made with changes of no more than 1.5 mg at weekly increments.
Maintenance: Oral, 0.75 to 12 mg a day; doses up to 6 mg are usually taken as a single dose with breakfast or the first main meal, while doses over 6 mg are usually taken as divided doses with meals.

Usual adult prescribing limits

12 mg daily.

Usual pediatric dose

Safety and efficacy have not been established.

Usual geriatric dose

Antidiabetic—
Initial: Oral, 0.75 to 3 mg per day with breakfast or the first main meal, with dosage being changed by no more than 1.5 mg at weekly increments.
Maintenance: See *Usual adult dose.*

Strength(s) usually available

U.S.—
Note: *Glynase PresTab* is formulated to divide easily in even halves by pressing gently on the scored area of the tablet.
1.5 mg (Rx) [*Glynase PresTab* (scored); GENERIC (may be scored)].
3 mg (Rx) [*Glynase PresTab* (scored); GENERIC (may be scored)].
4.5 mg (Rx) [GENERIC (may be scored)].
6 mg (Rx) [*Glynase PresTab* (scored); GENERIC].

Canada—
Not commercially available.

Packaging and storage

Store below 40 °C (104 °F), preferably between 15 and 30 °C (59 and 86 °F), in a well-closed container, unless otherwise specified by manufacturer.

Auxiliary labeling
- Avoid alcoholic beverages.
- Do not take other medicines without advice from your doctor.
- Avoid too much sun.

TOLAZAMIDE

Summary of Differences

Pharmacology/pharmacokinetics:
Other actions/effects—Has mild diuretic activity.
Protein binding—Very high, ionic.
Serum half-life—7 hours.
Duration of action—10 or 20 hours.
Precautions:
Drug interactions and/or related problems—Displacement from plasma proteins by other medications is more likely than with nonionic sulfonylureas.
Medical considerations/contraindications—Tolazamide may accumulate in patients with creatinine clearance less than 30 mL per minute (0.5 mL/second).

Additional Dosing Information

See also *General Dosing Information.*

When patients are transferred to tolazamide from another sulfonylurea antidiabetic medication (with the exception of chlorpropamide), no transition period is required. When transferring patients from chlorpropamide, caution should be exercised during the first 1 to 2 weeks because of the prolonged retention of chlorpropamide in the body.

During conversion from insulin therapy to tolazamide therapy, no gradual dosage adjustment usually is required for patients using less than 40 USP Units of insulin daily. Patients requiring 40 or more USP Units daily should receive a 50% reduction of insulin during the first few days, with gradual dosage adjustment of tolazamide as needed. Hospitalization for some patients on a higher insulin dosage may be required for uneventful conversion.

Oral Dosage Forms

TOLAZAMIDE TABLETS USP

Usual adult dose
Antidiabetic—
Initial: Oral, 100 to 250 mg once a day with breakfast or the first main meal, with dosage being changed by 100 to 250 mg at weekly intervals as needed.
Maintenance: Oral, 250 to 500 mg a day with breakfast or the first main meal; some patients may need less (100 mg a day) or more (up to 1000 mg a day). Doses greater than 500 mg should be divided and given two times a day with meals.

Usual adult prescribing limits
1 gram daily.

Usual pediatric dose
Safety and efficacy have not been established.

Usual geriatric dose
Antidiabetic—
Initial: Oral, 100 mg once a day in the morning with breakfast or the first main meal, with the dose being changed by 100 to 250 mg at weekly intervals as needed.
Note: Lower initial doses may be required in patients with medical problems that make them more sensitive to the effects of tolazamide.
Maintenance: See *Usual adult dose.*

Strength(s) usually available
U.S.—
100 mg (Rx) [*Tolinase* (scored); GENERIC (may be scored)].
250 mg (Rx) [*Tolinase* (scored); GENERIC (may be scored)].
500 mg (Rx) [*Tolinase* (scored); GENERIC (may be scored)].
Canada—
Not commercially available.

Packaging and storage
Store below 40 °C (104 °F), preferably between 15 and 30 °C (59 and 86 °F), unless otherwise specified by manufacturer. Store in a tight container.

Auxiliary labeling
- Avoid alcoholic beverages.
- Do not take other medicines without advice from your doctor.
- Avoid too much sun.

TOLBUTAMIDE

Summary of Differences

Pharmacology/pharmacokinetics:
Other actions/effects—Has mild antidiuretic activity.
Protein binding—Very high, ionic.
Serum half-life—4.5 to 6.5 hours.
Duration of action—6 to 12 hours.
Precautions:
Drug interactions and/or related problems—
Disulfiram-type reaction with concurrent alcohol use less likely with tolbutamide than with other antidiabetics. Also, displacement from plasma proteins by other medications is more likely than with nonionic sulfonylureas.
Metabolism of tolbutamide inhibited by sulfinpyrazone and phenylbutazone.
Laboratory value alterations—
Tolbutamide interferes with thyroidal uptake of I 123 and I 131.
Medical considerations/contraindications—
May be preferred for those patients with moderate renal function impairment but should be discontinued with renal failure.

Additional Dosing Information

See also *General Dosing Information.*

When patients are transferred to tolbutamide from another sulfonylurea antidiabetic medication (with the exception of chlorpropamide), no transition period is required. When transferring patients from chlorpropamide, caution should be exercised during the first 1 to 2 weeks because of the prolonged retention of chlorpropamide in the body.

During conversion from insulin therapy to tolbutamide therapy, no gradual dosage adjustment usually is required for patients using less than 20 USP Units of insulin daily. Patients using 20 to 40 USP Units require a 30 to 50% reduction in insulin the first day with gradual dosage adjustment as needed. Patients requiring more than 40 USP Units should receive a 20% reduction of insulin the first day with gradual dosage adjustment of tolbutamide as needed. Hospitalization for some patients on a higher insulin dosage may be required for uneventful conversion.

Oral Dosage Forms

TOLBUTAMIDE TABLETS USP

Usual adult dose
Antidiabetic—
Initial: Oral, 1000 to 2000 mg a day as single morning or divided doses.
Note: Lower initial doses may be required in patients with medical problems that make them more sensitive to the effects of tolbutamide.
Maintenance: Oral, 250 to 2000 mg a day as single morning or divided doses.

Usual adult prescribing limits
3000 mg a day.

Usual pediatric dose
Safety and efficacy have not been established.

Usual geriatric dose
Lower initial dose may be required. See *Usual adult dose.*

Strength(s) usually available
U.S.—
500 mg (Rx) [*Orinase* (scored); GENERIC (may be scored)].
Canada—
500 mg (Rx) [*Apo-Tolbutamide* (scored); *Novo-Butamide* (scored); *Orinase* (scored); GENERIC].
1000 mg (Rx) [*Orinase* (scored)].

Packaging and storage
Store below 40 °C (104 °F), preferably between 15 and 30 °C (59 and 86 °F), unless otherwise specified by manufacturer. Store in a well-closed container.

Preparation of dosage form
For patients who cannot take oral solids—Tolbutamide tablets may be dissolved in a glass of water and drunk. Additional water should then be added to the glass, stirred, and drunk to make sure all the medication is taken.

Auxiliary labeling
- Avoid alcoholic beverages.
- Do not take other medicines without advice from your doctor.
- Avoid too much sun.

Revised: 10/14/2004

Table 1. Pharmacology/Pharmacokinetics

Drug	V_D (L/kg)	Protein binding* (%)	Biotransformation (%)	Elimination half-life (hrs)	Time to peak (hrs)	Peak serum concentration		Duration of action (hrs)	Elimination (%)
						Concentration per mL	Dose (mg)		
Acetohexamide Hydroxyhexamide‡ (metabolite)	0.21	Very high, 65–90; Ionic	Hepatic, mainly; erythrocytes	1.3† 4.6–6	1.5–2 2–6	47 mcg 60 mcg	1000	8–24	Renal: 71 Fecal: 15
Chlorpropamide	0.09–0.27	Very high, >90; Ionic	Hepatic	36§ (range, 24–48)	2–4	N/A	N/A	24–72	Renal: In 96 hours: Unchanged—6–20 Active and inactive metabolites
Gliclazide	0.2	Very high, 94; Nonionic	Hepatic	10.4	4–6	5 mcg	3	24	Renal: Unchanged—<1 Metabolites, conjugates—60–70 Fecal: Metabolites, conjugates—10–20
Glimepiride	8.8	Very high, > 99.5	Hepatic	5 (following a single dose) 9.2 (following multiple doses)	2–3	N/A	N/A	N/A	Renal: 60 Fecal: 40
Glipizide	0.14–0.16	Very high, 99; Nonionic	Hepatic (no first-pass)	2–4		N/A	N/A		Renal: Unchanged—<10 Metabolites, inactive, and conjugates—80 Fecal: 10
immediate release					1–3			12–24	
extended release					6–12			24	
Glyburide	0.14–0.16	Very high, 99; Nonionic	Hepatic					24	Renal: 50 Metabolites, active—2 weak, short-lived Biliary: 50
Nonmicronized				6–10#	3.4–4.5	87.5 nanograms	5		
Micronized				4#	2.3–3.5	97.2 nanograms	3		
Tolazamide**	N/A	Very high, 94; Ionic	Hepatic	7	3–4			10–20	Renal: 85†† Metabolites, major—5 metabolites (potency 0–70%) Fecal: 7
Tolbutamide**	0.10	Very high, 96; Ionic	Hepatic	4.5–6.5	3–4	N/A		6–12	Renal: 100 Metabolites, inactive—75

*Primarily to albumin.

†Renal impairment prolongs acetohexamide half-life to 30 hours.

‡A primary metabolite for acetohexamide, hydroxyhexamide, accounts for 47 to 60% of dose and is 2.5 times more potent than its parent.

§A randomized crossover study of five phases conducted over a 2- to 3-week period demonstrated that the half-life of chlorpropamide can be affected by the pH of the urine; half-life is 69 ± 26 hours with acidic urine (pH 4.7 to 5.5) and 13 ± 3 hours with basic urine (pH 7.1 to 8.2).

#Micronized glyburide allows greater solubility, faster absorption, and, therefore, faster elimination; it is not bioequivalent to nonmicronized glyburide; micronized glyburide's area under the plasma concentration-time curve (AUC) is 568 ng•hr/mL and nonmicronized glyburide's AUC is 746 ng•hr/mL.

**Tolazamide is approximately 5 to 6.7 times more potent than tolbutamide and equal in potency to chlorpropamide on a milligram-per-milligram basis.

††The majority of a single dose of tolazamide is eliminated in urine within 24 hours and elimination is complete after 5 days. Less active metabolites include carboxytolazamide, hydroxytolazamide, and *p*-toulene sulfonamide.

ANTIDYSKINETICS Systemic

This monograph includes information on the following: 1) Benztropine; 2) Biperiden; 3) Ethopropazine; 4) Procyclidine; 5) Trihexyphenidyl.

INN:
Benztropine—Benzatropine
Ethopropazine—Profenamine

BAN:
Benztropine—Benzatropine
Trihexyphenidyl—Benzhexol

VA CLASSIFICATION (Primary): AU305

Commonly used brand name(s): *Akineton*[2]; *Apo-Benztropine*[1]; *Apo-Trihex*[5]; *Artane*[5]; *Artane Sequels*[5]; *Cogentin*[1]; *Kemadrin*[4]; *PMS Benztropine*[1]; *PMS Procyclidine*[4]; *PMS Trihexyphenidyl*[5]; *Parsidol*[3]; *Parsitan*[3]; *Procyclid*[4]; *Trihexane*[5]; *Trihexy*[5].

Note: For a listing of dosage forms and brand names by country availability, see *Dosage Forms* section(s).

Category

Antidyskinetic.

Indications

Note: Bracketed information in the *Indications* section refers to uses that are not included in U.S. product labeling.

Accepted

Parkinsonism (treatment)—Antidyskinetics are indicated in the treatment of mild cases of postencephalitic, arteriosclerotic, or idiopathic parkinsonism(paralysis agitans) in patients in whom anticholinergic therapy is not contraindicated. Antidyskinetics also are indicated as adjuncts to more potent medications to maximize improvement of symptoms. Procyclidine usually produces a more beneficial effect in conditions of rigidity than in those of tremor.

Extrapyramidal reactions, drug-induced (treatment)—Antidyskinetics are indicated in the control of extrapyramidal disorders(except tardive dyskinesia) due to central nervous system (CNS) drugs such as reserpine, phenothiazines, dibenzoxazepines, thioxanthenes, and butyrophenones. However, concomitant therapy with antipsychotics is not recommended beyond 3 months because extrapyramidal symptoms resulting from antipsychotic therapy usually resolve in 3 to 6 months and because prolonged, routine use of antidyskinetics with antipsychotics may predispose patients to the more serious neurological condition, tardive dyskinesia.

[Athetosis, congenital (treatment)][1] or
[Degeneration, hepatolenticular (treatment)][1]—Ethopropazine is used for the symptomatic treatment of hepatolenticular degeneration and congenital athetosis.

[1]Not included in Canadian product labeling.

Pharmacology/Pharmacokinetics

Physicochemical characteristics

Molecular weight—
Benztropine mesylate: 403.54.
Biperiden hydrochloride: 347.93.
Biperiden lactate: 401.54.
Ethopropazine hydrochloride: 348.93.
Procyclidine hydrochloride: 323.91.
Trihexyphenidyl hydrochloride: 337.93.

Mechanism of action/Effect

Specific mode of action is unknown, but it is thought that these agents partially block central (striatal) cholinergic receptors, thereby helping to balance cholinergic and dopaminergic activity in the basal ganglia; salivation may be decreased, and smooth muscle may be relaxed. Drug-induced extrapyramidal symptoms and those due to parkinsonism may be relieved, but tardive dyskinesia is not alleviated and may be aggravated by anticholinergic effects.

Other actions/effects

Benztropine and ethopropazine also have a slight antihistaminic and local anesthetic effect. Biperiden may have a slight effect on the cardiovascular and respiratory systems. Procyclidine and trihexyphenidyl have a direct antispasmodic effect on smooth muscle. In small doses trihexyphenidyl depresses the CNS, but larger doses may cause cerebral excitation.

Absorption

Well-absorbed from gastrointestinal tract.

Onset of action

Benztropine—
Oral: 1 to 2 hours.
Intramuscular or intravenous: Within a few minutes.
Biperiden—
Intramuscular: Average of 10 to 30 minutes.
Intravenous: Within a few minutes.
Trihexyphenidyl—
Oral: 1 hour.

Duration of action

Benztropine—Oral, intramuscular, or intravenous: 24 hours.

Biperiden—Intravenous: 1 to 8 hours.

Ethopropazine—Oral: 4 hours.

Procyclidine—Oral: 4 hours.

Trihexyphenidyl—Oral: 6 to 12 hours.

Precautions to Consider

Pregnancy/Reproduction

Pregnancy—Problems in humans have not been documented with benztropine, ethopropazine, procyclidine, or trihexyphenidyl.

For biperiden—Studies have not been done with biperiden in humans. Studies have not been done in animals.

FDA Pregnancy Category C.

Breast-feeding

It is not known whether antidyskinetics are distributed into breast milk. However, antidyskinetics may inhibit lactation.

Pediatrics

No information is available on the relationship of age to the effects of antidyskinetics in pediatric patients. However, it is known that pediatric patients exhibit increased sensitivity to other medications with anticholinergic properties.

Geriatrics

Chronic use of antidyskinetics may predispose geriatric patients to glaucoma.

Geriatric patients, especially those with arteriosclerotic changes, may respond to the usual doses of antidyskinetics, ethopropazine and procyclidine in particular, with mental confusion, disorientation, agitation, hallucinations, and psychotic-like symptoms.

Memory may become severely impaired in geriatric patients, especially those who already have memory problems, with the continued use of antidyskinetics since these drugs block the action of acetylcholine, which is responsible for many functions of the brain, including memory functions.

Dental

Prolonged use of antidyskinetics may decrease or inhibit salivary flow, thus contributing to the development of caries, periodontal disease, oral candidiasis, and discomfort.

Drug interactions and/or related problems

The following drug interactions and/or related problems have been selected on the basis of their potential clinical significance (possible mechanism in parentheses where appropriate)—not necessarily inclusive (» = major clinical significance):

Note: Combinations containing any of the following medications, depending on the amount present, may also interact with this medication.

» Alcohol or
» CNS depression-producing medications (See *Appendix II*)
(concurrent use with antidyskinetics may cause increased sedative effects)

Amantadine or
» Anticholinergics or other medications with anticholinergic action (See *Appendix II*) or
Monoamine oxidase (MAO) inhibitors, including furazolidone, procarbazine, and selegiline
(concurrent use may intensify anticholinergic effects of antidyskinetics because of the secondary anticholinergic activities of these medications; patients should be advised to report occurrence of gastrointestinal problems, fever, or heat intolerance promptly since paralytic ileus, hyperthermia, or heat stroke may occur with concurrent therapy)

Antidiarrheals, adsorbent
(simultaneous administration may reduce therapeutic effects of antidyskinetics because of particle adsorption; to avoid this effect, patients should be advised to allow at least 1 or 2 hours between doses of the different medications)

Carbidopa and levodopa or

Levodopa
(concurrent use of these medications with benztropine, procyclidine, or trihexyphenidyl may result in increased efficacy of levodopa; however, concurrent use is not recommended if there is a history of psychosis)

Chlorpromazine
(concurrent use of chlorpromazine with antidyskinetics may increase metabolism of chlorpromazine, resulting in decreased plasma concentration because of reduction in gastrointestinal motility)

Medical considerations/Contraindications

The medical considerations/contraindications included have been selected on the basis of their potential clinical significance (reasons given in parentheses where appropriate)—not necessarily inclusive (» = major clinical significance).

Risk-benefit should be considered when the following medical problems exist:

Cardiac arrhythmias
(increased risk of tachycardia)

» Cardiovascular instability
(increased risk of cardiac arrhythmias)

» Dyskinesia, tardive
(may be aggravated)

Extrapyramidal reactions, such as those resulting from phenothiazines or reserpine, in patients with mental disorders
(mental symptoms may be intensified, precipitating toxic psychosis)

» Glaucoma, angle-closure, or predisposition to
(mydriatic effect resulting in increased intraocular pressure may precipitate an acute attack of angle-closure glaucoma)

» Glaucoma, open-angle
(mydriatic effect may cause a slight increase in intraocular pressure; glaucoma therapy may need to be adjusted)

Hepatic function impairment
(metabolism may be altered)

Hypertension
(may be aggravated)

» Intestinal obstruction, complete, partial or history of
(decreased motility and tone may aggravate or precipitate obstruction)

» Myasthenia gravis
(condition may be aggravated because of inhibition of acetylcholine action)

Prostatic hypertrophy, moderate to severe or
» Urinary retention
(anticholinergic effect of antidyskinetics may precipitate or aggravate urinary retention)

Renal function impairment
(decreased elimination may increase risk of side effects)

Sensitivity to antidyskinetics (history of)

Patient monitoring

The following may be especially important in patient monitoring (other tests may be warranted in some patients, depending on condition; » = major clinical significance):

Intraocular pressure determinations
(recommended at periodic intervals during therapy, especially in patients with angle-closure and open-angle glaucoma)

Side/Adverse Effects

Note: Anticholinergic side effects that may occur with antidyskinetics are rarely severe and either disappear as therapy is continued, or diminish when the dose is reduced.

Anhidrosis and subsequent hyperthermia may occur with antidyskinetics when patients, especially geriatric, chronically ill, and alcoholic, are exposed to high environmental temperatures.

Ethopropazine is a phenothiazine derivative. Although the likelihood of ethopropazine causing such side effects as changes in vision, jaundice, rare hematologic reactions, and electrocardiogram (ECG) abnormalities associated with phenothiazines seems to be minimal, the possibility exists.

The following side/adverse effects have been selected on the basis of their potential clinical significance (possible signs and symptoms in parentheses where appropriate)—not necessarily inclusive:

Those indicating need for medical attention

Incidence rare

Allergic reaction (skin rash); ***confusion***—more frequent in the elderly or with high doses; ***increased intraocular pressure*** (eye pain)

Those indicating need for medical attention only if they continue or are bothersome

Incidence more frequent

Anticholinergic effects, mild (blurred vision; constipation; decreased sweating; difficult or painful urination, especially in older men; drowsiness; dryness of mouth, nose, or throat; increased sensitivity of eyes to light; nausea or vomiting)

Incidence less frequent or rare

False sense of well-being—especially in the elderly or with high doses; ***headache; loss of memory***—especially in the elderly; ***muscle cramps; nervousness; numbness or weakness in hands or feet; orthostatic hypotension*** (dizziness or lightheadedness when getting up from a lying or sitting position); ***soreness of mouth and tongue; stomach upset or pain; unusual excitement***—more frequent with high doses of trihexyphenidyl

Those indicating possible withdrawal symptoms and the need for medical attention if they occur after discontinuation of long-term therapy

Anxiety; extrapyramidal symptoms, recurrence or worsening of (difficulty in speaking or swallowing; loss of balance control; mask-like face; muscle spasms, especially of face, neck, and back; restlessness or desire to keep moving; shuffling walk; stiffness of arms or legs; trembling and shaking of hands and fingers; twisting movements of body)—especially after abrupt withdrawal of antidyskinetic medication; may require reinstatement of the antidyskinetic ***fast heartbeat; orthostatic hypotension*** (dizziness or lightheadedness when getting up from a lying or sitting position); ***trouble in sleeping***

Overdose

For specific information on the agents used in the management of antidyskinetics, see:
Barbiturates (Systemic) monograph;
Diazepam in *Benzodiazepines (Systemic)* monograph;
Physostigmine Salicylate (Systemic) monograph; and/or
Pilocarpine (Ophthalmic) monograph.

For more information on the management of overdose or unintentional ingestion, **contact a Poison Control Center** (see *Poison Control Center Listing*).

Clinical effects of overdose

The following effects have been selected on the basis of their potential clinical significance (possible signs and symptoms in parentheses where appropriate)—not necessarily inclusive:

Anticholinergic effects, severe (clumsiness or unsteadiness; severe drowsiness; severe dryness of mouth, nose, or throat; fast heartbeat; shortness of breath or troubled breathing; warmth, dryness, and flushing of skin); ***CNS depression*** (severe drowsiness); ***CNS stimulation*** (hallucinations, seizures, trouble in sleeping); ***toxic psychoses*** (mood or mental changes)—especially in patients with mental illness being treated with neuroleptic drugs

Treatment of overdose

Recommended treatment for overdose with antidyskinetics includes the following:

To decrease absorption—
Emesis or gastric lavage, except in precomatose, convulsive, or psychotic states.

Specific treatment—
Intramuscular or *slow* intravenous administration of 1 to 2 mg of physostigmine salicylate, repeated after 2 hours if needed (0.5 mg initially in children, repeated at five-minute intervals, up to a maximum of 2 mg), to reverse the cardiovascular and CNS toxic effects.
Administration of small doses of diazepam or a short-acting barbiturate to manage excitement.
Administration of pilocarpine 0.5%, to counteract mydriasis.

Supportive care—
Respiratory assistance and symptomatic support.
Patients in whom intentional overdose is confirmed or suspected should be referred for psychiatric consultation.

Patient Consultation

As an aid to patient consultation, refer to *Advice for the Patient, Antidyskinetics (Systemic)*

In providing consultation, consider emphasizing the following selected information (» = major clinical significance):

Before using this medication

» Conditions affecting use, especially:
Sensitivity to antidyskinetics (history of)
Breast-feeding—May inhibit lactation
Use in children—
Increased susceptibility to anticholinergic effects

Use in the elderly—Predisposition to glaucoma with chronic use; increased risk of mental confusion and other psychotic-like symptoms; impairment of memory

Dental—Decrease or inhibition of salivary flow

Other medications, especially other anticholinergics and CNS depressants

Other medical problems, especially cardiovascular instability, tardive dyskinesia, glaucoma, intestinal obstruction, myasthenia gravis, or urinary retention

Proper use of this medication

» Importance of not taking more medication than the amount prescribed

Taking with food to relieve gastric irritation

» Proper dosing

Missed dose: Taking as soon as possible; not taking if within 2 hours of next dose; not doubling doses

» Proper storage

Precautions while using this medication

Regular visits to physician to check progress during prolonged therapy; eye examination may also be needed

» Checking with physician before discontinuing medication; gradual dosage reduction may be necessary

» Avoiding use of alcohol or other CNS depressants

Avoiding use of antidiarrheal medications within 1 or 2 hours of taking this medication

Suspected overdose: Getting emergency help at once

Possible increased eye sensitivity to bright light

» Caution if drowsiness or blurred vision occurs

Caution when getting up suddenly from a lying or sitting position

» Caution during exercise and hot weather

Possible dryness of mouth; using sugarless gum or candy, ice, or saliva substitute for relief; checking with physician or dentist if dry mouth continues for more than 2 weeks

Side/adverse effects

Signs of potential side effects, especially allergic reaction, confusion, increased intraocular pressure, anticholinergic effects, or CNS depression or stimulation

General Dosing Information

For oral dosage forms only

Therapy should be initiated with a low dose because of cumulative action, and dosage should be increased gradually at 5- or 6-day intervals.

Titrated dosage is necessary to achieve the individual required therapeutic level, especially for geriatric patients, who tend to be more sensitive to anticholinergic effects, and patients receiving other medications.

During therapy, necessary dosage adjustments of antidyskinetic or other medication used concurrently should be made gradually to maintain proper control of the patient's condition.

Postencephalitic and younger parkinsonism patients often require and tolerate higher dosages than idiopathic, arteriosclerotic, or geriatric parkinsonism patients.

A drug-abuse potential exists with these medications as they may cause euphoria and hallucinations at higher dosages.

When an antidyskinetic is to be discontinued, dosage should be reduced gradually to prevent a sudden increase in adverse symptoms.

Diet/Nutrition

Antidyskinetics may be taken with or immediately after meals to lessen gastric irritation.

BENZTROPINE

Summary of Differences

Pharmacology/pharmacokinetics:

Other actions/effects—

Has slight antihistaminic and local anesthetic effect.

Onset of action—

Oral: 1 to 2 hours.

Intramuscular or intravenous: Within a few minutes.

Duration of action—

Oral, intramuscular, or intravenous: 24 hours.

Precautions:

Drug interactions and/or related problems—

May increase efficacy of levodopa if used concurrently; however, concurrent use not recommended if there is history of psychosis.

Additional Dosing Information

A single daily oral dose of benztropine at bedtime often provides maximum benefit for the patient because of the long duration of effect.

Oral Dosage Forms

BENZTROPINE MESYLATE TABLETS USP

Usual adult and adolescent dose

Parkinsonism—

Oral, 1 to 2 mg a day, the dosage being adjusted as needed and tolerated.

Note: Idiopathic parkinsonism—Therapy may be initiated in some patients with a single oral daily dose of 500 mcg (0.5 mg) to 1 mg at bedtime.

Postencephalitic parkinsonism—Therapy may be initiated in most patients with 2 mg a day, given once a day or in divided doses.

Drug-induced extrapyramidal reactions—

Oral, 1 to 4 mg one or two times a day. Or, 1 to 2 mg two or three times a day if drug-induced extrapyramidal reactions develop soon after initiation of treatment with neuroleptic drugs.

Usual adult prescribing limits

Up to 6 mg daily.

Usual pediatric dose

Parkinsonism or drug-induced extrapyramidal reactions—

Children up to 3 years of age: Use is not recommended.

Children 3 years of age and over: Dosage must be individualized by physician.

Usual geriatric dose

See *Usual adult and adolescent dose.*

Note: Geriatric patients may be more sensitive to the effects of the usual adult dose.

Strength(s) usually available

U.S.—

500 mcg (0.5 mg) (Rx) [*Cogentin* (scored); GENERIC].

1 mg (Rx) [*Cogentin* (scored); GENERIC].

2 mg (Rx) [*Cogentin* (scored); GENERIC].

Canada—

500 mcg (0.5 mg) (Rx) [*PMS Benztropine*].

1 mg (Rx) [*PMS Benztropine* (scored)].

2 mg (Rx) [*Apo-Benztropine* (double-scored); *Cogentin* (scored; lactose); *PMS Benztropine* (scored); GENERIC].

Packaging and storage

Store below 40 °C (104 °F), preferably between 15 and 30 °C (59 and 86 °F), in a well-closed container, unless otherwise specified by manufacturer.

Auxiliary labeling

- May cause drowsiness.
- Avoid alcoholic beverages.

Parenteral Dosage Forms

BENZTROPINE MESYLATE INJECTION USP

Usual adult and adolescent dose

Parkinsonism—

Intramuscular or intravenous, 1 to 2 mg a day, the dosage being adjusted as needed and tolerated.

Drug-induced extrapyramidal reactions—

Intramuscular or intravenous, 1 to 4 mg one or two times a day.

Usual adult prescribing limits

Up to 6 mg daily.

Usual pediatric dose

Parkinsonism or drug-induced extrapyramidal reactions—

Children up to 3 years of age: Use is not recommended.

Children 3 years of age and over: Dosage must be individualized by physician.

Usual geriatric dose

See *Usual adult and adolescent dose.*

Note: Geriatric patients may be more sensitive to the effects of the usual adult dose.

Strength(s) usually available

U.S.—

1 mg per mL (Rx) [*Cogentin* (sodium chloride 9 mg/mL)].

Canada—

1 mg per mL (Rx) [*Cogentin* (sodium chloride 9 mg/mL); GENERIC].

Packaging and storage

Store below 40 °C (104 °F), preferably between 15 and 30 °C (59 and 86 °F), unless otherwise specified by manufacturer. Protect from freezing.

BIPERIDEN

Summary of Differences

Pharmacology/pharmacokinetics:
Other actions/effects—
Slight cardiovascular and respiratory effects.
Side/adverse effects:
Has slight effect on cardiovascular and respiratory systems.

Oral Dosage Forms

BIPERIDEN HYDROCHLORIDE TABLETS USP

Usual adult and adolescent dose

Parkinsonism—
Oral, 2 mg three or four times a day, the dosage being adjusted as needed and tolerated.
Drug-induced extrapyramidal reactions—
Oral, 2 mg one to three times a day.

Usual adult prescribing limits

Parkinsonism—
Up to 16 mg daily.

Usual pediatric dose

Safety and efficacy have not been established.

Usual geriatric dose

See *Usual adult and adolescent dose.*

Note: Geriatric patients may be more sensitive to the effects of the usual adult dose.

Strength(s) usually available

U.S.—
2 mg (Rx) [*Akineton* (scored; corn syrup; lactose; magnesium stearate; potato starch; talc)].
Canada—
2 mg (Rx) [*Akineton*].

Packaging and storage

Store below 40 °C (104 °F), preferably between 15 and 30 °C (59 and 86 °F), unless otherwise specified by manufacturer. Store in a tight container.

Auxiliary labeling

- May cause drowsiness.
- Avoid alcoholic beverages.
- Keep container tightly closed.

Parenteral Dosage Forms

BIPERIDEN LACTATE INJECTION USP

Usual adult and adolescent dose

Drug-induced extrapyramidal reactions—
Intramuscular or slow intravenous, 2 mg repeated at half-hour intervals as needed and tolerated up to a total of four doses a day.

Usual pediatric dose

Drug-induced extrapyramidal reactions—
Intramuscular, initially 40 mcg (0.04 mg) per kg of body weight, or 1.2 mg per square meter of body surface; dose may be repeated at half-hour intervals if necessary, up to four doses a day.

Usual geriatric dose

See *Usual adult and adolescent dose.*

Note: Geriatric patients may be more sensitive to the effects of the usual adult dose.

Strength(s) usually available

U.S.—
5 mg per mL (Rx) [*Akineton* (1.4% sodium lactate)].
Canada—
Not commercially available.

Packaging and storage

Store below 40 °C (104 °F), preferably between 15 and 30 °C (59 and 86 °F), unless otherwise specified by manufacturer. Protect from light. Protect from freezing.

ETHOPROPAZINE

Summary of Differences

Indications:
Also used for the symptomatic treatment of hepatolenticular degeneration and congenital athetosis.
Pharmacology/pharmacokinetics:
Other actions/effects—
Has slight antihistaminic and local anesthetic effect.
Duration of action—
Oral: 4 hours.
Side/adverse effects:
May possess phenothiazine side effects, especially in high dosages.

Oral Dosage Forms

ETHOPROPAZINE HYDROCHLORIDE TABLETS USP

Usual adult and adolescent dose

Parkinsonism and
Drug-induced extrapyramidal reactions—
Oral, 50 mg one or two times a day, the dosage being increased as needed and tolerated. In severe cases, the dose may be increased gradually to a total of 500 to 600 mg a day.

Usual pediatric dose

Dosage has not been established.

Usual geriatric dose

See *Usual adult and adolescent dose.*

Note: Geriatric patients may be more sensitive to the effects of the usual adult dose.

Strength(s) usually available

U.S.—
10 mg (Rx) [*Parsidol*].
50 mg (Rx) [*Parsidol* (scored)].
Canada—
50 mg (Rx) [*Parsitan* (scored)].

Packaging and storage

Store below 40 °C (104 °F), preferably between 15 and 30 °C (59 and 86 °F), in a well-closed container, unless otherwise specified by manufacturer. Protect from light.

Auxiliary labeling

- May cause drowsiness.
- Avoid alcoholic beverages.

PROCYCLIDINE

Summary of Differences

Pharmacology/pharmacokinetics:
Other actions/effects—
Direct antispasmodic effect on smooth muscle.
Duration of action—
Oral: 4 hours.
Precautions:
Drug interactions and/or related problems—
May increase efficacy of levodopa if used concurrently; however, concurrent use not recommended if there is history of psychosis.
General dosing information:
Provides more beneficial effect in conditions of rigidity than in those of tremor.

Oral Dosage Forms

PROCYCLIDINE HYDROCHLORIDE ELIXIR

Usual adult and adolescent dose

Parkinsonism—
Oral, initially 2.5 mg three times a day after meals. If tolerated, the dosage may be gradually increased to 5 mg three times a day and, occasionally, 5 mg at bedtime.

Note: For patients being transferred from other therapy, 2.5 mg three times a day may be substituted for all or part of the original medication. The dose of procyclidine may be increased while the original medication is decreased until a level of maximum benefit is reached.

Drug-induced extrapyramidal reactions—
Oral, initially 2.5 mg three times a day, the dosage being increased in 2.5-mg increments per day as needed and tolerated.

Usual pediatric dose

Dosage has not been established.

Usual geriatric dose

See *Usual adult and adolescent dose.*

Note: Geriatric patients may be more sensitive to the effects of the usual adult dose.

Strength(s) usually available
U.S.—
Not commercially available.
Canada—
2.5 mg per 5 mL (Rx) [*Kemadrin* (alcohol 10%); *PMS Procyclidine* (spearmint-flavored); *Procyclid*].

Packaging and storage
Store below 40 °C (104 °F), preferably between 15 and 30 °C (59 and 86 °F), unless otherwise specified by manufacturer. Store in a tight container. Protect from freezing.

Auxiliary labeling
- May cause drowsiness.
- Avoid alcoholic beverages.
- Keep container tightly closed.

PROCYCLIDINE HYDROCHLORIDE TABLETS USP

Usual adult and adolescent dose
See *Procyclidine Hydrochloride Elixir*.

Usual pediatric dose
See *Procyclidine Hydrochloride Elixir*.

Usual geriatric dose
See *Procyclidine Hydrochloride Elixir*.

Strength(s) usually available
U.S.—
5 mg (Rx) [*Kemadrin* (scored)].
Canada—
2.5 mg (Rx) [*PMS Procyclidine* (scored)].
5 mg (Rx) [*Kemadrin* (scored); *PMS Procyclidine* (scored); *Procyclid* (scored)].

Packaging and storage
Store below 40 °C (104 °F), preferably between 15 and 30 °C (59 and 86 °F), unless otherwise specified by manufacturer. Store in a tight container.

Auxiliary labeling
- May cause drowsiness.
- Avoid alcoholic beverages.
- Keep container tightly closed.

TRIHEXYPHENIDYL

Summary of Differences

Pharmacology/pharmacokinetics:
Other actions/effects—
Direct antispasmodic effect on smooth muscle; small doses depress CNS; larger doses may cause cerebral excitation.
Onset of action—
Oral: 1 hour.
Duration of action—
Oral: 6 to 12 hours.
Precautions:
Drug interactions and/or related problems—
May increase efficacy of levodopa if used concurrently; however, concurrent use not recommended if there is history of psychosis.
Side/adverse effects:
Unusual excitement (with high doses).

Oral Dosage Forms

TRIHEXYPHENIDYL HYDROCHLORIDE EXTENDED-RELEASE CAPSULES USP

Usual adult and adolescent dose
Parkinsonism—
Oral, 5 mg a day after breakfast with an additional 5 mg taken twelve hours later as needed.

Note: This dosage form is usually utilized only after the patient has been stabilized on the conventional dosage forms.

Usual adult prescribing limits
Up to 15 mg daily.

Usual pediatric dose
Dosage has not been established.

Usual geriatric dose
See *Usual adult and adolescent dose*.

Note: Geriatric patients may be more sensitive to the effects of the usual adult dose.

Strength(s) usually available
U.S.—
5 mg (Rx) [*Artane Sequels*].
Canada—
5 mg (Rx) [*Artane Sequels*].

Packaging and storage
Store below 40 °C (104 °F), preferably between 15 and 30 °C (59 and 86 °F), in a tight container, unless otherwise specified by manufacturer.

Auxiliary labeling
- May cause drowsiness.
- Avoid alcoholic beverages.

TRIHEXYPHENIDYL HYDROCHLORIDE ELIXIR USP

Usual adult and adolescent dose
Parkinsonism—
Oral, 1 to 2 mg the first day, the dosage being increased by an additional 2 mg at three- to five-day intervals until the desired response is obtained or until the total dose per day reaches 6 to 10 mg, usually divided into three doses taken at mealtimes.
Note: Postencephalitic parkinsonism—A total dose of 12 to 15 mg per day may be required.

Drug-induced extrapyramidal reactions—
Oral, initially 1 mg a day, the dosage being increased as needed and tolerated or until the total daily dose reaches 5 to 15 mg.

Usual adult prescribing limits
Up to 15 mg daily.

Usual pediatric dose
Dosage has not been established.

Usual geriatric dose
See *Usual adult and adolescent dose.*

Note: Geriatric patients may be more sensitive to the effects of the usual adult dose.

Strength(s) usually available
U.S.—
2 mg per 5 mL (Rx) [*Artane* (lime-mint flavored); GENERIC].
Canada—
2 mg per 5 mL (Rx) [*Artane* (lime flavored); *PMS Trihexyphenidyl*].

Packaging and storage
Store below 40 °C (104 °F), preferably between 15 and 30 °C (59 and 86 °F), unless otherwise specified by manufacturer. Store in a tight container. Protect from freezing.

Auxiliary labeling
- May cause drowsiness.
- Avoid alcoholic beverages.
- Keep container tightly closed.

TRIHEXYPHENIDYL HYDROCHLORIDE TABLETS USP

Usual adult and adolescent dose
See *Trihexyphenidyl Hydrochloride Elixir USP*.

Usual adult prescribing limits
See *Trihexyphenidyl Hydrochloride Elixir USP*.

Usual pediatric dose
See *Trihexyphenidyl Hydrochloride Elixir USP*.

Usual geriatric dose
See *Trihexyphenidyl Hydrochloride Elixir USP*.

Strength(s) usually available
U.S.—
2 mg (Rx) [*Artane* (scored); *Trihexane; Trihexy;* GENERIC].
5 mg (Rx) [*Artane* (scored); *Trihexane; Trihexy;* GENERIC].
Canada—
2 mg (Rx) [*Apo-Trihex* (scored; sodium <1 mmol (0.113 mg)/2 mg); *Artane* (scored); *PMS Trihexyphenidyl* (sodium <1 mmol (0.113 mg)/2 mg)].
5 mg (Rx) [*Apo-Trihex* (scored; sodium <1 mmol (0.188 mg)/5 mg); *Artane* (scored); *PMS Trihexyphenidyl* (sodium <1 mmol (0.188 mg)/5 mg)].

Packaging and storage
Store below 40 °C (104 °F), preferably between 15 and 30 °C (59 and 86 °F), unless otherwise specified by manufacturer. Store in a tight container.

Auxiliary labeling
- May cause drowsiness.
- Avoid alcoholic beverages.
- Keep container tightly closed.

Revised: 05/11/1993

ANTIFUNGALS, AZOLE Systemic

This monograph includes information on the following: 1) Fluconazole; 2) Itraconazole; 3) Ketoconazole.

VA CLASSIFICATION (Primary/Secondary):
Fluconazole—AM700
Itraconazole—AM700
Ketoconazole—AM700/HS900; AN900

Commonly used brand name(s): *Diflucan*[1]; *Diflucan-150*[1]; *Nizoral*[3]; *Sporanox*[2].

Note: For a listing of dosage forms and brand names by country availability, see *Dosage Forms* section(s).

Category

Antiadrenal; antineoplastic (systemic)—Ketoconazole.
Antifungal (systemic)—Fluconazole; Itraconazole; Ketoconazole

Indications

Note: Bracketed information in the *Indications* section refers to uses that are not included in U.S. product labeling.

Accepted

Aspergillosis (treatment)—Itraconazole is indicated in the treatment of aspergillosis caused by *Aspergillus* species in patients who are intolerant of or refractory to amphotericin B therapy in both immunocompromised and non-immunocompromised patients.

Blastomycosis (treatment)—Itraconazole is indicated for the treatment of pulmonary and extrapulmonary blastomycosis caused by *Blastomyces dermatitidis* in immunocompromised and nonimmunocompromised patients. Ketoconazole[1] is also indicated in the treatment of blastomycosis.

Candidiasis (prophylaxis)—Fluconazole is indicated for the prophylaxis of candidiasis in patients undergoing bone marrow transplant who receive cytotoxic chemotherapy and/or radiation therapy.

Candidiasis, esophageal (treatment) or
Candidiasis, oropharyngeal (treatment)—Fluconazole, itraconazole, and ketoconazole are indicated for the treatment of esophageal and oropharyngeal candidiasis (thrush) caused by *Candida* species.

Candidiasis, disseminated (treatment)—Fluconazole and ketoconazole are indicated for the treatment of serious infections, including peritonitis, pneumonia, and urinary tract infections, caused by susceptible *Candida* species. [Fluconazole][1] is also indicated for the treatment of systemic infections caused by *Candida* species in neonates.

Candidiasis, mucocutaneous, chronic (treatment)—[Fluconazole][1], [itraconazole][1], and ketoconazole are indicated in the treatment of severe, chronic extensive mucocutaneous candidiasis caused by *Candida* species.

Candidiasis, vulvovaginal (treatment)—Fluconazole, [itraconazole][1], and [ketoconazole][1] are indicated in the treatment of vulvovaginal candidiasis caused by *Candida* species.

Chromomycosis (treatment)—[Itraconazole] and ketoconazole are indicated as secondary agents in the treatment of chromomycosis caused by *Cladosporium carrioni*, *Exophiala dermatitidis*, *Fonsecaea pedrosi*, *Fonsecaea compactum*, *Phialophora verrucosa*, *Rhinocladiella aquaspersa*, and *Rhinocladiella cerophilum*.

Coccidioidomycosis (treatment)—[Fluconazole][1] and [itraconazole][1] are indicated in the treatment of pulmonary and disseminated coccidioidomycosis caused by *Coccidioides immitis*. Ketoconazole is indicated as a secondary agent in the treatment of severe coccidioidomycosis.

Histoplasmosis (treatment)—Itraconazole is indicated for the treatment of histoplasmosis, including chronic cavitary pulmonary disease and disseminated, non-meningeal disease caused by *Histoplasma capsulatum*, in immunocompromised and nonimmunocompromised patients. Ketoconazole is also indicated in the treatment of pulmonary and disseminated histoplasmosis caused by *H. capsulatum*.

Meningitis, cryptococcal (treatment) or
Meningitis, cryptococcal (suppression)—Fluconazole is indicated for the treatment and suppression of cryptococcal meningitis. [Itraconazole][1] is indicated as an alternative agent as suppressive, maintenance therapy for cryptococcal meningitis.

Preliminary studies indicate that amphotericin B plus flucytosine are more efficacious than fluconazole in the primary treatment of cryptococcal meningitis in patients with acquired immunodeficiency syndrome (AIDS), although there was a greater incidence of toxicity with this combination. Another study found that amphotericin B alone was superior to fluconazole in the treatment of acute cryptococcal meningitis; however, fluconazole was better tolerated for maintenance therapy.

Neutropenia, febrile (treatment)—Itraconazole (injection and oral solution) is indicated for empiric therapy of febrile neutropenic patients with suspected fungal infections.

Onychomycosis (treatment)—[Fluconazole], itraconazole[1], and [ketoconazole] are indicated in nonimmunocompromised patients for the treatment of onychomycosis caused by *tinea unguium*, *Trichophyton* species and *Candida* species.

Paracoccidioidomycosis (treatment)—[Itraconazole] and ketoconazole are indicated in the treatment of paracoccidioidomycosis caused by *Paracoccidioides brasiliensis.*

Pityriasis versicolor (treatment)
Tinea corporis (treatment)
Tinea cruris (treatment) or
Tinea pedis (treatment)—Ketoconazole is indicated in the treatment of recalcitrant or very severe disfiguring or disabling pityriasis versicolor, tinea corporis, tinea cruris, and tinea pedis infections unresponsive to griseofulvin, or in patients allergic to or unable to tolerate griseofulvin. [Fluconazole][1] and [itraconazole] are used in the treatment of tinea corporis (ringworm of the body), tinea cruris (ringworm of the groin; jock itch), and tinea pedis (ringworm of the foot; athlete's foot).

[Carcinoma, prostatic (treatment)][1]—High-dose ketoconazole is indicated as a secondary antiandrogen agent in the treatment of advanced prostatic carcinoma.

[Cryptococcosis (treatment)][1]—Fluconazole and itraconazole are indicated in the treatment of extrameningeal cryptococcosis caused by *Cryptococcus neoformans.*

[Cushing's syndrome (treatment)][1]—High-dose ketoconazole is indicated as a secondary agent in the treatment of Cushing's syndrome.

[Hirsutism (treatment)][1]—Ketoconazole is indicated as an alternative (third or fourth line) agent in the treatment of hirsutism (Evidence rating: III). Ketoconazole has been shown to lower androgen levels and to decrease hair growth with long-term (> 6 months) use in hirsute women. However, some medical experts state that the potential benefits of treating hirsutism with ketoconazole do not outweigh the potential risks (including serious hepatotoxicity) because other less toxic agents are available.

[Histoplasmosis (suppression)][1]—Itraconazole is indicated for the suppression of disseminated histoplasmosis caused by *Histoplasma capsulatum*, in immunocompromised patients.

[Leishmaniasis, cutaneous (treatment)][1]—Itraconazole and ketoconazole are indicated for the treatment of cutaneous leishmaniasis.

[Neutropenia, febrile (prophylaxis)][1]—Fluconazole and itraconazole are indicated for the prophylaxis of febrile neutropenia in patients with hematologic malignancies..

In neutropenic patients treated for hematological malignancies with or without autologous stem cell transplantation, fluconazole and itraconazole in low doses result in a similar low frequency of fungal disease

[Neutropenia, febrile (treatment)][1]—Fluconazole is indicated in the treatment of febrile neutropenia when fungal infections are suspected or proven.

[Paronychia (treatment)][1]—Itraconazole and ketoconazole are indicated in the treatment of fungal paronychia.

[*Penicillium marneffei* infection (treatment)][1]—Itraconazole (in adults) and ketoconazole (in children) are indicated in the treatment of *P. marneffei* infection.

In certain parts of Southeast Asia and the southern part of China, *P. marneffei* infection is the third most common opportunistic infection in human immunodeficiency virus (HIV)-infected patients. *P. marneffei* infection was rare in the past; however, it has increased with the endemic of AIDS in the region. The reservoir of *P. marneffei* in nature is unknown; however, it seems likely that inhalation may be the route of entry of the organism leading to infection in humans. *P. marneffei* infection is a treatable disease; however, late diagnosis and treatment may be fatal. Itraconazole and ketoconazole are preferred for mild to moderately severe forms of the disease, whereas parenteral treatment with amphotericin B may be required for seriously ill patients. Recurrence of the disease is common; therefore, maintenance is recommended.

[Pneumonia, fungal (treatment)][1]—Fluconazole, itraconazole, and ketoconazole are indicated in the treatment of fungal pneumonia.

[Septicemia, fungal (treatment)][1]—Fluconazole, itraconazole, and ketoconazole are indicated in the treatment of fungal septicemia.

[Sporotrichosis, disseminated (treatment)]—Itraconazole and ketoconazole[1] are indicated in the treatment of disseminated sporotrichosis.

[Tinea barbae (treatment)] or

[Tinea capitis (treatment)][1]—Systemic ketoconazole is indicated, in combination with topical imidazoles, in the treatment of griseofulvin-resistant tinea barbae (ringworm of the beard) and tinea capitis (ringworm of the scalp).

[Tinea manuum (treatment)][1]—Fluconazole and itraconazole are indicated in the treatment of tinea manuum (ringworm of the hand).

Fluconazole is approved for the treatment of systemic candidal infections and is an appropriate, less toxic alternative to amphotericin B.

Fluconazole has been shown to be efficacious *in vivo* in the treatment of animals infected with candidiasis, cryptococcosis, histoplasmosis, coccidioidosis, blastomycosis, aspergillosis, and paracoccidioidosis. The *in vitro* susceptibility testing of fluconazole is affected by composition of the culture medium, pH, inoculum size, incubation temperature, and time. Because of this, published *in vitro* minimum inhibitory concentration (MIC) data vary widely, and a correlation between this and *in vivo* clinical efficacy cannot reliably be made.

Unaccepted

Ketoconazole is not effective in the treatment of fungal meningitis because it penetrates poorly into the cerebrospinal fluid (CSF). Also, it is not effective against *Aspergillus* or *Zygomycetes* (agents of mucormycosis) or in mycetoma.

---

[1]Not included in Canadian product labeling.

Pharmacology/Pharmacokinetics

See *Table 1* and *Table 2,* page 323.

Physicochemical characteristics

Molecular weight—
- Fluconazole: 306.28.
- Itraconazole: 705.64.
- Ketoconazole: 531.44.

Chemical class—
- Fluconazole: Triazole derivative.
- Itraconazole: Triazole derivative.
- Ketoconazole: Imidazole derivative.

Mechanism of action/Effect

Fungistatic; may be fungicidal, depending on concentration; azole antifungals interfere with cytochrome P450 enzyme activity, which is necessary for the demethylation of 14-alpha-methylsterols to ergosterol. Ergosterol, the principal sterol in the fungal cell membrane, becomes depleted. This damages the cell membrane, producing alterations in membrane functions and permeability. In *Candida albicans*, azole antifungals inhibit transformation of blastospores into invasive mycelial form.

Other actions/effects

High-dose ketoconazole therapy can interfere with the conversion of lanosterol to cholesterol, a major precursor of several hormones. It has been shown to suppress corticosteroid secretion and lower serum testosterone concentrations, which return to baseline values when ketoconazole is discontinued. Adrenocorticotropic hormone (ACTH)-induced serum corticosteroid concentrations and serum testosterone concentrations may be decreased by doses of 800 mg of ketoconazole daily; serum testosterone concentrations are abolished by doses of 1.6 grams of ketoconazole daily, leading to reduced libido and impotence, but return to baseline values when ketoconazole is discontinued.

Compared to ketoconazole, fluconazole and itraconazole have a very weak, noncompetitive inhibitory effect on the liver cytochrome P450 enzyme system, while maintaining a high affinity for fungal cytochrome P450 enzyme activity.

Fluconazole and itraconazole have not been reported to have antiandrogenic activity at currently used doses. Itraconazole has not affected cortisol metabolism in patients treated with clinically recommended doses; however, a decrease in cortisol synthesis was observed in a patient receiving high-dose itraconazole therapy (600 mg a day).

Distribution

Fluconazole—Fluconazole is widely distributed throughout the body, with good penetration into the cerebrospinal fluid (CSF) (ranging from 52 to 85% in patients with fungal meningitis), the eye, and peritoneal fluid.

Itraconazole—Highly lipophilic; extensively distributed to tissues, concentrating in fatty tissues, the omentum, the liver, and the kidneys. Aqueous fluids, such as the CSF, aqueous humor, and saliva, contain negligible concentrations of itraconazole. Itraconazole also does not distribute into peritoneal dialysate effluent. Exudates, such as pus, may have up to 3.5 times the simultaneous plasma concentration; tissues that are prone to fungal invasion, such as skin, lung tissue, and the female genital tract, have several times the plasma concentration.

Ketoconazole—Well distributed; distributed to inflamed joint fluid, saliva, bile, urine, breast milk, sebum, cerumen, feces, tendons, skin and soft tissues, and testes (small amounts); crosses the placenta; crosses the blood-brain barrier poorly; only negligible amounts reach the CSF. Although concentrations of 2.2 to 3 mcg per mL have been reported in the CSF with corresponding serum concentrations of 9 to 12 mcg per mL, most studies indicate that CSF concentrations > 1 mcg per mL are rare, regardless of dose.

Precautions to Consider

Cross-sensitivity and/or related problems

Patients allergic to one azole antifungal agent (fluconazole, itraconazole, ketoconazole) may also be allergic to the other antifungals in this family.

Carcinogenicity/Tumorigenicity

Fluconazole—Studies in rats and mice treated with oral doses of 2.5 to 10 mg per kg of body weight (mg/kg) per day (2 to 7 times the recommended human dose) for 24 months showed no carcinogenic potential. Male rats treated with 5 to 10 mg/kg per day had an increased incidence of hepatocellular adenomas.

Itraconazole—No evidence of carcinogenicity was found in mice given oral doses of up to 80 mg/kg per day, or approximately 10 times the maximum recommended human dose (MRHD), for 23 months. Male rats given 3 times the MRHD had a slightly increased incidence of soft tissue sarcoma. These sarcomas may have been a consequence of hypercholesterolemia, which is caused by chronic itraconazole administration in rats, but did not occur in dogs or humans. Female rats who were given 6.25 times the MRHD had an increased incidence of squamous cell carcinoma in the lung, compared to the untreated group, although the increase in this study was not statistically significant.

Ketoconazole—Long-term feeding studies in Swiss albino mice and in Wistar rats have not shown evidence of oncogenesis.

Mutagenicity

Fluconazole—Mutagenicity tests for fluconazole (with and without metabolic activation) in four strains of *Salmonella typhimurium* and in the mouse lymphoma L5178Y system were negative. Cytogenetic studies *in vivo* and *in vitro* showed no evidence of chromosomal mutations.

Itraconazole—Itraconazole produced no mutagenic effects when assayed in appropriate bacterial, non-mammalian and mammalian test systems.

Ketoconazole—Dominant lethal mutation tests have not shown mutation in any stage of germ cell development in male and female mice given single, oral doses of ketoconazole as high as 80 mg/kg. In addition, the Ames/ *Salmonella* microsomal activator tests have not shown evidence of mutagenicity.

Pregnancy/Reproduction

Fertility—*Fluconazole:* Fertility was not affected in male or female rats treated with oral daily doses of 5 to 20 mg/kg or parenteral doses of 5, 25, or 75 mg/kg, although the onset of parturition was slightly delayed with oral doses of 20 mg/kg.

Itraconazole: Itraconazole did not affect the fertility of male or female rats treated with oral doses of up to 5 times the MRHD, although parental toxicity was present at this dosage level.

Ketoconazole: Ketoconazole has been shown to decrease or abolish serum testosterone concentrations when used in high doses (e.g., 800 mg to 1.6 grams daily). Ketoconazole has also been shown to cause menstrual irregularities, oligospermia, azoospermia, impotence, and decreased male libido.

Pregnancy—

Fluconazole: There are no adequate and well controlled studies in pregnant women. There have been reports of infants with multiple congenital abnormalities when their mothers were treated for 3 or more months with high dose fluconazole (400 to 800 mg per day) therapy for coccidioidomycosis (an unindicated use). Fluconazole should be used in pregnancy only if the potential benefit justifies the possible risk to the fetus.

Maternal weight gain was impaired in pregnant rabbits administered oral fluconazole at doses ranging from 5 to 75 mg/kg per day. Abortions occurred at 75 mg/kg (20 to 60 times the recommended human dose); no adverse fetal effects were detected. Pregnant rats administered oral fluconazole showed impaired maternal weight gain and increased placental weight at 25 mg/kg. A slight increase in the number of stillborn pups and a decrease in neonatal survival were also seen at these doses. Supernumerary ribs, renal pelvis dilation, and delays in ossification were observed at doses of 25 mg/kg and higher. In rats, death of embryos and fetal abnormalities, including wavy ribs, cleft palate, and abnormal craniofacial ossification, occurred at doses ranging from 80 to 320 mg/kg (approximately 20 to 60 times the recommended human dose). These effects are consistent with the inhibition of estrogen synthesis in rats and may be a result of known effects of lowered estrogen on pregnancy, organogenesis, and parturition; this effect has not been observed in women treated with fluconazole.

FDA Pregnancy Category C

Itraconazole: Adequate and well-controlled studies in humans have not been done.

There is limited information on the use of itraconazole during pregnancy. During post-marketing experience, cases of congenital abnormalities including skeletal, genitourinary tract, cardiovascular and ophthalmic malformations as well as chromosomal and multiple malformations have been reported. A causal relationship with itraconazole has not been established.

Studies in rats found that itraconazole causes a dose-related increase in maternal toxicity, embryotoxicity, and teratogenicity, consisting of major skeletal defects, at doses approximately 5 to 20 times the MRHD. Studies in mice also found that itraconazole causes a dose-related increase in maternal toxicity, embryotoxicity, and teratogenicity, consisting of encephaloceles and/or macroglossia, at doses approximately 10 times the MRHD.

Itraconazole should be used during pregnancy only if the benefit outweighs the risk. Itraconazole should not be administered for the treatment of onychomycosis to pregnant patients or to women contemplating pregnancy. Women of childbearing potential should not receive itraconazole for treatment of onychomycosis unless they are using effective measures to prevent pregnancy and they begin therapy on the second or third day following onset of menses. Effective contraception should be continued throughout itraconazole therapy and for 2 months following the end of treatment.

FDA Pregnancy Category C

Ketoconazole: Ketoconazole crosses the placenta. Adequate and well-controlled studies in humans have not been done.

Studies in rats given doses of 80 mg/kg per day (10 times the MRHD) have shown ketoconazole to be teratogenic, causing syndactyly and oligodactyly. Ketoconazole has also been shown to be embryotoxic in rats given doses greater than 80 mg/kg during the first trimester.

FDA Pregnancy Category C

Labor—*Fluconazole:* Dystocia and prolongation of parturition were observed in a few pregnant rats given 20 and 40 mg/kg of intravenous fluconazole.

Ketoconazole: Ketoconazole has also been shown to cause dystocia in rats given doses greater than 10 mg/kg (greater than 1.25 times the MRHD) during the third trimester.

Breast-feeding

Fluconazole—Fluconazole is distributed into breast milk at concentrations similar to those in plasma.

Itraconazole—Itraconazole is distributed into breast milk. Therefore, expected benefits of therapy for the mother should be weighed against the potential risk of itraconazole exposure to the infant. U.S. Public Health Service Centers for Disease Control and Prevention advised HIV-infected women not to breast-feed to avoid potential transmission of HIV to uninfected infants.

Ketoconazole—Ketoconazole is distributed into breast milk.

Pediatrics

Fluconazole—Use of fluconazole in children younger than 6 months of age as well as 6 months of age and older with fungal infections is supported by evidence from adequate and well-controlled studies in adults, with additional data from pediatric pharmacokinetics studies and controlled clinical trials in pediatric patients. The safety profile of fluconazole in children has been studied in 577 children ages 1 day to 17 years who received doses ranging from 1 to 15 mg per kg of body weight per day for 1 to 1,616 days. Efficacy of fluconazole has not been established in infants less than 6 months of age. A small number of patients (29) ranging from 1 day to 6 months have been treated safely with fluconazole. Experience with neonates is limited to pharmacokinetic studies in premature newborns (gestational age 26 to 29 weeks). Pharmacokinetic information is not available for full-term infants.

Itraconazole—Appropriate studies on the relationship of age to the effects of itraconazole have not been performed in the pediatric population. Safety and efficacy have not been established. However, a small number of patients from 3 to 16 years of age have been treated with itraconazole capsules, 100 mg per day, for systemic fungal infections, and no serious adverse effects have been reported. Also, a small number of patients from 6 months to 12 years of age have been treated with itraconazole oral solution, 5 mg/kg per day, for systemic fungal infections, and no serious, unexpected adverse events have been reported. Long-term effects on bone growth in children are unknown. In three toxicology studies using rats, itraconazole induced bone defects at low dosage levels of 20 mg per kg of body weight per day (2.5 times MRHD). Induced defects included reduced bone plate activity, thinning of the large bones sona compacta, and increased bone fragility. At dosage levels of 80 mg per kg of body weight per day (10 times MRHD) or 160 mg per kg of body weight per day (20 times MRHD) over 6 months, itraconazole induced small tooth pulp with hypocellular appearance ins some rats.

Ketoconazole—Several cases of hepatitis have been reported in children who have taken ketoconazole. Appropriate studies on the relationship of age to the effects of ketoconazole have not been performed in children up to 2 years of age. However, no pediatrics-specific problems have been documented to date in children over 2 years of age.

Geriatrics

No information is available on the relationship of age to the effects of azole antifungals in geriatric patients. However, elderly patients are more likely to have an age-related decrease in renal function, which may require an adjustment in dosage or dosing interval in patients receiving fluconazole.

Fluconazole—There are no adequate and well controlled studies in patients aged 65 and older. Spontaneous reports of anemia and acute renal failure were more frequent among patients 65 years of age or older than in those between 12 and 65 years of age in post-marketing experience. Due to the voluntary nature of the reports and the natural increase in the incidence of anemia and renal failure in the elderly it is not possible to establish a causal relationship to drug exposure.

Drug interactions and/or related problems

The following drug interactions and/or related problems have been selected on the basis of their potential clinical significance (possible mechanism in parentheses where appropriate)—not necessarily inclusive (» = major clinical significance):

Note: Combinations containing any of the following medications, depending on the amount present, may also interact with this medication.

» Alcohol or
» Hepatotoxic medications, other (see *Appendix II*)

(concurrent use with ketoconazole may result in an increased incidence of hepatotoxicity; patients, especially those on prolonged administration or those with a history of liver disease, should be monitored carefully and should be advised to avoid alcoholic beverages and other hepatotoxins)

(concurrent ingestion of alcohol with ketoconazole has been reported to result in a disulfiram-like reaction, characterized by facial flushing; other symptoms may include difficult breathing, slight fever, and tightness of the chest; these effects subsided spontaneously within 24 hours with no lasting ill effects)

» Alprazolam or
» Diazepam or
» Midazolam or
» Triazolam

(concurrent use with itraconazole, or ketoconazole elevates the plasma concentration of oral midazolam or triazolam, which may potentiate and prolong their hypnotic and sedative effects; oral midazolam and triazolam should not be used in patients treated with ketoconazole and is **contraindicated** in patients treated with itraconazole; special precaution and patient monitoring is required in parenterally administered midazolam since the sedative effect may be prolonged)

(concurrent use of fluconazole and short-acting benzodiazepines, such as midazolam, may increase the concentration of the benzodiazepine and increase the psychomotor effects; consider decreasing the benzodiazepine dose and monitor the patient carefully for signs of increased benzodiazepine exposure)

» Antacids or
» Anticholinergics/antispasmodics or
» Histamine H_2-receptor antagonists or
» Omeprazole or
» Other proton pump inhibitors or
» Sucralfate

(these medications increase gastrointestinal pH; this may result in a marked reduction in absorption of itraconazole and ketoconazole; ketoconazole depends on stomach acid for dissolution and subsequent absorption; patients should be advised to take these medications at least 2 hours after taking itraconazole or ketoconazole; itraconazole should be administered with a cola beverage if patient is taking H_2-receptor antagonists or other gastric acid suppressors; antacids should be administered at least 1 hour before or 2 hours after administration of itraconazole)

» Antidiabetic agents, oral
(concurrent use of fluconazole or itraconazole with tolbutamide, chlorpropamide, glyburide, or glipizide has increased the plasma concen-
trations of these sulfonylurea agents; hypoglycemia has been noted; blood glucose concentrations should be monitored, and the dose of the oral hypoglycemic agent may need to be reduced)

» Astemizole or
» Terfenadine
(concurrent use of these medications with itraconazole, or ketoconazole is **contraindicated;** concurrent use of these antihistamines with itraconazole, or ketoconazole may result in elevated plasma concentrations of astemizole or terfenadine by inhibiting the cytochrome P450 enzyme metabolic pathways; this has led to cardiac arrhythmias, including QT prolongation, ventricular tachycardia, torsades de pointes, and death; in a small study, fluconazole was given with terfenadine and a small pharmacokinetic interaction was found; although no change in cardiac repolarization or accumulation of parent terfenadine was found, concurrent use of terfenadine with fluconazole at doses of 400 mg or greater per day is **contraindicated)**

» Atorvastatin or
» Cerivastatin or
» Lovastatin or
» Simvastatin
(concurrent use of itraconazole, capsules and injection, with lovastatin or simvastatin is **contraindicated**. Itraconazole inhibits the metabolism of atorvastatin, cerivastatin, lovastatin and simvastatin resulting in significantly elevated plasma concentrations of lovastatin or lovastatic acid, which have been associated with rhabdomyolysis; use of 3-hydroxy-3-methylglutaryl coenzyme A (HMG-CoA) reductase inhibitors that are metabolized by the cytochrome P450 enzyme system, such as atorvastatin, cerivastatin, lovastatin and simvastatin, should be temporarily discontinued during itraconazole therapy)

» Busulfan or
» Docetaxel or
» Vinca alkaloids
(itraconazole may inhibit the metabolism of these drugs)

Buspirone
(concomitant use with itraconazole may significantly increase buspirone plasma concentrations)

Calcium channel blockers, including
» Felodipine or
» Nifedipine or
» Verapamil
(concurrent use may result in edema, and dosage adjustment may be needed. caution should be used as itraconazole may inhibit the metabolism of calcium channel blockers, and calcium channel blockers can have a negative inotropic effect and may be additive to those of itraconazole)

» Carbamazepine
(may increase concentration of carbamazepine and decrease plasma concentration of itraconazole)

» Cisapride
(concurrent use of cisapride with fluconazole, itraconazole or oral ketoconazole is **contraindicated;** concurrent use of cisapride with these antifungals may inhibit the cytochrome P450 enzyme metabolic pathways, resulting in elevated plasma concentrations of cisapride; this has led to ventricular arrhythmias, including torsades de pointes and QT prolongation (with itraconazole), in patients taking cisapride and oral ketoconazole or itraconazole)

» Clarithromycin
(clarithromycin is a known inhibitor of CYP34A and may increase plasma concentrations of itraconazole)

» Cyclosporine or
» Sirolimus or
» Tacrolimus
(itraconazole, ketoconazole, and high doses of fluconazole have been reported to inhibit the metabolism of cyclosporine and tacrolimus; this may increase the plasma concentration of cyclosporine or tacrolimus to potentially toxic levels; a few studies have not found a significant interaction between fluconazole and cyclosporine; however, plasma cyclosporine concentrations should be monitored carefully in patients receiving any of the azole antifungals; the dose of cyclosporine may need to be reduced; it is currently recommended that the dose of cyclosporine be reduced by 50% when itraconazole is started; could increase sirolimus plasma concentrations if used concomitantly with itraconazole)

» CYP3A4 inducers
(may decrease itraconazole plasma concentrations making it not as effective when used concomitantly with CYP3A4 inducers; administration of these drugs with itraconazole is not recommended)

CYP3A4 inhibitors
(may increase itraconazole plasma concentrations; patients who must take itraconazole concomitantly with one of these drugs should be monitored closely for signs or symptoms of increased or prolonged pharmacologic effects of itraconazole)

» Didanosine (ddl)
(didanosine contains a buffer that increases gastrointestinal pH in order to increase its absorption; itraconazole and ketoconazole require an acidic environment for their optimal absorption; concurrent administration may result in a marked reduction in absorption of any of these medications; itraconazole and ketoconazole should be administered at least 2 hours before or 2 hours after didanosine is given)

» Digoxin
(itraconazole and ketoconazole may increase serum digoxin concentrations, leading to toxicity; digoxin concentrations should be monitored)

Disopyramide
(has potential to increase the QT interval at high plasma concentrations; caution advised with concomitant use of disopyramide and itraconazole)

» Dofetilide or
» Quinidine
(concurrent use of itraconazole with dofetilide or quinidine is **contraindicated;** coadministration with itraconazole may increase plasma concentrations of dofetilide or quinidine possibly resulting in serious cardiovascular events)

Drugs metabolized by CYP3A4 including:
Alfentanil or
Cilostazol or
Eletriptan or
Trimetrexate
(itraconazole may decrease elimination of these drugs resulting in increased plasma concentrations of these drugs; clinical monitoring for signs or symptoms of increased or prolonged pharmacologic effects is advised and caution should be used with concomitant use)

» Ergot alkaloids such as
Dihydroergotamine or
Ergometrine (ergonovine) or
Ergotamine or
Methylergometrine (methylergonovine)
(elevated concentrations of ergot alkaloids can cause ergotism, a risk for vasospasm potentially leading to cerebral ischemia and/or ischemia of the extremities; concomitant administration with itraconazole is **contraindicated)**

» Erythromycin
(concomitant use with azole antifungals showed an adjusted rate of sudden death from cardiac causes to be five times as high [incidence-rate ration, 5.35; 95% confidence interval, 1.72 to 16.64; $P=0.004$] as that among those who had used neither a CYP3A inhibitor nor any of the study antibiotic medications; concurrent use should be avoided)

Glucocorticosteroids such as
Budesonide or
Dexamethasone or
Methylprednisolone
(itraconazole may inhibit metabolism of certain glucocorticosteroids)

Halofantrine
(has potential to prolong QT interval at high plasma concentrations; caution advised when itraconazole and halofantrine are administered concomitantly)

Hydrochlorothiazide
(concurrent use of fluconazole with hydrochlorothiazide 50 mg for 10 days in volunteers resulted in a 41% increase in peak plasma concentration, and a 43% increase in the area under the plasma concentration-time curve [AUC] of fluconazole; this is thought to be due to a mean decrease of approximately 20% in the renal clearance of fluconazole)

» Indinavir or
» Ritonavir or

» Saquinavir
(concurrent use of ketoconazole or itraconazole with these drugs may increase concentration of protease inhibitor; indinavir and ritonavir may increase itraconazole concentration)

» Isoniazid or
» Rifampin
(concurrent use of rifampin may increase the metabolism of fluconazole, itraconazole, and ketoconazole, lowering their plasma concentrations; this may lead to clinical failure or relapse; concurrent use of isoniazid with ketoconazole has also been reported to decrease serum concentrations of ketoconazole; isoniazid or rifampin in not recommended to be given concurrently with azole antifungals)

» Levacetylmethadol (levomethadyl)
(known to prolong the QT interval and is metabolized by CYP3A4; concomitant use of itraconazole and levacetylmethadol could result in serious cardiovascular events and is, therefore, **contraindicated**)

Nevirapine
(concomitant administration is not recommended as there is the possibility of a significant reduction in bioavailability of itraconazole; studies have not been done with nevirapine and itraconazole, but studies done with ketoconazole have demonstrated that nevirapine induces the metabolism of ketoconazole, greatly reducing the bioavailability of ketoconazole)

» Phenobarbital or
» Phenytoin
(concurrent use may decrease itraconazole plasma concentrations, leading to treatment failure or clinical relapse)
(concurrent use with any azole antifungal may decrease the metabolism of phenytoin, resulting in increased plasma phenytoin concentrations; a 75% increase in the AUC of phenytoin was found in volunteers given 200 mg of fluconazole per day; concurrent use has also been reported to decrease the plasma concentration of azole antifungals, which may lead to treatment failure or relapse of the fungal infection; response to both medications should be monitored closely)

» Pimozide
(concurrent use of pimozide with itraconazole is **contraindicated;** concurrent use of pimozide with itraconazole may inhibit the cytochrome P450 enzyme metabolic pathways, resulting in elevated plasma concentrations of pimozide; cardiac arrhythmias, including QT prolongation, ventricular tachycardia, torsades de pointes, and death)

Polyenes including
Amphotericin B
(prior treatment with itraconazole, like other azoles, may reduce or inhibit activity of polyenes; clinical significance of this drug effect not clearly defined)

Rifabutin
(pharmacokinetic studies with fluconazole and rifabutin show that fluconazole appears to increase the serum concentration of rifabutin; however, this is not thought to have clinical significance, and rifabutin dosing does not need to be modified in patients receiving fluconazole)

Theophylline
(fluconazole has been found to increase serum theophylline concentrations by approximately 13%, which may lead to toxicity; theophylline concentrations should be monitored)

» Warfarin
(anticoagulant effects may be increased when warfarin is used concurrently with any azole antifungal, resulting in an increase in prothrombin time [PT]; PT must be monitored carefully in patients receiving warfarin and azole antifungals)

Laboratory value alterations

The following have been selected on the basis of their potential clinical significance (possible effect in parentheses where appropriate)—not necessarily inclusive (» = major clinical significance).

With physiology/laboratory test values
» Alanine aminotransferase (ALT [SGPT]) and
» Alkaline phosphatase and
» Aspartate aminotransferase (AST [SGOT]) and
» Bilirubin
(serum values may be elevated)

» Potassium, serum
(hypokalemia has occurred in approximately 2 to 6% of patients treated with oral itraconazole, and has resulted in ventricular fibrillation, especially at higher doses)

» Corticosteroid concentrations, serum, adrenocorticotropic hormone (ACTH)-induced and
» Testosterone concentrations, serum
(ACTH-induced serum corticosteroid concentrations and serum testosterone concentrations may be decreased by doses of 800 mg of ketoconazole daily; serum testosterone concentrations are abolished by doses of 1.6 grams of ketoconazole daily, but return to baseline values when ketoconazole is discontinued)

Medical considerations/Contraindications

The medical considerations/contraindications included have been selected on the basis of their potential clinical significance (reasons given in parentheses where appropriate)—not necessarily inclusive (» = major clinical significance).

Except under special circumstances, this medication should not be used when the following medical problem exists:

» Congestive heart failure (CHF) or
» Congestive heart failure, history of, or
» Ventricular dysfunction
(itraconazole capsules should not be used for treatment of *onychomycosis* in patients with a evidence of ventricular dysfunction such as congestive heart failure (CHF) or a history of CHF due to negative inotropic effects; continued use of itraconazole oral solution or injection should be reconsidered)

» Hypersensitivity to azole antifungals

Risk-benefit should be considered when the following medical problems exist:

» Achlorhydria or
» Hypochlorhydria
(may cause marked reduction in absorption of itraconazole and ketoconazole; patients with acquired immunodeficiency syndrome [AIDS] may have reduced itraconazole and ketoconazole absorption due to hypochlorhydria)

» Alcoholism, active or in remission or
» Hepatic function impairment
(azole antifungals are metabolized in the liver and may, infrequently, be hepatotoxic; azole antifungals, especially ketoconazole and itraconazole, should be used with caution in patients with pre-existing liver function impairment, those who have experienced liver toxicity with other medications, or a history of alcoholism)
(itraconazole has been associated with rare cases of serious hepatotoxicity, including liver failure and death; treatment should be discontinued and liver function testing performed if clinical signs or symptoms of liver disease develop; continued itraconazole use or reinstitution of treatment strongly discouraged unless there is a serious or life-threatening situation where expected benefit exceeds risk)
(ketoconazole has also been reported to cause a disulfiram-like reaction to alcohol, characterized by flushing, rash, peripheral edema, nausea, and headache; symptoms resolved within a few hours)

Congestive heart failure risk factors including:
Cardiac ischemia or
Chronic obstructive pulmonary disease or
Other edematous disorders or
Renal failure or
Valvular disease
(physicians should carefully review risks and benefits of itraconazole therapy in these patients)

Proarrhythmic conditions including:
Electrolyte abnormalities or
Heart disease, structural or
Medications, concomitant or
(use fluconazole with caution in patients with these potentially proarrhythmic conditions; rare cases of QT prolongation and torsades de pointes have been reported in seriously ill patients with multiple confounding risk factors)

» Renal function impairment
(because fluconazole is excreted through the kidneys, a reduction in dosage, or increase in dosing interval, is recommended in patients with renal function impairment)
(intravenous itraconazole contains the vehicle hydroxypropyl-beta-cyclodextrin, and elimination of the vehicle will be prolonged in patients with renal impairment)

Patient monitoring

The following may be especially important in patient monitoring (other tests may be warranted in some patients, depending on condition; » = major clinical significance):

Blood urea nitrogen or
Creatinine concentration, serum
(blood urea nitrogen or serum creatinine concentrations should be monitored as clinically indicated in patients taking fluconazole since patients with renal function impairment will require an adjustment in dosage)

Congestive heart failure signs and symptoms
(patients should be informed of CHF signs and symptoms and should be monitored; caution should be used; if CHF signs or symptoms appear during itraconazole administration, discontinue use)

» Hepatic function determinations
(liver function tests are recommended prior to treatment, monthly for 3 to 4 months after treatment is started, and periodically thereafter during treatment in patients receiving ketoconazole, and itraconazole; elevated serum enzyme values may occur without clinical hepatitis; however, ketoconazole or itraconazole should be discontinued if even minor abnormalities in enzyme values persist or worsen, or if they are accompanied by symptoms of hepatotoxicity; mild, transient increase in transaminases may occur with fluconazole and itraconazole therapy, and may, on rare occasion, progress to hepatotoxicity; liver function tests should be monitored periodically during treatment in all patients receiving continuous treatment for more than 1 month or any time a patient develops signs or symptoms suggestive of liver dysfunction; fluconazole and itraconazole should be discontinued if abnormal enzyme values persist or worsen, or if they are accompanied by symptoms of hepatotoxicity)

» Potassium, serum
(hypokalemia has occurred in patients treated with itraconazole, and has been associated with ventricular fibrillation)

Side/Adverse Effects

Note: In patients taking ketoconazole, hepatotoxicity, consisting primarily of hepatocellular damage or mixed hepatocellular and cholestatic changes, has been reported in approximately 1 in 10,000 exposed patients. It is usually, but not always, reversible upon discontinuation of ketoconazole, and fatalities have been reported rarely. It is considered to be an idiosyncratic reaction and can occur at any time during therapy. Females and patients over the age of 40 may be predisposed to hepatotoxicity. Several cases of hepatitis have also been reported in children.

Itraconazole has been associated with rare cases of serious hepatotoxicity, including liver failure and death. Some of these cases had neither pre-existing liver disease nor a serious underlying medical condition.

High-dose ketoconazole therapy has also been shown to suppress corticosteroid secretion. In addition, ketoconazole has been shown to lower serum testosterone concentrations at doses of 800 mg per day, and abolish concentrations at 1600 mg per day; these concentrations return to baseline values when ketoconazole is discontinued.

The overall incidence of side effects with fluconazole has been reported to be higher in human immunodeficiency virus (HIV)-infected patients (21%) than in those being treated with fluconazole who were not infected with HIV (13%); however, many patients in these studies were also receiving other medications known to be hepatotoxic or associated with exfoliative skin disorders, making a direct causal association with fluconazole difficult.

The following side/adverse effects have been selected on the basis of their potential clinical significance (possible signs and symptoms in parentheses where appropriate)—not necessarily inclusive:

Those indicating need for medical attention

Incidence less frequent

Hypersensitivity (fever and chills; skin rash or itching)

Incidence rare

Agranulocytosis (fever and sore throat)—for fluconazole; ***exfoliative skin disorders, including Stevens-Johnson syndrome*** (reddening, blistering, peeling, or loosening of skin and mucous membranes)—for fluconazole; ***hepatotoxicity*** (dark or amber urine; loss of appetite; pale stools; stomach pain; unusual tiredness or weakness; yellow eyes or skin); ***thrombocytopenia*** (unusual bleeding or bruising)—for fluconazole

Incidence not determined—Observed during clinical practice with itraconazole; estimates of frequency cannot be determined

Anaphylaxis, anaphylactoid and allergic reactions (cough; difficulty swallowing; dizziness; fast heartbeat; hives; itching; puffiness or swelling of the eyelids or around the eyes, face, lips or tongue; shortness of breath; skin rash; tightness in chest; unusual tiredness or weakness; wheezing); ***angioedema*** (large, hive-like swelling on face, eyelids, lips, tongue, throat, hands, legs, feet, sex organs); ***congestive heart failure*** (chest pain; decreased urine output; dilated neck veins; extreme fatigue; irregular breathing; irregular heartbeat; shortness of breath; swelling of face, fingers, feet, or lower legs; tightness in chest; troubled breathing; weight gain; wheezing); ***hepatitis*** (dark urine; general tiredness and weakness; light-colored stools; nausea and vomiting; upper right abdominal pain; yellow eyes and skin); ***hyperglycemia*** (abdominal pain; blurred vision; dry mouth; fatigue; flushed, dry skin; fruit-like breath odor; increased hunger; increased thirst; increased urination; nausea; sweating; troubled breathing; unexplained weight loss; vomiting); ***hypertriglyceridemia*** (large amount of triglyceride in the blood); ***hypokalemia*** (convulsions; decreased urine; dry mouth; irregular heartbeat; increased thirst; loss of appetite; mood changes; muscle pain or cramps; nausea or vomiting; numbness or tingling in hands, feet, or lips; shortness of breath; unusual tiredness or weakness); ***liver failure*** (headache; stomach pain; continuing vomiting; dark-colored urine; general feeling of tiredness or weakness; light-colored stools yellow eyes or skin); ***neutropenia*** (black, tarry, stools; chills; cough; fever; lower back or side pain; painful or difficult urination; pale skin; shortness of breath; sore throat; ulcers, sores, or white spots in mouth; unusual bleeding or bruising; unusual tiredness or weakness); ***peripheral edema*** (bloating or swelling of face, arms, hands, lower legs, or feet; rapid weight gain; tingling of hands or feet; unusual weight gain or loss); ***peripheral neuropathy*** (burning, numbness, tingling, or painful sensations; weakness in arms, hands, legs, or feet; unsteadiness or awkwardness); ***pruritus*** (itching skin); ***pulmonary edema*** (chest pain; difficult, fast, noisy breathing, sometimes with wheezing blue lips and fingernails; pale skin; increased sweating; coughing that sometimes produces a pink frothy sputum; shortness of breath; swelling in legs and ankles); ***Stevens-Johnson syndrome*** (blistering, peeling, loosening of skin; chills; cough; diarrhea; itching; joint or muscle pain; red, irritated eyes; red skin lesions, often with a purple center; sore throat; sores, ulcers, or white spots in mouth or on lips; unusual tiredness or weakness); ***urticaria*** (hives or welts; itching; redness of skin; skin rash)

Incidence not determined—Observed during clinical practice with fluconazole; estimates of frequency cannot be determined

angioedema (large, hive-like swelling on face, eyelids, lips, tongue, throat, hands, legs, feet, sex organs); ***hypercholesterolemia*** (large amount of cholesterol in the blood); ***hypertriglyceridemia*** (large amount of triglyceride in the blood); ***hypokalemia*** (convulsions; decreased urine; dry mouth; irregular heartbeat; increased thirst; loss of appetite; mood changes; muscle pain or cramps; nausea or vomiting; numbness or tingling in hands, feet, or lips; shortness of breath; unusual tiredness or weakness); ***leukopenia including; neutropenia*** (black, tarry, stools; chills; cough; fever; lower back or side pain; painful or difficult urination; pale skin; shortness of breath; sore throat; ulcers, sores, or white spots in mouth; unusual bleeding or bruising; unusual tiredness or weakness); ***QT prolongation*** (irregular heartbeat; fainting); ***pruritus*** (itching skin); ***seizures*** (convulsions; muscle spasm or jerking of all extremities; sudden loss of consciousness; loss of bladder control); ***torsades de pointes*** (chest pain or discomfort; irregular or slow heart rate; fainting; shortness of breath); ***toxic epidermal necrolysis*** (blistering, peeling, loosening of skin; chills; cough; diarrhea; itching; joint or muscle pain; red irritated eyes; red skin lesions, often with a purple center; sore throat; sores, ulcers, or white spots in mouth or on lips; unusual tiredness or weakness)

Those indicating need for medical attention only if they continue or are bothersome

Incidence less frequent

gastrointestinal disturbances (abdominal pain; constipation; loss of appetite; vomiting)

Incidence rare

Gynecomastia (enlargement of the breasts in males)—for ketoconazole; ***menstrual irregularities***—for ketoconazole; ***photophobia*** (increased sensitivity of the eyes to light)—for ketoconazole

Note: *Gynecomastia* and *impotence* are due to inhibition of testosterone and adrenal steroid synthesis.

Incidence not determined—Observed during clinical practice with itraconazole; estimates of frequency cannot be determined

Abdominal pain (stomach pain); ***alopecia*** (hair loss, thinning of hair); ***constipation*** (difficulty having a bowel movement [stool]); ***diarrhea; dizziness; dyspepsia*** (acid or sour stomach; belching; heartburn indigestion; stomach discomfort, upset or pain); ***headache; menstrual disorders*** (absent, missed, or irregular menstrual periods; stopping of menstrual bleeding); ***nausea; vomiting***

Incidence not determined—Observed during clinical practice with fluconazole; estimates of frequency cannot be determined

alopecia (hair loss, thinning of hair); ***dyspepsia*** (acid or sour stomach; belching; heartburn indigestion; stomach discomfort, upset or pain); ***dizziness; face edema*** (swelling of face); ***taste perversion*** (change in taste; bad unusual or unpleasant taste in mouth)

Patient Consultation

As an aid to patient consultation, refer to *Advice for the Patient, Antifungals, Azole (Systemic)*.

In providing consultation, consider emphasizing the following selected information (» = major clinical significance):

Before using this medication

» Conditions affecting use, especially:

Hypersensitivity to azole antifungals

Fertility—High doses of ketoconazole have been shown to cause menstrual irregularities, oligospermia, azoospermia, and impotence

Pregnancy—High doses of azole antifungals may cause maternal toxicity, embryotoxicity, and teratogenicity in animals

Breast-feeding—Fluconazole is distributed in human milk; use of fluconazole in nursing mothers is not recommended.

Contraindicated medications—Astemizole (with itraconazole or ketoconazole), cisapride (with fluconazole, itraconazole or oral ketoconazole), dofetilide, ergot alkaloids (with itraconazole), erythromycin (with itraconazole), levacetylmethadol (with itraconazole), lovastatin, midazolam (with itraconazole), pimozide (with itraconazole), quinidine (with itraconazole), simvastatin, terfenadine (with fluconazole ≥ 400 mg per day, itraconazole, or ketoconazole), and triazolam (with itraconazole).

Other medications, especially alcohol, alprazolam, antacids, anticholinergics/antispasmodics, oral antidiabetic agents, atorvastatin, barbiturates, long-acting, busulfan, carbamazepine, cerivastatin, clarithromycin, cyclosporine, CYP3A4 inducers, diazepam didanosine, digoxin, dihydropyridine calcium channel blockers, docetaxel, erythromycin, hepatotoxic medications, histamine H_2-receptor antagonists, indinavir, isoniazid, lovastatin, midazolam, nevirapine, omeprazole, phenobarbital, phenytoin, proton pump inhibitors, rifampin, ritonavir, saquinavir, simvastatin, sirolimus, sucralfate, tacrolimus, triazolam, verapamil, vinca alkaloids, or warfarin

Other medical problems, especially achlorhydria, alcoholism, CHF or history of, hepatic function impairment, hypochlorhydria, proarrhythmic conditions (fluconazole), renal function impairment or ventricular dysfunction

Proper use of this medication

» Taking itraconazole capsules with a full meal and ketoconazole with food to increase absorption

» Taking itraconazole oral solution on an empty stomach to increase absorption

Proper administration technique for oral liquids

Proper administration technique in achlorhydria

» Compliance with full course of therapy

» Importance of not missing doses and taking at evenly spaced times

» Proper dosing

Missed dose: Taking as soon as possible; not taking if almost time for next dose; not doubling doses

» Proper storage

Precautions while using this medication

Checking with physician if no improvement within a few days

» Not taking oral ketoconazole with terfenadine, cisapride, or astemizole, not taking itraconazole with astemizole, cisapride, dofetilide, pimozide, or quinidine, and not taking ≥ 400 mg per day of fluconazole with terfenadine; concurrent use may cause cardiac arrhythmias

» Avoiding intake of alcoholic beverages or other alcohol-containing preparations while taking ketoconazole because of increased risk of hepatotoxicity

» Avoiding use of antacids and other medications that increase gastrointestinal pH while taking itraconazole or ketoconazole; concurrent use may decrease the absorption of itraconazole or ketoconazole

Possible photophobic reactions when taking ketoconazole; wearing sunglasses and avoiding bright light to minimize potential eye discomfort

Side/adverse effects

Signs of potential side effects, especially agranulocytosis, exfoliative skin disorders, hepatotoxicity, and thrombocytopenia

Signs of potential side effects observed during clinical practice for fluconazole, especially angioedema, hypercholesterolemia, hypertriglyceridemia, hypokalemia, leukopenia, neutropenia, pruritus, QT prolongation, seizures, and torsades de pointes

Signs of potential side effects observed during clinical practice for itraconazole, especially anaphylaxis, anaphylactoid reactions, allergic reactions, angioedema, congestive heart failure, hepatitis, hyperglycemia, hypertriglyceridemia, hypokalemia, liver failure, neutropenia, peripheral edema, peripheral neuropathy, pruritus, pulmonary edema, Stevens-Johnson syndrome, and urticaria

---

FLUCONAZOLE

Summary of Differences

Indications:

Also indicated for the treatment of vulvovaginal candidiasis.

Pharmacology/pharmacokinetics:

Good penetration into the cerebrospinal fluid; 80% of an administered dose is eliminated as unchanged drug in the urine.

Precautions:

Medical considerations/contraindications—Dose may need to be adjusted in patients with renal function impairment.

Drug interactions and/or related problems—Use with oral antidiabetic agents has increased the plasma concentration of these sulfonylurea agents, leading to hypoglycemia. At fluconazole doses of 400 mg per day or greater, concurrent use with terfenadine is contraindicated and may increase the risk of cardiac arrhythmias, including torsades de pointes.

Side/adverse effects:

Increased risk of exfoliative skin disorders, including Stevens-Johnson syndrome, agranulocytosis, and thrombocytopenia.

Additional Dosing Information

Because oral fluconazole is almost completely bioavailable, the daily oral dose is the same as the intravenous dose.

Intravenous fluconazole should be administered at a maximum rate of approximately 200 mg per hour by continuous infusion.

The dose of fluconazole and the length of treatment should be based on the site of infection and the individual response to therapy. Treatment should be continued until clinical parameters and laboratory tests indicate that active fungal infection has subsided. Acquired immunodeficiency syndrome (AIDS) patients with cryptococcal meningitis or recurrent oropharyngeal candidiasis require maintenance therapy to prevent relapse.

Patients undergoing bone marrow transplantation in whom severe granulocytopenia is anticipated should start fluconazole prophylaxis several days before the anticipated onset of neutropenia, and continue treatment for seven days after the neutrophil count rises above 1000 cells per mm ^{3}.

Patients with impaired renal function who will receive multiple doses of fluconazole may require an adjustment in dose. An initial loading dose of 50 to 400 mg should be given. The daily dose, according to indication, should be modified as follows:

Creatinine clearance (mL/min)/(mL/sec)	Percent of recommended dose
> 50/0.83	100
≤50/ ≤0.83 (no dialysis)	50
Regular dialysis	100 after each dialysis

On dialysis days, the dose of fluconazole should be administered after hemodialysis has been performed since a single 3-hour dialysis period will reduce plasma fluconazole concentrations by approximately 50%.

These are suggested dose adjustments based on pharmacokinetics following administration of multiple doses. Further adjustments may be warranted depending on the clinical condition.

The pharmacokinetics of fluconazole has not been studied in children with renal insufficiency. Dosage reduction in children with renal insufficiency should parallel that recommended for adults.

Oral Dosage Forms

FLUCONAZOLE CAPSULES

Usual adult dose

Candidiasis, vulvovaginal—

Oral, 150 mg as a single dose.

Usual pediatric dose

Safety and efficacy have not been established for children up to 18 years of age.

Strength(s) usually available

U.S.—
Not commercially available.
Canada—
150 mg (Rx) [*Diflucan-150* (lactose)].

Packaging and storage

Store between 15 and 30 °C (59 and 86 °F).

FLUCONAZOLE FOR ORAL SUSPENSION

Usual adult and adolescent dose

Candidiasis (prophylaxis)—
Oral, 400 mg once a day. Fluconazole prophylaxis should start several days before the anticipated onset of neutropenia and continue for 7 days after neutrophil count rises above 1000 cells per cu mm in patients who are anticipated to have severe granulocytopenia (less than 500 neutrophils per cu mm).
Candidiasis, disseminated—
Oral, optimal therapeutic dosage and duration of therapy have not been established for systemic *Candida* infections including candidemia, disseminated candidiasis, and pneumonia. A small number of patients received doses up to 400 mg daily in open, noncomparative studies.
Oral, 50 to 200 mg have been used in open, noncomparative studies of small numbers of patients for the treatment of *Candida* urinary tract infections and peritonitis.
Candidiasis, esophageal—
Oral, 200 mg on the first day, then 100 mg once a day for at least three weeks and for at least two weeks following the resolution of symptoms. Doses of up to 400 mg once a day may be used depending on clinical response.
Candidiasis, oropharyngeal—
Oral, 200 mg on the first day, then 100 mg once a day for at least two weeks.
Candidiasis, vulvovaginal—
Oral, 150 mg as a single dose.
Meningitis, cryptococcal (treatment)—
Oral, 400 mg once a day until a clear clinical response is seen, then 200 to 400 mg once a day for at least ten to twelve weeks after the cerebrospinal fluid becomes culture-negative.
Note: Some clinicians prefer a loading dose of 400 mg two times a day for two days, then 400 mg a day for at least ten to twelve weeks after the cerebrospinal fluid becomes culture-negative.
Meningitis, cryptococcal (suppressive therapy)—
Oral, 200 mg once a day.
[Neutropenia, febrile (prophylaxis and treatment)][1]—
Oral, 50 mg two times a day until neutrophil levels had recovered to at least 1000/mcL for 7 days.
Note: Antifungal prophylaxis could be given continuously for up to 90 days for patients receiving multiple course of cytotoxic chemotherapy within this period. Clinical trials have demonstrated that high-dose and low-dose fluconazole are equally effective; however high-dose fluconazole was not superior to low-dose fluconazole.

Note: For dosage adjustment in patients with impaired renal function, see *Additional dosing information.*

Usual pediatric dose

[Candidiasis, disseminated][1]—
Neonates: Oral, 6 mg per kg of body weight (mg/kg) once a day. The dose may be reduced to 3 mg/kg once a day for neonates with reduced renal function.
Candidiasis, disseminated (treatment)—
Infants and children 6 months of age and older: Oral, 6 to 12 mg per kg of body weight once a day have been used in an open, noncomparative study of a small number of children.
Infants up to 6 months of age: Dosage has not been established.
Candidiasis, esophageal—
Infants and children 6 months of age and older: Oral, 6 mg per kg of body weight on the first day, followed by 3 mg per kg of body weight once daily. Doses up to 12 mg per kg of body weight per day may be used based on medical judgment of the patient's response. Patients with esophageal candidiasis should be treated for a minimum of three weeks and for at least 2 weeks following the resolution of symptoms.
Infants up to 6 months of age: Dosage has not been established.
Candidiasis, oropharyngeal—
Infants and children 6 months of age and older: Oral, 6 mg per kg of body weight on the first day, followed by 3 mg per kg of body weight once daily. Treatment should be administered for at least 2 weeks to decrease the likelihood of relapse.
Infants up to 6 months of age: Dosage has not been established.
Meningitis, cryptococcal (treatment)—
Infants and children 6 months of age and older: Oral, 12 mg per kg of body weight on the first day, followed by 6 mg per kg of body weight once daily. A dosage of 12 mg per kg of body weight once daily may be used, based on medical judgment of patient's response to therapy. The recommended duration of treatment for initial therapy of cryptococcal meningitis is 10 to 12 weeks after the cerebrospinal fluid becomes culture negative.
Infants up to 6 months of age: Dosage has not been established.
Meningitis, cryptococcal (suppressive therapy)—
Infants and children 6 months of age and older: Oral, 6 mg per kg of body weight once a day.
Infants up to 6 months of age: Dosage has not been established.
[Neutropenia, febrile (prophylaxis and treatment)][1]—
Studies have not been performed in persons younger than 18 years of age.
Note: Premature newborns (gestational age 26 to 29 weeks)—Based on the prolonged half-life seen in premature newborns, in the first 2 weeks of life, these children should receive the same dosage (mg/kg) as older children, but administered every 72 hours. After the first 2 weeks of life, these children should be dosed once daily.
Dose equivalency scheme for pediatric patients that should generally provide equivalent exposure as the dose indicated for adults:
- For adult dose of 100 mg, equivalent pediatric dose is 3 mg per kg of body weight.
- For adult dose of 200 mg, equivalent pediatric dose is 6 mg per kg of body weight.
- For adult dose of 400 mg, equivalent pediatric dose is 12 mg per kg of body weight. Absolute doses exceeding 600 mg per day are not recommended.

For dosage adjustment in children with impaired renal function, see *Additional dosing information.*

Usual pediatric prescribing limits

600 mg per day.

Strength(s) usually available

U.S.—
10 mg per mL (when reconstituted according to manufacturers instructions) (Rx) [*Diflucan* (sodium benzoate; sucrose)].
40 mg per mL (when reconstituted according to manufacturers instructions) (Rx) [*Diflucan* (sodium benzoate; sucrose)].
Canada—
10 mg per mL (when reconstituted according to manufacturers instructions) (Rx) [*Diflucan* (sodium benzoate; sucrose)].
40 mg per mL (when reconstituted according to manufacturers instructions) (Rx) [*Diflucan* (sodium benzoate; sucrose)].

Packaging and storage

Dry powder—Store below 86°F (30°C).
Reconstituted suspension—Store between 86 and 42 °F (30 and 5°C). Protect from freezing.

Stability

After reconstitution, suspensions retain their potency for 14 days.

Auxiliary labeling

- Shake well.
- You should take this medication exactly as prescribed. Do not skip or discontinue unless directed.
- Do not freeze.
- Discard unused drug after 14 days.

Note

When dispensing, include a calibrated liquid-measuring device.

FLUCONAZOLE TABLETS

Usual adult and adolescent dose

See *Fluconazole for Oral Suspension.*

Usual pediatric dose

See *Fluconazole for Oral Suspension.*

Strength(s) usually available

U.S.—
50 mg (Rx) [*Diflucan*].
100 mg (Rx) [*Diflucan*].
150 mg (Rx) [*Diflucan*].
200 mg (Rx) [*Diflucan*].

Canada—
50 mg (Rx) [*Diflucan*].
100 mg (Rx) [*Diflucan*].
200 mg (Rx) [*Diflucan*].

Packaging and storage

Store tablets below 30 °C (86 °F).

Auxiliary labeling

• You should take this medication exactly as prescribed. Do not skip or discontinue unless directed.

Parenteral Dosage Forms

FLUCONAZOLE INJECTION

Usual adult and adolescent dose

Candidiasis (prophylaxis)—
Intravenous, 400 mg once a day. Fluconazole prophylaxis should start several days before the anticipated onset of neutropenia and continue for 7 days after neutrophil count rises above 1000 cells per cu mm in patients who are anticipated to have severe granulocytopenia (less than 500 neutrophils per cu mm).

Candidiasis, disseminated—
Intravenous, optimal therapeutic dosage and duration of therapy have not been established for treatment of systemic *Candida* infections including candidemia, disseminated candidiasis, and pneumonia. Doses up to 400 mg daily have been used in open, noncomparative studies of small numbers of patients.
Intravenous, 50 to 200 mg have been used in open, noncomparative studies of small numbers of patients for the treatment of *Candida* urinary tract infections and peritonitis.

Candidiasis, esophageal—
Intravenous, 200 mg on the first day, then 100 mg once a day for at least three weeks and for at least two weeks following the resolution of symptoms. Doses of up to 400 mg once a day may be used depending on clinical response.

Candidiasis, oropharyngeal—
Intravenous, 200 mg on the first day, then 100 mg once a day for at least two weeks.

Meningitis, cryptococcal (treatment)—
Intravenous, 400 mg once a day until a clear clinical response is seen, then 200 to 400 mg once a day for at least ten to twelve weeks after the cerebrospinal fluid becomes culture-negative. The patient should be switched to fluconazole tablets when oral therapy can be administered.

Note: Some clinicians prefer a loading dose of 400 mg two times a day for two days, then 400 mg a day for at least ten to twelve weeks after the cerebrospinal fluid becomes culture-negative.

Meningitis, cryptococcal (suppressive therapy)—
Intravenous, 200 mg once a day.

Note: For dosage adjustment in patients with impaired renal function, see *Additional dosing information*.

Usual pediatric dose

[Candidiasis, disseminated][1]—
Neonates: Intravenous, 6 mg/kg once a day. The dose may be reduced to 3 mg/kg once a day for neonates with reduced renal function.

Note: USP experts recommend that amphotericin B as the first line agent for systemic candidiasis with fluconazole as an adjunct unless amphotericin B is contraindicated. Although oral fluconazole has been used in the treatment of systemic candidiasis, intravenous fluconazole may be the preferred dosage form, especially during initial treatment.

Candidiasis, disseminated (treatment)—
Infants and children 6 months of age and older: Oral, 6 to 12 mg per kg of body weight once a day have been used in an open, noncomparative study of a small number of children.
Infants up to 6 months of age: Dosage has not been established.

Candidiasis, esophageal—
Infants and children 6 months of age and older: Intravenous, 6 mg per kg of body weight on the first day, followed by 3 mg per kg of body weight once daily. Doses up to 12 mg per kg of body weight per day may be used based on medical judgment of the patient's response. Patients with esophageal candidiasis should be treated for a minimum of three weeks and for at least 2 weeks following the resolution of symptoms.
Infants up to 6 months of age: Dosage has not been established.

Candidiasis, oropharyngeal—
Infants and children 6 months of age and older: Intravenous, 6 mg per kg of body weight on the first day, followed by 3 mg per kg of body weight once daily. Treatment should be administered for at least 2 weeks to decrease the likelihood of relapse.
Infants up to 6 months of age: Dosage has not been established.

Meningitis, cryptococcal (treatment)—
Infants and children 6 months of age and older: Intravenous, 12 mg per kg of body weight on the first day, followed by 6 mg per kg of body weight once daily. A dosage of 12 mg per kg of body weight once daily may be used, based on medical judgment of patient's response to therapy. The recommended duration of treatment for initial therapy of cryptococcal meningitis is 10 to 12 weeks after the cerebrospinal fluid becomes culture negative.
Infants up to 6 months of age: Dosage has not been established.

Meningitis, cryptococcal (suppressive therapy)—
Infants and children 6 months of age and older: Intravenous, 6 mg per kg of body weight once a day.
Infants up to 6 months of age: Dosage has not been established.

[Neutropenia, febrile (prophylaxis and treatment)][1]—
Studies have not been performed in persons younger than 18 years of age.

Note: Premature newborns (gestational age 26 to 29 weeks)—Based on the prolonged half-life seen in premature newborns, in the first 2 weeks of life, these children should receive the same dosage (mg/kg) as older children, but administered every 72 hours. After the first 2 weeks of life, these children should be dosed once daily.

Dose equivalency scheme for pediatric patients that should generally provide equivalent exposure as the dose indicated for adults:
• For adult dose of 100 mg, equivalent pediatric dose is 3 mg per kg of body weight.
• For adult dose of 200 mg, equivalent pediatric dose is 6 mg per kg of body weight.
• For adult dose of 400 mg, equivalent pediatric dose is 12 mg per kg of body weight. Absolute doses exceeding 600 mg per day are not recommended.

For dosage adjustment in children with impaired renal function, see *Additional dosing information*.

Usual pediatric prescribing limits

600 mg per day.

Strength(s) usually available

U.S.—
200 mg in 100 mL (Rx) [*Diflucan* (56 mg dextrose per mL)].
200 mg in 100 mL (Rx) [*Diflucan* (9 mg sodium chloride per mL)].
400 mg in 200 mL (Rx) [*Diflucan* (56 mg dextrose per mL)].
400 mg in 200 mL (Rx) [*Diflucan* (9 mg sodium chloride per mL)].

Canada—
200 mg in 100 mL (Rx) [*Diflucan* (9 mg sodium chloride per mL)].
400 mg in 200 mL (Rx) [*Diflucan* (9 mg sodium chloride per mL)].

Packaging and storage

Store between 25 and 5 °C (77 and 41 °F). Brief exposure up to 40 °C (104 °F) does not adversely affect the product. Protect from freezing.

Viaflex® Plus plastic containers—Do not remove unit from overwrap until ready for use. The overwrap is a moisture barrier. The inner bag maintains the sterility of the product.

Incompatibilities

Intravenous admixtures of fluconazole and other medications are not recommended.

Note

Do not use plastic containers in series connections because an air embolism could result due to residual air being drawn from the primary container before administration of the fluid from the secondary container is complete.

Some opacity of the plastic due to moisture absorption during the sterilization process may be observed. This does not affect the solution quality or safety and will diminish gradually.

After removing the overwrap, check for minute leaks by squeezing the inner bag firmly. If a leak is found, discard solution as sterility may be impaired.

[1]Not included in Canadian product labeling.

ITRACONAZOLE

Summary of Differences

Precautions:
Drug interactions and/or related problems—
Antacids, anticholinergics/antispasmodics, histamine H_2-receptor antagonists, omeprazole, or sucralfate will increase the pH of the stomach and decrease the absorption of itraconazole.
Use with astemizole, cisapride, dofetilide, pimozide, quinidine, or terfenadine is contraindicated and may increase the risk of cardiac arrhythmias, including QT prolongation, ventricular tachycardia, torsades de pointes, and death.

Didanosine contains a buffer to increase its absorption; this will decrease the absorption of itraconazole since itraconazole needs an acidic environment.

Use with oral antidiabetic agents has increased the plasma concentration of these sulfonylurea agents, leading to hypoglycemia.

Use with carbamazepine, phenobarbital and phenytoin may decrease itraconazole plasma concentrations, leading to treatment failure or relapse.

Itraconazole may increase digoxin concentrations, leading to digoxin toxicity.

Use with atorvastatin, cerivastatin, lovastatin or simvastatin may increase the plasma concentrations of these cholesterol-lowering agents and may increase the risk of rhabdomyolysis.

Use with alprazolam, diazepam, midazolam or triazolam may potentiate the hypnotic and sedative effects of these benzodiazepines.

Use with nifedipine, felodipine, or verapamil may cause additive negative inotropic effects.

Use with macrolide antibiotics such as clarithromycin and erythromycin may cause increased plasma concentrations of itraconazole.

Use with erythromycin also showed an adjusted rate of sudden death from cardiac causes to be five times as high as that among those who had used neither a CYP3A inhibitor nor any of the study antibiotic medications; concurrent use should be avoided

Medical considerations/contraindications—

Achlorhydria or hypochlorhydria will decrease the absorption of itraconazole.

Additional Dosing Information

Itraconazole capsules and itraconazole oral solution are not bioequivalent; the two dosage forms should not be used interchangeably.

The dose of itraconazole and the length of treatment should be based on the site of infection and the individual response to therapy. Treatment may be continued for weeks or months until clinical parameters and laboratory tests indicate that active fungal infection has subsided.

Because patients with acquired immunodeficiency syndrome (AIDS) may have reduced absorption of itraconazole due to hypochlorhydria, they may require higher doses to achieve a clinical response.

Although studies did not provide for a loading dose, in life-threatening situations, a loading dose of 200 mg three times a day (600 mg per day) for the first 3 days is recommended, based on pharmacokinetic data.

Doses above 200 mg per day should be given in two divided doses.

Diet/Nutrition

Itraconazole capsules should be taken with a full meal to ensure maximal absorption of the medication.

Itraconazole oral solution should be taken on an empty stomach to increase absorption of the medication.

Oral Dosage Forms

Note: Bracketed uses in the *Dosage Forms* section refer to categories of use and/or indications that are not included in Us. product labeling.

ITRACONAZOLE CAPSULES

Usual adult and adolescent dose

Aspergillosis—

Oral, 200 mg one or two times a day with meals for at least three months.

Blastomycosis or
Histoplasmosis (treatment)—

Oral, 200 mg once a day with meals. The dose may be increased by 100 mg, up to a maximum of 400 mg a day, if there is no obvious improvement or if there is evidence of progressive fungal disease.

[Candidiasis, esophageal] or
[Candidiasis, oropharyngeal]—

Oral, 100 to 200 mg once a day with a meal for fourteen days; the dose for AIDS and neutropenic patients is increased to 200 mg for four weeks.

[Candidiasis, vulvovaginal][1]—

Oral, 200 mg once a day with a meal for three days.

[Chromomycosis]—

Oral, 100 to 200 mg once a day with a meal for three to six months.

[Coccidioidomycosis][1]—

Oral, 200 mg two times a day with meals for six weeks.

[Cryptococcosis (treatment)][1] or
[Meningitis, cryptococcal (suppression)][1]—

Oral, 200 mg two times a day with meals.

[Histoplasmosis (suppression)][1]—

Oral, 200 mg two times a day with meals.

[Neutropenia, febrile (prophylaxis and treatment)][1]—

Oral, 100 mg two times a day until neutrophil levels had recovered to at least 1000/mcL for 7 days.

Onychomycosis[1]—

Fingernails only: Oral, 200 mg two times a day with meals for one week; this treatment is suspended for three weeks, then resumed for one week.

Toenails with or without fingernail involvement: Oral, 200 mg once a day with meals for twelve consecutive weeks.

[Paracoccidioidomycosis]—

Oral, 100 mg once a day with a meal for six months.

[*Penicillium Marneffei* infection (treatment)][1]—

Oral, 400 mg two times a day for two months followed by 100 mg once a day for another month.

Note: Itraconazole has been shown to be effective in the initial treatment of *Penicillium Marneffei* infection; however, relapse after treatment is common and long-term suppressive treatment is recommended.

[Sporotrichosis]—

Oral, 100 mg once a day with a meal for three months.

[Tinea corporis] or
[Tinea cruris]—

Oral, 100 mg once a day with a meal for fifteen days.

[Tinea manuum][1] or
[Tinea pedis]—

Oral, 100 mg once a day with a meal for thirty days.

Usual pediatric dose

Safety and efficacy have not been established. However, a small number of patients 3 to 16 years of age have been treated with itraconazole capsules, 100 mg per day, for systemic fungal infections, and no serious adverse effects have been reported.

Strength(s) usually available

U.S.—

100 mg (Rx) [*Sporanox* (sucrose)].

Canada—

100 mg (Rx) [*Sporanox* (sugar spheres NF)].

Packaging and storage

Store below 40 °C (104 °F), preferably between 15 and 30 °C (59 and 86 °F), in a well-closed container.

Auxiliary labeling

- Take with food.
- Continue medicine for full time of treatment.
- Keep out of reach of children

ITRACONAZOLE ORAL SOLUTION

Usual adult and adolescent dose

Candidiasis, esophageal—

Oral, 100 mg once a day for a minimum of three weeks; treatment should continue for two weeks after resolution of symptoms.

Candidiasis, oropharyngeal—

Oral, 200 mg once a day for seven to fourteen days.

Note: For patients unresponsive or refractory to treatment with fluconazole, 100 mg two times a day for two to four weeks.

Neutropenia, febrile (treatment)—

Oral, 200 mg (20 mL) twice daily until resolution. Oral solution dosing follows the administration of the injectable dose. See *Itraconazole Injection* for injectable dosing to be administered prior to the oral solution.

Usual adult prescribing limits

For febrile neutropenia treatment, safety and efficacy for itraconazole use exceeding 28 days is not known.

Usual pediatric dose

Safety and efficacy have not been established. However, a small number of patients 6 months to 12 years of age have been treated with itraconazole oral solution, 5 mg per kg per day, for systemic fungal infections, and no unexpected serious adverse effects have been reported.

Strength(s) usually available

U.S.—

100 mg per 10 mL (Rx) [*Sporanox* (hydroxypropyl-beta-cyclodextrin [400 mg per mL]; sodium saccharin)].

Canada—

Note: Not commercially available.

Packaging and storage

Store at or below 25 °C (77 °F). Protect from freezing.

Preparation of dosage form
Proper use of dosage form—Itraconazole oral solution should be vigorously swished in the mouth, 10 mL at a time, for several seconds and swallowed.

Auxiliary labeling
- Take on an empty stomach.
- Keep out of reach of children

Parenteral Dosage Forms

ITRACONAZOLE INJECTION

Usual adult dose
Aspergillosis or
Blastomycosis or
Histoplasmosis (treatment)—
Intravenous, 200 mg twice a day for four doses followed by 200 mg once a day. Switch to oral itraconazole as soon as possible.

Note: Each intravenous dose should be infused over 1 hour. Not for intravenous, direct injection.

Neutropenia, febrile (treatment)—
Intravenous, 200 mg twice a day for the first four doses, followed by 200 mg once daily for up to 14 days. Intravenous dose should be infused over 1 hour. Treatment should be continued with itraconazole oral solution until resolution. See *Itraconazole Oral Solution* for dosing information following intravenous administration.

Usual adult prescribing limits
For febrile neutropenia treatment, safety and efficacy for itraconazole use exceeding 28 days is not known.

Usual pediatric dose
Safety and efficacy have not been established.

Strength(s) usually available
U.S.—
200 mg in 50 mL (Rx) [*Sporanox*].
Canada—
10 mg per mL (Rx) [*Sporanox* (kit)].

Packaging and storage
Store at or below 25 °C (77 °F). Protect from light and freezing.
After reconstitution, the diluted injection may be stored refrigerated (2 to 8 °C) or at room temperature (15 to 25 °C) for up to 48 hours, when protected from direct light.

Incompatibilities
Intravenous admixtures of itraconazole and other medications are not recommended.

[1]Not included in Canadian product labeling.

KETOCONAZOLE

Summary of Differences

Pharmacology/pharmacokinetics:
Ketoconazole has been shown to suppress corticosteroid secretion and lower serum testosterone concentrations.
Ketoconazole penetrates poorly into the cerebrospinal fluid.

Precautions:
Pregnancy/reproduction—
Ketoconazole may cause menstrual irregularities, oligospermia, azoospermia, impotence, and decreased male libido.
Drug interactions and/or related problems—
Alcohol and hepatotoxic medications may increase the risk of hepatotoxicity.
Antacids, anticholinergics/antispasmodics, histamine H_2-receptor antagonists, omeprazole, or sucralfate will increase the pH of the stomach and decrease the absorption of ketoconazole.
Use with astemizole, cisapride, or terfenadine is contraindicated and may increase the risk of cardiac arrhythmias, including torsades de pointes.
Didanosine contains a buffer to increase its absorption, which will decrease the absorption of ketoconazole.
Ketoconazole may increase digoxin concentrations, leading to digoxin toxicity.
Ketoconazole may increase plasma concentrations of indinavir; a dose reduction of indinavir is recommended.
Use with midazolam or triazolam may potentiate the hypnotic and sedative effects of these benzodiazepines.
Medical considerations/contraindications—
Achlorhydria or hypochlorhydria will decrease the absorption of ketoconazole.

Side/adverse effects:
Increased risk of hepatotoxicity and of side effects due to inhibition of testosterone and corticosteroid synthesis, such as menstrual irregularities, oligospermia, azoospermia, impotence, and decreased male libido.

Additional Dosing Information

In patients with achlorhydria or hypochlorhydria, higher serum concentrations may be achieved by taking the medication with an acidic drink. Ketoconazole may be dissolved in cola or seltzer water and swallowed, or the medication may be taken with a glass of cola or seltzer water. An alternative is to dissolve each tablet in 4 mL of 0.2 N hydrochloric acid. Patients may further dilute the resulting mixture in a small amount of water and should be instructed to drink it through a plastic or glass straw to avoid contact with the teeth. This should be followed by one-half glass (120 mL) of water, which is swished around in the mouth and swallowed.

Therapy should be continued for at least l to 2 weeks in candidiasis (3 to 5 days in vaginal candidiasis); for 1 to 8 weeks in dermatomycoses caused by yeasts or dermatophytes, and mycoses of hair and scalp; for 3 months to l year in paracoccidioidomycosis; and for 6 months or longer in other systemic mycoses. Chronic mucocutaneous candidiasis following a remission usually requires indefinite maintenance treatment to prevent relapse.

Diet/Nutrition
Ketoconazole may be taken with a meal or snack to minimize nausea or vomiting and to promote absorption.

Oral Dosage Forms

Note: Bracketed uses in the *Dosage Forms* section refer to categories of use and/or indications that are not included in U.S. product labeling.

KETOCONAZOLE ORAL SUSPENSION

Usual adult and adolescent dose
[Candidiasis, vulvovaginal][1]
Oral, 200 to 400 mg once a day for five days.
[Carcinoma, prostatic][1]—
Oral, 400 mg three times a day.
[Cushing's syndrome][1]
Oral, 600 mg to 1.2 grams a day.
[Paronychia][1]—
Oral, 200 to 400 mg once a day.
Pityriasis versicolor—
Oral, 200 mg once a day for five to ten days.
[Pneumonia, fungal][1] or
[Septicemia, fungal][1]—
Oral, 400 mg to 1 gram once a day.
For all other antifungal indications—
Oral, 200 to 400 mg once a day.

Usual adult prescribing limits
Antifungal—
1 gram a day.
[Antiadrenal; antineoplastic][1]—
1.2 grams a day

Usual pediatric dose
[Candidiasis, vulvovaginal][1]—
Children 2 years of age and older: Oral, 5 to 10 mg per kg of body weight once a day for five days.
Infants and children up to 2 years of age: Dosage has not been established.
[Paronychia][1] or
[*Penicillium Marneffei* infection][1] or
[Pneumonia, fungal][1] or
[Septicemia, fungal][1]—
Children 2 years of age and older: Oral, 5 to 10 mg per kg of body weight once a day.
Infants and children up to 2 years of age: Dosage has not been established.

Note: It is estimated that 6000–7200 human immunodeficiency virus (HIV)-infected children are born in Thailand every year. Many of these children will develop systemic *P. Marneffei* infection. Early diagnosis and prompt administration of antifungal treatment are crucial for improved outcome. Therefore, histologically or culture-proved *P. Marneffei* infection in HIV-infected children may be treated with ketoconazole.

For all other antifungal indications—
Children 2 years of age and older: Oral, 3.3 to 6.6 mg per kg of body weight once a day.

Infants and children up to 2 years of age: Dosage has not been established.

Strength(s) usually available

U.S.—

Not commercially available.

Canada—

100 mg per 5 mL (Rx) [*Nizoral* (sodium [≤ 0.55 mg per mL]; sodium benzoate; sucrose)].

Packaging and storage

Store below 40 °C (104 °F), preferably between 15 and 30 °C (59 and 86 °F), in a well-closed container. Protect from freezing.

Auxiliary labeling

- Shake well.
- Take with food.
- Avoid alcoholic beverages.
- May cause dizziness or drowsiness.
- Continue medicine for full time of treatment (antifungal only).

KETOCONAZOLE TABLETS USP

Usual adult and adolescent dose

See *Ketoconazole Oral Suspension.*

Usual adult prescribing limits

See *Ketoconazole Oral Suspension.*

Usual pediatric dose

See *Ketoconazole Oral Suspension.*

Strength(s) usually available

U.S.—

200 mg (Rx) [*Nizoral* (scored; lactose)].

Canada—

200 mg (Rx) [*Nizoral* (scored; lactose)].

Packaging and storage

Store below 40 °C (104 °F), preferably between 15 and 30 °C (59 and 86 °F). Store in a well-closed container.

Auxiliary labeling

- Take with food.
- Avoid alcoholic beverages.
- May cause dizziness or drowsiness.
- Continue medicine for full time of treatment (antifungal only).

[1]Not included in Canadian product labeling.

Revised: 01/04/2005
Developed: 11/14/1994

Table 1. Pharmacology/Pharmacokinetics*

Drug	Route of administration*	Bioavailability (%)	Vol_D	CSF/Serum concentrations (%)	Protein binding (%)	Metabolism
Fluconazole	IV, PO	90 (fasting)	0.7-1 L/kg	54-85 (patients with meningitis)	11	Hepatic†
Itraconazole	PO, capsules	40-55 (fasting) 90-100 (with food)	796 L	< 10	99	Hepatic‡
	IV, PO, oral solution	90-100 (fasting) 55 (with food)	796 L		99	Hepatic‡
Ketoconazole	PO	75 (with food)	0.36 L/kg	< 10	99	Hepatic

*IV = intravenous; PO = oral; Vol_D = apparent volume of distribution; CSF = cerebrospinal fluid; L/kg = liters per kilogram.
†Fluconazole is primarily excreted by the kidneys; however, a small amount of the drug undergoes hepatic metabolization.
‡Itraconazole is extensively metabolized by the liver, with more than 30 identifiable inactive metabolites. The major metabolite, hydroxyitraconazole, has antifungal activity.

Table 2. Pharmacology/Pharmacokinetics

Drug	Half-life (hr)		Time to peak serum concentration (hr)	Peak serum concentration after dose		Renal excretion (% unchanged)	Biliary excretion
	Normal renal function	Impaired renal function		mcg/mL	Dose		
Fluconazole	30 (adults) 14-20 (children)	98-125	1-2	4.5-8	100 mg	> 80	Yes; small amount
Itraconazole (capsules)	21 (single dose) 64 (steady state)		3-4	0.132* 0.234*	100 mg (with food) 200 mg (with food)	0.03	3-18%
Itraconazole (oral solution)	39 (steady state) 37 (steady state)		2.5 4.4	1.96* 1.43*	200 mg (fasting) 200 mg (with food)	0.03	
Itraconazole (injection)	35 (steady state)		1.0	2.9	200mg	0.03	3-18%
Ketoconazole	8		1-4	3.5	200 mg (with food)	2-4	Yes; primary route of elimination

*The plasma concentrations reported were measured by high performance liquid chromatography (HPLC), specific for itraconazole. When itraconazole in plasma is measured by a bioassay, values reported are approximately 3.3 times higher than those detected by HPLC due to the presence of the bioactive metabolite, hydroxyitraconazole.

ANTIFUNGALS, AZOLE Vaginal

This monograph includes information on the following: 1) Butoconazole†; 2) Clotrimazole; 3) Econazole*; 4) Miconazole; 5) Terconazole; 6) Tioconazole.

VA CLASSIFICATION (Primary): GU302

Commonly used brand name(s): *Canesten 1-Day Cream Combi-Pak*[2]; *Canesten 1-Day Therapy*[2]; *Canesten 3-Day Therapy*[2]; *Canesten 6-Day Therapy*[2]; *Canesten Combi-Pak 1-Day Therapy*[2]; *Canesten Combi-Pak 3-Day Therapy*[2]; *Clotrimaderm*[2]; *Ecostatin Vaginal Ovules*[3]; *FemCare*[2]; *Femizol-M*[4]; *Femstat 3*[1]; *GyneCure*[6]; *GyneCure Ovules*[6]; *GyneCure Vaginal Ointment Tandempak*[6]; *GyneCure Vaginal Ovules Tandempak*[6]; *Gyne-Lotrimin*[2]; *Gyne-Lotrimin Combination Pack*[2]; *Gyne-Lotrimin3*[2]; *Gyne-Lotrimin3 Combination Pack*[2]; *Miconazole-7*[4]; *Micozole*[4]; *Monazole 7*[4]; *Monistat 1*[6]; *Monistat 1 Combination Pack*[4]; *Monistat 3*[4]; *Monistat 3 Combination Pack*[4]; *Monistat 3 Dual-Pak*[4]; *Monistat 3 Vaginal Ovules*[4]; *Monistat 5 Tampon*[4]; *Monistat 7*[4]; *Monistat 7 Combination Pack*[4]; *Monistat 7 Dual-Pak*[4]; *Monistat 7 Vaginal Suppositories*[4]; *Mycelex Twin Pack*[2]; *Mycelex-7*[2]; *Mycelex-G*[2]; *Myclo-Gyne*[2]; *Novo-Miconazole Vaginal Ovules*[4]; *Terazol 3*[5]; *Terazol 3 Dual-Pak*[5]; *Terazol 3 Vaginal Ovules*[5]; *Terazol 7*[5]; *Vagistat-1*[6].

Note: For a listing of dosage forms and brand names by country availability, see *Dosage Forms* section(s).

*Not commercially available in U.S.
†Not commercially available in Canada.

Category

Antifungal (vaginal).

Indications

Accepted

Candidiasis, vulvovaginal (treatment)—Vaginal azoles are indicated in the local treatment of vulvovaginal candidiasis caused by *Candida albicans* and other species of *Candida* in pregnant (second and third trimesters only) and nonpregnant women. It is recommended that nonpregnant women self-medicate with nonprescription antifungal vaginal medications only if they have been diagnosed previously with vulvovaginal candidiasis and have the same symptoms. If symptoms recur within 2 months, women should seek professional medical care. Pregnant women treating vulvovaginal candidiasis with antifungal vaginal agents should use at least a 7-day treatment regimen and seek their physician's advice before using medication in the first trimester.

Not all species or strains of a particular organism may be susceptible to a specific vaginal azole.

Unaccepted

Vaginal azoles are not effective in the treatment of vulvovaginitis caused by other common pathogens such as *Trichomonas vaginalis*.

Pharmacology/Pharmacokinetics

Physicochemical characteristics

Chemical Group—
Imidazoles: Butoconazole, clotrimazole, econazole nitrate, miconazole nitrate, tioconazole.
Triazole: Terconazole.

Molecular weight—
Butoconazole nitrate: 474.80.
Clotrimazole: 344.85.
Econazole nitrate: 444.70.
Miconazole nitrate: 479.15.
Terconazole: 532.47.
Tioconazole: 387.72.

Mechanism of action/Effect

Fungistatic; may be fungicidal, depending on concentration; exact mechanism of action is unknown. Azoles inhibit biosynthesis of ergosterol or other sterols, damaging the fungal cell membrane and altering its permeability. As a result, loss of essential intracellular elements may occur.

Azoles also inhibit biosynthesis of triglycerides and phospholipids by fungi. In addition, azoles inhibit oxidative and peroxidative enzyme activity, resulting in intracellular buildup of toxic concentrations of hydrogen peroxide, which may contribute to deterioration of subcellular organelles and cellular necrosis. In *Candida albicans*, azoles inhibit transformation of blastospores into invasive mycelial form.

Terconazole—Triazoles are more slowly metabolized than imidazoles. Triazoles also affect sterol synthesis to a lesser degree.

Absorption

Butoconazole—Approximately 5.5% absorbed systemically following intravaginal administration.

Clotrimazole—3 to 10% estimated to be absorbed following intravaginal administration.

Econazole; miconazole; tioconazole—Small amounts absorbed systemically following intravaginal administration.

Terconazole—Approximately 5 to 8% absorbed in hysterectomized patients and approximately 12 to 16% absorbed in nonhysterectomized patients with tubal ligations.

Biotransformation

Clotrimazole—Rapidly metabolized to inactive metabolites.

Precautions to Consider

Carcinogenicity

Butoconazole; miconazole; terconazole; tioconazole—Long-term studies in animals have not been done.

Clotrimazole—Long-term studies of intravaginal clotrimazole in animals have not been done. However, a long-term study of oral clotrimazole in Wistar strains of rats has not shown that clotrimazole is carcinogenic.

Terconazole—Studies have not been done.

Mutagenicity

Butoconazole—Butoconazole has not been shown to be mutagenic in studies in appropriate indicator microorganisms.

Terconazole—Terconazole has not been shown to be mutagenic in studies for induction of microbial point mutations (Ames test), induction of cellular transformation, chromosomal breaks (micronucleus test), or in studies for dominant lethal mutations in mouse germ cells.

Tioconazole—No mutagenic or cytogenic effects were observed.

Pregnancy/Reproduction

Fertility—*Butoconazole*: Studies in rabbits or rats, given oral doses of up to 30 or 100 mg per kg of body weight (mg/kg) daily, respectively, have not shown that butoconazole causes impaired fertility.

Terconazole: Terconazole, given orally in doses of up to 40 mg/kg daily, has not been shown to cause impairment of fertility in female rats.

Pregnancy—Pregnant women treating vulvovaginal candidiasis with antifungal vaginal agents should use at least a 7-day treatment regimen. A decision to use antifungal vaginal agents during the first trimester should be based on risk-benefit status and on advice of the physician.

Butoconazole: Adequate and well-controlled studies in humans have not been done during the first trimester. Clinical studies in over 200 pregnant women, given butoconazole intravaginally for 3 or 6 days during the second and third trimesters, have not shown that butoconazole causes adverse effects on the fetus. Follow-up reports on infants born to these women have not shown that butoconazole causes any adverse effects.

Studies in rats, given intravaginal doses of 6 mg/kg daily (three to seven times the usual human dose) during organogenesis, have shown that butoconazole causes an increase in resorption rate and a decrease in litter size. Butoconazole was not shown to be teratogenic.

Studies in rats, given oral doses of up to 50 mg/kg daily throughout organogenesis, have not shown that butoconazole causes adverse effects on the fetus. The administration of oral doses of 100, 300, or 750 mg/kg daily has resulted in adverse effects (abdominal wall defects, cleft palate) on the fetus, although maternal stress was evident at these higher dosages.

Studies in rabbits, given oral doses (e.g., 150 mg/kg) that caused maternal stress, have not shown that butoconazole causes adverse effects on the fetus.

FDA Pregnancy Category C.

Clotrimazole: Adequate and well-controlled studies in humans have not been done during the first trimester. Reports on up to 177 pregnant females given clotrimazole intravaginally during the second and third trimesters have not shown that clotrimazole causes adverse effects on the fetus. Follow-up reports on 71 infants born to these females have not shown that clotrimazole causes any adverse effects.

Studies in rats, given repeated intravaginal doses of up to 100 mg/kg daily, have not shown that clotrimazole causes adverse effects on the fetus.

Studies in rats and mice, given repeated oral doses of 50 to 120 mg/kg, have shown that clotrimazole causes embryotoxicity (possibly secondary to maternal toxicity), impairment of mating, decreased litter size and number of viable young, and decreased survival to weaning. Studies in mice, rabbits, and rats, given oral doses of up to 200, 180, and 100 mg/kg, respectively, have not shown that clotrimazole is teratogenic.

FDA Pregnancy Category B.

Econazole: Adequate and well-controlled studies have not been performed in humans.

Miconazole: Clinical studies in over 500 pregnant females given miconazole intravaginally for 14 days have not shown that miconazole causes adverse effects on the fetus. Follow-up reports on infants born to these women have not shown that miconazole causes any adverse effects.

Miconazole crosses the placenta in animals. Studies in animals have shown that miconazole, given in oral doses of 80 mg/kg, causes embryotoxicity and fetotoxicity. Studies in rats have shown that miconazole, given orally, causes prolonged gestation, although this was not shown in studies using rabbits.

FDA Pregnancy Category B.

Terconazole: At oral doses less than or equal to 10 mg/kg, no embryotoxicity was seen in rats. Studies in rats given terconazole orally in doses of 10 mg/kg daily have shown that terconazole causes delayed fetal ossification. In studies in rats given 20 to 40 mg/kg orally during organogenesis, terconazole was shown to cause embryotoxicity (e.g., decreased litter size and number of viable young, reduced fetal weight, delayed ossification, and increased incidence of skeletal abnormalities). The skeletal changes observed (delayed ossification, short wavy ribs) were felt to be secondary to maternal toxicity or stress, which was evident from reduced body weight gain during most of the organogenesis period.

Terconazole has not been shown to be teratogenic in rats given oral doses of up to 40 mg/kg daily or given subcutaneous doses of up to 20 mg/kg daily, or in rabbits given doses of 20 mg/kg daily.

FDA Pregnancy Category C.

Tioconazole: Adequate and well-controlled studies have not been performed in humans.

In limited and uncontrolled clinical use in about 20 patients, a single dose administered at varying stages of pregnancy did not appear to interfere with normal progress of the pregnancy and delivery. However, 1-day treatment may not be effective in pregnant patients and is not recommended.

In studies in rats, adverse effects on parturition and/or fetal development were observed during local and systemic use.

FDA Pregnancy Category C.

Labor—Vaginal azoles have been shown to cause dystocia in rats when given through parturition.

Butoconazole: Butoconazole has not been shown to cause dystocia in rabbits given oral doses of up to 100 mg/kg.

Terconazole: Terconazole has not been shown to adversely affect parturition in rats given up to 40 mg/kg orally per day during pregnancy, up through 3 weeks of lactation.

Breast-feeding

It is not known whether vaginal azoles are distributed into breast milk. However, problems in humans have not been documented.

Pediatrics

No information is available on the relationship of age to the effects of vaginal azoles in pediatric patients. Safety and efficacy have not been established in children up to 12 years of age.

Geriatrics

Appropriate studies on the relationship of age to the effects of vaginal azoles have not been performed in the geriatric population. However, no geriatrics-specific problems have been documented to date.

Drug interactions and/or related problems

The following drug interactions and/or related problems have been selected on the basis of their potential clinical significance (possible mechanism in parentheses where appropriate)—not necessarily inclusive (» = major clinical significance):

For miconazole

» Warfarin
(concurrent use may cause bleeding and/or bruising)

Medical considerations/Contraindications

The medical considerations/contraindications included have been selected on the basis of their potential clinical significance (reasons given in parentheses where appropriate)—not necessarily inclusive (» = major clinical significance).

Risk-benefit should be considered when the following medical problem exists:
Allergy to azoles

Side/Adverse Effects

The following side/adverse effects have been selected on the basis of their potential clinical significance (possible signs and symptoms in parentheses where appropriate)—not necessarily inclusive:

Those indicating need for medical attention

Incidence less frequent
Vaginal burning, itching, discharge, or other irritation not present before therapy

Incidence rare
Hypersensitivity (skin rash or hives)

Those indicating need for medical attention only if they continue or are bothersome

Incidence less frequent or rare
Abdominal or stomach cramps or pain; burning or irritation of penis of sexual partner; headache

Patient Consultation

As an aid to patient consultation, refer to *Advice for the Patient, Antifungals, Azole (Vaginal).*

In providing consultation, consider emphasizing the following selected information (» = major clinical significance):

Before using this medication

» Conditions affecting use, especially:
Allergy to azoles
Pregnancy—Some animal studies have shown that vaginal azoles may be embryotoxic or fetotoxic; however, problems have not been documented in humans. Use of at least a 7-day treatment regimen is recommended for pregnant patients in the second and third trimesters instead of regimens of shorter duration; use of the medication in the first trimester should be based on risk-benefit status and on the advice of a physician
Labor—Vaginal azoles have been shown in some studies to cause dystocia when given through labor
Other medications, especially warfarin

Proper use of this medication

Reading patient instructions before using medication
Using at bedtime, unless otherwise directed by physician; retaining miconazole vaginal tampons overnight and removing them the following morning
Checking with physician before using applicator if pregnant
Using cream, which is packaged with some of the vaginal suppositories or tablets, by applying it externally to genitalia to treat genital itching
» Compliance with full course of therapy, even if menstruation begins
» Proper dosing
Missed dose: Inserting as soon as possible; not inserting if almost time for next dose
» Proper storage

Precautions while using this medication

Checking with physician if no improvement within 3 days, if symptoms do not disappear within 7 days, or if symptoms worsen during use of 1-, 3-, and 7-day treatment regimens; also, checking with physician if symptoms return within 2 months or if exposure to human immunodeficiency virus (HIV) occurs
Protecting clothing because of possible soiling with vaginal azoles; avoiding the use of unmedicated tampons
» *Using hygienic measures to cure infection and prevent reinfection:*
Wearing cotton panties instead of synthetic underclothes
Wearing only freshly washed underclothes
» Routine treatment of sexual partner is unnecessary unless male partner is experiencing symptoms of local itching or skin irritation of the penis
» Understanding that some vaginal products may contain oils that damage latex; avoiding concurrent use of latex products, such as condoms, diaphragms, and cervical caps, during treatment and for 3 days after discontinuing medication
» Checking with doctor before douching between doses to obtain recommendation for use and advice for proper procedure

Side/adverse effects

Signs of potential side effects, especially vaginal burning, itching, discharge, or other irritation not present before therapy, and hypersensitivity

General Dosing Information

Diagnosis of first-time users of vaginal azole antifungal agents should be made by physicians. Patients should consult a physician if symptoms return within 2 months or if exposure to HIV occurs. Recurring yeast infections may be a sign of other conditions, such as diabetes or impaired immune function. Recurring conditions or severe local vaginal infections may benefit from vaginal treatments of longer duration, such as 10 to 14 days, or from the use of appropriate oral medications instead.

If there is no response to therapy, the course of therapy may be repeated after other pathogens have been ruled out by potassium hydroxide (KOH) smears and cultures.

If sensitization or irritation occurs, treatment with vaginal azoles should be discontinued.

It is recommended that the patient wait 3 days after treatment with azole antifungal agents to resume using latex barrier devices such as condoms or diaphragms. The vehicles for some vaginal azole products contain lipid-based components. It is likely that many of these products affect the performance of latex contraceptive devices, such as cervical caps, condoms, or diaphragms.

Unmedicated tampons may absorb vaginal creams, ointments, or suppositories and are not recommended for use concurrently with vaginal azole antifungal agents.

For miconazole vaginal suppository

Complete relief following administration of one vaginal suppository may take up to 7 days to achieve.

For tioconazole ointment

Symptomatic relief following one dose of tioconazole ointment may take up to 7 days to achieve.

BUTOCONAZOLE

Vaginal Dosage Forms

BUTOCONAZOLE NITRATE CREAM (VAGINAL) USP

Usual adult and adolescent dose

Antifungal (vaginal)—

Nonpregnant patients: Intravaginal, 100 mg (1 applicatorful of a 2% cream) once a day at bedtime for three days. May be repeated for an additional three days if needed.

Pregnant patients (second and third trimesters only): Intravaginal, 100 mg (1 applicatorful of a 2% cream) once a day at bedtime for six days.

Usual pediatric dose

Children up to 12 years of age: Safety and efficacy have not been established.

Strength(s) usually available

U.S.—

Note: Packaging may include either three prefilled applicators or three cardboard applicators plus tube of cream.

2% (100 mg per applicatorful) (OTC) [*Femstat 3*].

Canada—

Not commercially available.

Packaging and storage

Store below 40 °C (104 °F), preferably between 15 and 30 °C (59 and 86 °F), unless otherwise specified by manufacturer. Store in a tight container. Protect from freezing.

Auxiliary labeling

- For vaginal use only.
- Continue medicine for full time of treatment.

Note

Include patient instructions when dispensing.

BUTOCONAZOLE NITRATE VAGINAL SUPPOSITORIES

Usual adult and adolescent dose

Antifungal (vaginal)—

Nonpregnant patients: Intravaginal, 100 mg once a day at bedtime for three days. May be repeated for an additional three days if needed.

Usual pediatric dose

Children up to 12 years of age: Safety and efficacy have not been established.

Strength(s) usually available

U.S.—

Not commercially available.

Canada—

Not commercially available.

Packaging and storage

Store below 40 °C (104 °F), preferably between 15 and 30 °C (59 and 86 °F), unless otherwise specified by manufacturer. Store in a well-closed container.

Auxiliary labeling

- For vaginal use only.
- Continue medicine for full time of treatment.

Note

Include patient instructions when dispensing.

CLOTRIMAZOLE

Vaginal Dosage Forms

CLOTRIMAZOLE CREAM (VAGINAL) USP

Usual adult and adolescent dose

Antifungal (vaginal)—

Intravaginal, 50 mg (1 applicatorful of a 1% vaginal cream) once a day, preferably at bedtime, for six to fourteen consecutive days; or

Intravaginal, 100 mg (1 applicatorful of a 2% vaginal cream) once a day, preferably at bedtime, for three days; or

Intravaginal, 500 mg (1 applicatorful of a 10% vaginal cream) as a single dose, preferably at bedtime.

Usual pediatric dose

Children up to 12 years of age: Safety and efficacy have not been established.

Strength(s) usually available

U.S.—

1% (50 mg per applicatorful) (OTC) [*FemCare; Gyne-Lotrimin; Mycelex-7;* GENERIC].

Canada—

1% (50 mg per applicatorful) (OTC) [*Canesten 6-Day Therapy; Clotrimaderm; Myclo-Gyne*].

2% (100 mg per applicatorful) (OTC) [*Canesten 3-Day Therapy; Clotrimaderm*].

10% (500 mg per applicatorful) (OTC) [*Canesten 1-Day Therapy; Canesten 1-Day Cream Combi-Pak*].

Note: Many of these products are packaged with one reusable vaginal applicator or more than one single-use vaginal applicator, or as prefilled vaginal applicators.

Combi-paks also contain a small tube of 1% clotrimazole cream for external application to genitals for treatment of itching.

Packaging and storage

Store between 2 and 30 °C (36 and 86 °F). Store in a collapsible tube or in a tight container.

Auxiliary labeling

- For vaginal use only.
- Continue medicine for full time of treatment.

Note

Include patient instructions when dispensing.

CLOTRIMAZOLE VAGINAL TABLETS USP

Usual adult and adolescent dose

Antifungal (vaginal)—

Nonpregnant patients: Intravaginal, 500 mg as a single dose, preferably at bedtime; 200 mg once a day, preferably at bedtime, for three consecutive days; or 100 mg once a day, preferably at bedtime, for six or seven consecutive days.

Pregnant patients: Intravaginal, 100 mg once a day, preferably at bedtime, for seven consecutive days.

Note: The three-day regimen is not effective in pregnant women.

In severe vulvovaginal candidiasis, single-dose treatment with clotrimazole 500-mg vaginal tablets may not be effective. Longer treatment with the 100- or 200-mg vaginal tablets or vaginal cream is recommended.

Usual pediatric dose

Children up to 12 years of age: Safety and efficacy have not been established.

Strength(s) usually available

U.S.—

100 mg (OTC) [*FemCare; Gyne-Lotrimin; Gyne-Lotrimin Combination Pack; Mycelex-7;* GENERIC].

200 mg (OTC) [*Gyne-Lotrimin3; Gyne-Lotrimin3 Combination Pack*].

500 mg (Rx) [*Mycelex-G; Mycelex Twin Pack*].

Canada—

100 mg (OTC) [*Myclo-Gyne*].

200 mg (OTC) [*Canesten Combi-Pak 3-Day Therapy*].

500 mg (OTC) [*Canesten Combi-Pak 1-Day Therapy*].

Note: Twin and combination packs and combi-paks also contain a small tube of 1% clotrimazole cream for external application to genitals for treatment of itching.

Packaging and storage

Store below 40 °C (104 °F), preferably between 15 and 30 °C (59 and 86 °F), unless otherwise specified by manufacturer. Store in a well-closed container.

Auxiliary labeling
- For vaginal use only.
- Continue medicine for full time of treatment.

Note
Include patient instructions when dispensing.

ECONAZOLE

Vaginal Dosage Forms

ECONAZOLE NITRATE VAGINAL SUPPOSITORIES

Usual adult and adolescent dose
Antifungal (vaginal)—
Intravaginal, 150 mg once a day at bedtime for three days. May be repeated if needed.

Usual pediatric dose
Children up to 12 years of age: Safety and efficacy have not been established.

Strength(s) usually available
U.S.—
Not commercially available.
Canada—
150 mg (Rx) [*Ecostatin Vaginal Ovules*].

Packaging and storage
Store below 30 °C (86 °F), in a well-closed container, unless otherwise specified by manufacturer.

Auxiliary labeling
- For vaginal use only.
- Continue medicine for full time of treatment.

Note
Include patient instructions when dispensing.

MICONAZOLE

Vaginal Dosage Forms

MICONAZOLE NITRATE VAGINAL CREAM

Usual adult and adolescent dose
Antifungal (vaginal)—
Intravaginal, 20 mg (one applicatorful) once a day at bedtime for seven days. May be repeated if needed.

Usual pediatric dose
Children up to 12 years of age: Safety and efficacy have not been established.

Strength(s) usually available
U.S.—
2% (OTC) [*Femizol-M; Miconazole-7; Monistat 7;* GENERIC].
Canada—
2% (OTC) [*Micozole; Monazole 7; Monistat 7*].

Note: Many of these products are packaged with one reusable vaginal applicator or more than one single-use vaginal applicator, or as prefilled vaginal applicators.

Packaging and storage
Store below 40 °C (104 °F), preferably between 15 and 30 °C (59 and 86 °F), unless otherwise specified by manufacturer. Store in a tight container. Protect from freezing.

Auxiliary labeling
- For vaginal use only.
- Continue medicine for full time of treatment.

Note
Include patient instructions when dispensing.

MICONAZOLE NITRATE VAGINAL SUPPOSITORIES USP

Usual adult and adolescent dose
Antifungal (vaginal)—
Intravaginal, 100 mg once a day at bedtime for seven days. May be repeated for seven days if needed; or
Intravaginal, 200 or 400 mg once a day at bedtime for three days. May be repeated if needed; or
Intravaginal, 1200 mg once a day at bedtime for one day.

Usual pediatric dose
Children up to 12 years of age: Safety and efficacy have not been established.

Strength(s) usually available
U.S.—
100 mg (OTC) [*Monistat 7; Monistat 7 Combination Pack;* GENERIC].
200 mg (OTC) [*Monistat 3 Combination Pack*].
200 mg (Rx) [*Monistat 3*].
1200 mg (OTC) [*Monistat 1 Combination Pack* (gelatin; glycerin; lecithin; white petrolatum)].
Canada—
100 mg (OTC) [*Monistat 7 Vaginal Suppositories; Monistat 7 Dual-Pak*].
400 mg (OTC) [*Monistat 3 Vaginal Ovules; Monistat 3 Dual-Pak; Novo-Miconazole Vaginal Ovules*].

Note: Dual-paks and combination packs also contain a small tube of 2% miconazole cream for external application to genitals for treatment of itching.

Packaging and storage
Store between 20 to 25 °C (68 to 77 °F). Store in a tight container.

Auxiliary labeling
- For vaginal use only.
- Continue medicine for full time of treatment.

Note
Include patient instructions when dispensing.

MICONAZOLE NITRATE VAGINAL TAMPONS

Usual adult and adolescent dose
Antifungal (vaginal)—
Intravaginal, 100 mg (1 tampon) once a day at bedtime for five consecutive days; retain vaginally overnight and remove tampon the following morning.

Usual pediatric dose
Children up to 12 years of age: Safety and efficacy have not been established.

Strength(s) usually available
U.S.—
Note: Available in California only.
5% (Rx) [*Monistat 5 Tampon*].
Canada—
Not commercially available.

Packaging and storage
Store below 40 °C (104 °F), preferably between 15 and 30 °C (59 and 86 °F), in a well-closed container, unless otherwise specified by manufacturer.

Auxiliary labeling
- For vaginal use only.
- Continue medicine for full time of treatment.

Note
Include patient instructions when dispensing.

TERCONAZOLE

Vaginal Dosage Forms

TERCONAZOLE VAGINAL CREAM

Usual adult and adolescent dose
Antifungal (vaginal)—
Intravaginal, 20 mg (1 applicatorful of a 0.4% cream) once a day at bedtime for seven days; or
Intravaginal, 40 mg (1 applicatorful of a 0.8% cream) once a day at bedtime for three days.

Usual pediatric dose
Children up to 12 years of age: Safety and efficacy have not been established.

Strength(s) usually available
U.S.—
0.4% (20 mg per applicatorful) (Rx) [*Terazol 7*].
0.8% (40 mg per applicatorful) (Rx) [*Terazol 3*].
Canada—
0.4% (20 mg per applicatorful) (Rx) [*Terazol 7*].
0.8% (40 mg per applicatorful) (Rx) [*Terazol 3*].

Packaging and storage
Store below 40 °C (104 °F), preferably between 15 and 30 °C (59 and 86 °F), in a well-closed container, unless otherwise specified by manufacturer. Protect from freezing.

Auxiliary labeling
- For vaginal use only.
- Continue medicine for full time of treatment.

Note
Include patient instructions when dispensing.

TERCONAZOLE VAGINAL SUPPOSITORIES

Usual adult and adolescent dose
Antifungal (vaginal)—
Intravaginal, 80 mg once a day at bedtime for three days.

Usual pediatric dose
Children up to 12 years of age: Safety and efficacy have not been established.

Strength(s) usually available
U.S.—
80 mg (Rx) [*Terazol 3*].
Canada—
80 mg (Rx) [*Terazol 3 Dual-Pak; Terazol 3 Vaginal Ovules*].

Note: Dual-paks also contain a small tube of 0.8% terconazole cream for external application to genitals for treatment of itching.

Packaging and storage
Store below 40 °C (104 °F), preferably between 15 and 30 °C (59 and 86 °F), in a well-closed container, unless otherwise specified by manufacturer.

Auxiliary labeling
- For vaginal use only.
- Continue medicine for full time of treatment.

Note
Include patient instructions when dispensing.

TIOCONAZOLE

Vaginal Dosage Forms

TIOCONAZOLE VAGINAL OINTMENT

Usual adult and adolescent dose
Antifungal (vaginal)—
Intravaginal, 300 mg (1 applicatorful of a 6.5% vaginal ointment) as a single dose, preferably at bedtime.

Note: Limited data suggest that a second dose one or two weeks later may be effective for those patients with residual symptoms after one dose.

Usual pediatric dose
Children up to 12 years of age: Safety and efficacy have not been established.

Strength(s) usually available
U.S.—
6.5% (OTC) [*Monistat 1; Vagistat-1*].
Canada—
6.5% (OTC) [*GyneCure; GyneCure Vaginal Ointment Tandempak*].

Note: Tandempaks also contain a small tube of 1% tioconazole cream for external application to genitals for treatment of itching.

Packaging and storage
Store below 40 °C (104 °F), preferably between 15 and 30 °C (59 and 86 °F), in a well-closed container, unless otherwise specified by manufacturer.

Auxiliary labeling
- For vaginal use only.

TIOCONAZOLE VAGINAL SUPPOSITORIES

Usual adult and adolescent dose
Antifungal (vaginal)—
Intravaginal, 300 mg, as a single dose, preferably at bedtime.

Note: Limited data suggest that a second dose one or two weeks later may be effective for those patients with residual symptoms after one dose.

Usual pediatric dose
Children up to 12 years of age: Safety and efficacy have not been established.

Strength(s) usually available
U.S.—
Not commercially available.
Canada—
300 mg (OTC) [*GyneCure Ovules; GyneCure Vaginal Ovules Tandempak*].

Note: Tandempaks also contain a small tube of 1% tioconazole cream for external application to genitals for treatment of itching.

Packaging and storage
Store below 40 °C (104 °F), preferably between 15 and 30 °C (59 and 86 °F), in a well-closed container, unless otherwise specified by manufacturer.

Auxiliary labeling
- For vaginal use only.

Note
Include patient instructions when dispensing.

Selected Bibliography

Doering PL, Santiago TM. Drugs for treatment of vulvovaginal candidiasis: comparative efficacy of agents and regimens [review]. Drug Intell Clin Pharm 1990; 24: 1078-83.

Revised: 01/19/2005

ANTIGLAUCOMA AGENTS, CHOLINERGIC, LONG-ACTING Ophthalmic

This monograph includes information on the following: 1) Demecarium†; 2) Echothiophate; 3) Isoflurophate†.

INN: Echothiophate—Ecothiopate Iodide

BAN: Isoflurophate—Dyflos

VA CLASSIFICATION (Primary/Secondary): OP118/OP900; DX900

Commonly used brand name(s): *Diflupyl*[3]; *Humorsol*[1]; *Phospholine Iodide*[2].

Other commonly used names are: DFP [isoflurophate], difluorophate [isoflurophate], dyflos [isoflurophate], and ecothiopate iodide [echothiophate].

Note: For a listing of dosage forms and brand names by country availability, see *Dosage Forms* section(s).

*Not commercially available in U.S.
†Not commercially available in Canada.

Category

Antiglaucoma agent (ophthalmic); cyclostimulant (accommodative esotropia); diagnostic aid (accommodative esotropia).

Indications

Accepted

Note: Because isoflurophate is not commercially available in the U.S. or Canada, the bracketed information and the use of the superscript 1 in this monograph reflect the lack of labeled (approved) indications for this medication in these countries.

Glaucoma (treatment)—Demecarium, echothiophate, and [isoflurophate][1], which are long-acting cholinesterase inhibitors, are potent miotics. Because of their toxicity, they should be reserved for use in patients with open-angle glaucoma or other chronic glaucomas not satisfactorily controlled with the short-acting miotics and other agents.

Glaucoma, open-angle (treatment): Demecarium, echothiophate, and [isoflurophate][1] are indicated in the treatment of chronic open-angle glaucoma.

Glaucoma, angle-closure, *after* iridectomy (treatment): Demecarium, echothiophate, and [isoflurophate][1] are indicated in the treatment of subacute or chronic angle-closure glaucoma following iridectomy if continued drug therapy is required and short-acting miotics and other agents are inadequate. Long-acting cholinesterase inhibitors are usually not recommended for use in angle-closure glaucoma *prior* to iridectomy, because they may increase the pupillary block. However, echothiophate may be indicated in subacute or chronic angle-closure glaucoma when surgery is refused or contraindicated in the informed patient who understands the increased risk of pupillary block.

Glaucoma, secondary (treatment): Echothiophate is indicated in the treatment of certain nonuveitic secondary types of glaucoma, especially glaucoma following cataract surgery.

Esotropia, accommodative (diagnosis) or
Esotropia, accommodative (treatment)—Demecarium, echothiophate, and [isoflurophate][1] are indicated in the diagnosis of accommodative esotropia. Demecarium and [isoflurophate][1] are indicated in the treat-

ment of accommodative esotropia uncomplicated by amblyopia (impairment of vision) or anisometropia (difference in the refractive power of the eyes). Echothiophate may be indicated in the treatment of concomitant esotropias with a significant accommodative component.

[1]Not included in Canadian product labeling.

Pharmacology/Pharmacokinetics

Physicochemical characteristics

Molecular weight—
- Demecarium bromide: 716.60.
- Echothiophate iodide: 383.23.
- Isoflurophate: 184.15.

Mechanism of action/Effect

Demecarium, echothiophate, and isoflurophate are indirect-acting parasympathomimetic agents, which are also known as cholinesterase inhibitors and anticholinesterases. Cholinesterase inhibitors prolong the effect of acetylcholine, which is released at the neuroeffector junction of parasympathetic postganglion nerves, by inactivating the cholinesterases that break it down. Echothiophate and isoflurophate primarily inactivate pseudocholinesterase and incompletely inactivate acetylcholinesterase, whereas demecarium inactivates both pseudocholinesterase and acetylcholinesterase. In the eye, this causes constriction of the iris sphincter muscle (causing miosis) and the ciliary muscle (affecting the accommodation reflex and causing a spasm of the focus to near vision). The outflow of the aqueous humor is facilitated, which leads to a reduction in intraocular pressure. Of the two actions, the effect on the accommodation reflex is the more transient and generally disappears before termination of the miosis.

Antiglaucoma agent (ophthalmic)—Cholinesterase inhibitors reduce intraocular pressure in both types of primary glaucoma (i.e., angle-closure glaucoma and open-angle glaucoma) primarily by lowering the resistance to the outflow of the aqueous humor. In angle-closure glaucoma, the abnormal contact between the peripheral iris and the peripheral cornea blocks the access of the anterior chamber of aqueous humor to the trabecular meshwork. In open-angle glaucoma, the block is between the trabecular meshwork and the canal of Schlemm. Effects on the volumes of the various intraocular vascular beds (e.g., those of the iris and the ciliary body) and on the rate of secretion of the aqueous humor into the posterior chamber may contribute secondarily to the lowering of pressure. Contraction of the ciliary muscle may act to increase tone and alignment of the trabecular meshwork, which improves outflow of aqueous humor through the meshwork to the canal of Schlemm. The longitudinal ciliary muscle is the major component; the iris sphincter is not relevant in open-angle glaucoma, but its contraction may improve (or worsen) angle-closure glaucoma. In angle-closure glaucoma, the outflow of the aqueous humor is facilitated by the drug-induced contraction of the iris sphincter muscle. This contraction prevents the iris from blocking the entrance to the trabecular space at the canal of Schlemm by lessening pupillary block. However, extreme miosis may actually increase pupillary block, thus worsening angle-closure glaucoma prior to iridectomy. In open-angle glaucoma, although there is no physical obstruction at the entrance to the trabecular space, the trabeculae, which are a meshwork of small-diameter pores, increase their resistance and lose their permeability.

Cyclostimulant (accommodative esotropia)—Cholinesterase inhibitors reduce the amount of convergence associated with a given amount of accommodation, thereby reducing the degree of esotropia.

Diagnostic aid (accommodative esotropia)—See *Cyclostimulant (accommodative esotropia)* above. An accommodative factor is demonstrated if the eyes become better aligned.

Onset of action

Miosis—Less than 1 hour.

Reduction in intraocular pressure—Within 4 hours.

Time to peak effect

Miosis—Within 2 hours.

Reduction in intraocular pressure—Within 24 hours.

Duration of action

Miosis—Up to 1 month.

Reduction in intraocular pressure—Up to 1 month, but usually 24 to 48 hours.

Precautions to Consider

Carcinogenicity/Mutagenicity

Studies have not been done for demecarium, echothiophate, and isoflurophate.

Pregnancy/Reproduction

Fertility—Studies have not been done for demecarium, echothiophate, and isoflurophate.

Pregnancy—

Demecarium and isoflurophate—

Use of demecarium and isoflurophate is not recommended during pregnancy, because of the toxicity of cholinesterase inhibitors in general. If pregnancy occurs while one of these medications is being administered, the patients should be advised of the potential hazard to the fetus.

FDA Pregnancy Category X.

Echothiophate—

Studies have not been done in humans. However, this ophthalmic medication may be systemically absorbed and should be administered to pregnant women only if clearly needed.

Studies have not been done in animals.

FDA Pregnancy Category C.

Note: Although the FDA Pregnancy Categories are different for the above medications, some experts believe that all three medications should be rated the same, namely, Category X.

Breast-feeding

Problems in humans have not been documented; however, these ophthalmic medications may be systemically absorbed. Because of the toxicity of cholinesterase inhibitors in general, and the potential for serious adverse reactions in the nursing infant, some clinicians believe that a decision should be made whether to discontinue nursing or discontinue the medication. Other clinicians believe that the concentration of medication in breast milk would be so minute that it would not present a problem.

Pediatrics

The iris cysts at the pupil margins that may occur following prolonged use of these medications occur frequently in children. The most common systemic effects, especially in children, are *nausea, vomiting, diarrhea,* and *stomach cramps* or *pain.* No other information is available on whether the risk of adverse effects is increased in children, except that one drop of medication will result in a greater systemic dose per kg of body weight in a child than in an adult. Because of the toxicity of these medications, they should be used with caution, after less toxic alternatives have been considered and/or found ineffective. Recommended doses should not be exceeded, and the patient should be carefully monitored during therapy.

Geriatrics

No information is available on whether the risk of adverse effects from long-acting cholinergic antiglaucoma agents is increased in the elderly. However, because of the toxicity of these medications, they should be used with caution, after less toxic alternatives have been considered and/or found ineffective. Recommended doses should not be exceeded, and the patient should be carefully monitored during therapy.

Drug interactions and/or related problems

The following drug interactions and/or related problems have been selected on the basis of their potential clinical significance (possible mechanism in parentheses where appropriate)—not necessarily inclusive (» = major clinical significance):

Note: Combinations containing any of the following medications, depending on the amount present, may also interact with this medication.

For echothiophate or isoflurophate only

Physostigmine, ophthalmic
(use of this medication prior to echothiophate or isoflurophate may partially block the effects of the latter medications and shorten their duration of action. Echothiophate and isoflurophate primarily inactivate pseudocholinesterase and incompletely inactivate acetylcholinesterase, whereas physostigmine and demecarium inactivate both pseudocholinesterase and acetylcholinesterase. Prior use of physostigmine inactivates the available acetylcholinesterase, thereby rendering it inaccessible to the incomplete inactivation by echothiophate or isoflurophate. This effect does not occur when physostigmine is given prior to demecarium, because both medications inactivate acetylcholinesterase, thereby producing an additive effect)

For demecarium, echothiophate, or isoflurophate

Anesthetics, mucosal-local, ester-derivative, such as benzocaine, butacaine, butamben, and tetracaine or
Anesthetics, parenteral-local, ester-derivative, such as chloroprocaine, procaine, propoxycaine, and tetracaine
(concurrent use with demecarium, echothiophate, or isoflurophate may inhibit the metabolism of these anesthetics, leading to prolonged anesthetic effect and increased risk of toxicity)

» Anticholinergics or other medications with anticholinergic activity (see *Appendix II*) or

» Antimyasthenics (see *Appendix II*) or
» Cholinesterase inhibitors, other, possibly including topical malathion
(concurrent use of these medications with demecarium, echothiophate, or isoflurophate is not recommended except under strict medical supervision, because of the possibility of additive toxicity; caution may also be warranted with topical application of malathion if excessive quantities of it are used)

Belladonna alkaloids, ophthalmic or
Cyclopentolate or
Tropicamide
(concurrent use of these parasympatholytics may antagonize the antiglaucoma and miotic actions of demecarium, echothiophate, or isoflurophate; however, tropicamide is expected to have little effect, since it is short acting)

Carbamate- or organophosphate-type insecticides or pesticides
(exposure of patients using demecarium, echothiophate, or isoflurophate to these preparations may increase the possibility of systemic effects due to absorption of the insecticide or pesticide through the respiratory tract or skin; patients should be advised to protect themselves from contact with such insecticides or pesticides during therapy with demecarium, echothiophate, or isoflurophate)

Cocaine
(inhibition of cholinesterase activity by demecarium, echothiophate, or isoflurophate reduces or slows cocaine metabolism, thereby increasing and/or prolonging cocaine's effects and increasing the risk of toxicity; cholinesterase inhibition may persist for weeks or months after demecarium, echothiophate, or isoflurophate has been discontinued)

Corticosteroids, ophthalmic
(chronic or intensive use of ophthalmic corticosteroids may increase intraocular pressure and decrease the efficacy of the antiglaucoma agents)

Edrophonium
(caution is recommended in administering edrophonium to patients with symptoms of myasthenic weakness who are also using demecarium, echothiophate, or isoflurophate; symptoms of cholinergic crisis [overdosage] may be similar to those occurring with myasthenic crisis [underdosage] and the patient's condition may be worsened by use of edrophonium)

» Succinylcholine
(demecarium, echothiophate, or isoflurophate may decrease plasma concentrations or activity of pseudocholinesterase, the enzyme that metabolizes succinylcholine, thereby enhancing the neuromuscular blockade of succinylcholine when it is used concurrently; cardiovascular collapse may occur; in addition, increased or prolonged respiratory depression or paralysis [apnea] may occur, which is of minor clinical significance while the patient is being mechanically ventilated; however, caution and careful monitoring of the patient are recommended during and following concurrent or sequential use, especially if there is a possibility of incomplete reversal of neuromuscular blockade postoperatively; these effects may be more pronounced in pediatric patients; the effects of this interaction may persist for several weeks or months after demecarium, echothiophate, or isoflurophate has been discontinued)

Medical considerations/Contraindications

The medical considerations/contraindications included have been selected on the basis of their potential clinical significance (reasons given in parentheses where appropriate)—not necessarily inclusive (» = major clinical significance).

Except under special circumstances, this medication should not be used when the following medical problems exist:

» Glaucoma, angle-closure, or predisposition to (except following iridectomy)
(medication may increase the narrowing of the angle)

» Glaucoma associated with iridocyclitis (anterior uveitis)
(medication may aggravate the inflammatory process and lead to the development of posterior synechiae)

» Sensitivity to the long-acting cholinergic antiglaucoma agent prescribed

» Uveitis, active
(medication may aggravate inflammation)

Risk-benefit should be considered when the following medical problems exist:

» Asthma, bronchial
(systemic absorption of medication may precipitate an attack)

» Bradycardia and hypotension, pronounced or
» Epilepsy or
» Gastrointestinal disturbances, spastic or
» Parkinsonism or
» Peptic ulcer or
» Urinary tract obstruction
(vagotonic effects of medication may worsen these conditions)

Down's syndrome (mongolism)
(echothiophate, and possibly demecarium or isoflurophate, may cause hyperactivity in these children)

Hypertension, systemic or
Hyperthyroidism
(systemic absorption of medication may cause paradoxical exacerbation of these conditions)

Iritis, quiescent or history of
(medication may activate latent iritis and aggravate the inflammatory process)

Myasthenia gravis
(medication may cause additive effects with antimyasthenic agents)

» Myocardial infarction, recent
(vagotonic effects may worsen cardiac function; medication may increase risk of cardiac arrhythmias)

» Retinal detachment, predisposition to or history of
(may result from drug-induced spasm of accommodation)

Surgery, intraocular
(intraocular surgery performed during the action of these medications may be complicated by hyphema and/or severe uveitis that is very difficult to manage; it is recommended that elective intraocular surgery not be performed until the full duration of action of these medications has elapsed)

Uveitis, quiescent or history of
(medication may activate latent uveitis and may predispose the patient to the development of posterior synechiae)

» Vagotonia, marked
(medication may increase vagotonic effects)

Patient monitoring

The following may be especially important in patient monitoring (other tests may be warranted in some patients, depending on condition; » = major clinical significance):

Gonioscopy
(recommended prior to, and soon after, initiation of therapy)

Intraocular pressure determinations
(recommended hourly for 3 or 4 hours initially, then at periodic intervals during therapy)

Ophthalmologic examinations
(recommended initially with close patient observation during the first 24 hours of therapy, then at periodic intervals for patients on prolonged therapy, since formation of iris cysts [especially in children], conjunctival thickening, obstruction of nasolacrimal canals, retinal detachment, and lens opacities may occur; also, the condition of the optic nerve should be monitored in patients with glaucoma)

Side/Adverse Effects

Note: Lens opacities and cataracts may occur following prolonged use of echothiophate, isoflurophate, and possibly demecarium. While there is strong evidence implicating the phosphorylating medications, echothiophate and isoflurophate, there is little or no similar evidence implicating the carbamylating medication, demecarium. If lens opacities occur, they may regress if therapy is discontinued early in their development; however, once cataracts are established, they often continue developing despite cessation of therapy. The incidence of cataracts appears to be directly related to the age of the patient and the concentration, frequency, and duration of the medication.

Retinal detachment has been reported in a few patients during the use of ophthalmic long-acting cholinergic antiglaucoma agents, such as demecarium, echothiophate, or isoflurophate.

Repeated administration of demecarium, echothiophate, or isoflurophate may cause depression of the concentration of cholinesterase in the serum and erythrocytes, resulting in systemic effects.

Iris cysts, conjunctival thickening, and obstruction of nasolacrimal canals may occur following prolonged use of demecarium, echothiophate, or isoflurophate, especially in children. If iris cysts occur and treatment with demecarium, echothiophate, or isoflurophate is continued, the cysts may enlarge and obscure the vision. In addition, rarely, the cysts may rupture or break free of the iris into the aqueous humor. The cysts usually decrease in size following discontinuation of the medication.

Activation of latent iritis or uveitis may occur following use of demecarium, echothiophate, or isoflurophate.

A paradoxical increase in intraocular pressure may occur following use of demecarium, echothiophate, or isoflurophate. This may be alleviated by the use of a sympathomimetic, such as phenylephrine.

The following side/adverse effects have been selected on the basis of their potential clinical significance (possible signs and symptoms in parentheses where appropriate)—not necessarily inclusive:

Those indicating need for medical attention

Incidence rare

Burning, redness, stinging, or other irritation of eyes; eye pain; retinal detachment (veil or curtain appearing across part of vision)

Symptoms of systemic absorption

Bradycardia (slow or irregular heartbeat); ***bronchospasm*** (shortness of breath, tightness in chest, or wheezing); ***hypotension, severe*** (unusual tiredness or weakness); ***increased sweating; loss of bladder control; muscle weakness; nausea, vomiting, diarrhea, or stomach cramps or pain; watering of mouth***

Note: The most common systemic effects, especially in children, are *nausea, vomiting, diarrhea,* and *stomach cramps* or *pain.*

Systemic absorption is rare with isoflurophate because systemic absorption from ointment bases is minimal and the isoflurophate that is absorbed is hydrolyzed in the circulation almost immediately.

Temporary discontinuation of the medication is recommended if symptoms of systemic absorption occur.

Those indicating need for medical attention only if they continue or are bothersome

Accommodative myopia (blurred vision or change in near or distance vision); ***browache; headache; miosis*** (difficulty in seeing at night or in dim light); ***twitching of eyelids; watering of eyes***

Overdose

For specific information on the agents used in the management of ophthalmic long-acting cholinergic antiglaucoma agents overdose, see:

- *Atropine* in *Anticholinergics/Antispasmodics (Systemic)* monograph; and/or
- *Diazepam* in *Benzodiazepines (Systemic)* monograph.

For more information on the management of overdose or unintentional ingestion, **contact a Poison Control Center** (see *Poison Control Center Listing*).

Clinical effects of overdose

Clinical effects of overdose may occur as a result of systemic absorption following unintentional ingestion, or from topical application in the eye, or excessive skin contact with demecarium, echothiophate, or rarely, with isoflurophate. These effects may occur in addition to those symptoms and signs of systemic absorption. The following effects have been selected on the basis of their potential clinical significance (possible signs and symptoms in parenthesis where appropriate)—not necessarily inclusive:

Cardiac arrhythmias; diarrhea; muscle weakness; profuse sweating; respiratory difficulties; shock; urinary incontinence

Treatment of overdose

Atropine sulfate injection is used as an antidote to the systemic cholinergic effects of demecarium, echothiophate, or isoflurophate.

For adults—Parenteral administration, intravenous if necessary, 0.4 to 0.6 mg or more. The use of much larger doses of atropine in treating anticholinesterase intoxication in adults has been reported as follows: intravenous, 2 to 6 mg initially, then 2 mg repeated every hour, or more often, until cholinergic symptoms disappear or signs of atropine toxicity appear. However, the risk of atropine intoxication increases when large doses are used, especially in sensitive individuals.

For infants and children younger than 12 years of age—Intravenous or intramuscular, 0.01 mg per kilogram repeated every two hours as needed until cholinergic symptoms disappear or signs of atropine toxicity appear. The maximum single dose should not exceed 0.4 mg.

Intravenous pralidoxime chloride (dose of 25 mg per kg of body weight [mg/kg]) may be used as an adjunct to atropine therapy to reverse the muscle paralysis caused by nicotinic effects of demecarium, echothiophate, or isoflurophate. The use of pralidoxime chloride for treating the systemic effects due to cholinesterase inhibitors is not intended to be a substitute for atropine therapy.

A short-acting barbiturate or diazepam may be administered for convulsions not controlled by atropine; however, the dosage of the barbiturate should be adjusted to avoid central respiratory depression.

Artificial respiration and maintenance of a clear airway are indicated for severe weakness or paralysis of muscles of respiration.

Patient Consultation

As an aid to patient consultation, refer to *Advice for the Patient, Antiglaucoma Agents, Cholinergic, Long-acting (Ophthalmic).*

In providing consultation, consider emphasizing the following selected information (» = major clinical significance):

Before using this medication

» Conditions affecting use, especially:

Sensitivity to demecarium, echothiophate, or isoflurophate

Pregnancy—Because of the toxicity of cholinesterase inhibitors in general, these medications are not recommended during pregnancy

Breast-feeding—Medications may be absorbed into the body and are not recommended during breast-feeding since they may cause adverse effects in nursing infants; a decision should be made whether to discontinue nursing or discontinue the medication

Use in children—The iris cysts that may occur following prolonged use of these medications occur frequently in children; also, children may be more sensitive to the effects of these medications, especially if they are absorbed into the body

Other medications, especially anticholinergics or other medications with anticholinergic activity; antimyasthenics; or other cholinesterase inhibitors, possibly including topical malathion

Recent exposure to pesticides or insecticides

Other medical problems, especially active uveitis, angle-closure glaucoma or glaucoma associated with iridocyclitis, bronchial asthma, epilepsy, marked vagotonia, parkinsonism, peptic ulcer, predisposition to or history of retinal detachment, pronounced bradycardia or hypotension, recent myocardial infarction, spastic gastrointestinal disturbances, or urinary tract obstruction

Proper use of this medication

Proper administration technique for ophthalmic solution; removing excess solution around eye with clean tissue, being careful not to touch eye; washing hands immediately after application to avoid possible systemic absorption; not touching applicator tip to any surface; keeping container tightly closed; applying the dose, or one of the two doses, at bedtime, since the solution may affect vision for several hours after administration

Proper administration technique for ophthalmic ointment; washing hands immediately after application to avoid possible systemic absorption; not washing tip of ointment tube or allowing it to touch moist surface, since medication loses efficacy when exposed to moisture; not touching applicator tip to any surface, wiping tip of ointment tube with clean tissue; keeping container tightly closed; applying at bedtime, since ointment causes blurred vision after administration

» Importance of not using more medication than the amount prescribed

» Not using ocular solutions or ointment that may have become contaminated through improper handling or administration

» Proper dosing

Waiting 15 minutes after instilling preparations containing demecarium prior to inserting soft contact lenses

Missed dose:

If dosing schedule is—

Every other day: Applying as soon as possible if remembered same day; if not remembered until the next day, applying it at that time, then skipping a day; not doubling doses

Once a day: Applying as soon as possible; if not remembered until next day, skipping missed dose and going back to regular dosing schedule; not doubling doses

More than once a day: Applying as soon as possible; if almost time for next dose, skipping missed dose and going back to regular dosing schedule; not doubling doses

» Proper storage

Precautions while using this medication

Regular visits to physician during therapy to check eye pressure and, for patients on prolonged therapy, to examine eyes

» Caution if any kind of surgery is required

» Caution if an ocular infection develops, or if ocular trauma occurs during therapy

» Caution in exposure to carbamate- or organophosphate-type insecticides or pesticides during therapy

» Making sure vision is clear before driving, using machines, or doing anything else that could be dangerous if not able to see well; caution because of possibility of decreased night vision, blurred vision or change in near or distance vision, or blurred vision for short time if using ointment

Side/adverse effects

Signs of potential side effects, especially burning, redness, stinging, or other irritation of the eyes; eye pain; retinal detachment; or symptoms of systemic absorption

General Dosing Information

To reduce the inconvenience of post-medication miosis, the daily dose or one of the daily doses of the medication may be administered at bedtime.

A stronger concentration may be required to produce adequate miosis and reduction in intraocular pressure in eyes with hazel or brown irides than in eyes with blue or light-colored irides because miotics are less effective in heavily pigmented eyes.

During initial therapy, close observation of the patient and frequent (hourly) tonometric examinations are recommended to ensure that no immediate rise in intraocular pressure occurs. Exams conducted at different times of the day will assist in the detection of inadequate control of intraocular pressure.

To reduce the incidence of iris cyst formation, the frequency of administration should be minimal in all patients, especially in children. In addition, the simultaneous administration of 2.5 to 10% ophthalmic phenylephrine with demecarium, echothiophate, or isoflurophate may prevent iris cyst formation. However, phenylephrine will not prevent iris cysts if the phenylephrine is administered several hours before or after demecarium, echothiophate, or isoflurophate. The 2.5% concentration of phenylephrine appears to be as effective as the 10% concentration and causes less burning upon administration.

Concurrent use of demecarium, echothiophate, or isoflurophate with epinephrine, a beta-adrenergic blocking agent, and/or a carbonic anhydrase inhibitor results in additive effects, thereby providing better control of glaucoma. Use of a reduced dose of demecarium, echothiophate, or isoflurophate may be possible. A dosage reduction of the miotic medication (i.e., demecarium, echothiophate, or isoflurophate) results in the patient experiencing less miosis and/or accommodative block. In addition, concomitant administration of 2.5 to 10% ophthalmic phenylephrine or 1 or 2% ophthalmic epinephrine may improve the visual acuity of some patients by dilating the miotic eye without increasing the intraocular pressure.

Tolerance to demecarium, echothiophate, or isoflurophate may develop with prolonged use. Effectiveness may be restored by changing to another miotic for a short time and then resuming the original medication.

Following long-term use of these medications, dilation of blood vessels and resulting greater permeability will increase postoperative inflammation and may increase the risk of hyphema during ophthalmic surgery; therefore, demecarium, echothiophate, or isoflurophate should be discontinued 2 to 3 weeks before eye surgery.

Temporary discontinuation of these medications is recommended if cardiac irregularities (e.g., arrhythmias) occur.

For the solution dosage forms only

Although some manufacturers recommend a dose of 2 drops of an ophthalmic solution at appropriate intervals, the conjunctival sac usually will hold only 1 drop. In addition, because of the potency of these medications and the possibility of systemic absorption, the smallest dose possible should be administered.

To avoid excessive systemic absorption, patient should press finger to the lacrimal sac during and for 1 or 2 minutes following instillation of medication.

DEMECARIUM

Summary of Differences

Precautions: Drug interactions and/or related problems—Physostigmine not listed as a precaution.

Ophthalmic Dosage Forms

DEMECARIUM BROMIDE OPHTHALMIC SOLUTION USP

Usual adult and adolescent dose

Antiglaucoma agent (ophthalmic)—

Topical, to the conjunctiva, 1 drop of a 0.125 or 0.25% solution one or two times a day.

Note: The usual dosage can vary from as much as 1 or 2 drops two times a day to as little as 1 or 2 drops two times a week. The 0.125% strength used twice a day usually results in optimal control of the diurnal variation in intraocular pressure, and is the preferred dosage for most open-angle glaucoma patients.

Cyclostimulant (accommodative esotropia)—

Topical, to the conjunctiva, 1 drop of a 0.125 or 0.25% solution once a day for two or three weeks, then 1 drop every two days for three or four weeks, at which time the patient's status should be re-evaluated. If improvement in the patient's clinical condition continues, the schedule may be reduced to 1 drop once a week, and eventually, to a trial without medication.

Note: In the treatment of esotropia uncomplicated by amblyopia or anisometropia, the patient's condition should be evaluated every four to twelve weeks. It is recommended that therapy be discontinued after four months if a dosage of 1 drop every two days is still required to control condition.

Diagnostic aid (accommodative esotropia)—

Topical, to the conjunctiva, 1 drop of a 0.125 or 0.25% solution once a day for two weeks, then 1 drop every two days for two or three weeks.

Usual pediatric dose

Antiglaucoma agent (ophthalmic)
Cyclostimulant (accommodative esotropia) or
Diagnostic aid (accommodative esotropia)—

For infants and young children: Use is not recommended.

Older children: See *Usual adult and adolescent dose*.

Note: Clinicians differ as to the age at which children may receive this medication, their recommendations ranging from 12 months to 15 years. Other clinicians feel that the lower end of the adult dose range, administered less frequently, may be used for infants and children.

Strength(s) usually available

U.S.—

Note: The preservative benzalkonium chloride may be absorbed by soft contact lenses. Patients wearing soft contact lenses should wait at least 15 minutes after instilling eye drop solutions containing demecarium prior to inserting lenses.

0.125% (Rx) [*Humorsol* (benzalkonium chloride 1:5000; sodium chloride)].

0.25% (Rx) [*Humorsol* (benzalkonium chloride 1:5000; sodium chloride)].

Canada—

Not commercially available.

Packaging and storage

Store below 40 °C (104 °F), preferably between 15 and 30 °C (59 and 86 °F), unless otherwise specified by manufacturer. Store in a tight, light-resistant container. Protect from freezing or excessive heat.

Auxiliary labeling

- For the eye.
- Keep container tightly closed.

ECHOTHIOPHATE

Ophthalmic Dosage Forms

ECHOTHIOPHATE IODIDE FOR OPHTHALMIC SOLUTION USP

Usual adult and adolescent dose

Antiglaucoma agent (ophthalmic)—

Topical, to the conjunctiva, 1 drop of a 0.03 to 0.25% solution one or two times a day.

Note: Twice-daily dosing provides optimal control of the diurnal variation in intraocular pressure.

For conditions requiring higher strengths of the ophthalmic solution, a brief trial with the 0.03% solution is recommended.

Cyclostimulant (accommodative esotropia)—

Topical, to the conjunctiva, 1 drop of a 0.03 to 0.125% solution once a day or every two days.

Diagnostic aid (accommodative esotropia)—

Topical, to the conjunctiva, 1 drop of a 0.125% solution once a day at bedtime for two or three weeks.

Usual pediatric dose

Antiglaucoma agent (ophthalmic)
Cyclostimulant (accommodative esotropia) or

Diagnostic aid (accommodative esotropia)—
For infants and young children: Use is not recommended.
Older children: See *Usual adult and adolescent dose*.

Note: Clinicians differ as to the age at which children may receive this medication, their recommendations ranging from 12 months to 15 years, with 2 years being the most frequently recommended age. Other clinicians feel that the lower end of the adult dose range, administered less frequently, may be used for infants and children.

Strength(s) usually available

U.S.—

0.03% (equivalent to 1.5 mg per 5 mL of sterile diluent) (Rx) [*Phospholine Iodide* (aluminum crimp seal is blue; in powder—potassium acetate 40 mg; in powder—sodium hydroxide; in powder—acetic acid; in diluent—chlorobutanol 0.55%; in diluent—mannitol 1.2%; in diluent—boric acid 0.06%; in diluent—sodium phosphate 0.026%)].

0.06% (equivalent to 3 mg per 5 mL of sterile diluent) (Rx) [*Phospholine Iodide* (aluminum crimp seal is red; in powder—potassium acetate 40 mg; in powder—sodium hydroxide; in powder—acetic acid; in diluent—chlorobutanol 0.55%; in diluent—mannitol 1.2%; in diluent—boric acid 0.06%; in diluent—sodium phosphate 0.026%)].

0.125% (equivalent to 6.25 mg per 5 mL of sterile diluent) (Rx) [*Phospholine Iodide* (aluminum crimp seal is green; in powder—potassium acetate 40 mg; in powder—sodium hydroxide; in powder—acetic acid; in diluent—chlorobutanol 0.55%; in diluent—mannitol 1.2%; in diluent—boric acid 0.06%; in diluent—sodium phosphate 0.026%)].

0.25% (equivalent to 12.5 mg per 5 mL of sterile diluent) (Rx) [*Phospholine Iodide* (aluminum crimp seal is yellow; in powder—potassium acetate 40 mg; in powder—sodium hydroxide; in powder—acetic acid; in diluent—chlorobutanol 0.55%; in diluent—mannitol 1.2%; in diluent—boric acid 0.06%; in diluent—sodium phosphate 0.026%)].

Canada—

0.06% (equivalent to 3 mg per 5 mL of sterile diluent) (Rx) [*Phospholine Iodide* (in powder—potassium acetate; in powder—sodium hydroxide; in powder—acetic acid; in diluent—mannitol; in diluent—hydrochloric acid; in diluent—sodium phosphate)].

0.125% (equivalent to 6.25 mg per 5 mL of sterile diluent) (Rx) [*Phospholine Iodide* (in powder—potassium acetate; in powder—sodium hydroxide; in powder—acetic acid; in diluent—mannitol; in diluent—hydrochloric acid; in diluent—sodium phosphate)].

0.25% (equivalent to 12.5 mg per 5 mL of sterile diluent) (Rx) [*Phospholine Iodide* (in powder—potassium acetate; in powder—sodium hydroxide; in powder—acetic acid; in diluent—mannitol; in diluent—hydrochloric acid; in diluent—sodium phosphate)].

Packaging and storage

Prior to reconstitution, store under refrigeration between 2 and 8 °C (36 and 46 °F). Reconstituted product may be stored between 15 and 30 °C (59 and 86 °F). Store in a tight container. Protect the reconstituted solution from freezing.

Preparation of dosage form

For reconstitution of echothiophate iodide powder, use only the diluent supplied by the manufacturer to provide for optimum stability. Use aseptic technique.

Stability

Reconstituted solution is stable for about 3 to 4 weeks at room temperature or for 3 to 6 months if refrigerated, depending on the manufacturer.

Auxiliary labeling

- For the eye.
- Beyond-use date.
- Keep container tightly closed.

ISOFLUROPHATE

Ophthalmic Dosage Forms

Note: Because isoflurophate is not commercially available in the U.S. or Canada, the bracketed uses and the use of the superscript 1 in this monograph reflect the lack of labeled (approved) indications for this medication in these countries.

ISOFLUROPHATE OPHTHALMIC OINTMENT USP

Usual adult and adolescent dose

[Antiglaucoma agent (ophthalmic)][1]—
Topical, to the conjunctiva, a thin strip (approximately 0.5 cm) of a 0.025% ointment once every three days to three times a day.

[Cyclostimulant (accommodative esotropia)][1]—
Topical, to the conjunctiva, a thin strip (approximately 0.5 cm) of a 0.025% ointment once a day at bedtime for two weeks, then once a week to once every two days, depending on the patient's condition, for two months.

Note: In the treatment of esotropia uncomplicated by anisometropia, it is recommended that therapy be discontinued if the patient's condition cannot be maintained on a dosage interval of at least every two days.

[Diagnostic aid (accommodative esotropia)][1]—
Topical, to the conjunctiva, a thin strip (approximately 0.5 cm) of a 0.025% ointment once a day at bedtime for two weeks.

Usual pediatric dose

[Antiglaucoma agent (ophthalmic)][1]
[Cyclostimulant (accommodative esotropia) or][1]
[Diagnostic aid (accommodative esotropia)][1]—
For infants and young children: Use is not recommended.
Older children: See *Usual adult and adolescent dose.*

Note: Clinicians differ as to the age at which children may receive this medication, their recommendations ranging from 12 months to 15 years, with 2 years being the most frequently recommended age. Other clinicians feel that the lower end of the adult dose range, administered less frequently, may be used for infants and children.

Strength(s) usually available

U.S.—
Not commercially available.

Canada—
Not commercially available.

France—
[*Diflupyl*].

Packaging and storage

Store below 40 °C (104 °F), preferably between 15 and 30 °C (59 and 86 °F), unless otherwise specified by manufacturer. Protect from freezing.

Stability

Isoflurophate hydrolyzes in the presence of water to form hydrofluoric acid and becomes inactivated.

Auxiliary labeling

- For the eye.
- Keep container tightly closed.

[1]Not included in Canadian product labeling.

Selected Bibliography

Havener, WH. Ocular pharmacology. 5th ed. St. Louis: Mosby; 1983. p. 261-418, 635-72.

Pavan-Langston D, editor. Manual of ocular diagnosis and therapy. 2nd ed. Boston: Little, Brown; 1985. p. 201-29.

Revised: 06/15/1999

ANTIHISTAMINES Systemic

This monograph includes information on the following: 1) Azatadine; 2) Brompheniramine; 3) Cetirizine; 4) Chlorpheniramine; 5) Clemastine; 6) Cyproheptadine; 7) Desloratadine; 8) Dexchlorpheniramine; 9) Dimenhydrinate; 10) Diphenhydramine; 11) Doxylamine†; 12) Fexofenadine; 13) Hydroxyzine; 14) Loratadine; 15) Phenindamine†.

Note: Products listed in this monograph contain single-entity antihistamines. For products containing antihistamines in combination with other medications, refer to *Antihistamines and Decongestants (Systemic)*, *Antihistamines, Decongestants, and Analgesics (Systemic)*, and *Cough/Cold Combinations (Systemic)*.

INN: Chlorpheniramine—Chlorphenamine

VA CLASSIFICATION (Primary/Secondary):
Azatadine—AH109
Brompheniramine—AH109
Cetirizine—AH109
Chlorpheniramine—AH109

Clemastine—AH109
Cyproheptadine—AH109
Desloratadine—AH102
Dexchlorpheniramine—AH109
Dimenhydrinate—AH109/CN550
Diphenhydramine
Oral—AH109/AU305; CN309; CN550; RE302
Parenteral—CN204
Doxylamine—AH109/CN309
Fexofenadine—AH102
Hydroxyzine—AH109/CN309
Loratadine—AH102
Phenindamine—AH109

Commonly used brand name(s): *Aerius*[7]; *Alavert*[14]; *Allegra*[12]; *Aller-Chlor*[4]; *AllerMax Caplets*[10]; *Allerdryl*[10]; *Aller-med*[10]; *Apo-Dimenhydrinate*[9]; *Apo-Hydroxyzine*[13]; *Atarax*[13]; *Banophen*[10]; *Banophen Caplets*[10]; *Benadryl*[10]; *Benadryl Allergy*[10]; *Bromphen*[2]; *Calm X*[9]; *Chlo-Amine*[4]; *Chlor-Trimeton*[4]; *Chlor-Trimeton Allergy*[4]; *Chlor-Trimeton Repetabs*[4]; *Chlor-Tripolon*[4]; *Chlorate*[4]; *Clarinex*[7]; *Claritin*[14]; *Claritin RediTabs*[14]; *Compoz*[10]; *Contac 12 Hour Allergy*[5]; *Dexchlor*[8]; *Dimetane*[2]; *Dimetapp Allergy Liqui-Gels*[2]; *Dinate*[9]; *Diphen Cough*[10]; *Diphenhist*[10]; *Diphenhist Captabs*[10]; *Dormarex 2*[10]; *Dramamine*[9]; *Dramanate*[9]; *Gen-Allerate*[4]; *Genahist*[10]; *Gravol*[9]; *Gravol Filmkote*[9]; *Gravol I/M*[9]; *Gravol I/V*[9]; *Gravol L/A*[9]; *Gravol Liquid*[9]; *Hydrate*[9]; *Hyrexin*[10]; *Hyzine-50*[13]; *Multipax*[13]; *Nasahist B*[2]; *Nervine Nighttime Sleep-Aid*[10]; *Nolahist*[15]; *Novo-Hydroxyzin*[13]; *Novo-Pheniram*[4]; *Nytol QuickCaps*[10]; *Nytol QuickGels*[10]; *Optimine*[1]; *PMS-Dimenhydrinate*[9]; *PediaCare Allergy Formula*[4]; *Periactin*[6]; *Phenetron*[4]; *Polaramine*[8]; *Polaramine Repetabs*[8]; *Reactine*[3]; *Siladryl*[10]; *Sleep-Eze D*[10]; *Sleep-Eze D Extra Strength*[10]; *Sleep-eze D Extra Strength*[10]; *Sominex*[10]; *Tavist*[5]; *Tavist-1*[5]; *Telachlor*[4]; *Teldrin*[4]; *Traveltabs*[9]; *Triptone Caplets*[9]; *Twilite Caplets*[10]; *Unisom Nighttime Sleep Aid*[11]; *Unisom SleepGels Maximum Strength*[10]; *Vistaril*[13]; *Zyrtec*[3].

Note: For a listing of dosage forms and brand names by country availability, see *Dosage Forms* section(s).

†Not commercially available in Canada.

Category

Antihistaminic (H_1-receptor)—Azatadine; Brompheniramine; Cetirizine; Chlorpheniramine; Clemastine; Cyproheptadine; Desloratadine; Dexchlorpheniramine; Dimenhydrinate; Diphenhydramine; Doxylamine; Fexofenadine; Hydroxyzine; Loratadine; Phenindamine.
Antianxiety agent—Hydroxyzine.
Antidyskinetic—Diphenhydramine.
Antiemetic—Dimenhydrinate; Diphenhydramine; Hydroxyzine (parenteral).
Antitussive—Diphenhydramine Elixir.
Antivertigo agent—Dimenhydrinate; Diphenhydramine.
Sedative-hypnotic—Diphenhydramine; Doxylamine; Hydroxyzine.
Appetite stimulant—Cyproheptadine.
Vascular headache suppressant—Cyproheptadine.
Antiasthmatic—Cetirizine; Loratadine

Indications

Note: Bracketed information in the *Indications* section refers to uses that are not included in U.S. product labeling.

Accepted

Rhinitis, perennial and seasonal allergic or vasomotor (prophylaxis and treatment) or
Conjunctivitis, allergic (prophylaxis and treatment)—Antihistamines are indicated in the prophylactic and symptomatic treatment of perennial and seasonal allergic rhinitis, vasomotor rhinitis, and allergic conjunctivitis due to inhalant allergens and foods.

Pruritus (treatment)
Urticaria (treatment)
Angioedema (treatment)
Dermatographism (treatment) or
Transfusion reactions, urticarial (treatment)—Antihistamines are indicated for the symptomatic treatment of pruritus associated with allergic reactions and of mild, uncomplicated allergic skin manifestations of urticaria and angioedema, in dermatographism, and in urticaria associated with transfusions. Cyproheptadine may be particularly useful for cold urticaria,dermatitis including neurodermatitis and neurodermatitis circumscripta, eczema, eczematoid dermatitis, mild local allergic reactions to insect bites, angioneurotic edema, drug and serum reactions, anogenital pruritus and pruritus of chickenpox. [Antihistamines are also used in the treatment of pruritus associated with pityriasis rosea.][1]

Sneezing (treatment) or
Rhinorrhea (treatment)—Antihistamines are indicated for the relief of sneezing and rhinorrhea associated with the common cold. However, controlled clinical studies have not demonstrated that antihistamines are significantly more effective than placebo in relieving cold symptoms. Non-sedating (i.e., second-generation) antihistamines are unlikely to be useful in the treatment of the common cold symptoms since they do not have clinically significant anticholinergic effects (e.g., drying effects on nasal mucosa).

Anaphylactic or anaphylactoid reactions (treatment adjunct)—Antihistamines are indicated as adjunctive therapy to epinephrine and other standard measures for anaphylactic reactions after the acute manifestations have been controlled, and to ameliorate the allergic reactions to blood or plasma.

Anxiety (treatment) and
Tension, psychosis-related (treatment)—Hydroxyzine is indicated for the relief of anxiety and tension associated with psychoneurosis and as an adjunct in organic disease states in which anxiety is manifested. The effectiveness of hydroxyzine as an antianxiety agent for long-term use (for example, more than 4 months) has not been assessed by systematic clinical studies.

Alcohol withdrawal (treatment)—Parenteral hydroxyzine is indicated in the acute or chronic alcoholic with anxiety withdrawal symptoms.

Parkinsonism (treatment)[1] or
Extrapyramidal reactions, drug-induced (treatment)[1]—Diphenhydramine is indicated for the symptomatic treatment of parkinsonism and drug-induced extrapyramidal reactions in elderly patients unable to tolerate more potent antidyskinetic medications, for mild cases of parkinsonism in other age groups and, in combination with centrally acting anticholinergic agents, for other cases of parkinsonism.

Cough (treatment)—Diphenhydramine hydrochloride syrup is currently indicated as a non-narcotic cough suppressant for control of cough due to colds or allergy.

Motion sickness (prophylaxis and treatment) or
Vertigo (treatment)—Dimenhydrinate and diphenhydramine are indicated for the prevention and treatment of the nausea, vomiting, dizziness, or vertigo of motion sickness.

Nausea or vomiting (prophylaxis and treatment)—Parenteral hydroxyzine is indicated for the control of nausea and vomiting, excluding nausea and vomiting of pregnancy.

Sedation—Diphenhydramine and hydroxyzine are indicated for their sedative and hypnotic effects and as preoperative medications.

Insomnia (treatment)—Diphenhydramine and doxylamine are indicated as nighttime sleep aids to help reduce the time to fall asleep in patients having difficulty falling asleep.

Analgesia adjunct, during surgery
Anesthesia, general, adjunct or
Anesthesia, local, adjunct—Parenteral hydroxyzine is useful as pre- and postoperative, and pre- and postpartum adjunctive medication to allow reduction in narcotic dosage, and to control anxiety and emesis.

[Appetite, lack of (treatment)]—Cyproheptadine is used as an appetite stimulant, in adults and children.

[Headache, vascular (treatment)]—Cyproheptadine is used for treatment of vascular headaches, such as migraine and histamine cephalalgia.

[Asthma, bronchial (treatment adjunct)][1]—Cetirizine, and loratadine are used as adjunctive treatment to asthma medications to reduce symptoms and improve bronchodilation in patients with mild atopic asthma.

Unaccepted

Cyproheptadine has been used in the treatment of Cushing's disease because of its pronounced antiserotonin properties, which may decrease corticotropin release. Cyproheptadine may also provide antidiarrheal action against intestinal hypermotility associated with the excessive production of serotonin in patients with carcinoid tumors, and in some other conditions involving the release of serotonin. However, there is no conclusive evidence of effectiveness for these uses.

[1]Not included in Canadian product labeling.

Pharmacology/Pharmacokinetics

Physicochemical characteristics

Chemical Group—
Ethanolamine derivatives: Clemastine; Dimenhydrinate (chlorotheophylline salt of diphenhydramine); Diphenhydramine; Doxylamine

Piperidine derivatives: Azatadine; Cyproheptadine; Desloratadine; Loratadine; Phenindamine; Piperazine derivative: Cetirizine (metabolite of hydroxyzine); Hydroxyzine
Propylamine derivatives (alkylamines): Brompheniramine; Chlorpheniramine; Dexchlorpheniramine

Molecular weight—
Azatadine maleate: 522.56.
Brompheniramine maleate: 435.32.
Cetirizine hydrochloride: 461.82.
Chlorpheniramine maleate: 390.87.
Clemastine fumarate: 459.97.
Cyproheptadine hydrochloride: 350.89.
Desloratadine: 310.8.
Dexchlorpheniramine maleate: 390.87.
Dimenhydrinate: 469.97.
Diphenhydramine hydrochloride: 291.82.
Doxylamine succinate: 388.46.
Hydroxyzine hydrochloride: 447.83.
Hydroxyzine pamoate: 763.29.
Loratadine: 382.89.
Phenindamine tartrate: 411.45.

pKa—
Azatadine maleate: 9.3.
Brompheniramine maleate: 3.59 and 9.12.
Chlorpheniramine maleate: 9.2.
Cyproheptadine hydrochloride: 9.3.
Desloratadine: 4.2 and 9.7.
Diphenhydramine hydrochloride: 9.
Doxylamine succinate: 5.8 and 9.3.
Hydroxyzine hydrochloride: 2.6 and 7.

Mechanism of action/Effect

Antihistaminic (H_1-receptor)—Antihistamines used in the treatment of allergy act by competing with histamine for H_1-receptor sites on effector cells. They thereby prevent, but do not reverse, responses mediated by histamine alone. Antihistamines antagonize, in varying degrees, most of the pharmacological effects of histamine, including urticaria and pruritus. Also, the anticholinergic actions of most antihistamines provide a drying effect on the nasal mucosa.

Antianxiety agent—Hydroxyzine's sedative action may be due to a suppression of activity in certain key regions of the subcortical area of the central nervous system (CNS). It is not a cortical depressant.

Antidyskinetic—The actions of diphenhydramine in parkinsonism and in drug-induced dyskinesias appear to be related to a central inhibition of the actions of acetylcholine, which are mediated via muscarinic receptors (anticholinergic action), and to its sedative effects.

Antiemetic; antivertigo agent—The mechanism by which some antihistamines exert their antiemetic, anti-motion sickness, and antivertigo effects is not precisely known but may be related to their central anticholinergic actions. They diminish vestibular stimulation and depress labyrinthine function. An action on the medullary chemoreceptive trigger zone may also be involved in the antiemetic effect.

Antitussive—Diphenhydramine suppresses the cough reflex by a direct effect on the cough center in the medulla of the brain.

Sedative-hypnotic—Most antihistamines cross the blood-brain barrier and produce sedation due to inhibition of histamine *N*-methyltransferase and blockage of central histaminergic receptors. Antagonism of other central nervous system receptor sites, such as those for serotonin, acetylcholine, and alpha-adrenergic stimulation, may also be involved. Central depression is not significant with cetirizine (low doses), desloratadine, or loratadine because they do not readily cross the blood-brain barrier. Also, they bind preferentially to peripheral H_1-receptors rather than to central nervous system H_1-receptors.

Appetite stimulant—Cyproheptadine competes with serotonin for receptor sites, thus blocking the responses to serotonin in vascular, intestinal, and other smooth muscles. It is possible that by altering serotonin activity in the appetite center of the hypothalamus, cyproheptadine stimulates appetite.

Vascular headache suppressant—Cyproheptadine's vascular headache suppressant effect is probably due to its antiserotonin action.

Antiasthmatic—Cetirizine, and loratadine have been shown to cause mild bronchodilation and also to block histamine-induced bronchoconstriction in asthmatic patients. Also, loratadine, have been shown to diminish exercise-induced bronchospasm and hyperventilation-induced bronchospasm. Cetirizine has not been shown to be uniformly effective in preventing allergen- or exercise-induced bronchoconstriction; however, due to its inhibition of late-phase eosinophil recruitment after local allergen challenge, it has been shown to be more effective, in higher doses, than other antihistamines in reducing the symptoms of pollen-induced asthma.

Other actions/effects

Anticholinergic—Antihistamines prevent responses to acetylcholine that are mediated via muscarinic receptors. The ethanolamine derivatives may show greater anticholinergic activity than the other classes of antihistamines. Loratadine, has no significant anticholinergic activity; cetirizine has minimal anticholinergic activity.

Anesthetic, local, dental—Antihistamines are structurally related to local anesthetics and have local anesthetic activity. Local anesthetics prevent the initiation and transmission of nerve impulses by decreasing the permeability of the nerve cell membrane to sodium ions. This action decreases the rate of depolarization of the membrane and prevents the generation of the action potential.

Absorption

Well absorbed after oral administration.

Note: Ingestion of food may enhance the absorption of loratadine by 40% and of its active metabolite by 15%.

Food may delay the rate, but not the extent of cetirizine absorption.

In one study involving patients 66 to 78 years of age the extent of absorption and peak plasma levels of loratadine and its metabolite were significantly higher (55%) than those in studies with younger patients.

Desloratadine's absorption is not affected by food. Renal impairment and hepatic impairment requires dosage adjustments due to increased AUC (area under the concentration time curve).

Protein binding

Cetirizine—93%.
Chlorpheniramine—72%.
Desloratadine—82 to 87%. 3-hydroxydesloratadine (active metabolite): 85 to 89%
Diphenhydramine—98 to 99%.
Loratadine—97% (at concentrations of 2.5 to 100 ng/mL). Descarboethoxyloratadine (active metabolite): 73 to 77% (at concentrations of 0.5 to 100 ng/mL).

Biotransformation

Hepatic (cytochrome P-450 system); some renal. Of the second-generation antihistamine, loratadine is metabolized by the hepatic cytochrome P-450 system and have active metabolites; however, cetirizine is minimally metabolized and excreted unchanged primarily through the kidneys.

Desloratadine is extensively metabolized to 3-hydroxydesloratadine, an active metabolite, which is subsequently glucuronidated. The enzymes responsible for the metabolism have not been identified.

Half-life

Elimination—
Azatadine—12 hours.
Brompheniramine—25 hours.
Cetirizine—8 hours (range, 6.5 to 10 hours).
In dialysis patients: 20 hours.
In children: 4.1 to 6 hours.
Chlorpheniramine—14 to 25 hours.
Desloratadine—27 hours.
Diphenhydramine—1 to 4 hours.
Hydroxyzine—20 to 25 hours.
Loratadine—3 to 20 hours (mean, 8.4 hours). Descarboethoxyloratadine (active metabolite): 8.8 to 92 hours (mean, 28 hours).

Note: In children, cetirizine, chlorpheniramine, and hydroxyzine have been found to have shorter elimination half-life values.

Onset of action

Oral—
Most first-generation antihistamines: 15 to 60 minutes.
Cetirizine: Histamine skin wheal studies—1 and 0.5 hours following 5 and 10 mg doses, respectively.
Desloratadine—Histamine skin wheal studies—within one hour.
Loratadine: Histamine skin wheal studies—1 to 3 hours.

Parenteral—
Dimenhydrinate: Intramuscular, 20 to 30 minutes.

Rectal—
Dimenhydrinate: 30 to 45 minutes.

Time to peak concentration

Oral—
Azatadine—4 hours.
Brompheniramine—2 to 5 hours.
Cetirizine—1 hour.
Chlorpheniramine—2 to 6 hours.
Clemastine—2 to 4 hours.
Desloratadine—approximately 3 hours.
Diphenhydramine—1 to 4 hours.

Loratadine—1.3 hours.
Descarboethoxyloratadine (active metabolite)—2.5 hours.

Time to peak effect

Oral—
Brompheniramine: 3 to 9 hours.
Chlorpheniramine: 6 hours.
Clemastine: 5 to 7 hours.
Loratadine: Histamine skin wheal studies—8 to 12 hours.

Duration of action

Ethanolamine derivatives—
6 to 8 hours.
Clemastine: 12 hours.
Dimenhydrinate: 3 to 6 hours.
Piperazine derivatives—
4 to 6 hours.
Cetirizine: Up to 24 hours.
Piperidine derivatives—
Azatadine: 12 hours.
Cyproheptadine: 8 hours.
Desloratadine: Histamine skin wheal study—Up to 24 hours.
Loratadine: Histamine skin wheal studies—At least 24 hours.
Phenindamine: 4 to 6 hours.
Propylamine derivatives—
4 to 8 hours.

Elimination

Most of the antihistamines studied (except cetirizine) are excreted as metabolites within 24 hours.
Cetirizine—
Approximately 60% of the total dose administered is excreted unchanged in urine within 24 hours; about 10% is excreted in feces.
Desloratadine—
Approximately 87% of a ^{14}C-desloratadine dose was equally recovered in urine and feces.
Loratadine—
Approximately 80% of the total dose administered is excreted equally in urine and feces in the form of metabolic products within 10 days. Twenty-seven percent of the total dose is excreted in the urine in the conjugated form within 24 hours.

Clearance

Cetirizine—
The weight-normalized, apparent total body clearance was 33% greater in children aged 7 to 12 years than in adults and 81% to 111% greater in children aged 2 to 5 years than in adults.
Patients with moderate renal impairment had a 70% decrease in clearance compared to normal volunteers.

Precautions to Consider

Cross-sensitivity and/or related problems

Patients sensitive to one of the antihistamines may be sensitive to others.

Carcinogenicity/Tumorigenicity/Mutagenicity

Long-term animal studies to evaluate carcinogenic, tumorigenic, or mutagenic potential of most antihistamines have not been performed.

Cetirizine—
In a 2-year study, cetirizine was not carcinogenic in rats given dietary doses up to 15 times the maximum recommended human daily oral dose for adults and 10 times the maximum recommended human daily oral dose for children on a mg/m^2 basis. In another 2-year study in male mice, cetirizine increased the incidence of benign liver tumors at a dose of 6 times the adult maximum recommended daily dose and 4 times the maximum pediatric dose on a mg/m^2 basis. The clinical significance of these findings during long-term use of cetirizine is not known.
Cetirizine was not mutagenic in the Ames test, and not clastogenic in the human lymphocyte assay, the mouse lymphoma assay, and the *in vivo* micronucleus test in rats.

Desloratadine—
The carcinogenic potential of desloratadine was assessed using loratadine studies.

Fexofenadine—
The carcinogenic and reproductive toxicity of fexofenadine were assessed using terfenadine# studies with adequate fexofenadine exposure. No evidence of carcinogenicity was observed in an 18 month study in mice and in a 24 month study in rats at oral doses of up to 150 mg/kg of terfenadine# (which led to fexofenadine exposures that were respectively approximately 3 to 5 times the exposure from the maximum recommended daily oral dose of fexofenadine in adults and children).
In *in vitro* (Bacterial Reverse Mutation, CHO/HGPRT Forward Mutation, and Rat Lymphocyte Chromosomal Aberration assays) and *in vivo* (Mouse Bone Marrow Micronucleus assay) tests, fexofenadine revealed no evidence of mutagenicity.

Loratadine—
In carcinogenicity studies, AUC data demonstrated that the exposure of mice given loratadine 40 mg/kg was 3.6 (loratadine) and 18 (active metabolite) times higher than that for a human given 10 mg/day. Exposure of rats given 25 mg/kg was 28 (loratadine) and 67 (active metabolite) times higher than that for a human given 10 mg/day. Male mice given 40 mg/kg had a significantly higher incidence of hepatocellular tumors (combined adenomas and carcinomas) than concurrent controls. In rats, a significantly higher incidence of hepatocellular tumors (combined adenomas and carcinomas) was observed in males given 10 mg/kg and males and females given 25 mg/kg. The clinical significance of these findings during long-term use of loratadine is not known.

Terfenadine#—
Studies in mice and rats have not shown evidence of tumorigenicity when terfenadine# was given in oral doses approximately 5 and 10 times the maximum recommended human daily dose on a mg per square meter of body surface area basis, respectively. Microbial and micronucleus test assays with terfenadine# have not shown evidence of mutagenesis.

Pregnancy/Reproduction

Pregnancy—Animal studies have suggested that meclizine and cyclizine, chemically related to antihistamines, might have a teratogenic potential

Azatadine, brompheniramine, chlorpheniramine, clemastine, cyproheptadine, dexchlorpheniramine, dimenhydrinate, and loratadine—
Well-controlled studies with azatadine, brompheniramine, chlorpheniramine, clemastine, cyproheptadine, dexchlorpheniramine, dimenhydrinate, and loratadine in humans have not been done.
Studies in animals have not shown that these medicines cause adverse effects on the fetus.
FDA Pregnancy Category B.

Cetirizine—
Adequate and well-controlled studies in humans have not been done. Cetirizine was not teratogenic in mice, rats, and rabbits.
FDA Pregnancy Category B.

Desloratadine—
Adequate and well-controlled studies in humans have not been done. Desloratadine was not teratogenic in rats at doses up to 48 mg/kg/day, or in rabbits at doses up to 60 mg/kg/day.
In a separate study, an increase in pre-implantation loss and a decreased number of implantations and fetuses were noted in female rats at 24 mg/kg. Reduced body weight and slow righting reflex were reported in pups at doses of 9 mg/kg/day or greater. Desloratadine had no effect on pup development at an oral dose of 3 mg/kg/day.
FDA Pregnancy Category C

Diphenhydramine—
Adequate and well-controlled studies in humans have not been done.
Studies in rats and rabbits at doses up to 5 times the human dose have revealed no evidence of impaired fertility or harm to the fetus.
FDA Pregnancy Category B.

Doxylamine—
The Food and Drug Administration has stated that human epidemiologic data have not produced convincing evidence that the doxylamine and pyridoxine combination, a medication previously prescribed to treat nausea and vomiting during pregnancy, causes diaphragmatic hernias or other birth defects.
FDA Pregnancy Category B.

Fexofenadine—
Adequate and well-controlled studies in humans have not been done.
Studies done in rats and rabbits showed no evidence of teratogenicity. Oral doses of terfenadine# up to 300 mg/kg (which led to fexofenadine exposures that were approximately 3 times the maximum recommended daily oral dose of fexofenadine in adults.
Nonteratogenic effects were seen as dose-related decreases in pup weight gain and survival were observed in rats exposed to an oral dose of 150 mg/kg of terfenadine# (approximately 3 times the maximum daily oral dose of fexofenadine in adults based on comparison of fexofenadine AUCs).
FDA Pregnancy Category C

Hydroxyzine—
Adequate and well-controlled studies in humans have not been done. However, hydroxyzine is not recommended for use in the early months of pregnancy since studies in rats have shown that it

causes fetal abnormalities when given in doses substantially above the human therapeutic range.

FDA Pregnancy Category C.

Breast-feeding

First-generation antihistamines may inhibit lactation because of their anticholinergic actions.

Small amounts of antihistamines are distributed into breast milk; use is not recommended in nursing mothers because of the risk of adverse effects, such as unusual excitement or irritability, in infants.

Desloratadine—

Desloratadine is distributed into breast milk

Cetirizine—

The extent of distribution into human breast milk is unknown. Studies in dogs indicated that approximately 3% of the dose is distributed into milk.

Loratadine—

Loratadine and its metabolite descarboethoxyloratadine are distributed into breast milk, achieving concentrations equivalent to plasma levels. In one study, approximately 0.03% of the administered dose was distributed into breast milk over 48 hours after maternal ingestion of a single oral dose of 40 mg.

Pediatrics

Use is not recommended in newborn or premature infants because this age group has an increased susceptibility to anticholinergic side effects, such as central nervous system (CNS) excitation, and an increased tendency toward convulsions.

A paradoxical reaction characterized by hyperexcitability may occur in children taking antihistamines.

Cetirizine, and loratadine—

Although adequate and well-controlled studies have not been done in the pediatric population, loratadine, is not likely, and cetirizine is less likely than first-generation antihistamines, to cause anticholinergic or significant CNS effects in children.

Desloratadine—

No information is available on the relationship of age to the effects of desloratadine in children under 12 years of age. Safety and efficacy have not been established.

Fexofenadine—

In two placebo controlled trials, the safety of fexofenadine in 6 to 11 year old pediatric patients was established for treatment of seasonal allergic rhinitis and was found to significantly reduce total symptom scores.

Based on a extrapolation of the demonstrated efficacy in adults, the safety of fexofenadine in 6 to 11 year old pediatric patients for the treatment of chronic idiopathic urticaria is established.

Adolescents

Desloratadine—

Desloratadine is approved for use in adolescents 12 years of age and older.

Geriatrics

Dizziness, sedation, confusion, and hypotension may be more likely to occur in geriatric patients taking antihistamines.

A paradoxical reaction characterized by hyperexcitability may occur in geriatric patients taking antihistamines.

Geriatric patients are especially susceptible to the anticholinergic side effects, such as dryness of mouth and urinary retention (especially in males), of the antihistamines. If these side effects occur and continue or are severe, medication should probably be discontinued.

Desloratadine, cetirizine, and loratadine—

Desloratadine, and Loratadine are not likely, and cetirizine is less likely than first-generation antihistamines, to cause anticholinergic or significant CNS effects in geriatric patients. However, because elderly patients are more likely to have age-related renal function impairment, cetirizine and loratadine may accumulate and cause anticholinergic or CNS effects when given in such patients at the usual adult dose.

Pharmacogenetics

Desloratadine has higher peak plasma concentration and area under the curve values in females compared with males and in African-Americans compared with Caucasian patients. However, no dosage adjustments are recommended in either case.

Dental

Prolonged use of antihistamines (except cetirizine, desloratadine, or loratadine) may decrease or inhibit salivary flow, thus contributing to the development of caries, periodontal disease, oral candidiasis, and discomfort.

#Products containing terfenadine were withdrawn from the U.S. market by the Food and Drug Administration in February 1998 and from the Canadian market by the Health Protection Branch, Health Canada in August 1998

Drug interactions and/or related problems

The following drug interactions and/or related problems have been selected on the basis of their potential clinical significance (possible mechanism in parentheses where appropriate)—not necessarily inclusive (» = major clinical significance):

Note: It is not likely that cetirizine, desloratadine, or loratadine will interact with most of the following medications because they lack significant anticholinergic and CNS actions. However, cetirizine and loratadine have been shown to cause dose-related CNS effects (e.g., sedation); and cetirizine has minimal anticholinergic effects.

Combinations containing any of the following medications, depending on the amount present, may also interact with this medication.

Antacids, magnesium or aluminum containing
(administration of fexofenadine within 15 minutes of an aluminum or magnesium containing antacid decreased fexofenadine AUC by 41% and C_{max} by 43%.)

» Alcohol or
» CNS depression-producing medications, other (see *Appendix II*)
(concurrent use may potentiate the CNS depressant effects of either these medications or antihistamines; also, concurrent use of maprotiline or tricyclic antidepressants may potentiate the anticholinergic effects of either antihistamines or these medications)

» Anticholinergics or other medications with anticholinergic activity (see *Appendix II*)
(anticholinergic effects may be potentiated when these medications are used concurrently with antihistamines; patients should be advised to report occurrence of gastrointestinal problems promptly since paralytic ileus may occur with concurrent therapy)

Apomorphine
(prior administration of dimenhydrinate, diphenhydramine, doxylamine, or hydroxyzine may decrease the emetic response to apomorphine in the treatment of poisoning)

Potent inhibitors of the cytochrome P450 enzyme system such as:
Erythromycin
Fluconazole
Itraconazole
Ketoconazole
Metronidazole
Miconazole
(concurrent use of these medications may increase plasma levels of loratadine; there are no reports to date of serious ventricular arrhythmias associated with increased plasma levels of loratadine)

(concurrent use of fexofenadine with co-administered ketoconazole and erythromycin may lead to increased plasma levels of fexofenadine, and may also enhance fexofenadine gastrointestinal absorption and decrease fexofenadine gastrointestinal excretion)

» Monoamine oxidase (MAO) inhibitors, including furazolidone and procarbazine
(concurrent use of MAO inhibitors with antihistamines may prolong and intensify the anticholinergic and CNS depressant effects of antihistamines; concurrent use is not recommended)

Ototoxic medications (see *Appendix II*)
(concurrent use with antihistamines may mask the symptoms of ototoxicity such as tinnitus, dizziness, or vertigo)

Photosensitizing medications, other
(concurrent use of these medications with antihistamines may cause additive photosensitizing effects)

Laboratory value alterations

The following have been selected on the basis of their potential clinical significance (possible effect in parentheses where appropriate)—not necessarily inclusive (» = major clinical significance).

With diagnostic test results
For all antihistamines
Skin tests using allergen extracts
(antihistamines may inhibit the cutaneous histamine response, thus producing false-negative results; it is recommended that antihistamines be discontinued at least 72 hours before testing begins [at least 1 week with loratadine])

For hydroxyzine (in addition to those listed for all antihistamines)
Urine 17-hydroxycorticosteroid determinations
(false increases have been reported with concurrent use of hydroxyzine)

With physiology/laboratory test values
For cyproheptadine
Amylase and
Prolactin
(serum concentrations may be increased when cyproheptadine is administered with thyrotropin-releasing hormone)

Medical considerations/Contraindications

The medical considerations/contraindications included have been selected on the basis of their potential clinical significance (reasons given in parentheses where appropriate)—not necessarily inclusive (» = major clinical significance).

Except under special circumstances, this medication should not be used when the following medical problems exist:

» Hepatic function impairment
(desloratadine dosage adjustment recommended due to increases in bioavailability, half-life, and area under the curve.)

» Renal function impairment
(Desloratadine dosage adjustment is recommended due to increases in plasma concentration and area under the curve)

Risk-benefit should be considered when the following medical problems exist:

» Bladder neck obstruction or
» Prostatic hypertrophy, symptomatic or
» Urinary retention, predisposition to
(anticholinergic effects may precipitate or aggravate urinary retention)

» Glaucoma, angle-closure, or predisposition to
(anticholinergic mydriatic effect resulting in increased intraocular pressure may precipitate an attack of angle-closure glaucoma)

Glaucoma, open-angle
(anticholinergic mydriatic effect may cause a slight increase in intraocular pressure; glaucoma therapy may need to be adjusted)

Hypersensitivity to the antihistamine used

Caution is recommended when dimenhydrinate, diphenhydramine, or hydroxyzine is used, since their antiemetic action may impede diagnosis of such conditions as appendicitis and obscure signs of toxicity from overdosage of other drugs.

For cyproheptadine
» Peptic ulcer, stenosing
» Pyloroduodenal obstruction
(anticholinergic effects of cyproheptadine may exacerbate these conditions)

For desloratadine
Metabolism of desloratadine, impaired
(slow metabolizers of desloratadine may be more susceptible to dose-related adverse events)

Side/Adverse Effects

The following side/adverse effects have been selected on the basis of their potential clinical significance (possible signs and symptoms in parentheses where appropriate)—not necessarily inclusive:

Those indicating need for medical attention

Incidence less frequent or rare

Anaphylaxis (cough; difficulty swallowing; dizziness; fast heartbeat; hives; itching; puffiness or swelling of the eyelids or around the eyes, face, lips or tongue; shortness of breath; skin rash; tightness in chest; unusual tiredness or weakness; wheezing); ***blood dyscrasias*** (sore throat; fever; unusual bleeding or bruising; unusual tiredness or weakness)—with azatadine, brompheniramine, cyproheptadine, and dexchlorpheniramine; ***cardiac arrhythmias/palpitations/tachycardia***(fast pounding or irregular heartbeat or pulse)—less frequent or rare with azatadine, cetirizine, clemastine, cyproheptadine, desloratadine, dexchlorpheniramine, diphenhydramine, or loratadine; ***cholestasis, hepatitis or other hepatic function abnormalities*** (abdominal or stomach pain; chills; clay-colored stools or dark urine; diarrhea; dizziness; fever; headache; itching); ***convulsions or seizures; edema*** (swelling); ***paresthesia or neuritis*** (burning; prickly sensations; tingling)—with cyproheptadine; ***urticaria*** (hives or welts; itching; redness of skin; skin rash)—with desloratadine

Those indicating need for medical attention only if they continue or are bothersome

Incidence more frequent

Drowsiness; dryness of mouth, nose, or throat; gastrointestinal upset, stomach pain, or nausea—with azatadine and diphenhydramine; ***headache***—with desloratadine; ***increased appetite or weight gain***—with, cyproheptadine; ***pharyngitis*** (body aches or pain; congestion; cough; dryness or soreness of throat; fever; hoarseness; runny nose; tender, swollen glands in neck; trouble in swallowing; voice changes)—with desloratadine; ***thickening of mucus***—with azatadine and cyproheptadine

Note: Tolerance to central nervous system effects may develop quickly with some antihistamines, so that sedation is no longer troublesome after a few days.

Incidence of sedation may increase when the recommended doses of loratadine are exceeded.

Incidence less frequent or rare

Blurred vision or any change in vision—with azatadine, cetirizine, cyproheptadine, diphenhydramine, and loratadine; ***confusion***—with azatadine, cetirizine, cyproheptadine, diphenhydramine, and loratadine; not reported with diphenhydramine; ***difficult or painful urination***—with azatadine, cetirizine, chlorpheniramine, cyproheptadine, dexclorpheniramine, and loratadine; ***dizziness***—except with brompheniramine and hydroxyzine; ***drowsiness***—with brompheniramine, chlorpheniramine; reported with high doses of desloratadine and loratadine; ***dryness of mouth, nose, or throat***—with cetirizine and loratadine; ***dysmenorrhea*** (difficult or painful menstruation)—with desloratadine; ***dyspepsia*** (acid or sour stomach; belching; heartburn; indigestion; stomach discomfort upset or pain)—with desloratadine; ***increased appetite or weight gain***—with cetirizine and loratadine; ***increased sweating***—with azatadine, cetirizine, chlorpheniramine, cyproheptadine, loratadine, and; ***fatigue*** (unusual tiredness or weakness)—with desloratadine; ***loss of appetite***—with cetirizine, chlorpheniramine, cyproheptadine, and loratadine; ***myalgia*** (joint pain; swollen joints; muscle aching or cramping; muscle pains or stiffness; difficulty in moving)—with desloratadine; ***nausea***—with desloratadine; ***paradoxical reaction*** (nightmares; unusual excitement, nervousness, restlessness, or irritability)—except with azatadine, chlorpheniramine, cyproheptadine, desloratadine, hydroxyzine, and loratadine; ***photosensitivity*** (increased sensitivity of skin to sun)—with azatadine, cetirizine, cyproheptadine, and loratadine; ***ringing or buzzing in ears***—with azatadine, cetirizine, cyproheptadine, and loratadine; ***skin rash***—with azatadine, brompheniramine, cetirizine, clemastine, cyproheptadine, and loratadine; ***gastrointestinal upset, stomach pain, or nausea***—with cetirizine, clemastine, cyproheptadine, and loratadine; ***tachycardia*** (fast heartbeat)—with azatadine, cetirizine, cyproheptadine, and loratadine; ***thickening of mucus***—with cyproheptadine, dexchlorpheniramine and diphenhydramine; ***abnormal coordination*** (clumsiness or unsteadiness); ***constipation; diarrhea; early menses; fatigue; tremor; vomiting***—with cyproheptadine

Note: *Confusion; difficult or painful urination; drowsiness; dizziness; and dryness of mouth, nose, or throat* are more likely to occur in the elderly.

Nightmares, unusual excitement, nervousness, restlessness, or irritability is more likely to occur in children and elderly patients.

Overdose

For more information on the management of overdose or unintentional ingestion, **contact a Poison Control Center** (see *Poison Control Center Listing*).

Clinical effects of overdose

Symptoms of overdose

Anticholinergic effects (clumsiness or unsteadiness; severe drowsiness; severe dryness of mouth, nose, or throat; flushing or redness of face; shortness of breath or troubled breathing)—especially with azatadine and clemastine; ***cardiac arrhythmias*** (fast or irregular heartbeat); less frequent with azatadine and clemastine; ***CNS depression*** (severe drowsiness); ***CNS stimulation*** (hallucinations, seizures, trouble in sleeping); ***hypotension*** (feeling faint); ***somnolence*** (sleepiness or unusual drowsiness)—especially with desloratadine

Note: *Anticholinergic* and *CNS stimulant* effects are more likely to occur in children with overdose. *Hypotension* may also occur in the elderly at usual doses.

Anticholinergic and CNS effects may be less likely to occur with, cetirizine, desloratadine or, loratadine, than with the first-generation antihistamines.

Treatment of overdose

Since there is no specific antidote for overdose with antihistamines, treatment is symptomatic and supportive.

To decrease absorption—
Induction of emesis (syrup of ipecac recommended); however, precaution against aspiration is necessary, especially in infants and children.

Gastric lavage (isotonic or 0.45% sodium chloride solution) if patient is unable to vomit within 3 hours of ingestion.

To enhance elimination—

Saline cathartics (milk of magnesia) are sometimes used.

Specific treatment—

Vasopressors to treat hypotension; however, epinephrine should not be used since it may further lower blood pressure.

Oxygen and intravenous fluids.

Precaution against use of stimulants (analeptic agents) because they may cause seizures.

Patient Consultation

As an aid to patient consultation, refer to *Advice for the Patient, Antihistamines (Systemic).*

In providing consultation, consider emphasizing the following selected information (» = major clinical significance):

Before using this medication

» Conditions affecting use, especially:

Sensitivity to any antihistamine

Pregnancy—Not taking during early months of pregnancy because of fetal abnormalities in studies in animals (for hydroxyzine only)

Breast-feeding—Use not recommended; may cause unusual excitement or irritability in nursing infant

Use in children—Increased susceptibility to anticholinergic side effects in newborn or premature infants; hyperexcitability (paradoxical reaction) may occur in children

Use in the elderly—Increased susceptibility to anticholinergic side effects; hyperexcitability (paradoxical reaction) may occur

Dental—Increased risk of dental problems because of decrease or inhibition of salivary flow

Other medications, especially alcohol or other CNS depressants, anticholinergics or other medications with anticholinergic activity, or MAO inhibitors

Other medical problems, especially angle closure glaucoma, bladder neck obstruction, hepatic or renal impairment (with desloratadine), prostatic hypertrophy, pyloroduodenal obstruction (with cyproheptadine), stenosing peptic ulcer (with cyproheptadine) or urinary retention.

Proper use of this medication

» Importance of not taking more medication than the amount recommended

» Proper dosing

Missed dose: If on scheduled dosing regimen—Using as soon as possible; not using if almost time for next dose; not doubling doses

» Proper storage

For oral dosage forms

Taking with food, water, or milk to minimize gastric irritation

Swallowing extended-release dosage forms whole

For injection dosage forms

Knowing correct administration technique for self-administration; checking with physician if necessary

For rectal dosage forms

Proper administration technique

For dimenhydrinate and diphenhydramine when used as antivertigo agent

Taking at least 30 minutes (preferably 1 to 2 hours) before traveling

Precautions while using this medication

Possible interference with skin tests using allergens; need to inform physician if using medication

May mask ototoxic effects of large doses of salicylates

» Avoiding use of alcohol or other CNS depressants

» Caution if drowsiness occurs

Possible dryness of mouth; using sugarless gum or candy, ice, or saliva substitute for relief; checking with physician or dentist if dry mouth continues for more than 2 weeks

For dimenhydrinate, diphenhydramine, or hydroxyzine:

Need to inform physician of use: Possible interference with diagnosis of appendicitis; may mask signs of toxicity from overdosage of other drugs

For diphenhydramine and doxylamine when used in the treatment of insomnia:

» Not using concurrently with other sedatives or tranquilizers

Side/adverse effects

Signs of potential side effects, especially anaphylaxis; blood dyscrasias, cardiac arrhythmias/palpitations/tachycardia, cholestasis, convulsions or seizures, dyspnea, edema, hepatitis or other hepatic function abnormalities, convulsions or seizures, paresthesia or neuritis; pruritus, rash, or urticaria)

General Dosing Information

For oral dosage forms only

Most antihistamines may be taken with food, water, or milk to lessen gastric irritation.

For parenteral dosage forms only

Intramuscular injections should be administered deeply into the muscle.

Intravenous injections should be administered slowly, preferably with the patient in a recumbent position.

For hydroxyzine—

Administration should be by deep intramuscular injection into a large muscle mass, preferably the upper outer quadrant of the buttock or the mid-lateral thigh.

Intramuscular injections should not be made into the lower or mid-third of the upper arm.

When used preoperatively or prepartum, narcotic requirements may be decreased as much as 50%.

Note: Products containing terfenadine were withdrawn from the U.S. market by the Food and Drug Administration in February 1998 and from the Canadian market by the Health Protection Branch, Health Canada in August 1998.

Note: Products containing astemizole were withdrawn from the U.S. and Canadian markets by the manufacturer in June 1999.

Note: Products containing tripelennamine were withdrawn from the U.S. and Canadian markets by the manufacturer in 1999.

AZATADINE

Summary of Differences

Pharmacology/pharmacokinetics:

Chemical group—Piperidine derivative.

pKa—9.3.

Half-life—12 hours.

Time to peak concentration—4 hours.

Duration of action—12 hours.

Side/adverse effects:

Potential for blood dyscrasias; more frequent gastrointestinal upset; no paradoxical reaction.

Oral Dosage Forms

AZATADINE MALEATE TABLETS USP

Usual adult and adolescent dose

Antihistaminic (H_1-receptor)—

Oral, 1 to 2 mg every eight to twelve hours as needed.

Usual pediatric dose

Antihistaminic (H_1-receptor)—

Children up to 12 years of age: Use is not recommended.

Children 12 years of age and over: Oral, 500 mcg (0.5 mg) to 1 mg two times a day as needed.

Usual geriatric dose

See *Usual adult and adolescent dose.*

Note: Geriatric patients may be more sensitive to the effects of the usual adult dose.

Strength(s) usually available

U.S.—

1 mg (Rx) [*Optimine* (scored)].

Canada—

1 mg (Rx) [*Optimine* (scored)].

Packaging and storage

Store below 40 °C (104 °F), preferably between 15 and 30 °C (59 and 86 °F), unless otherwise specified by manufacturer. Store in a well-closed container.

Auxiliary labeling

- May cause drowsiness.
- Avoid alcoholic beverages.

BROMPHENIRAMINE

Summary of Differences

Pharmacology/pharmacokinetics:

Chemical group—Propylamine derivative.

pKa—3.59 and 9.12.

Half-life—25 hours.

Time to peak concentration—2 to 5 hours.

Time to peak effect—3 to 9 hours.
Duration of action—4 to 8 hours.
Side/adverse effects:
Sedative effects less pronounced.
Potential for blood dyscrasias.

Oral Dosage Forms

BROMPHENIRAMINE MALEATE CAPSULES

Usual adult and adolescent dose
Antihistaminic (H_1-receptor)—
Oral, 4 mg every four to six hours as needed.

Usual adult prescribing limits
Up to 24 mg daily.

Usual pediatric dose
Antihistaminic (H_1-receptor)—
Children younger than 12 years of age: See *Brompheniramine Maleate Elixir USP*.
Children 12 years of age and over: Oral, 4 mg every four to six hours as needed.

Note: The available strength of the capsule may not conform to some of the recommended pediatric dosages.

Usual geriatric dose
See *Usual adult and adolescent dose*.

Note: Geriatric patients may be more sensitive to the effects of the usual adult dose.

Strength(s) usually available
U.S.—
4 mg (Rx) [*Dimetapp Allergy Liqui-Gels*].
Canada—
Not commercially available.

Packaging and storage
Store between 15 and 30 °C (59 and 86 °F), unless otherwise specified by manufacturer. Protect from freezing.

Auxiliary labeling
- May cause drowsiness.
- Avoid alcoholic beverages.

BROMPHENIRAMINE MALEATE ELIXIR USP

Usual adult and adolescent dose
See *Brompheniramine Maleate Capsules*.

Usual adult prescribing limits
See *Brompheniramine Maleate Capsules*.

Usual pediatric dose
Antihistaminic (H_1-receptor)—
Oral, 500 mcg (0.5 mg) per kg of body weight or 15 mg per square meter of body surface per day, in three or four divided doses, as needed; or for
Children 2 to 6 years of age: Oral, 1 mg every four to six hours as needed.
Children 6 to 12 years of age: Oral, 2 mg every four to six hours as needed.
Children 12 years of age and over: Oral, 4 mg every four to six hours as needed.

Note: Premature and full-term neonates—Use is not recommended.

Usual geriatric dose
See *Brompheniramine Maleate Capsules*.

Note: Geriatric patients may be more sensitive to the effects of the usual adult dose.

Strength(s) usually available
U.S.—
2 mg per 5 mL (Rx/OTC) [*Bromphen;* GENERIC].
2 mg per 5 mL (OTC) [GENERIC].
Canada—
2 mg per 5 mL (OTC) [*Dimetane* (alcohol 3%)].

Packaging and storage
Store below 40 °C (104 °F), preferably between 15 and 30 °C (59 and 86 °F), unless otherwise specified by manufacturer. Store in a well-closed, light-resistant container. Protect from freezing.

Auxiliary labeling
- May cause drowsiness.
- Avoid alcoholic beverages.
- Keep container tightly closed.

BROMPHENIRAMINE MALEATE TABLETS USP

Usual adult and adolescent dose
See *Brompheniramine Maleate Capsules*.

Usual pediatric dose
See *Brompheniramine Maleate Elixir USP*.

Note: The available strength of the tablet may not conform to some of the recommended pediatric dosages.

Usual geriatric dose
See *Brompheniramine Maleate Capsules*.

Note: Geriatric patients may be more sensitive to the effects of the usual adult dose.

Strength(s) usually available
U.S.—
Not commercially available.
Canada—
4 mg (OTC) [*Dimetane*].

Packaging and storage
Store below 40 °C (104 °F), preferably between 15 and 30 °C (59 and 86 °F), unless otherwise specified by manufacturer. Store in a tight container.

Auxiliary labeling
- May cause drowsiness.
- Avoid alcoholic beverages.

Parenteral Dosage Forms

BROMPHENIRAMINE MALEATE INJECTION USP

Usual adult and adolescent dose
Antihistaminic (H_1-receptor)—
Intramuscular, intravenous, or subcutaneous, 10 mg every eight to twelve hours as needed.

Usual adult prescribing limits
Up to 40 mg daily.

Usual pediatric dose
Antihistaminic (H_1-receptor)—
Children up to 12 years of age: Intramuscular, intravenous, or subcutaneous, 125 mcg (0.125 mg) per kg of body weight or 3.75 mg per square meter of body surface three or four times a day as needed.

Note: Premature and full-term neonates—Use is not recommended.

Usual geriatric dose
See *Usual adult and adolescent dose*.

Note: Geriatric patients may be more sensitive to the effects of the usual adult dose.

Strength(s) usually available
U.S.—
10 mg per mL (Rx) [*Nasahist B;* GENERIC].
Canada—
Not commercially available.

Packaging and storage
Store below 40 °C (104 °F), preferably between 15 and 30 °C (59 and 86 °F), unless otherwise specified by manufacturer. Protect from light. Protect from freezing.

Stability
Crystallization may occur if cooled below 0 °C (32 °F); but on warming to 30 °C (86 °F), the crystals will redissolve.

Additional information
The period of protection provided by a single dose ranges from three to twelve hours.

CETIRIZINE

Summary of Differences

Indications:
Used as treatment adjunct in asthma.
Pharmacology/pharmacokinetics:
Chemical group—Hydroxyzine metabolite.
Absorption—Decreased absorption rate, but not extent, with food.
Protein binding—93%.
Half-life—8 hours.
Time to peak concentration—1 hour.
Side/adverse effects:
Minimal sedative effects.

Oral Dosage Forms

CETIRIZINE HYDROCHLORIDE SYRUP

Usual adult and adolescent dose

Antihistaminic (H_1-receptor)—

Oral, 5 to 10 mg once a day.

Note: In patients with reduced creatinine clearance (< 31 mL per min) and with hepatic impairment, a dose of 5 mg once a day is recommended.

Usual adult prescribing limits

10 mg a day.

Usual pediatric dose

Antihistaminic (H_1-receptor)[1]—

Children up to 2 years of age: Safety and efficacy have not been established.

Children 2 to 6 years of age: Oral, 2.5 mg once a day. The dosage may be increased to a maximum daily dose of 5 mg, given as 5 mg once a day or 2.5 mg every 12 hours.

Children 6 years of age and older: Oral, 5 or 10 mg once a day.

Note: The dosage should be decreased in patients who have reduced renal function (creatinine clearance of 11–31 mL per minute) or hepatic function impairment. In patients up to 6 years of age with renal or hepatic dysfunction, cetirizine use is not recommended. For children 6 years of age and older, the lower dosage of 5 mg once a day should be used.

Usual geriatric dose

See *Usual adult and adolescent dose.*

Strength(s) usually available

U.S.—

5 mg per 5 mL (Rx) [*Zyrtec* (alcohol and dye free)].

Canada—

Not commercially available.

Packaging and storage

Store between 15 and 30 °C (59 and 86 °F), in a tight container, unless otherwise specified by the manufacturer.

Auxiliary labeling

- May cause drowsiness.
- Avoid alcoholic beverages.

CETIRIZINE HYDROCHLORIDE TABLETS

Usual adult and adolescent dose

Antihistaminic (H_1-receptor)—

See *Cetirizine Syrup.*

Usual pediatric dose

Antihistaminic (H_1-receptor)—

See *Cetirizine Syrup.*

Usual geriatric dose

See *Cetirizine Syrup.*

Strength(s) usually available

U.S.—

5 mg (Rx) [*Zyrtec* (dye free)].

10 mg (Rx) [*Zyrtec* (dye free)].

Canada—

10 mg (OTC) [*Reactine; Zyrtec*].

Packaging and storage

Store between 15 and 30 °C (59 and 86 °F), in a well-closed container, unless otherwise specified by manufacturer.

Auxiliary labeling

- May cause drowsiness.
- Avoid alcoholic beverages.

[1]Not included in Canadian product labeling.

CHLORPHENIRAMINE

Summary of Differences

Pharmacology/pharmacokinetics:

Chemical group—Propylamine derivative.

pKa—9.2.

Protein binding—72%.

Half-life—14 to 25 hours.

Time to peak concentration—2 to 6 hours.

Time to peak effect—6 hours.

Duration of action—4 to 8 hours.

Side/adverse effects:

Sedative effects less pronounced; no paradoxical reaction.

Oral Dosage Forms

CHLORPHENIRAMINE MALEATE EXTENDED-RELEASE CAPSULES USP

Usual adult and adolescent dose

Antihistaminic (H_1-receptor)—

Oral, 8 or 12 mg every eight to twelve hours as needed.

Usual pediatric dose

Antihistaminic (H_1-receptor)—

Children up to 12 years of age: Use is not recommended.

Children 12 years of age and over: Oral, 8 mg every twelve hours as needed.

Usual geriatric dose

See *Usual adult and adolescent dose.*

Note: Geriatric patients may be more sensitive to the effects of the usual adult dose.

Strength(s) usually available

U.S.—

8 mg (Rx) [*Telachlor;* GENERIC].

8 mg (OTC) [GENERIC].

12 mg (Rx) [*Telachlor;* GENERIC].

12 mg (OTC) [*Teldrin;* GENERIC].

Canada—

Not commercially available.

Packaging and storage

Store below 40 °C (104 °F), preferably between 15 and 30 °C (59 and 86 °F), unless otherwise specified by manufacturer. Store in a tight container.

Auxiliary labeling

- Swallow capsules whole.
- May cause drowsiness.
- Avoid alcoholic beverages.

CHLORPHENIRAMINE MALEATE SYRUP USP

Usual adult and adolescent dose

Antihistaminic (H_1-receptor)—

Oral, 4 mg every four to six hours as needed.

Usual adult prescribing limits

Up to 24 mg daily.

Usual pediatric dose

Antihistaminic (H_1-receptor)—

Oral, 87.5 mcg (0.0875 mg) per kg of body weight or 2.5 mg per square meter of body surface every six hours as needed; or for

Children up to 6 years of age: Use is not recommended.

Children 6 to 12 years of age: Oral, 2 mg three or four times a day as needed, not to exceed 12 mg per day.

Usual geriatric dose

See *Usual adult and adolescent dose.*

Note: Geriatric patients may be more sensitive to the effects of the usual adult dose.

Strength(s) usually available

U.S.—

1 mg per 5 mL (OTC) [*PediaCare Allergy Formula*].

2 mg per 5 mL (OTC) [*Aller-Chlor* (alcohol 7%); *Chlor-Trimeton* (alcohol 5%); GENERIC].

Canada—

2.5 mg per 5 mL (OTC) [*Chlor-Tripolon* (alcohol 7%)].

Packaging and storage

Store below 40 °C (104 °F), preferably between 15 and 30 °C (59 and 86 °F), unless otherwise specified by manufacturer. Store in a tight, light-resistant container. Protect from freezing.

Auxiliary labeling

- May cause drowsiness.
- Avoid alcoholic beverages.

CHLORPHENIRAMINE MALEATE TABLETS USP

Usual adult and adolescent dose

See *Chlorpheniramine Maleate Syrup USP.*

Usual pediatric dose

See *Chlorpheniramine Maleate Syrup USP.*

Usual geriatric dose
See *Chlorpheniramine Maleate Syrup USP*.

Note: Geriatric patients may be more sensitive to the effects of the usual adult dose.

Strength(s) usually available
U.S.—
4 mg (Rx) [*Phenetron* (scored); GENERIC].
4 mg (OTC) [*Aller-Chlor; Chlorate; Chlor-Trimeton* (scored); *Chlor-Trimeton Allergy; Gen-Allerate;* GENERIC].
Canada—
4 mg (OTC) [*Chlor-Tripolon* (scored); *Novo-Pheniram* (scored)].

Packaging and storage
Store below 40 °C (104 °F), preferably between 15 and 30 °C (59 and 86 °F), unless otherwise specified by manufacturer. Store in a tight container.

Auxiliary labeling
- May cause drowsiness.
- Avoid alcoholic beverages.

CHLORPHENIRAMINE MALEATE TABLETS (CHEWABLE) USP

Usual adult and adolescent dose
See *Chlorpheniramine Maleate Syrup USP*.

Usual pediatric dose
See *Chlorpheniramine Maleate Syrup USP*.

Usual geriatric dose
See *Chlorpheniramine Maleate Syrup USP*.

Note: Geriatric patients may be more sensitive to the effects of the usual adult dose.

Strength(s) usually available
U.S.—
2 mg (OTC) [*Chlo-Amine*].
Canada—
Not commercially available.

Packaging and storage
Store below 40 °C (104 °F), preferably between 15 and 30 °C (59 and 86 °F), unless otherwise specified by manufacturer. Store in a tight container.

Auxiliary labeling
- Chew before swallowing.
- May cause drowsiness.
- Avoid alcoholic beverages.

CHLORPHENIRAMINE MALEATE EXTENDED-RELEASE TABLETS

Usual adult and adolescent dose
See *Chlorpheniramine Maleate Extended-release Capsules USP*.

Usual pediatric dose
See *Chlorpheniramine Maleate Extended-release Capsules USP*.

Usual geriatric dose
See *Chlorpheniramine Maleate Extended-release Capsules USP*.

Note: Geriatric patients may be more sensitive to the effects of the usual adult dose.

Strength(s) usually available
U.S.—
8 mg (Rx) [*Phenetron;* GENERIC].
8 mg (OTC) [*Chlor-Trimeton Repetabs;* GENERIC].
12 mg (Rx) [*Phenetron* (sugar-coated); GENERIC].
12 mg (OTC) [*Chlor-Trimeton Repetabs* (sugar-coated); GENERIC].
Canada—
12 mg (OTC) [*Chlor-Tripolon*].

Packaging and storage
Store below 40 °C (104 °F), preferably between 15 and 30 °C (59 and 86 °F), in a well-closed container, unless otherwise specified by manufacturer.

Auxiliary labeling
- Swallow tablets whole.
- May cause drowsiness.
- Avoid alcoholic beverages.

Parenteral Dosage Forms

CHLORPHENIRAMINE MALEATE INJECTION USP

Usual adult and adolescent dose
Antihistaminic (H_1-receptor)—
Intramuscular, intravenous, or subcutaneous, 5 to 40 mg administered as a single dose as needed.

Usual adult prescribing limits
Up to 40 mg daily.

Usual pediatric dose
Antihistaminic (H_1-receptor)—
Subcutaneous, 87.5 mcg (0.0875 mg) per kg of body weight or 2.5 mg per square meter of body surface every six hours as needed.

Note: Premature and full-term neonates—Use is not recommended.

Usual geriatric dose
See *Usual adult and adolescent dose*.

Note: Geriatric patients may be more sensitive to the effects of the usual adult dose.

Strength(s) usually available
U.S.—
10 mg per mL (Rx) [GENERIC].
Canada—
10 mg per mL (Rx) [*Chlor-Tripolon*].

Packaging and storage
Store below 40 °C (104 °F), preferably between 15 and 30 °C (59 and 86 °F), unless otherwise specified by manufacturer. Protect from light. Protect from freezing.

Additional information
The 10-mg-per-mL solution may be administered intravenously, intramuscularly, or subcutaneously.

CLEMASTINE

Summary of Differences

Pharmacology/pharmacokinetics:
Chemical group—Ethanolamine derivative.
Other actions/effects—Greater anticholinergic activity.
Time to peak concentration—2 to 4 hours.
Time to peak effect—5 to 7 hours.
Duration of action—12 hours.

Oral Dosage Forms

CLEMASTINE FUMARATE SYRUP

Usual adult and adolescent dose
Antihistaminic (H_1-receptor)—
Oral, 1.34 mg two times a day or 2.68 mg one to three times a day as needed.

Note: Clemastine is indicated for dermatologic conditions at the 2.68-mg dosage level only.

Usual adult prescribing limits
Up to 8.04 mg daily.

Usual pediatric dose
Antihistaminic (H_1-receptor)—
Children up to 6 years of age: Dosage has not been established.
Children 6 to 12 years of age: Oral, 670 mcg (0.67 mg) to 1.34 mg two times a day, not to exceed 4.02 mg per day.

Note: Clemastine is indicated for dermatologic conditions at the 1.34-mg dosage level only.

Usual geriatric dose
See *Usual adult and adolescent dose*.

Note: Geriatric patients may be more sensitive to the effects of the usual adult dose.

Strength(s) usually available
U.S.—
0.67 mg per 5 mL (Rx) [*Tavist* (alcohol 5.5%); GENERIC].
Canada—
0.67 mg per 5 mL (OTC) [*Tavist* (alcohol 6.1%)].

Packaging and storage
Store below 25 °C (77 °F), preferably between 15 and 25 °C (59 and 77 °F), in a well-closed container, unless otherwise specified by manufacturer. Protect from freezing.

Auxiliary labeling
- May cause drowsiness.
- Avoid alcoholic beverages.

CLEMASTINE FUMARATE TABLETS USP

Usual adult and adolescent dose
See *Clemastine Fumarate Syrup*.

Note: Clemastine is indicated for dermatologic conditions at the 2.68-mg dosage level only.

Usual pediatric dose
See *Clemastine Fumarate Syrup.*

Note: Clemastine is indicated for dermatologic conditions at the 1.34-mg dosage level only.

Usual geriatric dose
See *Clemastine Fumarate Syrup.*

Note: Geriatric patients may be more sensitive to the effects of the usual adult dose.

Strength(s) usually available
U.S.—
1.34 mg (OTC) [*Contac 12 Hour Allergy; Tavist-1* (scored); GENERIC].
2.68 mg (Rx) [*Tavist* (scored); GENERIC].
Canada—
1 mg (base) (OTC) [*Tavist* (scored)].

Packaging and storage
Store between 15 and 30 °C (59 and 86 °F), unless otherwise specified by manufacturer. Store in a tight, light-resistant container.

Auxiliary labeling
- May cause drowsiness.
- Avoid alcoholic beverages.

CYPROHEPTADINE

Summary of Differences
Indications:
Also indicated in cold urticaria and used as an appetite stimulant in adults and children.
Pharmacology/pharmacokinetics:
Chemical group—Piperidine derivative.
pKa—9.3.
Other actions/effects—Serotonin antagonist.
Duration of action—8 hours.
Precautions:
Laboratory value alterations:
May increase serum amylase and serum prolactin concentrations when administered with thyrotropin-releasing hormone.
Side/adverse effects:
Potential for blood dyscrasias; no paradoxical reaction.

Oral Dosage Forms
Note: Bracketed uses in the *Dosage Forms* section refer to categories of use and/or indications that are not included in U.S. product labeling.

CYPROHEPTADINE HYDROCHLORIDE SYRUP USP

Usual adult and adolescent dose
Antihistaminic (H_1-receptor)—
Oral, initially 4 mg every eight hours, the dosage being increased as needed. For most patients the therapeutic range is 4 to 20 mg a day. However, doses up to 32 mg a day have been used occasionally.
[Vascular headache suppressant]—
Initial: Oral, 4 mg at the start of the attack, repeated after thirty minutes if necessary.
Maintenance: Oral, 4 mg every four to six hours.

Usual adult prescribing limits
32 mg per day

Usual pediatric dose
Antihistaminic (H_1-receptor)—
Children 2 to 6 years of age: Oral, 2 mg every eight to twelve hours as needed, not to exceed 12 mg per day.
Children 7 to 14 years of age: Oral, 2 mg every six to eight hours as needed, not to exceed 16 mg per day.

Note: Premature and full-term neonates—Use is not recommended.

Usual geriatric dose
See *Usual adult and adolescent dose.*

Note: Geriatric patients may be more sensitive to the effects of the usual adult dose.

Strength(s) usually available
U.S.—
Not commercially available.
Canada—
2 mg per 5 mL (OTC) [*Periactin* (alcohol 5%)].

Packaging and storage
Store below 40 °C (104 °F), preferably between 15 and 30 °C (59 and 86 °F), unless otherwise specified by manufacturer. Store in a tight container. Protect from freezing.

Auxiliary labeling
- May cause drowsiness.
- Avoid alcoholic beverages.

CYPROHEPTADINE HYDROCHLORIDE TABLETS USP

Usual adult and adolescent dose
Antihistaminic (H_1-receptor)—
Oral, initially 4 mg every eight hours, the dosage being increased as needed. For most patients the therapeutic range is 4 to 20 mg a day. However, doses up to 32 mg a day have been used occasionally.
[Appetite stimulant]—
Oral, 4 mg three times a day with meals.

Note: Treatment period to promote weight gain should not exceed six months.

[Vascular headache suppressant]—
Initial: Oral, 4 mg at the start of the attack, repeated after thirty minutes if necessary.
Maintenance: Oral, 4 mg every four to six hours.

Usual adult prescribing limits
500 mcg (0.5 mg) per kg of body weight daily.

Usual pediatric dose
Antihistaminic (H_1-receptor)—
Oral, 125 mcg (0.125 mg) per kg of body weight or 4 mg per square meter of body surface, every eight to twelve hours as needed or for
Children 2 to 6 years of age: Oral, 2 mg every eight to twelve hours as needed, not to exceed 12 mg per day.
Children 7 to 14 years of age: Oral, 4 mg every eight to twelve hours as needed, not to exceed 16 mg per day.
[Appetite stimulant]—
Children 2 to 6 years of age: Oral, initially 2 mg two or three times a day with meals. The dosage may be increased, if necessary, but not to exceed 8 mg a day.
Children 7 to 14 years of age: Oral, initially 2 mg three or four times a day with meals. The usual maintenance dose is 4 mg two or three times a day. The dosage may be increased, if necessary, but not to exceed 16 mg a day.

Note: Premature and full-term neonates—Use is not recommended.
Treatment period to promote weight gain should not exceed 3 months.

Usual geriatric dose
See *Usual adult and adolescent dose.*

Note: Geriatric patients may be more sensitive to the effects of the usual adult dose.

Strength(s) usually available
U.S.—
4 mg (Rx) [*Periactin* (scored); GENERIC].
Canada—
4 mg (OTC) [*Periactin* (scored)].

Packaging and storage
Store below 40 °C (104 °F), preferably between 15 and 30 °C (59 and 86 °F), unless otherwise specified by manufacturer. Store in a well-closed container.

Auxiliary labeling
- May cause drowsiness.
- Avoid alcoholic beverages.

DESLORATADINE

Summary of Differences
Indications:
Used for treatment of allergic rhinitis and chronic idiopathic urticaria.
Pharmacology/pharmacokinetics:
Chemical group—Piperidine derivative; metabolite of loratadine.
Molecular weight—310.8
pKa—Pyridine functional group; 4.2
pKa—Piperidine functional group; 9.7
Protein binding—desloratadine 82 to 87%; 3-hydroxydesloratadine (active metabolite): 85 to 89%
Half-life—27 hours.
Onset of action—Histamine skin wheal studies—within one hour.

Time to peak concentration—approximately 3 hours.
Duration of action—Histamine skin wheal studies—up to 24 hours.
Precautions:
Medical considerations/contraindications—hepatic and renal impairment cause increases in pharmacokinetic parameters requiring dosage adjustments.
Side/adverse effects:
May cause anaphylaxis, dry mouth, dysmenorrhea, dyspepsia, dyspnea, fatigue, edema, headache, myalgia, nausea, pharyngitis, pruritus, rash, somnolence, tachycardia or urticaria.

Oral Dosage Forms

DESLORATADINE TABLETS

Usual adult and adolescent dose
Rhinitis, allergic (treatment)—
Oral, 5 mg once daily.
Urticaria, idiopathic, chronic (treatment)—
Oral, 5 mg once daily.
Note: In patients with liver or renal impairment, U.S. prescribing information recommends a starting dose of Oral, 5 mg every other day.

Usual Pediatric Dose
Safety and efficacy have not been established.

Geriatric Dose
See *Usual adult and adolescent dose.*

Strength(s) usually available
U.S.—
5 mg (Rx) [*Clarinex*].
Canada—
5 mg (Rx) [*Aerius*].

Packaging and storage
Store between 2 and 25 °C (36 and 77 °F). Avoid exposure at or above 30 °C (86 °F). Heat sensitive. Protect from moisture.
Note: Canadian product information states to store between 15 and 30 °C.

Auxiliary labeling
- Do not use if you are breast-feeding. Contact your doctor or pharmacist.

DEXCHLORPHENIRAMINE

Summary of Differences

Pharmacology/pharmacokinetics:
Chemical group—Propylamine derivative.
Duration of action—4 to 8 hours.
Side/adverse effects:
Potential for blood dyscrasias; thickening of mucus less pronounced.

Oral Dosage Forms

DEXCHLORPHENIRAMINE MALEATE SYRUP USP

Usual adult and adolescent dose
Antihistaminic (H_1-receptor)—
Oral, 2 mg every four to six hours as needed.

Usual pediatric dose
Antihistaminic (H_1-receptor)—
Children up to 12 years of age: Oral, 150 mcg (0.15 mg) per kg of body weight or 4.5 mg per square meter of body surface per day, in four divided doses or for
Children 2 to 5 years of age: Oral, 500 mcg (0.5 mg) every four to six hours as needed.
Children 5 to 12 years of age: Oral, 1 mg every four to six hours as needed.
Note: Premature and full-term neonates—Use is not recommended.

Usual geriatric dose
See *Usual adult and adolescent dose.*
Note: Geriatric patients may be more sensitive to the effects of the usual adult dose.

Strength(s) usually available
U.S.—
2 mg per 5 mL (Rx) [*Polaramine* (alcohol 6%)].
Canada—
2 mg per 5 mL (OTC) [*Polaramine* (alcohol 5%)].

Packaging and storage
Store below 40 °C (104 °F), preferably between 15 and 30 °C (59 and 86 °F), unless otherwise specified by manufacturer. Store in a tight container. Protect from light. Protect from freezing.

Auxiliary labeling
- May cause drowsiness.
- Avoid alcoholic beverages.

DEXCHLORPHENIRAMINE MALEATE TABLETS USP

Usual adult and adolescent dose
See *Dexchlorpheniramine Maleate Syrup USP.*

Usual pediatric dose
See *Dexchlorpheniramine Maleate Syrup USP.*

Usual geriatric dose
See *Dexchlorpheniramine Maleate Syrup USP.*
Note: Geriatric patients may be more sensitive to the effects of the usual adult dose.

Strength(s) usually available
U.S.—
2 mg (Rx) [*Polaramine*].
Canada—
2 mg (OTC) [*Polaramine*].

Packaging and storage
Store below 40 °C (104 °F), preferably between 15 and 30 °C (59 and 86 °F), unless otherwise specified by manufacturer. Store in a tight container.

Auxiliary labeling
- May cause drowsiness.
- Avoid alcoholic beverages.

DEXCHLORPHENIRAMINE MALEATE EXTENDED-RELEASE TABLETS

Usual adult and adolescent dose
Antihistaminic (H_1-receptor)—
Oral, 4 or 6 mg every eight to twelve hours as needed.

Usual pediatric dose
Use is not recommended.

Usual geriatric dose
See *Usual adult and adolescent dose.*
Note: Geriatric patients may be more sensitive to the effects of the usual adult dose.

Strength(s) usually available
U.S.—
4 mg (Rx) [*Dexchlor; Polaramine Repetabs* (sugar-coated); GENERIC].
6 mg (Rx) [*Dexchlor; Polaramine Repetabs* (sugar-coated); GENERIC].
Canada—
6 mg (OTC) [*Polaramine Repetabs*].

Packaging and storage
Store below 40 °C (104 °F), preferably between 15 and 30 °C (59 and 86 °F), in a well-closed container, unless otherwise specified by manufacturer.

Auxiliary labeling
- Swallow tablets whole.
- May cause drowsiness.
- Avoid alcoholic beverages.

DIMENHYDRINATE

Summary of Differences

Category:
Also indicated as an antiemetic and antivertigo agent.
Pharmacology/pharmacokinetics:
Chemical group—Ethanolamine derivative.
Other actions/effects—Greater anticholinergic activity.
Duration of action—3 to 6 hours.
Precautions:
Drug interactions and/or related problems—May decrease emetic response to apomorphine.
Medical considerations/contraindications—May impede diagnosis of appendicitis; may obscure signs of overdose.

Additional Dosing Information

See also *General Dosing Information.*

When dimenhydrinate is used for prophylaxis of motion sickness, it should be taken at least 30 minutes, and preferably 1 or 2 hours, before exposure to conditions that may precipitate motion sickness.
For parenteral dosage form only
- Do not administer intra-arterially.

Oral Dosage Forms

DIMENHYDRINATE EXTENDED-RELEASE CAPSULES

Usual adult and adolescent dose

Antiemetic or
Antivertigo agent—
Oral, 1 capsule every twelve hours.

Usual pediatric dose

Use is not recommended.

Usual geriatric dose

See *Usual adult and adolescent dose.*

Note: Geriatric patients may be more sensitive to the effects of the usual adult dose.

Strength(s) usually available

U.S.—
Not commercially available.
Canada—
75 mg (25 mg for immediate release and 50 mg for extended release) (OTC) [*Gravol L/A*].

Packaging and storage

Store below 40 °C (104 °F), preferably between 15 and 30 °C (59 and 86 °F), in a well-closed container, unless otherwise specified by manufacturer.

Auxiliary labeling

- May cause drowsiness.
- Avoid alcoholic beverages.

DIMENHYDRINATE ORAL SOLUTION

Usual adult and adolescent dose

Antiemetic or
Antivertigo agent—
Oral, 50 to 100 mg every four to six hours.

Usual adult prescribing limits

400 mg per 24 hours.

Usual pediatric dose

Antiemetic or
Antivertigo agent—
Children 2 to 6 years of age: Oral, 12.5 to 25 mg every six to eight hours as needed, not to exceed 75 mg per day.
Children 6 to 12 years of age: Oral, 25 to 50 mg every six to eight hours as needed, not to exceed 150 mg per day.

Note: Premature and full-term neonates—Use is not recommended.

Usual geriatric dose

See *Usual adult and adolescent dose.*

Note: Geriatric patients may be more sensitive to the effects of the usual adult dose.

Strength(s) usually available

U.S.—
12.5 mg per 5 mL (OTC) [GENERIC].
Canada—
15 mg per 5 mL (OTC) [*Gravol Liquid* (alcohol-free)].

Packaging and storage

Store below 40 °C (104 °F), preferably between 15 and 30 °C (59 and 86 °F), unless otherwise specified by manufacturer. Store in a well-closed container.

Auxiliary labeling

- May cause drowsiness.
- Avoid alcoholic beverages.

DIMENHYDRINATE SYRUP USP

Usual adult and adolescent dose

See *Dimenhydrinate Oral Solution.*

Usual adult prescribing limits

See *Dimenhydrinate Oral Solution.*

Usual pediatric dose

See *Dimenhydrinate Oral Solution.*

Note: Premature and full-term neonates—Use is not recommended.

Usual geriatric dose

See *Dimenhydrinate Oral Solution.*

Note: Geriatric patients may be more sensitive to the effects of the usual adult dose.

Strength(s) usually available

U.S.—
12.5 mg per 5 mL (OTC) [*Dramamine;* GENERIC].
Canada—
15 mg per 5 mL (OTC) [*PMS-Dimenhydrinate*].

Packaging and storage

Store below 40 °C (104 °F), preferably between 15 and 30 °C (59 and 86 °F), unless otherwise specified by manufacturer. Store in a tight container. Protect from freezing.

Auxiliary labeling

- May cause drowsiness.
- Avoid alcoholic beverages.

DIMENHYDRINATE TABLETS USP

Usual adult and adolescent dose

See *Dimenhydrinate Oral Solution.*

Usual adult prescribing limits

See *Dimenhydrinate Oral Solution.*

Usual pediatric dose

See *Dimenhydrinate Oral Solution.*

Note: Premature and full-term neonates—Use is not recommended.

Usual geriatric dose

See *Dimenhydrinate Oral Solution.*

Note: Geriatric patients may be more sensitive to the effects of the usual adult dose.

Strength(s) usually available

U.S.—
50 mg (OTC) [*Calm X* (scored); *Dramamine* (scored); *Triptone Caplets;* GENERIC].
Canada—
15 mg (OTC) [*Gravol Filmkote*].
25 mg (OTC) [*Gravol Filmkote* (Junior Strength)].
50 mg (OTC) [*Apo-Dimenhydrinate; Gravol Filmkote; PMS-Dimenhydrinate; Traveltabs*].

Packaging and storage

Store below 40 °C (104 °F), preferably between 15 and 30 °C (59 and 86 °F), unless otherwise specified by manufacturer. Store in a well-closed container.

Auxiliary labeling

- May cause drowsiness.
- Avoid alcoholic beverages.

DIMENHYDRINATE TABLETS (CHEWABLE) USP

Usual adult and adolescent dose

See *Dimenhydrinate Oral Solution.*

Usual adult prescribing limits

See *Dimenhydrinate Oral Solution.*

Usual pediatric dose

See *Dimenhydrinate Oral Solution.*

Note: Premature and full-term neonates—Use is not recommended.

Usual geriatric dose

See *Dimenhydrinate Oral Solution.*

Note: Geriatric patients may be more sensitive to the effects of the usual adult dose.

Strength(s) usually available

U.S.—
50 mg (OTC) [*Dramamine* (scored)].
Canada—
15 mg (OTC) [*Gravol*].
50 mg (OTC) [*Gravol*].

Packaging and storage

Store below 40 °C (104 °F), preferably between 15 and 30 °C (59 and 86 °F), unless otherwise specified by manufacturer. Store in a well-closed container.

Auxiliary labeling

- May cause drowsiness.
- Avoid alcoholic beverages.

Parenteral Dosage Forms

DIMENHYDRINATE INJECTION USP

Usual adult and adolescent dose

Antiemetic or
Antivertigo agent—
Intramuscular, 50 mg repeated every four hours as needed.
Intravenous, 50 mg in 10 mL of 0.9% sodium chloride injection, administered slowly over a period of at least two minutes, repeated every four hours as needed.

Usual pediatric dose
Antiemetic or
Antivertigo agent—
Intramuscular, 1.25 mg per kg of body weight or 37.5 mg per square meter of body surface, every six hours as needed, not to exceed 300 mg per day.
Intravenous, 1.25 mg per kg of body weight or 37.5 mg per square meter of body surface, in 10 mL of 0.9% sodium chloride injection, administered slowly over a period of at least two minutes, every six hours as needed, not to exceed 300 mg per day.

Note: Premature and full-term neonates—Use is not recommended.

Usual geriatric dose
See *Usual adult and adolescent dose.*

Note: Geriatric patients may be more sensitive to the effects of the usual adult dose.

Strength(s) usually available
U.S.—
50 mg per mL (Rx) [*Dinate; Dramanate; Hydrate;* GENERIC].

Canada—

Note: The 50-mg-per-mL concentration is intended for intramuscular use. To use this concentration for intravenous administration, the solution must be further diluted at a ratio of at least 1:10 (10 mL of diluent for each 1 mL of dimenhydrinate) with a compatible intravenous solution, such as sterile saline or 5% dextrose in water.

10 mg per mL (Rx) [*Gravol I/V* (for intravenous administration only; ethyl alcohol)].
50 mg per mL (Rx) [*Gravol I/M* (for intramuscular administration; methylparaben; propylene glycol; propylparaben)].

Packaging and storage
Store below 40 °C (104 °F), preferably between 15 and 30 °C (59 and 86 °F), unless otherwise specified by manufacturer. Protect from freezing.

Rectal Dosage Forms

DIMENHYDRINATE SUPPOSITORIES

Usual adult and adolescent dose
Antiemetic or
Antivertigo agent—
Rectal, 50 to 100 mg every six to eight hours as needed.

Usual pediatric dose
Antiemetic or
Antivertigo agent—
Children up to 6 years of age: Dosage has not been established.
Children 6 to 8 years of age: Rectal, 12.5 to 25 mg every eight to twelve hours as needed.
Children 8 to 12 years of age: Rectal, 25 to 50 mg every eight to twelve hours as needed.
Children 12 years of age and over: Rectal, 50 mg every eight to twelve hours as needed.

Usual geriatric dose
See *Usual adult and adolescent dose.*

Note: Geriatric patients may be more sensitive to the effects of the usual adult dose.

Strength(s) usually available
U.S.—
Not commercially available.
Canada—
25 mg (OTC) [*Gravol*].

Packaging and storage
Store between 8 and 15 °C (46 and 59 °F), in a well-closed container, unless otherwise specified by manufacturer.

Auxiliary labeling
- May cause drowsiness.
- Avoid alcoholic beverages.

Note
When dispensing, include patient instructions.

DIPHENHYDRAMINE

Summary of Differences
Category:
Also indicated as an antidyskinetic, antiemetic, antitussive (syrup only), antivertigo agent, and a sedative-hypnotic.

Pharmacology/pharmacokinetics:
Chemical group—Ethanolamine derivative.
pKa—9.
Other actions/effects—Greater anticholinergic activity.
Protein binding—98 to 99%.
Half-life—1 to 4 hours.
Time to peak concentration—1 to 4 hours.
Duration of action—6 to 8 hours.

Precautions:
Drug interactions and/or related problems—May decrease emetic response to apomorphine.
Medical considerations/contraindications—May impede diagnosis of appendicitis; may obscure signs of overdose.

Side/adverse effects:
No confusion; sedative effects and gastrointestinal upset are more pronounced; thickening of mucus less pronounced.

Additional Dosing Information
See also *General Dosing Information.*

When diphenhydramine is used for prophylaxis of motion sickness, it should be taken at least 30 minutes, and preferably 1 or 2 hours, before exposure to conditions that may precipitate motion sickness.

Oral Dosage Forms

DIPHENHYDRAMINE HYDROCHLORIDE CAPSULES USP

Usual adult and adolescent dose
Antihistaminic (H_1-receptor)—
Oral, 25 to 50 mg every four to six hours as needed.
Antidyskinetic[1]—
For idiopathic and postencephalitic parkinsonism: Oral, 25 mg three times a day initially, the dose then being gradually increased to 50 mg four times a day if needed.
Antiemetic or
Antivertigo agent—
Oral, 25 to 50 mg every four to six hours as needed.
Sedative-hypnotic—
Oral, 50 mg twenty to thirty minutes before bedtime if needed.

Usual adult prescribing limits
Up to 300 mg daily.

Usual pediatric dose
Antihistaminic (H_1-receptor)—
Children up to 6 years of age: Oral, 6.25 to 12.5 mg every four to six hours.
Children 6 to 12 years of age: Oral, 12.5 to 25 mg every four to six hours, not to exceed 150 mg per day.
Antiemetic or
Antivertigo agent—
Oral, 1 to 1.5 mg per kg of body weight every four to six hours as needed, not to exceed 300 mg per day.

Note: The available strength of the capsule may not conform to some of the recommended pediatric dosages.

Usual geriatric dose
See *Usual adult and adolescent dose.*

Note: Geriatric patients may be more sensitive to the effects of the usual adult dose.

Strength(s) usually available
U.S.—
25 mg (Rx) [GENERIC].
25 mg (OTC) [*Banophen; Benadryl Allergy; Genahist; Nytol QuickCaps;* GENERIC].
50 mg (Rx) [GENERIC].
50 mg (OTC) [*Nytol QuickGels; Sleep-eze D Extra Strength; Unisom SleepGels Maximum Strength;* GENERIC].
Canada—
25 mg (Rx) [*Allerdryl*].
25 mg (OTC) [*Benadryl*].
50 mg (Rx) [*Allerdryl*].
50 mg (OTC) [*Benadryl*].

Packaging and storage
Store below 40 °C (104 °F), preferably between 15 and 30 °C (59 and 86 °F), unless otherwise specified by manufacturer. Store in a tight container.

Auxiliary labeling
- May cause drowsiness.
- Avoid alcoholic beverages.

DIPHENHYDRAMINE HYDROCHLORIDE ELIXIR USP

Usual adult and adolescent dose
See *Diphenhydramine Hydrochloride Capsules USP*.

Usual adult prescribing limits
See *Diphenhydramine Hydrochloride Capsules USP*.

Usual pediatric dose
Antihistaminic (H_1-receptor)—
Oral, 1.25 mg per kg of body weight or 37.5 mg per square meter of body surface, every four to six hours, not to exceed 300 mg a day or for
Children weighing up to 9.1 kg: Oral, 6.25 to 12.5 mg every four to six hours.
Children weighing 9.1 kg and over: Oral, 12.5 to 25 mg every four to six hours.
Antiemetic or
Antivertigo agent—
Oral, 1 to 1.5 mg per kg of body weight every four to six hours as needed, not to exceed 300 mg per day.
Antitussive—
Children up to 2 years of age: Dosage must be individualized by physician.
Children 2 to 6 years of age: Oral, 6.25 mg every four to six hours as needed, not to exceed 25 mg per day.
Children 6 to 12 years of age: Oral, 12.5 mg every four to six hours as needed, not to exceed 75 mg per day.
Note: Premature and full-term neonates—Use is not recommended.

Usual geriatric dose
See *Usual adult and adolescent dose*.

Note: Geriatric patients may be more sensitive to the effects of the usual adult dose.

Strength(s) usually available
U.S.—
12.5 mg per 5 mL (Rx) [GENERIC].
12.5 mg per 5 mL (OTC) [*Diphen Cough* (alcohol 5%); *Diphenhist; Genahist* (alcohol 14%); *Siladryl* (alcohol 5.6%); GENERIC].
Canada—
12.5 mg per 5 mL (OTC) [*Benadryl* (alcohol 14%)].

Packaging and storage
Store below 40 °C (104 °F), preferably between 15 and 30 °C (59 and 86 °F), unless otherwise specified by manufacturer. Store in a tight container. Protect from light. Protect from freezing.

Auxiliary labeling
- May cause drowsiness.
- Avoid alcoholic beverages.
- Keep container tightly closed.

DIPHENHYDRAMINE HYDROCHLORIDE TABLETS USP

Usual adult and adolescent dose
See *Diphenhydramine Hydrochloride Capsules USP*.

Usual adult prescribing limits
See *Diphenhydramine Hydrochloride Capsules USP*.

Usual pediatric dose
See *Diphenhydramine Hydrochloride Elixir USP*.

Usual geriatric dose
See *Diphenhydramine Hydrochloride Capsules USP*.

Note: Geriatric patients may be more sensitive to the effects of the usual adult dose.

Strength(s) usually available
U.S.—
25 mg (Rx) [GENERIC].
25 mg (OTC) [*Aller-med; Banophen Caplets; Benadryl; Diphenhist Captabs; Nervine Nighttime Sleep-Aid; Sleep-Eze D; Sominex*].
50 mg (Rx) [GENERIC].
50 mg (OTC) [*AllerMax Caplets; Compoz; Dormarex 2; Sleep-Eze D Extra Strength; Twilite Caplets*].
Canada—
Not commercially available.

Packaging and storage
Store below 40 °C (104 °F), preferably between 15 and 30 °C (59 and 86 °F), in a well-closed container, unless otherwise specified by manufacturer.

Auxiliary labeling
- May cause drowsiness.
- Avoid alcoholic beverages.

Parenteral Dosage Forms

DIPHENHYDRAMINE HYDROCHLORIDE INJECTION USP

Usual adult and adolescent dose
Antihistaminic (H_1-receptor) or
Antidyskinetic[1]—
Intramuscular or intravenous, 10 to 50 mg.
Antiemetic or
Antivertigo agent—
Intramuscular or intravenous, 10 mg initially, may be increased to 20 to 50 mg every two to three hours.

Usual adult prescribing limits
Up to 100 mg per dose or 400 mg daily.

Usual pediatric dose
Antihistaminic (H_1-receptor) or
Antidyskinetic—
Intramuscular, 1.25 mg per kg of body weight or 37.5 mg per square meter of body surface, four times a day, not to exceed 300 mg per day.
Antiemetic or
Antivertigo agent—
Intramuscular, 1 to 1.5 mg per kg of body weight every six hours, not to exceed 300 mg per day.
Note: Premature and full-term neonates—Use is not recommended.

Usual geriatric dose
See *Usual adult and adolescent dose*.

Note: Geriatric patients may be more sensitive to the effects of the usual adult dose.

Strength(s) usually available
U.S.—
10 mg per mL (Rx) [GENERIC].
50 mg per mL (Rx) [*Benadryl; Hyrexin;* GENERIC].
Canada—
50 mg per mL (Rx) [*Benadryl;* GENERIC].

Packaging and storage
Store below 40 °C (104 °F), preferably between 15 and 30 °C (59 and 86 °F), unless otherwise specified by manufacturer. Protect from light. Protect from freezing.

---

[1]Not included in Canadian product labeling.

DOXYLAMINE

Summary of Differences

Category:
Also indicated as a sedative-hypnotic.
Pharmacology/pharmacokinetics:
Chemical group—Ethanolamine derivative.
pKa—5.8 and 9.3.
Other actions/effects—Greater anticholinergic activity.
Duration of action—6 to 8 hours.
Precautions:
Drug interactions and/or related problems:
May decrease emetic response to apomorphine.

Oral Dosage Forms

DOXYLAMINE SUCCINATE TABLETS USP

Usual adult and adolescent dose
Antihistaminic (H_1-receptor)—
Oral, 12.5 to 25 mg every four to six hours as needed.
Sedative-hypnotic—
Oral, 25 mg thirty minutes before bedtime if needed.

Usual adult prescribing limits
Up to 150 mg daily.

Usual pediatric dose
Antihistaminic (H_1-receptor)—
Children up to 6 years of age: Use is not recommended.
Children 6 to 12 years of age: Oral, 6.25 to 12.5 mg every four to six hours as needed.

Sedative-hypnotic—
Use is not recommended.

Usual geriatric dose
See *Usual adult and adolescent dose.*

Note: Geriatric patients may be more sensitive to the effects of the usual adult dose.

Strength(s) usually available
U.S.—
25 mg (OTC) [*Unisom Nighttime Sleep Aid* (scored)].
Canada—
Not commercially available.

Packaging and storage
Store below 40 °C (104 °F), preferably between 15 and 30 °C (59 and 86 °F), unless otherwise specified by manufacturer. Store in a well-closed container. Protect from light.

Auxiliary labeling
- May cause drowsiness.
- Avoid alcoholic beverages.

FEXOFENADINE

Summary of Differences

Pharmacology/pharmacokinetics:
Chemical group—Metabolite of terfenadine
Half-life—14.4 hours.
Time to peak concentration—2.6 hours.

Oral Dosage Forms

FEXOFENADINE HYDROCHLORIDE CAPSULES

Usual adult and adolescent dose
Antihistaminic (H_1-receptor)—
Oral, 60 mg twice daily, or 180 mg once daily.
Urticaria, chronic idiopathic[1]—
Oral, 60 mg twice daily.

Note: For patients with decreased renal function, an initial dose of 60 mg once a day is recommended.

Usual pediatric dose
Antihistaminic (H_1-receptor)
Urticaria (treatment)[1]—
Children 12 years of age and older: See *Usual adult and adolescent dose*
Children 6 to 11 years of age: Oral, 30 mg twice daily.

Note: Capsules are not available in a 30 mg dose.

Children up to 6 years of age: Safety and efficacy have not been established.

Note: In Canada, not indicated for children younger than 12 years of age

Note: For pediatric patients with decreased renal function, an initial dose of 30 mg once a day is recommended

Strength(s) usually available
U.S.—
60 mg (Rx) [*Allegra* (croscarmellose sodium; magnesium stearate; gelatin; lactose; microcrystalline cellulose; pregelatinized starch)].
Canada—
60 mg (Rx) [*Allegra*].

Packaging and storage
Store at controlled room temperature 20–25°C (68–77 °F), preferably between 15 and 30 °C (59 and 86 °F). Protect from excessive moisture.

FEXOFENADINE HYDROCHLORIDE TABLETS

Usual adult and adolescent dose
Antihistaminic (H_1-receptor)
Urticaria (treatment)[1]—
See *Fexofenadine Hydrochloride Capsules*

Usual pediatric dose
Antihistaminic (H_1-receptor)
Urticaria (treatment)[1]—
See *Fexofenadine Hydrochloride Capsules*
Note: In Canada, not indicated for children younger than 12 years of age

Strength(s) usually available
U.S.—
30 mg (Rx) [*Allegra* (croscarmellose sodium; magnesium stearate; microcrystalline cellulose; pregelatinized starch)].
60 mg (Rx) [*Allegra* (croscarmellose sodium; magnesium stearate; microcrystalline cellulose; pregelatinized starch)].
180 mg (Rx) [*Allegra* (croscarmellose sodium; magnesium stearate; microcrystalline cellulose; pregelatinized starch)].
Canada—
60 mg (Rx) [*Allegra* (croscarmellose sodium; hydroxypropyl methylcellulose; iron oxide; lactose; magnesium stearate; microcrystalline cellulose; povidone; polyethylene glycol; silicon dioxide; starch; titanium dioxide)].

Packaging and storage
Store at controlled room temperature 20–25°C (68–77 °F), preferably between 15 and 30 °C (59 and 86 °F). Protect from excessive moisture.

[1]Not included in Canadian product labeling.

HYDROXYZINE

Summary of Differences

Category:
Also indicated in the treatment of anxiety and psychosis-related tension; antiemetic agent and sedative-hypnotic.
Pharmacology/pharmacokinetics:
Chemical group—Piperazine derivative.
pKa—Hydroxyzine hydrochloride: 2.6 and 7.
Half-life (elimination)—20 to 25 hours.
Duration of action—4 to 6 hours.
Precautions:
Pregnancy—Not taking during early months of pregnancy because of fetal abnormalities in studies in animals.
Drug interactions and/or related problems—May decrease emetic response to apomorphine.
Laboratory value alterations—False increases in urine 17-hydroxycorticosteroid determinations.
Medical considerations/contraindications—May impede diagnosis of appendicitis; may obscure signs of overdose.
Side/adverse effects:
No dizziness; no paradoxical reaction.

Oral Dosage Forms

HYDROXYZINE HYDROCHLORIDE CAPSULES

Usual adult and adolescent dose
Antianxiety agent or
Sedative-hypnotic—
Oral, 50 to 100 mg as a single dose.
Antihistaminic (H_1-receptor) or
Antiemetic—
Oral, 25 to 100 mg three or four times a day as needed.

Usual pediatric dose
Antianxiety agent or
Sedative-hypnotic—
Oral, 600 mcg (0.6 mg) per kg of body weight as a single dose.
Antihistaminic (H_1-receptor) or
Antiemetic—
Oral, 500 mcg (0.5 mg) per kg of body weight or 15 mg per square meter of body surface every six hours as needed; or for
Children up to 6 years of age: Oral, 30 to 50 mg a day in divided doses, or 12.5 mg every six hours as needed.
Children 6 to 12 years of age: Oral, 50 to 100 mg a day in divided doses, or 12.5 to 25 mg every six hours as needed.

Usual geriatric dose
See *Usual adult and adolescent dose.*

Note: Geriatric patients may be more sensitive to the effects of the usual adult dose.

Strength(s) usually available
U.S.—
Not commercially available.
Canada—
10 mg (Rx) [*Apo-Hydroxyzine; Novo-Hydroxyzin*].
25 mg (Rx) [*Apo-Hydroxyzine; Atarax; Multipax; Novo-Hydroxyzin*].
50 mg (Rx) [*Apo-Hydroxyzine; Multipax; Novo-Hydroxyzin*].

Packaging and storage

Store below 40 °C (104 °F), preferably between 15 and 30 °C (59 and 86 °F), unless otherwise specified by manufacturer.

Auxiliary labeling

- May cause drowsiness.
- Avoid alcoholic beverages.

HYDROXYZINE HYDROCHLORIDE SYRUP USP

Usual adult and adolescent dose

See *Hydroxyzine Hydrochloride Capsules.*

Usual pediatric dose

See *Hydroxyzine Hydrochloride Capsules.*

Usual geriatric dose

See *Hydroxyzine Hydrochloride Capsules.*

Note: Geriatric patients may be more sensitive to the effects of the usual adult dose.

Strength(s) usually available

U.S.—

10 mg per 5 mL (Rx) [*Atarax* (alcohol 0.5%); GENERIC].

Canada—

10 mg per 5 mL (Rx) [*Atarax*].

Packaging and storage

Store below 40 °C (104 °F), preferably between 15 and 30 °C (59 and 86 °F), unless otherwise specified by manufacturer. Store in a tight, light-resistant container. Protect from freezing.

Auxiliary labeling

- May cause drowsiness.
- Avoid alcoholic beverages.

HYDROXYZINE HYDROCHLORIDE TABLETS USP

Usual adult and adolescent dose

See *Hydroxyzine Hydrochloride Capsules.*

Usual pediatric dose

See *Hydroxyzine Hydrochloride Capsules.*

Usual geriatric dose

See *Hydroxyzine Hydrochloride Capsules.*

Note: Geriatric patients may be more sensitive to the effects of the usual adult dose.

Strength(s) usually available

U.S.—

10 mg (Rx) [*Atarax;* GENERIC].
25 mg (Rx) [*Atarax;* GENERIC].
50 mg (Rx) [*Atarax;* GENERIC].
100 mg (Rx) [*Atarax;* GENERIC].

Canada—

Not commercially available.

Packaging and storage

Store below 40 °C (104 °F), preferably between 15 and 30 °C (59 and 86 °F), unless otherwise specified by manufacturer. Store in a tight container.

Auxiliary labeling

- May cause drowsiness.
- Avoid alcoholic beverages.

HYDROXYZINE PAMOATE CAPSULES USP

Usual adult and adolescent dose

Antianxiety agent or
Sedative-hypnotic—

Oral, 50 to 100 mg as a single dose.

Antihistaminic (H_1-receptor) or
Antiemetic—

Oral, 25 to 100 mg three to four times a day as needed.

Usual pediatric dose

Antianxiety agent or
Sedative-hypnotic—

Oral, 600 mcg (0.6 mg) per kg of body weight as a single dose.

Antihistaminic (H_1-receptor) or
Antiemetic—

Oral, 500 mcg (0.5 mg) per kg of body weight or 15 mg per square meter of body surface every six hours as needed; or for

Children 6 years of age and over: Oral, 12.5 to 25 mg every six hours as needed.

Usual geriatric dose

See *Usual adult and adolescent dose.*

Note: Geriatric patients may be more sensitive to the effects of the usual adult dose.

Strength(s) usually available

U.S.—

The equivalent of hydroxyzine hydrochloride:
25 mg (Rx) [*Vistaril;* GENERIC].
50 mg (Rx) [*Vistaril;* GENERIC].
100 mg (Rx) [*Vistaril;* GENERIC].

Canada—

Not commercially available.

Packaging and storage

Store below 40 °C (104 °F), preferably between 15 and 30 °C (59 and 86 °F), in a well-closed container, unless otherwise specified by manufacturer.

Auxiliary labeling

- May cause drowsiness.
- Avoid alcoholic beverages.

HYDROXYZINE PAMOATE ORAL SUSPENSION USP

Usual adult and adolescent dose

See *Hydroxyzine Pamoate Capsules USP.*

Usual pediatric dose

Antianxiety agent or
Sedative-hypnotic—

Oral, 600 mcg (0.6 mg) per kg of body weight as a single dose.

Antihistaminic (H_1-receptor) or
Antiemetic—

Oral, 500 mcg (0.5 mg) per kg of body weight or 15 mg per square meter of body surface every six hours as needed; or for

Children up to 6 years of age: Oral, 12.5 mg every six hours as needed.

Children 6 years of age and over: Oral, 12.5 to 25 mg every six hours as needed.

Usual geriatric dose

See *Hydroxyzine Pamoate Capsules USP.*

Note: Geriatric patients may be more sensitive to the effects of the usual adult dose.

Strength(s) usually available

U.S.—

The equivalent of hydroxyzine hydrochloride:
25 mg per 5 mL (Rx) [*Vistaril*].

Canada—

Not commercially available.

Packaging and storage

Store below 40 °C (104 °F), preferably between 15 and 30 °C (59 and 86 °F), unless otherwise specified by manufacturer. Store in a tight, light-resistant container. Protect from freezing.

Auxiliary labeling

- Shake well.
- May cause drowsiness.
- Avoid alcoholic beverages.

Parenteral Dosage Forms

HYDROXYZINE HYDROCHLORIDE INJECTION USP

Usual adult and adolescent dose

Antianxiety agent—

Intramuscular, 50 to 100 mg, repeated as needed every four to six hours.

Sedative-hypnotic—

Intramuscular, 50 mg as a single dose.

Adjunct to narcotic medication: Intramuscular, 25 to 100 mg.

Antiemetic—

Intramuscular, 25 to 100 mg.

Usual pediatric dose

Adjunct to narcotic medication or
Antiemetic—

Intramuscular, 1 mg per kg of body weight, or 30 mg per square meter of body surface, as a single dose.

Usual geriatric dose

See *Usual adult and adolescent dose.*

Note: Geriatric patients may be more sensitive to the effects of the usual adult dose.

Strength(s) usually available

U.S.—

25 mg per mL (Rx) [*Vistaril;* GENERIC].

50 mg per mL (Rx) [*Hyzine-50; Vistaril;* GENERIC].

Canada—

50 mg per mL (Rx) [*Atarax;* GENERIC].

Packaging and storage

Store below 40 °C (104 °F), preferably between 15 and 30 °C (59 and 86 °F), unless otherwise specified by manufacturer. Protect from light. Protect from freezing.

LORATADINE

Summary of Differences

Indications:

Used as treatment adjunct in asthma.

Pharmacology/pharmacokinetics:

Chemical group—Piperidine derivative.

Other actions/effects—No significant anticholinergic activity. Mild bronchodilator.

Protein binding—97%.

Half-life—3 to 20 hours.

Onset of action—Histamine skin wheal studies—1 to 3 hours.

Time to peak concentration—1 to 2 hours.

Time to peak effect—Histamine skin wheal studies—8 to 12 hours.

Duration of action—Histamine skin wheal studies—At least 24 hours.

Side/adverse effects:

No paradoxical reaction; sedation more pronounced with large doses.

Oral Dosage Forms

LORATADINE SYRUP

Usual adult and adolescent dose

Antihistaminic (H_1-receptor)—Oral, 10 mg once a day.

Note: In patients with hepatic failure or decreased renal function (creatinine clearance < 30 mL per minute), the initial dose should be 10 mg every other day.

Usual pediatric dose

Antihistaminic (H_1-receptor)—

Children 2 to 6 years of age: Oral, 5 mg once a day.

Children 6 years of age and over: See *Usual adult and adolescent dose.*

Usual geriatric dose

See *Usual adult and adolescent dose.*

Strength(s) usually available

U.S.—

5 mg per 5 mL (OTC) [*Claritin*].

Canada—

5 mg per 5 mL (OTC) [*Claritin*].

Packaging and storage

Store between 2 and 30 °C (36 and 86 °F), in a well-closed container, unless otherwise specified by manufacturer.

LORATADINE TABLETS

Usual adult and adolescent dose

See *Loratadine Syrup.*

Usual pediatric dose

See *Loratadine Syrup.*

Usual geriatric dose

See *Loratadine Syrup.*

Strength(s) usually available

U.S.—

10 mg (OTC) [*Claritin* (scored); *Claritin RediTabs* (rapidly-disintegrating)].

10 mg (OTC) [*Alavert* (orally disintegrating)].

Canada—

10 mg (OTC) [*Claritin* (scored)].

Packaging and storage

Store below 40 °C (104 °F), preferably between 15 and 30 °C (59 and 86 °F), in a well-closed container, unless otherwise specified by manufacturer.

PHENINDAMINE

Summary of Differences

Pharmacology/pharmacokinetics:

Chemical group—Piperidine derivative.

Duration of action—4 to 6 hours.

Oral Dosage Forms

PHENINDAMINE TARTRATE TABLETS

Usual adult and adolescent dose

Antihistaminic (H_1-receptor)—

Oral, 25 mg every four to six hours as needed.

Usual adult prescribing limits

Up to 150 mg daily.

Usual pediatric dose

Antihistaminic (H_1-receptor)—

Children up to 6 years of age: Dosage must be individualized by physician.

Children 6 to 12 years of age: Oral, 12.5 mg every four to six hours as needed, not to exceed 75 mg per day.

Children 12 years of age and over: See *Usual adult and adolescent dose.*

Usual geriatric dose

See *Usual adult and adolescent dose.*

Note: Geriatric patients may be more sensitive to the effects of the usual adult dose.

Strength(s) usually available

U.S.—

25 mg (OTC) [*Nolahist* (scored)].

Canada—

Not commercially available.

Packaging and storage

Store below 40 °C (104 °F), preferably between 15 and 30 °C (59 and 86 °F), in a well-closed container, unless otherwise specified by manufacturer.

Auxiliary labeling

- May cause drowsiness.
- Avoid alcoholic beverages.

Revised: 06/05/2003

ANTIHISTAMINES AND DECONGESTANTS Systemic

NOTE: The *Antihistamines and Decongestants (Systemic)* monograph is maintained on the *USP DI* electronic data base. A copy of the most recent revision of the complete monograph can be accessed on the *USP DI* Updates Online website. See the front cover of book for details on accessing the site.

For information on the specific components of this combination, see the *USP DI* monographs for *Antihistamines (Systemic), Phenylephrine (Systemic), Phenylpropanolamine (Systemic),* and *Pseudoephedrine (Systemic),* and *Sympathominetic Agents—Cardiovascular Use (Systemic).*

The information that follows is selectively abstracted from the complete monograph and is provided to facilitate drug use review and patient counseling.

Note: Products containing phenylpropanolamine were removed from the U.S. and Canadian Markets in November 2000.

This monograph includes information on the following: 1) Acrivastine and Pseudoephedrine; 2) Azatadine and Pseudoephedrine; 3) Brompheniramine and Phenylephrine; 4) Brompheniramine and Pseudoephedrine; 5) Carbinoxamine and Pseudoephedrine; 6) Cetirizine and Pseudoephedrine; 7) Chlorpheniramine and Phenylephrine; 8) Chlorpheniramine, Phenyltoloxamine, and Phenylephrine; 9) Chlorpheniramine and Pseudoephedrine; 10) Chlorpheniramine, Pyrilamine, and Phenylephrine; 11) Dexbrompheniramine and Pseudoephedrine; 12) Diphenhydramine and Pseudoephedrine; 13) Loratadine and Pseudoephedrine; 14) Pheniramine and Phenylephrine; 15) Promethazine and Phenylephrine; 16) Triprolidine and Pseudoephedrine.

INN: Chlorpheniramine—Chlorphenamine

VA CLASSIFICATION (Primary): RE501

Note: Other combinations containing antihistamines and decongestants in addition to other ingredients are found in

Antihistamines, Decongestants, and Analgesics (Systemic); Antihistamines, Decongestants, and Anticholinergics (Systemic); and *Cough/Cold Combinations (Systemic).*

Note: For a listing of dosage forms and brand names by country availability, see *Dosage Forms* section(s).

Category

Antihistaminic (H_1-receptor)-decongestant.

Indications

Accepted

Congestion, nasal (treatment);
Sneezing (treatment); and
Rhinorrhea (treatment)—Antihistamine and decongestant combinations are indicated for the temporary relief of nasal and sinus congestion, sneezing, and rhinorrhea associated with the common cold and both seasonal and perennialallergic rhinitis.

The therapeutic effectiveness of oral phenylephrine as a nasal decongestant has been questioned, especially at the usual oral dose.

Note: Products containing terfenadine and pseudoephedrine were withdrawn from the U.S. market by the Food and Drug Administration in February 1998.

Note: In November 2000, the Food and Drug Administration (FDA) issued a public health warning regarding phenylpropanolamine (PPA) due to the risk of hemorrhagic stroke. The FDA, supported by the final report of The Hemorrhagic Stroke Project (HSP), requested that manufacturers voluntarily discontinue marketing products that contain PPA and that consumers work with their healthcare providers to select alternative products.

Patient Consultation

Note: Products containing phenylpropanolamine were removed from the U.S. and Canadian markets in November 2000.

As an aid to patient consultation, refer to *Advice for the Patient, Antihistamines and Decongestants (Systemic)*.

In providing consultation, consider emphasizing the following selected information (» = major clinical significance):

Before using this medication

» Conditions affecting use, especially:
- Sensitivity to any of the antihistamines or sympathomimetic amines
- Pregnancy—Studies in animals have shown that cetirizine and pseudoephedrine causes skeletal malformities and variants.
- Concern for the fetus and/or newborn infant only with high doses and long-term therapy;
- Breast-feeding—Antihistamines may cause excitement or irritability in nursing infants; high risk for infants from sympathomimetic amines
- Use in children—Increased susceptibility to anticholinergic effects of antihistamines and to vasopressor effects of sympathomimetic amines;
- Use in the elderly—Anticholinergic and CNS stimulant effects more likely to occur
- Other medications, especially anticholinergics; medicine for high blood pressure or depression; alcohol or CNS depression-producing medications, digitalis glycosides, and monoamine oxidase inhibitors (with cetirizine and pseudoephedrine).
- Other medical problems, especially cardiovascular disease, diabetes, hepatic function impairment, hypertension, hyperthyroidism, increased intraocular pressure, narrow angle glaucoma, prostatic hypertrophy, renal function impairment, or urinary retention

Proper use of this medication

» Importance of not taking more medication than the amount recommended

Taking with food, water, or milk to minimize gastric irritation

Swallowing extended-release dosage form whole

» Proper dosing

Missed dose: If on scheduled dosing regimen—Taking as soon as possible; not taking if almost time for next dose; not doubling doses

» Proper storage

Precautions while using this medication

Caution if skin tests using allergens required; possible interference with test results

May mask ototoxic effects of large doses of salicylates

» Avoiding use of alcohol or other CNS depressants

» Caution if drowsiness or dizziness occurs

» Caution if taking appetite suppressants

» Possible insomnia; taking the medication a few hours before bedtime

Possible dryness of mouth; using sugarless gum or candy, ice, or saliva substitute for relief; checking with dentist if dry mouth continues for more than 2 weeks.

For promethazine:

Possible interference with diagnosis of intestinal obstruction, brain tumor, or overdosage of toxic drugs; need to inform physician of use

Side/adverse effects

Signs of potential side effects, especially anaphylaxis, blood dyscrasias, cardiac arrhythmias, cholestasis, glomerulonephritis, hemolytic anemia, hepatitis, severe hypotension, orofacial dyskinesia, psychotic episodes, stillbirth, thrombocytopenia and tightness in chest

ANTIHISTAMINES AND DECONGESTANTS

Oral Dosage Forms

See *Table 1* below.

Strength(s) usually available

U.S.—

See *Table 1* below.

Revised: 06/05/2003

Table 1. Oral Dosage Forms

Note: Products containing phenylpropanolamine were removed from the U.S. and Canadian Markets in November 2000.
Content per capsule, tablet, or 5 mL, unless otherwise stated.

Brand or generic name [availability]	Antihistamines	Decongestants	Other content information as per product label	Usual adult and adolescent dose* prn	Usual pediatric dose prn	Packaging, storage, and auxiliary labeling†
Allerest Maximum Strength Tablets (OTC) [U.S.]	Chlorpheniramine maleate 2 mg	Pseudoephedrine HCl 30 mg		2 tabs q 4–6 hr (max 8 tabs/day)	6–12 yrs: 1 tab q 4–6 hr (max 4 tabs/day)	a
Allerphed Syrup USP (OTC) [U.S.]	Triprolidine HCl 1.25 mg	Pseudoephedrine HCl 30 mg		10 mL q 4–6 hr (max 40 mL/day)	6–12 yrs: 5 mL q 4–6 hr	b, e, f, g
Atrohist Pediatric Extended-release Capsules (Rx) [U.S.]	Chlorpheniramine maleate 4 mg	Pseudoephedrine HCl 60 mg		2 caps q 12 hr	6–12 yrs: 1 cap q 12 hr	b, g

Table 1. Oral Dosage Forms *(continued)*

Note: Products containing phenylpropanolamine were removed from the U.S. and Canadian Markets in November 2000.
Content per capsule, tablet, or 5 mL, unless otherwise stated.

Brand or generic name [availability]	Antihistamines	Decongestants	Other content information as per product label	Usual adult and adolescent dose* prn	Usual pediatric dose prn	Packaging, storage, and auxiliary labeling†
Atrohist Pediatric Suspension Dye Free Oral Suspension (Rx) [U.S.]	Chlorpheniramine tannate 2 mg, Pyrilamine tannate 12.5 mg	Phenylephrine tannate 5 mg		Intended for pediatric use	2–6 yrs: 2.5–5 mL, 6–12 yrs: 5–10 mL, q 12 hr	a, e, g, i
Benadryl Allergy Decongestant Liquid Medication Oral Solution (OTC) [U.S.]	Diphenhydramine HCl 12.5 mg	Pseudoephedrine HCl 30 mg	Alcohol free Sugar free	10 mL q 4–6 hr (max 40 mL/day)	6–12 yrs: 5 mL q 4–6 hr (max 20 mL/day)	c, e, g
Brofed Liquid Oral Solution (Rx) [U.S.]	Brompheniramine maleate 4 mg	Pseudoephedrine HCl 30 mg		10 mL q 8 hr (max 3 doses/day)	2–6 yrs: 2.5 mL, 6–12 yrs: 5 mL, q 8 hr (max 3 doses/day)	a, e, f, g
Bromadrine TR Extended-release Capsules (Rx) [U.S.]	Brompheniramine maleate 12 mg	Pseudoephedrine HCl 120 mg		1 cap q 12 hr		b, g
Bromfed Extended-release Capsules (Rx) [U.S.]	Brompheniramine maleate 12 mg	Pseudoephedrine HCl 120 mg		1 cap q 12 hr		a, g
Syrup (OTC) [U.S.]	Brompheniramine maleate 2 mg	Pseudoephedrine HCl 30 mg	Alcohol free	10 mL q 4–6 hr (max 40 mL/day)	6–12 yrs: 5 mL q 4–6 hr (max 20 mL/day)	b, e, f, g
Tablets (Rx) [U.S.]	Brompheniramine maleate 4 mg	Pseudoephedrine HCl 60 mg	Scored	1 tab q 4 hr (max 6 tabs/day)	6–12 yrs: ½ tab q 4 hr (max 3 tabs/day)	a, g
Bromfed-PD Extended-release Capsules (Rx) [U.S.]	Brompheniramine maleate 6 mg	Pseudoephedrine HCl 60 mg		1–2 caps q 12 hr	6–12 yrs: 1 cap q 12 hr	b, g
Bromfenex Extended-release Capsules (Rx) [U.S.]	Brompheniramine maleate 12 mg	Pseudoephedrine HCl 120 mg		1 cap q 12 hr		a, g
Bromfenex PD Extended-release Capsules (Rx) [U.S.]	Brompheniramine maleate 6 mg	Pseudoephedrine HCl 60 mg		1–2 caps q 12 hr	6–12 yrs: 1 cap q 12 hr	a, g
Brompheniramine Maleate and Pseudoephedrine HCl Extended-release Capsules (Rx) [U.S.]	Brompheniramine maleate 6 mg	Pseudoephedrine HCl 60 mg		1–2 caps q 12 hr	6–12 yrs: 1 cap q 12 hr	a, g
	Brompheniramine maleate 12 mg	Pseudoephedrine HCl 120 mg		1 cap q 12 hr		a, g
Chlordrine S.R. Extended-release Capsules (Rx) [U.S.]	Chlorpheniramine maleate 8 mg	Pseudoephedrine HCl 120 mg		1 cap q 12 hr		a, g
Chlorfed-A Extended-release Capsules (Rx) [U.S.]	Chlorpheniramine maleate 8 mg	Pseudoephedrine HCl 120 mg		1 cap q 12 hr		a, g
Chlorpheniramine Maleate and Pseudoephedrine HCl Extended-release Capsules (Rx) [U.S.]	Chlorpheniramine maleate 8 mg	Pseudoephedrine HCl 120 mg		1 cap q 12 hr		a, g
Chlor-Trimeton 4 Hour Relief Tablets (OTC) [U.S.]	Chlorpheniramine maleate 4 mg	Pseudoephedrine sulfate 60 mg	Lactose	1 tab q 4–6 hr (max 4 tabs/day)	6–12 yrs: ½ tab q 4–6 hr (max 2 tabs/day)	c, g

Table 1. Oral Dosage Forms *(continued)*

Note: Products containing phenylpropanolamine were removed from the U.S. and Canadian Markets in November 2000.
Content per capsule, tablet, or 5 mL, unless otherwise stated.

Brand or generic name [availability]	Antihistamines	Decongestants	Other content information as per product label	Usual adult and adolescent dose* prn	Usual pediatric dose prn	Packaging, storage, and auxiliary labeling†
Chlor-Trimeton 12 Hour Relief Extended-release Tablets (OTC) [U.S.]	Chlorpheniramine maleate 8 mg	Pseudoephedrine sulfate 120 mg	Lactose	1 tab q 12 hr (max 2 tabs/day)		c, g
Chlor-Trimeton Allergy-D 12 Hour Extended-release Tablets (OTC) [U.S.]	Chlorpheniramine maleate 8 mg	Pseudoephedrine sulfate 120 mg	Lactose	1 tab q 12 hr (max 2 tabs/day)		c, g
Claritin-D 12 Hour Extended-release Tablets (Rx) [U.S.]	Loratadine 5 mg	Pseudoephedrine sulfate 120 mg		1 tab q 12 hr (In renal function impairment [creatinine clearance <30 mL/min]: 1 tab q 24 hr)		d
Claritin-D 24 Hour Extended-release Tablets (Rx) [U.S.]	Loratadine 10 mg	Pseudoephedrine sulfate 240 mg		1 tab q 24 hr (In renal function impairment [creatinine clearance <30 mL/min]: 1 tab q 48 hr)		d
Claritin Extra Extended-release Tablets (OTC) [Canada]	Loratadine 5 mg	Pseudoephedrine sulfate 120 mg		1 tab q 12 hr		a
Colfed-A Extended-release Capsules (Rx) [U.S.]	Chlorpheniramine maleate 8 mg	Pseudoephedrine HCl 120 mg		1 cap q 12 hr		a, g
Comhist Tablets (Rx) [U.S.]	Chlorpheniramine maleate 2 mg, Phenyltoloxamine citrate 25 mg	Phenylephrine HCl 10 mg	Scored	1–2 tabs q 8 hr		a, g
CP Oral Oral Solution (Rx) [U.S.]	Carbinoxamine maleate 2 mg/mL	Pseudoephedrine HCl 25 mg/mL		Intended for pediatric use	1–3 mos: ¼ mL, 3–6 mos: ½ mL, 6–9 mos: ¾ mL, 9–18 mos: 1 mL, q 6 hr	a, e
Dallergy Jr. Extended-release Capsules (Rx) [U.S.]	Brompheniramine maleate 6 mg	Pseudoephedrine HCl 60 mg		2 caps q 12 hr (max 2 doses/day)	6–12 yrs: 1 cap q 12 hr (max 2 doses/day)	a, g
Deconamine Syrup (Rx) [U.S.]	Chlorpheniramine maleate 2 mg	Pseudoephedrine HCl 30 mg	Alcohol free Dye free	5–10 mL q 6–8 hr	2–6 yrs: 2.5 mL, 6–12 yrs: 2.5–5 mL, q 6–8 hr	b, g
Tablets (Rx) [U.S.]	Chlorpheniramine maleate 4 mg	Pseudoephedrine HCl 60 mg	Dye free Scored	1 tab q 6–8 hr	Not recommended See *Deconamine Syrup* and *Chewable Tablets*	b, g
Deconamine SR Extended-release Capsules (Rx) [U.S.]	Chlorpheniramine maleate 8 mg	Pseudoephedrine HCl 120 mg		1 cap q 12 hr	Not recommended See *Deconamine Syrup* and *Chewable Tablets*	b, g
Deconomed SR Extended-release Capsules (Rx) [U.S.]	Chlorpheniramine maleate 8 mg	Pseudoephedrine HCl 120 mg		1 cap q 12 hr		a, f, g

Table 1. Oral Dosage Forms *(continued)*

Note: Products containing phenylpropanolamine were removed from the U.S. and Canadian Markets in November 2000.
Content per capsule, tablet, or 5 mL, unless otherwise stated.

Brand or generic name [availability]	Antihistamines	Decongestants	Other content information as per product label	Usual adult and adolescent dose* prn	Usual pediatric dose prn	Packaging, storage, and auxiliary labeling†
Dexaphen SA Extended-release Tablets (Rx) [U.S.]	Dexbrompheniramine maleate 6 mg	Pseudoephedrine sulfate 120 mg		1 tab q 12 hr		a, g
Disobrom Extended-release Tablets (Rx) [U.S.]	Dexbrompheniramine maleate 6 mg	Pseudoephedrine sulfate 120 mg		1 tab q 12 hr		a, g
Disophrol Chronotabs Extended-release Tablets (OTC) [U.S.]	Dexbrompheniramine maleate 6 mg	Pseudoephedrine sulfate 120 mg	Sugar coated	1 tab q 12 hr (max 2 tabs/day)		c, g
Drixomed Extended-release Tablets (OTC) [U.S.]	Dexbrompheniramine maleate 6 mg	Pseudoephedrine sulfate 120 mg		1 tab q 12 hr (max 2 tabs/day)		c, f, g
Drixoral Extended-release Tablets (OTC) [Canada]	Dexbrompheniramine maleate 6 mg	Pseudoephedrine sulfate 120 mg	Sugar coated	1 tab q 8–12 hr		c, g
Drixoral Cold and Allergy Extended-release Tablets (OTC) [U.S.]	Dexbrompheniramine maleate 6 mg	Pseudoephedrine sulfate 120 mg	Lactose	1 tab q 12 hr (max 2 tabs/day)		c, g
Drixoral Night Tablets (OTC) [Canada]	Dexbrompheniramine maleate 2 mg	Pseudoephedrine sulfate 120 mg	Tartrazine free Available in a dual package that also contains *Drixoral N.D.*	1 tab hs		a, g
Drixtab Tablets (OTC) [Canada]	Dexbrompheniramine maleate 2 mg	Pseudoephedrine sulfate 60 mg	Tartrazine free	1 tab q 6–8 hr	6–12 yrs: ½ tab q 6–8 hr	a, g
Dura-Tap PD Extended-release Capsules (Rx) [U.S.]	Chlorpheniramine maleate 4 mg	Pseudoephedrine HCl 60 mg		2 caps q 12 hr	6–12 yrs: 1 cap q 12 hr	b, g
Ed A-Hist Oral Solution (Rx) [U.S.]	Chlorpheniramine maleate 4 mg	Phenylephrine HCl 10 mg	Alcohol 5%	5 mL q 6–8 hr	2–5 yrs: 1.25 mL, 6–12 yrs: 2.5 mL, q 6–8 hr	a, f, g
Extended-release Tablets (Rx) [U.S.]	Chlorpheniramine maleate 8 mg	Phenylephrine HCl 20 mg		1 tab q 12 hr		a, g
Hayfebrol Oral Solution (OTC) [U.S.]	Chlorpheniramine maleate 2 mg	Pseudoephedrine HCl 30 mg	Alcohol free Sugar free Dye free	10 mL q 6 hr	2–6 yrs: 2.5 mL, 6–12 yrs: 5 mL, q 6 hr	a, e, g
Histatab Plus Tablets (OTC) [U.S.]	Chlorpheniramine maleate 2 mg	Phenylephrine HCl 5 mg		2 tabs initially, then 1 tab q 4 hr		a, g
Iofed Extended-release Capsules (Rx) [U.S.]	Brompheniramine maleate 12 mg	Pseudoephedrine HCl 120 mg		1 cap q 12 hr		a, f, g
Iofed PD Extended-release Capsules (Rx) [U.S.]	Brompheniramine maleate 6 mg	Pseudoephedrine HCl 60 mg		1–2 caps q 12 hr	6–12 yrs: 1 cap q 12 hr	a, f, g
Kronofed-A Jr. Kronocaps Extended-release Capsules (Rx) [U.S.]	Chlorpheniramine maleate 4 mg	Pseudoephedrine HCl 60 mg	Dye free	1–2 caps q 12 hr	6–12 yrs: 1 cap q 12 hr	a, g
Kronofed-A Kronocaps Extended-release Capsules (Rx) [U.S.]	Chlorpheniramine maleate 8 mg	Pseudoephedrine HCl 120 mg	Dye free	1 cap q 12 hr		a, g

Table 1. Oral Dosage Forms *(continued)*

Note: Products containing phenylpropanolamine were removed from the U.S. and Canadian Markets in November 2000.

Content per capsule, tablet, or 5 mL, unless otherwise stated.

Brand or generic name [availability]	Antihistamines	Decongestants	Other content information as per product label	Usual adult and adolescent dose* prn	Usual pediatric dose prn	Packaging, storage, and auxiliary labeling†
Lodrane LD Extended-release Capsules (Rx) [U.S.]	Brompheniramine maleate 6 mg	Pseudoephedrine HCl 60 mg	Dye free	1–2 caps q 12 hr		a, g
Lodrane Liquid Oral Solution (Rx) [U.S.]	Brompheniramine maleate 4 mg	Pseudoephedrine HCl 60 mg	Dye free Sugar free Alcohol free		2–6 yrs: 1.25 mL 6–12 yrs: 2.5 mL ≥12 yrs: 5 mL q 4–6 hr	b, e, g
Mooredec Extended-release Tablets (Rx) [U.S.]	Carbinoxamine maleate 8 mg	Pseudoephedrine HCl 120 mg		1 tab q 12 hr		a, g
Nalex-A Extended-release Tablets (Rx) [U.S.]	Chlorpheniramine maleate 4 mg, Phenyltoloxamine citrate 40 mg	Phenylephrine HCl 20 mg	Lactose Scored	½–1 tab q 8–12 hr	6–12 yrs: ½ tab q 8–12 hr	a, f, g
ND Clear T.D. Extended-release Capsules (Rx) [U.S.]	Chlorpheniramine maleate 8 mg	Pseudoephedrine HCl 120 mg	Dye free	1 cap q 12 hr		a, g
Neo Citran A for Oral Solution (OTC) [Canada]	Pheniramine maleate 20 mg/pouch	Phenylephrine HCl 10 mg/pouch	Vitamin C 50 mg/pouch	1 pouch dissolved in 225 mL of hot water q 3–4 hr		a, g
Novafed A Extended-release Capsules (Rx) [U.S.]	Chlorpheniramine maleate 8 mg	Pseudoephedrine HCl 120 mg		1 cap q 12 hr		b, g
PediaCare Cold Formula Oral Solution (OTC) [U.S.]	Chlorpheniramine maleate 1 mg	Pseudoephedrine HCl 15 mg	Alcohol free Saccharin free	Intended for pediatric use	6–11 yrs: 10 mL q 4–6 hr	b, e, g
Poly Hist Forte Tablets (Rx) [U.S.]	Chlorpheniramine maleate 4 mg, Pyrilamine maleate 25 mg	Phenylephrine HCl 10 mg, HCl 50 mg		1 tab q 8–12 hr	6–12 yrs: ½ tab q 8–12 hr	b, f, g
Promethazine VC Phenylephrine HCl Syrup (Rx) [U.S.]	Promethazine HCl 6.25 mg	Phenylephrine HCl 5 mg	Alcohol 7%	5 mL q 4–6 hr	2–6 yrs: 1.25–2.5 mL, 6–12 yrs: 2.5–5 mL, q 4–6 hr	d, e, f, g
Promethazine VC Syrup (Rx) [U.S.]	Promethazine HCl 6.25 mg	Phenylephrine HCl 5 mg		5 mL q 4–6 hr (max 20 mL/day)	2–6 yrs: 1.25–2.5 mL, 6–12 yrs: 2.5–5 mL, q 4–6 hr	d, e, f, g
Prometh VC Syrup (Rx) [U.S.]	Promethazine HCl 6.25 mg	Phenylephrine HCl 5 mg	Alcohol 7%	5 mL q 4–6 hr (max 20 mL/day)	2–6 yrs: 1.25–2.5 mL, 6–12 yrs: 2.5–5 mL, q 4–6 hr	d, e, f, g
Pseudo-Chlor Extended-release Capsules (Rx) [U.S.]	Chlorpheniramine maleate 8 mg	Pseudoephedrine HCl 120 mg		1 cap q 12 hr		a, g
Rescon Extended-release Capsules (Rx) [U.S.]	Chlorpheniramine maleate 12 mg	Pseudoephedrine HCl 120 mg		1 cap q 12 hr		a, g
Rescon-ED Extended-release Capsules (Rx) [U.S.]	Chlorpheniramine maleate 8 mg	Pseudoephedrine HCl 120 mg		1 cap q 12 hr		a, g

Table 1. Oral Dosage Forms *(continued)*

Note: Products containing phenylpropanolamine were removed from the U.S. and Canadian Markets in November 2000.
Content per capsule, tablet, or 5 mL, unless otherwise stated.

Brand or generic name [availability]	Antihistamines	Decongestants	Other content information as per product label	Usual adult and adolescent dose* prn	Usual pediatric dose prn	Packaging, storage, and auxiliary labeling†
Rescon JR Extended-release Capsules (Rx) [U.S.]	Chlorpheniramine maleate 4 mg	Pseudoephedrine HCl 60 mg	Dye free	Intended for pediatric use	6–12 yrs: 1 cap q 12 hr	a, g
Respahist Extended-release Capsules (Rx) [U.S.]	Brompheniramine maleate 6 mg	Pseudoephedrine HCl 60 mg	Dye free	1–2 caps q 12 hr	6–12 yrs: 1 cap q 12 hr	a, f, g
Rhinosyn Oral Solution (OTC) [U.S.]	Chlorpheniramine maleate 4 mg	Pseudoephedrine HCl 60 mg	Alcohol 0.45%	5 mL q 4 hr		a, e, g
Rhinosyn-PD Oral Solution (OTC) [U.S.]	Chlorpheniramine maleate 2 mg	Pseudoephedrine HCl 30 mg	Alcohol 1.2%	10 mL q 4 hr		a, e, g
Rinade B.I.D. Extended-release Capsules (Rx) [U.S.]	Chlorpheniramine maleate 8 mg	Pseudoephedrine HCl 120 mg	Dye free	1 cap q 12 hr		a, g
Tablets (Rx) [U.S.]	Carbinoxamine maleate 4 mg	Pseudoephedrine HCl 60 mg		1 tab q 6 hr	6–12 yrs: 1 tab q 6 hr	a, g
Extended-release Tablets (Rx) [U.S.]	Carbinoxamine maleate 8 mg	Pseudoephedrine HCl 120 mg		1 tab q 12 hr		
Rondec Syrup (Rx) [U.S.]	Carbinoxamine maleate 4 mg	Pseudoephedrine HCl 60 mg	Alcohol free Sugar Free	5 mL q 6 hr	18 mos–6 yrs: 2.5 mL, 6–12 yrs: 5 mL, q 6 hr	a, e, g
Tablets (Rx) [U.S.]	Carbinoxamine maleate 4 mg	Pseudoephedrine HCl 60 mg	Film coated	1 tab q 6 hr	6–12 yrs: 1 tab q 6 hr	a, g
Rondec Chewable Chewable Tablets (Rx) [U.S.]	Brompheniramine maleate 4 mg	Pseudoephedrine HCl 60 mg	Aspartame	1 tab q 4 hr (max 6 tabs/day)	6-12 yrs: ½ tab q 4 hr (max 6 doses [3 tabs]/day)	a, g, j
Rondec Drops Oral Solution (Rx) [U.S.]	Carbinoxamine maleate 2 mg/mL	Pseudoephedrine HCl 25 mg/mL	Alcohol free	Intended for pediatric use	1–3 mos: ¼ mL, 3–6 mos: ½ mL, 6–9 mos: ¾ mL, 9–18 mos: 1 mL, q 6 hr	a, e, g
Rondec-TR Extended-release Tablets (Rx) [U.S.]	Carbinoxamine maleate 8 mg	Pseudoephedrine HCl 120 mg	Film coated	1 tab q 12 hr		a, g
R-Tannamine Tablets (Rx) [U.S.]	Chlorpheniramine tannate 8 mg, Pyrilamine tannate 25 mg	Phenylephrine tannate 25 mg		1–2 tabs q 12 hr		a, g
R-Tannamine Pediatric Oral Suspension (Rx) [U.S.]	Chlorpheniramine tannate 2 mg, Pyrilamine tannate 12.5 mg	Phenylephrine tannate 5 mg		Intended for pediatric use	2–6 yrs: 2.5–5 mL, 6–12 yrs: 5–10 mL, q 12 hr	a, e, g, i
R-Tannate Tablets (Rx) [U.S.]	Chlorpheniramine tannate 8 mg, Pyrilamine tannate 25 mg	Phenylephrine tannate 25 mg		1–2 tabs q 12 hr		a, g
Semprex-D Capsules (Rx) [U.S.]	Acrivastine 8 mg	Pseudoephedrine HCl 60 mg		1 cap q 4–6 hr (max 4 caps/day)		a, f, g
Silafed Syrup (OTC) [U.S.]	Triprolidine HCl 1.25 mg	Pseudoephedrine HCl 30 mg		10 mL q 4–6 hr (max 40 mL/day)	6–12 yrs: 5 mL q 4–6 hr (max 20 mL/day)	b, f, g

Table 1. Oral Dosage Forms *(continued)*

Note: Products containing phenylpropanolamine were removed from the U.S. and Canadian Markets in November 2000.
Content per capsule, tablet, or 5 mL, unless otherwise stated.

Brand or generic name [availability]	Antihistamines	Decongestants	Other content information as per product label	Usual adult and adolescent dose* prn	Usual pediatric dose prn	Packaging, storage, and auxiliary labeling†
Tanafed Oral Suspension (Rx) [U.S.]	Chlorpheniramine tannate 4.5 mg	Pseudoephedrine tannate 75 mg		10–20 mL q 12 hr	2–6 yrs: 2.5–5 mL (max 10 mL/day), 6–12 yrs: 5–10 mL (max 20 mL/day), q 12 hr	b, e, f, g, i
Trinalin Repetabs Extended-release Tablets (Rx) [U.S./Canada]	Azatadine maleate 1 mg	Pseudoephedrine sulfate 120 mg	Sugar coated	1 tab q 12 hr	Not recommended	c, g
Triotann Tablets (Rx) [U.S.]	Chlorpheniramine tannate 8 mg, Pyrilamine tannate 25 mg	Phenylephrine tannate 25 mg		1–2 tabs q 12 hr		a, g
Triotann Pediatric Oral Suspension (Rx) [U.S.]	Chlorpheniramine tannate 2 mg, Pyrilamine tannate 12.5 mg	Phenylephrine tannate 5 mg	Intended for pediatric use		2–6 yrs: 2.5–5 mL, 6–12 yrs: 5–10 mL, q 12 hr	a, e, g, i
Triotann-S Pediatric Oral Suspension (Rx) [U.S.]	Chlorpheniramine tannate 2 mg, Pyrilamine tannate 12.5 mg	Phenylephrine tannate 5 mg	Intended for pediatric use		2–6 yrs: 2.5–5 mL, 6–12 yrs: 5–10 mL, q 12 hr	a, e, g, i
Triprolidine HCl and Pseudoephedrine HCl Syrup USP (Rx) (OTC) [U.S.]	Triprolidine HCl 1.25 mg	Pseudoephedrine HCl 30 mg		10 mL q 4–6 hr (max 40 mL/day)	6–12 yrs: 5 mL q 4–6 hr	b, e, f, g
Tablets USP (Rx) (OTC) [U.S.]	Triprolidine HCl 2.5 mg	Pseudoephedrine HCl 60 mg		1 tab q 4–6 hr	6–12 yrs: ½ tab q 4–6 hr	b, f, g
Tri-Tannate Tablets (Rx) [U.S.]	Chlorpheniramine tannate 8 mg, Pyrilamine tannate 25 mg	Phenylephrine tannate 25 mg		1–2 tabs q 12 hr		a, g
ULTRAbrom Extended-release Capsules (Rx) [U.S.]	Brompheniramine maleate 12 mg	Pseudoephedrine HCl 120 mg		1 cap q 12 hr		a, g
ULTRAbrom PD Extended-release Capsules (Rx) [U.S.]	Brompheniramine maleate 6 mg	Pseudoephedrine HCl 60 mg		1–2 caps q 12 hr	6–12 yrs: 1 cap q 12 hr	a, g
Vasofrinic Oral Solution (OTC) [Canada]	Chlorpheniramine maleate 2 mg	Pseudoephedrine HCl 30 mg		5–10 mL q 6–8 hr	2–6 yrs: 2.5 mL, 6–12 yrs: 5 mL, q 6–8 hr	b, e, g
Zyrtec-D 12 Hour Extended-release Tablets (Rx) [U.S.]	Cetirizine hydrochloride, 5 mg,	Pseudoephedrine hydrochloride, 120 mg	Lactose	Adults and Children 12 years and older: 1 tablet twice daily		b

*Geriatric patients may be more sensitive to the effects of the usual adult dose.
†For appropriate *Packaging and storage* and *Auxiliary labeling* information refer to designated letters as follows:

a—Store below 40 °C (104 °F), preferably between 15 and 30 °C (59 and 86 °F), in a tight container, unless otherwise specified by manufacturer.
b—Store between 15 and 30 °C (59 and 86 °F), in a tight container, unless otherwise specified by manufacturer.
c—Store between 2 and 30 °C (36 and 86 °F), in a tight container, unless otherwise specified by manufacturer.
d—Store below 25 °C (77 °F), in a tight container, unless otherwise specified by manufacturer.
e—Protect from freezing.
f—Protect from light.
g—Auxiliary labeling:
• May cause drowsiness.
• Avoid alcoholic beverages.
h—Auxiliary labeling: • May be chewed.
i—Auxiliary labeling: • Shake well.
j—Color may change over time from pink to peach. This does not reflect any change in quality or potency of tablets.

ANTIHISTAMINES, DECONGESTANTS, AND ANALGESICS Systemic

NOTE: The *Antihistamines, Decongestants, and Analgesics (Systemic)* monograph is maintained on the *USP DI* electronic data base. A copy of the most recent revision of the complete monograph can be accessed on the *USP DI* Updates Online website. See the front cover of book for details on accessing the site.

For information on the specific components of this combination, see the *USP DI* monographs for *Acetaminophen (Systemic), Antihistamines (Systemic), Caffeine (Systemic), Phenylpropanolamine (Systemic), Pseudoephedrine (Systemic), Salicylates (Systemic),* and *Sympathomimetic Agents—Cardiovascular Use (Parenteral-Systemic).*

The information that follows is selectively abstracted from the complete monograph and is provided to facilitate drug use review and patient counseling.

Note: Products containing phenylpropanolamine were removed from the U.S. and Canadian Markets in November 2000.

This monograph includes information on the following: 1) Brompheniramine, Pseudoephedrine, and Acetaminophen; 2) Chlorpheniramine, Phenylephrine, and Acetaminophen; 3) Chlorpheniramine, Pseudoephedrine, and Acetaminophen; 4) Chlorpheniramine, Pyrilamine, Phenylephrine, and Acetaminophen; 5) Dexbrompheniramine, Pseudoephedrine, and Acetaminophen; 6) Diphenhydramine, Pseudoephedrine, and Acetaminophen; 7) Pheniramine, Phenylephrine, and Acetaminophen; 8) Pheniramine, Phenylephrine, Sodium Salicylate, and Caffeine; 9) Triprolidine, Pseudoephedrine, and Acetaminophen.

VA CLASSIFICATION (Primary): RE599

Note: Other combinations containing decongestants are found in *Antihistamines and Decongestants (Systemic), Antihistamines, Decongestants, and Anticholinergics (Systemic), Cough/Cold Combinations (Systemic),* and *Decongestants and Analgesics (Systemic).*

Commonly used brand name(s):

Note: For a listing of dosage forms and brand names by country availability, see *Dosage Forms* section(s).

Category

Antihistaminic (H_1-receptor)-decongestant-analgesic.

Indications

Accepted

Cold symptoms (treatment);
Congestion, nasal (treatment); and
Congestion, sinus (treatment)—Antihistamine, decongestant, and analgesic combinations are indicated for the temporary relief of nasal and sinus congestion and headaches, pains, and general discomfort due to colds, flu, or allergies. The antihistamine in these combinations may provide added relief of nasal congestion, rhinorrhea, and sneezing. It may also serve as an adjunct because of its anticholinergic drying effects.

The therapeutic effectiveness of oral phenylephrine as a nasal decongestant has been questioned, especially at the usual oral dose.

Note: In November 2000, the Food and Drug Administration (FDA) issued a public health warning regarding phenylpropanolamine (PPA) due to the risk of hemorrhagic stroke. The FDA, supported by the final report of The Hemorrhagic Stroke Project (HSP), requested that manufacturers voluntarily discontinue marketing products that contain PPA and that consumers work with their healthcare providers to select alternative products.

Patient Consultation

Note: Products containing phenylpropanolamine were removed from the U.S. and Canadian Markets in November 2000

As an aid to patient consultation, refer to Advice for the Patient, Antihistamines, Decongestants, and Analgesics (Systemic).

In providing consultation, consider emphasizing the following selected information (» = major clinical significance):

Before using this medication

» Conditions affecting use, especially:
Sensitivity to any of the medications in the combination being taken
Pregnancy—Concern for the fetus and/or newborn infant only with high doses and long-term therapy; use of aspirin-containing combinations not recommended during third trimester
Breast-feeding—Antihistamines may cause excitement or irritability in nursing infant; high risk for infants from sympathomimetic amines; also, concern with high doses and chronic use because of high salicylate intake by infant
Use in children—Increased susceptibility to anticholinergic effects of antihistamines and to vasopressor effects of sympathomimetic amines; hyperexcitability (paradoxical reaction) may occur; also, increased susceptibility to toxic effects of salicylates, especially if fever and dehydration present; possible association between aspirin usage and Reye's syndrome
Use in adolescents—Possible association between aspirin usage and Reye's syndrome
Use in the elderly—Anticholinergic and CNS stimulant effects more likely to occur; increased susceptibility to toxic effects of salicylates
Other medications, especially anticholinergics, medicine for high blood pressure or depression, or CNS depressants or stimulants
Other medical problems, especially alcoholism, cardiovascular disease, diabetes, gastritis or peptic ulcer (with salicylate-containing), hypertension, hyperthyroidism, or prostatic hypertrophy

Proper use of this medication

» Importance of not taking more medication than the amount recommended
Taking with food, water, or milk to minimize gastric irritation
Swallowing extended-release dosage form whole
» Not taking combinations containing aspirin if a strong vinegar-like odor is present
» Proper dosing
Missed dose: If on scheduled dosing regimen—Taking as soon as possible; not taking if almost time for next dose; not doubling doses
» Proper storage

Precautions while using this medication

Caution if skin tests using allergens required; possible interference with test results
Checking with physician if symptoms persist or become worse, or if high fever is present
» Avoiding alcoholic beverages or other CNS depressants while taking these medications; also, alcohol consumption may increase risk of salicylate-induced gastrointestinal toxicity and acetaminophen-induced liver toxicity
» Caution if drowsiness or dizziness occurs
» Possible insomnia; taking the medication a few hours before bedtime
» Caution if taking appetite suppressants
Need to inform physician or dentist of use of medication if any kind of surgery (including dental surgery) or emergency treatment is required
Possible dryness of mouth; using sugarless gum or candy, ice, or saliva substitute for relief; checking with dentist if dry mouth continues for more than 2 weeks
» Caution if other medications containing acetaminophen, aspirin, or other salicylates (including diflunisal) are used
» Suspected overdose: Getting emergency help at once
Not taking products containing aspirin for 5 days prior to any kind of surgery, unless otherwise directed by physician
Diabetics: Aspirin present in some combination formulations may cause false urine sugar test results with prolonged use of 8 or more 325-mg (5-grain) doses per day

Side/adverse effects

Signs of potential side effects, especially allergic reactions, anticholinergic effects, blood dyscrasias, jaundice (with acetaminophen-containing), and signs of gastrointestinal irritation or bleeding (with salicylate-containing)

ANTIHISTAMINES, DECONGESTANTS, AND ANALGESICS

Oral Dosage Forms

Note: Products containing phenylpropanolamine were removed from the U.S. and Canadian Markets in November 2000

See *Table 1,* page 359.

Strength(s) usually available

U.S.—
See *Table 1,* page 359.

Revised: 05/30/2002

Table 1. Oral Dosage Forms

Note: Content per capsule, tablet, or 5 mL, unless otherwise stated.

Brand or generic name [availability]	Antihistamines	Decongestants	Analgesics	Other content information as per product label	Usual adult and adolescent dose* (prn)	Usual pediatric dose (prn)	Packaging, storage, and auxiliary labeling†
Actifed Cold & Sinus Caplets Tablets (OTC) [U.S.]	Chlorpheniramine Maleate 2 mg	Pseudoephedrine HCl 30 mg	Acetaminophen 500 mg		2 tabs q 6 hr (max 8 tabs/day)	Not recommended	a, d
Actifed Plus Extra Strength Caplets Tablets (OTC) [Canada]	Triprolidine HCl 2.5 mg	Pseudoephedrine HCl 60 mg	Acetaminophen 500 mg	Scored	1 tab q 4–6 hr (max 4 tabs/day)		a, d
Alka-Seltzer Plus Cold Medicine Liqui-Gels Capsules (OTC) [U.S.]	Chlorpheniramine maleate 2 mg	Pseudoephedrine HCl 30 mg	Acetaminophen 500 mg		a, d		
Benadryl Allergy/ Sinus Headache Caplets Tablets (OTC) [U.S.]	Diphenhydramine HCl 12.5 mg	Pseudoephedrine HCl 30 mg	Acetaminophen 500 mg		2 tabs q 6 hr (max 8 tabs/day)		a, d
Children's Tylenol Cold Multi-Symptom Oral Solution (OTC) [U.S.]	Chlorpheniramine maleate 1 mg	Pseudoephedrine HCl 15 mg	Acetaminophen 160 mg	Sorbitol Alcohol free	Intended for pediatric use	2–5 yrs: 5 mL, 6–11 yrs: 10 mL, q 4–6 hr (max 4 doses/day)	a, c, d
Chewable Tablets (OTC) [U.S.]	Chlorpheniramine maleate 0.5 mg	Pseudoephedrine HCl 7.5 mg	Acetaminophen 80 mg	Phenylalanine 4 mg Scored	Intended for pediatric use	2–5 yrs: 2 tabs, 6–11 yrs: 4 tabs, q 4–6 hr (max 4 doses/day)	a, d
Comtrex Allergy-Sinus Tablets (OTC) [U.S.]	Chlorpheniramine maleate 2 mg	Pseudoephedrine HCl 30 mg	Acetaminophen 500 mg	Coated	2 tabs q 6 hr (max 8 tabs/day)		a, d
Comtrex Allergy-Sinus Caplets Tablets (OTC) [U.S.]	Chlorpheniramine maleate 2 mg	Pseudoephedrine HCl 30 mg	Acetaminophen 500 mg	Coated	2 tabs q 6 hr (max 8 tabs/day)		a, d
Contac Allergy/ Sinus Night Caplets Tablets (OTC) [U.S.]	Diphenhydramine HCl 50 mg	Pseudoephedrine HCl 60 mg	Acetaminophen 650 mg	In dual package that also contains *Contac Allergy/Sinus Day Caplets*	1 tab q 6 hr (max 4 tabs/day of any combination of Day or Night Caplets)		a, d
Dimetapp Cold & Fever Suspension Oral Suspension (OTC) [U.S.]	Brompheniramine maleate 1 mg	Pseudoephedrine HCl 15 mg	Acetaminophen 160 mg		Intended for pediatric use	6–11 mos: 2.5 mL, 12–23 mos: 5 mL, q 6–8 hr (max 4 doses/day); 2–6 yrs: 5 mL, 6–12 yrs: 10 mL, q 4 hr	a, c, d, e
Dristan Capsules (OTC) [Canada]	Chlorpheniramine maleate 2 mg	Phenylephrine HCl 5 mg	Acetaminophen 325 mg		2 caps or tabs q 4 hr (max 8 caps or tabs/day)	6–12 yrs: 1 cap or tab q 4 hr (max 4 caps or tabs/day)	a, d
Tablets (OTC) [Canada]							
Dristan Cold Multi-Symptom Formula Tablets (OTC) [U.S.]	Chlorpheniramine maleate 2 mg	Phenylephrine HCl 5 mg	Acetaminophen 325 mg		2 tabs q 4 hr		a, d
Dristan Extra Strength Caplets Tablets (OTC) [Canada]	Chlorpheniramine maleate 2 mg	Phenylephrine HCl 5 mg	Acetaminophen 500 mg		2 tabs q 4–6 hr (max 8 tabs/day)		a, d
Dristan Formula P Tablets (OTC) [Canada]	Pyrilamine maleate 12.5 mg	Phenylephrine HCl 5 mg	Aspirin 325 mg	Caffeine 16 mg Tartrazine-free	2 tabs q 4 hr	10–14 yrs: 1 tab q 4 hr	a, d

Table 1. Oral Dosage Forms *(continued)*

Note: Content per capsule, tablet, or 5 mL, unless otherwise stated.

Brand or generic name [availability]	Antihistamines	Decongestants	Analgesics	Other content information as per product label	Usual adult and adolescent dose* (prn)	Usual pediatric dose (prn)	Packaging, storage, and auxiliary labeling†
Drixoral Allergy-Sinus Extended-release Tablets (OTC) [U.S.]	Dexbrompheniramine maleate 3 mg	Pseudoephedrine sulfate 60 mg	Acetaminophen 500 mg		2 tabs q 12 hr		b, d
Drixoral Cold and Flu Extended-release Tablets (OTC) [U.S.]	Dexbrompheniramine maleate 3 mg	Pseudoephedrine sulfate 60 mg	Acetaminophen 500 mg		2 tabs q 12 hr		b, d
Kolephrin Caplets Tablets (OTC) [U.S.]	Chlorpheniramine maleate 2 mg	Pseudoephedrine HCl 30 mg	Acetaminophen 325 mg		2 tabs q 4–6 hr (max 8 tabs/day)	6–12 yrs: 1 tab q 4–6 hr (max 4 tabs/day)	a, d
ND-Gesic Tablets (OTC) [U.S.]	Chlorpheniramine maleate 1 mg, Pyrilamine maleate 8 mg Phenindemine tartrate 5 mg	Phenylephrine HCl 5 mg	Acetaminophen 300 mg	Sugar coated		a, d	
Neo Citran Nutrasweet for Oral Solution (OTC) [Canada]	Pheniramine maleate 20 mg per pouch	Phenylephrine HCl 10 mg per pouch	Acetaminophen 325 mg per pouch	Vitamin C 50 mg per pouch	1 pouch dissolved in 8 oz of hot water q 3–4 hr		a, d
Neo Citran Extra Strength Colds and Flu for Oral Solution (OTC) [Canada]	Pheniramine maleate 20 mg per pouch	Phenylephrine HCl 10 mg per pouch	Acetaminophen 600 mg per pouch	Vitamin C 50 mg per pouch	1 pouch dissolved in 8 oz of hot water q 3–4 hr		a, d
Scot-Tussin Original 5-Action Cold Formula Oral Solution (OTC) [U.S.]	Pheniramine maleate 13.3 mg	Phenylephrine HCl 4.2 mg	Sodium salicylate 83.3 mg	Caffeine citrate 25 mg; Sodium citrate 83.3 mg; Alcohol free; With or without sugar	5 mL q 3–4 hr (max 20 mL/day)	6–12 yrs: 2.5 mL q 3–4 hr	a, c, d
Sinarest Tablets (OTC) [U.S.]	Chlorpheniramine maleate 2 mg	Pseudoephedrine HCl 30 mg	Acetaminophen 325 mg		2 tabs q 4–6 hr (max 8 tabs/day)	6–12 yrs: 1 tab q 4–6 hr (max 4 tabs/day)	a
Sine-Off Sinus Medicine Caplets Tablets (OTC) [U.S.]	Chlorpheniramine maleate 2 mg	Pseudoephedrine HCl 30 mg	Acetaminophen 500 mg		2 tabs q 6 hr (max 8 tabs/day)		a, d
Singlet for Adults Tablets (OTC) [U.S.]	Chlorpheniramine maleate 4 mg	Pseudoephedrine HCl 60 mg	Acetaminophen 650 mg		1 tab q 6–8 hr (max 4 tabs/day)		a, d
Sinutab Extra Strength Caplets Tablets (OTC) [Canada]	Chlorpheniramine maleate 2 mg	Pseudoephedrine HCl 30 mg	Acetaminophen 500 mg		1–2 tabs q 4–6 hr (max 8 tabs/day)		a, d
Sinutab Regular Caplets Tablets (OTC) [Canada]	Chlorpheniramine maleate 2 mg	Pseudoephedrine HCl 30 mg	Acetaminophen 325 mg	Scored	2 tabs q 4–6 hr (max 8 tabs/day)	6–12 yrs: 1 tab q 4–6 hr (max 4 tabs/day)	a, d
TheraFlu/Flu and Cold Medicine for Oral Solution (OTC) [U.S.]	Chlorpheniramine maleate 4 mg per packet	Pseudoephedrine HCl 60 mg per packet	Acetaminophen 650 mg per packet		1 packet dissolved in 6-oz of hot water q 4 hr (max 4 doses/day)		a, d
TheraFlu/Flu and Cold Medicine for Sore Throat for Oral Solution (OTC) [U.S.]	Chlorpheniramine maleate 4 mg per packet	Pseudoephedrine HCl 60 mg per packet	Acetaminophen 1000 mg per packet		1 packet dissolved in 6-oz of hot water q 6 hr (max 4 doses/day)	Not recommended	a, d

Table 1. Oral Dosage Forms *(continued)*

Note: Content per capsule, tablet, or 5 mL, unless otherwise stated.

Brand or generic name [availability]	Antihistamines	Decongestants	Analgesics	Other content information as per product label	Usual adult and adolescent dose* (prn)	Usual pediatric dose (prn)	Packaging, storage, and auxiliary labeling†
Tylenol Allergy Sinus Medication Extra Strength Caplets Tablets (OTC) [Canada]	Chlorpheniramine maleate 2 mg	Pseudoephedrine HCl 30 mg	Acetaminophen 500 mg	Film-coated; Tartrazine-free	2 tabs q 6 hr (max 8 tabs/day)		a, d
Tylenol Allergy Sinus Medication Maximum Strength Caplets Tablets (OTC) [U.S.]	Chlorpheniramine maleate 2 mg	Pseudoephedrine HCl 30 mg	Acetaminophen 500 mg		2 tabs q 6 hr (max 8 tabs/day)	Not recommended	a, d
Tylenol Allergy Sinus Medication Maximum Strength Gelcaps Tablets (OTC) [U.S.]	Chlorpheniramine maleate 2 mg	Pseudoephedrine HCl 30 mg	Acetaminophen 500 mg		2 tabs q 6 hr (max 8 tabs/day)	Not recommended	a, d
Tylenol Allergy Sinus Medication Maximum Strength Geltabs Tablets (OTC) [U.S.]	Chlorpheniramine maleate 2 mg	Pseudoephedrine HCl 30 mg	Acetaminophen 500 mg		2 tabs q 6 hr (max 8 tabs/day)	Not recommended	a, d
Tylenol Allergy Sinus Night Time Medicine Maximum Strength Caplets Tablets (OTC) [U.S.]	Diphenhydramine HCl 25 mg	Pseudoephedrine HCl 30 mg	Acetaminophen 500 mg		2 tabs hs	Not recommended	a, d
Tylenol Cold Medication Children's Oral Solution (OTC) [Canada]	Chlorpheniramine maleate 1 mg	Pseudoephedrine HCl 15 mg	Acetaminophen 160 mg	Sorbitol; Alcohol-free	Intended for pediatric use	2–5 yrs: 5 mL, 6–12 yrs: 10 mL, q 4–6 hr (max 4 doses/day)	a, c, d
Chewable Tablets (OTC) [Canada]	Chlorpheniramine maleate 0.5 mg	Pseudoephedrine HCl 7.5 mg	Acetaminophen 80 mg	Phenylalanine; Scored	Intended for pediatric use	2–5 yrs: 2 tabs, 6–12 yrs: 4 tabs, q 4–6 hr (max 4 doses/day)	a, d
Tylenol Flu NightTime Medication Extra Strength Gelcaps Tablets (OTC) [Canada]	Diphenhydramine HCl 25 mg	Pseudoephedrine HCl 30 mg	Acetaminophen 500 mg		1–2 tabs q 6 hr (max 8 tabs/day)		a, d

*Geriatric patients may be more sensitive to the effects of usual adult dose.

†For appropriate *Packaging and storage* and *Auxiliary labeling* information refer to designated letters as follows:

a—Store below 40 °C (104 °F), preferably between 15 and 30 °C (59 and 86 °F), in a tight container, unless otherwise specified by manufacturer.
b—Store between 2 and 30 °C (36 and 86 °F), in a well-closed container, unless otherwise specified by manufacturer.
c—Protect from freezing.
d—Auxiliary labeling: • May cause drowsiness. • Avoid alcoholic beverages.
e—Auxiliary labeling: • Shake well.

ANTIHISTAMINES, DECONGESTANTS, AND ANTICHOLINERGICS Systemic

This monograph includes information on the following: 1) Chlorpheniramine, Phenylephrine, and Methscopolamine; 2) Chlorpheniramine, Pseudoephedrine, and Methscopolamine.

VA CLASSIFICATION (Primary): RE599

Note: For other combinations containing decongestants, see *Antihistamines and Decongestants (Systemic)*, *Antihistamines, Decongestants, and Analgesics (Systemic)*, *Cough/Cold Combinations (Systemic)*, and *Decongestants and Analgesics (Systemic)*.

Commonly used brand name(s):.

NOTE: The *Antihistamines, Decongestants, and Anticholinergics (Systemic)* monograph is maintained on the *USP DI* electronic data base. A copy of the most recent revision of the complete monograph can be accessed on the *USP DI* Updates Online website. See the front cover of book for details on accessing the site.

For information on the specific components of this combination, see the *USP DI* monographs for *Anticholinergics/Antispasmodics (Systemic)*, *Antihistamines (Systemic)*, *Phenylpropanolamine (Systemic)*, *Pseudoephedrine (Systemic)*, and *Sympathomimetic Agents—Cardiovascular Use (Systemic)*.

The information that follows is selectively abstracted from the complete monograph and is provided to facilitate drug use review and patient counseling.

Note: Products containing phenylpropanolamine were removed from the U.S. and Canadian Markets in November 2000

Note: For a listing of dosage forms and brand names by country availability, see *Dosage Forms* section(s).

Category

Antihistaminic (H_1-receptor)-decongestant-anticholinergic.

Indications

Accepted

Congestion, nasal (treatment)
Cold symptoms (treatment) and
Rhinitis, perennial and seasonal allergic or vasomotor (treatment)—Antihistamine, decongestant, and anticholinergic combinations are indicated in the symptomatic treatment of allergic rhinitis, sinusitis, and the common cold.

The therapeutic effectiveness of oral phenylephrine as a nasal decongestant has been questioned, especially at the usual oral dose.

Note: In November 2000, the Food and Drug Administration (FDA) issued a public health warning regarding phenylpropanolamine (PPA) due to the risk of hemorrhagic stroke. The FDA, supported by the final report of The Hemorrhagic Stroke Project (HSP), requested that manufacturers voluntarily discontinue marketing products that contain PPA and that consumers work with their healthcare providers to select alternative products.

Patient Consultation

As an aid to patient consultation, refer to *Advice for the Patient, Antihistamines, Decongestants, and Anticholinergics (Systemic)*.

Note: Products containing phenylpropanolamine were removed from the U.S. and Canadian Markets in November 2000.

In providing consultation, consider emphasizing the following selected information (» = major clinical significance):

Before using this medication

» Conditions affecting use, especially:

Sensitivity to any of the medications in the combination being taken

Pregnancy—In animal studies, pseudoephedrine caused reduced average weight, length, and rate of skeletal ossification in the fetus

Breast-feeding—Antihistamines may cause excitement or irritability in nursing infant; high risk to infants from sympathomimetic amines; possible inhibition of lactation

Use in children—Increased susceptibility to anticholinergic effects and to vasopressor effects; hyperexcitability (paradoxical reaction) may occur; increased response to anticholinergics in infants and children with spastic paralysis or brain damage; caution should be used in infants, especially newborn and premature infants, because of higher-than-usual risk of side/adverse effects of pseudoephedrine

Use in the elderly—Anticholinergic and CNS stimulant effects more likely to occur in older patients; danger of precipitating undiagnosed glaucoma; possible impairment of memory

Dental—Possible development of dental problems because of decreased salivary flow

Other medications, especially alcohol, other anticholinergics, beta-adrenergic blocking agents, CNS depressants or stimulants, cocaine, digitalis glycosides, medicine for high blood pressure or depression, monoamine oxidase (MAO) inhibitors, and potassium chloride

Other medical problems, especially cardiovascular disease, diabetes mellitus, hemorrhage, severe hypertension, hyperthyroidism, myasthenia gravis, obstruction in gastrointestinal or urinary tract, prostatic hypertrophy, tachycardia, urinary retention, and xerostomia

Proper use of this medication

» Importance of not taking more medication than the amount recommended

Taking with food, water, or milk to minimize gastric irritation

Swallowing extended-release dosage form whole

» Proper dosing

Missed dose: Taking as soon as possible; not taking if almost time for next dose; not doubling doses

» Proper storage

Precautions while using this medication

Checking with physician if symptoms persist or become worse, or if high fever is present

Caution if skin tests using allergens required; possible interference with test results

» Caution during exercise or hot weather; overheating may result in heat stroke

» Possible increased sensitivity of eyes to light

» Caution if blurred vision occurs

» Caution if drowsiness or dizziness occurs

» Possible insomnia; taking the medication a few hours before bedtime

» Caution if taking appetite suppressants

Need to inform physician or dentist of use of medication if any kind of surgery (including dental surgery or emergency treatment) is required

Possible dryness of mouth; using sugarless gum or candy, ice, or saliva substitute for relief; checking with dentist if dry mouth continues for more than 2 weeks

» Suspected overdose: Getting emergency help at once

Side/adverse effects

Signs of potential side effects, especially allergic reactions, severe anticholinergic effects, blood dyscrasias, CNS stimulation, severe drowsiness, hypertension, psychotic episodes, tightness in chest, convulsions, irregular or slow heartbeat, and shortness of breath or troubled breathing

ANTIHISTAMINES, DECONGESTANTS, AND ANTICHOLINERGICS

Oral Dosage Forms

Note: Products containing phenylpropanolamine were removed from the U.S. and Canadian Markets in November 2000.

See *Table 1* below.

Strength(s) usually available

U.S.—

See *Table 1* below.

Revised: 08/27/2002

Table 1. Oral Dosage Forms

Note: Content per capsule, tablet, or 5 mL, unless otherwise stated.

Brand or generic name [availability]	Antihistamines	Decongestants	Anticholinergics	Other information	Usual adult and adolescent dose* (prn)	Usual pediatric dose (prn)	Packaging, storage, and auxiliary labeling†
AH-chew Chewable Tablets (Rx) [U.S.]	Chlorpheniramine maleate 2 mg	Phenylephrine HCl 10 mg	Methscopolamine nitrate 1.25 mg	Scored	1–2 tabs q 4 hr	6–12 yrs: 1 tab q 4 hr	a, c, d
D.A. Chewable Chewable Tablets (Rx) [U.S.]	Chlorpheniramine maleate 2 mg	Phenylephrine HCl 10 mg	Methscopolamine nitrate 1.25 mg	Scored	1–2 tabs q 4 hr	6–12 yrs: 1 tab q 4 hr	a, c, d

Table 1. Oral Dosage Forms *(continued)*

Note: Content per capsule, tablet, or 5 mL, unless otherwise stated.

Brand or generic name [availability]	Antihistamines	Decongestants	Anticholinergics	Other information	Usual adult and adolescent dose* (prn)	Usual pediatric dose (prn)	Packaging, storage, and auxiliary labeling†
Dallergy Syrup (Rx) [U.S.]	Chlorpheniramine maleate 2 mg	Phenylephrine HCl 10 mg	Methscopolamine nitrate 0.625 mg		10 mL q 4–6 hr	6–12 yrs: 5 mL q 4–6 hr	a, b, d
Tablets (Rx) [U.S.]	Chlorpheniramine maleate 4 mg	Phenylephrine HCl 10 mg	Methscopolamine nitrate 1.25 mg	Scored	1 tab q 4–6 hr	6–12 yrs: ½ tab q 4–6 hr	a, d
Dura-Vent/DA Extended-release Tablets (Rx) [U.S.]	Chlorpheniramine maleate 8 mg	Phenylephrine HCl 20 mg	Methscopolamine nitrate 2.5 mg	Scored	1 tab q 12 hr	6–12 yrs: ½tab q 12 hr	a, d
Extendryl Syrup (Rx) [U.S.]	Chlorpheniramine maleate 2 mg	Phenylephrine HCl 10 mg	Methscopolamine nitrate 1.25 mg		10 mL q 4 hr	6–12 yrs: 5 mL q 4 hr	a, b, d
Chewable Tablets (Rx) [U.S.]	Chlorpheniramine maleate 2 mg	Phenylephrine HCl 10 mg	Methscopolamine nitrate 1.25 mg		2 tabs q 4 hr	6–12 yrs: 1 tab q 4 hr	a, c, d
Extendryl JR Extended-release Capsules (Rx) [U.S.]	Chlorpheniramine maleate 4 mg	Phenylephrine HCl 10 mg	Methscopolamine nitrate 1.25 mg		Intended for pediatric patients	6–12 yrs: 1 cap q 12 hr	a, d
Extendryl SR Extended-release Capsules (Rx) [U.S.]	Chlorpheniramine maleate 8 mg	Phenylephrine HCl 20 mg	Methscopolamine nitrate 2.5 mg		1 cap q 12 hr		a, d
Mescolor Extended-release Tablets (Rx) [U.S.]	Chlorpheniramine maleate 8 mg	Pseudoephedrine HCl 120 mg	Methscopolamine nitrate 2.5 mg	Scored Dye free	1 tab q 12 hr (max 2 tabs/ day)	6–12 yrs: ½ tab q 12 hr (max 1 tab/ day)	a,d
OMNIhist L.A. Extended-release Tablets (Rx) [U.S.]	Chlorpheniramine maleate 8 mg	Phenylephrine HCl 20 mg	Methscopolamine nitrate 2.5 mg	Scored	1 tab q 12 hr	6–12 yrs: ½ tab q 12 hr	a, d
Stahist Extended-release Tablets (Rx) [U.S.]	Chlorpheniramine maleate 8 mg	Phenylephrine HCl 25 mg Pseudoephedrine HCl 40 mg	Atropine sulfate 0.04 mg, Hyoscyamine sulfate 0.19 mg, Scopolamine HBr 0.01 mg	Scored Dye free		a, d	

*Geriatric patients may be more sensitive to the effects of usual adult dose.

†For appropriate *Packaging and storage* and *Auxiliary labeling* information refer to designated letters as follows:

a—Store below 40 °C (104 °F), preferably between 15 and 30 °C (59 and 86 °F), in a tight container, unless otherwise specified by manufacturer.
b—Protect from freezing.
c—May be chewed.
d—Auxiliary labeling: • May cause drowsiness. • Avoid alcoholic beverages.

ANTIHISTAMINES, PHENOTHIAZINE-DERIVATIVE
Systemic

Note: Products containing trimeprazine were withdrawn from the market by Allergan in July 1999

This monograph includes information on the following: 1) Methdilazine†; 2) Promethazine; 3) Trimeprazine.

INN: Trimeprazine—Alimemazine

VA CLASSIFICATION (Primary/Secondary):

Methdilazine—AH101
Promethazine—AH101/CN309; GA753
Trimeprazine—AH101

Commonly used brand name(s): *Anergan 25[2]; Anergan 50[2]; Antinaus 50[2]; Histantil[2]; Panectyl[3]; Pentazine[2]; Phenazine 25[2]; Phenazine 50[2]; Phencen-50[2]; Phenergan[2]; Phenergan Fortis[2]; Phenergan Plain[2]; Phenerzine[2]; Phenoject-50[2]; Pro-50[2]; Pro-Med 50[2]; Promacot[2]; Promet[2]; Prorex-25[2]; Prorex-50[2]; Prothazine[2]; Prothazine Plain[2]; Shogan[2]; Tacaryl[1]; V-Gan-25[2]; V-Gan-50[2]*.

Note: For a listing of dosage forms and brand names by country availability, see *Dosage Forms* section(s).

†Not commercially available in Canada.

Category

Antihistaminic (H_1-receptor)—Methdilazine; Promethazine; Trimeprazine.
Antiemetic—Promethazine.
Antivertigo agent—Promethazine.
Sedative-hypnotic—Promethazine; Trimeprazine.

Indications

Note: Products containing trimeprazine were voluntary withdrawn from the market by Allergan in July 1999

Accepted

Rhinitis, perennial and seasonal allergic or vasomotor (treatment) or
Conjunctivitis, allergic (treatment)—Antihistamines are indicated in the symptomatic treatment of perennial and seasonal allergic rhinitis, vasomotor rhinitis, and allergic conjunctivitis due to inhalant allergens and foods.

Pruritus (treatment)
Urticaria (treatment)
Angioedema (treatment)
Dermatographism (treatment) or
Transfusion reactions, urticarial (treatment)—Antihistamines are indicated for the symptomatic treatment of pruritus associated with allergic reactions and of mild, uncomplicated allergic skin manifestations of urticaria and angioedema, in dermatographism, and in urticaria associated with transfusions. Methdilazine is also indicated in the treatment of pruritus associated with pityriasis rosea.

Sneezing (treatment) or
Rhinorrhea (treatment)—Antihistamines are indicated for the relief of sneezing and rhinorrhea associated with the common cold. However, controlled clinical studies have not demonstrated that antihistamines are significantly more effective than placebo in relieving cold symptoms.

Anaphylactic or anaphylactoid reactions (treatment adjunct)—Antihistamines are indicated as adjunctive therapy to epinephrine and other standard measures for anaphylactic reactions after the acute manifestations have been controlled, and to ameliorate the allergic reactions to blood or plasma.

Motion sickness (prophylaxis and treatment) or
Vertigo (treatment)—Promethazine is indicated for the prevention and treatment of the nausea, vomiting, dizziness, or vertigo of motion sickness.

Nausea or vomiting (prophylaxis and treatment)—Promethazine is indicated in the control of nausea and vomiting associated with certain types of anesthesia and surgery.

Sedation—Promethazine and [trimeprazine][1] are indicated for preoperative and postoperative sedation in adults and children, obstetric sedation, and relief of apprehension and production of light sleep from which the patient can be easily aroused.

Pain, postoperative (treatment adjunct)—Promethazine is indicated as an adjunct to analgesics for control of postoperative pain.

Analgesia adjunct, during surgery
Anesthesia, general, adjunct or
Anesthesia, local, adjunct—Intravenous administration of promethazine is indicated in special surgical situations (such as repeated bronchoscopy, ophthalmic surgery, and poor-risk patients) in combination with reduced amounts of meperidine or other narcotic analgesics as an adjunct to anesthesia and analgesia.

Unaccepted

Antihistamines are contraindicated for use in the treatment of lower respiratory tract symptoms including asthma.

Antiemetics are not recommended for treatment of uncomplicated vomiting in pediatric patients. Their use should be limited to prolonged vomiting of known etiology.

---

[1]Not included in Canadian product labeling.

Pharmacology/Pharmacokinetics

Physicochemical characteristics

Chemical Group—Phenothiazine derivatives
Molecular weight—
Methdilazine hydrochloride: 332.89.
Promethazine hydrochloride: 320.88.
Trimeprazine tartrate: 746.98.
pKa—Promethazine: 9.1.

Mechanism of action/Effect

Antihistaminic (H_1-receptor)—Antihistamines used in the treatment of allergy act by competing with histamine for H_1-receptor sites on effector cells. They thereby prevent, but do not reverse, responses mediated by histamine alone. Antihistamines antagonize, in varying degrees, most of the pharmacological effects of histamine, including urticaria and pruritus. In addition, the anticholinergic actions of most antihistamines provide a drying effect on the nasal and oral mucosa.

Antiemetic; antivertigo—The mechanism by which some antihistamines exert their antiemetic, anti-motion sickness, and antivertigo effects is not precisely known but may be related to their central anticholinergic actions. They diminish vestibular stimulation and depress labyrinthine function. Activity on the medullary chemoreceptive trigger zone may also be involved in the antiemetic effect.

Sedative-hypnotic—Most antihistamines cross the blood-brain barrier and produce sedation due to inhibition of histamine *N*-methyltransferase and blockage of central histaminergic receptors. Antagonism of other central nervous system receptor sites, such as those for serotonin, acetylcholine, and alpha-adrenergic stimulation, may also be involved. Phenothiazines are thought to cause indirect reduction of stimuli to the brain stem reticular system.

Other actions/effects

Anticholinergic—Antihistamines prevent responses to acetylcholine that are mediated via muscarinic receptors.

Antiemetic—Methdilazine and trimeprazine also possess antiemetic properties. However, only promethazine is labeled for this indication.

Absorption

Well absorbed after oral administration.

Protein binding

Promethazine—High (65–90%).

Biotransformation

Hepatic; some renal.

Half-life

Elimination—Promethazine: 7 to 14 hours.

Onset of action

Oral—
15 to 60 minutes.
Parenteral—
Promethazine:
Intramuscular—20 minutes.
Intravenous—3 to 5 minutes.
Rectal—
Promethazine:
20 minutes.

Duration of action

Methdilazine—6 to 12 hours.

Promethazine—4 to 6 hours; may persist for up to 12 hours.

Trimeprazine—3 to 6 hours.

Elimination

Renal. Most of the antihistamines studied are excreted as metabolites within 24 hours.

Precautions to Consider

Cross-sensitivity and/or related problems

Patients sensitive to other phenothiazines may be sensitive to methdilazine, promethazine, and trimeprazine also.

Carcinogenicity/Tumorigenicity/Mutagenicity

Long-term animal studies to evaluate the carcinogenic, tumorigenic, or mutagenic potential of most antihistamines have not been performed.

Pregnancy/Reproduction

Pregnancy—Phenothiazines have been reported to cause jaundice and extrapyramidal symptoms in infants whose mothers received these medications during pregnancy.

For promethazine—

Adequate and well-controlled studies in humans have not been done. However, promethazine taken within 2 weeks prior to delivery may inhibit platelet aggregation in the newborn.

Studies in rats with doses 2.1 to 4.2 times the maximum recommended human daily dose have not shown that promethazine causes adverse effects on fetal development.

Promethazine should be used during pregnancy only if potential benefit justifies potential risk to the fetus.

FDA Pregnancy Category C.

Labor and delivery—For promethazine—May be used alone or as an adjunct to narcotic analgesics during labor. Labor and delivery data for promethazine is limited but does not show an appreciable effect on duration of labor nor an increased risk of need for intervention in the newborn. Effects on later newborn growth and development is unknown.

Breast-feeding

Small amounts of antihistamines may be distributed into breast milk; use is not recommended in nursing mothers because of the risk of adverse effects, such as unusual excitement or irritability, in infants.

Antihistamines may inhibit lactation because of their anticholinergic actions.

Some studies have indicated that the use of promethazine in children up to 2 years of age may be associated with the sudden infant death syndrome (SIDS) and an increase in sleep apnea, thus possibly increasing the risk to the nursing infant. Therefore, the use of phenothiazine-derivative antihistamines by nursing mothers should be discouraged until more studies have been performed to confirm the potential risk to the nursing infant.

Pediatrics

Use is not recommended in newborn or premature infants because this age group has an increased susceptibility to anticholinergic side effects, such as central nervous system (CNS) excitation, and an increased tendency toward convulsions.

A paradoxical reaction characterized by hyperexcitability may occur in children taking antihistamines.

The use of phenothiazine-derivative antihistamines is not recommended in infants up to 3 months of age, because of the possible absence or deficiency of detoxifying enzyme and inefficient renal function usually noted in this age group. Also, increased susceptibility to dystonias has been reported in newborn or premature infants, acutely ill or dehydrated children, and children with acute infections who have received phenothiazine medication.

Some studies have associated the use of promethazine with sudden infant death syndrome (SIDS) and with an increase in infant sleep apnea. Until more studies have been performed to confirm this potential risk, phenothiazine derivatives should not be used in children up to 2 years of age.

Post-marketing cases of respiratory depression, including fatalities, have been reported with use of promethazine in pediatric patients less than 2 years of age. A wide range of weight-based doses of promethazine have resulted in respiratory depression in these patients. Therefore, promethazine is **contraindicated** in pediatric patients less than 2 years of age. Promethazine should be used with caution in pediatric patients 2 years of age and older and the lowest effective dose be used.

In children with signs and symptoms suggestive of Reye's syndrome, phenothiazine-derivative antihistamines should not be used since the extrapyramidal symptoms that may occur, especially after parenteral administration of large doses, may be confused with the CNS signs of this syndrome, thus making diagnosis difficult.

Adolescents

In adolescents with signs and symptoms suggestive of Reye's syndrome, phenothiazine-derivative antihistamines should not be used since the extrapyramidal symptoms that may occur, especially after parenteral administration of large doses, may be confused with the CNS signs of this syndrome, thus making diagnosis difficult.

Geriatrics

Dizziness, sedation, confusion, and hypotension may be more likely to occur in geriatric patients taking antihistamines.

A paradoxical reaction characterized by hyperexcitability may occur in geriatric patients taking antihistamines.

Geriatric patients are especially susceptible to the anticholinergic side effects, such as dryness of the mouth and urinary retention (especially in males), of the antihistamines. If these side effects occur and continue or are severe, the medication should probably be discontinued.

Extrapyramidal signs, especially parkinsonism, akathisia, and persistent dyskinesia, may also be more likely to occur in geriatric patients, especially at the higher doses or with parenteral administration.

Dental

Prolonged use of antihistamines may decrease or inhibit salivary flow, especially in middle-aged or elderly patients, thus contributing to the development of caries, periodontal disease, oral candidiasis, and discomfort.

Involuntary orofacial muscle movement may result from extrapyramidal effects. These involuntary movements may result in occlusal adjustments, bite registrations, and treatment for bruxism being less reliable.

Drug interactions and/or related problems

The following drug interactions and/or related problems have been selected on the basis of their potential clinical significance (possible mechanism in parentheses where appropriate)—not necessarily inclusive (» = major clinical significance):

Note: Combination products containing any of the following medications, depending on the amount present, may also interact with this medication.

» Alcohol or
» CNS depression-producing medications, other (See *Appendix II*) or
» Respiratory depressants, other
(concurrent use may potentiate the CNS depressant effects of either these medications or antihistamines; also, concurrent use of maprotiline or tricyclic antidepressants may potentiate the anticholinergic effects of either antihistamines or these medications; concomitant use of promethazine with other respiratory depressants is associated with respiratory depression, and sometimes death, in pediatric patients; CNS depressants should be avoided or administered in reduced dosage to patients receiving promethazine)

Amphetamines
(concurrent use may decrease stimulant effects of amphetamines since phenothiazine derivatives produce alpha-adrenergic blockade)

» Anticholinergics or other medications with anticholinergic activity (See *Appendix II*)
(anticholinergic effects may be potentiated when these medications are used concurrently with antihistamines; patients should be advised to report occurrence of gastrointestinal problems promptly since paralytic ileus may occur with concurrent therapy)

Anticonvulsants, including barbiturates
(phenothiazine derivatives may lower the convulsion threshold; dosage adjustment of anticonvulsant medications may be necessary; potentiation of anticonvulsant effects does not occur)

Appetite suppressants
(concurrent use with phenothiazine derivatives may antagonize the anorectic effect of appetite suppressants)

Beta-adrenergic blocking agents, especially propranolol
(concurrent use with phenothiazine derivatives may result in increased plasma concentration of each medication because of inhibition of metabolism; this may result in additive hypotensive effects, irreversible retinopathy, cardiac arrhythmias, and tardive dyskinesia)

Bromocriptine
(concurrent use may increase serum prolactin concentrations and interfere with effects of bromocriptine; dosage adjustments of bromocriptine may be necessary)

Dopamine
(concurrent use may antagonize peripheral vasoconstriction produced by high doses of dopamine because of the alpha-adrenergic blocking action of phenothiazine derivatives)

Ephedrine or
Metaraminol or
Methoxamine
(alpha-adrenergic blocking action of phenothiazine derivatives may decrease the pressor response to these medications when used concurrently)

» Epinephrine
(alpha-adrenergic effects of epinephrine may be blocked when it is used concurrently with phenothiazine derivatives, possibly resulting in severe hypotension and tachycardia)

» Extrapyramidal reaction-causing medications, other (See *Appendix II*)
(concurrent use with phenothiazine derivatives may increase the severity and frequency of extrapyramidal effects)

Guanadrel or
Guanethidine
(neuronal uptake of these medications may be inhibited when they are used concurrently with phenothiazine derivatives, causing a decrease of their antihypertensive effect)

Hepatotoxic medications, other (See *Appendix II*)
(concurrent use of phenothiazine derivatives with other hepatotoxic medications may increase the potential for hepatotoxicity; patients, especially those on prolonged therapy or with a history of liver disease, should be carefully monitored)

Hypotension-producing medications, other (See *Appendix II*)
(concurrent use with phenothiazine derivatives may produce additive hypotensive effects)

» Levodopa
(antiparkinsonian effects of levodopa may be inhibited when used concurrently with phenothiazine derivatives because of blockade of dopamine receptors in the brain; levodopa has not been shown to be effective in phenothiazine-induced parkinsonism)

» Metrizamide, intrathecal
(concurrent use with phenothiazine derivatives may lower the seizure threshold; phenothiazine derivatives should be discontinued at least 48 hours before, and not resumed for at least 24 hours following, myelography)

» Monoamine oxidase (MAO) inhibitors, including furazolidone, procarbazine, and selegiline
(concurrent use of MAO inhibitors with antihistamines in general may prolong and intensify the anticholinergic and CNS depressant effects of antihistamines; concurrent use of MAO inhibitors with phenothiazine-derivative antihistamines may increase the risk of hypotension and extrapyramidal reactions; concurrent use is not recommended)

Ototoxic medications (See *Appendix II*)
(concurrent use with antihistamines may mask the symptoms of ototoxicity such as tinnitus, dizziness, or vertigo)

Quinidine
(concurrent use with phenothiazine-derivative antihistamines may result in additive cardiac effects)

Riboflavin
(requirements for riboflavin may be increased in patients receiving phenothiazine-derivative antihistamines)

Laboratory value alterations

The following have been selected on the basis of their potential clinical significance (possible effect in parentheses where appropriate)—not necessarily inclusive (» = major clinical significance).

With diagnostic test results

Glucose tolerance test
(an increase in glucose tolerance has been reported in patients receiving phenothiazine-derivative antihistamines)

Immunologic urine pregnancy tests
(may produce false-positive or false-negative results in patients receiving phenothiazine-derivative antihistamines, depending on the test used)

Skin tests using allergen extracts
(antihistamines may inhibit the cutaneous histamine response, thus producing false-negative results; it is recommended that antihistamines be discontinued at least 72 hours before testing begins)

Medical considerations/Contraindications

The medical considerations/contraindications included have been selected on the basis of their potential clinical significance (reasons given in parentheses where appropriate)—not necessarily inclusive (» = major clinical significance).

Except under special circumstances, this medication should not be used when the following medical problem exists:

» Comatose state or
» Hypersensitivity to phenothiazines
» Compromised respiratory function including:
» Chronic obstructive pulmonary disease or
» Sleep apnea
(promethazine use should be avoided in these patients due to the potential for respiratory depression, sometimes fatal, that is not directly related to individualized weight-based dosing which might otherwise permit safe administration.)

Risk-benefit should be considered when the following medical problems exist:

» Bladder neck obstruction or
» Prostatic hypertrophy, symptomatic or
» Urinary retention, predisposition to
(anticholinergic effects may precipitate or aggravate urinary retention)

Bone marrow depression
(increased risk of leukopenia and agranulocytosis)

Cardiovascular disease
(increased risk of transient hypotension)

» Encephalopathy or
» Reye's syndrome
(extrapyramidal symptoms that can occur secondary to promethazine administration may be confused with CNS signs of these undiagnosed primary diseases; promethazine use should be avoided in pediatric patients with signs and symptoms suggestive of Reye's syndrome or other hepatic diseases)

Epilepsy or
Seizure disorders
(administration of promethazine may lower seizure threshold and increase severity of seizures)

» Glaucoma, angle-closure or predisposition to
(mydriatic effect resulting in increased intraocular pressure may precipitate an attack of angle-closure glaucoma)

Glaucoma, narrow-angle or
Pyloroduodenal obstruction or
Stenosing peptic ulcer
(should be used with caution in these patients due to anticholinergic properties of antihistamines)

Glaucoma, open-angle
(mydriatic effect may cause a slight increase in intraocular pressure; glaucoma therapy may need to be adjusted)

Hepatic function impairment
(metabolism may be decreased; higher serum concentrations may increase sensitivity to CNS effects)

» Jaundice
(may be exacerbated with administration of promethazine)

Caution is recommended when phenothiazine-derivative antihistamines are used, since their antiemetic action may impede diagnosis of such conditions as appendicitis and obscure signs of toxicity from overdosage of other drugs.

Side/Adverse Effects

The following side/adverse effects have been selected on the basis of their potential clinical significance (possible signs and symptoms in parentheses where appropriate)—not necessarily inclusive:

Those indicating need for medical attention

Incidence less frequent or rare

Blood dyscrasias (sore throat; fever; unusual bleeding or bruising; unusual tiredness or weakness)

Incidence unknown

Agranulocytosis (cough or hoarseness; fever with or without chills; general feeling of tiredness or weakness; lower back or side pain; painful or difficult urination; sore throat; sores, ulcers, or white spots on lips or in mouth; unusual bleeding or bruising); ***angioneurotic edema*** (large, hive-like swelling on face, eyelids, lips, tongue, throat, hands, legs, feet, sex organs); ***apnea*** (bluish skin or lips; not breathing); ***bradycardia*** (chest pain or discomfort; lightheadedness, dizziness or fainting; shortness of breath; slow or irregular heartbeat; unusual tiredness); ***catatonic-like state*** (decreased awareness or responsiveness; mimicry of speech or movements; mutism; negativism; peculiar postures or movements, mannerisms or grimacing; severe sleepiness); ***convulsive seizures*** (convulsions; muscle spasm or jerking of all extremities; sudden loss of consciousness; loss of bladder control); ***disorientation*** (confusion about identity, place, and time); ***extrapyramidal symptoms*** (difficulty in speaking; drooling; loss of balance control; muscle trembling, jerking, or stiffness; restlessness; shuffling walk; stiffness of limbs; twisting movements of body; uncontrolled movements, especially of face, neck, and back); ***hallucinations*** (seeing, hearing, or feeling things that are not there); ***hysteria; increased blood pressure*** (headache; dizziness; weakness, numbness or tingling in arms or legs; trouble thinking, speaking or walking); ***jaundice*** (chills; clay-colored stools; dark urine; dizziness; fever; headache; itching; loss of appetite; nausea; abdominal or stomach pain; area rash; unpleasant breath odor; unusual tiredness or weakness; vomiting of blood; yellow eyes or skin); ***lassitude*** (unusual weak feeling; loss of strength or energy; muscle pain or weakness); ***leukopenia*** (black, tarry stools; chest pain; chills; cough; fever; painful or difficult urination; shortness of breath; sore throat; sores, ulcers, or white spots on lips or in mouth; swollen glands; unusual bleeding or bruising; unusual tiredness or weakness); ***neuroleptic malignant syndrome (NMS)*** (convulsions; difficulty in breathing; fast heartbeat; high fever; high or low blood pressure; increased sweating; loss of bladder control; severe muscle stiffness; unusually pale skin; tiredness); ***oculogyric crisis*** (fixed position of eye); ***respiratory depression*** (pale or blue lips, fingernails, or skin; difficult or troubled breathing; irregular, fast or slow, or shallow breathing; shortness of breath)—potentially fatal; ***thrombocytopenia*** (black, tarry stools; bleeding gums; blood in urine or stools; pinpoint red spots on skin; unusual bleeding or bruising); ***thrombocytopenic purpura*** (unusual bleeding or bruising; bloody nose; heavier menstrual periods; pinpoint red spots on skin; black, tarry stools; blood in urine; unusual tiredness or weakness; fever; skin rash); ***tinnitus*** (continuing ringing or buzzing or other unexplained noise in ears; hearing loss); ***tongue protrusion*** (sticking out of tongue); ***torticollis*** (uncontrolled twisting movements of neck); ***urticaria*** (hives or welts; itching; redness of skin; skin rash)

Note: *Neuroleptic malignant syndrome* is a potentially fatal symptom complex that has been reported with promethazine alone or in combination with antipsychotic drugs. Clinical manifestations include hyperpyrexia, muscle rigidity, altered mental status and evidence of autonomic instability. Diagnostic evaluation includes identifying cases where the clinical presentation includes both serious medical illness and untreated extrapyramidal signs and symptoms. Central anticholinergic toxicity, heat stroke, drug fever, and primary central nervous system pathology are other important considerations in differential diagnosis.

Those indicating need for medical attention only if they continue or are bothersome

Incidence more frequent

Drowsiness; thickening of mucus

Note: Sedative effects are more pronounced with promethazine and less pronounced with trimeprazine and methdilazine, in that order.

Incidence less frequent or rare

Blurred vision or any change in vision; burning or stinging of rectum—for promethazine rectal dosage form only; ***confusion***; ***difficult or painful urination; dizziness; dryness of mouth, nose, or throat; hypotension*** (feeling faint); ***increased sweating; loss of appetite; paradoxical reaction*** (nightmares; unusual excitement, nervousness, restlessness, or irritability); ***photosensitivity*** (increased sensitivity of skin to sun); ***ringing or buzzing in ears; skin rash; tachycardia*** (fast heartbeat)

Incidence not known

Asthma (cough; difficulty breathing; noisy breathing; shortness of breath; tightness in chest; wheezing); ***dermatitis*** (blistering, crusting, irritation, itching, or reddening of skin; cracked, dry, scaly skin; swelling); ***diplopia*** (double vision; seeing double); ***euphoria*** (false or unusual sense of well-being); ***faintness; excitation; faintness; fatigue*** (unusual tiredness or weakness); ***incoordination*** (lack of coordination); ***insomnia*** (sleeplessness; trouble sleeping; unable to sleep); ***nasal stuffiness; nausea; nervousness; sedation*** (drowsiness; sleepiness; relaxed and calm); ***somnolence*** (sleepiness or unusual drowsiness); ***tremors*** (shakiness); ***vomiting***

Note: *Confusion; difficult or painful urination; dizziness; drowsiness; and dryness of mouth, nose, or throat* are more likely to occur in the elderly.

Nightmares, unusual excitement, nervousness, restlessness, or irritability are more likely to occur in children and elderly patients.

Overdose

For specific information on the agents used in the management of phenothiazine-derivative antihistamines overdose, see:

- *Antidyskinetics (Systemic)* monograph;
- *Antihistamines (Systemic)* monograph;
- *Barbiturates (Systemic)* monograph; and/or
- *Ipecac (Oral-local)* monograph.

For more information on the management of overdose or unintentional ingestion, **contact a Poison Control Center** (see *Poison Control Center Listing*).

Clinical effects of overdose

The following effects have been selected on the basis of their potential clinical significance (possible signs and symptoms in parentheses where appropriate)—not necessarily inclusive:

Acute and chronic

Anticholinergic effects (clumsiness or unsteadiness; severe drowsiness; severe dryness of mouth, nose, or throat; flushing or redness of face; shortness of breath or troubled breathing); ***CNS depression*** (severe drowsiness); ***CNS stimulation*** (hallucinations; seizures; trouble in sleeping); ***extrapyramidal effects*** (muscle spasms, especially of neck and back; restlessness; shuffling walk; tic-like [jerky] movements of head and face; trembling and shaking of hands); ***hypotension, severe*** (feeling faint)

Note: *Anticholinergic* and *CNS stimulant* effects are more likely to occur in children with overdose. *Hypotension* may also occur in the elderly at usual doses.

Treatment of overdose

Since there is no specific antidote for overdose with antihistamines, treatment is symptomatic and supportive with possible utilization of the following:

To decrease absorption—

Induction of emesis (syrup of ipecac recommended); however, precaution against aspiration is necessary, especially in infants and children.

Gastric lavage (isotonic or 0.45% sodium chloride solution) if patient is unable to vomit within 3 hours of ingestion.

To enhance elimination—

Saline cathartics (milk of magnesia) are sometimes used.

Specific treatment—

Vasopressors to treat hypotension; however, epinephrine should not be used since it may further lower blood pressure.

Anticholinergic antiparkinson agents, diphenhydramine, or barbiturates, to control extrapyramidal reactions.

Precaution against use of stimulants (analeptic agents) because they may cause seizures.

Supportive care—

Oxygen and intravenous fluids.

Patient Consultation

Note: Products containing trimeprazine were voluntarily withdrawn from the market by Allergan in July 1999.

As an aid to patient consultation, refer to *Advice for the Patient, Antihistamines, Phenothiazine-derivative (Systemic)*.

In providing consultation, consider emphasizing the following selected information (» = major clinical significance):

Before using this medication

» Conditions affecting use, especially:

Hypersensitivity to the antihistamine used or to phenothiazine medications

Pregnancy—Not taking during the 2 weeks before delivery, to avoid possible inhibition of platelet aggregation in newborn; also, jaundice and extrapyramidal effects may occur in infant

Breast-feeding—Use not recommended; may cause unusual excitement or irritability in nursing infant; possible association with sudden infant death syndrome (SIDS) and sleep apnea

Use in children—Increased susceptibility to anticholinergic side effects in newborn or premature infants; hyperexcitability (paradoxical reaction) may occur in children; possible association with sudden infant death syndrome (SIDS) and sleep apnea; diagnosis of Reye's syndrome may be obscured if extrapyramidal effects occur; promethazine use **contraindicated** in children less than 2 years of age due to post-marketing cases of respiratory depression, including fatalities

Use in adolescents—Diagnosis of Reye's syndrome may be obscured if extrapyramidal effects occur

Use in the elderly—Increased susceptibility to CNS and anticholinergic side effects; hyperexcitability (paradoxical reaction) may occur; extrapyramidal symptoms more likely to occur

Dental—Increased risk of dental problems with prolonged use because of decrease or inhibition of salivary flow; involuntary orofacial muscle movements may result from extrapyramidal effects

Other medications, especially alcohol, other CNS depressants, or other respiratory depressants, anticholinergics, epinephrine, extrapyramidal reaction-causing medications, levodopa, MAO inhibitors, or metrizamide (intrathecal)

Other medical problems, especially comatose state, compromised respiratory function, chronic obstructive pulmonary disease, sleep apnea, bladder neck obstruction, prostatic hypertrophy, or urinary retention; encephalopathy, Reye's syndrome, angle-closure glaucoma (or predisposition to), jaundice (for parenteral promethazine)

Proper use of this medication

» Importance of not taking more medication than the amount recommended

» Proper dosing

Missed dose: If on scheduled dosing regimen—Using as soon as possible; not using if almost time for next dose; not doubling doses

» Proper storage

» Keeping out of reach of children

For oral dosage forms

Taking with food, water, or milk to minimize gastric irritation

Swallowing extended-release dosage forms whole

For injection dosage forms

Knowing correct administration technique for self-administration; checking with physician if necessary

For rectal dosage forms

Proper administration technique

For promethazine when used to prevent motion sickness

Taking 30 minutes to 1 hour before traveling

Precautions while using this medication

Possible interference with skin tests using allergens; need to inform physician of using medication

May mask ototoxic effects of large doses of salicylates

» Avoiding use of alcohol or other CNS depressants

» Caution if drowsiness occurs

Possible dryness of mouth; using sugarless gum or candy, ice, or saliva substitute for relief; checking with physician or dentist if dry mouth continues for more than 2 weeks

Need to inform physician of use: Possible interference with diagnosis of appendicitis; may mask signs of toxicity from overdosage of other drugs

Side/adverse effects

Signs of potential side effects, especially blood dyscrasias, agranulocytosis, angioneurotic edema, apnea, bradycardia, catatonic-like state, convulsive seizures, disorientation, extrapyramidal symptoms, hallucinations, hysteria, increased blood pressure, jaundice, lassitude, leukopenia, neuroleptic malignant syndrome (NMS), oculogyric crisis, respiratory depression, thrombocytopenia, thrombocytopenic purpura, tinnitus, tongue protrusion, torticollis, or urticaria

» Notifying physician immediately if symptoms of respiratory depression occur, especially pale or blue lips, fingernails, or skin; difficult or troubled breathing; irregular, fast or slow, or shallow breathing; shortness of breath

» Stopping medication and notifying physician immediately if symptoms of NMS appear, especially muscle rigidity, fever, difficult or fast breathing, seizures, fast heartbeat, increased sweating, loss of bladder control, unusually pale skin, unusual tiredness or weakness

General Dosing Information

For treatment of adverse events

Neuroleptic malignant syndrome (NMS)—
- Immediate discontinuation of phenothiazine
- Intensive symptomatic treatment and medical monitoring
- Treatment of any concomitant serious medical problems for which specific treatments are available
- Recurrences of NMS have been reported. Reintroduction of phenothiazine should be carefully considered.

For oral dosage forms only

Most antihistamines may be taken with food, water, or milk to lessen gastric irritation.

For parenteral dosage forms only

For promethazine—

The preferred route of administration is by deep intramuscular injection. Although intravenous administration is well tolerated, promethazine should not be administered in concentrations greater than 25 mg per mL and at a rate in excess of 25 mg per minute. Rapid intravenous administration of promethazine may produce a transient fall in blood pressure.

Intra-arterial administration is not recommended because of the possibility of severe arteriospasm and resultant gangrene; also, subcutaneous administration is not recommended, since chemical irritation has been noted and necrotic lesions have resulted on rare occasions.

METHDILAZINE

Summary of Differences

Indications: Used in the treatment of pruritus associated with pityriasis rosea.

Pharmacology/pharmacokinetics: Duration of action—6 to 12 hours.

Side/adverse effects: Least sedative effects.

Oral Dosage Forms

METHDILAZINE HYDROCHLORIDE SYRUP USP

Usual adult and adolescent dose

Antihistaminic (H_1-receptor)—

Oral, 8 mg every six to twelve hours as needed.

Usual pediatric dose

Antihistaminic (H_1-receptor)—

Children up to 3 years of age: Use is not recommended.

Children 3 to 12 years of age: Oral, 4 mg every six to twelve hours as needed.

Usual geriatric dose

See *Usual adult and adolescent dose.*

Note: Geriatric patients may be more sensitive to the effects of the usual adult dose.

Strength(s) usually available

U.S.—

4 mg per 5 mL (Rx) [*Tacaryl* (alcohol 7.37%)].

Canada—

Not commercially available.

Packaging and storage

Store below 40 °C (104 °F), preferably between 15 and 30 °C (59 and 86 °F), unless otherwise specified by manufacturer. Store in a tight, light-resistant container. Protect from freezing.

Auxiliary labeling

- May cause drowsiness.
- Avoid alcoholic beverages.

METHDILAZINE HYDROCHLORIDE TABLETS USP

Usual adult and adolescent dose

See *Methdilazine Hydrochloride Syrup USP.*

Usual pediatric dose

See *Methdilazine Hydrochloride Syrup USP.*

Usual geriatric dose

See *Usual adult and adolescent dose.*

Note: Geriatric patients may be more sensitive to the effects of the usual adult dose.

Strength(s) usually available

U.S.—

8 mg (Rx) [*Tacaryl* (scored)].

Canada—

Not commercially available.

Packaging and storage

Store below 40 °C (104 °F), preferably between 15 and 30 °C (59 and 86 °F), unless otherwise specified by manufacturer. Store in a tight, light-resistant container.

Auxiliary labeling

- May cause drowsiness.
- Avoid alcoholic beverages.

METHDILAZINE HYDROCHLORIDE TABLETS (CHEWABLE) USP

Usual adult and adolescent dose

See *Methdilazine Hydrochloride Syrup USP.*

Usual pediatric dose

See *Methdilazine Hydrochloride Syrup USP.*

Usual geriatric dose

See *Usual adult and adolescent dose.*

Note: Geriatric patients may be more sensitive to the effects of the usual adult dose.

Strength(s) usually available

U.S.—

4 mg (Rx) [*Tacaryl*].

Canada—

Not commercially available.

Packaging and storage

Store below 40 °C (104 °F), preferably between 15 and 30 °C (59 and 86 °F), unless otherwise specified by manufacturer. Store in a tight, light-resistant container.

Auxiliary labeling

- May cause drowsiness.
- Avoid alcoholic beverages.

PROMETHAZINE

Summary of Differences

Pharmacology/pharmacokinetics: Duration of action—Usually 4 to 6 hours.

Precautions: Use in children—Promethazine tablets and rectal suppositories **contraindicated** in children less than 2 years of age because of potential for fatal respiratory depression

Precautions: Medical considerations/contraindications—Caution needed in compromised respiratory function, epilepsy, jaundice, and Reye's syndrome.

Side/adverse effects: Most pronounced sedative effects; respiratory depression and neuroleptic malignant syndrome, both can be fatal

Oral Dosage Forms

PROMETHAZINE HYDROCHLORIDE SYRUP USP

Usual adult and adolescent dose

Antihistaminic (H_1-receptor)—

Oral, 10 to 12.5 mg four times a day before meals and at bedtime; or 25 mg at bedtime as needed.

Antiemetic—

Oral, 25 mg initially, then 10 to 25 mg every four to six hours as needed.

Antivertigo agent—

Oral, 25 mg two times a day as needed.

Note: For motion sickness, the initial 25-mg dose should be taken one-half to one hour before travel, and the dose repeated eight to twelve hours later, if necessary.

Sedative-hypnotic—
Oral, 25 to 50 mg for nighttime, presurgical, postsurgical, or obstetrical sedation.

Note: A 50-mg dose (with an equal amount of meperidine and an appropriate dose of an atropine-like drug) is used the night before surgery to relieve apprehension and produce sleep.

Usual adult prescribing limits
Up to 150 mg daily.

Usual pediatric dose
Children up to 2 years of age—
Use in **contraindicated** due to potential for respiratory depression, sometimes fatal.

Children 2 years of age and older—
Antihistaminic (H_1-receptor):
Oral, 125 mcg (0.125 mg) per kg of body weight or 3.75 mg per square meter of body surface every four to six hours, or 500 mcg per kg of body weight or 15 mg per square meter of body surface at bedtime as needed; or 5 to 12.5 mg three times a day or 25 mg at bedtime as needed.

Antiemetic:
Oral, 250 to 500 mcg (0.25 to 0.5 mg) per kg of body weight or 7.5 to 15 mg per square meter of body surface every four to six hours as needed; or 10 to 25 mg every four to six hours as needed.

Antivertigo agent:
Oral, 500 mcg (0.5 mg) per kg of body weight or 15 mg per square meter of body surface every twelve hours as needed; or 10 to 25 mg two times a day as needed.

Sedative-hypnotic:
Oral, 500 mcg (0.5 mg) to 1 mg per kg of body weight or 15 to 30 mg per square meter of body surface as needed; or 10 to 25 mg as needed.

Note: For preoperative sedation, children require doses of 1.1 mg per kg of body weight in combination with an equal dose of meperidine and the appropriate dose of an atropine-like drug.

For postoperative sedation, 10 to 25 mg may be used.

Usual geriatric dose
See *Usual adult and adolescent dose.*

Note: Geriatric patients may be more sensitive to the effects of the usual adult dose.

Strength(s) usually available
U.S.—
6.25 mg per 5 mL (Rx) [*Pentazine; Phenergan Plain* (alcohol 7%); *Prothazine Plain* (alcohol 7%); GENERIC].
25 mg per 5 mL (Rx) [*Phenergan Fortis* (alcohol 1.5%); GENERIC].

Canada—
10 mg per 5 mL (OTC) [*Phenergan* (alcohol 3%)].

Packaging and storage
Store below 40 °C (104 °F), preferably between 15 and 30 °C (59 and 86 °F), unless otherwise specified by manufacturer. Store in a tight, light-resistant container. Protect from freezing.

Auxiliary labeling
- May cause drowsiness. Be careful while driving or operating machinery. Use caution until you become familiar with its effects.
- Avoid alcoholic beverages.

PROMETHAZINE HYDROCHLORIDE TABLETS USP

Usual adult and adolescent dose
See *Promethazine Hydrochloride Syrup USP.*

Usual adult prescribing limits
Up to 150 mg daily.

Usual pediatric dose
See *Promethazine Hydrochloride Syrup USP.*

Usual geriatric dose
See *Usual adult and adolescent dose.*

Note: Geriatric patients may be more sensitive to the effects of the usual adult dose.

Strength(s) usually available
U.S.—
12.5 mg (Rx) [*Phenergan* (scored); GENERIC].
25 mg (Rx) [*Phenergan* (scored); *Promacot;* GENERIC].
50 mg (Rx) [*Phenergan;* GENERIC].

Canada—
10 mg (OTC) [*Phenergan* (scored)].
25 mg (OTC) [*Histantil* (film coated); *Phenergan* (film coated)].
50 mg (OTC) [*Histantil* (film coated); *Phenergan* (scored)].

Packaging and storage
Store below 40 °C (104 °F), preferably between 15 and 30 °C (59 and 86 °F), unless otherwise specified by manufacturer. Store in a tight, light-resistant container.

Auxiliary labeling
- May cause drowsiness. Be careful while driving or operating machinery. Use caution until you become familiar with its effects.
- Avoid alcoholic beverages.

Parenteral Dosage Forms

PROMETHAZINE HYDROCHLORIDE INJECTION USP

Usual adult and adolescent dose
Antihistaminic (H_1-receptor)—
Intramuscular or intravenous, 25 mg; may be repeated within two hours if necessary.

Antiemetic—
Intramuscular or intravenous, 12.5 to 25 mg every four hours as needed.

Sedative-hypnotic—
Intramuscular or intravenous, 25 to 50 mg for nighttime, presurgical, postsurgical, or obstetrical sedation.

Note: For preoperative and postoperative sedation, 25 to 50 mg of promethazine may be combined with appropriately reduced doses of analgesics and anticholinergics.

For obstetrical sedation, in the early stages of labor, 50 mg of promethazine will provide sedation and relief of apprehension. After labor is definitely established, 25 to 75 mg of promethazine may be administered with an appropriately reduced dose of an opioid analgesic, and may be repeated once or twice every four hours during the course of a normal labor.

Usual adult prescribing limits
Up to 150 mg daily.

Usual pediatric dose
Children up to 2 years of age—
Use is not recommended.

Children 2 years of age and older—
Antihistaminic (H_1-receptor):
Intramuscular, 125 mcg (0.125 mg) per kg of body weight or 3.75 mg per square meter of body surface every four to six hours or 500 mcg (0.5 mg) per kg of body weight or 15 mg per square meter of body surface at bedtime as needed; or 6.25 to 12.5 mg three times a day or 25 mg at bedtime as needed.

Antiemetic:
Intramuscular, 250 to 500 mcg (0.25 to 0.5 mg) per kg of body weight or 7.5 to 15 mg per square meter of body surface every four to six hours as needed; or 12.5 to 25 mg every four to six hours as needed.

Sedative-hypnotic:
Intramuscular, 500 mcg (0.5 mg) to 1 mg per kg of body weight as needed; or 12.5 to 25 mg as needed.

Note: For preoperative sedation, children require doses of 1.1 mg per kg of body weight in combination with an equal dose of meperidine and the appropriate dose of an atropine-like drug.

For postoperative sedation, 12.5 to 25 mg may be used.

Usual geriatric dose
See *Usual adult and adolescent dose.*

Note: Geriatric patients may be more sensitive to the effects of the usual adult dose.

Strength(s) usually available
U.S.—
25 mg per mL (Rx) [*Anergan 25; Phenazine 25; Phenergan; Prorex-25; Prothazine; Shogan; V-Gan-25;* GENERIC].
50 mg per mL (Rx) [*Anergan 50; Antinaus 50; Pentazine; Phenazine 50; Phencen-50; Phenergan; Phenerzine; Phenoject-50; Pro-50; Promacot; Pro-Med 50; Promet; Prorex-50; Prothazine; Shogan; V-Gan-50;* GENERIC].

Canada—
25 mg (base) per mL (Rx) [*Phenergan;* GENERIC].

Packaging and storage
Store below 40 °C (104 °F), preferably between 15 and 30 °C (59 and 86 °F), unless otherwise specified by manufacturer. Protect from light. Protect from freezing.

Stability
Do not use if discolored or if a precipitate is present.

Rectal Dosage Forms

PROMETHAZINE HYDROCHLORIDE SUPPOSITORIES USP

Usual adult and adolescent dose

Antihistaminic (H_1-receptor)—
Rectal, 25 mg; may be repeated in two hours if necessary.

Antiemetic—
Rectal, 25 mg initially, then 12.5 to 25 mg every four to six hours as needed.

Antivertigo agent—
Rectal, 25 mg two times a day as needed.

Sedative-hypnotic—
Rectal, 25 to 50 mg for nighttime, presurgical, postsurgical, or obstetrical sedation.

Note: A 50-mg dose (with an equal amount of meperidine and an appropriate dose of an atropine-like drug) is used the night before surgery to relieve apprehension and produce sleep.

Usual adult prescribing limits

Up to 150 mg daily.

Usual pediatric dose

Children up to 2 years of age—
Use in **contraindicated** due to potential for respiratory depression, sometimes fatal.

Children 2 years of age and older—
Antihistaminic (H_1-receptor):
Rectal, 125 mcg (0.125 mg) per kg of body weight or 3.75 mg per square meter of body surface every four to six hours, or 500 mcg (0.5 mg) per kg of body weight or 15 mg per square meter of body surface at bedtime as needed; or 6.25 to 12.5 mg three times a day or 25 mg at bedtime as needed.

Antiemetic:
Rectal, 250 to 500 mcg (0.25 to 0.5 mg) per kg of body weight or 7.5 to 15 mg per square meter of body surface every four to six hours as needed; or 12.5 to 25 mg every four to six hours as needed.

Antivertigo agent:
Rectal, 500 mcg (0.5 mg) per kg of body weight or 15 mg per square meter of body surface every twelve hours as needed; or 12.5 to 25 mg two times a day as needed.

Sedative-hypnotic:
Rectal, 500 mcg (0.5 mg) to 1 mg per kg of body weight or 15 to 30 mg per square meter of body surface as needed; or 12.5 to 25 mg as needed.

Note: For preoperative sedation, children require doses of 1.1 mg per kg of body weight in combination with an equal dose of meperidine and the appropriate dose of an atropine-like drug.
For postoperative sedation, 12.5 to 25 mg may be used.

Usual geriatric dose

See *Usual adult and adolescent dose.*

Note: Geriatric patients may be more sensitive to the effects of the usual adult dose.

Strength(s) usually available

U.S.—
12.5 mg (Rx) [*Phenergan*].
25 mg (Rx) [*Phenergan*].
50 mg (Rx) [*Phenergan;* GENERIC].

Canada—
Not commercially available.

Packaging and storage

Store between 2 and 8 °C (36 and 46 °F), in a tight, light-resistant container, unless otherwise specified by manufacturer.

Auxiliary labeling

- May cause drowsiness. Be careful while driving or operating machinery. Use caution until you become familiar with its effects.
- Avoid alcoholic beverages.

Note

Include patient instructions when dispensing.

Explain administration technique.

TRIMEPRAZINE

Summary of Differences

Pharmacology/pharmacokinetics: Duration of action—3 to 6 hours.

Oral Dosage Forms

Note: The dosing and strengths of the dosage forms available are expressed in terms of trimeprazine base (not the tartrate salt).

TRIMEPRAZINE TARTRATE EXTENDED-RELEASE CAPSULES

Strength(s) usually available

U.S.—

Note: Not commercially available

Canada—
Not commercially available.

Packaging and storage

Store below 40 °C (104 °F), preferably between 15 and 30 °C (59 and 86 °F), in a well-closed container, unless otherwise specified by manufacturer.

Auxiliary labeling

- May cause drowsiness.
- Avoid alcoholic beverages.

TRIMEPRAZINE TARTRATE SYRUP USP

Strength(s) usually available

U.S.—

Note: Not commercially available

Canada—
2.5 mg (base) per 5 mL (Rx) [*Panectyl* (alcohol 0.6%)].

Packaging and storage

Store below 40 °C (104 °F), preferably between 15 and 30 °C (59 and 86 °F), unless otherwise specified by manufacturer. Store in a tight, light-resistant container. Protect from freezing.

Auxiliary labeling

- May cause drowsiness.
- Avoid alcoholic beverages.

TRIMEPRAZINE TARTRATE TABLETS USP

Usual adult and adolescent dose

Antihistaminic (H_1-receptor)—
Oral, 2.5 mg (base) four times a day as needed.

Usual pediatric dose

Antihistaminic (H_1-receptor)—
Children up to 2 years of age: Use is not recommended.
Children 2 to 3 years of age: The available strength of the tablet may not conform to the recommended pediatric dosage. See *Trimeprazine Tartrate Syrup USP.*
Children 3 years of age and over: Oral, 2.5 mg (base) at bedtime or three times a day as needed.

Usual geriatric dose

See *Usual adult and adolescent dose.*

Note: Geriatric patients may be more sensitive to the effects of the usual adult dose.

Strength(s) usually available

U.S.—

Note: Not commercially available

Canada—
2.5 mg (base) (Rx) [*Panectyl*].
5 mg (base) (Rx) [*Panectyl*].

Packaging and storage

Store below 40 °C (104 °F), preferably between 15 and 30 °C (59 and 86 °F), unless otherwise specified by manufacturer. Store in a well-closed, light-resistant container.

Auxiliary labeling

- May cause drowsiness.
- Avoid alcoholic beverages.

Selected Bibliography

Simons FE, Simons KJ: H_1-receptor antagonist treatment of chronic rhinitis. J Allergy Clin Immunol 1988; 81: 975-80.

Simons FE, Simons KJ, Chung M, Yeh J. The comparative pharmacokinetics of H_1-receptor antagonists. Ann Allergy 1987 Dec; 59: 20-4.

Revised: 03/14/2005

ANTI-INFLAMMATORY DRUGS, NONSTEROIDAL Ophthalmic

This monograph includes information on the following: 1) Diclofenac; 2) Flurbiprofen; 3) Indomethacin*; 4) Suprofen†.

INN: Indomethacin—Indometacin

VA CLASSIFICATION (Primary/Secondary):
Diclofenac—OP302/OP900
Flurbiprofen—OP302/OP900
Indomethacin—OP302/OP900
Suprofen—OP900

Commonly used brand name(s): *Indocid*[3]; *Ocufen*[2]; *Profenal*[4]; *Voltaren Ophtha*[1]; *Voltaren Ophthalmic*[1].

Another commonly used name for indomethacin is indometacin.

Note: For a listing of dosage forms and brand names by country availability, see *Dosage Forms* section(s).

*Not commercially available in U.S.
†Not commercially available in Canada.

Category

Prostaglandin synthesis inhibitor, ophthalmic—Diclofenac; Flurbiprofen; Indomethacin; Suprofen.
Anti-inflammatory, nonsteroidal, ophthalmic—Diclofenac; Flurbiprofen; Indomethacin.
Miosis inhibitor, in ophthalmic surgery—Diclofenac; Flurbiprofen; Indomethacin; Suprofen

Indications

Note: Bracketed information in the *Indications* section refers to uses that are not included in U.S. product labeling.

Accepted

Inflammation, ocular (treatment)—Diclofenac is indicated to reduce postoperative inflammation following cataract surgery. [Diclofenac is also indicated in the treatment of conjunctivitis, keratoconjunctivitis, corneal ulcers, and posttraumatic inflammation of the cornea and conjunctiva, provided that these conditions are not associated with an ocular infection.] [Flurbiprofen] and indomethacin[1] are indicated to reduce inflammation of the anterior segment of the eye following ocular surgery or laser trabeculoplasty. However, flurbiprofen and indomethacin have produced inconsistent results in clinical studies and may not produce clinically significant reductions in postprocedure inflammation. In one study, these nonsteroidal anti-inflammatory drugs (NSAIDs) reduced conjunctival injection, but not the anterior chamber reaction, following argon laser trabeculoplasty.

Ophthalmic NSAIDs may be administered concurrently with an ophthalmic corticosteroid, if necessary. There is some evidence of a synergistic or additive effect when the two types of medication are used together.

Miosis, during ophthalmic surgery (prophylaxis)—[Diclofenac], flurbiprofen, indomethacin, and suprofen are indicated to inhibit intraoperative miosis, which may occur in response to surgical trauma despite preoperative establishment of mydriasis. These NSAIDs may facilitate cataract extraction and lens implantation. However, published clinical studies have shown small and variable effects on pupil size, and some investigators have reported flurbiprofen to be ineffective. Also, studies demonstrating that ophthalmic NSAIDs produce clinically significant inhibition of miosis in surgical procedures other than cataract surgery have not been published.

Use of ophthalmic NSAIDs to inhibit miosis during surgery does not eliminate the need for mydriatic agents prior to and during surgery.

Edema, cystoid macular, following cataract surgery (prophylaxis and treatment)—[Diclofenac] and indomethacin are indicated to reduce the occurrence and severity of cystoid macular edema following cataract surgery. These agents are usually used concurrently with an ophthalmic corticosteroid; clinical studies indicate that concurrent use of both types of medication provides a synergistic effect.

There is insufficient evidence to determine whether flurbiprofen or suprofen is effective in reducing cystoid macular edema following cataract surgery.

Photophobia, following incisional refractive surgery (treatment)—Diclofenac is indicated for the treatment of photophobia in patients who have undergone incisional refractive surgery.

[1]Not included in Canadian product labeling.

Pharmacology/Pharmacokinetics

Physicochemical characteristics

Chemical Group—
Anti-inflammatory drug, nonsteroidal (NSAID)—
Indoleacetic acid derivative—Indomethacin.
Phenylacetic acid derivative—Diclofenac.
Propionic acid derivatives—Flurbiprofen, suprofen.

Molecular weight—
Diclofenac sodium: 318.13.
Flurbiprofen sodium: 302.28.
Indomethacin: 357.79.
Suprofen: 260.31.

Mechanism of action/Effect

Ophthalmic NSAIDs inhibit the activity of the enzyme cyclo-oxygenase in ocular tissues, resulting in decreased formation of precursors of prostaglandins from arachidonic acid and subsequent inhibition of prostaglandin synthesis. These medications do not inhibit the actions of prostaglandins. Studies in animals have shown that trauma to the anterior segment of the eye, especially the iris, increases endogenous prostaglandin synthesis; that endogenous prostaglandins produce constriction of the iris sphincter independently of cholinergic mechanisms; and that endogenous prostaglandins may contribute to the development of intraocular inflammation by causing disruption of the blood–aqueous humor barrier, vasodilatation, increased vascular permeability, and leukocytosis. It is proposed that inhibition of prostaglandin synthesis in ocular tissues by ophthalmic NSAIDs decreases these effects, thereby reducing the severity of intraoperative miosis, signs and symptoms of postoperative inflammation, and postoperative cystoid macular edema (which may occur, independently of inflammation, because of prostaglandin-induced alterations in vascular permeability). Diclofenac and indomethacin have been shown to stabilize, or speed postoperative re-establishment of, the blood–aqueous humor barrier. However, the clinical consequences (benefit or harm) of this action in the treatment of postoperative inflammation have not been determined. Also, studies of flurbiprofen's or indomethacin's efficacy in reducing ocular inflammation following ophthalmic procedures have produced conflicting results. It is proposed that the anti-inflammatory activity of these medications may be limited, possibly because they do not inhibit the formation or activity of mediators of inflammation in the eye other than prostaglandins.

Other actions/effects

Clinical studies indicate that perioperative use of ophthalmic NSAIDs does not significantly affect intraocular pressure.

Ophthalmic NSAIDs may increase the risk of bleeding in ocular tissues following ophthalmic procedures; postoperative bleeding, including hyphema, has been documented with flurbiprofen.

Studies in animals have shown that ophthalmic flurbiprofen may delay wound healing following certain types of surgery. Diclofenac also may slow or delay healing postoperatively. However, ophthalmic suprofen did not delay wound healing in a study in animals.

The anti-inflammatory activity of ophthalmic NSAIDs may mask the onset and/or progression of ocular infections.

Absorption

Diclofenac—Studies suggest that limited, if any, systemic absorption occurs after a single application of up to 16 drops of a 0.1% solution.

Flurbiprofen—Flurbiprofen penetrates the cornea; significant systemic absorption may occur. In one study, 74% of the quantity of flurbiprofen applied to the conjunctiva appeared in the systemic circulation.

Indomethacin—The medication has not been detected in serum after ophthalmic administration. However, the possibility of significant systemic absorption must be considered, because a bronchospastic reaction has been reported in one asthmatic patient following ophthalmic administration of the medication.

Suprofen—No data regarding the extent of systemic absorption following ophthalmic application are available.

Precautions to Consider

Cross-sensitivity and/or related problems

Patients sensitive to aspirin or other systemically administered nonsteroidal anti-inflammatory drugs (NSAIDs) may be sensitive to ophthalmic NSAIDs also.

Carcinogenicity

Diclofenac—No evidence of carcinogenicity was found in long-term studies in rats or mice receiving up to 2 mg per kg of body weight (mg/kg) per day orally.

Flurbiprofen—No evidence of carcinogenicity was found in a 24-month study in rats receiving up to 4 mg/kg per day, a second 24-month study in rats receiving 12 mg/kg per day for 32 weeks followed by 5 mg/kg per day thereafter, or an 80-week study in mice receiving up to 12 mg/kg per day orally.

Indomethacin—No evidence of carcinogenicity was found in long-term studies in rats or mice receiving up to 1.5 mg/kg per day orally.

Suprofen—No evidence of carcinogenicity was found in long-term studies in rats or mice receiving up to 40 mg/kg per day orally.

Tumorigenicity

Diclofenac—A slight increase in the occurrence of benign mammary fibroadenomas was found in female rats, but the increase was not significant for this common rat tumor. No other evidence of tumorigenicity was found in rats receiving up to 2 mg/kg per day orally.

Flurbiprofen—No evidence of tumorigenicity was found in a 2-year study in rats receiving up to 12 mg/kg per day for 32 weeks, followed by up to 5 mg/kg per day orally for the remainder of the study period.

Indomethacin—No evidence of tumorigenicity was found in an 81-week study in rats receiving up to 1 mg/kg per day orally.

Suprofen—An increased incidence of benign hepatomas occurred in female mice receiving 40 mg/kg per day and in male mice receiving 2 mg/kg per day or more orally.

Mutagenicity

Diclofenac—No mutagenic activity was found in *in vitro* tests using mammalian cells or bacteria (with or without microsomal activation) or in various *in vivo* tests.

Flurbiprofen—Long-term mutagenicity studies have not been performed.

Indomethacin—No mutagenic activity was found in *in vitro* tests (Ames test or *E. coli*, with or without metabolic activation) or in *in vivo* tests (host-mediated assay, sex-linked recessive lethals in *Drosophila*, and micronucleus test in mice).

Suprofen—No mutagenic activity was found in the Ames, micronucleus, and dominant lethal tests.

Pregnancy/Reproduction

Fertility—*Diclofenac*: No impairment of fertility was found in reproduction studies in rats receiving up to 4 mg/kg per day orally.

Flurbiprofen: No impairment of fertility was found in reproduction studies in rats receiving up to 4 mg/kg per day orally.

Indomethacin: No impairment of fertility was found in a two-generation reproduction study in rats or in a two-litter reproduction study in rats receiving up to 0.5 mg/kg per day orally.

Suprofen: No impairment of fertility was found in reproduction studies in rats receiving up to 40 mg/kg per day. However, a slight reduction in fertility was found in rats receiving 80 mg/kg per day orally. Testicular atrophy and hypoplasia occurred in a 6-month study in dogs receiving 80 mg/kg per day and a 12-month study in rats receiving 40 mg/kg per day orally.

Pregnancy—Adequate and well-controlled studies with ophthalmic NSAIDs have not been performed in pregnant women. However, use of ophthalmic NSAIDs late in pregnancy is not recommended because oral NSAIDs caused premature closure of the ductus arteriosus in animal studies.

First trimester—

Diclofenac:

Diclofenac readily crosses the placenta.

No teratogenicity occurred in reproduction studies in mice receiving up to 20 mg/kg per day orally and in rats and rabbits receiving up to 10 mg/kg per day orally. However, maternal toxicity and embryotoxicity (reduced fetal weights and growth, reduced fetal survival) occurred in studies in rats receiving 2 or 4 mg/kg per day. Also, increases in resorption rates, decreased fetal weight, abnormal skeletal findings, and definite embryotoxicity occurred in studies in rabbits receiving 5 or 10 mg/kg per day orally.

FDA Pregnancy Category B.

Flurbiprofen:

Flurbiprofen crosses the placenta.

No teratogenicity occurred in reproduction studies in mice receiving up to 12 mg/kg per day, rats receiving up to 25 mg/kg per day, or rabbits receiving up to 7.5 mg/kg per day, orally. However, studies in rats have shown doses of 0.4 mg/kg per day or higher to be embryotoxic or embryocidal (causing reduced weight or slower fetal growth, increased stillbirths, and decreased pup survival). Also, stillbirths, retained fetuses, and/or fetal distress occurred in studies in rats receiving as little as 0.2 mg/kg per day. In addition, fetotoxicity related to maternal toxicity (gastrointestinal ulceration, retardation of weight gain, intrauterine hemorrhage, and maternal deaths) occurred in rats receiving 25 mg/kg per day from Days 1 through 20 of pregnancy. With lower doses (0.2, 0.675, or 2.25 mg/kg per day), such effects did not occur when the medication was discontinued on Day 17 of pregnancy. Maternal deaths due to gastrointestinal ulceration also occurred in rabbits receiving the medication.

FDA Pregnancy Category C.

Indomethacin:

Indomethacin crosses the placenta.

Studies in rats and mice have shown that indomethacin in doses of 4 mg/kg per day orally causes retarded ossification secondary to decreased average fetal weight. In other studies in mice, higher doses (5 to 15 mg/kg per day orally) caused maternal toxicity and death, increased fetal resorptions, and fetal malformations. Doses lower than 4 mg/kg per day produced no adverse effects in these studies.

Suprofen:

Studies in rats receiving 40 mg/kg or more per day, and rabbits receiving 80 mg/kg or more per day, orally have shown that suprofen causes an increased incidence of fetal resorption associated with maternal toxicity. In rats receiving 2.5 mg/kg or more per day orally, there was an increase in stillbirths and a decrease in pup survival.

FDA Pregnancy Category C.

Third trimester—

Diclofenac:

Studies in animals have shown that maternally toxic doses, administered orally, are associated with prolonged gestation and dystocia.

Flurbiprofen:

Studies in rats have shown that administration of 0.4 mg/kg or more per day orally causes prolonged gestation and delayed parturition.

Indomethacin:

Studies in rats and mice have shown that administration of 4 mg/kg per day orally during the last 3 days of gestation is associated with an increased incidence of neuronal necrosis in the diencephalon and some maternal and fetal deaths. Indomethacin also caused a slight delay in the onset of parturition in rats, but not in rabbits.

Suprofen:

Studies in rats have shown that suprofen causes a delay in parturition.

Breast-feeding

Although it is not known whether NSAIDs are distributed into breast milk after ophthalmic administration, it is known that orally administered diclofenac, indomethacin, and suprofen are distributed into human breast milk. It is not known whether orally administered flurbiprofen is distributed into breast milk. However, problems in humans have not been documented with any of these medications.

Pediatrics

Appropriate studies on the relationship of age to the effects of ophthalmic NSAIDs have not been performed in the pediatric population. Safety and efficacy have not been established.

Geriatrics

Studies performed to date have not demonstrated geriatrics-specific problems that would limit the usefulness of ophthalmic NSAIDs in the elderly.

Drug interactions and/or related problems

The following drug interactions and/or related problems have been selected on the basis of their potential clinical significance (possible mechanism in parentheses where appropriate)—not necessarily inclusive (» = major clinical significance):

Note: Combinations containing any of the following medications, depending on the amount present, may also interact with this medication.

Acetylcholine chloride or
Carbachol
(these medications may be less effective when administered after an ophthalmic NSAID has been used to inhibit miosis during ocular surgery; although the pharmacologic basis for the interaction has not been established, it has been suggested that NSAID-induced maintenance of a larger pupillary diameter during surgery, and the possibility that the duration of action of the NSAID may exceed that of acetylcholine chloride, may account for the apparent reduction in the ability of acetylcholine chloride to reverse mydriasis postoperatively)

Any medication that may interfere with blood clotting or prolong bleeding time, such as:
Anticoagulants, coumarin- or indandione-derivative or
Heparin or
Platelet aggregation inhibitors
(concurrent use with ophthalmic NSAIDs, which may also increase the bleeding tendency, may increase the risk of postoperative ocular bleeding)

Epinephrine (ophthalmic) and possibly other antiglaucoma agents
(the possibility should be considered that ophthalmic flurbiprofen may decrease the intraocular pressure-lowering effects of these medications; however, in one study, administration of ophthalmic flurbiprofen [1 drop every 10 minutes for 4 doses] had no effect on the intraocular pressure-lowering effect of 1% apraclonidine or 0.5% timolol)

Medical considerations/Contraindications

The medical considerations/contraindications included have been selected on the basis of their potential clinical significance (reasons given in parentheses where appropriate)—not necessarily inclusive (» = major clinical significance).

Risk-benefit should be considered when the following medical problems exist:

» Allergic reaction, such as anaphylaxis, bronchospasm, angioedema, allergic rhinitis, or urticaria, to aspirin or other systemic NSAIDs, history of
(possibility of cross-sensitivity)

Epithelial herpes simplex keratitis, active
(in one study in rabbits, ophthalmic flurbiprofen exacerbated herpes simplex keratitis [i.e., increased ulceration and conjunctivitis] and delayed healing; however, in another study in rabbits, neither flurbiprofen nor diclofenac exacerbated or prolonged acute herpes keratitis or prolonged viral shedding; although the risk of exacerbation or delayed healing of active epithelial herpes simplex keratitis in humans has not been determined, it is recommended that ophthalmic NSAIDs be administered with caution and in conjunction with an antiviral agent)

(suprofen is contraindicated in patients with active herpes simplex keratitis)

Epithelial herpes simplex keratitis, history of
(close monitoring of the patient following flurbiprofen administration is recommended because the risk of reactivation has not been determined)

(close monitoring of the patient following suprofen administration is recommended)

Hemophilia or other bleeding problems or coagulation defects or
Prolonged bleeding time
(increased risk of bleeding)

» Sensitivity to the ophthalmic NSAID considered for use

Soft contact lenses, use of
(wearing hydrogel soft contact lenses while using diclofenac is contraindicated because ocular irritation, such as redness and burning of the eye, may occur)

Side/Adverse Effects

Note: Oral administration of suprofen has caused acute flank pain and renal insufficiency, possibly manifestations of acute uric acid nephropathy. This reaction has occurred after ingestion of as few as 1 or 2 doses of 200 mg, > 25 times more than the total quantity of suprofen that would be administered over 2 days with recommended ophthalmic doses. The risk of such a reaction occurring after ophthalmic administration is unknown.

Keratitis, elevated intraocular pressure, corneal edema, chemosis, and anterior chamber reaction have also been reported with various ophthalmic nonsteroidal anti-inflammatory drugs (NSAIDs). Since these effects frequently occur following some types of ophthalmic procedures, a causal relationship has not been established.

The following side/adverse effects have been selected on the basis of their potential clinical significance (possible signs and symptoms in parentheses where appropriate)—not necessarily inclusive:

Those indicating need for medical attention

Incidence less frequent or rare

For diclofenac
Allergic reaction (itching; tearing)—in a patient hypersensitive to systemic NSAIDs; ***corneal opacity*** (blurred vision or other change in vision); ***discharge, ocular*** (sticky or matted eyelashes); ***facial edema*** (swelling of face); ***fever or chills; iritis*** (throbbing pain; tearing; sensitivity to light); ***nausea or vomiting; pain***

For flurbiprofen; ***Bleeding in eye; redness in eye***—not resulting from surgery and not present before use; ***fibrosis***

For indomethacin; ***Bronchospastic allergic reaction*** (shortness of breath; troubled breathing; tightness in chest; wheezing)—reported in an asthmatic patient; ***corneal epithelial defects, including corneal abrasion and punctate keratitis; redness in eye***—not resulting from surgery and not present before use; ***striate keratopathy***

For suprofen; ***Iritis*** (throbbing pain; tearing; sensitivity to light); ***punctate epithelial staining***

Note: *Eye pain* and *photophobia* have also been reported independently of iritis.

Those indicating need for medical attention only if they continue or are bothersome

Incidence more frequent
Dry eye; irritation, ocular (burning; stinging; itching; mild discomfort)

Incidence less frequent or rare
Asthenia (unusual weakness); ***headache; insomnia; miosis*** (smaller pupils [black part of eye]); ***mydriasis*** (bigger pupils [black part of eye]); ***rhinitis*** (runny or stuffy nose)

Overdose

For more information on the management of overdose or unintentional ingestion, **contact a Poison Control Center** (see *Poison Control Center Listing*).

Treatment of overdose

Recommended treatment in case of accidental ingestion consists of drinking large quantities of fluids to dilute the medication.

Patient Consultation

As an aid to patient consultation, refer to *Advice for the Patient, Anti-inflammatory Drugs, Nonsteroidal (Ophthalmic)*.

In providing consultation, consider emphasizing the following selected information (» = major clinical significance):

Before using this medication

» Conditions affecting use, especially:
Sensitivity to aspirin or other systemic nonsteroidal anti-inflammatory drugs (NSAIDs), or to the ophthalmic NSAID considered for use
Pregnancy—Diclofenac, flurbiprofen, and indomethacin known to cross the placenta when administered systemically
Breast-feeding—Indomethacin and suprofen known to be distributed into breast milk after oral administration

Proper use of this medication

Proper administration technique
Preventing contamination: Not touching dropper or applicator tip to any surface and keeping container tightly closed
» Importance of not using more medication than the amount prescribed
» Checking with physician before using medication for future eye problems
Proper dosing
Missed dose: Using as soon as possible; not using if almost time for next dose
» Proper storage

Precautions while using this medication

» For diclofenac: Not wearing soft contact lenses during treatment

Side/adverse effects

Signs of potential side effects, especially allergic reaction; corneal opacity; ocular discharge; facial edema; fever or chills; iritis; nausea or vomiting; pain, bleeding or redness in the eye; fibrosis; bronchospastic allergic reaction; corneal epithelial defects, including corneal abrasion, and punctate keratitis; striate keratopathy; and punctate epithelial staining.

General Dosing Information

When an ophthalmic nonsteroidal anti-inflammatory drug (NSAID) is used to prevent or reduce postoperative inflammation and/or cystoid macular edema, therapy should be started prior to the procedure. Ophthalmic NSAIDs are more effective in inhibiting the development of these complications than in treating them after they have fully developed.

DICLOFENAC

Additional Dosing Information

It is recommended that patients not wear hydrogel soft contact lenses during diclofenac therapy. Ocular irritation manifested by redness and burning has occurred in patients wearing this type of contact lens while using the medication.

Ophthalmic Dosage Forms

Note: Bracketed uses in the *Dosage Forms* section refer to categories of use and/or indications that are not included in U.S. product labeling.

DICLOFENAC SODIUM OPHTHALMIC SOLUTION

Usual adult dose

Anti-inflammatory, nonsteroidal, ophthalmic—

Treatment of inflammation following cataract surgery: Topical, to the conjunctiva, 1 drop in the affected eye four times a day, starting twenty-four hours postoperatively and continuing for the first two postoperative weeks. In some patients, treatment has been continued for six weeks or longer.

[Treatment of conjunctivitis, keratoconjunctivitis, corneal ulcers, or post-traumatic inflammation]: Topical, to the conjunctiva, 1 drop in the affected eye four to five times a day, depending on the severity of the disease.

[Miosis inhibitor, in ophthalmic surgery] or
[Prostaglandin synthesis inhibitor, ophthalmic]—

Prevention or reduction of intraoperative miosis and postoperative cystoid macular edema: Topical, to the conjunctiva, 1 drop in the affected eye, applied up to five times during the three hours prior to surgery; fifteen minutes, thirty minutes, and forty-five minutes postoperatively; then three to five times a day for as long as needed.

Photophobia, in incisional refractive surgery—

Topical, to the conjunctiva, 1 drop in the affected eye within one hour prior to surgery, then 1 drop within fifteen minutes after surgery, then 1 drop four times a day beginning four to six hours after surgery and continuing for up to three days as needed.

Usual pediatric dose

Safety and efficacy have not been established.

Strength(s) usually available

U.S.—

0.1% (1 mg per mL) (Rx) [*Voltaren Ophthalmic* (boric acid; edetate disodium 1 mg per mL; polyoxyl 35 castor oil; sorbic acid 2 mg per mL; tromethamine)].

Canada—

0.1% (1 mg per mL) (Rx) [*Voltaren Ophtha* (boric acid; cremophor EL; edetate disodium; sorbic acid; tromethamine [TRIS])].

Packaging and storage

Store between 15 and 30 °C (59 and 86 °F), protected from light and from freezing, unless otherwise directed by manufacturer.

Auxiliary labeling

- For the eye.

Note

Dispense in original unopened container.

FLURBIPROFEN

Ophthalmic Dosage Forms

Note: Bracketed uses in the *Dosage Forms* section refer to categories of use and/or indications that are not included in U.S. product labeling.

FLURBIPROFEN SODIUM OPHTHALMIC SOLUTION USP

Usual adult dose

Miosis inhibitor, in ophthalmic surgery—

Topical, to the conjunctiva, 1 drop every thirty minutes, beginning two hours prior to surgery, for a total of 4 drops.

[Anti-inflammatory, nonsteroidal, ophthalmic]—

Treatment of inflammation following ophthalmic surgery or laser trabeculoplasty: Topical, to the conjunctiva, 1 drop every four hours for one to three weeks.

Usual pediatric dose

Safety and efficacy have not been established.

Strength(s) usually available

U.S.—

0.03% (Rx) [*Ocufen* (polyvinyl alcohol 1.4%; edetate disodium; thimerosal 0.005%; potassium chloride; sodium chloride; sodium citrate; citric acid; hydrochloric acid and/or sodium hydroxide); GENERIC].

Canada—

0.03% (Rx) [*Ocufen* (citric acid; edetate disodium; hydrochloric acid and/or sodium hydroxide; polyvinyl alcohol; potassium chloride; sodium chloride; sodium citrate; thimerosal)].

Packaging and storage

Store below 40 °C (104 °F), preferably between 15 and 30 °C (59 and 86 °F), unless otherwise specified by manufacturer. Store in a tight container. Protect from freezing.

Auxiliary labeling

- For the eye.

Note

Dispense in original unopened container.

INDOMETHACIN

Additional Dosing Information

Because an ophthalmic dosage form of indomethacin is not commercially available in the U.S., ophthalmic preparations are being compounded extemporaneously in some pharmacies. Eye injuries resulting from *Pseudomonas* contamination have occurred following use of such preparations. Pharmacists are advised **not** to use the contents of commercially available indomethacin capsules in the preparation of ophthalmic indomethacin solutions or suspensions, because of a lack of data on stability, concentration, and possible effects of excipients. Also, the sterility of compounded preparations must be assured.

Ophthalmic Dosage Forms

INDOMETHACIN OPHTHALMIC SUSPENSION

Usual adult dose

Prostaglandin synthesis inhibitor, ophthalmic or
Miosis inhibitor, in cataract surgery—

Prevention or reduction of intraoperative miosis and postoperative cystoid macular edema: Topical, to the conjunctiva, 1 drop four times a day on the day prior to surgery, 1 drop forty-five minutes before surgery, then 1 drop four times a day for ten to twelve weeks postoperatively or as long as needed.

Usual pediatric dose

Safety and efficacy have not been established.

Strength(s) usually available

U.S.—

Not commercially available.

Canada—

1% (10 mg per mL) (Rx) [*Indocid* (lecithin; sodium bisulfite; sodium chloride; polysorbate 80; hydroxyethylcellulose; sorbitol; disodium edetate; benzalkonium chloride solution 0.02%; benzyl alcohol 0.25%; phenylethyl alcohol 0.25%)].

Packaging and storage

Store between 15 and 30 °C (59 and 86 °F), protected from light and from freezing, unless otherwise specified by manufacturer.

Auxiliary labeling

- For the eye.
- Shake well before using.

Note

Dispense in original unopened container.

SUPROFEN

Ophthalmic Dosage Forms

SUPROFEN OPHTHALMIC SOLUTION USP

Usual adult dose

Miosis inhibitor, in ophthalmic surgery—

Topical, to the conjunctiva, 2 drops three, two, and one hour prior to surgery. If desired, 2 drops may be applied every four hours while the patient is awake on the day prior to surgery.

Usual pediatric dose

Safety and efficacy have not been established.

Strength(s) usually available

U.S.—

1% (10 mg per mL) (Rx) [*Profenal* (thimerosal 0.005%; caffeine 2%; edetate disodium; dibasic sodium phosphate; monobasic sodium phosphate; sodium chloride; sodium hydroxide and/or hydrochloric acid)].

Canada—

Not commercially available.

Packaging and storage

Store below 40 °C (104 °F), preferably between 15 and 30 °C (59 and 86 °F), protected from freezing, unless otherwise directed by manufacturer.

Auxiliary labeling

- For the eye.

Note

Dispense in original unopened container.

Selected Bibliography

Keates RH, McGowan KA. Clinical trial of flurbiprofen to maintain pupillary dilation during cataract surgery. Ann Ophthalmol 1984; 16: 919-21.

Heinrichs DA, Leith AB. Effect of flurbiprofen on the maintenance of pupillary dilation during cataract surgery. Can J Ophthalmol 1990; 25: 239-42.

Stark WJ, Fagadau WR, Stewart RH, et al. Reduction of pupillary constriction during cataract surgery using suprofen. Arch Ophthalmol 1986; 104: 364-6.

Flach AJ. Cyclo-oxygenase inhibitors in ophthalmology. Surv Ophthalmol 1992; 36: 259-84.

Revised: 09/10/1998

ANTI-INFLAMMATORY DRUGS, NONSTEROIDAL Systemic

This monograph includes information on the following: 1) Diclofenac; 2) Diflunisal; 3) Etodolac†; 4) Fenoprofen; 5) Floctafenine*; 6) Flurbiprofen; 7) Ibuprofen; 8) Indomethacin; 9) Ketoprofen; 10) Meclofenamate†; 11) Mefenamic Acid; 12) Meloxicam; 13) Nabumetone; 14) Naproxen; 15) Oxaprozin; 16) Phenylbutazone; 17) Piroxicam; 18) Sulindac; 19) Tenoxicam*; 20) Tiaprofenic Acid*; 21) Tolmetin.

Note: See also individual *Ketorolac (Systemic)* monograph.

See also individual *Meloxicam (Systemic)* monograph.

See also *Indomethacin—For Patent Ductus Arteriosus (Systemic)* monograph.

See also *Anti-inflammatory Agents, Nonsteroidal (Ophthalmic)* monograph for information on ophthalmic use of diclofenac, flurbiprofen, and indomethacin.

See also *Salicylates (Systemic)* monograph for information on aspirin and other salicylates.

INN:

Etodolac—Etodolic acid.
Indomethacin—Indometacin.
Meclofenamate—Meclofenamic acid.

BAN: Meclofenamate—Meclofenamic acid.

JAN: Indomethacin—Indometacin.

VA CLASSIFICATION (Primary/Secondary):

Diclofenac—MS102/CN104; MS400; CN105
Diflunisal—MS102/CN104; MS400; CN105
Etodolac—MS102/CN104; MS400; CN105
Fenoprofen—MS102/CN104; MS400; CN105
Floctafenine—CN104/CN105; MS400
Flurbiprofen—MS102
Ibuprofen—MS102/CN104; CN850; MS400; CN105
Indomethacin—MS102/MS400; CN850; CN105; CV900
Ketoprofen—MS102/CN104; MS400; CN105
Meclofenamate—MS102/CN104; CN105
Mefenamic Acid—CN104/CN105
Meloxicam—MS102
Nabumetone—MS102
Naproxen—MS102/CN104; CN850; MS400; CN105
Oxaprozin—MS102
Phenylbutazone—MS102/MS400
Piroxicam—MS102/MS400
Sulindac—MS102/MS400
Tenoxicam—MS102
Tiaprofenic Acid—MS102
Tolmetin—MS102

Commonly used brand name(s): *Actiprofen Caplets*[7]; *Actron*[9]; *Advil*[7]; *Advil Caplets*[7]; *Advil, Children's*[7]; *Albert Tiafen*[20]; *Aleve*[14]; *Alka Butazolidin*[16]; *Anaprox*[14]; *Anaprox DS*[14]; *Ansaid*[6]; *Apo-Diclo*[1]; *Apo-Diflunisal*[2]; *Apo-Flurbiprofen*[6]; *Apo-Ibuprofen*[7]; *Apo-Indomethacin*[8]; *Apo-Keto*[9]; *Apo-Keto-E*[9]; *Apo-Napro-Na*[14]; *Apo-Napro-Na DS*[14]; *Apo-Naproxen*[14]; *Apo-Phenylbutazone*[16]; *Apo-Piroxicam*[17]; *Apo-Sulin*[18]; *Apo-Tenoxicam*[19]; *Bayer Select Ibuprofen Pain Relief Formula Caplets*[7]; *Butazolidin*[16]; *Cataflam*[1]; *Clinoril*[18]; *Cotylbutazone*[16]; *Cramp End*[7]; *Daypro*[15]; *Dolgesic*[7]; *Dolobid*[2]; *EC-Naprosyn*[14]; *Excedrin IB*[7]; *Excedrin IB Caplets*[7]; *Feldene*[17]; *Froben*[6]; *Froben SR*[6]; *Genpril*[7]; *Genpril Caplets*[7]; *Haltran*[7]; *Ibifon 600 Caplets*[7]; *Ibren*[7]; *Ibu*[7]; *Ibu-200*[7]; *Ibu-4*[7]; *Ibu-6*[7]; *Ibu-8*[7]; *Ibu-Tab*[7]; *Ibuprin*[7]; *Ibuprohm*[7]; *Ibuprohm Caplets*[7]; *Idarac*[5]; *Indocid*[8]; *Indocid SR*[8]; *Indocin*[8]; *Indocin SR*[8]; *Lodine*[3]; *Lodine XL*[3]; *Meclomen*[10]; *Medipren*[7]; *Medipren Caplets*[7]; *Midol IB*[7]; *Mobic*[12]; *Motrin*[7]; *Motrin Chewables*[7]; *Motrin, Children's*[7]; *Motrin, Children's Oral Drops*[7]; *Motrin, Junior Strength Caplets*[7]; *Motrin-IB*[7]; *Motrin-IB Caplets*[7]; *Nalfon*[4]; *Nalfon 200*[4]; *Naprelan*[14]; *Naprosyn*[14]; *Naprosyn-E*[14]; *Naprosyn-SR*[14]; *Naxen*[14]; *Novo-Difenac*[1]; *Novo-Difenac SR*[1]; *Novo-Diflunisal*[2]; *Novo-Flurprofen*[6]; *Novo-Keto-EC*[9]; *Novo-Methacin*[8]; *Novo-Naprox*[14]; *Novo-Naprox Sodium*[14]; *Novo-Naprox Sodium DS*[14]; *Novo-Pirocam*[17]; *Novo-Profen*[7]; *Novo-Sundac*[18]; *Novo-Tenoxicam*[19]; *Novo-Tolmetin*[21]; *Nu-Diclo*[1]; *Nu-Flurbiprofen*[6]; *Nu-Ibuprofen*[7]; *Nu-Indo*[8]; *Nu-Naprox*[14]; *Nu-Pirox*[17]; *Nuprin*[7]; *Nuprin Caplets*[7]; *Orudis*[9]; *Orudis KT*[9]; *Orudis-E*[9]; *Orudis-SR*[9]; *Oruvail*[9]; *PMS-Piroxicam*[17]; *Pamprin-IB*[7]; *Ponstan*[11]; *Ponstel*[11]; *Q-Profen*[7]; *Relafen*[13]; *Rhodis*[9]; *Rhodis-EC*[9]; *Rufen*[7]; *Surgam*[20]; *Surgam SR*[20]; *Synflex*[14]; *Synflex DS*[14]; *Tolectin 200*[21]; *Tolectin 400*[21]; *Tolectin 600*[21]; *Tolectin DS*[21]; *Trendar*[7]; *Voltaren*[1]; *Voltaren Rapide*[1]; *Voltaren SR*[1].

Other commonly used names are Etodolic acid [Etodolac], Indometacin [Indomethacin], Meclofenamic acid [Meclofenamate]

Note: For a listing of dosage forms and brand names by country availability, see *Dosage Forms* section(s).

*Not commercially available in U.S.
†Not commercially available in Canada.

Category

Note: All of these medications have analgesic, antipyretic, and anti-inflammatory actions; however, indications for specific agents may vary because of lack of specific testing and/or clinical-use data as well as the toxicity of the individual nonsteroidal anti-inflammatory drug (NSAID). **Clinically, most of these agents are used to treat a variety of painful and/or inflammatory conditions, both rheumatic and nonrheumatic, even though the specific uses are not listed in U.S. or Canadian product labeling.**

Antirheumatic (nonsteroidal anti-inflammatory)—Diclofenac; Diflunisal; Etodolac; Fenoprofen; Flurbiprofen; Ibuprofen; Indomethacin; Ketoprofen; Meclofenamate; Meloxicam; Nabumetone; Naproxen; Oxaprozin; Phenylbutazone; Piroxicam; Sulindac; Tenoxicam; Tiaprofenic Acid; Tolmetin.
Analgesic—Diclofenac; Diflunisal; Etodolac; Fenoprofen; Floctafenine; Ibuprofen; Ketoprofen; Meclofenamate; Mefenamic Acid; Naproxen.
Antigout agent—Diclofenac; Diflunisal; Etodolac; Fenoprofen; Floctafenine; Ibuprofen; Indomethacin; Ketoprofen; Naproxen; Phenylbutazone; Piroxicam; Sulindac.
Anti-inflammatory (nonsteroidal)—Flurbiprofen; Indomethacin; Naproxen; Sulindac; Tenoxicam.
Antipyretic—Ibuprofen; Indomethacin; Naproxen.
Antidysmenorrheal—Diclofenac; Flurbiprofen; Ibuprofen; Indomethacin; Ketoprofen; Meclofenamate; Mefenamic Acid; Naproxen; Piroxicam.
Vascular headache prophylactic—Fenoprofen; Ibuprofen; Indomethacin; Mefenamic Acid; Naproxen.
Vascular headache suppressant—Diclofenac; Diflunisal; Etodolac; Fenoprofen; Floctafenine; Ibuprofen; Indomethacin; Ketoprofen; Meclofenamate; Mefenamic Acid; Naproxen.
Prostaglandin synthesis inhibitor, renal (Bartter's syndrome)—Indomethacin

Indications

Note: Bracketed information in the *Indications* section refers to uses that are not included in U.S. product labeling.

Accepted

Rheumatic disease (treatment), such as:
Arthritis, rheumatoid
(Diclofenac, diflunisal, fenoprofen, flurbiprofen, ibuprofen, indomethacin, ketoprofen, meclofenamate, nabumetone, naproxen, oxaprozin, phenylbutazone[1], piroxicam, sulindac, tenoxicam, tiaprofenic acid, and tolmetin are indicated for the treatment of acute or chronic rheumatoid arthritis.)
Osteoarthritis
(Diclofenac, diflunisal, etodolac, fenoprofen, flurbiprofen, ibuprofen, indomethacin, ketoprofen, meclofenamate, meloxicam, nabumetone, naproxen, oxaprozin, phenylbutazone[1], piroxicam, sulindac, tenoxicam, tiaprofenic acid, and tolmetin are indicated for relief of acute or chronic osteoarthritis.)
Ankylosing spondylitis
(Diclofenac[1], [diflunisal][1], [fenoprofen][1], [flurbiprofen], [ibuprofen][1], indomethacin, [ketoprofen], naproxen, phenylbutazone, [piroxicam], sulindac, tenoxicam, and [tolmetin] are indicated for relief of acute or chronic ankylosing spondylitis.)
Arthritis, juvenile
(Ibuprofen, indomethacin[1], naproxen, and tolmetin are indicated for relief of acute or chronic juvenile arthritis.)
[Arthritis, psoriatic][1]
(Diflunisal, fenoprofen, ibuprofen, indomethacin, ketoprofen, meclofenamate, phenylbutazone, and tolmetin are used in the treatment of psoriatic arthritis.)
[Reiter's disease][1]
(Indomethacin is used in the treatment of Reiter's disease.)
[Rheumatic complications associated with Paget's disease of bone][1]
(Indomethacin is used in the treatment of this condition.)
Although NSAIDs may be required for relief of [rheumatic complications occurring in association with systemic lupus erythematosus (SLE)][1], extreme caution is recommended because patients with SLE may be predisposed toward NSAID-induced central nervous system (CNS) and/or renal toxicity. Several NSAIDs, including ibuprofen, sulindac, and tolmetin, have been shown to cause serious adverse effects, including aseptic meningitis, in patients with SLE. In addition, ibuprofen (although a causal relationship has not been established), meclofenamate, and phenylbutazone have rarely been reported to cause an SLE-like syndrome and/or to exacerbate pre-existing SLE.
NSAIDs do not affect the progressive course of some forms of rheumatic disease. Some patients with rheumatoid arthritis may need additional treatment.
Pain (treatment)—Diclofenac, diflunisal, etodolac, fenoprofen[1], floctafenine, ibuprofen, ketoprofen, meclofenamate, mefenamic acid, and naproxen are indicated for relief of mild to moderate pain, especially when anti-inflammatory actions may also be desired, e.g., following dental, obstetric, or orthopedic surgery, and for relief of musculoskeletal pain due to soft tissue athletic injuries (strains or sprains). Only immediate-release dosage forms are recommended for relief of acute pain because of their more rapid onset of action relative to delayed-release or extended-release dosage forms.

Mefenamic acid is indicated for relief of mild to moderate pain when therapy will not exceed 1 week.

Those NSAIDs indicated for relief of pain are also recommended for relief of mild to moderate bone pain caused by metastatic neoplastic disease. However, careful patient selection is necessary, especially in patients receiving chemotherapy, because of the potential gastrointestinal or renal toxicity and the platelet aggregation-inhibiting actions of these medications.

Gouty arthritis, acute (treatment) or
[Calcium pyrophosphate deposition disease, acute (treatment)][1]—[Diclofenac][1], [diflunisal][1], [etodolac], [fenoprofen][1], floctafenine[1], [ibuprofen][1], indomethacin, [ketoprofen][1], [meclofenamate], [mefenamic acid][1], naproxen[1], phenylbutazone, [piroxicam][1], and sulindac are indicated [or used] for relief of the pain and inflammation of acute gouty arthritis and [acute calcium pyrophosphate deposition disease (pseudogout; chondrocalcinosis articularis; synovitis, crystal-induced)][1]. Only immediate-release dosage forms are recommended for relief of acute attacks because of their more rapid onset of action relative to delayed-release or extended-release dosage forms.

[Long-term prophylactic use of an NSAID may decrease the incidence or severity of recurrent acute gout attacks, especially during the early months of antihyperuricemic therapy. The NSAIDs do not correct hyperuricemia (although diclofenac, diflunisal, etodolac, oxaprozin, and phenylbutazone have some uricosuric activity) and do not eliminate the need for administration of an antihyperuricemic agent for the long-term management of chronic gout. Colchicine is the recommended agent for preventing acute gout attacks because, in low (prophylactic) doses, it is less toxic for long-term use than NSAIDs. NSAIDs (other than phenylbutazone, which is *not recommended for long-term treatment*) should be used only for patients unable to tolerate even prophylactic doses of colchicine.]

Inflammation, nonrheumatic (treatment)—Most of the NSAIDs are indicated [or used] in the treatment of painful nonrheumatic inflammatory conditions, such as—[Flurbiprofen is indicated for relief of bursitis, tendinitis, and soft tissue injuries.] Indomethacin[1] and sulindac are indicated for treatment of bursitis and/or tendinitis of the shoulder. Naproxen is indicated for treatment of bursitis and/or tendinitis of any joint. Tenoxicam is indicated for treatment of tendinitis, bursitis, and periarthritis of the shoulders or hips. [Other NSAIDs, especially those approved by U.S. and/or Canadian regulatory agencies for relief of pain, are also used in the treatment of these and other painful inflammatory conditions.][1]
Fever (treatment)—Ibuprofen and naproxen[1] are indicated for reduction of fever.
[Fever, due to malignancy (treatment)][1]—Indomethacin (rapidly acting dosage forms only) is used to reduce fever in patients with Hodgkin's disease, other lymphomas, and hepatic metastases of solid tumors. Indomethacin should be used only after aspirin and acetaminophen have proven ineffective. If antipyretic therapy at an adequate dosage is not effective within 48 hours, indomethacin should be discontinued.
Dysmenorrhea (treatment)—Diclofenac, [flurbiprofen], ibuprofen, [indomethacin][1], ketoprofen, meclofenamate, mefenamic acid, naproxen, and [piroxicam] are indicated for relief of the pain and other symptoms of primary dysmenorrhea. [Other NSAIDs that have been approved by U.S. and/or Canadian regulatory agencies for relief of pain are also used to relieve dysmenorrhea.][1] Only immediate-release dosage forms are recommended for relief of dysmenorrhea because of their more rapid onset of action relative to delayed-release or extended-release dosage forms.

[Because of the high incidence of adverse effects with effective doses of indomethacin, it is recommended that indomethacin be used only for severe primary dysmenorrhea unresponsive to other, less toxic, NSAIDs.]

Hypermenorrhea (treatment)—Meclofenamate is indicated for treatment of idiopathic excessive menstrual bleeding. The absence of an underlying pathologic condition should be verified before meclofenamate therapy is instituted. [NSAIDs that are used for relief of dysmenorrhea (see *Dysmenorrhea*, above) may also decrease excessive menstrual blood loss caused by an intrauterine device in addition to relieving other symptoms.][1]
[Headache, vascular (prophylaxis)][1] or
[Headache, vascular (treatment)][1]—Diclofenac, diflunisal, etodolac, fenoprofen, floctafenine, ibuprofen, indomethacin, ketoprofen, meclofenamate, mefenamic acid, and naproxen are used to relieve (when taken at the first sign of onset) migraine headache or other vascular headaches. Fenoprofen, ibuprofen, indomethacin, and naproxen are also used chronically to prevent recurrence of such headaches. Fenopro-

fen, ibuprofen, indomethacin, mefenamic acid, and naproxen may also be taken prior to and during menstruation to prevent migraine associated with menstruation.

[Bartter's syndrome (treatment)][1]—Indomethacin is used in the treatment of Bartter's syndrome. However, its use in this condition has been associated with adverse effects, including pseudotumor cerebri. Because long-term therapy is required, it has been suggested that other, less toxic, NSAIDs may be suitable alternatives to indomethacin.

[Pericarditis][1]—Indomethacin (rapidly acting dosage forms only) is used to relieve pain, fever, and inflammation associated with pericarditis.

Unaccepted

Except in the treatment of ankylosing spondylitis, for which it is a treatment of choice, and Bartter's syndrome, indomethacin is not recommended as initial therapy because of its potential for causing severe side effects. Also, although indomethacin, like other NSAIDs, has analgesic and antipyretic activity, it should not be used indiscriminately (because of its toxicity) to relieve pain or reduce fever.

Phenylbutazone is not recommended as initial therapy for any indication. Because of its potential for causing severe side effects, including agranulocytosis and aplastic anemia, it should be used only after less toxic treatments (including other, less toxic, NSAIDs) have been found ineffective. In many countries, phenylbutazone is approved only for treatment of severe ankylosing spondylitis unresponsive to other NSAIDs. Use of phenylbutazone to relieve the pain and inflammation of acute painful shoulder (i.e., peritendinitis, capsulitis, or bursitis of that joint) is no longer FDA-approved. It is strongly recommended that use of phenylbutazone be restricted to short-term treatment of severe flares of rheumatic disease, gout, or calcium pyrophosphate deposition disease.

[1]Not included in Canadian product labeling.

Pharmacology/Pharmacokinetics

See *Table 1*, page 409.
See *Table 2*, page 411.

Physicochemical characteristics

Chemical Group—

Fenamate derivatives: Meclofenamate, mefenamic acid.Indoleacetic acid derivative: Indomethacin. Indomethacin is chemically related to the pyrroleacetic acid derivatives sulindac and tolmetin and to the pyranoindoleacetic acid derivative etodolac.

Naphthylalkanone derivative: Nabumetone.Oxicam derivative: Meloxicam, piroxicam, tenoxicam.

Phenylacetic acid derivative: Diclofenac.Propionic acid derivatives: Fenoprofen, flurbiprofen, ibuprofen, ketoprofen, naproxen, oxaprozin, tiaprofenic acid.

Pyranoindoleacetic acid: Etodolac. This medication is chemically related to the indoleacetic acid derivative indomethacin and to the pyrroleacetic acid derivatives sulindac and tolmetin.

Pyrazole derivative: Phenylbutazone.

Pyrroleacetic acid derivatives: Sulindac, tolmetin. These medications are chemically related to the indoleacetic acid derivative indomethacin and to the pyranoindoleacetic acid derivative etodolac.

Salicylic acid derivative: Diflunisal. However, diflunisal is not metabolized to salicylic acid *in vivo*

Molecular weight—

Diclofenac potassium: 334.24.
Diclofenac sodium: 318.13.
Diflunisal: 250.2.
Etodolac: 287.36.
Fenoprofen calcium: 558.64.
Floctafenine: 406.36.
Flurbiprofen: 244.26.
Ibuprofen: 206.28.
Indomethacin: 357.79.
Ketoprofen: 254.28.
Meclofenamate sodium: 336.15.
Mefenamic acid: 241.29.
Meloxicam: 351.4.
Nabumetone: 228.29 Active nabumetone metabolite 6-methoxy-2-naphthylacetic acid (6-MNA)—216.25.
Naproxen: 230.26.
Naproxen sodium: 252.24.
Oxaprozin: 293.32.
Phenylbutazone: 308.38.
Piroxicam: 331.35.
Sulindac: 356.41.
Tenoxicam: 337.37.
Tiaprofenic acid: 260.31.
Tolmetin sodium: 315.3.

Other characteristics—

Ketoprofen: Highly lipophilic.
Oxaprozin: Lipophilic.

pKa—

Diclofenac potassium: 4.0.
Diclofenac sodium: 4.0.
Diflunisal: 3.3.
Etodolac: 4.65.
Fenoprofen calcium: 4.5 (25 °C).
Flurbiprofen: 4.22.
Ibuprofen: 4.43.
Indomethacin: 4.5.
Ketoprofen: 5.94 (in methanol:water [3:1]).
Mefenamic acid: 4.2.
Meloxicam: 1.1 and 4.2.
Naproxen: 4.2.
Oxaprozin: 4.3.
Piroxicam: 1.8 and 5.1.
Tiaprofenic acid: 3.0.
Tolmetin sodium: 3.5.

Note: 6-MNA, the active metabolite of nabumetone, but not nabumetone itself, is acidic. Other NSAIDs not listed above are also acidic.

Mechanism of action/Effect

Nonsteroidal anti-inflammatory drugs (NSAIDs) inhibit the activity of the enzyme cyclo-oxygenase, resulting in decreased formation of precursors of prostaglandins and thromboxanes from arachidonic acid. Also, meclofenamate and mefenamic acid have been shown to inhibit competitively the actions of prostaglandins. Although the resultant decrease in prostaglandin synthesis and activity in various tissues may be responsible for many of the therapeutic (and adverse) effects of NSAIDs, other actions may also contribute significantly to the therapeutic effects of these medications.

Antirheumatic (nonsteroidal anti-inflammatory)—

Act via analgesic and anti-inflammatory mechanisms; the therapeutic effects are not due to pituitary-adrenal stimulation. These medications do not affect the progressive course of rheumatoid arthritis.

Analgesic—

May block pain impulse generation via a peripheral action that may involve reduction of the activity of prostaglandins, and possibly inhibition of the synthesis or actions of other substances that sensitize pain receptors to mechanical or chemical stimulation. The antibradykinin activity of ketoprofen may also be involved in relief of pain, because bradykinin has been shown to act together with prostaglandins to cause pain.

Antigout agent—

Act via analgesic and anti-inflammatory mechanisms; do not correct hyperuricemia.

Anti-inflammatory (nonsteroidal)—

Exact mechanisms have not been determined. NSAIDs may act peripherally in inflamed tissue, probably by reducing prostaglandin activity in these tissues and possibly by inhibiting the synthesis and/or actions of other local mediators of the inflammatory response. Inhibition of leukocyte migration, inhibition of the release and/or actions of lysosomal enzymes, and actions on other cellular and immunological processes in mesenchymal and connective tissue may be involved. Indomethacin has been shown to inhibit phosphodiesterase, with a resultant increase in intracellular cyclic adenosine monophosphate (cAMP) concentration. Ketoprofen has been shown to inhibit leukotriene synthesis, inhibit bradykinin activity, and stabilize lysosomal membranes.

Antipyretic—

Probably produce antipyresis by acting centrally on the hypothalamic heat-regulating center to produce peripheral vasodilation, resulting in increased blood flow through the skin, sweating, and heat loss. The central action probably involves reduction of prostaglandin activity in the hypothalamus.

Antidysmenorrheal—

By inhibiting the synthesis and activity of intrauterine prostaglandins (which are thought to be responsible for the pain and other symptoms of primary dysmenorrhea), NSAIDs decrease uterine contractility and uterine pressure, increase uterine perfusion, and relieve ischemic as well as spasmodic pain. The antibradykinin activity of ketoprofen may also be involved in relief of dysmenorrhea, because bradykinin has been shown to induce uterine contractions and to act together with prostaglandins to cause pain. Also, NSAIDs may relieve to some extent extrauterine symptoms (such as headache, nausea, and vomiting) that may be associated with excessive prostaglandin production.

Vascular headache prophylactic and suppressant—

Analgesic actions may be involved in relief of headache. Also, by reducing prostaglandin activity, NSAIDs may directly prevent or relieve certain types of headache thought to be caused by prostaglandin-induced dilation or constriction of cerebral blood vessels.

Prostaglandin synthesis inhibitor, renal—

Inhibition of renal prostaglandin synthesis probably is responsible for indomethacin's beneficial effect in patients with Bartter's syndrome, which is thought to be caused by excessive production of renal prostaglandins.

Other actions/effects

Most of the NSAIDs inhibit platelet aggregation. However, their antiplatelet effect, unlike that of aspirin, is reversible. Single doses of 4 to 10 mg of flurbiprofen inhibit platelet aggregation. Oxaprozin is as potent as aspirin in inhibiting platelet aggregation induced by epinephrine or collagen *in vitro*. With diflunisal, the effect is clinically significant only with greater-than-recommended daily doses. Also, usual doses of diclofenac, meclofenamate, mefenamic acid, or nabumetone (as determined after administration of 1000 mg per day for 7 to 10 days) may not significantly alter platelet aggregability. Recovery of platelet function may occur within 1 day after discontinuation of diclofenac, diflunisal, flurbiprofen, ibuprofen, indomethacin, or sulindac; 2 days after discontinuation of tolmetin; 4 days after discontinuation of naproxen; or 2 weeks following discontinuation of slowly eliminated agents such as oxaprozin or piroxicam.

Diclofenac, diflunisal, etodolac, oxaprozin, and phenylbutazone also have uricosuric activity.

Phenylbutazone also induces hepatic microsomal enzyme activity.

Studies have demonstrated that IgM rheumatoid factor production (which may be partially mediated by prostaglandins) may be decreased (but not totally inhibited) during NSAID therapy. However, because these medications do not affect the progressive course of rheumatoid arthritis, the clinical significance of this effect has not been determined.

It has been proposed that the gastrointestinal toxicity of NSAIDs may be caused primarily by reduction of the synthesis and activity of prostaglandins (which exert a protective effect on the gastrointestinal mucosa) because upper gastrointestinal toxicity has been reported following rectal or parenteral administration of some of these medications. However, when administered orally, some of these acidic medications probably also exert a direct irritant or erosive effect on the mucosa. Because nabumetone is a nonacidic prodrug, and the active metabolite 6-MNA is not formed until after absorption, the risk of serious upper gastrointestinal tract toxicity may be lower with nabumetone than with other NSAIDs. Also, in one study, gastric and duodenal prostaglandin concentrations were not altered by 4 weeks of administration of therapeutic doses of etodolac.

The renal toxicity associated with NSAIDs (i.e., decreased renal perfusion, sodium and fluid retention, and decreased renal function) may be caused by inhibition of renal prostaglandins, which are directly involved in the maintenance of renal hemodynamics and sodium and fluid balance. Renal prostaglandins are especially important in maintaining renal function in the presence of generalized vasoconstriction or volume depletion. Sulindac is a prodrug; its sulfide metabolite is the active substance. Because this active metabolite is not excreted via the kidneys, renal toxicity may be less likely with sulindac than with other NSAIDs. However, there have been reports of renal toxicity associated with sulindac therapy. Etodolac has been shown to decrease some measures of renal function, with maximum effects occurring within 1.5 to 2.5 hours after a dose. However, with administration of up to 500 mg every 12 hours, recovery of renal function occurred prior to administration of the next dose, even in patients with pre-existing mild to moderate renal function impairment (creatinine clearances ranging from 20 to 88 mL per minute). Whether more frequent administration of etodolac may cause cumulative effects on renal function has not been determined.

The analgesic, antipyretic, and anti-inflammatory effects of NSAIDs may mask symptoms of the onset and/or progression of an infection.

Therapeutic effect

When these medications are used in the treatment of arthritis, their analgesic actions may produce some relief of pain within the first day or two. Significant relief of other symptoms of inflammation usually occurs within a few days to a week; however, in severe cases, 2 weeks or more of continuous use may be required.

Drug and Indication	Onset of Action	Peak Effect	Duration of Action
Diclofenac			
Tablets			
Pain	30 min		Up to 8 hr
Diflunisal			
Pain	1 hr	2–3 hr	8–12 hr
Etodolac			
Pain	30 min	1–2 hr	
200 mg			4–5 hr
400 mg			5–6 hr, but 8–12 hr in some patients
Ibuprofen			
Fever		2-4 hr	
5 mg/kg			6 hr
10 mg/kg			8 hr or more
Pain	0.5 hr		4–6 hr
Indomethacin			
Gout	2–4 hr		
Heat, tenderness		2–3 days	
Swelling		3–5 days	
Meclofenamate			
Pain	1 hr		4–6 hr
Naproxen			
Gout		1–2 days	
Pain	1 hr	2–4 hr	Up to 7 hr
Piroxicam			
Gout	2–4 hr	3–5 days	24 hr

Synovial fluid concentrations

Studies with several of the NSAIDs have shown that these medications enter the synovial fluid and that, several hours after administration of a single dose, synovial fluid concentrations equal or exceed the simultaneously measured plasma concentration. In addition, there is some evidence that ketoprofen, oxaprozin, and possibly other NSAIDs, may accumulate in synovial fluid when administered chronically.

Drug and Dose	Concentration: Time to Peak (hr)	Concentration: Peak (mcg/mL)	Half-life* (hr)
Diclofenac	3†	0.28†	Up to 6
Etodolac‡	2.7–3.7	Total 2.6 Free (unbound) 44–84 nanograms/mL	6.5–7
Flurbiprofen			
100 mg†	5.2	4.4	4.6
Indomethacin			
50 mg	2	0.69	
Ketoprofen			
50 mg	2	0.7–0.9	
100 mg		0.7–0.9	
Nabumetone			
1000 mg	±8	20§; 35#	
Tenoxicam			
40 mg	10	1.82	
Tiaprofenic Acid			
Tablets			
200 mg†	4	5.3	
300 mg†	4	7.7	
Extended-release			
Capsules	8		8.6
Tolmetin			
400 mg†	2	5.6	6.9

*Elimination.

†Determined at steady-state, after administration of a single dose in patients receiving chronic therapy (for diclofenac—50 mg 3 times a day; for flurbiprofen—100 mg twice a day; for tiaprofenic acid—200 mg 3 times a day for 7 days or 300 mg twice a day for 7 days; for tolmetin—400 mg 4 times a day for 7 days).

‡Determined at steady-state.

§Single dose; simultaneous plasma concentration 36 mcg/mL.

#Multiple doses (1000 mg every 12 hours on the first day, then 1000 mg per day for 3 days); simultaneous plasma concentration 41 mcg/mL.

Precautions to Consider

Cross-sensitivity and/or related problems

Patients sensitive to one of the nonsteroidal anti-inflammatory drugs (NSAIDs), including aspirin, ketorolac, and NSAIDs no longer commercially available (such as oxyphenbutazone, suprofen, and zomepirac) may be sensitive to any of the other NSAIDs also.

NSAIDs may cause bronchoconstriction or anaphylaxis in aspirin-sensitive asthmatics, especially those with aspirin-induced nasal polyps, asthma, and other allergic reactions (the "aspirin triad").

Patients with bronchospastic reactions to aspirin may be desensitized to this effect by administration of initially small and gradually increasing doses of aspirin. Desensitization must be carried out by physicians who are experienced with the technique, in a facility having personnel, equipment, and medications immediately available for treatment of any adverse reaction to the medication (especially anaphylaxis or severe bronchospasm). Desensitization to aspirin also desensitizes the patient to other NSAIDs. However, unless aspirin or another NSAID is then administered on a daily basis, sensitivity to these medications redevelops within a few days.

Carcinogenicity

Diclofenac—

No oncogenic potential was demonstrated with diclofenac sodium in a 2-year carcinogenicity study in male mice given up to 0.3 mg per kg of body weight (mg/kg) (0.9 mg per square meter of body surface area [mg/m^2]) per day or in female mice given up to 1 mg/kg (3 mg/m^2) per day.

Diflunisal—

No effect on the incidence or type of neoplasia was found in a 105-week study in rats given up to 40 mg/kg per day (approximately 1.3 times the maximum recommended human dose [MRHD]) or in long-term studies in mice given up to 80 mg/kg per day (approximately 2.7 times the MRHD).

Etodolac—

No carcinogenicity was demonstrated in mice or rats receiving up to 15 mg/kg per day (corresponding to 45 mg/m^2 for mice and 89 mg/m^2 for rats) for 2 years or 18 months, respectively.

Floctafenine—

No effect on the incidence of neoplasia was found in studies in CD-1 mice receiving up to 240 mg/kg per day.

Flurbiprofen—

No evidence of carcinogenicity was found in an 80-week study in mice receiving up to 14 mg/kg per day or in a 2-year study in rats receiving up to 12 mg/kg per day for 32 weeks, then up to 5 mg/kg per day thereafter.

Indomethacin—

No evidence of carcinogenicity was found in studies in mice receiving up to 1.5 mg/kg per day for 62 to 88 weeks or in studies in rats receiving up to 1.5 mg/kg per day for 73 to 110 weeks.

Leukemia has been reported in a few patients receiving indomethacin; however, a causal relationship has not been established.

Ketoprofen—

No evidence of carcinogenicity was found in studies in mice receiving up to 32 mg/kg (96 mg/m^2) per day (approximately 0.5 times the MRHD based on body surface area).

Meclofenamate—

No evidence of carcinogenicity was found in an 18-month study in rats.

Meloxicam—

No carcinogenic effect was observed in a 104–week study in rats or in a 99–week study in mice.

Naproxen—

No evidence of carcinogenicity was found in a 24-month study in rats.

Oxaprozin—

An increased incidence of hepatic adenomas and carcinomas occurred in 2-year studies in male CD mice, but not in female CD mice or in rats, given oxaprozin. The significance of this species-specific finding is not known.

Phenylbutazone—

Leukemia has been reported in a few patients receiving phenylbutazone; however, a causal relationship has not been established.

Long-term studies in animals have not been done to determine whether phenylbutazone has carcinogenic activity.

Tenoxicam—

No evidence of carcinogenicity was found in an 80-week study in mice receiving up to 5 mg/kg per day or in a 104-week study in rats receiving up to 6 mg/kg per day.

Tiaprofenic acid—

No evidence of carcinogenicity was found in an 80-week study in mice receiving up to 30 mg/kg per day or in a 104-week study in rats receiving up to 30 mg/kg per day.

Tolmetin—

No evidence of carcinogenicity was found in an 18-month study in mice receiving up to 50 mg/kg per day or in a 24-month study in rats receiving up to 75 mg/kg per day.

Tumorigenicity

Diclofenac—

No tumorigenicity was demonstrated in studies in rats receiving up to 2 mg/kg per day (approximately the recommended human dose). Although there was a slight increase in benign mammary fibroadenomas in female rats given 0.5 mg/kg (3 mg/m^2) per day, the increase was not significant.

Flurbiprofen—

No tumorigenicity was demonstrated in a 2-year study in rats receiving up to 12 mg/kg per day for 32 weeks, then up to 5 mg/kg per day.

Indomethacin—

No tumorigenicity was demonstrated in an 81-week study in rats receiving up to 1 mg/kg per day.

Ketoprofen—

No tumorigenicity was demonstrated in studies in rats receiving 6 mg/kg (36 mg/m^2) per day for 81 weeks or lower doses for 104 weeks.

Nabumetone—

No tumorigenicity was demonstrated in 2-year studies in mice and rats.

Mutagenicity

Diclofenac—

No mutagenic activity was demonstrated in *in vitro* tests using mammalian cells or bacteria (with or without microsomal activation) or in *in vivo* tests, including dominant lethal and male germinal epithelial chromosomal studies in mice and nucleus anomaly and chromosomal aberration studies in Chinese hamsters.

Diflunisal—

No mutagenic activity was demonstrated in the dominant lethal assay, Ames microbial mutagen test, or V-79 Chinese hamster lung cell assay.

Etodolac—

No mutagenic activity was demonstrated in *in vitro* tests performed with *Salmonella typhimurium* and mouse lymphoma cells or in an *in vivo* mouse micronucleus test. However, in the *in vitro* human peripheral lymphocyte test, concentrations of 50 to 200 mcg per mL (mcg/mL) of etodolac produced an increase in the number of gaps (3 to 5.3% unstained regions in the chromatid without dislocation, compared with 2% in controls).

Indomethacin—

No mutagenic activity was demonstrated in *in vitro* tests (Ames test or *E. coli*, with or without metabolic activation) or in *in vivo* tests (host-mediated assay, sex-linked recessive lethals in *Drosophila*, and micronucleus test in mice).

Ketoprofen—

No mutagenic activity was demonstrated in the Ames test.

Meloxicam—

No mutagenic activity was demonstrated in the Ames test.

Nabumetone—

No mutagenic activity was demonstrated in the Ames test or in the mouse micronucleus test *in vivo*. However, chromosomal aberrations occurred in lymphocytes exposed *in vitro* to nabumetone or its active metabolite 6-methoxy-2-naphthylacetic acid (6-MNA) at concentrations of 80 mcg/mL (369.6 micromoles/L) or higher.

Oxaprozin—

No mutagenic activity was demonstrated in the Ames test, forward mutation testing in yeast and Chinese hamster ovary cells, DNA repair testing in Chinese hamster ovary cells, micronucleus testing in mouse bone marrow, chromosomal aberration testing in human lymphocytes, or cell transformation testing in mouse fibroblasts.

Phenylbutazone—

No mutagenic activity was demonstrated in tests in mice, Chinese hamsters, or rats given up to 33 times the maximum daily human dose, or in bacteria or fungi. However, *in vitro* tests using Chinese hamster fibroblast cells have shown that phenylbutazone concentrations exceeding 860 mg/L produce chromosome abnormalities. Although an increased incidence of chromosome anomalies has been reported in cultured leukocyte cells from patients receiving therapeutic doses of the medication, other similar studies in humans and in horses have yielded inconclusive or negative results.

Piroxicam—

No mutagenic activity was demonstrated (test systems used not specified).

Tenoxicam—

No mutagenic activity was demonstrated in studies in 3 bacterial systems and 4 eukaryotic test systems.

Tiaprofenic acid—
No mutagenic activity was demonstrated in the Ames test or in the micronucleus test in mice.

Tolmetin—
No mutagenic activity was demonstrated in the Ames test.

Pregnancy/Reproduction

Fertility—

Diclofenac—
No impairment of fertility was demonstrated in reproduction studies in rats receiving up to 4 mg/kg (24 mg/m^2) per day.

Diflunisal—
No impairment of fertility was demonstrated in reproduction studies in rats receiving up to 50 mg/kg per day.

Etodolac—
A reduction in the implantation of fertilized eggs was demonstrated in reproduction studies in rats receiving 8 mg/kg per day, but no impairment of fertility was demonstrated in male or female rats receiving up to 16 mg/kg (94 mg/m^2) per day.

Floctafenine—
No impairment of fertility was demonstrated in reproduction studies in rats receiving up to 160 mg/kg per day.

Flurbiprofen—
No impairment of fertility was demonstrated in reproduction studies in rats receiving 2.25 mg/kg per day.

Indomethacin—
No impairment of fertility was demonstrated in a 2-generation reproduction study in mice or in a 2-litter reproduction study in rats receiving up to 0.5 mg/kg per day.

Ketoprofen—
No impairment of fertility was demonstrated in reproduction studies in male rats receiving up to 9 mg/kg (54 mg/m^2) per day. However, a decrease in the number of implantation sites was demonstrated in female rats receiving 6 or 9 mg/kg (36 or 54 mg/m^2) per day. In other studies, high doses of ketoprofen caused abnormal spermatogenesis or inhibition of spermatogenesis in rats and dogs, and decreased testicular weight in dogs and baboons.

Mefenamic acid—
Impairment of fertility was demonstrated in reproduction studies in rats receiving 10 times the human dose.

Meloxicam—
No impairment of fertility was demonstrated in male or female rats receiving 4.9 times the human dose.

Nabumetone—
No impairment of fertility was demonstrated in male or female rats receiving 320 mg/kg (1888 mg/m^2) per day.

Naproxen—
No impairment of fertility was demonstrated in mice, rats, or rabbits receiving up to 6 times the human dose.

Oxaprozin—
No impairment of fertility was demonstrated in male or female rats receiving up to 200 mg/kg (1180 mg per square meter of body surface area [mg/m^2]) per day. For comparison, the usual human dose is about 17 mg/kg (629 mg/m^2) per day. However, testicular degeneration occurred in beagle dogs given 37.5 mg/kg (750 mg/m^2) or more per day for 42 days or longer. This finding did not occur in other species, and the clinical relevance to humans is unknown.

Phenylbutazone—
No impairment of fertility was demonstrated in reproduction studies in mice, Chinese hamsters, and rats receiving up to 33 times the maximum daily human dose.

Piroxicam and tolmetin—
No impairment of fertility was demonstrated in animal reproduction studies.

Tenoxicam—
No impairment of fertility was demonstrated in male rats receiving up to 8 mg per day for at least 63 days prior to mating. Administration of 8 mg per day, but not lower doses, to female rats from 14 days prior to, to 7 days after, mating resulted in a significant decrease in the number of corpora lutea and implantations, resulting in fewer live fetuses.

Tiaprofenic—
No impairment of fertility was demonstrated in reproduction studies in female or male rats receiving up to 20 mg/kg per day. However, an increased number of pre- and post-implantation losses was demonstrated in studies in female rats receiving 20 mg/kg per day, and a decrease in the number of implantation sites was demonstrated in studies in rabbits receiving 75 mg/kg per day.

Pregnancy—

First trimester—

Diclofenac:

Adequate and well-controlled studies in humans have not been done.

Diclofenac crosses the placenta in mice and rats. Studies in rats receiving 2 or 4 mg/kg per day have shown that diclofenac is embryotoxic (causing low birth weight, a slightly decreased growth rate, and failure to survive, especially with the higher dose). Also, in studies in rabbits receiving 5 or 10 mg/kg per day, diclofenac caused increases in the resorption rates, decreased fetal weights, abnormal skeletal findings, and definite embryotoxicity with the higher dose. However, no teratogenicity was demonstrated in reproduction studies in rabbits receiving up to 10 mg/kg (80 mg/m^2) per day, in mice receiving up to 20 mg/kg (60 mg/m^2) per day, or in rats receiving up to 10 mg/kg (60 mg/m^2) per day.

FDA Pregnancy Category B.

Diflunisal:

Adequate and well-controlled studies in humans have not been done.

Studies in animals have shown that diflunisal is teratogenic in rabbits (causing fetal vertebral and rib malformations at doses ranging from 40 to 50 mg/kg per day) but not in mice (in doses of 45 mg/kg per day) or rats (in doses of 100 mg/kg per day). Diflunisal also caused maternotoxicity and embryotoxicity (increased fetal resorptions) in rabbits receiving 60 mg/kg per day (2 times the maximum human dose).

FDA Pregnancy Category C.

Etodolac:

Adequate and well-controlled studies in humans have not been done.

Isolated alterations of limb development, including polydactyly (extra digits), oligodactyly (missing digits), syndactyly (digits attached by webbing), and unossified phalanges, occurred in rats receiving 2 to 14 mg/kg per day. Also, oligodactyly and synostosis of metatarsals occurred in rabbits receiving 2 to 14 mg/kg per day. However, the frequency and dosage group distribution in initial and repeated studies did not establish a clear drug- or dose-response relationship.

FDA Pregnancy Category C.

Fenoprofen, ibuprofen, and tolmetin:

Adequate and well-controlled studies in humans have not been done.

Studies in animals have not shown that these agents cause adverse effects on fetal development. Tolmetin was studied in rats and rabbits receiving up to 50 mg/kg (1.5 times the maximum human dose).

Tolmetin: FDA Pregnancy Category C.

Floctafenine:

Studies in mice receiving up to 320 mg/kg per day, rats receiving up to 240 mg/kg per day, and rabbits receiving up to 160 mg/kg per day have not shown that floctafenine is teratogenic. However, embryotoxicity (increased fetal losses in mice, decreased fetal weight in rats, and increased fetal losses in rabbits) was demonstrated with these high doses (but not at lower dosage levels).

Flurbiprofen:

Although adequate and well-controlled studies in humans have not been done, it has been shown that flurbiprofen crosses the placenta.

Studies in mice receiving up to 12 mg/kg per day, rats receiving up to 25 mg/kg per day, and rabbits receiving up to 7.5 mg/kg per day have not shown evidence of teratogenicity. However, studies in rats have shown doses of 0.4 mg/kg per day or higher to be embryocidal (causing reduced weight or slower fetal growth, increased stillbirths, and decreased pup survival). Also, stillbirths, retained fetuses, and/or fetal distress occurred in studies in rats receiving as little as 0.2 mg/kg per day. In addition, fetotoxicity related to maternal toxicity (gastrointestinal ulceration, retardation of weight gain, intrauterine hemorrhage, and maternal deaths) occurred in rats receiving 25 mg/kg per day from Days 1 through 20 of pregnancy. With lower doses (0.2, 0.675, or 2.25 mg/kg per day), such effects did not occur when the medication was discontinued on Day 17 of pregnancy. Maternal deaths due to gastrointestinal ulceration also occurred in rabbits receiving the medication.

FDA Pregnancy Category B.

Indomethacin:

Although studies in humans have not been done, it has been shown that indomethacin crosses the placenta.

Studies in rats and mice have shown that indomethacin (at a dosage of 4 mg/kg per day) causes decreased average fetal weight and retarded ossification. In other studies in mice, higher doses (5 to 15 mg/kg per day) caused maternal toxicity and death, increased fetal resorptions, and fetal malformations.

Ketoprofen:

Adequate and well-controlled studies in humans have not been done.

Studies in animals have not shown evidence of teratogenicity or embryotoxicity in mice receiving up to 12 mg/kg (36 mg/m^2) per day or in rats receiving up to 9 mg/kg (54 mg/m^2) per day. In studies in rabbits, maternally toxic doses were embryotoxic but not teratogenic.

FDA Pregnancy Category B.

Meclofenamate:

Adequate and well-controlled studies in humans have not been done.

Animal studies have shown meclofenamate to cause fetotoxicity, minor skeletal malformations (e.g., supernumerary ribs), and delayed ossification, but no major teratogenicity.

Mefenamic acid:

Although adequate and well-controlled studies in humans have not been done, it has been demonstrated that mefenamic acid metabolites readily cross the placenta.

Mefenamic acid caused increases in the number of resorptions in rabbits receiving 2.5 times the human dose and decreases in survival to weaning (possibly due to maternal neglect) in rats receiving 10 times the human dose. Although no fetal abnormalities were reported in these studies or in studies in dogs receiving up to 10 times the human dose, it has been recommended that mefenamic acid not be used during pregnancy.

FDA Pregnancy Category C.

Meloxicam:

Adequate and well-controlled studies in humans have not been done.

Meloxicam crosses the placenta in animals.

Meloxicam was not teratogenic in rats at a dose equivalent to 2.2 times the human dose when given throughout organogenesis. However, an increased incidence of embryolethality occurred when female rats were given half the human dose 2 weeks before mating and during early embryonic development. The number of live births and neonatal survival were reduced in rats give oral doses equivalent to 0.07 times the human dose during late gestation and lactation periods

Nabumetone:

Adequate and well-controlled studies in humans have not been done.

Nabumetone did not cause teratogenicity in rats receiving up to 400 mg/kg (2360 mg/m^2) per day or in rabbits receiving up to 300 mg/kg (3540 mg/m^2) per day. However, fetotoxicity (post-implantation losses) occurred in rats receiving 100 mg/kg (590 mg/m^2) per day or more. These doses are equivalent to the maximum recommended human dose of nabumetone.

FDA Pregnancy Category C.

Naproxen:

Adequate and well-controlled studies in humans have not been done.

Naproxen did not cause teratogenicity in rats, rabbits and mice receiving 0.23 times, 0.27 times, and 0.28 times the human systemic exposure, respectively. However, there is evidence that naproxen treatment given late in pregnancy to delay parturition has been associated with persistent pulmonary hypertension, renal dysfunction, and abnormal prostaglandin E levels in preterm infants. Because of this known effect on the human fetal cardiovascular system (closure of ductus arteriosus), naproxen use during the third trimester should be avoided.

FDA Pregnancy Category C.

Oxaprozin:

Adequate and well-controlled studies in humans have not been done.

Fetal malformations occurred infrequently in rabbits receiving 7.5 to 30 mg/kg per day (doses within the usual human dose range). However, no teratogenicity occurred in mice or rats receiving 50 to 200 mg/kg (225 to 900 mg/m^2) per day.

FDA Pregnancy Category C.

Phenylbutazone:

Adequate and well-controlled studies in humans have not been done.

Although studies in rats and rabbits have not shown that phenylbutazone (in doses up to 16 times the maximum daily human dose) is teratogenic, slightly reduced litter sizes were demonstrated in both species.

FDA Pregnancy Category C.

Piroxicam:

Studies in humans have not been done.

Studies in animals have not shown that piroxicam causes teratogenic effects in doses up to 10 mg/kg per day.

Sulindac:

Studies in humans have not been done.

Animal studies have shown that sulindac (at dosage levels of 20 and 40 mg/kg per day—2.5 and 5 times the MRHD) causes decreased average fetal weight and an increased number of deaths (observed on the first day of the postpartum period). Also, some studies in rabbits have shown a low incidence of visceral and skeletal malformations with sulindac. However, these effects did not occur in repeat studies using the same or higher dosages.

Tenoxicam:

Studies in mice receiving up to 8 mg/kg per day from Day 6 to Day 15 of gestation did not show tenoxicam to adversely affect the fetuses or neonates. Teratogenic effects did not occur in offspring of rats receiving up to 12 mg/kg per day from Day 7 to Day 17 of gestation. However, a higher mortality rate associated with panperitonitis, gastric lesions characteristic of NSAIDs, and uterine hemorrhage occurred in dams receiving 8 or 12 mg/kg, but not 4 mg/kg or less, per day. Tenoxicam was embryotoxic (causing increased resorptions), but not teratogenic, in rabbits receiving 32 mg/kg, but not 16 mg/kg or less, per day from Day 6 to Day 18 of gestation.

Tiaprofenic acid:

Tiaprofenic acid crosses the placenta.

Studies in mice receiving up to 100 mg/kg per day have not shown that the medication is teratogenic. However, an increase in the fetal loss rate was demonstrated in studies in mice receiving 100 mg/kg per day, rats receiving 10 or 25 (but not 5) mg/kg per day, and rabbits receiving 75 (but not 25 or 50) mg/kg per day.

Second and third trimesters—

All NSAIDs:

Although studies in humans have not been done with NSAIDs other than indomethacin, use of NSAIDs during the second half of pregnancy is not recommended because of possible adverse effects on the fetus, such as premature closure of the ductus arteriosus, which may lead to persistent pulmonary hypertension in the newborn. Studies in full-term pregnant rats have shown that diclofenac, fenoprofen, flurbiprofen, ibuprofen, indomethacin, ketoprofen, mefenamic acid, naproxen, and tolmetin have a strong constrictive effect on the fetal ductus arteriosus, whereas floctafenine, phenylbutazone, piroxicam, sulindac, and tiaprofenic acid have a moderate constrictive effect.

Animal studies have also shown that administration of NSAIDs during late pregnancy may cause prolonged gestation, dystocia, and delayed parturition, possibly because of decreased uterine contractility resulting from inhibition of uterine prostaglandins. Decreases in pup survival rates also have been reported. Studies with piroxicam and nabumetone (at a dose of 320 mg/kg per day) have indicated that dystocia may cause an increased mortality rate in both offspring and dams, and a study with tenoxicam showed a dose-dependent prolongation of gestation and decrease in neonatal viability with doses ranging between 0.5 and 2 mg/kg per day. Also, delayed and prolonged parturition was associated with decreased pup survival in studies with etodolac and with an increased number of stillbirths in studies with flurbiprofen and tiaprofenic acid. Administration of indomethacin to rats and mice during the last 3 days of gestation increased the incidence of neuronal necrosis in the diencephalon and caused maternal and fetal deaths. Administration of oxaprozin to rats during late pregnancy resulted in decreased pup survival, and administration of 3.5 times the maximum human daily dose of phenylbutazone to rats during late pregnancy and lactation resulted in an increased number of stillbirths and reduced survival of offspring. Studies in animals have also shown that administration of piroxicam during the third trimester may increase the risk of maternal gastrointestinal tract toxicity.

Indomethacin:

In addition to the adverse effects in animal studies described above, administration of indomethacin to pregnant women during the third trimester has caused closure of the ductus arteriosus, inhibition of platelet function resulting in bleeding, renal function impairment or failure with oligohydramnios, gastrointestinal bleeding or perforation, and myocardial degenerative changes in the fetus.

Labor and delivery—All NSAIDs—In rat studies with NSAIDs, as with other drugs known to inhibit prostaglandin synthesis, an increased incidence of dystocia, delayed parturition, and decrease pup survival occurred.

Labor and delivery—Naproxen-containing products—Not recommended in labor and delivery because, through its prostaglandin synthesis inhibitory effect, naproxen may adversely affect fetal circulation and inhibit uterine contractions, thus increasing the risk of uterine hemorrhage.

Breast-feeding

Problems in humans have not been documented with most of the NSAIDs.

Diclofenac—

Diclofenac is distributed into breast milk. In one study, long-term use of 150 mg per day produced concentrations of 100 nanograms per gram in the breast milk. An infant of 4 to 5 kg consuming one liter per day would therefore ingest approximately 0.03 mg/kg per day.

Diflunisal—

Diflunisal is distributed into breast milk. Concentrations may reach 2 to 7% of the maternal plasma concentration.

Etodolac, floctafenine, and tiaprofenic acid—

It is not known whether these medications are distributed into breast milk.

Fenoprofen and mefenamic acid—

Fenoprofen and mefenamic acid are distributed into breast milk in very small quantities.

Flurbiprofen—

Flurbiprofen is distributed into breast milk in very small quantities. In one study, the peak concentration of 0.09 mcg/mL occurred 3 hours following a single 100-mg dose. A maximum of 0.07% of the dose appeared in breast milk within 24 hours after administration. A nursing infant whose mother is taking 200 mg per day could receive approximately 0.1 mg of flurbiprofen per day.

Ibuprofen—

Studies in humans have failed to detect ibuprofen in breast milk using methodology capable of detecting the medication in a concentration of 1 mcg/mL. The maternal dosage was 400 mg four times a day.

Indomethacin—

Indomethacin is distributed into breast milk. Risk-benefit must be considered because convulsions were reported in one breast-fed infant whose mother received 200 mg of indomethacin per day, of which 0.5 to 2 mg per day was distributed into the breast milk.

Ketoprofen—

It is not known whether ketoprofen is distributed into human breast milk; however, in animal studies, the concentration in the milk of lactating dogs was 4 to 5% of the maternal plasma concentration. In other studies, no adverse effect on perinatal development was observed in offspring of rats receiving 9 mg/kg (54 mg/m^2) per day, corresponding to 1.5 times the MRHD based on weight or 0.3 times the MRHD based on body surface area.

Meclofenamate—

Trace amounts of meclofenamate are distributed into breast milk. Use of meclofenamate in nursing mothers is not recommended because animal studies have shown meclofenamate to interfere with normal development of the young before weaning.

Meloxicam—

Studies of distribution of meloxicam into human breast milk have not been done. However, meloxicam has been found in the milk of lactating rats at concentrations higher than those in plasma.

Nabumetone—

It is not known whether nabumetone or its metabolites are distributed into human breast milk. Problems in humans have not been documented. However, 6-MNA is distributed into the milk of lactating rats in concentrations approximately equal to those in plasma. Nabumetone is not recommended for use in nursing mothers because of possible adverse effects of prostaglandin synthesis drugs on neonates

Naproxen—

Naproxen is distributed into breast milk; concentrations may reach 1% of the maternal plasma concentration. The peak concentration in breast milk occurs 4 hours after a dose. Because of the possible adverse effects of prostaglandin-inhibiting drug on neonates, use in nursing mothers should be avoided.

Oxaprozin—

It is not known whether oxaprozin is distributed into human breast milk. However, it is distributed into the milk of lactating rats.

Phenylbutazone—

Phenylbutazone is distributed into breast milk; use by nursing mothers may cause severe adverse effects, including blood dyscrasias, in the infant.

Piroxicam—

Piroxicam is distributed into breast milk; concentrations may reach 1 to 3% of the maternal plasma concentration. Also, use of piroxicam by nursing mothers is not recommended because studies in rats have shown that piroxicam causes a dose-dependent inhibition of lactation.

Sulindac—

It is not known whether sulindac is distributed into human breast milk, but it is distributed into the milk of lactating rats.

Tolmetin—

Tolmetin is distributed into breast milk. In one study, an average concentration of 0.075 mcg/mL was measured, with the peak concentration occurring 1 hour following administration to the mother. The half-life in breast milk was 1.5 hours.

Pediatrics

Ibuprofen—

Appropriate studies performed to date have not demonstrated pediatrics-specific problems that would limit the usefulness of ibuprofen in children 6 months of age or older. Safety and efficacy in infants younger than 6 months of age have not been established.

Indomethacin—

Although appropriate studies have not been done in the pediatric population, no pediatrics-specific problems have been documented to date (with the immediate-release capsule or oral suspension dosage form; the extended-release dosage form is not recommended for pediatric patients). However, because of indomethacin's toxicity, it is recommended that its use be limited to patients unresponsive to (or intolerant of) other antirheumatic agents, that the patient be carefully monitored (especially for the presence of infection), and that the recommended pediatric doses not be exceeded.

Naproxen—

Studies in children 2 years of age and older with juvenile arthritis have shown higher incidences of naproxen-induced skin rash and increased bleeding time as compared with adults. Studies in children younger than 2 years of age have not been done.

Oxaprozin—

Although a study with oxaprozin has been conducted in patients 3 to 16 years of age, controlled studies have not been published. Preliminary evidence indicates that, although the risk of overt hepatotoxicity appears to be minimal, elevated aspartate aminotransferase (AST [SGOT]) values during oxaprozin therapy may occur more often in patients treated for juvenile arthritis than in patients treated for other forms of arthritic disease. Safety and efficacy in pediatric patients have not been established.

Phenylbutazone—

Because of phenylbutazone's toxicity, use in children younger than 15 years of age is not recommended.

Tolmetin—

Appropriate studies performed to date have not demonstrated pediatrics-specific problems that would limit the usefulness of tolmetin in children 2 years of age or older. Studies in children younger than 2 years of age have not been done.

Other NSAIDs—

No information is available on the relationship of age to the effects of these medications in pediatric patients. Safety, efficacy, and appropriate dosages have not been established.

Geriatrics

Use in the elderly—

All NSAIDs—

Whether geriatric patients are at increased risk of serious gastrointestinal toxicity during NSAID therapy has not been established. However, NSAID-induced gastrointestinal ulceration and/or bleeding may be more likely to cause serious consequences, including fatalities, in geriatric patients than in younger adults. In addition, elderly patients are more likely to have age-related renal function impairment, which may increase the risk of NSAID-induced hepatic or renal toxicity and may also require dosage reduction to prevent accumulation of the medication. Some clinicians recommend that geriatric patients, especially those 70 years of age or older, be given one half of the usual adult dose initially. Also, careful monitoring of the patient is recommended.

Etodolac—

Studies performed to date with 200 mg of etodolac twice a day have not shown differences in the pharmacokinetics of the medication in geriatric patients compared with younger adults. Also, studies with 600 mg of etodolac per day have not shown differences in the side effects profile of etodolac in geriatric patients compared with younger adults.

Flurbiprofen—

Studies have shown that the peak plasma concentration of flurbiprofen may be increased in females 74 to 94 years of age, but not in males 66 to 90 years of age.

Indomethacin—

In addition to the increased risks of therapy with any NSAID as described above, geriatric patients are more likely to develop adverse CNS effects, especially confusion, while taking indomethacin.

Ketoprofen—

Studies have shown that protein binding and clearance of ketoprofen may be reduced, leading to increased and prolonged serum concentration and elimination half-life.

Nabumetone—

Studies in geriatric patients have not shown differences in the efficacy or safety of nabumetone compared with younger adults. However, plasma concentrations of 6-MNA are higher in geriatric patients, and interpatient variability in the pharmacokinetic parameters for 6-MNA is greater in geriatric patients than in younger adults. Elderly patients also seem to tolerate ulceration or bleeding less well than other individuals and most spontaneous reports of fatal gastrointestinal events are in this population.

Naproxen—

Studies have shown that the unbound (free) fraction of naproxen, but not the total plasma concentration, may be increased in geriatric patients. The steady-state concentration of unbound naproxen may be almost doubled in geriatric patients as compared with younger adults. Caution is advised when high doses are required and some dose adjustment may be required in elderly patients, using the lowest effective dose.

Oxaprozin—

Studies have not demonstrated a need for adjustment of initial oxaprozin dosage in elderly patients on the basis of pharmacokinetic considerations.

The relationship of age to the risk of adverse effects in patients receiving oxaprozin has been examined using data from 3 studies in patients with rheumatoid arthritis and 1 study in patients with osteoarthritis. The data indicate that oxaprozin is more likely to cause a potentially significant decrease in renal function, adverse gastrointestinal effects, or a significant decrease in hemoglobin concentration in patients older than 60 years of age than in younger adults. Although it has also been reported, with other NSAIDs, that geriatric patients seem to be more susceptible to NSAID-induced hepatotoxicity, there were no significant age-related differences in measures of hepatic function in the 4 studies with oxaprozin.

Phenylbutazone—

In patients 60 years of age and over, therapy should be limited to short periods (not to exceed 1 week if possible) because of the high risk of severe, possibly fatal, toxic reactions. Specifically, the risk of aplastic anemia and agranulocytosis is increased in elderly patients.

Piroxicam—

Studies in geriatric patients have shown a tendency toward increased elimination half-life and steady-state plasma concentration in these patients, especially elderly females.

Tenoxicam—

The risk of hyperkalemia may be increased in elderly patients.

Tiaprofenic acid—

The risk of adverse renal effects reflected by hyperkalemia and/or an increase in blood urea nitrogen (BUN) may be increased in elderly patients; an increase in BUN occurred in 11.8% of elderly patients, but only 2.5% of all patients, in clinical trials.

Dental

NSAIDs may cause soreness, irritation, or ulceration of the oral mucosa. Most of the NSAIDs may rarely cause leukopenia and/or thrombocytopenia, which may result in an increased incidence of microbial infection, delayed healing, and gingival bleeding. If leukopenia or thrombocytopenia occurs, dental work should be deferred until blood counts have returned to normal, and patients should be instructed in proper oral hygiene, including caution in use of regular toothbrushes, dental floss, and toothpicks.

Surgical

Caution is recommended in patients who require surgery. Most NSAIDs inhibit platelet aggregation and may prolong bleeding time, which may increase intra- and postoperative bleeding. The risk may be lower with usual doses of diclofenac, diflunisal, meclofenamate, mefenamic acid, or nabumetone, which may not significantly alter platelet aggregability (although mefenamic acid–induced hypoprothrombinemia, if present, could be hazardous to the patient). Recovery of platelet function may occur within 1 day after discontinuation of diclofenac, diflunisal, flurbiprofen, ibuprofen, indomethacin, or sulindac; 2 days after discontinuation of tolmetin; 4 days after discontinuation of naproxen; or 2 weeks following discontinuation of slowly eliminated agents such as oxaprozin or piroxicam. Consideration should be given to discontinuing NSAID treatment for an appropriate length of time prior to elective surgery, depending on the potency and duration of effect of the individual agent on platelet aggregability. In particular, it is recommended that treatment with oxaprozin, which is as potent as aspirin in inhibiting platelet aggregation, be discontinued 1 to 2 weeks prior to elective surgery.

Drug interactions and/or related problems

The following drug interactions and/or related problems have been selected on the basis of their potential clinical significance (possible mechanism in parentheses where appropriate)—not necessarily inclusive (» = major clinical significance):

Note: Combinations containing any of the following medications, depending on the amount present, may also interact with this medication.

In addition to the interactions listed below, the possibility should be considered that additive or multiple effects leading to impaired blood clotting and/or increased risk of bleeding may occur if any NSAID is used concurrently with any medication having a significant potential for causing hypoprothrombinemia, thrombocytopenia, or gastrointestinal ulceration or hemorrhage.

Note: All of the following interactions have not been documented with every NSAID. However, they have been reported with several of these medications and should be considered potential precautions to the use of any NSAID, especially with chronic administration.

For all NSAIDs

ACE inhibitors

(reports suggest diminished antihypertensive effect of ACE inhibitors by NSAIDs and that NSAIDs use in patients receiving ACE inhibitors may potentiate renal disease states)

Acetaminophen

(prolonged concurrent use of acetaminophen with an NSAID may increase the risk of adverse renal effects; it is recommended that patients be under close medical supervision while receiving such combined therapy)

(concurrent use with diflunisal may also increase the risk of acetaminophen-induced hepatotoxicity because diflunisal may increase the acetaminophen plasma concentration by 50%)

» Alcohol or
» Corticosteroids, oral glucocorticoid or
» Corticotropin (chronic therapeutic use) or
» Potassium supplements

(concurrent use with an NSAID may increase the risk of gastrointestinal side effects, including ulceration or hemorrhage; however, concurrent use with a glucocorticoid or corticotropin in the treatment of arthritis may provide additional therapeutic benefit and permit reduction of glucocorticoid or corticotropin dosage)

(NSAIDs not substitute for corticosteroids or to treat corticosteroid insufficiency; abrupt corticosteroid discontinuation may lead to disease exacerbation; therapy should be tapered slowly if decision is made to discontinue corticosteroids observing patient for evidence of adverse events including adrenal insufficiency and arthritis symptom exacerbation)

» Anticoagulants, coumarin- or indanedione-derivative or
» Heparin or
» Thrombolytic agents, such as:
Alteplase
Anistreplase
Streptokinase
Urokinase or

Warfarin

(inhibition of platelet aggregation by NSAIDs, and the possibility of NSAID-induced gastrointestinal ulceration or bleeding, may be hazardous to patients receiving anticoagulant or thrombolytic therapy; although nabumetone may be less likely than other NSAIDs to increase the risk of bleeding because it may be less likely to cause gastrointestinal ulceration or hemorrhage and because it has minimal, if any, platelet aggregation-inhibiting activity, caution is recommended; also, with usual doses, diclofenac, diflunisal, meclofenamate, and mefenamic acid may be less likely than other NSAIDs to significantly alter platelet aggregability)

(diflunisal, etodolac, fenoprofen, floctafenine, flurbiprofen, indomethacin, meclofenamate, mefenamic acid, phenylbutazone, piroxicam, sulindac, tiaprofenic acid, and tolmetin have been reported to potentiate the effects of coumarin- or indanedione-derivative anticoagulants; the effect of floctafenine on coagulation test results becomes apparent only after 2 weeks of concurrent use; potentiation may result from displacement of the anticoagulant from protein-binding sites and, with phenylbutazone, from inhibition of the metabolism of the anticoagulant; concurrent use of phenylbutazone with an anticoagulant is not recommended; if another NSAID is used concurrently, coagulation tests should be monitored and anticoagulant dosage adjustments made, if necessary, when NSAID therapy is initiated or discontinued)

(caution should be used when administering warfarin with nabumetone since interactions have been seen with other NSAIDs)

Antidiabetic agents, oral or
Insulin

(NSAIDs may increase the hypoglycemic effect of these medications because prostaglandins are directly involved in regulatory mechanisms of glucose metabolism and possibly because of displacement of the oral antidiabetics from serum proteins; dosage adjustments of the antidiabetic agent may be necessary; glipizide and glyburide, due to their nonionic binding characteristics, may not be affected as much as the other oral antidiabetic agents; however, caution with concurrent use is recommended)

(diclofenac has also been reported to decrease the effects of these medications, leading to hyperglycemia)

Antihypertensives or
Diuretics, especially
» Triamterene

(increased monitoring of the response to an antihypertensive agent may be advisable when any NSAID is used concurrently because flurbiprofen, indomethacin, ibuprofen, naproxen, oxaprozin, and piroxicam have been shown to reduce or reverse the effects of antihypertensives, possibly by inhibiting renal prostaglandin synthesis and/or by causing sodium and fluid retention)

(NSAIDs may decrease the diuretic, natriuretic, and antihypertensive effects of diuretics, probably by inhibiting renal prostaglandin synthesis; flurbiprofen has also been shown to interfere with furosemide-induced kaliuresis; however, diflunisal does not decrease the diuretic effect of furosemide)

(indomethacin may block the increase in plasma renin activity [PRA] induced by bumetanide, furosemide, or indapamide)

(concurrent use of an NSAID and a diuretic may increase the risk of renal failure secondary to a decrease in renal blood flow caused by inhibition of renal prostaglandin synthesis; specifically, concurrent use of triamterene and indomethacin is not recommended because this combination has caused renal function impairment [azotemia and reduced creatinine clearance] and a few cases of renal failure requiring hemodialysis)

(concurrent use of a potassium-sparing diuretic with indomethacin or diclofenac, and possibly other NSAIDs, may increase the risk of hyperkalemia)

(diflunisal significantly increases the plasma concentration of hydrochlorothiazide and decreases the hyperuricemic effect of hydrochlorothiazide or furosemide)

» Aspirin or
NSAIDs, two or more concurrently, especially
» Diflunisal and indomethacin concurrently or
Salicylates other than aspirin and diflunisal

(concurrent use of two or more NSAIDs, including aspirin, is not recommended; concurrent therapy may increase the risk of gastrointestinal toxicity, including ulceration or hemorrhage, without providing additional symptomatic relief; specifically, concurrent use of diflunisal and indomethacin has resulted in fatal gastrointestinal hemorrhage)

(concurrent use of aspirin with other NSAIDs may also increase the risk of bleeding at sites other than the gastrointestinal tract because of additive inhibition of platelet aggregation)

(concurrent administration of two or more NSAIDs may alter the pharmacokinetic profile of at least one of the medications, which may alter the therapeutic effect and/or increase the risk of adverse effects; specifically, aspirin decreases protein binding of ketoprofen and etodolac [but does not alter etodolac clearance], increases plasma clearance of ketoprofen, interferes with the formation and excretion of ketoprofen conjugates, decreases concentrations of the active sulfide metabolite of sulindac, and decreases the bioavailability of diclofenac, diflunisal, fenoprofen, flurbiprofen [by 50%], ibuprofen [by 50% in multiple-dose studies], indomethacin [by 20%], meclofenamate, piroxicam [by 20%], a single dose of tenoxicam [by 20%], and tolmetin. Also, diflunisal decreases the renal clearance of indomethacin, resulting in significantly increased indomethacin plasma concentrations, and decreases the concentration of the active sulfide metabolite of sulindac by 33%. Although studies to determine whether phenylbutazone alters etodolac clearance have not been done, phenylbutazone has been shown *in vitro* to decrease the protein binding of etodolac, leading to an 80% increase in the concentration of unbound etodolac)

Bone marrow depressants (See *Appendix II*)

(leukopenic and/or thrombocytopenic effects of these medications may be increased with concurrent or recent therapy if an NSAID causes the same effects; dosage adjustment of the bone marrow depressant, if necessary, should be based on blood counts)

» Cefamandole or
» Cefoperazone or
» Cefotetan or
» Plicamycin or
» Valproic acid

(these medications may cause hypoprothrombinemia; in addition, plicamycin or valproic acid may inhibit platelet aggregation; concurrent use with an NSAID may increase the risk of bleeding because of additive interferences with platelet function and/or the potential occurrence of NSAID-induced gastrointestinal ulceration or hemorrhage)

Colchicine

(concurrent use with an NSAID may increase the risk of gastrointestinal ulceration or hemorrhage, and concurrent use with phenylbutazone may also increase the risk of adverse hematologic effects)

(inhibition of platelet aggregation by NSAIDs, added to colchicine's effects on blood clotting mechanisms [colchicine may cause thrombocytopenia with chronic use and clotting defects, including disseminated intravascular coagulation, with overdose], may increase the risk of bleeding at sites other than the gastrointestinal tract)

» Cyclosporine or
Gold compounds or
Nephrotoxic medications, other (See *Appendix II*)

(inhibition of renal prostaglandin activity by NSAIDs may increase the plasma concentration of cyclosporine and/or the risk of cyclosporine-induced nephrotoxicity; patients should be carefully monitored during concurrent use)

(the risk of adverse renal effects may also be increased when an NSAID is used concurrently with other nephrotoxic medications, possibly including gold compounds [although NSAIDs and gold compounds are commonly used concurrently in the treatment of arthritis])

Digitalis glycosides

(diclofenac and ibuprofen have been shown to increase serum digoxin concentrations, and indomethacin has increased digitalis concentrations in neonates being treated for patent ductus arteriosus; the possibility should be considered that some of the other NSAIDs may also increase digoxin concentrations, leading to an increased risk of digitalis toxicity; increased monitoring and dosage adjustments of the digitalis glycoside may be necessary during and following concurrent NSAID therapy; however, studies have failed to show that flurbiprofen, ketoprofen, piroxicam, or tenoxicam increases digoxin concentrations, and phenylbutazone may decrease digitalis concentrations [see individual *For phenylbutazone* listing, below])

» Lithium

(diclofenac, ibuprofen,indomethacin, meloxicam naproxen, and piroxicam have been reported to increase the steady-state concentration of lithium, possibly by decreasing its renal clearance; with indomethacin, the steady-state lithium concentration was increased by up to 50%; other NSAIDs may have a similar effect; increased monitoring of lithium concentrations is recommended during and following concurrent use)

» Methotrexate
(concurrent use with phenylbutazone may increase the risk of agranulocytosis or bone marrow depression and is not recommended)

(NSAIDs may decrease protein binding and/or renal elimination of methotrexate, resulting in increased and prolonged methotrexate plasma concentrations and an increased risk of toxicity, especially during high-dose methotrexate infusion therapy; indomethacin has caused toxicity with intermediate-dose methotrexate infusions; fatalities have been reported; it is recommended that NSAID therapy be withheld for varying periods of time, depending on the elimination half-life of the individual NSAID [12 to 24 hours for agents with a short elimination half-life to up to 10 or 12 days for agents with a very long elimination half-life] prior to administration of a high-dose methotrexate infusion [for indomethacin, an intermediate- or high-dose methotrexate infusion]; also, NSAID therapy should not be resumed following the infusion until the methotrexate plasma concentration has decreased to a nontoxic level, usually at least 12 hours)

(severe, sometimes fatal, methotrexate toxicity has also been reported when NSAIDs were used concurrently with low to moderate doses of methotrexate, including doses commonly used in the treatment of rheumatoid arthritis or psoriasis; caution in concurrent use is recommended, with dosage of methotrexate being adjusted as determined by monitoring the plasma methotrexate concentration and/or adequacy of the patient's renal function)

Photosensitizing medications, other
(concurrent use with photosensitizing NSAIDs may cause additive photosensitizing effects)

Platelet aggregation inhibitors, other (See *Appendix II*)
(concurrent use with an NSAID may increase the risk of bleeding because of additive inhibition of platelet aggregation, as well as the potential for NSAID-induced gastrointestinal ulceration or hemorrhage)

(concurrent use of sulfinpyrazone with NSAIDs may also increase the risk of gastrointestinal ulceration or hemorrhage)

» Probenecid
(concurrent use of probenecid with ketoprofen is not recommended; probenecid decreases ketoprofen's renal clearance [by approximately 66%] and protein binding [by 28%], and inhibits formation and renal clearance of ketoprofen conjugates, leading to greatly increased ketoprofen plasma concentration and risk of toxicity)

(probenecid has also been shown to decrease renal and biliary clearance of indomethacin, and to increase plasma concentrations of indomethacin and naproxen, leading to increased risk of toxicity and possibly to increased effectiveness of the NSAID; if concurrent use is necessary, it is recommended that these NSAIDs be administered in reduced dosage and that increases in dosage be made slowly and in small increments)

(probenecid may also decrease excretion and increase serum concentrations of other NSAIDs, possibly enhancing effectiveness and/or increasing the potential for toxicity; a decrease in dosage of the NSAID may be necessary if adverse effects occur)

(probenecid may increase the plasma concentration of sulindac and its sulfone metabolite, and slightly decrease the plasma concentration of the active sulfide metabolite)

For diflunisal (in addition to those listed for all NSAIDs)

Antacids
(concurrent chronic use may significantly decrease the plasma concentration of diflunisal)

For fenoprofen (in addition to those listed for all NSAIDs)

Antacids
(concurrent chronic use may significantly decrease the plasma concentration of fenoprofen)

Phenobarbital
(phenobarbital may increase metabolism of fenoprofen by inducing hepatic microsomal enzymes, leading to a decrease in the elimination half-life of fenoprofen; fenoprofen dosage adjustment may be required)

For indomethacin (in addition to those listed for all NSAIDs)

Aminoglycosides
(administration of indomethacin to neonates being treated for a patent ductus has decreased the renal clearance and increased the plasma concentration of concurrently administered aminoglycoside antibiotics; although not documented, similar effects may occur in other patients, leading to increased risk of toxicity; adjustment of aminoglycoside dosage may be required)

» Zidovudine
(indomethacin may competitively inhibit hepatic glucuronidation and decrease the clearance of zidovudine, possibly leading to potentiation of zidovudine toxicity; indomethacin toxicity may also be increased; concurrent use of the two medications should be avoided)

For naproxen (in addition to those listed for all NSAIDs)

H_2 blockers or
Intensive antacid therapy or
Sucralfate
(concomitant administration with delayed-release naproxen not recommended due to gastric pH elevating effects of these drugs)

Hydantoin or
Sulfonamide or
Sulfonylurea
(has potential for interaction; should be observed for dose adjustment if required)

Note: Phenylbutazone induces hepatic microsomal enzymes and is itself metabolized by the same enzymes. It has been reported to increase the metabolism of several medications metabolized by hepatic microsomal enzymes and to decrease the metabolism of others. Although not documented, it has been proposed that, in some cases, phenylbutazone may compete with other medications for the enzymes.

For phenylbutazone (in addition to those listed for all NSAIDs)

Alcohol
(concurrent use of alcohol with phenylbutazone may increase the potential for impairment of psychomotor skills)

Anticonvulsants, hydantoin, especially
» Phenytoin
(phenylbutazone may displace hydantoin anticonvulsants from their protein-binding sites and inhibit their metabolism, possibly leading to increased elimination half-life and toxicity; hydantoin dosage adjustment, based on monitoring of plasma concentrations and/or observed signs of toxicity, may be required)

Barbiturates or
Cortisone
(phenylbutazone may decrease the efficacy of these medications by inducing hepatic microsomal enzymes and increasing their metabolism; the possibility should be considered that corticosteroids other than cortisone may be similarly affected)

Cholestyramine
(cholestyramine may decrease absorption of phenylbutazone; administration of phenylbutazone 1 hour before or 4 to 6 hours after cholestyramine may decrease the risk of impaired absorption and of toxicity resulting from sudden increases in absorption and serum concentration of phenylbutazone if cholestyramine therapy is discontinued)

Contraceptives, estrogen-containing, oral
(concurrent long-term use with phenylbutazone may result in reduced contraceptive reliability and increased incidence of breakthrough bleeding)

Dermatitis-causing medications, especially
Chloroquine
Hydroxychloroquine
(concurrent use with phenylbutazone may increase the risk of severe dermatologic reactions)

» Digitalis glycosides, possibly excepting digoxin
(phenylbutazone may increase the hepatic metabolism of digitalis, leading to a decrease in digitalis serum concentration; digitalis glycoside dosage adjustment may be necessary during and following concurrent use)

Hepatic enzyme inducers, other (See *Appendix II*)
(hepatic enzyme inducers may increase phenylbutazone metabolism and decrease its half-life)

Methylphenidate
(methylphenidate may inhibit metabolism of phenylbutazone, leading to increased plasma concentrations and toxicity; dosage adjustments may be necessary)

» Penicillamine
(concurrent use with phenylbutazone may increase the risk of serious hematologic and/or renal adverse effects)

Sulfonamides
(sulfonamides may displace phenylbutazone from its protein binding sites and potentiate its effects; phenylbutazone has also been reported to potentiate the effects of sulfonamides)

Other medications, oral, especially:
» Ciprofloxacin
» Enoxacin

» Itraconazole
» Ketoconazole
» Lomefloxacin
» Norfloxacin
» Ofloxacin
» Tetracyclines, oral
(antacids present in buffered phenylbutazone formulations may decrease absorption of many other orally administered medications by forming nonabsorbable complexes and/or increasing intragastric pH; if used concurrently, buffered phenylbutazone should be taken at least 6 hours before or 2 hours after ciprofloxacin or lomefloxacin, 8 hours before or 2 hours after enoxacin, 2 hours after itraconazole, 3 hours before or after ketoconazole, 2 hours before or after norfloxacin or ofloxacin, 1 to 3 hours before or after tetracycline, and at least 1 to 2 hours before or after other orally administered medications)

For sulindac (in addition to those listed for all NSAIDs)
Antacids
(concurrent chronic use may significantly decrease the plasma concentration of sulindac)
Dimethyl sulfoxide (DMSO)
(topical application of DMSO to arthritic joints [not recommended because safety and efficacy are unproven] by patients receiving sulindac has been reported to cause peripheral neuropathy and to decrease the plasma concentration of sulindac's active metabolite, thereby decreasing its efficacy)

For tenoxicam (in addition to those listed for all NSAIDs)
Cholestyramine
(cholestyramine decreased the average half-life of an intravenous dose of tenoxicam from 67.4 to 31.9 hours and increased the apparent clearance of tenoxicam by 105%)

For tiaprofenic acid (in addition to those listed for all NSAIDs)
Anticonvulsants, hydantoin, especially
» Phenytoin
(tiaprofenic acid may displace hydantoin anticonvulsants from their protein-binding sites, which may lead to an increase in the concentration of the unbound fraction and to toxicity; hydantoin dosage adjustment, based on monitoring of plasma concentrations and/or observed signs of toxicity, may be required)

Laboratory value alterations

The following have been selected on the basis of their potential clinical significance (possible effect in parentheses where appropriate)—not necessarily inclusive (» = major clinical significance).

With diagnostic test results

For diflunisal
Salicylate concentrations, serum
(diflunisal may produce falsely elevated serum salicylate values determined via the Abbott TDx fluorescence polarization immunoassay, the Trinder colorimetric assay, or the Du Pont *aca* method, despite the fact that diflunisal is not metabolized to salicylate *in vivo*)

For etodolac
Bilirubin, urine, determinations
(phenolic metabolites of etodolac may cause false-positive test results)
Ketones, urine, determinations
(false-positive test results may occur with dipstick method of determination)

For fenoprofen
Triiodothyronine (T_3) determinations
(fenoprofen may interfere with total and free T_3 determinations in the Amerlex-M kit assay; thyroid-stimulating hormone, total thyroxine, and thyrotropin-releasing hormone test responses are not affected)

For indomethacin
Dexamethasone suppression test for endogenous depression
(indomethacin may produce false-negative test results [i.e., no indication of endogenous depression] because plasma cortisol concentration is reduced to a greater extent than with dexamethasone alone)
5-Hydroxyindoleacetic acid (5-HIAA), urinary, determinations
(false 5-HIAA concentration values may be measured via the Goldenberg modification of Undenfriend's method because indomethacin metabolites are structurally similar to 5-HIAA)

For ketoprofen
Albumin, urine, determinations and
Bile salts, urine, determinations and
17-Ketosteroid (17-KS), urine, determinations and
17-Hydroxycorticosteroid (17-OHCS), urine, determinations
(ketoprofen metabolites in urine may interfere with test procedures that rely on acid precipitation as an end point or on color reactions of carbonyl groups; no interference occurs in tests for urinary protein using commercially available dye-impregnated test strips)

For mefenamic acid
Bile, urinary, determinations
(false-positive test results may occur when the diazo tablet test is used; the Harrison test is not affected)

For naproxen
5-HIAA, urine, determinations
(naproxen may interfere with some assays)
Steroid, urine, determinations
(17-ketogenic steroid concentrations may be falsely increased by naproxen when *m*-dinitrobenzene reagent is used; although 17-hydroxycorticosteroid measurements are not significantly altered when the Porter-Silber test is used, naproxen therapy should be discontinued 72 hours before adrenal function tests are performed)

For phenylbutazone
Thyroid function tests
(phenylbutazone may decrease 24-hour ^{131}I thyroidal uptake [effect lasts about 14 days] or increase resin or red cell T_3 uptake)

For tolmetin
Protein, urine, determinations
(the metabolites of tolmetin in urine produce false-positive tests for urine protein when the sulfosalicylic acid method is used; no interference occurs in tests for urine protein when commercially available dye-impregnated reagent strips are used)

With physiology/laboratory test values
Bleeding time
(may be prolonged by most NSAIDs [with ketoprofen, by 3 to 4 minutes above baseline values] because of suppressed platelet aggregation; effects may persist for less than 1 day [flurbiprofen, ibuprofen, indomethacin, sulindac], 2 days [tolmetin], 4 days [naproxen], or 2 weeks [oxaprozin and piroxicam] following discontinuation of therapy)
(effects on platelet aggregation and bleeding time appear minimal with usual doses of diclofenac, meclofenamate, or mefenamic acid, up to 1000 mg twice a day of diflunisal, or up to 1000 mg per day of nabumetone)
Glucose concentrations
(decrease in blood glucose concentration has been reported with ibuprofen, indomethacin, and piroxicam)
(increase in blood glucose concentration has been reported with indomethacin, phenylbutazone, piroxicam, and sulindac)
(increase in urine glucose concentration has also been reported with indomethacin)
Hematocrit or
Hemoglobin
(values may be decreased, possibly because of gastrointestinal bleeding or microbleeding and/or hemodilution caused by fluid retention)
Leukocyte count and
Platelet count
(may be decreased)
Liver function tests, including:
Alkaline phosphatase, serum
Lactate dehydrogenase (LDH), serum
Transaminases, serum
(values may be increased; liver function test abnormalities may return to normal despite continued use; however, if significant abnormalities occur, clinical signs and symptoms consistent with liver disease develop, or systemic manifestations such as eosinophilia or rash occur, the medication should be discontinued)
(the incidence of significantly increased transaminase values is higher with diclofenac than with other NSAIDs; in clinical trials with diclofenac, elevations to more than 3 times the upper limit of normal occurred with overall rates of 2% in patients treated for 2 months and 4% in patients treated for 2 to 6 months; values in excess of 8 times the upper limit of normal occurred in approximately 1% of the patients)
Plasma renin activity (PRA)
(indomethacin has been reported to decrease PRA and to block the increase in PRA usually produced by bumetanide, furosemide, or indapamide)
Potassium, serum, concentrations
(may be increased)

Protein, urine (including albumin) concentrations
(increases have been reported with diclofenac, diflunisal, indomethacin, phenylbutazone, piroxicam, sulindac, tenoxicam, and tolmetin)

Renal function tests, including:
Blood urea nitrogen (BUN)
Creatinine, serum
Electrolyte, blood and urine, concentrations
Urine volume
(NSAIDs may decrease renal function, resulting in increased BUN, serum creatinine, and serum electrolyte concentrations and in decreased urine volume and urine electrolyte concentrations; however, in some cases, water retention may exceed that of sodium, resulting in dilutional hyponatremia)

Uric acid concentrations
(serum concentrations may be decreased and urine concentrations increased by diclofenac, diflunisal, etodolac, oxaprozin, and phenylbutazone; in clinical trials with etodolac, the serum concentration was usually decreased by 1 to 2 mg per 100 mL [59 to 118 micromoles/L] after 4 weeks of therapy with 600 to 1000 mg per day and the reduction was maintained during the study period)

For mefenamic acid only
Prothrombin time
(may be prolonged)

Medical considerations/Contraindications

The medical considerations/contraindications included have been selected on the basis of their potential clinical significance (reasons given in parentheses where appropriate)—not necessarily inclusive (» = major clinical significance).

Except under special circumstances, this medication should not be used when the following medical problems exist:

For all NSAIDs
» Allergic reaction, severe, such as anaphylaxis or angioedema, induced by aspirin or other NSAIDs, history of or
» Nasal polyps associated with bronchospasm, aspirin-induced
(high risk of severe allergic reactions because of cross-sensitivity)

For diclofenac (in addition to those listed for all NSAIDs)
» Blood dyscrasias, active or history of or
» Bone marrow depression
(diclofenac may induce or exacerbate these conditions)

For phenylbutazone (in addition to those listed for all NSAIDs)
» Blood dyscrasias, active or history of or
» Bone marrow depression
(phenylbutazone may induce or exacerbate these conditions)
» Cardiac disease, severe or
» Cardiac failure, incipient or
» Cardiopulmonary disease, severe
(sodium and fluid retention caused by phenylbutazone may increase plasma volume and the risk of edema, acute pulmonary edema, and cardiac decompensation)
» Hepatic disease, severe or
» Renal disease, severe
(increased phenylbutazone blood concentrations and potential for toxicity may result from decreased clearance; also, potential for adverse renal effects may be increased in the presence of pre-existing severe hepatic or renal disease)
» Peptic ulcer disease, active
(may be exacerbated; increased risk of perforation and/or bleeding)

Risk-benefit should be considered when the following medical problems exist:

For all NSAIDs
Allergic reaction, mild, such as allergic rhinitis, urticaria, or skin rash, induced by aspirin or other NSAIDs, history of
(possibility of cross-sensitivity)
Anemia or
Asthma
(may be exacerbated)
Conditions predisposing to and/or exacerbated by fluid retention, such as:
Compromised cardiac function
Congestive heart disease
Edema, pre-existing
Hypertension
Renal function impairment or failure
(NSAIDs may cause fluid retention and edema)
Conditions predisposing to gastrointestinal toxicity, such as:
Alcoholism, active or
» Gastrointestinal bleeding (GI), history of or
» Inflammatory or ulcerative disease of the upper or lower gastrointestinal tract, including Crohn's disease, diverticulitis, peptic ulcer disease, or ulcerative colitis, active or history of or
Tobacco use, or recent history of
(patients with prior history of of peptic ulcer disease or GI bleeding and who use NSAIDS have a greater than 10-fold risk for developing a GI bleed; NSAIDs should preferably not be given to patients with active peptic ulcer disease or gastrointestinal bleeding; if NSAID administration is considered essential, extreme caution should be used and an antiulcer regimen should be administered concurrently)
(caution and close supervision are also recommended for other patients in whom there is a significant risk of gastrointestinal toxicity; misoprostol or sucralfate should be considered as prophylaxis for those at high risk)
Congestive heart failure or
Diabetes mellitus or
Edema, pre-existing or
Extracellular volume depletion or
Sepsis
(increased risk of renal failure)
» Hemophilia or other bleeding problems including coagulation or platelet function disorders
(increased risk of bleeding because most NSAIDs inhibit platelet aggregation and may cause gastrointestinal ulceration or hemorrhage; although the risk of these problems is lower with nabumetone than with most other NSAIDs, caution is recommended)
Hepatic cirrhosis or
Hepatic function impairment
(risk of renal failure is increased in patients with hepatic function impairment)

(most NSAIDs are metabolized hepatically; impairment of metabolism may be particularly problematic for nabumetone, since metabolism to the active metabolite 6-MNA may be decreased sufficiently to reduce efficacy)

(although stable hepatic cirrhosis does not alter the clearance of etodolac, the possibility should be considered that unstable hepatic disease or severe hepatic function impairment may do so)

(hepatic function impairment, especially if associated with chronic alcoholic cirrhosis, produces variability in ketoprofen pharmacokinetics and reduces ketoprofen protein binding; the concentration of unbound ketoprofen may be doubled; caution and careful monitoring are recommended; also, only immediate-release ketoprofen dosage forms should be used if the patient's serum albumin is lower than 3.5 grams per deciliter)

(hepatic cirrhosis, especially if associated with chronic alcoholism, increases the concentration of unbound naproxen, even though the total plasma concentration may be decreased; the lowest effective dose should be administered and the patient carefully monitored; if systemic manifestations [eosinophilia, rash, etc.], liver or renal disease clinical signs and symptoms or persistent or worsening of abnormal liver tests occur, NSAID should be discontinued)

(although the clearance of oxaprozin is not altered by well-compensated hepatic cirrhosis, caution is recommended in patients with severe hepatic function impairment)

(biotransformation of sulindac to the active sulfide metabolite is slowed; however, biliary elimination of the metabolite is greatly decreased, leading to increased and prolonged plasma concentrations and increased risk of toxicity; the patient should be carefully monitored and dosage adjusted as necessary)

Renal function impairment
(increased risk of hyperkalemia and of adverse renal effects, including acute renal failure; especially careful monitoring of the patient is recommended)

(NSAIDs and/or their metabolites are excreted primarily via the kidneys; a reduction in dosage may be required to prevent accumulation)

(etodolac has not been shown to increase the risk of renal toxicity, and the pharmacokinetic profile of etodolac is not altered, when up to 500 mg of etodolac is administered every 12 hours to patients with mild to moderate renal function impairment; however, the possibility of renal toxicity associated with a reduction of renal prostaglandin synthesis leading to a decrease in renal blood flow cannot be discounted; caution and monitoring of patients considered to be at risk are recommended)

(in end-stage renal disease, conversion of sulindac to its active metabolite is decreased)

» Renal function impairment

(the risk of toxicity associated with accumulation of the NSAID and/or the risk of adverse renal effects may be higher with diflunisal, fenoprofen, indomethacin, and piroxicam than with other NSAIDs; individualization of dosage and especially careful monitoring of the patient are recommended)

(although less than 1% of the active 6-MNA metabolite of nabumetone is eliminated in the urine unchanged, and increased concentrations of 6-MNA were not measured after administration of a single dose, caution is recommended in patients with renal function impairment because the extent to which metabolites may accumulate and cause adverse effects has not been determined; in patients with moderate renal impairment [30 to 49 mL per minute] there is a 50% increase in unbound plasma 6-MNA; dose adjustment and careful monitoring of patients with moderate or severe renal insufficiency is necessary)

» Stomatitis

(may be induced by NSAIDs; this symptom of possible NSAID-induced blood dyscrasias may be masked by pre-existing stomatitis)

Systemic lupus erythematosus (SLE)

(patient may be predisposed to NSAID-induced central nervous system and/or renal adverse effects)

» Caution is also recommended in geriatric patients, who may be more likely to develop adverse hepatic or renal effects with these medications and in whom gastrointestinal ulceration or bleeding is more likely to cause serious consequences, including fatalities.

Caution is also recommended when an NSAID, especially fenoprofen, is used in patients who developed genitourinary tract problems such as dysuria, cystitis, hematuria, nephritis, or nephrotic syndrome during treatment with another NSAID.

The sodium content of diclofenac sodium, meclofenamate sodium, naproxen sodium, naproxen oral suspension, and tolmetin sodium should be considered when selecting an NSAID for patients who must restrict their sodium intake.

For diclofenac (in addition to those listed for all NSAIDs)

Porphyria, hepatic

(diclofenac may precipitate an acute attack)

For indomethacin (in addition to those listed for all NSAIDs)

Epilepsy or

» Mental depression or other psychiatric disturbances or

Parkinsonism

(indomethacin may aggravate these conditions)

For mefenamic acid (in addition to those listed for all NSAIDs)

» Hypoprothrombinemia, when prothrombin activity is 10 to 20% of normal

(increased risk of bleeding, since mefenamic acid may further increase the prothrombin time)

For naproxen (in addition to those listed for all NSAIDs)

Dehydration, considerable

(caution should be used; advisable to rehydrate patients first and then start naproxen therapy)

» Renal disease, advanced or

» Renal impairment, moderate to severe (creatinine <30 mL/min)

(naproxen treatment not recommended; however, if treatment must be initiated, close monitoring of patient's kidney function is advisable)

For phenylbutazone (in addition to those listed for all NSAIDs)

» Polymyalgia rheumatica or

» Temporal arteritis

(phenylbutazone may aggravate these conditions)

For sulindac (in addition to those listed for all NSAIDs)

» Renal calculus or history of

(renal calculi containing sulindac metabolites have occurred, rarely, in patients receiving sulindac; it is recommended that the medication be used with caution, and in conjunction with adequate fluid intake, in patients who may be predisposed to calculus formation)

For rectal administration (in addition to those listed as applying to oral use of the NSAIDs with rectal dosage forms)

» Bleeding, rectal or anal, active or recent history of or

» Hemorrhoids or

» Lesions, inflammatory, of anus or rectum or

» Proctitis or recent history of

(may be exacerbated or reactivated)

Patient monitoring

The following may be especially important in patient monitoring (other tests may be warranted in some patients, depending on condition; » = major clinical significance):

Blood urea nitrogen (BUN) determinations or

Creatinine concentrations, serum and/or

Potassium concentrations, serum

(monitoring may be required at periodic intervals during therapy, especially in patients with documented hepatic or renal function impairment, other patients known or suspected to be at risk for renal function impairment, and/or those taking diuretics concurrently; also, may be required if signs of possible renal toxicity, such as substantial increases in blood pressure, fluid retention, or rapid weight gain occur)

Complete physical examinations, including urinalyses

(recommended prior to and at regular frequent intervals during phenylbutazone therapy)

» Gastrointestinal bleeding

(can occur without warning; monitor for signs and symptoms of bleeding)

Hematocrit determinations and/or

Hemoglobin determinations and/or

Stool tests for occult blood loss

(may be performed at one- to six-month intervals to detect blood loss during prolonged therapy, depending on the individual patient's risk of developing gastrointestinal toxicity; however, these tests [unlike endoscopy, which is not recommended on a routine basis] are not capable of detecting ulcerations that are developing asymptomatically or of predicting whether severe gastrointestinal bleeding is likely to occur)

» Hematologic determinations

(recommended prior to initiation of phenylbutazone therapy and at regular intervals of 3 to 4 weeks during therapy for patients receiving the medication for periods longer than 1 week)

(although routine monitoring is not necessary during therapy with other NSAIDs, appropriate testing should be performed if symptoms of blood dyscrasias occur)

Liver function tests, especially determination of transaminase (AST [SGOT]; ALT [SGPT]) values

(may be required at periodic intervals during indomethacin therapy; also, it is recommended that hepatic function tests be performed within eight weeks following initiation of diclofenac therapy and periodically thereafter)

(may also be required at periodic intervals during therapy with other NSAIDs if the patient is known or suspected to be at increased risk of developing hepatic adverse effects)

(although routine monitoring is not necessary for most patients during therapy with NSAIDs other than diclofenac or indomethacin, appropriate tests should be performed if signs and/or symptoms of hepatotoxicity occur)

Ophthalmologic examinations

(may be required if vision problems such as blurred vision occur during therapy)

Upper gastrointestinal diagnostic tests

(recommended for patients with persistent or severe dyspepsia or other signs of possible gastrointestinal toxicity)

Side/Adverse Effects

In July 2005, the Food and Drug Administration (FDA) asked all manufacturers of NSAIDs to revise the labeling for their products to include a boxed warning, highlighting the potential for increased risk of cardiovascular (CV) events including stroke and the well described, serious potential life-threatening gastrointestinal (GI) bleeding associated with their use. See *Table 3*, page 413.

Note: *Hypersensitivity reactions* with these medications may be similar to those reported for aspirin, i.e., *rhinosinusitis/asthma* or *angioedema/urticaria. Anaphylaxis* has also been reported, both in aspirin-sensitive patients and in those without known hypersensitivity to any of these agents. The risk of anaphylaxis, characterized by respiratory distress, circulatory collapse, and angioedema and/or urticaria with or without pruritus, may be increased when previously discontinued therapy with one of these medications is reinstituted. Although anaphylaxis occurs rarely with these agents, several reports have indicated a higher incidence of anaphylactic reactions with tolmetin than with the others.

Other *hypersensitivity reactions* affecting multiple body systems have also been reported with several of the NSAIDs. A hypersensitivity syndrome consisting of fever and chills, skin rashes or other cutaneous manifestations, hepatotoxicity, renal toxicity (including renal failure), leukopenia, thrombocytopenia, eosinophilia, inflamed glands or lymph nodes, and arthralgias has been reported rarely with diflunisal and with sulindac. Fever, skin rashes, and arthralgias have also preceded fenoprofen-induced renal toxicity. In addition, a syndrome of fever and chills, nausea, vomiting, and abdominal pain has been reported with ibuprofen, and a serum sickness- or influenza-like syndrome that may consist of troubled breathing, arthralgias, fever and chills, fatigue, pruritus, and/or skin rash or other cutaneous manifestations, has been reported with ibuprofen (although a positive causal relationship has not been established), meclofenamate, phenylbutazone, piroxicam, and tolmetin.

The antipyretic, analgesic, and anti-inflammatory actions of NSAIDs may mask symptoms of the occurrence or worsening of infections. *Reactivation of latent pulmonary tuberculosis* has been reported in a few patients receiving indomethacin.

Two cases of *biliary obstruction* associated with sulindac therapy have been reported. The obstruction was caused in each case by the presence in the common bile duct of a "sludge" of crystals containing a sulindac metabolite.

Metabolic acidosis and *respiratory alkalosis* have also been reported rarely (incidences $< 1\%$) with phenylbutazone.

Patients 40 years of age and older may be more susceptible to the toxic effects of phenylbutazone. In patients 60 years of age and older, there is an increased risk of severe, possibly fatal, toxic reactions.

Phenylbutazone-induced *agranulocytosis* may occur with a rapid onset, especially in relatively young patients. *Aplastic anemia* may occur more frequently in patients receiving prolonged therapy, especially older female patients. Both *agranulocytosis* and *aplastic anemia* are more likely to occur in geriatric patients.

Because diflunisal is a salicylic acid derivative, the possibility that it may be associated with the development of *Reye's syndrome* in children, teenagers, or young adults with acute febrile illnesses, especially influenza or varicella, should be kept in mind.

Post-marketing side effects reported for naproxen include: menstrual disorders, pyrexia (chills and fever), congestive heart failure, hematemesis, colitis, abnormal liver function tests, nonpeptic gastrointestinal ulceration, ulcerative stomatitis, hyperglycemia, hypoglycemia, depression, dream abnormalities, insomnia, malaise, myalgia, muscle weakness, aseptic meningitis, cognitive dysfunction, eosinophilic pneumonitis, urticaria, and hyperkalemia.

Note: If skin fragility, blistering or other symptoms suggestive of pseudoporphyria occur, treatment should be discontinued and the patient monitored.

Overdose

For specific information on the agents used in the management of anti-inflammatory agents, nonsteroidal overdose, see:

- *Diazepam* in
- *Benzodiazepines (Systemic)* monograph;
- *Dopamine* or *Dobutamine* in *Sympathomimetic Agents—Cardiovascular Use (Parenteral-Systemic)* monograph; and/or
- *Vitamin K_1—Phytonadione* in *Vitamin K (Systemic)* monograph.

For more information on the management of overdose or unintentional ingestion, **contact a Poison Control Center** (see *Poison Control Center Listing*).

Clinical effects of overdose

The following effects have been selected on the basis of their potential clinical significance (possible signs and symptoms in parentheses where appropriate)—not necessarily inclusive:

Acute and chronic

For phenylbutazone

Bluish color of fingernails, lips, or skin; convulsions, especially in children; difficulty in hearing or ringing or buzzing in the ears; dizziness or lightheadedness; hallucinations; headache, severe and continuing; increase or decrease in blood pressure; mood or mental changes; nausea, vomiting, or stomach pain, severe; periorbital edema (swelling around the eyes); ***shortness of breath, troubled breathing, or unusually slow, fast, or irregular breathing; swelling of face, hands, feet, or lower legs***

Note: The lowest fatal doses reported for phenylbutazone are 14 grams (in an adult) and 2 grams (in a 3-year-old child). The highest doses reported to have been survived are 40 grams (in a young adult) and 5 grams (in a 3-year-old child).

Laboratory findings in overdose may reveal respiratory or metabolic acidosis or alkalosis, other electrolyte disturbances, impaired hepatic or renal function, and abnormalities of formed blood elements.

Late manifestations of massive overdosage may occur 2 to 7 days following ingestion and may include hepatomegaly, jaundice, electrocardiographic abnormalities, blood dyscrasias, and ulceration of the buccal or gastrointestinal mucosa.

For other NSAIDs

Note: The symptoms of overdose of most of the other NSAIDs have not been described as completely as for phenylbutazone. Reported symptoms have generally reflected the gastrointestinal, renal, and CNS toxicities of these medications. Following overdosage with a propionic acid derivative or indomethacin, patients may remain asymptomatic or experience only relatively mild *CNS effects* (e.g., lethargy, drowsiness) or *gastrointestinal symptoms* (e.g., abdominal pain, nausea, vomiting). However, more serious effects, such as *gastrointestinal hemorrhage, acute renal failure, convulsions,* and *coma* have been reported with these, as well as other, NSAIDs. *Convulsions* may be especially likely to occur following mefenamic acid overdose. Also, *hypoprothrombinemia* has been reported following overdose of several NSAIDs.

Treatment of overdose

To decrease absorption—Emptying the stomach via induction of emesis (in alert patients only) or gastric lavage. However, syrup of ipecac may induce symptoms similar to those of NSAID toxicity, which may complicate diagnosis, and is therefore not recommended for induction of emesis.

Administering activated charcoal. The efficacy of activated charcoal in decreasing absorption of these medications when given more than 2 hours (6 hours for piroxicam) following ingestion of the overdose has not been determined. However, there is some evidence that repeated administration of activated charcoal may interrupt enterohepatic circulation and/or bind any of the medication that has diffused from the circulation into the intestine, thereby increasing nonrenal excretion.

To enhance elimination—Administering antacids or other urinary alkalizers may increase diflunisal or sulindac excretion. Antacids may also relieve adverse gastrointestinal effects.

Inducing diuresis may be helpful in overdosage with fenoprofen, ibuprofen, or tolmetin; however, furosemide does not lower fenoprofen blood concentration.

Hemodialysis may be necessary to treat renal failure, but cannot be relied upon to decrease plasma concentrations of most NSAIDs because of their high degree of protein binding. Studies have shown that diclofenac and ketoprofen are dialyzable, but that diflunisal, etodolac, ibuprofen, indomethacin, and oxaprozin are not.

Specific treatment—

For severe hypotension plasma:

Use of volume expanders

For convulsions:

Diazepam or other appropriate benzodiazepine anticonvulsants. See the package insert or *Diazepam* in *Benzodiazepines (Systemic)* for specific dosing guidelines for use of this product.

For hypoprothrombinemia:

Use of Vitamin K_1. See the package insert or *Vitamin K_1—Phytonadione* in *Vitamin K (Systemic)* monograph for specific dosing guidelines for use of this product.

For prevention or reversal of early indications of, renal failure:

Use of dopamine plus dobutamine intravenously. See the package insert or *Dopamine* or *Dobutamine* in *Sympathomimetic Agents—Cardiovascular Use (Parenteral-Systemic)* monograph for specific dosing guidelines for use of this product.

Instituting symptomatic and other supportive treatment as necessary. Certain adverse effects of NSAIDs, including nephritis or nephrotic syndrome, thrombocytopenia, hemolytic anemia, and severe cutaneous or other hypersensitivity reactions, may respond to glucocorticoid administration.

Monitoring—The possibility must be considered that gastrointestinal ulceration or hemorrhage, and phenylbutazone-induced blood dyscrasias, may occur several days after ingestion of an overdose. Patients being discharged after initial treatment should be informed of possible presenting symptoms and advised to seek immediate treatment if they occur.

Supportive care—Monitoring and supporting vital functions. If respiratory support is required following phenylbutazone overdose, respiratory stimulants should not be used. Patients in whom intentional overdose is known or suspected should be referred for psychiatric consultation.

Patient Consultation

As an aid to patient consultation, refer to *Advice for the Patient, Anti-inflammatory Drugs, Nonsteroidal (Systemic)*.

In providing consultation, consider emphasizing the following selected information (» = major clinical significance):

Before using this medication

» Conditions affecting use, especially:

Hypersensitivity to aspirin or any of the nonsteroidal anti-inflammatory drugs (NSAIDs) or any component of the product

Pregnancy—Use of an NSAID during second half of pregnancy not recommended because of potential adverse effect on fetal blood flow and possible prolongation of pregnancy, dystocia, and difficult and/or delayed delivery

For naproxen: Use during third trimester should be avoided due to potential for premature closure of the ductus arteriosus

Breast-feeding—*For indomethacin:* Has caused convulsions in a nursing infant

For meclofenamate and piroxicam: These NSAIDs have caused adverse effects in animal studies

For naproxen: Use in nursing mothers should be avoided

For phenylbutazone: May cause blood dyscrasias or other adverse effects in the infant

For indomethacin: Because of toxicity, should be used with caution and only in patients unresponsive to less toxic NSAIDs

For naproxen: Skin rash more common in pediatric patients

For nabumetone: Not recommended for nursing mothers due to adverse effects in neonates

For phenylbutazone: Because of toxicity, not recommended in children < 15 years of age

Use in the elderly—Increased risk of toxicity; elderly patients seem to have lower tolerance of ulceration or bleeding and most reports of fatal GI events are in the elderly; initial dosage should be reduced and patients carefully monitored

Other medications, especially—

For all NSAIDs: Alcohol, anticoagulants, aspirin, cephalosporins that may induce hypoprothrombinemia, corticosteroids (oral), cyclosporine, lithium, methotrexate, plicamycin, potassium supplements, probenecid, triamterene, and valproic acid

For indomethacin (in addition to those applying to all NSAIDs): Zidovudine

For phenylbutazone (in addition to those applying to all NSAIDs): Digitalis, penicillamine, and phenytoin

For buffered phenylbutazone (in addition to those applying to all NSAIDs and to phenylbutazone): Ciprofloxacin, enoxacin, itraconazole, ketoconazole, lomefloxacin, norfloxacin, ofloxacin, and oral tetracyclines

For tiaprofenic acid (in addition to those applying to all NSAIDs): Phenytoin

Other medical problems, especially—

For all NSAIDs: Blood dyscrasias, bone marrow depression, cardiac or cardiopulmonary disease or predisposition to, clotting defects, hepatic disease, gastrointestinal bleeding or predisposition to, peptic ulcer or other inflammatory or ulcerative gastrointestinal tract disease or predisposition to, renal disease or predisposition to, and stomatitis

For indomethacin (in addition to those applying to all NSAIDs): Epilepsy, mental illness, and parkinsonism

For naproxen (in addition to those applying to all NSAIDs): Advanced renal disease or moderate to severe renal impairment

For nabumetone (in addition to those applying to all NSAIDs): Moderate to severe renal insufficiency

For phenylbutazone (in addition to those applying to all NSAIDs): Polymyalgia rheumatica and temporal arteritis

For sulindac (in addition to those applying to all NSAIDs): Renal calculus or history of

For rectal dosage forms (in addition to those applying to oral use of the NSAIDs with rectal dosage forms): Anal or rectal bleeding, hemorrhoids, inflammatory lesions of anus or rectum, and proctitis or recent history of

Proper use of this medication

For all NSAIDs

» Not taking more medication than prescribed or recommended on OTC package label

» For use in arthritis—Compliance with therapy; noticeable improvement in condition usually requires a few days to a week of treatment (but up to 2 weeks, and sometimes even longer, in severe cases) and maximum effectiveness may require several weeks of treatment

» Proper dosing

Missed dose (scheduled dosing): If dosing schedule is—

Once or twice a day: Taking as soon as possible if remembered within one or two hours after dose should have been taken; skipping dose if not remembered until later

More than twice a day: Taking as soon as possible; not taking if almost time for next dose; not doubling doses

» Proper storage

For all capsule and tablet dosage forms

Taking with a full glass of water and not lying down for 15 to 30 minutes after taking

For indomethacin, mefenamic acid, phenylbutazone, and piroxicam

» Taking oral dosage forms with meals or antacids (a magnesium- and aluminum-containing antacid may be preferred) to reduce gastrointestinal irritation

For flurbiprofen extended-release tablets, nabumetone, and naproxen extended-release tablets

Taking with food or antacids (a magnesium- and aluminum-containing antacid may be preferred) to reduce gastrointestinal irritation; taking with food also increases absorption

For immediate-release and extended-release oral dosage forms of NSAIDs not listed above

Taking with food or antacids (a magnesium- and aluminum-containing antacid may be preferred) to reduce gastrointestinal irritation, although when used for acute conditions (e.g., pain, gout, fever, or dysmenorrhea) the first 1 or 2 doses may be taken on an empty stomach to speed the onset of action

For oral suspensions

Not mixing suspension with an antacid or other liquid prior to use

For delayed-release (enteric-coated) or extended-release dosage forms, diflunisal tablets, and all phenylbutazone tablet formulations

Swallowing whole; not breaking, chewing or crushing before swallowing

For all suppository dosage forms

Proper administration technique

For indomethacin suppositories

Retaining in rectum for 1 full hour to ensure maximum absorption

For nonprescription use of ibuprofen or naproxen

» Reading patient information sheet provided in package

For phenylbutazone

» Taking for prescribed indications only; not taking to relieve other aches and pains

For mefenamic acid

» Not taking longer than 7 days at a time unless otherwise directed by physician

Precautions while using this medication

» Regular visits to physician during prolonged therapy

» Possibility that use of alcohol may increase the risk of ulceration and, with phenylbutazone, depressant effects

» Checking with physician if you consume 3 or more alcohol-containing beverages per day; alcohol consumption may increase the risk of NSAID-induced gastrointestinal toxicity

Not taking 2 or more NSAIDs, including ketorolac, concurrently, and not taking acetaminophen or aspirin or other salicylates for more than a few days while receiving NSAID therapy, unless concurrent use is prescribed by, and patient remains under the care of, a physician or dentist

» Importance of immediately reporting to physician symptoms of edema, gastrointestinal bleeding or ulceration, cardiovascular events, unusual weight gain, or skin rash

Caution if any surgery is required because of possible enhanced bleeding (although may be less of a problem with diclofenac, diflunisal, meclofenamate, mefenamic acid, and nabumetone)

Caution if confusion, dizziness or lightheadedness, drowsiness, or vision problems occur

» Possibility of photosensitivity

Possibility of gastrointestinal ulceration and bleeding

» Notifying physician immediately if influenza-like symptoms (chills, fever, or muscle aches and pains) occur shortly prior to or together with a skin rash; rarely, these symptoms may indicate a serious reaction to the medication

Possibility of anaphylaxis

For buffered phenylbutazone:

» Not taking within:

—6 hours before or 2 hours after ciprofloxacin or lomefloxacin

—8 hours before or 2 hours after enoxacin

—2 hours after itraconazole

—3 hours before or after ketoconazole
—2 hours before or after norfloxacin or ofloxacin
—1 to 3 hours before or after an oral tetracycline

For mefenamic acid:
Discontinuing use and checking with physician if severe diarrhea occurs

For nonprescription use of ibuprofen or naproxen:
Checking with health care professional if symptoms do not improve or if they worsen, if using for fever and fever lasts more than 3 days or returns, or if painful area is red or swollen

Side/adverse effects

» *Stopping medication and obtaining emergency treatment if symptoms of any of the following occur*

For all NSAIDs
Anaphylaxis, angioedema, or bronchospasm

» *Stopping medication and checking with physician immediately if symptoms of the following occur*

For all NSAIDs
Spitting up blood, unexplained nosebleeds, chest pain, convulsions, fainting, gastrointestinal ulceration or bleeding, and blood dyscrasias

For mefenamic acid (in addition to those applying to all NSAIDs)
Diarrhea

For phenylbutazone (in addition to those applying to all NSAIDs)
Edema

Signs and symptoms of other potential side effects, especially

For all NSAIDs
Dysarthria, hallucinations, aseptic meningitis, migraine, mood or mental changes, peripheral neuropathy, syncope, or other central nervous system effects; dermatitis (allergic or exfoliative), Stevens-Johnson syndrome, or other dermatologic effects; colitis, dysphagia, esophagitis, gastritis, gastroenteritis, or other digestive system effects; crystalluria, urinary tract irritation or infection, or other genitourinary effects; anemia or hypocoagulation; hepatitis; angiitis, fever, allergic rhinitis, or other hypersensitivity reactions not listed previously; loosening or splitting of fingernails; lymphadenopathy; vision problems, conjunctivitis, or other ocular effects; stomatitis, glossitis, or other oral/perioral effects; hearing problems or tinnitus; pancreatitis; and edema, hyperkalemia, polyuria, renal impairment or failure, or other renal effects

For indomethacin (in addition to those applying to all NSAIDs) Headache (severe), especially in the morning

Possibility that the following may occur many days or weeks after medication is discontinued

For phenylbutazone
Blood dyscrasias

General Dosing Information

The sodium content of diclofenac sodium, meclofenamate sodium, naproxen sodium, naproxen oral suspension, and tolmetin sodium should be considered when selecting a nonsteroidal anti-inflammatory drug (NSAID) for patients who must restrict their sodium intake. Also, the sucrose content of ibuprofen and naproxen suspensions must be considered when selecting an NSAID for patients who must restrict their sucrose intake.

Patients who do not respond to one NSAID may respond to another. In responsive patients, partial symptomatic relief of arthritic symptoms usually occurs within 1 or 2 weeks, although maximum effectiveness may occur only after several weeks of therapy.

A reduction of initial dosage, possibly to as low as one-half the usual adult dose, is recommended for geriatric patients, especially those 70 years of age or older. However, if the reduced dose fails to produce an adequate clinical response and the medication is well tolerated, dosage may be increased as required and tolerated.

A reduction of dosage may also be required to prevent accumulation of NSAIDs and/or their metabolites (some of which may be unstable and may be hydrolyzed to the parent compound when their excretion is delayed) in patients with renal function impairment.

Long-term use of NSAIDs in doses that approach or exceed maximum dosage recommendations should be considered only if the clinical benefit is increased sufficiently to offset the higher risk of gastrointestinal toxicity or other adverse effects.

To minimize the potential risk for an adverse gastrointestinal event, the lowest effective NSAID dose should be used for the shortest possible duration. For high-risk patients, alternate therapies that do not involve NSAIDs should be considered.

Indomethacin, mefenamic acid, phenylbutazone, and piroxicam should be administered immediately after meals or with food or antacids to reduce gastrointestinal irritation. Flurbiprofen extended-release capsules, nabumetone, or naproxen extended-release tablets should also be taken with food to increase absorption as well as reduce gastrointestinal irritation. The other NSAIDs (except for delayed-release [enteric-coated] and rectal dosage forms) are also preferably taken after meals or with food or antacids to reduce gastrointestinal irritation, especially during chronic use; however, for faster absorption when a rapid initial effect is required (as for analgesic or antipyretic use), the first 1 or 2 doses may be taken 30 minutes before meals or at least 2 hours after meals. If an antacid is taken concurrently, an aluminum- and magnesium-containing formulation may be preferred, since studies have shown that this formulation does not adversely affect absorption of most NSAIDs (See *Table 1*.

It is recommended that solid oral dosage forms of NSAIDs be taken with a full glass (240 mL) of water and that the patient remain in an upright position for 15 to 30 minutes after administration. These measures may reduce the risk of tablets or capsules becoming lodged in the esophagus, which has been reported to cause prolonged esophageal irritation and difficulty in swallowing in some patients receiving these medications.

In the treatment of primary dysmenorrhea, maximum benefit is achieved by initiating NSAID therapy as rapidly as possible after the onset of menses. Prophylactic therapy (i.e., starting NSAID administration a few days prior to the expected onset of the menstrual period) has not been found to provide additional therapeutic benefit.

Concurrent use of an NSAID with an opioid analgesic provides additive analgesia and may permit lower doses of the opioid analgesic to be utilized.

The analgesic activity of non-opioid analgesics is subject to a ceiling effect. Therefore, administration of an NSAID in higher-than-recommended analgesic doses may not provide additional therapeutic benefit in the treatment of pain not associated with inflammation.

In the treatment of arthritis, most of these agents have been shown to provide additional symptomatic relief when administered concurrently with gold compounds or glucocorticoids. NSAIDs may permit reduction of glucocorticoid dosage; however, reductions of glucocorticoid dosage, especially following long-term use, should be gradual to avoid symptoms associated with adrenal insufficiency or other manifestations of too-sudden withdrawal.

Naproxen-containing products should not be used concomitantly since they all circulate in the plasm as the naproxen anion.

DICLOFENAC

Summary of Differences

Indications:
Indicated for rheumatoid arthritis, osteoarthritis, and ankylosing spondylitis. Immediate-release tablets only indicated for pain and primary dysmenorrhea, and may also be used to relieve acute attacks of gout or calcium pyrophosphate deposition disease (pseudogout) and pain associated with nonrheumatic inflammatory conditions or vascular headaches.

Pharmacology/pharmacokinetics:
Physicochemical characteristics—Chemical group: A phenylacetic acid derivative.
Other actions/effects—
With usual doses, has lesser effect on platelet aggregation than most NSAIDs.
Also has uricosuric activity.
Biotransformation—Almost 50% of a dose eliminated via first-pass metabolism.
Half-life—Elimination: 1.2–2 hours.
Onset of action—Pain: Tablets—30 minutes.
Duration of action—Pain: Tablets—Up to 8 hours.

Precautions:
Pregnancy/reproduction—Embryotoxicity and other adverse effects, but not teratogenicity, demonstrated in animal studies.
Surgical—With recommended doses may be less likely than most other NSAIDs to increase perisurgical bleeding.
Drug interactions and/or related problems—
Also, reported to increase digoxin plasma concentrations.
Also, concurrent use with potassium-sparing diuretics may cause hyperkalemia.
Also, reported to decrease effects of antidiabetic agents or insulin.
Laboratory value alterations—
With usual doses is less likely than most other NSAIDs to increase bleeding time significantly.
Higher incidence of transaminase values being elevated to > 3 times the upper limit of normal than with other NSAIDs.

Also, may decrease plasma concentration and increase urine concentration of uric acid.
Medical considerations/contraindications—
Not recommended for patients with blood dyscrasias (or history of) or bone marrow depression.
Caution also required in patients with hepatic porphyria; may precipitate an acute attack.
Caution with diclofenac sodium-containing dosage forms in patients who must restrict their sodium intake.
Patient monitoring—Routine liver function tests recommended.
Side/adverse effects:
See *Table 3*.

Additional Dosing Information

See also *General Dosing Information*.

Diclofenac therapy should be discontinued if gastrointestinal bleeding or ulceration occurs.

For oral dosage forms only

The delayed-release tablets and the extended-release tablets are to be swallowed whole, not crushed or chewed.

Oral Dosage Forms

DICLOFENAC POTASSIUM TABLETS

Usual adult dose

Analgesic and
Antidysmenorrheal—
Oral, 50 mg three times a day as needed. If necessary, 100 mg may be administered for the first dose only.

Rheumatoid arthritis—
Oral, 150 to 200 mg per day in three or four divided doses, initially. After a satisfactory response has been obtained, dosage should be reduced to the minimum dose that provides continuing control of symptoms, usually 75 to 100 mg a day in three divided doses.

Osteoarthritis—
Oral, 100 to 150 mg per day in two or three divided doses, initially. After a satisfactory response has been obtained, dosage should be reduced to the minimum dose that provides continuing control of symptoms.

Ankylosing spondylitis[1]—
Oral, 100 to 125 mg a day in four or five divided doses, initially. After a satisfactory response has been obtained, dosage should be reduced to the minimum dose that provides continuing control of symptoms.

Usual adult prescribing limits

Analgesic and
Antidysmenorrheal—
Up to 200 mg on the first day, then 150 mg per day thereafter.

Rheumatoid arthritis—
225 mg per day.

Osteoarthritis—
150 mg per day; higher doses have not been studied.

Usual pediatric dose

Safety and efficacy have not been established.

Strength(s) usually available

U.S.—
25 mg (Rx) [*Cataflam* (calcium phosphate; colloidal silicon dioxide; iron oxides; magnesium stearate; microcrystalline cellulose; polyethylene glycol; povidone; sodium starch glycolate; starch; sucrose; talc; titanium dioxide)].
50 mg (Rx) [*Cataflam* (calcium phosphate; colloidal silicon dioxide; iron oxides; magnesium stearate; microcrystalline cellulose; polyethylene glycol; povidone; sodium starch glycolate; starch; sucrose; talc; titanium dioxide)].

Canada—
50 mg [*Voltaren Rapide* (carnauba wax; cellulose; colloidal silicon dioxide; corn starch; ferric oxide; magnesium stearate; polyethylene glycol; povidone; sodium carboxymethyl starch; sucrose; talc; titanium dioxide; tribasic calcium phosphate; white ink)].

Packaging and storage

Store below 30 °C (86 °F), in a tight container, unless otherwise directed by manufacturer. Protect from moisture.

Auxiliary labeling

- Take with food.
- Take with a full glass of water.
- Avoid alcoholic beverages.

DICLOFENAC SODIUM DELAYED-RELEASE TABLETS

Usual adult dose

Analgesic
and Antidysmenorrheal—
The delayed-release formulation is not recommended. See *Diclofenac Potassium Tablets*, which should be used for these indications.

Antirheumatic (nonsteroidal anti-inflammatory)—
See *Diclofenac Potassium Tablets*.

Usual pediatric dose

Safety and efficacy have not been established.

Strength(s) usually available

U.S.—
25 mg (Rx) [*Voltaren* (hydroxypropyl methylcellulose; iron oxide; lactose; magnesium stearate; methacrylic acid copolymer; microcrystalline cellulose; polyethylene glycol; povidone; propylene glycol; sodium hydroxide; sodium starch glycolate; talc; titanium dioxide; D&C Yellow #10 Aluminum Lake)].
50 mg (Rx) [*Voltaren* (hydroxypropyl methylcellulose; iron oxide; lactose; magnesium stearate; methacrylic acid copolymer; microcrystalline cellulose; polyethylene glycol; povidone; propylene glycol; sodium hydroxide; sodium starch glycolate; talc; titanium dioxide; FD&C Blue #1 Aluminum Lake)].
75 mg (Rx) [*Voltaren* (hydroxypropyl methylcellulose; iron oxide; lactose; magnesium stearate; methacrylic acid copolymer; microcrystalline cellulose; polyethylene glycol; povidone; propylene glycol; sodium hydroxide; sodium starch glycolate; talc; titanium dioxide)].

Canada—
25 mg (Rx) [*Apo-Diclo* (sodium <1 mmol [1.81 mg]); *Novo-Difenac; Nu-Diclo* (sodium <1 mmol); *Voltaren* (lactose; sodium < 1 mmol [2.03 mg])].
50 mg (Rx) [*Apo-Diclo* (sodium <1 mmol [3.62 mg]); *Novo-Difenac; Nu-Diclo* (sodium <1 mmol); *Voltaren* (lactose; sodium < 1 mmol [4.06 mg])].

Packaging and storage

Store below 30 °C (86 °F), in a tight container, unless otherwise specified by manufacturer. Protect from moisture.

Auxiliary labeling

- Swallow tablets whole.
- Take with a full glass of water.
- Avoid alcoholic beverages.

DICLOFENAC SODIUM EXTENDED-RELEASE TABLETS

Usual adult dose

Antirheumatic (nonsteroidal anti-inflammatory)—
Oral, 75 or 100 mg once a day, in the morning or evening, or 75 mg two times a day, in the morning and evening.

Note: The extended-release dosage form is not intended as initial therapy; the daily maintenance dose should be determined using an immediate- or delayed-release formulation. The extended-release dosage form may then be used, if desired, provided that the required dose can be achieved with the available strengths.

Usual pediatric dose

Safety and efficacy have not been established.

Strength(s) usually available

U.S.—
Not commercially available.

Canada—
75 mg (Rx) [*Voltaren SR* (sodium < 1 mmol [6.1 mg])].
100 mg (Rx) [*Novo-Difenac SR; Voltaren SR* (sodium < 1 mmol [8.13 mg])].

Packaging and storage

Store below 40 °C (104 °F), preferably between 15 and 30 °C (59 and 86 °F), unless otherwise specified by manufacturer.

Auxiliary labeling

- Take with food.
- Swallow tablets whole.
- Take with a full glass of water.
- Avoid alcoholic beverages.

Rectal Dosage Forms

DICLOFENAC SODIUM SUPPOSITORIES

Usual adult dose

Antirheumatic (nonsteroidal anti-inflammatory)—
Rectal, 50 or 100 mg, as a substitute for the last oral dose of the day.

Usual adult prescribing limits

Total daily dosage (oral and rectal) should not exceed 150 mg.

Usual pediatric dose
Safety and efficacy have not been established.

Strength(s) usually available
U.S.—
Not commercially available.
Canada—
50 mg (Rx) [*Voltaren* (sodium < 1 mmol [4.06 mg])].
100 mg (Rx) [*Voltaren* (sodium < 1 mmol [8.13 mg])].

Packaging and storage
Store below 40 °C (104 °F), preferably between 15 and 30 °C (59 and 86 °F), unless otherwise specified by manufacturer.

Auxiliary labeling
- Avoid alcoholic beverages.
- For rectal use.

[1]Not included in Canadian product labeling.

DIFLUNISAL

Summary of Differences

Indications:
Indicated for rheumatoid arthritis, osteoarthritis, ankylosing spondylitis, and psoriatic arthritis, and pain. May also be used to relieve acute attacks of gout or calcium pyrophosphate deposition disease (pseudogout), dysmenorrhea, and pain associated with nonrheumatic inflammatory conditions or vascular headaches.
Pharmacology/pharmacokinetics:
Physicochemical characteristics—Chemical group: A salicylate derivative, although not metabolized to salicylate *in vivo.*
Other actions/effects—
Platelet aggregation inhibition significant only with greater-than-recommended doses.
Also has uricosuric activity.
Half-life—Elimination: 8–12 hours; greatly prolonged by renal function impairment.
Onset of action—Pain: 1 hour.
Duration of action—Pain: 8–12 hours.
Precautions:
Pregnancy/reproduction—Embryotoxic and teratogenic effects demonstrated in rabbits, but not found to be teratogenic in mice.
Surgical—With recommended doses may be less likely than most other NSAIDs to increase perisurgical bleeding.
Drug interactions and/or related problems—
Also, may increase risk of acetaminophen-induced hepatotoxicity.
Also, chronic concurrent use of antacids significantly decreases diflunisal plasma concentration.
Diflunisal also increases plasma concentration of hydrochlorothiazide and decreases hyperuricemic effect of hydrochlorothiazide or furosemide, but has not been shown to decrease furosemide-induced diuresis.
Laboratory value alterations—
Interference with salicylate determinations; may cause falsely elevated salicylate values.
With usual doses is less likely than most other NSAIDs to increase bleeding time significantly.
May decrease plasma concentrations and increase urine concentrations of uric acid.
Medical considerations/contraindications—Higher risk than with most other NSAIDs in patients with renal function impairment.
Side/adverse effects:
Reported to cause a characteristic hypersensitivity syndrome.
Possibility of Reye's syndrome in children and adolescents with acute febrile illness should be considered (as with other salicylates).
See also *Table 3*.

Additional Dosing Information

See also *General Dosing Information.*

Administration of a 1-gram initial loading dose is recommended to provide faster onset of analgesic action, shorter time to peak analgesic effect, and greater peak analgesic action. For long-term use, the initial loading dose decreases the time needed to reach steady-state plasma concentrations; if a loading dose is not administered, 2 to 3 days may be required to evaluate changes in treatment regimens.

In patients with impaired renal function, especially if renal function is decreased to ½ the normal value or below, a reduction in dosage and/or an increase in the dosing interval may be necessary to prevent diflunisal accumulation.

Tablets are to be swallowed whole, not crushed or chewed.

Because diflunisal is not hydrolyzed to salicylic acid *in vivo*, serum salicylate concentration cannot be used as a guide to dosage or potential toxicity during therapy.

Oral Dosage Forms

DIFLUNISAL TABLETS USP

Usual adult dose
Rheumatoid arthritis or
Osteoarthritis—
Oral, 250 to 500 mg two times a day; dosage may be increased or decreased according to patient response.
Analgesic—
Oral, 1 gram initially, followed by 500 mg every eight to twelve hours as needed.

Note: For some patients, 500 mg initially followed by 250 mg every eight to twelve hours may be appropriate, depending on the severity of pain or the age, weight, or response of the patient.

Usual adult prescribing limits
Up to 1.5 grams daily.

Usual pediatric dose
Dosage has not been established.

Strength(s) usually available
U.S.—
250 mg (Rx) [*Dolobid;* GENERIC].
500 mg (Rx) [*Dolobid;* GENERIC (talc; titanium dioxide)].
Canada—
250 mg (Rx) [*Apo-Diflunisal; Dolobid; Novo-Diflunisal*].
500 mg (Rx) [*Apo-Diflunisal; Dolobid; Novo-Diflunisal*].

Packaging and storage
Store below 40 °C (104 °F), preferably between 15 and 30 °C (59 and 86 °F). Store in a well-closed container.

Auxiliary labeling
- Take with food.
- Swallow tablets whole.
- Take with a full glass of water.
- Avoid alcoholic beverages.

ETODOLAC

Summary of Differences

Indications:
Indicated for treatment of osteoarthritis and for pain. May also be used to relieve acute attacks of gout or calcium pyrophosphate deposition disease (pseudogout), dysmenorrhea, and pain associated with nonrheumatic inflammatory conditions or vascular headaches.
Pharmacology:
Physicochemical characteristics—Chemical group: A pyranoindoleacetic acid derivative.
Other actions/effects—Also has uricosuric activity.
Decreases renal function, but with administration of up to 500 mg every 12 hours recovery occurs prior to administration of next dose.
Half-life—Elimination:
Single dose—6–7 hours.
At steady-state—7.3±4 hours.
Onset of action—Pain: 30 minutes.
Time to peak effect—Pain: 1–2 hours.
Duration of action—Pain:
200-mg single dose—4–5 hours.
400-mg single dose—Generally 5–6 hours; up to 8–12 hours in some patients.
Precautions:
Pregnancy/reproduction—Alterations of limb development demonstrated in animal studies, but drug- or dose-response relationship not established.
Geriatrics—No differences relative to younger adults in pharmacokinetic profile with 200 mg twice a day or in side effects profile with 600 mg per day.
Laboratory value alterations—May cause false-positive test results in urinary bilirubin and urinary ketone determinations.
Decrease in serum uric acid concentration may be expected.
Medical considerations/contraindications: Significant problems have not been demonstrated in patients with mild to moderate renal function impairment receiving up to 500 mg every 12 hours.
Side/adverse effects:
See *Table 3.*

Oral Dosage Forms

ETODOLAC CAPSULES

Usual adult dose

Antirheumatic (nonsteroidal anti-inflammatory)—

Oral, 400 mg two or three times a day or 300 mg three or four times a day, initially. After a satisfactory response has been obtained, dosage should be individualized according to patient tolerance and response. Most patients are maintained on 600 to 1200 mg per day. However, as little as 200 mg two times a day has been effective in some patients.

Note: Although doses of up to 1 gram per day have been effective when administered in two divided doses (500 mg every twelve hours), administration on a three-dose-a-day schedule may provide greater benefit.

Analgesic—

Oral, 400 mg initially, then 200 to 400 mg every six to eight hours as needed. If a 400-mg dose fails to provide eight hours of analgesia, a regimen of 300 mg every six hours may be effective.

Usual adult prescribing limits

Patients weighing less than 60 kg—20 mg per kg of body weight per day.
Patients weighing 60 kg or more—1.2 grams per day.

Usual pediatric dose

Safety and efficacy have not been established.

Usual geriatric dose

See *Usual adult dose.*

Strength(s) usually available

U.S.—

200 mg (Rx) [*Lodine* (cellulose; gelatin; iron oxides; lactose; magnesium stearate; povidone; sodium lauryl sulfate; sodium starch glycolate; titanium dioxide)].

300 mg (Rx) [*Lodine* (cellulose; gelatin; iron oxides; lactose; magnesium stearate; povidone; sodium lauryl sulfate; sodium starch glycolate; titanium dioxide)].

Canada—

Not commercially available.

Packaging and storage

Store below 40 °C (104 °F), preferably between 15 and 30 °C (59 and 86 °F), unless otherwise specified by manufacturer.

Auxiliary labeling

- Take with food.
- Take with a full glass of water.
- Avoid alcoholic beverages.

ETODOLAC TABLETS

Usual adult dose

See *Etodolac Capsules.*

Usual adult prescribing limits

See *Etodolac Capsules.*

Usual pediatric dose

Safety and efficacy have not been established.

Usual geriatric dose

See *Etodolac Capsules.*

Strength(s) usually available

U.S.—

400 mg (Rx) [*Lodine* (cellulose; FD&C Yellow #10; FD&C Blue #2; FD&C Yellow #6; hydroxypropyl methylcellulose; lactose; magnesium stearate; polyethylene glycol; polysorbate 80; povidone; sodium starch glycolate; titanium dioxide)].

500 mg (Rx) [*Lodine* (cellulose; FD&C Yellow #10; FD&C Blue #2; FD&C Yellow #6; hydroxypropyl methylcellulose; lactose; magnesium stearate; polyethylene glycol; polysorbate 80; povidone; sodium starch glycolate; titanium dioxide)].

Canada—

Not commercially available.

Packaging and storage

Store below 40 °C (104 °F), preferably between 15 and 30 °C (59 and 86 °F), unless otherwise specified by manufacturer.

Auxiliary labeling

- Take with food.
- Take with a full glass of water.
- Avoid alcoholic beverages.

ETODOLAC EXTENDED-RELEASE TABLETS

Usual adult dose

Antirheumatic (nonsteroidal anti-inflammatory)—

Oral, 400 to 1000 mg once a day.

Usual adult prescribing limits

1000 mg a day.

Usual pediatric dose

Safety and efficacy have not been established.

Usual geriatric dose

See *Usual adult dose.*

Strength(s) usually available

U.S.—

400 mg (Rx) [*Lodine XL* (dibasic sodium phosphate; ethylcellulose; FD&C Red #40; FD&C Yellow #6; hydroxypropyl methylcellulose; lactose; magnesium stearate; polyethylene glycol; polysorbate 80; titanium dioxide)].

600 mg (Rx) [*Lodine XL* (dibasic sodium phosphate; ethylcellulose; FD&C Red #40; FD&C Yellow #6; hydroxypropyl cellulose; hydroxypropyl methylcellulose; iron oxide; lactose; magnesium stearate; polyethylene glycol; polysorbate 80; titanium dioxide)].

Canada—

Not commercially available.

Packaging and storage

Store below 40 °C (104 °F), preferably between 15 and 30 °C (59 and 86 °F), unless otherwise specified by manufacturer.

Auxiliary labeling

- Take with food.
- Take with a full glass of water.
- Avoid alcoholic beverages.

FENOPROFEN

Summary of Differences

Indications:

Indicated for rheumatoid arthritis, osteoarthritis, ankylosing spondylitis, and psoriatic arthritis; pain; and acute attacks of gout or calcium pyrophosphate deposition disease (pseudogout). May also be used to relieve dysmenorrhea and pain associated with nonrheumatic inflammatory conditions or vascular headaches. Also used for vascular headache prophylaxis.

Pharmacology/pharmacokinetics:

Physicochemical characteristics—Chemical group: A propionic acid derivative.

Half-life—Elimination: 3 hours.

Precautions:

Pregnancy/reproduction—No teratogenic or other adverse effects demonstrated in animal studies.

Drug interactions and/or related problems—Concurrent chronic use with antacids significantly decreases fenoprofen plasma concentration.

Also, phenobarbital may increase metabolism and decrease half-life of fenoprofen.

Laboratory value alterations—Interference with triiodothyronine (T_3) determinations using the Amerlex-M kit assay.

Medical considerations/contraindications—Higher risk than with most other NSAIDs in patients with renal function impairment.

Side/adverse effects:

See *Table 3.*

Additional Dosing Information

See also *General Dosing Information.*

In the treatment of arthritis, improvement in condition may occur within a few days, but 2 to 3 weeks of continuous use on a regular basis may be required for maximum effectiveness.

Oral Dosage Forms

Note: Bracketed uses in the *Dosage Forms* section refer to categories of use and/or indications that are not included in U.S. product labeling. The dosing and strengths of the available dosage forms are expressed in terms of the free acid (not the calcium salt).

FENOPROFEN CALCIUM CAPSULES USP

Usual adult dose

Antirheumatic (nonsteroidal anti-inflammatory)—

Oral, 300 to 600 mg (free acid), depending on the severity of the symptoms, three or four times a day, then adjusted as needed.

Note: Higher doses generally are required in rheumatoid arthritis than in osteoarthritis.

Analgesic[1] or
[Antidysmenorrheal][1]—
Oral, 200 mg (free acid) every four to six hours as needed.

Usual adult prescribing limits
Antirheumatic (nonsteroidal anti-inflammatory)—
Up to 3.2 grams (free acid) daily.

Usual pediatric dose
Safety and dosage have not been established.

Strength(s) usually available
U.S.—
200 mg (free acid) (Rx) [*Nalfon 200;* GENERIC].
300 mg (free acid) (Rx) [*Nalfon;* GENERIC].
Canada—
300 mg (free acid) (Rx) [*Nalfon*].

Packaging and storage
Store below 40 °C (104 °F), preferably between 15 and 30 °C (59 and 86 °F). Store in a well-closed container.

Auxiliary labeling
- Take with food.
- Take with a full glass of water.
- May cause drowsiness.
- Avoid alcoholic beverages.

FENOPROFEN CALCIUM TABLETS USP

Usual adult dose
See *Fenoprofen Calcium Capsules USP*.

Usual adult prescribing limits
See *Fenoprofen Calcium Capsules USP*.

Usual pediatric dose
Safety and dosage have not been established.

Strength(s) usually available
U.S.—
600 mg (free acid) (Rx) [*Nalfon* (scored); GENERIC].
Canada—
600 mg (free acid) (Rx) [*Nalfon*].

Packaging and storage
Store below 40 °C (104 °F), preferably between 15 and 30 °C (59 and 86 °F). Store in a well-closed container.

Auxiliary labeling
- Take with food.
- Take with a full glass of water.
- May cause drowsiness.
- Avoid alcoholic beverages.

[1]Not included in Canadian product labeling.

FLOCTAFENINE

Summary of Differences

Indications:
Indicated for relief of pain. May also be used to relieve acute attacks of gout or calcium pyrophosphate deposition disease (pseudogout), dysmenorrhea, and pain associated with nonrheumatic inflammatory conditions or vascular headaches.

Precautions:
Pregnancy/reproduction—Embryotoxicity but not teratogenicity demonstrated in animal studies.
Drug interactions and/or related problems—Floctafenine-induced increase in effect of coumarin- or indanedione-derivative anticoagulants may not become apparent until after 2 weeks of concurrent use.

Side/adverse effects:
See *Table 3*.

Additional Dosing Information

See also *General Dosing Information*.

Because the safety and efficacy of floctafenine for long-term administration has not been established, this medication is recommended for short-term use only.

Oral Dosage Forms

FLOCTAFENINE TABLETS

Usual adult dose
Analgesic—
Oral, 200 to 400 mg every six to eight hours, as needed.

Usual adult prescribing limits
Dosage should not exceed 1.2 grams per day.

Usual pediatric dose
Use is not recommended.

Strength(s) usually available
U.S.—
Not commercially available.
Canada—
200 mg (Rx) [*Idarac* (corn starch)].
400 mg (Rx) [*Idarac* (corn starch)].

Packaging and storage
Store below 40 °C (104 °F), preferably between 15 and 30 °C (59 and 86 °F), unless otherwise specified by manufacturer. Protect from light.

Auxiliary labeling
- Take with food.
- Take with a full glass of water.
- May cause drowsiness.
- Avoid alcoholic beverages.

FLURBIPROFEN

Summary of Differences

Indications:
Indicated for rheumatoid arthritis, osteoarthritis, ankylosing spondylitis, bursitis, tendinitis, soft tissue injuries, and dysmenorrhea.

Pharmacology/pharmacokinetics:
Physicochemical characteristics—Chemical group: A propionic acid derivative.
Half-life—Elimination: 5.7 hours.
Peak plasma concentration—Extended-release capsules: Increased by food.

Precautions:
Pregnancy/reproduction—Embryocidal and fetotoxic, but not teratogenic, effects demonstrated in animal studies.
Geriatrics—Peak plasma concentrations increased in elderly females.
Drug interactions and/or related problems—Studies failed to show that flurbiprofen increases digoxin plasma concentrations.

Side/adverse effects:
See *Table 3*.

Oral Dosage Forms

Note: Bracketed uses in the *Dosage Forms* section refer to categories of use and/or indications that are not included in U.S. product labeling.

FLURBIPROFEN EXTENDED-RELEASE CAPSULES

Usual adult dose
Antirheumatic (nonsteroidal anti-inflammatory)—
Oral, 200 mg once a day in the evening.

Note: The extended-release dosage form is not intended as initial therapy; the daily maintenance dose should be determined using the immediate-release formulation. The extended-release dosage form may then be used, if desired, provided that the required dose can be achieved with the available strength.

Usual pediatric dose
Safety and efficacy have not been established.

Strength(s) usually available
U.S.—
Not commercially available.
Canada—
200 mg (Rx) [*Froben SR*].

Packaging and storage
Store below 40 °C (104 °F), preferably between 15 and 30 °C (59 and 86 °F), unless otherwise specified by manufacturer.

Auxiliary labeling
- Take with food.
- Swallow capsules whole.
- Take with a full glass of water.
- Avoid alcoholic beverages.

FLURBIPROFEN TABLETS USP

Usual adult dose

Rheumatoid arthritis or
Osteoarthritis—
Oral, 200 to 300 mg a day in two to four divided doses, initially. Dosage may then be individualized according to the severity of the disease and patient response.

[Ankylosing spondylitis]—
Oral, 200 mg a day in four divided doses, initially, although some patients may require 250 to 300 mg a day.

Note: After a satisfactory response has been obtained, dosage should be decreased to the lowest dose that provides continuing control of symptoms.

[Antidysmenorrheal]—
Oral, 50 mg four times a day.

[Anti-inflammatory (nonsteroidal)]—
Oral, 50 mg every four to six hours as needed.

Usual adult prescribing limits

The maximum recommended single dose is 100 mg. Total daily dosage should not exceed 300 mg. This maximum dose is recommended for short-term use only, i.e., for initiation of therapy or for treating acute exacerbations of symptoms; it should not be used as a maintenance dose.

Usual pediatric dose

Safety and efficacy have not been established.

Strength(s) usually available

U.S.—
50 mg (Rx) [*Ansaid* (lactose); GENERIC].
100 mg (Rx) [*Ansaid* (lactose); GENERIC].

Canada—
50 mg (Rx) [*Ansaid; Apo-Flurbiprofen; Froben; Novo-Flurprofen; Nu-Flurbiprofen;* GENERIC].
100 mg (Rx) [*Ansaid; Apo-Flurbiprofen; Froben; Novo-Flurprofen; Nu-Flurbiprofen;* GENERIC].

Packaging and storage

Store below 40 °C (104 °F), preferably between 15 and 30 °C (59 and 86 °F), unless otherwise specified by manufacturer.

Auxiliary labeling

- Take with food.
- Take with a full glass of water.
- Avoid alcoholic beverages.

IBUPROFEN

Summary of Differences

Indications:
Indicated for rheumatoid arthritis, osteoarthritis, juvenile arthritis, and psoriatic arthritis; pain; gouty arthritis or calcium pyrophosphate deposition disease (pseudogout); fever; and dysmenorrhea. May also be used for prophylaxis and treatment of vascular headaches.

Pharmacology/pharmacokinetics:
Physicochemical characteristics—Chemical group: A propionic acid derivative.
Half-life—Elimination: 1.8–2 hours
Onset of action—Pain: 0.5 hour.
Time to peak effect—Fever: 2–4 hours.
Duration of action—
Fever:
5-mg/kg dose—6 hours.
10-mg/kg dose—8 hours or more.
Pain: 4–6 hours.

Precautions:
Pregnancy/reproduction—Teratogenic effects in animals have not been shown.
Breast-feeding—Methodology capable of detecting 1 mcg/mL failed to show that ibuprofen is distributed into breast milk.
Pediatrics—Studied in children 6 months of age and older; pediatrics-specific problems have not been demonstrated.
Drug interactions and/or related problems—Also, reported to increase digoxin plasma concentrations.
Laboratory value alterations—Also, may decrease blood glucose concentrations.

Side/adverse effects:
Reported to cause a characteristic hypersensitivity syndrome.
Reported to cause a serum sickness- or influenza-like syndrome.
See also *Table 3.*

Additional Dosing Information

See also *General Dosing Information.*

In the treatment of arthritis, improvement in condition may occur within 7 days, but 1 to 2 weeks of continuous use on a regular basis may be required for maximum effectiveness.

Oral Dosage Forms

IBUPROFEN ORAL SUSPENSION

Usual adult and adolescent dose

Antirheumatic (nonsteroidal anti-inflammatory)—
Oral, 1200 to 3200 mg a day in three or four divided doses. After a satisfactory response has been obtained, dosage should be reduced to the lowest maintenance dose that provides continuing control of symptoms.

Note: Higher doses generally are required in rheumatoid arthritis than in osteoarthritis.

Analgesic (mild to moderate pain)
Antipyretic or
Antidysmenorrheal—
Oral, 200 to 400 mg every four to six hours as needed.

Usual adult prescribing limits

Antirheumatic (nonsteroidal anti-inflammatory)—
Up to 3600 mg per day. The maximum dosage should be used only if the clinical benefit is increased sufficiently to offset the higher risk of adverse effects.

Analgesic
Antipyretic; or
Antidysmenorrheal—
For patient self-medication (over-the-counter use): Not to exceed 1200 mg per day.

Usual pediatric dose

Antirheumatic (nonsteroidal anti-inflammatory)—
Infants up to 6 months of age: Safety and efficacy have not been established.
Children 6 months to 12 years of age: Oral, initially 30 to 40 mg per kg of body weight a day in three or four divided doses, although 20 mg per kg of body weight per day may be sufficient for patients with mild disease. After a satisfactory response has been achieved, dosage should be reduced to the lowest dose needed to control disease activity.

Antipyretic—
Infants up to 6 months of age: Safety and efficacy have not been established.
Children 6 months to 12 years of age: Oral, 5 mg per kg of body weight for fevers less than 39.17 °C (102.5 °F) and 10 mg per kg of body weight for higher fevers. Dosage may be repeated, if necessary, at intervals of 4 to 6 hours or more.

Usual pediatric prescribing limits

Antirheumatic—
Oral, 50 mg per kg of body weight per day.

Antipyretic—
Oral, 40 mg per kg of body weight per day.

Strength(s) usually available

U.S.—
40 mg per mL (OTC) [*Motrin, Children's Oral Drops*].
40 mg per mL (Rx) [*Motrin, Children's Oral Drops*].
100 mg per 5 mL (OTC) [*Advil, Children's* (sucrose; cellulose gum; citric acid; disodium EDTA; FD&C Red #40; glycerin; microcrystalline cellulose; polysorbate 80; sodium benzoate; sorbitol; xanthan gum)].
100 mg per 5 mL (Rx) [*Advil, Children's* (sucrose; cellulose gum; citric acid; disodium EDTA; FD&C Red #40; glycerin; microcrystalline cellulose; polysorbate 80; sodium benzoate; sorbitol; xanthan gum)].
100 mg per 5 mL (OTC) [*Motrin, Children's* (sucrose; citric acid; glycerin; polysorbate 80; sodium benzoate; starch; xanthan gum; yellow #10; red #40)].
100 mg per 5 mL (Rx) [*Motrin, Children's* (sucrose; citric acid; glycerin; polysorbate 80; sodium benzoate; starch; xanthan gum; yellow #10; red #40)].

Canada—
Not commercially available.

Packaging and storage

Store between 15 and 30 °C (59 to 86 °F). Protect from freezing.

Auxiliary labeling
- Take with food or antacids.
- Shake well.
- Avoid alcoholic beverages.

IBUPROFEN TABLETS USP

Usual adult and adolescent dose
See *Ibuprofen Oral Suspension*.

Usual adult prescribing limits
See *Ibuprofen Oral Suspension*.

Usual pediatric dose
See *Ibuprofen Oral Suspension*.

Usual pediatric prescribing limits
See *Ibuprofen Oral Suspension*.

Strength(s) usually available
U.S.—

100 mg (Rx) [*Motrin, Junior Strength Caplets*].

100 mg (OTC) [*Motrin, Junior Strength Caplets*].

200 mg (OTC) [*Advil; Advil Caplets; Bayer Select Ibuprofen Pain Relief Formula Caplets; Cramp End; Excedrin IB; Excedrin IB Caplets; Genpril; Genpril Caplets; Haltran; Ibu-200; Ibuprin; Ibuprohm; Ibuprohm Caplets; Ibu-Tab; Medipren; Medipren Caplets; Midol IB; Motrin-IB; Motrin-IB Caplets; Nuprin; Nuprin Caplets; Pamprin-IB; Q-Profen; Trendar;* GENERIC].

300 mg (Rx) [*Motrin;* GENERIC].

400 mg (Rx) [*Dolgesic; Ibu; Ibu-4; Ibuprohm; Ibu-Tab; Motrin; Rufen;* GENERIC].

600 mg (Rx) [*Ibifon 600 Caplets; Ibren; Ibu; Ibu-6; Ibu-Tab; Motrin; Rufen;* GENERIC].

800 mg (Rx) [*Ibu; Ibu-8; Ibu-Tab; Motrin; Rufen;* GENERIC].

Canada—

200 mg (OTC) [*Actiprofen Caplets; Advil; Advil Caplets; Apo-Ibuprofen; Medipren Caplets; Motrin-IB; Motrin-IB Caplets; Novo-Profen;* GENERIC].

300 mg (Rx) [*Apo-Ibuprofen; Motrin; Novo-Profen; Nu-Ibuprofen;* GENERIC].

400 mg (Rx) [*Apo-Ibuprofen; Motrin; Novo-Profen; Nu-Ibuprofen;* GENERIC].

600 mg (Rx) [*Apo-Ibuprofen; Motrin; Novo-Profen; Nu-Ibuprofen;* GENERIC].

Packaging and storage
Store between 15 and 30 °C (59 and 86 °F), in a light-resistant container, unless otherwise specified by manufacturer. Store in a well-closed container.

Auxiliary labeling
- Take with food.
- Take with a full glass of water.
- May cause drowsiness.
- Avoid alcoholic beverages.

IBUPROFEN TABLETS (CHEWABLE)

Usual adult and adolescent dose
See *Ibuprofen Oral Suspension*.

Usual adult prescribing limits
See *Ibuprofen Oral Suspension*.

Usual pediatric dose
See *Ibuprofen Oral Suspension*.

Usual pediatric prescribing limits
See *Ibuprofen Oral Suspension*.

Strength(s) usually available
U.S.—

50 mg (Rx) [*Motrin Chewables*].

100 mg (Rx) [*Motrin Chewables*].

Canada—

Not commercially available.

Packaging and storage
Store between 15 and 30 °C (59 and 86 °F), in a well-closed, light-resistant container, unless otherwise specified by manufacturer.

Auxiliary labeling
- Take with food.
- Take with a full glass of water.
- May cause drowsiness.
- Avoid alcoholic beverages.

INDOMETHACIN

Summary of Differences

Indications:

Indicated for rheumatoid arthritis, osteoarthritis, ankylosing spondylitis, juvenile arthritis, psoriatic arthritis, Reiter's disease, and rheumatic complications associated with Paget's disease of bone; acute gouty arthritis and calcium pyrophosphate deposition disease (pseudogout); bursitis and tendinitis; fever associated with malignancy; dysmenorrhea; prevention and treatment of vascular headaches; Bartter's disease; and pericarditis.

Drug of first choice in ankylosing spondylitis; for other indications (except Bartter's syndrome), recommended only for patients unresponsive to less toxic NSAIDs or, in the case of fever, to other antipyretic agents.

Pharmacology/pharmacokinetics:

Physicochemical characteristics—Chemical group: An indoleacetic acid derivative.

Absorption—Oral: Capsules and oral suspension—90% of a dose absorbed within 4 hours.

Extended-release capsules—90% of a dose absorbed within 12 hours.

Rectal: 80 to 90% of a dose absorbed; incomplete absorption may result from failure to retain suppository in rectum for a full hour.

Half-life—Elimination: Average, about 4.5 hours; subject to substantial intersubject variability, possibly because of differences in enterohepatic circulation and subsequent reabsorption.

Onset of action—Gout: 2–4 hours.

Time to peak effect—Gout (capsules or oral suspension): 2–3 days for relief of heat and tenderness; 3–5 days for relief of swelling.

Precautions:

Pregnancy/reproduction—

First trimester: Crosses the placenta; fetotoxic, teratogenic, and other adverse effects demonstrated in animal studies.

Third trimester: Has caused closure of the ductus arteriosus, inhibition of platelet function resulting in bleeding, renal function impairment or failure with oligohydramnios, gastrointestinal bleeding or perforation, and myocardial degenerative changes in fetuses when given to pregnant women during the third trimester.

Breast-feeding—Distributed into breast milk; one report of convulsions in a breast-fed infant exposed to the medication.

Pediatrics—Recommended only for pediatric patients who are unresponsive to or intolerant of less toxic agents. Only immediate-release oral dosage forms should be used. Also, recommended doses should not be exceeded and the patient carefully monitored.

Geriatrics—Also, increased risk of adverse CNS effects, especially confusion.

Drug interactions and/or related problems—

Also, concurrent use with potassium-sparing diuretics may cause hyperkalemia.

Also, may block the increase in plasma renin activity induced by bumetanide, furosemide, or indapamide.

Also, concurrent use with zidovudine not recommended; toxicity of either or both of the medications may be increased.

Caution also recommended with aminoglycosides and digitalis glycosides; indomethacin has caused increased plasma concentrations of these medications in infants.

Laboratory value alterations—Also, may cause false-negative test results with dexamethasone suppression test for endogenous depression and one test for urinary 5-hydroxyindoleacetic acid (5-HIAA).

Also, may increase or decrease blood glucose concentrations.

Medical considerations/contraindications—

Higher risk than with most other NSAIDs in patients with renal function impairment.

Also, may aggravate epilepsy, mental depression or other mental disturbances, or parkinsonism.

Patient monitoring—Routine monitoring of liver function recommended.

Side/adverse effects:

See *Table 3*.

Additional Dosing Information

See also *General Dosing Information*.

Indomethacin should be administered in the lowest dose that provides symptomatic relief. Doses greater than 150 to 200 mg per day may increase the risk of adverse effects without providing additional clinical benefit. If therapy is to be continued after the acute phase of the disease has been controlled, periodic attempts should be made to reduce the dose to the lowest dose providing continuing control of symptoms.

If minor adverse effects occur, dosage should be reduced and the patient carefully monitored. If severe side effects occur, therapy should be discontinued.

For oral dosage forms only

Oral dosage forms of indomethacin should always be administered after meals or with food or an antacid to reduce gastrointestinal irritation. However, the oral suspension should not be mixed with an antacid or other liquid prior to use.

To facilitate dosage adjustment and assessment of patient tolerance of the medication, it is recommended that an immediate-release, rather than the extended-release, dosage form be used for initiation of therapy or to increase the daily dose. If the extended-release dosage form is used for initial therapy, or to increase the daily dose, careful observation of the patient is recommended.

For rectal dosage form only

To ensure maximum absorption, the suppository should be retained for at least one full hour after insertion.

Oral Dosage Forms

Note: Bracketed uses in the *Dosage Forms* section refer to categories of use and/or indications that are not included in U.S. product labeling.

INDOMETHACIN CAPSULES USP

Usual adult dose

Antirheumatic (nonsteroidal anti-inflammatory)—

Oral, initially 25 or 50 mg two to four times a day; if well tolerated, the dosage per day may be increased by 25 or 50 mg at weekly intervals until a satisfactory response is obtained or up to a maximum dose of 200 mg per day. After a satisfactory response has been achieved, dosage should be reduced to the lowest dose that provides continuing control of symptoms.

Note: In acute flare-ups of rheumatoid arthritis, dosage may be increased by 25 or 50 mg daily, as needed and tolerated.

For those arthritic patients who have persistent night pain and/or morning stiffness, up to 100 mg of the total daily dose may be given at bedtime. Lower bedtime doses may not provide adequate symptomatic relief.

A daily dose of less than 75 mg may not be effective in active inflammatory disease.

A daily dose of more than 150 to 200 mg may increase the risk of adverse effects without providing additional clinical benefit.

Antigout agent—

Oral, 100 mg initially, then 50 mg three times a day until pain is relieved, with the dosage then being reduced until medication is discontinued.

Anti-inflammatory (nonsteroidal)[1]—

75 to 150 mg per day in three or four divided doses.

Note: When used to treat conditions not requiring chronic therapy, such as acute bursitis or tendinitis of the shoulder, indomethacin should be discontinued when symptoms of inflammation have been controlled for several days. The usual length of treatment is 7 to 14 days.

[Antipyretic][1]—

Oral, 25 or 50 mg three or four times a day.

Usual adult prescribing limits

Oral, 200 mg a day.

Usual pediatric dose

Antirheumatic (nonsteroidal anti-inflammatory)—

Oral, 1.5 to 2.5 mg per kg of body weight per day, administered in three or four divided doses, up to a maximum of 4 mg per kg of body weight per day or 150 to 200 mg per day, whichever is less. After a satisfactory response has been obtained, dosage should be reduced to the lowest dose that provides continuing control of symptoms.

Strength(s) usually available

U.S.—

25 mg (Rx) [*Indocin* (lactose); GENERIC].
50 mg (Rx) [*Indocin* (lactose); GENERIC].

Canada—

25 mg (Rx) [*Apo-Indomethacin; Indocid* (lactose); *Novo-Methacin; Nu-Indo*].
50 mg (Rx) [*Apo-Indomethacin; Indocid* (lactose); *Novo-Methacin; Nu-Indo*].

Packaging and storage

Store below 40 °C (104 °F), preferably between 15 and 30 °C (59 and 86 °F). Store in a well-closed container.

Auxiliary labeling

- Take with food or antacids.
- Take with a full glass of water.
- Avoid alcoholic beverages.

INDOMETHACIN EXTENDED-RELEASE CAPSULES USP

Usual adult dose

Antirheumatic (nonsteroidal anti-inflammatory)—

Oral, 75 mg once a day, in the morning or at bedtime; may be increased to 75 mg two times a day if necessary.

Note: It is generally recommended that the daily maintenance dose be determined using the immediate-release formulation. The extended-release dosage form may then be used, if desired, provided that the required dose can be achieved with the available strength.

Careful observation of the patient for signs of intolerance is recommended if the extended-release capsule is used for initiating indomethacin therapy or for increasing the daily dose. Initiation of therapy with one extended-release capsule daily provides the maximum initial dose recommended by the manufacturer. Use of the extended-release capsule to increase the dose provides a greater-than-recommended increase in daily dosage.

Usual pediatric dose

Dosage has not been established.

Strength(s) usually available

U.S.—

75 mg (Rx) [*Indocin SR* (sugar); GENERIC].

Canada—

75 mg (Rx) [*Indocid SR* (sucrose)].

Packaging and storage

Store below 40 °C (104 °F), preferably between 15 and 30 °C (59 and 86 °F), unless otherwise specified by manufacturer. Store in a well-closed container.

Auxiliary labeling

- Take with food or antacids.
- Take with a full glass of water.
- Avoid alcoholic beverages.

Additional information

The extended-release capsules are designed to release 25 mg of indomethacin immediately and the remaining 50 mg over a 12-hour period.

INDOMETHACIN ORAL SUSPENSION USP

Usual adult dose

See *Indomethacin Capsules USP*.

Usual adult prescribing limits

See *Indomethacin Capsules USP*.

Usual pediatric dose

See *Indomethacin Capsules USP*.

Strength(s) usually available

U.S.—

25 mg per 5 mL (Rx) [*Indocin* (alcohol 1%); GENERIC].

Canada—

Not commercially available.

Packaging and storage

Store below 30 °C (86 °F). Store in a tight, light-resistant container. Protect from freezing.

Incompatibilities

Indomethacin is unstable in an alkaline medium and should not be mixed with antacids or other liquids having an alkaline pH.

Auxiliary labeling

- Take with food or antacids.
- Shake well.
- Avoid alcoholic beverages.

Rectal Dosage Forms

INDOMETHACIN SUPPOSITORIES USP

Usual adult dose

Antirheumatic (nonsteroidal anti-inflammatory)
Anti-inflammatory (nonsteroidal)[1]
Antigout agent or
[Antipyretic][1]—

Rectal, 50 mg up to four times a day.

Note: A daily dose of less than 75 mg may not be effective in active inflammatory disease.

For those arthritic patients who have persistent night pain and/or morning stiffness, up to 100 mg of the total daily dose may be given at bedtime. Lower bedtime doses may not provide adequate symptomatic relief.

A daily dose of more than 150 to 200 mg may increase the risk of adverse effects without providing additional clinical benefit.

Usual adult prescribing limits
Rectal or combined oral and rectal, 200 mg per day.

Usual pediatric dose
Antirheumatic (nonsteroidal anti-inflammatory)—
Rectal, 1.5 to 2.5 mg per kg of body weight per day, administered in 3 or 4 divided doses, up to a maximum of 4 mg per kg of body weight or 150 to 200 mg per day, whichever is less.

Strength(s) usually available
U.S.—
50 mg (Rx) [*Indocin* (butylated hydroxyanisole; butylated hydroxytoluene; edetic acid; glycerin; polyethylene glycol 3350; polyethylene glycol 8000; sodium chloride)].
Canada—
50 mg (Rx) [*Indocid*].
100 mg (Rx) [*Indocid*].

Packaging and storage
Store below 40 °C (104 °F), preferably between 15 and 30 °C (59 and 86 °F), unless otherwise specified by manufacturer. Store in a well-closed container. Protect from freezing.

Auxiliary labeling
- For rectal use.
- Avoid alcoholic beverages.

[1]Not included in Canadian product labeling.

KETOPROFEN

Summary of Differences

Indications:
Indicated for rheumatoid arthritis, osteoarthritis, ankylosing spondylitis, and psoriatic arthritis; pain; acute gouty arthritis and calcium pyrophosphate deposition disease (pseudogout); and dysmenorrhea. May also be used to relieve pain associated with nonrheumatic inflammatory disorders or vascular headaches.

Pharmacology/pharmacokinetics:
Physicochemical characteristics—Chemical group: A propionic acid derivative.
Half-life—Elimination:
Capsules—1.6 hours; increased by 26% in geriatric patients; also increased by renal function impairment.
Extended-release capsules—About 5.4 hours; higher value (relative to immediate-release capsules) represents prolonged absorption; increased by 54% in geriatric patients.
Extended-release tablets—About 3–4 hours; higher value (relative to immediate-release capsules) represents prolonged absorption.
Elimination—Dialyzable.

Precautions:
Pregnancy/reproduction—Fertility: Decreased number of implantation sites in female rats (but no effect on fertility in male rats); high doses caused abnormal spermatogenesis or impaired spermatogenesis in rats and dogs and decreased testicular weight in dogs and baboons.
First trimester: No teratogenicity demonstrated in animal studies; in rabbits, maternally toxic doses shown to be embryotoxic.
Geriatrics—Protein binding and clearance reduced in elderly people, leading to increased plasma concentration and prolonged half-life.
Drug interactions and/or related problems—
Probenecid may greatly increase ketoprofen plasma concentration and the risk of toxicity; concurrent use not recommended.
Studies failed to show that ketoprofen increases digoxin plasma concentration.
Laboratory value alterations—Interference with determinations of urinary albumin, bile salts, 17-ketosteroids, and 17-hydroxycorticosteroids via test procedures that rely on acid precipitation or on color reaction of carbonyl groups as an end point.

Side/adverse effects:
See *Table 3*.

Oral Dosage Forms

KETOPROFEN CAPSULES

Usual adult dose
Antirheumatic (nonsteroidal anti-inflammatory)—
Oral, 150 to 300 mg a day in three or four divided doses, usually 75 mg three times a day or 50 mg four times a day, initially, then adjusted according to patient response.
Analgesic or
Antidysmenorrheal—
Oral, 25 to 50 mg every six to eight hours as needed. Dosage may be increased if necessary, but single doses higher than 75 mg have not been shown to provide additional analgesia. In the treatment of dysmenorrhea, 75-mg doses may be more effective than lower doses.

Note: In patients with renal function impairment, a 33 to 50% reduction of dosage is recommended.

Note: The analgesic dosage for self-medication with ketoprofen using the over-the-counter product is 12.5 mg every four to six hours.

Usual adult prescribing limits
Oral, 300 mg a day in three or four divided doses.

Note: Risk/benefit must be considered when the maximum dose is prescribed because the incidence of gastrointestinal effects and headache is increased with administration of 300 mg per day (as compared with 200 mg per day).

Usual pediatric dose
Safety and efficacy have not been established.

Strength(s) usually available
U.S.—
25 mg (Rx) [*Orudis* (lactose); GENERIC].
50 mg (Rx) [*Orudis* (lactose); GENERIC].
75 mg (Rx) [*Orudis* (lactose); GENERIC].
Canada—
50 mg (Rx) [*Apo-Keto; Orudis; Rhodis*].

Packaging and storage
Store below 40 °C (104 °F), preferably between 15 and 30 °C (59 and 86 °F), in a tight container, unless otherwise specified by manufacturer.

Auxiliary labeling
- Take with food.
- Take with a full glass of water.
- Avoid alcoholic beverages.

KETOPROFEN EXTENDED-RELEASE CAPSULES

Usual adult dose
Antirheumatic (nonsteroidal anti-inflammatory)—
Oral, 150 or 200 mg once a day, in the morning or evening. Elderly or debilitated patients may require lower doses.

Note: The extended-release dosage form is not intended as initial therapy; the daily maintenance dose should be determined using an immediate- or delayed-release formulation. The extended-release dosage form may then be used, if desired, provided that the required dose can be achieved with the available strength(s).

Usual pediatric dose
Safety and efficacy have not been established.

Strength(s) usually available
U.S.—
100 mg (Rx) [*Oruvail*].
150 mg (Rx) [*Oruvail*].
200 mg (Rx) [*Oruvail*].
Canada—
150 mg (Rx) [*Oruvail*].
200 mg (Rx) [*Oruvail*].

Packaging and storage
Store below 40 °C (104 °F), preferably between 15 and 30 °C (59 and 86 °F), in a well-closed container, unless otherwise specified by manufacturer.

Auxiliary labeling
- Swallow capsule whole.
- Take with a full glass of water.
- Avoid alcoholic beverages.

Note
The extended-release capsule is formulated with delayed-release as well as extended-release characteristics. Dissolution of the contents of the capsules (coated pellets) does not occur until the medication reaches the alkaline pH of the small intestine.

KETOPROFEN DELAYED-RELEASE TABLETS

Usual adult dose
See *Ketoprofen Capsules*.

Usual adult prescribing limits
See *Ketoprofen Capsules*.

Usual pediatric dose
Safety and efficacy have not been established.

Strength(s) usually available
U.S.—
Not commercially available.
Canada—
50 mg (Rx) [*Apo-Keto-E; Novo-Keto-EC; Orudis-E; Rhodis-EC*].
100 mg (Rx) [*Apo-Keto-E; Novo-Keto-EC; Orudis-E; Rhodis-EC*].

Packaging and storage
Store below 40 °C (104 °F), preferably between 15 and 30 °C (59 and 86 °F), in a well-closed container, unless otherwise specified by manufacturer.

Auxiliary labeling
- Take with a full glass of water.
- Swallow tablets whole.
- Avoid alcoholic beverages.

KETOPROFEN EXTENDED-RELEASE TABLETS

Usual adult dose
See *Ketoprofen Extended-release Capsules*.

Usual pediatric dose
Safety and efficacy have not been established.

Strength(s) usually available
U.S.—
Not commercially available.
Canada—
200 mg (Rx) [*Orudis-SR;* GENERIC].

Packaging and storage
Store below 40 °C (104 °F), preferably between 15 and 30 °C (59 and 86 °F), in a well-closed container, unless otherwise specified by manufacturer.

Auxiliary labeling
- Take with food.
- Take with a full glass of water.
- Swallow tablets whole.
- Avoid alcoholic beverages.

KETOPROFEN TABLETS USP

Usual adult dose
See *Ketoprofen Capsules*.

Usual adult prescribing limits
See *Ketoprofen Capsules*.

Usual pediatric dose
Safety and efficacy have not been established.

Strength(s) usually available
U.S.—
12.5 mg (OTC) [*Orudis KT* (tartrazine); *Actron* (lactose)].
Canada—
Not commercially available.

Packaging and storage
Store below 40 °C (104 °F), preferably between 15 and 30 °C (59 and 86 °F), in a well-closed container, unless otherwise specified by manufacturer.

Auxiliary labeling
- Take with a full glass of water.
- Avoid alcoholic beverages.

Rectal Dosage Forms

KETOPROFEN SUPPOSITORIES

Usual adult dose
Antirheumatic (nonsteroidal anti-inflammatory)—
Rectal, 50 or 100 mg two times a day, in the morning and evening; or 50 or 100 mg in the evening in conjunction with oral administration during the day.

Usual adult prescribing limits
Rectal or combined oral and rectal, 300 mg a day.

Usual pediatric dose
Safety and efficacy have not been established.

Strength(s) usually available
U.S.—
Not commercially available.
Canada—
50 mg (Rx) [*Orudis*].
100 mg (Rx) [*Orudis; Rhodis*].

Packaging and storage
Store below 30 °C (86 °F), in a well-closed container, unless otherwise specified by manufacturer. Protect from freezing.

Auxiliary labeling
- For rectal use.
- Avoid alcoholic beverages.

MECLOFENAMATE

Summary of Differences

Indications:
Indicated for rheumatoid arthritis, osteoarthritis, psoriatic arthritis, pain, dysmenorrhea, and idiopathic hypermenorrhea. May also be used to relieve acute attacks of gout or calcium pyrophosphate deposition disease (pseudogout) and pain associated with nonrheumatic inflammatory conditions or vascular headaches.

Pharmacology/pharmacokinetics:
Physicochemical characteristics—Chemical group: A fenamate derivative.
Other actions/effects—With usual doses has lesser effect on platelet aggregation than most other NSAIDs.
Biotransformation—Hydroxymethyl metabolite has anti-inflammatory activity.
Half-life—Elimination:
Single dose—2 hours.
Multiple doses—3.3 hours.
Onset of action—Pain: 1 hour.
Duration of action—Pain: 4–6 hours.

Precautions:
Pregnancy/reproduction—Fetotoxicity and developmental abnormalities have been demonstrated in animals.
Breast-feeding—Use not recommended because animal studies have shown this agent to interfere with normal development of the young before weaning.
Surgical—With recommended doses may be less likely than most other NSAIDs to increase perisurgical bleeding.
Laboratory value alterations—With usual doses may be less likely than most other NSAIDs to increase bleeding time significantly.
Medical considerations/contraindications—Caution in patients on a sodium-restricted diet.

Side/adverse effects:
Reported to cause a serum sickness or influenza-like syndrome.
See also *Table 3*.

Additional Dosing Information

See also *General Dosing Information*.

Improvement in condition may occur within a few days, but 2 to 3 weeks of continuous use on a regular basis may be required for maximum effectiveness.

Gastrointestinal side effects may respond to a reduction in dosage; however, if severe adverse reactions occur, therapy should be discontinued.

Oral Dosage Forms

Note: The dosing and strengths of the available dosage form are expressed in terms of meclofenamic acid (not the sodium salt).

MECLOFENAMATE SODIUM CAPSULES USP

Usual adult dose
Antirheumatic (nonsteroidal anti-inflammatory)—
Oral, 200 mg (meclofenamic acid) a day, in three or four divided doses, initially. Dosage may be increased to up to 400 mg a day if necessary. After a satisfactory response has been obtained, dosage should be reduced to the lowest maintenance dose that provides continuing control of symptoms.
Analgesic—
Oral, 50 mg (meclofenamic acid) every four to six hours. If necessary, dosage may be increased to 100 mg every four to six hours.
Antidysmenorrheal and
Antihypermenorrheal—
Oral, 100 mg (meclofenamic acid) three times a day for up to six days.

Usual adult prescribing limits
Antirheumatic (nonsteroidal anti-inflammatory)
and analgesic—
Up to 400 mg daily.

Usual pediatric dose
Children up to 14 years of age—Safety and efficacy have not been established.

Strength(s) usually available
U.S.—
50 mg (meclofenamic acid) (Rx) [*Meclomen* (lactose); GENERIC].
100 mg (meclofenamic acid) (Rx) [*Meclomen* (lactose); GENERIC].
Canada—
Not commercially available.

Packaging and storage
Store between 15 and 30 °C (59 and 86 °F), unless otherwise specified by manufacturer. Store in a tight, light-resistant container.

Auxiliary labeling
- Take with food.
- Take with a full glass of water.
- Avoid alcoholic beverages.

MEFENAMIC ACID

Summary of Differences
Indications:
Indicated for short-term use (7 days or less) to relieve pain and dysmenorrhea. May also be used for acute attacks of gout or calcium pyrophosphate deposition disease (pseudogout), for pain associated with nonrheumatic inflammatory conditions or vascular headaches, and to prevent migraines associated with menstruation.
Pharmacology/pharmacokinetics:
Physicochemical characteristics—Chemical group: A fenamate derivative.
Other actions/effects—With usual doses has lesser effect on platelet aggregation than most other NSAIDs.
Half-life—Elimination: 2 hours
Precautions:
Pregnancy/reproduction—
Fertility: Decreased fertility demonstrated in rodents.
Pregnancy: Increased number of resorptions and decreased survival to weaning demonstrated in rodents.
Surgical—With usual doses may be less likely than other NSAIDs to inhibit platelet aggregation significantly, but has been reported to cause hypoprothrombinemia, which may increase the risk of perisurgical bleeding.
Laboratory value alterations—
Interference with urinary bile determinations via the diazo tablet test.
With usual doses is less likely than most other NSAIDs to increase bleeding time significantly because of lesser effect on platelet aggregation; however, may prolong prothrombin time.
Medical considerations/contraindications—Also, may exacerbate preexisting hypoprothrombinemia.
Side/adverse effects:
See *Table 3*.

Additional Dosing Information
See also *General Dosing Information.*

It is recommended that mefenamic acid therapy be discontinued promptly if diarrhea or a skin rash develops. Patients who develop diarrhea during mefenamic acid therapy are usually unable to tolerate the drug thereafter.

Mefenamic acid should not be used for more than 7 days at a time.

Oral Dosage Forms
MEFENAMIC ACID CAPSULES USP

Usual adult dose
Analgesic or
Antidysmenorrheal—
Oral, 500 mg initially, followed by 250 mg every six hours as needed.

Note: It is recommended that mefenamic acid be used for no longer than 7 days at a time.

Usual pediatric dose
Children up to 14 years of age—Safety and efficacy have not been established.

Strength(s) usually available
U.S.—
250 mg (Rx) [*Ponstel* (lactose; sodium benzoate)].
Canada—
250 mg (Rx) [*Ponstan* (lactose)].

Packaging and storage
Store below 40 °C (104 °F), preferably between 15 and 30 °C (59 and 86 °F). Store in a tight container.

Auxiliary labeling
- Take with food.
- Take with a full glass of water.
- May cause drowsiness.
- Avoid alcoholic beverages.

MELOXICAM

Summary of Differences
Indications:
Indicated for osteoarthritis.
Pharmacology/pharmacokinetics:
Physicochemical characteristics—Chemical group: An oxicam derivative.
Absorption—Neither rate nor extent affected by food
Half-life—Elimination: 15 to 20 hours.
Time to peak concentration—5 to 6 hours.
Precautions:
Pregnancy/reproduction—Increased embryolethality and reduced neonatal survival in rats.

Oral Dosage Forms
MELOXICAM TABLETS

Usual adult dose
Antirheumatic (nonsteroidal anti-inflammatory)—
Oral, 7.5 mg a day as a single dose. Dosage may be increased to 15 mg a day.

Usual adult prescribing limits
The maximum recommended daily dose is 15 mg.

Usual pediatric dose
Safety and efficacy have not been established

Usual geriatric dose
See *Usual adult dose*

Strength(s) usually available
U.S.—
7.5 mg (Rx) [*Mobic*].

Packaging and storage
Store between 15 and 30 °C (59 and 86 °F) in a dry place.

NABUMETONE

Summary of Differences
Indications:
Indicated for rheumatoid arthritis and osteoarthritis.
Pharmacology/pharmacokinetics:
Physicochemical characteristics—
Chemical group: A naphthylalkanone derivative.
Other characteristics:
Nabumetone (prodrug)—Nonacidic.
6-MNA (active metabolite)—Acidic.
Other actions/effects—With usual doses has lesser effect on platelet aggregation than most other NSAIDs.
Absorption—Rate and extent increased by food or milk.
Biotransformation—Metabolite 6-MNA, not nabumetone itself, is active substance.
Half-life (plasma)—Elimination: 6-MNA—23±3.7 hours; increased in geriatric patients to 30±8.1 hours (although values as high as 74 hours have been reported) and to 39 hours in patients with renal function impairment (creatinine clearance $<$ 30 mL/minute/1.73 cubic meters of body surface area).
Time to peak plasma concentration—6-MNA, at steady-state: Decreased by food; significantly delayed by hepatic cirrhosis.
Peak plasma concentration—6-MNA: Increased by food; may be increased in geriatric patients and substantially decreased in patients with hepatic cirrhosis.

Elimination—6-MNA: Significantly delayed by moderately severe renal function impairment (creatinine clearance < 30 mL/minute/1.73 cubic meters of body surface area).

Precautions:

Mutagenicity—Induced chromosomal aberrations in lymphocytes.

Pregnancy/reproduction—Fetotoxicity but not teratogenicity demonstrated in rats.

Geriatrics—Higher plasma concentrations and greater interpatient variability in pharmacokinetics of 6-MNA in geriatric patients.

Surgical—In doses up to 1000 mg per day may be less likely than most other NSAIDs to increase perisurgical bleeding.

Drug interactions and/or related problems—May be less likely than other NSAIDs to cause problems in patients receiving anticoagulant or thrombolytic therapy.

Medical considerations/contraindications—Hepatic function impairment may decrease biotransformation to active metabolite sufficiently to decrease efficacy.

Side/adverse effects:

Lower incidence of peptic ulceration and bleeding than with other NSAIDs.

See also *Table 3*.

Oral Dosage Forms

NABUMETONE TABLETS

Usual adult dose

Antirheumatic (nonsteroidal anti-inflammatory)—

Oral, initially 1000 mg a day, as a single dose (usually at night) or in two divided doses (in the morning and evening). Dosage may be increased, if necessary, to 1500 mg or 2000 mg a day in two divided doses. After a satisfactory response has been obtained, dosage should be individualized according to patient tolerance and response. The lowest dose that provides continuing control of symptoms should be used for maintenance.

Note: In patients with moderate renal insufficiency, the maximum starting dose should not exceed 750 mg once daily. Following careful monitoring of renal function the daily dose may be increased to a maximum of 1500 mg.

In patients with severe renal insufficiency, the maximum starting dose should not exceed 500 mg once daily. Following careful monitoring of renal function the daily dose may be increased to a maximum of 1000 mg.

Usual adult prescribing limits

Doses larger than 2000 mg a day have not been studied and are not recommended.

Note: 1500 mg and 1000 mg for patients with severe and moderate renal insufficiency, respectively

Usual pediatric dose

Safety and efficacy have not been established.

Usual geriatric dose

See *Usual adult dose*.

Strength(s) usually available

U.S.—

500 mg (Rx) [*Relafen* (hypromellose; microcrystalline cellulose; polyethylene glycol; polysorbate 80; sodium lauryl sulfate; sodium starch glycolate; titanium dioxide)].

750 mg (Rx) [*Relafen* (hypromellose; microcrystalline cellulose; polyethylene glycol; polysorbate 80; sodium lauryl sulfate; sodium starch glycolate; titanium dioxide; iron oxides)].

Canada—

500 mg (Rx) [*Relafen*].

Packaging and storage

Store between 15 and 30 °C (59 and 86 °F), in a well-closed container, unless otherwise specified by manufacturer.

Auxiliary labeling

- Take with food.
- Take with a full glass of water.
- Avoid alcoholic beverages.

NAPROXEN

Summary of Differences

Indications:

Indicated for rheumatoid arthritis, osteoarthritis, ankylosing spondylitis, and juvenile arthritis; pain; acute attacks of gout and calcium pyrophosphate deposition disease (pseudogout); bursitis and tendinitis; fever; and dysmenorrhea; and for prophylaxis and treatment of vascular headaches.

Pharmacology/pharmacokinetics:

Physicochemical characteristics—Chemical group: A propionic acid derivative.

Absorption—May be increased by sodium bicarbonate.

Half-life—Elimination: 13 hours.

Onset of action—Naproxen sodium: Pain—1 hour.

Time to peak plasma concentration—Extended-release tablets: Decreased by food.

Peak plasma concentration—Extended-release tablets: Increased by food.

Time to peak effect—Gout: 1–2 days.

Pain: 2–4 hours.

Duration of action—Pain: Up to 7 hours.

Precautions:

Pregnancy/reproduction—Teratogenic effects in animals have not been shown.

Pediatrics—Higher risk of skin rash and increases in bleeding time than in adults receiving the medication.

Laboratory value alterations—Interference with some assays for urinary 5-hydroxyindoleacetic acid (5-HIAA) and urinary 17-ketogenic steroids.

Medical considerations/contraindications—Caution with naproxen sodium and naproxen oral suspension for patients who must restrict their sodium intake.

Side/adverse effects:

See *Table 3*.

Additional Dosing Information

See also *General Dosing Information*.

In arthritis, improvement in condition may occur within 2 weeks, but 2 to 4 weeks of continuous use on a regular basis may be required for maximum effectiveness.

Naproxen should be administered in the lowest effective dose to geriatric patients, patients with hepatic function impairment, or patients with renal function impairment (especially if creatinine clearance is < 20 mL per minute).

Oral Dosage Forms

NAPROXEN ORAL SUSPENSION

Usual adult dose

Antirheumatic (nonsteroidal anti-inflammatory)—

Oral, 250, 375, or 500 mg two times a day, morning and evening.

Note: During long-term administration, dosage may be adjusted according to patient response; lower doses may suffice.

For acute exacerbations of rheumatic disease, dosage may be increased to up to 1.5 grams per day for limited periods. Use of this high dose requires that the clinical benefit be increased sufficiently to offset the potential increased risk of adverse effects.

Anti-inflammatory (nonsteroidal) or
Analgesic (mild to moderate pain) or
Antidysmenorrheal—

Oral, 500 mg initially, then 250 mg every six to eight hours as needed.

Antigout agent[1]—

Oral, 750 mg initially, then 250 mg every eight hours until the attack has subsided.

Usual adult prescribing limits

For mild to moderate pain and dysmenorrhea—

Up to a total dose of 1.25 grams daily.

Usual pediatric dose

Antirheumatic (nonsteroidal anti-inflammatory)—

Oral, 10 mg per kg of body weight per day, given in two divided doses.

Strength(s) usually available

U.S.—

125 mg per 5 mL (Rx) [*Naprosyn* (fumaric acid; imitation orange flavor; imitation pineapple flavor; magnesium aluminum silicate; methylparaben; sodium 8 mg [<1 mmol] per mL; sorbitol; sucrose)].

Canada—

125 mg per 5 mL (Rx) [*Naprosyn*].

Packaging and storage

Store below 40 °C (104 °F), preferably between 15 and 30 °C (59 and 86 °F), in a well-closed, light-resistant container, unless otherwise specified by manufacturer. Protect from freezing.

Auxiliary labeling
- Take with food.
- Shake well.
- Avoid alcoholic beverages.

NAPROXEN TABLETS USP

Usual adult dose
See *Naproxen Oral Suspension.*

Usual adult prescribing limits
See *Naproxen Oral Suspension.*

Usual pediatric dose
See *Naproxen Oral Suspension.*

Strength(s) usually available
U.S.—
250 mg (Rx) [*Naprosyn;* GENERIC].
375 mg (Rx) [*Naprosyn;* GENERIC].
500 mg (Rx) [*Naprosyn;* GENERIC].
Canada—
125 mg (Rx) [*Apo-Naproxen; Naprosyn* (lactose); *Naxen* (lactose); *Novo-Naprox; Nu-Naprox*].
250 mg (Rx) [*Apo-Naproxen; Naprosyn* (lactose); *Naxen* (lactose); *Novo-Naprox; Nu-Naprox*].
375 mg (Rx) [*Apo-Naproxen* (scored); *Naprosyn* (scored; lactose); *Naxen* (scored; lactose); *Novo-Naprox* (scored); *Nu-Naprox* (scored)].
500 mg (Rx) [*Apo-Naproxen* (scored); *Naprosyn* (scored; lactose); *Naxen* (scored; lactose); *Novo-Naprox* (scored); *Nu-Naprox* (scored)].

Packaging and storage
Store between 15 and 30 °C (59 and 86 °F). Store in a well-closed container.

Auxiliary labeling
- Take with food.
- Take with a full glass of water.
- May cause drowsiness.
- Avoid alcoholic beverages.

NAPROXEN DELAYED-RELEASE TABLETS

Usual adult dose
Ankylosing spondylitis (treatment) or
Antirheumatic or
Osteoarthritis (treatment)—
Oral, 375 or 500 mg two times a day, morning and evening.

Note: During long-term administration, dosage may be adjusted according to patient response; lower doses may suffice. The morning and evening doses do not have to be equal in size and the administration of the drug more frequently than twice daily is not necessary.

For acute exacerbations of rheumatic disease, dosage may be increased to up to 1500 mg per day for limited periods. Use of this high dose requires that the clinical benefit be increased sufficiently to offset the potential increased risk of adverse effects.

Usual adult prescribing limits
See *Naproxen Oral Suspension.*

Usual pediatric dose
See *Naproxen Oral Suspension.*

Strength(s) usually available
U.S.—
375 mg (Rx) [*EC-Naprosyn* (croscarmellose sodium; povidone; magnesium stearate; methacrylic acid copolymer; talc; triethyl citrate; sodium hydroxide; simethicone emulsion)].
500 mg (Rx) [*EC-Naprosyn* (croscarmellose sodium; povidone; magnesium stearate; methacrylic acid copolymer; talc; triethyl citrate; sodium hydroxide; simethicone emulsion)].
Canada—
250 mg (Rx) [*Naprosyn-E*].
375 mg (Rx) [*Naprosyn-E*].
500 mg (Rx) [*Naprosyn-E*].

Packaging and storage
Store between 15 and 30 °C (59 and 86 °F), unless otherwise directed by manufacturer.

Auxiliary labeling
- Swallow tablets whole. Do not crush or chew.
- Take with a full glass of water.
- Avoid alcoholic beverages.

NAPROXEN SODIUM TABLETS USP

Usual adult dose
Antirheumatic (nonsteroidal anti-inflammatory)—
Oral, 275 or 550 mg two times a day, morning and evening; or 275 mg in the morning and 550 mg in the evening.

Note: During long-term administration, dosage may be adjusted according to patient response; lower doses may suffice.

If necessary, dosage may be increased to up to 1650 mg per day for short periods. The use of this higher dose requires that the clinical benefit be increased sufficiently to offset the potential increased risk.

Anti-inflammatory (nonsteroidal) or
Analgesic (mild to moderate pain)—
Oral, 550 mg initially, then 275 mg every six to eight hours as needed.
Antigout agent[1]—
Oral, 825 mg initially, then 275 mg every eight hours until the attack has subsided.

Note: Delayed-release formula is not recommended for acute gout due to the delay in absorption.

Antidysmenorrheal—
Oral, 550 mg initially, then 275 mg every six to eight hours as needed.

Note: For patient self-medication (over-the-counter use) for pain, fever, or dysmenorrhea—Patients 12 years of age and older: Oral, 220 mg every eight to twelve hours while symptoms persist, or

Oral, 440 mg for the first dose only, followed by 220 mg twelve hours later and every eight to twelve hours thereafter as needed.

Usual adult prescribing limits
For mild to moderate pain and dysmenorrhea—
Up to a total dose of 1375 mg daily.

Note: For patient self-medication (over-the-counter use) for pain, fever, or dysmenorrhea—Not to exceed 2 tablets (220 mg each) in twenty-four hours for patients 65 years of age or older or 3 tablets in twenty-four hours for patients 12 to 65 years of age.

Usual pediatric dose
Pediatric strength not available. It is recommended that naproxen oral suspension or tablets be administered instead.

Strength(s) usually available
U.S.—
220 mg (equivalent to 200 mg of naproxen, with 20 mg of sodium) (OTC) [*Aleve* (magnesium stearate; microcrystalline cellulose; povidone; talc; Opadry YS-1-4215)].
275 mg (equivalent to 250 mg of naproxen, with 25 mg [approximately 1.1 mmol] of sodium) (Rx) [*Anaprox* (lactose); GENERIC].
550 mg (equivalent to 500 mg of naproxen, with 50 mg [approximately 2.2 mmol] of sodium) (Rx) [*Anaprox DS;* GENERIC].
Canada—
275 mg (equivalent to 250 mg of naproxen, with 25 mg [approximately 1.1 mmol] of sodium) (Rx) [*Anaprox* (lactose); *Apo-Napro-Na; Novo-Naprox Sodium; Synflex*].
550 mg (equivalent to 500 mg of naproxen, with 50 mg [approximately 2.2 mmol] of sodium) (Rx) [*Anaprox DS; Apo-Napro-Na DS; Novo-Naprox Sodium DS; Synflex DS*].

Packaging and storage
Store between 15 and 30 °C (59 and 86 °F). Store in a well-closed container.

Auxiliary labeling
- Take with food.
- Take with a full glass of water.
- May cause drowsiness.
- Avoid alcoholic beverages.

NAPROXEN SODIUM EXTENDED-RELEASE TABLETS

Usual adult dose
Antirheumatic (nonsteroidal anti-inflammatory)—
Oral, 750 to 1000 mg once a day in the morning or evening.
Analgesic or
Antidysmenorrheal or
Anti-inflammatory (nonsteroidal)—
Oral, 1000 mg once a day in the morning or evening.

Note: For patients who require greater analgesic benefit, 1500 mg once a day for a limited period may be given. Thereafter, the daily dose should not exceed 1000 mg.

Antigout—
Oral, initially 1000 to 1500 mg once a day in the morning or evening, followed by 1000 mg once a day, until attack has subsided.

Adult prescribing limits
1500 mg per day.

Usual pediatric dose
Safety and efficacy have not been established.

Usual geriatric dose
See *Usual adult dose.*

Strength(s) usually available
U.S.—
375 mg (Rx) [*Naprelan*].
500 mg (Rx) [*Naprelan*].
Canada—
750 mg (Rx) [*Naprosyn-SR*].

Packaging and storage
Store between 15 and 30 °C (59 and 86 °F), in a well-closed container, unless otherwise specified by manufacturer.

Auxiliary labeling
- Take with food.
- Take with a full glass of water.
- Swallow tablets whole.
- May cause drowsiness.
- Avoid alcoholic beverages.

Rectal Dosage Forms

NAPROXEN SUPPOSITORIES

Usual adult dose
Antirheumatic (nonsteroidal anti-inflammatory)—
Rectal, 500 mg at bedtime, administered in conjunction with oral administration during the day.

Usual adult prescribing limits
Total daily dose administered orally and rectally should not exceed 1.5 grams a day. The 1.5-gram daily dose is recommended only for short-term administration during acute exacerbations of rheumatic disease. Also, use of this high dose requires that the additional clinical benefit be sufficient to offset the potential increased risk of adverse effects.

Usual pediatric dose
Dosage has not been established.

Strength(s) usually available
U.S.—
Not commercially available.
Canada—
500 mg (Rx) [*Naprosyn; Naxen*].

Packaging and storage
Store below 40 °C (104 °F), preferably between 15 and 30 °C (59 and 86 °F), unless otherwise specified by manufacturer. Protect from freezing.

Auxiliary labeling
- For rectal use.
- Avoid alcoholic beverages.

[1]Not included in Canadian product labeling.

OXAPROZIN

Summary of Differences

Indications:
Indicated for rheumatoid arthritis and osteoarthritis.
Pharmacology/pharmacokinetics:
Physicochemical characteristics—Chemical group: A propionic acid derivative.
Other actions/effects—
Is as potent as aspirin as an inhibitor of platelet aggregation.
Also has uricosuric activity.
Half-life—Elimination:
600 mg per day—25 hours.
1200 mg per day—21 hours.
Peak plasma concentration—Accumulates with chronic dosing.
Precautions:
Carcinogenicity—Increased hepatic adenomas and carcinomas in male CD mice, but not in female CD mice or in rats.
Pregnancy/reproduction—Caused fetal malformations in rabbits with doses within the usual human therapeutic range, but not in mice or rats.
Pediatrics—Preliminary studies done in patients 3 to 16 years of age; elevated aspartate aminotransferase values occurred more frequently in patients treated for juvenile arthritis than for other forms of arthritis.
Geriatrics—Dosage adjustment not needed on basis of pharmacokinetic considerations. Studies showed increased occurrence of impaired renal function and of decreased hemoglobin concentration, but not of changes in hepatic function, in patients 60 years of age and older compared to younger adults.
Surgical—Recommended that oxaprozin be discontinued 1 to 2 weeks before elective surgery; may be more likely than most other NSAIDs to increase risk of perisurgical bleeding because of potent and prolonged inhibitory effect on platelet aggregation.
Laboratory value alterations—Also, may decrease plasma concentrations and increase urine concentrations of uric acid.
Side/adverse effects:
See *Table 3*.

Oral Dosage Forms

OXAPROZIN TABLETS

Usual adult dose
Rheumatoid arthritis—
Oral, 1200 mg per day, initially, then adjusted according to patient tolerance and response.
Osteoarthritis—
Oral, 1200 mg per day, initially, although a lower dose of 600 mg per day may be sufficient for mild disease or for patients of low body weight.

Note: Initial dosage must be individualized according to the severity of disease and patient variables such as body weight and renal function.

A single 1200-mg or 1800-mg loading dose may be administered to patients with normal renal function if necessary to speed the onset of action.

An initial dose of 600 mg per day is recommended for patients with renal function impairment. If this dose is well tolerated, higher doses may be administered if needed.

Doses of up to 1200 mg per day are usually administered once a day, but patients who are unable to tolerate a single dose of this size may tolerate divided doses.

Very severe arthritis may require doses higher than 1200 mg per day, which should be administered in two or three divided doses. It is recommended that these higher doses be reserved for patients weighing more than 50 kg who have normal hepatic and renal function and a low risk of peptic ulceration and who have not experienced adverse effects with lower doses.

After a beneficial response has been achieved, dosage should be reduced to the lowest dose that provides continuing control of symptoms.

Usual adult prescribing limits
Oral, 1800 mg per day or 26 mg per kg of body weight per day, whichever is lower, in two or three divided doses.

Usual pediatric dose
Safety and efficacy in children have not been established. However, one preliminary study in children 3 to 16 years of age used a starting dose of 10 mg per kg of body weight. The dose was increased to 20 mg per kg of body weight if necessary.

Strength(s) usually available
U.S.—
600 mg (Rx) [*Daypro* (scored)].
Canada—
600 mg (Rx) [*Daypro* (scored)].

Packaging and storage
Store below 30 °C (86 °F), preferably between 15 and 30 °C (59 and 86 °F), in a tight, light-resistant container, unless otherwise specified by manufacturer.

Note: Protect unit-dose packages from light.

Auxiliary labeling
- Take with food.
- Take with a full glass of water.
- Avoid alcoholic beverages.

PHENYLBUTAZONE

Summary of Differences

Indications:
Recommended only for short-term treatment of severe arthritic conditions, gout, or calcium pyrophosphate deposition disease (pseudogout) in patients unresponsive to less toxic NSAIDs. Not recommended as initial therapy for any indication.

Pharmacology/pharmacokinetics:
Physicochemical characteristics—Chemical group: A pyrazole derivative.
Other actions/effects—Also induces hepatic microsomal enzyme activity.
Also has uricosuric activity.
Biotransformation—Metabolized via hepatic microsomal enzymes. Metabolite oxyphenbutazone is active.
Half-life—Elimination: 54–99 (average, 77) hours; increased to 105 hours in geriatric patients.

Precautions:
Mutagenicity—High concentrations induced chromosome abnormalities in Chinese hamster fibroblast cells *in vitro*.
Pregnancy/reproduction—Fetotoxicity, but not teratogenicity, demonstrated in animal studies.
Breast-feeding—Distributed into breast milk; may cause blood dyscrasias or other adverse effects in nursing infants.
Pediatrics—Use in children up to 15 years of age not recommended.
Geriatrics—Also, increased risk of blood dyscrasias. Recommended that duration of treatment be limited to 1 week in patients 60 years of age and older.
Drug interactions and/or related problems—
Concurrent use with alcohol may also impair psychomotor skills.
Higher risk of bleeding with coumarin- or indanedione-derivative anticoagulants than with other NSAIDs because phenylbutazone inhibits the anticoagulant's metabolism; concurrent use not recommended.
Also, increased risk of toxicity with hydantoin anticonvulsants because phenylbutazone may displace them from protein-binding sites and inhibit their metabolism.
Also, by inducing hepatic microsomal enzymes, phenylbutazone may decrease effects of barbiturates, cortisone and possibly other corticosteroids, estrogen-containing oral contraceptives, and digitalis glycosides.
Also, increased risk of severe dermatologic reactions with other dermatitis-causing medications.
Also, cholestyramine may decrease absorption of phenylbutazone; recommend administering phenylbutazone 1 hour before or 4 to 6 hours after cholestyramine.
Also, increased risk of adverse hematologic effects if used concurrently with colchicine.
Also, other hepatic enzyme inducers may increase phenylbutazone metabolism and decrease its half-life.
Concurrent use with methotrexate may also increase risk of agranulocytosis or bone marrow depression.
Also, methylphenidate may inhibit phenylbutazone metabolism, leading to increased plasma concentration and risk of toxicity.
Also, concurrent use with penicillamine may increase risk of serious hematologic and/or renal adverse effects.
Also, concurrent use with sulfonamides may potentiate effects of either or both medications.
Also, antacids in buffered formulations may interfere with absorption of many other medications.
Laboratory value alterations—Interference with thyroid function tests, specifically, decreases 24-hour ^{131}I thyroidal uptake and increases resin or red cell triiodothyronine (T_3) uptake.
Also, may decrease blood glucose concentrations.
Also, may decrease plasma concentrations and increase urine concentrations of uric acid.
Medical considerations/contraindications—Also, not recommended in patients with blood dyscrasias (or history of), bone marrow depression, severe cardiac or cardiopulmonary disease or cardiac failure, severe hepatic or renal disease, or active peptic ulcer disease.
Also, may aggravate polymyalgia rheumatica or temporal arteritis.
Patient monitoring—Complete physical examinations, including urinalyses, and hematologic examinations recommended at regular intervals.

Side/adverse effects:
Higher risk of blood dyscrasias than with other NSAIDs, especially in geriatric patients.
Reported to cause a serum sickness- or influenza-like syndrome.
Blood dyscrasias may occur days or weeks after medication is discontinued.
See also *Table 3*.

Additional Dosing Information

See also *General Dosing Information*.

Because of its toxicity, phenylbutazone should be used in the minimum effective dosage and for the shortest possible time.

In geriatric patients, therapy should be limited to short periods, preferably not to exceed 1 week, because of the high risk of severe, possibly fatal, toxic reactions.

Phenylbutazone is generally better tolerated when administered with food to lessen gastric irritation.

If therapy is not effective within 1 week, the medication should be discontinued.

Edema may be dose-related and may be prevented in some patients by reducing the dosage.

Oral Dosage Forms

Note: Bracketed uses in the *Dosage Forms* section refer to categories of use and/or indications that are not included in U.S. product labeling.

PHENYLBUTAZONE CAPSULES USP

Usual adult dose

Rheumatoid arthritis[1]
or Osteoarthritis, acute attacks[1]
or Ankylosing spondylitis
[or Psoriatic arthritis]—
Oral, 300 to 600 mg a day in three or four divided doses.

Antigout agent—
Oral, initially 400 mg as a single dose; then 100 mg every four hours for approximately four days or until a satisfactory response is obtained, with the duration of therapy not exceeding one week.

Note: Some clinicians use a dose of 200 mg every four hours for approximately four days or until a satisfactory response is obtained, with the duration of therapy not exceeding two weeks.

Usual pediatric dose

Children up to 15 years of age—Use is not recommended.

Strength(s) usually available

U.S.—
100 mg (Rx) [*Cotylbutazone;* GENERIC].

Canada—
Not commercially available.

Packaging and storage

Store below 40 °C (104 °F), preferably between 15 and 30 °C (59 and 86 °F), unless otherwise specified by manufacturer. Store in a tight container.

Auxiliary labeling

- Take with food.
- Take with a full glass of water.
- Avoid alcoholic beverages.

PHENYLBUTAZONE TABLETS USP

Usual adult dose

See *Phenylbutazone Capsules USP*.

Usual pediatric dose

Children up to 15 years of age—Use is not recommended.

Strength(s) usually available

U.S.—
100 mg (Rx) [GENERIC].

Canada—
100 mg (Rx) [*Apo-Phenylbutazone; Butazolidin*].

Packaging and storage

Store below 40 °C (104 °F), preferably between 15 and 30 °C (59 and 86 °F), unless otherwise specified by manufacturer. Store in a tight container.

Auxiliary labeling

- Take with food.
- Swallow tablets whole.
- Take with a full glass of water.
- Avoid alcoholic beverages.

PHENYLBUTAZONE TABLETS BUFFERED

Usual adult dose

See *Phenylbutazone Capsules USP*.

Usual pediatric dose
Children up to 15 years of age—Use is not recommended.

Strength(s) usually available
U.S.—

Not commercially available.

Canada—

100 mg of phenylbutazone, with 150 mg of magnesium trisilicate and 100 mg of dried aluminum hydroxide gel (Rx) [*Alka Butazolidin*].

Packaging and storage
Store below 40 °C (104 °F), preferably between 15 and 30 °C (59 and 86 °F), in a tight container, unless otherwise specified by manufacturer.

Auxiliary labeling
- Take with food.
- Swallow tablets whole.
- Take with a full glass of water.
- Avoid alcoholic beverages.

[1]Not included in Canadian product labeling.

PIROXICAM

Summary of Differences
Indications:

Indicated for rheumatoid arthritis, osteoarthritis, ankylosing spondylitis, acute attacks of gout or calcium pyrophosphate deposition disease (pseudogout), and dysmenorrhea.

Pharmacology/pharmacokinetics:

Physicochemical characteristics—Chemical group: An oxicam derivative.

Half-life—Elimination: 50 hours, although values ranging from 14 to 158 hours have been reported. Increased in patients with renal function impairment. May also be increased in elderly patients, especially females.

Onset of action—Gout: 2–4 hours.

Peak effect time—Gout: 3–5 days.

Duration of action—Gout: 24 hours.

Precautions:

Pregnancy/reproduction—Teratogenic effects not demonstrated in animal studies.

Breast-feeding—Distributed into breast milk; use by breast-feeding mothers not recommended because piroxicam inhibits lactation in animals.

Geriatrics—Tendency toward increased half-life and steady-state concentrations, especially in females.

Drug interactions and/or related problems—Studies failed to show that piroxicam increases digoxin plasma concentrations.

Laboratory value alterations—Also, may increase or decrease blood glucose concentrations.

Medical considerations/contraindications—Higher risk than with most other NSAIDs in patients with renal function impairment.

Side/adverse effects:

Reported to cause a serum sickness- or influenza-like syndrome.

See also *Table 3*.

Additional Dosing Information
See also *General Dosing Information*.

Because steady-state plasma concentrations are not reached for 7 to 12 days following initiation of therapy, the effectiveness of therapy with piroxicam should not be assessed for 2 weeks.

Oral Dosage Forms
Note: Bracketed uses in the *Dosage Forms* section refer to categories of use and/or indications that are not included in U.S. product labeling.

PIROXICAM CAPSULES USP

Usual adult dose
Antirheumatic (nonsteroidal anti-inflammatory)—

Oral, 20 mg once a day or 10 mg two times a day.

[Antidysmenorrheal]—

Oral, 40 mg at the onset of symptoms on the first day only, then 20 mg once a day thereafter if necessary.

Usual pediatric dose
Dosage has not been established.

Strength(s) usually available
U.S.—

10 mg (Rx) [*Feldene* (lactose); GENERIC].

20 mg (Rx) [*Feldene* (lactose); GENERIC].

Canada—

10 mg (Rx) [*Apo-Piroxicam; Feldene* (lactose); *Novo-Pirocam; Nu-Pirox; PMS-Piroxicam*].

20 mg (Rx) [*Apo-Piroxicam; Feldene* (lactose); *Novo-Pirocam; Nu-Pirox; PMS-Piroxicam*].

Packaging and storage
Store below 30 °C (86 °F). Store in a tight, light-resistant container.

Auxiliary labeling
- Take after meals.
- Take with a full glass of water.
- Avoid alcoholic beverages.

Rectal Dosage Forms

PIROXICAM SUPPOSITORIES

Usual adult dose
Antirheumatic (nonsteroidal anti-inflammatory)—

Rectal, 20 mg once a day or 10 mg two times a day.

Usual adult prescribing limits
Rectal or combined oral and rectal—20 mg a day.

Usual pediatric dose
Dosage has not been established.

Strength(s) usually available
U.S.—

Not commercially available.

Canada—

10 mg (Rx) [*Feldene*].

20 mg (Rx) [*Feldene*].

Packaging and storage
Store below 40 °C (104 °F), preferably between 15 and 30 °C (59 and 86 °F), unless otherwise specified by manufacturer. Protect from freezing.

Auxiliary labeling
- For rectal use.
- Avoid alcoholic beverages.

SULINDAC

Summary of Differences
Indications:

Indicated for rheumatoid arthritis, osteoarthritis, ankylosing spondylitis, acute attacks of gout or calcium pyrophosphate deposition disease (pseudogout), bursitis, and tendinitis.

Pharmacology/pharmacokinetics:

Physicochemical characteristics—Chemical group: A pyrroleacetic acid derivative.

Biotransformation—Hepatic; sulfide metabolite, not sulindac itself, is active substance.

Half-life—Elimination:

Sulindac—7.8 hours.

Sulindac sulfide—16.4 hours.

Time to peak plasma concentration—Sulindac sulfide: Substantially delayed in patients with alcoholic hepatic disease.

Elimination: Less than 1% of a sulindac dose excreted via the kidneys as the active sulfide metabolite.

Precautions:

Pregnancy/reproduction—Fetotoxicity, and, in some studies, a low incidence of teratogenicity, have been demonstrated in animals.

Drug interactions and/or related problems—

Concurrent chronic use of antacids significantly decreases sulindac plasma concentration.

Decreased concentration of active sulfide metabolite of sulindac and peripheral neuropathy reported with concurrent (topical) use of dimethyl sulfoxide.

Laboratory value alterations—Also, may increase blood glucose concentrations.

Medical considerations/contraindications—

Hepatic function impairment may slow metabolism to, but also decrease biliary elimination of, the active sulfide metabolite; net result is increased and prolonged plasma concentration and higher risk of toxicity.

Also, caution and adequate fluid intake recommended for patients with renal calculi (or history of) because renal calculi containing sulindac metabolites have occurred in a few patients.

Side/adverse effects:

May be less likely than most other NSAIDs to cause renal toxicity.

Reported to cause biliary obstruction.

Reported to cause a characteristic hypersensitivity syndrome.

See also *Table 3*.

Additional Dosing Information

See also *General Dosing Information.*

In the treatment of arthritis, improvement in condition may occur within 7 days, but 2 to 3 weeks of continuous use on a regular basis may be required for maximum effectiveness.

Patients with impaired renal function may require lower doses.

Therapy for 7 days in acute gouty arthritis and for 7 to 14 days in acute painful shoulder is usually sufficient.

Oral Dosage Forms

SULINDAC TABLETS USP

Usual adult dose

Antirheumatic (nonsteroidal anti-inflammatory)—

Oral, 150 or 200 mg two times a day; may be increased or decreased, depending on patient response.

Note: Although some patients have received doses higher than 400 mg per day, such doses have not been fully evaluated and are not recommended.

Antigout agent—

Oral, 200 mg two times a day; dosage to be decreased according to patient response.

Anti-inflammatory (acute painful shoulder)—

Oral, 200 mg two times a day; dosage to be decreased according to patient response.

Usual pediatric dose

Safety and efficacy have not been established.

Strength(s) usually available

U.S.—

150 mg (Rx) [*Clinoril;* GENERIC].

200 mg (Rx) [*Clinoril* (scored); GENERIC (may be scored)].

Canada—

150 mg (Rx) [*Apo-Sulin* (scored); *Clinoril; Novo-Sundac* (scored)].

200 mg (Rx) [*Apo-Sulin* (scored); *Clinoril* (scored); *Novo-Sundac* (scored)].

Packaging and storage

Store below 40 °C (104 °F), preferably between 15 and 30 °C (59 and 86 °F). Store in a well-closed container.

Auxiliary labeling

- Take with food.
- Take with a full glass of water.
- Avoid alcoholic beverages.

TENOXICAM

Summary of Differences

Indications:

Indicated for rheumatoid arthritis, osteoarthritis, ankylosing spondylitis, bursitis, tendinitis, and periarthritis.

Pharmacology/pharmacokinetics:

Physicochemical characteristics—Chemical group: An oxicam derivative.

Half-life—Elimination: 72±26 (range, 32–110) hours.

Precautions:

Pregnancy/reproduction—

Fertility: Decreased number of corpora lutea and implantations in female rats, but no impairment of fertility in male rats, demonstrated in animal studies.

First trimester: Maternotoxicity (panperitonitis, gastric lesions, and uterine hemorrhage) and embryotoxicity, but not teratogenicity, demonstrated in animal studies.

Geriatrics—Also, risk of hyperkalemia may be increased in geriatric patients.

Drug interactions and/or related problems—

Studies failed to show that tenoxicam increases digoxin concentrations.

Also, cholestyramine administered in conjunction with intravenously administered tenoxicam shown to decrease half-life of tenoxicam from 67.4 to 31.9 hours and increase tenoxicam clearance by 105%.

Side/adverse effects:

See *Table 3*.

Oral Dosage Forms

TENOXICAM TABLETS

Usual adult dose

Antirheumatic (nonsteroidal anti-inflammatory)
and Anti-inflammatory (nonsteroidal)—

Oral, 20 mg once a day, at the same time each day. For some patients, 10 mg once a day may be sufficient. The smallest effective dose should be used.

Usual adult prescribing limits

20 mg per day. Higher doses may increase the risk of adverse effects without providing a significantly greater therapeutic response.

Usual pediatric dose

Children up to 16 years of age—Dosage has not been established.

Strength(s) usually available

U.S.—

Not commercially available.

Canada—

20 mg (Rx) [*Apo-Tenoxicam* (colloidal silicon dioxide; croscarmellose sodium; hydroxypropyl methylcellulose; lactose monohydrate; magnesium stearate; microcrystalline cellulose polydextrose; polyethylene glycol; titanium dioxide; yellow ferric oxide); GENERIC].

20 mg (Rx) [*Novo-Tenoxicam* (carnauba wax; cornstarch; dibutyl sebacate; ethylcellulose; hydroxypropyl methylcellulose; lactose; magnesium stearate; polydextrose; pregelatinized starch; sodium lauryl sulfate; synthetic yellow oxide; talc; titanium dioxide; triacetin); GENERIC].

Packaging and storage

Store between 15 and 30 °C (59 and 86 °F), unless otherwise specified by manufacturer.

Auxiliary labeling

- Take with food.
- Take with a full glass of water.
- Avoid alcoholic beverages.

TIAPROFENIC ACID

Summary of Differences

Indications:

Indicated for rheumatoid arthritis and osteoarthritis.

Pharmacology/pharmacokinetics:

Physicochemical characteristics—Chemical group: A propionic acid derivative.

Half-life—Elimination:

Single dose—Tablets: 1.7 hours; increased to 2.5 hours in geriatric patients.

At steady-state—Extended-release capsules (600 mg once a day): 4.2 hours.

Precautions:

Pregnancy/reproduction—

Fertility: Decreased number of implantation sites in female rabbits, but no effect on fertility in male or female rats.

First trimester:

Crosses the placenta.

Fetotoxicity, but not teratogenicity, demonstrated in animal studies.

Geriatrics—Substantially higher frequency of hyperkalemia and/or increased blood urea nitrogen documented in studies.

Drug interactions and/or related problems—Also, may displace hydantoin anticonvulsants from their protein-binding sites, possibly leading to increased hydantoin half-life and toxicity.

Side/adverse effects:

See *Table 3*.

Oral Dosage Forms

TIAPROFENIC ACID EXTENDED-RELEASE CAPSULES

Usual adult dose

Antirheumatic (nonsteroidal anti-inflammatory)—

Oral, 600 mg once a day, at the same time each day.

Usual pediatric dose

Safety and efficacy have not been established.

Strength(s) usually available

U.S.—

Not commercially available.

Canada—

300 mg (Rx) [*Surgam SR*].

Packaging and storage

Store below 40 °C (104 °F), preferably between 15 and 30 °C (59 and 86 °F), unless otherwise specified by manufacturer.

Auxiliary labeling

- Take with food.
- Swallow capsules whole.
- Take with a full glass of water.
- Avoid alcoholic beverages.

TIAPROFENIC ACID TABLETS

Usual adult dose

Rheumatoid arthritis—

Oral, 600 mg a day in two or three divided doses.

Osteoarthritis—

Oral, 600 mg a day in two or three divided doses, initially. After a satisfactory response has been obtained, dosage may be reduced. Some patients may be maintained on 300 mg a day in divided doses.

Usual adult prescribing limits

600 mg a day.

Usual pediatric dose

Safety and efficacy have not been established.

Strength(s) usually available

U.S.—

Not commercially available.

Canada—

200 mg (Rx) [*Albert Tiafen* (scored); *Surgam* (scored)].

300 mg (Rx) [*Albert Tiafen* (scored); *Surgam* (scored)].

Packaging and storage

Store below 40 °C (104 °F), preferably between 15 and 30 °C (59 and 86 °F), unless otherwise specified by manufacturer.

Auxiliary labeling

- Take with food.
- Take with a full glass of water.
- Avoid alcoholic beverages.

TOLMETIN

Summary of Differences

Indications:

Indicated for rheumatoid arthritis, osteoarthritis, ankylosing spondylitis, juvenile arthritis, and psoriatic arthritis.

Pharmacology/pharmacokinetics:

Physicochemical characteristics—Chemical group: A pyrroleacetic acid derivative.

Absorption—Extent decreased by food and milk.

Half-life—Elimination: 5 hours.

Precautions:

Pregnancy/reproduction—No teratogenicity or other adverse effects on fetal development demonstrated in animal studies.

Pediatrics—Studied in pediatric patients 2 years of age and older; no pediatrics-specific problems documented.

Laboratory value alterations—Interference with sulfosalicylic acid test method for urinary protein.

Medical considerations/contraindications—Caution in patients who must restrict their sodium intake.

Side/adverse effects:

Higher incidence of anaphylactic reactions than with other NSAIDs.

Reported to cause a serum sickness- or influenza-like syndrome.

See also *Table 3*.

Additional Dosing Information

See also *General Dosing Information*.

Improvement in condition may occur within 7 days, but 1 to 2 weeks of continuous use on a regular basis may be required for maximum effectiveness.

Oral Dosage Forms

Note: The dosing and strengths of the available dosage forms are expressed in terms of the free acid (not the sodium salt).

TOLMETIN SODIUM CAPSULES USP

Usual adult dose

Antirheumatic (nonsteroidal anti-inflammatory)—

Initial: Oral, 400 mg (free acid) three times a day, preferably including a dose in the morning and a dose at bedtime.

Maintenance: Rheumatoid arthritis—

Oral, 600 mg to 1.8 grams (free acid) a day in three or four divided doses.

Osteoarthritis—

Oral, 600 mg to 1.6 grams (free acid) a day in three or four divided doses.

Usual adult prescribing limits

Up to 2 grams (free acid) daily for rheumatoid arthritis or 1.6 grams (free acid) daily for osteoarthritis.

Usual pediatric dose

Antirheumatic (nonsteroidal anti-inflammatory)—

Children up to 2 years of age: Dosage has not been established.

Children 2 years of age and over: Initial—Oral, 20 mg (free acid) per kg of body weight a day in three or four divided doses.

Maintenance—Oral, 15 to 30 mg (free acid) per kg of body weight a day in divided doses.

Note: Doses higher than 30 mg (free acid) per kg of body weight per day have not been studied and therefore are not recommended.

Strength(s) usually available

U.S.—

400 mg (free acid, with 36 mg [1.568 mmol] of sodium) (Rx) [*Tolectin DS;* GENERIC].

Canada—

400 mg (free acid, with 36 mg [1.568 mmol] of sodium) (Rx) [*Novo-Tolmetin; Tolectin 400*].

Packaging and storage

Store below 40 °C (104 °F), preferably between 15 and 30 °C (59 and 86 °F). Store in a tight container.

Auxiliary labeling

- Take with food.
- Take with a full glass of water.
- Avoid alcoholic beverages.

TOLMETIN SODIUM TABLETS USP

Usual adult dose

See *Tolmetin Sodium Capsules USP*.

Usual adult prescribing limits

See *Tolmetin Sodium Capsules USP*.

Usual pediatric dose

See *Tolmetin Sodium Capsules USP*.

Strength(s) usually available

U.S.—

200 mg (free acid, with 18 mg [0.784 mmol] of sodium) (Rx) [*Tolectin 200* (scored); GENERIC].

600 mg (free acid, with 54 mg [2.352 mmol] of sodium) (Rx) [*Tolectin 600;* GENERIC].

Canada—

200 mg (free acid, with 18 mg [0.784 mmol] of sodium) (Rx) [*Tolectin 200* (scored)].

600 mg (free acid, with 54 mg [2.352 mmol] of sodium) (Rx) [*Tolectin 600*].

Packaging and storage

Store between 15 and 30 °C (59 and 86 °F). Store in a well-closed container.

Auxiliary labeling

- Take with food.
- Take with a full glass of water.
- Avoid alcoholic beverages.

Revised: 09/16/2005

Table 1. Pharmacology/Pharmacokinetics

	Absorption			Plasma Concentration			
Drug and Route	Rate (Factors that decrease)	Extent (Factors that decrease)	% Protein-Binding* (Factors that decrease)	Time to Peak (hr) [dose in mg]	Peak (mcg/mL) [dose in mg]	Time to Steady-State (days) [dose in mg/ doses per day]	Steady-State (mcg/mL) [dose in mg/ doses per day]
Diclofenac			>99				
Oral							
Tablets	Rapid (food)	Complete		1, range 0.33–2†; up to 3.6‡			
Delayed-release Tablets	Rapid (food)	Complete		2, range 0.25–4†; 6‡	0.7–1.1 [25] 1.5–1.6 [50]† 2 [75] Decreased 40% by food		
Extended-release Tablets				4			
Rectal	Rapid			0.5–2			
Diflunisal			>99				
Oral	Rapid (food)	Complete		2–3	41 [250] 87 [500] 124 [1000]		56 [250/2] 190 [500/2]
Etodolac			>99				
Oral	Rapid (food)§	Extensive		1.3, range 0.8–1.8†; 2.2–5.6‡ [200–600]; Steady-state 1.7±1.3	10–46 [200–600] Decreased 50% by food and 15–20% by antacids		16.5–19 [200/2]
Fenoprofen			99				
Oral	Rapid (food, milk)§			1–2 [600]† Increased by food	50 [600]† Decreased by food		
Floctafenine							
Oral	Rapid (food)			1–2		Within 3	
Flurbiprofen			99				
Oral							
Tablets	Rapid (food)			1.5; range 0.5–4	5–6; 8.7# [50] 10–15 [100]** Decreased by food		5–6 [50/3]
Extended-release Capsules				5.5†; 8.3‡	8.56 Increased by food	2–3 [200/1]	10.78 [200/1]
Ibuprofen			99				
Oral	Rapid (food)§			1.2–2.1	22–27 [200] 23–45 [400] 42–57 [600]†† 56–66 [800] Decreased up to 30% by food		
Indomethacin			99				
Oral							
Capsules; Oral Suspension	Rapid (food, antacids [Al- and/or Mg-containing])	Complete; 90% in 4 hr		0.5–2 [25]	0.8–2.5 [25] 2.5–4 [50]		1.4 [25/3] 2.8 [50/3]
Extended-release Capsules		90% in 12 hr		2–4.25 [75]	1.5–3 [75]		1.4 [75/1]
Rectal	Rapid	80–90‡‡					
Ketoprofen			99 (hepatic cirrhosis, advanced age)			<1	
Oral							
Capsules	Rapid (food, milk)§	Complete		0.5–2 [50] average 1.1† average 2‡	4.1 [50]†# 2.4 [50]‡#		
Extended-release Capsules	Slow	Almost complete		6–7†; 8–9‡	3.1±1.2†; 3.4±1.3‡ [200]		
Delayed-release Tablets	Delayed by ±1.5 hr			1.5–4 [50]			
Extended-release Tablets				5.5–8	Decreased 20% by high-fat meal		
Rectal§§				0.5–2			

Table 1. Pharmacology/Pharmacokinetics *(continued)*

Drug and Route	Absorption		% Protein-Binding* (Factors that decrease)	Plasma Concentration			
	Rate (Factors that decrease)	Extent (Factors that decrease)		Time to Peak (hr) [dose in mg]	Peak (mcg/mL) [dose in mg]	Time to Steady-State (days) [dose in mg/ doses per day]	Steady-State (mcg/mL) [dose in mg/ doses per day]
Meclofenamate Oral	Rapid (food)§	Complete (food)	>99	0.5–2	8–9 [100]		4.8, range 1.8-7.2 [100/3] Decreased by food
Mefenamic Acid Oral	Rapid			2.5 [250] 1–2 [500] 2–4 [1000]	3.6 [250] 3.5 [500] 10 [1000]	2 [1000/4]	20 [1000/4]
Meloxicam Oral	Rapid	Extensive	>99	4—5 [7.5]	1.05 [7.5]	5 [7.5/1]	
Nabumetone (prodrug) Oral	Increased by food, milk§	Increased by food, milk§					
6-methoxy-2-naphthylacetic acid (6-MNA) (active substance)			>99	Steady-state 3, range 1–12 [1000]##; 2.5, range 1–8 [2000] Decreased by food	24 [500]‡ 22–23†; 36–38‡# [1000]*** 64 [2000]	3 [500/2 or 1000/1]	18.5 [500/2]; trough 33, peak 52 [1000/1]#
Naproxen			>99 (hepatic cirrhosis, advanced age)				
Oral Tablets; Oral Suspension	Rapid (food, antacids [Al- and Mg-containing])†††	Complete		Naproxen: 2–4 [750] Sodium salt: 1–2 [825]	46.6 [375] 63.1 [500]‡‡‡ 90 [750]	2–2.5 (500/2)	55 [500/2]
Delayed-release Tablets				4.2-4.5 Decreased by antacids Increased by high-fat meal	47.9 [375] 58.2 [2×250] 60.7 [500]§§§		
Extended-release Tablets				9.7†; 7.7‡ [1000]	63.1†; 86.1‡ [1000]		
Oxaprozin			±99.9(renal impairment, congestive heart failure, hepatic cirrhosis)				
Oral	Relatively slow§ (food–slight effect)			3-5	70-80 [1200]	4-7	98-230 [600/1 or 1200/1] Accumulates with chronic dosing
Phenylbutazone Oral	Rapid		98	2–2.5	43 [300]		Phenylbutazone: up to 172 Oxyphenbutazone: up to 86
Piroxicam Oral	(food)§			3–5 [20]	1.5–2 [20]	7–12 [20/1]###	3–8 [20/1]****
Rectal				10 [20]			
Sulindac (prodrug) Oral	(food)§	90%		2† 3–4‡	1–2 [200]		
Sulindac sulfide (active substance)				1.7††††		4–5 [200/2]	4 [200/2]
Tenoxicam Oral	(food)§	Extensive§	98–99	1.25, range 0.5–6†	1.46–3.31† [20]		

Table 1. Pharmacology/Pharmacokinetics *(continued)*

Drug and Route	Absorption: Rate (Factors that decrease)	Absorption: Extent (Factors that decrease)	% Protein-Binding* (Factors that decrease)	Time to Peak (hr) [dose in mg]	Plasma Concentration: Peak (mcg/mL) [dose in mg]	Time to Steady-State (days) [dose in mg/ doses per day]	Steady-State (mcg/mL) [dose in mg/ doses per day]
Tiaprofenic Acid			98				
Oral							
Tablets	Rapid (food)§			0.5-1.5† Up to 2‡	26 [200] 50 [300]	Within 1 [200/ 3]	
Extended-release Capsules				Steady-state 4–8 [600/1]			
Tolmetin			>99				
Oral	Rapid (food)§	Almost complete (food, milk)		0.5–1	40 [400]† 20 [400]‡		

*To albumin.
†Taken on an empty stomach.
‡Taken with food.
§Absorption not affected by antacids, specifically: For fenoprofen, ibuprofen, ketoprofen, meclofenamate, piroxicam, sulindac, tolmetin—Aluminum- and magnesium-containing; For tiaprofenic acid—Aluminum-containing
#May be increased in geriatric patients (For flurbiprofen, geriatric females only).
**Decreased by 40% in patients with end-stage renal disease undergoing continuous ambulatory peritoneal dialysis.
††Decrease to 37 mcg/mL demonstrated in obese patients, probably because volume of distribution increased.
‡‡Failure to retain suppository in rectum for one full hour may be responsible for incomplete absorption.
§§Bioavailability 73–93% of that achieved with oral administration.
##Mean 8 hours in patients with hepatic cirrhosis. Not significantly different in geriatric patients than in younger adults.
***Administration of a second 1000-mg dose 12 hours after an initial 1000-mg dose produced peak concentrations of ±71 mcg/mL. Peak concentrations are significantly decreased (to as low as 18 mcg/mL) in patients with hepatic cirrhosis.
†††May be increased by concurrent administration of sodium bicarbonate.
‡‡‡Similar values reported with administration of 500-mg tablets to adults and with administration of 5 mg/kg of oral suspension to children 5 to 16 years of age with juvenile arthritis.
§§§Increased to 70.7 mcg/mL by concurrent administration with antacid.
###May be increased to 2 to 3 weeks if elimination half-life is greatly prolonged.
****May be increased if elimination half-life is greatly prolonged and/or renal function is impaired.
††††May be increased to 4 to 7 hours in patients with alcoholic hepatic disease.

Table 2. Pharmacology/Pharmacokinetics

Drug	Biotransformation	Half-Life: Distribution (hr)	Half-Life: Elimination (hr)	Renal Elimination: % of Dose	Renal Elimination: % Unchanged	Biliary/Fecal Elimination: % of Dose	Biliary/Fecal Elimination: % Unchanged
Diclofenac*	Hepatic; almost 50% eliminated via first-pass metabolism†		1.2–2	40–65	Little or none	35	Little or none
Diflunisal‡			8–12 22 (GFR 10–50)§# 60 (GFR 2–10)§# 115 (GFR <2)§#	80–95 in 72–96 hr 53 in 72 hr (GFR 10–50)§ 9.5 in 72 hr (GFR 2–10)§ 2.7 in 72 hr (GFR <2)§	<5	Little or none	
Etodolac‡	Hepatic, extensive. No significant first-pass metabolism	0.71±0.5, at steady-state	Single dose 6–7; Steady-state 7.3±4	72; 60% in 24 h	<1	16	
Fenoprofen	Hepatic		3	90 in 24 hr			
Floctafenine	Hepatic; rapid	1	8	40**		60**	
Flurbiprofen		3	5.7, range 2–12	88–98; 73 within 48 hr	20–25		
Ibuprofen‡	Hepatic		1.8–2	100 in 24 hr	<1		
Indomethacin‡	Hepatic	1	2.6–11.2 (average 4.5)††	60	10–20	33‡‡	1.5
Ketoprofen*	Primarily hepatic; glucuronide conjugation may also occur in other tissues	0.33	Capsules 1.6; Extended-release Capsules 5.4±2.2; Extended-release Tablets 3–4##	80 in 24 hr	Up to 10	***	
Meclofenamate	†††		2 (single dose) 3.3 (multiple doses)	66	Little or none	33	

Table 2. Pharmacology/Pharmacokinetics *(continued)*

Drug	Biotransformation	Half-Life		Renal Elimination		Biliary/Fecal Elimination	
		Distribution (hr)	Elimination (hr)	% of Dose	% Unchanged	% of Dose	% Unchanged
Mefenamic Acid	Hepatic		2	67		Up to 25	
Meloxicam	Hepatic, mainly by cytochrome P-450 2C9		15 –20	20	≤ 0.5	20	1.6
Nabumetone	Hepatic, with extensive first-pass metabolism. 35–38% of a 1000-mg dose metabolized to the active substance 6-MNA, which is further metabolized hepatically; bioavailability of 6-MNA decreased in patients with severe hepatic function impairment; bioavailability of unbound 6-NMA increased by 50% in patients with moderate renal insufficiency (creatinine clearance 30 to 49 mL per minute)		6-MNA: 23±3.7; 30±8.1‡‡‡	6-MNA: 80; 75 in 48 hr; complete in 168 hr; 32.5 in 96 hr§§§	6-MNA: <1		
Naproxen	Hepatic		13	95			
Oxaprozin‡	Hepatic, 65% via microsomal oxidation followed by glucuronic acid conjugation and 35% via direct glucuronic acid conjugation		Steady-state (mg/day) 25 (600) 21 (1200)###	65%, as glucuronide metabolites	Very small amounts	35%, as glucuronide metabolites	Very small amounts
Phenylbutazone	Slow, via hepatic microsomal enzymes		54–99 (average 77) 105****	61–75; may remain in body 7–10 days after last dose	Trace amounts	25–27	<5
Oxyphenbutazone (active metabolite)				4			
Piroxicam	Hepatic		50††††	66	<5	33	
Sulindac	Hepatic; sulfide metabolite, not sulindac itself, is active		7.8	50		‡‡	
Sulindac sulfide			16.4	<1		25‡‡	
Tenoxicam			72±28 (range, 32–110)	66	<0.5	17	
Tiaprofenic Acid			Tablets 1.7; 2.5**** Extended-release Capsules (at steady-state) 4.2	60	90	40	
Tolmetin	Hepatic	1–2	5	100 in 24 hr	Up to 17		

*Dialyzable.

†Some metabolites may be active.

‡Not dialyzable.

§In patients with renal function impairment. GFR=glomerular filtration rate in mL per minute, when specified.

#Reason for prolonged half-life is unclear because only small amounts are excreted unchanged. It has been proposed that biliary excretion of metabolites with subsequent hydrolysis to, and reabsorption of, the parent compound may occur in renal failure. Alternatively, slower renal excretion may permit hydrolysis of an unstable metabolite to the parent compound.

**Excretion (renal plus biliary/fecal) complete within 24 hours.

††Subject to large interindividual variation, possibly because of differences in enterohepatic circulation and subsequent reabsorption.

‡‡Undergoes extensive enterohepatic circulation.

§§Acyl-glucuronide conjugate is unstable; in patients with renal function impairment, this conjugate may accumulate and be deconjugated to the parent compound.

##Higher values for the extended-release dosage forms reflect prolonged absorption. In geriatric patients, values for the capsules and the extended-release capsules are prolonged by 26% and 54%, respectively. Also, values for the capsules may be prolonged to 3 hours in patients with mild renal function impairment and to 5 to 9 hours in patients with moderate to severe renal function impairment.

***Enterohepatic recirculation has been proposed to account for elimination of the other 40% of the dose; however, studies to confirm this possibility have not been done.

†††Hydroxymethyl metabolite has anti-inflammatory activity approximately 20% of that of the parent compound.

‡‡‡In geriatric patients, in whom values are especially subject to substantial interpatient variability; values as high as 74 hours have been measured. Also, increased to about 39 hours in patients with creatinine clearances <30 mL/minute/1.73 cubic meters of body surface area, but not in patients with lesser degrees of renal function impairment or in patients receiving hemodialysis.

§§§In patients with moderately severe renal function impairment (creatinine clearances 10–30 mL/min/1.73 cubic meters of body surface area).

###Several studies reported terminal elimination half-life values of 50 to 60 hours. However, these lower "accumulation" half-life values are recommended for use in clinical practice, e.g., for estimating time to reach steady-state, determining appropriate dosing intervals, and determining intervals for dosage adjustment.

****In geriatric patients.

††††Average; usual range 30 to 60 hours, but values ranging from 14 to 158 hours have been reported. Half-life may be especially prolonged in patients with renal function impairment.

Table 3. Side/Adverse Effects*

Legend:
I = Diclofenac; II = Diflunisal; III = Etodolac; IV = Fenoprofen;
V = Floctafenine; VI = Flurbiprofen; VII = Ibuprofen; VIII = Indomethacin;
IX = Ketoprofen; X = Meclofenamate; XI = Mefenamic Acid; XII = Nabumetone;
XIII = Naproxen; XIV = Oxaprozin; XV = Phenylbutazone; XVI = Piroxicam;
XVII = Sulindac; XVIII = Tenoxicam; XIX = Tiaprofenic Acid; XX = Tolmetin

	I	II	III	IV	V	VI	VII	VIII	IX	X	XI	XII	XIII	XIV	XV	XVI	XVII	XVIII	XIX	XX
Medical attention needed																				
Cardiovascular effects																				
Note: Many of these cardiovascular effects may occur secondary to NSAID-induced renal function impairment.																				
Angina pectoris or exacerbation of (chest pain)	L	U	U	U	U	R†	U	U	U	U	U	R†	U	U	U	R	U	U	R	U
Bleeding, other than gastrointestinal, including:																				
Hemoptysis (spitting blood)	U	U	U	U	U	U	U	U	R	U	U	U	U	U	U	U	U	U	U	U
Nosebleeds, unexplained	R	U	U	U	U	R	R†	R	R	U	U	U	U	U	U	R	R	R	L	R
Cardiac arrhythmias	L	U	R†	R†	U	R†	R†	R	R†	U	U	R†	U	U	U	U	R†	U	U	U
Chest pain	R†	R†	U	U	U	R	U	R	U	U	U	R	U	U	U	U	U	U	R	L
Congestive heart failure or exacerbation of (chest pain; shortness of breath; troubled breathing, tightness in chest, and/or wheezing; decrease in amount of urine; swelling of face, fingers, feet, or lower legs; unusual tiredness; weight gain)	R	U	R	U	U	R	R	R	R	U	U	U	R	U	R	R	R	U	R	R
Edema, pulmonary (shortness of breath, troubled breathing, tightness in chest, and/or wheezing)	U	U	U	R†	U	U	U	R	U	U	U	U	U	U	U	U	U	U	U	U
Increased blood pressure—may reach hypertensive levels	R	U	R	U	U	R	R	R	R	U	U	R†	U	R	R	R	R	R	U	M
Pericarditis (chest pain; fever with or without chills; shortness of breath, troubled breathing, and/or tightness in chest)	U	U	U	U	U	U	U	U	U	U	U	U	U	U	R	U	U	U	U	U
Central nervous system effects																				
Confusion	U	R	R†	L	U	R	R	R	R	U	U	R	R	L	R	R†	U	R	U	U
Convulsions	R†	U	U	R†	U	U	U	R	U	U	U	U	U	U	U	U	R	U	U	U
Dysarthria (trouble in speaking)	U	U	U	U	U	U	U	R	U	U	U	U	U	U	U	U	U	U	U	U
Forgetfulness	R†	U	U	U	U	L	U	R	R	U	U	U	U	U	U	U	U	U	U	U
Hallucinations	U	R	U	U	U	U	R†	R	R†	U	U	U	U	U	U	R†	U	U	U	U
Headache, severe, especially in the morning	U	U	U	U	U	U	U	M§	U	U	U	U	U	U	U	U	U	U	U	U
Meningitis, aseptic (severe headache, drowsiness, confusion, stiff neck and/or back, general feeling of illness, nausea)	R	U	U	U	U	R	R	U	U	U	U	U	R†	U	U	U	R	U	U	R
Migraine (headache, severe and throbbing, sometimes with nausea or vomiting)	U	U	U	U	U	U	U	U	R	U	U	U	U	U	U	U	U	U	U	U
Mood or mental changes, including:																				
Disorientation	U	R	U	R	U	U	U	U	U	U	U	U	U	U	U	U	U	U	R	U
Feeling of depersonalization or muzziness	U	U	U	U	U	U	U	R	U	U	U	U	U	U	U	U	U	U	U	U
Mental depression	R	R	L	R†	U	L	R	L	L	R†	‡	R	R	L	R	R	R	R	L	L
Psychotic reaction	R†	U	U	U	U	U	U	R	U	U	U	U	U	U	U	U	R	U	U	U
Neuropathy, peripheral (numbness, tingling, pain, or weakness in hands or feet)	R†	R†	U	U	U	U	R†	R	R	R†	U	U	R†	U	R†	R†	R	U	R	U
Syncope (fainting)	U	R†	R	U	U	U	U	R	U	U	U	R†	U	U	U	U	R	U	U	U

Table 3. Side/Adverse Effects* *(continued)*

Legend:
I = Diclofenac
II = Diflunisal
III = Etodolac
IV = Fenoprofen
V = Floctafenine
VI = Flurbiprofen
VII = Ibuprofen
VIII = Indomethacin
IX = Ketoprofen
X = Meclofenamate
XI = Mefenamic Acid
XII = Nabumetone
XIII = Naproxen
XIV = Oxaprozin
XV = Phenylbutazone
XVI = Piroxicam
XVII = Sulindac
XVIII = Tenoxicam
XIX = Tiaprofenic Acid
XX = Tolmetin

	I	II	III	IV	V	VI	VII	VIII	IX	X	XI	XII	XIII	XIV	XV	XVI	XVII	XVIII	XIX	XX
Dermatologic effects																				
Dermatitis, allergic																				
(bullous eruption/blisters)	R	U	R	U	U	U	R	U	R	U	U	R	U	U	U	R	U	U	U	U
(eczema)	U	U	U	U	R	R	U	U	U	U	U	U	U	U	U	U	U	U	R	U
(hives)	R	R	R	R	R	R	R	R	R	L	‡	R	M	R	R	R	U	R	U	R
(itching)	L	R	L	M	L	R	L	R	R	L	‡	M	R†	R	R	L	L	L	M	L
(skin rash)	L	M	L	M	L	L	M	R	L	M	L	M	M	M	L	L	M	L	M	L
Dermatitis, exfoliative (fever with or without chills; red, thickened, or scaly skin; swollen and/or painful glands; unusual bruising)	R†	R	U	R†	U	R	U	R	R	R	U	U	R	U	R	R	R	U	U	U
Desquamation (peeling of skin)	U	U	R†	U	U	U	U	U	U	U	U	U	U	U	U	R	U	U	U	U
Erythema (reddening of skin) ***or other skin discoloration***	U	U	U	U	U	U	U	U	R	U	U	U	U	U	U	R	U	U	R	U
Erythema multiforme (fever with or without chills; muscle cramps or pain; skin rash; sores, ulcers, or white spots on lips or in mouth)	R	R	U	U	U	U	R	R	U	R	U	R†	R†	U	R	R	R	U	U	R
Erythema nodosum (fever with or without chills; skin rash)	U	U	U	U	U	U	U	R	U	R†	U	U	U	U	R	U	U	U	U	U
Photosensitivity reactions resembling porphyria cutanea tarda and epidermyolysis bullosa (blistering, scarring, darkening or lightening of skin color)	U	U	U	U	U	U	U	U	U	U	U	R	R†	U	U	U	U	U	U	U
Stevens-Johnson syndrome (bleeding or crusting sores on lips; chest pain; fever with or without chills; muscle cramps or pain; skin rash; sores, ulcers, or white spots in mouth; sore throat)	R	R	R	R†	U	R	R	R	U	R	U	R†	R†	U	R	R	R	U	U	U
Toxic epidermal necrolysis (redness, tenderness, itching, burning, or peeling of skin; sore throat; fever with or without chills)	U	R	U	R†	U	R	R†	R	U	U	U	R	R†	U	R	R	R	U	U	R
Digestive system effects																				
Abdominal distention (swelling of abdomen)	L	U	U	U	U	U	U	R	U	U	U	U	U	U	R	U	U	R	U	U
Bleeding from rectum—with rectal dosage forms	‡	—	—	—	—	—	—	R	M	—	—	—	R	—	—	L	—	—	—	—
Colitis or exacerbation of or	R	U	R†	U	U	U	U	R	U	R	U	U	R	U	R	U	R	U	U	U
Enterocolitis or	U	U	U	U	U	U	U	R	U	U	U	U	U	U	U	U	U	U	R	U
Regional enteritis or exacerbation of (abdominal pain, cramping, or discomfort; bloody stools; diarrhea)	U	U	U	U	U	U	U	R	U	U	U	U	U	U	R	U	U	U	U	U
Dysphagia (difficulty in swallowing)	U	U	U	U	U	U	U	U	U	U	U	R	U	U	U	U	U	R	U	U
Esophagitis (burning feeling in throat or chest, difficulty in swallowing)	U	U	R†	U	U	R	U	R	U	U	U	U	U	U	R	U	U	R	U	U
Gastritis (burning feeling in chest or stomach, indigestion, tenderness in stomach area)	U	R	L	R	U	R	R	U	R	U	U	L	U	U	R	U	R	R	U	L
Gastroenteritis (severe abdominal pain, diarrhea, loss of appetite, nausea, weakness)	U	U	U	U	U	U	U	R	U	U	U	R	U	U	U	U	R	U	U	U
Gastrointestinal bleeding or hemorrhage—reported independently of gastrointestinal ulceration or perforation, including ***melena*** (bloody stools) and ***hematemesis*** (vomiting blood or material that looks like coffee grounds)**	R	R	L	R	M	L	R	R	R	R	U	R	R	R	R	R	R	R	R	R

Gastrointestinal perforation# and/or	U	R	U	R	U	U	R	R	R	R	U	U	R	U	U	R	R	U	U	R
Gastrointestinal ulceration#, including esophageal, gastric, or peptic ulceration, multiple gastrointestinal ulcerations, and perforation of pre-existing sigmoid lesions, e.g., diverticula, carcinoma (severe pain, cramping, or burning; bloody or black, tarry stools; vomiting of blood or material that looks like coffee grounds; severe and continuing nausea, heartburn, and/or indigestion)#	L	R	L	R	M	R	R	R	R	L	R	R	R	R	R	R	R	R	R	L
Note: *Intestinal ulceration* may lead to stenosis and obstruction. Also, paralytic ileus has been reported with meclofenamate, but a causal relationship has not been established.																				
Genitourinary effects																				
Bladder pain	U	U	U	U	U	U	U	U	U	U	U	U	U	U	U	U	U	U	R	U
Bleeding from vagina, unexplained, unexpected, and/or unusually heavy menstrual	R†	U	R†	U	U	R†	R†	R	R	U	U	U	R	R	U	U	R	U	R	U
Blood in urine	R†	U	R†	R	M	R	R	R	R	U	‡	U	R	R	R	R	R	R	U	R
Crystalluria, renal calculi, or ureteral obstruction (blood in urine; difficult, burning, or painful urination; severe pain in lower back, side, or abdomen)—with phenylbutazone, may be composed of uric acid crystals and with sulindac, may be composed of sulindac metabolites	U	U	R†	U	U	U	U	U	U	U	U	U	U	U	R	U	R	U	U	U
Cystitis or	R	R	R†	R	M	R	R	R†	L	U	R	U	R	U	U	R†	U	R	R	R
Urethritis or	U	U	U	U	M	U	U	U	U	U	U	U	U	U	U	U	U	U	U	U
Urinary tract infection (bloody or cloudy urine; difficult, burning, or painful urination; frequent urge to urinate)	U	U	U	U	U	M	U	U	U	U	U	U	U	U	U	U	U	U	U	L
Dysuria (burning, painful, or difficult urination)	U	R	L	L	M	U	U	U	U	U	R	U	U	U	U	R†	R	R	R	R
Frequent urge to urinate	R†	U	L	U	U	U	U	U	U	U	U	U	U	L	U	U	U	R	R	U
Incontinence (loss of bladder control)	U	U	U	U	U	R	U	U	U	U	U	U	U	U	U	U	U	U	R	U
Proteinuria (cloudy urine)	R	R	U	U	U	U	U	R	U	U	U	U	U	U	R	R	R	R	U	R
Strong-smelling urine	U	U	U	U	M	U	U	U	U	U	U	U	U	U	U	U	U	U	U	U
Hematologic effects																				
Agranulocytosis [granulocytopenia] (fever with or without chills; sores, ulcers, or white spots on lips or in mouth; sore throat)	R	R	U	R	U	U	R	R	R	R	R	R	R	U	R	U	R	U	U	R
Anemia (unusual tiredness or weakness)—may be associated with gastrointestinal bleeding or microbleeding or with hemodilution caused by fluid retention	R	U	R	U	U	R	R	R	R	R	L	R	U	R	R	L	U	R	U	L
Aplastic anemia [pancytopenia] (shortness of breath, troubled breathing, tightness in chest, and/or wheezing; sores, ulcers, or white spots on lips or in mouth; sore throat)	R	U	U	R	U	R	R	R	U	U	R	R	R†	U	R	R	R	U	U	U
Bone marrow depression—signs and symptoms are listed under individual entries for *Aplastic anemia* and *Thrombocytopenia*	U	U	U	U	U	U	U	R	U	U	R	U	U	U	R	R	R	U	U	U
Disseminated intravascular coagulation	U	U	U	U	U	U	U	R	U	U	U	U	U	U	U	U	U	U	U	U
Ecchymosis/bruising	R†	U	R	R	U	R	U	R	U	U	U	U	L	R	U	R	R	U	R	U
Eosinophilia	U	U	U	U	U	R	R	U	U	R	‡	U	R	U	U	L	U	U	U	U
Hemolytic anemia(troubled breathing, exertional; unusual tiredness or weakness)	R	R	U	R	U	R	R	R	R	R	R	U	R†	U	R	R†	R	U	U	U
Hypocoagulability (bleeding from cuts or scratches that lasts longer than usual)	U	U	U	U	U	U	U	U	R	U	R	U	U	U	U	U	U	U	U	U

Table 3. Side/Adverse Effects* *(continued)*

Legend:
I = Diclofenac; II = Diflunisal; III = Etodolac; IV = Fenoprofen;
V = Floctafenine; VI = Flurbiprofen; VII = Ibuprofen; VIII = Indomethacin;
IX = Ketoprofen; X = Meclofenamate; XI = Mefenamic Acid; XII = Nabumetone;
XIII = Naproxen; XIV = Oxaprozin; XV = Phenylbutazone; XVI = Piroxicam;
XVII = Sulindac; XVIII = Tenoxicam; XIX = Tiaprofenic Acid; XX = Tolmetin

	I	II	III	IV	V	VI	VII	VIII	IX	X	XI	XII	XIII	XIV	XV	XVI	XVII	XVIII	XIX	XX
Leukopenia [neutropenia] (usually asymptomatic; rarely, fever or chills, cough or hoarseness, lower back or side pain, painful or difficult urination)	R	U	R†	U	U	R	R	R	U	R	R	R	R	R	R	L	R	R	R	U
Petechia (pinpoint red spots on skin)	U	U	U	U	U	U	U	R	U	U	U	U	U	U	R	R	U	U	U	U
Purpura (bruises and/or red spots on skin)—may be associated with thrombocytopenia																				
Thrombocytopenia with or without purpura (usually asymptomatic; rarely, unusual bleeding or bruising; black, tarry stools; blood in urine or stools; pinpoint red spots on skin)	R	R	R	R	U	R	R	R	R	R	R	R	R	R	R	R	R	R	U	R
Hepatic effects, including:																				
Cholestatic hepatitis or jaundice (dark urine; fever; itching; light-colored stools; pain, tenderness, and/or swelling in upper abdominal area; skin rash; swollen glands)	U	R	R	R	U	R	U	U	U	R	U	R	U	U	R	U	R	U	U	U
Hepatitis or jaundice, toxic (loss of appetite, nausea, vomiting, yellow eyes or skin, swelling in upper abdominal area)	R	R	R	R	U	R	R	R	R	U	R	R	R	R	R	R	R	R	U	R
Hypersensitivity reactions See also *Dermatologic effects*																				
Anaphylaxis or anaphylactoid reactions (changes in facial skin color; skin rash, hives, and/or itching; fast or irregular breathing; puffiness or swelling of the eyelids or around the eyes; shortness of breath, troubled breathing, tightness in chest, and/or wheezing)—may include anaphylactic shock with sudden, severe decrease in blood pressure and collapse	R	R	U	R	R	R	R	R	R	U	U	R	R	R	R	R	R	U	U	R
Angiitis [vasculitis] (muscle pain, cramps, and/or weakness; shortness of breath, troubled breathing, tightness in chest, and/or wheezing; skin rash; spitting blood; unusual tiredness or weakness)	U	R	R	U	U	U	R†	R	U	U	U	R	R†	U	R	R	R	U	U	U
Angioedema (large, hive-like swellings on face, eyelids, mouth, lips, and/or tongue)	R	R	R	R	R	R	R†	R	U	U	U	R	R†	U	R	R	R	R	U	U
Bronchospastic allergic reactions (shortness of breath, troubled breathing, tightness in chest, and/or wheezing)	R	R	R	U	U	R	R	R	R	U	U	R†	U	U	R	R	R	R	U	U
Fever with or without chills	U	U	L	R†	U	R	U	R	U	U	U	R†	R	U	R	R	R	U	R	R
Hypersensitivity syndrome, multisystemic, diflunisal-induced, including dermatologic reactions; hematologic effects including eosinophilia, leukopenia, thrombocytopenia, and disseminated intravascular coagulation; jaundice; renal impairment or failure; and nonspecific signs and symptoms (disorientation, fever and chills, general feeling of illness or discomfort, loss of appetite, muscle and/or joint pain, swollen and/or painful glands)**	—	R	—	—	—	—	—	—	—	—	—	—	—	—	—	—	—	—	—	—

Hypersensitivity syndrome, multisystemic, sulindac-induced, including dermatologic reactions; conjunctivitis; hepatic failure and jaundice; pancreatitis; pneumonitis with or without pleural effusions (difficulty in breathing, coughing, tightness in chest, wheezing); ***hematologic effects including leukopenia, leukocytosis, eosinophilia, disseminated intravascular coagulation, and anemia; renal impairment or failure; and nonspecific signs and symptoms*** (chest pain, fast heartbeat, fever and chills, flushing, general feeling of illness or discomfort, low blood pressure, muscle and/or joint pain, sweating, tiredness)**	—	—	—	—	—	—	—	—	—	—	—	—	—	—	—	—	R	—	—	—
Laryngeal edema (shortness of breath or troubled breathing)	R	U	U	U	U	U	U	U	R	U	U	U	U	U	U	U	U	U	U	U
Loeffler syndrome [eosinophilic pneumonitis] (chest pain; fever with or without chills; shortness of breath, troubled breathing, tightness in chest, and/or wheezing; unusual weakness)	U	U	U	R†	U	U	U	U	U	U	U	R	R	U	U	U	U	U	U	U
Rhinitis, allergic (unexplained runny nose or sneezing)	U	U	U	U	U	L	R	U	R	U	U	U	U	U	U	U	U	U	R	U
Serum sickness-like reaction (fever with or without chills; muscle cramps, pain, and/or weakness; skin rash, hives, and/or itching; shortness of breath, troubled breathing, tightness in chest, and/or wheezing; swollen and/or painful glands)	U	U	U	U	U	U	R†	U	U	U	U	U	U	R	R	U	U	U	U	R
Systemic lupus erythematosus [SLE]-like syndrome (bloody or cloudy urine; chest pain; fever with or without chills; shortness of breath, troubled breathing, tightness in chest, and/or wheezing; skin rash, hives, and/or itching; sudden decrease in amount of urine; swelling of face, fingers, feet, and/or lower legs; swollen and/or painful glands; unusual weakness; rapid weight gain)	U	U	U	U	U	U	R†	U	U	R	U	U	U	U	R	U	U	U	U	U
Loosening or splitting of fingernails or other nail disorder	U	U	U	U	U	U	U	U	R	U	U	U	U	U	U	R†	U	R	R	U
Lymphadenopathy (swollen and/or painful glands)	U	U	U	U	U	R†	U	U	U	U	U	U	U	U	U	U	U	U	U	R
Muscle cramps or pain—not present before treatment and not related to condition being treated	U	R†	U	M	U	U	U	R	R	U	U	U	R	U	R	U	U	U	U	M
Ocular effects																				
Amblyopia, toxic, or	R†	U	U	U	U	U	R	U	U	U	U	U	U	U	R†	U	U	U	U	U
Corneal opacity or	U	U	U	U	U	R	U	U	U	U	U	U	U	U	U	U	U	U	U	U
Retinal or macular disturbances (blurred vision or other vision change)	U	U	U	U	U	U	U	R	U	R†	U	U	U	U	R†	U	R†	U	U	R†
Blurred or double vision or any change in vision	R	R	L	L	L	L	R	R	L	R†	‡	R	L	R	R†	R	R	R	R	L
Conjunctivitis (eye pain, redness, irritation, and/or swelling)	U	U	R†	U	U	R	R†	U	R	R†	U	U	U	R	U	U	U	R	R	U
Corneal deposits	U	U	U	U	U	U	U	R	U	U	U	U	U	U	U	U	U	U	U	U
Dry, irritated, or swollen eyes	U	U	U	U	U	R	R	U	R	R†	‡	U	U	U	R	U	U	U	R	U
Eye pain	U	U	U	U	U	U	U	R	R	U	U	U	U	U	U	U	U	U	U	U
Palpebral edema (swollen eyelids)	U	U	U	U	U	U	U	U	U	U	U	U	U	U	U	U	U	U	R	U
Retinal hemorrhage (red eyes)	U	U	U	U	U	R†	U	U	R	U	U	U	U	U	R†	U	U	U	U	U
Scotomata (change in vision)	R	U	U	U	U	U	R	U	U	U	U	U	U	U	R†	U	U	U	U	U
Oral/perioral effects																				
Gingival ulceration or	U	U	U	U	U	U	R	U	U	U	U	U	U	U	U	U	U	U	U	U
Stomatitis, aphthous (sores, ulcers, or white spots on lips or in mouth)	R	R	R	R†	U	R	R	R	L	L	U	L	L	R	R	L	R	R	L	R
Glossitis (irritated tongue)	U	U	U	U	U	U	U	U	U	U	U	R†	U	U	U	U	R	R	U	R
Swelling of lips and tongue	R	U	U	U	U	U	U	U	U	U	U	U	U	U	U	U	U	U	U	U

Table 3. Side/Adverse Effects* *(continued)*

Legend:
I = Diclofenac
II = Diflunisal
III = Etodolac
IV = Fenoprofen
V = Floctafenine
VI = Flurbiprofen
VII = Ibuprofen
VIII = Indomethacin
IX = Ketoprofen
X = Meclofenamate
XI = Mefenamic Acid
XII = Nabumetone
XIII = Naproxen
XIV = Oxaprozin
XV = Phenylbutazone
XVI = Piroxicam
XVII = Sulindac
XVIII = Tenoxicam
XIX = Tiaprofenic Acid
XX = Tolmetin

	I	II	III	IV	V	VI	VII	VIII	IX	X	XI	XII	XIII	XIV	XV	XVI	XVII	XVIII	XIX	XX
Otic effects																				
Decreased hearing or any change in hearing	R	U	R†	L	U	R†	R	R	R	U	U	U	L	R†	R	R†	R	R	U	R
Ringing or buzzing in ears	L	L	L	L	L	L	L	L	L	L	U	M	M	R	L	L	L	R	R	L
Pancreatitis (abdominal pain, fever with or without chills, swelling and/or tenderness in upper abdominal or stomach area)	R	U	U	R†	U	U	R	R	R†	U	R	R†	U	U	R†	R†	R	U	U	U
Renal effects																				
Fluid retention/edema (increased blood pressure; decrease in amount of urine; swelling of face, fingers, feet, and/or lower legs; rapid weight gain)	M	R	R	M	U	M	L	M	M	L	U	M	M	R	M	L	L	L	L	M
Glomerulitis or glomerulonephritis	U	U	U	U	U	U	U	U	U	U	U	U	U	U	R	R	U	U	U	U
Hyperkalemia (difficulty in speaking, low blood pressure, slow or irregular heartbeat, troubled breathing, severe weakness in arms or legs)	U	U	U	U	U	R†	U	R	U	U	U	U	U	U	U	R	U	U	L	U
Interstitial nephritis (bloody or cloudy urine; increased blood pressure; sudden decrease in amount of urine; swelling of face, fingers, feet, and/or lower legs; rapid weight gain)—may be hypersensitivity-mediated	R	R	R†	R	U	R	U	R	R	U	U	R	R	R	R	R	R	U	R	R
Nephrosis (sudden decrease in amount of urine; swelling of face, fingers, feet, and/or lower legs; rapid weight gain)	U	U	U	R	U	U	U	U	U	U	U	U	U	U	U	U	U	U	U	U
Nephrotic syndrome (cloudy urine, swelling of face)	R	R†	U	R	U	U	U	R	R	U	U	U	R	U	R	R	R	U	U	R
Oliguria/anuria (cessation of urination)—reported independently of renal impairment or failure	R	U	U	U	U	U	U	U	U	U	U	U	U	U	R	U	U	U	R	U
Polyuria (sudden, large increase in frequency and quantity of urine)	U	U	U	U	U	U	R	U	U	U	U	U	U	U	U	U	R	R	U	U
Renal impairment or failure (increased blood pressure; shortness of breath, troubled breathing, tightness in chest, and/or wheezing; sudden decrease in amount of urine; swelling of face, fingers, feet, and/or lower legs; continuing thirst; unusual tiredness or weakness; weight gain)	R	R	U	R	U	R	R	R	R	R	R	U	R	R	R	R	R	R	U	R
Renal papillary or tubular necrosis	U	U	U	U	U	U	R†	U	U	U	U	U	R	U	R	R	U	U	U	U
Shortness of breath or troubled breathing	R	R†	R†	M	U	R†	R	R	R	U	‡	R	M	U	R	R†	R	R	R	R
Thirst, continuing	U	U	R	U	L	U	U	U	R	U	U	U	L	U	U	U	U	U	U	U
Medical attention needed only if continuing or bothersome																				
Cardiovascular effects																				
Fast heartbeat	R†	U	U	L	L	L	R†	R	R	U	U	U	U	U	U	U	U	R	U	U
Flushing or hot flashes	R†	U	R	U	L	L	R	R	U	U	U	U	U	U	U	U	U	R	L	U
Increased sweating	R†	R	U	L	L	R†	U	L	L	U	‡	L	L	U	U	R	U	R	R	U
Pounding heartbeat	R†	R†	R	M	U	R	R	R	R	R†	R	R†	L	R†	U	R†	R	R	R	U

Central nervous system effects																				
Anxiety	U	U	U	U	U	L	U	U	U	U	U	R	U	U	U	U	U	U	R	U
Dizziness	L	L	M	M	M	L	M	M	L	M	‡	M	M	U	R	L	M	M	M	M
Drowsiness	R	L	R	M	M	L	R	L	L	U	‡	L	M	L	R	L	R	U	L	L
Headache, mild to moderate	M	M	M	M	M	M	L	M§	M	M	‡	M	M	U	R	L	L	M	M	M
Lightheadedness/vertigo	U	R	U	U	U	U	U	L	R	U	U	R	L	U	U	L	R	R	R	U
Nervousness or irritability	R	R	L	M	M	L	L	R	M	U	‡	L	U	U	R	R	L	R	U	L
Trembling or twitching	R†	U	U	L	U	L	U	U	U	U	U	R	U	U	L	U	U	U	L	U
Trouble in sleeping	R	L	R	L	M	L	R	R	L	R†	‡	L	R	L	U	R	R	R	R	L
Unusual weakness with no other signs or symptoms	R	L	M	M	L	L	U	R	U	R†	U	R	R	R	R	R†	R	R	R	M
Dermatologic effects																				
Photosensitive or photoallergic dermatologic reaction (severe sunburn; skin rash, redness, itching, and/or discoloration after exposure to sunlight)	R	R	R†	U	U	R	R†	R	R	U	U	R	R	R	R	R	R	R	U	U
Gastrointestinal effects																				
Abdominal cramps, pain, or discomfort, mild to moderate	M	M	M	L	M	M	M	M	M	M	M	M§	M	L	M	M	M§	U	M	M
Bitter taste or other taste change	R	U	U	R†	L	R	U	U	R	R†	U	R	U	R†	U	U	R	U	U	U
Bloated feeling or gas	L	L	M	L	L	L	L	R	M	M	L	M	U	L	R	L	L	L	L	M
Constipation	M	L	L	M	M	L	L	L	M	L	L	M	M	M	R	L	M	L	L	L
Decreased appetite or loss of appetite	R	R	R	L	L	L	L	R	L	L	‡	U	U	L	U	L	L	R	R	R
Diarrhea	M	M	M	L	M	M	L	L	M	M§	M††	M§	L	M	R	L	M	L	L	M
Epigastric pain or discomfort (stomach pain or discomfort, mild to moderate)	U	U	U	U	U	U	M	U	U	U	U	U	U	U	U	M	U	L	L	U
Heartburn	U	U	U	U	U	U	M	U	U	M	L	U	M	U	U	U	U	L	M	U
Indigestion	M	M	M	M§	M	M	L	M	M§	L	L	M§	L	M	L	L	M	M	M§	M
Nausea	M	M	M	M	M	M	M	M	M	M§	M	M	M	M	M	M	M	L	M	M§
Rectal irritation—with rectal dosage forms	‡	—	—	—	—	—	—	R	M	—	—	—	—	—	—	‡	—	—	—	—
Vomiting	R	L	R	L	U	L	L	L	L	U	U	L	R	L	R	R	L	R	M	M
General feeling of discomfort or illness	R	U	U	L	U	L	U	L	L	R†	U	R	R	R	U	L	U	R	U	U
Irritation, dryness, or soreness of mouth	R	L	R	L	L	R†	R	R	R	L	U	L	U	U	U	R	R	R	L	R
Muscle weakness	U	U	U	U	U	R†	U	R	U	U	U	U	R	U	U	U	R	R	U	L
Photophobia (increased sensitivity of eyes to light)	U	U	R	U	U	U	U	U	U	U	U	U	U	U	U	U	U	U	U	U
Weight loss, unexplained	R†	U	U	U	U	U	U	U	R	U	U	U	U	R	U	U	U	U	U	M

*Differences in frequency of occurrence may reflect either lack of clinical-use data or actual pharmacologic distinctions among agents (although their pharmacologic similarity suggests that side effects occurring with one may occur with the others). M=more frequent (3–9%); L=less frequent (1–3%); R=rare(<1%); U=unknown; unless otherwise specified.

†Has been reported, but a causal relationship has not been established.

‡Has been reported, but actual frequency of occurrence unknown.

§Frequency of occurrence 10% or higher.

#Serious gastrointestinal effects, including ulceration, perforation, and/or bleeding, may occur at any time, with or without warning signs and/or symptoms, during chronic therapy with nonsteroidal anti-inflammatory drugs (NSAIDs). The risk of NSAID-induced gastrointestinal toxicity may increase with the duration of therapy as well as with dosage. In clinical trials with nabumetone, peptic ulceration occurred in approximately 0.3%, 0.5%, and 0.8% of patients treated for 6 months, 1 year, and 2 years, respectively. In clinical trials with other NSAIDs, upper gastrointestinal tract ulceration, bleeding, or perforation occurred in approximately 1% of patients treated for 3 to 6 months and in approximately 2 to 4% of patients treated for 1 year. Risk factors that may increase the risk of NSAID-induced gastrointestinal toxicity, other than those associated with an increased risk of peptic ulcer disease in any patient, have not been identified.

**See also Dermatologic effects, Hematologic effects, Hepatic effects, and Renal effects for signs and symptoms of many of the reported components of this syndrome.

††Diarrhea occurring during mefenamic acid therapy requires medical attention.

ANTIMYASTHENICS Systemic

This monograph includes information on the following: 1) Ambenonium†; 2) Neostigmine; 3) Pyridostigmine.

VA CLASSIFICATION (Primary): AU300

Commonly used brand name(s): *Mestinon*[3]; *Mestinon Timespans*[3]; *Mestinon-SR*[3]; *Mytelase Caplets*[1]; *Prostigmin*[2]; *Regonol*[3].

Note: For a listing of dosage forms and brand names by country availability, see *Dosage Forms* section(s).

†Not commercially available in Canada.

Category

Note: Cholinergic (cholinesterase inhibitor) is the basic category; the other categories are specific categories of use.

Cholinergic (cholinesterase inhibitor)—Ambenonium; Neostigmine; Pyridostigmine; Antimyasthenic—Ambenonium; Neostigmine; Pyridostigmine; Antidote (to nondepolarizing neuromuscular block)—Neostigmine (parenteral only); Pyridostigmine (parenteral only); Diagnostic aid (myasthenia gravis)—Neostigmine (parenteral only).

Indications

Note: Bracketed information in the *Indications* section refers to uses that are not included in U.S. product labeling.

Accepted

Myasthenia gravis (treatment)—Ambenonium, neostigmine, and pyridostigmine are indicated in the treatment of myasthenia gravis. Ambenonium is used less commonly than neostigmine or pyridostigmine but may be preferred in patients hypersensitive to the bromide ion. Oral neostigmine or pyridostigmine is most useful in prolonged therapy where no difficulty in swallowing is present. In acute myasthenic crisis where difficulty in breathing and swallowing is present, the parenteral dosage form should be used and the patient transferred to the oral dosage form as soon as tolerated.

In the treatment of myasthenia gravis, other treatment (such as respiratory therapy and control of secondary infection) must be administered concurrently with the antimyasthenic.

Ileus, gastrointestinal, postoperative (prophylaxis and treatment); or
Urinary retention, postoperative (prophylaxis and treatment)—Parenteral neostigmine is indicated in the treatment of postoperative nonobstructive urinary retention. Although it is not commonly used, parenteral neostigmine may also be indicated for the prevention and treatment of postoperative gastrointestinal ileus and prevention of postoperative urinary retention.

Neuromuscular blockade, nondepolarizing (treatment)—Parenteral neostigmine and pyridostigmine are indicated as antidotes to tubocurarine and other nondepolarizing neuromuscular blocking agents.

[Myasthenia gravis (diagnosis)][1]—Parenteral neostigmine has been used as a diagnostic test for myasthenia gravis. Although edrophonium is usually considered the agent of first choice because of its rapid onset and brief duration of action, neostigmine is sometimes used to confirm the edrophonium response.

Unaccepted

Although parenteral neostigmine has been used as a screening test for pregnancy and in the treatment of delayed menstruation, these uses of neostigmine are obsolete.

[1]Not included in Canadian product labeling.

Pharmacology/Pharmacokinetics

See *Table 1*, page ■■■.

Physicochemical characteristics

Molecular weight—
Neostigmine bromide: 303.20.
Neostigmine methylsulfate: 334.39.
Pyridostigmine bromide: 261.12.

Other characteristics—
Neostigmine methylsulfate injection: pH approximately 5.9.
Pyridostigmine bromide injection: pH approximately 5.0.

Mechanism of action/Effect

Cholinergic (cholinesterase inhibitor)—
Antimyasthenics inhibit destruction of acetylcholine by acetylcholinesterase, thereby facilitating transmission of impulses across the myoneural junction. Cholinergic responses produced are miosis, bradycardia, increased tonus of intestinal and skeletal muscle, constriction of bronchi and ureters, and stimulation of secretion by salivary and sweat glands. In addition, these medications have a direct cholinomimetic effect on skeletal muscle. Neostigmine may also act on autonomic ganglion cells and neurons of the central nervous system (CNS).

Neostigmine prevents or relieves postoperative distention by stimulating gastric motility and increasing gastric tone, which probably represents a combination of actions at the ganglion cells of Auerbach's plexus and at the muscle fibers as a result of the preservation of acetylcholine released by the cholinergic preganglionic and postganglionic fibers, respectively.

Neostigmine prevents or relieves urinary retention by increasing the tone of the detrusor muscle of the urinary bladder to produce contractions strong enough to initiate micturition.

Antimyasthenic—
Muscle strength and response to repetitive nerve stimulation is increased as a result of these medications enhancing the peak effect and prolonging the duration of action of acetylcholine at the motor end plate.

Antidote (to nondepolarizing neuromuscular block)—
Since nondepolarizing neuromuscular blocking agents combine reversibly with the receptors, preventing access of acetylcholine, antagonism can be overcome by increasing the amount of agonist at the receptors; therefore, muscle paralysis induced by nondepolarizing neuromuscular blocking agents is reversed by neostigmine or pyridostigmine, which increases concentration of acetylcholine at the receptors.

Diagnostic aid (myasthenia gravis)—
By prolonging the duration of action of acetylcholine at the motor end plate, neostigmine increases muscle strength in patients with myasthenia gravis, whereas patients with other disorders develop either no increase in muscle strength or even a slight weakness and possibly fasciculations.

Absorption

Oral—Poorly absorbed from the gastrointestinal tract.
Parenteral—Intramuscular: Neostigmine is rapidly absorbed.

Precautions to Consider

Cross-sensitivity and/or related problems

Patients sensitive to bromides may be sensitive to neostigmine (oral) or pyridostigmine also.

Pregnancy/Reproduction

Pregnancy—Problems with cholinesterase inhibitors in the human fetus have not been documented; however, transient muscular weakness has occurred in about 20% of infants born to mothers who received these medications during pregnancy.

For neostigmine: Studies with neostigmine have not been done in either animals or humans.

FDA Pregnancy Category C.

Labor and delivery—Anticholinesterase agents may cause uterine irritability and induce premature labor when given intravenously to pregnant women near term.

Breast-feeding

Pyridostigmine is distributed into breast milk in concentrations of 36 to 113% of maternal plasma concentrations. It is not known whether ambenonium and neostigmine are distributed into breast milk. However, problems in humans have not been documented.

Pediatrics

Appropriate studies on the relationship of age to the effects of cholinesterase inhibitors have not been performed in the pediatric population. However, no pediatrics-specific problems have been documented to date.

Geriatrics

Extensive studies with cholinesterase inhibitors have not been performed in the geriatric population. However, in one study in which 14 out of 32 adult patients were over 60 years of age, the duration of antagonism of neuromuscular blockade by neostigmine and pyridostigmine in the elderly group was prolonged compared to younger patients.

Drug interactions and/or related problems

The following drug interactions and/or related problems have been selected on the basis of their potential clinical significance (possible mechanism in parentheses where appropriate)—not necessarily inclusive (» = major clinical significance):

Note: Combinations containing any of the following medications, depending on the amount present, may also interact with this medication.

Aminoglycosides, systemic or
Anesthetics, hydrocarbon inhalation, such as:
Chloroform
Cyclopropane
Enflurane
Halothane
Methoxyflurane
Trichloroethylene or
Anesthetics, parenteral-local, large doses or
Capreomycin or
Lidocaine, intravenous or
Lincomycins or
Polymyxins, such as colistimethate, colistin, and polymyxin B or
Quinine
(neuromuscular blocking action of these medications may antagonize the effect of antimyasthenics on skeletal muscle; temporary dosage adjustments of antimyasthenics may be necessary to control symptoms of myasthenia gravis during and following concurrent use)
(antimyasthenics, especially in large doses, may decrease the neuromuscular blocking activity of these medications)

Anesthetics, local, ester-derivative
(antimyasthenic agent-induced inhibition of plasma cholinesterase activity reduces the metabolism of these anesthetics, leading to increased risk of toxicity; it is recommended that local anesthetics that are not ester derivatives be used instead)

Anticholinergic agents, especially atropine and related compounds
(atropine may be used to reduce or prevent the muscarinic effects of antimyasthenics; however, routine concurrent use is not recommended since the muscarinic effects may be the first signs of overdose and masking them with atropine may prevent early recognition of cholinergic crisis)
(concurrent use of anticholinergics with antimyasthenics may further reduce intestinal motility; therefore, caution is recommended)

» Cholinesterase inhibitors, other, including demecarium, echothiophate, and isoflurophate, and possibly topical malathion
(concurrent use of other cholinesterase inhibitors with antimyasthenics is not recommended except under strict medical supervision because of the possibility of additive toxicity; caution may also be warranted with topical application of malathion if excessive quantities are used)

Edrophonium
(caution is recommended in administering edrophonium to patients with symptoms of myasthenic weakness who are also receiving antimyasthenics, since symptoms of cholinergic crisis [overdosage] may be similar to those occurring with myasthenic crisis [underdosage] and the patient's condition may be worsened by use of edrophonium)

» Guanadrel or
» Guanethidine or
» Mecamylamine or
» Trimethaphan
(these ganglionic-blocking medications may antagonize the effects of antimyasthenics when used concurrently, leading to increased muscle weakness, respiratory weakness, and/or difficulty in swallowing; the possibility should be considered that the antihypertensive effects of the ganglionic-blocking medication may also be decreased during concurrent use)

Neuromuscular blocking agents
(phase I block of depolarizing neuromuscular blocking agents such as succinylcholine may be prolonged when used concurrently with neostigmine or pyridostigmine; however, if a depolarizing neuromuscular blocking agent has been used over a prolonged period of time and the depolarization block has changed to a nondepolarization block, neostigmine or pyridostigmine may reverse the nondepolarization block)
(effects of nondepolarizing neuromuscular blocking agents are antagonized by parenteral neostigmine or pyridostigmine; this interaction may be used to therapeutic advantage to reverse muscle relaxation following surgery)
(neuromuscular blockade antagonizes the effect of antimyasthenics on skeletal muscle; temporary dosage adjustments of antimyasthenics may be required to control symptoms of myasthenia gravis following use of a neuromuscular blocking agent)

» Procainamide or
Quinidine
(neuromuscular blocking activity and/or secondary anticholinergic effects of these medications may antagonize the action of antimyasthenics; caution is recommended during concurrent use in patients with myasthenia gravis)

Medical considerations/Contraindications

The medical considerations/contraindications included have been selected on the basis of their potential clinical significance (reasons given in parentheses where appropriate)—not necessarily inclusive (» = major clinical significance).

Risk-benefit should be considered when the following medical problems exist:

Asthma, bronchial
(increase in bronchial secretions and other respiratory effects of antimyasthenics may aggravate condition)

Atelectasis, postoperative, or
Pneumonia
(may be exacerbated)

Cardiac dysrhythmias, especially bradycardia and atrioventricular (AV) block
(increased risk of cardiac arrhythmias)

» Intestinal or urinary tract obstruction, mechanical
(may be exacerbated)

Sensitivity to any of these medications or to bromides

» Urinary tract infections
(increase in urinary bladder muscle tone may aggravate symptoms)

» Caution is also recommended in the postsurgical patient because antimyasthenics may exacerbate respiratory problems caused by postoperative pain, sedation, retained secretions, or atelectasis. In the myasthenic patient, if a postoperative respiratory problem cannot be attributed to myasthenia gravis alone, mechanical ventilation is recommended.

Side/Adverse Effects

Note: Most common adverse reactions to cholinesterase inhibitors are caused by excessive cholinergic stimulation. These include both muscarinic and nicotinic effects.

Ambenonium produces fewer muscarinic side/adverse effects than neostigmine but more than pyridostigmine.

Neostigmine produces more severe muscarinic side effects than ambenonium or pyridostigmine.

Pyridostigmine may produce a significantly lower degree and incidence of bradycardia, salivation, and gastrointestinal stimulation than neostigmine.

The following side/adverse effects have been selected on the basis of their potential clinical significance (possible signs and symptoms in parentheses where appropriate)—not necessarily inclusive:

Those indicating need for medical attention

Incidence rare

Sensitivity to bromide ion of neostigmine or pyridostigmine (skin rash); ***thrombophlebitis*** (redness, swelling, or pain at injection site)—for pyridostigmine injection only

Those indicating need for medical attention only if they continue or are bothersome

Incidence more frequent

Muscarinic effects (diarrhea; increased sweating; increased watering of mouth; nausea or vomiting; stomach cramps or pain)

Incidence less frequent

Muscarinic effects (frequent urge to urinate; increase in bronchial secretions; unusually small pupils; unusual watering of eyes)

Overdose

For specific information on the agents used in the management of antimyasthenics overdose, see: *Atropine* in *Anticholinergics/Antispasmodics (Systemic)* monograph.

For more information on the management of overdose or unintentional ingestion, **contact a Poison Control Center** (see *Poison Control Center Listing*.

Clinical effects of overdose

The following effects have been selected on the basis of their potential clinical signifiance (possible signs and symptoms in parentheses where appropriate)—not necessarily inclusive:

Acute and chronic

CNS effects (clumsiness or unsteadiness; confusion; difficulty in breathing; seizures; slurred speech; unusual irritability, nervousness, restlessness, or fear); ***muscarinic effects*** (blurred vision; severe diarrhea; excessive increase in bronchial secretions or salivation; severe vomiting; shortness of breath; troubled breathing; wheezing, or tightness in chest; slow heartbeat; severe stomach cramps or pain; unusual tiredness or weakness); ***nicotinic effects*** (increasing muscle weakness or paralysis, especially in the arms, neck, shoulders, and tongue; muscle cramps or twitching)

Note: *Breathing problems* may also be caused by atelectasis.

Unusual tiredness or weakness may also be caused by hypokalemia resulting from severe diarrhea and vomiting.

In the myasthenic patient, *increased muscle weakness* may be caused by underdosage or resistance instead of by overdosage.

Note: Overdosage may induce cholinergic crisis,which is characterized by nicotinic effects in addition to intensified muscarinic effects.

In patients with myasthenia gravis or in the postoperative patient, cholinergic crisis may be difficult to distinguish from myasthenic crisis on a symptomatic basis because the principal symptom common to both is generalized muscle weakness. The time of onset of weakness may help determine whether the crisis is caused by overdosage or underdosage (or resistance). Weakness beginning about 1 hour after administration of antimyasthenic is probably overdosage while that occurring 3 or more hours after administration is probably underdosage or resistance.

If a differential diagnosis cannot be made on the basis of signs and symptoms, edrophonium may be used to distinguish cholinergic crisis from myasthenic crisisowever, caution is recommended because edrophonium will cause increased oropharyngeal secretions and further weakness in muscles of respiration in a cholinergic crisis. This may be especially critical in the postoperative patient.

Treatment of overdose

Recommended treatment for cholinergic crisis—

Prompt discontinuation of antimyasthenic.

Specific treatment—Use of intavenous atropine sulfate to counteract muscarinic effects.

Supportive care—May include establishment of endotracheal tube, if necessary.

Patient Consultation

As an aid to patient consultation, refer to *Advice for the Patient, Antimyasthenics (Systemic).*

In providing consultation, consider emphasizing the following selected information (» = major clinical significance):

Before using this medication

» Conditions affecting use, especially:
- Sensitivity to antimyasthenics or to bromides
- Pregnancy—Possible transient muscle weakness in newborns whose mothers received antimyasthenics during pregnancy
- Use in the elderly—In one study in a limited number of patients, duration of antagonism of neuromuscular blockade by neostigmine and pyridostigmine was prolonged
- Other medications, especially other cholinesterase inhibitors, guanadrel, guanethidine, mecamylamine, procainamide, or trimethaphan
- Other medical problems, especially intestinal or urinary tract blockage or, urinary tract infection

Proper use of this medication

Taking with food or milk to decrease possibility of side effects

» Importance of not taking more medication than the amount prescribed

For use in myasthenia gravis: Keeping daily record of dosing and effects on condition during initial therapy

Missed dose: Taking as soon as possible; not taking if almost time for next dose; not doubling doses

» Proper dosing

» Proper storage

Side/adverse effects

Signs of potential side effects, especially thrombophlebitis at injection site (for pyridostigmine only), and sensitivity

General Dosing Information

In myasthenia gravis, the dosage must be individualized according to the severity of the disease and the response of the patient.

To assist the physician in arranging an optimum therapeutic regimen in the treatment of myasthenia gravis, patients should keep a daily record of their condition.

Therapy in myasthenia gravis is frequently required day and night. Larger portions of the total daily dose may be taken at times of greater fatigue such as in the afternoons or at mealtimes.

Following prolonged therapy, myasthenic patients may become refractory to these medications. Responsiveness may be restored, especially when the resistance may have been caused by overdosage, by reducing the dosage or discontinuing the medication for a few days.

For parenteral dosage forms only

Patients should be closely observed for cholinergic reactions, especially when neostigmine or pyridostigmine is administered intravenously.

Atropine injection and antishock medication should always be readily available because of the possibility of hypersensitivity reactions.

When large doses of parenteral neostigmine or pyridostigmine are administered, as during reversal of muscle relaxants, prior or concurrent administration of atropine injection is recommended to counteract the muscarinic side effects.

Diet/Nutrition

Administration of oral forms of these medications with food or milk may decrease the muscarinic side effects by slowing down absorption of the medication and reducing serum peaks.

AMBENONIUM

Summary of Differences

Pharmacology/pharmacokinetics:

Has longer duration of action than neostigmine or pyridostigmine.

Side/adverse effects:

Produces fewer muscarinic side effects than neostigmine, but more than pyridostigmine.

Oral Dosage Forms

AMBENONIUM CHLORIDE TABLETS

Usual adult and adolescent dose

Antimyasthenic—

Oral, initially 5 mg three or four times a day, the dosage being adjusted as required at intervals of one to two days to avoid accumulation of medication and overdosage.

Note: When doses of more than 200 mg per day are administered, the patient should be closely observed for cholinergic reactions.

Usual pediatric dose

Antimyasthenic—

Oral, initially 300 mcg (0.3 mg) per kg of body weight or 10 mg per square meter of body surface per day (divided into three or four doses), the dosage being increased, if necessary, to 1.5 mg per kg of body weight or 50 mg per square meter of body surface per day (divided into three or four doses).

Usual geriatric dose

See *Usual adult and adolescent dose.*

Strength(s) usually available

U.S.—

10 mg (Rx) [*Mytelase Caplets* (scored; acacia; dibasic calcium phosphate; gelatin; lactose; magnesium stearate; starch; and sucrose)].

Canada—

Not commercially available.

Packaging and storage

Store below 40 °C (104 °F), preferably between 15 and 30 °C (59 and 86 °F), unless otherwise specified by manufacturer. Store in a tight container.

NEOSTIGMINE

Summary of Differences

Category: Parenteral neostigmine:

Also indicated as an antidote (to nondepolarizing neuromuscular block) and a diagnostic aid (myasthenia gravis).

Indications: Parenteral neostigmine:

Also indicated in the treatment of postoperative nonobstructive urinary retention.

May also be indicated for prevention and treatment of postoperative gastrointestinal ileus and prevention of postoperative urinary retention.

Pharmacology/pharmacokinetics:

Has shorter duration of action than ambenonium.

Precautions: Cross-sensitivity and/or related problems:
Oral neostigmine contains bromide ion to which some patients may be sensitive.
Side/adverse effects:
Produces more severe muscarinic side effects than ambenonium or pyridostigmine.

Additional Dosing Information

See also *General Dosing Information.*

Generally, 15 mg of neostigmine bromide administered orally is equivalent to 500 mcg (0.5 mg) of neostigmine methylsulfate administered parenterally.

For oral dosage forms only
- Neostigmine is poorly absorbed from the gastrointestinal tract following oral administration; therefore, much larger doses are required for oral than for parenteral use.
- Large oral doses should be avoided in conditions where there may be an increased absorption rate from the intestinal tract, in order to avoid possible toxicity.

For parenteral dosage forms only: When used as an antidote to nondepolarizing neuromuscular block
- It is recommended that the exact dose required be titrated, using a peripheral nerve stimulator device.
- Unless tachycardia is present, atropine (0.6 to 1 mg) should be administered concomitantly or several minutes before neostigmine to prevent bradycardia.
- In the presence of bradycardia, the pulse rate should be increased to about 80 per minute with atropine prior to administration of neostigmine.

When used as a diagnostic aid (myasthenia gravis)
- Significant improvement of muscle weakness occurring within several minutes to 1 hour following administration of neostigmine usually indicates myasthenia gravis. However, diagnosis also should include clinical and electromyographic (EMG) evaluation.

Oral Dosage Forms

NEOSTIGMINE BROMIDE TABLETS USP

Usual adult and adolescent dose

Antimyasthenic—
Initial—Oral, 15 mg every three to four hours, the dose and frequency of administration being adjusted as necessary.
Maintenance—Oral, 150 mg administered over a twenty-four-hour period, the intervals between doses being determined by response of the patient.

Note: The twenty-four-hour maintenance dose is highly variable among individuals.

Usual pediatric dose

Antimyasthenic—
Oral, 2 mg per kg of body weight or 60 mg per square meter of body surface per day, divided into six to eight doses.

Usual geriatric dose

See *Usual adult and adolescent dose.*

Strength(s) usually available

U.S.—
15 mg (Rx) [*Prostigmin* (scored; lactose); GENERIC].

Canada—
15 mg (Rx) [*Prostigmin* (scored; lactose)].

Packaging and storage

Store below 40 °C (104 °F), preferably between 15 and 30 °C (59 and 86 °F), unless otherwise specified by manufacturer. Store in a tight container.

Parenteral Dosage Forms

Note: Bracketed uses in the Dosage Forms section refer to categories of use and/or indications that are not included in U.S. product labeling.

NEOSTIGMINE METHYLSULFATE INJECTION USP

Usual adult and adolescent dose

Antimyasthenic—
Intramuscular or subcutaneous, 500 mcg (0.5); subsequent doses should be based on the patient's response.

Antidote (to nondepolarizing neuromuscular block)—
Intravenous, 500 mcg (0.5) to 2 mg administered slowly, repeated as required up to a total dose of 5 mg.

Note: Subsequent doses may be less than 500 mcg (0.5mg).

When neostigmine is administered intravenously, it is recommended that 600 mcg (0.6) to 1.2 mg of atropine sulfate be administered intravenously prior to or concurrently with neostigmine to counteract its muscarinic side effects.

Diagnostic aid (myasthenia gravis)[1]—
Intramuscular or subcutaneous, 1.5 mg administered simultaneously with 600 mcg (0.6 mg) of atropine

Note: Significant improvement of muscle weakness occurring within several minutes to one hour indicates myasthenia gravis.

Prevention of postoperative distention or urinary retention—
Intramuscular or subcutaneous, 250 mcg (0.25 mg) immediately following surgery, repeated every four to six hours for two or three days.

Treatment of postoperative distention—
Intramuscular or subcutaneous, 500 mcg (0.5 mg) as needed.

Treatment of urinary retention—
Intramuscular or subcutaneous, 500 mcg (0.5 mg); dose repeated every three hours for at least five doses after patient has voided or the bladder has been emptied.

Note: If urination does not occur within one hour following the initial 500–mcg (0.5–mg) dose, the patient should be catheterized.

Usual pediatric dose

Antimyasthenic—
Intramuscular or subcutaneous, 10 to 40 mcg (0.01 to 0.04 mg) per kg of body weight every two to three hours.

Note: A dose of 10 mcg (0.01 mg) of atropine per kg of body weight may be administered intramuscularly or subcutaneously with each dose or with alternate doses of neostigmine to counteract the muscarinic side effects.

Antidote (to nondepolarizing neuromuscular block)—
Intravenous, 40 mcg (0.04 mg) per kg of body weight administered with 20 mcg (0.02 mg) of atropine per kg of body weight.

[Diagnostic aid (myasthenia gravis)][1]—
Intramuscular, 40 mcg (0.04 mg) per kg of body weight or 1 mg per square meter of body surface per dose.
Intravenous, 20 mcg (0.02 mg) per kg of body weight or 500 mcg (0.5 mg) per square meter of body surface.

Usual geriatric dose

See *Usual adult and adolescent dose.*

Strength(s) usually available

U.S.—
0.25 mg per mL (1:4000) (Rx) [*Prostigmin* (parabens 0.2% [methyl and propyl]; sodium hydroxide); GENERIC].
0.5 mg per mL (1:2000) (Rx) [*Prostigmin* (parabens 0.2% [methyl and propyl]; sodium hydroxide—in 1–ml ampuls; phenol 0.45%; sodium acetate 0.02%; acetic acid; sodium hydroxide—in 10-mL vials); GENERIC].
1 mg per mL (1:1000) (Rx) [*Prostigmin* (phenol 0.45%; sodium acetate 0.02%; acetic acid; sodium hydroxide); GENERIC].

Canada—
0.5 mg per mL (1:2000) (Rx) [*Prostigmin* (methylparaben 1.8 mg; propylparaben 0.2 mg; sodium <0.01 mmol/mL—in 1–mL ampuls; phenol 0.45%; sodium acetate; acetic acid; sodium <0.01 mmol/mL—in 10-mL vials)].
1 mg per mL (1:1000) (Rx) [*Prostigmin* (phenol 0.45%; sodium acetate; acetic acid; sodium hydroxide; sodium <0.01 mmol/mL)].
2.5 mg per mL (1:400) (Rx) [*Prostigmin* (phenol 0.4%; sodium chloride; sodium hydroxide; sodium <0.01 mmol/mL)].

Packaging and storage

Store below 40 °C (104 °F), preferably between 15 and 30 °C (59 and 86 °F), unless otherwise specified by manufacturer. Protect from freezing. Protect from light.

[1]Not included in Canadian product labeling.

PYRIDOSTIGMINE

Summary of Differences

Category:
Parenteral pyridostigmine also indicated as an antidote (to nondepolarizing neuromuscular block).

Pharmacology/pharmacokinetics:
Generally has shorter duration of action than ambenonium and a slower onset and longer duration of action than neostigmine.

Precautions:
Cross-sensitivity and/or related problems—Contains bromide ion to which some patients may be sensitive.
Side/adverse effects:
May produce a significantly lower degree and incidence of bradycardia, salivation, and gastrointestinal stimulation than neostigmine.

Additional Dosing Information

See also *General Dosing Information.*

For oral dosage forms only:

- The syrup dosage form may be preferred for use in children and "brittle" myasthenic patients who require fractions of 60-mg doses. Also, the syrup is more easily swallowed, especially in the morning, by patients with bulbar involvement.
- It has been reported that the extended-release dosage form may pass intact through the gastrointestinal tract in patients with increased gastrointestinal activity or diarrhea. Use of other oral dosage forms may be required temporarily for continued control of symptoms.

Oral Dosage Forms

PYRIDOSTIGMINE BROMIDE SYRUP USP

Usual adult and adolescent dose

Antimyasthenic—
Initial—Oral, 30 to 60 mg every three to four hours, the dosage being adjusted as required.
Maintenance—Oral, 600 mg (range 60 mg to 1.5 grams) per day.

Usual pediatric dose

Antimyasthenic—
Oral, 7 mg per kg of body weight or 200 mg per square meter of body surface per day, divided into five or six doses.

Usual geriatric dose

See *Usual adult and adolescent dose.*

Strength(s) usually available

U.S.—
60 mg per 5 mL (Rx) [*Mestinon* (alcohol 5%; glycerin; lactic acid; sodium benzoate; sorbitol; sucrose; FD&C Red No. 40; FD&C Blue No. 1; flavors; water)].
Canada—
Not commercially available.

Packaging and storage

Store below 40 °C (104 °F), preferably between 15 and 30 °C (59 and 86 °F), unless otherwise specified by manufacturer. Store in a tight, light-resistant container. Protect from freezing.

PYRIDOSTIGMINE BROMIDE TABLETS USP

Usual adult and adolescent dose

See *Pyridostigmine Bromide Syrup USP.*

Usual pediatric dose

See *Pyridostigmine Bromide Syrup USP.*

Usual geriatric dose

See *Pyridostigmine Bromide Syrup USP.*

Strength(s) usually available

U.S.—
60 mg (Rx) [*Mestinon* (scored; lactose; silicon dioxide; stearic acid)].
Canada—
60 mg (Rx) [*Mestinon* (scored; lactose 272 mg)].

Packaging and storage

Store below 40 °C (104 °F), preferably between 15 and 30 °C (59 and 86 °F), unless otherwise specified by manufacturer. Store in a tight container.

PYRIDOSTIGMINE BROMIDE EXTENDED-RELEASE TABLETS

Usual adult and adolescent dose

Antimyasthenic—
Oral, 180 to 540 mg one or two times a day, with at least six hours between doses.

Note: For optimum control of symptoms, it may be necessary to administer the more rapidly acting regular tablet or syrup dosage form concurrently with extended-release therapy.

Extended-release preparations may increase the risk of cholinergic crisis and, therefore, are usually not recommended.

Usual pediatric dose

Dosage has not been established.

Usual geriatric dose

See *Usual adult and adolescent dose.*

Strength(s) usually available

U.S.—
180 mg (Rx) [*Mestinon Timespans* (carnauba wax; corn-derived proteins; magnesium stearate; silica gel; tribasic calcium phosphate)].
Canada—
180 mg (Rx) [*Mestinon-SR* (scored)].

Packaging and storage

Store below 40 °C (104 °F), preferably between 15 and 30 °C (59 and 86 °F), in a well-closed container, unless otherwise specified by manufacturer.

Auxiliary labeling

- Swallow tablets whole.

Parenteral Dosage Forms

PYRIDOSTIGMINE BROMIDE INJECTION USP

Usual adult and adolescent dose

Antimyasthenic—
Intramuscular or intravenous, 2 mg (approximately one-thirtieth of the usual oral dose) every two to three hours.
Antidote (to nondepolarizing neuromuscular block):—
Intravenous, 10 to 20 mg.

Note: Prior to administration of pyridostigmine, it is recommended that 600 mcg (0.6 mg) to 1.2 mg of atropine sulfate be given intravenously to counteract the muscarinic effects.

Usual pediatric dose

Antimyasthenic—
Neonates of myasthenic mothers—Intramuscular, 50 to 150 mcg (0.05 to 0.15 mg) per kg of body weight every four to six hours.

Usual geriatric dose

See *Usual adult and adolescent dose.*

Strength(s) usually available

U.S.—
5 mg per mL (Rx) [*Mestinon* (parabens 0.2% [methyl and propyl]; sodium citrate 0.02%; citric acid; sodium hydroxide); *Regonol* (benzyl alcohol 1%)].
Canada—
5 mg per mL (Rx) [*Regonol* (parabens 0.2% [methyl and propyl]; sodium citrate 0.02%; citric acid; sodium hydroxide)].

Packaging and storage

Store below 40 °C (104 °F), preferably between 15 and 30 °C (59 and 86 °F), unless otherwise specified by manufacturer. Protect from light. Protect from freezing.

Revised: 07/18/1994

Table 1. Pharmacology/Pharmacokinetics

Drug	Oral Bioavailability	Volume of Distribution V_D (L/kg)	Protein Binding	Biotrans- formation	Half-life Distribution (min)	Half-life Elimination (min)	Onset of Action (min)	Time to Peak Plasma Concentration (hr)	Peak Plasma Concentration (mcg/mL)	Peak Effect (min)	Duration of Action (hr)	Elimination (% excreted unchanged)	Clearance (L/hr/kg)
Ambenonium							20–30				3–8		
Neostigmine			Low (15–25%)	Plasma; hepatic								Renal (about 50)	
Oral	1–2%						45–75*	1–2	1–5†		3–6		
Parenteral							‡	0.5		30			
Intramuscular		0.74±0.2			3.6±1.2	77.4±48	20–30				2–4		0.55±0.14
Intravenous		0.37–1.08			5.4	24–79.2	4–8				2–4		0.24–1.0
Pyridostigmine			Not bound	Plasma; hepatic								Renal	
Oral	10–20%							1–2	40–60§	60–120			
Syrup, Tablets							30–45				3–6		
Extended-release Tablets							30–60				6–12		
Parenteral													
Intramuscular							<15				2–4		
Intravenous		1.03–1.76			7.2–8.4	63–112	2–5				2–4		0.52–1.0

*Peristaltic activity begins in 2 to 4 hours.
†Following a single 30-mg oral dose.
‡Peristaltic activity begins in 10 to 30 minutes.
§Following a single 60-mg oral dose.

ANTITHYROID AGENTS Systemic

This monograph includes information on the following: 1) Methimazole; 2) Propylthiouracil.

INN: Methimazole—Thiamazole

VA CLASSIFICATION (Primary): HS852

Commonly used brand name(s): *Propyl-Thyracil*[2]; *Tapazole*[1].

Note: For a listing of dosage forms and brand names by country availability, see *Dosage Forms* section(s).

Category

Antihyperthyroid agent.

Indications

Accepted

Hyperthyroidism (treatment)—Methimazole and propylthiouracil are indicated in the treatment of hyperthyroidism, including prior to surgery or radiotherapy, and as adjuncts in the treatment of thyrotoxicosis or thyroid storm. Propylthiouracil may be preferred over methimazole for use in thyroid storm, since propylthiouracil inhibits peripheral conversion of thyroxine [T_4] to triiodothyronine [T_3] .

Further studies are needed to establish the safety and efficacy of using propylthiouracil for the treatment of alcoholic liver disease.

Unaccepted

Efficacy of antithyroid medications has been inconsistent in the treatment of angina pectoris. These agents are probably useful for this purpose only in hyperthyroid patients with angina pectoris.

Antithyroid medications are not effective in the treatment of thyrotoxicosis resulting from exogenous thyroid hormone overdosage.

Pharmacology/Pharmacokinetics

Physicochemical characteristics

Chemical Group—Methimazole and propylthiouracil are thioamide derivatives.

Molecular weight—
- Methimazole: 114.16.
- Propylthiouracil: 170.23.

pKa—Propylthiouracil: 7.8.

Mechanism of action/Effect

Inhibit synthesis of thyroid hormone within the thyroid gland by serving as substrates for thyroid peroxidase, which catalyzes the incorporation of oxidized iodide into tyrosine residues in thyroglobulin molecules and couples iodotyrosines. This diverts iodine from the synthesis of thyroid hormones. Antithyroid agents do not interfere with the actions of exogenous thyroid hormone or inhibit the release of thyroid hormones. Therefore, stores of thyroid hormones must be depleted before clinical effects will be apparent. Antithyroid agents may also have moderating effects on the underlying immunologic abnormalities in hyperthyroidism due to Graves' disease (toxic diffuse goiter), but evidence on this point reported to date is inconclusive.

Propylthiouracil—
- Additionally, inhibits peripheral conversion of T_4 to T_3, which may theoretically make it more effective in the treatment of thyroid storm.

Absorption

Rapid.

Methimazole—
- Oral: Bioavailability 93%. Absorption may be unpredictably affected by food.
- Rectal: In one study in healthy subjects, absorption of extemporaneously compounded 60-mg rectal suppositories was similar to that of oral tablets.

Propylthiouracil—
- Oral: Bioavailability 65 to 75%.
- Rectal: In one study in healthy subjects, absorption of extemporaneously compounded 100-mg rectal suppositories was slower and less extensive than that of oral tablets ($AUC_{0\ to\ 8h}$: 23.77 ± 1.24 mcg•hr/mL [oral], 6.16 ± 2.07 mcg•hr/mL [rectal]).

Distribution

Both methimazole and propylthiouracil are actively concentrated by the thyroid.

Methimazole—Volume of distribution is approximately 0.6 liter per kilogram (L/kg) of body weight.

Propylthiouracil—Volume of distribution is approximately 0.4 L/kg of body weight.

Protein binding

Methimazole—Not significant.

Propylthiouracil—High (80%), primarily to albumin.

Biotransformation

Primarily hepatic; active metabolites of either compound have not been demonstrated.

Propylthiouracil—Primarily undergoes glucuronidation. Approximately 33% of an orally administered dose is metabolized by a first-pass effect.

Half-life

Methimazole—5 to 6 hours.

Propylthiouracil—1 to 2 hours.

Onset of action

Methimazole—In one study, substantial reductions in mean serum thyroxine and triiodothyronine concentrations were seen after 5 days of methimazole therapy at 40 mg per day.

Time to peak serum concentration

Methimazole—
- Oral/Rectal:
  - Approximately 30 to 60 minutes (occurrence of peak blood concentrations, after administration of a 60-mg rectal suppository or a 60-mg oral dose to healthy subjects).

Propylthiouracil—
- Oral:
  - 1.99 ± 0.26 hours (after administration of a 100-mg dose to healthy subjects).
- Rectal:
  - Solution—Approximately 3 hours (after administration of a 400-mg rectal dose of propylthiouracil in an aqueous solution of sodium phosphates to a patient with thyroid storm).
  - Suppository—4.72 ± 0.96 hours (after administration of a 100-mg suppository to healthy subjects).

Peak serum concentration

Methimazole—
- Oral:
  - 1.184 ± 0.12 mcg/mL (blood concentrations, after administration of a 60-mg dose to healthy subjects).
- Rectal:
  - 1.163 ± 0.15 mcg/mL (blood concentrations, after administration of a 60-mg suppository to healthy subjects).

Propylthiouracil—
- Oral:
  - 7.12 ± 0.48 mcg/mL (after administration of a 100-mg dose to healthy subjects).
- Rectal:
  - Solution—3.1 mcg/mL (approximate, after administration of a 400-mg rectal dose of propylthiouracil in an aqueous solution of sodium phosphates to a patient with thyroid storm).
  - Suppository—1.2 ± 0.31 mcg/mL (after administration of a 100-mg rectal suppository to healthy subjects).

Time to peak effect

Methimazole—7 weeks (average) to normalize serum T_3 and T_4 concentrations with use of 30 mg per day. In one study, 4 weeks (approximate) to normalize serum T_3 and T_4 concentrations with use of 40 mg per day.

Propylthiouracil—17 weeks (average) to normalize serum T_3 and T_4 concentrations with use of 300 mg per day.

Elimination

Methimazole—
- Less than 10% is excreted in the urine unchanged. Total body clearance is approximately 10 L per hour.

Propylthiouracil—
- Less than 1% is excreted in the urine unchanged. Total body clearance is approximately 7 L per hour.
- In dialysis: Elimination and pharmacokinetics are not significantly altered in hemodialysis. In one patient undergoing hemodialysis, 5% of a 200-mg oral dose was removed by 3 hours of hemodialysis; elimination rate was not significantly altered. Peak serum concentration was decreased (from 7.9 to 4.9 mcg/mL), although it remained within an approximate therapeutic range.

Precautions to Consider

Cross-sensitivity and/or related problems

Cross-sensitivity may occur frequently (in about 50% of patients) between antithyroid thioamide medications.

If a persistent or severe reaction necessitates withdrawal of one agent, therapy may be switched to the other, although there is a risk of cross-reactivity occurring. However, if agranulocytosis, thrombocytopenia, or hepatic dysfunction occurs, substitution with another thioamide is not recommended.

Carcinogenicity/Mutagenicity

Methimazole—In a two-year study, thyroid hyperplasia, adenoma, and carcinoma have developed in rats when given methimazole at doses of 3 and 18 mg per kg of body weight per day (mg/kg/day) (2 and 12 times the 15 mg/day maximum human maintenance dose calculated on the basis of surface area).

Propylthiouracil—Thyroid hyperplasia and carcinoma have occurred in laboratory animals treated with propylthiouracil for longer than 1 year. Similar effects are seen with continuous thyroid suppression with various antithyroid agents, dietary iodine deficiency, subtotal thyroidectomy, and ectopic thyrotropin-secreting pituitary tumors. Pituitary adenomas have also occurred.

Pregnancy/Reproduction

Pregnancy—Methimazole and propylthiouracil cross the placenta and can cause fetal hypothyroidism and goiter. However, the possible risks of adverse effects due to antithyroid agents must be weighed against the risks of possible adverse effects due to continuing hyperthyroidism during pregnancy. Propylthiouracil is considered by some clinicians as the agent of choice for women who require antithyroid medications during pregnancy. Propylthiouracil crosses the placenta less readily than methimazole, and the use of methimazole during pregnancy has been associated with several cases of scalp defects (aplasia cutis) in the infant. Rare instances of congenital defects including esophageal atresia with tracheoesophageal fistula and choanal atresia with absent/hypoplastic nipples have occurred in infants whose mothers were treated with methimazole during pregnancy. The reduced placental transfer of propylthiouracil is presumably due to its high level of serum protein binding and high level of ionization at a pH of 7.4.

The actual risk of fetal death, goiter, hypothyroidism, or certain congenital abnormalities with administration of antithyroid agents appears to be low, especially if maternal doses are low (for example, less than 100 to 150 mg of propylthiouracil or an equivalent dose of methimazole per day). Fetal goiters induced by antithyroid agents are generally not as large as iodide-induced fetal goiters and have not usually been reported to be obstructive. Fetal hypothyroidism and goiter usually occur when the antithyroid agents are used close to term, since the fetal thyroid does not begin to produce thyroid hormones until the 11th or 12th week of gestation. In long-term follow-up of some children exposed *in utero* to maternal therapeutic doses of propylthiouracil, gross abnormalities in development or diminished intellectual performance have not been observed.

It is recommended that antithyroid medication be prescribed at the lowest effective dose to maintain maternal thyroid function within the upper-normal range for normal pregnant women, especially during the last trimester, to reduce the risk of fetal and maternal hypothyroidism and goiter. Thyroid hyperfunction may diminish as pregnancy progresses, allowing a reduction in antithyroid dosage and, in some cases, withdrawal of antithyroid therapy 2 to 3 months before delivery. However, thyroid function may vary and dosing should be based on frequent and careful monitoring. Hyperthyroidism may recur soon after delivery. Because radioactive iodine is absolutely contraindicated during pregnancy, thyroidectomy may be very rarely required in refractory cases of hyperthyroidism or in patients who are noncompliant with the use of antithyroid medications.

Thyroid hormones are minimally transferred across the placenta and therefore have little protective effect on the fetus. They may also mask signs of remission of hyperthyroidism, resulting in fetal and maternal exposure to unnecessarily high doses of antithyroid agents. For these reasons, adjunctive treatment with thyroid hormones is not recommended during pregnancy.

Several case reports have been published in which antithyroid agents were given to a euthyroid mother of a hyperthyroid fetus. Fetal heart rate monitoring and ultrasound examinations were used to monitor fetal response. Fetal tachycardia was reduced and the infants were euthyroid at delivery. However, further data are needed regarding this form of therapy for fetal hyperthyroidism.

FDA Pregnancy Category D.

Breast-feeding

Small amounts of methimazole and propylthiouracil are distributed into breast milk. Maternal serum and breast milk concentrations of methimazole are nearly equal. Methimazole is contraindicated in nursing mothers. Postpartum patients should not breast feed their infants while receiving methimazole. Propylthiouracil is generally preferred over methimazole during lactation because methimazole is distributed into breast milk more readily (approximately ten-fold), presumably due to its insignificant level of protein binding and ionization. Serial monitoring of thyroid function (by measurement of serum thyrotropin and thyroxine concentrations) of the infant is advisable. However, some clinicians feel that small doses of methimazole (e.g., ≤ 10–15 mg per day) do not pose a significant risk to the infant if thyroid function is monitored frequently.

There is a theoretical risk of causing hypothyroidism and/or agranulocytosis in the infant with high maternal doses of antithyroid agents. Termination of breast-feeding may be necessary prior to initiation of high-dose therapy.

Pediatrics

Antithyroid agents are frequently used to treat hyperthyroidism in children. Children seem to respond to antithyroid agents as well as do adults. Pharmacokinetic studies conducted in children also did not reveal any differences unique to the pediatric population.

Caution is necessary in interpreting results of thyroid function tests in neonates, because serum concentrations of thyroid hormones are higher at birth than those of healthy children or adults and begin to fall to normal in the first week of life.

Adolescents

Antithyroid agents are frequently used to treat hyperthyroidism in adolescents. Adolescents seem to respond to antithyroid agents as well as do adults. Pharmacokinetic studies conducted in adolescents did not reveal any differences unique to the adolescent population.

Geriatrics

One study showed that agranulocytosis is more likely to occur in patients older than 40 years of age or in patients taking more than 40 mg of methimazole per day.

In one pharmacokinetic study, no significant differences were found for geriatric patients in certain pharmacokinetic parameters (e.g., Vd, Vd beta, Vd at steady state, area under the curve, and clearance). Rate of absorption was decreased (approximately one-third that of younger subjects) though there are no data regarding the clinical significance of this finding.

Geriatric patients with severe cardiac disease should be given antithyroid agents and/or beta-adrenergic blocking agents, such as propranolol, for 4 to 6 weeks prior to treatment with radioiodine to help reduce possible exacerbation of heart disease by radiation-induced thyroiditis. Antithyroid drugs must be discontinued at least 3 to 4 days prior to radioiodine treatment and should not be readministered until 1 week after treatment. However, a beta-adrenergic blocking agent may be used throughout the treatment period if needed.

Dental

The bone marrow depressant effects of antithyroid agents may result in an increased incidence of microbial infection, delayed healing, and gingival bleeding. If leukopenia or thrombocytopenia occurs, dental work should be deferred until blood counts have returned to normal, and patients should be instructed in proper oral hygiene, including caution in use of regular toothbrushes, dental floss, and toothpicks.

Drug interactions and/or related problems

The following drug interactions and/or related problems have been selected on the basis of their potential clinical significance (possible mechanism in parentheses where appropriate)—not necessarily inclusive (» = major clinical significance):

Note: Combinations containing any of the following medications, depending on the amount present, may also interact with this medication.

Aminophylline or
Oxtriphylline or
Theophylline
(hyperthyroid patients have exhibited increased metabolic clearance of aminophylline and theophylline, which returned to normal as the patients became euthyroid; decreased dose of aminophylline, oxtriphylline, or theophylline may be necessary as patients become euthyroid)

» Amiodarone or
» Iodinated glycerol or
» Iodine or
» Potassium iodide
(iodide or iodine excess may decrease response to antithyroid agents, requiring an increase in dosage or longer duration of therapy with antithyroid agents; amiodarone contains 37% iodine by weight, and therefore its use significantly increases iodine intake; iodine deficiency may increase response to antithyroid agents, requiring a decrease in dosage or shorter duration of therapy with antithyroid agents)

» Anticoagulants, coumarin- or indandione-derivative
(as thyroid and metabolic status of patient decreases toward normal, response to oral anticoagulants may decrease; however, if thioamide-induced hypoprothrombinemia occurs, anticoagulant effect may be enhanced; adjustment of oral anticoagulant dosage on the basis of prothrombin time is recommended)

» Beta-adrenergic blocking agents
(hyperthyroidism causes an increased clearance of beta blockers with a high extraction ratio; dose reduction may be necessary when patient becomes euthyroid.)

» Digitalis glycosides
(serum concentrations of digoxin and digitoxin have been reported to increase as the thyroid and metabolic status of patients taking antithyroid agents decreased; reduction in dosage of any digitalis glycoside may be necessary as patients become euthyroid)

» Sodium iodide I 131
(antithyroid agents may decrease thyroidal uptake of I 131; a rebound increase in uptake may occur up to 5 days after sudden withdrawal of the antithyroid agent)

Laboratory value alterations

The following have been selected on the basis of their potential clinical significance (possible effect in parentheses where appropriate)—not necessarily inclusive (» = major clinical significance).

With diagnostic test results
» Sodium iodide I 123 or
» Sodium iodide I 131 or
» Sodium pertechnetate Tc 99m
(antithyroid agents may decrease thyroidal uptake of I 123, I 131, or pertechnetate; withdrawal of the antithyroid agent 5 days or more before radioactive iodine uptake tests is necessary to prevent interference)

With physiology/laboratory test values
Alanine aminotransferase (ALT [SGPT]), serum concentrations and
Alkaline phosphatase, serum concentrations and
Aspartate aminotransferase (AST [SGOT]), serum concentrations and
Bilirubin, serum concentrations and
Lactate dehydrogenase (LDH), serum concentrations and
Prothrombin time (PT)
(may be increased; may indicate hepatotoxicity and be associated with splenomegaly)

Medical considerations/Contraindications

The medical considerations/contraindications included have been selected on the basis of their potential clinical significance (reasons given in parentheses where appropriate)—not necessarily inclusive (» = major clinical significance).

Except under special circumstances, this medication should not be used when the following medical problem exists:
» Severe adverse reaction or severe allergic reaction to either methimazole or propylthiouracil, or history of

Risk-benefit should be considered when the following medical problem exists:
» Hepatic function impairment
(elimination half-life may be prolonged, in proportion to the degree of hepatic insufficiency)

Patient monitoring

The following may be especially important in patient monitoring (other tests may be warranted in some patients, depending on condition; » = major clinical significance):

Leukocyte count, total and differential
(determinations recommended prior to initiation of treatment and if infection occurs)

Prothrombin time (PT)
(should be monitored during treatment with methimazole, especially before surgical procedures)

» Free thyroxine (T_4), by direct assay and/or
» Thyrotropin (TSH) by sensitive radioimmunoassay and/or
Total thyroxine (T_4), either by competitive protein-binding assay or by radioimmunoassay and/or
Total triiodothyronine (T_3) by radioimmunoassay
(determination of serum concentrations is recommended prior to initiation of therapy, at monthly intervals during initial therapy, then every 2 to 3 months; some clinicians recommend at least yearly follow-up for life in patients successfully treated with antithyroid medications; in patients treated with these agents who do not undergo thyroid ablation with sodium iodide I 131 or surgery, the risk of subsequent hypothyroidism is related to immunogenic thyroid disease itself, and not the medication; recurrence of hyperthyroidism is common)

Side/Adverse Effects

Note: Incidence of most adverse reactions is dose-related; most side effects occur within the first 4 to 8 weeks.

The following side/adverse effects have been selected on the basis of their potential clinical significance (possible signs and symptoms in parentheses where appropriate)—not necessarily inclusive:

Those indicating need for medical attention

Incidence more frequent
Fever, mild and transient; ***leukopenia*** (continuing or severe fever or chills, throat infection, cough, mouth sores, or hoarseness)—usually asymptomatic; ***skin rash or itching***

Note: Mild *leukopenias* occur more frequently in patients (12% of adults and 25% of children) treated with antithyroid agents. Also, approximately 10% of untreated hyperthyroid patients have leukocyte levels below 4000 per cubic millimeter.

Incidence of *skin rash or itching* is 3 to 5%. Usually consists of maculopapular eruptions. An allergic reaction occurs less frequently and may disappear spontaneously with continued treatment; appears to be dose-related. Skin rash may also be a sign of vasculitis.

Incidence less frequent
Agranulocytosis (continuing or severe fever or chills, throat infection, cough, mouth sores, or hoarseness); ***arthralgias or arthritis or vasculitis*** (pain, swelling, or redness in joints)—usually with propylthiouracil; ***lupus-like syndrome*** (fever or chills; general feeling of discomfort or illness or weakness)—usually with propylthiouracil; ***peripheral neuropathy*** (numbness or tingling of fingers, toes, or face)

Note: *Agranulocytosis* (incidence 0.4%) usually occurs during the first 3 months of therapy. May occur less predictably and with lower doses of propylthiouracil. Deaths due to agranulocytosis have been reported.

Incidence rare
Aplastic anemia (continuing or severe fever or chills, throat infection, cough, mouth sores, or hoarseness); ***hypoprothrombinemia (for propylthiouracil)***; ***or thrombocytopenia*** (rarely, increase in bleeding or bruising; black, tarry stools; blood in urine or stools; pinpoint red spots on skin)—usually asymptomatic; ***cholestatic jaundice*** (yellow eyes or skin)—for methimazole; ***hepatic necrosis*** (yellow eyes or skin)—primarily with propylthiouracil; ***interstitial pneumonitis*** (cough or shortness of breath)—with propylthiouracil; ***lymphadenopathy*** (swollen lymph nodes); ***sialadenopathy*** (swollen salivary glands); ***nephritis (for methimazole) or renal vasculitis (usually with propylthiouracil)*** (backache; increase or decrease in urination; swelling of feet or lower legs)

Note: *Jaundice* may persist for up to 10 weeks after drug discontinuance. Fatal *hepatic necrosis* has been reported with both agents.

Those indicating need for medical attention only if they continue or are bothersome

Incidence less frequent
Dizziness; loss of taste—for methimazole; ***nausea or vomiting***; ***stomach pain***

Overdose

For more information on the management of overdose or unintentional ingestion, **contact a Poison Control Center** (see *Poison Control Center Listing*).

Clinical effects of overdose

The following effects have been selected on the basis of their potential clinical significance (possible signs and symptoms in parentheses where appropriate)—not necessarily inclusive:

Changes in menstrual periods; coldness; constipation; dry, puffy skin; goiter (swelling in the front of the neck); ***headache***; ***listlessness or sleepiness; muscle aches; nausea or vomiting, severe***; ***unusual tiredness or weakness; weight gain, unusual***

Note: *Hypothyroidism* may be an unavoidable long-term sequela to hyperthyroidism.

Patient Consultation

As an aid to patient consultation, refer to *Advice for the Patient, Antithyroid Agents (Systemic)*.

In providing consultation, consider emphasizing the following selected information (» = major clinical significance):

Before using this medication

» Conditions affecting use, especially:
Allergies to any thioamide
Pregnancy—May be used but careful monitoring is necessary

Breast-feeding—Distributed into breast milk, although propylthiouracil is distributed in much lesser amounts; may continue breast-feeding with low doses and monitoring of infant

Other medications, especially iodides, coumarin- or indandione-derivative anticoagulants, amiodarone, beta-adrenergic blocking agents, digitalis glycosides, or radioiodide

Other medical problems, especially hepatic function impairment

Proper use of this medication

» Importance of not taking more or less medication than the amount prescribed

» Importance of not missing doses and, if taking more than one dose per day, of taking at evenly spaced intervals

Taking methimazole at same time in relation to meals every day

» Proper dosing

Missed dose: Taking as soon as possible; taking both doses together if almost time for next dose; checking with physician if more than one dose is missed

» Proper storage

Precautions while using this medication

» Importance of close monitoring by the physician

» Checking with physician before discontinuing medication

» Caution if any kind of surgery (including dental surgery) or emergency treatment is required, because of the risk of thyroid storm

» Checking with physician immediately if injury, infection, or other illness occurs, because of the risk of thyroid storm

Caution if any laboratory tests required; possible interference with test results

Side/adverse effects

Signs of potential side effects, especially fever, skin rash or itching, bone marrow depression, hepatic dysfunction, lupus-like syndrome, arthralgias, arthritis, nephritis (for methimazole), vasculitis, pneumonitis, lymphadenopathy, sialadenopathy, hypoprothrombinemia (for propylthiouracil), or peripheral neuropathy

General Dosing Information

Dosage must be adjusted to meet the individual requirements of each patient, on the basis of clinical response and results of thyroid function tests.

In some patients, once- or twice-a-day therapy may be associated with a decreased incidence of side effects and improved compliance, although divided daily doses may be more effective. If divided daily doses are given, they should be administered at evenly spaced intervals throughout the day. Methimazole has a longer duration of action and therefore may frequently be more effective than propylthiouracil in once-daily dosing.

Confirmation of remission may be by sensitive TSH assay, trial withdrawal of the medication, protirelin test, thyroid suppression test, or thyroid-stimulating immunogloglubin (TSI) titer.

Duration of treatment necessary to produce a prolonged remission varies from 6 months to several years, with an average duration of 1 to 2 years. Control of hyperthyroidism with medication is sometimes followed by a spontaneous remission. Premature withdrawal may result in exacerbation of hyperthyroidism, although some clinicians feel that treatment may be withdrawn as soon as a euthyroid state is obtained (usually within 4 to 5 months), with no problems of rebound.

Iodide is usually added to thioamide antithyroid therapy for 7 to 10 days prior to surgery to reduce the vascularity of the thyroid gland, thereby decreasing subsequent blood loss during surgery.

If an antithyroid agent is being used in severely hyperthyroid patients to improve their thyroid state prior to radioactive iodine therapy, the antithyroid medication must be discontinued 2 to 4 days before treatment to prevent impairment of radioactive iodine uptake. Antithyroid treatment may be resumed, if desired, 3 to 7 days after radioactive iodine treatment to hasten return to euthyroidism, until effects of the iodine are apparent.

Diet/Nutrition

Food may inconsistently alter the bioavailability of methimazole. It is recommended that methimazole be taken at the same time in relation to meals every day.

For treatment of adverse effects

Reduction in dosage or temporary withdrawal of antithyroid medication may be recommended if signs and symptoms of hypothyroidism occur. Some clinicians recommend adjunctive thyroid therapy (except during pregnancy) to prevent development of hypothyroidism. However, hypothyroidism may be an unavoidable long-term sequela to hyperthyroidism.

It is recommended that antithyroid therapy be discontinued promptly and supportive measures initiated if signs and symptoms of agranulocytosis, aplastic anemia, hepatic dysfunction, lupus-like syndrome, severe skin rash, swelling of cervical lymph nodes, or vasculitis occur. If laboratory examinations show only a mild leukopenia, periodic blood count monitoring without withdrawal or reduction in dosage may be sufficient. Mild reactions may not require withdrawal, although they may precede more serious reactions. Leukocyte production usually returns to normal within 1 to 2 weeks after withdrawal.

METHIMAZOLE

Summary of Differences

General dosing information: May be more suitable for once-daily administration.

Oral Dosage Forms

METHIMAZOLE TABLETS USP

Usual adult and adolescent dose

Hyperthyroidism—

Initial—

Mild hyperthyroidism—Oral, 15 mg a day as three equal divided daily doses.

Moderately severe hyperthyroidism—Oral, 30 to 40 mg a day as three equal divided daily doses.

Severe hyperthyroidism—Oral, 60 mg a day as three equal divided daily doses.

Maintenance—

Oral, 5 to 15 mg a day as three equal divided daily doses.

Thyrotoxic crisis—

Oral, 15 to 20 mg every four hours during the first day, as an adjunct to other measures.

Usual pediatric dose

Hyperthyroidism—

Initial: Oral, 0.4 mg per kg of body weight a day as three equal divided daily doses.

Maintenance: Oral, 0.2 mg per kg of body weight a day as three equal divided daily doses.

Strength(s) usually available

U.S.—

5 mg (Rx) [*Tapazole* (scored; lactose)].

10 mg (Rx) [*Tapazole* (scored; lactose)].

Canada—

5 mg (Rx) [*Tapazole* (scored)].

Packaging and storage

Store below 40 °C (104 °F), preferably between 15 and 30 °C (59 and 86 °F), unless otherwise specified by manufacturer. Store in a well-closed, light-resistant container.

Auxiliary labeling

• Take at the same time in relation to meals every day.

Rectal Dosage Forms

METHIMAZOLE SUPPOSITORIES

Usual adult and adolescent dose

Hyperthyroidism—

Initial: Thyrotoxic crisis—Rectal, 15 to 20 mg every four hours during the first day, as an adjunct to other measures, with the dosage being adjusted according to patient response.

Usual pediatric dose

Hyperthyroidism—

Initial: Thyrotoxic crisis—Rectal, 400 mcg (0.4 mg) per kg of body weight a day as one daily dose or as two divided daily doses.

Strength(s) usually available

U.S.—

Not commercially available. Compounding required for prescription.

Canada—

Not commercially available. Compounding required for prescription.

Packaging and storage

Store between 2 and 8 °C (36 and 46 °F). Store in a well-closed container. Protect from freezing.

Preparation of dosage form

A formulation that has been used for the extemporaneous compounding of methimazole suppositories is as follows:

• 1200 mg methimazole dissolved in 12 mL of distilled water
• 2 drops of Span 80
• Cocoa butter (warmed to 37 °C [98.6 °F]) of sufficient quantity to make 20 suppositories containing 60 mg methimazole each.

Auxiliary labeling
- Refrigerate.
- For rectal use only.

Note
Use of methimazole suppositories is generally reserved for treatment of thyrotoxic emergencies, in patients who are unable to tolerate oral medications. The efficacy of chronic rectal dosing with extemporaneously compounded formulations has not been established.

PROPYLTHIOURACIL

Summary of Differences
Precautions:

Pregnancy—May be preferred to methimazole, due to lower rate of placental transfer.

Breast-feeding—May be preferred to methimazole, due to a lower rate of distribution into breast milk.

Side/adverse effects:

Agranulocytosis may be less predictable, because it is usually not dose-related.

Oral Dosage Forms
PROPYLTHIOURACIL TABLETS USP
Usual adult and adolescent dose
Hyperthyroidism—

Initial—

Oral, 300 to 900 mg a day as one to four divided daily doses until the patient becomes euthyroid.

Note: Patients with severe hyperthyroidism may occasionally require up to 1.2 grams a day.

Maintenance—

Oral, 50 to 600 mg a day as one to four divided daily doses.

Thyrotoxic crisis—

Oral, 200 to 400 mg every four hours during the first day, as an adjunct to other measures, the dosage then being decreased as the crisis subsides.

Usual pediatric dose
Hyperthyroidism—

Initial—

Children 6 to 10 years of age—Oral, 50 to 150 mg a day as one to four divided daily doses.

Children 10 years of age and over—Oral, 50 to 300 mg a day as one to four divided daily doses.

Maintenance—

Oral, determined by response.

Neonatal thyrotoxicosis—

Oral, 10 mg per kg of body weight a day in divided daily doses.

Strength(s) usually available
U.S.—

50 mg (Rx) [GENERIC].

Canada—

50 mg (Rx) [*Propyl-Thyracil* (scored)].

100 mg (Rx) [*Propyl-Thyracil* (scored)].

Packaging and storage
Store below 40 °C (104 °F), preferably between 15 and 30 °C (59 and 86 °F), unless otherwise specified by manufacturer. Store in a well-closed container.

Auxiliary labeling
- Take at the same time in relation to meals every day.

Rectal Dosage Forms
PROPYLTHIOURACIL ENEMA
Usual adult and adolescent dose
Hyperthyroidism—

Initial: Thyrotoxic crisis—Rectal, 200 to 400 mg every four hours during the first day, as an adjunct to other measures, with the dosage being adjusted according to patient response.

Usual pediatric dose
Hyperthyroidism—

Initial: Thyrotoxic crisis—

Children 6 to 10 years of age: Rectal, 50 to 150 mg a day as one to four divided daily doses, with the dosage being adjusted according to patient response.

Children 10 years of age and over: Rectal, 50 to 300 mg a day as one to four divided daily doses, with the dosage being adjusted according to patient response.

Neonatal thyrotoxicosis: Rectal, 10 mg per kg of body weight a day in divided daily doses, with the dosage being adjusted according to patient response.

Strength(s) usually available
U.S.—

Not commercially available. Compounding required for prescription.

Canada—

Not commercially available. Compounding required for prescription.

Packaging and storage
Store between 2 and 8 °C (36 and 46 °F). Store in a well-closed container. Protect from freezing.

Preparation of dosage form
A formulation that has been used for the extemporaneous compounding of propylthiouracil enemas is as follows:
- 400 mg propylthiouracil (8-50 mg tablets)
- 60 mL aqueous sodium phosphates solution (*Fleet's Phospho-Soda*, pH 4.4 to 5.4).

Auxiliary labeling
- For rectal use only.

Note
Use of propylthiouracil enema is generally reserved for treatment of thyrotoxic emergencies, in patients who are unable to tolerate oral medications. The efficacy of chronic rectal dosing with extemporaneously compounded formulations has not been established.

PROPYLTHIOURACIL SUPPOSITORIES
Usual adult and adolescent dose
Hyperthyroidism—

Initial: Thyrotoxic crisis—Rectal, 200 to 400 mg every four hours during the first day, as an adjunct to other measures, with the dosage being adjusted according to patient response.

Usual pediatric dose
Hyperthyroidism—

Initial: Thyrotoxic crisis—

Children 6 to 10 years of age: Rectal, 50 to 150 mg a day as one to four divided daily doses, with the dosage being adjusted according to patient response.

Children 10 years of age and over: Rectal, 50 to 300 mg a day as one to four divided daily doses, with the dosage being adjusted according to patient response.

Neonatal thyrotoxicosis: Rectal, 10 mg per kg of body weight a day in divided daily doses, with the dosage being adjusted according to patient response.

Strength(s) usually available
U.S.—

Not commercially available. Compounding required for prescription.

Canada—

Not commercially available. Compounding required for prescription.

Packaging and storage
Store between 2 and 8 °C (36 and 46 °F). Store in a well-closed container. Protect from freezing.

Preparation of dosage form
A formulation that has been used for the extemporaneous compounding of propylthiouracil suppositories is as follows:
- 400 mg propylthiouracil (8-50 mg tablets) in
- Hardfat (Witepsol H15), of sufficient quantity to make 4 suppositories containing 100 mg each.

Auxiliary labeling
- For rectal use only.

Note
Use of propylthiouracil suppositories is generally reserved for treatment of thyrotoxic emergencies, in patients who are unable to tolerate oral medications. The efficacy of chronic rectal dosing with extemporaneously compounded formulations has not been established.

Selected Bibliography
Cooper DS. Antithyroid drugs. N Engl J Med 1984; 311(21): 1353-62.

Cooper DS. Which antithyroid drug? Am J Med 1986; 80(6): 1165-8.

Stockigt JR, Topliss DJ. Hyperthyroidism: current drug therapy. Drugs 1989; 37: 375-81.

Revised: 07/19/2001

ANTIVENIN (Crotalidae) POLYVALENT IMMUNE FAB (Ovine) Systemic

VA CLASSIFICATION (Primary): AD500

Commonly used brand name(s): *CroFab*.

Note: For a listing of dosage forms and brand names by country availability, see *Dosage Forms* section(s).

Category

Antivenin.

Indications

Accepted

Envenomation, pit viper (treatment)—Antivenin (*Crotalidae*) polyvalent immune Fab (ovine) is indicated for the treatment of minimal or moderate envenomation caused by bites of North American crotalid species, including the Western Diamondback rattlesnake (*Crotalus atrox*), Eastern Diamondback rattlesnake (*C. adamanteus*), Mojave rattlesnake (*C. scutulatus*), and Cottonmouth or Water Moccasin (*Agkistrodon piscivorus*). This medication is most effective when it is administered within 6 hours after envenomation.

Pharmacology/Pharmacokinetics

Physicochemical characteristics

Source—Antivenin (*Crotalidae*) polyvalent immune Fab (ovine) is a sterile, nonpyrogenic, purified, lyophilized preparation of ovine Fab (monovalent) immunoglobulin fragments obtained from the blood of healthy sheep flocks immunized with the venoms of one of the following crotalid snake species: Western Diamondback rattlesnake (*Crotalus atrox*), Eastern Diamondback rattlesnake (*C. adamanteus*), Mojave rattlesnake (*C. scutulatus*), and the Cottonmouth or Water Moccasin (*Agkistrodon piscivorus*). Each monospecific antivenin is prepared by fractionating the immunoglobulin from the ovine serum, digesting it with papain, and isolating the venom-specific Fab fragments on ion exchange and affinity chromatography columns. To obtain the final product, the four different monospecific antivenins are mixed together. The antivenin is standardized by biological assay on mice, based on its ability to neutralize the lethal action of each of the four immunogens.

Mechanism of action/Effect

Antivenin (*Crotalidae*) polyvalent immune Fab (ovine) is a venom-specific Fab fragment of immunoglobulin G (IgG) that binds and neutralizes venom toxins, facilitating their redistribution away from target tissues and their elimination from the body.

Half-life

Elimination—12 to 23 hours.

Precautions to Consider

Cross-sensitivity and/or related problems

Patients sensitive to sheep or any product of ovine origin may be sensitive to antivenin (*Crotalidae*) polyvalent immune Fab (ovine) also.

Carcinogenicity and mutagenicity

Studies have not been done in humans or animals.

Pregnancy/Reproduction

Pregnancy—Studies have not been done in humans. Antivenin (*Crotalidae*) polyvalent immune Fab (ovine) contains ethyl mercury from thimerosal. Although there are limited toxicology data on ethyl mercury, high dose and acute exposure to methyl mercury have been associated with neurological and renal toxicity. Developing fetuses are most at risk for toxicity.

Studies have not been done in animals.

FDA Pregnancy Category C.

Breast-feeding

It is not known whether antivenin (*Crotalidae*) polyvalent immune Fab (ovine) is distributed into human breast milk.

Pediatrics

Appropriate studies on the relationship of age to the effects of antivenin (*Crotalidae*) polyvalent immune Fab (ovine) have not been performed in the pediatric population. However, no dosage adjustment for age should be made, since the absolute venom dose following a snakebite is expected to be the same in children and adults. It should be noted that antivenin (*Crotalidae*) polyvalent immune Fab (ovine) contains ethyl mercury from thimerosal. Although there are limited toxicology data on ethyl mercury, high dose and acute exposure to methyl mercury have been associated with neurological and renal toxicity. Very young children are most at risk for toxicity.

Geriatrics

No information is available on the relationship of age to the effects of antivenin (*Crotalidae*) polyvalent immune Fab (ovine) in geriatric patients.

Medical considerations/Contraindications

The medical considerations/contraindications included have been selected on the basis of their potential clinical significance (reasons given in parentheses where appropriate)—not necessarily inclusive (» = major clinical significance).

Risk-benefit should be considered when the following medical problems exist:

» Envenomation, history of
(treatment with antivenin [*Crotalidae*] polyvalent immune Fab [ovine] may cause sensitization due to antibody formation; caution should be exercised when administering this medication to a patient who has previously been treated with it)

» Hypersensitivity to bromelain
(these patients may have an increased risk of developing an allergic reaction)

» Hypersensitivity to chymopapain or
» Hypersensitivity to papain or
» Hypersensitivity to papaya
(papain is used to cleave the immunoglobulin into fragments, therefore, trace amounts of papain or residues of inactivated papain may be present in antivenin [*Crotalidae*] polyvalent immune Fab [ovine]; patients hypersensitive to papain or related compounds may have an increased risk of developing an allergic reaction; use is not recommended unless the benefit outweighs the risk; however, if used, appropriate management for anaphylactic reactions must be readily available)

» Hypersensitivity to dust mites or
» Hypersensitivity to latex
(these allergens are similar in structure to papain, which may be present in trace amounts in antivenin [*Crotalidae*] polyvalent immune Fab [ovine]; these patients may have an increased risk of developing an allergic reaction)

Patient monitoring

The following may be especially important in patient monitoring (other tests may be warranted in some patients, depending on condition; » = major clinical significance):

» Allergic, anaphylactic, or anaphylactoid reaction
(close monitoring is recommended for all patients receiving antivenin [*Crotalidae*] polyvalent immune Fab [ovine]; appropriate treatment, including albuterol and intravenous antihistamines and epinepherine, should be readily available to manage a reaction if one should occur)

» Coagulopathy, recurrent
(when initial envenomation leads to coagulopathy, patients should be monitored for symptoms of recurrent coagulopathy for 1 week or longer)

Side/Adverse Effects

The following side/adverse effects have been selected on the basis of their potential clinical significance (possible signs and symptoms in parentheses where appropriate)—not necessarily inclusive:

Note: Because antivenin (*Crotalidae*) polyvalent immune Fab (ovine) is derived from animal protein, it is possible that an anaphylactic, anaphylactoid, or allergic reaction or a febrile response to the immune complexes may occur following treatment. Although during clinical trials, no patient experienced a severe anaphylactic reaction, it is recommended that all patients who receive this medication be closely monitored and that appropriate treatment be readily available to manage a reaction if one should occur. If a reaction does occur, administration of antivenin (*Crotalidae*) polyvalent immune Fab (ovine) should be immediately discontinued and appropriate treatment given.

Those indicating need for medical attention

Incidence more frequent

Coagulation disorder (unexplained bleeding or bruising)

Incidence less frequent

Allergic reaction, acute, including angioedema (large, hive-like swellings on the eyelids, face, lips, mouth, and/or tongue); ***bronchospasm with cough or wheezing; erythema*** (redness of skin); ***hy-***

potension (dizziness or lightheadedness); ***laryngeal edema*** (difficulty in swallowing); ***pruritus*** (itching of skin); ***stridor*** (noisy breathing); ***tachycardia*** (fast heartbeat); ***urticaria*** (hives or welts; itching of skin; skin rash); ***allergic reaction, delayed, including late serum reaction*** (pruritus; skin rash; urticaria); ***serum sickness*** (arthralgia; fever; myalgia; pruritus; skin rash); ***asthma*** (difficulty in breathing; shortness of breath; wheezing); ***cellulitis*** (chills; local pain, redness, and swelling; unusual tiredness or weakness); ***chest pain; ecchymosis*** (unusual bruising); ***wound infection*** (chills; discharge from wound; pain, tenderness, and warmth at wound site; unusual tiredness or weakness)

Those indicating need for medical attention only if they continue or are bothersome

Incidence more frequent

Nausea; pruritus (itching of skin); ***skin rash; urticaria*** (hives or welts; itching of skin; skin rash)

Incidence less frequent

Anorexia (loss of appetite); ***back pain; chills; cough; hypotension*** (dizziness or lightheadedness); ***myalgia*** (muscle pain); ***nervousness; paresthesia*** (burning, crawling, itching, numbness, prickling, "pins and needles", or tingling feelings)—circumoral or generalized; ***sputum, increased production; subcutaneous nodules*** (hard bumps under the skin)

Patient Consultation

As an aid to patient consultation, refer to *Advice for the Patient, Antivenin, Pit Viper—Sheep-derived (Systemic)*.

In providing consultation, consider emphasizing the following selected information (» = major clinical significance):

Before receiving this medication

» Conditions affecting use, especially:

Hypersensitivity to bromelain (pineapple enzyme), chymopapain, dust mites, latex, papain, papaya, or sheep or ovine products

Other conditions, especially history of envenomation

Proper use of this medication

» Proper dosing

Side/adverse effects

Signs of potential side effects, especially coagulation disorder, acute allergic reaction, delayed allergic reaction, asthma, cellulitis, chest pain, ecchymosis, and wound infection

General Dosing Information

In the management of poisonous snakebite, the following should be considered. Cooling may predispose tissues already jeopardized by the snake venom enzymes to severe necrosis when rewarmed. Therefore, under no circumstances should the affected area be cooled, and so-called cryotherapy is contraindicated. A tourniquet should not be applied as a first-aid measure, and excisional therapy is not recommended. Fasciotomy also should not be considered unless there is objective evidence of true compartment syndrome, in which case a surgical consultation should be obtained. For more information on the management of snake envenomation, contact a **Poison Control Center** (see *Poison Control Center Listing*.

Effectiveness of antivenin (*Crotalidae*) polyvalent immune Fab (ovine) is maximized when it is given within 6 hours of envenomation.

Skin testing is not required prior to administration of antivenin (*Crotalidae*) polyvalent immune Fab (ovine).

The initial intravenous infusion of antivenin (*Crotalidae*) polyvalent immune Fab (ovine) should proceed slowly over the first 10 minutes at a rate of 25 to 50 mL per hour (mL/hour), with careful observation for any sign of allergic reaction. If no reaction occurs, the infusion rate should be increased to 250 mL/hour until completion of the infusion.

Parenteral Dosage Forms

ANTIVENIN (CROTALIDAE) POLYVALENT IMMUNE FAB (OVINE)

Usual Adult Dose

Pit viper envenomation—

Initial: Intravenous, four to six vials over sixty minutes (at a rate of 25 to 50 mL per hour with close observation for an allergic reaction during the first ten minutes; if no allergic reaction develops, the rate may be increased to 250 mL per hour). Additional four- to six-vial doses should be given until control of the envenomation has been achieved.

Maintenance: Intravenous, two vials every six hours for up to eighteen hours (three doses). Additional two-vial doses may be given, if necessary.

Note: Initial control of the envenomation is defined as complete arrest of local manifestations and return of coagulation tests and systemic signs to normal.

Usual Pediatric Dose

See *Usual adult dose*.

Strength(s) usually available

U.S.—

One vial of antivenin neutralizes not less than 1350 mouse LD_{50} of *Crotalus atrox* (Western diamondback rattlesnake) venom; 800 mouse LD_{50} of *Crotalus adamanteus* (Eastern diamondback rattlesnake) venom; 5210 mouse LD_{50} of *Crotalus scutulatus* (Mojave rattlesnake) venom; and 460 mouse $LD_{50}$of *Agkistrodon piscivorus*(Cottonmouth or Water Moccasin) venom (Rx) [*CroFab* (dibasic sodium phosphate; sodium chloride; thimerosal [mercury $\leq$ 104.5 mcg])].

Packaging and storage

Store between 2 and 8°C (36 and 46°F). Do not freeze.

Preparation of dosage form

Each vial of antivenin (*Crotalidae*) polyvalent immune Fab (ovine) should be reconstituted with 10 mL of sterile water for injection. To avoid foaming, the contents of the vial should be mixed by gently swirling rather than by shaking. The reconstituted solution should be further diluted in 250 mL of 0.9% sodium chloride injection.

Stability

The reconstituted and diluted solutions should be used within 4 hours.

Developed: 07/5/2001

APOMORPHINE Systemic†

VA CLASSIFICATION (Primary): CN500

Commonly used brand name(s): *Apokyn*.

Note: For a listing of dosage forms and brand names by country availability, see *Dosage Forms* section(s).

†Not commercially available in Canada.

Category

Antiparkinsonian (dopamine agonist).

Indications

Accepted

Parkinsonism (treatment)—Apomorphine injection is indicated for the acute, intermittent treatment of hypomobililty, "off" episodes ("end-of-dose wearing off" and unpredictable "on/off"episodes) associated with advanced Parkinson's disease. Apomorphine injection has been studied as an adjunct to other medications.

Pharmacology/Pharmacokinetics

Physicochemical characteristics

Molecular weight—Apomorphine hydrochloride: 312.79.

Solubility—Soluble in water at 80 °C.

Mechanism of action/Effect

Apomorphine is a non-ergoline dopamine agonist with high *in vitro* binding affinity for the dopamine D_4 receptor and moderate affinity for the dopamine D_2, D_3, and D_5 receptors. Its precise mechanism of action is unknown; however, it is thought to be due to stimulation of post-synaptic dopamine D_2-type receptors within the caudate-putamen in the brain. In an animal model of Parkinson's disease, apomorphine has been shown to improve motor function. Specifically, apomorphine attenuates the motor deficits induced by lesions in the ascending nigrostriatal dopaminergic pathway with the neurotoxin 1-methyl-4-phenyl-1,2,3,6-tetrahydropyridine (MPTP) in primates.

Absorption

Rapid with bioavailability appearing to be equal to intravenous administration following subcutaneous administration into the abdominal wall

Exhibits linear pharmacokinetics over a 2 to 8-mg dose range in patients with idiopathic Parkinson's disease following a single subcutaneous injection into the abdominal wall

Distribution

Mean apparent volume of distribution (Vol_D)—218 L (123 to 404 L)

Biotransformation
Route of metabolism unknown
Potential routes include: sulfation, N-demethylation, glucuronidation and oxidation. In vitro, apomorphine undergoes rapid autooxidation.

Half-life
Terminal elimination: About 40 minutes (range about 30 to 60 minutes)

Time to peak concentration
Ranges from 10 to 60 minutes following subcutaneous injection

Elimination
Mean apparent clearance—223 L/hour (125 to 401 L/hour)

Precautions to Consider

Carcinogenicity
Carcinogenicity studies have not been conducted with apomorphine.

Mutagenicity
Apomorphine was mutagenic in the *in vitro* bacterial Ames test and the *in vitro* mammalian mouse lymphoma assay. Apomorphine was also clastogenic in the *in vitro* chromosomal aberration assay in human lymphocytes and the *in vitro* mouse lymphoma assays. Apomorphine was negative in the *in vivo* micronucleus assay in mice.

Pregnancy/Reproduction
Fertility—Studies in male rats given subcutaneous doses of 2 mg per kg of body weight (0.6 times the MRHD in a mg per m^2 basis) showed an adverse effect on fertility. In a 39-week study, cynomolgus monkeys given subcutaneous doses of 1 and 1.5 mg per kg of body weight (0.6 times and 1 time the MRHD in a mg per m^2 basis, respectively) showed a significant decrease in testis weight.

Pregnancy—Reproduction studies have not been conducted. Apomorphine should be given to a pregnant woman only if clearly needed.

FDA Pregnancy Category C

Breast-feeding
It is not known whether apomorphine is distributed into human milk. Because many drugs are distributed into human milk and because of the potential for serious adverse reactions in nursing infants from apomorphine, a decision should be made as to whether to discontinue nursing or to discontinue the drug, taking into account the importance of the drug to the mother.

Pediatrics
Safety and efficacy in pediatric patients have not been established.

Geriatrics
Appropriate studies performed to date have demonstrated that most adverse events were equally common in older and younger patients; however, older patients were more likely to experience confusion and hallucinations. Serious adverse events (i.e., life-threatening events or events resulting in hospitalization and/or increased disability) were also more common in older patients, with older patients being more likely to fall and experience bone and joint injuries, have cardiovascular events, develop respiratory disorders, and have gastrointestinal events.

Drug interactions and/or related problems
The following drug interactions and/or related problems have been selected on the basis of their potential clinical significance (possible mechanism in parentheses where appropriate)—not necessarily inclusive (» = major clinical significance):

Note: Combinations containing any of the following medications, depending on the amount present, may also interact with this medication.

» Alcohol
(should be avoided while taking apomorphine; effects of apomorphine on blood pressure may be increased with concomitant use)

» Antihypertensive medications (See *Appendix II*) or
» Vasodilators (especially nitrates)
(extra caution should be exercised; effects of apomorphine on blood pressure may be increased with concomitant use)

» Dopamine antagonists such as
Metoclopramide or
Neuroleptics including Butyrophenones or
Phenothiazines or
Thioxanthenes
(because apomorphine is a dopamine agonist, it is possible that effectiveness of apomorphine may be diminished with concomitant use)

» Drugs of the 5HT$_3$ antagonist class including:
Alosetron or
Dolasetron or
Granisetron or
Ondansetron or
Palonosetron
(concomitant use **contraindicated** based on reports of profound hypotension and loss of consciousness when apomorphine was administered with ondansetron)

» Drugs that prolong QT/QTc interval
(may increase risk of QT prolongation and torsades de pointes; caution recommended)

Sedating medications
(concurrent use may increase risk of drowsiness and sleepiness during daily activities)

Medical considerations/Contraindications
The medical considerations/contraindications included have been selected on the basis of their potential clinical significance (reasons given in parentheses where appropriate)—not necessarily inclusive (» = major clinical significance).

Except under special circumstances, this medication should not be used when the following medical problem exists:

» Hypersensitivity to apomorphine or its ingredients (including sodium metabisulfite)

Risk-benefit should be considered when the following medical problems exist:

» Bradycardia or
» Congenital prolongation of QT interval or
» Hypokalemia or
» Hypomagnesemia
(may increase risk of QT prolongation and torsades de pointes; caution recommended)

» Cardiovascular disease or
» Cerebrovascular disease
(extra caution should be used due to reports of coronary events with apomorphine use)

Dyskinesia, preexisting
(may be exacerbated with apomorphine use)

» Hepatic impairment
(caution should be exercised in patients with mild or moderate hepatic impairment due to increased C_{max} and AUC; studies of patients with severe hepatic impairment have not been done)

Major psychotic disorder
(if being treated with neuroleptics, patient should be treated with apomorphine only if potential benefits outweigh risk)

» Renal impairment
(starting dose reduction to 1 mg when administered to patients with mild or moderate renal impairment due to increased C_{max} and AUC; studies of patients with severe renal impairment have not been done)

Sleeping disorder
(could increase risk of drowsiness or sleepiness during daily activities)

Patient monitoring
The following may be especially important in patient monitoring (other tests may be warranted in some patients, depending on condition; » = major clinical significance):

» Apomorphine abuse
(rare reports of abuse by Parkinson's disease patients characterized by increasingly frequent dosing leading to hallucinations, dyskinesia, and abnormal behavior; prescribers should be vigilant for evidence of abuse such as use out of proportion to motor signs)

» Orthostatic hypotension
(Parkinson's disease patients may have impaired capacity to respond to orthostatic challenge sometimes brought on by dopamine agonists; careful monitoring for signs and symptoms, especially during dose escalation, and informing patient of this risk)

Side/Adverse Effects
A potential for apomorphine abuse has been rarely reported motivated by:

- An attempt to avoid all symptoms of all OFF events when OFF events occur frequently
- A psychosexual reaction related to the stimulation of penile erection and increase in libido. Adverse events reported in males with overuse include frequent penile erections, atypical sexual behavior, heightened libido, dyskinesias, agitation, confusion, and depression

Studies have not been conducted to evaluate the potential for dependence when apomorphine is used as acute (rescue) treatment of OFF episodes in the patients with ON/OFF or wearing-off effects associated with late stage Parkinson's disease.

The following side/adverse effects have been selected on the basis of their potential clinical significance (possible signs and symptoms in parentheses where appropriate)—not necessarily inclusive:

Those indicating need for medical attention

Incidence more frequent

Chest pain or pressure; confusion (mood or mental changes); ***dyskinesias*** (twitching, twisting, uncontrolled repetitive movements of tongue, lips, face, arms, or legs); ***edema*** (swelling); ***falling asleep during activity; hallucinations*** (seeing, hearing, or feeling things that are not there); ***postural hypotension*** (chills; cold sweats; confusion; dizziness, faintness, or lightheadedness when getting up from lying or sitting position)

Incidence less frequent

Angina (arm, back or jaw pain; chest pain or discomfort; chest tightness or heaviness; fast or irregular heartbeat; shortness of breath); ***cardiac arrest*** (stopping of heart; no blood pressure or pulse; unconsciousness); ***myocardial infarction*** (chest pain or discomfort; pain or discomfort in arms, jaw, back or neck; shortness of breath; nausea; sweating; vomiting); ***syncope*** (fainting)

Incidence rare

QT prolongation (irregular heartbeat; recurrent fainting)

Note: Although not reported with apomorphine, a symptom complex resembling the neuroleptic malignant syndrome (e.g., elevated temperature, muscular rigidity, altered consciousness, and autonomic instability) has been reported in association with rapid dose reduction, withdrawal of, or changes in antiparkinsonian therapy.

Fibrotic complications including retroperitoneal fibrosis, pulmonary infiltrates, pleural effusion, pleural thickening, and cardiac valvulopathy have been reported with ergot-derived dopaminergic agents. These complications may resolve when the drug is discontinued; however, complete resolution does not always occur. Although these adverse events are believed to be related to ergoline structure of these compounds, it is unknown whether other nonergot derived dopamine agonists can cause them.

Those indicating need for medical attention only if they continue or are bothersome

Incidence more frequent

Dizziness; drowsiness or somnolence (sleepiness); ***hypotension*** (blurred vision; confusion; dizziness, faintness, or lightheadedness when getting up from a lying or sitting position suddenly; sweating; unusual tiredness or weakness); ***injection site reactions*** (bleeding, blistering, burning, coldness, discoloration of skin, feeling of pressure, hives, infection, inflammation, itching, lumps, numbness, pain, rash, redness, scarring, soreness, stinging, swelling, tenderness, tingling, ulceration, or warmth at site); ***nausea and/or vomiting; rhinorrhea*** (runny nose); ***yawning***

Incidence rare

Priapism (painful or prolonged erection of the penis)

Overdose

For more information on the management of overdose or unintentional ingestion, **contact a poison control center** (see *Poison Control Center Listing*).

Clinical effects of overdose

A report of an accidental overdose of a 25 mg subcutaneous injection in a 62 year old man was published in the *Journal of Neurology, Neurosurgery, and Psychiatry* (1990), Volume 53, pages 96 to 102. After 3 minutes, the patient felt nauseated and lost consciousness for 20 minutes. Afterwards, he was alert with a heart rate of 40 per minute and a supine blood pressure of 90/50 and recovered completely within one hour.

Treatment of overdose

Supportive care—

Patients in whom intentional overdose is confirmed or suspected should be referred for psychiatric consultation.

Patient Consultation

As an aid to patient consultation, refer to *Advice for the Patient, Apomorphine (Systemic)*.

In providing consultation, consider emphasizing the following selected information (» = major clinical significance):

Before using this medication

» Conditions affecting use, especially:

Hypersensitivity to apomorphine or its ingredients (including sodium metabisulfite)

Pregnancy—Should be given to a pregnant woman only if clearly needed

Breast-feeding—Risk/benefit considerations

Use in children—Safety and efficacy not established

Use in the elderly—Older adults may be more likely to experience confusion and hallucinations, as well as other serious adverse effects.

Other medications, especially alcohol, antihypertensive medications, dopamine antagonists, drugs of the $5HT_3$ antagonist class, drugs that prolong QT/QTc interval, or vasodilators

Other medical problems, especially bradycardia, cardiovascular disease, cerebrovascular disease, congenital prolongation of QT interval, hepatic impairment, hypokalemia, hypomagnesemia, or renal impairment

Proper use of this medication

» Compliance with therapy; taking medication only as directed; not stopping medication unless ordered by physician

Importance of taking an antiemetic along with apomorphine to lessen symptoms of nausea and vomiting that may occur with apomorphine use

» Proper administration of the apomorphine pen and syringe

Changing injection site each time apomorphine is used

» Not using intravenously; subcutaneous use ONLY

» Proper dosing

Missed dose: Calling doctor or pharmacist for instructions

Proper storage

Precautions while using this medication

» Not drinking alcohol while taking apomorphine

» Counseling patient on potential for abuse; advising to contact doctor or go to emergency room immediately if side effects are stronger than usual

» Not taking medicines that may cause sleepiness while taking apomorphine

» Telling your doctor if sleepiness or falling asleep during the day is a problem while taking apomorphine

» Importance of not driving a car, operating machinery, or doing anything else that requires alertness until you know how apomorphine affects you as it may cause dizziness or fainting. Telling your doctor if you get dizzy or faint with apomorphine

» Getting up slowly from a sitting or lying position to avoid dizziness and faintness

Side/adverse effects

Signs of potential side effects, especially chest pain or pressure, confusion, dyskinesias, edema, hallucinations, postural hypotension, angina, cardiac arrest, myocardial infarction, syncope, or QT prolongation

General Dosing Information

The prescribed dose of apomorphine should always be expressed in mL to avoid confusion.

Apomorphine is indicated for subcutaneous administration only, NOT for IV. Patients and caregivers must receive detailed instructions in the preparation and injection of doses, with particular attention paid to the correct use of the dosing pen.

Apomorphine MUST be initiated with use of a concomitant antiemetic. Most antiemetic experience is with trimethobenzamide and this should generally be used. Trimethobenzamide (300 mg three times per day orally) should be started 3 days prior to the initial dose of apomorphine and continued at least during the first two months of therapy. For specific information regarding trimethobenzamide, see the *Trimethobenzamide (Systemic)* monograph.

If a single dose of apomorphine is ineffective for a particular OFF period, a second dose should not be given for that OFF episode. The efficacy of a second dose for a single OFF episode has not been systematically studied and the safety of re-dosing has not been characterized.

If there is a significant interruption in therapy (more than a week), apomorphine should be restarted on a 0.2 mL (2 mg) dose and gradually titrated to effect.

Parenteral Dosage Forms

APOMORPHINE HYDROCHLORIDE INJECTION

Usual adult dose

Parkinsonism (treatment)—

Subcutaneously, patients in an OFF state should be given a 0.2 mL (2 mg) test dose.

If the test dose is well tolerated, and a response is achieved: Starting dose should be 0.2 mL (2 mg) used on an as needed basis to treat existing OFF episodes. If needed the dose can be increased in 0.1 mL (1 mg) increments every few days on an outpatient basis.

Beyond this, the general principle guiding dosing (described in detail below) is to determine a dose (0.3 mL or 0.4 mL) that the patient will tolerate as a test dose under monitored conditions, and then begin an outpatient dosing trial (periodically assessing both efficacy and tolerability) using a dose 0.1 mL (1 mg) lower than the tolerated test dose.

If the test dose is well tolerated, but no response is achieved: A 0.4 mL (4 mg) test dose may be administered at the next observed OFF period, but no sooner than 2 hours after the initial test dose of 0.2 mL (2 mg). If the patient tolerates a test dose of 0.4 mL (4 mg), the starting dose should be 0.3 mL (3 mg) used on an as needed basis to treat existing OFF episodes. If needed the dose can be increased in 0.1 mL (1 mg) increments every few days on an outpatient basis.

If a patient does not tolerate a test dose of 0.4 mL (4 mg), a test dose of 0.3 mL (3 mg) may be administered during a separate OFF period, no sooner than 2 hours after the test dose of 0.4 mL (4 mg). If the patient tolerates the 0.3 mL (3 mg) test dose, the starting dose should be 0.2 mL (2 mg) used on an as needed basis to treat existing OFF episodes. If needed, and the 0.2 mL (2 mg) dose is tolerated, the dose can be increased to 0.3 mL (3 mg) after a few days. In such a patient, the dose should ordinarily not be increased to 0.4 mL (4 mg) on an out-patient basis.

Note: For patients with mild and moderate renal impairment, the testing dose and subsequently the starting dose should be reduced to 0.1 mL (1 mg).

Caution should be exercised when dosing mild and moderate hepatically impaired patients due to the increased C_{max} and AUC.

Usual adult prescribing limits
Up to 0.6 mL (6 mg) per dose. There is limited experience with single doses greater than 0.6 mL (6 mg), dosing more than 5 times per day and with total daily doses greater than 2 mL (20 mg).

Usual pediatric dose
Safety and efficacy have not been established in pediatric patients.

Usual geriatric dose
See *Usual adult dose.*

Strength(s) usually available
U.S.—

10 mg of apomorphine hydrochloride per 1 mL (Rx) [*Apokyn* (2-mL ampules and 3-mL cartridges; 1 mg sodium metabisulfite; water for injection; may contain sodium hydroxide and/or hydrochloric acid; 5 mg/mL benzyl alcohol [cartridges only])].

Packaging and storage
Store at 25 °C (77 °F); excursions permitted between 15 and 30 °C (59 and 86 °F).

Preparation of dosage form
The following are instructions for using the apomorphine pen:
- Remove the pen cap
- Unscrew the cartridge holder from the pen body
- Insert the apomorphine cartridge, metal cap first, into the cartridge holder
- Lower the pen body onto the cartridge holder so that the rod presses against the cartridge plunger. Screw the cartridge holder onto the pen body. Tighten the pieces until no gap remains and one of the arrow lines up with the marker on the pen body
- If a cartridge is already in the pen and the pen has been use; check the cartridge through the window in the cartridge holder to confirm that there is enough solution left in the cartridge to provide the next dose. If the cartridge plunger has reached the red line on the cartridge, remove that cartridge and insert a new cartridge into the pen before attaching the pen needle and preparing the dose.
- Remove the paper tab from the back of a new pen needle. Use a new needle for each injection. *Never reuse syringes and needles.*
- Holding the pen by the cartridge holder, push the pen needle unit onto the pen. Screw the threaded hub on the pen needle onto the cartridge holder with a turning motion as shown in the patient information leaflet. When the needle unit is attached, remove the outer shield that protects the needle with a gentle pull. Save the outer shield and use it to remove the needle from the pen after the injection is finished. Do not remove the inner needle shield at this time.
- To prime the pen, set the dose by turning the dose knob to 0.1 mL. This is important in order to get rid of any air bubbles in the cartridge.
- Remove the inner needle shield and with the needle pointing up, firmly push the injection button in as far as it will go and hold for at least 5 seconds. A small stream of medicine must come out of the end of the needle. If it does not, rest the dose per the previous step again and repeat this procedure until a small stream of medicine comes out the end of the needle. When medicine comes out of the end of the needle, the pen is primed and ready for use.
- To set the dose, turn the dose knob until the correct dose (i.e., number of mLs) for the dose is shown in the window.
- Inject the appropriate dose subcutaneously

The following are instructions on preparing syringes from an apomorphine ampule:
- Open the ampule by holding it upright and tapping the cap to force all the liquid into the body of the ampule
- Open the ampule by breaking off the ampule cap
- Use a 1 mL tuberculin syringe with a ½ inch needle.
- Use a new syringe and needle with each injection. *Never reuse syringes and needles.*
- Remove the protective cap from the syringe
- Insert the needle into the apomorphine in the open ampule. Pull back the syringe plunger to fill the syringe 0.2 to 0.3 mL past the dose
- Check for air bubbles. If bubbles are in the syringe, hold the syringe with the needle pointing up and tap the syringe with your finger to make them rise to the top. Then, slowly pull the syringe plunger 0.2 to 0.3 mL past the dose again and slowly push the syringe plunger until all the air bubbles are gone. Repeat this step, if needed, to get rid of air bubbles.
- Slowly push the syringe plunger to the line that matches your dose of apomorphine
- Use only if it is clear and colorless. Do not use apomorphine that is cloudy, green, or contains particles.

Stability
Apomorphine ampules should not be saved once opened.

Auxiliary labeling
- Please read patient information leaflet enclosed.
- Avoid alcohol while on this medication

Developed: 04/26/2006

APREPITANT Systemic†

VA CLASSIFICATION (Primary): GA609

Commonly used brand name(s): *Emend.*

Note: For a listing of dosage forms and brand names by country availability, see *Dosage Forms* section(s).

†Not commercially available in Canada.

Category
Antiemetic.

Indications

Accepted
Nausea and vomiting, cancer chemotherapy-induced (prophylaxis)—Aprepitant, in combination with other antiemetic agents, is indicated for the prevention of acute and delayed nausea and vomiting associated with initial and repeat courses of highly emetogenic cancer chemotherapy including high dose cisplatin.

Aprepitant, in combination with other antiemetic agents, is indicated for the prevention of nausea and vomiting associated with initial and repeat courses of moderately emetogenic cancer chemotherapy.

Pharmacology/Pharmacokinetics

Physicochemical characteristics
Molecular weight—Aprepitant: 534.43.

Solubility—Aprepitant is practically insoluble in water, sparingly soluble in ethanol and isopropyl acetate and slightly soluble in acetonitrile.

Mechanism of action/Effect
Antiemetic—Aprepitant is a selective, high-affinity antagonist of human substance P/neurokinin 1 (NK_1) receptors. Aprepitant has little or no affinity for serotonin ($5-HT_3$), dopamine, and corticosteroid receptors, the targets of existing therapies for chemotherapy-induced nausea and vomiting (CINV).

Aprepitant has been shown in animal models to inhibit emesis induced by cytotoxic chemotherapeutic agents, such as cisplatin, via central actions. Aprepitant augments the antiemetic activity of the $5-HT_3$-receptor antagonist ondansetron and the corticosteroid dexamethasone and inhibits both the acute and delayed phases of cisplatin-induced emesis.

Absorption
The mean absolute oral bioavailability of aprepitant is approximately 60% to 65%.
AUC—19.6-21.2 mcg hr per mL
The pharmacokinetics of aprepitant are nonlinear across the clinical dose range.

Distribution
Aprepitant crosses the placenta in animals. It has also been shown to cross the blood brain barrier in both animals and humans.

Volume of distribution (Vol_D)—Steady state: approximately 70 L.

Protein binding
Aprepitant: Very high (greater than 95%)—plasma protein

Biotransformation
Aprepitant is metabolized primarily by CYP3A4 with minor metabolism by CYP1A2 and CYP2C19. Metabolism occurs largely through oxidation at the morpholine ring and its side chains.

Half-life
Elimination—approximately 9 to 13 hours.

Time to peak concentration
Following oral administration—approximately 4 hours.

Peak plasma concentration:
C_{max}—1.4-1.6 mcg per mL.

Elimination
57%—urine (following a single 100 mg IV dose of [^{14}C]-aprepitant).
45%—feces (following a single 100 mg IV dose of [^{14}C]-aprepitant).
Renal—not renally excreted.

Note: The result may differ after oral administration.
In dialysis—not dialyzable.
Apparent plasma clearance 62 to 90 mL/min.

Precautions to Consider

Carcinogenicity/Tumorigenicity
Aprepitant produced thyroid follicular cell adenomas and carcinomas in male rats, thyroid follicular adenoma and hepatocellular adenoma in female rats, and skin fibrosarcomas in male mice following 2 years of exposure. Rats received oral doses of 0.05 to 125 mg per kg daily, with the highest dose producing systemic exposure of 0.4 to 1.4 times the human exposure at the recommended dose. Male rats developed adenomas at 5 to 125 mg per kg daily, and female rats developed adenomas at 25 and 125 mg per kg daily. Mice received oral doses of 2.2 and 2.7 times the human exposure at the recommended dose. Male mice developed skin fibrosarcomas at 125 and 500 mg per kg daily.

Mutagenicity
Aprepitant was not genotoxic in the Ames test, the human lymphoblastoid cell (TK6) mutagenesis test, the rat hepatocyte DNA strand break test, the Chinese hamster ovary cell chromosome aberration test and the mouse micronucleus test.

Pregnancy/Reproduction
Fertility—Aprepitant did not affect fertility or reproductive performance in male and female rats given doses up to the maximum feasible dose of 1000 mg per kg twice daily (producing exposure in male rats lower than the exposure at the recommended human dose and exposure in female rats about 1.6 times the human exposure).

Pregnancy—Teratology studies in rats and rabbits given oral doses of aprepitant about 1.6 and 1.4 times the human exposure at the recommended dose, respectively, revealed no evidence of harm to the fetus. Since there are no adequate and well controlled studies in humans, and animal studies are not always predictive of human response, aprepitant should only be administered during pregnancy if clearly needed.

FDA Pregnancy Category B

Breast-feeding
It is not known whether aprepitant is distributed into human breast milk. Aprepitant is not recommended for use while breast-feeding because of the potential for serious adverse effects in the nursing infant.

Pediatrics
Safety and effectiveness of aprepitant in patients less than 18 years old have not been established.

Geriatrics
Appropriate studies performed to date have not demonstrated geriatrics-specific problems that would limit the usefulness of aprepitant in the elderly. However, elderly patients are more likely to have a greater sensitivity to the adverse effects of aprepitant which may require caution. Dosage adjustment in the elderly is not necessary.

Pharmacogenetics
With oral aprepitant, no clinically significant difference in AUC (0–24 hours) was observed between males and females, or between Blacks, Hispanics, or Whites.

Drug interactions and/or related problems
The following drug interactions and/or related problems have been selected on the basis of their potential clinical significance (possible mechanism in parentheses where appropriate)—not necessarily inclusive (» = major clinical significance):

Aprepitant is an inducer, a moderate inhibitor, and substrate of CYP3A4. Aprepitant is also a CYP29C inducer.

Inhibition of CYP3A4 by aprepitant may result in elevated plasma concentrations of these concomitant medicines. The pharmacokinetic effect of aprepitant on orally administered CYP3A4 substrates is expected to be greater than the pharmacokinetic effect of aprepitant on intravenously administered CYP3A4 substrates.

Substrates for the P-glycoprotein transporter are unlikely to interact with aprepitant.

Note: Combinations containing any of the following medications, depending on the amount present, may also interact with this medication.

» Astemizole or
» Cisapride or
» Pimozide or
» Terfenadine
(use is contraindicated; inhibition of cytochrome P450 isoenzyme 3A4 [CYP3A4] by aprepitant could result in elevated plasma concentrations of these drugs potentially causing serious or life-threatening reactions)

» Benzodiazepines, such as
Alprazolam or
Midazolam or
Triazolam
(aprepitant may increase concentrations of these drugs)

Carbamazepine
(carbamazepine may induce aprepitant metabolism through CYP3A4 and reduce efficacy)

Enzyme CYP3A4 inhibitors, potent (see *Appendix II*) such as:
Clarithromycin or
Itraconazole or
Nefazodone or
Nelfinavir or
Ritonavir or
Troleandomycin
(administer with caution; strong CYP3A4 inhibitors may increase plasma concentration of aprepitant)

» Dexamethasone or
» Methylprednisolone
(when given orally may require a 50% dosage reduction when coadministered with aprepitant due to an increase in AUC; when given intravenously the methylprednisolone dose should be reduced approximately 25%)

Diltiazem
(diltiazem and aprepitant levels may be increased; caution is advised)

Chemotherapy agents metabolized by CYP3A4, (see *Appendix II*) including:
» Docetaxel or
» Etoposide or
» Ifosfamide or
» Imatinib or
» Irinotecan or
» Paclitaxel or
» Vinblastine, or
» Vincristine or
» Vinorelbine or
» Other chemotherapy agents
(careful monitoring and caution recommended when administering chemotherapy agents that are metabolized through CYP3A4 with aprepitant)

Ketoconazole
(concomitant use of ketoconazole and aprepitant is reported to increase aprepitant concentrations; caution is advised)

» Oral contraceptives
(efficacy of oral contraceptives may be reduced; alternative or back-up methods of contraception are advised)

Paroxetine
(levels of paroxetine and aprepitant may be decreased and reduce efficacy of both medicines)

Phenytoin
(aprepitant may induce phenytoin metabolism through CYP2C9; phenytoin may induce aprepitant metabolism through CYP3A4 and reduce aprepitant efficacy)

Rifampin
(may decrease aprepitant concentration and decrease efficacy)

Tolbutamide
(aprepitant may induce tolbutamide metabolism through CYP2C9)

» Warfarin
(International Normalized Ratio (INR) may be reduced; close monitoring is advised in the two week period following aprepitant administration)

Laboratory value alterations

The following have been selected on the basis of their potential clinical significance (possible effect in parentheses where appropriate)—not necessarily inclusive (» = major clinical significance).

With physiology/laboratory test values

Alanine aminotransferase, serum (ALT [SGPT]), or
Aspartate aminotransferase, serum (AST [SGOT]), or
Alkaline phosphatase, serum
(may be increased)

Blood glucose, serum
(may be increased)

Blood urea nitrogen or
Creatinine, serum or
Protein, urine
(may be increased)

Erythrocytes, urine or
Leukocytes, urine
(may be increased)

Hemoglobin
(may be decreased)

Sodium, serum
(may be decreased)

White blood cell, serum
(may be increased)

Medical considerations/Contraindications

The medical considerations/contraindications included have been selected on the basis of their potential clinical significance (reasons given in parentheses where appropriate)—not necessarily inclusive (» = major clinical significance).

Except under special circumstances, this medication should not be used when the following medical problem exists:

» Hypersensitivity to aprepitant or any of its components

Risk-benefit should be considered when the following medical problems exist:

» Hepatic function impairment, severe
(caution should be exercised; the safety of using aprepitant in patients with severe hepatic impairment has not been evaluated; however, aprepitant has been well tolerated in patients with mild to moderate hepatic impairment)

Side/Adverse Effects

The following side/adverse effects have been selected on the basis of their potential clinical significance (possible signs and symptoms in parentheses where appropriate)—not necessarily inclusive:

Those indicating need for medical attention

Incidence less frequent

Neutropenia (black or tarry stools, chills, cough, fever, lower back or side pain, painful or difficult urination, pale skin, shortness of breath, sore throat, ulcers, sores or white spots in mouth, unusual bleeding or bruising, unusual tiredness or weakness)

Incidence unknown

Angioedema (large, hive-like swelling on face, eyelids, lips, tongue, throat, hands, legs, feet, sex organs); ***bradycardia*** (chest pain or discomfort; lightheadedness; dizziness or fainting; shortness of breath, slow or irregular heartbeat; unusual tiredness); ***duodenal ulcer, perforating*** (burning upper abdominal pain; loss of appetite; nausea; vomiting); ***Steven-Johnson syndrome*** (blistering, peeling, loosening of skin; chills; cough; diarrhea; itching; joint or muscle pain; red irritated eyes; red skin lesions, often with a purple center; sore throat; sores, ulcers, or white spots in mouth or on lips; unusual tiredness or weakness); ***urticaria*** (hives or welts; itching; redness of skin, skin rash)

Those indicating need for medical attention only if they continue or are bothersome

Incidence more frequent

Anorexia (loss of appetite, weight loss); ***asthenia*** (lack or loss of strength); ***dehydration*** (confusion, decreased urination, dizziness, dry mouth, fainting, increase in heart rate, lightheadedness, rapid breathing, sunken eyes, thirst, unusual tiredness or weakness, wrinkled skin); ***diarrhea; dizziness; dyspepsia*** (acid or sour stomach; belching; heartburn; indigestion; stomach discomfort, upset, or pain); ***fatigue*** (unusual tiredness or weakness); ***heartburn; hiccups; nausea; stomatitis*** (swelling or inflammation of the mouth)

Incidence less frequent

Abdominal pain (stomach pain); ***epigastric discomfort*** (pain or discomfort in chest, upper stomach, or throat, heartburn); ***gastritis*** (burning feeling in chest or stomach, tenderness in stomach area, stomach upset, indigestion); ***hot flush; pharyngolaryngeal pain*** (sore throat)

Incidence unknown

Disorientation (confusion about identity, place, and time)

Overdose

For more information on the management of overdose or unintentional ingestion, **contact a poison control center** (see *Poison Control Center Listing*).

Clinical effects of overdose

The following effects have been selected on the basis of their potential clinical significance (possible signs and symptoms in parentheses where appropriate)—not necessarily inclusive:

Drowsiness (sleepiness); ***headache***

Treatment of overdose

There is no known specific antidote to aprepitant.

Drug induced emesis may not be effective due to the antiemetic activity of aprepitant

Aprepitant cannot be removed by hemodialysis

Supportive care—
In the event of an overdose aprepitant should be discontinued and general supportive treatment and monitoring should be provided
Patients in whom intentional overdose is confirmed or suspected should be referred for psychiatric consultation.

Patient Consultation

As an aid to patient consultation, refer to *Advice for the Patient, Aprepitant (Systemic)*.

In providing consultation, consider emphasizing the following selected information (» = major clinical significance):

Before using this medication

» Conditions affecting use, especially:
Hypersensitivity to aprepitant or any of its components
Pregnancy—Should be administered during pregnancy only if clearly needed
Breast-feeding—Use is not recommended; although not known if distributed into human breast milk, potential for serious adverse effects in nursing infant
Use in the elderly—Elderly patients may have a greater sensitivity to the adverse effects of aprepitant.
Other medications, especially alprazolam, astemizole, cisapride, dexamethasone, docetaxel, etoposide, ifosfamide, imatinib, irinotecan, methylprednisolone, midazolam, oral contraceptives, paclitaxel, pimozide, terfenadine, triazolam, vinblastine, vincristine, vinorelbine, or warfarin
Other medical problems, especially severe hepatic function impairment

Proper use of this medication

The importance of reading the package insert before starting therapy with aprepitant
The importance of reporting the use of any prescription or non-prescription medicine, or herbal products, because aprepitant may interact with some drugs including chemotherapy
» Proper dosing
Missed dose: Taking as soon as possible; not taking if almost time for next scheduled dose; not doubling doses
Proper storage

Side/adverse effects

Signs of potential side effects, especially angioedema, bradycardia, neutropenia, perforating duodenal ulcer, Steven-Johnson Syndrome, or urticaria

General Dosing Information

It is recommended that patients read the package insert before starting therapy with aprepitant.

Patients should be advised to report any prescription or non-prescription medicine, or herbal products that they are taking, because aprepitant may interact with some drugs including chemotherapy.

Aprepitant should be taken only as prescribed.

Dosage adjustment is not necessary for patients with renal insufficiency or patients with ESRD undergoing hemodialysis.

Dosage adjustment is not necessary for patients with mild to moderate hepatic insufficiency (Child-Pugh score 5 to 9). There are no clinical data in patients with severe hepatic insufficiency (Child-Pugh score greater than 9).

Aprepitant is given for three days as part of a regimen that includes ondansetron and dexamethasone given in combination.

Aprepitant is not recommended for chronic continuous use for the prevention of nausea and vomiting; safety and efficacy have not been established.

Diet/Nutrition

Aprepitant may be given at the same time as food or with no food.

Oral Dosage Forms

APREPITANT CAPSULES

Usual Adult Dose

Nausea and vomiting, cancer chemotherapy-induced (prophylaxis)—
Oral, 125 mg one hour prior to chemotherapy treatment (Day 1) and 80 mg once daily in the morning on Days 2 and 3.

Note: Aprepitant is given for three days as a part of a regimen that includes a corticosteroid and a 5–HT_3 antagonist.

Usual Pediatric Dose

Safety and efficacy have not been established.

Usual Geriatric Dose

See *Usual adult dose*.

Note: Geriatric patients may be more sensitive to the effects of the usual adult dose.

Strength(s) usually available

U.S.—
80 mg (Rx) [*Emend* (gelatin; hydroxypropyl cellulose; microcrystalline cellulose; sodium lauryl sulfate; sucrose; titanium dioxide)].
125 mg (Rx) [*Emend* (gelatin; hydroxypropyl cellulose; microcrystalline cellulose; red ferric oxide; sodium lauryl sulfate; sucrose; titanium dioxide; yellow ferric dioxide)].

Canada—
Not commercially available.

Packaging and storage

Store between 20 and 25 °C (68 and 77 °F). The desiccant should remain in the original bottle.

Auxiliary labeling

• Take with or without food.

Revised: 11/15/2005
Developed: 08/19/2003

APROBARBITAL—See *Barbiturates (Systemic)*

ARGATROBAN Systemic

VA CLASSIFICATION (Primary): BL119

Commonly used brand name(s):.

Note: For a listing of dosage forms and brand names by country availability, see *Dosage Forms* section(s).

Category

Anticoagulant.

Indications

Accepted

Heparin-induced thrombocytopenia (prophylaxis and treatment)—Argatroban is indicated for use as an anticoagulant for either prophylaxis or treatment of thrombosis in heparin-induced thrombocytopenia (HIT).

Thrombosis, percutaneous coronary intervention–related (prophylaxis)—Argatroban is indicated as an anticoagulant in patients with or at risk for heparin-induced thrombocytopenia undergoing percutaneous coronary intervention (PCI).

Unaccepted

The safety and effectiveness of argatroban for cardiac indications outside of percutaneous coronary intervention in patients with heparin-induced thrombocytopenia have not been established.

Pharmacology/Pharmacokinetics

Physicochemical characteristics

Source—Argatroban is a synthetic agent which is derived from L-arginine.
Molecular weight—526.66.

Mechanism of action/Effect

By reversibly binding to the thrombin active site, argatroban acts as a direct thrombin inhibitor. Without need of co-factor antithrombin III, argatroban inhibits thrombin-catalyzed or induced reactions, including fibrin formation, activation of coagulant factors V, VIII, and XIII; protein C; and platelet aggregation. Argatroban is selective for thrombin and has little to no effect on related serine proteases (i.e., trypsin, factor Xa, plasmin, kallikrein).

Distribution

Distribution mainly occurs throughout the extracellular fluid, with a steady-state distribution volume of 174 mL per kg (12.18 L in a 70 kg adult).

Protein binding

Moderate (54%); primarily to albumin (20%) and α_1-acid glycoprotein (34%).

Biotransformation

The majority of argatroban in the plasma remains unchanged from its original form. *In vitro* study of argatroban metabolism demonstrates that four metabolites result from hydroxylation and aromatization by cytochrome P450 enzymes in the liver. The resulting primary metabolite (M1) is 3 to 5 times weaker than the unchanged parent drug and represents between 0 –20% of the plasma concentration. The three other metabolites (M2–M4) have been detected in very small quantities in urine but have not been detected in plasma or feces. Argatroban's original mixture of *R* and *S* stereoisomers is not altered, maintaining the 65:35 ratio of each isomer form, respectively.

Half-life

Elimination—
39–51 minutes.

Onset of action

Anticoagulant effects are produced immediately upon infusion of argatroban, increasing as argatroban concentration rises.

Time to steady-state concentration

Typically, a steady-state concentration is reached in 1–3 hours.

Duration of action

Effects are maintained until drug infusion is discontinued or the dosage is altered.

Elimination

Biliary—Major route of metabolite elimination; approximately 14% of unchanged drug excreted via feces.
Renal—Low percentage (16%) of unchanged drug eliminated renally.

Precautions to Consider

Carcinogenicity/Mutagenicity

Long-term animal studies to identify the carcinogenicity of argatroban have not been performed.Mutagenicity was negative in the following tests: Ames test, Chinese hamster ovary cell forward mutation test, Chinese hamster lung fibroblast chromosome aberration test, rat hepatocyte and WI-38 human fetal lung cell unscheduled DNA synthesis tests, and the mouse micronucleus test.

Pregnancy/Reproduction

Fertility—No evidence of impaired fertility was found in argatroban animal studies using male and female rats with intravenous doses up to 0.3 times the maximum recommended human dose and in rabbits at intravenous doses up to 0.2 times the maximum recommended human dose.

Pregnancy—Adequate and well-controlled studies have not been done in humans. Because animal reproduction studies are not always predictive of human response, this drug should be used during pregnancy only if clearly needed.

No evidence of fetal harm was found in animal studies with male and female rats given intravenous argatroban doses of up to 0.3 times the maximum recommended human dose and in rabbits given intravenous doses of up to 0.2 times the maximum recommended human dose.

FDA Pregnancy Category B.

Breast-feeding

It is not known whether argatroban is distributed into human breast milk. However, experiments in rats demonstrated that argatroban is distributed into rat milk. Because many drugs are distributed into human milk and because of the potential for serious adverse reactions in nursing infants from argatroban, a decision should be made whether to discontinue nursing or to discontinue the drug, taking into account the importance of the drug to the mother.

Pediatrics

Appropriate studies on the relationship of age to the effects of argatroban have not been performed in the pediatric population. Safety and efficacy have not been established.

Geriatrics

Appropriate studies performed to date have not demonstrated geriatric-specific problems that would limit the usefulness of argatroban in the elderly.

Dental

Bleeding from gingival tissue may occur in anticoagulated patients.

Drug interactions and/or related problems

The following drug interactions and/or related problems have been selected on the basis of their potential clinical significance (possible mechanism in parentheses where appropriate)—not necessarily inclusive (» = major clinical significance):

Note: Combinations containing any of the following medications, depending on the amount present, may also interact with this medication.

» Anticoagulants, other or
» Antiplatelet agents or
» Thrombolytic agents
(the risk of bleeding may be increased with concurrent use)

Laboratory value alterations

The following have been selected on the basis of their potential clinical significance (possible effect in parentheses where appropriate)—not necessarily inclusive (» = major clinical significance).

With physiology/laboratory test values
» Hematocrit value or
» Hemoglobin concentration
(may be decreased)
» International Normalized Ratio (INR) or
» Prothrombin time (PT)
(concurrent use of argatroban with multiple doses of warfarin will result in prolonged INR and PT values compared with values obtained with warfarin alone)

Medical considerations/Contraindications

The medical considerations/contraindications included have been selected on the basis of their potential clinical significance (reasons given in parentheses where appropriate)—not necessarily inclusive (» = major clinical significance).

Except under special circumstances, this medication should not be used when the following medical problem exists:
» Hypersensitivity to argatroban or any of its components
» Overt major bleeding

Risk-benefit should be considered when the following medical problems exist:
» Anesthesia, spinal or
» Bleeding disorders, acquired or congenital or
» Gastrointestinal lesions or
» Hypertension, severe or
» Lumbar puncture, postprocedure or
» Major surgery, postoperative
(use of argatroban requires caution in these patients because they are at high risk for hemorrhage)
» Hepatic function impairment
(decreased clearance and increased elimination half-life; dosage reduction is recommended; after argatroban has been discontinued, reversal of anticoagulant effects may take longer than 4 hours)

Patient monitoring

The following may be especially important in patient monitoring (other tests may be warranted in some patients, depending on condition; » = major clinical significance):

» Activated clotting time (ACT)
(ACTs should be obtained before dosing, 5 to 10 minutes after intravenous direct dosing and after change in the infusion rate, and at the end of the percutaneous coronary intervention (PCI) procedure. Additional ACTs should be drawn about every 20 to 30 minutes during a prolonged procedure.)
» Activated partial thromboplastin time (aPTT)
(aPTT test recommended prior to therapy initiation, at two hours after therapy initiation, and at periodic intervals during treatment to confirm that aPTT is within desired therapeutic range; frequency varies according to clinical state, agent, dose, and other agents being used concurrently)
» Blood pressure measurementand
» Hematocrit value
(unexplained decreases may indicate hemorrhage; monitor periodically during therapy)
» International Normalized Ratio (INR)
(during combined therapy of warfarin and argatroban, the INR is increased, although there is not an increase in the vitamin K-dependent factor Xa activity. The relationship between the INR value obtained on warfarin alone and that obtained on combined therapy with argatroban plus warfarin is dependent upon the dose of argatroban and the thromboplastin reagent used; when the argatroban dose is greater than 2 mcg per kg of body weight [mcg/kg] per minute, the relationship between the values becomes less predictable)
(daily monitoring is recommended while argatroban and warfarin are administered concomitantly; a repeat INR is recommended 4 to 6 hours after discontinuation of argatroban; if the repeat value is below the desired therapeutic range for warfarin alone, argatroban therapy should be reinitiated and continued until the desired therapeutic range for warfarin alone is reached)
(to obtain the INR for warfarin alone when the dose of argatroban is greater than 2 mcg/kg per minute, the argatroban dose should be temporarily reduced to 2 mcg/kg per minute; the INR for combined therapy may then be obtained 4 to 6 hours after the argatroban dose was reduced)

Side/Adverse Effects

The following side/adverse effects have been selected on the basis of their potential clinical significance (possible signs and symptoms in parentheses where appropriate)—not necessarily inclusive:

Those indicating need for medical attention

Incidence more frequent
Cardiac arrest (chest pain; irregular heartbeat; heart failure); ***genitourinary hemorrhage and hematuria*** (blood in urine; lower back pain; pain or burning while urinating); ***hypotension*** (blurred vision; confusion; dizziness, faintness, or light-headedness when getting up from a lying or sitting position; sudden sweating; unusual tiredness or weakness)

Incidence less frequent
Gastrointestinal hemorrhage (black, tarry stools; bloody stools; vomiting of blood or material that looks like coffee grounds); ***ventricular tachycardia*** (fainting; fast, pounding, or irregular heartbeat or pulse; palpitations)

Those indicating need for medical attention only if they continue or are bothersome

Incidence more frequent
Diarrhea (increased bowel movements; loose stools); ***fever***

Incidence less frequent
Abdominal pain; coughing; hemoptysis (coughing or spitting up blood); ***nausea and vomiting***

Overdose

For more information on the management of overdose or unintentional ingestion, **contact a poison control center** (see *Poison Control Center Listing*).

Clinical effects of overdose

The following effects have been selected on the basis of their potential clinical significance (possible signs and symptoms in parentheses where appropriate)—not necessarily inclusive:

Excessive anticoagulation, with or without bleeding

Treatment of overdose

There is no known specific antidote to argatroban. If excessive anticoagulation occurs, either the dosage of argatroban should be decreased or therapy should be discontinued. Anticoagulation parameters usually return to baseline levels within 2 to 4 hours after argatroban has been discontinued. However, the return to baseline may be prolonged in patients with hepatic function impairment. If life-threatening bleeding occurs and it is suspected that the argatroban plasma concentration is unusually high, therapy should be immediately discontinued. Symptomatic and supportive therapy also should be provided.

To enhance elimination—

Approximately 20% of argatroban was cleared through dialysis when argatroban was administered as a continuous infusion (2 mcg per kg per minute) prior to and during a 4-hour hemodialysis session.

Monitoring—

Activated partial thromboplastin time (aPTT) and other coagulation tests should be performed.

General Dosing Information

No evidence of neutralizing antibodies was noted in the plasma of 12 healthy volunteers treated with argatroban over 6 days.

All parenteral anticoagulants should be discontinued before therapy with argatroban is initiated.

In case of dissection, impending abrupt closure, thrombus formation during the percutaneous coronary intervention (PCI) procedure, or inability to achieve or maintain an ACT over 300 seconds, additional intravenous direct doses of 150 mcg per kg of body weight may be administered and the infusion dose increased to 40 mcg per kg of body weight per minute. The ACT should be checked after each additional intravenous direct dose or change in the rate of infusion.

At the appropriate time, oral anticoagulation therapy may be initiated with the usual maintenance dose of warfarin. A loading dose is not recommended. Argatroban should be discontinued when the International Normalized Ratio (INR) for combined therapy is greater than 4.

If a patient requires anticoagulation after the PCI procedure, argatroban may be continued, but at a lower infusion dose.

Parenteral Dosage Forms

ARGATROBAN INJECTION

Note: **Argatroban injection is a concentrated solution and must be diluted 100-fold before administration.**

Usual adult dose

Prophylaxis and treatment of heparin-induced thrombosis—

Intravenous infusion, initially 2 mcg per kg of body weight per minute. Dose should then be adjusted to obtain a steady-state activated partial thromboplastin time (aPTT) value that is 1.5 to 3 times the baseline level.

Note: For patients with heparin-induced thrombocytopenia with hepatic impairment, the initial dose of argatroban should be reduced. For patients with moderate hepatic impairment, an initial dose of 0.5 mcg per kg of body weight per minute is recommended. The aPTT should be monitored closely, and the dosage should be adjusted as clinically indicated.

For patients with renal impairment, no dosage adjustment is necessary.

Treatment of percutaneous coronary intervention (PCI)–related thrombosis—

Intravenous infusion, initially 25 mcg per kg of body weight per minute and an intravenous direct injection of 350 mcg per kg administered via a large bore intravenous (IV) line over 3 to 5 minutes. Activated clotting time (ACT) should be checked 5 to 10 minutes after the intravenous direct dose is completed. The procedure may proceed if the ACT is greater than 300 seconds.

If the ACT is less than 300 seconds: An additional intravenous direct dose of 150 mcg per kg of body weight should be administered, the infusion dose increased to 30 mcg per kg of body weight per minute and the ACT checked 5 to 10 minutes later.

If the ACT is greater than 450 seconds: The infusion rate should be decreased to 15 mcg per kg of body weight per minute and the ACT checked 5 to 10 minutes later.

Once a therapeutic ACT (between 300 and 450 seconds) has been achieved, this infusion dose should be continued for the duration of the procedure.

Note: For PCI patients with clinically significant hepatic disease or AST/ALT levels ≥3 times the upper limit of normal, use of high doses of argatroban should be avoided. Such patients were not studied in PCI trials.

For patients with renal impairment, no dosage adjustment is necessary.

Usual adult prescribing limits

10 mcg per kg of body weight per minute. aPTT value should not exceed 100 seconds.

Usual Pediatric Dose

Safety and efficacy have not been established.

Usual Geriatric Dose

See *Usual adult dose.*

Usual geriatric prescribing limits

See *Usual adult prescribing limits.*

Strength(s) usually available

U.S.—

100 mg per mL (Rx) [GENERIC].

Packaging and storage

Unopened vials—Store in original cartons at 25 °C (77 °F), with excursions permitted between 15 and 30 °C (59 and 86 °F). Protect from freezing and from light.

Diluted solution—Store at 25 °C (77 °F). with excursions permitted between 15 and 30 °C (59 and 86 °F) in ambient indoor light, protected from direct sunlight, for up to 24 hours. Therefore, light-resistant measures such as foil protection for intravenous lines are unnecessary. Solutions are physically and chemically stable for up to 96 hours when protected from light and stored at controlled room temperature, 20 to 25 °C (68 to 77 °F), or at refrigerated conditions, between 2 and 8 °C (36 and 46 °F). Prepared solutions should not be exposed to direct sunlight.

Preparation of dosage form

Argatroban should be diluted in 0.9% Sodium Chloride Injection, 5% Dextrose Injection, or Lactated Ringer's Injection to a final concentration of 1 mg/mL. Each 2.5 mL vial should be diluted 100–fold by mixing with 250 mL of diluent. See the manufacturer's package insert for instructions.

Stability

Before solution preparation, examine the vial of argatroban concentrate which is slightly viscous, clear, and colorless to pale yellow. If concentrate is cloudy or contains an insoluble precipitate, the vial should be discarded.

No significant potency losses have been noted following simulated delivery of the solution through intravenous tubing.

Incompatibilities

Because adequate stability and compatibility studies have not been conducted with argatroban, it should not be mixed with other medications.

Revised: 05/10/2005
Developed: 10/19/2000

ARIPIPRAZOLE Systemic†

VA CLASSIFICATION (Primary): CN709

Commonly used brand name(s): *Abilify.*

Note: For a listing of dosage forms and brand names by country availability, see *Dosage Forms* section(s).

†Not commercially available in Canada.

Category

Antipsychotic.

Indications

Accepted

Bipolar mania (treatment)—Aripiprazole is indicated for the treatment of acute manic and mixed episodes associated with Bipolar Disorder. The effectiveness of aripiprazole for more than 6 weeks of treatment of an acute episode has not been established in controlled clinical trials.

Schizophrenia (treatment)—Aripiprazole is indicated for the treatment of schizophrenia. The effectiveness of aripiprazole for more than 26 weeks has not been evaluated in controlled trials.

Unaccepted

Aripiprazole is not approved for the treatment of patients with dementia-related psychosis.

Aripiprazole is not approved for the treatment of behavioral symptoms in elderly patients with dementia.

The effectiveness of aripiprazole for prophylactic use in mania has not been established in controlled clinical trials.

Pharmacology/Pharmacokinetics

Physicochemical characteristics

Chemical Group—Quinolinone derivative

Molecular weight—448.38.

Mechanism of action/Effect

Aripiprazole activity is presumably primarily due to the parent drug, aripiprazole, and to a lesser extent, to its major metabolite dehydro-aripiprazole, which has been shown to have affinities for D_2 receptors similar to the parent drug, and represents 40% of the parent drug exposure in plasma.

The exact mechanism of action is not known. It has been proposed that the efficacy of aripiprazole is mediated through a combination of partial agonist activity at dopamine D_2 and serotonin 5-HT_{1A} receptors, and antagonist activity at the serotonin 5-HT_{2A} receptor.

Aripiprazole exhibits a high affinity for dopamine D_2 and D_3, serotonin 5-HT_{1A} and 5-HT_{2A} receptors, moderate affinity for dopamine D_4, serotonin 5-HT_{2C} and 5-HT_7, alpha$_1$-adrenergic and histamine H_1 receptors, and moderate affinity for the serotonin reuptake site.

Other actions/effects

Actions at receptors other than D_2, 5-HT_{1A} and 5-HT_{2A} may explain some of the other clinical effects of aripiprazole, e.g., the orthostatic hypertension observed with aripiprazole may be explained by its antagonist activity at adrenergic alpha$_1$ receptors.

Absorption

Oral bioavailability: 87%

Aripiprazole is well absorbed and can be administered with or without food. Administration with a high-fat meal did not affect the C_{max} or AUC, but delayed T_{max} by 3 hours for aripiprazole, and 12 hours for dehydro-aripiprazole.

Distribution

Vol_D: 404 L or 4.9 L/kg following intravenous administration; indicating extensive extravascular distribution.

There was dose-dependent D_2-receptor occupancy indicating brain penetration of aripiprazole in healthy human volunteers administered 0.5 to 30 mg per day.

Protein binding

Very High (99%); bound to serum proteins, primarily to albumin.

Biotransformation

Aripiprazole is the predominant drug moiety in systemic circulation. At steady state, dehydro-aripiprazole, the active metabolite, represents about 40% of aripiprazole AUC in plasma.

Aripiprazole is metabolized primarily by dehydrogenation, hydroxylation, and N-dealkylation. Elimination is mainly through hepatic metabolism involving two isoenzymes, CYP2D6 and CYP3A4.

Half-life

Elimination: Aripiprazole 75 hours for extensive metabolizers (EM) and 146 hours for poor metabolizers (PM); Dehydro-aripiprazole: 94 hours

Time to peak concentration

Peak Plasma concentrations: within 3 to 5 hours

Steady State: within 14 days for both active moieties.

Elimination

Renal: 25%; less than 1% recovered unchanged

Fecal: 55%; approximately 18% recovered unchanged

Precautions to Consider

Carcinogenicity and Tumorigenicity

No tumorigenic potential was seen in male mice or rats. Pituitary gland adenomas, mammary gland adenocarcinomas, and adenocanthomas incidences increased in female mice dosed with 3 to 30 mg per kg per day (0.1 to 0.9 times the maximum recommended human dose [MRHD] based on AUC). In female rats, the incidence of mammary gland fibroadenomas was increased at a dose of 10 mg per kg per day (0.1 times the MRHD) and the incidence of adrenocortical carcinomas and combined adrenocortical adenomas and carcinomas were increased at an oral dose of 60 mg per kg per day (14 times the MRHD based on AUC).

Increases in serum prolactin levels were observed in female mice in a 13-week dietary study at doses associated with mammary gland and pituitary tumors, however serum prolactin increases were not seen in female rats given doses associated with mammary gland tumors in 4- and 13-week dietary studies. The relevance for human risk of the findings of prolactin-mediated endocrine tumors in rodents is unknown.

Mutagenicity

Aripiprazole and a metabolite (2,3-DCPP) were clastogenic in an *in vitro* chromosomal aberration assay in Chinese hamster lung cells with and without metabolic activation. A positive response was obtained in an *in vivo* micronucleus assay in mice, however the response was shown to be due to a mechanism not considered relevant to humans.

Pregnancy/Reproduction

Fertility—Adequate and well controlled studies in humans have not been done.

Studies in female rats given oral doses of aripiprazole 2, 6, and 20 mg per kg of body weight per day from 2 weeks prior to mating through day 7 of gestation found no impairment of fertility. However, estrus cycle irregularities and increased corpora lutea were seen at all doses and increased pre-implantation loss was seen at 6 and 20 mg/kg, and decreased fetal weight was seen at 20 mg/kg.

Male rats given doses of aripiprazole at 60 mg/kg from 9 weeks prior to mating through mating revealed disturbances in spermatogenesis and prostate atrophy was seen at doses of 40 and 60 mg/kg. However no impairment of fertility was seen at doses up to 60 mg/kg/day.

Pregnancy—Adequate and well controlled studies in humans have not been done.

Studies in pregnant rats and rabbits treated with oral doses of 3, 10 and 30 mg/kg/day (rats) and 10, 30 and 100 mg/kg/day (rabbits) have shown that aripiprazole causes developmental toxicity, including possible teratogenic effects.

FDA Pregnancy Category C

Labor and delivery—Adequate and well controlled studies in humans have not been done.

Breast-feeding

It is not known if aripiprazole is distributed in human breast milk. However, it is distributed into the milk of lactating rats. It is recommended that women receiving aripiprazole do not breast-feed.

Pediatrics

Safety and efficacy have not been established.

Geriatrics

Adequate and well controlled studies in humans have not been done.

According to an FDA Public Health Advisory, aripiprazole is not approved for the treatment of behavioral symptoms in elderly patients with dementia. Clinical studies of aripiprazole and other atypical antipsychotic drugs for treatment of behavioral symptoms in the elderly with dementia have shown a higher death rate associated with their use compared to patients receiving a placebo. Causes of death varied, but most seemed to be either heart-related (i.e., heart failure or sudden death) or from infections (i.e., pneumonia).

In clinical studies of dementia-related psychosis, there was an increased incidence of cerebrovascular adverse events (e.g., stroke, transient ischemic attack), including fatalities, in elderly patients ranging in age from 78 to 88 years of age treated with aripiprazole. Aripiprazole is not approved for the treatment of patients with dementia-related psychosis. The safety and efficacy of aripiprazole in the treatment of elderly patients with psychosis associated with Alzheimer's disease have not been established. If the healthcare professional elects to treat such patients with aripiprazole, vigilance should be exercised as elderly patients may be at increased risk for the emergence of difficulty swallowing or excessive somnolence, which may predispose them to accidental injury or aspiration.

Pharmacogenetics

Hydroxylation of aripiprazole via the cytochrome P450 2D6 (CYP2D6) isoenzyme is subject to genetic polymorphism. About 8% of Caucasians and a low percentage of Asians have little or no CYP2D6 activity and are considered poor metabolizers. Patients taking aripiprazole who have normal CYP2D6 activity (considered extensive metabolizers) have lower plasma concentrations of aripiprazole and higher concentrations of dehydro-aripiprazole (40% of aripiprazole AUC) than do patients who are poor metabolizers. Compared to persons with normal CYP2D6 activity, poor metabolizers have about an 80% increase in aripiprazole exposure and about a 30% decrease in exposure to the total active moieties from a given dose.

Coadministration of aripiprazole with known inhibitors of CYP2D6 in extensive metabolizers results in an 112% increase in aripiprazole plasma exposure and dosing adjustment is recommended.

Drug interactions and/or related problems

The following drug interactions and/or related problems have been selected on the basis of their potential clinical significance (possible mechanism in parentheses where appropriate)—not necessarily inclusive (» = major clinical significance):

Note: Both CYP3A4 and CYP2D6 are responsible for aripiprazole metabolism

Aripiprazole is **not** a substrate of CYP1A1, CYP1A2, CYP2A6, CYP2B6, CYP2C8, CYP2C9, CYP2C19, or CYP2E1 and does not undergo direct glucuronidation. This suggests that an interaction of enzyme inhibitors or enzyme inducers with aripiprazole or an interaction of other factors (like smoking) with aripiprazole is unlikely.

Aripiprazole does **not** inhibit or induce the CYP2D6 pathway.

Combinations containing any of the following medications, depending on the amount present, may also interact with this medication.

» Alcohol
(aripiprazole may potentiate the cognitive and motor effects of alcohol)

» Antihypertensive medications with $alpha_1$-adrenergic receptor antagonism
(hypotensive effects of these medications may be enhanced by aripiprazole)

» Carbamazepine or
» Other agents that induce CYP3A4
(may cause an increase in aripiprazole clearance and lower aripiprazole blood levels)

» Central nervous system (CNS) stimulation-producing medications (see *Appendix II*) or
» Central nervous system (CNS) depression-producing medications (see *Appendix II*)
(given the primary CNS effects of aripiprazole caution should be used when using other centrally acting drugs)

» CYP3A4 inhibitors including:
» Itraconazole or
» Ketoconazole
(may inhibit aripiprazole elimination and cause increased aripiprazole blood levels)

» CYP2D6 inhibitors including:
» Fluoxetine or
» Paroxetine or
» Quinidine
(may inhibit aripiprazole elimination and cause increased aripiprazole blood levels)

» Medications with anticholinergic activity (see *Appendix II*)
(concomitant administration may disrupt the ability to reduce core body temperature)

Laboratory value alterations

The following have been selected on the basis of their potential clinical significance (possible effect in parentheses where appropriate)—not necessarily inclusive (» = major clinical significance).

With physiology/laboratory test values

Blood glucose
(patients with a diagnosis of or risk factors for diabetes mellitus should undergo fasting blood glucose testing at the beginning of treatment and periodically during treatment)

Creatinine phosphokinase, serum
(elevated levels may be a sign of a potentially fatal symptom complex sometimes referred to as Neuroleptic Malignant Syndrome [NMS] which has been associated with administration of antipsychotic drugs, including aripiprazole)

Myoglobulin, urine
(presence in the urine may be a sign of NMS)

Medical considerations/Contraindications

The medical considerations/contraindications included have been selected on the basis of their potential clinical significance (reasons given in parentheses where appropriate)—not necessarily inclusive (» = major clinical significance).

Except under special circumstances, this medication should not be used when the following medical problem exists:

» Hypersensitivity to aripiprazole

Risk-benefit should be considered when the following medical problems exist:

Alcohol or drug abuse or dependence, history of
(patients should be carefully evaluated for a history of drug abuse; they should be closely monitored for signs of misuse or abuse such as development of tolerance, increases in dose, or drug-seeking behavior.)

Alzheimer's dementia or
Conditions that lower the seizure threshold or
Seizures, history of
(may increase incidence of seizure)

Aspiration pneumonia, risk or history of
(may increase risk of adverse events)

» Cardiovascular disease or
» Cerebrovascular disease or
» Conduction abnormalities or
» Dehydration or
» Heart failure or
» Hypovolemia or
» Ischemic heart disease, history of or
» Myocardial infarction, history of
(may increase the risk of orthostatic hypotension)

Conditions which may contribute to an elevation in core body temperature, such as
Exposure to extreme heat or
Strenuous exercise
(appropriate care is advised; disruption of the body's ability to reduce core body temperature has been attributed to antipsychotic agents)

» Diabetes mellitus or
» Risk factors for diabetes mellitus such as
Obesity or
Family history of diabetes
(increased risk of treatment-emergent hyperglycemia-related adverse events including ketoacidosis, hyperosmolar coma, or death in patients treated with atypical antipsychotics; patients should be monitored carefully)

Drug abuse or dependence, history of
(patients should be observed closely for signs of misuse or abuse of aripiprazole [e.g., development of tolerance, increases in dose, drug-seeking behavior)

» Neuroleptic Malignant Syndrome (NMS), history of
(reintroduction of drug therapy to patients recovering from NMS should be carefully considered; patients should be carefully monitored for recurrences of NMS)

Patient monitoring

The following may be especially important in patient monitoring (other tests may be warranted in some patients, depending on condition; » = major clinical significance):

Careful observation for early symptoms of tardive dyskinesia
(recommended at periodic intervals, especially in the elderly and patients on high or extended maintenance dosage; discontinuation of aripiprazole should be considered if early symptoms of tardive dyskinesia appear, since there is no known effective treatment)

Careful supervision of patients with suicidal tendencies
(recommended in high-risk patients since the possibility of a suicide attempt is inherent in schizophrenia and in bipolar disorder; prescriptions should be written for smallest quantity consistent with good patient management)

Hyperglycemia
(all patients should be monitored for symptoms of hyperglycemia including polydipsia, polyuria, polyphagia, and weakness; patients developing symptoms should undergo fasting blood glucose testing)

» Re-evaluation of the usefulness of aripiprazole therapy
(Patients should be periodically reassessed to determine the need for maintenance treatment; the effectiveness of long-term use [more than 6 months and 6 weeks for schizophrenia and bipolar mania, respectively] has not been systematically evaluated in clinical trials)

Retinal evaluation
(Adequate and well-controlled studies in humans have not been done.)
(Aripiprazole produced retinal degeneration in albino rats in animal chronic toxicity and carcinogenicity studies. The relevance of this finding to human risk is unknown.)

Side/Adverse Effects

The following side/adverse effects have been selected on the basis of their potential clinical significance (possible signs and symptoms in parentheses where appropriate)—not necessarily inclusive:

Those indicating need for medical attention

Incidence more frequent

Extrapyramidal syndrome (difficulty in speaking; drooling; loss of balance control; muscle trembling, jerking, or stiffness; restlessness; shuffling walk; stiffness of limbs; twisting movements of body; uncontrolled movements, especially of face, neck, and back)

Incidence less frequent

Hypertension (blurred vision; dizziness; nervousness; headache; pounding in the ears; slow or fast heartbeat)

Incidence rare

Neuroleptic malignant syndrome (convulsions; difficulty in breathing; fast heartbeat; high fever; high or low blood pressure; increased sweating; loss of bladder control; severe muscle stiffness; unusually pale skin; tiredness); ***seizures*** (convulsions; muscle spasm or jerking of all extremities; sudden loss of consciousness; loss of bladder control); ***Tardive dyskinesia*** (lip smacking or puckering; puffing of cheeks; rapid or worm-like movements of tongue; uncontrolled chewing movements; uncontrolled movements of arms and legs)

Incidence not determined—Observed during clinical practice; estimates of frequency can not be determined.

Anaphylactic reaction (cough; difficulty swallowing; dizziness; fast heartbeat; hives; itching, puffiness or swelling of the eyelids or around the eyes, face, lips or tongue; shortness of breath; skin rash; tightness in chest; unusual tiredness or weakness; wheezing); ***angioedema*** (large, hive-like swelling on face, eyelids, lips, tongue, throat, hands, legs, feet, sex organs); ***laryngospasm*** (shortness of breath; trouble in breathing; tightness in chest; or wheezing); ***pruritus*** (itching skin); ***urticaria*** (hives or welts; itching; redness of skin; skin rash)

Those indicating need for medical attention only if they continue or are bothersome

Incidence more frequent

Agitation (anxiety; nervousness; restlessness; irritability; dry mouth; shortness of breath; hyperventilation; trouble sleeping; irregular heartbeats; shaking); ***akathisia*** (inability to sit still; need to keep moving; restlessness); ***anxiety*** (fear; nervousness); ***asthenia*** (lack or loss of strength); ***constipation*** (difficulty having a bowel movement (stool)); ***dyspepsia*** (acid or sour stomach; belching; heartburn; indigestion; stomach discomfort, upset, or pain); ***headache; insomnia*** (sleeplessness; trouble sleeping; unable to sleep); ***lightheadedness; nausea; rash; somnolence*** (sleepiness or unusual drowsiness); ***vomiting; weight gain***

Incidence less frequent

Accidental injury; blurred vision; coughing; increased salivation; myalgia (joint pain; swollen joints; muscle aching or cramping; muscle pains or stiffness; difficulty in moving); ***fever; peripheral edema*** (bloating or swelling of face, arms, hands, lower legs, or feet; rapid weight gain; tingling of hands or feet; unusual weight gain or loss); ***pharyngitis*** (body aches or pain; congestion; cough; dryness or soreness of throat; fever; hoarseness; runny nose; tender, swollen glands in neck; trouble in swallowing; voice changes); ***rhinitis*** (stuffy nose; runny nose; sneezing); ***tremor***

Overdose

For more information on the management of overdose or unintentional ingestion, **contact a poison control center** (see *Poison Control Center Listing).*

Clinical effects of overdose

The following effects have been selected on the basis of their potential clinical significance (possible signs and symptoms in parentheses where appropriate)—not necessarily inclusive:

Acute

Asthenia (lack or loss of strength); ***diarrhea; extrapyramidal symptoms*** (difficulty in speaking; drooling; loss of balance control; muscle trembling, jerking, or stiffness; restlessness; shuffling walk; stiffness of limbs; twisting movements of body; uncontrolled movements, especially of face, neck, and back); ***loss of consciousness; nausea; somnolence*** (sleepiness or unusual drowsiness); ***tachycardia*** (fast, pounding, or irregular heartbeat or pulse); ***vomiting***

Treatment of overdose

To decrease absorption—

Early activated charcoal administration may be useful in partially preventing the absorption of aripiprazole.

Administration of 50 grams of activated charcoal one hour after a single 15-mg oral dose of aripiprazole decreased the mean AUC and C_{max} of aripiprazole by 50%.

To enhance elimination—

There is no information on the effect of hemodialysis in treating an overdose with aripiprazole. Because aripiprazole is highly bound to plasma proteins, hemodialysis is unlikely to be useful.

Specific treatment—

Treatment should be primarily symptomatic and supportive.

Monitoring—

An electrocardiogram should be obtained. Cardiac monitoring should be instituted in patients with QTc interval prolongation.

Careful monitoring of the patient by medical personnel is recommended until the patient recovers.

Supportive care—

Treatment should be symptomatic and supportive, including maintaining an adequate airway, oxygenation and ventilation, and management of symptoms.

Patients in whom intentional overdose is confirmed or suspected should be referred for psychiatric consultation.

Patient Consultation

As an aid to patient consultation, refer to *Advice for the Patient, Aripiprazole (Systemic).*

In providing consultation, consider emphasizing the following selected information (» = major clinical significance):

Before using this medication

» Conditions affecting use, especially:

Hypersensitivity to aripiprazole

Pregnancy—Studies in animals showed that aripiprazole causes developmental toxicity and possible teratogenic effects.

FDA Pregnancy Category C

Breast-feeding—Should not be given to nursing women because aripiprazole is distributed into the milk of rats.

Use in the elderly—Increased incidence of cerebrovascular adverse events (stroke, transient ischemic attack); safety and efficacy not established in Alzheimer's patients with psychosis associated with dementia; if healthcare professional elects to treat, vigilance should be exercised with attention to difficulty swallowing or excessive somnolence, which could predispose to accidental injury or aspiration; not approved for the treatment of behavioral disorders in elderly patients with dementia; associated with a higher death rate

Pharmacogenetics—Extensive metabolizers: Coadministration of aripiprazole with known inhibitors of CYP2D6 may result in increased aripiprazole plasma exposure.

Other medications especially, alcohol, antihypertensives, carbamazepine or other CYP3A4 inducers, central nervous system stimulants or depressants, ketoconazole or other CYP3A4 inhibitors, fluoxetine or other CYP2D6 inhibitors, or medications with anticholinergic activity

Other medical problems, especially neuroleptic malignant syndrome (NMS), cardiovascular disease, cerebrovascular disease, conduction abnormalities, dehydration, heart failure, hypovolemia, ischemic heart disease, myocardial infarction, diabetes mellitus or risk factors for diabetes mellitus

Proper use of this medication

Compliance with therapy; not taking more of less medicine than prescribed

Importance of being checked regularly by your physician

» Importance of caregivers contacting doctor and not giving this medicine for treatment of behavioral problems in elderly patients with dementia

Taking without regards to meals, as directed by physician

» Proper dosing

Missed dose: Taking as soon as possible; not taking if almost time for next scheduled dose; not doubling doses

Proper storage

Precautions while using this medication

Possible drowsiness, impaired judgement, thinking, or motor skills; caution when driving or operating machinery until familiar with the effects of aripiprazole

Possible orthostatic hypotension; rising slowly form a sitting or lying position

Avoiding overheating and dehydration as aripiprazole may impair ability to regulate core body temperature

Avoiding use of alcoholic beverages; not taking other CNS depressants unless prescribed by physician

Telling your doctor about all medications you are taking, prescription and nonprescription

This medicine may affect blood sugar levels. Also, the oral solution contains sugar.

Side/adverse effects

Signs of potential side effects, especially extrapyramidal syndrome, hypertension, neuroleptic malignant syndrome (NMS), seizures, or tardive dyskinesia

Signs of potential side effects observed during clinical practice, especially anaphylactic reaction, angioedema, laryngospasm, pruritus, or urticaria

General Dosing Information

For oral dosing forms:

Maintenance therapy—There is no evidence from controlled trials to determine how long a patient should remain on aripiprazole therapy. It is generally agreed that pharmacological treatment for episodes of acute schizophrenia should continue for 6 months or longer. And, both for maintenance of the initial response and for prevention of new bipolar manic episodes, there are no systematically obtained data to support the use of aripiprazole in treatment beyond 6 weeks.

Switching from other antipsychotics—Immediate discontinuation of the previous antipsychotic treatment may be acceptable for some patients with schizophrenia, more gradual discontinuation may be most appropriate for others. In all cases, the period of overlapping antipsychotic administration should be minimized.

Approximately 8% of Caucasians lack the capacity to metabolize CYP2D6 substrates and are classified as poor metabolizers (PM), whereas the rest are extensive metabolizers (EM). PMs have an 80% increase in aripiprazole exposure and about a 30% decrease in exposure to the active metabolite compared to EMs, resulting in about a 60% higher exposure to the total active moieties from a given dose of aripiprazole compared to EMs.

Patients should be advised that each mL of aripiprazole oral solution contains 400 mg of sucrose and 200 mg of fructose.

Diet/Nutrition
Aripiprazole can be taken without regard to meals.

Bioequivalence information
Oral solution can be given on a mg-per-mg basis in place of the 5-, 10-, 15-, or 20-mg tablet strengths. Solution doses can be substituted for tablet doses on a mg-per-mg basis up to 25 mg of the tablet. Patients receiving 30-mg tablets should receive 25 mg of the solution.

For treatment of adverse effects
Neuroleptic malignant syndrome (NMS)—Recommended treatment consists of the following:

- *Discontinuing aripiprazole and other drugs not essential to current therapy.*
- Providing intensive symptomatic treatment and medical monitoring.
- Treating any concomitant serious medical problems for which specific treatments are available.
- After recovery, giving careful consideration to the reintroduction of antipsychotic drug therapy in patients with severe psychosis requiring treatment, because of possible recurrence of NMS; closely monitoring patients in whom antipsychotic drug therapy is reintroduced after recovery from NMS.

Tardive dyskinesia—There is no known effective treatment. If signs and symptoms of tardive dyskinesia appear, discontinuation of aripiprazole treatment should be considered if clinically feasible. To minimize the occurrence of tardive dyskinesia, chronic antipsychotic treatment should be prescribed in the smallest effective dose for the shortest duration necessary to produce a satisfactory clinical response.

Oral Dosage Forms

ARIPIPRAZOLE ORAL SOLUTION

Usual adult dose
Bipolar mania (treatment)—

Oral, 25 mg once daily as starting dose. Maintenance treatment in longer-term (i.e., beyond 6 weeks) treatment has not been studied.

Schizophrenia—

Oral, 10 to 15 mg a day, once a day, without regard to food. Dose increases should not be made before 2 weeks.

Concomitant Therapy

- CYP3A4 inhibitors: Oral, dose reduction of aripiprazole by one-half of the usual dose when coadministered with ketoconazole and other CYP3A4 inhibitors
- CYP2D6 inhibitors: Oral, dose reduction of aripiprazole by one-half of the usual dose when coadministered with CYP2D6 inhibitors such as quinidine, fluoxetine or paroxetine
- CYP3A4 inducers: Oral, dose increase of aripiprazole by double (20 or 25 mg), additional doses should be based on clinical evaluation when combined with carbamazepine or other CYP3A4 inducers

Note: Aripiprazole dose should be appropriately adjusted to the usual recommended dose when concomitant therapy is discontinued.

Note: No dosage adjustments are recommended based on hepatic impairment, renal impairment, gender, or race.

Usual adult prescribing limits
Bipolar mania (treatment)—

Safety of doses above 25 mg per day has not been evaluated.

Usual pediatric dose
Safety and efficacy have not been established.

Usual geriatric dose
See *Usual adult dose.*

Strength(s) usually available
U.S.—

1 mg/mL (Rx) [*Abilify* (fructose; glycerin; dl-lactic acid; methylparaben; propylene glycol; propylparaben; sodium hydroxide; sucrose; purified water; natural orange cream flavor; other natural flavors)].

Canada—

Not commercially available

Packaging and storage
Store in a refrigerator at 2 °C to 8 °C (36 °F to 46 °F).

Stability
Open bottles of aripiprazole should be stored in a refrigerator and can be used for up to 6 months after opening.

Auxiliary labeling
- May cause drowsiness. Be careful while driving or operating machinery. Use caution until you become familiar with its effects.
- Avoid alcoholic beverages.

ARIPIPRAZOLE TABLETS

Usual adult dose
Bipolar mania (treatment)—

Oral, 30 mg once daily as starting dose. Maintenance treatment in longer-term (i.e., beyond 6 weeks) treatment has not been studied.

Schizophrenia—

Oral, 10 to 15 mg a day, once a day, without regard to food. Dose increases should not be made before 2 weeks.

Concomitant Therapy

- CYP3A4 inhibitors: Oral, dose reduction of aripiprazole by one-half of the usual dose when coadministered with ketoconazole and other CYP3A4 inhibitors
- CYP2D6 inhibitors: Oral, dose reduction of aripiprazole by one-half of the usual dose when coadministered with CYP2D6 inhibitors such as quinidine, fluoxetine or paroxetine
- CYP3A4 inducers: Oral, dose increase of aripiprazole by double (20 or 30 mg), additional doses should be based on clinical evaluation when combined with carbamazepine or other CYP3A4 inducers

Note: Aripiprazole dose should be appropriately adjusted to the usual recommended dose when concomitant therapy is discontinued.

Note: No dosage adjustments are recommended based on hepatic impairment, renal impairment, gender, or race.

Usual adult prescribing limits
Bipolar mania (treatment)—

Safety of doses above 30 mg per day has not been evaluated.

Usual pediatric dose
Safety and efficacy have not been established.

Usual geriatric dose
See *Usual adult dose.*

Strength(s) usually available
U.S.—

5 mg (Rx) [*Abilify* (lactose monohydrate; cornstarch; microcrystalline cellulose; hydroxypropyl cellulose; magnesium stearate; ferric oxide; FD&C Blue No. 2 Aluminum Lake)].

10 mg (Rx) [*Abilify* (lactose monohydrate; cornstarch; microcrystalline cellulose; hydroxypropyl cellulose; magnesium stearate; ferric oxide; FD&C Blue No. 2 Aluminum Lake)].

15 mg (Rx) [*Abilify* (lactose monohydrate; cornstarch; microcrystalline cellulose; hydroxypropyl cellulose; magnesium stearate; ferric oxide; FD&C Blue No. 2 Aluminum Lake)].

20 mg (Rx) [*Abilify* (lactose monohydrate; cornstarch; microcrystalline cellulose; hydroxypropyl cellulose; magnesium stearate; ferric oxide; FD&C Blue No. 2 Aluminum Lake)].

30 mg (Rx) [*Abilify* (lactose monohydrate; cornstarch; microcrystalline cellulose; hydroxypropyl cellulose; magnesium stearate; ferric oxide; FD&C Blue No. 2 Aluminum Lake)].

Canada—

Not commercially available

Packaging and storage
Store at 25 °C (77 °F), excursions permitted to 15 to 30 °C (59 to 86 °F).

Auxiliary labeling
- May cause drowsiness. Be careful while driving or operating machinery. Use caution until you become familiar with its effects.
- Avoid alcoholic beverages.

Revised: 05/04/2005
Developed: 06/02/2003

ARSENIC TRIOXIDE Systemic†

VA CLASSIFICATION (Primary): AN900

Commonly used brand name(s): *Trisenox*.

Note: For a listing of dosage forms and brand names by country availability, see *Dosage Forms* section(s).

†Not commercially available in Canada.

Category

Antineoplastic.

Indications

Accepted

Leukemia, acute promyelocytic (treatment)—Arsenic trioxide is indicated for induction of remission and consolidation in patients with acute promyelocytic leukemia (APL) who are refractory to, or have relapsed from, retinoid and anthracycline chemotherapy, and whose APL is characterized by the presence of the t(15;17) translocation or PML/RAR-alpha gene expression.

Acceptance not established

Multiple myeloma, relapsed/refractory—Arsenic trioxide has demonstrated limited activity as a single agent and in combination with melphalan and ascorbic acid in the treatment of refractory/relapsed multiple myeloma. Overall objective response rates were less than or equal to 33%. Efficacy was measured by decreases in serum or urine M protein levels.

Myelodysplastic Syndrome—Arsenic trioxide is being evaluated for use in myelodysplastic syndromes (MDS) in two clinical trials reporting interim analyses. Overall response rates of 24%-28% have been reported in low-risk patients and 12%-30% in high risk patients. Azacitidine, an FDA approved treatment for MDS, has an approximate response rate of 23%. Arsenic appears to be showing a similar response rate, however it is important to note that of 191 total patients enrolled in the trials, only 28 patients (all in the same trial) completed the protocol. Primary reasons for withdrawal from the treatment protocols were disease progression and adverse effects.

Pharmacology/Pharmacokinetics

Physicochemical characteristics

Molecular weight—197.8.

pH—7-9

Mechanism of action/Effect

The mechanism of action of arsenic trioxide is not well understood, however, *in vitro* studies indicate that morphological changes and DNA fragmentation characteristic of apoptosis occur in NB4 human promyelocytic leukemia cells following arsenic trioxide administration. Additionally, arsenic trioxide induces damage and degradation of the fusion protein PML/RAR-alpha.

Distribution

Arsenic is stored in the liver, kidneys, heart, lungs, hair, and nails.

Biotransformation

Hepatic; pentavalent arsenic reduced to the active trivalent arsenic via arsenate reductase; trivalent arsenic is methylated to monomethylarsonic acid, which is metabolized to dimethylarsinic acid via methyltransferase.

Elimination

Renal.

Precautions to Consider

Note: Acute promyelocytic leukemia (APL) is associated with thrombocytopenia and patients may present with disseminated intravascular coagulation (DIC) and bleeding. Caution with dental care is advised. Arsenic trioxide therapy may improve this condition.

Carcinogenicity

Human carcinogenicity studies have not been performed using *intravenous* arsenic trioxide, however, arsenic trioxide is a known human carcinogen.

Mutagenicity

Arsenic trioxide and arsenite salts have not been proven to be mutagenic to bacteria, yeast, or mammalian cells. *In vitro* studies using human fibroblasts, human lymphocytes, Chinese hamster ovary cells, and Chinese hamster V79 lung cells have demonstrated the clastogenicity of arsenite salts. The incidence of chromosomal aberrations and appearance of micronuclei in the bone marrow cells of mice is increased with the use of trivalent arsenic.

Pregnancy/Reproduction

Fertility—Studies in humans or animals have not been performed.

Pregnancy—Arsenic crosses the placenta and has been shown to cause adverse effects on the fetus in animals. Pregnant rats given 10 mg per kg of arsenic trioxide (10 times the recommended human daily dose on a mg per squared meter of body surface area basis) experienced an increased number of resorptions, and neural-tube defects, anophthalmia, and microphthalmia. Similar findings were noted in mice given arsenic doses up to 5 times the recommended human daily doses.

No studies have been done in pregnant women. Due to potential fetal harm and/or miscarriage, women of childbearing potential should avoid becoming pregnant.

FDA Pregnancy Category D.

Breast-feeding

Arsenic is distributed into human breast milk. Due to the possibility of serious adverse effects to the infant, a decision should be made as to whether to discontinue nursing or to discontinue the drug.

Pediatrics

Appropriate studies have not been performed on the relationship of age to the effects of arsenic trioxide in children up to 5 years of age. Safety and efficacy have not been established. Limited clinical data is available on the use of arsenic trioxide in pediatric patients 5 to 18 years of age.

Geriatrics

No information is available on the relationship of age to the effects of arsenic trioxide in geriatric patients. However, elderly patients are more likely to have age-related renal-function impairment, which may require caution in patients receiving arsenic trioxide.

Drug interactions and/or related problems

The following drug interactions and/or related problems have been selected on the basis of their potential clinical significance (possible mechanism in parentheses where appropriate)—not necessarily inclusive (» = major clinical significance):

Note: APL is associated with thrombocytopenia and presents a potential interaction with blood dyscrasia-causing medications (see Appendix II).

» Amphotericin B or
» Diuretics, potassium-depleting or
» QT interval-prolonging drugs, such as, or
  Antiarrhythmics
  Azole antifungals
  Antihistamines
  Antidepressants, tricyclic
  Fluoroquinolones
» Thioridazine
  (QT interval prolongation and complete AV block have been reported; the risk increases with concomitant use of other drugs which prolong the QT interval or cause electrolyte imbalances; if possible, any other drugs causing QT interval prolongation should be discontinued prior to treatment with arsenic trioxide)

Laboratory value alterations

The following have been selected on the basis of their potential clinical significance (possible effect in parentheses where appropriate)—not necessarily inclusive (» = major clinical significance).

With physiology/laboratory test values
  Alanine aminotransferase (ALT [SGPT]) values and
  Aspartate aminotransferase (AST [SGOT]) values
    (increases occurred in patients during clinical trials)

Medical considerations/Contraindications

The medical considerations/contraindications included have been selected on the basis of their potential clinical significance (reasons given in parentheses where appropriate)—not necessarily inclusive (» = major clinical significance).

Except under certain circumstances, this medication should not be used when the following medical problems exist:

» Hypersensitivity to arsenic

Risk-benefit should be considered when the following medical problems exist:

» Congestive heart failure or
» Hypokalemia or
» Hypomagnesemia or
» QT interval prolongation, preexisting or

» Torsades de pointes, history of
(arsenic trioxide has been reported to cause QT prolongation and complete AV block; these conditions should be corrected before the start of arsenic trioxide therapy)

» Renal insufficiency
(renal excretion is the main route of elimination of arsenic; caution is warranted)

Patient monitoring

The following may be especially important in patient monitoring (other tests may be warranted in some patients, depending on condition; » = major clinical significance):

» Absolute neutrophil count and
» Leukocyte counts and
» Platelet counts and
» Red blood cell counts
(recommended prior to initiation of therapy and twice weekly during induction and at least weekly during consolidation; frequency should increase if patient is clinically unstable)

» Electrocardiogram, 12–lead
(recommended prior to initiation of therapy and at weekly intervals during induction and consolidation; frequency should increase if patient is clinically unstable; if QTc exceeds 500 msec, corrective measures should be completed and ECG reassessed serially prior to initiation of therapy; QTc should be kept below 460 msec; QTc exceeding 500 msec during therapy should be reassessed and corrected and arsenic trioxide therapy discontinued until QTc falls below 460 msec)

Creatinine, serum and
» Electrolytes, serum
(recommended prior to initiation of therapy and twice weekly during induction and at least weekly during consolidation; frequency should increase if patient is clinically unstable; preexisting electrolyte abnormalities should be corrected prior to initiation of therapy; serum potassium levels should be kept above 4 mEq/dL and magnesium concentrations above 1.8 mg/dL)

» Syncope or
» Tachycardia
(patient should be hospitalized for monitoring, along with serum electrolytes and QTc interval)

Side/Adverse Effects

The following side/adverse effects have been selected on the basis of their potential clinical significance (possible signs and symptoms in parentheses where appropriate)—not necessarily inclusive:

Those indicating need for medical attention

Incidence more frequent (>50%)

Dyspnea (shortness of breath; difficult or labored breathing); ***hyperleukocytosis*** (chills; cough; eye pain; general feeling of illness; headache; sore throat; unusual tiredness); ***hypokalemia*** (convulsions; decreased urine; dry mouth; irregular heartbeat; increased thirst; loss of appetite; mood changes; muscle pain or cramps; nausea or vomiting; numbness or tingling in hands, feet, or lips; shortness of breath; unusual tiredness or weakness); ***tachycardia*** (rapid heartbeat)

Incidence less frequent (10–50%)

Acute promyelocytic leukemia (APL) differentiation syndrome (chest pain; chills; cough; difficult or labored breathing; fever; shortness of breath; sore throat; unusual tiredness or weakness; weight gain)—syndrome can be fatal; ***anemia; chest pain; hyperglycemia*** (blurred vision; dry mouth; fatigue; flushed, dry skin; fruit-like breath odor; increased hunger; increased thirst; increased urination; loss of consciousness; nausea; stomachache; sweating; troubled breathing; unexplained weight loss; vomiting); ***hyperkalemia*** (abdominal pain; nausea or vomiting; weakness); ***hypertension*** (high blood pressure); ***hypocalcemia*** (abdominal cramps; confusion; irregular heartbeats; muscle cramps in hands, arms, feet, legs, or face; numbness and tingling around the mouth, fingertips, or feet); ***hypomagnesemia*** (muscle trembling or twitching); ***hypotension*** (low blood pressure; dizziness or lightheadedness); ***hypoxia*** (bluish lips and skin); ***neutropenia, including febrile*** (black, tarry stools; chest pain; chills; cough; fever; painful or difficult urination; shortness of breath; sore throat; sores, ulcers, or white spots on lips or in mouth; swollen glands; unusual bleeding or bruising; unusual tiredness or weakness); ***palpitations*** (fast, irregular, pounding, or racing heartbeat or pulse); ***pleural effusion*** (chest pain; shortness of breath); ***QT interval prolongation*** (dizziness or fainting; fast or irregular heartbeat; pounding heartbeat); ***thrombocytopenia*** (black, tarry stools; chest pain; chills; cough; fever; painful or difficult urination; shortness of breath; sore throat; sores, ulcers, or white spots on lips or in mouth; swollen glands; unusual bleeding or bruising; unusual tiredness or weakness)—causal relationship most likely due to APL, not arsenic therapy; ***upper respiratory tract infection; wheezing***

Incidence rare (<10%)

Acidosis (drowsiness; severe nausea; continuing shortness of breath; troubled breathing); ***atrioventricular block*** (chest pain; dizziness; fainting; pounding, slow heartbeat; troubled breathing; unusual tiredness or weakness); ***coma*** (loss of consciousness); ***disseminated intravascular coagulation (DIC)*** (blood in stools; blood in urine; bluish color of fingernails, lips, skin, palms, or nail beds; bruising; excessive sweating; persistent bleeding or oozing from puncture sites, mouth, or nose)—causal relationship most likely due to APL, not arsenic therapy; ***gastrointestinal hemorrhage*** (black, tarry stools; bloody stools; vomiting of blood or material that looks like coffee grounds); ***hemorrhage*** (bleeding); ***hypersensitivity reaction, delayed or immediate*** (large hives; rash; shortness of breath or troubled breathing; swelling of eyelids, lips, or face); ***hypoglycemia*** (anxiety; behavior change similar to drunkenness; cold sweats; cool pale skin; fast heartbeat; headache; shakiness); ***oliguria*** (decrease in amount of urine); ***oral candidiasis*** (sore mouth or tongue; white patches in mouth and/or on tongue); ***renal dysfunction*** (decrease in urine output or decrease in urine-concentrating ability; cloudy urine); ***seizures*** (convulsions); ***sepsis*** (chills; fever; fast heartbeat)

Those indicating need for medical attention only if they continue or are bothersome

Incidence more frequent (>50%)

Abdominal pain; cough; diarrhea; fatigue (unusual tiredness or weakness); ***fever; headache; nausea and vomiting***

Incidence less frequent (10–50%)

Anorexia (loss of appetite); ***anxiety; arthralgia*** (joint and muscle pain); ***back pain; blurred vision; bone pain; constipation; dizziness; dermatitis*** (itchy, red skin; swelling); ***dyspepsia*** (acid or sour stomach; belching; heartburn; indigestion; stomach discomfort upset or pain); ***edema*** (rapid weight gain; bloating or swelling of face, hands, lower legs, and/or feet); ***ecchymosis*** (bruising); ***epistaxis*** (nosebleed); ***flushing; injection site pain, redness, and swelling; limb pain; insomnia*** (trouble sleeping or getting to sleep); ***myalgia*** (muscle pain); ***neck pain; mental depression; paresthesia*** (tingling, burning, or prickly sensations); ***pallor*** (pale skin); ***pruritus*** (itching); ***rigors*** (shivering chills); ***sinusitis*** (headache); ***sore throat; sweating; tremor; vaginal hemorrhage*** (heavy nonmenstrual vaginal bleeding); ***weakness; weight gain***

Incidence rare (<10%)

Abdominal distention (swelling of abdominal or stomach area); ***agitation; confusion; diarrhea, hemorrhagic*** (loose, bloody stools); ***dry eyes; dry mouth; earache; eye pain or redness; facial or eyelid edema*** (swelling or puffiness of face or eyelids); ***fecal or urinary incontinence*** (loss of bowel or bladder control); ***hemoptysis*** (coughing or spitting up blood); ***intermenstrual bleeding*** (uterine bleeding between menstrual periods); ***lymphadenopathy*** (swollen, painful, or tender lymph glands in neck, armpit, or groin); ***nasopharyngitis*** (cough; sore throat); ***night sweats; oral blistering*** (blisters inside mouth); ***petechiae*** (small red or purple spots on skin); ***tachypnea*** (rapid, shallow breathing); ***tinnitus*** (ringing in the ears); ***weight loss***

Overdose

For specific information on the agents used in the management of arsenic overdose, see:

- *Dimercaprol (Systemic)* monograph;
- *Penicillamine (Systemic)* monograph

For more information on the management of overdose or unintentional ingestion, **contact a poison control center** (see *Poison Control Center Listing*).

Clinical effects of overdose

The following effects have been selected on the basis of their potential clinical significance (possible signs and symptoms in parentheses where appropriate)—not necessarily inclusive:

Acute

Confusion; muscle weakness; seizures (convulsions)

Treatment of overdose

Specific treatment—

Administering dimercaprol 3 mg per kg of body weight intramuscularly every 4 hours until immediate life-threatening toxicity has subsided. Thereafter, penicillamine 250 mg orally up to 4 times daily may be given.

Discontinue arsenic therapy immediately.

Monitoring—

Monitoring cardiovascular function (ECG), electrolytes and blood counts

Supportive care—
Maintaining cardiac function
Patients in whom intentional overdose is confirmed or suspected should be referred for psychiatric consultation.

Patient Consultation

As an aid to patient consultation, refer to *Advice for the Patient, Arsenic Trioxide*.

In providing consultation, consider emphasizing the following selected information (» = major clinical significance):

Before using this medication

» Conditions affecting use, especially:
Hypersensitivity to arsenic
Arsenic is a known human carcinogen
Pregnancy—Not recommended for use during pregnancy
Breast-feeding—Distributed into human milk; not recommended for use in breast-feeding women
Use in children—Limited data in children above the age of 5
Other medications, especially amphotericin B, potassium-depleting diuretics, QT interval-prolonging agents such as antiarrhythmics, azole antifungals, antihistamines, fluoroquinolones, or tricyclic antidepressants, or thioridazine
Other medical problems, especially bone marrow suppression, congestive heart failure, hypokalemia, hypomagnesemia, QT interval prolongation, Torsades de pointes, or renal insufficiency

Proper use of this medication

» Proper dosing

Precautions while using this medication

» Regular visits to physician to monitor progress

» Precautions regarding thrombocytopenia: dental care, increased risk of infection and bleeding, or interactions with blood dyscrasia-causing medications, are necessary in patients with acute promyelocytic leukemia (APL); arsenic trioxide may improve these conditions

Caution if bone marrow depression occurs:

» Avoiding exposure to persons with infections, especially during periods of low blood counts; checking with physician immediately if fever or chills, cough or hoarseness, lower back or side pain, or painful or difficult urination occurs

» Checking with physician immediately if unusual bleeding or bruising; black, tarry stools; blood in urine or stools; or pinpoint red spots on skin occur

Caution in use of regular toothbrush, dental floss, or toothpick; physician, dentist, or nurse may suggest alternatives; checking with physician before having dental work done

Not touching eyes or inside of nose unless hands washed immediately before

Using caution to avoid accidental cuts with use of sharp objects such as safety razor or fingernail or toenail cutters

Avoiding contact sports or other situations where bruising or injury could occur

Side/adverse effects

Signs of potential side effects, especially acidosis, acute promyelocytic leukemia differentiation syndrome, anemia, atrioventricular block, chest pain, coma, disseminated intravascular coagulation, dyspnea, gastrointestinal hemorrhage, hemorrhage, hyperglycemia, hyperkalemia, hyperleukocytosis, hypertension, hypersensitivity reaction (delayed or immediate), hypocalcemia, hypoglycemia, hypokalemia, hypomagnesemia, hypoxia, neutropenia (including febrile), oliguria, oral candidiasis, palpitations, pleural effusion, QT interval prolongation, renal dysfunction, seizures, sepsis, tachycardia, thrombocytopenia, upper respiratory tract infection, or wheezing

General Dosing Information

Patients receiving arsenic trioxide should be under supervision of a physician experienced in treatment of acute leukemia.

Special precautions are recommended in patients who develop thrombocytopenia as a result of administration of arsenic trioxide. These may include extreme care in performing invasive procedures; regular inspection of intravenous sites, skin (including perirectal area), and mucous membrane surfaces for signs of bleeding or bruising; limiting frequency of venipuncture and avoiding intramuscular injections; testing urine, emesis, stool, and secretions for occult blood; care in the use of regular toothbrushes, dental floss, toothpicks, safety razors, and fingernail and toenail cutters; avoiding constipation; and using caution to prevent falls and other injuries. Such patients should avoid alcohol and aspirin intake because of the risk of gastrointestinal bleeding.

Safety considerations for handling this medication

There is limited but increasing evidence and concern that personnel involved in preparation and administration of parenteral antineoplastic agents may be at some risk because of the potential mutagenicity, teratogenicity, and/or carcinogenicity of these agents, although the actual risk is unknown. USP advisory panels recommend cautious handling both in preparation and disposal of antineoplastic agents. Precautions that have been suggested include:

- Use of a biological containment cabinet during reconstitution and dilution of parenteral medications and wearing of disposable surgical gloves, goggles, gowns, and masks.
- Pregnant personnel should not come in contact with antineoplastic medication containers or mixing supplies.
- Use of proper technique to prevent contamination of the medication, work area, and operator during transfer between containers (including proper training of personnel in this technique).
- Cautious and proper disposal of needles, syringes, vials, ampules, and unused medication.
- Use of proper technique in handling spills, including the use of dilute sodium hypochlorite solution (1% active chlorine) and water, and proper disposal of waste.

A number of medical centers have developed detailed guidelines for handling of antineoplastic agents.

For treatment of adverse effects

High-dose steroids have been used at the first suspicion of APL differentiation syndrome. Dexamethasone 10 mg intravenously should be given twice daily, irrespective of the leukocyte count, and continued for at least 3 days or longer until signs and symptoms have abated. In general, patients may continue to receive arsenic trioxide therapy during treatment of APL differentiation syndrome.

Parenteral Dosage Forms

ARSENIC TRIOXIDE INJECTION

Usual Adult Dose

Leukemia, acute promyelocytic—
Induction—Intravenous, 0.15 mg per kg of body weight daily, over 1 to 2 hours, until bone marrow remission occurs.
Consolidation—Intravenous, beginning 3 to 6 weeks after completion of induction, 0.15 mg per kg of body weight daily, over 1 to 2 hours, for 25 doses over a period of up to 5 weeks.

Usual adult prescribing limits

Induction; total induction dose should not exceed 60 doses.
Consolidation; 25 doses.

Note: Infusion duration may be extended up to 4 hours if acute vasomotor reactions are observed.

Usual Pediatric Dose

Safety and efficacy have not been established in children less than 5 years of age.

Limited clinical data is available on the use of the *Usual adult dose* in pediatric patients 5 to 18 years of age.

Usual Geriatric Dose

See *Usual adult dose.*

Usual geriatric prescribing limits

See *Usual adult prescribing limits.*

Strength(s) usually available

U.S.—
1 mg per 1 mL (Rx) [*Trisenox* (sodium hydroxide (1.2 mg/mL); hydrochloric acid)].

Packaging and storage

Store at 25 °C (77 °F). Protect from freezing.

Stability

After dilution, arsenic trioxide suspension is chemically and physically stable when stored for 24 hours at room temperature and 48 hours when refrigerated. Discard unused portion of vial.

Note

Arsenic trioxide should only be diluted in 5% Dextrose or 0.9% Sodium Chloride, USP.

Revised: 05/10/2006
Developed: 12/01/2000

ARTICAINE—See *Anesthetics (Parenteral-Local)*

ASPARAGINASE Systemic

VA CLASSIFICATION (Primary): AN900

Commonly used brand name(s): *Elspar; Kidrolase.*

Another commonly used name is colaspase.

Note: For a listing of dosage forms and brand names by country availability, see *Dosage Forms* section(s).

Category

Antineoplastic.

Indications

Note: Bracketed information in the *Indications* section refers to uses that are not included in U.S. product labeling.

Accepted

Leukemia, acute lymphocytic (treatment)—Asparaginase is indicated, in combination with other agents, for induction of remissions in acute lymphocytic leukemia (primarily in pediatric patients). It is recommended that asparaginase not be used as part of a maintenance regimen because of the rapid development of resistance (as cells develop the capability to synthesize asparagine) to the medication.

[Lymphomas, non-Hodgkin's (treatment)]—Asparaginase is used for treatment of lymphosarcoma and reticulum cell sarcoma (reticulosarcoma).

Pharmacology/Pharmacokinetics

Physicochemical characteristics

Source—Asparaginase is a high molecular weight enzyme obtained commercially from *Escherichia coli.*

Mechanism of action/Effect

Asparaginase breaks down extracellular asparagine, which is required for cell survival, to aspartic acid and ammonia. Normal cells are capable of synthesizing their own asparagine but certain malignant cells are not. Asparaginase interferes with protein synthesis and also with DNA and RNA synthesis, and appears to be cell cycle–specific for the G_1 phase of cell division. Cell death then results from fragmentation of the cell into membrane-bound particles that are eliminated by phagocytosis.

Other actions/effects

Has immunosuppressant activity in animals.

Distribution

Crosses the blood-brain barrier to only a limited extent; cerebrospinal fluid concentrations are less than 1% of concurrent plasma concentrations; slow sequestration by the reticuloendothelial system.

Half-life

Intramuscular—39 to 49 hours.

Intravenous—8 to 30 hours.

Onset of action

Blood concentrations of asparagine fall to undetectable levels almost immediately after administration of asparaginase. Normal or below-normal leukocyte counts are noted frequently within the first several days after treatment with asparaginase is started.

Time to peak plasma concentration

After intramuscular administration—14 to 24 hours.

Duration of action

Concentrations of asparagine in the blood remain low for 7 to 10 days after discontinuation of therapy with asparaginase.

Elimination

Unknown; only trace amounts appear in the urine following intravenous administration.

Precautions to Consider

Cross-sensitivity and/or related problems

In one study, cross-sensitivity between commercially available asparaginase and one product for investigational use derived from *Erwinia carotovora* was reported in 22.6% of patients. Allergic reactions included urticaria, tachypnea, wheezing, shortness of breath, pruritus, and tachycardia.

Carcinogenicity

Secondary malignancies are potential delayed effects of many antineoplastic agents, although it is not clear whether the effect is related to their mutagenic or immunosuppressive action. The effect of dose and duration of therapy is also unknown, although risk seems to increase with long-term use. Although information is limited, available data seem to indicate that the carcinogenic risk is greatest with the alkylating agents.

Intraperitoneal administration of 2500 Units of asparaginase per kg of body weight per day for 4 days reportedly caused a small increase in pulmonary adenomas in newborn Swiss mice.

Mutagenicity

Asparaginase was not found to be mutagenic at concentrations of 152 to 909 international units (IU) per plate in the Ames microbial mutagen test with or without metabolic activation.

Pregnancy/Reproduction

Pregnancy—Adequate and well-controlled studies in humans have not been done.

First trimester: It usually is recommended that use of antineoplastics, especially combination chemotherapy, be avoided whenever possible, especially during the first trimester. Although information is limited because of the relatively few instances of antineoplastic administration during pregnancy, the teratogenic and carcinogenic potential of these medications must be considered.

Other hazards to the fetus include adverse reactions seen in adults.

In general, use of a contraceptive is recommended during cytotoxic drug therapy.

Studies in mice and rats have shown that asparaginase, given in doses of greater than 1000 IU per kg of body weight (the recommended human dose), retards the weight gain of mothers and fetuses and causes resorptions, gross abnormalities, and skeletal abnormalities. Dose-dependent embryotoxicity and gross abnormalities also have been reported with intravenous administration of 50 or 100 IU of asparaginase per kg of body weight to pregnant rabbits on days 8 and 9 of gestation.

FDA Pregnancy Category C.

Breast-feeding

It is not known whether asparaginase is distributed into breast milk. Although very little information is available regarding distribution of antineoplastic agents into breast milk, breast-feeding is not recommended while asparaginase is being administered because of the risks to the infant (adverse effects, carcinogenicity).

Pediatrics

Appropriate studies performed to date have not demonstrated pediatrics-specific problems that would limit the usefulness of asparaginase in children. In fact, incidence of toxicity appears to be lower in pediatric patients than in adult patients.

Geriatrics

No information is available on the relationship of age to the effects of asparaginase in geriatric patients.

Dental

Asparaginase may cause stomatitis associated with considerable discomfort.

Drug interactions and/or related problems

The following drug interactions and/or related problems have been selected on the basis of their potential clinical significance (possible mechanism in parentheses where appropriate)—not necessarily inclusive (» = major clinical significance):

Note: Combinations containing any of the following medications, depending on the amount present, may also interact with this medication.

Allopurinol or
Colchicine or
» Probenecid or
» Sulfinpyrazone
(asparaginase may raise the concentration of blood uric acid; dosage adjustment of antigout agents may be necessary to control hyperuricemia and gout; allopurinol may be preferred to prevent or reverse asparaginase-induced hyperuricemia because of risk of uric acid nephropathy with uricosuric antigout agents)

Antidiabetic agents, sulfonylurea or
Insulin
(asparaginase may alter blood glucose concentrations; for adult-onset diabetics, dosage adjustment of hypoglycemic medications may be necessary during and after asparaginase therapy)

Corticosteroids, glucocorticoid, especially prednisone or
» Vincristine
(concurrent use may enhance the hyperglycemic effect of asparaginase and may increase the risk of neuropathy and disturbances in erythropoiesis; toxicity appears to be less pronounced when asparaginase is administered after vincristine and prednisone rather than before or with these medications)

Immunosuppressant medications, other, such as:
Azathioprine
Chlorambucil
Cyclophosphamide
Cyclosporine
Mercaptopurine
Muromonab-CD3 or
Radiation therapy
(concurrent use with asparaginase may increase the total effects of these medications and radiation therapy; dosage reduction may be required)

» Methotrexate
(asparaginase may block the effects of methotrexate by inhibiting cell replication; this inhibition of methotrexate's action appears to correlate with suppression of asparagine concentrations. Some studies indicate that administration of asparaginase 9 to 10 days before or within 24 hours after methotrexate administration does not produce this inhibition of antineoplastic effect and may reduce the gastrointestinal and hematological effects of methotrexate)

Vaccines, killed virus
(because normal defense mechanisms may be suppressed by asparaginase therapy, the patient's antibody response to the vaccine may be decreased. The interval between discontinuation of medications that cause immunosuppression and restoration of the patient's ability to respond to the vaccine depends on the intensity and type of immunosuppression-causing medication used, the underlying disease, and other factors; estimates vary from 3 months to 1 year)

» Vaccines, live virus
(because normal defense mechanisms may be suppressed by asparaginase therapy, concurrent use with a live virus vaccine may potentiate the replication of the vaccine virus, may increase the side/adverse effects of the vaccine virus, and/or may decrease the patient's antibody response to the vaccine; immunization of these patients should be undertaken only with extreme caution after careful review of the patient's hematologic status and only with the knowledge and consent of the physician managing the asparaginase therapy. The interval between discontinuation of medications that cause immunosuppression and restoration of the patient's ability to respond to the vaccine depends on the intensity and type of immunosuppression-causing medication used, the underlying disease, and other factors; estimates vary from 3 months to 1 year. Patients with leukemia in remission should not receive live virus vaccine until at least 3 months after their last chemotherapy. In addition, immunization with oral poliovirus vaccine should be postponed in persons in close contact with the patient, especially family members)

Laboratory value alterations

The following have been selected on the basis of their potential clinical significance (possible effect in parentheses where appropriate)—not necessarily inclusive (» = major clinical significance).

With diagnostic test results
Thyroid function tests
(results may be altered because asparaginase decreases serum thyroxine-binding globulin concentrations within 2 days after the first dose; concentrations return to normal within 4 weeks of the last dose of asparaginase)

With physiology/laboratory test values
Ammonia concentrations, blood and
Blood urea nitrogen (BUN) concentrations
(may be increased because of breakdown of asparagine)

Cholesterol
(serum concentrations may be reversibly decreased; increases and decreases of total lipids have occurred)

Medical considerations/Contraindications

The medical considerations/contraindications included have been selected on the basis of their potential clinical significance (reasons given in parentheses where appropriate)—not necessarily inclusive (» = major clinical significance).

Except under special circumstances, this medication should not be used when the following medical problems exist:

» Pancreatitis, or history of
(potentially fatal acute hemorrhagic pancreatitis has been associated with asparaginase treatment)

» Previous allergic reaction to asparaginase

Risk-benefit should be considered when the following medical problems exist:

» Chickenpox, existing or recent (including recent exposure) or
» Herpes zoster
(risk of severe generalized disease)

Diabetes mellitus
(asparaginase may increase blood glucose concentrations)

Gout, history of or
Urate renal stones, history of
(asparaginase may increase serum uric acid concentrations)

» Hepatic function impairment
(may be increased by asparaginase)

» Infection
(immunosuppressive effects)

» Caution should be used also in patients who have had previous cytotoxic drug therapy and radiation therapy.

Patient monitoring

The following may be especially important in patient monitoring (other tests may be warranted in some patients, depending on condition; » = major clinical significance):

» Amylase concentrations, serum and
Bone marrow aspiration studies and
» Central nervous system (CNS) function, clinical and
» Coagulation tests, plasma and
Glucose concentrations, blood and
Hepatic function and
Peripheral blood count and
Renal function and
Uric acid concentrations, serum
(recommended at the initiation of therapy and at frequent intervals during therapy)

Side/Adverse Effects

Note: Incidence of toxicity appears to be greater in adult patients than in pediatric patients.

The following side/adverse effects have been selected on the basis of their potential clinical significance (possible signs and symptoms in parentheses where appropriate)—not necessarily inclusive:

Those indicating need for medical attention

Incidence more frequent

Allergic reaction (trouble in breathing; joint pain; puffy face; skin rash or itching); ***decrease in blood clotting factors*** (unusual bleeding or bruising)—usually asymptomatic; ***hepatotoxicity, including fatty changes***—asymptomatic; ***pancreatitis*** (severe stomach pain with nausea and vomiting)

Note: *Allergic reactions* occur frequently and may be severe or even fatal. The risk is increased with repeated doses, but may occur on initial administration, including during desensitization.

An *allergic reaction* to a therapeutic dose may occur even after a negative reaction to the intradermal skin test. Rarely, an anaphylactic reaction to the intradermal skin test itself may occur.

Anaphylaxis may be less common after intramuscular than after intravenous administration in children with advanced leukemia (although incidence of mild allergic reactions may be increased), or when asparaginase is given in combination with immunosuppressive agents.

The most common and most marked *decreases in blood clotting factors* occur in fibrinogen and factors V and VIII, with a variable decrease in factors VII and IX. Bleeding is rare, but intracranial hemorrhage and fatal bleeding have been reported. A compensatory increase in fibrinolytic activity has also occurred.

Hepatotoxicity usually occurs within 2 weeks of start of treatment.

Incidence less frequent

CNS effects, reversible (confusion; drowsiness; hallucinations; mental depression; nervousness; unusual tiredness); ***hyperglycemia*** (frequent urination; unusual thirst); ***hyperuricemia or uric acid nephropathy*** (lower back or side pain; swelling of feet or lower legs); ***hypoalbuminemia or renal failure*** (swelling of feet or lower legs); ***stomatitis*** (sores in mouth and on lips)

Note: *CNS effects* occur mostly in adults, in whom incidence may be as high as 30 to 60%; they usually occur within the first day of treatment and subside 1 to 3 days after asparaginase is withdrawn.

Hyperglycemia resembles hyperosmolar, nonketotic hyperglycemia. It usually responds to withdrawal of asparaginase and appropriate treatment, but may occasionally be fatal.

Hyperuricemia or uric acid nephropathy occurs most commonly during initial treatment of patients with leukemia or lymphoma, as a result of rapid cell breakdown leading to elevated serum uric acid concentrations.

Azotemia, usually pre-renal, occurs frequently. Fatal *renal insufficiency* has been reported.

Incidence rare

Hyperthermia (fever or chills); ***immunosuppression*** (infection); ***intracranial hemorrhage or thrombosis*** (severe headache; inability to move arm or leg); ***leg vein thrombosis*** (pain in lower legs); ***leukopenia***

Note: *Leukopenia* may be marked but bone marrow depression is transient.

Hyperthermia may be fatal.

Those indicating need for medical attention only if they continue or are bothersome

Incidence more frequent

Hyperammonemia (mild headache; loss of appetite; nausea or vomiting; stomach cramps; weight loss)

Those indicating the need for medical attention if they occur after medication is discontinued

Intracranial hemorrhage or thrombosis (severe headache; inability to move arm or leg); ***pancreatitis*** (severe stomach pain with nausea and vomiting)

Patient Consultation

As an aid to patient consultation, refer to *Advice for the Patient, Asparaginase (Systemic).*

In providing consultation, consider emphasizing the following selected information (» = major clinical significance):

Before using this medication

» Conditions affecting use, especially:
- Sensitivity to asparaginase
- Pregnancy—Embryotoxicity and abnormalities reported in animals; advisability of using contraception; telling physician immediately if pregnancy is suspected
- Breast-feeding—Not recommended because of risk of serious side effects
- Other medications, especially probenecid, sulfinpyrazone, or previous cytotoxic drug or radiation therapy
- Other medical problems, especially chickenpox, herpes zoster, pancreatitis, hepatic function impairment, or infection

Proper use of this medication

Caution with combination therapy; taking each medication at the right time

Importance of ample fluid intake and subsequent increase in urine output to aid in excretion of uric acid

Possible nausea, vomiting, and loss of appetite; importance of continuing medication despite stomach upset

» Proper dosing

Precautions while using this medication

» Importance of close monitoring by physician

» Avoiding immunizations unless approved by physician; other persons in patient's household should avoid immunizations with oral poliovirus vaccine; avoiding persons who have taken oral poliovirus vaccine or wearing a protective mask that covers nose and mouth

Caution if thyroid function test required; possible interference with test results

Side/adverse effects

Importance of discussing possible adverse effects, including cancer, with physician

Signs of potential side effects, especially allergic reaction, decrease in blood clotting factors, hepatotoxicity, pancreatitis, CNS effects, hyperglycemia, hyperuricemia or uric acid nephropathy, hypoalbuminemia or renal failure, stomatitis, hyperthermia, immunosuppression, intracranial hemorrhage or thrombosis, leg vein thrombosis, and leukopenia

Asymptomatic side effects, including hepatotoxicity

Physician or nurse can help in dealing with side effects

General Dosing Information

It is recommended that asparaginase be administered to patients only in a hospital setting under the supervision of a physician experienced in cancer chemotherapy. It is also recommended that equipment and medications (including epinephrine, diphenhydramine, oxygen, and intravenous steroids) necessary for treatment of a possible anaphylactic reaction be immediately available during each administration of asparaginase.

A variety of dosage schedules and regimens of asparaginase, alone or in combination with other antitumor agents, are used. The prescriber may consult the medical literature as well as the manufacturer's literature in choosing a specific dosage.

Dosage must be adjusted to meet the individual requirements of each patient, on the basis of clinical response and appearance or severity of toxicity.

Although the intradermal skin test has not been found entirely reliable in predicting allergic reactions to asparaginase, it is recommended that this test be performed prior to the initial administration of asparaginase and when a week or more has passed between doses. The test solution is prepared by adding 5 mL of sterile water for injection or 0.9% sodium chloride injection to the 10,000–International Unit (IU) vial of asparaginase, shaking to dissolve, and withdrawing 0.1 mL of the resulting solution (2000 IU per mL) and injecting it into another vial containing 9.9 mL of diluent to produce a test solution containing approximately 20 IU per mL. An intradermal injection of 0.1 mL (about 2 IU) is administered and the site observed for 1 hour for the appearance of a wheal or erythema, which indicates a positive reaction.

It is recommended that a desensitization method of administration of the first dose be utilized in patients who have had a positive reaction to the intradermal skin test and on re-treatment of a patient with asparaginase. A recommended schedule begins with the intravenous administration of 1 IU and doubles the dosage every 10 minutes, provided no allergic reaction has occurred, until the accumulated total dosage equals the dosage for that day.

It is recommended that when asparaginase is administered intravenously, it be given over a period of not less than 30 minutes through the side arm of an already running infusion of 0.9% sodium chloride injection or 5% dextrose injection. Asparaginase should not be infused through a filter. However, if gelatinous fiber-like particles develop on standing, reconstituted asparaginase may be filtered through a 5-micron filter during administration without loss in potency. Use of a 0.2-micron filter may result in a loss of potency.

No more than 2 mL of asparaginase solution should be injected at a single intramuscular injection site.

Development of uric acid nephropathy in patients with leukemia or lymphoma may be prevented by adequate oral hydration and, in some cases, administration of allopurinol. Alkalinization of urine may be necessary if serum uric acid concentrations are elevated.

If pancreatitis occurs, it is recommended that asparaginase therapy be permanently discontinued.

Safety considerations for handling this medication

There is limited but increasing evidence and concern that personnel involved in preparation and administration of parenteral antineoplastics may be at some risk because of the potential mutagenicity, teratogenicity, and/or carcinogenicity of these agents, although the actual risk is unknown. USP advisory panels recommend cautious handling both in preparation and disposal of antineoplastic agents. Precautions that have been suggested include:
- Use of a biological containment cabinet during reconstitution and dilution of parenteral medications and wearing of disposable surgical gloves and masks.
- Use of proper technique to prevent contamination of the medication, work area, and operator during transfer between containers (including proper training of personnel in this technique).
- Cautious and proper disposal of needles, syringes, vials, ampuls, and unused medication.

A number of medical centers have developed detailed guidelines for handling of antineoplastic agents.

Combination chemotherapy

Asparaginase may be used in combination with other agents in various regimens. As a result, incidence and/or severity of side effects may be altered and different dosages (usually reduced) may be used.

Parenteral Dosage Forms

ASPARAGINASE FOR INJECTION

Usual adult dose

Acute lymphocytic leukemia—

Induction: Intravenous, 200 IU per kg of body weight a day for twenty-eight days.

Note: Because use of asparaginase in adults is primarily investigational at this time, the prescriber should consult the medical literature in choosing a specific dosage.

Usual pediatric dose

Acute lymphocytic leukemia—

Intramuscular, 6000 IU per square meter of body surface on days 4, 7, 10, 13, 16, 19, 22, 25, and 28 of the treatment period, in combination with vincristine and prednisone or

Intravenous, 1000 IU per kg of body weight per day for ten days beginning on day 22 of the treatment period, in combination with vincristine and prednisone.

Note: Many dosage regimens of asparaginase are in use at this time. A review of all of them is impossible in this space. Consultation of current medical literature is recommended. Use of asparaginase as the sole induction agent generally is not recommended unless combination therapy is considered inappropriate.

Strength(s) usually available

U.S.—

10,000 IU (Rx) [*Elspar* (mannitol 80 mg)].

Canada—

10,000 IU (Rx) [*Kidrolase*].

Packaging and storage

Store between 2 and 8 °C (36 and 46 °F).

Preparation of dosage form

Caution: Asparaginase is a contact irritant, and both the powder and solution should be handled with care to prevent inhalation of dust or vapors or contact with skin or mucous membranes (especially eyes). If accidental contact occurs, the affected area should be flushed with water for at least 15 minutes.

Elspar is reconstituted for intravenous use by adding 5 mL of sterile water for injection or 0.9% sodium chloride injection to a vial containing 10,000 IU of asparaginase and shaking to dissolve the medication. (Caution: Overly vigorous shaking may cause foaming and difficulty in withdrawing the contents of the vial.) Only a clear solution should be used. The resulting colorless solution, containing 2000 IU of asparaginase per mL, may be used for direct intravenous administration within 8 hours of reconstitution, provided the solution remains clear, or may be further diluted with 0.9% sodium chloride injection or 5% dextrose injection for administration by intravenous infusion. The infusion solution may also be used within 8 hours, provided it remains clear.

Elspar is reconstituted for intramuscular use by adding 2 mL of 0.9% sodium chloride injection to the 10,000-IU vial. The resulting solution should be used within 8 hours provided it remains clear.

If gelatinous fiber-like particles develop on standing, reconstituted *Elspar* may be filtered through a 5-micron filter during administration without loss in potency. Use of a 0.2-micron filter may result in a loss of potency.

Kidrolase is reconstituted for intramuscular or intravenous use by adding 4 mL of sterile water for injection to a vial containing 10,000 IU of asparaginase and rotating gently to dissolve the medication. (Caution: Rotate gently; do not shake.) The resulting solution may be further diluted with 0.9% sodium chloride injection or isotonic glucose solution for administration by intravenous infusion.

Stability

Elspar—Contains no preservative. Unused, reconstituted solution should be stored at 2 to 8 °C (36 to 46 °F) and discarded after 8 hours or sooner if it becomes cloudy.

Kidrolase—Unused, reconstituted solution may be stored at 2 to 8 °C (36 to 46 °F) for 14 days.

Revised: 09/26/1997

ASPIRIN—See *Salicylates (Systemic)*

ASPIRIN, BUFFERED—See *Salicylates (Systemic)*

ATAZANAVIR Systemic†

VA CLASSIFICATION (Primary): AM830

Commonly used brand name(s): *REYATAZ*.

Note: For a listing of dosage forms and brand names by country availability, see *Dosage Forms* section(s).

†Not commercially available in Canada.

Category

Antiviral (systemic).

Indications

Accepted

Human immunodeficiency virus (HIV) infection (treatment)—Atazanavir sulfate is indicated in combination with other antiretroviral agents for the treatment of HIV-1 infection.

The use of atazanavir sulfate may be considered in antiretroviral-treatment experienced adults with HIV strains that are expected to be susceptible to atazanavir sulfate by genotypic and phenotypic testing.

Pharmacology/Pharmacokinetics

Physicochemical characteristics

Molecular weight—

Atazanavir (sulfuric acid salt): 802.9.

Atazanavir (free base): 704.9.

pH—1.9 at 24 ± 3 °C

Solubility—slightly soluble in water (4 to 5 mg/mL, free base equivalent).

Mechanism of action/Effect

Atazanavir is an azapeptide HIV-1 protease inhibitor. It prevents formation of mature virions by selectively inhibiting the virus-specific processing of viral Gag and Gag-Pol polyproteins in HIV-1 infected cells

Absorption

Atazanavir is rapidly absorbed with a T_{max} of approximately 2.5 hours. Administration with food enhances bioavailability and reduces pharmacokinetic variability. A single dose of 400 mg with a light meal resulted in a 70% increase in AUC and 57% increase in C_{max} relative to the fasting state, while the same dose administered with a high fat meal resulted in a mean increase AUC of 35% with no change in C_{max} relative to the fasting state. Administration with either a light meal or high fat meal decreased the coefficient of variation of AUC and C_{max} by approximately one half compared to the fasting state

Distribution

In a multiple dose study in HIV infected patients given 400 mg once daily with a light meal for 12 weeks, atazanavir was found in cerebrospinal fluid and semen. The cerebrospinal fluid/plasma ratio for atazanavir (n=4) ranged between 0.0021 and 0.0226 and seminal fluid/plasma ratio (n=5) ranged between 0.11 and 4.42

Serum protein binding

High (86%); binds to alpha-1-acid glycoprotein and albumin

Biotransformation

Atazanavir is extensively metabolized in humans. *In vitro* studies suggest that atazanavir is metabolized by CYP3A. Atazanavir inhibits CYP3A and UGT1A1.

The major biotransformation pathways of atazanavir consist of monooxygenation and dioxygenation. Other minor biotransformation pathways for atazanavir or its metabolites consist of glucuronidation, N-dealkylation, hydrolysis, and oxygenation with dehydrogenation. Two minor metabolites in plasma have been characterized, however neither metabolite demonstrated *in vitro* antiviral activity.

Half-life

Adults (healthy and HIV infected)—

Elimination—approximately 7 hours (following a 400 mg daily dose with a light meal)

Hepatically impaired—

Elimination—12.1 hours (following a single 400 mg dose)

Time to peak concentration

Healthy patients—2.5 hours

HIV-Infected patients—2 hours

Peak plasma concentration

Healthy subjects—5199 nanograms/mL on Day 29 following a 400 mg daily dose with a light meal

HIV-Infected patients—2298 nanograms/mL on Day 29 following a 400 mg daily dose with a light meal

Elimination

Fecal; 79% total with approximately 20% of the administered dose unchanged drug

Renal; 13% total with approximately 7% of the administered dose unchanged drug

Precautions to Consider

Carcinogenicity/Mutagenicity

Long-term carcinogenicity studies of atazanavir in animals have not been completed. In an *in vitro* clastogenicity test using primary human lymphocytes atazanavir tested positive. However, atazanavir tested negative in the *in vitro* Ames reverse-mutation assay, *in vivo* micronucleus and DNA repair tests in rats, and *in vivo* damage test in rat duodenum.

Pregnancy/Reproduction

Fertility—No significant effects on mating, fertility, or early embryonic development were produced in rats given daily doses equal to or two times those at the human clinical dose of 400 mg/daily.

Pregnancy—*An Antiretroviral Pregnancy Registry has been established to monitor the maternal-fetal outcomes of pregnant women exposed to zalcitabine. Physicians are encouraged to register patients by calling (800) 258-4263.*

Adequate and well controlled studies in pregnant women have not been done. Atazanavir should be used in pregnancy only if the potential benefit to the mother justifies the potential risk to the fetus.

Cases of lactic acidosis syndrome, sometimes fatal, and symptomatic hyperlactatemia have been reported in patients (including pregnant women) receiving atazanavir in combination with nucleoside analogues. Nucleoside analogues are known to increase risk of of lactic acidosis syndrome.

Increased rates of hyperbilirubinemia has also occurred during treatment with atazanavir. It is not known if atazanavir treatment to the mother during pregnancy will exacerbate physiological hyperbilirubinemia and lead to kernicterus in neonates and young infants. Therefore, additional monitoring and alternative therapy should be considered in the prepartum period.

In studies with rabbits and rats given maternal doses producing drug exposure levels equal to or two times the human clinical dose of 400 mg once daily, atazanavir did not produce teratogenic effects. However pre- and postnatal studies in rats given a maternally toxic exposure levels, two times the human clinical dose caused weight loss or weight gain suppression in the offspring.

FDA Pregnancy Category B

Breast-feeding

It is not known whether atazanavir is distributed into human breast milk. However, atazanavir is distributed into the milk of rats. Because of both the potential for HIV transmission and the potential for serious adverse reactions in the nursing infant, mothers should be instructed not to breast-feed if receiving atazanavir.

Pediatrics

The use of atazanavir in pediatric population has not been established. Atazanavir should not be administered to children under the age of 3 months due to the risk of kernicterus.

Geriatrics

No information is available on the relationship of age to the effects of atazanavir in geriatric patients. However, elderly patients are more likely to have age related renal function impairment, which may require caution and monitoring in patients receiving atazanavir.

Pharmacogenetics

In studies done there were no clinically important pharmacokinetic differences due to gender, and there is insufficient data to determine whether there are any effects on race.

Drug interactions and/or related problems

The following drug interactions and/or related problems have been selected on the basis of their potential clinical significance (possible mechanism in parentheses where appropriate)—not necessarily inclusive (» = major clinical significance):

Atazanavir inhibits CYP3A and UGT1A1.

Note: Combinations containing any of the following medications, depending on the amount present, may also interact with this medication.

» Amiodarone, or
» Bepridil or
» Lidocaine (systemic), or
» Quinidine, or
(may increase antiarrhythmic drug concentration resulting in potential for serious or life-threatening adverse events; caution; concentration monitoring is recommended)

» Antiacids, or
» Buffered medicines
(lower plasma concentrations of atazanavir; atazanavir should be administered 2 hours before or 1 hour after taking these medicines)

» Atorvastatin
(may increase atorvastatin drug concentration resulting in increased risk of myopathy including rhabdomyolysis; use with caution)

» Cisapride, or
» Pimozide
(contraindicated; potential for serious or life-threatening events such as cardiac arrhythmias)

» Clarithromycin
(increased concentrations of clarithromycin may cause QTc prolongations; dose reduction of clarithromycin should be considered; concentrations of the active metabolite 14–OH clarithromycin are significantly reduced; increased concentrations of atazanavir; alternative therapy for indications other than infections due to *Mycobacteria avium* complex should be considered)

» Cyclosporine, or
» Sirolimus, or
» Tacrolimus
(may increase immunosuppressant drug concentration; monitoring for therapeutic concentrations of immunosuppressant agents is recommended when coadministered with atazanavir)

CYP3A inducer
(may increase the clearance of atazanavir resulting in lower plasma concentrations)

CYP3A inhibitor
(may increase atazanavir plasma concentrations)

» Didanosine
(coadministration decreases the exposure of atazanavir due to the increased pH caused by the buffers; because didanosine is given on an empty stomach and atazanavir is to be given with food, they should be administered at different times)

» Dihydroergotamine, or
» Ergonovine, or
» Ergotamine, or
» Methylergonovine, or
(contraindicated; potential for serious or life-threatening events such as acute ergot toxicity characterized by peripheral vasospasm and ischemia of the extremities and other tissues)

» Diltiazem
(may increase diltiazem and desacetyl-diltiazem concentrations; caution; a dose reduction of diltiazem should be considered and ECG monitoring is recommended)

» Efavirenz
(decreases atazanavir exposure; it is recommended that atazanavir with ritonavir should be coadministered with efavirenz)

» Felodipine, or
» Nicardipine, or
» Nifedipine, or
» Verapamil
(may increase calcium channel blocker drug concentration; caution; dose titration of calcium channel blocker should be considered and ECG monitoring is recommended)

» H_2-Receptor antagonists
(reduced plasma concentrations of atazanavir may result in loss of therapeutic effect and development of resistance, administer as far apart as possible, preferably 12 hours)

» Indinavir
(should not be administered concomitantly; associated with indirect hyperbilirubinemia)

» Irinotecan
(should not be administered concomitantly; inhibits UGT and may interfere with metabolism, resulting in increased irinotecan toxicities)

Ketoconazole or
Itraconazole
(use cautiously with atazanavir plus ritonavir; concomitant use may increase antifungal concentrations)

» Lovastatin, or
» Simvastatin
(should not be administered concomitantly; potential for serious reactions such as myopathy including rhabdomyolysis)

» Midazolam, or
» Triazolam
(contraindicated; potential for serious or life-threatening events such as prolonged or increased sedation or respiratory depression)

Nevirapine
(coadministration not recommended; may decrease atazanavir exposure)

» Oral contraceptives, containing ethinyl estradiol and norethindrone
(concentrations of oral contraceptives increase; alternate methods of non hormonal contraception are recommended)

» Proton-Pump Inhibitors
(concomitant use is not recommended; substantial decreases in atazanavir concentrations and reductions in its therapeutic effects)

» Rifabutin
(increases rifabutin concentrations; dose reduction of rifabutin is recommended)

» Rifampin
(decreases plasma concentrations and AUC of most protease inhibitors by approximately 90%; this may result in loss of therapeutic effect of atazanavir and development of viral resistance)

» Ritonavir
(increases atazanavir concentrations; reduce dose of atazanavir)

» Saquinavir
(increases saquinavir concentration; dosing for coadministration with respect to efficacy and safety have not been established)

» Sildenafil or
» Tadalafil or
» Vardenafil
(increase in PDE 5 inhibitor concentrations may result in adverse events such as hypotension, visual changes and priapism; caution; reduce dose of PDE 5 inhibitor and monitor for adverse events)

» St. John's wort
(should not be administered concomitantly; it may reduce the plasma concentrations of atazanavir, which may result in loss of therapeutic effects and development of resistance)

Tenofovir
(decrease atazanavir exposure; if tenofovir is coadministered with atazanavir, it is recommended that it be coadministered with ritonavir)

» Tricyclic antidepressants
(may increase tricyclic antidepressant drug concentrations resulting in potential for serious or life-threatening adverse events; caution; concentration monitoring is recommended)

» Voriconazole
(voriconazole should not be administered with atazanavir plus ritonavir; concomitant use of voriconazole with atazanavir (without ritonavir) may increase atazanavir concentrations)

» Warfarin
(may increase warfarin drug concentration which may result in the potential for serious or life-threatening bleeding event; caution; International Normalization Ratio [INR] should be monitored)

Medical considerations/Contraindications

The medical considerations/contraindications included have been selected on the basis of their potential clinical significance (reasons given in parentheses where appropriate)—not necessarily inclusive (» = major clinical significance).

Except under special circumstances, this medication should not be used when the following medical problem exists:

» Hypersensitivity to atazanavir or any of the ingredients contained in the tablet

Risk-benefit should be considered when the following medical problems exist:

» Atrioventricular (AV) conduction abnormalities, preexisting
(caution; atazanavir has been shown to prolong the PR interval of the electrocardiogram)

» Diabetes mellitus, or
» Hyperglycemia
(new-onset or exacerbation of preexisting diabetes may occur; initiation or dose adjustments of insulin or oral hypoglycemic agents may be required)

» Hemophilia, type A and B
(increased bleeding, including spontaneous skin hematomas and hemarthrosis may occur)

» Hepatic function impairment
(caution; atazanavir drug concentration may increase; reduce atazanavir dose in patients with moderate hepatic insufficiency; atazanavir should not be used in patients with severe hepatic insufficiency)

» Hepatitis B, or
» Hepatitis C, or
» Transaminase, elevated
(increased risk for developing further transaminase elevations or hepatic decompensations)

» Obesity
(Obesity and female gender are known risk factors for lactic acidosis in patients receiving atazanavir in combination with nucleoside analogues)

Patient monitoring

The following may be especially important in patient monitoring (other tests may be warranted in some patients, depending on condition; » = major clinical significance):

Alanine aminotransferase, serum (ALT [SGPT]), or
Aspartate aminotransferase, serum (AST [SGOT]), or
Alkaline phosphatase, serum or
Amylase or
Bilirubin, total or
Lipase
(monitor in patients with hepatitis B or C; elevations that occur with hyperbilirubinemia should be evaluated for alternative etiologies, and alternative therapy may be considered if jaundice or scleral icterus associated with bilirubin elevations present cosmetic concerns)

Electrocardiogram (ECG)
(atazanavir has been shown to prolong the PR interval of the electrocardiogram, there was no effect of atazanavir on the QTc interval; evaluate patients with symptoms of dizziness or light-headedness or patients on concomitant medications that may prolong the PR interval)

International Normalization Ratio (INR)
(monitoring recommended if atazanavir is coadministered with warfarin)

Side/Adverse Effects

The following side/adverse effects have been selected on the basis of their potential clinical significance (possible signs and symptoms in parentheses where appropriate)—not necessarily inclusive:

The redistribution or accumulation of body fat, including central obesity, dorsocervical fat enlargement (buffalo hump), peripheral wasting, breast enlargement, and "cushingoid appearance" have been reported in patients on protease inhibitor therapy. A causal relationship between these events and use of protease inhibitors has not been confirmed.

Cases of lactic acidosis syndrome (LAS), sometimes fatal, and symptomatic hyperlactatemia have been reported in patients receiving atazanavir in combination with nucleoside analogues, which are associated with increase risk of LAS. Obesity and female gender are also risk factors for LAS. The contribution of atazanavir to the risk of development of LAS has not been established.

Those indicating need for medical attention

Incidence not determined—Observed during clinical practice; estimates of frequency cannot be determined

Allergic reaction (chills; hives; fever; shortness of breath; tightness in chest; trouble in breathing; wheezing; skin rash; itching); ***diabetes mellitus or hyperglycemia*** (blurred vision; dry mouth; fatigue; flushed, dry skin; fruit-like breath odor; increased hunger; increased thirst; increased urination; loss of consciousness; nausea; stomachache; sweating; troubled breathing; unexplained weight loss; vomiting)—new onset or exacerbation of; ***hyperbilirubinemia*** (yellow eyes or skin)—usually asymptomatic; ***lactic acidosis*** (abdominal discomfort; decreased appetite; diarrhea; fast, shallow breathing; general feeling of discomfort; muscle pain or cramping; nausea; shortness of breath; sleepiness; unusual tiredness or weakness); ***PR interval prolongation*** (dizziness or lightheadedness)—usually asymptomatic

Those indicating need for medical attention only if they continue or are bothersome

Incidence more frequent

Abdominal pain (stomach pain); ***back pain; cough, increased; depression*** (discouragement; feeling sad or empty; irritability; lack of appetite; loss of interest or pleasure; tiredness; trouble concentrating; trouble sleeping); ***diarrhea; headache; jaundice*** (chills; clay-colored stools; dark urine; dizziness; fever; headache; itching; loss of appetite; nausea; abdominal or stomach pain; area rash; unpleasant breath odor; unusual tiredness or weakness; vomiting of blood; yellow eyes or skin); ***lipodystrophy*** (redistribution or accumulation of body fat); ***nausea; rash; scleral icterus*** (yellowing of eyes); ***vomiting***

Incidence less frequent

Arthralgia (pain in joints; muscle pain or stiffness; difficulty in moving); ***dizziness; fatigue*** (unusual tiredness or weakness); ***fever; insomnia*** (sleeplessness; trouble sleeping; unable to sleep); ***pain; peripheral neuropathy*** (burning, numbness, tingling, or painful sensations; weakness in arms, hands, legs, or feet; unsteadiness or awkwardness)

Overdose

For more information on the management of overdose or unintentional ingestion, **contact a poison control center** (see *Charcoal, Activated (Oral-Local)*).

Clinical effects of overdose

The following effects have been selected on the basis of their potential clinical significance (possible signs and symptoms in parentheses where appropriate)—not necessarily inclusive:

Bifascicular block—asymptomatic; ***jaundice*** (chills; clay-colored stools; dark urine; dizziness; fever; headache; itching; loss of appetite; nausea; abdominal or stomach pain; area rash; unpleasant breath odor; unusual tiredness or weakness; vomiting of blood; yellow eyes or skin); ***PR interval prolongation*** (dizziness or lightheadedness)—usually asymptomatic

Treatment of overdose

Treatment is essentially symptomatic and supportive, possibly including

To decrease absorption—
Emptying stomach with emesis or gastric lavage

To enhance elimination—
Administration of activated charcoal slurry

Monitoring—
Monitoring for cardiovascular function ECG
Monitoring of vital signs
Monitoring of the patient's clinical status

Supportive care—
There is no known specific antidote for overdose with atazanavir, treatment should be symptomatic and supportive
Dialysis is unlikely to be beneficial in significant removal of atazanavir since it is metabolized by the liver and highly protein bound
Patients in whom intentional overdose is confirmed or suspected should be referred for psychiatric consultation.

Patient Consultation

As an aid to patient consultation, refer to *Advice for the Patient, Atazanavir (Systemic)*.

In providing consultation, consider emphasizing the following selected information (» = major clinical significance):

Importance of diet

Importance of taking with a small meal or snack

Before using this medication

» Conditions affecting use, especially:
Hypersensitivity to atazanavir or any of its ingredients
Pregnancy—Atazanavir should be used during pregnancy only if the benefit to the mother outweighs the potential risk to the fetus
FDA Pregnancy Category B
Breast-feeding—Not recommended, because of the potential for serious adverse reactions and postnatal transmission of HIV to the nursing infant
Use in children—Safety and effectiveness have not been established in children; atazanavir should not be administered to children under the age of 3 months due to the risk of kernicterus
Other medications, especially amiodarone, antiacids, atorvastatin, bepridil, buffered medicines, cisapride, clarithromycin, didanosine, dihydroergotamine, diltiazem, efavirenz, ergonovine, ergotamine, ethinyl estradiol and norethindrone containing oral contraceptives, felodipine, H_2-receptor antagonists, indinavir, irinotecan, itraconazole, ketoconazole, systemic lidocaine, lovastatin, methylergonovine, midazolam, nicardipine, nifedipine, pimozide, proton-pump inhibitors, quinidine, rifabutin, rifampin, ritonavir, saquinavir, sildenafil, simvastatin, St. John's wort, tadalafil, triazolam, tricyclic antidepressants, vardenafil, verapamil, voriconazole, and warfarin
Other medical problems, especially preexisting atrioventricular conduction abnormalities, preexisting diabetes mellitus or hyperglycemia, hemophilia A, hemophilia B, hepatitis B, hepatitis C, hepatic function impairment, or obesity

Proper use of this medication

» Importance of taking with a small meal or snack
» Proper dosing
Missed dose: If you miss a dose of this medicine, take it as soon as you remember. However, if it is within 6 hours of your next dose, skip the missed dose and go back to your regular dosing schedule. Do not double doses. *It is very important that you do not miss any doses of atazanavir or your other anti-HIV medicines.*
Proper storage

Precautions while using this medication

» Because atazanavir may interact with other medications, not taking any other medications (prescription or nonprescription) without first consulting your physician
» Regular visits to physician for blood tests
» Monitoring of blood glucose concentrations in patients with preexisting diabetes mellitus (sugar diabetes) or hyperglycemia (high blood glucose).

Side/adverse effects

Signs of potential side effects, especially allergic reaction, diabetes mellitus or hyperglycemia, hyperbilirubinemia, lactic acidosis, or PR interval prolongation

General Dosing Information

For oral dosing forms:

Cross-resistance among protease inhibitors has been observed, resistance to atazanavir may not preclude the subsequent use of other protease inhibitors

Diet/Nutrition

Taking with food enhances absorption and reduces pharmacokinetic variability

Combination chemotherapy

Atazanavir is used in combination with other agents in various regimens. As a result, incidence and/or severity of side effects may be altered and different dosages (usually reduced) may be used

Oral Dosage Forms

ATAZANAVIR SULFATE CAPSULES

Usual adult dose

Human immunodeficiency virus (HIV) infection (treatment)—
Therapy-Naive Patients:Oral, 400 mg (two 200-mg capsules) once daily taken with food
Therapy-Experienced Patients: Oral, 300 mg once daily plus ritonavir 100 mg once daily taken with food
Concomitant TherapyClarithromycin: Oral, atazanavir 400 mg once daily taken with food, clarithromycin 50% dose reduction
Didanosine: Atazanavir should be given 2 hours before or 1 hour after didanosine
Diltiazem: Oral, atazanavir 400 mg once daily taken with food, diltiazem 50% dose reduction
Efavirenz: Oral, atazanavir 300 mg with ritonavir 100 mg and efavirenz 600 mg once daily taken with food
Rifabutin: Oral, atazanavir 400 mg in therapy-naive patients once daily taken with food, rifabutin 150 mg every other day or three time per week
Ritonavir: Oral; atazanavir 300 mg with ritonavir 100 mg once daily with food
Sildenafil: Oral, atazanavir 400 mg once daily taken with food, sildenafil 25 mg every 48 hours
Tadalafil: Oral, atazanavir 400 mg once daily taken with food, tadalafil 10 mg every 72 hours
Tenofovir: Oral, atazanavir 300 mg with 100 mg ritonavir and 300 mg tenofovir as a single dose with food, *Atazanavir without ritonavir should not be coadministered with tenofovir*
Vardenafil: Oral atazanavir 400 mg once daily taken with food, vardenafil 2.5 mg every 72 hours

Usual pediatric dose

Safety and effectiveness of atazanavir have not been established. Atazanavir should not be administered to children under the age of 3 months due to the risk of kernicterus

Usual geriatric dose

See *Usual adult dose.*

Strength(s) usually available

U.S.—
100 mg (base) (Rx) [*REYATAZ* (ammonium hydroxide; crospovidone; dehydrated alcohol; FD&C Blue #2; gelatin; isopropyl alcohol; lactose monohydrate; magnesium stearate; n-butyl alcohol; propylene glycol; shellac; simethicone; titanium dioxide)].
150 mg (base) (Rx) [*REYATAZ* (ammonium hydroxide; crospovidone; dehydrated alcohol; FD&C Blue #2; gelatin; isopropyl alcohol; lactose monohydrate; magnesium stearate; n-butyl alcohol; propylene glycol; shellac; simethicone; titanium dioxide)].
200 mg (base) (Rx) [*REYATAZ* (ammonium hydroxide; crospovidone; dehydrated alcohol; FD&C Blue #2; gelatin; isopropyl alcohol; lactose monohydrate; magnesium stearate; n-butyl alcohol; propylene glycol; shellac; simethicone; titanium dioxide)].

Packaging and storage

Store at 25 °C (77 °F); excursions permitted between 15 to 30°C (59 to 86°F), in a child resistant container.

Auxiliary labeling

- Ask your doctor or pharmacist before using non prescription drugs
- Take with food

Revised: 08/24/2004
Developed: 01/15/2004

ATENOLOL—See *Beta-adrenergic Blocking Agents (Systemic)*

ATOMOXETINE Systemic

VA CLASSIFICATION (Primary): CN900

Commonly used brand name(s): *Strattera.*

Note: For a listing of dosage forms and brand names by country availability, see *Dosage Forms* section(s).

Category

Attention deficit hyperactivity disorder therapy agent.

Indications

Accepted

Attention-deficit hyperactivity disorder (treatment)—Atomoxetine is indicated for the treatment of attention deficit hyperactivity disorder [ADHD]. Atomoxetine is an integral part of a total treatment program for ADHD that may include other measures (psychological, educational, and social) for some patients with this syndrome.

The effectiveness of atomoxetine for more than 9 weeks in child and adolescent patients and 10 weeks in adult patients has not been systematically evaluated. The physician who elects to use atomoxetine for extended periods should periodically reevaluate the long-term usefulness of atomoxetine for the individual patient.

Note: When remedial measures (i.e., appropriate educational placement and psychosocial intervention) alone are insufficient, the decision to prescribe atomoxetine will depend upon the physician's assessment of the chronicity and severity of the patient's symptoms.

Unaccepted

Atomoxetine is not intended for use in patients who exhibit symptoms secondary to environmental factors and/or other primary psychiatric disorders, including psychosis.

Pharmacology/Pharmacokinetics

Physicochemical characteristics

Chemical Group—Cyclic, propylamine-derivative
Molecular weight—291.82.
Solubility—27.8 mg/mL in water.

Mechanism of action/Effect

Selective norepinephrine reuptake inhibitor—The exact mechanism is unknown, but it is thought to be related to selective inhibition of the presynaptic norepinephrine transporter, as determined in *ex vivo* uptake and neurotransmitter depletion studies.

Other actions/effects

Atomoxetine was **not** associated with a pattern of response that suggested stimulant or euphoriant properties.

Absorption

Rapidly absorbed; absolute bioavailability 63% in extensive metabolizers (EMs) and 94% in poor metabolizers (PMs).

Can be administered with or without food; administration with a standard high-fat meal did not affect AUC but decreased the rate of absorption resulting a 37% lower C_{max} and a delayed T_{max} by 3 hours.

Distribution

Steady-state Vol_D (intravenous administration): 0.85 L/kg

Atomoxetine distributes primarily into total body water; Vol_D is similar across patient weight range after normalizing for body weight.

Protein binding

Very high (98%); primarily bound to albumin

Biotransformation

Liver: Extensively metabolized, primarily through the CYP2D6 enzymatic pathway. A fraction of the population (about 7% of Caucasians and 2% of African-Americans) are poor metabolizers (PMs) of CYP2D6 drugs. These individuals have reduced activity in this pathway resulting in 10-fold higher AUCs, 5-fold higher peak plasma concentrations, and slower elimination (plasma half-life of about 24 hours) of atomoxetine compared with those who have normal activity (extensive metabolizers [EMs]).

The major oxidative metabolite (regardless of CYP2D6) is 4-Hydroxyatomoxetine, which is glucuronidated. 4-Hydroxyatomoxetine is equipotent to atomoxetine as in inhibitor of the norepinephrine transporter but circulates in plasma at much lower concentrations (1% of atomoxetine concentration in EMs and 0.1% of atomoxetine concentration in PMs).

4-Hydroxyatomoxetine is primarily formed by CYP2D6, but in PMs 4-hydroxyatomoxetine is formed at a slower rate by several other cytochrome P450 enzymes. N-Desmethylatomoxetine is formed by CYP2C19 and other cytochrome P450 enzymes. N-Desmethylatomoxetine is formed by CYP2C19 and other cytochrome P450 enzymes, but has substantially less pharmacological activity compared with atomoxetine and circulates in plasma at lower concentrations (5% of atomoxetine concentration in EMs and 45% of atomoxetine concentration in PMs).

Half-life

Mean: 5.2 hours for EMs; 21.6 hours for PMs
4-hydroxyatomoxetine: approximately 6 to 8 hours in EMs
N-Desmethylatomoxetine: approximately 6 to 8 hours in EMs; 30 to 40 hours in PMs

Elimination

Renal: excreted mainly as 4-hydroxyatomoxetine-*O*-glucuronide; greater than 80%
Fecal: less than 17%
3% excreted unchanged

Precautions to Consider

Carcinogenicity

Atomoxetine was not carcinogenic in rats or mice.

Mutagenicity

Atomoxetine was negative in a battery of genotoxicity studies in animals. However, there was a slight increase in the percentage of Chinese hamster ovary cells with diplochromosomes.

N-desmethylatomoxetine hydrochloride was not mutagenic by the Ames test, mouse lymphoma assay, and unscheduled DNA synthesis test.

Pregnancy/Reproduction

Fertility—Studies in rats found no effect on fertility.

Pregnancy—Adequate and well controlled studies in humans have not been done. Atomoxetine should not be used during pregnancy unless the potential benefit justifies the potential risk to the fetus.

Studies in animals have shown that atomoxetine may cause a decrease in live fetuses and an increase in early resorptions in rabbits. Also noted in rabbits were slight increases in the incidences of atypical origin of carotid artery and absent subclavian artery at doses that caused slight maternal toxicity. A decrease in pup weight, pup survival, and fetal weight and an increase in the incidence of incomplete ossification of the vertebral arch in fetuses were observed in rats.

FDA Pregnancy Category C

Labor and delivery—The effect of atomoxetine on human labor and delivery is unknown.

Labor and delivery—In rats, parturition was not affected by atomoxetine.

Breast-feeding

Caution is advised if atomoxetine is administered to a nursing mother. It is not known if atomoxetine is distributed into human breast milk. However, atomoxetine and/or its metabolites were distributed into milk of rats.

Pediatrics

Safety and efficacy have not been established in pediatric patients less than 6 years of age.

The safety and effectiveness of atomoxetine for more than 9 weeks in child and adolescent patients has not been systematically evaluated. The physician who elects to use atomoxetine for extended periods should periodically reevaluate the long-term usefulness of atomoxetine for the individual patient.

An increased risk of suicidal thinking in children and adolescents being treated with atomoxetine was identified in a combined analysis of 12 short-term placebo-controlled trials. The trials involved a total of over 2200 patients, including 1357 receiving atomoxetine and 851 receiving placebo. Compared to no events in placebo-treated patients, the average risk of suicidal thinking was about 4 per thousand patients treated with atomoxetine. Anyone considering the use of atomoxetine in a child or adolescent for ADHD must balance the increased risk of suicidal thinking with the clinical need for atomoxetine. Close observation of patients receiving atomoxetine for clinical worsening, suicidal thinking or behaviors, or unusual changes in behavior is recommended.

Geriatrics
Safety and efficacy have not been established in the geriatric population.

Pharmacogenetics
Atomoxetine is extensively metabolized, primarily through the CYP2D6 enzymatic pathway. A fraction of the population (about 7% of Caucasians and 2% of African-Americans) are poor metabolizers (PMs) of CYP2D6 drugs. These individuals have reduced activity in this pathway resulting in 10-fold higher AUCs, 5-fold higher peak plasma concentrations, and slower elimination (plasma half-life of about 24 hours) of atomoxetine compared with those who have normal activity (extensive metabolizers [EMs]).

Drug interactions and/or related problems
The following drug interactions and/or related problems have been selected on the basis of their potential clinical significance (possible mechanism in parentheses where appropriate)—not necessarily inclusive (» = major clinical significance):

Atomoxetine did not cause clinically important induction or inhibition of cytochrome P450 enzymes, including CYP1A2, CYP3A, CYP2D6, and CYP2C9.

Note: Combinations containing any of the following medications, depending on the amount present, may also interact with this medication.

» Albuterol
(may increase heart rate and blood pressure)

» CYP2D6 inhibitors, potent including:
Fluoxetine or
Paroxetine or
Quinidine
(starting dose of atomoxetine should be reduced when potent CYP2D6 inhibitors are administered concomitantly with atomoxetine in extensive metabolizer [EM] individuals)

Midazolam
(AUC for midazolam may increase by up to 15%)

» Monoamine oxidase inhibitors (MAOIs)
(atomoxetine should not be taken with an MAOI or within 2 weeks after discontinuing an MAOI; concomitant use may result in serious adverse events, including hyperthermia, rigidity, myoclonus, autonomic instability with rapid fluctuations of vital signs, and mental status changes)

» Vasopressor agents
(atomoxetine should be used cautiously with vasopressor agents because of possible effects on blood pressure)

Laboratory value alterations
The following have been selected on the basis of their potential clinical significance (possible effect in parentheses where appropriate)—not necessarily inclusive (» = major clinical significance).

» Hepatic enzymes or
» Bilirubin, serum
(may be markedly elevated according to post-marketing experience in two reported cases; lab testing to determine these levels should be done upon first symptom or sign of liver dysfunction [e.g., pruritus, dark urine, jaundice, right upper quadrant tenderness, or unexplained "flu-like" symptoms]; should be discontinued and not restarted in these patients; these lab abnormalities may continue to worsen for several weeks after drug discontinuation)

Medical considerations/Contraindications
The medical considerations/contraindications included have been selected on the basis of their potential clinical significance (reasons given in parentheses where appropriate)—not necessarily inclusive (» = major clinical significance).

Except under special circumstances, this medication should not be used when the following medical problem exists:

» Hypersensitivity to atomoxetine or any of its components

Risk-benefit should be considered when the following medical problems exist:

» Cardiovascular disease or
» Cerebrovascular disease or
» Hypertension or
» Tachycardia
(may increase blood pressure and heart rate)

Conditions that would predispose to hypotension
(symptoms of postural hypotension have been reported; should be used with caution in these patients)

» Glaucoma, narrow angle
(may increase risk of mydriasis)

» Hepatic impairment
(may increase atomoxetine exposure (AUC); dosage adjustment may be necessary)

Patient monitoring
The following may be especially important in patient monitoring (other tests may be warranted in some patients, depending on condition; » = major clinical significance):

» Blood pressure
» Heart rate
(may be necessary to measure at baseline, following atomoxetine dose increases, and periodically while on therapy; may be especially important in patients with cardiovascular or cerebrovascular disease, hypertension, or tachycardia)

Careful supervision of patients for:
Clinical worsening, or
Abnormal behaviors (i.e., agitation, irritability), or
Suicidal thinking or behaviors, or
Unusual changes in behaviors
(recommended especially during the initial few months of a course of atomoxetine therapy, or at times of dose changes, either increases or decreases; monitoring should include daily observation by families and caregivers and frequent contact with the physician)

» Growth including:
Height
Weight
(measure at baseline and periodically during atomoxetine therapy; consider interrupting therapy in patients who are not growing or gaining weight during long-term therapy)

» Liver injury
(post-marketing experience indicate that atomoxetine can cause severe liver injury in rare cases; liver injury may occur several months after therapy is started; atomoxetine should be discontinued in patients with jaundice or laboratory evidence of liver injury and should not be restarted)

» Re-evaluation of the long-term usefulness of atomoxetine
(periodic evaluations for individual patients recommended; effectiveness for long term use [9 weeks in pediatric and adolescent patients and 10 weeks in adult patients] has not been systematically evaluated in controlled trials)

Side/Adverse Effects
Atomoxetine was not associated with a pattern of response that suggested stimulant or euphoriant properties.

In two post-marketing cases, severe liver injury was reported to be caused by atomoxetine. These two patients recovered from their liver injury and did not require a liver transplant. However, in a small percentage of patients, severe drug-related liver injury may progress to acute liver failure resulting in death or the need for a liver transplant.

The following side/adverse effects have been selected on the basis of their potential clinical significance (possible signs and symptoms in parentheses where appropriate)—not necessarily inclusive:

Those indicating need for medical attention
Incidence less frequent
Palpitations (irregular heartbeat)

Incidence rare
Allergic reactions, including; angioedema (large, hive-like swelling on face, eyelids, lips, tongue, throat, hands, legs, feet, sex organs); ***skin rash; urticaria*** (hives or welts; itching; redness of skin; skin rash)

Incidence not determined—Observed during clinical practice; estimates of frequency can not be determined
Liver injury, severe (pruritus; dark urine; persistent anorexia; yellow eyes or skin; influenza (flu)-like symptoms; right upper quadrant tenderness)

Those indicating need for medical attention only if they continue or are bothersome
Incidence more frequent
Abdominal pain, upper (stomach pain); ***appetite, decreased; constipation*** (difficulty having a bowel movement (stool)); ***cough; dizziness; dry mouth; dysmenorrhea*** (pain; cramps; heavy bleeding); ***dyspepsia*** (acid or sour stomach; belching; heartburn; indigestion; stomach discomfort, upset, or pain); ***erectile disturbance*** (loss in sexual ability, desire, drive, or performance; decreased interest in sexual intercourse; inability to have or keep an erection); ***fatigue*** (unusual tiredness or weakness); ***headache; insomnia*** (sleeplessness; trouble sleeping; unable to sleep); ***irritability; lethargy*** (unusual drowsiness, dullness, tiredness, weakness or feeling of sluggishness); ***libido, decreased*** (loss in sexual ability, desire, drive, or performance; de-

creased interest in sexual intercourse; inability to have or keep an erection); ***menstruation irregular, delayed menses, or menstrual disorder*** (change in pattern of monthly periods; change in amount of bleeding during periods; unusual stopping of menstrual bleeding; bleeding between periods); ***nausea; sinusitis*** (pain or tenderness around eyes and cheekbones; fever; stuffy or runny nose; headache; cough; shortness of breath or troubled breathing; tightness of chest or wheezing); ***somnolence*** (sleepiness or unusual drowsiness); ***urinary hesitation or retention*** (decrease in urine volume; decrease in frequency of urination; difficulty in passing urine [dribbling]; painful urination); ***vomiting***

Incidence less frequent

Crying; dermatitis (blistering, crusting, irritation, itching, or reddening of skin; cracked, dry, scaly skin; swelling); ***diarrhea; dreams, abnormal; ear infection*** (change in hearing; earache or pain in ear; ear drainage; fever); ***ejaculation failure or disorder*** (change or problem with discharge of semen); ***flatulence*** (bloated, full feeling; excess air or gas in stomach or intestines; passing gas); ***hot flushes*** (feeling of warmth redness of the face, neck, arms and occasionally, upper chest; sudden sweating); ***hypotension, orthostatic*** (chills; cold sweats; confusion; dizziness, faintness, or lightheadedness when getting up from lying or sitting position); ***impotence*** (loss in sexual ability, desire, drive, or performance; decreased interest in sexual intercourse; inability to have or keep an erection); ***influenza*** (chills; cough; diarrhea; fever; general feeling of discomfort or illness; headache; joint pain; loss of appetite; muscle aches and pains); ***mood swings; myalgia*** (joint pain; swollen joints; muscle aching or cramping; muscle pains or stiffness; difficulty in moving); ***orgasm, abnormal; paresthesia*** (burning, crawling, itching, numbness, prickling, “pins and needles”, or tingling feelings); ***prostatitis*** (back pain; chills; fever; frequent urination; groin pain; muscle aches; pain or burning with urination; swollen, tender prostate); ***pyrexia*** (fever); ***rhinorrhea*** (runny nose); ***rigors*** (feeling unusually cold; shivering); ***sleep disorder; sinus headache; sweating, increased; weight, decreased***

Overdose

For specific information on the agents used in the management of atomoxetine overdose, see *Charcoal, Activated (Oral-Local)* monograph.

For more information on the management of overdose or unintentional ingestion, **contact a poison control center** (see *Poison Control Center Listing).*

Clinical effects of overdose

There is limited clinical trial and postmarketing experience with atomoxetine acute and chronic overdoses. No fatal overdoses of atomoxetine alone have been reported. Commonly reported symptoms associated with acute and chronic overdoses are somnolence, agitation, hyperactivity, abnormal behavior, and gastrointestinal symptoms. Mydriasis, tachycardia, and dry mouth (signs and symptoms of sympathetic nervous system activation) has also been reported.

Treatment of overdose

To decrease absorption—

Gastric emptying and activated charcoal may prevent systemic absorption.

To enhance elimination—

Dialysis is not likely to be useful in the treatment of overdose because atomoxetine is highly protein-bound.

Specific treatment—

There is no specific antidote for atomoxetine overdose. Treatment is symptomatic and supportive.

See the package insert or *Charcoal, Activated (Oral-Local)* for specific dosing guidelines for use of this product.

Monitoring—

Monitoring vital signs and cardiac function is recommended.

Supportive care—

Treatment should be symptomatic and supportive. An airway should be established.

Patients in whom intentional overdose is confirmed or suspected should be referred for psychiatric consultation.

Patient Consultation

As an aid to patient consultation, refer to *Advice for the Patient, Atomoxetine (Systemic).*

In providing consultation, consider emphasizing the following selected information (» = major clinical significance):

Before using this medication

» Conditions affecting use, especially:

Hypersensitivity to atomoxetine or any of its components

Pregnancy—Adequate and well controlled studies in humans have not been done. Atomoxetine should not be used during pregnancy unless the potential benefit justifies the potential risk to the fetus.

FDA Pregnancy Category C

Breast-feeding—Caution is advised if atomoxetine is administered to a nursing mother. It is not known if atomoxetine is distributed into human breast milk. However, atomoxetine and/or its metabolites were distributed into milk of rats.

Use in children—Safety and efficacy have not been established in pediatric patients less than 6 years of age. Atomoxetine increases the risk of suicidal thinking in children and adolescents with ADHD.

Use in the elderly—Safety and efficacy have not been established in the geriatric population.

Pharmacogenetics—Atomoxetine is extensively metabolized, primarily through the CYP2D6 enzymatic pathway. A fraction of the population (about 7% of Caucasians and 2% of African-Americans) are poor metabolizers (PMs) of CYP2D6 drugs. These individuals have reduced activity in this pathway which may increase the incidence of some adverse effects.

Other medications, especially albuterol, potent CYP2D6 inhibitors such as fluoxetine, paroxetine, or quinidine, monoamine oxidase inhibitors (MAOIs), and vasopressor agents.

Other medical problems, especially cardiovascular disease, cerebrovascular disease, hypertension, tachycardia, narrow angle glaucoma, or hepatic impairment

Proper use of this medication

» Proper dosing

Missed dose: Taking as soon as possible; but not taking more than the prescribed total daily amount of atomoxetine in any 24-hour period.

Proper storage

Precautions while using this medication

» Regular visits to physician periodically to monitor progress and re-evaluate long-term usefulness of the drug

» Importance of contacting physician immediately if symptoms of severe liver injury occur (e.g., pruritus, dark urine, jaundice, right upper quadrant tenderness, or unexplained “flu-like symptoms)

» Importance of contacting physician immediately if increase in aggression or hostility

» May cause dizziness or lightheadedness. Using caution when driving a car or operating hazardous machinery until effects of medication are known.

» Talk to your doctor if you are nursing, pregnant, or thinking of becoming pregnant.

» Call your doctor right away if you get swelling, hives, or if you develop any symptoms that concern you.

Tell your doctor about all the medicines you take or plan to take, including prescription and nonprescription medicines, dietary supplements, and herbal remedies.

Do not give atomoxetine to other people, even if they have the same symptoms as you have.

Atomoxetine may be taken with or without food.

Possible dryness of mouth; using sugarless candy or gum, ice or saliva substitute for relief; checking with physician or dentist if dry mouth continues for more than 2 weeks.

Side/adverse effects

Signs of potential side effects, especially palpitations or allergic reactions

Signs of potential side effects observed during clinical practice, especially severe liver injury

General Dosing Information

Atomoxetine can be discontinued without being tapered.

Diet/Nutrition

May be given with or without food.

Oral Dosage Forms

ATOMOXETINE HYDROCHLORIDE CAPSULES

Usual adult and adolescent (over 70 kg body weight) dose

Attention deficit hyperactivity disorder (ADHD)—

Patients not currently using a strong CYP2D6 inhibitor (e.g., paroxetine, fluoxetine, quinidine)—

Oral, initially 40 mg once daily

Dosage may be increased after a minimum of 3 days to a target total daily dose of approximately 80 mg administered either as a single daily dose in the morning or as evenly divided doses in the morning and late afternoon/early evening. After two to four additional weeks, the dose may be increased to a maximum of 100 mg daily in patients who have not achieved an optimal response.

Patients using a strong CYP2D6 inhibitor (e.g., paroxetine, fluoxetine, quinidine)—

Oral, initially 40 mg once daily

Dosage should only be increased to the usual target dose of 80 mg per day if symptoms fail to improve after 4 weeks and the initial dose is well tolerated.

Note: The following dosing adjustments are recommended for patients with hepatic insufficiency (HI):

- For patients with moderate HI (Child-Pugh Class B)—initial and target dose should be reduced to 50% of the normal dose
- For patients with severe HI (Child-Pugh Class C)—initial and target dose should be reduced to 25% of the normal dose

Usual adult and adolescent prescribing limits

100 mg daily

Usual pediatric (up to 70 kg body weight) dose

Attention deficit hyperactivity disorder (ADHD)—

Patients not currently using a strong CYP2D6 inhibitor (e.g., paroxetine, fluoxetine, quinidine)—

Oral, initially 0.5 mg per kg of body weight once daily

Dosage may be increased after a minimum of 3 days to a target total daily dose of approximately 1.2 mg per kg of body weight either as a single daily dose in the morning or as evenly divided doses in the morning and late afternoon/early evening.

Patients currently using a strong CYP2D6 inhibitor (e.g., paroxetine, fluoxetine, quinidine)—

Oral, initially 0.5 mg per kg of body weight once daily

Dosage should only be increased to the usual target dose of 1.2 mg per kg of body weight per day if symptoms fail to improve after 4 weeks and the initial dose is well tolerated.

Note: The following dosing adjustments are recommended for patients with hepatic insufficiency (HI):

- For patients with moderate HI (Child-Pugh Class B)—initial and target dose should be reduced to 50% of the normal dose
- For patients with severe HI (Child-Pugh Class C)—initial and target dose should be reduced to 25% of the normal dose

Usual pediatric prescribing limits

1.4 mg per kg of body weight or 100 mg daily, whichever is less.

Usual geriatric dose

Safety and efficacy in geriatric patients have not been established.

Strength(s) usually available

U.S.—

10 mg (Rx) [*Strattera* (pregelatinized starch; dimethicone; gelatin; sodium lauryl sulfate; may contain FD&C Blue No. 2; may contain synthetic yellow iron oxide; may contain titanium dioxide; may contain red iron oxide; edible black ink)].

18 mg (Rx) [*Strattera* (pregelatinized starch; dimethicone; gelatin; sodium lauryl sulfate; may contain FD&C Blue No. 2; may contain synthetic yellow iron oxide; may contain titanium dioxide; may contain red iron oxide; edible black ink)].

25 mg (Rx) [*Strattera* (pregelatinized starch; dimethicone; gelatin; sodium lauryl sulfate; may contain FD&C Blue No. 2; may contain synthetic yellow iron oxide; may contain titanium dioxide; may contain red iron oxide; edible black ink)].

40 mg (Rx) [*Strattera* (pregelatinized starch; dimethicone; gelatin; sodium lauryl sulfate; may contain FD&C Blue No. 2; may contain synthetic yellow iron oxide; may contain titanium dioxide; may contain red iron oxide; edible black ink)].

60 mg (Rx) [*Strattera* (pregelatinized starch; dimethicone; gelatin; sodium lauryl sulfate; may contain FD&C Blue No. 2; may contain synthetic yellow iron oxide; may contain titanium dioxide; may contain red iron oxide; edible black ink)].

80 mg (Rx) [*Strattera* (pregelatinized starch; dimethicone; gelatin; sodium lauryl sulfate; may contain FD&C Blue No. 2; may contain synthetic yellow iron oxide; may contain titanium dioxide; may contain red iron oxide; edible black ink)].

100 mg (Rx) [*Strattera* (pregelatinized starch; dimethicone; gelatin; sodium lauryl sulfate; may contain FD&C Blue No. 2; may contain synthetic yellow iron oxide; may contain titanium dioxide; may contain red iron oxide; edible black ink)].

Canada—

10 mg (Rx) [*Strattera*].
18 mg (Rx) [*Strattera*].
25 mg (Rx) [*Strattera*].
40 mg (Rx) [*Strattera*].
60 mg (Rx) [*Strattera*].

Packaging and storage

Store at 25 °C (77 °F); excursions permitted to 15 to 30 °C (59 to 86 °F)

Auxiliary labeling

- May cause drowsiness. Be careful while driving or operating machinery. Use caution until you become familiar with its effects.
- This medication could be harmful during pregnancy. If you are pregnant or plan to be pregnant, you should consult your doctor about the use of this medication.
- Ask your doctor or pharmacist before using nonprescription drugs.

Revised: 10/03/2005
Developed: 09/22/2003

ATORVASTATIN—See *HMG-CoA Reductase Inhibitors (Systemic)*

ATORVASTATIN Systemic

VA CLASSIFICATION (Primary): CV351

Commonly used brand name(s): *Lipitor*.

Note: For a listing of dosage forms and brand names by country availability, see *Dosage Forms* section(s).

Category

Antihyperlipidemic; HMG-CoA reductase inhibitor.

Indications

Accepted

Coronary heart disease (prophylaxis)—In adult patients without clinically evident coronary heart disease, but with multiple risk factors for coronary heart disease such as age greater than or equal to 55 years, smoking, hypertension, low HDL-C, or family history of early coronary heart disease, atorvastatin is indicated to:

- Reduce the risk of myocardial infarction
- Reduce the risk of stroke
- Reduce the risk of revascularization procedures and angina

Coronary heart disease (prophylaxis)—In adult patients with type 2 diabetes and without clinically evident coronary heart disease, but with multiple risk factors for coronary heart disease such as retinopathy, albuminuria, smoking, or hypertension, atorvastatin is indicated to:

- Reduce the risk of myocardial infarction
- Reduce the risk of stroke

Hyperlipidemia (treatment)—Atorvastatin is indicated as an adjunct to diet to reduce elevated total cholesterol (total-C), low-density lipoprotein cholesterol (LDL-C), apolipoprotein B (apo B), and triglyceride (TG) concentrations in patients with primary hypercholesterolemia (heterozygous familial and nonfamilial) and mixed dyslipidemia (Fredrickson Types IIa and IIb).It is indicated as an adjunct to diet in the treatment of heterozygous familial hypercholesterolemia in boys and postmenarchal girls from 10 to 17 years of age if after an adequate trial of diet therapy the following findings are present:

- LDL-C remains greater than or equal to 190 mg/dL or
- LDL-C remains greater than or equal to 160 mg/dL and:
  - —there is a positive family history of premature cardiovascular disease or
  - —two or more other CVD risk factors are present in the pediatric patient

Homozygous familial hypercholesterolemia as an adjunct to other lipid-lowering treatments, such as low-density lipoprotein apheresis, or if such treatments are unavailable.

Primary dysbetalipoproteinemia (Fredrickson Type III) who do not respond adequately to diet.

Adjunct to diet for the treatment of patients with elevated serum triglyceride levels (Fredrickson Type IV).

For additional information on initial therapeutic guidelines related to the treatment of hyperlipidemia, see *Appendix III*.

Pharmacology/Pharmacokinetics

Physicochemical characteristics

Molecular weight—1209.42.

Solubility—Atorvastatin is very slightly soluble in distilled water, pH 7.4 phosphate buffer, and acetonitrile, slightly soluble in ethanol, and freely soluble in methanol. Atorvastatin is insoluble in aqueous solutions of pH 4 and below.

Mechanism of action/Effect

3-hydroxy-3-methylglutaryl coenzyme A (HMG-CoA) reductase inhibitors competitively inhibit the enzyme that catalyzes the conversion of HMG-CoA to mevalonate, the rate-limiting step in cholesterol biosynthesis. The primary site of action of HMG-CoA reductase inhibitors is the liver, which is the principal site of cholesterol synthesis and low-density lipoprotein clearance. Cholesterol and triglycerides circulate in the bloodstream as part of lipoprotein complexes. These complexes are composed of high-density lipoprotein (HDL), intermediate-density lipoprotein (IDL), low-density lipoprotein (LDL), and very-low-density lipoprotein (VLDL). In the liver, triglycerides (TG) and cholesterol are incorporated into VLDL, which is released into the plasma for transport to the peripheral tissues. LDL is formed from VLDL and is catabolized primarily through the LDL receptor. Elevated plasma concentrations of total cholesterol (total-C), LDL-cholesterol (LDL-C), and apolipoprotein B (apo B) promote human atherosclerosis and are risk factors for developing cardiovascular disease. Increased plasma concentrations of HDL-C are associated with decreased cardiovascular risk. Atorvastatin lowers plasma cholesterol and lipoprotein concentrations by inhibiting HMG-CoA reductase and cholesterol synthesis in the liver and by increasing the number of hepatic LDL receptors on the cell surface to enhance uptake and catabolism of LDL. Atorvastatin also reduces LDL production and the number of LDL particles. Atorvastatin reduces total-C, LDL-C, and apo B in patients with homozygous and heterozygous familial hypercholesterolemia (FH), nonfamilial forms of hypercholesterolemia, and mixed dyslipidemia. Atorvastatin also reduces VLDL-C and TG and produces variable increases in HDL-C and apolipoprotein A-1.

Absorption

Atorvastatin is rapidly absorbed, the extent of absorption increasing in proportion to the dose. The absolute bioavailability of atorvastatin is approximately 14%. Atorvastatin has a low systemic availability due to pre-systemic clearance in the gastrointestinal mucosa and/or hepatic first-pass metabolism. Food decreases the rate and extent of absorption by approximately 25% and 9%, respectively; although, LDL-C reduction is similar when atorvastatin is given with or without food. The concentration of atorvastatin in plasma (C_{max}) and the area under the plasma concentration-time curve (AUC) are lower by approximately 30% following evening administration when compared with morning administration. However, LDL-C reduction is the same, regardless of the time of day of administration. Grapefruit juice in large amounts, has been shown to interfere with the metabolism of atorvastatin, causing increases in C_{max} and AUC. It is recommended that atorvastatin not be administered with large amounts of grapefruit juice.

Distribution

Mean volume of distribution (Vol_D)—Approximately 381 liters.

Protein binding

Very high (≥ 98%).

Biotransformation

Atorvastatin undergoes extensive hepatic and/or extra-hepatic metabolism to form ortho- and parahydroxylated derivatives and various beta-oxidation products. It does not appear to undergo enterohepatic recirculation. Atorvastatin and its ortho- and parahydroxylated metabolites were found to have equal inhibitory effects on HMG-CoA reductase *in vitro*. The active metabolites are responsible for approximately 70% of the inhibition of HMG-CoA reductase. Studies *in vitro* suggest that atorvastatin is metabolized by the cytochrome P450 3A4 isozyme.

Half-life

Elimination—

Approximately 14 hours.

Time to peak concentration

1 to 2 hours.

Elimination

Primarily fecal (biliary).

Renal: < 2%.

In dialysis—

Although studies have not been performed, atorvastatin is not expected to be removed significantly by hemodialysis because of its extensive binding to plasma proteins.

Precautions to Consider

Carcinogenicity

In a 2-year study in mice, doses of 100, 200, or 400 mg per kg (mg/kg) of body weight per day resulted in a marked increase in liver adenomas in male mice given high doses and liver carcinomas in female mice given high doses. These events occurred at area under the plasma concentration-time curve ($AUC_{[0-24]}$) values of approximately six times the mean human plasma drug exposure after an 80-mg oral dose.

In a 2-year study in rats, doses of 10, 30, and 100 mg/kg per day resulted in rare muscle tumors. Rhabdomyosarcoma occurred in one female rat given high doses and fibrosarcoma occurred in another female rat given high doses. The high dose represents an $AUC_{(0-24)}$ value of approximately 16 times the mean human plasma drug exposure after an 80-mg oral dose.

Mutagenicity

No evidence of mutagenicity or clastogenicity was found in *in vitro* tests, with and without metabolic activation, including the Ames test with *Salmonella typhimurium* and *Escherichia coli*, the HGPRT forward mutation assay in Chinese hamster lung cells, the chromosomal aberration assay in Chinese hamster lung cells, or in the *in vivo* mouse micronucleus test.

Pregnancy/Reproduction

Fertility—No changes in fertility were observed in studies in rats given doses of up to 175 mg/kg (15 times the human exposure) of atorvastatin. In 2 of 10 rats given 100 mg/kg per day for 3 months (16 times the human exposure at the 80-mg dose), aplasia and aspermia in the epididymis resulted. Testis weights were significantly decreased with 30 and 100 mg/kg doses and epididymal weight was lower at 100 mg/kg. Doses of 100 mg/kg per day given to male rats for 11 weeks prior to mating resulted in decreases in sperm motility and spermatid head concentration and increases in the number of abnormal sperm. No adverse effects were observed on semen parameters or in reproductive organ histopathology in dogs given doses of 10, 40, or 120 mg/kg for 2 years.

Pregnancy—Atorvastatin therapy is *contraindicated* in pregnant women because it decreases cholesterol synthesis and possibly the synthesis of other biologically active substances, such as steroids and cell membranes, that are derived from cholesterol and are essential for fetal development.

There have been rare reports of congenital anomalies following intrauterine exposure to HMG-CoA reductase inhibitors. Severe congenital bone deformities, tracheo-esophageal fistula, and anal atresia (VATER association) were reported in a baby born to a woman who took the HMG-CoA reductase inhibitor lovastatin with dextroamphetamine sulfate during the first trimester of pregnancy. Atorvastatin should not be administered to women of childbearing potential when they are highly likely to conceive. If a woman becomes pregnant during atorvastatin therapy, the medication should be discontinued and the patient advised of the potential hazards to the fetus.

In rats, atorvastatin crosses the placenta and reaches a concentration in fetal liver tissue equal to that in maternal plasma. No evidence of teratogenicity was found in rats given doses of up to 300 mg/kg per day or in rabbits given doses of up to 100 mg/kg per day. These doses represent 30 and 20 times, respectively, the human exposure based on body surface area (mg/m^2).

Studies in rats given 20, 100, or 225 mg/kg per day, from gestation day 7 through lactation day 21 (weaning), have shown decreased pup survival at birth, neonate, weaning, and maturity in pups of mothers given doses of 225 mg/kg per day. On days 4 and 21, body weight was decreased in pups of mothers given doses of 100 mg/kg per day; body weight was decreased at birth and at days 4, 21, and 91 in pups of mothers given 225 mg/kg per day. Pup development was delayed, as determined by rotorod performance (mothers given 100 mg/kg per day) and acoustic startle (mothers given 225 mg/kg per day). Development was also delayed in pinnae detachment and eye opening (mothers given 225 mg/kg per day). These doses represent 6 times (100 mg/kg) and 22 times (225 mg/kg) the human exposure at 80 mg per day.

FDA Pregnancy Category X

Breast-feeding

While it is not known whether atorvastatin is distributed into breast milk, atorvastatin is *contraindicated* in women who are breast-feeding because inhibition of cholesterol synthesis may cause serious adverse effects in the nursing infant. Atorvastatin is distributed into the milk of lactating rats. Plasma and liver atorvastatin concentrations in nursing rat pups have reached 50% and 40%, respectively, of that in the mother's milk.

Pediatrics

Safety and effectiveness in patients 10 to 17 years of age with heterozygous familial hypercholesterolemia have been evaluated with a safety, tolerability, and adverse event profile similar to that of the placebo. There was no detectable effect on growth or sexual maturation in boys or on menstrual cycle length in girls. In an uncontrolled study, eight pediatric patients (none younger than 9 years of age) with homozygous familial hypercholesterolemia (FH) were treated with atorvastatin at doses of up to 80 mg per day for 1 year. No clinical or biochemical abnormalities were reported in these patients. Appropriate studies (controlled clinical trial) have not been performed on the relationship of the effect of atorvastatin with respect to age in prepubertal patients or patients younger than 10 years of age. The safety and efficacy of doses above 20 mg have not been studied in children. And, the long-term efficacy of atorvastatin therapy in childhood to reduce morbidity and mortality in adulthood has not been established.

Geriatrics

Use of atorvastatin in patients 65 years of age and older has not demonstrated geriatrics-specific problems that would limit the usefulness of atorvastatin in the elderly. Safety and efficacy of atorvastatin in 221 patients ≥ 70 years of age given doses of up to 80 mg per day were similar to those in younger patients. However, in healthy subjects ≥ 65 years of age, atorvastatin plasma concentrations (C_{max}) are higher and the AUC is greater by approximately 40% and 30%, respectively, compared with those in younger adults. Reduction of low-density lipoprotein cholesterol (LDL-C) is comparable to that in younger patients given equal doses of atorvastatin.

Pharmacogenetics

There is no clinically significant difference in LDL-C reduction with atorvastatin between men and women, although plasma concentrations of atorvastatin in women are approximately 20% higher for C_{max} and 10% lower for AUC, compared with those in men.

Surgical

Aorvastatin therapy should be temporarily withheld or discontinued in any patient having a risk factor, such as major surgery, predisposing to the development of renal failure secondary to rhabdomyolysis.

Drug interactions and/or related problems

The following drug interactions and/or related problems have been selected on the basis of their potential clinical significance (possible mechanism in parentheses where appropriate)—not necessarily inclusive (» = major clinical significance):

Note: Combinations containing any of the following medications, depending on the amount present, may also interact with this medication.

» Alcohol, substantial use of
(use of atorvastatin is contraindicated in patients with active liver disease or unexplained transaminase elevations)

Antacids, aluminum and magnesium hydroxide–containing
(plasma concentrations decreased by approximately 35% when atorvastatin was administered concurrently with an aluminum and magnesium hydroxide–containing antacid; however, reduction of LDL-C was not altered)

Note: for erythromycin: plasma concentrations of atorvastatin increased approximately 40% with coadministration of atorvastatin and erythromycin, a known inhibitor of cytochrome P450 3A4

» Azole antifungals or
» Cyclosporine or
» Erythromycin or
» Fibric acid derivatives or
» Niacin (nicotinic acid)
(risk of myopathy increased with concurrent administration of atorvastatin and these drugs; potential benefits and risks should be weighed and patients closely monitored for signs of myopathy)

Cimetidine or
Ketoconazole or
Spironolactone
(caution should be exercised if atorvastatin is administered concomitantly with these drugs that may decrease the levels or activity of endogenous steroid hormones)

Colestipol
(concurrent use may decrease plasma concentrations of atorvastatin by approximately 25%; however, LDL-C reduction may be greater with combination therapy than with either medication given alone)

» Digoxin
(concurrent administration may increase steady-state digoxin plasma concentrations by approximately 20%; patients taking digoxin and atorvastatin should be followed closely for evidence of digoxin toxicity)

Grapefruit juice in large amounts
(concurrent use with large amounts of grapefruit juice has been reported to significantly increase the serum concentrations and the area under the plasma concentration-time curve (AUC). In a study with 12 subjects, administration of grapefruit juice double-strength 200 mL three times a day resulted in a C_{max} decrease of about 24% of active atorvastatin compounds. An increase in AUC of active atorvastatin compounds was about 23%. The time to C_{max} (tmax) was increased from 1 hour to 4 hours. Grapefruit juice or other grapefruit products in large doses should not be taken before or after administration of atorvastatin)

Oral contraceptives
(coadministration increased AUC values for norethindrone and ethinyl estradiol by approximately 30% and 20%; these increases should be considered when selecting an oral contraceptive for a woman taking atorvastatin)

Laboratory value alterations

The following have been selected on the basis of their potential clinical significance (possible effect in parentheses where appropriate)—not necessarily inclusive (» = major clinical significance).

With physiology/laboratory test values

Creatine phosphokinase (CPK), serum
(increases of CPK > 10 times the upper limit of normal [ULN], accompanied by muscle aches or weakness, are associated with myopathy, such as rhabdomyolysis; atorvastatin should be discontinued if marked elevations of creatine phosphokinase occur)

Transaminases, serum
(elevations in liver enzyme values usually occur within the first 3 months of treatment; persistent increases [> three times ULN, occurring on two or more occasions] in transaminase values occurred in 0.7% of patients in clinical trials; elevations in transaminase values are not usually associated with clinical signs or symptoms, although one patient in clinical trials developed jaundice; if elevations in aspartate aminotransferase [AST (SGOT)] or alanine aminotransferase [ALT (SGPT)] are > three times the ULN and persist, atorvastatin dosage should be reduced or discontinued; patients should be monitored until the abnormal values are resolved)

Medical considerations/Contraindications

The medical considerations/contraindications included have been selected on the basis of their potential clinical significance (reasons given in parentheses where appropriate)—not necessarily inclusive (» = major clinical significance).

Except under special circumstances, this medication should not be used when the following medical problems exist:

» Hepatic disease, active, including
» Alcoholic liver disease, chronic or
» Childs-Pugh Index grade A disease or
» Childs-Pugh Index grade B disease or
» Elevations of transaminase values, unexplained, persistent
(the presence of hepatic disease may increase atorvastatin plasma concentrations. Plasma concentrations are significantly increased in patients with chronic alcoholic liver disease. In patients with Childs-Pugh Index grade A disease, C_{max} and AUC are each 4-fold greater. In patients with Childs-Pugh Index grade B disease, C_{max} and AUC are approximately 16- and 11-fold greater, respectively)

» Hypersensitivity to atorvastatin

Risk-benefit should be considered when the following medical problems exist:

» Electrolyte, endocrine, or metabolic disorders, severe or
» Hypotension or
» Infection, severe acute or
» Myopathy
» Seizures, uncontrolled or
» Surgery, major or
» Trauma
(these conditions may predispose a patient to the development of renal failure, secondary to rhabdomyolysis; atorvastatin should be discontinued or temporarily withheld)

Hepatic disease, history of
(elevations in transaminase values may occur)

Patient monitoring

The following may be especially important in patient monitoring (other tests may be warranted in some patients, depending on condition; » = major clinical significance):

Creatine phosphokinase (CPK), serum
(periodic determinations recommended in patients who develop muscle pain, tenderness, or weakness during therapy or if concurrently receiving azole antifungals, erythromycin, gemfibrozil, immunosuppressive drugs such as cyclosporine, or niacin)

» Hepatic function determinations
(recommended prior to initiation of treatment and at 12 weeks of treatment or at a dosage increase, and periodically, such as every 6 months, thereafter)

» Lipid concentrations, serum, primarily:
    Low-density lipoprotein cholesterol (LDL-C) and, if not available
    Total cholesterol (total-C)
        (determinations recommended within 2 to 4 weeks after initiation or at a dosage adjustment of atorvastatin)

Side/Adverse Effects

The following side/adverse effects have been selected on the basis of their potential clinical significance (possible signs and symptoms in parentheses where appropriate)—not necessarily inclusive:

Those indicating need for medical attention

Incidence less frequent or rare

Allergic reaction (cough; difficulty swallowing; dizziness; fast heartbeat; hives; itching; puffiness or swelling of the eyelids or around the eyes, face, lips or tongue; shortness of breath; skin rash; tightness in chest; unusual tiredness or weakness; wheezing); ***liver function abnormalities*** (persistent elevation of liver function tests); ***muscle disorders, such as leg cramps; myalgia, uncomplicated*** (muscle pain); ***myopathy and/or rhabdomyolysis*** (fever; muscle cramps, pain, stiffness, or weakness; unusual tiredness); ***and myositis*** (inflammation of muscle)

Note: The degradation of muscle occurs in *rhabdomyolysis*, resulting in the release of myoglobin into the urine, which can lead to acute renal failure. *Myopathy* and/or rhabdomyolysis should be considered if symptoms occur in conjunction with creatine phosphokinase (CPK) value increases $>$ 10 times the upper limit of normal.. The risk of myopathy increases when HMG-CoA reductase inhibitors are administered with azole antifungals, erythromycin, fibric acid derivatives, immunosuppressants such as cyclosporine, or niacin.. Patients should be monitored during the first months of therapy and during dosage increases of either drug, and should report immediately any unexplained symptoms of muscle pain, tenderness, or weakness, especially if accompanied by fever or malaise.

Incidence not determined—Observed during clinical practice; estimates of frequency can not be determined

Anaphylaxis (cough; difficulty swallowing; dizziness; fast heartbeat; hives; itching; puffiness or swelling of the eyelids or around the eyes, face, lips or tongue; shortness of breath; skin rash; tightness in chest; unusual tiredness or weakness; wheezing); ***angioneurotic edema*** (large, hive-like swelling on face, eyelids, lips, tongue, throat, hands, legs, feet, sex organs); ***bullous rashes*** (skin blisters); ***erythema multiforme*** (blistering, peeling, loosening of skin; chills; cough; diarrhea; fever; itching; joint or muscle pain; red irritated eyes; sore throat; sores, ulcers, or white spots in mouth or on lips; unusual tiredness or weakness); ***rhabdomyolysis*** (dark-colored urine; fever; muscle cramps or spasms; muscle pain or stiffness; unusual tiredness or weakness); ***Stevens-Johnson syndrome*** (blistering, peeling, loosening of skin; chills; cough; diarrhea; itching; joint or muscle pain; red irritated eyes; red skin lesions, often with a purple center sore; throat sores, ulcers, or white spots in mouth or on lips; unusual tiredness or weakness); ***toxic epidermal necrolysis*** (redness, tenderness, itching, burning, or peeling of skin red or irritated eyes; sore throat, fever, and chills)

Those indicating need for medical attention only if they continue or are bothersome

Incidence more frequent

Headache; infection (fever or chills; cough or hoarseness; lower back or side pain; painful or difficult urination); ***sinusitis*** (pain or tenderness around eyes and cheekbones; fever; stuffy or runny nose; headache; cough; shortness of breath or troubled breathing; tightness of chest or wheezing)

Incidence less frequent

Abdominal pain; accidental injury; asthenia (lack or loss of strength); ***back pain; constipation; diarrhea; dyspepsia*** (heartburn; indigestion; stomach discomfort); ***flatulence*** (belching; excessive gas); ***flu syndrome*** (chills; cough; diarrhea; fever; general feeling of discomfort or illness; headache; joint pain; loss of appetite; muscle aches and pains; nausea; runny nose; shivering; sore throat; sweating; trouble sleeping; unusual tiredness or weakness; vomiting); ***skin rash***

Incidence not determined—Observed during clinical practice, estimates of frequency can not be made

Abnormal dreams; acne; albuminuria (cloudy urine); ***alopecia*** (hair loss, thinning of hair); ***amblyopia*** (blurred vision; change in vision; impaired vision); ***amnesia; anemia*** (pale skin; troubled breathing with exertion; unusual bleeding or bruising; unusual tiredness or weakness); ***angina pectoris*** (arm, back or jaw pain; chest pain or discomfort; chest tightness or heaviness; fast or irregular heartbeat; shortness of breath; sweating; nausea); ***anorexia ; appetite increased; arrhthmia*** (dizziness; fainting; fast, slow, or irregular heartbeat); ***arthritis; asthma; biliary pain*** (upper abdominal pain); ***breast enlargement; bronchitis*** (cough producing mucus; difficulty breathing; shortness of breath; tightness in chest; wheezing); ***bursitis*** (pain and inflammation at the joints); ***cheilitis*** (chapped, red, or swollen lips; scaling, redness, burning, pain, or other signs of inflammation of lips); ***chest pain; colitis*** (stomach cramps; tenderness; pain; watery or bloody diarrhea; fever); ***contact dermatitis*** (blistering, burning, crusting, dryness, flaking of skin itching; scaling; severe redness, soreness swelling of skin); ***cystitis*** (bloody or cloudy urine; difficult; burning, or painful urination; frequent urge to urinate); ***deafness; depression; dizziness; dry eyes; dry mouth ; dry skin; dysphagia*** (difficulty swallowing); ***dyspnea*** (shortness of breath; difficult or labored breathing; tightness in chest; wheezing); ***dysuria*** (difficult or painful urination; burning while urinating); ***ecchymosis*** (bruising; large, flat, blue or purplish patches in the skin); ***eczema*** (skin rash encrusted, scaly and oozing); ***edema, face, generalized, peripheral*** (swelling); ***emotional lability*** (crying; depersonalization; dysphoria; euphoria; mental depression; paranoia; quick to react or overreact emotionally; rapidly changing moods); ***enteritis*** (diarrhea; stomach pain or cramps); ***epididymitis*** (chills; fever, pain in abdomen, groin, or scrotum; pain or burning with urination; swelling of scrotum); ***epistaxis*** (bloody nose); ***eructation*** (belching; bloated full feeling; excess air or gas in stomach); ***esophagitis*** (difficulty in swallowing; pain or burning in throat; chest pain; heartburn; vomiting; sores, ulcers, or white spots on lips or tongue or inside the mouth); ***facial paralysis*** (unable to move or feel face); ***fever; fibrocystic breast*** (lumps in breasts; painful or tender cysts in the breasts); ***gastritis*** (burning feeling in chest or stomach; tenderness in stomach area; stomach upset; indigestion); ***gastroenteritis*** (abdominal or stomach pain; diarrhea; loss of appetite; nausea; weakness); ***glaucoma*** (blindness; blurred vision; decreased vision; eye pain; headache; nausea or vomiting; tearing); ***glossitis*** (redness, swelling, or soreness of tongue); ***gout*** (ankle, knee or great toe joint pain; joint stiffness or swelling; lower back or side pain); ***hematuria*** (blood in urine); ***hemorrhage, rectal, gum, vaginal, uterine, eye*** (bleeding); ***hyperglycemia*** (abdominal pain; blurred vision; dry mouth; fatigue; flushed, dry skin; fruit-like breath odor; increased hunger; increased thirst; increased urination; nausea; sweating; troubled breathing; unexplained weight loss; vomiting); ***hyperkinesia*** (increase in body movements); ***hypertension; hypertonia*** (excessive muscle tone; muscle tension or tightness; muscle stiffness); ***hypesthesia*** (increased sensitivity to pain; increased sensitivity to touch; tingling in the hands and feet); ***hypoglycemia*** (anxiety; blurred vision; chills; cold sweats; coma; confusion; cool pale skin; depression; dizziness; fast heartbeat; headache; increased hunger; nausea; nervousness; nightmares; seizures; shakiness; slurred speech; unusual tiredness or weakness); ***impotence*** (loss in sexual ability, desire, drive, or performance; decreased interest in sexual intercourse; inability to have or keep an erection); ***incoordination; insomnia; kidney calculus*** (blood in urine; nausea and vomiting; pain in groin or genitals; sharp back pain just below ribs); ***leg cramps; libido decreased*** (loss in sexual ability, desire, drive, or performance decreased interest in sexual intercourse; inability to have or keep an erection); ***lymphadenopathy*** (swollen, painful, or tender lymph glands in neck, armpit, or groin); ***malaise*** (general feeling of discomfort or illness; unusual tiredness or weakness); ***melena*** (bloody, black, or tarry stools); ***metorrhagia*** (normal menstrual bleeding occurring earlier, possibly lasting longer than expected); ***migraine*** (headache, severe and throbbing); ***mouth ulceration; myasthenia*** (loss of strength or energy muscle pain or weakness); ***myositis*** (muscle pain unusual tiredness or weakness); ***nausea; neck rigidity*** (severe muscle stiffness); ***nephritis*** (bloody or cloudy urine, difficulty in breathing, drowsiness headache unusual tiredness or weakness nausea or vomiting blood in urine unusual weight gain swelling of face, feet, or lower legs); ***nocturia*** (waking to urinate at night; increased urge to urinate during the night); ***palpitation*** (fast, irregular, pounding, or racing heartbeat or pulse); ***pancreatitis*** (bloating; chills; constipation; darkened urine; fast heartbeat; fever; indigestion; loss of appetite; nausea; pains in stomach, side, or abdomen possibly radiating to the back; vomiting; yellow eyes or skin); ***parosmia*** (transient, mild, pleasant aromatic odor); ***paresthesia*** (burning, crawling, itching, numbness, prickling, "pins and needles", or tingling feelings); ***peripheral neuropathy*** (burning, numbness, tingling, or painful sensations; weakness in arms, hands, legs, or feet; unsteadiness or awkwardness); ***petechia*** (small red or purple spots on skin); ***phlebitis*** (bluish color changes in skin color; pain; tenderness; swelling of foot or leg); ***photosensitivity*** (blurred vision; change in color vision; difficulty seeing at night; increased sensitivity of eyes to sunlight); ***postural hypotension*** (chills; cold sweats; confusion; dizziness, faintness, or lightheadedness when getting up from lying or sitting position); ***pruritis*** (itching skin); ***refraction disorder*** (blurred vision); ***rhinitis*** (stuffy nose; runny nose sneezing); ***sebor-***

rhea (dandruff; oily skin); ***skin ulcer*** (sores on the skin); ***somnolence*** (sleepiness or unusual drowsiness); ***stomatitis*** (swelling or inflammation of the mouth); ***sweating; syncope*** (fainting); ***taste loss; taste perversion; tendinous contracture*** (difficulty moving body parts); ***tenesmus*** (frequent urge to defecate; straining while passing stool); ***tenosynovitis*** (joint or muscle pain or stiffness); ***thrombocytopenia*** (black, tarry stools; bleeding gums; blood in urine or stools; pinpoint red spots on skin; unusual bleeding or bruising); ***tinnitus*** (continuing ringing or buzzing or other unexplained noise in ears; hearing loss); ***torticollis*** (uncontrolled twisting movements of neck); ***ulcerative stomatitis*** (sores on inside of cheeks or gums, fever, feeling ill); ***urinary incontinence*** (loss of bladder control); ***urinary retention; urinary tract infection*** (bladder pain; bloody or cloudy urine; difficult, burning, or painful urination; frequent urge to urinate; lower back or side pain); ***urinary urgency; urticaria*** (hives or welts; itching; redness of skin; skin rash); ***vasodilation*** (feeling of warmth or heat; flushing or redness of skin, especially on face and neck; headache; feeling faint, dizzy, or light-headedness; sweating); ***vomiting; weight gain***

Overdose

For more information on the management of overdose or unintentional ingestion, **contact a Poison Control Center** (see *Poison Control Center Listing*).

Treatment of overdose

Treatment should be symptomatic and supportive.

Hemodialysis is *not* expected to significantly enhance atorvastatin clearance due to extensive drug binding to plasma proteins.

Patients in whom intentional overdose is confirmed or suspected should be referred for psychiatric consultation.

Patient Consultation

As an aid to patient consultation, refer to *Advice for the Patient, Atorvastatin (Systemic)*.

In providing consultation, consider emphasizing the following selected information (» = major clinical significance):

Before using this medication

» Conditions affecting use, especially:

Hypersensitivity to atorvastatin

Pregnancy—Contraindicated during pregnancy or in women planning to become pregnant while taking atorvastatin

Breast-feeding—Contraindicated in women who are breast-feeding

Use in children—Safety and effectiveness have been established in boys and postmenarchal girls 10 to 17 years of age for treating heterozygous familial hypercholesterolemia. Atorvastatin has not been studied in pre-pubertal patients, patients younger than 10 years of age, or doses above 20 mg in patients 10 to 17 years of age.

Surgical—Increased risk of development of renal failure secondary to rhabdomyolysis with major surgery

Other medications, especially alcohol (substantial use of), azole antifungals, cyclosporine, erythromycin, fibric acid derivatives, niacin, and digoxin

Other medical problems, especially active hepatic disease, including chronic alcoholic liver disease, Childs-Pugh Index grade A disease and Childs-Pugh Index grade B disease; hypotension; major surgery; severe acute infection; myopathy; severe electrolyte, endocrine, or metabolic disorders; trauma; uncontrolled seizures; or unexplained persistent elevations of transaminase values

Proper use of this medication

Compliance with therapy; taking medication at the same time each day to maintain the antihyperlipidemic effect

Compliance with prescribed diet during treatment

» Proper dosing

Missed dose: Taking as soon as possible; not taking if almost time for next dose; not doubling doses

» Proper storage

Precautions while using this medication

Regular visits to physician to check progress

Notifying physician immediately if pregnancy is suspected because of possible harm to the fetus

Caution if any kind of surgery (including dental surgery) or emergency treatment is required

Not taking over-the-counter niacin preparations without consulting physician because of increased risk of rhabdomyolysis

Not using alcohol excessively because elevations of liver enzymes may occur

Notifying physician immediately if unexplained muscle pain, tenderness, or weakness occurs, especially if accompanied by unusual tiredness or fever

Side/adverse effects

Signs of potential side effects, especially allergic reactions, liver function abnormalities, muscle disorders, such as leg cramps, uncomplicated myalgia, myopathy and/or rhabdomyolysis, and myositis

Signs of potential side effects observed during clinical practice, especially anaphylaxis, angioneurotic edema, bullous rashes, erythema multiforme, rhabdomyolysis, Stevens-Johnson syndrome, and toxic epidermal necrolysis

General Dosing Information

Clinical response to atorvastatin is seen within 2 weeks, and maximum response is usually achieved within 4 weeks and maintained during long-term therapy.

Prior to starting atorvastatin therapy, secondary causes for hypercholesterolemia, such as poorly controlled diabetes mellitus, hypothyroidism, nephrotic syndrome, dysproteinemias, obstructive liver disease, other medication therapy, and alcoholism should be excluded and a lipid profile performed to measure total cholesterol (total-C), low-density lipoprotein cholesterol (LDL-C), high-density lipoprotein cholesterol (HDL-C), and triglycerides (TG).

Atorvastatin may be used with bile acid binding resin for additive antihyperlipidemic effects.

Diet/Nutrition

Prior to treatment with atorvastatin, control of hypercholesterolemia with diet, exercise, weight reduction in obese patients, and treatment of underlying medical problems should be attempted. The patient should be placed on a standard cholesterol-lowering diet before receiving atorvastatin and should continue on this diet during treatment with atorvastatin.

Atorvastatin may be taken with or without food.

Grapefruit juice and grapefruit products in large doses should not be taken before or after administration of atorvastatin or the dose of atorvastatin should be reduced accordingly in order to avoid significant increases in plasma drug concentrations and the area under the atorvastatin plasma concentration-time curve (AUC).

Adolescent female patients should be counseled on appropriate contraceptive methods while on atorvastatin therapy.

For additional information on initial therapeutic guidelines related to the treatment of hyperlipidemia, see *Appendix III*.

Oral Dosage Forms

ATORVASTATIN CALCIUM TABLETS

Usual adult dose

Coronary heart disease (prophylaxis)—

Oral, 10 mg once per day.

Heterozygous familial and nonfamilial hypercholesterolemia and mixed dyslipidemia (Fredrickson Types IIa and IIb)—

Oral, initially 10 mg once a day. The dosage range is 10 to 80 mg once a day, to be administered at any time of the day, with or without food. After initiation or titration of atorvastatin, lipid concentrations should be measured within 2 to 4 weeks and the dosage adjusted accordingly.

Note: Dosage adjustment in patients with renal dysfunction is not necessary.

Note: The goal of therapy is to lower LDL-C. The National Cholesterol Education Program (NCEP) recommends that LDL-C concentrations be used to initiate and assess treatment response. Only if LDL-C concentrations are not available should total-C be used to monitor therapy.

Homozygous familial hypercholesterolemia—

Oral, 10 to 80 mg a day.

Note: Atorvastatin should be used in these patients as an adjunct to other lipid-lowering treatments, such as LDL apheresis, or if such treatments are unavailable.

Usual adult prescribing limits

80 mg a day.

Usual pediatric dose

Heterozygous familial hypercholesterolemia—

Oral, 10 mg per day in boys and postmenarchal girls 10 to 17 years of age. Adjustments should be made at intervals of 4 weeks or more.

Note: Atorvastatin has not been studied in prepubertal patients or patients younger than 10 years of age.

The goal of therapy is to lower LDL-C. The National Cholesterol Education Program (NCEP) recommends that LDL-C concentrations be used to initiate and assess treatment response.

Dosage adjustment in patients with renal dysfunction is not necessary.

Usual pediatric prescribing limit

Doses greater than 20 mg per day have not been studied in this patient population.

Strength(s) usually available

U.S.—

10 mg (Rx) [*Lipitor* (film-coated)].
20 mg (Rx) [*Lipitor* (film-coated)].
40 mg (Rx) [*Lipitor* (film-coated)].
80 mg (Rx) [*Lipitor* (film-coated)].

Canada—

10 mg (Rx) [*Lipitor* (film-coated; calcium carbonate; candelilla wax; croscarmellose sodium; hydroxypropyl methylcellulose; lactose monohydrate; magnesium stearate; microcrystalline cellulose; hydroxypropyl methylcellulose; polyethylene glycol; talc; titanium dioxide; polysorbate 80; simethicone emulsion)].

20 mg (Rx) [*Lipitor* (film-coated; calcium carbonate; candelilla wax; croscarmellose sodium; hydroxypropyl methylcellulose; lactose monohydrate; magnesium stearate; microcrystalline cellulose; hydroxypropyl methylcellulose; polyethylene glycol; talc; titanium dioxide; polysorbate 80; simethicone emulsion)].

40 mg (Rx) [*Lipitor* (film-coated; calcium carbonate; candelilla wax; croscarmellose sodium; hydroxypropyl methylcellulose; lactose monohydrate; magnesium stearate; microcrystalline cellulose; hydroxypropyl methylcellulose; polyethylene glycol; talc; titanium dioxide; polysorbate 80; simethicone emulsion)].

80 mg (Rx) [*Lipitor* (film-coated; calcium carbonate; candelilla wax; croscarmellose sodium; hydroxypropyl methylcellulose; lactose monohydrate; magnesium stearate; microcrystalline cellulose; hydroxypropyl methylcellulose; polyethylene glycol; talc; titanium dioxide; polysorbate 80; simethicone emulsion)].

Packaging and storage

Store at controlled room temperature between 20 and 25 °C (68 and 77 °F).

Auxiliary labeling

• This medication could be harmful if you are pregnant or breast-feeding. Consult your pharmacist or doctor about using this medication if you are pregnant, plan to become pregnant, or if you are breast-feeding.
• Ask your doctor or pharmacist before using nonprescription drugs.

Revised: 11/28/2005
Developed: 10/29/1997

ATOVAQUONE AND PROGUANIL Systemic

VA CLASSIFICATION (Primary): AP101

Commonly used brand name(s): *Malarone.*

Note: For a listing of dosage forms and brand names by country availability, see *Dosage Forms* section(s).

Category

Anti-protozoal.

Indications

General Considerations

Atovaquone and proguanil metabolite, cycloguanil, are active against the erythrocytic and exoerythrocytic stages of *Plasmodium* species. The combination product has been shown to exert increased efficacy in the treatment of malaria in both immune and nonimmune patients compared with either agent alone.

Accepted

Malaria (prophylaxis and treatment)—Atovaquone and proguanil combination is indicated for the prevention of malaria caused by susceptible strains of *P. falciparum* in adults and children. This combination is also indicated for use in geographical regions that have previously shown chloroquine resistance.

Atovaquone and proguanil combination is indicated for treatment of acute, uncomplicated malaria caused by susceptible strains of *P. falciparum.* It has been shown to be effective in geographical regions where resistance has diminished the efficacy of drugs such as amodiaquine, chloroquine, halofantrine, and mefloquine. However, atovaquone and proguanil combination may not be effective if malaria recurs following therapy.

Unaccepted

Safety and efficacy of atovaquone and proguanil combination have not been established for treatment of cerebral malaria or symptoms of severe, complicated malaria such as hyperparasitemia, pulmonary edema, or renal failure. Oral therapy is not recommended for treatment of such severe conditions.

Pharmacology/Pharmacokinetics

Physicochemical characteristics

Molecular weight—
Atovaquone: 366.84.
Proguanil: 290.22.

Mechanism of action/Effect

Atovaquone and proguanil interfere with two different pathways that are involved in the biosynthesis of pyrimidines required for parasitic nucleic acid replication.

Atovaquone selectivelyinhibits parasite mitochondrial electron transport.

Proguanil's primary mechanism is via its metabolite, cycloguanil. Dihydrofolate reductase is inhibited in the malaria parasite by cycloguanil and disrupts deoxythymidylate synthesis.

Absorption

Atovaquone—Considerable variability among individuals. Because of its lipophilicity and low aqueous solubility, dietary fat intake increases absorption rate and extent; area under the plasma concentration-time curve (AUC) increases 2 to 3 times and C_{max} 5 times over fasting.

Atovaquone Tablet—Total absolute bioavailability (taken with food): 23%

Proguanil—Extensive, regardless of food intake.

Distribution

Atovaquone—Vol_D: 3.5 L per kg

Proguanil—Vol_D: 42 L per kg

Protein binding

Atovaquone: Very high (99%)
Proguanil: High (75%)

Biotransformation

Atovaquone—
Indirect evidence suggests that atovaquone undergoes limited metabolism. However, no metabolite has been identified.

Proguanil—
Metabolized into cycloguanil (via CYP2C19) and 4-chlorophenylbiguanide.

Half-life

Atovaquone—Elimination: 2 to 3 days in adults; 1 to 2 days in children.

Proguanil—Elimination: 12 to 21 hours in adults and children; may be increased in patients who are slow metabolizers.

Elimination

Atovaquone—
Fecal: Greater than 94% was recovered unchanged over 21 days.
Renal: Less than 0.6% was excreted in the urine.

Proguanil—
Renal: Between 40 and 60%.

Precautions to Consider

Carcinogenicity/Mutagenicity

Atovaquone: Carcinogenicity studies done in rats were negative. Studies done in mice showed treatment-related increases in hepatocellular adenomas and hepatocellular carcinomas at doses ranging 5 to 8 times the average steady-state plasma concentrations used in humans for prevention of malaria. Atovaquone was found to be negative with or without metabolic activation in the Ames *Salmonella* mutagenicity assay, the mouse lymphoma mutagenesis assay, and the cultured human lymphocyte cytogenic assay. No evidence of genotoxicity was seen in the *in vivo* mouse micronucleus assay.

Proguanil: No evidence of a carcinogenic effect was observed in studies conducted in CD-1 mice (doses up to 1.51 times the average systemic human exposure base on AUC) and in Wistar Hannover rats (doses up to 1.12 times the average systemic human exposure). It was found to be negative or without metabolic activation in the Ames *Salmonella* mutagenicity assay and the Mouse Lymphoma mutagenesis assay. There was no evidence of genotoxicity in the *in vivo* Mouse Micronucleus assay.

Atovaquone and proguanil: There have been no genotoxicity studies done.

Pregnancy/Reproduction

Fertility—Effects of atovaquone and proguanil combination on male and female reproductivity are unknown.

Pregnancy—

Note: Falciparum malaria carries a higher risk of morbidity and mortality in pregnant women. Maternal death and fetal loss are both known complications. Personal protection and antimalarials should always be used by pregnant women who must travel to malaria-endemic areas.

Although proguanil inhibits parasitic dihydrofolate reductase, there are no clinical data indicating that folate supplementation diminishes medication efficacy. It is not necessary for women of childbearing age who are taking folate supplements to prevent neural tube defects to discontinue their use while taking atovaquone and proguanil combination.

Atovaquone: Not found to be teratogenic and did not cause reproductive toxicity in rats at maternal plasma concentrations up to 5 to 6.5 times the estimated human exposure. It did cause maternal toxicity in rabbits with plasma concentrations that were approximately 0.6 to 1.3 times the estimated human exposure. Decreased mean fetal body lengths, increased early resorption and post-implantation losses were found. It is not clear whether these effects were caused by atovaquone or were secondary to maternal toxicity. Concentrations in rabbit fetuses averaged 30% of the concurrent maternal plasma concentrations. After a single ^{14}C-radiolabeled dose, concentrations of radiocarbon in rat fetuses were 18% (middle gestation) and 60% (late gestation) of concurrent maternal plasma concentrations.

Atovaquone and proguanil: There are no adequate and well-controlled studies of atovaquone and proguanil in pregnant women. Not teratogenic in rats at plasma concentrations up to 1.7 and 0.1 times, respectively, the estimated human exposure during malaria treatment. In rabbits, it was not teratogenic or embryotoxic at concentrations up ot 0.34 and 0.82 times, respectively, the estimated human exposure during malaria treatment. Atovaquone and proguanil may be used if the potential benefit justifies the potential risk to the fetus.

FDA Pregnancy Category C.

Breast-feeding

Atovaquone: It is unknown whether atovaquone is distributed into human breast milk. However, a rat study showed concentrations were 30% of the concurrent atovaquone concentrations in maternal plasma.

Proguanil: Distributed into human breast milk in small quantities.

Atovaquone and proguanil: Caution should be used when prescribing to lactating women.

Pediatrics

Malaria (prophylaxis): There is no information on the relationship of age to the effects of atovaquone and proguanil in the pediatric population of patients who weigh less than 11 kg. Safety and efficacy have not been established in pediatrics weighing less than 11 kg.

Malaria (treatment): There is no information on the relationship of age to the effects of atovaquone and proguanil in the pediatric population of patients who weigh less than 5 kg. Safety and efficacy have not been established in pediatrics weighing less than 5 kg.

Geriatrics

Although appropriate studies on the relationship of age to the effects of atovaquone and proguanil combination have not been performed in the geriatric population, geriatrics-specific problems are not expected to limit the usefulness of atovaquone and proguanil in the elderly. However, elderly patients are more likely to have age-related renal function impairment, which may require caution in patients receiving this combination.

Drug interactions and/or related problems

The following drug interactions and/or related problems have been selected on the basis of their potential clinical significance (possible mechanism in parentheses where appropriate)—not necessarily inclusive (» = major clinical significance):

» Metoclopramide
(decreases bioavailability of atovaquone; use alternate antiemetics whenever possible)

» Rifabutin or
» Rifampin
(reduces atovaquone levels 34% and 50%, respectively; avoid concomitant use)

» Proguanil-containing medications
(concomitant use should be avoided)

» Tetracycline
(associated with approximately 40% reduction in plasma concentrations of atovaquone; closely monitor parasitemia in these patients)

Laboratory value alterations

The following have been selected on the basis of their potential clinical significance (possible effect in parentheses where appropriate)—not necessarily inclusive (» = major clinical significance).

With physiology/laboratory test values

Alanine aminotransferase (ALT [SGPT]) and
Aspartate aminotransferase (AST [SGOT]) and
(values may be increased, and persist up to 4 weeks after treatment.)

Medical considerations/Contraindications

The medical considerations/contraindications included have been selected on the basis of their potential clinical significance (reasons given in parentheses where appropriate)—not necessarily inclusive (» = major clinical significance).

Except under special circumstances, this medication should not be used when the following medical problem exists:

» Hypersensitivity to atovaquone, proguanil hydrochloride, or any component of the formulation.

» Severe renal impairment
(contraindicated in patients with creatinine clearance <30 mL per minute for prophylaxis of malaria; should be used with caution and risk-benefit considered for treatment of malaria)

Risk-benefit should be considered when the following medical problems exist:

» Diarrhea or vomiting
(absorption may be decreased; parasitemia should be monitored and antiemetic use considered; if severe or persistent then alternative malaria therapy should be considered)

Note: Relapse is common when treating *P. vivax*malaria

Failure of chemoprophylaxis or
Recrudescent *P. falciparum* infections
(treatment with a different blood schizonticide is recommended)

Side/Adverse Effects

The following side/adverse effects have been selected on the basis of their potential clinical significance (possible signs and symptoms in parentheses where appropriate)—not necessarily inclusive:

Those indicating need for medical attention

Incidence not determined—Observed during clinical practice; estimates of frequency can not be determined

Anaphylaxis (cough; difficulty swallowing; dizziness; fast heartbeat; hives; itching; puffiness or swelling of the eyelids or around the eyes, face, lips or tongue; shortness of breath; skin rash; tightness in chest; unusual tiredness or weakness; wheezing); ***angioedema*** (large, hive-like swelling on face, eyelids, lips, tongue, throat, hands, legs, feet, sex organs); ***erythema multiforme*** (blistering, peeling, loosening of skin; chills; cough; diarrhea; fever; itching; joint or muscle pain; red irritated eyes; sore throat; sores, ulcers, or white spots in mouth or on lips; unusual tiredness or weakness); ***photosensitivity*** (increased sensitivity of skin to sunlight; itching; redness or other discoloration of skin; severe sunburn; skin rash); ***psychotic events (such as hallucinations)*** (severe mental changes; [seeing, hearing, or feeling things that are not there]); ***rash; seizures*** (convulsions; muscle spasm or jerking of all extremities; sudden loss of consciousness; loss of bladder control); ***Stevens-Johnson syndrome*** (blistering, peeling, loosening of skin; chills; cough; diarrhea; itching; joint or muscle pain; red irritated eyes; red skin lesions, often with a purple center; sore throat; sores, ulcers, or white spots in mouth or on lips; unusual tiredness or weakness); ***urticaria*** (hives or welts; itching; redness of skin; skin rash)

Those indicating need for medical attention only if they continue or are bothersome

Incidence more frequent

Abdominal pain; asthenia (lack or loss of strength); ***back pain; cough; diarrhea; dreams; headache; myalgia*** (muscle pain); ***nausea; oral ulcers*** (sores in mouth); ***pruritus*** (itching skin); ***upper respiratory infection*** (cough; fever; sneezing; sore throat); ***vomiting***

Incidence less frequent

Anorexia (loss of appetite; weight loss); ***dizziness; dyspepsia*** (acid or sour stomach; belching; heartburn; indigestion; stomach discomfort, upset, or pain); ***fever; flu syndrome*** (chills; cough; diarrhea; fever; general feeling of discomfort or illness; headache; joint pain; loss of appetite; muscle aches and pains; nausea; runny nose; shivering; sore throat; sweating; trouble sleeping; unusual tiredness or weakness; vomiting); ***gastritis*** (burning feeling in chest or stomach; indigestion; stomach upset; tenderness in stomach area); ***insomnia*** (sleeplessness; trouble sleeping; unable to sleep); ***visual difficulties*** (blurred or loss of vision; disturbed color perception; night blindness; double vision; tunnel vision; halos around lights; overbright appearance of lights)

Rare

Anxiety (fear, nervousness); ***depression*** (discouragement; feeling sad or empty; irritability; lack of appetite; loss of interest or pleasure; tiredness; trouble concentrating; trouble sleeping)

Overdose

For more information on the management of overdose or unintentional ingestion, **contact a poison control center** (see *Poison Control Center Listing*).

Clinical effects of overdose

The following effects have been selected on the basis of their potential clinical significance (possible signs and symptoms in parentheses where appropriate)—not necessarily inclusive:

Note: There have been no known reports of overdosage of atovaquone and proguanil.

Note: The median lethal dose of atovaquone is higher than the mean oral dose tested in mice and rats (1825 mg per kg). Overdoses of up to 31,500 mg of atovaquone have been reported.

Note: Overdoses of 1500 mg of proguanil hydrochloride have been reported, followed by complete recovery, and doses as high as 700 mg twice daily have been taken over two weeks without serious toxicity.

Atovaquone

Rash

Proguanil

Aphthous ulceration, reversible (sores in mouth); ***epigastric discomfort*** (pain in chest, upper stomach or throat; heartburn); ***hair loss, reversible; hematologic side effects; scaling of the skin on palms or soles; vomiting***

Treatment of overdose

There is no known antidote for atovaquone, and it is unknown if it is dialyzable.

Treatment is primarily symptomatic and supportive.

Patients in whom intentional overdose is confirmed or suspected should be referred for psychiatric consultation.

Patient Consultation

As an aid to patient consultation, refer to *Advice for the Patient, Atovaquone and Proguanil (Systemic)*.

In providing consultation, consider emphasizing the following selected information (» = major clinical significance):

Before using this medication

» Conditions affecting use, especially:
- Hypersensitivity to atovaquone, proguanil hydrochloride, or any component of the formulation
- Pregnancy—Risk-benefit should be considered
- Breast-feeding—Caution should be used when administering to lactating women
- Use in children—Malaria prophylaxis: Safety and efficacy not established in children less than 11 kg
- Malaria treatment: Safety and efficacy not established in children less than 5 kg
- Use in the elderly—Caution due to the potential for age-related renal impairment
- Other medications, especially metoclopramide, proguanil hydrochloride containing drugs, rifabutin, rifampin and tetracycline
- Other medical problems, especially diarrhea or vomiting; recrudescent *P. falciparum* infections or failure of chemoprophylaxis; or severe renal impairment

Proper use of this medication

Taking medication at the same time each day

» Taking with food or a milky drink

» Repeating dose if vomiting occurs within 1 hour

Crushing tablet and mixing with condensed milk if difficulty in swallowing tablets

» Proper dosing

Missed dose: Taking as soon as possible; not doubling doses; contacting doctor for further instructions.

Proper storage

Precautions while using this medication

Personal protection measures to prevent malaria, such as:
- Remaining in air-conditioned or well-screened rooms to reduce human-mosquito contact
- Sleeping under mosquito netting; preferably impregnated with permethrin-containing insecticide
- Wearing suitable clothing (long-sleeved shirt or long trousers) to protect arms and legs when mosquitoes are out
- Applying mosquito repellents containing *N,N*–diethyl-*m*-toluamide (DEET) to uncovered areas of skin when mosquitoes are out
- Using a pyrethrum-containing flying insect spray to kill mosquitoes
- Notifying physician immediately if symptoms of anaphylaxis develop

Caution when exposed to sunlight because photosensitivity can occur, which may result in sunburn

Side/adverse effects

Signs of potential side effects observed during clinical practice, especially anaphylaxis, angioedema, erythema multiforme, photosensitivity, psychotic events (such as hallucinations), rash, seizures, Stevens-Johnson syndrome, or urticaria

General Dosing Information

Prophylactic treatment should start 1 to 2 days before entering the malaria-endemic area. It should be continued daily and extend until 7 days after return from the region.

The dose of atovaquone and proguanil combination should be repeated if vomiting occurs within 1 hour after administration.

Parasite relapse commonly occurred with *P. vivax* malaria, when it was treated with atovaquone and proguanil alone.

Diet/Nutrition

Atovaquone and proguanil combination should be taken at the same time each day with food or a milky drink.

Folate supplementation may continue during atovaquone and proguanil therapy.

Oral Dosage Forms

ATOVAQUONE AND PROGUANIL HYDROCHLORIDE TABLETS

Usual adult dose

Malaria (prophylaxis)—

Oral, 250 mg atovaquone and 100 mg proguanil (one adult strength tablet) per day, beginning 1–2 days prior to entering an endemic area and continuing daily until 7 days after return.

Malaria (treatment)—

Oral, 1 gram atovaquone and 400 mg proguanil (4 adult strength tablets) as a single dose daily for three consecutive days.

Note: For patients with severe renal impairment (creatinine clearance <30 mL per minute): Atovaquone/proguanil should not be used for malaria prophylaxis and should be used with caution and risk-benefit considerations in malaria treatment.

For patients with mild (creatinine clearance 50 to 80 mL per minute) or moderate (creatinine clearance 30 to 50 mL per minute) renal impairment: No dosage adjustments are needed.

For patients with severe hepatic impairment: No studies have been conducted.

For patients with mild or moderate hepatic impairment: No dosage adjustments are needed.

Usual pediatric dose

Malaria (prophylaxis)—

Oral, pediatric strength tablets, dose is based on body weight and is started 1–2 days prior to entrance into endemic area and continuing daily until 7 days after return.

11-20 kg: 62.5 mg atovaquone and 25 mg proguanil (1 pediatric strength tablet) daily.

21-30 kg: 125 mg atovaquone and 50 mg proguanil (2 pediatric strength tablets) as a single dose daily.

31-40 kg: 187.5 mg atovaquone and 75 mg proguanil (3 pediatric strength tablets) as a single dose daily.

greater than 40 kg: 250 mg atovaquone and 100 mg proguanil (1 adult strength tablet) as a single dose daily.

Malaria (treatment)—

Oral, dose is based on body weight as follows:

5-8 kg: 125 mg atovaquone and 50 mg proguanil (2 pediatric strength tablets) daily for 3 consecutive days.

9-10 kg: 187.5 mg atovaquone and 75 mg proguanil (3 pediatric strength tablets) daily for 3 consecutive days.

11-20 kg: 250 mg atovaquone and 100 mg proguanil (1 adult strength tablet) daily for 3 consecutive days.

21-30 kg: 500 mg atovaquone and 200 mg proguanil (2 adult strength tablets) as a single dose daily for 3 consecutive days.

31-40 kg: 750 mg atovaquone and 300 mg proguanil (3 adult strength tablets) as a single dose daily for 3 consecutive days.

greater than 40 kg: 1 gram atovaquone and 400 mg proguanil (4 adult strength tablets) as a single dose daily for 3 consecutive days.

Note: For children who may have difficulty swallowing tablets: atovaquone and proguanil tablets may be crushed and mixed with condensed milk just prior to administration.

Usual geriatric dose

See *Usual adult dose.*

Note: Caution should be exercised when this medication is used in geriatric patients because of the potential for age-related renal function impairment.

Strength(s) usually available

U.S.—

250 mg atovaquone, 100 mg proguanil hydrochloride (Rx) [*Malarone* (low-substituted hydroxypropyl cellulose; magnesium stearate; microcrystalline cellulose; poloxamer 188; povidone K30; and sodium starch glycolate)].

62.5 mg atovaquone, 25 mg proguanil hydrochloride (Rx) [*Malarone* (low-substituted hydroxypropyl cellulose; magnesium stearate; microcrystalline cellulose; poloxamer 188; povidone K30; sodium starch glycolate)].

Packaging and storage

Store at 25 °C (77 °F), excursions permitted to 15° to 30 ° (59° to 86°).

Auxiliary labeling

- Take with food or milk.

Revised: 02/23/2005
Developed: 11/03/2000

ATRACURIUM—See *Neuromuscular Blocking Agents (Systemic)*

ATROPINE—See *Anticholinergics/Antispasmodics (Systemic), Atropine (Ophthalmic)*

ATROPINE Ophthalmic

VA CLASSIFICATION (Primary): OP600

Commonly used brand name(s): *Atropair; Atropine Care; Atropine Sulfate S.O.P.; Atropisol; Atrosulf; I-Tropine; Isopto Atropine; Minims Atropine; Ocu-Tropine.*

Note: For a listing of dosage forms and brand names by country availability, see *Dosage Forms* section(s).

Category

Cycloplegic; mydriatic.

Indications

Note: Bracketed information in the *Indications* section refers to uses that are not included in U.S. product labeling.

Accepted

Refraction, cycloplegic—Atropine is indicated for measurement of refractive errors. Atropine is a commonly used cycloplegic for refraction in children up to 6 years of age and in children with convergent strabismus. It is not useful for refraction in adults, because of its long duration of action.

Uveitis (treatment)—Atropine is indicated for pupil dilation and ciliary muscle relaxation, which are desirable in acute inflammatory conditions of the iris and uveal tract.

[Synechiae, posterior (prophylaxis and treatment)]—Atropine may be used for pupil dilation to break posterior synechiae and decrease the possibility of serious complications resulting from synechiae. However, a more rapidly acting medication is usually used. Atropine may also be used to prevent formation of posterior synechiae.

[Mydriasis, preoperative and postoperative]—Atropine may be used for preoperative and postoperative mydriasis.

[Glaucoma, malignant (treatment)][1]—Atropine is used in the treatment of malignant (ciliary block) glaucoma, which may occur after inflammation, surgery, trauma, or use of miotics.

[1]Not included in Canadian product labeling.

Pharmacology/Pharmacokinetics

Mechanism of action/Effect

Atropine (a belladonna alkaloid) is an anticholinergic agent that blocks the responses of the sphincter muscle of the iris and the accommodative muscle of the ciliary body to stimulation by acetylcholine. Dilation of the pupil (mydriasis) and paralysis of accommodation (cycloplegia) result.

Duration of action

Long-acting; effects on accommodation may last 6 days; mydriasis may persist for 12 days.

Precautions to Consider

Cross-sensitivity and/or related problems

Patients sensitive to any of the other belladonna alkaloids may be sensitive to atropine also.

Carcinogenicity/Mutagenicity

Studies have not been done in either animals or humans to evaluate the carcinogenic or mutagenic potential of atropine.

Pregnancy/Reproduction

Fertility—Studies have not been done in either animals or humans to evaluate the potential of atropine impairing fertility.

Pregnancy—Studies have not been done in humans; however, ophthalmic atropine may be systemically absorbed.

Studies have not been done in animals.

FDA Pregnancy Category C.

Breast-feeding

Systemic atropine is distributed into breast milk in very small amounts. Ophthalmic atropine may be systemically absorbed and may possibly cause adverse effects, such as fast pulse, fever, or dry skin, in nursing infants of mothers using ophthalmic atropine.

Pediatrics

Atropine should not be used in children who have previously had a severe systemic reaction to atropine.

An increased susceptibility to atropine has been reported in infants and young children and in children with blond hair, blue eyes, Down's syndrome, spastic paralysis, or brain damage; therefore, atropine should be used with great caution in these patients.

The ointment dosage form is generally preferred for use in children, since use of the solution presents a greater chance of systemic absorption.

Geriatrics

Geriatric patients are more susceptible to the effects of atropine, thus increasing the potential for systemic side effects.

Drug interactions and/or related problems

The following drug interactions and/or related problems have been selected on the basis of their potential clinical significance (possible mechanism in parentheses where appropriate)—not necessarily inclusive (» = major clinical significance):

Note: Combinations containing any of the following medications, depending on the amount present, may also interact with this medication.

Anticholinergics or medications with anticholinergic activity, other (See *Appendix II*)
(if significant systemic absorption of ophthalmic atropine occurs, concurrent use of other anticholinergics or medications with anticholinergic activity may result in potentiated anticholinergic effects)

Antiglaucoma agents, cholinergic, long-acting, ophthalmic
(concurrent use with atropine may antagonize the antiglaucoma and miotic actions of ophthalmic long-acting cholinergic antiglaucoma agents, such as demecarium, echothiophate, and isoflurophate; concurrent use with atropine may also antagonize the antiaccommodative convergence effects of these medications when they are used for the treatment of strabismus)

Antimyasthenics or
Potassium citrate or
Potassium supplements
(if significant systemic absorption of ophthalmic atropine occurs, concurrent use may increase the chance of toxicity and/or side effects of these systemic medications because of the anticholinergic-induced slowing of gastrointestinal motility)

Carbachol or
Physostigmine or
Pilocarpine
(concurrent use with atropine may interfere with the antiglaucoma action of carbachol, physostigmine, or pilocarpine. Also, concur-

rent use may counteract the mydriatic effect of atropine; this counteraction may be used to therapeutic advantage)

CNS depression-producing medications (See *Appendix II*)
(if significant systemic absorption of ophthalmic atropine occurs, concurrent use of medications having CNS effects, such as antiemetic agents, phenothiazines, or barbiturates, may result in opisthotonos, convulsions, coma, and extrapyramidal symptoms)

Medical considerations/Contraindications

The medical considerations/contraindications included have been selected on the basis of their potential clinical significance (reasons given in parentheses where appropriate)—not necessarily inclusive (» = major clinical significance).

Except under special circumstances, this medication should not be used when the following medical problem exists:

» Severe systemic reaction to atropine, especially in children, history of

Risk-benefit should be considered when the following medical problems exist:

Brain damage, in children

Down's syndrome (mongolism), in children and adults

» Glaucoma, primary, or predisposition to angle closure

Keratoconus
(atropine may produce fixed dilated pupil)

Sensitivity to atropine

Spastic paralysis, in children

Synechiae between the iris and lens

Side/Adverse Effects

Note: An increased susceptibility to atropine has been reported in infants, young children, children with blond hair or blue eyes, adults and children with Down's syndrome, children with brain damage or spastic paralysis, and the elderly. This susceptibility increases the potential for systemic side effects.

Prolonged use of atropine may produce local irritation, resulting in follicular conjunctivitis, vascular congestion, edema, exudate, contact dermatitis, or an eczematoid dermatitis.

Severe reactions to atropine may occur and are evidenced by hypotension with progressive respiratory depression. Coma and death have been reported in the very young.

The following side/adverse effects have been selected on the basis of their potential clinical significance (possible signs and symptoms in parentheses where appropriate)—not necessarily inclusive:

Those indicating need for medical attention

Symptoms of systemic absorption
Clumsiness or unsteadiness; confusion or unusual behavior; dizziness; dryness of skin; fever; flushing or redness of face; hallucinations; skin rash; slurred speech; swollen stomach in infants; tachycardia (fast or irregular heartbeat); ***unusual drowsiness; tiredness or weakness; xerostomia*** (thirst or dryness of mouth)

Those indicating need for medical attention only if they continue or are bothersome

Blurred vision; eye irritation not present before therapy; increased sensitivity of eyes to light; swelling of the eyelids

Overdose

For specific information on the agents used in the management of ophthalmic atropine overdose, see:

- *Atropine* in *Anticholinergics/Antispasmodics (Systemic)* monograph;
- *Diazepam* in *Benzodiazepines (Systemic)* monograph; and/or
- *Physostigmine (Systemic)* monograph.

For more information on the management of overdose or unintentional ingestion, **contact a Poison Control Center** (see *Poison Control Center Listing*).

Treatment of overdose

For accidental ingestion, emesis or gastric lavage with 4% tannic acid solution is recommended.

For systemic effects, 0.2 to 1 mg (0.2 mg in children) physostigmine should be administered intravenously, as a dilution containing 1 mg in 5 mL of normal saline. The solution should be injected over a period of not less than 2 minutes. Dosage may be repeated every 5 minutes up to a total dose of 2 mg in children and 6 mg in adults in each 30-minute period.

Physostigmine is contraindicated in hypertensive reactions.

ECG monitoring is recommended during physostigmine administration.

Excitement may be controlled by diazepam or a short-acting barbiturate.

It is recommended that 1 mg of atropine be available for immediate injection if the physostigmine causes bradycardia, convulsion, or bronchoconstriction.

Supportive therapy may require oxygen and assisted respiration; cool water baths for fever, especially in children; and catheterization for urinary retention. In infants and small children, the body surface should be kept moist.

Patient Consultation

As an aid to patient consultation, refer to *Advice for the Patient, Atropine/Homatropine/Scopolamine (Ophthalmic)*.

In providing consultation, consider emphasizing the following selected information (» = major clinical significance):

Before using this medication

» Conditions affecting use, especially:
Sensitivity to atropine, homatropine, or scopolamine
Breast-feeding—Medication passes into the breast milk in very small amounts and may cause side effects, such as fast pulse, fever, or dry skin, in babies of nursing mothers using ophthalmic atropine
Use in children—Infants and young children and children with blond hair or blue eyes may be especially sensitive to the effects of atropine; this may increase the chance of side effects during treatment
Use in the elderly—Geriatric patients are more susceptible to the effects of atropine, thus increasing the potential for systemic side effects
Other medical problems, especially primary glaucoma or predisposition to angle closure

Proper use of this medication

Proper administration technique
Washing hands immediately after application to remove any medication that may be on them; if applying medication to infants or children, washing their hands immediately afterwards also, and not letting any medication get into their mouths; wiping off any medication that may have accidentally gotten on the infant or child, including his or her face and eyelids
Preventing contamination: Not touching applicator tip to any surface; keeping container tightly closed

» Importance of not using more medication than the amount prescribed

» Proper dosing
Missed dose:
If dosing schedule is—
Once a day: Applying as soon as possible if remembered same day; if remembered later, skipping missed dose and going back to regular dosing schedule; not doubling doses
More than once a day: Applying as soon as possible; if almost time for next dose, skipping missed dose and going back to regular dosing schedule; not doubling doses

» Proper storage

Precautions while using this medication

» Medication causes blurred vision and increased sensitivity of the eyes to light; checking with physician if these effects continue for longer than 14 days after discontinuation of atropine

Side/adverse effects

Signs of potential side effects, especially symptoms of systemic absorption

General Dosing Information

A stronger concentration may be required to produce adequate cycloplegia in eyes with hazel or brown irides than in eyes with blue or light-colored irides.

The ointment dosage form is generally preferred for use in children, since use of the solution presents a greater chance of systemic absorption.

For ointment dosage form only

If the ointment is used for refraction, it should be applied several hours prior to the examination; otherwise it may impair the transparency of the cornea and alter the regularity of its refraction.

For solution dosage form only

Although some manufacturers recommend a dose of 2 drops of an ophthalmic solution at appropriate intervals, the conjunctival sac will usually hold only 1 drop.

To avoid excessive systemic absorption, patient should press finger to the lacrimal sac during, and for 2 or 3 minutes following, instillation of the solution.

Ophthalmic Dosage Forms

Note: Bracketed uses in the *Dosage Forms* section refer to categories of use and/or indications that are not included in U.S. product labeling.

ATROPINE SULFATE OPHTHALMIC OINTMENT USP

Usual adult and adolescent dose

Uveitis—

Topical, to the conjunctiva, 0.3 to 0.5 cm of a l% ointment one or two times a day.

Usual pediatric dose

Cycloplegic refraction—

Topical, to the conjunctiva, 0.3 cm of the following concentrations three times a day for one to three days prior to refraction:

Children up to 2 years of age with blue irides—
0.5%.

Children up to 2 years of age with dark irides—
1%.

Children 2 years of age and over—
1%.

Uveitis

[Postoperative mydriasis]—

Topical, to the conjunctiva, 0.3 to 0.5 cm of a 0.5 or 1% ointment one to three times a day.

Strength(s) usually available

U.S.—

0.5% (Rx) [*Atropine Sulfate S.O.P.* (chlorobutanol 0.5%)].

1% (Rx) [*Atropair; Atropine Sulfate S.O.P.* (chlorobutanol 0.5%); *Ocu-Tropine;* GENERIC (may contain chlorobutanol)].

Canada—

1% (Rx) [GENERIC (may contain methylparaben, propylparaben)].

Packaging and storage

Store below 40 °C (104 °F), preferably between 15 and 30 °C (59 and 86 °F), in a tight container, unless otherwise specified by manufacturer. Protect from freezing.

Auxiliary labeling

- For the eye.
- Keep container tightly closed.

ATROPINE SULFATE OPHTHALMIC SOLUTION USP

Usual adult and adolescent dose

Uveitis—

Topical, to the conjunctiva, 1 drop of a 1% solution one or two times a day. In some cases, up to four doses a day may be required.

[To break posterior synechiae]—

Topical, to the conjunctiva, 1 drop of a 1 to 3% solution alternated with 1 drop of a 2.5 or 10% phenylephrine solution every ten minutes for three applications of each. Extreme caution should be used if 10% phenylephrine is administered.

[Mydriasis]—

Preoperative: Topical, to the conjunctiva, 1 drop of a 1% solution supplemented with 1 drop of a 2.5 or 10% phenylephrine solution, prior to surgery. Extreme caution should be used if 10% phenylephrine is administered.

Postoperative: Topical, to the conjunctiva, 1 drop of a 1 to 3% solution one to three times a day.

[Malignant (ciliary block) glaucoma][1]—

Initial: Topical, to the conjunctiva, 1 drop of a 1 to 3% solution administered concurrently with 1 drop of a 2.5 or 10% phenylephrine solution, three or four times a day. Extreme caution should be used if 10% phenylephrine is administered.

Maintenance: Topical, to the conjunctiva, 1 drop of a 1 to 3% solution once every other day or once a day.

Usual pediatric dose

Cycloplegic refraction—

Topical, to the conjunctiva, 1 drop of the following concentrations two times a day for one to three days prior to refraction:

Infants up to 1 year of age—
0.125%.

Children 1 to 5 years of age—
0.25%.

Children 5 years of age and over with blue irides—
0.25%.

Children 5 years of age and over with dark irides—
0.5 or 1%.

Uveitis—

Topical, to the conjunctiva, 1 drop of a 0.125 to 1% solution one to three times a day.

[Postoperative mydriasis]—

Topical, to the conjunctiva, 1 drop of a 0.5% solution one to three times a day or as determined by physician.

Strength(s) usually available

U.S.—

0.5% (Rx) [*Atropisol; Isopto Atropine* (benzalkonium chloride 0.01%)].

1% (Rx) [*Atropair; Atropine Care; Atropisol; Atrosulf; Isopto Atropine* (benzalkonium chloride 0.01%); *I-Tropine; Ocu-Tropine;* GENERIC (may contain chlorobutanol)].

2% (Rx) [*Atropisol;* GENERIC].

Canada—

1% (Rx) [*Atropisol* (benzalkonium chloride); *Isopto Atropine* (benzalkonium chloride); *Minims Atropine;* GENERIC (may contain benzalkonium chloride)].

Note: The 0.125 and 0.25% strengths are no longer commercially available; compounding required for prescriptions.

Packaging and storage

Store below 40 °C (104 °F), preferably between 15 and 30 °C (59 and 86 °F), unless otherwise specified by manufacturer. Store in a tight container. Protect from freezing.

Auxiliary labeling

- For the eye.
- Keep container tightly closed.

---

[1]Not included in Canadian product labeling.

Revised: 05/01/1995

AURANOFIN—See *Gold Compounds (Systemic)*

AUROTHIOGLUCOSE—See *Gold Compounds (Systemic)*

AZACITIDINE Systemic†

VA CLASSIFICATION (Primary): AN300

Commonly used brand name(s): *Vidaza.*

Note: For a listing of dosage forms and brand names by country availability, see *Dosage Forms* section(s).

†Not commercially available in Canada.

Category

Antineoplastic.

Indications

Accepted

Myelodysplastic syndrome (treatment)—Azacitidine is indicated for treatment of patients with the following myelodysplastic syndrome subtypes: refractory anemia or refractory anemia with ringed sideroblasts (if accompanied by neutropenia or thrombocytopenia or requiring transfusions), refractory anemia with excess blasts, refractory anemia with excess blasts in transformation, and chronic myelomonocytic leukemia.

Acceptance not established

Acute myelogenous leukemia—Large, historical cooperative trials have yielded response rates of 50-75% in patient with acute myelogenous leukemia (AML) receiving a standard induction regimen of cytarabine plus an anthracycline. Older patients (greater than 65 years old) and those with relapsed/refractory disease, are a more difficult population to treat, with only 30 to 50% of patients attaining responses. Several small, open-label trials have demonstrated azacitidine activity (0% to 75%) and tolerability in these settings. However, well-designed, large, randomized trials of azacitidine in the treatment of AML are lacking.

Acute myelogenous leukemia (pediatric)—Many small studies have demonstrated activity of azacitidine in the treatment of pediatric patients with acute myelogenous leukemia. Various patient populations (de novo, relapsed, refractory), treatment phases (induction, maintenance), and regimens have been used. Common toxicities associated with azacitidine-containing regimens include; infection, gastrointestinal (nausea, vomiting, diarrhea), and mucositis.

Pharmacology/Pharmacokinetics

Physicochemical characteristics

Source—Azacitidine is a pyrimidine nucleoside analog of cytidine.

Molecular weight—Azacitidine: 244.

Solubility—Azacitidine was found to be insoluble in acetone, ethanol, and methyl ethyl ketone; slightly soluble in ethanol/water (50/50), propylene glycol, and polyethylene glycol; sparingly soluble in water, water saturated octanol, 5% dextrose in water, N-methyl-2-pyrrolidone, normal saline and 5% tween in water, and soluble in dimethylsulfoxide (DMSO).

Mechanism of action/Effect

It is believed that azacitidine exerts its antineoplastic effects by causing hypomethylation of DNA and direct cytotoxicity on abnormal hematopoietic cells in the bone marrow. The cytotoxic effects cause cell death of rapidly dividing cells, including cancer cells that are no longer responsive to normal growth control mechanisms. Non-proliferating cells are relatively insensitive to these effects. Hypomethylation may restore normal function to genes that are critical for differentiation and proliferation. The required concentration of azacitidine for maximum inhibition of DNA methylation *in vitro* does not cause suppression of DNA synthesis.

Absorption

Rapidly absorbed after subcutaneous administration.

The bioavailability of subcutaneous azacitidine relative to IV azacitidine is 89%, based on area under the curve.

Distribution

Volume of distribution (Vol_D)—76 ± 26 L following IV dosing.

Half-life

Elimination—about 4 hours

Time to peak concentration

0.5 hour

Peak plasma concentration:

750 ± 403 ng/mL following subcutaneous administration

Elimination

Urinary: 85% following IV dosing, 50% following SC dosing; Fecal: <1%

Precautions to Consider

Carcinogenicity/Tumorigenicity

Studies were done in mice and rats to determine the carcinogenic and tumorigenic potential of azacitidine. Azacitidine was shown to induced tumors of the hematopoietic system in female mice, and increased the incidence of tumors in the lymphoreticular system, lung, mammary gland and skin at doses (approximately 8% of the recommended human daily dose on a mg/m^2 basis). Doses given to rats (approximately 20–80% of the recommended daily human dose), revealed an increased incidence of testicular tumors compared with controls.

Mutagenicity

Azacitidine was found to be mutagenic in bacterial and mammalian cell systems. The clastogenic effect was shown by the induction of micronuclei in L5178Y mouse cells and Syrian hamster embryo cells.

Pregnancy/Reproduction

Fertility—Studies in male mice given (approximately 9% of the recommended human daily dose on a mg/m^2 basis) daily for 3 days prior to mating with untreated female mice revealed both a decreased fertility and loss of offspring during subsequent embryonic and postnatal development. Treatment of male rats three times per week for 11 or 16 weeks at doses (approximately 20–40%, the recommended human daily dose) resulted in decreased weight of the testes and epididymides, and decreased sperm counts along with decreased pregnancy rates and increased loss of embryos in mated females. In a related study male rats treated for 16 weeks showed an increase in abnormal embryos in mated females when examined on day 2 of gestation.

Pregnancy—There are no adequate and well controlled studies in pregnant women using azacitidine. If this drug is used during pregnancy, or if the patient becomes pregnant while taking this drug, the patient should be apprised of the potential hazard to the fetus. However, women of child bearing potential should be advised to avoid becoming pregnant while receiving treatment with azacitidine.

Men should be advised not to father a child while receiving treatment with azacitidine.

Azacitidine crosses the placenta and may cause harm to the fetus. Risk benefit must be carefully considered when this medicine is required in life-threatening situations or in serious diseases for which other medications cannot be used or are ineffective.

Early embryotoxicity studies in mice given a single IP dose (approximately 8% of the recommended human daily dose) on gestation day 10, revealed a 44% frequency of intrauterine embryonal death. Developmental abnormalities in the brain have also been detected in mice when given azacitidine (approximately 4–16% of the recommended human daily dose) on or before gestation day 15. In rats azacitidine was clearly embryotoxic and caused multiple fetal abnormalities including CNS anomalies, limb anomalies and others including death when given doses (approximately 8% of the recommended human daily dose).

FDA Pregnancy Category D

Breast-feeding

It is not know whether azacitidine or its metabolites are distributed into human breast milk. Because of the potential for tumorigenicity shown in animal studies and the potential for serious adverse reactions, women treated with azacitidine should not nurse.

Pediatrics

Safety and effectiveness in pediatric patients have not been established.

Geriatrics

Appropriate studied performed to date have not demonstrated geriatrics-specific problems that would limit the usefulness of azacitidine in the elderly. However, elderly patients are more likely to have age-related renal function impairment which may require monitoring.

Drug interactions and/or related problems

The following drug interactions and/or related problems have been selected on the basis of their potential clinical significance (possible mechanism in parentheses where appropriate)—not necessarily inclusive (» = major clinical significance):

Note: Drug interaction studies with azacitidine have not been done.

Medical considerations/Contraindications

The medical considerations/contraindications included have been selected on the basis of their potential clinical significance (reasons given in parentheses where appropriate)—not necessarily inclusive (» = major clinical significance).

Except under special circumstances, this medication should not be used when the following medical problem exists:

» Hepatic tumors malignant, advanced
(use is contraindicated.)

» Hypersensitivity to azacitidine or mannitol.

Risk-benefit should be considered when the following medical problems exist:

» Hepatic function impairment, pre-existing
» Renal function impairment
(safety and efficacy have not been established)

Patient monitoring

The following may be especially important in patient monitoring (other tests may be warranted in some patients, depending on condition; » = major clinical significance):

» Complete blood count
(prior to each dosing cycle)

Liver function test, and
Serum creatinine
(should be obtained prior to initiation of therapy.)

Side/Adverse Effects

The following side/adverse effects have been selected on the basis of their potential clinical significance (possible signs and symptoms in parentheses where appropriate)—not necessarily inclusive:

Those indicating need for medical attention

Incidence more frequent

Anaphylactic reaction (cough; difficulty swallowing; dizziness; fast heartbeat; hives; itching; puffiness or swelling of the eyelids or around the eyes, face, lips or tongue; shortness of breath; skin rash; tightness in chest; unusual tiredness or weakness; wheezing); ***anemia*** (pale skin; troubled breathing with exertion; unusual bleeding or bruising; unusual tiredness or weakness); ***atelectasis*** (coughing; difficult breathing; fever; rapid heartbeat); ***cellulitis*** (itching, pain, redness, swelling, tenderness, warmth on skin); ***chest pain; dyspnea*** (shortness of breath; difficult or labored breathing; tightness in chest; wheezing); ***dyspnea exertional*** (shortness of breath; difficult or labored breathing; tightness in chest; wheezing); ***febrile neutropenia*** (black, tarry stools; chills; cough; fever; lower back or side pain; painful or difficult urination; pale skin; shortness of breath; sore throat; ulcers, sores, or white spots in mouth; unusual bleeding or bruising; unusual tiredness or weakness); ***herpes simplex*** (burning or stinging of skin; painful cold sores or blisters on lips, nose, eyes, or genitals); ***leukopenia*** (black, tarry stools; chest pain; chills; cough; fever; painful or difficult urination; shortness of breath; sore throat; sores, ulcers, or white spots on lips or in mouth; swollen glands; unusual bleeding or bruising; unusual tiredness or weakness); ***nasopharyngitis*** (stuffy or runny nose; muscle aches; unusual tiredness or weakness; fever; sore throat; headache); ***neutropenia*** (black, tarry, stools; chills; cough; fever; lower back or side pain; painful or difficult urination; pale skin; shortness of breath; sore throat; ulcers, sores, or white spots in mouth; unusual bleeding or bruising; unusual tiredness or weakness); ***pharyngitis*** (body aches or pain; congestion; cough; dryness or soreness of throat; fever; hoarseness; runny nose; tender, swollen glands in neck; trouble in swallowing; voice changes); ***pleural effusion*** (chest pain; shortness of breath); ***pneumonia*** (chest pain; cough; fever or chills; sneezing; shortness of breath; sore throat; troubled breathing; tightness in chest; wheezing); ***sinusitis*** (pain or tenderness around eyes and cheekbones; fever; stuffy or runny nose; headache; cough; shortness of breath or troubled breathing; tightness of chest or wheezing); ***thrombocytopenia*** (black, tarry stools; bleeding gums; blood in urine or stools; pinpoint red spots on skin; unusual bleeding or bruising); ***transfusion reaction*** (dizziness; fever or chills; facial swelling; headache; nausea or vomiting; shortness of breath; skin rash; weakness); ***upper respiratory tract infection*** (ear congestion; nasal congestion; chills; cough; fever; sneezing; or sore throat; body aches or pain; headache; loss of voice; runny nose; unusual tiredness or weakness; difficulty in breathing); ***urinary tract infection*** (bladder pain; bloody or cloudy urine; difficult, burning, or painful urination; frequent urge to urinate; lower back or side pain); ***wheezing***

Incidence unknown

Hepatic coma (change in consciousness; loss of consciousness); ***hypokalemia*** (convulsions; decreased urine; dry mouth; irregular heartbeat; increased thirst; loss of appetite; mood changes; muscle pain or cramps; nausea or vomiting; numbness or tingling in hands, feet, or lips; shortness of breath; unusual tiredness or weakness); ***renal failure*** (lower back/side pain; decreased frequency/amount of urine; bloody urine; increased thirst; loss of appetite; nausea; vomiting; unusual tiredness or weakness; swelling of face, fingers, lower legs; weight gain; troubled breathing; increased blood pressure); ***renal tubular acidosis*** (drowsiness; fatigue; headache; nausea; troubled breathing; vomiting); ***serum creatinine, elevated*** (increased blood creatinine)

Those indicating need for medical attention only if they continue or are bothersome

Incidence more frequent

Abdominal distention (swelling of abdominal or stomach area; full or bloated feeling or pressure in the stomach); ***abdominal pain*** (stomach pain); ***abdominal tenderness*** (soreness or discomfort to touch or pressure on stomach); ***anorexia*** (loss of appetite; weight loss); ***anxiety*** (fear; nervousness); ***appetite decreased; arthralgia*** (pain in joints; muscle pain or stiffness; difficulty in moving); ***back pain; breath sounds decreased; cardiac murmur*** (heart murmur); ***constipation*** (difficulty having a bowel movement (stool)); ***contusion*** (injury to tissue usually without laceration; bruise); ***cough; crackles lung; depression*** (discouragement; feeling sad or empty; irritability; lack of appetite; loss of interest or pleasure; tiredness; trouble concentrating; trouble sleeping); ***diarrhea; dizziness; dry skin; dyspepsia*** (acid or sour stomach; belching; heartburn; indigestion; stomach discomfort upset or pain); ***dysphagia*** (difficulty swallowing); ***dysuria*** (difficult or painful urination; burning while urinating); ***ecchymosis*** (bruising; large, flat, blue or purplish patches in the skin); ***edema, peripheral*** (swelling of hands, ankles, feet, or lower legs); ***epistaxis*** (bloody nose); ***erythema*** (flushing; redness of skin; unusually warm skin); ***fatigue*** (unusual tiredness or weakness); ***gingival bleeding*** (bleeding gums); ***headache; hematoma*** (collection of blood under skin; deep, dark purple bruise; itching; pain; redness or swelling); ***hemorrhoids*** (bleeding after defecation; uncomfortable swelling around anus); ***hypoesthesia*** (burning, crawling, itching, numbness, prickling, "pins and needles"; or tingling feelings); ***hypotension*** (blurred vision; confusion; dizziness, faintness, or lightheadedness when getting up from a lying or sitting position suddenly; sweating; unusual tiredness or weakness); ***injection site bruising; injection site erythema*** (abnormal redness of skin at injection site); ***injection site granuloma*** (inflamed tissue from infection at the site of injection); ***injection site pain; injection site pruritus*** (itching at injection site); ***injection site reaction*** (bleeding, blistering, burning, coldness, discoloration of skin, feeling of pressure, hives, infection, inflammation, itching, lumps, numbness, pain, rash, redness, scarring, soreness, stinging, swelling, tenderness, tingling, ulceration, or warmth at injection site); ***injection site swelling; insomnia*** (sleeplessness; trouble sleeping; unable to sleep); ***lethargy*** (unusual drowsiness; dullness, tiredness, weakness or feeling of sluggishness); ***loose stools; lymphadenopathy*** (swollen, painful, or tender lymph glands in neck, armpit, or groin); ***malaise*** (general feeling of discomfort or illness; unusual tiredness or weakness); ***mouth hemorrhage; muscle cramps; myalgia*** (joint pain; swollen joints; muscle aching or cramping; muscle pains or stiffness; difficulty in moving); ***nasal congestion*** (stuffy nose); ***nausea; night sweats; pain; pain in limb; pallor*** (paleness of skin); ***petechia*** (small red or purple spots on skin); ***petechia, oral mucosal*** (small red or purple spots in mouth); ***pitting edema*** (swelling with pits or depressions visible on skin); ***post-nasal drip; post procedural hemorrhage; pruritus*** (itching skin); ***pyrexia*** (fever); ***rales*** (small clicking, bubbling, or rattling sounds in the lung when listening with a stethoscope); ***rash; rhinorrhea*** (runny nose); ***rhonchi*** (trouble breathing; noisy breathing); ***rigors*** (feeling unusually cold; shivering); ***skin lesions*** (bumps on skin; rash on skin); ***skin nodules*** (small lumps under the skin); ***stomatitis*** (swelling or inflammation of the mouth); ***sweating increased; syncope*** (fainting); ***tachycardia*** (fast, pounding, or irregular heartbeat or pulse); ***tongue ulceration; upper abdominal pain; urticaria*** (hives or welts; itching; redness of skin; skin rash); ***vomiting; weakness; weight decreased***

Overdose

For more information on the management of overdose or unintentional ingestion, **contact a poison control center** (see *Poison Control Center Listing*).

Clinical effects of overdose

The following effects have been selected on the basis of their potential clinical significance (possible signs and symptoms in parentheses where appropriate)—not necessarily inclusive:

Diarrhea; nausea; vomiting

Treatment of overdose

There is no known specific antidote to azacitidine. Treatment is generally symptomatic and supportive.

Monitoring—

Monitor appropriate blood counts.

Supportive care—

Patients in whom intentional overdose is confirmed or suspected should be referred for psychiatric consultation.

Patient Consultation

As an aid to patient consultation, refer to *Advice for the Patient, Azacitidine (Systemic)*.

In providing consultation, consider emphasizing the following selected information (» = major clinical significance):

Before using this medication

» Conditions affecting use, especially:

Hypersensitivity to azacitidine or mannitol

Pregnancy—Use not recommended because of mutagenic, teratogenic, embryotoxic, and fetotoxic potential; advisability of using contraception; telling physician immediately if pregnancy is suspected

Breast-feeding—Not recommended because of risk of serious adverse effects

Use in children—Safety and effectiveness in pediatric patients have not been established.

Other medical problems, especially hepatic tumors, advanced malignant, hepatic function impairment, pre-existing, and renal function impairment.

Proper use of this medication

» Proper dosing

Missed dose: Not taking at all; not doubling doses; checking with physician

Proper storage

Precautions while using this medication

» Importance of close monitoring by the physician; periodic blood tests required to monitor blood counts

Side/adverse effects

Signs of potential side effects, especially anaphylactic reaction, anemia, atelectasis, cellulitis, chest pain, dyspnea, dyspnea exertional, febrile neutropenia, herpes simplex, hepatic coma, hypokalemia, leukopenia, nasopharyngitis, neutropenia, pharyngitis, sinusitis, pleural effusion, pneumonia, renal failure, renal tubular acidosis, serum creatinine, elevated, thrombocytopenia, transfusion reaction, upper respiratory tract infection, urinary tract infection, wheezing

General Dosing Information

Patients receiving azacitidine should be under the supervision of a physician experienced in cancer chemotherapy.

Azacitidine is administered subcutaneously. Doses greater than 4 mL should be divided equally into 2 syringes and injected into 2 separate sites. Rotate sites for each injection never going into an area where the site is tender, bruised, red or hard.

To ensure a homogeneous suspension the contents of the syringe must be resuspended by inverting the syringe 2–3 times and gently rolling the syringe between the palms for 30 seconds immediately prior to administration.

Safety considerations for handling this medication

There is limited but increasing evidence and concern that personnel involved in preparation and administration of parenteral antineoplastics may be at some risk because of the potential mutagenicity, teratogenicity, and/or carcinogenicity of these agents, although the actual risk is unknown. USP advisory panels recommend cautious handling both in preparation and disposal of antineoplastic agents. Precautions that have been suggested include:

- Use of a biological containment cabinet during reconstitution and dilution of parenteral medications and wearing of disposable surgical gloves and masks.
- Use of proper technique to prevent contamination of the medication, work area, and operator during transfer between containers (including proper training of personnel in this technique).
- Cautious and proper disposal of needles, syringes, vials, ampuls, and unused medication.

A number of medical centers have developed detailed guidelines for handling of antineoplastic agents.

Parenteral Dosage Forms

Note: Bracketed information in the *Indications* section refers to uses that are not included in U.S. product labeling.

Azacitidine For Injection

Usual adult dose

Antineoplastic—

Subcutaneously, 75 mg/m², daily for seven days, every four weeks

- ANC: < 0.5x10⁹/L; Platelets: < 25x10⁹/L; 50% of dose in next course.
- ANC: 0.5–1.5x10⁹/L; Platelets: <25–50x10⁹/L; 67% of dose in next course.
- ANC: > 1.5x10⁹/L; Platelets: > 50x10⁹/L; 100% of dose in next course.

Dosage adjustments based on hematologic laboratory values—

- WBC or platelet nadir % decrease in counts from baseline: 50–75%; Bone marrow biopsy cellularity at time of nadir: 30–60%; 100% dose in next course.
- WBC or platelet nadir % decrease in counts from baseline: > 75%; Bone marrow biopsy cellularity at time of nadir: 30–60%; 75% dose in next course.
- WBC or platelet nadir % decrease in counts from baseline: 50–75%; Bone marrow biopsy cellularity at time of nadir: 15–30%; 50% dose in next course.
- WBC or platelet nadir % decrease in counts from baseline: > 75%; Bone marrow biopsy cellularity at time of nadir: 15–30%; 50% dose in next course.
- WBC or platelet nadir % decrease in counts from baseline: 50–75%; Bone marrow biopsy cellularity at time of nadir: <15%; 33% dose in next course.
- WBC or platelet nadir % decrease in counts from baseline: > 75%; Bone marrow biopsy cellularity at time of nadir: <15%; 33% dose in next course.

For patients whose baseline counts are WBC < 3x10⁹/L, ANC < 1.5x10⁹/L, or < 75x10⁹/L, dose adjustments should be based on nadir counts and bone marrow biopsy cellularity at the time of the nadir as indicated below, unless there is a clear improvement in differentiation (percentage of mature granulocytes is higher and ANC is higher than at onset of that course) at the time of the next cycle, in which case the dose of the current treatment should be continued.

Note: If a nadir as defined above has occurred, the next course of treatment should be given 28 days after the start of the preceding course, provided that both the WBC and the platelet counts are >25% above and rising. If a >25% increase above the nadir is not seen by day 28, counts should be reassessed every 7 days. If a 25% increase is not seen by day 42, then the patient should be treated with 50% of the scheduled dose.

- If reductions in serum bicarbonate levels < 20 mEq/L occur: reduce dosage by 50% on the next course.
- If elevations of BUN or serum creatinine occur: delay treatment until values return to normal or baseline and then reduce dosage by 50% on the next course.

Dosage adjustments based on renal function and serum electrolytes—

Usual Pediatric Dose

Safety and efficacy have not been established.

Usual Geriatric Dose

See *Usual adult dose.*

Strength(s) usually available

U.S.—

100 mg as a sterile lyophilized powder per vial (Rx) [*Vidaza* (mannitol)].

Packaging and storage

Store at 25 °C (77 °F); excursions permitted to 15 to 30°C (59 to 86°F)

Preparation of dosage form

Caution should be exercised when handling and preparing azacitidine suspensions. If reconstituted azacitidine comes into contact with the skin immediately and thoroughly wash with soap and water. If it comes into contact with mucus membranes, flush thoroughly with water. Each vial of azacitidine must be reconstituted aseptically with 4 mL sterile water for injection. The diluent should be injected slowly into the vial. Invert the vial 2–3 times and gently rotate to achieve a uniform suspension. The suspension will be cloudy and contain azacitidine 25 mg/mL. See the manufacturer's package insert for instructions.

Stability

Reconstituted azacitidine may be stored for up to 1 hour at 25°C (77 °F) or for up to eight hours between 2 and 8°C (36 and 46°F). After removal from refrigerated conditions, the suspension may be allowed to equilibrate to room temperature for up to 30 minutes prior to administration.

The azacitidine vial is for single use and does not contain preservatives. Unused portions should be disposed of properly and not saved for future use.

Caution

Azacitidine is a cytotoxic drug. Caution should be exercised when handling and preparing azacitidine suspensions.

Revised: 07/19/2006
Developed: 08/17/2004

AZATADINE—See *Antihistamines (Systemic)*

AZATHIOPRINE Systemic

VA CLASSIFICATION (Primary/Secondary): IM403/MS109; GA400

Commonly used brand name(s): *Imuran.*

Note: For a listing of dosage forms and brand names by country availability, see *Dosage Forms* section(s).

Category

Immunosuppressant; antirheumatic (disease-modifying); bowel disease (inflammatory) suppressant; lupus erythematosus suppressant.

Indications

Note: Bracketed information in the *Indications* section refers to uses that are not included in U.S. product labeling.

Accepted

Transplant rejection, organ (prophylaxis)—Azathioprine is indicated as an adjunct for prevention of rejection in renal homotransplantation. [It is also indicated in the prevention of rejection in cardiac, hepatic, and pancreatic transplantation.]

Arthritis, rheumatoid (treatment)—Azathioprine is indicated for the management of severe, active, and erosive rheumatoid arthritis unresponsive to rest or conventional medications.

[Bowel disease, inflammatory (treatment)][1]
[Cirrhosis, biliary (treatment)][1]
[Dermatomyositis, systemic (treatment)][1]
[Glomerulonephritis (treatment)][1]
[Hepatitis, chronic active (treatment)][1]
[Lupus erythematosus, systemic (treatment)][1]
[Myasthenia gravis (treatment)][1]
[Myopathy, inflammatory (treatment)][1]
[Nephrotic syndrome (treatment)][1]
[Pemphigoid (treatment)][1] or

[Pemphigus (treatment)][1]—Azathioprine also is indicated in the treatment of other immunologic diseases including regional and ulcerative colitis, biliary cirrhosis, systemic dermatomyositis (polymyositis), glomerulonephritis, chronic active hepatitis, systemic lupus erythematosus (SLE), inflammatory myopathy, myasthenia gravis, nephrotic syndrome, pemphigus, and pemphigoid.

[1]Not included in Canadian product labeling.

Pharmacology/Pharmacokinetics

Physicochemical characteristics
Molecular weight—277.27.

Mechanism of action/Effect
The exact mechanism of immunosuppressive action is unknown since the exact mechanism of the immune response itself is complex and not completely understood. The immunosuppressive effects of azathioprine involve a greater suppression of delayed hypersensitivity and cellular cytotoxicity tests than of antibody responses. Azathioprine antagonizes purine metabolism and may inhibit synthesis of DNA, RNA, and proteins; it may also interfere with cellular metabolism and inhibit mitosis.

The mechanism of action of azathioprine in rheumatoid arthritis and other immunologic diseases is unknown but may be related to immunosuppression. Azathioprine has a steroid-sparing effect, which allows a reduction in steroid dose when the two are combined in chronic inflammatory diseases.

Absorption
Well absorbed from the gastrointestinal tract.

Protein binding
Low (30%).

Biotransformation
Largely converted to 6-mercaptopurine and 6-thioinosinic acid (active metabolites). Further metabolism—Hepatic, largely by xanthine oxidase, and in erythrocytes. Proportions of metabolites vary among individual patients.

Half-life
Approximately 5 hours (unchanged drug and metabolites).

Onset of action
In rheumatoid arthritis—6 to 8 weeks.
In other inflammatory disorders—4 to 8 weeks.

Time to peak concentration
Serum—1 to 2 hours.

Duration of action
Immunosuppressant—Clinical effects may persist for long periods after the medication is eliminated.

Elimination
Hepatic (biliary).
Renal (1 to 2% unchanged).
In dialysis—Partially removable by hemodialysis.

Precautions to Consider

Carcinogenicity
Azathioprine has been shown to be carcinogenic in animals and may be associated with an increased risk of development of carcinomas in humans, especially skin cancer and reticulum cell tumors or lymphomas in renal transplant patients and acute myelocytic leukemia and some solid tumors in rheumatoid arthritis patients. The risk of neoplastic toxicity appears to be lower in rheumatoid arthritis patients than in renal transplant patients; however, there is evidence that the risk is increased with prior use of alkylating agents.

Mutagenicity
Mutagenic effects have been reported in animals, and chromosomal abnormalities (reversible when azathioprine is discontinued) have been noted in humans.

Pregnancy/Reproduction
Fertility—Azathioprine has been reported to cause temporary depression in spermatogenesis and reduction in sperm viability and sperm count in mice at doses 10 times the human therapeutic dose; a reduced percentage of fertile matings occurred when animals received 5 mg per kg of body weight (mg/kg).

Pregnancy—Adequate and well-controlled studies in humans have not been done.

Azathioprine crosses the placenta.

Risk-benefit must be considered, especially during the first trimester, since azathioprine affects cell kinetics and can theoretically cause mutagenicity or teratogenicity.

There have been reports of limited immunologic abnormalities (lymphopenia, diminished immunoglobulin G [IgG] and immunoglobulin M [IgM] levels, cytomegalovirus [CMV] infection, and decreased thymic shadow; pancytopenia and severe immune deficiency) and other abnormalities (preaxial polydactyly in an infant whose mother received azathioprine and prednisone; meningomyelocele, bilateral dislocated hips, and bilateral *talipes equinovarus* in an infant whose father received azathioprine) in infants of renal homograft recipients treated with azathioprine.

Azathioprine is not recommended for use in pregnant women with rheumatoid arthritis.

Teratogenic effects (including skeletal malformations and visceral abnormalities) have been reported in rabbits and mice given doses equivalent to the human dose (5 mg/kg a day).

FDA Pregnancy Category D.

Breast-feeding
Azathioprine is distributed, at low concentrations, into breast milk. Use by nursing mothers is not recommended because of possible adverse effects (especially tumorigenicity) in the infant.

Pediatrics
Appropriate studies performed to date have not demonstrated pediatrics-specific problems that would limit the usefulness of azathioprine in children.

Geriatrics
Although appropriate studies on the relationship of age to the effects of azathioprine have not been performed in the geriatric population, geriatrics-specific problems are not expected to limit the usefulness of this medication in the elderly. However, elderly patients are more likely to have age-related renal function impairment, which may require reduced dosage in patients receiving azathioprine.

Dental
The bone marrow–depressant effects of azathioprine may result in an increased incidence of microbial infection, delayed healing, and gingival bleeding. Dental work, whenever possible, should be completed prior to initiation of therapy or deferred until blood counts have returned to normal. Patients should be instructed in proper oral hygiene during treatment, including caution in use of regular toothbrushes, dental floss, and toothpicks.

In addition, azathioprine rarely causes sores in the mouth and on the lips.

Drug interactions and/or related problems
The following drug interactions and/or related problems have been selected on the basis of their potential clinical significance (possible mechanism in parentheses where appropriate)—not necessarily inclusive (» = major clinical significance):

Note: Combinations containing any of the following medications, depending on the amount present, may also interact with this medication.

» Allopurinol
(allopurinol-induced inhibition of xanthine oxidase–mediated metabolism may result in greatly increased azathioprine activity and toxicity; concurrent use should be avoided if possible, especially in renal transplant patients, because of the high risk of 6-mercaptopurine [azathioprine metabolite] accumulation and consequent azathioprine toxicity if the transplanted kidney is rejected; if concurrent use is essential, it is recommended that azathioprine dosage be reduced to one quarter to one third of the usual dosage, the patient be carefully monitored, and subsequent dosage adjustments be based on patient response and evidence of toxicity)

Angiotensin-converting enzyme inhibitors
(increased risk of anemia and leukopenia)

Blood dyscrasia-causing medications (see *Appendix II*)
(leukopenic and/or thrombocytopenic effects of azathioprine may be increased with concurrent or recent therapy if these medications cause the same effects; dosage adjustment of azathioprine, if necessary, should be based on blood counts)

» Bone marrow depressants, other (see *Appendix II*) or
Radiation therapy
(concurrent use with azathioprine may increase the bone marrow depressant effects of these medications and radiation therapy; dosage reduction may be required; use prior to azathioprine therapy may be associated with an increased risk of development of neoplasms)

» Immunosuppressants, other, such as:
Chlorambucil

Corticosteroids, glucocorticoid
Cyclophosphamide
Cyclosporine
Mercaptopurine
Muromonab-CD3
(concurrent use with azathioprine may increase the risk of infection and development of neoplasms)

Vaccines, killed virus
(because normal defense mechanisms may be suppressed by azathioprine therapy, the patient's antibody response to the vaccine may be decreased. The interval between discontinuation of medications that cause immunosuppression and restoration of the patient's ability to respond to the vaccine depends on the intensity and type of immunosuppression-causing medication used, the underlying disease, and other factors; estimates vary from 3 months to 1 year)

» Vaccines, live virus
(because normal defense mechanisms may be suppressed by azathioprine therapy, concurrent use with a live virus vaccine may potentiate the replication of the vaccine virus, may increase the side/adverse effects of the vaccine virus, and/or may decrease the patient's antibody response to the vaccine; immunization of these patients should be undertaken only with extreme caution after careful review of the patient's hematologic status and only with the knowledge and consent of the physician managing the azathioprine therapy. The interval between discontinuation of medications that cause immunosuppression and restoration of the patient's ability to respond to the vaccine depends on the intensity and type of immunosuppression-causing medication used, the underlying disease, and other factors; estimates vary from 3 months to 1 year. Patients with leukemia in remission should not receive live virus vaccine until at least 3 months after their last chemotherapy. In addition, immunization with oral poliovirus vaccine should be postponed in persons in close contact with the patient, especially family members)

Warfarin
(activity of warfarin may be decreased; increased doses of warfarin may be needed)

Laboratory value alterations

The following have been selected on the basis of their potential clinical significance (possible effect in parentheses where appropriate)—not necessarily inclusive (» = major clinical significance).

With physiology/laboratory test values

Alanine aminotransferase (ALT [SGPT]) and
Alkaline phosphatase and
Amylase and
Aspartate aminotransferase (AST [SGOT]) and
Bilirubin
(serum values may be increased in association with toxic hepatitis and biliary stasis, primarily in allograft recipients; may also be increased as part of a gastrointestinal hypersensitivity reaction; uncommon in rheumatoid arthritis patients)

Albumin, plasma and
Hemoglobin and
Uric acid in blood and urine
(concentrations may be decreased)

Mean corpuscular volume (MCV)
(may be increased; occurs commonly, as a sign of macrocytosis)

Medical considerations/Contraindications

The medical considerations/contraindications included have been selected on the basis of their potential clinical significance (reasons given in parentheses where appropriate)—not necessarily inclusive (» = major clinical significance).

Risk-benefit should be considered when the following medical problems exist:

» Chickenpox, existing or recent (including recent exposure) or
» Herpes zoster
(risk of severe generalized disease)

» Gout
(because of interaction with allopurinol)

» Hepatic function impairment

» Infection

Pancreatitis

» Renal function impairment
(increased risk of hematologic toxicity; a lower dosage of azathioprine is recommended for patients with impaired renal function)

» Sensitivity to azathioprine

» Xanthine oxidase deficiency, severe
(reduced metabolism may result in increased azathioprine activity and toxicity)

» Caution should be used also in patients who have had previous cytotoxic drug therapy and radiation therapy.

Patient monitoring

The following may be especially important in patient monitoring (other tests may be warranted in some patients, depending on condition; » = major clinical significance):

» Complete blood counts
(recommended at least weekly during the first 2 months of therapy; frequency may be reduced to monthly once the patient is stabilized)

Side/Adverse Effects

Note: The risk of hematologic and neoplastic toxicity appears to be lower in rheumatoid arthritis patients because of the lower doses used. Bone marrow depression may be more severe in renal transplant patients whose hemografts are undergoing rejection.

The following side/adverse effects have been selected on the basis of their potential clinical significance (possible signs and symptoms in parentheses where appropriate)—not necessarily inclusive:

Those indicating need for medical attention

Incidence more frequent

Leukopenia or infection (fever or chills; cough or hoarseness; lower back or side pain; painful or difficult urination)—leukopenia is usually asymptomatic; ***megaloblastic anemia*** (unusual tiredness or weakness)

Note: *Leukopenia* may be severe or delayed and is dose-related. It is not correlated with therapeutic effect.

The incidence of *infection* in renal transplant patients is 30 to 60 times that in patients taking azathioprine for rheumatoid arthritis.

Infections may be fatal.

Incidence less frequent—dose-related

Hepatitis or biliary stasis—asymptomatic; ***thrombocytopenia*** (unusual bleeding or bruising; black, tarry stools; blood in urine or stools; pinpoint red spots on skin)—usually asymptomatic

Note: *Hepatotoxicity* usually occurs within 6 months of transplantation and usually is reversible on withdrawal of azathioprine. It is uncommon (incidence less than 1%) in rheumatoid arthritis patients. Hepatotoxicity occurs more frequently at dosages above 2.5 mg per kg of body weight (mg/kg) per day.

Thrombocytopenia may be severe or delayed and is dose-related.

Incidence rare

Gastrointestinal hypersensitivity reaction (severe nausea and vomiting with diarrhea; sudden fever; joint pain; sudden unusual feeling of discomfort or illness); ***hepatic veno-occlusive disease*** (stomach pain; swelling of feet or lower legs)—potentially fatal; ***hypersensitivity*** (fast heartbeat; sudden fever; muscle or joint pain; redness or blisters on skin); ***pancreatitis, hypersensitivity*** (severe stomach pain with nausea and vomiting); ***pneumonitis*** (cough; shortness of breath); ***sores in mouth and on lips***

Note: Symptoms of the *gastrointestinal hypersensitivity reaction* usually develop within the first several weeks of therapy and are reversible on withdrawal of azathioprine, although they will recur within hours after the first dose on rechallenge. *Hypotension* may occasionally occur. Hepatic enzymes may also be elevated.

Hypersensitivity reactions usually occur after at least 1 week of therapy and are reversible on withdrawal. The reaction may be more severe on rechallenge and can be fatal.

Those indicating need for medical attention only if they continue or are bothersome

Incidence more frequent

Loss of appetite; nausea or vomiting

Incidence less frequent

Skin rash

Those indicating the need for medical attention if they occur after medication is discontinued

Bone marrow depression, delayed (black, tarry stools; blood in urine; cough or hoarseness; fever or chills; lower back or side pain; painful or difficult urination; pinpoint red spots on skin; unusual bleeding or bruising)

Overdose

Clinical effects of overdose

The following effects have been selected on the basis of their potential clinical significance (possible signs and symptoms in parentheses where appropriate)—not necessarily inclusive:

Acute and/or chronic

Bleeding (pinpoint red spots on skin; unusual bleeding or bruising); ***diarrhea; leukopenia or infection*** (fever or chills; cough or hoarseness; lower back or side pain; painful or difficult urination); ***hepatotoxicity***—usually asymptomatic; however, liver function test abnormalities may occur; ***nausea; vomiting***

Treatment of overdose

There is no published literature establishing the superiority of any specific techniques to treat azathioprine overdose. Treatment of azathioprine overdose is supportive.

To decrease absorption—Although there is no literature on the usefulness of techniques to decrease absorption of azathioprine, gastric emptying within 30 minutes to 1 hour of ingestion may decrease systemic absorption.

To enhance elimination—Hemodialysis can be used to enhance elimination. In one study, 45% of ingested azathioprine was removed during 8 hours of hemodialysis.

Monitoring—White blood cell count and liver function tests should be monitored until the values return to normal. In one case of acute ingestion of 7500 mg of azathioprine, the values returned to normal after 6 days.

Patients in whom intentional overdose is confirmed or suspected should be referred for psychiatric consultation.

Patient Consultation

As an aid to patient consultation, refer to *Advice for the Patient, Azathioprine (Systemic).*

In providing consultation, consider emphasizing the following selected information (» = major clinical significance):

Before using this medication

» Conditions affecting use, especially:
- Sensitivity to azathioprine
- Pregnancy—Use not recommended because of mutagenic or teratogenic potential
- Breast-feeding—Not recommended because of risk of serious side effects
- Other medications, especially allopurinol or other immunosuppressants
- Other medical problems, especially chickenpox, gout, hepatic function impairment, herpes zoster, infection, pancreatitis, renal function impairment, or xanthine oxidase deficiency

Proper use of this medication

» Importance of not taking more or less medication than the amount prescribed

Caution with combination therapy; taking each medication at the right time

» Checking with physician before discontinuing medication

Possible nausea or vomiting; taking after meals or at bedtime to reduce stomach upset

Checking with physician if vomiting occurs shortly after dose is taken

» Proper dosing

Missed dose—
- If dosing schedule is once a day—Not taking missed dose and not doubling next one
- If dosing schedule is several times a day—Taking as soon as possible or doubling next dose; checking with physician if more than one dose is missed

» Proper storage

Precautions while using this medication

» Importance of close monitoring by physician

» Avoiding immunizations unless approved by physician; other persons in patient's household should avoid immunizations with oral poliovirus vaccine; avoiding other persons who have taken oral poliovirus vaccine or wearing a protective mask that covers nose and mouth

Caution if bone marrow depression occurs:

» Avoiding exposure to persons with bacterial or viral infections, especially during periods of low blood counts; checking with physician immediately if fever or chills, cough or hoarseness, lower back or side pain, or painful or difficult urination occurs

» Checking with physician immediately if unusual bleeding or bruising; black, tarry stools; blood in urine or stools; or pinpoint red spots on skin occur

Caution in use of regular toothbrush, dental floss, or toothpick; physician, dentist, or nurse may suggest alternatives; checking with physician before having dental work done

Not touching eyes or inside of nose unless hands washed immediately before

Using caution to avoid accidental cuts with use of sharp objects such as safety razor or fingernail or toenail cutters

Avoiding contact sports or other situations where bruising or injury could occur

Side/adverse effects

Importance of discussing possible effects, including cancer, with physician

Signs of potential side effects, especially leukopenia, infection, megaloblastic anemia, hepatitis, biliary stasis, thrombocytopenia, gastrointestinal hypersensitivity reaction, hepatic veno-occlusive disease, hypersensitivity, pancreatitis, pneumonitis, and sores in mouth and on lips

Asymptomatic side effects, including hepatotoxicity

General Dosing Information

Patients receiving azathioprine should be under supervision of a physician experienced in immunosuppressive therapy.

A variety of dosage schedules and regimens of azathioprine, alone or in combination with other immunosuppressive agents, are used. The prescriber may consult the medical literature as well as the manufacturer's literature in choosing a specific dosage.

Dosage must be adjusted to meet the individual requirements of each patient, on the basis of clinical response and appearance or severity of toxicity.

Cadaveric kidneys frequently develop a tubular necrosis with delayed onset of adequate function, necessitating a reduction in azathioprine dosage. If persistent negative nitrogen balance occurs, dosage should be reduced.

Because of the delayed action of azathioprine, dosage should be reduced or the medication withdrawn at the first sign of an abnormally large or persistent decrease in leukocyte count (to less than 3000 per cubic millimeter) or platelet count (to less than 100,000 per cubic millimeter) or other evidence of bone marrow depression. Therapy may be reinstituted at a lower dosage when leukocyte and platelet counts return to acceptable levels, usually after 7 to 10 days.

Special precautions are recommended in patients who develop thrombocytopenia as a result of administration of azathioprine. These may include extreme care in performing invasive procedures; regular inspection of intravenous sites, skin (including perirectal area), and mucous membrane surfaces for signs of bleeding or bruising; limiting frequency of venipuncture and avoiding intramuscular injections; testing urine, emesis, stool, and secretions for occult blood; care in use of regular toothbrushes, dental floss, toothpicks, safety razors, and fingernail and toenail cutters; avoiding constipation; and using caution to prevent falls and other injuries. Such patients should avoid alcohol and aspirin intake because of the risk of gastrointestinal bleeding. Platelet transfusions may be required.

Patients who develop leukopenia should be observed carefully for signs of infection. Antibiotic support may be required. In patients with neutropenia who develop fever, broad-spectrum antibiotic coverage should be initiated empirically, pending bacterial cultures and appropriate diagnostic tests.

If an infection develops, it must be treated promptly; reduction of azathioprine dosage and/or use of other drugs may be necessary.

If symptoms of toxic hepatitis or biliary stasis appear, azathioprine therapy may have to be withdrawn. Patients with existing hepatic function impairment should be monitored carefully and treated with conservative doses (some clinicians recommend an initial dose of two thirds the usual dose). If hepatic veno-occlusive disease is clinically suspected, it is recommended that azathioprine be permanently withdrawn.

If signs of homograft rejection occur, a larger dose may be necessary. However, the dose should not be increased to toxic levels. Other therapy should be considered if signs of homograft rejection persist.

For parenteral dosage forms

Azathioprine may be administered by intravenous push or infusion. Time for infusion is usually 30 to 60 minutes, but may range from 5 minutes to 8 hours.

Diet/Nutrition

Gastrointestinal upset may be reduced by giving oral azathioprine in divided doses or after meals.

Safety considerations for handling this medication

There is limited but increasing evidence and concern that personnel involved in preparation and administration of parenteral antineoplastics and immunosuppressants may be at some risk because of the potential mutagenicity, teratogenicity, and/or carcinogenicity of these agents, although the actual risk is unknown. USP advisory panels recommend cautious handling both in preparation and disposal of antineoplastic and immunosuppressant agents. Precautions that have been suggested include:

• Use of a biological containment cabinet during reconstitution and dilution of parenteral medications and wearing of disposable surgical gloves and masks.

• Use of proper technique to prevent contamination of the medication, work area, and operator during transfer between containers (including proper training of personnel in this technique).

• Cautious and proper disposal of needles, syringes, vials, ampuls, and unused medication.

A number of medical centers have developed detailed guidelines for handling of antineoplastic and immunosuppressant agents.

The manufacturer does not make any recommendations regarding the use of a biological containment cabinet or the wearing of disposable surgical gloves during reconstitution and dilution of azathioprine sodium for injection.

Oral Dosage Forms

Note: Bracketed uses in the *Dosage Forms* section refer to categories of use and/or indications that are not included in U.S. product labeling.

AZATHIOPRINE TABLETS USP

Usual adult and adolescent dose

Transplant rejection, organ (prophylaxis)—

Initial: Oral, 3 to 5 mg per kg of body weight or 120 mg per square meter of body surface area a day, one to three days before or at the time of surgery, the dosage being adjusted to maintain the homograft without causing toxicity.

Maintenance: Oral, 1 to 3 mg per kg of body weight or 45 mg per square meter of body surface area a day.

Rheumatoid arthritis or
[Bowel disease, inflammatory][1] or
[Cirrhosis, biliary][1] or
[Dermatomyositis, systemic][1] or
[Glomerulonephritis][1] or
[Hepatitis, chronic active][1] or
[Lupus erythematosus, systemic][1] or
[Myopathy, inflammatory][1] or
[Myasthenia gravis][1] or
[Nephrotic syndrome][1] or
[Pemphigoid][1] or
[Pemphigus][1]—

Initial: Oral, 1 mg per kg of body weight a day, the dosage being increased in increments of 500 mcg (0.5 mg) per kg of body weight a day after six to eight weeks, then every four weeks as necessary up to a maximum dose of 2.5 mg per kg of body weight a day.

Maintenance: Oral, the dosage being reduced to the minimum effective dose in decrements of 500 mcg (0.5 mg) per kg of body weight a day every four to eight weeks.

Usual pediatric dose

See *Usual adult and adolescent dose*.

Strength(s) usually available

U.S.—

50 mg (Rx) [*Imuran* (scored; lactose); GENERIC (scored)].

Canada—

50 mg (Rx) [*Imuran* (scored)].

Packaging and storage

Store below 40 °C (104 °F), preferably between 15 and 25 °C (59 and 77 °F), in a well-closed container. Protect from light.

Parenteral Dosage Forms

Note: The dosing and strengths of the dosage form available are expressed in terms of azathioprine base.

AZATHIOPRINE SODIUM FOR INJECTION USP

Usual adult and adolescent dose

Transplant rejection, organ (prophylaxis)—

Initial: Intravenous 3 to 5 mg (base) per kg of body weight a day prior to, during, or soon after surgery, the dosage being adjusted to maintain the homograft without causing toxicity.

Maintenance: Intravenous, 1 to 3 mg (base) per kg of body weight a day.

Usual pediatric dose

See *Usual adult and adolescent dose*.

Strength(s) usually available

U.S.—

100 mg (base) (Rx) [*Imuran* (lyophilized); GENERIC].

Canada—

100 mg (base) (Rx) [*Imuran* (lyophilized)].

Packaging and storage

Store below 40 °C (104 °F), preferably between 15 and 25 °C (59 and 77 °F). Protect from light.

Preparation of dosage form

Azathioprine Sodium for Injection USP is reconstituted for intravenous use by adding 10 mL of sterile water for injection to the vial and swirling to dissolve.

Reconstituted solutions may be further diluted for administration by intravenous infusion with 0.9% sodium chloride injection or 5% dextrose and 0.9% sodium chloride injection.

Stability

Reconstituted solutions of azathioprine are stable for 24 hours at room temperature. Although solutions may be stable for longer periods, because there is no preservative, use within 24 hours is recommended for reasons of sterility.

Incompatibilities

Mixing with alkaline solutions, especially on warming, may result in conversion to 6-mercaptopurine. Conversion to mercaptopurine also occurs in the presence of sulfhydryl compounds such as cysteine, glutathione, and hydrogen sulfide.

[1]Not included in Canadian product labeling.

Revised: 12/03/1998

AZELAIC ACID Topical†

VA CLASSIFICATION (Primary/Secondary): DE752/DE900

Commonly used brand name(s): *Azelex; Finevin*.

Note: For a listing of dosage forms and brand names by country availability, see *Dosage Forms* section(s).

†Not commercially available in Canada.

Category

Antiacne agent (topical); hypopigmentation agent (topical).

Indications

Note: Bracketed information in the *Indications* section refers to uses that are not included in U.S. product labeling.

Accepted

Acne vulgaris(treatment)—Azelaic acid is indicated in the treatment of mild to moderate acne vulgaris.

[Melasma (treatment)]—Azelaic acid has been used to treat melasma, caused by hyperfunctioning melanocytes. Azelaic acid will not similarly affect the function of normal melanocytes; thus, it will not lighten freckles.

Pharmacology/Pharmacokinetics

Physicochemical characteristics

Source—Dietary component (whole grain cereals and animal products).

Molecular weight—188.22.

Mechanism of action/Effect

Antiacne agent—

The mechanism of action is not fully known but it is thought that azelaic acid causes antibacterial effects by inhibiting the synthesis of cellular protein in aerobic and anaerobic microorganisms, especially *Propionibacterium acnes* and *Staphylococcus epidermidis*. Within aerobic microorganisms, azelaic acid reversibly inhibits a variety of oxidoreductive enzymes including tyrosinase, mitochondrial enzymes of the respiratory chain, thioredoxin reductase, 5-alpha-reductase, and DNA polymerases. In anaerobic microorganisms, glycolysis is disrupted.

Also, azelaic acid improves acne vulgaris by decreasing microcomedo formation and normalizing the keratin process. Azelaic acid may be effective against both inflamed and noninflamed lesions. Specifically, azelaic acid reduces the thickness of the stratum corneum, shrinks keratohyalin granules by reducing the amount and distribution of filaggrin (a component of keratohyalin) in epidermal layers, and lowers the number of keratohyalin granules.

Hypopigmentation agent—
Azelaic acid's antityrosinase and antimitochondrial enzymatic activities may interrupt the hyperactivity of normal melanocytes and their resulting growth in melasma, a localized macular hyperpigmentation of facial or nuchal skin. Use of azelaic acid to treat hyperpigmentation disorders due to hyperactivity of abnormal melanocytes has not been consistently successful. The hypopigmentation action of azelaic acid may result, to a lesser extent, from its ability to scavenge free radicals that can cause hyperactivity of melanocytes. Free radicals are a metabolic product of peroxidation of cell membrane lipids, produced when cells are irradiated with ultraviolet light, including sunlight. There is no depigmenting effect on normal melanocytes.

Other actions/effects

Azelaic acid is being studied for potential antimycotic and antiviral properties.

In time- and dose-dependent *in vitro* studies, azelaic acid has been shown to selectively penetrate rapidly growing human and murine tumor cells that are undifferentiated and possess chromosomal abnormalities while not affecting normal cells. The antiproliferative and cytotoxic effects are attributed to the antityrosinase and antimitochondrial activity of azelaic acid. Further *in vivo* studies are needed to fully characterize the clinical course of azelaic acid within these cell lines.

Absorption

One study found the following levels of penetration after a single application to human skin *in vitro*—
Stratum corneum: Approximately 3 to 5%.
Dermis and epidermis: Up to 10%.
Plasma: Approximately 4%.

Elimination

Renal, mainly unchanged.

Precautions to Consider

Carcinogenicity

Carcinogenic animal studies were deemed unnecessary because azelaic acid is normally found in the human diet and is not considered to be a carcinogenic substance.

Mutagenicity

The Ames test, hypoxanthine-guanine phosphoribosyltransferase (HGPRT) test in Chinese hamster ovary cells, human lymphocyte test, and dominant lethal assay in mice suggest that azelaic acid is nonmutagenic.

Pregnancy/Reproduction

Fertility—Adequate and well-controlled studies have not been done in humans.

Animal studies have shown no adverse effects.

Pregnancy—Systemically absorbed azelaic acid crosses the placenta; however, little systemic absorption of topical azelaic acid occurs. Adequate and well-controlled studies have not been done; problems in humans have not been documented.

In animal studies using toxic oral doses, embryotoxic effects occurred in Segment I and II studies of rats given doses of 2500 mg per kg of body weight (mg/kg) a day; similar effects were reported for Segment II studies in rabbits given doses of 150 to 500 mg/kg a day and monkeys given doses of 500 mg/kg a day. No teratogenic effects occurred. Animal studies using topical administration have not been done.

FDA Pregnancy Category B.

Breast-feeding

Azelaic acid may pass into breast milk, according to *in vitro* studies; however, the amount that is absorbed systemically from topical administration is insignificant and should not affect physiologic levels of azelaic acid. Problems in humans have not been documented.

Pediatrics

No information is available on the relationship of age to the effects of azelaic acid in pediatric patients. Safety and efficacy have not been established.

Geriatrics

No information is available on the relationship of age to the effects of azelaic acid in geriatric patients.

Medical considerations/Contraindications

The medical considerations/contraindications included have been selected on the basis of their potential clinical significance (reasons given in parentheses where appropriate)—not necessarily inclusive (» = major clinical significance).

Risk-benefit should be considered when the following medical problem exists:
Hypersensitivity to azelaic acid

Side/Adverse Effects

The following side/adverse effects have been selected on the basis of their potential clinical significance (possible signs and symptoms in parentheses where appropriate)—not necessarily inclusive:

Those indicating need for medical attention

Incidence rare
Hypopigmentation (white spots or lightening of treated areas of dark skin)—in patients with dark complexions

Note: Azelaic acid will consistently lighten hyperpigmented skin (skin that is darker than normal for a given individual) but will not typically lighten skin beyond its normal color. Rarely, patients with dark complexions may notice *hypopigmentation* of skin.

Those indicating need for medical attention only if they continue or are bothersome

Incidence more frequent
Desquamation (peeling of skin); ***dryness of skin; erythema*** (redness of skin); ***inflammatory reaction, mild*** (burning, stinging, or tingling of skin, mild)—1 to 5% with continued use; ***pruritus, mild*** (itching of skin)—1 to 5% with continued use

Note: *Mild burning, stinging, or tingling of skin* and *pruritus* may occur at the start of each treatment and may last 5 to 20 minutes, especially if skin is inflamed or broken, but lessens with continued use. Dosage may be reduced until skin irritation lessens.

Patient Consultation

As an aid to patient consultation, refer to *Advice for the Patient, Azelaic Acid (Topical).*

In providing consultation, consider emphasizing the following selected information (» = major clinical significance):

Before using this medication

» Conditions affecting use, especially:
Hypersensitivity to azelaic acid

Proper use of this medication

Applying a small amount of medication as a thin film to clean, dry skin; gently and thoroughly rubbing into the affected area
Washing hands well after applying
» Not applying to mucous membranes and, if accidental contact occurs, washing affected area well with water immediately
» Compliance with full course of treatment
» Proper dosing
Missed dose: Applying as soon as possible; not applying if almost time for next dose; not doubling doses
» Proper storage

Precautions while using this medication

Contacting health care professional if acne worsens or does not improve in the first 4 weeks or if medication causes too much redness, dryness, or peeling of skin

May take longer than 4 weeks before full improvement is noticed

Other topical medications may be used but recommend applying them at different times during the day

Conservative use of water-base cosmetics is permissible with use of azelaic acid

General Dosing Information

Some skin irritation may be expected with first use of topical azelaic acid; however, if skin irritation persists, dosage may be reduced to one time a day until irritation lessens. If skin irritation continues, azelaic acid treatment should be discontinued.

Patient should apply azelaic acid as a thin film to clean dry skin and rub into skin thoroughly. Improvement of acne or hyperpigmentation condition may take 4 weeks or longer.

Safety considerations for handling this medication

Wash hands thoroughly after handling topical azelaic acid.

Keep topical azelaic acid away from mouth, eyes, and other mucous membranes. If accidental contact occurs, large amounts of water should be used to wash affected area. If the eyes are involved and eye irritation persists after a thorough washing, contact a physician.

Topical Dosage Form

Note: Bracketed uses in the *Dosage Forms* section refer to categories of use and/or indications that are not included in U.S. product labeling.

AZELAIC ACID CREAM

Usual adult and adolescent dose

Antiacne agent or
[Hypopigmentation agent]—
Topical, to the affected area, two times a day (morning and evening).

Note: Initially, application once a day for a few days has been used for some patients sensitive to azelaic acid.

Usual pediatric dose

Safety and efficacy have not been established.

Strength(s) usually available

U.S.—
20% (Rx) [*Azelex*].
20% (Rx) [*Finevin*].
Canada—
Not commercially available.

Packaging and storage

Store below 40 °C (104 °F), preferably between 15 and 30 °C (59 and 86 °F), unless otherwise specified by manufacturer. Protect from freezing.

Auxiliary labeling

- External use only.

Note

Dermatologic use only; not for ophthalmic use.

Selected Bibliography

Breathnach AS. Pharmacological properties of azelaic acid. Clin Drug Invest 1995; 10(Suppl 2): 27-33.

Revised: 7/24/2001
Developed: 06/27/1996

AZELASTINE Nasal†

VA CLASSIFICATION (Primary): NT400
Commonly used brand name(s): *Astelin*.

Note: For a listing of dosage forms and brand names by country availability, see *Dosage Forms* section(s).

†Not commercially available in Canada.

Category

Antihistaminic (H_1-receptor), nasal.

Indications

Accepted

Rhinitis, seasonal allergic (treatment)—Azelastine is indicated for symptomatic treatment of seasonal allergic rhinitis, including rhinorrhea, sneezing, and nasal pruritus, in adults and children 5 years of age and older.

Rhinitis, vasomotor (treatment)—Azelastine is indicated for symptomatic treatment of vasomotor rhinitis including rhinorrhea, nasal congestion, and post nasal drip in adults and children 12 years of age and older.

Pharmacology/Pharmacokinetics

Physicochemical characteristics

Chemical Group—Phthalazinone derivative.
Molecular weight—418.37.
pH—
Saturated solution: 5 to 5.4.
Commercial product: 6.8 ± 0.3.
Solubility—Sparingly soluble in water, methanol, and propylene glycol and slightly soluble in ethanol, octanol, and glycerine.

Mechanism of action/Effect

Azelastine acts by competing with histamine for H_1-receptor sites on effector cells.

Absorption

Systemic bioavailability is approximately 40% after nasal administration.

Distribution

Vol_D—14.5 liters per kg of body weight.

Protein binding

Azelastine—High (88%).
Desmethylazelastine—Very high (97%).

Biotransformation

Hepatic, by oxidation via the cytochrome P450 enzyme system. The exact cytochrome P450 isoenzyme involved has not been determined, but a nonspecific P450 inhibitor (cimetidine) was found to raise mean concentrations of azelastine significantly; no pharmacokinetic interaction could be demonstrated with a known CYP3A4 inhibitor (erythromycin).

The major metabolite, desmethylazelastine, also has H_1-receptor antagonist activity. Desmethylazelastine is undetectable in plasma following single intranasal doses of azelastine but concentrations range from 20 to 50% of azelastine concentrations at the steady-state.

Half-life

Elimination—
Azelastine (after intravenous or oral administration)—22 hours.
Desmethylazelastine (after oral administration of azelastine)—54 hours.

Note: According to limited data, the metabolite profile is similar for oral and intranasal administration of azelastine.

Onset of action

In dose-ranging trials, nasal azelastine was found to produce a statistically significant decrease in allergic symptoms within 3 hours after the initial dose.

Time to peak concentration

Plasma—2 to 3 hours.

Peak plasma concentration

Oral administration of azelastine produces linear responses in the maximum plasma concentration (C_{max}) and area under the plasma concentration-time curve (AUC). However, administration of intranasal doses of more than 2 sprays per nostril for 29 days has been found to produce greater than proportional increases in the C_{max} and AUC.

In oral, single-dose studies, renal insufficiency (creatinine clearance less than 50 mL per minute) resulted in a 70 to 75% increase in the C_{max} and AUC compared with those in normal subjects, although the time to peak plasma concentration was unchanged.

Duration of action

12 hours.

Elimination

Fecal—75% (less than 10% unchanged) after oral administration.

Precautions to Consider

Carcinogenicity

Studies in rats and mice given oral doses of up to 30 and 25 mg per kg of body weight (mg/kg) per day, respectively (240 and 100 times the maximum recommended human daily intranasal dose on a mg per square meter of body surface area [mg/m^2] basis, respectively), found no evidence of carcinogenicity.

Mutagenicity

No evidence of mutagenicity caused by azelastine was found in the Ames test, DNA repair test, mouse lymphoma forward mutation assay, mouse micronucleus test, or chromosomal aberration test in rat bone marrow.

Pregnancy/Reproduction

Fertility—Studies in rats given oral doses of azelastine of up to 30 mg/kg per day (240 times the maximum recommended human daily intranasal dose on a mg/m^2 basis) found no effects on male or female fertility. However, at doses of 68.6 mg/kg per day (550 times the maximum recommended human daily intranasal dose on a mg/m^2 basis), duration of estrous cycles was prolonged and copulatory activity and the number of pregnancies were decreased. The numbers of corpora lutea and implantations were decreased, but the implantation ratio was not affected.

Pregnancy—Adequate and well-controlled studies in humans have not been done.

Studies in mice given an oral dose of 68.6 mg/kg per day (280 times the maximum recommended human daily intranasal dose on a mg/m^2 basis) found azelastine to be embryotoxic, fetotoxic, and teratogenic (external and skeletal abnormalities). Studies in rats given an oral dose of 30 mg/kg per day (240 times the maximum recommended human daily intranasal dose on a mg/m^2 basis) found delayed ossification (undeveloped metacarpus) and an increased incidence of 14th rib. At 68.6 mg/kg per day (550 times the maximum recommended human daily intranasal dose on a mg/m^2 basis), azelastine caused abortion and fetotoxic effects in rats.

It is recommended that risk-benefit be considered before using azelastine during pregnancy.

FDA Pregnancy Category C.

Breast-feeding
It is not known whether azelastine is distributed into breast milk.

Pediatrics
Appropriate studies performed to date have not demonstrated pediatrics-specific problems that would limit the usefulness of azelastine in children 5 years of age and older.

Geriatrics
Although studies on the relationship of age to the effects of azelastine have not been performed in the geriatric population, placebo-controlled clinical trials included a small number of patients over 60 years of age, and adverse effects in this group were similar to those in younger individuals.

Drug interactions and/or related problems
The following drug interactions and/or related problems have been selected on the basis of their potential clinical significance (possible mechanism in parentheses where appropriate)—not necessarily inclusive (» = major clinical significance):

Note: Combinations containing any of the following medications, depending on the amount present, may also interact with this medication.

» Alcohol or
» CNS depression-producing medications, other (see *Appendix II*)
(concurrent use may potentiate the CNS depressant effects of either these medications or azelastine)

» Cimetidine
(concurrent use with azelastine results in significantly increased plasma concentrations of azelastine, as a result of inhibition of cytochrome P450 by cimetidine)

Ketoconazole
(interferes with measurement of plasma azelastine concentrations)

Laboratory value alterations
The following have been selected on the basis of their potential clinical significance (possible effect in parentheses where appropriate)—not necessarily inclusive (» = major clinical significance).

Alanine aminotransferase (ALT [SGPT])
(serum values may rarely be increased)

Medical considerations/Contraindications
The medical considerations/contraindications included have been selected on the basis of their potential clinical significance (reasons given in parentheses where appropriate)—not necessarily inclusive (» = major clinical significance).

Risk-benefit should be considered when the following medical problems exist:

Renal function impairment
(plasma concentrations may be increased)

Sensitivity to azelastine

Side/Adverse Effects

Note: No significant effect on QT interval has been found in studies of orally or nasally administered azelastine at therapeutic doses.

The following side/adverse effects have been selected on the basis of their potential clinical significance (possible signs and symptoms in parentheses where appropriate)—not necessarily inclusive:

Those indicating need for medical attention
Incidence rare

Allergic reaction (skin rash, hives, or itching); ***bronchospasm*** (shortness of breath, tightness in chest, troubled breathing, or wheezing); ***cough; eye problems or pain*** (eye pain or redness or blurred vision or other change in vision); ***hematuria*** (blood in urine); ***stomatitis*** (sores in mouth or on lips); ***tachycardia*** (rapid heartbeat)

Those indicating need for medical attention only if they continue or are bothersome
Incidence more frequent

Bitter taste—incidence 19.7%; ***somnolence*** (drowsiness or sleepiness)

Incidence less frequent

Burning inside the nose; dizziness; dryness of mouth; epistaxis (bloody mucus or unexplained nosebleeds); ***fatigue*** (unusual tiredness or weakness); ***headache; myalgia*** (muscle aches or pain); ***nausea; pharyngitis*** (sore throat); ***sneezing, paroxysmal*** (sudden outbursts of sneezing); ***weight gain***

Overdose
For more information on the management of overdose or unintentional ingestion, **contact a Poison Control Center** (see *Poison Control Center Listing*).

Clinical effects of overdose
There have been no reported incidents of azelastine overdose in humans; however, acute overdose would not be expected to result in clinically significant adverse effects other than increased somnolence, since one bottle contains 17 mg of azelastine hydrochloride and single oral doses of up to 16 mg have not produced serious adverse effects.

In mice, oral doses of greater than 120 mg per kg of body weight (mg/kg) (480 times the maximum recommended human daily intranasal dose on a mg per square meter of body surface area [mg/m^2] basis) produced significant mortality, preceded by tremor, convulsions, decreased muscle tone, and salivation. In dogs, single doses as high as 10 mg/kg (270 times the maximum recommended human daily intranasal dose on a mg/m^2 basis) were well tolerated, but single doses of 20 mg/kg were lethal.

Treatment of overdose
General supportive measures.

Patient Consultation
As an aid to patient consultation, refer to *Advice for the Patient, Azelastine (Nasal)*.

In providing consultation, consider emphasizing the following selected information (» = major clinical significance):

Before using this medication
» Conditions affecting use, especially:

Sensitivity to azelastine

Pregnancy—Risk-benefit should be considered; teratogenic in animals

Use in children—Safety and efficacy not established in children up to 5 years of age

Other medications, especially alcohol or other CNS depressants or cimetidine

Proper use of this medication
Reading patient instructions carefully before using

Clearing nasal passages by blowing nose before use

Proper administration technique; reading patient directions carefully before use; before initial use, priming the pump with four sprays or until a fine mist appears; if not used for 3 or more days, priming the pump with two sprays or until a fine mist appears

Preventing contamination: Wiping tip of applicator with clean, damp tissue; replacing cap right after use

» Importance of not using more medication than the amount prescribed

» Proper dosing

Missed dose: Using as soon as possible; if almost time for next dose, skipping missed dose and going back to regular dosing schedule; not doubling doses

» Proper storage; storing upright at room temperature with pump tightly closed

Precautions while using this medication
» Avoiding use of alcohol or other CNS depressants

» Caution if dizziness or drowsiness occurs

» Avoiding spraying in the eyes

Side/adverse effects
Signs of potential side effects, especially allergic reaction, bronchospasm, cough, eye problems or pain, hematuria, stomatitis, or tachycardia

General Dosing Information
Before initial use, the pump should be primed with four sprays or until a fine mist appears. If not used for 3 or more days, the pump should be primed with two sprays or until a fine mist appears.

Prior to administration of azelastine, the nasal passages should be cleared.

Azelastine is dispensed in a package consisting of two bottles of medication (for a total of 200 metered sprays) and one pump assembly.

Nasal Dosage Forms

AZELASTINE HYDROCHLORIDE NASAL SOLUTION

Usual adult and adolescent dose
Rhinitis, seasonal allergic—

Intranasal, 1 or 2 sprays in each nostril two times a day.

Rhinitis, vasomotor—

Intranasal, 2 sprays in each nostril two times a day

Usual pediatric dose

Rhinitis, seasonal allergic—

Children 12 years of age and older: See *Usual adult and adolescent dose*.

Children 5 to 11 years of age: Intranasal, 1 spray in each nostril twice daily.

Children up to 5 years of age: Safety and efficacy have not been established.

Rhinitis, vasomotor—

Children 12 years of age and older: See *Usual adult and adolescent dose*

Children up to 12 years of age: Safety and efficacy have not been established.

Strength(s) usually available

U.S.—

137 mcg per metered spray (1 mg per mL; 100 metered sprays per bottle) (Rx) [*Astelin* (benzalkonium chloride 125 mcg per mL; edetate disodium; hydroxypropyl methylcellulose; citric acid; dibasic sodium phosphate; sodium chloride; purified water)].

Note: Azelastine is dispensed in a package consisting of two bottles of medication (for a total of 200 metered sprays) and one pump assembly.

Packaging and storage

Store between 20 and 25 °C (68 and 77 °F). Protect from freezing.

Stability

The expiration date on the bottles applies to the unopened bottles.

Once the pump assembly has been inserted into the first bottle of the dispensing package, the pump assembly (and any unused portion of either bottle) should be discarded after 3 months, but not to exceed the original expiration date.

Auxiliary labeling

- Avoid spraying in eyes.
- For the nose.

Revised: 04/26/2006
Developed: 11/11/1997

AZELASTINE Ophthalmic†

VA CLASSIFICATION (Primary): OP801

Commonly used brand name(s): *Optivar*.

Note: For a listing of dosage forms and brand names by country availability, see *Dosage Forms* section(s).

†Not commercially available in Canada.

Category

Antihistaminic (H_1—receptor), ophthalmic; antiallergic, ophthalmic; mast cell stabilizer, ophthalmic.

Indications

Accepted

Conjunctivitis, allergic (treatment)—Azelastine is indicated for the treatment of itching of the eye associated with allergic conjunctivitis.

Pharmacology/Pharmacokinetics

Physicochemical characteristics

Molecular weight—418.37.

pH—5–6.5.

Melting point—225°C.

Mechanism of action/Effect

Azelastine is a relatively selective histamine H_1 antagonist and an inhibitor of the release of histamine and other mediators from cells (e.g., mast cells) involved in the allergic response. Based on *in vitro* studies using human cell lines, inhibition of other mediators involved in allergic reactions (e.g., leukotrienes and platelet activating factor [PAF]) has been demonstrated with azelastine. Decreased chemotaxis and activation of eosinophils also has been demonstrated.

Absorption

After ocular administration, absorption of azelastine was relatively low. In a study involving symptomatic patients, the administered dosage of one drop per eye two to four times a day (0.06 to 0.12 mg) demonstrated patient plasma concentrations between 0.02 and 0.25 nanograms per mL after 56 treatment days.

Distribution

Volume of distribution (Vol_D) (based on intravenous and oral administration)—Steady state: 14.5 L per kg. It is unknown whether azelastine is excreted into human breast milk.

Protein binding

Based on intravenous and oral administration—

Azelastine: High (88%)

N-desmethylazelastine: Very high (97%)

Biotransformation

Based on intravenous and oral administration—Hepatic; resulting in one primary metabolite, N-desmethylazelastine, via oxidation by the cytochrome P450 enzyme system.

Half-life

Elimination (based on intravenous and oral administration)—22 hours.

Onset of action

Ophthalmic administration—Within 3 minutes of administration.

Duration of action

Ophthalmic administration—Approximately 8 hours.

Elimination

Fecal—75% (less than 10% unchanged) after oral administration.

Precautions to Consider

Carcinogenicity/Mutagenicity

Studies in rats and mice have shown that azelastine is not carcinogenic. This conclusion was reached after 24 months of oral administration of azelastine, with doses for rats up to 30 mg per kg per day and doses for mice up to 25 mg per kg per day. Respectively, these doses represent the equivalent of approximately 25,000 and 21,000 times greater than the maximum daily recommended ocular human dose. Mutagenicity findings were negative as verified by the following genotoxic tests: Ames test; DNA repair test; mouse lymphoma forward mutation assay; mouse micronucleus test; or chromosomal aberration test in rat bone marrow.

Pregnancy/Reproduction

Fertility—At oral doses of up to 25,000 times the maximum recommended ocular human dose, reproduction and fertility studies showed no effects on male or female rats.

Pregnancy—No adequate and well-controlled studies in pregnant women have been done.

Animal studies with mice and rats showed evidence of fetotoxic and teratogenic effects when given azelastine orally at doses of 68.6 mg per kg per day (57,000 times the recommended ocular human dose).

FDA Pregnancy Category C.

Breast-feeding

It is not known whether azelastine is distributed into human breast milk after ocular use.

Pediatrics

Appropriate studies on the relationship of age to the effects of azelastine have not been performed in children under 3 years of age. Safety and efficacy have not been established in this population.

Geriatrics

Appropriate studies performed to date have not demonstrated geriatrics-specific problems that would limit the usefulness of azelastine in the elderly.

Medical considerations/Contraindications

The medical considerations/contraindications included have been selected on the basis of their potential clinical significance (reasons given in parentheses where appropriate)—not necessarily inclusive (» = major clinical significance).

Risk-benefit should be considered when the following medical problems exist:

Hypersensitivity to azelastine

Side/Adverse Effects

The following side/adverse effects have been selected on the basis of their potential clinical significance (possible signs and symptoms in parentheses where appropriate)—not necessarily inclusive:

Those indicating need for medical attention

Incidence less frequent (1% to 10%)

Asthma (cough; difficulty breathing; noisy breathing; shortness of breath; tightness in chest; wheezing); ***dyspnea*** (shortness of breath; difficult or labored breathing; tightness in chest; wheezing)

Those indicating need for medical attention only if they continue or are bothersome

Incidence more frequent (greater than 10%)

Bitter taste in mouth; headaches; transient eye burning or stinging

Incidence less frequent (1% to 10%)

Conjunctivitis (redness, pain, swelling of eye, eyelid, or inner lining of eyelid; burning, dry or itching eyes; discharge; excessive tearing); ***eye pain; fatigue*** (unusual tiredness or weakness); ***influenza-like symptoms*** (chills; cough; diarrhea; fever; general feeling of discomfort or illness; headache; joint pain; loss of appetite; muscle aches and pains; nausea; runny nose; shivering; sore throat; sweating; trouble sleeping; unusual tiredness or weakness; vomiting); ***pharyngitis*** (body aches or pain; congestion; cough; dryness or soreness of throat; fever; hoarseness; runny nose; tender, swollen glands in neck; trouble in swallowing; voice changes); ***pruritus*** (itching skin); ***rhinitis*** (stuffy nose; runny nose; sneezing); ***temporary blurring vision***

Patient Consultation

As an aid to patient consultation, refer to *Advice for the Patient, Azelastine (Ophthalmic).*

In providing consultation, consider emphasizing the following selected information (» = major clinical significance):

Before using this medication

» Conditions affecting use, especially:
  Hypersensitivity to azelastine

Proper use of this medication

» Importance of removing contact lenses prior to administration of medication; not using if eyes are red or irritated due to contact lenses
» Proper administration technique for ophthalmic solution
» Preventing contamination: Not touching applicator tip to any surface; keeping container tightly closed
» Proper dosing
  Missed dose: Using as soon as possible; not using if almost time for next dose; using next dose at regularly scheduled time; not doubling doses
» Proper storage

Precautions while using this medication

» Checking with physician if symptoms do not improve or if condition worsens

Side/adverse effects

Signs of potential side effects, especially asthma and dyspnea

General Dosing Information

Because the preservative, benzalkonium chloride, may be absorbed by contact lenses, it is recommended that they be removed prior to administration of azelastine. The lenses may be reinserted 10 minutes after administration of the medication.

Azelastine should not be administered if eyes are red or irritated secondary to use of contact lenses.

Ophthalmic Dosage Forms

AZELASTINE HYDROCHLORIDE OPHTHALMIC SOLUTION

Usual Adult and Adolescent Dose

Allergic conjunctivitis—
Topical to the conjunctiva, 1 drop in the affected eye(s) 2 times per day.

Usual Pediatric Dose

Allergic conjunctivitis—
Children younger than 3 years of age: Safety and efficacy have not been established.
Children 3 years of age and older: See *Usual adult and adolescent dose.*

Usual Geriatric Dose

See *Usual adult and adolescent dose.*

Strength(s) usually available

U.S.—
0.5 mg (0.457 mg base) per mL (Rx) [*Optivar* (Benzalkonium chloride 0.125 mg; disodium edetate dihydrate; hydroxypropyl methylcellulose; sorbitol solution; sodium hydroxide; water for injection)].

Packaging and storage

Store upright between 2 and 25 °C (36 and 77 °F).

Auxiliary labeling

• For the eye.

Revised: 01/03/2001
Developed: 10/27/2000

AZITHROMYCIN Systemic

VA CLASSIFICATION (Primary): AM200

Commonly used brand name(s): *Zithromax.*

Note: For a listing of dosage forms and brand names by country availability, see *Dosage Forms* section(s).

Category

Antibacterial (systemic).

Indications

Note: Bracketed information in the *Indications* section refers to uses that are not included in U.S. product labeling.

General Considerations

Azithromycin is an azalide antibiotic, part of the macrolide family of antibacterials. It has *in vitro* activity against many gram-positive and gram-negative aerobic and anaerobic bacteria. It also has greater stability than erythromycin in the presence of acid.

Azithromycin is active against staphylococci, including *Staphylococcus aureus* and *Staphylococcus epidermidis*, as well as streptococci, such as *Streptococcus pyogenes* and *Streptococcus pneumoniae.* The minimum inhibitory concentration (MIC) of azithromycin is two to four times greater than that of erythromycin against staphylococcus and streptococcus. Most erythromycin-resistant strains of staphylococcus, enterococcus, and streptococcus, including methicillin-resistant *S. aureus*, are also resistant to azithromycin. Also, azithromycin is less potent than erythromycin and clarithromycin against erythromycin-sensitive enterococci.

Azithromycin has excellent activity against *Haemophilus influenzae*, being two to eight times more active than erythromycin and four to eight times more active than clarithromycin *in vitro.* MICs of 4 to 16 mcg per mL inhibit most *Escherichia coli*, *Salmonella*, *Shigella*, and *Aeromonas* species. *Pseudomonas aeruginosa*, *Klebsiella*, *Enterobacter*, *Citrobacter*, *Proteus*, *Providencia*, *Morganella*, and *Serratia* species are resistant to azithromycin.

Azithromycin is two- to fourfold more active than erythromycin against *Moraxella (Branhamella) catarrhalis.* Inhibition of anaerobes, such as *Clostridium perfringens*, is slightly better with azithromycin than with erythromycin, and azithromycin's inhibition of *Bacteroides fragilis* and other *Bacteroides* species is comparable to that of erythromycin. Azithromycin also has good *in vitro* activity against *Chlamydia trachomatis*, *Chlamydia pneumoniae*, *Mycoplasma pneumoniae*, *Legionella* species, *Borrelia burgdorferi*, *Ureaplasma urealyticum*, and *Gardnerella vaginalis.* Azithromycin has eightfold more activity than erythromycin against *Neisseria gonorrhoeae* and tenfold more activity against *Haemophilus ducreyi.* It has also been shown to inhibit *Toxoplasma gondii in vitro* and in animal models. However, no potentiation against *T. gondii* could be demonstrated when azithromycin was combined with pyrimethamine. Also, when azithromycin was administered as a single agent in the treatment of cerebral toxoplasmosis in two patients, it failed, although the patients responded to conventional treatment.

Accepted

Bronchitis, bacterial exacerbations (treatment) or
Otitis media, acute (treatment)—Azithromycin is indicated in the treatment of bacterial exacerbations of chronic bronchitis or acute otitis media due to *Haemophilus influenzae, Moraxella catarrhalis,* or *Streptococcus pneumoniae.* However, azithromycin is not recommended as the first line of therapy for otitis media.

Cervicitis, gonococcal (treatment)
Cervicitis, nongonococcal (treatment)
Urethritis, gonococcal (treatment) or
Urethritis, nongonococcal (treatment)—Azithromycin is indicated in the treatment of cervicitis or urethritis due to *Chlamydia trachomatis* or *Neisseria gonorrhoeae.*

Chancroid (treatment)—Azithromycin is indicated in the treatment of genital ulcer disease in men due to *Haemophilus ducreyi.*

Mycobacterium avium complex (MAC) disease, disseminated (prophylaxis)[1]—Azithromycin is indicated in the prevention of disseminated

MAC disease in patients with advanced human immunodeficiency virus (HIV) infection.

Pelvic inflammatory disease (treatment)[1]—Azithromycin is indicated in the treatment of pelvic inflammatory disease due to *Chlamydia trachomatis, Mycoplasma hominis*, or *Neisseria gonorrhoeae.*

Pharyngitis (treatment) or
Tonsillitis (treatment)—Azithromycin is indicated in the treatment of pharyngitis or tonsillitis due to *Streptococcus pyogenes.*

Pneumonia, community-acquired (treatment)—Azithromycin is indicated in the treatment of community-acquired pneumonia due to *Chlamydia pneumoniae*[1], *Haemophilus influenzae, Legionella pneumophila*[1], *Moraxella catarrhalis*[1], *Mycoplasma pneumoniae*[1], *Staphylococcus aureus*[1], or *Streptococcus pneumoniae.*

Skin and soft tissue infections (treatment)—Azithromycin is indicated in the treatment of uncomplicated skin and soft tissue infections due to *Staphylococcus aureus, Streptococcus agalactiae*, or *Streptococcus pyogenes.*

Sinusitis, acute, bacterial—Azithromycin is indicated for the treatment of acute bacterial sinusitis due to *Haemophilus influenzae, Moraxella catarrhalis*, or *Streptococcus pneumoniae*

[Trachoma (treatment)][1]—Azithromycin is indicated in the treatment of trachoma due to *Chlamydia trachomatis.*

Trachoma is the leading cause of preventable blindness. Programs to prevent blindness due to trachoma have been based on community-wide treatment with topical tetracycline. Single-dose azithromycin has been shown to be as effective as a 6–week course of topical tetracycline ointment in the treatment of active trachoma. Therefore, azithromycin is useful in establishing high compliance in the treatment of trachoma.

---

[1]Not included in Canadian product labeling.

Pharmacology/Pharmacokinetics

Physicochemical characteristics
Molecular weight—Azithromycin: 785.03.

Mechanism of action/Effect
Azithromycin binds to the 50S ribosomal subunit of the 70S ribosome of susceptible organisms, thereby inhibiting RNA-dependent protein synthesis.

Azithromycin is bactericidal for *Streptococcus pyogenes, Streptococcus pneumoniae*, and *Haemophilus influenzae;* it is bacteriostatic for staphylococci and most aerobic gram-negative species.

Absorption
For oral dosage forms—
- Rapidly absorbed; bioavailability is approximately 37%.
- Capsule form: Food decreases peak serum concentration (C_{max}) values by approximately 52% and area under the plasma concentration-time curve (AUC) values by approximately 43%.
- Tablet form: Food increases C_{max} values by approximately 23% and 34% for the 250- and 600-mg tablets, respectively, and has no effect on AUC values.
- Oral suspension form (for adults): Food increases C_{max} values by approximately 56% and has no effect on AUC values.

Distribution
Rapidly and widely distributed throughout the body. Concentrates intracellularly, resulting in tissue concentrations 10 to 100 times higher than those found in plasma or serum. Azithromycin is highly concentrated in phagocytes and fibroblasts. Phagocytes transport the drug to the site of infection and inflammation. Release of azithromycin from phagocytes is gradual, but it is enhanced by exposure to the cell membrane of bacteria. Release of azithromycin from fibroblasts is not enhanced by bacteria, but fibroblasts may act as reservoirs of the antibiotic, releasing azithromycin to phagocytes. Very low concentrations ($<$ 0.01 mcg per mL [mcg/mL]) have been detected in the cerebrospinal fluid of human subjects with noninflamed meninges; however, higher concentrations were found in brain tissue in animal studies.

Vol_D—For oral dosage forms, approximately 31 L per kg (steady-state). For parenteral dosage forms, approximately 33 L per kg (following 1000- to 4000-mg doses at a concentration of 1 mg/mL infused over a 2-hour period).

Protein binding
Varies with concentration—Very low to moderate; approximately 7% at 1 mcg/mL, to 50% at 0.02 to 0.05 mcg/mL.

Biotransformation
Hepatic; approximately 35% metabolized by demethylation. Up to 10 metabolites, which are thought to have no significant antimicrobial activity, may be found in the bile.

Half-life
Peripheral leukocytes—34 to 57 hours (mean) after a single dose of 1200 mg (two 600-mg tablets).

Serum—11 to 14 hours when measured between 8 and 24 hours after a single, oral dose of 500 mg; however, after several doses, the half-life is approximately the same as the half-life in tissues.

Tissue—2 to 4 days.

Time to peak concentration
Adult subjects—
- For oral dosage forms: 2.1 to 3.2 hours.
- For parenteral dosage forms: 1 to 2 hours.

Elderly subjects—3.8 to 4.4 hours.

Peak plasma concentration
For oral dosage forms, after a 500-mg loading dose on day 1, then 250 mg once a day on days 2 through 5—
- Day 1: Approximately 0.41 and 0.38 mcg/mL for healthy young and elderly adults, respectively.
- Day 5: Approximately 0.24 and 0.26 mcg/mL for healthy young and elderly adults, respectively.

For parenteral dosage forms—
- Approximately 1.1 mcg/mL after a 3-hour intravenous infusion of 500 mg at a concentration of 1 mg/mL.
- Approximately 3.6 mcg/mL after a 1-hour intravenous infusion of 500 mg at a concentration of 2 mg/mL.

Elimination
Over 50% of the dose is eliminated through biliary excretion as unchanged drug.

For oral dosage forms, approximately 4.5% of the dose is eliminated in the urine as unchanged drug within 72 hours.

For parenteral dosage forms, approximately 11 to 14% of the dose is eliminated in the urine as unchanged drug within 24 hours.

Precautions to Consider

Cross-sensitivity and/or related problems
Patients who are hypersensitive to erythromycin or other macrolides may also be hypersensitive to azithromycin.

Carcinogenicity
Long-term studies have not been done in animals to evaluate the carcinogenic potential of azithromycin.

Mutagenicity
Azithromycin was not found to be mutagenic in the mouse lymphoma assay, the human lymphoctye clastogenic assay, or the mouse bone marrow clastogenic assay.

Pregnancy/Reproduction
Fertility—Adequate and well-controlled studies in humans have not been done.

Reproduction studies done in rats and mice given azithromycin at doses of up to moderately maternally toxic levels (i.e., 200 mg per kg of body weight [mg/kg] per day) have found no evidence of impaired fertility. On a mg per square meter of body surface area (mg/m^2) basis, these doses are estimated to be four and two times the human daily dose of 500 mg in rats and mice, respectively.

Pregnancy—Adequate and well-controlled studies in humans have not been done.

Reproduction studies done in rats and mice given azithromycin at doses of up to moderately maternally toxic levels (i.e., 200 mg/kg per day) have found no evidence of harm to the fetus. On a mg/m^2 basis, these doses are estimated to be four and two times the human daily dose of 500 mg in rats and mice, respectively.

FDA Pregnancy Category B.

Breast-feeding
It is not known if azithromycin is distributed into breast milk.

Pediatrics
Appropriate studies on the relationship of age to the effects of parenteral azithromycin or of the capsule or tablet dosage form of oral azithromycin have not been performed in children up to 16 years of age. Safety and efficacy have not been established. However, the oral suspension dosage form of azithromycin is approved for use in infants and children 6 months of age and older.

Geriatrics
Pharmacokinetic data in healthy elderly subjects (65 to 85 years old) were similar to those for younger volunteers (18 to 40 years old). A higher peak concentration (by 30 to 50%) was found in elderly women; however, no significant accumulation occurred. Dosage adjustment does not appear to be necessary in older patients with normal renal and hepatic function.

Drug interactions and/or related problems

The following drug interactions and/or related problems have been selected on the basis of their potential clinical significance (possible mechanism in parentheses where appropriate)—not necessarily inclusive (» = major clinical significance):

Note: Combinations containing any of the following medications, depending on the amount present, may also interact with this medication.

» Antacids, aluminum- and magnesium-containing
(concurrent use with antacids decreases the peak serum concentration [C_{max}] of azithromycin by approximately 24%, but has no effect on the area under the plasma concentration-time curve [AUC]; oral azithromycin should be administered at least 1 hour before or 2 hours after aluminum- and magnesium-containing antacids)

Cyclosporine or
Digoxin or
Hexobarbital or
Phenytoin or
Terfenadine
(concurrent use with macrolide antibiotics has been associated with increased serum concentrations of cyclosporine, digoxin, hexobarbital, phenytoin, and terfenadine; patients concurrently receiving azithromycin and any of these medications should be monitored carefully)

Dihydroergotamine or
Ergotamine
(concurrent use with macrolide antibiotics has been associated with acute ergot toxicity characterized by severe peripheral vasospasm and dysesthesia; patients concurrently receiving azithromycin and either of these medications should be monitored carefully)

Nelfinavir
(close monitoring for known side effects of azithromycin, such as liver enzyme abnormalities and hearing impairment, is warranted)

Warfarin
(concurrent use with macrolide antibiotics has been associated with increased anticoagulant effects; prothrombin time should be monitored carefully in patients concurrently receiving azithromycin and warfarin)

Laboratory value alterations

The following have been selected on the basis of their potential clinical significance (possible effect in parentheses where appropriate)—not necessarily inclusive (» = major clinical significance).

With physiology/laboratory test values
Alanine aminotransferase (ALT [SGPT]) and
Aspartate aminotransferase (AST [SGOT]) and
Creatine kinase and
Gamma-glutamyltransferase and
Lactate dehydrogenase
(serum values may be increased)
Bilirubin and
Potassium, serum
(concentrations may be increased)

Medical considerations/Contraindications

The medical considerations/contraindications included have been selected on the basis of their potential clinical significance (reasons given in parentheses where appropriate)—not necessarily inclusive (» = major clinical significance).

Except under special circumstances, this medication should not be used when the following medical problem exists:

» Hypersensitivity to azithromycin, erythromycins, or other macrolides

Risk-benefit should be considered when the following medical problem exists:

» Hepatic function impairment
(because biliary excretion is the major route of elimination, caution should be used in patients with hepatic function impairment)

Side/Adverse Effects

Note: Rarely, serious allergic reactions, such as anaphylaxis and angioedema, have been reported in patients taking azithromycin. Despite discontinuation of azithromycin and successful symptomatic treatment of the allergic reactions, allergic symptoms soon recurred in some patients when the symptomatic therapy was discontinued. These patients require prolonged periods of observation and symptomatic treatment.

The following side/adverse effects have been selected on the basis of their potential clinical significance (possible signs and symptoms in parentheses where appropriate)—not necessarily inclusive:

Those indicating need for medical attention

Incidence more frequent—for injection form only
Thrombophlebitis (pain, redness, and swelling at site of injection)

Incidence rare
Acute interstitial nephritis (fever; joint pain; skin rash); ***allergic reactions*** (difficulty in breathing; swelling of face, mouth, neck, hands, and feet; skin rash); ***pseudomembranous colitis*** (abdominal or stomach cramps or pain, severe; abdominal tenderness; diarrhea, watery and severe, which may also be bloody; fever)

Those indicating need for medical attention only if they continue or are bothersome

Incidence less frequent
Gastrointestinal disturbances (abdominal pain; diarrhea, mild; nausea; vomiting)

Incidence rare
Dizziness; headache

Patient Consultation

As an aid to patient consultation, refer to *Advice for the Patient, Azithromycin (Systemic).*

In providing consultation, consider emphasizing the following selected information (» = major clinical significance):

Before using this medication

» Conditions affecting use, especially:
Hypersensitivity to azithromycin, erythromycins, or other macrolides
Other medications, especially aluminum- and magnesium-containing antacids
Other medical problems, especially hepatic function impairment

Proper use of this medication

Azithromycin capsules and pediatric oral suspension should be given at least 1 hour before or 2 hours after meals
Azithromycin tablets and adult single dose oral suspension may be taken with or without food
Compliance with full course of therapy
» Importance of not taking more medication than prescribed; importance of not discontinuing medication without checking with physician
» Proper dosing
Missed dose: Taking as soon as possible; not taking if almost time for next dose; not doubling doses
» Proper storage

Precautions while using this medication

Checking with physician if no improvement within a few days or if condition becomes worse

Side/adverse effects

Signs of potential side effects, especially thrombophlebitis, acute interstitial nephritis, allergic reactions, and pseudomembranous colitis

General Dosing Information

No adjustment in dose is required in patients with mild renal function impairment (creatinine clearance ≥ 40 mL per minute [0.67 mL per second]). No data are available on the use of azithromycin in patients with more severe renal function impairment.

Diet/Nutrition

Azithromycin capsules and oral suspension in dropper bottles (for children) should be given at least 1 hour before or 2 hours after meals.

Azithromycin tablets and oral suspension in 1-gram packets (for adults) may be taken with or without food.

Oral Dosage Forms

AZITHROMYCIN CAPSULES USP

Usual adult and adolescent dose

Bronchitis, bacterial exacerbations or
Pharyngitis, streptococcal or
Pneumonia, due to *Streptococcus pneumoniae* or *Haemophilus influenzae*, or
Skin and soft tissue infections, uncomplicated, due to *Staphylococcus aureus, Streptococcus agalactiae*, or *Streptococcus pyogenes* or
Tonsillitis, streptococcal—
Adults and adolescents 16 years of age and older: Oral, 500 mg as a single dose on the first day, then 250 mg once a day on days two through five.

Adolescents up to 16 years of age: Safety and efficacy have not been established.

Cervicitis, nongonococcal or
Urethritis, nongonococcal—
Adults and adolescents 16 years of age and older: Oral, 1000 mg as a single dose.
Adolescents up to 16 years of age: Safety and efficacy have not been established.

Usual pediatric dose
Children up to 16 years of age—Safety and efficacy have not been established.

Strength(s) usually available
U.S.—
Not Commercially available
Canada—
Not Commercially available

Packaging and storage
Store below 40 °C (104 °F), preferably between 15 and 30 °C (59 and 86 °F) in a well-closed container.

Auxiliary labeling
- Do not take with food.
- Continue medicine for full time of treatment.

AZITHROMYCIN FOR ORAL SUSPENSION USP

Usual adult and adolescent dose
Cervicitis, nongonococcal or
Chancroid, in men or
Urethritis, nongonococcal—
Oral, 1 gram as a single dose.
Cervicitis, gonococcal or
Urethritis, gonococcal—
Oral, 2 grams as a single dose.

Usual pediatric dose
Otitis media, acute or
Pneumonia, due to *Chlamydia pneumoniae*[1], *Haemophilus influenzae*, *Mycoplasma pneumoniae*[1], or *Streptococcus pneumoniae*—
Infants and children 6 months to 12 years of age: Oral, 10 mg per kg of body weight, up to 500 mg, on the first day, then 5 mg per kg of body weight, up to 250 mg, on days two through five.
Infants up to 6 months of age: Safety and efficacy have not been established.

Pharyngitis, streptococcal or
Tonsillitis, streptococcal—
Children 2 to 12 years of age: Oral, 12 mg per kg of body weight, up to 500 mg, once a day for five days.
Infants and children up to 2 years of age: Safety and efficacy have not been established.

[Trachoma (treatment)][1]—
Children 2 to 10 years of age: Oral, 20 mg per kg of body weight as a single dose.
Infants and children up to 2 years of age: Safety and efficacy have not been established.

Note: Depending on the severity of the trachoma and the initial clinical response, doses of azithromycin oral suspension may be repeated once every 28 days for a total of 6 doses.

Usual pediatric prescribing limits
500 mg per day for pharyngitis, tonsillitis, and the first day of dosing for otitis media and pneumonia.
250 mg per day for days two through five for otitis media and pneumonia.

Strength(s) usually available
U.S.—
100 mg per 5 mL (when reconstituted according to manufacturer's instructions) (available in 300-mg bottles) (Rx) [*Zithromax* (sucrose)].
200 mg per 5 mL (when reconstituted according to manufacturer's instructions) (available in 600-, 900-, and 1200-mg bottles) (Rx) [*Zithromax* (sucrose)].
1 gram (single dose packet) (Rx) [*Zithromax* (sucrose)].
Canada—
100 mg per 5 mL (when reconstituted according to manufacturer's instructions) (available in 300-mg bottles) (Rx) [*Zithromax* (sucrose)].
200 mg per 5 mL (when reconstituted according to manufacturer's instructions) (available in 600- and 900-mg bottles) (Rx) [*Zithromax* (sucrose)].
1 gram (single dose packet) (Rx) [*Zithromax* (sucrose)].

Packaging and storage
Prior to reconstitution, store between 5 and 30 °C (41 and 86 °F) in a tight container.
After reconstitution, the pediatric oral suspension should be stored between 5 and 30 °C (41 and 86 °F).

Preparation of dosage form
For the pediatric suspension—Add the indicated volume of water to the bottle and shake well.

Azithromycin content	Final concentration	Total volume of water to be added
300 mg	100 mg/5 mL	9 mL
600 mg	200 mg/5 mL	9 mL
900 mg	200 mg/5 mL	12 mL
1200 mg	200 mg/5 mL	15 mL

For the adult single dose packets—Empty the entire contents of the packet into a glass containing 2 ounces (approximately 60 mL) of water and mix thoroughly. The suspension should be consumed immediately. Add an additional 2 ounces of water to the glass, mix, and drink to assure complete consumption of the dose. This packet should not be used to administer doses other than 1000 mg of azithromycin.

Auxiliary labeling
For the pediatric suspension—
- Refrigerate.
- Shake well.
- Do not take with food.
- Continue medicine for full time of treatment.

For the adult single dose packets—
- Reconstitute before taking.

AZITHROMYCIN TABLETS

Usual adult and adolescent dose
Bronchitis, bacterial exacerbations or
Pharyngitis, streptococcal or
Pneumonia, due to *Chlamydia pneumoniae*[1], *Haemophilus influenzae*, *Mycoplasma pneumoniae*[1], or *Streptococcus pneumoniae* or
Skin and soft tissue infections or
Tonsillitis, streptococcal—
Adults and adolescents 16 years of age and older: Oral, 500 mg as a single dose on the first day, then 250 mg once a day on days two through five.
Adolescents up to 16 years of age: Safety and efficacy have not been established.

Cervicitis, nongonococcal or
Urethritis, nongonococcal—
Adults and adolescents 16 years of age and older: Oral, 1000 mg as a single dose.
Adolescents up to 16 years of age: Safety and efficacy have not been established.

Sinusitis, acute, bacterial—
500 mg a day for 3 days

Mycobacterium avium complex (MAC) disease, disseminated, prophylaxis[1]—
Adults and adolescents 16 years of age and older: Oral, 1200 mg once a week, alone or in combination with an approved dosing regimen of rifabutin.
Adolescents up to 16 years of age: Safety and efficacy have not been established.

Usual pediatric dose
Children up to 16 years of age—Safety and efficacy have not been established.

Strength(s) usually available
U.S.—
250 mg (Rx) [*Zithromax* (scored; lactose)].
500 mg (Rx) [*Zithromax* (scored; lactose)].
600 mg (Rx) [*Zithromax* (lactose)].
Canada—
250 mg (Rx) [*Zithromax* (scored; lactose)].

Packaging and storage
Store between 5 and 30 °C (41 and 86 °F).

Auxiliary labeling
- Continue medicine for full time of treatment.

Parenteral Dosage Form

AZITHROMYCIN FOR INJECTION

Note: Azithromycin for injection should be infused at a concentration of 1 mg per mL over a 3-hour period, or 2 mg per mL over a 1-hour period. Azithromycin should not be administered by bolus or intramuscular injection.

Usual adult and adolescent dose

Pelvic inflammatory disease[1]—

Adults and adolescents 16 years of age and older: Intravenous infusion, 500 mg as a single dose once a day for the first one or two days of a seven-day course of therapy.

Adolescents up to 16 years of age: Safety and efficacy have not been established.

Note: After the one- or two-day infusion therapy is complete, an oral dose of 250 mg should be administered once a day to complete the seven-day course of therapy.

Pneumonia[1], due to *Chlamydia pneumoniae*, *Haemophilus influenzae*, *Legionella pneumophila*, *Moraxella catarrhalis*, *Mycoplasma pneumoniae*, *Staphylococcus aureus*, or *Streptococcus pneumoniae*—

Adults and adolescents 16 years of age and older: Intravenous infusion, 500 mg as a single dose once a day for at least the first two days of a seven- to ten-day course of therapy.

Adolescents up to 16 years of age: Safety and efficacy have not been established.

Note: After the infusion therapy is complete, an oral dose of 500 mg should be administered once a day to complete the seven- to ten-day course of therapy.

Usual pediatric dose

Children up to 16 years of age—Safety and efficacy have not been established.

Strength(s) usually available

U.S.—

500 mg (Rx) [*Zithromax* (sodium hydroxide)].

Canada—

Not commercially available.

Preparation of dosage form

To prepare the initial solution for intravenous infusion, add 4.8 mL of sterile water for injection to each 500-mg vial and shake until all of the medication is dissolved. Further dilute this solution by transferring it into 250 or 500 mL of a suitable diluent (see manufacturer's package insert) to provide a final concentration of 2 or 1 mg per mL, respectively.

Stability

After reconstitution with sterile water for injection, the solution is stable for 24 hours when stored below 30 °C (86 °F). After dilution to 1 or 2 mg per mL in suitable diluent, solutions are stable for 24 hours at or below room temperature (30 °C [86 °F]), or for 7 days if stored at 5 °C (41 °F).

[1]Not included in Canadian product labeling.

Selected Bibliography

Drew RH, Gallis HA. Azithromycin—spectrum of activity, pharmacokinetics, and clinical applications. Pharmacotherapy 1992; 12(3): 161-73.

Revised: 08/17/2004

AZTREONAM Systemic†

VA CLASSIFICATION (Primary): AM119

Commonly used brand name(s): *Azactam*.

Note: For a listing of dosage forms and brand names by country availability, see *Dosage Forms* section(s).

†Not commercially available in Canada.

Category

Antibacterial (systemic).

Note: Aztreonam is a narrow-spectrum antibacterial that is only active against aerobic, gram-negative organisms.

Indications

Note: Bracketed information in the *Indications* section refers to uses that are not included in U.S. product labeling.

Accepted

Bronchitis (treatment) or

Pneumonia, gram-negative, bacterial (treatment)—Aztreonam is indicated as a secondary agent in the treatment of aerobic gram-negative bacterial bronchitis and pneumonia caused by *Enterobacter* species, *Escherichia coli*, *Haemophilus influenzae*, *Klebsiella pneumoniae*, *Proteus mirabilis*, *Pseudomonas aeruginosa*, and *Serratia marcescens*.

Skin and soft tissue infections (treatment)—Aztreonam is indicated as a secondary agent in the treatment of skin and soft tissue infections (including ulcers, burn wound infections, and postoperative wounds) caused by *Citrobacter* species, *Enterobacter* species, *E. coli*, *K. pneumoniae*, *P. mirabilis*, *Ps. aeruginosa*, and *S. marcescens*.

Cystitis (treatment) or

Urinary tract infections, bacterial (treatment)—Aztreonam is indicated as a secondary agent in the treatment of cystitis and complicated and uncomplicated urinary tract infections (including initial and recurrent pyelonephritis) caused by *Citrobacter* species, *Enterobacter cloacae*, *E. coli*, *Klebsiella oxytoca*, *K. pneumoniae*, *P. mirabilis*, *Ps. aeruginosa*, and *S. marcescens*.

Gynecologic infections (treatment)—Aztreonam is indicated as a secondary agent in the treatment of gynecologic infections (including endometritis and pelvic cellulitis) caused by *Enterobacter* species (including *E. cloacae*), *E. coli*, *K. pneumoniae*, and *P. mirabilis*.

Infections, surgically treated (treatment adjunct)—Aztreonam is indicated for adjunctive therapy to surgery for the management of infections, such as abscesses, infections complicating hollow viscous perforations, cutaneous infections, and infections of serous surfaces, caused by susceptible organisms.

Intra-abdominal infections (treatment)—Aztreonam is indicated as a secondary agent in the treatment of intra-abdominal infections (including peritonitis) caused by *Citrobacter* species (including *Citrobacter freundii*), *Enterobacter* species (including *E. cloacae*), *E. coli*, *Klebsiella* species (including *K. pneumoniae*), *Ps. aeruginosa*, and *Serratia* species (including *S. marcescens*).

Septicemia, bacterial (treatment)—Aztreonam is indicated as a secondary agent in the treatment of septicemia caused by *Enterobacter* species, *E. coli*, *K. pneumoniae*, *P. mirabilis*, *Ps. aeruginosa*, and *S. marcescens*.

[Bone and joint infections (treatment)]—Aztreonam is used as a secondary agent in the treatment of bone and joint infections caused by susceptible aerobic, gram-negative bacteria.

Aztreonam and aminoglycosides are synergistic *in vitro* against most strains of *Ps. aeruginosa*, many strains of Enterobacteriaceae, and other aerobic gram-negative bacilli.

Not all species or strains of a particular organism may be susceptible to aztreonam.

Unaccepted

Aztreonam is not effective against gram-positive organisms (e.g., *Staphylococcus aureus*, enterococci, *Streptococcus pneumoniae*) and anaerobes (e.g., *Bacteroides* species and *Clostridium* species).

Pharmacology/Pharmacokinetics

Physicochemical characteristics

Molecular weight—435.44.

Mechanism of action/Effect

Bactericidal; binds to penicillin-binding protein-3(PBP-3), which results in inhibition of bacterial cell wall synthesis, and often results ultimately in cell lysis and death; filamentation also occurs in Enterobacteriaceae and *Ps. aeruginosa;* does not induce beta-lactamase activity, but has a high degree of stability in the presence of bacterial beta-lactamases; does not bind appreciably to any essential PBPs in gram-positive or anaerobic organisms.

Absorption

Oral—Less than 1% absorbed from the gastrointestinal tract following oral administration.

Intramuscular—Completely absorbed following intramuscular administration.

Distribution

Rapidly and widely distributed to body fluids and tissues; distributed to bile; breast milk; bronchial secretions; and blister, pericardial, pleural, synovial, amniotic, peritoneal, and cerebrospinal fluids (inflamed meninges); also distributed to atrial appendages, endometrium, fallopian tubes, fat, femurs, gallbladder, kidneys, large intestine, liver, lungs, myometrium, ovaries, prostate, skeletal muscles, skin, and sternum; also crosses the placenta and enters fetal circulation.

Vol_D (steady state)—
Adults:
0.11 to 0.21 L per kg.
Burn patients:
Approximately 0.31 L per kg.
Pediatric patients:
Premature neonates—0.29 to 0.36 L per kg.
Neonates (up to 1 month old)—0.26 to 0.30 L per kg.
Infants and children (1 month to 12 years)—0.20 to 0.29 L per kg.
Cystic fibrosis patients—Approximately 0.25 L per kg.

Protein binding
Normal renal function—Moderate (56 to 60%).
Impaired renal function (creatinine clearance < 30 mL per min [0.50 mL per sec])—36 to 43%.

Biotransformation
Approximately 6 to 16% metabolized to inactive metabolites by hydrolysis of the beta-lactam bond, resulting in an open-ring compound.

Half-life
Adults—
Normal renal function:
1.4 to 2.2 hours.
Impaired renal function:
4.7 to 6 hours.
Impaired hepatic function:
Primary biliary cirrhosis—Approximately 2.2 hours.
Alcoholic cirrhosis—Approximately 3.4 hours.
In elderly males (65 to 75 years of age):
Slightly prolonged (2.1 hours).
Pediatric patients—
Premature neonates:
3.1 to 5.7 hours.
Neonates (up to 1 month old):
2.4 to 2.6 hours.
Infants and children (1 month to 12 years):
1.5 to 1.7 hours.
Cystic fibrosis patients:
1 to 1.3 hours.

Time to peak serum concentration
Intramuscular—Approximately 0.6 to 1.3 hours.

Time to peak bile concentration
Intravenous—Approximately 2.4 hours.

Peak serum concentration
Linear kinetics—
Adults:
Intramuscular—1 gram: 40 to 46.5 mcg per mL.
Intravenous injection—1 gram: Approximately 125 mcg per mL.
Intravenous infusion—1 gram: 90 to 164 mcg per mL.
Pediatric patients:
Intravenous injection (over 3 to 5 minutes)—30 mg per kg of body weight (mg/kg).
Premature neonates—Approximately 80 mcg per mL.
Neonates and children up to 12 years of age—90 to 120 mcg per mL.

Peak bile concentration
Approximately 43 mcg per mL following a 1-gram intravenous dose.

Urine concentration
Intramuscular—Approximately 500 and 1200 mcg per mL 2 hours following intramuscular doses of 500 mg and 1 gram, respectively.
Intravenous—Approximately 1100, 3500, and 6600 mcg per mL 2 hours following 30-minute intravenous infusions of 500 mg, 1 gram, and 2 grams, respectively.

Elimination
Renal—
Approximately 60 to 75% excreted unchanged in urine within 8 hours by active tubular secretion and glomerular filtration (in approximately equal amounts); excretion essentially complete within 12 hours; inactive metabolites also excreted in urine.
Biliary/fecal—
Excreted unchanged in feces following oral administration.
Approximately 1.5 to 3.5% (up to 12%) excreted unchanged in feces following parenteral administration; inactive metabolites also excreted in feces.
In dialysis—
Hemodialysis: A 4-hour period of hemodialysis reduces plasma aztreonam concentrations by 27 to 58%.
Peritoneal dialysis: Reduces plasma aztreonam concentrations by approximately 10%.

Precautions to Consider

Cross-sensitivity and/or related problems
Studies in rabbits have shown negligible cross-reactivity between antiaztreonam, antibenzylpenicillin, and anticephalothin antibodies.
In studies in normal volunteers, aztreonam was shown to be only weakly immunogenic in humans. Of 41 patients with immunoglobulin E (IgE) antibodies to one or more penicillin moieties, none reacted to aztreonam. In a study of 36 patients receiving multiple doses of aztreonam over a 7-day period, there were no IgE antibody responses. Only one patient had an immunoglobulin G (IgG) response. In a study of 22 patients with positive skin tests to penicillin reagents, three had positive skin tests to aztreonam. Of those three, one was negative on rechallenge and one was confirmed as positive. Of the 20 patients with negative aztreonam skin tests who received aztreonam, none showed immediate hypersensitivity reactions.
Since cross-reactivity only rarely occurs between aztreonam and beta-lactam antibacterials, aztreonam usually may be given without incident to patients with "rash-type" beta-lactam allergy. However, patients who have had immediate hypersensitivity (e.g., anaphylactic or urticarial) reactions to beta-lactams should be closely monitored while receiving aztreonam.

Carcinogenicity
Studies in animals have not been done.

Mutagenicity
Studies with aztreonam in several standard *in vivo* and *in vitro* laboratory models have shown no evidence of mutagenic potential at the chromosome or gene level.

Pregnancy/Reproduction
Fertility—Two-generation reproduction studies in rats given doses of up to 20 times the maximum recommended human dose (MRHD) prior to and during gestation and lactation have not shown any evidence of impaired fertility.

Pregnancy—Aztreonam crosses the placenta and enters the fetal circulation. Adequate and well-controlled studies in humans have not been done.
Studies in rats and rabbits given daily doses of up to 15 and 5 times the MRHD, respectively, have not shown that aztreonam is embryotoxic, fetotoxic, or teratogenic. Studies in rats given 15 times the MRHD during late gestation and lactation have not shown any aztreonam-induced changes.

FDA Pregnancy Category B.

Breast-feeding
Aztreonam is distributed into breast milk in concentrations that are less than 1% of maternal serum concentrations. However, aztreonam is not absorbed from the gastrointestinal tract.

Pediatrics
Clinical studies of aztreonam have shown that it is effective in pediatric patients and that the side effects seen in children are similar to those seen in adults. Neutropenia occurred at a higher incidence in patients younger than 2 years of age receiving 30 mg per kg (mg/kg) every 6 hours. In children 2 years of age and older receiving 50 mg/kg every 6 hours, increases of hepatic transaminases, AST and ALT, greater than three times the upper limit of normal were seen. The increased frequency of these adverse events may have been due to the severity of the illness treated or the use of higher doses of aztreonam.
Aztreonam is not indicated for skin and skin-structure infections believed or known to be due to *H. influenzae* type b or for septicemia in pediatric patients because of the lack of clinical data concerning the treatment of these infections with aztreonam in children.

Geriatrics
Studies performed to date have not demonstrated geriatrics-specific problems that would limit the usefulness of aztreonam in the elderly. However, elderly patients are more likely to have an age-related decrease in renal function, which may require a decrease in dosage in patients receiving aztreonam.

Laboratory value alterations
The following have been selected on the basis of their potential clinical significance (possible effect in parentheses where appropriate)—not necessarily inclusive (» = major clinical significance).
With diagnostic test results
Coombs' (antiglobulin) tests
(may become positive during therapy)
With physiology/laboratory test values

Alanine aminotransferase (ALT [SGPT]), serum and
Alkaline phosphatase, serum and
Aspartate aminotransferase (AST [SGOT]), serum and
Lactate dehydrogenase (LDH), serum
(values may be increased transiently during therapy)

Creatinine, serum
(concentration may be increased transiently during therapy)

Partial thromboplastin time (PTT) and
Prothrombin time (PT)
(may be prolonged during therapy)

Medical considerations/Contraindications

The medical considerations/contraindications included have been selected on the basis of their potential clinical significance (reasons given in parentheses where appropriate)—not necessarily inclusive (» = major clinical significance).

Except under special circumstances, this medication should not be used when the following medical problem exists:

» Previous allergic reaction to aztreonam

Risk-benefit should be considered when the following medical problems exist:

» Cirrhosis
(prolonged half-life; patients with cirrhosis may require a modest reduction in dose [20 to 25%] when receiving high-dose, long-term therapy with aztreonam)

» Hepatic function impairment
(appropriate monitoring is recommended during treatment with aztreonam for patients with impaired hepatic function)

» Renal function impairment
(it is recommended that aztreonam be administered at a reduced dosage to patients with impaired renal function)

Side/Adverse Effects

Note: Pseudomembranous colitis has been reported rarely with aztreonam and may range in severity from mild to life-threatening. Patients who develop diarrhea during or following adminstration of aztreonam should be evaluated for this diagnosis.

Toxic epidermal necrolysis has been reported rarely with the use of aztreonam in patients undergoing bone marrow transplantation. Other risk factors, such as graft-versus-host disease, sepsis, radiation therapy, and other concommitantly administered drugs, are thought to have contributed to the development of this reaction.

The following side/adverse effects have been selected on the basis of their potential clinical significance (possible signs and symptoms in parentheses where appropriate)—not necessarily inclusive:

Those indicating need for medical attention

Incidence less frequent

Hypersensitivity (anaphylaxis; skin rash, redness, or itching); ***thrombophlebitis*** (discomfort, inflammation, or swelling at the injection site)

Incidence rare

Chest pain; confusion; diarrhea; diplopia (seeing double); ***dyspnea or wheezing*** (difficulty in breathing); ***electrocardiogram (ECG) changes***—usually transient; ***fever; hematological reactions, such as pancytopenia*** (nosebleeds or other unusual bleeding or buising); ***neutropenia*** (chills; fever; sore throat); ***thrombocytopenia*** (unusual bleeding or bruising; black, tarry stools; blood in urine or stools; pinpoint red spots on skin); ***anemia*** (unusual tiredness or weakness); ***leukocytosis*** (sore throat; headache; general feeling of illness; chills; eye pain; cough; unusual tiredness); ***and thrombocytosis***—usually asymptomatic; ***hepatitis*** (dark urine; flu-like symptoms; general feeling of discomfort or illness; light gray–colored stools; loss of appetite; yellow skin or eyes); ***hypotension*** (dizziness or weakness); ***numbness of tongue; seizures; urticaria*** (hives); ***vaginal candidiasis or vaginitis*** (burning or itching of vagina; discharge from vagina); ***vertigo*** (dizziness)

Those indicating need for medical attention only if they continue or are bothersome

Incidence less frequent or rare

Altered sense of taste; breast tenderness; diaphoresis (increased sweating); ***flushing; gastrointestinal upset*** (abdominal or stomach cramps; nausea; vomiting); ***halitosis*** (bad breath); ***headache; insomnia*** (trouble in sleeping); ***mouth ulcers; muscular aches; nasal congestion; paresthesia*** (burning or prickling feeling of skin); ***petechiae or purpura*** (small, nonraised, round, purplish or red spots on skin); ***sneezing; tinnitus*** (ringing, buzzing, or noise in ear)

Overdose

If necessary, aztreonam may be cleared from the blood stream by hemodialysis and/or peritoneal dialysis.

For more information on the management of overdose or unintentional ingestion, contact a **Poison Control Center** (see *Poison Control Center Listing*).

Treatment of overdose

Recommended treatment consists of the following:

Specific treatment—If necessary, hemodialysis to clear aztreonam from the serum.

Supportive care—Patients in whom intentional overdose is confirmed or suspected should be referred for psychiatric consultation.

Patient Consultation

As an aid to patient consultation, refer to *Advice for the Patient, Aztreonam (Systemic)*.

In providing consultation, consider emphasizing the following selected information (» = major clinical significance):

Before receiving this medication

» Conditions affecting use, especially:
Allergy to aztreonam or anaphylaxis to beta-lactam antibiotics
Pregnancy—Aztreonam crosses the placenta and enters the fetal circulation
Breast-feeding—Aztreonam is distributed into breast milk
Other medical problems, especially cirrhosis, or hepatic or renal function impairment

Proper use of this medication

» Importance of receiving medication for full course of therapy and on regular schedule

» Proper dosing

Side/adverse effects

Signs of potential side effects, especially hypersensitivity, thrombophlebitis, chest pain, confusion, diarrhea, diplopia, dyspnea or wheezing, fever, hematological reactions, such as pancytopenia, neutropenia, thrombocytopenia, anemia, leukocytosis, and thrombocytosis, hepatitis, hypotension, numbness of tongue, seizures, urticaria, vaginal candidiasis or vaginitis, or vertigo

General Dosing Information

Before the organism responsible for the infection in seriously ill patients is identified, concommitant therapy with aztreonam and appropriate antibiotics is recommended for patients who are also at risk for having an infection due to gram-positive aerobic pathogens or anaerobic organisms. Therapy should be initiated that would treat the suspected organism appropriately. Cefoxitin and imipenem are not recommended as agents for concommitant therapy because *in vitro* studies show that they induce high levels of beta-lactamase production in some gram-negative aerobes, such as *Enterobacter* and *Pseudomonas* species, which may induce antagonism in many beta-lactam antibiotics including aztreonam.

The duration of aztreonam therapy is dependent on the severity of the infection. It is recommended that aztreonam be continued for at least 48 hours after the patient becomes asymptomatic or evidence of bacterial eradication is obtained. Some persistent infections may require treatment for several weeks. The use of smaller doses than those indicated is not recommended.

The use of aztreonam may promote the overgrowth of nonsusceptible organisms, such as fungi and the gram-positive organisms *Staphylococcus aureus* and *Streptococcus faecalis*. If superinfection occurs during therapy with aztreonam, appropriate measures should be taken.

Aztreonam may be administered intramuscularly or intravenously. Intramuscular doses should be injected into a large muscle, such as the upper outer quadrant of the gluteus maximus or lateral part of the thigh. In patients requiring single doses greater than 1 gram or in patients with bacterial septicemia, localized parenchymal abscesses, peritonitis, or other severe or life-threatening infections, the intravenous route is recommended.

Aztreonam may be administered slowly over a 3- to 5-minute period either by direct injection into a vein or by injection into the tubing of a suitable intravenous administration set. If a Y-type administration set is used, consideration should be given to the calculated required volume of aztreonam solution so that the entire dose of medication will be infused.

When aztreonam is infused intermittently with another drug with which it is not pharmaceutically compatible, the common delivery tube should be flushed both before and after aztreonam administration with an infusion solution compatible with both drugs. Simultaneous administration of the two drugs should be avoided.

Aztreonam may also be administered by intermittent intravenous infusion in 50 to 100 mL of a suitable fluid over a 20- to 60-minute period.

If aztreonam is administered via a volume-control administration set, the final dilution should not exceed 2% (20 mg per mL).

Because of the serious nature of infections caused by *Pseudomonas aeruginosa*, the recommended dose in the treatment of such infections is 2 grams every 6 to 8 hours.

Patients with renal function impairment may need an adjustment in dosage, based on creatinine clearance. Creatinine clearance (in mL per minute) may be calculated as follows:

Adult males—Creatinine clearance = [(140 − age) × (ideal body weight in kg)]/[72 × serum creatinine (mg per dL)].

Adult females—Creatinine clearance = [(140 − age) × (ideal body weight in kg)]/[72 × serum creatinine (mg per dL)] × 0.85.

Creatinine clearance may also be calculated in SI units (as mL per second) as follows:

Adult males—Creatinine clearance = [(140 − age) × (ideal body weight in kg)]/[50 × serum creatinine (micromoles per L)].

Adult females—Creatinine clearance = [(140 − age) × (ideal body weight in kg)]/[50 × serum creatinine (micromoles per L)] × 0.85.

For treatment of adverse effects

Recommended treatment consists of the following:

- Discontinuation of aztreonam and institution of supportive treatment (e.g., maintenance of ventilation and administration of epinephrine, pressor amines, antihistamines, corticosteroids) if serious hypersensitivity reactions or allergic reactions occur.
- Appropriate therapeutic measures should be initiated if pseudomembranous colitis occurs. Discontinuation of aztreonam usually is sufficient in mild cases; however, in moderate or severe cases treatment with fluids and electrolytes, protein supplements, and antibacterials also should be considered.

Parenteral Dosage Forms

AZTREONAM INJECTION

Usual adult and adolescent dose

Antibacterial—

Intravenous infusion over twenty to sixty minutes:

Moderately severe systemic infections—1 to 2 grams every eight to twelve hours.

Severe systemic or life-threatening infections—2 grams every six to eight hours.

Note: Urinary tract infections—Intravenous infusion over twenty to sixty minutes, 500 mg to 1 gram every eight to twelve hours.

Adults with impaired renal function require a reduction in dose as follows:

Creatinine clearance (mL/min)/ (mL/sec)	Dose: Loading dose	Dose: Maintenance dose (every 6–12 hours)
>30/0.5		See *Usual adult and adolescent dose*
10-30/0.17–0.5	1–2 grams	½ of the loading dose
<10/0.17	500 mg–2 grams	¼ of the loading dose; in serious or life-threatening infections, an additional ⅛ of the loading dose should be given after each hemodialysis period

Usual adult prescribing limits

8 grams daily.

Usual pediatric dose

Antibacterial—

See *Aztreonam for Injection USP.*

Note: The 1- and 2-gram strengths of Aztreonam Injection are single-dose units and are intended to be infused in their entirety. Since it is unlikely that the pediatric dose would correspond to either 1 or 2 grams exactly, it may be more practical to use the Aztreonam for Injection dosage form.

Usual pediatric prescribing limits

See *Aztreonam for Injection USP.*

Strength(s) usually available

U.S.—

Note: The 1- and 2-gram strengths are available in Galaxy® plastic containers as single-dose units.

1 gram in 50 mL (Rx) [*Azactam*].

2 grams in 50 mL (Rx) [*Azactam*].

Canada—

Not commercially available.

Packaging and storage

Do not store above −20 °C (−4 °F).

Preparation of dosage form

Thaw container at room temperature, 25 °C (77 °F), or in a refrigerator, 2 to 8 °C (36 to 46 °F), before administration, making sure that all ice crystals have melted. Precipitates may appear in the product in the frozen state that will dissolve with little or no agitation upon reaching room temperature.

Do not thaw bags by immersion in water baths or by heating in a microwave.

The bag should be inspected for leaks by squeezing the container. If leaks are discovered the container should be discarded since sterility may be impaired. The solution should be inspected visually and discarded if there is evidence of precipitates or discoloration. The solution should be clear and colorless to yellow in appearance.

Do not use plastic bags in series connections. This may result in air embolism because of residual air being drawn from the primary container before administration of the intravenous solution from the secondary container is complete.

For intravenous aztreonam infusion, the intravenous administration apparatus should be replaced at least once every 48 hours.

Stability

After thawing, solutions retain their potency for 48 hours at room temperature or for 14 days if refrigerated.

Once thawed, solutions should not be refrozen.

Do not use if the solution is cloudy or contains a precipitate.

Each plastic container is a single-dose unit. Any unused portion remaining in the container should be discarded.

Incompatibilities

Additives or other medication should not be added to, or infused simultaneously through, the same intravenous line. If the same intravenous line is used for infusion of another medication, the line should be flushed both before and after aztreonam infusion with an infusion solution compatible with both drugs.

AZTREONAM FOR INJECTION USP

Usual adult and adolescent dose

Antibacterial—

Intramuscular or intravenous:

Moderately severe systemic infections—1 to 2 grams every eight to twelve hours.

Severe systemic or life-threatening infections—2 grams every six to eight hours.

Note: Urinary tract infections—Intramuscular or intravenous, 500 mg to 1 gram every eight to twelve hours.

Adults with impaired renal function require a reduction in dose as follows:

Creatinine clearance (mL/min)/ (mL/sec)	Dose: Loading dose	Dose: Maintenance dose (every 6–12 hours)
>30/0.5		See *Usual adult and adolescent dose*
10–30/0.17–0.5	1–2 grams	½ of the loading dose
<10/0.17	500 mg–2 grams	¼ of the loading dose; in serious or life-threatening infections, an additional ⅛ of the loading dose should be given after each hemodialysis period

Usual adult prescribing limits

8 grams daily.

Usual pediatric dose

Antibacterial—

Intravenous:

Children up to 9 months of age—Safety and efficacy have not been established; however, the following doses have been reported in the literature: Infants up to 7 days of age—30 mg per kg of body weight every twelve hours. Infants 1 to 4 weeks of age—30 mg per kg of body weight every eight hours. Infants

4 weeks of age and older—30 mg per kg of body weight every six to eight hours.

Children 9 months to 16 years of age—The following doses are recommended for intravenous administration for pediatric patients with normal renal function: Mild to moderate infections—30 mg per kg of body weight every eight hours. Moderate to severe infections—30 mg per kg of body weight every six to eight hours.

Note: Higher doses may be required for cystic fibrosis patients.

Due to a lack of clinical data, the intramuscular route of administration is not recommended in pediatric patients.

Due to a lack of clinical data, aztreonam is not recommended for use in pediatric patients who have impaired renal function.

Children 16 years of age and older: See *Usual adult and adolescent dose.*

Usual pediatric prescribing limits

120 mg per kg of body weight per day.

Strength(s) usually available

U.S.—

Note: The 500-mg strength is available in 15-mL capacity single-dose vials. The 1-gram strength is available in 15-mL capacity single-dose vials and 100-mL capacity single-dose bottles for intravenous infusion. The 2-gram strength is available in 30-mL capacity single-dose vials and 100-mL capacity single-dose bottles for intravenous infusion.

500 mg (Rx) [*Azactam* (L-arginine, 780 mg per gram)].
1 gram (Rx) [*Azactam* (L-arginine, 780 mg per gram)].
2 grams (Rx) [*Azactam* (L-arginine, 780 mg per gram)].

Canada—
Not commercially available.

Packaging and storage

Prior to reconstitution, store below 40 °C (104 °F), preferably between 15 and 30 °C (59 and 86 °F), unless otherwise specified by manufacturer.

Preparation of dosage form

To prepare initial dilution for intramuscular use (15-mL or 30-mL vials), for each gram of aztreonam add at least 3 mL of sterile water for injection, bacteriostatic water for injection (preserved with benzyl alcohol or methylparabens and propylparabens), 0.9% sodium chloride injection, or bacteriostatic sodium chloride injection (preserved with benzyl alcohol).

To prepare initial dilution for direct intravenous use, add 6 to 10 mL of sterile water for injection to each 15-mL or 30-mL vial.

If the contents of a 15-mL or 30-mL capacity vial are to be transferred to an appropriate infusion solution, perform the initial dilution for intravenous infusion by adding at least 3 mL of sterile water for injection for each gram of aztreonam. The resulting solution may be further diluted in 0.9% sodium chloride injection, Ringer's injection, lactated Ringer's injection, dextrose injection (5 or 10%), dextrose and sodium chloride injection, sodium lactate injection (M/6), mannitol injection (5 or 10%), dextrose and lactated Ringer's injection, or other electrolyte-containing solutions (see manufacturer's package insert).

For reconstitution of 100-mL capacity infusion bottles, add at least 50 mL of suitable diluent (see manufacturer's package insert) for each gram of aztreonam. The final concentration should not exceed 2% (20 mg per mL). These solutions may be frozen immediately after constitution in the original container.

After addition of the diluent, contents of the vial should be shaken immediately and vigorously.

Aztreonam solutions should be inspected visually for discoloration or particulate matter.

Stability

Aztreonam vials are not intended for multiple-dose use. Unused solutions should be discarded.

Solutions range in color from colorless to light straw yellow, depending on the concentration and diluent.

Solutions may develop a slight pink tint on standing. This does not affect their potency.

After reconstitution for intramuscular use, solutions retain their potency for 48 hours at room temperature or for 7 days if refrigerated.

After reconstitution for intravenous use, solutions at concentrations not exceeding 2% (20 mg per mL) retain their potency for 48 hours at controlled room temperature (15 to 30 °C [59 to 86 °F]) or for 7 days if refrigerated at 2 to 8 °C (36 to 46 °F). Solutions at concentrations exceeding 2% (except those reconstituted with sterile water for injection and sodium chloride injection) should be used promptly after reconstitution. Solutions reconstituted with sterile water for injection or sodium chloride injection retain their potency for 48 hours at controlled room temperature or for 7 days if refrigerated.

Frozen solutions retain their potency for up to 3 months at −20 °C (−4 °F). Frozen solutions may be thawed at controlled room temperature or by storage in a refrigerator overnight. Solutions that have been thawed and maintained at controlled room temperature or under refrigeration should be used within 24 or 72 hours, respectively. Once thawed, solutions should not be refrozen.

Admixtures of aztreonam and clindamycin phosphate, gentamicin sulfate, tobramycin sulfate, or cefazolin sodium in 0.9% sodium chloride injection or 5% dextrose injection retain their potency for 48 hours at room temperature or for 7 days if refrigerated.

Admixtures of aztreonam and ampicillin sodium in 0.9% sodium chloride injection retain their potency for 24 hours at room temperature (25 °C [77 °F]) or for 48 hours if refrigerated at 4 °C (39 °F). Admixtures containing aztreonam and ampicillin sodium in 5% dextrose injection retain their potency for 2 hours at room temperature (25 °C [77 °F]) or for 8 hours if refrigerated at 4 °C (39 °F).

Admixtures of aztreonam and cloxacillin sodium or aztreonam and vancomycin hydrochloride in peritoneal dialysis solution containing 4.25% dextrose retain their potency for 24 hours at room temperature.

Incompatibilities

Admixtures of aztreonam and nafcillin sodium, cephradine, vancomycin, or metronidazole are incompatible.

In general, admixtures of aztreonam and other medications are not recommended. However, certain admixtures have been shown to be compatible (see *Stability*).

Revised: 03/23/1999

BACAMPICILLIN—See *Penicillins (Systemic)*

BACILLUS CALMETTE-GUÉRIN (BCG) LIVE Mucosal-Local

VA CLASSIFICATION (Primary): AN900

Commonly used brand name(s): *ImmuCyst; PACIS; TICE BCG; TheraCys.*

Note: For a listing of dosage forms and brand names by country availability, see *Dosage Forms* section(s).

Category

Antineoplastic.

Indications

Note: Bracketed information in the *Indications* section refers to uses that are not included in U.S. product labeling.

Accepted

Carcinoma, bladder (prophylaxis and treatment)—BCG is used intravesically for prophylaxis and treatment of primary (multifocal, high grade) and relapsed superficial transitional cell bladder carcinoma. It is used to reduce frequency of tumor recurrence after transurethral resection and to eliminate existing tumors, including [Ta and T1 tumors] and carcinoma in situ (CIS tumors) with or without associated papillary tumors. It is not indicated for treatment of papillary tumors occurring alone or for prevention of papillary tumors after transurethral resection.

Unaccepted

The product labeled for use only in treatment of bladder carcinoma is not intended to be used as an immunizing agent for the prevention of tuberculosis; the product labeled for both uses can be used for both. BCG is not a vaccine for the prevention of cancer.

Pharmacology/Pharmacokinetics

Physicochemical characteristics

Source—It is a live culture of the attenuated bacillus Calmette-Guérin strain of *Mycobacterium bovis.* Commercially available strains (which are substrains of the Pasteur Institute strain) include the Armand-Frapier, Connaught, Glaxo/Evans, and Tice substrains; of these, only the Connaught and Tice strains are approved for bladder carcinoma.

Mechanism of action/Effect

The effect of BCG against carcinoma is not completely understood. It may be related to an inflammatory response and possibly also to an immune response.

Intravesical BCG suspension produces a granulomatous response locally and in regional lymph nodes; the inflammatory response stimulates production of macrophages that have tumoricidal effects. The presence of interleukin-2, which is a substance produced by activated helper T lymphocytes and which activates natural killer cells, has also been noted in the urine of patients who responded to BCG treatment. However, the relationship of these effects to the antineoplastic effect of BCG is unknown.

Other actions/effects

Induces active immunity against tuberculosis by unknown mechanism; may involve stimulating the reticuloendothelial system (RES) to produce macrophages and other activated cells that prevent multiplication of virulent *Mycobacterium tuberculosis*.

Viability and immunogenicity may vary between strains and viability varies between lots of any one strain. With intracavitary BCG, positive conversion of tuberculin (purified protein derivative [PPD]) skin test occurs in a majority of patients, usually after 3 to 12 weeks. Positive conversion of PPD skin test, when it occurs, is usually not permanent, although duration is variable and sometimes long.

Precautions to Consider

Tumorigenicity

Two cases of nephrogenic adenoma (adenomatous metaplasia of the bladder), which is usually benign and believed to result from chronic irritation or trauma, have been reported.

Pregnancy/Reproduction

Pregnancy—Studies have not been done in humans.

Studies have not been done in animals.

FDA Pregnancy Category C.

Breast-feeding

It is not known whether intravesical BCG is distributed into breast milk. However, problems in humans have not been documented.

Pediatrics

No information is available on the relationship of age to the effects of BCG in pediatric patients. Safety and efficacy have not been established.

Geriatrics

Studies performed to date have not demonstrated geriatrics-specific problems that would limit the usefulness of BCG as an antineoplastic in the elderly.

Drug interactions and/or related problems

The following drug interactions and/or related problems have been selected on the basis of their potential clinical significance (possible mechanism in parentheses where appropriate)—not necessarily inclusive (» = major clinical significance):

Note: Combinations containing any of the following medications, depending on the amount present, may also interact with this medication.

Antimicrobial therapy
(potential negative effect on actions of BCG)

» Bone marrow depressants (see *Appendix II*) or
» Immunosuppressants or
» Radiation
(may impair immune response to BCG. The interval between discontinuation of medications that cause immunosuppression and restoration of the patient's ability to respond to BCG depends on the intensity and type of immunosuppression-causing therapy used, the underlying disease, and other factors; estimates vary from 3 months to 1 year. Also, may increase the risk of osteomyelitis or disseminated BCG infection)

» Vaccines, killed or live virus
(concurrent administration with BCG is not recommended; it is recommended that live virus vaccines be given 6 to 8 weeks after BCG; it is recommended that killed virus vaccines be given 7 days before or 10 days after BCG)

Laboratory value alterations

The following have been selected on the basis of their potential clinical significance (possible effect in parentheses where appropriate)—not necessarily inclusive (» = major clinical significance).

With physiology/laboratory test values

Hepatic function tests
(abnormalities have been reported rarely)

Tuberculin (purified protein derivative [PPD]) skin test
(positive conversion is produced in a majority of patients, usually after 3 to 12 weeks of intravesical BCG therapy; may complicate future interpretations of tuberculin skin test reactions in the diagnosis of suspected mycobacterial infections)

Microscopic examination of urine
(microscopic pyuria commonly seen; however, bacterial growth in urine is uncommon; returns to normal after completion of a course of BCG therapy)

Medical considerations/Contraindications

The medical considerations/contraindications included have been selected on the basis of their potential clinical significance (reasons given in parentheses where appropriate)—not necessarily inclusive (» = major clinical significance).

Except under special circumstances, this medication should not be used when the following medical problems exist:

» Fever
(BCG should not be administered until the cause has been determined; if fever is caused by infection, BCG should be withheld until the patient is afebrile and off all therapy)

» Urinary tract infection
(risk of disseminated BCG infection; increased severity of bladder irritation)

Risk-benefit should be considered when the following medical problems exist:

» Hematuria, gross, existing
(risk of disseminated BCG infection; caution is necessary especially if the hematuria is induced by recent biopsy or resection, and it is recommended that intravesical BCG not be given until gross hematuria has cleared; if hematuria is from the tumor itself, BCG can still be given, but with caution because irritable bladder symptoms may be increased)

» Impaired immune response
(decreased response to treatment; risk of osteomyelitis or disseminated BCG infection)

» Sensitivity to BCG live

Small bladder capacity
(increased incidence and severity of local irritation; in addition, therapy with BCG may rarely cause bladder contracture, which further decreases capacity)

Patient monitoring

The following may be especially important in patient monitoring (other tests may be warranted in some patients, depending on condition; » = major clinical significance):

» Bladder biopsy, cold cup
(recommended at regular intervals to assess response; also recommended for any suspicious area found by cystoscopy or cytology studies)

» Cystoscopy and
» Urine cytology studies
(recommended at regular intervals during and after treatment to assess response and confirm that the tumor is not progressing)

Hepatic function determinations
(recommended if persistent [e.g., 101 °F for longer than 2 days] or severe [e.g., greater than 103 °F] fever or continuing malaise occurs)

Needle biopsy of prostate in males
(recommended as indicated by presence of clinical signs of granulomatous prostatitis)

Tuberculin (PPD) skin test
(recommended before treatment and at periodic intervals during treatment. However, although it may predict responsiveness to BCG treatment in general, this is controversial and it is unlikely to provide a prognosis for a specific individual patient, especially since positive conversion does not occur in all patients who respond to BCG therapy)

Urine cultures
(recommended before and at periodic intervals during treatment; recommended if urinalysis or clinical symptoms suggest presence of urinary tract infection)

Side/Adverse Effects

Note: Side/adverse effects are usually mild to moderate and transient, but may be cumulative.

The following side/adverse effects have been selected on the basis of their potential clinical significance (possible signs and symptoms in parentheses where appropriate)—not necessarily inclusive:

Those indicating need for medical attention

Incidence more frequent

Bladder infection, secondary to bladder irritation—usually asymptomatic; ***bladder irritation*** (blood in urine; frequent urge to urinate;

increased frequency of urination; painful urination, severe or continuing); ***flu-like syndrome*** (fever and chills; joint pain; nausea and vomiting; in a few patients, has progressed to a severe systemic reaction with high fever, malaise, and anorexia); ***granulomatous prostatitis*** (appears as nodularity, enlargement, induration, and distortion of the prostate, which is clinically indistinguishable from prostatic carcinoma)—usually asymptomatic

Note: *Bladder infection* responds rapidly to antibiotic treatment.

Bladder irritation occurs in most patients, but is usually transient; may be severe in some patients. May predict antitumor response. Symptoms usually begin within 2 to 4 hours after a dose and last 24 to 72 hours. Granulomatous inflammation is seen on the histological examination; lesions that may be confused with tumors appear commonly within 4 weeks after BCG treatment; inflammation usually disappears within about 4 to 6 months after treatment.

Symptoms of the *flu-like syndrome* usually begin within 4 hours after a dose and last 24 to 72 hours.

Incidence rare

Allergic reaction or erythema nodosum (skin rash); ***BCG infection, disseminated, with lung or liver involvement*** (fever; cough); ***bladder contracture; hepatic function impairment***—asymptomatic; ***hypotension; leukopenia***—asymptomatic

Note: Symptoms of *disseminated BCG infection* may be difficult to distinguish from those of gram-negative sepsis or severe hypersensitivity reactions, or of progressing malignancy. Disseminated infection, with associated fever, may occur as late as 6 months or more after BCG therapy and may persist for 1 to 3 weeks after antituberculosis therapy is begun. It is usually diagnosed clinically based on the presence of fever (over 39 °C [103 °F] or persistently over 38 °C [101 °F] over 2 days) and chills, especially when associated with malaise and other systemic symptoms, negative blood and urine cultures, chest x-ray or computed tomography (CT) to exclude other pulmonary diseases, and hepatic function tests. Deaths have been reported.

Hepatic function impairment is usually mild and transient; abnormalities peak by 20 days and may persist months after BCG administration.

Those indicating need for medical attention only if they continue or are bothersome

Incidence more frequent

Burning, slight, during first void after treatment

Those indicating the need for medical attention if they occur after medication is discontinued

BCG infection, disseminated, with lung or liver involvement (fever; cough)

Patient Consultation

As an aid to patient consultation, refer to *Advice for the Patient, Bacillus Calmette-Guérin (BCG) Live (Mucosal-Local)*.

In providing consultation, consider emphasizing the following selected information (» = major clinical significance):

Before using this medication

» Conditions affecting use, especially:
- Sensitivity to BCG
- Other medications, especially bone marrow depressants or immunosuppressants or radiation therapy
- Other medical problems, especially fever, gross hematuria, impaired immune response, or urinary tract infection

Proper use of this medication

Emptying bladder before instillation of each dose

» Following physician's instructions for holding solution in bladder; holding in bladder for 2 hours; telling physician if unable to retain solution for prescribed time; physician may recommend lying down for 15 minutes each in prone and supine positions, and on each side, during first hour; sitting down while voiding

» Importance of ample fluid intake for several hours after instillation

Bacteria will be present in urine; treating all urine voided within 6 hours after each instillation with an equal volume of 5% hypochlorite solution (undiluted household bleach; usually 6 to 8 ounces) and allowing to stand for 15 minutes before flushing

» Proper dosing

Precautions while using this medication

Avoiding persons with active tuberculosis for 6 to 12 weeks after treatment; telling physician about any exposure to active tuberculosis

Avoiding immunizations unless approved by physician

Side/adverse effects

Signs of potential side effects, especially bladder infection, bladder irritation, flu-like syndrome, allergic reaction, erythema nodosum, disseminated BCG infection, bladder contracture, and hypotension

General Dosing Information

Patients receiving intravesical BCG should be under the supervision of a physician experienced in immunotherapy.

Prior to BCG administration, the bladder is emptied either by voiding or drainage through a urethral catheter inserted into the bladder under aseptic conditions. BCG is then instilled into the bladder by gravity flow via the catheter; the plunger should not be depressed to force the flow.

It is recommended that BCG instillation and equipment and materials used in preparation of the instillation be treated as biohazardous waste.

BCG should not be injected intravenously, subcutaneously, or intramuscularly.

Care and aseptic technique are necessary during administration of intravesical BCG therapy so as not to introduce contaminants into the urinary tract or to unduly traumatize the urinary mucosa.

If the physician believes that the bladder catheterization has been traumatic (e.g., associated with bleeding or possible false passage), instillation of BCG should be delayed by at least 1 week. However, beginning with the delayed dose, subsequent doses should be administered according to the original schedule (i.e., no doses should be omitted).

It is recommended that BCG therapy not be started until 7 to 14 days after bladder tumor resection or biopsy because fatalities from disseminated BCG infection have been reported with use of BCG after traumatic catheterization.

If development of systemic BCG infection is suspected, it is recommended that BCG be withheld and fast-acting antituberculosis therapy initiated.

Patients who do not respond after two 6-week courses of BCG therapy are not likely to respond, and consideration of alternative therapy is recommended.

Most severe adverse effects can be prevented or reduced in severity with prophylactic isoniazid treatment given for 3 days beginning the morning of BCG treatment. Some clinicians also recommend use of antihistamines and nonsteroidal anti-inflammatory agents.

Safety considerations for handling this medication

There is concern that personnel involved in preparation and administration of intravesical BCG may be at some risk because of the infectious potential of this agent, although the actual risk is unknown. USP advisory panels recommend cautious handling both in preparation and disposal of BCG for intravesical use. Precautions that have been suggested include:

- Use of a biological containment cabinet during reconstitution and dilution of parenteral medications and wearing of disposable surgical gloves and masks.
- Use of proper technique to prevent contamination of the medication, work area, and operator during transfer between containers (including proper training of personnel in this technique).
- Cautious and proper disposal of needles, syringes, vials, ampuls, and unused medication.

A number of medical centers have developed detailed guidelines for handling of antineoplastic and similar agents.

For treatment of adverse effects

Most adverse effects respond to a reduction in BCG dose or temporary interruption of therapy; however, in some patients withdrawal of BCG therapy may be necessary.

Mild bladder irritation can usually be treated symptomatically with phenazopyridine hydrochloride and antispasmodics such as propantheline bromide or oxybutynin.

Recommended treatment of moderate to severe bladder irritation and flu-like syndrome may consist of the following:

- Isoniazid.
- Antihistamines, such as diphenhydramine hydrochloride.
- Nonsteroidal anti-inflammatory agents; parenteral narcotic analgesics may be necessary for severe bladder irritation.

Recommended treatment of disseminated BCG infection with liver and lung involvement consists of the following:

- Triple-drug antituberculosis therapy or
- A fast-acting antituberculosis medication such as cycloserine.

No specific treatment of granulomatous prostatitis secondary to BCG therapy is required.

Topical Dosage Forms

BCG LIVE (CONNAUGHT STRAIN)

Usual adult dose

Bladder carcinoma—

Intracavitary, 1 vial (81 mg), reconstituted and then diluted with 50 mL of sterile, preservative-free 0.9% sodium chloride injection, to a final volume of 53 mL (less in patients with reduced bladder capacity), instilled into the empty bladder and retained for one to two hours (depending on irritative symptoms and the patient's ability to retain the solution). The procedure is repeated once a week for six weeks, followed by one treatment given at three, six, twelve, eighteen, and twenty-four months following the initial treatment or according to response.

Note: During the first hour after instillation, the patient may lie down for 15 minutes in the prone position, followed by the supine position, and on each side, then may be up for the second hour while the suspension is retained.

The patient voids in a seated position.

Usual pediatric dose

Safety and efficacy have not been established.

Strength(s) usually available

U.S.—

81 mg (dry weight) or 10.5 ± 8.7 × 10^8 colony-forming units (CFU) per vial (1 vial per package) (Rx) [*TheraCys* (monosodium glutamate 5% w/v plus diluent)].

Canada—

Approximately 3 × 10^8 colony-forming units (CFU) per vial (3 vials per package) (Rx) [*ImmuCyst* (monosodium glutamate 5% w/v plus diluent)].

Packaging and storage

Store between 2 and 8 °C (36 and 46 °F). Protect from light.

Preparation of dosage form

BCG live (Connaught strain) is reconstituted by adding to the vial 1 mL of diluent provided by manufacturer. The vial is then shaken gently until a fine, even suspension results. The suspension is then diluted in a suitable quantity of sterile, preservative-free 0.9% sodium chloride injection for administration.

Note: Aseptic technique must be used for reconstitution and dilution.

The product should not be handled by persons with a known immunologic deficiency.

Stability

Reconstituted suspension should be used immediately; otherwise, it should be refrigerated until use and should be discarded after 2 hours.

Note

Commercially available BCG strains are not interchangeable. *One product should not be substituted for another.* If patients are to be transferred from one to another, appropriate changes in dosage may be necessary.

Additional information

After usage, all equipment and materials used for instillation of BCG into the bladder should be placed immediately into plastic bags labeled as infectious waste and disposed of properly as biohazardous waste.

Any unused portion of reconstituted BCG, and urine voided for 6 hours after instillation, should be disinfected with an equal volume of 5% hypochlorite solution (undiluted household bleach) and allowed to stand for 15 minutes before being flushed.

BCG LIVE (MONTREAL STRAIN)

Usual adult dose

Bladder carcinoma—

Intracavitary, a single dose of 120 mg, reconstituted and then diluted with 50 mL of sterile, preservative-free 0.9% sodium chloride injection instilled into the bladder once a week for six weeks. The bladder should be drained via a urethral catheter under aseptic conditions prior to administration of the recommended dose. The induction therapy may be followed by a single instillation given at three, six, twelve, and twenty-four months following the initial treatment.

Note: During the first hour following instillation, the patient should lie down for 15 minutes in the prone position, supine position, and on each side. After this procedure, the patient should be allowed to be up; however, the suspension should be retained for another 60 minutes for a total of 2 hours. Some patients may not be able to retain the suspension for 2 hours and should be instructed to void in less time if necessary. At the end of treatment all patients should void in a seated position for safety reasons. Patients should be instructed to drink enough liquid after treatment to maintain adequate hydration.

Usual pediatric dose

Safety and efficacy have not been established.

Strength(s) usually available

U.S.—

2.4 to 12 x 10^8 colony-forming units (CFU) per vial (Rx) [*PACIS* (lactose 15% w/v)].

Canada—

2 to 10 × 10^6 colony-forming units (CFU) per vial (Rx) [*PACIS* (lactose 15% w/v plus diluent)].

Packaging and storage

Store between 2 and 8 °C (35 and 46 °F).

Protect from light.

Note: Freezing will not harm the BCG; however, the sterile diluent should not be used if it has been frozen. At no time should the lyophilized preparation be exposed to sunlight, direct or indirect.

Preparation of dosage form

BCG live (Montreal strain) is reconstituted by adding to the vial 1 mL of diluent provided by manufacturer. The diluent should be left in contact with BCG live for about 1 minute. Then the suspension should be mixed by withdrawing it into the syringe and expelling it gently back to into the vial two or three times. To prevent the formation of foam, the suspension should not be shaken. The suspension is then diluted in a suitable quantity of sterile, preservative-free 0.9% sodium chloride injection for administration.

BCG live (Montreal strain) is reconstituted by adding 1 mL of preservative-free 0.9% Sodium Chloride Injection to the ampule. The diluent should be left in contact with BCG live for about 1 minute. Then the suspension should be mixed by withdrawing it into the syringe and expelling it gently back to into the ampule two or three times. To prevent the formation of foam, the suspension should not be shaken. The suspension is then diluted in a suitable quantity of sterile, preservative-free 0.9% sodium chloride injection for administration

Note: BCG live (Montreal strain) should be handled as infectious material. Persons handling this product should wear masks and gloves. The product should not be handled by persons with a known immunologic deficiency.

Stability

BCG live (Montreal strain) should be used immediately after preparation.

Additional information

After usage, all equipment and materials used for instillation of BCG into the bladder should be placed immediately into plastic bags labeled as infectious waste and disposed of properly as biohazardous waste.

BCG VACCINE (TICE STRAIN) USP

Usual adult dose

Bladder carcinoma—

Intracavitary, 1 vial (1 to 8 × 10^8 colony-forming units [CFU]), reconstituted and then diluted to a total volume of 50 mL with sterile, preservative-free 0.9% sodium chloride injection (less in patients with reduced bladder capacity), instilled into the empty bladder and retained for one to two hours (depending on irritative symptoms and the patient's ability to retain the solution). The procedure is repeated once a week for six weeks; the schedule may be repeated once if circumstances warrant. This is followed by treatment at approximately monthly intervals for at least six to twelve months or according to response.

Note: During the first hour after instillation, the patient may lie for 15 minutes in the prone position, followed by the supine position, and on each side, then may be up for the second hour while the suspension is retained.

The patient voids in a seated position.

Usual pediatric dose

Safety and efficacy have not been established.

Strength(s) usually available

U.S.—

1 to 8 × 10^8 CFU or approximately 50 mg (wet weight) per vial, (Rx) [*TICE BCG* (lactose)].

Canada—

Not commercially available.

Packaging and storage

Store between 2 and 8 °C (36 and 46 °F). Protect from light.

Preparation of dosage form

BCG Vaccine USP (Tice Strain) is reconstituted by adding 1 mL of sterile, preservative-free 0.9% sodium chloride injection to ampul, drawing the mixture back into the syringe and expelling it into the ampul three times to mix it thoroughly (minimizes clumping of mycobacteria). The suspension is then diluted in a suitable quantity of sterile, preservative-free 0.9% sodium chloride injection for administration.

Note: Aseptic technique must be used for reconstitution and dilution.

The product should not be handled by persons with a known immunologic deficiency.

Stability

Reconstituted suspension should be used immediately and any unused portion discarded after 2 hours.

Additional information

After usage, all equipment and materials used for instillation of BCG into the bladder should be placed immediately into plastic bags labeled as infectious waste and disposed of properly as biohazardous waste.

Any unused portion of reconstituted BCG, and urine voided for 6 hours after instillation, should be disinfected with an equal volume of 5% hypochlorite solution (undiluted household bleach) and allowed to stand for 15 minutes before being flushed.

Revised: 08/17/2000

BACLOFEN Systemic

VA CLASSIFICATION (Primary/Secondary): MS200/CN103

Commonly used brand name(s): *Apo-Baclofen; Lioresal; Novo-Baclofen; Nu-Baclofen; PMS-Baclofen.*

Note: For a listing of dosage forms and brand names by country availability, see *Dosage Forms* section(s).

Category

Antispastic analgesic (in trigeminal neuralgia).

Indications

Note: Bracketed information in the *Indications* section refers to uses that are not included in U.S. product labeling.

Accepted

Spasticity (treatment)—Baclofen is indicated to relieve the signs and symptoms of spasticity caused by multiple sclerosis, spinal cord diseases, or spinal cord injury. It is especially useful in relieving flexor spasms and concomitant pain, clonus, and muscular rigidity. Baclofen may also improve bowel and bladder function in some patients with spinal lesions; however, it may not improve spastic stiff gait or manual dexterity.

[Neuralgia, trigeminal (treatment)][1]—Baclofen is used to reduce the number and severity of attacks of trigeminal neuralgia in patients who are not able to tolerate, or who have become refractory to the effects of, carbamazepine. In some patients, baclofen may provide additional benefit when used concurrently with carbamazepine.

Unaccepted

Baclofen should not be used in patients who require spasticity to sustain upright posture or balance in locomotion, or to obtain increased function.

Baclofen may not be effective, and is not recommended, in the treatment of patients with cerebrovascular accident, parkinsonism, cerebral palsy, or trauma-induced cerebral lesions.

Baclofen is not indicated in the treatment of skeletal muscle spasm caused by rheumatic disorders.

[1]Not included in Canadian product labeling.

Pharmacology/Pharmacokinetics

Physicochemical characteristics

Molecular weight—213.66.

Mechanism of action/Effect

The precise mechanism of action of baclofen has not been fully determined. It acts mainly at the spinal cord level to inhibit the transmission of both monosynaptic and polysynaptic reflexes, possibly by hyperpolarization of primary afferent fiber terminals resulting in antagonism of the release of putative excitatory transmitters (i.e., glutamic and aspartic acids). Actions at supraspinal sites may also be involved.

Other actions/effects

Baclofen has general central nervous system (CNS)–depressant actions.

Absorption

Rapid and extensive but subject to interpatient variation. Also, the rate and extent of absorption may decrease with increasing doses.

Protein binding

Low (30%).

Biotransformation

Hepatic; only about 15% of a dose is metabolized.

Half-life

2 to 4 hours.

Onset of action

Highly variable; may range from hours to weeks.

Time to peak concentration

Within 2 hours.

Peak serum concentration

500 to 600 nanograms per mL (nanograms/mL) (2.34 to 2.81 micromoles/L) following a 40-mg single dose; concentration remains above 200 nanograms/mL (0.94 micromoles/L) for 8 hours.

Therapeutic serum concentration

80 to 400 nanograms/mL (0.37 to 1.87 micromoles/L).

Elimination

Renal; 70 to 85% of a dose is excreted unchanged within 24 hours. Small amounts may also be excreted via the feces. About 40% of a dose is usually excreted within 6 hours, and excretion is usually complete within 3 days; however, with chronic use the rate of excretion is subject to interpatient variation.

Precautions to Consider

Pregnancy/Reproduction

Pregnancy—Studies have not been done in humans.

Some studies in rats have shown that baclofen increases the incidence of omphaloceles (ventral hernias) and incomplete sternebral ossification in the fetus when given in doses approximately 13 times the maximum recommended human dose (MRHD). However, these abnormalities did not occur in studies using mice or rabbits. Also, studies in rabbits have shown that baclofen causes an increased incidence of unossified phalangeal nuclei of forelimbs and hindlimbs in the fetus when given in doses approximately 7 times the MRHD. In addition, some studies in mice have shown that baclofen causes a reduction in fetal birth weight with consequent delays in skeletal ossification when given in doses 17 times or 34 times the MRHD.

Breast-feeding

Baclofen is distributed into breast milk. However, problems in humans have not been documented.

Pediatrics

No information is available on the relationship of age to the effects of baclofen in pediatric patients. Safety and efficacy in children up to 12 years of age have not been established.

Geriatrics

Geriatric patients may be especially at risk for the development of CNS toxicity, leading to hallucinations, confusion or mental depression, other psychiatric disturbances, or incapacitating sedation, during baclofen therapy. Also, elderly patients are more likely to have age-related renal function impairment, which may require a reduction of dosage in patients receiving baclofen.

Drug interactions and/or related problems

The following drug interactions and/or related problems have been selected on the basis of their potential clinical significance (possible mechanism in parentheses where appropriate)—not necessarily inclusive (» = major clinical significance):

Note: Combinations containing any of the following medications, depending on the amount present, may also interact with this medication.

Antidepressants, tricyclic
(concurrent use with baclofen may result in pronounced muscle hypotonia; caution is recommended)

Antidiabetic agents, oral or
Insulin
(baclofen may increase blood glucose concentrations; dosage adjustments of these medications and/or of baclofen may be necessary during and after concurrent therapy)

Antihypertensives or
Other hypotension-producing medications
(concurrent use with baclofen may increase the risk of hypotension; dosage adjustment of the antihypertensive agent may be needed)

Carbidopa and levodopa
(concurrent use with baclofen may result in mental confusion, hallucinations, or agitation)

» CNS depression-producing medications, other (see *Appendix II*) or
» Monoamine oxidase (MAO) inhibitors, including furazolidone, procarbazine, and selegiline
(concurrent use may result in increased CNS-depressant and hypotensive effects; caution is recommended and dosage of one or both agents should be reduced)

Neuromuscular blocking agents
(concurrent use with neuromuscular blocking agents may enhance the effects of baclofen)

Laboratory value alterations

The following have been selected on the basis of their potential clinical significance (possible effect in parentheses where appropriate)—not necessarily inclusive (» = major clinical significance).

With physiology/laboratory test values
Alanine aminotransferase (ALT [SGPT]) and
Alkaline phosphatase and
Aspartate aminotransferase (AST [SGOT])
(values may be increased)

Glucose, blood
(concentration may be increased)

Medical considerations/Contraindications

The medical considerations/contraindications included have been selected on the basis of their potential clinical significance (reasons given in parentheses where appropriate)—not necessarily inclusive (» = major clinical significance).

Risk-benefit should be considered when the following medical problems exist:

Cerebral lesions or
Cerebrovascular accident
(increased risk of CNS, respiratory, or cardiovascular depression; ataxia; and psychiatric disturbances such as hallucinations, euphoria, and mental excitation, confusion, or depression)

Diabetes mellitus
(baclofen may increase blood glucose concentrations)

Epilepsy
(baclofen may cause deterioration of seizure control, electroencephalographic [EEG] changes)

Psychiatric disorders, pre-existing
(increased risk of baclofen-induced psychiatric disturbances)

» Renal function impairment
(baclofen may accumulate; reduction in dosage may be required)

Sensitivity to baclofen

Caution is required in geriatric patients, who may be especially susceptible to baclofen-induced CNS toxicity and who are more likely than younger adults to have renal function impairment.

Patient monitoring

The following may be especially important in patient monitoring (other tests may be warranted in some patients, depending on condition; » = major clinical significance):

Electroencephalogram (EEG) and clinical state determinations
(increased or periodic monitoring recommended for epileptic patients because baclofen may cause deterioration of seizure control and EEG changes in these patients)

Side/Adverse Effects

Note: Chronic administration of baclofen to female rats has caused a dose-related increase in the incidence of ovarian cysts and in enlarged and/or hemorrhagic adrenal glands.

Many of the CNS, visual, and genitourinary side effects listed below may be symptoms associated with the underlying spastic disease rather than baclofen-induced.

The following side/adverse effects have been selected on the basis of their potential clinical significance (possible signs and symptoms in parentheses where appropriate)—not necessarily inclusive:

Those indicating need for medical attention

Incidence less frequent or rare
Bloody or dark urine; chest pain; CNS toxicity (visual and auditory hallucinations; mental depression or other mood changes; ringing or buzzing in ears); ***dermatitis, allergic*** (skin rash or itching); ***ovarian cysts***—up to 5% of the female population using baclofen; ***syncope*** (fainting)

Those indicating need for medical attention only if they continue or are bothersome

Incidence more frequent
CNS effects (drowsiness [up to 63%]; dizziness or lightheadedness [up to 15%]; weakness [up to 15%]; confusion [up to 11%]); ***muscle weakness***—may be caused by CNS effect or become apparent if baclofen-induced reduction of muscle tone unmasks existing paresis; ***nausea***—4 to 12%

Incidence less frequent or rare
CNS effects (clumsiness, unsteadiness, trembling, or other problems with muscle control; false sense of well-being; headache [up to 8%]; muscle pain; numbness or tingling in hands or feet; slurred speech or other speech problems; trouble in sleeping [up to 7%]; unexplained muscle stiffness; unusual excitement; unusual tiredness [up to 4%]); ***constipation***—2 to 6%; ***difficult or painful urination or decrease in amount of urine; fluid retention*** (swelling of ankles; weight gain); ***frequent urge to urinate or uncontrolled urination***—2 to 6%; ***gastrointestinal irritation*** (abdominal or stomach pain or discomfort; diarrhea); ***loss of appetite; low blood pressure***—up to 9%; ***pounding heartbeat; sexual problems in males; stuffy nose***

Those indicating need for medical attention and/or reinstitution of therapy if they occur after medication is abruptly discontinued

Convulsions; hallucinations, visual and auditory; increased spasticity; mood or mental changes such as paranoid ideation or manic psychosis; unusual nervousness or restlessness

Overdose

For specific information on the agents used in the management of baclofen overdose, see *Atropine* in *Anticholinergics/Antispasmodics (Systemic)* monograph.

For more information on the management of overdose or unintentional ingestion, **contact a Poison Control Center** (see *Poison Control Center Listing*).

Clinical effects of overdose

The following effects have been selected on the basis of their potential clinical significance (possible signs and symptoms in parentheses where appropriate)—not necessarily inclusive:

Acute and chronic
CNS toxicity (blurred or double vision; convulsions; miosis; mydriasis; severe muscle weakness; strabismus); ***respiratory depression*** (shortness of breath or unusually slow or troubled breathing); ***vomiting***

Treatment of overdose

To decrease absorption—May include emptying the stomach by induction of emesis and/or gastric lavage.

Specific treatment—Administration of atropine has been recommended to increase ventilation, heart rate, blood pressure, and core body temperature. See the package insert or *Atropine* in *Anticholinergics/Antispasmodics (Systemic)* monograph.

Supportive care—May include maintaining adequate respiratory exchange. Respiratory stimulants should *not* be used. Patients in whom intentional overdose is confirmed or suspected should be referred for psychiatric consultation.

Patient Consultation

As an aid to patient consultation, refer to *Advice for the Patient, Baclofen (Systemic)*.

In providing consultation, consider emphasizing the following selected information (» = major clinical significance):

Before using this medication

» Conditions affecting use, especially:
Sensitivity to baclofen
Use in the elderly—Increased risk of adverse CNS effects
Other medications, especially other CNS depression-producing medications

Proper use of this medication
» Proper dosing
Missed dose: Taking if remembered within an hour or so; not taking if not remembered within an hour; not doubling doses
» Proper storage

Precautions while using this medication
» Checking with physician before discontinuing medication; gradual dosage reduction is necessary
» Avoiding alcohol or other CNS depressants
» Caution if drowsiness, dizziness, visual disturbances, or impaired coordination occur

Diabetics: May increase blood sugar concentrations

Side/adverse effects
Convulsions, hallucinations, mood or mental changes, increased spasticity, seizures, or unusual nervousness or restlessness may occur following abrupt withdrawal
Signs and symptoms of potential side effects, especially bloody or dark urine, chest pain, CNS toxicity, allergic dermatitis, and syncope

General Dosing Information

Side effects may be minimized by initiating therapy with low doses, which should be increased gradually until the desired response is obtained.

If the desired response is not achieved after a reasonable trial period, the medication should be slowly withdrawn.

Lower doses may be required in patients with renal function impairment.

Convulsions, hallucinations, other psychiatric disturbances, and exacerbation of spasticity have occurred following abrupt withdrawal of baclofen; gradual reduction of dosage over a period of 1 to 2 weeks or more is recommended before the medication is discontinued.

Oral Dosage Forms

Note: Bracketed uses in the *Dosage Forms* section refer to categories of use and/or indications that are not included in U.S. product labeling.

BACLOFEN TABLETS USP

Usual adult and adolescent dose
Antispastic and
[Analgesic (in trigeminal neuralgia)][1]—
Oral, 5 mg three times a day initially, then increased by increments of 5 mg per dose every three days until the desired response is achieved.

Note: A smoother response may be achieved in some patients if the total daily dose is given in four divided doses.

Usual adult prescribing limits
80 mg daily.

Note: Higher doses may be required in some patients.

Usual pediatric dose
Safety and efficacy have not been established.

Strength(s) usually available
U.S.—
10 mg (Rx) [*Lioresal* (scored); GENERIC].
20 mg (Rx) [*Lioresal* (scored); GENERIC].
Canada—
10 mg (Rx) [*Apo-Baclofen; Lioresal* (scored); *Novo-Baclofen; Nu-Baclofen; PMS-Baclofen*].
20 mg (Rx) [*Apo-Baclofen; Lioresal* (scored); *Novo-Baclofen; Nu-Baclofen; PMS-Baclofen*].

Packaging and storage
Store below 40 °C (104 °F), preferably between 15 and 30 °C (59 and 86 °F). Store in a well-closed container.

Auxiliary labeling
- May cause drowsiness.
- Avoid alcoholic beverages.

[1]Not included in Canadian product labeling.

Revised: 05/19/1999

BALSALAZIDE Systemic†

VA CLASSIFICATION (Primary): GA400

Commonly used brand name(s): *Colazal*.

Note: For a listing of dosage forms and brand names by country availability, see *Dosage Forms* section(s).

†Not commercially available in Canada.

Category

Bowel disease (inflammatory) suppressant.

Indications

Accepted
Ulcerative colitis (treatment)—Balsalazide is indicated for the treatment of mildly to moderately active ulcerative colitis.

Pharmacology/Pharmacokinetics

Physicochemical characteristics
Molecular weight—437.32.

Mechanism of action/Effect
Mesalamine (5–aminosalicylic acid), a therapeutically active byproduct cleaved from balsalazide by bacterial azoreduction, is created in the colon and acts to diminish colon inflammation by inhibiting the production of arachidonic acid metabolites.

Absorption
Low variable; intact balsalazide is poorly absorbed systemically

Protein binding
Very high (≥ 99%)

Biotransformation
Cleaved in the colon via bacterial azoreduction to 5–aminosalicylic acid (5–ASA) and 4–aminobenzoyl-beta-alanine, the inactive carrier moiety.

Half-life
Could not be determined because of the great variability in the balsalazide plasma concentration versus time profiles of the healthy subjects studies.

Time to peak concentration
Approximately 1 to 2 hours after single oral doses of 1.5 grams or 2.25 grams.

Elimination
Renal—Less than 1% of dose recovered as parent compound, 25% of dose recovered as N-acetylated metabolites.
Feces—Less than 1% of dose recovered as parent compound, 65% of dose recovered as N-acetylated metabolites, 5–ASA and carrier moiety.

Precautions to Consider

Cross-sensitivity and/or related problems
Patients allergic to salicylates may also be allergic to balsalazide.

Carcinogenicity/Tumorigenicity
Rats given balsalazide disodium orally at doses up to 2 grams per kg of body weight per day (2.4 times the recommended human dose on a body surface area basis for a 50-kg person of average height) for 24 months did not exhibit any tumorigenic effects.

Mutagenicity
Long–term studies evaluating the mutagenic potential of balsalazide disodium in humans have not been done. Genotoxicity was detected in the in vitro Chinese hamster lung cell (CH V79/HGPRT) forward mutation test.However, the genotoxic potential of balsalazide disodium was not demonstrated in the following tests: the Ames test, the human lymphocyte chromosomal aberration test, the mouse lymphoma cell (L5178Y/TK+/-) forward mutation test, or the mouse micronucleus test. Four–aminobenzoyl–β–alanine, a metabolite of balsalazide was shown to be genotoxic in the human lymphocyte chromosomal aberration test and non–genotoxic in the Ames test and the mouse lymphoma cell (L5178Y/TK+/-) forward mutation test. N–acetyl–4–aminobenzoyl–β–alanine, another metabolite of balsalazide, was not shown to be genotoxic in any of the three previously mentioned tests done on 4–aminobenzoyl–β–alanine.

Pregnancy/Reproduction

Fertility—Adequate and well-controlled studies in humans have not been done. Fertility was not affected when rats and rabbits were administered balsalazide disodium at oral doses up to 2 grams per kg of body weight per day (2.4 and 4.7 times the recommended human dose based on body surface area, respectively).

Pregnancy—Adequate and well controlled studies have not been done in humans.

No evidence of teratogenicity was found when rats and rabbits were administered up to 2 grams per kg of body weight per day (2.4 and 4.7 times the recommended human dose based on body surface area, respectively) of balsalazide disodium.

FDA Pregnancy Category B.

Breast-feeding

It is not known whether balsalazide is distributed into breast milk.

Pediatrics

No information is available on the relationship of age to the effects of balsalazide in the pediatric population. Safety and efficacy have not been established.

Geriatrics

No information is available on the relationship of age to the effects of balsalazide in geriatric patients. However, elderly patients are more likely to have age-related renal function impairment, which may require caution in elderly patients receiving balsalazide.

Laboratory value alterations

The following have been selected on the basis of their potential clinical significance (possible effect in parentheses where appropriate)—not necessarily inclusive (» = major clinical significance).

With physiology/laboratory test values

Alanine aminotransferase (ALT [SGPT]) and
Alkaline phosphatase and
Aspartate aminotransferase (AST [SGOT]) and
Bilirubin and
Gamma-glutamyl transferase (GGT) and
Lactate dehydrogenase (LDH)
(enzyme elevations were reported in post marketing clinical studies)

Medical considerations/Contraindications

The medical considerations/contraindications included have been selected on the basis of their potential clinical significance (reasons given in parentheses where appropriate)—not necessarily inclusive (» = major clinical significance).

Risk-benefit should be considered when the following medical problems exist:

Hypersensitivity to salicylates, mesalamine, or any other components of balsalazide disodium.

Pyloric stenosis.
(prolonged gastric retention of balsalazide capsules may occur)

Renal function impairment, or history of
(Although there have been no reports of renal toxicity in patients who have taken balsalazide or nephrotoxic effects in rats and dogs given the equivalent of 21 times the recommended human dose, other mesalamine products have been shown to cause renal toxicity in animals and patients; therefore, caution is warranted)

Side/Adverse Effects

Note: In clinical trials, 3 cases of exacerbation of the symptoms of colitis, possibly related to balsalazide treatment, have been reported in 259 patients receiving balsalazide at a dose of 6.75 grams per day.

The following side/adverse effects have been selected on the basis of their potential clinical significance (possible signs and symptoms in parentheses where appropriate)—not necessarily inclusive:

Those indicating need for medical attention only if they continue or are bothersome

Incidence more frequent

Abdominal pain; diarrhea

Incidence less frequent or rare

anorexia (loss of appetite); ***Arthralgia*** (joint pain); ***constipation; coughing; cramps; dry mouth; dyspepsia*** (heart burn or upset stomach); ***fatigue; fever; flatulence; flu-like disorder; insomnia*** (trouble sleeping or getting to sleep); ***jaundice*** (yellowish skin); ***myalgia*** (muscle pain); ***pharyngitis*** (flu–like symptoms); ***rhinitis*** (stuffy nose); ***urinary tract infection*** (blood in urine; lower back pain; pain or burning while urinating)

Note: In post marketing studies, hepatotoxicity, including *jaundice*, elevated liver function tests, and hepatocellular damage, have been reported. Although some of these cases were fatal, no fatalities were found in these events.

Overdose

For more information on the management of overdose or unintentional ingestion, **contact a poison control center** (see *Poison Control Center Listing*).

Treatment of overdose

There are no reported cases of an overdose with balsalazide disodium. However, a 3-year-old boy who ingested 2 grams of another mesalamine product was treated with ipecac and activated charcoal with no adverse reactions. If an overdose does occur, treatment should be primarily symptomatic and supportive with special attention paid to the correction of electrolyte levels.

Supportive care—Patients in whom overdose is confirmed or suspected should be referred for psychiatric consultation.

Patient Consultation

As an aid to patient consultation, refer to *Advice for the Patient, Balsalazide (Systemic)*.

In providing consultation, consider emphasizing the following selected information (» = major clinical significance):

Before using this medication

» Conditions affecting use, especially:
Sensitivity to balsalazide, balsalazide metabolites, or salicylates

Proper use of this medication

» Proper dosing
Missed dose: Taking as soon as possible; not taking if almost time for next scheduled dose; not doubling doses
Proper storage

Precautions while using this medication

» Regular visits to physician to check progress
» Contacting physician if condition gets worse

General Dosing Information

For oral dosing forms:

The recommended dose, frequency, and length of treatment should not be exceeded.

Oral Dosage Forms

BALSALAZIDE DISODIUM CAPSULES

Usual Adult Dose

Ulcerative colitis, active (treatment)—
Oral, three 750-mg balsalazide capsules three times a day for a total daily dose of 6.75 grams for a duration of eight weeks. Treatment may last up to twelve weeks in some patients.

Usual adult prescribing limits

The safety and effectiveness of balsalazide disodium treatments over a period of time greater than 12 weeks has not been established.

Usual Pediatric Dose

Safety and efficacy have not been established.

Usual Geriatric Dose

See *Usual adult dose*.

Strength(s) usually available

U.S.—
750 milligram (Rx) [*Colazal* (colloidal silicon dioxide; magnesium stearate)].

Packaging and storage

Store at 25 °C (77 °F), excursions permitted to 15°C–30°C (59°F–86°F)

Developed: 11/10/2000

BARBITURATES Systemic

This monograph includes information on the following: 1) Amobarbital; 2) Aprobarbital†; 3) Butabarbital; 4) Mephobarbital; 5) Metharbital†; 6) Pentobarbital; 7) Phenobarbital; 8) Secobarbital; 9) Secobarbital and Amobarbital.

VA CLASSIFICATION (Primary/Secondary):

Amobarbital Oral—CN301
Amobarbital Parenteral—CN301/CN400
Aprobarbital Oral—CN301
Butabarbital Oral—CN301
Mephobarbital Oral—CN400
Metharbital Oral—CN400
Pentobarbital Oral—CN301
Pentobarbital Parenteral—CN301/CN400
Phenobarbital Oral—CN301/CN400; GA900
Phenobarbital Parenteral—CN301/CN400; GA900
Secobarbital Oral—CN301
Secobarbital Parenteral—CN301/CN400

Note: Controlled substances in the U.S. and Canada as follows:

Drug	U.S.	Canada
Amobarbital	II	C
Aprobarbital	III	
Butabarbital	III	C
Mephobarbital	IV	C
Pentobarbital		
Oral	II	C
Parenteral	II	C
Rectal	III	C
Phenobarbital	IV	C
Secobarbital		
Oral	II	C
Parenteral	II	
Secobarbital and Amobarbital	II	C

Commonly used brand name(s): *Alurate*[2]; *Amytal*[1]; *Ancalixir*[7]; *Barbita*[7]; *Busodium*[3]; *Butalan*[3]; *Butisol*[3]; *Gemonil*[5]; *Luminal*[7]; *Mebaral*[4]; *Nembutal*[6]; *Nova Rectal*[6]; *Novopentobarb*[6]; *Novosecobarb*[8]; *Sarisol No. 2*[3]; *Seconal*[8]; *Solfoton*[7]; *Tuinal*[9].

Note: For a listing of dosage forms and brand names by country availability, see *Dosage Forms* section(s).

*Not commercially available in U.S.
†Not commercially available in Canada.

Category

Sedative-hypnotic—Amobarbital; Aprobarbital; Butabarbital; Pentobarbital; Phenobarbital (parenteral only); Secobarbital.

Anticonvulsant—Amobarbital (parenteral only); Mephobarbital; Metharbital; Pentobarbital (parenteral only); Phenobarbital; Secobarbital (parenteral only).

Antihyperbilirubinemic—Phenobarbital

Indications

Note: Bracketed information in the *Indications* section refers to uses that are not included in U.S. product labeling.

Accepted

Anesthesia, adjunct—Amobarbital, butabarbital, pentobarbital, phenobarbital (parenteral), and secobarbital are indicated for use as preoperative medication to help reduce anxiety and facilitate induction of anesthesia.

Narcoanalysis—Amobarbital (parenteral) may be indicated in narcoanalysis.

Epilepsy, tonic-clonic seizure pattern (treatment) or
Epilepsy, simple partial seizure pattern (treatment)—Phenobarbital, a long-acting barbiturate, is indicated as long-term anticonvulsant therapy for the treatment of generalized tonic-clonic and simple partial (cortical focal) seizures; mephobarbital and metharbital, also long-acting barbiturates, may be indicated as alternatives to phenobarbital.

Convulsions (treatment)
Seizures (prophylaxis and treatment)
Status epilepticus (treatment) or
Tetanus (treatment adjunct)—Parenteral barbiturates, especially phenobarbital, are indicated in the emergency treatment of certain acute convulsive episodes such as those associated with status epilepticus, eclampsia, meningitis, and toxic reactions to strychnine. They are also indicated as adjunctive treatment for acute convulsive episodes associated with tetanus.

Phenobarbital is used in the prophylaxis and treatment of febrile seizures.[1]

[Hyperbilirubinemia (prophylaxis and treatment)][1]—Phenobarbital (oral and parenteral) is used in the prevention and treatment of hyperbilirubinemia in neonates. It is used also to lower bilirubin concentrations in patients with congenital nonhemolytic unconjugated hyperbilirubinemia or chronic intrahepatic cholestasis.

[Ischemia, cerebral (treatment)][1] or
[Hypertension, cerebral (treatment)][1]—Pentobarbital (parenteral) is used for induction of coma to protect the brain from various states, including ischemia and increased intracranial pressure that follow stroke and head trauma; however, this use is controversial and further studies are needed.

Amobarbital, aprobarbital, butabarbital, pentobarbital, phenobarbital, secobarbital, and secobarbital and amobarbital have been used for the short-term treatment of insomnia; however, they generally *have been replaced* by benzodiazepines. If barbiturates are used, they are not recommended for long-term use since they appear to lose their effectiveness in sleep induction and maintenance after 2 weeks or less.

Amobarbital, aprobarbital, butabarbital, mephobarbital, pentobarbital, phenobarbital, and secobarbital have also been used for routine sedation to relieve anxiety, tension, and apprehension; however, barbiturates generally *have been replaced* by benzodiazepines for daytime sedation.

Unaccepted

Amobarbital (parenteral) has been used as a diagnostic aid in schizophrenia but it generally has been replaced by other agents.

Amobarbital (parenteral) has also been used in the management of catatonic and negativistic reactions; however, phenothiazines generally are more appropriate therapy for catatonic reactions. It has also been used in the management of manic reactions, although benzodiazepines and lithium are usually preferred.

[Phenobarbital (oral and parenteral) has been used in the treatment of familial, senile, or essential action tremors; however, it generally has been replaced by other agents, such as benzodiazepines and beta-adrenergic blockers.]

[1]Not included in Canadian product labeling.

Pharmacology/Pharmacokinetics

See *Table 1*, page 509.

Physicochemical characteristics

Molecular weight—
Amobarbital: 226.27.
Amobarbital sodium: 248.26.
Aprobarbital: 210.23.
Butabarbital sodium: 234.23.
Mephobarbital: 246.27.
Metharbital: 198.22.
Pentobarbital: 226.27.
Pentobarbital sodium: 248.26.
Phenobarbital: 232.24.
Phenobarbital sodium: 254.22.
Secobarbital sodium: 260.27.

Mechanism of action/Effect

Barbiturates act as nonselective depressants of the central nervous system (CNS), capable of producing all levels of CNS mood alteration from excitation to mild sedation, hypnosis, and deep coma. In sufficiently high therapeutic doses, barbiturates induce anesthesia. Recent studies have suggested that the sedative-hypnotic and anticonvulsant effects of barbiturates may be related to their ability to enhance and/or mimic the inhibitory synaptic action of gamma-aminobutyric acid (GABA).

Sedative-hypnotic—

Barbiturates depress the sensory cortex, decrease motor activity, alter cerebral function, and produce drowsiness, sedation, and hypnosis. Although the mechanism of action has not been completely established, the barbiturates appear to have a particular effect at the level of the thalamus where they inhibit ascending conduction in the reticular formation, thus interfering with the transmission of impulses to the cortex.

The mechanism of action of pentobarbital in protecting the brain from ischemia and intracranial pressure is not completely understood; however, it is related to pentobarbital's anesthetic action (produced by sufficiently high dosage) and possibly to the depression of neuronal activity and metabolism.

Anticonvulsant—

Barbiturates are believed to act by depressing monosynaptic and polysynaptic transmission in the CNS. They also increase the threshold for electrical stimulation of the motor cortex.

Antihyperbilirubinemic—

Phenobarbital lowers serum bilirubin concentrations probably by induction of glucuronyl transferase, the enzyme which conjugates bilirubin.

Other actions/effects

Barbiturates have little analgesic action at subanesthetic doses and may increase reaction to painful stimuli.

Although phenobarbital, mephobarbital, and metharbital are the only barbiturates effective as anticonvulsants in subhypnotic doses, all of the barbiturates exhibit anticonvulsant activity in anesthetic doses.

Barbiturates are respiratory depressants; the degree of respiratory depression is dose-dependent.

Barbiturates have been shown to reduce the rapid eye movement (REM) phase of sleep or dreaming stage. Also, Stages III and IV sleep (slow-wave sleep, SWS) are decreased.

Animal studies have shown that barbiturates cause reduction in the tone and contractility of the uterus, ureters, and urinary bladder; however, concentrations required to produce this effect in humans are not attained with sedative-hypnotic doses.

Barbiturates have been shown to induce liver microsomal enzymes, thereby increasing and altering the metabolism of other medications or compounds.

Absorption

Absorbed in varying degrees following oral, parenteral, or rectal administration.

Barbiturate sodium salts are absorbed more rapidly than the free acids because of rapid dissolution.

The rate of absorption is increased if barbiturates are taken well diluted or on an empty stomach.

Distribution

Rapidly distributed to all tissues and fluids with high concentrations in the brain, liver, and kidneys.

Lipid solubility is the primary factor in distribution within the body. The more lipid soluble the barbiturate, the more rapidly it penetrates all tissues of the body; phenobarbital has the lowest lipid solubility and secobarbital the highest.

Biotransformation

Hepatic, primarily by the hepatic microsomal enzyme system.

About 75% of a single oral dose of mephobarbital is metabolized to phenobarbital in 24 hours.

Metharbital is metabolized to barbital.

Onset of action

Oral or rectal—Varies from 20 to 60 minutes.

Intramuscular—Slightly faster than for oral or rectal.

Intravenous—Ranges from almost immediately for pentobarbital sodium to 5 minutes for phenobarbital sodium.

Therapeutic serum concentration

Anticonvulsant—Phenobarbital: 10 to 40 mcg per mL (43 to 172 micromoles/L).

Note: The optimal blood phenobarbital concentration should be determined by response in seizure control and the appearance of toxic effects.

To achieve blood concentrations considered therapeutic in children, higher-per-kg dosages of phenobarbital and most other anticonvulsants generally are required.

Time to peak effect

Phenobarbital—Maximal CNS depression may not occur for 15 minutes or more after intravenous administration of phenobarbital sodium.

Precautions to Consider

Cross-sensitivity and/or related problems

Patients sensitive to one of the barbiturates may be sensitive to other barbiturates also.

Carcinogenicity/Tumorigenicity/Mutagenicity

For butabarbital and secobarbital—No long-term studies in animals have been done to determine the carcinogenic and mutagenic potential of butabarbital or secobarbital.

For pentobarbital—Adequate studies have not been done in humans or animals to determine the carcinogenic potential of pentobarbital.

For phenobarbital—Studies in animals have shown that phenobarbital is carcinogenic in mice and rats following lifetime administration. It produced benign and malignant liver cell tumors in mice and benign liver cell tumors very late in life in rats. A study in humans did not provide sufficient evidence that phenobarbital is carcinogenic in humans.

Pregnancy/Reproduction

Fertility—For butabarbital: No long-term studies in animals have been done to determine the effects of butabarbital on fertility.

Pregnancy—Barbiturates readily cross the placenta following oral or parenteral administration. They are distributed throughout fetal tissues, the highest concentrations being found in the placenta, fetal liver, and brain. Following parenteral administration, fetal blood concentration approaches maternal blood concentration. Barbiturates have been shown to cause an increased incidence of fetal abnormalities. Risk-benefit must be carefully considered when the medication is required in life-threatening situations or in serious diseases for which other medications cannot be used or are ineffective.

Third trimester: Use of barbiturates throughout the last trimester of pregnancy may cause physical dependence with resulting withdrawal symptoms in the neonate. In infants suffering from long-term exposure in utero, the acute withdrawal syndrome of seizures and hyperirritability has been reported to occur from birth to a delayed onset of up to 14 days.

Use of long-acting barbiturates, especially phenobarbital, as anticonvulsants during pregnancy is reportedly associated with a neonatal coagulation defect that may cause bleeding during the early neonatal period (usually within 24 hours of birth). This coagulation defect is characterized by decreased concentrations of vitamin K-dependent clotting factors and prolongation of the prothrombin time and/or the partial thromboplastin time. Vitamin K should be given to the mother during delivery and to the infant (intramuscularly or subcutaneously) immediately after birth.

Also, one study in humans has suggested that prenatal exposure to barbiturates may be associated with an increased incidence of brain tumors.

FDA Pregnancy Category D.

Labor and delivery—Barbiturates in hypnotic doses do not appear to inhibit uterine activity; however, full anesthetic doses of barbiturates decrease the force and frequency of uterine contractions.

Labor and delivery—Use of barbiturates during labor may cause respiratory depression in the neonate, especially the premature neonate, because of immature hepatic function.

Labor and delivery—If barbiturates are used during labor and delivery, it is recommended that resuscitation equipment be readily available.

Breast-feeding

Barbiturates are distributed into breast milk; use by nursing mothers may cause CNS depression in the infant.

Pediatrics

Some children may react to barbiturates with paradoxical excitement.

Geriatrics

Geriatric patients may react to usual doses of barbiturates with excitement, confusion, or mental depression.

The risk of barbiturate-induced hypothermia may be increased in elderly patients, especially with high doses or in acute overdose of barbiturates.

In addition, elderly patients are more likely to have age-related hepatic or renal function impairment, which may require a reduction of dosage in patients receiving a barbiturate.

Drug interactions and/or related problems

The following drug interactions and/or related problems have been selected on the basis of their potential clinical significance (possible mechanism in parentheses where appropriate)—not necessarily inclusive (» = major clinical significance):

Note: Combinations containing any of the following medications, depending on the amount present, may also interact with this medication.

Acetaminophen

(therapeutic effects of acetaminophen may be decreased when the medication is used concurrently in patients receiving chronic barbiturate therapy because of increased metabolism resulting from induction of hepatic microsomal enzymes; also, risk of hepatotoxicity with single toxic doses or prolonged use of high doses of acetaminophen may be increased in alcoholics or in patients regularly using hepatic enzyme inducers such as barbiturates)

Addictive medications, other, especially CNS depressants with habituating potential

(prolonged concurrent use may increase the risk of habituation; caution is recommended)

» Adrenocorticoids, glucocorticoid and mineralocorticoid or
Chloramphenicol or
» Corticotropin or
Cyclosporine or
Dacarbazine or
Digitalis glycosides or
Metronidazole or
Quinidine
(effects may be decreased when these medications are used concurrently with barbiturates, especially phenobarbital, because of enhanced metabolism resulting from induction of hepatic microsomal enzymes; dosage adjustment of these medications, with the exception of digoxin, may be necessary)

» Alcohol or
» CNS depression-producing medications, other (See *Appendix II*)
(concurrent use may increase the CNS depressant effects of either these medications or barbiturates; caution is recommended and dosage of one or both agents should be reduced)

Amphetamines
(concurrent use may cause a delay in the intestinal absorption of phenobarbital)

Anesthetics, halogenated hydrocarbon
(chronic use of barbiturates prior to enflurane, halothane, or methoxyflurane anesthesia may increase anesthetic metabolism leading to increased risk of hepatotoxicity)
(chronic use of barbiturates prior to methoxyflurane anesthesia may increase formation of nephrotoxic metabolites leading to increased risk of nephrotoxicity)

» Anticoagulants, coumarin- or indandione-derivative
(effects may be decreased when these medications are used concurrently with barbiturates because of increased metabolism resulting from induction of hepatic microsomal enzymes; also, bleeding may result when the barbiturate is discontinued; periodic prothrombin-time determinations may be required to determine if dosage adjustments of anticoagulants are necessary)

Anticonvulsants, hydantoin
(concurrent use with barbiturates appears to produce variable and unpredictable effects on the metabolism of hydantoin anticonvulsants; blood concentrations of hydantoin anticonvulsants should be closely monitored when these medications are used concurrently)

Anticonvulsants, succinimide or
» Carbamazepine
(concurrent use with barbiturates may result in increased metabolism, leading to decreased serum concentrations and reduced elimination half-lives of carbamazepine or succinimide anticonvulsants because of induction of hepatic microsomal enzyme activity; monitoring of serum concentrations as a guide to dosage is recommended, especially when carbamazepine or a succinimide anticonvulsant is added to or withdrawn from an existing regimen)

Antidepressants, tricyclic
(effects of tricyclic antidepressants may be decreased when these medications are used concurrently with barbiturates, especially phenobarbital, because of increased metabolism resulting from induction of hepatic microsomal enzymes)

Calcium channel blocking agents
(caution is advised during titration of calcium channel blocker dosage for those patients taking medication known to promote hypotension, such as barbiturate preanesthetics, since the combination may result in excessive hypotension)

Carbonic anhydrase inhibitors
(osteopenia induced by barbiturates, especially phenobarbital, may be enhanced when carbonic anhydrase inhibitors are used concurrently; it is recommended that patients receiving concurrent therapy be monitored for early signs of osteopenia and that the carbonic anhydrase inhibitor be discontinued and appropriate treatment initiated if necessary)

» Contraceptives, estrogen-containing, oral
(concurrent use with barbiturates, especially phenobarbital, may result in reduced contraceptive reliability because of accelerated estrogen metabolism caused by induction of hepatic microsomal enzymes; use of a nonhormonal method of birth control or a progestin-only oral contraceptive may be necessary)

Cyclophosphamide
(concurrent use with barbiturates, especially phenobarbital, may induce microsomal metabolism to increase formation of alkylating metabolites of cyclophosphamide, thereby reducing the half-life and increasing the leukopenic activity of cyclophosphamide)

Disopyramide
(concurrent use with barbiturates, especially phenobarbital, may reduce serum disopyramide to ineffective concentrations; therefore, monitoring of its serum concentrations is necessary during concurrent therapy)

» Divalproex sodium or
» Valproic acid
(concurrent use may decrease the metabolism of barbiturates, resulting in increased serum concentrations, which may lead to increased CNS depression and neurological toxicity; barbiturate serum concentrations should be monitored to determine if dosage adjustment is necessary when these medications are used concurrently; also, the half-life of valproic acid may be decreased and dosage adjustment may be necessary)
(in addition, phenobarbital may enhance valproic acid hepatotoxicity, presumably through the formation of hepatotoxic valproate metabolites)

Doxycycline
(half-life of doxycycline may be shortened when this medication is used concurrently with barbiturates, especially phenobarbital, probably because of increased metabolism resulting from induction of hepatic microsomal enzymes; this effect may continue for up to 2 weeks after barbiturate therapy is discontinued; adjustment of doxycycline dosage during and after therapy or substitution of another tetracycline may be necessary)

Fenoprofen
(concurrent use with phenobarbital may decrease the elimination half-life of fenoprofen, possibly because of increased metabolism resulting from induction of hepatic microsomal enzyme activity; fenoprofen dosage adjustment may be required)

Griseofulvin
(absorption may be decreased when this medication is used concurrently with barbiturates, especially phenobarbital, resulting in decreased serum concentrations; although the effect of decreased serum concentrations on therapeutic response has not been established, concurrent use preferably should be avoided)

Guanadrel or
Guanethidine
(concurrent use with barbiturates may aggravate orthostatic hypotension)

Haloperidol
(concurrent use with barbiturate anticonvulsants may cause a change in the pattern and/or frequency of epileptiform seizures; dosage adjustments of anticonvulsants may be necessary; serum concentrations of haloperidol may be significantly reduced)

Hypothermia-producing medications, other (See *Appendix II*)
(concurrent use with barbiturates in high doses or acute overdose may increase the risk of hypothermia)

Ketamine
(concurrent use of ketamine, especially in high doses or when rapidly administered, with barbiturate preanesthetics may increase the risk of hypotension and/or respiratory depression)

Leucovorin
(large doses may counteract the anticonvulsant effects of barbiturate anticonvulsants)

Levothyroxine
(concurrent use of barbiturates may increase hepatic degradation of levothyroxine, which may result in increased requirements; dosage adjustment may be necessary)

Loxapine or
Phenothiazines or
Thioxanthenes
(may lower the seizure threshold; dosage adjustment of barbiturate anticonvulsants may be necessary)
(concurrent use of chlorpromazine with phenobarbital has been shown to increase the metabolism of chlorpromazine; therefore, phenobarbital may decrease serum concentrations of phenothiazines when used concurrently)

Maprotiline
(in addition to possibly enhancing CNS depressant effects, concurrent use of maprotiline may lower the convulsive threshold, at high doses, and decrease the effects of barbiturate anticonvulsants)

Methylphenidate
(concurrent use may increase serum concentrations of barbiturate anticonvulsants, especially phenobarbital, because of metabolism inhibition, possibly resulting in toxicity; dosage adjustment of the barbiturate anticonvulsant may be necessary)

Mexiletine
(concurrent use with barbiturates may accelerate metabolism and result in decreased plasma concentrations of mexiletine; plasma concentrations of mexiletine should be monitored during concurrent use to ensure efficacy is maintained)

Monoamine oxidase (MAO) inhibitors, including furazolidone, pargyline, and procarbazine
(concurrent use may prolong the CNS depressant effects of barbiturates, probably because metabolism of the barbiturate is inhibited)
(concurrent use with barbiturate anticonvulsants may cause a change in the pattern of epileptiform seizures; dosage adjustment of the barbiturate anticonvulsant may be necessary)

Phenylbutazone
(concurrent use may decrease the efficacy of barbiturates by inducing hepatic microsomal enzymes and increasing their metabolism; also, hepatic enzyme inducers such as barbiturates may increase phenylbutazone metabolism and decrease its half-life)

Posterior pituitary
(concurrent use with barbiturates may increase the risk of cardiac arrhythmias and coronary insufficiency)

Primidone
(although concurrent use with barbiturate anticonvulsants is rarely indicated, since primidone is metabolized to phenobarbital, it may cause a change in the pattern of epileptiform seizures because of altered medication metabolism and also increase the sedative effect of either primidone or the barbiturate anticonvulsant; decreases in primidone dosage may be necessary)

Rifampin
(concurrent use with rifampin may enhance the metabolism of hexobarbital by induction of hepatic microsomal enzymes, resulting in lower serum concentrations; there are conflicting data on rifampin's effect on phenobarbital; dosage adjustment may be required)

Vitamin D
(effects may be reduced by barbiturates, especially phenobarbital, because of accelerated metabolism by hepatic microsomal enzyme induction; vitamin D supplementation may be required in patients on long-term barbiturate anticonvulsant therapy to prevent osteomalacia, although rickets is rare)

Xanthines, such as:
Aminophylline
Caffeine
Oxtriphylline
Theophylline
(concurrent use with barbiturates, especially phenobarbital, may increase metabolism of the xanthines [except dyphylline] by induction of hepatic microsomal enzymes, resulting in increased theophylline clearance; also, concurrent use may antagonize hypnotic effects of barbiturates)

Laboratory value alterations

The following have been selected on the basis of their potential clinical significance (possible effect in parentheses where appropriate)—not necessarily inclusive (» = major clinical significance).

With diagnostic test results

Cyanocobalamin Co 57
(absorption of radioactive cyanocobalamin may be impaired by concurrent use of barbiturate anticonvulsants, especially phenobarbital)

Metyrapone test
(increased metabolism of metyrapone by an hepatic enzyme inducer such as a barbiturate may decrease the response to metyrapone)

Phentolamine test
(barbiturates may cause a false-positive phentolamine test; it is recommended that all medications be withdrawn at least 24 hours, preferably 48 to 72 hours, prior to a phentolamine test)

With physiology/laboratory test values

Bilirubin, serum
(concentrations may be decreased in neonates, in patients with congenital nonhemolytic unconjugated hyperbilirubinemia, and in epileptics; this effect is presumably due to induction of glucuronyl transferase, the enzyme responsible for the conjugation of bilirubin)

Medical considerations/Contraindications

The medical considerations/contraindications included have been selected on the basis of their potential clinical significance (reasons given in parentheses where appropriate)—not necessarily inclusive (» = major clinical significance).

Except under special circumstances, this medication should not be used when the following medical problem exists:

» Porphyria, acute intermittent or variegata, or history of
(barbiturates may aggravate symptoms by inducing enzymes responsible for porphyrin synthesis)

Risk-benefit should be considered when the following medical problems exist:

Anemia, severe
(may be complicated by barbiturate-induced respiratory depression, especially with phenobarbital)

Asthma, history of
(hypersensitivity reactions such as bronchospasm more likely to occur in these patients)

Diabetes mellitus, especially with phenobarbital

» Drug abuse or dependence, history of
(predisposition of patient to habituation and dependence)

» Hepatic coma, premonitory signs of, or
Hepatic function impairment
(barbiturates metabolized in liver; medication should be administered with caution and, initially, in reduced dosage)

Hyperkinesis
(condition may be exacerbated)

Hyperthyroidism
(symptoms may be exacerbated because barbiturates displace thyroxine from plasma proteins)

Hypoadrenalism, borderline
(systemic effects of exogenous hydrocortisone and endogenous cortisol may be diminished by barbiturates)

Mental depression and/or
Suicidal tendencies
(condition may be exacerbated, especially in elderly patients)

» Pain, acute or chronic
(paradoxical excitement may be induced or important symptoms may be masked)

Renal function impairment, especially with intermediate- and long-acting barbiturates
(barbiturates excreted primarily by kidneys; dosage reduction may be necessary)

» Respiratory disease involving dyspnea or obstruction, particularly status asthmaticus
(serious ventilatory depression may occur)

» Sensitivity to barbiturate prescribed
(in patients sensitive to barbiturates, severe hepatic damage can occur from ordinary doses and is usually associated with dermatitis and involvement of parenchymatous organs)

Caution should be used also in debilitated patients because they may react to usual doses with marked excitement, mental depression, and confusion

For parenteral dosage forms only

Cardiac disease
(adverse circulatory reactions may occur with intravenous administration, especially with too-rapid administration)

Hypertension
(hypotension may occur with intravenous administration, especially in these patients; slow administration usually prevents this occurrence)

Patient monitoring

The following may be especially important in patient monitoring (other tests may be warranted in some patients, depending on condition; » = major clinical significance):

Folate concentrations, serum
(determinations recommended periodically because of increased folate requirements of patients on long-term anticonvulsant therapy with phenobarbital and possibly mephobarbital)

Hematopoietic function and
Hepatic function and
Renal function
(determinations recommended at periodic intervals during prolonged barbiturate therapy)

Barbital concentrations, serum
(determinations recommended when clinically indicated during metharbital therapy)

Phenobarbital concentrations, serum
(determinations recommended as clinically indicated when phenobarbital or mephobarbital is used as an anticonvulsant)

Side/Adverse Effects

Note: Exfoliative dermatitis and Stevens-Johnson syndrome, possibly fatal, may occur rarely as hypersensitivity reactions to barbiturates. If dermatologic reactions occur, the barbiturate should be discontinued.

Severe respiratory depression, apnea, laryngospasm, bronchospasm, or hypertension may occur with intravenous administration of barbiturates, especially if administered too rapidly.

Prolonged barbiturate therapy may result in osteopenia or rickets.

Barbiturate dependence may occur, especially following prolonged use of high doses. The characteristics of dependence include: a strong desire or need to continue taking the barbiturate; a tendency to increase the dose; a psychological dependence on the effects of the medication; and a physical dependence on the effects of the medication requiring its presence for maintenance of homeostasis and resulting in an abstinence syndrome when the barbiturate is discontinued. Symptoms of withdrawal are related to the pharmacokinetics of the specific barbiturate and can be severe and may even cause death.

The following side/adverse effects have been selected on the basis of their potential clinical significance (possible signs and symptoms in parentheses where appropriate)—not necessarily inclusive:

Those indicating need for medical attention

Incidence less frequent

Sensitivity to barbiturates (confusion)—especially in geriatric or debilitated patients; ***mental depression***—especially in geriatric or debilitated patients; ***paradoxical reaction*** (unusual excitement)—especially in children or geriatric or debilitated patients

Incidence rare

Agranulocytosis (sore throat and/or fever); ***allergic reaction*** (skin rash or hives; swelling of eyelids, face, or lips; wheezing or tightness in chest)—especially in patients who have asthma, urticaria, angioedema, and similar conditions; ***exfoliative dermatitis*** (fever; red, thickened, or scaly skin); ***hallucinations; hypotension or megaloblastic anemia*** (unusual tiredness or weakness)—with chronic barbiturate use; ***Stevens-Johnson syndrome*** (bleeding sores on lips; chest pain; muscle or joint pain; painful sores, ulcers, or white spots in mouth; skin rash or hives; sore throat or fever); ***thrombocytopenia*** (unusual bleeding or bruising); ***thrombophlebitis*** (soreness, redness, swelling, or pain at injection site)—for parenteral dosage forms only

With prolonged or chronic use

Hepatic damage (yellow eyes or skin); ***osteopenia or rickets*** (bone pain, tenderness, or aching; loss of appetite; muscle weakness; unusual weight loss)

Those indicating need for medical attention only if they continue or are bothersome

Incidence more frequent

Clumsiness or unsteadiness; dizziness or lightheadedness; drowsiness; "hangover" effect

Incidence less frequent

Anxiety or nervousness; constipation; feeling faint; headache; irritability; nausea or vomiting; nightmares or trouble in sleeping

Those indicating possible barbiturate withdrawal and need for medical attention if they occur after medication is discontinued

Minor symptoms—may occur within 8 to 12 hours and usually occur in the following sequence:

Anxiety or restlessness; muscle twitching; trembling of hands; weakness; dizziness; vision problems; nausea; vomiting; trouble in sleeping, increased dreaming, or nightmares; orthostatic hypotension (feeling faint; lightheadedness)

Major symptoms—may occur within 16 hours and last up to 5 days

Convulsions; hallucinations

Note: Intensity of withdrawal symptoms gradually declines over a period of approximately 15 days.

Overdose

For specific information on the agents used in the management of barbiturate overdose, see:

- *Charcoal, Activated (Oral-Local)* monograph; and/or
- *Ipecac (Oral-Local)* monograph.

For more information on the management of overdose or unintentional ingestion, **contact a Poison Control Center** (see *Poison Control Center Listing*).

Clinical effects of overdose

The following effects have been selected on the basis of their potential clinical significance (possible signs and symptoms in parentheses where appropriate)—not necessarily inclusive:

Acute

Confusion, severe; decrease in or loss of reflexes; drowsiness, severe; fever; hypothermia (low body temperature); ***shortness of breath or slow or troubled breathing; slow heartbeat; slurred speech; staggering; unusual movements of the eyes; weakness, severe***

Note: In acute barbiturate overdosage, CNS and respiratory depression may progress to Cheyne-Stokes respiration, areflexia, slight constriction of the pupils (in severe toxicity, pupils may be dilated), oliguria, tachycardia, lowered body temperature, and coma. Typical shock syndrome (apnea, circulatory collapse, respiratory arrest, and death) may occur.

In extreme barbiturate overdosage, all electrical activity in the brain may cease. In this case an electroencephalogram (EEG) may be "flat," but this does not necessarily indicate clinical death since, unless hypoxic damage occurs, this effect is fully reversible.

Complications in barbiturate overdosage such as pneumonia, pulmonary edema, cardiac arrhythmias, congestive heart failure, and renal failure may occur.

In acute overdosage, the blood barbiturate concentration for some of the barbiturates relative to the degree of CNS depression in nontolerant persons is as follows:

See *Table 2*, page 509.

Chronic

Confusion, severe; irritability, continuing; poor judgment; trouble in sleeping

Treatment of overdose

Treatment of barbiturate overdose is primarily supportive and consists of the following

To decrease absorption—

If the patient is conscious and has not lost the gag reflex, emesis may be induced with ipecac syrup; care should be taken to prevent pulmonary aspiration of vomitus. After vomiting is completed, 30 to 60 grams of activated charcoal in a glass of water or sorbitol may be administered to prevent absorption and increase excretion of the barbiturate.

If emesis is contraindicated, gastric lavage may be performed with a cuffed endotracheal tube in place with the patient face down. Activated charcoal should be left in the stomach and a saline cathartic may be administered.

To enhance elimination—

If renal function is normal, forced diuresis may help to eliminate the barbiturate.

Alkalinization of the urine increases renal excretion of some barbiturates, especially phenobarbital, also aprobarbital, and mephobarbital (which is metabolized to phenobarbital).

Although hemodialysis or hemoperfusion is not recommended as a routine procedure, it may be used in severe barbiturate poisoning or if the patient is anuric or in shock.

Monitoring—

Vital signs and fluid balance should be monitored.

Supportive care—

An adequate airway should be maintained, with assisted respiration and administration of oxygen as needed.

Blood pressure and body temperature should be maintained.

Fluid therapy and other standard treatment for shock should be administered, if necessary.

A vasopressor may be required if hypotension occurs.

Fluid or sodium overload should be avoided, especially if cardiovascular status is decreased.

Chest physiotherapy should be administered.

If pneumonia is suspected, appropriate cultures should be taken and antibiotics should be administered.

Also, appropriate care should be taken to prevent hypostatic pneumonia, decubiti, aspiration, and other complications that may occur with altered states of consciousness.

Patients in whom intentional overdose is known or suspected should be referred for psychiatric consultation.

Patient Consultation

As an aid to patient consultation, refer to *Advice for the Patient, Barbiturates (Systemic)*.

In providing consultation, consider emphasizing the following selected information (» = major clinical significance):

Before using this medication

» Conditions affecting use, especially:
Sensitivity to barbiturates
Pregnancy—Barbiturates readily cross placenta; increase in incidence of fetal abnormalities (FDA Pregnancy Category D); use during third trimester of pregnancy may cause physical dependence with resulting withdrawal symptoms in neonate; long-acting barbiturates associated with neonatal coagulation defect that may cause bleeding during early neonatal period; use during labor may cause respiratory depression in neonate
Breast-feeding—Barbiturates distributed into breast milk; use by nursing mothers may cause CNS depression in infant
Use in children—Children may react to barbiturates with paradoxical excitement
Use in the elderly—Elderly patients may react to usual doses of barbiturates with excitement, confusion, or mental depression; risk of barbiturate-induced hypothermia may be increased in elderly patients; elderly patients more likely to have age-related hepatic or renal function impairment, which may require a dosage reduction of barbiturates
Other medications, especially alcohol, adrenocorticoids, corticotropin, other CNS depression-producing medications, coumarin- or indandione-derivative anticoagulants, carbamazepine, divalproex sodium, estrogen-containing contraceptives, or valproic acid
Other medical problems, especially history of drug abuse or dependence, premonitory signs of hepatic coma, acute or chronic pain, or respiratory disease involving dyspnea or obstruction (particularly status asthmaticus)
Caution if any laboratory tests required; possible interference with results of metyrapone test.

Proper use of this medication

» Importance of not using more medication than the amount prescribed because of habit-forming potential
» Not increasing dose if medication appears less effective after a few weeks; checking with physician
» For anticonvulsant use: Compliance with therapy; not missing any doses
» Proper dosing
Missed dose: If on scheduled dosing regimen—Taking as soon as possible; not taking if almost time for next dose; not doubling doses
Proper administration
For extended-release dosage form
Swallowing capsule or tablet whole
Not breaking, crushing, or chewing
For suppository dosage form
Proper administration technique
» Proper storage

Precautions while using this medication

Regular visits to physician to check progress during prolonged therapy
Checking with physician before discontinuing medication after prolonged use; gradual dosage reduction may be necessary to avoid the possibility of withdrawal symptoms
» Avoiding use of alcohol or other CNS depressants
» Suspected psychological or physical dependence: Checking with physician
» Suspected overdose: Getting emergency help at once
» Caution if dizziness, lightheadedness, or drowsiness occurs
» Use of another or additional method of contraception if taking estrogen-containing oral contraceptives concurrently

Side/adverse effects

Signs of potential side effects, especially allergic reaction or intolerance to barbiturate, blood dyscrasias, exfoliative dermatitis, hallucinations, hepatic damage (with prolonged or chronic use), mental depression, paradoxical reaction, osteopenia or rickets (with prolonged or chronic use), or Stevens-Johnson syndrome
Unusual excitement may be more likely to occur in children and in elderly or very ill patients
Confusion and mental depression may be more likely to occur in elderly or very ill patients

General Dosing Information

Dosage of the barbiturates must be individualized, based on the patient's age, weight, and condition.

In patients with impaired hepatic function, lower doses should be used initially. Lower doses may be required also in patients with impaired renal function.

Patients on dialysis may require an increase in dosage.

Tolerance may occur with repeated administration of the barbiturates, especially of the long-acting ones and with large doses of the shorter-acting ones.

Prolonged administration of barbiturates as hypnotics generally is not recommended because they have not been shown to be effective for a period of more than 2 weeks.

Prolonged uninterrupted use of barbiturates, particularly the short-acting ones, may result in psychic or physical dependence.

Chronic use of barbiturates at doses 3 to 4 times the therapeutic concentration will usually produce physical dependence in about 75% of patients.

Daily administration in excess of 400 mg of pentobarbital or secobarbital for approximately 90 days is likely to produce some degree of physical dependence; a dosage of 600 to 800 mg taken for at least 35 days is sufficient to produce withdrawal seizures. The average daily dose for the barbiturate addict generally is about 1.5 grams.

Barbiturates should be withdrawn gradually in order to avoid the possibility of precipitating withdrawal symptoms.

To minimize the possibility of acute or chronic overdosage, the least possible quantity of a barbiturate should be prescribed and dispensed at any one time.

The toxic dose of barbiturates varies but generally an oral dose of 1 gram of most barbiturates produces serious poisoning in an adult. Death commonly occurs after 2 to 10 grams of ingested barbiturate.

Diet/Nutrition

Patients on long-term anticonvulsant therapy with phenobarbital and possibly mephobarbital may have increased folic acid requirements. In addition, patients on long-term therapy may require supplements of vitamin D to prevent osteomalacia.

For parenteral dosage forms only

Prior to administration, parenteral solutions should be inspected visually for particulate matter and discoloration, if possible.

For intravenous injections, it is preferable to use the larger veins to minimize the risk of irritation and the possibility of resulting thrombosis. Administration into varicose veins is not recommended because of poor circulation in these veins.

Intravenous injections should be administered slowly and patients should be carefully monitored during administration. This requires maintenance of blood pressure, respiration, and cardiac function and recording of vital signs. Equipment for resuscitation and artificial ventilation should be readily available.

Intramuscular injections should be administered deeply into large muscles, such as the gluteus maximus or vastus lateralis because superficial intramuscular injection may be painful and may produce sterile abscesses or sloughs.

No more than 5 mL, regardless of drug concentration, should be injected intramuscularly at any one site because of possible tissue irritation.

Parenteral solutions of barbiturate salts are highly alkaline; therefore, caution should be used to avoid perivascular extravasation or intra-arterial injection, since extravasation may cause local tissue damage with subsequent necrosis and intra-arterial injection may cause spasm, severe pain, and possibly gangrene.

For rectal dosage forms only

Barbiturates may be administered rectally when oral or parenteral administration may be undesirable. If the rectal dosage form is not available, the soluble sodium salt of the barbiturate may be incorporated in a retention enema.

To assure accuracy in dosage, suppositories should not be divided.

Rectal administration of barbiturates is not recommended for status epilepticus; intravenous injection is the preferred route of administration for this condition.

For treatment of dependence

Treatment of dependence consists of the following

- Gradual withdrawal of the barbiturate.
- An example of the different withdrawal regimens used (all of which require an extended period of time) involves substituting a 30-mg dose of phenobarbital for each 100- to 200-mg dose of the barbiturate that the patient has been taking. The total daily amount of phenobarbital then is administered as a single dose or in 3 or 4 divided doses, not to exceed 600 mg per day. If signs of withdrawal occur on the first day of treatment, a loading dose of 100 to 200 mg of phenobarbital may be administered intramuscularly in addition to the oral dose. After stabilization on phenobarbital, the total daily dose is decreased by 30 mg a day as long as withdrawal is proceeding smoothly. This regimen may be modified by initiating treatment at the patient's regular dosage level and decreasing the daily dosage by 10% if tolerated by the patient.

• For infants physically dependent on barbiturates, initially a dose of 3 to 10 mg of phenobarbital per kg of body weight per day may be given. After withdrawal symptoms (hyperactivity, disturbed sleep, tremors, hyperreflexia) are relieved, the dosage of phenobarbital should be gradually decreased and completely withdrawn over a 2-week period.

• Also, barbiturate withdrawal may be accomplished with benzodiazepines, such as diazepam.

For treatment of adverse effects

For extravasation into subcutaneous tissues—Recommended treatment includes

• Application of moist heat to affected area.

• Injection of a 0.5% procaine solution into the affected area.

For accidental intra-arterial injection—Recommended treatment includes

• Release of tourniquet or restrictive garments to permit dilution of injected medication.

• Injection of 10 mL of a 1% procaine solution into the artery and, if necessary, brachial plexus block to relieve spasm.

• Anticoagulant therapy may prevent thrombosis.

• Supportive treatment.

AMOBARBITAL

Summary of Differences

Category:

Parenteral amobarbital also may be indicated as an anticonvulsant.

Indications:

Parenteral amobarbital also may be indicated in narcoanalysis; and has been used in diagnosis of schizophrenia and for catatonic, negativistic, and manic reactions, but generally has been replaced by other agents.

Pharmacology/pharmacokinetics:

Long-acting barbiturate—

Onset of action: 60 minutes or longer.

Duration of action: 10 to 12 hours.

Protein binding—

Moderate.

Additional Dosing Information

See also *General Dosing Information.*

For parenteral dosage forms only

The rate of intravenous injection should not exceed 100 mg per minute for adults or 60 mg per square meter of body surface per minute for children. Faster rates of administration may cause serious respiratory depression.

Superficial intramuscular or subcutaneous injections may be painful and may produce sterile abscesses or sloughs.

Oral Dosage Forms

AMOBARBITAL TABLETS USP

Usual adult dose

Sedative-hypnotic—

Hypnotic—

Oral, 65 to 200 mg at bedtime.

Sedative—

Daytime—Oral, 50 to 300 mg a day in divided doses.

Note: Geriatric and debilitated patients may react to usual doses with excitement, confusion, or mental depression. Lower doses may be required in these patients.

Usual pediatric dose

Sedative-hypnotic—

Hypnotic—

Dosage has not been established.

Sedative—

Daytime—Oral, 2 mg per kg of body weight or 60 mg per square meter of body surface three times a day.

Preoperative—Oral, 2 to 6 mg per kg of body weight, up to a maximum of 100 mg per dose.

Strength(s) usually available

U.S.—

Not commercially available.

Canada—

30 mg (Rx) [*Amytal*].

100 mg (Rx) [*Amytal*].

Packaging and storage

Store below 40 °C (104 °F), preferably between 15 and 30 °C (59 and 86 °F), unless otherwise specified by manufacturer. Store in a well-closed container.

Auxiliary labeling

• Avoid alcoholic beverages.

• May cause drowsiness.

Note

Controlled substance in the U.S. and Canada.

AMOBARBITAL SODIUM CAPSULES USP

Usual adult dose

Sedative-hypnotic—

Hypnotic—

Oral, 65 to 200 mg at bedtime.

Sedative—

Daytime—Oral, 50 to 300 mg a day in divided doses.

During labor—Oral, 200 to 400 mg, repeated every one to three hours, if necessary, up to a total dose of 1 gram.

Preoperative—Oral, 200 mg one to two hours before surgery.

Note: Geriatric and debilitated patients may react to usual doses with excitement, confusion, or mental depression. Lower doses may be required in these patients.

Usual pediatric dose

Sedative-hypnotic—

Hypnotic—

Dosage has not been established.

Sedative—

Daytime—Oral, 2 mg per kg of body weight or 60 mg per square meter of body surface three times a day.

Preoperative—Oral, 2 to 6 mg per kg of body weight, up to a maximum of 100 mg per dose.

Strength(s) usually available

U.S.—

200 mg (Rx) [*Amytal;* GENERIC].

Canada—

200 mg (Rx) [*Amytal*].

Packaging and storage

Store below 40 °C (104 °F), preferably between 15 and 30 °C (59 and 86 °F), unless otherwise specified by manufacturer. Store in a tight container.

Auxiliary labeling

• Avoid alcoholic beverages.

• May cause drowsiness.

Note

Controlled substance in the U.S. and Canada.

Parenteral Dosage Forms

AMOBARBITAL SODIUM STERILE USP

Usual adult dose

Sedative-hypnotic—

Hypnotic—

Intramuscular or intravenous, 65 to 200 mg.

Sedative—

Intramuscular or intravenous, 30 to 50 mg two or three times a day.

Anticonvulsant—

Intravenous, 65 to 500 mg.

Note: Geriatric and debilitated patients may react to usual doses with excitement, confusion, or mental depression. Lower doses may be required in these patients.

Usual adult prescribing limits

Intramuscular, up to 500 mg per dose.

Intravenous, up to 1 gram per dose.

Usual pediatric dose

Sedative-hypnotic—

Hypnotic—

Children up to 6 years of age:

Intramuscular, 2 to 3 mg per kg of body weight per dose.

Children 6 years of age and over:

Intramuscular, 2 to 3 mg per kg of body weight per dose.

Intravenous, 65 to 500 mg per dose.

Sedative—

Preoperative:

Intravenous, 65 to 500 mg or 3 to 5 mg per kg of body weight per dose.

Anticonvulsant—
Children up to 6 years of age—
Intramuscular or intravenous, 3 to 5 mg per kg of body weight or 125 mg per square meter of body surface per dose.

Children 6 years of age and over—
Intravenous, 65 to 500 mg per dose.

Strength(s) usually available
U.S.—
500 mg (Rx) [*Amytal*].
Canada—
500 mg (Rx) [*Amytal*].

Packaging and storage
Prior to reconstitution, store below 40 °C (104 °F), preferably between 15 and 30 °C (59 and 86 °F), unless otherwise specified by manufacturer.

Preparation of dosage form
Solutions of amobarbital sodium should be prepared aseptically with sterile water for injection. For preparation of various concentrations of solutions for injection, see the manufacturer's package insert.

Stability
After reconstitution, solution should be used within 30 minutes since amobarbital sodium hydrolyzes in solution or upon exposure to air. Solution should not be used if it does not become absolutely clear within 5 minutes after reconstitution or if a precipitate forms after the solution clears.

Note
Controlled substance in the U.S. and Canada.

APROBARBITAL

Summary of Differences

Pharmacology/pharmacokinetics:
Intermediate-acting barbiturate—
Onset of action: 45 to 60 minutes.
Duration of action: 6 to 8 hours.
Protein binding—
Low.

Oral Dosage Forms

APROBARBITAL ELIXIR

Usual adult dose
Sedative-hypnotic—
Hypnotic: Oral, 40 to 160 mg at bedtime.
Sedative: Daytime—Oral, 40 mg three times a day.

Note: Geriatric and debilitated patients may react to usual doses with excitement, confusion, or mental depression. Lower doses may be required in these patients.

Usual pediatric dose
Dosage has not been established.

Strength(s) usually available
U.S.—
40 mg per 5 mL (Rx) [*Alurate* (alcohol 20%; dextrose; saccharin; sorbitol; sucrose; FD&C Yellow No. 6; FD&C Red No. 40)].
Canada—
Not commercially available.

Packaging and storage
Store below 40 °C (104 °F), preferably between 15 and 30 °C (59 and 86 °F), in a tight, light-resistant container, unless otherwise specified by manufacturer. Protect from freezing.

Auxiliary labeling
- Avoid alcoholic beverages.
- May cause drowsiness.
- Keep container tightly closed.

Note
Controlled substance in the U.S.

BUTABARBITAL

Summary of Differences

Pharmacology/pharmacokinetics:
Intermediate-acting barbiturate—
Onset of action: 45 to 60 minutes.
Duration of action: 6 to 8 hours.
Protein binding—
Low.

Oral Dosage Forms

BUTABARBITAL SODIUM ELIXIR USP

Usual adult dose
Sedative-hypnotic—
Hypnotic—
Oral, 50 to 100 mg at bedtime.
Sedative—
Daytime—Oral, 15 to 30 mg three or four times a day.
Preoperative—Oral, 50 to 100 mg sixty to ninety minutes before surgery.

Note: Geriatric and debilitated patients may react to usual doses with excitement, confusion, or mental depression. Lower doses may be required in these patients.

Usual pediatric dose
Sedative-hypnotic—
Hypnotic—
Dosage must be individualized by physician.
Sedative—
Daytime—Oral, 2 mg per kg of body weight or 60 mg per square meter of body surface three times a day.
Preoperative—Oral, 2 to 6 mg per kg of body weight, up to a maximum of 100 mg per dose.

Strength(s) usually available
U.S.—
30 mg per 5 mL (Rx) [*Busodium; Butalan; Butisol* (alcohol [by volume] 7%; tartrazine); GENERIC].
Canada—
Not commercially available.

Packaging and storage
Store below 40 °C (104 °F), preferably between 15 and 30 °C (59 and 86 °F), unless otherwise specified by manufacturer. Store in a tight container. Protect from freezing.

Auxiliary labeling
- Avoid alcoholic beverages.
- May cause drowsiness.
- Keep container tightly closed.

Note
Controlled substance in the U.S.

BUTABARBITAL SODIUM TABLETS USP

Usual adult dose
See *Butabarbital Sodium Elixir USP*.

Usual pediatric dose
See *Butabarbital Sodium Elixir USP*.

Strength(s) usually available
U.S.—
15 mg (Rx) [*Busodium; Butisol* (scored); GENERIC].
30 mg (Rx) [*Busodium; Butisol* (scored; tartrazine); *Sarisol No. 2;* GENERIC].
50 mg (Rx) [*Butisol* (scored; tartrazine)].
100 mg (Rx) [*Busodium; Butisol* (scored); GENERIC].
Canada—
15 mg (Rx) [*Butisol* (scored; sodium 2 mg)].
30 mg (Rx) [*Butisol* (scored; sodium 3 mg; tartrazine)].
100 mg (Rx) [*Butisol* (scored; sodium 10 mg)].

Packaging and storage
Store below 40 °C (104 °F), preferably between 15 and 30 °C (59 and 86 °F), unless otherwise specified by manufacturer. Store in a well-closed container.

Auxiliary labeling
- Avoid alcoholic beverages.
- May cause drowsiness.

Note
Controlled substance in the U.S. and Canada.

MEPHOBARBITAL

Summary of Differences

Category:
Indicated only as an anticonvulsant.

Pharmacology/pharmacokinetics:
Biotransformation—
About 75% of a single dose metabolized to phenobarbital in 24 hours.
Long-acting barbiturate—
Onset of action: 60 minutes or longer.
Duration of action: 10 to 12 hours.
Patient consultation:
Compliance with therapy when used as an anticonvulsant.

Additional Dosing Information

See also *General Dosing Information.*
In epilepsy
- Therapy with mephobarbital should begin with small doses, the dosage being gradually increased over a period of 4 to 5 days until the optimum dosage is determined.
- When used to replace another anticonvulsant, the dosage of mephobarbital should be gradually increased while the dosage of the other medication is maintained initially and then gradually decreased in order to maintain seizure control.
- Mephobarbital may be alternated with phenobarbital therapy.
- When used in conjunction with phenytoin, the dose of phenytoin may need to be reduced, but the full dose of mephobarbital may be given.
- Mephobarbital should be withdrawn slowly in order to avoid precipitating seizures or status epilepticus. When the dosage is to be reduced to a maintenance level or discontinued, the amount should be reduced over a period of 4 to 5 days or possibly longer.

Oral Dosage Forms

MEPHOBARBITAL TABLETS USP

Usual adult dose
Anticonvulsant—
Oral, 200 mg at bedtime to 600 mg a day in divided doses.
Sedative-hypnotic—
Sedative: Daytime—Oral, 32 to 100 mg three or four times a day.
Note: Geriatric and debilitated patients may react to usual doses with excitement, confusion, or mental depression. Lower doses may be required in these patients.

Usual pediatric dose
Anticonvulsant—
Children up to 5 years of age: Oral, 16 to 32 mg three or four times a day.
Children 5 years of age and over: Oral, 32 to 64 mg three or four times a day.
Sedative-hypnotic—
Sedative: Daytime—Oral, 16 to 32 mg three or four times a day.

Strength(s) usually available
U.S.—
32 mg (Rx) [*Mebaral* (scored; lactose; starch; stearic acid; talc)].
50 mg (Rx) [*Mebaral* (lactose; starch; stearic acid; talc)].
100 mg (Rx) [*Mebaral* (lactose; starch; stearic acid; talc)].
Canada—
30 mg (Rx) [*Mebaral* (lactose 65 mg)].
100 mg (Rx) [*Mebaral* (lactose 59 mg)].

Packaging and storage
Store below 40 °C (104 °F), preferably between 15 and 30 °C (59 and 86 °F), unless otherwise specified by manufacturer. Store in a well-closed container.

Auxiliary labeling
- Avoid alcoholic beverages.
- May cause drowsiness.

Note
Controlled substance in the U.S. and Canada.

METHARBITAL

Summary of Differences

Category:
Indicated only as an anticonvulsant.
Pharmacology/pharmacokinetics:
Biotransformation—
Metabolized to barbital.
Long-acting barbiturate—
Onset of action: 60 minutes or longer.
Duration of action: 10 to 12 hours.
Patient consultation:
Compliance with therapy.

Additional Dosing Information

See also *General Dosing Information.*
Metharbital should be withdrawn gradually in order to avoid the possibility of precipitating seizures or status epilepticus.
When used to replace or supplement other anticonvulsant therapy, the dosage of metharbital should be gradually increased while the dosage of the other medication is maintained initially and then gradually decreased in order to maintain seizure control.

Oral Dosage Forms

METHARBITAL TABLETS

Usual adult dose
Anticonvulsant—
Oral, initially 100 mg one to three times a day, the dosage being increased up to 800 mg per day, if necessary.
Note: Geriatric and debilitated patients may react to usual doses with excitement, confusion, or mental depression. Lower doses may be required in these patients.

Usual pediatric dose
Anticonvulsant—
Oral, 50 mg one to three times a day; or 5 to 15 mg per kg of body weight per day in divided doses.

Strength(s) usually available
U.S.—
Not commercially available.
Canada—
Not commercially available.
In other countries—
100 mg [*Gemonil* (scored; lactose)].

Packaging and storage
Store below 40 °C (104 °F), preferably between 15 and 30 °C (59 and 86 °F), unless otherwise specified by manufacturer. Store in a tight container.

Auxiliary labeling
- Avoid alcoholic beverages.
- May cause drowsiness.

PENTOBARBITAL

Summary of Differences

Category:
Parenteral pentobarbital also may be indicated as an anticonvulsant.
Indications:
Parenteral pentobarbital also used to protect brain from ischemia and increased intracranial pressure that follow stroke and head trauma.
Pharmacology/pharmacokinetics:
Short-acting barbiturate—
Onset of action: 10 to 15 minutes.
Duration of action: 3 to 4 hours.
Protein binding—
Moderate to high.

Additional Dosing Information

See also *General Dosing Information.*
When administered during labor, doses greater than 200 mg may cause respiratory depression in the newborn.

For parenteral dosage forms only
The injection is for intramuscular or intravenous use only; it is not recommended for subcutaneous administration.
Intravenous injections should be made slowly, not to exceed 50 mg per minute, to avoid adverse respiratory and circulatory reactions.

Oral Dosage Forms

PENTOBARBITAL ELIXIR USP

Usual adult dose
Sedative-hypnotic—
Hypnotic—
Oral, 100 mg (pentobarbital sodium) at bedtime.
Sedative—
Daytime—Oral, 20 mg (pentobarbital sodium) three or four times a day.

Note: Geriatric and debilitated patients may react to usual doses with excitement, confusion, or mental depression. Lower doses may be required in these patients.

Usual pediatric dose

Sedative-hypnotic—
- Hypnotic—
  - Dosage must be individualized by physician.
- Sedative—
  - Daytime—Oral, 2 to 6 mg (pentobarbital sodium) per kg of body weight per day.
  - Preoperative—Oral, 2 to 6 mg (pentobarbital sodium) per kg of body weight, up to a maximum of 100 mg per dose.

Strength(s) usually available

U.S.—
- 20 mg of pentobarbital sodium (18.2 mg of pentobarbital) per 5 mL (Rx) [*Nembutal* (alcohol 18%)].

Canada—
- Not commercially available.

Packaging and storage

Store below 40 °C (104 °F), preferably between 15 and 30 °C (59 and 86 °F), unless otherwise specified by manufacturer. Store in a tight container. Protect from freezing.

Auxiliary labeling

- Avoid alcoholic beverages.
- May cause drowsiness.
- Keep container tightly closed.

Note

Controlled substance in the U.S.

PENTOBARBITAL SODIUM CAPSULES USP

Usual adult dose

Sedative-hypnotic—
- Hypnotic: Oral, 100 mg at bedtime.
- Sedative: Preoperative—Oral, 100 mg.

Note: Geriatric and debilitated patients may react to usual doses with excitement, confusion, or mental depression. Lower doses may be required in these patients.

Usual pediatric dose

Sedative-hypnotic—
- Hypnotic: Dosage must be individualized by physician.
- Sedative: Preoperative—Oral, 2 to 6 mg per kg of body weight, up to a maximum of 100 mg per dose.

Strength(s) usually available

U.S.—
- 50 mg (Rx) [*Nembutal*; GENERIC].
- 100 mg (Rx) [*Nembutal* (tartrazine); GENERIC].

Canada—
- 100 mg (Rx) [*Nembutal* (tartrazine); *Novopentobarb*].

Packaging and storage

Store below 40 °C (104 °F), preferably between 15 and 30 °C (59 and 86 °F), unless otherwise specified by manufacturer. Store in a tight container.

Auxiliary labeling

- Avoid alcoholic beverages.
- May cause drowsiness.

Note

Controlled substance in the U.S. and Canada.

Parenteral Dosage Forms

PENTOBARBITAL SODIUM INJECTION USP

Usual adult dose

Sedative-hypnotic—
- Hypnotic—
  - Intramuscular, 150 to 200 mg.
  - Intravenous, 100 mg initially; after one minute, additional small doses may be administered at one-minute intervals, if necessary, up to a total of 500 mg.
- Sedative—
  - Preoperative—Intramuscular, 150 to 200 mg.

Anticonvulsant—
- Intravenous, 100 mg initially; after one minute, additional small doses may be administered at one-minute intervals, if necessary, up to a total of 500 mg.

Note: Geriatric and debilitated patients may react to usual doses with excitement, confusion, or mental depression. Lower doses may be required in these patients.

Usual pediatric dose

Sedative-hypnotic—
- Hypnotic—
  - Intramuscular, 2 to 6 mg per kg of body weight, up to a maximum of 100 mg per dose.
  - Intravenous, 50 mg initially; after one minute, additional small doses may be administered at one-minute intervals, if necessary, until desired effect is obtained.
- Sedative—
  - Preoperative—Intramuscular, 2 to 6 mg per kg of body weight, up to a maximum of 100 mg per dose.

Anticonvulsant—
- Intramuscular or intravenous, 50 mg initially; after one minute, additional small doses may be administered at one-minute intervals, if necessary, until desired effect is obtained.

Strength(s) usually available

U.S.—
- 50 mg per mL (Rx) [*Nembutal* (alcohol 10%; propylene glycol 40% v/v); GENERIC].

Canada—
- 50 mg per mL (Rx) [*Nembutal* (alcohol 10%; propylene glycol 40%)].

Packaging and storage

Store below 40 °C (104 °F), preferably between 15 and 30 °C (59 and 86 °F), unless otherwise specified by manufacturer. Protect from freezing.

Stability

Do not use if solution is discolored or contains a precipitate.

Note

Controlled substance in the U.S. and Canada.

Rectal Dosage Forms

PENTOBARBITAL SODIUM SUPPOSITORIES

Usual adult dose

Sedative-hypnotic—
- Hypnotic—
  - Rectal, 120 to 200 mg at bedtime.
- Sedative—
  - Daytime—Rectal, 30 mg two to four times a day.

Note: Geriatric and debilitated patients may react to usual doses with excitement, confusion, or mental depression. Lower doses may be required in these patients.

Usual pediatric dose

Sedative-hypnotic—
- Hypnotic—
  - Children up to 2 months of age: Dosage has not been established.
  - Children 2 months to 1 year of age (4.5 to 9 kg): Rectal, 30 mg.
  - Children 1 to 4 years of age (9 to 18 kg): Rectal, 30 or 60 mg.
  - Children 5 to 12 years of age (18 to 36 kg): Rectal, 60 mg.
  - Children 12 to 14 years of age (36 to 50 kg): Rectal, 60 or 120 mg.
- Sedative—
  - Daytime:
    - Rectal, 2 mg per kg of body weight or 60 mg per square meter of body surface three times a day.
  - Preoperative:
    - Children up to 2 months of age: Dosage has not been established.
    - Children 2 months to 1 year of age: Rectal, 30 mg.
    - Children 1 to 4 years of age: Rectal, 30 or 60 mg.
    - Children 5 to 12 years of age: Rectal, 60 mg.
    - Children 12 to 14 years of age: Rectal, 60 or 120 mg.

Strength(s) usually available

U.S.—
- 30 mg (Rx) [*Nembutal* (semisynthetic glycerides)].
- 60 mg (Rx) [*Nembutal* (semisynthetic glycerides)].
- 120 mg (Rx) [*Nembutal* (semisynthetic glycerides)].
- 200 mg (Rx) [*Nembutal* (semisynthetic glycerides)].

Canada—
- 25 mg (Rx) [*Nova Rectal* (in a polyethylene glycol base)].
- 50 mg (Rx) [*Nova Rectal* (in a polyethylene glycol base)].

Packaging and storage

Store between 2 and 15 °C (36 and 59 °F), in a well-closed container, unless otherwise specified by manufacturer.

Auxiliary labeling

- For rectal use only.
- Avoid alcoholic beverages.

- May cause drowsiness.
- Refrigerate.

Note
Controlled substance in the U.S. and Canada.

PHENOBARBITAL

Summary of Differences
Category:
Also indicated as an anticonvulsant.
Oral and parenteral phenobarbital also used as an antihyperbilirubinemic; and has been used as an antitremor agent, although generally has been replaced by benzodiazepines and beta-adrenergic blockers.

Pharmacology/pharmacokinetics:
Distribution—
Distributed less rapidly than other barbiturates because it has lowest lipid solubility.
Time to peak effect—
Maximal CNS depression may not occur for 15 minutes or more after intravenous administration.
Long-acting barbiturate—
Onset of action: 60 minutes or longer.
Duration of action: 10 to 12 hours.
Protein binding—
Low to moderate.

Patient consultation:
Compliance with therapy when used as an anticonvulsant.

Additional Dosing Information
See also *General Dosing Information.*
In epilepsy
- In children, higher-per-kg dosage of phenobarbital and most other anticonvulsants generally are required to achieve blood concentrations considered therapeutic.
- Several weeks of phenobarbital therapy may be required to achieve maximum antiepilepsy effects.
- Phenobarbital should be withdrawn slowly in order to avoid precipitating seizures or status epilepticus.
- When phenobarbital is replaced by another anticonvulsant, the dosage of phenobarbital should be maintained initially and then reduced gradually while, at the same time, the dosage of the replacement medication is increased gradually in order to maintain seizure control.
- When administered intravenously, phenobarbital sodium may require 15 minutes or more to attain peak concentrations in the brain; therefore, it is important to use the minimal dosage required and to wait for the anticonvulsant effect to develop before administering a second dose, in order to avoid the possibility of severe barbiturate-induced depression.

For parenteral dosage forms only
Sterile phenobarbital sodium may be administered subcutaneously after reconstitution, but phenobarbital sodium injection is not recommended for subcutaneous use.

The rate of the intravenous injection should not exceed 60 mg per minute. Faster rates of administration may cause serious respiratory depression.

Following intravenous administration, up to 30 minutes may be required for maximum effect.

Bioequivalence information
For phenobarbital tablets—
Bioavailability differences between generic products from different manufacturers have been reported in the past. However, no controlled studies systematically comparing the large number of tablets commercially available from different manufacturers have been conducted. In two studies published in 1979 and 1984 comparing phenobarbital tablets from different manufacturers in male volunteers, there were no significant differences in mean peak plasma concentrations (C_{max}) or relative area under the plasma concentration-time curve (AUC); however, statistically significant delays in reaching time of peak concentration (t_{max}) were demonstrated among products. In response to the potential problem of bio-inequivalence, official dissolution standards were changed, and problems have not been documented in the years following establishment of these standards. The current standard excludes slow-dissolving tablets.

Oral Dosage Forms
Note: Bracketed uses in the *Dosage Forms* section refer to categories of use and/or indications that are not included in U.S. product labeling.

PHENOBARBITAL CAPSULES

Usual adult dose
Anticonvulsant—
Oral, 60 to 250 mg (base) per day, as a single dose or in divided doses.
Sedative-hypnotic—
Hypnotic: Oral, 100 to 320 mg (base) at bedtime.
Sedative: Daytime—Oral, 30 to 120 mg (base) in two or three divided doses a day.
[Antihyperbilirubinemic][1]—
Oral, 30 to 60 mg (base) three times a day.

Note: Geriatric and debilitated patients may react to usual doses with excitement, confusion, or mental depression. Lower doses may be required in these patients.

Usual pediatric dose
Anticonvulsant—
Oral, 1 to 6 mg (base) per kg of body weight per day, as a single dose or in divided doses.
Sedative-hypnotic—
Hypnotic—
Dosage must be individualized by physician.
Sedative—
Daytime—Oral, 2 mg (base) per kg of body weight or 60 mg per square meter of body surface three times a day.
Preoperative—Oral, 1 to 3 mg (base) per kg of body weight.
[Antihyperbilirubinemic][1]—
Neonates: Oral, 5 to 10 mg (base) per kg of body weight per day for the first few days after birth.
Children up to 12 years of age: Oral, 1 to 4 mg (base) per kg of body weight three times a day.

Strength(s) usually available
U.S.—
15 mg (Rx) [*Solfoton*].
Canada—
Not commercially available.

Packaging and storage
Store below 40 °C (104 °F), preferably between 15 and 30 °C (59 and 86 °F), in a well-closed container, unless otherwise specified by manufacturer.

Auxiliary labeling
- Avoid alcoholic beverages.
- May cause drowsiness.

Note
Controlled substance in the U.S.

PHENOBARBITAL ELIXIR USP

Usual adult dose
See *Phenobarbital Capsules.*

Usual pediatric dose
See *Phenobarbital Capsules.*

Strength(s) usually available
U.S.—
20 mg per 5 mL (Rx) [GENERIC].
Canada—
20 mg per 5 mL (Rx) [*Ancalixir*].

Packaging and storage
Store below 40 °C (104 °F), preferably between 15 and 30 °C (59 and 86 °F), unless otherwise specified by manufacturer. Store in a tight, light-resistant container. Protect from freezing.

Auxiliary labeling
- Avoid alcoholic beverages.
- May cause drowsiness.
- Keep container tightly closed.

Note
Controlled substance in the U.S. and Canada.

PHENOBARBITAL TABLETS USP
Note: Bioavailability differences between products from different manufacturers have been reported in the past. However, no controlled studies systematically comparing the large number of tablets commercially available from different manufacturers have been conducted. In two studies published in 1979 and 1984 comparing phe-

nobarbital tablets from different manufacturers in male volunteers, there were no significant differences in mean peak plasma concentrations (C_{max}) or relative area under the plasma concentration-time curve (AUC); however, statistically significant delays in reaching time of peak concentration (T_{max}) were demonstrated among products. In response to the potential problem of bio-inequivalence, official dissolution standards were changed, and problems have not been documented in the years following establishment of these standards. The current standard excludes slow-dissolving tablets.

Usual adult dose
See *Phenobarbital Capsules*.

Usual pediatric dose
See *Phenobarbital Capsules*.

Strength(s) usually available
U.S.—
8 mg (Rx) [GENERIC].
15 mg (Rx) [*Barbita; Solfoton;* GENERIC].
30 mg (Rx) [GENERIC].
60 mg (Rx) [GENERIC].
100 mg (Rx) [GENERIC].
Canada—
15 mg (Rx) [GENERIC].
30 mg (Rx) [GENERIC].
60 mg (Rx) [GENERIC].
100 mg (Rx) [GENERIC].

Packaging and storage
Store below 40 °C (104 °F), preferably between 15 and 30 °C (59 and 86 °F), unless otherwise specified by manufacturer. Store in a well-closed container.

Auxiliary labeling
- Avoid alcoholic beverages.
- May cause drowsiness.

Note
Controlled substance in the U.S. and Canada.

Parenteral Dosage Forms

Note: Bracketed uses in the *Dosage Forms* section refer to categories of use and/or indications that are not included in U.S. product labeling.

PHENOBARBITAL SODIUM INJECTION USP

Usual adult dose
Anticonvulsant—
Intravenous, 100 to 320 mg, repeated if necessary up to a total dose of 600 mg during a twenty-four-hour period.
Status epilepticus: Intravenous (slow), 10 to 20 mg per kg of body weight, repeated if necessary.
Sedative-hypnotic—
Hypnotic—
Intramuscular or intravenous, 100 to 325 mg.
Sedative—
Daytime—Intramuscular or intravenous, 30 to 120 mg a day in two or three divided doses.
Preoperative—Intramuscular, 130 to 200 mg sixty to ninety minutes before surgery.

Note: Geriatric and debilitated patients may react to usual doses with excitement, confusion, or mental depression. Lower doses may be required in these patients.

Usual pediatric dose
Anticonvulsant—
Initial: Intravenous, 10 to 20 mg per kg of body weight as a single loading dose.
Maintenance: Intravenous, 1 to 6 mg per kg of body weight per day.
Status epilepticus: Intravenous, 15 to 20 mg per kg of body weight, administered over a period of ten to fifteen minutes.
Sedative-hypnotic—
Hypnotic: Dosage must be individualized.
Sedative: Preoperative—Intramuscular or intravenous, 1 to 3 mg per kg of body weight, sixty to ninety minutes prior to surgery.
[Antihyperbilirubinemic][1]—
Intramuscular, 5 to 10 mg per kg of body weight per day for the first few days after birth.

Strength(s) usually available
U.S.—
30 mg per mL (Rx) [GENERIC].
60 mg per mL (Rx) [GENERIC].
65 mg per mL (Rx) [GENERIC].
130 mg per mL (Rx) [*Luminal* (alcohol 10%; propylene glycol 67.8% by volume); GENERIC].
Canada—
30 mg per mL (Rx) [GENERIC].
120 mg per mL (Rx) [GENERIC].

Packaging and storage
Store below 40 °C (104 °F), preferably between 15 and 30 °C (59 and 86 °F), unless otherwise specified by manufacturer. Protect from freezing.

Stability
Do not use if solution is discolored or contains a precipitate.

Note
Controlled substance in the U.S. and Canada.

PHENOBARBITAL SODIUM STERILE USP

Usual adult dose
Anticonvulsant—
Intravenous, 100 to 320 mg, repeated if necessary up to a total dose of 600 mg during a twenty-four-hour period.
Status epilepticus: Intravenous (slow), 10 to 20 mg per kg of body weight, repeated if necessary.
Sedative-hypnotic—
Hypnotic—
Intramuscular, intravenous, or subcutaneous, 100 to 325 mg.
Sedative—
Daytime—Intramuscular, intravenous, or subcutaneous, 30 to 120 mg a day in two or three divided doses.
Preoperative—Intramuscular, 130 to 200 mg sixty to ninety minutes before surgery.

Note: Geriatric and debilitated patients may react to usual doses of barbiturates with excitement, confusion, or mental depression. Lower doses may be required in these patients.

Usual pediatric dose
Anticonvulsant—
Initial: Intravenous, 10 to 20 mg per kg of body weight as a single loading dose.
Maintenance: Intravenous, 1 to 6 mg per kg of body weight per day.
Status epilepticus: Intravenous, 15 to 20 mg per kg of body weight, administered over a period of ten to fifteen minutes.
Sedative-hypnotic—
Hypnotic: Dosage must be individualized.
Sedative: Preoperative—Intramuscular, 1 to 3 mg per kg of body weight.
[Antihyperbilirubinemic][1]—
Intramuscular, 5 to 10 mg per kg of body weight per day for the first few days after birth.

Strength(s) usually available
U.S.—
120 mg (Rx) [GENERIC].
Canada—
Not commercially available.

Packaging and storage
Prior to reconstitution, store below 40 °C (104 °F), preferably between 15 and 30 °C (59 and 86 °F), unless otherwise specified by manufacturer.

Preparation of dosage form
Solutions of phenobarbital sodium for subcutaneous or intramuscular injection may be prepared by dissolving 120 mg of anhydrous phenobarbital sodium powder in 1 mL of sterile water for injection. For intravenous use, 120 mg of anhydrous phenobarbital sodium powder should be dissolved in 3 mL of sterile water for injection. When solutions are prepared, the sterile water for injection should be introduced slowly into the vial by means of a sterile syringe. Several minutes may be required for the medication to dissolve completely; solution should not be injected if it has not become clear after 5 minutes.

Stability
After reconstitution, solution should be used within thirty minutes since phenobarbital hydrolyzes in solution or upon exposure to air. Solution should not be used if it does not become absolutely clear within 5 minutes after reconstitution or if a precipitate forms after the solution clears.

Note
Controlled substance in the U.S.

[1]Not included in Canadian product labeling.

SECOBARBITAL

Summary of Differences

Category:
Parenteral secobarbital also may be indicated as an anticonvulsant (in tetanus).

Pharmacology/pharmacokinetics:
Distribution—
Distributed more rapidly than other barbiturates because it has highest lipid solubility.
Short-acting barbiturate—
Onset of action: 10 to 15 minutes.
Duration of action: 3 to 4 hours.
Protein binding—
Moderate to high.

Additional Dosing Information

See also *General Dosing Information.*

For parenteral dosage forms only

The rate of the intravenous injection should not exceed 50 mg per 15-second period. Faster rates of administration may cause respiratory depression or apnea, laryngospasm, or vasodilation with fall in blood pressure.

For rectal dosage forms only

To prepare a solution for rectal administration, dilute the commercially available 5% secobarbital sodium injection with lukewarm tap water to a concentration of 10 to 15 mg per mL (1 to 1.5%).

Oral Dosage Forms

SECOBARBITAL SODIUM CAPSULES USP

Usual adult dose

Sedative-hypnotic—
Hypnotic—
Oral, 100 mg at bedtime.
Sedative—
Daytime—Oral, 30 to 50 mg three or four times a day.
Preoperative—Oral, 200 to 300 mg one to two hours before surgery.

Note: Geriatric and debilitated patients may react to usual doses with excitement, confusion, or mental depression. Lower doses may be required in these patients.

Usual pediatric dose

Sedative-hypnotic—
Sedative—
Daytime—Oral, 2 mg per kg of body weight or 60 mg per square meter of body surface three times a day.
Preoperative—Oral, 2 to 6 mg per kg of body weight, up to a maximum of 100 mg per dose, one to two hours before surgery.

Strength(s) usually available

U.S.—
100 mg (Rx) [*Seconal;* GENERIC].
Canada—
50 mg (Rx) [*Seconal*].
100 mg (Rx) [*Novosecobarb; Seconal*].

Packaging and storage

Store below 40 °C (104 °F), preferably between 15 and 30 °C (59 and 86 °F), unless otherwise specified by manufacturer. Store in a tight container.

Auxiliary labeling

- Avoid alcoholic beverages.
- May cause drowsiness.

Note

Controlled substance in the U.S. and Canada.

Parenteral Dosage Forms

SECOBARBITAL SODIUM INJECTION USP

Usual adult dose

Sedative-hypnotic—
Hypnotic—
Intramuscular, 100 to 200 mg.
Intravenous, 50 to 250 mg.
Sedative—
Dentistry—Intramuscular, 1.1 to 2.2 mg per kg of body weight ten to fifteen minutes before procedure.
Nerve block—Intravenous, 100 to 150 mg.
Anticonvulsant (in tetanus)—
Intramuscular or intravenous, 5.5 mg per kg of body weight, repeated every three to four hours as needed.

Note: Geriatric and debilitated patients may react to usual doses of barbiturates with excitement, confusion, or mental depression. Lower doses may be required in these patients.

Usual pediatric dose

Sedative-hypnotic—
Hypnotic—
Intramuscular:
3 to 5 mg per kg of body weight or 125 mg per square meter of body surface, up to a maximum of 100 mg per dose.
Rectal, the following doses as a 1 to 1.5% solution:
Children weighing up to 40 kg: 5 mg per kg of body weight.
Children weighing 40 kg and over: 4 mg per kg of body weight.
Sedative—
Preoperative:
Intramuscular, 4 to 5 mg per kg of body weight.
Anticonvulsant (in tetanus)—
Intramuscular or intravenous, 3 to 5 mg per kg of body weight or 125 mg per square meter of body surface per dose.

Strength(s) usually available

U.S.—
50 mg per mL (Rx) [GENERIC].
Canada—
Not commercially available.

Packaging and storage

Store between 2 and 8 °C (36 and 46 °F). Protect from light.

Preparation of dosage form

Secobarbital sodium injection may be administered in a concentration of 50 mg per mL or it may be diluted with sterile water for injection, 0.9% sodium chloride injection, or Ringer's injection.

Stability

Do not use if solution is discolored or contains a precipitate.

Note

Controlled substance in the U.S.

SECOBARBITAL AND AMOBARBITAL

Oral Dosage Forms

SECOBARBITAL SODIUM AND AMOBARBITAL SODIUM CAPSULES USP

Usual adult dose

Sedative-hypnotic—
Oral, 1 capsule at bedtime or one hour preoperatively.

Note: Geriatric and debilitated patients may react to usual doses with excitement, confusion, or mental depression. Lower doses may be required in these patients.

Usual pediatric dose

Dosage has not been established.

Strength(s) usually available

U.S.—
50 mg of secobarbital and 50 mg of amobarbital (Rx) [*Tuinal*].
100 mg of secobarbital and 100 mg of amobarbital (Rx) [*Tuinal*].
Canada—
50 mg of secobarbital and 50 mg of amobarbital (Rx) [*Tuinal*].
100 mg of secobarbital and 100 mg of amobarbital (Rx) [*Tuinal*].

Packaging and storage

Store below 40 °C (104 °F), preferably between 15 and 30 °C (59 and 86 °F), unless otherwise specified by manufacturer. Store in a well-closed container.

Auxiliary labeling

- Avoid alcoholic beverages.
- May cause drowsiness.

Note

Controlled substance in the U.S. and Canada.

Revised: 08/15/1995

Table 1. Pharmacology/Pharmacokinetics

Drug	Protein Binding* (%)	Half-life (hr)		Onset of Action† (min)	Duration of Action‡ (hr)	Elimination/% Excreted Unchanged§
		Range	Mean			
Long-acting				60 or longer	10–12	
Mephobarbital#		11–67	34			Renal
Metharbital						Renal/2%; 20% excreted as barbital
Phenobarbital	Low to Moderate (20–45)	53–118**	79			Renal/25–50%
Intermediate-acting				45–60	6–8	
Amobarbital	Moderate (61)	16–40	25			Renal/<1%
Aprobarbital	Low (20)	14–34	24			Renal/25–50%
Butabarbital	Low (26)	34–42	††			Renal/<1%
Short-acting				10–15	3–4	
Pentobarbital	Moderate to High (60–70)	15–50	‡‡			Renal/<1%
Secobarbital	Moderate to High (46–70)	15–40	28			Renal/5%

*Bound to plasma and tissue proteins to a varying degree; binding increases proportionate to lipid solubility

†Following oral administration. Phenobarbital has the slowest, and secobarbital the fastest, onset of action

‡Following oral administration. Duration of action is related to the rate at which the barbiturates are redistributed throughout the body and is variable among individuals and in the same individual from time to time. Phenobarbital has the longest, and secobarbital the shortest, duration of action

§Metabolic products are excreted in the urine and, less commonly, in the feces. Inactive metabolites are excreted as conjugates of glucuronic acid. Peritoneal dialysis and hemodialysis remove phenobarbital from the body; serum phenobarbital concentrations should be determined during and after peritoneal dialysis and hemodialysis

#Activity due mostly to accumulation of phenobarbital

**Half-life is 60 to 180 hours in children (half-life 48 hours or less for newborns)

††One manufacturer states that the half-life of butabarbital is 100 hours

‡‡Dose-dependent; the mean half-life of elimination is 50 and 22 hours following a 50- and 100-mg dose, respectively

Table 2. General Dosing Information

Drug	Onset/Duration of Action	Barbiturate Blood Concentrations (mcg/mL) Categories of Degree of CNS Depression*				
		(1)	(2)	(3)	(4)	(5)
Pentobarbital	Fast/short	≤2	0.5–3	10–15	12–25	15–40
Secobarbital	Fast/short	≤2	0.5–5	10–15	15–25	15–40
Amobarbital	Intermediate/intermediate	≤3	2–10	30–40	30–60	40–80
Butabarbital	Intermediate/intermediate	≤5	3–25	40–60	50–80	60–100
Phenobarbital	Slow/long	≤10	5–40	50–80	70–120	100–200

*Categories of degree of CNS depression in nontolerant persons:

(1) Under the influence and appreciably impaired for purposes of driving a motor vehicle or performing tasks requiring alertness and unimpaired judgment and reaction time.
(2) Sedated, therapeutic range, calm, relaxed, and easily aroused.
(3) Comatose, difficult to arouse, and significant respiratory depression.
(4) Comparable with death in aged or ill persons or in presence of obstructed airway, other toxic agents, or exposure to cold.
(5) Usual lethal concentration, the upper end of the range includes those who received some supportive treatment

BECLOMETHASONE—See *Corticosteroids (Inhalation-Local), Corticosteroids (Nasal), Corticosteroids (Topical)*

BELLADONNA—See *Anticholinergics/Antispasmodics (Systemic)*

BELLADONNA ALKALOIDS AND BARBITURATES Systemic

This monograph includes information on the following: 1) Atropine, Hyoscyamine, Scopolamine, and Phenobarbital; 2) Atropine and Phenobarbital; 3) Belladonna and Butabarbital.

VA CLASSIFICATION (Primary): GA802

Note: Atropine, Hyoscyamine, Scopolamine, and Phenobarbital combination and Hyoscyamine, Scopolamine, and Phenobarbital combination are controlled substances in Canada.

Commonly used brand name(s): *Antrocol[2]; Barbidonna[1]; Barbidonna No. 2[1]; Barophen[1]; Bellalphen[1]; Butibel[3]; Donnamor[1]; Donnapine[1]; Donnatal[1]; Donnatal Extentabs[1]; Donnatal No. 2[1]; Donphen[1]; Hyosophen[1]; Kinesed[1]; Malatal[1]; Relaxadon[1]; Spaslin[1]; Spasmolin[1]; Spasmophen[1]; Spasquid[1]; Susano[1].*

NOTE: The *Belladonna Alkaloids and Barbiturates (Systemic)* monograph is maintained on the *USP DI* electronic data base. A copy of the most recent revision of the complete monograph can be accessed on the *USP DI* Updates Online website. See the front cover of book for details on accessing the site.

For information on the specific components of this combination, see the *USP DI* monographs for *Anticholinergics/Antispasmodics (Systemic)* and *Barbiturates (Systemic)*.

The information that follows is selectively abstracted from the complete monograph and is provided to facilitate drug use review and patient counseling.

Note: For a listing of dosage forms and brand names by country availability, see *Dosage Forms* section(s).

Category

Anticholinergic-sedative.

Indications

Accepted

Ulcer, peptic (treatment adjunct) or

Bowel syndrome, irritable (treatment adjunct)—FDA has classified these medications as possibly effective for use as adjunctive therapy in the treatment of peptic ulcer and irritable bowel syndrome (irritable colon, spastic colon, mucous colitis).

Note: Less than effective classification requires the submission of adequate and well-controlled studies in order to provide substantial evidence of effectiveness. In the past, FDA has notified manufacturers of the possible withdrawal from the market of products containing a combination of an anticholinergic and a sedative because their efficacy as fixed combinations had not been proven in adequately designed clinical trials. To date, no final action has been taken.

Unaccepted

Anticholinergic and sedative combinations have been used as adjuncts in the treatment of acute enterocolitis; however, their use for this condition is controversial since they cause a reduction in gastrointestinal motility resulting in retention of the causative organism or toxin and the consequent prolongation of symptoms.

Patient Consultation

As an aid to patient consultation, refer to *Advice for the Patient, Belladonna Alkaloids and Barbiturates (Systemic)*.

In providing consultation, consider emphasizing the following selected information (» = major clinical significance):

Before using this medication

» Conditions affecting use, especially:
- Sensitivity to any of the belladonna alkaloids or barbiturates
- Pregnancy—Use not recommended because belladonna alkaloids and barbiturates cross placenta; barbiturates may cause fetal abnormalities; phenobarbital may cause neonatal hemorrhage
- Breast-feeding—Distributed into breast milk; possible inhibition of lactation
- Use in children—Increased susceptibility to toxic effects of anticholinergics; increased response in infants and children with spastic paralysis or brain damage; risk of increased body temperature in hot weather; hyperexcitability (paradoxical reaction); hyperkinesis may be induced in hypersensitive children
- Use in the elderly—Increased susceptibility to mental and other toxic effects of anticholinergics and barbiturates; danger of precipitating undiagnosed glaucoma; possible impairment of memory
- Dental—Possible development of dental problems because of decreased salivary flow
- Other medications, especially adrenocorticoids or corticotropin, other anticholinergics, antacids, anticoagulants, antidiarrheals, ketoconazole, CNS depressants, MAO inhibitors, or potassium chloride
- Other medical problems, especially gastrointestinal obstructive disease, glaucoma, hepatic function impairment, renal function impairment, or urinary retention

Proper use of this medication

Taking dose 30 to 60 minutes before meals unless otherwise directed by physician

» Importance of not taking more medication than the amount prescribed

» Proper dosing

Missed dose: Taking as soon as possible; not taking if almost time for next dose; not doubling doses

» Proper storage

Precautions while using this medication

» Avoiding use of alcohol or other CNS depressants

Not taking antacids and antidiarrheal medications within 1 hour of taking this medication

» Caution during exercise and hot weather; overheating may result in heat stroke

Possible increased sensitivity of eyes to light

» Caution if drowsiness or blurred vision occurs

Possible dryness of mouth, nose, and throat; using sugarless candy or gum, ice, or saliva substitute for relief; checking with physician or dentist if dry mouth continues for more than 2 weeks

Side/adverse effects

Signs of potential side effects, especially agranulocytosis, allergic reaction, hepatitis, increased intraocular pressure, and thrombocytopenia

ATROPINE, HYOSCYAMINE, SCOPOLAMINE, AND PHENOBARBITAL

Oral Dosage Forms

ATROPINE SULFATE, HYOSCYAMINE SULFATE (or HYOSCYAMINE HYDROBROMIDE), SCOPOLAMINE HYDROBROMIDE, AND PHENOBARBITAL CAPSULES

Usual adult and adolescent dose

Anticholinergic-sedative—

Oral, 1 or 2 capsules two to four times a day, the dosage being adjusted as needed and tolerated.

Usual pediatric dose

Dosage must be individualized by physician.

Usual geriatric dose

See *Usual adult and adolescent dose.*

Note: Geriatric patients may be more sensitive to the effects of the usual adult dose.

Strength(s) usually available

U.S.—

Note: Strengths of individual components may vary slightly among products of different manufacturers.

19.4 mcg (0.0194 mg) of atropine sulfate, 104 mcg (0.104 mg) of hyoscyamine sulfate (or hydrobromide), 6.5 mcg (0.0065 mg) of scopolamine hydrobromide, and 16 mg of phenobarbital (Rx) [*Donnatal* (lactose); *Hyosophen*].

Canada—

Not commercially available.

Auxiliary labeling

- May cause drowsiness.
- Avoid alcoholic beverages.

ATROPINE SULFATE, HYOSCYAMINE SULFATE (or HYOSCYAMINE HYDROBROMIDE), SCOPOLAMINE HYDROBROMIDE, AND PHENOBARBITAL ELIXIR

Usual adult and adolescent dose

Anticholinergic-sedative—

Oral, 5 to 10 mL three or four times a day, the dosage being adjusted as needed and tolerated.

Usual pediatric dose

Anticholinergic-sedative—

Children 4.5 to 9 kg of body weight: Oral, 0.5 to 0.75 mL every four to six hours.

Children 9 to 13.5 kg of body weight: Oral, 1.0 to 1.5 mL every four to six hours.

Children 13.5 to 22.5 kg of body weight: Oral, 1.5 to 2 mL every four to six hours.

Children 22.5 to 36.5 kg of body weight: Oral, 2.5 to 3.75 mL every four to six hours.

Children 36.5 to 45.4 kg of body weight: Oral, 3.75 to 5 mL every four to six hours.

Children 45.4 kg of body weight and over: Oral, 5 to 7.5 mL every four to six hours.

Note: Dosage must be adjusted for each patient as needed and tolerated.

Usual geriatric dose

See *Usual adult and adolescent dose.*

Note: Geriatric patients may be more sensitive to the effects of the usual adult dose.

Strength(s) usually available

U.S.—

Note: Contain 23% alcohol.

19.4 mcg (0.0194 mg) of atropine sulfate, 103.7 mcg (0.1037 mg) of hyoscyamine sulfate (or hydrobromide), 6.5 mcg (0.0065 mg) of scopolamine hydrobromide, and 16 mg of phenobarbital, per 5 ml (Rx) [*Barophen; Donnamor; Donnapine; Donnatal; Hyosophen; Spasmophen; Spasquid; Susano*].

34 mcg (0.034 mg) of atropine sulfate, 174 mcg (0.174 mg) of hyoscyamine sulfate (or hydrobromide), 10 mcg (0.01 mg) of scopolamine hydrobromide, and 21.6 mg of phenobarbital, per 5 mL (Rx) [*Barbidonna* (alcohol 15%)].

Canada—

Note: Strengths of individual components may vary slightly among products of different manufacturers.

19 mcg (0.019 mg) of atropine sulfate, 104 mcg (0.104 mg) of hyoscyamine sulfate, 7 mcg (0.007 mg) of scopolamine hydrobromide, and 16.2 mg of phenobarbital, per 5 ml (Rx) [*Donnatal* (alcohol 23%)].

Auxiliary labeling
- May cause drowsiness.
- Avoid alcoholic beverages.
- Keep container tightly closed.

ATROPINE SULFATE, HYOSCYAMINE SULFATE (or HYOSCYAMINE HYDROBROMIDE), SCOPOLAMINE HYDROBROMIDE, AND PHENOBARBITAL TABLETS

Usual adult and adolescent dose
Anticholinergic-sedative—
Oral, 1 or 2 tablets two to four times a day, the dosage being adjusted as needed and tolerated.

Usual pediatric dose
Dosage must be individualized by physician.

Usual geriatric dose
See *Usual adult and adolescent dose.*

Note: Geriatric patients may be more sensitive to the effects of the usual adult dose.

Strength(s) usually available
U.S.—
19.4 mcg (0.0194 mg) of atropine sulfate, 104 mcg (0.104 mg) of hyoscyamine sulfate (or hydrobromide), 6.5 mcg (0.0065 mg) of scopolamine hydrobromide, and 16 mg of phenobarbital (Rx) [*Bellalphen; Donnapine; Donnatal; Malatal; Relaxadon; Spaslin; Spasmolin; Susano;* GENERIC].
19.4 mcg (0.0194) of atropine sulfate, 104 mcg (0.104 mg) of hyoscyamine sulfate, 6.5 mcg (0.0065 mg) of scopolamine hydrobromide, and 32 mg of phenobarbital (Rx) [*Donnatal No. 2*].
20 mcg (0.02 mg) of atropine sulfate, 100 mcg (0.1 mg) of hyoscyamine sulfate (or hydrobromide), 6.0 mcg (0.006 mg) of scopolamine hydrobromide, and 15 mg of phenobarbital (Rx) [*Donphen; Spasmophen*].
25 mcg (0.025 mg) of atropine sulfate, 128.6 mcg (0.1286 mg) of hyoscyamine sulfate (or hydrobromide), 7.4 mcg (0.0074 mg) of scopolamine hydrobromide, and 16 mg of phenobarbital (Rx) [*Barbidonna*].
25 mcg (0.025 mg) of atropine sulfate, 128.6 mcg (0.1286 mg) of hyoscyamine sulfate (or hydrobromide), 7.4 mcg (0.0074 mg) of scopolamine hydrobromide, and 32 mg of phenobarbital (Rx) [*Barbidonna No. 2*].
Canada—
Note: Strengths of individual components may vary slightly among products of different manufacturers.
19 mcg (0.019 mg) of atropine sulfate, 104 mcg (0.104 mg) of hyoscyamine sulfate, 7 mcg (0.007 mg) of scopolamine hydrobromide, and 16.2 mg of phenobarbital (Rx) [*Donnatal*].

Auxiliary labeling
- May cause drowsiness.
- Avoid alcoholic beverages.

ATROPINE SULFATE, HYOSCYAMINE SULFATE, SCOPOLAMINE HYDROBROMIDE, AND PHENOBARBITAL CHEWABLE TABLETS

Usual adult and adolescent dose
Anticholinergic-sedative—
Oral, 1 or 2 tablets three or four times a day, the dosage being adjusted as needed and tolerated.

Usual pediatric dose
Anticholinergic-sedative—
Children up to 2 years of age: Use is not recommended.
Children 2 to 12 years of age: Oral, ½ to 1 tablet three or four times a day, the dosage being adjusted as needed and tolerated.

Usual geriatric dose
See *Usual adult and adolescent dose.*

Note: Geriatric patients may be more sensitive to the effects of the usual adult dose.

Strength(s) usually available
U.S.—
120 mcg (0.12 mg) of atropine sulfate, 120 mcg (0.12 mg) of hyoscyamine sulfate, 7 mcg (0.007 mg) of scopolamine hydrobromide, and 16 mg of phenobarbital (Rx) [*Kinesed*].
Canada—
Not commercially available.

Auxiliary labeling
- May be chewed or swallowed with liquids.
- May cause drowsiness.
- Avoid alcoholic beverages.

ATROPINE SULFATE, HYOSCYAMINE SULFATE, SCOPOLAMINE HYDROBROMIDE, AND PHENOBARBITAL EXTENDED-RELEASE TABLETS

Usual adult and adolescent dose
Anticholinergic-sedative—
Oral, 1 tablet every eight to twelve hours, the dosage being adjusted as needed and tolerated.

Usual pediatric dose
Use is not recommended.

Usual geriatric dose
See *Usual adult and adolescent dose.*

Note: Geriatric patients may be more sensitive to the effects of the usual adult dose.

Strength(s) usually available
U.S.—
58.2 mcg (0.0582 mg) of atropine sulfate, 311.1 mcg (0.3111 mg) of hyoscyamine sulfate, 19.5 mcg (0.0195 mg) of scopolamine hydrobromide, and 48.6 mg of phenobarbital (Rx) [*Donnatal Extentabs*].
Canada—
58.2 mcg (0.0582 mg) of atropine sulfate, 311.1 mcg (0.3111 mg) of hyoscyamine sulfate, 19.5 mcg (0.0195 mg) of scopolamine hydrobromide, and 48.6 mg of phenobarbital (Rx) [*Donnatal Extentabs*].

Auxiliary labeling
- Swallow tablets whole.
- May cause drowsiness.
- Avoid alcoholic beverages.

ATROPINE AND PHENOBARBITAL

Oral Dosage Forms

ATROPINE SULFATE AND PHENOBARBITAL CAPSULES

Usual adult and adolescent dose
Anticholinergic-sedative—
Oral, 1 or 2 capsules two to four times a day, the dosage being adjusted as needed and tolerated.

Usual pediatric dose
Dosage must be individualized by physician.

Usual geriatric dose
See *Usual adult and adolescent dose.*

Note: Geriatric patients may be more sensitive to the effects of the usual adult dose.

Strength(s) usually available
U.S.—
195 mcg (0.195 mg) of atropine sulfate and 16 mg of phenobarbital (Rx) [*Antrocol*].
Canada—
Not commercially available.

Auxiliary labeling
- May cause drowsiness.
- Avoid alcoholic beverages.

ATROPINE SULFATE AND PHENOBARBITAL ELIXIR

Usual adult and adolescent dose
Anticholinergic-sedative—
Oral, 5 to 10 mL three or four times a day, the dosage being adjusted as needed and tolerated.

Usual pediatric dose
Anticholinergic-sedative—
Children 7 to 14 kg of body weight: Oral, 0.5 to 1 mL every four to six hours.
Children 14 to 21 kg of body weight: Oral, 1 to 1.5 mL every four to six hours.
Children 21 to 28 kg of body weight: Oral, 1.5 to 2 mL every four to six hours.
Children 28 to 35 kg of body weight: Oral, 2 to 2.5 mL every four to six hours.

Children 41 kg of body weight and over: Oral, 3 mL every four to six hours.

Note: Dosage must be adjusted for each patient as needed and tolerated.

Usual geriatric dose
See *Usual adult and adolescent dose.*

Note: Geriatric patients may be more sensitive to the effects of the usual adult dose.

Strength(s) usually available
U.S.—
195 mcg (0.195 mg) of atropine sulfate and 16 mg of phenobarbital, per 5 mL (Rx) [*Antrocol* (alcohol 20%)].
Canada—
Not commercially available.

Auxiliary labeling
- May cause drowsiness.
- Avoid alcoholic beverages.
- Keep container tightly closed.

ATROPINE SULFATE AND PHENOBARBITAL TABLETS

Usual adult and adolescent dose
Anticholinergic-sedative—
Oral, 1 or 2 tablets three or four times a day, the dosage being adjusted as needed and tolerated.

Usual pediatric dose
Dosage must be individualized by physician.

Usual geriatric dose
See *Usual adult and adolescent dose.*

Note: Geriatric patients may be more sensitive to the effects of the usual adult dose.

Strength(s) usually available
U.S.—
195 mcg (0.195 mg) of atropine sulfate and 16 mg of phenobarbital (Rx) [*Antrocol*].
Canada—
Not commercially available.

Auxiliary labeling
- May cause drowsiness.
- Avoid alcoholic beverages.

BELLADONNA AND BUTABARBITAL

Oral Dosage Forms

BELLADONNA EXTRACT AND BUTABARBITAL SODIUM ELIXIR

Usual adult and adolescent dose
Anticholinergic-sedative—
Oral, 5 to 10 mL three or four times a day, the dosage being adjusted as needed and tolerated.

Usual pediatric dose
Anticholinergic-sedative—
Children up to 6 years of age: Oral, 1.25 to 2.5 mL three or four times a day, the dosage being adjusted as needed and tolerated.
Children 6 to 12 years of age: Oral, 2.5 to 5 mL three or four times a day, the dosage being adjusted as needed and tolerated.

Usual geriatric dose
See *Usual adult and adolescent dose.*

Note: Geriatric patients may be more sensitive to the effects of the usual adult dose.

Strength(s) usually available
U.S.—
15 mg of belladonna extract and 15 mg of butabarbital sodium, per 5 mL (Rx) [*Butibel* (alcohol 7%)].
Canada—
Not commercially available.

Auxiliary labeling
- May cause drowsiness.
- Avoid alcoholic beverages.
- Keep container tightly closed.

BELLADONNA EXTRACT AND BUTABARBITAL SODIUM TABLETS

Usual adult and adolescent dose
Anticholinergic-sedative—
Oral, 1 or 2 tablets three or four times a day, the dosage being adjusted as needed and tolerated.

Usual pediatric dose
Dosage must be individualized by physician.

Usual geriatric dose
See *Usual adult and adolescent dose.*

Note: Geriatric patients may be more sensitive to the effects of the usual adult dose.

Strength(s) usually available
U.S.—
15 mg of belladonna extract and 15 mg of butabarbital sodium (Rx) [*Butibel*].
Canada—
Not commercially available.

Auxiliary labeling
- May cause drowsiness.
- Avoid alcoholic beverages.

Revised: 08/09/2000

BENAZEPRIL—See *Angiotensin-converting Enzyme (ACE) Inhibitors (Systemic)*

BENDROFLUMETHIAZIDE—See *Diuretics, Thiazide (Systemic)*

BENZALKONIUM CHLORIDE—See *Spermacides (Vaginal)*

BENZOCAINE—See *Anesthetics (Mucosal-Local), Anesthetics (Topical)*

BENZOCAINE AND MENTHOL—See *Anesthetics (Topical)*

BENZODIAZEPINES Systemic

This monograph includes information on the following: 1) Alprazolam; 2) Bromazepam*; 3) Chlordiazepoxide; 4) Clobazam*; 5) Clonazepam; 6) Clorazepate; 7) Diazepam; 8) Estazolam†; 9) Flurazepam; 10) Halazepam†; 11) Ketazolam†; 12) Lorazepam; 13) Nitrazepam*; 14) Oxazepam; 15) Prazepam†; 16) Quazepam†; 17) Temazepam; 18) Triazolam.

VA CLASSIFICATION (Primary/Secondary):
Alprazolam
Oral—CN302
Bromazepam
Oral—CN302
Chlordiazepoxide
Oral—CN302
Chlordiazepoxide
Parenteral—CN302
Clobazam
Oral—CN400
Clonazepam
Oral—CN302/CN400
Clorazepate
Oral—CN302/CN400
Diazepam
Oral—CN302/CN400; MS200
Diazepam
Parenteral—CN302/CN400; MS200
Diazepam
Rectal—CN400

Estazolam
Oral—CN302
Flurazepam
Oral—CN302
Halazepam
Oral—CN302
Ketazolam
Oral—CN302
Lorazepam
Oral—CN302/MS200
Lorazepam
Parenteral—CN302/CN400; MS200; GA609
Nitrazepam
Oral—CN302/CN400
Oxazepam
Oral—CN302
Prazepam
Oral—CN302
Quazepam
Oral—CN302
Temazepam
Oral—CN302
Triazolam
Oral—CN302

Note: Controlled substance classification
U.S.: Schedule IV (all of the benzodiazepines in this monograph)

Commonly used brand name(s): *Alprazolam Intensol*[1]; *Alti-Alprazolam*[1]; *Alti-Bromazepam*[2]; *Alti-Clonazepam*[5]; *Alti-Triazolam*[18]; *Apo-Alpraz*[1]; *Apo-Chlordiazepoxide*[3]; *Apo-Clonazepam*[5]; *Apo-Clorazepate*[6]; *Apo-Diazepam*[7]; *Apo-Flurazepam*[9]; *Apo-Lorazepam*[12]; *Apo-Oxazepam*[14]; *Apo-Temazepam*[17]; *Apo-Triazo*[18]; *Ativan*[12]; *Clonapam*[5]; *Dalmane*[9]; *Diastat*[7]; *Diazemuls*[7]; *Diazepam Intensol*[7]; *Dizac*[7]; *Doral*[16]; *Frisium*[4]; *Gen-Alprazolam*[1]; *Gen-Bromazepam*[2]; *Gen-Clonazepam*[5]; *Gen-Triazolam*[18]; *Halcion*[18]; *Klonopin*[5]; *Lectopam*[2]; *Librium*[3]; *Lorazepam Intensol*[12]; *Mogadon*[13]; *Niravam*[1]; *Novo-Alprazol*[1]; *Novo-Clopate*[6]; *Novo-Dipam*[7]; *Novo-Flupam*[9]; *Novo-Lorazem*[12]; *Novo-Poxide*[3]; *Novo-Temazepam*[17]; *Novo-Triolam*[18]; *Novoxapam*[14]; *Nu-Alpraz*[1]; *Nu-Loraz*[12]; *PMS-Clonazepam*[5]; *PMS-Diazepam*[7]; *Paxipam*[10]; *ProSom*[8]; *Restoril*[17]; *Rivotril*[5]; *Serax*[14]; *Somnol*[9]; *Tranxene*[6]; *Tranxene T-Tab*[6]; *Tranxene-SD*[6]; *Tranxene-SD Half Strength*[6]; *Valium*[7]; *Vivol*[7]; *Xanax*[1]; *Xanax TS*[1].

Note: For a listing of dosage forms and brand names by country availability, see *Dosage Forms* section(s).

---

*Not commercially available in U.S.
†Not commercially available in Canada.

Category

Note: **All of the benzodiazepines have similar pharmacologic actions; however, clinical uses among specific agents may vary because of actual pharmacokinetic differences, availability of specific testing, and/or availability of clinical-use data.**

Antianxiety agent—Alprazolam; Bromazepam; Chlordiazepoxide; Clorazepate; Diazepam; Halazepam; Ketazolam; Lorazepam; Oxazepam; Prazepam.

Sedative-hypnotic—Alprazolam; Bromazepam; Chlordiazepoxide; Clonazepam; Clorazepate; Diazepam; Estazolam; Flurazepam; Halazepam; Ketazolam; Lorazepam; Nitrazepam; Oxazepam; Prazepam; Quazepam; Temazepam; Triazolam.

Amnestic—Diazepam (parenteral only); Lorazepam (parenteral only).

Anticonvulsant—Clobazam; Clonazepam; Clorazepate; Diazepam; Lorazepam (parenteral only); Nitrazepam.

Antipanic agent—Alprazolam; Chlordiazepoxide (parenteral only); Clonazepam; Diazepam; Lorazepam.

Skeletal muscle relaxant adjunct—Diazepam; Lorazepam.

Antitremor agent—Alprazolam; Chlordiazepoxide (oral only); Diazepam (oral only); Lorazepam (oral only).

Antiemetic, in cancer chemotherapy—Lorazepam (parenteral only)

Indications

Note: Because ketazolam and prazepam are not commercially available in the U.S. or Canada, the bracketed information and the use of the superscript 1 in this monograph reflect the lack of labeled (approved) indications for these medications.

Bracketed information in the *Indications* section refers to uses that are not included in U.S. product labeling.

Accepted

Anxiety (treatment)—Alprazolam, bromazepam, chlordiazepoxide, clorazepate, diazepam, halazepam, [ketazolam][1], lorazepam, oxazepam, and [prazepam][1] are indicated for the management of anxiety disorders or for the short-term relief of the symptoms of anxiety. Chlordiazepoxide, [oral diazepam][1], and sublingual or intramuscular lorazepam are indicated for treatment of preoperative apprehension and anxiety.

Benzodiazepines are not indicated for the treatment of anxiety or tension associated with the stress of everyday life. Effectiveness of these medications for long-term management of anxiety has not been assessed in systematic clinical studies. The medication's efficacy in an individual patient should be reassessed at periodic intervals.

Anxiety associated with mental depression (treatment adjunct)[1]—Alprazolam, lorazepam (oral), and oxazepam are also indicated for the adjunctive management of anxiety associated with mental depression. Effectiveness of these medications for long-term use has not been assessed in systematic clinical studies. The medication's efficacy in an individual patient should be reassessed at periodic intervals.

Alcohol withdrawal (treatment)—Chlordiazepoxide, clorazepate, diazepam, [lorazepam][1], and oxazepam are indicated for the relief of acute alcohol withdrawal symptoms such as acute agitation, tremor, impending or acute delirium tremens, and hallucinosis.

Anesthesia, adjunct—Parenteral chlordiazepoxide and parenteral diazepam are indicated as premedication to relieve anxiety and tension in patients who are to undergo surgical procedures. Also, parenteral lorazepam is indicated in adults as preanesthetic medication to produce sedation, relief of anxiety, and anterograde amnesia.

Amnesia, in cardioversion or
Anxiety, in cardioversion (treatment)—Parenteral diazepam is indicated for intravenous administration prior to cardioversion to relieve anxiety and tension and to produce anterograde amnesia.

Amnesia, in endoscopic procedures or
Anxiety, in endoscopic procedures (treatment adjunct)—Parenteral diazepam and [parenteral lorazepam][1] are indicated as adjuncts prior to endoscopic procedures if apprehension, anxiety, or acute stress reactions are present and to diminish patient's recall of the procedure. Safety and efficacy have not been established for the use of diazepam prior to bronchoscopy or laryngoscopy.

[Sedation, conscious][1]—Parenteral diazepam is used in dentistry to relieve anxiety and produce amnesia in prolonged or difficult dental procedures. It is used frequently with a local anesthetic.

Insomnia (treatment)—Estazolam, flurazepam, nitrazepam, quazepam, temazepam, and triazolam are indicated for the short-term treatment of insomnia characterized by difficulty in falling asleep, frequent nocturnal awakenings, and/or early morning awakenings. Lorazepam[1] is indicated for insomnia due to anxiety or transient situational stress. Other benzodiazepines, such as [alprazolam][1], bromazepam[1], [diazepam][1], [ketazolam][1], [halazepam], and [prazepam][1], are also used in the treatment of insomnia. Failure of insomnia to remit after 7 to 10 days of treatment may indicate the presence of a primary psychiatric or medical illness. Worsening of insomnia or the emergence of new abnormalities of thinking or behavior may be the consequence of an unrecognized psychiatric or physical disorder.

[Short- and intermediate-acting benzodiazepine hypnotics may be useful in the prevention or treatment (short-term) of transient insomnia associated with a sudden sleep schedule change, such as occurs in trans-meridian travel and shift-work rotation.][1]

Convulsions (treatment adjunct) or
Status epilepticus (treatment adjunct)—Diazepam injection, sterile emulsion[1], and [diazepam for rectal solution][1] are indicated as adjuncts in status epilepticus and severe recurrent convulsive seizures. Lorazepam injection is indicated for the treatment of status epilepticus as part of a complex and sustained intervention that may include support of vital functions, administration of additional anticonvulsant medications, and/or correction of acute causes of status epilepticus. These medications are not recommended for maintenance anticonvulsant therapy; therefore, once seizures are controlled, appropriate maintenance anticonvulsant therapy should be instituted.

Convulsive disorders (treatment adjunct)—Oral diazepam[1] is indicated as short-term (7 to 14 days) adjunctive therapy in convulsive disorders. It is not useful as sole therapy in convulsive disorders. [Clonazepam may be effective as an adjunct in convulsive disorders such as eclamptic convulsions, infantile spasms, reading epilepsy, and startle-induced seizures.][1]

Epilepsy (treatment adjunct)—Clobazam is indicated as an adjunct in the treatment of patients with epilepsy who are not adequately stabilized by their current anticonvulsant therapy.

Diazepam rectal gel is indicated to control bouts of increased seizure activity in patients with refractory epilepsy who are on stable regimens of antiepileptic medications. Diazepam rectal gel may be administered in the home by a competent caregiver who has been instructed in its proper use and who can distinguish the characteristic seizure clusters that may be treated with diazepam rectal gel from the patient's usual seizure activity.

Epilepsy, Lennox-Gastaut syndrome (treatment) or
Epilepsy, akinetic seizure pattern (treatment) or
Epilepsy, myoclonic seizure pattern (treatment)—Clonazepam is indicated for use alone or, more frequently, as an adjunct in the treatment of the Lennox-Gastaut syndrome (petit mal variant), akinetic seizures, and myoclonic seizures.

Nitrazepam also is indicated for the treatment of myoclonic seizures.

[Epilepsy, myoclonic seizure pattern (treatment adjunct)][1]—Oral diazepam is used as adjunctive therapy in myoclonus. It is not useful as sole therapy in this condition.

Epilepsy, absence seizure pattern (treatment)—Clonazepam may be useful in the treatment of absence (petit mal) seizures refractory to the succinimide anticonvulsants or valproic acid.

Epilepsy, simple partial seizure pattern (treatment adjunct)[1] or
Epilepsy, complex partial seizure pattern (treatment adjunct)[1]—Clorazepate is indicated as adjunctive therapy in the management of partial seizures.

[Epilepsy, simple partial seizure pattern (treatment)][1] or
[Epilepsy, complex partial seizure pattern (treatment)][1]—Clonazepam may be effective in refractory seizures such as complex partial (psychomotor, temporal lobe) or elementary partial (focal) seizures.

[Epilepsy, tonic-clonic seizure pattern (treatment)][1]—Clonazepam may be effective in tonic-clonic (grand mal) seizures. However, when clonazepam is used in patients in whom several types of seizure disorders coexist, it may increase the incidence or, rarely, precipitate the onset of generalized tonic-clonic (grand mal) seizures; addition of another anticonvulsant and/or an increase in dosage may be required.

Panic disorders (treatment)—Alprazolam, [chlordiazepoxide (parenteral)], clonazepam[1], [diazepam][1], and [lorazepam][1] are used in the treatment of panic disorders.

[Agoraphobia][1]—Alprazolam is used in the treatment of agoraphobia.

Spasm, skeletal muscle (treatment adjunct)—Diazepam and [lorazepam][1] are indicated as adjunctive therapy for the relief of skeletal muscle spasm due to reflex spasm of local pathology (such as inflammation of the muscles or joints, or secondary to trauma); spasticity caused by upper motor neuron disorders (such as cerebral palsy and paraplegia); athetosis; stiff-man syndrome; and tetanus. [Diazepam also is used to relieve spasms of facial muscles associated with problems of occlusion and temporomandibular joint disorders.][1]

[Nausea and vomiting, cancer chemotherapy-induced (prophylaxis)][1]—Lorazepam injection, alone or in combination with other agents, reduces the severity and duration of nausea and vomiting associated with emetogenic cancer chemotherapy. In addition, lorazepam-induced amnesia can reduce anticipatory anxiety, nausea, and vomiting.

[Headache, tension (treatment)]—Chlordiazepoxide, diazepam[1], lorazepam[1], and possibly other benzodiazepines[1] are used in the treatment of tension headache.

[Tremors (treatment)][1]—Oral alprazolam, chlordiazepoxide, diazepam, and lorazepam are also used in the treatment of familial, senile, or essential action tremors.

---

[1]Not included in Canadian product labeling.

Pharmacology/Pharmacokinetics

See *Table 1*, page 535.

Physicochemical characteristics

Molecular weight—
- Alprazolam: 308.77.
- Bromazepam: 316.16.
- Chlordiazepoxide: 299.76.
- Chlordiazepoxide hydrochloride: 336.22.
- Clonazepam: 315.72.
- Clorazepate dipotassium: 408.93.
- Diazepam: 284.75.
- Estazolam: 294.74.
- Flurazepam hydrochloride: 460.81.
- Halazepam: 352.74.
- Ketazolam: 368.82.
- Lorazepam: 321.16.
- Nitrazepam: 281.27.
- Oxazepam: 286.72.
- Prazepam: 324.81.
- Quazepam: 386.8.
- Temazepam: 300.75.
- Triazolam: 343.22.

Mechanism of action/Effect

In general, benzodiazepines act as depressants of the central nervous system (CNS), producing all levels of CNS depression from mild sedation to hypnosis to coma, depending on dose.

Although the precise mechanisms of action have not been completely established, it is believed that benzodiazepines enhance or facilitate the action of gamma-aminobutyric acid (GABA), the major inhibitory neurotransmitter in the CNS, by causing it to bind more tightly to the GABA type A ($GABA_A$) receptor.

Benzodiazepines reportedly act as agonists at the benzodiazepine receptors, which have been shown to form a component of a functional supramolecular unit known as the benzodiazepine-GABA receptor-chloride ionophore complex. This receptor complex, which resides on neuronal membranes, functions mainly in the gating of the chloride channel. Activation of the GABA receptor results in the opening of the chloride channel, allowing the flow of chloride ions into the neuron. This results in hyperpolarization, which inhibits firing of the neuron and translates into decreased neuronal excitability, thus attenuating the effects of subsequent depolarizing excitatory transmitters. Benzodiazepines reportedly increase the frequency of chloride channel opening. There is also evidence that benzodiazepines may act at GABA-independent receptors.

Antianxiety agent; sedative-hypnotic—Believed to stimulate GABA receptors in the ascending reticular activating system. Since GABA is inhibitory, receptor stimulation increases inhibition and blocks both cortical and limbic arousal following stimulation of the brain stem reticular formation.

Amnestic—Mechanism of action has not been determined. However, as may occur with all sedative-hypnotic medications, preanesthetic doses of diazepam and lorazepam impair recent memory and interfere with the establishment of the memory trace, thus producing anterograde amnesia for events occurring while therapeutic concentrations of the benzodiazepine are present.

Anticonvulsant—Hyperpolarization, which is enhanced by benzodiazepines, reduces the ability of the neuron to depolarize to the threshold required to produce an action potential. Thus, the seizure threshold is raised. Benzodiazepines suppress the spread of seizure activity produced by epileptogenic foci in the cortex, thalamus, and limbic structures but do not abolish the abnormal discharge of the focus.

Skeletal muscle relaxant adjunct—The exact mechanism of action of benzodiazepines has not been completely established but these medications appear to produce skeletal muscle relaxation primarily by inhibiting spinal polysynaptic afferent pathways; however, monosynaptic afferent pathways may also be inhibited. Benzodiazepines may also directly depress motor nerve and muscle function.

Absorption

Following oral administration—Benzodiazepines are well absorbed from the gastrointestinal tract, usually within 1 to 2 hours. Diazepam and clorazepate are among the most rapidly absorbed, and prazepam and oxazepam are the least rapidly absorbed.

Following intramuscular administration—Lorazepam absorption is rapid and complete, whereas chlordiazepoxide and diazepam absorption may be slow and erratic, depending upon the site of administration. When diazepam is injected into the deltoid muscle, absorption is usually rapid and complete.

Following rectal administration—Absorption of diazepam rectal solution and rectal gel is rapid.

Biotransformation

Hepatic.

Long half-life benzodiazepines—

Chlordiazepoxide, flurazepam, halazepam, ketazolam, and quazepam are metabolized by oxidation to active, as well as inactive, metabolites before final inactivation as glucuronide conjugates.

Diazepam undergoes hepatic demethylation and hydroxylation, involving the cytochrome P450 2C19 (CYP2C19) and CYP3A4 isoenzymes, followed by glucuronidation. Only one active metabolite, desmethyldiazepam, is present in clinically significant concentrations.

Clorazepate and prazepam are metabolized in the stomach and liver, respectively, to desmethyldiazepam as a result of first-pass biotransformation prior to entering systemic circulation.

Short to intermediate half-life benzodiazepines—

Alprazolam undergoes hydroxylation, which is catalyzed by the CYP3A isoenzymes, and is eliminated as glucuronide conjugates. One of alprazolam's metabolites has one half of the biological activity of alprazolam, but is present in very low plasma concentrations.

Bromazepam undergoes hepatic microsomal oxidation and is eliminated primarily as glucuronide conjugates.

Clobazam undergoes hepatic demethylation and hydroxylation to active and inactive metabolites before inactivation by conjugation.

Clonazepam and nitrazepam undergo hepatic nitro-reduction to inactive metabolites. Clonazepam also undergoes oxidative hydroxylation and CYP3A isoenzymes may play an important role in clonazepam's metabolism.

Estazolam undergoes oxidative metabolism and hydroxylation to metabolites with little activity and low plasma concentrations in comparison with the parent compound.

Lorazepam, oxazepam, and temazepam are metabolized by direct conjugation with glucuronic acid.

Triazolam undergoes hepatic microsomal oxidation to inactive hydroxylated metabolites that are eliminated primarily as glucuronide conjugates.

Accumulation

During repeated dosing with long half-life benzodiazepines, there is accumulation of the parent compound and/or any pharmacologically active metabolites. Accumulation continues until a steady-state plasma concentration is reached, which usually takes 5 days to 2 weeks after initiation of therapy. Following termination of treatment, drug elimination is slow since active metabolites may remain in the blood for several days or even weeks, possibly resulting in persistent effects.

During repeated dosing with short to intermediate half-life benzodiazepines, accumulation is minimal, and a steady-state plasma concentration is usually attained within a few days after initiation of therapy. Following termination of treatment, blood concentrations are subclinical in 24 hours and return rapidly to zero (in about 4 days or less).

Onset of action

After single oral doses, onset of action depends largely upon absorption rate. After multiple doses, effects depend partly upon rate and extent of drug accumulation, which in turn relate to elimination half-life and clearance.

Duration of action

After single oral doses, duration of action depends upon rate and extent of drug distribution, as well as rate of elimination once distribution is complete. After multiple doses, effects depend partly upon rate and extent of drug accumulation, which in turn relate to elimination half-life and clearance. The duration of clinical effects of the benzodiazepines is not always predictable from the elimination half-life.

Precautions to Consider

Cross-sensitivity and/or related problems

Patients sensitive to one of the benzodiazepines may be sensitive to the other benzodiazepines also.

Carcinogenicity/Tumorigenicity

Alprazolam—In a 24-month study in rats, alprazolam at doses of up to 150 times the maximum recommended human dose (MRHD) showed no evidence of carcinogenic potential.

Clobazam—Hepatomas, thyroid adenomas, and malignancies of the liver and thyroid gland were seen in rodent studies; the significance of this finding to humans is unknown.

Clonazepam—Studies on carcinogenic potential have not been done.

Diazepam—An increased incidence of liver tumors was seen in male mice and rats following oral administration of diazepam to mice and rats of both sexes at doses that were approximately 6 and 12 times, respectively, the MRHD (1 mg per kg of body weight [mg/kg] per day) on a mg per square meter of body surface area (mg/m^2) basis for 80 and 104 weeks, respectively.

Estazolam—Studies of 24-months duration in mice and rats showed no evidence of tumorigenicity. However, the female mice given 3 and 10 mg/kg per day of estazolam over the 2-year period showed an increase in hyperplastic liver nodules; the significance of this finding is unknown.

Halazepam—In oral oncogenicity studies in rats and mice, halazepam at doses 5 to 50 times the usual daily human dose of 120 mg showed no evidence of carcinogenicity.

Lorazepam—In an 18-month study in rats, lorazepam showed no evidence of carcinogenic potential.

Oxazepam—A 24-month study in rats given oxazepam at doses 30 times the MRHD showed an increase in benign thyroid follicular cell tumors, testicular interstitial cell adenomas, and prostatic adenomas. In a 9-month study in mice, oxazepam in doses 35 to 100 times the usual daily human dose caused dose-related increases in liver adenomas, some of which were classified as carcinomas after microscopic examination.

Quazepam—Oral oncogenicity studies in mice and hamsters showed no evidence of carcinogenicity.

Temazepam—Long-term studies in mice and rats showed no evidence of carcinogenicity. However, hyperplastic liver nodules occurred in female mice at the highest dose used (160 mg/kg per day); the clinical significance of this finding is unknown.

Triazolam—In a 24-month study in mice, triazolam in doses up to 4000 times the human dose showed no evidence of carcinogenic potential.

Mutagenicity

Alprazolam—Mutagenicity was not demonstrated in appropriate tests on mice or bacteria.

Estazolam—Mutagenicity was not demonstrated in appropriate tests on mice, rats, and bacteria.

Diazepam—Data are insufficient to determine mutagenic potential.

Halazepam—Halazepam demonstrated no mutagenic activity in the Ames test.

Lorazepam, oxazepam, and temazepam—Studies on mutagenic potential have not been done.

Quazepam—Mutagenicity was not demonstrated in tests on mice or bacteria.

Pregnancy/Reproduction

Pregnancy—

All benzodiazepines—

Chlordiazepoxide, clonazepam, diazepam, estazolam, flurazepam, lorazepam, nitrazepam, temazepam, and triazolam cross the placenta. Alprazolam, bromazepam, clorazepate, halazepam, ketazolam, oxazepam, prazepam, and quazepam are assumed to cross the placenta because of their similarity to the other benzodiazepines.

First trimester—Chlordiazepoxide and diazepam have been reported to increase the risk of congenital malformations when used during the first trimester of pregnancy. Because of the similarity of the benzodiazepines, the other benzodiazepines are assumed to be associated with this increased risk also. Risk-benefit must be considered carefully. However, since the use of benzodiazepines (with the possible exception of anticonvulsant use) is rarely a matter of urgency, it should be avoided during pregnancy, especially during the first trimester. The possibility that a woman of childbearing potential may already be pregnant should be considered when initiating benzodiazepine treatment.

When benzodiazepines are used as anticonvulsants, risk-benefit must be considered. Reports suggest an increased incidence of congenital abnormalities in children whose mothers used anticonvulsants during pregnancy, although anticonvulsant medications have not been definitively shown to have a causative role and other factors, such as the epileptic condition itself, may be involved. The severity of the seizure disorder and the potential harm to the mother or fetus in the event of a seizure must be considered when deciding whether to continue anticonvulsant treatment during pregnancy.

Regular use of benzodiazepines during pregnancy may cause physical dependence with resulting withdrawal symptoms in the neonate.

Use of benzodiazepine hypnotics during the last weeks of pregnancy has resulted in neonatal CNS depression, neonatal flaccidity, feeding difficulties, hypothermia, and respiratory problems.

Chlordiazepoxide—

Reproduction studies in rats showed that chlordiazepoxide, at doses of 10, 20, and 80 mg per kg of body weight (mg/kg) per day, caused no congenital anomalies or adverse effects on the growth of the newborn animal. However, another study with chlordiazepoxide at doses of 100 mg/kg per day showed a significant decrease in the fertilization rate and a decrease in the viability and body weight of offspring, which may have been due to the sedative effect; also, one neonate in each of the first and second matings in this study showed skeletal deformities.

FDA pregnancy category not presently included in product labeling.

Clonazepam—

Studies in rabbits have shown that clonazepam in oral doses of 0.2 to 10 mg/kg per day (low dose approximately 0.2 times the maximum recommended human dose [MRHD] for seizure disorders and approximately equivalent to the MRHD for panic disorder, on a mg/m^2 basis), given during organogenesis, caused a non–dose-related increased incidence of cleft palates, open eyelids, fused sternebrae, and limb defects.

Withdrawal of clonazepam anticonvulsant prior to or during pregnancy should be considered only when seizures are mild and infrequent in the absence of the medication and where the possibility of status epilepticus and withdrawal symptoms is considered low.

FDA Pregnancy Category D.

Diazepam—

Rodent studies have shown that single oral doses ≥ eight times the MRHD of 1 mg/kg per day on a mg/m^2 basis, administered during organogenesis, are teratogenic. Cleft palate and exencephaly were the most commonly and consistently reported malformations. Also, long-term changes in cellular immune response, brain neurochemistry, and behavior were seen in offspring of rodents given diazepam during pregnancy in doses similar to human clinical doses.

FDA Pregnancy Category D.

Lorazepam—

Studies in rabbits have shown that lorazepam causes fetal resorption and increased fetal loss at oral doses of 40 mg/kg and intravenous doses of 4 mg/kg and higher; lorazepam was also shown to cause anomalies in rabbits without relationship to dosage.

FDA Pregnancy Category D (parenteral).

Quazepam—

Reproduction studies in mice given 66 to 400 times the human dose of quazepam showed minor developmental variations including delayed ossification of the sternum, vertebrae, distal phalanges, and supraoccipital bones. Studies in mice given 60 to 180 times the human dose showed slight reductions in the pregnancy rate.

FDA Pregnancy Category X.

Temazepam—

Studies in rats have shown that temazepam causes an increased incidence of fetal resorption at doses of 30 and 120 mg/kg, and an increased occurrence of rudimentary ribs (considered skeletal variants) at doses of 240 mg/kg or higher. Increased nursling mortality was seen in rats when oral doses of 60 mg/kg per day were given to the dam during the perinatal-postnatal period. Also, studies in rabbits have shown that temazepam causes an increased incidence of the 13th rib variant at doses of 40 mg/kg or higher, and occasional abnormalities such as exencephaly and fusion or asymmetry of ribs without relationship to dosage.

FDA Pregnancy Category X.

Alprazolam; Halazepam—FDA Pregnancy Category D.

Estazolam; Triazolam—FDA Pregnancy Category X.

Clorazepate, flurazepam, and oxazepam—

FDA pregnancy categories not presently included in product labeling.

Labor—*All benzodiazepines*: Use of benzodiazepines just prior to or during labor may cause neonatal flaccidity.

Delivery—*Diazepam*: When diazepam is administered in doses of more than 30 mg (especially intramuscularly or intravenously) to women within 15 hours before delivery, the neonate may develop apnea, hypotonia, hypothermia, a reluctance to feed, and impaired metabolic response to cold stress.

Breast-feeding

Chlordiazepoxide, diazepam, halazepam, quazepam, and their metabolites, including desmethyldiazepam (which is also the metabolite of clorazepate and prazepam) are distributed into breast milk; clobazam and nitrazepam are distributed into breast milk also; alprazolam, clonazepam, flurazepam, lorazepam, oxazepam, temazepam, and/or their metabolites are assumed to be distributed into breast milk because of their similarity to the other benzodiazepines. Although studies in humans have not been done, studies in rats have shown that bromazepam, estazolam, ketazolam, triazolam, and their metabolites are distributed into the milk of rats.

Chronic use of diazepam by nursing mothers has been reported to cause lethargy and weight loss in the infants. Since neonates metabolize benzodiazepines more slowly than adults and accumulation of the benzodiazepine and/or its metabolites may occur, use by nursing mothers may cause sedation, feeding difficulties, and/or weight loss in the infant.

Pediatrics

All benzodiazepines—Children, especially the very young, are usually more sensitive to the CNS effects of benzodiazepines. Prolonged CNS depression may be produced in the neonate because of inability to biotransform the benzodiazepine into inactive metabolites.

Clonazepam—Risk-benefit must be considered in the long-term use of clonazepam to treat seizure disorders in pediatric patients because of the possibility that adverse effects on physical or mental development may occur and may not become apparent for many years.

Geriatrics

Geriatric patients are usually more sensitive to the CNS effects of benzodiazepines. It is recommended that dosage be limited to the smallest effective dose and increased gradually, if necessary, to decrease the possibility of development of ataxia, dizziness, and oversedation, which may lead to falls and other accidents. A retrospective case-control study has shown that elderly patients receiving long-acting benzodiazepines are more likely than those receiving short-acting benzodiazepines to suffer falls and fall-related fractures. However, both groups had an increased risk of these sequelae as compared to older patients who did not receive benzodiazepines or who received other short-acting sedative-hypnotics.

The half-lives of benzodiazepines may be longer in elderly than in younger patients.

Parenteral administration of benzodiazepines may be more likely to cause apnea, hypotension, bradycardia, or cardiac arrest in geriatric patients.

Pharmacogenetics

Diazepam—3 to 5% of white patients have little or no cytochrome P450 2C19 (CYP2C19) activity and are poor metabolizers of diazepam.

Drug interactions and/or related problems

The following drug interactions and/or related problems have been selected on the basis of their potential clinical significance (possible mechanism in parentheses where appropriate)—not necessarily inclusive (» = major clinical significance):

Note: The cytochrome P450 2C19 (CYP2C19) isoenzyme is known to be involved in diazepam's metabolism. Medications that inhibit CYP2C19, such as cimetidine, quinidine, and tranylcypromine, may decrease the rate of elimination of diazepam. Likewise, medications that induce CYP2C19, such as rifampin, may increase the rate of diazepam's elimination.

The CYP3A isoenzymes are known to be involved in the metabolism of alprazolam, clonazepam, diazepam, and triazolam. Concurrent use with medications that inhibit CYP3A isoenzymes, other than those listed below, should be undertaken with caution, and reduction in benzodiazepine dosage should be considered.

Combinations containing any of the following medications, depending on the amount present, may also interact with this medication.

Addictive medications, other, especially CNS depressants with habituating potential
(prolonged concurrent use may increase the risk of habituation; caution is recommended)

» Alcohol or
» CNS depression-producing medications, other (see *Appendix II*)
(CNS depressant effects may be potentiated and the risk of apnea may be increased; use of alcohol during treatment with a benzodiazepine is not recommended; caution is recommended when another CNS depression-producing medication is used with a benzodiazepine, and dosage of one or both agents should be reduced)
(when a benzodiazepine is used with an opioid analgesic, the dosage of the opioid analgesic should be reduced by at least one third and administered in small increments)

Antacids
(concurrent use may delay, but not reduce, the absorption of chlordiazepoxide and diazepam; whether this effect applies to other benzodiazepines has not been determined)
(concurrent use with clorazepate may decrease the rate of conversion of clorazepate to desmethyldiazepam, but does not affect the degree of absorption)

Antidepressants, tricyclic
(in addition to possibly increasing CNS depressant effects, concurrent use with alprazolam in doses of up to 4 mg per day has been reported to increase steady-state plasma concentrations of imipramine and desipramine by an average of 31% and 20%, respectively; however, the clinical significance of these changes is unknown)

Carbamazepine
(induction of hepatic microsomal enzyme activity by carbamazepine may result in increased rate of metabolism, decreased serum concentrations, and reduced elimination half-lives of benzodiazepines metabolized via the hepatic enzyme system, such as clonazepam; carbamazepine concentrations may be increased during concurrent use with a benzodiazepine; monitoring of carbamazepine blood concentrations as a guide to dosage is recommended, especially when carbamazepine is added to or withdrawn from existing benzodiazepine therapy)

Cimetidine or
Contraceptives, estrogen-containing, oral or

Diltiazem or
Disulfiram or
Erythromycin or
Fluoxetine or
» Fluvoxamine or
Grapefruit juice or
» Nefazodone or
Propoxyphene or
Ranitidine or
Verapamil

(concurrent use may inhibit the hepatic metabolism of benzodiazepines that are metabolized by oxidation, resulting in delayed elimination and increased plasma concentrations; however, the hepatic metabolism of benzodiazepines that undergo direct glucuronide conjugation, such as lorazepam, oxazepam, and temazepam, is probably not affected)

(concurrent use of cimetidine or oral, estrogen-containing contraceptives may inhibit the hepatic metabolism of benzodiazepines that are metabolized primarily by nitro-reduction, such as nitrazepam, possibly resulting in delayed elimination, prolonged elimination half-life, and, during long-term use, increased serum concentrations)

(alprazolam's peak plasma concentration [C_{max}] has been almost doubled during concurrent use of cimetidine, fluvoxamine, or nefazodone; also, decreased psychomotor performance has been demonstrated during concurrent use of fluvoxamine; dosage reductions of alprazolam may be required [initial reductions of 50% are recommended in patients receiving fluvoxamine or nefazodone]; alprazolam's C_{max} has been increased by approximately 50% during concurrent use of fluoxetine or propoxyphene; also, psychomotor performance has been decreased during concurrent use of fluoxetine)

(diazepam and desmethyldiazepam clearances have been reduced and patient psychomotor performance has been impaired during concurrent use of fluvoxamine; concurrent use is not recommended due to the potential for accumulation of diazepam and desmethyldiazepam)

(triazolam's area under the plasma concentration-time curve [AUC] has been increased 22 and 27 times during concurrent use of ketoconazole and itraconazole, respectively; concurrent use is not recommended; triazolam's AUC was increased fourfold and patient psychomotor performance was impaired during concurrent use of nefazodone; reductions in initial triazolam dosage of 75% are recommended in patients receiving nefazodone; triazolam's C_{max} and half-life [$t_{1/2}$] have been doubled during concurrent use of cimetidine or erythromycin; dosage reductions may be necessary; triazolam's C_{max}, $t_{1/2}$, and AUC have been increased during concurrent use of ranitidine; caution is recommended; plasma concentration, AUC, and $t_{1/2}$ of triazolam have been increased by coadministration with grapefruit juice)

(due to inhibition of CYP3A estazolam should be avoided in patients receiving these drugs, especially ketoconazole and itraconazole)

Clozapine

(collapse, sometimes accompanied by respiratory depression or arrest, has been reported in a few patients receiving clozapine concurrently with benzodiazepines. Caution is advised when clozapine is administered concomitantly with any agent that may depress respiration, and the dosage of clozapine should be titrated upward slowly. Some clinicians have recommended that benzodiazepines be discontinued at least 1 week prior to initiation of therapy with clozapine)

Fentanyl derivatives

(premedication with diazepam or lorazepam may decrease the dose of a fentanyl derivative required for induction of anesthesia and decrease the time to loss of consciousness with induction doses; also, administration of diazepam or lorazepam prior to or during surgery may decrease risk of patient recall of surgical events postoperatively; however, these potential benefits must be weighed against the potential risks of concurrent use, such as an increased risk of severe hypotension associated with decreases in systemic vascular resistance, increased risk of respiratory depression, and delayed recovery time, especially when the benzodiazepine is administered intravenously)

Hypotension-producing medications, other (see *Appendix II*)

(concurrent use may potentiate the hypotensive effects of benzodiazepine preanesthetics used in surgery; dosage adjustments may be necessary)

(concurrent use of mecamylamine or trimethaphan with benzodiazepine preanesthetics used in surgery may potentiate the hypotensive response, with increased risk of severe hypotension, shock, and cardiovascular collapse during surgery)

(caution is advised during titration of calcium channel blocker dosage for those patients taking medication known to promote hypotension, such as benzodiazepine preanesthetics, since the combination may result in excessive hypotension)

Isoniazid

(concurrent use may inhibit the elimination of diazepam and triazolam, resulting in increased plasma concentrations; whether this effect applies to other benzodiazepines has not been determined; dosage adjustment may be necessary)

» Itraconazole or
» Ketoconazole

(use is contraindicated)

Levodopa

(concurrent use with benzodiazepines may decrease the therapeutic effects of levodopa)

Omeprazole

(concurrent use of omeprazole may prolong the elimination of diazepam)

Probenecid

(concurrent use may impair glucuronide conjugation of lorazepam, oxazepam, or temazepam, resulting in increased effects and possibly excessive sedation)

Rifampin

(concurrent use may enhance the elimination of diazepam, resulting in decreased plasma concentrations; whether this effect applies to other benzodiazepines has not been determined; dosage adjustment may be necessary)

Scopolamine, systemic

(concurrent use of scopolamine with parenteral lorazepam is reported to have no added beneficial effect and their combined effect may increase the incidence of sedation, hallucination, and irrational behavior)

» Tubing, infusion, plastic

(diazepam adheres to plastic infusion tubing; if parenteral diazepam must be administered through tubing, it should be injected as closely as possible to the insertion point)

Zidovudine

(concurrent use with benzodiazepines may, in theory, competitively inhibit hepatic glucuronidation and decrease the clearance of zidovudine; the toxicity of zidovudine potentially could be increased)

Laboratory value alterations

The following have been selected on the basis of their potential clinical significance (possible effect in parentheses where appropriate)—not necessarily inclusive (» = major clinical significance).

With diagnostic test results

Metyrapone test

(chlordiazepoxide may interfere with the assay for urine 17-ketosteroids or 17-ketogenic steroids; in addition, the response to metyrapone may be decreased)

Sodium iodide I 123 and
Sodium iodide I 131

(benzodiazepines may decrease thyroidal uptake of I 123 and I 131)

Medical considerations/Contraindications

The medical considerations/contraindications included have been selected on the basis of their potential clinical significance (reasons given in parentheses where appropriate)—not necessarily inclusive (» = major clinical significance).

Except under special circumstances, this medication should not be used when the following medical problem exists:

» Glaucoma, acute narrow angle

(use is contraindicated)

» Hypersensitivity to the benzodiazepine prescribed or to any other benzodiazepine or any component of the product

Risk-benefit should be considered when the following medical problems exist:

» Alcohol intoxication, acute, with depressed vital signs

(additive CNS depression)

» Coma or
» Shock

(hypnotic or hypotensive effects may be prolonged or intensified by benzodiazepines administered parenterally)

Drug abuse or dependence, history of

(patients predisposed to habituation and dependence)

Epilepsy or
Seizures, history of
(initiation or abrupt withdrawal of clonazepam or diazepam therapy may increase frequency and/or severity of tonic-clonic [grand mal] seizures; use of intravenous diazepam for absence [petit mal] status or Lennox-Gastaut syndrome [petit mal variant] status may precipitate tonic status epilepticus)
(abrupt withdrawal of clonazepam or diazepam used to treat these disorders may precipitate seizures or status epilepticus)

» Glaucoma, open angle
(may use benzodiazepines if patient is receiving appropriate glaucoma therapy)

Hepatic function impairment
(elimination half-life may be prolonged; minimal effect with oxazepam, lorazepam, and temazepam)

Hyperkinesis
(paradoxical reactions may occur)

Hypoalbuminemia
(may predispose patient to higher incidence of sedative side effects, especially with chlordiazepoxide and diazepam)

Mental depression, severe
(suicidal tendencies may be present; protective measures may be necessary; also benzodiazepines, when used alone, may increase depression; episodes of hypomania and mania reported with use of alprazolam in patients with mental depression)

» Myasthenia gravis
(condition may be exacerbated)

Organic brain disorders
(patients may be more prone to disinhibition and CNS depressant effects of benzodiazepines)

Porphyria
(condition may be exacerbated with the use of chlordiazepoxide)

Psychoses
(benzodiazepines are rarely effective as primary treatment for psychosis; also, paradoxical reactions may be more likely to occur in psychotic patients)

» Pulmonary disease, severe chronic obstructive
(compromised respiratory function may be exacerbated and increased salivation and bronchial secretions occurring with benzodiazepine use may cause problems in these patients; deaths occurring shortly after beginning treatment with alprazolam have been reported rarely in patients with severe pulmonary disease)

Renal function impairment
(accumulation of renally excreted metabolites may occur)

Sleep apnea, established or suspected
(condition may be exacerbated)

Swallowing abnormality, in children
(condition may be exacerbated because drooling and aspiration induced by benzodiazepines, such as nitrazepam, may delay cricopharyngeal relaxation; patient should be closely monitored)

Caution should also be used in surgical or nonambulatory patients because of the cough-suppressant effects of clonazepam.

Patient monitoring

The following may be especially important in patient monitoring (other tests may be warranted in some patients, depending on condition; » = major clinical significance):

Assessment of amount and frequency of medication use
(recommended at periodic intervals during long-term therapy to detect signs of dependence or abuse)

Reassessment of medication's efficacy as an antianxiety agent or a sedative-hypnotic
(recommended at periodic intervals during therapy; see *Indications*)

Side/Adverse Effects

Note: Although not all of these side effects have been attributed specifically to each benzodiazepine, a potential exists for their occurrence during the use of any benzodiazepine.

Psychological or physical dependence and tolerance may occur with benzodiazepine use, especially with high-dose or prolonged use.

Geriatric and debilitated patients, children (especially the very young), and patients with hepatic disease or low serum albumin are usually more sensitive to the CNS effects of benzodiazepines.

Parenteral administration of benzodiazepines may cause apnea, hypotension, bradycardia, or cardiac arrest, especially in geriatric or severely ill patients and in patients with limited pulmonary reserve or unstable cardiovascular status or if intravenous administration of medication is too rapid.

Parenteral benzodiazepines have produced hypotension or muscular weakness in some patients, especially when used concurrently with narcotics, barbiturates, or alcohol.

Coughing, depressed respiration, dyspnea, hyperventilation, laryngospasm, and pain in throat and chest have been reported when parenteral diazepam was administered in peroral endoscopic procedures.

The following side/adverse effects have been selected on the basis of their potential clinical significance (possible signs and symptoms in parentheses where appropriate)—not necessarily inclusive:

Those indicating need for medical attention

Incidence less frequent

Anterograde amnesia (lack of memory of events taking place after benzodiazepine is taken); ***anxiety; confusion***—especially in the elderly and in patients with cerebral impairment; ***mental depression; tachycardia/palpitation*** (fast, pounding, or irregular heartbeat)

Note: *Anterograde amnesia* may be dose-related and may occur at a higher rate with triazolam than with other benzodiazepines. "Traveler's amnesia," which occurs in people taking benzodiazepines to avoid jet lag, may be associated with allowing insufficient time for sleep and/or concomitant use of alcohol.

Daytime *anxiety*, as well as wakefulness during the last third of the night, may develop over several weeks of nightly dosing with short to intermediate half-life benzodiazepines. These effects are thought to be due to the development of tolerance or adaptation, which leads to a relative deficiency of benzodiazepine receptor binding between nightly doses.

Incidence rare

Abnormal thinking; including delusions (false beliefs that cannot be changed by facts); ***depersonalization*** (loss of sense of reality); ***or disorientation; allergic reaction*** (skin rash or itching); ***behavior changes; including bizarre behavior; or decreased inhibition; blood dyscrasias, including agranulocytosis*** (chills, fever, sore throat; unusual tiredness or weakness); ***anemia*** (unusual tiredness or weakness); ***leukopenia*** (chills, fever, sore throat); ***neutropenia*** (chills, fever, and/or sore throat; ulcers or sores in mouth or throat, continuing; unusual tiredness or weakness); ***thrombocytopenia*** (unusual bleeding or bruising); ***extrapyramidal effects, dystonic*** (uncontrolled movements of body, including the eyes); ***hepatic dysfunction*** (yellow eyes or skin); ***hypotension*** (low blood pressure); ***muscle weakness; paradoxical reactions; including agitation; aggressive behavior; hallucinations*** (seeing, hearing, or feeling things that are not there); ***hostility or rage*** (outbursts of anger); ***insomnia*** (trouble in sleeping); ***unusual excitement, irritability, or nervousness; phlebitis or venous thrombosis*** (redness, swelling, or pain at injection site)—for parenteral dosage forms only; ***seizures***

Note: *Behavioral disturbances* associated with clonazepam are more likely to occur in children or in patients with pre-existing brain damage and/or mental retardation or a history of behavioral or psychiatric disturbances; if these effects occur, the medication should be discontinued.

Paradoxical reactions have occurred most often in patients who were receiving additional CNS-active medications, or who had underlying psychiatric conditions, a history of violent or aggressive behavior, a history of alcohol or substance abuse, or a history of unusual reactions to sedatives or alcohol. Benzodiazepine treatment should be discontinued if a paradoxical reaction occurs.

Incidence of *phlebitis* or *venous thrombosis* is more common with diazepam, less common with lorazepam, and rare with chlordiazepoxide.

There may be an increased incidence and severity of *seizures*, especially on initiation or abrupt withdrawal of clonazepam and diazepam, in patients with epilepsy or history of seizures.

Those indicating need for medical attention only if they continue or are bothersome

Incidence more frequent

Ataxia (clumsiness or unsteadiness)—especially in elderly or debilitated patients; ***dizziness or lightheadedness; drowsiness, including residual daytime drowsiness when used as a hypnotic***—especially in elderly or debilitated patients; ***slurred speech***

Note: *Ataxia* and *drowsiness* are dose-related and are most severe during initial therapy. They may decrease in severity or disappear with continued or long-term therapy.

Residual daytime drowsiness is dose-related.

Incidence less frequent or rare

Abdominal or stomach cramps or pain; blurred vision or other changes in vision; changes in libido (changes in sexual desire or ability); ***constipation; diarrhea; dryness of mouth or increased thirst; euphoria*** (false sense of well-being); ***headache; increased bronchial secretions or excessive salivation*** (watering of mouth); ***muscle spasm; nausea or vomiting; problems with urination; tremor*** (trembling or shaking); ***unusual tiredness or weakness***

Note: *Increased bronchial secretions* and *excessive salivation* may pose a risk of aspiration in infants and young children, and in elderly or bedridden patients as well as in patients with chronic respiratory disease.

Those indicating possible withdrawal and the need for medical attention if they occur (usually within 2 to 3 days with short to intermediate half-life benzodiazepines and 10 to 20 days with long half-life benzodiazepines) after medication is discontinued

Incidence more frequent

Insomnia (trouble in sleeping); ***irritability; nervousness***

Note: When a benzodiazepine has been used as a hypnotic, withdrawal of the medication may cause a transient recurrence of symptoms known as *rebound insomnia*. Rebound insomnia may be more severe than the insomnia that originally led to treatment.

Incidence less frequent

Abdominal or stomach cramps; confusion; depersonalization (loss of sense of reality); ***increased sweating; mental depression; muscle cramps; nausea or vomiting; perceptual disturbances, including hyperacusis*** (increased sense of hearing); ***hypersensitivity to touch and pain; parasthesias*** (tingling, burning, or prickly sensations); ***or photophobia*** (sensitivity of eyes to light); ***tachycardia*** (fast or pounding heartbeat); ***tremor*** (trembling or shaking)

Incidence rare

Convulsions; delirium (confusion as to time, place, or person); ***hallucinations; paranoid symptoms*** (feelings of suspicion and distrust)

Note: *Withdrawal symptoms* are more common and often more severe in patients who have received high doses of a benzodiazepine over a prolonged period of time. However, symptoms have occurred following abrupt discontinuation of benzodiazepines that have been taken continuously, at therapeutic doses, for as few as 1 to 2 weeks. Abrupt discontinuation increases the chance of developing withdrawal symptoms, including life-threatening seizures. In some patients, withdrawal symptoms have occurred during gradual discontinuation or tapering of benzodiazepines. Withdrawal symptoms may be more likely to occur following the use of short-acting benzodiazepines than following the use of long-acting benzodiazepines.

Overdose

For specific information on the agents used in the management of benzodiazepine overdose, see:

- *Charcoal, Activated (Oral-Local)* monograph;
- *Dopamine* and/or *Metaraminol* and/or *Norepinephrine* in *Sympathomimetic Agents—Cardiovascular Use (Parenteral-Systemic)* monograph; and/or
- *Flumazenil (Systemic)* monograph.

For more information on the management of overdose or unintentional ingestion, **contact a Poison Control Center** (see *Poison Control Center Listing*).

Clinical effects of overdose

Note: Serious sequelae are rare unless other drugs or alcohol have been coingested. However, deaths have occurred after overdoses of benzodiazepines alone. Also, when benzodiazepines have been coingested with alcohol, deaths have occurred at benzodiazepine and alcohol plasma concentrations that were less than those usually associated with death by overdose with either agent alone.

The following effects have been selected on the basis of their potential clinical significance (possible signs and symptoms in parentheses where appropriate)—not necessarily inclusive:

Confusion, continuing; decreased reflexes; drowsiness, severe, or coma; seizures; shakiness; slow heartbeat; slurred speech, continuing; staggering; troubled breathing; weakness, severe

Treatment of overdose

To decrease absorption—

If the patient is conscious (and not at risk of becoming obtunded, comatose, or convulsing based on ingestion), emesis should be induced mechanically or with emetics; also, activated charcoal may be administered orally to increase clearance as well as decrease absorption of the benzodiazepine.

If the patient is unconscious, gastric lavage may be performed with a cuffed endotracheal tube in place to prevent aspiration of vomitus.

To enhance elimination—

Intravenous fluids may be administered to promote diuresis.

Specific treatment—

After airway, ventilation, and intravenous access have been secured, flumazenil, a specific benzodiazepine receptor antagonist, may be administered to reverse sedative effects. Patients must be monitored for the return of sedation after the administration of flumazenil. Flumazenil may precipitate seizures, especially in patients who have been using benzodiazepines long-term or who have coingested a cyclic antidepressant. Because of the risk of seizure induction, flumazenil use is not recommended in epileptic patients who have been treated with benzodiazepines.

Oxygen should be administered if respiration is depressed.

Hypotension may be controlled, if necessary, by intravenous administration of vasopressors such as dopamine, norepinephrine, or metaraminol.

Monitoring—

Respiration, pulse, and blood pressure should be monitored.

Supportive care—

Maintenance of adequate pulmonary ventilation is essential.

Intravenous fluids should be administered to maintain blood pressure.

Patients in whom intentional overdose is confirmed or suspected should be referred for psychiatric consultation.

Note: If excitation occurs, barbiturates should *not* be used since they may exacerbate excitation and/or prolong CNS depression.

Dialysis is of no known value in the treatment of benzodiazepine overdose.

Patient Consultation

As an aid to patient consultation, refer to *Advice for the Patient, Benzodiazepines (Systemic)*.

In providing consultation, consider emphasizing the following selected information (» = major clinical significance):

Before using this medication

» Conditions affecting use, especially:

Hypersensitivity to benzodiazepines or any other component of the product

Pregnancy—Benzodiazepines reported to increase risk of congenital malformations when used during first trimester of pregnancy; chronic use may cause physical dependence in the neonate with resulting withdrawal symptoms; use during last weeks of pregnancy may cause neonatal CNS depression; use just prior to or during labor may cause neonatal flaccidity

Breast-feeding—Some benzodiazepines and their metabolites distributed into breast milk and others may be distributed into breast milk; use by nursing mothers may cause sedation, and possibly feeding difficulties and weight loss in the infant

Use in children—Children, especially the very young, usually more sensitive to CNS effects of benzodiazepines

Use in the elderly—Elderly patients usually more sensitive to CNS effects of benzodiazepines

Other medications, especially other CNS depression-producing medications, fluvoxamine, itraconazole, ketoconazole, or nefazodone

Other medical problems, especially acute angle-closure glaucoma, myasthenia gravis, or severe chronic obstructive pulmonary disease

Proper use of this medication

For caregiver administering diazepam rectal gel

Discussing with patient's physician when to use and proper administration

Discussing with patient's physician when to summon emergency help

Carefully reading instructions supplied with medication before use is needed

Monitoring patient after administration as instructed by physician

Proper administration

For extended-release dosage form of clorazepate

(Swallowing tablets whole)

(Not crushing, breaking, or chewing)

For concentrated oral solution dosage form of alprazolam, diazepam, or lorazepam

(Measuring each dose with dropper provided with medication)

(Diluting dose with liquid or semisolid food such as water, soda or soda-like beverages, applesauce, or pudding is recommended)

(Consuming entire mixture immediately; not saving for later use)

For sublingual tablet dosage form of lorazepam
(Not chewing or swallowing tablet whole)
(Dissolving slowly under tongue; not swallowing for at least 2 minutes to allow sufficient absorption)
For oral disintegrating tablet dosage form of alprazolam
(Removing tablet from the bottle with dry hands just prior to administration)
(Immediately placing the tablet on top of the tongue where it will disintegrate, and be swallowed with saliva)
(Administering with liquid is not necessary)
(Discarding the other half of a scored tablet if only half was used because it may not remain stable)
» Importance of not taking more medication than the amount prescribed, because of habit-forming potential
» Not increasing dose if medication is less effective after a few weeks; checking with physician

For anticonvulsant use when on a regular dosing regimen
» Compliance with therapy; not missing any doses

For hypnotic use
» Taking only when schedule will allow a full night's sleep, to avoid amnesia and residual daytime sedation

For flurazepam only
» Maximum effectiveness of medication may not occur until 2 or 3 nights after initiation of therapy
» Proper dosing
Missed dose: If on scheduled dosing regimen (e.g., for epilepsy)—Taking right away if remembered within an hour or so; if remembered later, not taking at all; not doubling doses
» Proper storage
For alprazolam oral disintegrating tablets—Discarding any cotton that was included in the bottle and resealing the bottle tightly to prevent introducing moisture that might cause the tablets to disintegrate

Precautions while using this medication
Regular visits to physician to check progress during prolonged therapy (and during initial therapy for anticonvulsant use) and to evaluate need to continue benzodiazepine use

For anticonvulsant use:
Carrying medical identification card or bracelet during therapy

For sedative-hypnotic use:
Checking with physician if feel need to use medication for more than 7 to 10 days
Possibility of rebound insomnia after discontinuing medication
» Checking with physician if physical or psychological dependence is suspected
» Checking with physician before discontinuing medication after high-dose or prolonged use; gradual dosage reduction may be necessary to avoid the possibility of withdrawal symptoms and, in patients with epilepsy or history of seizures, the possibility of precipitating seizures
» Avoiding use of alcohol or other CNS depressants during therapy
» Suspected overdose: Getting emergency help at once
Caution if any laboratory tests required; possible interference with results of metyrapone test
» Not driving, riding a bicycle, or operating machinery until effects of medication are known or until effects of acute use have worn off, including residual daytime effects after use to treat insomnia, because of possible drowsiness, dizziness, lightheadedness, clumsiness, or unsteadiness; may be especially important for elderly patients

Side/adverse effects
Signs of potential side effects, especially anterograde amnesia, anxiety, confusion, mental depression, abnormal thinking, allergic reaction, behavior changes, blood dyscrasias, extrapyramidal symptoms, hepatic dysfunction, hypotension, muscle weakness, paradoxical reactions, or seizures
Most side/adverse effects are more likely to occur in children, especially the very young, and in elderly patients; these patients are usually more sensitive to effects of benzodiazepines
For patients receiving chlordiazepoxide, diazepam, or lorazepam injection: Checking with physician if redness, swelling, or pain at injection site occurs
Possibility of withdrawal symptoms

General Dosing Information
The possibility that a woman of childbearing potential may already be pregnant should be considered when initiating benzodiazepine treatment.

Geriatric or debilitated patients, children, or patients with hepatic or renal function impairment or low serum albumin should receive decreased initial dosage since elimination of benzodiazepines, especially those with long half-lives, may be decreased in these patients, resulting in increased CNS side effects such as oversedation, dizziness, or impaired coordination.

Benzodiazepines may suppress respiration, especially in the elderly, the very ill, the very young, and patients with limited pulmonary reserve. Lower doses may be required for these patients. Deaths occurring shortly after beginning treatment with alprazolam have been reported rarely in patients with severe pulmonary disease.

Optimal dosage of benzodiazepines varies with diagnosis and patient response. Individual dosage adjustments are important. The minimum effective dose should be used for the shortest period, with the need for continuing therapy with benzodiazepines reviewed regularly.

If daytime anxiety appears in a patient being treated for insomnia, discontinuation of the benzodiazepine should be considered.

Prolonged use and/or use of large doses of benzodiazepines increases the risk of developing psychological or physical dependence. However, withdrawal symptoms, including seizures, have occurred after short-term use at recommended doses of alprazolam. The risk of dependence among patients taking > 4 mg per day of alprazolam may be greater than among patients taking lower doses.

When a benzodiazepine is discontinued after treatment with a dose higher than the lowest dose for more than a few weeks, the medication should be withdrawn gradually to lessen the possibility of precipitating withdrawal symptoms, especially in patients with a history of seizures.

Depressed patients with suicidal tendencies, particularly those who use alcohol excessively, should not have access to large quantities of benzodiazepines.

For parenteral dosage forms only
Following administration of parenteral dosage forms, patients should be kept under observation for a period of 3 to 8 hours or longer, based on the patient's clinical response and rate of recovery.

Too rapid intravenous administration may result in apnea, hypotension, bradycardia, or cardiac or respiratory arrest.

Inadvertent intra-arterial injection of benzodiazepines may produce arteriospasm, resulting in gangrene.

When parenteral benzodiazepines are to be administered intravenously, equipment necessary to support respiration should be immediately available and a patent airway should be maintained. This may be especially important in the elderly and in children.

For treatment of dependence
Some clinicians substitute a long-acting benzodiazepine for short-acting agents before withdrawal is attempted.

Benzodiazepines should be tapered gradually, since there is some evidence that some withdrawal symptoms may be lessened in severity or avoided by gradual dosage reduction. Withdrawal schedules ranging from 4 to 16 weeks are usually suggested; however, some practitioners believe withdrawal should be completed within 2 weeks, thus exposing patients to withdrawal symptoms for a shorter length of time.

When necessary, the benzodiazepine may be reinstituted or another benzodiazepine may be substituted, at doses sufficient to suppress withdrawal symptoms, until restabilization allows continuance of the dosage taper, possibly at a slower rate.

ALPRAZOLAM

Summary of Differences
Category:
In addition to being indicated as an antianxiety agent, indicated as an antipanic agent and used as an antitremor agent.

Indications:
Also indicated for adjunctive management of anxiety associated with mental depression.

Pharmacology/pharmacokinetics:
Short to intermediate half-life benzodiazepine.
Accumulation is minimal during repeated dosing.
Steady-state plasma concentration usually attained within a few (2 to 3) days.
Elimination rapid following discontinuation of therapy.

Precautions:
Drug interactions and/or related problems—Elevation of steady-state plasma concentrations of imipramine and desipramine reported with concurrent use of alprazolam.

Medical considerations/contraindications—Episodes of hypomania and mania reported with use of alprazolam in patients with mental depression; deaths shortly after alprazolam therapy initiation reported rarely in patients with severe pulmonary disease.

Additional Dosing Information

See also *General Dosing Information.*

Dosage should be reduced gradually when therapy is discontinued or the daily dosage is decreased. It is suggested that the daily dosage be decreased by no more than 500 mcg (0.5 mg) every 3 days. However, some patients may need a slower reduction in dosage.

The occurrence of early morning anxiety or the emergence of anxiety symptoms between doses of alprazolam in panic disorder patients may reflect the development of tolerance, or a time interval between doses that exceeds the duration of clinical action of the administered dose. The manufacturer states that when these effects occur, the prescribed dose is presumed to be insufficient to maintain plasma levels above those needed to prevent relapse, rebound, or withdrawal symptoms over the course of the interdosing interval; they recommend that the same total daily dose be administered in more frequently divided doses.

Oral Dosage Forms

ALPRAZOLAM ORAL SOLUTION

Usual adult dose

Antianxiety agent—

Oral, initially 250 to 500 mcg (0.25 to 0.5 mg) three times a day, the dosage being titrated to the needs of the patient up to a maximum total dose of 4 mg per day.

Note: Debilitated patients—Oral, initially 250 mcg (0.25 mg) two or three times a day, the dosage being increased as needed and tolerated.

The starting dosage may be decreased if adverse effects occur.

Antipanic or [anti-agoraphobic][1] agent—

Oral, initially 500 mcg (0.5 mg) three times a day, the dosage being increased as needed and tolerated up to a maximum of 10 mg per day.

Usual pediatric dose

Antianxiety or antipanic agent—

Children younger than 18 years of age: Safety and efficacy have not been established.

Usual geriatric dose

Antianxiety agent—

Oral, initially 250 mcg (0.25 mg) two or three times a day, the dosage being increased as needed and tolerated.

Strength(s) usually available

U.S.—

0.1 mg per mL (Rx) [GENERIC].

1 mg per mL (Rx) [*Alprazolam Intensol*].

Canada—

Not commercially available.

Packaging and storage

Store between 15 and 30 °C (59 and 86 °F), unless otherwise specified by manufacturer. Store in a tight, light-resistant container.

Preparation of dosage form

For concentrated oral solution (1 mg per mL)—Measure dose with calibrated dropper provided with product. It is recommended that each dose be gently stirred into liquid or semi-solid food, such as water, soda or soda-like beverage, applesauce, or pudding, immediately before taking. Entire mixture should be consumed; no mixture should be stored for later use.

Auxiliary labeling

- Avoid alcoholic beverages.
- May cause drowsiness.

Note

Patient or caregiver should be instructed in proper measurement and, for concentrated oral solution (1 mg per mL), preparation of dose.

Controlled substance in the U.S.

ALPRAZOLAM TABLETS USP

Usual adult dose

See *Alprazolam Oral Solution.*

Usual pediatric dose

See *Alprazolam Oral Solution.*

Usual geriatric dose

See *Alprazolam Oral Solution.*

Strength(s) usually available

U.S.—

Note: The multi-scored 2-mg tablet can be broken to provide doses of 0.5 or 1 mg.

0.25 mg (Rx) [*Xanax* (scored; lactose; sodium benzoate); GENERIC (may be scored)].

0.5 mg (Rx) [*Xanax* (scored; docusate sodium; lactose; sodium benzoate); GENERIC (may be scored)].

1 mg (Rx) [*Xanax* (scored; docusate sodium; lactose; sodium benzoate); GENERIC (may be scored)].

2 mg (Rx) [*Xanax* (multi-scored; docusate sodium; lactose; sodium benzoate); GENERIC].

Canada—

Note: The triscored 2-mg tablet can be broken into four equal parts of 0.5 mg each.

0.25 mg (Rx) [*Alti-Alprazolam* (scored; lactose); *Apo-Alpraz* (scored; sodium < 0.14 mg); *Gen-Alprazolam* (lactose); *Novo-Alprazol; Nu-Alpraz* (scored; sodium < 0.14 mg); *Xanax* (scored; lactose)].

0.5 mg (Rx) [*Alti-Alprazolam* (scored; lactose); *Apo-Alpraz* (scored; sodium < 0.14 mg); *Gen-Alprazolam* (lactose); *Novo-Alprazol; Nu-Alpraz* (scored; sodium < 0.14 mg); *Xanax* (scored; lactose)].

1 mg (Rx) [*Gen-Alprazolam* (lactose); *Xanax* (scored; lactose)].

2 mg (Rx) [*Gen-Alprazolam* (lactose); *Xanax TS* (triscored; lactose)].

Packaging and storage

Store between 15 and 30 °C (59 and 86 °F), unless otherwise specified by manufacturer. Store in a tight, light-resistant container.

Auxiliary labeling

- Avoid alcoholic beverages.
- May cause drowsiness.

Note

Controlled substance in the U.S.

ALPRAZOLAM ORAL DISINTEGRATING TABLETS

Usual adult dose

See *Alprazolam Oral Solution.*

Usual pediatric dose

See *Alprazolam Oral Solution.*

Usual geriatric dose

See *Alprazolam Oral Solution.*

Strength(s) usually available

U.S.—

0.25 mg (Rx) [*Niravam* (colloidal silicon dioxide; corn starch; crospovidone; magnesium stearate; mannitol; methacrylic acid copolymer; microcrystalline cellulose; natural and artificial orange flavor; sucralose; sucrose; yellow iron oxide)].

0.5 mg (Rx) [*Niravam* (colloidal silicon dioxide; corn starch; crospovidone; magnesium stearate; mannitol; methacrylic acid copolymer; microcrystalline cellulose; natural and artificial orange flavor; sucralose; sucrose; yellow iron oxide)].

1 mg (Rx) [*Niravam* (colloidal silicon dioxide; corn starch; crospovidone; magnesium stearate; mannitol; methacrylic acid copolymer; microcrystalline cellulose; natural and artificial orange flavor; sucralose; sucrose)].

2 mg (Rx) [*Niravam* (colloidal silicon dioxide; corn starch; crospovidone; magnesium stearate; mannitol; methacrylic acid copolymer; microcrystalline cellulose; natural and artificial orange flavor; sucralose; sucrose)].

Canada—

Not commercially available

Packaging and storage

Store between 20 and 25 °C (68 and 77 °F), excursions permitted between 15 and 30 °C (59 and 86 °F). Protect from moisture.

Stability

If only one half of a scored tablet is used for dosing, the unused portion of the tablet should be discarded immediately because it may not remain stable.

Discard any cotton that was included in the bottle and reseal the bottle tightly to prevent introducing moisture that might cause the tablets to disintegrate.

Auxiliary labeling

- Keep in the original container. Close container tightly after use.

Additional information

Proper handling/administration—Just prior to administration, with dry hands, remove the tablet from the bottle. Immediately place the tablet on top of the tongue where it will disintegrate, and be swallowed with saliva. Administration with liquid is not necessary.

[1]Not included in Canadian product labeling.

BROMAZEPAM

Summary of Differences

Category:
Indicated only as an antianxiety agent.

Pharmacology/pharmacokinetics:
Short to intermediate half-life benzodiazepine.
Accumulation is minimal during repeated dosing.
Steady-state plasma concentration usually attained within a few (2 to 3) days.
Elimination rapid following discontinuation of therapy.

Oral Dosage Forms

BROMAZEPAM TABLETS

Usual adult dose

Antianxiety agent—
Oral, 6 to 30 mg per day in divided doses.

Note: Dosages of up to 60 mg may be used in severe cases.

Debilitated patients—Initial daily dosage should not exceed 3 mg in divided doses, the dosage being carefully adjusted as needed and tolerated.

Usual pediatric dose

Antianxiety agent—
Children younger than 18 years of age: Safety and efficacy have not been established.

Usual geriatric dose

Antianxiety agent—
Oral, initially up to 3 mg per day, the dosage being carefully adjusted as needed and tolerated.

Strength(s) usually available

U.S.—
Not commercially available.

Canada—
1.5 mg (Rx) [*Alti-Bromazepam* (scored; lactose); *Gen-Bromazepam* (scored; lactose); *Lectopam* (scored; lactose 96 mg)].
3 mg (Rx) [*Alti-Bromazepam* (scored; lactose); *Gen-Bromazepam* (scored; lactose); *Lectopam* (scored; lactose 94 mg)].
6 mg (Rx) [*Alti-Bromazepam* (scored; lactose); *Gen-Bromazepam* (scored; lactose); *Lectopam* (scored; lactose 91 mg)].

Packaging and storage

Store below 40 °C (104 °F), preferably between 15 and 30 °C (59 and 86 °F), in a well-closed container, unless otherwise specified by manufacturer.

Auxiliary labeling

- Avoid alcoholic beverages.
- May cause drowsiness.

CHLORDIAZEPOXIDE

Summary of Differences

Category:
In addition to being indicated as an antianxiety agent and a sedative-hypnotic, oral chlordiazepoxide is used as an antitremor agent and parenteral chlordiazepoxide is used as an antipanic agent.

Indications:
Also indicated for relief of acute alcohol withdrawal symptoms and as a preoperative medication.
Also used in treatment of tension headache.

Pharmacology/pharmacokinetics:
Absorption of intramuscular chlordiazepoxide may be slow and erratic.
Long half-life benzodiazepine.
Accumulation of chlordiazepoxide and its active metabolites is significant during repeated dosing.
Steady-state plasma concentration usually attained in 5 days to 2 weeks.
Elimination slow since metabolites remain in blood for several days or even weeks.

Precautions:
Drug interactions and/or related problems—
Antacids may delay the rate of but not reduce the extent of absorption of chlordiazepoxide.
Medical considerations/contraindications—
Hypoalbuminemia may predispose patient to an increased incidence of sedative side effects.
Porphyria may be exacerbated by use of chlordiazepoxide.

Side/adverse effects:
Intravenous chlordiazepoxide less likely to cause phlebitis or venous thrombosis than diazepam or lorazepam.

Additional Dosing Information

See also *General Dosing Information*.

For parenteral dosage forms only

Intramuscular injections should be administered deeply into the muscle; absorption may be slow and erratic, but effects are usually seen in 15 to 30 minutes.

When more rapid effect is mandatory, chlordiazepoxide hydrochloride solution prepared with sterile physiological saline (0.9% sodium chloride injection) or sterile water for injection may be administered intravenously.

Intravenous administration of the intramuscular preparation is not recommended by the manufacturer because of the air bubbles that may form when the intramuscular diluent is added to the chlordiazepoxide hydrochloride powder.

Intravenous injections should be administered slowly over a 1-minute period.

The chlordiazepoxide hydrochloride solution prepared with sterile physiological saline (0.9% sodium chloride injection) or sterile water for injection should not be administered intramuscularly because of pain on injection.

Oral Dosage Forms

CHLORDIAZEPOXIDE HYDROCHLORIDE CAPSULES USP

Usual adult dose

Antianxiety agent—
Oral, 5 to 25 mg three or four times a day.

Note: Debilitated patients—Oral, 5 mg two to four times a day, the dosage being increased gradually as needed and tolerated.

Sedative-hypnotic—
Alcohol withdrawal: Oral, initially 50 to 100 mg, repeated as needed, up to 400 mg per day, the dosage then reduced to maintenance levels.

Usual pediatric dose

Antianxiety agent—
Children younger than 6 years of age: Safety and efficacy have not been established.
Children 6 years of age and older: Oral, 5 mg two to four times a day, the dosage being increased, if necessary, to 10 mg two or three times a day.

Usual geriatric dose

Antianxiety agent—
Oral, 5 mg two to four times a day, the dosage being increased gradually as needed and tolerated.

Strength(s) usually available

U.S.—
5 mg (Rx) [*Librium* (lactose; gelatin capsule shells may contain methyl and propyl parabens and potassium sorbate); GENERIC].
10 mg (Rx) [*Librium* (lactose; gelatin capsule shells may contain methyl and propyl parabens and potassium sorbate); GENERIC].
25 mg (Rx) [*Librium* (lactose; gelatin capsule shells may contain methyl and propyl parabens and potassium sorbate); GENERIC].

Canada—
5 mg (Rx) [*Apo-Chlordiazepoxide; Novo-Poxide* (lactose)].
10 mg (Rx) [*Apo-Chlordiazepoxide; Novo-Poxide* (lactose)].
25 mg (Rx) [*Apo-Chlordiazepoxide; Novo-Poxide* (lactose)].

Packaging and storage

Store below 40 °C (104 °F), preferably between 15 and 30 °C (59 and 86 °F), unless otherwise specified by manufacturer. Store in a tight, light-resistant container.

Auxiliary labeling

- Avoid alcoholic beverages.
- May cause drowsiness.

Note
Controlled substance in the U.S.

Parenteral Dosage Forms

Note: Bracketed uses in the *Dosage Forms* section refer to categories of use and/or indications that are not included in U.S. product labeling.

CHLORDIAZEPOXIDE HYDROCHLORIDE FOR INJECTION USP

Usual adult dose
Antianxiety agent—
Intramuscular or intravenous, initially 50 to 100 mg, then 25 to 50 mg three or four times a day, if necessary.
Preoperative: Intramuscular, 50 to 100 mg one hour prior to surgery.
Sedative-hypnotic—
Alcohol withdrawal: Intramuscular or intravenous, initially 50 to 100 mg, repeated in two to four hours, if necessary.
[Antipanic agent]—
Intramuscular or intravenous, initially 50 to 100 mg, repeated in four to six hours if necessary.
Note: Debilitated patients—Intramuscular or intravenous, 25 to 50 mg per dose.

Usual adult prescribing limits
300 mg per day.

Usual pediatric dose
Antianxiety agent or
Sedative-hypnotic—
Children younger than 12 years of age: Safety and efficacy have not been established.
Children 12 years of age and older: Intramuscular or intravenous, 25 to 50 mg per dose.

Usual geriatric dose
Antianxiety agent or
Sedative-hypnotic—
Intramuscular or intravenous, 25 to 50 mg per dose.

Strength(s) usually available
U.S.—
100 mg, with 2 mL of special intramuscular diluent (Rx) [*Librium* (benzyl alcohol 1.5%; polysorbate 80 4%; propylene glycol 20%; maleic acid 1.6%; sodium hydroxide)].
Canada—
Not commercially available.

Packaging and storage
Prior to reconstitution, store below 40 °C (104 °F), preferably between 15 and 30 °C (59 and 86 °F), unless otherwise specified by manufacturer. Protect from light.
Note: Chlordiazepoxide injectable diluent should be stored between 2 and 8 °C (36 and 46 °F).

Preparation of dosage form
Solutions of chlordiazepoxide hydrochloride for intramuscular or intravenous use should be prepared immediately before administration.
To prepare solution for intramuscular use, add 2 mL of the special intramuscular diluent (supplied by manufacturer) to the ampul containing 100 mg of chlordiazepoxide hydrochloride. The diluent solution should not be used if it is opalescent or hazy. The diluent should be added carefully to the ampul of powder to avoid bubble formation. Agitate the ampul gently until the powder is completely dissolved.
To prepare solution for intravenous use, add 5 mL of 0.9% sodium chloride injection or sterile water for injection to the ampul containing 100 mg of chlordiazepoxide hydrochloride. Agitate the ampul gently until the powder is completely dissolved.

Stability
If the diluent is stored at room temperature, it will remain stable for 18 to 20 months rather than until the expiration date, which reflects a stability period of 36 months. As the diluent alters, it develops slight opalescence; do not use if opalescent. Stability of diluent will not be affected by 2 to 4 weeks at room temperature.
After reconstitution, solution should be used immediately.
Any unused portion of the solution should be discarded.
Sterilization by heating should not be done.

Caution
Use of diluents containing benzyl alcohol is not recommended for preparation of medications for use in neonates (first 30 days of postnatal life). A fatal toxic syndrome consisting of metabolic acidosis, CNS depression, respiratory problems, renal failure, hypotension, and possibly seizures and intracranial hemorrhages has been associated with this use.

Note
Controlled substance in the U.S.

CLOBAZAM

Summary of Differences

Category:
Indicated as an anticonvulsant only.
Pharmacology/pharmacokinetics:
Intermediate half-life benzodiazepine.

Additional Dosing Information

See also *General Dosing Information*.
Daily dosages of up to 30 mg may be taken as a single dose at bedtime. If the daily dosage is divided, the larger portion should be taken at bedtime.
There have been reports of development of tolerance to the anticonvulsant effects of clobazam with continuous, long-term use. There are insufficient data to predict which patients will develop tolerance or when this might occur. Some studies in catamenial epilepsy have indicated that efficacy may be maintained with intermittent use. However, long-term results from intermittent-use studies are not available.

Oral Dosage Forms

CLOBAZAM TABLETS

Usual adult dose
Anticonvulsant—
Oral, initially 5 to 15 mg per day. Dosage may be increased gradually as needed.
Note: Dosage should be reduced in patients with impaired hepatic or renal function.

Usual adult prescribing limits
80 mg per day.

Usual pediatric dose
Anticonvulsant—
Children younger than 2 years of age: Oral, initially 0.5 to 1 mg per kg of body weight per day.
Children 2 to 16 years of age: Oral, initially 5 mg per day. Dosage may be increased at five-day intervals.

Usual pediatric prescribing limits
Children 2 to 16 years of age—40 mg per day.

Strength(s) usually available
U.S.—
Not commercially available.
Canada—
10 mg (Rx) [*Frisium* (scored; lactose)].

Packaging and storage
Store in original container at room temperature, below 25 °C (77 °F), unless otherwise specified by manufacturer.

Auxiliary labeling
- May cause drowsiness or dizziness.
- Avoid alcoholic beverages.

CLONAZEPAM

Summary of Differences

Category:
In addition to being indicated as an anticonvulsant, indicated as an antipanic agent.
Pharmacology/pharmacokinetics:
Intermediate half-life benzodiazepine.
Precautions:
Pregnancy—
Increased incidence of congenital abnormalities in children whose mothers used anticonvulsants during pregnancy; studies in animals have shown that clonazepam causes a non–dose-related increased incidence of cleft palates, open eyelids, fused sternebrae, and limb defects; withdrawal of clonazepam prior to or during pregnancy should be considered only when seizures are mild and infrequent in absence of medication and the

possibility of status epilepticus and withdrawal symptoms is considered low.

Pediatrics—

It is possible that long-term use of clonazepam may result in adverse effects on physical or mental development that may not become apparent for many years.

Medical considerations/contraindications—

Initiation or abrupt withdrawal of clonazepam in patients with epilepsy or a history of seizures may precipitate seizures or status epilepticus.

Caution should be used in surgical or non-ambulatory patients because of cough suppressant effects of clonazepam.

Additional Dosing Information

See also *General Dosing Information.*

In some studies, up to 30% of patients have shown loss of anticonvulsant activity after a few (often within 3) months of therapy; dosage adjustment may restore efficacy of clonazepam.

In order to maintain seizure control when clonazepam is used to replace other anticonvulsant therapy, the dosage of clonazepam should be increased gradually while the dosage of the other medication is decreased gradually; when clonazepam is used to supplement other anticonvulsant therapy, the dosage of clonazepam should be increased gradually until seizure activity is controlled adequately and then the dosage of the other medication may be decreased gradually if necessary.

Also, clonazepam should be withdrawn gradually, especially in patients being treated for epilepsy and in patients who have received long-term, high-dose therapy, since abrupt withdrawal may precipitate seizures or status epilepticus. During withdrawal of clonazepam, the simultaneous administration of another anticonvulsant may be indicated in patients with epilepsy. The manufacturer recommends clonazepam dosage be decreased by 0.125 mg two times a day every 3 days.

Oral Dosage Forms

CLONAZEPAM TABLETS USP

Usual adult dose

Anticonvulsant—

Oral, initially up to 500 mcg (0.5 mg) three times a day; the dosage may be increased in increments of 500 to 1000 mcg (0.5 to 1 mg) every three days until seizures are controlled or until side effects prevent any further increase.

Note: Maintenance dose must be individualized, depending on patient's response.

Antipanic agent[1]—

Oral, initially 250 mcg (0.25 mg) two times a day, the dosage being increased to 1000 mcg (1 mg) per day after three days in most patients. The dosage may be increased in increments of 125 to 250 mcg (0.125 to 0.25 mg) two times a day every three days until panic disorder is controlled or until side effects prevent further dosage increases. One dose may be taken at bedtime to minimize daytime somnolence.

Note: A fixed-dose study comparing dosages of 1, 2, 3, and 4 mg per day in the treatment of panic disorder found that a dosage of 1000 mcg (1 mg) per day was the most effective and best tolerated dosage for most patients.

Usual adult prescribing limits

Anticonvulsant—

20 mg per day.

Antipanic agent[1]—

4 mg per day.

Usual pediatric dose

Anticonvulsant—

Infants and children younger than 10 years of age or less than 30 kg of body weight: Oral, initially 10 to 30 mcg (0.01 to 0.03 mg), not to exceed 50 mcg (0.05 mg), per kg of body weight per day in two or three divided doses, the dosage being increased by no more than 250 to 500 mcg (0.25 to 0.5 mg) every third day until a maintenance dose of 100 to 200 mcg (0.1 to 0.2 mg) per kg of body weight per day is reached or until seizures are controlled or side effects prevent a further increase.

Note: The daily dose should be divided into three equal doses, if possible. If doses are not divided equally, the largest dose should be given at bedtime.

Antipanic agent[1]—

Safety and efficacy have not been established in children up to 18 years of age.

Strength(s) usually available

U.S.—

0.5 mg (Rx) [*Klonopin* (scored; lactose); GENERIC (may be scored)].

1 mg (Rx) [*Klonopin* (lactose); GENERIC (may be scored)].

2 mg (Rx) [*Klonopin* (lactose); GENERIC (may be scored)].

Canada—

0.25 mg (Rx) [*PMS-Clonazepam* (lactose)].

0.5 mg (Rx) [*Alti-Clonazepam* (scored; lactose); *Apo-Clonazepam* (scored); *Clonapam* (scored; lactose); *Gen-Clonazepam; PMS-Clonazepam* (scored; lactose); *Rivotril* (scored; lactose 122 mg)].

1 mg (Rx) [*Clonapam* (scored; lactose); *PMS-Clonazepam* (lactose)].

2 mg (Rx) [*Alti-Clonazepam* (cross-scored; lactose); *Apo-Clonazepam* (scored); *Clonapam* (scored; lactose); *Gen-Clonazepam; PMS-Clonazepam* (lactose); *Rivotril* (scored; lactose 122 mg)].

Packaging and storage

Store between 15 and 30 °C (59 and 86 °F). Store in a tight, light-resistant container.

Auxiliary labeling

- Avoid alcoholic beverages.
- May cause drowsiness.

Note

Controlled substance in the U.S.

---

[1]Not included in Canadian product labeling.

CLORAZEPATE

Summary of Differences

Category:

In addition to being indicated as an antianxiety agent and a sedative-hypnotic, indicated as an anticonvulsant.

Indications:

Also indicated for relief of acute alcohol withdrawal symptoms.

Pharmacology/pharmacokinetics:

Drug precursor; metabolized to desmethyldiazepam before absorption.

Orally, one of most rapidly absorbed benzodiazepines.

Long half-life benzodiazepine.

Accumulation of active metabolites is significant during repeated dosing.

Steady-state plasma concentration usually attained in 5 days to 2 weeks.

Elimination slow since metabolites remain in blood for several days or even weeks.

Precautions:

Drug interactions and/or related problems—

Antacids may decrease rate of conversion to desmethyldiazepam but do not affect degree of absorption.

Additional Dosing Information

See also *General Dosing Information.*

When used for alcohol withdrawal, excessive reductions in the total amount of medication administered on successive days should be avoided.

Oral Dosage Forms

CLORAZEPATE DIPOTASSIUM CAPSULES

Usual adult and adolescent dose

Antianxiety agent—

Oral, 7.5 to 15 mg two to four times a day; or 15 mg initially, as a single dose at bedtime, the dosage being adjusted as needed and tolerated.

Note: Debilitated patients—Oral, initially 3.75 to 15 mg per day, the dosage being increased gradually as needed and tolerated.

Sedative-hypnotic—

Alcohol withdrawal: Oral, 30 mg initially, followed by 15 mg two to four times a day the first day; 15 mg three to six times a day the second day; 7.5 to 15 mg three times a day the third day; 7.5 mg two to four times a day the fourth day; and thereafter, 3.75 mg two to four times a day. Discontinue when patient's condition is stable.

Anticonvulsant[1]—

Oral, initially up to 7.5 mg three times a day, the dosage being increased by no more than 7.5 mg per week, not to exceed 90 mg per day.

Usual adult prescribing limits

90 mg per day.

Usual pediatric dose
Children younger than 9 years of age: Safety and efficacy have not been established.
Anticonvulsant[1]—
Children 9 to 12 years of age: Oral, initially up to 7.5 mg two times a day, the dosage being increased by no more than 7.5 mg per week, not to exceed 60 mg per day.
Children 12 years of age and older: See *Usual adult and adolescent dose.*

Usual geriatric dose
Antianxiety agent—
Oral, initially 3.75 to 15 mg per day, the dosage being increased gradually as needed and tolerated.

Strength(s) usually available
U.S.—
Not commercially available.
Canada—
3.75 mg (Rx) [*Apo-Clorazepate; Novo-Clopate; Tranxene*].
7.5 mg (Rx) [*Apo-Clorazepate; Novo-Clopate; Tranxene*].
15 mg (Rx) [*Apo-Clorazepate; Novo-Clopate*].

Packaging and storage
Store below 40 °C (104 °F), preferably between 15 and 30 °C (59 and 86 °F), in a tight, light-resistant container, unless otherwise specified by manufacturer.

Auxiliary labeling
- Avoid alcoholic beverages.
- May cause drowsiness.

CLORAZEPATE DIPOTASSIUM TABLETS USP

Usual adult and adolescent dose
See *Clorazepate Dipotassium Capsules.*

Usual adult prescribing limits
See *Clorazepate Dipotassium Capsules.*

Usual pediatric dose
See *Clorazepate Dipotassium Capsules.*

Usual geriatric dose
See *Clorazepate Dipotassium Capsules.*

Strength(s) usually available
U.S.—
3.75 mg (Rx) [*Tranxene T-Tab* (scored); GENERIC (may be scored)].
7.5 mg (Rx) [*Tranxene T-Tab* (scored); GENERIC (may be scored)].
15 mg (Rx) [*Tranxene T-Tab* (scored); GENERIC (may be scored)].
Canada—
Not commercially available.

Packaging and storage
Store between 15 and 30 °C (59 and 86 °F), in a tight, light-resistant container, unless otherwise specified by manufacturer.

Stability
Clorazepate dipotassium degrades in the presence of moisture. One of the degradation products is carbon dioxide gas, which tends to cause the tablets to "blow apart" and disintegrate very rapidly. The drug is also sensitive to heat and light. Pharmacists are advised to retain the desiccant when opening a new stock bottle of the product. If it is necessary to repackage the drug into unit doses, it is recommended that pharmacists be certain that the packaging materials used for unit-dose containers will produce a Class A package as defined in the USP. Multiple-dose containers should meet USP "tight" and "light-resistant" specifications. Pharmacists should consider using desiccant packets when dispensing a large number of tablets in a multiple-dose container. If shipping or mailing prescriptions, pharmacists should take into account these instability problems. Patients should be warned not to expose the product to moisture, light, or heat, and, when possible, to keep the tablets in the original containers.

Auxiliary labeling
- Avoid alcoholic beverages.
- May cause drowsiness.

Note
Controlled substance in the U.S.

CLORAZEPATE DIPOTASSIUM EXTENDED-RELEASE TABLETS

Usual adult and adolescent dose
Not intended for initiation of therapy. Single daily dose of 11.25 mg may be substituted for prompt-release dosage forms in patients already stabilized on a dosage of 3.75 mg three times a day. Single daily dose of 22.5 mg may be substituted for prompt-release dosage forms in patients already stabilized on a dosage of 7.5 mg three times a day.

Usual pediatric dose
Children younger than 9 years of age—Safety and efficacy have not been established.
Children 9 to 12 years of age—See *Usual adult and adolescent dose.*

Usual geriatric dose
See *Usual adult and adolescent dose.*

Strength(s) usually available
U.S.—
11.25 mg (Rx) [*Tranxene-SD Half Strength* (lactose; potassium carbonate; potassium chloride; castor oil wax; magnesium stearate; magnesium oxide; talc; FD&C Blue #2)].
22.5 mg (Rx) [*Tranxene-SD* (iron oxide; lactose; potassium carbonate; potassium chloride; castor oil wax; magnesium stearate; magnesium oxide; talc)].
Canada—
Not commercially available.

Packaging and storage
Store between 15 and 30 °C (59 and 86 °F), in a tight, light-resistant container, unless otherwise specified by manufacturer.

Stability
Clorazepate dipotassium degrades in the presence of moisture. One of the degradation products is carbon dioxide gas, which tends to cause the tablets to "blow apart" and disintegrate very rapidly. The drug is also sensitive to heat and light. Pharmacists are advised to retain the desiccant when opening a new stock bottle of the product. If it is necessary to repackage the drug into unit doses, it is recommended that pharmacists be certain that the packaging materials used for unit-dose containers will produce a Class A package as defined in the USP. Multiple-dose containers should meet USP "tight" and "light-resistant" specifications. Pharmacists should consider using desiccant packets when dispensing a large number of tablets in a multiple-dose container. If shipping or mailing prescriptions, pharmacists should take into account these instability problems. Patients should be warned not to expose the product to moisture, light, or heat, and, when possible, to keep the tablets in the original containers.

Auxiliary labeling
- Avoid alcoholic beverages.
- May cause drowsiness.
- Swallow tablets whole.

Note
Clorazepate dipotassium extended-release tablets are not intended to be used to initiate therapy, but to provide ease of dosing in patients who are already stabilized on clorazepate dipotassium at a dosage that allows direct substitution of the extended-release tablet for the prompt-release dosage forms.

Controlled substance in the U.S.

[1]Not included in Canadian product labeling.

DIAZEPAM

Summary of Differences

Category:
In addition to being indicated as an antianxiety agent and a sedative-hypnotic, indicated as an anticonvulsant and a skeletal muscle relaxant adjunct and used as an antipanic agent.
Parenteral diazepam also indicated as an amnestic.
Oral diazepam also used as an antitremor agent.

Indications:
Also indicated for relief of acute alcohol withdrawal symptoms, for the treatment of status epilepticus, and as a preoperative medication.
Parenteral diazepam also indicated as an adjunct prior to endoscopic procedures; indicated prior to cardioversion; and used in dentistry to produce conscious sedation.
Also used to relieve spasms of facial muscles associated with problems of occlusion and temporomandibular joint disorders, and for the treatment of tension headache.

Pharmacology/pharmacokinetics:
Orally, the most rapidly absorbed benzodiazepine.
Absorption of intramuscular diazepam may be slow and erratic, depending upon administration site; usually rapid and complete when injected into the deltoid muscle.
Absorption of rectal diazepam gel or solution is rapid.
Long half-life benzodiazepine.
Accumulation of diazepam and its active metabolites is significant during repeated dosing.

Steady-state plasma concentration usually attained in 5 days to 2 weeks.
Elimination slow since metabolites remain in blood for several days or even weeks.

Precautions:
Sensitivity—
Sterile emulsion dosage form contains soybean oil.
Pregnancy—
Administration (especially intramuscular or intravenous) in doses of more than 30 mg within 15 hours before delivery may cause apnea, hypotonia, hypothermia, a reluctance to feed, and impaired metabolic response to cold stress in the neonate.
Drug interactions and/or related problems—
Antacids may delay but not reduce the absorption of diazepam.
Premedication with diazepam may decrease dose of a fentanyl derivative required for induction of anesthesia and decrease time to loss of consciousness with induction doses.
Diazepam in parenteral dosage forms adheres to plastic infusion tubing.
Isoniazid may inhibit elimination of diazepam, resulting in increased plasma concentrations.
Rifampin may enhance elimination of diazepam, resulting in decreased plasma concentrations.
Medical considerations/contraindications—
Initiation or abrupt withdrawal of diazepam in patients with epilepsy or a history of seizures may precipitate seizures or status epilepticus. Use of intravenous diazepam for absence status or Lennox-Gastaut syndrome status may precipitate tonic status epilepticus.
Hypoalbuminemia may predispose patient to increased incidence of sedative side effects.

Side/adverse effects:
Intravenous diazepam more likely to cause phlebitis or venous thrombosis than chlordiazepoxide or lorazepam.

Additional Dosing Information

See also *General Dosing Information.*

For oral dosage forms only

When diazepam is used as an adjunct in treating convulsive disorders, the possibility of an increase in the frequency and/or severity of generalized tonic-clonic (grand mal) seizures may require an increase in dosage of standard anticonvulsant medication. Also, abrupt withdrawal of diazepam may result in a temporary increase in the frequency and/or severity of seizures.

For parenteral dosage forms only

Intravenous administration of diazepam is usually preferred, since absorption may be slow and erratic following intramuscular administration depending upon site of injection.

If intramuscular injections of diazepam are used, they should be administered deeply into the deltoid muscle.

For intravenous injections of diazepam, small veins such as those on the back of the hand or wrist should not be used and care should be taken to avoid intra-arterial administration or extravasation in order to reduce the possibility of venous thrombosis, phlebitis, local irritation, swelling, and, rarely, vascular impairment.

For intravenous injections, the medication should be injected slowly into a large vein, taking at least 1 minute for each 5 mg (1 mL) of medication given, due to the risk of thrombophlebitis.

When subsequent doses are administered within 1 to 4 hours, consideration should be given to the possibility that active metabolites may still be present from the initial dose.

Continuous intravenous infusion of diazepam is not recommended because of the possibility of precipitation of diazepam in intravenous fluids and adsorption of the medication to the plastic of infusion bags and tubing.

If diazepam cannot be administered by direct intravenous injection, it may be injected slowly through an infusion tubing as close as possible to the insertion point to minimize adsorption of the medication to the plastic tubing.

When intravenous diazepam is used to control seizures, a significant proportion of patients will return to seizure activity and will require additional doses.

When parenteral diazepam is used for peroral endoscopic procedures, the use of a topical anesthetic and availability of necessary countermeasures are recommended since these procedures may cause an increase in cough reflex and laryngospasm.

For rectal gel dosage form only

Diazepam rectal gel should be administered only by caregivers who are able to distinguish the distinct cluster of seizures to be treated, or the events accompanying their onset, from the patient's usual seizure activity, and who understand which seizure manifestations may or may not be treated with diazepam rectal gel. The caregiver also must be competent in the proper administration of the rectal gel and in monitoring the patient's response, including recognizing when professional medical attention is required.

Caregivers should be instructed to notify the physician immediately of any signs that are not typical of the patient's characteristic seizure episode.

Oral Dosage Forms

DIAZEPAM ORAL SOLUTION

Usual adult dose

Antianxiety agent—
Oral, 2 to 10 mg two to four times a day.
Sedative-hypnotic—
Alcohol withdrawal: Oral, 10 mg three or four times during the first twenty-four hours, the dosage being decreased to 5 mg three or four times a day as needed.
Anticonvulsant—
Oral, 2 to 10 mg two to four times a day.
Skeletal muscle relaxant adjunct—
Oral, 2 to 10 mg three or four times a day.

Note: Debilitated patients—Oral, 2 to 2.5 mg one or two times a day, the dosage being increased gradually as needed and tolerated.

Usual pediatric dose

Antianxiety agent or
Anticonvulsant or
Skeletal muscle relaxant adjunct—
Children younger than 6 months of age: Use is not recommended.
Children 6 months of age and older: Oral, 1 to 2.5 mg, or 40 to 200 mcg (0.04 to 0.2 mg) per kg of body weight, or 1.17 to 6 mg per square meter of body surface area, three or four times a day, the dosage being increased gradually as needed and tolerated.

Usual geriatric dose

Antianxiety agent or
Sedative-hypnotic or
Anticonvulsant or
Skeletal muscle relaxant adjunct—
Oral, 2 to 2.5 mg one or two times a day, the dosage being increased gradually as needed and tolerated.

Strength(s) usually available

U.S.—
5 mg per mL (Rx) [*Diazepam Intensol*].
5 mg per 5 mL (Rx) [GENERIC].
Canada—
1 mg per mL (Rx) [*PMS-Diazepam*].

Packaging and storage

Store below 40 °C (104 °F), preferably between 15 and 30 °C (59 and 86 °F), in a well-closed container, unless otherwise specified by manufacturer. Protect from freezing.

Preparation of dosage form

For concentrated oral solution (5 mg per mL)—Measure dose with calibrated dropper provided with product. It is recommended that each dose be mixed with liquid or soft food, such as water, juice, soda, pudding, or applesauce, immediately before taking. The entire mixture should be consumed; none of the mixture should be stored for later use.

Auxiliary labeling

- Avoid alcoholic beverages.
- May cause drowsiness.

Note

Patient or caregiver should be instructed in proper measurement of the dose and, for concentrated oral solution (5 mg per mL), preparation of the dose.

Controlled substance in the U.S.

DIAZEPAM TABLETS USP

Usual adult dose

See *Diazepam Oral Solution.*

Usual pediatric dose

See *Diazepam Oral Solution.*

Usual geriatric dose

See *Diazepam Oral Solution.*

Strength(s) usually available

U.S.—
2 mg (Rx) [*Valium* (scored); GENERIC].
5 mg (Rx) [*Valium* (scored); GENERIC].
10 mg (Rx) [*Valium* (scored); GENERIC].

Canada—
2 mg (Rx) [*Apo-Diazepam* (scored); *Novo-Dipam* (scored); *Vivol* (double-scored; lactose; sodium < 1 mmol [trace])].
5 mg (Rx) [*Apo-Diazepam* (scored); *Novo-Dipam* (scored); *Valium* (scored; lactose); *Vivol* (double-scored; lactose; sodium < 1 mmol [trace])].
10 mg (Rx) [*Apo-Diazepam* (scored); *Novo-Dipam* (scored); *Valium* (scored; lactose 100 mg); *Vivol* (double-scored; lactose; sodium < 1 mmol [trace])].

Packaging and storage
Store below 40 °C (104 °F), preferably between 15 and 30 °C (59 and 86 °F), unless otherwise specified by manufacturer. Store in a tight, light-resistant container.

Auxiliary labeling
- Avoid alcoholic beverages.
- May cause drowsiness.

Note
Controlled substance in the U.S.

Parenteral Dosage Forms

DIAZEPAM INJECTION USP

Usual adult dose
Antianxiety agent—
Preoperative medication: Dosage must be individualized; however, as a general guideline—Intramuscular or intravenous, 5 to 10 mg prior to surgery.
Anxiety disorders or symptoms of anxiety: Intramuscular or intravenous, 2 to 10 mg (2 to 5 mg for moderate symptoms; 5 to 10 mg for severe symptoms), the dose being repeated in three or four hours, if necessary.
Sedative-hypnotic—
Alcohol withdrawal: Intramuscular or intravenous, initially 10 mg, followed by 5 to 10 mg in three or four hours, if necessary.
Amnestic—
Cardioversion: Intravenous, 5 to 15 mg five to ten minutes prior to the procedure.
Endoscopic procedures: Intravenous (preferred route), up to 20 mg, the dosage being titrated to give the desired sedative response and administered immediately prior to the procedure. Intramuscular, 5 to 10 mg approximately thirty minutes prior to the procedure.
Anticonvulsant—
Status epilepticus and severe recurrent convulsive seizures: Intravenous, initially 5 to 10 mg, the dose being repeated, if necessary, at ten- to fifteen-minute intervals up to a cumulative dose of 30 mg. If necessary, regimen may be repeated in two to four hours.
Note: The intravenous route of administration is preferred; however, if intravenous administration is impossible, the intramuscular route of administration may be used.
Some clinicians have used continuous intravenous infusions of diazepam in the treatment of selected patients with status epilepticus refractory to initial treatment. However, this method of administration is problematic due to inherent adsorption problems with plastic infusion bags and tubing.
Skeletal muscle relaxant adjunct—
Muscle spasm: Intramuscular or intravenous, initially 5 to 10 mg, the dose being repeated in three or four hours, if necessary. For tetanus, larger doses may be required.
Note: Debilitated patients—Intramuscular or intravenous, initially 2 to 5 mg per dose, the dosage being increased gradually as needed and tolerated.

Usual pediatric dose
Neonates 30 days of age and younger—Safety and efficacy have not been established.
Anticonvulsant—
Status epilepticus and severe recurrent convulsive seizures:
Infants older than 30 days of age and children younger than 5 years of age—Intravenous (slow), 200 to 500 mcg (0.2 to 0.5 mg) every two to five minutes up to a cumulative dose of 5 mg.
If necessary, regimen may be repeated in two to four hours.
Children 5 years of age and older—Intravenous (slow), 1 mg every two to five minutes up to a cumulative dose of 10 mg. If necessary, regimen may be repeated in two to four hours.
Note: The intravenous route of administration is preferred; however, if intravenous administration is impossible, the intramuscular route of administration may be used.

Skeletal muscle relaxant adjunct—
Tetanus:
Infants older than 30 days of age and children younger than 5 years of age—Intramuscular or intravenous, 1 to 2 mg, the dose being repeated every three or four hours as needed.
Children 5 years of age and older—Intramuscular or intravenous, 5 to 10 mg, the dose being repeated every three or four hours as needed.
Note: In general, when the intravenous route is used in infants and children, it is recommended that the medication be administered slowly over a three-minute period in a dose not to exceed 250 mcg (0.25 mg) per kg of body weight. After an interval of fifteen to thirty minutes, a second dose may be administered. After an additional interval of fifteen to thirty minutes, a third dose may be administered. If the third administration does not provide relief of symptoms, adjunctive treatment appropriate to the condition being treated should be considered.

Usual geriatric dose
Antianxiety agent or
Sedative-hypnotic or
Amnestic or
Anticonvulsant or
Skeletal muscle relaxant adjunct—
Intramuscular or intravenous, initially 2 to 5 mg per dose, the dosage being increased gradually as needed and tolerated.

Strength(s) usually available
U.S.—
5 mg per mL (Rx) [*Valium* (benzoic acid; benzyl alcohol 1.5%; ethyl alcohol 10%; propylene glycol 40%; sodium benzoate 5%); GENERIC].
Canada—
5 mg per mL (Rx) [*Valium* (benzyl alcohol 16 mg; ethyl alcohol 80 mg; propylene glycol 414 mg; sodium < 1 mmol; sodium benzoate; benzoic acid)].

Packaging and storage
Store below 40 °C (104 °F), preferably between 15 and 30 °C (59 and 86 °F), unless otherwise specified by manufacturer. Protect from light. Protect from freezing.

Stability
Do not mix or dilute this medication with other solutions, intravenous fluids, or medications, because the resulting admixtures are unstable.
Diazepam is adsorbed to the plastic of intravenous infusion bags and tubing.

Incompatibilities
Diazepam injection is physically incompatible with aqueous solutions.

Caution
Medications containing benzyl alcohol are not recommended for use in neonates (first 30 days of postnatal life). A fatal toxic syndrome consisting of metabolic acidosis, CNS depression, respiratory problems, renal failure, hypotension, and possibly seizures and intracranial hemorrhages has been associated with this use.

Note
Controlled substance in the U.S.

DIAZEPAM EMULSION STERILE

Usual adult dose
Antianxiety agent—
Preoperative medication: Dosage must be individualized; however, as a general guideline—Intramuscular or intravenous, 10 mg one to two hours prior to surgery.
Anxiety disorders or symptoms of anxiety: Intramuscular or intravenous, 2 to 10 mg (2 to 5 mg for moderate symptoms; 5 to 10 mg for severe symptoms), the dose being repeated in three or four hours, if necessary.
Anticonvulsant[1]—
Status epilepticus and severe recurrent convulsive seizures[1]: Intravenous, 5 to 10 mg, the dose being repeated at ten- to fifteen-minute intervals, if needed, up to a cumulative dose of 30 mg. Regimen may be repeated in two to four hours, if needed, keeping in mind the persistence of active metabolites in the circulation.
Sedative-hypnotic—
Alcohol withdrawal: Intramuscular or intravenous, initially 10 mg, followed by 5 to 10 mg in three or four hours, if necessary.
Amnestic—
Cardioversion: Intravenous, 5 to 15 mg ten to twenty minutes prior to the procedure.
Endoscopic procedures: Intramuscular or intravenous, 5 to 10 mg about thirty minutes prior to procedure. Intravenous dose may be titrated to desired sedative response with slow administration immediately prior to the procedure; although ≤ 10 mg is generally

adequate, up to 20 mg may be given, particularly when no concomitant narcotics are administered.

Skeletal muscle relaxant adjunct—
Muscle spasm: Intramuscular or intravenous, initially 5 to 10 mg, the dose being repeated in three or four hours, if necessary. Larger doses may be required in tetanus.

Note: Debilitated patients and patients receiving other sedative medications—Intramuscular or intravenous, initially 2 to 5 mg per dose, the dosage being increased gradually as needed and tolerated.

Usual pediatric dose

Antianxiety agent or
Amnestic—
Neonates 30 days of age and younger: Safety and efficacy have not been established.
Infants and children older than 30 days of age: Dosage must be individualized.

Anticonvulsant[1]—
For status epilepticus and severe recurrent convulsive seizures[1]: Neonates 30 days of age and younger—Safety and efficacy have not been established. Infants older than 30 days of age and children younger than 5 years of age—Intravenous, 0.2 to 0.5 mg, administered slowly. May be repeated every two to five minutes, if needed, up to a cumulative dose of 5 mg. Regimen may be repeated in two to four hours, if needed, keeping in mind the persistence of active metabolites in the circulation. Children 5 years of age and older—Intravenous, 1 mg, administered slowly. May be repeated every two to five minutes, if needed, up to a cumulative dose of 10 mg. Regimen may be repeated in two to four hours, if needed, keeping in mind the persistence of active metabolites in the circulation.

Skeletal muscle relaxant adjunct—
For tetanus[1]: Neonates 30 days of age and younger—Safety and efficacy have not been established. Infants older than 30 days of age and children younger than 5 years of age—Intravenous, 1 to 2 mg, administered slowly. May be repeated every three to four hours, if needed. Children 5 years of age and older—Intravenous, 5 to 10 mg, administered slowly. May be repeated every three to four hours, if needed.

Note: In general, when the intravenous route is used in infants and children, it is recommended that the medication be administered slowly over a three-minute period in a dose not to exceed 250 mcg (0.25 mg) per kg of body weight. After an interval of fifteen to thirty minutes, a second dose may be administered. After an additional interval of fifteen to thirty minutes, a third dose may be administered. If the third administration does not provide relief of symptoms, adjunctive treatment appropriate to the condition being treated should be considered.

Usual geriatric dose

Antianxiety agent or
Anticonvulsant[1] or
Sedative-hypnotic or
Amnestic or
Skeletal muscle relaxant adjunct—
Intramuscular or intravenous, initially 2 to 5 mg per dose, the dosage being increased gradually as needed and tolerated.

Strength(s) usually available

U.S.—
5 mg per mL (Rx) [*Dizac* (fractionated soybean oil 150 mg/mL; deacetylated monoglycerides 50 mg/mL; fractionated egg yolk phospholipids 12 mg/mL; glycerin 22 mg/mL; water for injection; sodium hydroxide)].

Canada—
5 mg per mL (Rx) [*Diazemuls* (acetylated monoglycerides 50 mg/mL; purified egg phospholipids 12 mg/mL; purified soybean oil 150 mg/mL; glycerol 22 mg/mL; sodium hydroxide)].

Note: Sterile diazepam emulsion is an oil/water emulsion with a pH of approximately 8.

Packaging and storage

Store below 25 °C (77 °F), unless otherwise specified by manufacturer. Protect from freezing. Protect from light.

Preparation of dosage form

When administered intravenously, sterile diazepam emulsion should be administered without prior dilution or mixing with other products or solutions. However, it may be mixed or diluted with its emulsion base (*Intralipid* or *Nutralipid*) but the admixture should be used within 6 hours.

Stability

Sterile diazepam emulsion contains no preservatives and can support rapid microbial growth. Administration should be completed within 6 hours after the ampul has been opened.

Mixing or diluting sterile diazepam emulsion with products or solutions other than its own emulsion base (*Intralipid* or *Nutralipid*) may destabilize the emulsion. Although such an effect may not be recognized on visual inspection, it may result in potentially serious adverse reactions.

Incompatibilities

Sterile diazepam emulsion is incompatible with morphine and glycopyrrolate.

Infusion sets containing polyvinyl chloride should not be used for administration of sterile diazepam emulsion.

Note

For administration of sterile diazepam emulsion, polyethylene-lined or glass infusion sets and polyethylene/polypropylene plastic syringes are recommended.

Sterile diazepam emulsion should not be administered through a filter with a pore size of less than 5 microns, because the emulsion may be broken down.

Strict aseptic technique is required in the handling of sterile diazepam emulsion.

Controlled substance in the U.S.

Rectal Dosage Forms

DIAZEPAM FOR RECTAL SOLUTION

Usual adult and adolescent dose

Anticonvulsant—
Status epilepticus and severe recurrent convulsive seizures: Rectal, 150 to 500 mcg (0.15 to 0.5 mg) of diazepam per kg of body weight, up to a maximum of 20 mg per dose.

Usual pediatric dose

Anticonvulsant—
Status epilepticus and severe recurrent convulsive seizures: Rectal, 200 to 500 mcg (0.2 to 0.5 mg) of diazepam per kg of body weight.

Usual geriatric dose

Rectal, 200 to 300 mcg (0.2 to 0.3 mg) of diazepam per kg of body weight.

Strength(s) usually available

U.S.—
Not commercially available.

Canada—
Not commercially available.

Packaging and storage

Store below 40 °C (104 °F), preferably between 15 and 30 °C (59 and 86 °F), unless otherwise specified by manufacturer. Protect from light. Protect from freezing.

Preparation of dosage form

For rectal administration, Diazepam Injection USP has been used. The parenteral preparation may be instilled via a cannula or catheter fitted to the syringe or directly from a needleless 1-mL syringe inserted 4 to 5 centimeters into the rectum to allow for optimum absorption. Alternatively, a dilution of Diazepam Injection USP with propylene glycol to make a solution containing 1 mg of diazepam per mL has been used.

Stability

Do not mix or dilute this medication with other solutions, intravenous fluids, or medications, because the resulting admixtures are unstable.

Diazepam is adsorbed to the plastic of intravenous infusion bags and tubing.

Incompatibilities

Diazepam injection is physically incompatible with aqueous solutions.

DIAZEPAM RECTAL GEL

Usual adult and adolescent dose

Anticonvulsant—
Rectal, 200 mcg (0.2 mg) per kg of body weight rounded up to the next available unit dose. Dose may be repeated, if needed, in four to twelve hours.

Note: Geriatric or debilitated patients—Rounding down to the next available unit dose is recommended to avoid ataxia and oversedation.

Usual pediatric dose

Anticonvulsant—
Children younger than 2 years of age: Safety and efficacy have not been established.

Children 2 to 6 years of age: Rectal, 500 mcg (0.5 mg) per kg of body weight rounded up to the next available unit dose. Dose may be repeated, if needed, in four to twelve hours.

Children 6 to 12 years of age: Rectal, 300 mcg (0.3 mg) per kg of body weight rounded up to the next available unit dose. Dose may be repeated, if needed, in four to twelve hours.

Children 12 years of age and older: See *Usual adult and adolescent dose.*

Strength(s) usually available

U.S.—

2.5 mg with pediatric (4.4 cm) rectal tip size (Rx) [*Diastat* (propylene glycol; ethyl alcohol 10%; hydroxypropyl methylcellulose; sodium benzoate; benzyl alcohol 1.5%; benzoic acid; water)].

5 mg with pediatric (4.4 cm) rectal tip size (Rx) [*Diastat* (propylene glycol; ethyl alcohol 10%; hydroxypropyl methylcellulose; sodium benzoate; benzyl alcohol 1.5%; benzoic acid; water)].

10 mg with pediatric (4.4 cm) rectal tip size (Rx) [*Diastat* (propylene glycol; ethyl alcohol 10%; hydroxypropyl methylcellulose; sodium benzoate; benzyl alcohol 1.5%; benzoic acid; water)].

10 mg with adult (6 cm) rectal tip size (Rx) [*Diastat* (propylene glycol; ethyl alcohol 10%; hydroxypropyl methylcellulose; sodium benzoate; benzyl alcohol 1.5%; benzoic acid; water)].

15 mg with adult (6 cm) rectal tip size (Rx) [*Diastat* (propylene glycol; ethyl alcohol 10%; hydroxypropyl methylcellulose; sodium benzoate; benzyl alcohol 1.5%; benzoic acid; water)].

20 mg with adult (6 cm) rectal tip size (Rx) [*Diastat* (propylene glycol; ethyl alcohol 10%; hydroxypropyl methylcellulose; sodium benzoate; benzyl alcohol 1.5%; benzoic acid; water)].

Canada—

Not commercially available.

Packaging and storage

Store between 15 and 30 °C (59 and 86 °F), unless otherwise specified by manufacturer.

Auxiliary labeling

- May cause drowsiness.
- For rectal use only.

Caution

Medications containing benzyl alcohol are not recommended for use in neonates (first 30 days of postnatal life). A fatal toxic syndrome consisting of metabolic acidosis, CNS depression, respiratory problems, renal failure, hypotension, and possibly seizures and intracranial hemorrhages has been associated with this use.

It is recommended that diazepam rectal gel be used no more frequently than every 5 days, and no more than five times a month.

Note

Caregiver must be instructed in the proper use of diazepam rectal gel, including when use is appropriate, how to administer, how to monitor the patient after administration, and when immediate medical attention is required.

Administration instructions for caregiver should be included with each prescription dispensed.

If a child requires a dose of 15 mg and the pediatric rectal tip size is desired, unit doses of 5 and 10 mg must be dispensed since the 15 mg unit dose is available only in the adult rectal tip size.

Controlled substance in the U.S.

Additional information

The 2.5 mg unit dose size is intended for more precise dose titration or for the partial replacement of a dose that is expelled by the patient.

[1]Not included in Canadian product labeling.

ESTAZOLAM

Summary of Differences

Category:

Indicated only as a sedative-hypnotic.

Indications:

May be useful in prevention or treatment of transient insomnia associated with sudden sleep schedule changes.

Pharmacology/pharmacokinetics:

Intermediate half-life benzodiazepine.

Small degree of accumulation during repeated dosing.

Steady-state plasma concentration usually attained within a few days.

Intermediate rate of elimination following discontinuation of therapy.

Oral Dosage Forms

ESTAZOLAM TABLETS

Usual adult dose

Sedative-hypnotic—

Oral, initially 1 mg at bedtime. A dose of 2 mg may be necessary in some patients.

Usual pediatric dose

Sedative-hypnotic—

Children younger than 18 years of age: Safety and efficacy have not been established.

Usual geriatric dose

Sedative-hypnotic—

Oral, initially 1 mg at bedtime. Dosage increases should be made cautiously.

Note: Small or debilitated older patients may be started at 0.5 mg.

Strength(s) usually available

U.S.—

1 mg (Rx) [*ProSom* (scored; lactose); GENERIC (may be scored)].

2 mg (Rx) [*ProSom* (scored; lactose); GENERIC (may be scored)].

Canada—

Not commercially available.

Packaging and storage

Store below 30 °C (86 °F), in a well-closed container, unless otherwise specified by manufacturer.

Auxiliary labeling

- Avoid alcoholic beverages.
- May cause daytime drowsiness.

Note

Controlled substance in the U.S.

FLURAZEPAM

Summary of Differences

Category:

Indicated only as a sedative-hypnotic.

Pharmacology/pharmacokinetics:

Drug precursor; parent drug does not reach systemic circulation in significant amounts.

Long half-life benzodiazepine.

Accumulation of active metabolites is significant during repeated dosing.

Steady-state plasma concentration usually attained in 7 to 10 days.

Elimination slow since metabolites remain in blood for several days.

Additional Dosing Information

See also *General Dosing Information.*

Flurazepam is increasingly effective on the second or third night of consecutive use, and for one or two nights after medication is discontinued both sleep latency and total wake time may still be decreased.

Oral Dosage Forms

FLURAZEPAM HYDROCHLORIDE CAPSULES USP

Usual adult dose

Sedative-hypnotic—

Oral, 15 or 30 mg at bedtime.

Note: The usual adult dose is 30 mg, but 15 mg may be sufficient for some patients.

Debilitated patients—Oral, initially 15 mg at bedtime, the dosage being increased as needed and tolerated.

Usual pediatric dose

Sedative-hypnotic—

Children younger than 15 years of age: Safety and efficacy have not been established.

Usual geriatric dose

Sedative-hypnotic—

Oral, initially 15 mg at bedtime, the dosage being increased as needed and tolerated.

Strength(s) usually available

U.S.—

15 mg (Rx) [*Dalmane* (lactose; gelatin capsules may contain methyl and propyl parabens); GENERIC].

30 mg (Rx) [*Dalmane* (lactose; gelatin capsules may contain methyl and propyl parabens); GENERIC].

Canada—
15 mg (Rx) [*Apo-Flurazepam; Dalmane* (lactose 276 mg; methylparaben; propylparaben); *Novo-Flupam*].
30 mg (Rx) [*Apo-Flurazepam; Dalmane* (lactose 263 mg; methylparaben; propylparaben); *Novo-Flupam*].

Packaging and storage
Store below 40 °C (104 °F), preferably between 15 and 30 °C (59 and 86 °F), unless otherwise specified by manufacturer. Store in a tight, light-resistant container.

Auxiliary labeling
- Avoid alcoholic beverages.
- May cause daytime drowsiness.

Note
Controlled substance in the U.S.

FLURAZEPAM HYDROCHLORIDE TABLETS

Usual adult dose
See *Flurazepam Hydrochloride Capsules USP*.

Usual pediatric dose
See *Flurazepam Hydrochloride Capsules USP*.

Usual geriatric dose
See *Flurazepam Hydrochloride Capsules USP*.

Strength(s) usually available
U.S.—
Not commercially available.
Canada—
15 mg (Rx) [*Somnol* (scored; lactose)].
30 mg (Rx) [*Somnol* (scored; lactose)].

Packaging and storage
Store between 8 and 15 °C (46 and 59 °F), in a well-closed container, unless otherwise specified by manufacturer.

Auxiliary labeling
- Avoid alcoholic beverages.
- May cause daytime drowsiness.

HALAZEPAM

Summary of Differences

Category:
Indicated only as an antianxiety agent.
Pharmacology/pharmacokinetics:
Long half-life benzodiazepine.
Accumulation of active metabolite is significant during repeated dosing.
Steady-state plasma concentration usually attained in 5 days to 2 weeks.
Elimination slow since metabolite remains in blood for several days or even weeks.

Oral Dosage Forms

HALAZEPAM TABLETS

Usual adult dose
Antianxiety agent—
Oral, 20 to 40 mg three or four times a day. Dosage may be adjusted upward or downward after several days if needed. The optimal dosage is usually 80 to 160 mg per day.
Note: Debilitated patients—Oral, 20 mg one or two times a day, the dosage being adjusted as needed and tolerated.

Usual pediatric dose
Antianxiety agent—
Children younger than 18 years of age: Safety and efficacy have not been established.

Usual geriatric dose
Antianxiety agent—
Oral, 20 mg one or two times a day, the dosage being adjusted as needed and tolerated.

Strength(s) usually available
U.S.—
20 mg (Rx) [*Paxipam* (scored; lactose)].
40 mg (Rx) [*Paxipam* (scored; lactose)].
Canada—
Not commercially available.

Packaging and storage
Store between 2 and 30 °C (36 and 86 °F), in a well-closed container, unless otherwise specified by manufacturer.

Auxiliary labeling
- Avoid alcoholic beverages.
- May cause drowsiness.

Note
Controlled substance in the U.S.

KETAZOLAM

Summary of Differences

Category:
Formerly indicated in Canada as an antianxiety agent only.
Pharmacology/pharmacokinetics:
Long half-life benzodiazepine.
Accumulation of active metabolites is significant during repeated dosing.
Steady-state plasma concentration usually attained in 7 to 10 days.
Elimination slow since metabolites remain in blood for several days.

Oral Dosage Forms

KETAZOLAM CAPSULES

Usual adult dose
[Antianxiety agent][1]—
Oral, 15 mg one or two times a day, the dosage being increased in 15-mg increments as needed and tolerated.
Note: Debilitated patients—The recommended initial dosage is one half the lowest recommended initial adult dosage.

Usual pediatric dose
[Antianxiety agent][1]—
Children younger than 18 years of age: Safety and efficacy have not been established.
Note: Use in infants is not recommended.

Usual geriatric dose
[Antianxiety agent][1]—
Oral, 15 mg once a day, the dosage being increased in 15-mg increments as needed and tolerated.

Strength(s) usually available
U.S.—
Not commercially available.
Canada—
Not commercially available.

Packaging and storage
Store below 40 °C (104 °F), preferably between 15 and 30 °C (59 and 86 °F), in a well-closed container, unless otherwise specified by manufacturer.

Auxiliary labeling
- Avoid alcoholic beverages.
- May cause drowsiness.

[1]Not included in Canadian product labeling.

LORAZEPAM

Summary of Differences

Category:
In addition to being indicated as an antianxiety agent and a sedative-hypnotic, lorazepam is indicated as an amnestic and an anticonvulsant (parenteral only), and is used as an antiemetic in cancer chemotherapy (parenteral only), an antipanic agent, an antitremor agent (oral only), and a skeletal muscle relaxant adjunct.
Indications:
Oral lorazepam also indicated for adjunctive management of anxiety associated with mental depression.
Parenteral lorazepam also indicated as a preanesthetic medication and for the treatment of status epilepticus; and used as an adjunct prior to endoscopic procedures and as prophylaxis of cancer chemotherapy-induced nausea and vomiting.
Oral and parenteral lorazepam also used for relief of acute alcohol withdrawal symptoms and for treatment of tension headache.
Pharmacology/pharmacokinetics:
Absorption of intramuscular lorazepam is rapid and complete.
Short to intermediate half-life benzodiazepine.
Accumulation is minimal during repeated dosing.
Steady-state plasma concentration usually attained within a few (2 to 3) days.
Elimination rapid following discontinuation of therapy.

Precautions:
Drug interactions and/or related problems—
Cimetidine, oral estrogen-containing contraceptives, diltiazem, disulfiram, erythromycin, fluoxetine, fluvoxamine, grapefruit juice, itraconazole, ketoconazole, nefazodone, propoxyphene, ranitidine, and verapamil, which inhibit the oxidative metabolism of benzodiazepines, are less likely to affect lorazepam, which undergoes glucuronide conjugation.
Premedication with lorazepam may decrease dose of a fentanyl derivative required for induction of anesthesia and reduce time to loss of consciousness with induction doses.
Probenecid may impair glucuronide conjugation of lorazepam, resulting in increased effects and possibly excessive sedation.
Medical considerations/contraindications—
Prolongation of elimination half-life due to hepatic function impairment may be minimal with lorazepam.
Side/adverse effects:
Intravenous lorazepam more likely than chlordiazepoxide but less likely than diazepam to cause phlebitis or venous thrombosis.

Additional Dosing Information

See also *General Dosing Information.*

For sublingual tablets only

Do not swallow for at least 2 minutes to allow sufficient time for absorption.

For parenteral dosage forms only

Immediately prior to intravenous use, lorazepam injection must be diluted with an equal amount of a compatible diluent such as sterile water for injection, 0.9% sodium chloride injection, or 5% dextrose injection.

Following proper dilution, the medication may be injected directly into the vein or into the tubing of an intravenous infusion.

Intravenous injection should be made slowly and with repeated aspiration.

The rate of the intravenous injection should not exceed 2 mg per minute.

Intra-arterial injection and perivascular extravasation should be avoided. Intra-arterial injection may produce arteriospasm, possibly resulting in gangrene.

When administered intramuscularly, the injection (undiluted) should be injected deeply into the muscle mass.

When parenteral lorazepam is used for peroral endoscopic procedures, the use of topical or regional anesthesia is recommended to minimize the reflex activity associated with such procedures.

When lorazepam is administered intravenously as premedication prior to regional or local anesthesia, potential excessive sleepiness or drowsiness may interfere with patient cooperation in determining levels of anesthesia. This is more likely to occur when doses greater than 0.05 mg per kg of body weight (mg/kg) are given and narcotic analgesics are used concomitantly with recommended doses.

Oral Dosage Forms

LORAZEPAM ORAL CONCENTRATE USP

Usual adult and adolescent dose

Antianxiety agent—
Oral, 1 to 3 mg two or three times a day.
Sedative-hypnotic—
Oral, 2 to 4 mg as a single dose at bedtime.

Note: Debilitated patients—Oral, initially 1 to 2 mg per day in divided doses, the dosage being increased gradually as needed and tolerated.

Usual adult prescribing limits

10 mg per day.

Usual pediatric dose

Antianxiety agent or
Sedative-hypnotic[1]—
Children younger than 12 years of age: Safety and efficacy have not been established.

Strength(s) usually available

U.S.—
2 mg per mL (Rx) [*Lorazepam Intensol*].
Canada—
Not commercially available.

Packaging and storage

Store between 2 and 8 °C (36 and 46 °F), unless otherwise specified by manufacturer. Store in a well-closed container. Protect from light.

Preparation of dosage form

The manufacturer recommends that each dose be mixed with water, juice, soda or soda-like beverages, or semisolid food, such as applesauce or pudding. The entire amount of the mixture should be consumed immediately after mixing; no part of the mixture should be saved for later use.

Auxiliary labeling

- Refrigerate.
- Avoid alcoholic beverages.
- May cause drowsiness.

Note

The patient or caregiver should be instructed in proper measurement of the dose using the calibrated dropper provided with the medication, and in preparation of the dose.

Controlled substance in the U.S.

LORAZEPAM TABLETS USP

Usual adult and adolescent dose

Antianxiety agent—
Oral, 1 to 3 mg two or three times a day.
Note: Debilitated patients—Oral, initially 0.5 to 2 mg per day in divided doses, the dosage being increased gradually as needed and tolerated.
Sedative-hypnotic[1]—
Oral, 2 to 4 mg as a single dose at bedtime.
Note: Elderly and debilitated patients may require a lower dose.

Usual pediatric dose

Antianxiety agent or
Sedative-hypnotic[1]—
Children younger than 12 years of age: Safety and efficacy have not been established.

Usual geriatric dose

Antianxiety agent—
Oral, initially 0.5 to 2 mg per day in divided doses, the dosage being increased gradually as needed and tolerated.

Strength(s) usually available

U.S.—
0.5 mg (Rx) [*Ativan* (lactose); GENERIC (may be scored)].
1 mg (Rx) [*Ativan* (scored; lactose); GENERIC (may be scored)].
2 mg (Rx) [*Ativan* (scored; lactose); GENERIC (may be scored)].
Canada—
0.5 mg (Rx) [*Apo-Lorazepam* (sodium $<$ 1 mmol [0.06 mg]); *Ativan* (lactose); *Novo-Lorazem; Nu-Loraz* (sodium $<$ 1 mmol [0.06 mg])].
1 mg (Rx) [*Apo-Lorazepam* (scored; sodium $<$ 1 mmol [0.13 mg]); *Ativan* (scored; lactose); *Novo-Lorazem* (scored); *Nu-Loraz* (scored; sodium $<$ 1 mmol [0.13 mg])].
2 mg (Rx) [*Apo-Lorazepam* (scored; sodium $<$ 1 mmol [0.16 mg]); *Ativan* (scored; lactose); *Novo-Lorazem* (scored); *Nu-Loraz* (scored; sodium $<$ 1 mmol [0.16 mg])].

Packaging and storage

Store between 15 and 30 °C (59 and 86 °F), unless otherwise specified by manufacturer. Store in a tight, light-resistant container.

Auxiliary labeling

- Avoid alcoholic beverages.
- May cause drowsiness.

Note

Controlled substance in the U.S.

LORAZEPAM SUBLINGUAL TABLETS

Usual adult dose

Antianxiety agent—
Sublingual, 2 to 3 mg per day in divided doses, the dosage being adjusted as needed, usually not exceeding 6 mg per day.
Note: Debilitated patients—Sublingual, initially 500 mcg (0.5 mg) per day, the dosage being gradually adjusted as necessary.
Preoperative: Sublingual, 50 mcg (0.05 mg) per kg of body weight, up to a maximum of 4 mg, one to two hours before surgery.

Usual pediatric dose

Antianxiety agent—
Children younger than 18 years of age: Safety and efficacy have not been established.

Usual geriatric dose

Antianxiety agent—
Sublingual, initially 500 mcg (0.5 mg) per day, the dosage being gradually adjusted as necessary.

Strength(s) usually available

U.S.—
Not commercially available.
Canada—
0.5 mg (Rx) [*Ativan* (lactose)].
1 mg (Rx) [*Ativan* (lactose)].
2 mg (Rx) [*Ativan* (lactose)].

Packaging and storage

Store below 40 °C (104 °F), preferably between 15 and 30 °C (59 and 86 °F), in a well-closed container, unless otherwise specified by manufacturer.

Auxiliary labeling
- Dissolve tablets under tongue.
- Avoid alcoholic beverages.
- May cause drowsiness.

Parenteral Dosage Forms

Note: Bracketed uses in the *Dosage Forms* section refer to categories of use and/or indications that are not included in U.S. product labeling.

LORAZEPAM INJECTION USP

Usual adult dose
Antianxiety agent or
Sedative-hypnotic or
Amnestic—

Intramuscular, 50 mcg (0.05 mg) per kg of body weight, up to a maximum of 4 mg. Dose should be administered at least two hours prior to surgery for optimum amnestic effect.

Intravenous, initially 44 mcg (0.044 mg) per kg of body weight or a total dose of 2 mg, whichever is less. For greater amnestic effect, up to 50 mcg (0.05 mg) per kg of body weight, not to exceed a maximum of 4 mg, may be administered. Dose should be administered fifteen to twenty minutes prior to surgery for optimum amnestic effect.

Anticonvulsant—

Status epilepticus: Intravenous, initially 4 mg administered slowly (at a rate not to exceed 2 mg per minute). If seizures continue or recur after ten to fifteen minutes, the dose may be repeated. If seizure control is not evident after another ten to fifteen minutes, other measures to control status epilepticus should be used. The total cumulative dose should not exceed 8 mg of lorazepam in a twelve-hour period. Experience with additional doses is extremely limited.

[Antiemetic, in cancer chemotherapy][1]—

Intravenous, initially 2 mg thirty minutes before initiation of chemotherapy, followed by 2 mg every four hours as needed.

Usual pediatric dose
Antianxiety agent or
Sedative-hypnotic or
Anticonvulsant or
Amnestic—

Children younger than 18 years of age: Safety and efficacy have not been established.

Strength(s) usually available
U.S.—

2 mg per mL (Rx) [*Ativan* (benzyl alcohol 2%; polyethylene glycol 400 0.18 mL in propylene glycol); GENERIC].

4 mg per mL (Rx) [*Ativan* (benzyl alcohol 2%; polyethylene glycol 400 0.18 mL in propylene glycol); GENERIC].

Canada—

4 mg per mL (Rx) [*Ativan* (benzyl alcohol 2%; polyethylene glycol 18%; propylene glycol 80%)].

Packaging and storage
Store between 2 and 8 °C (36 and 46 °F), unless otherwise specified by manufacturer. Protect from light. Protect from freezing.

Preparation of dosage form
For intravenous administration—Immediately prior to use, lorazepam injection must be diluted with an equal volume of a compatible diluent, such as sterile water for injection, 0.9% sodium chloride injection, or 5% dextrose injection.

Stability
Do not use if solution is discolored or contains a precipitate.

Incompatibilities
Lorazepam injection is physically incompatible with buprenorphine injection.

Caution
Medications containing benzyl alcohol are not recommended for use in neonates (first 30 days of postnatal life). A fatal toxic syndrome consisting of metabolic acidosis, CNS depression, respiratory problems, renal failure, hypotension, and possibly seizures and intracranial hemorrhages has been associated with this use.

Note
Controlled substance in the U.S.

[1]Not included in Canadian product labeling.

NITRAZEPAM

Summary of Differences

Category:

In addition to being indicated as a sedative-hypnotic, indicated as an anticonvulsant.

Pharmacology/pharmacokinetics:

Absorption of nitrazepam is rapid.
Short to intermediate half-life benzodiazepine.
Accumulation is minimal during repeated dosing.
Steady-state plasma concentration usually attained within a few (2 to 3) days.
Elimination rapid following discontinuation of therapy.

Precautions:

Drug interactions and/or related problems—Cimetidine or oral estrogen-containing contraceptives may inhibit the nitro-reduction of nitrazepam, resulting in delayed elimination and prolonged elimination half-life; serum concentrations may also be increased during long-term use.

Medical considerations/contraindications—Nitrazepam may delay cricopharyngeal relaxation, exacerbating swallowing abnormalities in children.

Oral Dosage Forms

NITRAZEPAM TABLETS

Usual adult dose
Sedative-hypnotic—

Oral, 5 or 10 mg at bedtime.

Note: Debilitated patients—Oral, initially 2.5 mg, the dosage being increased as needed and tolerated up to 5 mg.

Usual pediatric dose
Sedative-hypnotic—

Dosage has not been established.

Anticonvulsant—

Children up to 30 kg: Oral, initially the dosage should be below the usual recommended dosage range of 300 mcg (0.3 mg) to 1 mg per kg of body weight per day given in three divided doses, to determine response and tolerance. The dosage may be increased above the recommended range gradually, as needed and tolerated.

Note: If doses are not equally divided, the larger dose should be given at bedtime.

Usual geriatric dose
Sedative-hypnotic—

Oral, initially 2.5 mg, the dosage being increased as needed and tolerated up to 5 mg.

Strength(s) usually available
U.S.

Not commercially available.

Canada—

5 mg (Rx) [*Mogadon* (scored; lactose)].
10 mg (Rx) [*Mogadon* (scored; lactose)].

Packaging and storage
Store below 40 °C (104 °F), preferably between 15 and 30 °C (59 and 86 °F), in a well-closed container, unless otherwise specified by manufacturer. Protect from light.

Auxiliary labeling
- Avoid alcoholic beverages.
- May cause drowsiness.

OXAZEPAM

Summary of Differences

Indications:

Also indicated for adjunctive management of anxiety associated with mental depression and relief of acute alcohol withdrawal symptoms.

Pharmacology/pharmacokinetics:

Orally, one of least rapidly absorbed benzodiazepines.
Short to intermediate half-life benzodiazepine.
Accumulation is minimal during repeated dosing.
Steady-state plasma concentration usually attained within a few days.
Elimination rapid following discontinuation of therapy.

Precautions:

Drug interactions and/or related problems—

Cimetidine, oral estrogen-containing contraceptives, diltiazem, disulfiram, erythromycin, fluoxetine, fluvoxamine, grapefruit juice, itraconazole, ketoconazole, nefazodone, propoxyphene, ranitidine, and verapamil, which inhibit the oxidative metabolism of benzodiazepines, are less likely to affect oxazepam, which undergoes glucuronide conjugation.

Probenecid may impair glucuronide conjugation of oxazepam, resulting in increased effects and possibly excessive sedation.

Medical considerations/contraindications—
Prolongation of elimination half-life due to hepatic function impairment may be minimal with oxazepam.

Oral Dosage Forms

OXAZEPAM CAPSULES USP

Usual adult dose
Antianxiety agent—
Oral, 10 to 30 mg three or four times a day.
Sedative-hypnotic—
Alcohol withdrawal: Oral, 15 or 30 mg three or four times a day.

Usual pediatric dose
Antianxiety agent or
Sedative-hypnotic—
Children younger than 6 years of age: Safety and efficacy have not been established.
Children 6 to 12 years of age: Dosage has not been established.

Usual geriatric dose
Antianxiety agent—
Oral, initially 10 mg three times a day, the dosage being increased as needed and tolerated to 15 mg three or four times a day.

Strength(s) usually available
U.S.—
10 mg (Rx) [*Serax* (lactose); GENERIC].
15 mg (Rx) [*Serax* (lactose); GENERIC].
30 mg (Rx) [*Serax* (lactose); GENERIC].
Canada—
Not commercially available.

Packaging and storage
Store below 40 °C (104 °F), preferably between 15 and 30 °C (59 and 86 °F), in a well-closed container, unless otherwise specified by manufacturer.

Auxiliary labeling
- Avoid alcoholic beverages.
- May cause drowsiness.

Note
Controlled substance in the U.S.

OXAZEPAM TABLETS USP

Usual adult dose
See *Oxazepam Capsules USP*.

Usual pediatric dose
See *Oxazepam Capsules USP*.

Usual geriatric dose
Antianxiety agent—
Oral, initially 10 mg three times a day, the dosage being increased as needed and tolerated to 15 mg three or four times a day. Alternatively, an initial dosage of 5 mg one or two times a day has been recommended.

Strength(s) usually available
U.S.—
15 mg (Rx) [*Serax* (tartrazine; lactose); GENERIC].
Canada—
10 mg (Rx) [*Apo-Oxazepam* (scored); *Novoxapam* (scored); *Serax* (scored; lactose)].
15 mg (Rx) [*Apo-Oxazepam* (scored); *Novoxapam* (scored); *Serax* (scored; lactose)].
30 mg (Rx) [*Apo-Oxazepam* (scored; sodium < 1 mmol [0.49 mg]); *Novoxapam* (scored); *Serax* (scored; lactose)].

Packaging and storage
Store below 40 °C (104 °F), preferably between 15 and 30 °C (59 and 86 °F), in a well-closed container, unless otherwise specified by manufacturer.

Auxiliary labeling
- Avoid alcoholic beverages.
- May cause drowsiness.

Note
Controlled substance in the U.S.

PRAZEPAM

Summary of Differences

Category:
Formerly indicated in the U.S. as an antianxiety agent only.

Pharmacology/pharmacokinetics:
Drug precursor; metabolized to desmethyldiazepam before reaching systemic circulation.
Orally, one of least rapidly absorbed benzodiazepines.
Long half-life benzodiazepine.
Accumulation of active metabolites is significant during repeated dosing.
Steady-state plasma concentration usually attained in 5 days to 2 weeks.
Elimination slow since metabolites remain in blood for several days.

Oral Dosage Forms

PRAZEPAM CAPSULES USP

Usual adult dose
[Antianxiety agent][1]—
Oral, 10 mg three times a day (range, 20 to 60 mg per day); or 20 to 40 mg at bedtime.
Note: Debilitated patients—Oral, initially 10 to 15 mg per day in divided doses, the dosage being increased gradually as needed and tolerated.

Usual pediatric dose
[Antianxiety agent][1]—
Children younger than 18 years of age: Safety and efficacy have not been established.

Usual geriatric dose
[Antianxiety agent][1]—
Oral, initially 10 to 15 mg per day in divided doses, the dosage being increased gradually as needed and tolerated.

Strength(s) usually available
U.S.—
Not commercially available.
Canada—
Not commercially available.

Packaging and storage
Store between 15 and 30 °C (59 and 86 °F), unless otherwise specified by manufacturer. Store in a tight, light-resistant container.

Auxiliary labeling
- Avoid alcoholic beverages.
- May cause drowsiness.

[1]Not included in Canadian product labeling.

QUAZEPAM

Summary of Differences

Category:
Indicated only as a sedative-hypnotic.
Pharmacology/pharmacokinetics:
Long half-life benzodiazepine.
Accumulation of active metabolites may occur during repeated dosing.
Steady-state plasma concentrations usually attained within 7 to 13 days.
Elimination slow since metabolites remain in blood for several days.

Oral Dosage Forms

QUAZEPAM TABLETS

Usual adult dose
Sedative-hypnotic—
Oral, initially 15 mg, the dose being reduced to 7.5 mg as needed.
Note: Debilitated patients—Because of increased sensitivity to benzodiazepines, it is suggested that the nightly dose be reduced after one or two nights of treatment.

Usual pediatric dose
Sedative-hypnotic—
Children younger than 18 years of age: Safety and efficacy have not been established.

Usual geriatric dose
Sedative-hypnotic—
Oral, initially 15 mg, the dose being reduced to 7.5 mg after one or two nights.

Strength(s) usually available
U.S.—
7.5 mg (Rx) [*Doral* (lactose)].
15 mg (Rx) [*Doral* (lactose)].
Canada—
Not commercially available.

Packaging and storage
Store between 15 and 30 °C (59 and 86 °F), in a tight container, unless otherwise specified by manufacturer.

Auxiliary labeling
- Avoid alcoholic beverages.
- May cause daytime drowsiness.

Note
Controlled substance in the U.S.

TEMAZEPAM

Summary of Differences
Category:
Indicated only as a sedative-hypnotic.
Indications:
May be useful in prevention or treatment of transient insomnia associated with sudden sleep schedule changes.
Pharmacology/pharmacokinetics:
Short to intermediate half-life benzodiazepine.
Accumulation is minimal during repeated dosing.
Steady-state plasma concentration usually attained within a few (about 3) days.
Elimination rapid following discontinuation of therapy.
Precautions:
Drug interactions and/or related problems—
Cimetidine, oral estrogen-containing contraceptives, diltiazem, disulfiram, erythromycin, fluoxetine, fluvoxamine, grapefruit juice, itraconazole, ketoconazole, nefazodone, propoxyphene, ranitidine, and verapamil, which inhibit the oxidative metabolism of the benzodiazepines, are less likely to affect temazepam, which undergoes glucuronide conjugation.
Probenecid may impair glucuronide conjugation of temazepam, resulting in increased effects and possibly excessive sedation.
Medical considerations/contraindications—
Prolongation of elimination half-life due to hepatic function impairment may be minimal with temazepam.

Oral Dosage Forms

TEMAZEPAM CAPSULES USP

Usual adult dose
Sedative-hypnotic—
Oral, usually 15 mg at bedtime, although 7.5 mg may be sufficient for some patients and others may need 30 mg.

Note: In transient insomnia, 7.5 mg may be sufficient to improve sleep latency.
Debilitated patients—Oral, initially 7.5 mg, the dosage being adjusted as needed and tolerated.

Usual pediatric dose
Sedative-hypnotic—
Children younger than 18 years of age: Safety and efficacy have not been established.

Usual geriatric dose
Sedative-hypnotic—
Oral, initially 7.5 mg, the dosage being adjusted as needed and tolerated.

Strength(s) usually available
U.S.—
7.5 mg (Rx) [*Restoril* (lactose); GENERIC].
15 mg (Rx) [*Restoril* (lactose); GENERIC].
30 mg (Rx) [*Restoril* (lactose); GENERIC].
Canada—
15 mg (Rx) [*Apo-Temazepam; Novo-Temazepam; Restoril* (lactose)].
30 mg (Rx) [*Apo-Temazepam; Novo-Temazepam; Restoril* (lactose)].

Packaging and storage
Store between 15 and 30 °C (59 and 86 °F), in a tight, light-resistant container, unless otherwise specified by manufacturer.

Auxiliary labeling
- Avoid alcoholic beverages.
- May cause daytime drowsiness.

Note
Controlled substance in the U.S.

TRIAZOLAM

Summary of Differences
Category:
Indicated only as a sedative-hypnotic.
Indications:
May be useful in prevention or treatment of transient insomnia associated with sudden sleep schedule change.
Pharmacology/pharmacokinetics:
Short half-life benzodiazepine.
Accumulation is minimal during repeated dosing.
Elimination rapid following discontinuation of therapy.
Precautions:
Drug interactions and/or related problems—
Itraconazole and ketoconazole greatly increase the area under the plasma concentration-time curve (AUC) of triazolam; concurrent use is not recommended.
Nefazodone increases the AUC of triazolam fourfold, resulting in impairment of psychomotor function; a 75% reduction in triazolam dosage is recommended during concurrent use.
Cimetidine and erythromycin may inhibit the hepatic metabolism of triazolam, resulting in increased plasma concentrations and delayed clearance of triazolam; dosage reductions may be necessary.
Isoniazid may inhibit the elimination of triazolam, resulting in increased plasma concentrations.
Side/adverse effects:
Anterograde amnesia may be more likely to occur with triazolam than with most other benzodiazepines.
Because of the potency of triazolam, symptoms of overdose may occur at doses as low as 2 mg.

Oral Dosage Forms

TRIAZOLAM TABLETS USP

Usual adult dose
Sedative-hypnotic—
Oral, 125 to 250 mcg (0.125 to 0.25 mg) at bedtime.

Note: A dose of 500 mcg (0.5 mg) may be necessary in some patients. However, this dose should be reserved for patients who do not respond adequately to lower doses, since the risk of side effects increases with dosage increases.
Debilitated patients—Oral, initially 125 mcg (0.125 mg) at bedtime, the dosage being increased as needed and tolerated.

Usual pediatric dose
Sedative-hypnotic—
Children younger than 18 years of age: Safety and efficacy have not been established.

Usual geriatric dose
Sedative-hypnotic—
Oral, initially 125 mcg (0.125 mg) at bedtime, the dosage being increased as needed and tolerated.

Strength(s) usually available
U.S.—
125 mcg (0.125 mg) (Rx) [*Halcion* (docusate sodium; lactose; sodium benzoate); GENERIC (may contain docusate sodium, lactose, and/or sodium benzoate)].
250 mcg (0.25 mg) (Rx) [*Halcion* (scored; docusate sodium; lactose; sodium benzoate); GENERIC (may be scored; may contain docusate sodium, lactose, and/or sodium benzoate)].
Canada—
125 mcg (0.125 mg) (Rx) [*Alti-Triazolam* (scored; docusate sodium; erythrosine sodium; lactose); *Apo-Triazo* (scored; sodium < 1 mmol [0.32 mg]); *Gen-Triazolam* (scored); *Halcion* (scored; docusate sodium; lactose); *Novo-Triolam* (scored); GENERIC].
250 mcg (0.25 mg) (Rx) [*Alti-Triazolam* (scored; docusate sodium; lactose); *Apo-Triazo* (scored; sodium < 1 mmol [0.32 mg]); *Gen-Triazolam* (scored); *Halcion* (scored; docusate sodium; lactose); *Novo-Triolam* (scored); GENERIC].

Packaging and storage
Store between 15 and 30° C (59 and 86° F), unless otherwise specified by manufacturer. Store in a tight, light-resistant container.

Auxiliary labeling
- Avoid alcoholic beverages.
- May cause daytime drowsiness.

Note
Controlled substance in the U.S.

Revised: 02/24/2005

Table 1. Pharmacology/Pharmacokinetics

Note: Whether the half-life of a benzodiazepine is considered to be long, intermediate, or short is determined by the half-lives of any active metabolites, as well as the half-life of the parent compound.

Drug	Protein binding (%)	Half-life* (hr)	Major active metabolites (half-life in hr)	Time to peak plasma concentration† (oral dose) (hr)	Elimination‡ (% excreted unchanged)
Long half-life					
Chlordiazepoxide	Very high (96)	5–30	Desmethylchlordiazepoxide (18) Demoxepam (14–95) Desmethyldiazepam (40–120) Oxazepam (5–15)	0.5–4	Renal (1–2); 3–6% as conjugate
Clorazepate§	Desmethyldiazepam: Very high (95–98)	—	Desmethyldiazepam (40–120) Oxazepam (5–15)	0.5–2	Renal; fecal
Diazepam	Very high (98)	20–80#	Desmethyldiazepam (40–120) Temazepam (8–15) Oxazepam (5–15)	1–2 (injection: IM, 0.5–1.5; IV, within 0.25) (sterile emulsion: IM, > 2; IV, 0.13–0.25) (rectal gel: 1.5)	Renal
Flurazepam§**	Desalkylflurazepam: Very high (97)	2.3	Desalkylflurazepam (47–100) *N*-1-hydroxyethylflurazepam (2–4)	0.5–1	Renal
Halazepam	Very high (97)	14	Desmethyldiazepam (40–120)	1–3	Renal (< 1)
Ketazolam	Very high (93)	2	Desmethyldiazepam (40–120) *N*-methylketazolam (34–52) Diazepam (20–80)#	3	Renal; fecal < 1%
Prazepam§	Desmethyldiazepam: Very high (95–98)	—	Desmethyldiazepam (40–120) Oxazepam (5–15)	Desmethyldiazepam (single dose): 2.5–6	Renal
Quazepam	Very high (> 95)	39	Desalkylflurazepam (47–100) 2-oxoquazepam (39)	2	Renal (trace); fecal
Short to intermediate half-life					
Alprazolam	High (80)	11 (6.3–26.9)	None	1–2	Renal
Bromazepam	High (70)	12 (8–19)	None	1–4	Renal
Clobazam	High (85)	18 (10–30)	*N*-desmethylclobazam 42 (36–46)	1–4	Renal
Clonazepam	High (85)	18–50	None	1–2††	Renal (< 2)
Estazolam	Very high (93)	10–24	None	2 (0.5–6)	Renal (< 5)
Lorazepam‡‡	High (85)	10–20	None	1–6 (IM, 1–1.5; sublingual, 1)	Renal
Nitrazepam	High (87)	30 (18–57)	None	2–3	Renal (about 1); fecal
Oxazepam	Very high (97)	5–15	None	1–4	Renal; fecal
Temazepam	Very high (96)	8–15	None	1–2	Renal (< 1)§§
Triazolam	High (89)	1.5–5.5	None	≤ 2	Renal (small amount)§§

*Elimination half-lives may be prolonged in children, especially premature and newborn infants, geriatric patients, and patients with hepatic disease; however, metabolic clearance of short to intermediate half-life benzodiazepines, especially lorazepam, oxazepam, temazepam, and triazolam, is affected less by age and hepatic disease than that of the long half-life benzodiazepines. The elimination half-life does not always predict the duration of clinical effects.

†With multiple dosing, steady-state plasma concentrations of long half-life benzodiazepines usually are achieved within 5 days to 2 weeks and those of short to intermediate half-life benzodiazepines within a few days.

‡Benzodiazepines are not significantly removed from the body by hemodialysis.

§Prodrugs or drug precursors; do not reach circulation in clinically significant amounts.

#Increases with age from approximately 20 hours in a 20-year-old patient to approximately 80 hours in an 80-year-old patient.

**Maximum effectiveness as a hypnotic may not be achieved for 2 to 3 days.

††Following a single dose; in some patients peak concentrations may not be achieved for 4 to 8 hours.

‡‡Peak amnestic effect: IM, within 2 hours; IV, 15 to 20 minutes.

§§Appears to be biphasic in its time course.

BENZONATATE Systemic

VA CLASSIFICATION (Primary): RE302

Commonly used brand name(s): *Tessalon.*

Note: For a listing of dosage forms and brand names by country availability, see *Dosage Forms* section(s).

Category

Antitussive.

Indications

Accepted

Cough (treatment)—Benzonatate is indicated for the symptomatic relief of nonproductive cough. It is used to provide relief of acute cough due to minor throat and bronchial irritation occurring with colds or inhaled irritants.

Pharmacology/Pharmacokinetics

Physicochemical characteristics

Molecular weight—603.7.

Mechanism of action/Effect

Suppresses cough through a peripheral action, anesthetizing the stretch or cough receptors of vagal afferent fibers, which are located in the respiratory passages, lungs, and pleura; also, may suppress transmission of the cough reflex by a central mechanism, at the level of the medulla.

Other actions—

Local anesthetic activity when applied topically to the mucosa.

Onset of action

Usually within 15 to 20 minutes.

Duration of action

Up to 8 hours.

Elimination

As with other ester-type local anesthetics (e.g., tetracaine) to which benzonatate is chemically related, excretion may be primarily via metabolism, followed by renal excretion of metabolites.

Precautions to Consider

Cross-sensitivity and/or related problems

Patients sensitive to tetracaine or other ester-type local anesthetics may also be sensitive to benzonatate.

Pregnancy/Reproduction

Pregnancy—Studies have not been done in humans.

Studies have not been done in animals.

FDA Pregnancy Category C.

Breast-feeding

It is not known whether benzonatate is distributed into breast milk. However, problems in humans have not been documented.

Pediatrics

Appropriate studies have not been performed in children up to 10 years of age. However, benzonatate should not be used in infants and young children since numbness of the mouth, tongue, and pharynx may occur, which may cause swallowing difficulty and aspiration. Children should be instructed not to chew or suck on the capsule before swallowing it since the mouth and throat may become numb from contact with the benzonatate within the capsule and choking may occur.

Geriatrics

No information is available on the relationship of age to the effects of benzonatate in geriatric patients.

Drug interactions and/or related problems

The following drug interactions and/or related problems have been selected on the basis of their potential clinical significance (possible mechanism in parentheses where appropriate)—not necessarily inclusive (» = major clinical significance):

Note: Combinations containing any of the following medications, depending on the amount present, may also interact with this medication.

Central nervous system (CNS) depression-producing medications, other (see *Appendix II*)
(concurrent use may potentiate the CNS depressant effects of these medications or benzonatate)

Medications, other
(concurrent use of benzonatate with other medications has resulted rarely in bizarre behavior, including confusion and visual hallucinations)

Medical considerations/Contraindications

The medical considerations/contraindications included have been selected on the basis of their potential clinical significance (reasons given in parentheses where appropriate)—not necessarily inclusive (» = major clinical significance).

Risk-benefit should be considered when the following medical problems exist:

» Cough, productive
(inhibition of cough reflex may lead to retention of secretions)

Sensitivity to benzonatate or topical anesthetics

Side/Adverse Effects

The following side/adverse effects have been selected on the basis of their potential clinical significance (possible signs and symptoms in parentheses where appropriate)—not necessarily inclusive:

Those indicating need for medical attention

Incidence rare

Confusion—may occur with concurrent use of other medications; ***hypersensitivity reactions, severe, such as bronchospasm*** (shortness of breath, troubled breathing, tightness in chest, or wheezing); ***laryngospasm*** (difficulty in speaking or breathing); ***or cardiovascular collapse***—possibly related to local anesthesia caused by sucking or chewing the capsule rather than swallowing it whole; ***visual hallucinations*** (seeing things that are not there)—may occur with concurrent use of other medications

Those indicating need for medical attention only if they continue or are bothersome

Incidence less frequent or rare

Constipation; dizziness, mild; drowsiness, mild; headache; nausea or vomiting; pruritus (itching); ***sensation of burning in the eyes; skin rash; stuffy nose***

Overdose

For more information on the management of overdose or unintentional ingestion, **contact a Poison Control Center** (see *Poison Control Center Listing*).

Clinical effects of overdose

The following effects have been selected on the basis of their potential clinical significance (possible signs and symptoms in parentheses where appropriate)–not necessarily inclusive:

Acute and/or chronic

CNS stimulation (convulsions; restlessness; trembling); ***oropharyngeal anesthesia***—if capsules are chewed or dissolved in mouth

Note: *CNS stimulation* may cause tremors and restlessness that may develop into clonic convulsions followed by profound CNS depression.

In some cases, deliberate or accidental overdose has resulted in death.

Treatment of overdose

Specific treatment—Treatment consists of gastric lavage and liberal administration of activated charcoal slurry. Even for conscious patients, protection against aspiration of gastric contents is required because of the possibility of depressed cough and gag reflexes. A short-acting intravenous barbiturate in the smallest effective dose should be used if convulsions are present. Respiratory, cardiovascular, and renal function support are also essential in the treatment of severe intoxication from benzonatate overdosage. CNS stimulants should be avoided.

Supportive care—Patients in whom intentional overdose is confirmed or suspected should be referred for psychiatric consultation.

Patient Consultation

As an aid to patient consultation, refer to *Advice for the Patient, Benzonatate (Systemic)*.

In providing consultation, consider emphasizing the following selected information (» = major clinical significance):

Before using this medication

» Conditions affecting use, especially:
Sensitivity to benzonatate or topical anesthetics
Use in children—Importance of children not chewing or sucking on the capsule before swallowing it; if the medication contained in the capsules comes in contact with the mouth, the mouth and throat may become numb and choking may occur
Other medical problems, especially a productive cough

Proper use of this medication

» Not chewing or sucking on capsules; swallowing whole to avoid local anesthetic effect and choking
» Proper dosing
Missed dose: Taking as soon as possible; not taking if almost time for next dose; not doubling doses
» Proper storage

Precautions while using this medication

Checking with physician if cough persists after medication has been used for 7 days or if high fever, skin rash, or continuing headache is present with cough

Side/adverse effects

Signs of potential side effects, especially confusion, bronchospasm, laryngospasm, cardiovascular collapse, and visual hallucinations

General Dosing Information

It is recommended that the capsules not be chewed or sucked on before they are swallowed. Release of benzonatate from the capsule may produce temporary local anesthesia of the oral mucosa and choking may occur. In addition, severe hypersensitivity reactions have occurred.

For treatment of adverse effects

Severe hypersensitivity reactions, such as bronchospasm, laryngospasm, or cardiovascular collapse, have occurred and may be related to local anesthesia caused by sucking or chewing the capsule rather than swallowing it whole. Severe reactions have required treatment with vasopressor agents and use of supportive measures.

Oral Dosage Forms

BENZONATATE CAPSULES USP

Usual adult and adolescent dose

Antitussive—
Oral, 100 mg three times a day, as needed.

Usual adult prescribing limits

600 mg per day.

Usual pediatric dose

Antitussive—
Children up to 10 years of age: Dosage has not been established.
Children 10 years of age and older: See *Usual adult and adolescent dose.*

Usual geriatric dose

See *Usual adult and adolescent dose.*

Strength(s) usually available

U.S.—
100 mg (Rx) [*Tessalon;* GENERIC].
Canada—
100 mg (OTC) [*Tessalon*].

Packaging and storage

Store below 40 °C (104 °F), preferably between 15 and 30 °C (59 and 86 °F), in a tight, light-resistant container.

Auxiliary labeling

• Do not chew or suck on capsule.

Selected Bibliography

Irwin RS, Curley FJ, Pratter MR. The effects of drugs on cough. Eur J Respir Dis Suppl 1987; 153: 173-81.
Irwin RS, Curley FJ, Bennett FM. Appropriate use of antitussives and protussives. Drugs 1993; 46(1): 80-91.

Revised: 08/13/1998

BENZPHETAMINE—See *Appetite Suppressants (Systemic)*

BENZTROPINE—See *Antidyskinetics (Systemic)*

BEPRIDIL—See *Calcium Channel Blocking Agents (Systemic)*

BETA-ADRENERGIC BLOCKING AGENTS Ophthalmic

This monograph includes information on the following: 1) Betaxolol; 2) Carteolol†; 3) Levobetaxolol†; 4) Levobunolol; 5) Metipranolol†; 6) Timolol.

VA CLASSIFICATION (Primary): OP110

Commonly used brand name(s): *AKBeta*[4]; *Apo-Timop*[6]; *Betagan*[4]; *Betaxon*[3]; *Betimol*[6]; *Betoptic*[1]; *Betoptic S*[1]; *Novo-Levobunolol*[4]; *Novo-Timol*[6]; *Ocupress*[2]; *Ophtho-Bunolol*[4]; *OptiPranolol*[5]; *Tim-AK*[6]; *Timoptic*[6]; *Timoptic in Ocudose*[6]; *Timoptic-XE*[6].

Note: For a listing of dosage forms and brand names by country availability, see *Dosage Forms* section(s).

†Not commercially available in Canada.

Category

Antiglaucoma agent (ophthalmic).

Indications

Note: Bracketed information in the *Indications* section refers to uses that are not included in U.S. product labeling.

Accepted

Glaucoma, open-angle (treatment) or
Hypertension, ocular (treatment)—Ophthalmic beta-adrenergic blocking agents are indicated in the treatment of chronic open-angle glaucoma. They also may be used in the treatment of ocular hypertension. They may be used alone or in combination with other antiglaucoma agents.

Ophthalmic beta-adrenergic blocking agents have been used as long-term ocular hypotensive therapy in glaucoma patients who have undergone laser trabeculectomy and in some cases of secondary glaucoma. They are well tolerated in aphakic glaucoma patients and in glaucoma patients who wear hard or soft contact lenses.

[Glaucoma, angle-closure (treatment adjunct)]—Betaxolol[1], carteolol, levobetaxolol, levobunolol[1], metipranolol, and timolol may be used in conjunction with miotics to reduce intraocular pressure in acute and chronic angle-closure glaucoma. However, the ophthalmic beta-adrenergic blocking agent's action alone is unlikely to terminate an acute attack of angle-closure glaucoma, because the agent produces little or no constriction of the pupil. Constriction of the pupil is necessary to pull the iris away from the trabeculum to relieve blockage of the trabecular meshwork.

[Glaucoma, angle-closure, *during* or *after* iridectomy (treatment)][1] or
[Glaucoma, malignant (treatment)][1]—Ophthalmic beta-adrenergic blocking agents may be used to lower intraocular pressure in the treatment of angle-closure glaucoma *during* or *after* iridectomy and in the treatment of malignant glaucoma.

Note: Ophthalmic preparations of betaxolol and levobetaxolol may be especially useful in the treatment of glaucoma in patients with pulmonary disease because they are relatively selective beta-1-adrenergic antagonists. Although ophthalmic betaxolol can have significant effects on pulmonary function in persons with pulmonary disease, it appears to do so much less frequently than nonselective beta-adrenergic antagonists. Ophthalmic levobetaxolol is expected to show a similar sparing of pulmonary function.

[1]Not included in Canadian product labeling.

Pharmacology/Pharmacokinetics

Physicochemical characteristics

Molecular weight—
Betaxolol hydrochloride: 343.89.
Carteolol hydrochloride: 328.84.
Levobetaxolol hydrochloride: 343.89.
Levobunolol: 327.85.
Metipranolol: 309.41.
Timolol maleate: 432.49.

pH—
Metipranolol hydrochloride ophthalmic solution: 5 to 5.8
Levobetaxolol hydrochloride ophthalmic suspension: 5.5 to 7.5

Mechanism of action/Effect

Betaxolol and levobetaxolol are cardioselective (beta-1-adrenergic) receptor blocking agents Carteolol, levobunolol, metipranolol, and timolol are beta-1 and beta-2 (nonselective) adrenergic blocking agents. The exact mechanism of the ocular hypotensive action of ophthalmic beta-adrenergic blocking agents has not been established. However, it appears that the ophthalmic beta-adrenergic blocking agents reduce aqueous humor production, as demonstrated by tonography and fluorophotometry. A slight increase in aqueous humor outflow may be an additional mechanism.

Other actions/effects

Ophthalmic beta-adrenergic blocking agents, if systemically absorbed, are capable of producing beta-adrenergic receptor blockade in the bronchi and bronchioles. (This is less likely to occur with ophthalmic betaxolol or levobetaxolol because they are relatively selective beta-1-adrenergic blocking agents.) This action results in an increase in airway resistance because of unopposed parasympathetic activity. This effect is in keeping with the beta-2-adrenergic blocking action of these medications. It is possible that carteolol, because of its partial beta-agonist activity, may have less of a beta-blockade effect than the other ophthalmic beta-2-adrenergic blocking agents; however, the possible protection conferred by the beta-agonist effect has not been clinically evaluated. Betaxolol 1% solution, when compared to a placebo, was not shown to have a significant effect on pulmonary function as measured by forced expiratory volume in 1 second (FEV_1), forced vital capacity (FVC), and FEV_1/VC. However, in clinical use, ophthalmic betaxolol has caused a worsening of respiratory symptoms in some patients with pulmonary disease.

Ophthalmic beta-adrenergic blocking agents, if systemically absorbed, are also capable of reducing heart rate, myocardial contractility, and cardiac output, resulting in bradycardia and hypotension, in both healthy individuals and patients with heart disease. This is in keeping with the beta-1-adrenergic blocking action of these medications.

The ophthalmic beta-adrenergic blocking agents do not have significant membrane-stabilizing (local anesthetic) activity.

Ophthalmic beta-adrenergic blocking agents reduce normal as well as elevated intraocular pressure (IOP), whether or not it is accompanied by glaucoma.

Ophthalmic beta-adrenergic blocking agents have little or no effect on pupil size or accommodation compared with miosis produced by cholinergic agents.

Absorption

Ophthalmic beta-adrenergic blocking agents may be systemically absorbed.

Half-life

Levobetaxolol—Approximately 20 hours.

Onset of action

Betaxolol, levobetaxolol, metipranolol, and timolol—Within 30 minutes following a single dose.

Levobunolol—Within 1 hour following a single dose.

Peak serum concentration

Timolol maleate ophthalmic solution—0.46 nanogram per mL following morning dosing and 0.35 nanogram per mL following afternoon dosing.

Timolol maleate gel-forming ophthalmic solution—0.28 nanogram per mL following morning dosing.

Time to peak effect

Betaxolol, carteolol, levobetaxolol, and metipranolol—Approximately 2 hours following a single dose. This applies to both betaxolol ophthalmic solution and suspension.

Levobunolol—Between 2 and 6 hours following a single dose.

Timolol—Within 1 to 2 hours following a single dose.

Duration of action

Betaxolol and levobetaxolol—12 hours, following a single dose of either the ophthalmic solution or suspension.

Carteolol—More than 6 to 8 hours.

Levobunolol and timolol—A significant lowering of intraocular pressure may be maintained for up to 24 hours following a single dose.

Metipranolol—A reduction in intraocular pressure can be demonstrated 24 hours following a single dose.

Precautions to Consider

Cross-sensitivity and/or related problems

Patients sensitive to any of the ophthalmic or systemic beta-adrenergic blocking agents, such as acebutolol, atenolol, betaxolol, bisoprolol, carteolol, labetalol, levobetaxolol, levobunolol, metipranolol, metoprolol, nadolol, oxprenolol, penbutolol, pindolol, propranolol, sotalol, or timolol, may be sensitive to any other beta-adrenergic blocking agent also.

Patients sensitive to sulfites may be sensitive to levobunolol hydrochloride ophthalmic solution which contains sodium metabisulfite.

Carcinogenicity

Betaxolol—In lifetime studies in mice and rats, betaxolol has not been shown to be carcinogenic when administered orally at doses of 6, 20, or 60 mg per kg of body weight (mg/kg) per day (mice) and at doses of 3, 12, or 48 mg/kg per day (rats).

Carteolol—In 2-year studies in mice and rats, carteolol has not been shown to be carcinogenic when administered orally at doses of up to 40 mg/kg per day.

Metipranolol—In lifetime studies, metipranolol has not been shown to be carcinogenic when administered orally to mice at doses of 5, 50, and 100 mg/kg per day and to rats at doses of up to 70 mg/kg per day.

Timolol—In a lifetime study in mice, timolol increased the incidence of malignant pulmonary tumors and mammary adenocarcinomas in female mice when administered orally at doses of 500 mg/kg per day, but not at 5 or 50 mg/kg per day.

Tumorigenicity

Betaxolol, carteolol, and levobetaxolol—Unknown.

Levobunolol—In a lifetime study, levobunolol increased the incidence of benign leiomyomas in female mice when administered orally at doses of 200 mg/kg per day (14,000 times the recommended human dose for glaucoma), but did not produce this effect at doses of 12 or 50 mg/kg per day (850 and 3500 times the human dose). In a 2-year study in rats, levobunolol increased the incidence of benign hepatomas in male rats when administered orally at doses 12,800 times the recommended human dose for glaucoma. Similar differences were not observed in rats when levobunolol was administered at oral doses equivalent to 350 to 2000 times the recommended human dose for glaucoma.

Metipranolol—In lifetime studies, female mice had an increased number of pulmonary adenomas when they were given metipranolol at an oral dose of 5 mg/kg per day. However, doses of 50 and 100 mg/kg per day did not produce this effect.

Timolol—In a 2-year study in rats, timolol increased the incidence of adrenal pheochromocytomas in male rats when administered orally at doses of 300 mg/kg per day (which are 250 times the maximum recommended human oral dose of 30 mg [1 drop of ophthalmic timolol contains about 1/150th of this dose or about 0.2 mg of timolol]). However, similar effects were not observed in rats when timolol was administered at oral doses equivalent to 20 or 80 times the maximum recommended human oral dose. In a lifetime study in mice, timolol increased the incidence of benign pulmonary tumors and benign uterine polyps in female mice when administered orally at doses of 500 mg/kg per day. However, doses of 5 and 50 mg/kg per day did not produce this effect. In addition, timolol increased the overall incidence of neoplasms in female mice at oral doses of 500 mg/kg per day.

Mutagenicity

Betaxolol—*In vitro* and *in vivo* bacterial and mammalian cell assays have not shown betaxolol to be mutagenic.

Carteolol—Carteolol was not shown to be mutagenic in the Ames test and recombinant (rec)-assay and in the *in vivo* cytogenetic and dominant lethal assays.

Levobetaxolol—Potential mutagenicity was shown *in vitro* in the Chinese Hamster Ovarian Cell sister chromatid exhange assay, in the presence of metabolic activation systems.

Levobunolol—In microbiological and mammalian *in vitro* and *in vivo* assays, levobunolol was not shown to be mutagenic.

Metipranolol—Metipranolol was nonmutagenic in *in vivo* and *in vitro* bacterial and mammalian cell assays.

Timolol—Timolol was not shown to be mutagenic when tested *in vivo* (mouse) in the micronucleus test and cytogenetic assay (at doses up to 800 mg/kg) and *in vitro* in a neoplastic cell transformation assay (up to 0.1 mg per mL).

Pregnancy/Reproduction

Fertility—*Betaxolol*: Studies in rabbits and rats have shown that betaxolol, administered at oral doses above 12 mg/kg and 128 mg/kg, respectively, causes drug-related postimplantation loss.

Carteolol: Studies in rats and mice have not shown that carteolol causes any adverse effects on male and female fertility when administered at doses of up to 150 mg/kg per day.

Levobetaxolol: Reproduction and fertility studies in rabbits showed evidence of drug related postimplantation loss at doses of levobetaxolol 12 mg/kg per day.

Levobunolol: Reproduction and fertility studies in rats showed no adverse effects on male or female fertility when levobunolol was administered at doses of up to 1800 times the recommended human dose for glaucoma.

Metipranolol: Reproduction and fertility studies on metipranolol in rats and mice showed no adverse effect on female or male fertility at oral doses of up to 25 mg/kg per day and 50 mg/kg per day, respectively.

Timolol: Reproduction and fertility studies in rats have not shown that timolol causes any adverse effects on male and female fertility when administered at doses of up to 125 times the maximum recommended human oral dose.

Pregnancy—

Betaxolol—

Adequate and well-controlled studies in humans have not been done.

In animal studies, betaxolol was not shown to cause teratogenic effects or other adverse effects on reproduction at subtoxic doses.

FDA Pregnancy Category C.

Carteolol—

Adequate and well-controlled studies in humans have not been done.

In rabbits and rats, carteolol, administered in doses approximately 1052 and 5264 times the maximum recommended human oral dose of 10 mg per 70 kg of body weight per day, respectively, resulted in maternotoxicity, increased incidence of fetal resorptions, and decreased fetal weights. In rats, carteolol, administered in doses approximately 212 times the maximum recommended human oral dose, resulted in a dose-related increase in wavy ribs in the developing rat fetus. However, in mice, carteolol, administered in doses up to approximately 1052 times the maximum recommended human oral dose, did not result in wavy ribs.

FDA Pregnancy Category C.

Levobetaxolol—

Adequate and well-controlled studies in humans have not been done.

Sternebrae malformations were observed in rabbits administered levobetaxolol 4 mg/kg per day.

FDA Pregnancy Category C.

Levobunolol—

Adequate and well-controlled studies in humans have not been done.

Although levobunolol has been shown to cause fetotoxicity in rabbits when administered at doses equivalent to 200 and 700 times the recommended dose for the treatment of glaucoma, similar studies in rats have not shown levobunolol to cause fetotoxic effects when administered at doses of up to 1800 times the human dose for glaucoma. Moreover, in teratogenicity studies in rats, levobunolol was not shown to cause fetal malformations when administered at doses of up to 25 mg/kg per day (1800 times the recommended human dose for glaucoma). Also, levobunolol was not shown to have adverse effects on the postnatal development of animal offspring.

FDA Pregnancy Category C.

Metipranolol—

Adequate and well-controlled studies in humans have not been done.

No metipranolol-related effects were reported for the segment II teratology study in fetal rats when metipranolol was administered orally to pregnant rats in doses of up to 50 mg/kg per day during organogenesis. However, metipranolol has been shown to increase fetal resorption, fetal death, and delayed development when administered orally to pregnant rabbits at 50 mg/kg during organogenesis.

FDA Pregnancy Category C.

Timolol—

Although adequate and well-controlled studies in humans have not been done, timolol may be absorbed systemically.

Studies in rats have shown that timolol at doses of up to 50 mg/kg per day (50 times the maximum recommended human oral dose) causes delayed fetal ossification; however, there were no adverse effects on postnatal development of offspring. Teratogenic studies in mice and rabbits have not shown that timolol at doses of up to 50 mg/kg per day causes fetal malformations. In mice, timolol at doses of 1 gram per kg per day (1000 times the maximum recommended human oral dose) was maternotoxic and resulted in increased incidence of fetal resorptions. In rabbits, timolol at doses 100 times the maximum recommended human oral dose caused increased incidence of fetal resorptions but not maternotoxicity.

FDA Pregnancy Category C.

Breast-feeding

Betaxolol—Systemic betaxolol is distributed into breast milk in large enough quantities to have pharmacological effects. However, it is not known whether ophthalmic betaxolol is distributed into breast milk and problems in humans have not been documented.

Carteolol—It is not known whether systemic or ophthalmic carteolol is distributed into human breast milk; however, carteolol has been shown to be distributed into animal milk.

Levobetaxolol—It is not known whether ophthalmic levobetaxolol is distributed into human breast milk.

Levobunolol—It is not known whether ophthalmic levobunolol is distributed into breast milk. However, problems in humans have not been documented.

Metipranolol—It is not known whether ophthalmic metipranolol is distributed into breast milk. However, problems in humans have not been documented.

Timolol—Systemic timolol is distributed into breast milk. Problems in humans have not been documented for ophthalmic timolol; however, ophthalmic timolol may be systemically absorbed and distributed into the breast milk, possibly causing serious adverse reactions in the infants of nursing mothers.

Pediatrics

Although appropriate studies on the relationship of age to the effects of beta-adrenergic blocking agents, including the ophthalmic blocking agents, have not been performed in the pediatric population, infants should be treated cautiously and monitored for signs of dyspnea. In addition, the use of nasolacrimal occlusion should be emphasized for both infants and children.

Geriatrics

Although appropriate studies on the relationship of age to the effects of ophthalmic beta-adrenergic blocking agents have not been performed in the geriatric population, no geriatrics-specific problems have been documented to date. However, if significant systemic absorption of ophthalmic beta-adrenergic blocking agents occurs, the same geriatrics-related problems may occur that are possible with the systemic beta-adrenergic blocking agents. These include bradycardia, increased myocardial depression because of reduced metabolic and excretory capabilities in many elderly patients, and the increased risk of beta-adrenergic blocking agent-induced hypothermia in elderly patients.

In addition, elderly patients are more likely to have age-related peripheral vascular disease, which may require caution in patients receiving beta-adrenergic blocking agents.

Surgical

Gradual withdrawal of ophthalmic beta-adrenergic blocking agent therapy may be advisable prior to general anesthesia because of the beta-adrenergic blocking agent-induced suppression of the cardiac response to beta-adrenergically mediated sympathetic reflex stimuli.

Drug interactions and/or related problems

The following drug interactions and/or related problems have been selected on the basis of their potential clinical significance (possible mechanism in parentheses where appropriate)—not necessarily inclusive (» = major clinical significance):

Note: Combinations containing any of the following medications, depending on the amount present, may also interact with this medication.

Information concerning interactions between ophthalmic beta-adrenergic blocking agents and other medications is still limited. Some of the following potential interactions apply to beta-adrenergic blocking agents in general and are stated for cautionary reference until additional information specific to the ophthalmic beta-adrenergic blocking agents is available.

Allergen immunotherapy or
Allergenic extracts for skin testing
(if significant systemic absorption of ophthalmic beta-adrenergic blocking agents occurs, concurrent use of these agents in patients using ophthalmic beta-adrenergic blocking agents may increase the potential for serious systemic reaction or anaphylaxis)

Amiodarone
(if significant systemic absorption of ophthalmic beta-adrenergic blocking agents occurs, concurrent use may potentiate bradycardia, sinus arrest, and atrioventricular [AV] block, especially in patients with underlying sinus function impairment)

Anesthetics, hydrocarbon inhalation, such as:
Chloroform
Cyclopropane
Enflurane
Halothane
Isoflurane
Methoxyflurane

Trichloroethylene
(if significant systemic absorption of ophthalmic beta-adrenergic blocking agents occurs, concurrent use of hydrocarbon inhalation anesthetics may increase the risk of myocardial depression and hypotension because the beta-adrenergic blockade reduces the ability of the heart to respond to beta-adrenergically mediated sympathetic reflex stimuli; if it is necessary to reverse the effects of beta-adrenergic blocking agents during surgery, agonists, such as dobutamine, dopamine, isoproterenol, or norepinephrine, may be used but should be administered with caution, especially in patients receiving halothane. Some clinicians recommend gradual withdrawal of beta-adrenergic blocking agents 48 hours prior to elective surgery; however, this recommendation is controversial)

Antidiabetic agents, oral or
Insulin
(systemic beta-adrenergic blocking agents may affect diabetes mellitus therapy. This may also occur with ophthalmic beta-adrenergic blocking agents if there is significant systemic absorption. Nonselective beta-adrenergic blocking agents impair glycogenolysis and the hyperglycemic response to endogenous epinephrine, leading to persistence of hypoglycemia. Also, beta-adrenergic blocking agents, especially nonselective agents, decrease the release of insulin in response to hyperglycemia. Dosage adjustment of the antidiabetic agent may be required to avoid a severe hypoglycemic reaction. In addition, beta-adrenergic blocking agents may complicate patient monitoring by masking symptoms of hypoglycemia caused by epinephrine, such as increased heart rate and increased blood pressure, but not dizziness and sweating. Although selective or relatively selective beta-adrenergic blocking agents usually cause fewer problems with blood glucose levels, they may still mask symptoms of hypoglycemia)

Beta-adrenergic blocking agents, systemic
(if significant systemic absorption of ophthalmic beta-adrenergic blocking agents occurs, concurrent use of these medications may result in an additive effect on intraocular pressure or in additive systemic effects of beta-adrenergic blockade)

Calcium channel blocking agents
(if significant systemic absorption of ophthalmic beta-adrenergic blocking agents occurs, concurrent use of calcium channel blocking agents, such as bepridil, diltiazem, flunarizine, isradipine, nicardipine, nifedipine, nimodipine, and verapamil, may result in atrioventricular conduction disturbances, left ventricular failure, and hypotension; in some patients, if a calcium antagonist is necessary, nicardipine or nifedipine may be preferred because they have less effect on heart rate and conduction, although they may also cause greater hypotension; concurrent use of calcium channel blockers and ophthalmic beta-adrenergic blocking agents should be used with care in patients with impaired cardiac function)

Catecholamine-depleting medications, such as the rauwolfia alkaloids:
Alseroxylon
Deserpidine
Rauwolfia serpentina
Reserpine
(if significant systemic absorption of ophthalmic beta-adrenergic blocking agents occurs, concurrent use of catecholamine-depleting medications may result in additive and possibly excessive beta-adrenergic blockade; although this effect is largely theoretical, close observation is recommended, since bradycardia and marked hypotension may occur)

Cimetidine
(if significant systemic absorption of ophthalmic beta-adrenergic blocking agents occurs, concurrent use with cimetidine may reduce the clearance of hepatically metabolized beta-adrenergic blocking agents, resulting in elevations of plasma concentrations)

Clonidine
(if significant systemic absorption of ophthalmic beta-adrenergic blocking agents occurs during concurrent use, discontinuation of clonidine therapy may increase the risk of clonidine-withdrawal hypertensive crisis; ideally, beta-adrenergic blocking agents should be discontinued several days before clonidine is discontinued; blood pressure control may also be impaired when the two are combined)

Cocaine
(cocaine may inhibit the therapeutic effects of systemic beta-adrenergic blocking agents, and may also have this effect on ophthalmic beta-adrenergic blocking agents)
(concurrent use of cocaine with systemic beta-adrenergic blocking agents may increase the risk of hypertension, excessive bradycardia, and possibly heart block because beta-adrenergic blockade may leave cocaine's alpha-adrenergic activity unopposed. This may also occur with ophthalmic beta-adrenergic blocking agents if significant systemic absorption of the ophthalmic beta-adrenergic blocking agent occurs)

Contrast media, iodinated
(if significant systemic absorption of ophthalmic beta-adrenergic blocking agents occurs, concurrent use with intravenous contrast media may increase the risk of moderate to severe anaphylaxis; these reactions may be refractory to treatment. There was no consensus among USP experts as to whether or not this interaction was clinically significant)

Fentanyl and derivatives
(preoperative chronic use of ophthalmic beta-adrenergic blocking agents [with the possible exception of betaxolol] may increase the risk of initial bradycardia following induction doses of fentanyl or any of its derivatives)

Flecainide
(if significant systemic absorption of ophthalmic beta-adrenergic blocking agents occurs, concurrent use may result in additive negative cardiac inotropic effects, especially, or perhaps only, in patients with cardiac problems)

Hypotension-producing medications, other (See *Appendix II*)
(if significant systemic absorption of ophthalmic beta-adrenergic blocking agents [with the possible exception of betaxolol and levobetaxolol] occurs, concurrent use may potentiate the hypotensive effects of these medications)

Methacholine
(if significant systemic absorption of ophthalmic beta-adrenergic blocking agents occurs, methacholine inhalation challenge should not be performed, since the reaction to methacholine may be exaggerated or prolonged and may not respond as rapidly to treatment with bronchodilators)

Nicotine
(nicotine increases the metabolism of beta-adrenergic blocking agents; if significant systemic absorption of ophthalmic beta-adrenergic blocking agents occurs, patients undergoing smoking cessation may experience an increase in the frequency of side/adverse effects caused by the blocking agents because of the subsequent decrease in the blocking agents" metabolism. There was no consensus among USP experts as to whether or not this interaction was clinically significant)

Phenothiazines
(if significant systemic absorption of ophthalmic beta-adrenergic blocking agents occurs, concurrent use may result in an increased plasma concentration of either the phenothiazine or the ophthalmic beta-adrenergic blocking agent because of inhibition of metabolism. This may result in additive hypotensive effects, irreversible retinopathy, cardiac arrhythmias, or tardive dyskinesia. There was no consensus among USP experts as to whether or not this interaction was clinically significant)

Phenytoin, intravenous
(if significant systemic absorption of ophthalmic beta-adrenergic blocking agents occurs, concurrent use may cause additive cardiac depressant effects. There was no consensus among USP experts as to whether or not this interaction was clinically significant)

Quinidine
(beta-adrenergic blocking effects of timolol may be potentiated because quinidine inhibits cytochrome P450 CYP2D6)

Sympathomimetics, systemic
(if significant systemic absorption of ophthalmic beta-adrenergic blocking agents occurs, concurrent use may result in inhibition of the beta-adrenergic effects of sympathomimetics; depending on the type of sympathomimetic, this inhibition will occur with the beta-1-adrenergic cardiac effects and/or the beta-2-adrenergic bronchodilating effect; betaxolol and levobetaxolol will block primarily the beta-1-adrenergic effects)
(concurrent use of norepinephrine may result in mutual inhibition of therapeutic effects)

Xanthines, such as:
Aminophylline
Caffeine
Dyphylline
Oxtriphylline
Theophylline
(if significant systemic absorption of ophthalmic beta-adrenergic blocking agents [with the possible exception of betaxolol] occurs,

concurrent use may result in inhibition of therapeutic effects of xanthines; in addition, concurrent use of xanthines [except dyphylline] with the ophthalmic beta-adrenergic blocking agents [with the possible exception of betaxolol] may decrease theophylline clearance, especially in patients with increased theophylline clearance induced by smoking; concurrent use requires careful monitoring)

(concurrent use with caffeine may result in inhibition of caffeine's therapeutic effect)

Medical considerations/Contraindications

The medical considerations/contraindications included have been selected on the basis of their potential clinical significance (reasons given in parentheses where appropriate)—not necessarily inclusive (» = major clinical significance).

Except under special circumstances, this medication should not be used when the following medical problems exist:

» Asthma, bronchial (or history of) or
» Pulmonary disease, obstructive, severe chronic
(severe respiratory reactions, including death due to bronchospasm, have been reported in patients with asthma, following administration of the ophthalmic beta-adrenergic blocking agents. Although betaxolol (and, possibly, levobetaxolol)appears to have a minimal effect on pulmonary function, caution should be used in patients with severe restriction of pulmonary function)

» Cardiac failure, overt or
» Cardiogenic shock or
» Heart block, 2nd- or 3rd-degree atrioventricular (AV) or
» Sinus bradycardia
(risk of further myocardial depression may occur with the use of the ophthalmic beta-adrenergic blocking agents)

» Previous allergic reaction to the ophthalmic beta-adrenergic blocking agent prescribed

Risk-benefit should be considered when the following medical problems exist:

» Allergic reactions, severe, history of
(risk of developing unresponsiveness to usual doses of epinephrine used to treat anaphylactic reactions)

» Bronchitis, nonallergenic or chronic or
» Emphysema or
» Pulmonary function impairment, other
(use of the ophthalmic beta-adrenergic blocking agents may promote bronchospasm and block bronchodilation produced by endogenous and exogenous catecholamine stimulation of beta-2-receptors. Although the effects of betaxolol on pulmonary function have been shown in some studies to be minimal in patients with reactive airway disease, there have been reports of asthmatic attacks and pulmonary distress during betaxolol treatment)

Cerebrovascular insufficiency
(potential effects on blood pressure and pulse; if signs of reduced cerebral blood flow occur following initiation of therapy, alternative therapy should be considered)

» Congestive heart failure
(risk of further depression of myocardial contractility)

» Cardiac failure, history of or
Heart block, history of
(possible risk of myocardial depression; treatment should be discontinued at first signs of cardiac failure)

» Diabetes mellitus, especially labile diabetes or
» Hypoglycemia
(ophthalmic beta-adrenergic blocking agents may mask some signs and symptoms of hypoglycemia, such as tachycardia and tremor, although they do not mask dizziness and sweating)

» Hyperthyroidism
(ophthalmic beta-adrenergic blocking agents may mask certain signs and symptoms of hyperthyroidism; abrupt withdrawal may precipitate a thyroid storm)

Myasthenia gravis
(beta-adrenergic blockade may potentiate muscle weakness related to certain myasthenic symptoms, such as diplopia, ptosis, and generalized weakness)

Patient monitoring

The following may be especially important in patient monitoring (other tests may be warranted in some patients, depending on condition; » = major clinical significance):

Intraocular pressure determination
(recommended during, and following, the first month of therapy during which stabilization of the pressure-lowering response to the ophthalmic beta-adrenergic blocking agent usually occurs; thereafter, intraocular pressure should be determined as necessary)

Side/Adverse Effects

Note: Even in patients *without* a history of cardiac failure, continued depression of the myocardium with beta-blockers, including ophthalmic beta-adrenergic blocking agents, over a period of time can lead to cardiac failure, if significant systemic absorption occurs. However, betaxolol, levobetaxolol, and metipranolol may be less likely to cause myocardial depression. At the first sign or symptom of cardiac failure, the ophthalmic beta-adrenergic blocking agent should be discontinued.

Although ophthalmic beta-adrenergic blocking agents have minimal membrane-stabilizing (local anesthetic) action,decreased corneal sensitivity may occur following prolonged use, and has been reported rarely with the use of betaxolol, levobunolol, and timolol, but not with the use of metipranolol. In contrast, carteolol has been reported to occasionally cause increased corneal sensitivity.

Because of the relative selectivity of betaxolol and levobetaxolol for beta-1-adrenergic receptor inhibition,betaxolol and levobetaxolol may have less potential for systemic side/adverse effects than have the other ophthalmic beta-adrenergic blocking agents, which are nonselective beta-1 and beta-2 adrenergic receptor inhibitors. This may be especially important for patients for whom beta-2 adrenergic blockade could be harmful.

The ophthalmic suspension dosage form of betaxolol appears to be less irritating to the eye than the ophthalmic solution dosage form, although eye irritation occurs more frequently than other side effects with both dosage forms.

The side effects listed below have been reported for one or more of the ophthalmic beta-adrenergic blocking agents. However, all of these side effects are possible with any of the ophthalmic beta-adrenergic blocking agents. In addition, since the ophthalmic beta-adrenergic blocking agents may be systemically absorbed, any of the side effects that are possible for the systemic beta-adrenergic blocking agents are also theoretically possible for the ophthalmic beta-adrenergic blocking agents.

A slight reduction in resting heart rate has been observed in patients receiving ophthalmic timolol maleate. In patients receiving timolol maleate ophthalmic solution, a mean reduction of 2.9 beats per minute with a standard deviation of 10.2 was observed. In patients receiving the gel-forming ophthalmic solution of timolol maleate, a mean reduction of 0.8 beat per minute at twenty-four hours postdose and 3.8 beats per minute at two hours postdose was observed.

The following side/adverse effects have been selected on the basis of their potential clinical significance (possible signs and symptoms in parentheses where appropriate)—not necessarily inclusive:

Those indicating need for medical attention

Incidence more frequent

Conjunctival hyperemia (redness of eyes or inside of eyelids)—reported for carteolol, frequency 25%

Incidence less frequent or rare

Anisocoria (different size pupils of the eyes)—reported for betaxolol; ***blepharitis*** (irritation or inflammation of eyelid)—reported for metipranolol and timolol; ***blepharoconjunctivitis*** (irritation or inflammation of eye and eyelid)—reported for carteolol and levobunolol; ***cataracts*** (blurred or decreased vision)—reported for levobetaxolol only; ***conjunctivitis*** (irritation or inflammation of eye)—reported for metipranolol and timolol; ***corneal punctate keratitis*** (irritation or inflammation of eye)—reported for betaxolol; ***dermatitis of eyelid*** (irritation or inflammation of eyelid)—reported for metipranolol; ***edema*** (swelling of eye or eyelid)—reported for carteolol and metipranolol; ***iridocyclitis*** (irritation or inflammation of eye)—reported for levobunolol; ***keratitis*** (irritation or inflammation of eye)—reported for betaxolol and timolol; ***blepharoptosis*** (droopy upper eyelid)—reported for carteolol and timolol; ***corneal staining*** (discoloration of the eyeball)—reported for betaxolol and carteolol; ***decreased corneal sensitivity***—reported for betaxolol, levobunolol, and timolol; ***diplopia*** (seeing double)—reported for timolol; ***eye pain***—reported for betaxolol suspension; ***glossitis*** (redness or irritation of the tongue)—reported for betaxolol; ***vision disturbances*** (blurred vision or other change in vision)—reported for betaxolol suspension, carteolol, metipranolol, and timolol; ***vitreous disorders***—reported for levobetaxolol only

Symptoms of systemic absorption

Allergic reaction (skin rash, hives, or itching)—reported for all except levobunolol; ***alopecia*** (hair loss)—reported for betaxolol, levobetaxolol, and timolol; ***anxiety or nervousness***—reported for levobetaxolol andmetipranolol; ***arthritis or myalgia*** (muscle or joint aches or pain)—reported for levobetaxolol and metipranolol; ***ataxia*** (clumsiness or unsteadiness)—reported for levobunolol only; ***breast abscess*** (breast pain)—reported for levobetaxolol only; ***change in taste***—reported for carteolol and levobetaxolol; ***chest pain***—reported for timolol only; ***confusion or mental depression***—reported for betaxolol, metipranolol, and timolol; ***congestive heart failure*** (swelling of feet, ankles, or lower legs)—reported for betaxolol and timolol; ***coughing, wheezing, or troubled breathing, especially in patients with predisposition to bronchoconstriction***—reported for all; ***cystitis*** (bloody or cloudy urine; difficult, burning, or painful urination)—reported for levobetaxolol only; ***diarrhea***—reported for timolol only; ***dizziness or feeling faint***—reported for all; ***drowsiness***—reported for metipranolol and timolol; ***ear pain***—reported for levobetaxolol only; ***epistaxis*** (bleeding nose)—reported for metipranolol and timolol; ***gout*** (ankle, knee, or great toe joint pain; ankle, knee, or great toe joint swelling; lower back or side pain)—reported for levobetaxolol only; ***hallucinations***—reported for timolol only; ***headache***—reported for all; ***heartblock***—reported for betaxolol, levobetaxolol, and timolol; ***hypercholesterolemia***—reported for levobetaxolol only; ***hyperlipidemia***—reported for levobetaxolol only; ***hypertension***—reported for levobetaxolol, metipranolol, and timolol; ***hypertonia*** (muscle tightness or stiffness)—reported for levobetaxolol only; ***hypotension*** (confusion; faintness; light-headedness)—reported for levobetaxolol only; ***impotence*** (decreased sexual ability)—reported for timolol only; ***infection*** (chills; fever)—reported for levobetaxolol only; ***insomnia*** (trouble in sleeping)—reported for betaxolol and carteolol; ***irregular, slow, or pounding heartbeat***—reported for all; ***nasal congestion*** (stuffy nose)—reported for timolol only; ***nausea or vomiting***—reported for metipranolol and timolol; ***otitis media*** (earache; ringing or buzzing in ears)—reported for levobetaxolol only; ***paresthesia*** (burning or prickling feeling on body)—reported for timolol only; ***pharyngitis*** (dryness or soreness of throat; hoarseness)—reported for levobetaxolol only; ***psoriasis*** (red, scaling, or crusted skin)—reported for levobetaxolol only; ***rhinitis or sinusitis*** (runny nose)—reported for carteolol, levobetaxolol, metipranolol, and timolol; ***systemic lupus erythematosus***—reported for timolol only; ***tachycardia*** (fast, pounding, or irregular heartbeat)—reported for levobetaxolol only; ***tinnitus*** (ringing in the ears)—reported for levobetaxolol and timolol; ***toxic epidermal necrolysis*** (raw or red areas of the skin)—reported for betaxolol only; ***unusual tiredness or weakness***—reported for all; ***vascular anomoly***—reported for levobetaxolol only; ***vertigo*** (dizziness; feeling of constant movement of self or surroundings)—reported for levobetaxolol only

Those indicating need for medical attention only if they continue or are bothersome

Incidence more frequent

Blurred vision, transient—reported for levobetaxolol and the timolol maleate gel-forming solution; usually lasts from thirty seconds to five minutes; ***decreased night vision***—reported for carteolol; ***stinging of eye or other eye irritation, transient upon administration of medication***—reported for betaxolol, levobetaxolol, levobunolol, and metipranolol

Incidence less frequent or rare

Browache—reported with carteolol and metipranolol; ***constipation***—reported for levobetaxolol only; ***corneal sensitivity***—reported for carteolol; ***crusting of eyelashes***—reported with betaxolol suspension; ***dermatitis*** (blistering, crusting, irritation, itching, or reddening of skin; dry, scaly skin)—reported for levobetaxolol only; ***dryness of eye***—reported with betaxolol suspension and timolol; ***dyspepsia*** (acid or sour stomach; belching; heartburn; indigestion)—reported for levobetaxolol only; ***foreign body sensation*** (feeling of having something in the eye)—reported with betaxolol; ***increased sensitivity of eye to light***—reported for betaxolol, carteolol, and metipranolol; ***redness, itching, stinging, burning, or watering of eye or other eye irritation***—reported for all; more frequent for carteolol and levobunolol; ***tendinitis*** (inflammation, pain, or swelling in muscles)—reported for levobetaxolol only

Overdose

For specific information on the agents used in the management of ophthalmic beta-adrenergic blocking agents overdose, see:

- *Aminophylline* in *Bronchodilators, Theophylline-derivative (Systemic)* monograph;
- *Atropine* in *Anticholinergics/Antispasmodics (Systemic)* monograph;
- *Charcoal, Activated (Oral-Local)* monograph;
- *Digitalis Glycosides (Systemic)* monograph;
- *Dobutamine* in *Sympathomimetic Agents-Cardiovascular Use (Parenteral-Systemic)* monograph;
- *Dopamine* in *Sympathomimetic Agents-Cardiovascular Use (Parenteral-Systemic)* monograph;
- *Glucagon (Systemic)* monograph;
- *Isoproterenol* in *Sympathomimetic Agents-Cardiovascular Use (Parenteral-Systemic)* monograph;
- *Norepinephrine* in *Sympathomimetic Agents-Cardiovascular Use (Parenteral-Systemic)* monograph; and/or
- *Theophylline* in *Bronchodilators, Theophylline-derivative (Systemic)* monograph.

For more information on the management of overdose or unintentional ingestion, **contact a Poison Control Center** (see *Poison Control Center Listing*).

Treatment of overdose

If an ophthalmic overdose occurs, immediately flush the eyes with warm tap water.

If an ophthalmic beta-adrenergic blocking agent is accidentally ingested, activated charcoal or gastric lavage may be appropriate to decrease further absorption.

For symptoms of systemic toxicity, the medication should be discontinued. Depending on severity of toxicity, the following supportive and symptomatic treatments should be utilized if necessary: For bradycardia: Atropine (0.25 to 2 mg) should be administered intravenously to induce vagal blockade. If bradycardia persists, intravenous isoproterenol hydrochloride may be administered with caution. A transvenous cardiac pacemaker may be used, if necessary. For hypotension: Glucagon and sympathomimetic pressor agents, such as dobutamine, dopamine, or norepinephrine, may be used. (See *Drug interactions and/or related problems* for precautions in use of sympathomimetic vasopressors.) For bronchospasm: Isoproterenol hydrochloride should be administered. Additional therapy with a beta-2-agonist or a theophylline derivative may be used, if necessary. For cardiac failure, acute: Digitalis, diuretics, and oxygen should be administered immediately. Intravenous aminophylline may be used in refractory cases. Also, glucagon hydrochloride may be used, if necessary. For heart block, second or third degree: Isoproterenol hydrochloride or a transvenous cardiac pacemaker should be used.

Patient Consultation

As an aid to patient consultation, refer to *Advice for the Patient, Beta-adrenergic Blocking Agents (Ophthalmic).*

In providing consultation, consider emphasizing the following selected information (» = major clinical significance):

Before using this medication

» Conditions affecting use, especially:

Allergy to any of the beta-adrenergic blocking agents, either ophthalmic or systemic, such as acebutolol, atenolol, betaxolol, bisoprolol, carteolol, labetalol, levobetaxolol, levobunolol, metipranolol, metoprolol, nadolol, oxprenolol, penbutolol, pindolol, propranolol, sotalol, or timolol

Pregnancy—Ophthalmic beta-adrenergic blocking agents may be absorbed into the body. Studies in animals have not shown that betaxolol, levobunolol, metipranolol, or timolol causes birth defects. However, very large doses of carteolol given by mouth to pregnant rats have been shown to cause wavy ribs in rat babies. In addition, some studies in animals have shown that beta-adrenergic blocking agents increase the chance of death in the animal fetus

Use in children—Infants may be especially sensitive to the effects of ophthalmic beta-adrenergic blocking agents, thus increasing the risk of side effects

Use in the elderly—If significant systemic absorption of ophthalmic beta-adrenergic blocking agents occurs, the chance of side effects during treatment may be increased, since elderly people are especially sensitive to the effects of these medications

Other medical problems, especially bronchial asthma, or history of, severe chronic obstructive pulmonary disease, overt cardiac failure, 2nd- or 3rd-degree atrioventricular (AV) heart block, cardiogenic shock, sinus bradycardia, history of severe allergic reactions, nonallergenic or chronic bronchitis, emphysema or other pulmonary function impairment, congestive heart failure, history of cardiac failure, diabetes mellitus, spontaneous hypoglycemia, or hyperthyroidism

Proper use of this medication

» Proper administration technique; using nasolacrimal occlusion is especially important in infants and children

Preventing contamination: Not touching applicator tip to any surface; keeping container tightly closed

Proper use of levobunolol having compliance cap

Proper use of gel-forming timolol solution

» Importance of not using more medication than the amount prescribed

Importance of removing soft contact lenses prior to administration for products containing benzalkonium chloride as a preservative

» Proper dosing

Missed dose: If dosing schedule is—

Once a day: Applying as soon as possible; not applying if not remembered until next day; applying regularly scheduled dose

More than once a day: Applying as soon as possible; not applying if almost time for next dose; applying next dose at regularly scheduled time

» Proper storage

Precautions while using this medication

Regular visits to physician to check eye pressure during therapy

Checking with physician immediately if having ocular surgery, if trauma to the eye occurs, or an eye infection develops to determine if the present multidose container should continue to be used

Caution when driving or using machinery because of possible blurred vision

» Caution if any kind of surgery (including dental surgery) or emergency treatment is required

» Diabetic patients: May mask some signs of hypoglycemia, such as increased pulse rate and trembling, but not dizziness and sweating; also, may cause decreased or sometimes increased blood glucose concentrations

Possible photophobia: Wearing sunglasses and avoiding too much exposure to bright light

Side/adverse effects

Signs of potential side effects, especially conjunctival hyperemia, anisocoria, blepharitis, blepharoconjunctivitis, cataracts, conjunctivitis, corneal punctate keratitis, dermatitis of eyelid, edema, iridocyclitis, keratitis, blepharoptosis, corneal staining, decreased corneal sensitivity, diplopia, eye pain, glossitis, vision disturbances, vitreous disorders, or symptoms of systemic absorption

General Dosing Information

Although some manufacturers recommend a dose of 2 drops of an ophthalmic solution at appropriate intervals, the conjunctival sac will usually hold 1 drop or less.

When one ophthalmic beta-adrenergic blocking agent is used to replace another, the original beta-blocker may be discontinued simultaneously with initiation of therapy with the new one.

When an ophthalmic beta-adrenergic blocking agent is used to replace a single antiglaucoma agent other than another beta-blocker, the other antiglaucoma agent may be continued on the first day that the new beta-blocker is used but can be discontinued on the second day.

When an ophthalmic beta-adrenergic blocking agent is used to replace several concomitantly administered antiglaucoma agents, the patient's dosage should be individualized as required. If any of the other antiglaucoma agents used is a beta-blocker, it can be discontinued before the new ophthalmic beta-adrenergic blocking agent is added to the regimen. The other antiglaucoma agents being used may be continued on the first day that the new beta-blocker is used but one of the agents should be discontinued on the second day. Then the remaining antiglaucoma agents may be decreased or discontinued according to the patient's response. Additional adjustments usually should involve only one agent at a time and should be made at intervals of not less than one week.

Ophthalmic beta-adrenergic blocking agents may be used concurrently with direct and indirect cholinergic agonists (e.g., pilocarpine, echothiophate, carbachol), beta-agonists (e.g., ophthalmic epinephrine or dipivefrin), or systemic carbonic anhydrase inhibitors (such as acetazolamide), if necessary to control intraocular pressure.

In patients scheduled for major surgery, some practitioners recommend that beta-adrenergic blocking agents be gradually withdrawn 48 hours prior to surgery because beta-adrenergic receptor blockade impairs the ability of the heart to respond to beta-adrenergically mediated reflex stimuli. This recommendation is controversial. However, since ophthalmic beta-adrenergic blocking agents may be absorbed systemically, gradual withdrawal of the medication should be considered for patients undergoing elective surgery because prolonged severe hypotension during anesthesia has occurred in some patients receiving systemic beta-adrenergic blocking agents. If necessary during surgery, the effects of beta-adrenergic blocking agents may be reversed by sufficient doses of agonists, such as isoproterenol, dopamine, dobutamine, or norepinephrine.

To help reduce systemic side effects, the patient can be instructed to close the eyes gently and apply pressure to the inner canthus of each eye in order to block lacrimal drainage through the tear ducts after instillation of the ophthalmic drops.

Products containing benzalkonium chloride as a preservative may be absorbed by soft contact lenses. Contact lenses should be removed prior to the administration of benzalkonium chloride-containing products. Lenses may be reinserted fifteen minutes after administration.

BETAXOLOL

Summary of Differences

Indications:

Betaxolol may be especially useful in the treatment of glaucoma in patients with pulmonary disease.

Pharmacology/pharmacokinetics:

Mechanism of action/effect—Betaxolol is a cardioselective (beta-1-adrenergic) receptor blocking agent.

Other actions/effects—Betaxolol is less likely to produce significant beta-adrenergic receptor blockade in the bronchi and bronchioles.

Duration of action—12 hours.

Fertility:

Studies in rabbits and rats have shown that betaxolol, at oral doses above 12 mg/kg and 128 mg/kg, respectively, causes drug-related postimplantation loss.

Breast-feeding:

Systemic betaxolol is distributed into breast milk in large enough quantities to have pharmacological effects. However, it is not known whether ophthalmic betaxolol is distributed into breast milk and problems in humans have not been documented.

Ophthalmic Dosage Forms

BETAXOLOL HYDROCHLORIDE OPHTHALMIC SOLUTION USP

Note: The dosing and strength usually available are expressed in terms of betaxolol base.

Usual adult and adolescent dose

Ophthalmic antiglaucoma agent—

Topical, to the conjunctiva, 1 drop of a 0.5% solution of betaxolol (base) two times a day.

Usual pediatric dose

Safety and efficacy have not been established.

Strength(s) usually available

U.S.—

0.5% (5 mg base; 5.6 mg as hydrochloride) (Rx) [*Betoptic* (benzalkonium chloride 0.01%; edetate disodium; sodium chloride; hydrochloric acid; sodium hydroxide)].

Canada—

Not commercially available.

Packaging and storage

Store below 40 °C (104 °F), preferably between 15 and 30 °C (59 and 86 °F), in a tight container, unless otherwise specified by manufacturer. Protect from freezing.

Auxiliary labeling

- For the eye.
- Keep container tightly closed.

BETAXOLOL HYDROCHLORIDE OPHTHALMIC SUSPENSION

Usual adult and adolescent dose

Ophthalmic antiglaucoma agent—

Topical, to the conjunctiva, 1 drop of a 0.25% suspension of betaxolol (base) two times a day.

Usual pediatric dose

Safety and efficacy have not been established.

Strength(s) usually available

U.S.—

0.25% (2.5 mg base; 2.8 mg as hydrochloride) (Rx) [*Betoptic S* (benzalkonium chloride 0.01%; mannitol; poly(styrene-divinyl benzene) sulfonic acid; Carbomer 934P; edetate disodium; hydrochloric acid; sodium hydroxide)].

Canada—

0.25% (2.5 mg base; 2.8 mg as hydrochloride) (Rx) [*Betoptic S* (benzalkonium chloride; mannitol; poly(styrene-divinyl benzene) sulfonic acid; carbomer 934P; edetate disodium; hydrochloric acid and/or sodium hydroxide)].

Packaging and storage
Store below 40 °C (104 °F), preferably between 15 and 30 °C (59 and 86 °F), in a well-closed container, unless otherwise specified by manufacturer. Protect from freezing.

Auxiliary labeling
- Shake well.
- For the eye.
- Keep container tightly closed.

CARTEOLOL

Summary of Differences

Pharmacology/pharmacokinetics:
Other actions/effects—Carteolol has intrinsic sympathomimetic activity.
Duration of action—More than 6 to 8 hours.

Pregnancy:
In rabbits and rats, carteolol, administered in doses approximately 1052 and 5264 times the maximum recommended human oral dose of 10 mg per 70 kg of body weight per day, respectively, resulted in maternotoxicity, increased incidence of fetal resorptions, and decreased fetal weights. In rats, carteolol, administered in doses approximately 212 times the maximum recommended human oral dose, resulted in a dose-related increase in wavy ribs in the developing rat fetus. However, in mice, carteolol, administered in doses up to approximately 1052 times the maximum recommended human oral dose, did not result in wavy ribs.

Breast-feeding:
It is not known whether systemic or ophthalmic carteolol is distributed into human breast milk; however, carteolol has been shown to be distributed into animal milk.

Ophthalmic Dosage Forms

CARTEOLOL HYDROCHLORIDE OPHTHALMIC SOLUTION

Usual adult and adolescent dose
Ophthalmic antiglaucoma agent—
Topical, to the conjunctiva, 1 drop two times a day.

Usual pediatric dose
Safety and efficacy have not been established.

Strength(s) usually available
U.S.—
1% (10 mg carteolol hydrochloride per mL) (Rx) [*Ocupress* (benzalkonium chloride 0.005%; sodium chloride; monobasic sodium phosphate; dibasic sodium phosphate)].
Canada—
Not commercially available.

Packaging and storage
Store between 15 and 25 °C (59 and 77 °F), in a well-closed container, unless otherwise specified by manufacturer. Protect from light. Protect from freezing.

Auxiliary labeling
- For the eye.
- Keep container tightly closed.

LEVOBETAXOLOL

Summary of Differences

Indications:
Levobetaxolol is expected to be effective for the treatment of glaucoma in patients with pulmonary reactive airway disease.

Pharmacology/pharmacokinetics:
Mechanism of action/effect—Levobetaxolol is a cardioselective (beta-1-adrenergic) receptor blocking agent.
Levobetaxolol is expected to produce less beta-adrenergic receptor blockade in the bronchi and bronchioles.
Onset of action—30 minutes.
Duration of action—12 hours.
Time to peak effect—2 hours.

Fertility:
Post-implantation loss was observed in rabbits given oral levobetaxolol in doses of 12 mg/kg per day.

Pregnancy:
Sternebrae malformations were observed in rabbits given oral levobetaxolol in doses of 4 mg/kg per day.

Breast feeding:
It is not known whether ophthalmic levobetaxolol is distributed into human breast milk.

Ophthalmic Dosage Forms

LEVOBETAXOLOL HYDROCHLORIDE OPHTHALMIC SUSPENSION

Note: The dosing and strength usually available are expressed in terms of levobetaxolol base.

Usual adult dose
Ophthalmic antiglaucoma agent—
Topical, to the conjunctiva, 1 drop of a 0.5% suspension of levobetaxolol (base) two times a day.

Usual pediatric dose
Safety and efficacy have not been established.

Usual geriatric dose
See *Usual adult dose.*

Strength(s) usually available
U.S.—
0.5% (5 mg base; 5.6 mg as hydrochloride (Rx) [*Betaxon* (benzalkonium chloride 0.01%; mannitol; poly(styrene-divinyl benzene) sulfonic acid; Carbomer 974P; boric acid; N-lauroylsarcosine; edetate disodium; hydrochloric acid or tromethamine [to adjust pH]; purified water)].
Canada—
Not commercially available.

Packaging and storage
Store upright between 4 and 25 °C (39 and 77 °F). Protect from light.

Auxiliary labeling
- For the eye.
- Protect from light.
- Shake well before using.

LEVOBUNOLOL

Summary of Differences

Pharmacology/pharmacokinetics:
Onset of action—Within 1 hour.
Time to peak effect—Between 2 and 6 hours.
Duration of action—Up to 24 hours.

Pregnancy:
Although levobunolol has been shown to cause fetotoxicity in rabbits when administered at doses equivalent to 200 and 700 times the recommended dose for the treatment of glaucoma, similar studies in rats have not shown levobunolol to cause fetotoxic effects when administered at doses of up to 1800 times the human dose for glaucoma. Moreover, in teratogenicity studies in rats, levobunolol was not shown to cause fetal malformations when administered at doses of up to 25 mg/kg per day (1800 times the recommended human dose for glaucoma). Also, levobunolol was not shown to have adverse effects on the postnatal development of animal offspring.

Ophthalmic Dosage Forms

LEVOBUNOLOL HYDROCHLORIDE OPHTHALMIC SOLUTION USP

Usual adult and adolescent dose
Ophthalmic antiglaucoma agent—
Topical, to the conjunctiva, 1 drop of a 0.25% solution two times a day or 1 drop of a 0.5% solution once a day.

Note: In patients with more severe or uncontrolled glaucoma, the 0.5% solution may be administered two times a day.

Usual adult prescribing limits
Dosages above 1 drop of a 0.5% solution two times a day are generally not more effective.

Usual pediatric dose
Safety and efficacy have not been established.

Strength(s) usually available
U.S.—
0.25% (Rx) [*AKBeta; Betagan* (polyvinyl alcohol 1.4%; benzalkonium chloride 0.004%; sodium metabisulfite; edetate disodium; dibasic sodium phosphate; monobasic potassium phosphate; sodium chloride; hydrochloric acid; sodium hydroxide); GENERIC].
0.5% (Rx) [*AKBeta; Betagan* (polyvinyl alcohol 1.4%; benzalkonium chloride 0.004%; sodium metabisulfite; edetate disodium; dibasic

sodium phosphate; monobasic potassium phosphate; sodium chloride; hydrochloric acid; sodium hydroxide); GENERIC].

Canada—

0.25% (Rx) [*Betagan* (polyvinyl alcohol; benzalkonium chloride 0.004%; sodium metabisulfite; edetate disodium; dibasic sodium phosphate; monobasic potassium phosphate; sodium chloride; hydrochloric acid and/or sodium hydroxide); *Novo-Levobunolol; Ophtho-Bunolol* (benzalkonium chloride 0.004%; edetate disodium; polyvinyl alcohol; monobasic potassium phosphate; sodium chloride; sodium metabisulfite; dibasic sodium phosphate; sodium hydroxide or hydrochloric acid)].

0.5% (Rx) [*Betagan* (polyvinyl alcohol; benzalkonium chloride 0.004%; sodium metabisulfite; edetate disodium; dibasic sodium phosphate; monobasic potassium phosphate; sodium chloride; hydrochloric acid; sodium hydroxide); *Novo-Levobunolol; Ophtho-Bunolol* (benzalkonium chloride 0.004%; edetate disodium; polyvinyl alcohol; monobasic potassium phosphate; sodium chloride; sodium metabisulfite; dibasic sodium phosphate; sodium hydroxide or hydrochloric acid)].

Packaging and storage

Store below 40 °C (104 °F), preferably between 15 and 30 °C (59 and 86 °F), in a tight container, unless otherwise specified by manufacturer. Protect from light. Protect from freezing.

Auxiliary labeling

- For the eye.
- Keep container tightly closed.

METIPRANOLOL

Summary of Differences

Pharmacology/pharmacokinetics: Duration of action—More than 24 hours.

Pregnancy: No metipranolol-related effects were reported for the segment II teratology study in fetal rats when metipranolol was administered orally to pregnant rats in doses of up to 50 mg/kg per day during organogenesis. However, metipranolol has been shown to increase fetal resorption, fetal death, and delayed development when administered orally to pregnant rabbits at 50 mg/kg during organogenesis.

Ophthalmic Dosage Forms

METIPRANOLOL HYDROCHLORIDE OPHTHALMIC SOLUTION

Note: The dosing and strengths usually available are expressed in terms of metipranolol base.

Usual adult and adolescent dose

Ophthalmic antiglaucoma agent—

Topical, to the conjunctiva, 1 drop of a 0.3% solution of metipranolol (base) two times a day.

Usual adult prescribing limits

Dosages above 1 drop of a 0.3% solution two times a day are not known to be of benefit.

Usual pediatric dose

Safety and efficacy have not been established.

Strength(s) usually available

U.S.—

0.3% (3 mg base per mL) (Rx) [*OptiPranolol* (benzalkonium chloride 0.004%; glycerin; sodium chloride; edetate disodium; povidone; hydrochloric acid and/or sodium hydroxide)].

Canada—

Not commercially available.

Packaging and storage

Store below 40 °C (104 °F), preferably between 15 and 30 °C (59 and 86 °F), in a well-closed container, unless otherwise specified by manufacturer. Protect from freezing.

Auxiliary labeling

- For the eye.
- Keep container tightly closed.

TIMOLOL

Summary of Differences

Pharmacology/pharmacokinetics: Duration of action—Up to 24 hours.

Carcinogenicity: In a lifetime study in mice, timolol increased the incidence of malignant pulmonary tumors and mammary adenocarcinomas in female mice when administered orally at doses of 500 mg/kg per day, but not at 5 or 50 mg/kg per day.

Pregnancy: Studies in rats have shown that timolol at doses of up to 50 mg/kg per day (50 times the maximum recommended human oral dose) causes delayed fetal ossification; however, there were no adverse effects on postnatal development of offspring. Teratogenic studies in mice and rabbits have not shown that timolol at doses of up to 50 mg/kg per day causes fetal malformations. In mice, timolol at doses of 1 gram per kg per day (1000 times the maximum recommended human oral dose) was maternotoxic and resulted in increased incidence of fetal resorptions. In rabbits, timolol at doses 100 times the maximum recommended human oral dose caused increased incidence of fetal resorptions but not maternotoxicity.

Breast-feeding: Systemic timolol is distributed into breast milk. Problems in humans have not been documented for ophthalmic timolol; however, ophthalmic timolol may be systemically absorbed and distributed into the breast milk, possibly causing serious adverse reactions in the infants of nursing mothers.

Side/adverse effects: Transient blurred vision was reported frequently with the timolol maleate gel-forming solution. The blurred vision typically lasts from thirty seconds to five minutes.

General dosing information: The gel-forming timolol ophthalmic solution should be inverted and shaken one time prior to each use. If other topically administered ophthalmic medications are required, they should be administered at least ten minutes before the administration of the gel-forming timolol ophthalmic solution. When patients were transferred from the twice-daily administration of timolol maleate solution to the once-daily administration of timolol maleate gel-forming solution, the effect on ocular hypertension has remained consistant.

Ophthalmic Dosage Forms

TIMOLOL HEMIHYDRATE OPHTHALMIC SOLUTION

Note: The dosing and strengths usually available are expressed in terms of timolol base.

Usual adult and adolescent dose

Ophthalmic antiglaucoma agent—

Topical, to the conjunctiva, 1 drop of a 0.25 or 0.5% solution of timolol (base) twice a day.

Usual pediatric dose

Ophthalmic antiglaucoma agent—

Safety and efficacy have not been established.

Strength(s) usually available

U.S.—

0.25% (2.5 mg base; 2.56 mg as hemihydrate) (Rx) [*Betimol* (benzalkonium chloride 0.01%; monosodium phosphate dihydrate; disodium phosphate dihydrate)].

0.5% (5 mg base; 5.12 mg as hemihydrate) (Rx) [*Betimol* (benzalkonium chloride 0.01%; monosodium phosphate dihydrate; disodium phosphate dihydrate)].

Canada—

Not commercially available in Canada.

Packaging and storage

Store between 15 and 30 °C (59 and 86 °F). Protect from freezing. Protect from light.

Auxiliary labeling

- For the eye.
- Keep container tightly closed.

TIMOLOL MALEATE OPHTHALMIC SOLUTION USP

Note: The dosing and strengths usually available are expressed in terms of timolol base.

Usual adult and adolescent dose

Ophthalmic antiglaucoma agent—

Topical, to the conjunctiva, 1 drop of a 0.25 or 0.5% solution of timolol (base) one or two times a day.

Usual pediatric dose

Ophthalmic antiglaucoma agent—

Infants and children up to 10 years of age: Topical, to the conjunctiva, 1 drop of a 0.25% solution of timolol (base) one or two times a day.

Children 10 years of age and older: See *Usual adult and adolescent dose.*

Note: Nasolacrimal occlusion should be emphasized to patient.

Strength(s) usually available

U.S.—

0.25% (2.5 mg base; 3.4 mg as maleate) (Rx) [*Timoptic* (benzalkonium chloride 0.01%; monobasic sodium phosphate; dibasic sodium phosphate; sodium hydroxide); *Timoptic in Ocudose* (monobasic sodium phosphate; dibasic sodium phosphate; sodium hydroxide); GENERIC].

0.5% (5 mg base; 6.8 mg as maleate) (Rx) [*Timoptic* (benzalkonium chloride 0.01%; monobasic sodium phosphate; dibasic sodium phosphate; sodium hydroxide); *Timoptic in Ocudose* (monobasic sodium phosphate; dibasic sodium phosphate; sodium hydroxide); GENERIC].

Canada—

0.25% (2.5 mg base; 3.4 mg as maleate) (Rx) [*Apo-Timop* (benzalkonium chloride; monobasic sodium phosphate; dibasic sodium phosphate; sodium hydroxide); *Novo-Timol; Timoptic* (benzalkonium chloride; monobasic sodium phosphate; dibasic sodium phosphate; sodium hydroxide); GENERIC].

0.5% (5 mg base; 6.8 mg as maleate) (Rx) [*Apo-Timop* (benzalkonium chloride; monobasic sodium phosphate; dibasic sodium phosphate; sodium hydroxide); *Novo-Timol; Tim-AK* (benzalkonium chloride; dibasic sodium phospate; monobasic sodium phosphate; sodium chloride; sodium hydroxide); *Timoptic* (benzalkonium chloride; monobasic sodium phosphate; dibasic sodium phosphate; sodium hydroxide); GENERIC].

Packaging and storage

Store between 15 and 30 °C (59 and 86 °F), in a tight container, unless otherwise specified by manufacturer. Protect from freezing. Protect from light.

Auxiliary labeling

- For the eye.
- Keep container tightly closed.

TIMOLOL MALEATE EXTENDED-RELEASE OPHTHALMIC SOLUTION (GEL-FORMING)

Note: The dosing and strengths usually available are expressed in terms of timolol base.

Usual adult and adolescent dose

Ophthalmic antiglaucoma agent—

Topical, to the conjunctiva, 1 drop of a 0.25 or 0.5% solution of timolol (base) once a day.

Usual pediatric dose

Ophthalmic antiglaucoma agent—

Safety and efficacy have not been established.

Strength(s) usually available

U.S.—

0.25% (2.5 mg base; 3.4 mg as maleate) (Rx) [*Timoptic-XE* (benzododecinium bromide 0.012%; gellan gum; tromethamine; mannitol)].

0.5% (5 mg base; 6.8 mg as maleate) (Rx) [*Timoptic-XE* (benzododecinium bromide 0.012%; gellan gum; tromethamine; mannitol)].

Canada—

0.25% (2.5 mg base; 3.4 mg as maleate) (Rx) [*Timoptic-XE* (benzododecinium bromide; gellan gum; tromethamine; mannitol)].

0.5% (5 mg base; 6.8 mg as maleate) (Rx) [*Timoptic-XE* (benzododecinium bromide; gellan gum; tromethamine; mannitol)].

Packaging and storage

Store between 15 and 25 °C (59 and 77 °F). Protect from freezing. Protect from light.

Auxiliary labeling

- For the eye.
- Keep container tightly closed.
- Shake once before use.

Selected Bibliography

For levobunolol

Gonzalez JP, Clissold SP. Ocular levobunolol. A review of its pharmacodynamic and pharmacokinetic properties, and therapeutic efficacy. Drugs 1987 Dec; 34(60): 648-61.

For timolol

Novack GD. Ophthalmic beta-blockers since timolol. Surv Ophthalmol 1987 Mar-Apr; 31(5): 307-27.

For betaxolol

Buckley MMT, et al. Ocular betaxolol. A review of its pharmacological properties, and therapeutic efficacy in glaucoma and ocular hypertension. Drugs 40. Auckland, New Zealand: ADIS Drug Information Services, 1990.

For metipranolol

Battershill PE, Sorkin EM. Ocular metipranolol. A preliminary review of its pharmacodynamic and pharmacokinetic properties, and therapeutic efficacy in glaucoma and ocular hypertension. Drugs 1988 Nov; 36(5): 601-15.

General

Bauer K, et al. Assessment of systemic effects of different ophthalmic beta-blockers in healthy volunteers. Clin Pharmacol Ther 1991 Jun; 49(6): 658-64.

Brooks AM, Gillies WE. Ocular beta-blockers in glaucoma management. Clinical pharmacological aspects. Drugs Aging 1992 May-Jun; 2(3): 208-21.

For carteolol

Chrisp P, Sorkin EM. Ocular carteolol. A review of its pharmacological properties, and therapeutic use in glaucoma and ocular hypertension. Drugs Aging 1992 Jan-Feb; 2(1): 58-77.

Revised: 05/25/2000

BETA-ADRENERGIC BLOCKING AGENTS Systemic

This monograph includes information on the following: 1) Acebutolol; 2) Atenolol; 3) Betaxolol†; 4) Bisoprolol†; 5) Carteolol†; 6) Labetalol; 7) Metoprolol; 8) Nadolol; 9) Oxprenolol*; 10) Penbutolol†; 11) Pindolol; 12) Propranolol; 13) Sotalol; 14) Timolol.

VA CLASSIFICATION (Primary/Secondary):

Acebutolol—CV100/CV250; CV300; CV409; CV900; CN900
Atenolol—CV100/CV250; CV300; CV409; CV900; CN105; CN900
Betaxolol—CV100/CV409
Bisoprolol—CV100/CV409
Carteolol—CV100/CV409
Labetalol—CV100/CV250; CV409
Metoprolol—CV100/CV250; CV300; CV409; CV900; CN105; CN900
Nadolol—CV100/CV250; CV300; CV409; CV900; CN105; CN900
Oxprenolol—CV100/CV250; CV300; CV409; CV900; CN900
Penbutolol—CV100/CV409
Pindolol—CV100/CV250; CV409; CN900
Propranolol—CV100/CV250; CV300; CV409; CV900; CN105; CN900
Sotalol—CV100/CV250; CV300; CV409; CV900; CN900
Timolol—CV100/CV250; CV300; CV409; CV900; CN105; CN900; OP111

Commonly used brand name(s): *Apo-Atenolol*[2]; *Apo-Metoprolol*[7]; *Apo-Metoprolol (Type L)*[7]; *Apo-Propranolol*[12]; *Apo-Timol*[14]; *Betaloc*[7]; *Betaloc Durules*[7]; *Betapace*[13]; *Blocadren*[14]; *Cartrol*[5]; *Corgard*[8]; *Detensol*[12]; *Inderal*[12]; *Inderal LA*[12]; *Kerlone*[3]; *Levatol*[10]; *Lopresor*[7]; *Lopresor SR*[7]; *Lopressor*[7]; *Monitan*[1]; *Normodyne*[6]; *Novo-Atenol*[2]; *Novo-Pindol*[11]; *Novo-Timol*[14]; *Novometoprol*[7]; *Novopranol*[12]; *Nu-Metop*[7]; *Sectral*[1]; *Slow-Trasicor*[9]; *Sotacor*[13]; *Syn-Nadolol*[8]; *Syn-Pindolol*[11]; *Tenormin*[2]; *Toprol-XL*[7]; *Trandate*[6]; *Trasicor*[9]; *Visken*[11]; *Zebeta*[4]; *pms Propranolol*[12].

Note: For a listing of dosage forms and brand names by country availability, see *Dosage Forms* section(s).

*Not commercially available in U.S.
†Not commercially available in Canada.

Category

Note: All of the beta-adrenergic blocking agents have similar pharmacologic actions; however, clinical uses among specific agents may vary because of pharmacologic or pharmacokinetic differences, availability of specific testing, and/or availability of clinical-use data.

Antiadrenergic—Acebutolol; Atenolol; Betaxolol; Carteolol; Labetalol; Metoprolol; Nadolol; Oxprenolol; Penbutolol; Pindolol; Propranolol; Sotalol; Timolol.

Antianginal—Acebutolol; Atenolol; Carteolol; Labetalol; Metoprolol; Nadolol; Oxprenolol; Penbutolol; Pindolol; Propranolol; Sotalol; Timolol.

Antiarrhythmic—Acebutolol; Atenolol; Metoprolol; Nadolol; Oxprenolol; Propranolol; Sotalol; Timolol.

Antihypertensive—Acebutolol; Atenolol; Betaxolol; Bisoprolol; Carteolol; Labetalol; Metoprolol; Nadolol; Oxprenolol; Penbutolol; Pindolol; Propranolol; Sotalol; Timolol.

Hypertrophic cardiomyopathy therapy adjunct—Acebutolol; Atenolol; Metoprolol; Nadolol; Oxprenolol; Pindolol; Propranolol; Sotalol; Timolol.

Myocardial infarction prophylactic and therapy—Acebutolol; Atenolol; Metoprolol; Nadolol; Oxprenolol; Propranolol; Sotalol; Timolol.

Neuroleptic-induced akathisia therapy—Betaxolol; Metoprolol; Nadolol; Propranolol.

Pheochromocytoma therapy adjunct—Acebutolol; Atenolol; Labetalol; Metoprolol; Nadolol; Oxprenolol; Propranolol; Sotalol; Timolol.
Vascular headache prophylactic—Atenolol; Metoprolol; Nadolol; Propranolol; Timolol.
Antitremor agent—Acebutolol; Atenolol; Metoprolol; Nadolol; Oxprenolol; Pindolol; Propranolol; Sotalol; Timolol.
Antianxiety therapy adjunct—Acebutolol; Metoprolol; Oxprenolol; Propranolol; Sotalol; Timolol.
Thyrotoxicosis therapy adjunct—Acebutolol; Atenolol; Metoprolol; Nadolol; Oxprenolol; Propranolol; Sotalol; Timolol.
Antiglaucoma agent—Timolol

Indications

Note: Bracketed information in the *Indications* section refers to uses that are not included in U.S. product labeling.

Accepted

Angina pectoris, chronic (treatment)—[Acebutolol], atenolol, [carteolol], [labetalol][1], metoprolol, nadolol, oxprenolol[1], [penbutolol], [pindolol], propranolol, [sotalol], and [timolol] are indicated in the treatment of classic angina pectoris, also referred to as "effort-associated angina."

Arrhythmias, cardiac (prophylaxis and treatment)—Propranolol is indicated in the control and correction of supraventricular arrhythmias, ventricular tachycardias, digitalis-induced tachyarrhythmias, and catecholamine-induced tachyarrhythmias during anesthesia (with extreme caution because of possible additive myocardial depression with general anesthesia). Propranolol by intravenous injection is recommended only in the treatment of cardiac arrhythmias that occur while the patient is unable to receive oral medication, or when a rapid and observable effect is desired. [Acebutolol][1], [atenolol][1], [metoprolol][1], [nadolol][1], oxprenolol[1], sotalol[1], and [timolol][1] are also used for their antiarrhythmic effects, especially in supraventricular arrhythmias and ventricular tachycardias. Acebutolol[1] is indicated in the control and correction of premature ventricular contractions.

Hypertension (treatment)—Acebutolol, atenolol, betaxolol, bisoprolol, carteolol, labetalol, metoprolol, nadolol, oxprenolol, penbutolol, pindolol, propranolol, [sotalol], and timolol are indicated in the treatment of hypertension when used alone or in combination with other antihypertensive medication.

Parenteral labetalol is indicated for treatment of severe hypertension. Intravenous metoprolol and propranolol are not recommended for the management of hypertensive emergencies. However, intravenous propranolol has proven useful in controlling hypertension during anesthesia and surgery.

For additional information on initial therapeutic guidelines related to the treatment of hypertension, see *Appendix III*.

Cardiomyopathy, hypertrophic (treatment)—[Acebutolol][1], [atenolol][1], [metoprolol][1], [nadolol][1], oxprenolol[1], [pindolol][1], propranolol, [sotalol][1], and [timolol][1] are indicated in the management of angina, palpitations, and syncope associated with hypertrophic subaortic stenosis.

Myocardial infarction (treatment and prophylaxis)—[Acebutolol][1], atenolol[1], metoprolol, [nadolol][1], oxprenolol[1], propranolol, [sotalol][1], and timolol are indicated in clinically stable patients recovering from an initial definite or suspected acute myocardial infarction in order to reduce cardiovascular mortality and to decrease the risk of reinfarction.

Pheochromocytoma (treatment adjunct)—Propranolol is indicated in the management of symptoms of tachycardia due to excessive beta-receptor stimulation in pheochromocytoma. However, it should be used only after primary treatment with an alpha-adrenergic blocking agent (since use without concomitant alpha-blockade could lead to serious blood pressure elevation). [Acebutolol][1], [atenolol][1], [labetalol (with caution)][1], [metoprolol][1], [nadolol][1], oxprenolol[1], [sotalol][1], and [timolol][1] also may be used.

Headache, vascular (prophylaxis)—Propranolol and timolol are indicated for reducing frequency and severity of migraine headaches but are not recommended for treatment of acute attacks. [Atenolol][1], [metoprolol][1], and [nadolol][1] are also useful for prophylaxis of migraine. A beta-adrenergic blocking agent is the drug of choice for vascular headache prophylaxis.

Tremors (treatment)—Propranolol is indicated in the treatment of essential, familial, and senile tremors. Propranolol also has been used to reduce the agitation and tremors of alcohol withdrawal. [Acebutolol][1], [atenolol][1], [metoprolol][1], [nadolol][1], oxprenolol[1], [pindolol][1], [sotalol][1], and [timolol][1] also may be used to treat tremors. Propranolol is the drug of choice for treatment of essential tremor.

Anxiety (treatment adjunct)—[Propranolol][1] is used to control the physical manifestations of anxiety such as tachycardia and tremor. It is not particularly useful for chronic anxiety or panic attacks but is most useful for reducing anxiety and improving performance in specific stressful situations. [Acebutolol][1], [metoprolol][1], oxprenolol[1], [sotalol][1], and [timolol][1] also have been used for this purpose.

Thyrotoxicosis (treatment adjunct)—[Propranolol][1] has been effective in the short-term preoperative management of thyrotoxic crises (until thioamide therapy is effective) by reducing symptoms such as fever, tachycardia, and hyperkinesia. There is no effect on the hormone production of the thyroid. Abrupt withdrawal of beta-blocker treatment may provoke "thyroid storm." [Acebutolol][1], [atenolol][1], [metoprolol][1], [nadolol][1], oxprenolol[1], [sotalol][1], and [timolol][1] are also used for thyrotoxicosis.

Mitral valve prolapse syndrome (treatment)—[Acebutolol][1], [atenolol][1], [metoprolol][1], [nadolol][1], oxprenolol[1], [pindolol][1], [propranolol][1], [sotalol][1], and [timolol][1] are used in the treatment of mitral valve prolapse syndrome.

[Hypotension, controlled (induction and maintenance)][1]—Parenteral labetalol is used to produce controlled hypotension during surgery to reduce bleeding into the surgical field.

[Glaucoma, open-angle (treatment)][1]—Timolol is used to lower intraocular pressure in the treatment of open-angle glaucoma.

[Neuroleptic-induced akathisia (treatment)][1]—Propranolol may be used to relieve the somatic and subjective symptoms associated with neuroleptic-induced akathisia (NIA). Betaxolol, metoprolol, and nadolol have also been used for NIA.

Note: In addition, metoprolol is indicated for the treatment of stable, symptomatic (NYHA Class II or III) heart failure of ischemic, hypertensive, or cardiomyopathic origin. It was studied in patients already receiving ACE inhibitors, diuretics, and, in the majority of cases, digitalis. In this population, metoprolol decreased the rate of mortality plus hospitalization, largely through a reduction in cardiovascular mortality and hospitalizations for heart failure.

[1]Not included in Canadian product labeling.

Pharmacology/Pharmacokinetics

See *Table 1*, page 563.

Physicochemical characteristics

Molecular weight—
- Acebutolol: 336.43.
- Atenolol: 266.34.
- Betaxolol hydrochloride: 343.89.
- Bisoprolol fumarate: 766.97.
- Carteolol hydrochloride: 328.84.
- Labetalol hydrochloride: 364.87.
- Metoprolol succinate: 652.83.
- Metoprolol tartrate: 684.82.
- Nadolol: 309.40.
- Oxprenolol hydrochloride: 301.81.
- Penbutolol sulfate: 680.94.
- Pindolol: 248.32.
- Propranolol hydrochloride: 295.81.
- Sotalol hydrochloride: 308.82.
- Timolol maleate: 432.49.

pKa—
- Acebutolol: 9.20.
- Carteolol: 9.74.
- Labetalol: 9.45.
- Metoprolol: 9.68.
- Nadolol: 9.67.
- Penbutolol: 9.3.
- Timolol: Approximately 9 in water at 25 °C.

Lipid solubility—
- Acebutolol: Low
- Atenolol: Very low (log partition coefficient for octanol/water=0.23)
- Bisoprolol: Moderate (equally hydrophilic and lipophilic)
- Carteolol: Low
- Labetalol: Low
- Metoprolol: Moderate
- Nadolol: Low
- Oxprenolol: Moderate
- Penbutolol: Moderate
- Pindolol: Moderate
- Propranolol: High
- Sotalol: Low
- Timolol: Moderate

Mechanism of action/Effect

Beta-adrenergic blocking agents block the agonistic effect of the sympathetic neurotransmitters by competing for receptor binding sites. When they predominantly block the beta-1 receptors in cardiac tissue, they are said to be cardioselective. When they block both beta-1 receptors and beta-2 receptors (primarily located in tissues other than cardiac), they are said to be nonselective. In general, so-called cardioselective beta-adrenergic blocking agents are relatively cardioselective—at lower doses they block beta-1 receptors only but begin to block beta-2 receptors as the dose increases.

Some beta-adrenergic blocking agents also have intrinsic sympathomimetic activity (ISA or partial agonist activity), which is the ability to cause weak stimulation of beta-adrenergic receptors while simultaneously blocking the effect of endogenous catecholamines; however, the significance of this property has not been established. Possession of ISA theoretically may result in fewer adverse effects related to unopposed beta blockade (e.g., bradycardia, heart block, bronchoconstriction, peripheral vascular constriction), but studies have not proven clinical benefit. Pindolol exhibits the most ISA of the beta-adrenergic blocking agents currently available; carteolol, oxprenolol, and penbutolol have moderate ISA; acebutolol has mild to moderate ISA; and the other members of the group have little, if any, such activity.

Propranolol possesses moderate membrane-stabilizing (quinidine-like) activity; acebutolol, betaxolol, metoprolol, and oxprenolol have slight activity. The other beta-adrenergic blocking agents of this group show little, if any, such activity. At one time membrane-stabilizing activity was thought to be related to the antiarrhythmic effect, but it is no longer considered to be significant because it occurs only at very high (much greater than therapeutic) doses.

Antianginal—
- Reduction in myocardial oxygen demand through negative chronotropic and inotropic effects.

Antiarrhythmic—
- May involve beta-blockade–induced reduction in the rate of spontaneous firing of sinus and ectopic pacemakers and slowing of atrioventricular (AV) nodal conduction. In the Vaughan Williams classification of antiarrhythmics, beta-adrenergic blocking agents are considered to be class II agents.

Antihypertensive—
- The precise mechanism of antihypertensive effect is not known. Possible mechanisms include reduced cardiac output, decreased sympathetic outflow to peripheral vasculature, and inhibition of renin release by the kidneys; with labetalol, may also be related to reduced peripheral vascular resistance as a result of alpha-adrenergic blockade.

Hypertrophic cardiomyopathy therapy adjunct—
- Reduction of elevated outflow pressure gradient, which is exacerbated by beta-receptor stimulation.

Myocardial infarction therapy and prophylactic—
- Possible reduction in severity of myocardial ischemia by decrease of myocardial oxygen requirements; postinfarction mortality may also be reduced through an antiarrhythmic action.

Vascular headache prophylactic—
- Involves several mechanisms, including prevention of arterial dilation through beta-blockade, blockade of catecholamine-induced platelet aggregation and lipolysis, reduction of platelet adhesiveness, prevention of coagulation factor elevation during epinephrine release, promotion of oxygen release to tissues, and inhibition of renin secretion.

Antitremor agent—
- Precise mechanism not known, but antitremor effect may be mediated predominantly by peripheral beta-2 receptor mechanisms.

Antianxiety therapy adjunct—
- Precise mechanism unknown; however, thought to involve improvement of somatic symptoms secondary to beta-blockade.

Thyrotoxicosis therapy adjunct—
- Unknown, but probably related to reduction of symptoms such as tremor, tachycardia, and elevated blood pressure caused by increased sensitivity to catecholamines.

Other actions/effects

Labetalol also has selective alpha-1-adrenergic blocking effects, which lead to vasodilation, reduced peripheral vascular resistance, and postural hypotension.

Precautions to Consider

Note: In general, because of the similarity of effect and because the cardioselectivity of beta-1 blockers is relative, the same precautions, especially drug interactions and medical problems, apply to all beta-adrenergic blocking agents.

Carcinogenicity/Tumorigenicity

Acebutolol—Studies in rats and mice given up to 300 mg per kg of body weight (mg/kg) per day (equivalent to 15 times the maximum recommended human dose) found no evidence of carcinogenicity. Diacetolol, the major metabolite, also did not produce evidence of carcinogenicity in rats given up to 1800 mg/kg per day.

Atenolol—Two 18- to 24-month studies in rats and one study for up to 18 months in mice given up to 150 times the maximum recommended human antihypertensive dose found no evidence of carcinogenicity. However, a 24-month study in rats given up to 750 times the maximum recommended human antihypertensive dose revealed increased incidences of benign adrenal medullary tumors in males and females, mammary fibroadenomas in females, and anterior pituitary adenomas and thyroid parafollicular cell carcinomas in males.

Betaxolol—Studies in mice given up to 60 mg/kg per day orally (up to 90 times the maximum recommended human dose based on 60-kg body weight) and in rats given up to 48 mg/kg per day orally (up to 72 times the maximum recommended human dose) found no evidence of carcinogenicity.

Bisoprolol—Studies in mice and rats given 625 and 312 times, respectively, the maximum recommended human dose by weight found no evidence of carcinogenicity.

Carteolol—A 2-year study in rats and mice given 280 times the maximum recommended human dose (10 mg per 70 kg of body weight per day) found no evidence of carcinogenicity.

Labetalol—Studies for 18 months in mice and 2 years in rats found no evidence of carcinogenicity.

Metoprolol—A 1-year study in dogs given up to 105 mg/kg per day orally, a 2-year study in rats given up to 800 mg/kg per day orally, and a 21-month study in mice given up to 750 mg/kg per day orally found no evidence of carcinogenicity, although the incidence of small benign adenomas of the lung was higher in the treated female mice. A repeat of the 21-month study in mice found no increased incidence of any type of tumor.

Nadolol—A 2-year study in rats and mice found no evidence of carcinogenicity.

Oxprenolol—Long-term studies in mice and rats found no evidence of carcinogenicity.

Penbutolol—A 21-month study in mice and a 2-year study in rats at doses up to 500 times the maximum recommended human dose found no evidence of carcinogenicity.

Pindolol—Two-year studies in rats and mice found no evidence of carcinogenicity at doses as high as 50 and 100 times, respectively, the maximum recommended human dose.

Propranolol—Eighteen-month studies in rats and mice given up to 150 mg/kg per day found no evidence of carcinogenicity.

Timolol—A 2-year study found an increased incidence of adrenal pheochromocytomas in male rats given 300 times (but not 25 or 80 times) the maximum recommended human dose. Another study found an increased incidence of benign and malignant pulmonary tumors and benign uterine polyps in female mice given 500 (but not 5 or 50) mg/kg per day and an increase in mammary adenocarcinomas associated with elevations in serum prolactin at 500 mg/kg per day.

Mutagenicity

Acebutolol—Ames mutagenicity studies with acebutolol and diacetolol were negative.

Atenolol—Mutagenicity studies were negative.

Betaxolol—Betaxolol was not found to be mutagenic in a variety of *in vitro* and *in vivo* bacterial and mammalian cell assays.

Bisoprolol—Bisoprolol was not found to be mutagenic in a variety of *in vitro* and *in vivo* assays.

Carteolol—Carteolol was not found to be mutagenic in the Ames test, recombinant (rec)-assay, *in vivo* cytogenetics tests, and dominant lethal assay.

Labetalol—Labetalol was not found to be mutagenic in dominant lethal assays in rats and mice or in modified Ames tests.

Metoprolol—Metoprolol was not found to be mutagenic in several tests, including a dominant lethal study in mice, chromosome studies in somatic cells, a *Salmonella* /mammalian-microsome mutagenicity test, and a nucleus anomaly test in somatic interphase nuclei.

Penbutolol—Penbutolol was not found to be mutagenic in the *Salmonella* mutagenicity test (Ames test), the point mutation induction test (*Saccharomyces*), or the micronucleus test.

Timolol— *In vivo* (mouse) and *in vitro* mutagenicity studies were negative; in Ames tests, some changes were seen, but not enough to make the test positive.

Pregnancy/Reproduction

Fertility— *Acebutolol:* No adverse effect on fertility was observed in male or female rats given up to 240 mg/kg per day of acebutolol and 1000 mg/kg per day of diacetolol.

Atenolol: No adverse effect on fertility was observed in male or female rats given 100 times the maximum recommended human dose.

Betaxolol: No adverse effect on fertility or mating performance was observed in male or female rats given 380 times the maximum recommended human dose.

Bisoprolol: No adverse effect on fertility was observed in rats given 375 times the maximum recommended human dose by weight.

Carteolol: No adverse effect on fertility was observed in male or female rats and mice given 1052 times the maximum recommended human dose.
Metoprolol: No adverse effect on fertility was observed in rats given up to 55.5 times the maximum human daily dose of 450 mg.
Nadolol: No adverse effect on fertility was observed in rats given nadolol.
Pindolol: Mortality and decreased weight gain were observed in male rats given 100 mg/kg per day. Decreased mating was associated with atrophy and/or decreased spermatogenesis at 30 mg/kg per day. Mating behavior decreased and offspring mortality increased in females given 100 mg/kg per day and 30 mg/kg per day. In addition, there was an increase in prenatal mortality at a dose of 10 mg/kg per day, although there was not a clear dose-response relationship. In females necropsied on the 15th day of gestation, an increased resorption rate was observed at a dose of 100 mg/kg per day.
Propranolol: No adverse effect on fertility was observed in animal studies.
Timolol: No adverse effect on fertility was observed in male or female rats at doses up to 125 times the maximum recommended human dose.

Pregnancy—Beta-adrenergic blocking agents cross the placenta. The safety of these agents in pregnancy is not fully established. Fetal and neonatal bradycardia, hypotension, hypoglycemia, and respiratory depression have been reported with administration of a cardioselective or a noncardioselective beta-adrenergic blocking agent to pregnant women. In addition, intrauterine growth retardation has been reported rarely with atenolol and nadolol. However, other reports seem to indicate successful treatment of maternal hypertension during pregnancy with no apparent effects on the fetus or neonate.

Acebutolol—
Acebutolol was not teratogenic in rats or rabbits given up to 31.5 and 6.8 times, respectively, the maximum recommended therapeutic dose in a 60-kg human. However, slight fetal growth retardation occurred in rabbits given 135 mg/kg per day. An elevation in postimplantation loss was seen in rabbit dams given 450 mg/kg per day of diacetolol.
FDA Pregnancy Category B.

Atenolol—
Atenolol can cause fetal harm when administered to a pregnant woman. Atenolol crosses the placental barrier and appears in cord blood. Atenolol administration starting in the second trimester has been associated with small birth weights. Neonates born to mothers who are receiving atenolol may be at risk of hypoglycemia and bradycardia. Caution should be exercised when atenolol is administered during pregnancy and the patient should be apprised of the potential hazard to the fetus.
Dose-related increases in embryo/fetal resorptions were observed in rats given atenolol in doses greater than or equal to 25 times the maximum recommended human antihypertensive dose. This effect was not seen in rabbits given 12.5 times the maximum recommended human antihypertensive dose.
FDA Pregnancy Category D.

Betaxolol—
Administration of betaxolol to pregnant rats in doses up to 600 times the maximum recommended human dose was associated with increased postimplantation loss, reduced litter size and weight, and increased incidence of skeletal and visceral abnormalities, which may or may not have resulted from maternal drug toxicity. In another study, betaxolol, given at doses of up to 300 times the maximum recommended human dose, was associated with an increase in resorptions, but no teratogenicity. Administration of 380 times the maximum recommended human dose caused a marked increase in total litter loss within 4 days postpartum. A marked increase in postimplantation loss, but no teratogenicity, was observed in pregnant rabbits given up to 54 times the maximum recommended human dose.
FDA Pregnancy Category C.

Bisoprolol—
Bisoprolol was not teratogenic in rats or rabbits given 375 and 31 times, respectively, the maximum recommended human dose by weight. However, there was an increase in late resorptions in rats given bisoprolol at doses 125 times the maximum recommended human dose by weight.
FDA Pregnancy Category C.

Carteolol—
Increased resorptions and decreased fetal weights occurred in rabbits and rats given maternally toxic doses 1052 and 5264 times, respectively, the maximum recommended human dose. A dose-related increase in fetal wavy ribs was seen in pregnant rats given 212 times the maximum recommended human dose. However, this was not observed in mice given up to 1052 times the maximum recommended human dose.
FDA Pregnancy Category C.

Labetalol—
Teratogenic effects were not seen in rats and rabbits given 6 and 4 times, respectively, the maximum recommended human dose. Administration of labetalol to rats during late gestation through weaning at doses up to 2 to 4 times the maximum recommended human dose resulted in decreased neonatal survival.
FDA Pregnancy Category C.

Metoprolol—
Increased postimplantation loss and decreased neonatal survival were observed in rats given up to 55.5 times the maximum human daily dose of 450 mg. No evidence of teratogenicity was seen in animal studies.
FDA Pregnancy Category C.

Nadolol—
Evidence of embryotoxicity and fetotoxicity was found in rabbits given up to 10 times the maximum indicated human dose. However, these effects were not seen in rats or hamsters. Teratogenic effects were not seen in any of these species.
FDA Pregnancy Category C.

Pindolol—
No evidence of embryotoxicity or teratogenicity was found in rats and rabbits given doses exceeding 100 times the maximum recommended human dose.
FDA Pregnancy Category B.

Propranolol—
Embryotoxicity occurred in animals given 10 times the maximum recommended human dose.
FDA Pregnancy Category C.

Timolol—
No evidence of fetal malformations was observed in mice and rabbits given up to 50 times the maximum recommended human dose. In rats, at similar doses, delayed fetal ossification was observed, but there were no adverse effects on postnatal development of offspring. Increased fetal resorptions were seen in mice and rabbits given 1000 and 100 times, respectively, the maximum recommended human dose.
FDA Pregnancy Category C.

Breast-feeding

Acebutolol (and diacetolol), atenolol, betaxolol, labetalol, metoprolol, nadolol, oxprenolol, pindolol, propranolol, sotalol, and timolol are distributed into breast milk. It is not known whether bisoprolol, carteolol, and penbutolol are distributed into breast milk. Cyanosis and bradycardia resulted from maternal therapy with atenolol in one breast-fed neonate; hypotension, bradycardia, and transient tachypnea resulted from maternal acebutolol therapy in another. Infants of mothers who are receiving atenolol while breast-feeding may be at risk for hypoglycemia and bradycardia. Caution should be exercised when atenolol is administered to a nursing woman.Adverse neonatal effects resulting from maternal ingestion of other beta-adrenergic blocking agents have not been reported. Although the risk appears to be small, breast-fed infants should be monitored for signs of beta-adrenergic blockade, especially bradycardia, hypotension, respiratory distress, and hypoglycemia.

Pediatrics

Use of beta-adrenergic blocking agents in a limited number of neonates, infants, and children has not demonstrated pediatrics-specific problems that would limit the usefulness of these medications in children.
For *atenolol* and *metoprolol*: Safety and effectiveness in pediatric patients have not been established.

Geriatrics

Beta-adrenergic blocking agents have been used safely and efficaciously in elderly patients. However, elderly patients may be more susceptible to some adverse effects of these agents. Beta-adrenergic blocking agents have been reported to cause or exacerbate mental impairment in the elderly. However, other evidence suggests that these agents do not produce significant lethargy or impairment in mental performance. It is possible that the likelihood of central nervous system (CNS) effects may be related to lipophilicity of the beta-adrenergic blocking agent. However, this relationship has not been conclusively established.
Elderly patients are more likely to have age-related peripheral vascular disease, which may require caution in patients receiving beta-adrenergic blocking agents. In addition, the risk of beta-blocker–induced hypothermia may be increased in elderly patients.

Surgical

The necessity or desirability of withdrawing beta-blocking therapy prior to major surgery is controversial. The impaired ability of the heart to respond to reflex adrenergic stimuli may augment the risks of general anesthesia and surgical procedures.

Drug interactions and/or related problems

The following drug interactions and/or related problems have been selected on the basis of their potential clinical significance (possible mechanism in parentheses where appropriate)—not necessarily inclusive (» = major clinical significance):

Note: Combinations containing any of the following medications, depending on the amount present, may also interact with this medication.

Information concerning interactions between beta-adrenergic blocking agents and other medications is still limited. Therefore, some of the following potential interactions are stated for cautionary reference until additional information is available.

» Allergen immunotherapy or
» Allergenic extracts for skin testing
(use of these agents in patients taking beta-adrenergic blocking agents may increase the potential for serious systemic reaction or anaphylaxis; if possible, another medication should be substituted for a beta-adrenergic blocking agent in patients on allergen immunotherapy; allergen immunotherapy for conditions that are not life-threatening should be avoided in patients who cannot discontinue beta-adrenergic blocking agent therapy)

Amiodarone
(concurrent administration with beta-adrenergic blocking agents may result in additive depressant effects on conduction and negative inotropic effects, especially in patients with underlying sinus node dysfunction or atrioventricular node dysfunction)

Anesthetics, hydrocarbon inhalation, such as:
Chloroform
Cyclopropane
Enflurane
» Halothane
Isoflurane
Methoxyflurane
Trichloroethylene
(concurrent use with beta-adrenergic blocking agents may increase the risk of myocardial depression and hypotension because beta-blockade reduces the ability of the heart to respond to beta-adrenergically mediated sympathetic reflex stimuli; if necessary to reverse the effects of beta-adrenergic blocking agents during surgery, agonists such as dobutamine, dopamine, isoproterenol, or norepinephrine may be used but should be administered with caution. In patients scheduled for major surgery, most practitioners believe the risk of precipitating myocardial infarction following abrupt cessation of beta-adrenergic blocking agent therapy prior to surgery outweighs the risks of continuing therapy while compensating for medication effects by anesthetic techniques)
(high concentrations of halothane [3% or above] or high concentrations of other halogenated hydrocarbon anesthetics should not be used when labetalol is used to produce controlled hypotension during anesthesia because of the risk of excessive hypotension, large reduction in cardiac output, and increase in central venous pressure)

» Antidiabetic agents, oral or
» Insulin
(concurrent use with beta-adrenergic blocking agents may impair glycemic control; there may be an increased risk of hyperglycemia secondary to a slight deterioration in carbohydrate metabolism and peripheral insulin resistance; beta-adrenergic blocking agents may impair recovery from hypoglycemia in diabetics because they block the effects of catecholamines, which promote glycogenolysis and mobilize glucose in response to hypoglycemia; beta-adrenergic blocking agents also may mask certain symptoms of developing hypoglycemia such as increases in pulse rate and blood pressure, thus complicating patient monitoring; labetalol and selective or relatively selective beta-adrenergic blocking agents, such as acebutolol, atenolol, betaxolol, bisoprolol, or metoprolol, may cause fewer problems with blood glucose levels, especially at lower dosages, although they may still mask the symptoms of hypoglycemia)

Anti-inflammatory drugs, nonsteroidal (NSAIDs), especially indomethacin
(NSAIDs may reduce the antihypertensive effects of beta-adrenergic blocking agents, possibly by inhibiting renal prostaglandin synthesis and/or causing sodium and fluid retention)

Beta-adrenergic blocking agents, ophthalmic
(if significant systemic absorption of the ophthalmic beta-adrenergic blocking agent occurs, concurrent use may result in an additive effect either on intraocular pressure or on systemic effects of beta-blockade)

» Calcium channel blocking agents or
» Clonidine or
Diazoxide or
» Guanabenz or
Reserpine or
Hypotension-producing medications, other, (See *Appendix II*) with the exception of monoamine oxidase (MAO) inhibitors
(blood pressure control may be impaired when clonidine or guanabenz is used concurrently with a beta-adrenergic blocking agent; potentiation of antihypertensive effect should be anticipated when other hypotension-producing medications are used concurrently; although combinations of antihypertensive agents and/or diuretics are often used for therapeutic advantage, dosage adjustment may be needed when any hypotension-producing medication is added to or withdrawn from a regimen including a beta-adrenergic blocking agent)
(symptomatic bradycardia, with or without serious hemodynamic effects, has been reported during concurrent use of diltiazem or verapamil with systemic beta-adrenergic blocking agents; although these effects may occur in the absence of overt pre-existing sinoatrial disease, older patients and patients with left ventricular dysfunction or sinoatrial or atrioventricular conduction abnormalities may be at increased risk; concurrent use of nifedipine with beta-adrenergic blocking agents, although usually well tolerated, may produce excessive hypotension and in rare cases may increase the possibility of congestive heart failure)
(calcium channel blocking agents may decrease the hepatic metabolism of propranolol, metoprolol, and possibly other beta-adrenergic blocking agents with substantial hepatic biotransformation; although the clinical significance of this effect appears to be minimal, caution is warranted given the potential for additive cardiodepressant effects during concurrent use)
(concurrent use of diazoxide with beta-adrenergic blocking agents prevents the tachycardia produced by diazoxide but may also increase the hypotensive effects)
(concurrent use of reserpine with beta-adrenergic blocking agents may result in additive and possibly excessive beta-adrenergic blockade; close observation is recommended since bradycardia and hypotension may occur)

Cimetidine
(cimetidine may reduce the clearance of hepatically metabolized beta-adrenergic blocking agents, resulting in elevations of plasma concentrations)

» Cocaine
(cocaine may inhibit the therapeutic effects of beta-adrenergic blocking agents)
(although beta-adrenergic blocking agents are recommended to reduce tachycardia, myocardial ischemia, and/or arrhythmias induced by cocaine, concurrent use of a beta-adrenergic blocking agent with cocaine may increase the risk of hypertension, excessive bradycardia, and possibly heart block, because beta-adrenergic blockade may leave cocaine's alpha-adrenergic activity unopposed; the risk of these adverse effects may be decreased with labetalol because labetalol also has some alpha-adrenergic blocking activity, although its beta-adrenergic blocking activity predominates)

Contrast media, iodinated
(concurrent use of beta-adrenergic blocking agents with intravenous contrast media may increase the risk of moderate to severe anaphylaxis; an anaphylactic event may be refractory to treatment)

Estrogens
(concurrent use may decrease the antihypertensive effect of beta-adrenergic blocking agents because estrogen-induced fluid retention may lead to increased blood pressure)

Fentanyl and derivatives
(preoperative chronic use of systemic beta-adrenergic blocking agents may decrease the frequency and/or severity of hypertensive responses to surgery, especially during sternotomy and sternal spread in cardiac or coronary artery surgery; however, chronic preoperative use of systemic beta-adrenergic blocking agents may also increase the risk of initial bradycardia following induction doses of fentanyl or any of its derivatives)

Flecainide
(although there have been no reports of adverse effects during concurrent administration of flecainide with the beta-adrenergic blocking agents, caution is recommended because of the potential for additive negative inotropic effects, especially in patients with compromised left ventricular function [ejection fraction $< 30\%$])

Lidocaine
(concurrent use with beta-adrenergic blocking agents may reduce lidocaine elimination and increase the risk of lidocaine toxicity because of reduced hepatic blood flow; lidocaine dosage should be adjusted on the basis of serum lidocaine concentrations)

Monoamine oxidase (MAO) inhibitors, including furazolidone, procarbazine, and selegiline
(significant hypertension theoretically may occur up to 14 days following discontinuation of the MAO inhibitor; although sufficient clinical reports are lacking, concurrent use with beta-adrenergic blocking agents is not recommended)

Neuromuscular blocking agents, nondepolarizing
(beta-adrenergic blocking agents may potentiate and prolong the action of nondepolarizing neuromuscular blocking agents when used concurrently; careful postoperative monitoring of the patient may be necessary following concurrent or sequential use, especially if there is a possibility of incomplete reversal of neuromuscular blockade)

Nicotine chewing gum or
Smoking deterrents, other or
Smoking, tobacco, cessation of
(smoking cessation may increase therapeutic effects of propranolol by decreasing metabolism, thereby increasing serum concentrations; dosage adjustments may be necessary)

Nitroglycerin
(labetalol reduces the reflex tachycardia caused by nitroglycerin and may increase the antihypertensive effect)

Phenothiazines
(concurrent use with beta-adrenergic blocking agents results in an increased plasma concentration of each medication)

Phenytoin
(concurrent use of propranolol, and probably other beta-adrenergic blocking agents, with intravenous phenytoin may produce additive cardiac depressant effects)

Phenoxybenzamine or
Phentolamine
(concurrent use with labetalol may result in additive alpha-adrenergic blocking effects)

Propafenone
(concurrent use with metoprolol or propranolol may result in significant increases in plasma concentrations and half-life of propranolol and metoprolol, without affecting plasma propafenone concentrations; dosage reduction of the beta-adrenergic blocking agent may be necessary)

» Sympathomimetics
(concurrent use of beta-adrenergic blocking agents with sympathomimetic amines having beta-adrenergic stimulant activity may result in mutual inhibition of therapeutic effects; for sympathomimetic agents with beta-adrenergic effects, beta-blockade may antagonize beta-1-adrenergic cardiac effects [dobutamine, dopamine] or the beta-2-adrenergic bronchodilating effect [albuterol, ethylnorepinephrine, isoetharine, isoproterenol, metaproterenol, terbutaline] or both [isoproterenol]; use of a cardioselective beta-1-adrenergic blocker [atenolol, betaxolol, or metoprolol] or labetalol [because of its alpha-blocking activity] at low doses may prevent antagonism of the bronchodilating effect)

(sympathomimetic agents with both alpha- and beta-adrenergic effects [amphetamines, ephedrine, epinephrine, metaraminol, norepinephrine, phenylephrine, pseudoephedrine], beta-blockade may result in unopposed alpha-adrenergic activity with a risk of hypertension and excessive bradycardia and possible heart block; risk should be less with labetalol because of its alpha-blocking activity; beta-blockade also antagonizes the bronchodilating effect of ephedrine and epinephrine)

» Xanthines, especially aminophylline or theophylline
(concurrent use with beta-adrenergic blocking agents may result in mutual inhibition of therapeutic effects; in addition, concurrent use with the xanthines [except dyphylline] may decrease xanthine clearance, especially in patients with increased theophylline clearance induced by smoking; concurrent use requires careful monitoring)

Laboratory value alterations

The following have been selected on the basis of their potential clinical significance (possible effect in parentheses where appropriate)—not necessarily inclusive (» = major clinical significance).

With diagnostic test results

Amphetamine determinations, urinary
(labetalol may produce false-positive results when commercially available assay methods [thin-layer chromatographic assay or radioenzymatic assay] are used; during labetalol therapy, positive results should be confirmed with more specific methods, such as a gas chromatographic-mass spectrometer technique)

Catecholamine determinations
(urinary concentrations of catecholamines and/or their metabolites [metanephrine, normetanephrine, vanillylmandelic acid] may be falsely increased by labetalol when measured by fluorimetric or photometric methods; a specific method, such as high performance liquid chromatography assay with solid phase extraction, should be used instead)

Glaucoma screening test
(may be interfered with by systemic beta-blockade, which reduces intraocular pressure)

Radionuclide ventriculography
(beta-adrenergic blocking agents may blunt the exercise-induced changes in cardiac function in the evaluation of coronary artery disease by decreasing heart rate)

With physiology/laboratory test values

Alkaline phosphatase, serum and
Lactate dehydrogenase (LDH), serum and
Transaminases, serum
(may be increased by acebutolol, labetalol, or metoprolol; it is recommended that labetalol be withdrawn if jaundice or laboratory signs of hepatic function impairment occur)

Antinuclear antibody (ANA) titers
(may be increased by beta-adrenergic blocking agents; dose-related)

Blood glucose concentrations
(nonselective beta-adrenergic blocking agents impair glycogenolysis and the hyperglycemic response to endogenous epinephrine, leading to persistence of hypoglycemia and delayed recovery of blood glucose to normal levels, especially in diabetics; studies have shown no such effect in resting nondiabetics with therapeutic doses; beta-adrenergic blocking agents, especially nonselective agents, decrease the release of insulin in response to hyperglycemia; effects on blood glucose may be less likely with labetalol or cardioselective agents such as acebutolol, betaxolol, atenolol, and metoprolol, especially at lower doses)

Blood urea nitrogen (BUN) (usually in patients with severe heart disease) and
Potassium concentrations, serum and
Uric acid concentrations, serum
(may be increased)

Lipoproteins, serum and
Triglycerides, serum
(concentrations may be increased)

Medical considerations/Contraindications

The medical considerations/contraindications included have been selected on the basis of their potential clinical significance (reasons given in parentheses where appropriate)—not necessarily inclusive (» = major clinical significance).

Note: In general, because of the similarity of effect and because the cardioselectivity of beta-1 blockers is relative, the same precautions apply to all beta-adrenergic blocking agents.

Except under special circumstances, this medication should not be used when the following medical problems exist:

For all indications

» Cardiac failure, decompensated or
» Cardiogenic shock or
» Heart block, 2nd- or 3rd-degree atrioventricular (AV) block or
» Sick sinus syndrome (unless a permanent pacemaker is in place) or
» Sinus bradycardia (heart rate less than 45 beats per minute)
(risk of further myocardial depression; risk may be less with carteolol, labetalol, oxprenolol, penbutolol, and pindolol; metoprolol is contraindicated in patients with sick sinus syndrome unless a permanent pacemaker is in place; beta-adrenergic blocking agents may be used with extreme caution in some patients with cardiac failure [e.g., high output failure associated with thyrotoxicosis])

» Hypersensitivity to the beta-blocker prescribed or to any other beta-blocker or any component of the product

For use in myocardial infarction

» Hypotension
(patients dependent on sympathetic stimulation to maintain adequate cardiac output and blood pressure, such as patients with

hypotension in the setting of myocardial infarction, may not benefit from beta-adrenergic blockade; studies of beta-adrenergic blockade in the treatment of myocardial infarction excluded patients with systolic pressures less than 100 mm Hg)

Risk-benefit should be considered when the following medical problems exist:

For all beta-adrenergic blocking agents

» Allergy, history of or

» Asthma, bronchial or

» Emphysema or nonallergenic bronchitis

(beta-adrenergic blocking agents may promote bronchospasm and block the bronchodilating effect of epinephrine; cardioselective agents such as acebutolol, atenolol, betaxolol, bisoprolol, and metoprolol, or agents with ISA such as carteolol, oxprenolol, penbutolol, or pindolol are theoretically less likely to cause such effects when used at lower doses; labetalol may also pose less risk of bronchoconstriction; however, caution is necessary with all beta-adrenergic blocking agents)

(severity and duration of anaphylactic reactions to allergens and allergen immunotherapy may be increased in some patients being treated with beta-adrenergic blocking agents; if possible, another medication should be substituted for a beta-adrenergic blocking agent in patients receiving allergen immunotherapy, or, for conditions that are not life-threatening, allergen immunotherapy should be avoided in patients who cannot discontinue beta-adrenergic blocking agent therapy; caution is also recommended during skin testing in patients on beta-adrenergic blocking agents)

» Congestive heart failure

(risk of further depression of myocardial contractility; labetalol and agents with ISA such as carteolol, oxprenolol, penbutolol, pindolol, and possibly acebutolol may theoretically be associated with less risk and may be used with caution in patients who are well-compensated)

» Diabetes mellitus

(beta-adrenergic blocking agents may mask tachycardia associated with hypoglycemia, but not dizziness and sweating; beta-adrenergic blocking agents may adversely affect recovery from hypoglycemia and impair peripheral circulation; these effects may theoretically be more likely with the noncardioselective agents and less likely with labetalol and cardioselective agents)

Hepatic function impairment

(metabolism of beta-adrenergic blocking agents that undergo hepatic metabolism may be decreased; patients with impaired hepatic function may require lower doses of beta-adrenergic blocking agents [exceptions are atenolol, betaxolol, carteolol, metoprolol (except in severe impairment), and nadolol, which require no dosage adjustment]; such reduction in dosage frequently applies to geriatric patients, many of whom have reduced hepatic function)

» Hyperthyroidism

(beta-adrenergic blocking agents may mask tachycardic symptoms; abrupt withdrawal may intensify symptoms)

» Ischemic heart disease

(following abrupt cessation of certain beta-blocking agent therapy, exacerbations of angina pectoris and, in some cases, myocardial infarction have occurred; when discontinuing chronically administered metoprolol, particularly in patients with ischemic heart disease, dosage should be gradually reduced over a 1 to 2 week period and patient should be carefully monitored; if angina markedly worsens or acute coronary insufficiency develops, administration of beta-blocker should be reinstate promptly, at least temporarily, and other measures appropriate for management of unstable angina should be taken; patients should be warned against interruption or discontinuation of therapy without physician's advice; because coronary artery disease is common and may be unrecognized, it my be prudent not to discontinue therapy abruptly even in patients treated only for hypertension)

» Mental depression, or history of

(although the association between beta-adrenergic blocking agents and depression is not fully established, these medications should be used cautiously in these patients)

Major surgery

(necessity of withdrawing beta-blocking therapy prior to major surgery is controversial; impaired ability of the heart to respond to reflex adrenergic stimuli may augment risks of general anesthesia and surgical procedures)

Myasthenia gravis

(beta-adrenergic blocking agents may potentiate a myasthenic condition, including muscle weakness and double vision)

Peripheral vascular disease

(caution should be exercised; beta-blockers can precipitate or aggravate symptoms of arterial insufficiency in patients with this condition)

Pheochromocytoma

(an alpha-blocking agent should be initiated prior to use of any beta-blocking agent)

Psoriasis

(may be exacerbated)

Renal function impairment

(may impair beta-adrenergic blocking agent clearance; risk of reduced renal blood flow; patients with impaired renal function may require reduced doses of beta-adrenergic blocking agents [exceptions are labetalol, metoprolol, oxprenolol, penbutolol, pindolol (unless impairment is severe), propranolol, and timolol, which require no dosage adjustment]; such reduction in dosage frequently applies to geriatric patients, many of whom have reduced renal function; specific dosage recommendations, where available, are included in the *Dosage Forms* section for the particular agent)

For all beta-adrenergic blocking agents except labetalol

Raynaud's syndrome and other peripheral vascular diseases

(beta-adrenergic blocking agents may reduce peripheral circulation and worsen these conditions; cardioselective agents such as acebutolol, atenolol, betaxolol, bisoprolol, metoprolol, or agents with ISA such as acebutolol, carteolol, oxprenolol, penbutolol, or pindolol are theoretically less likely to produce adverse effect)

Patient monitoring

The following may be especially important in patient monitoring (other tests may be warranted in some patients, depending on condition; » = major clinical significance):

Blood cell counts and

Blood glucose concentrations (for diabetic patients) and

» Cardiac function monitoring and

Hepatic function determinations and

» Pulse rate determinations and

Renal function determinations

(may be required at periodic intervals)

» Blood pressure and

» Electrocardiogram (ECG) and

» Heart rate

(should be carefully monitored during intravenous administration)

» Blood pressure determinations

(recommended at periodic intervals to monitor efficacy and safety of therapy in patients being treated for hypertension; selected patients may be trained to perform blood pressure measurements at home and report the results at regular physician visits)

Side/Adverse Effects

While taking beta-blockers, patients with a history of severe anaphylactic reactions to a variety of allergens may be more reactive to repeated challenge, either accidental, diagnostic, or therapeutic. Such patients may be unresponsive to the usual doses of epinephrine use to treat allergic reaction.

The following side/adverse effects have been selected on the basis of their potential clinical significance (possible signs and symptoms in parentheses where appropriate)—not necessarily inclusive:

Those indicating need for medical attention

Incidence less frequent

Bradycardia, symptomatic (dizziness); ***bronchospasm*** (difficulty breathing and/or wheezing); ***congestive heart failure*** (swelling of ankles, feet, and/or lower legs; shortness of breath); ***mental depression; reduced peripheral circulation*** (cold hands and feet)—except labetalol

Note: Risk of *bronchospasm or reduced peripheral circulation* is theoretically reduced with acebutolol, atenolol, betaxolol, bisoprolol, carteolol, metoprolol, oxprenolol, penbutolol, or pindolol.

Mental depression is usually reversible and mild, but may progress to catatonia.

Incidence rare

Allergic reaction (skin rash); ***arrhythmias*** (irregular heartbeat); ***back pain or joint pain; chest pain; confusion***—especially in the elderly; ***hallucinations; hepatotoxicity*** (dark urine, yellow eyes or skin)—for acebutolol, bisoprolol, or labetalol; ***leukopenia*** (fever, sore throat); ***orthostatic hypotension*** (dizziness or lightheadedness when getting up from a lying or sitting position); ***psoriasiform eruption*** (red, scaling, or crusted skin); ***thrombocytopenia*** (unusual bleeding and bruising)

Note: *Hepatotoxicity* is usually reversible; however, hepatic necrosis and death have been reported with labetalol.

The following post-marketing side effects for metoprolol have been reported: increased sweating and photosensitivity.

Those indicating need for medical attention only if they continue or are bothersome

Incidence more frequent

Decreased sexual ability; drowsiness—especially with higher doses; ***trouble in sleeping; unusual tiredness or weakness***

Incidence less frequent

Anxiety and/or nervousness; constipation; diarrhea; nasal congestion (stuffy nose); ***nausea or vomiting; stomach discomfort***

Incidence rare

Changes in taste; dry, sore eyes; frequent urination—for acebutolol or carteolol; ***itching of skin; nightmares and vivid dreams; numbness and/or tingling of fingers, toes, or skin, especially the scalp***—for labetolol

Those indicating the need for medical attention if they occur after medication is discontinued

Arrhythmias (fast or irregular heartbeat)

chest pain; general feeling of discomfort, illness, or weakness; headache; shortness of breath, sudden; sweating; trembling

Overdose

For more information on the management of overdose or unintentional ingestion, **contact a Poison Control Center** (see *Poison Control Center Listing*).

Clinical effects of overdose

The following effects have been selected on the basis of their potential clinical significance (possible signs and symptoms in parentheses where appropriate)—not necessarily inclusive:

Bradycardia; dizziness, severe, or fainting; hypotension; irregular heartbeat; difficulty breathing; bluish-colored fingernails or palms of hands; or seizures

Treatment of overdose

Decreased absorption—Gastric lavage and administration of activated charcoal.

Specific treatment—

Atropine: May be administered for severe bradycardia in the presence of hypotension.

Diazepam or lorazepam: May be used intravenously to treat associated seizures.

Dobutamine, dopamine, epinephrine, norepinephrine, or isoproterenol: May be administered for chronotropic and inotropic support and treatment of severe hypotension. However, the effects of sympathomimetic agents may be inhibited by the presence of significant beta-blockade. Therefore, hypotension and ensuing pump failure may be refractory to treatment with catecholamines.

Glucagon: Glucagon has been used effectively in the treatment of bradycardia and hypotension in beta-adrenergic blocking agent overdose. Glucagon demonstrates major inotropic and less dramatic chronotropic effects. These effects appear to be independent of the beta-adrenergic receptor. Therefore, glucagon may be an advantageous alternative treatment to reverse the hemodynamic depression of beta-adrenergic blocking agent overdose.

Transvenous pacing: May be necessary for heart block.

Other therapy: May include furosemide or digitalis glycoside for pulmonary edema or cardiac failure; or a beta-2 agonist such as isoproterenol and/or a theophylline derivative for bronchospasm.

There is limited evidence that calcium chloride may be effective in improving myocardial contractility and hemodynamic status. It is speculated that hypocalcemia resulting from beta-adrenergic blocking agent overdose may contribute to a decline in myocardial contractility.

Patient Consultation

As an aid to patient consultation, refer to *Advice for the Patient, Beta-adrenergic Blocking Agents (Systemic)*.

In providing consultation, consider emphasizing the following selected information (» = major clinical significance):

Before using this medication

» Conditions affecting use, especially:

Hypersensitivity to the beta-blocker prescribed or any other beta-blocker or to any component of the product

Pregnancy—Beta-adrenergic blocking agents cross the placenta; risk of hypoglycemia, respiratory depression, bradycardia, and hypotension in the fetus and neonate

Breast-feeding—Beta-adrenergic blocking agents pass into breast milk; bradycardia, cyanosis, hypoglycemia, hypotension, and tachypnea have been reported in breast-fed infants whose mothers ingested atenolol or acebutolol

Use in the elderly—Older patients may be more susceptible to some side/adverse effects; increased risk of beta-blocker–induced hypothermia

Surgical—May increase risks of general anesthesia and surgical procedures

Other medications, especially allergen immunotherapy and allergenic extracts used for skin testing, oral antidiabetic agents, insulin, calcium channel blocking agents, clonidine, guanabenz, cocaine, MAO inhibitors, sympathomimetics, or xanthines

Other medical problems, especially decompensated cardiac failure, cardiogenic shock, 2nd- or 3rd- degree AV block, sick sinus syndrome, sinus bradycardia, ischemic heart disease, hypotension (when used in myocardial infarction), history of allergy, bronchial asthma, emphysema or nonallergenic bronchitis, congestive heart failure, diabetes mellitus, hyperthyroidism, or mental depression

Proper use of this medication

Proper administration of extended-release dosage forms: Swallowing whole without crushing, breaking (except with metoprolol succinate), or chewing

Proper use of concentrated oral propranolol solution

Measuring with calibrated dropper

(Mixing with liquid or semi-solid food such as water, juices, soda or soda-like beverages, applesauce, and puddings; making sure entire dose is taken)

(Not storing after mixing)

Checking pulse, if directed to do so by physician, and notifying physician if pulse falls below the rate designated by physician

Taking medication at the same time(s) each day to maintain the therapeutic effect

» Importance of not missing doses, especially with schedules of one dose per day

» Proper dosing

Missed dose: Taking as soon as possible; not taking at all if within 4 hours of next scheduled dose (8 hours for atenolol, betaxolol, carteolol, labetalol, nadolol, penbutolol, sotalol, or extended-release oxprenolol or propranolol); not doubling doses

» Proper storage

For use as an antihypertensive

Possible need for control of weight and diet, especially sodium intake

» Compliance with therapy; patient may not experience symptoms of hypertension; importance of taking medication only as directed and keeping appointments with physician, even if feeling well

» Does not cure, but helps control hypertension; possible need for lifelong therapy; checking with physician before discontinuing medication; serious consequences of untreated hypertension

Precautions while using this medication

Making regular visits to physician to check progress

» Checking with physician before discontinuing medication; gradual dosage reduction may be necessary

Having enough medication on hand to get through weekends, holidays, and vacations; possibly carrying second written prescription for emergency use

Carrying medical identification card during therapy

» Consulting with physician if sign or symptoms of worsening heart failure such as weight gain or increasing shortness of breath occur

» Caution if any kind of surgery (including dental surgery) or emergency treatment is required

» Diabetics: May mask signs and symptoms of hypoglycemia or may cause increased blood glucose concentrations or prolong hypoglycemia

» Caution when driving or doing things requiring alertness, because of possible drowsiness, dizziness, or lightheadedness

Caution during exposure to cold weather because of possible increased sensitivity to cold

Possible skin photosensitivity reported in post-marketing experience; avoiding unprotected exposure to sun; using protective clothing and sun block product; avoiding use of sunlamp, tanning bed, or tanning booth

» Caution against overexertion in response to decreased chest pain

Caution if any laboratory tests required; possible interference with test results

Patients with allergies to foods, medications, or stinging insect venom: Possible increase in severity of allergic reactions; checking with physician immediately if severe allergic reaction occurs

For use as an antihypertensive:

» Not taking other medications, especially nonprescription sympathomimetics, unless discussed with physician

For oral labetalol only:

» Caution when getting up suddenly from a lying or sitting position, especially during initiation of therapy or when dosage is increased

» Caution in using alcohol, while standing for long periods or exercising, and during hot weather because of enhanced orthostatic hypotensive effects

For parenteral labetalol only:

» Lying down during injection and for up to 3 hours after getting injection, then getting up gradually

Side/adverse effects

Signs of potential side effects, especially bradycardia, breathing difficulty and/or wheezing, congestive heart failure, mental depression, reduced peripheral circulation, allergic reaction, arrhythmias, back pain or joint pain, chest pain, confusion, hallucinations, hepatotoxicity, leukopenia, psoriasiform eruption, thrombocytopenia, and withdrawal reaction

Signs of potential side effects observed during clinical practice of metoprolol, especially increased sweating and photosensitivity

For labetalol: Transient scalp tingling may occur, usually at beginning of treatment

General Dosing Information

Although plasma concentrations of beta-adrenergic blocking agents can be ascertained, there is not always a predictable relationship between plasma concentration and pharmacological effects. Pharmacological effects have been observed when plasma concentrations were not discernible. Therefore, titration of dosage with measurement of heart rate and blood pressure is used to guide therapy.

In some patients, once-daily dosing is effective.

When beta-adrenergic blocking agent therapy is discontinued in patients concurrently receiving clonidine or guanabenz, the beta-adrenergic blocking agent should be gradually discontinued several days before the clonidine or guanabenz is gradually discontinued in order to avoid clonidine- or guanabenz-withdrawal hypertensive crisis.

For oral dosage forms only

When a beta-adrenergic blocking agent must be withdrawn from established therapy *(especially in patients with ischemic heart disease)*, it is recommended that the dosage be reduced gradually to minimize risk of exacerbation of angina or development of myocardial infarction. Dosage reduction should occur over a period of approximately 2 weeks. During this time the patient should avoid vigorous physical activity in order to minimize the danger of infarction or arrhythmias. If signs of withdrawal (e.g., angina) occur, beta-adrenergic blocking agent therapy should be reinstated temporarily and then carefully withdrawn after the patient has stabilized.

It is recommended that beta-adrenergic blocking agent therapy be withdrawn if drug-induced mental depression occurs.

Diet/Nutrition

Oral beta-adrenergic blocking agents may be taken either with food or on an empty stomach. Studies indicate that bioavailability of labetalol, propranolol, and possibly metoprolol may be enhanced by administration with food, which may slow the hepatic metabolism of the medication. Bioavailability of acebutolol, atenolol, nadolol, oxprenolol, penbutolol, and pindolol are not affected by food intake. Concurrent food intake may slow carteolol absorption, but does not affect bioavailability. Sotalol does not undergo significant first-pass metabolism. Food, especially milk and milk products, may reduce the bioavailability of sotalol.

ACEBUTOLOL

Summary of Differences

Pharmacology/pharmacokinetics:

Mechanism of action/Effect—Mild to moderate intrinsic sympathomimetic activity (ISA); relatively cardioselective; low lipid solubility.

Absorption—Bioavailability significantly reduced by first-pass metabolism but effect not reduced because of active metabolite.

Protein binding—Low.

Elimination—Removable by hemodialysis.

Precautions:

Medical considerations/contraindications—Dosage reduction necessary in hepatic function and renal function impairment.

Side/adverse effects:

Theoretical reduced risk of bronchospasm, hypoglycemia, and peripheral vasoconstriction because of cardioselectivity.

Oral Dosage Forms

ACEBUTOLOL HYDROCHLORIDE CAPSULES

Usual adult dose

Antiarrhythmic—

Oral, 200 mg two times a day, the dosage being adjusted according to response, generally in the range of 600 to 1200 mg per day.

Antihypertensive—

Oral, initially 400 mg per day as a single dose or in two divided daily doses, the dosage being adjusted according to response, with maintenance doses usually in the range of 400 to 800 mg per day.

Note: Geriatric patients may have increased or decreased sensitivity to the effects of the usual adult dose.

It is recommended that the dosage of acebutolol be reduced in patients with renal function impairment as follows:

Creatinine clearance (mL/min/1.73m)	% of normal dose to be given
<50	50
<25	25

Usual geriatric prescribing limits

In geriatric patients, daily doses should not exceed a total of 800 mg.

Usual pediatric dose

Dosage has not been established.

Strength(s) usually available

U.S.—

200 mg (Rx) [*Sectral;* GENERIC].

400 mg (Rx) [*Sectral;* GENERIC].

Canada—

Not commercially available.

Packaging and storage

Store below 40 °C (104 °F), preferably between 15 and 30 °C (59 and 86 °F), in a well-closed container, unless otherwise specified by manufacturer.

Auxiliary labeling

- Do not take other medicine without your doctor's advice.

Note

Check refill frequency to determine compliance in hypertensive patients.

ACEBUTOLOL HYDROCHLORIDE TABLETS

Usual adult dose

Antianginal[1]—

Oral, initially 200 mg two times a day, the dosage being adjusted according to response, generally in the range of 600 to 1200 mg per day.

Antihypertensive—

Oral, initially 100 mg two times a day, the dosage being adjusted weekly according to response, up to a maximum of 400 mg two times a day.

Antiarrhythmic[1]—

Oral, 200 mg two times a day, the dosage being adjusted according to response.

Usual pediatric dose

Dosage has not been established.

Strength(s) usually available

U.S.—

Not commercially available.

Canada—

100 mg (Rx) [*Monitan; Sectral* (scored)].

200 mg (Rx) [*Monitan* (scored); *Sectral* (scored)].

400 mg (Rx) [*Monitan* (scored); *Sectral* (scored)].

Packaging and storage

Store below 40 °C (104 °F), preferably between 15 and 30 °C (59 and 86 °F), in a well-closed container, unless otherwise specified by manufacturer.

Auxiliary labeling

- Do not take other medicines without your doctor's advice.

Note

Check refill frequency to determine compliance in hypertensive patients.

---

[1]Not included in Canadian product labeling.

ATENOLOL

Summary of Differences

Pharmacology/pharmacokinetics:
- Mechanism of action/Effect—Relatively cardioselective (beta-1); very low lipid solubility.
- Biotransformation—Minimal hepatic metabolism.
- Protein binding—Very low to low.
- Elimination—Removable by hemodialysis.

Precautions:
- Medical considerations/contraindications—Dosage reduction necessary in renal function impairment but not necessary in hepatic function impairment.

Side/adverse effects:
- Theoretical reduced risk of bronchospasm, hypoglycemia, and peripheral vasoconstriction when daily dosage is in the lower range, because of cardioselectivity.

Oral Dosage Forms

ATENOLOL TABLETS

Usual adult dose

Antianginal—
Oral, initially 50 mg once a day, the dosage being increased gradually to 100 mg a day after one week if necessary and tolerated. Some patients may require up to 200 mg a day.

Antihypertensive—
Oral, initially 25 to 50 mg once a day, the dosage being increased to 50 to 100 mg a day after two weeks if necessary and tolerated.

Myocardial infarction—
In patients who tolerate the full intravenous dose: Oral, initially 50 mg ten minutes after the last intravenous dose, followed by another 50 mg twelve hours later. A dose of 100 mg once a day or 50 mg two times a day may then be given for six to nine days or until discharge from the hospital.

Note: Geriatric patients may have increased or decreased sensitivity to the effects of the usual adult dose.

For elderly patients and patients with renal function impairment, the following maximum doses are recommended:

Creatinine clearance (mL/min/1.73 m²)	Maximum dose
15–35	50 mg per day
<15	25 mg per day

For some renally-impaired or elderly patients being treated for hypertension, a lower starting dose of 25 mg given as one tablet daily may be required. If this 25 mg dose is used, assessment of efficacy must be made carefully. This should include a blood pressure measurement ('trough' blood pressure) just prior to the next dose to ensure that the treatment effect is present for a full 24 hours. Data are not available on dose adjustments for other indications.

Patients on hemodialysis should be given 25 or 50 mg after each dialysis *under hospital supervision* as marked falls in blood pressure can occur.

Usual pediatric dose

Dosage has not been established.

Strength(s) usually available

U.S.—
- 25 mg (Rx) [*Tenormin;* GENERIC].
- 50 mg (Rx) [*Tenormin* (scored); GENERIC].
- 100 mg (Rx) [*Tenormin;* GENERIC].

Canada—
- 50 mg (Rx) [*Apo-Atenolol; Novo-Atenol; Tenormin* (scored); GENERIC].
- 100 mg (Rx) [*Apo-Atenolol; Novo-Atenol; Tenormin* (scored); GENERIC].

Packaging and storage

Store below 40 °C (104 °F), preferably between 15 and 30 °C (59 and 86 °F), in a well-closed container, unless otherwise specified by manufacturer. Protect from light.

Auxiliary labeling

- Do not take other medicine without your doctor's advice.

Note

Check refill frequency to determine compliance in hypertensive patients.

Parenteral Dosage Forms

ATENOLOL INJECTION

Usual adult dose

Myocardial infarction—
Early treatment: Intravenous, 5 mg (over five minutes), the dose being repeated ten minutes later.

Note: Geriatric patients may have increased or decreased sensitivity to the effects of the usual adult dose.

In patients who tolerate the full intravenous dose (10 mg), oral atenolol treatment should be initiated ten minutes after the last intravenous dose.

For patients with severe renal function impairment, the following maximum doses are recommended:

Creatinine clearance (mL/min/1.73m)	Maximum dose
15–35	50 mg per day
<15	50 mg every second day

Usual pediatric dose

Dosage has not been established.

Strength(s) usually available

U.S.—
- 500 mcg (0.5 mg) per mL (Rx) [*Tenormin*].

Canada—
- Not commercially available.

Packaging and storage

Store between 2 and 30 °C (36 and 86 °F), unless otherwise specified by manufacturer. Protect from light. Protect from freezing.

BETAXOLOL

Summary of Differences

Pharmacology/pharmacokinetics:
- Mechanism of action/Effect—Relatively cardioselective; moderate lipid solubility.
- Protein binding—Moderate.
- Elimination—Not removable by hemodialysis.

Precautions:
- Medical considerations/contraindications—Dosage reduction may be recommended in renal function impairment; dosage reduction not necessary in hepatic function impairment.

Oral Dosage Forms

BETAXOLOL TABLETS

Usual adult dose

Antihypertensive—
Oral, 10 mg once a day initially, the dosage being doubled, if necessary, after seven to fourteen days.

Note: Geriatric patients may have increased or decreased sensitivity to the effects of the usual adult dose. An initial dose of 5 mg should be considered for elderly patients.

For patients with renal function impairment who are undergoing hemodialysis, an initial dose of 5 mg once a day is recommended, increased by 5 mg a day every fourteen days, as necessary, up to a maximum daily dose of 20 mg.

Usual pediatric dose

Dosage has not been established.

Strength(s) usually available

U.S.—
- 10 mg (Rx) [*Kerlone* (scored)].
- 20 mg (Rx) [*Kerlone*].

Canada—
- Not commercially available.

Packaging and storage

Store below 40 °C (104 °F), preferably between 15 and 30 °C (59 and 86 °F), unless otherwise specified by manufacturer.

Auxiliary labeling

- Do not take other medicine without your doctor's advice.

Note

Check refill frequency to determine compliance in hypertensive patients.

BISOPROLOL

Summary of Differences

Pharmacology/pharmacokinetics:
Mechanism of action/Effect—Relatively cardioselective (beta-1).
Protein binding—Low.
Precautions:
Breast-feeding—Not known if distributed into breast milk.

Oral Dosage Forms

BISOPROLOL FUMARATE TABLETS

Usual adult dose
Antihypertensive—
Oral, initially 5 mg once a day, the dosage being increased to 10 mg once a day if hypertension is not adequately controlled.

Note: An initial dose of 2.5 mg once a day may be appropriate for some patients, especially patients with bronchospastic disease.

Usual adult prescribing limits
20 mg once a day.

Usual pediatric dose
Dosage has not been established.

Strength(s) usually available
U.S.—
5 mg (Rx) [*Zebeta* (scored)].
10 mg (Rx) [*Zebeta*].
Canada—
Not commercially available.

Packaging and storage
Store below 40 °C (104 °F), preferably between 15 and 30 °C (59 and 86 °F), in a tight container, unless otherwise specified by manufacturer.

Auxiliary labeling
- Do not take other medicine without your doctor's advice.

Note
Check refill frequency to determine compliance in hypertensive patients.

CARTEOLOL

Summary of Differences

Pharmacology/pharmacokinetics:
Mechanism of action/Effect—Moderate intrinsic sympathomimetic activity (ISA); nonselective; low lipid solubility.
Biotransformation—Minimal hepatic metabolism (one active metabolite).
Protein binding—Low.
Precautions:
Breast-feeding—Not known if distributed into breast milk.
Medical considerations/contraindications—Dosage reduction necessary in renal function impairment but not necessary in hepatic function impairment.
Side/adverse effects:
Theoretical reduced risk of bronchospasm, heart failure, and peripheral vasoconstriction because of ISA.

Oral Dosage Forms

CARTEOLOL HYDROCHLORIDE TABLETS

Usual adult dose
Antihypertensive—
Oral, initially 2.5 mg once a day, the dosage being adjusted according to response, up to a maximum of 10 mg once a day.

Note: Geriatric patients may have increased or decreased sensitivity to the effects of the usual adult dose.
It is recommended that the dosage interval be increased in patients with renal function impairment as follows:

Creatinine clearance (mL/min)	Dosage interval (hrs)
>60	24
20–60	48
<20	72

Usual adult prescribing limits
10 mg per day.

Usual pediatric dose
Dosage has not been established.

Strength(s) usually available
U.S.—
2.5 mg (Rx) [*Cartrol* (lactose)].
5 mg (Rx) [*Cartrol* (lactose)].
Canada—
Not commercially available.

Packaging and storage
Store below 40 °C (104 °F), preferably between 15 and 30 °C (59 and 86 °F), in a well-closed container, unless otherwise specified by manufacturer.

Auxiliary labeling
- Do not take other medicine without your doctor's advice.

Note
Check refill frequency to determine compliance in hypertensive patients.

LABETALOL

Summary of Differences

Pharmacology/pharmacokinetics:
Mechanism of action/Effect—Also has selective alpha-1-adrenergic blocking effects; nonselective beta-blocker; low lipid solubility.
Absorption—Bioavailability significantly reduced by first-pass metabolism and enhanced by concurrent administration with food.
Protein binding—Moderate.
Elimination—Not removable by hemodialysis.
Precautions:
Medical considerations/contraindications—May not exacerbate Raynaud's phenomenon or other peripheral vascular diseases; dosage reduction necessary in hepatic function impairment but not necessary in renal function impairment.
Side/adverse effects:
Possible reduced risk of bradycardia, bronchoconstriction, cardiac failure, hypoglycemia, and peripheral vasoconstriction, and increased incidence of postural hypotension.

Additional Dosing Information

See also *General Dosing Information.*

The hypotensive effect of labetalol may be especially pronounced when the patient is standing. If feasible, blood pressure should be taken in the supine position, after standing for 10 minutes, and immediately after exercise. Dosage increases should be made only if there has been no decrease in the standing blood pressure from previous levels.

Hospitalized patients should not be discharged until the effect of labetalol on their standing blood pressure has been determined.

Dosage reduction is indicated if the patient has excessive orthostatic fall in pressure and/or normal supine pressure.

Appropriate laboratory testing is recommended at the first sign and/or symptom of hepatotoxicity; if there is laboratory evidence of hepatotoxicity, it is recommended that labetalol be permanently withdrawn.

For parenteral dosage form

Labetalol hydrochloride injection may be administered as a direct intravenous injection (over a 2-minute period) or by continuous intravenous infusion.

When labetalol is administered by continuous intravenous infusion, it is recommended that it be administered by means of an infusion pump, a micro-drip regulator, or a similar device to allow precise adjustment of the flow rate.

To reduce the chance of postural hypotension, patients should remain supine for up to 3 hours after receiving parenteral labetalol. Ambulation should not be permitted until the ability of the patient to tolerate the upright position has been determined.

Oral Dosage Forms

LABETALOL HYDROCHLORIDE TABLETS USP

Usual adult dose
Antihypertensive—
Initial: Oral, 100 mg two times a day, the dosage being adjusted in increments of 100 mg two times a day every two or three days until the desired response is achieved.
Maintenance: Oral, 200 to 400 mg two times a day.

Note: Labetalol may be administered in three divided daily doses if necessary because of side effects such as nausea or dizziness.

In severe hypertension, doses of 1.2 to 2.4 grams per day, in two or three divided doses, may be needed.

Geriatric patients may have increased or decreased sensitivity to the effects of the usual adult dose.

Usual pediatric dose
Dosage has not been established.

Strength(s) usually available
U.S.—
100 mg (Rx) [*Normodyne* (scored); *Trandate* (scored)].
200 mg (Rx) [*Normodyne* (scored); *Trandate* (scored)].
300 mg (Rx) [*Normodyne; Trandate* (scored)].
Canada—
100 mg (Rx) [*Trandate* (scored)].
200 mg (Rx) [*Trandate* (scored)].

Packaging and storage
Store between 2 and 30 °C (36 and 86 °F), unless otherwise specified by manufacturer. Store in a tight, light-resistant container.

Auxiliary labeling
- Do not take other medicines without your doctor's advice.

Note
Check refill frequency to determine compliance in hypertensive patients.

Parenteral Dosage Forms

LABETALOL HYDROCHLORIDE INJECTION USP

Usual adult dose
Antihypertensive—
Intravenous, 20 mg (0.25 mg per kg of body weight for an 80-kg patient) injected slowly over a two-minute period; additional injections of 40 mg and 80 mg may be given at ten-minute intervals until the desired blood pressure is achieved or a total of 300 mg has been given; or
Intravenous infusion, administered at a rate of 2 mg per minute, the dosage being adjusted according to response; the total dose necessary may range from 50 to 300 mg.

Note: Geriatric patients may have increased or decreased sensitivity to the effects of the usual adult dose.

Usual pediatric dose
Dosage has not been established.

Strength(s) usually available
U.S.—
5 mg per mL (Rx) [*Normodyne; Trandate*].
Canada—
5 mg per mL (Rx) [*Trandate*].

Packaging and storage
Store between 2 and 30 °C (36 and 86 °F), unless otherwise specified by manufacturer. Protect from light. Protect from freezing.

Preparation of dosage form
Labetalol hydrochloride may be prepared for administration by continuous intravenous infusion by either of the following methods—
Adding 200 mg to 160 mL of a commonly used intravenous fluid to produce 200 mL of solution containing 1 mg of labetalol hydrochloride per mL; or
Adding 200 mg to 250 mL of intravenous fluid to produce about 300 mL of solution containing approximately 2 mg of labetalol hydrochloride per 3 mL.

METOPROLOL

Summary of Differences

Pharmacology/pharmacokinetics:
Mechanism of action/Effect—Relatively cardioselective (beta-1); moderate lipid solubility.
Absorption—Bioavailability significantly reduced by first-pass metabolism.
Protein binding—Low.
Elimination—Not removable by hemodialysis.
Precautions:
Medical considerations/contraindications—No dosage reduction necessary in hepatic function impairment (unless severe) or renal function impairment.
Side/adverse effects:
Theoretical reduced risk of bronchospasm, hypoglycemia, and peripheral vasoconstriction when daily dosage does not exceed 200 mg, because of cardioselectivity; increased risk of central nervous system (CNS) side effects because of lipid solubility and relative ease of penetration into CNS.

Oral Dosage Forms

Note: Bracketed uses in the *Dosage Forms* section refer to categories of use and/or indications that are not included in U.S. product labeling.

METOPROLOL SUCCINATE EXTENDED-RELEASE TABLETS

Usual adult dose
Antihypertensive—
Oral, 25 to 100 mg once a day, the dosage being increased at weekly (or longer) intervals as needed and tolerated up to a total of 400 mg a day.
Antianginal—
Oral, 100 mg once a day, the dosage being increased gradually at weekly intervals as needed and tolerated up to a maximum of 400 mg a day.
Heart failure (treatment)—
Oral, 25 mg once daily for two weeks in patients with NYHA Class II heart failure and 12.5 mg once daily in patients with more severe heart failure. Dose should then be doubled every two weeks to the highest dosage level tolerated by the patient or up to 200 mg

Note: Dosage must be individualized and closely monitored during up-titration. Prior to initiation of metoprolol succinate, the dosing of diuretics, ACE inhibitors, and digitalis (if used) should be stabilized.

If transient worsening of heart failure occurs, it may be treated with increased doses of diuretics, and it may also be necessary to lower the metoprolol succinate dose or temporarily discontinue it. The dose should not be increased until symptoms of worsening heart failure have been stabilized. Initial difficulty with titration should not preclude later attempts to introduce metoprolol succinate. If heart failure patients experience symptomatic bradycardia, the dose of metoprolol succinate should be reduced.

[Vascular headache prophylactic][1]—
Oral, 200 mg once a day.

Note: Geriatric patients may have increased or decreased sensitivity to the effects of the usual adult dose.

Usual pediatric dose
Safety and efficacy have not been established.

Strength(s) usually available
U.S.—
25 mg (Rx) [*Toprol-XL* (scored; silicon dioxide; cellulose compounds; sodium stearyl fumarate; polyethylene glycol; titanium dioxide; paraffin)].
50 mg (Rx) [*Toprol-XL* (scored; silicon dioxide; cellulose compounds; sodium stearyl fumarate; polyethylene glycol; titanium dioxide; paraffin)].
100 mg (Rx) [*Toprol-XL* (scored; silicon dioxide; cellulose compounds; sodium stearyl fumarate; polyethylene glycol; titanium dioxide; paraffin)].
200 mg (Rx) [*Toprol-XL* (scored; silicon dioxide; cellulose compounds; sodium stearyl fumarate; polyethylene glycol; titanium dioxide; paraffin)].
Canada—
Not commercially available.

Packaging and storage
Store at 25 °C (77 °F), excursions permitted between 15 and 30 °C (59 and 86 °F), unless otherwise specified by manufacturer. Store in a tight container.

Auxiliary labeling
- Do not take other medicine without your doctor's advice.

Note
Check refill frequency to determine compliance in hypertensive patients.

METOPROLOL TARTRATE TABLETS USP

Usual adult dose
Antianginal
Antihypertensive—
Oral, initially 100 mg a day in single (hypertension) or divided (angina or hypertension) doses, the dosage being increased at one-week intervals as needed and tolerated up to a total of 450 mg a day if necessary.

Note: To maintain satisfactory blood pressure control, some patients may require division of the total daily dose into three separate doses.

Myocardial infarction—
Early treatment: Oral, 50 mg (for patients who tolerate the full intravenous dose) or 25 to 50 mg (for patients who do not tolerate the

full intravenous dose) every six hours starting fifteen minutes after the last intravenous dose or as soon as clinical condition allows. This dosage is continued for forty-eight hours, followed by

Late treatment: Oral, 100 mg two times a day for at least three months and possibly for as long as one to three years.

[Vascular headache prophylactic][1]—

Oral, 50 to 100 mg two to four times a day.

Note: Geriatric patients may have increased or decreased sensitivity to the effects of the usual adult dose.

Usual pediatric dose
Dosage has not been established.

Strength(s) usually available
U.S.—

50 mg (Rx) [*Lopressor* (scored); GENERIC].

100 mg (Rx) [*Lopressor* (scored); GENERIC].

Canada—

50 mg (Rx) [*Apo-Metoprolol* (scored); *Apo-Metoprolol (Type L); Betaloc* (scored); *Lopresor* (scored); *Novometoprol* (scored); *Nu-Metop;* GENERIC].

100 mg (Rx) [*Apo-Metoprolol* (scored); *Apo-Metoprolol (Type L); Betaloc* (scored); *Lopresor* (scored); *Novometoprol* (scored); *Nu-Metop;* GENERIC].

Packaging and storage
Store between 15 and 30 °C (59 and 86 °F), unless otherwise specified by manufacturer. Store in a tight, light-resistant container.

Auxiliary labeling
• Do not take other medicine without your doctor's advice.

Note
Check refill frequency to determine compliance in hypertensive patients.

METOPROLOL TARTRATE EXTENDED-RELEASE TABLETS

Usual adult dose
Antianginal

Antihypertensive—

Oral, 100 to 400 mg administered once a day for maintenance of established dosage requirements.

Note: Geriatric patients may have increased or decreased sensitivity to the effects of the usual adult dose.

Usual pediatric dose
Dosage has not been established.

Strength(s) usually available
U.S.—

Not commercially available.

Canada—

100 mg (Rx) [*Lopresor SR*].

200 mg (Rx) [*Betaloc Durules; Lopresor SR*].

Packaging and storage
Store below 40 °C (104 °F), preferably between 15 and 30 °C (59 and 86 °F), unless otherwise specified by manufacturer. Store in a light-resistant container.

Auxiliary labeling
• Do not take other medicine without your doctor's advice.

Note
Check refill frequency to determine compliance in hypertensive patients.

Parenteral Dosage Forms

METOPROLOL TARTRATE INJECTION USP

Usual adult dose
Myocardial infarction—

Early treatment: Intravenous (rapid), 5 mg every two minutes for three doses.

Note: Geriatric patients may have increased or decreased sensitivity to the effects of the usual adult dose.

Usual pediatric dose
Dosage has not been established.

Strength(s) usually available
U.S.—

1 mg per mL (Rx) [*Lopressor;* GENERIC].

Canada—

1 mg per mL (Rx) [*Betaloc* (sodium chloride 45 mg per mL); *Lopresor* (sodium chloride 45 mg per mL)].

Packaging and storage
Store below 40 °C (104 °F), preferably between 15 and 30 °C (59 and 86 °F), unless otherwise specified by manufacturer. Protect from light. Protect from freezing.

[1]Not included in Canadian product labeling.

NADOLOL

Summary of Differences
Pharmacology/pharmacokinetics:

Mechanism of action/Effect—Nonselective; low lipid solubility.

Biotransformation—Not hepatically metabolized.

Protein binding—Very low to low.

Elimination—Removable by hemodialysis.

Precautions:

Medical considerations/contraindications—Dosage reduction or increased dosing intervals recommended in renal function impairment; dosage reduction not necessary in hepatic function impairment.

Oral Dosage Forms
Note: Bracketed uses in the *Dosage Forms* section refer to categories of use and/or indications that are not included in U.S. product labeling.

NADOLOL TABLETS USP

Usual adult dose
Antianginal—

Oral, 40 mg once a day initially, the dosage being increased by 40 to 80 mg at three- to seven-day intervals as needed and tolerated up to a total of 240 mg a day if necessary.

Antihypertensive—

Oral, initially 40 mg once a day, the dosage being increased in increments of 40 to 80 mg at one-week intervals as needed and tolerated up to a total of 320 mg a day if necessary.

[Vascular headache prophylactic][1]—

Oral, 20 to 40 mg once a day initially, the dosage being gradually increased as tolerated up to 120 mg per day if necessary.

Note: Geriatric patients may have increased or decreased sensitivity to the effects of the usual adult dose.

Because of the long half-life, once-a-day dosage is sufficient to provide stable plasma concentrations; however, such steady-state concentrations may not be achieved for up to 5 days following initiation of therapy or change of dose.

For patients with renal function impairment, the following dosage adjustments are recommended:

Creatinine clearance (mL/min/1.73m)	Dosage interval (hours)
>50	24
31–50	24–36
10–30	24–48
<10	40–60

Usual pediatric dose
Dosage has not been established.

Strength(s) usually available
U.S.—

20 mg (Rx) [*Corgard* (scored); GENERIC].

40 mg (Rx) [*Corgard* (scored); GENERIC].

80 mg (Rx) [*Corgard* (scored); GENERIC].

120 mg (Rx) [*Corgard* (scored); GENERIC].

160 mg (Rx) [*Corgard* (scored); GENERIC].

Canada—

40 mg (Rx) [*Corgard* (scored); *Syn-Nadolol* (scored); GENERIC].

80 mg (Rx) [*Corgard* (partially scored); *Syn-Nadolol* (partially scored); GENERIC].

160 mg (Rx) [*Corgard* (scored); *Syn-Nadolol* (scored); GENERIC].

Packaging and storage
Store between 15 and 30 °C (59 and 86 °F), unless otherwise specified by manufacturer. Store in a tight, light-resistant container.

Auxiliary labeling
• Do not take other medicine without your doctor's advice.

Note
Check refill frequency to determine compliance in hypertensive patients.

[1]Not included in Canadian product labeling.

OXPRENOLOL

Summary of Differences

Pharmacology/pharmacokinetics:
Mechanism of action/Effect—Moderate intrinsic sympathomimetic activity (ISA); nonselective; moderate lipid solubility.
Absorption—Bioavailability significantly reduced by first-pass metabolism.
Protein binding—High.
Precautions:
Medical considerations/contraindications—Dosage reduction necessary in hepatic function impairment but not necessary in renal function impairment.
Side/adverse effects:
Theoretical reduced risk of bronchospasm, heart failure, and peripheral vasoconstriction because of ISA.

Oral Dosage Forms

Note: Dosage and strengths of the dosage forms available are expressed in terms of the hydrochloride salt.

OXPRENOLOL TABLETS USP

Usual adult dose
Antihypertensive—
Oral, 20 mg three times a day initially, the dosage being increased in increments of 60 mg per day every one to two weeks until the desired response is achieved, usually in the range of 120 to 320 mg a day.
Note: Once the optimal daily dose has been reached, twice-daily dosing may be used.
Geriatric patients may have increased or decreased sensitivity to the effects of the usual adult dose.

Usual adult prescribing limits
480 mg per day.

Usual pediatric dose
Dosage has not been established.

Strength(s) usually available
U.S.—
Not commercially available.
Canada—
20 mg (hydrochloride) (Rx) [*Trasicor*].
40 mg (hydrochloride) (Rx) [*Trasicor* (scored)].
80 mg (hydrochloride) (Rx) [*Trasicor* (scored)].

Packaging and storage
Store below 40 °C (104 °F), preferably between 15 and 30 °C (59 and 86 °F), in a well-closed container, unless otherwise specified by manufacturer. Protect from light.

Auxiliary labeling
• Do not take other medicine without your doctor's advice.

Note
Check refill frequency to determine compliance in hypertensive patients.

OXPRENOLOL EXTENDED-RELEASE TABLETS USP

Usual adult dose
Antihypertensive—
Oral, usually 120 to 320 mg a day administered once a day in the morning for maintenance of established dosage requirements.
Note: Geriatric patients may have increased or decreased sensitivity to the effects of the usual adult dose.

Usual pediatric dose
Dosage has not been established.

Strength(s) usually available
U.S.—
Not commercially available.
Canada—
80 mg (hydrochloride) (Rx) [*Slow-Trasicor* (lactose)].
160 mg (hydrochloride) (Rx) [*Slow-Trasicor* (lactose)].

Packaging and storage
Store below 40 °C (104 °F), preferably between 15 and 30 °C (59 and 86 °F), in a well-closed container, unless otherwise specified by manufacturer. Protect from light.

Auxiliary labeling
• Do not take other medicine without your doctor's advice.

Note
Check refill frequency to determine compliance in hypertensive patients.

PENBUTOLOL

Summary of Differences

Pharmacology/pharmacokinetics:
Mechanism of action/Effect—Moderate intrinsic sympathomimetic activity (ISA); high lipid solubility; nonselective.
Biotransformation—Although hepatically metabolized, penbutolol undergoes no significant first-pass effect.
Protein binding—High to very high.
Elimination—Not removable by hemodialysis.
Precautions:
Breast-feeding—Not known whether distributed into breast milk.
Medical considerations/contraindications—Dosage reduction necessary in hepatic function impairment but not necessary in renal function impairment.
Side/adverse effects:
Theoretical reduced risk of bronchospasm, heart failure, and peripheral vasoconstriction because of ISA.

Oral Dosage Forms

PENBUTOLOL SULFATE TABLETS

Usual adult dose
Antihypertensive—
Oral, 20 mg once a day.
Note: Geriatric patients may have increased or decreased sensitivity to the effects of the usual adult dose.

Usual pediatric dose
Dosage has not been established.

Strength(s) usually available
U.S.—
20 mg (Rx) [*Levatol* (scored; lactose)].
Canada—
Not commercially available.

Packaging and storage
Store below 40 °C (104 °F), preferably between 15 and 30 °C (59 and 86 °F), in a well-closed container, unless otherwise specified by manufacturer. Protect from light.

Auxiliary labeling
• Do not take other medicine without your doctor's advice.

Note
Check refill frequency to determine compliance in hypertensive patients.

PINDOLOL

Summary of Differences

Pharmacology/pharmacokinetics:
Mechanism of action/Effect—Exhibits the most intrinsic sympathomimetic activity (ISA) of beta-blockers currently available; moderate lipid solubility; nonselective.
Biotransformation—Although hepatically metabolized, pindolol undergoes no significant first-pass effect.
Protein binding—Moderate.
Precautions:
Medical considerations/contraindications—Dosage reduction necessary in hepatic function and severe renal function impairment.
Side/adverse effects:
Theoretical reduced risk of bronchospasm, heart failure, and peripheral vasoconstriction because of ISA; overdose may produce tachycardia and hypertension.

Oral Dosage Forms

Note: Bracketed uses in the *Dosage Forms* section refer to categories of use and/or indications that are not included in U.S. product labeling.

PINDOLOL TABLETS USP

Usual adult dose
Antihypertensive—
Oral, initially 5 mg two times a day, the dosage being increased in increments of 10 mg per day at two- or three-week intervals as needed and tolerated up to a maximum of 45 mg a day (Canada) or 60 mg a day (U.S.).
Note: Many hypertensive patients require a maintenance dose of only 5 mg of pindolol two times a day to provide an adequate reduction in blood pressure.

Once the optimal daily dose has been reached, once-daily dosing may be used.

Geriatric patients may have increased or decreased sensitivity to the effects of the usual adult dose.

[Antianginal]—
Oral, 5 mg three times a day, the dosage being increased at one to two week intervals up to a maximum of 40 mg per day.

Usual adult prescribing limits
45 mg a day (Canada) or 60 mg a day (U.S.).

Usual pediatric dose
Dosage has not been established.

Strength(s) usually available
U.S.—
5 mg (Rx) [*Visken* (scored); GENERIC].
10 mg (Rx) [*Visken* (scored); GENERIC].
Canada—
5 mg (Rx) [*Novo-Pindol; Syn-Pindolol; Visken* (scored); GENERIC].
10 mg (Rx) [*Novo-Pindol; Syn-Pindolol; Visken* (scored); GENERIC].
15 mg (Rx) [*Novo-Pindol; Syn-Pindolol; Visken* (scored); GENERIC].

Packaging and storage
Store below 40 °C (104 °F), preferably between 15 and 30 °C (59 and 86 °F), in a well-closed container, unless otherwise specified by manufacturer. Protect from light.

Auxiliary labeling
- Do not take other medicine without your doctor's advice.

Note
Check refill frequency to determine compliance in hypertensive patients.

PROPRANOLOL

Summary of Differences

Pharmacology/pharmacokinetics:
Mechanism of action/Effect—Nonselective; high lipid solubility.
Absorption—Bioavailability significantly reduced by first-pass metabolism.
Protein binding—Very high.
Elimination—Not removable by hemodialysis.
Precautions:
Medical considerations/contraindications—Dosage reduction necessary in hepatic function impairment but not necessary in renal function impairment.
Side/adverse effects:
Increased risk of CNS side effects because of high lipid solubility and ease of penetration into CNS.

Oral Dosage Forms

Note: Bracketed uses in the *Dosage Forms* section refer to categories of use and/or indications that are not included in U.S. product labeling.

PROPRANOLOL HYDROCHLORIDE EXTENDED-RELEASE CAPSULES USP

Usual adult dose
Antihypertensive—
Oral, 80 mg once a day, the dosage being increased gradually up to 160 mg once a day. Doses up to 640 mg per day may be needed in some patients.
Antianginal—
Oral, 80 mg once a day, the dosage being increased gradually at three- to seven-day intervals as needed up to 320 mg per day.
Vascular headache prophylaxis—
Oral, 80 mg once a day, the dosage being increased gradually as needed up to 240 mg once a day.

Note: Geriatric patients may have increased or decreased sensitivity to the effects of the usual adult dose.

Usual pediatric dose
Dosage has not been established.

Strength(s) usually available
U.S.—
60 mg (Rx) [*Inderal LA;* GENERIC].
80 mg (Rx) [*Inderal LA;* GENERIC].
120 mg (Rx) [*Inderal LA;* GENERIC].
160 mg (Rx) [*Inderal LA;* GENERIC].
Canada—
60 mg (Rx) [*Inderal LA* (sulfites)].
80 mg (Rx) [*Inderal LA* (sulfites)].
120 mg (Rx) [*Inderal LA* (sulfites)].
160 mg (Rx) [*Inderal LA* (sulfites)].

Packaging and storage
Store below 40 °C (104 °F), preferably between 15 and 30 °C (59 and 86 °F), unless otherwise specified by manufacturer. Protect from light.

Auxiliary labeling
- Do not take other medicine without your doctor's advice.

Note
Check refill frequency to determine compliance in hypertensive patients.

PROPRANOLOL HYDROCHLORIDE ORAL SOLUTION

Usual adult dose
Antianginal—
Oral, 80 to 320 mg per day given in two, three, or four divided doses.
Antiarrhythmic—
Oral, 10 to 30 mg three or four times a day, the dosage being adjusted as needed and tolerated.
Antihypertensive—
Oral, 40 mg two times a day, the dosage being increased gradually as needed and tolerated, usually 120 to 240 mg a day; doses up to a total of 640 mg a day may be necessary (a total daily dose of 1 gram has been used by some clinicians).
Hypertrophic cardiomyopathy therapy adjunct—
Oral, 20 to 40 mg three or four times a day, the dosage being adjusted as needed and tolerated.
Myocardial infarction—
Oral, 180 to 240 mg a day in divided doses.
Pheochromocytoma therapy adjunct—
Oral, 20 mg three times a day to 40 mg three or four times a day (as necessary for sufficient beta-blockade) for three days prior to surgery, concomitantly with alpha-adrenergic blocking medication (should *never* be started until alpha-adrenergic blockade is at least partially established). Doses of 30 to 160 mg per day in divided doses have been used for management of inoperable tumor.
Vascular headache prophylactic—
Oral, 20 mg four times a day initially, the dosage being increased gradually as needed and tolerated up to a total of 240 mg a day if necessary.
Antitremor agent—
Oral, 40 mg two times a day, the dosage being adjusted as needed and tolerated, up to 120 mg a day; occasionally, doses up to 320 mg a day may be needed.
[Antianxiety therapy adjunct][1]—
Oral, 10 to 80 mg thirty to ninety minutes prior to the anxiety-provoking activity.
[Thyrotoxicosis therapy adjunct][1]—
Oral, 10 to 40 mg three or four times a day, the dosage being adjusted as needed and tolerated.

Note: Twice-daily or, in some patients, once-daily dosing may be effective for use as an antianginal, antihypertensive, or for myocardial infarction.

Geriatric patients may have increased or decreased sensitivity to the effects of the usual adult dose.

Usual pediatric dose
Antiarrhythmic
Antihypertensive—
Initial: Oral, 500 mcg (0.5 mg) to 1 mg per kg of body weight per day in two to four divided doses has been used as an initial dose, the dosage being adjusted as necessary to treat hypertension and prevent supraventricular tachycardia.
Maintenance: Oral, 2 to 4 mg per kg per day in two divided doses.

Strength(s) usually available
U.S.—
4 mg per mL (Rx) [GENERIC].
8 mg per mL (Rx) [GENERIC].
80 mg per mL (concentrated; must be diluted) (Rx) [GENERIC].
Canada—
Not commercially available.

Packaging and storage
Store below 40 °C (104 °F), preferably between 15 and 30 °C (59 and 86 °F), in a well-closed container, unless otherwise specified by manufacturer. Protect from light. Protect from freezing.

Preparation of dosage form
Propranolol concentrated oral solution is prepared for administration by mixing it with a liquid such as water, juice, or soda or soda-like bev-

erage. After the patient drinks the mixture, the glass should be rinsed with more liquid to make sure all the medication is taken. Propranolol concentrated oral solution may also be mixed with semi-solid food such as applesauce or pudding.

Auxiliary labeling

- Do not take other medicine without your doctor's advice.

Note

Check refill frequency to determine compliance in hypertensive patients.

PROPRANOLOL HYDROCHLORIDE TABLETS USP

Usual adult dose

See *Propranolol Hydrochloride Oral Solution.*

Usual pediatric dose

See *Propranolol Hydrochloride Oral Solution.*

Strength(s) usually available

U.S.—

10 mg (Rx) [*Inderal* (scored); GENERIC].
20 mg (Rx) [*Inderal* (scored); GENERIC (may be scored)].
40 mg (Rx) [*Inderal* (scored); GENERIC (may be scored)].
60 mg (Rx) [*Inderal* (scored); GENERIC (may be scored)].
80 mg (Rx) [*Inderal* (scored); GENERIC (may be scored)].
90 mg (Rx) [*Inderal* (scored); GENERIC (may be scored)].

Canada—

10 mg (Rx) [*Apo-Propranolol* (scored); *Detensol* (scored); *Inderal* (scored); *Novopranol* (scored); *pms Propranolol* (scored); GENERIC].
20 mg (Rx) [*Apo-Propranolol* (scored); *Novopranol* (scored); *Inderal* (scored); GENERIC].
40 mg (Rx) [*Apo-Propranolol* (scored); *Detensol* (scored); *Inderal* (scored); *Novopranol* (scored); *pms Propranolol* (scored); GENERIC].
80 mg (Rx) [*Apo-Propranolol* (scored); *Detensol* (scored); *Inderal* (scored); *Novopranol* (scored); *pms Propranolol* (scored); GENERIC].
120 mg (Rx) [*Apo-Propranolol* (scored); *Inderal* (scored); *Novopranol* (scored); *pms Propranolol* (scored); GENERIC].

Packaging and storage

Store below 40 °C (104 °F), preferably between 15 and 30 °C (59 and 86 °F), unless otherwise specified by manufacturer. Store in a well-closed, light-resistant container.

Auxiliary labeling

- Do not take other medicine without your doctor's advice.

Note

Check refill frequency to determine compliance in hypertensive patients.

Parenteral Dosage Forms

PROPRANOLOL HYDROCHLORIDE INJECTION USP

Usual adult dose

Antiarrhythmic—

Intravenous, 1 to 3 mg administered at a rate not to exceed 1 mg per minute, repeated after two minutes and again after four hours if necessary.

Note: An intravenous dose of one-tenth the oral dose may be used to temporarily replace oral dosing in patients undergoing surgery.

Geriatric patients may have increased or decreased sensitivity to the effects of the usual adult dose.

Usual pediatric dose

Antiarrhythmic—

Slow intravenous, 10 to 100 mcg (0.01 to 0.1 mg) per kg of body weight (up to a maximum of 1 mg per dose), repeated every six to eight hours if necessary.

Strength(s) usually available

U.S.—

1 mg per mL (Rx) [*Inderal;* GENERIC].

Canada—

1 mg per mL (Rx) [*Inderal*].

Packaging and storage

Store below 40 °C (104 °F), preferably between 15 and 30 °C (59 and 86 °F), unless otherwise specified by manufacturer. Store in a light-resistant container. Protect from freezing.

[1]Not included in Canadian product labeling.

SOTALOL

Summary of Differences

Pharmacology/pharmacokinetics:

Mechanism of action/Effect—Nonselective; no intrinsic sympathomimetic activity (ISA) or membrane-stabilizing activity; low lipid solubility.

Protein binding—Not protein bound.

Elimination—Removable by hemodialysis.

Oral Dosage Forms

Note: Bracketed uses in the *Dosage Forms* section refer to categories of use and/or indications that are not included in U.S. product labeling.

SOTALOL HYDROCHLORIDE TABLETS

Usual adult dose

[Antianginal]

[Antihypertensive]—

Initial: Oral, 80 mg two times a day, the dosage being increased in increments of 80 mg two times a day at weekly intervals as needed and tolerated.

Maintenance: Oral, 160 mg two times a day.

Note: Once-daily dosing may be effective in patients taking a total daily maintenance dose of 320 mg or less.

Geriatric patients may have increased or decreased sensitivity to the effects of the usual adult dose.

Antiarrhythmic[1]—

Initial: Oral, 80 mg two times a day, the dosage being increased gradually.

Maintenance: Oral, 160 to 320 mg per day, given in two or three divided doses.

Note: It is recommended that the dosage interval be increased in patients with renal function impairment as follows:

Creatinine clearance (mL/min)	Dosage interval (hrs)
>60	12
30–60	24
10–30	36–48
<10	Dosage and dosing interval must be individualized

Usual adult prescribing limits

For life-threatening arrhythmias—640 mg per day.
For other indications—480 mg per day.

Usual pediatric dose

Dosage has not been established.

Strength(s) usually available

U.S.—

80 mg (Rx) [*Betapace* (scored)].
120 mg (Rx) [*Betapace*].
160 mg (Rx) [*Betapace* (scored)].
240 mg (Rx) [*Betapace* (scored)].

Canada—

160 mg (Rx) [*Sotacor* (scored)].

Packaging and storage

Store below 40 °C (104 °F), preferably between 15 and 30 °C (59 and 86 °F), in a well-closed container, unless otherwise specified by manufacturer.

Auxiliary labeling

- Do not take other medicines without your doctor's advice.

Note

Check refill frequency to determine compliance in hypertensive patients.

[1]Not included in Canadian product labeling.

TIMOLOL

Summary of Differences

Pharmacology/pharmacokinetics:

Mechanism of action/Effect—Nonselective; no significant intrinsic sympathomimetic activity (ISA); moderate lipid solubility.

Absorption—Bioavailability significantly reduced by first-pass metabolism.

Protein binding—Very low.
Elimination—Not removable by hemodialysis.

Precautions:
Medical considerations/contraindications—Dosage reduction necessary in hepatic function impairment but not necessary in renal function impairment.

Oral Dosage Forms

Note: Bracketed uses in the *Dosage Forms* section refer to categories of use and/or indications that are not included in U.S. product labeling.

TIMOLOL MALEATE TABLETS USP

Usual adult dose

Antihypertensive
[Antianginal]—
Initial: Oral, 10 mg two times a day initially, the dosage being increased at one-week intervals as needed and tolerated.
Maintenance: Oral, usually 20 to 40 mg per day; doses up to 60 mg per day divided into two doses may be necessary.

Myocardial infarction[1]—
Oral, 10 mg two times a day prophylactically against reinfarction in clinically stable patients. Treatment is initiated one to four weeks following initial infarction.

Vascular headache prophylactic—
Oral, 10 mg two times a day initially; maintenance, 20 mg a day (may be given as a single daily dose); maximum dose is 30 mg per day (10 mg in the morning and 20 mg at night).

Note: Geriatric patients may have increased or decreased sensitivity to the effects of the usual adult dose.

Usual pediatric dose

Dosage has not been established.

Strength(s) usually available

U.S.—
5 mg (Rx) [*Blocadren;* GENERIC].
10 mg (Rx) [*Blocadren* (scored); GENERIC].
20 mg (Rx) [*Blocadren* (scored); GENERIC].

Canada—
5 mg (Rx) [*Apo-Timol* (scored); *Blocadren* (scored); *Novo-Timol;* GENERIC].
10 mg (Rx) [*Apo-Timol* (scored); *Blocadren* (scored); *Novo-Timol;* GENERIC].
20 mg (Rx) [*Apo-Timol; Blocadren* (scored); *Novo-Timol;* GENERIC].

Packaging and storage

Store below 40 °C (104 °F), preferably between 15 and 30 °C (59 and 86 °F), unless otherwise specified by manufacturer. Store in a well-closed, light-resistant container.

Auxiliary labeling

• Do not take other medicine without your doctor's advice.

Note

Check refill frequency to determine compliance in hypertensive patients.

[1]Not included in Canadian product labeling.

Selected Bibliography

Prichard BN, Tomlinson B. The additional properties of beta adrenoreceptor blocking drugs. J Cardiovasc Pharmacol 1986; 8(Suppl 4): S1-S15.

For betaxolol

Beresford R, Heel RC. Betaxolol. A review of its pharmacodynamic and pharmacokinetic properties, and therapeutic efficacy in hypertension. Drugs 1986; 31: 6-28.

For bisoprolol

Lancaster SG, Sorkin EM. Bisoprolol. A preliminary review of its pharmacodynamic and pharmacokinetic properties, and therapeutic efficacy in hypertension and angina pectoris. Drugs 1988; 36: 256-85.

For sotalol

Singh BN, Deedwania P, Nademanee K, Ward A, Sorkin EM. Sotalol. A review of its pharmacodynamic and pharmacokinetic properties, and therapeutic use. Drugs 1987; 34: 311-49.

General

Gerber JG, Nies AS. Beta-adrenergic blocking drugs. Ann Rev Med 1985; 36: 145-64.

Drayer DE. Lipophilicity, hydrophilicity, and the central nervous system side effects of beta blockers. Pharmacother 1987; 7(4): 87-91.

For acebutolol

Singh BN, Thoden WR, Wahl J. Acebutolol: a review of its pharmacology, pharmacokinetics, clinical uses, and adverse effects. Pharmacother 1986 Mar/Apr; 6: 45-63.

Anonymous. Acebutolol. Med Lett Drugs Ther 1985 Jul 5; 27: 58-9.

De Bono G, Kaye CM, Roland E, Summers AJH. Acebutolol: ten years of experience. Am Heart J 1985 May; 109: 1211-23.

For carteolol

Luther RR, Glassman HN, Jordan DC, et al. Long-term treatment of angina pectoris with carteolol. J Int Med Res 1986; 14: 167-74.

Luther RR, Maurath CJ, Klepper MJ, et al. Carteolol treatment of essential hypertension. J Int Med Res 1986; 14: 175-84.

For labetalol

Blakey B, Williams LL, Lopez LM, Stein GH. Labetalol HCl: alpha- and beta-blocking properties may offer advantages over pure beta-blockers. Hosp Form 1987 Oct; 22: 864-9.

Weintraub M, Evans P. Labetalol: an alpha-blocker for treatment of hypertension. Hosp Form 1984 Apr; 19: 295-305.

MacCarthy EP, Bloomfield SS. Labetalol: a review of its pharmacology, pharmacokinetics, clinical uses, and adverse effects. Pharmacother 1983 Jul/Aug; 3: 193-219.

For oxprenolol

Weintraub M, Standish R. Oxprenolol: a nonselective beta blocking agent with intrinsic sympathomimetic activity. Hosp Form 1984 May; 19: 359-65.

For penbutolol

Marone C, Perisic M, Borer M. Antihypertensive efficacy and tolerance of penbutolol. Results of a cooperative study in 227 patients. Curr Med Res Opin 1985; 9: 417-25.

Revised: 07/13/2005

Table 1. Pharmacology/Pharmacokinetics

Drug	Site of Effect	Oral Absorption (%)	Protein Binding	Biotransformation	Half-life (hr)	Time to Peak Effect—Single dose (hr)	Elimination (% unchanged)	Removable by Hemodialysis
Acebutolol	Beta-1*	70†	Low (26%)	Hepatic‡	3–4‡	2.5‡	30–40% Renal; 50–60% Biliary/fecal	Yes
Atenolol	Beta-1*	50–60	Very low to low (6–16%)	Hepatic (minimal)	6–7§	2–4	85–100% Renal	Yes**
Betaxolol	Beta-1*	80–89†	Moderate (50–55%)	Hepatic	14–22§	3–4	>80% (15) Renal	No
Bisoprolol	Beta-1	80–90	Low (26–33%)	Hepatic	9–12		Renal (50) <2% Fecal	No
Carteolol	Beta-1; Beta-2	85	Low (23–30%)	Hepatic (minimal)	6§	1–3	Renal (50–70)	?
Labetalol	Beta-1; Beta-2	100†	Moderate (50%)	Hepatic	6–8 (oral); 5.5 (IV)	2–4 (oral); 5 min (IV)	55–60% (<5) Renal; Biliary/fecal	No
Metoprolol	Beta-1*	95†	Low (12%)	Hepatic	3–7§	1–2 (oral—regular); 6–12 (oral—long-acting); 20 min (IV)	Renal (3–10)	No
Nadolol	Beta-1; Beta-2	30	Very low to low (4 to 30%)	None	20–24§	4	Renal (70)	Yes
Oxprenolol	Beta-1; Beta-2	90†	High (80%)	Hepatic	1.3–1.5	?	Renal (<5)	?
Penbutolol	Beta-1; Beta-2	100	High to very high (80–98%)	Hepatic	5§	1.5–3	90% (0) Renal	No
Pindolol	Beta-1; Beta-2	90–100	Moderate (40%)	Hepatic	3–4§	1–2	Renal (40)	?
Propranolol	Beta-1; Beta-2	90†	Very high (93%)	Hepatic	3–5	1–1.5	Renal (<1)	No
Sotalol	Beta-1; Beta-2	> 80	None	Hepatic	7–18§	2–3	Renal (75)	Yes
Timolol	Beta-1; Beta-2	90†	Very low (<10%)	Hepatic	4	1–2	Renal (20); Fecal	No

*Cardioselectivity tends to diminish with increased dosage.

†First-pass metabolism results in a decrease (usually significant) in bioavailability. Acebutolol—The effect is not reduced because of the active metabolite. Bioavailability of acebutolol may be increased 2-fold in the elderly because of reduced first-pass metabolism and renal function. Betaxolol—First-pass effect is small.

‡Acebutolol—Major metabolite (diacetolol) is pharmacologically active and even more cardioselective than acebutolol; time to peak effect is 3.5 hours; the half-life of diacetolol is 8 to 13 hours.

§Atenolol—Increased to 16–27 hours or more in patients with renal function impairment (up to 144 hours when severe). Betaxolol—Increased by approximately 33% in hepatic function impairment, but clearance unchanged.—Approximately doubled in renal function impairment; dosage reduction necessary. Carteolol—Prolonged in renal failure. Metoprolol—No change in renal failure. Nadolol—Increased in renal failure. Penbutolol—Increased in renal failure. Pindolol—Varies from 2.5 to more than 30 hours in patients with hepatic function impairment.—Increased to 3 to 11.5 hours in patients with renal function impairment.—Increased to an average of 7 hours (and as high as 15 hours) in the elderly. Sotalol—Increased in renal failure.

**Atenolol—Patients should receive 50 mg of atenolol after each dialysis and remain under supervision since marked hypotension may occur.

BETA-ADRENERGIC BLOCKING AGENTS AND THIAZIDE DIURETICS Systemic

This monograph includes information on the following: 1) Atenolol and Chlorthalidone; 2) Bisoprolol and Hydrochlorothiazide; 3) Metoprolol and Hydrochlorothiazide; 4) Nadolol and Bendroflumethiazide; 5) Pindolol and Hydrochlorothiazide; 6) Propranolol and Hydrochlorothiazide; 7) Timolol and Hydrochlorothiazide.

VA CLASSIFICATION (Primary): CV408

Commonly used brand name(s): *Corzide[4]; Corzide 40/5[4]; Corzide 80/5[4]; Inderide[6]; Inderide LA[6]; Lopressor HCT[3]; Tenoretic[1]; Tenoretic 100[1]; Tenoretic 50[1]; Timolide[7]; Timolide 10-25[7]; Viskazide[5]; Ziac[2]*.

NOTE: The *Beta-adrenergic Blocking Agents and Thiazide Diuretics (Systemic)* monograph is maintained on the *USP DI* electronic data base. A copy of the most recent revision of the complete monograph can be accessed on the *USP DI* Updates Online website. See the front cover of book for details on accessing the site.

For information on the specific components of this combination, see the *USP DI* monographs for *Beta-adrenergic Blocking Agents (Systemic)* and *Diuretics, Thiazide (Systemic)*.

The information that follows is selectively abstracted from the complete monograph and is provided to facilitate drug use review and patient counseling.

Note: For a listing of dosage forms and brand names by country availability, see *Dosage Forms* section(s).

Category

Antihypertensive.

Indications

Accepted

Hypertension (treatment)—Beta-adrenergic blocking agent (beta-blocker) and thiazide diuretic combinations are indicated in the management of hypertension.

Fixed-dosage combinations generally are not recommended for initial therapy, but are utilized in maintenance therapy after the required dose is established, in order to increase convenience, economy, and patient compliance.

For additional information on initial therapeutic guidelines related to the treatment of hypertension, see *Appendix III*.

Patient Consultation

As an aid to patient consultation, refer to *Advice for the Patient, Beta-adrenergic Blocking Agents and Thiazide Diuretics (Systemic)*.

In providing consultation, consider emphasizing the following selected information (» = major clinical significance):

Before using this medication

» Conditions affecting use, especially:

Sensitivity to the beta-adrenergic blocking agent prescribed, or to any thiazide diuretic or other sulfonamide-type medications

Pregnancy—Risk of hypoglycemia, respiratory depression, bradycardia, and hypotension with beta-adrenergic blocking agents; thiazide diuretics may cause jaundice, thrombocytopenia, hypokalemia in infant

Breast-feeding—Distributed into breast milk; not known for bisoprolol

Use in the elderly—Increased sensitivity to effects; increased risk of beta-blocker-induced hypothermia

Other medications, especially allergen immunotherapy or skin testing, oral antidiabetic agents, calcium channel blocking agents, clonidine, cocaine, digitalis glycosides, guanabenz, insulin, lithium, MAO inhibitors, sympathomimetics, or xanthines

Other medical problems, especially anuria or severe renal function impairment, bronchial asthma, cardiogenic shock, congestive heart failure, diabetes mellitus, emphysema or nonallergenic bronchitis, history of allergy, hyperthyroidism, hypotension, mental depression, overt cardiac failure, second or third degree AV block, or sinus bradycardia

Proper use of this medication

Possible need for control of weight and diet, especially sodium intake

» Compliance with therapy; patient may not experience symptoms of hypertension; importance of taking medication only as directed and keeping appointments with physician, even if feeling well

» Does not cure, but helps control hypertension; possible need for lifelong therapy; serious consequences of untreated hypertension

Proper administration of extended-release dosage forms: Swallowing whole without crushing, breaking, or chewing

Getting into habit of taking at same time each day to help increase compliance

Checking pulse as directed (checking with physician if less than 50 beats per minute)

Diuretic effects of the medication and timing of doses to minimize inconvenience of diuresis

» Importance of not missing doses, especially with schedules of one dose per day

» Proper dosing

Missed dose: Taking as soon as possible; not taking at all if within 4 hours of next scheduled dose (8 hours for atenolol and chlorthalidone, nadolol and bendroflumethiazide, or extended-release propranolol and hydrochlorothiazide); not doubling doses

» Proper storage

Precautions while using this medication

Regular visits to physician to check progress

» Checking with physician before discontinuing medication; gradual dosage reduction may be necessary

Having enough medication on hand to get through weekends, holidays, and vacations; possibly carrying second written prescription for emergency use

Carrying medical identification during therapy

» Not taking other medications, especially nonprescription sympathomimetics, unless discussed with physician

» Caution if any kind of surgery (including dental surgery) or emergency treatment is required

» Diabetics: May mask signs and symptoms of hypoglycemia or cause increased blood glucose concentrations

» Possibility of hypokalemia; possible need for additional potassium in diet; not changing diet without first checking with physician

To prevent dehydration, checking with physician if severe nausea, vomiting, or diarrhea occurs and continues

» Caution when driving or doing things requiring alertness, because of possible drowsiness, dizziness, or lightheadedness

Caution during exposure to cold weather because of possible increased sensitivity to cold

Possible skin photosensitivity; avoiding unprotected exposure to sun; using protective clothing and sun block product; avoiding use of sunlamp, tanning bed, or tanning booth

Caution if any laboratory tests required; possible interference with test results

Patients with allergies to foods, medications, or stinging insect venom: Possible increase in severity of allergic reactions; checking with physician immediately if severe allergic reaction occurs

Side/adverse effects

Signs of potential side effects, especially electrolyte imbalance, bradycardia, bronchospasm, congestive heart failure, mental depression, reduced peripheral circulation, allergic reaction, arrhythmias, agranulocytosis, back pain, joint pain, chest pain, cholecystitis, pancreatitis, confusion (especially in elderly), hallucinations, hepatotoxicity, hyperuricemia, gout, leukopenia, psoriasiform eruption, and thrombocytopenia

---

ATENOLOL AND CHLORTHALIDONE

Summary of Differences

Atenolol:

Pharmacology/pharmacokinetics—

Mechanism of action/effect: Relatively cardioselective (beta-1); very low lipid solubility.

Biotransformation: Minimal hepatic metabolism.

Elimination: Removable by hemodialysis.

Precautions—

Medical considerations/contraindications: Dosage reduction necessary in renal function impairment but not necessary in hepatic function impairment.

Side/adverse effects—

Theoretical reduced risk of bronchospasm, hypoglycemia, and peripheral vasoconstriction because of cardioselectivity.

Chlorthalidone:

Pharmacology/pharmacokinetics—

Although not chemically the same, chlorthalidone has the same actions as the thiazide diuretics.

Oral Dosage Forms

ATENOLOL AND CHLORTHALIDONE TABLETS

Usual adult dose

Antihypertensive—

Oral, 1 or 2 tablets once a day, as determined by individual titration with the component agents.

Note: Geriatric patients may have increased or decreased sensitivity to the effects of the usual adult dose.

Usual pediatric dose

Dosage has not been established.

Strength(s) usually available

U.S.—

50 mg of atenolol and 25 mg of chlorthalidone (Rx) [*Tenoretic 50* (scored); GENERIC].

100 mg of atenolol and 25 mg of chlorthalidone (Rx) [*Tenoretic 100*; GENERIC].

Canada—

50 mg of atenolol and 25 mg of chlorthalidone (Rx) [*Tenoretic* (scored)].

100 mg of atenolol and 25 mg of chlorthalidone (Rx) [*Tenoretic* (scored)].

Auxiliary labeling

- Do not take other medicines without your doctor's advice.

BISOPROLOL AND HYDROCHLOROTHIAZIDE

Summary of Differences

Bisoprolol:
Pharmacology/pharmacokinetics—
Mechanism of action/effect: Relatively cardioselective (beta-1).
Protein binding: Low.
Precautions—
Breast-feeding: Not known if distributed into breast milk.

Oral Dosage Forms

BISOPROLOL FUMARATE AND HYDROCHLOROTHIAZIDE TABLETS

Usual adult dose
Antihypertensive—
Oral, 1 or 2 tablets once a day, as determined by individual titration with the component agents.

Note: Geriatric patients may have increased or decreased sensitivity to the effects of the usual adult dose.

Usual pediatric dose
Dosage has not been established.

Strength(s) usually available
U.S.—
2.5 mg of bisoprolol and 6.25 mg of hydrochlorothiazide (Rx) [*Ziac*].
5 mg of bisoprolol and 6.25 mg of hydrochlorothiazide (Rx) [*Ziac*].
10 mg of bisoprolol and 6.25 mg of hydrochlorothiazide (Rx) [*Ziac*].
Canada—
Not commercially available.

Auxiliary labeling
- Do not take other medicine without your doctor's advice.

METOPROLOL AND HYDROCHLOROTHIAZIDE

Summary of Differences

Metoprolol:
Pharmacology/pharmacokinetics—
Mechanism of action/effect: Relatively cardioselective (beta-1); moderate lipid solubility.
Absorption: Bioavailability significantly reduced by first-pass metabolism.
Elimination: Not removable by hemodialysis.
Precautions—
Medical considerations/contraindications: No dosage reduction necessary in hepatic function impairment (unless severe) or renal function impairment.
Side/adverse effects—
Theoretical reduced risk of bronchospasm, hypoglycemia, and peripheral vasoconstriction when daily dosage does not exceed 200 mg, because of cardioselectivity; increased risk of central nervous system (CNS) side effects because of lipid solubility and relative ease of penetration into CNS.

Oral Dosage Forms

METOPROLOL TARTRATE AND HYDROCHLOROTHIAZIDE TABLETS USP

Usual adult dose
Antihypertensive—
Oral, 1 or 2 tablets a day, as a single dose or in divided doses, as determined by individual titration with the component agents.

Note: Geriatric patients may have increased or decreased sensitivity to the effects of the usual adult dose.

Usual pediatric dose
Dosage has not been established.

Strength(s) usually available
U.S.—
50 mg of metoprolol tartrate and 25 mg of hydrochlorothiazide (Rx) [*Lopressor HCT* (scored; lactose)].
100 mg of metoprolol tartrate and 25 mg of hydrochlorothiazide (Rx) [*Lopressor HCT* (scored; lactose)].
100 mg of metoprolol tartrate and 50 mg of hydrochlorothiazide (Rx) [*Lopressor HCT* (scored; lactose)].
Canada—
Not commercially available.

Auxiliary labeling
- Do not take other medicines without your doctor's advice.

NADOLOL AND BENDROFLUMETHIAZIDE

Summary of Differences

Nadolol:
Pharmacology/pharmacokinetics—
Mechanism of action/effect: Nonselective (blocks both beta-1 and beta-2 adrenergic receptors); low lipid solubility.
Biotransformation: Not hepatically metabolized.
Elimination: Removable by hemodialysis.
Precautions—
Medical considerations/contraindications: Dosage reduction or increased dosing intervals recommended in renal function impairment; dosage reduction not necessary in hepatic function impairment.

Oral Dosage Forms

NADOLOL AND BENDROFLUMETHIAZIDE TABLETS USP

Usual adult dose
Antihypertensive—
Oral, 1 tablet once a day, as determined by individual titration with the component agents.

Note: Geriatric patients may have increased or decreased sensitivity to the effects of the usual adult dose.

Usual pediatric dose
Dosage has not been established.

Strength(s) usually available
U.S.—
40 mg of nadolol and 5 mg of bendroflumethiazide (Rx) [*Corzide 40/5* (scored; lactose)].
80 mg of nadolol and 5 mg of bendroflumethiazide (Rx) [*Corzide 80/5* (scored; lactose)].
Canada—
40 mg of nadolol and 5 mg of bendroflumethiazide (Rx) [*Corzide* (scored)].
80 mg of nadolol and 5 mg of bendroflumethiazide (Rx) [*Corzide* (scored)].

Auxiliary labeling
- Do not take other medicines without your doctor's advice.

PINDOLOL AND HYDROCHLOROTHIAZIDE

Summary of Differences

Pindolol:
Pharmacology/pharmacokinetics—
Mechanism of action/effect: Nonselective (blocks both beta-1 and beta-2 adrenergic receptors); exhibits the most intrinsic sympathomimetic activity (ISA) of beta-blockers currently available; moderate lipid solubility.
Biotransformation: Although hepatically metabolized, undergoes no significant first-pass effect.
Precautions—
Medical considerations/contraindications: Dosage reduction necessary in hepatic function impairment and severe renal function impairment.
Side/adverse effects—
Theoretical reduced risk of bronchospasm, heart failure, and peripheral vasoconstriction because of ISA; overdose may produce tachycardia and hypertension.

Oral Dosage Forms

PINDOLOL AND HYDROCHLOROTHIAZIDE TABLETS

Usual adult dose
Antihypertensive—
Oral, 1 or 2 tablets once a day, as determined by individual titration with the component agents.

Note: Geriatric patients may have increased or decreased sensitivity to the effects of the usual adult dose.

Usual pediatric dose
Dosage has not been established.

Strength(s) usually available
U.S.—
Not commercially available.
Canada—
10 mg of pindolol and 25 mg of hydrochlorothiazide (Rx) [*Viskazide*].
10 mg of pindolol and 50 mg of hydrochlorothiazide (Rx) [*Viskazide*].

Auxiliary labeling
- Do not take other medicines without your doctor's advice.

PROPRANOLOL AND HYDROCHLOROTHIAZIDE

Summary of Differences
Propranolol:
Pharmacology/pharmacokinetics—
Mechanism of action/effect: Nonselective (blocks both beta-1 and beta-2 adrenergic receptors); high lipid solubility.
Absorption: Bioavailability significantly reduced by first-pass metabolism.
Elimination: Not removable by hemodialysis.
Precautions—
Medical considerations/contraindications: Dosage reduction necessary in hepatic function impairment but not necessary in renal function impairment.
Side/adverse effects—
Increased risk of CNS side effects because of high lipid solubility and ease of penetration into CNS.

Oral Dosage Forms

PROPRANOLOL HYDROCHLORIDE AND HYDROCHLOROTHIAZIDE EXTENDED-RELEASE CAPSULES USP

Usual adult dose
Antihypertensive—
Oral, 1 capsule a day, as determined by individual titration with the component agents.
Note: Geriatric patients may have increased or decreased sensitivity to the effects of the usual adult dose.

Usual pediatric dose
Dosage has not been established.

Strength(s) usually available
U.S.—
80 mg of propranolol hydrochloride and 50 mg of hydrochlorothiazide (Rx) [*Inderide LA* (lactose)].
120 mg of propranolol hydrochloride and 50 mg of hydrochlorothiazide (Rx) [*Inderide LA* (lactose)].
160 mg of propranolol hydrochloride and 50 mg of hydrochlorothiazide (Rx) [*Inderide LA* (lactose)].
Canada—
Not commercially available.

Auxiliary labeling
- Do not take other medicines without your doctor's advice.

PROPRANOLOL HYDROCHLORIDE AND HYDROCHLOROTHIAZIDE TABLETS USP

Usual adult dose
Antihypertensive—
Oral, 1 or 2 tablets two times a day, as determined by individual titration with the component agents.
Note: Geriatric patients may have increased or decreased sensitivity to the effects of the usual adult dose.

Usual pediatric dose
Dosage has not been established.

Strength(s) usually available
U.S.—
40 mg of propranolol hydrochloride and 25 mg of hydrochlorothiazide (Rx) [*Inderide* (scored); GENERIC (may be scored)].
80 mg of propranolol hydrochloride and 25 mg of hydrochlorothiazide (Rx) [*Inderide* (scored); GENERIC (may be scored)].
Canada—
40 mg of propranolol hydrochloride and 25 mg of hydrochlorothiazide (Rx) [*Inderide* (scored)].
80 mg of propranolol hydrochloride and 25 mg of hydrochlorothiazide (Rx) [*Inderide* (scored)].

Auxiliary labeling
- Do not take other medicines without your doctor's advice.

TIMOLOL AND HYDROCHLOROTHIAZIDE

Summary of Differences
Timolol:
Pharmacology/pharmacokinetics—
Mechanism of action/effect: Nonselective (blocks both beta-1 and beta-2 adrenergic receptors); no significant intrinsic sympathomimetic activity (ISA); moderate lipid solubility.
Absorption: Bioavailability significantly reduced by first-pass metabolism.
Elimination: Not removable by hemodialysis.
Precautions—
Medical considerations/contraindications: Dosage reduction necessary in hepatic function impairment but not necessary in renal function impairment.

Oral Dosage Forms

TIMOLOL MALEATE AND HYDROCHLOROTHIAZIDE TABLETS USP

Usual adult dose
Antihypertensive—
Oral, 1 tablet two times a day or 2 tablets once a day, as determined by individual titration with the component agents.
Note: Geriatric patients may have increased or decreased sensitivity to the effects of the usual adult dose.

Usual pediatric dose
Dosage has not been established.

Strength(s) usually available
U.S.—
10 mg of timolol maleate and 25 mg of hydrochlorothiazide (Rx) [*Timolide 10-25*].
Canada—
10 mg of timolol maleate and 25 mg of hydrochlorothiazide (Rx) [*Timolide*].

Auxiliary labeling
- Do not take other medicine without your doctor's advice.

Revised: 08/12/1998

BETAMETHASONE—See *Corticosteroids—Glucocorticoid Effects (Systemic), Corticosteroids (Ophthalmic), Corticosteroids (Otic), Corticosteroids (Rectal), Corticosteroids (Topical)*

BETAXOLOL—See *Beta-adrenergic Blocking Agents (Ophthalmic), Beta-adrenergic Blocking Agents (Systemic)*

BETHANECHOL Systemic

VA CLASSIFICATION (Primary): AU300
Commonly used brand name(s): *Duvoid; Urabeth; Urecholine.*
Note: For a listing of dosage forms and brand names by country availability, see *Dosage Forms* section(s).

Category
Cholinergic.

Indications
Note: Bracketed information in the *Indications* section refers to uses that are not included in U.S. product labeling.

Accepted
Urinary retention (treatment)—Although it generally has been replaced by more effective agents, bethanechol is indicated for the treatment of acute postoperative nonobstructive urinary retention and for neurogenic atony of the urinary bladder with retention.
[Atony, postoperative, gastric (treatment)][1] or

[Megacolon, congenital (treatment)][1]—Bethanechol is used in certain cases of gastric atony or stasis, and is also used in selected cases of congenital megacolon.

[Reflux, gastroesophageal (treatment)]—Oral bethanechol is used for treatment of gastroesophageal reflux associated with decreased pressure of the lower esophageal sphincter.

---

[1]Not included in Canadian product labeling.

Pharmacology/Pharmacokinetics

Physicochemical characteristics

Molecular weight—196.68.

Mechanism of action/Effect

Bethanechol is a muscarinic cholinomimetic, which acts at cholinergic receptors in the smooth muscle of the urinary bladder and gastrointestinal tract. It increases the tone of the detrusor urinae muscle, producing an increase in the intravesical pressure. It may initiate micturition and empty the bladder; however, its clinical effectiveness in such conditions as voiding dysfunction has not been fully established. It also stimulates gastric and intestinal motility, and increases lower esophageal sphincter pressure.

Other actions/effects

Following oral or subcutaneous administration, cardiovascular effects and nicotinic activity are minimal.

Onset of action

Oral–Within 30 to 90 minutes.

Subcutaneous–Within 5 to 15 minutes.

Time to peak effect

Oral–About 1 hour.

Subcutaneous–Within 15 to 30 minutes.

Duration of action

Oral—Up to 6 hours, depending on dose.

Subcutaneous—About 2 hours.

Precautions to Consider

Pregnancy/Reproduction

Pregnancy—Adequate and well-controlled studies in humans have not been done.

Studies have not been done in animals.

FDA Pregnancy Category C.

Breast-feeding

It is not known whether bethanechol is distributed into breast milk.

Pediatrics

Appropriate studies on the relationship of age to the effects of bethanechol have not been performed in the pediatric population. However, no pediatrics-specific problems have been documented to date.

Geriatrics

Appropriate studies on the relationship of age to the effects of bethanechol have not been performed in the geriatric population. However, geriatric-specific problems that would limit the usefulness of this medication in the elderly are not expected.

Drug interactions and/or related problems

The following drug interactions and/or related problems have been selected on the basis of their potential clinical significance (possible mechanism in parentheses where appropriate)—not necessarily inclusive (» = major clinical significance):

Note: Combinations containing any of the following medications, depending on the amount present, may also interact with this medication.

Cholinergics, other, especially cholinesterase inhibitors
(concurrent use may increase the effects of either these medications or bethanechol and increase the potential for toxicity)

Ganglionic blocking agents, such as mecamylamine, pentolinium, and trimethaphan
(concurrent use with bethanechol may produce a critical fall in blood pressure, which is usually preceded by severe abdominal symptoms)

Procainamide or
Quinidine
(concurrent use may antagonize the cholinergic effects of bethanechol)

Laboratory value alterations

The following have been selected on the basis of their potential clinical significance (possible effect in parentheses where appropriate)—not necessarily inclusive (» = major clinical significance).

With physiology/laboratory test values

Amylase, serum, and
Lipase, serum
(concentrations may be increased because bethanechol stimulates pancreatic secretion and constricts the sphincter of Oddi)

Aspartate aminotransferase, serum (AST [SGOT])
(concentrations may be increased because bethanechol impairs excretion by causing contractions in the sphincter of Oddi)

Medical considerations/Contraindications

The medical considerations/contraindications included have been selected on the basis of their potential clinical significance (reasons given in parentheses where appropriate)—not necessarily inclusive (» = major clinical significance).

Risk-benefit should be considered when the following medical problems exist:

» Asthma, bronchial, active or latent
(bethanechol may cause bronchospasm and may precipitate asthmatic attack)

Atrioventricular conduction defects
(bethanechol may aggravate this condition by decreasing the rate of conduction)

» Bradycardia, pronounced
(bethanechol slows heart rate and may exacerbate the condition)

» Hypotension
(bethanechol may reduce blood pressure)

» Conditions in which increased muscular activity of the gastrointestinal tract or urinary bladder might be harmful, such as:
Anastomosis
Bladder surgery, recent
Gastrointestinal resection

» Conditions in which strength or integrity of gastrointestinal or bladder wall is questionable or

» Gastrointestinal obstruction or
Urinary tract obstruction
(increased muscular activity of the gastrointestinal tract or urinary bladder may be harmful)

» Coronary artery disease, especially occlusion
(bethanechol may decrease coronary blood flow)

Epilepsy
(although no causal relationship has been established, seizures have been reported in patients receiving bethanechol)

Hypertension
(bethanechol may cause sudden fall in blood pressure)

» Hyperthyroidism
(risk of atrial fibrillation may be increased)

» Peptic ulcer
(bethanechol may aggravate symptoms probably by increasing acid secretion and/or by increasing gastric motility)

Parkinsonism or
Vagotonia, marked
(bethanechol may exacerbate these conditions)

» Peritonitis
(bethanechol may increase cramping and exacerbate the condition and increase patient discomfort)

Sensitivity to bethanechol

Side/Adverse Effects

Note: In addition to those side/adverse effects needing medical attention listed below, other severe symptoms of cholinergic overstimulation such as circulatory collapse, hypotension, bloody diarrhea, shock, or sudden cardiac arrest are likely to occur in cases of hypersensitivity or overdosage, and may occur rarely after subcutaneous administration.

The following side/adverse effects have been selected on the basis of their potential clinical significance (possible signs and symptoms in parentheses where appropriate)—not necessarily inclusive:

Those indicating need for medical attention

Incidence rare—more frequent with subcutaneous injection

Shortness of breath, wheezing, or tightness in chest, especially in patients with predisposition to bronchoconstriction

Those indicating need for medical attention only if they continue or are bothersome

Incidence less frequent or rare—more frequent with subcutaneous injection

Belching; blurred vision or change in near or distance vision; diarrhea; frequent urge to urinate

With high doses
CNS stimulation (sleeplessness, nervousness, or jitters); *orthostatic hypotension* (dizziness or lightheadedness; feeling faint); *parasympathetic stimulation* (headache; increased salivation or sweating; nausea or vomiting; redness or flushing of skin or feeling of warmth; stomach discomfort or pain); *seizures*

Overdose

For specific information on the agents used in the management of bethanechol overdose, see:
- *Atropine* in *Anticholinergics/Antispasmodics monograph.*

For more information on the management of overdose or unintentional ingestion, **contact a Poison Control Center** (see *Poison Contol Center Listing*).

Treatment of overdose

Specific treatment—
Treatment consists of subcutaneous administration of atropine in doses of 500 mcg (0.5 mg) to 1 mg for adults and 10 mcg (0.01 mg) per kg of body weight for infants and children, repeated as needed every 2 hours. In emergencies, intravenous injection of atropine may be used to counteract severe toxic cardiovascular or bronchoconstrictor effects of bethanechol.

Patient Consultation

As an aid to patient consultation, refer to *Advice for the Patient, Bethanechol (Systemic).*

In providing consultation, consider emphasizing the following selected information (» = major clinical significance):

Before using this medication

» Conditions affecting use, especially:
Sensitivity to bethanechol
Other medical problems, especially anastomosis, recent bladder surgery or gastrointestinal resection; asthma; pronounced bradycardia or hypotension; coronary artery disease; hyperthyroidism; peptic ulcer; peritonitis; or conditions in which the strength or integrity of the gastrointestinal or bladder wall is in question or in the presence of mechanical obstruction; or marked vagotonia

Proper use of this medication

» Taking medication on an empty stomach to minimize the possibility of nausea and vomiting, unless otherwise directed by physician
» Importance of not taking more medication than the amount prescribed
» Proper dosing
Missed dose: Taking if remembered within an hour or so; not taking if remembered after 2 or more hours; not doubling doses
» Proper storage

Precautions while using this medication

Caution when getting up suddenly from a lying or sitting position

Side/adverse effects

Signs of potential side effects, especially shortness of breath, wheezing, or tightness in chest

General Dosing Information

For oral dosage forms only

Preferably, bethanechol should be taken on an empty stomach to minimize the possibility of nausea and vomiting.

For parenteral dosage forms only

Bethanechol injection is for subcutaneous use *only.* It should *not* be given intravenously or intramuscularly because severe symptoms of cholinergic overstimulation may occur, and the selectivity of bethanechol's action may be decreased.

After administration of bethanechol, the patient should be observed for 30 minutes to 1 hour for possible severe reactions, and a syringe containing a dose of atropine should be immediately available during this period.

Oral Dosage Forms

Note: Bracketed uses in the *Dosage Forms* section refer to categories of use and/or indications that are not included in U.S. product labeling.

BETHANECHOL CHLORIDE TABLETS USP

Usual adult and adolescent dose

Cholinergic—
Oral, 25 to 50 mg three or four times a day.

Note: The minimum effective dose may be determined by administering 5 or 10 mg initially and repeating the same dose at one- to two-hour intervals until a satisfactory response is obtained or up to a maximum of 50 mg; or by administering 10 mg initially, and repeating with 25 mg and then 50 mg at six-hour intervals until the desired response is obtained.

[Treatment of gastroesophageal reflux]—
Oral, 10 to 25 mg four times a day, after meals and at bedtime.

Usual pediatric dose

Cholinergic—
Oral, 0.6 mg per kg of body weight a day in 3 or 4 divided doses.

[Treatment of gastroesophageal reflux]—
Oral, 0.4 mg per kg of body weight a day in 4 divided doses or 3 mg per square meter of body surface every eight hours.

Usual geriatric dose

See *Usual adult and adolescent dose.*

Strength(s) usually available

U.S.—
5 mg (Rx) [*Urabeth; Urecholine;* GENERIC (may be scored)].
10 mg (Rx) [*Duvoid* (scored); *Urabeth; Urecholine* (scored); GENERIC (may be scored)].
25 mg (Rx) [*Duvoid* (scored); *Urabeth; Urecholine* (scored); GENERIC (may be scored)].
50 mg (Rx) [*Duvoid* (scored); *Urabeth; Urecholine* (scored); GENERIC (may be scored)].

Canada—
10 mg (Rx) [*Duvoid* (scored); *Urecholine* (scored)].
25 mg (Rx) [*Duvoid* (scored); *Urecholine* (scored)].
50 mg (Rx) [*Duvoid* (scored)].

Packaging and storage

Store below 40 °C (104 °F), preferably between 15 and 30 °C (59 and 86 °F), unless otherwise specified by manufacturer. Store in a tight container.

Parenteral Dosage Forms

BETHANECHOL CHLORIDE INJECTION USP

Usual adult and adolescent dose

Cholinergic—
Subcutaneous, 5 mg three or four times a day as needed.

Note: The minimum effective dose may be determined by administering 2.5 mg initially and repeating the same dose at 15- to 30-minute intervals up to a maximum of four doses until a satisfactory response is obtained.

Single doses of 10 mg may be required. However, such a large dose may cause severe side effects and should be used only after single doses of 2.5 to 5 mg have proven to be ineffective.

Usual pediatric dose

Cholinergic—
Subcutaneous, 0.2 mg per kg of body weight a day in 3 or 4 divided doses.

Usual geriatric dose

See *Usual adult and adolescent dose.*

Strength(s) usually available

U.S.—
5 mg per mL (Rx) [*Urecholine*].

Canada—
5 mg per mL (Rx) [*Urecholine*].

Packaging and storage

Store below 40 °C (104 °F), preferably between 15 and 30 °C (59 and 86 °F), unless otherwise specified by manufacturer. Protect from freezing.

Note

For subcutaneous use only. Discard unused portion.

Revised: 06/27/1994

BEVACIZUMAB Systemic

VA CLASSIFICATION (Primary): AN900

Commonly used brand name(s): *Avastin.*

Note: For a listing of dosage forms and brand names by country availability, see *Dosage Forms* section(s).

Category

Antineoplastic; monoclonal antibody; vascular endothelial growth factor (VEGF) inhibitor.

Indications

Accepted

Carcinoma, colorectal (treatment)—Bevacizumab in combination with intravenous 5–fluorouracil-based chemotherapy is indicated for first-line treatment of patients with metastatic carcinoma of the colon or rectum

[Metastatic breast carcinoma, HER2-negative disease, first line therapy in combination with paclitaxel]—Bevacizumab-containing regimens have demonstrated anti-tumor activity in patients with metastatic breast cancer. Interim analysis of the Eastern Oncology Cooperative Group (E2100) phase III trial assessing the addition of paclitaxel to bevacizumab as first-line therapy in mostly HER2-negative metastatic breast cancer patients yielded improvements in response rates, progression-free survival, and a trend toward improved survival.

[Non-squamous non small cell lung cancer, advanced/metastatic, first-line treatment, in combination with paclitaxel and carboplatin][1]—Combination chemotherapy regimens including bevacizumab have demonstrated activity in the treatment of patients with non-small cell lung cancer. Interim results from a phase II/III trial [abstract] and a single published phase II trial, indicate improved response rates, time to progression, and overall survival in patients receiving paclitaxel/carboplatin in combination with bevacizumab. Common bevacizumab grade 3/4 toxicities include: neutropenia, thrombocytopenia, hypertension, and hemorrhage. These trials demonstrate that it is imperative that selection criteria be followed (e.g., no brain metastases, no hemoptysis, no history of bleeding, no anticoagulation).

Acceptance not established

Colorectal cancer, advanced/metastatic, relapsed, in combination therapy

Data are inconclusive for the use of bevacizumab plus a new chemotherapy regimen in patients with relapsed metastatic colorectal cancer. Trials suggest benefit, however, issues such as poor study design, low response rates, bevacizumab-naive patients, and an unmet primary endpoint, all question the applicability of these data to current practice. The BOND 2.5 trial, designed to evaluate a bevacizumab-containing regimen in the relapsed metastatic setting in patients previously exposed to bevacizumab is eagerly awaited.

Metastatic renal cell carcinoma—Time to progression was prolonged in one phase II study of high-dose bevacizumab (10 milligrams/kilogram); survival was not affected.

Data from a randomized, placebo-controlled, phase II trial of adult patients with metastatic renal cell carcinoma indicate a prolonged time to progression of disease with bevacizumab therapy. Patients were randomized to placebo, low-dose bevacizumab (3 milligrams (mg)/kilogram (kg), or high-dose bevacizumab therapy (10 mg/kg). Median time to progression increased from 2.5 months in the placebo group to 4.8 months in the high-dose bevacizumab group (P less than 0.001); no difference was noted between the placebo and low-dose group. However, few objective responses, all of which were partial responses, were noted (n = 4 (10%); 95% CI, 2.9,24.2). Eventual tumor escape from VEGF blockade occurred in most patients (due to alternative proangiogenic pathways or insufficient blockade of VEGF by bevacizumab). Hence, survival (as of 2/2003) was not significantly different among all three groups. A pilot study containing a cohort of patients from the above study was later conducted. Patients randomized to placebo from the above study were administered either low-dose bevacizumab or bevacizumab plus thalidomide, a known antiangiogenic agent. No objective responses or differences in progression-free survival between groups were reported.

Further Phase III randomized trials are needed to assess the role of VEGF inhibitors in the treatment of renal cell cancer.

Metastatic renal cell carcinoma, combination therapy—Bevacizumab has demonstrated some activity in combination with erlotinib in the treatment of metastatic renal cancer. Median survival of 11 months was reported in the interim analysis of a phase II trial with 63 nephrectomized patients enrolled. This survival time is comparable to treatment with nephrectomy and interferon alfa-2b. Interim analysis shows a progression free survival rate in patients with CR/PR of 80%. Another small trial (n=38) showed a partial response rate of 9% using bevacizumab, erlotinib, and imatinib in interim analysis. The combination of bevacizumab, erlotinib, and imatinib shows no increased efficacy when retrospectively compared to bevacizumab/erlotinib.

[1]Not included in Canadian product labeling.

Pharmacology/Pharmacokinetics

Physicochemical characteristics

Source—Produced in Chinese Hamster Ovary mammalian cell expression system in a nutrient medium containing the antibiotic gentamicin.

Molecular weight—149 kilodaltons.

pH—6.2 (solution for intravenous infusion)

Mechanism of action/Effect

Bevacizumab binds VEGF and prevents the interaction of VEGF to its receptors on the surface of endothelial cells. The interaction of VEGF with its receptors leads to endothelial cell proliferation and new blood vessel formation in *in vitro* models of angiogenesis.

Half-life

20 (11 to 50) days

Time to steady state concentration

100 days

Precautions to Consider

Carcinogenicity

No carcinogenicity data are available for bevacizumab in animals or humans.

Pregnancy/Reproduction

Fertility—Bevacizumab may impair fertility. Dose-related decreases in ovarian and uterine weights, endometrial proliferation, number of menstrual cycles, and arrested follicular development or absent corpora lutea were observed in female cynomolgus monkeys treated with 10 or 50 mg per kg of bevacizumab for 13 to 26 weeks. Trends suggestive of reversibility were noted following a 4–12–week recovery period.

Pregnancy—Adequate and well controlled studies in humans have not been done. Bevacizumab should be used during pregnancy or in any woman not employing adequate contraception only if the potential benefit justifies the potential risk to the fetus. Since bevacizumab exposure may continue for a prolonged time after discontinuation of bevacizumab patients should be counseled about not becoming pregnant in the period following discontinuation.

Studies in rabbits have shown that bevacizumab may cause decreases in maternal and fetal body weights, an increased number of fetal resorptions, and an increased incidence of specific gross and skeletal fetal alterations. Adverse fetal outcomes were observed at all doses tested.

FDA Pregnancy Category C

Breast-feeding

Although very little information is available regarding distribution of antineoplastic agents into breast milk, breast-feeding is not recommended during chemotherapy or for a prolonged period following the use of bevacizumab because of the potential risks to the infant.

Pediatrics

Appropriate studies have not been performed on the relationship of age to the effects of bevacizumab in the pediatric population. Safety and efficacy have not been established. However, studies on juvenile cynomolgus monkeys found an increased incidence and severity of physeal dysplasia.

Geriatrics

Appropriate studies performed to date have not demonstrated geriatrics-specific problems that would limit the usefulness of bevacizumab in the elderly. However, elderly patients have been shown to have a higher incidence of some adverse effects.

Pharmacogenetics

Males have been shown to have a higher clearance and maximum concentration of bevacizumab than females

Dental

The leukopenic and thrombocytopenic effects of bevacizumab may result in an increased incidence of microbial infection delayed healing and gingival bleeding. If leukopenia or thrombocytopenia occurs, dental work should be deferred until blood counts have returned to normal and patients should be instructed in proper oral hygiene, including caution in use of regular toothbrushes, dental floss, and toothpicks.

Surgical

Surgical—Not to be initiated in for at least 28 days following major surgery; surgical incision must be fully healed prior to initiation; therapy should be discontinued several weeks prior to elective surgery.

Laboratory value alterations

The following have been selected on the basis of their potential clinical significance (possible effect in parentheses where appropriate)—not necessarily inclusive (» = major clinical significance).

With physiology/laboratory test values—

» Protein, urine

(bevacizumab should be interrupted for ≥ 2 g of proteinuria per 24 hours and resumed when proteinuria is ≤ 2 g per 24 hours)

Medical considerations/Contraindications

The medical considerations/contraindications included have been selected on the basis of their potential clinical significance (reasons given in parentheses where appropriate)—not necessarily inclusive (» = major clinical significance).

Except under special circumstances, this medicine should not be used when the following medical problem exists:

» Hypersensitivity

Risk-benefit should be considered when the following medical problems exist:

Congestive heart failure
(may result in patients who have received prior anthracyclines and or left chest wall irradiation; the safety of continuation or resumption of bevacizumab in patients with cardiac dysfunction has not been studied.)

» Gastrointestinal perforations or
» Wound healing complications
(may result in the development of gastrointestinal perforation and wound dehiscence, in some instances resulting in fatality; treatment should be permanently discontinued in the presence of these conditions)

» Hemoptysis or
Hemorrhage
(risk may be increased; patients with recent history of hemoptysis should not receive bevacizumab; patients with serious hemorrhage should permanently discontinue bevacizumab and receive aggressive medical management of hemorrhage.)

Hepatic impairment or
Renal impairment
(no studies have examined the effects of bevacizumab in patients with these conditions)

» Hypertension, severe or
» Hypertensive crisis
(permanently discontinue bevacizumab in patients with hypertensive crisis; temporarily suspend bevacizumab in patients with severe hypertension that is not controlled with medical management)

» Nephrotic syndrome
(bevacizumab should be discontinued in patients with this condition)

» Thromboembolic events, including:
» Angina or
» Cerebral infarction or
» Myocardial infarction or
» Transient ischemic attacks
(risk may be increased; may be fatal in some instances)

Patient monitoring

The following may be especially important in patient monitoring (other tests may be warranted in some patients, depending on condition; » = major clinical significance):

» Blood pressure
(conducted every 2 or 3 weeks during treatment; those who develop hypertension may require more frequent monitoring)

Urinalysis
(serial urinalyses should be used to monitor for the development or worsening of proteinuria; bevacizumab should be interrupted for ≥ 2 g of proteinuria per 24 hours and resumed when proteinuria is ≤ 2 g per 24 hours)

Side/Adverse Effects

The following side/adverse effects have been selected on the basis of their potential clinical significance (possible signs and symptoms in parentheses where appropriate)—not necessarily inclusive:

Those indicating need for medical attention

Incidence more frequent

Abdominal pain; asthenia (lack or loss of strength); ***bilirubinemia*** (yellow skin; unusual tiredness or weakness); ***colitis*** (stomach cramps; tenderness; pain; watery or bloody diarrhea; fever); ***congestive heart failure*** (chest pain; decreased urine output; dilated neck veins; extreme fatigue; irregular breathing; irregular heartbeat; shortness of breath; swelling of face, fingers, feet, or lower legs; tightness in chest; troubled breathing; weight gain; wheezing); ***diarrhea; deep vein thrombosis*** (pain, redness, or swelling in arm or leg); ***dyspnea*** (shortness of breath; difficult or labored breathing; tightness in chest; wheezing); ***exfoliative dermatitis*** (cracks in the skin; loss of heat from the body; red, swollen skin, scaly skin); ***gastrointestinal hemorrhage*** (black, tarry stools; bloody stools; vomiting of blood or material that looks like coffee grounds); ***hypertension*** (high blood pressure); ***hypokalemia*** (convulsions; decreased urine; dry mouth; irregular heartbeat; increased thirst; loss of appetite; mood changes; muscle pain or cramps; nausea or vomiting; numbness or tingling in hands, feet, or lips; shortness of breath; unusual tiredness or weakness); ***leukopenia*** (black, tarry stools; chest pain; chills; cough; fever; painful or difficult urination; shortness of breath; sore throat; sores, ulcers, or white spots on lips or in mouth; swollen glands; unusual bleeding or bruising; unusual tiredness or weakness); ***neutropenia; pain; proteinuria*** (cloudy urine); ***thrombocytopenia*** (black, tarry stools; bleeding gums; blood in urine or stools; pinpoint red spots on skin; unusual bleeding or bruising); ***upper respiratory infection*** (ear congestion; nasal; congestion; chills; cough, fever, sneezing, or sore throat; body aches or pain; headache; loss of voice; runny nose; unusual tiredness or weakness; difficulty in breathing); ***vomiting; wound healing complications***

Incidence less frequent

constipation (difficulty having a bowel movement (stool)); ***intra-abdominal thrombosis*** (stomach tenderness, pain, swelling, or warmth); ***syncope*** (fainting); ***vaginal hemorrhage*** (heavy nonmenstrual vaginal bleeding)

Incidence rare

Anastomotic ulceration (abdominal or stomach pain; cramping or burning; black, tarry stools; constipation; diarrhea; vomiting of blood or material that looks like coffee grounds; nausea; heartburn; indigestion); ***hyponatremia*** (coma; confusion; convulsions; decreased urine output; dizziness; fast or irregular heartbeat; headache; increased thirst; muscle pain or cramps; nausea or vomiting; shortness of breath; swelling of face, ankles, or hands; unusual tiredness or weakness); ***intestinal necrosis*** (black, tarry stools; bloody stools; vomiting of blood or material that looks like coffee grounds); ***intestinal obstruction*** (abdominal pain, severe constipation nausea vomiting); ***mesenteric venous occlusion*** (abdominal pain, usually after eating a meal; constipation; diarrhea; nausea; vomiting); ***pancytopenia*** (high fever; chills; unexplained bleeding or bruising; bloody, black, or tarry stools; pale skin; unusual tiredness or weakness; cough; shortness of breath; sores, ulcers, or white spots on lips or in mouth; swollen glands); ***polyserositis*** (abdominal pain; chest pain; fever; shortness of breath); ***ureteral stricture*** (difficult or painful urination; frequent urge to urinate)

Those indicating need for medical attention only if they continue or are bothersome

Incidence more frequent

Abnormal gait (change in walking and balance; clumsiness or unsteadiness); ***anorexia*** (loss of appetite; weight loss); ***bleeding gums; confusion; dizziness; dry mouth; dry skin; dyspepsia*** (acid or sour stomach; belching; heartburn; indigestion; stomach discomfort, upset or pain); ***epistaxis*** (bloody nose); ***excess lacrimation*** (excess flow of tears); ***flatulence; headache; hypotension*** (low blood pressure); ***myalgia*** (muscle pain); ***nail disorder*** (discoloration of fingernails or toenails); ***skin discoloration; skin ulcer*** (sores on the skin); ***stomatitis*** (swelling or inflammation of the mouth); ***taste disorder*** (change in taste; bad, unusual or unpleasant (after)taste); ***urinary frequency/urgency; voice alteration; weight loss***

Those not indicating need for medical attention

Incidence more frequent

Alopecia (hair loss; thinning of hair)

Patient Consultation

As an aid to patient consultation, refer to *Advice for the Patient, Bevacizumab (Systemic).*

In providing consultation, consider emphasizing the following selected information (» = major clinical significance):

Before using this medication

» Conditions affecting use, especially:
Hypersensitivity to bevacizumab or any of its components
Pregnancy—Not recommended for use during pregnancy
Breast-feeding—Not recommended
Use in the elderly—Elderly patients may be at higher risk for adverse effects.
Surgical—Treatment should not be initiated in patients that have had recent surgery and therapy should be discontinued several weeks prior to elective surgery.
Other medical problems, especially angina, cerebral infarction, gastrointestinal perforations, hemoptysis, hypertension, hypertensive crisis, myocardial infarction, transient ischemic attack, or wound healing complications

Proper use of this medication

» Proper dosing
Proper storage

Precautions while using this medication

» Regular visits to physician to check progress

Side/adverse effects

Signs of potential side effects, especially abdominal pain, asthenia, diarrhea, dyspnea, exfoliative dermatitis, severe hypertension, hypokalemia, gastrointestinal hemorrhage, leukopenia, neutropenia, pain, proteinuria, upper respiratory infection, vomiting, wound healing complications, constipation, gastrointestinal hemorrhage, intra-abdominal thrombosis, syncope, anastomotic ulceration, hyponatremia, intestinal necrosis, intestinal obstruction, pancytopenia, polyserositis, thrombocytopenia, ureteral stricture, or vaginal hemorrhage

General Dosing Information

For parenteral dosing forms:

Special precautions are recommended in patients who develop thrombocytopenia as a result of administration of bevacizumab. These may include: extreme care in performing invasive procedures; regular inspection of intravenous sites, skin (including perirectal area), and mucous membrane surfaces for signs of bleeding or bruising; limiting frequency of venipuncture and avoiding intramuscular injections; testing urine, emesis, stool and secretions for occult blood; care in use of toothbrushes, dental floss, toothpicks, safety razors, and fingernail and toenail cutters; avoiding constipation; and using caution to prevent falls and other injuries. Such patients should avoid alcohol and any aspirin intake because of the risk of gastrointestinal bleeding. Platelet transfusions may be required

Patients who develop leukopenia should be observed carefully for signs of infection. Antibiotic support may be required. In neutropenic patients who develop fever, broad-spectrum antibiotic coverage should be initiated empirically, pending bacterial cultures and approach diagnostic tests.

Safety considerations for handling this medication

There is limited but increasing evidence and concern that personnel involved in preparation and administration of parenteral antineoplastics may be at some risk because of the potential mutagenicity, teratogenicity, and/or carcinogenicity of these agents, although the actual risk is unknown. USP advisory panels recommend cautious handling both in preparation and disposal of antineoplastic agents. Precautions that have been suggested include:

• Use of a biological containment cabinet during reconstitution and dilution of parenteral medications and wearing of disposable surgical gloves and masks.

• Use of proper technique to prevent contamination of the medication, work area, and operator during transfer between containers (including proper training of personnel in this technique).

• Cautious and proper disposal of needles, syringes, vials, ampuls, and unused medication.

A number of medical centers have developed detailed guidelines for handling of antineoplastic agents.

Combination chemotherapy

Bevacizumab may be used in combination with other agents in various regimens. As a result, incidence and/or severity of side effects may be altered and different dosages (usually reduced) may be used. For example, bevacizumab is part of the following chemotherapeutic combination:

—irinotecan, 5–fluorouracil, and leucovorin.

For specific dosages and schedules, consult the literature. For information regarding each agent, consult the individual monographs.

Parenteral Dosage Forms

Note: Bracketed information in the *Indications* section refers to uses that are not included in U.S. product labeling.

BEVACIZUMAB INJECTION

Usual adult dose

Carcinoma, colorectal—

Intravenous infusion, 5 mg per kg of body weight over 90 min once every 14 days until disease progression is detected. Subsequent doses may be infused over 60 and 30 minutes if well tolerated

[Non-squamous non small cell lung cancer, advanced/metastatic, first-line treatment, in combination with paclitaxel and carboplatin][1]—

Intravenous infusion, 15 mg per kg of body weight in combination with paclitaxel 200 mg per square meter and carboplatin (area under the curve of 6) each given intravenously once every three weeks.

Usual pediatric dose

Safety and effectiveness in pediatric patients have not been established.

Usual geriatric dose

See *Usual adult dose.*

Strength(s) usually available

U.S.—

100 mg of bevacizumab per 4–mL vial of sterile solution (Rx) [*Avastin* (alpha, alpha-trehalose dihydrate; sodium phosphate (monobasic, monohydrate); sodium phosphate (dibasic, anhydrous); polysorbate 20; Water for Injection, USP)].

400 mg of bevacizumab per 16–mL vial of sterile solution [*Avastin* (alpha, alpha-trehalose dihydrate; sodium phosphate (monobasic, monohydrate); sodium phosphate (dibasic, anhydrous); polysorbate 20; Water for Injection, USP)].

Packaging and storage

Store between 2 and 8 °C (36 and 46 °F), in a tight container. Protect from light. Protect from freezing. Diluted solutions for infusion may be stored up to 8 hours

Preparation of dosage form

Bevacizumab should be diluted with Sodium Chloride Injection, USP by a healthcare professional. See the manufacturer's package insert for instructions.

Incompatibilities

Bevacizumab injections should not be administered or mixed with dextrose solutions.

[1]Not included in Canadian product labeling.

Revised: 05/12/2006
Developed: 02/23/2005

BEXAROTENE Systemic†

VA CLASSIFICATION (Primary): AN900

Commonly used brand name(s): *Targretin.*

Note: For a listing of dosage forms and brand names by country availability, see *Dosage Forms* section(s).

†Not commercially available in Canada.

Category

Antineoplastic.

Indications

Accepted

Lymphoma, cutaneous T–cell (treatment)—Bexarotene is indicated in the treatment of cutaneous manifestations of cutaneous T–cell lymphoma in patients who are refractory to at least one prior systemic therapy.

Note: The USP medical experts have chosen to *not include* bexarotene as treatment of non-small cell lung carcinoma. There is insufficient information to make any assessment at this time. Reevaluation will occur when phase III comparison data is available.

Pharmacology/Pharmacokinetics

Physicochemical characteristics

Molecular weight—348.48.

Mechanism of action/Effect

Bexarotene is a retinoid that selectively binds to and activates retinoid X receptor subtypes (RXRα, RXRβ, RXRγ), which modulates transcription and expression of genes that control the process of cellular differentiation and proliferation in cells. Bexarotene inhibits the growth of some tumor cell lines of hematopoietic and squamous cell origin *in vitro* and induces tumor regression *in vivo* in some animal models. Its exact mechanism of action in the treatment of cutaneous T-cell lymphoma is unknown.

Absorption

Maximal absorption of bexarotene occurs at approximately two hours after oral administration. Following a fat-containing meal, area under the plasma concentration-time curve (AUC) and peak plasma concentration (C_{max}) resulting from a 300 milligram (mg) dose were 35% and 48% higher, respectively, than after administration of a glucose solution.

Protein binding

Very high (>99%)

Biotransformation

Four known metabolites: 6–hydroxybexarotene, 7–hydroxybexarotene, 6–oxo-bexarotene, and 7–oxo-bexarotene.

Oxidative metabolites formed via CYP 3A4 and then glucuronidated. *In vitro* studies have revealed retinoid receptor activation by the oxidative metabolites, however the relative contribution of the parent and any metabolites to the efficacy and safety of bexarotene is unknown.

Half-life
Terminal half-life—
Seven hours.

Elimination
Primarily hepatobiliary.

Precautions to Consider

Cross-sensitivity and/or related problems
The manufacturer recommends caution when administering bexarotene to patients with a known hypersensitivity to retinoids. No clinical reports of cross-sensitivity have been noted at this time.

Carcinogenicity/Tumorigenicity
Long-term studies in animals have not been conducted.

Mutagenicity
Bexarotene was not mutagenic in the Ames assay or the mouse lymphoma assay, nor was it clastogenic in the mouse micronucleus test.

Pregnancy/Reproduction
Fertility—Fertility studies have not been conducted. Oral bexarotene doses of 1.5 mg per kg of body weight (mg/kg) per day (resulting in an area under the plasma concentration-time curve (AUC) value that was approximately one-fifth the AUC value at the recommended human daily dose) for 91 days produced testicular degeneration in dogs.

Pregnancy—Bexarotene must not be given to a woman who is pregnant or who intends to become pregnant. It is recommended that women of childbearing potential be advised to avoid becoming pregnant during treatment because of the potential risks to the fetus. If a woman becomes pregnant during treatment, bexarotene must be discontinued immediately and the woman given appropriate counseling.

Administration of bexarotene to a female patient requires that the following criteria be met:

• Two reliable forms of contraception (one non-hormonal form) should be used simultaneously for 1 month prior to the initiation, during, and for at least 1 month after discontinuation, of bexarotene therapy.

• A negative pregnancy test with a sensitivity of at least 50 milli International Units per liter (mIU/L) should be obtained within 1 week before treatment is started. Bexarotene therapy should be initiated on the second or third day of a normal menstrual period.

• Pregnancy testing and contraception counseling should be repeated on a monthly basis during treatment.

Male patients with sexual partners who are pregnant, possibly pregnant, or who could become pregnant must use condoms during sexual intercourse during bexarotene therapy and for at least 1 month after the last dose of the drug.

Bexarotene caused malformations when given orally to pregnant rats on days 7 through 17 of gestation. Developmental abnormalities, including incomplete ossification at 4 mg/kg per day and cleft palate, depressed eye bulge/microphthalmia, and small ears at 16 mg/kg per day, occurred. The 4 mg/kg per day dose produces an AUC value in rats that is approximately one-third the AUC in humans at the recommended daily dose. Developmental mortality occurred at doses greater than 10 mg/kg per day. The no-effect dose for fetal effects in rats was 1 mg/kg per day, which produces an AUC value approximately one-sixth of the AUC in humans at the recommended daily dose.

FDA Pregnancy Category X.

Breast-feeding
It is not known whether bexarotene is distributed into human breast milk. However, breast-feeding is not recommended during treatment because of the potential risks to the infant.

Pediatrics
The safety and efficacy of bexarotene in pediatric patients have not been established.

Geriatrics
Appropriate studies performed to date have not demonstrated geriatrics-specific problems that would limit the usefulness of bexarotene in the elderly. In clinical trials, 64% of the total patients with cutaneous T-cell lymphoma were 60 years or older, while 33% of patients were 70 years or older. No overall differences in safety were observed between patients 70 years or older and younger patients; however, greater sensitivity of some older patients to bexarotene cannot be ruled out.

Dental
The bone marrow depressant effects of bexarotene may result in an increased incidence of microbial infection, delayed healing, and gingival bleeding. Dental work, whenever possible, should be completed prior to initiation of therapy or deferred until blood counts have returned to normal. Patients should be instructed in proper oral hygiene during treatment, including caution in use of regular toothbrushes, dental floss, and toothpicks.

Drug interactions and/or related problems
The following drug interactions and/or related problems have been selected on the basis of their potential clinical significance (possible mechanism in parentheses where appropriate)—not necessarily inclusive (» = major clinical significance):

Note: Combinations containing any of the following medications, depending on the amount present, may also interact with this medication.

» Blood dyscrasia-causing medications (see *Appendix II*)
(leukopenic and/or thrombocytopenic effects of bexarotene may be increased with concurrent or recent therapy if these medications cause the same effects; dosage adjustment of the bone marrow depressant, if necessary, should be based on blood counts)

» Bone marrow depressants, other (see *Appendix II*) or
» Radiation therapy
(additive bone marrow depression may occur; dosage reduction may be required when two or more bone marrow depressants, including radiation, are used concurrently or consecutively)

Contraceptives, hormonal
(concomitant use may result in a increase of the rate of metabolism and a reduction in the plasma concentration of contraceptives; use of two forms of contraception (one non-hormonal) is strongly suggested.)

» Cytochrome P450 3A4 enzyme inducers, such as:
Phenobarbital or
Phenytoin or
Rifampin
(may cause a reduction in plasma bexarotene concentrations)

» Cytochrome P450 3A4 enzyme inhibitors, such as:
Erythromycin or
Grapefruit juice or
Itraconazole or
Ketoconazole
(may cause an increase in plasma bexarotene concentrations)

» Gemfibrozil
(concomitant use with gemfibrozil is not recommended since it can substantially increase plasma bexarotene concentrations)

» Insulin or
» Insulin secretion enhancers such as sulfonylureas or
» Insulin sensitizers
(bexarotene may enhance action of these agents, resulting in hypoglycemia; use caution with concomitant use)

» Tamoxifen
(concomitant use with tamoxifen in women with breast cancer, progressing on tamoxifen therapy, resulted in a modest decrease in plasma concentrations of tamoxifen; occurred through possible cytochrome P450 induction)

» Vitamin A
(use should be limited to ≤ 15,000 International Units daily; may cause additive toxic effects in higher doses)

Vaccines, killed virus
(because normal defense mechanisms may be suppressed by bexarotene therapy, the patient's antibody response to the vaccine may be decreased. The interval between discontinuation of medications that cause immunosuppression and restoration of the patient's ability to respond to the vaccine depends on the intensity and type of immunosuppression-causing medication used, the underlying disease, and other factors; estimates vary from 3 months to 1 year)

» Vaccines, live virus
(because normal defense mechanisms may be suppressed by bexarotene therapy, concurrent use with a live virus vaccine may potentiate the replication of the vaccine virus, may increase the side/adverse effects of the vaccine virus, and/or may decrease the patient's antibody response to the vaccine; immunization of these patients should be undertaken only with extreme caution after careful review of the patient's hematologic status and only with the knowledge and consent of the physician managing the bexarotene therapy. The interval between discontinuation of medications that

cause immunosuppression and restoration of the patient's ability to respond to the vaccine depends on the intensity and type of immunosuppression-causing medication used, the underlying disease, and other factors; estimates vary from 3 months to 1 year. Immunization with oral poliovirus vaccine should be postponed in persons in close contact with the patient, especially family members)

Laboratory value alterations

The following have been selected on the basis of their potential clinical significance (possible effect in parentheses where appropriate)—not necessarily inclusive (» = major clinical significance).

With diagnostic test results

CA125 assay values
(may be increased in patients with ovarian cancer)

With physiology/laboratory test values

» Alanine aminotransferase (ALT [SGPT]) and
» Aspartate aminotransferase (AST [SGOT]) and
» Bilirubin and
Lactate dehydrogenase
(elevations in liver function tests were observed in 5 to 7% (SGOT [AST]), 2 to 9% (SGPT [ALT]), and 0 to 6% (bilirubin) of patients; increases appear to be dose dependent; values returned to normal within 1 month in 80% of patients after a decrease in dose or discontinuation of therapy; bexarotene therapy should be suspended or discontinued if elevations beyond three times normal persist)

Alkaline phosphatase
(values may be abnormal)

Calcium, serum
(concentrations may be decreased)

Glucose, blood
(concentrations may be increased)

» Cholesterol, total, serum, and
» Triglycerides, fasting, serum
(may be significantly increased during bexarotene therapy; fasting triglyceride concentrations greater than 2.5 times the upper limit of normal were observed in 70% of patients and cholesterol increases greater than 300 mg per deciliter (mg/dL) were observed in 60 to 75% of patients; the effects on triglyceride and total cholesterol were reversible with discontinuation of therapy and were generally mitigated by dose reduction or concomitant antilipemic therapy)

Hemoglobin
(concentrations may be abnormal)

High density lipoproteins (HDL)
(may be significantly decreased during bexarotene therapy; decreases to ≤ 25 mg/dL have been reported in 55 to 90% of patients; the effect on HDL cholesterol was reversible with discontinuation of therapy and was generally mitigated by dose reduction or concomitant antilipemic therapy)

Potassium, serum
(concentrations may be increased)

Sodium, blood
(concentrations may be increased or decreased)

Thyroid-stimulating hormone (TSH) and
Thyroxine (T_4), total
(bexarotene therapy may induce biochemical evidence of or clinical hypothyroidism in half of all patients treated; TSH and total T_4 levels were decreased in about 60 and 45% of patients, respectively; thyroid hormone supplements should be considered in patients with laboratory evidence of hypothyroidism)

White blood cell counts (WBC)
(bexarotene therapy may induce reversible leukopenia/neutropenia; leukopenia in the range of 1000 to < 3000 WBC per cubic millimeter (WBC/mm^3) occurred in 18 to 43% of patients; the time to onset of leukopenia was generally 4 to 8 weeks and in most patients was explained by neutropenia; the incidence of U.S. National Cancer Institute [NCI] grades 3 and 4 neutropenia was 12% and 4%, respectively; leukopenia/neutropenia resolved after dose reduction or discontinuation of therapy on average within 30 days in 93% of patients with cutaneous T-cell lymphoma and 82% of patients with non-cutaneous T-cell lymphoma; leukopenia/neutropenia were rarely associated with severe sequelae or serious adverse events)

Medical considerations/Contraindications

The medical considerations/contraindications included have been selected on the basis of their potential clinical significance (reasons given in parentheses where appropriate)—not necessarily inclusive (» = major clinical significance).

Except under special circumstances, this medication should not be used when the following medical problems exist:

» Hypersensitivity to bexarotene or other retinoids

» Pregnancy

Risk-benefit should be considered when the following medical problems exist:

» Bone marrow depression, existing

» Chickenpox, existing or recent (including recent exposure) or
» Herpes zoster
(risk of severe generalized disease)

Cataracts
(bexarotene may cause new cataracts or worsening of previous cataracts)

» Diabetes mellitus
(bexarotene may contribute to hypoglycemia in patients being treated for diabetes with insulin, insulin secretion enhancers, or insulin sensitizers; caution should be used)

» Hepatic dysfunction
(may cause significant decreases in bexarotene clearance; caution should be used)

» Hyperlipidemia, uncontrolled
(bexarotene may cause significant increases in serum lipids)

» Infection

» Pancreatitis, history of or
» Risk factors for pancreatitis, such as:
Alcohol consumption, excessive or
Biliary tract disease or
Diabetes mellitus, uncontrolled or
Hyperlipidemia, uncontrolled or
Hypertriglyceridemia causing medications or
Pancreas toxic medications or
(bexarotene therapy may precipitate pancreatitis by increasing triglyceride levels; acute pancreatitis has been reported in patients receiving bexarotene; use of bexarotene in patients with risk factors for pancreatitis is not generally recommended)

Photosensitivity
(mild phototoxicity manifested as sunburn and skin sensitivity to sunlight was reported in patients receiving bexarotene who were exposed to direct sunlight)

Renal dysfunction
(pharmacokinetics may be altered in patients with renal insufficiency)

Note: Caution should be used also in patients who have had previous cytotoxic drug therapy or radiation therapy.

Patient monitoring

The following may be especially important in patient monitoring (other tests may be warranted in some patients, depending on condition; » = major clinical significance):

» Alanine aminotransferase (ALT [SGPT]) and
» Aspartate aminotransferase (AST [SGOT]) and
» Bilirubin and
Lactate dehydrogenase
(measurements should be taken at baseline and one, two, and four weeks after initiation of treatment, then every eight weeks for duration of treatment; bexarotene therapy should be suspended or discontinued if elevations beyond three times the upper limit of normal persist)

» Lipid panel, fasting
(fasting blood lipid determinations should be performed at baseline and then weekly until the lipid response to bexarotene is established (usually within 2–4 weeks), with continued monitoring every eight weeks; fasting triglyceride levels should be normalized prior to initiating bexarotene therapy; triglyceride levels should be maintained below 400 mg/dL; if fasting triglyceride levels become elevated during treatment, antilipemic therapy should be instituted and the dose of bexarotene should be reduced or suspended, if necessary; in clinical trials, 60% of patients were given antilipemic drugs (48% of patients received atorvastatin); use of gemfibrozil is not recommended due to a potential drug interaction)

Ophthalmologic exam
(recommended in patients who experience visual difficulties during therapy)

Thyroid function tests
(baseline measurements with periodic monitoring during therapy)

» White blood cell count with differential and
» Platelet count
(baseline measurements with periodic monitoring during therapy)

Side/Adverse Effects

The following side/adverse effects have been selected on the basis of their potential clinical significance (possible signs and symptoms in parentheses where appropriate)—not necessarily inclusive:

Those indicating need for medical attention

Incidence more frequent (10% or higher)

Anemia, hypochromic (unusual tiredness or weakness)—more frequent at doses > 300 mg per square meter of body surface area daily; ***exfoliative dermatitis*** (skin rash or other skin and mucous membrane lesions)—more frequent at doses >300 mg per square meter of body surface area daily; ***fever***—more frequent at doses >300 mg per square meter of body surface area daily; ***hyperlipemia or hypercholesterolemia*** (increase in lipid or cholesterol levels); ***hypothyroidism*** (coldness; dry, puffy skin; unusual tiredness; weight gain); ***increased lactic dehydrogenase; infection, bacterial*** (fever or chills; cough or hoarseness; lower back or side pain; painful or difficult urination); ***leukopenia*** (fever or chills; cough or hoarseness; lower back or side pain; painful or difficult urination); ***peripheral edema*** (swelling of the arms, feet, hands, or legs)

Incidence less frequent (less than 10%)

Bilirubinemia (yellow eyes or skin); ***elevated hepatic enzymes; pancreatitis*** (severe stomach pain with nausea or vomiting); ***pneumonia*** (fever or chills; cough; shortness of breath)

Those indicating need for medical attention only if they continue or are bothersome

Incidence more frequent (10% or higher)

Abdominal pain—more frequent at doses of 300 mg per square meter of body surface area daily; ***alopecia*** (hair loss)—more frequent at doses >300 mg per square meter of body surface area daily; ***anorexia*** (loss of appetite)—more frequent at doses >300 mg per square meter of body surface area daily; ***asthenia*** (loss of strength or energy; tiredness or weakness); ***back pain***—more frequent at doses >300 mg per square meter of body surface area daily; ***chills***—more frequent at doses >300 mg per square meter of body surface area daily; ***diarrhea***—more frequent at doses >300 mg per square meter of body surface area daily; ***dry skin***—more frequent at doses of 300 mg per square meter of body surface area daily; ***flu-like syndrome*** (chills and fever; diarrhea; cough; general feeling of discomfort or illness)—more frequent at doses >300 mg per square meter of body surface area daily; ***insomnia*** (trouble in sleeping)—more frequent at doses >300 mg per square meter of body surface area daily; ***headache; nausea***—more frequent at doses of 300 mg per square meter of body surface area daily; ***rash; vomiting***—more frequent at doses >300 mg per square meter of body surface area daily

Overdose

For more information on the management of overdose or unintentional ingestion, **contact a poison control center** (see *Poison Control Center Listing*).

Note: Bexarotene has been given to patients with advanced cancer in doses of up to 1000 mg per square meter of body surface area per day without acute toxic effects. No cases of overdose have been reported.

Treatment of overdose

Supportive care should be made available.

Patients in whom intentional overdose is confirmed or suspected should be referred for psychiatric consultation.

Patient Consultation

As an aid to patient consultation, refer to *Advice for the Patient, Bexarotene (Systemic)*.

In providing consultation, consider emphasizing the following selected information (» = major clinical significance):

Before using this medication

» Conditions affecting use, especially:
Sensitivity to bexarotene or other retinoids
Pregnancy—Avoiding pregnancy during treatment; need to use two forms of reliable contraception (one should be non-hormonal) simultaneously starting 1 month prior to initiation of therapy and continuing at least 1 month after discontinuation of treatment; use of condoms by male patients
Breast-feeding—Not recommended because of risk of serious side effects in nursing infants
Other medications, especially other blood dyscrasia-causing medications, other bone marrow depressants, previous cytotoxic drug or radiation therapy, medications that induce hepatic metabolism such as phenobarbital, phenytoin, and rifampin; medications or substances that inhibit hepatic metabolism such as erythromycin, grapefruit juice, itraconazole, and ketoconazole; gemfibrozil, insulin, insulin secretion enhancers such as sulfonylureas, insulin sensitizers, tamoxifen, or vitamin A
Other medical problems, especially chickenpox, existing bone marrow depression, herpes zoster, diabetes mellitus, hepatic dysfunction, uncontrolled hyperlipidemia, infection, history of pancreatitis or risk of developing pancreatitis

Proper use of this medication

» Taking with a meal
» Proper dosing
Missed dose: Taking as soon as possible; not taking if almost time for next dose; not doubling doses
» Proper storage

Precautions while using this medication

» Regular visits to physician to assess effectiveness
» Avoiding immunizations unless approved by physician; other persons in patient's household should avoid immunizations with oral poliovirus vaccine; avoiding persons who have taken oral poliovirus vaccine, or wearing a protective mask that covers nose and mouth

Caution if bone marrow depression occurs:
» Avoiding exposure to persons with infections, especially during periods of low blood counts; checking with physician immediately if fever or chills, cough or hoarseness, lower back or side pain, or painful or difficult urination occurs
» Checking with physician immediately if unusual bleeding or bruising; black, tarry stools; blood in urine or stools; or pinpoint red spots on skin occur
Caution in use of regular toothbrush, dental floss, or toothpick; physician, dentist, or nurse may suggest alternatives; checking with physician before having dental work done
Not touching eyes or inside of nose unless hands washed immediately before
Using caution to avoid accidental cuts with use of sharp objects such as safety razor or fingernail or toenail cutters
Avoiding contact sports or other situations where bruising or injury could occur
Possible photosensitivity reactions

Side/adverse effects

Signs of potential side effects including hypochromic anemia, exfoliative dermatitis, fever, hyperlipemia or hypercholesterolemia, hypothyroidism, increased lactic dehydrogenase, bacterial infection, leukopenia, peripheral edema, bilirubinemia, elevated hepatic enzymes, pancreatitis, or pneumonia

General Dosing Information

Patients receiving bexarotene should be under supervision of a physician experienced in cancer chemotherapy.

Treatment should continue for as long as the patient continues to receive benefit.

Special precautions are recommended in patients who develop thrombocytopenia as a result of administration of bexarotene. These may include extra care in performing invasive procedures, regular inspection of intravenous sites, skin (including perirectal area), and mucous membrane surfaces for signs of bleeding or bruising; limiting frequency of venipuncture and avoiding intramuscular injections; testing urine, emesis, stool, and secretions for occult blood; care in use of regular toothbrushes, dental floss, toothpicks, safety razors, and fingernail and toenail cutters; avoiding constipation; and using caution to prevent falls and other injuries. Such patients should avoid alcohol and aspirin intake because of the risk of gastrointestinal bleeding. Platelet transfusion may be required.

Patients who develop leukopenia should be observed carefully for signs of infection. Antibiotic support may be required. In neutropenic patients who develop fever, broad-spectrum antibiotic coverage should be initiated empirically, pending bacterial cultures and appropriate diagnostic tests.

Bexarotene should be taken with a meal.

Diet/Nutrition

Patients should avoid drinking grapefruit juice while receiving bexarotene treatment.

Oral Dosage Forms

BEXAROTENE CAPSULES

Usual adult dose

Lymphoma, cutaneous T–cell—

Initial, oral, 300 mg per square meter of body surface area per day in a single dose with a meal. May be decreased to 200 mg per square meter of body surface area per day, then to 100 mg per square meter of body surface area per day, or temporarily suspended if patient exhibits signs of toxicity. Once toxicity is controlled, the dose may be retitrated upwards. If there is no tumor response after eight weeks of therapy and if the initial dose of 300 mg per square meter of body surface area per day is well-tolerated, the dose may be increased to 400 mg per square meter of body surface area per day with careful monitoring.

Usual adult prescribing limits

400 mg per square meter of body surface area per day.

Usual pediatric dose

Safety and efficacy have not been established.

Usual geriatric dose

See *Usual adult dose*

Strength(s) usually available

U.S.—

75 mg (Rx) [*Targretin* (polyethylene glycol 400 NF; polysorbate 20 NF; povidone USP; butylated hydroxyanisole NF)].

Packaging and storage

Store at 2–25 °C (36–77 °F). Avoid exposure to high temperatures and humidity once the bottle is opened. Protect from light.

Auxiliary labeling

- Take with food.
- Keep out of reach of children.

Revised: 11/07/2003
Developed: 03/30/2000

BEXAROTENE Topical†

VA CLASSIFICATION (Primary): DE900

Commonly used brand name(s): *Targretin.*

Note: For a listing of dosage forms and brand names by country availability, see *Dosage Forms* section(s).

†Not commercially available in Canada.

Category

Antineoplastic (topical).

Indications

Accepted

Lymphoma, cutaneous T-cell (treatment)—Bexarotene administered topically is indicated for the treatment of cutaneous lesions in patients with cutaneous T-cell lymphoma, stage 1A and 1B, who have refractory or persistent disease after other therapies, or who have not tolerated other therapies.

Pharmacology/Pharmacokinetics

Physicochemical characteristics

Molecular weight—348.48.

Solubility—Bexarotene is insoluble in water and slightly soluble in vegetable oils and ethanol, USP..

Mechanism of action/Effect

Bexarotene is a retinoid that selectively binds and activates retinoid X receptor subtypes (RXRα, RXRβ, RXRγ). Once activated, these receptors function as transcription factors that regulate the expression of genes that control cellular differentiation and proliferation. The exact mechanism of action of bexarotene in the treatment of cutaneous T-cell lymphoma is unknown, but it inhibits the growth *in vitro* of some tumor cell lines of hematopoietic and squamous cell origin. It also induces tumor regression *in vivo* in some animal models.

Absorption

The generally low plasma bexarotene concentrations (less than 5 ng/mL and not exceeding 55 ng/mL) indicate that, in patients receiving low to moderate doses, there is a low potential for significant systemic absorption. The quantifiable amount of absorption increased with an increase in percent body surface area treated and increasing quantity of bexarotene applied. The uptake of topical bexarotene by organs and tissues has not been evaluated.

Protein binding

Very highly (>99%)

Biotransformation

Following oral administration of bexarotene four oxidative metabolites have been identified in the plasma: 6– and 7–hydroxy-bexarotene and 6– and 7–oxo-bexarotene, formed by the cytochrome P450 3A4 pathway. When bexarotene is applied topically, the contribution of the parent and any metabolite to the efficacy and safety is unknown.

Onset of action

After therapy is initiated a response may be seen as soon as four weeks, but most patients require longer application to achieve further benefit. In one study the longest time to onset of response was 392 days.

Elimination

Primarily hepatobiliary.

Precautions to Consider

Cross-sensitivity and/or related problems

Bexarotene should be used with caution in patients with a known hypersensitivity to other retinoids. However, no clinical instances of cross-reactivity have been noted.

Carcinogenicity

Long-term studies in animals have not been conducted.

Mutagenicity

Bexarotene was not mutagenic to bacteria (Ames assay) or mammalian cell (mouse lymphoma assay). Bexarotene was not clastogenic *in vivo* (micronucleus test in mice).

Pregnancy/Reproduction

Fertility—Bexarotene caused testicular degeneration when oral doses of 1.5 milligrams per kilogram per day (mg/kg/day) were given to dogs for 91 days.

Pregnancy—Bexarotene is contraindicated during pregnancy. Studies in animals have shown that bexarotene causes serious adverse effects in the fetus. Male patients with sexual partners who are pregnant, possibly pregnant, or who could become pregnant must use condoms during sexual intercourse while applying bexarotene and for at least one month after the last dose of drug.

Two reliable forms of contraception should be used, unless abstinence is followed, simultaneously for 1 month prior to the initiation, during, and for at least 1 month after discontinuation, of bexarotene therapy.

A negative pregnancy test should be obtained within 1 week prior to initiation of topical bexarotene therapy. A pregnancy test should be repeated monthly while on topical bexarotene therapy.

Animal studies with orally administered bexarotene in pregnant rats was shown to cause developmental abnormalities (incomplete ossification, cleft palate, depressed eye bulge/microphthalmia, and small ears) at dosages of 4 mg to 16 mg/kg/day. At dosages of greater than 10 mg/kg/day bexarotene caused developmental mortality. Plasma bexarotene concentrations after topical administration were generally less than one-hundredth the maximum plasma concentration (C_{max}) associated with dysmorphogenesis in rats, although some patients had levels that were approximately one-eighth of the C_{max} associated with dysmorphogenesis in rats.

FDA Pregnancy Category X.

Breast-feeding

It is not known whether bexarotene is distributed into breast milk; however because of the potential for serious adverse reactions in nursing infants from bexarotene, a decision should be made whether to discontinue nursing or to discontinue the drug, taking into account the importance of bexarotene to the mother.

Pediatrics

No information is available. Appropriate studies have not been performed on the relationship of age to the effects of bexarotene in the pediatric population. Safety and efficacy have not been established.

Geriatrics

Appropriate studies performed to date have not demonstrated geriatrics-specific problems that would limit the usefulness of bexarotene in the elderly. In clinical studies, with 38% of the tested population over 65 years of age, there were no overall differences in response, but greater sensitivity of some older individuals to bexarotene cannot be ruled out.

Pharmacogenetics
Pharmacokinetic differences as a result of gender or race could not be assessed in clinical trials due to immeasurable plasma concentrations (<1 ng/ml).

Drug interactions and/or related problems
The following drug interactions and/or related problems have been selected on the basis of their potential clinical significance (possible mechanism in parentheses where appropriate)—not necessarily inclusive (» = major clinical significance):

» DEET (N,N-diethyl-m-toluamide)
(increased DEET toxicity in concurrent use)

» Vitamin A supplementation
(Concomitant use of vitamin A supplements in amounts >15,000 IU/day should be avoided to decrease the potential for additive toxic effects)

Note: Systemic interactions with gemfibrozil and cytochrome P450 3A4 inhibitors, such as ketoconazole, itraconazole, erythromycin, and grapefruit juice are unlikely, due to the low systemic exposure with topical bexarotene. Any increases in plasma bexarotene that occur are unlikely to be of sufficient magnitude to result in adverse effects.

Medical considerations/Contraindications
The medical considerations/contraindications included have been selected on the basis of their potential clinical significance (reasons given in parentheses where appropriate)—not necessarily inclusive (» = major clinical significance).

Except under special circumstances, this medication should not be used when the following medical problem exists:

» Hypersensitivity to Bexarotene or other components of the product

» Pregnancy

Risk-benefit should be considered when the following medical problems exist:

Hepatic dysfunction
(may lead to significant decreases in bexarotene clearance; caution should be used)

» Photosensitivity
(may have the potential for photosensitization; minimize exposure to sunlight and artificial ultraviolet light during the use of topical bexarotene)

Renal dysfunction
(urinary elimination is a minor excretory pathway (< 1% of an orally administered dose), but because renal insufficiency can result in significant protein binding changes, the pharmacokinetics of bexarotene, which is highly protein bound, may be altered in patients with renal insufficiency.)

Patient monitoring
The following may be especially important in patient monitoring (other tests may be warranted in some patients, depending on condition; » = major clinical significance):

» Pregnancy Test
(A negative pregnancy test [such as serum beta-human chorionic gonadotropin, beta-HCG] with a sensitivity of at least 50 mIU/L should be obtained within one week prior to bexarotene use. The pregnancy test must be repeated at monthly intervals while the patient remains on bexarotene)

Side/Adverse Effects
The following side/adverse effects have been selected on the basis of their potential clinical significance (possible signs and symptoms in parentheses where appropriate)—not necessarily inclusive:

Those indicating need for medical attention
Incidence more frequent

Asthenia (lack or loss of strength); ***edema*** (decreased urination: rapid weight gain, bloating); ***exfoliative dermatitis*** (blisters on skin; chills; fever; general feeling of discomfort or illness; red, thickened, or scaly skin; swollen and/or painful glands; unusual bruising); ***hyperlipemia*** (increase in lipid levels); ***leukopenia*** (sore throat; fever); ***lymphadenopathy*** (swollen, painful, or tender lymph glands in neck, armpit, or groin); ***maculopapular rash*** (skin rash with lesions); ***paresthesia*** (burning, crawling, itching, numbness, prickling, "pins and needles", or tingling feelings); ***peripheral edema*** (bloating or swelling of face, hands, lower legs, and/or feet); ***skin disorder*** (skin inflammations; scratch; sticky or tacky sensation)

Those indicating need for medical attention only if they continue or are bothersome
Incidence more frequent

Contact dermatitis (blistering, burning, crusting, dryness, flaking of skin, itching, scaling, severe redness, soreness, swelling of skin); ***cough increased; headache; infection*** (fever or chills; cough or hoarseness; lower back or side pain; painful or difficult urination); ***pain; pharyngitis*** (sore throat); ***pruritus*** (itching skin; itching of lesion); ***rash; sweating***

Patient Consultation
As an aid to patient consultation, refer to *Advice for the Patient, Bexarotene (Topical).*

In providing consultation, consider emphasizing the following selected information (» = major clinical significance):

Before using this medication
» Conditions affecting use, especially:
Hypersensitivity to bexarotene or other retinoids
Pregnancy—Avoiding pregnancy during treatment; need to use two forms of reliable contraception simultaneously starting 1 month prior to initiation of therapy and continuing at least 1 month after discontinuation of treatment; use of condoms by male patients
Breast-feeding—Not recommended because of risk of serious side effects in nursing infants
Other medication, especially DEET (N,N-diethyl-m-toluamide) or vitamin A
Other medical problems, especially photosensitivity

Proper use of this medication
» Proper application technique
To use
Avoid normal skin and mucosal membranes
Wash hands immediately after applying or use applicator stick
Dry before covering with clothes; no occlusive dressing
» Proper dosing
Applying as soon as possible; not applying if almost time for next scheduled dose; not doubling doses
Proper storage

Precautions while using this medication
» Regular visits to physician to check progress
Possible photosensitivity reactions, minimize or avoid exposure to natural or artificial sunlight (tanning beds or UVA/B treatment)
Not taking Vitamin A supplements exceeding 15,000 IU/day

Side/adverse effects
Signs of potential side effects, especially asthenia, edema, exfoliative dermatitis, hyperlipemia, leukopenia, lymphadenopathy, maculopapular rash, paresthesia, peripheral edema, or skin disorders

General Dosing Information
Topical application
Bexarotene for topical use, is not intended for systemic use. Therapy should be continued as long as the patient is deriving benefit.

A sufficient amount of bexarotene should be applied to cover the lesion with a generous coating. Occlusive dressings should not be used. Allow to dry before covering with clothing. Avoid application of bexarotene to normal, unaffected skin surrounding the lesions to avoid irritation. Do not apply near mucosal surfaces of the body. Avoid exposure to sunlight. If application site toxicity occurs, the frequency of application can be reduced or temporarily discontinued for a few days until the symptoms subside.

Diet/Nutrition
Diet and NutritionSince bexarotene is metabolized by cytochrome P450 3A4, the consumption of grapefruit juice should be avoided to decrease the possibility of an increase in bexarotene plasma concentrations.

Patients should be advised to limit vitamin A intake to ≤15,000 IU/day.

Safety considerations for handling this medication
Avoid contact with normal skin to decrease irritation.

Topical Dosage Forms
BEXAROTENE GEL
Usual adult dose
Cutaneous T-cell lymphoma (Stage 1A and 1B)—
Topical, to the skin, applied to generously cover the lesion, once every other day for the first week. Increase the application frequency at weekly intervals to once daily, then twice daily, then three times

daily and finally four times daily, dependent upon individual lesion tolerance. Usually, a dosing frequency of two to four times per day is tolerated. If severe irritation occurs, reduce the frequency or temporarily discontinue for a few days until symptoms subside.

Usual adult prescribing limits
Up to four times daily.

Usual pediatric dose
Safety and effectiveness in pediatric patients have not been established

Usual geriatric dose
See *Usual adult dose.*

Usual geriatric prescribing limits
See *Usual adult prescribing limits.*

Strength(s) usually available
U.S.—
1% (Rx) [*Targretin* (dehydrated alcohol; polyethylene glycol 400; hydroxypropyl cellulose; butylated hydroxytoluene)].
Canada—
Not commercially available.

Packaging and storage
Store at 25 °C (77 °F), with excursions permitted between 15 and 30 °C (59 and 86 °F). Protect from light. Avoid exposure to high temperatures and humidity after the tube is opened.

Auxiliary labeling
- Use protection against sun and avoid use of sunlamp or tanning booth.
- For topical use only.
- Keep from heat and light.

Revised: 10/15/2001
Developed: 09/07/2001

BICALUTAMIDE—See *Antiandrogens, Nonsteroidal (Systemic)*

BIMATOPROST Ophthalmic†

VA CLASSIFICATION (Primary): OP116
Commonly used brand name(s): *Lumigan.*
Note: For a listing of dosage forms and brand names by country availability, see *Dosage Forms* section(s).

†Not commercially available in Canada.

Category
Antiglaucoma agent (ophthalmic); antihypertensive, ocular.

Indications

Accepted
Glaucoma, open-angle (treatment) or
Hypertension, ocular (treatment)—Bimatoprost is indicated for the treatment of elevated intraocular pressure (IOP) in patients with ocular hypertension or open-angle glaucoma who are intolerant of similar medications or not responsive (failed to achieve target IOP determined after multiple measurements over time) to another intraocular pressure lowering medication.

Acceptance not established
Ophthalmic bimatoprost has not been studied in patients with angle-closure, inflammatory, or neovascular glaucoma.

Pharmacology/Pharmacokinetics

Physicochemical characteristics
Chemical Group—Prostaglandin analog (synthetic)
Molecular weight—415.58.
Solubility—Very soluble in ethanol and methanol, and slightly soluble in water.
pH—6.8 to 7.8.

Mechanism of action/Effect
Antiglaucoma agent—Bimatoprost, a prostamide or synthetic prostaglandin analog, is thought to lower intraocular pressure (IOP) by increasing the outflow of aqueous humor through both the trabecular meshwork and uveoscleral drainage systems.

Absorption
Bimatoprost is systemically absorbed when administered to the eye.

Distribution
Volume of distribution (Vol_D)—Steady state: 0.67 L per kg. Bimatoprost is moderately distributed into body tissues, with most remaining in the plasma. It is unknown whether bimatoprost is excreted into human breast milk.

Protein binding
High (approximately 88%)

Biotransformation
Bimatoprost is the main circulating species in systemic blood but then undergoes oxidation, N-deethylation and glucuronidation to form a variety of metabolites.

Half-life
Intravenous administration—Elimination half-life of approximately 45 minutes.

Onset of action
Ophthalmic administration—Reduction of IOP starts after approximately four hours.

Peak plasma concentration:
Intravenous administration—Peak plasma concentration of unchanged bimatoprost was 12.2 nanograms per mL.

Time to peak effect
Ophthalmic administration—Reached after eight to twelve hours.

Elimination
Fecal, after intravenous administration—25%.
Renal, after intravenous administration—Up to 67%.

Total blood clearance
1.5 L per hour per kilogram.

Precautions to Consider

Carcinogenicity
Studies have not been performed.

Tumorigenicity
Studies have not been performed.

Mutagenicity
Bimatoprost was not mutagenic or clastogenic in the Ames test, in the mouse lymphoma test, or in the *in vivo* mouse micronucleus tests.

Pregnancy/Reproduction
Fertility—Bimatoprost did not impair fertility in male or female rats up to doses of 0.6 mg per kg per day, or approximately 103 times the recommended human exposure based on blood AUC levels.

Pregnancy—Adequate and well-controlled studies in humans have not been done.

In embryo/fetal development studies in pregnant mice and rats, abortion occurred at 33 or 97 times the intended human exposure, based on blood AUC levels. At doses of 41 times the intended human exposure (based on blood AUC levels), the gestation length was reduced in the dams, the incidence of dead fetuses, late resorptions, peri- and postnatal pup mortality was increased, and pup body weights were reduced.

FDA Pregnancy Category C

Breast-feeding
It not known whether bimatoprost is distributed into human breast milk. However, in animal studies, bimatoprost is distributed in breast milk.
It is recommended that caution should be exercised when given to a nursing woman.

Pediatrics
Appropriate studies have not been performed on the relationship of age to the effects of bimatoprost in the pediatric population. Safety and efficacy have not been established.

Geriatrics
Appropriate studies on the relationship of age to the effects of bimatoprost have not been performed in the geriatric population. However, no geriatrics-specific problems have been documented to date.

Medical considerations/Contraindications
The medical considerations/contraindications included have been selected on the basis of their potential clinical significance (reasons given in parentheses where appropriate)—not necessarily inclusive (» = major clinical significance).

Except under special circumstances, this medication should not be used when the following medical problem exists:
» Hypersensitivity to bimatoprost or benzalkonium chloride

Risk-benefit should be considered when the following medical problems exist:

» Aphakia or
» Macular edema or
» Pseudophakia
(macular edema, including cystoid macular edema, has been reported during treatment with bimatoprost; use with caution in aphakic patients, pseudophakic patients with a torn posterior lens capsule, or patients with risk factors for macular edema)

Hepatic function impairment or
Renal function impairment
(although studies with bimatoprost have not been done in patients with hepatic or renal function impairment, use with caution in these patients)

Iritis or
Uveitis
(bimatoprost should be used with caution in patients with active intraocular inflammation [iritis/uveitis])

Patient monitoring

The following may be especially important in patient monitoring (other tests may be warranted in some patients, depending on condition; » = major clinical significance):

Ophthalmic examinations
(patients should be examined regularly and, depending on the clinical situation, treatment may be stopped if increased brown pigmentation of iris occurs)

Side/Adverse Effects

Note: Bimatoprost may gradually change eye color by increasing the number of melanosomes (pigment granules) in the melanocytes, thereby increasing the amount of brown pigment in the iris. The long-term effects on the melanocytes, the consequences of potential injury to the melanocytes, and the possibility of deposition of pigment granules to other areas of the eye are not known. The change in iris color occurs slowly and may not be noticeable for several months to years. In addition, bimatoprost has been reported to cause increased pigmentation of the periorbital tissue (eyelid). Also, bimatoprost may gradually change eyelashes. The changes to the lashes include increased length, thickness, pigmentation, and the number of lashes. Patients should be advised of all the effects listed above and informed that if only one eye is treated with the medication, only one eye will be affected (heterochromia between the eyes). The changes in pigmentation and eyelash growth may be permanent.

Macular edema, including cystoid macular edema, has been reported during treatment with bimatoprost, mainly in patients with aphakia, in patients with pseudophakia who have a torn posterior lens capsule, or in patients with known risk factors for macular edema. It is recommended that bimatoprost be used with caution in these patients.

The following side/adverse effects have been selected on the basis of their potential clinical significance (possible signs and symptoms in parentheses where appropriate)—not necessarily inclusive:

Those indicating need for medical attention

Incidence less frequent (3 – 10% of patients)

Asthenia (lack or loss of strength)—up to 5% of patients; ***blepharitis*** (redness, swelling, and/or itching of eyelid); ***cataract*** (blindness; blurred vision; decreased vision)—in approximately 3 to 10% of patients; ***eye pain; eyelash darkening*** (darker eyelashes); ***eyelid erythema*** (redness of eyelid); ***infection*** (fever or chills)—primarily colds and upper respiratory infections, in approximately 10% of patients; ***pigmentation of the periocular skin*** (color changes in skin around eyes); ***superficial punctate keratitis*** (feeling of something in eye; sensitivity of eyes to light); ***visual disturbance*** (blurred vision or other change in vision)

Incidence rare (up to 3% of patients)

Allergic conjunctivitis (itching, redness, swelling, or other sign of eye or eyelid irritation); ***conjunctival edema*** (swelling and/or redness of eye and lining of eyelid); ***intraocular inflammation, such as iritis*** (eye pain, tearing, sensitivity or eye to light, redness of eye, or blurred vision or other change in vision); ***iris pigmentation increases*** (eye color changes)

Those indicating need for medical attention only if they continue or are bothersome

Incidence more frequent (15–45% of patients)

Conjunctival hyperemia (redness of the white part of eyes or inside of eyelids); ***growth of eyelashes; ocular pruritus*** (itching eye)

Incidence less frequent (3 – 10% of patients)

Foreign body sensation (feeling of having something in the eye); ***headaches***—up to 5% of patients; ***hirsutism*** (increase in hair growth)—up to 5% of patients; ***ocular burning*** (burning sensation in eyes); ***ocular dryness*** (dry eyes); ***ocular irritation*** (red, sore eyes)

Incidence rare (up to 3% of patients)

Asthenopia (eye strain); ***eye discharge; photophobia*** (increased sensitivity of eyes to sunlight); ***tearing***

Overdose

For more information on the management of overdose or unintentional ingestion, **contact a poison control center** (see *Poison Control Center Listing*).

Treatment of overdose

Supportive care—
No information is available on overdosage in humans. Treatment is generally symptomatic.
Patients in whom intentional overdose is confirmed or suspected should be referred for psychiatric consultation.

Patient Consultation

As an aid to patient consultation, refer to *Advice for the Patient, Bimatoprost (Ophthalmic)*

In providing consultation, consider emphasizing the following selected information (» = major clinical significance):

Before using this medication

» Conditions affecting use, especially:
Hypersensitivity to bimatoprost or benzalkonium chloride
Pregnancy—Not recommended for use during pregnancy
Breast-feeding—Use caution when giving to a nursing woman
Other medical problems, especially aphakia; macular edema, including cystoid macular edema, risk factors for; and pseudophakia

Proper use of this medication

» Using medication only as directed; not using more of it or using it more often than directed

Waiting at least 5 minutes between use of two different ophthalmic preparations to prevent second medication from "washing out" the first one

Removing contact lenses prior to administration of bimatoprost; reinserting lenses, if desired, at least 15 minutes after administration

» Proper administration technique; preventing contamination; not touching applicator tip to any surface

» Proper dosing
Missed dose: Using as soon as possible; not taking if almost time for next scheduled dose; not doubling doses

Proper storage

Precautions while using this medication

Regular visits to physician to check progress during therapy

» Checking with physician if signs of ocular allergic reaction occur

» Checking with physician about possible need for a fresh bottle of medication to use in case of surgery, injury, or infection

» Temporary blurring of vision may occur following administration; caution in driving or operating machinery

» Possibility of iris of eye becoming more brown in color; in addition, possibility of the darkening of eyelid skin color; also, possibility of increased length, thickness, pigmentation, and the number of lashes; iris, eyelid, and lash pigmentation and other lash changes may be permanent even if medication is stopped; the color and lash changes will occur only to the eye being treated; if only one eye is treated, there is a possibility of having differently colored eyes and differently appearing eyelashes

Possibility of medication causing eyes to become more sensitive to light than they are normally

Side/adverse effects

Signs of potential side effects, especially blurred vision, cataract, infection (such as colds and upper respiratory infections), increased length, thickness, pigmentation, and number of eyelashes, iris discoloration, pigmentation of the periocular skin

General Dosing Information

Bimatoprost may be used alone or in combination with other antiglaucoma agents. If more than one ophthalmic medication is used, the medications should be administered at least 5 minutes apart.

Bimatoprost contains benzalkonium chloride, which may be absorbed by contact lenses. Contact lenses should be removed prior to administration of bimatoprost. Lenses may be reinserted 15 minutes after administration.

Once-daily dosing of bimatoprost should not be exceeded. More frequent administration may decrease the intraocular pressure-lowering effect of the medication.

Ophthalmic Dosage Forms

BIMATOPROST OPHTHALMIC SOLUTION

Usual Adult Dose

Glaucoma, open-angle (treatment)

Hypertension, ocular (treatment)—

Topical, to the conjunctiva, 1 drop in the affected eye(s) once a day, in the evening.

Usual adult prescribing limits

No more than one dose per day.

Usual Pediatric Dose

Glaucoma, open-angle (treatment)

Hypertension, ocular (treatment)—

Safety and efficacy have not been established.

Usual Geriatric Dose

See *Usual adult dose.*

Strength(s) usually available

U.S.—

0.03% (0.3 mg per mL) (Rx) [*Lumigan* (benzalkonium chloride, 0.05 mg; citric acid; purified water; sodium chloride; sodium phosphate, dibasic; sodium hydroxide (and/or hydrochloric acid) for adjusting pH)].

Canada—

Not commercially available.

Packaging and storage

Store between 15° and 25 °C (59° and 77 °F).

Auxiliary labeling

• For the eye.

Developed: 07/24/2001

BIPERIDEN—See *Antidyskinetics (Systemic)*

BISACODYL—See *Laxatives (Local)*

BISMUTH SUBSALICYLATE, METRONIDAZOLE, AND TETRACYCLINE—FOR *H. pylori* Systemic

VA CLASSIFICATION (Primary): GA303

Commonly used brand name(s): *Helidac.*

NOTE: The *Bismuth Subsalicylate, Metronidazole, and Tetracycline—for H. pylori (Systemic)* monograph is maintained on the *USP DI* electronic database. A copy of the most recent revision of the complete monograph can be accessed on the *USP DI* Updates Online website. See the front cover of book for details on accessing the site. The information that follows is selectively abstracted from the complete monograph and is provided to facilitate drug use review and patient counseling.

Note: For a listing of dosage forms and brand names by country availability, see *Dosage Forms* section(s).

Category

Antiulcer agents.

Indications

General Considerations

The information in this monograph is specific only to the use of these products as indicated in this combination package. These products are intended only for use as described. The individual medications contained in this package should not be used alone or in combination for other purposes. For information on use of the individual components when dispensed as individual medications outside this combined use for treating *Helicobacter pylori* -associated duodenal ulcer, refer to the monographs for each individual agent.

Accepted

Duodenal ulcer, active (treatment)—Bismuth subsalicylate, metronidazole, and tetracycline, administered in combination with a histamine H_2-receptor antagonist, are indicated for the treatment of patients with an active duodenal ulcer associated with *Helicobacter pylori* infection. Eradication of *H. pylori* has been shown to reduce the risk of ulcer recurrence.

Patients who are still infected with *H. pylori* following treatment with this combination plus a histamine H_2-receptor antagonist should be considered to have *H. pylori* resistant to metronidazole, and should not be re-treated with a regimen containing metronidazole.

Patient Consultation

As an aid to patient consultation, refer to *Advice for the Patient, Bismuth Subsalicylate, Metronidazole, and Tetracycline—For H. Pylori (Systemic).*

In providing consultation, consider emphasizing the following selected information (» = major clinical significance):

Before using this medication

» Conditions affecting use, especially:

Sensitivity to bismuth subsalicylate, aspirin, or other salicylates; metronidazole or other nitroimidazole derivatives; or any of the tetracyclines

Pregnancy—Use is not recommended during pregnancy since tetracycline may cause permanent discoloration of the teeth and enamel hypoplasia in the fetus; animal studies have shown tetracycline to be embryotoxic

Breast-feeding—Metronidazole and tetracycline are distributed into breast milk

Use in children—Tetracycline should not be used in children younger than 8 years of age because of risk of permanent tooth discoloration or enamel hypoplasia; bismuth subsalicylate should not be used in children and adolescents who have or are recovering from chickenpox or influenza, as it may mask early signs of Reye's syndrome

Dental—Tetracycline should not be used during pregnancy or in children younger than 8 years of age because of risk of permanent tooth discoloration or enamel hypoplasia

Surgical—Tetracycline used concurrently with methoxyflurane may result in fatal renal toxicity

Other medications, especially alcohol; antacids; anticoagulants; antidiabetic agents; aspirin or other salicylates; disulfiram; hepatic enzyme inducers; hepatic enzyme inhibitors; insulin; methoxyflurane; milk or other dairy products; oral contraceptives; other medicines containing calcium, iron, magnesium, or zinc; penicillin; or sodium bicarbonate

Other medical problems, especially hepatic function impairment or renal function impairment

Proper use of this medication

Understanding patient instructions in package

Compliance with full course of therapy

» Proper dosing

Missed dose: Continuing on regular dosing schedule until the medication is finished; not doubling doses; checking with physician if more than four doses are missed

» Proper storage

Precautions while using this medication

» Avoiding use of aspirin and other salicylates

» Avoiding milk, milk formulas, and other dairy products within 1 to 2 hours of tetracycline

» Avoiding antacids or sodium bicarbonate within 1 to 2 hours of tetracycline; avoiding iron preparations within 2 to 3 hours of tetracycline

» Avoiding use of alcohol

» Caution if dizziness or lightheadedness occurs

» Using an alternative or additional means of contraception if currently taking oral contraceptives

» Possible photosensitivity reactions

Side/adverse effects

Signs of potential side effects, especially abdominal pain, diarrhea, melena, nausea, dizziness, paresthesia, vomiting, dysphagia, gastrointestinal hemorrhage, glossitis, hypertension, myocardial infarction, pain, photosensitivity reaction, rheumatoid arthritis, seizures, skin rash, stomatitis, and syncope

Darkening of tongue and grayish-black stools caused by bismuth subsalicylate may be alarming to patient although medically insignificant

Oral Dosage Forms

BISMUTH SUBSALICYLATE CHEWABLE TABLETS, METRONIDAZOLE TABLETS, AND TETRACYCLINE CAPSULES

Note: Each day's therapy is contained on a blister card and contains eight bismuth subsalicylate 262.4-mg chewable tablets, four metronidazole 250-mg tablets, and four tetracycline 500-mg capsules. They must be taken in combination with a histamine H_2-receptor antagonist.

Usual adult dose

Duodenal ulcer associated with *H. pylori*—

Oral, 525 mg bismuth subsalicylate, 250 mg metronidazole, and 500 mg tetracycline, taken four times a day (with meals and at bedtime) for fourteen days, in combination with the appropriate dose of a histamine H_2-receptor antagonist.

Note: Each bismuth subsalicylate tablet should be chewed and swallowed. The metronidazole tablet and the tetracycline capsule should be swallowed with a full glass (eight ounces) of water.

Usual pediatric dose

Safety and efficacy of this therapy in pediatric patients infected with *H. pylori* have not been established.

Usual geriatric dose

See *Usual adult dose*.

Strength(s) usually available

U.S.—

Eight bismuth subsalicylate 262.4-mg chewable tablets, four metronidazole 250-mg tablets, and four tetracycline 500-mg capsules per card (Rx) [*Helidac* (each blister card contains one day's dosage, fourteen days" therapy [fourteen cards] per carton)].

Auxiliary labeling

- Follow patient instructions included with the product.

Revised: 07/28/1998

BISOPROLOL—See *Beta-adrenergic Blocking Agents (Systemic)*

BITOLTEROL—See *Bronchodilators, Adrenergic (Inhalation-Local)*

BLENDERIZED ENTERAL NUTRITION FORMULAS—See *Enteral Nutrition Formulas (Systemic)*

BLEOMYCIN Systemic

VA CLASSIFICATION (Primary/Secondary): AN200/DE600

Commonly used brand name(s): *Blenoxane*.

Note: For a listing of dosage forms and brand names by country availability, see *Dosage Forms* section(s).

Category

Antineoplastic.

Indications

Note: Bracketed information in the *Indications* section refers to uses that are not included in U.S. product labeling.

Accepted

Carcinoma, head and neck (treatment)
Carcinoma, laryngeal (treatment)
[Carcinoma, paralaryngeal (treatment)]
[Carcinoma, esophageal (treatment)][1]
[Carcinoma, thyroid (treatment)][1]
Carcinoma, cervical (treatment)
Carcinoma, penile (treatment)
[Carcinoma, skin (treatment)]
Carcinoma, vulvar (treatment) or
Carcinoma, testicular (treatment)—Bleomycin is indicated for treatment of squamous cell carcinomas of the head and neck (including the mouth, tongue, tonsil, nasopharynx, oropharynx, sinus, palate, lip, buccal mucosa, gingiva, epiglottis, and larynx and paralarynx), cervix, penis, skin, and vulva. It is also indicated for treatment of testicular carcinoma (including embryonal cell carcinoma, choriocarcinoma, and teratocarcinoma), esophageal, and thyroid carcinomas.

Lymphomas, Hodgkin's (treatment) or
Lymphomas, non-Hodgkin's (treatment)—Bleomycin is indicated for treatment of Hodgkin's and non-Hodgkin's lymphomas.

[Kaposi's sarcoma, acquired immunodeficiency syndrome (AIDS)-associated (treatment)][1]—Bleomycin is indicated in the treatment of AIDS-associated Kaposi's sarcoma.

[Osteosarcoma (treatment)][1]—Bleomycin is indicated in the treatment of osteosarcoma.

[Malignant effusions, peritoneal (treatment)][1]
[Malignant effusions, pericardial (treatment)][1] or
Malignant effusions, pleural (treatment)—Bleomycin is indicated, by intracavitary administration, for treatment of peritoneal, pericardial, and pleural effusions.

[Melanoma, malignant (treatment)][1]—Bleomycin is indicated as reasonable medical therapy for the treatment of malignant melanoma (Evidence rating: IA).

[Tumors, germ cell, ovarian (treatment)][1]—Bleomycin is indicated for treatment of germ cell ovarian tumors.

[Tumors, trophoblastic, gestational (treatment)][1]—Bleomycin is indicated for treatment of gestational trophoblastic tumors.

[Mycosis fungoides (treatment)][1]—Bleomycin is indicated, in combination with other agents, for treatment of advanced stage mycosis fungoides.

[Verruca vulgaris (treatment)][1]—Bleomycin is indicated, by intralesional injection, for treatment of severe, recalcitrant common warts (verrucae vulgaris) not responding to conventional treatment.

Extreme caution is recommended in use of bleomycin for nonneoplastic conditions because of potential carcinogenicity with long-term use of this agent.

[1]Not included in Canadian product labeling.

Pharmacology/Pharmacokinetics

Physicochemical characteristics

Hygroscopic; inactivated *in vitro* by agents containing sulfhydryl groups, hydrogen peroxide, and ascorbic acid.

Mechanism of action/Effect

Bleomycin is classed as an antibiotic but is not used as an antimicrobial agent. Although bleomycin is effective against both cycling and noncycling cells, it seems to be most effective in the G_2 phase of cell division. Its exact mechanism of antineoplastic action is unknown but may involve binding to DNA, inducing lability of the DNA structure, and reduced synthesis of DNA, and, to a lesser extent, RNA and proteins.

Absorption

Approximately 45% of a dose is absorbed into the systemic circulation following intrapleural or intraperitoneal administration.

Protein binding

Very low (1%).

Biotransformation

Unknown; probably by enzyme degradation in tissues (based on animal studies). Tissue enzyme activity varies, which may determine toxicity and antitumor effect of bleomycin; enzyme activity is high in the liver and kidneys, as well as in bone marrow and lymph nodes, but is low in the skin and lungs. It is not known if any metabolites are active.

Half-life

Creatinine clearance greater than 35 mL per minute—115 minutes.

Creatinine clearance less than 35 mL per minute—Increases exponentially as creatinine clearance decreases.

Elimination

Renal, 60 to 70%, largely as unchanged drug; markedly reduced in renal failure.

In dialysis—Probably not dialyzable.

Precautions to Consider

Carcinogenicity/Mutagenicity

Secondary malignancies are potential delayed effects of many antineoplastic agents, although it is not clear whether the effect is related to their mutagenic or immunosuppressive action. The effects of dose and duration of therapy are also unknown, although risk seems to increase with long-term use.

Carcinostatic antibiotics have been shown to be carcinogenic in animals, and have been associated with an increased risk of development of secondary carcinomas in humans.

Bleomycin has not been found to be mutagenic according to the Ames test. However, chromosomal aberrations were reported in bone marrow cells and spermatogonia of mice given very high doses.

Pregnancy/Reproduction

Fertility—Gonadal suppression, resulting in amenorrhea or azoospermia, may occur in patients taking antineoplastic therapy, especially with the alkylating agents. In general, these effects appear to be related to dose and length of therapy and may be irreversible. Prediction of the degree of testicular or ovarian function impairment is complicated by the common use of combinations of several antineoplastics, which makes it difficult to assess the effects of individual agents.

Pregnancy—First trimester: It is usually recommended that use of antineoplastics, especially combination chemotherapy, be avoided whenever possible, especially during the first trimester. Although information is limited because of the relatively few instances of antineoplastic administration during pregnancy, the mutagenic, teratogenic, and carcinogenic potential of these medications must be considered.

Other hazards to the fetus include adverse reactions seen in adults.

In general, use of a contraceptive is recommended during cytotoxic drug therapy.

Bleomycin has been found to be teratogenic in mice given intraperitoneal doses of 0.6 to 5 Units per kg of body weight on days 7 to 12 of gestation; increased fetal resorptions occurred at doses of 3 and 5 Units per kg of body weight.

Breast-feeding

Although very little information is available regarding distribution of antineoplastic agents into breast milk, breast-feeding is not recommended while bleomycin is being administered because of the risks to the infant (adverse effects, mutagenicity, carcinogenicity).

Pediatrics

Appropriate studies on the relationship of age to the effects of bleomycin have not been performed in the pediatric population. However, no pediatrics-specific problems have been documented to date.

Geriatrics

Although appropriate studies on the relationship of age to the effects of bleomycin have not been performed in the geriatric population, there may be an increased risk of pulmonary toxicity in the elderly (over 70 years of age). In addition, elderly patients are more likely to have age-related renal function impairment, which may require reduction of dosage in patients receiving bleomycin.

Dental

Bleomycin may cause mild stomatitis.

Drug interactions and/or related problems

The following drug interactions and/or related problems have been selected on the basis of their potential clinical significance (possible mechanism in parentheses where appropriate)—not necessarily inclusive (» = major clinical significance):

» Anesthetics, general
(use in patients previously treated with bleomycin may result in rapid pulmonary deterioration because bleomycin causes sensitization of lung tissue to oxygen; even with concentrations of inspired oxygen considered to be safe, pulmonary fibrosis may develop postoperatively)

Antineoplastics, other or
Radiation therapy
(concurrent use may result in increased bleomycin toxicity, including bone marrow depression, which is rarely caused by bleomycin alone, and mucosal and pulmonary toxicity; dosage adjustment may be necessary)

Cisplatin
(cisplatin-induced renal function impairment may result in delayed clearance and bleomycin toxicity even at low doses; caution is recommended because of the frequent combined use of these two agents)

Vincristine
(sequential administration prior to bleomycin arrests cells in mitosis so that they are more susceptible to bleomycin; frequently used to therapeutic advantage)

Medical considerations/Contraindications

The medical considerations/contraindications included have been selected on the basis of their potential clinical significance (reasons given in parentheses where appropriate)—not necessarily inclusive (» = major clinical significance).

Risk-benefit should be considered when the following medical problems exist:

Hepatic function impairment
(potential hepatotoxicity)

» Pulmonary function impairment

Raynaud's phenomenon or
Vascular disease, peripheral
(for intralesional use in treatment of warts; local Raynaud's phenomenon reported in fingers injected with bleomycin)

» Renal function impairment, severe—creatinine clearance less than 25 to 35 mL per minute
(toxicity of bleomycin may be increased; it is recommended that dosage of bleomycin be reduced in patients with renal function impairment)

Sensitivity to bleomycin

» Caution should be used also in patients who have had previous cytotoxic drug therapy or radiation therapy (especially chest irradiation), as well as in patients who smoke, because of the increased risk of pulmonary toxicity.

Patient monitoring

» Auscultation of the lungs and
» Chest x-ray
(recommended prior to initiation of therapy and at periodic intervals during therapy)

Blood urea nitrogen (BUN) concentrations and
Creatinine concentrations, serum
(determinations recommended prior to initiation of therapy and at periodic intervals during therapy; frequency varies according to clinical state, agent, dose, and other agents being used concurrently)

» Pulmonary function studies, including single-breath carbon monoxide diffusion capacity (DLco) and forced vital capacity
(recommended at frequent intervals during therapy to detect early asymptomatic interstitial damage; however, DLco results are sometimes difficult to interpret because of the effects of weakness and anemia or the presence of an extensive lung tumor or effusion. Therapy with bleomycin should be discontinued at the first sign of pulmonary changes [for example, if forced vital capacity is reduced to 75% or less or DLco to 40% or less of pretreatment level]; if the changes are determined to be drug-related, bleomycin therapy should not be resumed)

Side/Adverse Effects

Note: There is some evidence that administration of bleomycin by continuous intravenous infusion over 24 hours rather than intermittently may be associated with less pulmonary and idiosyncratic toxicity, although mucocutaneous toxicity may be increased.

The main reported side effect with intralesional use is local burning or pain within 24 to 48 hours after injection. Blackening and eschar occur at the site of the lesion within 1 or 2 weeks and healing usually occurs within 2 to 3 weeks without scarring. Cases of urticaria, nail loss, and Raynaud's phenomenon have also been reported.

When bleomycin is used in combination with vinblastine for testicular carcinoma, vasospasm is a common vascular toxicity.

The following side/adverse effects have been selected on the basis of their potential clinical significance (possible signs and symptoms in parentheses where appropriate)—not necessarily inclusive:

Those indicating need for medical attention

Incidence more frequent

Fever and chills; pneumonitis, progressing to pulmonary fibrosis (cough; shortness of breath); ***stomatitis, mild*** (sores in mouth and on lips)—due to mucocutaneous toxicity

Note: *Fever and chills* occur in approximately 20 to 60% of patients, usually 3 to 6 hours after administration, last 4 to 12 hours, and become less frequent with continued use.

Pulmonary toxicity occurs in 10 to 40% of treated patients, usually 4 to 10 weeks after initiation of treatment; approximately 1% of treated patients have died of pulmonary fibrosis. Pulmonary toxicity is age- and dose-related, occurring most frequently in patients over 70 years of age and/or receiving a total dose greater than 400 Units (although it has been reported with doses as low as 20 to 60 Units). It may be irreversible and fatal; however, there is some evidence that in patients who survive, symptoms and pulmonary function parameters return to normal in approximately 2 years. It occurs at lower doses in patients who have received other antineoplastics or thoracic irradiation; mortality may be as high as 10% in patients who have received pulmonary irradiation. A low-dose allergic pneumonitis has also been reported.

The earliest signs of *pulmonary toxicity* are a decrease in diffusion capacity and fine rales. On chest x-ray, pneumonitis is seen as nonspecific patchy opacities, usually of the lower lung fields. Pulmonary function tests show a decrease in total lung volume and a decrease in vital capacity.

Incidence less frequent

Idiosyncratic reaction (confusion; faintness; fever and chills; wheezing)

Note: The *idiosyncratic reaction* occurs in approximately 1% of treated patients (1 to 6% of lymphoma patients). If not promptly treated, it may progress to sweating, dehydration, hypotension, and renal failure or cardiorespiratory collapse. It usually occurs at doses of 25 Units per square meter of body surface area or greater, although it has occurred with a dose of 7.5 Units. May be immediate or delayed by several hours, and occurs after the first or second dose.

Incidence rare

Hepatic toxicity—seen as changes in hepatic function tests; ***pleuropericarditis*** (sudden severe chest pain); ***renal toxicity***—seen as changes in renal function tests; ***vascular toxicity, including cerebral arteritis, cerebrovascular accident, myocardial infarction, and/or thrombotic microangiopathy*** (sudden weakness in arms or legs; sudden, severe chest pain)

Those indicating need for medical attention only if they continue or are bothersome

Incidence more frequent

Mucocutaneous toxicity (darkening or thickening of skin; itching of skin; skin rash or colored bumps on fingertips, elbows, or palms; skin redness or tenderness; dark stripes on skin; swelling of fingers; less frequently, changes in fingernails or toenails); ***vomiting and loss of appetite***

Note: *Skin toxicity* occurs in 25 to 50% of treated patients, usually 2 to 4 weeks after initiation of therapy; it appears to be related to cumulative dose and usually develops after 150 to 200 Units have been given.

Vomiting and loss of appetite occur in 15 to 30% of treated patients.

Incidence less frequent

Weight loss

Those not indicating need for medical attention

Incidence less frequent

Loss of hair

Note: *Loss of hair* begins after several weeks, with regrowth occurring several months later.

Those indicating the need for medical attention if they occur after medication is discontinued

Pulmonary toxicity (cough; shortness of breath)

Note: *Pulmonary toxicity* may occur up to 1 month after bleomycin is discontinued.

Patient Consultation

As an aid to patient consultation, refer to *Advice for the Patient, Bleomycin (Systemic)*.

In providing consultation, consider emphasizing the following selected information (» = major clinical significance):

Before using this medication

» Conditions affecting use, especially:

Sensitivity to bleomycin

Pregnancy—Use not recommended because of mutagenic, teratogenic, and carcinogenic potential; advisability of using contraception; telling physician immediately if pregnancy is suspected

Breast-feeding—Not recommended because of risk of serious side effects

Use in the elderly—Increased risk of pulmonary toxicity

Other medications, especially previous cytotoxic drug or radiation therapy

Other medical problems, especially pulmonary function impairment, severe renal function impairment, or history of smoking

Proper use of this medication

Caution in taking combination therapy; taking each medication at the proper time

Frequency of nausea, vomiting, and loss of appetite; importance of continuing medication despite stomach upset

» Proper dosing

Precautions while using this medication

» Importance of close monitoring by physician

» Caution if any kind of surgery (including dental surgery) or emergency treatment is required

Side/adverse effects

Signs of potential side effects, especially fever and chills, pneumonitis, pulmonary fibrosis, mild stomatitis due to mucocutaneous toxicity, idiosyncratic reaction, hepatic toxicity, pleuropericarditis, renal toxicity, or vascular toxicity, including cerebral arteritis, cerebrovascular accident, myocardial infarction, and/or thrombotic microangiopathy

Physician or nurse can help in dealing with side effects

Possibility of hair loss; normal hair growth should return after treatment has ended (may take several months)

Pulmonary toxicity more likely in smokers

General Dosing Information

See also *Patient monitoring*.

It is recommended that bleomycin be administered to patients under supervision of a physician experienced in cancer chemotherapy. It is also recommended that equipment and medications (including epinephrine, oxygen, diphenhydramine, and intravenous corticosteroids) necessary for treatment of a possible anaphylactic reaction be readily available at each administration of bleomycin.

A variety of dosage schedules, routes, and regimens of bleomycin, alone or in combination with other antitumor agents, are used. The prescriber may consult the medical literature in choosing a specific dosage or route.

Because of the risk of an idiosyncratic reaction in lymphoma patients, one test dose of 1 or 2 Units or less of bleomycin (base) given 2 to 4 hours prior to initiation of therapy at regular dosage may be used, although the test dose does not always detect reactors.

Some clinicians recommend premedication of patients receiving bleomycin with acetaminophen, steroids, and diphenhydramine hydrochloride to reduce drug fever and the risk of anaphylaxis.

Bleomycin may be administered intravenously or intra-arterially slowly over a period of 10 minutes, or may be further diluted with 50 to 100 mL of the initial diluent for administration by regional infusion.

It is recommended that the dosage of bleomycin be reduced in patients with renal function impairment (creatinine clearance less than 25 to 35 mL per minute). For example, dosage may be adjusted as follows:

Serum creatinine (mg/dL)	Serum creatinine (micromoles per liter)	Fraction of normal dose to be given
1.5–2	130–180	1/2
2.5–4	180–350	1/4
4–6	350–530	1/5
6–10	530–900	1/10–1/20

Safety considerations for handling this medication

There is limited but increasing evidence and concern that personnel involved in preparation and administration of parenteral antineoplastics may be at some risk because of the potential mutagenicity, teratogenicity, and/or carcinogenicity of these agents, although the actual risk is unknown. USP advisory panels recommend cautious handling both in preparation and disposal of antineoplastic agents. Precautions that have been suggested include:

- Use of a biological containment cabinet during reconstitution and dilution of parenteral medications and wearing of disposable surgical gloves and masks.

• Use of proper technique to prevent contamination of the medication, work area, and operator during transfer between containers (including proper training of personnel in this technique).

• Cautious and proper disposal of needles, syringes, vials, ampuls, and unused medication.

A number of medical centers have developed detailed guidelines for handling of antineoplastic agents.

Combination chemotherapy

Bleomycin is usually used in combination with other agents in various regimens. As a result, incidence and/or severity of side effects may be altered and different dosages (usually reduced) may be used. For example, bleomycin is part of the following chemotherapeutic combination (a commonly used acronym is in parentheses):

—doxorubicin, bleomycin, vinblastine, and dacarbazine (ABVD).

For specific dosages and schedules, consult the literature. For information regarding each agent, consult the individual monographs.

For treatment of adverse effects

Treatment of the idiosyncratic reaction is symptomatic and may consist of volume expansion, pressor agents, antihistamines, and corticosteroids.

Parenteral Dosage Forms

Note: Bracketed uses in the *Dosage Forms* section refer to categories of use and/or indications that are not included in U.S. product labeling.

A Unit of bleomycin is equal to the formerly used milligram activity. The term milligram activity is a misnomer and was changed to Units to be more precise.

BLEOMYCIN FOR INJECTION USP

Note: The doses and strength of the available dosage form are expressed in terms of bleomycin base (not the sulfate salt).

Usual adult and adolescent dose

Squamous cell carcinoma

Non-Hodgkin's lymphomas

Testicular carcinoma—

Intramuscular, intravenous, or subcutaneous, 0.25 to 0.5 Units (base) per kg of body weight or 10 to 20 Units per square meter of body surface area one or two times a week or

Intravenous infusion, continuous, 0.25 Units (base) per kg of body weight or 15 Units per square meter of body surface area per day (over twenty-four hours) for four to five days.

Hodgkin's lymphomas—

Initially, intramuscular, intravenous, or subcutaneous, 0.25 to 0.5 Units (base) per kg of body weight or 10 to 20 Units per square meter of body surface area one or two times a week.

Maintenance: Intramuscular or intravenous, after a 50% response occurs, 1 Unit (base) a day or 5 Units a week.

Squamous cell carcinoma of the head, neck, or uterine cervix—

Regional arterial infusion, 30 to 60 Units (base) a day over a period of one to twenty-four hours.

[Esophageal carcinoma][1] or

[Germ cell ovarian tumors][1] or

[Gestational trophoblastic tumors][1] or

[Kaposi's sarcoma, AIDS-associated][1] or

[Malignant melanoma][1] or

[Mycosis fungoides][1] or

[Osteosarcoma][1] or

[Paralaryngeal carcinoma][1] or

[Skin carcinoma][1] or

[Thyroid carcinoma][1]—

Consult medical literature and manufacturer's literature for information on appropriate dosage.

[Malignant effusions][1]—

Intrapleural, 15 to 120 Units (base) in 100 mL of sodium chloride injection, instilled, and after twenty-four hours, removed.

Intraperitoneal, 60 to 120 Units (base) in 100 mL of sodium chloride injection, instilled, and after twenty-four hours, removed.

[Verruca vulgaris][1]—

Intralesional, 0.2 to 0.8 Units (base) (according to size) one or more times at intervals of two to four weeks, up to a maximum total dose of 2 Units, using a solution of 15 Units of Sterile Bleomycin Sulfate USP in 15 mL of 0.9% sodium chloride injection or water for injection.

Usual adult prescribing limits

Because of the risk of pulmonary toxicity, total doses exceeding 225 to 400 Units (base) (less in patients with renal or pulmonary function impairment) should be given with great caution. If bleomycin is administered intrapleurally or intraperitoneally, one half of the administered dose should be counted towards this total.

Usual pediatric dose

See *Usual adult and adolescent dose*.

Strength(s) usually available

U.S.—

15 Units (base) (Rx) [*Blenoxane*].

Canada—

15 Units (base) (Rx) [*Blenoxane*].

Packaging and storage

Store between 2 and 8 °C (36 and 46 °F).

Preparation of dosage form

Sterile bleomycin sulfate may be prepared for intramuscular or subcutaneous use by dissolving the contents of the vial (15 Units [base]) in 1 to 5 mL of sterile water for injection, 0.9% sodium chloride for injection, or bacteriostatic water for injection.

U.S.—Sterile Bleomycin Sulfate USP may be prepared for intravenous use by dissolving the contents of the vial (15 Units [base]) in 5 mL or more of 0.9% sodium chloride injection.

Canada—Sterile bleomycin sulfate may be prepared for intravenous or intra-arterial use by dissolving the contents of the vial (15 Units [base]) in 5 to 20 mL of 0.9% sodium chloride for injection.

Use of diluents containing benzyl alcohol is not recommended for preparation of medications for use in neonates. A fatal toxic syndrome consisting of metabolic acidosis, central nervous system (CNS) depression, respiratory problems, renal failure, hypotension, and possibly seizures and intracranial hemorrhages has been associated with this use.

Stability

U.S.—Reconstituted solutions of Sterile Bleomycin Sulfate USP in 0.9% sodium chloride injection are stable for 24 hours at room temperature, or for at least 14 days if refrigerated.

Canada—Reconstituted solutions are stable for 8 hours at room temperature and at least 48 hours when refrigerated.

---

[1]Not included in Canadian product labeling.

Selected Bibliography

DeVita VT, Hellman S, Rosenberg SA, editors. Cancer: principles and practice of oncology. 5th ed. Philadelphia: Lippincott-Raven; 1997.

Revised: 07/08/1998

BORTEZOMIB Systemic†

VA CLASSIFICATION (Primary): AN300

Commonly used brand name(s): *Velcade*.

Note: For a listing of dosage forms and brand names by country availability, see *Dosage Forms* section(s).

†Not commercially available in Canada.

Category

Antineoplastic.

Indications

Accepted

Multiple myeloma (treatment)—Bortezomib for injection is indicated for the treatment of multiple myeloma patients who have received at least 1 prior therapy.

[Mantle cell lymphoma, second line therapy[1]]—Mantle cell lymphoma (MCL) represents approximately 6% of all lymphomas. It has the poorest long-term survival of all lymphoma subtypes, with a median survival of only 3 years. Overall response rates of approximately 70% with complete remissions in 20 to 40% have been reported. CHOP-like regimens (cyclophosphamide, doxorubicin, vincristine, prednisone) represent the standard therapeutic approach. Fludarabine-based regimens, CHOP plus rituximab, and HyperCVAD (fractionated cyclophosphamide, doxorubicin, vincristine, dexamethasone) with or without stem cell transplantation are also commonly used. Similarly, no consensus exists for treatment of patients with relapsed MCL. Therapeutic options include peripheral blood stem cell transplant, allogeneic stem cell transplant, fludarabine-based regimens, and even repeated courses of CHOP-like chemotherapy. Innovative approaches such as thalidomide, flavopiridol, m-TOR inhibitors, and bortezomib have demonstrated preclinical activity in pretreated MCL patients.

Promising data have emerged for the use of bortezomib in patients with MCL. In four, single-agent, phase II, open label, trials response rates ranged from 30% to 50% with durations exceeding 6 months in heavily pretreated patients. All studies reported reasonable toxicity profiles, with gastrointestinal, thrombocytopenia, neutropenia, fatigue, dizziness, neuropathy, and myalgia being the most common.

[1]Not included in Canadian product labeling.

Pharmacology/Pharmacokinetics

Physicochemical characteristics

Molecular weight—384.24.

Solubility—Bortezomib as the monomeric boronic acid is soluble in water, 3.3–3.8 mg/mL in a pH range of 2–6.5.

Mechanism of action/Effect

Bortezomib is a reversible inhibitor of the chymotrypsin-like activity of the 26S proteasome in mammalian cells. The 26S proteasome degrades ubiquitinated proteins responsible in regulating intracellular concentrations of specific proteins, thereby maintaining homeostasis within cells. Inhibition of the 26S proteasome prevents this targeted proteolysis, thereby affecting multiple signaling cascades within the cell. This disruption of normal homeostatic mechanisms can lead to cell death. Experiments have shown that bortezomib is cytotoxic to many types of cancer cells *in vitro*. In non-clinical tumor models bortezomib caused a delay in *in vivo* tumor growth including multiple myeloma.

Protein binding

High (83%)—over the concentration range of 100–1000 ng/ml.

Biotransformation

Bortezomib is primarily oxidatively metabolized via cytochrome P450 enzymes 3A4, 2D6, 2C19, 2C9, and 1A2. The major metabolic pathway is deboronation to form two deboronated metabolites that subsequently undergo hydroxylation to several metabolites. Deboronated-bortezomib metabolites are inactive as 26S proteasome inhibitors.

Half-life

Elimination—9–15 hours

Peak plasma concentration

509 ng/mL (range = 109–1300 mg/mL) following intravenous administration of 1.3 mg per square meter of body surface area.

Elimination

Elimination of bortezomib in humans has not been characterized.

Precautions to Consider

Carcinogenicity

Carcinogenicity studies have not been conducted with bortezomib.

Mutagenicity

Bortezomib showed clastogenic activity in the *in vitro* chromosomal aberration assay using Chinese hamster ovary cells and was not genotoxic when tested in the *in vitro* mutagenicity assay (Ames test) and *in vivo* micronucleus assay in mice.

Pregnancy/Reproduction

Fertility—Fertility studies with bortezomib were not performed but evaluation of reproductive tissues has been performed in general toxicity studies. In the 6-month rat toxicity study, degenerative effects in the ovary were observed at doses 1/4 of the recommended clinical dose and degenerative changes in the testes occurred at 1.2 mg per m^2. Bortezomib could have a potential effect on either male or female fertility.

Pregnancy—Adequate and well-controlled studies in humans have not been done. Women of childbearing potential should avoid becoming pregnant while being treated with bortezomib. If bortezomib is used during pregnancy, or if the patient becomes pregnant while receiving this drug, the patient should be apprised of the potential hazard to the fetus.

Pregnant rabbits given bortezomib at doses approximately half the clinical dose experienced significant post-implantation loss and decreased number of live fetuses. Live fetuses from these liters also showed significant decreases in fetal weight.

In nonclinical developmental toxicity studies done in rats and rabbits given doses approximately half the clinical dose, bortezomib was not teratogenic.

FDA Pregnancy Category D

Breast-feeding

It is not known whether bortezomib is distributed in human milk. Because many drugs are distributed in human milk and because of the potential for serious adverse reactions in nursing infants from bortezomib, women should be advised against breast-feeding while being treated with bortezomib.

Pediatrics

No information is available on the relationship of age to the effects of bortezomib in the pediatric population. Safety and efficacy have not been established.

Geriatrics

Appropriate studies performed to date have not demonstrated geriatrics-specific problems that would limit the usefulness of bortezomib in the elderly. However, elderly patients are more likely to have age related medical problems which may require caution, adjustment in dosage or dosing interval in patients receiving bortezomib.

In clinical trials, patients aged 65 years or older had a lower response rate (19% versus 32% in patients under 65 years) and a greater incidence of Grade 3 or 4 events (85% versus 80% in patients aged 51 to 65 years and 74% in patients aged 50 years and under).

Pharmacogenetics

The effects of age, gender, and race on the pharmacokinetics of bortezomib have not been evaluated.

Drug interactions and/or related problems

The following drug interactions and/or related problems have been selected on the basis of their potential clinical significance (possible mechanism in parentheses where appropriate)—not necessarily inclusive (» = major clinical significance):

Note: No formal drug interaction studies have been done with bortezomib.

In vitro studies indicate that bortezomib is primarily a substrate of cytochrome P450 3A4, 2C19, and 1A2.

» Amiodarone, or
» Antivirals, or
» Isoniazid, or
» Nitrofurantoin, or
» Statins
(caution; concomitant use with bortezomib may increase the chance of peripheral neuropathy)

Antidiabetic agents, oral
(may require close monitoring of blood glucose levels and adjustment of antidiabetic medication dose with concomitant use; reports of hypoglycemia and hyperglycemia during clinical trials in diabetic patients receiving oral hypoglycemics)

CYP3A4 inducers or
CYP3A4 inhibitors
(should be closely monitored for either toxicities or reduced efficacy with concomitant use)

» Medicines associated with hypotension
(caution; management of orthostatic/postural hypotension may include adjustment of antihypertensive medications, hydration or administration of mineralocorticoids)

Medical considerations/Contraindications

The medical considerations/contraindications included have been selected on the basis of their potential clinical significance (reasons given in parentheses where appropriate)—not necessarily inclusive (» = major clinical significance).

Except under special circumstances, this medication should not be used when the following medical problem exists:

» Hypersensitivity to bortezomib, boron or mannitol

Risk-benefit should be considered when the following medical problems exist:

» Dehydration, or
» Syncope, history of
(caution; bortezomib treatment can cause orthostatic/postural hypotension; management of orthostatic/postural hypotension may include adjustment of antihypertensive medications, hydration, or administration of mineralocorticoids)

» Heart disease
(bortezomib may result in the acute development or exacerbation of congestive heart failure in patients with risk factors for or existing heart disease; patients at risk should be closely monitored)

» Hepatic impairment
(patients with hepatic impairment may be at increased risk of toxicity)

» Peripheral neuropathy
(patients may experience new symptoms or worsening symptoms during treatment with bortezomib)

Renal impairment
(patients with renal impairment (creatinine clearance less then 13 mL/min and on hemodialysis) may be at increased risk of toxicity)

» Tumor lysis syndrome
(patients at risk of tumor lysis syndrome should be monitored closely and appropriate precautions taken)

Patient monitoring

The following may be especially important in patient monitoring (other tests may be warranted in some patients, depending on condition; » = major clinical significance):

» Blood count, complete
(monitor frequently throughout treatment)

Blood glucose levels
(diabetic patients may require close monitoring and adjustment of antidiabetic medication dose)

» Peripheral neuropathy
(monitor for signs and symptoms of neuropathy such as burning sensation, hyperesthesia, hypesthesia, paresthesia, discomfort or neuropathic pain.)

» Platelet count
(monitor platelet count prior to each dose of bortezomib; therapy should be held when platelet count is < 25,000 per microliter and reinitiated at a reduced dose)

Side/Adverse Effects

The following side/adverse effects have been selected on the basis of their potential clinical significance (possible signs and symptoms in parentheses where appropriate)—not necessarily inclusive:

Those indicating need for medical attention

Incidence more frequent

Anemia (pale skin; troubled breathing with exertion; unusual bleeding or bruising; unusual tiredness or weakness); ***dehydration*** (confusion; decreased urination; dizziness; dry mouth; fainting; increase in heart rate; lightheadedness; rapid breathing; sunken eyes; thirst; unusual tiredness or weakness; wrinkled skin); ***dysesthesia*** (burning, crawling, itching, numbness, prickling, "pins and needles", or tingling feelings); ***dyspnea*** (shortness of breath; difficult or labored breathing; tightness in chest; wheezing); ***herpes zoster*** (painful blisters on trunk of body); ***hypotension*** (blurred vision, confusion, dizziness, faintness, or lightheadedness when getting up from a lying or sitting position suddenly; sweating; unusual tiredness or weakness); ***neutropenia*** (black, tarry, stools; chills; cough; fever; lower back or side pain; painful or difficult urination; pale skin; shortness of breath; sore throat; ulcers, sores, or white spots in mouth; unusual bleeding or bruising; unusual tiredness or weakness); ***paresthesias*** (burning, crawling, itching, numbness, prickling, "pins and needles", or tingling feelings); ***peripheral neuropathy*** (burning, numbness, tingling, or painful sensations; weakness in arms, hands, legs, or feet; unsteadiness or awkwardness); ***pneumonia*** (chest pain, cough, fever or chills, sneezing, shortness of breath, sore throat, troubled breathing, tightness in chest, wheezing); ***pyrexia*** (fever); ***thrombocytopenia*** (black, tarry stools; bleeding gums; blood in urine or stools; pinpoint red spots on skin; unusual bleeding or bruising); ***upper respiratory tract infection*** (ear congestion; nasal congestion; chills; cough; fever; sneezing, or sore throat; body aches or pain; headache; loss of voice; runny nose; unusual tiredness or weakness; difficulty in breathing)

Incidence not determined—Observed during clinical practice; estimates of frequency can not be determined

Acute pancreatitis (bloating; chills; constipation; darkened urine; fast heartbeat; fever; indigestion; loss of appetite; nausea; pains in stomach, side, or abdomen, possibly radiating to the back; vomiting; yellow eyes or skin); ***atrioventricular block complete*** (chest pain; dizziness; fainting; pounding, slow heartbeat; troubled breathing; unusual tiredness or weakness); ***cardiac tamponade*** (shortness of breath); ***deafness bilateral; disseminated intravascular coagulation*** (blood in stools; blood in urine; bruising; confusion; coughing or vomiting blood; persistent bleeding or oozing from puncture sites, mouth, or nose; rash; shortness of breath); ***dysautonomia*** (difficult or painful urination; dizziness or lightheadedness, especially when getting up from a lying or sitting position; fast heartbeat); ***encephalopathy*** (agitation; back pain; blurred vision; coma; confusion; dizziness; drowsiness; fever; hallucinations; headache; irritability; mood or mental changes; seizures; stiff neck; unusual tiredness or weakness; vomiting); ***hepatitis*** (dark urine; general tiredness and weakness; light-colored stools; nausea and vomiting; upper right abdominal pain; yellow eyes and skin); ***ischemic colitis*** (abdominal pain and tenderness; bloody stools; rectal bleeding)

Those indicating need for medical attention only if they continue or are bothersome

Incidence more frequent

Abdominal pain (stomach pain); ***arthralgia*** (pain in joints; muscle pain or stiffness; difficulty in moving); ***asthenic conditions*** (fatigue; malaise; weakness); ***anxiety*** (fear, nervousness); ***appetite decreased; back pain; blurred vision; Bone pain; constipation*** (difficulty having a bowel movement (stool)); ***cough; diarrhea; dizziness; dysgeusia*** (loss of taste; change in taste); ***dyspepsia*** (acid or sour stomach; belching; heartburn; indigestion, stomach discomfort, upset or pain); ***edema*** (swelling); ***headache; insomnia*** (sleeplessness; trouble sleeping; unable to sleep); ***muscle cramps; myalgia*** (joint pain, swollen joints; muscle aching or cramping; muscle pains or stiffness; difficulty in moving); ***nausea; pain in limb; pruritus*** (itching skin); ***rash; rigors*** (feeling unusually cold; shivering); ***vomiting***

Overdose

For more information on the management of overdose or unintentional ingestion, **contact a poison control center** (see *Poison Control Center Listing*).

Clinical effects of overdose

No cases of overdosage with bortezomib were reported during clinical trials. Single doses of up to 2.0 mg per square meter of body surface area per week have been administered in adults.

Treatment of overdose

There is no known specific antidote to bortezomib. Treatment is generally symptomatic and supportive.

Monitoring—
Monitoring vital signs.

Supportive care—
Maintaining blood pressure.
Maintaining body temperature.
Patients in whom intentional overdose is confirmed or suspected should be referred for psychiatric consultation.

Patient Consultation

As an aid to patient consultation, refer to *Advice for the Patient, Bortezomib (Systemic)*.

In providing consultation, consider emphasizing the following selected information (» = major clinical significance):

Before using this medication

» Conditions affecting use, especially:
Hypersensitivity to bortezomib, boron or mannitol
Pregnancy—Should use effective contraceptive to avoid pregnancy and if pregnancy occurs, physician should be contacted immediately
Breast-feeding—Should be advised against breast-feeding while being treated with bortezomib
Other medications, especially amiodarone, antivirals, isoniazid, nitrofurantoin, statins or medicines associated with hypotension.
Other medical problems, especially dehydration, heart disease, hepatic impairment, or peripheral neuropathy, renal impairment, risk of tumor lysis syndrome, or history of syncope

Proper use of this medication

» Proper injection technique
» Safe handling technique
» Proper dosing
Missed dose: Discuss with physician
Proper storage

Precautions while using this medication

Importance of discussing possible side effects with physician

» Caution if dizziness or drowsiness occurs; not driving, using machines, or anything else that requires alertness while taking bortezomib and for 24 hours after discontinuing it

» Drinking plenty of fluids to avoid dehydration and telling doctor if symptoms of dizziness or lightheadedness occur

Diabetic patients: Checking blood sugar level often if taking an oral antidiabetic medication while taking bortezomib and contacting doctor if any unusual changes

Side/adverse effects

Signs of potential side effects, especially anemia, dehydration, dysesthesias, dyspnea, herpes zoster, hypotension, neutropenia, paresthesias, peripheral neuropathy, pneumonia, pyrexia, thrombocytopenia, or upper respiratory tract infection

Signs of potential side effects observed during clinical practice, especially acute pancreatitis, atrioventricular block complete, cardiac tamponade, deafness bilateral, disseminated intravascular coagulation, dysautonomia, encephalopathy, hepatitis, or ischemic colitis

General Dosing Information

Patients receiving bortezomib should be under supervision of a physician experienced in cancer chemotherapy.

Patients should be advised regarding appropriate measures to avoid dehydration while on bortezomib therapy.

Patients should seek medical advice if symptoms of dizziness, lightheadedness or fainting spells occur.

Therapy should be withheld at the onset of any Grade 3 nonhematological or Grade 4 hematological toxicities excluding neuropathy. Once symptoms have resolved therapy may be reinstituted at a 25% reduced dose (1.3 mg/m²/dose reduced to 1 mg/m²/dose, 1 mg/m²/dose reduced to 0.7 mg/m²/dose).

Safety considerations for handling this medication

There is limited but increasing evidence and concern that personnel involved in preparation and administration of parenteral antineoplastics may be at some risk because of the potential mutagenicity, teratogenicity, and/or carcinogenicity of these agents, although the actual risk is unknown. USP advisory panels recommend cautious handling both in preparation and disposal of antineoplastic agents. Precautions that have been suggested include:

- Use of a biologic containment cabinet during reconstitution and dilution of parenteral medications and wearing of disposable surgical gloves and masks.
- Use of proper technique to prevent contamination of the medication, work area, and operator during transfer between containers (including proper training of personnel in this technique).
- Cautious and proper disposal of needles, syringes, vials, ampuls, and unused medication.

A number of medical centers have developed detailed guidelines for handling of antineoplastic agents.

Treatment of adverse effects

Treatment of nausea, diarrhea, constipation, and vomiting may require use of antiemetic and antidiarrheal medications. To prevent dehydration, fluid and electrolyte replacement should be administered.

Parenteral Dosage Forms

BORTEZOMIB FOR INJECTION

Usual adult and adolescent dose

Antineoplastic—

Patients with no symptoms or with Grade 1 symptoms of peripheral neuropathy (paresthesias and/or loss of reflexes without pain or loss of function)—

Intravenous, 1.3 mg/m²/dose as a bolus intravenous injection twice weekly for two weeks (days 1, 4, 8, and 11) followed by a 10–day rest period (days 12–21). For extended therapy of more than 8 cycles, administer on standard schedule or on a maintenance schedule of once weekly for 4 weeks (days 1, 8, 15, and 22) followed by a 13-day rest period (days 23 to 35). At least 72 hours should elapse between consecutive doses.

Patients with Grade 1 with pain or Grade 2 symptoms of peripheral neuropathy (interfering with function but not with activities of daily living)—

Intravenous, 1 mg/m²/dose as a bolus intravenous injection twice weekly for two weeks (days 1, 4, 8, and 11) followed by a 10–day rest period (days 12–21). At least 72 hours should elapse between consecutive doses.

Patients with Grade 2 with pain or Grade 3 symptoms of peripheral neuropathy (interfering with activities of daily living)—

Withhold bortezomib therapy until toxicity resolves. When toxicity resolves reinitiate with a reduced intravenous dose of 0.7 mg/m² once per week.

Patients with Grade 4 symptoms of peripheral neuropathy (permanent sensory loss that interferes with function)—

Discontinue use of treatment.

Dose modification and reinitiation of therapy for toxicities excluding neuropathy—

Bortezomib therapy should be withheld at the onset of any Grade 3 non-hematological or Grade 4 hematological toxicities excluding neuropathy. Once the symptoms of toxicity have resolved, bortezomib may be reinitiated at a 25% reduced dose.

- from 1.3 mg per square meter of body surface area per dose to 1 mg per square meter of body surface area per dose
- from 1 mg per square meter of body surface area per dose to 0.7 mg per square meter of body surface area per dose

Usual pediatric dose

Safety and efficacy have not been established.

Usual geriatric dose

See *Usual adult and adolescent dose*..

Strength(s) usually available

U.S.—

3.5 mg as a sterile lyophilized powder (Rx) [*Velcade* (preservative-free; mannitol)].

Packaging and storage

Unopened vials may be stored at controlled room temperature 25 °C (77 °F); excursions permitted from 15 to 30 °C (59 to 86 °F). When reconstituted as directed, bortezomib may be stored at 25 °C (77 °F). Protect from freezing or excessive heat. Protect from light.

Preparation of dosage form

Each vial of bortezomib for injection must be reconstituted with 3.5 mL of normal saline (0.9% sodium chloride injection) prior to use. The reconstituted solution should be clear and colorless, if any discoloration or particulate matter is observed, do not use. See the manufacturer's package insert for instructions.

Stability

Unopened vials of bortezomib are stable until the date indicated on the package when stored in the original package protected from light. Reconstituted bortezomib should be administered within 8 hours of preparation. The reconstituted material may be stored in the original vial and/or the syringe prior to administration. The product may be stored for up to 8 hours in a syringe; however, total storage time for the reconstituted material must not exceed 8 hours when exposed to normal indoor lighting.

Auxiliary labeling

- May caused dizziness or drowsiness. Be careful while driving or operating machinery.

Note

Caution; avoid contact with skin during handling and preparation of bortezomib. Proper aseptic technique, gloves and protective clothing should be used.

Revised: 08/01/2005
Developed: 12/18/2003

BOSENTAN Systemic

VA CLASSIFICATION (Primary): CV900

Commonly used brand name(s): *Tracleer.*

Note: For a listing of dosage forms and brand names by country availability, see *Dosage Forms* section(s).

Category

Antihypertensive, (pulmonary); Endothelin receptor antagonist.

Indications

Note: Bracketed information in the indications section refers to uses that are not included in the U.S. product labeling.

Accepted

Pulmonary arterial hypertension—Bosentan is indicated for the treatment of pulmonary arterial hypertension in patients with WHO Class III or IV symptoms, to improve exercise ability and decrease the rate of clinical worsening

[Pulmonary hypertension secondary to scleroderma]—Bosentan is indicated for the treatment of pulmonary hypertension secondary to scleroderma.

Pharmacology/Pharmacokinetics

Physicochemical characteristics

Chemical Group—Pyrimidine
Molecular weight—569.64.

Mechanism of action/Effect

Bosentan is a dual endothelin receptor antagonist. Endothelin-1 (ET-1) is a neurohormone, and a potent vasoconstrictor with the ability to promote fibrosis, cell proliferation and tissue remodeling. The effects of which are mediated by binding to ET_A and ET_B receptors in the endothelium and vascular smooth muscle. ET-1 concentrations are elevated in plasma and lung tissue of patients with pulmonary arterial hypertension, suggesting a pathogenic role for ET-1 in this disease.

Bosentan exerts a specific and competitive antagonist at endothelin receptor types ET_A and ET_B, with a slightly higher affinity for ET_A than ET_B receptors. Bosentan decreases both pulmonary and systemic vascular resistance resulting in increased cardiac output without increasing heart rate.

Absorption
Absolute bioavailability—approximately 50%
Absorption is unaffected by food

Distribution
Volume of distribution (Vol_D—approximately 18 liters

Protein binding
Very high (greater than 98%); bound mainly to albumin

Biotransformation
Bosentan is metabolized in the liver by cytochrome P450 isoenzymes (CYP3A4 and CYP2C9) resulting in three metabolites, one of which, Ro 48-5033, is pharmacologically active and may contribute 10 to 20% to the total activity of the parent compound. Bosentan is an inducer of CYP2C9, CYP3A4 and possibly CYP2C19.

In patients with severe renal impairments (creatine clearance 15–30 mL per min) the plasma concentrations of the three metabolites were increased about 2 fold compared to patients with normal renal function. Differences do not appear to be clinically significant since less than 3% of an administered dose is excreted in the urine.

Half-life
Approximately 5 hours

Time to peak concentration
Approximately 3 to 5 hours

Time to steady state concentration
Approximately 3 to 5 days

Peak serum concentration
Plasma concentration—

A 30 to 40% increased bosentan exposure was observed in patients with severe chronic heart failure. The pharmacokinetics of bosentan was not studied in patients with pulmonary arterial hypertension, but exposure is expected to be greater.

Elimination
Biliary—eliminated by biliary excretion following metabolism in the liver.Total clearance after a single intravenous dose is about 8 L per hr.

Renal—Less than 3% of oral dose is recovered in urine.

Precautions to Consider

Carcinogenicity
Two years of dietary administration of bosentan to mice produced an increased incidence of hepatocellular adenomas and carcinomas in males at doses as low as 450 mg per kg of body weight per day (about 8 times the maximum recommended human dose [MRHD] of 125 mg twice daily on a mg per m^2 basis). In the same study, doses greater than 2000 mg per kg of body weight per day (about 32 times the MRHD) were associated with an increased incidence of colon adenomas in both males and females.

In rats, oral administration of bosentan for two years produced a small, significant increase in the combined incidence of thyroid follicular cell adenomas and carcinomas in male rats treated at doses of 3000 mg per kg of body weight per day, about 600 times the human oral therapeutic dose in a 50 kg patient. In this same study, there was evidence for a mild thyroid hormonal imbalance induced by bosentan in rats

In a two year study in rats, the administration of bosentan was associated with an increased incidence of brain astrocytomas in males at doses as low as 500 mg per kg of body weight per day (about 16 times the MRHD).

Mutagenicity
In a comprehensive study using *in vitro* tests (microbial mutagenesis assay, unscheduled DNA synthesis assay, V-79 mammalian cell mutagenesis assay and human lymphocyte assay) and an *in vivo* mouse micronucleus assay there was no evidence for any mutagenic or clastogenic activity of bosentan.

Pregnancy/Reproduction
Fertility—In animal studies in which male and female rats were treated with bosentan at oral doses of up to 1500 mg per kg of body weight per day (50 times the MRHD on a mg per m^2 basis) or intravenous doses up to 40 mg per kg of body weight per day, showed no effects on sperm count, sperm motility, mating performance or fertility. An increased incidence of testicular tubular atrophy was observed in rats given bosentan orally at doses as low as 125 mg per kg of body weight per day (about 4 times the MRHD and the lowest doses tested) for two years but not at doses as high as 1500 mg per kg of body weight per day (about 50 times the MRHD) for 6 months. Effects on sperm count and motility were evaluated only in much shorter duration fertility studies in which males had been exposed to the drug for 4 to 6 weeks.

An increased incidence of tubular atrophy was not observed in mice treated for 2 years at doses up to 4500 mg per kg of body weight per day (about 75 times the MRHD) or in dogs treated up to 500 mg per kg of body weight per day (about 50 times the MRHD).

Note: Many endothelin receptor antagonists have profound effects on the histology and function of the testes in animals. These drugs have been shown to induce atrophy of the seminiferous tubules of the testes and to reduce sperm counts and male fertility in rats when administered for longer than 10 weeks. Where studied, testicular tubular atrophy and decreases in male fertility observed with endothelin receptor antagonists appear irreversible.

Pregnancy—Bosentan is expected to cause fetal harm if administered to pregnant women and should not be used during pregnancy. Although there are no data on the use of bosentan in pregnant women, it is very likely that bosentan will produce major birth defects if used by pregnant women, as this effect has been seen consistently when administered to animals. Pregnancy must be excluded before the start of treatment, and follow up pregnancy tests should be obtained monthly in women of childbearing potential. Women should not rely on hormonal contraception, including oral, injectable, transdermal, and implantable contraceptives as the sole means of contraception because these may not be effective. For more information, see *Drug interactions and/or related problems*.

In animal studies bosentan has been shown to teratogenic in rats when given doses greater than or equal to 60 mg per kg of body weight per day (twice the maximum recommended human oral dose of 125 mg twice a day on an mg per m^2 basis). Bosentan rat studies showed dose-dependent teratogenicity when given at doses about 6 times the human oral therapeutic dose in a 50 kg patient. In an embryo-fetal toxicity study in rats, bosentan showed teratogenic effects, including malformations of the head, mouth, face and large blood vessels-Bosentan increased stillbirths and pup mortality at oral doses of 60 and 300 mg per kg of body weight per day (2 and 10 times, respectively, the maximum recommended human dose on a mg per m^2 basis). No birth defects were observed in rabbits at a dose of up to 1500 mg per kg of body weight per day, where plasma concentrations were lower than those reached in the rat.

FDA Pregnancy Category X

Breast-feeding
It is not known whether bosentan is distributed into breast milk. Because many drugs are distributed into breast milk, breast-feeding while taking bosentan is not recommended.

Pediatrics
No information is available on the relationship of age to the effects of bosentan in the pediatric population. Safety and efficacy have not been established.

Geriatrics
Appropriate studies on the relationship of age to the effects of bosentan have not been performed in the geriatric population. However, elderly patients are more likely to have age-related medical problems including renal and liver function impairment. Caution should be used when administering bosentan to the elderly patients.

Drug interactions and/or related problems
The following drug interactions and/or related problems have been selected on the basis of their potential clinical significance (possible mechanism in parentheses where appropriate)—not necessarily inclusive (» = major clinical significance):

Note: Combinations containing any of the following medications, depending on the amount present, may also interact with this medication.

» Concomitant administration of:
» CYP2C9 inhibitor (i.e. amiodarone, fluconazole) and
» CYP3A4 inhibitor (e.g., itraconazole, ketoconazole, ritonavir)
(concomitant administration of a CYP2C9 and CYP3A4 inhibitor with bosentan may lead to large increases in bosentan plasma concentrations; co-administration of this combination with bosentan is not recommended)

» Cyclosporine A
(cyclosporine A coadministered with bosentan results in decreases in plasma concentration of cyclosporine A by approximately 50% and increases the trough concentrations of bosentan by approximately 30-fold; concomitant use is contraindicated)

» Hormonal contraceptives (implantable) or
» Hormonal contraceptives (injectable) or
» Hormonal contraceptives (oral) or

» Hormonal contraceptives (transdermal)
(possibility of failure when co-administered with bosentan; an alternate or additional method of contraception should be considered; women should not rely on hormonal contraception alone)

» Hypoglycemic agents, oral, such as
» Glyburide
(oral hypoglycemic agents which are metabolized by CYP2C9 or CYP3A4 are expected to have reduced plasma concentrations; patients may experience the possibility of worsened glucose control)
(glyburide coadministered with bosentan results in increases the risk of elevated liver aminotransferases; decreases the plasma concentration of glyburide by approximately 40%; decreases the plasma concentration of bosentan by approximately 30%; concomitant use is **contraindicated**)

» Ketoconazole
(ketoconazole coadministered with bosentan, 125 mg twice daily, results in increases in the plasma concentration of bosentan approximately 2-fold; no dose adjustments for bosentan are recommended but increased effects should be considered)

Sildenafil
(multiple doses of 125 mg bosentan twice daily and 80 mg sildenafil three times daily in healthy subjects showed a 63% reduction of sildenafil plasma concentrations and 50% increased bosentan plasma concentrations; dose adjustments are not necessary; this recommendation is true for sildenafil in treatment of pulmonary arterial hypertension or erectile dysfunction)

» Statins, such as
» Atorvastatin or
» Lovastatin or
» Simvastatin
(statins that are significantly metabolized by CYP3A4, such as lovastatin and atorvastatin when coadministered with bosentan may have reduced plasma concentrations; the possibility of reduced statin efficacy should be considered; patients using CYP3A4 metabolized statins should have cholesterol levels monitored after bosentan is initiated to see whether a dose adjustment of the statin is needed)
(simvastatin coadministered with bosentan results in decreases in plasma concentrations of simvastatin, and its active β-hydroxy acid metabolite, by approximately 50%; plasma concentrations of bosentan were not affected)

Tacrolimus
(caution should be exercised with concomitant use)

Warfarin
(warfarin coadministered with bosentan [oral 500 mg twice daily for 6 days] results in a decrease the plasma concentration of both S-warfarin and R-warfarin by 29 and 38%, respectively; the need to change the warfarin dose during clinical studies due to changes in INR or due to adverse events was similar among bosentan and placebo treated patients)

Laboratory value alterations

The following have been selected on the basis of their potential clinical significance (possible effect in parentheses where appropriate)—not necessarily inclusive (» = major clinical significance).

With physiology/laboratory test values

» Liver function tests such as
» Alanine aminotransferase (ALT [SGPT]), serum and
» Aspartate aminotransferase (AST [SGOT]), serum
(bosentan causes at least a 3 fold (upper limit of normal; ULN) elevation of liver aminotransferases (ALT and AST) in about 11% of patients accompanied by elevated bilirubin in a small number of cases; the combination of hepatocellular injury and increases in total bilirubin is a marker for potential serious liver injury.)
(the elevations of AST and/or ALT are dose dependent, occur both early and late in treatment, usually progress slowly and typically, asymptomatic, and to date have been reversible after treatments interruption or cessation; these aminotransferase elevations may reverse spontaneously while continuing treatment with bosentan)

» Hematologic tests such as
» Hemoglobin and
» Hematocrit
(bosentan causes a dose related decrease in hemoglobin and hematocrit; the explanation for the change in hemoglobin is not known, but it does not appear to be hemorrhage or hemolysis)
(the overall mean decrease in hemoglobin concentration for bosentan-treated patients was 0.9 g per dL [change to end treatment]; most of this decrease of hemoglobin concentration was detected during the first few weeks of treatment and hemoglobin levels stabilized by 4 to 12 weeks of treatment)
(in clinical studies, marked decreases in hemoglobin (> 15% decrease from baseline resulting in values < 11 g per dL) were observed in 6% of bosentan treated patients compared to 3% of placebo treated patients; a decrease in hemoglobin concentration by at least 1 g per dL was observed in 57% bosentan treated patients compared to 29% of placebo treated patients)

Medical considerations/Contraindications

The medical considerations/contraindications included have been selected on the basis of their potential clinical significance (reasons given in parentheses where appropriate)—not necessarily inclusive (» = major clinical significance).

Except under special circumstances, this medication should not be used when the following medical problem exists:

» Hypersensitivity to bosentan or any component of the medication

» Liver impairment, moderate or severe
(bosentan should generally be avoided in patients with moderate or severe liver impairment; elevations of aminotransferases and bilirubin are markers for potential serious liver injury; bosentan use should generally be avoided in patients with baseline values of liver transaminases greater than 3 times the upper limit of normal (ULN) because monitoring liver injury may be more difficult; when the total bilirubin is increased to greater than 2 times the ULN, treatment should be discontinued)

Risk-benefit should be considered when the following medical problems exist :

Liver impairment, mild
(caution should be exercised when administering to patients with mild liver impairment)

Patient monitoring

The following may be especially important in patient monitoring (other tests may be warranted in some patients, depending on condition; » = major clinical significance):

Cholesterol monitoring
(patients using CYP3A4 metabolized statins should have cholesterol levels monitored after bosentan is initiated to determine whether the statin dose adjustments are necessary)

» Hematocrit monitoring
(hemoglobin concentration recommended at one month; every 3 months of treatment; every 3 months thereafter; if a marked decrease in hemoglobin concentration occurs, further evaluation should be undertaken to determine the cause and need for specific treatment)

» Liver aminotransferases, such as
» Alanine aminotransferase (ALT [SGPT]), serum and
» Aspartate aminotransferase (AST [SGOT]), serum
(bosentan treatment should be stopped when liver aminotransferase elevations are accompanied by clinical symptoms of liver injury such as, nausea, vomiting, fever, abdominal pain, jaundice, increases of bilirubin greater than 2 times ULN or unusual lethargy or fatigue)
(liver aminotransferase levels must be measured prior to initiation of treatment then every month for the duration of treatment; if elevated aminotransferase levels are observed, changes in monitoring and treatment must be initiated:
• >3 and ≤5 x ULN—confirm by another aminotransferase test; if confirmed, reduce daily dose or interrupt treatment and continue to monitor at least every two weeks; if levels return to pre-treatment values, continue or reintroduce treatment.
• >5 and ≤8 x ULN—confirm by another aminotransferase test; if confirmed, stop treatment and monitor levels at least every two week; if levels return to pre-treatment values, continue or consider reintroduction of treatment
• >8 x ULN—treatment should be stopped and reintroduction of bosentan should not be considered
(bosentan reintroduced at a starting dose and aminotransferase levels must then be checked within 3 days after re-introduction, then again after 2 weeks and thereafter as needed)

» Pregnancy testing
(prior to initiation of bosentan therapy the possibility of pregnancy must be excluded; either the patient is not sexually active or has a negative urine or serum pregnancy test performed during the first 5 days of a normal menstrual period and at least 11 days after the last unprotected act of sexual intercourse)
(monthly serum pregnancy tests should be obtained in women of childbearing potential after initial dosing)

(immediate pregnancy testing should be performed if there is any delay in the onset of menses or any other reason to suspect pregnancy)

Side/Adverse Effects

The following side/adverse effects have been selected on the basis of their potential clinical significance (possible signs and symptoms in parentheses where appropriate)—not necessarily inclusive:

Those indicating need for medical attention

Incidence more frequent

Hepatic dysfunction (dark urine; light-colored stools; loss of appetite; nausea and vomiting; unusual tiredness; yellow eyes or skin; fever with or without chills; stomach pain); ***hypotension*** (blurred vision; confusion; dizziness; faintness or lightheadedness when getting up from a lying or sitting position; sudden sweating; unusual tiredness or weakness)

Incidence less frequent

Edema (swelling)

Incidence not determined—Observed during clinical practice; estimates of frequency can not be determined

Fluid retention (decrease in amount of urine; noisy, rattling breathing; shortness of breath; swelling of fingers, hands, feet, or lower legs; troubled breathing at rest; weight gain)—in patients with pulmonary hypertension occurring within weeks after starting bosentan; ***hepatic cirrhosis*** (yellow eyes or skin)—after prolonged [>12 months] therapy with bosentan in patients with multiple co-morbidities and drug therapies; ***hypersensitivity*** (fast heartbeat; fever; hives; itching; irritation; hoarseness; joint pain, stiffness or swelling; rash; redness of skin; shortness of breath; swelling of eyelids, face, lips, hands, or feet; tightness in chest; troubled breathing or swallowing; wheezing); ***pulmonary edema*** (chest pain; difficult, fast, noisy breathing, sometimes with wheezing; blue lips and fingernails; pale skin; increased sweating; coughing that sometimes produces a pink frothy sputum; shortness of breath; swelling in legs and ankles); ***pulmonary veno-occlusive disease (PVOD)*** (shortness of breath, fatigue on exertion, fainting, coughing up blood); ***rash***

Note: If signs of pulmonary edema should occur when taking bosentan, the possibility of associated PVOD should be considered.

The contribution of bosentan in rare cases of unexplained hepatic cirrhosis could not be excluded.

Those indicating need for medical attention only if they continue or are bothersome

Incidence more frequent

Edema, lower limb (swelling of the legs); ***flushing*** (feeling of warmth; redness of the face, neck, arms, and occasionally upper chest); ***headache; nasopharyngitis*** (stuffy or runny nose; muscle aches; unusual tiredness or weakness; fever; sore throat; headache); ***palpitations*** (fast, irregular, pounding, or racing heartbeat or pulse)

Incidence less frequent

Dyspepsia (acid or sour stomach; belching; heartburn; indigestion; stomach discomfort upset or pain); ***fatigue*** (unusual tiredness or weakness); ***pruritus*** (itching skin)

Overdose

For more information on the management of overdose or unintentional ingestion, **contact a poison control center** (see *Poison Control Center Listing*).

Clinical effects of overdose

The following effects have been selected on the basis of their potential clinical significance (possible signs and symptoms in parentheses where appropriate)—not necessarily inclusive:

Headache; heart rate, increases; hypotension (blurred vision; confusion; dizziness; faintness, or lightheadedness when getting up from a lying or sitting position; sudden sweating; unusual tiredness or weakness); ***nausea; vomiting***

Bosentan has been given as a single dose of up to 2400 mg in normal volunteers or up to 2000 mg per day for 2 months without any major clinical consequences.

In a cyclosporine A interaction study in which doses of 500 and 1000 mg twice a day of bosentan were given concomitantly with cyclosporine A, trough plasma concentrations of bosentan increased 30 fold, but no serious adverse events occurred.

Treatment of overdose

Specific treatment—

There is no specific antidote for bosentan. Treatment should be symptomatic and supportive.

Monitoring—

Supportive care—For massive overdosage active cardiovascular support is recommended. Patients in whom intentional overdose is confirmed or suspected should be referred for psychiatric consultation.

Patient Consultation

As an aid to patient consultation, refer to *Advice for the Patient, Bosentan (Systemic)*.

In providing consultation, consider emphasizing the following selected information (» = major clinical significance):

Before using this medication

» Conditions affecting use, especially:

Hypersensitivity to bosentan or any component of the medication

Pregnancy—Contraindicated during pregnancy; is expected to cause fetal harm if administered to pregnant women

Other medications, especially concomitant use of CYP2C9 and CYP3A4 inhibitors, cyclosporine A, hormonal contraceptives (implantable, injectable, oral, and transdermal), ketoconazole, oral hypoglycemic agents (such as glyburide), statins (such as atorvastatin, lovastatin and simvastatin)

Other medical problems, especially moderate or severe liver dysfunction.

Laboratory value alterations, especially liver function tests such as alanine aminotransferase (ALT [SGPT]), aspartate aminotransferase (AST [SGOT]) and hematocrit.

Proper use of this medication

Patient monitoring especially hematocrit, liver aminotransferases (ALT [SGPT] and AST [SGOT]) and pregnancy testing.

» Proper dosing; calling Access Program prior to starting treatment; special considerations in patients with low body weight and tapering dose with discontinuation of therapy.

Missed dose: Taking as soon as possible; not taking if almost time for next scheduled dose; not doubling doses

Proper storage

Precautions while using this medication

» Notifying physician immediately if there is any delay in onset of menses or any other reason to suspect pregnancy because of possible harm to the fetus.

» Not using hormonal contraceptives, including oral, injectable, transdermal, and implantable contraceptives as the sole means of contraception while taking this medicine

» Notifying physician immediately if dark urine, light-colored stools, loss of appetite, nausea and vomiting, unusual tiredness, yellow eyes or skin, fever with or without chills, or stomach pain, these symptoms may indicate potential liver injury.

Side/adverse effects

Signs of potential side effects, especially hepatic dysfunction, hypotension and edema.

Signs of potential side effects observed during clinical practice, especially fluid retention, hepatic cirrhosis, hypersensitivity, pulmonary edema, pulmonary veno-occlusive disease, and rash

General Dosing Information

Bosentan is recommended to be taken in the morning and evening, with or without food

Hormonal contraceptives, including implantable, injectable, oral, and transdermal contraceptives may not be reliable in the presence of bosentan and should not be used as the sole contraceptive method in patients receiving bosentan. Input from a gynecologist or similar expert on adequate contraception should be sought as needed.

Treatment of adverse events

Fluid retention—Pulmonary hypertension patients presenting with fluid retention may require intervention with a diuretic fluid management, or hospitalization for decompensating heart failure.

Pulmonary edema—The possibility of pulmonary veno-occlusive disease (PVOD) should be considered and bosentan should be discontinued.

Oral Dosage Forms

Note: Bracketed information in the *Indications* section refers to uses that are not included in U.S. product labeling.

Note: ***Due to the potential for liver injury and fetal injury in pregnant women, Tracleer may only be prescribed through the Tracleer Access Program by calling 1–866–228–3546.*** Adverse events can also be reported directly via this number.

BOSENTAN TABLETS

Usual adult dose

Antihypertension, (pulmonary)

[Antihypertension, pulmonary, secondary to scleroderma]—

Oral, initially; 62.5 mg twice a day for 4 weeks, then increased to the maintenance dose 125 mg twice a day.

Note: In patients with a body weight below 40 kg but who are over 12 years of age, the recommended oral, initial and maintenance dose is 62.5 mg twice a day.

No dosing adjustment is needed for renally impaired patients.

Caution should be exercised in dosing patients with mildly impaired liver impairment.

Bosentan should generally be avoided in patients with moderate or severe liver impairment.

Discontinuation of treatment—

There is limited experience with abrupt discontinuation of bosentan. To avoid the potential for clinical deterioration, gradual dose reduction of 62.5 mg twice a day for 3 to 7 days should be considered.

Usual adult prescribing limits

Doses above 125 mg orally, twice a day do not appear to confer additional benefit sufficient to offset the increased risk of liver injury.

Usual pediatric dose

Safety and efficacy have not been established.

Usual geriatric dose

Dose selection for elderly patients should be cautious due to the greater frequency of geriatric-specific problems.

Strength(s) usually available

U.S.—

62.5 mg (Rx) [*Tracleer* (corn starch, ethylcellulose, glyceryl behenate, hydroxypropylmethylcellulose, iron oxide red, iron oxide yellow, magnesium stearate, povidone, pregelatinized starch, sodium starch glycolate, talc, titanium dioxide, and triacetin)].

125 mg (Rx) [*Tracleer* (corn starch, ethylcellulose, glyceryl behenate, hydroxypropylmethylcellulose, iron oxide red, iron oxide yellow, magnesium stearate, povidone, pregelatinized starch, sodium starch glycolate, talc, titanium dioxide, and triacetin)].

Canada—

62.5 mg (Rx) [*Tracleer* (corn starch, ethylcellulose, glyceryl behenate, hydroxypropylmethylcellulose, iron oxide red, iron oxide yellow, magnesium stearate, povidone, pregelatinized starch, sodium starch glycolate, talc, titanium dioxide, and triacetin)].

125 mg (Rx) [*Tracleer* (corn starch, ethylcellulose, glyceryl behenate, hydroxypropylmethylcellulose, iron oxide red, iron oxide yellow, magnesium stearate, povidone, pregelatinized starch, sodium starch glycolate, talc, titanium dioxide, and triacetin)].

Packaging and storage

Store between 20 and 25°C (68 and 77 °F). Excursions are permitted between 15 and 30°C (59 and 86°F). USP controlled room temperature.

Auxiliary labeling

- This medication could be harmful during pregnancy. If you are pregnant or plan to be pregnant, you should consult your doctor about the use of this medication.
- Please read patient information leaflet enclosed

Revised: 02/15/2006
Developed: 11/13/2002

BOTULINUM TOXIN TYPE A
Parenteral-Local

VA CLASSIFICATION (Primary/Secondary): OP900/MS300

Commonly used brand name(s): *Botox*.

Note: For a listing of dosage forms and brand names by country availability, see *Dosage Forms* section(s).

Category

Neuromuscular blocking agent.

Indications

Note: Bracketed information in the *Indications* section refers to uses that are not included in U.S. product labeling.

General Considerations

This product contains a derivative of human blood, albumin. Human blood-derived products carry an extremely remote risk for transmission of viral diseases. In addition, there is a theoretical risk for transmission of Creutzfeldt-Jakob disease (CJD). No cases of transmission of viral diseases or CJD have ever been identified for albumin.

Accepted

Blepharospasm (treatment) or

Strabismus (treatment)—Botulinum toxin type A is indicated for the treatment of strabismus, including horizontal strabismus up to 50 prism diopters, vertical strabismus, and persistent VI nerve palsy of 1 month or longer duration, and for blepharospasm associated with dystonia, including benign essential blepharospasm or VII nerve disorders.

Hyperhidrosis (treatment)[1]—Botulinum toxin type A is indicated for the treatment of severe primary axillary hyperhidrosis that is inadequately managed with topical agents. Patients should be evaluated for potential causes of secondary hyperhidrosis (e.g., hyperthyroidism) to avoid symptomatic treatment.

Spasmodic torticollis (cervical dystonia) (treatment)—Botulinum toxin type A is indicated for the treatment of cervical dystonia in adults to decrease the severity of abnormal head position and neck pain associated with cervical dystonia.

[Hemifacial spasm (treatment)][1]

[Facial spasm (treatment)][1]

[Spasmodic dysphonia (treatment)][1] or—Botulinum toxin type A is also used to treat the above-listed dystonias or dysphonias.

[Dystonia, focal hand (treatment)][1]—Botulinum toxin type A is indicated for the treatment of focal hand dystonia, including writer's cramp and musician's cramp (Evidence rating: III).

[Facial wrinkles, hyperfunctional (treatment)][1]—Botulinum toxin type A is indicated for the treatment of hyperfunctional wrinkles of the upper face, including glabellar frown lines, deep forehead wrinkles, and periorbital wrinkles (crow's feet) (Evidence rating: I).

[Frey's syndrome (treatment)][1]—Botulinum toxin type A is indicated for the treatment of Frey's syndrome (gustatory sweating) (Evidence rating: III).

[Hyperhidrosis (treatment)][1]—Botulinum toxin type A is indicated for the treatment of hyperhidrosis of the palms (Evidence rating: III).

[Lower limb spasticity, in multiple sclerosis patients]—Botulinum toxin type A (BTX-A) minimizes lower limb muscle spasticity in patients with multiple sclerosis. Randomized, double-blind, placebo-controlled clinical trials with BTX-A have demonstrated improved muscle tone, reduced the extent of hip adductor spasticity, and improved hygiene care. In addition, a case-series and several open-label trials (in abstract format) have suggested that BTX-A increases range of movement, improves ability to climb stairs, and improves muscle pain. Effects on muscle weakness are conflicting. BTX-A is generally safe and well tolerated. The benefits of long-term use are unknown.

[Upper limb spasticity, in stroke patients]—Botulinum toxin A provides benefit in minimizing muscle spasticity caused by stroke; however, most data do not demonstrate a benefit in functional ability, joint range of motion, activities of daily living, and muscle pain. When disability and care taker burden were the primary outcomes in stroke patients with upper limb spasticity, significant benefits were demonstrated. The benefits of long-term use are unknown. Botulinum toxin A is generally safe and well tolerated. One disadvantage is potential muscle weakness, which is dose related.

Acceptance not established

Botulinum toxin type A is of doubtful efficacy for the following indications, or multiple injections over time may be required: deviations over 50 prism diopters, restrictive strabismus, Duane's syndrome with lateral rectus muscle weakness, and secondary strabismus caused by prior surgical over-recession of the antagonist muscle.

Botulinum toxin type A has been used to treat *temporomandibular disorder* (TMD), including recurrent temporomandibular joint (TMJ) disorder (Evidence rating: III). Although botulinum toxin type A may be effective in the treatment of TMD, more comparative clinical studies need to be performed before recommending its use.

Detrusor sphincter dyssynergia—Limited clinical trials have found inconsistent results with botulinum toxin A (BTX-A) in the treatment of patients with detrusor sphincter dyssynergia (DSD) due to various etiologies. A double-blind, placebo-controlled clinical trial in patients with DSD due to multiple sclerosis found no differences in efficacy between BTX-A and placebo in the primary endpoint of post-residual urine volume or in any subjective endpoints, while few other objective secondary endpoints were significantly improved. Open-label, time-series clinical trials in patients with DSD due to spinal cord injury have found improvements in urodynamic parameters and/or subjective clinical improvement. BTX-A was well-tolerated in clinical trials, with few reports of urethral bleeding and incontinence.

Lower limb spasticity, in pediatric patients with cerebral palsy—A number of clinical trials have evaluated the effects of botulinum toxin A (BTX A) in the treatment of lower limb spasticity in children with cerebral palsy. Randomized, controlled clinical trials have tested BTX-A against placebo, casting, in combination with casting versus casting alone, and in combination with physical therapy versus physical therapy alone. Variable and conflicting results have been reported across trials, with one of the few long-term trials suggesting a detrimental effect of BTX-A in combination with casting compared to casting alone.

Lower limb spasticity, in stroke patients—The efficacy of botulinum toxin A (BTX-A) in the treatment of patients with lower limb spasticity due to stroke has been evaluated in double-blind, comparative clinical trials, a double-blind, dose-ranging trial, and several open-label single-arm clinical trials. Results from one double-blind, placebo-controlled trial found that treatment with BTX-A significantly improved patients' subjective spasticity scores over placebo. Differences in objective scores between BTX-A and placebo were not reported, and results were not stratified according to the etiology of spasticity. Differences in distance covered in a 2-minute walking test, the primary endpoint, for another double-blind, placebo-controlled trial, and secondary outcomes (step length, step rate, gonometry, and Rivermead Motor Assessment) were not significantly different between BTX-A and placebo. However, BTX-A significantly improved other secondary endpoints (use of walking aids and calf spasticity) at various doses and time points. In a comparative clinical trial, BTX-A significantly improved Ashworth scores compared to phenol at weeks 2 and 4, but not a weeks 8 and 12. Several open-label, single-arm trials and a dose-ranging trial all report improved spasticity scores over baseline with the administration of BTX-A in various muscles of the lower limbs in patients post-stroke. BTX-A is well tolerated.

Neurogenic detrusor overactivity, refractory to standard treatment—Botulinum toxin A (BTX-A) has been studied for the treatment of refractory neurogenic detrusor overactivity in one randomized, double-blind, placebo-controlled clinical trial and in multiple, single-arm, open-label, time-series. The effect of BTX-A on daily incontinence episodes, urodynamics, and catheterization frequency compared to placebo was inconsistent across doses of 200 and 300 units and across time points ranging from 2 to 24 weeks. Open-label time-series also inconsistently showed improvements across time points with BTX-A in incontinence, urodynamics, anticholinergic use, and patient satisfaction. BTX-A was generally well-tolerated, but associated with transient muscle weakness, transient urinary retention, and hematuria.

Oromandibular dystonia—Small, open-label clinical trials have shown subjective benefits with botulinum toxin A injections for the treatment of oromandibular dystonia (OMD). Validated, standardized assessments are lacking in the treatment of OMD and are necessary to evaluate the effect of treatments for OMD. Dysphagia was a common adverse effect seen in clinical trials of botulinum toxin A in patients with OMD.

Spasticity, in patients with traumatic brain injury—Open-label clinical trials have shown benefit with botulinum toxin A injections for the treatment of muscle spasticity of the upper and lower limbs due to traumatic brain injury (TBI). However, only one randomized, double-blind, placebo-controlled trial has been conducted in this patient population and it failed to demonstrate a benefit over casting alone in lower limb spasticity due to TBI. The benefits of long-term use are unknown. Botulinum toxin A is generally safe and well tolerated.

Upper limb spasticity, in pediatric patients with cerebral palsy—Clinical trials evaluating the effects of botulinum toxin A (BTX-A) in the treatment of upper limb spasticity in children with cerebral palsy (CP) have produced conflicting and variable results. A randomized, double-blind, placebo-controlled clinical trial reported inconsistent, significant improvements in some aspects of muscle tone and range of motion of the thumb, wrist, and elbow, wrist resonance, and grasp and release function. A randomized, controlled clinical trial found no differences in active range of motion, muscle tone, function, or velocity between BTX-A plus intensive rehabilitation or intensive rehabilitation alone. A significant improvement in one (weight-bearing) of the four domains of the QUEST (Quality of Upper Extremities Test) was found with BTX-A plus occupational therapy (OT) versus OT alone in a randomized, single-blind, controlled clinical trial. However, this trial failed to show any differences in grip strength, muscle tone, or passive range of motion between groups. Open-label clinical trials evaluation BTX-A have reported improved muscle tone, caregiver ratings, and range of movement. BTX-A was generally well tolerated with a few exceptions of excessive weakness.

Unaccepted

Botulinum toxin type A is ineffective in chronic paralytic strabismus except to reduce antagonist contracture in conjunction with surgical repair.

[1]Not included in Canadian product labeling.

Pharmacology/Pharmacokinetics

Physicochemical characteristics

Botulinum toxin type A is a sterile, lyophilized form of purified botulinum toxin type A that is produced from a culture of the Hall strain of *Clostridium botulinum*.

Mechanism of action/Effect

Botulinum toxin type A blocks neuromuscular conduction by binding to receptor sites on motor nerve terminals, entering the nerve terminals, and inhibiting the release of acetylcholine. When injected intramuscularly in therapeutic doses, botulinum toxin type A produces a localized chemical denervation muscle paralysis. When the muscle is chemically denervated, it atrophies and may develop extrajunctional acetylcholine receptors. There is evidence that the nerve can sprout and reinnervate the muscle, thereby reversing the weakness. The paralytic effect on muscles injected with botulinum toxin type A reduces the excessive, abnormal contractions associated with blepharospasm. In the treatment of strabismus, it is postulated that the administration of botulinum toxin type A affects muscle pairs by inducing an atrophic lengthening of the injected muscle and a corresponding shortening of the muscle's antagonist. Following peri-ocular injection of botulinum toxin type A, distant muscles show electrophysiologic changes, but no clinical weakness or other clinical change, for a period of several weeks or months, corresponding to the duration of local clinical paralysis.

Onset of action

In the treatment of blepharospasm, the initial effect of the injections is seen within 3 days and the effect reaches a peak 1 to 2 weeks after treatment.

In the treatment of strabismus, the initial doses typically create paralysis of injected muscles beginning 1 or 2 days after injection and increasing in intensity during the first week.

Duration of action

In the treatment of blepharospasm, each treatment lasts approximately 3 months.

In the treatment of strabismus, the paralysis lasts for 2 to 6 weeks and gradually resolves over an additional 2 to 6 weeks.

In the treatment of hemifacial spasm, treatment may last 6 months.

Precautions to Consider

Carcinogenicity

Long-term studies in animals have not been done to evaluate the carcinogenic potential of botulinum toxin type A.

Pregnancy/Reproduction

Pregnancy—There are no adequate and well-controlled studies of botulinum toxin type A in pregnant women. Botulinum toxin type A should only be used during pregnancy if the potential benefit justifies the potential risk to the fetus. The patient should be apprised of the potential risks, including abortion or fetal malformations which have been observed in rabbits, if botulinum toxin type A is used during pregnancy or if the patient becomes pregnant while taking this medication.

FDA Pregnancy Category C.

Breast-feeding

It is not known whether botulinum toxin type A is distributed into breast milk. However, problems in humans have not been documented.

Pediatrics

Appropriate studies on the relationship of age to the effect of botulinum toxin type A have not been performed in children up to 12 years of age for treatment of blepharospasm or strabismus, or up to age of 16 years of age for cervical dystonia or up to the age of 18 years for hyperhidrosis.

Geriatrics

Appropriate studies on the relationship of age to the effects of botulinum toxin type A have not been performed in the geriatric population. Dose selection for an elderly patient should be cautious, usually starting at the low end of the dosing range, reflecting the greater frequency of decreased hepatic, renal or cardiac function, and of concomitant disease or other drug therapy.

Drug interactions and/or related problems

The following drug interactions and/or related problems have been selected on the basis of their potential clinical significance (possible mechanism in parentheses where appropriate)—not necessarily inclusive (» = major clinical significance):

Note: Combinations containing any of the following medications, depending on the amount present, may also interact with this medication.

Aminoglycoside antibiotics or

Other agents interfering with neuromuscular transmission, such as:
Curare-like compounds
(may potentiate the effects of botulinum toxin type A)
Botulinum neurotoxin serotype, other
(the effect of administering different botulinum neurotoxin serotypes at the same time or within several months of each other is unknown; excessive neuromuscular weakness may be exacerbated by administration of another botulinum toxin prior to the resolution of the effects of a previously administered botulinum toxin)

Medical considerations/Contraindications

The medical considerations/contraindications included have been selected on the basis of their potential clinical significance (reasons given in parentheses where appropriate)—not necessarily inclusive (» = major clinical significance).

Except under special circumstances, this medication should not be used when the following medical problem exists:

» Hypersensitivity to botulinum toxin type A injection or any ingredient in the formulation
(use is contraindicated)
» Infection at the proposed injection site(s)
(use is contraindicated in the presence of infection at the proposed injection site or sites)

Risk-benefit should be considered when the following medical problems exist:

Cardiac or other medical conditions that may worsen with rapidly increasing activity
(patients with blepharospasm may have been sedentary for a long time; sedentary patients should be cautioned to resume activity slowly and carefully following the administration of botulinum toxin type A)
Dysphagia
(use may exacerbate this condition; dysphagia may be severe enough to warrant the insertion of a gastric feeding tube to decrease the risk of aspiration pneumonia in patients with dysphagia)
Infection with *Clostridium botulinum* toxin, history of
(persons with a previous episode of botulism poisoning may have produced antibodies that may interfere with botulinum toxin type A therapy)
Inflammation at the proposed injection site(s) or
Excessive weakness or atrophy present in the target muscle(s)
(use with caution in patients with these conditions)
Neuromuscular disorders, pre-existing, such as:
Peripheral motor neuropathic diseases, such as:
Amyotrophic lateral sclerosis or
Motor neuropathy or
Neuromuscular junctional disorders, such as:
Lambert-Eaton syndrome or
Myasthenia gravis
(use with caution in patients with these conditions; these patients may be at increased risk of clinically significant systemic effects including dysphagia and respiratory compromise from typical doses of botulinum toxin type A)
VII nerve disorders
(use of botulinum toxin type A injection of the orbicularis muscle may lead to corneal exposure, persistent epithelial defect, and corneal ulceration, especially in patients with VII nerve disorders; careful testing of corneal sensation in eyes previously operated upon, avoidance of injection into the lower lid area to avoid ectropion, and vigorous treatment of any epithelial defect should be employed, such as protective drops, ointment, therapeutic soft contact lenses, or closure of the eye by patching or other means.)

Side/Adverse Effects

Note: Treatment with botulinum toxin type A may cause the body to produce antibodies against the toxin. This may reduce the effectiveness of continued therapy. To forestall this, the dose of botulinum toxin type A should be kept as low as possible, and in any case below 200 units given in a one-month period.

Two persons previously incapacitated by blepharospasm experienced cardiac collapse within 3 weeks following treatment with botulinum toxin type A. The collapse was attributed to physical overexertion. Sedentary patients should be cautioned to resume activity slowly and carefully following treatment with botulinum toxin type A.

During the treatment of strabismus, retrobulbar hemorrhages sufficient to compromise retinal circulation have occurred from needle penetrations into the orbit. It is recommended that appropriate instruments to decompress the orbit be accessible.

Ocular (globe) penetrations by needles have also occurred. An ophthalmoscope should be available to diagnose this condition.

The injection procedure for the treatment of strabismus has also caused scleral perforations, vitreous hemorrhage, and pupillary change consistent with ciliary ganglion damage (Adie's pupil).

During the treatment of blepharospasm, reduced blinking as a result of injection of botulinum toxin type A into the orbicularis muscle can lead to corneal exposure, persistent epithelial defect, and corneal ulceration, especially in patients with VII nerve disorders. In one case, in an aphakic eye, reduced blinking resulted in corneal perforation that subsequently required corneal grafting. Careful testing of corneal sensation in eyes previously operated upon, avoidance of injection into the lower lid area in order to avoid ectropion, and vigorous treatment of any epithelial defect should be employed. Treatment for the above problems may include protective drops, ointment, therapeutic soft contact lenses, or closure of the eye by patching or other means.

The following side/adverse effects have been selected on the basis of their potential clinical significance (possible signs and symptoms in parentheses where appropriate)—not necessarily inclusive:

Those indicating need for medical attention

Incidence more frequent
After treatment for blepharospasm
Keratoconjunctivitis sicca (dryness of the eye); ***lagophthalmos*** (inability to close the eyelid completely)

Incidence less frequent or rare
After treatment for blepharospasm
Decreased blinking; ectropion (turning outward of the edge of the eyelid); ***entropion*** (turning inward of the edge of the eyelid); ***keratitis*** (irritation of the cornea [colored portion] of the eye)

Those indicating need for medical attention only if they continue or are bothersome

Incidence more frequent
After treatment for blepharospasm
Ecchymosis (blue or purplish bruise on eyelid); ***irritation or watering of the eye; photophobia*** (sensitivity of the eye to light); ***ptosis*** (drooping of the upper eyelid)
After treatment for cervical dystonia
Dysphagia (difficulty swallowing); ***headache; neck pain; upper respiratory infection*** (ear congestion; nasal congestion; chills; cough, fever, sneezing, or sore throat; body aches or pain; headache; loss of voice; runny nose; unusual tiredness or weakness; difficulty in breathing)
After treatment for horizontal strabismus
Ptosis (drooping of the upper eyelid)—In trials, the average incidence was 10 to 20%; the incidence of ptosis was much less after inferior rectus injection (less than 1%) and much greater after superior rectus injection (30 to 40%); less than 1% of patients had ptosis lasting more than 180 days; ***vertical deviation*** (eye pointing upward or downward instead of straight ahead)—In trials, the incidence was 10 to 20%; 2% of patients had vertical deviation greater than 2 prism diopters lasting more than 180 days
After treatment for primary axillary hyperhidrosis
Anxiety (fear; nervousness); ***back or neck pain; fever; flu syndrome*** (chills; cough; diarrhea; fever; general feeling of discomfort or illness; headache; joint pain; loss of appetite; muscle aches and pains; nausea; runny nose; shivering; sore throat; sweating; trouble sleeping; unusual tiredness or weakness; vomiting); ***headache; infection*** (fever or chills; cough or hoarseness; lower back or side pain; painful or difficult urination); ***injection site pain; injection site hemorrhage*** (heavy bleeding from place where shot was given); ***pharyngitis*** (body aches or pain; congestion; cough; dryness or soreness of throat; fever; hoarseness; runny nose; tender, swollen glands in neck; trouble in swallowing; voice changes); ***pruritus*** (itching skin); ***sweating, non-axillary*** (sweating, not from armpits)

Incidence less frequent
After treatment for blepharospasm or strabismus
Skin rash, diffuse; swelling of the eyelid skin following injection into the eyelid—may last several days
After treatment for horizontal strabismus
Diplopia (double vision); ***past-pointing or spatial disorientation*** (difficulty finding the location of objects)

Incidence rare (less than 1%)
After treatment for blepharospasm
Diplopia (double vision)

Patient Consultation

As an aid to patient consultation, refer to *Advice for the Patient, Botulinum Toxin Type A (Parenteral-Local).*

In providing consultation, consider emphasizing the following selected information (» = major clinical significance):

Before using this medication

» Conditions affecting use, especially:

Hypersensitivity to botulinum toxin type A or any ingredient in the formulation

Pregnancy—There are no adequate or well-controlled studies in pregnant women. Tell your doctor if you are pregnant or if you plan to become pregnant.

Breast-feeding—It is not know if this medication is distributed to human breast milk. Tell your doctor if you are nursing.

Use in children—Safety and effectiveness have not been established in children below the age of 12 years for treatment of blepharospasm or strabismus, below the age of 16 years for treatment of cervical dystonia, or below the age of 18 years for the treatment of hyperhidrosis.

Use in the elderly—There are no adequate or well-controlled studies in patients aged 65 years and over. Dose selection should be cautious, usually starting at the low end of the dosing range.

Other medical problems, especially infection at the proposed injection site(s).

Proper use of this medication

» Proper dosing

Precautions while using this medication

Tell your doctor right away if you have difficulty swallowing, speaking, or breathing.

Increasing activities slowly and carefully to allow the heart and body time to strengthen; checking with physician before starting any exercise program

Side/adverse effects

Signs of potential side effects, especially keratoconjunctivitis sicca, lagophthalmos, decreased blinking, ectropion, entropion, and keratitis

General Dosing Information

The cumulative dose of botulinum toxin type A in the treatment of either strabismus or blepharospasm should not exceed 200 units (U) in a one-month period.

Physicians administering botulinum toxin type A should understand the standard electromyographic techniques as well as the relevant neuromuscular and orbital anatomy and any alterations to the anatomy because of prior surgical procedures.

For treatment of blepharospasm

For blepharospasm, the diluted medication is injected using a sterile, 27- to 30-gauge needle without electromyographic guidance.

For treatment of strabismus

For strabismus, botulinum toxin type A is intended for injection into extraocular muscles utilizing the electrical activity recorded from the tip of the injection needle as a guide to placement within the target muscle. Injection without surgical exposure or electromyographic guidance should not be attempted.

The injection should be prepared by drawing into a sterile 1 mL tuberculin syringe an amount of the properly diluted toxin that is slightly greater than the intended dose. Any air bubbles should be expelled from the syringe barrel and the syringe should be attached to the electromyographic injection needle, which is preferably a 1½-inch, 27-gauge needle. The injection volume that is in excess of the intended dose should be expelled through the needle; this assures patency of the needle and confirms that there is no syringe-needle leakage. A new, sterile needle and syringe should be used to enter the vial on each occasion for dilution or removal of the medication.

To prepare the eye for the injection, it is recommended that several drops of a local anesthetic and an ocular decongestant be administered several minutes prior to injection.

For treatment of adverse effects

Recommended treatment consists of the following:

• Should accidental injection or oral ingestion occur, the person should be medically supervised for up to several weeks for signs or symptoms of systemic weakness or muscle paralysis.

• An antitoxin is available in the event of immediate knowledge of an overdose or misinjection. The antitoxin will not reverse any botulinum toxin induced muscle weakness effects already apparent by the time of antitoxin administration. **Immediately contact Allergan for additional information at 800-433-8871 from 8 a.m. to 4 p.m. Pacific Time or at 714-246-5954 for a recorded message at other times.**

A vial containing 100 U of lyophilized *Clostridium botulinum* toxin type A is considered to be below the estimated dose for systemic toxicity in humans weighing 6 kg (13.2 lb) or greater.

Parenteral Dosage Forms

Note: Bracketed uses in the Dosage Forms section refer to categories of use and/or indications that are not included in U.S. product labeling.

BOTULINUM TOXIN TYPE A FOR INJECTION

Usual adult and adolescent dose

Blepharospasm—

Intramuscularly, initially, 1.25 to 2.5 U (using 0.05 to 0.1 mL volume at each site) injected into the medial and lateral pre-tarsal orbicularis oculi of the upper lid and into the lateral pre-tarsal orbicularis oculi of the lower lid. An additional 2.5 to 5 U may be injected into the orbital portion of the orbicularis oculi at the zygomatic arch.

Note: In general, the initial effect of the injections is seen within three days and the effect reaches a peak one to two weeks after treatment.

Each treatment lasts approximately three months, following which the procedure can be repeated.

At subsequent treatment sessions, the dose may be increased up to twofold if the response from the initial treatment is considered insufficient, which is usually defined as an effect that does not last longer than two months. There appears to be little benefit from injecting more than 5 U per site. In addition, some tolerance may occur when the medication is used in treating blepharospasm if the treatments are administered more frequently than every three months. Also, it is rare to have the effect be permanent.

Hyperhidrosis, primary axillary[1]—

Intradermally, 50 Units per axilla.

The area to be injected should be defined using standard staining techniques, such as Minor's Iodine-Starch Test. Using a 30-gauge needle, 50 Units of botulinum toxin type A is injected intradermally in 2.5- to 5-Unit (0.1 to 0.2 mL of botulinum toxin type A 100 Units per 4 mL) aliquots to each axilla evenly distributed in 10 to 15 multiple sites approximately 1 to 2 cm apart.

Subsequent injections for hyperhidrosis should be administered when the clinical effect of a previous injection diminishes.

[Lower limb spasticity, in multiple sclerosis patients]—

Dose depends on muscle injected and preparation (BOTOX® or DYSPORT®).

Spasmodic torticollis (cervical dystonia)—

Intramuscularly, the dosage should be individualized based on the patient's head and neck position, localization of pain and muscle hypertrophy, individual patient response. and adverse event history.

Intramuscularly, the initial dose for a patient without prior use of botulinum toxin type A should be at a lower dose, with subsequent dosing adjusted based on individual response. The total dose injected into the sternocleidomastoid muscles should be limited to 100 Units or less to decrease the occurrence of dysphagia.

Intramuscular, the mean botulinum toxin type A dose administered to patients who had extended histories of receiving and tolerating botulinum toxin type A injections in the phase 3 study was 236 Units. The 25th to 75th percentile range was 198 to 300 Units. The dose was divided among the affected muscles.

Note: For injections into superficial muscles, a 25-, 27-, or 30-gauge needle may be used, and a 22-gauge needle may be used for deeper musculature. Localization of the involved muscles with electromyographic guidance may be useful.

Clinical improvement usually begins within the first two weeks after injection. Maximum clinical benefit occurs at approximately six weeks post-injection. Most subjects in the phase 3 study returned to pre-treatment status by 3 months post-treatment.

The use of multiple injection sites allows botulinum toxin type A to have more uniform contact with the innervation areas of the dystonic muscle and are especially useful in larger muscles. The optimal number of injection sites is dependent upon the size of the muscle to be chemically denervated.

Dosage Guide—

Note: This dosing table is intended to provide guidelines for the injection of botulinum toxin type A in the treatment of cervical dystonia. This information is provided as guidance for the initial injection since the extent of muscle hypertrophy and the muscle groups involved in the dystonic posture may change over time, necessitating alterations in the dose of botulinum toxin type A and the muscles to be injected. The exact dosage and the sites to be injected should be individualized for each patient.

Dosage Guide			
Classification of Cervical Dystonia	Muscle Groupings	Total Dosage	Number of Sites
Type I—Head rotated toward side of shoulder elevations	Sternocleidomastoid	50–100 U	at least 2 sites
	Levator scapulae	50 U	1 or 2 sites
	Scalene	25–50 U	1 or 2 sites
	Splenius capitis	25–75 U	1 to 3 sites
	Trapezius	25–100 U	1 to 8 sites
Type II—Head rotation only	Sternocleidomastoid	25–100 U	at least 2 sites if > 25 U given
Type III—Head tilted toward side of shoulder elevation	Sternocleidomastoid	25–100 U	at posterior border; at least 2 sites if > 25 U given
	Levator scapulae	25–100 U	at least 2 sites
	Scalene	25–75 U	at least 2 sites
	Trapezius	25–100 U	1 to 8 sites
Type IV—Bilateral posterior cervical muscle spasm with elevation of the face	Splenius capitis and cervicis	50–200 U	2 to 8 sites; treat bilaterally

Strabismus—

Vertical muscles; or horizontal strabismus of less than 20 prism diopters—

Intramuscularly, initially, 1.25 to 2.5 units (U) into any one muscle.

Horizontal strabismus of 20 to 50 prism diopters—

Intramuscularly, initially, 2.5 to 5 U into any one muscle.

Persistent VI nerve palsy of one month duration or longer—

Intramuscularly, initially, 1.25 to 2.5 U into the medial rectus muscle.

Note: The volume of botulinum toxin type A injected for treatment of strabismus should be between 0.05 to 0.15 mL per muscle.

For initial treatment of strabismus—Use the lower of the initial doses for treatment of small deviations. Use the larger doses only for large deviations. The initial doses typically create paralysis of injected muscles beginning one or two days after injection and increasing in intensity during the first week. The paralysis usually lasts for two to six weeks and gradually resolves over an additional two to six weeks. Overcorrections lasting more than six months have been rare. About one half of patients will require subsequent doses because of inadequate paralytic response of the muscle to the initial dose, or because of mechanical factors, such as large deviations or restrictions, or because of the lack of binocular motor fusion to stabilize the alignment.

For subsequent treatment of residual or recurrent strabismus—

It is recommended that patients be reexamined seven to fourteen days after each injection to assess the effect of that dose. Patients who experience adequate paralysis of the target muscle and who require subsequent injections should receive a dose comparable to the initial dose. Subsequent doses for patients experiencing incomplete paralysis of the target muscle may be increased up to twice the previously administered dose. Subsequent injections should not be administered until the effects of the previous dose have dissipated, as evidenced by substantial function in the injected and adjacent muscles.

The maximum recommended dose as a single injection into any one muscle is 25 U.

[Upper limb spasticity in stroke]—

Dose depends on muscle injected and preparation (BOTOX® or DYSPORT®).

Usual pediatric dose

Blepharospasm or Strabismus:

Infants and children up to 12 years of age—Safety and efficacy have not been established.

Children 12 years of age and older—See *Usual adult and adolescent dose.*

Cervical dystonia or Hyperhidrosis:

Infants and children up to 16 years of age—Safety and efficacy have not been established.

Children 16 years of age and older—See *Usual adult and adolescent dose.*

Strength(s) usually available

U.S.—

100 units of vacuum-dried *Clostridium botulinum* type A neurotoxin complex (Rx) [*Botox* (0.5 mg human albumin)].

Canada—

100 units of lyophilized *Clostridium botulinum* toxin type A (Rx) [*Botox* (0.5 mg human albumin)].

Note: One unit corresponds to the calculated median lethal intraperitoneal dose (LD/50) in mice.

Packaging and storage

Unopened vials—Should be stored in a refrigerator between 2 and 8 °C (36 and 46 °F) for up to 24 months. Do not use after the expiration date on the vial.

Reconstituted product—Store in a refrigerator between 2 and 8 °C (36 and 46 °F); administer within 4 hours of reconstitution

Preparation of dosage form

Botulinum toxin type A for injection should be reconstituted with sterile non-preserved normal saline, such as 0.9% sodium chloride injection.

Amount of Diluent Added	Resulting dose in Units per 0.1 mL
1 mL	10 U
2 mL	5 U
4 mL	2.5 U
8 mL	1.25 U

Dilution Table—

Note: The dilutions and doses listed below are calculated for an injection volume of 0.1 mL. A decrease or increase in the dose is also possible by administering a smaller or larger injection volume; from 0.05 mL (50% decrease in dose) to 0.15 mL (50% increase in dose).

Stability

Botulinum toxin type A is denatured by bubbling or similar violent agitation; the diluent should be injected into the vial gently.

Discard the vial if its vacuum does not pull the diluent into the vial.

The lyophilized medication and the diluent to be used contain no preservatives.

The medication should be administered within 4 hours after reconstitution and should be stored in a refrigerator during those 4 hours. The date and time of reconstitution should be recorded on the vial.

Reconstituted botulinum toxin type A is clear, colorless, and free of particulate matter. The solution should be discarded if it is discolored or contains particulate matter.

Note

Vials of BOTOX® have a holographic film on the vial label that contains the name "Allergan" within the horizontal lines of rainbow color. If you do not see the lines of rainbow color or the name "Allergan", do not use the product and contact Allergan for additional information at 800-890-4345 from 8 a.m. to 4 p.m. Pacific Time.

[1]Not included in Canadian product labeling.

Revised: 05/31/2006

BOTULINUM TOXIN TYPE B Parenteral-Local

VA CLASSIFICATION (Primary): MS300

Commonly used brand name(s): *Myobloc.*

Note: For a listing of dosage forms and brand names by country availability, see *Dosage Forms* section(s).

Category

Neuromuscular blocking agent.

Indications

Accepted

Cervical dystonia (treatment)—Botulinum toxin type B is indicated for the treatment of patients with cervical dystonia to reduce the severity of abnormal head position and neck pain associated with cervical dystonia.

Acceptance not established

Upper Limb Spasticity—The data describing the treatment of limb spasticity with botulinum toxin type B (BTX-B) are limited and inconclusive. In a single, randomized, placebo-controlled trial, BTX-B did not demonstrate a benefit in reducing muscle tone in the elbow, wrist or finger flexors in post-stroke patients. However, some published and unpublished small open-label trials suggest efficacy. BTX-B appeared safe and well tolerated.

Pharmacology/Pharmacokinetics

Physicochemical characteristics

Source—Botulinum toxin type B is a sterile liquid form of purified botulinum toxin type B that is produced by fermentation of the bacterium *Clostridium botulinum* type B (Bean strain) and exists in a noncovalent association with hemagglutinin and nonhemagglutinin proteins as a neurotoxin complex.
pH—5.6
Specific activity—70 to 130 units per nanogram.

Mechanism of action/Effect

Botulinum toxin type B is a purified neurotoxin that acts at the neuromuscular junction to produce flaccid paralysis. It inhibits the release of acetylcholine in a three-step process that involves neurospecific binding of the toxin via its heavy chain; internalization of the toxin by receptor-mediated endocytosis; and cleavage of the synaptic Vesicle Associated Membrane Protein (VAMP or synaptobrevin), which is a component of the protein complex that is responsible for docking and fusion of the synaptic vesicle to the presynaptic membrane, a step that is necessary for neurotransmitter release.

Duration of Effect

Between 12 and 16 weeks for patients in clinical studies, on doses of 5000 units or 10,000 units.

Precautions to Consider

Carcinogenicity

Long-term studies have not been done in humans or in animals to evaluate the carcinogenic potential of botulinum toxin type B.

Pregnancy/Reproduction

Fertility—Long-term studies have not been done in humans or in animals.

Pregnancy—Studies have not been done in humans.
Studies have not been done in animals.

FDA Pregnancy Category C.

Breast-feeding

It is not known whether botulinum toxin type B is distributed into breast milk.

Pediatrics

No information is available on the relationship of age to the effects of botulinum toxin type B in the pediatric population. Safety and efficacy have not been established.

Geriatrics

Appropriate studies on the relationship of age to the effects of botulinum toxin type B have not been performed in the geriatric population. However, patients between the ages of 65 and 75 years were enrolled in clinical trials and geriatrics-specific problems that would limit the usefulness of this medication in this population are not expected.

Drug interactions and/or related problems

The following drug interactions and/or related problems have been selected on the basis of their potential clinical significance (possible mechanism in parentheses where appropriate)—not necessarily inclusive (» = major clinical significance):

Note: Combinations containing any of the following medications, depending on the amount present, may also interact with this medication.

Aminoglycosides or
Neuromuscular blocking agents, other, nondepolarizing, such as tubocurarine or
Other agents interfering with neuromuscular transmission
(may potentiate the effects of botulinum toxin type B)

Botulinum neurotoxin serotypes, other
(effects of administration of different botulinum neurotoxin serotypes concurrently or within 4 months of each other are not known)
(neuromuscular paralysis may be potentiated by concurrent administration or by overlapping administration of different botulinum neurotoxin serotypes)

Medical considerations/Contraindications

The medical considerations/contraindications included have been selected on the basis of their potential clinical significance (reasons given in parentheses where appropriate)—not necessarily inclusive (» = major clinical significance).

Risk-benefit should be considered when the following medical problems exist:

» Hypersensitivity to any of the ingredients in the formulation
Neuromuscular junctional disorders, such as:
Amyotrophic lateral sclerosis (ALS or Lou Gehrig disease)
Motor neuropathy or
Peripheral motor neuropathic diseases, such as:
Eaton-Lambert syndrome
Myasthenia gravis
(risk of systemic effects, including severe dysphagia and respiratory compromise, may be increased; caution is recommended)

Side/Adverse Effects

Note: There were no cases of botulism reported in patients receiving botulinum toxin type B during clinical trials. However, if botulism is suspected, it may be necessary to hospitalize the patient so that respiratory function and systemic weakness or paralysis can be monitored.

The following side/adverse effects have been selected on the basis of their potential clinical significance (possible signs and symptoms in parentheses where appropriate)—not necessarily inclusive:

Those indicating need for medical attention

Dysphagia (difficulty swallowing); ***infection***

Note: In rare cases, *dysphagia* has been severe enough to necessitate the insertion of a gastric feeding tube. Also, at least one patient developed aspiration pneumonia and subsequently died after developing *dysphagia.*

Those indicating need for medical attention only if they continue or are bothersome

Incidence more frequent

Arthraglia (pain, swelling, or redness in joints; muscle pain or stiffness; difficulty in moving); ***asthenia*** (lack or loss of strength); ***back pain; cough; dry mouth; dizziness; dyspepsia*** (acid or sour stomach; belching; heartburn; indigestion; stomach discomfort, upset, or pain); ***flu syndrome*** (chills; cough; diarrhea; fever; general feeling of discomfort or illness; headache; joint pain; loss of appetite; muscle aches and pains; nausea; runny nose; shivering; sore throat; sweating; trouble sleeping; unusual tiredness or weakness; vomiting); ***headache; injection site pain; nausea; neck pain; mysathenia*** (loss of strength or energy; muscle pain or weakness); ***pain; pain related to cervical dystonia and torticollis; torticollis*** (abnormal head position)

Overdose

For more information on the management of overdose or unintentional ingestion, **contact a poison control center** (see *Poison Control Center Listing*).

Treatment of overdose

In the event of an overdose, antitoxin may be administered. Contact the manufacturer for additional information and your State Health Department to process a request for antitoxin through the Centers for Disease Control and Prevention (CDC) in Atlanta, Georgia. The antitoxin will not reverse any botulinum toxin–induced muscle weakness effects already apparent by the time of antitoxin administration.

Monitoring—
Patients should be monitored for up to several weeks for signs and symptoms of systemic weakness or paralysis. Symptoms are not likely to present immediately following overdose.

Supportive care—
Patients in whom intentional overdose is confirmed or suspected should be referred for psychiatric consultation.

Patient Consultation

As an aid to patient consultation, refer to *Advice for the Patient, Botulinum Toxin Type B (Parenteral-Local).*

In providing consultation, consider emphasizing the following selected information (» = major clinical significance):

Before using this medication

» Conditions affecting use, especially:

Hypersensitivity to botulinum toxin or any ingredient in the formulation.

Proper use of this medication

» Proper dosing

Side/adverse effects

Signs of potential side effects, especially dysphagia and infection

General Dosing Information

Botulinum toxin type B should be administered by a health care provider that is familiar and experienced in treating patients with cervical dystonia.

Botulinum toxin type B contains albumin. A theoretical risk for the transmission of viral diseases such as Creutzfeldt-Jakob disease is a remote possibility, although no cases have ever been identified.

Units of biological activity of botulinum toxin type B cannot be compared to or converted into units of other types of botulinum toxin, or any other toxin assessed with other specific assay methods.

Parenteral Dosage Forms

BOTULINUM TOXIN TYPE B INJECTION

Usual adult dose

Cervical dystonia—

Prior history of toleration of botulinum toxin injections

Intramuscular, 2500 to 5000 units divided among affected muscles.

No prior history of tolerating botulinum toxin injections

Intramuscular, initial dose should be lower than those who have history of tolerating botulinum injections. Subsequent injections should be adjusted according to each patient's individual response.

Usual pediatric dose

Safety and efficacy have not been established.

Usual geriatric dose

See *Usual adult dose.*

Strength(s) usually available

U.S.—

2500 units of *Clostridium botulinum* toxin type B (Rx) [*Myobloc* (albumin human 0.05% per mL; sodium succinate 0.01 M per mL; sodium chloride 0.1 M per mL)].

5000 units of *Clostridium botulinum* toxin type B (Rx) [*Myobloc* (albumin human 0.05% per mL; sodium succinate 0.01 M per mL; sodium chloride 0.1 M per mL)].

10,000 units of *Clostridium botulinum* toxin type B (Rx) [*Myobloc* (albumin human 0.05% per mL; sodium succinate 0.01 M per mL; sodium chloride 0.1 M per mL)].

Packaging and storage

Store in a refrigerator between 2 and 8 °C (36 and 46 °F). Do not freeze.

Preparation of dosage form

Botulinum toxin type B may be diluted with normal saline. Once diluted, it must be used within 4 hours.

Stability

Botulinum toxin type B can be stored for up to 48 months when it is refrigerated.

Auxiliary labeling

- Do not shake.

Revised: 02/23/2006
Developed: 02/20/2001

BRIMONIDINE Ophthalmic

VA CLASSIFICATION (Primary): OP114

Commonly used brand name(s): *Alphagan P*.

Note: For a listing of dosage forms and brand names by country availability, see *Dosage Forms* section(s).

Category

Antiglaucoma agent (ophthalmic); antihypertensive, ocular.

Indications

Accepted

Glaucoma, open-angle (treatment) or

Hypertension, ocular (treatment)—Brimonidine is indicated for the lowering of intraocular pressure in patients with open-angle glaucoma or ocular hypertension.

Pharmacology/Pharmacokinetics

Physicochemical characteristics

Molecular weight—442.24.

Other characteristics—The pH of brimonidine tartrate ophthalmic solution is 6.3 to 6.5.

Mechanism of action/Effect

Brimonidine is a relatively selective alpha$_2$-adrenergic agonist. It appears to act by decreasing aqueous humor production and increasing aqueous outflow.

Other actions/effects

Brimonidine has minimal cardiovascular or pulmonary effects after application to the conjunctiva.

Absorption

Some systemic absorption occurs after ocular instillation.

Half-life

For systemically absorbed brimonidine—Approximately 3 hours.

Time to peak plasma concentration

Approximately 1 to 4 hours after ocular instillation.

Time to peak effect

Approximately 2 hours.

Elimination

For systemically absorbed brimonidine—Primarily renal, as unchanged brimonidine and metabolites.

Precautions to Consider

Carcinogenicity

Brimonidine was not carcinogenic in a 21-month study in mice given oral doses of 2.5 mg per kg of body weight (mg/kg) per day or in a 2-year study in rats given oral doses of 1 mg/kg per day. These doses provided plasma concentrations equivalent to 77 and 118 times, respectively, the human plasma concentration occurring after ocular instillation of a recommended dose.

Mutagenicity

Brimonidine was not mutagenic in several *in vitro* and *in vivo* studies including the Ames test, host-mediated assay, chromosomal aberration test in Chinese hamster ovary (CHO) cells, dominant lethal assay, and cytogenetic studies in mice.

Pregnancy/Reproduction

Fertility—Brimonidine did not impair fertility in rats given oral doses of 0.66 mg/kg, which produced plasma concentrations equivalent to 100 times the human plasma concentration occurring after ocular instillation of multiple doses.

Pregnancy—Studies in humans have not been done. Brimonidine should be used during pregnancy only if the potential benefit to the mother justifies the potential risk to the fetus.

Animal studies have shown that limited quantities of brimonidine cross the placenta and enter the fetal circulation. However, no harm to the fetus occurred in rats given oral doses of 0.66 mg/kg of brimonidine, which produced plasma concentrations equivalent to 100 times the human plasma concentration occurring after ocular instillation of multiple doses.

FDA Pregnancy Category B.

Breast-feeding

It is not known whether brimonidine is distributed into human breast milk. However, brimonidine was detected in breast milk in animal studies. A decision should be made whether to discontinue nursing or to discontinue the drug, taking into account the importance of the drug to the mother.

Pediatrics

The safety and efficacy of brimonidine tartrate ophthalmic solution have not been established in pediatric patients below the age of 2 years. It is not recommended for use in pediatric patients under the age of 2 years.

Geriatrics

No overall differences in safety or effectiveness have been observed between elderly and other adult patients.

Drug interactions and/or related problems

The following drug interactions and/or related problems have been selected on the basis of their potential clinical significance (possible mechanism in parentheses where appropriate)—not necessarily inclusive (» = major clinical significance):

Note: Combinations containing any of the following medications, depending on the amount present, may also interact with this medication.

Antihypertensives or
Beta-adrenergic blocking agents or
Other cardiovascular agents
(although ophthalmic brimonidine had little effect on pulse or blood pressure in clinical studies, caution in concurrent use with these medications is recommended because alpha-adrenergic agonists such as brimonidine may decrease pulse rate and blood pressure)

Central nervous system (CNS) depressants
(caution in concurrent use is recommended because of the possibility of additive CNS depression)

» Monoamine oxidase (MAO) inhibitors
(brimonidine is contraindicated during, or within 14 days following, the administration of an MAO inhibitor)

Tricyclic antidepressants
(whether tricyclic antidepressants may interfere with the ocular antihypertensive effect of ophthalmic brimonidine has not been determined, but they have been reported to decrease the antihypertensive effect of systemic clonidine)
(although the effect of ophthalmic brimonidine on systemic catecholamine concentrations has not been determined, caution is recommended in its concurrent use with tricyclic antidepressants because the antidepressants may alter the metabolism and uptake of circulating catecholamines)

Medical considerations/Contraindications

The medical considerations/contraindications included have been selected on the basis of their potential clinical significance (reasons given in parentheses where appropriate)—not necessarily inclusive (» = major clinical significance).

Except under special circumstances, this medication should not be used when the following medical problem exists:

» Hypersensitivity to brimonidine or any component of the medication

Risk-benefit should be considered when the following medical problems exist:

» Cardiovascular disease, severe or
Cerebral insufficiency or
Coronary insufficiency or
Hypotension, orthostatic or
Raynaud's disease or
Thromboangiitis obliterans
(caution is advised, although ocular instillation of brimonidine had minimal effect on blood pressure in clinical trials)

Hepatic function impairment or
Renal function impairment
(caution is recommended because studies have not been done in patients with these conditions)

Mental depression
(caution is recommended; some patients experienced mental depression during clinical trials with brimonidine)

Patient monitoring

The following may be especially important in patient monitoring (other tests may be warranted in some patients, depending on condition; » = major clinical significance):

» Intraocular pressure
(should be monitored regularly to determine that an adequate response to treatment is achieved and maintained; in clinical trials the efficacy of brimonidine decreased over time in some patients)

Side/Adverse Effects

The following side/adverse effects have been selected on the basis of their potential clinical significance (possible signs and symptoms in parentheses where appropriate)–not necessarily inclusive:

Those indicating need for medical attention

Incidence more frequent (10 to 30%)

Allergic reaction (redness of eye or inner lining of eyelid; swelling of eyelid; itching; tearing); ***conjunctival follicles; headache; ocular hyperemia*** (redness of eye)

Incidence less frequent (9% or lower)

Ache or pain in eye; blepharitis (redness, swelling, and/or itching of eyelid); ***blepharoconjunctivitis*** (drainage from the eye; redness, swelling, and/or itching of eye and eyelid); ***blurred vision or other change in vision; cataract*** (blindness; blurred vision; decreased vision); ***conjunctival discharge*** (oozing in eye); ***conjunctival hemorrhage*** (bloody eye); ***corneal erosion; dizziness; dyspnea*** (shortness of breath; difficult or labored breathing; tightness in chest; wheezing); ***edema of conjunctiva or eyelid*** (swelling of eye or eyelid); ***foreign body sensation*** (feeling of something in the eye); ***gastrointestinal symptoms*** (nausea or vomiting); ***hypotension*** (blurred vision; confusion; dizziness, faintness, or lightheadedness when getting up from a lying or sitting position suddenly; sweating; unusual tiredness or weakness); ***increased blood pressure; mental depression; muscle pain; superficial punctate keratopathy*** (blurred vision or other change in vision); ***syncope*** (fainting); ***upper respiratory symptoms*** (runny or stuffy nose; sneezing); ***vitreous detachment*** (seeing flashes or sparks of light; seeing floating spots before the eyes or a veil or curtain appearing across part of vision); ***vitreous disorder*** (change in vision; seeing floating spots before the eyes; looking through water); ***vitreous floaters*** (seeing floating dark spots or material before eyes)

Incidence not determined—Observed during clinical practice; estimates of frequency cannot be determined

Apnea (bluish lips or skin; not breathing); ***bradycardia*** (chest pain or discomfort; lightheadedness; dizziness or fainting; shortness of breath; slow or irregular heartbeat; unusual tiredness); ***tachycardia*** (fast, pounding, or irregular heartbeat or pulse); ***vasodilation*** (feeling of warmth or heat; flushing or redness of skin, especially on face and neck; headache; feeling faint, dizzy, or light-headedness; sweating)

Note: Apnea, bradycardia, hypotension, hypothermia, hypotonia, and somnolence have been reported in infants receiving brimonidine tartrate ophthalmic solutions.

Those indicating need for medical attention only if they continue or are bothersome

Incidence more frequent (10 to 30%)

Burning, stinging, or tearing; drowsiness or tiredness; dryness of mouth

Incidence less frequent (9% or lower)

Anxiety; blurred vision; bronchitis (cough producing mucus; difficulty breathing; shortness of breath; tightness in chest; wheezing); ***conjunctival blanching*** (paleness of eye or inner lining of eyelid); ***corneal staining*** (discoloration of white part of eye); ***cough; crusting on eyelid or corner of eye; dizziness; dryness of eye; dyspepsia*** (acid or sour stomach; belching; heartburn; indigestion; stomach discomfort, upset, or pain); ***epiphora*** (watery eye); ***eye irritation or pain*** (red, sore, or painful eyes); ***eyelid erythema*** (redness of eyelid); ***fatigue*** (unusual tiredness or weakness); ***flu syndrome*** (chills; cough; diarrhea; fever; general feeling of discomfort or illness; headache; joint pain; loss of appetite; muscle aches and pains; nausea; runny nose; shivering; sore throat; sweating; trouble sleeping; unusual tiredness or weakness; vomiting); ***gastrointestinal disorder*** (diarrhea; loss of appetite; nausea or vomiting; stomach pain, fullness, or discomfort; indigestion; passing of gas); ***headache; hypercholesterolemia*** (large amount of cholesterol in the blood); ***keratitis*** (eye irritation, redness, or pain); ***lid disorder; muscle weakness; pharyngitis*** (body aches or pain; congestion; cough; dryness or soreness of throat; fever; hoarseness; runny nose; tender, swollen glands in neck; trouble in swallowing; voice changes); ***photophobia*** (increased sensitivity of eye to light); ***pounding heartbeat; rash; rhinitis*** (stuffy nose; runny nose; sneezing); ***sinus infection or sinusitis*** (pain or tenderness around eyes and cheekbones; fever; stuffy or runny nose; headache; cough; shortness of breath or troubled breathing; tightness of chest or wheezing); ***taste changes; trouble in sleeping; visual field defect*** (blurred vision; decrease or change in vision); ***worsened visual acuity*** (decreased vision)

Incidence not determined—Observed during clinical practice; estimates of frequency cannot be determined

Erythema (flushing, redness of skin; unusually warm skin); ***eyelid pruritus*** (itchy eyelid); ***iritis*** (sensitivity to light; tearing; throbbing pain); ***keratoconjunctivitis sicca*** (dryness of the eye); ***miosis*** (constricted, pinpoint, or small pupils [black part of eye]); ***nausea***

Overdose

There is no experience with brimonidine overdose. For information on the management of overdose or unintentional ingestion, **contact a Poison Control Center** (see *Poison Control Center Listing*).

Treatment of overdose

Treatment may consist of maintaining a patent airway and other supportive measures required to relieve observed symptoms.

Patient Consultation

As an aid to patient consultation, refer to *Advice for the Patient, Brimonidine (Ophthalmic).*

In providing consultation, consider emphasizing the following selected information (» = major clinical significance)

Before using this medication

» Conditions affecting use, especially:
Hypersensitivity to brimonidine or any other component of the medication
Pregnancy—Risk benefit considerations
Breast-feeding—Risk benefit considerations
Use in children—Safety and efficacy not established in children less than 2 years of age
Other medications, especially monoamine oxidase inhibitors
Other medical problems, especially severe cardiovascular disease

Proper use of this medication

Waiting at least 5 minutes between instillation of two different ophthalmic solutions
Proper administration technique; using a second drop if necessary; not touching applicator tip to any surface; keeping container tightly closed
» Importance of not using more medication than the amount prescribed
» Proper dosing
Missed dose: Using as soon as possible; not using if almost time for next dose; using next dose at regularly scheduled time; not doubling doses
» Proper storage

Precautions while using this medication

» Regular visits to physician to check eye pressure during therapy
» Medication may cause dizziness, drowsiness, or tiredness; using caution when driving, using machines, or doing anything else requiring alertness
» Contacting physician immediately if syncope occurs
» Soft contact lens users: Preservative in product may be absorbed by soft contact lenses; waiting at least 15 minutes after instilling medication before inserting lenses
Possible photophobia; wearing sunglasses or avoiding bright light

Side/adverse effects

Signs of potential side effects, especially allergic reaction, conjunctival follicles, headache, ocular hyperemia, ache or pain in eye, blepharitis, blepharoconjunctivitis, blurred vision or other change in vision, cataract, conjunctival discharge, conjunctival hemorrhage, corneal erosion, dizziness, dyspnea, edema of conjunctiva or eyelid, foreign body sensation, gastrointestinal symptoms, hypotension, increased blood pressure, mental depression, muscle pain, superficial punctate keratopathy, syncope, upper respiratory symptoms, vitreous detachment, vitreous disorder, or vitreous floaters
Signs of potential side effects observed during clinical practice, especially apnea, bradycardia, tachycardia, or vasodilation

General Dosing Information

The intraocular pressure (IOP) lowering effect of brimonidine decreases over time. Although the onset of loss of effect is variable, in clinical studies some patients experienced inadequate control of IOP during the first month of treatment.

Brimonidine ophthalmic solution may be used concomitantly with other topical ophthalmic drug products to lower intraocular pressure. If more than one topical ophthalmic product is being used, the products should be administered at least 5 minutes apart.

Ophthalmic Dosage Forms

BRIMONIDINE TARTRATE OPHTHALMIC SOLUTION

Usual adult dose

Open-angle glaucoma or
Ocular hypertension—
Topical, to the conjunctiva, 1 drop in the affected eye(s) three times a day, approximately 8 hours apart.

Usual pediatric dose

For children 2 years of age and older, see *Usual adult dose*.
Safety and efficacy have not been established in children less than 2 years of age.

Strength(s) usually available

U.S.—
0.1% (Rx) [*Alphagan P* (sodium carboxymethylcellulose; sodium borate; boric acid; sodium chloride; potassium chloride; calcium chloride; magnesium chloride; Purite® as a preservative; purified water; hydrochloric acid and/or sodium hydroxide to adjust pH)].
0.15% (Rx) [*Alphagan P* (sodium carboxymethylcellulose; sodium borate; boric acid; sodium chloride; potassium chloride; calcium chloride; magnesium chloride; Purite® as a preservative; purified water; hydrochloric acid and/or sodium hydroxide to adjust pH)].
0.2% (2 mg of brimonidine tartrate, equivalent to 1.32 mg of brimonidine base, per mL) (Rx) [GENERIC].

Packaging and storage

Store at 15 to 25 °C (59 to 77 °F).

Auxiliary labeling

• For the eye.

Revised: 09/13/2005
Developed: 04/01/1997

BRINZOLAMIDE Ophthalmic

VA CLASSIFICATION (Primary): OP112

Commonly used brand name(s): *Azopt*.

Note: For a listing of dosage forms and brand names by country availability, see *Dosage Forms* section(s).

Category

Antiglaucoma agent (ophthalmic).

Indications

Accepted

Glaucoma, open-angle (treatment) or
Hypertension, ocular (treatment)—Brinzolamide is indicated in the treatment of elevated intraocular pressure in patients with ocular hypertension or open-angle glaucoma.

Acceptance not established

Ophthalmic brinzolamide has not been studied in patients with acute angle-closure glaucoma.

Pharmacology/Pharmacokinetics

Physicochemical characteristics

Chemical Group—Sulfonamide.
Molecular weight—383.5.
pH—Brinzolamide ophthalmic suspension: 7.5.
Solubility—Insoluble in water, very soluble in methanol, and soluble in ethanol.

Mechanism of action/Effect

Brinzolamide is a sulfonamide and a carbonic anhydrase inhibitor. Carbonic anhydrase is an enzyme found in many tissues of the body, including the eye. Carbonic anhydrase catalyzes the reversible reaction involving the hydration of carbon dioxide and the dehydration of carbonic acid. In humans, carbonic anhydrase exists as a number of isoenzymes, the most active of which is carbonic anhydrase II. Carbonic anhydrase II is found primarily in red blood cells, but it also appears in other tissues.

Antiglaucoma agent—Brinzolamide inhibits human carbonic anhydrase II. Inhibition of carbonic anhydrase in the ciliary processes of the eye decreases aqueous humor secretion, presumably by slowing the formation of bicarbonate ions, with subsequent reduction in sodium and fluid transport. The result is a reduction in intraocular pressure, and thereby a reduction in the risk of optic nerve damage and glaucomatous visual field loss. In clinical studies of up to 3 months in duration in patients with glaucoma or ocular hypertension, brinzolamide had an intraocular pressure (IOP)–lowering effect of approximately 4 or 5 mm of mercury (mm Hg).

Other actions/effects

When brinzolamide was administered orally in doses of 1 mg twice a day for up to 32 weeks to healthy volunteers, inhibition of carbonic anhydrase II activity at steady state was approximately 70 to 75%, which was less than the degree of inhibition considered to be necessary for a pharmacological effect on renal function and respiration in healthy persons. (The oral dose of 1 mg twice daily approximates the amount of medication delivered systemically by ophthalmic administration of 1% brinzolamide to both eyes three times per day, and simulates systemic drug and metabolite concentrations similar to those achieved with long-term ophthalmic dosing.)

Absorption

Brinzolamide is systemically absorbed when applied to the eye. In a study designed to simulate systemic absorption during long-term ophthalmic administration, healthy subjects were given 1 mg of oral brinzolamide twice a day for up to 32 weeks. (The oral dose of 1 mg twice daily closely approximates the amount of medication delivered systemically by ophthalmic administration of 1% brinzolamide in both eyes three times a day). Saturation of red blood cell carbonic anhydrase II by brinzolamide (concentrations of approximately 20 micromolar) was reached within 4 weeks, and steady-state accumulation of the metabolite *N*-desethyl brinzolamide in red blood cells (6 to 30 micromolar) was reached within 20 to 28 weeks.

Distribution
During chronic dosing, brinzolamide accumulates in red blood cells by binding to carbonic anhydrase II. The *N*-desethyl metabolite also accumulates in red blood cells by binding primarily to carbonic anhydrase I in the presence of brinzolamide. Plasma concentrations of brinzolamide and the *N*-desethyl metabolite are generally below the minimum assay limit of 10 nanograms per mL.

Protein binding
Moderate (approximately 60%).

Biotransformation
To an *N*-desethyl metabolite that binds mainly to carbonic anhydrase I in the presence of brinzolamide.

Half-life
Following ophthalmic administration—In whole blood, approximately 111 days.

Elimination
Renal, primarily as unchanged drug. Metabolites *N*-desethyl brinzolamide and, in lower concentrations, the *N*-desmethoxypropyl and *O*-desmethyl metabolites also appear in the urine.

Precautions to Consider

Cross-sensitivity and/or related problems
Patients sensitive to sulfonamides may also be sensitive to brinzolamide.

Carcinogenicity
Studies have not been done.

Mutagenicity
No evidence of mutagenicity was found in the *in vivo* mouse micronucleus assay, the *in vivo* sister chromatid exchange assay, or the Ames *Escherichia coli* test. The *in vitro* mouse lymphoma forward mutation assay was negative in the absence of microsomal activation, but positive in the presence of activation.

Pregnancy/Reproduction
Fertility—Studies in male and female rats at doses of up to 18 mg per kg of body weight (mg/kg) per day (375 times the recommended human ophthalmic dose) found no adverse effects on fertility.

Pregnancy—Adequate and well-controlled studies in humans have not been done.

Radiolabeled brinzolamide has been found to cross the placenta and appear in the fetal tissues and blood in pregnant rats. Studies in rabbits at oral brinzolamide doses of 1, 3, and 6 mg/kg per day (20, 62, and 125 times the recommended human ophthalmic dose, respectively) found maternal toxicity at the 6 mg/kg per day dose and a significant increase in the number of fetal variations (such as accessory skull bones) that was only slightly higher than the historic value at 1 and 6 mg/kg. Studies in female rats at oral doses of 18 mg/kg per day (375 times the recommended human ophthalmic dose) during gestation found statistically decreased body weights of fetuses that were proportional to the reduced maternal weight gain, with no statistically significant effects on organ or tissue development. Increases in unossified sternebrae, reduced ossification of the skull, and unossified hyoid that occurred at 6 and 18 mg/kg were not statistically significant. No treatment-related malformations have been seen.

It is recommended that risk-benefit be considered before using ophthalmic brinzolamide during pregnancy.

FDA Pregnancy Category C.

Breast-feeding
It is not known whether ophthalmic brinzolamide passes into human breast milk. A study in lactating rats at an oral dose of 15 mg/kg per day (312 times the recommended human ophthalmic dose) found decreases in body weight gain in offspring during lactation. When radiolabeled oral brinzolamide was administered to lactating rats, radioactivity was found in milk at concentrations below those in the blood and plasma.

It is recommended that risk-benefit be considered before patients breastfeed during treatment with ophthalmic brinzolamide.

Pediatrics
Safety and efficacy have not been established.

Geriatrics
No information is available on the relationship of age to the effects of brinzolamide in geriatric patients.

Drug interactions and/or related problems
The following drug interactions and/or related problems have been selected on the basis of their potential clinical significance (possible mechanism in parentheses where appropriate)—not necessarily inclusive (» = major clinical significance):

Note: Combinations containing any of the following medications, depending on the amount present, may also interact with this medication.

» Carbonic anhydrase inhibitors, oral
(potential additive systemic effect; concurrent use is not recommended)

Salicylates, high doses
(acid-base and electrolyte alterations have not been reported with the use of ophthalmic brinzolamide; however, in patients treated with oral carbonic anhydrase inhibitors, rare cases of adverse effects have occurred with concurrent high-dose salicylate therapy)

Medical considerations/Contraindications
The medical considerations/contraindications included have been selected on the basis of their potential clinical significance (reasons given in parentheses where appropriate)—not necessarily inclusive (» = major clinical significance).

Risk-benefit should be considered when the following medical problems exist:

Hepatic function impairment
(although studies with brinzolamide have not been done in patients with hepatic function impairment, caution is advised when brinzolamide is administered to these patients)

» Renal function impairment, severe (creatinine clearance less than 30 mL per minute)
(although studies with brinzolamide have not been done in patients with renal function impairment, brinzolamide is eliminated renally, and the risk of side effects may be increased because of decreased elimination; use is not recommended)

» Sensitivity to brinzolamide

Side/Adverse Effects

Note: Because it is absorbed systemically, there is a possibility that ophthalmic brinzolamide could cause serious side effects associated with other sulfonamides, including Stevens-Johnson syndrome, toxic epidermal necrolysis, fulminant hepatic necrosis, agranulocytosis, aplastic anemia, and other blood dyscrasias.

Carbonic anhydrase activity has been observed in both the cytoplasm and around the plasma membranes of the corneal endothelium. The effect of continued administration of ophthalmic brinzolamide on the corneal endothelium has not been fully evaluated.

The following side/adverse effects have been selected on the basis of their potential clinical significance (possible signs and symptoms in parentheses where appropriate)—not necessarily inclusive:

Those indicating need for medical attention
Incidence less frequent

Blepharitis (redness or soreness of eyelid); ***dermatitis*** (skin rash); ***feeling of something in the eye; headache; hyperemia*** (redness of the eye); ***keratitis*** (eye redness, irritation, or pain); ***ocular discharge*** (discharge from the eye); ***ocular pain*** (eye pain)

Incidence rare

Allergic reaction, ocular (itching, redness, swelling, or other sign of eye or eyelid irritation); ***alopecia*** (hair loss); ***chest pain; conjunctivitis*** (redness of inner lining of eyelid); ***diplopia*** (seeing double); ***dizziness; dyspnea*** (shortness of breath); ***hypertonia*** (excessive muscle tone); ***keratoconjunctivitis*** (eye redness, irritation, or pain); ***keratopathy*** (eye redness, irritation, or pain); ***kidney pain; pharyngitis*** (sore throat); ***urticaria*** (hives)

Those indicating need for medical attention only if they continue or are bothersome
Incidence more frequent

Bitter, sour, or other unusual taste; blurred vision, transient, after application

Incidence less frequent

Burning, stinging, or discomfort when medicine is applied; dry eye; rhinitis (runny nose)

Overdose

For more information on the management of overdose or unintentional ingestion, **contact a Poison Control Center** (see *Poison Control Center Listing*).

Clinical effects of overdose
No human data are available. However, electrolyte imbalance, acidosis, and possible nervous system effects may occur with oral overdose.

Treatment of overdose
Monitoring of serum electrolyte concentrations (especially potassium) and blood pH is recommended.

Patient Consultation
As an aid to patient consultation, refer to *Advice for the Patient, Brinzolamide (Ophthalmic)*.

In providing consultation, consider emphasizing the following selected information (» = major clinical significance):

Before using this medication
» Conditions affecting use, especially:
- Sensitivity to brinzolamide or other sulfonamides
- Pregnancy—Crosses the placenta in animals; maternal and fetal toxicity occurs in animals administered large doses of medication
- Breast-feeding—Risk-benefit should be considered
- Other medicines, especially oral carbonic anhydrase inhibitors
- Other medical problems, especially renal function impairment

Proper use of this medication
Shaking medication before each use

Proper administration technique; preventing contamination of medication in bottle

» Importance of using medication only as directed

Waiting 10 minutes between use of two different ophthalmic preparations to prevent "washing out" of the first one

» Proper dosing

Missed dose: Using as soon as possible; not using if almost time for next dose; not doubling doses

» Proper storage

Precautions while using this medication
Regular visits to physician to check progress during therapy

» Checking with physician if signs of ocular allergic reaction occur

Removing soft contact lenses before instillation of suspension; may be reinserted 15 minutes after instillation

» Checking with physician about possible need for a fresh bottle of medication to use in case of surgery, injury, or infection

» Temporary blurring of vision may occur following administration; caution in driving or operating machinery

Side/adverse effects
Signs of potential side effects, especially blepharitis, dermatitis, feeling of something in the eye, headache, hyperemia, keratitis, ocular discharge, ocular pain, ocular allergic reaction, alopecia, chest pain, conjunctivitis, diplopia, dizziness, dyspnea, hypertonia, keratoconjunctivitis, keratopathy, kidney pain, pharyngitis, or urticaria

General Dosing Information
Because of the preservative benzalkonium chloride, the manufacturer recommends that patients remove soft contact lenses before instillation of brinzolamide. Lenses may be reinserted 15 minutes after instillation.

Brinzolamide may be used concurrently with other medications instilled in the eye to lower intraocular pressure. However, the medications should be administered at least 10 minutes apart.

It is recommended that brinzolamide be discontinued if signs of hypersensitivity or other serious reactions occur.

Ophthalmic Dosage Forms
BRINZOLAMIDE OPHTHALMIC SUSPENSION
Usual adult dose
Antiglaucoma agent (ophthalmic)—

Topical, to the conjunctiva, 1 drop in the affected eye(s) three times a day.

Usual pediatric dose
Antiglaucoma agent (ophthalmic)—

Safety and efficacy have not been established.

Strength(s) usually available
U.S.—

1% (Rx) [*Azopt* (benzalkonium chloride 0.01%; mannitol; carbomer 974P; tyloxapol; edetate disodium; sodium chloride; hydrochloric acid and/or sodium hydroxide)].

Packaging and storage
Store between 4 and 30 °C (39 and 86 °F).

Auxiliary labeling
- For the eye.
- Shake well before using.

Developed: 08/06/1998

BROMAZEPAM—See *Benzodiazepines (Systemic)*

BROMFENAC Ophthalmic

VA CLASSIFICATION (Primary): OP302

Commonly used brand name(s): *Xibrom*.

Note: For a listing of dosage forms and brand names by country availability, see *Dosage Forms* section(s).

Category
Anti-inflammatory, nonsteroidal (ophthalmic).

Indications
Accepted
Inflammation, ocular (treatment)—Bromfenac ophthalmic solution is indicated for the treatment of postoperative inflammation in patients who have undergone cataract extraction.

Pharmacology/Pharmacokinetics
Physicochemical characteristics
Molecular weight—Bromfenac sodium: 383.17.

pH—8.3

Osmolality—300 mOsmol per kg

Mechanism of action/Effect
Bromfenac is a nonsteroidal anti-inflammatory drug (NSAID) that has anti-inflammatory activity. The mechanism of action is thought to be due to its ability to block prostaglandin synthesis by inhibiting cyclooxygenase 1 and 2. Prostaglandins have been shown to be mediators of certain kinds of intraocular inflammation. Prostaglandins produce disruption of the blood-aqueous humor barrier, vasodilation, increased vascular permeability, leukocytosis, and increased intraocular pressure in the eye.

Steady-state plasma concentration
Below the limit of quantification (50 ng per mL)

Precautions to Consider
Cross-sensitivity and/or related problems
There is the potential for cross-sensitivity to acetylsalicylic acid, phenylacetic acid derivatives, and other NSAIDs. Caution should be used if individuals have exhibited sensitivities to these drugs.

Carcinogenicity
Studies in rats and mice given oral doses of bromfenac up to 0.6 mg per kg per day (360 times the recommended human ophthalmic dose [RHOD] of 1.67 mcg per kg in 60 kg person on a mg per kg basis) and 5 mg per kg per day (3000 times the RHOD), respectively, revealed no significant increases in tumor incidence.

Mutagenicity
Bromfenac did not show mutagenic potential in various mutagenicity studies, including the reverse mutation, chromosomal aberration, and micronucleus tests.

Pregnancy/Reproduction
Fertility—No impairment of fertility was seen when bromfenac was administered orally to male and female rats at doses up to 0.9 mg per kg per day and 0.3 mg per kg per day, respectively (540 and 180 times the RHOD, respectively).

Pregnancy—Adequate and well controlled studies in humans have not been done. Because animal reproduction studies are not always predictive of human response, this drug should be used during pregnancy only if the potential benefit justifies the potential risk to the fetus. The use of bromfenac ophthalmic solution should be avoided during late pregnancy due to known effects of prostaglandin biosynthesis-inhibiting drugs on the fetal cardiovascular system (closure of ductus arteriosis).

Reproduction studies in rats given 0.9 mg per kg per day (540 times RHOD) caused embryo-fetal lethality, increased neonatal mortality, and reduced postnatal growth. Pregnant rabbits treated with 7.5 mg per kg per day caused post-implantation loss.

FDA Pregnancy Category C

Breast-feeding
It is not known whether bromfenac is distributed into breast milk. However, caution should be exercised when this ophthalmic solution is administered to nursing women. Problems in humans have not been documented.

Pediatrics
No information is available on the relationship of age to the effects of bromfenac in pediatric patients below the age of 18. Safety and efficacy have not been established.

Geriatrics
Appropriate studies on the relationship of age to the effects of bromfenac have not been performed in the geriatric population. However, no geriatrics-specific problems have been documented to date.

Drug interactions and/or related problems
The following drug interactions and/or related problems have been selected on the basis of their potential clinical significance (possible mechanism in parentheses where appropriate)—not necessarily inclusive (» = major clinical significance):

Note: Combinations containing any of the following medications, depending on the amount present, may also interact with this medication.

Corticosteroids, topical
(concomitant use of these medicines may increase the potential for healing problems)

Medicines that prolong bleeding time
(concomitant use may cause increased bleeding, use with caution)

Medical considerations/Contraindications
The medical considerations/contraindications included have been selected on the basis of their potential clinical significance (reasons given in parentheses where appropriate)—not necessarily inclusive (» = major clinical significance).

Except under special circumstances, this medication should not be used when the following medical problem exists:

» Hypersensitivity to bromfenac or any of its components, including sulfite
(may cause allergic-type reactions including anaphylactic symptoms and life-threatening or less severe asthmatic episodes in certain susceptible people)

Risk-benefit should be considered when the following medical problems exist:

Bleeding tendencies, ocular
(ocularly applied NSAIDs may cause increased bleeding of ocular tissues)

Corneal denervation or
Corneal epithelial defects or
Diabetes mellitus or
Ocular surface diseases (e.g., dry eye syndrome) or
Ocular surgeries, complicated or
Ocular surgeries, multiple within a short period of time or
Rheumatoid arthritis
(may be at increased risk for corneal adverse events)

Patient monitoring
The following may be especially important in patient monitoring (other tests may be warranted in some patients, depending on condition; » = major clinical significance):

Corneal epithelial breakdown
(patients developing this condition should discontinue use of bromfenac and be monitored closely for corneal health)

Side/Adverse Effects
The following side/adverse effects have been selected on the basis of their potential clinical significance (possible signs and symptoms in parentheses where appropriate)—not necessarily inclusive:

Those indicating need for medical attention
Incidence not determined—Observed during clinical practice, estimates of frequency can not be determined

Corneal epithelial breakdown (blurred vision or other change in vision)

Those indicating need for medical attention only if they continue or are bothersome
Incidence more frequent

Abnormal sensation in eye; burning or stinging of the eye; conjunctival hyperemia (increase in blood flow to the whites of the eyes); ***eye irritation; eye pain; eye pruritus*** (itching of the eyes); ***eye redness; headache; iritis*** (sensitivity to light; tearing; throbbing pain)

Incidence not determined—Observed during clinical practice, estimates of frequency can not be determined

Corneal erosion (eye irritation or redness); ***corneal perforation*** (blurred vision or other change in vision); ***corneal thinning*** (blurred vision or other change in vision); ***corneal ulceration*** (eye irritation or redness); ***keratitis*** (eye redness, irritation, or pain)

Patient Consultation
As an aid to patient consultation, refer to *Advice for the Patient, Bromfenac (Ophthalmic)*.

In providing consultation, consider emphasizing the following selected information (» = major clinical significance):

Before using this medication
» Conditions affecting use, especially:

Hypersensitivity to acetylsalicylic acid, phenylacetic acid derivatives, and other NSAIDs

Mutagenicity—Bromfenac did not show mutagenic potential in various mutagenicity studies

Pregnancy—Studies in rats and rabbits have revealed some potential adverse effects on the fetus.

Use in children—Safety and efficacy have not been established

Other medical problems, especially hypersensitivity to bromfenac or sulfites

Proper use of this medication
» Proper dosing

Missed dose: Taking as soon as possible; then returning to regular schedule.

Proper storage

Side/adverse effects
Signs of potential side effects, especially corneal epithelial breakdown

General Dosing Information
Bromfenac should not be administered while wearing contact lenses.

Use of ophthalmic NSAIDs more than 24 hours prior to surgery or use beyond 14 days post surgery may increase patient risk for the occurrence and severity of corneal adverse events.

Ophthalmic Dosage Forms
BROMFENAC SODIUM HYDRATE
Usual adult dose
Inflammation, ophthalmic—

Topical, to the conjunctiva, one drop of solution to the affected eye twice daily beginning 24 hours after cataract surgery and continuing for 2 weeks

Usual pediatric dose
Safety and efficacy have not been established.

Usual geriatric dose
See *Usual adult dose*.

Strength(s) usually available
U.S.—

0.9 mg per mL (free acid) (Rx) [*Xibrom* (benzalkonium chloride; boric acid; disodium edetate; polysorbate; povidone; sodium borate; sodium sulfite anhydrous; sodium hydroxide; purified water, USP)].

Packaging and storage
Store between 15 and 25 °C (59 and 77 °F)

Auxiliary labeling
- For the eye.

Developed: 06/13/2005

BROMOCRIPTINE Systemic

VA CLASSIFICATION (Primary/Secondary): AU900/HS900

Commonly used brand name(s): *Alti-Bromocriptine; Apo-Bromocriptine; Parlodel; Parlodel SnapTabs.*

Note: For a listing of dosage forms and brand names by country availability, see *Dosage Forms* section(s).

Category
Dopamine agonist; antihyperprolactinemic; infertility therapy adjunct; lactation inhibitor; antidyskinetic; growth hormone suppressant (acromegaly); neuroleptic malignant syndrome therapy.

Indications

Note: Bracketed information in the *Indications* section refers to uses that are not included in U.S. product labeling.

Accepted

Prolactinomas, pituitary (treatment)—Bromocriptine is indicated in the treatment of prolactin-secreting pituitary tumors in men and women. Bromocriptine is usually considered to be the treatment of choice for microadenomas and for macroadenomas including those with visual defects. However, surgery may be required to treat macroadenomas in those patients who either cannot take bromocriptine or who exhibit a poor therapeutic response to bromocriptine. Bromocriptine may also be used as an adjunct to radiotherapy when the tumor is inoperable.

[Bromocriptine is used by some clinicians in the treatment of visual field defects that develop during pregnancy. Visual field defects that respond to bromocriptine are secondary to pituitary adenoma enlargement.][1]

Amenorrhea, secondary, due to hyperprolactinemia (treatment) or
Galactorrhea due to hyperprolactinemia (treatment) or
Hypogonadism, male, due to hyperprolactinemia (treatment) or
Infertility due to hyperprolactinemia (treatment)—Bromocriptine is indicated in the short-term symptomatic treatment of amenorrhea and/or galactorrhea or male or female infertility associated with hyperprolactinemia. Its usefulness in normoprolactinemic amenorrhea or anovulation is controversial.

[Lactation, after second- or third-trimester pregnancy loss (prophylaxis)][1]—Bromocriptine can be used in selected individuals for the prevention of physiological lactation and breast engorgement after stillbirth, neonatal death, or abortion. However, in many patients, breast engorgement is a benign, self-limited condition, which may respond to breast support and mild analgesics, such as acetaminophen and ibuprofen. Once bromocriptine has been discontinued, 18 to 40% of patients experience rebound symptoms of breast secretion, congestion, or engorgement. Also, the relative risk of all of bromocriptine's rare, severe, or life-threatening side effects, which have included strokes, seizures, and myocardial infarction, has yet to be determined.

Parkinsonism (treatment)—Bromocriptine is indicated, usually as an adjunct to levodopa/carbidopa therapy, in the treatment of the signs and symptoms of idiopathic or postencephalic parkinsonism.

Acromegaly (treatment)—Bromocriptine is indicated in the treatment of some cases of acromegaly, usually as an adjunct to surgery or radiotherapy. There are some reports that patients who respond may have elevated prolactin as well as elevated growth hormone concentrations.

[Neuroleptic malignant syndrome (treatment)][1]—Although controlled clinical trials have not been conducted, bromocriptine is sometimes used as adjunctive therapy in the treatment of neuroleptic malignant syndrome. Individual case reports and the known pharmacological activity of bromocriptine indicate that it may have some utility in the treatment of this disorder, as well as a lower incidence of side effects, as compared with other modes of therapy for this condition.

Unaccepted

The routine use of bromocriptine for suppression of postpartum lactation is not recommended.

---

[1]Not included in Canadian product labeling.

Pharmacology/Pharmacokinetics

Physicochemical characteristics

Chemical Group—Bromocriptine is an ergot alkaloid derivative.
Molecular weight—750.70.

Mechanism of action/Effect

Dopamine agonist
Antihyperprolactinemic
Infertility therapy adjunct and
Lactation inhibitor—Reduction of serum prolactin concentrations by direct inhibition of release of prolactin from the anterior pituitary gland through binding to dopamine type 2 (D_2) receptors, resulting in restoration of testicular or ovarian function and suppression of lactation.

Antidyskinetic—In high doses, stimulation of post-synaptic dopamine type 2 (D_2) receptors in the neostriatum of the central nervous system (CNS); may also decrease dopamine turnover. At low doses, bromocriptine may worsen dyskinesia by stimulating presynaptic dopamine receptors. Is most effective when used concurrently with levodopa, as stimulation of D_1 receptors by levodopa enhances the antidyskinetic effects of postsynaptic D_2 receptor stimulation by bromocriptine.

Growth hormone suppressant (acromegaly)—Suppression of secretion and reduction of elevated growth hormone serum concentrations.

Neuroleptic malignant syndrome therapy—Some evidence exists that neuroleptic malignant syndrome may result from depletion of dopamine or blockade of dopamine receptors in the nigrostriatal, hypothalamic, and mesolimbic cortical pathways. Bromocriptine stimulates these dopamine receptors.

Absorption

Approximately 28% of an oral dose is absorbed from the gastrointestinal tract, but because of first-pass metabolism, only 6% reaches the systemic circulation unchanged.

Protein binding

Very high (90 to 96% to serum albumin).

Biotransformation

Hepatic.

Half-life

Biphasic—
4 to 4.5 hours (alpha phase).
15 hours (terminal).

Onset of action

Single dose—
Serum prolactin-lowering effect: 2 hours.
Antiparkinsonism effect: 30 to 90 minutes.
Growth hormone-lowering effect: 1 to 2 hours.

Time to peak concentration

1 to 3 hours.

Time to peak effect

Serum prolactin-lowering effect—8 hours (after a single dose).

Note: The maximum obtainable reduction in serum prolactin occurs after approximately 4 weeks of continuous therapy. The average duration of therapy required to reinitiate menses is 6 to 8 weeks. In the treatment of galactorrhea, a significant reduction in lactation usually occurs within 6 to 7 weeks, with cessation of lactation occurring by 12 to 13 weeks. Suppression of postpartum lactation requires 2 to 3 weeks of therapy; some clinicians believe that 3 weeks of therapy is necessary to prevent rebound lactation.

Antiparkinsonism effect—2 hours (after a single dose).

Growth hormone-lowering effect—A clinical response occurs within 4 to 8 weeks with continuous therapy.

Duration of action

Serum prolactin-lowering effect—Approximately 24 hours (after a single dose).

Note: Serum prolactin concentrations usually return to pretreatment levels within 2 months after bromocriptine is discontinued.

Growth hormone-lowering effect—4 to 8 hours.

Elimination

As metabolites—
Biliary: Approximately 95%.
Renal: 2.5 to 5.5%.

Precautions to Consider

Cross-sensitivity and/or related problems

Patients sensitive to other ergot derivatives may be sensitive to this medication also.

Pregnancy/Reproduction

Fertility—Restoration of fertility may result in pregnancy with possible enlargement of a pituitary adenoma, leading to visual field defects, headaches, and excessive nausea and vomiting in the mother.

In general, use of a nonhormonal contraceptive is recommended in patients being treated for hyperprolactinemia until normal ovulatory menstrual cycles are established. At that time, contraception can be discontinued in patients desiring pregnancy, with careful monitoring to avoid inadvertent administration of bromocriptine after pregnancy is diagnosed.

Pregnancy—Bromocriptine is not generally recommended for use during pregnancy; however, it has been used in the treatment of acromegaly, Parkinson's disease, or prolactinoma in pregnant patients when deemed medically necessary. For patients who develop pregnancy-related hypertension or have recently developed hypertensive disorders of pregnancy, withdrawal of bromocriptine is recommended, unless discontinuation is considered medically contraindicated.

Large and long-term studies performed in humans have found no increased incidence of birth defects. In clinical use, successful pregnancies have occurred in humans taking bromocriptine both before conception and for periods ranging from the first 2 to 3 weeks to the full length of the pregnancy.

FDA Pregnancy Category B.

Postpartum—
Bromocriptine should not be used during the postpartum period in women with a history of coronary artery disease or other severe cardiovascular conditions, unless withdrawal of bromocriptine is considered medically contraindicated. If bromocriptine is used during the postpartum period, the patient should be monitored for adverse events. Although causal relationship between bromocriptine and these adverse events has not been established, serious events that have occurred during bromocriptine treatment are seizures with or without hypertension, stroke, and myocardial infarction. Many postpartum patients who had seizures or strokes during bromocriptine therapy experienced severe headaches with possible visual disturbances for hours or days before the event occurred.

Breast-feeding
This medication should not be administered to mothers who intend to breast-feed, since bromocriptine interferes with lactation.

Pediatrics
Appropriate studies on the relationship of age to the effects of bromocriptine have not been performed in the pediatric population. Safety and efficacy have not been established.

Adolescents
Appropriate studies performed to date have not demonstrated adolescent-specific problems that would limit the use of bromocriptine in adolescents 15 years of age and older. However, appropriate studies to establish safety and efficacy in adolescents younger than 15 years of age have not been performed.

Geriatrics
Appropriate studies on the relationship of age to the effects of bromocriptine have not been performed in the geriatric population. However, clinical experience with the use of bromocriptine has shown that CNS effects may occur more frequently in the elderly.

Dental
Use of large doses of bromocriptine (for example, in the treatment of acromegaly or parkinsonism) may decrease or inhibit salivary flow, thus contributing to the development of caries, periodontal disease, oral candidiasis, and discomfort.

Drug interactions and/or related problems
The following drug interactions and/or related problems have been selected on the basis of their potential clinical significance (possible mechanism in parentheses where appropriate)—not necessarily inclusive (» = major clinical significance):

Note: Combinations containing any of the following medications, depending on the amount present, may also interact with this medication.

» Alcohol
(disulfiram-like reaction may occur, including chest pain, confusion, fast or pounding heartbeat, flushing or redness of face, sweating, nausea, vomiting, throbbing headache, blurred vision, and severe weakness)

Clarithromycin or
» Erythromycin or
Troleandomycin
(concurrent use of erythromycin caused a 268% increase in bromocriptine's area under the plasma concentration-time curve (AUC) when standardized to body weight and a 4.7-fold increase in the peak bromocriptine plasma concentration (C_{max}). Patients should be monitored for bromocriptine toxicity if erythromycin is used concurrently. Although not reported, similar increases may be expected for clarithromycin or troleandomycin)

» Ergot alkaloids, other, or derivatives, including
Dihydroergotamine
Ergonovine
Methylergonovine
Methysergide
(although there is no conclusive evidence of a drug interaction, rarely occurring cases of hypertension associated with the use of bromocriptine may be aggravated with use of ergot alkaloids or its derivatives)

Haloperidol or
Loxapine or
Methyldopa or
Metoclopramide or
Molindone or
Monoamine oxidase (MAO) inhibitors, including furazolidone, procarbazine, and selegiline or
Phenothiazines or
Pimozide or
Reserpine or
» Risperidone or
Thioxanthenes
(may increase serum prolactin concentrations and interfere with effects of bromocriptine; dosage adjustment of bromocriptine may be necessary)

Hypotension-producing medications, other (See *Appendix II*)
(concurrent use may result in additive hypotensive effects; antihypertensive dosage adjustment may be necessary)

Levodopa
(bromocriptine may produce additive effects, allowing reduction in levodopa dosage)

» Ritonavir
(bromocriptine serum concentrations can increase threefold when given with ritonavir; 50% reduction of bromocriptine dose is recommended if the combination is necessary)

Laboratory value alterations
The following have been selected on the basis of their potential clinical significance (possible effect in parentheses where appropriate)—not necessarily inclusive (» = major clinical significance).

With physiology/laboratory test values
Growth hormone
(plasma concentrations may be transiently increased in individuals with normal concentrations, paradoxically reduced in patients with acromegaly)

Medical considerations/Contraindications
The medical considerations/contraindications included have been selected on the basis of their potential clinical significance (reasons given in parentheses where appropriate)—not necessarily inclusive (» = major clinical significance).

Risk-benefit should be considered when the following medical problems exist:
Hepatic function impairment
(metabolism may be reduced; dosage reduction may be required)

Hypertension, or history of or
Hypertension, pregnancy-induced, history of
(may be aggravated; cautious use and monitoring of blood pressure are indicated with these conditions)

Psychiatric disorders
(may be exacerbated)

Sensitivity to bromocriptine or other ergot alkaloids

Patient monitoring
The following may be especially important in patient monitoring (other tests may be warranted in some patients, depending on condition; » = major clinical significance):

» Blood pressure measurements
(recommended especially when used for suppression of postpartum lactation; commonly decreases or rarely increases)

» Imaging studies of sella turcica
(recommended prior to initiation of therapy for all patients with hyperprolactinemia, to rule out possible pituitary tumor, and once a year during therapy to detect enlargement of a tumor; after one or two years of therapy, this examination may be performed less frequently in asymptomatic patients)

» Pregnancy test
(recommended in patients being treated for amenorrhea once menses resumes, whenever a menstrual period is missed)

» Prolactin, serum
(measurement of serum concentrations is recommended monthly during initial treatment and twice yearly during maintenance treatment of hyperprolactinemia to assess effectiveness of bromocriptine)

Visual field assessment
(recommended if clinically indicated during pregnancy after treatment with bromocriptine in case of enlargement of a previously detected macroadenoma)

For treatment of female infertility
Anterior pituitary function
(complete evaluation may be warranted prior to initiation of treatment for infertility)

» Evaluation of ovulation, including:
Daily basal body temperature and/or
Progesterone, serum and/or
Use of ovulation prediction test kits and

» Prolactin, serum
(measurement of baseline serum prolactin concentration is recommended, with subsequent measurements as needed, along

with other tests as may be appropriate for the evaluation and treatment of female infertility)

For treatment of male infertility

FSH, serum and
LH, serum and
Prolactin, serum and
Testosterone, serum
(baseline serum concentration measurements recommended to rule out other causes of infertility and at 3- to 6-month intervals thereafter)

Prolactin, serum
(measurement of serum concentrations is recommended at 4- to 6-week intervals until normal levels are established, then at 3- to 6-month intervals)

Sperm counts
(recommended at periodic intervals beginning 3 months after initiation of treatment)

For treatment of acromegaly

» Growth hormone or
Insulin-like growth factor I concentrations (IGF-I), serum
(measurement of serum concentrations is recommended at periodic intervals to assess efficacy and aid in dosage adjustment)

Physical examination
(periodic examination, especially assessing changes in ring size, heel pad thickness, or soft-tissue volume)

Side/Adverse Effects

Note: The most common side effects occur on initiation of therapy. Most side effects occurring with continuous therapy are dose-related.

Long-term treatment (6 to 36 months) with bromocriptine mesylate has rarely been associated with pulmonary infiltrates, pleural effusion, and thickening of the pleura. These occurred in a few patients taking doses ranging from 20 to 100 mg per day. When bromocriptine was discontinued, the changes slowly reversed toward normal.

The following side/adverse effects have been selected on the basis of their potential clinical significance (possible signs and symptoms in parentheses where appropriate)—not necessarily inclusive:

Those indicating need for medical attention

Incidence less frequent

Confusion; dyskinesia (uncontrolled movements of the body, such as the face, tongue, arms, hands, head, and upper body); ***hallucinations***

Note: *Confusion, dyskinesia,* or *hallucinations* are usually associated with use of high doses but may occur in 20 to 25% of patients being treated for parkinsonism, even at low doses, and may persist for a week or more after bromocriptine is withdrawn.

Incidence rare

Myocardial infarction (severe chest pain; fainting; fast heartbeat; increased sweating; continuing or severe nausea and vomiting; nervousness; unexplained shortness of breath; weakness); ***seizures or strokes*** (atypical headache; vision changes, such as blurred vision or temporary blindness; sudden weakness)

Note: There have been a few reports of *myocardial infarction* occurring in patients treated with bromocriptine, including patients that were treated with bromocriptine to suppress lactation, although a direct causal relationship has not been established.

There have been a number of reports of postpartum hypertension, *seizures,* and *strokes* as well as reports of fatalities occurring in patients treated with bromocriptine to suppress lactation; however, further studies are being conducted to determine if a causal relationship exists between the incidence of hypertension, strokes, and seizures and the use of bromocriptine for suppression of lactation. Mean onset of the reactions was 9 days postpartum. The cases of cerebrovascular accident were all associated with hypertension. Use of bromocriptine should be re-evaluated in those patients who experience unexplained headaches and therapy discontinued if headache is severe and atypical.

With high doses

Cerebrospinal fluid rhinorrhea (continuing runny nose)—in patients treated for pituitary macroadenomas; ***fainting***—has also occurred with low doses used in postpartum patients; ***gastrointestinal hemorrhage or peptic ulcer*** (black, tarry stools; blood in vomit; severe or continuing stomach pain); ***retroperitoneal fibrosis*** (continuing or severe abdominal or stomach pain; increased frequency of urination; continuing loss of appetite; lower back pain; continuing or severe nausea and vomiting; weakness)—with long-term use

Those indicating need for medical attention only if they continue or are bothersome

Incidence more frequent

Hypotension, especially orthostatic hypotension (dizziness or lightheadedness, especially when getting up from a lying or sitting position); ***nausea***

Note: *Hypotension* occurs frequently, but is symptomatic only in 1 to 5% of patients (8% of postpartum patients). Rarely, hypotension may be severe. A "first-dose phenomenon" has been reported.

Incidence less frequent—more frequent with high doses (for example, when used for acromegaly or parkinsonism)

Constipation; diarrhea; drowsiness or tiredness; dry mouth; leg cramps at night; loss of appetite; mental depression; Raynaud's phenomenon (tingling or pain in fingers or toes when exposed to cold); ***stomach pain; stuffy nose; vomiting***

Patient Consultation

As an aid to patient consultation, refer to *Advice for the Patient, Bromocriptine (Systemic).*

In providing consultation, consider emphasizing the following selected information (» = major clinical significance):

Before using this medication

» Conditions affecting use, especially:
Sensitivity to bromocriptine or other ergot alkaloids
Pregnancy—Use is not generally recommended
Breast-feeding—Will prevent lactation in mothers who intend to breast-feed
Use in the elderly—CNS effects may occur more frequently
Dental—Reduced salivary flow caused by large doses may contribute to dental disorders
Other medications, especially alcohol, ergot alkaloids or derivatives, erythromycin, risperidone, or ritonavir

Proper use of this medication

Taking with meals or milk to reduce gastrointestinal irritation; taking dose at bedtime or the first doses vaginally to better tolerate nausea

» Proper dosing
Missed dose: Taking if remembered within 4 hours; otherwise not taking at all; not doubling doses

» Proper storage

Precautions while using this medication

Regular visits to physician to check progress

» Caution when driving or doing jobs requiring alertness because of possible drowsiness or dizziness

Dizziness may be more likely to occur after initial dose; taking first dose at bedtime or lying down; getting up slowly from sitting or lying position; taking first dose vaginally, if necessary

» Possible dryness of mouth; using sugarless gum or candy, ice, or saliva substitute for relief; checking with physician or dentist if dry mouth continues for more than 2 weeks

Checking with physician before reducing dosage or discontinuing medication

» Possibility of disulfiram-like reaction with alcohol

For treatment of acromegaly, amenorrhea, infertility, galactorrhea, or pituitary prolactinomas in females of child-bearing potential:

Advisability of using nonhormonal contraception during therapy or, when using bromocriptine for female infertility, until normal menstrual cycle is established; patients desiring pregnancy should discuss with physician proper time to discontinue use of contraception; telling physician immediately if pregnancy is suspected

» Telling physician right away if symptoms of enlargement of pituitary tumor (blurred vision, sudden headache, severe nausea and vomiting) occur

Side/adverse effects

Signs of potential side effects, especially CNS effects, fainting, myocardial infarction, seizures, gastrointestinal hemorrhage, peptic ulcer, retroperitoneal fibrosis, rhinorrhea, and strokes

General Dosing Information

Incidence and severity of side effects (especially nausea) may be reduced by initiating therapy at a low dose (for example, 1.25 mg at bedtime) and increasing gradually (increments of 2.5 mg every 14 to 28 days for parkinsonism and 3 to 7 days for other indications) to the minimum effective dose, and by administering bromocriptine with food. Also, dizziness and nausea may be better tolerated by administering some or all of the dose at bedtime or by administering one or more of the initial doses intravaginally. Since no first-pass effect occurs with a vaginal dose, a reduced first dose may be warranted in some cases and certainly with subsequent doses because higher serum concentrations may result.

Bromocriptine is used rarely to prevent postpartum lactation because of the risk of significant hypotension and other adverse effects. If it is used, the medication should be given only after the patient's vital signs are stable and no sooner than 4 hours after delivery.

Treatment of hyperprolactinemia with bromocriptine may be symptomatic rather than curative. Following withdrawal, rebound amenorrhea usually occurs within 4 to 24 weeks and galactorrhea within 2 to 12 weeks. Pituitary adenoma regrowth and increase in serum prolactin concentrations may occur after withdrawal of bromocriptine. Elevated growth hormone concentrations will also return when the medication is withdrawn if the cause of acromegaly is not eliminated.

Oral Dosage Forms

Note: Bracketed uses in the *Dosage Forms* section refer to categories of use and/or indications that are not included in U.S. product labeling.

BROMOCRIPTINE MESYLATE CAPSULES USP

Note: For doses less than 5 mg, use *Bromocriptine Mesylate Tablets USP*.

Usual adult dose

Amenorrhea, secondary, due to hyperprolactinemia or
Galactorrhea due to hyperprolactinemia or
Hypogonadism, male, due to hyperprolactinemia or
Infertility due to hyperprolactinemia—

Initial: Oral, 1.25 to 2.5 mg at bedtime with a snack. Dosage may be increased by 2.5 mg every three to seven days as needed to a total of 5 to 7.5 mg a day taken in divided doses with meals.

Maintenance: Oral, 2.5 mg two or three times a day with meals. Doses of up to 15 mg have been used.

Prolactinomas, pituitary—

Initial: Oral, 1.25 mg two or three times a day with meals. Dosage adjustment is gradual over several weeks to 10 to 20 mg a day taken in divided doses with meals. Occasionally, higher doses may be required.

Maintenance: Oral, 2.5 to 20 mg a day taken in divided doses with meals.

Parkinsonism—

Initial: Oral, 1.25 mg one or two times a day with meals; for single doses, at bedtime with a snack is preferred. Dosage may be increased by 2.5 mg increments every fourteen to twenty-eight days.

Maintenance: Oral, 2.5 to 40 mg a day, taken in divided doses with meals. Although higher doses have been used, safety and efficacy have not been established with doses greater than 100 mg a day.

Acromegaly—

Initial: Oral, 1.25 to 2.5 mg at bedtime with a snack for 3 days; dosage may be increased by 1.25 or 2.5 mg every three to seven days up to 30 mg a day taken in divided doses with meals or at bedtime with a snack.

Maintenance: Oral, 10 to 30 mg a day taken in divided doses with meals or at bedtime with a snack. Up to 100 mg per day has been used.

[Lactation suppression][1]—

Initial: Oral, 2.5 mg twice a day taken with meals. Patient may begin medication only after vital signs stabilize and no sooner than four hours after delivery.

Maintenance: Oral, 2.5 to 7.5 mg a day taken in divided doses with meals or at bedtime with a snack for fourteen days. Has been used for up to twenty-one days if needed.

[Neuroleptic malignant syndrome][1]—

Initial: Oral, 5 mg once a day taken at bedtime with a snack; dosage adjustment titrated according to patient response by 2.5 mg increments a day as needed, taken in divided doses with meals or at bedtime with a snack.

Maintenance: Oral, up to 20 mg a day taken in divided doses with meals or at bedtime with a snack.

Usual adult prescribing limits

Parkinsonism—40 mg a day.
Other indications—20 mg a day.

Note: Although higher doses have been used, safety and efficacy have not been established with doses greater than 100 mg a day.

Usual pediatric dose

Children up to 15 years of age: Dosage has not been established.
Children 15 years of age and older: See *Usual adult dose*.

Strength(s) usually available

U.S.—
5 mg (Rx) [*Parlodel* (lactose; sodium bisulfite)].

Canada—
5 mg (Rx) [*Parlodel* (lactose)].

Packaging and storage

Store below 25 °C (77 °F), unless otherwise specified by manufacturer. Store in a tight, light-resistant container.

Auxiliary labeling

- Avoid alcoholic beverages.
- Take with meals or milk.
- May cause drowsiness.

Note

Unit-dose repackaging by any process involving heat is not recommended.

BROMOCRIPTINE MESYLATE TABLETS USP

Note: For doses 5 mg or greater, consider using *Bromocriptine Mesylate Capsules USP*.

Usual adult dose

See *Bromocriptine Mesylate Capsules USP*.

Usual pediatric dose

See *Bromocriptine Mesylate Capsules USP*.

Strength(s) usually available

U.S.—
2.5 mg (Rx) [*Parlodel SnapTabs* (scored; lactose); GENERIC].

Canada—
2.5 mg (Rx) [*Alti-Bromocriptine; Apo-Bromocriptine; Parlodel* (scored; lactose); GENERIC].

Packaging and storage

Store below 25 °C (77 °F), unless otherwise specified by manufacturer. Store in a tight, light-resistant container.

Auxiliary labeling

- Avoid alcoholic beverages.
- Take with meals or milk.
- May cause drowsiness.

Note

Unit-dose repackaging by any process involving heat is not recommended.

[1]Not included in Canadian product labeling.

Selected Bibliography

Ho Ky, Thorner Mo. Therapeutic applications of bromocriptine in endocrine and neurological diseases. Drugs 1988; 36: 67-82.

The American Fertility Society. Guideline for practice: The use of bromocriptine. Birmingham: American Fertility Society, 1991.

Revised: 08/20/1997

BROMPHENIRAMINE—See *Antihistamines (Systemic)*

BRONCHODILATORS, ADRENERGIC Inhalation-Local

Note: Products containing bitolterol were withdrawn from the market by Elan Pharmaceuticals in November 2001.

Note: Products containing salmeterol xinafoate with chlorofluorocarbons (CFCs) as an inhalation aerosol were withdrawn from the market by GlaxoSmithKline in June 2003.

This monograph includes information on the following: 1) Albuterol; 2) Bitolterol†; 3) Epinephrine; 4) Fenoterol*; 5) Formoterol; 6) Isoetharine†; 7) Isoproterenol; 8) Metaproterenol; 9) Pirbuterol; 10) Procaterol*; 11) Salmeterol*; 12) Terbutaline.

INN: Albuterol—Salbutamol

BAN:
Albuterol—Salbutamol
Epinephrine—Adrenaline
Formoterol—Eformoterol

JAN:
Albuterol—Salbutamol
Formoterol—Formoterol Fumarate
Metaproterenol—Orciprenaline

VA CLASSIFICATION (Primary/Secondary):
Albuterol—RE120
Bitolterol—RE120

Epinephrine—RE120/RE900
Fenoterol—RE120
Formoterol—RE120
Isoetharine—RE120
Isoproterenol—RE120
Metaproterenol—RE120
Pirbuterol—RE120
Procaterol—RE120
Racepinephrine—RE120
Salmeterol—RE120
Terbutaline—RE120

Commonly used brand name(s): *Adrenalin Chloride*[3]; *Airet*[1]; *Alupent*[8]; *Apo-Salvent*[1]; *Arm-a-Med Isoetharine*[6]; *Arm-a-Med Metaproterenol*[8]; *AsthmaNefrin*[3]; *Asthmahaler Mist*[3]; *Berotec*[4]; *Beta-2*[6]; *Brethaire*[12]; *Bricanyl Turbuhaler*[12]; *Bronkaid Mist*[3]; *Bronkaid Suspension Mist*[3]; *Bronkometer*[6]; *Bronkosol*[6]; *Dey-Lute Isoetharine*[6]; *Dey-Lute Metaproterenol*[8]; *Foradil*[5]; *Gen-Salbutamol Sterinebs P.F.*[1]; *Isuprel*[7]; *Isuprel Mistometer*[7]; *Maxair*[9]; *Maxair Autohaler*[9]; *Medihaler-Iso*[7]; *Nephron*[3]; *Novo-Salmol*[1]; *Oxeze Turbuhaler*[5]; *Oxeze Turbuhaler Foradil*[5]; *Primatene Mist*[3]; *Pro-Air*[10]; *Proventil*[1]; *Proventil HFA*[1]; *S-2*[3]; *Serevent*[11]; *Serevent Diskhaler*[11]; *Serevent Diskus*[11]; *Vaponefrin*[3]; *Ventodisk*[1]; *Ventolin*[1]; *Ventolin HFA*[1]; *Ventolin Nebules*[1]; *Ventolin Nebules P.F.*[1]; *Ventolin Rotacaps*[1]; *microNefrin*[3].

Other commonly used names are:
Adrenaline [Epinephrine]
Orciprenaline [Metaproterenol]
Salbutamol [Albuterol]

Note: For a listing of dosage forms and brand names by country availability, see *Dosage Forms* section(s).

*Not commercially available in U.S.
†Not commercially available in Canada.

Category

Bronchodilator—Albuterol; Bitolterol; Epinephrine; Fenoterol; Formoterol; Isoetharine; Isoproterenol; Metaproterenol; Pirbuterol; Procaterol; Salmeterol; Terbutaline.

Croup therapy agent—Epinephrine; Racepinephrine

Indications

Note: Products containing salmeterol xinafoate with chlorofluorocarbons (CFCs) as an inhalation aerosol were withdrawn from the market by GlaxoSmithKline in June 2003.

Note: Bracketed information in the *Indications* section refers to uses that are not included in U.S. product labeling.

Note: Products containing bitolterol were withdrawn from the market by Elan Pharmaceuticals in November 2001.

Accepted

Asthma (treatment)—Formoterol is indicated for long-term maintenance treatment of asthma in patients with reversible obstructive airway disease, including patients with symptoms of nocturnal asthma, who are using optimal corticosteroid treatment and experiencing regular or frequent breakthrough symptoms requiring regular use of short-acting bronchodilators.

Bronchospasm, asthma-associated (treatment)—Albuterol, bitolterol, fenoterol, metaproterenol, pirbuterol, procaterol, and terbutaline are indicated as bronchodilators for the treatment of bronchospasm associated with asthma.

Adrenergic bronchodilators that are more selective for the beta$_2$-receptor and have a longer duration of action are preferred; therefore, epinephrine, isoetharine, and isoproterenol are generally not recommended for this indication.

Bronchospasm, asthma-associated (prophylaxis)—Salmeterol and formoterol are indicated to prevent bronchospasm and reduce the frequency of acute asthma exacerbations in patients with chronic asthma who require regular treatment with an inhaled shorter-acting beta-adrenergic bronchodilator. Patients treated with formoterol should be receiving corticosteroid treatment. Salmeterol may be used with or without concurrent inhaled or systemic corticosteroid therapy. During therapy with salmeterol or formoterol, it is important for patients to have a fast-acting inhaled beta-adrenergic bronchodilator available for relief of acute attacks.

Generally, regularly scheduled, daily use of short-acting beta$_2$-agonists is not recommended.

Bronchospasm, exercise-induced (prophylaxis)—Albuterol, [bitolterol], formoterol[1][pirbuterol], procaterol, salmeterol[1], and [terbutaline][1] are indicated for the prevention of exercise-induced bronchospasm. With use of salmeterol and formoterol, it is important for patients to also have a fast-acting inhaled beta-adrenergic bronchodilator available for relief of acute attacks. Adrenergic bronchodilators that are more selective for the beta$_2$-receptor and have a longer duration of action are preferred; therefore, epinephrine, isoetharine, and isoproterenol are generally not recommended for this indication.

Bronchospasm, chronic bronchitis-associated (prophylaxis and treatment)

Bronchospasm, pulmonary emphysema-associated (prophylaxis and treatment)

Bronchospasm, chronic obstructive pulmonary disease-associated (prophylaxis and treatment)—Albuterol, bitolterol, fenoterol, metaproterenol, pirbuterol, procaterol, salmeterol, and terbutaline are indicated as bronchodilators for the treatment of bronchospasm associated with chronic obstructive airway disease, including bronchitis and pulmonary emphysema. Patients may benefit from the addition of regularly scheduled doses of a beta$_2$-agonist to ipratropium. Adrenergic bronchodilators that are more selective for the beta$_2$-receptor and have a longer duration of action are preferred; therefore, epinephrine, isoetharine, and isoproterenol are generally not recommended for these indications.

Chronic obstructive pulmonary disease [COPD] (treatment)—Formoterol and salmeterol are indicated as long-term, twice-daily administration in the treatment of patients with chronic obstructive pulmonary disease including chronic bronchitis and emphysema.

Croup (treatment)—Racepinephrine and nebulized [epinephrine][1] are indicated in the treatment of postintubation and viral croup to temporarily reduce mucosal edema, thereby relieving acute respiratory distress.

[Hyperkalemia (treatment)][1]—Albuterol is indicated as a temporary treatment option for hyperkalemia in acute situations in pediatric patients.

Acceptance not established

Although albuterol, epinephrine, and racepinephrine have been used for treatment of *acute bronchiolitis in infants*, data are insufficient to prove that these medications are effective for this indication. Some studies indicate modest, short-term benefit; however, other results are conflicting.

There is insufficient data to show that albuterol is beneficial for the treatment of *hyperkalemia in adults*.

Unaccepted

Salmeterol is not indicated for the treatment of acute or breakthrough asthma symptoms when rapid bronchodilation is needed because of its slower onset of action compared to shorter-acting adrenergic bronchodilators.

Formoterol is not indicated in the treatment of acute asthma attacks and should not be used in patients whose asthma can be managed by occasional use of short-acting inhaled beta$_2$-agonists.

Neither formoterol nor salmeterol therapy should be initiated in patients with significantly worsening or acutely deteriorating asthma(rapid worsening over hours to days).

[1]Not included in Canadian product labeling.

Pharmacology/Pharmacokinetics

Physicochemical characteristics

Molecular weight—
Albuterol: 239.32.
Albuterol sulfate: 576.71.
Bitolterol mesylate: 557.67.
Epinephrine: 183.21.
Epinephrine bitartrate: 333.30.
Fenoterol hydrobromide: 303.36.
Formoterol fumarate dihydrate: 840.9.
Isoetharine hydrochloride: 275.78.
Isoetharine mesylate: 335.42.
Isoproterenol sulfate: 556.64.
Metaproterenol sulfate: 520.60.
Pirbuterol acetate: 300.36.
Procaterol hydrochloride: 326.82.
Salmeterol xinafoate: 603.76.
Terbutaline sulfate: 548.66.

Mechanism of action/Effect

Bronchodilator—Adrenergic bronchodilators act by stimulating beta$_2$-adrenergic receptors in the lungs to relax bronchial smooth muscle, thereby relieving bronchospasm. This action is believed to result from increased production of cyclic adenosine 3,5-monophosphate (cyclic 3,5-AMP; cAMP) and ensuing reduction in intracellular calcium concentration caused by activation of the enzyme adenylate cyclase that catalyzes the conversion of adenosine triphosphate (ATP) to cAMP. Increased cAMP concentrations, in addition to relaxing bronchial smooth muscle, inhibit release of mediators of immediate hypersensitivity from cells, especially from mast cells.

Croup therapy agent—Epinephrine has alpha-adrenergic stimulating effects that produce constriction of arteries and veins. The resulting decreased mucosal edema is thought to be the mechanism by which epinephrine and racepinephrine are beneficial in the treatment of croup. The *L*-isomer of racepinephrine is the primary active isomer.

Other actions/effects

Albuterol, bitolterol, fenoterol, formoterol, isoetharine, pirbuterol, procaterol, salmeterol, and terbutaline have a relatively high degree of selectivity for beta$_2$-adrenergic receptors. Data indicate that there is a population of beta$_2$-receptors in the human heart existing in a concentration between 10 and 50% of the cardiac beta-adrenergic receptors; stimulation of these receptors produces tachycardia. Stimulation of beta$_2$-receptors located in skeletal muscle causes muscle tremor.

Epinephrine, isoproterenol, and metaproterenol have significant beta$_1$-adrenergic activity in the heart, resulting in an increased rate and force of cardiac contractions.

Other effects of epinephrine include alpha- and beta$_2$-receptor–mediated stimulation of glycogenolysis and gluconeogenesis.

Limited *in vitro* and *in vivo* animal studies and allergen challenge studies in asthmatics demonstrate that some adrenergic bronchodilators have inhibitory effects on several inflammatory response mediators. However, these medications are not considered to have clinically relevant anti-inflammatory effects.

Absorption

Systemic absorption is rapid following aerosol administration; however, serum concentrations at recommended doses are very low or unmeasurable.

Biotransformation

Bitolterol—A prodrug hydrolyzed by esterases in tissue and blood to the active compound colterol.

Onset of action

Albuterol, bitolterol, epinephrine, fenoterol, formoterol, isoetharine, isoproterenol, metaproterenol, pirbuterol, procaterol, and terbutaline—Rapid, within 5 minutes.

Salmeterol—Approximately 10 to 20 minutes.

Time to peak effect

Epinephrine, isoetharine, and isoproterenol—Within 5 to 15 minutes.

Albuterol, bitolterol, fenoterol, metaproterenol, pirbuterol, procaterol, and terbutaline—Within 30 to 90 minutes; however, for albuterol, fenoterol, pirbuterol, and terbutaline, 75% of maximal effect is achieved within 5 minutes.

Salmeterol—3 to 4 hours; however, approximately 80% of the maximal increase in forced expiratory volume in 1 second (FEV$_1$) occurs within 1 hour after administration.

Duration of action

Short-acting (less than 3 hours)—Epinephrine, isoetharine, and isoproterenol.

Intermediate-acting (3 to 6 hours)—Albuterol, bitolterol, fenoterol, metaproterenol, pirbuterol, procaterol, and terbutaline.

Long-acting—Formoterol and salmeterol: Approximately 12 hours.

Note: It is believed that the sustained pharmacological action of salmeterol is due to its lipophilicity and long *N*-substituted side chain. The side chain has been shown to bind to the exo-site, an area in the beta$_2$-receptor adjacent to the active site. The phenylethanolamine portion of the salmeterol molecule is then in position to associate with and dissociate from the receptor's active site. This theory is supported by the fact that the pharmacologic effect of salmeterol *in vitro* is rapidly and completely reversed by beta-receptor antagonism and resumes once the antagonist is removed.

Precautions to Consider

Carcinogenicity/Tumorigenicity/Mutagenicity

Albuterol—A 2-year study in rats showed that albuterol, administered orally in doses that provided 93, 463, and 2315 times the maximum inhalational dose for a human weighing 50 kilograms (kg), caused a dose-related increase in the incidences of benign leiomyomas of the mesovarium. An 18-month study in mice and a lifetime study in hamsters showed no evidence of tumorigenicity. Studies with albuterol showed no evidence of mutagenesis.

Bitolterol—No tumorigenicity was observed in a 2-year study in rats given oral doses that provided 12 or 62 times the maximal daily human inhalational dose for the inhalation solution, or 23 or 114 times the maximal daily human dose for the metered-dose inhaler, or in an 18-month study in mice given oral doses that provided up to 312 times the maximal daily human inhalational dose for the inhalation solution, or 568 times the maximal daily human dose for the metered-dose inhaler. Bitolterol was not mutagenic in Ames Salmonella and mouse lymphoma mutation assays *in vitro.*

Epinephrine and fenoterol—Studies to evaluate the carcinogenic, tumorigenic, or mutagenic potential of epinephrine and fenoterol have not been done. There is no evidence from human data that use of these medications may cause problems.

Formoterol—An increase in the frequency of uterine leiomyomas of the uterus was observed in mice given oral formoterol and of leiomyomas of the mesovarium in rats given formoterol by inhalation. *In vitro* and *in vivo* studies showed no mutagenic effects of formoterol.

Isoetharine—No evidence of carcinogenicity was observed in chronic toxicity studies in dogs given doses up to the equivalent of approximately 200 times the dose for a 70 kg human for 12 months or in rats given doses of up to the equivalent of approximately 450 times the dose for a 70 kg human.

Isoproterenol—Isoproterenol has not been evaluated for carcinogenicity or mutagenicity.

Metaproterenol—An 18-month study in mice given doses equivalent to 320 and 640 times the maximum recommended dose for a 50 kg human showed an increase in benign ovarian tumors. In a 2-year study in rats given 640 times the maximum recommended human dose, a nonsignificant incidence of benign mesovarian leiomyomas was noted. Mutagenic studies have not been conducted.

Pirbuterol—When administered orally to rats for 24 months and to mice for 18 months in doses equivalent to 200 times the maximum human inhalation dose, no evidence of carcinogenicity was observed. In a 12-month study in rats, direct intragastric administration of pirbuterol in doses equivalent to 6250 times the maximum recommended daily inhalation dose for humans resulted in no increased incidence of tumorigenicity. Studies with pirbuterol showed no evidence of mutagenicity.

Procaterol—A 23-month study in mice given procaterol orally showed no increased incidence of tumorigenicity. When administered orally to rats at doses of 5, 50, and 500 mg per kg per day, a dose-related incidence of mesovarian leiomyomas was observed. Procaterol has not been shown to be mutagenic.

Salmeterol—An 18-month study in mice showed that salmeterol, administered orally in doses that provided 9 and 63 times the human exposure (based on comparison of area under the plasma concentration-time curves [AUCs]), caused a dose-related increase in the incidences of smooth muscle hyperplasia, cystic glandular hyperplasia, leiomyomas of the uterus, and ovarian cysts. A 24-month study in rats given salmeterol orally and by inhalation in doses approximately 55 and 215 times, respectively, the recommended human clinical dose based on mg per square meter of body surface area (mg/m^2) showed dose-related increases in the incidences of mesovarian leiomyomas and ovarian cysts. Similar results have been reported with other beta-adrenergic bronchodilators. Salmeterol produced no significant carcinogenic effects in mice receiving doses that provided 1.3 times the human exposure based on AUC comparison, or in rats given 15 times the recommended human clinical dose based on mg/m^2. Salmeterol was not mutagenic in *in vitro* tests in microbial or mammalian genes or in human lymphocytes or in an *in vivo* rat micronucleus test.

Terbutaline—A 2-year study in rats given oral doses equivalent to 1042, 10,417, 20,833, and 41,667 times the recommended daily human adult dose showed dose-related increases in leiomyomas of the mesovarium. The incidence of ovarian cysts was significantly increased at all doses except the highest dose, and mesovarium hyperplasia was increased significantly at 10,417 and 41,667 times the recommended daily human adult dose. A 21-month study in mice given oral doses equivalent to 104, 1042, and 4167 times the recommended daily human adult dose showed no evidence of carcinogenicity. Studies to evaluate mutagenicity have not been done.

Pregnancy/Reproduction

Fertility—*Albuterol, bitolterol, pirbuterol, procaterol, salmeterol, and terbutaline:* Reproduction studies in rats showed no significant effects on fertility after administration of these agents.

Formoterol: Fertility was significantly reduced in male rats given oral formoterol 15 mg/kg but not in those given lower doses. Fertility of female rats was not affected by formoterol, even at the high dose.

Isoetharine, isoproterenol, and metaproterenol: Studies with isoetharine, isoproterenol, and metaproterenol have not been done.

Pregnancy—

All adrenergic bronchodilators—

Although adequate and well-controlled studies in pregnant women have not been done with inhaled adrenergic bronchodilators, albuterol, bitolterol, fenoterol, isoetharine, isoproterenol, metaproterenol, pirbuterol, procaterol, salmeterol, and terbutaline (but not epinephrine) are used in pregnancy when any potential risk that may be associated with treatment is preferable to the risk of placental hypoxemia from uncontrolled pulmonary disease. Extensive use of adrenergic bronchodilators during pregnancy has provided no evidence that the sympathomimetic class effects seen in animal studies are relevant to human use.

Albuterol—

Adequate and well-controlled studies in humans have not been done.

Albuterol has been shown to be teratogenic in mice given doses equivalent to 14 times the human dose. Studies in mice given albuterol subcutaneously at doses comparable to 1.15, 11.5, and 115 times the maximum inhalation dose for a 50-kg human showed cleft palate formation in 0%, 4.5%, and 9.3% of fetuses, respectively. When rabbits were given oral albuterol at doses corresponding to 2315 times the maximum inhalation dose for a 50-kg human, cranioschisis occurred in 37% of their fetuses.

FDA Pregnancy Category C.

Bitolterol—

Adequate and well-controlled studies in humans have not been done.

No teratogenic effects were seen in rats and rabbits after administration of oral doses of bitolterol of up to 361 and 557 times the maximal daily human inhalation dose, or in mice after administration of oral doses of bitolterol of up to 188 and 284 times the maximal daily human inhalation doses, for the inhalation solution and the metered-dose inhaler, respectively. When bitolterol was injected subcutaneously into mice at doses of 2, 10, and 20 mg per kg of body weight, the incidence of cleft palate was 5.7%, 3.8%, and 3.3%, respectively.

FDA Pregnancy Category C.

Epinephrine—

Adequate and well-controlled studies in humans have not been done. Epinephrine crosses the placenta and, although systemic concentrations are generally low following inhalation therapy, epinephrine usually should be avoided during pregnancy due to its alpha-adrenergic effects; safer and more effective $beta_2$-adrenergic bronchodilators are preferred. The Collaborative Perinatal Project monitored 189 mother-child pairs exposed to subcutaneous epinephrine during the first trimester as well as anytime during pregnancy. An association was found between first trimester use and the incidence of fetal malformations. An association was also found between use anytime during pregnancy and the incidence of inguinal hernia. Interpretation of these data is complicated in that the severity of the mother's asthma may contribute to the effects on the fetus.

Epinephrine has been shown to be teratogenic in rats when given systemically in doses of about 25 times the human dose.

FDA Pregnancy Category C.

Fenoterol—

Adequate and well-controlled studies in humans have not been done. Direct blood and tissue studies in humans showed that the levels of fenoterol and its conjugates were 10 to 20 times lower in the fetus than in maternal tissues.

Autoradiographic studies in pregnant rats showed no detectable amounts of fenoterol in the fetus. Direct blood and tissue studies in several animal species showed that levels of fenoterol and its conjugates were 10 to 20 times lower in the fetus than in maternal tissues.

FDA Pregnancy Category B.

Formoterol—

Adequate and well-controlled studies in humans have not been done.

In studies of rats given formoterol 0.004 to 1.2 mg/kg by inhalation, no undesirable effects on fetal development were observed. However, maternal weight gain was greater in treated rats than in control rats and in proportion to dose. Also, a dose-related tachycardia was observed.

In studies of rabbits given a range of dosages by oral gavage, no undesirable effects were observed at doses up to 3.5 mg/kg. At 60 mg/kg (7000 to 11000 times the recommended human exposure), there was an increase in occurrence of fetal hepatic cysts.

Isoetharine—

Studies have not been done in humans.

Studies have not been done in animals.

FDA Pregnancy Category C.

Isoproterenol—

Adequate and well-controlled studies have not been done in humans.

Studies performed in rats and rabbits at inhaled doses comparable to 15 times the human dose have not shown harm to the fetus.

FDA Pregnancy Category B.

Metaproterenol—

Adequate and well-controlled studies in humans have not been done.

Metaproterenol has been shown to be teratogenic and embryocidal in rabbits when given orally in doses comparable to 620 times the human inhalation dose. Effects included skeletal abnormalities and hydrocephalus with bone separation. Studies in mice, rats, and rabbits showed no teratogenic or embryocidal effects at doses corresponding to 310 times the recommended human inhalation dose.

FDA Pregnancy Category C.

Pirbuterol—

Adequate and well-controlled studies in humans have not been done.

Studies performed in rats and rabbits given inhaled pirbuterol at doses of up to 12 and 16 times the maximum human inhalation dose, respectively, showed no teratogenic effects.

FDA Pregnancy Category C.

Procaterol—

Adequate and well-controlled studies have not been done in humans.

Studies in rabbits and rats given large doses of inhaled procaterol showed no teratogenic or embryocidal effects.

Salmeterol—

Adequate and well-controlled studies have not been done in humans.

In rats, maternal exposure to salmeterol at doses of up to approximately 160 times the recommended human clinical dose based on mg per square meter of body surface (mg/m^2) produced no significant effects. However, Dutch rabbit fetuses exposed to high concentrations of salmeterol *in utero* developed effects considered to be characteristic of beta-adrenergic stimulation (i.e., precocious eyelid openings, cleft palate, sternebral fusion, limb and paw flexures, and delayed ossification of the frontal cranial bones). No significant effects occurred at 12 times the recommended human clinical dose based on AUC comparisons. In New Zealand rabbits, exposure to oral doses approximately 1600 times the recommended human clinical dose based on mg/m^2 produced only delayed ossification of frontal bones.

FDA Pregnancy Category C.

Terbutaline—

Adequate and well-controlled studies in humans have not been done.

Studies in rats and mice at doses of up to 1042 times the human dose showed no teratogenic effects.

FDA Pregnancy Category B.

Labor and delivery—Beta-adrenergic agonists have been shown to decrease uterine contractions when administered systemically. This effect is unlikely with inhaled beta-adrenergic bronchodilators.

Breast-feeding

It is not known whether albuterol, bitolterol, epinephrine, fenoterol, formoterol, isoetharine, isoproterenol, metaproterenol, pirbuterol, procaterol, salmeterol, or terbutaline is distributed into the breast milk of humans.

Salmeterol is distributed into the milk of lactating rats in concentrations similar to those in plasma.

Formoterol, administered orally, is distributed into the milk of lacatating rats.

Pediatrics

Some children up to 5 years old may have difficulty using a metered dose or powder inhaler device correctly; therefore, use of an inhalation solution may be more appropriate. A spacer device is recommended for use with metered dose inhalers.

Albuterol, bitolterol, epinephrine, isoproterenol, metaproterenol, pirbuterol, procaterol, salmeterol, and terbutaline—Use of these medications in children has not demonstrated pediatrics-specific problems that would limit their usefulness.

Fenoterol—Appropriate studies on the relationship of age to the effects of fenoterol have not been performed in the pediatric population.

Formoterol—Appropriate studies on the relationship of age to the effects of formoterol have not been performed in children under 12 years of age.

Isoetharine—Use of isoetharine in children is not recommended.

Geriatrics

Although not clearly proven, airway responsiveness to these medications may change with age. Additionally, older patients may also be more sensitive to the side effects of beta$_2$-agonists, including tremor and tachycardia, especially those with preexisting ischemic heart disease.

Albuterol, bitolterol, epinephrine, fenoterol, isoetharine, isoproterenol, metaproterenol, pirbuterol, procaterol, and terbutaline—Appropriate studies on the relationship of age to the effects of these agents have not been performed in the geriatric population. However, no geriatric-specific problems have been documented to date.

Salmeterol—Clinical studies have been conducted in 241 patients 65 years of age and older. No apparent differences in the efficacy and safety of salmeterol were observed in these patients compared with younger patients.

Drug interactions and/or related problems

The following drug interactions and/or related problems have been selected on the basis of their potential clinical significance (possible mechanism in parentheses where appropriate)—not necessarily inclusive (» = major clinical significance):

Note: Because adrenergic bronchodilators produce low systemic concentrations following oral aerosol or powder inhalation when compared to serum concentrations following systemic administration, drug interactions known to occur with sympathomimetics as a class, especially with those possessing alpha-adrenoceptor activity, are unlikely to occur with use of albuterol, bitolterol, epinephrine, fenoterol, formoterol, isoetharine, isoproterenol, metaproterenol, pirbuterol, procaterol, salmeterol, or terbutaline at recommended doses.

Combinations containing any of the following medications, depending on the amount present, may also interact with this medication.

» Beta-adrenergic blocking agents, ophthalmic
(ophthalmic beta-adrenergic blocking agents are absorbed systemically via the nasolacrimal duct. Respiratory complications associated with the use of timolol have been reported and include bronchospasm, dyspnea, wheezing, decreased pulmonary function, and respiratory failure; therefore, concurrent use may result in inhibition of the beta-adrenergic effects of the adrenergic bronchodilators and worsening of bronchospasm)

» Beta-adrenergic blocking agents, systemic
(concurrent use with adrenergic bronchodilators may result in mutual inhibition of therapeutic effects; beta-blockade may antagonize the bronchodilating effect of these bronchodilators; although antagonists with beta$_1$-selectivity may be less antagonistic, extreme caution is recommended if these agents are used in patients with bronchospasm because beta-adrenergic blocking agents may induce bronchospasm; use of a nonselective beta-blocking agent also allows for alpha-adrenergic receptor stimulation when epinephrine is administered, which may result in increased vascular resistance when epinephrine aerosol is used in higher-than-recommended doses)

Corticosteroids,
Diuretics, non potassium-sparing, or
Methylxanthines
(concomitant treatment with corticosteroids, xanthine derivatives, or diuretics may potentiate a possible hypokalemic effect of formoterol, especially in patients with severe asthma)

» Disopyramide
» Quinidine
» Phenothiazines
» Procainamide
(can prolong the QTc-interval and increase the risk of ventricular arrhythmia when used with formoterol)

Monoamine oxidase inhibitors or
Tricyclic antidepressants
(the action of salmeterol on the vascular system may be potentiated by these agents; caution should be used with concurrent administration or when salmeterol is given within 2 weeks of discontinuing these agents. Concomitant treatment with formoterol can prolong the QTc-interval and increase the risk of ventricular arrhythmia)

Laboratory value alterations

The following have been selected on the basis of their potential clinical significance (possible effect in parentheses where appropriate)—not necessarily inclusive (» = major clinical significance).

With physiology/laboratory test values

Electrocardiogram
(transient ventricular premature contractions, atrial arrhythmia, inverted T waves, junctional rhythm, and prolongation of the QTc interval are reported rarely with adrenergic bronchodilators; effects may be more pronounced following nebulization, frequent use of higher doses or an overdose, or with use of fenoterol; arrhythmias may also result from hypoxia or hypokalemia)

Glucose, blood
(concentrations may be increased, possibly due to glycogenolysis; clinically significant changes may be more pronounced following nebulization or with frequent use of higher doses or an overdose)

Potassium, serum
(concentrations may be decreased, possibly through intracellular shunting; the decrease is dose-related, is usually transient, and may not require supplementation; effects may be more pronounced following nebulization, frequent use of higher doses or an overdose, or use of fenoterol)

Medical considerations/Contraindications

The medical considerations/contraindications included have been selected on the basis of their potential clinical significance (reasons given in parentheses where appropriate)—not necessarily inclusive (» = major clinical significance).

Risk-benefit should be considered when the following medical problems exist:

Allergy to lactose or milk
(formoterol powder for inhalation contains lactose)

Cardiac arrhythmias or
» Coronary insufficiency
(rarely, inhaled adrenergic bronchodilators, especially epinephrine, may make these conditions worse. Formoterol is contraindicated in patients with tachyarrhythmias)

Hypertension, not optimally controlled
(rarely, inhaled epinephrine may make this condition worse)

Hyperthyroidism, not optimally controlled, or
Pheochromocytoma, diagnosed or suspected
(signs or symptoms of excessive beta-adrenergic stimulation are more likely to occur)

» Sensitivity to an adrenergic bronchodilator

» Sensitivity to sulfites contained in some isoetharine, isoproterenol, and racepinephrine solutions for inhalation

Patient monitoring

The following may be especially important in patient monitoring (other tests may be warranted in some patients, depending on condition; » = major clinical significance):

Pulmonary function monitoring
(objective measures of lung function are essential for diagnosis and for guiding therapeutic decision-making in the treatment of asthma; measurement of forced expiratory airflow, using a spirometer or a peak expiratory flowmeter, is recommended at periodic intervals)

Side/Adverse Effects

Note: The side effects of aerosolized adrenergic bronchodilators are due primarily to systemic absorption of the medication, which is limited with usual doses. Higher doses or administration via nebulization is more likely to be associated with side effects than are lower doses.

Fatalities have been reported in association with excessive use of inhaled sympathomimetics. The exact cause of death is unknown. Whether the fatalities are associated with disease severity, substandard quality of care, and/or patient noncompliance has not been established.

For salmeterol xinafoate inhalation aerosol, data from a large 28-week placebo-controlled US study that compared the safety of salmeterol with the safety of placebo added to usual asthma therapy showed a significant increase in asthma-related deaths in patients receiving salmeterol compared with placebo (13 deaths out of 13, 176 patients versus 3 deaths out of 13, 179 patients).

For side effects more commonly seen with an overdose, see the *Overdose* section of this monograph.

The following side/adverse effects have been selected on the basis of their potential clinical significance (possible signs and symptoms in parentheses where appropriate)—not necessarily inclusive:

Those indicating need for medical attention

Incidence rare

Bronchospasm, paradoxical or hypersensitivity-induced (shortness of breath; troubled breathing; tightness in chest; wheezing); ***dermatitis, hypersensitivity-induced*** (angioedema [swelling of face, lips, or eyelids]; skin rash; urticaria [hives]); ***laryngeal spasm, irritation, or swelling*** (feeling of choking)—with salmeterol; ***sensitivity reaction to sulfites*** (chest pain; dizziness, severe, or feeling faint; flushing or redness of skin, continuing; skin rash, hives, or itching;

swelling of face, lips, or eyelids; wheezing or difficulty in breathing)—for isoetharine, isoproterenol, and racepinephrine inhalation solutions containing sulfites

Incidence not known

Asthma, significantly worsening or acutely deteriorating (cough; difficulty breathing; noisy breathing; shortness of breath; tightness in chest; wheezing)—in patients taking salmeterol

Those indicating need for medical attention only if they continue or are bothersome

Incidence more frequent

Fast heartbeat; headache; nervousness; trembling

Incidence less frequent

Coughing or other bronchial irritation; dizziness or light-headedness; dryness or irritation of mouth or throat

Incidence rare

Chest discomfort or pain; drowsiness or fatigue (weakness); ***hypokalemia; increase in blood pressure***—with epinephrine; ***irregular heartbeat; muscle cramps or twitching; nausea and/or vomiting; oropharyngeal irritation*** (irritation of throat or mouth); ***restlessness; trouble in sleeping***

Those not indicating need for medical attention

Incidence more frequent

Pinkish to red coloration of saliva—with isoproterenol

Incidence less frequent

Taste changes

Overdose

Although uncommon, fatalities have been reported in association with excessive use of inhaled sympathomimetics. The exact cause of death is unknown. Whether the fatalities are associated with disease severity, substandard quality of care, and/or patient noncompliance has not been established.

For specific information on the agents used in the management of adrenergic bronchodilator overdose, see:

- *Beta-adrenergic Blocking Agents (Systemic)* monograph.

For more information on the management of overdose, **contact a Poison Control Center** (see *Poison Control Center Listing*).

Clinical effects of overdose

Note: The following effects are more likely to occur following oral or parenteral overdose with an adrenergic bronchodilator; however, they may occur following overdose via inhalation, if sufficient systemic concentrations of medication are achieved.

The following effects have been selected on the basis of their potential clinical significance (possible signs and symptoms in parentheses where appropriate)—not necessarily inclusive:

Acute overdose

More common

Hyperglycemia; hypokalemia; hypotension (dizziness or lightheadedness); ***lactic acidosis; tachycardia*** (fast heartbeat, continuing); ***trembling, continuing; vomiting***

Less common

Agitation; chest pain—with epinephrine; ***headache***—with epinephrine; ***hypercalcemia; hypertension***—with epinephrine; ***hypophosphatemia; leukocytosis; peripheral vasoconstriction***—with epinephrine; ***respiratory alkalosis***

Rare

Hallucinations—with nebulized albuterol; ***paranoia***—with nebulized albuterol; ***seizures***; ***tachyarrhythmias*** (fast and irregular heartbeat, continuing)

Chronic overdose

More common

Hypotension (dizziness or lightheadedness); ***tachycardia*** (fast heartbeat, continuing); ***trembling, continuing; vomiting***

Less common

Agitation; chest pain—with epinephrine; ***headache***—with epinephrine; ***hypertension***—with epinephrine; ***peripheral vasoconstriction***—with epinephrine

Rare

Seizures; tachyarrhythmias (fast and irregular heartbeat, continuing)

Treatment of overdose

Specific treatment—

Therapy with any adrenergic bronchodilator should be stopped.

For tachyarrhythmias—Administering a cardioselective beta-adrenergic blocking agent, if necessary; however, caution is needed because beta-adrenergic blocking agents can induce bronchospasm.

Monitoring—

Monitoring the patient carefully, especially for cardiovascular status.

Supportive care—

Patients in whom intentional overdose is confirmed or suspected should be referred for psychiatric evaluation.

Patient Consultation

Note: Bitolterol was withdrawn from the market by Elan Pharmaceuticals in November 2001.

Note: Products containing salmeterol xinafoate with chlorofluorocarbons (CFCs) as an inhalation aerosol were withdrawn from the market by GlaxoSmithKline in June 2003.

As an aid to patient consultation, refer to *Advice for the Patient, Bronchodilators, Adrenergic (Inhalation)*.

In providing consultation, consider emphasizing the following selected information (» = major clinical significance):

Before using this medication

» Conditions affecting use, especially:

Sensitivity to sympathomimetics or sulfites contained in some isoetharine, isoproterenol, and racepinephrine solutions for inhalation

Allergy to lactose contained in formoterol powder for inhalation

Pregnancy—Risk/benefit assessment; use of epinephrine is generally avoided

Breast-feeding—Risk/benefit assessment

Other medications, especially beta-adrenergic blocking agents, disopyramide, quinidine, phenothiazines, and procainamide

Other medical problems, especially cardiovascular disease

Proper use of this medication

For all adrenergic bronchodilators

» Reading patient instructions carefully before using

» Importance of not using more medication than prescribed

» Proper dosing

Missed dose: If used regularly, using as soon as possible; resuming regular schedule; not doubling doses

» Proper storage

For formoterol and salmeterol

» Importance of not using this medication to treat acute symptoms

» Having a rapid-acting inhaled beta-adrenergic bronchodilator available for symptomatic relief of acute asthma attacks

» Not using more than two times a day or less than 12 hours apart

» Importance of not stopping or reducing oral corticosteroids when initiating treatment with formoterol or salmeterol

» Missed dose: If used regularly, using as soon as possible; resuming regular schedule; not doubling doses; using rapid-acting inhaled bronchodilator if symptoms occur before next dose is due

For epinephrine

Not self-medicating without a diagnosis of asthma and follow-up by a physician, or unless directed by a physician if previously hospitalized for asthma; if taking a prescription drug for asthma, not using unless told to do so by physician

For inhalation aerosol dosage form

Avoiding contact with the eyes

Testing or priming inhaler before using first time if required

Proper administration technique

Technique for using spacer with inhaler

Proper cleaning procedure for inhaler

Saving inhaler, refill canister may be available

For powder for inhalation dosage form

Knowing correct administration technique for using inhaler

For inhalation solution dosage form

Knowing correct administration technique for using in a nebulizer

Not using if solution is discolored or cloudy

Not mixing with another inhalation solution in nebulizer unless directed

Precautions while using this medication

For all adrenergic bronchodilators:

Regular visits to physician to check progress during therapy

» Checking with physician immediately if difficulty in breathing persists after use of this medication or if condition becomes worse

» For patients also using anti-inflammatory medication, checking with physician before stopping or reducing anti-inflammatory therapy

For salmeterol:

» Checking with physician if using four or more inhalations per day of a rapid-acting beta-adrenergic bronchodilator for two or more consecutive days or more than one canister (200 inhalations per canister) in an eight-week period

For albuterol, bitolterol, epinephrine, fenoterol, isoetharine, isoproterenol, metaproterenol, pirbuterol, procaterol, and terbutaline:

» Checking with physician immediately if more inhalations than usual of a rapid-acting beta-adrenergic bronchodilator are needed to relieve an acute attack

» If not using anti-inflammatory medication: checking with physician if using a rapid-acting beta-adrenergic bronchodilator to relieve symptoms more than two times per week

» If using anti-inflammatory medication: checking with physician if using more than one canister per month of a rapid-acting beta-adrenergic bronchodilator to relieve symptoms

Side/adverse effects

Signs of potential side effects, especially laryngeal spasm, irritation, or swelling, paradoxical bronchospasm, hypersensitivity, or significantly worsening or acutely deteriorating asthma

General Dosing Information

For emergency department and hospital treatment of acute, severe bronchospasm associated with asthma, inhaled short-acting $beta_2$-agonist therapy using the higher dose and administered either as three treatments within the first hour or by continuous nebulization is recommended. Studies have shown that administration of high doses (6 to 12 puffs) of a short-acting $beta_2$-agonist via metered-dose inhaler with a spacer can produce equivalent bronchodilation when compared with nebulizer therapy. For outpatient management of an asthma exacerbation, two to four puffs of a short-acting $beta_2$-adrenergic bronchodilator via metered-dose inhaler every 20 minutes, for up to 1 hour if needed, or a single dose via nebulization is recommended as initial treatment.

Long-acting adrenergic bronchodilators SHOULD NOT be initiated in patients with significantly worsening or acutely deteriorating asthma, which may be a life-threatening condition. They should not be used to treat acute symptoms. ***It is crucial to inform patients of this and prescribe an inhaled short-acting $beta_2$-agonist for this purpose as well as warn them that increasing inhaled $beta_2$-agonist is a signal of deteriorating asthma.***

Long-acting adrenergic bronchodilators are not a substitute for inhaled or oral corticosteroids. Corticosteroids ***should not be stopped or reduced*** when long-acting adrenergic bronchodilators are initiated.

The use of a spacer device with many adrenergic bronchodilators may be beneficial, especially for young children and older adults. By reducing the need for proper coordination of timing of inhalation with activation of the inhaler and reducing the velocity and mean diameter of the aerosol particles, a spacer reduces the amount of medication deposited in the upper airways and increases the amount deposited in the lower respiratory tract in patients with poor technique.

For dilution of adrenergic bronchodilator solutions for inhalation, only products that do not contain benzyl alcohol, preferably preservative-free products, should be used.

A metered-dose inhaler (MDI) should be primed before it is used for the first time or if it has not recently been used. The amount of medication in a dose from a MDI product may depend on how much time has elapsed since the preceding dose and the position in which the inhaler has been stored. One study found that the medication content of single sprays of albuterol MDI ranged between 23 and 208% of the label claim. Additionally, this study suggests that initial sprays from a new canister contain higher albuterol content than the final sprays from the same canister. Single, unprimed doses (doses taken 4 hours or more after the last spray) from canisters stored in the upright position and activated after 4 or 16 hours averaged a higher medication content than single, unprimed doses from canisters stored with the valve down. Primed sprays (those sprays that were taken within minutes of a previous spray), whether stored with the valve up or valve down, contained a mean of 92% of labeled medication content of single sprays of albuterol MDI. Specific information about when to prime an inhaler, other than the first time it is used, as well as the number of sprays that should be performed, remains to be defined. For salmeterol, the recommendation is to prime the inhaler if it has not been used for 4 weeks or longer, and that four priming sprays should be performed.

The contents of metered dose inhalers should generally not be floated in water to assess the contents since this method may not reliably predict the amount of medication remaining in the canister. A record should be kept of the number of inhalations used.

It is not clear whether clinically significant tachyphylaxis or tolerance to the bronchodilator effects of rapid-acting beta-adrenergic bronchodilators develops with repeated use. For longer-acting salmeterol, a 12-month study demonstrated that regular use does not lead to a loss of bronchodilatory effect. Decreased bronchoprotection was reported in one 8-week study in which the effects of salmeterol on bronchodilation and on airway hyperresponsiveness to methacholine were studied in a small number of asthmatics. In another study, duration of salmeterol's protective effect against exercise-induced bronchospasm, another potential marker of tolerance, decreased over a 4-week period in some patients. Systemic administration of corticosteroids has been shown to alter $beta_2$-receptor function on lymphocytes to prevent and reverse tolerance; however, the effect of inhaled or systemic corticosteroids on changes in bronchodilator responses in asthmatics is less clear. There is some evidence that inhaled corticosteroids are unable to prevent tolerance to long-acting $beta_2$-agonists.

As a way to protect the stratospheric ozone layer, the manufacture of chlorofluorocarbons (CFCs) is being phased out. The 1987 Montreal Protocol, an international treaty that is enforced in the U.S. by the Clean Air Act, banned CFC use as of January 1, 1996. CFC-containing inhalers have been granted a temporary exemption so that alternative propellants can be developed.

ALBUTEROL

Additional Dosing Information

See also *General Dosing Information*.

Bioequivalence information

Unless a generic albuterol metered-dose inhaler has proven bioequivalence, one product should not be substituted for another without the concurrence of the prescribing physician. Generic albuterol metered-dose inhalers distributed by Zenith Goldline and Dey Laboratories may be substituted for *Ventolin.* The generic product distributed by Warrick Pharmaceuticals may only be substituted for *Proventil.*

Inhalation Dosage Forms

Note: The doses and strengths of the available dosage forms are expressed in terms of albuterol (not the sulfate salt).

Note: Bracketed used in the *Dosage Forms* section refers to categories of use and/or indications that are not included in the U.S. product labeling.

ALBUTEROL INHALATION AEROSOL

Note: Unless a generic albuterol metered-dose inhaler has proven bioequivalence, one product should not be substituted for another without the concurrence of the prescribing physician. Generic albuterol metered-dose inhalers distributed by Zenith Goldline and Dey Laboratories may be substituted for *Ventolin.* The generic product distributed by Warrick Pharmaceuticals may only be substituted for *Proventil.*

Usual adult and adolescent dose

Bronchodilator—

Oral inhalation, 2 inhalations (180 or 200 mcg albuterol) every four to six hours. For some patients, 1 inhalation (90 or 100 mcg) every four hours may be sufficient.

Bronchospasm, exercise-induced (prophylaxis)—

Oral inhalation, 2 inhalations (180 or 200 mcg) fifteen minutes prior to exercise.

Usual pediatric dose

Bronchodilator—

Children up to 4 years of age: Dosage has not been established.

Children 4 years of age and over: See *Usual adult and adolescent dose.*

Bronchospasm, exercise-induced (prophylaxis)—

Children up to 4 years of age: Dosage has not been established.

Children 4 years of age and over: See *Usual adult and adolescent dose.*

[Hyperkalemia][1]—

For patients weighing less than 25 kg: Oral inhalation, 2.5 mg.

For patients weighing 25 kg or more: Oral inhalation, 5 mg.

Strength(s) usually available

U.S.—

90 mcg albuterol per metered spray (Rx) [*Proventil* (dichlorodifluoromethane; trichloromonofluoromethane; oleic acid); *Ventolin* (dichlorodifluoromethane; trichloromonofluoromethane; oleic acid)].

Canada—

100 mcg albuterol per metered spray (Rx) [*Apo-Salvent; Novo-Salmol; Ventolin*].

Note: In Canada, metered dose inhalers are labeled according to the amount of medication delivered from the valve; in the U.S., metered dose inhalers are labeled according to the amount of medication delivered at the mouthpiece or actuator.

Packaging and storage

Store below 40 °C (104 °F), preferably between 15 and 30 °C (59 and 86 °F), unless otherwise specified by manufacturer.

Auxiliary labeling

- For oral inhalation only.
- Shake well before using.

Note
Include patient instructions when dispensing.

ALBUTEROL SULFATE INHALATION AEROSOL

Usual adult and adolescent dose
Bronchodilator—
Oral inhalation, 2 inhalations (180 mcg albuterol) every four to six hours. For some patients, 1 inhalation (90 mcg) every four hours may be sufficient.
Bronchospasm, exercise-induced (prophylaxis)—
Oral inhalation, 2 inhalations (180 mcg albuterol) fifteen to thirty minutes prior to exercise.

Usual pediatric dose
Bronchodilator—
Children up to 4 years of age: Dosage has not been established.
Children 4 years of age and over: See *Usual adult and adolescent dose*.
Bronchospasm, exercise-induced (prophylaxis)—
Children up to 4 years of age: Dosage has not been established.
Children 4 years of age and over: See *Usual adult and adolescent dose*.

Strength(s) usually available
U.S.—
90 mcg (albuterol) per metered spray [*Proventil HFA* (CFC-free; hydrofluoroalkane-134a [1,1,1,2 tetrafluoroethane]; oleic acid; ethanol)].
90 mcg (albuterol) per metered spray [*Ventolin HFA* (CFC-free; hydrofluoroalkane-134a [1,1,1,2 tetrafluoroethane])].
Canada—
Not commercially available.

Packaging and storage
Store between 15 and 25 °C (59 and 77 °F).

Auxiliary labeling
- For oral inhalation only.
- Shake well before using.

Note
Include patient instructions when dispensing.

ALBUTEROL SULFATE INHALATION SOLUTION

Usual adult and adolescent dose
Bronchodilator—
Oral inhalation, administered by nebulization, 2.5 mg (albuterol), delivered over approximately five to fifteen minutes, repeated every four to six hours.

Usual pediatric dose
Bronchodilator—
Neonates and infants: Oral inhalation, administered by nebulization, 0.05 to 0.15 mg (albuterol) per kg of body weight delivered over approximately five to fifteen minutes, repeated every four to six hours.
Children up to 12 years of age: Oral inhalation, administered by nebulization, 1.25 to 2.5 mg delivered over approximately five to fifteen minutes, repeated every four to six hours if necessary.
Children 12 years of age and over: See *Usual adult and adolescent dose*.

Strength(s) usually available
U.S.—
0.83 mg (albuterol) per mL (Rx) [*Airet; Proventil* (benzalkonium chloride); *Ventolin Nebules*].
5 mg (albuterol) per mL (Rx) [*Proventil* (benzalkonium chloride); *Ventolin* (benzalkonium chloride)].
Canada—
0.5 mg (albuterol) per mL (Rx) [*Ventolin Nebules P.F.*].
1 mg (albuterol) per mL (Rx) [*Gen-Salbutamol Sterinebs P.F.; Ventolin Nebules P.F.*].
2 mg (albuterol) per mL (Rx) [*Gen-Salbutamol Sterinebs P.F.; Ventolin Nebules P.F.*].
5 mg (albuterol) per mL (Rx) [*Apo-Salvent* (benzalkonium chloride); *Ventolin* (benzalkonium chloride)].

Packaging and storage
Store below 40 °C (104 °F), preferably between 15 and 30 °C (59 and 86 °F), unless otherwise specified by manufacturer.

Preparation of dosage form
For preparation of the inhalation solution, diluents containing benzyl alcohol or preservatives other than benzalkonium chloride are not recommended since the safety of these preservatives has not been established for inhalation therapy.
The 0.5-, 0.83-, 1-, and 2-mg-per-mL solutions do not require dilution prior to administration. The 5-mg-per-mL solution is concentrated and must be diluted in 2.5 mL of sterile 0.9% sodium chloride solution prior to administration.

Stability
Albuterol inhalation solution is compatible with cromolyn and ipratropium inhalation solutions for up to 1 hour.

Auxiliary labeling
For oral inhalation only.

Note
Include patient instructions when dispensing.

ALBUTEROL SULFATE POWDER FOR INHALATION

Usual adult and adolescent dose
Bronchodilator—
Oral inhalation, 200 or 400 mcg every four to six hours.
Bronchospasm, exercise-induced (prophylaxis)—
Oral inhalation, 200 mcg, fifteen minutes before exercise.

Usual pediatric dose
Bronchodilator—
Children up to 4 years of age: Dosage has not been established.
Children 4 years of age and over: See *Usual adult and adolescent dose*.

Strength(s) usually available
U.S.—
200 mcg per capsule (Rx) [*Ventolin Rotacaps* (lactose)].
Canada—
200 mcg per blister or capsule (Rx) [*Ventodisk; Ventolin Rotacaps* (lactose)].
400 mcg per blister or capsule (Rx) [*Ventodisk; Ventolin Rotacaps* (lactose)].

Packaging and storage
Store below 40 °C (104 °F), preferably between 15 and 30 °C (59 and 86 °F), in a well-closed container, unless otherwise specified by manufacturer.

Auxiliary labeling
- For oral inhalation only.

Note
Include patient instructions when dispensing.
Use of albuterol powder for inhalation requires a special device that separates the capsule into halves or pierces the blister and releases the medication.

---

[1]Not included in Canadian product labeling.

BITOLTEROL

Note: Products containing bitolterol were withdrawn from the U.S. market by the manufacturer in November 2001.

Summary of Differences

Pharmacology/pharmacokinetics: Biotransformation—A prodrug hydrolyzed by esterases in tissue and blood to the active compound colterol.

Inhalation Dosage Forms

Note: Bracketed uses refer to categories of use and/or indications that are not included in U.S. product labeling.

BITOLTEROL MESYLATE INHALATION AEROSOL

Usual adult and adolescent dose
Bronchodilator—
Oral inhalation, 2 inhalations (740 mcg) every eight hours, or 2 inhalations (740 mcg) administered at least one to three minutes apart, followed by 1 additional inhalation (370 mcg) if needed. Dosage per day should not exceed 2 inhalations (740 mcg) every four hours or 3 inhalations (1.11 mg) every six hours.
[Bronchospasm, exercise-induced (prophylaxis)]—
Oral inhalation, 2 inhalations (740 mcg) five minutes prior to exercise.

Usual pediatric dose
Bronchodilator—
See *Usual adult and adolescent dose*.
[Bronchospasm, exercise-induced (prophylaxis)]—
Oral inhalation, 1 or 2 inhalations (370 or 740 mcg) five minutes prior to exercise.

Strength(s) usually available
U.S.—
Not commercially available.
Note: Withdrawn from the U.S. market in November 2001.
Canada—
Not commercially available.

Packaging and storage
Store between 15 and 30 °C (59 and 86 °F).

Auxiliary labeling
• For oral inhalation only.

Note
Include patient instructions when dispensing.

BITOLTEROL MESYLATE INHALATION SOLUTION

Usual adult and adolescent dose
Bronchodilator—
Oral inhalation:
Continuous flow nebulization—2.5 milligrams (mg) (range, 1.5 to 3.5 mg), diluted and delivered over ten to fifteen minutes, three to four times per day, not less than four hours apart.
Intermittent flow nebulization—1 milligram (mg) (range, 0.5 to 1.5 mg), diluted and delivered over ten to fifteen minutes, three to four times per day, not less than four hours apart.

Usual adult and adolescent prescribing limits
The maximum daily dose should not exceed 8 mg with intermittent flow nebulization or 14 mg with continuous flow nebulization.

Usual pediatric dose
Children up to 12 years of age: Dosage has not been established.
Children 12 years of age and over: See *Usual adult and adolescent dose*.

Strength(s) usually available
U.S.—
Not commercially available.
Note: Withdrawn from the U.S. market in November 2001.
Canada—
Not commercially available.

Packaging and storage
Store between 15 and 30 °C (59 and 86 °F).

Preparation of dosage form
Bitolterol inhalation solution should be diluted to 2 to 4 mL with sterile 0.9% sodium chloride solution.

Stability
Bitolterol inhalation solution should not be mixed with other medications, such as cromolyn sodium or acetylcysteine, at clinically recommended doses due to chemical and/or physical incompatibilities.

EPINEPHRINE

Summary of Differences

Indications:
Epinephrine and racepinephrine inhalation also indicated in treatment of postintubation and infectious croup.
Pharmacology/pharmacokinetics:
Epinephrine also has alpha- and beta$_1$-adrenergic receptor action.
Duration of action: Short-acting.
Pregnancy:
Not recommended during pregnancy because of alpha-adrenergic agonist activity.
Medical considerations/contraindications:
May worsen heart conditions or hypertension.

Inhalation Dosage Forms

Note: The doses and strengths of the available dosage forms are expressed in terms of epinephrine (not the bitartrate or chloride salt).
Effective June 19, 1996, the Food and Drug Administration amended the final monograph for over-the-counter bronchodilator products by removing *pressurized metered-dose aerosol inhaler* dosage forms containing epinephrine and epinephrine bitartrate. Initial introduction of such a product now requires an application for approval of safety and efficacy. Products that are currently marketed contain a chlorofluorocarbon (CFC) propellant and will be phased out when the temporary exemption for CFCs expires.

EPINEPHRINE INHALATION AEROSOL USP

Usual adult and adolescent dose
Bronchodilator—
Oral inhalation, 1 inhalation (200 to 275 mcg), repeated after at least one minute, if necessary; subsequent dose(s) should not be administered for at least three hours.

Usual pediatric dose
Bronchodilator—
Children up to 4 years of age: Dosage must be individualized by physician.
Children 4 years of age and over: See *Usual adult and adolescent dose.*

Strength(s) usually available
U.S.—
0.125% (OTC).
0.5% (200 mcg per metered spray) (OTC).
0.5% (220 mcg per metered spray) (OTC) [*Primatene Mist* (alcohol 34%; fluorocarbons)].
0.5% (250 mcg per metered spray) (OTC) [*Bronkaid Mist* (alcohol 33%; dichlorodifluoromethane; dichlorotetrafluoroethane)].
Canada—
Not commercially available.

Packaging and storage
Store below 40 °C (104 °F), preferably between 15 and 30 °C (59 and 86 °F), unless otherwise specified by manufacturer.

EPINEPHRINE INHALATION SOLUTION USP

Usual adult and adolescent dose
Bronchodilator—
Oral inhalation, 10 drops administered by hand-bulb nebulizer, 1 to 3 inhalations. Doses should not be repeated more often than every three hours.

Usual pediatric dose
Bronchodilator—
Children up to 4 years of age: Dosage must be individualized by physician.
Children 4 years of age and over: See *Usual adult and adolescent dose.*

Strength(s) usually available
U.S.—
1% (epinephrine) (OTC) [*Adrenalin Chloride* (benzethonium chloride; sodium bisulfite)].
Canada—
Not commercially available.
Note: The solution intended for oral inhalation is more concentrated than those intended for injection and is not to be given parenterally.

Packaging and storage
Store below 40 °C (104 °F), preferably between 15 and 30 °C (59 and 86 °F), unless otherwise specified by manufacturer, in a tight, light-resistant container.

Stability
When exposed to air, the solution will turn pinkish to brownish in color because of oxidation. Also, light, heat, alkalies, and certain metals (for example, copper, iron, zinc) may promote deterioration. Do not use if solution is pinkish to brownish in color or contains a precipitate.

Auxiliary labeling
• For oral inhalation only.

EPINEPHRINE BITARTRATE INHALATION AEROSOL USP

Usual adult and adolescent dose
Bronchodilator—
Oral inhalation, 1 inhalation (160 mcg epinephrine) repeated after one minute, if necessary; subsequent dose(s) should not be administered for at least three hours.

Usual pediatric dose
Bronchodilator—
Children up to 4 years of age: Dosage must be individualized by physician.
Children 4 years of age and over: See *Usual adult and adolescent dose.*

Strength(s) usually available
U.S.—
300 mcg (160 mcg [epinephrine]) per metered spray (OTC) [*Asthmahaler Mist* (dichlorodifluoromethane; dichlorotetrafluoroethane; trichloromonofluoromethane); *Bronkaid Suspension Mist*].
Canada—
Not commercially available.

Packaging and storage
Store below 40 °C (104 °F), preferably between 15 and 30 °C (59 and 86 °F), unless otherwise specified by manufacturer.

RACEPINEPHRINE INHALATION SOLUTION USP

Usual adult and adolescent dose
Bronchodilator—
Oral inhalation, administered by hand-bulb nebulization, 0.5 mL (approximately 10 drops) to provide 1 to 3 inhalations, repeated after three hours if necessary.
Oral inhalation, administered by jet nebulization, 0.2 to 0.5 mL (approximately 4 to 10 drops) of diluted solution, delivered over approximately fifteen minutes, repeated every three or four hours.

Usual pediatric dose

Bronchodilator—

Children up to 4 years of age: Dosage must be individualized by physician.

Children 4 years of age and over: See *Usual adult and adolescent dose.*

Croup—

Oral inhalation, administered by nebulization, 0.05 mL per kg of body weight, diluted to 3 mL with 0.9% sodium chloride solution, delivered over approximately fifteen minutes, repeated not more frequently than every two hours, if needed.

Usual pediatric prescribing limits

Croup—

0.5 mL per dose.

Strength(s) usually available

U.S.—

2% (OTC) [*Vaponefrin* (sodium metabisulfite; chlorobutanol; benzoic acid; glycerin)].

2.25% (epinephrine) (OTC) [*AsthmaNefrin* (sodium bisulfite; benzoic acid; chlorobutanol); *microNefrin* (sodium bisulfite; potassium metabisulfite; chlorobutanol; benzoic acid; propylene glycol); *Nephron; S-2* (sodium bisulfite; potassium metabisulfite; chlorobutanol; benzoic acid; propylene glycol)].

Canada—

2.25% (epinephrine) (OTC) [*Vaponefrin* (sodium metabisulfite)].

Packaging and storage

Store below 40 °C (104 °F), preferably between 15 and 30 °C (59 and 86 °F), unless otherwise specified by manufacturer, in a tight, light-resistant container.

Preparation of dosage form

If administered via hand-bulb nebulizer, racepinephrine inhalation solution does not require dilution; however, if administered via jet nebulizer, it should be diluted to a volume of 3 to 5 mL with sterile 0.9% sodium chloride solution.

Stability

When exposed to air, the solution will turn pinkish to brownish in color because of oxidation. Also, light, heat, alkalies, and certain metals (for example, copper, iron, zinc) may promote deterioration. Do not use if solution is pinkish to brownish in color or contains a precipitate.

FENOTEROL

Inhalation Dosage Forms

FENOTEROL HYDROBROMIDE INHALATION AEROSOL

Usual adult and adolescent dose

Bronchodilator—

Oral inhalation, 2 inhalations (100 or 200 mcg), three to four times a day, if necessary, but not to be administered more often than every four hours. Dosage should not exceed 8 inhalations *of the 100 mcg per metered spray formulation* or 6 inhalations *of the 200 mcg per metered spray* formulation per day.

Usual pediatric dose

Bronchodilator—

Children up to 12 years of age: Dosage has not been established.

Children 12 years of age and over: See *Usual adult and adolescent dose.*

Strength(s) usually available

U.S.—

Not commercially available.

Canada—

100 mcg per metered spray (Rx) [*Berotec* (monofluorotrichloromethane; dichlorotetrafluoroethane; dichlorodifluoromethane)].

200 mcg per metered spray (Rx) [*Berotec* (monofluorotrichloromethane; dichlorotetrafluoroethane; dichlorodifluoromethane)].

Packaging and storage

Store below 40 °C (104 °F), preferably between 15 and 30 °C (59 and 86 °F), unless otherwise specified by manufacturer.

Auxiliary labeling

- For oral inhalation only.
- Shake well before using.

Note

Include patient instructions when dispensing.

FENOTEROL HYDROBROMIDE INHALATION SOLUTION

Usual adult and adolescent dose

Bronchodilator—

Oral inhalation, administered via nebulization, 0.5 mg to 1 mg (up to 2.5 mg in some cases) of diluted solution, delivered over ten to fifteen minutes. Dosage may be repeated every six hours, if necessary.

Usual pediatric dose

Bronchodilator—

Children up to 12 years of age: Dosage has not been established.

Children 12 years of age and over: See *Usual adult and adolescent dose.*

Strength(s) usually available

U.S.—

Not commercially available.

Canada—

1 mg per mL (Rx) [*Berotec* (benzalkonium chloride)].

Packaging and storage

Store below 40 °C (104 °F), preferably between 15 and 30 °C (59 and 86 °F), in a well-closed container, unless otherwise specified by manufacturer.

Preparation of dosage form

Fenoterol inhalation solution should be diluted to 5 mL with sterile 0.9% sodium chloride solution.

Auxiliary labeling

- For oral inhalation only.

FORMOTEROL

Summary of Differences

Indications:

Indicated for long-term treatment of asthma in patients 5 years of age and older with reversible obstructive airways, including patients with symptoms of nocturnal asthma, who are receiving corticosteroid treatment and who experience regular or frequent exacerbations of symptoms that require use of a short-acting bronchodilator. Formoterol is *not indicated* for the treatment of acute bronchospasm. Formoterol treatment *should not be initiated* in patients with significantly worsening or acutely deteriorating asthma (rapid worsening over hours or days).

Corticosteroids should not be stopped when formoterol is prescribed.

Pharmacology/pharmacokinetics:

Onset of action—1 to 3 minutes

Duration of action—Long-acting (12 hours)

Inhalation Dosage Forms

FORMOTEROL FUMARATE DIHYDRATE POWDER FOR INHALATION

Usual adult and adolescent dose

Bronchodilator—

Oral inhalation, 12 micrograms (mcg) two times a day, morning and evening, approximately 12 hours apart.

Note: Canadian product information states that some patients may need up to 24 mcg every 12 hours.

Adult and adolescent dosing limits

Bronchodilator—

Adults: Not to exceed 24 mcg a day

Note: Canadian product information states that up to 24 mcg twice daily can be prescribed.

Adolescents: Not to exceed 24 mcg a day.

Usual pediatric dose

Children 5 years and older: See *Usual adult and adolescent dose.*

Safety and efficacy in children under 5 years of age not established.

Note: Canadian product information states that in children 6 years of age and older: See *Usual adult and adolescent dose*

Strength(s) usually available

U.S.—

12 mcg per metered dose (Rx) [*Foradil* (lactose)].

Canada—

6 micrograms (mcg) per inhalation (Rx) [*Oxeze Turbuhaler* (The rotating knob of the Turbuhaler is light turquoise; lactose)].

12 micrograms (mcg) per inhalation (Rx) [*Oxeze Turbuhaler Foradil* (The rotating knob of the Turbuhaler is dark turquoise; lactose)].

12 micrograms (mcg) per capsule for inhalation (Rx) [*Foradil* (lactose)].

Packaging and storage
Prior to dispensing—store in a refrigerator, 2° to 8°C (36° to 46°F)
After dispensing to patient—store at 20° to 25°C (68° to 77°F)

Note: Canadian product information states to store between 15 and 25 °C

Auxiliary labeling
- For oral inhalation only
- Protect from heat and moisture

ISOETHARINE

Summary of Differences
Pharmacology/pharmacokinetics: Duration of action—short-acting.
Precautions: Pediatrics—Use in children not recommended.

Inhalation Dosage Forms

ISOETHARINE INHALATION SOLUTION USP

Usual adult dose
Bronchodilator—
Oral inhalation, administered via nebulization, 2.5 to 10 mg, delivered over approximately fifteen to twenty minutes, repeated every four hours, if needed.

Usual pediatric dose
Use is not recommended.

Strength(s) usually available
U.S.—
0.062% (HCl) (Rx) [*Arm-a-Med Isoetharine*].
0.08% (Rx) [*Dey-Lute Isoetharine*].
0.1% (Rx) [*Dey-Lute Isoetharine*].
0.125% (Rx) [*Arm-a-Med Isoetharine*].
0.167% (Rx) [*Arm-a-Med Isoetharine*].
0.17% (Rx) [*Dey-Lute Isoetharine*].
0.2% (Rx) [*Arm-a-Med Isoetharine*].
0.25% (Rx) [*Arm-a-Med Isoetharine; Dey-Lute Isoetharine*].
1% (Rx) [*Beta-2* (sodium bisulfite); *Bronkosol* (acetone sodium bisulfite; glycerin; parabens; sodium chloride; sodium citrate)].

Canada—
Not commercially available.

Packaging and storage
Store below 40 °C (104 °F), preferably between 15 and 30 °C (59 and 86 °F), unless otherwise specified by manufacturer, in a tight, light-resistant container.

Preparation of dosage form
For preparation of the inhalation solution, diluents containing benzyl alcohol or preservatives other than benzalkonium chloride are not recommended since the safety of these preservatives has not been established for inhalation therapy.

The 0.062 to 0.25% solutions do not require dilution prior to administration. The 1% solution is concentrated and must be diluted with 1 to 4 mL of sterile 0.9% sodium chloride solution prior to administration.

Stability
Do not use if solution is pinkish or darker than slightly yellow in color or if it contains a precipitate.

Auxiliary labeling
- For oral inhalation only.

ISOETHARINE MESYLATE INHALATION AEROSOL USP

Usual adult and adolescent dose
Bronchodilator—
Oral inhalation, 1 or 2 inhalations (340 or 680 mcg) repeated every four hours as needed.

Usual pediatric dose
Use is not recommended.

Strength(s) usually available
U.S.—
0.61% (340 mcg per metered spray) (Rx) [*Bronkometer*].

Canada—
Not commercially available.

Packaging and storage
Store below 40 °C (104 °F), preferably between 15 and 30 °C (59 and 86 °F), unless otherwise specified by manufacturer.

Auxiliary labeling
- For oral inhalation only.
- **Note:** Include patient instructions when dispensing.

ISOPROTERENOL

Summary of Differences
Pharmacology/pharmacokinetics:
Isoproterenol also has $beta_1$-adrenergic receptor activity.
Duration of action: Short-acting.

Side/adverse effects:
Pinkish to red coloration of saliva.

Inhalation Dosage Forms

ISOPROTERENOL INHALATION SOLUTION USP

Usual adult and adolescent dose
Bronchodilator—
Oral inhalation, administered via nebulization, 2.5 mg diluted, and delivered over approximately ten to twenty minutes, repeated every four hours if needed.

Usual pediatric dose
Bronchodilator—
Oral inhalation, administered via nebulization, 0.05 to 0.1 mg per kg up to 1.25 mg diluted, and delivered over approximately ten to twenty minutes, repeated every four hours if needed.

Strength(s) usually available
U.S.—
0.25% (2.5 mg per mL) (Rx).
0.5% (5 mg per mL) (Rx) [*Isuprel* (sodium metabisulfite; chlorobutanol; citric acid; glycerin; sodium chloride); GENERIC (may contain sodium bisulfite)].
1% (10 mg per mL) (Rx) [*Isuprel* (sodium metabisulfite; chlorobutanol; saccharin; sodium chloride; sodium citrate; citric acid)].

Canada—
0.5% (5 mg per mL) (Rx) [*Isuprel* (chlorobutanol)].

Packaging and storage
Store below 40 °C (104 °F), preferably between 15 and 30 °C (59 and 86 °F), unless otherwise specified by manufacturer, in a tight, light-resistant container.

Preparation of dosage form
Isoproterenol inhalation solution should be diluted with 1.5 to 2 mL of sterile 0.9% sodium chloride solution.

Stability
When exposed to air, alkalies, or metals, isoproterenol solutions turn pinkish to brownish in color because of oxidation. Do not use if solution is pinkish to brownish in color or contains a precipitate.

Auxiliary labeling
- For oral inhalation only.

ISOPROTERENOL HYDROCHLORIDE INHALATION AEROSOL USP

Usual adult and adolescent dose
Bronchodilator—
Oral inhalation, 1 inhalation (120 to 131 mcg) repeated after two to five minutes if necessary, every three to four hours.

Usual pediatric dose
Bronchodilator—
Children up to 12 years of age: Use is not recommended.
Children 12 years of age and over: See *Usual adult and adolescent dose*.

Strength(s) usually available
U.S.—
120 mcg per metered spray (Rx).
131 mcg per metered spray (Rx) [*Isuprel Mistometer* (alcohol 33%; ascorbic acid; dichlorodifluoromethane; dichlorotetrafluoroethane)].

Canada—
125 mcg per metered spray (Rx) [*Isuprel Mistometer* (ethyl alcohol; ascorbic acid; inert propellants)].

Packaging and storage
Store below 40 °C (104 °F), preferably between 15 and 30 °C (59 and 86 °F), unless otherwise specified by manufacturer.

Auxiliary labeling
- For oral inhalation only.
- Shake well before using.

Note
Include patient instructions when dispensing.

ISOPROTERENOL SULFATE INHALATION AEROSOL USP

Usual adult and adolescent dose
Bronchodilator—
Oral inhalation, 1 inhalation (80 mcg) repeated after two to five minutes if necessary, every four to six hours.

Usual pediatric dose
Bronchodilator—
Children up to 12 years of age: Dosage has not been established.
Children 12 years of age and over: See *Usual adult and adolescent dose.*

Strength(s) usually available
U.S.—
80 mcg per metered spray (Rx) [*Medihaler-Iso* (dichlorodifluoromethane; dichlorotetrafluoroethane; trichloromonofluoromethane; sorbitan trioleate)].
Canada—
Not commercially available.

Packaging and storage
Store below 40 °C (104 °F), preferably between 15 and 30 °C (59 and 86 °F), unless otherwise specified by manufacturer.

Auxiliary labeling
- For oral inhalation only.
- Shake well before using.

Note
Include patient instructions when dispensing.

METAPROTERENOL

Summary of Differences
Pharmacology/pharmacokinetics: Has significant beta$_1$-adrenergic activity.

Inhalation Dosage Forms

METAPROTERENOL SULFATE INHALATION AEROSOL USP

Usual adult and adolescent dose
Bronchodilator—
Oral inhalation, 2 or 3 inhalations (1.3 to 1.95 mg) every three to four hours, not to exceed 12 inhalations per day.

Usual pediatric dose
Bronchodilator—
Children up to 12 years of age: Oral inhalation, 1 to 3 inhalations (0.65 to 1.95 mg) every three to four hours, not to exceed 12 inhalations per day.
Children 12 years of age and over: See *Usual adult and adolescent dose.*

Strength(s) usually available
U.S.—
650 mcg per metered spray (Rx) [*Alupent* (dichlorodifluoromethane; dichlorotetrafluoroethane; trichloromonofluoromethane; sorbitan trioleate)].
Canada—
750 mcg per metered spray (Rx) [*Alupent* (dichlorodifluoromethane; dichlorotetrafluoroethane; trichloromonofluoromethane; sorbitan trioleate)].

Note: In Canada, metered dose inhalers are labeled according to the amount of medication delivered from the valve; in the U.S., metered dose inhalers are labeled according to the amount of medication delivered at the mouthpiece or actuator.

Packaging and storage
Store below 40 °C (104 °F), preferably between 15 and 25 °C (59 and 77 °F), unless otherwise specified by manufacturer.

Auxiliary labeling
- For oral inhalation only.
- Shake well before using.

Note
Include patient instructions when dispensing.

METAPROTERENOL SULFATE INHALATION SOLUTION USP

Usual adult and adolescent dose
Bronchodilator—
Oral inhalation, administered via nebulization, 15 mg (range 10 to 15 mg), repeated three or four times a day, not more often than every four hours.

Usual pediatric dose
Bronchodilator—
Children up to 6 years of age: Oral inhalation, administered via nebulization, 5 to 15 mg, repeated three or four times a day, not more often than every four hours.
Children 6 years of age and over: See *Usual adult and adolescent dose.*

Strength(s) usually available
U.S.—
0.4% (Rx) [*Alupent; Arm-a-Med Metaproterenol; Dey-Lute Metaproterenol*].
0.6% (Rx) [*Alupent; Arm-a-Med Metaproterenol; Dey-Lute Metaproterenol*].
5% (Rx) [*Alupent* (benzalkonium chloride)].
Canada—
5% (Rx) [*Alupent*].

Packaging and storage
Store below 40 °C (104 °F), preferably between 15 and 30 °C (59 and 86 °F), unless otherwise specified by manufacturer, in a tight, light-resistant container.

Preparation of dosage form
For preparation of the inhalation solution, diluents containing benzyl alcohol or preservatives other than benzalkonium chloride are not recommended since the safety of these preservatives has not been established for inhalation therapy.

The 0.4% and 0.6% solutions require no dilution prior to administration. The 5% solution is concentrated and must be diluted in approximately 2.5 mL of sterile 0.9% sodium chloride solution prior to administration.

Stability
Do not use solution if its color is pinkish or darker than slightly yellow or if it contains a precipitate.

Metaproterenol inhalation solution is compatible with cromolyn inhalation solution for up to 1 hour.

Auxiliary labeling
- For oral inhalation only.

PIRBUTEROL

Inhalation Dosage Forms
Note: Bracketed uses refer to categories of use and/or indications that are not included in U.S. product labeling.
The doses and strengths of the available dosage forms are expressed in terms of pirbuterol (not the acetate salt).

PIRBUTEROL ACETATE INHALATION AEROSOL

Usual adult and adolescent dose
Bronchodilator—
Oral inhalation, 1 or 2 inhalations (200 or 400 mcg pirbuterol) every four to six hours, not to exceed a total dose of 12 inhalations (2.4 mg) per day.
[Bronchospasm, exercise-induced (prophylaxis)]—
Oral inhalation, 2 inhalations (400 mcg pirbuterol) five minutes prior to exercise.

Usual pediatric dose
Bronchodilator—
See *Usual adult and adolescent dose.*

Strength(s) usually available
U.S.—
200 mcg (pirbuterol) per metered spray (Rx) [*Maxair* (dichlorodifluoromethane; trichloromonofluoromethane; sorbitan trioleate); *Maxair Autohaler* (dichlorodifluoromethane; trichloromonofluoromethane; sorbitan trioleate)].
Canada—
250 mcg (pirbuterol) per metered spray (Rx) [*Maxair*].

Note: *Maxair Autohaler* is a breath-activated inhaler, which automatically releases a spray of medicine when the patient inhales.

Packaging and storage
Store below 40 °C (104 °F), preferably between 15 and 30 °C (59 and 86 °F), unless otherwise specified by manufacturer.

Auxiliary labeling
- For oral inhalation only.
- Shake well before using.

Note
Include patient instructions when dispensing.

PROCATEROL

Inhalation Dosage Forms

PROCATEROL HYDROCHLORIDE HEMIHYDRATE INHALATION AEROSOL

Usual adult and adolescent dose
Bronchodilator—
Oral inhalation, 1 or 2 inhalations (10 or 20 mcg) three times a day.
Bronchospasm, exercise-induced (prophylaxis)—
Oral inhalation, 1 or 2 inhalations (10 or 20 mcg) at least fifteen minutes before exertion.

Usual pediatric dose
Bronchodilator—
See *Usual adult and adolescent dose*.

Strength(s) usually available
U.S.—
Not commercially available.
Canada—
10 mcg per metered spray (Rx) [*Pro-Air* (monofluorotrichloromethane; tetrafluorodichloroethane; difluorodichloromethane)].

Note: Each canister provides at least 200 inhalations.

Packaging and storage
Store below 40 °C (104 °F), preferably between 15 and 30 °C (59 and 86 °F), unless otherwise specified by manufacturer.

Auxiliary labeling
- For oral inhalation only.
- Shake well before using.

Note
Include patient instructions when dispensing.

SALMETEROL

Summary of Differences

Indications:
Salmeterol is *not indicated* for the treatment of acute or breakthrough asthma symptoms when rapid bronchodilation is needed because of its slower onset of action compared to shorter-acting adrenergic bronchodilators.
Salmeterol therapy *should not be initiated* in patients with significantly worsening or acutely deteriorating asthma (rapid worsening over hours to days).

Pharmacology/pharmacokinetics:
Onset of action—Approximately 10 to 20 minutes.
Time to peak effect—3 to 4 hours; however, approximately 80% of the maximal increase in forced expiratory volume in 1 second (FEV_1) occurs within 1 hour after administration.
Duration of action—Approximately 12 hours.

Inhalation Dosage Forms

Note: The doses and strengths of the available dosage forms are expressed in terms of salmeterol (not the xinafoate salt).

SALMETEROL XINAFOATE INHALATION AEROSOL

Usual adult and adolescent dose
Bronchospasm, asthma-associated (prophylaxis)—
Oral inhalation, 2 inhalations (42 or 50 mcg salmeterol) two times a day, morning and evening, approximately twelve hours apart.
Bronchospasm, exercise-induced (prophylaxis)[1]—
Oral inhalation, 2 inhalations (42 mcg salmeterol) at least thirty to sixty minutes before exercise.
Bronchospasm, chronic obstructive pulmonary disease-associated, including chronic bronchitis and emphysema (prophylaxis)—
Oral inhalation, 2 inhalations (42 or 50 mcg salmeterol) twice daily approximately 12 hours apart.

Note: Patients receiving chronic therapy should not use additional salmeterol for prevention of exercise-induced bronchospasm. Patients using salmeterol for exercise-induced bronchospasm should not use additional doses for twelve hours after each prophylactic administration.

Usual pediatric dose
Bronchospasm, asthma-associated (prophylaxis)—
Children up to 12 years of age: Dosage has not been established.
Children 12 years of age and over: See *Usual adult and adolescent dose*.
[Children 4 years of age and older: 2 inhalations (50 mcg salmeterol) twice daily.]
Bronchospasm, exercise-induced (prophylaxis)—
Children up to 12 years of age: Dosage has not been established.
Children 12 years of age and over: See *Usual adult and adolescent dose*.

Strength(s) usually available
U.S.—
25 mcg salmeterol per metered spray (Rx) [*Serevent* (trichlorofluoromethane; dichlorodifluoromethane; soya lecithin)].
Canada—
25 mcg (salmeterol) per metered spray (Rx) [*Serevent* (dichlorodifluoromethane; lecithin; trichlorofluoromethane)].

Note: In Canada, metered dose inhalers are labeled according to the amount of salmeterol delivered at the valve; in the U.S., metered dose inhalers are labeled according to the amount of salmeterol delivered at the mouthpiece or actuator.

Packaging and storage
Store between 15 and 30°C (59 and 86°F). Store canister with nozzle down.

Auxiliary labeling
- For oral inhalation only.
- Shake well before using.

Note
Include patient instructions when dispensing.

SALMETEROL XINAFOATE POWDER FOR INHALATION

Usual adult and adolescent dose
Bronchospasm, asthma-associated (prophylaxis)—
Oral inhalation, the contents of one blister (50 mcg salmeterol) two times a day.
Bronchospasm, exercise-induced (prophylaxis)—
Oral inhalation, the contents of one blister (50 mcg salmeterol) at least 30 minutes before exercise.
Bronchospasm, chronic obstructive pulmonary disease-associated, including chronic bronchitis and emphysema (prophylaxis)—
Oral inhalation, the contents of one blister (50 mcg salmeterol) twice daily.

Usual pediatric dose
Bronchospasm, asthma-associated (prophylaxis)—
Children 4 years of age and over: See *Usual adult and adolescent dose*.
Children up to 4 years of age: Safety and efficacy have not been established.
Bronchospasm, exercise-induced (prophylaxis)—
Children 4 years of age and over: See *Usual adult and adolescent dose*.
Children up to 4 years of age: Safety and efficacy have not been established.

Strength(s) usually available
U.S.—
50 mcg (delivering 47 mcg) salmeterol per blister (Rx) [*Serevent Diskus* (lactose)].
Canada—
50 mcg salmeterol per blister (Rx) [*Serevent Diskus* (lactose)].
50 mcg salmeterol per blister (Rx) [*Serevent Diskhaler* (lactose)].

Packaging and storage
Store at controlled room temperature, 20 to 25°C (68 to 77°F) in a dry place away from direct heat or sunlight.

Auxiliary labeling
- For oral inhalation only.

Note
Use of salmeterol powder for inhalation requires a special device that pierces the blister and releases the medication. Include patient instructions when dispensing.

---
[1]Not included in Canadian product labeling.

TERBUTALINE

Inhalation Dosage Forms

Note: Bracketed uses refer to categories of use and/or indications that are not included in U.S. product labeling.

TERBUTALINE SULFATE INHALATION AEROSOL USP

Usual adult and adolescent dose

Bronchodilator—

Oral inhalation, 2 inhalations (400 mcg) every four to six hours.

Note: In Canada, the recommended dose from the *breath-actuated dry powder inhaler* is 1 inhalation (500 mcg), repeated after five minutes if needed. Doses should not exceed 6 inhalations per day.

[Bronchospasm, exercise-induced (prophylaxis)][1]—

Oral inhalation, 2 inhalations (400 mcg) five to fifteen minutes prior to exercise.

Usual pediatric dose

Bronchodilator—

See *Usual adult and adolescent dose.*

Strength(s) usually available

U.S.—

200 mcg per metered spray (Rx) [*Brethaire* (dichlorodifluoromethane; dichlorotetrafluoroethane; trichloromonofluoromethane)].

Canada—

Note: *Bricanyl Turbuhaler* is a *breath-actuated dry powder inhaler*, which automatically releases a dose of terbutaline, without carrier powders or propellants, when the patient inhales.

500 mcg per metered spray (Rx) [*Bricanyl Turbuhaler*].

Packaging and storage

Store below 40 °C (104 °F), preferably between 15 and 30 °C (59 and 86 °F), unless otherwise specified by manufacturer.

Auxiliary labeling

- For oral inhalation only.
- Shake well before using.

Note

Include patient instructions when dispensing.

[1]Not included in Canadian product labeling.

Selected Bibliography

Jenne JW, Tashkin DP. Beta-adrenergic agonists. In: Weiss EB, Stein M, editors. Bronchial asthma—mechanisms and therapeutics. Boston: Little, Brown and Co; 1993. p. 746-83.

National Asthma Education and Prevention Program. Expert panel report II. Guidelines for the diagnosis and management of asthma. National Heart, Lung, and Blood Institute, Feb 1997. Available from: http://www.nhlbi.nih.gov/nhlbi/lung/asthma/prof/asthgdln.htm.

Nelson H. Beta-adrenergic bronchodilators. N Engl J Med 1995; 333: 499-506.

Revised: 09/19/2005

BRONCHODILATORS, ADRENERGIC Systemic

This monograph includes information on the following: 1) Albuterol; 2) Ephedrine; 3) Epinephrine; 4) Isoproterenol; 5) Metaproterenol; 6) Terbutaline.

Note: For information regarding use of sympathomimetics for cardiovascular indications, see the *Sympathomimetic Agents—Cardiovascular Use (Parenteral-Systemic)* monograph.

For information regarding use of epinephrine in combination with local anesthetics as an adjunct to local or regional anesthesia, see the *Anesthetics (Parenteral-Local)* monograph.

INN: Albuterol—Salbutamol

BAN:

Albuterol—Salbutamol
Epinephrine—Adrenaline

JAN:

Albuterol—Salbutamol
Metaproterenol—Orciprenaline

VA CLASSIFICATION (Primary/Secondary):

Albuterol—RE125
Epinephrine—RE190/CN205; AD900; GU900; BL116
Isoproterenol—RE190
Metaproterenol—RE125
Terbutaline
Oral—RE125
Parenteral—RE190/GU650

Note: Ephedrine is categorized as a Schedule V controlled substance in several states in order to help prevent abuse. In addition to being abused as a stimulant, ephedrine also can be chemically manipulated to produce illicit designer drugs, such as methcathinone (cat) and methamphetamine (crank).

Commonly used brand name(s): *Adrenalin*[3]; *Alupent*[5]; *Ana-Guard*[3]; *Brethine*[6]; *Bricanyl*[6]; *EpiPen*[3]; *EpiPen Auto-Injector*[3]; *EpiPen Jr.*[3]; *EpiPen Jr. Auto-Injector*[3]; *Isuprel*[4]; *Proventil*[1]; *Proventil Repetabs*[1]; *Ventolin*[1]; *Volmax*[1].

Other commonly used names are:

Adrenaline [Epinephrine]
Orciprenaline [Metaproterenol]
Salbutamol [Albuterol]

Note: For a listing of dosage forms and brand names by country availability, see *Dosage Forms* section(s).

Category

Bronchodilator—Albuterol; Epinephrine; Isoproterenol; Metaproterenol; Terbutaline.
Anesthetic, local and regional, adjunct—Epinephrine.
Antiallergic, systemic—Epinephrine.
Tocolytic—Terbutaline.
Priapism reversal agent—Epinephrine.
Antihemorrhagic, dental—Epinephrine

Indications

Accepted

Asthma, bronchial (treatment)
Bronchitis (treatment)
Bronchospasm (treatment) or
Emphysema, pulmonary (treatment)—Albuterol, subcutaneous or intramuscular epinephrine, metaproterenol, and terbutaline are indicated for the symptomatic treatment of bronchial asthma and for treatment of reversible bronchospasm that may occur in association with bronchitis, pulmonary emphysema, and other obstructive airway diseases.

Inhaled albuterol and terbutaline are the initial drugs of choice for treatment of acute bronchospasm because they provide faster delivery of medication to the lungs and fewer systemic side effects. The agents that are less selective for the beta$_2$ receptor (epinephrine, isoproterenol, metaproterenol) generally are not recommended because of their potential for excessive cardiac stimulation, especially at high doses. Use of albuterol oral solution or syrup is not recommended for treatment of acute bronchospasm.

Oral beta$_2$-adrenergic receptor agonists may be useful in children who are unable to handle use of inhalers.

Long-acting oral beta$_2$-adrenergic receptor agonists may be useful for control of nocturnal asthma symptoms, however, inhaled long-acting beta$_2$-adrenergic receptor agonists generally are preferred because they have fewer side effects associated with their use.

Isoproterenol injection is indicated for treatment of bronchospasm occurring during anesthesia. However, use of intravenous isoproterenol is not generally recommended for treatment of asthma because of the danger of myocardial toxicity.

Allergic reactions (treatment)
Anaphylactic or anaphylactoid reactions (treatment) or
Angioedema (treatment)—Epinephrine injection is indicated for the emergency treatment of severe (Type 1) allergic reactions (anaphylaxis or anaphylactoid reactions) to insect stings or bites, animal sera, foods, drugs, and other allergens, as well as for treatment of idiopathic or exercise-induced anaphylaxis. Epinephrine is the treatment of choice for these indications. (For additional information regarding use of epinephrine in anaphylactic shock, see the *Sympathomimetic Agents—Cardiovascular Use [Parenteral-Systemic]* monograph.)

Epinephrine injection may be self-administered by patients with a history of an anaphylactic reaction as soon as exposure occurs and/or with onset of symptoms (including flushing, apprehension, syncope, tachycardia, thready or unobtainable pulse associated with a fall in blood pressure, convulsions, vomiting, diarrhea and abdominal cramps, involuntary voiding, wheezing, dyspnea due to laryngeal spasm, pruritus, rashes, urticaria, or angioedema)Patients should seek medical attention from a physician or medical facility as soon as possible following the self-administration of epinephrine.

Anesthesia, local, adjunct or

Anesthesia, regional, adjunct—Epinephrine is indicated for concurrent use with a local anesthetic to decrease the rate of vascular absorption in order to localize and prolong the action of the local anesthetic. The addition of epinephrine to local anesthetics for injection into areas of the body served by end arteries or with otherwise limited blood supply (fingers, toes, nose, ears, penis) usually is not recommended because of the risk that vasoconstriction will cause sloughing of tissue. (For additional information regarding use of epinephrine in combination with local anesthetics, see the *Anesthetics [Parenteral-Local]* monograph.)

[Labor, premature (treatment)][1]—Terbutaline is indicated parenterally as initial tocolytic treatment to suppress premature labor and delay premature delivery. Although there is a risk of adverse effects (including maternal tachycardia, arrhythmias, hyperglycemia, hypotension, hypokalemia, pulmonary edema, and myocardial ischemia, and fetal tachycardia and reactive neonatal hypoglycemia) and the manufacturer's product labeling states that use during labor is not recommended, USP DI Advisory Panels agree that use for this indication is safe and effective.

[Priapism (treatment)][1]—Epinephrine is indicated by intracavernosal injection to treat priapism, although phenylephrine is considered to be the drug of first choice because it has no direct beta-adrenergic effects.

[Hemorrhage, gingival (treatment)][1] or

[Hemorrhage, pulpal (treatment)][1]—Epinephrine-impregnated retraction cords are used to control minor gingival bleeding in order to facilitate obtaining accurate dental impressions. However, there is a risk of unpredictable systemic absorption, especially from abraded surfaces. It is recommended that epinephrine retraction cords be used with caution in patients with cardiovascular disease.

Epinephrine also is applied topically, in dilute solutions, directly to gingival or pulpal tissues to control minor local hemorrhage.

[Hyperkalemia (treatment)][1]—Albuterol is indicated as a temporary treatment option for hyperkalemia in acute situations in pediatric patients.

Acceptance not established

The evidence to support use of terbutaline in *maintenance treatment of premature labor* is limited and conflicting, but seems to indicate that terbutaline administration does not significantly prolong pregnancy. Despite the routine use of terbutaline as a tocolytic agent, USP DI Advisory Panels agree that safety and efficacy are not established for this indication.

There is insufficient data to show that albuterol is beneficial for the treatment of *hyperkalemia in adults*.

Unaccepted

Although ephedrine has been used as a *bronchodilator*, a *nasal decongestant*, and to treat *urinary incontinence*, it has been generally replaced by safer and more effective medications.

---

[1]Not included in Canadian product labeling.

Pharmacology/Pharmacokinetics

Physicochemical characteristics

Molecular weight—
- Albuterol: 239.32.
- Albuterol sulfate: 576.7.
- Ephedrine sulfate: 428.55.
- Epinephrine: 183.21.
- Isoproterenol hydrochloride: 247.72.
- Metaproterenol sulfate: 520.60.
- Terbutaline sulfate: 548.66.

Mechanism of action/Effect

Sympathomimetic agents mimic, to varying degrees, the actions of endogenous catecholamines by stimulating adrenergic receptors. Stimulation of adrenergic receptors may occur directly (e.g., epinephrine) or indirectly via norepinephrine release (e.g., ephedrine), or effects may be mixed. Relative stimulation of alpha- and beta-adrenergic receptors and selectivity of effect ($alpha_1$, $alpha_2$, $beta_1$, $beta_2$) vary with individual agents, which leads to variation in effects.

Albuterol—Primarily stimulates $beta_2$-adrenergic receptors, with some minor $beta_1$-adrenergic activity.

Ephedrine—Stimulates both alpha- and beta-adrenergic receptors. Also, stimulates the release of other catecholamines, specifically norepinephrine.

Epinephrine—Potent stimulant of both alpha- and beta-adrenergic receptors.

Isoproterenol—Stimulates both $beta_2$- and $beta_1$-adrenergic receptors.

Metaproterenol—Somewhat selective for $beta_2$-adrenergic receptors, with some $beta_1$-adrenergic activity.

Terbutaline—Primarily stimulates $beta_2$-adrenergic receptors, with some minor $beta_1$-adrenergic activity.

All of these beta-adrenoceptor agonists have at least one asymmetric carbon atom and as a result exist in two or more stereoisomeric forms. The biological activity of racemic sympathomimetics is primarily the result of the (R)-enantiomer, whereas the (S)-enantiomer, though apparently lacking in therapeutic effect, may play a role in the undesirable action observed with adrenergic bronchodilators of inducing airway hyperreactivity or hyperresponsiveness (paradoxical bronchospasm).

Bronchodilator—Adrenergic bronchodilators act by stimulating $beta_2$-adrenergic receptors in the lungs to relax bronchial smooth muscle, thereby relieving bronchospasm.

Anesthetic (local) adjunct—Epinephrine acts on alpha-adrenergic receptors in the skin and mucous membranes to produce vasoconstriction. Vasoconstriction decreases the rate of vascular absorption of the local anesthetic used with epinephrine, prolonging the duration of action and possibly decreasing the risk of toxicity due to the anesthetic.

Antiallergic—Epinephrine acts on alpha-adrenergic receptors to counteract vasodilation, particularly peripheral vessel vasodilation, and on beta-adrenergic receptors to inhibit the release of mediators of immediate hypersensitivity, such as histamine and leukotrienes, from mast cells.

Tocolytic—Beta-adrenergic stimulation by terbutaline relaxes uterine muscle, decreasing uterine contractibility and inhibiting preterm labor.

Priapism reversal agent—Epinephrine-induced vasoconstriction reverses priapism.

Antihemorrhagic, dental—Vasoconstriction by epinephrine reduces minor bleeding during dental procedures.

Other actions/effects

Stimulation of $beta_1$ and $beta_2$-adrenergic receptors in the heart produces tachycardia and causes an increase in the rate and force of cardiac contractions.

Stimulation of $beta_2$ receptors located in skeletal muscle causes muscle tremorand the dilation of skeletal muscle vasculature, which may result in decreased peripheral resistance.

Beta-adrenergic stimulation may inhibit contractions of the pregnant uterus.

$Beta_2$-adrenergic stimulation also enhances glycogenolysis and gluconeogenesis, which may lead to hyperglycemia.

$Beta_2$-adrenergic stimulation of Na^+/K^+-ATPase may cause an intracellular potassium shift, leading to hypokalemia.

Alpha-adrenergic stimulation causes vasoconstriction that can lead to hypertension.

Albuterol—

Albuterol primarily stimulates $beta_2$-adrenergic receptors, although it has some minor $beta_1$-adrenergic activity.

Ephedrine—

Ephedrine stimulates both alpha- and beta-adrenergic receptors and enhances the release of endogenous norepinephrine from sympathetic neurons, resulting in increased systolic and diastolic blood pressure and increased cardiac output. Ephedrine also stimulates the central nervous system (CNS), although to a lesser extent than does amphetamine.

Epinephrine—

Epinephrine is a potent non-selective stimulant of both alpha- and beta-adrenergic receptors. At very low doses (less than 0.01 mcg per kg of body weight per minute [mcg/kg/minute]), epinephrine may stimulate $beta_2$-adrenergic receptors and decrease blood pressure through dilatation of skeletal muscle vasculature. At doses of 0.04 to 0.1 mcg/kg/minute, stimulation of $beta_1$- and $beta_2$-adrenergic receptors predominates, increasing heart rate, cardiac output, and stroke volume and decreasing peripheral vascular resistance. At doses exceeding 0.2 mcg/kg/minute, stimulation of alpha-adrenergic receptors produces vasoconstriction and increased total peripheral resistance. Doses exceeding 0.3 mcg/kg/minute decrease renal blood flow, gastrointestinal motility, pyloric tone, and splanchnic vascular bed perfusion.

Epinephrine has significant beta-adrenergic activity in the heart, resulting in an increased rate and force of cardiac contractions. Epinephrine increases conduction velocity in the myocardium and increases ectopic pacemaker activity. Myocardial oxygen demand also is increased.

Isoproterenol—

Isoproterenol is a nonselective beta-adrenergic receptor agonist. It is a potent inotrope and chronotrope ($beta_1$-adrenergic effects produce increased rate and force of cardiac contractions), increasing cardiac output despite a reduction in mean blood pressure due to peripheral vasodilation.

Metaproterenol—

Metaproterenol stimulates both $beta_1$- and $beta_2$-adrenergic receptors. Metaproterenol has significant $beta_1$-adrenergic activity in the heart, resulting in an increased rate and force of cardiac contractions.

Terbutaline—

Terbutaline primarily stimulates $beta_2$-adrenergic receptors, although it also has some minor $beta_1$-adrenergic activity.

Absorption

Albuterol—

Rapidly and well absorbed following oral administration.

Extended-release tablets: Availability is approximately 80% of that for tablets after a single dose, regardless of whether or not taken with food, but is 100% of that for immediate-release tablets at steady-state. Food decreases the rate of absorption without affecting bioavailability.

Ephedrine—

Rapidly and completely absorbed following parenteral administration.

Epinephrine—

Well absorbed following subcutaneous or intramuscular administration. Absorption is slower after subcutaneous administration, but vigorous massage of the injection site will speed absorption. Rapidly absorbed through the lung capillary bed after injection into the endotracheal tube directly into the bronchial tree.

Isoproterenol—

Rapidly absorbed following parenteral administration.

Metaproterenol—

Oral: Less than 10% absorbed intact.

Terbutaline—

Oral: 30 to 70%; food reduces bioavailability by one third.

Subcutaneous: More rapidly absorbed than with oral administration. Systemic availability is approximately 100%.

Biotransformation

Albuterol—

Metabolized through sulfate conjugation to its inactive 4'-*O*-sulphate ester by phenol sulphotransferase (PST). The (R)-enantiomer of albuterol is preferentially metabolized (ten fold) by PST compared to the (S)-enantiomer of albuterol.

Ephedrine—

Hepatic, slow (small amounts). Metabolites include p-hydroxyephedrine, p-hydroxynorephedrine, norephedrine, and their conjugates.

Epinephrine—

Hepatic and other tissues, rapid, by monoamine oxidase (MAO) and COMT. After becoming fixed in tissues, epinephrine is enzymatically inactivated to metanephrine or 3,4-dihydroxyphenylglycoaldehyde (DOPGAL), both of which undergo further metabolism and/or sulfate or glucuronide conjugation and are eliminated in the urine in the form of sulfates and glucuronides. Vanillylmandelic acid (VMA) formation results from the combined action of MAO and COMT; VMA also is detectable in the urine. Any circulating epinephrine not enzymatically deactivated is deactivated by reuptake at synaptic receptor sites.

Isoproterenol—

Hepatic and other tissues, by COMT as well as PST. The 3'-*O*-methyl metabolite is a weak beta-adrenergic receptor antagonist.

Metaproterenol—

By sulfate conjugation in the gastrointestinal tract.

Terbutaline—

Oral: Gastrointestinal and hepatic, 60% metabolized by first-pass metabolism; no known active metabolites.

Subcutaneous: Approximately one third metabolized, to inactive metabolites.

Half-life

Elimination—

Albuterol: 3.8 to 6 hours.

Ephedrine: About 3 hours at urinary pH 5 and about 6 hours at urinary pH 6.3.

Isoproterenol: 0.05 hour.

Terbutaline: 3 to 4 hours.

Onset of action

Albuterol—

Tablets: Within 30 minutes.

Epinephrine—

Intravenous: Immediate.

Subcutaneous: Bronchodilation—Within 5 to 10 minutes.

Metaproterenol—

Within 30 minutes.

Terbutaline—

Oral:

Measurable change in flow rate—Within 30 minutes.

Improvement in pulmonary function—Within 60 to 120 minutes

Subcutaneous:

Measurable change in flow rate—Within 5 minutes.

Improvement in pulmonary function—Within 15 minutes.

Time to peak concentration

Albuterol—

Syrup: Within 2 hours.

Tablets: 2 to 3 hours.

Terbutaline—

Oral: Serum—After single dose: 30 minutes to 5 hours.

Subcutaneous: Plasma—15 to 30 minutes.

Peak plasma concentration

Albuterol—

Syrup: 18 nanograms per mL after a 4 mg dose.

Tablets: 18 nanograms per mL after a single 4 mg dose; 6.7 nanograms per mL after dosing with 2 mg every 6 hours; 14.8 nanograms per mL after dosing with 4 mg every 6 hours.

Extended-release tablets: 6.5 nanograms per mL after dosing with 4 mg every 12 hours.

Terbutaline—

Oral: Average of approximately 1 nanogram per mL after each 1 mg administered to fasting adults.

Subcutaneous: Mean, 7.6 nanograms per mL after a 0.5 mg dose.

Time to peak effect

Albuterol—

Tablets: 2 to 3 hours.

Epinephrine—

Bronchodilation: Within 20 minutes following subcutaneous administration.

Terbutaline—

Oral: 120 to 180 minutes.

Subcutaneous: Within 30 to 60 minutes.

Duration of action

Albuterol—

Oral solution: 4 to 6 hours.

Extended-release tablets: Up to 12 hours.

Ephedrine—

Pressor and cardiac effects: 1 hour following intramuscular or subcutaneous administration.

Epinephrine—

Injection: Short, following subcutaneous or intramuscular administration.

Isoproterenol—

1 to 2 hours.

Metaproterenol—

Approximately 4 hours.

Terbutaline—

Oral:

Clinically significant decrease in airway and pulmonary resistance—At least 4 hours.

Significant bronchodilator activity, as measured by various pulmonary function determinations (airway resistance, MMEFR, PEFR)—Up to 8 hours.

Subcutaneous:

Clinically significant bronchodilator activity—90 minutes to 4 hours. The duration is comparable to that found with equimilligram doses of epinephrine.

Elimination

Albuterol—

Renal, 69 to 90% (60% as the metabolite).

Fecal, 4%.

Ephedrine—

Renal, mostly unchanged. Rate of urinary excretion is dependent on urinary pH; percentage of drug and metabolites excreted is increased by acidification of urine and decreased by alkalinization of urine.

Epinephrine—

Renal, largely as inactivated compounds, with the remainder either partly unchanged or as sulfate or glucuronide conjugates. VMA is also detected in urine.

Metaproterenol—
Fecal.
Terbutaline—
Oral: Renal.
Subcutaneous: Renal, unchanged (majority of drug).
In dialysis—
Albuterol:
There is insufficient evidence to determine whether albuterol is removable by dialysis.
Ephedrine:
It is not known whether ephedrine is removable by dialysis.
Isoproterenol:
It is not known whether isoproterenol is removable by dialysis.
Terbutaline:
It is not known whether terbutaline is removable by dialysis.

Precautions to Consider

Carcinogenicity/Tumorigenicity

Albuterol—Studies in Sprague-Dawley rats for 2 years at dietary doses of 2, 10, and 50 mg per kg of body weight (mg/kg) (corresponding to 1/2, 3, and 15 times, respectively, the maximum recommended daily oral dose for adults on a mg per square meter of body surface area basis (mg/m^2) or 2/5, 2, and 10 times, respectively, the maximum recommended daily oral dose for children on a mg/m^2 basis) found significant dose-related increases in the incidence of benign leiomyomas of the mesovarium. Studies in CD-1 mice for 18 months at dietary doses of up to 500 mg/kg (approximately 65 times the maximum recommended daily oral dose for adults on a mg/m^2 basis or approximately 50 times the maximum recommended daily oral dose for children on a mg/m^2 basis) and in Golden hamsters for 22 months at dietary doses of up to 50 mg/kg (approximately 7 times the maximum recommended daily oral dose for adults and children on a mg/m^2 basis) found no evidence of tumorigenicity.

Epinephrine—Studies have not been done.

Isoproterenol—Long-term studies have not been done. However, there are no reports of carcinogenic effects in humans.

Metaproterenol—Studies in mice for 18 months at doses corresponding to 31 and 62 times the maximum recommended human dose (MRHD) (based on a 50 kg individual) found a significant increase in benign hepatic adenomas in males and benign ovarian tumors in females. A study in rats for 2 years at doses 62 times the MRHD found a nonsignificant incidence of benign leiomyomata of the mesovarium.

Terbutaline—Two-year studies in Sprague-Dawley rats at doses of 50, 500, 1000, and 2000 mg/kg (corresponding to 167, 1667, 3333, and 6667 times the recommended daily human adult oral dose, respectively) found drug-related changes in the female genital system, including dose-related increases in leiomyomas of the mesovarium. In addition, dose-related increases in the incidence of ovarian cysts were seen at all dose levels except 2000 mg/kg. A 21-month study in mice at oral doses of 5, 50, and 200 mg/kg (corresponding to 17, 167, and 667 times the recommended daily adult oral dose, respectively) found no evidence of carcinogenicity.

Mutagenicity

Mutagenicity—

Albuterol—No evidence of mutagenicity was found in the Ames test with or without metabolic activation using tester strains *Salmonella typhimurium* TA1537, TA1538, and TA98 or *Escherichia coli* WP2, WP2uvrA, and WP67. No forward mutation occurred in yeast strain *Saccharomyces cerevisiae* S9 nor any mitotic gene conversion in yeast *S. cerevisiae* JD1 with or without metabolic activation. Results of fluctuation assays in *S. typhimurium* TA98 and *E. coli* WP2, both with metabolic activation, were negative. Albuterol was not found to be clastogenic in a human peripheral lymphocyte assay or in an AH1 strain mouse micronucleus assay at intraperitoneal doses of up to 200 mg/kg.

Epinephrine—Studies have not been done.

Isoproterenol—Studies have not been done.

Metaproterenol—Studies have not been done.

Terbutaline—Studies have not been done.

Pregnancy/Reproduction

Pregnancy—

Albuterol—

Adequate and well-controlled studies in humans have not been done. Albuterol crosses the placenta. In a surveillance study of 1090 Michigan Medicaid recipients whose newborns were exposed to albuterol during the first trimester, 43 major defects were expected and 48 were observed (including cardiovascular defects, oral clefts, spina bifida, limb reduction defects, hypospadias, and polydactyly). Only with the occurrence of polydactyly was there a suggestion of a possible association; however, the mother's disease severity and concurrent medication use may also have been a factor.

Albuterol may delay preterm labor. Caution is recommended with use for bronchospasm in pregnant patients because of possible interference with uterine contractility.

Albuterol also has been reported to cause maternal and fetal tachycardia and hyperglycemia (especially in patients with diabetes), as well as maternal hypotension, acute congestive heart failure, pulmonary edema, and death.

Studies in mice at subcutaneous doses corresponding to 0.2 times the maximum human (child weighing 21 kg) oral dose found teratogenicity. In CD-1 mice, cleft palate occurred in 5 of 111 fetuses (4.5%) at a dose of 0.25 mg/kg and in 10 of 108 fetuses (9.3%) at a dose of 2.5 mg/kg (approximately 3/100 and 3/10 the maximum recommended daily oral dose for adults on a mg/m^2 basis, respectively). Cleft palate also occurred in 22 of 72 fetuses (30.5%) in a control group treated with isoproterenol 2.5 mg/kg subcutaneously (approximately 3/10 the maximum recommended daily oral dose for adults on a mg/m^2 basis)

A study in Stride Dutch rabbits at oral doses of 50 mg/kg (approximately 25 times the maximum recommended daily oral dose for adults on a mg/m^2 basis) found cranioschisis in 7 of 19 (37%) fetuses.

FDA Pregnancy Category C.

Ephedrine—

Although adequate and well-controlled studies in humans have not been done, the Collaborative Perinatal Project monitored 373 and 873 mother-child pairs exposed to ephedrine during their first trimester and any time during pregnancy, respectively. For use in the first trimester, an association was found between sympathomimetic drugs as a class and minor malformations, inguinal hernia, and clubfoot.

Studies in animals have not been done.

Ephedrine is contraindicated when maternal blood pressure exceeds 130/80 mmHg.

FDA Pregnancy Category C.

Epinephrine—

Epinephrine crosses the placenta. Although adequate and well-controlled studies in humans have not been done, the Collaborative Perinatal Project monitored 189 mother-child pairs having first trimester exposure to epinephrine. A statistically significant association was found between first trimester use and both major and minor malformations. An association also was found with inguinal hernia after both first trimester use and use any time during pregnancy. Although not specified, these data may reflect the mother's asthma severity.

A surveillance study of 35 Michigan Medicaid recipients whose newborns were exposed to epinephrine during the first trimester showed no association between use of the drug and the development of congenital defects.

Theoretically, the alpha-adrenergic effects of epinephrine could cause a decrease in uterine blood flow, and one case of fetal anoxic damage has been reported after intravenous administration.

Studies in rats at doses of 25 times the human dose have found that epinephrine causes teratogenicity.

Epinephrine is contraindicated when maternal blood pressure exceeds 130/80 mm Hg.

Epinephrine, administered subcutaneously, may be considered in acute, severe exacerbations of asthma, following the unsuccessful use of other therapies.

FDA Pregnancy Category C.

Isoproterenol—

Adequate and well-controlled studies in humans have not been done. In a surveillance study of 16 Michigan Medicaid recipients whose newborns were exposed to isoproterenol during the first trimester, 0.7 major defects were expected and one major defect (oral cleft) was observed. The Collaborative Perinatal Project monitored 31 mother-child pairs who had first trimester exposure to isoproterenol. No association was found between use of the drug and subsequent development of congenital defects. For use in the first trimester, an association was found between sympathomimetic drugs as a class and minor malformations, inguinal hernia, and clubfoot.

The beta-adrenergic effects of isoproterenol may result in inhibition of contractions of the pregnant uterus.

Studies in animals found evidence of teratogenicity.

FDA Pregnancy Category C.

Metaproterenol—

Adequate and well-controlled studies in humans have not been done. In a surveillance study of 361 Michigan Medicaid recipients whose newborns were exposed to metaproterenol during the first trimester, 15 major birth defects were expected and 17 were observed. Only with the occurrence of polydactyly was there a suggestion of a possible association; however, the mother's disease severity and concurrent medication use may also have been a factor.

Metaproterenol can also cause maternal and fetal tachycardia, as well as maternal hyperglycemia and hypotension and fetal hypoglycemia.

Studies in rabbits at oral doses of 100 mg/kg, corresponding to 62 times the MRHD, found teratogenicity and embryotoxicity (including skeletal abnormalities, hydrocephalus, and skull bone separation). Studies in mice at oral doses of 50 mg/kg (31 times the MRHD) also found embryotoxicity. Other studies in rabbits, rats, and mice found no teratogenic, embryotoxic, or fetotoxic effects.

FDA Pregnancy Category C.

Terbutaline—

Adequate and well-controlled studies in humans have not been done.

Terbutaline crosses the placenta. Studies using single intravenous doses found umbilical blood concentrations ranging from 11 to 48% of maternal blood concentrations.

In a surveillance study of 149 Michigan Medicaid recipients whose newborns were exposed to terbutaline during the first trimester, six major defects were expected and seven occurred (including three cardiovascular defects and one oral cleft). The data did not support an association between the medication and congenital defects.

Terbutaline can cause transient maternal and fetal tachycardia, as well as maternal hyperglycemia (followed by an increase in serum insulin concentrations) and hypotension and fetal hypoglycemia. There has been a single report of myocardial necrosis in an infant, possibly caused by catecholamine excess, and one unexplained intrapartum fetal death.

Studies in mice at subcutaneous doses of up to 1.1 mg/kg (corresponding to 4 times the human oral dose or 110 times the human subcutaneous dose) and in rats at oral doses of up to 50 mg/kg (corresponding to 167 times the human oral dose) found no harmful effects on the fetus.

FDA Pregnancy Category B.

Labor and delivery—

Albuterol—

There have been reports of delayed preterm labor after administration of albuterol. Although albuterol has been used for initial treatment to suppress premature labor and delay premature delivery, caution is recommended because of the potential for adverse effects (including maternal tachycardia, hyperglycemia, and hypotension and fetal tachycardia and hypoglycemia).

Epinephrine—

May delay the second stage of labor. Doses sufficient to reduce uterine contractions may cause prolonged uterine atony with hemorrhage.

Isoproterenol—

Decreases uterine contractility in humans and animals.

Metaproterenol—

Decreases uterine contractility.

Terbutaline—

Terbutaline delays preterm labor. Although terbutaline is being used for initial treatment to suppress premature labor and delay premature delivery, caution is recommended because of the potential for adverse effects (including maternal tachycardia, hyperglycemia, and hypotension and fetal tachycardia and hypoglycemia).

Breast-feeding

Albuterol—It is not known whether albuterol is distributed into human breast milk.

Ephedrine—It is not known whether ephedrine is distributed into human breast milk. Irritability, excessive crying, and disturbed sleeping pattern were reported in the breast-fed infant of a mother taking a long-acting preparation containing *d*-isoephedrine and dexbrompheniramine; the symptoms resolved when breast-feeding was discontinued.

Epinephrine—Epinephrine is distributed into human breast milk. Risk-benefit should be considered because of potential adverse effects in the nursing infant.

Isoproterenol—It is not known whether isoproterenol is distributed into human breast milk. However, risk-benefit should be considered.

Metaproterenol—It is not known whether metaproterenol is distributed into human breast milk. However, risk-benefit should be considered.

Terbutaline—Terbutaline is distributed into breast milk, although no adverse effects have been reported in nursing infants. Risk-benefit should be considered before breast-feeding during treatment with terbutaline.

Pediatrics

In infants with asthma, response to beta$_2$-adrenergic receptor agonist therapy can be variable and may not be a reliable predictor of satisfactory outcome.

Albuterol—The safety and efficacy of albuterol tablets in children younger than 6 years of age have not been established. The safety and efficacy of albuterol oral solution or syrup in children under 2 years of age have not been established.The incidence of excitement and nervousness may be increased in children 2 to 6 years of age.

Ephedrine—Use has been replaced by safer and more effective agents.

Isoproterenol—Appropriated studies on the relationship of age to the effects of isoproterenol have not been performed in the pediatric population. However, no pediatrics-specific problems have been documented to date.

Metaproterenol—Safety and efficacy of the tablets in children younger than 6 years of age have not been established. Safety and efficacy of the syrup in children younger than 6 years of age have been established in only a limited number of patients.

Terbutaline—Safety and efficacy in children younger than 6 years of age have not been established.

Geriatrics

Older adults, especially those with pre-existing ischemic heart disease, may be more sensitive to the effects of beta-adrenergic receptor agonists, including tremor, hypertension, hypokalemia, and tachycardia. In general, use of inhaled beta$_2$-adrenergic receptor agonists is preferred because they cause fewer systemic side effects than beta$_2$-adrenergic receptor agonists delivered by other routes of administration.

Because of the risk of cardiac stimulation, use of subcutaneous bronchodilators is recommended only in life-threatening situations, with careful electrocardiogram (ECG) monitoring.

Ephedrine—The possibility of urinary retention, especially in elderly males with prostatism, as a result of contraction of the bladder sphincter should be kept in mind.

Dental

Unpredictable systemic absorption can occur with topical application of epinephrine to the gingival or pulpal tissues.

Drug interactions and/or related problems

The following drug interactions and/or related problems have been selected on the basis of their potential clinical significance (possible mechanism in parentheses where appropriate)—not necessarily inclusive (» = major clinical significance):

Note: Combinations containing any of the following medications depending on the amount present, may also interact with this medication.

Acidifiers, urinary
(may decrease the half-life of ephedrine by decreasing tubular reabsorption, which may lead to decreased effects)

Alkalizers, urinary
(may increase the half-life and decrease elimination of ephedrine by increasing tubular reabsorption, which may lead to increased effects)

Alpha-adrenergic blocking agents, such as:
Doxazosin
Labetalol
Phenoxybenzamine
Phentolamine
Prazosin
Terazosin
Tolazoline or
Other medications with alpha-adrenergic blocking action, such as:
Haloperidol
Phenothiazines
Thioxanthenes
(concurrent use may antagonize the peripheral vasoconstriction and hypertensive effects of sympathomimetic agents; phentolamine may be used for therapeutic benefit, such as in ephedrine overdose)

» Anesthetics, hydrocarbon inhalation, such as:
Chloroform

Enflurane
Halothane
Methoxyflurane
(administration of sympathomimetic agents, especially ephedrine, epinephrine, or isoproterenol, to patients receiving these anesthetics may increase the risk of severe atrial and ventricular arrhythmias because these anesthetics greatly sensitize the myocardium to the effects of sympathomimetic agents; arrhythmias may respond to administration of a beta-blocking agent; use of a pressor drug with less severe cardiac-stimulating effects should be considered)

» Antidepressants, tricyclic
(tricyclic antidepressants block reuptake of sympathomimetic agents in the neuron, which may increase the pressor response to direct-acting sympathomimetic agents and decrease sensitivity to indirect-acting sympathomimetic agents; caution is recommended with concurrent use)
(may add to the QTc interval prolongation caused by beta-adrenergic receptor agonists)

Antidiabetic agents, oral or
Insulin
(concurrent use with epinephrine may result in decreased effects of these medications because epinephrine increases blood glucose by inhibiting glucose uptake by peripheral tissues and promotes glycogenolysis; increased doses of these medications may be required)

Antihypertensives
(sympathomimetic agents may increase blood pressure and interfere with the hypotensive effects of these medications; the patient should be carefully monitored to confirm that the desired effect is being obtained)
(concurrent use of epinephrine with guanadrel or guanethidine may increase the pressor effect of epinephrine as a result of inhibition of sympathomimetic uptake by adrenergic neurons, possibly resulting in hypertension and cardiac arrhythmias)
(ephedrine may decrease the hypotensive effects of guanadrel or guanethidine by causing displacement from and inhibiting uptake by adrenergic neurons)
(concurrent use with methyldopa may decrease the hypotensive effect of methyldopa and potentiate the pressor effect of sympathomimetic agents)
(guanethidine, methyldopa, or reserpine may reduce the pressor response to indirectly-acting sympathomimetic agents such as ephedrine by reducing the amount of norepinephrine in sympathetic nerve endings)

Astemizole or
Cisapride or
Terfenadine or
Medications that prolong the QTc interval, other
(may add to the QTc interval prolongation caused by beta-adrenergic receptor agonists)

» Beta-adrenergic blocking agents, ophthalmic
(ophthalmic beta-adrenergic blocking agents are absorbed systemically via the nasolacrimal duct; respiratory complications associated with the use of timolol have been reported and include bronchospasm, dyspnea, wheezing, decreased pulmonary function, and respiratory failure; therefore, concurrent use may result in inhibition of the beta-adrenergic effects of the adrenergic bronchodilators and worsening of bronchospasm)

» Beta-adrenergic blocking agents, systemic
(may block the cardiostimulating and bronchodilating effects of sympathomimetic agents and can cause bronchospasm on their own; concurrent use in asthmatic patients can lead to severe asthmatic attacks and is not recommended; it is recommended that patients receiving treatment for both bronchospastic disease and hypertension receive an alternative medication to a beta-blocker for the hypertension)
(the use of epinephrine may be hazardous in patients who are receiving nonselective beta-adrenergic blocking agents since its unopposed actions on vascular $alpha_1$-adrenergic receptors may lead to severe hypertension and cerebral hemorrhage; epinephrine retraction cords, used in the treatment of gingival or pulpal hemorrhage, should be avoided in patients taking beta-adrenergic blocking agents due to the potential systemic vasoconstriction)

» Cocaine, mucosal-local
(in addition to increasing CNS stimulation, concurrent use with sympathomimetic agents may increase the cardiovascular effects of either or both medications and the risk of adverse effects)
(concurrent use of epinephrine with cocaine [especially intranasal application of epinephrine and cocaine, which is potentially lethal] is not recommended because of the high risk of hypertensive episodes and cardiac arrhythmias; also, concurrent topical use of cocaine and epinephrine is unnecessary because epinephrine does not provide additional local vasoconstriction, slow absorption of cocaine from the mucosa, or prolong cocaine's duration of action)

» Diatrizoates or
» Iothalamate or
» Ioversol or
» Ioxaglate
(neurologic effects, including paraplegia, may increase during aortography when these agents are administered after vasopressor agents used to increase contrast; this increase is due to contraction of vessels in the splanchnic circulation, which forces more of the contrast material into the vessels leading to the spine and spinal cord)

Digitalis glycosides
(a single dose of albuterol has been reported to result in a 16 to 22% decrease in serum digoxin concentrations in patients who have received digoxin for 10 days; although the clinical significance in obstructive airway disease has not been established, monitoring of serum digoxin concentrations is recommended)
($beta_2$-adrenergic–induced hypokalemia could lead to digitalis toxicity)
(concurrent use with sympathomimetic agents possessing $beta_1$-adrenergic activity may increase the risk of cardiac arrhythmias; caution and close ECG monitoring are very important if concurrent use is necessary)

Ergot alkaloids
(concurrent use with sympathomimetic agents may result in enhanced vasoconstriction and pressor effects; concurrent use of ergotamine may produce peripheral vascular ischemia and gangrene and is not recommended)

Hypokalemia-causing medications, other (see *Appendix II*)
(possibility of increased effects, especially with high doses of sympathomimetic agents; monitoring of serum potassium concentrations and cardiac function is recommended with concurrent use)

» Medications that sensitize the myocardium to the actions of sympathomimetic agents (e.g., digitalis glycosides, quinidine)
(caution is recommended with concurrent use because sympathomimetic agents can cause arrhythmias; caution and close ECG monitoring are very important if concurrent use is necessary)

» Monoamine oxidase (MAO) inhibitors, including furazolidone, procarbazine, and selegiline
(pressor effects of indirect-acting sympathomimetic agents may be potentiated; indirect-acting sympathomimetics cause the release of catecholamines, which accumulate in intraneuronal storage sites during MAO inhibitor therapy, and may result in severe hypertension, headache, and hyperpyrexia that could lead to hypertensive crisis; extreme caution is recommended when indirect-acting sympathomimetic agents are given during or within 2 weeks after therapy with these agents)

» Sympathomimetic agents, other
(concurrent use may result in increased effects, including unwanted cardiovascular effects, and is not recommended; however, one sympathomimetic may be substituted for another once the effects of the preceding medication have subsided; this also does not preclude use of an aerosol adrenergic bronchodilator for relief of acute bronchospasm in patients receiving chronic oral adrenergic bronchodilator therapy)

Theophylline
(Enhanced toxicity, especially cardiotoxicity has been reported with use with sympathomimetic agents, particularly isoproterenol; concurrent use with ephedrine may result in increased nausea, nervousness, and insomnia; isoproterenol increases theophylline clearance resulting in decreased theophylline concentrations; theophylline plasma concentrations should be monitored)

» Thyroid hormones
(concurrent use may increase the effects of these medications or thyroid hormone; thyroid hormones enhance the risk of coronary insufficiency when sympathomimetic agents are administered to patients with coronary artery disease)

Laboratory value alterations

The following have been selected on the basis of their potential clinical significance (possible effect in parentheses where appropriate)—not necessarily inclusive (» = major clinical significance).

With physiology/ laboratory test values
» Blood pressure and
» Heart rate
(may be increased)
Electrocardiogram (ECG) changes, including:
T-wave flattening
QTc-interval prolongation
ST-segment depression
(arrythmias may occur, usually following hypokalemia)
» Glucose
(blood glucose concentrations may be increased)
Hepatic enzymes
(serum values may be increased with high doses of terbutaline)
Lactic acid
(serum values may be increased; may result in severe metabolic acidosis after prolonged use or overdose of epinephrine)
» Potassium
(serum concentrations may be decreased, possibly as a result of intracellular shunting)

Medical considerations/Contraindications

The medical considerations/contraindications included have been selected on the basis of their potential clinical significance (reasons given in parentheses where appropriate)—not necessarily inclusive (» = major clinical significance).

Risk-benefit should be considered when the following medical problems exist:

For all sympathomimetics
» Cardiac disease, including:
Cardiac arrhythmias, especially tachyarrhythmias or
Ischemic heart disease
(beta-adrenergic receptor agonists can cause arrhythmias and ECG changes, including T-wave flattening, QTc-interval prolongation, and ST-segment depression)
(epinephrine may precipitate or aggravate angina pectoris or may produce potentially fatal ventricular arrhythmias)
(isoproterenol increases cardiac oxygen requirements while decreasing effective coronary artery perfusion)
» Diabetes mellitus
(sympathomimetic agents can cause hyperglycemia, followed by increased insulin concentrations, which may aggravate pre-existing diabetes mellitus and ketoacidosis; increased insulin or hypoglycemic medication doses may be required; concurrent administration of sympathomimetic agents and corticosteroids may exaggerate this hyperglycemic effect)
» Hypertension or
» Hyperthyroidism
(sympathomimetic agents can cause significant increases in systolic and diastolic blood pressure)
(incidence of side/adverse effects may be increased)
» Seizures, history of
(may exacerbate condition)
» Sensitivity to the sympathomimetic prescribed

For albuterol extended-release tablets (in addition to the above)
Gastrointestinal narrowing, pre-existing
(there have been rare reports of gastrointestinal obstruction from the delivery system for albuterol extended-release tablets)

For ephedrine or epinephrine (in addition to the above)
» Cerebral arteriosclerosis or
» Brain damage, organic
(vasoconstriction caused by epinephrine may reduce cerebral blood flow)
Glaucoma, narrow-angle
(may be exacerbated by sympathomimetic agents with alpha$_1$-adrenergic activity)
Parkinson's disease
(rigidity and tremor may worsen temporarily after epinephrine administration)
Prostatic hypertrophy
(urinary retention may occur with ephedrine administration as a result of vesical sphincter spasm)
» Psychoneurotic disorders
(symptoms may worsen with epinephrine administration)
» Shock, nonasthmatic (i.e., cardiogenic, traumatic, or hemorrhagic)
(administration of epinephrine is not recommended)

For isoproterenol (in addition to the above)
» Cardiac disease, organic, including organic disease of the atrioventricular (AV) node and its branches
(isoproterenol may paradoxically worsen heart block or precipitate Adams-Stokes attacks during normal sinus rhythm or transient block)

For metaproterenol (in addition to the above)
Sensitivity to parabens
(formulations of metaproterenol sulfate oral syrup contain parabens)

Patient monitoring

The following may be especially important in patient monitoring (other tests may be warranted in some patients, depending on condition; » = major clinical significance):

For all indications
» ECG
(recommended routinely, especially with high doses, although cardiac arrhythmias can occur with epinephrine even at therapeutic doses)
Potassium concentrations, serum
(monitoring of serum potassium concentrations may be appropriate, especially in patients taking other medications that may induce hypokalemia, such as non-potassium-sparing diuretics)

For use as a bronchodilator
» Arterial blood gas determinations
(arterial blood gas measurements are recommended if PEF is 150 L per minute or less)
» Pulmonary function studies, including:
Peak expiratory flow (PEF)
Spirometry
(recommended at regular intervals to monitor progress)

Side/Adverse Effects

Note: Most side/adverse effects are mild and transient.
Tolerance to the side/adverse effects usually develops within weeks or lesswith regular use, although it does not occur consistently.

The following side/adverse effects have been selected on the basis of their potential clinical significance (possible signs and symptoms in parentheses where appropriate)–not necessarily inclusive:

Those indicating need for medical attention

Incidence more frequent
Palpitation (pounding heartbeat); ***tachycardia*** (fast heartbeat)
Note: For isoproterenol, doses sufficient to cause *tachycardia* with greater than 130 beats per minute may increase the risk of inducing ventricular arrhythmias. Such increases may also increase cardiac workload and oxygen requirements, which may adversely affect the failing heart or the heart with a significant degree of arteriosclerosis.

Incidence rare
Adams-Stokes attacks (fainting)—for isoproterenol; ***allergic reactions; including angioedema*** (hoarseness; large hive-like swellings on eyelids, face, genitals, hands or feet, lips, throat, tongue; sudden trouble in swallowing or breathing); ***bronchospasm*** (trouble in breathing); ***oropharyngeal edema*** (tightness in throat; trouble in breathing); ***skin rash; or urticaria*** (hives); ***bronchospasm, paradoxical*** (shortness of breath)—for albuterol or terbutaline; ***cardiac arrhythmias*** (fast or irregular heartbeat); ***chest pain; hypokalemia*** (irregular heartbeat; muscle cramps or pain; unusual tiredness or weakness); ***severe reaction; including erythema multiforme*** (reaction starting with chills; fever; general feeling of illness; muscle aches or pains; sore throat; and/or nausea with or without vomiting; followed by sores, ulcers, or white spots in mouth or on lips; skin rash or sores; hives; and/or itching); ***and Stevens-Johnson syndrome*** (bleeding or crusting sores on lips; chest pain; fever with or without chills; muscle cramps or pain; painful eyes; painful sores, ulcers, or white spots in mouth; skin rash; sore throat; red or irritated eyes)—with oral albuterol in children; ***hypertension*** (increase in blood pressure)—asymptomatic; more common for epinephrine; ***psychoneurotic disorders; including psychomotor agitation; disorientation; impairment of memory; assaultive behavior; panic; hallucinations; suicidal or homicidal tendencies; schizophrenic-type thought disorder; or paranoid delusions*** (mental problems)—for epinephrine; ***seizures***—for terbutaline; ***urinary hesitation or retention*** (trouble in urinating)—more common for terbutaline
Note: In a few patients, presumably with organic disease of the AV node and its branches, isoproterenol injection has been reported to precipitate *Adams-Stokes* attacks during normal sinus rhythm or transient heart block.
Cardiac arrhythmias induced by epinephrine have included fatal ventricular fibrillation.

Paradoxical bronchospasm may be life-threatening.

For ephedrine or epinephrine, excessive doses or inadvertent intravenous administration of usual subcutaneous doses can cause acute *hypertension*. Rapid increases in arterial blood pressure can lead to cerebral hemorrhage, especially in elderly patients, or to angina pectoris, aortic rupture, hemiplegia, or subarachnoid hemorrhage.

Seizures also may occur with overdose of other sympathomimetic agents.

Urinary hesitation occurs as the result of vesical sphincter spasm. *Urinary retention* may develop in males with prostatism.

Those indicating need for medical attention only if they continue or are bothersome

Incidence more frequent

Anxiety—for epinephrine; ***headache; nervousness; tremor***

Incidence less frequent

Dizziness; insomnia (trouble in sleeping); ***muscle cramps; nausea; sweating; vertigo*** (feeling of constant movement of self or surroundings); ***vomiting***

Overdose

For specific information on the agents used in the management of bronchodilators, adrenergic overdose, see:

- *Anesthetics, Barbiturate (Systemic)*monograph;
- *Anesthetics, Inhalation (Systemic)* monograph;
- *Anticonvulsants, Hydantoin (Systemic) monograph;*
- *Barbiturates (Systemic)* monograph;
- *Benzodiazepines (Systemic)* monograph;
- *Beta-adrenergic Blocking Agents (Systemic)* monograph;
- *Charcoal, Activated (Oral-Local)* monograph;
- *Ipecac (Oral-Local)* monograph;
- *Nitroprusside (Systemic)* monograph;
- *Phentolamine (Systemic)* monograph;
- *Sympathomimetic Agents—Cardiovascular Use (Parenteral-Systemic)* monograph.

For more information on the managment of overdose or unintentional ingestion, *contact a Poison Control Center* (see *Poison Control Center Listing*).

Clinical effects of overdose

Note: In general, symptoms of overdose reflect excessive beta-adrenergic stimulation or exaggeration of side/adverse effects. In addition, ephedrine or epinephrine overdose would be expected to produce alpha-adrenergic effects.

The following effects have been selected on the basis of their potential clinical significance (possible signs and symptoms in parentheses where appropriate)–not necessarily inclusive:

Acute

For albuterol, isoproterenol, metaproterenol, and terbutaline

Angina; arrhythmias; dizziness; dry mouth; fatigue; headache; hyperglycemia (followed by rebound hypoglycemia); hypertension or hypotension; hypokalemia; insomnia; malaise; nausea; nervousness; palpitation; seizures; tachycardia (with rates up to 200 beats per minute); tremor

For ephedrine

Blurred vision; chills; dilated pupils; fever; gasping respirations; hypertension, followed by hypotension accompanied by anuria; irritability; nausea; nervousness; opisthotonos; personality changes, including craving for the medication; pulmonary edema; respiratory failure; seizures; spasms; suicidal behavior; tachyarrhythmias; tachycardia; vomiting

Note: *Hypertension* occurs initially, and may be followed by *hypotension* (when depletion of norepinephrine from nerves endings ends pressor effects) and *anuria*. Suddenly elevated blood pressure may lead to cerebrovascular hemorrhage.

The *craving for the medication* is psychological.

The probable lethal dose in adults is 50 mg per kg of body weight (mg/kg). The minimum lethal dose in children up to 2 years of age is approximately 200 mg.

For epinephrine

Arterial blood pressure elevation, extreme; bradycardia, transient, followed by tachycardia; coldness of skin; dyspnea; headache; metabolic acidosis; myocardial infarct; pallor, extreme; pulmonary edema; renal failure; vomiting

Note: Suddenly *elevated arterial blood pressure* may lead to cerebrovascular hemorrhage, particularly in elderly patients, or to angina pectoris, aortic rupture, hemiplegia, or subarachnoid hemorrhage.

With *pulmonary edema*, peripheral vascular constriction together with cardiac stimulation may lead to fatalities.

Tachycardia may be accompanied by potentially fatal cardiac arrhythmias, including ventricular fibrillation. Ventricular premature contractions may occur within 1 minute after injection, followed by multilocal ventricular tachycardia (prefibrillation rhythm); subsidence of ventricular effects may be followed by atrial tachycardia and occasionally by atrioventricular (AV) block.

Chronic

For ephedrine

Anxiety and tension, possibly leading to psychosis; nasal congestion, chronic

Note: *Anxiety and tension* may progress to psychosis.

Nasal congestion occurs as a result of prolonged exposure of the nasal mucosa to the medication.

Prolonged abuse can lead to a syndrome resembling an anxiety state (including symptoms of paranoid schizophrenia and other physical signs including tachycardia, poor nutrition and hygiene, fever, cold sweat, and dilated pupils).

Treatment of overdose

Albuterol—

Withdrawal of albuterol.

Symptomatic treatment.

For tachyarrhythmias—Judicious use of a cardioselective beta-adrenergic blocking agent, if necessary; however, caution is necessary because of the possible induction of bronchospasm by the beta-blocker.

Ephedrine—

Protect the patient's airway and support ventilation and perfusion.

Monitor and maintain, within acceptable limits, the patient's vital signs, blood gases, and serum electrolytes.

Decrease absorption from the gastrointestinal tract with activated charcoal (may be more effective than emesis or lavage); consider charcoal instead of or in addition to gastric emptying; repeated doses of charcoal may hasten elimination of absorbed drug. (It is important to safeguard the patient's airway during these procedures.)

For marked hypertension, consider use of nitroprusside or phentolamine infusion.

For hypotension, consider use of intravenous fluids, elevation of the legs, or inotropic vasopressors such as norepinephrine.

For life-threatening supraventricular or ventricular tachycardias, treat with slow intravenous administration of propranolol, with continuous monitoring of the ECG and vital signs.

For seizures, consider use of diazepam, phenytoin, or phenobarbital. For refractory seizures, general anesthesia with thiopental or halothane and paralysis with a neuromuscular blocking agent may be necessary.

Epinephrine—

Because epinephrine is rapidly inactivated in the body, treatment is primarily supportive.

Pressor effects may be counteracted by rapidly acting vasodilators or alpha-adrenergic blocking agents. If prolonged hypotension follows this treatment, it may be necessary to administer another pressor (e.g., norepinephrine).

If pulmonary edema interferes with respiration, treatment with a rapidly acting alpha-adrenergic blocking agent (e.g., phentolamine) and/or intermittent positive-pressure respiration is recommended.

For arrhythmias, consider administration of a beta-adrenergic blocking agent (e.g., propranolol).

For metabolic acidosis or renal failure, use suitable corrective measures.

Isoproterenol—

Reduce the rate of administration or discontinue the injection until the patient's condition stabilizes.

Monitor blood pressure, pulse, respiration, and ECG.

Metaproterenol—

Discontinue metaproterenol.

Symptomatic treatment.

Terbutaline—

If the patient is alert, empty the stomach by inducing emesis, followed by gastric lavage.

If the patient is unconscious, secure the airway with a cuffed endotracheal tube before beginning lavage (and do not induce emesis).

Instillation of activated charcoal slurry may help reduce absorption.

Maintain adequate respiratory exchange.
Provide cardiac and respiratory support.
Continue observation until the patient is symptom-free.

Patient Consultation

As an aid to patient consultation, refer to *Advice for the Patient, Bronchodilators, Adrenergic (Oral/Injection).*

In providing consultation, consider emphasizing the following selected information (» = major clinical significance):

Before using this medication

» Conditions affecting use, especially:
- Sensitivity to the sympathomimetic prescribed
- Pregnancy—Possible malformations including inguinal hernia and clubfoot; teratogenicity with epinephrine; risks with pre-existing hypertension or hyperglycemia
- Labor and/or delivery—
- Beta-adrenergiic receptor agonists may decrease uterine contractions and delay labor
- Breast-feeding—Epinephrine and terbutaline distributed into breast milk; consider risk-benefit for all agents
- Use in the elderly—May be more sensitive to tremor, hypertension, or tachycardia, especially those patients with pre-existing ischemic heart disease
- Other medications, especially tricyclic antidepressants, MAO inhibitors, ophthalmic or systemic beta-adrenergic blocking agents, cocaine, medications that sensitize the myocardium to the actions of sympathomimetic agents, other sympathomimetic agents, or thyroid hormones
- Other medical problems, especially cardiac arrhythmias, ischemic heart disease, diabetes mellitus, hypertension, hyperthyroidism, history of seizures, cerebral arteriosclerosis (for epinephrine), organic brain damage (for epinephrine), psychoneurotic disorders (for epinephrine), or organic heart disease (for isoproterenol)

Proper use of this medication

» Compliance with therapy; importance of not using more medication than prescribed

Proper administration of extended-release albuterol tablets: Swallowing tablets whole without breaking, crushing, or chewing

» Proper dosing

Missed dose: If taken regularly, taking as soon as possible; not taking if almost time for next dose; not doubling doses

» Proper storage

For use as a bronchodilator

» Having a rapid-acting inhaled beta-adrenergic bronchodilator available for symptomatic relief of acute asthma attacks

For epinephrine

Knowing correct administration technique
With intramuscular use:
- Injecting into the thigh
- Not injecting into the buttock to avoid vasoconstriction

Not using if solution is discolored or cloudy
Keeping medication on hand and checking expiration date regularly

For epinephrine for emergency treatment of allergic reactions

» Using medication at first sign of allergic reaction
» Notifying physician immediately and/or going to nearest hospital emergency room

If stung by an insect, carefully removing insect's stinger to avoid additional venom from being released from the sac; applying ice packs or sodium bicarbonate soaks, if available, to area stung

For epinephrine auto-injector

» Reading patient instructions carefully before needed

Importance of not removing safety cap before ready to use
Knowing correct administration technique—
- Removing gray safety cap
- Placing black tip on the side of the thigh (mid-thigh area) at right angle to leg
- Pressing hard into thigh until auto-injector functions; holding in place several seconds; removing and discarding properly
- Massaging injection site for 10 seconds

Precautions while using this medication

» Regular visits to physician to check progress during therapy
» Not taking other medications, especially nonprescription sympathomimetic agents, unless discussed with physician

Patients with diabetes: May increase blood glucose concentrations

For use as a bronchodilator:

» Checking with physician immediately if more doses than usual are needed, or if using a rapid-acting inhaled beta-adrenergic bronchodilator to relieve symptoms more than two times per week (for mild asthma) or daily (for moderate to severe persistent asthma)

For epinephrine:

» Checking with physician immediately if severe pain occurs at injection site

For epinephrine auto-injector:

» Avoiding accidental injection into the hands or feet due to the potential for vasocontriction in these areas; getting emergency attention immediately if this occurs

Side/adverse effects

Signs of potential side effects, especially palpitation, tachycardia, Adams-Stokes attacks (for isoproterenol), allergic reactions, paradoxical bronchospasm (for albuterol or terbutaline), cardiac arrhythmias, chest pain, erythema multiforme or Stevens-Johnson syndrome (for oral albuterol in children), hypertension, psychoneurotic disorders (for epinephrine), seizures (for terbutaline), and urinary retention

Albuterol extended-release tablets: Shell may appear in stool

General Dosing Information

For use in asthma

Daily use or increasing frequency of use of supplemental short-acting inhaled $beta_2$-adrenergic receptor agonists may indicate a loss of asthma control and the need for an adjustment in therapy.

There is some evidence of development of tolerance to the bronchodilating effects of beta-adrenergic receptor agonists (due to down regulation of beta-adrenergic receptors), although clinical significance has not been established.

For treatment of adverse effects

Recommended treatment consists of the following:
- Pressor effects, marked—Administration of rapidly acting vasodilators such as nitrites or alpha-adrenergic blocking agents.

ALBUTEROL

Summary of Differences

Pharmacology/pharmacokinetics: Primarily stimulates $beta_2$-adrenergic receptors, with some minor $beta_1$-adrenergic activity.

Pediatrics: Increased incidence of excitement and nervousness in children 2 to 6 years of age.

Medical considerations/contraindications: Caution in use of extended-release tablets in patients with pre-existing gastrointestinal narrowing.

Side/adverse effects: Paradoxical bronchospasm may occur rarely.

Erythema multiforme and Stevens-Johnson syndrome reported rarely with oral albuterol in children.

Additional Dosing Information

Switching to albuterol sulfate extended-release tablets from maintenance therapy with albuterol sulfate tablets or syrup is acceptable. For example, a dose of one 4-mg extended-release tablet every twelve hours is comparable to a dose of one 2-mg tablet every six hours. Multiples of this regimen up to the maximum recommended daily dose also apply.

Withdrawal of albuterol may be necessary if cardiovascular effects (e.g., hypertension, tachycardia) occur.

It is recommended that albuterol be withdrawn immediately and alternative therapy be instituted, if paradoxical bronchospasm occurs.

Oral Dosage Forms

ALBUTEROL SULFATE ORAL SOLUTION

Note: Dose and strength of albuterol sulfate oral solution are expressed in terms of the base.

Usual adult and adolescent dose

Bronchodilator—

Oral, 2 to 4 mg (base) three or four times a day.

Note: Patients sensitive to beta-adrenergic stimulation should receive an initial dose of 2 mg (base) three or four times a day, increased gradually as needed and tolerated.

Usual adult and adolescent prescribing limits

32 mg (base) per day.

Usual pediatric dose

Bronchodilator—

Children up to 2 years of age: Safety and efficacy have not been established.

Children 2 to 6 years of age: Oral, 100 mcg (0.1 mg) (base) per kg of body weight (up to a maximum of 2 mg) three to four times a day.

Note: Safety and efficacy for chronic therapy have not been established.

Children 6 to 12 years of age—Oral, 2 mg (base) three or four times a day.

Children 12 years of age and older—See *Usual adult and adolescent dose.*

Usual pediatric prescribing limits
Children 2 to 6 years of age—
400 mcg (0.4 mg) (base) per kg of body weight per day in divided doses.
Children 6 to 12 years of age—
8 mg (base) per day in divided doses.
Children 12 years of age and over—
See *Usual adult and adolescent prescribing limits.*

Usual geriatric dose
Bronchodilator—
Initial: Oral, 2 mg (base) three or four times a day.

Strength(s) usually available
U.S.—
Not commercially available.
Canada—
400 mcg (0.4 mg) (base) per mL (Rx) [*Ventolin*].

Packaging and storage
Store at or below 25 °C (77 °F).

ALBUTEROL SULFATE SYRUP

Note: Dose and strength of albuterol sulfate syrup are expressed in terms of the base.

Usual adult and adolescent dose
Bronchodilator—
Oral, 2 to 4 mg (base) three or four times a day. Dosage may be increased gradually, as needed and tolerated, up to a maximum of 8 mg four times a day.

Note: Patients sensitive to beta-adrenergic stimulation should receive an initial dose of 2 mg (base) three or four times a day, increased gradually as needed and tolerated.

Usual adult and adolescent prescribing limits
32 mg (base) per day in divided doses.

Usual pediatric dose
Bronchodilator—
Children up to 2 years of age: Safety and efficacy have not been established.
Children 2 to 6 years of age: Oral, 100 mcg (0.1 mg) (base) per kg of body weight (up to a maximum of 2 mg) three times a day. Dosage may be increased gradually as needed and tolerated, to a maximum of 4 mg three times a day.
Children 6 to 14 years of age: Oral, 2 mg (base) three or four times a day. Dosage may be increased gradually as needed and tolerated, to a maximum of 24 mg per day in divided doses.
Children 14 years of age and older: See *Usual adult and adolescent dose.*

Usual pediatric prescribing limits
Children 2 to 6 years of age: 4 mg (base) three times a day.
Children 6 to 14 years of age: 24 mg (base) per day in divided doses.
Children 14 years of age and older: See *Usual adult and adolescent prescribing limits.*

Usual geriatric dose
Bronchodilator—
Oral, 2 mg (base) three or four times a day, adjusted as needed and tolerated.

Strength(s) usually available
U.S.—
400 mcg (0.4 mg) (base) per mL (Rx) [*Proventil; Ventolin;* GENERIC].
Canada—
Not commercially available.

Packaging and storage
Store between 2 and 30 °C (36 and 86 °F), unless otherwise specified by manufacturer.

ALBUTEROL SULFATE TABLETS

Note: Dose and strength of albuterol sulfate tablets are expressed in terms of the base.

Usual adult and adolescent dose
Bronchodilator—
Oral, 2 to 4 mg (base) three or four times a day. Dosage may be increased gradually, as needed and tolerated, up to a maximum of 8 mg four times a day.

Note: Patients sensitive to beta-adrenergic stimulation should receive an initial dose of 2 mg (base) three or four times a day, increased gradually to a maximum of 8 mg three or four times a day if needed and tolerated.

Usual adult and adolescent prescribing limits
32 mg (base) per day in divided doses.

Usual pediatric dose
Bronchodilator—
Children up to 6 years of age: Safety and efficacy have not been established.
Children 6 to 12 years of age: Oral, 2 mg (base) three or four times a day.
Children 12 years of age and older: See *Usual adult and adolescent dose.*

Usual pediatric prescribing limits
Children 6 to 12 years of age: 24 mg (base) per day in divided doses.
Children 12 years of age and older: See *Usual adult and adolescent prescribing limits.*

Usual geriatric dose
Bronchodilator—
Oral, 2 mg (base) three or four times a day. Dosage may be increased gradually, as needed and tolerated, up to a maximum of 8 mg three or four times a day.

Strength(s) usually available
U.S.—
2 mg (base) (Rx) [*Proventil* (lactose); GENERIC].
4 mg (base) (Rx) [*Proventil* (lactose); GENERIC].
Canada—
Not commercially available.

Packaging and storage
Store between 2 and 25 °C (36 and 77 °F), unless otherwise specified by manufacturer.

ALBUTEROL SULFATE EXTENDED-RELEASE TABLETS

Note: Dose and strength of albuterol sulfate extended-release tablets are expressed in terms of the base.

Usual adult and adolescent dose
Bronchodilator—
Oral, 4 to 8 mg (base) every twelve hours.

Note: In unusual circumstances, such as in adults of low body weight, an initial dose of 4 mg (base) every twelve hours is sufficient, with progression to 8 mg every twelve hours according to response.

If control of reversible airway obstruction is not achieved with the recommended dose, and other asthma therapy is already optimized, the initial dose may be cautiously increased stepwise under the control of the supervising physician to a maximum dose of 32 mg (base) per day in divided doses (i.e., 16 mg every twelve hours).

Usual adult and adolescent prescribing limits
32 mg (base) per day in divided doses (i.e., 16 mg [base] every twelve hours).

Usual pediatric dose
Bronchodilator—
Children up to 6 years of age: Safety and efficacy have not been established.
Children 6 to 12 years of age: Oral, 4 mg (base) every twelve hours.

Note: If control of reversible airway obstruction is not achieved with the recommended dose, and other asthma therapy is already optimized, the initial dose may be cautiously increased stepwise under the control of the supervising physician to a maximum dose of 24 mg (base) per day in divided doses (i.e., 12 mg [base] every twelve hours).

Children 12 years of age and older: See *Usual adult and adolescent dose.*

Usual pediatric prescribing limits
Children 6 to 12 years of age—
24 mg (base) per day in divided doses (i.e., 12 mg [base] every twelve hours).
Children 12 years of age and older—
See *Usual adult and adolescent prescribing limits.*

Strength(s) usually available
U.S.—
4 mg (base) (Rx) [*Proventil Repetabs* (lactose; sugar); *Volmax*].
8 mg (base) (Rx) [*Volmax*].
Canada—
Not commercially available.

Packaging and storage
Store between 2 and 30 °C (36 and 86 °F), unless otherwise specified by manufacturer.

Auxiliary labeling
• Swallow whole.

Parenteral Dosage Forms
Note: Bracketed used in the *Dosage Forms* section refers to categories of use and/or indications that are not included in the U.S. product labeling.

ALBUTEROL SULFATE INJECTION
Note: Dose and strength of albuterol sulfate injection are expressed in terms of the base.

Usual adult dose
Severe bronchospasm and status asthmaticus—
Intramuscular, 500 mcg (0.5 mg) (base) (8 mcg per kg of body weight) every four hours as required.
Intravenous bolus (over two to five minutes), 250 mcg (0.25 mg) (base) (4 mcg per kg of body weight, repeated after fifteen minutes if necessary.
Intravenous infusion (continuous), 5 mcg (0.005 mg) (base) per minute, increased to 10 mcg per minute and then 20 mcg per minute at fifteen- to thirty-minute intervals, if necessary.

Usual adult prescribing limits
Intramuscular: 2 mg (base) per day.
Intravenous bolus: 1 mg (base) per day.

Usual pediatric dose
Dosage has not been established.
[Hyperkalemia][1]—
Continuous infusion, 0.1 mcg (base) per kg of body weight per minute. Or, intravenous bolus, 4.5 mcg (base) per kg body weight over fifteen to twenty minutes.

Strength(s) usually available
U.S.—
Not commercially available.
Canada—
50 mcg (0.05 mg) (base) per mL (Rx) [*Ventolin* (for bolus intravenous injection; sulfuric acid and/or hydrochloric acid)].
500 mcg (0.5 mg) (base) per mL (Rx) [*Ventolin* (for intramuscular injection; sulfuric acid and/or hydrochloric acid)].
1 mg (base) per mL (Rx) [*Ventolin* (for intravenous infusion; sulfuric acid and/or hydrochloric acid)].

Packaging and storage
Store between 15 and 30 °C (59 and 86 °F), unless otherwise specified by manufacturer. Protect from light.

Preparation of dosage form
Albuterol injection (for intravenous infusion) is prepared for administration by diluting 5 mg (base) in 500 mL of a chosen intravenous solution to produce a solution containing 10 mcg (0.01 mg) (base) of albuterol per mL. *This solution must not be injected undiluted; the concentration should be reduced by 50% before administration.* Acceptable intravenous solutions include water for injection, sodium chloride injection, dextrose injection, or sodium chloride and dextrose injection.

Stability
It is recommended that all unused intravenous infusion solutions be discarded 24 hours after preparation.

Incompatibilities
It is recommended that albuterol sulfate injection not be mixed in the same syringe or infused with any other medication.

Auxiliary labeling
• Must be diluted before administration (for solution for intravenous infusion).

Note
Solution for intravenous infusion must be diluted appropriately before administration.

---

[1]Not included in Canadian product labeling.

EPHEDRINE

Summary of Differences
Unaccepted indications: Ephedrine has been used as a bronchodilator, a nasal decongestant, and to treat urinary incontinence; however, it has been generally replaced by safer and more effective medications.

Pharmacology/pharmacokinetics: Stimulates both alpha- and beta-adrenergic receptors. It is also indirect-acting (stimulates release of endogenous norepinephrine from sympathetic neurons, resulting in increased blood pressure and cardiac output). Stimulates CNS.
Drug interactions: Urinary acidifiers or alkalizers, guanadrel, guanethidine.
Medical considerations/contraindications: Brain damage, organic; cerebral arteriosclerosis; glaucoma, narrow-angle; prostatic hypertrophy.

Additional Dosing Information
Some tolerance to the effects of ephedrine occurs, but not addiction. Temporary withdrawal of ephedrine restores responsiveness to the medication.

Oral Dosage Forms
EPHEDRINE SULFATE CAPSULES USP

Usual adult dose
Use has been generally replaced by safer and more effective agents.

Usual pediatric dose
Use has been generally replaced by safer and more effective agents.

Strength(s) usually available
U.S.—
25 mg (OTC) [GENERIC].
50 mg (OTC) [GENERIC].
Canada—
Not commercially available.

Packaging and storage
Store between 15 and 30 °C (59 and 86 °F), unless otherwise specified by manufacturer.

Parenteral Dosage Forms
EPHEDRINE SULFATE INJECTION USP

Usual adult dose
Use has been generally replaced by safer and more effective agents.

Usual pediatric dose
Use has been generally replaced by safer and more effective agents.

Strength(s) usually available
U.S.—
25 mg per mL (Rx) [GENERIC].
50 mg per mL (Rx) [GENERIC].
Canada—
50 mg per mL (Rx) [GENERIC].

Packaging and storage
Store between 15 and 30 °C (59 and 86 °F), unless otherwise specified by manufacturer. Protect from light.

EPINEPHRINE

Summary of Differences
Indications: Allergic reactions, severe; anaphylaxis; anesthesia (local or regional) adjunct; priapism; gingival or pulpal hemorrhage.
Pharmacology/pharmacokinetics: Potent stimulant of both alpha- and beta-adrenergic receptors. Direct-acting.
Drug interactions: Insulin, oral antidiabetic agents, cocaine.
Medical considerations/contraindications: Cardiac disease; cerebral arteriosclerosis; organic brain damage; glaucoma, narrow angle; Parkinson's disease; psychoneurotic disorders; nonasthmatic shock.
Laboratory value alterations: Lactic acid serum values may be increased, which may result in severe metabolic acidosis after prolonged use or overdose of epinephrine.
Side/adverse effects: Hypertension and anxiety are more common. Psychoneurotic disorders occur rarely.
Parenteral administration initially may produce constriction of renal blood vessels and decreased urine formation.
Repeated local injections can cause necrosis at sites of injection as a result of vascular constriction.

Additional Dosing Information
The 1:1000 strength is *only* for subcutaneous or intramuscular use, further dilution to at least 1:10,000 (some clinicians prefer a dilution of 1:100,000) is required before intravenous administration.

The 1:1000 strength may be given by subcutaneous or intramuscular injection. In children, the intramuscular route is preferred due to faster absorption from this route. It is recommended that subcutaneous injection sites be rotated to avoid necrosis from vascular constriction at the injection site.

Injection of epinephrine into areas of the body served by end arteries or with otherwise limited blood supply (fingers, toes, nose, ears, penis) usually is not recommended because of the risk that vasoconstriction will cause sloughing of tissue.

When given intramuscularly, epinephrine should be injected only into the anterolateral aspect of the thigh or the deltoid region of the arm. It should not be injected into the buttock.

Inadvertent vascular administration should be avoided. Accidental intravenous injection of usual subcutaneous doses may lead to cerebral hemorrhage as a result of a sudden sharp rise in blood pressure. Epinephrine should not be administered by intra-arterial injection because marked vasoconstriction may lead to gangrene.

Accidental injection into the hands or feet should be avoided, and requires immediate emergency treatment, because it may lead to loss of blood flow to the affected area. Administration of phentolamine is recommended to treat digital vasoconstriction caused by local administration of epinephrine.

Tolerance may occur with prolonged use.

For additional information regarding use of epinephrine for treatment of anaphylactic shock, see the *Sympathomimetic Agents—Cardiovascular Use (Parenteral-Systemic)* monograph.

Parenteral Dosage Forms

EPINEPHRINE INJECTION

Usual adult and adolescent dose

Allergic reactions, severe or
Anaphylaxis—

Subcutaneous or intramuscular, 300 to 500 mcg (0.3 to 0.5 mg), repeated, if necessary, every ten to twenty minutes for up to three doses.

Intravenous (slow and cautious), 100 to 250 mcg (0.1 to 0.25 mg).

Note: Intravenous administration may be necessary if shock develops, which could reduce absorption of subcutaneous epinephrine.

Only a 1:10,000 epinephrine should be used for intravenous administration.

Bronchospasm, acute—

Subcutaneous, 10 mcg (0.01 mg) per kg of body weight (up to 300 to 500 mcg [0.3 to 0.5 mg]), repeated every twenty minutes as required for up to three doses or

Intravenous (slow and cautious), 100 to 250 mcg (0.1 to 0.25 mg).

Note: Only a 1:10,000 epinephrine solution should be used for intravenous administration.

If an intravenous route cannot be established and the patient has been intubated, the intravenous dose (of the 1:10,000 injection) can be injected via the endotracheal tube directly into the bronchial tree.

Anesthetic (local or regional) adjunct—

For use with local or regional anesthetics: A final concentration of 1:200,000 (5 mcg [0.005 mg] per mL) is recommended for infiltration. However, concentrations may vary depending on the anesthetic agent used.

For use with intraspinal anesthetics: 200 to 400 mcg (0.2 to 0.4 mg) may be mixed with spinal anesthetic agents.

Usual pediatric dose

Allergic reactions, severe or
Anaphylaxis—

Subcutaneous or intramuscular, 10 mcg (0.01 mg) per kg of body weight (up to a maximum of 300 mcg [0.3 mg] per dose), repeated every fifteen minutes if needed for up to three doses.

Bronchospasm, acute—

Subcutaneous, 10 mcg (0.01 mg) per kg of body weight (up to a maximum of 300 mcg [0.3 mg] per dose). The dose may be repeated every fifteen minutes for three or four doses or every four hours as necessary.

Anesthetic (local or regional) adjunct—

For use with local or regional anesthetics: A final concentration of 1:200,000 (5 mcg [0.005 mg] per mL) is recommended for infiltration. However, concentrations may vary depending on the anesthetic agent used.

Usual pediatric prescribing limits

Subcutaneous: 300 mcg (0.3 mg) per dose.

Strength(s) usually available

U.S.—

Note: The 1:10,000 strength is intended only for adult use; it is not recommended for pediatric use. It is also meant for intravenous administration.

Note: The 1:1000 strength is for intramuscular or subcutaneous use only; it *must* be diluted to a 1:10,000 strength for intravenous administration.

Although these preparations contain sulfites, this factor should not prevent the use of epinephrine in life-threatening hypersensitivity reactions or asthma attacks in patients who are sensitive to sulfites.

100 mcg (0.1 mg) per mL (1:10,000) (Rx) [GENERIC (sodium chloride)].

500 mcg (0.5 mg) per mL (1:2000) (0.15 mg per injector) (Rx) [*EpiPen Jr. Auto-Injector* (sodium chloride; sodium metabisulfite; hydrochloric acid)].

1 mg per mL (1:1000) (Rx) [*Adrenalin* (sodium bisulfite); *Ana-Guard* (sodium chloride; chlorobutanol; sodium bisulfite); *EpiPen Auto-Injector* (0.3 mg per injector; sodium chloride; sodium metabisulfite; hydrochloric acid); GENERIC].

Canada—

Note: The 1:10,000 strength is intended only for adult use; it is not recommended for pediatric use. It is also meant for intravenous administration.

Note: The 1:1000 strength is for intramuscular or subcutaneous use only; it *must* be diluted to a 1:10,000 strength for intravenous administration.

Although these preparations contain sulfites, this factor should not prevent the use of epinephrine in life-threatening hypersensitivity reactions or asthma attacks in patients who are sensitive to sulfites.

100 mcg (0.1 mg) per mL (1:10,000) (Rx) [GENERIC].

500 mcg (0.5 mg) per mL (1:2000) (Rx) [*EpiPen Jr.* (sodium chloride; sodium metabisulfite; hydrochloric acid)].

1 mg per mL (1:1000) (Rx) [*Adrenalin* (sulfites); *EpiPen* (sodium chloride; sodium metabisulfite; hydrochloric acid); GENERIC].

Packaging and storage

Store between 15 and 25 °C (59 and 77 °F), unless otherwise specified by manufacturer. Protect from light. Protect from freezing.

Preparation of dosage form

Epinephrine injection 1:1000 may be prepared for intravenous or intrapleural administration by adding one part of the 1:1000 strength to ten parts of sterile water for injection, producting a 1:10,000 solution.

Epinephrine injection 1:10,000 may be used undiluted for intravenous or intrapleural administration.

Stability

Epinephrine is readily oxidized, turning pink from oxidation to adrenochrome and then brown from the formation of polymers. The solution should not be used if it has a pinkish or slightly darker than yellow color or contains a precipitate.

Incompatibilities

Epinephrine is readily destroyed by alkalies, as well as by oxidizing agents (oxygen, chlorine, bromine, iodine, permanganates, chromates, nitrites, and salts of easily reducible metals, especially iron).

Auxiliary labeling

- For subcutaneous or intramuscular use only (for the 1:1000 strength).

Caution

The 1:1000 strength should *not* be used for intravenous administration. Only a 1:10,000 strength may be given intravenously.

Note

For auto-injector—Include patient instructions when dispensing.

ISOPROTERENOL

Summary of Differences

Pharmacology/pharmacokinetics: Nonselective beta-adrenergic receptor agonist.

Medical considerations/contraindications: Caution also is required in patients with organic cardiac disease, including organic disease of the AV node and its branches.

Side/adverse effects: Rarely, Adams-Stokes attacks.

Additional Dosing Information

If the heart rate increases to greater than 110 beats per minute, it may be advisable to decrease the rate of infusion or temporarily discontinue the infusion.

Parenteral Dosage Forms

ISOPROTERENOL HYDROCHLORIDE INJECTION USP

Usual adult dose

Bronchospasm during anesthesia—

Intravenous (rapid), 10 to 20 mcg (0.01 to 0.02 mg), repeated as necessary.

Usual pediatric dose

Bronchospasm—

Intravenous infusion, 0.1 to 2 mcg (0.0001 to 0.002 mg) per kg of body weight per minute, starting at the minimum dose and increasing the dose every five to ten minutes until the effective dose is reached or toxicity occurs.

Usual pediatric prescribing limits

2 mcg (0.002 mg) per kg of body weight per minute.

Strength(s) usually available

U.S.—

200 mcg (0.2 mg) per mL (1:5000) (Rx) [*Isuprel* (lactic acid; sodium chloride; sodium lactate; sodium metabisulfite); GENERIC].

Canada—

200 mcg (0.2 mg) per mL (1:5000) (Rx) [*Isuprel* (lactic acid; sodium chloride; sodium lactate; sodium metabisulfite); GENERIC].

Packaging and storage

Store between 8 and 15 °C (46 and 59 °F), unless otherwise specified by manufacturer. Protect from light. Protect from freezing.

Preparation of dosage form

For bolus intravenous administration, 200 mcg (0.2 mg) of isoproterenol hydrochloride injection is diluted to 10 mL with 5% dextrose injection or 0.9% sodium chloride injection, producing a solution containing 20 mcg (0.02 mg) of isoproterenol hydrochloride per mL.

For administration by intravenous infusion to pediatric patients, the desired dose is added to 100 mL of 5% dextrose injection.

Stability

It is recommended that the injection not be used if it is pinkish or darker than slightly yellow in color or contains a precipitate.

METAPROTERENOL

Summary of Differences

Pharmacology/pharmacokinetics: Somewhat selective for beta$_2$-adrenergic receptors; also has beta$_1$-adrenergic activity, including significant beta$_1$-adrenergic activity in the heart.

Medical considerations/contraindications: Sensitivity to parabens; formulations of metaproterenol sulfate syrup contain parabens.

Oral Dosage Forms

METAPROTERENOL SULFATE SYRUP USP

Usual adult dose

Bronchodilator—

Oral, 20 mg three or four times a day, adjusted as needed.

Usual pediatric dose

Bronchodilator—

Children up to 6 years of age: Safety and efficacy have been demonstrated in a limited number of patients. Daily doses of 1.3 to 2.6 mg per kg of body weight (mg/kg) have been well tolerated.

Children 6 to 9 years of age or

Children weighing less than 27 kilograms: Oral, 10 mg three or four times a day.

Children 9 years of age or older or

Children weighing more than 27 kilograms: Oral, 20 mg three or four times a day.

Strength(s) usually available

U.S.—

200 mcg (0.2 mg) per mL (Rx) [*Alupent;* GENERIC].

Canada—

200 mcg (0.2 mg) per mL (Rx) [*Alupent*].

Packaging and storage

Store between 15 and 30 °C (59 and 86 °F), unless otherwise specified by manufacturer. Protect from light.

METAPROTERENOL SULFATE TABLETS USP

Usual adult dose

Bronchodilator—

Oral, 20 mg three or four times a day, adjusted as needed.

Usual pediatric dose

Bronchodilator—

Children up to 6 years of age: Safety and efficacy have not been established.

Children 6 to 9 years of age or

Children weighing less than 27 kilograms: Oral, 10 mg three or four times a day.

Children 9 years of age or older or

Children weighing more than 27 kilograms: Oral, 20 mg three or four times a day.

Strength(s) usually available

U.S.—

10 mg (Rx) [*Alupent* (lactose); GENERIC].

20 mg (Rx) [*Alupent* (lactose); GENERIC].

Canada—

20 mg (Rx) [*Alupent* (lactose)].

Packaging and storage

Store between 15 and 30 °C (59 and 86 °F), unless otherwise specified by manufacturer. Protect from light.

TERBUTALINE

Summary of Differences

Indications: Premature labor.

Pharmacology/pharmacokinetics: Primarily stimulates beta$_2$-adrenergic receptors, with some minor beta$_1$-adrenergic activity.

Laboratory value alterations: Hepatic enzymes may be increased with high doses of terbutaline.

Side/adverse effects: Paradoxical bronchospasm may occur rarely; difficulty in urinating is more common.

Oral Dosage Forms

TERBUTALINE SULFATE TABLETS USP

Usual adult and adolescent dose

Bronchodilator—

Oral, 5 mg three times a day, at approximately six-hour intervals (while the patient is awake). If unacceptable side effects occur, the dose may be decreased to 2.5 mg three times a day.

Usual adult prescribing limits

15 mg per day.

Usual pediatric dose

Bronchodilator—

Children up to 6 years of age: Safety and efficacy have not been established.

Children 6 to 12 years of age: Oral, 50 to 75 mcg (0.05 to 0.075 mg) per kg of body weight three times a day, at approximately six-hour intervals (while the patient is awake).

Children 12 to 15 years of age: Oral, 2.5 mg three times a day, at approximately six-hour intervals (while the patient is awake).

Children 15 years of age and older: See *Usual adult and adolescent dose.*

Usual pediatric prescribing limits

Children 6 to 11 years of age: 150 mcg (0.15 mg) per kg of body weight per dose or up to a total of 5 mg per day.

Children 12 to 15 years of age: 7.5 mg per day.

Strength(s) usually available

U.S.—

2.5 mg (Rx) [*Brethine* (lactose); *Bricanyl* (lactose)].

5 mg (Rx) [*Brethine* (lactose); *Bricanyl* (lactose)].

Canada—

2.5 mg (Rx) [*Bricanyl* (scored; lactose)].

5 mg (Rx) [*Bricanyl* (scored; lactose)].

Packaging and storage

Store between 15 and 30 °C (59 and 86 °F), unless otherwise specified by manufacturer. Protect from light.

Parenteral Dosage Forms

TERBUTALINE SULFATE INJECTION USP

Usual adult dose

Bronchodilator—

Subcutaneous (injected into the lateral deltoid area), 250 mcg (0.25 mg), repeated in fifteen to thirty minutes if significant clinical improvement has not occurred.

Note: If the patient does not respond after a second dose, other therapeutic measures should be considered.

[Tocolytic][1]—
Subcutaneous, 250 mcg (0.25 mg) every one to six hours or
Intravenous infusion, 10 mcg (0.01 mg) per minute, the dose being increased by 5 mcg (0.005 mg) per minute every ten minutes until contractions stop or a maximum dose of 25 mcg (0.025 mg) per minute is reached.

Usual adult prescribing limits

Bronchodilator—
500 mcg (0.5 mg) in a four-hour period.

Usual pediatric dose

Bronchodilator—
Children up to 6 years of age—Safety and efficacy have not been established.
Children 6 to 12 years of age—Subcutaneous, 5 to 10 mcg (0.005 to 0.01 mg) per kg of body weight, repeated every fifteen to twenty minutes for up to three doses.
Children 12 years of age or older—Subcutaneous, 250 mcg (0.25 mg), repeated in fifteen to thirty minutes if significant clinical improvement has not occurred.

Note: If the patient does not respond after a second dose, other therapeutic measures should be considered.

Usual pediatric prescribing limits

Children 6 to 12 years of age: 400 mcg (0.4 mg) per dose.
Children 12 years of age or older: 500 mcg (0.5 mg) in a four-hour period.

Strength(s) usually available

U.S.—
1 mg per mL (Rx) [*Bricanyl* (sodium chloride; hydrochloric acid)].
Canada—
Not commercially available.

Packaging and storage

Store between 15 and 30 °C (59 and 86 °F), unless otherwise specified by manufacturer. Protect from light. Protect from freezing.

[1]Not included in Canadian product labeling.

Selected Bibliography

National Asthma Education and Prevention Program. Expert panel report II: guidelines for the diagnosis and management of asthma. National Heart, Lung, and Blood Institute, Feb 1997. Component 3. Available from: http//www.nhlbi.nih.gov/nhlbi/lung/asthma/prof/asthgdln.htm

National Asthma Program. Report of the working group on asthma and pregnancy: management of asthma during pregnancy. National Heart, Lung, and Blood Institute, September 1993 (NIH Publication No. 93-3279). Available from gopher://fido.nhlbi.nih.gov/55/nhlbi/health/lung/asthma/prof/apa/astpreg.htm

National Asthma Education and Prevention Program. NAEPP working group report: considerations for diagnosing and managing asthma in the elderly. National Heart, Lung, and Blood Institute, 1996 (NIH Publication No. 96-3662). Available from: http://www.nhlbi.nih.gov/nhlbi/lung/asthma/prof/as_elder.txt

Revised: 06/17/2002

BRONCHODILATORS, THEOPHYLLINE Systemic

This monograph includes information on the following: 1) Aminophylline; 2) Oxtriphylline; 3) Theophylline.

INN: Oxtriphylline—Choline theophyllinate
BAN: Oxtriphylline—Choline theophyllinate
JAN: Oxtriphylline—Choline theophylline
VA CLASSIFICATION (Primary/Secondary):

Aminophylline
- Injection—RE140/RE900
- Oral solution—RE140/RE190; RE900
- Tablets—RE140/RE190
- Extended-release tablets—RE140/RE190

Oxtriphylline—RE140/RE190

Theophylline
- Capsules—RE140/RE190
- Extended-release capsules—RE140/RE190
- Elixir—RE140/RE190; RE900
- Oral solution—RE140/RE190; RE900
- Syrup—RE140/RE190; RE900
- Tablets—RE140/RE190
- Extended-release tablets—RE140/RE190

Theophylline in Dextrose—RE140/RE900

Commonly used brand name(s): *Aerolate Sr*[3]; *Apo-Oxtriphylline*[2]; *Apo-Theo LA*[3]; *Asmalix*[3]; *Choledyl*[2]; *Choledyl SA*[2]; *Elixophyllin*[3]; *Lanophyllin*[3]; *PMS Theophylline*[3]; *PMS-Oxtriphylline*[2]; *Phyllocontin*[1]; *Phyllocontin-350*[1]; *Pulmophylline*[3]; *Quibron-T Dividose*[3]; *Quibron-T/SR Dividose*[3]; *Respbid*[3]; *Slo-Bid Gyrocaps*[3]; *Slo-Phyllin*[3]; *T-Phyl*[3]; *Theo-24*[3]; *Theo-Dur*[3]; *Theo-SR*[3]; *Theo-Time*[3]; *Theo-X*[3]; *Theobid Duracaps*[3]; *Theochron*[3]; *Theolair*[3]; *Theolair SR*[3]; *Theolair-SR*[3]; *Theovent Long-Acting*[3]; *Truphylline*[1]; *Truxophyllin*[3]; *Uni-Dur*[3]; *Uniphyl*[3].

Note: For a listing of dosage forms and brand names by country availability, see *Dosage Forms* section(s).

Category

Bronchodilator—Aminophylline; Oxtriphylline; Theophylline.
Asthma prophylactic—Aminophylline; Oxtriphylline; Theophylline.
Stimulant, respiratory—Aminophylline Injection USP; Aminophylline Oral Solution USP; Theophylline Elixir; Theophylline Oral Solution; Theophylline Syrup.
Antidote (to dipyridamole toxicity)—Aminophylline Injection USP

Indications

Note: Bracketed information in the *Indications* section refers to uses that are not included in U.S. product labeling.

Accepted

Asthma, bronchial (prophylaxis and treatment)—Aminophylline, oxtriphylline, and theophylline are indicated for the prevention and treatment of bronchial asthma symptoms. They improve pulmonary function and reduce the frequency and severity of symptoms such as wheezing, cough, shortness of breath, or dyspnea.

Some studies have shown that theophylline does not provide additional benefit in the initial treatment of *acute* airway obstruction when optimal therapy is provided with inhaled or injected beta-2-adrenergic bronchodilators and systemic glucocorticoids in patients not already receiving a methylxanthine. Although patients hospitalized with asthma may benefit from administration of aminophylline or theophylline, these medications should not be relied upon to produce immediate bronchodilation, even if therapeutic theophylline concentrations are rapidly achieved.

Aminophylline, oxtriphylline, and theophylline may benefit those patients with an inadequate response to anti-inflammatory medications and beta-adrenergic bronchodilators; however, theophylline bronchodilators are not considered to be first-line therapy.

Bronchitis, chronic (treatment)
Emphysema, pulmonary (treatment) or
Pulmonary disease, chronic obstructive, other (treatment)—Aminophylline, oxtriphylline, and theophylline may be indicated in the treatment of reversible airway obstruction associated with chronic bronchitis, emphysema, or other chronic obstructive pulmonary disease.

[Apnea, neonatal (treatment adjunct)][1]—Aminophylline oral solution and injection and theophylline oral liquids are used in the treatment of idiopathic apnea in neonates, characterized by cessation of respiration that lasts 20 seconds or longer. Aminophylline or theophylline should be considered in addition to administration of oxygen, sensory stimulation, or low pressure nasal continuous positive airway pressure.

Toxicity, dipyridamole (treatment)[1]—Parenteral aminophylline is used to reverse the adenosine-mediated adverse effects of dipyridamole, such as angina pectoris, ventricular arrhythmias, bronchospasm, and severe hypotension.

Unaccepted

Parenteral aminophylline and theophylline have been used in the treatment of Cheyne-Stokes respiration. However, there is insufficient evidence to establish the efficacy of these medications for this indication.

[1]Not included in Canadian product labeling.

Pharmacology/Pharmacokinetics

Physicochemical characteristics

Source—
Aminophylline: Theophylline compound with ethylenediamine.
Oxtriphylline: The choline salt of theophylline.

Molecular weight—
Aminophylline: 420.43.
Oxtriphylline: 283.33.
Theophylline: 198.18.

Mechanism of action/Effect

The exact mechanism of action by which theophylline produces its pharmacologic effect is unknown; it is likely to involve multiple mechanisms.

Bronchodilator; asthma prophylactic—Theophylline directly relaxes smooth muscle in the bronchial airways and pulmonary blood vessels.

This action is believed to be mediated by selective inhibition of specific phosphodiesterases (PDEs), which in turn produces an increase in intracellular cyclic 3′, 5′-adenosine monophosphate (cyclic AMP). *In vitro* study results demonstrate that the PDE isoenzyme types III and IV may play a primary role. Inhibition of these isoenzymes may also mediate certain theophylline side effects such as emesis, hypotension, and tachycardia. Theophylline also demonstrates adenosine receptor antagonism, which may contribute to its effect on bronchial airways.

Respiratory stimulant—Theophylline is believed to stimulate the medullary respiratory center, presumably by increasing sensitivity to the stimulatory actions of carbon dioxide.

Antidote (to dipyridamole toxicity)—Involves antagonism of the coronary vasodilatory effects of the increased concentrations of adenosine produced by intravenous administration of dipyridamole during myocardial perfusion studies.

Other actions/effects

Theophylline may attenuate airway hyperreactivity associated with the late phase response that is induced by inhaled allergens by an undefined mechanism which is not attributable to PDE inhibition or adenosine antagonism. Theophylline also has been reported to increase the number and activity of suppressor T-cells in the peripheral blood. Whether these actions are clinically relevant is not clear.

Theophylline may produce other physiologic effects such as transient diuresis, stimulation of cardiac muscle, improved contractility of the diaphragm, reduction of systemic and pulmonary vascular resistance, increased gastric acid secretion, central nervous system stimulation, and cerebral vasoconstriction.

Absorption

Immediate-release capsule, liquid, or tablet dosage forms—Rapidly and completely absorbed. The rate of absorption may be slowed by concurrent ingestion of food or magnesium-containing antacids; however, the effect on the extent of absorption is generally not clinically significant.

Delayed-release tablets—Enteric coating provides delayed and possibly incomplete absorption compared with immediate-release dosage forms.

Extended-release capsules or tablets—The rate of absorption varies among different formulations and is slower than with immediate-release products; the extent of absorption may also vary. Significant intra- and interindividual differences in absorption have been reported. Serum concentration fluctuations are most apparent in patients demonstrating increased theophylline clearance. Co-administration of antacids or food may only slow the rate of absorption from some extended-release formulations, while significantly altering the extent of absorption from others. Some formulations designed for once-a-day administration may be substantially affected by food.

Intramuscular—Slow absorption; medication may precipitate at the injection site.

Suppository—Slow and unreliable absorption.

Distribution

Theophylline distributes rapidly into peripheral non-adipose tissues and body water, including breast milk and cerebrospinal fluid. It freely crosses the placenta. The apparent volume of distribution (Vol_D) for theophylline averages 0.45 L per kg of body weight (L/kg) and ranges from 0.3 to 0.7 L/kg (30 to 70% of ideal body weight) in both adults and children. The Vol_D may be increased, probably due to altered protein binding, in premature neonates, adults with cirrhosis, patients with uncorrected acidemia, elderly patients, pregnant women during the third trimester, critically ill patients, mechanically ventilated adults, and children with protein-calorie malnutrition.

Protein binding

Moderate (40%). Primarily to albumin. Patients with reduced protein binding may have low total serum theophylline concentrations when unbound theophylline is in the therapeutic range.

Biotransformation

Aminophylline and oxtriphylline—

Release free theophylline at physiologic pH.

Theophylline—

Hepatic; no first-pass effect. Believed to occur over multiple parallel pathways, mediated by cytochrome P-450 isoenzymes P-4501A2, P-4503A3, and P-4502E1. In neonates, several of these pathways are undeveloped but mature slowly over the first year of life. Caffeine is a minor active metabolite, except in premature neonates and children less than 6 months of age, in whom caffeine's extremely long half-life results in significant accumulation. The half-life of caffeine shortens over the first 6 months of life because of maturation of its metabolic pathway. Thereafter, caffeine does not accumulate in older children and adults. Major inactive metabolites in adults and children older than 6 months of age are 1,3-dimethyluric acid, 3-methylxanthine, and 1-methyluric acid.

Theophylline approximates first-order elimination kinetics, where serum concentrations follow a log-linear decay. However, zero-order kinetics, where elimination becomes dependent on the serum concentration, can be observed in patients at therapeutic concentrations. This is probably due to capacity limitations of the hepatic enzymes that metabolize theophylline, and is clinically relevant for some patients in that a small change in theophylline dosage may result in a disproportionately large change in serum concentration.

Half-life

Elimination half-life and total body clearance values for theophylline in various patients are as follows—

Patient characteristics	Half-life Mean (Range)* (hr)	Total body clearance Mean (Range)* (mL/kg/min)
Age		
Premature neonates		
3–15 days†	30 (17–43)	0.29 (0.09–0.49)
25–57 days†	20 (9.4–30.6)	0.64 (0.04–1.2)
Term infants	(25–26.5)	
1–2 days†	11 (6–29)	
3–26 weeks†		
Children		
1–4 yrs	3.4 (1.2–5.6)	1.7 (0.5–2.9)
4–12 yrs		1.57 (0.83–2.31)
13–15 yrs		0.88 (0.38–1.38)
6–17 yrs‡	3.7 (1.5–5.9)	1.4 (0.2–2.6)
Adults§	8.2 (6.1–12.8)	0.65 (0.27–1.03)
Elderly#	9.8 (1.6–18)	0.41 (0.21–0.61)
Concurrent illness or altered physiologic state		
Acute pulmonary edema	19 (3.1–82)**	0.33 (0.07–2.35)**
COPD††	11 (9.4–12.6)	0.54 (0.44–0.64)
COPD and cor pulmonale		0.48 (0.08–0.88)
Cystic fibrosis‡‡	6 (1.8–10.2)	1.25 (0.31–2.19)
Fever§§	7 (1–13)	
Hepatic disease		
Acute hepatitis	19.2 (16.6–21.8)	0.35 (0.25–0.45)
Cholestasis	14.4 (5.7–31.8)	0.65 (0.25–1.45)
Cirrhosis	32 (10–56)**	0.31 (0.1–0.7)**
Hyperthyroidism	4.5 (3.7–5.6)	0.8 (0.68–0.97)
Hypothyroidism	11.6 (8.2–25)	0.38 (0.13–0.57)
Pregnancy		
First trimester	8.5 (3.1–13.9)	
Second trimester	8.8 (3.9–13.8)	
Third trimester	13.3 (8.4–17.6)	
Sepsis##	18.8 (6.3–24.1)	0.46 (0.19–1.9)

*Reported or estimated range (mean ±2 SD) where actual range not reported.

†Postnatal age.

‡Elimination half-life and total body clearance gradually become slower until adult values are reached.

§Otherwise healthy, nonsmoking asthmatics.

#Nonsmokers with normal cardiac, liver, and renal function; 70 to 85 years of age.

**Median.

††Stable; older than 60 years of age; at least 1 year since stopped smoking.

‡‡Patients 14 to 28 years of age.

§§Associated with acute viral respiratory illness in children 9 to 15 years of age.

##With multi-organ failure.

Time to peak concentration

Theophylline—

Immediate-release capsules, tablets, or oral solution: 1 to 2 hours.

Delayed-release tablets: Approximately 4 hours.

Extended-release capsules and tablets: 4 to 13 hours depending upon the specific product.

Therapeutic serum concentration

Bronchodilator—

For most patients, a conservative goal of therapy would be to target peak steady-state serum concentrations in the range of 5 to 15 mcg/mL (27.5 to 82.5 micromoles/L). Although improved pulmonary function is evident over the range of 5 to 20 mcg/mL (27.5 to 110 micromoles/L), concentrations at the upper end of the therapeutic range may be associated with an increased potential for toxicity. When serum concentrations exceed 20 mcg/mL (110 micromoles/L), the probability of toxicity increases.

Respiratory stimulant—

Neonatal apnea: Steady-state peak serum concentrations of 5 to 12 mcg per mL (27.5 to 66 micromoles per L).

Elimination

Theophylline—

Renal; approximately 10% excreted unchanged in the urine in adults; amount excreted unchanged may reach 50% in neonates.

In dialysis: Charcoal hemoperfusion increases theophylline clearance 2 to 4 times. Hemodialysis and peritoneal dialysis are estimated to increase theophylline clearance by approximately 50% and 30%, respectively.

Precautions to Consider

Carcinogenicity/Tumorigenicity

Long-term studies have not been done in humans. The results of long-term carcinogenicity studies performed in mice and rats are pending.

Mutagenicity

Theophylline has not been shown to be mutagenic in Ames salmonella, *in vivo* and *in vitro* cytogenetics, micronucleus and Chinese hamster ovary test systems.

Pregnancy/Reproduction

Fertility—Studies in rodents have shown that theophylline impairs fertility in mice given oral doses approximately 1 to 3 times the human dose on a mg per square meter of body surface area (mg/m^2), and in rats given oral doses approximately 2 times the human dose on a mg/m^2 basis.

Pregnancy—Although adequate and well-controlled studies in pregnant women have not been done, these medications are used in pregnancy when the risk of treatment is preferable to the risk of placental hypoxemia from uncontrolled pulmonary disease. The Collaborative Perinatal Project monitored 193 mother-child pairs exposed to theophylline during the first trimester and found no evidence of association with teratogenicity.

Theophylline crosses the placenta; cord blood concentrations are approximately equal to the maternal serum concentration. Because of this, higher-than-recommended serum concentrations during pregnancy may result in potentially dangerous serum theophylline and caffeine concentrations in the neonate. Tachycardia, irritability, jitteriness, and vomiting have been reported; therefore, neonates of mothers taking these medications during pregnancy should be monitored for signs of theophylline toxicity.

Theophylline clearance is reported to be lower in the third trimester, which may necessitate more frequent theophylline serum concentration determinations and possible dosage reductions.

Theophylline was not teratogenic in mice or rats given oral doses approximately 2 and 3 times the recommended human dose on a mg/m^2 basis, respectively. Embryotoxicity was observed in rats given 220 mg per kg of body weight, in the absence of maternal toxicity.

FDA Pregnancy Category C.

Labor—Theophylline has been shown to slightly inhibit uterine contractions.

Breast-feeding

Less than 1% of a maternal theophylline dose distributes into breast milk; this may cause irritability in the infant.

Pediatrics

Caution is recommended in neonates and children less than 1 year of age, especially in premature neonates and in infants less than 3 months of age with renal function impairment, because theophylline clearance is reduced, resulting in lower dosage requirements. Clearance progressively increases over the first year of life, remains constant during the subsequent 9 years, and gradually declines to mean adult values by 16 years of age.

Geriatrics

Caution is recommended when aminophylline, oxtriphylline, or theophylline is used in patients older than 60 years of age. Theophylline clearance in healthy adults older than 60 years of age is 30% lower than in healthy younger adults. These patients may require adjustment in dosage or dosing interval. Severe signs or symptoms of toxicity resulting from chronic overdose are more common in elderly patients, occurring in 65% of patients 60 years of age or older with serum theophylline concentrations > 30 mcg per mL (165 micromoles per L).

Drug interactions and/or related problems

The following drug interactions and/or related problems have been selected on the basis of their potential clinical significance (possible mechanism in parentheses where appropriate)—not necessarily inclusive (» = major clinical significance):

Note: Combinations containing any of the following medications, depending on the amount present, may also interact with this medication.

Pharmacokinetic interactions

Medications that decrease theophylline clearance

(the medications listed in the table below probably decrease theophylline clearance by inhibition of one or more hepatic cytochrome P-450 isoenzyme; changes in clearance of approximately 25% or greater can have clinical significance; monitoring of serum theophylline concentrations and/or dosage adjustments are strongly recommended when concurrent use of these medications with aminophylline, oxtriphylline, or theophylline is initiated or discontinued

	Medication	Decrease in Clearance (avg. %)	Increase in Serum Concentration (avg. %)*
	Alcohol†	25	33
	Allopurinol‡	20	25
»	Cimetidine	33	33–50
	Contraceptives, estrogen-containing, oral	25–34	33–50
	Disulfiram§	21–33	25–50
	Fluoroquinolone antibiotics#		
»	Ciprofloxacin	20–40	25–66
»	Enoxacin	40–70	66–300
»	Fluvoxamine	100	>300
»	Interferon alpha, recombinant	10–50	11–100
	Macrolide antibiotics**		
»	Clarithromycin	20	25
»	Erythromycin	5–35	5–50
»	Troleandomycin	25–50††	33–100
	Methotrexate‡‡	15–25	18–33
»	Mexiletine	43	75
	Propafenone		40§§
»	Pentoxifylline		30 (0–95)
»	Propranolol	30–50	40–100
»	Tacrine	50	100
»	Thiabendazole	66	>200
»	Ticlopidine	37	60
	Verapamil	14–23	16–30

*Calculation based on reported change in clearance if actual change not reported.

†3 mL of whiskey per kg of body weight as a single dose decreased clearance up to 24 hrs.

‡≥600 mg per day.

§Dose-dependent, 250 and 500 mg.

#Norfloxacin, lomefloxacin, and ofloxacin are not considered to significantly decrease theophylline clearance.

**Azithromycin does not appear to alter theophylline clearance.

††Once-daily dose decreases clearance by average of 25%.

‡‡Low-dose intramuscular regimen of 15 mg per week.

§§Beta-2-antagonist effect may decrease effect of theophylline.

Medications that increase theophylline clearance

(the medications listed in the table below probably increase theophylline clearance by induction of one or more hepatic cytochrome P-450 isoenzyme; changes in clearance of approximately 25% or greater can have clinical significance; monitoring of serum theophylline concentrations and/or dosage adjustments are strongly recommended when concurrent use of these medications with aminophylline, oxtriphylline, or theophylline is initiated or discontinued

	Medication	Increase in Clearance (avg. %)	Decrease in Serum Concentration (avg. %)*
	Aminoglutethimide	18–43	15–30
	Carbamazepine	33	25
	Isoproterenol, intravenous	21	17
»	Moricizine	44–66	30–40
	Phenobarbital	33	25
»	Phenytoin	35–75	25–43
»	Rifampin	64–100	40–50

*Calculation based on reported change in clearance if actual change not reported.)

Pharmacodynamic or other drug interactions

Adenosine

(concurrent use with theophylline may antagonize the cardiovascular effects of adenosine; larger doses of adenosine may be required or alternative therapy should be used)

Benzodiazepines
(theophylline may reverse benzodiazepine sedation; caution is recommended when starting or stopping either medication)

» Beta-adrenergic blocking agents, including ophthalmic agents
(concurrent use with theophylline may result in inhibition of its bronchodilator effect; although agents with beta-1-selectivity may be less antagonistic, extreme caution is recommended if beta-adrenergic blocking agents are used in patients with bronchospasm)

Ephedrine
(concurrent use with theophylline may result in increased frequency of nausea, nervousness, or insomnia)

» Halothane
(ventricular arrhythmias have been reported when halothane is used concurrently with theophylline)

» Ketamine
(concurrent use with theophylline may lower the seizure threshold)

Lithium
(concurrent use of lithium with theophylline may increase renal elimination of lithium, thus decreasing its therapeutic effect)

Neuromuscular blocking agents, nondepolarizing
(concurrent use with theophylline may antagonize neuromuscular blocking effects; a larger dose of neuromuscular blocking agent may be required)

» Smoking tobacco or marijuana
(induces the hepatic metabolism of theophylline, resulting in increased clearance and decreased serum concentrations. Passive smoking may also increase theophylline clearance. Induction is attributed to the polyaromatic hydrocarbons in smoke. Following cessation of cigarette smoking, theophylline clearance begins to decrease after 1 week; however, normalization may require 6 months to 2 years. Dosage adjustments and/or additional theophylline serum determinations may be necessary when smoking is started or stopped)

Sucralfate
(concurrent use with aminophylline, oxtriphylline, or theophylline may result in adsorption of the theophylline bronchodilator if medications are administered less than 2 hours apart)

Laboratory value alterations

The following have been selected on the basis of their potential clinical significance (possible effect in parentheses where appropriate)—not necessarily inclusive (» = major clinical significance).

With diagnostic test results

» Dipyridamole-assisted myocardial perfusion studies
(the theophylline bronchodilators reverse the effects of dipyridamole on myocardial blood flow, thereby interfering with test results; dipyridamole-assisted myocardial perfusion studies should not be performed if therapy with aminophylline, oxtriphylline, or theophylline cannot be withheld for 36 hours prior to the test)

With physiology/laboratory test values

Cholesterol and
Free cortisol excretion, urinary and
Free fatty acids and
Glucose, plasma and
HDL and HDL/LDL ratio and
Uric acid, plasma
(concentrations may be increased by theophylline serum concentrations within the therapeutic range)

Triiodothyronine, serum
(concentration may be transiently decreased by theophylline serum concentrations within the therapeutic range)

Medical considerations/Contraindications

The medical considerations/contraindications included have been selected on the basis of their potential clinical significance (reasons given in parentheses where appropriate)—not necessarily inclusive (» = major clinical significance).

Risk-benefit should be considered when the following medical problems exist:

» Acute pulmonary edema or
» Congestive heart failure or
Fever, sustained or
» Hepatic disease or
» Hypothyroidism, not optimally controlled or
» Sepsis
(theophylline clearance may be decreased, resulting in increased theophylline serum concentrations)

(the extent to which fever, as opposed to other complicating factors such as acute viral illness, affects theophylline clearance is controversial; however, some practitioners recommend additional monitoring and/or dose reduction when the body temperature is 102 °F or greater for at least 24 hours, or when a lower temperature elevation persists for a longer period)

Gastritis, active or
Peptic ulcer disease, active
(may be exacerbated because theophylline increases gastric acid secretion)

Gastroesophageal reflux
(theophylline may decrease lower esophageal sphincter pressure, resulting in increased gastroesophageal reflux)

» Seizure disorder
(aminophylline, oxtriphylline, or theophylline may lower the seizure threshold; caution is recommended unless the patient is receiving appropriate anticonvulsant therapy)

Tachyarrhythmias
(condition may be exacerbated at higher theophylline serum concentrations)

» Sensitivity to a theophylline bronchodilator or ethylenediamine

Patient monitoring

The following may be especially important in patient monitoring (other tests may be warranted in some patients, depending on condition; » = major clinical significance):

Caffeine concentrations, serum
(determinations may be required in neonates; usually necessary only if adverse effects occur when the serum theophylline concentration is within the therapeutic range)

Pulmonary function tests
(objective measures of lung function are essential for diagnosis and for guiding therapeutic decision making in asthma; measurement of forced expiratory airflow, using a spirometer or a peak expiratory flowmeter, is recommended at periodic intervals)

» Theophylline concentrations
(dosage requirements are usually guided by measurement of the peak serum concentration obtained at the expected time of the peak, depending upon the specific product characteristics; the frequency of determinations should relate to the specific clinical situation)

(theophylline determinations are recommended when initiating therapy, before increasing the dose when a patient fails to exhibit the expected results, at the appearance of any adverse reaction, whenever any change in physiologic state or medication known to alter theophylline elimination occurs, and upon the addition of any new medication with an unknown effect on theophylline elimination; also recommended at least every 6 to 12 months in stable patients)

(blood samples obtained for guidance of therapy should be collected during steady-state conditions, which are generally reached after 48 to 72 hours of treatment, provided that the medication is taken at regular intervals, with no missed or extra doses. Steady-state conditions may not be reached for up to 5 days in patients with factors known to decrease theophylline clearance. On each occasion, blood samples should be obtained during the same dosing interval, due to the diurnal variation in the absorption of these medications)

(for intravenous therapy, concentrations may be determined 30 to 60 minutes after an intravenous loading dose, approximately 8 to 12 hours after initiating continuous intravenous therapy, and at approximately 24-hour intervals during continuous intravenous therapy)

(trough concentration may be useful when evaluating serum concentration-time profiles; determinations may be performed just before the next dose or, for once-daily evening administration of an extended-release product, the morning following a dose)

(caution is recommended in interpreting serum theophylline concentrations in patients with low albumin; total serum theophylline concentrations may be low when unbound theophylline is in the therapeutic range; measurement of unbound serum theophylline concentration provides a more reliable basis for dosage adjustment)

(caution is recommended in interpreting the results of rapid theophylline immunoassays for uremic patients, because falsely high values may occur. Also, when theophylline concentration is determined via high pressure liquid chromatography, sulfamethoxazole may cause inaccurate test results and large doses of ampicillin, cephalothin, or acetazolamide may cause falsely high concentrations. Determinations via specific immunoassay or high pressure liquid chromatography are not affected by caffeine or dyphylline. However, when theophylline is measured via spectrophotometry, caffeine [including caffeine-containing substances such as chocolate, coffee, tea, colas, or medications] or acetaminophen may cause falsely high concentrations)

Note: Concentrations in saliva are approximately 60% of serum concentrations; however, the saliva-to-serum concentration ratio may not remain constant within the same patient; caution is recommended in use and interpretation of the data without the use of special techniques.

Side/Adverse Effects

Note: The less severe signs or symptoms of toxicity, such as continuing or severe abdominal pain, agitation, confusion or change in behavior, diarrhea, hematemesis, hypotension, trembling, and continued vomiting, do not always precede the more serious ones such as sinus tachycardia, ventricular arrhythmias, or seizures. Patients with chronic overdosage have a greater risk for serious toxicity at lower serum concentrations than patients with acute single overdosage. Severe signs or symptoms of toxicity resulting from chronic overdose are more common in elderly patients, occurring in 65% of patients 60 years of age or older with serum theophylline concentrations > 30 mcg/mL (165 micromoles/L). For additional information about acute or chronic overdose, refer to the *Overdose* section of this monograph.

Although some studies do not support the suggestion that theophylline has an adverse effect on behavioral and cognitive function in children, differences in individual response have been reported; monitoring for these effects may be advisable.

The following side/adverse effects have been selected on the basis of their potential clinical significance (possible signs and symptoms in parentheses where appropriate)—not necessarily inclusive:

Those indicating need for medical attention

Incidence less frequent

Gastroesophageal reflux (heartburn; vomiting)

Note: Aminophylline, oxtriphylline, or theophylline may relax the gastroesophageal sphincter; however, if *vomiting* occurs, theophylline toxicity should be considered.

Incidence rare

For aminophylline only

Dermatitis, ethylenediamine hypersensitivity-induced (hives; skin rash; sloughing of skin)

Note: *Ethylenediamine hypersensitivity-induced dermatitis* can appear up to 48 hours after administration of aminophylline.

Those indicating need for medical attention only if they continue or are bothersome

Incidence less frequent

Headache; increased urination; insomnia (trouble in sleeping); ***nausea; nervousness; tachycardia*** (fast heartbeat); ***trembling***

Note: These caffeine-like side effects may occur at therapeutic theophylline serum concentrations, especially if the concentrations are rapidly attained. Tolerance generally develops within 1 or 2 weeks; however, the symptoms may persist in < 3% of children and < 10% of adults with chronic therapy despite therapeutic serum theophylline concentrations. Starting therapy at a low dose and slowly increasing the dose by no more than 25% at no less than 3-day intervals until the desired daily dose is reached may prevent the caffeine-like side effects.

For parenteral aminophylline and theophylline—with too rapid intravenous administration;

Anxiety; headache; nausea; vomiting

Note: *Hypotension and cardiac arrest have been reported following rapid direct administration through a central venous catheter.*

Overdose

For specific information on the agents used in the management of theophylline overdose, see:

- *Anesthetics, Inhalation (Systemic)* monograph;
- *Benzodiazepines (Systemic)* monograph;
- *Charcoal, Activated (Oral-Local)* monograph;
- *Metoclopramide (Systemic)* monograph;
- *Neuromuscular Blocking Agents (Systemic)* monograph;
- *Ondansetron (Systemic)* monograph;
- *Phenobarbital* in *Barbiturates (Systemic)* monograph;
- *Polyethylene Glycol and Electrolytes (Local)* monograph; and/or
- *Thiopental* in *Anesthetics, Barbiturate (Systemic)* monograph.

For more information on the management of overdose or unintentional ingestion, **contact a Poison Control Center** (see *Poison Control Center Listing*).

Theophylline is associated with a significant potential for toxicity because of its narrow therapeutic index. The upper limit of the therapeutic serum concentration range is considered to be 20 mcg per mL (mcg/mL) (110 micromoles per L [micromoles/L]). Clinical symptoms of toxicity become evident in some patients with serum concentrations above 15 mcg/mL (82.5 micromoles/L), and increase in frequency when 20 mcg/mL (110 micromoles/L) is exceeded. Less severe toxicities do not always precede major toxicities. Serum theophylline concentrations do not always predict who will experience life-threatening toxicity. Theophylline demonstrates concentration-dependent elimination kinetics as its metabolic pathways become saturated, resulting in prolonged elimination.

Theophylline overdose is associated with significant morbidity and mortality, primarily due to the development of arrhythmias or seizures. Patients who develop seizures are at the highest risk for further morbidity and mortality from associated hypoxia, acidosis, rhabdomyolysis, or myoglobinuric renal failure. The type of theophylline overdose has significant influence on clinical outcome. Chronic theophylline overdose appears to be associated with a greater frequency of seizures and arrhythmias at lower theophylline concentrations, when compared with acute overdose outcomes; this is especially true in patients older than 60 years of age. Although there is a lack of correlation between serum theophylline concentrations and clinical course of a chronic overdose, serum theophylline concentrations > 40 mcg/mL (220 micromoles/L) are considered potentially life-threatening. Following an acute overdose, serum theophylline concentrations of > 90 mcg/mL (495 micromoles/L) are associated with major toxicity, especially seizures. The onset and duration of theophylline toxicity vary and depend on the formulation used, the route of administration, the amount ingested, time since the ingestion, and the patient's theophylline elimination capacity.

Clinical effects of overdose

The following effects have been selected on the basis of their potential clinical significance (possible signs and symptoms in parentheses where appropriate)—not necessarily inclusive:

Acute and chronic effects

Abdominal pain, continuing or severe; agitation (nervousness or restlessness, continuing); ***confusion or change in behavior; diarrhea; hematemesis*** (dark or bloody vomit); ***hyperglycemia; hypokalemia; hypotension*** (dizziness; lightheadedness); ***metabolic acidosis; seizures*** (convulsions); ***tachyarrhythmias*** (fast and irregular heartbeat); ***tachycardia*** (fast heartbeat); ***trembling, continuing; vomiting***

Treatment of overdose

There is no antidote for theophylline overdose. Treatment is symptomatic and supportive.

To decrease absorption—

Regardless of the route or mode of exposure resulting in toxicity, oral activated charcoal (OAC) should be administered. OAC binds medication remaining in the gastrointestinal tract and decreases serum concentrations by interrupting enteroenteric recirculation of theophylline. Use of an aqueous activated charcoal preparation is recommended. If the total dose of OAC is not tolerated, more frequent administration of smaller doses, slow instillation through a nasogastic tube, or concurrent use of an antiemetic may be tried.

The initial dose of charcoal may be followed by a single dose of sorbitol if the charcoal is not pre-mixed with sorbitol. Caution is recommended when giving more than a single dose of sorbitol since frequent administration may result in dehydration and electrolyte imbalance secondary to diarrhea. Sorbitol is reported to be more effective than magnesium-containing cathartics and is not associated with hypermagnesemia; however, the role of cathartics is questionable.

Ipecac syrup should generally be avoided in the management of theophylline overdoses.

Gastric lavage is generally not necessary if the patient has vomited. Lavage may provide some benefit if performed via a large bore orogastric tube less than 1 hour after a large ingestion. This procedure may not be very effective for large, poorly soluble tablets.

Whole bowel irrigation with polyethylene glycol and electrolyte combination may be of some value if performed early in the treatment of large ingestions of extended-release dosage forms. Whole bowel irrigation with polyethylene glycol and electrolytes may also be useful when theophylline serum concentrations rapidly increase or when high concentrations persist despite other methods of removal.

To enhance elimination—

Repeated doses of OAC will at least double theophylline clearance and should be continued throughout the course of toxicity, until the patient is asymptomatic and serum concentration is below 20 mcg/mL (110 micromoles/L).

Extracorporeal elimination of theophylline by charcoal hemoperfusion is the most effective means of increasing theophylline clearance. Hemodialysis is less effective; however, it may be used if hemoperfusion is unavailable. Peritoneal dialysis is considered ineffective. Controversy exists about when to initiate extracorporeal elimination. It may be indicated when serum theophylline concentrations are approaching 90 mcg/mL (495 micromoles/L) in an acute overdose or when serum theophylline concentrations are greater than 40 mcg/mL (220 micromoles/L) in a chronic overdose or in certain patients with other significant risk factors, such as age greater than 60 years or presence of complicating illness. In addition, use of extracorporeal elimination is recommended in the presence of intractable seizures or life-threatening cardiovascular symptoms, regardless of serum concentration.

Nausea or vomiting—

The presence of nausea or vomiting should not cause postponement of OAC administration. Antiemetic therapy with metoclopramide or ondansetron, administered intravenously, may be useful. See the package insert or the *Metoclopramide (Systemic)* or *Ondansetron (Systemic)* monograph for specific dosing guidelines for use of these products. Phenothiazine antiemetics such as prochlorperazine or perphenazine should be avoided since they can lower the seizure threshold.

Seizures—

Seizures associated with serum concentrations > 30 mcg/mL (165 micromoles/L) are often resistant to anticonvulsant therapy and may produce a toxic encephalopathy and permanent brain damage if not rapidly controlled. An intravenous benzodiazepine is the drug of choice. See the package insert or the *Benzodiazepines (Systemic)* monograph for specific dosing guidelines for use of these products.

If seizures are repetitive or seizure prophylaxis is indicated in selected patients at high risk for theophylline-induced seizures, intravenous phenobarbital may be administered. In animal studies, the prophylactic use of phenobarbital in therapeutic doses has delayed the onset of theophylline-induced seizures and reduced mortality. There are no controlled studies in humans. See the package insert or the *Barbiturates (Systemic)* monograph for specific dosing guidelines for use of this product. Phenytoin is considered ineffective.

Should use of a benzodiazepine and phenobarbital fail to control seizure activity, the addition of the barbiturate anesthetic agent, thiopental, may be considered. Use of a neuromuscular blocking agent may also be considered to decrease the muscular manifestations of persistent seizures. General anesthesia should be used with caution because fluorinated volatile anesthetics may sensitize the myocardium to endogenous catecholamines released by theophylline. Enflurane appears less likely to be associated with this effect than does halothane. See the package insert or the *Anesthetics, Inhalation (Systemic)*, *Anesthetics, Barbiturate (Systemic)*, and/or *Neuromuscular Blocking Agents (Systemic)* monographs for specific dosing guidelines for use of these products.

Ventricular tachyarrhythmias—

Ventricular tachyarrhythmias considered to be life-threatening require antiarrhythmic therapy specific for the type of arrhythmia.

Monitoring—

Serial theophylline serum concentrations should be obtained to guide and assess treatment decisions. Serial monitoring should continue at periodic intervals after treatment has been discontinued until it is clear that the serum concentration is no longer rising. Serious rebound theophylline toxicity has been reported, due to bezoar formation composed of undissolved extended-release tablets.

All monitoring interventions should be continued until the serum concentration remains below 20 mcg/mL (110 micromoles/L) and the patient is asymptomatic.

Abdominal physical examination should be performed to determine the presence of distention and/or the absence of bowel sounds when repeated doses of OAC are administered. Arterial blood gases, electrocardiograph, serum electrolytes and glucose, stool output, and vital signs should also be monitored as required.

Supportive care—

Respiration should be supported by airway management, oxygen administration, or mechanical ventilation as required, especially if higher doses of a benzodiazepine, phenobarbital, or a neuromuscular blocking agent are used.

Standard measures should be used to manage hypotension and metabolic complications.

Patients in whom intentional overdose is known or suspected should be referred for psychiatric consultation.

Patient Consultation

As an aid to patient consultation, refer to *Advice for the Patient, Bronchodilators, Theophylline (Systemic)*.

In providing consultation, consider emphasizing the following selected information (» = major clinical significance):

Before using this medication

» Conditions affecting use, especially:

Sensitivity to theophylline bronchodilators or to ethylenediamine in aminophylline

Pregnancy—Crosses placenta; decreased elimination during third trimester may require more frequent serum concentration determinations

Breast-feeding—Distributes into breast milk; may result in irritability in infants

Use in children—Decreased theophylline clearance in children less than 1 year of age, especially neonates and infants less than 3 months of age with renal function impairment, results in lower dosage requirements; initially, use in children less than 1 year of age may require more frequent serum concentration determinations

Use in the elderly—Possible decreased theophylline clearance in patients 60 years of age or older may result in lower dosage requirements; severe signs or symptoms of toxicity are more common in these patients following chronic overdose that results in serum concentrations > 30 mcg per mL (165 micromoles per L)

Other medications, especially beta-adrenergic blocking agents; cimetidine; ciprofloxacin; clarithromycin; enoxacin; erythromycin; fluvoxamine; mexiletine; moricizine; pentoxifylline; phenytoin; rifampin; tacrine; thiabendazole; ticlopidine; or troleandomycin

Other medical problems, especially congestive heart failure, convulsions (seizures), hepatic disease, or hypothyroidism

Proper use of this medication

» Proper administration

For liquids and immediate-release capsules or tablets: Taking on an empty stomach with a glass of water for faster absorption or, if necessary, taking with meals or immediately after meals to lessen gastrointestinal irritation, unless otherwise directed

For once-a-day dosage forms: Taking the medication either in the morning at least 1 hour before eating or in the evening with or without food, depending on the specific product; taking consistently with or without food; taking at approximately the same time each day

For enteric-coated or delayed-release tablet dosage form: Swallowing tablets whole; not breaking (unless scored for breakage), crushing, or chewing

For extended-release dosage forms: Swallowing capsules whole or opening capsules and sprinkling contents on soft food, then swallowing without crushing or chewing; not breaking (unless scored for breakage), crushing, or chewing tablets; taking on an empty stomach with a glass of water for faster absorption or, if necessary, taking with meals or immediately after meals to lessen gastrointestinal irritation, unless otherwise directed

» Importance of not using more than amount prescribed

» Compliance with therapy; not missing doses

» Proper dosing

Missed dose: Taking as soon as possible; not taking if almost time for next dose; not doubling doses

» Proper storage

Precautions while using this medication

» Regular visits to physician required to check progress, including blood levels

» Not changing brands or dosage forms without first checking with physician

» Notifying physician of factors that may alter theophylline concentrations, such as:

—fever (≥102 °F ≥ 24 hours or a lower temperature elevation for a longer period)

—other medicines started or stopped

—smoking started or stopped

—an extended change in diet

Caution in eating or drinking large amounts of caffeine-containing foods or beverages during therapy with this medication

Side/adverse effects

Signs of potential side effects, especially heartburn and/or vomiting, hives, skin rash, and sloughing of skin

Signs of toxicity

General Dosing Information

The bronchodilator action of aminophylline, oxtriphylline, and theophylline depends upon their theophylline content. The anhydrous theophylline content of various theophylline salts is as follows:
Aminophylline anhydrous—86%.
Aminophylline dihydrate—79%.
Oxtriphylline—64%.
Theophylline monohydrate—91%.

Theophylline does not distribute into fatty tissue; therefore, all dosages should be calculated on the basis of lean (ideal) body weight.

The recommended doses are given as a guideline for use in the average patient. Dosage of aminophylline, oxtriphylline, or theophylline must be adjusted to meet the individual requirements of each patient on the basis of product selected, patient characteristics, clinical response, and steady-state serum theophylline concentrations.

Administration of a single loading dose of theophylline is intended to produce a serum concentration in the therapeutic range as quickly as possible. A theophylline loading dose may be considered for all patient groups, including neonates. Although the intravenous route of administration provides the most rapid effect, immediate-release oral liquids, tablets, or capsules may also be used. Delayed- or extended-release dosage forms should not be used when rapid achievement of a therapeutic serum theophylline concentration is required.

Before a loading dose is administered, it is extremely important to determine the time, amount, dosage form, and route of administration of previous doses of aminophylline, oxytriphylline, or theophylline.

Once the desired theophylline serum concentration is obtained with a loading dose, it can be maintained with an oral or intravenous dosage form.

The goal of chronic therapy is to obtain maximum potential benefit with minimal risk of adverse effects. Transient caffeine-like side effects and excessively high serum concentrations can be avoided in most patients by starting with a lower dose and slowly increasing the dose by 25% at three-day intervals, approximately.

For final dosage adjustment in chronic therapy after serum theophylline measurement, the following dosage adjustments are recommended:

Steady-state Peak Serum Theophylline Concentration (mcg/mL)	Recommended Dosage Adjustment
Below 9.9	If *clinically indicated*, about 25% increase to nearest dose increment; recheck serum theophylline concentration after 3 days for further dosage adjustment
10–14.9	If *clinically indicated*, maintain dose and recheck serum theophylline concentration at 6- to 12-month intervals; if symptoms are not controlled, consider adding additional medication to treatment regimen
15–19.9	Consider 10% decrease in dose to increase margin of safety even if current dosage is tolerated
20–24.9	Decrease dose by 25% even if no adverse effects are present; recheck serum theophylline concentration after 3 days
25–30	Omit next dose; 25% decrease in subsequent doses even if no adverse effects are present; recheck serum theophylline concentration after 3 days; if symptomatic, consider whether overdose treatment is indicated
> 30	Treatment of overdose may be indicated; when theophylline is resumed, decrease subsequent dose by at least 50%; recheck serum theophylline concentration after 3 days

Note: If asthma is well controlled and there are no side effects or intervening factors that would alter dose requirements, follow-up serum concentration measurements can be obtained at 6- to 12-month intervals. However, **whenever a patient develops nausea, vomiting, CNS stimulation or any other symptom of theophylline toxicity, even if another cause is suspected (e.g., viral gastroenteritis), the next dose should be withheld and a serum concentration measurement obtained.** In addition, various drug interactions and physiologic abnormalities can alter theophylline elimination and require serum concentration measurement and/or dose adjustment.

For oral dosage forms only

The dosing frequency should be individualized. When rapidly absorbed dosage forms such as liquids or immediate-release capsules or tablets are used, dosing to maintain therapeutic serum concentrations usually requires administration every 6 hours, especially in children and smoking adults. A dosing interval of up to 8 hours may be appropriate in some nonsmoking adults, elderly or debilitated patients, and neonates due to a slower clearance rate. In premature neonates and patients with hepatic disease, dosing every 12 hours or longer will usually provide relatively constant serum concentrations.

Patients requiring higher-than-usual doses (i.e., patients with rapid clearance rates) may be more effectively controlled during chronic therapy by being given extended-release dosage forms. These products have the potential to achieve relatively constant serum concentrations with 12-hour dosing intervals. Patients who metabolize theophylline rapidly may require an extended-release product every 8 hours. Patients who metabolize theophylline at a normal or slow rate (elimination half-life longer than 8 hours) are potential candidates for once-a-day formulations.

Alcohol-free liquid dosage forms are generally preferred.

For patients who have difficulty in swallowing, some extended-release capsules may be opened and the contents sprinkled on a spoonful of soft, cold food such as applesauce or pudding, then taken without chewing.

For parenteral dosage forms only

Therapy can be converted from an intravenous to an oral product by dividing the total daily dose that produced the desired steady-state peak serum concentration into equal parts, and giving in amounts and at intervals appropriate for the product. The intravenous infusion can usually be discontinued when the first oral dose of medication is administered. Extreme caution is recommended if intravenous and oral therapy are overlapped, since this practice may lead to inadvertent theophylline toxicity.

Use of intravenous aminophylline or theophylline should be reassessed after 24 to 72 hours. Oral therapy should be substituted for intravenous therapy as soon as the patient is able to take medication orally.

Diet/Nutrition

Dietary changes are of clinical importance only if a sustained and extreme change in the usual eating pattern occurs. High-carbohydrate, low-protein diets have been shown to decrease theophylline elimination. Low-carbohydrate, high-protein diets and daily ingestion of charcoal-broiled beef have been shown to increase theophylline elimination.

Large amounts of caffeine-containing foods or beverages should be avoided, since they may increase CNS stimulant effects of theophylline bronchodilators.

Bioequivalence information

For oral dosage forms only—

The formulation selected for maintenance therapy can have an important effect on the serum concentration-time profile. Selection of a theophylline product must be based upon the specific clinical indication, the absorption characteristics of the formulation, and the rate of theophylline elimination in the individual patient. Immediate-release oral formulations can generally be used interchangeably since they are not considered to have clinically important differences in rates of absorption. However, many brands of extended-release theophylline products have clinically important differences in their extent and/or rate of absorption. Different extended-release products having the same strength of active ingredient may not be equivalent due to formulation differences. Even with reliably absorbed extended-release formulations, a minority of patients can have marked day-to-day variations in absorption. When this occurs, alternative therapy should be considered.

Due to the significant variability in extended-release product characteristics, pharmacists should not substitute one brand for another without consulting the prescribing physician unless the product has proven bioequivalence, so that theophylline serum concentrations can be appropriately monitored.

AMINOPHYLLINE

Summary of Differences

Category:
Aminophylline (injection, oral solution) is also used as a respiratory stimulant in neonatal apnea; aminophylline injection is used as an antidote to dipyridamole toxicity.

Pharmacology/pharmacokinetics:
Aminophylline is a theophylline compound with ethylenediamine.
Aminophylline releases free theophylline at physiologic pH.

Side/adverse effects:

Ethylenediamine in aminophylline may cause hives, skin rash, or sloughing of skin.

General dosing information:

Aminophylline anhydrous contains about 86% of anhydrous theophylline.

Aminophylline dihydrate contains about 79% of anhydrous theophylline.

Additional Dosing Information

See also *General Dosing Information.*

The recommended doses are given as a guideline for use in the average patient. Dosage of aminophylline must be adjusted to meet the individual requirements of each patient on the basis of product selected, patient characteristics, clinical response, and steady-state serum theophylline concentrations.

For parenteral dosage forms only

Intramuscular administration of aminophylline injection is not recommended since precipitation may occur at the site of injection, resulting in severe local pain and slow absorption.

Aminophylline may be administered by direct intravenous injection or by intravenous infusion; however, it is recommended that intravenous aminophylline be administered slowly, at a rate *not exceeding* 25 mg per minute.

For rectal dosage forms only

USP DI Advisory Panels do not recommend the use of aminophylline suppositories because of the potential for slow and unreliable absorption. The suppositories may also cause local irritation.

Oral Dosage Forms

Note: Bracketed uses in the *Dosage Forms* section refer to categories of use and/or indications that are not included in U.S. product labeling.

AMINOPHYLLINE ORAL SOLUTION USP

Usual adult dose

Bronchodilator—

Loading dose—

For patients *not* currently receiving theophylline preparations—Oral, the equivalent of 5 mg of anhydrous theophylline per kg of lean (ideal) body weight as a single dose to provide an average peak serum concentration of 10 mcg per mL (55 micromoles per L), range 5 to 15 mcg per mL (27.5 to 82.5 micromoles per L).

For patients currently receiving theophylline preparations—Obtaining a serum theophylline concentration prior to administering a partial loading dose is recommended. Once the theophylline concentration is known, the loading dose for theophylline is based on the principle that each 0.5 mg of theophylline per kg of lean (ideal) body weight will result in a 1 mcg per mL increase in serum theophylline concentration.

Maintenance—

Oral, the equivalent of anhydrous theophylline, initially, 300 mg per day. After three days, the dosage may be increased, if tolerated, to 400 mg per day. After three more days, the dosage may be increased, if tolerated, to 600 mg per day without measurement of serum concentration.

The total daily adult dose is administered in three or four divided doses given about six to eight hours apart. Patients with risk factors for impaired theophylline clearance may require a dosing interval of every twelve hours. Young adult smokers and patients with more rapid metabolism may require a dosing interval of every six hours.

Note: **If the 600-mg-per-day dose is to be maintained or exceeded, monitoring of serum theophylline concentration and patient response is recommended to achieve the optimal therapeutic aminophylline dosage and minimize the risk of toxicity.**

Usual pediatric dose

Bronchodilator—

Loading dose—

For patients not currently receiving theophylline preparations—Infants and children up to 16 years of age: Oral, the equivalent of 5 mg of anhydrous theophylline per kg of lean (ideal) body weight as a single dose to provide an average peak serum concentration of 10 mcg per mL (55 micromoles per L), range 5 to 15 mcg per mL (27.5 to 82.5 micromoles per L).

For patients currently receiving theophylline preparations—Obtaining a serum theophylline concentration prior to administering a partial loading dose is recommended. Once the theophylline concentration is known, the loading dose for theophylline is based on the principle that each 0.5 mg of theophylline per kg of lean (ideal) body weight will result in a 1 mcg per mL increase in serum theophylline concentration.

Maintenance—

Premature infants, postnatal age less than 24 days—Oral, the equivalent of 1 mg of anhydrous theophylline per kg of body weight every twelve hours.

Premature infants, postnatal age 24 days and older—Oral, the equivalent of 1.5 mg of anhydrous theophylline per kg of body weight every twelve hours.

Full-term infants, postnatal age up to 52 weeks—Oral, the equivalent of anhydrous theophylline: total daily dose in mg per kg of body weight = (0.2)(postnatal age in weeks) + 5.

Note: For full-term infants up to 26 weeks of age, divide the total daily dose into three equal amounts administered eight hours apart.

For full-term infants 26 to 52 weeks of age, divide the total daily dose into four equal amounts administered six hours apart.

Children 1 year of age and older, weighing less than 45 kg—Oral, the equivalent of anhydrous theophylline, 12 to 14 mg per kg of body weight, *up to a maximum of 300 mg*, per day in divided doses. The dosage may be increased, if tolerated, after three days to 16 mg per kg of body weight, *up to a maximum of 400 mg*, per day. After three more days, if tolerated, the dosage may be increased to 20 mg per kg of body weight, *up to a maximum of 600 mg*, per day. The total daily dose is administered in four to six divided doses and given every four to six hours.

Children weighing more than 45 kg—See *Usual adult dose.*

Note: **If the above maintenance dose is to be maintained or exceeded, monitoring of serum theophylline concentration and patient response is recommended to achieve the optimal therapeutic aminophylline dosage and minimize the risk of toxicity.**

[Respiratory stimulant (neonatal apnea)][1]—

Loading dose—

For patients *not* currently receiving theophylline preparations—Oral, the equivalent of 5 mg of anhydrous theophylline per kg of lean (ideal) body weight as a single dose to provide an average peak serum concentration of 10 mcg per mL (55 micromoles per L), range 5 to 15 mcg per mL (27.5 to 82.5 micromoles per L).

For patients currently receiving theophylline preparations—Obtaining a serum theophylline concentration prior to administering a partial loading dose is recommended. Once the theophylline concentration is known, the loading dose for theophylline is based on the principle that each 0.5 mg of theophylline per kg of lean (ideal) body weight will result in a 1 mcg per mL increase in serum theophylline concentration.

Maintenance—

Premature infants, postnatal age less than 24 days—Oral, the equivalent of 1 mg of anhydrous theophylline per kg of body weight every twelve hours.

Premature infants, postnatal age 24 days and older—Oral, the equivalent of 1.5 mg of anhydrous theophylline per kg of body weight every twelve hours.

Note: **If the above maintenance dose is to be maintained or exceeded, monitoring of serum theophylline concentration and patient response is recommended to achieve the optimal therapeutic aminophylline dosage and minimize the risk of toxicity.**

Strength(s) usually available

U.S.—

105 mg of anhydrous aminophylline (equivalent to 90 mg of anhydrous theophylline) per 5 mL (Rx) [GENERIC].

Canada—

Not commercially available.

Packaging and storage

Store between 15 and 30 °C (59 and 86 °F), unless otherwise specified by manufacturer. Store in a tight container.

AMINOPHYLLINE TABLETS USP

Usual adult dose

See *Aminophylline Oral Solution USP.*

Usual pediatric dose

Bronchodilator—

Loading dose—

For patients not currently receiving theophylline preparations—Infants and children up to 16 years of age: Oral, the equivalent of 5 mg of anhydrous theophylline per kg of lean (ideal) body weight as a single dose to provide an average peak serum concentration of 10 mcg per mL (55 micromoles per L), range 5 to 15 mcg per mL (27.5 to 82.5 micromoles per L).

For patients currently receiving theophylline preparations—Obtaining a serum theophylline concentration prior to administering a partial loading dose is recommended. Once the theophylline concentration is known, the loading dose for theophylline is based on the principle that each 0.5 mg of theophylline per kg of lean (ideal) body weight will result in a 1 mcg per mL increase in serum theophylline concentration.

Maintenance—

Premature infants, postnatal age less than 24 days—Oral, the equivalent of 1 mg of anhydrous theophylline per kg of body weight every twelve hours.

Premature infants, postnatal age 24 days and older—Oral, the equivalent of 1.5 mg of anhydrous theophylline per kg of body weight every twelve hours.

Full-term infants, postnatal age up to 52 weeks—Oral, the equivalent of anhydrous theophylline: total daily dose in mg per kg of body weight = (0.2)(postnatal age in weeks) + 5.

Note: For full-term infants up to 26 weeks of age, divide the total daily dose into three equal amounts administered eight hours apart.

For full-term infants 26 to 52 weeks of age, divide the total daily dose into four equal amounts administered six hours apart.

Children 1 year of age and older, weighing less than 45 kg—Oral, the equivalent of anhydrous theophylline, 12 to 14 mg per kg of body weight, *up to a maximum of 300 mg*, per day in divided doses. The dosage may be increased, if tolerated, after three days to 16 mg per kg of body weight, *up to a maximum of 400 mg*, per day. After three more days, if tolerated, the dosage may be increased to 20 mg per kg of body weight, *up to a maximum of 600 mg*, per day. The total daily dose is administered in four to six divided doses and given every four to six hours.

Children weighing more than 45 kg—See *Usual adult dose*.

Note: **If the above maintenance dose is to be maintained or exceeded, monitoring of serum theophylline concentration and patient response is recommended to achieve the optimal therapeutic aminophylline dosage and minimize the risk of toxicity.**

Strength(s) usually available

U.S.—

100 mg of hydrous aminophylline (equivalent to 79 mg of anhydrous theophylline) (Rx) [GENERIC (may be scored)].

200 mg of hydrous aminophylline (equivalent to 158 mg of anhydrous theophylline) (Rx) [GENERIC (may be scored)].

Canada—

100 mg of hydrous aminophylline (equivalent to 79 mg of anhydrous theophylline) (Rx) [GENERIC (may be scored)].

200 mg of hydrous aminophylline (equivalent to 158 mg of anhydrous theophylline) (Rx) [GENERIC (may be scored)].

Packaging and storage

Store below 40 °C (104 °F), preferably between 15 and 30 °C (59 and 86 °F), unless otherwise specified by manufacturer. Store in a tight container.

AMINOPHYLLINE EXTENDED-RELEASE TABLETS

Usual adult dose

Bronchodilator—

Oral, the equivalent of anhydrous theophylline, initially, 300 mg per day. If tolerated, the dosage may be increased after three days, to 400 mg per day. After three more days, the dosage may be increased, if tolerated, to 600 mg per day without measurement of serum concentration. One-half of the daily dose may be given at twelve-hour intervals. However, certain patients metabolize theophylline more rapidly, especially the young and those who smoke, and may require dosing at eight-hour intervals.

Note: **If the 600-mg-per-day dose is to be maintained or exceeded, monitoring of serum theophylline concentration and patient response is recommended to achieve the optimal therapeutic aminophylline dosage and minimize the risk of toxicity.**

Usual pediatric dose

Bronchodilator—

Children up to 6 years of age: Use is not recommended.

Children 6 to 16 years of age: See *Usual adult dose*.

Strength(s) usually available

U.S.—

225 mg of hydrous aminophylline (equivalent to 178 mg of anhydrous theophylline) (Rx) [*Phyllocontin* (scored)].

Canada—

225 mg of hydrous aminophylline (equivalent to 182.25 mg of anhydrous theophylline) (Rx) [*Phyllocontin* (scored)].

350 mg of hydrous aminophylline (equivalent to 283.5 mg of anhydrous theophylline (Rx) [*Phyllocontin-350* (scored)].

Packaging and storage

Store below 40 °C (104 °F), preferably between 15 and 30 °C (59 and 86 °F), in a well-closed container, unless otherwise specified by manufacturer.

Parenteral Dosage Forms

Note: Bracketed uses in the *Dosage Forms* section refer to categories of use and/or indications that are not included in U.S. product labeling.

AMINOPHYLLINE INJECTION USP

Usual adult dose

Bronchodilator—

Loading dose—

For patients *not* currently receiving theophylline preparations—Intravenous, the equivalent of 5 mg of anhydrous theophylline per kg of lean (ideal) body weight as a single dose, infused over twenty to thirty minutes, to provide an average peak serum concentration of 10 mcg per mL (55 micromoles per L), range 5 to 15 mcg per ml (27.5 to 82.5 micromoles per L).

For patients currently receiving theophylline preparations—Obtaining a serum theophylline concentration prior to administering a partial loading dose is recommended. Once the theophylline concentration is known, the loading dose for theophylline is based on the principle that each 0.5 mg of theophylline per kg of lean (ideal) body weight will result in a 1 mcg per mL increase in serum theophylline concentration.

Maintenance—

Young adult smokers—Intravenous infusion, the equivalent of anhydrous theophylline, 700 mcg (0.7 mg) per kg of body weight per hour.

Otherwise healthy nonsmoking adults—Intravenous infusion, the equivalent of anhydrous theophylline, 400 mcg (0.4 mg) per kg of body weight per hour.

Older patients and patients with cardiac decompensation, cor pulmonale, or hepatic function impairment—Intravenous infusion, the equivalent of anhydrous theophylline, 200 mcg (0.2 mg) per kg of body weight per hour.

Note: **If the above maintenance dose is to be maintained or exceeded, monitoring of serum theophylline concentration and patient response is recommended to achieve the optimal therapeutic aminophylline dosage and minimize the risk of toxicity.**

Antidote (to dipyridamole toxicity)[1]—

Intravenous, the equivalent of 50 to 100 mg (range, 50 mg up to a maximum dose of 250 mg) administered over thirty to sixty seconds.

Usual pediatric dose

Bronchodilator—

Loading dose—

For patients not currently receiving theophylline preparations—Children up to 16 years of age: Intravenous, the equivalent of 5 mg of anhydrous theophylline per kg of lean (ideal) body weight as a single dose over twenty to thirty minutes to provide an average peak serum concentration of 10 mcg per mL (55 micromoles per L), range 5 to 15 mcg per mL (27.5 to 82.5 micromoles per L).

For patients currently receiving theophylline preparations—Obtaining a serum theophylline concentration prior to administering a partial loading dose is recommended. Once the theophylline concentration is known, the loading dose for theophylline is based on the principle that each 0.5 mg of theophylline per kg of lean (ideal) body weight will result in a 1 mcg per mL increase in serum theophylline concentration.

Maintenance—

Premature infants, postnatal age less than 24 days—Intravenous, the equivalent of 1 mg of anhydrous theophylline per kg of body weight every twelve hours.

Premature infants, postnatal age 24 days and older—Intravenous, the equivalent of 1.5 mg of anhydrous theophylline per kg of body weight every twelve hours.

Full-term infants, postnatal age up to 52 weeks—Intravenous, the equivalent of anhydrous theophylline, total daily dose in mg per kg of body weight = (0.2)(postnatal age in weeks) + 5.

For full-term infants up to 26 weeks of age, divide the total daily dose into three equal amounts administered eight hours apart. For full-term infants 26 to 52 weeks of age, divide the total daily dose into four equal amounts administered six hours apart.

Note: May also be administered to infants less than 1 year as an intravenous infusion, the equivalent of anhydrous theophylline, dose in mg per kg of body weight per hour = (0.008)(age in weeks) + 0.21.

Children 1 to 9 years of age—Intravenous infusion, the equivalent of anhydrous theophylline, 800 mcg (0.8 mg) per kg of body weight per hour.

Children 9 to 16 years—Intravenous infusion, the equivalent of anhydrous theophylline, 700 mcg (0.7 mg) per kg of body weight per hour.

Note: **If the above maintenance dose is to be maintained or exceeded, monitoring of serum theophylline concentration and patient response is recommended to achieve the optimal therapeutic aminophylline dosage and minimize the risk of toxicity.**

[Respiratory stimulant (neonatal apnea)][1]—

Loading dose—

For patients *not* currently receiving theophylline preparations—Intravenous, the equivalent of 5 mg of anhydrous theophylline per kg of lean (ideal) body weight as a single dose over twenty to thirty minutes to provide an average peak serum concen0 tration of 10 mcg per mL (55 micromoles per L), range 5 to 15 mcg per mL (27.5 to 82.5 micromoles per L).

For patients currently receiving theophylline preparations: Obtaining a serum theophylline concentration prior to administering a partial loading dose is recommended. Once the theophylline concentration is known, the loading dose for theophylline is based on the principle that each 0.5 mg of theophylline per kg of lean (ideal) body weight will result in a 1 mcg per mL increase in serum theophylline concentration.

Maintenance—

Premature infants, postnatal age less than 24 days—Intravenous, the equivalent of 1 mg of anhydrous theophylline per kg of body weight every twelve hours.

Premature infants, postnatal age 24 days and older—Intravenous, the equivalent of 1.5 mg of anhydrous theophylline per kg of body weight every twelve hours.

Note: **If the above maintenance dose is to be maintained or exceeded, monitoring of serum theophylline concentration and patient response is recommended to achieve the optimal therapeutic aminophylline dosage and minimize the risk of toxicity.**

Strength(s) usually available

U.S.—

25 mg of hydrous aminophylline (equivalent to 19.7 mg of anhydrous theophylline) per mL (Rx) [GENERIC].

Canada—

25 mg of hydrous aminophylline (equivalent to 19.7 mg of anhydrous theophylline) per mL (Rx) [GENERIC].

50 mg of hydrous aminophylline (equivalent to 39.4 mg of anhydrous theophylline) per mL (Rx) [GENERIC].

Packaging and storage

Store below 40 °C (104 °F), preferably between 15 and 30 °C (59 and 86 °F), unless otherwise specified by manufacturer. Protect from light. Protect from freezing.

Preparation of dosage form

To dilute the injection for intravenous administration, dextrose 5% in water, sodium chloride, or dextrose-sodium chloride combinations may be used.

Stability

A slight yellowing of the solution can occur when aminophylline is added to some dextrose-containing solutions. Because the aminophylline content remains constant, the discoloration is believed to result from the decomposition of dextrose.

Aminophylline solutions whose concentration does not exceed 40 mg/mL are reported to be stable for at least 48 hours at 77 °F (25 °C).

Incompatibilities

Although aminophylline has been reported to precipitate in acidic media, this generally does not apply to the dilute solutions for intravenous infusions.

No additives should be made directly to the same intravenous bag or bottle of aminophylline because dosages are titrated to response, and because admixture incompatibilities exist with a number of other medications.

Doxapram hydrochloride is reported to be incompatible with aminophylline when combined in the same syringe.

Medications that are incompatible when injected into Y-sites of administration sets with a continuous infusion of aminophylline include amiodarone hydrochloride, ciprofloxacin, diltiazem hydrochloride, dobutamine hydrochloride, hydralazine hydrochloride, and ondansetron hydrochloride.

Rectal Dosage Forms

AMINOPHYLLINE SUPPOSITORIES USP

Note: **USP DI Advisory Panels do not recommend the use of Aminophylline Suppositories USP because of the potential for slow and unreliable absorption.**

Strength(s) usually available

U.S.—

250 mg of hydrous aminophylline (equivalent to 197.5 mg of anhydrous theophylline) (Rx) [*Truphylline;* GENERIC].

500 mg of hydrous aminophylline (equivalent to 395 mg of anhydrous theophylline) (Rx) [*Truphylline;* GENERIC].

Canada—

Not commercially available.

---

[1]Not included in Canadian product labeling.

OXTRIPHYLLINE

Summary of Differences

Pharmacology/pharmacokinetics:

Oxtriphylline is the choline salt of theophylline.

Oxtriphylline releases free theophylline at physiologic pH.

General dosing information:

Oxtriphylline contains about 64% of anhydrous theophylline.

Additional Dosing Information

See also *General Dosing Information.*

The recommended doses are given as a guideline for use in the average patient. Dosage of oxtriphylline must be adjusted to meet the individual requirements of each patient on the basis of product selected, patient characteristics, clinical response, and steady-state serum theophylline concentrations.

Oral Dosage Forms

OXTRIPHYLLINE ORAL SOLUTION USP

Usual adult dose

Bronchodilator—

Loading dose—

For patients *not* currently receiving theophylline preparations—Oral, the equivalent of 5 mg of anhydrous theophylline per kg of lean (ideal) body weight as a single dose to provide an average peak serum concentration of 10 mcg per mL (55 micromoles per L), range 5 to 15 mcg per mL (27.5 to 82.5 micromoles per L).

For patients currently receiving theophylline preparations—Obtaining a serum theophylline concentration prior to administering a partial loading dose is recommended. Once the theophylline concentration is known, the loading dose for theophylline is based on the principle that each 0.5 mg of theophylline per kg of lean (ideal) body weight will result in a 1 mcg per mL increase in serum theophylline concentration.

Maintenance—

Oral, the equivalent of anhydrous theophylline, initially, 300 mg per day. After three days, the dosage may be increased, if tolerated, to 400 mg per day. After three more days, the dosage may be increased, if tolerated, to 600 mg per day without measurement of serum concentration.

The total daily adult dose is administered in three or four divided doses given about six to eight hours apart. Patients with risk factors for impaired theophylline clearance may require a dosing interval of every twelve hours. Young adult smokers and patients with more rapid metabolism may require a dosing interval of every six hours.

Note: **If the 600-mg-per-day dose is to be maintained or exceeded, monitoring of serum theophylline concentration and patient response is recommended to achieve**

the optimal therapeutic oxtriphylline dosage and minimize the risk of toxicity.

Usual pediatric dose

Use is not recommended in children due to high alcohol content.

Strength(s) usually available

U.S.—
Not commercially available.
Canada—
100 mg (equivalent to 64 mg of anhydrous theophylline) per 5 mL (Rx) [*Choledyl* (alcohol 20%); *PMS-Oxtriphylline* (alcohol 20%)].

Packaging and storage

Store below 40 °C (104 °F), preferably between 15 and 30 °C (59 and 86 °F), unless otherwise specified by manufacturer. Store in a tight container. Protect from freezing.

OXTRIPHYLLINE SYRUP

Usual adult dose

See *Oxtriphylline Oral Solution USP.*

Usual pediatric dose

Bronchodilator—
Loading dose—
For patients not currently receiving theophylline preparations—Infants and children up to 16 years of age: Oral, the equivalent of 5 mg of anhydrous theophylline per kg of lean (ideal) body weight as a single dose to provide an average peak serum concentration of 10 mcg/mL (55 micromoles per L), range 5 to 15 mcg per mL (27.5 to 82.5 micromoles per L).
For patients currently receiving theophylline preparations—Obtaining a serum theophylline concentration prior to administering a partial loading dose is recommended. Once the theophylline concentration is known, the loading dose for theophylline is based on the principle that each 0.5 mg of theophylline per kg of lean (ideal) body weight will result in a 1 mcg per mL increase in serum theophylline concentration.
Maintenance—
Premature infants, postnatal age less than 24 days—Oral, the equivalent of 1 mg of anhydrous theophylline per kg of body weight every twelve hours.
Premature infants, postnatal age 24 days and older—Oral, the equivalent of 1.5 mg of anhydrous theophylline per kg of body weight every twelve hours.
Full-term infants, postnatal age up to 52 weeks—Oral, the equivalent of anhydrous theophylline: Total daily dose in mg per kg of body weight = (0.2)(postnatal age in weeks) + 5.
Note: For full-term infants up to 26 weeks of age, divide the total daily dose into three dosing intervals, eight hours apart.
For full-term infants 26 to 52 weeks of age, divide the total daily dose into four dosing intervals six hours apart.
Children 1 year of age and older, but weighing less than 45 kg—Oral, the equivalent of anhydrous theophylline, 12 to 14 mg per kg of body weight, *up to a maximum of 300 mg*, per day in divided doses. The dosage may be increased, if tolerated, after three days to 16 mg per kg of body weight, *up to a maximum of 400 mg per day*. After three more days, if tolerated, the dosage may be increased to 20 mg per kg of body weight *up to a maximum of 600 mg per day*. The total daily dose is administered in four to six divided doses given every four to six hours.
Children weighing more than 45 kg—See *Usual adult dose*.
Note: **If the above maintenance dose is to be maintained or exceeded, monitoring of serum theophylline concentration and patient response is recommended to achieve the optimal therapeutic oxtriphylline dosage and minimize the risk of toxicity.**

Strength(s) usually available

U.S.—
Not commercially available.
Canada—
50 mg (equivalent to 32 mg of anhydrous theophylline) per 5 mL (Rx) [*Choledyl; PMS-Oxtriphylline*].

Packaging and storage

Store below 40 °C (104 °F), preferably between 15 and 30 °C (59 and 86 °F), in a tight container, unless otherwise specified by manufacturer. Protect from freezing.

OXTRIPHYLLINE TABLETS

Usual adult dose

See *Oxtriphylline Oral Solution USP.*

Usual pediatric dose

See *Oxtriphylline Syrup.*

Strength(s) usually available

U.S.—
Not commercially available.
Canada—
100 mg (equivalent to 64 mg of anhydrous theophylline) (Rx) [*Apo-Oxtriphylline*].
200 mg (equivalent to 128 mg of anhydrous theophylline) (Rx) [*Apo-Oxtriphylline; Choledyl*].
300 mg (equivalent to 192 mg of anhydrous theophylline) (Rx) [*Apo-Oxtriphylline*].

Packaging and storage

Store below 40 °C (104 °F), preferably between 15 and 30 °C (59 and 86 °F), unless otherwise specified by manufacturer. Store in a tight container.

OXTRIPHYLLINE DELAYED-RELEASE TABLETS USP

Usual adult dose

Bronchodilator—
Oral, the equivalent of anhydrous theophylline, initially, 300 mg per day. If tolerated, the dosage may be increased after three days to 400 mg per day. After three more days, the dosage may be increased, if tolerated, to 600 mg per day without measurement of serum concentration. The total daily adult dose is administered in three or four divided doses given about six to eight hours apart. Patients with risk factors for impaired theophylline clearance may require a dosing interval of every twelve hours. Young adult smokers and patients with more rapid metabolism may require a dosing interval of every six hours.

Usual pediatric dose

Bronchodilator—
Children up to 6 years of age: Use is not recommended in children up to 6 years of age since this age group may not be capable of swallowing the tablets whole.
Children 6 to 16 years of age: See *Usual adult dose.*

Strength(s) usually available

U.S.—
100 mg (equivalent to 64 mg of anhydrous theophylline) (Rx) [*Choledyl* (enteric, sugar-coated)].
200 mg (equivalent to 127 mg of anhydrous theophylline) (Rx) [*Choledyl* (enteric, sugar-coated)].
Canada—
Not commercially available.

Packaging and storage

Store below 40 °C (104 °F), preferably between 15 and 30 °C (59 and 86 °F), unless otherwise specified by manufacturer. Store in a tight container.

Auxiliary labeling

- Swallow tablets whole.

OXTRIPHYLLINE EXTENDED-RELEASE TABLETS USP

Usual adult dose

Bronchodilator—
Oral, the equivalent of anhydrous theophylline, initially, 300 mg per day. If tolerated, the dosage may be increased after three days to 400 mg per day. After three more days, the dosage may be increased, if tolerated, to 600 mg per day without measurement of serum concentration. One-half of the daily dose may be given at twelve-hour intervals. However, certain patients metabolize theophylline more rapidly, especially the young and those that smoke, and may require dosing at eight-hour intervals.
Note: **If the 600-mg-per-day dose is to be maintained or exceeded, monitoring of serum theophylline concentration and patient response is recommended to achieve the optimal therapeutic oxtriphylline dosage and minimize the risk of toxicity.**

Usual pediatric dose

Bronchodilator—
Children up to 6 years of age: Use is not recommended.
Children 6 to 16 years of age: See *Usual adult dose.*

Strength(s) usually available

U.S.—
400 mg (equivalent to 254 mg of anhydrous theophylline) (Rx) [*Choledyl SA* (confectioner's sugar)].
600 mg (equivalent to 382 mg of anhydrous theophylline) (Rx) [*Choledyl SA* (confectioner's sugar)].
Canada—
400 mg (equivalent to 254 mg of anhydrous theophylline) (Rx) [*Choledyl SA* (scored)].
600 mg (equivalent to 382 mg of anhydrous theophylline) (Rx) [*Choledyl SA* (scored)].

Packaging and storage
Store below 40 °C (104 °F), preferably between 15 and 30 °C (59 and 86 °F), unless otherwise specified by manufacturer. Store in a tight container.

THEOPHYLLINE

Summary of Differences
Category: Theophylline oral liquids are also used as a respiratory stimulant in neonatal apnea.

Additional Dosing Information
See also *General Dosing Information.*

The recommended doses are given as a guideline for use in the average patient. Dosage of theophylline must be adjusted to meet the individual requirements of each patient on the basis of product selected, patient characteristics, clinical response, and steady-state serum theophylline concentrations.

For parenteral dosage forms only
The rate of administration of theophylline and dextrose injection should *not exceed* 25 mg per minute.

Oral Dosage Forms
Note: Bracketed uses in the *Dosage Forms* section refer to categories of use and/or indications that are not included in U.S. product labeling.

THEOPHYLLINE CAPSULES USP

Usual adult dose
Bronchodilator—

Loading dose—

For patients *not* currently receiving theophylline preparations—Oral, the equivalent of 5 mg of anhydrous theophylline per kg of lean (ideal) body weight as a single dose to provide an average peak serum concentration of 10 mcg per mL (55 micromoles per L), range 5 to 15 mcg per mL (27.5 to 82.5 micromoles per L).

For patients currently receiving theophylline preparations—Obtaining a serum theophylline concentration prior to administering a partial loading dose is recommended. Once the theophylline concentration is known, the loading dose for theophylline is based on the principle that each 0.5 mg of theophylline per kg of lean (ideal) body weight will result in a 1 mcg per mL increase in serum theophylline concentration.

Maintenance—

Oral, the equivalent of anhydrous theophylline, initially, 300 mg per day. After three days, the dosage may be increased, if tolerated, to 400 mg per day. After three more days, the dosage may be increased, if tolerated, to 600 mg per day without measurement of serum concentration.

The total daily adult dose is administered in three or four divided doses given about six to eight hours apart. Patients with risk factors for impaired theophylline clearance may require a dosing interval of every twelve hours. Young adult smokers and patients with more rapid metabolism may require a dosing interval of every six hours.

Note: **If the 600-mg-per-day dose is to be maintained or exceeded, monitoring of serum theophylline concentration and patient response is recommended to achieve the optimal therapeutic theophylline dosage and minimize the risk of toxicity.**

Usual pediatric dose
Bronchodilator—

Loading dose—

For patients *not* currently receiving theophylline preparations—Infants and children up to 16 years of age: Oral, the equivalent of 5 mg of anhydrous theophylline per kg of lean (ideal) body weight as a single dose to provide an average peak serum concentration of 10 mcg per mL (55 micromoles per L), range 5 to 15 mcg per mL (27.5 to 82.5 micromoles per L).

For patients currently receiving theophylline preparations—Obtaining a serum theophylline concentration prior to administering a partial loading dose is recommended. Once the theophylline concentration is known, the loading dose for theophylline is based on the principle that each 0.5 mg of theophylline per kg of lean (ideal) body weight will result in a 1 mcg per mL increase in serum theophylline concentration.

Maintenance—

Children 1 year of age and older, weighing less than 45 kg—Oral, the equivalent of anhydrous theophylline, 12 to 14 mg per kg of body weight, *up to a maximum of 300 mg,* per day in divided doses. The dosage may be increased, if tolerated, after three days to 16 mg per kg of body weight, *up to a maximum of 400 mg,* per day. After three more days, if tolerated, the dosage may be increased to 20 mg per kg of body weight *up to a maximum of 600 mg,* per day. The total daily dose is administered in four to six divided doses given every four to six hours.

Children weighing more than 45 kg—See *Usual adult dose.*

Note: **If the 600-mg-per-day dose is to be maintained or exceeded, monitoring of serum theophylline concentration and patient response is recommended to achieve the optimal therapeutic theophylline dosage and minimize the risk of toxicity.**

Strength(s) usually available
U.S.—

100 mg (equivalent of anhydrous theophylline) (Rx) [*Elixophyllin;* GENERIC].

200 mg (equivalent of anhydrous theophylline) (Rx) [*Elixophyllin;* GENERIC].

300 mg (equivalent of anhydrous theophylline) (Rx) [GENERIC].

Canada—

Not commercially available.

Packaging and storage
Store below 40 °C (104 °F), preferably between 15 and 30 °C (59 and 86 °F), unless otherwise specified by manufacturer. Store in a well-closed container.

THEOPHYLLINE EXTENDED-RELEASE CAPSULES USP
Note: Due to the significant variability in extended-release product characteristics, pharmacists should not substitute one brand for another without consulting the prescribing physician unless the product has proven bioequivalence, so that theophylline serum concentrations can be appropriately monitored.

Usual adult dose
Bronchodilator—

Oral, the equivalent of anhydrous theophylline, initially, 300 mg per day. If tolerated, the dosage may be increased after three days to 400 mg per day. After three more days, the dosage may be increased, if tolerated, to 600 mg per day without measurement of serum concentration. One-half of the daily theophylline dose may be given at twelve-hour intervals. However, certain patients metabolize theophylline more rapidly, especially the young and those that smoke, and may require dosing at eight-hour intervals.

Note: **If the 600-mg-per-day dose is to be maintained or exceeded, monitoring of serum theophylline concentration and patient response is recommended to achieve the optimal therapeutic theophylline dosage and minimize the risk of toxicity.**

Usual pediatric dose
Bronchodilator—

Children 1 year of age and older, weighing less than 45 kg: Oral, the equivalent of anhydrous theophylline, 12 to 14 mg per kg of body weight, *up to a maximum of 300 mg,* per day in divided doses. The dosage may be increased, if tolerated, after three days to 16 mg per kg of body weight, *up to a maximum of 400 mg,* per day. After three more days, if tolerated, the dosage may be increased to 20 mg per kg of body weight *up to a maximum of 600 mg,* per day. One-half of the daily theophylline dose may be given as aminophylline at twelve-hour intervals. However, younger patients may require dosing at eight-hour intervals.

Children weighing more than 45 kg: See *Usual adult dose.*

Note: **If the 600-mg-per-day dose is to be maintained or exceeded, monitoring of serum theophylline concentration and patient response is recommended to achieve the optimal therapeutic theophylline dosage and minimize the risk of toxicity.**

Strength(s) usually available
U.S.—

50 mg (equivalent of anhydrous theophylline) (Rx) [*Slo-Bid Gyrocaps*].

75 mg (equivalent of anhydrous theophylline) (Rx) [*Slo-Bid Gyrocaps*].

100 mg (equivalent of anhydrous theophylline) (Rx) [*Slo-Bid Gyrocaps; Theo-24*].

125 mg (equivalent of anhydrous theophylline) (Rx) [*Slo-Bid Gyrocaps; Theovent Long-Acting*].

200 mg (equivalent of anhydrous theophylline) (Rx) [*Slo-Bid Gyrocaps; Theo-24*].

250 mg (equivalent of anhydrous theophylline) (Rx) [*Theovent Long-Acting*].

260 mg (equivalent of anhydrous theophylline) (Rx) [*Aerolate Sr; Theobid Duracaps*].
300 mg (equivalent of anhydrous theophylline) (Rx) [*Slo-Bid Gyrocaps; Theo-24*].
400 mg (equivalent of anhydrous theophylline) (Rx) [*Theo-24*].

Canada—
50 mg (equivalent of anhydrous theophylline) (Rx) [*Slo-Bid Gyrocaps*].
100 mg (equivalent of anhydrous theophylline) (Rx) [*Slo-Bid Gyrocaps*].
200 mg (equivalent of anhydrous theophylline) (Rx) [*Slo-Bid Gyrocaps*].
300 mg (equivalent of anhydrous theophylline) (Rx) [*Slo-Bid Gyrocaps*].

Packaging and storage

Store below 40 °C (104 °F), preferably between 15 and 30 °C (59 and 86 °F), unless otherwise specified by manufacturer. Store in a well-closed container.

Additional information

Certain extended-release capsules may be opened and the contents sprinkled on soft food immediately prior to ingestion, then swallowed without crushing or chewing. Capsule contents should not be subdivided.

THEOPHYLLINE ELIXIR

Usual adult dose

See *Theophylline Capsules USP*.

Usual pediatric dose

Use is not recommended in children due to the high alcohol content.

Strength(s) usually available

U.S.—
27 mg (equivalent of anhydrous theophylline) per 5 mL (Rx) [*Asmalix* (alcohol 20%); *Elixophyllin* (alcohol 20%); *Lanophyllin* (alcohol 20%); *Truxophyllin;* GENERIC].

Canada—
27 mg (equivalent of anhydrous theophylline) per 5 mL (Rx) [*PMS Theophylline* (alcohol 18%); *Pulmophylline* (alcohol 20% [v/v]); GENERIC].

Packaging and storage

Store below 40 °C (104 °F), preferably between 15 and 30 °C (59 and 86 °F), in a tight container, unless otherwise specified by manufacturer. Protect from freezing.

Stability

Exposure to cold temperatures may cause theophylline crystallization to occur. At room temperature the crystals redissolve and solution gradually clears.

Auxiliary labeling

• Do not refrigerate.

THEOPHYLLINE ORAL SOLUTION

Usual adult dose

See *Theophylline Capsules USP*.

Usual pediatric dose

Bronchodilator—
Loading dose—
For patients not currently receiving theophylline preparations—Infants and children up to 16 years of age: Oral, the equivalent of 5 mg of anhydrous theophylline per kg of lean (ideal) body weight as a single dose to provide an average peak serum concentration of 10 mcg per mL (55 micromoles per L), range 5 to 15 mcg per mL (27.5 to 82.5 micromoles per L).
For patients currently receiving theophylline preparations—Obtaining a serum theophylline concentration prior to administering a partial loading dose is recommended. Once the theophylline concentration is known, the loading dose for theophylline is based on the principle that each 0.5 mg of theophylline per kg of lean (ideal) body weight will result in a 1 mcg per mL increase in serum theophylline concentration.

Maintenance—
Premature infants, postnatal age less than 24 days—Oral, the equivalent of 1 mg of anhydrous theophylline per kg of body weight every twelve hours.
Premature infants, postnatal age 24 days and older—Oral, the equivalent of 1.5 mg of anhydrous theophylline per kg of body weight every twelve hours.
Full-term infants, postnatal age up to 52 weeks—Oral, the equivalent of anhydrous theophylline: total daily dose in mg per kg of body weight = (0.2)(postnatal age in weeks) + 5.

Note: For full-term infants up to 26 weeks of age, divide the total daily dose into three equal amounts administered eight hours apart.

For full-term infants 26 to 52 weeks of age, divide the total daily dose into four equal amounts administered six hours apart.

Children 1 year of age and older, weighing less than 45 kg: Oral, the equivalent of anhydrous theophylline, 12 to 14 mg per kg of body weight, *up to a maximum of 300 mg*, per day in divided doses. The dosage may be increased, if tolerated, after three days to 16 mg per kg of body weight, *up to a maximum of 400 mg*, per day. After three more days, if tolerated, the dosage may be increased to 20 mg per kg of body weight *up to a maximum of 600 mg*, per day. The total daily dose is administered in four to six divided doses given every four to six hours.
Children weighing more than 45 kg: See *Usual adult dose*.

Note: **If the above maintenance dose is to be maintained or exceeded, monitoring of serum theophylline concentration and patient response is recommended to achieve the optimal therapeutic theophylline dosage and minimize the risk of toxicity.**

[Respiratory stimulant (neonatal apnea)][1]—
Loading dose—
For patients *not* currently receiving theophylline preparations—Infants and children up to 16 years of age: Oral, the equivalent of 5 mg of anhydrous theophylline per kg of lean (ideal) body weight as a single dose to provide an average peak serum concentration of 10 mcg per mL (55 micromoles per L), range 5 to 15 mcg per mL (27.5 to 82.5 micromoles per L).
For patients currently receiving theophylline preparations—Obtaining a serum theophylline concentration prior to administering a partial loading dose is recommended. Once the theophylline concentration is known, the loading dose for theophylline is based on the principle that each 0.5 mg of theophylline per kg of lean (ideal) body weight will result in a 1 mcg per mL increase in serum theophylline concentration.

Maintenance—
Premature infants, postnatal age less than 24 days—Oral, the equivalent of 1 mg of anhydrous theophylline per kg of body weight every twelve hours.
Premature infants, postnatal age 24 days and older—Oral, the equivalent of 1.5 mg of anhydrous theophylline per kg of body weight every twelve hours.

Note: **If the above maintenance dose is to be maintained or exceeded, monitoring of serum theophylline concentration and patient response is recommended to achieve the optimal therapeutic theophylline dosage and minimize the risk of toxicity.**

Strength(s) usually available

U.S.—
27 mg (equivalent of anhydrous theophylline) per 5 mL (Rx) [*Theolair;* GENERIC].

Canada—
27 mg (equivalent of anhydrous theophylline) per 5 mL (Rx) [*Theolair*].

Packaging and storage

Store below 40 °C (104 °F), preferably between 15 and 30 °C (59 and 86 °F), in a well-closed container, unless otherwise specified by manufacturer. Protect from freezing.

Stability

Exposure to cold temperatures may cause theophylline crystallization to occur. At room temperature the crystals redissolve and solution gradually clears.

Auxiliary labeling

• Do not refrigerate.

THEOPHYLLINE SYRUP

Usual adult dose

See *Theophylline Capsules USP*.

Usual pediatric dose

See *Theophylline Oral Solution*.

Strength(s) usually available

U.S.—
27 mg (equivalent of anhydrous theophylline) per 5 mL (Rx) [*Slo-Phyllin*].

Canada—
Not commercially available.

Packaging and storage
Store below 40 °C (104 °F), preferably between 15 and 30 °C (59 and 86 °F), in a well-closed container, unless otherwise specified by manufacturer. Protect from freezing.

Stability
Exposure to cold temperatures may cause theophylline crystallization to occur. At room temperature the crystals redissolve and solution gradually clears.

Auxiliary labeling
- Do not refrigerate.

THEOPHYLLINE TABLETS USP

Usual adult dose
See *Theophylline Capsules USP*.

Usual pediatric dose
See *Theophylline Capsules USP*.

Strength(s) usually available
U.S.—

100 mg (equivalent of anhydrous theophylline) (Rx) [*Slo-Phyllin* (scored); GENERIC].

125 mg (equivalent of anhydrous theophylline) (Rx) [*Theolair* (scored)].

200 mg (equivalent of anhydrous theophylline) (Rx) [*Slo-Phyllin* (scored); GENERIC].

250 mg (equivalent of anhydrous theophylline) (Rx) [*Theolair* (scored)].

300 mg (equivalent of anhydrous theophylline) (Rx) [*Quibron-T Dividose* (scored); GENERIC].

Canada—

125 mg (equivalent of anhydrous theophylline) (Rx) [*Theolair* (scored)].

250 mg (equivalent of anhydrous theophylline) (Rx) [*Theolair* (scored)].

Packaging and storage
Store below 40 °C (104 °F), preferably between 15 and 30 °C (59 and 86 °F), unless otherwise specified by manufacturer. Store in a well-closed container.

THEOPHYLLINE EXTENDED-RELEASE TABLETS

Note: Due to the significant variability in extended-release product characteristics, pharmacists should not substitute one brand for another without consulting the prescribing physician unless the product has proven bioequivalence, so that theophylline serum concentrations can be appropriately monitored.

Usual adult dose
Bronchodilator—Oral, the equivalent of anhydrous theophylline, initially, 300 mg per day. If tolerated, the dosage may be increased after three days, to 400 mg per day. After three more days, the dosage may be increased, if tolerated, to 600 mg per day without measurement of serum concentration. One-half the daily theophylline dose may be given at twelve hour intervals. However, certain patients metabolize theophylline more rapidly, especially the young and those that smoke, and may require dosing at eight hour intervals.

Note: **If the 600-mg-per-day dose is to be maintained or exceeded, monitoring of serum theophylline concentration and patient response is recommended to achieve the optimal therapeutic theophylline dosage and minimize the risk of toxicity.**

Usual pediatric dose
Bronchodilator—

Children 1 year of age and older, weighing less than 45 kg: Oral, the equivalent of anhydrous theophylline, 12 to 14 mg per kg of body weight, *up to a maximum of 300 mg*, per day in divided doses. The dosage may be increased, if tolerated, after three days to 16 mg per kg of body weight, *up to a maximum of 400 mg*, per day. After three more days, if tolerated, the dosage may be increased to 20 mg per kg of body weight *up to a maximum of 600 mg*, per day. One-half of the daily theophylline dose may be given at twelve-hour intervals. However, younger patients may require dosing at eight-hour intervals.

Children weighing more than 45 kg: See *Usual adult dose*.

Children 6 to 16 years of age: See *Usual adult dose*.

Strength(s) usually available
U.S.—

100 mg (equivalent of anhydrous theophylline) (Rx) [*Theochron* (scored); *Theo-Dur* (scored); *Theo-Time; Theo-X;* GENERIC].

200 mg (equivalent of anhydrous theophylline) (Rx) [*Theochron* (scored); *Theo-Dur* (scored); *Theolair-SR* (scored); *Theo-Time; Theo-X; T-Phyl* (scored); GENERIC].

250 mg (equivalent of anhydrous theophylline) (Rx) [*Respbid* (scored); *Theolair-SR* (scored)].

300 mg (equivalent of anhydrous theophylline) (Rx) [*Quibron-T/SR Dividose* (scored); *Theochron* (scored); *Theo-Dur* (scored); *Theolair-SR* (scored); *Theo-Time; Theo-X;* GENERIC].

400 mg (equivalent of anhydrous theophylline) (Rx) [*Uni-Dur* (scored); *Uniphyl* (scored)].

450 mg (equivalent of anhydrous theophylline) (Rx) [*Theo-Dur* (scored); GENERIC (may be scored)].

500 mg (equivalent of anhydrous theophylline) (Rx) [*Respbid* (scored); *Theolair-SR* (scored)].

600 mg (equivalent of anhydrous theophylline) (Rx) [*Uni-Dur* (scored)].

Canada—

100 mg (equivalent of anhydrous theophylline) (Rx) [*Apo-Theo LA* (scored); *Theochron* (scored); *Theo-Dur* (scored)].

200 mg (equivalent of anhydrous theophylline) (Rx) [*Apo-Theo LA* (scored); *Theochron* (scored); *Theo-Dur* (scored); *Theolair-SR* (scored); *Theo-SR* (scored)].

250 mg (equivalent of anhydrous theophylline) (Rx) [*Theolair SR* (scored)].

300 mg (equivalent of anhydrous theophylline) (Rx) [*Apo-Theo LA* (scored); *Quibron-T/SR Dividose* (scored); *Theochron* (scored); *Theo-Dur* (scored); *Theolair-SR* (scored); *Theo-SR* (scored)].

400 mg (equivalent of anhydrous theophylline) (Rx) [*Uniphyl* (scored)].

450 mg (equivalent of anhydrous theophylline) (Rx) [*Theo-Dur* (scored)].

500 mg (equivalent of anhydrous theophylline) (Rx) [*Theolair-SR* (scored)].

600 mg (equivalent of anhydrous theophylline) (Rx) [*Uniphyl* (scored)].

Packaging and storage
Store below 40 °C (104 °F), preferably between 15 and 30 °C (59 and 86 °F), in a well-closed container, unless otherwise specified by manufacturer.

Auxiliary labeling
- Swallow tablets whole, unless otherwise directed.

Parenteral Dosage Forms

Note: Bracketed uses in the *Dosage Forms* section refer to categories of use and/or indications that are not included in U.S. product labeling.

THEOPHYLLINE IN DEXTROSE INJECTION USP

Usual adult dose
Bronchodilator—

Loading dose—

For patients *not* currently receiving theophylline preparations—Intravenous, the equivalent of 5 mg of anhydrous theophylline per kg of lean (ideal) body weight as a single dose, infused over 20 to 30 minutes, to provide an average peak serum concentration of 10 mcg per mL (55 micromoles per L), range 5 to 15 mcg per mL (range 27.5 to 82.5 micromoles per L).

For patients currently receiving theophylline preparations—Obtaining a serum theophylline concentration prior to administering a partial loading dose is recommended. Once the theophylline concentration is known, the loading dose for theophylline is based on the principle that each 0.5 mg of theophylline per kg of lean (ideal) body weight will result in a 1 mcg per mL increase in serum theophylline concentration.

Maintenance—

Young adult smokers—Intravenous infusion, the equivalent of anhydrous theophylline: 700 mcg (0.7 mg) per kg of body weight per hour

Otherwise healthy nonsmoking adults—Intravenous infusion, the equivalent of anhydrous theophylline: 400 mcg (0.4 mg) per kg of body weight per hour.

Older patients and patients with cardiac decompensation, cor pulmonale, or hepatic function impairment—Intravenous infusion, the equivalent of anhydrous theophylline: 200 mcg (0.2 mg) per kg of body weight per hour.

Note: **If the above maintenance dose is to be maintained or exceeded, monitoring of serum theophylline concentration and patient response is recommended to achieve the optimal therapeutic theophylline dosage and minimize the risk of toxicity.**

Usual pediatric dose
Bronchodilator—

Loading dose—

For patients *not* currently receiving theophylline preparations—

Children 1 to 16 years of age: Intravenous, the equivalent of 5 mg of anhydrous theophylline per kg of lean (ideal) body weight as a single dose over twenty to thirty minutes to provide an average peak serum concentration of 10 mcg per mL (55 micromoles per L), range 5 to 15 mcg per mL (27.5 to 82.5 micromoles per L).

For patients currently receiving theophylline preparations—Obtaining a serum theophylline concentration prior to administering a partial loading dose is recommended. Once the theophylline concentration is known, the loading dose for theophylline is based on the principle that each 0.5 mg of theophylline per kg of lean (ideal) body weight will result in a 1 mcg per mL increase in serum theophylline concentration.

Maintenance—

Full-term infants, postnatal age up to 52 weeks—Intravenous infusion, the equivalent of anhydrous theophylline: Dose in mg per kg of body weight per hour = (0.008)(age in weeks) + 0.21.

Children 1 to 9 years of age—Intravenous infusion, the equivalent of anhydrous theophylline: 800 mcg (0.8 mg) per kg of body weight per hour.

Children 9 to 16 years—Intravenous infusion, the equivalent of anhydrous theophylline: 700 mcg (0.7 mg) per kg of body weight per hour.

Note: **If the above maintenance dose is to be maintained or exceeded, monitoring of serum theophylline concentration and patient response is recommended to achieve the optimal therapeutic theophylline dosage and minimize the risk of toxicity.**

Strength(s) usually available

U.S.—

Theophylline in 5% dextrose injection (Rx) [GENERIC] contains the following amounts of anhydrous theophylline:

Volume (approx.) mL	Theophylline Anhydrous	
	Total mg	mg/mL
50	200	4
100	200	2
100	400	4
250	400	1.6
250	800	3.2
500	400	0.8
500	800	1.6
1000	400	0.4
1000	800	0.8

Canada—

Theophylline in 5% dextrose injection (Rx) [GENERIC] contains the following amounts of anhydrous theophylline:

Volume (approx.) mL	Theophylline Anhydrous	
	Total mg	mg/mL
50	200	4
100	200	2
100	400	4
250	400	1.6
500	400	0.8
500	800	1.6
1000	400	0.4
1000	800	0.8

Packaging and storage

Store below 40 °C (104 °F), preferably between 15 and 30 °C (59 and 86 °F), unless otherwise specified by manufacturer. Protect from freezing.

Stability

Theophylline and dextrose solutions contain no bacteriostatic, antimicrobial agent, or added buffer; they are intended only for single-dose administration. When smaller doses are required, the unused portion should be discarded.

Incompatibilities

No additives should be made to theophylline and dextrose injection because dosages are titrated to response.

Hetastarch has been shown to be incompatible with theophylline in dextrose solution when injected into Y-sites of administration sets.

[1]Not included in Canadian product labeling.

Selected Bibliography

Edwards DJ, Zarowitz BJ, Slaughter RL. Theophylline. In: Evans WE, Schentag JJ, Jusko WJ, editors. Applied Pharmacokinetics: principles of therapeutic drug monitoring. Vancouver, WA: Applied Therapeutics, 1992: 13-1–13-38.

Weinberger MM. Methylxanthines. In: Weiss EB, Stein M, editors. Bronchial asthma—mechanisms and therapeutics. Boston: Little, Brown and Co, 1993: 746-83.

National Asthma Education Program. Expert Panel Report. Guidelines for the diagnosis and management of asthma. National Heart, Lung and Blood Institute, 1991.

Revised: 8/11/1995

BUDESONIDE—See *Corticosteroids—Glucocorticoid Effects (Systemic), Corticosteroids (Inhalation-Local), Corticosteroids (Nasal), Corticosteroids (Rectal)*

BUMETANIDE—See *Diuretics, Loop (Systemic)*

BUPIVACAINE—See *Anesthetics (Parenteral-Local)*

BUPROPION Systemic

INN: Amfebutamone

VA CLASSIFICATION (Primary/Secondary): CN609/AD600

Commonly used brand name(s): *Wellbutrin; Wellbutrin SR; Wellbutrin XL; Zyban.*

Note: For a listing of dosage forms and brand names by country availability, see *Dosage Forms* section(s).

Category

Antidepressant; smoking cessation adjunct.

Indications

Accepted

Depressive disorder, major (treatment)—Bupropion is indicated for the treatment of major depression. Treatment of acute depressive episodes typically requires 6 to 12 months of antidepressant therapy. Patients with recurrent or chronic depression may require long-term treatment.

Nicotine dependence (treatment adjunct)—The sustained-release formulation of bupropion is indicated as an aid to smoking cessation treatment. A smoking cessation program should include behavioral interventions, counseling, and/or other support services.

Unaccepted

Bupropion is not approved for use in treating bipolar depression.

Pharmacology/Pharmacokinetics

Physicochemical characteristics

Chemical Group—Aminoketone. Bupropion is structurally related to phenylethylamines and closely resembles diethylpropion.

Molecular weight—Bupropion hydrochloride: 276.21.

Solubility—Highly soluble in water.

Mechanism of action/Effect

Antidepressant—

Although the exact mechanism of antidepressant action is unclear, it is thought to be mediated by bupropion's noradrenergic and/or dopaminergic effects. Bupropion is a weak inhibitor of neuronal uptake of norepinephrine, serotonin, and dopamine, although inhibition of uptake occurs at doses higher than those required for bupropion's antidepressant effects. Hydroxybupropion, an active metabolite of bupropion, has weak norepinephrine reuptake blocking activity but it reaches concentrations high enough to produce significant norepinephrine blockade and may have clinically significant antidepressant effects. Animal studies have suggested that bupropion's antidepressant activity may be mediated through noradrenergic pathways involving the locus ceruleus. Bupropion and hydroxybupropion reduce the firing rates of noradrenergic neurons in the locus ceruleus in a dose-dependent manner; this action is similar to that of the tricyclic antidepressants.

Bupropion shows little affinity for the serotonergic transport system, and it does not inhibit monoamine oxidase.

Smoking cessation adjunct—

Although the exact mechanism of smoking cessation action is unclear, it is thought to be mediated by bupropion's noradrenergic and/or dopaminergic effects. Bupropion increases extracellular dopamine concentrations in the nucleus accumbens, as do all known addictive substances including nicotine. The nucleus accumbens, a part of the mesolimbic dopamine system, may be an important component of the neural circuitry of reward. Also, as nicotine concentrations drop with abstinence, the firing rates of noradrenergic neurons in the locus ceruleus increase, which may be the basis of withdrawal symptoms. Bupropion and its active metabolite, hydroxybupropion, reduce the firing rates of noradrenergic neurons in the locus ceruleus in a dose-dependent manner.

Other actions/effects
Although animal studies indicate that bupropion may be an inducer of hepatic microsomal enzymes, a study in humans using a dosage of 150 mg three times a day for 14 days found no evidence of autoinduction.

May produce dose-related central nervous system (CNS) stimulation.

Absorption
Approximately 80%; rapidly absorbed from the gastrointestinal tract; however, extensive presystemic metabolism limits bioavailability. Food increases extent of absorption insignificantly.

Distribution
Readily crosses the blood-brain barrier and placenta; a study of one subject demonstrated that bupropion and its metabolites are distributed into breast milk.

Protein binding
Bupropion—High (84%), to human plasma proteins.
Hydroxybupropion—High (77%).

Biotransformation
Bupropion is extensively metabolized, including presystemic metabolism. Three metabolites have shown activity in animal studies. Hydroxybupropion, formed principally by the cytochrome P450 2B6 (CYP2B6) isoenzyme, is comparable in potency to bupropion. Threohydrobupropion and erythrohydrobupropion, amino-alcohol isomers formed by hydroxylation and/or reduction, are one tenth to one half as potent as bupropion.

Half-life
Distribution—
3 to 4 hours.

Elimination—
Bupropion: Single-dose mean, approximately 14 (range, 8 to 24) hours. Single-dose studies demonstrate a first-order elimination pattern with a mean total body clearance of approximately 2 liters per hour per kilogram of body weight.
Bupropion: Steady-state mean, 21 ± 9 hours.
Hydroxybupropion: Mean, approximately 20 hours.

Onset of action
Antidepressant—1 to 3 weeks; full effect may require 4 or more weeks to achieve.

Time to peak concentration
Prompt-release formulation—
Bupropion: Approximately 1.5 hours, followed by biphasic decline.
Hydroxybupropion: Approximately 3 hours.

Extended-release formulation—
Bupropion: Approximately 3 hours.
Hydroxybupropion: Approximately 6 hours.

Time to steady-state concentration
Bupropion—Within 5 days.
Hydroxybupropion—Within 8 days.

Steady-state plasma concentration
Mean maximum concentration of bupropion was 136 nanograms per mL (0.492 micromoles per L) in healthy volunteers following a 150-mg dose of the extended-release tablet every 12 hours. Peak plasma concentration of hydroxybupropion at steady-state is approximately 10 times that of bupropion.

Elimination
Renal—
Less than 1% excreted in urine unchanged. Over 60% excreted as metabolites within 24 hours, over 80% within 96 hours.

Fecal—
Less than 10% excreted in feces, primarily as metabolites.

Precautions to Consider

Carcinogenicity
In a lifetime study of rats, there was an increase in nodular proliferative lesions of the liver at doses of 100 mg to 300 mg per kg of body weight (mg/kg; approximately 3 to 10 times the maximum recommended human dose [MRHD] on a mg per square meter of body surface area [mg/m^2] basis) a day. However, whether such lesions may be precursors of neoplasms of the liver has not been resolved. Similar lesions were not seen in studies with mice given doses of up to 150 mg/kg a day (approximately two times the MRHD on a mg/m^2 basis).

Tumorigenicity
Studies in rodents showed no increase in malignant tumors of the liver or other organs.

Mutagenicity
In two of five strains in the Ames bacterial mutagenicity test, bupropion produced a mutation rate of two to three times the control mutation rate. In one of three *in vivo* bone marrow cytogenetic studies in rats, bupropion produced chromosomal aberrations.

Pregnancy/Reproduction
Fertility—Studies in rats and rabbits given doses of up to 300 mg/kg a day have shown no evidence of impaired fertility.

Pregnancy—Adequate and well-controlled studies in humans have not been done. However, bupropion readily crosses the placenta.

Studies in rats and rabbits given doses of up to 15 to 45 times the human daily dose have not shown that bupropion causes adverse effects in the fetus. In rabbits, two studies showed a slightly increased incidence of fetal abnormalities; however, there was no increase in any specific abnormality. Because animal reproduction studies are not always predictive of human response, bupropion should be used during pregnancy only if clearly needed.

Note: To monitor fetal outcomes of pregnant women exposed to bupropion, the manufacturer maintains a Bupropion Pregnancy Registry. Health care providers are encouraged to register patients by calling 1–800–336–2176.

FDA Pregnancy Category B.

Labor and delivery—The effect of bupropion on labor and delivery in humans is unknown.

Breast-feeding
Bupropion accumulates in breast milk, and the potential exists for serious adverse reactions (such as seizures) in the infant.

The milk-to-plasma ratio of bupropion in one nursing mother who was receiving 100 mg of the prompt-release formulation of bupropion three times a day ranged from 2.51 to 8.58 over 6 hours, with the peak breast-milk concentration occurring 2 hours after bupropion dosing. The bupropion metabolite threohydrobupropion also accumulated in breast milk, with a milk-to-plasma ratio ranging from 1.23 to 1.57 over the same 6 hours. Hydroxybupropion concentrations in milk did not exceed corresponding plasma concentrations at any of the measure times. Neither bupropion nor its metabolites were detectable in serum taken from the infant, a 14-month-old boy, 3.75 hours after nursing, which occurred 9.5 hours after the mother's last dose of bupropion. No adverse effects were observed in the infant.

Because of the potential for serious adverse reactions in nursing infants from bupropion, a decision should be made whether to discontinue nursing or to discontinue the drug, taking into account the importance of the drug to the mother.

Pediatrics
There is not sufficient evidence to establish safety and efficacy of bupropion in children up to 18 years of age. Bupropion is not approved for use in treating any indications in the pediatric population.

Antidepressants increase the risk of suicidal thinking and behavior (suicidality) in children and adolescents with major depressive disorder (MDD) and other psychiatric disorders. Anyone considering the use of bupropion or any other antidepressant in a child or adolescent must balance this risk with the clinical need.

Pooled analyses of short-term placebo controlled trials of nine antidepressant drugs in children and adolescents with MDD, obsessive compulsive disorder, or other psychiatric disorders have revealed a greater risk of adverse events representing suicidality during the first few months of treatment in those receiving antidepressants.

Geriatrics
In general, studies that included patients 60 years of age and older have not demonstrated geriatrics-specific problems that would limit the usefulness of bupropion in the elderly. However, one pharmacokinetic study has suggested that the elderly may be at increased risk for accumulation of bupropion and its metabolites. Older patients are known to be more sensitive to the anticholinergic, sedative, and cardiovascular side effects of antidepressants. In addition, elderly patients are more likely to have age-related renal or hepatic function impairment, which may require dosage adjustment in patients receiving bupropion.

Drug interactions and/or related problems
The following drug interactions and/or related problems have been selected on the basis of their potential clinical significance (possible

mechanism in parentheses where appropriate)—not necessarily inclusive (» = major clinical significance):

Note: The cytochrome P450 2B6 (CYP2B6) isoenzyme is involved in the metabolism of bupropion to its active metabolite hydroxybupropion. A potential exists for interactions between bupropion and medications that affect CYP2B6, such as orphenadrine and cyclophosphamide.

Combinations containing any of the following medications, depending on the amount present, may also interact with this medication.

» Alcohol
(concurrent use of or the cessation of chronic use of alcohol during therapy may lower the seizure threshold and increase the risk of seizures; patients should be advised to minimize alcohol consumption or avoid the use of alcohol completely)

Enzyme inducers, hepatic, cytochrome P450 (see *Appendix II*)
(concurrent use with bupropion may increase the metabolism of bupropion; a study in patients receiving chronic carbamazepine therapy showed significant decreases in bupropion peak plasma concentration and area under the plasma concentration-time curve [AUC] and increases in hydroxybupropion peak plasma concentration and AUC; a study in cigarette smokers showed no effect of smoking on the pharmacokinetics of bupropion)

Enzyme inhibitors, hepatic, cytochrome P450 (see *Appendix II*)
(these medications may inhibit hepatic microsomal enzymes, thereby decreasing metabolism and increasing serum concentrations of bupropion, thus increasing the risk of seizures; a study in patients receiving chronic valproic acid therapy showed no change in bupropion concentrations but increases in hydroxybupropion peak concentration and AUC)

Levodopa
(concurrent use with bupropion may result in a greater incidence of adverse effects; small initial doses of bupropion and gradual dosage increases are recommended during concurrent therapy)

» Monoamine oxidase (MAO) inhibitors, including furazolidone, procarbazine, and selegiline
(concurrent use of bupropion with these medications may increase the risk of acute toxicity of bupropion and is **contraindicated**; a medication-free interval of at least 14 days should elapse between discontinuation of the MAO inhibitor and initiation of bupropion therapy)

Nicotine
(although a nicotine transdermal system may be used concurrently with bupropion in the treatment of nicotine dependence, the combination has been associated with hypertension; blood pressure should be monitored in patients receiving this combination)

» Ritonavir
(although there is no experience with the combination, ritonavir has a high affinity for several cytochrome P450 isoenzymes and may increase bupropion plasma concentrations, thus increasing the risk of seizures; concurrent use should be approached with caution until more information is available)

» Seizure-threshold–lowering medications, other, such as:
Antidepressants, tricyclic or
Clozapine or
Corticosteroids, glucocorticoid and/or mineralocorticoid or
Fluoxetine or
Haloperidol or
Lithium or
Loxapine or
Maprotiline or
Molindone or
Phenothiazines or
Theophylline, or
Thioxanthenes or
Trazodone
(concurrent use of these medications with bupropion may increase the risk of major motor seizures; in addition, changes in treatment regimen, such as abrupt discontinuation of a benzodiazepine, may precipitate a seizure)

Laboratory value alterations

The following have been selected on the basis of their potential clinical significance (possible effect in parentheses where appropriate)—not necessarily inclusive (» = major clinical significance).

With physiology/laboratory test values
White blood cell count
(decreased by 10 to 14% during the first 2 months of therapy in one study; unknown clinical significance)

Medical considerations/Contraindications

The medical considerations/contraindications included have been selected on the basis of their potential clinical significance (reasons given in parentheses where appropriate)—not necessarily inclusive (» = major clinical significance).

Except under special circumstances, this medication should not be used when the following medical problems exist:

» Abrupt discontinuation of alcohol or sedatives (including benzodiazepines)

» Anorexia nervosa, or history of or
» Bulimia, or history of
(increased risk of seizures in patients with current or prior diagnosis of these conditions)

» Hypersensitivity to bupropion or its components

» Seizure disorders
(increased risk of seizures)

Risk-benefit should be considered when the following medical problems exist:

» Bipolar disorder or risk of
(may increase likelihood of precipitation of a mixed/manic episode in these patients; prior to initiating bupropion treatment, patient should be adequately screened to determine if they are at risk for bipolar disorder; such screening should include a detailed psychiatric history, including a family history of suicide, bipolar disorder, and depression.)

» CNS tumor or
» Head trauma or
» Neurologic impairment, including developmental delay, or
» Spontaneous seizures, history of
(increased risk of seizures)

Drug abuse
(patients with a history of amphetamine or stimulant abuse may be attracted to bupropion because of its mild amphetamine-like activity, especially at higher doses; however, risk of seizures has prevented adequate testing)

(risk of seizures may be increased in patients with addiction to opiates, cocaine, or stimulants)

» Heart disease
(higher plasma concentrations of the active metabolites of bupropion may occur in patients with left ventricular dysfunction; in a short-term study of 36 patients with left ventricular impairment, ventricular arrhythmias, and/or conduction disease, mean systolic supine blood pressure readings increased by 5 ± 10 mm Hg, mean diastolic supine blood pressure readings increased by 3 ± 5 mm Hg, and two patients with mild hypertension at baseline discontinued use due to exacerbation of hypertension)

» Hepatic function impairment or
» Renal function impairment
(metabolism or excretion may be altered; bupropion treatment should be initiated at a reduced dosage and patient should be monitored closely)

Hypertension
(may be exacerbated)

Psychosis, especially schizoaffective disorder, depressed
(latent psychosis or mania may be activated in susceptible patients)

Patient monitoring

The following may be especially important in patient monitoring (other tests may be warranted in some patients, depending on condition; » = major clinical significance):

Blood pressure
(recommended in patients who are using a nicotine transdermal system concurrently with bupropion and in patients with baseline hypertension)

Careful supervision of depressed patients including those with:
Abnormal behaviors (i.e., agitation, panic attacks, hostility) or
Clinical worsening of their depression or
Suicidal ideation and behavior (suicidality)
(recommended especially during early treatment phase before peak effectiveness of bupropion is achieved or at the time of increases or decreases in dose; prescribing the smallest number of tablets necessary for good patient management is recommended to decrease the risk of overdose; consideration should be given to changing the therapeutic regimen, including possibly discontinuing the medicine, in patients whose depression is persistently worse or whose emergent suicidality or

other symptoms are severe, abrupt in onset, or were not part of the patient's presenting symptoms)

Side/Adverse Effects

The following side/adverse effects have been selected on the basis of their potential clinical significance (possible signs and symptoms in parentheses where appropriate)—not necessarily inclusive:

Those indicating need for medical attention

Incidence more frequent

Agitation; anxiety

Incidence less frequent

Headache, severe; skin rash, hives, or itching; tinnitus (buzzing or ringing in ears)

Incidence rare

Fainting; neuropsychiatric effects, including confusion; delusions (false beliefs that are not changed by facts); ***hallucinations*** (seeing, hearing, or feeling things that are not there); ***paranoia*** (extreme distrust); ***or trouble in concentrating; seizures***—especially with higher doses

Note: The risk of *seizures* with bupropion may be greater than with other antidepressants. Seizures occur more frequently at higher doses. The incidence with use of the extended-release formulation is approximately 0.1% (3/3100 patients) at doses of up to 300 mg a day, and 0.4% (4/1000 patients) at a dose of 400 mg a day. With the use of the prompt-release formulation, seizure frequencies of 0.4% (13/3200 patients) at doses of 300 to 450 mg a day and almost tenfold higher at doses between 450 mg and 600 mg a day have been reported.

Incidence not determined—Observed during clinical practice, estimates of frequency can not be determined

Akathisia (psychomotor restlessness) (inability to sit still; need to keep moving; restlessness); ***hostility (aggressiveness)*** (anger; attack; assault; force); ***hypomania or mania*** (actions that are out of control; irritability; nervousness; talking, feeling, and acting with excitement); ***impulsivity; irritability; panic attacks*** (anxiety, chest pain or discomfort, fast or pounding heartbeat, sweating)

Those indicating need for medical attention only if they continue or are bothersome

Incidence more frequent

Abdominal pain; anorexia (decrease in appetite); ***constipation; dizziness; dryness of mouth; increased sweating; insomnia*** (trouble in sleeping); ***myalgia*** (muscle pain); ***nausea or vomiting; pharyngitis*** (sore throat); ***tremor*** (trembling or shaking); ***weight loss, unusual***

Note: *Dryness of mouth* and *insomnia* may be dose-related. Avoiding taking bupropion at bedtime may help to relieve insomnia.

Incidence less frequent or rare

Blurred vision; drowsiness; palpitation (feeling of fast or irregular heartbeat); ***taste perversion*** (change in sense of taste); ***unusual feeling of well-being; urinary frequency***

Overdose

For specific information on the agents used in the management of bupropion overdose, see:

- *Benzodiazepines (Systemic)* monograph; and/or
- *Charcoal, Activated (Oral-Local)* monograph.

For more information on the management of overdose or unintentional ingestion, **contact a Poison Control Center** (see *Poison Control Center Listing*).

Clinical effects of overdose

Note: Deaths have occurred following massive overdose with bupropion alone.

The following effects have been selected on the basis of their potential clinical significance (possible signs and symptoms in parentheses where appropriate)—not necessarily inclusive:

Acute

Hallucinations (seeing, hearing, or feeling things that are not there); ***loss of consciousness; nausea; seizures; tachycardia*** (fast heartbeat)—possibly progressing to bradycardia or asystole; ***vomiting***

Note: *Seizures* occur in about one third of bupropion overdose cases.

Treatment of overdose

To decrease absorption—In comatose or stuporous patients, initiation of airway intubation followed by gastric lavage within the first 12 hours of ingestion, when absorption is not yet complete. Administration of activated charcoal every 6 hours within the first 12 hours of ingestion. Ipecac syrup should not be used to induce vomiting because of the possibility of seizures.

Specific treatment—Treatment of seizures with an intravenous benzodiazepine, although seizures may be resistant to benzodiazepine treatment.

Monitoring—Monitoring ECG and EEG for at least 48 hours. Monitoring acid-base and electrolyte balance in patients presenting in status epilepticus.

Supportive care—Maintenance of patent airway and adequate ventilation. Patients in whom intentional overdose is confirmed or suspected should be referred for psychiatric consultation.

Note: Diuresis, dialysis, and hemoperfusion are not likely to be of benefit due to the slow diffusion of bupropion and its metabolites from tissue to plasma.

Patient Consultation

As an aid to patient consultation, refer to *Advice for the Patient, Bupropion (Systemic)*.

In providing consultation, consider emphasizing the following selected information (» = major clinical significance):

Before using this medication

» Conditions affecting use, especially:

Hypersensitivity to bupropion or any of its components

Pregnancy—Crosses placenta; should be used during pregnancy only if clearly needed

Breast-feeding—Accumulates in breast milk; because of potential for serious adverse effects in the infant, use is not recommended

Contraindicated medications—MAO inhibitors

Other medications, especially alcohol, other seizure-threshold–lowering medications, or ritonavir

Other medical problems, especially abrupt discontinuation of alcohol or sedatives (including benzodiazepines), anorexia nervosa, bipolar disorder or risk of, bulimia, CNS tumor, head trauma, heart disease, hepatic or renal function impairment, history of spontaneous seizures, neurologic impairment, or seizure disorders

Proper use of this medication

» Compliance with therapy; not taking more or less medication than prescribed

» Taking doses of prompt-release tablets at least 4 hours apart; taking doses of sustained-release tablets at least 8 hours apart; taking extended-release tablets at least 24 hours apart to avoid occurrence of seizures

» Swallowing sustained-release and extended-release tablets whole; not crushing, breaking, or chewing

Taking with food if needed to lessen gastrointestinal irritation

For smoking cessation

Taking bupropion for 7 or more days prior to the date on which smoking will be discontinued

Participating in smoking cessation support program, including behavioral interventions, counseling, and/or other support

For mental depression

May require 4 weeks or longer for optimal antidepressant effects

Continuing to take bupropion after feeling better, as directed by physician, to help prevent recurrence

» Proper dosing

Missed dose: For extended-release, sustained-release, and prompt-release tablets—Skipping the missed dose and returning to regular dosing schedule; not doubling doses

» Proper storage

Precautions while using this medication

Regular visits to physician to check progress during therapy

» Importance of patient or caregiver notifying physician immediately if any signs of abnormal behavior, worsening depression or suicidality occur

» Not taking bupropion within 14 days of taking an MAO inhibitor

» Not taking bupropion under different brand names or same brand name with different formulations concurrently, because of dose-dependent incidence of seizures

» Minimizing or avoiding consumption of alcoholic beverages to reduce the risk of seizures

» Possible dizziness, drowsiness, or euphoria; caution when driving, using machinery, or doing other things requiring alertness and judgment

Side/adverse effects

Signs of potential side effects, especially agitation; anxiety; severe headache; skin rash, hives, or itching; tinnitus; fainting; neuropsychiatric effects; or seizures

Signs of potential side effects observed during clinical practice, especially akathisia, hostility, hypomania, impulsivity, irritability, mania, or panic attacks

General Dosing Information

Bupropion is marketed under different brand names for different approved indications; patients should not receive bupropion under different brand names or same brand name with different formulations concurrently due to the dose-dependent incidence of seizures.

To reduce the risk of agitation, anxiety, and insomnia, which are more frequent at initiation of therapy, increases in dosage must be made gradually.

Seizures occur more frequently at higher doses; the incidence with use of the sustained-release formulation is approximately 0.1% (3/3100 patients) at doses of up to 300 mg a day, and 0.4% (4/1000 patients) at a dose of 400 mg a day. With use of the prompt-release formulation, seizure frequencies of 0.4% (13/3200 patients) at doses of 300 to 450 mg a day and almost tenfold higher at doses between 450 mg and 600 mg a day have been reported. Seizure incidence with extended-release bupropion, while not formally evaluated in clinical trials, may be similar to that of prompt-release and sustained-release formulations.

Patients being treated for nicotine dependence should continue to smoke during the first week of treatment with bupropion to allow the medication to reach steady-state plasma concentrations. A target date for discontinuation of smoking should be set for the second week of treatment. Bupropion treatment should be continued for 7 to 12 weeks. Longer treatment may be considered in individual patients. If significant progress toward abstinence is not seen by the seventh week of therapy, the current attempt to quit smoking is unlikely to be successful and discontinuation of bupropion should be considered.

Full antidepressant action may not be evident for 4 weeks or longer.

Acute episodes of depression may require several months or longer of sustained therapy beyond response to the acute episode. It is unknown whether or not the dose of bupropion needed for maintenance treatment is identical to the dose needed to achieve an initial response. Patients should be periodically reassessed to determine the need for maintenance treatment and the appropriate dose for such treatment.

When switching patients from one formulation of bupropion (prompt-, sustained-, or extended-release), the same total daily dose should be administered when possible.

Potentially suicidal patients should not have access to large quantities of this medication since depressed patients, particularly those who use alcohol excessively, may continue to exhibit suicidal tendencies until significant improvement occurs.

Diet/Nutrition

Bupropion may be taken with food to lessen gastrointestinal irritation.

Bioequivalence information

At steady-state, the prompt-release, the sustained-release, and the extended-release formulations of bupropion hydrochloride are bioequivalent with respect to both rate and extent of absorption.

For prevention of seizures

The risk of seizures may be reduced if:

- The total daily dose of the prompt-release formulation or the extended-release formulation (once daily) does not exceed 450 mg and the total daily dose of the sustained-release formulation does not exceed 400 mg when used as an antidepressant and 300 mg when used as an aid to smoking cessation.
- Each single dose of the prompt-release formulation or the sustained-release formulation, when used as an aid to smoking cessation, does not exceed 150 mg, and each single dose of the sustained-release formulation does not exceed 200 mg when used as an antidepressant.
- Doses of the prompt-release formulation are taken at least 4 hours apart, doses of the sustained-release formulation are taken at least 8 hours apart, and doses of the extended-release formulation are taken at least 24 hours apart.
- The dosage is increased gradually.
- Caution is used in patients with a history of seizures, cranial trauma, or other predisposition to seizures, and during concurrent use with other medications or treatment regimens, such as the abrupt discontinuation of benzodiazepines, that may lower the seizure threshold.

Bupropion should be discontinued and not restarted in patients who experience a seizure while on treatment.

For treatment of adverse effects

Recommended treatment consists of the following:

- For agitation, anxiety, or insomnia—Lowering dosage, and then increasing it gradually as needed and tolerated. Temporary sedative-hypnotic medication may be necessary, but is usually not required beyond the first week of treatment. Avoiding a bedtime bupropion dose may minimize insomnia. If effects are severe, discontinuation of bupropion may be necessary.
- For nausea and vomiting—Taking with meals, or decreasing and then gradually increasing the dosage.

Oral Dosage Forms

BUPROPION HYDROCHLORIDE EXTENDED-RELEASE TABLETS once-daily

Usual adult dose

Antidepressant—

Oral, initially 150 mg once daily in the morning. If this dose is adequately tolerated, an increase to the 300-mg target dose given once daily may be made as early as day 4 of dosing. There should be an interval of at least 24 hours between successive doses. An increase in dosage to the maximum of 450 mg per day given as a single dose may be considered for patients in whom no clinical improvement is noted after several weeks of treatment at 300 mg per day.

Note: Extended-release bupropion should be used with extreme caution in patients with severe hepatic cirrhosis. Dose should not exceed 150 mg every other day in these patients. Caution should be used in patients with mild to moderate hepatic impairment and a reduced frequency and/or dose should be considered in these patients.

Extended-release bupropion should be used with caution in patients with renal impairment and a reduced frequency and/or dose should be considered.

Usual adult prescribing limits

Antidepressant—

450 mg per day.

Usual pediatric dose

Safety and efficacy have not been established in children younger than 18 years of age.

Strength(s) usually available

U.S.—

150 mg (Rx) [*Wellbutrin XL* (carnauba wax; ethylcellulose aqueous dispersion; glyceryl behenate; methacrylic acid copolymer dispersion; polyvinyl alcohol; polyethylene glycol; povidone; silicon dioxide; triethyl citrate)].

300 mg (Rx) [*Wellbutrin XL* (carnauba wax; ethylcellulose aqueous dispersion; glyceryl behenate; methacrylic acid copolymer dispersion; polyvinyl alcohol; polyethylene glycol; povidone; silicon dioxide; triethyl citrate)].

Packaging and storage

Store at 25 °C (77 °F) excursions permitted to 15 to 30 °C (59 to 86 °F).

Auxiliary labeling

- Avoid alcoholic beverages.
- Swallow tablet whole. Do not break or chew.

Additional information

Bupropion is marketed under different brand names for different approved indications; patients should not receive bupropion under different brand names or same brand name with different formulations concurrently due to the dose-dependent incidence of seizures.

BUPROPION HYDROCHLORIDE SUSTAINED-RELEASE TABLETS

Usual adult dose

Antidepressant—

Oral, initially 150 mg once a day in the morning for three days, then 150 mg two times a day if well tolerated. If no improvement is seen after several weeks, dosage may be increased to 200 mg two times a day.

Note: Doses should be taken at least eight hours apart to reduce the risk of seizures.

Smoking cessation adjunct—

Oral, initially 150 mg once a day for three days, then 150 mg two times a day for seven to twelve weeks.

Note: Doses should be taken at least eight hours apart to reduce the risk of seizures.

Usual adult prescribing limits

Antidepressant—

400 mg per day, with no single dose exceeding 200 mg.

Smoking cessation adjunct—

300 mg per day, with no single dose exceeding 150 mg.

Usual pediatric dose
Safety and efficacy have not been established in children younger than 18 years of age.

Strength(s) usually available
U.S.—
100 mg (Rx) [*Wellbutrin SR* (carnauba wax; cysteine hydrochloride; FD&C Blue No. 1 Lake; hydroxypropyl methylcellulose; magnesium stearate; microcrystalline cellulose; polyethylene glycol; polysorbate 80; titanium dioxide)].
150 mg (Rx) [*Wellbutrin SR* (carnauba wax; cysteine hydrochloride; FD&C Blue No. 2 Lake; FD&C Red No. 40 Lake; hydroxypropyl methylcellulose; magnesium stearate; microcrystalline cellulose; polyethylene glycol; polysorbate 80; titanium dioxide); *Zyban* (carnauba wax; cysteine hydrochloride; FD&C Blue No. 2 Lake; FD&C Red No. 40 Lake; hydroxypropyl methylcellulose; magnesium stearate; microcrystalline cellulose; polyethylene glycol; polysorbate 80; titanium dioxide)].

Canada—
100 mg (Rx) [*Wellbutrin SR* (carnauba wax; cysteine hydrochloride; FD&C Blue No. 1 Lake; hydroxypropyl methylcellulose; magnesium stearate; microcrystalline cellulose; polyethylene glycol; polysorbate 80; titanium dioxide)].
150 mg (Rx) [*Wellbutrin SR* (carnauba wax; cysteine hydrochloride; FD&C Blue No. 2 Lake; FD&C Red No. 40 Lake; hydroxypropyl methylcellulose; magnesium stearate; microcrystalline cellulose; polyethylene glycol; polysorbate 80; titanium dioxide); *Zyban* (carnauba wax; cysteine hydrochloride; FD&C Blue No. 2 Lake; FD&C Red No. 40 Lake; hydroxypropyl methylcellulose; magnesium stearate; microcrystalline cellulose; polyethylene glycol; polysorbate 80; titanium dioxide)].

Packaging and storage
Store at controlled room temperature, 20 to 25 °C (68 to 77 °F), in a tight, light-resistant container, unless otherwise specified by manufacturer.

Auxiliary labeling
- Avoid alcoholic beverages.
- Swallow tablet whole. Do not break or chew.

Additional information
Bupropion is marketed under different brand names for different approved indications; patients should not receive bupropion under different brand names or the same brand name with different formulations concurrently due to the dose-dependent incidence of seizures.

Note: Bupropion hydrochloride may have a characteristic odor.

BUPROPION HYDROCHLORIDE TABLETS

Usual adult dose
Antidepressant—
Oral, initially 100 mg two times a day, the dosage being increased gradually, no sooner than three days after beginning therapy, to 100 mg three times a day as needed and tolerated.

Note: Doses should be taken at least four hours apart to reduce the risk of seizures.

Usual adult prescribing limits
450 mg per day, with no single dose exceeding 150 mg.

Usual pediatric dose
Safety and efficacy have not been established in children younger than 18 years of age.

Strength(s) usually available
U.S.—
75 mg (Rx) [*Wellbutrin* (D&C Yellow No. 10 Lake; FD&C Yellow No. 6 Lake; hydroxypropyl cellulose; hydroxypropyl methylcellulose; light mineral oil; microcrystalline cellulose; talc; titanium dioxide)].
100 mg (Rx) [*Wellbutrin* (FD&C Red No. 40 Lake; FD&C Yellow No. 6 Lake; hydroxypropyl cellulose; hydroxypropyl methylcellulose; light mineral oil; microcrystalline cellulose; talc; titanium dioxide)].

Canada—
Not commercially available.

Packaging and storage
Store below 40 °C (104 °F), preferably between 15 and 30 °C (59 and 86 °F), unless otherwise specified by manufacturer.

Auxiliary labeling
- Avoid alcoholic beverages.

Additional information
Bupropion is marketed under different brand names for different approved indications; patients should not receive bupropion under different brand names or the same brand name with different formulations concurrently due to the dose-dependent incidence of seizures.

Note: Bupropion hydrochloride may have a characteristic odor.

Revised: 01/07/2005

BUSPIRONE Systemic

VA CLASSIFICATION (Primary): CN304

Commonly used brand name(s): *BuSpar; BuSpar DIVIDOSE; Bustab.*

Note: For a listing of dosage forms and brand names by country availability, see *Dosage Forms* section(s).

Category
Antianxiety agent.

Indications

General Considerations
The efficacy of buspirone in the treatment of generalized anxiety of moderate severity has been shown to be comparable to that of benzodiazepines such as diazepam, clorazepate, alprazolam, and lorazepam. However, unlike the benzodiazepines, buspirone appears to lack potential for physical dependence or abuse.

Buspirone has been shown to cause less sedation than other antianxiety agents, especially at lower doses. Therefore, it may be a useful alternative to other antianxiety agents in the treatment of generalized anxiety, particularly in patients hypersensitive to the sedative effects of the other agents.

Accepted
Anxiety (treatment)—Buspirone is indicated for the management of anxiety disorders or the short-term relief of the symptoms of anxiety. However, buspirone usually is not indicated for the treatment of anxiety or tension associated with the stress of everyday life.

The effectiveness of buspirone in the management of anxiety for more than 3 to 4 weeks has not been shown in controlled studies. However, buspirone has not been shown to cause adverse effects different from those seen with short-term use when used for up to 1 year. If buspirone is used for extended periods of time, efficacy of the medication should be reassessed at periodic intervals.

Acceptance not established
Buspirone has shown some effectiveness in small uncontrolled studies as an adjunct to antidepressant medications in the treatment of mental depression (Evidence rating: C-3).

Small uncontrolled studies and case reports indicate buspirone may be effective as a treatment of aggressive behavior in patients with neurological disorders or damage (Evidence rating: C-3).

Pharmacology/Pharmacokinetics

Physicochemical characteristics
Chemical Group—Azaspirodecanedione (an azapirone). Buspirone is not chemically or pharmacologically related to benzodiazepines, barbiturates, or other sedative/antianxiety agents.

Molecular weight—Buspirone hydrochloride: 421.97.

Solubility—Buspirone hydrochloride is very water soluble.

Mechanism of action/Effect
The exact mechanism of action of buspirone has not been determined. The medication is believed to have a unique anxioselective action, since it has no anticonvulsant or muscle relaxant activity and does not appear to cause physical dependence or significant sedation. Buspirone has a high affinity for serotonin 5-HT_{1A} receptors. Serotonin 5-HT_{1A} receptors are found in high concentrations in the dorsal raphe nucleus of the brain, where they are considered to be presynaptic, and in the hippocampal and cortical regions of the brain, where they are considered to be postsynaptic. Buspirone acts as an agonist at presynaptic 5-HT_{1A} receptors, causing decreased firing of serotonergic neurons in the dorsal raphe nucleus, and decreased serotonin synthesis and release. Buspirone acts as a partial agonist at postsynaptic 5-HT_{1A} receptors. Buspirone also has been shown to have a moderate affinity for brain dopamine D_2 receptors, where it acts as a weak antagonist both pre- and postsynaptically. It has no significant affinity for benzodiazepine receptors and does not affect gamma-aminobutyric acid (GABA) binding. The neuronal reuptake of monoamines is not blocked by buspirone. Some studies have suggested that buspirone may have indirect effects on other neurotransmitter systems.

In contrast to the benzodiazepines, the spontaneous firing rate of noradrenergic cells in the locus ceruleus is increased rather than decreased by buspirone. Differences in dependence and tolerance between benzodiazepines and buspirone are due to these site-specific differences.

Other actions/effects
Although increases in plasma prolactin and growth hormone concentrations to more than two times the upper limit of normal were seen in healthy male volunteers given buspirone in single doses of 30 mg or higher, these increases did not occur in another study using a buspirone dosage of 10 mg three times a day for 28 days.

Absorption
Rapidly and completely absorbed from the gastrointestinal tract; however, extensive first-pass metabolism limits the bioavailability of buspirone to approximately 4%. Although concurrent administration of food slows the rate of absorption of buspirone, the presence of food increases the amount of unchanged buspirone reaching systemic circulation.

Distribution
Apparent Vol_D—Healthy adult males: 5.3 ± 2.6 L per kg (L/kg).

Protein binding
Plasma—Very high (95%); about 70% is bound to albumin, and 30% is bound to $alpha_1$-acid glycoprotein. Although buspirone is highly protein-bound, it does not displace tightly protein-bound medications, such as warfarin, phenytoin, and propranolol, *in vitro*. However, buspirone does displace digoxin *in vitro*.

Biotransformation
Hepatic. Buspirone is rapidly metabolized and undergoes extensive first-pass metabolism. It is metabolized primarily by oxidation, producing several hydroxylated derivatives, and dealkylation. The *N*-dealkylated metabolite, 1-pyrimidinylpiperazine (1-PP), is pharmacologically active. In animal studies, 1-PP has been shown to have about one fourth the anxiolytic activity of buspirone.

A study on the effects of pretreatment with erythromycin or itraconazole on buspirone pharmacokinetics indicated that the cytochrome P450 3A4 (CYP3A4) isoenzyme plays a significant role in buspirone metabolism.

Half-life
Elimination—

Mean, about 2 to 3 hours following single oral doses of 10 to 40 mg or a single intravenous dose of 1 mg in healthy males. Mean elimination half-life has ranged from 2 to 11 hours in other studies.

Onset of action
May require up to 4 weeks to reach maximal effect, although some improvement may be seen in 1 week. Since buspirone does not cause muscle relaxation or significant sedation, patient may not immediately notice effects of medication.

Time to peak plasma concentration
40 to 90 minutes following single oral doses of 20 mg; less than 1 hour following single oral doses of 10 mg.

Peak plasma concentration
1 to 6 nanograms per mL following single oral doses of 20 mg. Following oral administration, plasma concentrations of unchanged buspirone are very low and vary about tenfold among individuals. One study in 15 subjects suggests that buspirone may exhibit nonlinear pharmacokinetics. Therefore, blood concentrations after dosage increases or multiple dosing may be higher than predicted by single-dose studies.

Elimination
Clearance of a single 1-mg dose of buspirone in eight healthy males was 28 mL per kg of body weight per minute (mL/kg/min).

Renal—

29 to 63% of the dose was excreted in urine within 24 hours in a single-dose study; less than 1% as unchanged drug.

Fecal—

18 to 38% of the dose was excreted in feces in a single-dose study.

In dialysis—

In six anuric patients, hemodialysis either decreased or had no effect on buspirone clearance.

Precautions to Consider

Carcinogenicity
Buspirone was not shown to be carcinogenic when it was administered to rats during a 24-month study at doses approximately 133 times the maximum recommended human dose (MRHD) or to mice during an 18-month study at doses approximately 167 times the MRHD.

Mutagenicity
Buspirone was not shown to induce point mutations, with or without metabolic activation, in five strains of *Salmonella typhimurium* (Ames test) or mouse lymphoma L5178YTK+ cell cultures, nor was DNA damage observed with buspirone in Wi-38 human cells. Also, chromosomal abnormalities did not occur in bone marrow cells of mice given one or five daily doses of buspirone.

Pregnancy/Reproduction
Fertility—Reproduction studies in rats and rabbits showed no impairment of fertility when buspirone was administered at doses approximately 30 times the maximum recommended human dose (MRHD).

Pregnancy—Adequate and well-controlled studies in humans have not been done.

Reproduction studies in rats and rabbits did not show buspirone to cause fetal damage when the medication was administered at doses approximately 30 times the MRHD.

FDA Pregnancy Category B.

Labor and delivery—Reproduction studies in rats have not shown buspirone to cause any adverse effects during labor and delivery.

Breast-feeding
Problems in humans have not been documented. However, buspirone and its metabolites are distributed into the milk of rats.

Pediatrics
Appropriate studies on the relationship of age to the effects of buspirone have not been performed in children up to 18 years of age. Safety and efficacy have not been established.

Geriatrics
Although buspirone has not been systematically evaluated in older patients, clinical studies performed in several hundred elderly patients have not demonstrated geriatrics-specific problems that would limit the usefulness of buspirone in the elderly.

Drug interactions and/or related problems
The following drug interactions and/or related problems have been selected on the basis of their potential clinical significance (possible mechanism in parentheses where appropriate)—not necessarily inclusive (» = major clinical significance):

Note: In one pharmacokinetics study, eight healthy females received erythromycin or itraconazole, at therapeutic doses, or placebo for four days. On the fourth day, a single 10-mg dose of buspirone was given and a series of blood samples was drawn. Buspirone area under the plasma concentration-time curve (AUC) and mean maximum plasma concentration (C_{max}) were greatly increased in the erythromycin and itraconazole pretreated subjects, indicating that the cytochrome P450 3A4 (CYP3A4) isoenzyme, which these medications inhibit, plays a significant role in buspirone metabolism. Interactions with medications that inhibit CYP3A4, other than those listed below, should be considered.

Combinations containing any of the following medications, depending on the amount present, may also interact with this medication.

Digoxin
(may be displaced from serum protein binding sites when used concurrently with buspirone; however, the clinical significance is unknown)

» Erythromycin or
» Itraconazole
(after pretreatment with erythromycin and itraconazole, C_{max} of buspirone was increased 5-fold and 13-fold, respectively, and AUC of buspirone was increased 6-fold and 19-fold, respectively, in eight healthy female volunteers, probably due to decreased first-pass metabolism; also, an increased incidence of adverse effects was observed; decreased buspirone dosage is recommended)

» Monoamine oxidase (MAO) inhibitors, including furazolidone, procarbazine, and more than 10 mg a day of selegiline
(elevations in blood pressure have been reported when buspirone was added to regimens that included MAO inhibitors)

Medical considerations/Contraindications
The medical considerations/contraindications included have been selected on the basis of their potential clinical significance (reasons given in parentheses where appropriate)—not necessarily inclusive (» = major clinical significance).

Risk-benefit should be considered when the following medical problems exist:

» Hepatic function impairment
(buspirone clearance is decreased in patients with impaired hepatic function; careful monitoring is recommended, and dosage adjustments may be necessary)

Renal function impairment
(clearance of buspirone or its active metabolite, 1-pyrimidinylpiperazine [1-PP], may be decreased in patients with impaired renal function)

Sensitivity to buspirone

Side/Adverse Effects

Note: Buspirone appears to lack potential for physical dependence or abuse.

Studies have shown that buspirone causes less sedation than other antianxiety agents (about one third of that occurring with benzodiazepines) and does not produce significant functional impairment. However, the CNS effects of buspirone in any individual patient may not be predictable.

Withdrawal symptoms or rebound anxiety has not been reported when the medication was abruptly discontinued.

The following side/adverse effects have been selected on the basis of their potential clinical significance (possible signs and symptoms in parentheses where appropriate)—not necessarily inclusive:

Those indicating need for medical attention

Incidence rare

Chest pain; confusion; fast or pounding heartbeat; fever; mental depression; neurologic effects (incoordination; muscle weakness; numbness, tingling, pain, or weakness in hands or feet; stiffness of arms or legs; uncontrolled movements of the body); ***skin rash or hives; sore throat***

Those indicating need for medical attention only if they continue or are bothersome

Incidence more frequent

Dizziness or lightheadedness—especially when getting up from a sitting or lying position; ***headache; nausea; syndrome of restlessness*** (restlessness, nervousness, or unusual excitement)

Note: *Syndrome of restlessness* may occur shortly after buspirone therapy is initiated, and may be due to increased central noradrenergic activity or to dopaminergic effects.

Incidence less frequent or rare

Blurred vision; clamminess or sweating; decreased concentration; diarrhea; drowsiness—more frequent with doses > 20 mg per day; ***dryness of mouth; insomnia*** (trouble in sleeping); ***nightmares; or vivid dreams; musculoskeletal effects*** (muscle pain, spasms, cramps, or stiffness); ***ringing in the ears; unusual tiredness or weakness***

Overdose

For more information on the management of overdose or unintentional ingestion, **contact a Poison Control Center** (see *Poison Control Center Listing*).

Clinical effects of overdose

Note: Buspirone is minimally toxic in overdose.

The following effects have been selected on the basis of their potential clinical significance (possible signs and symptoms in parentheses where appropriate)—not necessarily inclusive:

Acute

Dizziness or lightheadedness; drowsiness, severe, or loss of consciousness; stomach upset, including nausea or vomiting; unusually small pupils

Treatment of overdose

There is no known specific antidote to buspirone. Treatment is generally symptomatic and supportive.

To decrease absorption—Immediate (within 1 to 1.5 hours of ingestion) gastric lavage may be used.

Monitoring—Monitoring of respiration, pulse, and blood pressure is recommended. Patient should be observed for the development of extrapyramidal symptoms or behavior disturbances such as panic or mania.

Supportive care—Patients in whom intentional overdose is confirmed or suspected should be referred for psychiatric consultation.

Patient Consultation

As an aid to patient consultation, refer to *Advice for the Patient, Buspirone (Systemic).*

In providing consultation, consider emphasizing the following selected information (» = major clinical significance):

Before using this medication

» Conditions affecting use, especially:
- Sensitivity to buspirone
- Other medications, especially erythromycin, itraconazole, and monoamine oxidase (MAO) inhibitors
- Other medical problems, especially hepatic function impairment

Proper use of this medication

» Importance of not using more medication than the amount prescribed

One to two weeks of therapy may be required before antianxiety effect is noticeable

» Proper dosing

Missed dose: Taking as soon as possible; not taking if almost time for next dose; not doubling doses

» Proper storage

Precautions while using this medication

Regular visits to physician to check progress during prolonged therapy

» Caution in driving or operating machinery until effects of medication are known

» Suspected overdose: Getting emergency help at once

Side/adverse effects

Signs of potential side effects, especially chest pain, confusion, fast or pounding heartbeat, fever, mental depression, neurologic effects, skin rash or hives, and sore throat

General Dosing Information

Since buspirone does not exhibit cross-tolerance with benzodiazepines and other common sedative/hypnotic agents, the medication will not block the withdrawal syndrome associated with discontinuation of therapy with these agents. Therefore, prior to initiating therapy with buspirone, these agents should be withdrawn gradually, especially in patients who have been chronically using these CNS depressants.

A study that evaluated 120 patients meeting *Diagnostic and Statistical Manual of Mental Disorders, Third edition, Revised* (DSM IIIR) criteria for generalized anxiety disorder who had received buspirone 10 mg three times a day or 15 mg two times a day found no significant difference in efficacy or safety between the two regimens.

One to two weeks of therapy may be required before the antianxiety effect of buspirone is noticeable, as compared to the immediate effect of benzodiazepines.

Oral Dosage Forms

BUSPIRONE HYDROCHLORIDE TABLETS USP

Usual adult dose

Antianxiety agent—

Oral, initially 5 mg two or three times a day, or 7.5 mg two times a day, the dosage being increased by 5 mg per day at two- to three-day intervals until the desired response is obtained.

Note: The usual therapeutic dosage is 20 to 30 mg a day.

Usual adult prescribing limits

60 mg per day.

Usual pediatric dose

Safety and efficacy have not been established in children under 18 years of age.

Usual geriatric dose

Antianxiety agent—

See *Usual adult dose.*

Strength(s) usually available

U.S.—

Note: The 15-mg tablet may be divided to provide doses of 5, 7.5, 10, or 15 mg.

5 mg (Rx) [*BuSpar* (scored; colloidal silicon dioxide; lactose; magnesium stearate; microcrystalline cellulose; sodium starch glycolate)].

10 mg (Rx) [*BuSpar* (scored; colloidal silicon dioxide; lactose; magnesium stearate; microcrystalline cellulose; sodium starch glycolate)].

15 mg (Rx) [*BuSpar DIVIDOSE* (multi-scored; colloidal silicon dioxide; lactose; magnesium stearate; microcrystalline cellulose; sodium starch glycolate)].

Canada—

5 mg (Rx) [*BuSpar* (scored; lactose anhydrous); *Bustab*].

10 mg (Rx) [*BuSpar* (scored; lactose anhydrous); *Bustab*].

Packaging and storage

Store between 15 and 30 °C (59 and 86 °F), in a tight, light-resistant container, unless otherwise specified by manufacturer.

Auxiliary labeling

- May cause dizziness or drowsiness.

Selected Bibliography

Fulton B, Brogden RN. Buspirone: an updated review of its clinical pharmacology and therapeutic applications. CNS Drugs 1997 Jan; 7(1): 68-88.

Revised: 03/17/1998

BUSULFAN Systemic

VA CLASSIFICATION (Primary): AN100

Commonly used brand name(s): *Busulfex; Myleran.*

Note: For a listing of dosage forms and brand names by country availability, see *Dosage Forms* section(s).

Category

Antineoplastic.

Indications

Note: Bracketed information in the *Indications* section refers to uses that are not included in U.S. product labeling.

Accepted

Leukemia, chronic myelogenous (myeloid, myelocytic, granulocytic) (treatment)—Busulfan is indicated for palliative treatment of chronic myelogenous leukemia. It is not useful in the blastic crisis phase.

Conditioning regimen (treatment adjunct)—Busulfan injection is indicated in combination with cyclophosphamide as a conditioning regimen prior to allogeneic hematopoietic progenitor cell transplantation for treatment of chronic myelogenous leukemia.

[Leukemia, acute nonlymphocytic (treatment)][1]—Busulfan is used for treatment of acute nonlymphocytic leukemia.

[1]Not included in Canadian product labeling.

Pharmacology/Pharmacokinetics

Physicochemical characteristics

Molecular weight—246.29.

pH—3.4 to 3.9, for a > 0.5% solution in 0.9% sodium chloride USP or 5% dextrose in water USP.

Solubility—Soluble in water at 0.1 gram/L.

Mechanism of action/Effect

Busulfan is a bifunctional alkylating agent of the alkylsulfonate type and is cell cycle-phase nonspecific. Its mechanism of action is not clear but is thought to consist of alkylation and cross-linking of strands of DNA and myelosuppression.

Absorption

Mean bioavailability—80% (60 to 100% range) for adults; 68% (37 to 99%) for 8 children 1.5 to 6 years of age

No data available on effect of food on busulfan bioavailability.

AUC—269 ng hr/mL (after dose normalization to 4 mg)

Completely absorbed from the gastrointestinal tract. Radioactivity is detected in the blood ½ to 2 hours after oral administration of radiolabeled busulfan.

Distribution

Busulfan distributes equally into both plasma and cerebrospinal fluid.

Protein binding

Low (32.4%)irreversible binding to plasma elements, primarily to albumin.

Biotransformation

Occurs in the liver; metabolized by enzymatic activity to at least 12 inactive metabolites, including: tetrahydrothiphene, tetrahydrothiphene 12-oxide, sulfolane, and 3-hydroxysulfolane

Half-life

Terminal elimination—about 2.6 hours

Onset of action

A clinical response usually begins within 1 to 2 weeks after initiation of therapy.

Peak plasma concentration

C_{max}—30 ng/mL (after dose normalization to 2 mg); 68.2 ng/mL (after dose normalization to 4 mg)

Time to peak effect

T_{max}—about 0.9 hours

Elimination

Renal, slow, 30% in 48 hours, almost entirely as metabolites.

In dialysis—There has been one report that busulfan is dialyzable; however, dialysis is likely to have minimal effect because of poor water solubility of busulfan and prolonged retention of metabolites.

Precautions to Consider

Carcinogenicity

Secondary malignancies are potential delayed effects of many antineoplastic agents, although it is not clear whether the effect is related to their mutagenic or immunosuppressive action. The effect of dose and duration of therapy is also unknown, although risk seems to increase with long-term use. Although information is limited, available data seem to indicate that the carcinogenic risk is greatest with the alkylating agents.

Busulfan has been associated with development of acute leukemia in humans.

Mutagenicity

Busulfan is mutagenic in mice. It has been reported to cause chromosome aberrations in human cells.

Pregnancy/Reproduction

Fertility—Gonadal suppression, resulting in amenorrhea or azoospermia, may occur in patients taking antineoplastic therapy, especially with the alkylating agents. In general, these effects appear to be related to dose and length of therapy and may be irreversible. Prediction of the degree of testicular or ovarian function impairment is complicated by the common use of combinations of several antineoplastics, which makes it difficult to assess the effects of individual agents.

Busulfan produces sterility in the male and female offspring of rats due to germinal cell aplasia in testes and ovaries. It has also been associated with impairment of gonadal function in humans (ovarian suppression and amenorrhea with menopausal symptoms in premenopausal patients; sterility, azoospermia, and testicular atrophy in males).

Pregnancy—Adequate and well-controlled studies in humans have not been done. Although several successful pregnancies have been reported, one case of neonatal abnormalities has been reported in which the mother received radiation and combination chemotherapy including busulfan. In addition, there have been reports of small infants, especially after use of busulfan during the third trimester, and there is one report of mild anemia and neutropenia at birth after maternal administration of busulfan from the eighth week of pregnancy to term.

First trimester: It is usually recommended that use of antineoplastics, especially combination chemotherapy, be avoided whenever possible, especially during the first trimester. Although information is limited because of the relatively few instances of antineoplastic administration during pregnancy, the mutagenic, teratogenic, and carcinogenic potential of these medications must be considered.

Other hazards to the fetus include adverse reactions seen in adults.

In general, use of a contraceptive is recommended during cytotoxic drug therapy.

Teratogenic anomalies have occurred in the offspring of mice, rats, and rabbits, including cleft palate, heart vessel, rib, and vertebral anomalies, and malformations in the musculoskeletal system, body weight gain, and size.

FDA Pregnancy Category D.

Breast-feeding

Although very little information is available regarding distribution of antineoplastic agents into breast milk, breast-feeding is not recommended during chemotherapy because of the risks to the infant (adverse effects, mutagenicity, carcinogenicity). It is not known whether busulfan is distributed into breast milk.

Pediatrics

Safety and efficacy have not been established. Clearance has been demonstrated to be greater in children than in adults, necessitating the development of alternative dosing regimens. Cardiac tamponade has been reported for patients with thalassemia receiving high doses of oral busulfan and cyclophosphamide.

Geriatrics

Appropriate studies on the relationship of age to the effects of busulfan have not been performed in the geriatric population. However, geriatrics-specific problems that would limit the usefulness of this medication in the elderly are not expected.

Dental

The bone marrow depressant effects of busulfan may result in an increased incidence of microbial infection, delayed healing, and gingival bleeding. Dental work, whenever possible, should be completed prior to initiation of therapy or deferred until blood counts have returned to normal. Patients should be instructed in proper oral hygiene during

treatment, including caution in use of regular toothbrushes, dental floss, and toothpicks.

Busulfan may also cause stomatitis associated with considerable discomfort.

Drug interactions and/or related problems

The following drug interactions and/or related problems have been selected on the basis of their potential clinical significance (possible mechanism in parentheses where appropriate)—not necessarily inclusive (» = major clinical significance):

Note: Combinations containing any of the following medications, depending on the amount present, may also interact with this medication.

» Acetaminophen
(reduced busulfan clearance may occur if acetaminophen is administered <72 hours before or at the same time as busulfan)

Allopurinol or
Colchicine or
» Probenecid or
» Sulfinpyrazone
(busulfan may raise the concentration of blood uric acid; dosage adjustment of antigout agents may be necessary to control hyperuricemia and gout; allopurinol may be preferred to prevent or reverse busulfan-induced hyperuricemia because of risk of uric acid nephropathy with uricosuric antigout agents)

» Blood dyscrasia-causing medications (see *Appendix II*)
(leukopenic and/or thrombocytopenic effects of busulfan may be increased with concurrent or recent therapy if these medications cause the same effects; dosage adjustment of busulfan, if necessary, should be based on blood counts)

» Bone marrow depressants, other (see *Appendix II*) or
» Radiation therapy
(additive bone marrow depression may occur; dosage reduction may be required when two or more bone marrow depressants, including radiation, are used concurrently or consecutively)

» Cytotoxic therapy
(busulfan-induced pulmonary toxicity may be additive to effect produced by other cytotoxic agents)

» Epileptogenic drugs
(seizures have been reported with busulfan; caution should be exercised when administering busulfan to patients receiving other potentially epileptogenic drugs)

» Itraconazole
(decreased busulfan clearance of up to 25% may occurmonitor for busulfan toxicity)

» Phenytoin
(increased busulfan clearance of 15% or more may occur)

Vaccines, killed virus
(because normal defense mechanisms may be suppressed by busulfan therapy, the patient's antibody response to the vaccine may be decreased. The interval between discontinuation of medications that cause immunosuppression and restoration of the patient's ability to respond to the vaccine depends on the intensity and type of immunosuppression-causing medication used, the underlying disease, and other factors; estimates vary from 3 months to 1 year)

» Vaccines, live virus
(because normal defense mechanisms may be suppressed by busulfan therapy, concurrent use with a live virus vaccine may potentiate the replication of the vaccine virus, may increase the side/adverse effects of the vaccine virus, and/or may decrease the patient's antibody response to the vaccine; immunization of these patients should be undertaken only with extreme caution after careful review of the patient's hematologic status and only with the knowledge and consent of the physician managing the busulfan therapy. The interval between discontinuation of medications that cause immunosuppression and restoration of the patient's ability to respond to the vaccine depends on the intensity and type of immunosuppression-causing medication used, the underlying disease, and other factors; estimates vary from 3 months to 1 year. Patients with leukemia in remission should not receive live virus vaccine until at least 3 months after their last chemotherapy. In addition, immunization with oral poliovirus vaccine should be postponed in persons in close contact with the patient, especially family members)

Laboratory value alterations

The following have been selected on the basis of their potential clinical significance (possible effect in parentheses where appropriate)—not necessarily inclusive (» = major clinical significance).

With diagnostic test results
Cytology studies of lung, bladder, breast, or uterine cervix tissue
(cytologic dysplasia caused by busulfan may be severe enough to cause difficulty in interpretation)

With physiology/laboratory test values
Alkaline phosphatase, serum and
Alanine aminotransferase (ALT [SGPT]), serum and
Aspartate transaminase (AST [SGOT]), serum and
Billirubin, serum
(levels may be increased)

Complete blood count with differential, blood and
Neutrophils, blood and
Platelets, blood
(counts may be decreased)

Calcium, serum and
Magnesium, serum and
Potassium, serum
(concentrations may be decreased)

Busulfan, plasma and
Creatinine, serum and
Blood urea nitrogen and
Glucose, serum and
Uric acid in blood and urine
(concentrations may be increased)

Medical considerations/Contraindications

The medical considerations/contraindications included have been selected on the basis of their potential clinical significance (reasons given in parentheses where appropriate)—not necessarily inclusive (» = major clinical significance).

Except under special circumstances, this medication should not be used when the following medical problems exist:

» Definitive diagnosis of chronic myelogenous leukemia not firmly established

» Hypersensitivity to busulfan or any other component of the preparation

Risk-benefit should be considered when the following medical problems exist:

» Bone marrow depression

» Chemotherapy, previous or
» Cytotoxic therapy, previous (marrow function recovering) or
» Irradiation, prior
(busulfan should be used with extreme caution and exceptional vigilance in patients whose bone marrow reserve may have been compromised by these conditions; bone marrow failure resulting in severe pancytopenia can result)

» Chickenpox, existing or recent (including recent exposure) or
» Herpes zoster
(risk of severe generalized disease)

» Gout, history of or
» Urate renal stones, history of
(risk of hyperuricemia)

Hepatic impairment or
Renal impairment
(caution should be used due to a lack of studies in these groups)

» Infection

» Seizures, history of or
» Head trauma
(caution should be exercised; prophylactic anticonvulsant therapy should be started prior to initiating busulfan injection)

» Thalassemia
(cardiac tamponade, preceded by abdominal pain and vomiting, has been reported in pediatric patients receiving busulfan and cyclophosphamide therapy)

Patient monitoring

The following may be especially important in patient monitoring (other tests may be warranted in some patients, depending on condition; » = major clinical significance):

Alanine aminotransferase values, serum and
Alkaline phosphatase values, serum and
Bilirubin concentrations, serum
(recommended at periodic intervals to detect possible hepatotoxicity, including hepatic veno-occlusive disease and recommended daily through transplant day 28 with busulfan injection for bone marrow transplantation)

» Hematocrit or hemoglobin and
» Leukocyte count, total and, if appropriate, differential and
Neutrophil count, absolute and

Platelet count
(determinations recommended prior to initiation of therapy and at periodic intervals during therapy; frequency varies according to clinical state, agent, dose, and other agents being used concurrently; because of severe and delayed myelosuppression caused by busulfan, frequent monitoring is necessary so that therapy can be withdrawn promptly when indicatedand recommended daily with busulfan injection, until engraftment is complete)

Uric acid concentrations, serum
(recommended prior to initiation of therapy and at periodic intervals during therapy; frequency varies according to clinical state, agent, dose, and other agents being used concurrently)

Side/Adverse Effects

Note: Many "side effects" of antineoplastic therapy are unavoidable and represent the medication's pharmacologic action. Some of these (for example, leukopenia and thrombocytopenia) are actually used as parameters to aid in individual dosage titration.

Busulfan can cause cellular dysplasia in many tissues, including lungs, lymph nodes, pancreas, thyroid, adrenal gland, liver, bone marrow, bladder, breast, and uterine cervix.

Seizures have been reported in 2 of 130 patients receiving very high investigational doses (1 mg per kg of body weight [mg/kg] four times a day for four days, total dose 16 mg/kg).

Hepatic veno-occlusive disease, which may be life threatening, has been reported in patients receiving busulfan, usually in combination with cyclophosphamide or other chemotherapeutic agents prior to bone marrow transplantation. Possible risk factors for the development of this disease include a total busulfan dose exceeding 16 mg per kg of body weight based on ideal body weight and concurrent use of multiple alkylating agents.

Continuous treatment with a combination of busulfan and thioguanine in approximately 330 patients was associated with esophageal varices along with abnormal hepatic function tests and evidence of nodular regenerative hyperplasia on liver biopsy in 12 patients after six to forty-five months of therapy. No hepatic toxicity was found in the busulfan alone arm of the study.

The following side/adverse effects have been selected on the basis of their potential clinical significance (possible signs and symptoms in parentheses where appropriate)—not necessarily inclusive:

Those indicating need for medical attention

Incidence more frequent (> 50%)

Anemia; bone marrow failure (chest pain; chills; cough or hoarseness; fever; lower back or side pain; painful or difficult urination; shortness of breath; sores, ulcers, or white spots on lips or in mouth; swollen glands; unusual bleeding or bruising; unusual tiredness or weakness); ***leukopenia; or infection*** (fever or chills; cough or hoarseness; lower back or side pain; painful or difficult urination)—usually asymptomatic, anemia and leukopenia occur in 100% of patients; ***stomatitis*** (inflammation of the oral mucosa)—occurs with busulfan injection; ***thrombocytopenia*** (unusual bleeding or bruising; black, tarry stools; blood in urine or stools; pinpoint red spots on skin)—occurs in 100% of patients

Note: Onset of *leukopenia* is usually 10 to 15 days after initiation of therapy (leukocyte counts usually increase transiently before this), with nadir of white cell count at 11 to 30 days; white cell counts may continue to fall for more than 1 month after withdrawal but usually recover within 12 to 20 weeks.

Bone marrow depression may be severe and progressive, leading to pancytopenia. Recovery from pancytopenia after withdrawal of busulfan may take 1 month to 2 years.

Symptoms of *bone marrow depression* may also indicate transformation of chronic myelocytic leukemia into the acute blastic form.

Incidence less frequent (5–50%)—occurring with long-term use or high dosage

Allergic reaction (fast or irregular breathing; puffiness or swelling around face; shortness of breath; sudden, severe decrease in blood pressure)—occurs with busulfan injection; ***chest pain; dyspnea*** (shortness of breath); ***edema*** (swelling of fingers, hands, arms, lower legs, or feet)—occurs with busulfan injection; ***hyperuricemiaor uric acid nephropathy*** (joint pain; lower back or side pain; swelling of feet or lower legs); ***tachycardia*** (rapid heartbeat); ***thrombosis*** (tingling in lower legs, hands, or feet); ***vasodilation*** (dizziness; light-headedness; sweating)

Note: *Hyperuricemia or uric acid nephropathy* occurs most commonly during initial treatment of patients with leukemia, as a result of rapid cell breakdown which leads to elevated serum uric acid concentrations.

Incidence rare (< 5%)

Bronchopulmonary dysplasia with pulmonary fibrosis (fever; cough; shortness of breath); ***cataracts*** (blurred vision)—occur after prolonged administration; ***esophagitis*** (heartburn; difficulty swallowing); ***hematemesis*** (vomiting blood); ***pancreatitis*** (severe upper abdominal and back pain)

Incidence not determined—Observed during clinical practice; estimates of frequency can not be determined

Aplastic anemia (chest pain; chills; cough; fever; headache; shortness of breath; sores, ulcers, or white spots on lips or in mouth; swollen or painful glands; tightness in chest; unusual bleeding or bruising; unusual tiredness or weakness; wheezing); ***centrilobular sinusoidal fibrosis*** (abdominal pain; feeling of fullness in upper abdomen; bleeding from the esophagus; vomiting); ***corneal thinning*** (blurred vision or other change in vision); ***hepatic veno-occlusive disease*** (bloated abdomen; pain and fullness in right upper abdomen; weight gain; yellow eyes and skin); ***hepatocellular atrophy*** (abdominal pain; bloating of abdomen; dark urine; light-colored stools; nausea and vomiting; yellow eyes or skin); ***hepatocellular necrosis*** (abdominal or stomach pain; black, tarry stools; chills; light-colored stools; dark urine; dizziness; fever; headache; itching; loss of appetite; nausea; rash; unpleasant breath odor; unusual tiredness or weakness; vomiting of blood; yellow eyes or skin); ***hyperbilirubinemia*** (yellow eyes or skin); ***lens changes*** (changes in lenses of eyes); ***mucositis*** (cracked lips; diarrhea; difficulty in swallowing; sores, ulcers, or white spots on lips, tongue, or inside mouth); ***pneumonia*** (chest pain; cough; fever or chills; sneezing; shortness of breath; sore throat; troubled breathing; tightness in chest; wheezing); ***pulmonary toxicity*** (cough or shortness of breath); ***rash; sepsis*** (chills; confusion; dizziness; lightheadedness; fainting; fast heartbeat; fever; rapid, shallow breathing)

Note: In post-marketing, an increased local cutaneous reaction has been observed in patients receiving radiotherapy soon after busulfan.

Those indicating need for medical attention only if they continue or are bothersome

Incidence more frequent (> 50%)

Abdominal pain; amenorrhea and ovarian suppression (missed or irregular menstrual periods); ***anorexia*** (loss of appetite and weight loss); ***anxiety***—occurs with busulfan injection; ***asthenia*** (general fatigue; muscle pain)—occurs with busulfan injection; ***diarrhea; headache***—occurs with busulfan injection; ***insomnia*** (trouble in sleeping)—occurs with busulfan injection; ***nausea; rash; vomiting***

Incidence less frequent (5 –50%)—occurring with long-term use

Confusion; constipation; darkening of skin—5 to 10%; ***depression; dry mouth; epistaxis*** (bloody nose); ***inflammation at injection site; pain; pharyngitis or cough*** (sore throat or cough); ***pruritus*** (itching); ***rhinitis*** (stuffy nose; runny nose; sneezing)

Note: All of the above, as well as darkening of skin, may occur after prolonged therapy and may resemble adrenocortical insufficiency, although adrenocortical function is not suppressed in most patients. Symptoms are sometimes reversible on withdrawal of busulfan. Adrenal responsiveness to exogenous adrenocorticotropic hormone (ACTH) is usually normal, but pituitary function testing with metyrapone has shown blunted urinary 17-hydroxycorticosteroid excretion in some patients that returned to normal when busulfan was discontinued.

Those indicating the need for medical attention if they occur after medication is discontinued

Bone marrow depression; pancytopenia; or thrombocytopenia (unusual bleeding or bruising; black, tarry stools; blood in urine or stools; pinpoint red spots on skin; fever or chills; cough or hoarseness; lower back or side pain; painful or difficult urination); ***pulmonary fibrosis*** (fever; cough; shortness of breath)

Overdose

For more information on the management of overdose or unintentional ingestion, **contact a Poison Control Center** (see *Poison Control Center Listing*).

Clinical effects of overdose

The following effects have been selected on the basis of their potential clinical significance (possible signs and symptoms in parentheses where appropriate)—not necessarily inclusive:

Acute

Bone marrow hypoplasia/aplasia; pancytopenia

Treatment of overdose

Induction of vomiting or gastric lavage followed by administration of charcoal if ingestion of oral busulfan is recent.

Glutathione—Consider as treatment of overdose based on busulfan metabolism by conjugation with glutathione

Hematopoietic progenitor cell transplantation—In the absence of hematopoietic progenitor cell transplantation, the normal dosage of busulfan injection constitutes an overdose of busulfan.

Dialysis—There has been one report that busulfan is dialyzable.

Monitoring of hematologic status and supportive measures if necessary.

Patient Consultation

As an aid to patient consultation, refer to *Advice for the Patient, Busulfan (Systemic).*

In providing consultation, consider emphasizing the following selected information (» = major clinical significance):

Before using this medication

» Conditions affecting use, especially:
- Hypersensitivity to busulfan or any component of the preparation
- Pregnancy—Use not recommended because of mutagenic, teratogenic, and carcinogenic potential; advisability of using contraception; telling physician immediately if pregnancy is suspected
- Breast-feeding—Not recommended because of risk of serious side effects
- Other medications, especially acetaminophen, itraconazole, blood dyscrasia-causing medications, epileptogenic drugs, live vaccines, phenytoin, probenecid, sulfinpyrazone, other bone marrow depressants, or previous cytotoxic drug therapy or radiation therapy
- Other medical problems, especially bone marrow depression, chickenpox, definitive diagnosis of chronic myelogenous leukemia not firmly established, herpes zoster, or other infections gout, head injury or history of seizures, previous chemotherapy, thalassemia, urate kidney stones

Proper use of this medication

» Importance of not taking more or less medication than the amount prescribed

Taking each dose at the same time each day to ensure uniform effect

Importance of ample fluid intake and subsequent increase in urine output to aid in excretion of uric acid

» Possible nausea and vomiting; importance of continuing medication despite stomach upset

Checking with physician if vomiting occurs shortly after dose is taken

» Proper dosing

Missed dose: Not taking at all; not doubling doses

» Proper storage

Precautions while using this medication

» Importance of close monitoring by the physician

» Avoiding immunizations unless approved by physician; other persons in patient's household should avoid immunizations with oral poliovirus vaccine; avoiding persons who have taken oral poliovirus vaccine or wearing a protective mask that covers nose and mouth

Caution if bone marrow depression occurs:

» Avoiding exposure to persons with infections, especially during periods of low blood counts; checking with physician immediately if fever or chills, cough or hoarseness, lower back or side pain, or painful or difficult urination occurs

» Checking with physician immediately if unusual bleeding or bruising; black, tarry stools; blood in urine or stools; or pinpoint red spots on skin occur

Caution in use of regular toothbrush, dental floss, or toothpick; physician, dentist, or nurse may suggest alternatives; checking with physician before having dental work done

Not touching eyes or inside of nose unless hands washed immediately before

Using caution to avoid accidental cuts with use of sharp objects such as safety razor or fingernail or toenail cutters

Avoiding contact sports or other situations where bruising or injury might occur

Caution if any laboratory tests required; possible interference with tissue study results

Importance of proper handling and disposal of cancer drugs

Side/adverse effects

May cause adverse effects such as lung or blood problems; importance of discussing possible effects with physician

Signs of potential side effects, especially allergic reaction, anemia, bronchopulmonary dysplasia with pulmonary fibrosis, cataracts, chest pain, dyspnea, edema, esophagitis, hematemesis, hyperuricemia, infection, leukopenia, stomatitis, thrombocytopenia, tachycardia, thrombosis, uric acid nephropathy, and vasodilation

Signs of potential side effects observed during clinical practice, especially aplastic anemia, centrilobular sinusoidal fibrosis, corneal thinning, hepatic veno-occlusive disease, hepatocellular atrophy, hepatocellular necrosis, hyperbilirubinemia, lens changes, mucositis, pneumonia, rash, and sepsis

Physician or nurse can help in dealing with side effects

General Dosing Information

Patients receiving busulfan should be under supervision of a physician experienced in cancer chemotherapy.

Dosage must be adjusted to meet the individual requirements of each patient, based on clinical response and degree of bone marrow depression.

Development of uric acid nephropathy in patients with leukemia may be prevented by adequate oral hydration and, in some cases, administration of allopurinol. Alkalinization of urine may be necessary if serum uric acid concentrations are elevated.

Busulfan therapy should be discontinued at the first sign of interstitial pulmonary fibrosis.

Busulfan injection should be administered only under supervision of a physician who is experienced in allogeneic hematopoietic stem cell transplantation and in the use of antineoplastic agents

Dosing busulfan injection based on actual body weight, ideal body weight or other factors can produce significant differences in busulfan injection clearance among lean, normal and obese patients. The dose of busulfan injection is based on ideal body weight (IBW) or actual body weight, whichever is lower. For obese or severely obese patients, busulfan injection should be administered based on adjusted ideal body weight (AIBW) as follows:

IBW (males) = 50 + 0.91 × (height in cm − 152)

IBW (females) = 45 + 0.91 × (height in cm − 152)

AIBW = IBW + 0.25 × (actual weight in kg − IBW)

Rapid infusion of busulfan injection is not recommended. Infusion pumps should be used to administer busulfan injection solution. Before and after each infusion, flush the catheter line with approximately 5 mL of 0.9% Sodium Chloride Injection, USP or 5% Dextrose Injection, USP.

Busulfan is known to cross the blood brain barrier and induce seizures. In cases in which other anticonvulsants must be used, busulfan plasma levels should be monitored.

If high-dose busulfan is prescribed, patients should be given prophylactic anticonvulsant therapy, administration preferably with a benzodiazepine rather than an enzyme-inducing anticonvulsant (e.g., phenytoin). Phenytoin use may result in a decrease in the myeloablative effect of busulfan due to increased busulfan clearance. (See *Drug interactions*)

Because of the delayed effect, it is recommended that busulfan therapy be discontinued or dosage reduced at the first sign of a sudden large decrease in leukocyte (particularly granulocyte) count to prevent irreversible bone marrow depression.

Special precautions are recommended in patients who develop thrombocytopenia as a result of administration of busulfan. These may include extreme care in performing invasive procedures; regular inspection of intravenous sites, skin (including perirectal area), and mucous membrane surfaces for signs of bleeding or bruising; limiting frequency of venipuncture and avoiding intramuscular injections; testing urine, emesis, stool, and secretions for occult blood; care in use of regular toothbrushes, dental floss, toothpicks, safety razors, and fingernail and toenail cutters; avoiding constipation; and using caution to prevent falls and other injuries. Such patients should avoid alcohol and aspirin intake because of the risk of gastrointestinal bleeding. Platelet transfusions may be required.

Patients who develop leukopenia should be observed carefully for signs of infection. Antibiotic support may be required. In neutropenic patients who develop fever, broad-spectrum antibiotic coverage should be initiated empirically, pending bacterial cultures and appropriate diagnostic tests.

Safety considerations for handling this medication

There is limited but increasing evidence and concern that personnel involved in preparation and administration of parenteral antineoplastic agents may be at some risk because of the potential mutagenicity, teratogenicity, and/or carcinogenicity of these agents, although the actual risk is unknown. USP advisory panels recommend cautious handling both in preparation and disposal of antineoplastic agents. Precautions that have been suggested include:

- Use of a biological containment cabinet during reconstitution and dilution of parenteral medications and wearing of disposable surgical gloves and masks.
- Use of proper technique to prevent contamination of the medication,

work area, and operator during transfer between containers (including proper training of personnel in this technique).
• Cautious and proper disposal of needles, syringes, vials, ampuls, and unused medication.

A number of medical centers have developed detailed guidelines for handling of antineoplastic agents.

Oral Dosage Forms

BUSULFAN TABLETS USP

Usual adult dose

Chronic myelocytic leukemia—

Induction—

Oral, 1.8 mg per square meter of body surface or 60 mcg (0.06 mg) per kg of body weight a day until the white cell count falls below 15,000 cells per cubic millimeter. Usual dosage range is 4 to 8 mg per day but may range from 1 to 12 mg per day. During remission, treatment is resumed when a monthly white cell count reaches 50,000 cells per cubic millimeter.

Note: Since the rate of fall of the leukocyte count is dose related, daily doses exceeding 4 mg per day should be reserved for patients with the most compelling symptoms; the greater the total daily dose, the greater is the possibility of inducing bone marrow aplasia

A decrease in the leukocyte count is not usually seen during the first 10 to 15 days of treatment; the leukocyte count may actually increase during this period and it should not be interpreted as resistance to the drug, nor should the dose be increased. Since the leukoctye count may continue to fall for more than 1 month after discontinuing busulfan, it is important that busulfan be discontinued *prior to the total leukocyte count falling into the normal range.*Some patients may be unusually sensitive to busulfan and develop myelosuppression more rapidly than usual. Therefore, frequent and careful monitoring of blood counts is necessary. The total leukocyte count decreases exponentially at a constant busulfan dose, so a weekly plot of leukocyte count on semi-logarithmic graph paper can aid in predicting when leukocyte counts will reach 15,000 and busulfan should be discontinued. With the recommended dose of busulfan, a normal leukocyte count is usually achieved in 12 to 20 weeks.

Maintenance—

Oral, 1 to 3 mg per day.

Note: Maintenance therapy with busulfan is recommended only when a remission is shorter than 3 months.

Usual pediatric dose

Chronic myelocytic leukemia—

Induction: Oral, 60 (0.06 mg) per kg of body weight or 1.8 per square meter of body surface per day.

Note: Dosage is titrated to reduce and maintain a leukocyte count of about 20,000 cells per cubic millimeter.

Strength(s) usually available

U.S.—

2 mg (Rx) [*Myleran* (scored; hypromellose; lactose, anhydrous; magnesium stearate; pregelatinized starch; triacetin; titanium dioxide)].

Canada—

2 mg (Rx) [*Myleran* (scored)].

Packaging and storage

Store at 25 °C (77 °F), preferably between 15 and 30 °C (59 and 86 °F), unless otherwise specified by manufacturer.

Auxiliary labeling

• Caution: Chemotherapy. Handle and dispose of properly.

Parenteral Dosage Forms

BUSULFAN INJECTION

Usual adult dose

Chronic myelocytic leukemia—Conditioning regimen: Intravenous (over two hours), 0.8 mg per kg of ideal or actual body weight (whichever is lower), every six hours, for four days, for a total of 16 doses, in combination with 60 mg of cyclophosphamide per kg of body weight daily for two days, given over one hour, starting six hours after the last dose of busulfan is administered.

Note: For obese or severely obese patients, busulfan injection should be administered based on adjusted ideal body weight.

Strength(s) usually available

U.S.—

6 mg/ml (Rx) [*Busulfex* (N,N-dimethylacetamide 33% W/W, polyethylene glycol 400 67% W/W)].

Packaging and storage

Store between 2 and 8 °C (36 and 46 °F).

Preparation of dosage form

Busulfan injection should be diluted with either 0.9% sodium chloride USP or 5% dextrose in water USP, maintaining a diluent concentration that is 10 times the volume of busulfan. Final busulfan concentration should be ≥ 0.5 mg/mL.

Remove the calculated volume of busulfan injection with a syringe fitted with a needle and the five micron nylon filter supplied with the ampule. Remove the needle and filter and replace with a new needle. Dispense the contents of the syringe into an intravenous bag (or syringe) already containing the calculated amount of either 0.9% sodium chloride or 5% dextrose in water. Make sure the drug flows into and through the solution. Always add busulfan injection to the diluent and not diluent to busulfan injection. Mix thoroughly by inverting several times.

Stability

Diluted solutions of busulfan injection are stable at room temperature (25 °C) for up to eight hours but the infusion must be completed by that time. When refrigerated (2-8 °C), diluted solutions of busulfan injection are stable for up to 12 hours but the infusion must be completed within that time.

Note: Dimethylacetamide (DMA), the solvent used in the busulfan injection formulation, can cause increased transaminases and neurologic symptoms. The contribution of DMA to neurologic and hepatic toxicities observed with busulfan injection is unknown.

Selected Bibliography

Murphy CP, Harden EA, Thompson JM. Generalized seizures secondary to high-dose busulfan therapy. Ann Pharmacother 1992; 26: 30-1.

Revised: 08/29/2005

BUTABARBITAL—See *Barbiturates (Systemic)*

BUTAMBEN—See *Anesthetics (Topical)*

BUTOCONAZOLE—See *Antifungals, Azole (Vaginal)*

BUTORPHANOL—See *Opioid (Narcotic) Analgesics (Systemic)*

BUTORPHANOL Nasal-Systemic

VA CLASSIFICATION (Primary): CN101

Note: Controlled substance classification

U.S.: Schedule II

Commonly used brand name(s): *Stadol NS.*

Note: For information on parenteral administration of butorphanol, see *Opioid (Narcotic) Analgesics (Systemic).*

Note: For a listing of dosage forms and brand names by country availability, see *Dosage Forms* section(s).

Category

Analgesic.

Indications

Accepted

Pain (treatment)—Intranasal butorphanol is indicated for relief of pain requiring treatment with an opioid analgesic. Butorphanol has been used to relieve moderate to severe pain following cesarean section, arthroscopic or abdominal surgery, and episiotomy.

Acceptance not established

Intranasal butorphanol may be appropriate for use as alternative therapy for migraine headache pain that has not responded to other abortive agents. However, more comparative clinical studies with first-line agents in the treatment of acute migraine headaches need to be done to determine the role of intranasal butorphanol as an alternative therapy.

Unaccepted

Intranasal butorphanol has not been evaluated, and is therefore not recommended, for relief of labor pain or for use as an adjunct to anesthesia.

Pharmacology/Pharmacokinetics

Physicochemical characteristics

Source—Synthetic.

Chemical Group—An opioid analgesic of the phenanthrene series.

Molecular weight—477.56.

Mechanism of action/Effect

Butorphanol is a mixed agonist/antagonist opioid analgesic. It has agonist activity at the kappa opioid receptor and mixed agonist and antagonist activity at the mu opioid receptor. Because of its antagonist activity, withdrawal symptoms may occur if a patient dependent on another opioid is abruptly transferred to butorphanol.

A 2-mg dose of intranasal butorphanol produces analgesic and/or respiratory depressant effects equivalent to those produced by 2 mg of intravenous butorphanol, 10 mg of intramuscular morphine or methadone, or 75 mg of intramuscular meperidine.

Note: See *Opioid (Narcotic) Analgesics (Systemic)* for additional information on the mechanisms of action of opioid analgesics.

Other actions/effects

Butorphanol has cardiovascular effects that tend to increase cardiac work. It produces alterations in cardiovascular resistance and capacitance that may lead to increases in left ventricular pressure, diastolic pressure, systemic arterial pressure, pulmonary arterial pressure, and pulmonary wedge pressure.

Butorphanol shares the central nervous system (CNS) depressant and respiratory depressant effects of other opioid analgesics.

Butorphanol also alters bronchomotor tone, gastrointestinal secretory and motor activity, and bladder sphincter activity; suppresses the cough reflex; stimulates emesis; and produces miosis.

Absorption

After intranasal administration, absolute bioavailability averages 60 to 70%, although mean values of 48% and 75% have been determined for elderly females and elderly males, respectively.

Nasal mucosal blood vessels are surrounded by adrenergic nerves, and stimulation of adrenergic receptor produces a decrease in blood content and blood flow by vasoconstriction. However, concurrent use of a nasal vasoconstrictor (e.g., oxymetazoline) decreases the rate, but not the extent, of absorption. A study evaluating patients with rhinitis found that inflammation of the nasal mucosa and secretions from the nasal gland did not effect the rate or extent of absorption of transnasal butorphanol.

Distribution

Butorphanol crosses the blood-brain barrier and the placenta and is distributed into breast milk.

Protein binding

High (approximately 80%), with plasma concentrations of up to 7 nanograms per mL (nanograms/mL).

Biotransformation

Hepatic; extensive, primarily to hydroxybutorphanol and, to a lesser extent, to norbutorphanol. These metabolites have some analgesic activity in animal models; possible analgesic activity in humans has not been investigated.

Half-life

Elimination—
- Normal renal function:
  - Young adults (20 to 40 years of age)—4.74 ± 1.57 (range, 2.89 to 8.79) hours.
  - Elderly adults (> 65 years of age)—6.56 ± 1.51 (range, 3.75 to 9.17) hours.
- Renal function impairment (creatinine clearance < 30 mL per minute): Approximately 10.5 hours.

Onset of action

Within 15 minutes, but may be delayed if administered concurrently with or immediately following a nasal vasoconstrictor (e.g., oxymetazoline).

Time to peak concentration

Approximately 30 to 60 minutes.

Peak serum concentration

Following a 1-mg dose—1.04 ± 0.4 (range, 0.35 to 1.97) nanograms/mL, in young adults with normal renal function. Values in individuals older than 65 years of age are more variable, ranging from 0.1 to 2.68 nanograms/mL, but mean values are not significantly different than in young adults. Single-dose values in patients with renal function impairment (creatinine clearance < 30 mL per minute) are not significantly different than those in individuals with normal renal function.

Time to steady-state serum concentration

Within 2 days, when administered at 6-hour intervals.

Time to peak effect

1 to 2 hours.

Duration of action

4 to 5 hours.

Elimination

Renal—Approximately 70 to 80% of a dose; 5% of a dose as unchanged butorphanol, 49% of a dose as hydroxybutorphanol, and < 5% of a dose as norbutorphanol.

Biliary/fecal: Approximately 15% of a dose.

Precautions to Consider

Carcinogenicity

The carcinogenic potential of butorphanol has not been adequately studied.

Mutagenicity

No genotoxicity was demonstrated in assays in *Salmonella typhimurium* or *Escherichia coli*, or in unscheduled DNA synthesis and repair assays in cultured human fibroblast cells.

Pregnancy/Reproduction

Fertility—A reduced pregnancy rate occurred in rats given 160 mg per kg of body weight (mg/kg) per day (944 mg per square meter of body surface area [mg/m^2] per day) orally, but not in rats given 2.5 mg/kg per day (14.75 mg/m^2) per day subcutaneously.

Pregnancy—Adequate and well-controlled studies in humans have not been done.

No teratogenicity occurred in reproduction studies in mice, rats, and rabbits given butorphanol during organogenesis. However, the rate of stillbirths was increased in pregnant rats given 1 mg/kg (5.9 mg/m^2) subcutaneously. Also, postimplantation losses were increased in rabbits given 60 mg/kg (10.2 mg/m^2) orally.

FDA Pregnancy Category C.

Labor—Intranasally administered butorphanol has not been studied, and is therefore not recommended, for relief of labor pain.

Breast-feeding

Butorphanol has been detected in breast milk after intramuscular administration of 2 mg 4 times a day, producing estimated concentrations of 4 micrograms per mL (mcg/mL). Although there is no experience with intranasal administration of butorphanol in nursing women, it should be assumed that similar quantities are distributed into breast milk. However, the amount of butorphanol that might be ingested by a nursing infant is probably clinically insignificant.

Pediatrics

No information is available on the relationship of age to the effects of butorphanol in patients up to 18 years of age. Safety and efficacy have not been established.

Geriatrics

Studies in patients 65 years of age and older indicate that absorption may be decreased in elderly females, but not in elderly males. Butorphanol clearance is decreased in geriatric patients, resulting in a prolonged elimination half-life. Results from a long-term clinical trial also indicate that older individuals may be more sensitive to butorphanol-induced side effects. In particular, these patients may be less able than younger adults to tolerate dizziness that occurs during treatment. Due to the increase in sensitivity to the butorphanol induced side effects, it is recommended that the dosage and dosing interval be adjusted in elderly patients.

Drug interactions and/or related problems

The following drug interactions and/or related problems have been selected on the basis of their potential clinical significance (possible

mechanism in parentheses where appropriate)—not necessarily inclusive (» = major clinical significance):

Note: Combinations containing any of the following medications, depending on the amount present, may also interact with this medication

See *Opioid (Narcotic) Analgesics (Systemic)* for additional drug interactions that apply to use of butorphanol.

» Alcohol or
» CNS depression-producing medications, other (See *Appendix II*)
(concurrent use with opioid analgesics may result in increased CNS and/or respiratory depressant effects; the lowest effective dosage regimen for intranasal butorphanol should be used)

Decongestants, sympathomimetic, nasal
(vasoconstriction induced by these medications decreases the rate, but not the extent, of butorphanol absorption through the nasal mucosa; a slower onset of action should be anticipated if butorphanol is administered concurrently with or immediately following a decongestant)

Enzyme inducers, hepatic, cytochrome P450 (See *Appendix II*) or
Enzyme inhibitors, hepatic, various (See *Appendix II*)
(effects of these medications on the pharmacokinetics of butorphanol have not been established; dose or frequency of administration of butorphanol may need to be adjusted during concurrent use)

» Opioid analgesics, other
(patients who have been receiving long-term treatment with other opioid analgesics may experience withdrawal symptoms if abruptly transferred to butorphanol)

Laboratory value alterations

The following have been selected on the basis of their potential clinical significance (possible effect in parentheses where appropriate)—not necessarily inclusive (» = major clinical significance).

With physiology/laboratory test values
Cerebrospinal fluid pressure
(may be increased secondary to carbon dioxide retention)

Medical considerations/Contraindications

The medical considerations/contraindications included have been selected on the basis of their potential clinical significance (reasons given in parentheses where appropriate)—not necessarily inclusive (» = major clinical significance).

Except under special circumstances, this medication should not be used when the following medical problems exist:

» CNS disease affecting respiratory function or
» Pulmonary disease affecting respiratory function or control or
» Respiratory depression, pre-existing
(risk of precipitating, or exacerbating pre-existing, respiratory depression)

» Physical dependence on other opioid analgesics
(butorphanol may precipitate withdrawal symptoms)

Risk-benefit should be considered when the following medical problems exist:

» Cardiovascular disease, including:
Coronary insufficiency or
Myocardial infarction, acute or
Ventricular function abnormalities
(butorphanol may increase the work of the heart, especially the pulmonary circuit, and should be administered only if the potential benefit clearly outweighs the potential risks)

Drug abuse, history of or
Emotional instability
(patient predisposition to drug abuse)

Head injury or
Increased intracranial pressure
(caution is recommended because butorphanol may increase cerebrospinal fluid pressure and may also cause miosis and alterations in mental state that may interfere with assessment of the clinical course of the patient)

Hepatic function impairment or
Renal function impairment
(clearance of butorphanol may be altered; it is recommended that the medication be given at 6- to 8-hour intervals, initially, until the patient's response has been characterized. Also, subsequent doses should be determined by patient response rather than scheduled at fixed intervals)

Sensitivity to butorphanol

Tolerance to other opioid analgesics, possibility of
(caution is recommended when patients receiving these medications are transferred to butorphanol because of difficulty in assessing the degree to which tolerance may have developed)

Note: See *Opioid (Narcotic) Analgesics (Systemic)* for additional medical considerations/contraindications that apply to use of butorphanol.

Side/Adverse Effects

Note: A 2-mg dose of butorphanol produces respiratory depression equivalent to that caused by 10 mg of intramuscular morphine. In contrast to a pure opioid agonist such as morphine, which produces dose-related respiratory depression, butorphanol produces limited depression that reaches a plateau or ceiling at doses two to three times the analgesic dose. The duration, but not the depth, of butorphanol-induced respiratory depression is increased when these higher doses are given.

In addition to the side/adverse effects listed below, apnea or shallow breathing, convulsions, delusions, edema, hypertension, and mental depression have been reported during butorphanol therapy (incidence of each < 1%). However, a causal relationship has not been established.

Intranasal butorphanol can produce drug dependence and may potentially be abused. Studies have found the abuse potential to be similar to intramuscular butorphanol.

The following side/adverse effects have been selected on the basis of their potential clinical significance (possible signs and symptoms in parentheses where appropriate)—not necessarily inclusive:

Those indicating need for medical attention

Incidence more frequent (3 to 9%)
Difficulty in breathing; nosebleeds; runny nose; sinus congestion; sore throat; tinnitus (ringing or buzzing in ears); ***upper respiratory infection*** (fever; sneezing)

Note: Several side/adverse effects that are listed individually according to their reported frequencies of occurrence (bronchitis, cough, nasal congestion, runny nose, sinus congestion, sinusitis, sore throat) may also occur in conjunction with an *upper respiratory infection*.

Incidence less frequent (1 to 3%)
Blurred vision; bronchitis (congestion in chest; cough; difficult or painful breathing); ***cough; ear pain; itching; sinusitis*** (sinus congestion with pain)

Incidence rare (< 1%)
Decrease in blood pressure; difficulty in urinating; fainting; hallucinations; skin rash or hives

Those indicating need for medical attention only if they continue or are bothersome

Incidence more frequent (3 to 9% or as indicated)
Confusion; constipation; dizziness—incidence 19%; ***drowsiness***—incidence 43%; ***dry mouth; headache; irritation inside nose; loss of appetite; nasal congestion***—incidence 13%; ***nausea or vomiting; sweating or clammy feeling; trouble in sleeping; unpleasant taste; vasodilation*** (flushing); ***weakness, severe***

Incidence less frequent (1 to 3%) or rare (< 1%)
Anxiety; behavior changes; burning, crawling, or prickling feeling on skin; false sense of well-being; feeling hot; floating feeling; nervousness, sometimes with restlessness; pounding heartbeat; stomach pain; strange dreams; trembling

Those indicating possible withdrawal and/or the need for medical attention if they occur after medication is discontinued

Anxiety; diarrhea; nervousness and restlessness

Note: See *Opioid (Narcotic) Analgesics (Systemic)* for additional signs and symptoms typical of opioid withdrawal.

Overdose

For specific information on the agents used in the management of butorphanol overdose, see *Naloxone (Systemic)* monograph.

For more information on the management of overdose or unintentional ingestion, **contact a Poison Control Center** (see *Poison Control Center Listing*).

Clinical effects of overdose

The following effects have been selected on the basis of their potential clinical significance (possible signs and symptoms in parentheses where appropriate)—not necessarily inclusive:

Acute and chronic
Cold, clammy skin; confusion; convulsions; low blood pressure; pinpoint pupils of eyes; severe dizziness, drowsiness, nervousness, restlessness, or weakness; slow heartbeat; slow or troubled breathing; unconsciousness

Note: Excessive administration of transnasal butorphanol may cause saturation of the nasal mucosa and limited absorption. However, overdose occurs when butorphanol is administered after desaturation of the nasal mucosa.

Treatment of overdose

Primary importance should be given to maintaining adequate ventilation. Assessing the patient's respiratory status and, if necessary, administering oxygen or otherwise assisting respiration are essential. Provision of an artificial airway may be necessary in the presence of coma.

Specific treatment—Administering naloxone if necessary. See the package insert or *Naloxone (Systemic)* for specific dosing guidelines for naloxone.

Monitoring—Continuous monitoring of mental status, responsiveness, and vital signs is recommended. Oxygenation may be monitored via pulse oximetry.

Supportive care—Supportive measures include establishing intravenous lines, maintaining peripheral perfusion and normal body temperature, and treating hypotension. Patients in whom intentional overdose is confirmed or suspected should be referred for psychiatric consultation.

Patient Consultation

In providing consultation, consider emphasizing the following selected information (» = major clinical significance):

Before using this medication

» Conditions affecting use, especially:
- Sensitivity to butorphanol
- Pregnancy—Safe use in pregnancy has not been established
- Breast-feeding—Probably distributed into breast milk
- Use in the elderly—Lower dosage regimen recommended because of increased susceptibility to effects of opioids and prolonged butorphanol half-life in geriatric patients
- Other medications, especially other CNS depressants, including alcohol and, other opioid analgesics
- Other medical problems, especially cardiovascular disease, CNS or pulmonary disease affecting respiratory function, physical dependence on other opioid analgesics or pre-existing respiratory depression

Proper use of this medication

» Reading patient instructions carefully
» Importance of not using more medication than the amount prescribed

Priming the unit
» Removing protective cover and clip
» Keeping sprayer pointed away from patient, other people, or pets while priming
» Prior to first use, pumping the activator 7 or 8 times until a fine, wide spray appears
» Repriming by pumping the activator 1 or 2 times if unit has not been used in 48 hours

Proper administration
» Blowing nose gently
» To obtain a 1-mg dose, inserting spray unit into a nostril, closing off the other nostril with index finger, tilting head slightly forward and spraying once, sniffing gently with mouth closed
» Removing unit from nostril, tilting head back, then sniffing gently again
» To obtain a 2-mg dose, repeating procedure for obtaining a 1-mg dose using the other nostril
» Replacing protective cover and clip after use
» Proper dosing
(if on scheduled dosing)
Missed dose: Using as soon as possible; not using if almost time for next dose
» Proper storage

Precautions while using this medication

» Avoiding use of alcoholic beverages or other CNS depressants during therapy, unless prescribed or otherwise approved by physician
» Caution if dizziness, drowsiness, lightheadedness, impairment of physical or mental abilities, or false sense of well-being occurs
» Possibility of hypotension and syncope, especially during the first hour after administration; avoiding activities in which these effects could be hazardous
Caution if any kind of surgery (including dental surgery) or emergency treatment is required
Possible dryness of mouth; using sugarless candy or gum, ice, or saliva substitute for relief; checking with physician or dentists if dry mouth continues for more than 2 weeks
Checking with physician before discontinuing medication after prolonged use; gradual dosage reduction may be necessary to avoid withdrawal symptoms
» Suspected overdose: Getting emergency help at once

Side/adverse effects

Checking with physician if difficulty in breathing, nosebleeds, runny nose, sinus congestion, sore throat, tinnitus, upper respiratory infection, blurred vision, bronchitis, cough, ear pain, itching, sinusitis, decrease in blood pressure, difficulty in urinating, fainting, hallucinations, or skin rash or hives occurs

General Dosing Information

Dosage of butorphanol should be based on the patient's age, body weight, physical status, underlying pathological condition, and other medications being used concurrently.

Nasal Dosage Forms

BUTORPHANOL TARTRATE NASAL SOLUTION

Usual adult dose

Analgesic—

Nongeriatric adults with normal hepatic and renal function: Intranasal, 1 mg (one spray in one nostril). If adequate pain relief is not achieved within sixty to ninety minutes, another 1-mg dose may be administered. This two-dose sequence may be repeated in three to four hours as needed. Alternatively, if pain is severe and the patient will be able to remain recumbent if drowsiness or dizziness occurs, a 2-mg dose (one spray in each nostril) may be administered. This dose may be repeated every three or four hours. The increased risk of adverse effects must be kept in mind if this higher dose is used.

Patients with impaired hepatic or renal function: Intranasal, 1 mg (one spray in one nostril). If adequate pain relief is not achieved within ninety minutes to two hours, another 1-mg dose may be given. Subsequent doses should be administered according to patient response rather than at fixed intervals, but generally at not less than six-hour intervals.

Usual pediatric dose

Safety and efficacy in patients up to 18 years of age have not been established.

Usual geriatric dose

Analgesic—Intranasal, 1 mg (one spray in one nostril). If adequate pain relief is not achieved within ninety minutes to two hours, another 1-mg dose may be given. Subsequent doses should be administered according to patient response rather than at fixed intervals, but generally at not less than six-hour intervals.

Strength(s) usually available

U.S.—

1% (10 mg per mL; 1 mg per metered spray) (Rx) [*Stadol NS* (benzethonium chloride; sodium chloride; purified water; sodium hydroxide and/or hydrochloric acid to adjust pH)].

Canada—

1% (10 mg per mL; 1 mg per metered spray) (Rx) [*Stadol NS* (benzethonium chloride; citric acid; sodium chloride; purified water; sodium hydroxide and/or hydrochloric acid to adjust pH)].

Note: Each container provides an average of 14 to 15 doses (1 mg each). If frequent repriming is necessary, only 8 to 10 doses may be obtained from the unit.

Packaging and storage

Store below 30 °C (86 °F), unless otherwise specified by manufacturer.

Auxiliary labeling

- May cause drowsiness.
- Avoid alcoholic beverages.

Note

Controlled substance in the U.S.

Additional information

At the time of dispensing, the pharmacist should replace the screw cap on the bottle of nasal solution with the spray pump included in the package without removing the clear cover from the pump. The unit should be returned to the child-resistant vial before being given to the patient.

Revised: 03/30/1998

CABERGOLINE Systemic

VA CLASSIFICATION (Primary/Secondary): AU900/HS900

Commonly used brand name(s): *Dostinex*.

Note: For a listing of dosage forms and brand names by country availability, see *Dosage Forms* section(s).

Category

Dopamine agonist; antihyperprolactinemic.

Indications

Accepted

Hyperprolactinemic disorders (treatment) or

Prolactinomas, pituitary (treatment)—Cabergoline is indicated in the treatment of hyperprolactinemic disorders due to pituitary adenomas or to idiopathic etiology.

Acceptance not established

There are insufficient data to show that cabergoline is safe and effective for *suppression of postpartum lactation*. The routine use of medication to suppress postpartum lactation has become controversial and some medical experts now regard this practice as obsolete.

There are insufficient data to show that cabergoline is safe and effective for the *treatment of Parkinson's disease*.

Pharmacology/Pharmacokinetics

Physicochemical characteristics

Chemical Group—Cabergoline is an ergoline (ergot alkaloid derivative).

Molecular weight—451.62.

Mechanism of action/Effect

Cabergoline is a long-acting, selective dopamine receptor agonist, exhibiting high affinity for D_2 receptors and low affinity for D_1, alpha$_1$- and alpha$_2$-adrenergic, and serotonin (5-hydroxytryptamine$_1$ and 5-hydroxytryptamine$_2$) receptors. Cabergoline inhibits the synthesis and release of prolactin from the anterior pituitary by directly stimulating the D_2 receptors of the pituitary lactotrophs in a dose-related fashion. While cabergoline doses up to 2 mg inhibited prolactin in healthy volunteers, similar inhibition did not occur for the other anterior pituitary hormones, including growth hormone, follicle-stimulating hormone, luteinizing hormone, corticotropin, and thyroid-stimulating hormone. Cabergoline did not affect serum cortisol concentrations.

Absorption

Exhibits first-pass effect; absolute bioavailability is unknown.

Distribution

Extensive tissue distribution; cabergoline concentrations are at least 100 times greater in the pituitary than in the serum. Studies done in rats showed significant concentrations of cabergoline in the mammary glands and uterine wall, and that cabergoline crosses the placenta.

Protein binding

Moderate (40 to 42%), in a concentration-independent manner. Cabergoline's protein binding is unlikely to be influenced by concomitant treatment with other protein-bound medications.

Biotransformation

Hepatic—Cabergoline undergoes hydrolysis to inactive metabolites without causing hepatic enzyme induction or inhibition; cytochrome P450–mediated metabolism is minimal. Although mild to moderate hepatic function impairment does not alter pharmacokinetic values for cabergoline, severe hepatic function impairment (Child-Pugh score greater than 10) can substantially increase the values of C_{max} and area under the plasma concentration-time curve (AUC).

Half-life

Elimination—63 to 69 hours.

Time to peak concentration

Within 3 hours.

Peak serum concentration

30 to 70 picograms/mL (66.4 to 155 picomoles/L), reported in healthy volunteers taking single doses of 0.5 to 1.5 mg cabergoline. The steady-state serum concentration in patients using multiple weekly doses is expected to be 2 to 3 times higher than that reported for single doses.

Time to peak effect

48 hours (single 0.6-mg dose of cabergoline in hyperprolactinemic patients).

Duration of action

Up to 14 days (single 0.6-mg dose of cabergoline in hyperprolactinemic patients).

Elimination

At 20 days for five healthy patients given single doses—
- Fecal: 60%.
- Renal: 22% (4% unchanged).

Nonrenal clearance was 3.2 L per minute in healthy adults. Renal clearance was 0.08 L per minute, similar to that of hyperprolactinemic patients. Moderate-to-severe renal insufficiency did not alter cabergoline's pharmacokinetics.

Precautions to Consider

Cross-sensitivity and/or related problems

Patients sensitive to other ergot derivatives may be sensitive to cabergoline also.

Carcinogenicity/tumorigenicity

In studies of mice, a slight increase in cervical and uterine leiomyomas and uterine leiomyosarcomas occurred when cabergoline was given in doses seven times the maximum recommended human dose (MRHD)—a dose based on the body surface area (BSA) of a 50-kg human. Cabergoline, when given to rats at doses four times greater than the MRHD, caused a slight increase in interstitial cell adenomas and malignant tumors of the uterus and cervix. The relevance of these findings to humans is not clear because of the hormonal differences between humans and animals.

Mutagenicity

Cabergoline was not found to be mutagenic in a series of *in vitro* tests, including the Ames test, gene mutation assay, chromosomal aberration test in human lymphocytes, and a DNA damage and repair test in bacteria. Cabergoline also produced a negative mouse bone marrow micronucleus test.

Pregnancy/Reproduction

Fertility—Cabergoline doses equal to one twenty-eighth of the MRHD inhibited conception in studies of female rats.

Pregnancy—Adequate and well-controlled studies in humans have not been done. Cabergoline is not recommended for use during pregnancy.

Cabergoline crosses the placenta in animals. Researchers studied cabergoline's effect on reproduction in mice, rats, and rabbits. Maternotoxicity, but not teratogenicity, occurred in studies of mice given doses of cabergoline 55 times greater than the MRHD (based on body surface area of a 50-kg human). When given doses of cabergoline equal to one seventh of the MRHD, rats experienced embryofetal loss after embryo implantation. Similar studies in rabbits given doses 19 times greater than the MRHD produced maternotoxicity, exhibited as reduced food intake and body weight loss. Doses 150 times greater than the MRHD produced fetal malformations in rabbits in one study, a result not reproduced in another study using doses 300 times greater than the MRHD. The relevance of these findings to humans is not clear since prolactin affects the reproductive cycles of animals and humans differently.

FDA Pregnancy Category B.

Breast-feeding

It is not known if cabergoline is distributed into breast milk. Cabergoline should not be used in breast-feeding women or women planning to begin breast-feeding within a short period of time since it inhibits lactation by suppressing prolactin release.

In a study in rats, continued treatment of female rats with cabergoline beginning 6 days before parturition resulted in arrested pup growth and death of the litter due to the decreased amount of available maternal milk.

Pediatrics

Appropriate studies on the relationship of age to the effects of cabergoline have not been performed in the pediatric population. Safety and efficacy have not been established.

Geriatrics

No information is available on the relationship of age to the effects of cabergoline in geriatric patients. Safety and efficacy have not been established.

Drug interactions and/or related problems

The following drug interactions and/or related problems have been selected on the basis of their potential clinical significance (possible

mechanism in parentheses where appropriate)—not necessarily inclusive (» = major clinical significance):

Note: Combinations containing any of the following medications, depending on the amount present, may also interact with this medication.

Antihypertensives, including
  Methyldopa
  Reserpine
  (concurrent use may result in additive hypotensive effects; dosage adjustment of the antihypertensive agent may be needed)

» Dopaminergic blocking agents, including metoclopramide or
» Neuroleptics, including
  Haloperidol
  Phenothiazines
  Thioxanthenes
  (cabergoline may interfere with the dopamine-blocking effects of these medications, reducing their effectiveness and exacerbating the patient's underlying condition; dosage adjustment of either medication may be necessary)

Medical considerations/Contraindications

The medical considerations/contraindications included have been selected on the basis of their potential clinical significance (reasons given in parentheses where appropriate)—not necessarily inclusive (» = major clinical significance).

Except under special circumstances, this medication should not be used when the following medical problems exist:

» Eclampsia, or history of or
» Hypertension, uncontrolled or
» Preeclampsia, or history of
  (may aggravate these conditions; although cabergoline usually lowers blood pressure, rarely, blood pressure can increase)
» Hepatic function impairment, severe
  (metabolism may be reduced with severe hepatic function impairment; dosage reduction may be required if cabergoline is used)

Risk-benefit should be considered when the following medical problems exist:

Hepatic function impairment, mild to moderate
  (although mild to moderate hepatic function impairment does not decrease cabergoline metabolism, special hepatic function and serum prolactin monitoring as a precaution may be warranted; a lower dose of cabergoline may be needed if condition worsens)

Sensitivity to cabergoline or other ergot derivatives

Patient monitoring

The following may be especially important in patient monitoring (other tests may be warranted in some patients, depending on condition; » = major clinical significance):

Blood pressure measurements
  (initial doses of cabergoline above 1 mg can cause orthostatic hypotension; monitoring for possible hypotensive effects may be needed)

Prolactin, serum
  (periodic monitoring of serum prolactin concentrations is needed during treatment, after each dosing interval, or when cabergoline is discontinued to assess efficacy of treatment. If serum prolactin levels are normal for 6 months, cabergoline can be discontinued. Patient monitoring should be continued to assess if or when to reinstate the antihyperprolactinemic treatment)

Side/Adverse Effects

Note: Side effects for cabergoline are dose-related. Patients using cabergoline for Parkinson's disease, an unlabeled use, receive much higher doses than do those patients with a hyperprolactinemic condition. At doses up to 11.5 mg of cabergoline a day, patients with Parkinson's disease have experienced the following additional side effects: dyskinesia, hallucinations, heart failure, pleural effusion, pulmonary fibrosis, gastric or duodenal ulcer, and, in one case, constrictive pericarditis.

The following side/adverse effects have been selected on the basis of their potential clinical significance (possible signs and symptoms in parentheses where appropriate)—not necessarily inclusive:

Those indicating need for medical attention

Incidence less frequent—4 or 5%

Abdominal pain; vertigo (sensation of motion, usually whirling, either of oneself or of one's surroundings)

Incidence rare—≤ 1%

Anorexia (loss of appetite associated with weight loss or gain); ***edema, periorbital*** (vision changes); ***edema, peripheral*** (swelling of hands, ankles, or feet); ***impaired concentration; syncope or hypotension*** (fainting or lightheadedness when getting up from a lying or sitting position; unusually fast heartbeat)—especially orthostatic hypotension

Those indicating need for medical attention only if they continue or are bothersome

Incidence more frequent

Asthenia (weakness)—incidence 6%; ***constipation***—incidence 7%; ***dizziness***—incidence 17%; ***dyspepsia*** (stomach discomfort following meals)—incidence 4%; ***headache***—incidence 26%; ***nausea***—incidence 29%

Incidence less frequent—< 3%

Diarrhea; dryness of mouth; flatulence (stomach or intestinal gas); ***flu-like symptoms*** (general feeling of discomfort or illness; runny nose; sore throat); ***hot flashes; insomnia*** (trouble in sleeping); ***mental depression; muscle or joint pain; paresthesia*** (unusual feeling of burning or stinging of skin); ***pruritus*** (itching of skin); ***somnolence*** (sleepiness); ***toothache; vomiting***

Those not indicating need for medical attention

Incidence less frequent—< 1%

Acne; increased libido (increased sex drive)

Overdose

For more information on the management of overdose or unintentional ingestion, **contact a Poison Control Center** (see *Poison Control Center Listing*).

Clinical effects of overdose

The following effects have been selected on the basis of their potential clinical significance (possible signs and symptoms in parentheses where appropriate)—not necessarily inclusive:

Hallucinations; nasal congestion; syncope (fainting; lightheadedness; palpitations)

Treatment of overdose

Monitoring—Blood pressure measurements.

Patients in whom intentional overdose is known or suspected should be referred for psychiatric consultation.

Patient Consultation

As an aid to patient consultation, refer to *Advice for the Patient, Cabergoline (Systemic)*.

In providing consultation, consider emphasizing the following selected information (» = major clinical significance):

Before using this medication

» Conditions affecting use, especially:
  Sensitivity to cabergoline or other ergot derivatives
  Carcinogenicity/tumorigenicity—Studies in mice showed slight increase in cervical and uterine leiomyomas and uterine leiomyosarcomas; studies in rats showed a slight increase in malignant tumors of the uterus and cervix and interstitial cell adenomas. Relevancy to humans is not known because prolactin affects animals and humans differently
  Pregnancy—Not recommended for use during pregnancy
  Breast-feeding—Not known if cabergoline is distributed into breast milk; will prevent lactation in mothers who breast-feed or are planning to begin breast-feeding soon
  Other medications, especially dopaminergic blocking agents and neuroleptics
  Other medical problems, especially eclampsia (or history of), severe hepatic function impairment, hypertension (uncontrolled), or preeclampsia (or history of)

Proper use of this medication

Compliance with therapy: Importance of not taking more or less medication than the amount prescribed

» Proper dosing

Missed dose: Taking as soon as possible within 1 or 2 days; if missed dose is not remembered until time of next dose, doubling the dose if medication is generally well-tolerated, without causing nausea. If not well-tolerated, discussing with health care professional before taking missed dose

» Proper storage

Precautions while using this medication

Regular visits to physician to check progress

» Caution when driving or doing jobs requiring alertness because of possible drowsiness or dizziness

Checking with physician immediately if pregnancy is suspected

Getting up slowly from sitting or lying position to decrease the incidence of dizziness, lightheadedness, or vertigo

Side/adverse effects
Signs of potential side effects, especially abdominal pain, vertigo, anorexia, periorbital or peripheral edema, impaired concentration, or syncope or hypotension

General Dosing Information

The use of cabergoline for longer than 24 months has not been established. After the patient's serum prolactin level is normal for 6 months, cabergoline may be discontinued. Treatment of hyperprolactinemia may be symptomatic rather than curative; reinitiation of an antihyperprolactinemic agent may be needed.

Oral Dosage Forms

CABERGOLINE TABLETS

Usual adult dose
Antihyperprolactinemic—
Oral, 0.25 mg two times a week. In accordance with patient's serum prolactin level, dosage may be increased in increments of 0.25 mg, up to 1 mg two times a week, waiting at least four weeks between each dosage increase.

Usual adult prescribing limits
2 mg a week.

Usual pediatric dose
Antihyperprolactinemic—
Safety and efficacy have not been established.

Usual geriatric dose
Antihyperprolactinemic—
See *Usual adult dose.*

Strength(s) usually available
U.S.—
0.5 mg (Rx) [*Dostinex* (scored; lactose)].

Packaging and storage
Store below 40 °C (104 °F), preferably between 15 and 30 °C (59 and 86 °F), unless otherwise specified by manufacturer.

Revised: 03/05/2001
Developed: 06/26/1997

CAFFEINE Systemic

This monograph includes information on the following: 1) Caffeine; 2) Citrated Caffeine; 3) Caffeine and Sodium Benzoate†.

VA CLASSIFICATION (Primary/Secondary):
Caffeine—CN809/RE900
Caffeine, Citrated—CN809/RE900
Caffeine and Sodium Benzoate—CN809

Commonly used brand name(s): *Cafcit*[2]; *Caffedrine Caplets*[1]; *Dexitac Stay Alert Stimulant*[1]; *Enerjets*[1]; *Keep Alert*[1]; *Maximum Strength SnapBack Stimulant Powders*[1]; *NoDoz Maximum Strength Caplets*[1]; *Pep-Back*[1]; *Quick Pep*[1]; *Ultra Pep-Back*[1]; *Vivarin*[1]; *Wake-Up*[1].

Note: For a listing of dosage forms and brand names by country availability, see *Dosage Forms* section(s).

†Not commercially available in Canada.

Category

Central nervous system stimulant—Caffeine; Citrated Caffeine; Caffeine and Sodium Benzoate.
Analgesia adjunct—Caffeine.
Respiratory stimulant adjunct—Caffeine; Citrated Caffeine

Indications

Note: Bracketed information in the *Indications* section refers to uses that are not included in U.S. product labeling.

Accepted

Fatigue or
Drowsiness (treatment)—Caffeine is used as a mild central nervous system stimulant to help restore mental alertness or wakefulness when fatigue or drowsiness is experienced.

Apnea, neonatal (treatment adjunct)—Caffeine or citrated caffeine (but not caffeine and sodium benzoate combination) is indicated in the short-term management of neonatal apnea, especially apnea of prematurity, which is characterized by periodic breathing and apneic episodes of more than 15 seconds accompanied by cyanosis and bradycardia, in infants between 28 and 33 weeks gestational age. Other treatments include increased stimulation (cutaneous, vestibular, or proprioceptive), nasal continuous positive airway pressure (CPAP), increased environmental oxygen, and artificial ventilation. Determination of which therapy is to be undertaken is based upon the assessment of each individual patient's clinical status and therapeutic requirement. Caffeine may be considered a desirable alternative to theophylline when initiating therapy for premature neonatal apnea because some infants are unable to convert theophylline to caffeine, a major metabolite of theophylline in neonates. Caffeine also has a wider therapeutic index than theophylline. Caffeine therapy in the management of apnea is usually required for only a few weeks and rarely for more than a few months, since the apnea usually resolves by about 34 to 36 weeks' gestational age.

[Apnea, infant, postoperative (prophylaxis)]—Caffeine or citrated caffeine is indicated for the prevention of postoperative apnea in former preterm infants.

[Electroconvulsive therapy (ECT) (treatment adjunct)]—Caffeine pretreatment is indicated to augment ECT by increasing seizure duration and reducing the need for increases in stimulus intensity.

Caffeine is used in combination with ergotamine to treat vascular headaches such as migraine and cluster headaches (histaminic cephalalgia, migrainous neuralgia, Horton's headache).

Caffeine is also used, and has been shown to be effective, as an analgesic adjunct in combination with aspirin or acetaminophen and aspirin to enhance pain relief, although it has no analgesic activity of its own. However, caffeine's efficacy as an analgesic adjunct in combination with acetaminophen alone has been questioned.

Unaccepted

Caffeine and sodium benzoate combination has been used in conjunction with other supportive measures to treat respiratory depression associated with overdose with central nervous system (CNS) depressants such as narcotic analgesics or alcohol; however, because of the availability of specific antagonists, such as flumazenil and naloxone, and caffeine's questionable benefit and transient effect, most authorities believe caffeine should not be used for these conditions and, therefore, recommend other supportive therapy.

Caffeine is used in combination with other agents such as analgesics and diuretics to relieve tension and fluid retention associated with menstruation; however, its usefulness for this purpose is in doubt because of its minimal diuretic action.

Pharmacology/Pharmacokinetics

Physicochemical characteristics

Source—Coffee, tea, some soft drinks, cocoa or chocolate, and kola nuts. May also be synthesized from urea or dimethylurea.
Chemical Group—Methylated xanthine.
Molecular weight—
Caffeine (anhydrous): 194.19.
Citrated caffeine: 386.31.
Sodium benzoate: 144.11.
pH—
Citrated caffeine injection: 4.7.
Caffeine and sodium benzoate injection: Between 6.5 and 8.5.

Mechanism of action/Effect

Central nervous system stimulant—Caffeine stimulates all levels of the CNS, although its cortical effects are milder and of shorter duration than those of amphetamines. In larger doses, caffeine stimulates medullary, vagal, vasomotor, and respiratory centers, promoting bradycardia, vasoconstriction, and increased respiratory rate. This action was previously believed to be due primarily to increased intracellular cyclic 3′,5′-adenosine monophosphate (cyclic AMP) following inhibition of phosphodiesterase, the enzyme that degrades cyclic AMP. More recent studies indicate that caffeine exerts its physiological effects in large part through antagonism of central adenosine receptors.

Analgesia adjunct—Caffeine constricts cerebral vasculature with an accompanying decrease in cerebral blood flow and in the oxygen tension of the brain. It has been suggested that the addition of caffeine to aspirin or aspirin and acetaminophen combinations may help to relieve headache by providing a more rapid onset of action and/or enhanced pain relief with a lower dose of the analgesic. In some patients, caffeine may reduce headache pain by reversing caffeine withdrawal symptoms. Recent studies with ergotamine indicate that the enhancement of effect by the addition of caffeine may be due to improved gastrointestinal absorption of ergotamine when administered with caffeine.

Respiratory stimulant adjunct—Although the exact mechanism of action has not been completely established, caffeine, as other methylxanthines, is believed to act primarily through stimulation of the medullary respiratory center. This action is seen in certain pathophysiological states, such as in Cheyne-Stokes respiration and in apnea of preterm infants, and when respiration is depressed by certain drugs, such as barbiturates and opioids. Methylxanthines appear to increase the sensitivity of the respiratory center to the stimulatory actions of carbon dioxide, increasing alveolar ventilation, thereby reducing the severity and frequency of apneic episodes.

Other actions/effects

Cardiac—Caffeine produces a positive inotropic effect on the myocardium and a positive chronotropic effect on the sinoatrial node, causing transient increases in heart rate, force of contraction, and cardiac output. Low concentrations of caffeine may produce small decreases in heart rate, possibly as a result of stimulation of the medullary vagal nuclei. At higher concentrations, caffeine produces definite tachycardia and sensitive persons may experience other arrhythmias, such as premature ventricular contractions.

Vascular—Caffeine causes constriction of cerebral vasculature with an accompanying decrease in cerebral blood flow and in the oxygen tension in the brain. Caffeine also causes an increase in systemic vascular resistance, resulting in an increase in blood pressure. These effects are believed to be mediated by blockade of adenosine-induced vasodilation and activation of the sympathetic nervous system.

Skeletal muscles—Caffeine stimulates voluntary skeletal muscle, possibly by inducing the release of acetylcholine, increasing the force of contraction and decreasing muscle fatigue. This stimulation of diaphragmatic muscles decreases the work of breathing.

Gastrointestinal secretions—Caffeine causes secretion of both pepsin and gastric acid from parietal cells.

Renal—Caffeine increases renal blood flow and glomerular filtration rate and decreases proximal tubular reabsorption of sodium and water, resulting in a mild diuresis.

Caffeine also inhibits uterine contractions, increases plasma and urinary catecholamine concentrations, and transiently increases plasma glucose by stimulating glycogenolysis and lipolysis.

In neonates, caffeine causes a 25% increase in oxygen consumption, blood vessel dilatation, cerebral vessel vasoconstriction, and smooth muscle relaxation.

Absorption

Readily absorbed after oral or parenteral administration. Absorption of methylxanthines relates more to lipophilicity than to water solubility.

Distribution

Rapidly distributed to all body compartments; readily crosses the placenta and blood-brain barrier. Volume of distribution (Vol_D) in adults ranges from 0.4 to 0.6 liter per kg of body weight (L/kg). Vol_D in neonates averages between 0.78 and 0.92 L/kg.

Protein binding

Low (25 to 36%).

Biotransformation

Hepatic. In adults, about 80% of a dose of caffeine is metabolized to paraxanthine (1,7-dimethylxanthine), about 10% is metabolized to theobromine (3,7-dimethylxanthine), and about 4% is metabolized to theophylline (1,3-dimethylxanthine). These compounds are further demethylated to monomethylxanthines and then to methyl uric acids. In premature neonates, cytochrome P450 1A2 is involved in caffeine biotransformation; however, caffeine metabolism is limited due to hepatic enzyme immaturity. In the neonate, caffeine and theophylline are interconverted, with caffeine concentrations measuring approximately 25% of theophylline concentrations after theophylline administration and theophylline concentrations measuring approximately 3% to 8% of caffeine concentrations after caffeine administration.

Half-life

Adults—3 to 7 hours.

Neonates—65 to 130 hours. Decreases to adult values by 4 to 9 months post-term and is inversely proportional to gestational/postconceptual age.

Note: Half-life is increased in pregnant women and in patients with cirrhosis.

Time to peak plasma concentration

In adults—50 to 75 minutes following oral administration.

In preterm neonates—30 to 120 minutes following oral administration of 10 mg of caffeine base per kg of body weight.

Peak plasma concentration

6 to 10 mg per L following oral administration of 10 mg of caffeine base per kg of body weight to preterm neonates.

Therapeutic plasma concentration

5 to 25 mcg per mL (25.8 to 128.8 micromoles per L).

Elimination

Adults—Renal; primarily as metabolites; about 1 to 2% excreted unchanged.

Neonates—Renal; about 85% excreted unchanged.

Precautions to Consider

Cross-sensitivity and/or related problems

Patients sensitive to other xanthines (aminophylline, dyphylline, oxtriphylline, theobromine, theophylline) may be sensitive to caffeine also.

Pregnancy/Reproduction

Pregnancy—Caffeine crosses the placenta and achieves blood and tissue concentrations in the fetus that are similar to maternal concentrations. Studies in humans have shown that heavy caffeine consumption by pregnant women may increase the risk of spontaneous abortion and intrauterine growth retardation. Also, excessive intake of caffeine by pregnant women has resulted in fetal arrhythmias. It is therefore recommended that pregnant women limit their intake of caffeine to less than 300 mg (3 cups of coffee) per day.

Studies in animals have shown that caffeine causes skeletal abnormalities in the digits and phalanges when given in doses equivalent to the caffeine content of 12 to 24 cups of coffee daily throughout pregnancy or when given in very large single doses (i.e., 50 to 100 mg per kg of body weight), and causes retarded skeletal development when given in lower doses.

FDA Pregnancy Category C.

Breast-feeding

Caffeine is distributed into breast milk in very small amounts. Although the concentration of caffeine in breast milk is 1% of the mother's plasma concentration, caffeine can accumulate in the infant. The infant may show signs of caffeine stimulation such as hyperactivity and wakefulness when a breast-feeding mother drinks as much as 6 to 8 cups of caffeine-containing beverages. It is recommended that nursing mothers limit their intake of caffeine-containing beverages to 1 to 2 cups per day and avoid taking over-the-counter caffeine capsules or tablets. At recommended doses of caffeine-containing analgesic combinations, concentration in the infant is considered to be insignificant.

Pediatrics

With the exception of infants, appropriate studies on the relationship of age to the effects of caffeine have not been performed in children up to 12 years of age; however, no pediatrics-specific problems have been documented to date.

Caffeine and sodium benzoate injection is not recommended in neonatal apnea because the benzoate may interact competitively with bilirubin at the albumin binding site, which could cause or increase jaundice. In addition, elevated serum concentrations of benzyl alcohol and benzoate have been associated with neurological disturbances, hypotension, gasping respirations, and metabolic acidosis.

Geriatrics

No information is available on the relationship of age to the effects of caffeine in geriatric patients.

Drug interactions and/or related problems

The following drug interactions and/or related problems have been selected on the basis of their potential clinical significance (possible mechanism in parentheses where appropriate)—not necessarily inclusive (» = major clinical significance):

Note: Combinations containing any of the following medications, depending on the amount present, may also interact with this medication.

Adenosine
(effects of adenosine are antagonized by caffeine; larger doses of adenosine may be required, or adenosine may be ineffective)

Barbiturates or
Primidone
(concurrent use of barbiturates or primidone [because of the phenobarbital metabolite] with caffeine may increase the metabolism of caffeine by induction of hepatic microsomal enzymes, resulting in increased clearance of caffeine; in addition, concurrent use may antagonize the hypnotic or anticonvulsant effects of the barbiturates)

Beta-adrenergic blocking agents, systemic or
Beta-adrenergic blocking agents, ophthalmic
(concurrent use of beta-blocking agents, including ophthalmic agents [significant systemic absorption possible], with caffeine may result in mutual inhibition of therapeutic effects)

Bronchodilators, adrenergic
(concurrent use with caffeine may result in additive CNS stimulation and other additive toxic effects)

» Caffeine-containing beverages (coffee, tea, or soft drinks) or
» Caffeine-containing medications, other or
» CNS stimulation-producing medications, other (see *Appendix II*)
(excessive CNS stimulation causing nervousness, irritability, insomnia, or possibly convulsions or cardiac arrhythmias may occur; close observation is recommended)

Calcium supplements
(concurrent use with excessive amounts of caffeine may inhibit absorption of calcium)

Cimetidine
(decreased hepatic metabolism of caffeine results in delayed elimination and increased blood concentrations)

Ciprofloxacin or
Enoxacin or
Norfloxacin
(hepatic metabolism and clearance of caffeine may be reduced, increasing the risk of caffeine-related CNS stimulation)

Contraceptives, oral
(concurrent use may decrease caffeine metabolism)

Disulfiram
(concurrent use may reduce the elimination rate of caffeine by inhibiting its metabolism; recovering alcoholic patients on disulfiram therapy are best advised to avoid the use of caffeine to prevent the possibility of complicating alcohol withdrawal by caffeine-induced cardiovascular and cerebral excitation)

Erythromycin or
Troleandomycin
(concurrent use may reduce the hepatic clearance of caffeine)

Hydantoin anticonvulsants, especially phenytoin
(concurrent use of phenytoin may increase the clearance of caffeine)

Lithium
(concurrent use with caffeine increases urinary excretion of lithium, possibly reducing its therapeutic effect)

Mexiletine
(concurrent use with caffeine reduces the elimination of caffeine by up to 50% and may increase the potential for adverse effects)

» Monoamine oxidase (MAO) inhibitors, including furazolidone, procarbazine, and selegiline
(large amounts of caffeine may produce dangerous cardiac arrhythmias or severe hypertension because of the sympathomimetic side effects of caffeine; concurrent use with small amounts of caffeine may produce tachycardia and a mild increase in blood pressure)

Smoking, tobacco
(concurrent use of tobacco increases the elimination rate of caffeine)

Xanthines, other, such as:
Aminophylline or
Dyphylline or
Oxtriphylline or
Theobromine or
Theophylline
(caffeine may decrease the clearance of theophylline and possibly other xanthines, increasing the potential for additive pharmacodynamic and toxic effects)

Laboratory value alterations

The following have been selected on the basis of their potential clinical significance (possible effect in parentheses where appropriate)—not necessarily inclusive (» = major clinical significance).

With diagnostic test results

Dipyridamole- or adenosine-assisted cardiac diagnostic studies
(caffeine antagonizes the effects of dipyridamole and adenosine on myocardial blood flow, thereby interfering with test results; patients should be instructed to avoid ingesting caffeine [from a dietary or medicinal source] for 8 to 12 hours prior to the test)

Urate measurements, serum
(false-positive elevations when measured by the Bittner method)

Vanillylmandelic acid (VMA) and
Catecholamines, including norepinephrine and epinephrine and
5-hydroxyindoleacetic acid
(urine concentrations are slightly increased; high urinary concentrations of VMA or catecholamines may result in a false-positive diagnosis of pheochromocytoma or neuroblastoma; caffeine intake should be avoided during tests)

With physiology/laboratory test values

Blood urea nitrogen
(may be elevated following overdose)

Glucose, blood
(concentrations may be increased; glucose tolerance may be impaired in neonates and in patients with diabetes)

Medical considerations/Contraindications

The medical considerations/contraindications included have been selected on the basis of their potential clinical significance (reasons given in parentheses where appropriate)—not necessarily inclusive (» = major clinical significance).

Risk-benefit should be considered when the following medical problems exist:

» Anxiety disorders, including agoraphobia and panic attacks
(increased risk of anxiety, nervousness, fear, nausea, palpitations, rapid heartbeat, restlessness, and trembling)

» Cardiac disease, severe
(high doses not recommended because of increased risk of tachycardia or extrasystoles, which may lead to heart failure)

» Hepatic function impairment
(half-life of caffeine may be prolonged, leading to toxic accumulation)

» Hypertension or
» Insomnia
(may be potentiated)

Seizure disorders, in neonates
(caution is recommended because seizures have been reported following toxic doses)

Sensitivity to caffeine or other xanthines

Patient monitoring

The following may be especially important in patient monitoring (other tests may be warranted in some patients, depending on condition; » = major clinical significance):

For neonatal apnea

Caffeine concentrations, plasma or serum
(determinations recommended prior to initiation of therapy in infants previously treated with theophylline and in infants born to mothers who consumed caffeine prior to delivery, 24 hours after loading dose, then 1 to 2 times a week; alternatively, some clinicians recommend checking caffeine concentrations every 2 weeks once the infant has been stabilized)

Glucose concentrations, serum
(hyperglycemia and hypoglycemia have been reported in neonates receiving citrated caffeine)

Theophylline concentrations, serum
(determinations may be indicated in the presence of adverse effects possibly caused by conversion of caffeine to theophylline in the neonate)

Side/Adverse Effects

The following side/adverse effects have been selected on the basis of their potential clinical significance (possible signs and symptoms in parentheses where appropriate)—not necessarily inclusive:

Those indicating need for medical attention

Incidence more frequent

CNS stimulation, excessive (dizziness; fast heartbeat; irritability, nervousness, or severe jitters—in neonates; tremors; trouble in sleeping); ***gastrointestinal irritation*** (diarrhea; nausea; vomiting); ***hyperglycemia*** (blurred vision; drowsiness; dry mouth; flushed, dry skin; fruit-like breath odor; increased urination [frequency and volume]; ketones in urine; loss of appetite; stomachache, nausea, or vomiting; tiredness; troubled breathing [rapid and deep]; unconsciousness; unusual thirst)—in neonates; ***hypoglycemia*** (anxiety; blurred vision; cold sweats; confusion; cool, pale skin; drowsiness; excessive hunger; fast heartbeat; nausea; nervousness; restless sleep; shakiness; unusual tiredness or weakness)—in neonates

Incidence rare

Necrotizing enterocolitis (abdominal distention; dehydration; diarrhea, bloody; irritability; unusual tiredness or weakness; vomiting)—in neonates

Those indicating need for medical attention only if they continue or are bothersome

Incidence more frequent

CNS stimulation, mild (nervousness or jitters); ***gastrointestinal irritation, mild*** (nausea)

Those indicating possible withdrawal if they occur after medication is abruptly discontinued after prolonged use

Anxiety; dizziness; headache; irritability; muscle tension; nausea; nervousness; stuffy nose; unusual tiredness

Overdose

For specific information on the agents used in the management of caffeine overdose, see:
- *Antacids (Oral-Local)* monograph;
- *Charcoal, Activated (Oral-Local)*monograph;
- *Diazepam* in *Benzodiazepines (Systemic)* monograph;
- *Ipecac (Oral-Local)* monograph;
- *Magnesium sulfate* in *Laxatives (Local)* monograph;
- *Phenobarbital* in *Barbiturates (Systemic)* monograph; and/or
- *Phenytoin* in *Anticonvulsants, Hydantoin (Systemic)* monograph.

For more information on the management of overdose or unintentional ingestion, **contact a poison control center** (see *Poison Control Center Listing*).

Clinical effects of overdose

The following effects have been selected on the basis of their potential clinical significance (possible signs and symptoms in parentheses where appropriate)—not necessarily inclusive:

Abdominal or stomach pain; agitation, anxiety, excitement, or restlessness; confusion or delirium; dehydration; fast or irregular heartbeat; fever; frequent urination; headache; increased sensitivity to touch or pain; irritability; leukocytosis—in neonates; ***muscle trembling or twitching; nausea and vomiting, sometimes with blood; opisthotonos*** (hyperextension of the body with head and heels bent backward and body bowed forward)—in neonates; ***painful, swollen abdomen or vomiting***—in neonates; ***ringing or other sounds in ears; seeing flashes of "zig-zag" lights; seizures, usually tonic-clonic seizures***—in acute overdose; ***tachypnea; trouble in sleeping; whole body tremors***—in neonates

Treatment of overdose

Treatment of acute overdose—

Acute caffeine toxicity has been reported rarely. Treatment is primarily symptomatic and supportive.

To decrease absorption—

Induction of emesis with ipecac syrup and/or gastric lavage if caffeine has been ingested within 4 hours in amounts over 15 mg per kg of body weight (mg/kg) and emesis has not been induced by caffeine.

Administration of activated charcoal may be useful within the first 4 hours if precautions are taken to minimize the risk of aspiration; magnesium sulfate cathartic may also be useful.

To enhance elimination—

Hemoperfusion is usually more effective than dialysis. Use of exchange transfusion in neonates, if necessary.

Specific treatment—

Control of CNS stimulation or seizures with intravenous diazepam, phenobarbital, or phenytoin.

Administration of antacids and iced saline lavage for hemorrhagic gastritis.

Supportive care—

Maintenance of fluid and electrolyte balance. Maintenance of ventilation and oxygenation. Patients in whom intentional overdose is confirmed or suspected should be referred for psychiatric consultation.

Patient Consultation

As an aid to patient consultation, refer to *Advice for the Patient, Caffeine (Systemic)*.

In providing consultation, consider emphasizing the following selected information (» = major clinical significance):

Before using this medication

» Conditions affecting use, especially:

Sensitivity to caffeine or other xanthines (aminophylline, dyphylline, oxtriphylline, theobromine, theophylline)

Pregnancy—Crosses placenta; excessive use during pregnancy may result in spontaneous abortion, intrauterine growth retardation, or fetal arrhythmias; animal studies have shown skeletal abnormalities with large doses and retarded skeletal development with lower doses

Breast-feeding—Distributed into breast milk in small amounts but accumulates in infant and may cause hyperactivity and wakefulness; nursing mothers should limit intake of caffeine from all sources

Use in children—Caffeine and sodium benzoate injection is not recommended in neonates because of the benzoate content. However, caffeine citrate may be used safely

Other medications, especially caffeine-containing medications or beverages, other CNS stimulation-producing medications, or monoamine oxidase (MAO) inhibitors

Other medical problems, especially anxiety disorders including agoraphobia and panic attacks, severe cardiac disease, hepatic function impairment, hypertension, or insomnia

Proper use of this medication

» Importance of not taking more medication and not taking it more often than directed because of increased risk of side effects and habit-forming potential; should be used only occasionally

Proper administration of powder: Stirring contents of packet into water or other beverage or placing on tongue and following with water or other beverage

For the oral solution: Using each vial only for one dose; discarding unused portion of medication; following manufacturer's instructions

» Caution if tolerance develops; not increasing dose

» Proper dosing

» Proper storage

Precautions while using this medication

» Checking with physician if fatigue or drowsiness persists or recurs often

Possible interference with cardiac diagnostic studies

Caution in concurrently drinking large amounts of coffee, tea, or colas or using other medications containing caffeine since amount of caffeine in medication is about the same as in a cup of coffee

Importance of knowing amounts of caffeine in common foods and beverages

» Discontinuing caffeine-containing medications and foods if fast pulse, dizziness, or pounding heartbeat occurs

Not taking too close to bedtime

Side/adverse effects

Signs of potential side effects, especially excessive CNS stimulation, gastrointestinal irritation, hyperglycemia or hypoglycemia (in neonates), and necrotizing enterocolitis (in neonates)

General Dosing Information

With prolonged use, habituation or psychological dependence and tolerance to cardiovascular, diuretic, and stimulant effects may occur.

A dose of caffeine powder should be stirred into water or other beverage or placed on the tongue and followed with water or other beverage.

Citrated caffeine oral solution for use in neonatal apnea is not available commercially but must be prepared extemporaneously from citrated caffeine powder. Caffeine tablets may also be crushed and made into an oral suspension. Caffeine citrate powder may be combined with lactose to add to infant feedings.

Citrated caffeine injection should not be administered intramuscularly because of its acidic nature (pH 4.7). It may be administered intravenously.

Caffeine and sodium benzoate injection is not recommended in neonatal apnea because of the benzoate content.

Diet/Nutrition

The amount of caffeine from dietary sources is as follows:
Coffee, brewed—40 to 180 mg per cup.
Coffee, instant—30 to 120 mg per cup.
Coffee, decaffeinated—3 to 5 mg per cup.
Tea, brewed American—20 to 90 mg per cup.
Tea, brewed imported—25 to 110 mg per cup.
Tea, instant—28 mg per cup.
Tea, canned iced—22 to 36 mg per 12 ounces.
Cola and other soft drinks, caffeine-containing—36 to 90 mg per 12 ounces.
Cola and other soft drinks, decaffeinated—0 mg per 12 ounces.
Cocoa—4 mg per cup.
Chocolate, milk—3 to 6 mg per ounce.
Chocolate, bittersweet—25 mg per ounce.

CAFFEINE

Oral Dosage Forms

Note: Bracketed uses in the *Dosage Forms* section refer to categories of use and/or indications that are not included in U.S. product labeling.

CAFFEINE POWDER

Usual adult and adolescent dose

Fatigue; drowsiness—

Oral, 200 mg, the dosage to be repeated no sooner than every three or four hours, as needed.

Usual adult prescribing limits

1.6 grams a day.

Usual pediatric dose

Fatigue; drowsiness—

Children up to 12 years of age: Use is not recommended.

Strength(s) usually available

U.S.—

200 mg per packet (OTC) [*Maximum Strength SnapBack Stimulant Powders*].

Canada—

Not commercially available.

Packaging and storage

Store below 40 °C (104 °F), preferably between 15 and 30 °C (59 and 86 °F), unless otherwise specified by manufacturer. Protect from moisture.

Auxiliary labeling

- Do not take at bedtime.

CAFFEINE TABLETS

Usual adult and adolescent dose

Fatigue; drowsiness—

Oral, 100 to 200 mg (anhydrous caffeine), the dosage to be repeated no sooner than every three or four hours, as needed.

Usual adult prescribing limits

1 gram a day.

Usual pediatric dose

Fatigue; drowsiness—

Children up to 12 years of age: Use is not recommended.

[Neonatal apnea]—

Initial: Oral, 10 mg (anhydrous caffeine) per kg of body weight.

Maintenance: Oral, 2.5 mg (anhydrous caffeine) per kg of body weight a day, starting twenty-four hours after the initial dose, to maintain a serum concentration of 5 to 25 mcg per mL (25.8 to 128.8 micromoles per L).

Note: Caffeine tablets may be crushed and made into an oral suspension for use in neonatal apnea.

Strength(s) usually available

U.S.—

75 mg (anhydrous caffeine) (OTC) [*Enerjets*].

100 mg (anhydrous caffeine) (OTC) [*Pep-Back*].

150 mg (anhydrous caffeine) (OTC) [*Quick Pep*].

200 mg (anhydrous caffeine) (OTC) [*Caffedrine Caplets; Dexitac Stay Alert Stimulant; Keep Alert; NoDoz Maximum Strength Caplets* (scored); *Ultra Pep-Back; Vivarin*].

Canada—

100 mg (caffeine alkaloid) (OTC) [*Wake-Up*].

Packaging and storage

Store below 40 °C (104 °F), preferably between 15 and 30 °C (59 and 86 °F), in a well-closed container, unless otherwise specified by manufacturer.

Auxiliary labeling

- Do not take at bedtime.

CAFFEINE, CITRATED

Oral Dosage Forms

Note: Bracketed uses in the *Dosage Forms* section refer to categories of use and/or indications that are not included in U.S. product labeling.

CITRATED CAFFEINE ORAL SOLUTION

Usual pediatric dose

Neonatal apnea—

Initial: Oral, 20 mg (10 mg of anhydrous caffeine and 10 mg of anhydrous citric acid) per kg of body weight.

Maintenance: Oral, 5 mg (2.5 mg of anhydrous caffeine and 2.5 mg of anhydrous citric acid) per kg of body weight a day, starting twenty-four hours after the initial dose, to maintain a serum concentration of 5 to 25 mcg per mL (25.8 to 128.8 micromoles per L).

Note: Premature neonates may require a smaller dose.

Strength(s) usually available

U.S.—

20 mg caffeine citrate (10 mg caffeine base) per mL (Rx) [*Cafcit* (citric acid monohydrate 5 mg; sodium citrate dihydrate 8.3 mg; Water for Injection)].

Canada—

Dosage form not commercially available. Compounding required.

Packaging and storage

Store between 15 and 30 °C (59 and 86 °F)

Preparation of dosage form

Compounded product—Ten grams of citrated caffeine powder should be dissolved in 250 mL of sterile water for irrigation and stirred until completely clear; then flavoring should be added (simple syrup and cherry syrup 2:1) to make 500 mL. The final concentration is 20 mg (10 mg of anhydrous caffeine and 10 mg of anhydrous citric acid) per mL.

Stability

Compounded product as described above is stable for 3 months at room temperature.

Auxiliary labeling

- For single use only. Discard unused portion.

Note

Citrated caffeine powder may also be combined with lactose and added to infant feedings.

Additional information

Dispense patient instructions portion of the package insert with the prescription

Parenteral Dosage Forms

CITRATED CAFFEINE INJECTION

Usual pediatric dose

Neonatal apnea—

Initial: Intravenous, 20 mg (10 mg of caffeine base) per kg of body weight.

Maintenance: Intravenous, 5 mg (2.5 mg of caffeine base) per kg of body weight every twenty-four hours, starting twenty-four hours after the initial dose, to maintain a serum concentration of 5 to 25 mcg per mL (25.8 to 128.8 micromoles per L).

Strength(s) usually available

U.S.—

20 mg caffeine citrate (10 mg caffeine base) per mL (Rx) [*Cafcit* (citric acid 5 mg; sodium citrate dihydrate 8.3 mg; Water for Injection)].

Canada—

Dosage form not commercially available. Compounding required.

Packaging and storage

Store between 15 –30 °C (59 –86 °F)

Preparation of dosage form

Compounded product—Ten grams of citrated caffeine powder should be dissolved in 250 mL of sterile water for injection and transferred to a 500-mL empty evacuated container (EEC). The container should be filled with sterile water to the 500-mL mark and filtered through a 0.22-micron filter into another 500-mL EEC. Then the solution should be transferred to 10-mL vials and autoclaved at 121 °C (250 °F) for 15 minutes and allowed to cool. The resulting concentration is 20 mg (10 mg of anhydrous caffeine and 10 mg of anhydrous citric acid) per mL.

Stability

Compounded product as described above is stable for 3 months at room temperature.

Commercially available product is chemically stable for 24 hours at room temperature when combined with the following:

- Aminosyn crystalline amino acid solution 8.5%
- calcium gluconate injection, USP 10% (0.465 mEq of Ca^{+2}per mL
- dextrose injection, USP 5%
- dextrose injection, USP 50%
- dopamine HCl injection, USP 40 mg per mL diluted to 0.6 mg per mL with dextrose injection, USP 5%
- fentanyl citrate injection, USP 50 mcg per mL diluted to 10 mcg per mL with dextrose injection, USP 5%
- heparin sodium injection, USP 1000 units per mL diluted to 1 unit per mL with dextrose injection, USP 5%
- Intralipid IV fat emulsion 20%

Additional information

Commercially available product is preservative free.

CAFFEINE AND SODIUM BENZOATE

Parenteral Dosage Forms

CAFFEINE AND SODIUM BENZOATE INJECTION USP

Usual adult and adolescent dose

CNS stimulant—

Intramuscular or intravenous, up to a maximum of 500 mg (250 mg of anhydrous caffeine and 250 mg of sodium benzoate), as needed and tolerated.

Usual adult prescribing limits

2.5 grams (1.25 grams of anhydrous caffeine and 1.25 grams of sodium benzoate) a day.

Usual pediatric dose

Dosage has not been established.

Note: Use not recommended in neonatal apnea because of benzoate content.

Strength(s) usually available

U.S.—

250 mg (125 mg of anhydrous caffeine and 125 mg of sodium benzoate) per mL (Rx).

Canada—

Not commercially available.

Packaging and storage

Store below 40 °C (104 °F), preferably between 15 and 30 °C (59 and 86 °F), unless otherwise specified by manufacturer.

Selected Bibliography

Nehlig A, Daval J-L, Debry G. Caffeine and the central nervous system: mechanisms of action, biochemical, metabolic and psychostimulant effects. Brain Res Brain Res Rev 1992; 17: 139-70.

Revised: 05/25/2000

CAFFEINE, CITRATED—See *Caffeine (Systemic)*

CALCIFEDIOL—See *Vitamin D and Analogs (Systemic)*

CALCIPOTRIENE Topical

INN: Calcipotriol; BAN: Calcipotriol

VA CLASSIFICATION (Primary): DE802

Commonly used brand name(s): *Dovonex*.

Another commonly used name is MC 903.

NOTE: The *Calcipotriene (Topical)* monograph is maintained on the *USP DI* electronic database. A copy of the most recent revision of the complete monograph can be accessed on the *USP DI* Updates Online website. See the front cover of book for details on accessing the site.

The information that follows is selectively abstracted from the complete monograph and is provided to facilitate drug use review and patient counseling.

Note: For a listing of dosage forms and brand names by country availability, see *Dosage Forms* section(s).

Category

Antipsoriatic (topical).

Indications

Note: Bracketed information in the *Indications* section refers to uses that are not included in U.S. product labeling.

Accepted

Psoriasis (treatment)—Calcipotriene cream and ointment are indicated for the treatment of [mild] to moderate plaque psoriasis. [Calcipotriene cream and ointment also may be used in the treatment of extensive or severe chronic plaque psoriasis. However, its use in this type of psoriasis is generally not recommended because of increased risk of hypercalcemia, secondary to excessive absorption of the medication when there is extensive skin involvement. If calcipotriene is to be used for severe extensive psoriasis, it is necessary to monitor the serum and urinary calcium levels at regular intervals.]

[Calcipotriene ointment is also used in combination with ultraviolet B light (UVB) phototherapy in the treatment of psoriasis.]

Psoriasis, of scalp (treatment)—Calcipotriene topical solution is indicated to treat chronic, moderately severe psoriasis of the scalp.

Patient Consultation

As an aid to patient consultation, refer to *Advice for the Patient, Calcipotriene (Topical)*.

In providing consultation, consider emphasizing the following selected information (» = major clinical significance):

Before using this medication

» Conditions affecting use, especially:

Hypersensitivity to calcipotriene or to other components of the preparation

Study with mice exposed to ultra-violet radiation (UVR) and topically applied calcipotriene showed a reduction in time required for UVR to induce skin tumor formation suggesting that calcipotriene may enhance UVR effect to induce skin tumors

Pregnancy—Calcipotriene probably crosses placenta. Human studies have not been done; in animal studies, high oral doses have caused incomplete skeletal development and skeletal abnormalities in fetuses

Use in children—Safety and efficacy have not been established. Children are at greater risk of developing adverse systemic effects than adults when treated with topical medications; however, problems in bone and calcium metabolism did not occur in 43 children between 2 and 14 years of age treated for 8 weeks with topical calcipotriene applied to less than 30% of their body surface areas

Use in the elderly—Skin-related side effects may be more severe when they occur in patients over 65 years of age

Other medical problems, especially hypercalcemia, hypercalciuria, hypervitaminosis D, acute psoriatic eruptions on the scalp (for topical solution), or nephrolithiasis

Proper use of this medication

» For external use only and not for ophthalmic, oral, or intravaginal use; using this medication only as directed by physician

Compliance with full course of therapy

» Not using more than 100 grams of cream or ointment or 60 mL of solution per week or a total dose of more than 5 mg of calcipotriene a week

» Avoiding contact of medication with face, eyes, mucous membranes, or uninvolved skin; washing medication off with water if it accidentally gets onto face, into eyes or mucous membranes, or onto normal skin surrounding the psoriatic area(s)

Applying medication sparingly in folds of skin because of risk of irritation of skin where there is natural occlusion

Washing hands after application to avoid inadvertently transferring medication onto face or uninvolved areas of the skin

Not using medication for any skin disorder other than that for which it was prescribed

For cream and ointment dosage forms

» Applying enough medication to cover affected area(s) of skin and rubbing in gently and completely; avoiding use of occlusive dressing

» When ointment is used in combination with ultraviolet B light (UVB) phototherapy, applying medication after ultraviolet light exposure. This avoids the vehicle's UV-blocking action. Also, UV light can inactivate calcipotriene.

For solution dosage form

Properly preparing scalp before application by combing and removing scaly debris, parting hair for easy access to scalp lesions; applying medication only to visible lesions; rubbing it in gently and completely; not applying on acute psoriatic eruptions

» Proper dosing

Missed dose: Applying as soon as possible; not applying if almost time for next dose; not doubling doses

» Proper storage

Precautions while using this medication

Medication may cause transient irritation of lesions and surrounding uninvolved skin after application; not scratching irritated skin

» Discontinuing use and checking with physician if irritation persists, or if facial rash or other problems develop

While using this medication, visiting physician regularly for monitoring of serum and urine calcium levels

» Possible skin photosensitivity; avoiding unprotected exposure to sun; using protective clothing; using a sun block product that includes protection against both UVA-caused photosensitivity reactions and UVB-caused sunburn reactions; avoiding use of sunlamp, tanning bed, or tanning booth

» Importance of physician limiting or avoiding use of phototherapy in patients who use calcipotriene

Checking with physician if skin problem has not improved (usually within 2 to 8 weeks) or if skin condition becomes worse

Side/adverse effects

Signs of potential side effects, especially dermatitis, skin rash, worsening of psoriasis, atrophy of skin, folliculitis, hypercalcemia, and hypercalciuria

Topical Dosage Forms

CALCIPOTRIENE CREAM

Usual adult dose

Psoriasis—
Topical, to the affected area(s) of skin, two times a day. Efficacy of treatment beyond eight weeks has not been established.

Usual adult prescribing limits

100 grams of cream per week, or a total dose of 5 mg of calcipotriene per week when using more than one formulation.

Usual pediatric dose

Safety and efficacy have not been established.

Usual geriatric dose

See *Usual adult dose.*

Strength(s) usually available

U.S.—
0.005% (Rx) [*Dovonex* (cetearyl alcohol; ceteth-20; diazolidinyl urea; dichlorobenzyl alcohol; dibasic sodium phosphate; edetate disodium; glycerin; mineral oil; petrolatum; water)].

Canada—
0.005% (Rx) [*Dovonex* (cetomacrogol 1000; chlorallyhexaminium chloride [dowicil 200]; disodium edetate; disodium phosphate dihydrate; glycerol 85%; liquid paraffin; purified water; white soft paraffin)].

Auxiliary labeling

• For external use only.

CALCIPOTRIENE OINTMENT

Usual adult dose

Psoriasis—
Topical, to the affected area(s) of skin, one or two times a day. Efficacy of treatment beyond eight weeks has not been established.

Usual adult prescribing limits

100 grams of ointment per week or a total dose of 5 mg of calcipotriene per week when more than one formulation is used.

Usual pediatric dose

Safety and efficacy have not been established.

Usual geriatric dose

See *Usual adult dose.*

Strength(s) usually available

U.S.—
0.005% (Rx) [*Dovonex* (dibasic sodium phosphate; edetate disodium; mineral oil; petrolatum; propylene glycol; tocopherol; steareth-2; water)].

Canada—
0.005% (Rx) [*Dovonex* (disodium edetate; disodium phosphate dihydrate; D,L-alpha-tocopherol; liquid paraffin; polyoxyethylene-(2)-stearyl ether; propylene glycol; purified water; white soft paraffin)].

Auxiliary labeling

• For external use only.
• Avoid contact in or around eyes
• Avoid extended exposure to sunlight or tanning beds while using this drug. Severe burns may result.
• Keep out of reach of children

CALCIPOTRIENE SOLUTION

Usual adult dose

Psoriasis, of scalp—
Topical, to the scalp lesions, two times a day. Efficacy of treatment beyond eight weeks has not been established.

Usual adult prescribing limits

60 mL of solution per week, or a total dose of 5 mg of calcipotriene per week when other formulations are used.

Usual pediatric dose

Safety and efficacy have not been established.

Usual geriatric dose

See *Usual adult dose.*

Strength(s) usually available

U.S.—
0.005% (Rx) [*Dovonex* (hydroxypropyl cellulose; isopropanol 51% v/v; menthol; propylene glycol; sodium citrate; water)].

Canada—
0.005% (Rx) [*Dovonex* (hydroxypropyl cellulose; isopropanol; levomenthol; propylene glycol; purified water; sodium citrate)].

Auxiliary labeling

• For external use only.

Revised: 07/13/2005

CALCITONIN Nasal-Systemic

VA CLASSIFICATION (Primary): HS900

Commonly used brand name(s): *Fortical; Miacalcin.*

Note: For a listing of dosage forms and brand names by country availability, see *Dosage Forms* section(s).

Category

Bone resorption inhibitor; osteoporosis therapy.

Indications

Accepted

Osteoporosis, postmenopausal (treatment adjunct)—Intranasal calcitonin-salmon is indicated for the treatment of osteoporosis in women who are more than 5 years postmenopause and have low bone mass relative to healthy premenopausal women. It is used in conjunction with an adequate intake of calcium (1000 mg of elemental calcium a day) and vitamin D (400 IU a day). Calcitonin should be reserved for patients who refuse or cannot tolerate estrogens or those in whom estrogens are contraindicated.

Intranasal calcitonin has been shown to increase spinal bone mass in postmenopausal women with established osteoporosis, but not in early postmenopausal women.

Pharmacology/Pharmacokinetics

Mechanism of action/Effect

Osteoporosis—Studies using injectable calcitonin have found that it inhibits bone resorption by reducing the number and/or function of osteoclasts. With prolonged injectable calcitonin use, there is a persistent, smaller decrease in the rate of bone resorption. *In vitro* studies using injectable calcitonin-salmon have found an inhibition of osteoclast function with loss of the ruffled osteoclast border that is responsible for resorption of bone. *In vitro* studies indicate that calcitonin may augment bone formation by increasing osteoblastic activity. Long-term studies indicate that injectable calcitonin therapy results in the formation of bone that is of normal quality.

Other actions/effects

There is a slight decrease in serum calcium concentrations associated with intranasal calcitonin-salmon use; however, serum calcium remains within normal limits.

Injectable calcitonin increases the excretion of filtered phosphate, calcium, and sodium by inhibiting their tubular reabsorption.

Short-term administration of injectable calcitonin decreases the volume and acidity of gastric juice, the content of trypsin and amylase, and the volume of pancreatic juice. However, studies have not been conducted with intranasal calcitonin.

Absorption

Rapidly absorbed by the nasal mucosa.

Half-life

Elimination—43 minutes after intranasal administration.

Time to peak concentration

Approximately 31 to 39 minutes after intranasal administration.

Precautions to Consider

Cross-sensitivity and/or related problems

Although not specifically reported for intranasal calcitonin-salmon, patients who are allergic to proteins may be allergic to calcitonin, because calcitonin is a protein. Its use in not recommended in patients with suspected sensitivity to calcitonin who show a positive response to skin testing prior to initiating therapy.

Carcinogenicity
A 1-year toxicity study in Sprague-Dawley and Fischer 344 rats given subcutaneous calcitonin-salmon at doses of 80 IU per kg of body weight a day (16 to 19 times the recommended human parenteral dose and approximately 130 to 160 times the recommended human intranasal dose based on body surface area) found an increased incidence of nonfunctioning pituitary adenomas. It was suggested that calcitonin-salmon reduced the latency period for development of pituitary adenomas that do not produce hormones, probably through the perturbation of physiologic processes involved in the evolution of this commonly occurring endocrine lesion in the rat. Although calcitonin-salmon reduced the latency period, it did not induce the hyperplastic or neoplastic process.

Mutagenicity
Calcitonin-salmon was found nonmutagenic in studies using *Salmonella typhimurium* (five strains) and *Escherichia coli* (two strains), both with and without rat liver metabolic activation. Calcitonin-salmon also was found nonmutagenic in an *in vitro* chromosome aberration test in mammalian V79 cells of the Chinese hamster.

Pregnancy/Reproduction
Pregnancy—Adequate and well-controlled studies in humans have not been done. Intranasal calcitonin-salmon is not indicated for use in pregnancy.

Reproduction studies in rabbits given injectable calcitonin-salmon in doses ranging from 8 to 33 times the recommended human parenteral dose and 70 to 278 times the recommended human intranasal dose based on body surface area showed a decrease in fetal birth weights. Since calcitonin does not cross the placenta, these effects may have been due to metabolic effects on the pregnant animal.

FDA Pregnancy Category C.

Breast-feeding
It is not known whether intranasal calcitonin-salmon is distributed into human breast milk. Because many drugs are distributed into human milk, nursing women should not use intranasal calcitonin. Calcitonin has been shown to inhibit lactation in animals.

Pediatrics
There are no data to support the use of intranasal calcitonin-salmon in children.

Geriatrics
Appropriate studies performed to date have not demonstrated geriatrics-specific problems that would limit the usefulness of intranasal calcitonin-salmon in the elderly.

Drug interactions and/or related problems
The following drug interactions and/or related problems have been selected on the basis of their potential clinical significance (possible mechanism in parentheses where appropriate)—not necessarily inclusive (» = major clinical significance):

Bisphosphonates, such as alendronate, etidronate, and pamidronate
(prior bisphosphonate use has been reported to reduce the antiresorptive response to intranasal calcitonin-salmon in patients with Paget's disease; however, this effect has not been assessed in postmenopausal women)

Medical considerations/Contraindications
The medical considerations/contraindications included have been selected on the basis of their potential clinical significance (reasons given in parentheses where appropriate)—not necessarily inclusive (» = major clinical significance).

Except under special circumstances, this medication should not be used when the following medical problem exists:

» Allergy to proteins (or history of) or
» Clinical sensitivity to calcitonin
(serious systemic allergic reactions [e.g., bronchospasm, swelling of the tongue or throat, anaphylactic shock, death due to anaphylaxis] have been reported with use of nasal injectable calcitonin-salmon; skin testing should be considered prior to treatment of patients with suspected sensitivity to calcitonin-salmon)

Patient monitoring
The following may be especially important in patient monitoring (other tests may be warranted in some patients, depending on condition; » = major clinical significance):

Alkaline phosphatase, serum and
Hydroxyproline, urinary
(effects of intranasal calcitonin-salmon on these markers of bone turnover have not been consistently demonstrated in studies of women with postmenopausal osteoporosis; therefore, these parameters alone should not be used to determine clinical response to calcitonin-salmon; values should decrease with treatment)

Bone mass
(periodic measurements of vertebral bone mass are recommended during treatment to document stabilization of bone loss or increases in bone density; bone mass values should increase with treatment)

Nasal examinations
(nasal examinations should be performed before treatment begins, and at any time that nasal complaints occur; mucosal alterations or transient nasal conditions have been reported in up to 9% of patients receiving intranasal calcitonin-salmon; the examination should consist of visualization of the nasal mucosa, turbinates, and septum and assessment of mucosal blood vessel status; therapy should be discontinued temporarily to allow healing if small ulcers occur, and discontinued permanently if severe ulceration [e.g., ulcers greater than 1.5 mm in diameter, ulcers that penetrate below the mucosa, or ulcers associated with heavy bleeding] occurs)

Urinalysis
(periodic examinations of urine sediment should be considered, since coarse granular casts containing renal tubular epithelial cells were found in the urine of individuals receiving injectable calcitonin-salmon while at bedrest; no urine sediment abnormalities were found in ambulatory patients receiving injectable calcitonin-salmon)

Side/Adverse Effects
The following side/adverse effects have been selected on the basis of their potential clinical significance (possible signs and symptoms in parentheses where appropriate)—not necessarily inclusive:

Those indicating need for medical attention
Incidence more frequent (3 to 12%)

Nasal symptoms, specifically development of crusts; dryness; epistaxis (nose bleeds); ***inflammation; irritation; itching; redness; rhinitis*** (runny nose); ***sores or wounds on nasal mucosa; or tenderness***

Note: Patients who develop these nasal symptoms should be examined by their physicians. Development of ulcers on the nasal mucosa may require temporary or permanent discontinuation of intranasal calcitonin-salmon.

Incidence less frequent (1 to 3%)

Angina (chest pain); ***bronchospasm*** (wheezing or troubled breathing, severe); ***cystitis*** (bloody or cloudy urine; difficult, burning, or painful urination; frequent urge to urinate); ***hypertension*** (dizziness; headaches, severe or continuing); ***lymphadenopathy*** (swollen glands); ***respiratory tract infection, upper*** (chest pain; chills; cough; ear congestion or pain; fever; head congestion; hoarseness or other voice changes; nasal congestion; runny nose; sneezing; sore throat)

Incidence rare (< 1%)

Allergic reactions, specifically hives, itching, or skin rash

Those indicating need for medical attention only if they continue or are bothersome
Incidence more frequent (3 to 12%)

Arthralgia (joint pain); ***back pain; headache***

Incidence less frequent (1 to 3%) or rare (< 1%)

Abdominal pain; conjunctivitis (burning, dry, or itching eyes); ***constipation; diarrhea; dizziness; dyspepsia*** (upset stomach); ***fatigue*** (unusual tiredness or weakness); ***flu-like symptoms; flushing; lacrimation, unusual*** (unusual tearing of eyes); ***mental depression; myalgia*** (muscle pain); ***nausea; skin rash***

Overdose
For specific information on the agents used in the management of intranasal calcitonin-salmon overdose, see the *Calcium Supplements (Systemic)* monograph.

For more information on the management of overdose or unintentional ingestion, **contact a Poison Control Center** (see *Poison Control Center Listing*).

Treatment of overdose
Specific treatment—Administering parenteral calcium if hypocalcemic tetany develops.

Supportive care—Patients in whom intentional overdose is confirmed or suspected should be referred for psychiatric consultation.

Patient Consultation
As an aid to patient consultation, refer to *Advice for the Patient, Calcitonin (Nasal-Systemic)*.

In providing consultation, consider emphasizing the following selected information (» = major clinical significance):

Before using this medication

» Conditions affecting use, especially:
Allergies (history of) or sensitivity to calcitonin or other proteins
Pregnancy—Not indicated for use during pregnancy
Breast-feeding—Lactation inhibited in animal studies; should not be used by nursing women
Use in children—No data to support use

Proper use of this medication

» Reading patient instructions carefully
» Importance of not using more medication than the amount prescribed
» Importance of not reactivating pump before daily dose

Assembling the unit (Note: If unit has been assembled by health care professional, this step is not necessary)

» Removing bottle from refrigerator and allowing it to reach room temperature
» Lifting up plastic tab and pulling metal safety seal off bottle
» Keeping bottle upright while removing rubber stopper from bottle
» Holding pump unit while removing opaque plastic protective cap from bottom of unit
» Holding bottle upright while inserting nasal spray pump unit into bottle
» Turning pump unit clockwise and tightening until securely fastened

Priming the unit (for first-time use of unit only)

» Holding bottle upright while removing clear protective cap from nozzle
» Depressing the two white side arms several times until a faint spray is emitted

Proper administration

» Blowing nose gently before using spray
» Keeping head in upright position and placing nozzle firmly into one nostril
» Depressing pump toward bottle one time
» Not inhaling while spraying
» Replacing plastic cap
» Proper dosing
Missed dose: Using as soon as possible; not using if almost time for next dose
» Proper storage

Side/adverse effects

Signs of potential side effects, especially nasal symptoms; angina; bronchospasm; cystitis; hypertension; lymphadenopathy; respiratory tract infection, upper; and allergic reaction

General Dosing Information

Skin testing should be considered prior to treatment of patients with suspected sensitivity to calcitonin-salmon. The manufacturer's recommendation for preparing the solution for skin testing is as follows:

- Prepare a dilution of 10 IU per mL by withdrawing 0.05 mL of calcitonin-salmon into a tuberculin syringe.
- Fill syringe to 1 mL with 0.9% sodium chloride injection. Mix well.
- Discard 0.9 mL and inject 0.1 mL intracutaneously on the inner forearm.
- Observe injection site 15 minutes after injection.
- A positive response is considered to be the appearance of erythema or a wheal that is more than mild.

Before priming the pump and using a new bottle, the bottle should be allowed to reach room temperature.

Nasal Dosage Form

CALCITONIN-SALMON NASAL SOLUTION

Usual adult and adolescent dose

Postmenopausal osteoporosis—
Intranasal, 200 IU (one metered spray in one nostril) a day, alternating nostrils daily.

Strength(s) usually available

U.S.—
200 IU per metered spray (Rx) [*Fortical* (sodium chloride; citric acid; phenylethyl alcohol; benzyl alcohol; polysorbate 80; hydrochloric acid or sodium hydroxide as necessary to adjust pH; purified water); *Miacalcin*].

Packaging and storage

The unopened container should be stored between 2 and 8 °C (36 and 46 °F). Protect from freezing.

Store opened bottle in an upright position for up to 30 days at 20 to 25 °C; excursions permitted to 15 to 30 °C (59 to 86 °F).

Preparation of dosage form

To prime (activate) the pump—

- Before administration of first dose, allow bottle to reach room temperature.
- Remove the protective cap and clip from the bottle.
- To prime the pump, hold the bottle upright and depress the two side arms of the pump toward the bottle at least 5 times until a full spray is produced.
- The pump is primed once the first full spray is emitted.
- To administer, nozzle should be carefully placed into the nostril with the head in the upright position and the pump firmly depressed toward the bottle.
- The pump should NOT be primed before each daily use.

Stability

Once the pump has been activated, the bottle may be kept at room temperature until the medication is finished. Opened or unopened bottles left at room temperature for more than 30 days must be discarded.

Revised: 09/08/2005
Developed: 03/23/1998

CALCITONIN-HUMAN—See *Calcitonin (Systemic)*

CALCITONIN-SALMON—See *Calcitonin (Systemic)*

CALCITRIOL—See *Vitamin D and Analogs (Systemic)*

CALCIUM ACETATE—See *Calcium Supplements (Systemic)*

CALCIUM ACETATE Systemic

VA CLASSIFICATION (Primary): TN402

Commonly used brand name(s): *PhosLo*.

Note: For a listing of dosage forms and brand names by country availability, see *Dosage Forms* section(s).

Category

Antihyperphosphatemic.

Indications

Accepted

Hyperphosphatemia (treatment)—Calcium acetate is indicated in patients with end-stage renal failure to lower serum phosphate concentrations. It does not promote aluminum absorption.

Pharmacology/Pharmacokinetics

Physicochemical characteristics

Molecular weight—158.17.

Mechanism of action/Effect

Calcium acetate, when taken with meals, combines with dietary phosphate to form insoluble calcium phosphate, which is excreted in the feces.

Absorption

Data from healthy subjects and renal dialysis patients under various conditions indicate that after oral administration of calcium acetate, approximately 40% is absorbed in the fasting state and approximately 30% is absorbed in the nonfasting state.

Elimination

Fecal.

Precautions to Consider

Carcinogenicity

Long-term studies to evaluate carcinogenic potential of calcium acetate have not been performed.

Pregnancy/Reproduction

Fertility—Studies have not been done in either humans or animals.

Pregnancy—Studies in humans have not been done.

Studies in animals have not been done.

FDA Pregnancy Category C.

Breast-feeding
It is not known whether calcium acetate is distributed into breast milk.

Pediatrics
No information is available on the relationship of age to the effects of calcium acetate in pediatric patients. Safety and efficacy have not been established.

Geriatrics
No information is available on the relationship of age to the effects of calcium acetate in geriatric patients.

Drug interactions and/or related problems
The following drug interactions and/or related problems have been selected on the basis of their potential clinical significance (possible mechanism in parentheses where appropriate)—not necessarily inclusive (» = major clinical significance):

Note: Combinations containing any of the following, depending on the amount present, may also interact with this medication.

» Calcium-containing foods or preparations, including dietary supplements or antacids
(concurrent use may cause hypercalcemia; dietary calcium should be estimated daily initially and intake adjusted as needed)

» Digitalis glycosides
(concurrent use is not recommended because calcium acetate may cause hypercalcemia, which could precipitate cardiac arrhythmias)

Tetracyclines, oral
(concurrent administration may decrease the bioavailability of tetracyclines)

Medical considerations/Contraindications
The medical considerations/contraindications included have been selected on the basis of their potential clinical significance (reasons given in parentheses where appropriate)—not necessarily inclusive (» = major clinical significance).

Except under special circumstances, this medication should not be used when the following medical problem exists:

» Hypercalcemia
(calcium acetate may exacerbate the condition)

Risk-benefit should be considered when the following medical problem exists:

Sensitivity to calcium acetate

Patient monitoring
The following may be especially important in patient monitoring (other tests may be warranted in some patients, depending on condition; » = major clinical significance):

Calcium concentrations, serum and
Phosphate concentrations, serum
(serum calcium concentrations should be monitored twice a week early in the treatment during the dosage adjustment period; serum calcium concentrations > 10.5 mg per dL (mg/dL) indicate mild hypercalcemia and serum concentrations > 12 mg/dL indicate severe hypercalcemia; the product of the serum calcium concentration and the serum phosphate concentration should not exceed 66; if hypercalcemia develops, calcium acetate should be discontinued or the dosage reduced, depending on the severity of hypercalcemia; serum phosphate concentrations should be monitored periodically and the dosage adjusted as needed to keep concentrations below 6 mg per dL)

Side/Adverse Effects
The following side/adverse effects have been selected on the basis of their potential clinical significance (possible signs and symptoms in parentheses where appropriate)—not necessarily inclusive:

Those indicating need for medical attention
Incidence rare

Hypercalcemia, mild (constipation; loss of appetite; nausea or vomiting); ***hypercalcemia, severe*** (confusion; full or partial loss of consciousness; incoherent speech)

Note: *Mild hypercalcemia* may be asymptomatic.

Those indicating need for medical attention only if they continue or are bothersome
Incidence less frequent

Nausea; pruritus (itching)

Note: *Pruritus* may represent an allergic reaction.

Overdose
For more information on the management of overdose or unintentional ingestion, **contact a Poison Control Center** (see *Poison Control Center Listing*).

Clinical effects of overdose
The following effects have been selected on the basis of their potential clinical significance (possible signs and symptoms in parentheses where appropriate)—not necessarily inclusive:

Acute and/or chronic

Hypercalcemia, mild (constipation; loss of appetite; nausea and vomiting); ***hypercalcemia, severe*** (confusion; full or partial loss of consciousness; incoherent speech)

Note: *Mild hypercalcemia* may be asymptomatic.
Chronic *hypercalcemia* may lead to vascular calcification or other soft-tissue calcification.

Treatment of overdose
Mild hypercalcemia may be controlled by reducing the dose of calcium acetate or temporarily discontinuing therapy. Calcium acetate therapy should be discontinued in severe hypercalcemia.

To enhance elimination—Severe hypercalcemia should be treated by hemodialysis.

Monitoring—If chronic hypercalcemia develops, radiographic evaluation of the suspected anatomical region may detect soft-tissue calcification.

Supportive care—Patients in whom intentional overdose is confirmed or suspected should be referred for psychiatric consultation.

Patient Consultation
As an aid to patient consultation, refer to *Advice for the Patient, Calcium Acetate (Systemic)*.

In providing consultation, consider emphasizing the following selected information (» = major clinical significance):

Before using this medication
» Conditions affecting use, especially:
Other medications, especially calcium-containing foods or preparations or digitalis glycosides
Other medical problems, especially hypercalcemia

Proper use of this medication
Taking with meals
» Proper dosing
Missed dose: Taking as soon as possible; not taking if almost time for next dose; not doubling doses
» Proper storage

Precautions while using this medication
Importance of close monitoring by physician
» Avoiding concurrent use with calcium-containing preparations, including dietary supplements and antacids
» Estimating daily dietary calcium intake and adjusting if needed

Side/adverse effects
Signs of potential side effects, especially mild and severe hypercalcemia

General Dosing Information
Most patients require 3 to 4 tablets with each meal.

Diet/Nutrition
Calcium acetate should be taken with meals.

Daily intake of dietary calcium should be estimated initially and adjusted if needed.

Oral Dosage Forms

CALCIUM ACETATE TABLETS

Usual adult and adolescent dose
Antihyperphosphatemic—
Oral, 2 tablets three times a day with meals. The dosage may be increased gradually to keep serum phosphate concentrations below 6 mg per dL.

Usual pediatric dose
Safety and efficacy have not been established.

Strength(s) usually available
U.S.—
169 mg elemental calcium (667 mg calcium acetate) (Rx) [*PhosLo*].

Packaging and storage
Store below 40 °C (104 °F), preferably between 15 and 30 °C (59 and 86 °F), unless otherwise specified by the manufacturer.

Auxiliary labeling
- Take with meals.

Developed: 03/23/1998

CALCIUM CARBONATE—See *Antacids (Oral-Local), Calcium Supplements (Systemic)*

CALCIUM CHANNEL BLOCKING AGENTS Systemic

This monograph includes information on the following: 1) Amlodipine; 2) Bepridil†; 3) Diltiazem; 4) Felodipine; 5) Flunarizine*; 6) Isradipine†; 7) Nicardipine†; 8) Nifedipine; 9) Nimodipine; 10) Verapamil.

VA CLASSIFICATION (Primary/Secondary):

Amlodipine—CV200/CV250; CV409
Bepridil—CV200/CV250
Diltiazem—CV200/CV250; CV300; CV409
Felodipine—CV200/CV409
Flunarizine—CV200/CN105
Isradipine—CV200/CV409
Nicardipine—CV200/CV250; CV409
Nifedipine—CV200/CV250; CV409
Nimodipine—CV200
Verapamil—CV200/CN105; CV250; CV300; CV409; CV900

Commonly used brand name(s): *Adalat*[8]; *Adalat CC*[8]; *Adalat PA*[8]; *Adalat XL*[8]; *Apo-Diltiaz*[3]; *Apo-Nifed*[8]; *Apo-Verap*[10]; *Calan*[10]; *Calan SR*[10]; *Cardene*[7]; *Cardizem*[3]; *Cardizem CD*[3]; *Cardizem LA*[3]; *Cardizem SR*[3]; *Dilacor-XR*[3]; *DynaCirc*[6]; *Isoptin*[10]; *Isoptin SR*[10]; *Nimotop*[9]; *Norvasc*[1]; *Novo-Diltazem*[3]; *Novo-Nifedin*[8]; *Novo-Veramil*[10]; *Nu-Diltiaz*[3]; *Nu-Nifed*[8]; *Nu-Verap*[10]; *Plendil*[4]; *Procardia*[8]; *Procardia XL*[8]; *Renedil*[4]; *Sibelium*[5]; *Syn-Diltiazem*[3]; *Vascor*[2]; *Verelan*[10]; *Verelan PM*[10].

Note: For a listing of dosage forms and brand names by country availability, see *Dosage Forms* section(s).

*Not commercially available in U.S.
†Not commercially available in Canada.

Category
Antianginal—Amlodipine; Bepridil; Diltiazem; Felodipine; Isradipine; Nicardipine; Nifedipine; Verapamil.
Antiarrhythmic—Diltiazem; Verapamil.
Antihypertensive—Amlodipine; Diltiazem; Felodipine; Isradipine; Nicardipine; Nifedipine; Verapamil.
Hypertrophic cardiomyopathy therapy adjunct—Verapamil.
Subarachnoid hemorrhage therapy—Flunarizine; Nicardipine; Nimodipine.
Vascular headache prophylactic—Flunarizine; Verapamil

Indications
Note: Bracketed information in the *Indications* section refers to uses that are not included in U.S. product labeling.

Accepted
Angina pectoris, chronic (treatment)—Amlodipine,bepridil, diltiazem, [felodipine], [isradipine], nicardipine, nifedipine, and verapamil are indicated in the management of classic angina (chronic stable angina or effort-associated angina) with no evidence of vasospasm. Nicardipine, amlodipine [and other calcium channel blocking agents] may be used alone or in combination, with caution, with beta-adrenergic blocking agents.

Amlodipine, diltiazem, [felodipine], [isradipine], [nicardipine], nifedipine, and verapamil are also indicated in the management of vasospastic angina (Prinzmetal's variant, or at-rest angina) or unstable angina in patients who are unable to tolerate or whose symptoms are not relieved by adequate doses of beta-adrenergic blocking agents or organic nitrates. They are generally indicated when vasospastic angina is confirmed by: (a) the classical pattern accompanied by elevation of ST segment; (b) ergonovine-induced angina or coronary artery spasm; or (c) coronary artery spasm demonstrated by angiography, although they may also be used when a vasospastic component is indicated but not confirmed (e.g., where pain has a variable threshold on exertion or in unstable angina where electrocardiographic findings are compatible with intermittent vasospasm).

Tachycardia, supraventricular (treatment and prophylaxis)—Verapamil and parenteral diltiazem are indicated in the treatment of supraventricular tachyarrhythmias. Diltiazem and verapamil produce rapid conversion to sinus rhythm of paroxysmal supraventricular tachycardia (including those associated with accessory bypass tracts, such as Wolff-Parkinson-White [W-P-W] or Lown-Ganong-Levine [L-G-L] syndrome) in patients who do not respond to vagal maneuvers when the atrioventricular (AV) node is required for reentry to sustain tachycardia. Parenteral diltiazem and verapamil also produce temporary control of rapid ventricular rate in atrial flutter or atrial fibrillation. Oral verapamil is indicated, alone or in association with digitalis, for control of ventricular rate at rest and during stress in patients with chronic atrial flutter and/or atrial fibrillation (not otherwise controllable with digitalis), and for prophylaxis of repetitive paroxysmal supraventricular tachycardia. Diltiazem and verapamil do not produce class I, II, or III antiarrhythmic effects.

Hypertension (treatment)—Amlodipine, diltiazem, felodipine, isradipine, nicardipine, nifedipine, and verapamil are indicated, alone or in combination with other agents, for treatment of hypertension.

For additional information on initial therapeutic guidelines related to the treatment of hypertension, see *Appendix III*.

[Cardiomyopathy, hypertrophic (treatment adjunct)]—Verapamil is used in the treatment of hypertrophic cardiomyopathy to relieve ventricular outflow obstruction. However, extreme caution is recommended when hypertrophic cardiomyopathy is complicated by left ventricular obstruction, high pulmonary wedge pressure, paroxysmal nocturnal dyspnea or orthopnea, sinoatrial (SA) nodal function impairment, or severe heart block.

Raynaud's phenomenon (treatment)—[Felodipine], [isradipine], [nicardipine], and [nifedipine][1] are used for symptomatic treatment of Raynaud's phenomenon.

Subarachnoid hemorrhage-associated neurologic deficits (treatment)—Nimodipine is indicated for improvement of neurological outcome by reducing the incidence and severity of ischemic deficits in patients with subarachnoid hemorrhage from ruptured congenital intracranial aneurysms who are in good neurological condition post-ictus (e.g., Hunt and Hess Grades I–III). [Flunarizine] and [nicardipine] are also used for this indication.

Headache, vascular (prophylaxis)—Flunarizine and [verapamil] are indicated for reducing frequency and severity of vascular headaches, but are not recommended for treatment of acute attacks.

Acceptance not established
A preliminary study and case report suggest diltiazem may be used in pediatric patients for the treatment of *pulmonary hypertension*. However, data are insufficient to establish safety and efficacy of diltiazem for this indication.

Unaccepted
Sublingual use of nifedipine capsules for hypertensive crisis is not recommended because it has been associated with severe hypotension, acute myocardial infarction, stroke, and death.

[1]Not included in Canadian product labeling.

Pharmacology/Pharmacokinetics

Physicochemical characteristics
Molecular weight—

Amlodipine besylate: 567.1.
Bepridil hydrochloride: 421.02.
Diltiazem hydrochloride: 450.98.
Felodipine: 384.26.
Flunarizine hydrochloride: 477.42.
Isradipine: 371.39.
Nicardipine hydrochloride: 515.99.
Nifedipine: 346.34.
Nimodipine: 418.45.
Verapamil hydrochloride: 491.07.

Mechanism of action/Effect
These agents are calcium-ion influx inhibitors (slow-channel blocking agents). Although their mechanism is not completely understood, they are thought to inhibit calcium ion entry through select voltage-sensitive areas termed "slow channels" across cell membranes. By reducing intracellular calcium concentration in cardiac and vascular smooth muscle cells, they dilate coronary arteries and peripheral arteries and arterioles, and may reduce heart rate, decrease myocardial contractility (negative inotropic effect), and slow atrioventricular (AV) nodal conduction. Serum calcium concentrations are unchanged, although

there is some evidence that elevated serum calcium concentrations may alter the therapeutic effect of verapamil.

Calcium channel blocking agents may be classified into subgroups according to structure—

Bepridil.

Benzothiazepine (diltiazem).

Diphenylpiperazine (flunarizine).

Dihydropyridine (amlodipine,felodipine, isradipine, nicardipine, nifedipine, nimodipine).

Diphenylalkylamine (verapamil).

Effects within each subgroup are generally the same—

Bepridil is a nonselective calcium channel blocking agent that affects both cardiac and smooth muscle. It also inhibits the fast sodium inward current in myocardial and vascular smooth muscle.

Piperazine derivatives act on vascular smooth muscle, with few or no direct myocardial effects.

Dihydropyridines are selective for vascular smooth muscle compared with myocardium and therefore act primarily as vasodilators. Hypotensive effects are accompanied by reflex tachycardia. However, amlodipine appears to have no significant effect on the sinoatrial (SA) or atrioventricular (AV) node in humans.

Diltiazem (a benzothiazepine) and verapamil (a diphenylalkylamine) are less selective vasodilators that also have direct effects on the myocardium, including depression of sinoatrial (SA) and atrioventricular (AV) nodal conduction.

See *Table 1*, page 688.

Antianginal—

Dilation of the peripheral vasculature reduces systemic pressure or cardiac afterload, which results in lessened myocardial wall tension and reduced oxygen requirements of the myocardial tissues. In vasospastic angina, a relaxation of coronary arteries and arterioles and inhibition of coronary artery spasm improves blood flow and oxygen supply to myocardial tissues. May also be related to enhanced left ventricular diastolic relaxation and decreased wall stiffness (improved diastolic compliance).In vasospastic angina, amlodipine blocks constriction and restores blood flow in coronary arteries and arterioles in response to calcium, potassium, epinephrine, serotonin, and thromboxane A_2 analog in human coronary vessels *in vitro*.

Antiarrhythmic—

The inhibited influx of calcium ions in cardiac tissues prolongs the effective refractory period and results in slowed AV nodal conduction. Normal sinus rhythm is usually not affected, except in some elderly patients or patients with sick sinus syndrome, in whom calcium channel blockade may interfere with sinus-node impulse generation and may induce sinus or sinoatrial block. Normal atrial action potential or intraventricular conduction are not altered, but in depressed atrial fibers amplitude, velocity of depolarization, and conduction velocity are decreased. The antegrade effective refractory period of the accessory bypass tract may be shortened.

Antihypertensive—

Reduction of total peripheral vascular resistance as a result of vasodilation.

Hypertrophic cardiomyopathy therapy adjunct—

Improvement of left ventricular outflow. May also be related to enhanced left ventricular diastolic relaxation and decreased wall stiffness.

Subarachnoid hemorrhage therapy—

Theoretically, nimodipine may prevent cerebral arterial spasm following subarachnoid hemorrhage, but that has not been confirmed by arteriography. Its exact mechanism of action in treatment of neurologic deficits caused by subarachnoid hemorrhage is not known.

Vascular headache prophylactic—

By inhibiting the vasoconstriction that occurs in the prodromal phase, calcium channel blockade may relieve or prevent reactive vasodilation.

Other actions/effects

Inhibition of platelet aggregation. Decrease in esophageal contraction amplitude. Diltiazem and verapamil may inhibit cytochrome P450 metabolism, thereby inhibiting the metabolism of other medications or compounds. Flunarizine has antihistaminic effects. Isradipine has diuretic effects. Verapamil decreases gastrointestinal transit time.

Absorption

Amlodipine—bioavailability 64 to 90% absorption, not affected by food.

Bepridil—Rapid and complete; bioavailability 60 to 70% because of first-pass metabolism; rate, but not extent of absorption, is reduced in the presence of food.

Diltiazem—Well absorbed; bioavailability approximately 40% because of first-pass metabolism; bioavailability may increase with chronic use and increasing dose (i.e., bioavailability is nonlinear).

Felodipine—Almost completely absorbed; bioavailability approximately 20% because of first-pass metabolism. Bioavailability is not affected in the presence of food; however, bioavailability more than doubled when felodipine was taken with doubly concentrated grapefruit juice as compared to when it was taken with water or orange juice (a similar, but lesser, effect is also seen with other dihydropyridines).

Flunarizine—Well absorbed.

Isradipine—Absorption is 90 to 95%; bioavailability approximately 15 to 24% because of first-pass metabolism; rate, but not extent, of absorption is reduced in the presence of food.

Nicardipine—Completely absorbed; bioavailability approximately 35% because of first-pass metabolism.

Nifedipine—Rapidly and completely absorbed; bioavailability approximately 60 to 75% because of first-pass metabolism. Bioavailability of extended-release formulations may be 10 to 15% lower than that of immediate-release formulations, but plasma concentrations are more stable, with smaller fluctuations over the dosing interval. Bioavailability of both formulations is increased with hepatic function impairment. Rate, but not extent, of absorption of *Procardia XL* may be reduced in the presence of food.

Nimodipine—Rapidly absorbed. Because of extensive first-pass metabolism, bioavailability is only about 13% (significantly increased [up to double the peak serum concentration] in patients with hepatic function impairment). The effect of food on absorption is unknown.

Verapamil—More than 90% of an oral dose is absorbed; bioavailability approximately 20 to 35% because of first-pass metabolism; bioavailability of oral verapamil may increase with chronic use and increasing dose (i.e., bioavailability is nonlinear).

Distribution

Bepridil—In breast milk: Concentration is approximately one-third serum concentration.

Protein binding

Amlodipine—Very high (93%).

Bepridil—Very high (more than 99%).

Diltiazem—High (70 to 80%, 35 to 40% to albumin).

Felodipine—Very high (more than 99%).

Flunarizine—Very high (99%).

Isradipine—Very high (95%).

Nicardipine—Very high (more than 95%).

Nifedipine—Very high (92 to 98%).

Nimodipine—Very high (over 95%); independent of concentration.

Verapamil—Very high (approximately 90%).

Biotransformation

Hepatic; extensive and rapid, with a prominent first-pass effect.

Amlodipine—Extensive hepatic metabolism; 90% converted to inactive metabolites.

Bepridil—At least 17 metabolites, 1 or more of which may have cardiovascular activity.

Diltiazem—By cytochrome P450 mixed function oxidase. A major metabolite, detected following oral and continuous intravenous administration but not rapid intravenous administration, is desacetyl diltiazem, which has one quarter to one half the coronary dilatation activity of the parent compound.

Felodipine—Six metabolites, accounting for 23% of an oral dose, have been identified; none has significant vasodilating activity.

Isradipine—Completely metabolized; six metabolites identified.

Nifedipine—No known active metabolites.

Verapamil—Principal metabolite is norverapamil, which has approximately 20% of the hypotensive cardiovascular activity of verapamil; 11 other metabolites occur only in trace amounts.

Half-life

Amlodipine (biphasic)—

Elimination—

Terminal: 30 to 50 hours

Bepridil (biphasic)—

Distribution—

Approximately 2 hours.

Elimination—

Terminal: Average, 42 hours (range, 26 to 64 hours).

Dosing interval: Less than 24 hours.

Diltiazem—

Oral (biphasic):

Extended-release capsules—

Cardizem CD: Apparent—5 to 8 hours.

Cardizem SR: Apparent—5 to 7 hours.

Tablets—

Early: 20 to 30 minutes.

Terminal: Approximately 3.5 hours (5 to 8 hours with high and repetitive dosage).
Intravenous:
Approximately 3.4 hours.
Felodipine (polyphasic)—
Terminal:
11 to 16 hours.
Flunarizine—
19 days.
Isradipine (biphasic)—
Early: 1.5 to 2 hours.
Terminal: About 8 hours.
Nicardipine (biphasic)—
Early: 2 to 4 hours.
Terminal: 8.6 hours.
Nifedipine—
Approximately 2 hours.
Extended-release tablets—
Adalat CC: Terminal—Approximately 7 hours
Adalat PA: Terminal—6 to 12 hours
Adalat XL, Procardia XL: Not available. The gastrointestinal therapeutic system (GITS) is designed to deliver nifedipine by zero-order systemic absorption over a period of approximately 18 hours.
Nimodipine—
Terminal: 8 to 9 hours. Earlier, more rapid elimination rates (equivalent to a half-life of 1 to 2 hours) necessitate frequent dosing.
Verapamil—
Oral:
Single dose—Range, 2.8 to 7.4 hours.
Repetitive dosage—Range, 4.5 to 12 hours (half-life is increased because of saturation of hepatic enzyme systems as plasma verapamil concentrations increase).
Intravenous (biphasic):
Early—About 4 minutes.
Terminal—2 to 5 hours.

Onset of action

Diltiazem—
Oral:
Extended-release capsules—2 to 3 hours.
Tablets—30 to 60 minutes.
Parenteral:
Rapid intravenous injection—
Reduction in heart rate or conversion of paroxysmal supraventricular tachycardia to sinus rhythm: Within 3 minutes.
Felodipine—
Within 2 to 5 hours.
Isradipine—
2 to 3 hours.
Nifedipine—
Oral:
Capsules—20 minutes.
Verapamil—
Oral:
1 to 2 hours.
Intravenous:
Antiarrhythmic—Within 1 to 5 minutes and usually less than 2 minutes.
Hemodynamic—Within 3 to 5 minutes.

Time to peak concentration

Amlodipine—
6 to 12 hours.
Bepridil—
2 to 3 hours.
Diltiazem—
Oral (wide individual variation in concentrations achieved):
Extended-release capsules—
Cardizem CD: 10 to 14 hours.
Cardizem SR: 6 to 11 hours.
Tablets—
2 to 3 hours.
Felodipine—
2.5 to 5 hours. Peak plasma concentrations at steady state are about 20% higher than after a single dose.
Flunarizine—
2 to 4 hours.
Isradipine—
About 1.5 hours.
Nicardipine—
30 minutes to 2 hours (mean, 1 hour).
Nifedipine—
Capsules:
About 30 to 60 minutes.
Extended-release tablets:
Adalat CC—2.5 to 5 hours
Adalat PA—4 hours.
Adalat XL, Procardia XL—Approximately 6 hours.
Nimodipine—
Within 1 hour.
Verapamil—
Oral:
Extended-release capsules—7 to 9 hours.
Tablets—1 to 2 hours (wide individual variation in concentrations achieved).
Extended-release tablets—5 to 7 hours.

Time to peak effect

Amlodipine—
Time to steady-state plasma concentration: 7 to 8 days.
Bepridil—
Time to steady-state plasma concentration: 8 days.
Diltiazem—
Antihypertensive: Multiple doses—Within 2 weeks.
Antiarrhythmic: Rapid intravenous injection—Hypotension or reduction in heart rate: Within 2 to 7 minutes.
Flunarizine—
Multiple doses: Several weeks.
Isradipine—
Antihypertensive: Multiple doses—2 to 4 weeks.
Nicardipine—
Single dose: 1 to 2 hours.
Verapamil—
Oral: About 30 to 90 minutes. The maximum effects from oral dosage are usually evident sometime during the first 24 to 48 hours of therapy (for some patients the time may be slightly extended because the half-life of verapamil tends to increase during this period).
Intravenous: Within 3 to 5 minutes after completion of injection.

Elimination

Amlodipine—
Renal: 60% as metabolites and 10% as unchanged amlodipine.
Bepridil—
Renal: 70% (none unchanged).
Biliary/fecal: 22% (none unchanged).
In dialysis: Not removable by hemodialysis.
Diltiazem—
Biliary and renal (2 to 4% unchanged).
In dialysis: Does not appear to be removable by hemodialysis or peritoneal dialysis.
Felodipine—
Renal: 70% (less than 0.5% unchanged).
Biliary/fecal: 10% (less than 0.5% unchanged).
Flunarizine—
Drug and metabolites: Very slow and prolonged.
Biliary/fecal: Less than 6% in the first 48 hours.
Renal: Less than 0.2% in the first 48 hours.
Isradipine—
Renal: 60 to 65% (none unchanged).
Biliary/fecal: 25 to 30% (none unchanged).
In dialysis: No information, but not likely to be removable by hemodialysis because of plasma protein binding.
Nicardipine—
Renal: 60% (less than 1% unchanged).
Biliary/fecal: 35%.
Nifedipine—
Renal: 80% (as metabolites), only traces unchanged.
Biliary/fecal: 20% (as metabolites).
In dialysis: Does not appear to be removed by hemodialysis or chronic ambulatory peritoneal dialysis; however, plasmapheresis may be beneficial.
Nimodipine—
Renal (less than 1% unchanged).
Biliary/fecal.
In dialysis: Because of extensive protein binding, unlikely to be significantly removed by hemodialysis or peritoneal dialysis.
Verapamil—
Renal:
As conjugated metabolites—70% as metabolites and 3 to 4% unchanged within 5 days.
Unmetabolized—3%.

Biliary/fecal:
9 to 16%.
In dialysis:
Not removable by hemodialysis.

Precautions to Consider

Carcinogenicity/Mutagenicity

For amlodipine—

No evidence of carcinogenicity was found in rats or mice given dosages of 0.5, 1.25, and 2.5 mg per kg of body weight (mg/kg) per day for 2 years.

No mutagenicity was found in studies at either the gene or chromosome level.

For bepridil—

A lifetime study in mice at doses up to 60 times the maximum recommended human dose (MRHD) (based on a 60-kg subject) found no evidence of carcinogenicity. A lifetime study in rats at doses 20 times the usual recommended human dose found unilateral follicular adenomas of the thyroid.

Mutagenicity studies (micronucleus test for chromosomal effects, liver microsome activated bacterial assay for mutagenicity, Chinese hamster ovary cell assay for mutagenicity, sister chromatid exchange assay) were negative.

For diltiazem—

A 24-month study with diltiazem in rats and a 21-month study in mice found no evidence of carcinogenicity.

There was no mutagenic response in *in vitro* bacterial tests.

For felodipine—

A 2-year study in rats at doses of 7.7, 23.1, or 69.3 mg per kg of body weight (mg/kg) per day (up to 28 times the MRHD [based on a 50-kg subject]) found an increased incidence of benign interstitial cell tumors of the testes (Leydig cell tumors) in males, probably secondary to a reduction in testicular testosterone and corresponding increase in serum luteinizing hormone (which have not been observed in humans). In addition, a dose-related increase in the incidence of focal squamous cell hyperplasia in the esophageal groove of both males and females at all doses (humans have no anatomical structure comparable to the esophageal groove). Felodipine was not carcinogenic and did not increase the incidence of Leydig cell tumors in mice at doses up to 138.6 mg/kg per day (28 times the MRHD [based on a 50-kg subject]) for periods up to 80 and 99 weeks in males and females, respectively; no effect on the esophageal groove occurred.

Mutagenicity studies (Ames test, mouse lymphoma forward mutation assay, mouse micronucleus test, human lymphocyte chromosome aberration assay) were negative.

For flunarizine—

A 24-month study in 4 groups of 50 male and 50 female Wistar rats at doses of 0, 5, 20, or 40 mg/kg per day (the 40-mg/kg group received 80 mg/kg for the first 2 months) did not produce an effect on tumor rate or type; however, the validity of the study is questionable because of an extremely high mortality rate (more than 90% in the males and 80% in the females).

Mutagenicity studies (Ames test, sister chromatid exchange test in human lymphocytes, sex-linked recessive lethal test in *Drosophila melanogaster*, micronucleus test in male rats, dominant lethal test in male and female mice) were negative.

For isradipine—

A 2-year study in male rats at doses of 2.5, 12.5, or 62.5 mg/kg per day (approximately 6, 31, and 156 times the MRHD, respectively, based on a 50-kg subject) found a dose-dependent increase in the incidence of benign Leydig cell tumors and testicular hyperplasia relative to untreated control animals; these findings were replicated in a subsequent study. A 2-year study in mice at doses of 6, 38, and 200 times the MRHD found no evidence of oncogenicity.

Mutagenicity studies were negative.

For nicardipine—

A 2-year study in rats with nicardipine at dosage levels of 5, 15, or 45 mg/kg per day found a dose-dependent increase in thyroid hyperplasia and neoplasia (follicular adenoma/carcinoma). One- and three-month studies in the rat suggest that the mechanism for this effect is a nicardipine-induced reduction in plasma thyroxine (T_4) concentrations with a resulting increase in thyroid-stimulating hormone (TSH) concentrations, which is known to cause hyperstimulation of the thyroid; in rats on an iodine-deficient diet, one month of nicardipine administration produced thyroid hyperplasia that was prevented by T_4 supplementation. Studies in mice for up to 18 months at doses up to 100 mg/kg per day and in dogs for 1 year at doses up 25 mg/kg per day found no evidence of neoplasia of any tissue and no evidence of thyroid changes. No effects of nicardipine on thyroid function (plasma T_4 and TSH) have been reported in humans.

No evidence of mutagenicity was found in a battery of genotoxicity tests conducted on microbial indicator organisms, in micronucleus tests in mice and hamsters, or in a sister chromatid exchange study in hamsters.

For nifedipine—

Nifedipine was not shown to be carcinogenic when administered orally to rats for 2 years.

In vivo mutagenic tests were negative.

For nimodipine—

A 2-year study in rats found an increased incidence of adenocarcinoma of the uterus and Leydig-cell adenoma of the testes, but the increases were not significant. A 91-week study in mice found no evidence of carcinogenicity, although the life expectancy was shortened.

Mutagenicity studies, including the Ames, micronucleus, and dominant lethal tests, have been negative.

For verapamil—

A 2-year study in rats with verapamil at doses up to 12 times the MRHD found no evidence of carcinogenicity.

There was no mutagenic response in the Ames test in 5 test strains at 3 mg per plate with or without metabolic activation.

Pregnancy/Reproduction

Fertility—

Amlodipine—

No effects were seen on the fertility of rats treated with amlodipine at doses up to 10 mg per kg per day, which represents 8 times the maximum recommended human dose.

For felodipine—

No significant effect on reproductive performance was found in male or female rats given doses of 3.8, 9.6, or 26.9 mg/kg per day.

For flunarizine—

In studies in male and female Wistar rats at doses of 0 and approximately 10, 40, and 160 mg/kg given for 60 days pre-mating in the males or 14 days pre-mating and 21 days of gestation in the females, treated animals were mated with non-treated animals. In treated females at the highest dose, there were no pregnancies and a large number of deaths; at the 40-mg/kg dose, there was decreased weight gain during pregnancy, decreased rate of pregnancy, increase in the number of resorbed fetuses, decreased litter size, and decreased weight of pups at birth. In non-treated females mated with treated males, a slight increase in resorption was seen only at the highest dose.

For nifedipine—

Reduced fertility occurred in rats given 30 times the maximum recommended human dose (MRHD) prior to mating.

Pregnancy—

For amlodipine—

Adequate and well-controlled studies have not been done in humans.No evidence of teratogenicity or other embryo/fetal toxicity was observed in rats or rabbits given up to 10 mg/kg during periods of major organogenesis. However, in rats the number of intrauterine deaths increased about five-fold, and litter size was significantly decreased by 50%.

FDA Pregnancy Category C.

For bepridil—

Adequate and well-controlled studies in humans have not been done.

Studies in rats at maternal doses of 37 times the MRHD found reduced litter size at birth and decreased pup survival during lactation. No teratogenicity was observed in rats or rabbits at the same dose.

FDA Pregnancy Category C.

For diltiazem—

Well-controlled studies in humans have not been done.

Studies in mice, rats, and rabbits, using doses of diltiazem 5 to 10 times greater than the recommended daily dose on a mg/kg basis, resulted in embryo and fetal deaths, reduced neonatal survival rates, and skeletal abnormalities. In addition, there was an increased incidence of stillbirths at doses of 20 or more times the recommended human dose. Diltiazem should be used in pregnant women only if potential benefit justifies potential risk to the fetus.

FDA Pregnancy Category C.

For felodipine—

Adequate and well-controlled studies in humans have not been done.

Studies in rabbits at doses of 0.46, 1.2, 2.3, and 4.6 mg/kg per day (from 0.4 to 4 times the MRHD [based on a 50-kg subject] on a mg per square meter of body surface area basis) found digital anomalies consisting of reduction in size and degree of ossification of the terminal phalanges in the fetuses. Frequency and severity of the changes were dose-related and occurred even at the lowest dose. These changes are similar to those occurring with other dihydropyridines and may be the result of compromised uterine blood flow. The anomalies did not occur in rats; abnormal position of the distal phalanges (but not reduction in size of the terminal phalanges) occurred in about 40% of cynomolgus monkey fetuses.

Studies in rats at doses of 9.6 mg/kg per day (4 times the MRHD [based on a 50-kg subject] on a mg per square meter of body surface area basis) produced a prolongation of parturition with a difficult labor and an increased frequency of fetal and early postnatal deaths.

Studies in rabbits at doses greater than or equal to 1.2 mg/kg per day (equal to the MRHD on a mg per square meter of body surface area basis) found significant enlargement (in excess of normal) of the mammary glands during pregnancy, which regressed during lactation. These effects were not observed in rats or monkeys.

FDA Pregnancy Category C.

For flunarizine—

Studies in humans have not been done.

There was a slight increase in resorptions and decrease in number of live fetuses in female Wistar rats given 40 mg/kg, with no effects seen at doses of 0, 10, or 20 mg/kg; there was no evidence of teratogenicity. There was a dose-related increase in the number of resorptions in New Zealand rabbits given doses of 0, 2.5, or 10 mg/kg from day 6 to day 18 of pregnancy, with a corresponding decrease in number of live births; there was no evidence of teratogenicity.

For isradipine—

Studies in humans have not been done.

Studies in rats at doses of 6, 20, or 60 mg/kg per day produced a significant reduction in maternal weight gain at the highest dose (150 times the MRHD), but with no lasting effects on the mother or offspring. Studies in rabbits at doses of 1, 3, or 10 mg/kg per day (2.5, 7.5, and 25 times the MRHD, respectively) found decreased maternal weight gain and increased fetal resorptions at the two highest doses. There was no evidence of embryotoxicity at doses that were not maternotoxic and no evidence of teratogenicity at any dose. With peri- and postnatal administration of doses of 20 and 60 mg/kg per day, reduced maternal weight gain during late pregnancy was associated with reduced birth weights and decreased peri- and postnatal pup survival.

FDA Pregnancy Category C.

For nicardipine—

Adequate and well-controlled studies in humans have not been done.

Studies in Japanese White rabbits at doses of 150 mg/kg per day during organogenesis (but not at doses of 50 mg/kg per day [25 times the MRHD]) found nicardipine to be embryocidal and to cause marked body weight gain suppression in the treated doe. Studies in rats with nicardipine at doses 50 times the MRHD found no evidence of embryolethality or teratogenicity, but dystocia, reduced birth weights, reduced neonatal survival, and reduced neonatal weight gain occurred.

FDA Pregnancy Category C.

For nifedipine—

Adequate and well-controlled studies in humans have not been done.

Nifedipine has been shown to be teratogenic in rodents and embryotoxic (increased fetal resorptions, reduced fetal weight, increase in stunted forms, increased fetal deaths, and decreased fetal survival) in rodents and rabbits at doses 30 times and 3 to 10 times the MRHD, respectively. In pregnant monkeys, small placentas and underdeveloped chorionic villi occurred at two thirds and two times the MRHD. In rats, three times or more the MRHD caused prolongation of pregnancy.

FDA Pregnancy Category C.

For nimodipine—

Adequate and well-controlled studies in humans have not been done.

Two studies in Himalayan rabbits found an increased incidence of teratogenic malformations in the fetuses at doses of 1 and 10 (but not 3) mg/kg per day given on days 6 through 18 of pregnancy; in these same studies, stunted fetuses were found at doses of 1 and 10 (but not 3) mg/kg per day in one study, and only at 1 mg/kg per day in the other. Studies in Long Evans rats at doses of 100 mg/kg per day given on days 6 through 15 found embryotoxicity, including fetal resorption and stunted fetal growth. In other rat studies, doses of 30 mg/kg per day from days 16 to 20 or 21 produced an increased incidence of skeletal variation, stunted fetuses, and stillbirths, but no malformations.

FDA Pregnancy Category C.

For verapamil—

Adequate and well-controlled studies in humans have not been done.

Verapamil crosses the placenta and can be detected in umbilical vein blood at delivery. Occasionally, rapid intravenous injection of verapamil in humans may cause maternal hypotension resulting in fetal distress.

Studies in rats, using doses of verapamil up to 6 times the recommended daily dose for humans, resulted in embryo deaths and slowed growth.

FDA Pregnancy Category C.

Breast-feeding

For all calcium channel blocking agents—

Although problems in humans have not been documented, bepridil, nifedipine, and verapamil, and possibly other calcium channel blocking agents, are distributed into breast milk.

For diltiazem—

Diltiazem is distributed into human breast milk. If diltiazem treatment is necessary, breast-feeding should be discontinued

For felodipine and amlodipine only—

It is not known whether felodipine or amlodipine is distributed into breast milk in humans.

For flunarizine only—

It is not known whether flunarizine is distributed into breast milk in humans; however, it is distributed into the milk of dogs, at concentrations much higher than in plasma.

For nimodipine only—

It is not known whether nimodipine is distributed into breast milk in humans; however, nimodipine and/or its metabolites have been found in the milk of treated rats, at concentrations much higher than maternal plasma concentrations.

Pediatrics

For all calcium channel blockers—

Although appropriate studies on the relationship of age to the effects of calcium channel blocking agents have not been performed in the pediatric population, pediatrics-specific problems that would limit the usefulness of calcium channel blocking agents in children are not expected. However, in rare instances, severe adverse hemodynamic effects have occurred after intravenous administration of verapamil in neonates and infants.

For amlodipine—

Safety and efficacy have not been established in children younger than 6 years of age.

Geriatrics

Use in the elderly—

For nimodipine, verapamil, and possibly other calcium channel blocking agents—

Half-life of calcium channel blocking agents may be increased in the elderly as a result of decreased clearance.

For amlodipine only—

Due to a decreased clearance of amlodipine with a resulting increase in AUC of 40 to 60%, a lower initial dose may be required.

For diltiazem only—

Although appropriate studies on the relationship of age to the effects of diltiazem have not been performed in the geriatric population, no geriatrics-specific problems have been documented to date. However, dose selection for an elderly patient should be cautious, usually starting at the low end of the dosing range, reflecting the greater frequency of decreased hepatic, renal, or cardiac function, and of concomitant disease or other drug therapy.

For felodipine only—

Plasma concentrations increase with age. Mean clearance at mean age of 76 was found to be only 45% of that at mean age of 26.

For isradipine only—

Bioavailability may be increased in patients over 65 years of age.

For nicardipine only—
Studies in patients 65 years of age and older found no difference in half-life or protein binding from that in young normal volunteers.

For nimodipine only—
Risk of hypotension may be increased.

For all calcium channel blocking agents—
Elderly patients are more likely to have age-related renal function impairment, which may require caution in patients receiving calcium channel blocking agents.

Pharmacogenetic differences with amlodipine

In clinical trials there was a greater incidence of edema, flushing and palpitations seen in women than in men

Dental

Gingival enlargement is a rare side effect that has been reported with amlodipine, diltiazem, felodipine, nifedipine, and verapamil. It usually starts as gingivitis or gum inflammation in the first 1 to 9 months of treatment. A strictly enforced program of teeth cleaning by a professional combined with plaque control by the patient will minimize growth rate and severity of gingival enlargement. Periodontal surgery may be indicated in some cases, and should be followed by careful plaque control to inhibit recurrence of gum enlargement.

Drug interactions and/or related problems

The following drug interactions and/or related problems have been selected on the basis of their potential clinical significance (possible mechanism in parentheses where appropriate)—not necessarily inclusive (» = major clinical significance):

Note: Information concerning interactions between calcium channel blocking agents and other medications is still limited. Therefore, some of the following potential interactions are stated for cautionary reference until additional information is available.

Combinations containing any of the following medications, depending on the amount present, may also interact with these medications.

Anesthetics, hydrocarbon inhalation
(concurrent use with calcium channel blocking agents may produce additive hypotension; although calcium channel blocking agents may be useful to prevent supraventricular tachycardias, hypertension, or coronary spasm during surgery, caution is recommended during use)

Anti-inflammatory drugs, nonsteroidal (NSAIDs), especially indomethacin
(indomethacin, and possibly other NSAIDs, may antagonize the antihypertensive effect of calcium channel blocking agents by inhibiting renal prostaglandin synthesis and/or by causing sodium and fluid retention; the patient should be carefully monitored to confirm that the desired effect is being obtained. Amlodipine was not affected by coadministration with NSAIDs.)

Aspirin
(in a few reported cases, concomitant use with verapamil led to increased bleeding times greater than with aspirin alone)

Benzodiazepines such as
Midazolam or
Triazolam
(concomitant use with diltiazem increases AUC, C_{max}, and elimination half-life of the benzodiazepine; can result in increased clinical effects [e.g., prolonged sedation of midazolam and triazolam)

» Beta-adrenergic blocking agents, systemic or ophthalmic
(concurrent use of oral dosage forms with oral bepridil, diltiazem, or verapamil or intravenous verapamil usually results in no serious negative inotropic, chronotropic, or dromotropic effects. However, caution and careful monitoring are necessary since the additive effect may prolong sinoatrial [SA] and atrioventricular [AV] conduction [which may lead to severe hypotension, bradycardia, and cardiac failure], especially in patients with impaired ventricular function or abnormal cardiac conduction or sinus node depression. When verapamil and beta-adrenergic blocking agents are to be given intravenously, they should be administered at least a few hours apart since they may have additive depressant effects on myocardial contractility or SA or AV conduction, and asystole has been reported with concurrent use)

(In clinical trials amlodipine has been safely administered with beta-adrenergic blocking agents.)

(in a single small study, diltiazem was reported to significantly increase the bioavailability of propranolol; in other studies, verapamil was found to decrease clearance of both metoprolol and propranolol, with a variable effect on atenolol)

(concurrent use with dihydropyridines, although usually well tolerated, may produce excessive hypotension, and in rare cases may increase the possibility of congestive heart failure. Occasionally, angina has occurred upon initiation of nicardipine or nifedipine therapy, especially after recent abrupt discontinuation of beta-adrenergic blocking agent therapy. If possible, it is recommended that beta-adrenergic blocking agent dosage be discontinued gradually, but especially before nicardipine or nifedipine therapy is begun. However, if concurrent use is necessary, nicardipine or nifedipine may be preferred over other calcium channel blocking agents in some patients because both have less effect on heart rate and conduction)

(if significant systemic absorption of an ophthalmic beta-adrenergic blocking agent occurs, concurrent use of calcium channel blocking agents may result in atrioventricular conduction disturbances, left ventricular failure, and hypotension; in some patients, if a calcium antagonist is necessary, nicardipine or nifedipine may be preferred because both have less effect on heart rate and conduction, although they may also cause greater hypotension; concurrent use of calcium channel blocking agents and ophthalmic beta-adrenergic blocking agents should be avoided in patients with impaired cardiac function)

Calcium supplements
(concurrent use in quantities sufficient to elevate serum calcium concentrations above normal may reduce the response to verapamil and probably other calcium channel blocking agents)

» Carbamazepine or
» Cyclosporine or
» Quinidine or
Theophylline or
Valproate
(diltiazem or verapamil may inhibit cytochrome P450 metabolism, resulting in increased concentrations and toxicity of these medications)

(an idiosyncratic reaction has been reported in which concurrent use of nifedipine and quinidine resulted in significantly reduced serum quinidine concentrations; caution is recommended when nifedipine therapy is initiated or discontinued in a patient stabilized on quinidine)

Cimetidine
(concurrent use may result in accumulation of the calcium channel blocking agent as a result of inhibition of first-pass metabolism; caution and careful titration of the calcium channel blocking agent dose is recommended on initiation of therapy in patients receiving cimetidine; ranitidine and famotidine do not appear to significantly affect calcium channel blocking agent metabolismAmlodipine was not affected by coadministration with cimetidine.)

» Digitalis glycosides
(concurrent use of digoxin with some calcium channel blocking agents [especially verapamil and, to a lesser extent, bepridil, diltiazem, and nifedipine] has been reported to increase the serum concentration of digoxin; the effect of verapamil on digoxin kinetics is enhanced in patients with hepatic function impairment; felodipine significantly increased peak plasma concentrations of digoxin, although there was no significant change in the area under the plasma concentration-time curve [AUC]; amlodipine, isradipine and nicardipine do not appear to have a significant effect. Digoxin serum concentrations should be monitored and dosage may need to be altered when concurrent dosage of the calcium channel blocking agent is initiated, changed, or discontinued. Concurrent use of oral digitalis preparations with oral diltiazem or verapamil or intravenous verapamil has resulted in no serious adverse effects when patients were closely monitored; however, both groups of medications slow AV conduction. Patients receiving them concurrently should be monitored for AV block or excessive bradycardia, especially during the first week of concurrent dosage. To avoid toxicity, dosage reduction of digitalis glycoside may be necessary)

» Disopyramide or
Flecainide
(disopyramide should not be administered within 48 hours before or 24 hours following verapamil administration since both medications possess negative inotropic properties; deaths have been reported; caution is also recommended when disopyramide is used concurrently with diltiazem, nicardipine, or nifedipine; caution is also recommended when flecainide is used concurrently with a calcium channel blocking agent)

» Erythromycin
(concomitant use with diltiazem or verapamil showed an adjusted rate of sudden death from cardiac causes to be five times as high [incidence-rate ration, 5.35; 95% confidence interval, 1.72 to 16.64; P=0.004] as that among those who had used neither a CYP3A inhibitor nor any of the study antibiotic medications; concurrent use should be avoided)

Estrogens
(estrogen-induced fluid retention tends to increase blood pressure; the patient should be carefully monitored to confirm that the desired effect is being obtained)

» Grapefruit juice
(concurrent administration with 200 mL of grapefruit juice has been shown to increase felodipine plasma concentration more than two-fold by inhibiting first-pass metabolism in the gastrointestinal wall and/or the liver; a lesser effect also has been seen with two other dihydropyridines, nifedipine and nisoldipine. There are no effects seen with the concurrent use of amlodipine.)

Highly protein-bound medications, such as:
Anticoagulants, coumarin- and indandione-derivative or
Anticonvulsants, hydantoin or
Anti-inflammatory drugs, nonsteroidal or
Quinine or
Salicylates or
Sulfinpyrazone
(caution is advised when these medications are used concurrently with nifedipine or verapamil since changes in serum concentrations of the free, unbound medications may occur)

» Hypokalemia-producing medications, such as:
Amphotericin B, parenteral or
Carbonic anhydrase inhibitors or
Corticosteroids, glucocorticoid, especially those with significant mineralocorticoid activity or
Corticosteroids, mineralocorticoid or
Corticotropin (ACTH) or
Diuretics, potassium-depleting (such as bumetanide, ethacrynic acid, furosemide, indapamide, mannitol, or thiazides) or
Sodium phosphates
(risk of bepridil-induced arrhythmias may be increased)

Hypotension-producing medications, other (see *Appendix II*)
(antihypertensive effects may be potentiated when these medications are used concurrently with hypotension-producing calcium channel blocking agents; although some antihypertensive and/or diuretic combinations are frequently used for therapeutic advantage, when any hypotension-producing medication is used concurrently dosage adjustments may be necessary)

Lithium
(concurrent use with calcium channel blocking agents may result in neurotoxicity in the form of nausea, vomiting, diarrhea, ataxia, tremors, and/or tinnitus; caution is recommended)

Lovastatin
(concomitant use with diltiazem increases mean lovastatin AUC and C_{max} by 3 to 4 times)

Neuromuscular blocking agents
(verapamil may potentiate the activity of curare-like and depolarizing neuromuscular blocking agents; dosage reduction of either or both medications may be necessary during concurrent use)

Phenobarbital
(may increase clearance of verapamil)

Prazosin, and possibly other alpha-adrenergic blocking agents
(concurrent use with calcium channel blocking agents may produce an increased hypotensive effect, possibly related to impairment of compensatory responses by alpha-blockade and/or inhibition of prazosin metabolism by calcium channel blocking agents; caution is recommended)

» Procainamide or
» Quinidine or
» Other medications causing Q-T interval prolongation
(risk of increased Q-T interval prolongation)

(caution is recommended when procainamide or quinidine is used with a calcium channel blocking agent since both groups of medications possess negative inotropic properties)

» Rifampin, and possibly other hepatic enzyme inducers
(rifampin may reduce the bioavailability of oral verapamil by induction of first-pass metabolism; other calcium channel blocking agents may also be affected, depending on the extent of first-pass metabolism)

Sympathomimetics
(concurrent use may reduce antihypertensive effects of calcium channel blocking agents; the patient should be carefully monitored to confirm that the desired effect is being obtained)

Tacrolimus
(concomitant use with felodipine may increase blood concentration of tacrolimus; when given together, tacrolimus blood concentration should be followed and tacrolimus dose may need to be adjusted)

Laboratory value alterations

The following have been selected on the basis of their potential clinical significance (possible effect in parentheses where appropriate)—not necessarily inclusive (» = major clinical significance).

With physiology/laboratory test values
Antinuclear antibody (ANA) titers and
Direct Coombs test, with or without hemolytic anemia
(positive results have been reported during nifedipine therapy)

Arterial blood pressure
(may be reduced by calcium channel blocking agents [except bepridil and flunarizine])

Electrocardiograph (ECG) effects
P-R interval
(may be increased by diltiazem and verapamil)

Note: Increase tends to be proportional to serum concentration.

Q-T interval
(may be increased by bepridil)

T-wave morphology
(may be altered by bepridil)

Hepatic enzymes
may rarely be increased after several days of therapy; concentrations return to normal upon withdrawal of therapy

Prolactin
serum concentrations may be slightly increased by flunarizine

Note: Total serum calcium concentrations are not affected by the calcium channel blocking agents.

Medical considerations/Contraindications

The medical considerations/contraindications included have been selected on the basis of their potential clinical significance (reasons given in parentheses where appropriate)—not necessarily inclusive (» = major clinical significance).

See *Table 2,* page 688.

Patient monitoring

The following may be especially important in patient monitoring (other tests may be warranted in some patients, depending on condition; » = major clinical significance):

» Blood pressure determinations and
» ECG readings and
» Heart rate determinations
(recommended primarily during dosage titration or when dosage is increased from established maintenance dosage level, or during addition of medications affecting cardiac conduction or blood pressure; also recommended during intravenous verapamil administration)

(blood pressure determinations are recommended at periodic intervals in patients being treated for hypertension; selected patients may be trained to perform blood pressure measurements at home and report the results at regular physician visits)

Hepatic function determinations or
Renal function determinations
(may be required at periodic intervals during long-term therapy)

For bepridil
Potassium concentrations, serum
(recommended at periodic intervals during therapy to watch for hypokalemia)

For nimodipine
Neurological examinations
(recommended at periodic intervals during treatment)

For verapamil
PR interval prolongation, abnormal or
Other signs of pharmacologic effects
(careful monitoring in patients with impaired hepatic function)

Side/Adverse Effects

See *Table 3,* page 690.

Patient Consultation

As an aid to patient consultation, refer to *Advice for the Patient, Calcium Channel Blocking Agents (Systemic)*.

In providing consultation, consider emphasizing the following selected information (» = major clinical significance):

Before using this medication

» Conditions affecting use, especially:
Hypersensitivity to the calcium channel blocking agent prescribed
Pregnancy—High doses in animals cause birth defects, prolonged pregnancy, poor bone development, and stillbirth
Use in children—Safety and efficacy not established in pediatric patients for most calcium channel blockers; for amlodipine—safety and efficacy not established for children younger than 6 years of age
Use in the elderly—Elderly patients may be more sensitive to effects
Other medications, especially parenteral amphotericin B (for bepridil), beta-adrenergic blocking agents, carbamazepine, carbonic anhydrase inhibitors, corticosteroids (for bepridil), cyclosporine, digitalis glycosides, disopyramide, erythromycin (for diltiazem and verapamil), grapefruit juice potassium-depleting diuretics (for bepridil), procainamide, or quinidine
Other medical problems, especially arrhythmias (for bepridil), myocardial infarction or pulmonary congestion (diltiazem), other cardiovascular problems, or hypokalemia (for bepridil)

Proper use of this medication

» Compliance with therapy; importance of not taking more medication than amount prescribed

» Proper dosing
Missed dose: Taking as soon as possible; not taking if almost time for next scheduled dose; not doubling doses

» Proper storage

For amlodipine
Possible need for control of weight and diet, especially sodium intake

For bepridil
If nausea occurs, may be taken with meals or at bedtime

For extended-release diltiazem capsules and tablets
Swallowing capsules whole without crushing or chewing
» Caution if switching brands; one is for once-daily dosing and one is for twice-daily dosing

For extended-release verapamil capsules
Swallowing capsules whole without crushing or chewing
(Sprinkling entire contents of capsule on applesauce and taking right away if difficulty swallowing a capsule)

For extended-release felodipine or nifedipine tablets
Swallowing tablets whole, without breaking, crushing, or chewing
For *Adalat XL* and *Procardia XL*—Patient may notice empty shell in stool left over after medication is absorbed
Taking *Adalat CC* on an empty stomach

For extended-release verapamil tablets
Swallowing tablets whole, without crushing or chewing; 240-mg tablet may be broken in half on instructions from physician
Taking with food or milk

For felodipine
Importance of not taking felodipine with grapefruit juice

For use as an antihypertensive
Importance of diet; possible need for sodium restriction and/or weight reduction
» Patient may not experience symptoms of hypertension; importance of taking medication even if feeling well
» Does not cure, but helps control hypertension; possible need for lifelong therapy; serious consequences of untreated hypertension

Precautions while using this medication

Regular visits to physician to check progress during therapy

Checking with physician before discontinuing medication; gradual dosage reduction may be necessary

» Discussing exercise or physical exertion limits with physician; reduced occurrence of chest pain may tempt patient to be overactive

Possible headache; checking with physician if continuing or severe

» Maintaining good dental hygiene and seeing dentist frequently for teeth cleaning to prevent tenderness, bleeding, and gum enlargement

For use as an antihypertensive:
» Not taking other medications, especially nonprescription sympathomimetics, unless discussed with physician

For patients taking bepridil, diltiazem, or verapamil:
» Checking pulse as directed; checking with physician if less than 50 beats per minute

For patients taking flunarizine:
Caution when driving or doing other things requiring alertness because of risk of drowsiness

Side/adverse effects

Signs of potential side effects, especially angina, arrhythmias, congestive heart failure or pulmonary edema, extrapyramidal effects (for flunarizine), galactorrhea (for flunarizine), peripheral edema, tachycardia, bradycardia, excessive hypotension, gingival enlargement, allergic reaction, mental depression (for flunarizine), arthritis (for nifedipine), thrombocytopenia, and transient blindness (for nifedipine)

General Dosing Information

The results of several meta-analyses of clinical trials in post-myocardial infarction patients and patients with angina and of observational studies in hypertensive patients have suggested that taking short-acting nifedipine may increase the risk of adverse cardiovascular events and/or mortality, especially when given in high doses. Consequently, the National Heart, Lung, and Blood Institute (NHLBI) recommends that short-acting nifedipine be used with extreme caution in the treatment of hypertension or angina, especially when given in higher doses. Other drugs, such as beta-adrenergic blocking agents and diuretics, have been found to reduce the risk of major cardiovascular events and mortality in the treatment of hypertension and are recommended as preferred treatment by *The Fifth Report of the Joint National Committee on Detection, Evaluation, and Treatment of High Blood Pressure*.

Amlodipine will not protect against the consequences of abrupt beta-blocker withdrawal; gradual beta-blocker dose reduction is recommended

For oral dosage forms only

Oral dosage must be titrated for each patient as needed and tolerated.

Concurrent administration of nitroglycerin sublingually or long-acting nitrates with calcium channel blocking agents may produce an additive antianginal effect. Nitroglycerin may be used sublingually as required to abort acute angina attacks during calcium channel blocking agent therapy. Nitrate medication may be used during calcium channel blocking agent therapy for angina prophylaxis.

Although no "rebound effect" has been reported upon discontinuation of calcium channel blocking agents, a gradual decrease of dosage with physician supervision is recommended.

Diet/Nutrition

Concurrent administration of felodipine with 200 mL of grapefruit juice has been shown to increase felodipine plasma concentration more than twofold by inhibiting first-pass metabolism in the gastrointestinal wall and/or the liver; a lesser effect also has been seen with two other dihydropyridines, nifedipine and nisoldipine

Amlodipine, unlike other dihyropyridine calcium channel blockers, showed no changes in pharmacokinetics when administered with grapefruit juice

For treatment of overdose or acute adverse effects

The following treatments have been proven effective for the indicated adverse effect:

• Hypotension, symptomatic—Intravenous fluids. Intravenous dopamine or dobutamine, calcium chloride, isoproterenol, metaraminol, or norepinephrine. For parenteral verapamil, placement of patient in Trendelenburg position.

• Tachycardia, rapid ventricular rate in patients with antegrade conduction in atrial flutter fibrillation, and accessory pathway with Wolff-Parkinson-White or Lown-Ganong-Levine syndrome—Direct-current cardioversion or intravenous procainamide. Intravenous fluids given by slow-drip.

• Bradycardia, rarely second- or third-degree atrioventricular (AV) block, with a few patients progressing to asystole—Intravenous atropine, isoproterenol, norepinephrine, or calcium chloride or use of electronic cardiac pacemaker.

AMLODIPINE

Summary of Differences

Pharmacology/pharmacokinetics:
Dihydropyridine structure
Selective calcium channel blocking agent; selectively inhibits calcium influx in cardiac and vascular smooth muscle
Amlodipine has not been associated with a negative inotropic effect when administered in therapeutic doses. It appears to have no significant effect on the sinoatrial (SA) or atrioventricular (AV) node in humans.

Precautions:

Medical considerations/contraindications—Caution should be exercised when administering with any other peripheral vasodilator particularly in patients with severe aortic stenosis. In general, calcium channel blockers should be used with caution in patients with heart failure. Caution should be exercised when administering amlodipine to patients with severe hepatic impairment.

Patients with severe obstructive coronary artery disease have rarely experienced an increased risk of acute myocardial infarction or increased frequency, duration and/or severity of angina during the initiation of amlodipine therapy or at the time of a dosage increase.

Side/adverse effects:

Differences in frequencies are due to differences in pharmacological effects. Also causes edema (common), headache, arrhythmias, including ventricular tachycardia and atrial fibrillation (rare).

Note: In clinical trials there was a greater incidence of edema, flushing and palpitations seen in women than in men.

Note: During postmarketing reporting there has been an association between amlodipine therapy and jaundice and hepatic enzyme elevations (mostly consistent with cholestasis or hepatitis) requiring hospitalization in some patients.

Drug Interactions:

Unlike other dihyropyridine calcium channel blockers, amlodipine showed no changes in pharmacokinetics when administered with grapefruit juice

Unlike other drugs metabolized by cytochrome P450, amlodipine levels was not affected by inhibitors of the enzyme such as cimetidine. Amlodipine did not affect the levels of digoxin or cyclosporin, nor did it change the warfarin-induced prothrombin response time.

Oral dosage forms

AMLODIPINE BESYLATE TABLETS

Usual adult dose

Antianginal or antihypertensive—

Oral, 5 or 10 mg once a day.

Note: An initial antihypertensive dose of 2.5 mg once a day is recommended for small, fragile or elderly patients, patients with hepatic insufficiency, or when adding amlodipine to other antihypertensive therapy.

Note: In general, titration should proceed over 7 to 14 days. Titration may proceed more rapidly if clinically warranted provided the patient is assessed frequently. Most patients will require 10 mg daily for adequate effect.

Usual adult prescribing limits

10 mg daily.

Usual pediatric dose

Antihypertensive—

Children younger than 6 years of age—Safety and efficacy have not been established.

Children 6 years of age and older—Oral, 2.5 to 5 mg once daily.

Usual geriatric dose

See *Usual adult dose*.

Strength(s) usually available

U.S.—

2.5 mg (Rx) [*Norvasc* (microcrystalline cellulose; dibasic calcium phosphate anhydrous; sodium starch glycolate; magnesium stearate)].

5 mg (Rx) [*Norvasc* (microcrystalline cellulose; dibasic calcium phosphate anhydrous; sodium starch glycolate; magnesium stearate)].

10 mg (Rx) [*Norvasc* (microcrystalline cellulose; dibasic calcium phosphate anhydrous; sodium starch glycolate; magnesium stearate)].

Canada—

2.5 mg (Rx) [*Norvasc* (microcrystalline cellulose; dibasic calcium phosphate anhydrous; sodium starch glycolate; magnesium stearate)].

5 mg (Rx) [*Norvasc* (microcrystalline cellulose; dibasic calcium phosphate anhydrous; sodium starch glycolate; magnesium stearate)].

10 mg (Rx) [*Norvasc* (microcrystalline cellulose; dibasic calcium phosphate anhydrous; sodium starch glycolate; magnesium stearate)].

Packaging and storage

Store at controlled room temperature, preferably between 15 and 30 °C (59 and 86 °F), in a tight, light-resistant container.

BEPRIDIL

Summary of Differences

Pharmacology/pharmacokinetics:

Nonselective calcium channel blocking agent; also affects fast sodium inward current.

Depresses sinoatrial (SA) and atrioventricular (AV) nodes; negative inotropic effect; causes bradycardia.

Precautions:

Laboratory value alterations—Increases Q-T interval and alters T-wave morphology.

Medical considerations/contraindications—Contraindicated in patients with history of serious ventricular arrhythmias or Q-T interval prolongation. Also, contraindicated in patients with second- or third-degree atrioventricular (AV) block or sinoatrial (SA) nodal function impairment, except in patients with a functioning artificial ventricular pacemaker. Extreme caution necessary in patients with hypokalemia.

Side/adverse effects:

Differences in frequencies are due to differences in pharmacological effects. Also causes agranulocytosis (rare); arrhythmias, including torsades de pointes (less common).

Oral Dosage Forms

BEPRIDIL HYDROCHLORIDE TABLETS

Usual adult dose

Antianginal—

Oral, initially 200 mg once a day, the dosage being increased after ten days, if necessary, to 300 mg once a day.

Usual adult prescribing limits

400 mg daily.

Usual pediatric dose

Safety and efficacy have not been established.

Usual geriatric dose

See *Usual adult dose*.

Strength(s) usually available

U.S.—

200 mg (Rx) [*Vascor*].

300 mg (Rx) [*Vascor*].

400 mg (Rx) [*Vascor*].

Canada—

Not commercially available.

Packaging and storage

Store below 40 °C (104 °F), preferably between 15 and 30 °C (59 and 86 °F), in a well-closed container, unless otherwise specified by manufacturer. Protect from light.

DILTIAZEM

Summary of Differences

Pharmacology/pharmacokinetics:

Benzothiazepine structure.

Depresses sinoatrial (SA) and atrioventricular (AV) nodes; little or no negative inotropic effect; usually does not significantly alter heart rate, but may cause slight bradycardia.

Precautions:

Laboratory value alterations—Increases P-R interval.

Medical considerations/contraindications—Contraindicated in patients with second- or third-degree atrioventricular (AV) block, sinoatrial (SA) nodal function impairment, myocardial infarction and pulmonary congestion, or Wolff-Parkinson-White or Lown-Ganong-Levine syndrome accompanied by atrial flutter or fibrillation, except in patients with a functioning artificial ventricular pacemaker.

Side/adverse effects:

Differences in frequencies are due to differences in pharmacological effects.

Additional Dosing Information

See also *General Dosing Information*.

Dermatologic side effects usually disappear even with continued use. However, if skin eruptions persist, it is recommended that diltiazem therapy be withdrawn, since progression to erythema multiforme and/or exfoliative dermatitis or Stevens-Johnson syndrome have been reported rarely.

Oral Dosage Forms

Note: Bracketed uses in the *Dosage Forms* section refer to categories of use and/or indications that are not included in U.S. product labeling.

DILTIAZEM HYDROCHLORIDE EXTENDED-RELEASE CAPSULES

Usual adult and adolescent dose

Antihypertensive—

Cardizem CD or *Dilacor-XR*: Oral, 180 to 240 mg once a day, the dosage being adjusted after fourteen days as needed and tolerated.

Note: The total daily dose usually ranges from 240 to 360 mg.

Cardizem SR: Oral, initially 60 to 120 mg two times a day, the dosage being adjusted after fourteen days as needed and tolerated.

Note: Geriatric patients may be more sensitive to the effects of the usual adult dose.

Usual adult prescribing limits

360 mg daily.

Usual pediatric dose

Dosage has not been established.

Strength(s) usually available

U.S.—

60 mg (Rx) [*Cardizem SR* (sucrose); GENERIC].

90 mg (Rx) [*Cardizem SR* (sucrose); GENERIC].

120 mg (Rx) [*Cardizem CD; Cardizem SR* (sucrose); *Dilacor-XR;* GENERIC].

180 mg (Rx) [*Cardizem CD* (sucrose); *Dilacor-XR*].

240 mg (Rx) [*Cardizem CD* (sucrose); *Dilacor-XR*].

300 mg (Rx) [*Cardizem CD* (sucrose)].

Canada—

90 mg (Rx) [*Cardizem SR*].

120 mg (Rx) [*Cardizem SR*].

Packaging and storage

Store below 40 °C (104 °F), preferably between 15 and 30 °C (59 and 86 °F), in a well-closed container, unless otherwise specified by manufacturer.

Auxiliary labeling

- Do not take other medicines without physician's advice.

Note

Check refill frequency to determine compliance in hypertensive patients.

Cardizem CD and *Cardizem SR* can be used interchangeably on a total daily mg-per-mg dosing basis.

DILTIAZEM HYDROCHLORIDE EXTENDED-RELEASE TABLETS

Usual adult and adolescent dose

Angina (treatment)—

Cardizem LA: Oral, 180 mg once daily, may be increased at 7 to 14-day intervals if adequate response is not obtained.

Antihypertensive—

Cardizem LA: Oral, 180 to 240 mg once daily, the dosage being adjusted after fourteen days as needed and tolerated.

Usual adult prescribing limits

Angina (treatment): 360 mg daily; doses above 360 mg confer no additional benefit.

Antihypertensive: 540 mg daily

Usual pediatric dose

Safety and efficacy have not been established.

Strength(s) usually available

U.S.—

120 mg (Rx) [*Cardizem LA* (carnauba wax; colloidal silicon dioxide; croscarmellose sodium; hydrogenated vegetable oil; hypromellose; magnesium stearate; microcrystalline cellulose; microcrystalline wax; pregelatinized starch; polyacrylate dispersion 30%; polyethylene glycol; polydextrose; polysorbate; povidone; simethicone; sucrose stearate; titanium dioxide; triacetin)].

180 mg (Rx) [*Cardizem LA* (carnauba wax; colloidal silicon dioxide; croscarmellose sodium; hydrogenated vegetable oil; hypromellose; magnesium stearate; microcrystalline cellulose; microcrystalline wax; pregelatinized starch; polyacrylate dispersion 30%; polyethylene glycol; polydextrose; polysorbate; povidone; simethicone; sucrose stearate; titanium dioxide; triacetin)].

240 mg (Rx) [*Cardizem LA* (carnauba wax; colloidal silicon dioxide; croscarmellose sodium; hydrogenated vegetable oil; hypromellose; magnesium stearate; microcrystalline cellulose; microcrystalline wax; pregelatinized starch; polyacrylate dispersion 30%; polyethylene glycol; polydextrose; polysorbate; povidone; simethicone; sucrose stearate; titanium dioxide; triacetin)].

300 mg (Rx) [*Cardizem LA* (carnauba wax; colloidal silicon dioxide; croscarmellose sodium; hydrogenated vegetable oil; hypromellose; magnesium stearate; microcrystalline cellulose; microcrystalline wax; pregelatinized starch; polyacrylate dispersion 30%; polyethylene glycol; polydextrose; polysorbate; povidone; simethicone; sucrose stearate; titanium dioxide; triacetin)].

360 mg (Rx) [*Cardizem LA* (carnauba wax; colloidal silicon dioxide; croscarmellose sodium; hydrogenated vegetable oil; hypromellose; magnesium stearate; microcrystalline cellulose; microcrystalline wax; pregelatinized starch; polyacrylate dispersion 30%; polyethylene glycol; polydextrose; polysorbate; povidone; simethicone; sucrose stearate; titanium dioxide; triacetin)].

420 mg (Rx) [*Cardizem LA* (carnauba wax; colloidal silicon dioxide; croscarmellose sodium; hydrogenated vegetable oil; hypromellose; magnesium stearate; microcrystalline cellulose; microcrystalline wax; pregelatinized starch; polyacrylate dispersion 30%; polyethylene glycol; polydextrose; polysorbate; povidone; simethicone; sucrose stearate; titanium dioxide; triacetin)].

Packaging and storage

Store below 25 °C (77 °F), preferably between 15 and 30 °C (59 and 86 °F) in a tight, light resistant container. Avoid excessive humidity and temperatures above 30 °C (86 °F).

Auxiliary labeling

- Do not take other medicines without physician's advice.
- Swallow whole. Do not crush or chew.

Note

Check refill frequency to determine compliance in hypertensive patients.

Cardizem CD and *Cardizem SR* can be used interchangeably on a total daily mg-per-mg dosing basis.

Additional information

Cardizem LA tablets should be taken about the same time once each day either in the morning or at bedtime. The time of dosing should be considered when making dose adjustments based on trough effects.

DILTIAZEM HYDROCHLORIDE TABLETS USP

Usual adult and adolescent dose

Antianginal or

[Antihypertensive][1]—

Oral, initially 30 mg three or four times a day, the dosage being increased gradually at one- or two-day intervals as needed and tolerated.

Note: Geriatric patients may be more sensitive to the effects of the usual adult dose.

Usual adult prescribing limits

360 mg daily.

Usual pediatric dose

Dosage has not been established.

Strength(s) usually available

U.S.—

30 mg (Rx) [*Cardizem;* GENERIC].

60 mg (Rx) [*Cardizem* (scored); GENERIC].

90 mg (Rx) [*Cardizem* (scored); GENERIC].

120 mg (Rx) [*Cardizem* (scored); GENERIC].

Canada—

30 mg (Rx) [*Apo-Diltiaz; Cardizem; Novo-Diltazem; Nu-Diltiaz; Syn-Diltiazem;* GENERIC].

60 mg (Rx) [*Apo-Diltiaz; Cardizem* (scored); *Novo-Diltazem* (scored); *Nu-Diltiaz; Syn-Diltiazem* (scored); GENERIC].

90 mg (Rx) [*Cardizem*].

120 mg (Rx) [*Cardizem*].

Packaging and storage

Store below 40 °C (104 °F), preferably between 15 and 30 °C (59 and 86 °F), unless otherwise specified by manufacturer. Store in a tight container. Protect from light.

Auxiliary labeling

- Do not take other medicines without physician's advice.

Note

Check refill frequency to determine compliance in hypertensive patients.

Parenteral Dosage Forms

DILTIAZEM HYDROCHLORIDE INJECTION

Usual adult and adolescent dose

Antiarrhythmic—

Intravenous (rapid), 250 mcg (0.25 mg) per kg of actual body weight administered slowly over a two-minute period with continuous ECG and blood pressure monitoring. If response is not adequate, 350 mcg (0.35 mg) per kg of actual body weight may be administered fifteen minutes after completion of initial dose. Subsequent doses should be individualized.

Note: Some patients may respond to an initial dose of 150 mcg (0.15 mg) per kg of actual body weight, although the duration of action may be shorter.

Intravenous infusion, continuous (for continued reduction of heart rate [up to twenty-four hours] in patients with atrial fibrillation or atrial flutter), initially 10 mg per hour beginning immediately after the last rapid intravenous dose. The rate of infusion may be increased in increments of 5 mg per hour as needed, up to a maximum rate of 15 mg per hour.

Note: Some patients may respond to an initial rate of 5 mg per hour.

Usual pediatric dose

Safety and efficacy have not been established.

Strength(s) usually available

U.S.—

5 mg per mL (Rx) [*Cardizem;* GENERIC].

Canada—

5 mg per mL (Rx) [*Cardizem;* GENERIC].

Packaging and storage

Store between 2 and 8 °C (36 and 46 °F), unless otherwise specified by manufacturer. May be stored at room temperature for 1 month; destroy after 1 month at room temperature. Protect from freezing.

Preparation of dosage form

Diltiazem hydrochloride injection may be prepared for administration by continuous intravenous infusion by diluting the appropriate quantity in the desired volume of 0.9% sodium chloride injection, 5% dextrose injection, or 5% dextrose in 0.45% sodium chloride injection, and mixing thoroughly, as follows:

Diluent volume	Quantity of cardizem injection	Final concentrations	Administration Dose*	Administration Infusion rate
100 mL	125 mg (25 mL)	1.0 mg/mL	10 mg/hr 15 mg/hr	10 mL/hr 15 mL/hr
250 mL	250 mg (50 mL)	0.83 mg/mL	10 mg/hr 15 mg/hr	12 mL/hr 18 mL/hr
500 mL	250 mg (50 mL)	0.45 mg/mL	10 mg/hr 15 mg/hr	22 mL/hr 33 mL/hr

*5 mg/hr may be appropriate for some patients.

Stability

After dilution for administration by intravenous infusion, diltiazem hydrochloride injection should be refrigerated until use and should be used within 24 hours.

Incompatibilities

Diltiazem hydrochloride injection is physically incompatible with furosemide solution.

[1]Not included in Canadian product labeling.

FELODIPINE

Summary of Differences

Pharmacology/pharmacokinetics:

Dihydropyridine structure.

Potent peripheral vasodilator; does not depress sinoatrial (SA) or atrioventricular (AV) node; reflex increase in heart rate in response to vasodilation masks negative inotropic effect.

Precautions:

Medical considerations/contraindications—No caution necessary in renal function impairment.

Side/adverse effects:

Differences in frequencies are due to differences in pharmacological effects.

Oral Dosage Forms

FELODIPINE EXTENDED-RELEASE TABLETS

Usual adult dose

Antihypertensive—

Initial: Oral, 5 mg once a day, the dosage being adjusted as needed, usually at intervals of not less than two weeks.

Maintenance: Oral, 5 to 10 mg once a day.

Antianginal—

Oral, 10 mg once a day.

Note: Geriatric patients may be more sensitive to the effects of the usual adult dose.

Usual adult prescribing limits

20 mg once a day.

Usual pediatric dose

Safety and efficacy have not been established.

Strength(s) usually available

U.S.—

2.5 mg [*Plendil*].

5 mg (Rx) [*Plendil*].

10 mg (Rx) [*Plendil*].

Canada—

2.5 mg [*Plendil; Renedil*].

5 mg (Rx) [*Plendil; Renedil*].

10 mg (Rx) [*Plendil; Renedil*].

Packaging and storage

Store below 30 °C (86 °F), unless otherwise specified by manufacturer. Store in a tight container. Protect from light.

Auxiliary labeling

- Do not take other medicines without physician's advice.

Note

Check refill frequency to determine compliance in hypertensive patients.

FLUNARIZINE

Summary of Differences

Indications:

Indicated for prophylaxis of migraine.

Pharmacology/pharmacokinetics:

Diphenylpiperazine structure.

Does not depress sinoatrial (SA) or atrioventricular (AV) node; no negative inotropic effect; no reflex increase in heart rate; no antihypertensive effect.

Cerebroselective.

Precautions:

Medical considerations/contraindications—Caution required in patients with history of mental depression or with Parkinsonian syndrome or other extrapyramidal disorders.

Side/adverse effects:

Differences in frequencies are due to differences in pharmacological effects. Also causes parkinsonian extrapyramidal effects (less common), galactorrhea (rare), mental depression (less common), drowsiness (more common), dryness of mouth (less common), increased appetite and/or weight gain (more common).

Oral Dosage Forms

FLUNARIZINE HYDROCHLORIDE CAPSULES

Usual adult dose

Vascular headache prophylactic—

Oral, 10 mg once a day in the evening.

Note: Geriatric patients may be more sensitive to the effects of the usual adult dose.

Usual pediatric dose

Dosage has not been established.

Strength(s) usually available

U.S.—

Not commercially available.

Canada—

5 mg (Rx) [*Sibelium*].

Packaging and storage

Store below 40 °C (104 °F), preferably between 15 and 30 °C (59 and 86 °F), in a well-closed container, unless otherwise specified by manufacturer. Protect from light.

ISRADIPINE

Summary of Differences

Pharmacology/pharmacokinetics:
Dihydropyridine structure.
Potent peripheral vasodilator; does not depress sinoatrial (SA) or atrioventricular (AV) node; reflex increase in heart rate in response to vasodilation masks negative inotropic effect.

Side/adverse effects:
Differences in frequencies are due to differences in pharmacological effects.

Oral Dosage Forms

ISRADIPINE CAPSULES

Usual adult dose

Antihypertensive—
Oral, initially 2.5 mg two times a day, alone or in combination with a thiazide diuretic, the dosage being increased, if necessary, in increments of 5 mg per day at two- to four-week intervals.

Note: Geriatric patients may be more sensitive to the effects of the usual adult dose.

Usual adult prescribing limits

10 mg two times a day.

Usual pediatric dose

Safety and efficacy have not been established.

Strength(s) usually available

U.S.—
2.5 mg (Rx) [*DynaCirc*].
5 mg (Rx) [*DynaCirc*].

Canada—
Not commercially available.

Packaging and storage

Store below 40 °C (104 °F) between 15 and 30 °C (59 and 86 °F), unless otherwise specified by manufacturer. Store in a tight container. Protect from light.

Auxiliary labeling

- Do not take other medicines without physician's advice.

Note

Check refill frequency to determine compliance in hypertensive patients.

NICARDIPINE

Summary of Differences

Pharmacology/pharmacokinetics:
Dihydropyridine structure.
Potent peripheral vasodilator; does not depress sinoatrial (SA) or atrioventricular (AV) node; reflex increase in heart rate in response to vasodilation masks negative inotropic effect.

Precautions:
Geriatrics—No change in half-life or protein binding.
Medical considerations/contraindications—Caution necessary in patients with acute cerebral infarction or hemorrhage.

Side/adverse effects:
Differences in frequencies are due to differences in pharmacological effects.

Oral Dosage Forms

NICARDIPINE HYDROCHLORIDE CAPSULES

Usual adult and adolescent dose

Antianginal or
Antihypertensive—
Oral, initially 20 mg three times a day, the dosage being adjusted as needed and tolerated.

Usual pediatric dose

Dosage has not been established.

Strength(s) usually available

U.S.—
20 mg (Rx) [*Cardene;* GENERIC].
30 mg (Rx) [*Cardene;* GENERIC].

Canada—
Not commercially available

Packaging and storage

Store between 15 and 25 °C (59 and 77 °F), in a well-closed, light-resistant container, unless otherwise specified by manufacturer.

Auxiliary labeling

- Do not take other medicines without physician's advice.

Note

Check refill frequency to determine compliance in hypertensive patients.

NIFEDIPINE

Summary of Differences

Pharmacology/pharmacokinetics:
Dihydropyridine structure.
Potent peripheral vasodilator; does not depress sinoatrial (SA) or atrioventricular (AV) node; reflex increase in heart rate in response to vasodilation masks negative inotropic effect.

Precautions:
The results of several meta-analyses of clinical trials in post-myocardial infarction patients and patients with angina and of observational studies in hypertensive patients have suggested that taking short-acting nifedipine may increase the risk of adverse cardiovascular events and/or mortality, especially when given in high doses. Consequently, the National Heart, Lung, and Blood Institute (NHLBI) recommends that short-acting nifedipine be used with extreme caution in the treatment of hypertension or angina, especially at higher doses. Other drugs, such as beta-adrenergic blocking agents and diuretics, have been found to reduce the risk of major cardiovascular events and mortality in the treatment of hypertension and are recommended as preferred treatment by *The Fifth Report of the Joint National Committee on Detection, Evaluation, and Treatment of High Blood Pressure.*

Side/adverse effects:
Differences in frequencies are due to differences in pharmacological effects. Also causes arthritis associated with elevated antinuclear antibody (ANA) titers (rare), transient blindness at peak plasma concentrations (rare).

Additional Dosing Information

See also *General Dosing Information.*

In solution, degradation of nifedipine occurs more rapidly at 25 °C (77 °F) than at 4 °C (39 °F). However, when nifedipine solutions are protected from light and refrigerated, concentrations of nifedipine decline to approximately 90% of the original concentrations within 6 hours of preparation. It is recommended that extemporaneous preparations be made immediately before use.

Oral Dosage Forms

Note: Bracketed uses in the *Dosage Forms* section refer to categories of use and/or indications that are not included in U.S. product labeling.

NIFEDIPINE CAPSULES USP

Usual adult and adolescent dose

Antianginal or
[Antihypertensive][1]—
Essential hypertension: Oral, initially 10 mg three times a day, the dosage being increased over a seven- to fourteen-day period as needed and tolerated.

Note: For hospitalized patients under close supervision, dosage may be increased by 10-mg increments over four- to six-hour periods until symptoms are controlled.

When justified by symptom frequency and/or severity, dosage titration may be accomplished over a three-day period (medication given three times a day and increased stepwise from 10 mg to 20 mg, then to 30 mg per dose as needed and tolerated), but only if the patient is monitored frequently.

Geriatric patients may be more sensitive to the effects of the usual adult dose.

Usual adult prescribing limits

Single dose, up to 30 mg; total daily dose, up to 180 mg (a total daily dose greater than 120 mg is rarely required).

Usual pediatric dose

Dosage has not been established.

Strength(s) usually available

U.S.—
10 mg (Rx) [*Adalat; Procardia;* GENERIC].
20 mg (Rx) [*Adalat; Procardia;* GENERIC].

Canada—
5 mg (Rx) [*Adalat*].
10 mg (Rx) [*Adalat; Apo-Nifed; Novo-Nifedin; Nu-Nifed*].

Packaging and storage

Store between 15 and 25 °C (59 and 77 °F), unless otherwise specified by manufacturer. Store in a tight, light-resistant container.

Auxiliary labeling

- Do not take other medicines without physician's advice.

Note

Check refill frequency to determine compliance in hypertensive patients.

NIFEDIPINE EXTENDED-RELEASE TABLETS

Usual adult and adolescent dose

Antianginal—
Adalat XL or *Procardia XL*—
Oral, 30 or 60 mg once a day, the dosage being adjusted over a seven- to fourteen-day period as needed and tolerated.

Antihypertensive—
Adalat CC—
Initial—Oral, 30 mg once a day.
Maintenance—Oral, 30 to 60 mg once a day, the dosage being adjusted over a seven- to fourteen-day period as needed and tolerated.

Note: *Adalat CC* should be taken on an empty stomach.

Adalat PA—
Initial—Oral, 10 or 20 mg two times a day. The full antihypertensive effect may not be apparent for three weeks; therefore, a dosage increase, if needed, should occur at three-week intervals.
Maintenance—Oral, 20 mg two times a day.

Note: Geriatric patients may be more sensitive to the effects of the usual adult dose.

Adalat XL—
Initial—Oral, 30 or 60 mg once a day, the dosage being adjusted over a seven- to fourteen-day period as needed and tolerated.
Maintenance—Oral, 60 to 90 mg once daily.

Procardia XL—
Oral, 30 or 60 mg once a day, the dosage being adjusted over a seven- to fourteen-day period as needed and tolerated

Usual adult prescribing limits

Antianginal—
90 mg a day (*Adalat XL*, *Procardia XL*).

Antihypertensive—
90 mg a day (*Adalat CC*), or 80 mg a day (*Adalat PA*), or 120 mg a day (*Adalat XL*, *Procardia XL*)

Usual pediatric dose

Dosage has not been established.

Strength(s) usually available

U.S.—
30 mg (Rx) [*Adalat CC; Procardia XL*].
60 mg (Rx) [*Adalat CC; Procardia XL*].
90 mg (Rx) [*Adalat CC; Procardia XL*].

Canada—
10 mg [*Adalat PA*].
20 mg [*Adalat PA*].
30 mg [*Adalat XL*].
60 mg [*Adalat XL*].

Note: Although similar in appearance to conventional tablets, *Adalat XL* and *Procardia XL* consist of an osmotically active drug core surrounded by a semipermeable membrane which is designed to release nifedipine at a constant rate over 24 hours; following the release of the drug, the insoluble tablet shell is eliminated in the feces.

Packaging and storage

Store below 40 °C (104 °F), preferably between 15 and 30 °C (59 and 86 °F), in a well-closed container, unless otherwise specified by manufacturer.

Auxiliary labeling

- Do not take other medicines without physician's advice.

Adalat CC
- Do not take other medicines without physician's advice.
- Take on empty stomach.

Note

Check refill frequency to determine compliance in hypertensive patients.

[1]Not included in Canadian product labeling.

NIMODIPINE

Summary of Differences

Indications:
Indicated for treatment of subarachnoid hemorrhage-associated neurologic deficits.

Pharmacology/pharmacokinetics:
Dihydropyridine structure.
Potent peripheral vasodilator; does not depress sinoatrial (SA) or atrioventricular (AV) node; no negative inotropic effect; reflex increase in heart rate in response to vasodilation occurs.
Cerebroselective.

Side/adverse effects:
Differences in frequencies are due to differences in pharmacological effects. Also causes thrombocytopenia (rare).

Oral Dosage Forms

NIMODIPINE CAPSULES

Usual adult dose

Subarachnoid hemorrhage-associated neurologic deficits—
Oral, 60 mg every four hours, beginning within ninety-six hours after the subarachnoid hemorrhage and continuing for twenty-one days.

Note: In patients with hepatic function impairment, dosage should be reduced to 30 mg every four hours, with close monitoring of blood pressure and heart rate.
Geriatric patients may be more sensitive to the effects of the usual adult dose.

Usual pediatric dose

Dosage has not been established.

Strength(s) usually available

U.S.—
30 mg (Rx) [*Nimotop*].

Canada—
30 mg (Rx) [*Nimotop*].

Packaging and storage

Store between 15 and 30 °C (59 and 86 °F), in a well-closed container, unless otherwise specified by manufacturer. Protect from light. Protect from freezing.

Preparation of dosage form

For patients who cannot take oral solids—
For patients who cannot swallow, a hole may be made in both ends of the capsule with an 18 gauge needle and the contents of the capsule withdrawn into a syringe, and then emptied into the patient's nasogastric tube and washed down the tube with 30 mL of 0.9% sodium chloride solution.

VERAPAMIL

Summary of Differences

Indications:
Indicated for treatment of supraventricular tachyarrhythmias; oral dosage form indicated for prophylaxis.
Also used to treat hypertrophic cardiomyopathy.

Pharmacology/pharmacokinetics:
Diphenylalkylamine structure.
Depresses sinoatrial (SA) and atrioventricular (AV) nodes; usually does not significantly alter heart rate but may cause bradycardia; negative inotropic effect countered by reduction in afterload.

Precautions:
Pediatrics—In rare instances, severe adverse hemodynamic effects have occurred after intravenous administration of verapamil in neonates and infants.
Laboratory value alterations—Prolongs P-R interval in serum concentrations greater than 30 nanograms per mL.
Medical considerations/contraindications—Contraindicated in patients with second- or third-degree atrioventricular (AV) block, sinoatrial (SA) nodal function impairment, or Wolff-Parkinson-White or Lown-Ganong-Levine syndrome accompanied by atrial flutter or fibrillation, except in patients with a functioning artificial ventricular pacemaker. Caution necessary in patients with neuromuscular transmission deficiency, and wide-complex ventricular tachycardia (with intravenous use).

Side/adverse effects:
Differences in frequencies are due to differences in pharmacological effects.

Additional Dosing Information

See also *General Dosing Information.*

Dermatologic side effects usually disappear even with continued use. However, if skin eruptions persist, it is recommended that verapamil therapy be withdrawn, since progression to erythema multiforme has been reported rarely.

For parenteral dosage forms only

Parenteral dosage is indicated in the management of cardiac arrhythmias with close monitoring. Emergency equipment and medications should be readily available.

Oral Dosage Forms

Note: Bracketed uses in the *Dosage Forms* section refer to categories of use and/or indications that are not included in U.S. product labeling.

VERAPAMIL TABLETS USP

Note: The dosing and strengths of verapamil are expressed in terms of hydrochloride salt.

Usual adult and adolescent dose

Antianginal
Antiarrhythmic
Antihypertensive or[1]
[Hypertrophic cardiomyopathy therapy adjunct]—

Oral, initially 80 to 120 mg (HCl) three times a day, the dosage being increased at daily or weekly intervals as needed and tolerated.

Note: An initial dose of 40 mg (HCl) three times a day is recommended in patients who may have an increased response to verapamil (e.g., those with hepatic function impairment, elderly patients, patients with poor left ventricular function).

The total daily dose usually ranges from 240 to 480 mg.

Because of prolongation of the half-life with repeated dosing, decreased frequency of dosing may be possible; dosage should be individualized.

Geriatric patients may be more sensitive to the effects of the usual adult dose.

Usual adult prescribing limits

480 mg (HCl) daily in divided doses; has been used in doses up to 720 mg per day in the treatment of hypertrophic cardiomyopathy.

Usual pediatric dose

For infants less than 1 year and children 1 to 15 years of age—Oral, 4 to 8 mg (HCl) per kg of body weight per day in divided doses.

Usual geriatric dose

Oral, initially 40 mg (HCl) three times a day, the dosage being adjusted as needed and tolerated.

Strength(s) usually available

U.S.—
40 mg (HCl) (Rx) [*Calan; Isoptin* (scored); GENERIC].
80 mg (HCl) (Rx) [*Calan* (scored); *Isoptin* (scored); GENERIC].
120 mg (HCl) (Rx) [*Calan* (scored); *Isoptin* (scored); GENERIC].

Canada—
80 mg (HCl) (Rx) [*Apo-Verap; Isoptin; Novo-Veramil; Nu-Verap;* GENERIC].
120 mg (HCl) (Rx) [*Apo-Verap; Isoptin; Novo-Veramil; Nu-Verap;* GENERIC].

Packaging and storage

Store below 40 °C (104 °F), preferably between 15 and 30 °C (59 and 86 °F), unless otherwise specified by manufacturer. Store in a tight container. Protect from light.

Auxiliary labeling

- Do not take other medicines without physician's advice.

Note

Check refill frequency to determine compliance in hypertensive patients.

VERAPAMIL HYDROCHLORIDE EXTENDED-RELEASE CAPSULES

Usual adult and adolescent dose

Antihypertensive—

Oral, initially 240 mg once a day, the dosage being increased in increments of 120 mg per day at daily or weekly intervals as needed and tolerated.

Note: An initial dose of 120 mg per day is recommended in patients who may have an increased response to verapamil (e.g., elderly, small people, etc.).

The total daily dose usually ranges from 240 to 480 mg.

Geriatric patients may be more sensitive to the effects of the usual adult dose.

Usual pediatric dose

Dosage has not been established.

Strength(s) usually available

U.S.—
120 mg (Rx) [*Verelan*].
180 mg (Rx) [*Verelan*].
240 mg (Rx) [*Verelan*].
360 mg (Rx) [*Verelan*].

Canada—
120 mg (Rx) [*Verelan*].
180 mg (Rx) [*Verelan*].
240 mg (Rx) [*Verelan*].

Packaging and storage

Store below 40 °C (104 °F), preferably between 15 and 30 °C (59 and 86 °F), unless otherwise specified by manufacturer. Store in a tight container. Protect from light.

Auxiliary labeling

- Do not take other medicines without physician's advice.

Note

Check refill frequency to determine compliance in hypertensive patients.

VERAPAMIL HYDROCHLORIDE EXTENDED-RELEASE CAPSULES CONTROLLED-ONSET

Usual adult and adolescent dose

Antihypertensive—

Oral, initially 200 mg once daily at bedtime with dosage being increased in increments of 100 mg per day based on therapeutic efficacy and safety evaluated approximately 24 hours after dosing.

Note: An initial dose of 100 mg per day is recommended in patients who may have an increased response to verapamil (e.g., elderly, small people, etc.).

Total daily dose usually ranges from 200 to 400 mg.

Geriatric patients may be more sensitive to the effects of the usual adult dose.

Usual pediatric dose

Dosage has not been established.

Strength(s) usually available

U.S.—
100 mg (Rx) [*Verelan PM* (controlled-onset; D&C Red #28; FD&C Blue #1; FD&C red #40; fumaric acid; gelatin; povidone; shellac; silicon dioxide; sodium lauryl sulfate; starch; sugar spheres; talc; titanium dioxide)].
200 mg (Rx) [*Verelan PM* (controlled-onset; D&C Red #28; FD&C Blue #1; FD&C red #40; fumaric acid; gelatin; povidone; shellac; silicon dioxide; sodium lauryl sulfate; starch; sugar spheres; talc; titanium dioxide)].
300 mg (Rx) [*Verelan PM* (controlled-onset; D&C Red #28; FD&C Blue #1; FD&C red #40; fumaric acid; gelatin; povidone; shellac; silicon dioxide; sodium lauryl sulfate; starch; sugar spheres; talc; titanium dioxide)].

Packaging and storage

Store below 25 °C (77 °F), preferably between 15 and 30 °C (59 and 86 °F) in a tight, light resistant container. Avoid excessive humidity.

Preparation of dosage form

If patient has difficulty swallowing, capsule contents can be sprinkled on applesauce for immediate use. Pellets should not be crushed or chewed.

Auxiliary labeling

- Do not take other medicines without physician's advice.
- Swallow whole. Do not crush or chew.

Note

Check refill frequency to determine compliance in hypertensive patients.

VERAPAMIL HYDROCHLORIDE EXTENDED-RELEASE TABLETS

Usual adult and adolescent dose

Antihypertensive—

Oral, initially 180 mg once a day in the morning with food, the dosage being increased at daily or weekly intervals as needed and tolerated in the following order: 240 mg once a day in the morning; 180 mg every twelve hours or 240 mg in the morning and 120 mg in the evening; 240 mg every twelve hours.

Note: Lower initial doses (e.g., 120 mg per day) may be necessary in patients with a potential increased response to verapamil.

Calan SR and *Isoptin SR* 240 mg tablets may be broken in half, but should not be crushed or chewed.

Geriatric patients may be more sensitive to the effects of the usual adult dose.

Usual pediatric dose
Dosage has not been established.

Strength(s) usually available
U.S.—
- 120 mg (Rx) [*Calan SR; Isoptin SR*].
- 180 mg (Rx) [*Calan SR; Isoptin SR*].
- 240 mg (Rx) [*Calan SR* (scored); *Isoptin SR* (scored)].

Canada—
- 120 mg (Rx) [*Isoptin SR*].
- 180 mg (Rx) [*Isoptin SR*].
- 240 mg (Rx) [*Isoptin SR* (scored)].

Packaging and storage
Store below 40 °C (104 °F), preferably between 15 and 30 °C (59 and 86 °F), unless otherwise specified by manufacturer. Store in a tight, light-resistant container.

Auxiliary labeling
- Take with meals or milk.
- Do not take other medicines without physician's advice.

Note
Check refill frequency to determine compliance in hypertensive patients.

Parenteral Dosage Forms

VERAPAMIL INJECTION USP
Note: The dosing and strengths of verapamil are expressed in terms of hydrochloride salt.

Usual adult dose
Intravenous, initially 5 to 10 mg (HCl) (or 75 to 150 mcg [0.075 to 0.15 mg] per kg of body weight) administered slowly over a two-minute period with continuous ECG and blood pressure monitoring. If response is not adequate, 10 mg (or 150 mcg [0.15 mg] per kg of body weight) may be administered thirty minutes after completion of initial dose.

Note: In geriatric patients, the intravenous dose should be administered slowly over a three-minute period to minimize undesired effects.

Usual pediatric dose
The following doses should be administered slowly over a two-minute period, with continuous ECG monitoring. If response is not adequate, a repeat dose may be administered thirty minutes after completion of initial dose.

Infants up to 1 year of age—Initially, 100 to 200 mcg (HCl) (0.1 to 0.2 mg) per kg of body weight (usual single dose range, 0.75 to 2 mg).

Children 1 to 15 years of age—Initially, 100 to 300 mcg (HCl) (0.1 to 0.3 mg) per kg of body weight (usual single dose range, 2 to 5 mg) not to exceed a total of 5 mg. For repeat dose, thirty minutes after initial dose, do not exceed 10 mg as a single dose.

Strength(s) usually available
U.S.—
- 2.5 mg (HCl) per mL (Rx) [*Isoptin;* GENERIC (sodium chloride 8.5 mg per mL)].

Canada—
- 2.5 mg (HCl) per mL (Rx) [*Isoptin;* GENERIC].

Packaging and storage
Store between 15 and 30 °C (59 and 86 °F), unless otherwise specified by manufacturer. Protect from light. Protect from freezing.

Stability
Verapamil hydrochloride injection is physically and chemically compatible with Ringer's injection or 5% dextrose or 0.9% sodium chloride injection.

Incompatibilities
Verapamil hydrochloride injection is physically incompatible with albumin, amphotericin B injection, hydralazine hydrochloride injection, and sulfamethoxazole and trimethoprim injection. Precipitation of verapamil hydrochloride will occur in any solution with a pH greater than 6.

---

[1]Not included in Canadian product labeling.

Selected Bibliography
Pickard JD, Murray GD, Illingworth R, et al. Effect of oral nimodipine on cerebral infarction and outcome after subarachnoid hemorrhage: British aneurysm nimodipine trial. Br Med J 1989 Mar 11; 298: 636-42.

General
Freedman DD, Waters DD. "Second generation" dihydropyridine calcium antagonists. Greater vascular selectivity and some unique applications. Drugs 1987; 34: 578-98.

Tracy TS, Black CD. Calcium modulators: future agents, future uses. Drug Intell Clin Pharm 1987 Jul/Aug; 21: 575-83.

Lam YW. Calcium metabolism, calcium-channel blocking agents, and hypertension management. Drug Intell Clin Pharm 1988 Sep; 22: 659-71.

Bepridil
Flaim SF, Cummings DM. Bepridil hydrochloride: a review of its pharmacologic properties. Curr Ther Res 1986 Apr; 39: 568-97.

Bepridil and nicardipine
Hasegawa GR. Nicardipine, nitrendipine, and bepridil: new calcium antagonists for cardiovascular disorders. Clin Pharm 1988 Feb; 7: 97-108.

Diltiazem
McAuley BJ, Schroeder JS. The use of diltiazem hydrochloride in cardiovascular disorders. Pharmacother 1982 May/Jun; 2: 121-33.

Chaffman M, Brogden RN. Diltiazem. A review of its pharmacological properties and therapeutic efficacy. Drugs 1985 May; 29: 387-454.

Felodipine
Yedinak KC, Lopez LM. Felodipine: a new dihydropyridine calcium-channel antagonist. DICP Ann Pharmacother 1991 Nov; 25: 1193-1206.

Flunarizine
Holmes B, Brogden RN, Heel RC, et al. Flunarizine: a review of its pharmacodynamic and pharmacokinetic properties and therapeutic use. Drugs 1984; 27: 6-44.

Isradipine
Fitton A, Benfield P. Isradipine. A review of its pharmacodynamic and pharmacokinetic properties, and therapeutic use in cardiovascular disease. Drugs 1990; 40(1): 31-74.

Nicardipine
Sorkin EM, Clissold SP. Nicardipine. A review of its pharmacodynamic and pharmacokinetic properties, and therapeutic efficacy, in the treatment of angina pectoris, hypertension and related cardiovascular disorders. Drugs 1987; 33: 296-345.

Nifedipine
Ferlinz J. Nifedipine in myocardial ischemia, systemic hypertension, and other cardiovascular disorders. Ann Intern Med 1986 Nov; 105: 714-29.

Nimodipine
Allen GS, et al. A controlled trial of nimodipine in acute ischemic stroke. N Engl J Med 1988 Jan 28; 318: 203-7.

Petruk K, et al. Nimodipine treatment in poor-grade aneurysm patients. Results of a multicenter, double-blind, placebo-controlled trial. J Neurosurg 1988; 68: 505-17.

Verapamil
Baky SH, Singh BN. Verapamil hydrochloride: Pharmacological properties and role in cardiovascular therapeutics. Pharmacother 1982 Nov/Dec; 2: 328-53.

Revised: 01/19/2005

Table 1. Pharmacology/Pharmacokinetics

Legend*:
I = Bepridil
II = Diltiazem
III = Felodipine
IV = Flunarizine
V = Isradipine
VI = Nicardipine
VII = Nifedipine
VIII = Nimodipine
IX = Verapamil
X = Amlodipine

Hemodynamic effect	I	II	III	IV	V	VI	VII	VIII	IX	X
Peripheral vasodilation	+	+	++	+	++	++	++	++	+	++
Heart rate	D	D	I†	N	I†	I†	I†	I†	D	N
Depression of sinoatrial (SA) or atrioventricular (AV) nodal conduction	+	+	–	–	–	–	–	–	+	–
Negative inotropic effect	+‡	+/–	+/–‡	–	+/–‡	+/–‡	+/–‡	+/–‡	+‡	–
Antihypertensive effect	–	+	+	–	+	+	+	+	+	+
Cerebrovascular selectivity				+		+		+		

*Legend: I = Increase; D = Decrease; N = No effect; + = Some effect; ++ = Significant effect; – = No effect.
†Reflex increase occurs in response to vasodilating action. Isradipine causes only a slight increase or no change.
‡Bepridil's negative inotropic effect is small and tends to occur at high doses. For felodipine, isradipine, nicardipine, nifedipine, and nimodipine, the effect is masked by the reflex increase in heart rate. The effect of verapamil is countered by a reduction in afterload.

Table 2. Medical Considerations/Contraindications

The medical considerations/contraindications included have been selected on the basis of their potential clinical significance (reasons given in parentheses where appropriate)—not necessarily inclusive (» = major clinical significance).

Legend:
I = Bepridil
II = Diltiazem
III = Felodipine
IV = Flunarizine
V = Isradipine
VI = Nicardipine
VII = Nifedipine
VIII = Nimodipine
IX = Verapamil
X = Amlodipine

	I	II	III	IV	V	VI	VII	VIII	IX	X
Except under special circumstances, this medication should not be used when the following medical problems exist:										
» Arrhythmias, ventricular, serious, history of or » Q-T interval prolongation, history of (increased risk of bepridil-induced arrhythmias)	✓									
» Heart block—2nd- or 3rd- degree atrioventricular (AV) block, except in patients with a functioning artificial ventricular pacemaker (use of calcium channel blocking agent may lead to excessive bradycardia)	✓	✓							✓	
» Hypersensitivity to the calcium channel blocking agent prescribed		✓							✓	
» Hypotension, severe	✓	✓	✓		✓	✓	✓	✓	✓	✓
» Myocardial infarction, acute, with pulmonary congestion documented by x-ray on admission (associated heart failure may be acutely worsened by administration of diltiazem; use is **contraindicated**)		✓								
» Sinoatrial (SA) nodal function impairment (sick sinus syndrome) except in patients with functioning artificial ventricular pacemaker (use of calcium channel blocking agent may lead to severe hypotension, bradycardia, and asystole)	✓	✓							✓	
» Wolff-Parkinson-White or Lown-Ganong-Levine syndrome accompanied by atrial flutter or fibrillation, except in patients with a functioning artificial ventricular pacemaker (use of a calcium channel blocking agent for treatment of atrial fibrillation or flutter may precipitate severe ventricular arrhythmias)		✓							✓	
Risk-benefit should be considered when the following medical problems exist:										
Aortic stenosis, severe (increased risk of heart failure when a calcium channel blocking agent is initiated, because of fixed impedance to flow across aortic valve)		✓				✓	✓		✓	✓
» Bradycardia, extreme, or » Heart failure (reduced sinus node and AV node activity may be worsened) Note: When not severe or rate-related, heart failure should be controlled with digitalization and diuretics before administration of a calcium channel blocking agent. Heart failure, severe or moderately severe (pulmonary wedge pressure above 20 mm of mercury, ejection fraction less than 30%), may be acutely worsened by administration of a calcium channel blocking agent.	✓	✓							✓	
Bradycardia, extreme, or Heart failure (because these agents have a slight negative inotropic effect, caution is recommended)			✓		✓	✓	✓	✓		✓

Table 2. Medical Considerations/Contraindications

The medical considerations/contraindications included have been selected on the basis of their potential clinical significance (reasons given in parentheses where appropriate)—not necessarily inclusive (» = major clinical significance).

Legend:
I = Bepridil
II = Diltiazem
III = Felodipine
IV = Flunarizine
V = Isradipine
VI = Nicardipine
VII = Nifedipine
VIII = Nimodipine
IX = Verapamil
X = Amlodipine

	I	II	III	IV	V	VI	VII	VIII	IX	X
» Cardiac conduction abonomalities (patients with this condition were excluded from clinical studies)		✓								
» Cardiogenic shock	✓	✓	✓		✓	✓	✓	✓	✓	
Cerebral infarction or hemorrhage, acute						✓				
Hepatic function impairment (clearance and duration of effect may be prolonged; clearance of felodipine is reduced to about 60%; half-life of nicardipine may be increased to 19 hours in patients with severe hepatic function impairment; half-life of verapamil may be increased to 14 to 16 hours and plasma clearance reduced to about 30% of normal; dosage reduction may be necessary)	✓	✓	✓	✓	✓	✓	✓	✓	✓	✓
» Hypokalemia (risk of bepridil-induced arrhythmias may be increased)	✓									
Hypotension, mild to moderate (tendency to hypotension is augmented by the peripheral vasodilating effect of the calcium channel blocking agent)		✓	✓		✓	✓	✓	✓	✓	
Mental depression, history of (flunarizine may precipitate mental depression)				✓						
» Myocardial infarction, acute, with pulmonary congestion documented by x-ray on admission (associated heart failure may be acutely worsened by administration of a calcium channel blocking agent)	✓	✓							✓	
Myocardial infarction, acute, with pulmonary congestion documented by x-ray on admission (because these agents have a slight negative inotropic effect, there is a possibility that associated heart failure may be acutely worsened)			✓		✓	✓	✓	✓		
Narrowing of the gastrointestinal tract, pathologic or iatrogenic, severe (passage of the nondeformable extended-release nifedipine system [*Procardia XL*] may be impaired; obstructive symptoms may occur)							✓			
Neuromuscular transmission deficiency (verapamil has been reported to decrease neuromuscular transmission in patients with Duchenne's muscular dystrophy, and to prolong recovery from the neuromuscular blocking agent vecuronium; dosage reduction may be required)									✓	
Parkinsonian syndrome or Extrapyramidal disorders, other (flunarizine may produce parkinsonian extrapyramidal symptoms not responsive to antiparkinsonian medications)				✓						
Renal function impairment (possible reduced clearance of the calcium channel blocking agent or metabolites, although half-life is only slightly increased; dosage adjustment may be necessary) (plasma concentrations of felodipine are unchanged; although reduced excretion results in increased concentrations of metabolites, they are inactive)	✓	✓	✓		✓	✓	✓		✓	
» Sensitivity to the calcium channel blocking agent prescribed	✓		✓	✓	✓	✓	✓	✓		✓
Ventricular tachycardia, wide-complex (risk of ventricular fibrillation if intravenous diltiazem or verapamil administered)		✓							✓	
» Ventricular function, impaired (patients with this condition were excluded from clinical studies)		✓								

Table 3. Side/Adverse Effects

Note: Side/adverse effects tend to be dose-related and occur most frequently during periods of dosage titration.

Although not reported to occur in humans, lenticular changes and cataracts have developed during chronic dosage with verapamil in beagles. These effects resulted from daily dosage of 30 mg and more per kg of body weight and are considered likely to be species-specific.

A possible hyperglycemic effect has been reported with nicardipine (at a daily dose of 40 mg) and nifedipine therapy (when the daily dosage exceeds 60 mg). No significant effect on fasting serum glucose has been seen with felodipine.

Depression of atrioventricular (AV) and sinoatrial (SA) nodal conduction by bepridil, diltiazem, and verapamil may result in asymptomatic first-degree block and transient sinus bradycardia, sometimes accompanied by nodal escape rhythms.

Use of verapamil for hypertrophic cardiomyopathy, especially in patients with pre-existing risk factors, has resulted in serious side effects (including pulmonary edema, sinus bradycardia, severe hypotension, second-degree AV block, and sudden death).

The following side/adverse effects have been selected on the basis of their potential clinical significance (possible signs and symptoms in parentheses where appropriate)—not necessarily inclusive:*

Legend:
I = Bepridil
II = Diltiazem
III = Felodipine
IV = Flunarizine
V = Isradipine
VI = Nicardipine
VII = Nifedipine
VIII = Nimodipine
IX = Verapamil
X = Amlodipine

Side/adverse effect	I	II	III	IV	V	VI	VII	VIII	IX	X
Medical attention needed										
Agranulocytosis—not symptomatic	R	U	U	U	U	U	U	U	U	X
Allergic reaction (skin rash) Note: May disappear, even with continued diltiazem use. Rarely, may progress to erythema multiforme (diltiazem, verapamil), exfoliative dermatitis (diltiazem), or Stevens-Johnson syndrome (diltiazem, verapamil).	R	L	L	R	L	R	R	R	L	L
Angina (chest pain)—may occur about 30 minutes after administration Note: Rarely, especially in patients with severe obstructive coronary artery disease, increased frequency, duration, and/or severity of angina or acute myocardial infarction have occurred when therapy is initiated or dosage increased.	U	R	L	U	L	L	R	U	R	R
Arrhythmias, including torsades de pointes—usually asymptomatic	L	U	U	U	U	U	U	U	U	R
Arthritis (painful, swollen joints)—associated with elevated ANA titers	U	U	U	U	U	U	R	U	U	X
Blindness, transient, at peak plasma concentration	U	U	U	U	U	U	R	U	U	X
Bradycardia less than 50 beats per minute; rarely, 2nd- or 3rd- degree AV block, with a few patients progressing to asystole (slow heartbeat)	L	R	X	U	X	X	X	X	L	R
Congestive heart failure or pulmonary edema, possible (breathing difficulty, coughing, or wheezing)	L	L	U	U	R	R	L	R	L	X
Extrapyramidal effects, parkinsonian (loss of balance control, mask-like face, shuffling walk, stiffness of arms or legs, trembling and shaking of hands and fingers, trouble in speaking or swallowing) Note: Symptoms are not responsive to antiparkinsonian medications, but are reversible on withdrawal of flunarizine.	U	R	U	L	U	U	U	U	U	R
Galactorrhea (unusual secretion of milk)	U	U	U	R	U	U	U	U	R	X
Gingival enlargement (bleeding, tender, or swollen gums)	U	R	R	U	U	U	R	U	R	R
Hypotension—usually not symptomatic; not orthostatic	R	L	R	U	L	L	L	L	L	R
Hypotension, excessive (fainting)	R	R	R	U	R	R	R	R	R	R
Mental depression	U	R	R	L	U	U	U	U	U	R
Peripheral edema (swelling of ankles, feet, or lower legs)	R	L	M	U	L	L	M	L	L	M
Tachycardia (irregular or fast, pounding heartbeat) Note: In patients receiving verapamil, rapid ventricular rate may occur in patients with atrial flutter/fibrillation and an accessory AV pathway as with Wolff-Parkinson-White, or Lown-Ganong-Levine syndrome; in patients receiving felodipine, isradipine, nicardipine, nifedipine, or nimodipine, reflex tachycardia may occur because of its hypotensive effect.	X	R	L	U	L	L	L	R	R	R
Thrombocytopenia—not symptomatic	U	R	U	U	U	U	U	R	U	R
Medical attention needed only if continuing or bothersome										
Constipation	L	L	L	U	R	R	L	U	L	R
Diarrhea	M	L	L	U	L	R	U	L	U	R
Dizziness or lightheadedness	M	L	L	L	L	L	M	L	L	L
Drowsiness	U	R	U	M	U	R	U	U	U	X
Dryness of mouth	U	R	R	L	U	R	U	U	U	R
Flushing and feeling of warmth	U	L	L	U	L	M	M	R	R	L
Headache	L	L	M	U	M	L	M	L	L	M
Increased appetite and/or weight gain	U	U	U	M	U	U	U	U	U	R
Nausea	M	L	L	L	L	L	M	L	L	L
Unusual tiredness or weakness	L	L	L	L	L	L	L	U	L	L

*Differences in frequency of occurrence may reflect either lack of clinical-use data or actual pharmacologic distinctions among agents (although their pharmacologic similarity suggests that side effects occurring with one may occur with the others). M = more frequent; L = less frequent; R = rare; U = unknown; X = does not occur.

CALCIUM CHLORIDE—See *Calcium Supplements (Systemic)*

CALCIUM CITRATE—See *Calcium Supplements (Systemic)*

CALCIUM GLUBIONATE—See *Calcium Supplements (Systemic)*

CALCIUM GLUCEPTATE—See *Calcium Supplements (Systemic)*

CALCIUM GLUCEPTATE AND CALCIUM GLUCONATE—See *Calcium Supplements (Systemic)*

CALCIUM GLUCONATE—See *Calcium Supplements (Systemic)*

CALCIUM GLYCEROPHOSPHATE AND CALCIUM LACTATE—See *Calcium Supplements (Systemic)*

CALCIUM LACTATE—See *Calcium Supplements (Systemic)*

CALCIUM LACTATE-GLUCONATE AND CALCIUM CARBONATE—See *Calcium Supplements (Systemic)*

CALCIUM PANTOTHENATE—See *Pantothenic Acid (Systemic)*

CALCIUM PHOSPHATE, DIBASIC—See *Calcium Supplements (Systemic)*

CALCIUM PHOSPHATE, TRIBASIC—See *Calcium Supplements (Systemic)*

CANDESARTAN Systemic

VA CLASSIFICATION (Primary/Secondary): CV805/CV409

Commonly used brand name(s): *Atacand*.

Note: For a listing of dosage forms and brand names by country availability, see *Dosage Forms* section(s).

Category

Antihypertensive.

Indications

Accepted

Heart failure (treatment)—Candesartan is indicated for the treatment of heart failure (NYHA class II-IV and ejection fraction ≤40%) to reduce cardiovascular death and to reduce heart failure hospitalizations. Candesartan also has an added effect on these outcomes when used with an ACE inhibitor.

Hypertension (treatment)—Candesartan is indicated for the treatment of hypertension. It may be used alone or in combination with other antihypertensive medications.

For additional information on initial therapeutic guidelines related to the treatment of hypertension, see *Appendix III*.

Pharmacology/Pharmacokinetics

Physicochemical characteristics

Molecular weight—Candesartan cilexetil: 610.67.

Mechanism of action/Effect

Candesartan is a nonpeptide angiotensin II antagonist that selectively blocks the binding of angiotensin II to the AT_1 receptors in tissues such as vascular smooth muscle and the adrenal gland. In the renin-angiotensin system, angiotensin I is converted by angiotensin-converting enzyme (ACE) to form angiotensin II. Angiotensin II stimulates the adrenal cortex to synthesize and secrete aldosterone, which decreases the excretion of sodium and increases the excretion of potassium. Angiotensin II also acts as a vasoconstrictor in vascular smooth muscle. By blocking the binding of angiotensin II to the AT_1 receptors, candesartan causes vasodilation and decreases the effects of aldosterone. The negative feedback regulation of angiotensin II on renin secretion also is inhibited, resulting in a rise in plasma renin concentrations and a consequent rise in angiotensin II plasma concentrations; however, these effects do not counteract the blood pressure-lowering effect that occurs.

Absorption

Absolute bioavailability of candesartan from the administered prodrug, candesartan cilexetil, has been estimated to be about 15%.

Food with a high fat content does not affect the bioavailability of candesartan from candesartan cilexetil (see *Biotransformation* section).

Distribution

Vol_D—0.13 L per kg (L/kg). Candesartan does not penetrate red blood cells. In rats, distribution across the blood-brain barrier is poor.

Protein binding

Very high (> 99%).

Biotransformation

During absorption from the gastrointestinal tract, candesartan cilexetil undergoes rapid and complete ester hydrolysis to form the active drug, candesartan. Elimination of candesartan is primarily as unchanged drug in the urine and, by the biliary route, in the feces. Minor hepatic metabolism of candesartan occurs by *O*-deethylation to form an inactive metabolite.

Half-life

Elimination—
Approximately 9 hours.

Time to peak concentration

3 to 4 hours.

Elimination

After oral administration—
- Renal—33%.
- Fecal (biliary)—67%.

After intravenous administration—
- Renal—59%.
- Fecal (biliary)—36%.

In dialysis—
Candesartan is not removable by hemodialysis.

Precautions to Consider

Carcinogenicity

No evidence of carcinogenicity was found when candesartan cilexetil was given to mice (via diet) or rats (via gavage) for up to 104 weeks in doses of up to 100 and 1000 mg per kg of body weight (mg/kg) per day, respectively. These doses represent approximately 7 and more than 70 times the maximum recommended human daily dose (MRHDD) of 32 mg, respectively.

Mutagenicity

Candesartan and its O-deethyl metabolite tested positive for genotoxicity in the *in vitro* Chinese hamster lung (CHL) chromosomal aberration assay. Neither compound tested positive in the Ames microbial mutagenesis assay or the *in vitro* mouse lymphoma cell assay. Candesartan was also evaluated *in vivo* in the mouse micronucleus test and *in vitro* in the Chinese hamster ovary (CHO) gene mutation assay, in both cases with negative results. Candesartan cilexetil was evaluated in the Ames test, the *in vitro* mouse lymphoma cell and rat hepatocyte unscheduled DNA synthesis assays and the *in vivo* mouse micronucleus test, in each case with negative results. Candesartan cilexetil was not evaluated in the CHL chromosomal aberration or CHO gene mutation assay.

Pregnancy/Reproduction

Fertility—No impairment of fertility or reproductive performance was found in male or female rats given oral doses of up to 300 mg/kg per day. This dose represents 83 times the MRHDD of 32 mg on a body surface area basis.

Pregnancy—Medications that act directly on the renin-angiotensin system can cause fetal and neonatal morbidity and mortality when administered to pregnant women during the second and third trimesters. Candesartan should be discontinued as soon as possible when pregnancy is detected, unless no alternative therapy can be used. In the latter instance, serial ultrasound examinations should be performed to assess the intra-amniotic environment. If oligohydramnios is observed, candesartan should be discontinued unless it is considered lifesaving for the mother. Perinatal diagnostic tests, such as contraction-stress testing (CST), a nonstress test (NST), or biophysical profiling (BPP) may be appropriate during the applicable week of pregnancy. However, oligohydramnios may not appear until after the fetus has sustained irreversible damage.

Fetal exposure to drugs that act directly on the renin-angiotensin system during the second and third trimesters can cause hypotension, reversible or irreversible renal failure, anuria, neonatal skull hypoplasia, and death in the fetus or neonate. Maternal oligohydramnios, which may result from decreased fetal renal function, has been reported, and is associated with fetal limb contractures, craniofacial deformation, and hypoplastic lung development. Other adverse effects that have been reported are prematurity, intrauterine growth retardation, and patent ductus arteriosus, although it is not clear how these effects are related to drug exposure. When limited to the first trimester, exposure to this medication does not appear to be associated with these adverse effects.

Infants exposed in utero to angiotensin II receptor antagonists should be closely observed for hypotension, oliguria, and hyperkalemia. Oliguria should be treated with support of blood pressure and renal perfusion. Dialysis or exchange transfusion may be necessary to reverse hypotension and/or substitute for disordered renal function.

Studies in pregnant rats given oral daily doses of ≥ 10 mg per kg of candesartan during late gestation and continued through lactation resulted in reduced survival and an increase in the incidence of hydronephrosis in the offspring. The 10-mg/kg dose represents 2.8 times the MRHDD of 32 mg on a mg/m^2 basis, assuming a 50-kg patient.

Studies in pregnant rabbits given oral, maternally toxic (based on a reduction in body weight and death) daily doses of 3 mg/kg of candesartan resulted in no adverse effects on fetal survival, fetal weight, or external, visceral, or skeletal development in the offspring of surviving dams. This dose represents approximately 1.7 times the MRHDD on a mg/m^2 basis.

No maternal toxicity or adverse effects on fetal development were observed in pregnant mice given oral doses of up to 1000 mg/kg per day of candesartan. This dose represents approximately 138 times the MRHDD on a mg/m^2 basis.

FDA Pregnancy Category C (first trimester).

FDA Pregnancy Category D (second and third trimesters).

Breast-feeding

It is not known whether candesartan is distributed into human breast milk. However, candesartan is distributed into the milk of lactating rats. Because of the potential for adverse effects in the nursing infant, a decision should be made whether to discontinue nursing or discontinue the drug, taking into account the importance of the drug to the mother.

Pediatrics

No information is available on the relationship of age to the effects of candesartan in pediatric patients. Safety and efficacy have not been established.

Geriatrics

Use of candesartan in patients 65 years of age and older (21% of patients in clinical studies) has not demonstrated geriatrics-specific problems that would limit the usefulness of candesartan in the elderly, but greater sensitivity in older patients cannot be ruled out. And, in addition to monitoring of serum creatinine, potassium, and blood pressure during dose escalation and periodically thereafter, greater sensitivity of some older individuals with heart failure must be considered. However, in clinical studies, the peak plasma concentration (C_{max}) and area under the plasma concentration-time curve (AUC) increased by 50 and 80%, respectively, when compared with those in younger patients. In a placebo-controlled trial of about 200 elderly hypertensive patients, candesartan was well tolerated.

Pharmacogenetics

Black patients have a somewhat smaller response to the blood pressure-lowering effects of candesartan.

Drug interactions and/or related problems

The following drug interactions and/or related problems have been selected on the basis of their potential clinical significance (possible mechanism in parentheses where appropriate)—not necessarily inclusive (» = major clinical significance):

Note: Combinations containing any of the following medications, depending on the amount present, may also interact with this medication.

ACE inhibitors or
Diuretics, potassium-sparing such as
Spironolactone
(in heart failure patients treated with candesartan, hyperkalemia may occur especially when taken concomitantly with these drugs)

Diuretics
(concurrent use with candesartan may have additive hypotensive effects)

Lithium
(serum lithium level increases and toxicity have been reported with concomitant use; careful monitoring of serum lithium levels recommended with concomitant use)

Laboratory value alterations

The following have been selected on the basis of their potential clinical significance (possible effect in parentheses where appropriate)—not necessarily inclusive (» = major clinical significance).

With physiology/laboratory test values

Blood urea nitrogen (BUN) and
Creatinine, serum
(minor increases in concentrations have occurred infrequently in patients treated with candesartan; serum creatinine increases may occur in heart failure patients treated with candesartan)
(in heart failure patients treated with candesartan, increases in serum creatinine may occur that may require a dosage reduction or discontinuation of the diuretic or candesartan and volume repletion; in clinical studies, mean increase of 0.2 mg per dL in serum creatinine)

Hematocrit and
Hemoglobin
(in clinical studies, small decreases in hemoglobin and hematocrit values of approximately 0.2 gram per dL and 0.5 volume percent, respectively, occurred in patients treated with candesartan; in heart failure patients, small decreases in hemoglobin and hematocrit values of 0.5 g per dL and 1.6%, respectively; candesartan therapy was discontinued in three patients who experienced either anemia, leukopenia, or thrombocytopenia during these studies)

Liver function tests
(in clinical studies, elevations of liver enzymes and/or serum bilirubin occurred infrequently in candesartan-treated patients; five patients discontinued candesartan because of abnormal liver function test values [all had elevated liver enzyme values and two had mildly elevated total bilirubin, although one (of the two) was diagnosed with Hepatitis A])

Potassium, serum
(in clinical studies, a mean increase of 0.1 mEq per L [mEq/L] occurred in patients treated with candesartan; one patient with congestive heart failure and concurrently receiving spironolactone was withdrawn from the trial for hyperkalemia [serum potassium of 7.5 mEq/L])
(in heart failure patients treated with candesartan, hyperkalemia may occur; mean increase of 0.15 mEq per L in clinical studies)

Uric acid, serum
(hyperuricemia occurred in 0.6% of patients treated with candesartan in clinical studies)

Medical considerations/Contraindications

The medical considerations/contraindications included have been selected on the basis of their potential clinical significance (reasons given in parentheses where appropriate)—not necessarily inclusive (» = major clinical significance).

Except under special circumstances, this medication should not be used when the following medical problem exists:

» Hypersensitivity to candesartan or any component of the product

Risk-benefit should be considered when the following medical problems exist:

Dehydration (sodium or volume depletion, due to excessive perspiration, vomiting, diarrhea, prolonged diuretic therapy, dialysis, or dietary salt restriction)
(a reduction in salt or fluid volume may increase the risk of symptomatic hypotension)

Heart failure
(caution should be observed when initiating candesartan in heart failure patients; these patients commonly have some reduction in

blood pressure when given candesartan; may require a temporary reduction in dose and/or diuretic and volume repletion)

Hepatic function impairment, severe or moderate
(no information is available on the use of candesartan in patients with severe hepatic function impairment; significant increases in candesartan AUC and C_{max} in patients with moderate hepatic impairment; lower initiating dose should be considered)

Renal artery stenosis, unilateral or bilateral or
Renal function impairment
(increases in candesartan serum concentrations have occurred in patients with renal function impairment; in patients with severe renal function impairment [creatinine clearance < 30 mL per minute (mL/min)], the area under the plasma concentration-time curve [AUC] and peak plasma concentration [C_{max}] were approximately doubled during repeated dosing in clinical trials. Increases in serum creatinine or blood urea nitrogen [BUN] have occurred in patients with unilateral or bilateral renal artery stenosis and treated with angiotensin-converting enzyme [ACE] inhibitors; similar increases may also occur in patients treated with candesartan. Changes in renal function as a result of therapy with angiotensin receptor–antagonists in patients susceptible to changes in the renin-angiotensin-aldosterone system [such as patients with severe congestive heart failure] have been associated with oliguria, progressive azotemia, acute renal failure, and/or death; increases in serum creatinine may require a temporary reduction in dose and/or diuretic and volume repletion)

Patient monitoring

The following may be especially important in patient monitoring (other tests may be warranted in some patients, depending on condition; » = major clinical significance):

» Blood pressure measurements
(periodic monitoring is necessary for titration of dose according to the patient's response)

Creatinine serum
(recommended during dose escalation and periodically thereafter, especially in heart failure patients)

Potassium serum
(recommended during dose escalation and periodically thereafter in patients with heart failure)

Renal function and
Volume status
(should always be assessed in patients with heart failure being evaluated for candesartan treatment)

Side/Adverse Effects

The following side/adverse effects have been selected on the basis of their potential clinical significance (possible signs and symptoms in parentheses where appropriate)—not necessarily inclusive:

Those indicating need for medical attention

Incidence rare

Angina pectoris (arm, back or jaw pain, chest pain or discomfort, chest tightness or heaviness, fast or irregular heartbeat, shortness of breath, sweating, nausea); ***Angioedema*** (large, hive-like swelling on face, eyelids, lips, tongue, throat, hands, legs, feet, sex organs); ***Hyperuricemia or gout*** (joint pain, lower back or side pain, swelling of feet or lower legs); ***hypotension*** (dizziness, lightheadedness, or fainting)—usually seen in volume- or salt-depleted patients; ***leukopenia*** (cough or hoarseness; chills or fever; lower back or side pain; painful or difficult urination)—usually asymptomatic; ***myocardial infarction*** (chest pain or discomfort, pain or discomfort in arms, jaw, back or neck, shortness of breath, nausea, sweating, vomiting); ***thrombocytopenia*** (nosebleeds or bleeding gums)

Incidence not determined—Observed during clinical practice, estimates of frequency cannot be determined

Abnormal hepatic function (dark urine, light-colored stools, loss of appetite, nausea and vomiting, unusual tiredness, yellow eyes or skin, fever with or without chills, stomach pain); ***agranulocytosis*** (cough or hoarseness, fever with or without chills, general feeling of tiredness or weakness, lower back or side pain. painful or difficult urination, sore throat, sores, ulcers, or white spots on lips or in mouth, unusual bleeding or bruising); ***hepatitis*** (dark urine, general tiredness and weakness, light-colored stools, nausea and vomiting, upper right abdominal pain, yellow eyes and skin); ***hyperkalemia*** (abdominal pain, confusion, irregular heartbeat, nausea or vomiting, nervousness, numbness or tingling in hands, feet, or lips, shortness of breath, difficult breathing, weakness or heaviness of legs); ***hyponatremia*** (coma, confusion, convulsions, decreased urine output, dizziness, fast or irregular heartbeat, headache, increased thirst, muscle pain or cramps, nausea or vomiting, shortness of breath, swelling of face, ankles, or hands, unusual tiredness or weakness); ***neutropenia*** (black, tarry stools; chills; cough; fever; lower back or side pain; painful or difficult urination; pale skin; shortness of breath; sore throat; ulcers, sores, or white spots in mouth; unusual bleeding or bruising; unusual tiredness or weakness); ***renal impairment/failure*** (lower back/side pain, decreased frequency/amount of urine, bloody urine, increased thirst, loss of appetite, nausea, vomiting, unusual tiredness or weakness, swelling of face, fingers, lower legs, weight gain, troubled breathing, increased blood pressure); ***urticaria*** (hives or welts, itching, redness of skin, skin rash)

Those indicating need for medical attention only if they continue or are bothersome

Incidence less frequent

Back pain; dizziness; headache; pharyngitis (sore throat); ***rhinitis*** (stuffy nose); ***upper respiratory tract infection*** (coughing; ear congestion or pain; fever; head congestion; nasal congestion; runny nose; sneezing; sore throat)

Incidence not determined—Observed during clinical practice, estimates of frequency cannot be determined

Pruritus (itching skin)

Note: In clinical trials, the side effects that most often resulted in the discontinuation of candesartan were *headache* (incidence 0.6%) and *dizziness* (incidence 0.3%).

Overdose

For more information on the management of overdose or unintentional ingestion, **contact a Poison Control Center** (see *Poison Control Center Listing*).

Clinical effects of overdose

The following effects have been selected on the basis of their potential clinical significance (possible signs and symptoms in parentheses where appropriate)—not necessarily inclusive:

Acute and/or chronic

Bradycardia (slow heartbeat)—as a result of parasympathetic (vagal) stimulation; ***dizziness; hypotension*** (dizziness, lightheadedness, or fainting); ***tachycardia*** (fast heartbeat)

Treatment of overdose

Candesartan can not be removed by hemodialysis.

Treatment should be symptomatic and supportive.

Supportive care—Patients in whom intentional overdose is confirmed or suspected should be referred for psychiatric consultation.

Patient Consultation

As an aid to patient consultation, refer to *Advice for the Patient, Candesartan (Systemic)*.

In providing consultation, consider emphasizing the following selected information (» = major clinical significance):

Before using this medication

» Conditions affecting use, especially:
Hypersensitivity to candesartan or any of its components
Candesartan tested positive for genotoxicity in the *in vitro* Chinese hamster lung (CHL) chromosomal aberration assay
Pregnancy—Fetal and neonatal hypotension, skull hypoplasia, renal failure, and death have been reported; candesartan should be discontinued as soon as possible when pregnancy is detected
Breast-feeding—Candesartan is distributed into the milk of lactating rats; not recommended in mothers who are breast-feeding
Use in the elderly—Area under the plasma concentration-time curve (AUC) and peak plasma concentration (C_{max}) may be increased; greater sensitivity in older patients cannot be ruled out; monitoring of serum creatinine, potassium, and blood pressure due to greater sensitivity of some older individuals with heart failure
Pharmacogenetics—Black patients may have a somewhat smaller therapeutic response

Proper use of this medication

» Compliance with therapy; taking medication at the same time each day to maintain the antihypertensive effect

» Proper dosing
Missed dose: Taking as soon as possible; not taking if almost time for next scheduled dose; not doubling doses

» Proper storage

Precautions while using this medication

Visiting the physician regularly to check progress
Notifying physician immediately if pregnancy is suspected
Not taking other medications without consulting the physician

Caution when driving or doing other things requiring alertness, because of possible dizziness

Checking with physician if severe nausea, vomiting, or diarrhea occurs and continues to prevent dehydration and hypotension

Caution when exercising or during exposure to hot weather, because of the risk of dehydration and hypotension due to reduced fluid volume

Side/adverse effects

Signs of potential side effects, especially angina pectoris, angioedema, hyperuricemia, hypotension, leukopenia, myocardial infarction, and thrombocytopenia

Signs of potential side effects observed during clinical practice, especially abnormal hepatic function, agranulocytosis, hepatitis, hyperkalemia, hyponatremia, neutropenia, renal impairment/failure, and urticaria

General Dosing Information

Dosage must be adjusted, on the basis of clinical response, to meet the individual requirements of each patient.

No initial dosage adjustment is necessary for elderly patients, for patients with mildly impaired renal function, or for patients with mildly impaired hepatic function

Diet/Nutrition

Candesartan may be taken with or without food.

For treatment of adverse effects

Recommended treatment consists of the following:

- Treatment of symptomatic hypotension involves placing the patient in a supine position and, if needed, administering normal saline intravenously.

Oral Dosage Forms

CANDESARTAN CILEXETIL TABLETS

Usual adult dose

Antihypertensive—

Oral, initially 16 mg once a day, when used as monotherapy in patients who are not volume-depleted. Candesartan may be administered once or twice daily with total daily doses ranging from 8 to 32 mg. Larger doses do not appear to have a greater antihypertensive effect. The antihypertensive effect is considerable within two weeks of candesartan therapy, and maximal antihypertensive effect usually is attained within four to six weeks of therapy. If blood pressure is not controlled by candesartan alone, a diuretic may be added.

Patients with volume depletion (e.g., from diuretic treatment) and/or renal function impairment should be closely monitored during initiation of therapy and may require a lower dose.

Note: In patients with moderate hepatic impairment, consideration should be given to initiation of candesartan at a lower dose. No initial dosage adjustment is necessary in patients with mild hepatic impairment

Heart failure (treatment)—

Oral, initial dose of 4 mg once daily with a target dose of 32 mg once daily. This is achieved by doubling the dose at approximately 2-week intervals, as tolerated by the patient.

Note: In heart failure patients with symptomatic hypotension, a temporary reduction in candesartan dose, or diuretic, or both, and volume repletion may be necessary.

Usual adult prescribing limits

32 mg per day.

Usual pediatric dose

Safety and efficacy have not been established.

Strength(s) usually available

U.S.—

4 mg (Rx) [*Atacand* (carboxymethylcellulose calcium; corn starch; hydroxypropyl cellulose; lactose; magnesium stearate; polyethylene glycol)].

8 mg (Rx) [*Atacand* (carboxymethylcellulose calcium; corn starch; ferric oxide; hydroxypropyl cellulose; lactose; magnesium stearate; polyethylene glycol)].

16 mg (Rx) [*Atacand* (carboxymethylcellulose calcium; corn starch; ferric oxide; hydroxypropyl cellulose; lactose; magnesium stearate; polyethylene glycol)].

32 mg (Rx) [*Atacand* (carboxymethylcellulose calcium; corn starch; ferric oxide; hydroxypropyl cellulose; lactose; magnesium stearate; polyethylene glycol)].

Packaging and storage

Store at 25 °C (77 °F); excursions permitted between 15 and 30 °C (59 and 86 °F). Store in tight container.

Auxiliary labeling

- Do not take other medicines without your doctor's advice.

Revised: 04/11/2006
Developed: 11/23/1998

CANDESARTAN AND HYDROCHLOROTHIAZIDE Systemic

VA CLASSIFICATION (Primary/Secondary): CV408/ CV805/CV701

Commonly used brand name(s): *Atacand HCT 16-12.5; Atacand HCT 32-12.5.*

NOTE: The *Candesartan and Hydrochlorothiazide (Systemic)* monograph is maintained on the *USP DI* electronic data base. A copy of the most recent revision of the complete monograph can be accessed on the *USP DI* Updates Online website. See the front cover of book for details on accessing the site.

For information on the specific components of this combination, see the *USP DI* monographs for *Candesartan (Systemic),* and *Diuretics, Thiazide (Systemic).*

The information that follows is selectively abstracted from the complete monograph and is provided to facilitate drug use review and patient counseling.

Note: For a listing of dosage forms and brand names by country availability, see *Dosage Forms* section(s).

Category

Antihypertensive.

Indications

Accepted

Hypertension (treatment)—The combination of candesartan and hydrochlorothiazide is indicated for the treatment of hypertension. The fixed dose combination is not indicated for initial therapy.

For additional information on initial therapeutic guidelines related to the treatment of hypertension, see *Appendix III.*

Patient Consultation

As an aid to patient consultation, refer to *Advice for the Patient, Candesartan and Hydrochlorothiazide (Systemic).*

In providing consultation, consider emphasizing the following selected information (» = major clinical significance):

Before using this medication

» Conditions affecting use, especially:

Hypersensitivity to candesartan, hydrochlorothiazide, any component of candesartan and hydrochlorothiazide combination, or sulfonamide-type medications.

Pregnancy—Not recommended for use during pregnancy; can cause fetal and neonatal morbidity and mortality

Breast-feeding—Hydrochlorothiazide is distributed into human breast milk

Other medications, especially lithium; potassium supplements or substances containing high concentrations of potassium, or salt substitutes

Other medical problems, especially: anuria, congestive heart failure, renal artery stenosis, renal function impairment, and systemic lupus erythematosus.

Proper use of this medication

Compliance with therapy; taking medication at the same time each day to maintain the therapeutic effect

» Possible need for control of weight and diet, especially sodium intake; risks associated with sodium depletion; not taking potassium supplements or salt substitutes containing potassium unless approved by physician

» Importance of taking medication even if feeling well; possible life-long therapy; checking with physician before discontinuing medication

May be taken with other antihypertensive agents; with or without food

» Proper dosing

Missed dose: Taking as soon as possible; not taking if almost time for next scheduled dose; not doubling doses

Proper storage

Precautions while using this medication

» Regular visits to physician

» Notifying physician immediately if pregnancy is suspected

Not taking other medications without consulting the physician, especially nonprescription sympathomimetics

Caution when driving or doing other things requiring alertness, because of possible dizziness, especially during the first days of therapy; notifying physician if it occurs; discontinuing the medication and notifying physician if syncope occurs

To prevent dehydration and hypotension, checking with physician if severe nausea, vomiting, or diarrhea occurs and continues

Caution when exercising or during exposure to hot weather, because of the risk of dehydration and hypotension due to reduced fluid volume

» Caution in using alcohol because of the risk of dehydration and hypotension due to reduced fluid volume

Diabetics: May increase blood sugar levels

Side/adverse effects

Signs of potential side effects, especially dizziness or lightheadedness, electrolyte imbalance, upper respiratory tract infection, angina, angioedema, and myocardial infarction

Oral Dosage Forms

CANDESARTAN CILEXETILAND HYDROCHLOROTHIAZIDE TABLETS

Usual Adult Dose

Antihypertensive—

Oral, 1 or 2 tablets (16-12.5 mg tablet) or 1 tablet (32-12.5 mg tablet) once a day as determined by individual titration with the component agents.

Note: Candesartan and hydrochlorothiazide combination is not recommended in patients with renal impairment of creatinine clearance ≤ 30 mL per minute.

Caution is recommended in patients with hepatic impairment when receiving hydrochlorothiazide.

Usual adult prescribing limits

32 mg of candesartan daily

Usual Pediatric Dose

Safety and efficacy have not been established.

Usual geriatric dose

See *Usual adult dose*

Strength(s) usually available

U.S.—

16 mg candesartan cilexetil and 12.5 mg hydrochlorothiazide (Rx) [*Atacand HCT 16-12.5* (calcium carboxymethylcellulose; corn starch; ferric oxide (reddish brown); ferric oxide yellow; hydroxypropyl cellulose; lactose monohydrate; magnesium stearate; polyethylene glycol 8000)].

32 mg candesartan cilexetil and 12.5 mg hydrochlorothiazide (Rx) [*Atacand HCT 32-12.5* (calcium carboxymethylcellulose; corn starch; ferric oxide yellow; hydroxypropyl cellulose; lactose monohydrate; magnesium stearate; polyethylene glycol 8000)].

Auxiliary labeling

• May cause drowsiness.

Developed: 01/08/2001

CAPECITABINE Systemic

VA CLASSIFICATION (Primary): AN300

Commonly used brand name(s): *Xeloda.*

Note: For a listing of dosage forms and brand names by country availability, see *Dosage Forms* section(s).

Category

Antineoplastic.

Indications

Note: Bracketed information in the *Indications* section refers to uses that are not included in U.S. product labeling.

Accepted

Carcinoma, breast (treatment)—Capecitabine is indicated for treatment of metastatic breast carcinoma that is resistant to both paclitaxel and an anthracycline-containing chemotherapy regimen (i.e., has progressed during, or relapsed within 6 months following completion of, treatment). It is also indicated for treating patients whose disease is resistant to paclitaxel and who should not receive further anthracycline therapy (for example, patients who have received cumulative doses of 400 mg per square meter of body surface area of doxorubicin or doxorubicin equivalents).

Capecitabine is also indicated in combination with docetaxel for the treatment of patients with metastatic breast cancer after failure of prior anthracycline-containing chemotherapy.

Carcinoma, colorectal (treatment)—Capecitabine is indicated as first-line treatment of patients with metastatic colorectal carcinoma when treatment with fluoropyrimidine therapy alone is preferred. Combination therapy has shown a survival benefit comparable to 5-FU/leucovorin monotherapy. Monotherapy with capecitabine has not shown a survival benefit over 5–FU/leucovorin.

Capecitabine is indicated as a single agent for adjuvant treatment in patients with Dukes' C colon cancer who have undergone complete resection of the primary tumor when treatment with fluoropyrimidine therapy alone is preferred. Capecitabine was non-inferior to 5-fluorouracil and leucovorin (5-FU/LV) for disease-free survival (DFS). Although neither capecitabine nor combination chemotherapy prolongs overall survival (OS), combination chemotherapy has been demonstrated to improve disease-free survival compared to 5-FU/LV. Physicians should consider these results when prescribing single-agent capecitabine in the adjuvant treatment of Dukes' C colon cancer.

Capecitabine is also indicated, [in combination with oxaliplatin][1], for the first-line treatment of nonresectable, advanced, or metastatic colon or rectal carcinoma. Prior adjuvant or palliative 5–FU-based chemotherapy and radiation therapy are permitted.

Acceptance not established

Metastatic colorectal cancer, capecitabine in combination with irinotecan—Published data on the combination of irinotecan and oral capecitabine in patients with metastatic colorectal cancer are limited. However, efficacy, tolerability, and convenience have been reported with this combination in several abstracts. In three published phase II studies, patients with advanced or metastatic colorectal cancer treated with varying doses/schedules of irinotecan plus intermittent capecitabine obtained overall objective response rates and median time to progression of approximately 40% and 6 months, respectively. Adverse events were consistent with reports in the literature for continuous 5-fluorouracil and irinotecan. Despite the fact that the results of these studies are similar to those of two, large, randomized trials of bolus or infusional 5-fluorouracil (5-FU) with irinotecan, additional phase III trials are needed.

Use of capecitabine for the treatment of unresectable, locally advanced and/or metastatic pancreatic carcinoma has not been established, due to insufficient data supporting efficacy. Awaiting phase III trial results to define the role of capecitabine in combination with gemcitabine. There is insufficient data available comparing capecitabine, as a single agent, to gemcitabine or to 5–FU with radiation therapy.

Pancreatic cancer, locally advanced or metastatic, first-line therapy, in combination with gemcitabine—Clinical trials evaluating the addition of capecitabine to gemcitabine for the first-line treatment of locally advanced or metastatic pancreatic cancer have found conflicting results. Two phase 3 clinical trials have randomized the combination using various doses of gemcitabine and capecitabine versus standard gemcitabine monotherapy. One phase 3 study, available as an abstract and presentation, found no differences in survival or response between treatment groups while the other phase 3 trial, available as an abstract reporting interim results, found significant improvements in overall survival and response rates in favor of the gemcitabine plus capecitabine arm. In addition, a randomized phase 2 clinical trial reported no differences in efficacy between gemcitabine plus capecitabine versus standard gemcitabine alone. Additional phase 2 clinical trials, in abstract form, have supported the activity of gemcitabine plus capecitabine in pancreatic cancer. Grades 3 or 4 hematologic toxicity appear to be consistent between treatment arms, while the incidences of grades 3 or 4 diarrhea, nausea, vomiting, and hand-foot syndrome appear to be higher in the combination arm in one phase 3 trial but similar in the other. Mild to moderate stomatitis, diarrhea, and hand-foot syndrome were more common in the gemcitabine plus capecitabine.

[1]Not included in Canadian product labeling.

Pharmacology/Pharmacokinetics

Physicochemical characteristics

Chemical Group—A fluoropyrimidine carbamate.
Molecular weight—359.35.
Solubility—In water: 26 mg per mL at 20 °C.

Mechanism of action/Effect

Capecitabine is relatively noncytotoxic *in vitro;* its activity occurs after *in vivo* conversion to 5-fluorouracil (5-FU; fluorouracil), which in turn is converted to two active metabolites, 5-fluoro-2-deoxyuridine monophosphate (FdUMP) and 5-fluorouridine triphosphate (FUTP). The cytotoxic effect is produced by two different mechanisms. First, FdUMP and the folate cofactor N^{5-10}-methylenetetrahydrofolate bind to thymidylate synthase to form a ternary complex, thereby inhibiting thymidylate formation. Thymidylate is the precursor of thymidine triphosphate, which is essential for DNA synthesis; deficiency of this precursor leads to inhibition of cell division. Second, nuclear transcriptional enzymes can incorporate FUTP instead of uridine triphosphate during RNA synthesis, resulting in a metabolic error that interferes with RNA processing and protein synthesis.

Absorption

Readily absorbed. Both the rate and extent of absorption are decreased by concurrent administration with food.

Protein binding

Moderate (less than 60%), primarily to albumin (approximately 35%). Binding is not concentration-dependent.

Biotransformation

Capecitabine—

Initially hepatic, hydrolyzed via a carboxylesterase to 5′-deoxy-5-fluorocytidine (5′-DFCR), which in turn is first converted to 5′-deoxy-5-fluorouridine (5′-DFUR) and then hydrolyzed to the active substance, fluorouracil, by cytidine deaminase and thymidine phosphorylase, respectively. These enzymes are found in most tissues, including tumors. Thymidine phosphorylase is expressed in higher concentrations by some human carcinomas than by surrounding normal tissues.

Fluorouracil—

Metabolized in normal and tumor cells to the active metabolites FdUMP and FUTP. Also, metabolized by dihydropyrimidine dehydrogenase to 5-fluoro-5,6-dihydro-fluorouracil (FUH_2), which is much less toxic. This compound is further metabolized by cleavage of the pyrimidine ring to yield 5-fluoro-ureido-propionic acid (FUPA), which undergoes further cleavage to produce alpha-fluoro-beta-alanine (FBAL).

Half-life

Elimination—

For both capecitabine and fluorouracil: Approximately 45 minutes.

Time to peak concentration

In blood—Approximately 1.5 hours for capecitabine and 2 hours for fluorouracil. Peak concentrations of both substances are delayed by 1.5 hours when capecitabine is administered concurrently with food.

Peak blood concentration

There is wide interpatient variability (> 85%) in the maximum concentration (C_{max}) and area under the plasma concentration-time curve (AUC) for fluorouracil.

In studies with doses ranging between 500 and 3500 mg per square meter of body surface area (mg/m^2) per day, the pharmacokinetics of capecitabine and 5′-DFCR were dose-proportional and did not change over time. However, the increases in the AUCs of fluorouracil and 5′-DFUR were greater than proportional to the increase in dose, and the AUC of fluorouracil was 34% higher on day 14 than on day 1. In 13 patients with mild to moderate hepatic function impairment given single doses of 1255 mg/m^2 of capecitabine, C_{max} and AUC values for the parent compound were 60% higher than in patients with normal hepatic function, but values for fluorouracil were not affected.

When capecitabine is administered concurrently with food, C_{max} values for capecitabine and fluorouracil are decreased by 60% and 35%, respectively, and AUC values are reduced by 43% and 21%, respectively.

Elimination

Renal, more than 70% of a capecitabine dose as drug-related species (approximately 50% as FBAL).

In dialysis—

Although there is no clinical experience, it is possible that 5′-DFUR (the low-molecular weight capecitabine metabolite that is the immediate precursor of fluorouracil) may be removable by dialysis.

Precautions to Consider

Cross-sensitivity and/or related problems

Patients sensitive to fluorouracil may also be sensitive to capecitabine.

Carcinogenicity

Long-term studies in animals have not been done.

Mutagenicity

Capecitabine was not found to be mutagenic in *in vitro* bacterial tests (Ames test) or in mammalian cells (Chinese hamster V79/HPRT gene mutation assay). It was clastogenic to human peripheral blood lymphocytes *in vitro* but not to mouse bone marrow (micronucleus test) *in vivo*.

Fluorouracil causes mutations in bacteria and yeast and causes chromosomal abnormalities in the mouse micronucleus test *in vivo*.

Pregnancy/Reproduction

Fertility—Studies in female mice given oral doses of 760 mg per kg of body weight (mg/kg) per day found a reversible disturbance of estrus and a subsequent decrease in fertility; in mice that did become pregnant, no fetuses survived. The same dose in male mice produced degenerative changes in the testes, including decreases in the number of spermatocytes and spermatids. In mice, this dose produces area under the plasma concentration-time curve (AUC) values for the immediate precursor of fluorouracil (5′-deoxy-5-fluorouridine [5′-DFUR]) that are approximately 0.7 times the corresponding values in humans taking the recommended daily dose.

Pregnancy—Adequate and well-controlled studies in women have not been done. It is recommended that women of childbearing potential be advised to avoid becoming pregnant during treatment because of the potential risks to the fetus. Also, if the medication is used during pregnancy, or the patient becomes pregnant during treatment, the patient should be informed of the potential risks.

Capecitabine caused teratogenicity (cleft palate, anophthalmia, microphthalmia, oligodactyly, polydactyly, syndactyly, kinky tail, dilation of cerebral ventricles) and embryolethality in mice given doses of 198 mg/kg per day (producing AUC values for 5′-DFUR approximately 0.2 times the corresponding value in humans taking the recommended daily dose) during the period of organogenesis. It also caused fetal deaths in monkeys given 90 mg/kg per day (producing AUC values for 5′-DFUR approximately 0.6 times the corresponding value in humans taking the recommended daily dose) during organogenesis.

FDA Pregnancy Category D.

Breast-feeding

It is not known whether capecitabine is distributed into human breast milk. However, breast-feeding is not recommended during treatment because of the potential risks to the infant.

Pediatrics

Studies on the relationship of age to the effects of capecitabine have not been performed in the pediatric population. Safety and efficacy in patients younger than 18 years of age have not been established.

Geriatrics

Geriatric patients may be pharmacodynamically more sensitive to the toxic effects of capecitabine than younger adults. In particular, the risk of severe (National Cancer Institute [NCI] grade 3 or 4) gastrointestinal adverse effects (diarrhea, nausea, vomiting) may be increased in patients 80 years of age and older. Patients 60 years of age and older are independently predisposed to an increased risk of coagulopathy.. Careful monitoring is recommended. Pharmacokinetic studies have not been performed in the geriatric population.

Dental

Capecitabine may cause stomatitis. In clinical trials, stomatitis occurred in up to 24%, and was severe enough to decrease food intake substantially (NCI grade 3) in 4 to 7%, of the patients.

Drug interactions and/or related problems

The following drug interactions and/or related problems have been selected on the basis of their potential clinical significance (possible mechanism in parentheses where appropriate)—not necessarily inclusive (» = major clinical significance):

Note: Combinations containing any of the following medications, depending on the amount present, may also interact with this medication.

Antacids, aluminum and magnesium-containing
(administration of an aluminum and magnesium-containing antacid immediately after capecitabine in 12 patients produced small increases in blood concentrations of capecitabine and the metabolite 5′-deoxy-5-fluorocytidine [5′-DFCR], but did not affect the concentrations of other major metabolites)

» Anticoagulants, coumarin-derivative, such as warfarin and phenprocoumon
(altered coagulation parameters and/or bleeding, including death-have been reported in patients receiving capecitabine and coumarin-derived anticoagulants; these events occurred within several days to several months after concurrent therapy was initiated and, in a few cases, within one month after stopping capecitabine; patients receiving oral anticoagulants should be routinely monitored for alterations in their prothrombin time (PT) or International Normalized ratio (INR); coumarin-derivative anticoagulant dose may need to be reduced when administered concomitantly with capecitabine)

Blood dyscrasia-causing medications
(leukopenia and/or thrombocytopenic effects of capecitabine may be increased with concurrent or recent therapy if these medications cause the same effects; dosage adjustment of capecitabine if necessary, should be based on blood counts)

» Bone marrow depressants, other or
» Radiation therapy
(additive bone marrow depression, including severe dermatitis and/or mucositis, may occur; dosage reduction may be required when two or more bone marrow depressants, including radiation, are used concurrently or consecutively)

CYP2C9 substrates
(Although no formal drug-drug interaction studies between capecitabine and CYP2C9 substrates other than warfarin have been conducted, care should be exercised during coadministration)

Leucovorin
(concurrent use may increase the therapeutic and toxic effects of fluorouracil as a result of increased concentrations; fatalities as a result of severe enterocolitis, diarrhea, and dehydration have been reported in elderly patients who received the two medications concurrently)

Phenytoin or
Fosphenytoin
(plasma concentrations and associated clinical symptoms may increase as a result of concurrent use with capecitabine; dose of phenytoin or fosphenytoin may need to be reduced with concomitant use)

Vaccines, killed virus
(because normal defense mechanisms may be suppressed by capecitabine therapy, the patient's antibody response to the vaccine may be decreased. The interval between discontinuation of medications that cause immunosuppression and restoration of the patient's ability to respond to the vaccine depends on the intensity and type of immunosuppression-causing medication used, the underlying disease, and other factors; estimates vary from 3 months to 1 year)

» Vaccines, live virus
(because normal defense mechanisms may be suppressed by capecitabine therapy, concurrent use with a live virus vaccine may potentiate the replication of the vaccine virus, may increase the side/adverse effects of the vaccine virus, and/or may decrease the patient's antibody response to the vaccine; immunization of these patients should be undertaken only with extreme caution after careful review of the patient's hematologic status and only with the knowledge and consent of the physician managing the capecitabine therapy. The interval between discontinuation of medications that cause immunosuppression and restoration of the patient's ability to respond to the vaccine depends on the intensity and type of immunosuppression-causing medication used, the underlying disease, and other factors; estimates vary from 3 months to 1 year. In addition, immunization with oral poliovirus vaccine should be postponed in persons in close contact with the patient, especially family members)

Laboratory value alterations

The following have been selected on the basis of their potential clinical significance (possible effect in parentheses where appropriate)—not necessarily inclusive (» = major clinical significance).

With physiology/laboratory test values
Alkaline phosphatase and
Alanine aminotransferase (ALT [SGPT]) and
Aspartate aminotransferase (AST [SGOT]) and
Bilirubin
(elevations of serum bilirubin and concurrent increases in alkaline phosphatase and/or transaminase concentrations may occur, especially in patients with hepatic metastases)

Magnesium
Potassium
(hypomagnesemia or hypokalemia can occur with capecitabine treatment)

» Prothrombin time or INR
(elevations in INR values by as much as 91% have been observed in cancer patients on concomitant capecitabine and warfarin therapy)

Triglycerides
(elevated levels of triglycerides may occur with capecitabine use)

Medical considerations/Contraindications

The medical considerations/contraindications included have been selected on the basis of their potential clinical significance (reasons given in parentheses where appropriate)—not necessarily inclusive (» = major clinical significance).

Except under certain circumstances, this medication should not be used when the following medical problem exists:

» Dihydropyrimidine dehydrogenase (DPD) deficiency or
» Hypersensitivity to capecitabine or to any of its components or
» Hypersensitivity to 5-fluorouracil
(capecitabine use contraindicated)

» Renal function impairment, severe
(capecitabine use contraindicated; high rate of grade III-IV adverse events in patients with creatinine clearance < 30 mL/min)

Risk-benefit should be considered when the following medical problems exist:

» Bone marrow depression, existing or
Cancer
(predisposes patients to an increased risk of coagulopathy)

» Chickenpox, existing or recent, or
» Herpes zoster
(risk of severe generalized disease)

Coronary artery disease, history of
(fluorinated pyrimidine therapy has been associated with cardiotoxicity, which may be more common in patients with a prior history of coronary artery disease)

Cytoxic drug or radiation therapy, previous
(caution should be used)

» Hepatic function impairment
(caution is recommended because blood concentrations and AUC values for capecitabine may be increased, and the risk of grade 3 or 4 hyperbilirubinemia with concurrent increases in alkaline phosphatase and/or transaminases is higher, in patients with mild to moderate hepatic function impairment due to hepatic metastases; no information is available for patients with severe hepatic function impairment)

» Infection
» Renal function impairment, moderate
(greater incidence of treatment-related grade III-IV adverse events in patients with creatinine clearance 30-50 mL/min; starting dose is reduced to 75% of the recommended starting dose)

Patient monitoring

The following may be especially important in patient monitoring (other tests may be warranted in some patients, depending on condition; » = major clinical significance):

Hepatic function
(monitoring recommended in patients with pre-existing hepatic function impairment because of the increased risk of hyperbilirubinemia and associated increases in alkaline phosphatase and/or transaminase values; temporary withdrawal of treatment is recommended if hyperbilirubinemia of NCI grade 2 [serum bilirubin 1.5 times normal values] or higher occurs. If treatment is reinstated after hyperbilirubinemia has resolved, a reduction in dosage may be needed)

» Neutropenia
(neutrophil count should be monitored; patients who develop a fever of 100.5°F or greater or other evidence of potential infection should be instructed to call their physician)

» Prothrombin time or INR
(patients receiving concomitant capecitabine and oral coumarin-derivative anticoagulant therapy should have their anticoagulant response monitored closely and with great frequency and anticoagulant dose adjustments made accordingly)

» Renal function
(monitoring for grade II-IV severe adverse events in patients with creatinine clearance 30-50 mL/min (moderate impairment) to < 30 mL/min (severe impairment); dose adjustments or treatment interruption if necessary)

Side/Adverse Effects

The following side/adverse effects have been selected on the basis of their potential clinical significance (possible signs and symptoms in parentheses where appropriate)—not necessarily inclusive:

Those indicating need for medical attention

Incidence more frequent

Abdominal or stomach pain; anemia (unusual tiredness or weakness)—usually asymptomatic; ***diarrhea, moderate or severe; hand-and-foot syndrome*** (blistering, peeling, redness, and/or swelling of palms of hands or bottoms of feet; numbness, pain, tingling, or unusual sensations in palms of hands or bottoms of feet); ***hyperbilirubinemia*** (yellow eyes or skin); ***lymphopenia*** (fever or chills; cough or hoarseness; lower back or side pain; painful or difficult urination); ***neutropenia***—usually asymptomatic; ***stomatitis*** (pain, redness, and/or swelling in mouth and on lips; sores or ulcers in mouth and on lips); ***thrombocytopenia***—usually asymptomatic

Note: *Diarrhea* is one of the dose-limiting toxicities of capecitabine. It may be severe and lead to dehydration. In clinical trials, diarrhea of any grade occurred in at least 50% of the patients, but was severe in relatively few, with National Cancer Institute (NCI) grades 3 and 4 diarrhea occurring in fewer than 12% and 3% of the patients, respectively. The median time to first occurrence of NCI grade 2 or higher diarrhea was 31 (range, 1 to 322) days.

Hand-and-foot syndrome (also known as palmar-plantar erythrodysesthesia or chemotherapy-induced acral erythema) may result in severe discomfort that interferes with the patient's ability to work or perform activities of daily living. A reaction of such severity requires immediate medical attention.

Bone marrow depression during treatment with capecitabine resulted in *anemia*, *neutropenia*, or *thrombocytopenia* in up to 74%, 26%, and 24%, respectively, of the patients in clinical trials. However, each of these hematologic toxicities reached a severity of NCI grade 3 or 4 in only 4% or fewer, and grade 3 or 4 coagulation disorders, pancytopenia, or thrombocytopenic purpura each occurred in only 0.2%, of the patients.

Incidence less frequent or rare

Angina pectoris (chest pain); ***ataxia*** (clumsiness or unsteadiness; problems with coordination); ***atrial fibrillation*** (fast or irregular heartbeat; dizziness; fainting); ***bone marrow depression*** (bleeding and bruising; sore throat and fever; unusual tiredness or weakness); ***bradycardia*** (chest pain or discomfort; lightheadedness; dizziness or fainting; shortness of breath; slow or irregular heartbeat; unusual tiredness); ***bronchitis*** (cough producing mucus; difficulty breathing; shortness of breath; tightness in chest; wheezing); ***bronchopneumonia*** (chest pain; cough; fever or chills; sneezing; shortness of breath; sore throat; troubled breathing; tightness in chest; wheezing); ***bronchospasm; dyspnea; or respiratory distress*** (shortness of breath, troubled breathing, tightness in chest, or wheezing); ***cardiomyopathy*** (fast or irregular heartbeat; shortness of breath or troubled breathing; tiredness or weakness, severe); ***cardiotoxicity*** (chest pain or discomfort; fast or irregular heartbeat; shortness of breath; swelling of the feet and lower legs; troubled breathing); ***cerebrovascular accident*** (blurred vision; headache, sudden and severe; inability to speak; seizures; slurred speech; temporary blindness; weakness in arm and/or leg on one side of the body, sudden and severe); ***chest mass*** (unusual lump or swelling in the chest); ***cholestatic hepatitis; hepatic fibrosis; or hepatitis*** (dark urine; fever; itching; light-colored stools; pain, tenderness, and/or swelling in upper abdominal area; skin rash; swollen glands; yellow eyes or skin); ***coagulation disorder*** (problems with bleeding or clotting); ***collapse; conjunctivitis*** (redness, pain, swelling of eye, eyelid, or inner lining of eyelid; burning, dry or itching eyes; discharge; excessive tearing); ***dysarthria*** (trouble in speaking; slurred speech; changes in patterns and rhythms of speech); ***dysphasia*** (loss of ability to use or understand speech or language); ***edema*** (swelling of face, fingers, feet, or lower legs); ***encephalopathy*** (agitation; back pain; blurred vision; coma; confusion; dizziness; drowsiness; fever; hallucinations; headache; irritability; mood or mental changes; seizures; stiff neck; unusual tiredness or weakness; vomiting); ***epistaxis*** (unexplained nosebleeds); ***extrasystoles*** (extra heartbeats); ***fever; fungal infection (including candidiasis)*** (itching in genital or other skin areas; scaling; white patches in the mouth or throat or on the tongue; white patches with diaper rash); ***gastric ulcer*** (loss of appetite; nausea; stomach bloating, burning, cramping, or pain; vomiting; weight loss); ***gastrointestinal hemorrhage*** (black, tarry stools; bloody stools; vomiting of blood or material that looks like coffee grounds); ***gastrointestinal tract toxicity*** (abdominal or stomach cramping or pain, severe; bloody or black, tarry stools; constipation or diarrhea, severe; difficulty in swallowing or pain in back of throat or chest when swallowing; vomiting blood or material that looks like coffee grounds); ***hemorrhage*** (bleeding gums; coughing up blood; difficulty in breathing or swallowing; dizziness; headache; increased menstrual flow or vaginal bleeding; nosebleeds; paralysis; prolonged bleeding from cuts; red or dark brown urine; red or black, tarry stools; shortness of breath); ***hemoptysis*** (coughing or spitting up blood); ***hypokalemia*** (convulsions; decreased urine; dry mouth; irregular heartbeat; increased thirst; loss of appetite; mood changes; muscle pain or cramps; nausea or vomiting; numbness or tingling in hands, feet, or lips; shortness of breath; unusual tiredness or weakness); ***hypomagnesemia*** (drowsiness; loss of appetite; mood or mental changes; muscle spasms; [tetany] or twitching seizures; nausea or vomiting; trembling; unusual tiredness or weakness); ***hypotension*** (decreased blood pressure); ***hypertension*** (increased blood pressure); ***hypertriglyceridemia*** (large amount of triglyceride in the blood); ***idiopathic thrombocytopenia purpura*** (unusual bleeding or bruising; bloody nose; heavier menstrual periods; pinpoint red spots on skin; black, tarry stools; blood in urine; unusual tiredness or weakness; fever; skin rash); ***ileus*** (abdominal pain, severe constipation, severe vomiting); ***infection*** (cough or hoarseness; fever or chills; lower back or side pain; painful or difficult urination; sneezing; sore throat; stuffy nose; white spots in mouth or throat)—rarely, may be associated with neutropenia; ***keratoconjunctivitis*** (eye redness; irritation; or pain); ***leukopenia*** (black, tarry stools; chest pain; chills; cough; fever; painful or difficult urination; shortness of breath; sore throat; sores, ulcers, or white spots on lips or in mouth; swollen glands; unusual bleeding or bruising; unusual tiredness or weakness); ***loss of consciousness; lymphoedema*** (swelling of lymph nodes); ***myocarditis*** (chest pain or discomfort; fever and chills; fast heartbeat; trouble breathing); ***nausea***—severe enough to cause loss of appetite; ***pancytopenia*** (high fever; chills; unexplained bleeding or bruising; bloody, black, or tarry stools; pale skin; unusual tiredness or weakness; cough; shortness of breath; sores, ulcers, or white spots on lips or in mouth; swollen glands); ***pericardial effusion*** (chest pain or discomfort; shortness of breath); ***phlebitis; thrombophlebitis; or deep vein thrombosis*** (hot, red skin on feet or legs; painful, swollen feet or legs); ***pneumonia*** (chest pain; cough; fever or chills; sneezing; shortness of breath; sore throat; troubled breathing; tightness in chest; wheezing); ***pulmonary embolism*** (shortness of breath or troubled breathing; pain in chest); ***renal impairment*** (lower back/side pain; decreased frequency/amount of urine; bloody urine; increased thirst; loss of appetite; nausea; vomiting; unusual tiredness or weakness; swelling of face, fingers, lower legs; weight gain; troubled breathing; increased blood pressure); ***sepsis*** (chills; confusion; dizziness; lightheadedness; fainting; fast heartbeat; fever; rapid, shallow breathing); ***tachycardia*** (fast, pounding, or irregular heartbeat or pulse); ***thrombocytopenic purpura*** (unusual bleeding or bruising; black, tarry stools; blood in urine or stools; pinpoint red spots on skin); ***toxic dilation of intestine*** (bloating; constipation; loss of appetite; nausea or vomiting; stomach pain); ***ventricular extrasystoles*** (extra heartbeats); ***viral infection*** (chills; cough or hoarseness; fever; cold; flu-like symptoms); ***vomiting***—two or more episodes in 24 hours

Note: *Gastrointestinal toxicity* may affect any area of the gastrointestinal tract and may result in colitis, duodenitis, esophagitis, gastritis, gastrointestinal or rectal bleeding, hematemesis, intestinal obstruction, or necrotizing enterocolitis.

Reported *infections* include oral, esophageal, or gastrointestinal candidiasis; upper respiratory tract infection; urinary tract infection; bronchitis, pneumonia, or bronchopneumonia; and sepsis. Each of these occurred in fewer than 5%, and was severe (NCI grade 3 or 4) in only 0.2% (0.4% for sepsis), of the patients in clinical trials.

Reported neurologic effects (in addition to *ataxia*) include decrease or loss of consciousness and encephalopathy.

Incidence not determined—Observed during clinical practice, estimates of frequency can not be determined

Hepatic failure (headache; stomach pain; continuing vomiting; dark-colored urine; general feeling of tiredness or weakness; light-colored stools; yellow eyes or skin)

Those indicating need for medical attention only if they continue or are bothersome

Incidence more frequent

Constipation, mild or moderate; dermatitis (skin rash or itching); ***diarrhea, mild; loss of appetite; nausea; unusual tiredness; vomiting***

Note: NCI grade 2 or greater *nausea* or *vomiting* requires immediate medical attention.

Incidence less frequent

Anorexia (loss of appetite, weight loss); ***arthralgia*** (pain in joints; muscle pain or stiffness; difficulty in moving); ***back pain; changes in fingernails or toenails; dehydration*** (confusion; decreased urination; dizziness; dry mouth; fainting; increase in heart rate; lightheadedness; rapid breathing; sunken eyes; thirst; unusual tiredness or weakness; wrinkled skin); ***dizziness; dyspepsia*** (heartburn); ***eye irritation*** (red, sore eyes); ***fatigue; headache; insomnia*** (trouble in sleeping); ***myalgia*** (muscle pain); ***pain; pain in limb; paresthesia*** (burning, crawling, itching, numbness, prickling, "pins and needles", or tingling feelings); ***photosensitivity*** (increased sensitivity of skin to sunlight); ***pyrexia*** (fever); ***radiation recall syndrome*** (pain and redness of skin at place of earlier radiation treatment); ***weakness***

Incidence rare

Abdominal distension (swelling of abdominal or stomach area; full or bloated feeling or pressure in the stomach); ***abnormal coordination*** (clumsiness or unsteadiness); ***arthritis*** (pain, swelling, or redness in joints; muscle pain or stiffness; difficulty in moving); ***ascites*** (stomach pain and bloating); ***asthma*** (cough; difficulty breathing; noisy breathing; shortness of breath; tightness in chest; wheezing); ***bone pain; cachexia*** (general physical wasting or malnutrition associated with severe illness); ***confusion*** (mood or mental changes); ***cough; depression*** (discouragement; feeling sad or empty; irritability; lack of appetite; loss of interest or pleasure; tiredness; trouble concentrating; trouble sleeping); ***difficulty in walking; dysphagia*** (difficulty in swallowing); ***fibrosis; gastroenteritis*** (abdominal or stomach pain; diarrhea; loss of appetite; nausea; weakness); ***gastrointestinal motility disorder*** (constipation; full feeling in abdomen; passing less gas; stomach cramps or pain); ***hoarseness*** (rough, scratchy sound to voice); ***hot flushes; impaired balance; increased weight; influenza-like illness*** (chills; cough; diarrhea; fever; general feeling of discomfort or illness; headache; joint pain; loss of appetite; muscle aches and pains; nausea; runny nose; shivering; sore throat; sweating; trouble sleeping; unusual tiredness or weakness; vomiting); ***irritability; laryngitis*** (cough; dryness or soreness of throat; hoarseness; trouble in swallowing; voice changes); ***muscle weakness; nail disorder*** (discoloration of fingernails or toenails); ***proctalgia*** (pain in rectum); ***pruritus*** (itching skin); ***sedation*** (drowsiness; sleepiness; relaxed and calm); ***skin discoloration*** (change in color of treated skin); ***skin ulceration*** (sores on the skin); ***sweating increased; thirst; tremor*** (trembling or shaking of hands or feet, shakiness in legs, arms, hands, feet); ***vertigo*** (dizziness or lightheadedness; feeling of constant movement of self or surroundings; sensation of spinning)

Overdose

For more information on the management of overdose or unintentional ingestion, **contact a Poison Control Center** (see *Poison Control Center Listing*).

Clinical effects of overdose

The following effects have been selected on the basis of their potential clinical significance (possible signs and symptoms in parentheses where appropriate)—not necessarily inclusive:

Acute and chronic

Bone marrow depression (black, tarry stools; blood in urine or stools; cough or hoarseness; fever or chills; lower back or side pain; painful or difficult urination; pinpoint red spots on skin; unusual bleeding or bruising); ***diarrhea; gastrointestinal tract toxicity*** (abdominal or stomach pain, severe; bloody or black, tarry stools; constipation or diarrhea, severe; difficulty in swallowing or pain in back of throat or chest when swallowing; nausea or vomiting, severe; vomiting blood or material that looks like coffee grounds); ***nausea; vomiting***

Treatment of overdose

Supportive care—Appropriate care to address the clinical manifestations.

Dialysis may be effective in removing circulating 5′-DFUR, the low-molecular weight metabolite that is the immediate precursor of fluorouracil.

Patient Consultation

As an aid to patient consultation, refer to *Advice for the Patient, Capecitabine (Systemic)*

In providing consultation, consider emphasizing the following selected information (» = major clinical significance):

Before using this medication

» Conditions affecting use, especially:
- Sensitivity to capecitabine or fluorouracil
- Pregnancy—Avoiding pregnancy during treatment; telling physician immediately if pregnancy is suspected
- Breast-feeding—Not recommended because of risk of serious side effects
- Use in the elderly—Possible increased sensitivity to gastrointestinal adverse effects
- Increased risk of coagulopathy
- Other medications, especially bone marrow depressants, live virus vaccines, coumarin-derivative anticoagulants, or previous cytotoxic drug therapy or radiation therapy
- Other medical problems, especially dihydropyrimidine dehydrogenase (DPD) deficiency; existing bone marrow depression; existing or recent chicken pox; hepatic function impairment; herpes zoster infection; hypersensitivity to capecitabine or any of its components; hypersensitivity to 5-fluorouracil; infection; moderate renal function impairment; or severe renal function impairment

Proper use of this medication

Taking within 30 minutes after a meal

Swallowing tablets with water

» Proper dosing

Missed dose: Not taking at all; not doubling doses; checking with physician

» Proper storage

Precautions while using this medication

» Importance of close monitoring by the physician

» Importance of monitoring prothrombin time or INR in patients on coumarin-derived anticoagulants

» Notifying physician immediately if fever of 100.5 °F or higher, or other evidence of an infection, occurs

» Stopping treatment and notifying physician immediately if symptoms indicative of NCI grade 2 (or higher) diarrhea, hand-and-foot syndrome, nausea, vomiting, or stomatitis occurs

» Avoiding immunizations unless approved by physician; other persons in patient's household should avoid immunizations with oral poliovirus vaccine; avoiding other persons who have taken oral poliovirus vaccine or wearing a protective mask that covers nose and mouth

Caution if bone marrow depression occurs:

» Avoiding exposure to persons with infections, especially during periods of low blood counts; checking with physician immediately if fever or chills, cough or hoarseness, lower back or side pain, or painful or difficult urination occur

» Checking with physician immediately if unusual bleeding or bruising; black tarry stools; blood in urine or stools; or pinpoint red spots on skin occur

Caution in use of regular toothbrush, dental floss, or toothpick; physician, dentist, or nurse may suggest alternatives; checking with physician before having dental work done

Not touching eyes or inside of nose unless hands washed immediately before

Using caution to avoid accidental cuts with use of sharp objects such as safety razor or fingernail or toenail cutters

Avoiding contact sports or other situations where bruising or injury could occur

Side/adverse effects

May cause adverse effects such as blood problems, hand-and-foot syndrome, and gastrointestinal tract toxicity; importance of discussing possible effects with physician

Signs of potential side effects, especially abdominal or stomach pain; anemia; diarrhea (moderate or severe); hand-and-foot-syndrome; hyperbilirubinemia; lymphopenia; neutropenia; stomatitis; thrombocytopenia; angina; ataxia; atrial fibrillation; bone marrow depression; bradycardia; bronchitis; bronchopneumonia; bronchospasm, dyspnea, or respiratory distress; cardiomyopathy; cardiotoxicity; cerebrovascular accident; chest mass; cholestatic hepatitis, hepatic fibrosis, or hepatitis; coagulation disorder; collapse; conjunctivitis; dysarthria; dysphasia; edema; encephalopathy; epistaxis; extrasystoles; fever; fungal infection (including candidiasis); gastric ulcer; gastrointestinal hemorrhage; gastrointestinal tract toxicity; hemorrhage; hemoptysis; hypokalemia; hypomagnesemia; hypotension; hypertension; hypertriglyceridemia; idiopathic thrombocytopenia purpura; ileus; infection; keratoconjunctivitis; leukopenia; loss of consciousness; lymphoedema; myocarditis; nausea (severe enough to cause loss of appetite); pancytopenia; pericardial effusion; phlebitis, thrombophlebitis, or deep venous thrombosis; pneumonia; pulmonary embolism; renal impairment; thrombocytopenic purpura; toxic dilation of intestine; ventricular extrasystoles; viral infection; or vomiting (two or more episodes in 24 hours)

Signs of potential side effects observed during clinical practice, especially hepatic failure

Physician or nurse can help in dealing with side effects

General Dosing Information

Patients receiving capecitabine should be under the supervision of a physician experienced in cancer chemotherapy.

Dosage must be adjusted to meet the individual requirements of each patient, based on appearance or severity of toxicity.

It is recommended that capecitabine be taken within 30 minutes after a meal and that the tablets be swallowed with water.

It is recommended that capecitabine be discontinued immediately if any of the following occur:

Diarrhea, grade 2 (an increase of 4 to 6 stools per day or nocturnal stools) or greater.

Hand-and-foot syndrome, grade 2 (painful erythema and swelling of the palms of the hands and/or the bottoms of the feet that results in discomfort affecting daily living activities) or greater.

Hyperbilirubinemia, grade 2 (bilirubin concentrations 1.5 times normal) or greater.

Nausea, grade 2 (sufficient to result in significantly decreased food intake, but the patient is able to eat intermittently) or greater.

Vomiting, grade 2 (2 to 5 episodes in a 24-hour period) or greater.

Stomatitis, grade 2 (painful erythema, edema, or ulcers of the mouth or tongue) or greater.

Once the effect has resolved or decreased to grade 1, capecitabine therapy may be reinstituted (depending on the number of times that the problem has occurred), but a reduction of dosage may be required.

For treatment of adverse effects

Patients should be carefully monitored for toxicity. Toxicity due to capecitabine administration may be managed by symptomatic treatment, dose interruptions and adjustment of capecitabine dose. Once the dose has been reduced it should not be increased at a later time.

Withdrawal of capecitabine therapy is recommended for NCI grade 2 or higher adverse effects; dosage adjustment may be necessary if treatment is reinstituted.

For NCI grade 2 or higher diarrhea: Standard antidiarrheal treatment (e.g., loperamide). Severe diarrhea requires careful monitoring and possibly fluid and electrolyte replacement for dehydration.

For NCI grade 2 or higher nausea, vomiting, hand-and-foot syndrome, or stomatitis: Symptomatic treatment is recommended.

Oral Dosage Forms

Note: Bracketed uses in the *Dosage Forms* section refer to categories of use and/or indications that are not included in U.S. product labeling.

CAPECITABINE TABLETS

Usual adult dose

Carcinoma, breast or
Carcinoma, colorectal (treatment)—

Capecitabine as monotherapyOral, 2500 mg per square meter (mg/m^2) of body surface per day, in two divided doses (approximately twelve hours apart) within 30 minutes after the end of a meal. This dose is given for two weeks, followed by a one-week rest period, i.e., as three-week cycles.

Because several doses and regimens using capecitabine, [*in combination with oxaliplatin*][1], as first-line treatment of colorectal carcinoma, are showing activity, no individual dose/regimen is listed here. Consult the medical literature and/or experts in the field of oncology for more information.

Capecitabine in combination with docetaxelOral, 1250 mg/m^2 twice daily for 2 weeks followed by a 1-week rest period, combined with docetaxel at 75 mg/m^2 as a 1-hour intravenous infusion every 3 weeks. Premedication should be started prior to docetaxel administration for patients receiving the capecitabine plus docetaxel combination. See the docetaxel manufacturer's package insert for information regarding premedication.

The following table displays the amount in mg per dose by body surface area and the number of tablets to be taken at each dose.

Surface Area (m^2)	Amount Per Dose (mg)	No. of 150-mg tablets per dose	No. of 500-mg tablets per dose
≤1.25	1500	0	3
1.26 to 1.37	1650	1	3
1.38 to 1.51	1800	2	3
1.52 to 1.65	2000	0	4
1.66 to 1.77	2150	1	4
1.78 to 1.91	2300	2	4
1.92 to 2.05	2500	0	5
2.06 to 2.17	2650	1	5
≥2.18	2800	2	5

Note: The development of adverse effects may require adjustment of capecitabine dosage, depending on severity (as graded according to NCI common toxicity criteria) as follows:

Grade 1 toxicity—No interruption or modification of therapy is needed.

Grade 2 toxicity—Therapy should be interrupted until the effect has resolved or improved to the grade 1 level, then reinstituted (or not) according to the following guidelines:

After a first occurrence—Treatment may be reinstituted using 100% of the starting dose.

After a second occurrence—Treatment may be reinstituted using 75% of the starting dose.

After a third occurrence—Treatment may be reinstituted using 50% of the starting dose.

After a fourth occurrence—Treatment should be discontinued permanently.

Grade 3 toxicity—Therapy should be interrupted until the effect has resolved or improved to the grade 1 level, then reinstituted (or not) according to the following guidelines:

After a first occurrence—Treatment may be reinstituted using 75% of the starting dose.

After a second occurrence—Treatment may be reinstituted using 50% of the starting dose.

After a third occurrence—Treatment should be discontinued permanently.

Grade 4 toxicity—Based on clinician judgement, treatment may be withdrawn permanently or, after the effect has resolved or improved to the grade 0 to 1 level, reinstituted using 50% of the starting dose.

Note: The following is a list of dose modifications for capecitabine/docetaxel combination therapy in the event of adverse events, depending on severity (as graded according to NCI common toxicity criteria: (Doses of capecitabine missed during a capecitabine/docetaxel treatment cycle are not to be replaced. During capecitabine/docetaxel treatment, prophylaxis for toxicities should be implemented where possible.)

Grade 1 toxicity—No interruption or modification of therapy is needed.

Grade 2 toxicity—Therapy should be interrupted until the effect has resolved or improved to the grade 0 to 1 level, then reinstituted (or not) according to the following guidelines:

After a first occurrence—Treatment may be reinstituted using 100% of the capecitabine and docetaxel starting dose.

After a second occurrence—Treatment may be reinstituted using 75% of the capecitabine starting dose and 55 mg/m^2 docetaxel.

After a third occurrence—Treatment may be reinstituted using 50% of the capecitabine starting dose and the docetaxel discontinued.

After a fourth occurrence—Treatment should be discontinued permanently.

Grade 3 toxicity—Therapy should be interrupted until the effect has resolved or improved to the grade 1 level, then reinstituted (or not) according to the following guidelines:

After a first occurrence—Treatment may be reinstituted using 75% of the starting dos and 55 mg/m^2 docetaxel.

After a second occurrence—Treatment may be reinstituted using 50% of the capecitabine starting dose and the docetaxel discontinued.

After a third occurrence—Treatment should be discontinued permanently.

Grade 4 toxicity—Based on clinician judgement, treatment may be withdrawn permanently or, after the effect has resolved or improved to the grade 0 to 1 level, reinstituted using 50% of the capecitabine starting dose.

Note: Hepatic impairment, mild to moderate (due to liver metastases): No starting dose adjustment is necessary. However, patients should be carefully monitored.

Hepatic impairment, severe: Has not been studied

Renal impairment, mild (creatinine clearance of 51 to 80 mL per minute [using Cockroft and Gault equation]): No starting dose adjustment is necessary.

Renal impairment, moderate (creatinine clearance of 30 to 50 mL per minute): Dose reduction to 75% of the capecitabine starting dose when used as monotherapy or in combination with docetaxel (from 1250 mg/m^2 to 950 mg/m^2 twice daily) is recommended

Usual pediatric dose
Safety and efficacy in children younger than 18 years of age have not been established.

Usual geriatric dose
Caution should be exercised in monitoring the effects of capecitabine in the elderly. Insufficient data are available to provide a dosage recommendation.

Strength(s) usually available
U.S.—

150 mg (Rx) [*Xeloda* (anhydrous lactose; croscarmellose sodium; hydroxypropyl methylcellulose; magnesium stearate; microcrystalline cellulose; talc; titanium dioxide; synthetic red and yellow iron oxides)].

500 mg (Rx) [*Xeloda* (anhydrous lactose; croscarmellose sodium; hydroxypropyl methylcellulose; magnesium stearate; microcrystalline cellulose; talc; titanium dioxide; synthetic red and yellow iron oxides)].

Canada—

150 mg (Rx) [*Xeloda* (croscarmellose sodium; hydroxypropyl methylcellulose; lactose anhydrous; magnesium stearate; microcrystalline cellulose; talc; titanium dioxide; synthetic red and yellow iron oxides)].

500 mg (Rx) [*Xeloda* (croscarmellose sodium; hydroxypropyl methylcellulose; lactose anhydrous; magnesium stearate; microcrystalline cellulose; talc; titanium dioxide; synthetic red and yellow iron oxides)].

Packaging and storage
Store between 15 and 30 °C (59 and 86 °F), preferably at 25 °C (77 °F), in a tight container.

Auxiliary labeling
- Take with meals.
- Take with water.
- This medication could be harmful if you are pregnant or breast-feeding. Consult your pharmacist or doctor about using this medication if you are pregnant, plan to become pregnant, or if you are breast-feeding.
- Keep out of reach of children

[1]Not included in Canadian product labeling.

Revised: 07/19/2006
Developed: 06/25/1998

CAPTOPRIL—See *Angiotensin-converting Enzyme (ACE) Inhibitors (Systemic)*

CARBACHOL Ophthalmic

VA CLASSIFICATION (Primary): OP118

Commonly used brand name(s): *Carbastat; Carboptic; Isopto Carbachol; Miostat.*

Another commonly used name is carbamylcholine.

Note: For a listing of dosage forms and brand names by country availability, see *Dosage Forms* section(s).

Category
Antiglaucoma agent (ophthalmic)—Carbachol Ophthalmic Solution USP; Miotic—Carbachol Intraocular Solution USP; Carbachol Ophthalmic Solution USP.

Indications
Note: Bracketed information in the *Indications* section refers to uses that are not included in U.S. product labeling.

Accepted
Miosis induction, during surgery—Carbachol intraocular solution is indicated to produce pupillary miosis during surgery.

Glaucoma, open-angle (treatment)—Carbachol ophthalmic solution is indicated for lowering intraocular pressure in the treatment of chronic open-angle glaucoma. It is especially useful as a replacement drug, particularly in eyes that have become intolerant of, or resistant to, pilocarpine.

[Glaucoma, angle-closure (treatment)][1]—Carbachol ophthalmic solution is used for emergency treatment of angle-closure glaucoma; however, pilocarpine is usually preferred.

[Glaucoma, angle-closure, *during* or *after* iridectomy (treatment)][1]—Carbachol ophthalmic solution is used in the treatment of angle-closure glaucoma during or after iridectomy.

[Glaucoma, secondary (treatment)][1]—Carbachol ophthalmic solution is used in the treatment of secondary glaucoma if there is no active intraocular inflammation present.

Hypertension, ocular, postsurgical (treatment)[1]—Carbachol intraocular solution is indicated to reduce the intensity of intraocular pressure elevation in the first twenty-four hours after cataract surgery.

[1]Not included in Canadian product labeling.

Pharmacology/Pharmacokinetics

Physicochemical characteristics
Molecular weight—182.65.

Mechanism of action/Effect
Carbachol is a parasympathomimetic that directly stimulates cholinergic receptors. It may also act indirectly by promoting release of acetylcholine and by a weak anticholinesterase action. Carbachol produces contraction of the iris sphincter muscle resulting in pupillary constriction (miosis), constriction of the ciliary muscle resulting in increased accommodation, and a reduction in intraocular pressure associated with decreased resistance to aqueous humor outflow.

In chronic open-angle glaucoma, the exact mechanism by which carbachol lowers intraocular pressure is not precisely known; however, contraction of the ciliary muscle apparently opens the intertrabecular spaces and facilitates aqueous humor outflow.

In angle-closure glaucoma, constriction of the pupil apparently pulls the iris away from the trabeculum, thereby relieving blockage of the trabecular meshwork.

Onset of action
Ophthalmic solution—Miosis: Within 10 to 20 minutes.

Time to peak effect
Intraocular solution—Miosis: Within 2 to 5 minutes.

Ophthalmic solution—Reduction in intraocular pressure: Within 4 hours.

Duration of action
Intraocular solution—
Miosis: About 24 hours.
Ophthalmic solution—
Miosis: About 4 to 8 hours.
Reduction in intraocular pressure: About 8 hours.

Precautions to Consider

Carcinogenicity
Long-term animal studies have not been done.

Pregnancy/Reproduction
Pregnancy—Studies have not been done in humans. However, carbachol may be systemically absorbed.

Studies have not been done in animals.

FDA Pregnancy Category C.

Breast-feeding
Carbachol may be systemically absorbed. It is not known whether carbachol is distributed into breast milk. However, problems in humans have not been documented.

Pediatrics
Appropriate studies on the relationship of age to the effects of carbachol have not been performed in the pediatric population. However, no pediatrics-specific problems have been documented to date.

Geriatrics
Appropriate studies on the relationship of age to the effects of carbachol have not been performed in the geriatric population. However, no geriatrics-specific problems have been documented to date.

Drug interactions and/or related problems
The following drug interactions and/or related problems have been selected on the basis of their potential clinical significance (possible mechanism in parentheses where appropriate)—not necessarily inclusive (» = major clinical significance):

Note: Combinations containing any of the following medications, depending on the amount present, may also interact with this medication.

Belladonna alkaloids, ophthalmic or
Cyclopentolate
(concurrent use of these medications may interfere with the antiglaucoma action of carbachol. Also, concurrent use with carbachol

counteracts the mydriatic effects of these medications; this counteraction may be used to therapeutic advantage)

Flurbiprofen, ophthalmic
(ophthalmic carbachol may be ineffective when administered following ophthalmic flurbiprofen; the pharmacologic basis for this interference is not known)

Medical considerations/Contraindications

The medical considerations/contraindications included have been selected on the basis of their potential clinical significance (reasons given in parentheses where appropriate)—not necessarily inclusive (» = major clinical significance).

Risk-benefit should be considered when the following medical problems exist:

Asthma, bronchial
Cardiac failure, acute
Corneal abrasion or injury
(possible excessive absorption of medication, which can produce systemic toxicity)
Gastrointestinal spasm
Hyperthyroidism
» Iritis, acute, or other conditions in which pupillary constriction is undesirable
Parkinson's disease
Peptic ulcer, active
Sensitivity to carbachol
Urinary tract obstruction

Patient monitoring

The following may be especially important in patient monitoring (other tests may be warranted in some patients, depending on condition; » = major clinical significance):

Intraocular pressure determinations
(recommended at periodic intervals during therapy when carbachol is used in the treatment of glaucoma)

Side/Adverse Effects

Note: Corneal clouding, persistent bullous keratopathy, and post-operative iritis following cataract extraction have been reported occasionally when carbachol intraocular solution was used during cataract surgery.

With the exception of retinal detachment, the following side effects have not been reported following the use of carbachol intraocular solution.

The following side/adverse effects have been selected on the basis of their potential clinical significance (possible signs and symptoms in parentheses where appropriate)—not necessarily inclusive:

Those indicating need for medical attention

Incidence rare
Retinal detachment (veil or curtain appearing across part of vision)

Symptoms of systemic absorption
Asthma (shortness of breath, wheezing, or tightness in chest); ***cardiac arrhythmia*** (irregular heartbeat); ***diarrhea, stomach cramps or pain, or vomiting; flushing or redness of face; frequent urge to urinate; hypotension*** (unusual tiredness or weakness); ***increased sweating; syncope*** (fainting); ***watering of mouth***

Those indicating need for medical attention only if they continue or are bothersome

Incidence more frequent
Blurred vision or change in near or distance vision; eye pain; stinging or burning of the eye

Incidence less frequent
Headache; irritation or redness of eyes; twitching of eyelids

Overdose

For specific information on the agents used in the management of ophthalmic carbachol overdose, see:

- *Atropine* in *Anticholinergics/Antispasmodics (Systemic)* monograph.

For more information on the management of overdose or unintentional ingestion, **contact a Poison Control Center** (see *Poison Control Center Listing*).

Treatment of overdose

Atropine sulfate injection is used as an antidote to the systemic effects of carbachol.

Patient Consultation

As an aid to patient consultation, refer to *Advice for the Patient, Carbachol (Ophthalmic)*.

In providing consultation, consider emphasizing the following selected information (» = major clinical significance):

Before using this medication

» Conditions affecting use, especially:
Sensitivity to carbachol
Other medical problems, especially acute iritis or other conditions in which pupillary constriction is undesirable

Proper use of this medication

For the ophthalmic solution
» Importance of not using more medication than the amount prescribed
Proper administration technique
Washing hands immediately after applying eye drops
Preventing contamination: Not touching applicator tip to any surface; keeping container tightly closed
» Proper dosing
Missed dose: Applying as soon as possible; not applying if almost time for next dose; applying next dose at regularly scheduled time
» Proper storage

Precautions while using this medication

For the ophthalmic solution:
Regular visits to physician to check eye pressure during therapy
» Caution if driving or doing anything else at night or in dim light
» Caution if blurred vision or change in near or distance vision occurs

Side/adverse effects

Signs of potential side effects, especially retinal detachment or symptoms of systemic absorption

General Dosing Information

For ophthalmic solution

Although some manufacturers recommend a dose of 2 drops of an ophthalmic solution at appropriate intervals, the conjunctival sac will usually hold only 1 drop.

More frequent instillation or use of a stronger solution may be required to produce an adequate reduction in intraocular pressure in eyes with hazel or brown irides than is needed in eyes with blue or light-colored irides.

To avoid excessive systemic absorption, patient should press finger to the lacrimal sac during and for 1 or 2 minutes following instillation of medication.

Tolerance to carbachol may develop with prolonged use. Effectiveness may be restored by changing to another miotic for a short time and then resuming the original medication.

Ophthalmic Dosage Forms

CARBACHOL INTRAOCULAR SOLUTION USP

Usual adult and adolescent dose

Miotic—
Intraocular irrigation, no more than 0.5 mL of a 0.01% solution instilled into the anterior chamber.

Antihypertensive agent, ocular, postsurgical—
Intraocular irrigation, no more than 0.5 mL of a 0.01% solution instilled into the anterior chamber.

Note: The intraocular solution may be instilled before or after securing sutures.

Usual pediatric dose

See *Usual adult and adolescent dose.*

Usual geriatric dose

See *Usual adult and adolescent dose.*

Strength(s) usually available

U.S.—
0.01% (Rx) [*Carbastat; Miostat*].

Canada—
0.01% (Rx) [*Carbastat; Miostat*].

Packaging and storage

Store between 15 and 30 °C (59 and 86 °F), in a tight container. Protect from freezing.

Auxiliary labeling

- For single-dose intraocular use only.
- Discard unused portion.

CARBACHOL OPHTHALMIC SOLUTION USP

Usual adult and adolescent dose

Antiglaucoma agent (ophthalmic)—

Topical, to the conjunctiva, 1 drop of a 0.75 to 3% solution one to three times a day.

Usual pediatric dose

See *Usual adult and adolescent dose.*

Usual geriatric dose

See *Usual adult and adolescent dose.*

Strength(s) usually available

U.S.—

0.75% (Rx) [*Isopto Carbachol* (benzalkonium chloride 0.005%)].
1.5% (Rx) [*Isopto Carbachol* (benzalkonium chloride 0.005%)].
2.25% (Rx) [*Isopto Carbachol* (benzalkonium chloride 0.005%)].
3% (Rx) [*Carboptic; Isopto Carbachol* (benzalkonium chloride 0.005%)].

Canada—

1.5% (Rx) [*Isopto Carbachol* (benzalkonium chloride)].
3% (Rx) [*Isopto Carbachol* (benzalkonium chloride)].

Packaging and storage

Store below 40 °C (104 °F), preferably between 15 and 30 °C (59 and 86 °F), unless otherwise specified by manufacturer. Store in a tight container. Protect from freezing.

Auxiliary labeling

- For the eye.
- Keep container tightly closed.

Revised: 09/11/1998

CARBAMAZEPINE Systemic

VA CLASSIFICATION (Primary/Secondary): CN400/CN103; CN900; HS900

Commonly used brand name(s): *Apo-Carbamazepine; Atretol; Carbatrol; Epitol; Equetro; Novo-Carbamaz; Nu-Carbamazepine; Taro-Carbamazepine; Taro-Carbamazepine CR; Tegretol; Tegretol CR; Tegretol Chewtabs; Tegretol-XR.*

Note: For a listing of dosage forms and brand names by country availability, see *Dosage Forms* section(s).

Category

Anticonvulsant; antineuralgic (specific pain syndromes); antimanic; antidiuretic; antipsychotic.

Indications

Note: Bracketed information in the *Indications* section refers to uses that are not included in U.S. product labeling.

Accepted

Bipolar disorder (treatment)—Carbamazepine is indicated for the treatment of acute manic and mixed episodes associated with Bipolar I disorder.

Epilepsy (treatment)—Carbamazepine is indicated for the treatment of partial seizures with simple or complex symptomatology (psychomotor, temporal lobe); generalized tonic-clonic seizures (grand mal); mixed seizure patterns that include the above; or other partial or generalized seizures.

Carbamazepine is a first-choice anticonvulsant because of its relatively low behavioral and psychological toxicity and the rarity of serious adverse effects.

Neuralgia, trigeminal (treatment)—Carbamazepine is indicated for relief of pain due to true trigeminal neuralgia (tic douloureux) and glossopharyngeal neuralgia.

[Bipolar disorder (prophylaxis)]—Carbamazepine is used alone or in combination with lithium and/or antidepressants or antipsychotic agents to treat patients with manic-depressive illness who are unresponsive to, or cannot tolerate, lithium or neuroleptics alone.

[Pain, neurogenic, other (treatment)][1]—Carbamazepine may also be used in some patients to relieve the lightning pains of tabes dorsalis; neuralgic pain associated with multiple sclerosis, acute idiopathic neuritis (Guillain-Barré syndrome), peripheral diabetic neuropathy, phantom limb, restless leg syndrome (Ekbom's syndrome), and hemifacial spasm; post-traumatic neuropathy or neuralgia; and postherpetic neuralgia.

[Diabetes insipidus, central partial (treatment)][1]—Carbamazepine is used alone or with other agents such as clofibrate or chlorpropamide in the treatment of partial central diabetes insipidus.

[Alcohol withdrawal (treatment)][1]—Carbamazepine is used for the detoxification of alcoholics. It has been found to be effective in rapidly relieving anxiety and distress of acute alcohol withdrawal and for such symptoms as seizures, hyperexcitability, and sleep disturbances.

[Psychotic disorders (treatment)][1]—Carbamazepine has been shown to be effective in certain psychiatric disorders including schizoaffective illness, resistant schizophrenia, and dyscontrol syndrome associated with limbic system dysfunction.

Unaccepted

Carbamazepine is not a simple analgesic and should not be used to relieve general aches or pains.

Carbamazepine is *not* indicated for atypical or generalized absence seizures (petit mal) or myoclonic or atonic seizures.

Although carbamazepine has also been reported to relieve dystonic attacks in children, reduce migraine attacks, and relieve intractable hiccups in some patients, its therapeutic efficacy in such cases has not been established.

Carbamazepine should not be used prophylactically during long periods of remission in trigeminal neuralgia.

[1]Not included in Canadian product labeling.

Pharmacology/Pharmacokinetics

Physicochemical characteristics

Chemical Group—Tricyclic iminostilbene derivative. Structurally resembles the psychoactive agents imipramine, chlorpromazine, and maprotiline; shares some structural features with the anticonvulsant agents phenytoin, clonazepam, and phenobarbital.

Molecular weight—236.27.

pKa—7.

Mechanism of action/Effect

Anticonvulsant—Exact mechanism unknown; may act postsynaptically by limiting the ability of neurons to sustain high frequency repetitive firing of action potentials through enhancement of sodium channel inactivation; in addition to altering neuronal excitability, may act presynaptically to block the release of neurotransmitter by blocking presynaptic sodium channels and the firing of action potentials, which in turn decreases synaptic transmission.

Antineuralgic—Exact mechanism unknown; may involve gamma-aminobutyric acid ($GABA_B$) receptors, which may be linked to calcium channels.

Antidiuretic—Exact mechanism unknown; may exert a hypothalamic effect on the osmoreceptors mediated via secretion of antidiuretic hormone (ADH), or may have a direct effect on the renal tubule.

Antimanic; antipsychotic—Exact mechanism unknown; may be related to either the anticonvulsant or the antineuralgic effects of carbamazepine, or to its effects on neurotransmitter modulator systems.

Other actions/effects

Anticholinergic, antidepressant, neuromuscular transmission–inhibiting, and antiarrhythmic actions have been reported.

Absorption

Slow and variable, but almost completely absorbed from gastrointestinal tract.

Distribution

Apparent volume of distribution (Vol_D)—

Carbamazepine: Ranges from 0.8 to 2 L per kg.
Carbamazepine-10,11–epoxide: Ranges from 0.59 to 1.5 L per kg.

In breast milk—

May reach 60% of the maternal plasma concentration.

Protein binding

Carbamazepine—Moderate (55 to 59% in children, 76% in adults).
Carbamazepine-10,11–epoxide—Moderate (50%).

Biotransformation

Hepatic (97%); may induce its own metabolism. One metabolite, carbamazepine-10,11–epoxide, has anticonvulsant, antidepressant, and antineuralgic activity.

Half-life

Carbamazepine—

Initial single dose: May range from 25 to 65 hours.
Chronic dosing: May decrease to 8 to 29 hours (average 12 to 17 hours) because of autoinduction of metabolism.

Carbamazepine-10,11–epoxide—

5 to 8 hours.

Onset of action
Anticonvulsant effect—Varies from hours to days, depending on individual patient. A stable therapeutic concentration may require a month to achieve due to autoinduction of metabolism.
Relief of pain of trigeminal neuralgia—8 to 72 hours.
Antimanic response—Usually 7 to 10 days.

Time to peak concentration
Suspension—1.5 hours following chronic administration.
Tablets—4 to 5 hours following chronic administration.
Extended-release capsules—5.9 (range, 4.1 to 7.7) hours following chronic administration.
Extended-release tablets—3 to 12 hours following chronic administration.

Therapeutic plasma concentrations
4 to 12 mcg per mL (16.9 to 50.8 micromoles per L) (in adults); variations due to autoinduction of metabolism.

Elimination
Renal—72% (3% as unchanged drug).
Fecal—28%.
Clearance values ranged from 0.011 to 0.021 L per hour per kg following a single dose of carbamazepine in healthy volunteers, and from 0.025 to 0.540 L per hour per kg following multiple dosing in healthy volunteers and epilepsy patients.

Note: Large interindividual differences in apparent plasma half-life and total body clearance are related to the phenomenon of autoinduction, which reaches different levels in different individuals. Autoinduction may lead to time-dependent kinetics, in which clearance values increase with time and higher doses are required to maintain the same plasma concentrations. In healthy volunteers, it is estimated that a plateau for autoinduction is reached after 20 to 30 days; in epileptic patients, however, the time course may differ due to previous induction by other medications.

Although the pharmacokinetic parameters of carbamazepine disposition are similar in children and adults, there is a poor correlation between plasma concentrations and carbamazepine dose in children. Carbamazepine is more rapidly metabolized to the active 10,11–epoxide metabolite in younger age groups than in adults. In children younger than 15 years of age, there is an inverse relationship between the carbamazepine-10,11–epoxide to carbamazepine ratio (CBZ-E/CBZ) and increasing age.

Precautions to Consider

Cross-sensitivity and/or related problems
Patients who are sensitive to tricyclic antidepressants may be sensitive to carbamazepine also. Carbamazepine should not be given to such patients.

Carcinogenicity/Tumorigenicity
Carbamazepine is considered carcinogenic in Sprague-Dawley rats because doses of 25, 75, and 250 mg per kg per day for 2 years caused a dose-related increase in the incidence of hepatocellular tumors in females and of benign interstitial cell adenomas in the testes of males. The significance of these findings for use of carbamazepine in humans is not known.

Pregnancy/Reproduction
Pregnancy—Carbamazepine crosses the placenta. Although adequate and well-controlled studies in humans have not been done, there have been reports of babies prenatally exposed to carbamazepine having small head circumferences, low birth weights, craniofacial defects, fingernail hypoplasia, developmental delays, and spina bifida. When it is essential to continue carbamazepine therapy during pregnancy, serum carbamazepine concentrations must be monitored closely, since adverse effects in the fetus have been associated with high blood concentrations.Risk-benefit must be carefully considered when this medication is required in life-threatening situations or in serious diseases for which other medications cannot be used or are ineffective.
Studies in animals have shown that carbamazepine caused kinked ribs in 1.5% of the offspring of rats receiving 250 mg per kg. Also, carbamazepine caused cleft palate, deformities of the foot, or anophthalmos in about 3% of the offspring of rats receiving 650 mg per kg. These doses are 10 to 25 times the human daily dose.

FDA Pregnancy Category D.
Also, it must be kept in mind that other anticonvulsants used during pregnancy have been implicated in birth defects in infants born to epileptic mothers. In addition, retrospective studies have suggested that there may be a higher incidence of teratogenic effects with the use of combinations of anticonvulsants than with monotherapy.

Delivery—To prevent neonatal bleeding disorders, administration of vitamin K to the mother during the last weeks of pregnancy has been recommended.

Breast-feeding
Carbamazepine is distributed into breast milk. Concentrations in breast milk and in the plasma of nursing infants have been reported to reach 60% of the maternal plasma concentration. Therefore, the possibility exists that carbamazepine may cause adverse effects in the nursing infant. In animal studies, nursing rats showed a lack of weight gain and an unkempt appearance with maternal doses of 200 mg per kg. Because of the potential for serious adverse reactions in nursing infants from carbamazepine, a decision should be made whether to discontinue nursing or to discontinue the drug, taking into account the importance of the drug to the mother.

Pediatrics
Epilepsy—Appropriate studies have not been performed in children up to 6 years of age. However, behavioral changes are more likely to occur in children.
Bipolar disorder—Safety and efficacy have not been established in pediatric patients.

Geriatrics
Geriatric patients may be more susceptible to carbamazepine-induced confusion or agitation, atrioventricular (AV) heart block, syndrome of inappropriate antidiuretic hormone (SIADH), and bradycardia than younger patients.

Dental
The leukopenic and thrombocytopenic effects of carbamazepine may result in an increased incidence of microbial infection, delayed healing, and gingival bleeding. If leukopenia or thrombocytopenia occurs, dental work should be deferred until blood counts have returned to normal. Patient instruction in proper oral hygiene should include caution in use of regular toothbrushes, dental floss, and toothpicks.

Surgical
Carbamazepine antagonizes the effects of nondepolarizing muscle relaxants, such as pancuronium. Patients should be monitored closely for more rapid recovery from neuromuscular blockade than expected.

Drug interactions and/or related problems
The following drug interactions and/or related problems have been selected on the basis of their potential clinical significance (possible mechanism in parentheses where appropriate)—not necessarily inclusive (» = major clinical significance):

Note: Carbamazepine should not be used in combination with any other medications containing carbamazepine.

Hepatic cytochrome P450 3A4 has been identified as the major isoform responsible for the metabolism of carbamazepine to carbamazepine-10,11–epoxide. Medications that inhibit or induce the CYP3A4 isoenzymes may alter carbamazepine plasma concentrations. Similarly, carbamazepine may inhibit or induce the metabolism of other medications, thus altering their plasma concentrations.

Note: Combinations containing any of the following medications, depending on the amount present, may also interact with this medication.

Acetaminophen
(risk of hepatotoxicity with single toxic doses or prolonged use of high doses of acetaminophen may be increased, and therapeutic effects of acetaminophen may be decreased, in patients taking hepatic enzyme-inducing agents such as carbamazepine)

Aminophylline or
Oxtriphylline or
Theophylline
(concurrent use with carbamazepine may stimulate hepatic metabolism of the xanthines [except dyphylline], resulting in increased theophylline clearance)

» Anticoagulants, coumarin- or indandione-derivative
(anticoagulant effects may be decreased because of induction of hepatic microsomal enzyme activity, resulting in increased anticoagulant metabolism leading to decreased anticoagulant plasma concentrations and elimination half-life; dosage adjustments based on monitoring of prothrombin time may be necessary during and after carbamazepine therapy)

» Anticonvulsants, hydantoin or
» Anticonvulsants, succinimide or
» Barbiturates or
» Benzodiazepines metabolized via hepatic microsomal enzymes, especially clonazepam or
» Primidone or

» Valproic acid
(concurrent use with carbamazepine may result in increased metabolism, leading to decreased serum concentrations and reduced elimination half-lives of these medications because of induction of hepatic microsomal enzyme activity; monitoring of serum concentrations as a guide to dosage is recommended, especially when any of these medications or carbamazepine is added to or withdrawn from an existing regimen)

(valproic acid may prolong the half-life and reduce the protein-binding of carbamazepine; the concentration of the active 10,11-epoxide metabolite may be increased)

(in addition, use of carbamazepine in combination with other anticonvulsants has been reported to be associated with an increased risk of congenital defects and with an alteration of thyroid function)

» Antidepressants, tricyclic or
Clozapine or
Haloperidol or
Loxapine or
Maprotiline or
Molindone or
Phenothiazines or
Pimozide or
Thioxanthenes
(concurrent use of these agents with carbamazepine may enhance the central nervous system [CNS]–depressant effects of carbamazepine, lower the seizure threshold, and decrease the anticonvulsant effects of carbamazepine; dosage adjustments may be necessary to control seizures; anticholinergic effects may be potentiated, leading to confusion and delirium)

(also, concurrent use of haloperidol, and possibly other neuroleptics, with carbamazepine may decrease plasma concentrations of the neuroleptic by about 60% with or without adverse clinical effects; close observation of patient for clinical signs of ineffectiveness of the neuroleptic is recommended; dosage adjustment may be necessary)

Anti-malarial drugs such as
Chloroquine or
Mefloquine
(may antagonize carbamazepine activity; dose adjustment may be necessary)

Carbonic anhydrase inhibitors
(concurrent use may increase the risk of carbamazepine-induced osteopenia; it is recommended that patients receiving concurrent therapy be monitored for early signs of osteopenia and that the carbonic anhydrase inhibitor be discontinued and appropriate treatment initiated if necessary)

Chlorpropamide or
Desmopressin or
Lypressin or
Posterior pituitary or
Thiazide diuretics, when used for their paradoxical antidiuretic activity in the treatment of diabetes insipidus, or
Vasopressin
(concurrent use with carbamazepine may potentiate the antidiuretic effect, leading to a lower sodium concentration and causing adverse effects that include increased seizure activity; a reduction in dosage of either or both medications may be necessary for optimal therapeutic effect in the treatment of diabetes insipidus)

» Cimetidine
(concurrent use may result in increased plasma concentrations of carbamazepine by delaying its clearance, leading to carbamazepine toxicity)

Cisplatin or
Doxorubicin or
Rifampin
(concurrent use with carbamazepine may cause an increased rate of metabolism of carbamazepine, resulting in decreased plasma concentrations)

(rifampin also increases the plasma concentrations of the 10,11–epoxide metabolite)

» Clarithromycin
(administration of carbamazepine with clarithromycin has been shown to significantly increase the plasma concentration of carbamazepine; carbamazepine plasma concentrations should be monitored)

» Clomipramine
(increased clomipramine plasma levels with concomitant use; dose decrease for clomipramine may be necessary)

» CNS acting drugs (see *Appendix II)* or
» Alcohol
(caution should be used with concomitant use due to CNS effect of carbamazepine)

» Contraceptives, estrogen-containing, oral or
Cyclosporine or
Dacarbazine or
Digitalis glycosides, with the possible exception of digoxin or
Disopyramide or
» Estrogens, including estramustine or
Levothyroxine or
Methadone or
Mexiletine or
» Quinidine
(concurrent use may decrease the effects of these medications because of increased metabolism resulting from induction of hepatic microsomal enzyme activity; dosage adjustments may be necessary)

(in addition, concurrent use of oral, estrogen-containing contraceptives with carbamazepine may result in breakthrough bleeding and contraceptive failure due to the increased rate of hepatic enzyme metabolism of steroids induced by carbamazepine; the dose of the estrogenic substance in the oral contraceptive may be increased to diminish bleeding and decrease the risk of conception; parenteral medroxyprogesterone or nonhormonal methods of birth control may be considered as alternatives)

» Corticosteroids
(concurrent use may decrease the corticosteroid effect because of increased corticosteroid metabolism resulting from induction of hepatic microsomal enzymes)

CYP1A2 substrates including:
Mirtazapine or
Olanzapine or
Quetiapine or
Tramadol or
Triazolam or
Warfarin or
Zonisamide
(concurrent use with carbamazepine may decrease plasma levels of these substrates)

CYP3A4 inhibitors including:
Dalfopristin or
Grapefruit juice or
Nefazodone or
Nicotinamide or
Protease inhibitors or
Quinine or
Quinupristin or
Valproate or
Zileuton
(may increase plasma levels of carbamazepine; dose reduction of carbamazepine may be necessary with concomitant use)

» Delavirdine
(may lead to loss of virologic response and possible resistance to *Rescriptor* or to the class of non-nucleoside reverse transcriptase inhibitors)

Danazol or
» Diltiazem or
Felodipine or
Loratadine or
Niacinamide or
Terfenadine or
» Verapamil
(concurrent use of these agents with carbamazepine may inhibit carbamazepine metabolism, resulting in increased plasma concentrations and toxicity)

(carbamazepine toxicity may be delayed for several weeks after initiation of danazol therapy; carbamazepine dosage may need to be reduced)

(it is recommended that nifedipine be used as an alternative to verapamil or diltiazem)

Doxycycline
(concurrent use may decrease plasma concentration and elimination half-life of doxycycline because of induction of hepatic microsomal enzyme activity; if concurrent use cannot be avoided,

doxycycline plasma concentrations or the therapeutic response to doxycycline should be closely monitored and dosage adjustments made as necessary)

Enflurane or
Halothane or
Methoxyflurane
(chronic use of a hepatic enzyme-inducing agent such as carbamazepine prior to anesthesia may increase the metabolism of these anesthetics, leading to an increased risk of hepatotoxicity)
(formation of nephrotoxic metabolites of methoxyflurane may be increased by chronic use of a hepatic enzyme-inducing agent such as carbamazepine prior to anesthesia, leading to increased risk of nephrotoxicity)
(in addition, cardiac arrhythmias may occur, possibly due to sensitization of the myocardium resulting from increased concentrations of norepinephrine)

» Erythromycin or
Troleandomycin
(concurrent use of these agents with carbamazepine may inhibit carbamazepine metabolism, resulting in increased plasma concentrations and toxicity; it is recommended that an alternate antibiotic to erythromycin or troleandomycin be used)

» Felbamate
(concurrent use may decrease carbamazepine plasma concentrations by about 20 to 30% and increase carbamazepine-10,11–epoxide plasma concentrations by about 60%, leading to an increase in adverse effects; enzyme induction by carbamazepine may lead to decreased felbamate plasma concentrations; carbamazepine dosage should be reduced by 20 to 33% when felbamate therapy is initiated, and plasma concentrations of carbamazepine should be monitored with further dosage adjustments made as clinically necessary)

Folic acid
(requirements for folic acid may be increased in patients receiving anticonvulsant therapy)

Fluoxetine or
» Fluvoxamine
(concurrent use with carbamazepine may inhibit the metabolism of carbamazepine, resulting in increased plasma concentrations and toxicity; carbamazepine plasma concentrations should be monitored)

Influenza virus vaccine
(concurrent use with carbamazepine may inhibit carbamazepine metabolism, resulting in increased plasma concentrations and toxicity; carbamazepine plasma concentrations may be increased on days 7 to 14 after influenza virus vaccination; dosage adjustments of carbamazepine based on the patient's clinical status and plasma carbamazepine concentrations may be necessary)

» Isoniazid
(carbamazepine may induce microsomal metabolism of isoniazid, increasing formation of a reactive intermediate and leading to hepatotoxicity; also, isoniazid administration may result in elevated plasma concentrations of carbamazepine and possible toxicity)

Isotretinoin
(concurrent use with carbamazepine alters the bioavailability and/or clearance of carbamazepine and its active 10,11–epoxide metabolite; plasma concentrations should be monitored)

» Itraconazole and
» Ketoconazole
(concurrent use with carbamazepine may inhibit the metabolism of carbamazepine, resulting in increased plasma concentrations and toxicity)
(concurrent use of carbamazepine with itraconazole may decrease itraconazole plasma concentrations, leading to treatment failure or relapse)

» Lamotrigine
(concurrent use with carbamazepine increases the clearance of lamotrigine; initial lamotrigine dosage and rate of lamotrigine dosage escalation should be based on concomitant anticonvulsant therapy; monitoring of plasma concentrations of lamotrigine and carbamazepine should be considered, especially during dosage adjustments)
(an increased incidence of CNS adverse effects, including ataxia, blurred vision, diplopia, dizziness, or increased excitation, may occur with concomitant use of lamotrigine; dose reduction of either lamotrigine or carbamazepine may decrease these effects)

Lithium
(concurrent use may decrease the antidiuretic effect of carbamazepine and increase the neurotoxic side effects even at nontoxic blood concentrations of both lithium and carbamazepine; however, the concurrent use of lithium with carbamazepine may be synergistic in the treatment of patients with manic-depressive illness who fail to respond to either drug alone)

Mebendazole
(in patients receiving high oral doses of mebendazole for treatment of tissue-dwelling organisms such as *Echinococcus multilocularis* or *granulosus* [Hydatid disease], carbamazepine has been shown to lower plasma mebendazole concentrations by induction of hepatic microsomal enzymes and to impair the therapeutic response; if carbamazepine is being used for seizures, replacement with another anticonvulsant is recommended; treatment of intestinal helminths such as whipworms or hookworms does not appear to be affected by the rate of hepatic metabolism of mebendazole)

Metoclopramide
(concurrent use with carbamazepine may increase the risk of neurotoxic side effects, even if plasma concentrations remain in the therapeutic range)

» Monoamine oxidase (MAO) inhibitors, including furazolidone and procarbazine
(concurrent use with carbamazepine has resulted in hyperpyretic crises, hypertensive crises, severe convulsions, and death; a medication-free interval of at least 14 days is recommended between discontinuation of MAO inhibitor therapy and initiation of carbamazepine therapy, or vice versa)
(MAO inhibitors may also cause a change in the pattern of epileptiform seizures in patients receiving carbamazepine as an anticonvulsant)

Pancuronium
(carbamazepine antagonizes the effects of nondepolarizing muscle relaxants; dosage of the muscle relaxant may need to be increased; patients should be monitored closely for more rapid recovery from neuromuscular blockade than expected)

Praziquantel
(one small, single-dose, controlled study found that epileptic patients taking carbamazepine had significantly lower plasma concentrations of praziquantel [7.9% of the control group]; this effect is thought to be due to induction of the cytochrome P450 microsomal enzyme system by carbamazepine; patients on carbamazepine may require a larger dose of praziquantel)

» Propoxyphene
(concurrent use with carbamazepine may inhibit carbamazepine metabolism, resulting in increased plasma concentrations and toxicity; an analgesic other than propoxyphene should be used)

» Risperidone
(chronic administration of carbamazepine may increase the clearance of risperidone)

Tiagabine
(tiagabine clearance is increased by 60% in patients taking carbamazepine)

Topiramate
(when these two medications were given concurrently, the mean carbamazepine area under the plasma concentration-time curve [AUC] was unchanged or changed by less than 10%, whereas the AUC of topiramate was decreased by 40%)

Laboratory value alterations

The following have been selected on the basis of their potential clinical significance (possible effect in parentheses where appropriate)—not necessarily inclusive (» = major clinical significance).

With diagnostic test results
» Metyrapone test
(increased metabolism of metyrapone by a hepatic enzyme inducer such as carbamazepine may decrease the response to metyrapone)

Pregnancy test
(false-negative results may occur with the use of tests that determine human chorionic gonadotropin [HCG])

With physiology/laboratory test values
Alanine aminotransferase (ALT [SGPT]), serum, and
Alkaline phosphatase, serum, and
Aspartate aminotransferase (AST [SGOT]), serum
(values may be increased)

Bilirubin, serum and
Blood urea nitrogen (BUN)
(concentrations may be increased)

Cholesterol, serum and
High-density lipoprotein cholesterol, serum and

Triglyceride, serum
(concentrations may occasionally be increased)

Free cortisol, urine
(may be increased)

Glucose, urine and
Protein (albumin), urine
(may be detected in the urine)

Ionized calcium, serum
(concentrations may be decreased)

Thyroid hormones
(serum concentrations of T_3, free T_4, and free T_4 index may be decreased due to increased hepatic metabolism of hormones during long-term therapy with carbamazepine; thyroid size may be increased as a compensatory mechanism)

Medical considerations/Contraindications

The medical considerations/contraindications included have been selected on the basis of their potential clinical significance (reasons given in parentheses where appropriate)—not necessarily inclusive (» = major clinical significance).

Except under special circumstances, this medication should not be used when the following medical problems exist:

» Absence seizures, atypical or generalized or
» Atonic seizures or
» Myoclonic seizures
(increased risk of generalized seizures)

» Atrioventricular (AV) heart block or
» Blood disorders characterized by serious abnormalities in blood count, platelets, or serum iron or
» Bone marrow depression, history of
(increased risk of exacerbation)

» Hypersensitivity to carbamazepine or
» Hypersensitivity to any of the tricyclic compounds, such as
Amitriptyline or
Desipramine or
Imipramine or
Nortriptyline or
Protriptyline

Risk-benefit should be considered when the following medical problems exist:

Alcoholism, active
(CNS depression may be potentiated; in addition, the metabolism of carbamazepine may be accelerated)

Behavioral disorders
(latent psychosis may be activated, or agitation or confusion may be produced in elderly patients, especially when carbamazepine is used concurrently with other medications)

Cardiac damage, including organic heart disease and congestive heart disease or
Coronary artery disease
(may be exacerbated)

Diabetes mellitus
(elevated urine glucose concentrations may occur)

Glaucoma or
Increased intraocular pressure
(may be exacerbated because of mild anticholinergic effects of carbamazepine)

Hematologic reactions, adverse, to other medications, history of
(patients may be especially at risk for carbamazepine-induced bone marrow depression)

Hepatic function impairment
(increased risk of liver damage)

Hyponatremia, dilutional, caused by syndrome of inappropriate antidiuretic hormone (SIADH) secretion or other conditions such as hypopituitarism, hypothyroidism, or adrenocortical insufficiency or
Urinary retention
(may be exacerbated)

Renal function impairment
(excretion of carbamazepine may be altered)

Caution is also advised in administration to patients who have had interrupted courses of therapy with carbamazepine.

Patient monitoring

The following may be especially important in patient monitoring (other tests may be warranted in some patients, depending on condition; » = major clinical significance):

» Blood counts, complete (CBCs), including platelet and possibly reticulocyte counts and
» Iron concentrations, serum
(determinations recommended prior to initiation of therapy as a baseline. Patients who develop low or decreased white blood cell or platelet counts during the course of treatment should be monitored closely and carbamazepine discontinued if there is any evidence of significant bone marrow depression)

BUN determinations and
Ophthalmologic examinations, including slit-lamp funduscopy and tonometry, where indicated, and
Urinalysis, complete
(recommended prior to initiation of therapy and at periodic intervals during therapy)

» Carbamazepine concentrations, plasma
(determinations recommended periodically as a guide to efficacy and safety; plasma concentrations of 6 to 12 mcg per mL [25 to 51 micromoles per L] are optimal for anticonvulsant activity and, in rare cases, concentrations may go up to 16 mcg per mL [68 micromoles per L]; when used to treat psychiatric disorders, carbamazepine plasma concentrations of 8 to 12 mcg per mL [34 to 51 micromoles per L] are optimal; taking sample prior to the morning dose to determine lowest daily concentration is suggested)

Careful supervision of patients at high risk for suicide
(recommended since possibility of suicide attempt is inherent with bipolar disorder; prescribing the least amount of medication necessary for good patient management is recommended to decrease risk of overdose)

Electrocardiogram (ECG) readings and
Electrolyte concentrations, serum
(determinations recommended prior to therapy and periodically during therapy because of possibility of hyponatremia)

» Ionized calcium concentrations, serum
(recommended every 6 months or if seizure frequency increases after weeks or months of carbamazepine therapy, since hypocalcemia decreases seizure threshold)

Liver function tests
(recommended prior to initiation of therapy and at periodic intervals during therapy; discontinuation of carbamazepine should be considered immediately upon evidence of aggravated liver function impairment or new disease)

Side/Adverse Effects

Note: Carbamazepine-induced stimulation of antidiuretic hormone (ADH) release may cause water retention resulting in significant volume expansion and dilutional hyponatremia (syndrome of inappropriate secretion of antidiuretic hormone). Patients reporting lethargy, weakness, nausea, vomiting, confusion or hostility, neurological abnormalities, stupor, or increased seizure frequency should be suspected of being hyponatremic, although many of these symptoms may also be associated with other carbamazepine-induced side effects.

Aplastic anemia and *agranulocytosis* have been reported in association with carbamazepine use. Studies demonstrate that the risk of developing these reactions is 5 to 8 times greater than in the general population. However, the overall risk of these reactions in the untreated general population is low (i.e. 6 patients per one million population per year for agranulocytosis and 2 patients per one million population per year for aplastic anemia).

A case of aseptic meningitis accompanied by myoclonus and peripheral eosinophilia has been reported in a patient taking carbamazepine in conjunction with other medications; rechallenge with carbamazepine resulted in recurrence of meningitis.

The following side/adverse effects have been selected on the basis of their potential clinical significance (possible signs and symptoms in parentheses where appropriate)—not necessarily inclusive:

Those indicating need for medical attention

Incidence more frequent

CNS toxicity, including blurred or double vision; or nystagmus (continuous back-and-forth eye movements)

Incidence less frequent

Allergic reaction; Stevens-Johnson syndrome; or toxic epidermal necrolysis (skin rash, hives, or itching); ***anxiety*** (fear; nervousness); ***ataxia*** (shakiness and unsteady walk; unsteadiness; trembling; or other problems with muscle control or coordination); ***behavioral changes***—especially in children; ***chest pain; depersonalization*** (feeling of unreality; sense of detachment from self or body); ***depression*** (discouragement; feeling sad or empty; irritability; lack of appetite; loss of interest or pleasure; tiredness; trouble concentrating; trouble sleeping); ***diarrhea, severe; extrapyramidal symptoms*** (difficulty in speaking; drooling; loss of balance control; muscle trembling, jerking, or stiffness; restlessness; shuffling walk; stiffness of limbs; twisting movements of body; uncontrolled movements, especially of face, neck, and back); ***hyponatremia, dilutional, or water intoxication (SIADH)*** (confusion, agitation, or hostility, especially in the elderly; continuing headache; increase in seizure frequency; severe nausea and vomiting; unusual drowsiness; weakness); ***infection*** (fever or chills; cough or hoarseness; lower back or side pain; painful or difficult urination); ***manic depressive reaction*** (sudden, wide mood swings); ***manic reaction*** (actions that are out of control; irritability; nervousness; talking, feeling, and acting with excitement); ***suicide ideation or attempt*** (thoughts or attempts of killing oneself); ***systemic lupus erythematosus (SLE)-like syndrome*** (skin rash, hives, or itching; fever; sore throat; bone or joint pain; unusual tiredness or weakness)

Note: The risk of *hyponatremia* and *SIADH* appears to increase with patient age and serum concentration of carbamazepine; *hyponatremia* seemingly does not occur in children.

Incidence rare

Adenopathy or lymphadenopathy (swollen glands); ***blood dyscrasias, including aplastic anemia*** (shortness of breath, troubled breathing, wheezing, or tightness in chest; sores, ulcers, or white spots on lips or in mouth; swollen or painful glands; unusual bleeding or bruising); ***agranulocytosis*** (chills; fever; sore throat; unusual tiredness or weakness); ***eosinophilia*** (fever); ***leukopenia*** (usually asymptomatic; rarely, fever or chills; cough or hoarseness; lower back or side pain; painful or difficult urination); ***pancytopenia*** (nosebleeds or other unusual bleeding or bruising); ***and thrombocytopenia*** (usually asymptomatic; rarely, unusual bleeding or bruising; black, tarry stools; blood in urine or stools; pinpoint red spots on skin); ***bone marrow depression*** (chills; fever; sore throat; unusual bleeding or bruising); ***cardiovascular effects, including arrhythmias*** (fast, slow, or irregular heartbeat); ***atrioventricular (AV) heart block*** (unusual weakness; pounding heartbeat; troubled breathing; fainting); ***bradycardia*** (slow heartbeat); ***congestive heart failure*** (chest pain; troubled breathing; swelling of feet or lower legs; rapid weight gain); ***edema*** (swelling of face, hands, feet, or lower legs); ***hypertension, increased*** (high blood pressure); ***hypotension*** (low blood pressure); ***and syncope*** (fainting); ***CNS toxicity*** (difficulty in speaking or slurred speech; mental depression with restlessness and nervousness; rigidity; ringing, buzzing, or other unexplained sounds in the ears; trembling; uncontrolled body movements; visual hallucinations); ***hypersensitivity hepatitis*** (darkening of urine; pale stools; yellow eyes or skin); ***hypocalcemia*** (increase in seizure frequency; muscle or abdominal cramps); ***renal toxicity, renal failure, acute, or water intoxication (SIADH)*** (frequent urination; sudden decrease in amount of urine; swelling of feet or lower legs); ***paresthesias or peripheral neuritis*** (numbness, tingling, pain, or weakness in hands and feet); ***porphyria, acute intermittent*** (darkening of urine); ***pulmonary hypersensitivity*** (fever; troubled breathing; cough; shortness of breath; tightness in chest; wheezing); ***thrombophlebitis*** (pain, tenderness, bluish color, or swelling of leg or foot)

Note: Geriatric patients and those with a defective conduction system may be especially susceptible to *AV heart block* or *bradycardia* with carbamazepine.

Hypocalcemia may lead to osteopenia as a direct effect of carbamazepine on bone metabolism.

Those indicating need for medical attention only if they continue or are bothersome

Incidence more frequent, especially during initiation of therapy

Clumsiness or unsteadiness; confusion; dizziness, mild, or lightheadedness; drowsiness, mild; nausea or vomiting, mild

Incidence less frequent or rare

Accidental injury; aching joints or muscles, or leg cramps; alopecia (loss of hair); ***amnesia*** (loss of memory; problems with memory); ***anorexia*** (loss of appetite); ***asthenia*** (lack or loss of strength); ***back pain; constipation; diaphoresis*** (increased sweating); ***diarrhea; dryness of mouth; dyspepsia*** (acid or sour stomach; belching; heartburn; indigestion; stomach discomfort, upset, or pain); ***glossitis or stomatitis*** (irritation or soreness of tongue or mouth); ***headache; increased sensitivity of skin to sunlight; pruritus*** (itching skin); ***rash; sexual problems in males; somnolence*** (sleepiness or unusual drowsiness); ***speech disorder*** (difficulty in speaking); ***stomach pain or discomfort; unusual tiredness or weakness***

Overdose

Note: For specific information on the agents used in the management of carbamazepine overdose, see:

- *Barbiturates (Systemic)* monograph;
- *Benzodiazepines (Systemic)* monograph;
- *Charcoal, Activated (Oral-Local)* monograph; and/or
- *Laxatives (Local)* monograph.

For more information on the management of overdose or unintentional ingestion, **contact a Poison Control Center** (see *Poison Control Center Listing*).

Clinical effects of overdose

The following effects have been selected on the basis of their potential clinical significance (possible signs and symptoms in parentheses where appropriate)—not necessarily inclusive:

Anuria, oliguria, or urinary retention (sudden decrease in amount of urine); ***cardiovascular effects, including conduction disorders or tachycardia*** (fast or irregular heartbeat); ***convulsions***—especially in small children; ***dizziness, severe; drowsiness, severe; dysmetria*** (poor control in body movements—for example, when reaching or stepping); ***hyperreflexia, followed by hyporeflexia*** (overactive reflexes, followed by underactive reflexes); ***hypertension or hypotension*** (high or low blood pressure); ***motor restlessness; muscular twitching; mydriasis*** (large pupils); ***nausea or vomiting, severe; neurological effects, including ataxia*** (clumsiness or unsteadiness); ***athetoid movements or ballism*** (abnormal body movements); ***opisthotonus*** (body spasm in which head and heels are bent backward and body bowed forward); ***respiratory depression*** (irregular, slow, or shallow breathing); ***shock*** (fainting); ***tremor***

Note: Signs and symptoms of acute toxicity may occur 1 to 3 hours following ingestion of an overdose. Neurological and neuromuscular symptoms predominate, followed by cardiovascular toxicity. Symptoms resemble those observed following overdose with tricyclic antidepressants. Cardiotoxic effects are more likely to occur in elderly and cardiopathic patients.

Laboratory findings in overdosage may indicate leukocytosis, reduced leukocyte count, glycosuria, acetonuria, and electroencephalogram (EEG) dysrhythmias.

Treatment of overdose

Recommended treatment consists of the following:

To decrease absorption—Induction of emesis or gastric lavage, followed by administration of activated charcoal or laxatives to reduce further absorption.

To enhance elimination—Forced diuresis may accelerate elimination. Dialysis is indicated only in severe poisoning associated with renal failure. In small children, severe poisoning may require replacement transfusion.

Specific treatment—For hypotension and shock, elevation of patient's legs and administration of a plasma volume expander. Use of a vasopressor may be considered if other measures are insufficient. Administration of a benzodiazepine or a barbiturate as required for seizures. The fact that these agents may aggravate respiratory depression (especially in children), hypotension, and coma must be considered. Also, barbiturates or benzodiazepines should not be used if the patient has taken a monoamine oxidase inhibitor within the previous 14 days.

Monitoring—Monitoring of respiration, cardiac function, blood pressure, body temperature, pupillary reflexes, and kidney and bladder function for several days.

Supportive care—Maintenance of a patent airway with tracheal intubation, artificial respiration, and/or administration of oxygen. Patients in whom intentional overdose is confirmed or suspected should be referred for psychiatric consultation.

Patient Consultation

As an aid to patient consultation, refer to *Advice for the Patient, Carbamazepine (Systemic)*.

In providing consultation, consider emphasizing the following selected information (» = major clinical significance):

Before using this medication

» Conditions affecting use, especially:

Hypersensitivity to tricyclic antidepressants or carbamazepine

Pregnancy—Crosses placenta; babies reportedly born with small head circumference, low birth weight, craniofacial defects, fingernail hypoplasia, developmental delays, and spina bifida; animal studies have shown rib anomalies, cleft palate, foot deformities, or anophthalmos with doses 10 to 25 times the human dose. Risk-benefit should be carefully considered in pregnant women due to potential for fetal harm.

Breast-feeding—Distributed into breast milk; animal studies have shown lack of weight gain and unkempt appearance of young at high doses; risk-benefit should be considered in nursing women

Use in children—Epilepsy—Appropriate studies have not been done in children up to 6 years of age; behavior changes more likely to occur in children

Bipolar disorder—Safety and efficacy not established

Use in the elderly—Elderly more likely to have confusion or agitation, AV heart block, SIADH, or bradycardia than are younger people

Dental—Increased incidence of blood dyscrasias that cause infection, delayed healing, or gingival bleeding; proper oral hygiene necessary

Surgical—Recovery from neuromuscular blockade induced by nondepolarizing muscle relaxants such as pancuronium may be more rapid than expected due to antagonism by carbamazepine

Other medications, especially alcohol, anticoagulants, other anticonvulsants, tricyclic antidepressants, barbiturates, benzodiazepines metabolized via hepatic microsomal enzymes (especially clonazepam), cimetidine, clarithromycin, clomipramine, CNS acting drugs, oral estrogen-containing contraceptives, corticosteroids, delavirdine, diltiazem, erythromycin, estrogens, isoniazid, fluvoxamine, itraconazole, ketoconazole, lamotrigine, MAO inhibitors, propoxyphene, quinidine, risperidone, or verapamil

Other medical problems, especially absence, atonic, or myoclonic seizures; AV heart block; blood disorders; or bone marrow depression

Proper use of this medication

» Not drinking grapefruit juice or eating grapefruit

» Taking with food to lessen gastrointestinal irritation

» Compliance with therapy; not taking more or less medication than prescribed

» Not using medication for minor aches and pains

» Importance of informing physician of use or any changes in use of other prescription, non-prescription or herbal products

» Proper dosing

Missed dose: Taking as soon as possible; not taking if almost time for next dose; not doubling doses; calling physician if more than one dose a day is missed

» Proper storage; not storing tablet dosage forms in bathroom or other high-moisture areas due to loss of potency and effectiveness

For use in epilepsy

» Checking with physician before discontinuing medication; gradual dosage reduction may be necessary to prevent seizures or status epilepticus

Precautions while using this medication

» Regular visits to physician to check progress of therapy

» Avoiding the use of alcoholic beverages and other CNS depressants while taking this medicine

» Contacting physician immediately if fever, sore throat, rash, ulcers in the mouth, easy bruising, petechial or purpuric hemorrhage occur; these could be signs of a potential hematologic problem

» Possible drowsiness, dizziness, lightheadedness, blurred or double vision, weakness, or muscular incoordination; caution when driving or using machinery, or doing jobs requiring alertness and coordination

» Possible skin photosensitivity; avoiding unprotected exposure to sun; using protective clothing; using a sun block product that includes protection against both UVA-caused photosensitivity reactions and UVB-caused sunburn reactions; avoiding use of sunlamp, tanning bed, or tanning booth

» Using different or additional means of birth control than estrogen-containing oral contraceptives

Diabetic patients: May increase urine sugar concentrations

Caution if any laboratory tests required; possible interference with results of metyrapone or pregnancy tests

» Caution if any kind of surgery, dental treatment, or emergency treatment is needed

Carrying medical identification card or bracelet during therapy

Side/adverse effects

Signs of potential side effects, especially CNS toxicity, allergic reaction, Stevens-Johnson syndrome, toxic epidermal necrolysis, anxiety, ataxia, behavioral changes, chest pain, depersonalization, depression, severe diarrhea, extrapyramidal symptoms, dilutional hyponatremia or water intoxication (SIADH), SLE-like syndrome, infection, manic depressive reaction, manic reaction, suicide ideation or attempt, adenopathy or lymphadenopathy, blood dyscrasias, bone marrow depression, cardiovascular effects, hypersensitivity, hepatitis, hypocalcemia, renal toxicity or failure, paresthesias or peripheral neuritis, porphyria, pulmonary hypersensitivity, or thrombophlebitis

General Dosing Information

Before prescribing carbamazepine, the physician should be thoroughly familiar with prescribing information, particularly regarding use with other drugs, especially those which accentuate toxicity potential, and a detailed history and physical examination should be made.

Side effects may be minimized by initiating therapy with low doses, which should be increased gradually at weekly intervals until an adequate response is obtained; administering carbamazepine with meals, and giving the total daily dosage in 3 or 4 divided doses may also minimize side effects.

When carbamazepine is added to existing anticonvulsant therapy, it should be added gradually while the other anticonvulsants are maintained or gradually decreased, except for phenytoin, which may have to be increased.

The maintenance dosage of carbamazepine may need to be increased progressively over the first few weeks of treatment to avoid low plasma carbamazepine concentrations caused by autoinduction.

Abrupt discontinuation in a responsive epileptic patient may result in convulsions and possibly status epilepticus; gradual withdrawal is recommended.

Therapy should be discontinued if cardiovascular reactions or skin rashes occur, or if evidence of significant bone marrow depression develops.

When carbamazepine is used as an antineuralgic in specific pain syndromes, *an attempt should be made at least once every few months to reduce dosage or discontinue therapy* if the patient is totally free of pain.

Carbamazepine suspension should not be administered simultaneously with other liquid medications or diluents because of the possibility of precipitation of an orange rubbery mass. This phenomenon has been observed after mixing carbamazepine suspension with chlorpromazine solution or with liquid forms of thioridazine hydrochloride.

Diet/Nutrition

Carbamazepine suspension and tablets should be taken with food to lessen gastrointestinal irritation. Carbamazepine extended-release capsules may be taken with or without food. The contents of carbamazepine extended-release capsules may also be sprinkled over food (such as a teaspoonful of applesauce or other similar food products); the capsule or its contents should not be crushed or chewed.

The requirements for folic acid may be increased in patients receiving anticonvulsant therapy.

Bioequivalence information

Administration of carbamazepine suspension results in higher peak serum concentrations than does the same dose administered as tablets. It is recommended that doses of the suspension be initially lower and be increased more slowly than doses of the tablets to avoid side effects.

For treatment of adverse effects

Treatment of bone marrow depression includes the following:

- Discontinuing carbamazepine therapy.
- Daily CBC, platelet, and reticulocyte counts.
- Performing a bone marrow aspiration and trephine biopsy immediately and repeating with sufficient frequency to monitor recovery.
- Considering other studies that may be helpful, including white cell and platelet antibodies; ^{59}Fe—ferrokinetic studies; peripheral blood cell typing; cytogenic studies on marrow and peripheral blood; bone marrow culture studies for colony-forming units; hemoglobin electrophoresis for A^2 and F hemoglobin; and serum folic acid and B_{12} concentrations. If aplastic anemia develops, specialized consultation should be sought for appropriate monitoring and treatment.

Oral Dosage Forms

Note: Bracketed uses in the *Dosage Forms* section refer to categories of use and/or indications that are not included in U.S. product labeling.

CARBAMAZEPINE ORAL SUSPENSION USP

Usual adult and adolescent dose

Anticonvulsant—

Initial: Oral, 100 mg four times a day on the first day, the dosage being increased by up to 200 mg a day at weekly intervals. Some clinicians recommend initiating therapy at 100 mg a day and increasing to full therapeutic dosage slowly at weekly intervals to avoid side effects and potential noncompliance.

Maintenance: Oral, usually 800 mg to 1.2 grams a day.

Antineuralgic—

Initial: Oral, 50 mg four times a day on the first day, the dosage being increased by up to 200 mg a day, using increments of 50 mg four times a day only as needed until pain is relieved.

Maintenance: Oral, 200 mg to 1.2 grams a day (average 400 to 800 mg a day) in divided doses.

[Antidiuretic][1]—

Oral, 300 to 600 mg a day if used as sole therapy; or 200 to 400 mg a day if used concurrently with other antidiuretic agents.

[Antimanic][1] or

[Antipsychotic][1]—

Oral, initially 200 to 400 mg a day in divided doses, the dosage being gradually increased at weekly intervals up to a maximum of 1.6 grams a day as needed and tolerated according to clinical response.

Note: Whenever possible, total daily dosage should be given in 3 or 4 divided doses.

Usual adult and adolescent prescribing limits

Anticonvulsant—

Patients 12 to 15 years of age—

Dosage should generally not exceed 1 gram a day.

Patients 15 years of age and over—

Dosage should generally not exceed 1.2 grams a day. In rare instances, doses of up to 1.6 grams a day have been used in adults.

Antineuralgic—

Dosage should not exceed 1.2 grams a day.

Usual pediatric dose

Anticonvulsant—

Children up to 6 years of age—

Initial—Oral, 10 to 20 mg per kg of body weight a day in two or three divided doses, the dosage being increased by up to 100 mg a day at weekly intervals as needed and tolerated.

Maintenance—Oral, adjusted to the minimum effective dosage, usually 250 to 350 mg a day, and generally not exceeding 400 mg or 35 mg per kg of body weight a day.

Children 6 to 12 years of age—

Initial—Oral, 50 mg four times a day on the first day, the dosage being increased by up to 100 mg a day at weekly intervals until the best response is obtained.

Maintenance—Oral, adjusted to the minimum effective dosage, usually 400 to 800 mg a day.

Note: Dosage generally should not exceed 1 gram a day.

Whenever possible, total daily dosage should be given in 3 or 4 divided doses.

Strength(s) usually available

U.S.—

100 mg per 5 mL (Rx) [*Tegretol* (citrus-vanilla flavor; sorbitol; sucrose)].

Canada—

100 mg per 5 mL (Rx) [*Tegretol* (citrus-vanilla flavor; sorbitol; sucrose)].

Packaging and storage

Store below 30 °C (86 °F), in a tight, light-resistant container, unless otherwise specified by manufacturer. Protect from freezing.

Incompatibilities

Tegretol suspension should not be administered simultaneously with other liquid medicinal agents or diluents.

Auxiliary labeling

- Grapefruit and grapefruit juice should not be taken with this medication
- Shake well before using.
- May cause drowsiness.
- Take with meals.

CARBAMAZEPINE TABLETS USP

Usual adult and adolescent dose

Anticonvulsant—

Initial: Oral, 200 mg two times a day on the first day, the dosage being increased by up to 200 mg a day at weekly intervals until the best response is obtained. Some clinicians recommend initiating therapy at 100 mg a day and increasing to full therapeutic dosage slowly at weekly intervals to avoid side effects and potential noncompliance.

Maintenance: Oral, adjusted to the minimum effective dosage, usually 600 mg to 1.6 grams a day.

Antineuralgic—

Initial: Oral, 100 mg two times a day on the first day, the dosage being increased by up to 200 mg a day, using increments of 100 mg every twelve hours only as needed until pain is relieved.

Maintenance: Oral, 200 mg to 1.2 grams a day (average 400 to 800 mg a day) in divided doses.

[Antidiuretic][1]—

Oral, 300 to 600 mg a day if used as sole therapy; or 200 to 400 mg a day if used concurrently with other antidiuretic agents.

[Antimanic][1] or

[Antipsychotic][1]—

Oral, initially 200 to 400 mg a day in divided doses, the dosage being gradually increased at weekly intervals up to a maximum of 1.6 grams a day as needed and tolerated according to clinical response.

Note: Whenever possible, total daily dosage should be given in 3 or 4 divided doses.

Usual adult and adolescent prescribing limits

Anticonvulsant—

Patients 12 to 15 years of age—

Dosage should generally not exceed 1 gram a day.

Patients 15 years of age and over—

Dosage should generally not exceed 1.2 grams a day. In rare instances, doses of up to 1.6 grams a day have been used in adults.

Antineuralgic—

Dosage should not exceed 1.2 grams a day.

Usual pediatric dose

Anticonvulsant—

Children up to 6 years of age—

Initial—Oral, 10 to 20 mg per kg of body weight a day in two or three divided doses, the dosage being increased by up to 100 mg a day at weekly intervals as needed and tolerated.

Maintenance—Oral, adjusted to the minimum effective dosage, usually 250 to 350 mg a day, and generally not exceeding 400 mg or 35 mg per kg of body weight a day.

Children 6 to 12 years of age—

Initial—Oral, 100 mg two times a day on the first day, the dosage being increased by 100 mg a day at weekly intervals until the best response is obtained.

Maintenance—Oral, adjusted to the minimum effective dosage, usually 400 to 800 mg a day.

Note: Dosage generally should not exceed 1 gram a day.

Whenever possible, total daily dosage should be given in 3 or 4 divided doses.

Strength(s) usually available

U.S.—

200 mg (Rx) [*Atretol* (scored); *Epitol* (scored); *Tegretol* (scored); GENERIC (scored)].

Canada—

200 mg (Rx) [*Apo-Carbamazepine* (double-scored); *Novo-Carbamaz* (scored); *Nu-Carbamazepine* (double-scored); *Taro-Carbamazepine* (double-scored); *Tegretol* (double-scored)].

Packaging and storage

Store below 40 °C (104 °F), preferably between 15 and 30 °C (59 and 86 °F), unless otherwise specified by manufacturer. Store in a tight container.

Auxiliary labeling

- Grapefruit and grapefruit juice should not be taken with this medication
- May cause drowsiness.
- Take with meals.
- Store in a dry place.
- Protect from moisture.

CARBAMAZEPINE TABLETS (CHEWABLE) USP

Usual adult and adolescent dose

See *Carbamazepine Tablets USP*.

Usual adult and adolescent prescribing limits

See *Carbamazepine Tablets USP*.

Usual pediatric dose

See *Carbamazepine Tablets USP*.

Strength(s) usually available

U.S.—

100 mg (Rx) [*Epitol* (scored); *Tegretol* (scored; sucrose); GENERIC (scored)].

Canada—

100 mg (Rx) [*Tegretol Chewtabs* (scored)].

200 mg (Rx) [*Tegretol Chewtabs* (scored)].

Packaging and storage

Store below 40 °C (104 °F), preferably between 15 and 30 °C (59 and 86 °F), unless otherwise specified by manufacturer. Store in a tight container.

Auxiliary labeling
- Grapefruit and grapefruit juice should not be taken with this medication
- May cause drowsiness.
- Take with meals.
- May be chewed.
- Store in a dry place.
- Protect from moisture.

CARBAMAZEPINE EXTENDED-RELEASE CAPSULES

Usual adult and adolescent dose
Anticonvulsant—

Initial: Oral, 200 mg two times a day, the dosage being increased gradually as needed and tolerated. Some clinicians recommend increasing to full therapeutic dosage slowly at weekly intervals to avoid side effects and potential noncompliance.

Maintenance: Oral, adjusted to the minimum effective dosage, usually 800 to 1200 mg a day.

Antineuralgic—

Initial: Oral, 200 mg on the first day, the dosage being increased by up to 200 mg a day every twelve hours only as needed until pain is relieved.

Maintenance: Oral, 200 mg to 1.2 grams a day (average 400 to 800 mg a day) in divided doses.

Note: As soon as pain relief is maintained, the dosage should be reduced to the minimum effective dose.

Attempts should be made at intervals of not more than 3 months to reduce or discontinue use.

Bipolar disorder (treatment)—

Initial: Oral, 200 mg twice daily. Dose adjustment should be made in 200 mg daily increments up to 1600 mg to achieve optimal clinical response.

Usual adult and adolescent prescribing limits
Anticonvulsant—

Patients 12 to 15 years of age—

Dosage should generally not exceed 1 gram a day.

Patients 15 years of age and over—

Dosage should generally not exceed 1.2 grams a day. In rare instances, doses of up to 1.6 grams a day have been used in adults.

Antineuralgic—

Dosage should not exceed 1.2 grams a day.

Bipolar disorder (treatment)—

Doses higher than 1600 mg per day have not been studied.

Usual pediatric dose
Anticonvulsant—

Children up to 12 years of age

Oral, doses of immediate-release carbamazepine of 400 mg or greater may be converted to the same total daily dose of extended-release carbamazepine capsules using the twice a day regimen. Ordinarily, optimal clinical response is achieved at daily doses below 35 mg per kg of body weight.

Note: When seizure relief is maintained, the dosage should be reduced gradually to the lowest effective dose.

If satisfactory clinical response has not been achieved, plasma concentrations of carbamazepine should be measured to determine whether they are in the therapeutic range.

Dosage generally should not exceed 1 gram a day.

Strength(s) usually available
U.S.—

200 mg (Rx) [*Carbatrol*].

300 mg (Rx) [*Carbatrol*].

100 mg (Rx) [*Equetro* (citric acid; colloidal silicon dioxide; lactose monohydrate; microcrystalline cellulose; polyethylene glycol; povidone; sodium lauryl sulfate; talc; triethyl citrate; gelatin; FD&C Blue #2; yellow iron oxide; titanium dioxide)].

200 mg (Rx) [*Equetro* (citric acid; colloidal silicon dioxide; lactose monohydrate; microcrystalline cellulose; polyethylene glycol; povidone; sodium lauryl sulfate; talc; triethyl citrate; yellow iron oxide; gelatin; FD&C Blue #2; titanium dioxide)].

300 mg (Rx) [*Equetro* (citric acid; colloidal silicon dioxide; lactose monohydrate; microcrystalline cellulose; polyethylene glycol; povidone; sodium lauryl sulfate; talc; triethyl citrate; FD&C Blue #2; titanium dioxide)].

Canada—

Not commercially available.

Packaging and storage
Store at controlled room temperature, preferably between 15 and 25 °C (59 and 77 °F), in a tight container, unless otherwise specified by manufacturer. Protect from light.

Preparation of dosage form
For patients who cannot take oral solids—Individual doses may be sprinkled over soft foods, such as applesauce, immediately before use.

Auxiliary labeling
- Grapefruit and grapefruit juice should not be taken with this medication
- May cause drowsiness.
- Swallow whole. Do not crush or chew.
- Tell your doctor about all medications you are taking, prescription and non-prescription

CARBAMAZEPINE EXTENDED-RELEASE TABLETS

Usual adult and adolescent dose
Anticonvulsant—

Initial: Oral, 100 to 200 mg one or two times a day with meals, the dosage being increased gradually as needed and tolerated. Some clinicians recommend initiating therapy at 100 mg a day and increasing to full therapeutic dosage slowly at weekly intervals to avoid side effects and potential noncompliance.

Maintenance: Oral, adjusted to the minimum effective dosage, usually 800 to 1200 mg a day.

Antineuralgic—

Oral, initially 100 mg two times a day on the first day, the dosage being increased by 200 mg a day (in increments of 100 mg every twelve hours) only as needed and tolerated until pain is relieved.

Note: As soon as pain relief is maintained, the dosage should be reduced to the minimum effective dose.

Attempts should be made at intervals of not more than 3 months to reduce or discontinue use.

Usual adult and adolescent prescribing limits
Anticonvulsant—

Patients 12 to 15 years of age—

Dosage should generally not exceed 1 gram a day.

Patients 15 years of age and over—

Dosage should generally not exceed 1.2 grams a day. In rare instances, doses of up to 1.6 grams a day have been used in adults.

Antineuralgic—

Dosage should not exceed 1.2 grams a day.

Usual pediatric dose
Anticonvulsant—

Children 6 to 12 years of age

Oral, initially 100 mg one to two times on the first day, the dosage being increased gradually by 100 mg a day as needed and tolerated until the best response is obtained.

Note: When seizure relief is maintained, the dosage should be reduced gradually to the lowest effective dose.

Dosage generally should not exceed 1 gram a day.

Strength(s) usually available
U.S.—

100 mg (Rx) [*Tegretol-XR*].

200 mg (Rx) [*Tegretol-XR*].

400 mg (Rx) [*Tegretol-XR*].

Canada—

200 mg (Rx) [*Taro-Carbamazepine CR; Tegretol CR* (scored)].

400 mg (Rx) [*Taro-Carbamazepine CR; Tegretol CR* (scored)].

Packaging and storage
Store below 40 °C (104 °F), preferably between 15 and 30 °C (59 and 86 °F), in a tight container, unless otherwise specified by manufacturer.

Auxiliary labeling
- Grapefruit and grapefruit juice should not be taken with this medication
- May cause drowsiness.
- Take with meals.
- Swallow whole. Do not crush or chew.

[1]Not included in Canadian product labeling.

Revised: 01/19/2005

CARBENICILLIN—See *Penicillins (Systemic)*

CARBIDOPA AND LEVODOPA Systemic

PEN: Co-Careldopa
VA CLASSIFICATION (Primary): CN500
Commonly used brand name(s): *Apo-Levocarb; Atamet; Nu-Levocarb; Parcopa; Sinemet; Sinemet CR 25-100; Sinemet CR 50-200.*
Note: For a listing of dosage forms and brand names by country availability, see *Dosage Forms* section(s).

Category

Antidyskinetic.

Indications

General Considerations

Levodopa is administered most commonly in combination with a peripheral decarboxylase inhibitor (PDI), such as carbidopa, to maximize the amount of levodopa available to enter the brain and to lessen adverse effects (such as nausea, vomiting, and hypotension) caused by the peripheral decarboxylation of levodopa to dopamine. Levodopa currently is a mainstay of therapy for symptomatic treatment of Parkinson's disease. However, complications to long-term levodopa therapy appear commonly, and the majority of patients experience serious adverse effects including motor fluctuations, dyskinesias, and neuropsychiatric effects. Fluctuations in response to levodopa therapy represent a significant problem in the long-term management of patients with Parkinson's disease. Later stage motor complications are related to the severity and duration of the underlying disease, as well as to treatment-related factors such as the dose of levodopa therapy.

Patients who develop response fluctuations to levodopa therapy appear to lack the capacity to buffer fluctuations in plasma levels of levodopa. One theory to explain the mechanism of fluctuation is that chronic, sporadic stimulation of striatal postsynaptic dopaminergic receptors from exogenous levodopa administration results in changes downstream from the nigrostriatal dopamine system; residual dopaminergic neurons, attempting to compensate for loss of degenerated neurons, accelerate dopamine formation and rapidly release it, rather than retaining it in storage vesicles. In addition, nondopaminergic neurons and other cells that possess significant decarboxylase activity become increasingly important sources of intrasynaptic dopamine. Once synthesized in these cells, dopamine is immediately released, resulting in intrasynaptic dopamine concentrations that reflect the marked swings in levodopa availability and in the ensuing motor fluctuations.

Therapeutic responses to levodopa therapy include a short-duration response, in which improvement in motor disability lasts a few hours after the administration of a single dose of levodopa, and a long-duration response, in which antiparkinsonian effects may last for many hours or days following discontinuation of levodopa.

Controversies exist regarding the optimal time to initiate therapy with levodopa and the optimal use of other antiparkinsonian medications throughout the disease process.

Accepted

Parkinsonism (treatment)—Carbidopa and levodopa combination is indicated in the treatment of idiopathic Parkinson's disease, postencephalitic parkinsonism, or symptomatic parkinsonism, which may follow injury to the nervous system by carbon monoxide intoxication or manganese intoxication, to permit achievement of symptomatic relief with a lower dosage of levodopa than with levodopa alone. Also, it permits a smoother and more rapid dosage titration, reduces nausea and vomiting, and allows concurrent administration of pyridoxine when necessary.

Pharmacology/Pharmacokinetics

See also *Levodopa (Systemic).*

Physicochemical characteristics

Chemical Group—
Levodopa: Levorotatory isomer of dihydroxyphenylalanine (L-DOPA), which is the metabolic precursor of dopamine.
Carbidopa: Hydrazine analog of levodopa.

Molecular weight—
Levodopa: 197.19.
Carbidopa: 244.25.

Solubility—
Levodopa: 66 mg in 40 mL of water.
Carbidopa: Slightly soluble in water.

Other properties—
In the presence of moisture, levodopa is oxidized by atmospheric oxygen and darkens.

Mechanism of action/Effect

Normal motor function depends on the synthesis and release of dopamine by neurons projecting from substantia nigra to corpus striatum. The progressive degeneration of these neurons that occurs in Parkinson's disease disrupts the nigrostriatal pathway and results in diminished levels of the intrasynaptic neurotransmitter dopamine. Striatal dopamine levels in symptomatic Parkinson's disease are decreased by 60 to 80%.

Levodopa—Striatal dopaminergic neurotransmission may be enhanced by exogenous supplementation of dopamine through administration of dopamine's precursor, levodopa. A small percentage of each levodopa dose crosses the blood-brain barrier and is decarboxylated to dopamine. This newly formed dopamine then is available to stimulate dopaminergic receptors, thus compensating for the depleted supply of endogenous dopamine.

Carbidopa—Inhibits the peripheral decarboxylation of levodopa, thus decreasing its conversion to dopamine in peripheral tissues. This results in higher plasma levels of levodopa and, consequently, an increased availability of levodopa for transport across the blood-brain barrier, where it undergoes decarboxylation to the neurotransmitter dopamine.

Other actions/effects

Levodopa's metabolite, dopamine, stimulates beta-adrenergic cardiac receptors, interacts with the chemoreceptor zone in the area postrema, located outside the blood-brain barrier, and promotes release of pituitary growth hormone.

Absorption

Carbidopa—
Carbidopa is poorly absorbed; its oral bioavailability is 40 to 70%.

Levodopa—
Levodopa is rapidly absorbed from the proximal small intestine by the large neutral amino acid (LNAA) transport carrier system. This transport system is a saturable, sodium-independent, facilitated mechanism for aromatic and branched chain amino acids. The capacity of the transport system is limited, and levodopa must compete for energy-dependent proximal small bowel absorption sites. Stomach and intestinal walls contain abundant levels of the L-aromatic amino acid decarboxylase (AAAD) enzyme, which degrades levodopa, and thus serves as a significant barrier to the absorption of intact levodopa; only about 30% of an orally administered dose reaches the circulation as intact levodopa. However, concomitant administration of a peripheral decarboxylase inhibitor, such as carbidopa, will enhance the absorption of levodopa.

High gastric acidity, delayed stomach emptying time, and the presence of certain other amino acids, such as those that occur after digestion of a protein-containing meal, may prevent absorption of levodopa. Intense exercise and other activity that diverts blood flow from the mesenteric circulation also may delay levodopa absorption.

Carbidopa and levodopa combination—
Tablets: Absorption is rapid and virtually complete in 2 to 3 hours.
Extended-release tablets: Absorption is gradual and continuous for 4 to 5 hours, although the majority of the dose is absorbed in 2 to 3 hours.
Absorption may be impaired by a high-protein diet.

Bioavailability of carbidopa and levodopa extended-release tablets—
Approximately 70 to 75% relative to the immediate-release tablets.
Increased somewhat in the presence of food.
Two half tablets approximately 20% more bioavailable than one intact tablet.

Note: Liquid formulations of carbidopa and levodopa combination have been extemporaneously compounded in an attempt to minimize absorption problems. The liquid preparation is absorbed slightly faster than carbidopa and levodopa tablets, and antiparkinsonian effects may take effect more quickly than with the tablets. Thus, the liquid preparation may be useful in patients who are extremely sensitive to small changes in the dose of levodopa, such as those experiencing erratic motor control (e.g., severe oscillations between "on" and "off" periods). (See *Side/Adverse Effects* section and *Preparation of dosage form* section.)

Distribution

Levodopa—Widely distributed to most body tissues, but not to the central nervous system (CNS) because of extensive metabolism in the periphery. Levodopa crosses biological membranes, including the intestinal epithelium and the blood-brain barrier, by means of the LNAA transport system. This system is the saturable, stereospecific, facilitated transport mechanism for large neutral amino acids, including those from dietary protein intake. The transport rate across the blood-brain barrier is dependent upon the plasma concentration of levodopa and the concentration of competing amino acids. The flux of amino acids across the blood-brain barrier is bidirectional; the net flux of unmetabolized levodopa is from the brain into the plasma as levodopa plasma concentrations fall.

Carbidopa—Does not cross the blood-brain barrier.

Biotransformation

Levodopa—95% of an administered oral dose of levodopa is pre-systemically decarboxylated to dopamine by the L-aromatic amino acid decarboxylase (AAAD) enzyme in the stomach, lumen of the intestine, kidney, and liver. This converted portion of dopamine cannot cross the blood-brain barrier to exert its effects on the brain. Dopamine remaining in the periphery is believed responsible for many levodopa adverse effects, including cardiac arrhythmias and gastrointestinal upset. Levodopa also may be methoxylated by the hepatic catechol-*O*-methyltransferase (COMT) enzyme system to 3-*O*-methyldopa (3-OMD), which cannot be converted to central dopamine. 3-OMD has a long half-life and competes with levodopa for the same transport mechanism across the blood-brain barrier.

When the portion of the remaining intact levodopa does cross the blood-brain barrier, it is decarboxylated to dopamine, which is normally stored in presynaptic terminals of dopaminergic neurons in the striatum. After release into the synapse, dopamine is transported back into the dopaminergic terminals by the presynaptic uptake mechanism, or is further metabolized by monoamine oxidase (MAO) or COMT. The actions of levodopa in the brain are affected by the rate and extent of cerebral conversion to dopamine, the rate of movement of the synthesized dopamine to the striatal receptors, and the rate of inactivation of newly synthesized dopamine.

Carbidopa—Unlike levodopa, carbidopa is not a substrate for dopa decarboxylase; it does inhibit the metabolism of levodopa in the gastrointestinal tract and plasma by blocking dopa decarboxylase, thus increasing the absorption and plasma concentrations of levodopa.

Half-life

Levodopa: 0.75 to 1.5 hours.

3-O-methyldopa (3-OMD): 15 hours; accumulation will occur during chronic dosing.

Carbidopa—1 to 2 hours. When given in combination with levodopa, carbidopa increases levodopa's plasma half-life to about 1.5 hours.

Time to peak concentration

Peak levodopa concentrations at steady state—

Carbidopa and levodopa tablets:

0.5 to 0.7 hours.

Carbidopa and levodopa extended-release tablets:

2.1 to 2.4 hours.

Note: Peak plasma concentrations of levodopa are increased when the extended-release tablets are administered with food.

Plasma concentrations of levodopa fluctuate less with the extended-release tablets than with the immediate release tablets.

Extended-release tablets have a delayed onset of action of two to three times that of the immediate-release tablets.

Elimination

Levodopa—Renal, 70 to 80% of dose eliminated within 24 hours, largely as dopamine metabolites. Homovanillic acid (HVA) is a major urinary metabolite, accounting for 13 to 42% of the ingested dose of levodopa in twenty-four hour urine samples. Unchanged levodopa accounts for less than 1% of an administered dose. Some of the eliminated metabolites may color the urine red; oxidation that occurs when urine is exposed to air will cause it to darken.

Fecal, 2% of dose.

Carbidopa—Renal; 30% of dose of carbidopa excreted unchanged in urine within 24 hours. When given in combination with levodopa, the amount of levodopa excreted unchanged in urine is increased by about 6%.

Precautions to Consider

Carcinogenicity

In a two-year bioassay of carbidopa and levodopa, no evidence of carcinogenicity was found in rats that received doses of approximately two times the maximum daily human dose of carbidopa and four times the maximum daily human dose of levodopa.

Pregnancy/Reproduction

Fertility—No effects on fertility were found in reproduction studies done in rats receiving approximately two times the maximum daily human dose of carbidopa and four times the maximum daily human dose of levodopa.

Pregnancy—Adequate and well-controlled studies in humans have not been done. However, case studies have reported that levodopa crosses the placenta and is metabolized in the fetal tissues.

Reproduction studies in rodents have shown that levodopa, when given in doses in excess of 200 mg per kg of body weight (mg/kg) per day, depresses fetal and postnatal growth and viability. Also, studies in rabbits have shown that levodopa alone or in combination with carbidopa causes visceral and skeletal malformations.

FDA Pregnancy Category C.

Breast-feeding

Levodopa is distributed into breast milk. Although problems in humans have not been documented, breast-feeding is not recommended because of the potential for side effects in the infant.

Also, levodopa may inhibit lactation.

Pediatrics

Appropriate studies on the relationship of age to the effects of carbidopa and levodopa have not been performed in children up to 18 years of age. Safety and efficacy have not been established.

Geriatrics

Smaller doses may be required in geriatric patients since they may have reduced tolerance to the effects of levodopa. Similarly, patients with Alzheimer's disease are more sensitive to usual doses of levodopa.

Geriatric patients, especially those with osteoporosis, who respond to levodopa therapy should resume normal activity gradually and with caution because increased mobility may increase risk of fractures.

Central nervous system (CNS) effects, such as anxiety, confusion, or nervousness, are more common in geriatric patients receiving anticholinergic antiparkinsonian medications in addition to levodopa.

Dental

Involuntary movements of jaws may result in poor retention of full dentures; dosage reduction may be required.

Surgical

If general anesthesia is required and the administration of carbidopa and levodopa combination is interrupted temporarily, the patient should be observed for symptoms of a neuroleptic malignant-like syndrome.

Drug interactions and/or related problems

The following drug interactions and/or related problems have been selected on the basis of their potential clinical significance (possible mechanism in parentheses where appropriate)—not necessarily inclusive (» = major clinical significance):

Note: Combinations containing any of the following medications, depending on the amount present, may also interact with this medication.

Amantadine or
Benztropine or
Procyclidine or
Trihexyphenidyl
(concurrent use may result in increased efficacy of levodopa; however, concurrent use is not recommended if there is a history of psychosis)

» Anesthetics, hydrocarbon inhalation
(administration prior to anesthesia with these agents may result in cardiac arrhythmias because of increased endogenous dopamine concentration; carbidopa and levodopa combination should be discontinued 6 to 8 hours before the administration of these anesthetics, especially halothane)

Benzodiazepines
(concurrent use may decrease the therapeutic effects of levodopa)

Bromocriptine
(may produce additive effects, allowing reduction in levodopa dosage)

» Cocaine
(concurrent use with levodopa may increase the risk of cardiac arrhythmias; if use of cocaine is necessary in patients receiving levodopa, it is recommended that cocaine be administered with caution, in reduced dosage, and in conjunction with electrocardiographic monitoring)

Dopamine D_2 receptor antagonists
Droperidol or
» Haloperidol or
Loxapine or
Molindone or
Papaverine or
» Phenothiazines or
» Risperidone or

» Thioxanthenes
(agents that block the dopamine receptors in the brain, such as traditional antipsychotics, may antagonize the effects of levodopa)
(reported sporadic cases of a symptom complex resembling neuroleptic malignant syndrome [NMS] in association with dose reductions or withdrawals of therapy with carbidopa/levodopa combination, especially if patient is receiving neuroleptics; these patients should be observed carefully during abrupt dose reduction or discontinuation)

Foods, especially high-protein
(concurrent or previous ingestion of food may decrease the absorption of levodopa from the gastrointestinal tract, consequently delaying its effect; in addition, proteins in food may be degraded into amino acids that compete with levodopa for transport across the intestinal epithelium and the blood-brain barrier, resulting in a decreased or erratic response to levodopa; however, rather than cutting down on daily protein intake to avoid this effect, it has been recommended that the intake of proteins be distributed equally throughout the day. Alternatively, some clinicians recommend a redistribution diet for selected patients for a limited time during which all protein intake is in the evening meal, as patients would be minimally affected by any ensuing "off" period (see *Side/Adverse Effects*); diets with austere restrictions in total daily protein intake (≤ 10 grams) have been shown to reduce the magnitude of response fluctuations and may benefit some patients, but are often unpalatable and may result in a negative nitrogen balance if not carefully monitored; a recommended dietary allowance of 0.8 gram of protein per kg of body weight a day is thought to be a sufficient and safe restriction that does not affect the levodopa dose-response relationship)

Hypotension-producing medications, other (see *Appendix II*)
(concurrent use with levodopa may result in an increased hypotensive effect)

Iron salts or
Vitamin/mineral preparations containing iron salts
(iron salts may chelate with levodopa, resulting in decreased absorption and lower serum levels of levodopa, and thus reduce its efficacy)

Methyldopa
(concurrent use with levodopa may alter the antiparkinsonian effects of levodopa and may also produce additive toxic CNS effects such as psychosis)

Metoclopramide
(metoclopramide may worsen Parkinson's disease through inhibition of CNS dopamine receptors; conversely, levodopa may antagonize the effects of metoclopramide by increasing the amount of available dopamine)

» Monoamine oxidase (MAO) inhibitors, including furazolidone, procarbazine, and selegiline
(although high doses [300 to 400 mg a day] of carbidopa in combination with levodopa may help suppress the hypertensive reactions caused by concurrent use with MAO inhibitors, it is recommended that MAO inhibitors be discontinued for at least 2 weeks prior to initiation of carbidopa and levodopa combination therapy)

Rauwolfia alkaloids
(rauwolfia alkaloids cause dopamine depletion in the brain, decreasing the effects of levodopa; dosage adjustments of either or both medications may be necessary)

» Selegiline or
Tolcapone
(although sometimes used in conjunction with carbidopa and levodopa combination, selegiline or tolcapone may have additive effects; selegiline may enhance levodopa-induced dyskinesias, nausea, orthostatic hypotension, confusion, and hallucinations; levodopa dosage should be reduced within 2 to 3 days after the initiation of therapy with selegilineor tolcapone)

Tricyclic antidepressants
(rare reports of adverse reactions, including hypertension and dyskinesia resulting from concomitant use with carbidopa and levodopa combination)

Laboratory value alterations

The following have been selected on the basis of their potential clinical significance (possible effect in parentheses where appropriate)—not necessarily inclusive (» = major clinical significance).

With diagnostic test results

Catecholamines, plasma and urine or
Metanephrines, plasma and urine
(test results are unreliable)

Coombs' (antiglobulin) test
(occasionally becomes positive after long-term levodopa therapy)

Glucose, urine
(tests using copper reduction methods may cause false-positive results; tests using glucose oxidase methods may cause false-negative results)

Gonadorelin test
(levodopa may elevate serum gonadotropin concentrations)

Ketones, urine
(tests using dipstick or test tape methods may cause false-positive results)

Protein, urine
(use of the Lowery test may cause false-positive results)

Thyroid function determinations
(chronic use of levodopa may inhibit the TSH response to protirelin)

Uric acid, serum and urine
(tests may show high concentrations with colorimetric measurements, but not with uricase)

With physiology/laboratory values

Alanine aminotransferase (ALT [SGPT]) and
Alkaline phosphatase and
Aspartate aminotransferase (AST [SGOT]) and
Bilirubin and
Lactate dehydrogenase (LDH) and
Protein-bound iodine (PBI)
(serum concentrations may be increased)

Blood urea nitrogen (BUN)
(concentrations may be increased)

Hematocrit or
Hemoglobin or
White blood cell counts
(values may be decreased)

Note: Concentrations of BUN, creatinine, and uric acid, although elevated during carbidopa and levodopa therapy, are elevated to a lesser degree than when levodopa is used alone.

Medical considerations/Contraindications

The medical considerations/contraindications included have been selected on the basis of their potential clinical significance (reasons given in parentheses where appropriate)—not necessarily inclusive (» = major clinical significance).

Except under special circumstances, this medication should not be used when the following medical problem exists:

» Glaucoma, narrow-angle

» Hypersensitivity to carbidopa, levodopa, or any component of the product

» Melanoma, history of, or
» Skin lesions, suspicious, undiagnosed
(levodopa may activate a malignant melanoma)

Risk-benefit should be considered when the following medical problems exist:

» Bronchial asthma, emphysema, and other severe pulmonary diseases
(respiratory effects of levodopa may aggravate condition)

» Cardiovascular disease, severe
(increased risk of cardiac arrhythmias)

Convulsive disorders, history of
(use of levodopa may precipitate seizures)

Diabetes mellitus
(use of levodopa may adversely affect control of glucose in blood)

Endocrine diseases
(use of levodopa may adversely affect hypothalamus or pituitary function)

» Glaucoma, angle-closure, or predisposition to
(mydriatic effect resulting in increased intraocular pressure may precipitate an acute attack of angle closure glaucoma)

Glaucoma, open-angle, chronic
(mydriatic effect may cause a slight increase in intraocular pressure; glaucoma therapy may need to be adjusted)

Hepatic function impairment

Mental depression or
Psychosis
(increased risk of developing suicidal tendencies and/or suicidal ideation; also, conditions may be aggravated by neuropsychiatric effects of levodopa)

» Myocardial infarction, history of, with residual atrial, nodal, or ventricular arrhythmias
(use of levodopa may precipitate or aggravate condition)

» Neuroleptic malignant syndrome (NMS)
(patients with a history of NMS may be at greater risk of this condition recurring with combination carbidopa/levodopa use)

» Peptic ulcer, history of
(increased risk of upper gastrointestinal hemorrhage)

» Renal function impairment
(use of levodopa may lead to urinary retention)

Patient monitoring

The following may be especially important in patient monitoring (other tests may be warranted in some patients, depending on condition; » = major clinical significance):

Blood cell counts and
Hemoglobin determinations and
Hepatic function determinations and
Ophthalmologic examinations for glaucoma and monitoring of intraocular pressure in patients with open angle glaucoma and
Renal function determinations
(recommended at periodic intervals for patients on long-term levodopa therapy)

Cardiovascular monitoring
(recommended at periodic intervals for patients on long-term therapy)

» Neuroleptic malignant syndrome [NMS]
(reported sporadic cases of a symptom complex resembling NMS in association with dose reductions or withdrawal of carbidopa/levodopa therapy; patients should be observed carefully with abrupt dose reduction or discontinuation, especially if patient is receiving neuroleptics)

Side/Adverse Effects

Note: Carbidopa, in doses used to inhibit peripheral decarboxylation of levodopa, has no significant ability to produce side effects. However, it allows certain CNS side effects of levodopa, such as dyskinesias and mental effects, to develop sooner and at lower levodopa doses because of the resultant greater efficiency per dose of levodopa.

A syndrome resembling neuroleptic malignant syndrome, which includes intermittent dystonia alternating with substantial agitation, hyperthermia and mental changes, has been reported after the abrupt reduction or discontinuation of levodopa therapy. Neurological findings, including muscle rigidity, involuntary movements, altered consciousness, mental status changes; other disturbances such as autonomic dysfunction, tachycardia, tachypnea, sweating, hypertension, hypotension, laboratory findings, such as creatine phosphokinase elevation, leukocytosis, myoglobinuria, and increased serum myoglobin have been reported. Early diagnosis of this condition is important for the appropriate management of these patients. Considering NMS as a possible diagnosis and ruling out other acute illnesses is essential.

Although carbidopa and levodopa combination is the most commonly used antiparkinsonian medication, complications to long-term levodopa therapy appear commonly and include motor fluctuations, dyskinesias, and neuropsychiatric problems. Fifty percent or more of patients who have received levodopa for 5 years experience motor fluctuations; after 10 years or more of treatment, up to 90% of patients may be affected.

Periods of therapeutic response in terms of antiparkinsonian effects are termed "on" periods; "off" periods are periods of suboptimal response where the patient experiences a worsening of parkinsonian symptoms. Motor fluctuations include predictable "wearing off" periods, unpredictable "off" periods, and various abnormal involuntary movements. End-of-dose deterioration or "wearing off" periods (predictable periods of immobility or greater severity of other parkinsonian symptoms when medications wear off) usually have a close temporal relationship to the timing of antiparkinsonian medication. "On-off" fluctuations are sudden unpredictable shifts between "on" and "off" periods that are unrelated to the timing of antiparkinsonian medication; relatively small changes in circulating levodopa, and thus in striatal dopamine, can induce large shifts in dopaminergic transmission and ultimately in motor function.

Dyskinesias may include peak-dose (or square-wave) dyskinesias (appearing during maximum effect), biphasic dyskinesias (appearing at beginning and end of dosing period), and focal or generalized dystonia. The severity of dyskinesias increases with time, as the distribution of abnormal movements spreads, and the degree of abnormal movements increases. Dyskinesias are dose-dependent, and the dose threshold decreases as Parkinson's disease progresses.

Random oscillations include transient episodes of "freezing" or motor blocks, where initiation or continuation of a motor act such as walking is arrested for a few seconds. "Yo-yoing" is unpredictable oscillations between choreic dyskinesia and Parkinsonian rigidity; patients may progress from severe dyskinesias to rigidity, or have an acceptable response to medication for part of the day ("ons") and be intermittently disabled by periods of suboptimal response ("offs") or dyskinesias.

Neuropsychiatric effects may occur in up to two-thirds of patients on long-term levodopa therapy and may be related to the activation of dopamine receptors in nonstriatal regions of the brain, especially the cortical and limbic regions. These mental and behavioral changes include confusion, agitation, hallucinations, irritability, panic, paranoid delusions, mental depression, dementia, mania, and psychosis; euphoria, hypersexuality, or hypomania may occur during "on" periods.

The following side/adverse effects have been selected on the basis of their potential clinical significance (possible signs and symptoms in parentheses where appropriate)—not necessarily inclusive:

Those indicating need for medical attention

Incidence more frequent

Agitation; anxiety; ataxia (clumsiness or unsteadiness); ***bruxism*** (clenching or grinding of teeth); ***choreiform and/or dystonic movements*** (unusual and uncontrolled movements of the body, including the face, tongue, arms, hands, head, and upper body); ***confusion; delusions*** (abnormal thinking: holding false beliefs that cannot be changed by fact); ***dizziness; dysphagia*** (difficulty swallowing); ***euphoria*** (false sense of well-being); ***fatigue*** (unusual tiredness or weakness); ***feeling faint; hallucinations*** (seeing, hearing, or feeling things that are not there); ***increased hand tremor; malaise*** (general feeling of discomfort or illness); ***nausea or vomiting; peripheral neuropathy*** (numbness, burning, tingling, or prickling sensations); ***sialorrhea*** (excessive watering of mouth); ***weakness***

Note: *Hallucinations* are usually visual and, at early stages, non-threatening.

Nausea and vomiting may occur frequently in early carbidopa and levodopa therapy, with tolerance being gradually achieved during continued use. The concurrent use of carbidopa with levodopa often reduces the frequency and severity of nausea and vomiting, although approximately 15% of patients continue to experience these side effects.

Incidence less frequent

Blepharospasm (increased blinking or spasms of eyelids); ***blurred vision; cardiac irregularities*** (fast, irregular, or pounding heart beat); ***diplopia*** (double vision); ***hot flashes; mydriasis*** (dilated pupils); ***neuropsychiatric effects, including paranoid ideation, psychotic episodes, and mental depression with or without suicidal tendencies*** (mood or mental changes); ***orthostatic hypotension*** (dizziness or lightheadedness when getting up from a lying or sitting position); ***palpitations*** (fast or pounding heart beat); ***skin rash; trismus*** (difficulty opening mouth); ***unusual weight gain or loss; urinary incontinence*** (loss of bladder control); ***urinary retention*** (difficult urination)

Note: *Cardiac arrhythmias, palpitations,* and *urinary retention* may become less frequent when levodopa is administered concomitantly with a peripheral decarboxylase inhibitor, such as carbidopa.

Incidence rare

Agranulocytosis (chills; fever; sore throat; unusual tiredness or weakness); ***duodenal ulcer*** (stomach pain); ***edema*** (swelling of face; swelling of feet or lower legs; unusual weight gain); ***gastrointestinal bleeding*** (bloody or black, tarry stools; severe stomach pain; vomiting of blood or material that looks like coffee grounds); ***hemolytic anemia*** (back, leg, or stomach pain; fever; loss of appetite; pale skin; unusual tiredness or weakness); ***hypertension*** (high blood pressure); ***oculogyric crisis*** (inability to move eyes); ***phlebitis*** (pain, tenderness, or swelling of foot or leg); ***priapism*** (prolonged, painful, inappropriate penile erection); ***seizures*** (convulsions)

Note: A causal relationship between the use of levodopa or carbidopa and levodopa combination and *seizures* has not been established.

Those indicating need for medical attention only if they continue or are bothersome

Incidence more frequent

Abdominal pain; anorexia (loss of appetite); ***dryness of mouth; flatulence*** (passing gas); ***nightmares***

Note: *Nightmares* may become less frequent when levodopa is combined with carbidopa because of the reduced levodopa dose requirements and reduced conversion to peripheral dopamine.

Incidence less frequent

Constipation; diarrhea; flushing of skin; headache; hiccups; increased sweating; insomnia (trouble in sleeping); ***muscle twitching; unusual tiredness or weakness***

Note: *Constipation* may become less frequent when levodopa is combined with a peripheral decarboxylase inhibitor.

Those not indicating need for medical attention

Incidence less frequent

Bitter taste; burning sensation of tongue; darkening in color of urine, saliva, or sweat

Overdose

For information on the management of overdose or unintentional ingestion, **contact a Poison Control Center** (see *Poison Control Center Listing*).

Clinical effects of overdose

Blepharospasm (increased blinking or spasms of eyelids)—possible early sign of overdose

Treatment of overdose

Since there is no specific antidote for acute overdose with carbidopa and levodopa, treatment is symptomatic and supportive, with possible utilization of the following

To decrease absorption—Immediate gastric lavage.

Monitoring—Electrocardiographic monitoring for development of arrhythmias.

Specific treatment—

Antiarrhythmic medication, if necessary.

Pyridoxine is not effective in reversing the actions of carbidopa and levodopa combination.

The value of dialysis in the treatment of overdose is not known.

Supportive care—

Judicious use of intravenous fluids.

Maintenance of airway.

Patients in whom intentional overdose is confirmed or suspected should be referred for psychiatric consultation.

Patient Consultation

As an aid to patient consultation, refer to *Advice for the Patient, Levodopa (Systemic).*

In providing consultation, consider emphasizing the following selected information (» = major clinical significance):

Before using this medication

» Conditions affecting use, especially:

Hypersensitivity to carbidopa and/or levodopa or any component of the product

Pregnancy—No studies in humans; depressed growth and malformations in animal studies

Breast-feeding—Levodopa is distributed into breast milk; may inhibit lactation

Use in the elderly—Reduced tolerance to effects of levodopa; caution in resuming normal activity, especially in patients with osteoporosis; CNS effects more common with concurrent use of anticholinergic agents

Dental—Possible difficulty in retention of full dentures

Other medications, especially cocaine, haloperidol, hydrocarbon inhalation anesthetics, MAO inhibitors, phenothiazines, selegiline, and thioxanthenes; high-protein foods

Other medical problems, especially severe cardiovascular disease, glaucoma (narrow angle), melanoma (history of or suspected), mental depression, myocardial infarction with residual arrhythmias, peptic ulcer (history of), psychosis, severe pulmonary diseases, renal function impairment, skin lesions (suspicious, undiagnosed), or urinary retention

Proper use of this medication

» Taking with meals or snacks for the first few months until tolerance to gastrointestinal effects develops; later, taking on an empty stomach for maximal absorption

» Compliance with therapy; taking medication only as directed; not stopping medication unless ordered by physician

» Maximum effectiveness of medication may not occur for several weeks or months after therapy is initiated

» Proper dosing

Missed dose: Taking as soon as possible; skipping dose if next scheduled dose is within 2 hours; not doubling doses

» Proper storage

Precautions while using this medication

Caution if any kind of surgery (including dental surgery) or emergency treatment is required

For patients with diabetes—May interfere with urine tests for sugar and ketones

» Caution if drowsiness occurs

» Caution when getting up suddenly from lying or sitting position; dizziness and fainting may occur

» Caution in resuming normal physical activities when condition has improved, especially for geriatric patients

Side/adverse effects

Signs of potential side effects, especially agitation; anxiety; ataxia; bruxism; choreiform and/or dystonic movements; confusion; delusions; dizziness; dysphagia; euphoria; fatigue; feeling faint; hallucinations; increased hand tremor; malaise; nausea or vomiting; peripheral neuropathy; sialorrhea; weakness; blepharospasm; blurred vision; cardiac irregularities; diplopia; hot flashes; mydriasis; neuropsychiatric effects, including paranoid ideation, psychotic episodes, and mental depression with or without suicidal tendencies; orthostatic hypotension; palpitations; skin rash; trismus; unusual weight gain or loss; urinary incontinence; urinary retention; agranulocytosis; duodenal ulcer; edema; gastrointestinal bleeding; hemolytic anemia; hypertension; oculogyric crisis; phlebitis; priapism; seizures

Occasional darkening of urine, saliva, or sweat may be alarming to patient although medically insignificant

General Dosing Information

Carbidopa and levodopa therapy must be individualized and dosage gradually titrated to the desired therapeutic level in order to minimize adverse effects. An interval of at least 3 days is recommended between dosage adjustments of carbidopa and levodopa. The therapeutic range of carbidopa and levodopa combination is narrower than that of levodopa, owing to its greater milligram potency. Therefore, dosage adjustments should be made in small increments and the recommended dosage ranges generally should not be exceeded. The treatment goal should be to achieve maximal benefit without inducing dyskinesias. The appearance of involuntary movements may be a sign of levodopa toxicity, and may require dose reduction.

End-of-dose deterioration or "wearing off" periods usually have a close temporal relationship to the timing of levodopa administration. These effects may be alleviated for a time by shortening the dosing interval and reducing the size of individual doses. However, compliance may be poor if the dosage regimen becomes too complex. Extended-release formulations of carbidopa and levodopa combination may be useful in the early stages of the wearing-off phenomenon, as they could typically add 60 to 90 minutes to the response duration compared with the immediate-release formulation. Since the bioavailability of the extended-release formulation is less than that of the immediate-release form, a dose increase of 20 to 30% may be required. Use of the extended-release form in the later stages of Parkinson's disease should be avoided, as it may induce prolonged dopaminergic side effects such as dyskinesia and psychosis.

Benefits from initiation of levodopa therapy, although sometimes evident from the first dose, commonly increase over several weeks despite a fixed dosage regimen. Generally it takes 2 weeks for the final effects of a given change in levodopa treatment to "equilibrate" in the body so that the results of a dosage change can be assessed.

Postencephalitic and geriatric patients often require and tolerate lower dosage levels than other parkinsonism patients.

Patients who fail to respond to the carbidopa and levodopa combination may have an atypical parkinsonism. Many patients with atypical parkinsonism still receive some benefit from small doses of levodopa.

Levodopa must be discontinued at least 12 hours before the carbidopa and levodopa combination dosage is begun. Levodopa may be discontinued in the evening and the carbidopa and levodopa combination started the following morning.

The concurrent administration of carbidopa may permit the dose of levodopa to be reduced by up to 75% with no decrease in therapeutic results. Use of carbidopa and levodopa combination permits an earlier response to therapy than use of levodopa alone, and also decreases the incidence of nausea, vomiting, and cardiac arrhythmias. At least

75 to 100 mg of carbidopa per day is needed to block the peripheral decarboxylation of levodopa. A lesser amount of carbidopa renders the patient more likely to experience adverse reactions to levodopa, such as nausea and vomiting. Rarely, doses of carbidopa as high as 300 mg a day are needed to functionally inhibit peripheral decarboxylase activity.

Because both therapeutic and adverse responses occur more rapidly with carbidopa and levodopa combination than with levodopa alone, patients should be monitored closely during the dose adjustment period. Involuntary movements occur more rapidly with the combination than with levodopa. Occurrence of involuntary movements may require dosage reduction. Blepharospasm may be a useful early sign of excess dosage in some patients.

When a patient is switched from the immediate-release form to the extended-release form of carbidopa and levodopa combination, dosage must be titrated carefully, and the patient should be kept on the new regimen for at least 3 to 5 days before further dosage changes are made.

The absorption of the extended-release formulation of carbidopa and levodopa is sometimes considered to be unpredictable. This is because levodopa absorption takes place over a limited length of the small intestine, and delivery to this region is controlled by the rate of gastric emptying and factors influencing gastric motility; these factors (e.g., too slow or too fast a release rate from the stomach or a rate of transit through the small intestine) can adversely affect the amount of levodopa absorbed from the extended-release dosage form.

Other antiparkinsonian medications may be used concomitantly with or preceding carbidopa and levodopa therapy. Gradual dosage reduction of these medications is recommended during initiation of therapy with carbidopa and levodopa, and after optimum dosage is reached, to maintain proper control of the patient's condition.

When carbidopa and levodopa combination is to be discontinued, dosage should be tapered gradually to prevent the occurrence of a syndrome that resembles the neuroleptic malignant syndrome. Careful patient monitoring after withdrawal of carbidopa and levodopa will allow early diagnosis and treatment of neuroleptic malignant-like syndrome.

Diet/Nutrition

Carbidopa reduces the adverse effect of pyridoxine on levodopa. A daily carbidopa dose of 100 mg will eliminate the clinical significance of this interaction.

Peripheral decarboxylation of levodopa to dopamine causes gastrointestinal side effects such as nausea and vomiting, but concomitant administration with carbidopa will reduce this effect. Levodopa may be given with meals or snacks for the first few months of therapy until tolerance to these side effects develops. Later, levodopa should be given on an empty stomach for maximal absorption; administering levodopa on an empty stomach facilitates absorption and reduces competition with dietary proteins. Also, standardizing the administration of levodopa with regard to meal times will optimize the rate of gastric emptying. Some clinicians consider administering the levodopa dose 1 hour before or after eating food to be a practical approach.

High-protein diets should be avoided because protein degradation products compete with levodopa for transport across the intestinal epithelium and blood-brain barrier, resulting in a decreased or erratic response to levodopa. Patients experiencing response fluctuations may be more susceptible to the interference that protein-containing meals have on the effectiveness of levodopa. Strategies for reducing the competitive effects from dietary proteins include:

- Assuring that the intake of normal amounts of protein be distributed equally throughout the day.
- Introducing the redistribution diet, where protein intake is restricted to the evening meal only.
- Imposing austere restrictions on total daily protein intake ($\leq$ 10 grams) for limited times in selected patients.
- Adherence to a recommended dietary allowance of 0.8 gram of protein per kilogram of body weight per day which seems to be a sufficient and safe restriction that does not affect the levodopa dose-response relationship.

Bioequivalence information

Because carbidopa and levodopa extended-release tablets are 25 to 30% systemically less bioavailable than Carbidopa and Levodopa Tablets USP (immediate-release), increased daily doses of the extended-release tablets may be required to achieve the same level of symptomatic relief.

For treatment of adverse effects

Immediate relief of nausea and vomiting may sometimes be obtained by reducing the daily dose, giving smaller individual doses at more frequent intervals, or having patient take each dose with food. High-protein foods should be avoided since they may decrease levodopa's effect (See *Drug interactions and/or related problems*). After tolerance to nausea and vomiting develops, carbidopa and levodopa combination should be taken on an empty stomach to maximize absorption and reduce competition with dietary proteins. In some patients, as much as 200 to 300 mg of carbidopa per day may be needed to eliminate levodopa-induced nausea.

Management of neuroleptic malignant syndrome (NMS) should include:

- Intensive symptomatic treatment and medical monitoring and
- Treatment of any concomitant serious medical problems for which specific treatments are available. Dopamine agonists, such as bromocriptine, and muscle relaxants, such as dantrolene, are often used in the treatment of NMS. However, there effectiveness has not been demonstrated in controlled studies.

Oral Dosage Forms

CARBIDOPA AND LEVODOPA TABLETS USP

Usual adult dose

Antidyskinetic—

For patients not being converted from levodopa therapy—

Oral, initially, 10 mg of carbidopa and 100 mg of levodopa three or four times a day or 25 mg of carbidopa and 100 mg of levodopa three times a day, the dosage per day being increased gradually at one- or two-day intervals as needed and tolerated.

For patients being converted from levodopa therapy (levodopa must be discontinued for at least twelve hours prior to conversion to carbidopa and levodopa therapy):

Patients who require less than 1.5 grams of levodopa per day—Oral, 10 mg of carbidopa and 100 mg of levodopa or 25 mg of carbidopa and 100 mg of levodopa three or four times a day initially, the dosage per day being increased gradually at one- or two-day intervals as needed and tolerated.

Patients who require more than 1.5 grams of levodopa per day—Oral, 25 mg of carbidopa and 250 mg of levodopa three or four times a day initially, the dosage per day being increased gradually at one- or two-day intervals as needed and tolerated.

Note: Postencephalitic patients may be more sensitive to the effects of the usual adult dose.

For patients being converted from levodopa therapy, the initial dose of carbidopa and levodopa per day should provide approximately 20 to 25% of the total dosage of levodopa per day previously required.

Usual adult prescribing limits

200 mg of carbidopa and 2 grams of levodopa in combination daily.

Note: Additional levodopa may be administered alone if it is required and tolerated.

Usual pediatric dose

Children up to 18 years of age—Safety and efficacy have not been established.

Usual geriatric dose

See *Usual adult dose*.

Note: Geriatric patients may be more sensitive to the effects of the usual adult dose.

Strength(s) usually available

U.S.—

10 mg of carbidopa and 100 mg of levodopa (Rx) [*Sinemet* (scored); GENERIC].

25 mg of carbidopa and 100 mg of levodopa (Rx) [*Atamet* (scored); *Sinemet* (scored); GENERIC].

25 mg of carbidopa and 250 mg of levodopa (Rx) [*Atamet* (scored); *Sinemet* (scored); GENERIC].

Canada—

10 mg of carbidopa and 100 mg of levodopa (Rx) [*Apo-Levocarb* (scored); *Nu-Levocarb; Sinemet;* GENERIC].

25 mg of carbidopa and 100 mg of levodopa (Rx) [*Apo-Levocarb* (scored); *Nu-Levocarb; Sinemet* (scored); GENERIC].

25 mg of carbidopa and 250 mg of levodopa (Rx) [*Apo-Levocarb* (scored); *Nu-Levocarb; Sinemet* (scored); GENERIC].

Packaging and storage

Store below 40 °C (104 °F), preferably between 15 and 30 °C (59 and 86 °F), unless otherwise specified by manufacturer. Store in a well-closed, light-resistant container.

Preparation of dosage form

A liquid formulation of levodopa may be prepared extemporaneously for use in dosage titration in patients who are extremely sensitive to small changes in dose. One formula uses ten crushed tablets of carbidopa 25 mg and levodopa 100 mg, and 1 gram of ascorbate, dissolved in one liter of water. A fresh solution must be prepared daily.

Auxiliary labeling
- May darken urine, saliva, or sweat.

CARBIDOPA AND LEVODOPA ORAL DISINTEGRATING TABLETS USP

Usual adult dose
Antidyskinetic—
See *Carbidopa and Levodopa Tablets*

Usual adult prescribing limits
See *Usual adult prescribing limits for Carbidopa and Levodopa Tablets.*

Usual pediatric dose
Children up to 18 years of age—Safety and efficacy have not been established.

Usual geriatric dose
See *Usual adult dose for Carbidopa and Levodopa Tablets.*

Strength(s) usually available
U.S.—
10 mg of carbidopa and 100 mg of levodopa (Rx) [*Parcopa* (orally disintegrating tablets; aspartame; citric acid; crospovidone; magnesium stearate; mannitol; microcrystalline cellulose; natural and artificial mint flavor; sodium bicarbonate; FD&C blue #2 HT aluminum lake)].
25 mg of carbidopa and 100 mg of levodopa (Rx) [*Parcopa* (orally disintegrating tablets; aspartame; citric acid; crospovidone; magnesium stearate; mannitol; microcrystalline cellulose; natural and artificial mint flavor; sodium bicarbonate; yellow 10 iron oxide)].
25 mg of carbidopa and 250 mg of levodopa (Rx) [*Parcopa* (orally disintegrating tablets; aspartame; citric acid; crospovidone; magnesium stearate; mannitol; microcrystalline cellulose; natural and artificial mint flavor; sodium bicarbonate; FD&C blue #2 HT aluminum lake)].

Packaging and storage
Store at 20 and 25 °C (68 and 77 °F), excursions permitted between 15 and 30 °C (59 and 86 °F). Protect from moisture and light. Store in a well-closed, light-resistant container.

Auxiliary labeling
- May darken urine, saliva, or sweat.

Additional information
Instructions for use/handling of carbidopa and levodopa orally disintegrating tablets: Just prior to administration, gently remove the tablet from the bottle with dry hands. Immediately place the tablet on top of the tongue where it will dissolve in seconds, then swallow with saliva. Administration with liquid is not necessary.

CARBIDOPA AND LEVODOPA EXTENDED-RELEASE TABLETS

Usual adult dose
Antidyskinetic—
Initial dosage—
For patients not receiving levodopa therapy:
Mild to moderate disease—
Oral, initially, 50 mg of carbidopa and 200 mg of levodopa twice a day, at intervals of at least 6 hours.

For patients currently treated with conventional carbidopa-levodopa preparations:
Dosage with the extended-release tablets should be substituted at an amount that provides approximately 10% more levodopa per day, although this may need to be increased to 30% more levodopa per day based on clinical response. The interval between doses of the extended-release tablets should be 4 to 8 hours during the waking day, although a few patients may require more frequent dosing.
Guidelines for initial conversion from Carbidopa and Levodopa Tablets USP (immediate-release) to carbidopa and levodopa extended-release tablets are as follows:

Total daily dose of levodopa (mg)	Suggested dosage regimen of carbidopa and levodopa extended-release tablets (based on levodopa content)
300–400	200 mg twice a day
500–600	300 mg twice a day or 200 mg three times a day
700–800	A total of 800 mg in 3 or more divided doses (e.g., 300 mg a.m., 300 mg early p.m., and 200 mg later p.m.)
900–1000	A total of 1000 mg in 3 or more divided doses (e.g., 400 mg a.m., 400 mg early p.m., and 200 mg later p.m.)

For patients currently treated with levodopa without a decarboxylase inhibitor:
Levodopa must be discontinued at least twelve hours before initiating therapy with carbidopa and levodopa extended-release tablets. The extended-release tablets should be substituted at a dosage of approximately 25% of the previous levodopa dosage.
Mild to moderate disease: Oral, initially, 50 mg of carbidopa and 200 mg of levodopa twice a day.

Maintenance dosing—
Depending upon therapeutic response, doses and dosing intervals may be increased or decreased following initiation of therapy. An interval of at least 3 days between dosage adjustments is recommended. Most patients have been adequately treated with 400 to 1600 mg of levodopa per day, administered as divided doses at intervals ranging from 4 to 8 hours. A few patients may require higher doses (12 or more tablets per day) and shorter intervals (less than 4 hours), but this is usually not recommended.
When the extended-release tablets are given at less than 4-hour intervals, and/or if the divided doses are not equal, the smaller doses should be given at the end of the day.
Carbidopa and Levodopa Tablets USP (immediate-release) may be added to the dosage regimen in selected patients with advanced disease who need additional levodopa for a brief time during daytime hours. Usually one-half or one tablet of carbidopa 10 mg and levodopa 100 mg or carbidopa 25 mg and levodopa 100 mg is added.

Note: Cutting or breaking an extended-release form of carbidopa and levodopa combination will cause a more rapid onset of action.

Usual adult prescribing limits
The equivalent of 2400 mg of levodopa.

Usual pediatric dose
Children up to 18 years of age—Safety and efficacy have not been established.

Usual geriatric dose
See *Usual adult dose.*

Strength(s) usually available
U.S.—
25 mg of carbidopa and 100 mg of levodopa (Rx) [*Sinemet CR 25-100*].
50 mg of carbidopa and 200 mg of levodopa (Rx) [*Sinemet CR 50-200* (scored)].

Canada—
25 mg of carbidopa and 100 mg of levodopa (Rx) [*Sinemet CR 25-100*].
50 mg of carbidopa and 200 mg of levodopa (Rx) [*Sinemet CR 50-200* (scored)].

Packaging and storage
Store below 40 °C (104 °F), preferably between 15 and 30 °C (59 and 86 °F), unless otherwise specified by manufacturer. Store in a well-closed, light-resistant container.

Auxiliary labeling
- May darken urine, saliva, or sweat.
- Do not chew or crush tablets.

Revised: 09/23/2004

CARBIDOPA, ENTACAPONE AND LEVODOPA Systemic†

VA CLASSIFICATION (Primary): CN500

Commonly used brand name(s): *Stalevo 100; Stalevo 150; Stalevo 50.*

Note: For a listing of dosage forms and brand names by country availability, see *Dosage Forms* section(s).

†Not commercially available in Canada.

Category
Antidyskinetic.

Indications

Accepted

Parkinsonism (treatment)—Carbidopa, entacapone and levodopa combination is indicated in the treatment of idiopathic Parkinson's disease. It is used to substitute (with equivalent strength of each of the three components) for immediate release carbidopa/levodopa and entacapone previously administered as individual products and/or to replace immediate-release carbidopa/levodopa therapy (without entacapone) when patients experience the signs and symptoms of end-of-dose "wearing-off" (only for patients taking a total daily dose of levodopa of 600 mg or less and not experiencing dyskinesias).

Pharmacology/Pharmacokinetics

Physicochemical characteristics

Molecular weight—

Carbidopa: 244.3; Tablet content is anhydrous carbidopa: 226.3.
Entacapone: 305.3.
Levodopa: 197.2.

Mechanism of action/Effect

Carbidopa—When levodopa is administered orally it is rapidly decarboxylated to dopamine in extracerebral tissues so that only a small portion of a given dose is transported unchanged to the central nervous system. Carbidopa inhibits the decarboxylation of peripheral levodopa, making more levodopa available for transport to the brain. When coadministered with levodopa, carbidopa increases plasma levels of levodopa and reduces the amount of levodopa required to produce a given response by about 75%. Carbidopa prolongs the plasma half-life of levodopa from 50 minutes to 1.5 hours and decreases plasma and urinary dopamine and its major metabolite, homovanillic acid. The T_{max} of levodopa, however, was unaffected by the coadministration.

Entacapone—Entacapone is a selective and reversible inhibitor of catechol-O-methyltransferase (COMT). In mammals, COMT is distributed throughout various organs with the highest activities in the liver and kidney. COMT also occurs in neuronal tissues, especially in glial cells. COMT catalyzes the transfer of the methyl group of S-adenosyl-L-methionine to the phenolic group of substrates that contain a catechol structure. Physiological substrates of COMT include DOPA, catecholamines (dopamine, norepinephrine, and epinephrine) and their hydroxylated metabolites. The function of COMT is the elimination of biologically active catechols and some other hydroxylated metabolites. When decarboxylation of levodopa is prevented by carbidopa, COMT becomes the major metabolizing enzyme for levodopa, catalyzing its metabolism to 3-methoxy-4-hydroxy-L-phenylalanine (3-OMD).

When entacapone is given in conjunction with levodopa and carbidopa, plasma levels of levodopa are greater and more sustained than after administration of levodopa and carbidopa alone. It is believed that at a given frequency of levodopa administration, these more sustained plasma levels of levodopa result in more constant dopaminergic stimulation in the brain, leading to greater effects on the signs and symptoms of Parkinson's disease. The higher levodopa levels may also lead to increased levodopa adverse effects, sometimes requiring a decrease in the dose of levodopa.

When 200 mg entacapone is coadministered with levodopa/carbidopa, it increases levodopa plasma exposure (AUC) by 35%-40% and prolongs its elimination half-life in Parkinson's disease patients from 1.3 to 2.4 hours. Plasma levels of the major COMT-mediated dopamine metabolite, 3-methoxy-4-hydroxy-L-phenylalanine (3-OMD), are also markedly decreased proportionally with increasing dose of entacapone.

In animals, while entacapone enters the CNS to a minimal extent, it has been shown to inhibit central COMT activity. In humans, entacapone inhibits the COMT enzyme in peripheral tissues. The effects of entacapone on central COMT activity in humans have not been studied.

Levodopa—Current evidence indicates that symptoms of Parkinson's disease are related to depletion of dopamine in the corpus striatum. Administration of dopamine is ineffective in the treatment of Parkinson's disease apparently because it does not cross the blood-brain barrier. However, levodopa, the metabolic precursor of dopamine, does cross the blood-brain barrier, and presumably is converted to dopamine in the brain. This is thought to be the mechanism whereby levodopa relieves symptoms of Parkinson's disease.

Absorption

The food-effect on the carbidopa, entacapone and levodopa combination has not been evaluated.

Carbidopa—

Slightly more slowly than compared with levodopa and entacapone; mean AUC range is from 170 to 700 ng hr per mL, with different strengths providing 12.5 mg, 25 mg, or 37.5 mg of carbidopa.

Entacapone—

Rapidly absorbed; AUC is 1250 to 1450 ng hr per mL after administration of different carbidopa, entacapone and levodopa combination therapy strengths all providing 200 mg of entacapone.

Levodopa—

Rapidly absorbed; Since levodopa competes with certain amino acids for transport across the gut wall, the absorption of levodopa may be impaired in some patients on a high protein diet. Meals rich in large neutral amino acids may delay and reduce the absorption of levodopa.

AUC ranges from 1040 to 3770 ng hr per mL, depending on strength of tablet.

Distribution

Levodopa and entacapone—Distribution volume is moderately small.

Protein binding

Carbidopa—

Moderate (36%); plasma protein.

Entacapone—

Very high (98%); plasma protein over the concentration range of 0.4-50 mcg per mL; binds mainly to serum albumin.

Levodopa—

Low (10–30%); plasma protein.

Biotransformation

Carbidopa—

Carbidopa is metabolized to two main metabolites: α-methyl–3-methoxy-4-hydroxyphenylpropionic acid and α-methyl-3,4-dihydroxyphenylpropionic acid.

Entacapone—

The main metabolic pathway is isomerization to the cis-isomer, the only active metabolite.

Levodopa—

Levodopa is extensively metabolized to various metabolites. Two major pathways are decarboxylation by dopa decarboxylase (DDC) and O-methylation by catechol-O-methyltransferase (COMT).

Half-life

Due to short elimination half-lives, no true accumulation of levodopa or entacapone occurs when they are administered repeatedly.

Carbidopa—

Elimination: 1.6 to 2 hours (range 0.7-4 hours).

Entacapone—

Elimination: 0.8 to 1 hour (0.3-4.5 hours).

Levodopa—

Elimination: 1.7 hours (range 1.1-3.2 hours).

Time to peak concentration

Levodopa T_{max}: 1.1 to 1.5 hours, depending upon tablet strength.

Peak plasma concentration

Carbidopa—

C_{max} ranged from about 40 to 125 ng per mL

Entacapone—

C_{max}: 1200 ng per mL

Levodopa—

C_{max}: 470 to 1270 ng per mL; depending on tablet strength

Elimination

Carbidopa—

The 2 main metabolites are primarily eliminated in the urine unchanged or as glucuronide conjugates. Unchanged carbidopa accounts for 30% of the total urinary excretion.

Entacapone—

Entacapone is almost completely metabolized prior to excretion with only a very small amount (0.2% of dose) found unchanged in urine. The main metabolic pathway is isomerization to the cis-isomer, the only active metabolite. Entacapone and the cis-isomer are eliminated in the urine as glucuronide conjugates. The glucuronides account for 95% of all urinary metabolites (70% as parent and 25% as cis-isomer glucuronides). The glucuronide conjugate of the cis-isomer is inactive. After oral administration of a ^{14}C-labeled dose of entacapone, 10% of labeled parent and metabolite is excreted in urine and 90% in feces.

Special Populations

Hepatic impairment—While there are no studies on the pharmacokinetics of carbidopa and levodopa in patients with hepatic impairment, carbidopa, entacapone and levodopa combination should be administered cautiously to patients with biliary obstruction or hepatic disease since biliary excretion appears to be the major route of excretion of entacapone and hepatic impairment had a significant effect on the pharmacokinetics of entacapone when 200 mg entacapone was administered alone.

Entacapone: Hepatic impairment had a significant effect on the pharmacokinetics of entacapone when 200 mg entacapone was administered alone. A single 200 mg dose of entacapone, without levodopa/dopa decarboxylase inhibitor coadministration, showed approximately two-fold higher AUC and C_{max} values in patients with a history of alcoholism and hepatic impairment (n=10) compared to normal subjects (n=10). All patients had biopsy-proven liver cirrhosis caused by alcohol. According to Child-Pugh grading 7 patients with liver disease had mild hepatic impairment and 3 patients had moderate hepatic impairment. As only about 10% of the entacapone dose is excreted in urine, as parent compound and conjugated glucuronide, biliary excretion appears to be the major route of excretion of this drug. Consequently, carbidopa, entacapone and levodopa combination should be administered with care to patients with biliary obstruction or hepatic disease.

Renal disease—Carbidopa, entacapone and levodopa combination should be administered cautiously to patients with severe renal disease. There are no studies on the pharmacokinetics of levodopa and carbidopa in patients with renal impairment.

Entacapone: No important effects of renal function on the pharmacokinetics of entacapone were found. The pharmacokinetics of entacapone have been investigated after a single 200 mg entacapone dose, without levodopa/dopa decarboxylase inhibitor coadministration, in a specific renal impairment study. There were three groups: normal subjects (n=7; creatinine clearance >1.12 mL/sec/1.73 m^2), moderate impairment (n=10; creatinine clearance ranging from 0.60-0.89 mL/sec/1.73 m^2), and severe impairment (n=7; creatinine clearance ranging from 0.20-0.44 mL/sec/1.73 m^2).

Elderly—Carbidopa, entacapone and levodopa combination has not been studied in Parkinson's disease patients or in healthy volunteers older than 75 years old. In the pharmacokinetics studies conducted in healthy volunteers following single dose of carbidopa/levodopa/entacapone (as carbidopa, entacapone and levodopa combination or as separate carbidopa/levodopa and entacapone tablets.

Carbidopa: There is no significant difference in the C_{max} and AUC of carbidopa, between younger (45-60 years) and elderly subjects (60-75 years).

Entacapone: The AUC of entacapone is significantly (on average, 15%) higher in elderly (60-75 years) than younger subjects (45-60 years). There is no significant difference in the C_{max} of entacapone between younger (45-60 years) and elderly subjects (60-75 years).

Levodopa: The AUC of levodopa is significantly (on average 10%-20%) higher in elderly (60-75 years) than younger subjects (45-60 years). There is no significant difference in the C_{max} of levodopa between younger (45-60 years) and elderly subjects (60-75 years).

Gender—The bioavailability of levodopa is significantly higher in females when given with or without carbidopa and/or entacapone

Carbidopa: There is no gender difference in the pharmacokinetics of carbidopa.

Entacapone: There is no gender difference in the pharmacokinetics of entacapone.

Levodopa: The plasma exposure (AUC and C_{max}) of levodopa is significantly higher in females than males (on average, 40% for AUC and 30% for C_{max}). These differences are primarily explained by body weight. Other published literature showed significant gender effect (higher concentrations in females) even after correction for body weight.

Precautions to Consider

Carcinogenicity/Mutagenicity

In a two-year bioassay of carbidopa and levodopa combination, no evidence of carcinogenicity was found in rats receiving doses of approximately two times the maximum daily human dose of carbidopa and four times the maximum daily human dose of levodopa.

Two-year carcinogenicity studies of entacapone were conducted in mice and rats. Rats were treated once daily by oral gavage with entacapone doses of 20, 90, or 400 mg per kg. An increased incidence of renal tubular adenomas and carcinomas was found in male rats treated with the highest dose of entacapone. Plasma exposures (AUC) associated with this dose were approximately 20 times higher than estimated plasma exposures of humans receiving the maximum recommended daily dose of entacapone (MRDD = 1600 mg). Mice were treated once daily by oral gavage with doses of 20, 100 or 600 mg per kg of body weight of entacapone (0.05, 0.3, and 2 times the MRDD for humans on a mg per m^2 basis). Because of a high incidence of premature mortality in mice receiving the highest dose of entacapone, the mouse study is not an adequate assessment of carcinogenicity. Although no treatment related tumors were observed in animals receiving the lower doses, the carcinogenic potential of entacapone has not been fully evaluated.

The carcinogenic potential of entacapone administered in combination with carbidopa-levodopa has not been evaluated.

Mutagenicity

Carbidopa was positive in the Ames test in the presence and absence of metabolic activation, was mutagenic in the *in vitro* mouse lymphoma/thymidine kinase assay in the absence of metabolic activation, and was negative in the *in vivo* mouse micronucleus test.

Entacapone was mutagenic and clastogenic in the *in vitro* mouse lymphoma/thymidine kinase assay in the presence and absence of metabolic activation, and was clastogenic in cultured human lymphocytes in the presence of metabolic activation. Entacapone, either alone or in combination with carbidopa-levodopa, was not clastogenic in the *in vivo* mouse micronucleus test or mutagenic in the bacterial reverse mutation assay (Ames test).

Pregnancy/Reproduction

Fertility—In reproduction studies with carbidopa and levodopa combination, no effects on fertility were found in rats receiving doses of approximately two times the maximum daily human dose of carbidopa and four times the maximum daily human dose of levodopa.

Entacapone did not impair fertility or general reproductive performance in rats treated with up to 700 mg per kg of body weight per day (plasma AUCs 28 times those in humans receiving the MRDD). Delayed mating, but no fertility impairment, was evident in female rats treated with 700 mg per kg of body weight per day of entacapone.

Pregnancy—Adequate and well-controlled studies in humans have not been done. There is no experience from clinical studies regarding the use of carbidopa, entacapone and levodopa in pregnant women. Therefore, carbidopa, entacapone and levodopa should be used during pregnancy only if the potential benefit justifies the potential risk to the fetus.

It has been reported from individual cases that levodopa crosses the human placental barrier, enters the fetus, and is metabolized. Carbidopa concentrations in fetal tissue appeared to be minimal.

Carbidopa and levodopa combination caused both visceral and skeletal malformations in rabbits at all doses and ratios of carbidopa and levodopa tested, which ranged from 10 times and 5 times the maximum recommended human dose of carbidopa-levodopa to 20 times and 10 times the maximum recommended human dose of carbidopa and levodopa, respectively. There was a decrease in the number of live pups delivered by rats receiving approximately two times the maximum recommended human dose of carbidopa and approximately five times the maximum recommended human dose of levodopa during organogenesis. No teratogenic effects were observed in mice receiving up to 20 times the maximum recommended human dose of carbidopa and levodopa combination.

In embryofetal development studies, entacapone was administered to pregnant animals throughout organogenesis at doses of up to 1000 mg per kg of body weight per day in rats and 300 mg per kg of body weight per day in rabbits. Increased incidences of fetal variations were evident in litters from rats treated with the highest dose, in the absence of overt signs of maternal toxicity. The maternal plasma drug exposure (AUC) associated with this dose was approximately 34 times the estimated plasma exposure in humans receiving the maximum recommended daily dose (MRDD) of 1600 mg. Increased frequencies of abortions and late/total resorptions and decreased fetal weights were observed in the litters of rabbits treated with maternotoxic doses of 100 mg per kg of body weight per day (plasma AUCs 0.4 times those in humans receiving the MRDD) or greater. There was no evidence of teratogenicity in these studies.

However, when entacapone was administered to female rats prior to mating and during early gestation, an increased incidence of fetal eye anomalies (macrophthalmia, microphthalmia, anophthalmia) was observed in the litters of dams treated with doses of 160 mg per kg of body weight per day (plasma AUCs 7 times those in humans receiving the MRDD) or greater, in the absence of maternotoxicity. Administration of up to 700 mg per kg of body weight per day (plasma AUCs 28 times those in humans receiving the MRDD) to female rats during the latter part of gestation and throughout lactation, produced no evidence of developmental impairment in the offspring.

FDA Pregnancy Category C

Breast-feeding

It is not known whether carbidopa, entacapone and levodopa is distributed into human breast milk. In animal studies, carbidopa and entacapone were distributed into maternal rat milk. Because many drugs are distributed in human milk, caution should be exercised when carbidopa, entacapone and levodopa is administered to a nursing woman.

Pediatrics

No information is available on the relationship of age to the effects of carbidopa, entacapone and levodopa in the pediatric population. Safety and efficacy have not been established in pediatric patients.

Geriatrics

No information is available on the relationship of age to the effects of carbidopa, entacapone and levodopa in the geriatric population. Carbidopa, entacapone and levodopa have not been studied in Parkinson's disease patients or in healthy volunteers older than 75 years old. Elderly patients are more likely to have age related problems such as decreased hepatic, renal, or cardiac function, concomitant diseases or other drug therapy. Dose selection should be cautious.

Drug interactions and/or related problems

The following drug interactions and/or related problems have been selected on the basis of their potential clinical significance (possible mechanism in parentheses where appropriate)—not necessarily inclusive (» = major clinical significance):

Note: Combinations containing any of the following medications, depending on the amount present, may also interact with this medication.

Ampicillin or
Chloramphenicol or
Cholestyramine or
Erythromycin or
Probenecid or
Rifampicin
(Drugs known to interfere with biliary excretion, glucuronidation, and intestinal beta-glucuronidase should be used with caution; as most entacapone excretion is via the bile.))

Anti-hypertensive agents
(symptomatic postural hypotension has occurred when carbidopa-levodopa was added to the treatment of a patient receiving anti-hypertensive drugs; when therapy with carbidopa, entacapone and levodopa combination is started, dosage adjustment of the anti-hypertensive drug may be required.)

» COMT metabolized drugs, such as
» Alpha-methyldopa or
» Apomorphine or
» Bitolterol or
» Dobutamine or
» Dopamine or
» Epinephrine or
» Isoetharine or
» Isoproterenol or
» Norepinephrine
(should be administered with caution in patients receiving entacapone regardless of the route of administration (including inhalation), as their interaction may result in increased heart rates, possibly arrhythmias, and excessive changes in blood pressure.)

Dopamine D2 receptor antagonists, such as
Butyrophenones or
Phenothiazines or
Risperidone
(may reduce the therapeutic effects of levodopa.)

Foods, high-protein
(change in diet to foods that are high in protein may delay the absorption of levodopa and may reduce the amount taken up in the circulation; excessive acidity also delays stomach emptying, thus delaying the absorption of levodopa.)

Iron salts
(may reduce the amount of levodopa available to the body and may reduce the clinical effectiveness and bioavailability of the carbidopa, entacapone and levodopa combination therapy; clinical relevance is unclear.)

Isoniazid
(may reduce the therapeutic effects of levodopa.)

Metoclopramide
(although metoclopramide may increase the bioavailability of levodopa by increasing gastric emptying, metoclopramide may also adversely affect disease control by its dopamine receptor antagonistic properties.)

» Non-selective MAO inhibitors, such as
» Phenelzine or
» Tranylcypromine
(as with carbidopa and levodopa combination, nonselective monoamine oxidase [MAO] inhibitors are contraindicated for use with carbidopa, entacapone and levodopa combination; these inhibitors must be discontinued at least two weeks prior to initiating therapy with carbidopa, entacapone and levodopa combination; carbidopa, entacapone and levodopa combination may be administered concomitantly with the manufacturer's recommended dose of MAO inhibitors with selectivity for MAO type B [e.g., selegiline HCl])
(Monoamine oxidase [MAO] and COMT are the two major enzyme systems involved in the metabolism of catecholamines. It is theoretically possible, therefore, that the combination of entacapone and a non-selective MAO inhibitor [e.g., phenelzine and tranylcypromine] would result in inhibition of the majority of the pathways responsible for normal catecholamine metabolism.)

Phenytoin or
Papaverine
(beneficial effects of levodopa in Parkinson's disease have been reported to be reversed by phenytoin and papaverine; patients taking these drugs with carbidopa-levodopa should be carefully observed for loss of therapeutic response.)

Pyridoxine
(carbidopa, entacapone and levodopa combination can be given to patients receiving supplemental pyridoxineoral coadministration of 10 to 25 mg of pyridoxine hydrochloride (vitamin B6) with levodopa may reverse the effects of levodopa by increasing the rate of aromatic amino acid decarboxylation; carbidopa inhibits this action of pyridoxine; therefore, carbidopa, entacapone and levodopa combination can be given to patients receiving supplemental pyridoxine.)

Tricyclic antidepressants
(rare reports of adverse reactions, including hypertension and dyskinesia, resulting from the concomitant use of tricyclic antidepressants and carbidopa-levodopa.)

Laboratory value alterations

The following have been selected on the basis of their potential clinical significance (possible effect in parentheses where appropriate)—not necessarily inclusive (» = major clinical significance).

With diagnostic test results

Catecholamines, plasma and urine
(test results are unreliable)

Coombs' (antiglobulin) test
(positive tests have been reported)

Glucose, urine
(carbidopa, entacapone and levodopa combination may cause a false-positive reaction for urinary ketone bodies when a test tape is used for determination of ketonuria; this reaction will not be altered by boiling the urine specimen; false-negative tests may result with the use of glucose-oxidase methods of testing for glucosuria.)

Growth hormone
(levodopa may increase levels)

Iron
(decreased iron in serum has been reported)

Ketones, urine
(tests using test tape or glucose-oxidase methods may cause false-positive results)

Prolactin
(levodopa may depress secretion)

With physiology/laboratory test values

Alanine aminotransferase (ALT [SGPT]) and
Alkaline phosphatase and
Aspartate aminotransferase (AST [SGOT]) and
Bilirubin and
Glucose, serum and
Lactate dehydrogenase (LDH)
(serum concentrations may be increased)

Blood urea nitrogen (BUN) or
Creatinine or
Uric acid
(commonly, levels are lower during administration of carbidopa, entacapone and levodopa combination than with administration of levodopa; abnormalities in blood urea nitrogen (BUN) tests may also be seen)

Hematocrit or
Hemoglobin or
Serum potassium or
White blood cell count
(values may be decreased)

Bacteria or
Blood in the urine
(abnormalities may be seen)

Protein, urine
(may be present)

Medical considerations/Contraindications

The medical considerations/contraindications included have been selected on the basis of their potential clinical significance (reasons given in parentheses where appropriate)—not necessarily inclusive (» = major clinical significance).

Except under special circumstances, this medication should not be used when the following medical problem exists:

» Hypersensitivity to any component of the tablet (carbidopa, entacapone or levodopa) of the drug or any of its excipients

» Narrow-angle glaucoma
(use of carbidopa, entacapone and levodopa combination is contraindicated in patients with narrow-angle glaucoma)

» Melanoma, history of, or
» Skin lesions, undiagnosed
(levodopa may activate malignant melanoma, carbidopa, entacapone and levodopa combination should not be used in patients with suspicious, undiagnosed skin lesions or a history of melanoma)

Risk-benefit should be considered when the following medical problems exist:

Biliary obstruction
(caution should be exercised when administering carbidopa, entacapone and levodopa combination to patients with biliary obstruction as entacapone is excreted mostly via the bile.)

Bronchial asthma, or
Cardiovascular disease, severe, or
Endocrine disease or
Hepatic disease or
Pulmonary disease, severe, or
Renal disease
(carbidopa, entacapone and levodopa combination should be administered cautiously to patients with severe cardiovascular or pulmonary disease, bronchial asthma, renal, hepatic or endocrine disease.)

Dyskinesia
(entacapone may potentiate the dopaminergic side effects of levodopa and may therefore exacerbate preexisting dyskinesia; although decreasing the dose of levodopa may ameliorate this side effect, many patients in controlled trials continued to experience frequent dyskinesias despite a reduction in their dose of levodopa; the rates of withdrawal for dyskinesia were 1.5% and 0.8% for 200 mg entacapone and placebo, respectively)

Hepatic impairment
(should be treated with caution; the AUC and C_{max} of entacapone approximately doubled in patients with documented liver disease compared to controls.)

» Myocardial infarction, history of, with residual atrial, nodal, or ventricular arrhythmias
(as with levodopa, care should be exercised in administering carbidopa, entacapone and levodopa combination to patients with this condition)

Peptic ulcer, history of
(as with levodopa, treatment with carbidopa, entacapone and levodopa combination may increase the possibility of upper gastrointestinal hemorrhage in patients with a history of peptic ulcer.)

Psychoses, past or current
(should be treated with caution as carbidopa, levodopa and entacapone may cause mental disturbances; these reactions are thought to be due to increased brain dopamine following administration of levodopa; all patients should be observed carefully for the development of depression with concomitant suicidal tendencies.)

» Wide-angle glaucoma
(may be treated cautiously with carbidopa, levodopa and entacapone combination provided the intraocular pressure is well controlled and the patient is monitored carefully for changes in intraocular pressure during therapy)

Patient monitoring

The following may be especially important in patient monitoring (other tests may be warranted in some patients, depending on condition; » = major clinical significance):

Cardiac function
(patients with a history of myocardial infarction who have residual atrial, nodal, or ventricular arrhythmias should have cardiac function monitored carefully during the period of initial dosage adjustment, in a facility with provisions for intensive cardiac care)

Cardiovascular function and
Hematopoietic function and
Hepatic function and
Renal function
(monitoring recommended during extended therapy)

CNS effects
(because carbidopa as well as entacapone permits more levodopa to reach the brain and more dopamine to reach the brain and more dopamine to be formed, certain adverse CNS effects, e.g., dyskinesia (involuntary movements) may occur at lower dosages and sooner with levodopa preparations containing carbidopa and entacapone than with levodopa alone; the occurrence of dyskinesias may require dosage reduction.)

Depression
(all patients should be observed carefully for the development of depression with concomitant suicidal tendencies.)

Intraocular pressure
(patients with wide-angle glaucoma should be monitored carefully for changes in intraocular pressure during therapy.)

Neuroleptic Malignant Syndrome (NMS)
(patients should be observed carefully when the dosage of carbidopa, entacapone and levodopa is reduced abruptly or discontinued, especially if the patient is receiving neuroleptics.)

Side/Adverse Effects

The following side/adverse effects have been selected on the basis of their potential clinical significance (possible signs and symptoms in parentheses where appropriate)—not necessarily inclusive:

Hypotension/syncope—In the large controlled trials of entacapone, approximately 1.2% and 0.8% of 200 mg entacapone and placebo patients treated also with levodopa/dopa decarboxylase inhibitor, respectively, reported at least one episode of syncope. Reports of syncope were generally more frequent in patients in both treatment groups who had an episode of documented hypotension (although the episodes of syncope, obtained by history, were themselves not documented with vital sign measurement).

Diarrhea—In clinical trials of entacapone, diarrhea developed in 60 of 603 (10%) and 16 of 400 (4%) of patients treated with 200 mg of entacapone or placebo in combination with levodopa/dopa decarboxylase inhibitor, respectively. In patients treated with entacapone, diarrhea was generally mild to moderate in severity (8.6%) but was regarded as severe in 1.3%. Diarrhea resulted in withdrawal in 10 of 603 (1.7%) patients, 7 (1.2%) with mild and moderate diarrhea and 3 (0.5%) with severe diarrhea. Diarrhea generally resolved after discontinuation of entacapone. Two patients with diarrhea were hospitalized. Typically, diarrhea presents within 4 to 12 weeks after entacapone is started, but it may appear as early as the first week and as late as many months after the initiation of treatment.

Hallucinations—Dopaminergic therapy in Parkinson's disease patients has been associated with hallucinations. In clinical trials of entacapone, hallucinations developed in approximately 4% of patients treated with 200 mg entacapone or placebo in combination with levodopa/dopa decarboxylase inhibitor. Hallucinations led to drug discontinuation and premature withdrawal from clinical trials in 0.8% and 0% of patients treated with 200 mg entacapone and placebo, respectively. Hallucinations led to hospitalization in 1% and 0.3% of patients in the 200 mg entacapone and placebo groups, respectively.

Dyskinesia—Entacapone may potentiate the dopaminergic side effects of levodopa and may therefore cause and/or exacerbate preexisting dyskinesia. Although decreasing the dose of levodopa may ameliorate this side effect, many patients in controlled trials continued to experience frequent dyskinesias despite a reduction in their dose of levodopa. The rates of withdrawal for dyskinesia were 1.5% and 0.8% for 200 mg entacapone and placebo, respectively.

Rhabdomyolysis—Cases of severe rhabdomyolysis have been reported with entacapone when used in combination with levodopa. The complicated nature of these cases makes it impossible to determine what role, if any, entacapone played in their pathogenesis. Severe prolonged motor activity including dyskinesia may account for rhabdomyolysis. One case, however, included fever and alteration of consciousness. It is therefore possible that the rhabdomyolysis may be a result of the syndrome described in Hyperpyrexia and confusion below.

Hyperpyrexia and confusion—Cases of a symptom complex resembling the neuroleptic malignant syndrome characterized by elevated temperature, muscular rigidity, altered consciousness, and elevated CPK have been reported in association with the rapid dose reduction or withdrawal of other dopaminergic drugs. No cases have been reported following the abrupt withdrawal or dose reduction of entacapone treatment during clinical studies.

Fibrotic complications—Cases of retroperitoneal fibrosis, pulmonary infiltrates, pleural effusion, and pleural thickening have been reported in some patients treated with ergot derived dopaminergic agents. These complications may resolve when the drug is discontinued, but complete resolution does not always occur. Although these adverse events are believed to be related to the ergoline structure of these compounds, whether other, nonergot derived drugs (e.g., entacapone, levodopa) that increase dopaminergic activity can cause them is unknown. It should be noted that the expected incidence of fibrotic complications is so low that even if entacapone caused these complications at rates similar to those attributable to other dopaminergic therapies, it is unlikely that it would have been detected in a cohort of the size exposed to entacapone. Four cases of pulmonary fibrosis were reported during clinical development of entacapone; three of these patients were also treated with pergolide and one with bromocriptine. The duration of treatment with entacapone ranged from 7 to 17 months.

Renal toxicity—In a one-year toxicity study, entacapone (plasma exposure 20 times that in humans receiving the maximum recommended daily dose of 1600 mg) caused an increased incidence of nephrotoxicity in male rats that was characterized by regenerative tubules, thickening of basement membranes, infiltration of mononuclear cells and tubular protein casts. These effects were not associated with changes in clinical chemistry parameters, and there is no established method for monitoring for the possible occurrence of these lesions in humans. Although this toxicity could represent a species-specific effect, there is not yet evidence that this is so.

Those indicating need for medical attention

More frequent—Entacapone

Dyskinesia (twitching, twisting, uncontrolled repetitive movements of tongue, lips, face, arms, or legs)

Incidence unknown—Carbidopa and Levodopa and/or Levodopa alone

Agranulocytosis (cough or hoarseness; fever with or without chills; general feeling of tiredness or weakness; lower back or side pain; painful or difficult urination; sore throat; sores, ulcers, or white spots on lips or in mouth; unusual bleeding or bruising); ***anemia*** (pale skin; troubled breathing with exertion; unusual bleeding or bruising; unusual tiredness or weakness)—hemolytic and non-hemolytic; ***angioedema*** (large, hive-like swelling on face, eyelids, lips, tongue, throat, hands, legs, feet, sex organs); ***ataxia*** (shakiness and unsteady walk; unsteadiness. trembling, or other problems with muscle control or coordination); ***chest pain; cardiac irregularities*** (chest pain or discomfort; fast, irregular, or pounding heart beat; shortness of breath); ***convulsions*** (seizures); ***extrapyramidal disorder*** (difficulty in speaking; drooling; loss of balance control; muscle trembling, jerking, or stiffness; restlessness; shuffling walk; stiffness of limbs; twisting movements of body; uncontrolled movements, especially of face, neck, and back); ***fibrotic complications including; pleural effusion*** (chest pain; shortness of breath); ***pleural thickening*** (shortness of breath; chest pain or tightness); ***pulmonary infiltrates*** (cough; chest pain; unusual tiredness or weakness); ***retroperitoneal fibrosis*** (fever; general feeling of illness; loss of appetite; lower abdominal pain; lower back pain; nausea; vomiting); ***gastrointestinal bleeding*** (bloody or black, tarry stools; vomiting of blood or material that looks like coffee grounds; severe stomach pain; constipation); ***Henoch Schonlein purpura*** (blood in urine; bloody or black, tarry stools; fever; large, flat, blue or purplish patches in the skin; painful knees and ankles; raised red swellings on the skin, the buttocks, legs or ankles; stomach pain); ***Horner's syndrome, latent, activation of*** (constricted pupil; drooping eyelid (ptosis); and facial dryness); ***hyperpyrexia*** (fever); ***leukopenia*** (black, tarry stools; chest pain; chills; cough; fever; painful or difficult urination; shortness of breath; sore throat; sores, ulcers, or white spots on lips or in mouth; swollen glands; unusual bleeding or bruising; unusual tiredness or weakness); ***malignant melanoma*** (new mole; change in size, shape or color of existing mole; mole that leaks fluid or bleeds); ***myocardial infarction*** (chest pain or discomfort; pain or discomfort in arms, jaw, back or neck; shortness of breath; nausea; sweating; vomiting); ***neuroleptic malignant syndrome*** (convulsions; difficulty in breathing; fast heartbeat; high fever; high or low blood pressure; increased sweating; loss of bladder control; severe muscle stiffness; unusually pale skin tiredness); ***oculogyric crisis*** (fixed position of eye); ***phlebitis*** (bluish color; changes in skin color; pain, tenderness and swelling of foot or leg); ***psychotic episodes*** (severe mental changes; hallucinations [seeing, hearing, or feeling things that are not there])—including delusions, hallucinations and paranoid ideation; ***rhabdomyolysis*** (dark-colored urine; fever; muscle cramps or spasms; muscle pain or stiffness; unusual tiredness or weakness); ***thrombocytopenia*** (black, tarry stools; bleeding gums; blood in urine or stools; pinpoint red spots on skin; unusual bleeding or bruising)

Those indicating need for medical attention only if they continue or are bothersome

More frequent—Entacapone

Abdominal pain (stomach pain); ***constipation*** (difficulty having a bowel movement (stool)); ***diarrhea; dizziness; fatigue*** (unusual tiredness or weakness); ***hyperkinesia*** (increase in body movements); ***hypokinesia*** (absence of or decrease in body movement); ***nausea; urine discoloration***

Less frequent—Entacapone

Agitation (anxiety; nervousness; restlessness; irritability; dry mouth; shortness of breath; hyperventilation; trouble sleeping; irregular heartbeats; shaking); ***anxiety*** (fear; nervousness); ***asthenia*** (lack or loss of strength); ***back pain; bacterial infection; dry mouth; dyspepsia*** (acid or sour stomach; belching; heartburn; indigestion; stomach discomfort, upset or pain); ***dyspnea*** (shortness of breath; difficult or labored breathing; tightness in chest; wheezing); ***flatulence*** (bloated, full feeling; excess air or gas in stomach or intestines; passing gas); ***gastritis*** (burning feeling in chest or stomach; tenderness in stomach area; stomach upset; indigestion); ***gastrointestinal disorders*** (abdominal or stomach cramps; discomfort; pain; back pain; constipation; diarrhea; indigestion; loss of appetite; nausea or vomiting; swollen mouth and tongue; unpleasant taste; urge to have bowel movement; vomiting); ***increased sweating; purpura*** (pinpoint red or purple spots on skin)—including Henoch-Schonlein; ***somnolence*** (sleepiness or unusual drowsiness); ***taste perversion*** (bitter, sour or unusual taste in mouth); ***vomiting***

Incidence unknown—Carbidopa and Levodopa and/or Levodopa alone

Abdominal pain and distress; agitation (anxiety; nervousness; restlessness; irritability; dry mouth; shortness of breath; hyperventilation; trouble sleeping; irregular heartbeats; shaking); ***alopecia*** (hair loss; thinning of hair); ***anorexia*** (loss of appetite; weight loss); ***anxiety*** (fear; nervousness); ***asthenia*** (lack or loss of strength); ***back pain; bizarre breathing patterns; blepharospasm*** (increased blinking; twitching of eyelids); ***blurred vision; bradykinetic episodes*** (slow movement; slow reflexes); ***bruxism*** (clenching, gnashing, or grinding teeth); ***bullous lesions*** (large, hard skin blisters); ***burning sensation of the tongue; confusion*** (mood or mental changes); ***constipation*** (difficulty having a bowel movement (stool)); ***cough; dark saliva; dark sweat; dark urine; decreased mental acuity; depression*** (discouragement; feeling sad or empty; irritability; lack of appetite; loss of interest or pleasure; tiredness; trouble concentrating; trouble sleeping)—with or without development of suicidal tendencies; ***dementia*** (poor insight and judgment; problems with memory or speech; trouble recognizing objects; trouble thinking and planning; trouble walking); ***diarrhea; dilated pupils*** (enlarged pupils); ***diplopia*** (double vision; seeing double); ***disorientation*** (confusion about identity, place, and time); ***dizziness; dream abnormalities***—including nightmares; ***dry mouth; duodenal ulcer development*** (burning and upper abdominal pain; loss of appetite; nausea; vomiting); ***dyspepsia*** (acid or sour stomach; belching; heartburn; indigestion; stomach discomfort upset or pain); ***dysphagia*** (difficulty swallowing); ***dyspnea*** (shortness of breath; difficult or labored breathing; tightness in chest; wheezing); ***edema*** (swelling); ***euphoria*** (false or unusual sense of well-being); ***failing; faintness*** (feeling like you will pass out); ***fatigue*** (unusual tiredness or weakness); ***flatulence*** (bloated full feeling; excess air or gas in stomach or intestines; passing gas); ***flushing; gait disorders*** (walking in unusual manner); ***gastrointestinal pain; headache; heartburn*** (pain in the chest below the breastbone; belching; feeling of indigestion); ***hiccups; hoarseness; hot flashes*** (feeling of warmth; redness of the face, neck, arms and occasionally upper chest; sudden sweating); ***hypertension*** (blurred vision; dizziness; nervousness; headache; pounding in the ears; slow or fast heartbeat); ***hypotension*** (blurred vision; confusion; dizziness, faintness, or lightheadedness when getting up from a lying or sitting position suddenly; sweating; unusual tiredness or weakness); ***increased sweating; insomnia*** (sleeplessness; trouble sleeping; unable to sleep); ***libido, increased*** (increased interest in sexual ability, desire, drive, or performance; increased interest in sexual intercourse); ***leg pain; malaise*** (general feeling of discomfort or illness; unusual tiredness or weakness); ***memory impairment*** (being forgetful); ***muscle cramps; muscle twitching; nervousness; numbness; orthostatic hypotension*** (chills; cold sweats; confusion; dizziness, faintness, or lightheadedness when getting up from lying or sitting position); ***palpitation*** (fast, irregular, pounding, or racing heartbeat or pulse); ***paresthesia*** (burning, crawling, itching, numbness, prickling, "pins and needles", or tingling feelings); ***peripheral neuropathy*** (burning, numbness, tingling, or painful sensations weakness in arms, hands, legs, or feet, unsteadiness or awkwardness); ***pharyngeal pain; priapism*** (painful or prolonged erection of the penis); ***pruritus*** (itching skin); ***sense of stimulation; shoulder pain; sialorrhea*** (excessive watering of mouth); ***somnolence*** (sleepiness or unusual drowsiness); ***syncope*** (fainting); ***taste***

alterations; tremor, increased; trismus (difficulty opening the mouth; lockjaw; muscle spasm, especially of neck and back); ***upper respiratory tract infection*** (ear congestion; nasal congestion; chills; cough; fever; sneezing; sore throat; body aches or pain; headache; loss of voice; runny nose; unusual tiredness or weakness; difficulty in breathing); ***urinary frequency; urinary incontinence; urinary retention; urinary tract infection*** (bladder pain; bloody or cloudy urine; difficult, burning, or painful urination; frequent urge to urinate; lower back or side pain); ***urticaria*** (hives or welts; itching; redness of skin; skin rash); ***vomiting; weight gain; weight loss***

Overdose

For more information on the management of overdose or unintentional ingestion, **contact a poison control center** (see *Poison Control Center Listing*).

Management of acute overdosage with carbidopa, levodopa and entacapone is the same as management of acute overdosage with levodopa and entacapone.

There are very few cases of overdosage with levodopa reported in the published literature. Based on the limited available information, the acute symptoms of levodopa/dopa decarboxylase inhibitor overdosage can be expected to arise from dopaminergic overstimulation. Doses of a few grams may result in CNS disturbances, with an increasing likelihood of cardiovascular disturbance (e.g. hypotension, tachycardia) and more severe psychiatric problems at higher doses. An isolated report of rhabdomyolysis and another of transient renal insufficiency suggest that levodopa overdosage may give rise to systemic complications, secondary to dopaminergic overstimulation.

There have been no reported cases of either accidental or intentional overdose with entacapone tablets. However, COMT inhibition by entacapone treatment is dose-dependent. A massive overdose of entacapone may theoretically produce a 100% inhibition of the COMT enzyme in people, thereby preventing the O-methylation of endogenous and exogenous catechols.

The highest single dose of entacapone administered to humans was 800 mg, resulting in a plasma concentration of 14.1 micrograms per mL The highest daily dose given to humans was 2400 mg, administered in one study as 400 mg six times daily with carbidopa-levopoda for 14 days in 15 Parkinson's disease patients, and in another study as 800 mg t.i.d. for 7 days in 8 healthy volunteers. At this daily dose, the peak plasma concentrations of entacapone averaged 2 microgram per mL (at 45 min., compared to 1 and 1.2 micrograms per mL with 200 mg entacapone at 45 min). Abdominal pain and loose stools were the most commonly observed adverse events during this study. Daily doses as high as 2000 mg entacapone have been administered as 200 mg 10 times daily with carbidopa-levodopa or benserazide-levodopa for at least 1 year in 10 patients, for at least 2 years in 8 patients and for at least 3 years in 7 patients. Overall, however, clinical experience with daily doses above 1600 mg is limited.

Treatment of overdose

Since there is no specific antidote for acute overdose, treatment is symptomatic and supportive, with possible utilization of the following:

To decrease absorption—Immediate gastric lavage and repeated doses of charcoal over time. This may hasten the elimination of entacapone in particular, by decreasing its absorption/reabsorption from the GI tract.

Hospitalization is advised.

Monitoring—Electrocardiographic monitoring for development of arrhythmias. The patient should be carefully observed for the development of arrhythmias.

The possibility that the patient may have taken other drugs, increasing the risk of drug interactions (especially catechol-structured drugs) should be taken into consideration.

Specific treatment—

Antiarrhythmic therapy, if necessary.

Pyridoxine is not effective in reversing the actions of carbidopa and levodopa combination.

To date, no experience has been reported with dialysis; hence, its value in overdosage is not known. Hemodialysis or hemoperfusion is unlikely to reduce entacapone levels due to its high binding to plasma proteins.

Supportive care—

Judicious use of intravenous fluids.

Maintenance of airway.

The adequacy of the respiratory, circulatory and renal systems should be carefully monitored and appropriate supportive measures employed.

Patients in whom intentional overdose is confirmed or suspected should be referred for psychiatric consultation.

Patient Consultation

As an aid to patient consultation, refer to *Advice for the Patient, Carbidopa, Entacapone and Levodopa (Systemic)*.

In providing consultation, consider emphasizing the following selected information (» = major clinical significance):

Importance of diet

A change in diet to foods that are high in protein may delay the absorption of levodopa and may reduce the amount taken up in the circulation and may reduce the clinical effectiveness of the therapy

Iron salts (such as in multi-vitamin tablets) may also reduce the amount of levodopa available to the body and may reduce the clinical effectiveness of the therapy

Excessive acidity also delays stomach emptying, thus delaying the absorption of levodopa and may reduce the clinical effectiveness of the therapy

Before using this medication

» Conditions affecting use, especially:

Hypersensitivity to any component of the tablet (carbidopa, entacapone or levodopa) or any of its excipients

Carcinogenicity/Mutagenicity—The carcinogenic potential of entacapone administered in combination with carbidopa-levodopa has not been evaluated.

Carbidopa was shown to be mutagenic and entacapone was shown to be mutagenic and clastogenic

Pregnancy—Studies have not been done in humans; should be used during pregnancy only if the potential benefit justifies the potential risk to the fetus

Breast-feeding—Caution should be exercised when administering to nursing women

Use in children—Safety and efficacy have not been established in pediatric patients.

Use in the elderly—Carbidopa, entacapone and levodopa have not been studied in Parkinson's disease patients or in healthy volunteers older than 75 years old; dose selection should be cautious

Other medications, especially alpha-methyldopa, apomorphine, bitolterol, dobutamine, dopamine, epinephrine, isoetharine, isoproterenol, norepinephrine, phenelzine, tranylcypromine

Other medical problems, especially narrow-angle glaucoma, history of melanoma, history of myocardial infarction with residual atrial, nodal, or ventricular arrhythmias, undiagnosed skin lesions, wide-angle glaucoma

Proper use of this medication

Compliance with therapy; taking medication exactly as directed; not stopping medication unless ordered by physician; not adding additional antiparkinsonian medications without first consulting the physician.

Understanding that sometimes a "wearing-off" effect may occur at the end of the dosing interval. The physician should be notified for possible treatment adjustments if such response poses a problem to patient's every day life.

This medicine is a standard-release formulation of carbidopa-levodopa combined with entacapone that is designed to begin release of ingredients within 30 minutes after ingestion.

Occasionally, dark color (red, brown, or black) may appear in saliva, urine, or sweat after ingestion of this medicine. Although the color appears to be clinically insignificant, garments may become discolored.

A change in diet to foods that are high in protein may delay the absorption of levodopa and may reduce the amount taken up in the circulation. Excessive acidity also delays stomach emptying, thus delaying the absorption of levodopa; these factors may reduce the clinical effectiveness; Importance of discussing this with your doctor.

If taking multi-vitamin tablets discuss this with your doctor.

» Proper dosing

» Do not break tablets; swallow whole

» Do not take more than one tablet at any one time

Missed dose: Taking as soon as possible; not taking if almost time for next scheduled dose; not doubling doses

» Proper storage

Precautions while using this medication

Understanding that postural (orthostatic) hypotension (with or without symptoms) such as dizziness, nausea, syncope, and sweating may develop. Hypotension may occur more frequently during initial therapy or when total daily levodopa dosage is increased

Caution should be used when rising rapidly after sitting or lying down, especially if you have been doing so for prolonged periods; Use extra caution during the beginning of treatment with carbidopa, entacapone and levodopa combination

Caution if dizziness or drowsiness occurs; not driving, using machines, or doing anything else that requires alertness while taking carbidopa, entacapone and levodopa combination

Importance of using this medicine carefully when taking other CNS depressants as there is the possibility of additive sedative effects

Possibility that nausea may occur, especially at the initiation of treatment

Understanding possibility of hallucinations or increase in dyskinesia

Importance of notifying physician if patient intends to breast-feed or is breast-feeding an infant

Importance of notifying physician if patient becomes pregnant or intend to become pregnant during therapy

Side/adverse effects

Signs of potential side effects, especially angioedema, agranulocytosis, anemia, ataxia, chest pain, cardiac irregularities, convulsions, extrapyramidal disorder, fibrotic complications including pleural effusion, pleural thickening, pulmonary infiltrates and retroperitoneal fibrosis, gastrointestinal bleeding, Henoch-Schonlein purpura, Horner's syndrome (latent, activation of), leukopenia, malignant melanoma, myocardial infarction, neuroleptic malignant syndrome, oculogyric crisis, phlebitis, psychotic episodes, and thrombocytopenia.

General Dosing Information

For oral dosing forms:

Parkinson's disease is a progressive, neurodegenerative disorder of the extrapyramidal nervous system affecting the mobility and control of the skeletal muscular system. Its characteristic features include resting tremor, rigidity, and bradykinetic movements.

Maintenance of carbidopa, entacapone and levodopa treatment:

- Therapy should be individualized and adjusted for each patient according to the desired therapeutic response.
- Individual tablets should not be fractionated and only one tablet should be administered at each dosing interval.
- When less levodopa is required, the total daily dosage of carbidopa-levodopa should be reduced by either decreasing the strength of carbidopa, entacapone and levodopa combination at each administration or by decreasing the frequency of administration by extending the time between doses.
- When more levodopa is required, the next higher strength of carbidopa, entacapone and levodopa combination should be taken and/or the frequency of doses should be increased, up to a maximum of 8 times daily and not to exceed the maximum daily dose recommendations as outlined above.

Addition of other Antiparkinsonian Medications—Standard drugs for Parkinson's disease may be used concomitantly while carbidopa, entacapone and levodopa combination is being administered, although dosage adjustments may be required.

Interruption of therapy—Sporadic cases of a symptom complex resembling Neuroleptic Malignant Syndrome (NMS) have been associated with dose reductions and withdrawal of levodopa preparations. Patients should be observed carefully if abrupt reduction or discontinuation of carbidopa, entacapone and levodopa combination is required, especially if the patient is receiving neuroleptics. If general anesthesia is required, carbidopa, entacapone and levodopa combination may be continued as long as the patient is permitted to take fluids and medication by mouth. If therapy is interrupted temporarily, the patient should be observed for symptoms resembling NMS, and the usual daily dosage may be administered as soon as the patient is able to take oral medication.

Physical and psychological dependence—Carbidopa, entacapone and levodopa has not been systematically studied, in animal or humans, for its potential for abuse, tolerance or physical dependence. In premarketing clinical experience, carbidopa and levodopa combination did not reveal any tendency for a withdrawal syndrome or any drug-seeking behavior. However, there are rare postmarketing reports of abuse and dependence of medications containing levodopa. In general, these reports consist of patients taking increasing doses of medication in order to achieve a euphoric state.

Discontinuation—Prescribers should exercise caution when discontinuing carbidopa, levodopa and entacapone combination treatment. When considered necessary, withdrawal should proceed slowly. If a decision is made to discontinue treatment with carbidopa, levodopa and entacapone combination, recommendations include monitoring the patient closely and adjusting other dopaminergic treatments as needed. This syndrome should be considered in the differential diagnosis for any patient who develops a high fever or severe rigidity. Tapering entacapone has not been systematically evaluated.

Hormone levels—Of the ingredients in carbidopa, entacapone and levodopa combination, levodopa is known to depress prolactin secretion and increase growth hormone levels.

Generally speaking, carbidopa, entacapone and levodopa should be used as a substitute for patients already stabilized on equivalent doses of carbidopa and levodopa combination and entacapone. However, some patients who have been stabilized on a given dose of carbidopa and levodopa combination may be treated with carbidopa, entacapone and levodopa if a decision has been made to add entacapone.

The optimum daily dosage of carbidopa, entacapone and levodopa must be determined by careful titration in each patient. Carbidopa, entacapone and levodopa tablets are available in three strengths, each in a 1:4 ratio of carbidopa to levodopa and combined with 200 mg of entacapone in a standard release formulation.

Therapy should be individualized and adjusted according to the desired therapeutic response. Studies show that peripheral dopa decarboxylase is saturated by carbidopa at approximately 70 mg to 100 mg a day. Patients receiving less than this amount of carbidopa are more likely to experience nausea and vomiting. Experience with total daily dosages of carbidopa greater than 200 mg is limited. Clinical experience with daily doses above 1600 mg of entacapone is limited. It is recommended that no more than one carbidopa, entacapone and levodopa combination tablet be taken at each dosing administration.

For treatment of adverse effects

The addition of carbidopa to levodopa reduces the peripheral effects (nausea, vomiting) due to decarboxylation of levodopa; however, carbidopa does not decrease the adverse reactions due to the central effects of levodopa. Because carbidopa as well as entacapone permits more levodopa to reach the brain and more dopamine to be formed, certain adverse CNS effects, e.g., dyskinesia (involuntary movements) may occur at lower dosages and sooner with levodopa preparations containing carbidopa and entacapone than with levodopa alone.

Sporadic cases of a symptom complex resembling NMS have been reported in association with dose reductions or withdrawal of therapy with carbidopa and levodopa combination. Therefore, patients should be observed carefully when the dosage of carbidopa, entacapone and levodopa combination is reduced abruptly or discontinued, especially if the patient is receiving neuroleptics. NMS is an uncommon but life-threatening syndrome characterized by fever or hyperthermia. Neurological findings, including muscle rigidity, involuntary movements, altered consciousness, mental status changes; other disturbances, such as autonomic dysfunction, tachycardia, tachypnea, sweating, hyper- or hypotension; laboratory findings, such as creatine phosphokinase elevation, leukocytosis, myoglobinuria, and increased serum myoglobin have been reported. The early diagnosis of this condition is important for the appropriate management of these patients. Considering NMS as a possible diagnosis and ruling out other acute illnesses (e.g., pneumonia, systemic infection, etc.) is essential. This may be especially complex if the clinical presentation includes both serious medical illness and untreated or inadequately treated extrapyramidal signs and symptoms (EPS). Other important considerations in the differential diagnosis include central anticholinergic toxicity, heat stroke, drug fever, and primary central nervous system (CNS) pathology. The management of NMS should include: 1) intensive symptomatic treatment and medical monitoring and 2) treatment of any concomitant serious medical problems for which specific treatments are available. Dopamine agonists, such as bromocriptine, and muscle relaxants, such as dantrolene, are often used in the treatment of NMS, however, their effectiveness has not been demonstrated in controlled studies.

Oral Dosage Forms

CARBIDOPA, ENTACAPONE AND LEVODOPA TABLETS

Usual adult dose

Antidyskinetic—

For patients being converted from carbidopa-levodopa therapy and entacapone therapy—

Patients who are currently treated with entacapone 200 mg with each dose of standard release carbidopa-levodopa: Oral, can be directly switched to the corresponding strength of carbidopa, entacapone and levodopa combination that contains the same amounts of levodopa and carbidopa.

Note: There is no experience in transferring patients currently treated with formulations of carbidopa-levodopa other than immediate release carbidopa-levodopa with a 1:4 ratio (controlled-release formulations, or standard release preparations with a 1:10 ratio of carbidopa-levodopa) and entacapone to carbidopa, entacapone and levodopa combination.

For patients not being currently treated with entacapone tablets from carbidopa-levodopa to carbidopa, entacapone and levodopa combination—

Oral, Initially it is recommended that patients first be titrated individually with a carbidopa-levodopa product (ratio 1:4) and an entacapone product, and then transferred to a corresponding dose of carbidopa, entacapone and levodopa combination once the patient's status has stabilized.

Oral, In patients who take a total daily levodopa dose up to 600 mg, and who do not have dyskinesias, an attempt can be made to transfer to the corresponding daily dose of carbidopa, entacapone and levodopa combination. A reduction of carbidopa-levodopa or entacapone may be necessary however, this may not be possible with the carbidopa, entacapone and levodopa fixed dose combination.

Note: In patients with Parkinson's disease who experience the signs and symptoms of end-of-dose "wearing-off" on their current standard-release carbidopa-levodopa treatment, clinical experience shows that patients with a history of moderate or severe dyskinesias or taking more than 600 mg of levodopa per day are likely to require a reduction in daily levodopa dose when entacapone is added to their treatment. Since entacapone prolongs and enhances the effects of levodopa, therapy should be individualized and adjusted if necessary according to the desired therapeutic response.

Note: Patients with hepatic impairment should be treated with caution. The AUC and C_{max} of entacapone approximately doubled in patients with documented liver disease, compared to controls. However, these studies were conducted with single-dose entacapone without levodopa/dopa decarboxylase inhibitor coadministration, and therefore the effects of liver disease on the kinetics of chronically administered entacapone have not been evaluated.

Usual adult prescribing limits
Eight tablets per day.

Usual pediatric dose
Children up to 18 years of age—Safety and efficacy have not been established.

Usual geriatric dose
See *Usual adult dose*.

Strength(s) usually available
U.S.—

12.5 mg of carbidopa, 50 mg of levodopa and 200 mg of entacapone (Rx) [*Stalevo 50* (corn starch; croscarmellose sodium; glycerol 85%; hypromellose; magnesium stearate; mannitol; polysorbate 80; povidone; sucrose; red iron oxide; titanium dioxide; yellow iron oxide.)].

25 mg of carbidopa, 100 mg of levodopa and 200 mg of entacapone (Rx) [*Stalevo 100* (corn starch; croscarmellose sodium; glycerol 85%; hypromellose; magnesium stearate; mannitol; polysorbate 80; povidone; sucrose; red iron oxide; titanium dioxide; yellow iron oxide.)].

37.5 mg of carbidopa, 150 mg of levodopa and 200 mg of entacapone (Rx) [*Stalevo 150* (corn starch; croscarmellose sodium; glycerol 85%; hypromellose; magnesium stearate; mannitol; polysorbate 80; povidone; sucrose; red iron oxide; titanium dioxide; yellow iron oxide.)].

Canada—

Not commercially available.

Packaging and storage
Store at 25°C (77°F); excursions permitted to 15°C to 30°C (59°F to 86°F).

Auxiliary labeling
- May cause drowsiness. Be careful while driving or operating machinery. Use caution until you become familiar with its effects.
- May change color of skin or body fluids.
- Do not crush or chew.
- Swallow whole.

Developed: 07/13/2004

CARBONIC ANHYDRASE INHIBITORS Systemic

This monograph includes information on the following: 1) Acetazolamide; 2) Dichlorphenamide†; 3) Methazolamide.

INN: Dichlorphenamide—Diclofenamide

VA CLASSIFICATION (Primary/Secondary):

Acetazolamide—CV703/OP113; CN400; MS900; GU900
Dichlorphenamide—CV703/OP113
Methazolamide—CV703/OP113

Commonly used brand name(s): *Acetazolam*[1]; *Ak-Zol*[1]; *Apo-Acetazolamide*[1]; *Daranide*[2]; *Dazamide*[1]; *Diamox*[1]; *Diamox Sequels*[1]; *MZM*[3]; *Neptazane*[3]; *Storzolamide*[1].

Note: For a listing of dosage forms and brand names by country availability, see *Dosage Forms* section(s).

†Not commercially available in Canada.

Category
Antiglaucoma agent (systemic)—Acetazolamide; Dichlorphenamide; Methazolamide.

Anticonvulsant—Acetazolamide (tablets and injection).

Altitude sickness (acute) prophylactic and therapeutic agent—Acetazolamide.

Antiparalytic (familial periodic paralysis)—Acetazolamide.

Diuretic, urinary alkalinizing—Acetazolamide (parenteral).

Antiurolithic (uric acid calculi; cystine calculi)—Acetazolamide Tablets USP

Indications
Note: Bracketed information in the *Indications* section refers to uses that are not included in U.S. product labeling.

Accepted
Glaucoma, open-angle (treatment)
Glaucoma, secondary (treatment)
Glaucoma, angle-closure (treatment) or
[Glaucoma, malignant (treatment)]—Carbonic anhydrase inhibitors are indicated primarily as adjuncts to other agents in the treatment of open-angle (chronic simple) glaucoma and secondary glaucoma, and to lower intraocular pressure prior to surgery for some types of glaucoma.

These medications should not be used for long-term therapy in non-congestive angle-closure (closed-angle) glaucoma; organic closure of the angle may occur while the worsening condition is masked by the lowered intraocular pressure.

[Acetazolamide is used to lower intraocular pressure in the treatment of malignant (ciliary block) glaucoma, which may occur after inflammation, surgery, trauma, or use of miotics.]

Epilepsy, absence seizure pattern (treatment)
Epilepsy, tonic-clonic seizure pattern (treatment)
Epilepsy, mixed seizure pattern (treatment)
Epilepsy, simple partial seizure pattern (treatment) or
Epilepsy, myoclonic seizure pattern (treatment)—Acetazolamide is indicated as an adjunct to other anticonvulsants in the management of absence seizures (petit mal), generalized tonic-clonic seizures (grand mal), mixed seizure patterns, simple partial seizure patterns, and myoclonic seizure patterns. It may be especially useful for intermittent therapy in females who experience increased seizure activity at the time of menstruation.

Altitude sickness (prophylaxis)[1] or
Altitude sickness (treatment)[1]—Oral acetazolamide is indicated to decrease the incidence and/or severity of symptoms (such as headache, nausea, shortness of breath, dizziness, drowsiness, and fatigue) associated with acute altitude sickness in mountain climbers who are attempting rapid ascent and in those who are very susceptible to altitude sickness despite gradual ascent. Gradual ascent is desirable for prevention of acute altitude sickness even when acetazolamide is used. However, prompt descent may still be necessary if severe manifestations of acute altitude sickness, such as pulmonary edema or cerebral edema, occur.

[Paralysis, familial periodic (treatment)][1]—Acetazolamide is used to treat both the hypokalemic and hyperkalemic forms of familial periodic paralysis. It terminates the acute attacks and, with chronic use, prevents their recurrence. It may be the drug of choice in the hypokalemic form of the condition.

[Toxicity, weakly acidic medications (treatment)]—Parenteral acetazolamide is used to produce a forced alkaline diuresis as a method of increasing the elimination of certain weakly acidic medications.

[Renal calculi, uric acid (prophylaxis)][1] or
[Renal calculi, cystine (prophylaxis)][1]—Oral acetazolamide is used to alkalinize the urine as a means of preventing the occurrence or recurrence of uric acid renal stones, especially in patients receiving uricosuric antigout agents, or of cystine renal stones.

Unaccepted

Acetazolamide has also been used to prevent or counteract metabolic alkalosis, including that which may occur following open-heart surgery; however, it is no longer used for these indications.

Acetazolamide has also been used as a diuretic in the treatment of edema due to congestive heart disease and drug-induced edema. However, it has been replaced by newer diuretics for these indications.

[1]Not included in Canadian product labeling.

Pharmacology/Pharmacokinetics

Physicochemical characteristics

Molecular weight—
- Acetazolamide—222.24.
- Acetazolamide sodium—244.22.
- Dichlorphenamide—305.15.
- Methazolamide—236.26.

Mechanism of action/Effect

Nonbacteriostatic sulfonamide derivatives. Inhibition of the enzyme carbonic anhydrase decreases formation of hydrogen and bicarbonate ions from carbon dioxide and water and reduces the availability of these ions for active transport. These agents reduce plasma bicarbonate concentration and increase plasma chloride concentration, producing systemic metabolic acidosis. Although all of these medications may produce diuresis with acute or intermittent administration, loss of diuretic effect occurs with chronic administration. Therefore, dichlorphenamide and methazolamide are not used as diuretics, and acetazolamide is now being used only to produce alkaline diuresis in certain cases of drug overdose. Methazolamide has less diuretic effect and less influence on urinary bicarbonate than do other carbonic anhydrase inhibitors with doses used in glaucoma.

Antiglaucoma agent—
- Lowers intraocular pressure by decreasing the production of aqueous humor by 50 to 60%. The mechanism is not completely understood but probably involves a decrease of the bicarbonate ion concentration in ocular fluids. These agents have no effect on the facility of aqueous outflow. The ocular action is independent of any diuretic action.

Acetazolamide—
- Anticonvulsant:
  - Mechanism of action has not been fully determined. Inhibition of carbonic anhydrase in the central nervous system (CNS) may increase carbon dioxide tension, resulting in a retardation of neuronal conduction. The production of systemic metabolic acidosis may also be involved. This action is independent of any diuretic action.
- Altitude sickness, acute, prophylactic and therapeutic agent:
  - May act by producing metabolic acidosis resulting in increased respiratory drive and arterial oxygen tension and/or by causing diuresis.
  - In clinical trials, pulmonary function, such as minute ventilation, expired vital capacity, and peak flow, was greater in climbers treated with acetazolamide, whether they had acute altitude sickness or were asymptomatic. Acetazolamide-treated climbers also had less difficulty sleeping.
- Antiparalytic (for familial periodic paralysis):
  - May stabilize muscle membranes against abnormal fluxes of potassium ions. Alternatively, may produce metabolic acidosis resulting in prevention of the intracellular shift of potassium.
- Diuretic, urinary alkalinizing:
  - Induces alkaline diuresis by lowering hydrogen ion concentration in the renal tubule and increasing excretion of bicarbonate, sodium, potassium, and water. This increases the solubility in urine of weakly acidic drugs and promotes their excretion.
- Antiurolithic:
  - Alkalinization of the urine increases the solubility in urine of uric acid and cystine, thereby reducing the formation of uric acid- or cystine-containing renal stones.

Absorption

Well absorbed; methazolamide absorbed more slowly than acetazolamide or dichlorphenamide.

Protein binding

Acetazolamide—Very high (90%).
Methazolamide—Moderate.

Half-life

Acetazolamide (tablets)—10 to 15 hours.
Methazolamide—14 hours.

Time to peak concentration

Acetazolamide tablets—2 to 4 hours after a 500-mg dose.
Acetazolamide extended-release capsules—8 to 12 hours after a 500-mg dose.

Peak serum concentration

Acetazolamide tablets—12 to 27 mcg per mL with a 500-mg dose.

Acetazolamide extended-release capsules—6 mcg per mL with a 500-mg dose.

Elimination

Acetazolamide—Renal; as unchanged drug; 90 to 100% of a dose is excreted within 24 hours after administration of oral tablets or intravenous injection; 47% of a dose is excreted within 24 hours after administration of extended-release capsules.

Dichlorphenamide—Unknown.

Methazolamide—Renal; 15 to 30% excreted unchanged. Remainder unknown.

Effects on intraocular pressure

Drug	Onset of Action	Peak Effect	Duration of Action (hr)
Acetazolamide			
Extended-release capsules	2 hr	8–12 hr	18–24
Tablets	1–1.5 hr	2–4 hr	8–12
Intravenous	2 min	15 min	4–5
Dichlorphenamide			
Tablets	0.5–1 hr	2–4 hr	6–12
Methazolamide			
Tablets	2–4 hr	6–8 hr	10–18

Precautions to Consider

Cross-sensitivity and/or related problems

Patients sensitive to antibacterial sulfonamides, thiazide diuretics, or other sulfonamide-derivative diuretics may be sensitive to carbonic anhydrase inhibitors also.

Carcinogenicity

Long-term studies in animals have not been conducted using carbonic anhydrase inhibitors.

Mutagenicity

Acetazolamide—In a bacterial mutagenicity assay, acetazolamide was not mutagenic when evaluated with and without metabolic activation.

Methazolamide—In the Ames bacterial test, methazolamide was not mutagenic.

Pregnancy/Reproduction

Fertility—*Acetazolamide:* Acetazolamide had no effect on fertility of male and female rats administered oral daily doses of up to 4 times the recommended human dose of 1000 mg in a 50 kg individual.

Dichlorphenamide and *methazolamide:* Long-term studies in animals have not been conducted.

Pregnancy—Adequate and well-controlled studies have not been done using carbonic anhydrase inhibitors in humans.

Acetazolamide—
- Acetazolamide has been shown to cause limb defects in mice, rats, hamsters, and rabbits.
- FDA Pregnancy Category C.

Dichlorphenamide and methazolamide—
- Dichlorphenamide and methazolamide, when given in large doses, have been shown to cause skeletal anomalies in rats.
- FDA Pregnancy Category C.

Breast-feeding

Because of the potential for serious adverse reactions, a decision should be made whether to discontinue nursing during therapy with carbonic anhydrase inhibitors.

Acetazolamide—Acetazolamide may be distributed into breast milk.

Dichlorphenamide and *methazolamide*—It is not known whether dichlorphenamide or methazolamide is distributed into breast milk.

Pediatrics

Appropriate studies on the relationship of age to the effects of carbonic anhydrase inhibitors have not been performed in the pediatric population. However, no pediatrics-specific problems have been documented to date.

Geriatrics

No information is available on the relationship of age to the effects of carbonic anhydrase inhibitors in geriatric patients. However, elderly patients are more likely to have age-related renal function impairment, which may require caution in patients receiving these medications.

Dental

Acetazolamide may cause facial paresthesia, such as numbness, tingling, or burning feeling of the mouth, tongue, or lips. Other carbonic anhydrase inhibitors may cause similar side effects.

Drug interactions and/or related problems

The following drug interactions and/or related problems have been selected on the basis of their potential clinical significance (possible mechanism in parentheses where appropriate)—not necessarily inclusive (» = major clinical significance):

Note: Combinations containing any of the following medications, depending on the amount present, may also interact with this medication.

Corticosteroids, glucocorticoid, especially with significant mineralocorticoid activity or
Corticosteroids, mineralocorticoid or
Amphotericin B, parenteral or
Corticotropin, especially prolonged therapeutic use
(concurrent use with carbonic anhydrase inhibitors may result in severe hypokalemia and should be undertaken with caution; serum potassium concentrations and cardiac function should be monitored during concurrent use)

(concurrent use of corticosteroids or corticotropin with acetazolamide sodium may increase the risk of hypernatremia and/or edema because these medications cause sodium and fluid retention; the risk with corticosteroids or corticotropin may depend on the patient's sodium requirement as determined by the condition being treated)

(the possibility should be considered that concurrent chronic use of corticosteroids or corticotropin with carbonic anhydrase inhibitors may increase the risk of hypocalcemia and osteoporosis because these medications increase calcium excretion)

» Amphetamines or
Anticholinergics, especially atropine and related compounds or
» Mecamylamine or
» Quinidine
(therapeutic and/or side effects may be enhanced or prolonged when these medications are used concurrently with carbonic anhydrase inhibitors, especially acetazolamide, as a result of decreased excretion caused by alkalinization of urine; concurrent use with mecamylamine is not recommended; dosage adjustments of the other medications may be needed when carbonic anhydrase inhibitor therapy is initiated or discontinued or if the dosage is changed)

Antidiabetic agents, oral or
Insulin
(hypoglycemic response may be decreased during concurrent use because carbonic anhydrase inhibitors may cause hyperglycemia and glycosuria in diabetic patients; dosage adjustments may be required)

Barbiturates, especially phenobarbital or
Carbamazepine or
Phenytoin or other hydantoin anticonvulsants or
Primidone
(osteopenia induced by these agents may be enhanced; it is recommended that patients receiving concurrent therapy be monitored for early signs of osteopenia and that the carbonic anhydrase inhibitor be discontinued and appropriate treatment initiated if necessary)

Ciprofloxacin
(urinary alkalizers, such as carbonic anhydrase inhibitors, may reduce the solubility of ciprofloxacin in the urine; patients should be observed for signs of crystalluria and nephrotoxicity)

Digitalis glycosides
(concurrent use with carbonic anhydrase inhibitors may enhance the possibility of digitalis toxicity associated with hypokalemia)

Diuretics, other
(diuretic effects may be enhanced during concurrent therapy; however, the hypokalemic and hyperuricemic effects of many diuretics may also be enhanced during concurrent therapy)

Ephedrine
(urine alkalinization induced by carbonic anhydrase inhibitors may increase the half-life of ephedrine and prolong its duration of action, especially if the urine remains alkaline for several days or longer; dosage adjustment of ephedrine may be necessary)

Mannitol or
Urea
(concurrent use with carbonic anhydrase inhibitors may lead to increased reduction of intraocular pressure as well as increased diuresis)

» Methenamine
(efficacy may be reduced because alkaline urine produced by carbonic anhydrase inhibitors inhibits methenamine conversion to formaldehyde, which is the active bacteriostatic derivative of methenamine; concurrent use is not recommended)

Mexiletine
(marked alkalinization of urine by carbonic anhydrase inhibitors may retard renal excretion of mexiletine)

Neuromuscular blocking agents, nondepolarizing
(hypokalemia induced by carbonic anhydrase inhibitors may enhance the blockade of nondepolarizing neuromuscular blocking agents, possibly leading to increased or prolonged respiratory depression or paralysis [apnea]; serum potassium concentration determinations may be necessary prior to administration of a nondepolarizing neuromuscular blocking agent)

Salicylates
(the risk of salicylate intoxication in patients receiving large doses of salicylates may be increased during concurrent therapy because metabolic acidosis induced by carbonic anhydrase inhibitors may increase penetration of salicylate into the brain. Anorexia, tachypnea, lethargy, coma, and death have been reported with concurrent use of high-dose aspirin and carbonic anhydrase inhibitors. In addition, the increased risk of severe metabolic acidosis and salicylate toxicity should be considered if acetazolamide is used to produce forced alkaline diuresis in the treatment of salicylate overdose. With average doses of salicylates, alkalinization of the urine results in increased salicylate excretion and decreased salicylate plasma concentrations)

Laboratory value alterations

The following have been selected on the basis of their potential clinical significance (possible effect in parentheses where appropriate)—not necessarily inclusive (» = major clinical significance).

With diagnostic test results

Urine 17-hydroxysteroid (17-OHCS) determinations
(may produce false-positive results by interfering with absorbance in the modified Glenn-Nelson technique)

Urine protein determinations
(may produce false-positive results with bromophenol blue test reagent and with sulfosalicylic acid, heat and acetic acid, and nitric acid ring test methods because of alkalinization of urine)

With physiology/laboratory test values

Ammonia concentrations, blood and
Bilirubin concentrations, serum and
Urobilinogen concentrations, urine
(may be increased)

Bicarbonate concentrations, plasma
(usually are decreased)

Calcium concentrations, urine
(may be increased or unchanged)

Chloride concentrations, plasma
(may be increased, especially with acetazolamide)

Citrate concentrations, urine
(may be decreased; in combination with increased or unchanged urine calcium concentrations may result in renal calculi and ureteral colic)

Glucose concentrations, blood and
Glucose concentrations, urine
(may be increased, especially in diabetic or prediabetic patients receiving acetazolamide; patients not predisposed to diabetes are not significantly affected)

Iodine uptake by the thyroid gland
(may be decreased in hyperthyroid patients or those with normal thyroid function but not in hypothyroid patients)

Potassium concentrations, serum
(may be decreased, especially when therapy is initiated or with intermittent dosage; with continuous therapy, serum potassium concentrations usually return to normal)

Uric acid concentrations, serum
(may be increased; rarely, gout may be exacerbated)

Medical considerations/Contraindications

The medical considerations/contraindications included have been selected on the basis of their potential clinical significance (reasons

given in parentheses where appropriate)—not necessarily inclusive (» = major clinical significance).

Risk-benefit should be considered when the following medical problems exist:

» Adrenal gland failure or adrenocortical insufficiency (Addison's disease)
(patients more susceptible to electrolyte imbalances)

Diabetes mellitus
(may increase blood and urine sugar concentrations)

Gout, except when used to prevent uric acid calculi in patients receiving uricosuric antigout agents or

» Hyperchloremic acidosis or

» Hypokalemia, hyponatremia, or other electrolyte imbalance or
Respiratory acidosis
(may be exacerbated)

» Hepatic disease, including cirrhosis, or impairment
(patients more susceptible to electrolyte imbalances; increased risk of hepatic coma and hepatotoxicity)

Impaired alveolar ventilation due to pulmonary disease, edema, infection, or obstruction
(respiratory acidosis may be induced or increased)

» Renal failure, disease, or impairment
(excessively high plasma concentrations may result and the acidosis of renal failure may be aggravated)

» Renal calculi, calcium-containing, or history of
(may be exacerbated or induced during therapy)

Sensitivity to carbonic anhydrase inhibitors

Patient monitoring

The following may be especially important in patient monitoring (other tests may be warranted in some patients, depending on condition; » = major clinical significance):

Complete blood cell (CBC) count
Platelet count
(baseline CBC and platelet counts recommended prior to initiating therapy and at regular intervals during therapy. If significant changes occur, medication should be promptly discontinued and appropriate therapy instituted)

» Electrolyte concentrations, serum
(recommended prior to initiation of therapy and at periodic intervals during therapy, especially in patients for whom hypokalemia or other electrolyte imbalances would be detrimental, such as those with hepatic cirrhosis or those receiving potassium-wasting medications or digitalis)

Urologic examinations
(may be necessary to detect possible renal problems, especially crystalluria or renal calculi)

Side/Adverse Effects

Note: Serious side/adverse effects occur infrequently; many of the serious adverse effects are those that are common to all sulfonamide derivatives, such as Stevens-Johnson syndrome, toxic epidermal necrolysis, fulminant hepatic necrosis, agranulocytosis, aplastic anemia, and other blood dyscrasias. Rarely, these serious adverse effects have caused fatalities. Many side effects are dose-related and may respond to a reduction of dosage.

Hypokalemia may occur if diuresis is brisk and may be especially likely to occur if hepatic cirrhosis is present, if potassium intake is inadequate, or if other potassium-wasting drugs are used concurrently. Potassium supplementation may be necessary in some patients.

Severe metabolic acidosis or acidotic coma may occur rarely during long-term carbonic anhydrase inhibitor therapy and may be corrected by administration of bicarbonate.

The following side/adverse effects have been selected on the basis of their potential clinical significance (possible signs and symptoms in parentheses where appropriate)—not necessarily inclusive:*

Legend:
I = Acetazolamide
II = Dichlorphenamide
III = Methazolamide

	I	II	III
Medical attention needed			
Acidosis (shortness of breath, troubled breathing)#	R	R	R
Blood dyscrasias (fever and sore throat, unusual bruising or bleeding)†	R	R	R
Bloody or black, tarry stools	R	R	R
Cholestatic jaundice (darkening of urine, pale stools, yellow eyes or skin)	R	U	U
Clumsiness or unsteadiness	R	R	R
Confusion	R	R	R
Convulsions	R	R	R
Crystalluria, renal calculus, or sulfonamide-like nephrotoxicity (blood in urine, difficult urination, pain in lower back, pain or burning while urinating, sudden decrease in amount of urine)†	L	L	L
Hypersensitivity (fever, hives, itching, skin rash or sores)	R	R	R
Hypokalemia (dryness of mouth, increased thirst, irregular heartbeats, mood or mental changes, muscle cramps or pain, nausea or vomiting, unusual tiredness or weakness, weak pulse)‡	R	R	R
Mental depression	L	L	L
Nearsightedness§	R	R	R
Ringing or buzzing in ears	R	R	R
Severe muscle weakness or trembling	R	R	R
Unusual tiredness or weakness**	M	M	M
Medical attention needed only if continuing or bothersome			
Constipation	U	R	U
Diarrhea	M	M	M
Dizziness or lightheadedness	U	L	L
Drowsiness	L	L	L
Feeling of choking or lump in throat	U	R	U
General feeling of discomfort or illness	M	M	M
Headache	R	R	R
Increase in frequency of urination or amount of urine	M	M	R
Increased sensitivity of eyes to sunlight	R	U	R
Loss of appetite	M	M	M
Loss of taste and smell	R	R	R
Metallic taste in mouth	M	M	M
Nausea or vomiting	M	M	M
Nervousness or irritability	U	R	U
Numbness, tingling, or burning in hands, fingers, feet, toes, mouth, tongue, lips, or anus†	M	M	M
Weight loss	M	M	M

*Acetazolamide is the most widely used carbonic anhydrase inhibitor; most of the data concerning side effects have been reported for that medication. The comparatively infrequent reports of side effects with other agents of this group may reflect their less frequent usage rather than actual reduced incidence. The pharmacologic similarity of these medications suggests that side effects occurring with one may potentially occur with the others. However, many side effects may not occur with the same severity or frequency with all carbonic anhydrase inhibitors, and patients unable to tolerate one of these medications may be able to tolerate another. Frequency of side effects (generalized): M = more frequent; L = less frequent; R = rare; U = unknown.

†May be more likely to occur with acetazolamide and least likely to occur with methazolamide.

‡May be more likely to occur with dichlorphenamide.

§Transient myopia may occur when therapy is initiated and usually responds to a reduction in dosage or withdrawal of therapy. Transient myopia may not recur if therapy is restarted.

#May be less likely to occur with dichlorphenamide.

**Usually part of a general feeling of malaise induced by these agents but should be evaluated because rarely may indicate acidosis, blood dyscrasias, or hypokalemia.

Patient Consultation

As an aid to patient consultation, refer to *Advice for the Patient, Carbonic Anhydrase Inhibitors (Systemic).*

In providing consultation, consider emphasizing the following selected information (» = major clinical significance):

Before using this medication

» Conditions affecting use, especially:

Sensitivity to carbonic anhydrase inhibitors, antibacterial sulfonamides, thiazide diuretics, or other sulfonamide-derivative diuretics

Pregnancy—Studies in animals have shown teratogenic (skeletal anomalies) and embryocidal effects

Breast-feeding—Use is not recommended, because these medicines may be distributed into breast milk and have the potential for serious adverse reactions

Other medications, especially amphetamines, mecamylamine, methenamine, or quinidine

Other medical problems, especially adrenal gland failure or adrenocortical insufficiency; hepatic disease, including cirrhosis or impairment; hyperchloremic acidosis; hypokalemia, hyponatremia, or other electrolyte imbalance; renal calculi, calcium-containing, or history of; or renal failure, disease, or impairment

Proper use of this medication

» Importance of not taking more medication than the amount prescribed

Taking medication with meals to lessen gastrointestinal upset

How to minimize inconvenience of unwanted diuresis

» Proper dosing

Missed dose: Taking as soon as possible; not taking if almost time for next dose; not doubling doses

» Proper storage

Precautions while using this medication

» Caution if drowsiness, dizziness, lightheadedness, or tiredness occurs

Regular visits to physician to check progress during therapy

» Possibility of hypokalemia

Diabetics: May increase blood and urine glucose concentrations

Importance of adequate fluid intake during therapy to help prevent kidney stones

Checking with physician before discontinuing acetazolamide (when used as anticonvulsant); gradual dosage reduction may be desirable

Side/adverse effects

Signs of potential side effects, especially acidosis; blood dyscrasias; bloody or black, tarry stools; cholestatic jaundice; clumsiness or unsteadiness; confusion; convulsions; crystalluria, renal calculus, sulfonamide-like nephrotoxicity; hypersensitivity; hypokalemia; mental depression; nearsightedness; ringing or buzzing in ears; severe muscle weakness or trembling; or unusual tiredness or weakness

General Dosing Information

Carbonic anhydrase inhibitors are usually used concurrently with other antiglaucoma agents including miotics, mydriatics, and osmotic agents.

Dosage should be adjusted according to the requirements and response of the individual patient as indicated by measurement of ocular tension and symptomatology.

Carbonic anhydrase inhibitors may be given with meals to minimize gastrointestinal upset.

Maintenance of a high fluid intake may be advisable, especially in patients with hypercalciuria or gout, to reduce the risk of renal calculi.

Patients unable to tolerate one carbonic anhydrase inhibitor because of side effects may be able to tolerate another.

If a satisfactory lowering of intraocular pressure is not achieved or maintained with one carbonic anhydrase inhibitor, one of the other agents in this group may provide a beneficial effect.

It is recommended that various brands of acetazolamide marketed by different manufacturers not be used interchangeably unless data indicating therapeutic equivalence are available; bioequivalence problems have been reported.

It is recommended that carbonic anhydrase inhibitor therapy be discontinued if hematopoietic reactions, fever, skin rash, or renal problems occur.

If potassium supplementation is needed in a patient receiving a carbonic anhydrase inhibitor, the fact that plasma chloride concentration may be elevated should be kept in mind and a potassium preparation chosen that does not contain chloride.

ACETAZOLAMIDE

Summary of Differences

Indications: Also indicated as an anticonvulsant, to prevent or reduce severity of symptoms of acute altitude sickness, to treat toxicity caused by weakly acidic medications, to treat familial periodic paralysis, and to prevent uric acid or cystine renal calculi.

Side effects: See *Side/Adverse Effects.*

Additional Dosing Information

See also *General Dosing Information.*

When acetazolamide is added to existing anticonvulsant therapy, an initial daily dose of 4 to 5 mg per kg of body weight per day in addition to existing medication is recommended. Dosage may be increased as necessary. Changes from other anticonvulsants to acetazolamide or withdrawal of acetazolamide therapy should be gradual to prevent increased seizure activity and possible status epilepticus.

Tolerance to the anticonvulsant effect of acetazolamide develops rapidly, over weeks or months in some patients.

For oral dosage forms only:

- Both the acetazolamide tablets and extended-release capsules are indicated for use in glaucoma and for prophylaxis and treatment of acute altitude sickness. Although the extended release capsules may be better tolerated than the acetazolamide tablets or the tablets of the other carbonic anhydrase inhibitors, they may be less effective in some patients.

For parenteral dosage forms only:

- Direct intravenous administration is preferred; intramuscular injection is not recommended, because it is painful due to the alkaline pH of the solution.
- Parenteral administration is usually used when the patient cannot take oral medication or when a rapid initial intraocular pressure-lowering action is necessary. Therapy is usually continued with oral acetazolamide, depending on the patient's condition and response.

Oral Dosage Forms

Note: Bracketed uses in the *Dosage Forms* section refer to categories of use and/or indications that are not included in U.S. product labeling.

ACETAZOLAMIDE EXTENDED-RELEASE CAPSULES

Usual adult and adolescent dose

Antiglaucoma agent—

Oral, 500 mg two times a day, in the morning and evening.

Note: In the treatment of glaucoma, dosage greater than 1 gram per day usually does not produce an increased effect.

Altitude sickness, acute, prophylactic and therapeutic agent[1]—

Oral, 500 mg one or two times a day.

Note: During rapid ascent, such as in rescue or military operations, 1,000 mg a day is recommended. Therapy should preferably be initiated 24 to 48 hours before ascent and, while at high altitude, continued for 48 hours or longer as necessary to control symptoms.

The use of acetazolamide for rapid ascent does not obviate the need for prompt descent if severe forms of high altitude sickness, such as high altitude pulmonary edema (HAPE) or high altitude cerebral edema, occur.

Usual pediatric dose

Safety and efficacy have not been established.

Strength(s) usually available

U.S.—

500 mg (Rx) [*Diamox Sequels*].

Canada—

500 mg (Rx) [*Diamox Sequels*].

Packaging and storage

Store between 15 and 30 °C (59 and 86 °F), in a well-closed container, unless otherwise specified by manufacturer.

Auxiliary labeling

- May cause drowsiness.

ACETAZOLAMIDE TABLETS USP

Usual adult and adolescent dose

Antiglaucoma agent—

Open-angle glaucoma—

Initial—Oral, 250 mg one to four times a day.

Maintenance—To be titrated according to patient response; lower doses may be sufficient.

Secondary glaucoma and preoperative lowering of intraocular pressure—

Oral, 250 mg every four hours. Some patients may respond to 250 mg two times a day. In some acute cases, an initial dose of 500 mg followed by 125 or 250 mg every four hours may be preferable.

Malignant (ciliary block) glaucoma—

Oral, 250 mg four times a day to reduce intraocular pressure.

Anticonvulsant—

Oral, 4 to 30 mg (usually 10 mg initially) per kg of body weight a day in up to 4 divided doses; usually 375 mg to 1 gram a day.

Altitude sickness, acute, prophylactic and therapeutic agent[1]—

Oral, 250 mg two to four times a day.

Note: During rapid ascent, such as in rescue or military operations, 1,000 mg a day is recommended. Therapy should preferably be initiated 24 to 48 hours before ascent and, while at high altitude, continued for 48 hours or longer as necessary to control symptoms.

The use of acetazolamide for rapid ascent does not obviate the need for prompt descent if severe forms of high altitude sickness, such as high altitude pulmonary edema (HAPE) or high altitude cerebral edema, occur.

[Antiparalytic][1]—

Oral, 250 mg to 1.5 grams a day in divided doses.

[Antiurolithic][1]—

Oral, 250 mg daily at bedtime.

Note: For use as an anticonvulsant or in open-angle glaucoma, dosage greater than 1 gram per day usually does not produce an increased effect.

Usual pediatric dose

Glaucoma—

Oral, 8 to 30 mg per kg of body weight, usually 10 to 15 mg per kg, or 300 to 900 mg per square meter of body surface area a day in divided doses.

Anticonvulsant—

See *Usual adult and adolescent dose.*

Strength(s) usually available

U.S.—

125 mg (Rx) [*Diamox* (scored); GENERIC].

250 mg (Rx) [*Ak-Zol; Dazamide; Diamox* (scored); *Storzolamide;* GENERIC].

Canada—

250 mg (Rx) [*Acetazolam; Apo-Acetazolamide; Diamox*].

Packaging and storage

Store between 15 and 30 °C (59 and 86 °F), in a well-closed container, unless otherwise specified by manufacturer.

Preparation of dosage form

For pediatric patients or adults unable to swallow tablets—An acetazolamide oral suspension may be prepared by crushing acetazolamide tablets and suspending the resultant powder in a highly flavored syrup (cherry, raspberry, chocolate, etc.). Up to 500 mg may be suspended in 5 mL of syrup, but a suspension containing 250 mg per 5 mL is more palatable. Such a suspension is stable for 1 week. Refrigeration may improve the taste but does not increase or lengthen stability. Elixirs or other vehicles containing alcohol or glycerin will not provide a palatable suspension.

Auxiliary labeling

- May cause drowsiness.

Parenteral Dosage Forms

Note: Bracketed uses in the *Dosage Forms* section refer to categories of use and/or indications that are not included in U.S. product labeling.

ACETAZOLAMIDE SODIUM STERILE USP

Usual adult and adolescent dose

Antiglaucoma agent—

For rapid initial lowering of intraocular pressure: Intravenous, the equivalent of acetazolamide—500 mg.

Note: Parenteral administration may be repeated in two to four hours in some acute cases, but therapy is usually continued with oral acetazolamide, depending on the patient's response.

[Diuretic (urinary alkalinizing)]—

Intravenous, 5 mg per kg of body weight or as required to achieve and maintain a forced alkaline diuresis.

Note: For other uses or when the patient is unable to take oral medication, acetazolamide may be given parenterally in dosages equivalent to those recommended for the oral tablets. (See *Acetazolamide Tablets USP.*)

Usual pediatric dose

Antiglaucoma agent—

Acute glaucoma: Intravenous, the equivalent of acetazolamide—5 to 10 mg per kg of body weight every six hours.

[Diuretic (urinary alkalinizing)]—

Intravenous, the equivalent of acetazolamide: 5 mg per kg of body weight or 150 mg per square meter of body surface area once a day in the morning for one or two days alternated with a drug-free day.

Strength(s) usually available

U.S.—

500 mg (Rx) [*Diamox;* GENERIC].

Canada—

500 mg (Rx) [*Diamox*].

Packaging and storage

Prior to reconstitution, store below 40 °C (104 °F), preferably between 15 and 30 °C (59 and 86 °F), unless otherwise specified by manufacturer.

Preparation of dosage form

Sterile Acetazolamide Sodium USP is reconstituted for parenteral use by adding at least 5 mL of Sterile Water for Injection USP to the vial and shaking to dissolve. A solution prepared using 5 mL of diluent contains the equivalent of 100 mg of acetazolamide per mL.

Stability

After reconstitution, solutions retain their potency for 1 week if refrigerated. However, because they contain no preservative, use within 24 hours is strongly recommended.

[1]Not included in Canadian product labeling.

DICHLORPHENAMIDE

Summary of Differences

Side effects: See *Side/Adverse Effects.*

Oral Dosage Forms

DICHLORPHENAMIDE TABLETS USP

Usual adult and adolescent dose

Antiglaucoma agent—

Initial: 100 to 200 mg for the first dose followed by 100 mg every twelve hours until the desired response is obtained.

Maintenance: 25 to 50 mg one to three times a day.

Usual pediatric dose

Safety and efficacy have not been established.

Strength(s) usually available

U.S.—

50 mg (Rx) [*Daranide* (scored)].

Canada—

Not commercially available.

Packaging and storage

Store below 40 °C (104 °F), preferably between 15 and 30 °C (59 and 86 °F), in a well-closed container, unless otherwise specified by manufacturer.

Auxiliary labeling

- May cause drowsiness.

METHAZOLAMIDE

Summary of Differences

Side effects: See *Side/Adverse Effects.*

Oral Dosage Forms

METHAZOLAMIDE TABLETS USP

Usual adult and adolescent dose

Antiglaucoma agent—

Oral, 50 to 100 mg two or three times a day.

Usual pediatric dose

Safety and efficacy have not been established.

Strength(s) usually available

U.S.—

25 mg (Rx) [*MZM; Neptazane;* GENERIC].

50 mg (Rx) [*MZM; Neptazane* (scored); GENERIC].

Canada—

50 mg (Rx) [*Neptazane*].

Packaging and storage

Store between 15 and 30 °C (59 and 86 °F), in a well-closed container, unless otherwise specified by manufacturer.

Auxiliary labeling

• May cause drowsiness.

Revised: 01/24/1995

CARBOPLATIN Systemic

VA CLASSIFICATION (Primary): AN900

Commonly used brand name(s): *Paraplatin; Paraplatin-AQ.*

Note: For a listing of dosage forms and brand names by country availability, see *Dosage Forms* section(s).

Category

Antineoplastic.

Indications

Note: Bracketed information in the *Indications* section refers to uses that are not included in U.S. product labeling.

Accepted

Carcinoma, ovarian, epithelial (treatment)—Carboplatin is indicated for palliative treatment of epithelial ovarian carcinoma refractory to standard chemotherapy that did or did not include cisplatin. It is also indicated for initial treatment of advanced ovarian carcinoma in established combination with other approved chemotherapeutic agents.

Carboplatin is indicated, in combination with paclitaxel, for the [treatment of fallopian tube and peritoneal carcinomas, of ovarian origin][1].

[Carcinoma, breast (treatment)][1]—Carboplatin is indicated, in combination with paclitaxel, for the first-line treatment of locally advanced and/or metastatic breast carcinoma. Trastuzumab may be added to this combination, in HER2/neu positive patients. Prior adjuvant chemotherapy is allowed (not chemotherapy for advanced or metastatic disease). Use in combination with a high-dose chemotherapy regimen (e.g., STAMP-V) is now rarely used.

[Carcinoma, bladder (treatment)][1]—Carboplatin is indicated for use in combination with other chemotherapeutic agents at some point in the treatment of advanced transitional-cell bladder (urothelial) carcinoma. Carboplatin can be a less toxic alternative for patients for whom cisplatin is not an option.

[Carcinoma, endometrial (treatment)][1]—Carboplatin is indicated as reasonable medical therapy in the treatment of endometrial carcinoma. (Evidence rating: IIID)

[Carcinoma, esophageal (treatment)][1]—Carboplatin is indicated for use in combination with paclitaxel at some point in the treatment of esophageal carcinoma and adenocarcinoma. Carboplatin is a reasonable substitution for cisplatin., Use is also appropriate in the treatment of gastroesophageal (GE) junction adenocarcinomas.

[Carcinoma, lung, small cell (treatment)][1]

[Carcinoma, lung, non-small cell (treatment)][1]

[Carcinoma, head and neck (treatment)][1]

[Carcinoma, testicular (treatment)][1] or

[Seminoma (treatment)][1]—Carboplatin is indicated for treatment of small cell and non-small cell lung carcinoma, head and neck tumors, nonseminomatous testicular carcinoma, and seminoma.

[Carcinoma, unknown primary site (treatment)][1]—Carboplatin is indicated for the first-line treatment of carcinoma of unknown primary site (CUPS), as part of a combination regimen with paclitaxel and etoposide. There was not a clear consensus by the USP medical experts. Some of the experts are hesitant about the use of this regimen and suggest that individual case factors (e.g. metastatic sites, disease factors, patient characteristics, etc.) be considered when choosing an appropriate treatment.

[Retinoblastoma (treatment)][1]—Carboplatin is indicated as reasonable medical therapy in the treatment of retinoblastoma. (Evidence rating: IIID)

[Tumors, brain, primary (treatment)][1]—Carboplatin is indicated for treatment of primary brain tumors.

[Lymphomas, Hodgkin's (treatment)][1]

[Lymphomas, non-Hodgkin's (treatment)][1]—Carboplatin is indicated, in combination with ifosfamide and etoposide (ICE regimen), for the treatment of Hodgkin's and non-Hodgkin's lymphomas.

[Malignant melanoma (treatment)][1]—Carboplatin is indicated for treatment of malignant melanoma.

Acceptance not established

Use of carboplatin for the treatment of cervical carcinoma has not been established.

Use of carboplatin for the treatment of merkle cell carcinoma has not been established. Even though this is a rare tumor, more data is needed showing single-agent activity or contribution when added to combination therapy.

Use of carboplatin for the treatment of gastric carcinomas has not been established, due to insufficient data supporting efficacy as a single agent and an undefined role in combination chemotherapy. Studies with larger sample sizes are needed.

Unaccepted

Carboplatin is not indicated as single-agent therapy for the 2nd- or 3rd-line treatment of breast carcinoma.

Note: The USP medical experts chose to *not include* carboplatin as single-agent therapy for the 1st-line treatment of breast carcinoma.

The USP medical experts chose to *not include* carboplatin for the treatment of hormone-refractory prostate cancer (HRPC). There is not enough medical literature or clinical experience to consider this indication.

The USP medical experts chose to *not include* carboplatin for the treatment of acute leukemias, as a single agent or in combination therapy. There is insufficient information offering evidence of increased activity or reduced toxicity over standard agents.

[1]Not included in Canadian product labeling.

Pharmacology/Pharmacokinetics

Physicochemical characteristics

Molecular weight—371.26.

Mechanism of action/Effect

Carboplatin resembles an alkylating agent. Although the exact mechanism of action is unknown, action is thought to be similar to that of the bifunctional alkylating agents, that is, possible cross-linking and interference with the function of DNA. It is cell cycle-phase nonspecific.

Protein binding

Very low; however, platinum from carboplatin is irreversibly bound to plasma proteins and is slowly eliminated with a minimum half-life of 5 days.

Biotransformation

By hydrolysis in solution (aquation), at a rate slower than occurs with cisplatin, to the active species that reacts with DNA.

Half-life

Alpha phase—1.1 to 2 hours.

Beta phase—2.6 to 5.9 hours.

Elimination

Renal (71% within 24 hours at creatinine clearances of 60 mL per minute and greater).

Precautions to Consider

Cross-sensitivity and/or related problems

Patients sensitive to cisplatin or other platinum-containing compounds may be sensitive to carboplatin also.

Carcinogenicity

Secondary malignancies are potential delayed effects of many antineoplastic agents, although it is not clear whether the effect is related to their mutagenic or immunosuppressive action. The effect of dose and duration of therapy is also unknown, although risk seems to increase with long-term use. Although information is limited, available data seem to indicate that the carcinogenic risk is greatest with the alkylating agents.

Mutagenicity

Both *in vivo* and *in vitro* studies have shown carboplatin to be mutagenic.

Pregnancy/Reproduction

Fertility—Gonadal suppression, resulting in amenorrhea or azoospermia, may occur in patients taking antineoplastic therapy, especially with the alkylating agents. In general, these effects appear to be related to dose and length of therapy and may be irreversible. Prediction of the degree of testicular or ovarian function impairment is complicated by the common use of combinations of several antineoplastics, which makes it difficult to assess the effects of individual agents.

Pregnancy—Carboplatin is embryotoxic and teratogenic in rats.

First trimester: It is usually recommended that use of antineoplastics, especially combination chemotherapy, be avoided whenever possible, especially during the first trimester. Although information is limited because of the relatively few instances of antineoplastic administration during pregnancy, the mutagenic, teratogenic, and carcinogenic potential of these medications must be considered.

Other hazards to the fetus include adverse reactions seen in adults.

In general, use of a contraceptive is recommended during cytotoxic drug therapy.

FDA Pregnancy Category D.

Breast-feeding

Although very little information is available regarding distribution of antineoplastic agents into breast milk, breast-feeding is not recommended while carboplatin is being administered because of the risks to the infant (adverse effects, mutagenicity, carcinogenicity). It is not known whether carboplatin is distributed into breast milk.

Pediatrics

No information is available on the relationship of age to the effects of carboplatin in pediatric patients.

Geriatrics

Incidence of peripheral neurotoxicity is increased and myelotoxicity may be more severe in patients older than 65 years of age. In addition, elderly patients are more likely to have age-related renal function impairment, which may require dosage reduction and careful monitoring of blood counts in patients receiving carboplatin.

Dental

The bone marrow depressant effects of carboplatin may result in an increased incidence of microbial infection, delayed healing, and gingival bleeding. Dental work, whenever possible, should be completed prior to initiation of therapy or deferred until blood counts have returned to normal. Patients should be instructed in proper oral hygiene during treatment, including caution in use of regular toothbrushes, dental floss, and toothpicks.

Carboplatin rarely may also cause mucositis or stomatitis associated with considerable discomfort.

Drug interactions and/or related problems

The following drug interactions and/or related problems have been selected on the basis of their potential clinical significance (possible mechanism in parentheses where appropriate)—not necessarily inclusive (» = major clinical significance):

Note: Combinations containing any of the following medications, depending on the amount present, may also interact with this medication.

Blood dyscrasia-causing medications (see *Appendix II*)
(leukopenic and/or thrombocytopenic effects of carboplatin may be increased with concurrent or recent therapy if these medications cause the same effects; dosage adjustment of carboplatin, if necessary, should be based on blood counts)

» Bone marrow depressants, other (see *Appendix II*) or
Radiation therapy
(concurrent use may increase the total effects of these medications and radiation therapy; dosage reduction is recommended)

Cisplatin
(incidence of carboplatin-induced neurotoxicity or ototoxicity is increased in patients previously treated with cisplatin; use of carboplatin worsens pre-existing cisplatin-induced neurotoxicity [in about 30% of those patients] or ototoxicity; additive nephrotoxicity has not been reported)

Nephrotoxic medications, other (see *Appendix II*) or
Ototoxic medications, other (see *Appendix II*)
(concurrent and/or sequential administration may increase the potential for ototoxicity and nephrotoxicity)

Vaccines, killed virus
(because normal defense mechanisms may be suppressed by carboplatin therapy, the patient's antibody response to the vaccine may be decreased. The interval between discontinuation of medications that cause immunosuppression and restoration of the patient's ability to respond to the vaccine depends on the intensity and type of immunosuppression-causing medication used, the underlying disease, and other factors; estimates vary from 3 months to 1 year)

» Vaccines, live virus
(because normal defense mechanisms may be suppressed by carboplatin therapy, concurrent use with a live virus vaccine may potentiate the replication of the vaccine virus, may increase the side/adverse effects of the vaccine virus, and/or may decrease the patient's antibody response to the vaccine; immunization of these patients should be undertaken only with extreme caution after careful review of the patient's hematologic status and only with the knowledge and consent of the physician managing the carboplatin therapy. The interval between discontinuation of medications that cause immunosuppression and restoration of the patient's ability to respond to the vaccine depends on the intensity and type of immunosuppression-causing medication used, the underlying disease, and other factors; estimates vary from 3 months to 1 year. In addition, immunization with oral poliovirus vaccine should be postponed in persons in close contact with the patient, especially family members)

Laboratory value alterations

The following have been selected on the basis of their potential clinical significance (possible effect in parentheses where appropriate)—not necessarily inclusive (» = major clinical significance).

With physiology/laboratory test values

Bilirubin concentrations, serum and
Alkaline phosphatase values, serum and
Aspartate aminotransferase (AST [SGOT]) values, serum
(may be increased; increases are usually mild and are reversible in 50% of cases; severe abnormalities occur at carboplatin doses of more than four times the recommended dose)

Blood urea nitrogen (BUN) concentrations and
Creatinine concentrations, serum
(may be increased, indicating nephrotoxicity; usually mild; reversible in about 50% of cases)

Calcium and
Magnesium and
Potassium and
Sodium
(serum concentrations may be decreased)

Medical considerations/Contraindications

The medical considerations/contraindications included have been selected on the basis of their potential clinical significance (reasons given in parentheses where appropriate)—not necessarily inclusive (» = major clinical significance).

Risk-benefit should be considered when the following medical problems exist:

Ascites or
Pleural effusion
(increased risk of toxicity)

Bleeding, significant

» Bone marrow depression

» Chickenpox, existing or recent (including recent exposure) or
» Herpes zoster
(risk of severe generalized disease)

Hearing impairment

» Infection

» Renal function impairment
(reduced elimination; increased bone marrow depression; incidence and severity of nephrotoxicity may be increased. A lower dosage of carboplatin is recommended in patients with impaired renal function and careful monitoring of blood counts between courses is recommended)

Sensitivity to carboplatin

» Caution should be used also in patients who have had previous cytotoxic drug therapy or radiation therapy.

Patient monitoring

The following may be especially important in patient monitoring (other tests may be warranted in some patients, depending on condition; » = major clinical significance):

Audiometric testing
(recommended prior to initiation of therapy and if ototoxicity is suspected during therapy)

Blood urea nitrogen (BUN) concentrations and
» Creatinine clearance and
Creatinine concentrations, serum
(recommended prior to initiation of therapy and before each course of carboplatin to adjust dosage and detect renal toxicity)

Calcium concentrations, serum and
Magnesium concentrations, serum and
Potassium concentrations, serum and
Sodium concentrations, serum
(recommended at periodic intervals during therapy)

» Hematocrit or hemoglobin and
» Leukocyte count, total and, if appropriate, differential, and
» Platelet count
(determinations recommended prior to initiation of therapy and at periodic intervals during therapy; frequency varies according to clinical state, agent, dose, and other agents being used concurrently)

Neurologic function studies
(recommended prior to initiation of therapy and at periodic intervals during therapy)

Side/Adverse Effects

Note: Many "side effects" of antineoplastic therapy are unavoidable and represent the medication's pharmacologic action. Some of these (for example, leukopenia and thrombocytopenia) are actually used as parameters to aid in individual dosage titration.

Carboplatin infrequently causes mild renal toxicity, which may be detected initially only by means of renal function tests.

The following side/adverse effects have been selected on the basis of their potential clinical significance (possible signs and symptoms in parentheses where appropriate)—not necessarily inclusive:

Those indicating need for medical attention

Incidence more frequent—dose-related

Anemia (unusual tiredness or weakness)—usually asymptomatic; ***leukopenia or neutropenia*** (fever or chills; cough or hoarseness; lower back or side pain; painful or difficult urination)—usually asymptomatic; ***pain at site of injection; thrombocytopenia*** (unusual bleeding or bruising; black, tarry stools; blood in urine or stools; pinpoint red spots on skin)—usually asymptomatic

Note: *Anemia* may be cumulative; transfusions are frequently necessary.

With *leukopenia and thrombocytopenia*, nadir of leukocyte and platelet counts occurs after 21 days and counts usually recover by 30 days after a dose. Nadir of granulocyte counts usually occurs after 21 to 28 days and counts usually recover by day 35.

Leukopenia and thrombocytopenia are dose-dependent and cumulative; in a small percentage of patients (less than 10%) they are unpredictable.

Incidence less frequent

Allergic reaction (skin rash or itching; wheezing); ***peripheral neurotoxicity*** (numbness or tingling in fingers or toes); ***ototoxicity*** (ringing in ears)—usually asymptomatic

Note: An *allergic reaction* occurs within minutes of administration.

Neurotoxicity may be cumulative.

With *ototoxicity,* hearing loss usually occurs first with high frequencies (above speech tones) and may be unilateral or bilateral.

Incidence rare

Blurred vision; mucositis or stomatitis (sores in mouth and on lips)

Those indicating need for medical attention only if they continue or are bothersome

Incidence more frequent

Asthenia (unusual tiredness or weakness); ***nausea and vomiting***

Note: Less frequently, *asthenia* may be related to anemia.

Nausea and vomiting occur in about 65% of patients; these are severe in about one third of those. Nausea alone occurs in about 10 to 15% of patients. Symptoms usually begin 6 to 12 hours after a dose, and vomiting may persist for 24 hours. May be treated or prevented by antiemetic medication.

Incidence less frequent

Constipation or diarrhea; loss of appetite

Those not indicating need for medical attention

Incidence less frequent

Loss of hair

Patient Consultation

As an aid to patient consultation, refer to *Advice for the Patient, Carboplatin (Systemic).*

In providing consultation, consider emphasizing the following selected information (» = major clinical significance):

Before using this medication

» Conditions affecting use, especially:

Sensitivity to cisplatin or other platinum-containing compounds, or to carboplatin

Pregnancy—Use not recommended because of mutagenic, teratogenic, and carcinogenic potential; advisability of using contraception; telling physician immediately if pregnancy is suspected

Breast-feeding—Not recommended because of risk of serious side effects

Use in the elderly—Increased incidence of peripheral neurotoxicity and severity of myelotoxicity

Other medications, especially other bone marrow depressants or previous cytotoxic drug or radiation therapy

Other medical problems, especially chickenpox, herpes zoster, other infections, or renal function impairment

Proper use of this medication

Caution if taking combination therapy; taking each medication at the right time

Frequency of nausea and vomiting; importance of continuing medication despite stomach upset

» Proper dosing

Precautions while using this medication

» Importance of close monitoring by the physician

» Avoiding immunizations unless approved by physician; other persons in patient's household should avoid immunizations with oral poliovirus vaccine; avoiding persons who have taken oral poliovirus vaccine within the past several months or wearing a protective mask that covers nose and mouth

Caution if bone marrow depression occurs:

» Avoiding exposure to persons with infections, especially during periods of low blood counts; checking with physician immediately if fever or chills, cough or hoarseness, lower back or side pain, or painful or difficult urination occurs

» Checking with physician immediately if unusual bleeding or bruising; black, tarry stools; blood in urine or stools; or pinpoint red spots on skin occur

Caution in use of regular toothbrush, dental floss, or toothpick; physician, dentist, or nurse may suggest alternatives; checking with physician before having dental work done

Not touching eyes or inside of nose unless hands washed immediately before

Using caution to avoid accidental cuts with use of sharp objects such as safety razor or fingernail or toenail cutters

Avoiding contact sports or other situations where bruising or injury might occur

Side/adverse effects

May cause adverse effects such as ear and kidney problems, blood problems, and cancer; importance of discussing possible effects with physician

Signs of potential side effects, especially anemia, leukopenia or neutropenia, pain at site of injection, thrombocytopenia, allergic reaction, peripheral neurotoxicity, ototoxicity, blurred vision, and mucositis or stomatitis

Physician or nurse can help in dealing with side effects

Possibility of hair loss; normal hair growth should resume after treatment has ended

General Dosing Information

It is recommended that carboplatin be administered to patients under supervision of a physician experienced in cancer chemotherapy. It is also recommended that equipment and medications (including epinephrine, oxygen, antihistamines, and intravenous corticosteroids) necessary for treatment of a possible anaphylactic reaction be readily available at each administration of carboplatin.

Dosage must be adjusted to meet the individual requirements of each patient, on the basis of clinical response and appearance or severity of toxicity.

Carboplatin may be used in combination with other agents in various regimens. As a result, incidence and/or severity of side effects may be altered and different dosages (usually reduced) may be used.

It is recommended that carboplatin be administered as an intravenous infusion, usually over 15 to 60 minutes. No pre- or post-treatment hydration or forced diuresis is required.

Carboplatin has also been administered as a continuous intravenous infusion over 24 hours or by dividing the total dose into five consecutive daily pulse doses; this method of administration appears to reduce nausea and vomiting but not nephrotoxicity or ototoxicity.

It is recommended that courses of carboplatin be administered no more frequently than every 4 weeks to allow recovery of bone marrow.

Administration of subsequent doses of carboplatin is not recommended before platelet levels return to at least 100,000 per cubic millimeter and leukocyte levels to at least 2000 per cubic millimeter.

Special precautions are recommended in patients who develop thrombocytopenia as a result of administration of carboplatin. These may include extreme care in performing invasive procedures; regular inspection of intravenous sites, skin (including perirectal area), and mucous membrane surfaces for signs of bleeding or bruising; limiting frequency of venipuncture and avoiding intramuscular injections; testing urine, emesis, stool, and secretions for occult blood; care in use of regular toothbrushes, dental floss, toothpicks, safety razors, and fingernail and toenail cutters; avoiding constipation; and using caution to prevent falls and other injuries. Such patients should avoid alcohol and aspirin intake because of the risk of gastrointestinal bleeding. Platelet transfusions may be required.

Patients who develop leukopenia should be observed carefully for signs of infection. Antibiotic support may be required. In neutropenic patients who develop fever, broad-spectrum antibiotic coverage should be initiated empirically, pending bacterial cultures and appropriate diagnostic tests.

Safety considerations for handling this medication

There is limited but increasing evidence and concern that personnel involved in preparation and administration of parenteral antineoplastics may be at some risk because of the potential mutagenicity, teratogenicity, and/or carcinogenicity of these agents, although the actual risk is unknown. USP advisory panels recommend cautious handling both in preparation and disposal of antineoplastic agents. Precautions that have been suggested include:

- Use of a biological containment cabinet during reconstitution and dilution of parenteral medications and wearing of disposable surgical gloves and masks.
- Use of proper technique to prevent contamination of the medication, work area, and operator during transfer between containers (including proper training of personnel in this technique).
- Cautious and proper disposal of needles, syringes, vials, ampuls, and unused medication.
- A number of medical centers have developed detailed guidelines for handling of antineoplastic agents.

Parenteral Dosage Forms

Note: Bracketed uses in the *Dosage Forms* section refer to categories of use and/or indications that are not included in U.S. product labeling.

Note: The Calvert formula has been widely used to individualize carboplatin dosing and it permits targeting at an acceptable level of toxicity, based on the individual patient's renal function. Total Dose (mg) = (target AUC [mg per mL x min]) × (GFR [mL per minute] + 25). AUC (area under the plasma concentration-time curve) and GFR (glomerular filtration rate) are used.

CARBOPLATIN FOR INJECTION

Usual adult dose

Carcinoma, ovarian, epithelial—

Initial: Intravenous, according to the formula, Total dose (mg) = (target AUC) × (GFR + 25) where AUC (area under the plasma concentration-time curve) is expressed in mg per mL x min and GFR (glomerular filtration rate) is expressed in mL per minute.

The target AUC of 4 to 6 mg per mL x min using carboplatin monotherapy appears to provide the most appropriate dose range in previously treated patients.

Additional dosing option: Advanced, initial treatment—Intravenous, 300 mg per square meter of body surface area once every four weeks (day 1) for six cycles, in combination with cyclophosphamide 600 mg per square meter of body surface area intravenously once every four weeks (day 1) for six cycles.

Refractory to other chemotherapy: Intravenous, 360 mg per square meter of body surface area once every four weeks (day 1).

Note: An initial dose of 250 mg per square meter of body surface area is recommended in patients with creatinine clearance of 41 to 59 mL per minute; an initial dose of 200 mg per square meter of body surface area is recommended in patients with creatinine clearance of 16 to 40 mL per minute.

A suggested dosage adjustment schedule for subsequent doses is:

Nadir after prior dose (cells per cubic millimeter)		% of Prior dose to be given
Neutrophils	Platelets	
>2000	>100,000	125
500–2000	50,000–100,000	100
<500	<50,000	75

Note: Only one dose escalation should be made.

Geriatric patients may require lower doses.

For the [treatment of fallopian tube and peritoneal carcinomas of ovarian origin][1], patients have benefited from intravenous doses of carboplatin AUC 5 to 6 mg per mL x min, in combination with paclitaxel 135 to 175 mg/m² (by 3–hour infusion), every 21 days, for 5 to 9 treatment cycles. Duration of paclitaxel infusion may be adjusted from 1 hour to 24 hours, depending on toxicity.

[Carcinoma, bladder][1] or
[Carcinoma, endometrial][1] or
[Carcinoma, head and neck][1] or
[Carcinoma, lung, non-small cell][1] or
[Carcinoma, lung, small cell][1] or
[Malignant melanoma][1] or
[Retinoblastoma][1] or
[Seminoma][1] or
[Tumors, brain, primary][1]—

Consult medical literature or manufacturer's literature for information on dosage.

[Carcinoma, breast][1]—

Because several doses and regimens using carboplatin and paclitaxel (plus trastuzumab in HER2/neu positive disease) are showing activity, no individual dose/regimen is listed here. Consult the medical literature and/or experts in the field of oncology for information on dosage.

[Carcinoma, esophageal][1]—

Patients have benefited from intravenous doses of AUC 5 to 6 mg per mL x min, for up to 6 treatment cycles.

[Carcinoma, unknown primary site][1]—

Patients have benefited from an intravenous dose of AUC 6 mg per mL x min, on day 1 of a 21–day treatment cycle, combined with intravenous paclitaxel and oral etoposide, for 4 to 8 cycles.

[Lymphomas, Hodgkin's][1] or
[Lymphomas, non-Hodgkin's][1]—

As part of the ICE regimen (i.e., ifosfamide and etoposide), patients have benefited from intravenous doses of 750 to 1800 mg/m² (total dose). Using the Calvert formula, an intravenous dose of AUC 5 mg per mL x min (maximum 800 mg), every 14 days, for 3 cycles has provided benefit.

Usual pediatric dose

Dosage has not been established.

Strength(s) usually available

U.S.—

50 mg (Rx) [*Paraplatin* (mannitol, equal quantity by weight)].
150 mg (Rx) [*Paraplatin* (mannitol, equal quantity by weight)].
450 mg (Rx) [*Paraplatin* (mannitol, equal quantity by weight)].

Canada—

50 mg (Rx) [*Paraplatin* (mannitol, equal quantity by weight)].
150 mg (Rx) [*Paraplatin* (mannitol, equal quantity by weight)].
450 mg (Rx) [*Paraplatin* (mannitol, equal quantity by weight)].

Packaging and storage

Store between 15 and 30 °C (59 and 86 °F), unless otherwise specified by manufacturer. Protect from light.

Preparation of dosage form

Carboplatin for injection is reconstituted for intravenous use by adding 5, 15, or 45 mL of sterile water for injection, 5% dextrose injection, or 0.9% sodium chloride injection to the 50-mg, 150-mg, or 450-mg vial, respectively, producing a solution containing 10 mg of carboplatin per mL. The resulting solution may be further diluted to a concentration as low as 500 mcg (0.5 mg) per mL with 5% dextrose injection or 0.9% sodium chloride injection if further dilution for administration by intravenous infusion is required.

Stability

Reconstituted solutions of carboplatin are stable for 8 hours at 25 °C (77 °F).

Caution—A black platinum precipitate will form if carboplatin comes in contact with aluminum.

Incompatibilities
Do not use needles, intravenous sets, or equipment containing aluminum for administration since carboplatin is incompatible with aluminum.

CARBOPLATIN INJECTION

Usual adult dose
See *Carboplatin for injection.*

Usual pediatric dose
Dosage has not been established.

Strength(s) usually available
U.S.—
Not commercially available.
Canada—
10 mg per mL (Rx) [*Paraplatin-AQ*].

Packaging and storage
Store between 15 and 30 °C (59 and 86 °F), unless otherwise specified by manufacturer. Protect from light. Protect from freezing.

Stability
Caution—A black platinum precipitate will form if carboplatin comes in contact with aluminum.

Incompatibilities
Do not use needles, intravenous sets, or equipment containing aluminum for administration since carboplatin is incompatible with aluminum.

[1]Not included in Canadian product labeling.

Revised: 04/23/2004
Developed: 09/02/1999

CARISOPRODOL—See *Skeletal Muscle Relaxants (Systemic)*

CARMUSTINE Systemic

VA CLASSIFICATION (Primary/Secondary): AN100/DE600

Commonly used brand name(s): *BiCNU*.

Another commonly used name is BCNU.

Note: For a listing of dosage forms and brand names by country availability, see *Dosage Forms* section(s).

Category
Antineoplastic.

Indications
Note: Bracketed information in the *Indications* section refers to uses that are not included in U.S. product labeling.

Accepted
Tumors, brain, primary (treatment)
[Carcinoma, gastric (treatment)] or
[Carcinoma, colorectal (treatment)]—Carmustine is indicated as palliative therapy as a single agent or in combination therapy for treatment of primary brain tumors (glioblastoma, brain stem glioma, medulloblastoma, astrocytoma, ependymoma, and metastatic brain tumors) and for gastric and colorectal carcinoma.

Lymphomas, Hodgkin's (treatment) or
Lymphomas, non-Hodgkin's (treatment)—Carmustine is indicated for treatment of Hodgkin's disease and non-Hodgkin's lymphomas. Carmustine is indicated as secondary therapy in combination with other approved drugs in patients who relapse while being treated with primary therapy, or who fail to respond to primary therapy.

Multiple myeloma (treatment)—Carmustine is indicated for treatment of multiple myeloma, in combination with prednisone.

[Melanoma, malignant (treatment)]—Carmustine is used for treatment of disseminated malignant melanoma, in combination with vincristine sulfate.

[Mycosis fungoides (treatment)][1]—Carmustine is used topically for treatment of mycosis fungoides.

[Waldenström's macroglobulinemia (treatment)][1]—Carmustine is used for treatment of Waldenström's macroglobulinemia.

[1]Not included in Canadian product labeling.

Pharmacology/Pharmacokinetics

Physicochemical characteristics
Molecular weight—214.05.

Mechanism of action/Effect
Carmustine is an alkylating agent of the nitrosourea type. Carmustine and/or its metabolites alkylate and interfere with the function of DNA and RNA and are also capable of cross-linking DNA. It is cell cycle-phase nonspecific. Carmustine may also act by protein modification.

Distribution
Crosses the blood-brain barrier (because of high lipid solubility and relative lack of ionization at physiological pH).

Biotransformation
Hepatic; rapid (active metabolites).

Half-life
Biologic—Approximately 15 to 30 minutes.
Chemical—Approximately 5 minutes.
Metabolites may persist in the plasma for several days, which may explain the delayed hematologic toxicity.

Elimination
Renal—60 to 70% (less than 1% unchanged); some enterohepatic circulation believed to occur.
Fecal—1%.
Respiratory—10% (as carbon dioxide).

Precautions to Consider

Carcinogenicity/Mutagenicity
Secondary malignancies are potential delayed effects of many antineoplastic agents, although it is not clear whether the effect is related to their mutagenic or immunosuppressive action. The effect of dose and duration of therapy is also unknown, although risk seems to increase with long-term use. Although information is limited, available data seem to indicate that the carcinogenic risk is greatest with the alkylating agents.

Carmustine is carcinogenic in rats and mice at doses approximating the clinical dose and has been associated with development of secondary malignancies, including acute leukemia, in humans.

Pregnancy/Reproduction
Fertility—Gonadal suppression, resulting in amenorrhea or azoospermia, may occur in patients taking antineoplastic therapy, especially with the alkylating agents. In general, these effects appear to be related to dose and length of therapy and may be irreversible. Prediction of the degree of testicular or ovarian function impairment is complicated by the common use of combinations of several antineoplastics, which makes it difficult to assess the effects of individual agents.

Carmustine affects fertility in male rats at doses somewhat higher than the human dose.

Pregnancy—Adequate and well-controlled studies in humans have not been done.

First trimester: It is usually recommended that use of antineoplastics, especially combination chemotherapy, be avoided whenever possible, especially during the first trimester. Although information is limited because of the relatively few instances of antineoplastic administration during pregnancy, the mutagenic, teratogenic, and carcinogenic potential of these medications must be considered.

Other hazards to the fetus include adverse reactions seen in adults.

In general, use of a contraceptive is recommended during cytotoxic drug therapy.

Carmustine is embryotoxic and teratogenic in rats and embryotoxic in rats and rabbits at doses equivalent to the human dose.

FDA Pregnancy Category D.

Breast-feeding
It is not known whether carmustine is distributed into milk. Although very little information is available regarding distribution of antineoplastic agents into breast milk, breast-feeding is not recommended while carmustine is being administered because of the risks to the infant (adverse effects, mutagenicity, carcinogenicity).

Pediatrics
Appropriate studies on the relationship of age to the effects of carmustine have not been performed in the pediatric population. However, pediatrics-specific problems that would limit the usefulness of this medication in children are not expected.

Delayed, sometimes fatal, pulmonary fibrosis has been reported to occur up to 15 years after treatment with carmustine in childhood and early adolescence in cumulative doses ranging from 770 to 1800 mg per square meter of body surface in combination with cranial radiotherapy for intracranial tumors.

Geriatrics
No information is available on the relationship of age to the effects of carmustine in geriatric patients. However, geriatric patients are more likely to have age-related renal function impairment, which may require caution in patients receiving carmustine.

Dental
The bone marrow depressant effects of carmustine may result in an increased incidence of microbial infection, delayed healing, and gingival bleeding. Dental work, whenever possible, should be completed prior to initiation of therapy or deferred until blood counts have returned to normal. Patients should be instructed in proper oral hygiene during treatment, including caution in use of regular toothbrushes, dental floss, and toothpicks.
Carmustine may also cause stomatitis associated with considerable discomfort.

Drug interactions and/or related problems
The following drug interactions and/or related problems have been selected on the basis of their potential clinical significance (possible mechanism in parentheses where appropriate)—not necessarily inclusive (» = major clinical significance):
Note: Combinations containing any of the following medications, depending on the amount present, may also interact with this medication.

Blood dyscrasia-causing medications (see *Appendix II*)
(leukopenic and/or thrombocytopenic effects of carmustine may be increased with concurrent or recent therapy if these medications cause the same effects; dosage adjustment of carmustine, if necessary, should be based on blood counts)

» Bone marrow depressants, other (see *Appendix II*) or
Radiation therapy
(additive bone marrow depression may occur; dosage reduction may be required when two or more bone marrow depressants, including radiation, are used concurrently or consecutively)

Hepatotoxic medications, other (see *Appendix II*) or
Nephrotoxic medications, other (see *Appendix II*)
(concurrent use with carmustine may result in enhanced hepatotoxicity or nephrotoxicity; either or both medications should be discontinued at the first sign of impairment)

Vaccines, killed virus
(because normal defense mechanisms may be suppressed by carmustine therapy, the patient's antibody response to the vaccine may be decreased. The interval between discontinuation of medications that cause immunosuppression and restoration of the patient's ability to respond to the vaccine depends on the intensity and type of immunosuppression-causing medication used, the underlying disease, and other factors; estimates vary from 3 months to 1 year)

» Vaccines, live virus
(because normal defense mechanisms may be suppressed by carmustine therapy, concurrent use with a live virus vaccine may potentiate the replication of the vaccine virus, may increase the side/adverse effects of the vaccine virus, and/or may decrease the patient's antibody response to the vaccine; immunization of these patients should be undertaken only with extreme caution after careful review of the patient's hematologic status and only with the knowledge and consent of the physician managing the carmustine therapy. The interval between discontinuation of medications that cause immunosuppression and restoration of the patient's ability to respond to the vaccine depends on the intensity and type of immunosuppression-causing medication used, the underlying disease, and other factors; estimates vary from 3 months to 1 year. Immunization with oral poliovirus vaccine should also be postponed in persons in close contact with the patient, especially family members)

Laboratory value alterations
The following have been selected on the basis of their potential clinical significance (possible effect in parentheses where appropriate)—not necessarily inclusive (» = major clinical significance).
With physiology/laboratory test values
Alkaline phosphatase values, serum and
Aspartate aminotransferase (AST [SGOT]) values, serum and
Bilirubin concentrations, serum
(may be increased, indicating hepatotoxicity)
Blood urea nitrogen (BUN)
(concentrations may be increased, indicating nephrotoxicity)

Medical considerations/Contraindications
The medical considerations/contraindications included have been selected on the basis of their potential clinical significance (reasons given in parentheses where appropriate)—not necessarily inclusive (» = major clinical significance).

Risk-benefit should be considered when the following medical problems exist:
» Bone marrow depression
» Chickenpox, existing or recent (including recent exposure) or
» Herpes zoster
(risk of severe generalized disease)
Hepatic function impairment
(carmustine may cause mild hepatotoxicity)
» Infection
» Pulmonary function impairment, existing or history of
» Renal function impairment
» Sensitivity to carmustine
» Caution should be used also in patients who have had previous cytotoxic drug therapy or radiation therapy, especially to the mediastinum, and in patients who smoke, because of the possible increased risk of pulmonary toxicity.

Patient monitoring
The following may be especially important in patient monitoring (other tests may be warranted in some patients, depending on condition; » = major clinical significance):
Alanine aminotransferase (ALT [SGPT]) values, serum and
Aspartate aminotransferase (AST [SGOT]) values, serum and
Bilirubin concentrations, serum and
Lactate dehydrogenase (LDH) values, serum
(recommended prior to initiation of therapy and at periodic intervals during therapy; frequency varies according to clinical state, agent, dose, and other agents being used concurrently)
Blood urea nitrogen (BUN) concentrations and
Creatinine concentrations, serum
(recommended prior to initiation of therapy and at periodic intervals during therapy; frequency varies according to clinical state, agent, dose, and other agents being used concurrently)
» Hematocrit or hemoglobin and
» Leukocyte count, total and, if appropriate, differential and
» Platelet count
(determinations recommended prior to initiation of therapy and at periodic intervals during therapy; frequency varies according to clinical state, agent, dose, and other agents being used concurrently)
» Pulmonary function studies
(recommended prior to initiation of therapy and at frequent intervals during systemic therapy)
Uric acid concentrations, serum
(recommended prior to initiation of therapy and at periodic intervals during therapy; frequency varies according to clinical state, agent, dose, and other agents being used concurrently)

Side/Adverse Effects

Note: Many "side effects" of antineoplastic therapy are unavoidable and represent the medication's pharmacologic action. Some of these (for example, leukopenia and thrombocytopenia) are actually used as parameters to aid in individual dosage titration.
Encephalomyelopathy has been reported in patients who have received high-dose carmustine therapy.
Ocular toxicity has been associated with intra-arterial use.

The following side/adverse effects have been selected on the basis of their potential clinical significance (possible signs and symptoms in parentheses where appropriate)—not necessarily inclusive:

Those indicating need for medical attention
Incidence more frequent
Leukopenia or infection (fever or chills; cough or hoarseness; lower back or side pain; painful or difficult urination)—usually asymptomatic; ***phlebitis*** (pain or redness at site of injection); ***pneumonitis or pulmonary fibrosis*** (cough; shortness of breath); ***thrombocytopenia*** (unusual bleeding or bruising; black, tarry stools; blood in urine or stools; pinpoint red spots on skin)—usually asymptomatic

Note: Maximum *leukopenia* occurs about 5 to 6 weeks after a dose. Recovery usually occurs within 6 to 7 weeks but may take up to 10 to 12 weeks after prolonged therapy. Severity of bone marrow depression varies and determines subsequent dosage of carmustine.
Burning at the injection site is associated with rapid intravenous infusion; true thrombosis is rare.

Pneumonitis or pulmonary fibrosis was initially thought to occur after high cumulative doses (greater than 1200 to 1400 mg per square meter of body surface) or several courses (greater than 5) or months of therapy; however, there have been several reports of pulmonary toxicity after only 1 or 2 courses or low doses. Symptoms may be insidious or acute in onset, and damage may be reversible or irreversible. Fatalities have occurred. The relationship of pulmonary toxicity to dose is not yet clear and other factors (previous radiation to mediastinum, concurrent administration of cyclophosphamide or agents associated with pulmonary toxicity, history of lung disease or smoking) may be significant. Delayed pulmonary fibrosis has been reported to occur up to 15 years after treatment with carmustine in childhood and early adolescence in cumulative doses ranging from 770 to 1800 mg per square meter of body surface in combination with cranial radiotherapy for intracranial tumors. Chest x-rays demonstrated pulmonary hypoplasia with upper zone contraction, gallium scans were normal, and thoracic computed tomography (CT) scans demonstrated an unusual pattern of upper zone fibrosis. Late reduction of pulmonary function was noted in a substantial number of cases. This form of lung fibrosis may be slowly progressive and has been fatal in some cases.

Maximum *thrombocytopenia* occurs about 4 to 5 weeks after a dose. Recovery usually occurs within 6 to 7 weeks but may take up to 10 to 12 weeks after prolonged therapy. Severity of bone marrow depression varies and determines subsequent dosage of carmustine.

Incidence less frequent

Anemia (unusual tiredness or weakness); ***flushing of face; stomatitis*** (sores in mouth and on lips)

Note: *Flushing of face* is caused by rapid intravenous infusion. Flushing occurs within 2 hours after a dose and persists approximately 4 hours.

Incidence rare

Hepatotoxicity—asymptomatic; ***renal toxicity and failure*** (decrease in urination; swelling of feet or lower legs)

Note: *Renal toxicity and failure* usually occur in patients who have received large cumulative doses after prolonged therapy, but has occasionally been reported with lower cumulative doses.

Those indicating need for medical attention only if they continue or are bothersome

Incidence more frequent

Nausea and vomiting

Note: *Nausea and vomiting* occur within 2 hours after a dose and usually last 4 to 6 hours; dose-related.

Incidence less frequent

Central nervous system (CNS) toxicity (dizziness; trouble in walking); ***diarrhea; discoloration of skin along vein of injection; loss of appetite; skin rash and itching; trouble in swallowing***

Those not indicating need for medical attention

Incidence less frequent

Loss of hair

Those indicating the need for medical attention if they occur after medication is discontinued

Bone marrow depression (fever or chills; cough or hoarseness; lower back or side pain; painful or difficult urination; unusual bleeding or bruising; black, tarry stools; blood in urine or stools; pinpoint red spots on skin); ***pneumonitis or pulmonary fibrosis*** (cough or shortness of breath)

Note: Cumulative *myelosuppression* may occur with repeated doses.

Patient Consultation

As an aid to patient consultation, refer to *Advice for the Patient, Carmustine (Systemic).*

In providing consultation, consider emphasizing the following selected information (» = major clinical significance):

Before using this medication

» Conditions affecting use, especially:
- Sensitivity to carmustine
- Pregnancy—Use not recommended because of mutagenic, teratogenic, and carcinogenic potential; advisability of using contraception; telling physician immediately if pregnancy is suspected
- Breast-feeding—Not recommended because of risk of serious side effects
- Other medications, especially other bone marrow depressants, or previous cytotoxic drug therapy or radiation therapy
- Other medical problems, especially chickenpox, herpes zoster, infection, pulmonary function impairment, renal function impairment, or smoking

Proper use of this medication

Caution in taking combination therapy; taking each medication at the right time

Frequency of nausea and vomiting; importance of continuing medication despite stomach upset

» Proper dosing

Precautions while using this medication

» Importance of close monitoring by the physician

» Avoiding immunizations unless approved by physician; other persons in patient's household should avoid immunizations with oral poliovirus vaccine; avoiding persons who have taken oral poliovirus vaccine or wearing a protective mask that covers nose and mouth

Caution if bone marrow depression occurs:

» Avoiding exposure to persons with infections, especially during periods of low blood counts; checking with physician immediately if fever or chills, cough or hoarseness, lower back or side pain, or painful or difficult urination occurs

» Checking with physician immediately if unusual bleeding or bruising; black, tarry stools; blood in urine or stools; or pinpoint red spots on skin occur

Caution in use of regular toothbrush, dental floss, or toothpick; physician, dentist, or nurse may suggest alternatives; checking with physician before having dental work done

Not touching eyes or inside of nose unless hands washed immediately before

Using caution to avoid accidental cuts with use of sharp objects such as safety razor or fingernail or toenail cutters

Avoiding contact sports or other situations where bruising or injury could occur

» Possibility of local tissue injury and scarring if infiltration of intravenous solution occurs; telling doctor or nurse right away about redness, pain, or swelling at injection site

Side/adverse effects

Importance of discussing possible adverse effects, including cancer, with physician

Signs of potential side effects, especially leukopenia, infection, phlebitis, pneumonitis, pulmonary fibrosis, thrombocytopenia, anemia, flushing of face, stomatitis, and renal toxicity and failure

Asymptomatic side effects, including leukopenia, thrombocytopenia, and hepatotoxicity

Physician or nurse can help in dealing with side effects

Possibility of hair loss; growth should return after treatment has ended

Pulmonary toxicity more likely to occur in smokers

General Dosing Information

Patients receiving carmustine should be under supervision of a physician experienced in cancer chemotherapy.

A variety of dosage schedules and regimens of carmustine, alone or in combination with other antitumor agents, are used. The prescriber may consult the medical literature as well as the manufacturer's literature in choosing a specific dosage.

Dosage of carmustine subsequent to the initial course should be adjusted to meet the individual requirements of each patient, based on hematologic response of the patient to the previous dose. An additional course of carmustine should be given only after circulating blood elements have returned to acceptable levels (leukocytes above 4000 per cubic millimeter and platelets above 100,000 per cubic millimeter).

Because of the delayed and cumulative bone marrow suppression caused by carmustine, the medication should be given no more frequently than every 6 weeks.

Some cross-resistance has been reported between carmustine and lomustine.

Frequency and duration of nausea and vomiting may be reduced in some patients by administration of antiemetics prior to dosing.

Intravenous infusion solutions should be administered over 1 to 2 hours to prevent irritation at the injection site. Some clinicians also recommend flushing the line with 5 to 10 mL of 0.9% sodium chloride injection or 5% dextrose injection both before and after administration of carmustine.

Special precautions are recommended in patients who develop thrombocytopenia as a result of administration of carmustine. These may include extreme care in performing invasive procedures; regular inspection of intravenous sites, skin (including perirectal area), and mucous membrane surfaces for signs of bleeding or bruising; limiting frequency of venipuncture and avoiding intramuscular injections; testing urine, emesis, stool, and secretions for occult blood; care in use of regular toothbrushes, dental floss, toothpicks, safety razors, and fingernail and toenail cutters; avoiding constipation; and using caution to prevent falls and other injuries. Such patients should avoid alcohol and aspirin intake because of the risk of gastrointestinal bleeding. Platelet transfusions may be required.

Patients who develop leukopenia should be observed carefully for signs of infection. Antibiotic support may be required. In neutropenic patients who develop fever, broad-spectrum antibiotic coverage should be initiated empirically, pending bacterial cultures and appropriate diagnostic tests.

Carmustine has been injected intra-arterially (hepatic artery) in the investigational treatment of hepatic tumors in a dose of 200 mg per square meter of body surface administered over 20 to 60 minutes.

Safety considerations for handling this medication

There is limited but increasing evidence and concern that personnel involved in preparation and administration of parenteral antineoplastics may be at some risk because of the potential mutagenicity, teratogenicity, and/or carcinogenicity of these agents, although the actual risk is unknown. USP advisory panels recommend cautious handling both in preparation and disposal of antineoplastic agents. Precautions that have been suggested include:

- Use of a biological containment cabinet during reconstitution and dilution of parenteral medications and wearing of disposable surgical gloves and masks.
- Use of proper technique to prevent contamination of the medication, work area, and operator during transfer between containers (including proper training of personnel in this technique).
- Cautious and proper disposal of needles, syringes, vials, ampuls, and unused medication.
- A number of medical centers have developed detailed guidelines for handling of antineoplastic agents.

Combination chemotherapy

Carmustine may be used in combination with other agents in various regimens. As a result, incidence and/or severity of side effects may be altered and different dosages (usually reduced) may be used. For example, carmustine is part of the following chemotherapeutic combination:

—carmustine, cyclophosphamide, vinblastine, procarbazine, and prednisone (BCVPP).

For specific dosages and schedules, consult the literature. For information regarding each agent, consult the individual monographs.

Parenteral Dosage Forms

Note: Bracketed uses in the *Dosage Forms* section refer to categories of use and/or indications that are not included in U.S. product labeling.

CARMUSTINE FOR INJECTION

Usual adult and adolescent dose

Tumors, brain, primary or
[Carcinoma, colorectal or]
[Carcinoma, gastric] or
Lymphomas, Hodgkin's or
Lymphomas, non-Hodgkin's or
Multiple myeloma or
[Melanoma, malignant]—

Intravenous, 150 to 200 mg per square meter of body surface as a single dose every six to eight weeks, or 75 to 100 mg per square meter of body surface on two successive days every six weeks, or 40 mg per square meter of body surface on five successive days every six weeks.

A suggested dosage adjustment schedule for subsequent doses is:

Nadir after Prior Dose (cells per cubic millimeter)		% of Prior Dose to Be Given
Leukocytes	Platelets	
>4000	>100,000	100
3000–3999	75,000–99,999	100
2000–2999	25,000–74,999	70
<2000	<25,000	50

Usual pediatric dose

See *Usual adult and adolescent dose.*

Strength(s) usually available

U.S.—

100 mg (Rx) [*BiCNU*].

Canada—

100 mg (Rx) [*BiCNU*].

Packaging and storage

Store between 2 and 8 °C (36 and 46 °F), unless otherwise specified by manufacturer. Exposure of the dry material to temperatures of 30.5 to 32 °C (86.9 to 89.6 °F) or above will cause the drug to decompose and liquefy, appearing as an oily film in the bottom of the vial; if this occurs, the vial must be discarded.

Preparation of dosage form

Carmustine for injection is reconstituted for intravenous use by adding 3 mL of sterile diluent (dehydrated alcohol injection) supplied by the manufacturer to dissolve it, then adding 27 mL of sterile water for injection, producing a clear, colorless solution containing 3.3 mg of carmustine per mL.

Reconstituted solutions may be further diluted with 0.9% sodium chloride injection or 5% dextrose injection for administration by intravenous infusion.

Stability

Reconstituted solutions are stable for 8 hours at 25 °C (77 °F) or 24 hours at 4 °C (39 °F). Reconstituted solutions diluted further for administration by infusion are stable for 48 hours when refrigerated and an additional 8 hours at 25 °C (77 °F) under normal room fluorescent light. Freezing does not alter the potency. Because the product contains no preservative, it should not be used as a multiple-dose vial.

Note

Avoid contact of the reconstituted solution with skin and eyes; it will cause burning and brown staining of skin. If accidental contact with skin or mucosa occurs, the area should be washed immediately and thoroughly with soap and water.

Revised: 09/30/1997

CARTEOLOL—See *Beta-adrenergic Blocking Agents (Ophthalmic), Beta-adrenergic Blocking Agents (Systemic)*

CARVEDILOL Systemic

VA CLASSIFICATION (Primary/Secondary): CV100/CV409

Commonly used brand name(s): *Coreg.*

Note: For a listing of dosage forms and brand names by country availability, see *Dosage Forms* section(s).

Category

Antihypertensive; congestive heart failure treatment adjunct.

Indications

Accepted

Congestive heart failure (treatment)—Carvedilol is indicated for the treatment of mild-to-severe heart failure of ischemic or cardiomyopathic origin, usually in addition to diuretics, ACE inhibitor, and digitalis, to increase survival and, also, to reduce the risk of hospitalization.

Hypertension (treatment)—Carvedilol is indicated, either alone or in combination with other antihypertensive agents, such as thiazide diuretics, in the treatment of essential hypertension.

For additional information on initial therapeutic guidelines related to the treatment of hypertension, see *Appendix III.*

Left ventricular dysfunction, post-myocardial infarction (treatment)—Carvedilol is indicated to reduce cardiovascular mortality in clinically stable patients who have survived the acute phase of a myocardial infarction and have a left ventricular ejection fraction of ≤40% (with or without symptomatic heart failure).

Pharmacology/Pharmacokinetics

Physicochemical characteristics

Molecular weight—406.5.

Mechanism of action/Effect

Carvedilol is a nonselective beta-adrenergic blocking agent with alpha$_1$-adrenergic blocking activity and no intrinsic sympathomimetic activity. The exact mechanism of the antihypertensive effect produced by beta-adrenergic blockade is not known, but may involve suppression of renin production. The beta-adrenergic blocking activity of carvedilol decreases cardiac output, exercise- and/or isoproterenol-induced tachycardia, and reflex orthostatic tachycardia. The alpha$_1$-adrenergic blocking activity of carvedilol blunts the pressor effect of phenylephrine, causes vasodilation, and reduces peripheral vascular resistance. The effect of alpha$_1$-adrenergic blockade is a reduction in standing blood pressure (more than supine), potentiating symptoms of postural hypotension and possibly syncope.

The mechanism by which carvedilol produces a beneficial effect in congestive heart failure is not known, but may be attributable to beta-adrenergic blockade and vasodilation.

Absorption
Carvedilol is rapidly and extensively absorbed. Absolute bioavailability of carvedilol is 25 to 35%, due to significant first-pass metabolism. Food slows the rate of absorption but does not appear to affect the extent of the bioavailability of carvedilol.

Distribution
Volume of distribution (Vol_D)—Steady-state: Approximately 115 L.

Protein binding
Very high (98%), primarily to albumin; concentration-independent.

Biotransformation
Hepatic; carvedilol is extensively metabolized, primarily by aromatic ring oxidation and glucuronidation by the cytochrome P450 2D6 enzyme. Other isozymes, such as P450 2C9 and P450 3A4, are involved to a lesser extent. Three active metabolites with beta-receptor blocking activity are produced by demethylation and hydroxylation at the phenol ring. The active metabolites show weak vasodilating (alpha$_1$-antagonist) activity when compared with carvedilol; however, in preclinical studies, the beta-blockade effect of the 4′-hydroxyphenyl metabolite was found to be approximately 13 times more potent than that of carvedilol.

Half-life
Elimination—

Apparent mean terminal: 7 to 10 hours; may be affected by induction or inhibition of cytochrome P450 enzymes.

Elimination
Fecal (biliary).

In dialysis—

Carvedilol does not appear to be cleared significantly by hemodialysis.

Precautions to Consider

Carcinogenicity
No evidence of carcinogenicity was found in 2-year studies in rats and mice given doses of up to 75 mg per kg of body weight (mg/kg) per day (12 times the maximum recommended human dose [MRHD] on a mg per square meter of body surface area [mg/m^2] basis) and 200 mg/kg per day (16 times the MRHD on a mg/m^2 basis), respectively.

Mutagenicity
Mutagenicity was not detected in the Ames test or the CHO/HGPRT assay. Clastogenicity was not detected in the *in vitro* hamster micronucleus or the *in vivo* human lymphocyte cell tests.

Pregnancy/Reproduction
Fertility—Impaired fertility was observed in rats given doses ≥ 200 mg/kg per day (≥ 32 times the MRHD on a mg/m^2 basis). Administration of carvedilol at this dose was associated with a reduced number of successful matings, prolonged mating time, significantly fewer corpora lutea and implants per dam, and complete resorption of 18% of the litters.

Pregnancy—Adequate and well-controlled studies in humans have not been done. Carvedilol should be used during pregnancy only if the potential benefit justifies the potential risk to the fetus.

Reproduction studies in rats and rabbits revealed increased postimplantation loss in rats at doses of 300 mg/kg per day (50 times the MRHD on a mg/m^2 basis) and in rabbits at doses of 75 mg/kg per day (25 times the MRHD on a mg/m^2 basis). In rats, a decrease in fetal body weight and an increase in the frequency of fetuses with delayed skeletal development (missing or stunted 13th rib) also occurred.

FDA Pregnancy Category C.

Breast-feeding
It is not known whether carvedilol is distributed into breast milk.

Studies in lactating rats treated with 10 times the MRHD (as mg per m^2) and above during the last trimester through day 22 of lactation have shown that carvedilol and/or its metabolites were distributed into milk and caused an increased mortality in rat neonates. Because of the potential for a serious reaction in nursing infants from beta-adrenergic blockade (bradycardia), a decision should be made about whether to discontinue nursing or to discontinue carvedilol. The effects of other alpha- and beta-blocking agents have included perinatal and neonatal distress.

Pediatrics
No information is available on the relationship of age to the effects of carvedilol in pediatric patients. Safety and efficacy in pediatric patients have not been established.

Geriatrics
Use of carvedilol in patients 65 years of age and older has not demonstrated geriatric-specific problems that would limit the usefulness of carvedilol in the elderly. However, plasma levels of carvedilol in the elderly are about 50% higher on the average as compared with younger subjects, and the incidence of dizziness as a side effect is higher in the elderly than in younger patients.

Pharmacogenetics
In clinical trials, black patients with hypertension were less responsive to the antihypertensive beta-adrenergic blocking effects of carvedilol than nonblack patients.

Patients who are poor metabolizers of debrisoquin, a marker for the cytochrome P450 2D6 isozyme, may experience two- to threefold increases in carvedilol plasma concentrations, increasing the risk of adverse effects.

Surgical
Use of carvedilol perioperatively with anesthetic agents, such as cyclopropane, ether, and trichloroethylene, may further depress myocardial function.

Drug interactions and/or related problems
The following drug interactions and/or related problems have been selected on the basis of their potential clinical significance (possible mechanism in parentheses where appropriate)—not necessarily inclusive (» = major clinical significance):

Note: Combinations containing any of the following medications, depending on the amount present, may also interact with this medication.

Anesthetics, general, such as:
Cyclopropane
Ether
Trichloroethylene
(concurrent use with carvedilol may further depress myocardial function)

» Antidiabetic agents, sulfonylurea or
» Insulin
(concurrent use with carvedilol may increase the serum glucose-lowering effects of insulin and sulfonylurea antidiabetic agents; regular monitoring of blood glucose is recommended when using carvedilol and insulin or sulfonylurea antidiabetic agents concurrently)

» Calcium channel blocking agents, especially
Diltiazem or
Verapamil
(concurrent use of carvedilol with diltiazem has resulted in isolated cases of conduction disturbances; electrocardiogram and blood pressure measurements are recommended when carvedilol is used concurrently with calcium channel blocking agents)

Catecholamine-depleting agents, such as:
Monoamine oxidase inhibitors
Reserpine
(concurrent use of carvedilol with drugs that can deplete catecholamines may cause hypotension and bradycardia)

Clonidine
(concurrent use with carvedilol may have additive blood pressure- and heart rate-lowering effects)

» Cyclosporine
(modest increases in mean trough cyclosporine concentration observed with concomitant use; recommended close monitoring of cyclosporine concentrations after carvedilol therapy initiation and dose adjustment of cyclosporine as appropriate)

Digoxin
(in hypertensive patients, concurrent use with carvedilol increased steady-state area under the plasma concentration-time curve [AUC] and trough concentrations of digoxin by 14% and 16%, respectively; slowing of atrioventricular [AV] conduction may be additive; monitoring of plasma digoxin concentrations is recommended when carvedilol is used concurrently)

Enzyme inducers, hepatic, cytochrome P450 (see *Appendix II*), such as
Rifampin or

Enzyme inhibitors, hepatic, cytochrome P450 (see *Appendix II*), such as:
Cimetidine
Fluoxetine
Paroxetine
Propafenone
Quinidine
(concurrent use may affect the metabolism and pharmacokinetics of carvedilol by inducing or inhibiting cytochrome P450 enzymes; in healthy male subjects, concurrent use of rifampin decreased the AUC and peak plasma concentration [C_{max}] of carvedilol by about 70%; in healthy male subjects, concurrent use of cimetidine increased the steady-state AUC of carvedilol by 30% with no change in C_{max})

Laboratory value alterations

The following have been selected on the basis of their potential clinical significance (possible effect in parentheses where appropriate)—not necessarily inclusive (» = major clinical significance).

With physiology/laboratory test values
Bilirubin concentrations, serum or
Transaminase values, serum
(increases have occurred rarely; carvedilol should be withdrawn if laboratory signs of liver injury or jaundice occur)

Creatinine, serum
(value may be increased)

Glucose, serum
(beta-adrenergic blocking agents, e.g., carvedilol, increase the serum glucose–lowering effects of insulin and sulfonylurea antidiabetic agents and delay the recovery of serum glucose levels; however, in patients with both diabetes and congestive heart failure, hyperglycemia may be worsened; in clinical trials with congestive heart failure patients, the incidence of hyperglycemia was 12.2%)

Prothrombin
(may be decreased)

Medical considerations/Contraindications

The medical considerations/contraindications included have been selected on the basis of their potential clinical significance (reasons given in parentheses where appropriate)—not necessarily inclusive (» = major clinical significance).

Except under special circumstances, this medication should not be used when the following medical problems exist:

» Asthma, bronchial or
» Bronchospastic conditions, related
(carvedilol aggravates bronchial asthma and related bronchospastic conditions by blocking endogenous and exogenous beta agonists; two cases of death from status asthmaticus have been reported in patients receiving a single dose of carvedilol)

» Atrioventricular (AV) block, 2nd- or 3rd-degree or
» Bradycardia, severe or
» Cardiogenic shock or
» Sick sinus syndrome, without a pacemaker
(risk of further depression of myocardial contractility and conduction)

» Cardiac failure, decompensated, severe, requiring intravenous inotropic therapy, New York Heart Association (NYHA) class IV
(in clinical trials, area under the plasma concentration-time curve [AUC] and time to peak plasma concentration [C_{max}] increased by 50 to 100% in six patients with NYHA class IV heart failure; myocardial contractility may be further depressed in these patients)

» Hepatic function impairment, clinically manifested
(because carvedilol is hepatically metabolized, blood concentrations may be increased approximately four- to sevenfold following a single dose)

» Hypersensitivity to carvedilol or any of its components

Risk-benefit should be considered when the following medical problems exist:

» Anaphylactic reaction to a variety of allergens, severe, history of
(administration of beta-adrenergic blocking agents may make these patients more reactive to allergen exposure and less responsive to the usual doses of epinephrine used to treat the allergic reaction)

Angina, Prinzmetal's variant
(nonselective beta-adrenergic blocking agents, such as carvedilol, may provoke chest pain in patients with this condition; caution should be used)

» Bronchospastic conditions, nonallergic, such as:
Chronic bronchitis and
Emphysema
(because carvedilol blocks the effect of endogenous and exogenous beta-adrenergic agonists, nonallergic bronchospastic conditions may be aggravated by carvedilol; only the smallest effective dose of carvedilol should be used, if it is used at all; in clinical trials, patients with congestive heart failure and bronchospastic disease received carvedilol only if treatment of their bronchospastic condition did not require oral or inhaled medication)

Congestive heart failure, if accompanied by:
Hypotension (systolic blood pressure < 100 mm Hg) or
Ischemic heart disease or
Renal insufficiency or
Vascular disease, diffuse
(patients with these conditions may be at risk for worsening of renal function if treated with carvedilol; renal function should be monitored and a dosage adjustment or discontinuation of carvedilol may be necessary if renal function deteriorates; heart failure may be worsened or fluid retention may occur when the dosage of carvedilol is increased; in such cases, dosages of diuretics should be increased, and carvedilol dosage increases should be postponed until the patient is clinically stable; carvedilol dosage may need to be reduced or temporarily discontinued in such cases. The AUC and C_{max} may be increased in patients with congestive heart failure)

» Diabetes or
» Hypoglycemia
(beta-adrenergic blocking agents may mask symptoms of hypoglycemia, especially tachycardia; insulin-induced hypoglycemia may be potentiated and the recovery of serum glucose levels may be delayed; in patients with diabetes and congestive heart failure, hyperglycemia may be worsened with use of carvedilol; blood glucose concentrations should be monitored at each dosage adjustment)

» Hyperthyroidism
(beta-adrenergic blocking agents, such as carvedilol, may mask symptoms of hyperthyroidism, such as tachycardia; abrupt withdrawal of beta-adrenergic blocking agents may potentiate symptoms of hyperthyroidism or precipitate thyroid storm)

Peripheral vascular disease
(carvedilol may precipitate or aggravate symptoms of arterial insufficiency)

Pheochromocytoma
(in patients with this condition, therapy with alpha-adrenergic blocking agents should be initiated prior to beta-adrenergic blocking therapy; although carvedilol has both alpha- and beta-adrenergic blocking activity, there is no experience with use of carvedilol in this condition)

Renal function impairment
(increases in carvedilol plasma concentrations of approximately 40 to 50%, based on mean AUC data, were reported in patients with moderate to severe renal function impairment; peak plasma levels were approximately 12 to 26% higher in patients with renal function impairment)

Patient monitoring

The following may be especially important in patient monitoring (other tests may be warranted in some patients, depending on condition; » = major clinical significance):

» Blood pressure determinations, standing systolic
(measurements should be taken about 1 hour after dosing as a guide for tolerance and after 7 to 14 days to determine whether a dose increase is needed; monitoring is recommended when carvedilol is used concurrently with calcium channel blocking agents)

Blood glucose concentrations
(for diabetic patients)

» Discontinuation of carvedilol therapy
(patients with coronary artery disease should be advised against abrupt discontinuation of carvedilol therapy; severe exacerbation of angina and occurrence of myocardial infarction and ventricular arrhythmias have been reported in angina patients following abrupt beta blocker therapy discontinuation; with planned discontinuation of carvedilol, patients should be carefully observed and physical activity limited; discontinuation should occur over 1 to 2 weeks if possible; if angina worsens or acute coronary insufficiency develops, prompt reinstitution of carvedilol is recommended, at least temporarily; because coronary artery disease is common and may be unrecognized, it may be prudent not to discontinue therapy abruptly even in patients treated only for hypertension or heart failure)

Electrocardiogram (ECG) determinations
(monitoring is recommended when carvedilol is used concurrently with calcium channel blocking agents, such as diltiazem and verapamil, because of the possibility of cardiac conduction disturbances)

» Heart rate determinations
(in clinical trials in hypertensive patients, heart rate decreased by 7.5 beats per minute with a 50-mg per day dose of carvedilol; if heart rate drops below 55 beats per minute, the carvedilol dosage should be reduced)

Hepatic function determinations
(monitoring may be necessary)

Renal function determinations
(monitoring may be necessary, especially in patients with congestive heart failure, during dosage increases)

Side/Adverse Effects

Use of carvedilol in patients with congestive heart failure has resulted in deterioration of renal function. Renal function returned to baseline when carvedilol was discontinued. Other rare side/adverse effects that have occurred with carvedilol therapy are complete atrioventricular (AV) block, bundle branch block, and myocardial ischemia.

The following side/adverse effects have been selected on the basis of their potential clinical significance (possible signs and symptoms in parentheses where appropriate)—not necessarily inclusive:

Those indicating need for medical attention

Incidence more frequent

Allergy—increased sensitivity to allergens; ***bradycardia*** (slow heartbeat)—incidence 2% in patients with hypertension and 9% in patients with congestive heart failure; ***chest pain***—incidence 14.4% in patients with congestive heart failure; ***dizziness***—incidence 6% in patients with hypertension and 32% in patients with congestive heart failure; ***dyspnea*** (shortness of breath); ***edema, generalized*** (generalized swelling); ***edema, peripheral*** (swelling of feet, ankles, or lower legs); ***hypotension*** (dizziness, lightheadedness, or fainting); ***pain***—incidence 8.6% in patients with congestive heart failure; ***syncope*** (fainting); ***weight increase***—incidence 9.7% in patients with congestive heart failure; may be a sign of fluid retention and worsening of heart failure

Note: *Hypotension* and postural hypotension were reported in 9.7% and *syncope* was reported in 3.4% of patients with congestive heart failure. In patients with hypertension, postural hypotension was reported in 1.8% and syncope in 0.1%. These problems may occur following the initial dose or at the time of a dosage increase.

Incidence less frequent

Albuminuria (cloudy urine); ***angina pectoris*** (arm, back or jaw pain; chest pain or discomfort; chest tightness or heaviness; fast or irregular heartbeat; shortness of breath; sweating; nausea); ***atrioventricular (AV) block*** (chest pain; dizziness; fainting, pounding, slow heartbeat; troubled breathing; unusual tiredness or weakness); ***cerebrovascular accident*** (blurred vision; headache sudden and severe; inability to speak; seizures; slurred speech; temporary blindness; weakness in arm and/or leg on one side of the body, sudden and severe); ***depression, mental; diabetes mellitus*** (blurred vision; dry mouth; fatigue; flushed, dry skin; fruit-like breath odor; increased hunger; increased thirst; increased urination; loss of consciousness; nausea; stomachache; sweating; troubled breathing; unexplained weight loss; vomiting); ***edema, dependent*** (swelling of legs and feet); ***fever***—incidence 3.1% in patients with congestive heart failure; ***fluid overload*** (decrease in amount of urine; noisy, rattling breathing; shortness of breath; swelling of fingers, hands, feet, or lower legs; troubled breathing at rest; weight gain); ***gout*** (ankle, knee or great toe joint pain; joint stiffness or swelling; lower back or side pain); ***hematuria*** (blood in urine); ***hepatic injury*** (pruritus; dark urine; persistent anorexia; yellow eyes or skin; influenza (flu)-like symptoms; right upper quadrant tenderness); ***hypercholesterolemia*** (large amount of cholesterol in the blood); ***hyperglycemia*** (abdominal pain; blurred vision; dry mouth; fatigue; flushed, dry skin; fruit-like breath odor; increased hunger; increased thirst; increased urination; nausea; sweating; troubled breathing; unexplained weight loss; vomiting); ***hyperkalemia*** (abdominal pain; confusion; irregular heartbeat; nausea or vomiting; nervousness; numbness or tingling in hands, feet, or lips; shortness of breath; difficult breathing; weakness or heaviness of legs); ***hypertension*** (blurred vision; dizziness; nervousness; headache; pounding in the ears; slow or fast heartbeat); ***hyperuricemia*** (joint pain, stiffness, or swelling; lower back, side, or stomach pain; swelling of feet or lower legs); ***hypervolemia*** (blurred vision; cough; dizziness; fast or slow heartbeat; headache; rapid breathing; shortness of breath; swelling of lower legs or arms; weight gain); ***hypoglycemia*** (anxiety; blurred vision; chills; cold sweats; coma; confusion; cool pale skin; depression; dizziness; fast heartbeat; headache; increased hunger; nausea; nervousness; nightmares; seizures; shakiness; slurred speech; unusual tiredness or weakness); ***hyponatremia*** (coma; confusion; convulsions; decreased urine output; dizziness; fast or irregular heartbeat; headache; increased thirst; muscle pain or cramps; nausea or vomiting; shortness of breath; swelling of face, ankles, or hands; unusual tiredness or weakness); ***hypovolemia*** (blurred vision; confusion; dizziness, faintness, or lightheadedness when getting up from a lying or sitting position suddenly; sweating; unusual tiredness or weakness); ***melena*** (bloody, black, or tarry stools); ***palpitation*** (irregular heartbeat); ***postural hypotension*** (chills; cold sweats; confusion; dizziness, faintness, or lightheadedness when getting up from lying or sitting position); ***purpura*** (pinpoint red or purple spots on skin); ***renal insufficiency*** (lower back/side pain; decreased frequency /amount of urine; bloody urine; increased thirst; loss of appetite; nausea; vomiting; unusual tiredness or weakness; swelling of face, fingers, lower legs; weight gain; troubled breathing; increased blood pressure); ***thrombocytopenia*** (unusual bleeding or bruising)

Note: Mild, reversible *hepatic injury* with minimal symptoms has been reported after short- and long-term therapy with carvedilol. Carvedilol should be discontinued if jaundice or laboratory evidence of hepatic injury occurs.

Incidence not determined—Observed during clinical practice; estimates of frequency can not be determined

Aplastic anemia (chest pain; chills; cough; fever; headache; shortness of breath; sores, ulcers, or white spots on lips or in mouth; swollen or painful glands; tightness in chest; unusual bleeding or bruising; unusual tiredness or weakness; wheezing)

Those indicating need for medical attention only if they continue or are bothersome

Incidence more frequent

Back pain; diarrhea; fatigue (unusual tiredness or weakness); ***paresthesia*** (prickling or tingling sensation)

Incidence less frequent

Abdominal pain; abnormal vision (changes in vision); ***arthralgia*** (joint pain); ***arthritis*** (pain, swelling, or redness in joint; muscle pain or stiffness; difficulty in moving); ***asthenia*** (lack or loss of strength); ***blurred vision; cough increased; flu syndrome*** (chills; cough; diarrhea; fever; general feeling of discomfort or illness; headache; joint pain; loss of appetite; muscle aches and pains; nausea; runny nose; shivering; sore throat; sweating; trouble sleeping; unusual tiredness or weakness; vomiting); ***gastrointestinal pain*** (abdominal or stomach pain; diarrhea; nausea; vomiting); ***glycosuria*** (sugar in the urine); ***headache; hypesthesia*** (burning, crawling, itching, numbness, prickling, "pins and needles", or tingling feelings); ***hypotonia*** (unusual weak feeling; loss of strength or energy; muscle pain or weakness); ***impotence*** (loss in sexual ability, desire, drive, or performance; decreased interest in sexual intercourse; inability to have or keep an erection); ***insomnia*** (trouble in sleeping); ***lacrimation, decreased*** (decreased tearing)—in patients who wear contact lenses; ***myalgia*** (muscle pain); ***malaise*** (general feeling of discomfort or illness; unusual tiredness or weakness); ***muscle cramps; nausea; periodontitis*** (bleeding gums; loose teeth; persistent breath odor or bad taste in your mouth; redness and swelling of gums;); ***peripheral vascular disorder*** (cold hands and feet); ***pharyngitis*** (sore throat); ***rales*** (small clicking, bubbling, or rattling sounds in the lung when listening with a stethoscope); ***rhinitis*** (stuffy or runny nose); ***somnolence*** (sleepiness or unusual drowsiness); ***sweating, increased; vertigo*** (dizziness or lightheadedness; feeling of constant movement of self or surroundings, sensation of spinning); ***vomiting; weight loss***

Overdose

For specific information on the agents used in the management of carvedilol overdose, see:

- *Aminophylline* in *Bronchodilators, Theophylline (Systemic)* monograph;
- *Atropine* in *Anticholinergics/Antispasmodics (Systemic)* monograph;
- *Bronchodilators, Adrenergic (Inhalation-Local)* monograph;
- *Bronchodilators, Adrenergic (Systemic)* monograph;
- *Clonazepam* and *Diazepam* in
- *Benzodiazepines (Systemic)* monograph;
- *Dobutamine*,
- *Epinephrine*, *Isoproterenol*, and *Norepinephrine* in *Sympathomimetic Agents—Cardiovascular Use (Parenteral-Systemic)* monograph; and/or
- *Glucagon (Systemic)* monograph.

For more information on the management of overdose or unintentional ingestion, **contact a Poison Control Center** (see *Poison Control Center Listing*).

Clinical effects of overdose

The following effects have been selected on the basis of their potential clinical significance (possible signs and symptoms in parentheses where appropriate)—not necessarily inclusive:

Acute and chronic

Bradycardia, severe; bronchospasm; cardiac arrest; cardiac insufficiency; cardiogenic shock; hypotension, severe; lapses of consciousness; respiratory problems; seizures, generalized; vomiting

Treatment of overdose

For symptoms of shock (with severe intoxication), treatment with antidotes must be continued for an appropriate length of time consistent with the 7- to 10-hour half-life of carvedilol. Treatment is symptomatic and supportive and may include the following:

Monitoring—

The patient should be placed in a supine position and observed and treated under intensive care conditions.

To decrease absorption—

If overdose was recently ingested, gastric lavage or drug-induced emesis may be used.

Specific treatment—

For excessive bradycardia—Intravenous atropine may be used. If bradycardia is resistant to therapy, pacemaker therapy is recommended.

For bronchospasm—Intravenous or inhaled beta-adrenergic sympathomimetics or intravenous aminophylline is recommended.

For cardiovascular support—Intravenous glucagon or sympathomimetics such as dobutamine, isoproterenol, or epinephrine may be used.

For peripheral vasodilation—Epinephrine or norepinephrine with continuous monitoring is recommended.

For seizures—Intravenous diazepam or clonazepam is recommended.

Supportive care—

Patients in whom intentional overdose is confirmed or suspected should be referred for psychiatric consultation.

Patient Consultation

As an aid to patient consultation, refer to *Advice for the Patient, Carvedilol (Systemic)*.

In providing consultation, consider emphasizing the following selected information (» = major clinical significance):

Before using this medication

» Conditions affecting use, especially:

Hypersensitivity to carvedilol or any of its components

Pregnancy—Risk/benefit considerations

Breast-feeding—Not recommended in mothers who are breast-feeding because of potential for serious reaction in nursing infant

Other medications, especially sulfonylurea antidiabetic agents; calcium channel blocking agents, especially diltiazem or verapamil; cyclosporine; or insulin

Other medical problems, especially bronchial asthma or related bronchospastic conditions; atrioventricular block, 2nd- or 3rd-degree; bradycardia, severe; history of severe anaphylactic reaction to a variety of allergens; bronchospastic conditions, nonallergic; cardiac failure, decompensated, NYHA class IV; cardiogenic shock; diabetes or hypoglycemia; hepatic function impairment, clinically evident; hyperthyroidism; or sick sinus syndrome, without a pacemaker

Proper use of this medication

Taking medication at the same time each day to maintain the therapeutic effect

Taking medication with food

Not interrupting or discontinuing medication without consulting the physician

» Proper dosing

Missed dose: Taking as soon as possible; not taking if almost time for next dose; not doubling doses

» Proper storage

Precautions while using this medication

Making regular visits to physician to check progress

Not taking other medications unless discussed with physician

Caution when driving or doing other tasks requiring alertness, because of the possible dizziness, lightheadedness, or fainting due to postural hypotension

Caution when standing quickly because of possible drop in blood pressure, which may result in dizziness or fainting; sitting or lying down may help alleviate these symptoms

Checking with physician if experiencing dizziness or faintness; a dosage adjustment may be necessary

Caution if any kind of surgery (including dental surgery) or emergency treatment is required

For diabetic patients—Checking with physician if any changes in blood sugar concentrations occur

For congestive heart failure patients—Checking with physician if experiencing weight gain or increasing shortness of breath, because of possible worsening of heart failure

For patients who wear contact lenses—Checking with physician if decreased lacrimation occurs

Side/adverse effects

Signs of potential side effects, especially allergy; bradycardia; chest pain; dizziness; dyspnea; edema, generalized; edema, peripheral; hypotension; pain; syncope; weight increase; fever; albuminuria; angina pectoris; atrioventricular (AV) block; cerebrovascular accident; depression, mental; diabetes mellitus; edema, dependent; fluid overload; gout; hematuria; hepatic injury; hypercholesterolemia; hyperglycemia; hyperkalemia; hypertension; hyperuricemia; hypervolemia; hypoglycemia; hyponatremia; hypovolemia; melena; palpitation; postural hypotension; purpura; renal insufficiency; and thrombocytopenia

Signs of potential side effects observed during clinical practice, especially aplastic anemia

General Dosing Information

Dosage must be individualized and closely monitored by a physician during up-titration. Dosage must be adjusted to meet the individual requirements of each patient, on the basis of clinical response.

When concurrent carvedilol and clonidine treatment is to be discontinued, carvedilol should be discontinued before clonidine is discontinued. Clonidine should be withdrawn gradually; dosage should be decreased over several days.

When carvedilol is discontinued, its dosage should be tapered over a 1- to 2-week period, especially in patients with ischemic heart disease.

If the patient's pulse rate drops to below 55 beats per minute, the dosage of carvedilol should be reduced.

Hypotensive effects may be additive and orthostatic hypotension may be exaggerated when carvedilol therapy is added to diuretic therapy, or vice versa.

Diet/Nutrition

Taking carvedilol with food may slow the rate of absorption and minimize the risk of orthostatic hypotension.

Oral Dosage Forms

CARVEDILOL TABLETS

Usual adult dose

Congestive heart failure—

Initial: Oral, 3.125 mg two times a day for two weeks, taken with food. If tolerated, the dose may be increased to 6.25 mg two times a day. The dosage may then be doubled every two weeks to the highest dose tolerated by the patient.

At each dosage increase, the patient should be observed for one hour for signs of dizziness or lightheadedness.

In patients currently receiving digitalis, diuretics, and/or angiotensin-converting enzyme (ACE) inhibitors, the dosages of these medications should be stabilized prior to starting carvedilol therapy. Before each carvedilol dosage increase, tolerability of carvedilol should be determined by evaluation of the patient for symptoms of worsening heart failure, vasodilation (dizziness, lightheadedness, symptomatic hypotension), or bradycardia. Transient worsening of heart failure may be treated with increased doses of diuretics or it may be necessary to lower the carvedilol dose or temporarily discontinue it. Symptoms of vasodilation may respond to a reduction in the dose of diuretics or ACE inhibitors, and, if still not relieved, a reduction in the carvedilol dose. The dose of carvedilol should not be increased until symptoms of worsening heart failure or vasodilation have stabilized.

Hypertension—

Initial: Oral, 6.25 mg two times a day, taken with food. Dose should be maintained for seven to fourteen days and then increased to

12.5 mg two times a day, if tolerated, if blood pressure is not adequately controlled (based on trough blood pressure). If after the new dose is maintained for seven to fourteen days blood pressure is still not controlled, the dose may be increased to 25 mg two times a day, if tolerated. Standing systolic blood pressure taken one hour after dosing may be used as a guide for tolerance.

Maintenance: Oral, 6.25 to 25 mg two times a day. The full antihypertensive effect occurs within seven to fourteen days.

Left ventricular dysfunction, post-myocardial infarction (treatment)—

Initial: Oral, 6.25 mg twice daily. Dose should be increased after 3 to 10 days, based on tolerability, to 12.5 mg twice daily, then again to the target dose of 25 mg twice daily. A lower starting dosage may be used (3.125 mg twice daily) and/or, the rate of up-titration may be slowed if clinically indicated (e.g., due to low blood pressure or heart rate, or fluid retention). Patients should be maintained on lower doses if higher doses are not tolerated.

Note: Carvedilol should not be given to patients with severe hepatic impairment.

Usual adult prescribing limits

Congestive heart failure—

25 mg two times a day in patients weighing less than 85 kg (187 lbs) and 50 mg two times a day in patients weighing more than 85 kg.

Hypertension—

25 mg two times a day.

Usual pediatric dose

Children younger than 18 years of age—Safety and efficacy have not been established.

Strength(s) usually available

U.S.—

3.125 mg (Rx) [*Coreg*].
6.25 mg (Rx) [*Coreg*].
12.5 mg (Rx) [*Coreg*].
25 mg (Rx) [*Coreg*].

Packaging and storage

Store between 15 and 30 °C (59 and 86 °F) in a tight, light-resistant container. Protect from moisture.

Auxiliary labeling

- Do not take other medicines without your doctor's advice.
- Take with food.

Revised: 06/08/2005
Developed: 08/13/1998

CASANTHRANOL—See *Laxatives (Local)*

CASCARA SAGRADA—See *Laxatives (Local)*

CASPOFUNGIN Systemic

VA CLASSIFICATION (Primary): AM700

Commonly used brand name(s): *Cancidas*.

Note: For a listing of dosage forms and brand names by country availability, see *Dosage Forms* section(s).

Category

Antifungal (systemic).

Indications

General Considerations

Caspofungin is active *in vitro* against *Aspergillus fumigatus, A. flavus, A. terreus. Candida albicans, C. glabrata, C guilliermondii, C. krusei, C. parapsilosis*, and *C. tropicalis*

In vitro resistance to caspofungin by *Aspergillus* species has not been studied. Clinical experience is limited, however, drug resistance has not been seen in patients with invasive aspergillosis.

Accepted

Aspergillosis, invasive (treatment)—Caspofungin is indicated in the treatment of invasive aspergillosis in patients who are refractory to or intolerant of other therapies, including amphotericin B (lipid and nonlipid formulations) and/or itraconazole.

Candidiasis, disseminated (treatment) or
Candidiasis, esophageal (treatment) or
Candidiasis, intra-abdominal abscesses (treatment) or
Candidiasis, peritonitis (treatment) or
Candidiasis, pleural space infections (treatment)—Caspofungin is indicated for the treatment of candidemia and the following *Candidiasis* infections: esophageal, intra-abdominal abscesses, peritonitis, and plural space infections.

Fungal infection, presumed, in febrile neutropenia (treatment)—Caspofungin is indicated for the empirical therapy for presumed fungal infections in febrile, neutropenic patients.

Acceptance not established

The safety and efficacy of caspofungin as initial therapy for invasive aspergillosis has not been established.

Caspofungin has not been studied in endocarditis, osteomyelitis, and meningitis due to *Candida*.

Pharmacology/Pharmacokinetics

Physicochemical characteristics

Molecular weight—1213.42.

Solubility—Freely soluble in water and methanol, slightly soluble in ethanol.

pH—approximately 6.6

Mechanism of action/Effect

Caspofungin inhibits the synthesis of β (1,3)-D-glucan, an essential component of the cell wall of filamentous fungi.

Distribution

Following administration of a single 70-mg irradiated dose, approximately 92% of the administered radioactivity was distributed into tissues within 36 to 48 hours.

Distribution into red blood cells is minimal.

Protein binding

Very high (97%); predominantly to albumin

Biotransformation

Slowly metabolized by hydrolysis and N-acetylation; also undergoes spontaneous chemical degradation and further hydrolysis to constitutive amino acids and their degredates, including dihydroxyhomotyrosine and N-acetyl-dihydroxyhomotyrosine.

Half-life

Initial—9 to 11 hours (β phase)
Additional—40 to 50 hours (γ phase)

Elimination

Fecal—35% as drug or metabolites.
Renal—41% as drug (approximately 1.4% unchanged) or metabolites.
In dialysis—Not removed by hemodialysis.

Precautions to Consider

Carcinogenicity

No long term studies have been done in humans or animals to evaluate the carcinogenic potential of caspofungin.

Mutagenicity

Caspofungin did not show mutagenic or genotoxic potential in the following *in vitro* assays: bacterial (Ames) and mammalian cell mutagenesis assays, the alkaline elution/rat hepatocyte DNA strand break test, and the chromosome aberration assay in Chinese hamster ovary cells.

Caspofungin was not genotoxic when assessed in the mouse bone marrow chromosomal test at doses up to 12.5 mg per kg of body weight (mg/kg) (equivalent to a human dose of 1 mg/kg based on body surface area comparisons), administered intravenously.

Pregnancy/Reproduction

Fertility—Fertility and reproductive performance were not affected by the intravenous administration of caspofungin to rats at doses up to 5 mg/kg. At 5 mg/kg, exposures were similar to those seen in patients treated with the 70-mg dose.

Pregnancy—Adequate and well-controlled studies have not been done in humans. Caspofungin should be used during pregnancy only if potential benefit justifies potential risk to the fetus.

Caspofungin crosses the placenta in rats and rabbits and was detected in the plasma of fetuses of pregnant animals who were dosed with caspofungin.

Caspofungin was shown to be embryotoxic in rats and rabbits. Findings in rats included incomplete ossification of the skull and torso and an increased incidence of cervical rib. Increased incidence of incomplete ossifications of the talus and calcaneus was seen in rabbits. Increases in resorptions in rats and rabbits and periimplantation losses in rats were also seen. These findings were seen at doses which produced exposures similar to those in patients who were treated with a 70-mg dose.

FDA Pregnancy Category C.

Breast-feeding
It is not known whether caspofungin is distributed into human breast milk. Because caspofungin was found in the breast milk of lactating rats it should be used with caution when administered to nursing women.

Pediatrics
No information is available on the relationship of age to the effects of caspofungin in the pediatric population. Safety and efficacy have not been established.

Geriatrics
Although appropriate studies on the relationship of age to the effects of caspofungin have not been performed in the geriatric population, no geriatrics-specific problems have been documented to date. However, some elderly patients may be more sensitive to the effects of caspofungin, which may require caution in the use of this medication.

Pharmacogenetics
Plasma concentrations of caspofungin in healthy men and women were similar following a single 70-mg dose. After 13 daily 50-mg doses, plasma concentrations were slightly elevated in women. No dosage adjustment is needed based on gender.

No clinically significant differences were found among Caucasians, Blacks and Hispanics. No dosage adjustment is needed based on race.

Drug interactions and/or related problems
The following drug interactions and/or related problems have been selected on the basis of their potential clinical significance (possible mechanism in parentheses where appropriate)—not necessarily inclusive (» = major clinical significance):

Note: Combinations containing any of the following medications, depending on the amount present, may also interact with this medication.

» Cyclosporine
(concomitant administration can cause elevated alanine aminotransferase [ALT] and aspartate aminotransferase [AST] values/ ould only be used concomitantly in those patients for whom the potential benefit outweighs the potential risk; patients who develop abnormal liver function tests with concomitant therapy should be monitored and risk/benefit assessment of continued therapy evaluated)

Carbamazepine or
Dexamethasone or
Efavirenz or
Nevirapine or
Phenytoin or
Rifampin
(concomitant use with these medications may result in clinically significant reductions in caspofungin concentrations; these interactions are theoretical based upon linear regression analyses and there are presently no data from clinical studies to support the existence of this interaction; however, it may be necessary to increase the dosage of caspofungin in patients who do not respond to therapy)

» Tacrolimus
(concomitant use may result in decreased tacrolimus blood concentrations; monitoring of tacrolimus concentrations is recommended, and dosage adjustments may be required)

Laboratory value alterations
The following have been selected on the basis of their potential clinical significance (possible effect in parentheses where appropriate)—not necessarily inclusive (» = major clinical significance).

With physiology/laboratory test values
Alanine aminotransferase and
Alkaline phosphatase and
Aspartate aminotransferase and
Bilirubin, serum and
Eosinophil count
(values may be increased)

Bicarbonate, serum and
Magnesium, serum and
Potassium, serum
(concentration may be decreased)

Hematocrit and
Hemoglobin
(value may be decreased)

Blood urea
Creatinine, serum and
Protein, urine and
Red blood cells, urine
(concentrations may be increased)

Medical considerations/Contraindications
The medical considerations/contraindications included have been selected on the basis of their potential clinical significance (reasons given in parentheses where appropriate)—not necessarily inclusive (» = major clinical significance).

Except under special circumstances, this medication should not be used when the following medical problem exists:

» Hypersensitivity to any component of this product

Risk-benefit should be considered when the following medical problem exists:

» Hepatic function impairment, moderate to severe
(caspofungin plasma concentrations may be increased; dosage adjustment is recommended in patients with moderate hepatic function impairment [Child-Pugh score of 7 to 9]; there has been no clinical experience with caspofungin use in patients with severe hepatic function impairment [Child-Pugh score > 9])

Patient monitoring
The following may be especially important in patient monitoring (other tests may be warranted in some patients, depending on condition; » = major clinical significance):

Hepatic function
(patients who develop abnormal liver function tests during caspofungin therapy should be monitored for evidence of worsening hepatic function and assessed for risk/benefit of continuing therapy)

» Tacrolimus concentrations
(because concurrent use of caspofungin and tacrolimus may result in decreased tacrolimus blood concentrations, standard monitoring is recommended in patients receiving these medications concurrently)

Side/Adverse Effects
Note: Possible histamine-mediated symptoms, including reports of rash, facial swelling, pruritus, sensation of warmth, or bronchospasm have been reported in clinical studies. Anaphylaxis has been reported during administration of caspofungin.

An isolated, serious adverse experience of *hyperbilirubinemia* was reported and considered possibly related to caspofungin.

The following side/adverse effects have been selected on the basis of their potential clinical significance (possible signs and symptoms in parentheses where appropriate)—not necessarily inclusive:

Those indicating need for medical attention
Incidence more frequent

Infused vein complications (pain or redness at site of injection); ***phlebitis/thrombophlebitis*** (changes in skin color; pain, tenderness, or swelling of foot or leg)

Incidence less frequent

Anemia (pale skin; troubled breathing with exertion; unusual bleeding or bruising; unusual tiredness or weakness); ***edema, facial*** (swelling or puffiness of face); ***hyperbilirubinemia*** (yellow eyes or skin); ***hypokalemia*** (convulsions; decreased urine; dry mouth; irregular heartbeat; increased thirst; loss of appetite; mood changes; muscle pain or cramps; nausea or vomiting; numbness or tingling in hands, feet, or lips; shortness of breath; unusual tiredness or weakness); ***renal insufficiency*** (lower back/side pain; decreased frequency/amount of urine; bloody urine; increased thirst; loss of appetite; nausea; vomiting; unusual tiredness or weakness; swelling of face, fingers, lower legs; weight gain; troubled breathing; increased blood pressure)

Incidence not determined—Observed during clinical practice, estimates of frequency can not be determined

Hepatic dysfunction (dark urine; light-colored stools; loss of appetite; nausea and vomiting; unusual tiredness; yellow eyes or skin; fever with or without chills; stomach pain); ***hypercalcemia*** (abdominal pain; confusion; constipation; depression; dry mouth; headache; incoherent speech; increased urination; loss of appetite; metallic taste; muscle weakness; nausea; thirst; unusual tiredness; vomiting; weight loss); ***peripheral edema*** (bloating or swelling of face, arms, hands, lower legs, or feet; rapid weight gain; tingling of hands or feet; unusual weight gain or loss)

Those indicating need for medical attention only if they continue or are bothersome
Incidence less frequent

Fever; flushing; nausea; vomiting

Patient Consultation

As an aid to patient consultation, refer to *Advice for the Patient, Caspofungin (Systemic).*

In providing consultation, consider emphasizing the following selected information (» = major clinical significance):

Before using this medication

» Conditions affecting use, especially:
Hypersensitivity to caspofungin or any ingredients in the formulation.
Pregnancy—Risk/benefit should be considered in administering to a pregnant woman
Breast-feeding—Because many drugs are distributed into human milk, caution should be exercised when administering caspofungin to a nursing woman.
Other medications, especially cyclosporine or tacrolimus
Other medical problems, especially moderate to severe hepatic function impairment

Proper use of this medication

» Proper dosing

Side/adverse effects

Signs of potential side effects, especially infused vein complications, phlebitis/thrombophlebitis, anemia, facial edema, hyperbilirubinemia, hypokalemia, or renal insufficiency

Signs of potential side effects observed during clinical practice, especially hepatic dysfunction, hypercalcemia, and peripheral edema

General Dosing Information

Caspofungin should be administered by slow intravenous infusion over a period of 1 hour.

Caspofungin is NOT for direct intravenous injection.

The duration of therapy should be individualized based upon the severity of the patient's disease, recovery from immunosuppression, and clinical response. In clinical trials, patient were treated for a mean of 33.7 (range 1 to 162) days.

Parenteral Dosage Forms

CASPOFUNGIN ACETATE FOR INJECTION

Usual adult dose

Antifungal—
Intravenous infusion, Initial loading dose on day one is 70 mg, followed by 50 mg daily dose thereafter.

Candidiasis, disseminated (treatment) or
Candidiasis, intra-abdominal abscesses (treatment) or
Candidiasis, peritonitis (treatment) or
Candidiasis, pleural space infections (treatment)—
Intravenous infusion, Initial loading dose on day one is 70 mg, followed by 50 mg daily dose thereafter. Generally, therapy should continue for at least 14 days after the last positive culture.

Candidiasis, esophageal—
Intravenous infusion, 50 mg daily dose. A 70-mg loading dose has not been studied with this indication.

Fungal infection, presumed, in febrile neutropenia (treatment)—
Intravenous infusion, Initial loading dose on day one is 70 mg, followed by 50 mg daily dose thereafter. Treatment should continue for at least 7 days after neutropenia and clinical symptoms are resolved. If clinical response warrants, daily dose may be increased to 70 mg.

Note: Coadministration with efavirenz, nevirapine, phenytoin, rifampin, dexamethasone, or carbamazepine may warrant an increase in the daily dose to 70 mg, following the usual 70-mg loading dose.

In patients with moderate hepatic function impairment (Child-Pugh score of 7 to 9), the daily dose should be decreased to 35 mg, following the usual 70-mg loading dose.

Usual adult prescribing limits

70 mg daily.

Usual pediatric dose

Safety and efficacy have not been established.

Usual geriatric dose

See *Usual adult dose.*

Usual geriatric prescribing limits

See *Usual adult prescribing limits*

Strength(s) usually available

U.S.—
50 mg (Rx) [*Cancidas* (glacial acetic acid; 26 mg mannitol; sodium hydroxide; 39 mg sucrose)].
70 mg (Rx) [*Cancidas* (glacial acetic acid; 36 mg mannitol; sodium hydroxide; 54 mg sucrose)].

Packaging and storage

Store lyophilized cake/powder between 2 and 8 °C (36 and 46 °F)
Store reconstituted concentrate and infusion solution at or below 25 °C (77 °F).

Preparation of dosage form

Preparation of the 70 mg Day 1 loading-dose infusion
- Equilibrate the refrigerated vial to room temperature.
- Aseptically add 10.5 mL of 0.9% Sodium Chloride Injection into the vial. This reconstituted solution can be stored for up to one hour at ≤25°C (≤77°F).
- Aseptically transfer 10 mL of the reconstituted solution to an IV bag (or bottle) containing 250 mL 0.9% Sodium Chloride Injection. (If a 70 mg vial is unavailable see the instructions below for *Alternative Infusion Preparation Methods, Preparation of a 70 mg Day 1 Loading Dose from two 50 mg vials.*

Preparation of the daily 50 mg infusion
- Equilibrate the refrigerated vial to room temperature.
- Aseptically add 10.5 mL of 0.9% Sodium Chloride Injection into the vial. This reconstituted solution can be stored for up to one hour at ≤25°C (≤77°F).
- Aseptically transfer 10 mL of the reconstituted solution to an IV bag (or bottle) containing 250 mL 0.9% Sodium Chloride Injection. (If a reduced infusion volume is medically necessary see the instructions below for *Alternative Infusion Preparation Methods, Preparation of a 50 mg daily doses at reduced volume.*

Alternative Infusion Preparation Methods—Preparation of the 70 mg 1 Day loading dose from two 50 mg vials
- Reconstitute two 50 mg vials with 10.5 mL of diluent each.
- Aseptically transfer a total of 14 mL of the reconstituted solution from the two vials into 250 mL of 0.9% Sodium Chloride Injection.

Alternative Infusion Preparation Methods—Preparation of the 50 mg daily doses at reduced volume
- When medically necessary, the 50-mg daily doses can be prepared by adding 10 mL of reconstituted solution to 100 mL of 0.9% Sodium Chloride Injection.

Alternative Infusion Preparation Methods—Preparation of the 35 mg daily dose for patients with moderate Hepatic Insufficiency
- Reconstitute one 50 mg vial (see above *Preparation of the daily 50 mg infusion)*
- Aseptically transfer 7 mL of the reconstituted solution from the vial to 250 mL of 0.9% Sodium Chloride Injection, or, if medically necessary, to 100 mL of 0.9% Sodium Chloride Injection.

Stability

Reconstituted concentrate—may be stored below 25°C (77°F) for one hour prior to the preparation of the patient infusion solution.
Diluted product—final patient infusion solution in the IV bag or bottle can be stored below 25°C (77°F) for 24 hours.

Incompatibilities

Do not mix or co-infuse with any other medications. Do not use diluents containing dextrose.

Caution

Do not use if solution is cloudy or has precipitated. Visually inspect the reconstituted solution prior to infusion.

Revised: 09/08/2005
Developed: 03/19/2001

CASTOR OIL—See *Laxatives (Local)*

CEFACLOR—See *Cephalosporins (Systemic)*

CEFADROXIL—See *Cephalosporins (Systemic)*

CEFAMANDOLE—See *Cephalosporins (Systemic)*

CEFAZOLIN—See *Cephalosporins (Systemic)*

CEFDINIR—See *Cephalosporins (Systemic)*

CEFDITOREN Systemic

VA CLASSIFICATION (Primary): AM117

Commonly used brand name(s): *Spectracef*.

NOTE: The *Cefditoren (Systemic)* monograph is maintained on the *USP DI* electronic data base. A copy of the most recent revision of the complete monograph can be accessed on the *USP DI* Updates Online website. See the front cover of book for details on accessing the site.

For information on the specific components of this combination, see the *USP DI* monographs for *Cephalosporins (Systemic)*.

The information that follows is selectively abstracted from the complete monograph and is provided to facilitate drug use review and patient counseling.

Note: For a listing of dosage forms and brand names by country availability, see *Dosage Forms* section(s).

Category

Antibacterial (systemic).

Indications

Accepted

Bacterial exacerbation of chronic bronchitis, acute (treatment)—Cefditoren is indicated for the treatment of acute bacterial exacerbation of chronic bronchitis caused by *Haemophilus influenzae* (including β-lactamase-producing strains), *Haemophilus parainfluenzae* (including β-lactamase-producing strains), *Streptococcus pneumoniae* (penicillin-susceptible strains only), or *Moraxella catarrhalis* (including β-lactamase-producing strains)

Pharyngitis (treatment) or
Tonsillitis (treatment)—Cefditoren is indicated for the treatment of pharyngitis and tonsillitis caused by *Streptococcus pyogenes*.

Skin and skin–structure infections, uncomplicated (treatment)—Cefditoren is indicated for the treatment of uncomplicated skin and skin–structure infections caused by *Staphylococcus aureus* (including β-lactamase-producing strains) or *Streptococcus pyogenes*.

Unaccepted

Cefditoren has not been studied for the prevention of rheumatic fever following *Streptococcus pyogenes* pharyngitis or tonsillitis.

Patient Consultation

As an aid to patient consultation, refer to *Advice for the Patient, Cefditoren (Systemic)*.

In providing consultation, consider emphasizing the following selected information (» = major clinical significance):

Before using this medication

» Conditions affecting use, especially:
  Hypersensitivity to cefditoren
  Allergies to cefditoren, other cephalosporins,
  Allergies to any other substances, such as milk protein, foods, preservatives, or dyes.
  Other medical problems, especially carnitine deficiency or renal function impairment

Proper use of this medication

Taking medication with food
» Compliance with full course of therapy
» Importance of not missing doses and of taking at evenly spaced times
» Proper dosing
Missed dose: Taking as soon as possible; not taking if almost time for next scheduled dose; not doubling doses
Proper storage

Precautions while using this medication

Checking with physician if no improvement of symptoms within a few days
» For severe diarrhea, checking with physician before taking any antidiarrheals; checking with physician or pharmacist if mild diarrhea continues or worsens

Side/adverse effects

Signs of potential side effects, especially leukopenia, pseudomembranous colitis, or thrombocythemia.

Oral Dosage Forms

CEFDITOREN PIVOXIL TABLETS

Usual Adult and Adolescent Dose

Bacterial exacerbation of chronic bronchitis, acute—
  Oral, 400 mg twice daily for 10 days

Pharyngitis or
Skin and skin structure infections, uncomplicated or
Tonsillitis—
  Oral, 200 mg twice daily for 10 days.
  Renal function impairment, moderate (creatinine clearance: 30 to 49 mL per minute per 1.73 square meters of body surface area): It is recommended that not more than 200 mg twice daily be administered to patients with moderate renal impairment.
  Renal function impairment, severe (creatinine clearance less than 30 mL/minute/1.73 m^2: It is recommended that not more than 200 mg daily be administered to patients with moderate renal impairment.

Usual Pediatric Dose

Infants and children up to 12 years of age—Safety and efficacy have not been established.

Children 12 years of age or older—See usual adult and adolescent dose.

Usual Geriatric Dose

See *Usual adult and adolescent dose*.

Strength(s) usually available

U.S.—
  200 mg (Rx) [*Spectracef* (croscarmellose sodium; carnauba wax; D&C Red No. 27; D-mannitol; FD&C Blue No. 1; hydroxypropyl cellulose; hydroxypropyl methylcellulose; magnesium stearate; polyethylene glycol; propylene glycol; shellac; sodium caseinate; sodium tripolyphosphate; titanium dioxide)].

Auxiliary labeling

• Take with food

Revised: 02/06/2002
Developed: 12/20/2001

CEFEPIME—See *Cephalosporins (Systemic)*

CEFIXIME—See *Cephalosporins (Systemic)*

CEFONICID—See *Cephalosporins (Systemic)*

CEFOPERAZONE—See *Cephalosporins (Systemic)*

CEFOTAXIME—See *Cephalosporins (Systemic)*

CEFOTETAN—See *Cephalosporins (Systemic)*

CEFOXITIN—See *Cephalosporins (Systemic)*

CEFPODOXIME—See *Cephalosporins (Systemic)*

CEFPROZIL—See *Cephalosporins (Systemic)*

CEFTAZIDIME—See *Cephalosporins (Systemic)*

CEFTIBUTEN—See *Cephalosporins (Systemic)*

CEFTIZOXIME—See *Cephalosporins (Systemic)*

CEFTRIAXONE—See *Cephalosporins (Systemic)*

CEFUROXIME—See *Cephalosporins (Systemic)*

CEFUROXIME Systemic

VA CLASSIFICATION (Primary): AM117

Commonly used brand name(s): *Zinacef*.

Note: For a listing of dosage forms and brand names by country availability, see *Dosage Forms* section(s).

Category

Antibacterial (Systemic).

Indications

Accepted

Bone and joint infections (treatment)—Cefuroxime is indicated for the treatment of bone and joint infections caused by *Staphylococcus aureus* (penicillinase and non-penicillinase producing strains).

Gonorrhea (treatment)—Cefuroxime is indicated for the treatment of uncomplicated and disseminated gonococcal infections due to *Neisseria gonorrhoeae* (penicillinase and non-penicillinase producing strains) in both males and females.

Lower respiratory tract infections, including pneumonia (treatment)—Cefuroxime is indicated for the treatment of lower respiratory tract infections, including pneumonia, caused by *Streptococcus pneumoniae, Haemophilus influenzae* (including ampicillin-resistant strains), *Klebsiella* spp., *Staphylococcus aureus* (penicillinase and non-penicillinase producing strains), *Streptococcus pyogenes*, and *Escherichia coli*.

Meningitis (treatment)—Cefuroxime is indicated for the treatment of Meningitis caused by *Streptococcus pneumoniae, Haemophilus influenzae* (including ampicillin-resistant strains), *Neisseria meningitidis*, and *Staphylococcus aureus* (penicillinase and non-penicillinase producing strains).

Septicemia (treatment)[1]—Cefuroxime is indicated for the treatment of Septicemia caused by *Staphylococcus aureus* (penicillinase and non-penicillinase producing strains), *Streptococcus pneumoniae, Escherichia coli, Haemophilus influenzae* (including ampicillin-resistant strains), and *Klebsiella* spp.

Skin and Skin-Structure Infections (treatment)—Cefuroxime is indicated for the treatment of skin and skin-structure infections caused by *Staphylococcus aureus* (penicillinase and non-penicillinase producing strains), *Streptococcus pyogenes, Escherichia coli, Klebsiella* spp., and *Enterobacter* spp.[1]

Urinary Tract Infections (treatment)—Cefuroxime is indicated for the treatment of urinary tract infections caused by *Escherichia coli*, and *Klebsiella* spp.

Note: The preoperative prophylactic administration of cefuroxime may prevent the growth of susceptible disease-causing bacteria and thereby may reduce the incidence of certain postoperative infections in patients undergoing surgical procedures that are classified as clean-contaminated or potentially contaminated procedures.

In the absence of microbiological study results, cefuroxime may be started. Cefuroxime has been shown to be effective in treating susceptible mixed infections of strains of both aerobic and anaerobic organisms.

In cases of confirmed or suspected gram positive or gram negative sepsis or in patients with other serious infections in which the causative organism has not been identified, cefuroxime may be used concomitantly with an aminoglycoside.

The perioperative use of cefuroxime has been effective during open heart surgery.

Unaccepted

Gram positive aerobes—Most strains of enterococci, e.g., *Enterococcus faecalis* (formerly *Streptococcus faecalis*), are resistant to cefuroxime. Methicillin-resistant staphylococci and *Listeria monocytogenes* are resistant to cefuroxime.

Gram negative aerobes—Some strains of *Morganella morganii, Enterobacter cloacae* and *Citrobacter* spp. have been shown by ***in vitro*** tests to be resistant to cefuroxime. ***Pseudomonas, Campylobacter*** spp., ***Acinetobacter calcoaceticus*** and most strains of *Serratia* spp. and ***Proteus vulgaris*** are resistant to most first and second generation cephalosporins.

Anaerobes—***Clostridium difficile*** and most strains of ***Bacteroides fragilis*** are resistant to cefuroxime.

[1]Not included in Canadian product labeling.

Pharmacology/Pharmacokinetics

Physicochemical characteristics

Molecular weight—446.4.

pH—

6 to 8.5–freshly reconstituted solutions

5 to 7.5–thawed solutions.

Osmolality—Solution 300 mOsmol per kg

Mechanism of action/Effect

Bactericidal against a wide range of gram positive and gram negative aerobes and anaerobic organisms; the action of cefuroxime results from inhibition of cell-wall synthesis and is highly stable in the presence of beta-lactamases. Cefuroxime is detectable in therapeutic concentrations in cerebrospinal fluid, pleural fluid, joint fluid, bile, sputum, bone and aqueous humor.

Protein binding

Moderate: 50% to serum protein

Half-life

80 minutes following either intramuscular or intravenous injections

There was no evidence of accumulation of cefuroxime in the serum following intravenous administration of 1.5 gm dose every 8 hours to normal volunteers.

Time to peak concentration

Intramuscular: 45 minutes following a 750 mg dose

Intravenous: 15 minutes following doses of 750 mg and 1.5 gm

Peak serum concentration

Intramuscular: 27 mcg per mL following a 750 mg dose

Intravenous: 50 mcg per mL following a 750 mg dose; 100 mcg per mL following a 1.5 gm dose

Elimination

Renal—approximately 89%

Dialysis—cefuroxime is dialyzable via hemodialysis and peritoneal dialysis.

Concomitant use with probenecid

Concomitant administration with probenecid slows tubular secretion, decreases renal clearance by approximately 40%, increases peak serum levels by approximately 30%, and increases the serum half life by approximately 30%.

Precautions to Consider

Cross-sensitivity and/or related problems

Patients allergic to one cephalosporin or cephamycin may be allergic to other cephalosporins or cephamycins also.

Patients allergic to penicillins, penicillin derivatives, or penicillamine may be allergic to cephalosporins or cephamycins also. Cephalosporin cross reactivity is approximately 3 to 7 % in patients with a documented history of penicillin allergy. Although cephalosporins have been administered without incident to some patients with rash type penicillin allergy, caution is recommended when cephalosporins are administered to patients with a history of penicillin anaphylaxis since anaphylaxis may also occur after cephalosporin administration.

Carcinogenicity and Mutagenicity

Although lifetime studies in animals have not been performed to evaluate carcinogenic potential, no mutagenic activity was found for cefuroxime in the mouse lymphoma assay and a battery of bacterial mutation tests. Positive results were obtained in an *in vitro* chromosome aberration assay, however, negative results were found in an *in vivo* micronucleus test at doses up to 10 gm per kg.

Pregnancy/Reproduction

Fertility—Reproduction studies in mice at doses up to 3200 mg per kg per day (3.1 times the recommended maximum human dose based on mg per m^2 of body surface area) have revealed no impairment of fertility. Other reproductive studies have revealed no impairment of fertility in animals.

Pregnancy—Adequate and well controlled studies in humans have not been done.

In mice and rabbits, reproductive studies have shown that cefuroxime causes no adverse effects on the fetus. In mice, doses up to 6400 mg per kg of body weight per day (6.3 times the recommended maximum human dose based on mg per m^2 of body surface area) where administered. In rabbits, doses up to 400 mg per kg of body weight per day (2.1 times the recommended maximum human dose based on mg per m^2 of body surface area) where administered.

FDA Pregnancy Category B

Breast-feeding

Cefuroxime is distributed into breast milk in low concentrations 0.5 mg per L. Caution should be used when cefuroxime is administered to nursing mothers.

Pediatrics

US product information is approved for use in children over 3 months of age. Safety and effectiveness in pediatric patients three months of age and below has not been established. However, it is known that other members of the cephalosporin class have a prolonged drug half-life resulting from accumulation of drug in newborn infants.

Canadian product information is approved for use in neonates up to one month of age and children age 1 month to 12 years. Noting that in the first few weeks of life, the serum half life can be 3 to 5 times that in adults.

Geriatrics

In clinical studies of 1914 subjects, 47% were aged 65 and older and 22% were 75 years of age and over, there were no overall differences in safety or effectiveness between these subjects and younger subjects. Other reported clinical experience has not identified differences in responses between the elderly and younger patients but greater susceptibility of some older individuals to drug effects cannot be ruled out. Elderly patients are more likely to have decreased renal function; care should be taken in dose selection and it may be useful to monitor renal function.

Drug interactions and/or related problems

The following drug interactions and/or related problems have been selected on the basis of their potential clinical significance (possible mechanism in parentheses where appropriate)—not necessarily inclusive (» = major clinical significance):

Note: Combinations containing any of the following medications, depending on the amount present, may also interact with this medication.

» Aminoglycoside antibiotics
(may result in nephrotoxicity)

» Diuretics, potent
(administration may adversely affect renal function thereby affecting cefuroxime elimination)

» Probenecid
(concomitant administration with probenecid slows tubular secretion, decreases renal clearance by approximately 40%, increases peak serum levels by approximately 30%, and increases the serum half life by approximately 30%.)

Laboratory value alterations

The following have been selected on the basis of their potential clinical significance (possible effect in parentheses where appropriate)—not necessarily inclusive (» = major clinical significance).

With diagnostic test results

» Coombs' tests
(a positive reaction may occur)

» Copper reduction tests including:
Benedict's solution or
CLINITEST® tablets or
Fehling's solution
(a false positive reaction for glucose in the urine may occur; enzyme based tests for glycosuria are reliable.)

» Ferricyanide test
(a false negative result for blood plasma glucose may occur; blood plasma glucose levels should be determined by using either the glucose oxidase or hexokinase method.)

With physiology/laboratory test values

Alanine aminotransferase (ALT[SGPT]) or
Alkaline phosphatase or
Aspartase aminotransferase (AST[SGOT]) or
Bilirubin, serum or
Lactate dehydrogenase (LDH)
(transient rise in values has been reported)

Blood urea nitrogen (BUN) or
Creatinine clearance or
Creatinine, serum
(elevations in serum creatinine and /or BUN and a decreased creatinine clearance; relationship to cefuroxime is unknown)

Cerebrospinal fluid
(persistence of positive cultures have been noted at 18 to 36 hours; clinical relevance is unknown)

Hemoglobin or
Hematocrit
(a decrease in values has been observed along with transient eosinophilia)

» Prothrombin
(cephalosporins may be associated with a fall in prothrombin activity. Those at risk include patients with renal or hepatic impairments, or poor nutritional state, as well as patients receiving a protracted course of antimicrobial therapy and patients previously stabilized on anticoagulant therapy.)

Medical considerations/Contraindications

The medical considerations/contraindications included have been selected on the basis of their potential clinical significance (reasons given in parentheses where appropriate)—not necessarily inclusive (» = major clinical significance).

Except under special circumstances, this medication should not be used when the following medical problem exists:

» Hypersensitivity to cefuroxime or any other cephalosporin.

Risk-benefit should be considered when the following medical problems exist:

» Colitis, history of or
» Gastrointestinal disease, history of
(may aggravate symptoms)

Hepatic impairment or
Poor nutritional state or
Renal impairment
(may be associated with a fall in prothrombin activity; exogenous Vitamin K should be administered as indicated)

» Hypersensitivity to penicillins or
» Allergic reaction to other agents or other drugs
(previous hypersensitivity reactions to penicillins must be identified prior to administration; give cautiously to penicillin-sensitive patients; give cautiously to any patient with demonstrated any allergic reaction, particularly to any drug.)

» Renal insufficiency, transient or persistent
(may lead to high and prolonged serum antibiotic concentrations; the total daily dose should be reduced)

Patient monitoring

The following may be especially important in patient monitoring (other tests may be warranted in some patients, depending on condition; » = major clinical significance):

Bacteriologic appraisal
(frequent appraisal is necessary during therapy of chronic urinary tract infection and may be required for several months post therapy)

Prothrombin time
(may reduce prothrombin activity; patients with renal or hepatic impairment, poor nutritional state, as well as patients receiving a protracted course of antimicrobial therapy, and patients previously stabilized on anticoagulant therapy are at high risk)

» Pseudomembranous colitis
(monitor patient for development of diarrhea subsequent to cefuroxime therapy)

» Renal function evaluation
(rarely produces alterations in kidney function; evaluations are especially recommended in seriously ill patients receiving the maximum doses)

» Superinfection
(prolonged use may result in overgrowth of nonsusceptible organisms; careful observation is essential)

Side/Adverse Effects

The following side/adverse effects have been selected on the basis of their potential clinical significance (possible signs and symptoms in parentheses where appropriate)—not necessarily inclusive:

Note: Pseudomembranous colitis has been reported with nearly all antibacterial agents, including cefuroxime, and may range in severity from mild to life threatening. It is important to consider this diagnosis in patients who present with diarrhea subsequent to the administration of antibacterial agents

Those indicating need for medical attention

Incidence more frequent

Eosinophilia (black, tarry stools; chest pain; chills; cough; fever; painful or difficult urination; shortness of breath; sore throat; sores, ulcers, or white spots on lips or in mouth; swollen glands; unusual bleeding or bruising; unusual tiredness or weakness)

Incidence less frequent

hypersensitivity reaction (difficulty in breathing or swallowing; fast heartbeat; shortness of breath; skin itching, rash, or redness; swelling of face, throat, or tongue); ***pseudomembranous colitis*** (abdominal or stomach cramps; pain; bloating; abdominal tenderness; diarrhea, watery and severe, which may also be bloody; fever; increased thirst; nausea or vomiting; unusual tiredness or weakness; unusual weight loss); ***seizure*** (muscle spasm or jerking of all extremities; sudden loss of consciousness); ***thrombophlebitis*** (bluish color; changes in skin color; pain, tenderness, swelling of foot or leg); ***urticaria*** (hives or welts; itching; redness of skin; skin rash)

Incidence rare

Anaphylaxis (cough; difficulty swallowing; dizziness; fast heartbeat; hives; itching; puffiness or swelling of the eyelids or around the eyes, face, lips or tongue; shortness of breath; skin rash; tightness in chest; unusual tiredness or weakness; wheezing); ***epidermal necrolysis, toxic*** (redness, tenderness, itching, burning, or peeling of skin; red or irritated eyes; sore throat; fever; chills); ***erythema multiforme*** (blistering, peeling, loosening of skin; chills; cough; diarrhea; fever; itching; joint or muscle pain; red, irritated eyes; sore throat; sores; ulcers or white spots in mouth or on lips; unusual tiredness or weakness); ***hearing loss, mild to moderate; interstitial nephritis*** (bloody or cloudy urine; greatly decreased frequency of urination or amount of urine); ***leukopenia or neutropenia*** (black, tarry stools; chest pain; chills; cough; fever; painful or difficult urination; shortness of breath; sore throat; sores, ulcers, or white spots on lips or in mouth; swollen glands; unusual bleeding or bruising; unusual tiredness or weakness); ***Stevens-Johnson syndrome*** (blistering, peeling, loosening of skin; chills; cough; diarrhea; itching; joint or muscle pain; red, irritated eyes; red skin lesions, often with a purple center; sore throat; sores, ulcers, or white spots in mouth or on lips; unusual tiredness or weakness); ***thrombocytopenia*** (black, tarry stools; chest pain; chills; cough; fever; painful or difficult urination; shortness of breath; sore throat; sores, ulcers, or white spots on lips or in mouth; swollen glands; unusual bleeding or bruising; unusual tiredness or weakness)

Incidence unknown—reported during post marketing

Agranulocytosis (cough or hoarseness; fever with or without chills; general feeling of tiredness or weakness; lower back or side pain; painful or difficult urination; sore throat; sores, ulcers, or white spots on lips or in mouth; unusual bleeding or bruising); ***angioedema*** (large, hive-like swelling on face, eyelids, lips, tongue, throat, hands, legs, feet, sex organs); ***seizures; pancytopenia*** (high fever; chills; unexplained bleeding or bruising; bloody, black, or tarry stools; pale skin; unusual tiredness or weakness; cough; shortness of breath; sores, ulcers, or white spots on lips or in mouth; swollen glands)

Those indicating need for medical attention only if they continue or are bothersome

Incidence less frequent

Diarrhea; gastrointestinal problems (bloating; diarrhea; gas; loss of appetite; nausea; stomach pain; vomiting); ***nausea; pruritus*** (itching skin)

Incidence rare

Drug fever

Overdose

For more information on the management of overdose or unintentional ingestion, **contact a poison control center** (see *Poison Control Center Listing).*

Clinical effects of overdose

Overdose can cause cerebral irritation leading to convulsions.

Treatment of overdose

Specific treatment—

Serum levels of cefuroxime can be reduced by hemodialysis and peritoneal dialysis.

Supportive care—

Treatment should be symptomatic and supportive

Patients in whom intentional overdose is confirmed or suspected should be referred for psychiatric consultation.

Patient Consultation

As an aid to patient consultation, refer to *Advice for the Patient, Cefuroxime (Systemic).*

In providing consultation, consider emphasizing the following selected information (» = major clinical significance):

Before using this medication

» Conditions affecting use, especially:

Sensitivity to cefuroxime, other cephalosporins, penicillins or allergy to other drugs or agents

Breast-feeding—Distributed into breast milk

Use in children—U.S. product information—Safety and effectiveness not established in pediatric patients age 3 months and younger.

Canadian product information—Approved in neonates under one month of age and in infants and children 1 month to 12 years of age

Other medications, especially aminoglycoside antibiotics, potent diuretics, probenecid

Other medical problems, especially history of colitis or gastrointestinal disease, and transient or persistent renal insufficiency

Proper use of this medication

Patient monitoring, especially pseudomembranous colitis, renal function evaluation and signs of superinfection

» Proper dosing, especially reduced dosing in renal insufficiency.

Missed dose: Taking as soon as possible; not taking if almost time for next dose; do not double dose

» Proper storage

Precautions while using this medication

» Laboratory tests especially possible interference with test results including Coombs test, copper reductions tests (including Benedict's solution, Clinitest or Fehling's solution), ferricyanide test, and prothrombin levels.

Notifying physician immediately if diarrhea develops subsequent to administration of cefuroxime; may be symptomatic of pseudomembranous colitis.

Side/adverse effects

Signs of potential side effects, especially anaphylaxis, agranulocytosis, angioedema, eosinophilia, epidermal necrolysis, erythema multiforme, mild to moderate hearing loss, interstitial nephritis, leukopenia, neutropenia, pancytopenia, pseudomembranous colitis, seizure, Stevens-Johnson syndrome, thrombocytopenia, thrombophlebitis, toxic epidermal necrolysis, and urticaria

General Dosing Information

Parenteral drug products should be inspected visually for particulate matter and discoloration before administration whenever solution and container permit.

May be administered intravenously or by deep intramuscular injections into a large muscle mass such as the gluteus or lateral part of the thigh.

The intravenous route is preferred for patients with bacterial septicemia or other severe or life-threatening infections or for patients who may be poor risks because of lowered resistance, particularly if shock is present or impending.

For direct intermittent intravenous administration (bolus), slowly inject the solution into a vein over a period of 3 to 5 minutes, or give through the tubing system by which the patient is also receiving other intravenous solutions.

For short intravenous infusion administer over a period of approximately 30 minutes.

Clinical microbiological studies in skin and skin-structure infections frequently reveal the growth of susceptible strains of both aerobic and anaerobic organisms. Cefuroxime has been used successfully in these mixed infections in which several organisms have been isolated. Appropriate cultures and susceptibility studies should be performed to determine the susceptibility of the causative organisms to cefuroxime. Therapy may be started while awaiting the results of these studies; however, once these results become available, the antibiotic treatment should be adjusted accordingly.

A course of oral antibiotics may be administered when appropriate following the completion of parenteral administration of cefuroxime.

As with antibiotic therapy in general, administration of cefuroxime should be continued for a minimum of 48 to 72 hours after the patient becomes asymptomatic or after evidence of bacterial eradication has been obtained. A minimum of 10 days of treatment is recommended in infections caused by *Streptococcus pyogenes* in order to guard against the risk of rheumatic fever or glomerulonephritis.

In the treatment of chronic urinary tract infection, frequent bacteriologic and clinical appraisal may be required for several months after therapy has been completed. Persistent infections may require treatment for several weeks and doses smaller than those indicated should not be used.

In staphylococcal and other infections involving a collection of pus, surgical drainage should be carried out where indicated.

Treatment of side and adverse effects

Pseudomembranous colitis—mild cases usually respond to drug discontinuation alone. In moderate to severe cases, consideration should be given to management with fluids and electrolytes, protein supplementation, and treatment with an antibacterial drug clinically effective against *Clostridium difficile*, which is one primary cause of antibiotic associated colitis. Other causes of colitis should also be considered.

Parenteral Dosage Forms

Note: The dosing and strengths of the dosage forms available are expressed in terms of cefuroxime base (not the sodium salt).

CEFUROXIME FOR INJECTION USP

Note: For adults: a reduced dosage must be employed when renal function is impaired.

Creatinine clearance (mL/min)/(mL/sec)	Dose (base)
> 20/0.33	750 mg to 1.5 grams every 8 hours
10–20/0.17–0.33	750 mg every 12 hours
< 10/0.17	750 mg every 24 hours
Hemodialysis patients	750 mg at the end of each dialysis period

Usual Adult Dose

Intravenous or intramuscular, 750 mg to 1.5 gm of cefuroxime every 8 hours, usually for 5 to 10 days.

Canadian product information suggests a duration for 5 to 14 days.

Bone and joint infections (treatment),
Gonococcal infections, disseminated, severe or complicated (treatment)[1],
Pneumonia, severe or complicated (treatment),
Skin and skin-structure infections, severe or complicated (treatment)[1],
Urinary tract infections, severe or complicated (treatment)[1]—
Intravenous, 1.5 gm every 8 hours

Gonococcal infections, disseminated (treatment),[1]
Pneumonia, uncomplicated (treatment),
Skin and skin-structure infections (treatment),
Urinary tract infections, uncomplicated (treatment)—
Intravenous, 750 mg every 8 hours

Gonococcal infection, uncomplicated (treatment)—
Intramuscular, 1.5 gm given as one dose at 2 different sites; administer with 1 gm of oral probenecid

Meningitis, bacterial (treatment)—
Intravenous, up to 3 gm every 8 hours

Perioperative prophylaxis—
Open heart surgery patients: Intravenous, 1.5 gm at the induction of anesthesia, then 1.5 grams every twelve hours, for a total of 6 grams.
Surgical procedures, clean-contaminated or potentially contaminated: Intravenous 1.5 gm dose just before surgery (0.5 to 1 hour prior to initial incision). Thereafter, 750 mg intravenously or intramuscularly every 8 hours when the procedure is prolonged.
In Canada after surgery, 750 mg intravenously or intramuscularly at 8 hours and 16 hours when the procedure is prolonged. Continued prophylactic administration of any antibiotic does not appear to be associated with a reduced incidence of subsequent infection, but will increase the possibility of adverse reactions and the development of bacterial resistance.

Other infections—
Less susceptible organisms or life-threatening infections:[1] Intravenous, 1.5 gm every 6 hours.
[Severe or life threatening infections:]—Intravenous, 1.5 gm every 8 hours (4.5gm per day)

Note: A minimum of 10 days of treatment is recommended in infections caused by *Streptococcus pyrogens* in order to guard against the risk of rheumatic fever or glomerulonephritis.

Usual adult prescribing limits

Bacterial Meningitis-Up to 3 gm of cefuroxime every 8 hours.

Usual Pediatric Dose

For those three months of age and older: Intravenous, 50 to 150 mg per kg of body weight per day in equally divided doses every 6 to 8 hours. A higher dosage of 100 mg per kg of body weight per day (not to exceed the maximum adult dosage) should be used for the more severe or serious infections.

[Neonates (up to 1 month of age)]—Intravenous, 30 to 100 mg per kg of body weight per day in 2 or 3 equally divided doses. Note that in the first few weeks of life, the serum half-life of cefuroxime can be 3 to 5 times that in adults.

[Infants and children (1 month to 12 years)]—Intravenous, 30 to 100 mg per kg of body weight per day in 3 or 4 equally divided doses. A dose of 60 mg per kg of body weight per day is appropriate for most infections.

Note: Pediatric patients with renal insufficiency, the frequency of dosing should be modified consistent with the recommendations for adults.

Bone and joint infections (treatment)—
For those three months of age and older—Intravenous, 150 mg per kg of body weight per day (not exceeding the maximum adult dosage) in equally divided doses every 8 hours. In clinical trials a course of oral antibiotics was administered to pediatric patients following the completion of parenteral administration
[Infants and children (1 month to 12 years)]—Intravenous, 70 to 150 mg per kg of body weight per day every 8 hours. In clinical trials a course of oral antibiotics was administered to pediatric patients following the completion of parenteral administration

Meningitis, bacterial (treatment)—
For those 3 months of age and older—Intravenous, 200 to 240 mg per kg of body weight per day in equally divided doses every 6 to 8 hours.
[Infants and children (1 month to 12 years)]—Intravenous, 200 to 240 mg per kg of body weight per day in 3 or 4 equally divided doses.
[Neonates (up to 1 month of age)]—Intravenous, 100 mg per kg of body weight per day in 2 or 3 equally divided doses.

Usual pediatric prescribing limits

For those three months of age and older: See *Usual adult prescribing limits*.

Usual Geriatric Dose

See *Usual adult dose*.

Usual geriatric prescribing limits

See *Usual adult prescribing limits*.

Strength(s) usually available

U.S.—

Note: Zinacef contains 54.2 mg (2.4 mEq) of sodium per gram of cefuroxime activity.

750 mg vial (Rx) [*Zinacef* (sodium)].
1.5 gm vial (Rx) [*Zinacef* (sodium)].
7.5 gm vial (Rx) [*Zinacef* (sodium)].
750 mg ADD-Vantage vial (Rx) [*Zinacef* (sodium)].
1.5 gm ADD-Vantage vial (Rx) [*Zinacef* (sodium)].
750 mg infusion pack (Rx) [*Zinacef* (sodium)].
1.5 gm infusion pack (Rx) [*Zinacef* (sodium)].

Canada—
750 mg vial (Rx) [*Zinacef*].
1.5 gm vial (Rx) [*Zinacef*].
7.5 gm vial (Rx) [*Zinacef* (sodium)].

Packaging and storage

When dry, store between 59 and 86°F (15 and 30°C). Protect from light. When frozen, store at or below -4°F (-20°C)

Preparation of dosage form

For intramuscular use:
• Each 750 mg vial of cefuroxime should be constituted with 3 mL of Sterile Water for Injection. Shake gently to disperse. Results in 220 mg per mL *suspension* for injection.

For intravenous use:
• Each 750 mg vial should be constituted with 8 mL of Sterile Water for Injection. Results in 90 mg per mL solution for injection
• Each 1.5 gm vial should be constituted with 16 mL of Sterile Water for Injection. Results in 90 mg per mL solution for injection
• Each bulk 7.5 gm vial should be constituted with 77 mL of Sterile Water for Injection. Results in 95 mg per mL (750 mg per 8 mL) of solution for injection.

• Dilute solutions—Each 750 mg and 1.5 gm infusion packs should be constituted with 100 mL of Sterile Water for Injection, 5% Dextrose Injection, or 0.9% Sodium Chloride Injection. The 750 mg infusion pack results in 7.5 mg per mL of solution for injection. The 1.5 gm infusion pack results in 15 mg per mL of solution for injection.

• Dilute solutions may be further diluted to concentrations between 1 and 30 mg per mL in the following solutions: 0.9% Sodium Chloride Injection; 1/6 M Sodium Lactate Injection; Ringer's Injection, USP; Lactated Ringer's Injection, USP; 5% Dextrose and 0.9% Sodium Chloride Injection; 5% Dextrose Injection; 5 % Dextrose and 0.45% Sodium Chloride Injection; 5% Dextrose and 0.225% Sodium Chloride Injection; 10% Dextrose Injection; and 10% Invert Sugar in Water for Injection.

See the manufacturer's package insert for any additional instructions.

Stability

Solutions of cefuroxime range in color from light yellow to amber, depending on the concentration and diluent used.

ADD-Vantage diluent containers and activated to dissolve the drug are stable for 24 hours at room temperature or for 7 day under refrigeration (5° C). Joined vials that have not been activated may be used within a 14 day period. Freezing solutions in the ADD-Vantage system is not recommended.

Suspensions and solutions of reconstituted 750 mg or 1.5 gm vials should be used within 24 hours when stored at room temperature and within 48 hours when stored in refrigeration (5° C). The 7.5 gm bulk containers are stable for 24 hours at room temperature and 7 days under refrigeration (5° C)

Frozen solutions of 750 mg, or 1.5 gm vials properly reconstituted or 8 or 16 mL from the 7.5 gm bulk vial, which are subsequently diluted to 50 or 100 mL in Baxter Viaflex Mini-bags are stable for 6 months when stored at -20° C.

Thawed solutions may be stored for 24 hours at room temperature or for up to 7 days in refrigeration. Once thawed solutions should not be refrozen. Do not force thaw by immersion in water baths or by microwave irradiation.

Cefuroxime powder as well as solutions and suspensions tend to darken depending on conditions, without adversely affecting product potency.

Bulk packages after initial withdrawal must be discarded within 24 hours.

Solutions diluted to concentrations between 1 and 30 mg per mL will lose not more than 10% activity for 24 hours at room temperature or for at least 7 days under refrigeration.

Incompatibilities

Solutions of cefuroxime should not be added to solutions of aminoglycoside antibiotics because of potential interaction. However, if concurrent therapy is indicated, each of these antibiotics can be administered separately.

Sodium Bicarbonate Injection USP is not recommended for the dilution of cefuroxime.

CEFUROXIME INJECTION USP

Note: For Adults: A reduced dosage must be employed when renal function is impaired.

Creatinine clearance (mL/min)/(mL/sec)	Dose (base)
$> 20/0.33$	750 mg to 1.5 grams every 8 hours
10–20/0.17–0.33	750 mg every 12 hours
$< 10/0.17$	750 mg every 24 hours
Hemodialysis patients	750 mg at the end of each dialysis period

Patients on hemodialysis should receive a further dose at the end of the dialysis.

Usual Adult Dose

Intravenous, 750 mg to 1.5 gm of cefuroxime every 8 hours, usually for 5 to 10 days.

Canadian product information suggests a duration for 5 to 14 days.

Bone and joint infections (treatment),
Gonococcal infections, disseminated, severe or complicated (treatment)[1],
Pneumonia, severe or complicated (treatment),
Skin and skin-structure infections, severe or complicated (treatment)[1],
Urinary tract infections, severe or complicated (treatment)[1]—
Intravenous, 1.5 gm every 8 hours

Gonococcal infections, disseminated (treatment),[1]
Pneumonia, uncomplicated (treatment),
Skin and skin-structure infections (treatment),
Urinary tract infections, uncomplicated (treatment)—
Intravenous, 750 mg every 8 hours

Meningitis, bacterial (treatment)—
Intravenous, up to 3 gm every 8 hours

Perioperative prophylaxis—
Open heart surgery patients: Intravenous, 1.5 gm at the induction of anesthesia, then 1.5 grams every twelve hours, for a total of 6 grams.
Surgical procedures, clean-contaminated or potentially contaminated: Intravenous 1.5 gm dose just before surgery (0.5 to 1 hour prior to initial incision). Thereafter, 750 mg intravenously every 8 hours when the procedure is prolonged.
In Canada after surgery, 750 mg intravenously at 8 hours and 16 hours when the procedure is prolonged. Continued prophylactic administration of any antibiotic does not appear to be associated with a reduced incidence of subsequent infection, but will increase the possibility of adverse reactions and the development of bacterial resistance.

Other infections—
Less susceptible organisms or life-threatening infections:[1] Intravenous, 1.5 gm every 6 hours.
[Severe or life threatening infections:]—Intravenous, 1.5 gm every 8 hours (4.5gm per day)

Note: A minimum of 10 days of treatment is recommended in infections caused by *Streptococcus pyrogens* in order to guard against the risk of rheumatic fever or glomerulonephritis.

Usual adult prescribing limits

See *Usual adult prescribing limits: Cefuroxime for injection*

Usual Pediatric Dose

See *Usual Pediatric Dose: Cefuroxime for injection*

Usual pediatric prescribing limits

For those three months of age and older See *Usual adult prescribing limits: Cefuroxime for injection*

Usual Geriatric Dose

See *Usual adult dose: Cefuroxime for injection.*

Usual geriatric prescribing limits

See *Usual adult prescribing limits: Cefuroxime for injection.*

Strength(s) usually available

U.S.—

Note: The plastic container is fabricated from a specially designed multilayer plastic, PL 2040. Solutions are in contact with polyethylene layer of this container and can leach out certain chemical components of the plastic in very small amounts within the expiration period. The suitability of the plastic has been confirmed in tests in animals according to USP biological tests for plastic containers as well as by tissue culture toxicity studies.

750 mg as frozen, iso-osmotic, sterile, nonpyrogenic solution in a plastic container (Rx) [*Zinacef* (Dextrose Hydrous, USP 1.4 gm; Sodium Citrate Hydrous, USP 300 mg; sodium 111 mg (4.8 mEq); hydrochloric acid; sodium hydroxide)].

1.5 gm as frozen, iso-osmotic, sterile, nonpyrogenic solution in a plastic container (Rx) [*Zinacef* (Sodium Citrate Hydrous, USP 600 mg; sodium 222 mg (9.7 mEq); hydrochloric acid; sodium hydroxide)].

Canada—
Not commercially available

Packaging and storage

Store frozen below -20° C.

Preparation of dosage form

Thaw container at room temperature (25°C) or under refrigeration (5°C). Do not force thaw by immersion in water baths or by microwave irradiation.

Do not use plastic containers in series connections. Such use could result in air embolism due to residual air being drawn from the primary container before administration of the fluid for the secondary container is complete.

Mix after solution has reached room temperature. Check or minute leaks by squeezing bag firmly. Discard bag if leaks are found as sterility may be impaired.

Do not add supplementary medication.

Do not use unless solution is clar and seal is intact.

Stability

Solutions of premixed cefuroxime range in color from light yellow to amber.

Components of the solution may precipitate in the frozen state and will dissolve upon reaching room temperature with little or no agitation. Potency is not affected.

Thawed solutions may be stored for 24 hours at room temperature or for up to 28 days in refrigeration. Once thawed, solutions should not be refrozen.

Incompatibilities
Solutions of cefuroxime should not be added to solutions of aminoglycoside antibiotics because of potential interaction. However, if concurrent therapy is indicated, each of these antibiotics can be administered separately.

[1]Not included in Canadian product labeling.

Developed: 11/21/2002

CELECOXIB Systemic

VA CLASSIFICATION (Primary/Secondary): MS102/CN104

Commonly used brand name(s): *Celebrex.*

Note: For a listing of dosage forms and brand names by country availability, see *Dosage Forms* section(s).

Category
Analgesic; Antidysmenorrheal; Antirheumatic (nonsteroidal anti-inflammatory).

Indications

Accepted
Ankylosing spondylitis[1]—Celecoxib is indicated to relieve the signs and symptoms of ankylosing spondylitis

Arthritis, rheumatoid (treatment); or

Osteoarthritis (treatment)—Celecoxib is indicated to relieve the signs and symptoms of rheumatoid arthritis and osteoarthritis.

Dysmenorrhea, primary (treatment)—Celecoxib is indicated for relief of the pain of primary dysmenorrhea.

Familial adenomatous polyposis [FAP] (treatment)[1]—Celecoxib is indicated to reduce the number of adenomatous colorectal polyps in patients with FAP, as an adjunct to usual care.

Note: It is not known whether there is a clinical benefit from a reduction in the number of colorectal polyps in FAP patients; it is not known if the effects of celecoxib treatment will persist after celecoxib is discontinued; the safety and efficacy of celecoxib treatment in patients with FAP beyond six months is not known.

Pain, acute (treatment)[1]—Celecoxib is indicated for relief of acute pain rated as moderate to severe, such as following dental or orthopedic surgery.

[1]Not included in Canadian product labeling.

Pharmacology/Pharmacokinetics

Physicochemical characteristics
Molecular weight—381.38.

Mechanism of action/Effect
Celecoxib is a nonsteroidal anti-inflammatory drug (NSAID) with anti-inflammatory, analgesic, and antipyretic therapeutic effects. It has been proposed that celecoxib inhibits the activity of the enzyme cyclooxygenase-2 (COX-2), resulting in a decreased formation of precursors of prostaglandins. However, unlike most NSAIDs, celecoxib does not inhibit cyclooxygenase-1 (COX-1) isoenzyme in humans at therapeutic concentrations.

Other actions/effects
Celecoxib has anti-inflammatory and antipyretic actions that, together with its analgesic effects, may mask the onset and/or progression of an infection.

Absorption
Rapid. Administration of celecoxib with a high-fat meal resulted in a 1- to 2-hour delay in the peak plasma concentration level and a 10 to 20% increase in the area under the plasma concentration-time curve (AUC). Celecoxib may be coadministered with meals without altering the dosing schedule based on the timing of meals.

Protein binding
Very high (97%).

Biotransformation
Hepatic via cytochrome P450 C9 enzymes to inactive metabolites.

Half-life
Approximately 11 hours.

Time to peak concentration
Approximately 3 hours.

Peak serum concentration
Following a single 200-mg dose—705 nanograms per mL.

Elimination
Approximately 57% and 27% of a radioactive celecoxib dose is eliminated in the feces and urine, respectively. Less than 3% is excreted in the feces and urine unchanged. The primary metabolite in the feces and urine is carboxylic acid metabolite (73% of dose).

Precautions to Consider

Cross-sensitivity and/or related problems
Celecoxib may cause bronchoconstriction or anaphylaxis in aspirin-sensitive asthmatics, especially those with aspirin-induced nasal polyps, asthma, and other allergic reactions (the "aspirin triad").

Patients sensitive to other nonsteroidal anti-inflammatory drugs, aspirin, sulfonamides, or related compounds may be sensitive to celecoxib also.

Carcinogenicity
In a 2-year carcinogenicity study in male and female rats given oral doses of celecoxib of up to 200 mg per kg of body weight (mg/kg) and 10 mg/kg, respectively (approximately two to four times the human exposure based on the area under the plasma concentration-time curve [AUC] at 200 mg twice a day), no carcinogenic effects were observed. In a 2-year carcinogenicity study in male and female mice receiving oral doses of celecoxib of up to 25 mg/kg and 50 mg/kg, respectively (approximately equal to the human exposure based on the AUC at 200 mg twice a day), no carcinogenic effects were observed.

Mutagenicity
Celecoxib was not mutagenic in the Ames test or the mutation assay in Chinese hamster ovary (CHO) cells. No clastogenic effect was observed in the chromosome aberration assay in CHO cells or in an *in vivo* micronucleus test in rat bone marrow.

Pregnancy/Reproduction
Fertility—There was no evidence of impairment of fertility in reproduction studies in female rats receiving oral doses of celecoxib of up to 600 mg/kg per day (approximately 11 times the human exposure at 200 mg twice a day based on the AUC).

Pregnancy—Adequate and well-controlled studies in humans have not been done. Celecoxib may cause premature closure of the ductus arteriosus. Therefore, use of celecoxib is not recommended during late pregnancy.

No teratogenic effects were observed in rabbits receiving oral doses of celecoxib at 60 mg/kg per day (equal to the human exposure at 200 mg twice a day of celecoxib based on the AUC). However, there was an increase in malformations of the ribs and sternebrae at oral doses of celecoxib at 150 mg/kg and greater per day. In one of two rat studies, a dose-dependent increase in diaphragmatic hernias was observed in rats receiving oral doses of celecoxib at 30 mg/kg and greater per day.

In rats receiving oral doses of celecoxib of up to 50 mg/kg and greater, pre-implantation and post-implantation losses and reduced embryo/fetal survival were reported. These changes were expected with inhibition of prostaglandin synthesis, but not at clinical exposures. However, these changes are not the result of permanent alteration in female reproductive function.

FDA Pregnancy Category C.

Labor and delivery—The effect of celecoxib on labor and delivery in pregnant women is unknown.

Labor and delivery—No evidence of delayed labor or parturition was found in rats receiving oral doses of celecoxib of up to 100 mg/kg (approximately seven times the human exposure based on AUC at 200 mg twice a day).

Breast-feeding
It is not known whether celecoxib is distributed into human breast milk. However, celecoxib may potentially cause serious adverse effects in the nursing infant. Celecoxib is distributed into the milk of lactating rats at concentrations similar to those in plasma.

Pediatrics
No information is available on the relationship of age to the effects of celecoxib in pediatric patients. Safety and efficacy have not been established.

Geriatrics
Appropriate studies performed to date have not demonstrated geriatrics-specific problems that would limit the use of celecoxib in geriatric patients. In pharmacokinetic studies, elderly patients 65 years of age and older demonstrated increases in the AUC and C_{max} (50% and 40%, respectively) compared with those in younger patients. Due to their

lower body weight, elderly females had a higher AUC and C_{max} compared with elderly males.

Reported adverse effects were higher in elderly patients, but no substantial differences in safety and efficacy were observed between the elderly and younger patients. However, there have been more spontaneous post-marketing reports of fatal GT events and acute renal failure in the elderly than in younger patients. The lowest effective dose for the shortest possible duration is recommended in elderly patients to minimize the potential risks for gastrointestinal ulceration or bleeding.

Drug interactions and/or related problems

The following drug interactions and/or related problems have been selected on the basis of their potential clinical significance (possible mechanism in parentheses where appropriate)—not necessarily inclusive (» = major clinical significance):

Note: Combinations containing any of the following medications, depending on the amount present, may also interact with this medication.

Note: Patients receiving celecoxib therapy who are known or suspected to be P450 2C9 poor metabolizers based on previous history may have abnormally high plasma levels of celecoxib due to reduced metabolic clearance. Therefore, celecoxib should be administered with caution in these patients.

Angiotensin-converting enzyme (ACE) inhibitors
(concurrent use with celecoxib may decrease the antihypertensive effects of ACE inhibitors; also, risk of renal failure is increased in patients taking these medications)

Antacids, aluminum- or magnesium-containing
(the administration of celecoxib with an aluminum- or magnesium-containing antacid has been reported to result in a 37% decrease in the peak plasma concentration and a 10% decrease in the area under the plasma concentration-time curve [AUC] of celecoxib)

» Aspirin or
Corticosteroids, oral
(concurrent use with celecoxib may result in celecoxib-induced gastrointestinal ulceration or other gastrointestinal complications; can be used with low dose aspirin)

Diuretics, thiazide or
Furosemide
(nonsteroidal anti-inflammatory drugs may decrease the natriuretic effects of diuretics, possibly by inhibiting renal prostaglandin synthesis; also, risk of renal failure is increased in patients taking these medications)

» Fluconazole
(in clinical trials, concurrent administration of fluconazole 200 mg daily resulted in a twofold increase in plasma concentration of celecoxib; the increase in plasma concentration of celecoxib was due to the inhibition of celecoxib metabolism via P450 2C9 by fluconazole; therefore, if celecoxib is coadministered with fluconazole, the dose of celecoxib should be initiated at the lowest recommended dose)

» Lithium
(a 17% increase in the plasma concentration of lithium has been reported in patients receiving lithium 450 mg twice a day with celecoxib 200 mg twice a day compared with patients receiving lithium alone; therefore, monitoring of lithium concentrations is recommended when treatment is initiated and when treatment with celecoxib is discontinued)

Warfarin or
Anticoagulants
(clinical studies reported that celecoxib does not alter the anticoagulant effects of warfarin; since patients receiving warfarin are at increased risk of bleeding complications and post-marketing experience includes serious bleeding events, caution is recommended with concurrent use)

Laboratory value alterations

The following have been selected on the basis of their potential clinical significance (possible effect in parentheses where appropriate)—not necessarily inclusive (» = major clinical significance).

With physiology/laboratory test values
Alanine aminotransferase (ALT [SGPT]) and
Alkaline phosphatase and
Aspartate aminotransferase (AST [SGOT]) and
Creatinine and
Non protein nitrogen
(serum values may be increased; liver function test abnormalities may return to normal despite continued use; however, if significant abnormalities occur, clinical signs and symptoms consistent with liver disease develop, or systemic manifestations such as eosinophilia or rash occur, use of celecoxib should be discontinued)

Blood urea nitrogen (BUN) and
Chloride
(concentrations may be increased)

Phosphate
(concentrations may be decreased)

Medical considerations/Contraindications

The medical considerations/contraindications included have been selected on the basis of their potential clinical significance (reasons given in parentheses where appropriate)—not necessarily inclusive (» = major clinical significance).

Except under special circumstances, this medication should not be used when the following medical problems exist:

» Allergic reaction, severe, such as anaphylaxis or angioedema, induced by aspirin, other NSAIDs, or sulfonamide-derived medications, history of or

» Nasal polyps associated with bronchospasm, aspirin-induced
(high risk of severe allergic reaction)

» Coronary artery bypass graft (CABG) surgery
(use is contraindicated for treatment of perioperative pain in the setting of CABG surgery)

» Hypersensitivity to celecoxib

Risk-benefit should be considered when the following medical problems exist:

Anemia
(may be exacerbated)

» Asthma, pre-existing
(may be exacerbated; caution is recommended)

Alcoholism, active or
» Gastrointestinal bleeding, active or prior history of or
» Peptic ulcer disease, active or pre-existing or
Tobacco use, or recent history of
(celecoxib should be used with extreme caution in patients with peptic ulcer disease or gastrointestinal bleeding; dosage adjustment is recommended to minimize potential risk of gastrointestinal bleeding)

» Cardiovascular disease
(may be at greater risk of serious cardiovascular thrombotic events, myocardial infarction, and stroke; risk may increase with duration of use)

Conditions predisposing to and/or exacerbated by fluid retention, such as:
Compromised cardiac heart function or
Congestive heart disease or
Edema, pre-existing or
Hypertension
(celecoxib may cause fluid retention or edema; risk of renal failure is increased in patients with congestive heart disease)

Extracellular volume depletion, especially associated with pre-existing renal disease
(prior to initiating therapy with celecoxib, patients should be rehydrated; caution is recommended in patients with pre-existing renal disease)

» Hepatic function impairment
(risk of renal failure is increased in these patients; careful monitoring is recommended)
(studies have shown increased area under the plasma concentration-time curve in patients with mild and moderate hepatic impairment [40% and 180%, respectively]; therefore, dosage adjustment and careful monitoring are recommended in patients with moderate hepatic impairment; however, use in patients with severe hepatic impairment is not recommended)

» Renal function impairment
(studies have shown a 40% decrease in the celecoxib AUC in patients with renal function impairment compared with healthy volunteers; caution is recommended in patients with renal function impairment)
(long-term studies in patients with severe renal disease have not been done; use of celecoxib is not recommended in these patients; however, if celecoxib is used in patients with severe renal impairment, close monitoring is recommended)

Patient monitoring

The following may be especially important in patient monitoring (other tests may be warranted in some patients, depending on condition; » = major clinical significance):

Alanine aminotransferase (ALT [SGPT]) and

Aspartate aminotransferase (AST [SGOT])
(careful monitoring is recommended in patients with signs and symptoms of hepatic function impairment; if elevations persist, discontinuation of therapy may be necessary)

Complete blood count and chemistry profile
(careful monitoring should be conducted periodically)

Gastrointestinal bleeding or ulceration
(monitoring for signs or symptoms of gastrointestinal bleeding is recommended)

Hematocrit or
Hemoglobin
(monitoring is recommended in patients who have developed signs and symptoms of anemia or blood loss during prolonged therapy with celecoxib)

Side/Adverse Effects

In July 2005, the Food and Drug Administration (FDA) asked all manufacturers of NSAIDs, including celecoxib, to revise the labeling for their products to include a boxed warning, highlighting the potential for increased risk of cardiovascular (CV) events including stroke and the well described, serious potential life-threatening gastrointestinal (GI) bleeding associated with their use. CV events with celecoxib use include myocardial infarction, cerebrovascular accident, and death.

The following side/adverse effects have been selected on the basis of their potential clinical significance (possible signs and symptoms in parentheses where appropriate)—not necessarily inclusive:

Those indicating need for medical attention

Incidence more frequent

Edema (swelling of face, fingers, feet, and/or lower legs); ***skin rash; upper respiratory tract infection*** (cough; fever; sneezing; sore throat)

Incidence less frequent or rare

Allergic reaction (cough, difficulty swallowing, dizziness, fast heartbeat, hives, itching, puffiness or swelling of the eyelids or around the eyes, face, lips or tongue, shortness of breath skin rash tightness in chest, unusual tiredness or weakness, wheezing); ***anemia*** (pale skin, troubled breathing with exertion, unusual bleeding or bruising, unusual tiredness or weakness); ***angina*** (arm, back or jaw pain, chest pain or discomfort, chest tightness or heaviness, fast or irregular heartbeat, shortness of breath, sweating, nausea); ***breast neoplasm*** (abnormal growth in breast); ***bronchitis*** (congestion in chest; cough); ***chest pain; coronary artery disorder*** (arm, back or jaw pain, chest pain or discomfort, chest tightness or heaviness, fast or irregular heartbeat, shortness of breath, sweating, nausea); ***diabetes mellitus*** (blurred vision dry mouth fatigue flushed, dry skin fruit-like breath odor increased hunger increased thirst increased urination loss of consciousness nausea stomachache sweating troubled breathing unexplained weight loss vomiting); ***dyspnea*** (shortness of breath); ***eructation; gastritis*** (burning feeling in chest or stomach; tenderness in stomach area); ***gastroenteritis*** (severe stomach pain; diarrhea; loss of appetite; nausea; weakness); ***gastrointestinal bleeding or ulceration*** (bloody or black, tarry stools; vomiting of blood or material that looks like coffee grounds); ***glaucoma*** (blindness blurred vision; decreased vision; eye pain; headache; nausea or vomiting; tearing); ***herpes simplex*** (burning or stinging of skin painful cold sores or blisters on lips, nose, eyes, or genitals); ***herpes zoster*** (painful blisters on trunk of body); ***hypertension, aggravated*** (high blood pressure); ***infection, bacterial*** (confusion fever headache stiff neck); ***infection, fungal*** (confusion fever headache stiff neck); ***infection, soft tissue*** (confusion fever headache stiff neck); ***infection, viral*** (confusion fever headache stiff neck); ***melena; moniliasis*** (skin rash cracks in skin at the corners of mouth soreness or redness around fingernails and toenails); ***myocardial infarction*** (chest pain or discomfort; pain or discomfort in arms, jaw, back or neck; shortness of breath; nausea; sweating; vomiting); ***neuralgia*** (nerve pain); ***neuropathy*** (burning, tingling, numbness or pain in the hands, arms, feet, or legs sensation of pins and needles stabbing pain); ***otitis media*** (earache, redness or swelling in ear); ***pneumonia*** (chest pain cough fever or chills sneezing shortness of breath sore throat troubled breathing tightness in chest wheezing); ***tachycardia*** (fast heartbeat); ***vaginal hemorrhage*** (heavy nonmenstrual vaginal bleeding); ***weight gain, unusual***

Incidence Rare—Occurring in less than 0.1% of patients

Acute renal failure; agranulocytosis (cough or hoarseness; fever with or without chills; general feeling of tiredness or weakness; lower back or side pain; painful or difficult urination; sore throat; sores, ulcers, or white spots on lips or in mouth; unusual bleeding or bruising); ***angioedema*** (large, hive-like swelling on face, eyelids, lips, tongue, throat, hands, legs, feet, sex organs); ***aplastic anemia*** (chest pain; chills; cough; fever; headache; shortness of breath; sores, ulcers, or white spots on lips or in mouth; swollen or painful glands; tightness in chest; unusual bleeding or bruising; unusual tiredness or weakness; wheezing); ***aseptic meningitis; cerebrovascular accident*** (blurred vision; headache; sudden and severe inability to speak; seizures slurred speech; temporary blindness; weakness in arm and/or leg on one side of the body, sudden and severe); ***colitis*** (stomach cramps; tenderness; pain; watery or bloody diarrhea; fever); ***congestive heart failure*** (chest pain; decreased urine output; dilated neck veins; extreme fatigue; irregular breathing; irregular heartbeat; shortness of breath; swelling of face, fingers, feet, or lower legs; tightness in chest; troubled breathing; weight gain; wheezing); ***deep venous thrombosis*** (pain, redness, or swelling in arm or leg); ***epidermal necrolysis, toxic*** (redness, tenderness, itching, burning, or peeling of skin red; irritated eyes sore throat; fever; chills); ***exfoliative dermatitis*** (cracks in the skin; loss of heat from the body; red, swollen skin; scaly skin); ***hepatitis*** (dark urine; general tiredness and weakness; light-colored stools; nausea and vomiting; upper right abdominal pain; yellow eyes and skin); ***intracranial hemorrhage*** (confusion,headache; sudden severe weakness; nausea and vomiting); ***jaundice*** (chills; clay-colored stools; dark urine; dizziness; fever; headache; itching; loss of appetite; nausea; abdominal or stomach pain; area rash; unpleasant breath odor; unusual tiredness or weakness; vomiting of blood; yellow eyes or skin); ***liver failure; pancytopenia*** (high fever; chills; unexplained bleeding or bruising; bloody, black, or tarry stools; pale skin; unusual tiredness or weakness; cough; shortness of breath; sores, ulcers, or white spots on lips or in mouth; swollen glands); ***peripheral gangrene*** (cold, pale or a bluish color skin of the fingers or toes; itching skin; numbness or tingling of the fingers or toes; pain in the fingers or toes); ***pulmonary embolism*** (anxiety; chest pain; cough; fainting; fast heartbeat; sudden shortness of breath or troubled breathing; dizziness or lightheadedness); ***sepsis*** (chills; confusion; dizziness; lightheadedness; fainting; fast heartbeat; fever; rapid, shallow breathing); ***Stevens-Johnson syndrome*** (blistering, peeling, loosening of skin; chills; cough; diarrhea; itching; joint or muscle pain; red irritated eyes; red skin lesions, often with a purple center sore throat sores, ulcers, or white spots in mouth or on lips; unusual tiredness or weakness); ***suicide; syncope; thrombophlebitis*** (changes in skin color; pain, tenderness, swelling of foot or leg); ***vasculitis*** (redness, soreness or itching skin; fever; sores, welting or blisters); ***ventricular fibrillation*** (fainting; fast, slow, or irregular heartbeat; shortness of breath; unusual tiredness or weakness)

Those indicating need for medical attention only if they continue or are bothersome

Incidence more frequent

Back pain; diarrhea; dizziness; dyspepsia (heartburn); ***flatulence*** (gas); ***headache; insomnia*** (inability to sleep); ***nausea; pharyngitis*** (pain or burning in throat); ***rhinitis*** (runny nose); ***sinusitis*** (stuffy or runny nose; headache); ***stomach pain***

Incidence less frequent

Abdominal pain; albuminuria; alopecia (hair loss, thinning of hair); ***anxiety; anorexia*** (decreased appetite); ***appetite increased; arthralgia*** (joint or muscle pain or stiffness); ***arthrosis*** (degenerative disease of the joint); ***asthenia*** (loss of energy or weakness); ***blurred vision; breast pain; breast fibroadenosis*** (lumps in breasts; painful or tender cysts in the breasts); ***bronchospasm*** (cough difficulty breathing noisy breathing shortness of breath tightness in chest wheezing); ***bone disorder*** (bone deformity; decrease in height; difficulty in moving or walking; headache; loss of hearing; pain in back, ribs, arms, or legs; redness or swelling in arms or legs); ***cataract; cellulitis*** (itching pain redness swelling tenderness warmth on skin); ***cholelithiasis*** (abdominal fullness; gaseous abdominal pain; recurrent fever; yellow eyes or skin); ***conjunctivitis*** (redness, pain, swelling of eye, eyelid, or inner lining of eyelid burning, dry or itching eyes discharge excessive tearing); ***constipation; coughing; cyst; cystitis*** (bloody or cloudy urine difficult, burning, or painful urination frequent urge to urinate); ***deafness; depression; dermatitis*** (blistering, crusting, irritation, itching, or reddening of skin cracked, dry, scaly skin swelling); ***diverticulitis*** (abdominal pain or tenderness; fever); ***dry mouth; dry skin; dysmenorrhea*** (pain, cramps, heavy bleeding); ***dysphagia*** (difficulty swallowing); ***dysuria*** (difficult or painful urination burning while urinating); ***earache; ecchymosis*** (bruising large, flat, blue or purplish patches in the skin); ***epistaxis*** (bloody nose); ***eye pain; esophagitis*** (pain or burning in throat); ***fatigue*** (unusual tiredness); ***fever; hematuria*** (blood in urine); ***hemorrhoids*** (bleeding after defecation uncomfortable swelling around anus); ***hiatal hernia*** (heartburn; vomiting); ***hot flashes*** (sudden sweating and feelings of warmth); ***hypercholesterolemia*** (large amount of cholesterol in the blood); ***hyperglycemia*** (abdominal pain, blurred vision dry mouth fatigue flushed, dry skin fruit-like breath odor increased hunger increased thirst increased urination nausea sweating troubled breathing unexplained weight loss vomiting); ***hypokalemia*** (abdominal pain confusion irregular heartbeat nausea or vomiting nervousness numbness or tingling in hands, feet, or lips shortness of breath difficult breathing weakness or heaviness of legs); ***hypertonia*** (excessive muscle tone, muscle tension or tightness, muscle stiffness); ***hypoesthesia*** (burning, crawling, itching, numbness, prickling, "pins and needles", or tingling feelings); ***hypoglycemia*** (anxiety; blurred vision; chills; cold sweats; coma; confusion; cool, pale skin; depression; dizziness; fast heartbeat; headache; increased hunger; nausea; nervousness; nightmares; seizures; shakiness; slurred speech; unusual tiredness or weakness); ***hyponatremia*** (coma; confusion; convulsions; decreased urine output; dizziness; fast or irregular heartbeat; headache; increased thirst; muscle pain or cramps; nausea or vomiting; shortness of breath; swelling of face, ankles, or hands; unusual tiredness or weakness); ***influenza-like symptoms*** (chills; fever; muscle aches and pains); ***injection site reaction*** (bleeding, blistering, burning, coldness, discoloration of skin, feeling of pressure, hives, infection, inflammation, itching, lumps, numbness, pain, rash, redness, scarring, soreness, stinging, swelling, tenderness, tingling, ulceration, or warmth at site); ***increased sweating; laryngitis*** (cough dryness or soreness of throat hoarseness trouble in swallowing voice changes); ***leg cramps; leukopenia*** (black, tarry stools; chest pain; chills; cough; fever; painful or difficult urination; shortness of breath; sore throat; sores, ulcers, or white spots on lips or in mouth; swollen glands; unusual bleeding or bruising; unusual tiredness or weakness); ***menstrual disorder*** (painful menstruation; absence of menstruation); ***micturition*** (trouble in holding or releasing urine; painful urination); ***migraine*** (headache, severe and throbbing); ***myalgia*** (muscle pain); ***nail disorder; neck stiffness; nervousness; palpitations*** (pounding heartbeat); ***paresthesias*** (numbness or tingling in fingers and/or toes); ***somnolence*** (sleepiness); ***photosensitivity reaction*** (increased sensitivity of skin to sunlight itching redness or other discoloration of skin severe sunburn skin rash); ***prostatic disorder; pruritus; reflux*** (heartburn; vomiting); ***skin disorder; skin nodule*** (small lumps under the skin); ***stomatitis*** (swelling or inflammation of the mouth); ***synovitis*** (joint or muscle pain or stiffness); ***taste perversion*** (change in sense of taste); ***tear abnormality; tendonitis*** (joint pain or stiffness); ***tenesmus*** (frequent urge to defecate straining while passing stool); ***thrombocythemia*** (pain, warmth, or burning in fingers, toes and legs, headache, dizziness, problems with vision or hearing with vision or hearing); ***tinnitus*** (buzzing or ringing noise in ears); ***tooth disorder; urinary incontinence*** (loss of bladder control); ***urinary tract infection*** (pain or burning while urinating); ***urticaria*** (hives or welts itching redness of skin skin rash); ***vaginitis*** (itching of the vagina or genital area pain during sexual intercourse thick, white vaginal discharge with no odor or with a mild odor); ***vertigo*** (dizziness); ***vomiting***

Incidence rare

Ageusia (loss of sense of taste); ***anaphylactoid reaction*** (cough; difficulty swallowing; dizziness; fast heartbeat; hives; itching; puffiness or swelling of the eyelids or around the eyes, face, lips or tongue; shortness of breath; skin rash; tightness in chest; unusual tiredness or weakness; wheezing); ***anosmia*** (loss of sense of smell); ***ataxia*** (shakiness and unsteady walk, unsteadiness. trembling, or other problems with muscle control or coordination); ***erythema multiforme*** (blistering, peeling, loosening of skin; chills; cough; diarrhea; fever; itching; joint or muscle pain; red irritated eyes; sore throat; sores, ulcers, or white spots in mouth or on lips; unusual tiredness or weakness); ***esophageal perforation*** (chest pain; troubled breathing; swelling of the neck; vomiting); ***ileus*** (abdominal pain; severe constipation; severe vomiting); ***interstitial nephritis*** (bloody or cloudy urine; fever, skin rash, swelling of feet or lower legs; greatly decreased frequency of urination or amount of urine,); ***intestinal obstruction*** (abdominal pain, severe constipation; nausea; vomiting); ***intestinal perforation*** (severe abdominal pain, cramping, burning; bloody, black, or tarry stools; trouble breathing; vomiting of material that looks like coffee grounds; severe and continuing nausea, heartburn, and/or indigestion); ***pancreatitis*** (bloating; chills; constipation; darkened urine; fast heartbeat; fever; indigestion; loss of appetite; nausea; pains in stomach, side, or abdomen, possibly radiating to the back; vomiting; yellow eyes or skin); ***thrombocytopenia*** (black, tarry stools; bleeding gums; blood in urine or stools; pinpoint red spots on skin; unusual bleeding or bruising)

Overdose

For specific information on the agents used in the management of celecoxib overdose, see:

- *Charcoal, Activated (Oral-Local)* monograph.

For more information on the management of overdose or unintentional ingestion, **contact a Poison Control Center** (see *Poison Control Center Listing*).

Clinical effects of overdose

The following effects have been selected on the basis of their potential clinical significance (possible signs and symptoms in parentheses where appropriate)—not necessarily inclusive:

Acute and/or chronic

Acute renal failure (shortness of breath, troubled breathing, tightness in chest and/or wheezing; sudden decrease in the amount of urine; swelling of face, fingers, and/or lower legs; continuing thirst; unusual tiredness or weakness; weight gain); ***coma; drowsiness; epigastric pain*** (stomach pain); ***gastrointestinal bleeding*** (bloody or black, tarry stools; vomiting of blood or material that looks like coffee grounds); ***hypertension*** (dizziness; headache, severe or continuing); ***lethargy*** (unusual feeling of tiredness or weakness); ***nausea and/or vomiting; respiratory depression*** (difficulty breathing)

Treatment of overdose

To decrease absorption—Emptying the stomach via induction of emesis. Administering activated charcoal.

To enhance elimination—Administering an osmotic cathartic within 4 hours of ingestion with symptoms or following a large overdose. Hemodialysis is not effective due to celecoxib's high protein binding.

Supportive care—Monitoring and supporting vital functions. Patients in whom intentional overdose is confirmed or suspected should be referred for psychiatric consultation.

Patient Consultation

As an aid to patient consultation, refer to *Advice for the Patient, Celecoxib (Systemic)*.

In providing consultation, consider emphasizing the following selected information (» = major clinical significance):

Before using this medication

» Conditions affecting use, especially:
 Sensitivity to celecoxib
 Allergies to aspirin, any other nonsteroidal anti-inflammatory drugs (NSAIDs), or sulfonamide-type medications
 Pregnancy—Use of celecoxib during late pregnancy is not recommended because of possible dystocia and prolonged parturition
 Breast-feeding—Celecoxib may potentially cause adverse effects in the nursing infant
 Other medications, especially aspirin, corticosteroids, anticoagulants, lithium, or fluconazole
 Other medical problems, especially allergic reaction induced by aspirin, other nonsteroidal anti-inflammatory drugs (NSAIDs), or sulfonamide-type drugs; aspirin-induced nasal polyps associated with bronchospasm; asthma (pre-existing); bleeding (active or prior history of); peptic ulcer disease (active or prior history of) cardiovascular disease; CABG surgery; congestive heart failure; hepatic function impairment; or renal function impairment

Proper use of this medication

» Not taking more medication than prescribed
» Proper dosing
 Missed dose: Taking as soon as possible; not taking if almost time for next dose; not doubling doses
» Proper storage

Precautions while using this medication

» Regular visits to physician during prolonged therapy
» Possibility that use of alcohol may increase the risk of ulceration
» Not taking two or more NSAIDs, including ketorolac, concurrently, and not taking acetaminophen or aspirin or other salicylates for more than a few days while receiving NSAID therapy, unless concurrent use is prescribed by, and patient remains under the care of, a physician or dentist
» Importance of immediately reporting to physician symptoms of edema, gastrointestinal bleeding or ulceration, cardiovascular events, unusual weight gain, or skin rash
» Notifying physician immediately if symptoms of hepatotoxicity occur, such as fever, fatigue, itching of the skin, lethargy, nausea, or stomach pain
» Possibility of anaphylaxis

Side/adverse effects

Signs of potential side effects, especially anemia, angina, breast fibroadenosis, breast neoplasm, chest pain, coronary artery disorder, diabetes mellitus, diverticulitis, dysmenorrhea, edema, herpes simplex, herpes zoster, hiatal hernia, hypertension, aggravated, infection, moniliasis, neuralgia, neuropathy, pneumonia, prostatic disorder, skin rash, upper respiratory tract infection, bronchitis, dyspnea, gastritis, gastroenteritis, gastrointestinal bleeding or ulceration, influenza-like symptoms, unusual weight gain, and vaginal hemorrhage

General Dosing Information

Physicians should monitor patients for signs and symptoms of gastrointestinal bleeding.

Celecoxib should not be substituted for corticosteroid treatment or treatment of corticosteroid insufficiency. Patients should be slowly tapered off of corticosteroid therapy, if discontinuation of therapy is needed.

Celecoxib has not been shown to reduce colorectal, duodenal or other familial adenomatous polyposis (FAP)-related cancers, or the need for endoscopic surveillance, prophylactic or other FAP-related surgery.

Oral Dosage Forms

CELECOXIB CAPSULES

Usual adult dose

Ankylosing spondylitis—

Oral, 200 mg in single or divided dose, may be increased to 400 mg after 6 weeks if no effect is observed.

Arthritis, rheumatoid—

Oral, 100 to 200 mg twice a day.

Dysmenorrhea—

Oral, 400 mg initially, followed by a 200 mg dose if needed on the first day, then 200 mg twice a day as needed.

Familial adenomatous polyposis [FAP]—

Oral, 400 mg twice a day to be taken with food.

Osteoarthritis—

Oral, 200 mg daily as a single dose or 100 mg twice a day.

Pain—

Oral, 400 mg initially, followed by a 200 mg dose if needed on the first day, then 200 mg twice a day as needed.

Note: The dose of celecoxib should be reduced by approximately 50% in patients with moderate hepatic impairment.

Usual pediatric dose

Safety and efficacy have not been established.

Usual geriatric dose

See *Usual adult dose*.

Note: It is recommended that therapy with celecoxib be initiated at the lowest recommended dose in elderly patients less than 50 kg of body weight.

Strength(s) usually available

U.S.—

100 (Rx) [*Celebrex* (croscarmellose sodium; edible inks; gelatin; lactose monohydrate; magnesium stearate; povidone; sodium lauryl sulfate; titanium dioxide)].

200 (Rx) [*Celebrex* (croscarmellose sodium; edible inks; gelatin; lactose monohydrate; magnesium stearate; povidone; sodium lauryl sulfate; titanium dioxide)].

400 (Rx) [*Celebrex* (croscarmellose sodium; edible inks; gelatin; lactose monohydrate; magnesium stearate; povidone; sodium lauryl sulfate; titanium dioxide)].

Canada—

100 (Rx) [*Celebrex* (croscarmellose sodium; edible inks; gelatin; lactose monohydrate; magnesium stearate; povidone; sodium lauryl sulfate; titanium dioxide)].

200 (Rx) [*Celebrex* (croscarmellose sodium; edible inks; gelatin; lactose monohydrate; magnesium stearate; povidone; sodium lauryl sulfate; titanium dioxide)].

Packaging and storage

Store at 25 °C (77 °F), unless otherwise specified by manufacturer.

Revised: 10/21/2005
Developed: 04/16/1999

CEPHALEXIN—See *Cephalosporins (Systemic)*

CEPHALOSPORINS Systemic

Note: Products containing cefixime were withdrawn from the U.S. market by Wyeth in October 2002

This monograph includes information on the following: 1) Cefaclor; 2) Cefadroxil; 3) Cefamandole; 4) Cefazolin; 5) Cefdinir†; 6) Cefditoren†; 7) Cefepime; 8) Cefixime*; 9) Cefonicid†; 10) Cefoperazone†; 11) Cefotaxime; 12) Cefotetan; 13) Cefoxitin; 14) Cefpodoxime†; 15) Cefprozil; 16) Ceftazidime; 17) Ceftibuten†; 18) Ceftizoxime; 19) Ceftriaxone; 20) Cefuroxime; 21) Cephalexin; 22) Cephalothin*; 23) Cephapirin†; 24) Cephradine†.

VA CLASSIFICATION (Primary):

Cefaclor—AM116
Cefadroxil—AM115
Cefamandole—AM116
Cefazolin—AM115
Cefdinir—AM117
Cefditoren—AM117
Cefepime—AM118
Cefixime—AM117
Cefonicid—AM116
Cefoperazone—AM117
Cefotaxime—AM117
Cefotetan—AM116
Cefoxitin—AM116
Cefpodoxime—AM117
Cefprozil—AM116
Ceftazidime—AM117
Ceftibuten—AM117
Ceftizoxime—AM117
Ceftriaxone—AM117
Cefuroxime—AM116
Cephalexin—AM115
Cephalothin—AM115
Cephapirin—AM115
Cephradine—AM115

Commonly used brand name(s): *Ancef*[4]; *Apo-Cefaclor*[1]; *Apo-Cephalex*[21]; *Ceclor*[1]; *Ceclor CD*[1]; *Cedax*[17]; *Cefadyl*[23]; *Cefizox*[18]; *Cefobid*[10]; *Cefotan*[12]; *Ceftin*[20]; *Cefzil*[15]; *Ceporacin*[22]; *Ceptaz*[16]; *Claforan*[11]; *Duricef*[2]; *Fortaz*[16]; *Keflex*[21]; *Keflin*[22]; *Keftab*[21]; *Kefurox*[20]; *Kefzol*[4]; *Mandol*[3]; *Maxipime*[7]; *Mefoxin*[13]; *Monocid*[9]; *Novo-Lexin*[21]; *Nu-Cephalex*[21]; *Omnicef*[5]; *PMS-Cephalexin*[21]; *Rocephin*[19]; *Spectracef* ™[6]; *Suprax*[8]; *Tazicef*[16]; *Tazidime*[16]; *Vantin*[14]; *Velosef*[24]; *Zinacef*[20].

Note: For a listing of dosage forms and brand names by country availability, see *Dosage Forms* section(s).

---

*Not commercially available in U.S.
†Not commercially available in Canada.

Category

Antibacterial (systemic).

Indications

Note: Products containing cefixime were withdrawn from the U.S. market by Wyeth in October 2002

Note: Bracketed information in the *Indications* section refers to uses that are not included in U.S. product labeling.

General Considerations

Cephalosporins have been classified by "generation" based on their spectrum of antibacterial activity, providing a useful, although somewhat arbitrary, means of grouping the many cephalosporins available. Several of the newer cephalosporins with an expanded spectrum of activity do not fit into any one generation but overlap into others. These medications have been placed into the generation that most closely describes their antibacterial spectrum.

First-generation cephalosporins include cefadroxil, cefazolin, cephalexin, cephalothin, cephapirin, and cephradine.

Second-generation cephalosporins include cefaclor, cefamandole, cefonicid, cefotetan, cefoxitin, cefprozil, and cefuroxime.

Third-generation cephalosporins include cefdinir, cefditoren, cefixime, cefoperazone, cefotaxime, cefpodoxime, ceftazidime, ceftibuten, ceftizoxime, and ceftriaxone.

The fourth-generation cephalosporin is cefepime.

Selection of any antimicrobial agent usually is based on the organism(s) that is present or most likely to be present, site(s) of infection, resistance patterns, and the side effects, cost, and pharmacokinetic properties of the cephalosporin. (See also *Table 1* and *Table 2*.)

First-generation cephalosporins have the highest degree of activity compared with other cephalosporins against most gram-positive bacteria, including beta-lactamase-producing *Staphylococcus aureus* and most streptococci; exceptions include methicillin-resistant staphylococci and penicillin-resistant *Streptococcus pneumoniae*. No cephalosporin is effective against *Enterococcus faecalis*, *Enterococcus faecium*, or

Listeria monocytogenes infections. Gram-negative bacteria coverage is generally limited to *Escherichia coli*, *Klebsiella pneumoniae*, and *Proteus mirabilis*; cephalothin, cephapirin, and cephradine are also active, although poorly, against *Haemophilus influenzae*. Cephalothin and cefazolin have similar spectra of activity *in vitro*. Although cefazolin is more active against *E. coli* and *Klebsiella* species, it is more susceptible to staphylococcal penicillinases than is cephalothin. Cephalexin, cefadroxil, and cephradine all have very similar activities *in vitro* and are available only in an oral dosage form.

First-generation cephalosporins are used to treat bacterial endocarditis, bone and joint infections, otitis media, pneumonia, septicemia, skin and soft tissue infections, including burn wound infections, and urinary tract infections caused by susceptible bacterial organisms. They are not effective in treating meningitis. These medications are possible alternatives to the penicillins for staphylococcal and nonenterococcal streptococcal infections, including pneumonias, bone and joint infections, and bacterial endocarditis. Cefazolin is the preferred agent for use in perioperative prophylaxis because of its longer half-life. Because first-generation cephalosporins provide inconsistent coverage against gram-negative bacilli, their empiric use as therapy for nosocomial infections is not recommended.

Second-generation cephalosporins have enhanced activity, compared with the first-generation cephalosporins, against *E. coli*, *Klebsiella* species, and *P. mirabilis;* in addition, they have greater activity *in vitro* against a larger number of gram-negative bacteria, including *H. influenzae*, indole-positive *Proteus*, *Moraxella (Branhamella) catarrhalis*, *Neisseria meningitidis*, *Neisseria gonorrhoeae*, and some strains of *Serratia* and *Enterobacter* species. *Serratia* and *Enterobacter* species may induce beta-lactamases that inactivate the drug after a period of exposure to the cephalosporin, producing a resistance that may be expressed late; this resistance may not be detectable by disc sensitivity techniques. The second-generation cephalosporins have slightly less or variable activity against most gram-positive cocci, and none have activity against *Acinetobacter* species or *Pseudomonas aeruginosa*.

Cefaclor and cephalexin have comparable activity *in vitro* against most gram-positive cocci; however, cefaclor has better activity than cephalexin against *H. influenzae*, *E. coli*, *M. catarrhalis*, and *P. mirabilis*. Cefamandole, cefonicid, and cefuroxime all have similar activities *in vitro*. However, cefuroxime may be more stable against plasmid-encoded beta-lactamases (e.g., TEM-1) than is cefamandole, and cefonicid has less activity *in vitro* against *S. aureus*. Cefuroxime sodium is the only second-generation cephalosporin to penetrate into the cerebrospinal fluid (CSF). Cefprozil has *in vitro* activity that covers a broad range of organisms, including many gram-positive and gram-negative organisms that are typically covered by first-generation cephalosporins. It also has good activity against *H. influenzae*, *M. catarrhalis*, *Citrobacter diversus*, penicillinase-producing strains of *N. gonorrhoeae*, and *P. mirabilis*.

Second-generation cephalosporins are used in the treatment of bone and joint infections, pneumonia, septicemia, skin and soft tissue infections, including burn wound, and urinary tract infections caused by susceptible bacterial organisms. Cefuroxime has been used to treat meningitis caused by *S. pneumoniae*, *H. influenzae* (including ampicillin-resistant strains), and *N. meningitidis*, although third-generation cephalosporins have better penetration into the CSF. Also, delayed sterilization of the CSF has been reported in children being treated with cefuroxime for bacterial meningitis. Because cefaclor has good activity against many strains of *H. influenzae*, it is used in the treatment of amoxicillin-resistant otitis media and sinusitis. This is also true of cefuroxime axetil, an oral prodrug that is hydrolyzed to cefuroxime after absorption. It has been used to treat mild to moderate bronchitis, Lyme disease, otitis media, pharyngitis and tonsillitis, sinusitis, skin and soft tissue infections, uncomplicated gonococcal urethritis, and urinary tract infections. Cefprozil is also used to treat bronchitis, otitis media, pharyngitis and tonsillitis, sinusitis, and skin and soft tissue infections.

Cefoxitin and cefotetan have the greatest activity of all the cephalosporins against anaerobes, particularly the *Bacteroides fragilis* group. Cefoxitin has the greatest stability in the presence of beta-lactamases produced by the *B. fragilis* group. Cefotetan has activity similar to that of cefoxitin against *B. fragilis*, but cefotetan has greater activity than cefoxitin against aerobic gram-negative bacilli in general. Most strains of *Bacteroides distasonis*, *Bacteroides ovatus*, and *Bacteroides thetaiotaomicron* are resistant to cefotetan *in vitro*. Many of the second- and third-generation cephalosporins that are active against anaerobic organisms are not effective against resistant strains of the *B. fragilis* group.

Cefoxitin and cefotetan are used primarily in the treatment of mixed aerobic-anaerobic bacterial infections, including aspiration pneumonia, diabetic foot infections, intraabdominal infections, and female pelvic infections. They are also used prophylactically to help prevent perioperative infections that may result from colorectal surgery and appendectomies, and in the treatment of penicillin-resistant strains of gonorrhea.

Most third-generation cephalosporins have a high degree of stability in the presence of beta-lactamases (penicillinases and cephalosporinases), and, therefore, have excellent activity against a wide spectrum of gram-negative bacteria, including penicillinase-producing strains of *N. gonorrhoeae* and most Enterobacteriaceae (*Citrobacter*, *E. coli*, *Enterobacter*, *Klebsiella*, *Morganella*, *Proteus*, *Providencia*, and *Serratia* species). However, third-generation cephalosporins in general are susceptible to hydrolysis by chromosomally encoded beta-lactamases. Cefdinir has no activity against *Enterobacter* species. Cefoperazone tends to have slightly less activity against Enterobacteriaceae than the other third-generation cephalosporins because of its greater susceptibility to plasmid-encoded beta-lactamases (e.g., TEM-1, TEM-2). Strains of *P. aeruginosa*, *Serratia*, and *Enterobacter* species may develop resistance to the cephalosporin after a period of exposure due to induction of beta-lactamases. The third-generation cephalosporins are generally not as active against gram-positive cocci as are the first- and second-generation cephalosporins. Cefotaxime, ceftizoxime, and ceftriaxone all have similar activity *in vitro*. Cefixime, one of three oral third-generation cephalosporins, has the most activity of all oral cephalosporins against *Streptococcus pyogenes*, *S. pneumoniae*, and all gram-negative bacilli, including beta-lactamase-producing strains of *H. influenzae*, *M. catarrhalis*, and *N. gonorrhoeae*. Cefixime has little activity against staphylococci. Cefpodoxime is also an oral third-generation cephalosporin; its spectrum of activity is very similar to that of cefixime, except that cefpodoxime also has some activity against *S. aureus* and *Staphylococcus saprophyticus*. Most species of *Enterobacter*, *Enterococcus*, *Pseudomonas*, *Morganella*, and *Serratia* are resistant to cefpodoxime. Ceftibuten is the oral third-generation cephalosporin that is most resistant to beta-lactamases. It has a broad spectrum of activity *in vitro* against many gram-negative and selected gram-positive microorganisms, including *H. influenzae*, *M. catarrhalis*, *S. pneumoniae*, and *S. pyogenes*.

Ceftazidime has the greatest activity of the third-generation cephalosporins against *P. aeruginosa*. Cefoperazone is less effective than ceftazidime, but more effective than cefotaxime, against *P. aeruginosa*. The other third-generation cephalosporins tend to have variable activity against this pathogen. Cefdinir and cefixime have no activity against *Pseudomonas* species.Cefoperazone achieves higher biliary concentrations than the other third-generation cephalosporins but has poor CSF penetration.

Cefditoren has activity against *Haemophilus influenzae* (including β-lactamase-producing strains), *Haemophilus parainfluenzae* (including β-lactamase-producing strains), *Moraxella catarrhalis* (including β-lactamase-producing strains), *Staphylococcus aureus* (including β-lactamase-producing strains), *Streptococcus pneumoniae* (penicillin–susceptible strains only), and *Streptococcus pyogenes*.

Third-generation cephalosporins and aminoglycosides (amikacin, gentamicin, netilmicin, or tobramycin) are synergistic *in vitro* against certain susceptible and resistant strains of *P. aeruginosa* as well as *Serratia marcescens* and other Enterobacteriaceae, including *Enterobacter cloacae*, *E. coli*, *K. pneumoniae*, and *P. mirabilis*.

Third-generation cephalosporins are used in the treatment of serious gram-negative bacterial infections, including bone and joint infections, female pelvic infections, intraabdominal infections, gram-negative pneumonia, septicemia, skin and soft tissue infections, including burn wound infections, and complicated urinary tract infections caused by susceptible organisms. Cefotaxime, ceftazidime, ceftizoxime, and ceftriaxone are used to treat meningitis in both children and adults. Single-dose cefixime, cefotaxime, cefpodoxime, ceftizoxime, and ceftriaxone have been found to be effective in the treatment of uncomplicated gonorrhea; single-dose ceftriaxone is used to treat acute otitis media; and cefuroxime axetil, [ceftriaxone], and [cefotaxime] are also effective in the treatment of Lyme disease.

The fourth-generation cephalosporin cefepime generally is more resistant to hydrolysis by beta-lactamases than are the third-generation cephalosporins. However, some medical experts group cefepime with the third-generation cephalosporins. Cefepime is stable against plasmid-encoded beta-lactamases (e.g., TEM-1, TEM-2, SHV-1) and is also relatively resistant to the inducible chromosomally encoded beta-lactamases; in addition, it penetrates rapidly into gram-negative bacteria and targets multiple essential penicillin-binding proteins. These properties of cefepime make it a useful agent in treating infections caused by many Enterobacteriaceae, including *Citrobacter freundii* and *E. cloacae*, that are resistant to other cephalosporins. Although cefepime has similar activity to ceftazidime against *P. aeruginosa* and other gram-negative bacteria, cefepime is less active than ceftazidime against other *Pseudomonas* species and *Stenotrophomonas (Pseudomonas) maltophilia*. The activity against gram-positive microorganisms is similar for cefepime, cefotaxime, and ceftriaxone. Cefepime is inactive against, methicillin-resistant staphylococci, penicillin-resistant pneumococci, most strains of *Clostridium difficile*, and most strains of enterococci such as *Enterococcus faecalis*.

Cefepime is effective in the treatment of complicated intraabdominal infections, pneumonia, uncomplicated skin and soft tissue infections, complicated and uncomplicated urinary tract infections, and in the empiric treatment of febrile neutropenia. [It is also used in the treatment of bronchitis and septicemia.]

Accepted

Biliary tract infections (treatment)[1]—Cefazolin is indicated in the treatment of biliary tract infections caused by susceptible organisms.

Bone and joint infections (treatment)—[Cefaclor][1], [cefadroxil][1], cefamandole, cefazolin, [cefixime][1], cefonicid[1], [cefoperazone][1], cefotaxime[1], cefotetan, cefoxitin, [cefpodoxime][1], [cefprozil][1], ceftazidime, ceftizoxime, ceftriaxone, cefuroxime, cephalexin, [cephalothin], cephapirin[1], and [cephradine][1] are indicated in the treatment of bone and joint infections caused by susceptible organisms.

Bronchitis (treatment)—Cefaclor, cefixime, cefprozil[1], and cefuroxime axetil are indicated in the treatment of secondary bacterial infections of acute bronchitis caused by susceptible organisms.

Bronchitis, bacterial exacerbations (treatment)—Cefaclor[1], cefdinir, cefditoren[1] [cefepime], cefixime[1], cefpodoxime[1], cefprozil[1], ceftibuten[1], and cefuroxime axetil[1] are indicated in the treatment of bacterial exacerbations of chronic bronchitis caused by susceptible organisms.

Endocarditis, bacterial (treatment)—Cefazolin, [cephalothin], cephapirin[1], and [cephradine][1] are indicated in the treatment of bacterial endocarditis caused by susceptible organisms.

Genitourinary tract infections (treatment)—Cefazolin, cefoperazone[1], cefotaxime, cephalexin, [cephalothin], and cephradine[1] are indicated in the treatment of genitourinary tract infections, including epididymitis and prostatitis.

Gonorrhea, disseminated (treatment)[1]—Cefuroxime is indicated in the treatment of disseminated gonorrhea.

Gonorrhea, uncomplicated (treatment)—Cefixime, cefotaxime, cefpodoxime[1], ceftizoxime[1], ceftriaxone, cefuroxime, and cefuroxime axetil are indicated in the treatment of uncomplicated gonorrhea.

Impetigo (treatment)[1]—Cefadroxil, cefuroxime axetil, and [cephalexin] (Evidence rating: III) are indicated in the treatment of impetigo.

Intraabdominal infections (treatment)—Cefamandole, cefepime, cefoperazone[1], cefotaxime, cefotetan, cefoxitin, ceftazidime, ceftizoxime, ceftriaxone, and [cephalothin] are indicated in the treatment of intraabdominal infections caused by susceptible organisms.

Lyme disease (treatment)[1]—[Cefotaxime], [ceftriaxone], and cefuroxime axetil are indicated in the treatment of Lyme disease.

Meningitis (treatment)—Cefotaxime, ceftazidime, ceftizoxime[1], ceftriaxone, and cefuroxime are indicated in the treatment of meningitis caused by susceptible organisms.

Although indicated, cefuroxime is no longer considered a medication of choice in the treatment of bacterial meningitis due to its poor coverage of penicillin-resistant *S. pneumoniae* and subsequent therapeutic failures.

Neutropenia, febrile (treatment)—Cefepime and [ceftazidime][1] are indicated for empiric treatment of febrile neutropenia.

In patients at high risk for severe infection, including patients with a history of recent bone marrow transplantation, with hypotension at presentation, with an underlying hematologic malignancy, or with severe or prolonged neutropenia, antimicrobial therapy alone may not be appropriate.

Otitis media (treatment)—Cefaclor, [cefadroxil][1], [cefazolin][1], cefdinir, cefixime, cefpodoxime[1], cefprozil, ceftibuten[1], ceftriaxone[1], cefuroxime axetil, cephalexin, [cephalothin][1], [cephapirin][1], and cephradine[1] are indicated in the treatment of otitis media caused by susceptible organisms.

Pelvic infections, female (treatment)—Cefoperazone[1], cefotaxime, cefotetan, cefoxitin, cefpodoxime[1], ceftazidime[1], ceftizoxime[1], and ceftriaxone[1] are indicated in the treatment of female pelvic infections caused by susceptible organisms.

Perioperative infections (prophylaxis)—Cefamandole[1], cefazolin, cefonicid[1], cefotaxime, cefotetan, cefoxitin, ceftriaxone, cefuroxime, [cephalothin], and cephapirin[1] are indicated for the prophylaxis of perioperative infections caused by susceptible organisms.

Pharyngitis, bacterial (treatment) or Tonsillitis (treatment)—Cefaclor, cefadroxil, cefdinir, cefditoren[1] cefixime, cefpodoxime[1], cefprozil, ceftibuten[1], cefuroxime axetil, cephalexin, and cephradine[1] are indicated in the treatment of bacterial pharyngitis and tonsillitis caused by susceptible organisms.

Penicillin is the usual medication of choice in the treatment of streptococcal infections, including the prophylaxis of rheumatic fever. These cephalosporins are generally effective in the eradication of streptococci from the nasopharynx; however, substantial data establishing the efficacy of cephalosporins in the prevention of subsequent rheumatic fever are not available at present.

Pneumonia, bacterial (treatment)—Cefaclor, [cefadroxil], cefamandole, cefazolin, cefdinir, cefepime, cefotaxime, cefoxitin, cefpodoxime[1], [cefprozil][1], ceftazidime, ceftriaxone[1], cefuroxime, [cefuroxime axetil], [cephalothin], and cephradine[1] are indicated in the treatment of bacterial pneumonia caused by susceptible organisms.

Pulmonary infections, in cystic fibrosis (treatment)—[Cefaclor], [cefamandole], and ceftazidime[1] are indicated in the treatment of pulmonary infections due to susceptible organisms in patients with cystic fibrosis.

Septicemia, bacterial (treatment)—Cefamandole, cefazolin, [cefepime], cefonicid[1], cefoperazone[1], cefotaxime, [cefotetan][1], cefoxitin, ceftazidime, ceftizoxime, ceftriaxone, cefuroxime[1], [cephalothin], cephapirin[1], and [cephradine][1] are indicated in the treatment of bacterial septicemia caused by susceptible organisms.

Sinusitis (treatment)—Cefdinir, [cefixime], cefprozil, and cefuroxime axetil are indicated in the treatment of sinusitis due to susceptible organisms.

Skin and soft tissue infections (treatment)—Cefaclor, cefadroxil, cefamandole, cefazolin, cefdinir, cefditoren[1], cefepime, [cefixime][1], cefonicid[1], cefoperazone[1], cefotaxime, cefotetan, cefoxitin, cefpodoxime[1], cefprozil, ceftazidime, ceftizoxime, ceftriaxone, cefuroxime, cefuroxime axetil, cephalexin, [cephalothin], cephapirin[1], and cephradine[1] are indicated in the treatment of skin and soft tissue infections caused by susceptible organisms.

Urinary tract infections, bacterial (treatment)—Cefaclor, cefadroxil, cefamandole, cefazolin, cefepime, cefixime, cefonicid[1], cefoperazone[1], cefotaxime, cefotetan, cefoxitin, cefpodoxime[1], [cefprozil], ceftazidime, ceftizoxime, ceftriaxone, cefuroxime, cefuroxime axetil[1], cephalexin, [cephalothin], cephapirin[1], and cephradine[1] are indicated in the treatment of bacterial urinary tract infections caused by susceptible organisms.

Ventriculitis (treatment)—Cefotaxime is indicated in the treatment of ventriculitis caused by susceptible organisms.

[Endocarditis, bacterial (prophylaxis)][1]—Cefadroxil, cefazolin, and cephalexin are indicated in the prevention of bacterial endocarditis caused by susceptible organisms. However, cefazolin and cephalexin are not recommended for genitourinary tract procedures.

[Melioidosis (treatment)][1]—Ceftazidime is indicated for the treatment of melioidosis.

Melioidosis is an infection with *Burkholderia pseudomallei*, previously known as *Pseudomonas pseudomallei*. It is endemic in areas of southeast Asia and the northern part of Australia. Melioidosis causes acute and chronic pulmonary disease, abscesses of the skin and internal organs, meningitis, brain abscess and cerebritis, and acute fulminant rapidly fatal sepsis. Infection with *B. pseudomallei* has a high mortality rate. It is more common among adults, individuals with diabetes, and individuals with chronic renal disease, but it can occur in normal hosts and children. Melioidosis can reactivate years after primary infection and result in chronic or acute life-threatening disease. Melioidosis should be considered as a potential diagnosis for any patient with exposure to areas of endemicity.

[Sinusitis, amoxicillin-resistant (treatment)][1]—Cefaclor is used in the treatment of sinusitis resistant to amoxicillin.

Unaccepted

None of the cephalosporins is considered to be effective against enterococci, *Listeria* species, chlamydia, *Clostridium difficile*, or methicillin-resistant *Staphylococcus epidermidis* or *S. aureus*.

---

[1]Not included in Canadian product labeling.

Pharmacology/Pharmacokinetics

See *Table 1*, page 789.

See *Table 2*, page 791.

Physicochemical characteristics

Molecular weight—

Cefaclor: 385.83.

Cefadroxil: 381.41.

Cefamandole nafate: 512.51.

Cefazolin sodium: 476.5.
Cefdinir: 395.42.
Cefditoren: 620.73.
Cefepime: 480.57.
Cefepime hydrochloride: 571.51.
Cefixime: 507.51.
Cefonicid sodium: 586.54.
Cefoperazone sodium: 667.66.
Cefotaxime sodium: 477.46.
Cefotetan disodium: 619.6.
Cefoxitin sodium: 449.44.
Cefpodoxime proxetil: 557.61.
Cefprozil: 407.45.
Ceftazidime: 636.67.
Ceftibuten: 410.43.
Ceftizoxime sodium: 405.39.
Ceftriaxone sodium: 661.61.
Cefuroxime axetil: 510.4.
Cefuroxime sodium: 446.38.
Cephalexin: 365.41.
Cephalothin sodium: 418.43.
Cephapirin sodium: 445.46.
Cephradine: 349.41.

Mechanism of action/Effect

Bactericidal; action depends on ability to reach and bind penicillin-binding proteins located in bacterial cytoplasmic membranes. Cephalosporins inhibit bacterial septum and cell wall synthesis, probably by acylation of membrane-bound transpeptidase enzymes. This prevents cross-linkage of peptidoglycan chains, which is necessary for bacterial cell wall strength and rigidity. Also, cell division and growth are inhibited, and elongation of susceptible bacteria and lysis frequently occur. Rapidly dividing bacteria are those most susceptible to the action of cephalosporins.

Distribution

Widely distributed throughout the body and reach therapeutic concentrations in most tissues and body fluids, including synovial, pericardial, pleural, and peritoneal fluids; bile; sputum; and urine. Also distributed into bone, the gallbladder, the myocardium, and skin and soft tissue. Most cephalosporins cross the placenta and are distributed into breast milk.

Cefoperazone and ceftriaxone reach the highest concentration in bile. Cefuroxime and ceftazidime reach the highest levels in the aqueous humor. Cefotaxime, ceftazidime, ceftizoxime, ceftriaxone, and cefuroxime are the only cephalosporins to achieve therapeutic concentrations in the cerebrospinal fluid (CSF).

Time to peak bile concentration

Cefoperazone—1 to 3 hours.
Cefditoren—1.5 to 3 hours

Bile concentration

Cefixime—Approximately 56.9 mcg per mL following a single 200-mg oral dose.

Cefoperazone—Approximately 65, 1940, and 6000 mcg per mL 0.5, 1, and 3 hours, respectively, following a 2-gram intravenous bolus dose.

Precautions to Consider

Cross-sensitivity and/or related problems

Patients allergic to one cephalosporin or cephamycin may be allergic to other cephalosporins or cephamycins also.

Patients allergic to penicillins, penicillin derivatives, or penicillamine may be allergic to cephalosporins or cephamycins also. Cephalosporin cross-reactivity is approximately 3 to 7% in patients with a documented history of penicillin allergy. Although cephalosporins have been administered without incident to some patients with rash-type penicillin allergy, caution is recommended when cephalosporins are administered to patients with a history of penicillin anaphylaxis since anaphylaxis may also occur after cephalosporin administration.

Carcinogenicity

Cefaclor, cefadroxil, cefazolin, cefdinir, cefditoren, cefepime, cefixime, cefonicid, cefoperazone, cefotaxime, cefotetan, cefoxitin, cefpodoxime, cefprozil, ceftazidime, ceftibuten, ceftizoxime, ceftriaxone, cefuroxime, cefuroxime axetil, and cephradine—Long-term studies in animals to evaluate the carcinogenic potential of these cephalosporins have not been done.

Mutagenicity

Cefaclor, cefadroxil, cefazolin, cefoxitin, and cephradine—Long-term studies in animals to evaluate the mutagenic potential of cefaclor, cefadroxil, cefazolin, cefoxitin, and cephradine have not been done.

Cefdinir, cefditoren, cefepime, cefixime, cefonicid, cefoperazone, cefotaxime, cefotetan, cefpodoxime, cefprozil, ceftazidime, ceftibuten, ceftizoxime, ceftriaxone, cefuroxime, and cefuroxime axetil—Studies have not shown that these cephalosporins are mutagenic.

Pregnancy/Reproduction

Fertility—

Cefamandole, cefditoren, cefoperazone, and cefotetan—

Adequate and well-controlled studies in humans have not been done.

Beta-lactam antibacterials containing the *N*-methylthiotetrazole (NMTT) side chain have not been shown to cause adverse effects on fertility in rats exposed *in utero*, in neonatal rats (4 days of age or younger) that were treated prior to initiation of spermatogenesis, or in older rats (more than 40 days of age) after exposure for up to 6 months. Beta-lactam antibacterials containing the NMTT side chain have been shown to cause delayed maturation of the testicular germinal epithelium when given to neonatal rats during initial spermatogenic development (6 to 40 days of age), although the effect was slight in rats given 30 to 100 mg per kg of body weight (mg/kg) daily. However, in those neonatal rats given 1000 mg/kg per day (approximately 5 to 20 times the usual human dose), delayed maturation was pronounced and was associated with decreased testicular weight, arrested spermatogenesis, a reduced number of germinal cells, and vacuolation of Sertoli's cell cytoplasm. In addition, some neonatal rats given 1000 mg/kg per day from days 6 to 40 were infertile after reaching sexual maturity.

Other cephalosporins—

Adequate and well-controlled studies in humans have not been done.

However, studies in animals have not shown that these cephalosporins cause impaired fertility.

Pregnancy—

Cefamandole, cefoperazone, and cefotetan—

Cefamandole, cefoperazone, and cefotetan cross the placenta. Adequate and well-controlled studies in humans have not been done.

Studies in mice, rats, and monkeys given doses of up to 10 times the usual human dose have not shown that cefamandole, cefoperazone, or cefotetan causes adverse effects in the fetus.

FDA Pregnancy Category B.

Cefdinir—

Adequate and well-controlled studies in humans have not been done.

Studies in rats given oral doses up to 70 times the recommended human dose or rabbits given oral doses up to 0.7 times the human dose have not shown that cefdinir is teratogenic. However, decrease in fetal and offspring weight was observed.

FDA Pregnancy Category B.

Cefditoren and Cefoxitin—

Cefoxitin crosses the placenta. Adequate and well-controlled studies in humans have not been done.

Studies in rats and mice given parenteral doses of approximately 1 to 7.5 times the maximum recommended human dose have not shown that cefoxitin is teratogenic or fetotoxic. However, a slight decrease in fetal weight was observed. Studies in rabbits have shown that cefoxitin, although not teratogenic, causes a high incidence of abortion and maternal death.

FDA Pregnancy Category B.

Cefotaxime—

Cefotaxime crosses the placenta. Adequate and well-controlled studies in humans have not been done.

Studies in rats given parenteral cefotaxime have not shown that cefotaxime is teratogenic or fetotoxic. However, a slight decrease in fetal and neonatal weight was observed.

FDA Pregnancy Category B.

Other cephalosporins—

Cephalosporins cross the placenta. Adequate and well-controlled studies in humans have not been done.

However, studies in animals have not shown that these cephalosporins cause adverse effects in the fetus.

FDA Pregnancy Category B—Cefaclor, cefadroxil, cefazolin, cefepime, cefixime, cefonicid, cefpodoxime, cefprozil, ceftazidime, ceftibuten, ceftizoxime, ceftriaxone, cefuroxime, cefuroxime axetil, cephalexin, cephapirin, and cephradine.

Breast-feeding

Cefadroxil, cefditoren, cefixime, and ceftibuten—It is not known whether cefadroxil, cefixime, or ceftibuten is distributed into breast milk. However, problems in humans have not been documented to date.

Cefdinir—Cefdinir was not detected in human breast milk following administration of a single 600-mg dose.

Other cephalosporins—Other cephalosporins are distributed into breast milk, usually in low concentrations. However, problems in humans have not been documented to date.

Pediatrics

All cephalosporins—Lower metabolic and/or renal clearance of cephalosporins, with resulting prolonged half-life, has been reported in newborn infants. However, ceftriaxone has been found to have a shorter half-life in infants than it does in adults.

Cefaclor and cefazolin—Appropriate studies on the relationship of age to the effects of cefaclor or cefazolin have not been performed in premature infants and infants up to 1 month of age. However, no pediatrics-specific problems have been documented to date in children 1 month of age and older.

Cefamandole—Appropriate studies on the relationship of age to the effects of cefamandole have not been performed in premature infants and infants up to 6 months of age. However, no pediatrics-specific problems have been documented to date in children 6 months of age and older.

Cefoperazone and cefotetan—Appropriate studies on the relationship of age to the effects of cefoperazone or cefotetan have not been performed in the pediatric population.

Cefdinir, cefixime, cefprozil, and ceftibuten—Appropriate studies on the relationship of age to the effects of cefdinir, cefixime, cefprozil, or ceftibuten have not been performed in children up to 6 months of age.

Cefditoren—Safety and efficacy have not been established in patients less than 12 years of age.

Cefonicid—Cefonicid has been used in children 1 year of age and older, and no pediatrics-specific problems have been documented to date.

Cefoxitin—In children 3 months of age and older, higher doses of cefoxitin have been associated with an increased incidence of eosinophilia and elevated aspartate aminotransferase (AST [SGOT]).

Cefpodoxime—Appropriate studies on the relationship of age to the effects of cefpodoxime have not been performed in children up to 5 months of age.

Ceftazidime L-arginine—The safety of the arginine component of ceftazidime L-arginine has not been established in children. If treatment with ceftazidime is indicated for children younger than 12 years of age, the ceftazidime sodium product should be used.

Ceftizoxime—Although studies have been done in children up to 6 months of age, ceftizoxime is not indicated for use in this age group. In children 6 months of age and older, the use of ceftizoxime has been associated with transient elevated eosinophil counts and increased concentrations of alanine aminotransferase (ALT [SGPT]), aspartate aminotransferase (AST [SGOT]), and creatine kinase (CK).

Ceftriaxone—Because ceftriaxone is very highly bound to plasma proteins, it may be more likely than some other cephalosporins to displace bilirubin from serum albumin. Ceftriaxone should be used with caution in hyperbilirubinemic neonates, especially premature neonates.

Cefuroxime, cefuroxime axetil, and cephapirin—Appropriate studies on the relationship of age to the effects of cefuroxime, cefuroxime axetil, and cephapirin have not been performed in children up to 3 months of age. However, no pediatrics-specific problems have been documented to date in children 3 months of age and older.

Cephradine—Appropriate studies on the relationship of age to the effects of cephradine have not been performed in children up to 9 months of age. However, no pediatrics-specific problems have been documented to date in children 9 months of age and older.

Other cephalosporins—Appropriate studies on the relationship of age to the effects of these cephalosporins have not been performed in the pediatric population. However, no pediatrics-specific problems have been documented to date.

Geriatrics

Cephalosporins have been used in the geriatric population, and no geriatrics-specific problems have been documented to date. However, elderly patients are more likely to have an age-related decrease in renal function, which may require an adjustment in dosage and/or dosing interval in patients receiving cephalosporins.

Dental

Long-term therapy with cephalosporins may allow for the overgrowth of *Candida albicans*, resulting in oral candidiasis.

Drug interactions and/or related problems

The following drug interactions and/or related problems have been selected on the basis of their potential clinical significance (possible mechanism in parentheses where appropriate)—not necessarily inclusive (» = major clinical significance):

Note: Combinations containing any of the following medications, depending on the amount present, may also interact with this medication.

» Alcohol

(concurrent use of alcohol with cefamandole, cefoperazone, or cefotetan is not recommended since these cephalosporins, because of their NMTT side chain, may inhibit the enzyme acetaldehyde dehydrogenase, resulting in accumulation of acetaldehyde in the blood)

(disulfiram-like effects such as abdominal or stomach cramps, facial flushing, headache, hypotension, nausea, palpitations, shortness of breath, sweating, tachycardia, or vomiting may occur following ingestion of alcohol or administration of intravenous alcohol-containing solutions; these effects usually occur within 15 to 30 minutes following ingestion of alcohol and usually subside spontaneously over several hours)

(patients should be advised not to drink alcoholic beverages, take alcohol-containing medications, or receive intravenous alcohol-containing solutions while receiving these cephalosporins and for several days after discontinuing them)

» Aminoglycoside antibiotics

(for cefuroxime: may result in nephrotoxicity)

Antacids or
Ranitidine or
Histamine H_2-receptor antagonists, other

(concurrent use of high doses of antacids or H_2-receptor antagonists with cefpodoxime decreases absorption of cefpodoxime by 27 to 32%, and decreases peak plasma levels by 24 to 42%)

(concurrent use of ranitidine with ceftibuten increases the plasma concentration of ceftibuten by 23% and systemic exposure by 16%; the clinical relevance of these increases is not known)

(the extent of absorption of cefaclor and cefdinir are decreased with concurrent use of aluminum hydroxide–or magnesium-containing antacids; cefaclor should not be taken within 1 hour of taking these antacids; cefdinir should not be taken within 2 hours of taking these antacids)

» Anticoagulants, coumarin- or indandione-derivative, or
» Heparin or
» Thrombolytic agents

(concurrent use of these medications with cefamandole, cefditoren, cefoperazone, or cefotetan may increase the risk of bleeding because of the NMTT side chain on these medications; however, critical illness, poor nutritional status, and the presence of liver disease may be more important risk factors for hypoprothrombinemia and bleeding; because all cephalosporins can inhibit vitamin K synthesis by suppressing gut flora, prophylactic vitamin K therapy is recommended when any of these medications is used for prolonged periods in malnourished or seriously ill patients; dosage adjustments of anticoagulants may be necessary during and after therapy with cefamandole, cefoperazone, or cefotetan; concurrent use of any of these three cephalosporins with thrombolytic agents may increase the risk of severe hemorrhage and is not recommended)

(an increased anticoagulant effect has been reported with concurrent use of cefaclor and oral anticoagulants)

» Diuretics, potent

(administration may adversely affect renal function thereby affecting cefuroxime elimination)

» Iron

(iron supplements, including multivitamins that contain iron, interfere with the absorption of cefdinir; cefdinir should not be taken within 2 hours of an iron supplement; iron-fortified infant formula does not significantly interfere with the absorption of cefdinir; cefdinir and iron-fortified formula can be administered concurrently)

Nephrotoxic medications (see *Appendix II*)

(cephalothin has been associated with an increased incidence of nephrotoxicity when used concurrently with aminoglycosides; this effect has rarely been seen with other commercially available cephalosporins used at appropriate doses; the potential for increased nephrotoxicity exists when cephalosporins are used with other nephrotoxic medications, such as loop diuretics, especially in patients with preexisting renal function impairment; renal function should be monitored carefully in patients receiving cephalosporins and aminoglycosides concurrently)

» Platelet aggregation inhibitors, other (see *Appendix II*)
(hypoprothrombinemia induced by large doses of salicylates and/or cephalosporins, and the gastrointestinal ulcerative or hemorrhagic potential of nonsteroidal anti-inflammatory drugs [NSAIDs], salicylates, or sulfinpyrazone may increase the risk of hemorrhage)

» Probenecid
(probenecid decreases renal tubular secretion of those cephalosporins excreted by this mechanism, resulting in increased and prolonged cephalosporin serum concentrations, prolonged elimination half-life, and increased risk of toxicity; probenecid has no effect on the excretion of cefoperazone, ceftazidime, or ceftriaxone; however, other cephalosporins and probenecid might be used concurrently in the treatment of infections, such as sexually transmitted diseases [STDs], or other infections in which high and/or prolonged antibiotic serum and tissue concentrations are required)

Laboratory value alterations

The following have been selected on the basis of their potential clinical significance (possible effect in parentheses where appropriate)—not necessarily inclusive (» = major clinical significance).

With diagnostic test results

» Coombs' (antiglobulin) tests
(a positive Coombs' reaction appears frequently in patients who receive large doses of a cephalosporin; hemolysis rarely occurs, but has been reported; test may become positive in neonates whose mothers received cephalosporins before delivery)

Copper reduction tests including Benedict's solution or CLINITEST®
tablets or
Fehling's solution
(false positive reactions for glucose in the urine may occur following treatment with cefditoren or cefuroxime.)

Corticosteroids, urinary
(high concentrations of cefoxitin in the urine may produce false increases in the measurement of urinary 17-hydroxycorticosteroids by the Porter-Silber reaction)

Creatinine, serum and urine
(cefotetan, cefoxitin, or cephalothin may falsely elevate test values when Jaffe's reaction method is used; serum samples should not be obtained within 2 hours after administration)

» Ferricyanide test
(cefuroxime may cause a false negative result for blood plasma glucose; blood plasma glucose levels should be determined by using either the glucose oxidase or hexokinase method.)

Glucose, blood
(cefprozil, cefuroxime, or cefuroxime axetil may give false-negative test results with ferricyanide tests; glucose enzymatic or hexokinase tests are recommended to determine blood glucose concentrations)

» Glucose, urine
(most cephalosporins [cefaclor, cefamandole, cefazolin, cefdinir, cefepime, cefixime, cefoperazone, cefotetan, cefoxitin, cefprozil, ceftazidime, cefuroxime, cefuroxime axetil, cephalexin, cephalothin, cephapirin, cephradine] may produce false-positive or falsely elevated test results with copper-reduction tests [Benedict's, Fehling's, or *Clinitest*]; glucose enzymatic tests, such as *Clinistix* and *Tes-Tape*, are not affected)

Ketones, urine
(cefdinir and cefixime may produce a false-positive reaction for ketones in the urine with tests using nitroprusside; tests using nitroferricyanide are not affected)

Protein, urine
(cefamandole may produce false-positive test results for proteinuria with acid and denaturation-precipitation tests)

» Prothrombin time (PT)
(may be prolonged; cephalosporins may inhibit vitamin K synthesis by suppressing gut flora; also, ceftazidime and cephalosporins with the NMTT side chain [cefamandole, cefoperazone, cefotetan] have been associated with an increased incidence of hypoprothrombinemia; patients who are critically ill, malnourished, or have liver function impairment may be at the highest risk of bleeding)

With physiology/laboratory test values

Alanine aminotransferase (ALT [SGPT]) or
Alkaline phosphatase or
Aspartate aminotransferase (AST [SGOT]) or
Lactate dehydrogenase (LDH)
(serum values may be increased)

Bilirubin, serum or
Blood urea nitrogen (BUN) or
Creatinine, serum
(concentrations may be increased)

Carnitine or
Hematocrit
(values may decrease during therapy)

Cerebrospinal fluid
(for cefuroxime: persistence of positive cultures have been noted at 18 to 36 hours; clinical relevance is unknown)

Complete blood count (CBC) or
Platelet count
(transient leukopenia, neutropenia, agranulocytosis, thrombocytopenia, eosinophilia, lymphocytosis, and thrombocytosis have been seen on rare occasions)

» Prothrombin time
(prothrombin time should be monitored in patients with hepatic or renal impairment, or poor nutritional state, as well as patients receiving a protracted course of antimicrobial therapy, and patients previously stabilized on anticoagulant therapy)

Medical considerations/Contraindications

The medical considerations/contraindications included have been selected on the basis of their potential clinical significance (reasons given in parentheses where appropriate)—not necessarily inclusive (» = major clinical significance).

Except under special circumstances, this medication should not be used when the following medical problem exists:

» Previous allergic reaction (anaphylaxis) to penicillins, penicillin derivatives, penicillamine, or cephalosporins

Risk-benefit should be considered when the following medical problems exist:

» Carnitine deficiency
(cefditoren increases renal excretion of carnitine)

» Colitis, history of or
» Gastrointestinal disease, history of, especially ulcerative colitis, regional enteritis, or antibiotic-associated colitis
(cephalosporins may cause pseudomembranous colitis)

» Bleeding disorders, history of
(cefamandole, cefoperazone, and cefotetan, which contain the NMTT side chain, have been associated with an increased risk of bleeding; however, all cephalosporins may cause hypoprothrombinemia and, potentially, bleeding)

» Hepatic function impairment or
Poor nutritional state
(cefoperazone is primarily excreted in bile; may also cause elevated AST [SGOT], ALT [SGPT], and alkaline phosphatase; it is recommended that patients with both severe liver disease and significant renal disease receive a reduced dosage of cefoperazone)
(for cefuroxime: may be associated with a fall in prothrombin activity; exogenous Vitamin K should be administered as indicated)

Phenylketonuria
(cefprozil for oral suspension contains 28 mg of phenylalanine per 5 mL)

» Renal function impairment
(many cephalosporins are excreted renally; a reduced dosage is recommended in patients with renal function impairment receiving cefadroxil, cefamandole, cefazolin, cefdinir, cefepime, cefixime, cefonicid, cefotaxime, cefotetan, cefoxitin, cefpodoxime, cefprozil, ceftazidime, ceftibuten, ceftizoxime, cefuroxime, cephalothin, cephapirin, and cephradine)

Patient monitoring

The following may be especially important in patient monitoring (other tests may be warranted in some patients, depending on condition; » = major clinical significance):

For all cephalosporins

Bleeding time and/or
» Prothrombin time (PT)
(determinations may be required in selected patients prior to and during therapy since hypoprothrombinemia and decreased vitamin K-dependent clotting factors may occur on rare occasion, resulting in significant hemorrhage; administration of vitamin K promptly reverses the hypoprothrombinemia, which usually occurs in elderly, debilitated, malnourished, or other seriously ill patients with deficient vitamin K stores; prophylactic daily or periodic administration of vitamin K may be required, especially in such patients receiving cefamandole, cefoperazone, or cefotetan)

For cefuroxime
Bacteriologic appraisal
(frequent appraisal is necessary during therapy of chronic urinary tract infection and may be required for several months post therapy)

» Renal function evaluation
(rarely produces alterations in kidney function; evaluations are especially recommended in seriously ill patients receiving the maximum doses)

» Superinfection
(prolonged use may result in overgrowth of nonsusceptible organisms; careful observation is essential)

For antibiotic-associated pseudomembranous colitis (AAPMC)
Stool examinations
(cytotoxin assays of stool samples to document the presence of *Clostridium difficile* and/or its cytotoxin, which can be neutralized by *Clostridium sordellii* antitoxin, may be required prior to treatment in patients with AAPMC; however, *C. difficile* and its cytotoxin may persist following treatment with oral vancomycin, cholestyramine, bacitracin, or metronidazole, despite clinical improvement; follow-up cytotoxin assays are generally not recommended with complete clinical improvement)

Side/Adverse Effects

The following side/adverse effects have been selected on the basis of their potential clinical significance (possible signs and symptoms in parentheses where appropriate)—not necessarily inclusive:

Those indicating need for medical attention

Incidence more frequent

Eosinophilia (black, tarry stools; chest pain; chills; cough; fever; painful or difficult urination; shortness of breath; sore throat; sores, ulcers, or white spots on lips or in mouth; swollen glands; unusual bleeding or bruising; unusual tiredness or weakness)

Incidence less frequent or rare

Hypersensitivity reactions (fever; skin itching, rash, or redness; swelling)—has occurred with many cephalosporins, but has been reported more commonly with cefazolin; ***hypoprothrombinemia*** (unusual bleeding or bruising)—more frequent for cefamandole, cefoperazone, and cefotetan; ***pseudomembranous colitis*** (abdominal or stomach cramps and pain, severe; abdominal tenderness; diarrhea, watery and severe, which may also be bloody; fever); ***thrombophlebitis*** (pain, redness, and swelling at site of injection); ***urticaria*** (hives or welts; itching; redness of skin; skin rash)

Incidence rare

Allergic reactions, specifically anaphylaxis (bronchospasm; hypotension); ***Epidermal necrolysis, toxic*** (blistering, peeling, loosening of skin; chills; cough; diarrhea; itching; joint or muscle pain; red irritated eyes; red skin lesions, often with a purple center; sore throat; sores, ulcers, or white spots in mouth or on lips; unusual tiredness or weakness); ***erythema multiforme or Stevens-Johnson syndrome*** (blistering, peeling, or loosening of skin and mucous membranes, which may involve the eyes or other organ systems); ***hearing loss***—has occurred rarely in pediatric patients being treated for meningitis, but more frequently with cefuroxime; ***hemolytic anemia, immune, drug-induced*** (unusual tiredness or weakness; yellowing of the eyes or skin)—has occurred with many cephalosporins, but has been reported more commonly with cefotetan; ***leukopenia, neutropenia, or thrombocytopenia*** (black, tarry stools; chest pain; chills; cough; fever; painful or difficult urination; shortness of breath; sore throat; sores, ulcers, or white spots on lips or in mouth; swollen glands; unusual bleeding or bruising; unusual tiredness or weakness); ***renal dysfunction*** (decrease in urine output or decrease in urine-concentrating ability); ***serum sickness-like reactions*** (fever; joint pain; skin rash)—may be more frequent with cefaclor; ***seizures***—especially with high doses and in patients with renal function impairment

Note: Since the risk of serum sickness-like reaction to cefaclor may be as high as 0.5%, it is recommended that another cephalosporin or a similar medication, such as loracarbef, be substituted as appropriate.

For ceftriaxone only; ***Biliary "sludge" or pseudolithiasis*** (anorexia; epigastric pain; nausea and vomiting)—more likely when administered by intravenous bolus over 3 to 5 minutes

Incidence unknown

Agranulocytosis (cough or hoarseness; fever with or without chills; general feeling of tiredness or weakness; lower back or side pain; painful or difficult urination; sore throat; sores, ulcers, or white spots on lips or in mouth; unusual bleeding or bruising); ***aplastic anemia*** (chest pain; chills; cough; fever; headache; shortness of breath; sores, ulcers, or white spots on lips or in mouth; swollen or painful glands; tightness in chest; unusual bleeding or bruising; unusual tiredness or weakness; wheezing); ***hemorrhage*** (bleeding gums; coughing up blood; difficulty in breathing or swallowing; dizziness; headache; increased menstrual flow or vaginal bleeding; nosebleeds; paralysis; prolonged bleeding from cuts; red or dark brown urine; red or black, tarry stools; shortness of breath); ***Hepatic dysfunction, including cholestasis*** (abdominal or stomach pain; chills; clay-colored stools; dark urine; diarrhea; dizziness; fever; headache; itching; loss of appetite; nausea; rash; unpleasant breath odor; unusual tiredness or weakness; vomiting of blood; yellow eyes or skin); ***pancytopenia*** (high fever; chills; unexplained bleeding or bruising; bloody, black, or tarry stools; pale skin; unusual tiredness or weakness; cough; shortness of breath; sores, ulcers, or white spots on lips or in mouth; swollen glands); ***superinfection*** (fever or chills; cough or hoarseness; lower back or side pain; painful or difficult urination); ***toxic nephropathy*** (bloody or cloudy urine; difficult or painful urination; sudden decrease in amount of urine)

For cefuroxime
Angioedema (large, hive-like swelling on face, eyelids, lips, tongue, throat, hands, legs, feet, sex organs)

Those indicating need for medical attention only if they continue or are bothersome

Incidence more frequent—less frequent with some cephalosporins

Gastrointestinal reactions (abdominal cramps; diarrhea, mild; nausea or vomiting); ***headache; oral candidiasis*** (sore mouth or tongue); ***stool changes***—with cefixime; ***vaginal candidiasis*** (vaginal itching and discharge)

Incidence less frequent or rare

Dizziness; drug fever; dyspepsia (acid or sour stomach; belching; heartburn; indigestion; stomach discomfort, upset or pain); ***flatulence*** (bloated full feeling; excess air or gas in stomach or intestines; passing gas); ***genital pruritus*** (itching or pain of the genital area)—with cefixime use; ***pruritus*** (itching skin); ***skin rash; vaginitis*** (itching of the vagina or genital area; pain during sexual intercourse; thick, white vaginal discharge with no odor or with a mild odor)

Those indicating possible pseudomembranous colitis and the need for medical attention if they occur after medication is discontinued

Abdominal or stomach cramps and pain, severe; abdominal tenderness; diarrhea, watery and severe, which may also be bloody; fever

Overdose

For more information on the management of overdose or unintentional ingestion, **contact a poison control center** (see *Poison Control Center Listing*).

Treatment of overdose

To decrease absorption—Activated charcoal may aid in decreasing the absorption of cefaclor and cephalexin; gastric lavage may be used to decrease the absorption of cefixime.

To enhance elimination—Hemodialysis may be used to aid in the removal of cefamandole, cefdinir, cefepime, cefotetan, cefpodoxime, cefprozil, ceftibuten, cefuroxime axetil, and cephalothin; peritoneal dialysis may also be used for cefpodoxime and cefuroxime axetil.

There is no known specific antidote to ceftriaxone and cefixime. Treatment is generally symptomatic and supportive.

Supportive care—Patients in whom intentional overdose is confirmed or suspected should be referred for psychiatric consultation.

Patient Consultation

Note: Products containing cefixime were withdrawn from the U.S. market by Wyeth in October 2002

As an aid to patient consultation, refer to *Advice for the Patient, Cephalosporins (Systemic)*.

In providing consultation, consider emphasizing the following selected information (» = major clinical significance):

Before using this medication

» Conditions affecting use, especially:
Allergies to penicillins, penicillin derivatives, penicillamine, or cephalosporins
Pregnancy—Cephalosporins cross the placenta
Breast-feeding—Most cephalosporins are distributed into breast milk; however, it is not known whether cefadroxil, cefditoren, cefixime, or ceftibuten is distributed into breast milk; no problems in humans have been documented
Use in children—Accumulation of cephalosporins, with resulting prolonged half-life, has been reported in newborn infants. Cefoxitin and ceftizoxime have been associated with an increased inci-

dence of eosinophilia and elevated aspartate aminotransferase (AST [SGOT]). Ceftizoxime also has been associated with elevated alanine aminotransferase (ALT [SGPT]) and creatine kinase (CK). Ceftriaxone should be used with caution in hyperbilirubinemic neonates since it may be more likely than other cephalosporins to displace bilirubin from serum albumin

Other medications, especially alcohol, anticoagulants, heparin, other platelet aggregation inhibitors, probenecid, or thrombolytic agents

Other medical problems, especially a history of bleeding disorders; a history of gastrointestinal disease, such as colitis; hepatic function impairment; low carnitine levels; or renal function impairment

Proper use of this medication

Taking on a full or empty stomach, or taking with food if gastrointestinal irritation occurs; cefaclor extended-release tablets, cefditoren, cefpodoxime proxetil, and cefuroxime axetil oral suspension should be taken with food; ceftibuten oral suspension should be taken on an empty stomach.

Proper administration technique for oral liquids; not using after expiration date

» Compliance with full course of therapy, especially in streptococcal infections

» Importance of not missing doses and of taking at evenly spaced times

» Proper dosing

Missed dose: Taking as soon as possible; not taking if almost time for next dose; not doubling doses

» Proper storage

Precautions while using this medication

Checking with physician if no improvement of symptoms within a few days

» Diabetics: False-positive reactions with copper-reduction tests for urine glucose may occur

» Patients with phenylketonuria (PKU): Cefprozil oral suspension contains phenylalanine

» For severe diarrhea, checking with physician before taking any antidiarrheals; for mild diarrhea, kaolin- or attapulgite-containing, but not other, antidiarrheals may be tried; checking with physician or pharmacist if mild diarrhea continues or worsens

» Avoiding alcoholic beverages or other alcohol-containing preparations while receiving, and for several days after discontinuing, cefamandole, cefoperazone, or cefotetan

Not taking antacids within 1 hour of taking cefaclor or within 2 hours of taking cefdinir

Side/adverse effects

Signs of potential side effects, especially eosinophilia, hypersensitivity reactions, hypoprothrombinemia, pseudomembranous colitis, thrombophlebitis, urticaria, erythema multiforme or Stevens-Johnson syndrome, hearing loss, drug-induced hemolytic anemia, leukopenia, neutropenia, thrombocytopenia, renal dysfunction, serum sickness-like reactions, seizures, biliary sludge or pseudolithiasis, agranulocytosis, aplastic anemia, hemorrhage, hepatic dysfunction including cholestasis, pancytopenia, superinfection, toxic nephropathy, or angioedema

General Dosing Information

Therapy should be continued for at least 10 days in group A beta-hemolytic streptococcal infections to help prevent the occurrence of acute rheumatic fever or glomerulonephritis.

For oral dosage forms only

Most cephalosporins may be taken either on a full or empty stomach. Taking them with food may help if gastrointestinal irritation occurs. Cefaclor extended-release tablets, cefpodoxime proxetil, and cefuroxime axetil oral suspension should be taken with food. Ceftibuten oral suspension should be taken on an empty stomach, 2 hours before or 1 hour after a meal.

For parenteral dosage forms only

Perioperative (preoperative, intraoperative, and postoperative) prophylactic administration of parenteral cephalosporins usually should be discontinued within 24 hours following surgery.

For treatment of adverse effects

For antibiotic-associated pseudomembranous colitis (AAPMC)—

Some patients may develop AAPMC, caused by *Clostridium difficile* toxin, during or following administration of cephalosporins. Mild cases may respond to discontinuation of the drug alone. Moderate to severe cases may require fluid, electrolyte, and protein replacement.

In cases not responding to the above measures or in more severe cases, oral doses of metronidazole, bacitracin, cholestyramine, or vancomycin may be used. Oral vancomycin is effective in doses of 125 to 500 mg every 6 hours for 7 to 10 days. The dose of metronidazole is 250 to 500 mg every 8 hours; cholestyramine, 4 grams four times a day; and bacitracin, 25,000 units, orally, four times a day for 5 to 10 days. Recurrences are not uncommon and may be treated with a second course of these medications.

Cholestyramine and colestipol resins have been shown to bind *C. difficile* toxin *in vitro*. If cholestyramine or colestipol resin is administered in conjunction with oral vancomycin, the medications should be administered several hours apart since the resins have been shown to bind oral vancomycin also.

In addition, AAPMC may result in severe watery diarrhea, which may occur during therapy or up to several weeks after therapy is discontinued. If diarrhea occurs, administration of antiperistaltic antidiarrheals (e.g., atropine and dephenoxylate combination, loperamide, opiates) is not recommended since they may delay the removal of toxins from the colon, thereby prolonging and/or worsening damage to the colon because of toxin retention.

If hypersensitivity reactions occur, cephalosporins should be discontinued and the patient should be treated with the usual agents (antihistamines, corticosteroids, or epinephrine or other pressor amines), oxygen, and airway management, including intubation.

If seizures occur, cephalosporins should be discontinued. Anticonvulsants may be administered if clinically indicated.

CEFACLOR

Summary of Differences

Category: Second-generation cephalosporin.

Indications: Good activity against *Haemophilus influenzae*. Used for amoxicillin-resistant sinusitis.

Drug interactions: Increased anticoagulant effect with oral anticoagulants.

Side/adverse effects: Serum sickness-like reactions more common.

Additional Dosing Information

Renal function impairment usually does not require a reduction in dose.

Cefaclor should not be taken within 1 hour of taking antacids.

Cefaclor extended-release tablets 500 mg two times a day are bioequivalent to the capsule formulation 250 mg three times a day, but are not bioequivalent to other cefaclor formulations 500 mg three times a day.

Extended-release tablets should be taken with food. They should not be cut, crushed, or chewed.

Oral Dosage Forms

Note: Bracketed uses in the *Dosage Forms* section refer to categories of use and/or indications that are not included in U.S. product labeling.

CEFACLOR CAPSULES USP

Usual adult and adolescent dose

[Bronchitis] or
Pharyngitis or
Pneumonia or
Skin and soft tissue infections, due to *Staphylococcus aureus* or *Streptococcus pyogenes* or
Tonsillitis or
Urinary tract infections—
Oral, 250 to 500 mg every eight hours.

Usual adult prescribing limits

2 grams per day; however, 4 grams per day have been administered.

Usual pediatric dose

This dosage form is usually not used for children. See *Cefaclor for Oral Suspension USP*.

Usual geriatric dose

See *Usual adult and adolescent dose*.

Strength(s) usually available

U.S.—
250 mg (Rx) [*Ceclor*].
500 mg (Rx) [*Ceclor*].

Canada—
250 mg (Rx) [*Apo-Cefaclor; Ceclor*].
500 mg (Rx) [*Apo-Cefaclor; Ceclor*].

Packaging and storage

Store below 40 °C (104 °F), preferably between 15 and 30 °C (59 and 86 °F), unless otherwise specified by manufacturer. Store in a tight container.

Auxiliary labeling
- Continue medicine for full time of treatment.

CEFACLOR FOR ORAL SUSPENSION USP

Usual adult and adolescent dose
See *Cefaclor Capsules USP*.

Usual adult prescribing limits
See *Cefaclor Capsules USP*.

Usual pediatric dose
[Bronchitis] or
Pneumonia or
Skin and soft tissue infections, due to *Staphylococcus aureus* or *Streptococcus pyogenes* or
Urinary tract infections—
Infants and children 1 month of age and older: Oral, 6.7 to 13.4 mg per kg of body weight every eight hours.
Infants up to 1 month of age: Safety and efficacy have not been established.
Otitis media or
Pharyngitis or
Tonsillitis—
Infants and children 1 month of age and older: Oral, 6.7 to 13.4 mg per kg of body weight every eight hours; or 10 to 20 mg per kg of body weight every twelve hours.
Infants up to 1 month of age: Safety and efficacy have not been established.

Usual pediatric prescribing limits
Doses of up to 60 mg per kg of body weight per day have been used. However, in older children, the maximum dose should not exceed 1.5 grams per day.

Usual geriatric dose
See *Cefaclor Capsules USP*.

Strength(s) usually available
U.S.—
125 mg per 5 mL (when reconstituted according to manufacturer's instructions) (available in 75- and 150-mL bottles) (Rx) [*Ceclor* (sucrose); GENERIC (may contain sucrose)].
187 mg per 5 mL (when reconstituted according to manufacturer's instructions) (available in 50- and 100-mL bottles) (Rx) [*Ceclor* (sucrose); GENERIC (may contain sucrose)].
250 mg per 5 mL (when reconstituted according to manufacturer's instructions) (available in 75- and 150-mL bottles) (Rx) [*Ceclor* (sucrose); GENERIC (may contain sucrose)].
375 mg per 5 mL (when reconstituted according to manufacturer's instructions) (available in 50- and 100-mL bottles) (Rx) [*Ceclor* (sucrose); GENERIC (may contain sucrose)].
Canada—
125 mg per 5 mL (when reconstituted according to manufacturer's instructions) (available in 100- and 150-mL bottles) (Rx) [*Apo-Cefaclor; Ceclor* (sucrose)].
250 mg per 5 mL (when reconstituted according to manufacturer's instructions) (available in 100- and 150-mL bottles) (Rx) [*Apo-Cefaclor; Ceclor* (sucrose)].
375 mg per 5 mL (when reconstituted according to manufacturer's instructions) (available in 70- and 100-mL bottles) (Rx) [*Apo-Cefaclor; Ceclor* (sucrose)].

Packaging and storage
Prior to reconstitution, store below 40 °C (104 °F), preferably between 15 and 30 °C (59 and 86 °F), unless otherwise specified by manufacturer. Store in a tight container.

Preparation of dosage form
See manufacturer's labeling for instructions.

Stability
After reconstitution, suspensions retain their potency for 14 days if refrigerated.

Auxiliary labeling
- Refrigerate.
- Shake well.
- Continue medicine for full time of treatment.
- Beyond-use date.

Note
When dispensing, include a calibrated liquid-measuring device.

CEFACLOR EXTENDED-RELEASE TABLETS

Usual adult and adolescent dose
Bronchitis or
Bronchitis, bacterial exacerbations—
Adults and adolescents 16 years of age and older: Oral, 500 mg every twelve hours for seven days.
Adolescents up to 16 years of age: Safety and efficacy have not been established.
Pharyngitis or
Tonsillitis—
Adults and adolescents 16 years of age and older: Oral, 375 mg every twelve hours for ten days.
Adolescents up to 16 years of age: Safety and efficacy have not been established.
Skin and soft tissue infections, uncomplicated, due to *Staphylococcus aureus*—
Adults and adolescents 16 years of age and older: Oral, 375 mg every twelve hours for seven to ten days
Adolescents up to 16 years of age: Safety and efficacy have not been established.

Usual pediatric dose
Children up to 16 years of age—Safety and efficacy have not been established.

Usual geriatric dose
See *Usual adult and adolescent dose.*

Strength(s) usually available
U.S.—
375 mg (Rx) [*Ceclor CD* (mannitol)].
500 mg (Rx) [*Ceclor CD* (mannitol)].
Canada—
Not commercially available.

Packaging and storage
Store at room temperature (15 to 30 °C [59 to 86 °F]).

Auxiliary labeling
- Take with food.
- Swallow whole.
- Continue medicine for full time of treatment.

CEFADROXIL

Summary of Differences
Category: First-generation cephalosporin.

Additional Dosing Information
May be taken with food.

Oral Dosage Forms
Note: Bracketed uses in the *Dosage Forms* section refer to categories of use and/or indications that are not included in U.S. product labeling.

CEFADROXIL CAPSULES USP

Usual adult and adolescent dose
[Endocarditis, prophylaxis][1]—
Oral, 2 grams one hour prior to the start of surgery.
Pharyngitis or
Tonsillitis—
Oral, 500 mg every twelve hours, or 1 gram once a day, for ten days.
[Pneumonia]—
Oral, 500 mg to 1 gram every twelve hours.
Skin and soft tissue infections—
Oral, 500 mg every twelve hours; or 1 gram once a day.
Urinary tract infections, uncomplicated—
Oral, 500 mg or 1 gram every twelve hours; or 1 or 2 grams once a day.
Note: After an initial loading dose of 1 gram, adults with impaired renal function may require a reduction in dose as follows:

Creatinine clearance (mL/min)/(mL/sec)	Dose
> 50/0.83	See *Usual adult and adolescent dose*
25–50/0.42–0.83	500 mg every 12 hours
10–25/0.17–0.42	500 mg every 24 hours
0–10/0–0.17	500 mg every 36 hours

Usual adult prescribing limits
4 grams per day.

Usual pediatric dose
This dosage form usually is not used for children. See *Cefadroxil for Oral Suspension USP*.

Usual pediatric prescribing limits
2 grams for prophylaxis of endocarditis.

Usual geriatric dose
See *Usual adult and adolescent dose.*

Strength(s) usually available
U.S.—
500 mg (Rx) [*Duricef*].
Canada—
500 mg (Rx) [*Duricef* (lactose)].

Packaging and storage
Store below 40 °C (104 °F), preferably between 15 and 30 °C (59 and 86 °F), unless otherwise specified by manufacturer. Store in a tight container.

Auxiliary labeling
- Continue medicine for full time of treatment.

CEFADROXIL FOR ORAL SUSPENSION USP

Usual adult and adolescent dose
See *Cefadroxil Capsules USP*.

Usual pediatric dose
[Endocarditis, prophylaxis][1]—
Oral, 50 mg per kg of body weight one hour prior to the start of surgery.
Impetigo[1] or
Pharyngitis or
Tonsillitis—
Oral, 15 mg per kg of body weight every twelve hours, or 30 mg per kg of body weight once a day, for ten days.
Skin and soft tissue infections or
Urinary tract infections—
Oral, 15 mg per kg of body weight every twelve hours.

Usual pediatric prescribing limits
See *Cefadroxil Capsules USP*.

Usual geriatric dose
See *Cefadroxil Capsules USP*.

Strength(s) usually available
U.S.—
125 mg per 5 mL (when reconstituted according to manufacturer's instructions) (available in 50- and 100-mL bottles) (Rx) [*Duricef* (sodium benzoate; sucrose)].
250 mg per 5 mL (when reconstituted according to manufacturer's instructions) (available in 50- and 100-mL bottles) (Rx) [*Duricef* (sodium benzoate; sucrose)].
500 mg per 5 mL (when reconstituted according to manufacturer's instructions) (available in 50-, 75-, and 100-mL bottles) (Rx) [*Duricef* (sodium benzoate; sucrose)].
Canada—
Not commercially available.

Packaging and storage
Prior to reconstitution, store below 40 °C (104 °F), preferably between 15 and 30 °C (59 and 86 °F), unless otherwise specified by manufacturer. Store in a tight container.

Preparation of dosage form
The bottle should be tapped to loosen the powder. The indicated volume of water should be added in two portions, shaking well after each addition.

Bottle size	Total volume of water to be added
50 mL	34 mL
75 mL	51 mL
100 mL	67 mL

Stability
After reconstitution, suspensions retain their potency for 14 days if refrigerated.

Auxiliary labeling
- Refrigerate.
- Shake well.
- Continue medicine for full time of treatment.
- Beyond-use date.

Note
When dispensing, include a calibrated liquid-measuring device.

CEFADROXIL TABLETS USP

Usual adult and adolescent dose
See *Cefadroxil Capsules USP*.

Usual adult prescribing limits
See *Cefadroxil Capsules USP*.

Usual pediatric dose
This dosage form usually is not used for children. See *Cefadroxil for Oral Suspension USP*.

Usual geriatric dose
See *Cefadroxil Capsules USP*.

Strength(s) usually available
U.S.—
1 gram (Rx) [*Duricef*].
Canada—
Not commercially available.

Packaging and storage
Store below 40 °C (104 °F), preferably between 15 and 30 °C (59 and 86 °F), unless otherwise specified by manufacturer. Store in a tight container.

Auxiliary labeling
- Continue medicine for full time of treatment.

[1]Not included in Canadian product labeling.

CEFAMANDOLE

Summary of Differences

Category: Second-generation cephalosporin.
Pharmacology/pharmacokinetics: Contains *N*-methylthiotetrazole (NMTT) side chain.
Precautions: Drug interactions and/or related problems—Interacts with alcohol (disulfiram-like reaction), oral anticoagulants, and other medications that affect blood clotting.
Laboratory value alterations—May produce false-positive test results for proteinuria with acid and denaturation-precipitation tests.
Medical considerations/contraindications—Caution required in patients with history of bleeding problems.
Patient monitoring—PT determinations may be required.
Side/adverse effects: May cause unusual bleeding or bruising.

Parenteral Dosage Forms

Note: The dosing and strengths of the dosage forms available are expressed in terms of cefamandole base (not the nafate salt).

CEFAMANDOLE NAFATE FOR INJECTION USP

Usual adult and adolescent dose
Perioperative prophylaxis[1]—
Cesarean-section patients: Intramuscular or intravenous, 1 or 2 grams (base) as soon as the umbilical cord is clamped.
Other surgery patients: Intramuscular or intravenous, 1 or 2 grams (base) one-half to one hour prior to the start of surgery; and 1 or 2 grams every six hours following surgery for twenty-four to forty-eight hours.
Pneumonia, uncomplicated or
Skin and soft tissue infections—
Intramuscular or intravenous, 500 mg (base) every six hours.
Urinary tract infections—
Intramuscular or intravenous, 500 mg to 1 gram (base) every eight hours.
For all other infections—
Severe: Intramuscular or intravenous, 1 gram (base) every four to six hours.
Life-threatening: Intramuscular or intravenous, up to 2 grams (base) every four hours.

Note: After an initial loading dose of 1 to 2 grams (base), adults with impaired renal function may require a reduction in dose as follows:

Creatinine clearance (mL/min)/(mL/sec)	Dose (base)	
	Severe infections	Life-threatening infections (maximum)
> 80/1.33	1–2 grams every 6 hours	2 grams every 4 hours
50–80/0.83–1.33	750 mg–1.5 grams every 6 hours	1.5 grams every 4 hours; or 2 grams every 6 hours
25–50/0.42–0.83	750 mg–1.5 grams every 8 hours	1.5 grams every 6 hours; or 2 grams every 8 hours
10–25/0.17–0.42	500 mg–1 gram every 8 hours	1 gram every 6 hours; or 1.25 grams every 8 hours
2–10/0.03–0.17	500–750 mg every 12 hours	670 mg every 8 hours; or 1 gram every 12 hours
< 2/0.03	250–500 mg every 12 hours	500 mg every 8 hours; or 750 mg every 12 hours

Usual adult prescribing limits
12 grams (base) per day.

Usual pediatric dose
Perioperative prophylaxis[1]—
Infants and children 3 months of age and older: Intramuscular or intravenous, 12.5 to 25 mg (base) per kg of body weight one-half to one hour prior to the start of surgery; and 12.5 to 25 mg per kg of body weight every six hours following surgery for twenty-four to forty-eight hours.
Premature infants and infants up to 3 months of age: Dosage has not been established.
Mild to moderate infections—
Infants and children 1 month of age and older: Intramuscular or intravenous, 8.3 to 33.3 mg (base) per kg of body weight every four to eight hours.
Premature infants and infants up to 1 month of age: Dosage has not been established.
Severe infections—
Infants and children 1 month of age and older: Intramuscular or intravenous, 25 to 50 mg (base) per kg of body weight every four to eight hours.
Premature infants and infants up to 1 month of age: Dosage has not been established.

Usual pediatric prescribing limits
150 mg (base) per kg of body weight, or the maximum adult and adolescent dose, per day.

Usual geriatric dose
See *Usual adult and adolescent dose*.

Usual geriatric prescribing limits
1.5 grams (base) every six hours for patients older than seventy-five years of age, even if serum creatinine concentrations are normal.

Strength(s) usually available
U.S.—
1 gram (base) (Rx) [*Mandol* (sodium 3.3 mEq per gram)].
2 grams (base) (Rx) [*Mandol* (sodium 3.3 mEq per gram)].
Canada—
1 gram (base) (Rx) [*Mandol* (sodium 3.3 mEq per gram)].
2 grams (base) (Rx) [*Mandol* (sodium 3.3 mEq per gram)].

Packaging and storage
Prior to reconstitution, store below 40 °C (104 °F), preferably between 15 and 30 °C (59 and 86 °F), unless otherwise specified by manufacturer.

Preparation of dosage form
To prepare initial dilution for intramuscular use, 3 mL of sterile water for injection, bacteriostatic water for injection, 0.9% sodium chloride injection, or bacteriostatic sodium chloride injection should be added to each 1-gram vial, or 6 mL of diluent should be added to each 2-gram vial. Also, up to 10 mL of 0.5 to 2% lidocaine hydrochloride injection (without epinephrine) may be added to each 1-gram vial.
To prepare initial dilution for direct intermittent intravenous use, 10 mL of sterile water for injection, 5% dextrose injection, or 0.9% sodium chloride injection should be added to each 1-gram vial, or 20 mL of diluent should be added to each 2-gram vial. The resulting solution may be administered over a 3- to 5-minute period.
To prepare initial dilution for continuous intravenous infusion, 10 mL of sterile water for injection should be added to each 1-gram vial, or 20 mL of diluent should be added to each 2-gram vial. The resulting solution may be further diluted in suitable diluents (see manufacturer's package insert).
For reconstitution of piggyback infusion bottles or pharmacy bulk vials, see manufacturer's labeling for instructions.

Stability
After reconstitution, solutions retain their potency for 24 hours at room temperature (25 °C [77 °F]) or for 96 hours if refrigerated (5 °C [41 °F]).
If frozen immediately after reconstitution with sterile water for injection, 5% dextrose injection, or 0.9% sodium chloride injection, solutions retain their potency in the original container for 6 months at −20 °C (−4 °F). After being warmed to a maximum of 37 °C (98.6 °F), the solution should not be heated after thawing is complete. Once thawed, solutions should not be refrozen.
Solutions range in color from light yellow to amber depending on the concentration and diluent used. Solutions should not be used if they are of a different color or if they contain a precipitate.
Caution—During storage at room temperature, carbon dioxide develops inside the vial after reconstitution. This is of little or no consequence if the solution is added to sufficient quantities of intravenous fluids. However, if reconstituted cefamandole nafate is repackaged into certain types of syringes, continued production of carbon dioxide may cause leakage, or the rubber closure may be forced out of the barrel of the syringe. Therefore, syringes should be filled immediately prior to use.

Incompatibilities
The admixture of beta-lactam antibacterials (penicillins and cephalosporins) and aminoglycosides may result in substantial mutual inactivation. If they are administered concurrently, they should be administered in separate sites. Do not mix them in the same intravenous bag or bottle.
Since cefamandole nafate contains sodium carbonate, it may be incompatible with magnesium or calcium ions (including Ringer's injection and lactated Ringer's injection).

Additional information
Cefamandole nafate is rapidly hydrolyzed to cefamandole after initial dilution. Both compounds have microbiologic activity *in vivo*.
A solution containing 1 gram in 22 mL of sterile water for injection is isotonic.

[1]Not included in Canadian product labeling.

CEFAZOLIN

Summary of Differences

Category: First-generation cephalosporin.

Parenteral Dosage Forms

Note: Bracketed uses in the *Dosage Forms* section refer to categories of uses and/or indications that are not included in U.S. product labeling.
The dosing and strengths of the dosage forms available are expressed in terms of cefazolin base (not the sodium salt).

CEFAZOLIN INJECTION USP

Usual adult and adolescent dose
[Endocarditis, prophylaxis][1]—
Intravenous infusion, 1 gram (base) one-half hour prior to the start of surgery.
Perioperative prophylaxis—
Intravenous infusion, 1 gram (base) one-half to one hour prior to the start of surgery; 500 mg to 1 gram during surgery; and 500 mg to 1 gram every six to eight hours following surgery for up to twenty-four hours.
Pneumonia, pneumococcal—
Intravenous infusion, 500 mg (base) every twelve hours.
Urinary tract infections, acute, uncomplicated—
Intravenous infusion, 1 gram (base) every twelve hours.
For all other infections—
Mild: Intravenous infusion, 250 to 500 mg (base) every eight hours.
Moderate to severe: Intravenous infusion, 500 mg to 1 gram (base) every six to eight hours.
Severe to life-threatening: Intravenous infusion, 1 to 1.5 grams (base) every six hours.

Note: After an initial loading dose appropriate to the severity of the infection, adults with impaired renal function may require a reduction in dose as follows:

Creatinine clearance (mL/min)/(mL/sec)	Dose (base)
≥ 55/0.92	See *Usual adult and adolescent dose*
35–54/0.58–0.9	Full dose every 8 hours or less frequently
11–34/0.18–0.57	One half the usual dose every 12 hours
≤ 10/0.17	One half the usual dose every 18–24 hours

Usual adult prescribing limits
6 grams (base) per day; however, doses of up to 12 grams per day have been used in rare instances.

Usual pediatric dose
[Endocarditis, prophylaxis][1]—
Intravenous infusion, 25 mg (base) per kg of body weight one-half hour prior to the start of surgery.
For all other infections—
Infants and children 1 month of age and older: Intravenous infusion, 6.25 to 25 mg (base) per kg of body weight every six hours; or 8.3 to 33.3 mg per kg of body weight every eight hours.
Neonates and infants up to 1 month of age: Intravenous infusion, 20 mg (base) per kg of body weight every eight to twelve hours.

Note: After an initial loading dose, children with impaired renal function may require a reduction in dose as follows:

Creatinine clearance (mL/min)/(mL/sec)	Dose (base)
> 70/1.17	See *Usual pediatric dose*
40–70/0.67–1.17	7.5–30 mg per kg of body weight every 12 hours
20–40/0.33–0.67	3.1–12.5 mg per kg of body weight every 12 hours
5–20/0.08–0.33	2.5–10 mg per kg of body weight every 24 hours

Usual pediatric prescribing limits
1 gram (base) for prophylaxis of bacterial endocarditis.

Usual geriatric dose
See *Usual adult and adolescent dose.*

Usual geriatric prescribing limits
500 mg (base) every eight hours for patients older than seventy-five years of age, even if serum creatinine concentrations are normal.

Strength(s) usually available
U.S.—
500 mg (base) per 50 mL (Rx) [*Ancef* (sodium 2 mEq per gram)].
1 gram (base) per 50 mL (Rx) [*Ancef* (sodium 2 mEq per gram)].
Canada—
Not commercially available.

Packaging and storage
Store between −25 and −10 °C (−13 and 14 °F), unless otherwise specified by manufacturer.

Preparation of dosage form
The container should be thawed at room temperature (25 °C [77 °F]) or under refrigeration (5 °C [41 °F]) before administration, making sure that all ice crystals have melted. Thawing should not be forced by immersion in water baths or by microwave irradiation.
Do not use minibags in series connections. This may result in air embolism because of residual air being drawn from the primary container before administration of intravenous solution from the secondary container is complete.

Stability
After thawing, solutions retain their potency for 48 hours at room temperature or for 30 days if refrigerated at 5 °C (41 °F). Once thawed, solutions should not be refrozen.
Do not use if the solution is cloudy or contains a precipitate.

Incompatibilities
The admixture of cefazolin sodium injection with other medications, including pentamidine isethionate, is not recommended.
The admixture of beta-lactam antibacterials (penicillins and cephalosporins) and aminoglycosides may result in substantial mutual inactivation. If they are administered concurrently, they should be administered at separate sites. Do not mix them in the same intravenous bag or bottle.

CEFAZOLIN FOR INJECTION USP

Usual adult and adolescent dose
[Endocarditis, prophylaxis][1]—
Intramuscular or intravenous, 1 gram (base) one-half hour prior to the start of surgery.
Perioperative prophylaxis—
Intramuscular or intravenous, 1 gram (base) one-half to one hour prior to the start of surgery; 500 mg to 1 gram during surgery; and 500 mg to 1 gram every six to eight hours following surgery for up to twenty-four hours.
Pneumonia, pneumococcal—
Intramuscular or intravenous, 500 mg (base) every twelve hours.
Urinary tract infections, acute, uncomplicated—
Intramuscular or intravenous, 1 gram (base) every twelve hours.
For all other infections—
Mild: Intramuscular or intravenous, 250 to 500 mg (base) every eight hours.
Moderate to severe: Intramuscular or intravenous, 500 mg to 1 gram (base) every six to eight hours.
Severe to life-threatening: Intramuscular or intravenous, 1 to 1.5 grams (base) every six hours.

Note: Adults with renal function impairment may require a reduction in dose. See *Cefazolin Injection USP*.

Usual adult prescribing limits
See *Cefazolin Injection USP.*

Usual pediatric dose
[Endocarditis, prophylaxis][1]—
Intramuscular or intravenous, 25 mg (base) per kg of body weight one-half hour prior to the start of surgery.
For all other infections—
Infants and children 1 month of age and older: Intramuscular or intravenous, 6.25 to 25 mg (base) per kg of body weight every six hours; or 8.3 to 33.3 mg (base) per kg of body weight every eight hours.
Neonates and infants up to 1 month of age: Intravenous infusion, 20 mg (base) per kg of body weight every eight to twelve hours.

Note: Children with renal function impairment may require a reduction in dose. See *Cefazolin Injection USP*.

Usual pediatric prescribing limits
See *Cefazolin Injection USP.*

Usual geriatric dose
See *Cefazolin Injection USP.*

Usual geriatric prescribing limits
See *Cefazolin Injection USP.*

Strength(s) usually available
U.S.—
500 mg (base) (may be available in ADD-Vantage® vials) (Rx) [*Ancef* (sodium 46 mg per gram); *Kefzol* (sodium 46 mg per gram); GENERIC].
1 gram (base) (may be available in ADD-Vantage® vials) (Rx) [*Ancef* (sodium 46 mg per gram); *Kefzol* (sodium 46 mg per gram); GENERIC].
5 grams (base) (Rx) [*Ancef* (sodium 46 mg per gram)].
10 grams (base) (Rx) [*Ancef* (sodium 46 mg per gram); *Kefzol* (sodium 46 mg per gram); GENERIC].
Canada—
50 mg (base) (may be available in Add-Vantage® vials) (Rx) [*Kefzol*].
500 mg (base) (may be available in ADD-Vantage® vials) (Rx) [*Ancef* (sodium 46 mg per gram); *Kefzol;* GENERIC].
1 gram (base) (also may be available in ADD-Vantage® vials) (Rx) [*Ancef* (sodium 46 mg per gram); *Kefzol;* GENERIC].
10 grams (base) (Rx) [*Ancef* (sodium 46 mg per gram); *Kefzol;* GENERIC].

Packaging and storage
Prior to reconstitution, store below 40 °C (104 °F), preferably between 15 and 30 °C (59 and 86 °F), unless otherwise specified by manufacturer.

Preparation of dosage form
To prepare initial dilution for intramuscular use, 2 mL of sterile water for injection should be added to each 500-mg vial, or 2.5 mL of diluent should be added to each 1-gram vial.
To prepare initial dilution for intravenous use, 2 mL of sterile water for injection should be added to each 500-mg vial, or 2.5 mL of diluent should be added to each 1-gram vial. For direct intravenous use further dilute with approximately 5 to 10 mL of sterile water for injection (see manufacturer's labeling instructions), and the resulting solution may be administered over a 3- to 5-minute period. For intermittent or continuous intravenous use, the solution may be further diluted in 50 to 100 mL of suitable diluent (see manufacturer's package insert).
For reconstitution of piggyback infusion bottles, pharmacy bulk vials, and dual-compartment vials, see manufacturer's labeling for instructions.

Stability
Prior to reconstitution, powders in their original containers are stable for up to 24 months.
After reconstitution, solutions retain their potency for 24 hours at room temperature or for 10 days if refrigerated (5 °C [41 °F]).
Reconstituted solutions may range in color from pale yellow to yellow without a change in potency.

Incompatibilities
The admixture of cefazolin with other medications, including pentamidine isethionate, is not recommended.
The admixture of beta-lactam antibacterials (penicillins and cephalosporins) and aminoglycosides may result in substantial mutual inactivation. If they are administered concurrently, they should be administered at separate sites. Do not mix them in the same intravenous bag or bottle.

[1]Not included in Canadian product labeling.

CEFDINIR

Summary of Differences

Category: Third-generation cephalosporin. One of three oral third-generation cephalosporins.
Laboratory values: May produce false-positive reaction for ketones in urine with tests using nitroprusside.

Additional Dosing Information

Iron supplements including iron containing multivitamins decrease the absorption of cefdinir. Administration of cefdinir should be taken at least 2 hours before or after the iron supplement. Iron-fortified infant formula can be administered concurrently with cefdinir because it does not significantly interfere with the absorption of cefdinir.

The capsule and oral suspension dosage form may be taken with or without food.

Oral Dosage Forms

CEFDINIR FOR ORAL SUSPENSION

Usual adult and adolescent dose

Chronic bronchitis, acute exacerbations
Pharyngitis/tonsillitis or
Sinusitis, acute maxillary—
Oral, 300 mg every 12 hours; or 600 mg every 24 hours. Duration of treatment is 10 days except for pharyngitis/tonsillitis when 300 mg every 12 hours is taken then the duration is 5 to 10 days.

Pneumonia, community-acquired or
Skin and skin structure infections, uncomplicated—
Oral, 300 mg every 12 hours. Treatment duration is 10 days.

Note: Patients with renal function impairment require a dose reduction. For adults with a creatinine clearance of < 30 mL/min the dose of cefdinir should be 300 mg once daily. In patients maintained on chronic hemodialysis, the recommended dose is 300 mg every other day with a supplemental dose (300 mg) at the conclusion of each hemodialysis session.

Usual pediatric dose

Otitis media, acute bacterial or
Pharyngitis/tonsillitis or
Sinusitis, acute maxillary—
Infants and children 6 months to 12 years of age: Oral, 7 mg per kg of body weight every twelve hours; or 14 mg per kg of body weight once a day. Duration of treatment is 10 days except for otitis media and pharyngitis/tonsillitis when doses of 7 mg per kg of body weight every 12 hours is administered then the duration is 5 to 10 days.
Infants up to 6 months of age: Dosage has not been established.

Skin and skin structure infections, uncomplicated—
Infants and children 6 months to 12 years of age: Oral, 7 mg per kg of body weight every 12 hours for 10 days.
Infants up to 6 months of age: Dosage has not been established.

Note: Patients with renal function impairment require a dose reduction. For pediatric patients with a creatinine clearance of < 30 mL/min/1.73 m^2, the dose of cefdinir should be 7 mg per kg of body weight (up to 300 mg) given once daily. In pediatric patients maintained on chronic hemodialysis, the recommended dose is 7 mg per kg body weight every other day and a supplemental dose (7 mg per kg of body weight) at the conclusion of each hemodialysis session.

Usual pediatric prescribing limits

600 mg per day.

Usual geriatric dose

See *Usual adult and adolescent dose*.

Strength(s) usually available

U.S.—
125 mg per 5 mL (when reconstituted according to manufacturer's instructions) (available in 60– and 100–mL bottles) (Rx) [*Omnicef* (sucrose, NF 2.86 gm per 5 mL; citric acid, USP; sodium citrate, USP; sodium benzoate, NF; xanthan gum, NF; guar gum, NF; artificial strawberry and cream flavors; silicon dioxide, NF; magnesium stearate, NF)].

Packaging and storage

Prior to reconstitution, store at 25° C (77° F); excursions permitted to 15°–30° C (59°–86° F).

Preparation of dosage form

The bottle should be tapped to loosen the powder. The indicated volume of water should be added in two portions, shaking well after each addition.

Final Concentration	Bottle size	Total volume of water to be added
125 mg/5 mL	60 mL	38 mL
125 mg/5 mL	100 mL	63 mL

Stability

After reconstitution, the suspension can be stored at room temperature (25° C [77° F]). The container should be shaken well before each administration. The suspension may be used for 10 days, after which any unused portion must be discarded.

Auxiliary labeling

- Shake well.
- Continue medicine for full time of treatment.
- Beyond-use date.

Note

When dispensing, include a calibrated liquid-measuring device.

CEFDINIR CAPSULES

Usual adult and adolescent dose

See *Cefdinir for Oral Suspension*.

Usual pediatric dose

See *Cefdinir for Oral Suspension*.

Usual geriatric dose

See *Cefdinir for Oral Suspension*.

Strength(s) usually available

U.S.—
300 mg (Rx) [*Omnicef* (carboxymethylcellulose calcium, NF; polyoxyl 40 stearate, NF; magnesium stearate, NF; silicon dioxide, NF)].

Packaging and storage

Store the capsules at 25° C (77° F); excursions permitted to 15°–30° C (59°–86° F).

Auxiliary labeling

- Continue medicine for full time of treatment.

CEFDITOREN

Summary of Differences

Category: Third-generation cephalosporin.

Oral Dosage Form

CEFDITOREN TABLETS

Usual adult and adolescent dose

Bacterial exacerbation of chronic bronchitis, acute—
Oral, 400 mg twice daily for ten days

Pharyngitis or
Skin and skin structure infections, uncomplicated or
Tonsillitis—
Oral, 200 mg twice daily for ten days

Usual pediatric dose

Safety and efficacy have not been established in children less than 12 years of age

Usual geriatric dose

See *Usual adult and adolescent dose*.

Strength(s) usually available

U.S.—
200 mg [*Spectracef*™ (croscarmellose sodium; sodium caseinate; D-mannitol; magnesium stearate; sodium triphosphate; hydroxypropyl methylcellulose; hydroxypropyl cellulose; titanium dioxide; polyethylene glycol; carnauba wax; FD&C Blue No. 1; D&C Red No. 27; shellac; and propylene glycol)].

CEFEPIME

Summary of Differences

Category: Fourth-generation cephalosporin.

Additional Dosing Information

Cefepime should be administered over a period of 30 minutes.

Parenteral Dosage Forms

Note: Bracketed uses is the *Dosage Forms* section refer to categories of use and/or indications that are not included in U.S. product labeling.

The dosing and strengths of the dosage form available are expressed in terms of cefepime base (not the hydrochloride salt).

CEFEPIME HYDROCHLORIDE FOR INJECTION

Usual adult and adolescent dose

intraabdominal infections, complicated—
Intravenous, 2 grams (base), in combination with metronidazole, every twelve hours for seven to ten days.

[Septicemia] or
Skin and soft tissue infections, uncomplicated, moderate to severe or
Urinary tract infections, severe—
Intravenous, 2 grams (base) every twelve hours for ten days.
Neutropenia, febrile—
Intravenous, 2 grams (base) every eight hours for seven days or until resolution of neutropenia.

Note: In patients whose fever resolves but who remain neutropenic for more than seven days, the need for continued antimicrobial therapy should be re-evaluated frequently.

Pneumonia, moderate to severe—
Intravenous, 1 to 2 grams (base) every twelve hours for ten days.
Urinary tract infections, mild to moderate—
Intramuscular or intravenous, 500 mg to 1 gram (base) every twelve hours for seven to ten days.

Note: After an initial loading dose equal to that of patients with normal renal function, patients with renal function impairment may require a reduction in dose as follows:

Creatinine clearance (mL/min)/(mL/sec)	Recommended dosing schedule for normal renal function, based on severity of infection			
> 60/1	500 mg every 12 hours	1 gram every 12 hours	2 grams every 12 hours	2 grams every 8 hours
	Recommended maintenance dosing schedule for renal function impairment, based on severity of infection			
30–60/0.5–1	500 mg every 24 hours	1 gram every 24 hours	2 grams every 24 hours	2 grams every 12 hours
11–29/0.18–0.49	500 mg every 24 hours	500 mg every 24 hours	1 gram every 24 hours	2 grams every 24 hours
< 11/0.18	250 mg every 24 hours	250 mg every 24 hours	500 mg every 24 hours	1 gram every 24 hours
Hemodialysis patients	Repeat the initial dose at the completion of each dialysis session.			
Peritoneal dialysis patients	Administer normally recommended dose at 48-hour intervals.			

Usual pediatric dose

Pneumonia, moderate to severe or
Skin and skin structure infection, moderate to severe, uncomplicated or—
Urinary tract infection, mild or moderate, uncomplicated or complicated—
Infants and children 2 months to 16 years of age (up to 40 kg of body weight): Intravenous, 50 mg per kg of body weight every 12 hours for 10 days (7 to 10 days for urinary tract infection).
Urinary tract infection, severe, uncomplicated or complicated—
Infants and children 2 months to 16 years of age (up to 40 kg of body weight): Intravenous or intramuscular, 50 mg per kg of body weight every 12 hours for 7 to 10 days.

Note: Intramuscular route of administration is indicated only for mild to moderate, uncomplicated or complicated urinary tract infections due to Escherichia coli in the event that intramuscular administration is determined to be the more appropriate drug administration route.

Febrile neutropenia, empiric therapy—
Infants and children 2 months to 16 years of age (up to 40 kg of body weight): Intravenous, 50 mg per kg of body weight every 8 hours for 7 days or until resolution of neutropenia.

Note: In patients whose fever resolves but who remain neutropenic for more than seven days, the need for continued antimicrobial therapy should be re-evaluated frequently.

Usual pediatric prescribing limits

The maximum pediatric dose should not exceed the dose recommended for adults.

Usual geriatric dose

See *Usual adult and adolescent dose*.

Strength(s) usually available

U.S.—
500 mg (base) (Rx) [*Maxipime* (L-arginine 725 mg per gram)].
1 gram (base) (also available in ADD-Vantage® vials) (Rx) [*Maxipime* (L-arginine 725 mg per gram)].
2 grams (base) (also available in ADD-Vantage® vials) (Rx) [*Maxipime* (L-arginine 725 mg per gram)].

Canada—
500 mg (base) (Rx) [*Maxipime* (L-arginine 725 mg per gram)].
1 gram (base) (Rx) [*Maxipime* (L-arginine 725 mg per gram)].
2 grams (base) (Rx) [*Maxipime* (L-arginine 725 mg per gram)].

Packaging and storage

Prior to reconstitution, store between 2 and 25 °C (36 and 77 °F). Protect from light.

Preparation of dosage form

To prepare initial dilution for intramuscular use, 1.3 mL of sterile water for injection, 0.9% sodium chloride injection, 5% dextrose injection, 0.5% or 1% lidocaine hydrochloride, or sterile bacteriostatic water for injection containing either parabens or benzyl alcohol should be added to each 500-mg vial, or 2.4 mL of diluent should be added to each 1-gram vial.

To prepare initial dilution for intravenous administration, 5 mL of suitable diluent (see manufacturer's labeling instructions) should be added to each 500-mg vial, or 10 mL of diluent should be added to each 1- or 2-gram vial. The resulting solution should be further diluted in 50 to 100 mL of a suitable diluent and administered over a period of 30 minutes.

For reconstitution of piggyback infusion bottles and ADD-Vantage® vials, dilute in 50 or 100 mL of suitable diluent (see manufacturer's labeling instructions), and administer over a period of 30 minutes.

Stability

After reconstitution, intramuscular solutions, intravenous solutions at concentrations from 1 to 40 mg per mL, and ADD-Vantage® vials at concentrations from 10 to 20 mg per mL retain their potency for up to 24 hours at room temperature (20 to 25 °C [68 to 77 °F]) or for 7 days if refrigerated (2 to 8 °C [36 to 46 °F]).

Solutions range in color from colorless to amber.

Incompatibilities

Cefepime should not be added to ampicillin solutions of a strength greater than 40 mg per mL, or to aminophylline, gentamicin, metronidazole, netilmicin, tobramycin, or vancomycin solutions. If these medications are administered concurrently with cefepime, they should be administered at separate sites.

CEFIXIME

Summary of Differences

Category: Third-generation cephalosporin. One of three oral third-generation cephalosporins.

Laboratory values: May produce false-positive reaction for ketones in urine with tests using nitroprusside.

Additional Dosing Information

The oral suspension form of cefixime results in higher peak blood concentrations than the tablet when administered at the same dose. Therefore, the tablet should not be substituted for the oral suspension in the treatment of otitis media.

Oral Dosage Forms

CEFIXIME FOR ORAL SUSPENSION USP

Usual adult and adolescent dose

Bronchitis or
Bronchitis, bacterial exacerbations[1] or
Pharyngitis or
Tonsillitis or
Urinary tract infections, uncomplicated—
Oral, 200 mg every twelve hours; or 400 mg once a day.
Gonorrhea, cervical or urethral, uncomplicated—
Oral, 400 mg as a single dose.

Note: Patients with renal function impairment may require a reduction in dose as follows:

Creatinine clearance (mL/min)/(mL/sec)	Dose
> 60/1	See *Usual adult and adolescent dose*
21–60/0.35–1 or hemodialysis patients	75% of standard dosage at standard dosing interval
< 20/0.33 or CAPD patients	50% of standard dosage at standard dosing interval

Usual pediatric dose

Bronchitis or
Bronchitis, bacterial exacerbations[1] or
Otitis media or

Pharyngitis or
Tonsillitis or
Urinary tract infections, uncomplicated—
Children 50 kg of body weight and over: See *Usual adult and adolescent dose.*
Infants and children 6 months to 12 years of age and up to 50 kg of body weight: Oral, 4 mg per kg of body weight every twelve hours; or 8 mg per kg of body weight once a day.
Infants up to 6 months of age: Dosage has not been established.

Usual geriatric dose
See *Usual adult and adolescent dose.*

Strength(s) usually available
U.S.—

Note: Products containing cefixime were withdrawn from the U.S. market by Wyeth in October 2002

Not commercially available

Canada—
100 mg per 5 mL (when reconstituted according to manufacturer's instructions) (available in 50-, 75-, and 100-mL bottles) (Rx) [*Suprax* (sodium benzoate; sucrose)].

Packaging and storage
Prior to reconstitution, store below 40 °C (104 °F), preferably between 15 and 30 °C (59 and 86 °F), unless otherwise specified by manufacturer. Store in a tight container.

Preparation of dosage form
The bottle should be tapped to loosen the powder. The indicated volume of water should be added in two portions, shaking well after each addition.

Bottle size	Total volume of water to be added
50 mL	36 mL
75 mL	52 mL
100 mL	69 mL

Stability
After reconstitution, suspension retains its potency for 14 days at room temperature or if refrigerated.

Auxiliary labeling
- Does not require refrigeration.
- Shake well.
- Continue medicine for full time of treatment.
- Beyond-use date.

Note
When dispensing, include a calibrated liquid-measuring device.

CEFIXIME TABLETS USP

Usual adult and adolescent dose
See *Cefixime for Oral Suspension USP.*

Usual pediatric dose
See *Cefixime for Oral Suspension USP.*

Note: Otitis media should be treated with cefixime for oral suspension since the suspension results in higher peak blood levels than the tablet when administered at the same dose.

Usual geriatric dose
See *Cefixime for Oral Suspension USP.*

Strength(s) usually available
U.S.—

Note: Products containing cefixime were withdrawn from the U.S. market by Wyeth in October 2002

Not commercially available

Canada—
400 mg (Rx) [*Suprax* (scored)].

Packaging and storage
Store below 40 °C (104 °F), preferably between 15 and 30 °C (59 and 86 °F), unless otherwise specified by manufacturer. Store in a tight container.

Auxiliary labeling
- Continue medicine for full time of treatment.

[1]Not included in Canadian product labeling.

CEFONICID

Summary of Differences
Category: Second-generation cephalosporin.

Additional Dosing Information
Intramuscular doses of 2 grams should be administered as divided doses in different sites.

Parenteral Dosage Forms
Note: The dosing and strengths of the dosage forms available are expressed in terms of cefonicid base (not the sodium salt).

CEFONICID INJECTION USP

Usual adult and adolescent dose
Perioperative prophylaxis[1]—
Cesarean-section patients: Intramuscular or intravenous, 1 gram (base) as soon as the umbilical cord is clamped.
Other surgical patients: Intramuscular or intravenous, 1 gram (base) one hour prior to the start of surgery.
Urinary tract infections, uncomplicated[1]—
Intramuscular or intravenous, 500 mg (base) every twenty-four hours.
For all other infections[1]—
Mild to moderate: Intramuscular or intravenous, 1 gram (base) every twenty-four hours.
Severe to life-threatening: Intramuscular or intravenous, 2 grams (base) every twenty-four hours.

Note: After an initial loading dose of 7.5 mg (base) per kg of body weight, adults with impaired renal function may require a reduction in dose as follows:

Creatinine clearance (mL/min)/(mL/sec)	Dose (base)	
	Mild to moderate infections	Severe infections
≥ 80/1.33	See *Usual adult and adolescent dose*	See *Usual adult and adolescent dose*
60–79/1–1.31	10 mg/kg every 24 hours	25 mg/kg every 24 hours
40–59/0.67–0.98	8 mg/kg every 24 hours	20 mg/kg every 24 hours
20–39/0.33–0.65	4 mg/kg every 24 hours	15 mg/kg every 24 hours
10–19/0.17–0.32	4 mg/kg every 48 hours	15 mg/kg every 48 hours
5–9/0.08–0.15	4 mg/kg every 3 to 5 days	15 mg/kg every 3 to 5 days
< 5/0.08	3 mg/kg every 3 to 5 days	4 mg/kg every 3 to 5 days

Usual pediatric dose
Antibacterial—
Safety and efficacy have not been established; however, cefonicid has been used in children 1 year of age and older, and no pediatrics-specific problems have been reported.

Usual geriatric dose
See *Usual adult and adolescent dose.*

Usual geriatric prescribing limits
25 mg (base) every twenty-four hours for patients older than seventy-five years of age, even if serum creatinine concentrations are normal.

Strength(s) usually available
U.S.—
500 mg (base) (Rx) [*Monocid* (sodium 3.7 mEq per gram)].
1 gram (base) (Rx) [*Monocid* (sodium 3.7 mEq per gram)].
10 grams (base) (Rx) [*Monocid* (sodium 3.7 mEq per gram)].
Canada—
Not commercially available.

Packaging and storage
Prior to reconstitution, store in the refrigerator (2 to 8 °C [36 to 46 °F]). Protect from light.

Preparation of dosage form
To prepare initial dilution for intramuscular or intravenous use, 2 mL of sterile water for injection should be added to each 500-mg vial, or 2.5 mL of diluent should be added to each 1-gram vial. For direct intravenous use, the resulting solution may be administered over a 3- to 5-minute period. For intravenous infusions, the resulting solution may be further diluted in 50 to 100 mL of suitable fluids (see manufacturer's package insert).

For reconstitution of piggyback infusion bottles or pharmacy bulk vials, see manufacturer's labeling for instructions.

Stability

After reconstitution for intramuscular or intravenous use, solutions retain their potency for 24 hours at room temperature or for 72 hours if refrigerated at 5 °C (41 °F).

Slight yellowing of cefonicid solutions does not affect their potency.

Incompatibilities

The admixture of beta-lactam antibacterials (penicillins and cephalosporins) and aminoglycosides may result in substantial mutual inactivation. If they are administered concurrently, they should be administered in separate sites. Do not mix them in the same intravenous bag or bottle.

Additional information

A solution containing 1 gram in 18 mL of sterile water for injection is isotonic.

---

[1]Not included in Canadian product labeling.

CEFOPERAZONE

Summary of Differences

Category: Third-generation cephalosporin.

Pharmacology/pharmacokinetics: Achieves high biliary concentrations.

Contains *N*-methylthiotetrazole (NMTT) side chain.

Precautions: Drug interactions and/or related problems—Interacts with alcohol (disulfiram-like reaction), oral anticoagulants, and other medications that affect blood clotting. Does not interact with probenecid.

Medical considerations/contraindications—Caution required in patients with history of bleeding problems, and in patients with both severe hepatic function impairment and renal dysfunction.

Patient monitoring—PT determinations may be required.

Side/adverse effects—May cause unusual bleeding or bruising.

Additional Dosing Information

Cefoperazone should be administered intramuscularly, by intermittent intravenous infusion over a 15- to 30-minute period, or by continuous intravenous infusion. Rapid bolus injection is not recommended.

Patients with impaired renal function generally do not require a reduction in dose since cefoperazone is excreted primarily in the bile. Also, patients with impaired hepatic function or biliary obstruction who are not receiving maximum doses generally do not require a reduction in dose since a corresponding increase in renal excretion (up to 90% or more) usually compensates, to a large degree, for reduced biliary excretion.

Patients with combined renal and hepatic function impairment require a reduction in dose since cefoperazone is not significantly metabolized and toxic serum concentrations may occur.

Parenteral Dosage Forms

Note: The dosing and strengths of the dosage forms available are expressed in terms of cefoperazone base (not the sodium salt).

CEFOPERAZONE INJECTION USP

Usual adult dose

Mild to moderate infections[1]—

Intravenous infusion, 1 to 2 grams (base) every twelve hours.

Severe infections[1]—

Intravenous infusion, 2 to 4 grams (base) every eight hours; or 3 to 6 grams every twelve hours.

Note: Adults with impaired hepatic function and/or biliary obstruction should not receive more than 4 grams (base) per day.

Adults with combined hepatic and renal function impairment should not receive more than 1 to 2 grams (base) per day.

In patients who are receiving hemodialysis treatments, a dose should be administered following hemodialysis.

Usual adult prescribing limits

12 grams (base) per day. However, up to 16 grams per day have been given by continuous infusion in severely immunocompromised patients without adverse effect.

Usual pediatric dose

Safety and efficacy have not been established.

Usual geriatric dose

See *Usual adult and adolescent dose*.

Strength(s) usually available

U.S.—

1 gram in 50 mL (base) (Rx) [*Cefobid* (sodium 1.5 mEq per gram)].
2 grams in 50 mL (base) (Rx) [*Cefobid* (sodium 1.5 mEq per gram)].

Canada—

Not commercially available.

Packaging and storage

Store between −25 and −10 °C (−13 and 14 °F), unless otherwise specified by manufacturer.

Preparation of dosage form

The container should be thawed at room temperature (25 °C [77 °F]) or under refrigeration (5 °C [41 °F]) before administration, making sure that all ice crystals have melted. Thawing should not be forced by immersion in water baths or by microwave irradiation.

Do not use minibags in series connections. This may result in air embolism because of residual air being drawn from the primary container before administration of intravenous solution from the secondary container is complete.

Stability

After thawing, solutions retain their potency for 48 hours at room temperature or for 14 days if refrigerated at 5 °C (41 °F). Once thawed, solutions should not be refrozen.

Do not use if the solution is cloudy or contains a precipitate.

Incompatibilities

The admixture of cefoperazone with other medications, including pentamidine isethionate, is not recommended.

The admixture of beta-lactam antibacterials (penicillins and cephalosporins) and aminoglycosides may result in substantial mutual inactivation. If they are administered concurrently, they should be administered in separate sites. Do not mix them in the same intravenous bag or bottle.

CEFOPERAZONE FOR INJECTION USP

Usual adult dose

Mild to moderate infections[1]—

Intramuscular or intravenous, 1 to 2 grams (base) every twelve hours.

Severe infections[1]—

Intramuscular or intravenous, 2 to 4 grams (base) every eight hours; or 3 to 6 grams every twelve hours.

Note: Adults with impaired hepatic function and/or biliary obstruction should not receive more than 4 grams (base) per day.

Adults with combined hepatic and renal function impairment should not receive more than 1 to 2 grams (base) per day.

In patients who are receiving hemodialysis treatments, a dose should be administered following hemodialysis.

Usual adult prescribing limits

See *Cefoperazone Injection USP*.

Usual pediatric dose

See *Cefoperazone Injection USP*.

Usual geriatric dose

See *Usual adult and adolescent dose*.

Strength(s) usually available

U.S.—

1 gram (base) (Rx) [*Cefobid* (sodium 1.5 mEq per gram)].
2 grams (base) (Rx) [*Cefobid* (sodium 1.5 mEq per gram)].
10 grams (base) (Rx) [*Cefobid* (sodium 1.5 mEq per gram)].

Canada—

Not commercially available.

Packaging and storage

Prior to reconstitution, store below 40 °C (104 °F), preferably between 15 and 30 °C (59 and 86 °F), unless otherwise specified by manufacturer. Protect from light.

Preparation of dosage form

To prepare initial dilution for intramuscular use resulting in final concentrations of less than 250 mg per mL, any suitable diluent (see manufacturer's package insert) may be used.

To prepare initial dilution for intramuscular use resulting in final concentrations of 250 mg per mL, 2.8 mL of sterile water for injection should be added to each 1-gram vial and shaken well until dissolution is complete. Then 1 mL of 2% lidocaine hydrochloride injection (without epinephrine) should be added and mixed well. Add 5.4 mL of sterile water for injection and 1.8 mL of 2% lidocaine hydrochloride injection to each 2-gram vial in the above manner. When a diluent other than lidocaine hydrochloride injection is used, follow the manufacturer's labeling instructions.

To prepare initial dilution for intramuscular use resulting in final concentrations of 333 mg per mL, 2 mL of sterile water for injection should be added to each 1-gram vial and shaken well until dissolution is complete. Then 0.6 mL of 2% lidocaine hydrochloride injection (without epinephrine) should be added and mixed well. Add 3.8 mL of sterile water for injection and 1.2 mL of 2% lidocaine hydrochloride injection to each 2-gram vial in the above manner. When a diluent other than lidocaine hydrochloride injection is used, follow the manufacturer's labeling instructions.

To prepare initial dilution for intravenous use, a minimum of 2.8 mL (5 mL preferred) of a suitable diluent (see manufacturer's package insert) should be added for each gram of cefoperazone. For intermittent infusion, the resulting solution should be further diluted in a suitable diluent (see manufacturer's package insert) and administered over a 15- to 30-minute period. For continuous infusion, the resulting solution should be further diluted to a final concentration of 2 to 25 mg per mL.

The solution should be allowed to stand following reconstitution. This allows the foam to dissipate, thus permitting visual inspection for complete dissolution. Vigorous and prolonged shaking may be required for complete dissolution, especially at higher concentrations (> 333 mg per mL). The maximum solubility of cefoperazone is approximately 475 mg per mL of compatible diluent.

For reconstitution of piggyback infusion bottles, see manufacturer's labeling for instructions.

Stability

After reconstitution, solutions stored in bacteriostatic water for injection containing benzyl alcohol or parabens, most dextrose-containing injections, dextrose and sodium chloride injection, lactated Ringer's injection, 0.5% lidocaine hydrochloride injection, 0.9% sodium chloride injection, or other electrolyte-containing injections (see manufacturer's package insert) at concentrations of 2 to 300 mg per mL retain their potency for 24 hours at room temperature (15 to 25 °C [59 to 77 °F]) or for 5 days if refrigerated at 2 to 8 °C (36 to 46 °F).

Solutions stored in 5% dextrose injection, or 5% dextrose and 0.2 or 0.9% sodium chloride injection at concentrations of 2 or 50 mg per mL, respectively, retain their potency for 3 weeks if frozen at −20 to −10 °C (−4 to 14 °F).

Solutions stored in 0.9% sodium chloride injection or sterile water for injection at concentrations of 300 mg per mL retain their potency for 5 weeks if frozen at −20 to −10 °C (−4 to 14 °F).

Frozen solutions should be thawed at room temperature prior to use. Once thawed, solutions should not be refrozen.

Solutions may vary in color from colorless to straw yellow, depending on concentration.

Incompatibilities

The admixture of cefoperazone with other medications, including pentamidine isethionate, is not recommended.

The admixture of beta-lactam antibacterials (penicillins and cephalosporins) and aminoglycosides may result in substantial mutual inactivation. If they are administered concurrently, they should be administered in separate sites. Do not mix them in the same intravenous bag or bottle.

[1]Not included in Canadian product labeling.

CEFOTAXIME

Summary of Differences

Category: Third-generation cephalosporin.

Additional Dosing Information

Intramuscular doses of 2 grams should be administered as divided doses in different sites.

Parenteral Dosage Forms

Note: The dosing and strengths of the dosage forms available are expressed in terms of cefotaxime free acid.

CEFOTAXIME INJECTION USP

Usual adult and adolescent dose

Perioperative prophylaxis—

Cesarean section patients: Intravenous infusion, 1 gram (free acid) as soon as the umbilical cord is clamped; then 1 gram every six hours for a maximum of two doses.

Other surgery patients: Intravenous infusion, 1 gram (free acid) one-half to one and one-half hours prior to the start of surgery.

Septicemia—

Intravenous infusion, 2 grams (free acid) every six to eight hours.

For all other infections—

Uncomplicated: Intravenous infusion, 1 gram (free acid) every twelve hours.

Moderate to severe: Intravenous infusion, 1 to 2 grams (free acid) every eight hours.

Life-threatening: Intravenous infusion, 2 grams (free acid) every four hours.

Note: For patients with renal function impairment (< 20 mL per minute), one half the *Usual adult and adolescent dose* should be used at the same dosing intervals given above.

Usual adult prescribing limits

12 grams (free acid) per day.

Usual pediatric dose

Antibacterial—

Neonates up to 1 week of age: Intravenous infusion, 50 mg (free acid) per kg of body weight every twelve hours.

Neonates 1 to 4 weeks of age: Intravenous infusion, 50 mg (free acid) per kg of body weight every eight hours.

Infants and children 1 month of age and older up to 50 kg of body weight: Intravenous infusion, 8.3 to 30 mg (free acid) per kg of body weight every four hours; or 12.5 to 45 mg per kg of body weight every six hours.

Children 50 kg of body weight and over: See *Usual adult and adolescent dose*.

Usual pediatric prescribing limits

Infants and children up to 50 kg of body weight should not exceed 180 mg (free acid) per kg of body weight per day.

Children 50 kg of body weight and over should not exceed 12 grams (free acid) per day.

Usual geriatric dose

See *Usual adult and adolescent dose*.

Strength(s) usually available

U.S.—

1 gram (free acid) in 50 mL (Rx) [*Claforan* (sodium 2.2 mEq per gram)].

2 grams (free acid) in 50 mL (Rx) [*Claforan* (sodium 2.2 mEq per gram)].

Canada—

Not commercially available.

Packaging and storage

Store between −25 and −10 °C (−13 and 14 °F), unless otherwise specified by manufacturer.

Preparation of dosage form

The container should be thawed at room temperature or under refrigeration (at or below 5 °C [41 °F]) before administration, making sure that all ice crystals have melted. Thawing should not be forced by immersion in water baths or by microwave irradiation.

Do not use minibags in series connections. This may result in air embolism because of residual air being drawn from the primary container before administration of intravenous solution from the secondary container is complete.

Stability

After thawing, solutions retain their potency for 24 hours at room temperature (22 °C [72 °F]) or for 10 days if refrigerated at 5 °C (41 °F). Once thawed, solutions should not be refrozen.

Do not use if the solution is cloudy or contains a precipitate.

Incompatibilities

The admixture of cefotaxime with other medications, including pentamidine isethionate, is not recommended.

The admixture of beta-lactam antibacterials (penicillins and cephalosporins) and aminoglycosides may result in substantial mutual inactivation. If they are administered concurrently, they should be administered in separate sites. Do not mix them in the same intravenous bag or bottle.

CEFOTAXIME FOR INJECTION USP

Usual adult and adolescent dose

Gonorrhea, cervical or urethral or

Gonorrhea, rectal, in females—

Intramuscular, 500 mg (free acid) as a single dose.

Gonorrhea, rectal, in males—

Intramuscular, 1 gram (free acid) as a single dose.

Perioperative prophylaxis—

Cesarean section patients: Intravenous, 1 gram (free acid) as soon as the umbilical cord is clamped; then 1 gram, intramuscularly or intravenously, every six hours for a maximum of two doses.

Other surgery patients: Intramuscular or intravenous, 1 gram (free acid) one-half to one and one-half hours prior to the start of surgery.

Septicemia—

Intravenous, 2 grams (free acid) every six to eight hours.

For all other infections—

Uncomplicated: Intramuscular or intravenous, 1 gram (free acid) every twelve hours.

Moderate to severe: Intramuscular or intravenous, 1 to 2 grams (free acid) every eight hours.

Life-threatening: Intravenous, 2 grams (free acid) every four hours.

Note: For patients with renal function impairment (< 20 mL per minute), one half the

Usual adult and adolescent dose should be used at the same dosing interval given above.

Usual adult prescribing limits
See *Cefotaxime Injection USP*.

Usual pediatric dose
For bacterial infections—

Neonates up to 1 week of age: Intravenous, 50 mg (free acid) per kg of body weight every twelve hours.

Neonates 1 to 4 weeks of age: Intravenous, 50 mg (free acid) per kg of body weight every eight hours.

Infants and children 1 month of age and older up to 50 kg of body weight: Intramuscular or intravenous, 8.3 to 30 mg (free acid) per kg of body weight every four hours; or 12.5 to 45 mg per kg of body weight every six hours.

Children 50 kg of body weight and over: See *Usual adult and adolescent dose*.

Usual pediatric prescribing limits
See *Cefotaxime Injection USP*.

Usual geriatric dose
See *Usual adult and adolescent dose*.

Strength(s) usually available
U.S.—

500 mg (free acid) (Rx) [*Claforan* (sodium 2.2 mEq per gram)].

1 gram (free acid) (available in ADD-Vantage® vials) (Rx) [*Claforan* (sodium 2.2 mEq per gram)].

2 grams (free acid) (available in ADD-Vantage® vials) (Rx) [*Claforan* (sodium 2.2 mEq per gram)].

10 grams (free acid) (Rx) [*Claforan* (sodium 2.2 mEq per gram)].

Canada—

500 mg (free acid) (Rx) [*Claforan*].

1 gram (free acid) (also available in ADD-Vantage® vials) (Rx) [*Claforan*].

2 grams (free acid) (Rx) [*Claforan*].

Packaging and storage
Prior to reconstitution, store below 30 °C (86 °F), preferably between 15 and 30 °C (59 and 86 °F). Protect from excessive light.

Preparation of dosage form
To prepare initial dilution for intramuscular use, 2, 3, or 5 mL of sterile water for injection or bacteriostatic water for injection should be added to each 500-mg, 1-gram, or 2-gram vial, respectively.

To prepare initial dilution for intravenous use, 10 mL of sterile water for injection should be added to each 500-mg, 1-gram, or 2-gram vial. For direct intravenous use, the resulting solution should be administered over a 3- to 5-minute period.

For reconstitution of piggyback infusion bottles or pharmacy bulk vials, see manufacturer's labeling for instructions.

Caution—Use of diluents containing benzyl alcohol is not recommended for preparation of medications for use in neonates. A fatal toxic syndrome consisting of metabolic acidosis, central nervous system (CNS) depression, respiratory problems, renal failure, hypotension, and possibly seizures and intracranial hemorrhages has been associated with this use.

Stability
After reconstitution for intramuscular use, solutions retain at least 90% of their potency for 12 hours at room temperature (22 °C [72 °F]), for at least 5 days in plastic syringes or 7 days in the original container if refrigerated (5 °C [41 °F]), or for 13 weeks if frozen.

After reconstitution for intravenous use, solutions retain at least 90% of their potency for 12 hours (2-gram vial) or for 24 hours (500-mg and 1-gram vials) at room temperature, for at least 5 days in plastic syringes or 7 days in the original container if refrigerated, or for 13 weeks in plastic syringes or the original container if frozen. Reconstituted solutions further diluted up to 1000 mL in suitable diluents (see manufacturer's package insert) retain their potency for 24 hours at room temperature or for at least 5 days if refrigerated.

Frozen solutions should be thawed at room temperature before use. Once thawed, solutions should not be refrozen.

Reconstituted solutions exhibit maximum stability at pH 5 to 7. Therefore, sterile cefotaxime sodium should not be reconstituted with diluents having a pH above 7.5 (e.g., sodium bicarbonate injection).

Solutions range in color from pale yellow to light amber, depending on the concentration and diluent used. However, solutions tend to darken during storage. This does not affect their potency when stored per manufacturer's recommendations.

Incompatibilities
The admixture of cefotaxime with other medications, including pentamidine isethionate, is not recommended.

The admixture of beta-lactam antibacterials (penicillins and cephalosporins) and aminoglycosides may result in substantial mutual inactivation. If they are administered concurrently, they should be administered in separate sites. Do not mix them in the same intravenous bag or bottle.

Additional information
A solution containing 1 gram in 14 mL of sterile water for injection is isotonic.

CEFOTETAN

Summary of Differences

Category: Cephamycin; second-generation cephalosporin.

Indications: Good activity against anaerobic organisms.

Pharmacology/pharmacokinetics: Contains *N*-methylthiotetrazole (NMTT) side chain.

Precautions: Drug interactions and/or related problems—Interacts with alcohol (disulfiram-like reaction), oral anticoagulants, and other medications that affect blood clotting.

Laboratory value alterations—May falsely elevate serum and urine creatinine concentrations when Jaffe's reaction method is used.

Medical considerations/contraindications—Caution required in patients with history of bleeding problems.

Patient monitoring—PT determinations may be required.

Side/adverse effects: May cause unusual bleeding or bruising.

Parenteral Dosage Forms

Note: The dosing and strengths of the dosage forms available are expressed in terms of cefotetan base (not the disodium salt).

CEFOTETAN INJECTION

Note: Cefotetan injection should be administered over a period of 20 to 60 minutes.

Usual adult and adolescent dose
Perioperative prophylaxis—

Cesarean section patients: Intravenous infusion, 1 or 2 grams (base) as soon as the umbilical cord is clamped.

Other surgical patients: Intravenous infusion, 1 or 2 grams (base) one-half to one hour prior to the start of surgery.

Skin and soft tissue infections—

Mild to moderate, due to *Klebsiella pneumoniae*: Intravenous infusion, 1 or 2 grams (base) every twelve hours for five to ten days.

Mild to moderate, due to other organisms: Intravenous infusion, 1 gram (base) every twelve hours for five to ten days; or 2 grams every twenty-four hours for five to ten days.

Severe: Intravenous infusion, 2 grams (base) every twelve hours for five to ten days.

Urinary tract infections—

Intravenous infusion, 500 mg (base) every twelve hours for five to ten days; or 1 or 2 grams every twelve or twenty-four hours for five to ten days.

For all other infections—

Mild to moderate: Intravenous infusion, 1 or 2 grams (base) every twelve hours for five to ten days.

Severe: Intravenous infusion, 2 grams (base) every twelve hours for five to ten days.

Life-threatening: Intravenous infusion, 3 grams (base) every twelve hours for five to ten days.

Note: Adults with renal function impairment may require a reduction in dose as follows:

Creatinine clearance (mL/min)/(mL/sec)	Dose (base) determined by type and severity of infection
> 30/0.5	See *Usual adult and adolescent dose*
10–30/0.17–0.5	Usual adult dose every 24 hours; or one half the usual adult dose every 12 hours
< 10/0.17	Usual adult dose every 48 hours; or one fourth the usual adult dose every 12 hours
Hemodialysis patients	One fourth the usual adult dose every 24 hours on the days between hemodialysis sessions; and one half the usual adult dose on the day of hemodialysis

Usual adult prescribing limits
6 grams (base) per day.

Usual pediatric dose
Safety and efficacy have not been established.

Usual geriatric dose
See *Usual adult and adolescent dose.*

Strength(s) usually available
U.S.—
1 gram (base) in 50 mL [*Cefotan* (sodium 3.5 mEq per gram)].
2 grams (base) in 50 mL [*Cefotan* (sodium 3.5 mEq per gram)].
Canada—
Not commercially available.

Packaging and storage
Store at −20 °C (−4 °F).

Preparation of dosage form
The container should be thawed at room temperature (25 °C [77 °F]) or under refrigeration (5 °C [41 °F]) before administration. Thawing should not be forced by immersion in water baths or microwave irradiation.
Do not use minibags in series connections. This may result in air embolism because of residual air being drawn from the primary container before administration of intravenous solution from the secondary container is complete.

Stability
After thawing, solutions retain their potency for 48 hours at room temperature, or for 21 days if refrigerated. Once thawed, solutions should not be refrozen.
Do not use if the solution is cloudy or contains a precipitate.

Incompatibilities
The admixture of beta-lactam antibacterials (penicillins and cephalosporins) and aminoglycosides may result in substantial mutual inactivation. If they are administered concurrently, they should be administered in separate sites. Do not mix them in the same intravenous bag or bottle.

CEFOTETAN FOR INJECTION USP

Usual adult and adolescent dose
Perioperative prophylaxis—
Cesarean section patients: Intravenous, 1 or 2 grams (base) as soon as the umbilical cord is clamped.
Other surgical patients: Intravenous, 1 or 2 grams (base) one-half to one hour prior to the start of surgery.
Skin and soft tissue infections—
Mild to moderate, due to *Klebsiella pneumoniae*: Intramuscular or intravenous, 1 or 2 grams (base) every twelve hours for five to ten days.
Mild to moderate, due to other organisms: Intramuscular or intravenous, 1 gram (base) every twelve hours for five to ten days; or 2 grams, intravenously, every twenty-four hours for five to ten days.
Severe: Intravenous, 2 grams (base) every twelve hours for five to ten days.
Urinary tract infections—
Intramuscular or intravenous, 500 mg (base) every twelve hours, or 1 or 2 grams every twelve or twenty-four hours, for five to ten days.
For all other infections—
Mild to moderate: Intramuscular or intravenous, 1 or 2 grams (base) every twelve hours for five to ten days.
Severe: Intravenous, 2 grams (base) every twelve hours for five to ten days.
Life-threatening: Intravenous, 3 grams (base) every twelve hours for five to ten days.

Note: Adults with renal function impairment may require a reduction in dose. See *Cefotetan Injection.*

Usual adult prescribing limits
See *Cefotetan Injection.*

Usual pediatric dose
Safety and efficacy have not been established.

Usual geriatric dose
See *Usual adult and adolescent dose.*

Strength(s) usually available
U.S.—
1 gram (base) (available in ADD-Vantage® vials) (Rx) [*Cefotan* (sodium 3.5 mEq per gram)].
2 grams (base) (available in ADD-Vantage® vials) (Rx) [*Cefotan* (sodium 3.5 mEq per gram)].
10 grams (base) (Rx) [*Cefotan* (sodium 3.5 mEq per gram)].
Canada—
1 gram (base) (Rx) [*Cefotan* (sodium 3.4 mEq per gram)].
2 grams (base) (Rx) [*Cefotan* (sodium 3.4 mEq per gram)].

Packaging and storage
Prior to reconstitution, do not store above 22 °C (72 °F), unless otherwise specified by manufacturer. Protect from light.

Preparation of dosage form
To prepare initial dilution for intramuscular use, 2 mL of sterile water for injection, bacteriostatic water for injection, 0.9% sodium chloride injection, or 0.5 or 1% lidocaine hydrochloride injection (without epinephrine) should be added to each 1-gram vial, or 3 mL of diluent should be added to each 2-gram vial.
To prepare initial dilution for intravenous use, 10 mL of sterile water for injection should be added to each 1-gram vial, or 10 to 20 mL of diluent should be added to each 2-gram vial. For direct intermittent intravenous use, the resulting solution should be administered over a 3- to 5-minute period.
For reconstitution of piggyback infusion bottles, add 50 to 100 mL of 5% dextrose injection or 0.9% sodium chloride injection to each bottle. If the Y-type method of administration is used, the primary infusion should be temporarily discontinued during infusion of cefotetan.
For reconstitution of ADD-Vantage® vials, see manufacturer's package labeling for instructions.

Stability
After reconstitution for intramuscular or intravenous use, solutions retain their potency for 24 hours at room temperature (25 °C [77 °F]), for 96 hours if refrigerated at 5 °C (41 °F), or for at least 1 week if frozen at −20 °C (−4 °F). Solutions stored in disposable glass or plastic syringes retain their potency for 24 hours at room temperature or for 96 hours if refrigerated.
Frozen solutions should be thawed at room temperature prior to use. Thawed solutions retain their potency for the time periods indicated above. Once thawed, solutions should not be refrozen.
After reconstitution of ADD-Vantage® vials, solutions retain their potency for 24 hours at room temperature. Solutions in ADD-Vantage® vials should not be refrigerated or frozen.
Solutions range from colorless to yellow in color, depending on the concentration.

Incompatibilities
The admixture of beta-lactam antibacterials (penicillins and cephalosporins) and aminoglycosides may result in substantial mutual inactivation. If they are administered concurrently, they should be administered in separate sites. Do not mix them in the same intravenous bag or bottle.

CEFOXITIN

Summary of Differences

Category: Cephamycin; second-generation cephalosporin.
Indications: Good activity against anaerobic organisms.
Precautions:
Pediatrics—Higher doses associated with increased incidence of eosinophilia and elevated AST (SGOT).
Laboratory value alterations—May falsely elevate serum and urine creatinine concentrations when Jaffe's reaction method is used.

Parenteral Dosage Forms

Note: The dose and strengths of the dosage forms available are expressed in terms of cefoxitin base (not the sodium salt).

CEFOXITIN INJECTION USP

Usual adult and adolescent dose
Mild or uncomplicated infections—
Intravenous, 1 gram (base) every six to eight hours.
Moderately severe or severe infections—
Intravenous, 1 gram (base) every four hours; or 2 grams every six to eight hours.
Life-threatening infections—
Intravenous, 2 grams (base) every four hours; or 3 grams every six hours.
Perioperative prophylaxis—
Cesarean section patients: Intravenous, 2 grams (base) as soon as the umbilical cord is clamped; or 2 grams as soon as the umbilical cord is clamped, and 2 grams four and eight hours after the first dose.
Other surgical patients: Intravenous, 2 grams (base) one-half to one hour prior to the start of surgery, and 2 grams every six hours after the first dose for up to twenty-four hours.

Note: After an initial loading dose of 1 to 2 grams (base), adults with impaired renal function may require a reduction in dose as follows:

Creatinine clearance (mL/min)/(mL/sec)	Dose (base)
> 50/0.83	See *Usual adult and adolescent dose*
30–50/0.5–0.83	1–2 grams every 8–12 hours
10–29/0.17–0.48	1–2 grams every 12–24 hours
5–9/0.08–0.15	500 mg–1 gram every 12–24 hours
< 5/0.08	500 mg–1 gram every 24–48 hours

Usual pediatric dose

Perioperative prophylaxis—

Intravenous infusion, 30 to 40 mg (base) per kg of body weight one-half to one hour prior to the start of surgery; and 30 to 40 mg per kg of body weight every six hours after the first dose for up to twenty-four hours.

For all other infections—

Infants and children 3 months of age and older: Intravenous infusion, 13.3 to 26.7 mg (base) per kg of body weight every four hours; or 20 to 40 mg per kg of body weight every six hours.

Infants 1 to 3 months of age: Intravenous infusion, 20 to 40 mg (base) per kg of body weight every six to eight hours.

Infants 1 to 4 weeks of age: Intravenous infusion, 20 to 40 mg (base) per kg of body weight every eight hours.

Premature infants weighing 1500 grams or over to neonates up to 1 week of age: Intravenous infusion, 20 to 40 mg (base) per kg of body weight every twelve hours.

Note: Pediatric patients with renal function impairment should receive a modified dose and a modified frequency of dosing consistent with the recommendations for adults. See *Usual adult and adolescent dose*.

Usual pediatric prescribing limits

12 grams (base) per day.

Usual geriatric dose

See *Usual adult and adolescent dose*.

Usual geriatric prescribing limits

2 grams (base) every eight hours for patients older than seventy-five years of age, even if serum creatinine concentrations are normal.

Strength(s) usually available

U.S.—

1 gram in 50 mL (Rx) [*Mefoxin* (sodium 2.3 mEq per gram)].

2 grams in 50 mL (Rx) [*Mefoxin* (sodium 2.3 mEq per gram)].

Canada—

Not commercially available.

Packaging and storage

Store between −25 and −10 °C (−13 and 14 °F), unless otherwise specified by manufacturer.

Preparation of dosage form

The container should be thawed at room temperature (25 °C [77 °F]) or under refrigeration (2 to 8 °C [36 to 46 °F]) before administration, making sure that all ice crystals have melted. Thawing should not be forced by immersion in water baths or by microwave irradiation.

Do not use minibags in series connections. This may result in air embolism because of residual air being drawn from the primary container before administration of intravenous solution from the secondary container is complete.

Stability

After thawing, solutions retain their potency for 24 hours at room temperature or for 21 days if refrigerated at 2 to 8 °C (36 to 46 °F). Once thawed, solutions should not be refrozen.

Do not use if the solution is cloudy or contains a precipitate.

Incompatibilities

The admixture of cefoxitin with other medications, including pentamidine isethionate, is not recommended.

The admixture of beta-lactam antibacterials (penicillins and cephalosporins) and aminoglycosides may result in substantial mutual inactivation. If they are administered concurrently, they should be administered in separate sites. Do not mix them in the same intravenous bag or bottle.

CEFOXITIN FOR INJECTION USP

Usual adult and adolescent dose

See *Cefoxitin Injection USP*.

Usual pediatric dose

See *Cefoxitin Injection USP*.

Usual pediatric prescribing limits

See *Cefoxitin Injection USP*.

Usual geriatric dose

See *Cefoxitin Injection USP*.

Usual geriatric prescribing limits

See *Cefoxitin Injection USP*.

Strength(s) usually available

U.S.—

1 gram (available in ADD-Vantage® vials) (Rx) [*Mefoxin* (sodium 2.3 mEq per gram)].

2 grams (available in ADD-Vantage® vials) (Rx) [*Mefoxin* (sodium 2.3 mEq per gram)].

10 grams (Rx) [*Mefoxin* (sodium 2.3 mEq per gram)].

Canada—

1 gram (also may be available in ADD-Vantage® vials) (Rx) [*Mefoxin* (sodium 2.3 mEq per gram); GENERIC].

2 grams (also may be available in ADD-Vantage® vials) (Rx) [*Mefoxin* (sodium 2.3 mEq per gram); GENERIC].

10 grams (Rx) [*Mefoxin* (sodium 2.3 mEq per gram)].

Packaging and storage

Prior to reconstitution, store below 40 °C (104 °F), preferably between 15 and 30 °C (59 and 86 °F), unless otherwise specified by manufacturer.

Preparation of dosage form

To prepare initial dilution for intravenous use, at least 10 mL of sterile water for injection, bacteriostatic water for injection, 0.9% sodium chloride injection, or 5% dextrose injection should be added to each 1-gram vial, or 10 or 20 mL of diluent should be added to each 2-gram vial. For continuous intravenous infusion, the resulting solution may be further diluted in 50 to 1000 mL of suitable diluent (see manufacturer's package insert).

To prepare initial dilution for direct intermittent intravenous use, 10 mL of sterile water for injection should be added to each 1- or 2-gram vial. The resulting solution should be administered over a 3- to 5-minute period.

For reconstitution of piggyback infusion bottles or pharmacy bulk vials, see manufacturer's labeling for instructions.

Caution—Use of diluents containing benzyl alcohol is not recommended for preparation of medications for use in neonates. A fatal toxic syndrome consisting of metabolic acidosis, CNS depression, respiratory problems, renal failure, hypotension, and possibly seizures and intracranial hemorrhages has been associated with this use.

Stability

After reconstitution for intravenous use to a concentration of 1 gram per 10 mL with sterile water for injection, bacteriostatic water for injection, 0.9% sodium chloride injection, or 5% dextrose injection, solutions retain their potency for 6 hours at room temperature, or for 7 days if refrigerated (below 5 °C). Initial dilutions retain their potency for an additional 18 hours at room temperature or for an additional 48 hours if refrigerated when diluted in 50 to 1000 mL of suitable diluents (see manufacturer's package insert).

Solutions range from clear to light amber in color but tend to darken depending on storage conditions. This does not affect their potency.

Incompatibilities

The admixture of cefoxitin with other medications, including pentamidine isethionate, is not recommended.

The admixture of beta-lactam antibacterials (penicillins and cephalosporins) and aminoglycosides may result in substantial mutual inactivation. If they are administered concurrently, they should be administered in separate sites. Do not mix them in the same intravenous bag or bottle.

CEFPODOXIME

Summary of Differences

Category: Third-generation cephalosporin, with broad *in vitro* activity. One of three oral third-generation cephalosporins.

Precautions: Drug interactions and/or related problems—Interacts with antacids and histamine H_2-receptor antagonists.

Additional Dosing Information

The tablet dosage form should be taken with food.

The oral suspension dosage form may be taken with or without food.

Oral Dosage Forms

Note: The dosing and strengths of the dosage forms available are expressed in terms of cefpodoxime base (not the proxetil salt).

CEFPODOXIME PROXETIL FOR ORAL SUSPENSION

Usual adult and adolescent dose

Gonorrhea, cervical[1] or urethral[1] or
Gonorrhea, rectal, in women[1]—
Oral, 200 mg (base) as a single dose.
Pharyngitis[1] or
Tonsillitis[1]—
Oral, 100 mg (base) every twelve hours for five to ten days.
Pneumonia, community-acquired[1]—
Oral, 200 mg (base) every twelve hours for fourteen days.
Skin and soft tissue infections[1]—
Oral, 400 mg (base) every twelve hours for seven to fourteen days.
Urinary tract infections, uncomplicated[1]—
Oral, 100 mg (base) every twelve hours for seven days.

Note: Adults with renal function impairment may require a reduction in dose as follows:

Creatinine clearance (mL/min)/(mL/sec)	Dosing interval
≥ 30/0.5	Every 12 hours
<30/0.5	Every 24 hours
Hemodialysis patients	3 times a week after hemodialysis

Usual pediatric dose

Otitis media[1]—
Infants and children 5 months to 12 years of age: Oral, 10 mg (base) per kg of body weight, up to 400 mg, every twenty-four hours for ten days; or 5 mg per kg of body weight, up to 200 mg, every twelve hours for ten days.
Infants up to 5 months of age: Safety and efficacy have not been established.
Pharyngitis[1] or
Tonsillitis[1]—
Infants and children 5 months to 12 years of age: Oral, 5 mg (base) per kg of body weight, up to 100 mg, every twelve hours for five to ten days.
Infants up to 5 months of age: Safety and efficacy have not been established.

Usual pediatric prescribing limits

For otitis media, 400 mg per day. For pharyngitis or tonsillitis, 200 mg per day.

Usual geriatric dose

See *Usual adult and adolescent dose.*

Strength(s) usually available

U.S.—
50 mg (base) per 5 mL (when reconstituted according to manufacturer's instructions) (available in 50-, 75-, and 100-mL bottles) (Rx) [*Vantin* (lactose; sodium benzoate; sucrose)].
100 mg (base) per 5 mL (when reconstituted according to manufacturer's instructions) (available in 50-, 75-, and 100-mL bottles) (Rx) [*Vantin* (lactose; sodium benzoate; sucrose)].
Canada—
Not commercially available.

Packaging and storage

Prior to reconstitution, store between 15 and 30 °C (59 and 86 °F), unless otherwise specified by manufacturer. Store in a tight container.

Preparation of dosage form

The bottle should be tapped to loosen the granules. The total volume of water should be added in two portions, shaking well after each addition.

Final concentration	Bottle size	Total volume of water to be added
50 mg/5 mL	100 mL	58 mL
	75 mL	44 mL
	50 mL	29 mL
100 mg/5 mL	100 mL	57 mL
	75 mL	43 mL
	50 mL	29 mL

Stability

After reconstitution, suspension retains its potency for 14 days if refrigerated at 2 to 8 °C (36 to 46 °F).

Auxiliary labeling

- Refrigerate.
- Shake well.
- May be taken with or without food.
- Continue medicine for full time of treatment.
- Beyond-use date.

Note

When dispensing, include a calibrated liquid-measuring device.

CEFPODOXIME PROXETIL TABLETS

Usual adult and adolescent dose

Bronchitis, bacterial exacerbations[1]—
Oral, 200 mg (base) every twelve hours for ten days.
Gonorrhea, cervical[1] or urethral[1] or
Gonorrhea, rectal, in women[1]—
Oral, 200 mg (base) as a single dose.
Pharyngitis[1] or
Tonsillitis[1]—
Oral, 100 mg (base) every twelve hours for five to ten days.
Pneumonia, community-acquired[1]—
Oral, 200 mg (base) every twelve hours for fourteen days.
Skin and soft tissue infections[1]—
Oral, 400 mg (base) every twelve hours for seven to fourteen days.
Urinary tract infections, uncomplicated[1]—
Oral, 100 mg (base) every twelve hours for seven days.

Usual pediatric dose

This dosage form usually is not used for children. See *Cefpodoxime Proxetil for Oral Suspension.*

Usual geriatric dose

See *Usual adult and adolescent dose.*

Strength(s) usually available

U.S.—
100 mg (base) (Rx) [*Vantin* (lactose)].
200 mg (base) (Rx) [*Vantin* (lactose)].
Canada—
Not commercially available.

Packaging and storage

Store between 15 and 30 °C (59 and 86 °F), unless otherwise specified by manufacturer. Store in a tight container.

Auxiliary labeling

- Continue medicine for full time of treatment.
- Take with food.

[1]Not included in Canadian product labeling.

CEFPROZIL

Summary of Differences

Category: Second-generation cephalosporin, with broad *in vitro* activity.
Precautions: Medical considerations/contraindications—Cefprozil for oral solution contains 28 mg of phenylalanine per 5 mL.

Oral Dosage Forms

Note: Bracketed uses in the *Dosage Forms* section refer to categories of use and/or indications that are not included in U.S. product labeling.

CEFPROZIL FOR ORAL SUSPENSION USP

Usual adult and adolescent dose

Bronchitis[1] or
Bronchitis, bacterial exacerbations[1]—
Oral, 500 mg every twelve hours for ten days.
Pharyngitis or
Tonsillitis—
Oral, 500 mg every twenty-four hours for ten days.
Sinusitis, acute—
Oral, 250 or 500 mg every twelve hours for ten days.
Skin and soft tissue infections—
Oral, 250 or 500 mg every twelve hours for ten days; or 500 mg every twenty-four hours for ten days.
[Urinary tract infections, uncomplicated]—
Oral, 500 mg every twenty-four hours.

Note: Adults with renal function impairment may require a reduction in dose as follows:

Creatinine clearance (mL/min)/(mL/sec)	Usual dose (%)
≥ 30/0.5	100
0–30/0–0.5	50
Hemodialysis patients	100, after hemodialysis

Usual pediatric dose
Otitis media—
Infants and children 6 months to 12 years of age: Oral, 15 mg per kg of body weight every twelve hours for ten days.
Infants up to 6 months of age: Safety and efficacy have not been established.
Pharyngitis or
Tonsillitis—
Children 2 to 12 years of age: Oral, 7.5 mg per kg of body weight every twelve hours for ten days.
Infants and children up to 2 years of age: Safety and efficacy have not been established.
Sinusitis, acute—
Infants and children 6 months to 12 years of age: Oral, 7.5 or 15 mg per kg of body weight every twelve hours for ten days.
Infants up to 6 months of age: Safety and efficacy have not been established.
Skin and soft tissue infections—
Children 2 to 12 years of age: Oral, 20 mg per kg of body weight every twenty-four hours for ten days.
Infants and children up to 2 years of age: Safety and efficacy have not been established.

Usual pediatric prescribing limits
1 gram per day.

Usual geriatric dose
See *Usual adult and adolescent dose.*

Strength(s) usually available
U.S.—
125 mg per 5 mL (when reconstituted according to manufacturer's instructions) (available in 50-, 75-, and 100-mL bottles) (Rx) [*Cefzil* (phenylalanine 28 mg per 5 mL; sodium benzoate; sodium chloride; sucrose)].
250 mg per 5 mL (when reconstituted according to manufacturer's instructions) (available in 50-, 75-, and 100-mL bottles) (Rx) [*Cefzil* (phenylalanine 28 mg per 5 mL; sodium benzoate; sodium chloride; sucrose)].
Canada—
125 mg per 5 mL (when reconstituted according to manufacturer's instructions) (available in 75- and 100-mL bottles) (Rx) [*Cefzil* (phenylalanine 28 mg per 5 mL; sodium benzoate; sodium chloride; sucrose)].
250 mg per 5 mL (when reconstituted according to manufacturer's instructions) (available in 75- and 100-mL bottles) (Rx) [*Cefzil* (phenylalanine 28 mg per 5 mL; sodium benzoate; sodium chloride; sucrose)].

Packaging and storage
Prior to reconstitution, store between 15 and 30 °C (59 and 86 °F), unless otherwise specified by manufacturer. Store in a tight container.

Preparation of dosage form
The bottle should be tapped to loosen the granules. The total volume of water indicated below should be added in two portions, shaking well after each addition.

Bottle size	Total volume of water to be added
50 mL	36 mL
75 mL	54 mL
100 mL	72 mL

Stability
After reconstitution, suspension retains its potency for 14 days if refrigerated.

Auxiliary labeling
- Refrigerate.
- Shake well.
- Continue medicine for full time of treatment.
- Beyond-use date.

Note
When dispensing, include a calibrated liquid-measuring device.

CEFPROZIL TABLETS USP

Usual adult and adolescent dose
See *Cefprozil for Oral Suspension USP.*

Usual pediatric dose
See *Cefprozil for Oral Suspension USP.*

Usual pediatric prescribing limits
See *Cefprozil for Oral Suspension USP.*

Usual geriatric dose
See *Cefprozil for Oral Suspension USP*

Strength(s) usually available
U.S.—
250 mg (Rx) [*Cefzil*].
500 mg (Rx) [*Cefzil*].
Canada—
250 mg (Rx) [*Cefzil*].
500 mg (Rx) [*Cefzil*].

Packaging and storage
Store between 15 and 30 °C (59 and 86 °F), unless otherwise specified by manufacturer. Store in a tight container.

Auxiliary labeling
- Continue medicine for full time of treatment.

[1]Not included in Canadian product labeling.

CEFTAZIDIME

Summary of Differences

Category: Third-generation cephalosporin.
Indications: Good activity against *Pseudomonas aeruginosa.*
Precautions: Drug interactions and/or related problems—Does not interact with probenecid.

Additional Dosing Information

Patients with impaired hepatic function do not require a reduction in dose.

Parenteral Dosage Forms

Note: The dosing and strengths of the dosage form available are expressed in terms of ceftazidime base (not the sodium salt).

CEFTAZIDIME INJECTION USP

Usual adult and adolescent dose
Bone and joint infections—
Intravenous infusion, 2 grams (base) every twelve hours.
Intraabdominal infections or
Meningitis or
Pelvic infections, female[1] or
Septicemia—
Intravenous infusion, 2 grams (base) every eight hours.
Pneumonia, uncomplicated or
Skin and soft tissue infections—
Intravenous infusion, 500 mg to 1 gram (base) every eight hours.
[Melioidosis][1]—
Intravenous, 120 mg per kg of body weight per day administered every eight hours
Pulmonary infections in cystic fibrosis, due to *Pseudomonas*[1]—
Intravenous infusion, 30 to 50 mg (base) per kg of body weight every eight hours, up to 6 grams per day.
Urinary tract infections, complicated—
Intravenous infusion, 500 mg (base) every eight to twelve hours.
Urinary tract infections, uncomplicated—
Intravenous infusion, 250 mg (base) every twelve hours.
For all other infections, severe to life-threatening, especially in immunocompromised patients—
Intravenous infusion, 2 grams (base) every eight hours.

Note: After an initial loading dose of 1 gram, adults with impaired renal function (including dialysis patients) may require a reduction in dose as follows:

Creatinine clearance (mL/min)/(mL/sec)	Dose (base)
> 50/0.83	See *Usual adult and adolescent dose*
31–50/0.52–0.83	1 gram every 12 hours
16–30/0.27–0.5	1 gram every 24 hours
6–15/0.1–0.25	500 mg every 24 hours
< 5/0.08	500 mg every 48 hours
Hemodialysis patients	1 gram after each hemodialysis period
Peritoneal dialysis patients	500 mg every 24 hours

Usual pediatric dose
For bacterial infections—
Neonates up to 4 weeks of age: Intravenous infusion, 30 mg (base) per kg of body weight every twelve hours.

Infants and children 1 month to 12 years of age: Intravenous infusion, 30 to 50 mg (base) per kg of body weight every eight hours.

Usual pediatric prescribing limits
6 grams (base) per day.

Usual geriatric dose
See *Usual adult and adolescent dose.*

Usual geriatric prescribing limits
1 gram (base) every twenty-four hours for patients older than seventy-five years of age, even if serum creatinine concentrations are normal.

Strength(s) usually available
U.S.—

1 gram in 50 mL (Rx) [*Fortaz* (sodium 2.3 mEq per gram)].
2 grams in 50 mL (Rx) [*Fortaz* (sodium 2.3 mEq per gram)].

Canada—

Not commercially available.

Packaging and storage
Store between −25 and −10 °C (−13 and 14 °F), unless otherwise specified by manufacturer.

Preparation of dosage form
The container should be thawed at room temperature (25 °C [77 °F]) or under refrigeration (5 °C [41 °F]) before administration, making sure that all ice crystals have melted. Thawing should not be forced by immersion in water bath or by microwave irradiation.

Do not use minibags in series connections. This may result in air embolism because of residual air being drawn from the primary container before administration of intravenous solution from the secondary container is complete.

Stability
After thawing, solutions retain their potency for 24 hours at room temperature or for 7 days if refrigerated. Once thawed, solutions should not be refrozen.

Do not use if the solution is cloudy or contains a precipitate.

Incompatibilities
The admixture of ceftazidime with other medications, including aminophylline, amsacrine, fluconazole, idarubicin hydrochloride, pentamidine isethionate, sargramostim, and vancomycin, is not recommended.

The admixture of beta-lactam antibacterials (penicillins and cephalosporins) and aminoglycosides may result in substantial mutual inactivation. If they are administered concurrently, they should be administered in separate sites. Do not mix them in the same intravenous bag or bottle.

Vancomycin is physically incompatible with ceftazidime and a precipitate may form, depending on the concentration. Therefore, the intravenous lines should be flushed between the administration of these two medications if they are to be given through the same tubing.

CEFTAZIDIME FOR INJECTION USP

Usual adult and adolescent dose
Bone and joint infections—

Intravenous, 2 grams (base) every twelve hours.

Intraabdominal infections or
Meningitis or
Pelvic infections, female[1] or
Septicemia—

Intravenous, 2 grams (base) every eight hours.

[Melioidosis][1]—

Intravenous, 120 mg per kg of body weight per day administered every eight hours

Pneumonia, uncomplicated or
Skin and soft tissue infections—

Intramuscular or intravenous, 500 mg to 1 gram (base) every eight hours.

Pulmonary infections in cystic fibrosis, due to *Pseudomonas*[1]—

Intravenous, 30 to 50 mg (base) per kg of body weight every eight hours, up to 6 grams per day.

Urinary tract infections, complicated—

Intramuscular or intravenous, 500 mg (base) every eight to twelve hours.

Urinary tract infections, uncomplicated—

Intramuscular or intravenous, 250 mg (base) every twelve hours.

For all other infections, severe to life-threatening, especially in immunocompromised patients—

Intravenous, 2 grams (base) every eight hours.

Note: Adults with renal function impairment may require a reduction in dose. See *Ceftazidime Injection USP*.

Usual pediatric dose
Meningitis—

Infants and children 1 month to 12 years of age: Intravenous, 50 mg (base) per kg of body weight every eight hours.

Neonates up to 1 month of age: Intravenous, 25 to 50 mg (base) per kg of body weight every twelve hours.

For all other infections—

Infants and children 1 month to 12 years of age: Intravenous, 30 to 50 mg (base) per kg of body weight every eight hours.

Neonates up to 4 weeks of age: Intravenous, 30 mg (base) per kg of body weight every twelve hours.

Note: The safety of the arginine component in the ceftazidime L-arginine formulation has not been established for neonates, infants, or children up to 12 years of age. If treatment with ceftazidime is indicated, the sodium formulation should be used.

Usual pediatric prescribing limits
See *Ceftazidime Injection USP*.

Usual geriatric dose
See *Usual adult and adolescent dose.*

Usual geriatric prescribing limits
See *Ceftazidime Injection USP*.

Strength(s) usually available
U.S.—

500 mg (Rx) [*Fortaz* (sodium 2.3 mEq per gram); *Tazidime* (sodium 2.3 mEq per gram)].

1 gram (may be available in ADD-Vantage® vials) (Rx) [*Ceptaz* (L-arginine 349 mg per gram); *Fortaz* (sodium 2.3 mEq per gram); *Tazicef* (sodium 2.3 mEq per gram); *Tazidime* (sodium 2.3 mEq per gram)].

2 grams (may be available in ADD-Vantage® vials) (Rx) [*Ceptaz* (L-arginine 349 mg per gram); *Fortaz* (sodium 2.3 mEq per gram); *Tazicef* (sodium 2.3 mEq per gram); *Tazidime* (sodium 2.3 mEq per gram)].

6 grams (Rx) [*Fortaz* (sodium 2.3 mEq per gram); *Tazicef* (sodium 2.3 mEq per gram); *Tazidime* (sodium 2.3 mEq per gram)].

10 grams (Rx) [*Ceptaz* (L-arginine 349 mg per gram)].

Canada—

500 mg (Rx) [*Fortaz; Tazidime* (sodium 2.3 mEq per gram)].

1 gram (also may be available in ADD-Vantage® vials) (Rx) [*Ceptaz* (L-arginine); *Fortaz; Tazidime* (sodium 2.3 mEq per gram)].

2 grams (also may be available in ADD-Vantage® vials) (Rx) [*Ceptaz* (L-arginine); *Fortaz; Tazidime* (sodium 2.3 mEq per gram)].

6 grams (Rx) [*Fortaz; Tazidime* (sodium 2.3 mEq per gram)].

10 grams (Rx) [*Ceptaz* (L-arginine)].

Packaging and storage
Prior to reconstitution, store between 15 and 30 °C (59 and 86 °F), unless otherwise specified by manufacturer. Protect from light.

Preparation of dosage form
To prepare solution for intramuscular use, 1.5 mL of suitable diluent (see manufacturer's package insert) should be added to each 500-mg vial, or 3 mL of diluent should be added to each 1-gram vial.

To prepare initial dilution for intravenous use, 3 or 5 mL of suitable diluent (see manufacturer's package insert) should be added to each 500-mg vial, or 10 mL of diluent should be added to each 1- or 2-gram vial, according to manufacturer's labeling instructions. For direct intermittent intravenous use, the resulting solution should be administered slowly over a 3- to 5-minute period. For intravenous infusion, the resulting solution may be further diluted in suitable fluids according to the manufacturer's labeling instructions.

For reconstitution of piggyback infusion bottles and pharmacy bulk vials, see manufacturer's labeling for instructions. If the Y-type method of administration is used, the primary infusion should be temporarily discontinued during infusion of ceftazidime.

After reconstitution of the sodium carbonate formulation, carbon dioxide is formed, causing positive pressure inside the vial. This may require venting.

Do not use minibags in series connections. This may result in air embolism because of residual air being drawn from the primary container before administration of intravenous solution from the secondary container is complete.

Caution—Use of diluents containing benzyl alcohol is not recommended for preparation of medications for use in neonates. A fatal toxic syndrome consisting of metabolic acidosis, CNS depression, respiratory problems, renal failure, hypotension, and possibly seizures and intracranial hemorrhages has been associated with this use.

Stability
After reconstitution for intramuscular use with sterile water for injection, bacteriostatic water for injection, or lidocaine hydrochloride injection,

solutions retain their potency for at least 18 hours at room temperature or for 7 days if refrigerated. Solutions that are frozen immediately after reconstitution in the original container retain their potency for at least 3 months at −20 °C (−4 °F).

After reconstitution for intravenous use, solutions retain their potency for at least 18 hours at room temperature or for 7 days if refrigerated. Solutions that are frozen immediately after reconstitution with sterile water for injection in the original container retain their potency for at least 3 months at −20 °C (−4 °F).

Once thawed, solutions should not be refrozen. Thawed solutions retain their potency for at least 8 hours at room temperature or for at least 4 days if refrigerated.

Intravenous infusions at concentrations from 1 to 40 mg per mL retain their potency for at least 18 hours at room temperature or for 7 days if refrigerated, when stored in suitable fluids (see manufacturer's package insert). However, storage in sodium bicarbonate injection is not recommended since ceftazidime is less stable in sodium bicarbonate than in other fluids.

Solutions range in color from light yellow to amber, depending on the diluent and volume. Ceftazidime powder and solutions tend to darken, depending on storage conditions. This does not affect their potency.

Incompatibilities

The admixture of ceftazidime with other medications, including pentamidine isethionate, is not recommended.

The admixture of beta-lactam antibacterials (penicillins and cephalosporins) and aminoglycosides may result in substantial mutual inactivation. If they are administered concurrently, they should be administered in separate sites. Do not mix them in the same intravenous bag or bottle.

Vancomycin is physically incompatible with ceftazidime and a precipitate may form, depending on the concentration. Therefore, the intravenous lines should be flushed between the administration of these two medications if they are to be given through the same tubing.

[1]Not included in Canadian product labeling.

CEFTIBUTEN

Summary of Differences

Category: Third-generation. One of three oral third-generation cephalosporins.

Additional Dosing Information

The capsule and oral suspension dosage forms are bioequivalent.

The oral suspension should be taken at least 2 hours before or 1 hour after a meal.

Oral Dosage Forms

CEFTIBUTEN CAPSULES

Usual adult and adolescent dose

Bronchitis, bacterial exacerbations[1] or
Otitis media[1] or
Pharyngitis[1] or
Tonsillitis[1]—

Oral, 400 mg once a day for ten days.

Note: Adults with renal function impairment may require a reduction in dose as follows:

Creatinine clearance (mL/min)/(mL/sec)	Dosing: Capsules	Dosing: Oral suspension
> 50/0.83	See *Usual adult and adolescent dose*	9 mg/kg once every 24 hours
30−49/0.5−0.82	200 mg once every 24 hours	4.5 mg/kg once every 24 hours
5−29/0.1−0.49	100 mg once every 24 hours	2.25 mg/kg once every 24 hours

For patients undergoing hemodialysis two or three times a week, a single dose of 400 mg (capsules) or 9 mg/kg, up to 400 mg (oral suspension), may be administered at the end of each hemodialysis session.

Usual adult and adolescent prescribing limits

400 mg per day.

Usual pediatric dose

This dosage form usually is not used for children. See *Ceftibuten for Oral Suspension.*

Usual geriatric dose

See *Usual adult and adolescent dose.*

Strength(s) usually available

U.S.—

400 mg (Rx) [*Cedax* (benzyl alcohol; butylparaben; methylparaben; propylparaben)].

Canada—

Not commercially available.

Packaging and storage

Store between 2 and 25 °C (36 and 77 °F) in a tight container.

Auxiliary labeling

- Continue medicine for full time of treatment.

CEFTIBUTEN FOR ORAL SUSPENSION

Usual adult and adolescent dose

See *Ceftibuten Capsules.*

Usual adult and adolescent prescribing limits

See *Ceftibuten Capsules.*

Usual pediatric dose

Otitis media[1] or
Pharyngitis[1] or
Tonsillitis[1]—

Infants and children 6 months to 12 years of age: Oral, 9 mg per kg of body weight once a day for ten days.

Infants up to 6 months of age: Safety and efficacy have not been established.

Usual pediatric prescribing limits

400 mg per day.

Usual geriatric dose

See *Ceftibuten Capsules.*

Strength(s) usually available

U.S.—

90 mg per 5 mL (when reconstituted according to manufacturer's instructions) (available in 30-, 60-, 90-, and 120-mL bottles) (Rx) [*Cedax* (sodium benzoate; sucrose 1 gram per 5 mL)].

180 mg per 5 mL (when reconstituted according to manufacturer's instructions) (available in 30-, 60-, and 120-mL bottles) (Rx) [*Cedax* (sodium benzoate; sucrose 1 gram per 5 mL)].

Canada—

Not commercially available.

Packaging and storage

Store between 2 and 25 °C (36 and 77 °F).

Preparation of dosage form

The bottle should be tapped to loosen the powder. The total volume of water indicated below should be added in two portions, shaking well after each addition.

Final concentration	Bottle size	Total amount of water
90 mg/5 mL	30 mL	28 mL
	60 mL	53 mL
	90 mL	78 mL
	120 mL	103 mL
180 mg/5 mL	30 mL	28 mL
	60 mL	53 mL
	120 mL	103 mL

Stability

After reconstitution, the suspension may be stored for up to 14 days between 2 and 8 °C (36 and 46 °F).

Auxiliary labeling

- Refrigerate.
- Shake well.
- Take on an empty stomach, at least 2 hours before or 1 hour after meals.
- Continue medicine for full time of treatment.
- Beyond-use date.

[1]Not included in Canadian product labeling.

CEFTIZOXIME

Summary of Differences

Category: Third-generation cephalosporin.

Precautions: Pediatrics—Associated with transient elevation in eosinophils, ALT (SGPT), AST (SGOT), and CK.

Additional Dosing Information

Intramuscular doses of 2 grams should be administered as divided doses in different sites.

Parenteral Dosage Forms

Note: The dosing and strengths of the dosage forms available are expressed in terms of ceftizoxime base (not the sodium salt).

CEFTIZOXIME INJECTION USP

Usual adult and adolescent dose

Pelvic inflammatory disease[1]—
Intravenous infusion, 2 grams (base) every eight hours.

Urinary tract infections, uncomplicated—
Intravenous infusion, 500 mg (base) every twelve hours.

For all other infections—
Mild to moderate: Intravenous infusion, 1 gram (base) every eight to twelve hours.
Severe or refractory: Intravenous infusion, 1 gram (base) every eight hours; or 2 grams every eight to twelve hours.
Life-threatening: Intravenous infusion, 3 to 4 grams (base) every eight hours.

Note: Dosages of up to 2 grams every four hours have been given for life-threatening infections.

After an initial loading dose of 500 mg to 1 gram (base), adults with impaired renal function may require a reduction in dose as follows:

Creatinine clearance (mL/min)/(mL/sec)	Dose (base)	
	Less severe infections	Life-threatening infections
≥80/1.33	See *Usual adult and adolescent dose*	See *Usual adult and adolescent dose*
50–79/0.83–1.32	500 mg every 8 hours	750 mg to 1.5 grams every 8 hours
5–49/0.08–0.82	250 to 500 mg every 12 hours	500 mg to 1 gram every 12 hours
0–4/0–0.07	500 mg every 48 hours; or 250 mg every 24 hours	500 mg to 1 gram every 48 hours; or 500 mg every 24 hours

Usual pediatric dose

For bacterial infections—
Children 6 months of age and older: Intravenous infusion, 50 mg (base) per kg of body weight every six to eight hours.
Infants up to 6 months of age: Safety and efficacy have not been established.

Usual pediatric prescribing limits

200 mg (base) per kg of body weight (not to exceed the maximum adult dose for serious infection).

Usual geriatric dose

See *Usual adult and adolescent dose.*

Usual geriatric prescribing limits

1.5 grams (base) for patients older than seventy-five years of age, even if serum creatinine concentrations are normal.

Strength(s) usually available

U.S.—
1 gram (base) per 50 mL (Rx) [*Cefizox* (sodium 2.6 mEq per gram)].
2 grams (base) per 50 mL (Rx) [*Cefizox* (sodium 2.6 mEq per gram)].

Canada—
Not commercially available.

Packaging and storage

Store between −25 and −10 °C (−13 and 14 °F), unless otherwise specified by manufacturer.

Preparation of dosage form

The container should be thawed at room temperature (25 °C [77 °F]) or under refrigeration (5 °C [41 °F]) before administration, making sure that all ice crystals have melted. Thawing should not be forced by immersion in water baths or by microwave irradiation.

Do not use minibags in series connections. This may result in air embolism because of residual air being drawn from the primary container before administration of intravenous solution from the secondary container is complete.

Stability

After thawing, solutions retain their potency for 48 hours at room temperature or for 28 days if refrigerated at 5 °C (41 °F). Once thawed, solutions should not be refrozen.

Do not use if the solution is cloudy or contains a precipitate.

Incompatibilities

The admixture of beta-lactam antibacterials (penicillins and cephalosporins) and aminoglycosides may result in substantial mutual inactivation. If they are administered concurrently, they should be administered in separate sites. Do not mix them in the same intravenous bag or bottle.

CEFTIZOXIME FOR INJECTION USP

Usual adult and adolescent dose

Gonorrhea, uncomplicated[1]—
Intramuscular, 1 gram (base) as a single dose.

Pelvic inflammatory disease[1]—
Intravenous, 2 grams (base) every eight hours.

Urinary tract infections, uncomplicated—
Intramuscular or intravenous, 500 mg (base) every twelve hours.

For all other infections—
Mild to moderate: Intramuscular or intravenous, 1 gram (base) every eight to twelve hours.
Severe or refractory: Intramuscular or intravenous, 1 gram (base) every eight hours; or 2 grams every eight to twelve hours.
Life-threatening: Intravenous, 3 to 4 grams (base) every eight hours.

Note: Dosages of up to 2 grams (base) every four hours have been given for life-threatening infections.

Adults with renal function impairment may require a reduction in dose. See *Ceftizoxime Injection USP*.

Usual pediatric dose

For bacterial infections—
Children 6 months to 12 years of age: Intramuscular or intravenous, 50 mg (base) per kg of body weight every six to eight hours.
Infants and children up to 6 months of age: Safety and efficacy have not been established.

Usual pediatric prescribing limits

See *Ceftizoxime Injection USP*.

Usual geriatric dose

See *Usual adult and adolescent dose.*

Usual geriatric prescribing limits

See *Ceftizoxime Injection USP*.

Strength(s) usually available

U.S.—
500 mg (base) (Rx) [*Cefizox* (sodium 2.6 mEq per gram)].
1 gram (base) (Rx) [*Cefizox* (sodium 2.6 mEq per gram)].
2 grams (base) (Rx) [*Cefizox* (sodium 2.6 mEq per gram)].
10 grams (base) (Rx) [*Cefizox* (sodium 2.6 mEq per gram)].

Canada—
1 gram (base) (Rx) [*Cefizox* (sodium 2.6 mEq per gram)].
2 grams (base) (Rx) [*Cefizox* (sodium 2.6 mEq per gram)].

Packaging and storage

Prior to reconstitution, store below 40 °C (104 °F), preferably between 15 and 30 °C (59 and 86 °F), unless otherwise specified by manufacturer. Protect from excess light.

Preparation of dosage form

To prepare initial dilution for intramuscular use, 1.5, 3, or 6 mL of sterile water for injection should be added to each 500-mg, 1-gram, or 2-gram vial, respectively.

To prepare initial dilution for intravenous use, 5, 10, or 20 mL of sterile water for injection should be added to each 500-mg, 1-gram, or 2-gram vial, respectively. For direct intravenous use, the resulting solution should be administered slowly over a 3- to 5-minute period. For continuous or intermittent infusions, the resulting solution should be further diluted in 50 to 100 mL of suitable fluids (see manufacturer's package insert).

For reconstitution of piggyback infusion bottles and pharmacy bulk vials, see manufacturer's labeling for instructions.

Stability

After reconstitution for intramuscular or intravenous use with suitable diluents (see manufacturer's package insert), solutions retain their potency for 24 hours at room temperature or for 48 to 96 hours (see manufacturer's package insert) if refrigerated at 5 °C (41 °F).

Solutions may vary in color from yellow to amber. This does not affect their potency.

Incompatibilities

The admixture of beta-lactam antibacterials (penicillins and cephalosporins) and aminoglycosides may result in substantial mutual inactivation. If they are administered concurrently, they should be administered in separate sites. Do not mix them in the same intravenous bag or bottle.

Additional information

A solution containing 1 gram in 13 mL of sterile water for injection is isotonic.

[1]Not included in Canadian product labeling.

CEFTRIAXONE

Summary of Differences

Category: Third-generation cephalosporin.

Pharmacology/pharmacokinetics: Long half-life; may be dosed once a day.

Precautions: Pediatrics—Should be used with caution when administered to hyperbilirubinemic neonates, especially premature neonates.

Drug interactions and/or related problems—Does not interact with probenecid.

Side/adverse effects: Associated with "biliary sludge" or pseudolithiasis.

Additional Dosing Information

Patients with impaired hepatic function do not generally require a reduction in dose. However, in patients with both impaired hepatic and renal function, the daily dose should not exceed 2 grams.

Intravenous infusion should be administered over a period of 30 minutes.

Parenteral Dosage Forms

Note: The dosing and strengths of the dosage forms available are expressed in terms of ceftriaxone base (not the sodium salt).

CEFTRIAXONE SODIUM INJECTION

Usual adult and adolescent dose

Perioperative prophylaxis—
Intravenous infusion, 1 gram (base) one-half to two hours prior to the start of surgery.

For all other infections—
Intravenous infusion, 1 to 2 grams (base) every twenty-four hours; or 500 mg to 1 gram every twelve hours.

Usual adult and adolescent prescribing limits

4 grams (base) per day.

Usual pediatric dose

Meningitis—
Intravenous infusion, 100 mg (base) per kg of body weight, up to 4 grams, on the first day; then 100 mg per kg of body weight every twenty-four hours, or 50 mg per kg of body weight every twelve hours, up to 4 grams per day, for seven to fourteen days.

Skin and soft tissue infections—
Intravenous infusion, 50 to 75 mg (base) per kg of body weight every twenty-four hours, or 25 to 37.5 mg per kg of body weight every twelve hours, up to 2 grams per day.

For all other infections, serious—
Intravenous infusion, 25 to 37.5 mg (base) per kg of body weight every twelve hours, up to 2 grams per day.

Usual pediatric prescribing limits

4 grams (base) per day for meningitis, and 2 grams per day for all other infections.

Usual geriatric dose

See *Usual adult and adolescent dose.*

Strength(s) usually available

U.S.—
1 gram (base) in 50 mL (Rx) [*Rocephin* (sodium 3.6 mEq per gram)].
2 grams (base) in 50 mL (Rx) [*Rocephin* (sodium 3.6 mEq per gram)].

Canada—
Not commercially available.

Packaging and storage

Store at or below -20 °C (-4 °F)

The thawed solution is stable for 21 days under refrigeration (5 °C or 21 °F) or 72 hours at room temperature (25 °C or 77 °F).

Preparation of dosage form

The container should be thawed at room temperature before administration, making sure that all ice crystals have melted.

Do not use minibags in series connections. This may result in air embolism because of residual air being drawn from the primary container before administration of intravenous solution from the secondary container is complete.

Stability

Once thawed, solutions should not be refrozen.

Do not use if the solution is cloudy or contains a precipitate.

Incompatibilities

The admixture of ceftriaxone with other medications, including pentamidine isethionate, or with labetalol hydrochloride is not recommended.

The admixture of beta-lactam antibacterials (penicillins and cephalosporins) and aminoglycosides may result in substantial mutual inactivation. If they are administered concurrently, they should be administered in separate sites. Do not mix them in the same intravenous bag or bottle.

The admixture of ceftriaxone and vancomycin and fluconazole are physically incompatible. When concomitantly administering ceftriaxone by intermittent intravenous infusion it is recommended that they be given sequentially, with thorough flushing of the intravenous lines (with one of the compatible fluids) between administrations.

Do not add supplementary medication to frozen solutions of ceftriaxone. Ceftriaxone solutions should not be physically mixed with or piggybacked into solutions containing other antimicrobial drugs or into diluent solutions other than those reported to be compatible.

CEFTRIAXONE SODIUM FOR INJECTION

Usual adult and adolescent dose

Gonorrhea, uncomplicated—
Intramuscular, 250 mg (base) as a single dose.

Perioperative prophylaxis—
Intravenous, 1 gram (base) one-half to two hours prior to the start of surgery.

For all other infections—
Intramuscular or intravenous, 1 to 2 grams (base) every twenty-four hours; or 500 mg to 1 gram every twelve hours.

Usual adult prescribing limits

See *Ceftriaxone Sodium Injection.*

Usual pediatric dose

Meningitis—
Intramuscular or intravenous, 100 mg (base) per kg of body weight, up to 4 grams, on the first day; then 100 mg per kg of body weight every twenty-four hours, or 50 mg per kg of body weight every twelve hours, up to 4 grams per day, for seven to fourteen days.

Otitis media[1]—
Intramuscular, 50 mg (base) per kg of body weight, up to 1 gram, as a single dose.

Skin and soft tissue infections—
Intramuscular or intravenous, 50 to 75 mg (base) per kg of body weight every twenty-four hours, or 25 to 37.5 mg per kg of body weight every twelve hours, up to 2 grams per day.

For all other serious infections—
Intramuscular or intravenous, 25 to 37.5 mg (base) per kg of body weight every twelve hours, up to 2 grams per day.

Usual pediatric prescribing limits

See *Ceftriaxone Sodium Injection.*

Usual geriatric dose

See *Usual adult and adolescent dose.*

Strength(s) usually available

U.S.—
250 mg (base) (Rx) [*Rocephin* (sodium 3.6 mEq per gram)].
500 mg (base) (Rx) [*Rocephin* (sodium 3.6 mEq per gram)].
1 gram (base) (also available in ADD-Vantage® vials) (Rx) [*Rocephin* (sodium 3.6 mEq per gram)].
2 grams (base) (also available in ADD-Vantage® vials) (Rx) [*Rocephin* (sodium 3.6 mEq per gram)].
10 grams (base) (Rx) [*Rocephin* (sodium 3.6 mEq per gram)].

Canada—
250 mg (base) (Rx) [*Rocephin* (sodium 3.6 mEq per gram)].
1 gram (base) (also available in ADD-Vantage® vials) (Rx) [*Rocephin* (sodium 3.6 mEq per gram)].
2 grams (base) (Rx) [*Rocephin* (sodium 3.6 mEq per gram)].
10 grams (base) (Rx) [*Rocephin* (sodium 3.6 mEq per gram)].

Packaging and storage

Prior to reconstitution, store below 25 °C (77 °F), preferably between 15 and 30 °C (59 and 86 °F), unless otherwise specified by manufacturer. Protect from light.

Preparation of dosage form

To prepare initial dilution for intramuscular use, 0.9 mL of sterile water for injection, 0.9% sodium chloride injection, 5% dextrose injection, bacteriostatic water for injection (with 0.9% benzyl alcohol), or 1% lidocaine hydrochloride injection (without epinephrine) should be added to each 250-mg vial, 1.8 mL of diluent should be added to each 500-mg vial, 3.6 mL of diluent should be added to each 1-gram vial, or 7.2 mL of diluent should be added to each 2-gram vial to provide a concentration of approximately 250 mg per mL. Alternatively, to reduce the volume of intramuscular injection, a solution of 350 mg per mL may be prepared by adding 1 mL of diluent to each 500-mg vial, 2.1 mL of diluent to each 1-gram vial, or 4.2 mL of diluent to each 2-gram vial. The 350-mg-per-mL solution is bioequivalent to a 250-mg-per-mL solution.

To prepare initial dilution for intravenous use, 2.4 mL of appropriate diluent (see manufacturer's package insert) should be added to each 250-mg vial, 4.8 mL of diluent should be added to each 500-mg vial, 9.6 mL of diluent should be added to each 1-gram vial, or 19.2 mL of diluent should be added to each 2-gram vial to provide a concentration of approximately 100 mg per mL. The reconstituted solution may be further diluted to 50 or 100 mL with an appropriate diluent for intravenous infusion.

For reconstitution of piggyback infusion bottles and pharmacy bulk vials, see manufacturer's labeling for instructions.

Caution—Use of diluents containing benzyl alcohol is not recommended for preparation of medications for use in neonates. A fatal toxic syndrome consisting of metabolic acidosis, CNS depression, respiratory problems, renal failure, hypotension, and possibly seizures and intracranial hemorrhages has been associated with this use.

Stability

After reconstitution for intramuscular use, solutions retain at least 90% of their potency for 1 to 2 days at room temperature (25 °C [77 °F]) or for 3 to 10 days if refrigerated at 4 °C (39 °F), depending on concentration and diluent.

After reconstitution for intravenous use, solutions retain at least 90% of their potency for 2 days at room temperature (25 °C [77 °F]) or for 10 days if refrigerated at 4 °C (39 °F), when stored in glass or polyvinyl chloride (PVC) containers in suitable diluents (see manufacturer's package insert).

After reconstitution for intravenous use with 5% dextrose injection or 0.9% sodium chloride injection, solutions at concentrations of 10 to 40 mg per mL retain their potency for 26 weeks at −20 °C (−4 °F) when stored in PVC or polyolefin containers. Frozen solutions should be thawed at room temperature. Once thawed, solutions should not be refrozen.

Solutions may vary in color from light yellow to amber, depending on length of time in storage, concentration, and diluent.

Incompatibilities

The admixture of ceftriaxone with other medications, including pentamidine isethionate, or with labetalol hydrochloride is not recommended.

The admixture of beta-lactam antibacterials (penicillins and cephalosporins) and aminoglycosides may result in substantial mutual inactivation. If they are administered concurrently, they should be administered in separate sites. Do not mix them in the same intravenous bag or bottle.

The admixture of ceftriaxone and vancomycin and fluconazole are physically incompatible. When concomitantly administering ceftriaxone by intermittent intravenous infusion it is recommended that they be given sequentially, with thorough flushing of the intravenous lines (with one of the compatible fluids) between administrations.

[1]Not included in Canadian product labeling.

CEFUROXIME

Summary of Differences

Category: Second-generation cephalosporin.

Pharmacology/pharmacokinetics: Cefuroxime oral suspension reaches only 91% of the area under the plasma concentration-time curve (AUC) and 71% of the peak serum concentration that cefuroxime tablets reach.

Parenteral cefuroxime is the only second-generation cephalosporin to adequately penetrate into the CSF; however, sterilization is delayed compared with third-generation cephalosporins.

Precautions: Laboratory value alteration—May give false-positive test results with Coombs' test, copper reduction tests (including Benedict's solution, Clinitest®, and Fehling's solution); a false negative for ferricyanide blood glucose test and a fall in prothrombin levels

Additional Dosing Information

For oral dosage forms only:

- Cefuroxime axetil tablets may be given without regard to meals; however, absorption is enhanced when they are given with food.
- Cefuroxime axetil oral suspension should be taken with food.
- Cefuroxime axetil tablets and oral suspension are not bioequivalent and are not substitutable on a mg-per-mg basis.

Oral Dosage Forms

Note: Bracketed uses in the *Dosage Forms* section refer to categories of use and/or indications that are not included in U.S. product labeling.

The dosing and strengths of the dosage forms available are expressed in terms of cefuroxime base (not the axetil salt).

CEFUROXIME AXETIL FOR ORAL SUSPENSION

Usual adult and adolescent dose

The oral suspension usually is used only for children. See *Cefuroxime Axetil Tablets USP*.

Usual pediatric dose

Impetigo[1] or
Otitis media, acute or
Sinusitis, acute bacterial maxillary—

Infants and children 3 months to 12 years of age: Oral, 15 mg (base) per kg of body weight every twelve hours, up to 1000 mg per day, for ten days.

Infants up to 3 months of age: Safety and efficacy have not been established.

Pharyngitis or
Tonsillitis—

Infants and children 3 months to 12 years of age: Oral, 10 mg (base) per kg of body weight every twelve hours, up to 500 mg per day, for ten days.

Infants up to 3 months of age: Safety and efficacy have not been established.

Usual pediatric prescribing limits

500 mg per day for pharyngitis and tonsillitis, and 1000 mg per day for impetigo otitis media and sinusitis.

Strength(s) usually available

U.S.—

125 mg per 5 mL (when reconstituted according to manufacturer's instructions) (available in 50- and 100-mL bottles) (Rx) [*Ceftin* (sucrose)].

250 mg per 5 mL (when reconstituted according to manufacturer's instructions) (available in 50- and 100-mL bottles) (Rx) [*Ceftin* (sucrose)].

Canada—

125 mg per 5 mL (when reconstituted according to manufacturer's instructions) (available in 70- and 100-mL bottles) (Rx) [*Ceftin* (sucrose)].

250 mg single dose packets (Rx) [*Ceftin* (sucrose)].

Packaging and storage

Prior to reconstitution, store between 2 and 30 °C (36 and 86 °F), in a well-closed container, unless otherwise specified by manufacturer.

Preparation of dosage form

Cefuroxime axetil should not be reconstituted with milk, hot water, or other hot fluids.

For the oral suspension—The bottle should be shaken to loosen the powder. The total amount of water for reconstitution should be added as indicated below. The solution should be shaken vigorously to reconstitute.

Final concentration	Labeled volume after reconstitution	Total volume of water to be added
125 mg/5 mL	50 mL	20 mL
	70 mL	27 mL
	100 mL	37 mL
250 mg/5 mL	50 mL	19 mL
	100 mL	35 mL

For the single dose packets—Empty the contents of the packet into a glass. Add 10 mL or more of cold water; apple, grape, or orange juice; or lemonade. Stir well and consume the entire volume immediately.

Stability

After reconstitution, suspension retains its potency for 10 days if refrigerated or stored at room temperature (between 2 and 25 °C [36 and 77 °F]).

Auxiliary labeling

- Take with food.
- Does not require refrigeration.
- Continue medicine for full time of treatment.
- Shake well.
- Beyond-use date.

Note

When dispensing, include a calibrated liquid-measuring device.

CEFUROXIME AXETIL TABLETS USP

Usual adult and adolescent dose

Bronchitis, bacterial exacerbations[1] or
Skin and soft tissue infections—
Oral, 250 or 500 mg (base) two times a day for ten days.
Bronchitis—
Oral, 250 or 500 mg (base) two times a day for five to ten days.
Gonorrhea, uncomplicated—
Oral, 1000 mg (base) as a single dose.
Lyme disease, early[1]—
Oral, 500 mg (base) two times a day for twenty days.
Pharyngitis or
Sinusitis, acute maxillary or
Tonsillitis—
Oral, 250 mg (base) two times a day for ten days.
[Pneumonia]—
Oral, 500 mg (base) two times a day.
Urinary tract infections, uncomplicated[1]—
Oral, 250 mg (base) two times a day for seven to ten days.

Usual pediatric dose

Otitis media, acute or
Sinusitis, acute bacterial maxillary—
Children who can swallow tablets whole: Oral, 250 mg (base) two times a day for ten days.
Children who cannot swallow tablets whole: See *Cefuroxime Axetil for Oral Suspension.*
Pharyngitis or
Tonsillitis—
Children who can swallow tablets whole: Oral, 250mg (base) two times a day for ten days.
Children who cannot swallow tablets whole: See *Cefuroxime Axetil for Oral Suspension.*

Usual geriatric dose

See *Usual adult and adolescent dose.*

Strength(s) usually available

U.S.—
250 mg (base) (Rx) [*Ceftin* (methylparaben; propylparaben)].
500 mg (base) (Rx) [*Ceftin* (methylparaben; propylparaben)].
Canada—
250 mg (base) (Rx) [*Ceftin* (methylparaben; propylparaben)].
500 mg (base) (Rx) [*Ceftin* (methylparaben; propylparaben)].

Packaging and storage

Store between 15 and 30 °C (59 and 86 °F), unless otherwise specified by manufacturer. Store in a tight container.

Auxiliary labeling

- Continue medicine for full time of treatment.

Parenteral Dosage Forms

Note: The dosing and strengths of the dosage forms available are expressed in terms of cefuroxime base (not the sodium salt).

CEFUROXIME INJECTION USP

Usual adult and adolescent dose

General dose—
Intravenous, 750 mg to 1.5 gm of cefuroxime every 8 hours, usually for 5 to 10 days. Canadian product information states usual duration of treatment is for 5 to 14 days.
Bone and joint infections (treatment)
Gonococcal infections, disseminated, severe or complicated (treatment)[1]
Pneumonia, severe or complicated (treatment)
Skin and skin-structure infections, severe or complicated (treatment),[1]
Urinary tract infections, severe or complicated (treatment)[1]—
Intravenous infusion, 1.5 grams (base) every eight hours.
Gonococcal infections, disseminated[1] or
Pneumonia, uncomplicated or
Skin and soft tissue infections or
Urinary tract infections, uncomplicated—
Intravenous infusion, 750 mg (base) every eight hours.
Meningitis, bacterial—
Intravenous infusion, up to 3 grams (base) every eight hours.
Perioperative prophylaxis—
Open heart surgery patients: Intravenous infusion, 1.5 grams (base) at the induction of anesthesia, then 1.5 grams every twelve hours, for a total of 6 grams.
Other surgery patients: Intravenous infusion, 1.5 grams (base) one-half to one hour prior to the start of surgery, then 750 mg every eight hours thereafter.
For all other infections—
Life-threatening or less susceptible organisms: Intravenous infusion, 1.5 grams (base) every six hours. Canadian product information states for severe or life threatening infections, intravenous 1.5 gm every 8 hours (4.5 gm per day).

Note: Adults with impaired renal function may require a reduction in dose as follows:

Creatinine clearance (mL/min)/(mL/sec)	Dose (base)
> 20/0.33	750 mg to 1.5 grams every 8 hours
10–20/0.17–0.33	750 mg every 12 hours
< 10/0.17	750 mg every 24 hours
Hemodialysis patients	750 mg at the end of each dialysis period

Usual adult prescribing limits

Bacterial Meningitis-Up to 3 gm of cefuroxime every 8 hours.

Usual pediatric dose

General dose—
For those three months of age and older: Intravenous, 50 to 150 mg per kg of body weight per day in equally divided doses every 6 to 8 hours. A higher dosage of 100 mg per kg of body weight per day (not to exceed the maximum adult dosage) should be used for the more severe or serious infections.
[Neonates (up to 1 month of age)]—Intravenous, 30 to 100 mg per kg of body weight per day in 2 or 3 equally divided doses. Note that in the first few weeks of life, the serum half-life of cefuroxime can be 3 to 5 times that in adults.
[Infants and children (1 month to 12 years)]—Intravenous, 30 to 100 mg per kg of body weight per day in 3 or 4 equally divided doses. A dose of 60 mg per kg of body weight per day is appropriate for most infections.
Note: Pediatric patients with renal insufficiency the frequency of dosing should be modified consistent with the recommendations for adults.
Bone and joint infections (treatment)—
For those three months of age and older—Intravenous, 150 mg per kg of body weight per day (not exceeding the maximum adult dosage) in equally divided doses every 8 hours. In clinical trials a course of oral antibiotics was administered to pediatric patients following the completion of parenteral administration
[Infants and children (1 month to 12 years)]—Intravenous, 70 to 150 mg per kg of body weight per day every 8 hours. In clinical trials a course of oral antibiotics was administered to pediatric patients following the completion of parenteral administration
Meningitis, bacterial (treatment)—
For those 3 months of age and older—Intravenous, 200 to 240 mg per kg of body weight per day in equally divided doses every 6 to 8 hours.
[Infants and children (1 month to 12 years)]—Intravenous, 200 to 240 mg per kg of body weight per day in 3 or 4 equally divided doses.
[Neonates (up to 1 month of age)]—Intravenous, 100 mg per kg of body weight per day in 2 or 3 equally divided doses.
Note: Pediatric patients with impaired renal function may require a reduction in the frequency of dosing consistent with adult dosing recommendations in renal impairment. See *Usual adult and adolescent dose.*

Usual pediatric prescribing limits

Up to the maximal adult dosage for the indication.See *Usual adult prescribing limits.*

Usual geriatric dose

See *Usual adult and adolescent dose*

Strength(s) usually available

U.S.—
Note: The plastic container is fabricated from a specially designed multilayer plastic, PL 2040. Solutions are in contact with polyethylene layer of this container and can leach out certain chemical components of the plastic in very small amounts within the expiration period. The suitability of the plastic has been confirmed in tests in animals according to USP biological tests for plastic containers as well as by tissue culture toxicity studies.
750 mg as frozen, iso-osmotic, sterile, nonpyrogenic solution in a plastic container (Rx) [*Zinacef* (Dextrose Hydrous, USP 1.4 gm; Sodium Citrate Hydrous, USP 300 mg; sodium 111 mg (4.8 mEq); hydrochloric acid; sodium hydroxide)].
1.5 gm as frozen, iso-osmotic, sterile, nonpyrogenic solution in a plastic container (Rx) [*Zinacef* (Sodium Citrate Hydrous, USP 600 mg; sodium 222 mg (9.7 mEq); hydrochloric acid; sodium hydroxide)].
Canada—
Not commercially available.

Packaging and storage
Store frozen below -20° C

Preparation of dosage form
The container should be thawed at room temperature (25 °C [77 °F]) or under refrigeration (5 °C [41 °F]) before administration, making sure that all ice crystals have melted. Thawing should not be forced by immersion in water baths or by microwave irradiation.Do not force thaw by immersion in water baths or by microwave irradiation
Do not use minibags in series connections. This may result in air embolism because of residual air being drawn from the primary container before administration of intravenous solution from the secondary container is complete.
Mix after solution has reached room temperature. Check or minute leaks by squeezing bag firmly. Discard bag if leaks are found as sterility may be impaired.
Do not add supplementary medication.
Do not use unless solution is clar and seal is intact.

Stability
After thawing, solutions retain their potency for 24 hours at room temperature or for 28 days if refrigerated at 5 °C (41 °F). Once thawed, solutions should not be refrozen.
Do not use if the solution is cloudy or contains a precipitate.
Components of the solution may precipitate in the frozen state and will dissolve upon reaching room temperature with little or no agitation. Potency is not affected.
Solution ranges in color from light yellow to amber.

Incompatibilities
The admixture of cefuroxime with other antibacterials is not recommended.
The admixture of beta-lactam antibacterials (penicillins and cephalosporins) and aminoglycosides may result in substantial mutual inactivation. If they are administered concurrently, they should be administered in separate sites. Do not mix them in the same intravenous bag or bottle.

CEFUROXIME FOR INJECTION USP

Usual adult and adolescent dose
General dose—
Intravenous or intramuscular, 750 mg to 1.5 gm of cefuroxime every 8 hours, usually for 5 to 10 days. Canadian product information states usual duration of treatment is for 5 to 14 days.
Bone and joint infections (treatment) or
Gonococcal infections, disseminated, severe or complicated (treatment)[1] or
Pneumonia, severe or complicated (treatment) or
Skin and skin-structure infections, severe or complicated (treatment),[1] or
Urinary tract infections, severe or complicated (treatment)[1]—
Intramuscular or intravenous, 1.5 grams (base) every eight hours.
Gonococcal infections, disseminated[1] or
Pneumonia, uncomplicated or
Skin and soft tissue infections or
Urinary tract infections, uncomplicated—
Intramuscular or intravenous, 750 mg (base) every eight hours.
Gonorrhea, uncomplicated—
Intramuscular, 1.5 grams (base) as a single dose at two different sites, in combination with 1 gram of oral probenecid.
Meningitis, bacterial—
Intravenous, up to 3 grams (base) every eight hours.
Perioperative prophylaxis—
Open heart surgery patients: Intravenous, 1.5 grams (base) at the induction of anesthesia, then 1.5 grams every twelve hours, for a total of 6 grams.
Other surgery patients: Intravenous, 1.5 grams (base) one-half to one hour prior to the start of surgery, then 750 mg (intramuscularly or intravenously) every eight hours thereafter.
In Canada after surgery, 750 mg intravenously or intramuscularly at 8 hours and 16 hours when the procedure is prolonged. Continued prophylactic administration of any antibiotic does not appear to be associated with a reduced incidence of subsequent infection, but will increase the possibility of adverse reactions and the development of bacterial resistance.
For all other infections—
Severe or complicated: Intramuscular or intravenous, 1.5 grams (base) every eight hours.
Life-threatening or less susceptible organisms: Intramuscular or intravenous, 1.5 grams (base) every six hours. Canadian product information states for severe or life threatening infections, intravenous 1.5 gm every 8 hours (4.5 gm per day)

Note: Adults with renal function impairment may require a reduction in dose. See *Cefuroxime Sodium Injection USP*.

Usual adult prescribing limits
Bacterial Meningitis-Up to 3 gm of cefuroxime every 8 hours.

Usual pediatric dose
General dose—
For those three months of age and older: Intravenous, 50 to 150 mg per kg of body weight per day in equally divided doses every 6 to 8 hours. A higher dosage of 100 mg per kg of body weight per day (not to exceed the maximum adult dosage) should be used for the more severe or serious infections.
[Neonates (up to 1 month of age)]—Intravenous, 30 to 100 mg per kg of body weight per day in 2 or 3 equally divided doses. Note that in the first few weeks of life, the serum half-life of cefuroxime can be 3 to 5 times that in adults.
[Infants and children (1 month to 12 years)]—Intravenous, 30 to 100 mg per kg of body weight per day in 3 or 4 equally divided doses. A dose of 60 mg per kg of body weight per day is appropriate for most infections.

Note: Pediatric patients with renal insufficiency the frequency of dosing should be modified consistent with the recommendations for adults.

Bone and joint infections (treatment)—
For those three months of age and older—Intravenous, 150 mg per kg of body weight per day (not exceeding the maximum adult dosage) in equally divided doses every 8 hours. In clinical trials a course of oral antibiotics was administered to pediatric patients following the completion of parenteral administration
[Infants and children (1 month to 12 years)]—Intravenous, 70 to 150 mg per kg of body weight per day every 8 hours. In clinical trials a course of oral antibiotics was administered to pediatric patients following the completion of parenteral administration
Meningitis, bacterial (treatment)—
For those 3 months of age and older—Intravenous, 200 to 240 mg per kg of body weight per day in equally divided doses every 6 to 8 hours.
[Infants and children (1 month to 12 years)]—Intravenous, 200 to 240 mg per kg of body weight per day in 3 or 4 equally divided doses.
[Neonates (up to 1 month of age)]—Intravenous, 100 mg per kg of body weight per day in 2 or 3 equally divided doses.

Note: Pediatric patients with renal function impairment may require a reduction in the frequency of dosing consistent with adult dosing recommendations in renal impairment. See *Cefuroxime Sodium Injection USP*.

Usual pediatric prescribing limits
Up to the maximal adult dosage for the indication.See *Cefuroxime Injection USP, Usual adult prescribing limits.*

Usual geriatric dose
See *Usual adult and adolescent dose.*

Strength(s) usually available
U.S.—

Note: Zinacef contains 54.2 mg (2.4 mEq) of sodium per gram of cefuroxime activity.

750 mg (also may be available in ADD-Vantage® vials) (Rx) [*Kefurox* (sodium 2.4 mEq per gram); *Zinacef* (sodium 2.4 mEq per gram); GENERIC].
1.5 grams (also may be available in ADD-Vantage® vials) (Rx) [*Kefurox* (sodium 2.4 mEq per gram); *Zinacef* (sodium 2.4 mEq per gram); GENERIC].
7.5 grams (Rx) [*Kefurox* (sodium 2.4 mEq per gram); *Zinacef* (sodium 2.4 mEq per gram); GENERIC].
750 mg infusion pack (Rx) [*Zinacef* (sodium)].
1.5 gm infusion pack (Rx) [*Zinacef* (sodium)].
Canada—
750 mg (also may be available in ADD-Vantage® vials) (Rx) [*Kefurox* (sodium 2.4 mEq per gram); *Zinacef*].
1.5 grams (also may be available in ADD-Vantage® vials) (Rx) [*Kefurox* (sodium 2.4 mEq per gram); *Zinacef*].
7.5 grams (Rx) [*Kefurox* (sodium 2.4 mEq per gram); *Zinacef*].

Packaging and storage
Prior to reconstitution, store below 40 °C (104 °F), preferably between 15 and 30 °C (59 and 86 °F), unless otherwise specified by manufacturer. Protect from light.
When frozen, store at or below -4°F (-20°C)

Preparation of dosage form
To prepare initial dilution for intramuscular use, 3 or 3.6 mL of sterile water for injection (see manufacturer's labeling instructions) should be added to each 750-mg vial and the entire volume withdrawn to provide a concentration of approximately 220 mg per mL.

To prepare initial dilution for intravenous use, see manufacturer's labeling instructions. For direct intermittent intravenous use, the resulting solution should be administered slowly over a 3- to 5-minute period. For infusion, each 750-mg or 1.5-gram dose may be diluted with 50 to 100 mL of appropriate diluent (see manufacturer's package insert).

For reconstitution of piggyback infusion bottles and pharmacy bulk vials, see manufacturer's labeling for instructions. If the Y-type method of administration is used, the primary infusion should be temporarily discontinued during infusion of cefuroxime.

Stability

After reconstitution for intramuscular use, suspensions retain their potency for 24 hours at room temperature or for 48 hours if refrigerated at 5 °C (41 °F).

ADD-Vantage diluent containers and activated to dissolve the drug are stable for 24 hours at room temperature or for 7 days under refrigeration (5° C). Joined vials that have not been activated may be used within a 14 day period. Freezing solutions in the ADD-Vantage system is not recommended.

After reconstitution for intravenous use, solutions retain their potency for 24 hours at room temperature or for 48 hours if refrigerated at 5 °C (41 °F). The 7.5 gm bulk containers are stable for 24 hours at room temperature and 7 days under refrigeration (5° C) Solutions stored in polyvinyl chloride (PVC) minibags in 50 or 100 mL of 5% dextrose injection or 0.9% sodium chloride injection retain their potency for 6 months at −20 °C (−4 °F).

Frozen solutions should be thawed at room temperature. Thawing should not be forced by immersion in water baths or by microwave irradiation. Thawed solutions retain their potency for up to 24 hours at room temperature or for 7 days if refrigerated.

Intravenous infusions at concentrations of 7.5 and 15 mg per mL in sterile water for injection, 5% dextrose injection, or 0.9% sodium chloride injection retain their potency for 24 hours at room temperature or for 7 days if refrigerated. Use of sodium bicarbonate is not recommended for dilution.

Solutions may vary in color from light yellow to amber, depending on concentration and diluent. In addition, cefuroxime powder, suspensions, and solutions tend to darken, depending on storage conditions. This does not affect their potency.

Incompatibilities

The admixture of beta-lactam antibacterials (penicillins and cephalosporins) and aminoglycosides may result in substantial mutual inactivation. If they are administered concurrently, they should be administered in separate sites. Do not mix them in the same intravenous bag or bottle.

Sodium Bicarbonate Injection USP is not recommended for the dilution of cefuroxime.

---

[1]Not included in Canadian product labeling.

CEPHALEXIN

Summary of Differences

Category: First-generation cephalosporin.

Additional Dosing Information

When daily doses greater than 4 grams are required, parenteral cephalosporins should be considered.

No dosage adjustment is necessary for renal function impairment.

Oral Dosage Forms

Note: Bracketed uses in the *Dosage Forms* section refer to categories of use and/or indications that are not included in U.S. product labeling.

CEPHALEXIN CAPSULES USP

Usual adult and adolescent dose

Cystitis, uncomplicated or
Pharyngitis or
Skin and soft tissue infections or
Tonsillitis—
Oral, 500 mg every twelve hours.

Note: Treatment of cystitis should be administered only to adults and adolescents 15 years of age and older, and should continue for seven to fourteen days.

[Endocarditis, prophylaxis][1]—
Oral, 2 grams as a single dose one hour prior to the start of surgery.

For all other infections—
Mild to moderate: Oral, 250 mg every six hours.
Severe: Oral, up to 1 gram every six hours.

Usual adult prescribing limits

4 grams per day.

Usual pediatric dose

This dosage form usually is not used for children. See *Cephalexin for Oral Suspension USP*.

Usual geriatric dose

See *Usual adult and adolescent dose*.

Strength(s) usually available

U.S.—
250 mg (Rx) [*Keflex;* GENERIC].
500 mg (Rx) [*Keflex;* GENERIC].

Canada—
250 mg (Rx) [*Novo-Lexin*].
500 mg (Rx) [*Novo-Lexin*].

Packaging and storage

Store below 40 °C (104 °F), preferably between 15 and 30 °C (59 and 86 °F), unless otherwise specified by manufacturer. Store in a tight container. Protect from light.

Auxiliary labeling

- Continue medicine for full time of treatment.

CEPHALEXIN FOR ORAL SUSPENSION USP

Usual adult and adolescent dose

See *Cephalexin Capsules USP*.

Usual adult prescribing limits

See *Cephalexin Capsules USP*.

Usual pediatric dose

[Endocarditis, prophylaxis][1]—
Children over 40 kg of body weight: See *Usual adult and adolescent dose*.
Children 1 year of age and older, and up to 40 kg of body weight: Oral, 50 mg per kg of body weight one hour prior to the start of surgery.

[Impetigo][1]—
Oral, 15 mg per kg of body weight three times per day for ten days.

Otitis media—
Children over 40 kg of body weight: See *Usual adult and adolescent dose*.
Children 1 year of age and older, and up to 40 kg of body weight: Oral, 18.75 to 25 mg per kg of body weight every six hours.

Pharyngitis or
Skin and soft tissue infections or
Tonsillitis—
Children over 40 kg of body weight: See *Usual adult and adolescent dose*.
Children 1 year of age and older, and up to 40 kg of body weight: Oral, 12.5 to 25 mg per kg of body weight every twelve hours.

For all other infections—
Children over 40 kg of body weight: See *Usual adult and adolescent dose*.
Children 1 year of age and older, and up to 40 kg of body weight: Mild to moderate—Oral, 12.5 to 25 mg per kg of body weight every twelve hours; or 6.25 to 12.5 mg per kg of body weight every six hours. Severe—Oral, 25 to 50 mg per kg of body weight every twelve hours; or 12.5 to 25 mg per kg of body weight every six hours.
Infants and children 1 month to 1 year of age: Oral, 6.25 to 12.5 mg per kg of body weight every six hours.

Usual pediatric prescribing limits

2 grams for prophylaxis of bacterial endocarditis.

Usual geriatric dose

See *Cephalexin Capsules USP*.

Strength(s) usually available

U.S.—
125 mg per 5 mL (when reconstituted according to manufacturer's instructions) (may be available in 100- and 200-mL bottles) (Rx) [*Keflex* (sucrose); GENERIC (may contain sucrose)].
250 mg per 5 mL (when reconstituted according to manufacturer's instructions) (may be available in 100- and 200-mL bottles) (Rx) [*Keflex* (sucrose); GENERIC (may contain sucrose)].

Canada—
125 mg per 5 mL (when reconstituted according to manufacturer's instructions) (may be available in 100-, 150-, and 200-mL bottles)

(Rx) [*Keflex* (sodium); *Novo-Lexin* (sodium); *PMS-Cephalexin* (sodium)].

250 mg per 5 mL (when reconstituted according to manufacturer's instructions) (may be available in 100-, 150-, and 200-mL bottles) (Rx) [*Keflex*(sodium); *Novo-Lexin* (sodium); *PMS-Cephalexin* (sodium)].

Packaging and storage
Prior to reconstitution, store below 40 °C (104 °F), preferably between 15 and 30 °C (59 and 86 °F), unless otherwise specified by manufacturer. Store in a tight container.

Preparation of dosage form
See manufacturer's labeling for instructions.

Stability
After reconstitution, suspensions retain their potency for 14 days if refrigerated.

Auxiliary labeling
- Refrigerate.
- Shake well.
- Continue medicine for full time of treatment.
- Beyond-use date.

Note
When dispensing, include a calibrated liquid-measuring device.

CEPHALEXIN TABLETS USP

Usual adult and adolescent dose
See *Cephalexin Capsules USP*.

Usual adult prescribing limits
See *Cephalexin Capsules USP*.

Usual pediatric dose
This dosage form usually is not used for children. See *Cephalexin for Oral Suspension USP*.

Usual geriatric dose
See *Cephalexin Capsules USP*.

Strength(s) usually available
U.S.—
250 mg (Rx) [GENERIC (may be scored)].
500 mg (Rx) [GENERIC (may be scored)].
Canada—
250 mg (Rx) [*Apo-Cephalex* (scored); *Keflex; Novo-Lexin; Nu-Cephalex; PMS-Cephalexin*].
500 mg (Rx) [*Apo-Cephalex* (scored); *Keflex; Novo-Lexin; Nu-Cephalex; PMS-Cephalexin*].

Packaging and storage
Store below 40 °C (104 °F), preferably between 15 and 30 °C (59 and 86 °F), unless otherwise specified by manufacturer. Store in a tight container.

Auxiliary labeling
- Continue medicine for full time of treatment.

CEPHALEXIN HYDROCHLORIDE TABLETS USP

Usual adult dose
See *Cephalexin Capsules USP*.

Usual adult prescribing limits
See *Cephalexin Capsules USP*.

Usual pediatric dose
Safety and efficacy have not been established.

Usual geriatric dose
See *Cephalexin Capsules USP*.

Strength(s) usually available
U.S.—
500 mg (Rx) [*Keftab* (sucrose)].
Canada—
Not commercially available.

Packaging and storage
Store between 15 and 30 °C (59 and 86 °F), unless otherwise specified by manufacturer. Store in a tight container.

Auxiliary labeling
- Continue medicine for full time of treatment.

[1]Not included in Canadian product labeling.

CEPHALOTHIN

Summary of Differences

Category: First-generation cephalosporin.
Precautions: Drug interactions and/or related problems—May be more likely to interact with nephrotoxic medications.
Laboratory value alterations—May falsely elevate serum and urine creatinine concentrations when Jaffe's reaction method is used.

Additional Dosing Information

Since pain, induration, tenderness, and elevated temperature may occur on intramuscular administration, cephalothin should be administered by deep intramuscular injection or by intravenous injection.

When intravenous doses greater than 6 grams daily are given for more than 3 days, thrombophlebitis may occur. To help minimize the incidence of thrombophlebitis, larger veins may be used.

Parenteral Dosage Forms

Note: Bracketed uses in the *Dosage Forms* section refer to categories of use and/or indications that are not included in U.S. product labeling.

The dosing and strengths of the dosage forms available are expressed in terms of cephalothin base (not the sodium salt).

CEPHALOTHIN FOR INJECTION USP

Usual adult and adolescent dose
[Furunculosis, with cellulitis] or
[Pneumonia, uncomplicated] or
[Urinary tract infections]—
Intramuscular or intravenous, 500 mg (base) every six hours.
[Perioperative prophylaxis]—
Intravenous, 2 grams (base) one-half to one hour prior to the start of surgery; 2 grams during surgery; and 2 grams every six hours following surgery for up to forty-eight hours.
[For all other infections]—
Intramuscular or intravenous, 500 mg to 2 grams (base) every four to six hours.

Note: After an initial loading dose of 1 to 2 grams (base), adults with renal function impairment may require a reduction in dose as follows:

Creatinine clearance (mL/min)/(mL/sec)	Dose (base)
> 80/1.33	See *Usual adult and adolescent dose*
50–80/0.83–1.33	Up to 2 grams every 6 hours
25–50/0.42–0.83	Up to 1.5 grams every 6 hours
10–25/0.17–0.42	Up to 1 gram every 6 hours
2–10/0.03–0.17	Up to 500 mg every 6 hours
<2/0.03	Up to 500 mg every 8 hours

Usual adult prescribing limits
12 grams (base) per day.

Usual pediatric dose
[For bacterial infections]—
Intramuscular or intravenous, 13.3 to 26.6 mg (base) per kg of body weight every four hours; or 20 to 40 mg per kg of body weight every six hours.

Usual geriatric dose
See *Usual adult and adolescent dose*.

Strength(s) usually available
U.S.—
Not commercially available.
Canada—
1 gram (base) (may be available in ADD-Vantage® vials) (Rx) [*Ceporacin; Keflin* (sodium 2.8 mEq per gram)].

Packaging and storage
Prior to reconstitution, store below 40 °C (104 °F), preferably between 15 and 30 °C (59 and 86 °F), unless otherwise specified by manufacturer.

Preparation of dosage form
To prepare initial dilution for intramuscular use, 4.5 mL of sterile water for injection should be added to each 1-gram vial.
To prepare initial dilution for intravenous use, 10 mL of sterile water for injection, 5% dextrose injection, or 0.9% sodium chloride injection should be added to each 1-gram vial. For direct or intermittent use, the resulting solution should be administered over a 3- to 5-minute period. For continuous infusion, the resulting solution should be further diluted in suitable fluids (see manufacturer's package insert).

Stability
After reconstitution, solutions retain their potency for 8 hours at room temperature or for 72 hours if refrigerated. Solutions reconstituted with bacteriostatic diluent and used for intramuscular administration retain their potency for up to 7 days when refrigerated.
Concentrated solutions will darken in color, especially at room temperature. However, slight discoloration does not affect potency.

Incompatibilities
The admixture of beta-lactam antibacterials (penicillins and cephalosporins) and aminoglycosides may result in substantial mutual inactivation. If they are administered concurrently, they should be administered in separate sites. Do not mix them in the same intravenous bag or bottle.

CEPHAPIRIN

Summary of Differences
Category: First-generation cephalosporin.

Additional Dosing Information
Cephapirin should be administered by deep intramuscular injection or by intravenous injection only.

Parenteral Dosage Forms
Note: The dosing and strengths of the dosage forms available are expressed in terms of cephapirin base (not the sodium salt).

CEPHAPIRIN FOR INJECTION USP

Usual adult and adolescent dose
Perioperative prophylaxis[1]—
Intramuscular or intravenous, 1 to 2 grams (base) one-half to one hour prior to the start of surgery; 1 to 2 grams during surgery; and 1 to 2 grams every six hours following surgery for up to twenty-four hours.
Skin and soft tissue infections[1] or
Urinary tract infections[1]—
Intramuscular or intravenous, 500 mg (base) every four to six hours.
For all other infections[1]—
Serious: Intramuscular or intravenous, 1 gram (base) every four to six hours.
Very serious or life-threatening: Intravenous, up to 12 grams (base) per day.

Note: Patients with impaired renal function (moderately severe oliguria or serum creatinine above 5 mg per 100 mL) may receive 7.5 to 15 mg (base) per kg of body weight every twelve hours.
Patients with severely reduced renal function and who are to be dialyzed should receive 7.5 to 15 mg (base) per kg of body weight just prior to dialysis and every twelve hours thereafter.

Usual adult prescribing limits
12 grams (base) per day.

Usual pediatric dose
For bacterial infections[1]—
Infants up to 3 months of age: Dosage has not been established.
Infants and children 3 months of age and older: Intramuscular or intravenous, 10 to 20 mg (base) per kg of body weight every six hours.

Usual geriatric dose
See *Usual adult and adolescent dose*.

Strength(s) usually available
U.S.—
500 mg (base) (Rx) [*Cefadyl* (sodium 2.36 mEq per gram)].
1 gram (base) (Rx) [*Cefadyl* (sodium 2.36 mEq per gram)].
2 grams (base) (Rx) [*Cefadyl* (sodium 2.36 mEq per gram)].
4 grams (base) (Rx) [*Cefadyl* (sodium 2.36 mEq per gram)].
20 grams (base) (Rx) [*Cefadyl* (sodium 2.36 mEq per gram)].
Canada—
Not commercially available.

Packaging and storage
Prior to reconstitution, store below 40 °C (104 °F), preferably between 15 and 30 °C (59 and 86 °F), unless otherwise specified by manufacturer.

Preparation of dosage form
To prepare initial dilution for intramuscular use, 1 mL of sterile water for injection or bacteriostatic water for injection should be added to each 500-mg vial, or 2 mL of diluent should be added to each 1-gram vial.
To prepare initial dilution for intravenous use, 10 mL or more of bacteriostatic water for injection, dextrose injection, or 0.9% sodium chloride injection should be added to each 500-mg, 1-gram, or 2-gram vial. For direct injection, the resulting solution should be administered slowly over a 3- to 5-minute period. For intermittent infusion, the resulting solution should be diluted with suitable fluids (see manufacturer's package insert).
For reconstitution of pharmacy bulk vials or piggyback infusion bottles, see manufacturer's labeling for instructions.

Stability
After reconstitution, solutions retain their potency for 12 to 48 hours at room temperature (25 °C [77 °F]), depending on the diluent, or for 10 days if refrigerated at 4 °C (39 °F). Color changes during the indicated storage times do not affect potency.
If frozen immediately after reconstitution with sterile water for injection, bacteriostatic water for injection containing either benzyl alcohol or parabens, 0.9% sodium chloride injection, or 5% dextrose injection, solutions retain their potency for up to 60 days at −15 °C (5 °F). After thawing at room temperature, solutions retain their potency for at least 12 hours at room temperature or for 10 days if refrigerated at 4 °C (39 °F).
At concentrations of 2 to 30 mg per mL in suitable fluids (see manufacturer's package insert), intravenous infusions retain their potency for 24 hours at room temperature. At a concentration of 4 mg per mL in suitable fluids (see manufacturer's package insert), intravenous infusions retain their potency for 10 days if refrigerated or for 14 days if frozen at −15 °C (5 °F). After thawing at room temperature, these infusions retain their potency for 24 hours at room temperature.

Incompatibilities
The admixture of beta-lactam antibacterials (penicillins and cephalosporins) and aminoglycosides may result in substantial mutual inactivation. If they are administered concurrently, they should be administered in separate sites. Do not mix them in the same intravenous bag or bottle.

---
[1]Not included in Canadian product labeling.

CEPHRADINE

Summary of Differences
Category: First-generation cephalosporin.

Additional Dosing Information
May be taken with or without food.

Oral Dosage Forms

CEPHRADINE CAPSULES USP

Usual adult and adolescent dose
Pneumonia, lobar[1] or
Prostatitis[1] or
Urinary tract infections, serious[1]—
Oral, 500 mg every six hours; or 1 gram every twelve hours.
Respiratory tract infections, other than lobar pneumonia[1] or
Skin and soft tissue infections[1]—
Oral, 250 mg every six hours; or 500 mg every twelve hours.
Urinary tract infections, uncomplicated[1]—
Oral, 500 mg every twelve hours.
For all other infections, severe or chronic[1]—
Oral, up to 1 gram every six hours.

Note: Adults with impaired renal function may require a reduction in dose as follows:

Creatinine clearance (mL/min)/(mL/sec)	Dose
> 20/0.33	500 mg every 6 hours
5–20/0.08–0.33	250 mg every 6 hours
< 5/0.08	250 mg every 12 hours
Chronic intermittent hemodialysis patients	250 mg at the start of hemodialysis; 250 mg after 12 hours; and 250 mg 36–48 hours after start

Usual adult prescribing limits
4 grams per day.

Usual pediatric dose
This dosage form usually is not used for children. See *Cephradine for Oral Suspension USP*.

Usual geriatric dose
See *Usual adult and adolescent dose*.

Strength(s) usually available
U.S.—
250 mg (Rx) [*Velosef* (lactose); GENERIC].
500 mg (Rx) [*Velosef* (lactose); GENERIC].

Canada—
Not commercially available.

Packaging and storage

Store below 30 °C (86 °F), preferably between 15 and 30 °C (59 and 86 °F), unless otherwise specified by manufacturer. Store in a tight container.

Auxiliary labeling

- Continue medicine for full time of treatment.

CEPHRADINE FOR ORAL SUSPENSION USP

Usual adult and adolescent dose

See *Cephradine Capsules USP*.

Usual adult prescribing limits

See *Cephradine Capsules USP*.

Usual pediatric dose

Otitis media, due to *Haemophilus influenzae*[1]—
Infants and children 9 months of age and older: Oral, 18.75 to 25 mg per kg of body weight every six hours; or 37.5 to 50 mg per kg of body weight every twelve hours.
Infants up to 9 months of age: Oral, 18.75 to 25 mg per kg of body weight every six hours.

For all other infections[1]—
Infants and children 9 months of age and older: Mild or moderate—Oral, 6.25 to 12.5 mg per kg of body weight every six hours; or 12.5 to 25 mg per kg of body weight every twelve hours. Severe or chronic—Oral, up to 1 gram every six hours.
Infants up to 9 months of age: Mild or moderate—Oral, 6.25 to 12.5 mg per kg of body weight every six hours. Severe—Oral, up to 1 gram every six hours.

Note: Pediatric patients with renal function impairment may require a reduction in dose proportional to their weight and severity of infection.

Usual pediatric prescribing limits

4 grams per day.

Usual geriatric dose

See *Cephradine Capsules USP*.

Strength(s) usually available

U.S.—
125 mg per 5 mL (when reconstituted according to manufacturer's instructions) (available in 100- and 200-mL bottles) (Rx) [*Velosef* (sucrose); GENERIC (may contain sucrose)].
250 mg per 5 mL (when reconstituted according to manufacturer's instructions) (available in 100- and 200-mL bottles) (Rx) [*Velosef* (sucrose); GENERIC (may contain sucrose)].

Canada—
Not commercially available.

Packaging and storage

Prior to reconstitution, store below 40 °C (104 °F), preferably between 15 and 30 °C (59 and 86 °F), unless otherwise specified by manufacturer. Store in a tight container.

Preparation of dosage form

See manufacturer's labeling instructions.

Stability

After reconstitution, suspensions retain their potency for 7 days at room temperature or for 14 days if refrigerated.

Auxiliary labeling

- Refrigerate.
- Shake well.
- Continue medicine for full time of treatment.
- Beyond-use date.

Note

When dispensing, include a calibrated liquid-measuring device.

[1]Not included in Canadian product labeling.

Revised: 11/17/2004

Table 1. Pharmacology/Pharmacokinetics

Drug	Bioavailability (%)	Half-life (hr) Normal renal function	Half-life (hr) Impaired renal function	Time to peak serum concentration (hr)	Peak serum concentration after dose mcg/mL	Peak serum concentration after dose Dose	Peak urine concentration after dose mcg/mL	Peak urine concentration after dose Dose
First generation								
Cefadroxil	95	1.5	20–25					
Oral				1.5–2	16	500 mg	1800	500 mg
					28	1 gram		
Cefazolin		1.4–2*	40–70					
IM					17	250 mg	2400	500 mg
					38	500 mg	4000	1 gram
					64	1 gram		
IV				End of infusion	188	1 gram		
Cephalexin	95	0.9–1.5	20–40					
Oral				1–2	9	250 mg	1000	250 mg
					18	500 mg	2200	500 mg
					32	1 gram	5000	1 gram
Cephalothin		0.5–1†	3–18					
IM				0.5	10	500 mg	800	500 mg
					20	1 gram	2500	1 gram
IV				0.25–0.5	30	1 gram		
					80–100	2 grams		
Cephapirin		0.5–0.8	1.5–2.7					
IM				0.5–1	9	500 mg	900	500 mg
					16	1 gram		
IV				End of infusion	35	500 mg		
					67	1 gram		
					129	2 grams		
Cephradine	95	1.3	6–15					
Oral				1‡	9	250 mg	1600	250 mg
					17	500 mg	3200	500 mg
					24	1 gram	4000	1 gram

Table 1. Pharmacology/Pharmacokinetics *(continued)*

Drug	Bioavailability (%)	Half-life (hr) Normal renal function	Half-life (hr) Impaired renal function	Time to peak serum concentration (hr)	Peak serum concentration after dose mcg/mL	Peak serum concentration after dose Dose	Peak urine concentration after dose mcg/mL	Peak urine concentration after dose Dose
Second generation								
Cefaclor	95	0.6–0.9	2.3–2.8					
Capsules, oral suspension				0.5–1‡	7	250 mg	600	250 mg
					13	500 mg	900	500 mg
					23	1 gram	1900	1 gram
Extended-release tablets				2.5–2.7	3.7§	375 mg		
					8.2§	500 mg		
Cefamandole		0.5–1.2	3–11					
IM				0.5–2	13	500 mg	254	500 mg
					25	1 gram	1357	1 gram
IV				End of infusion	139	1 gram	750	1 gram
					240	2 grams	1380	2 grams
					533	3 grams		
					666	4 grams		
Cefonicid		3.5–4.5	17–56					
IM				1	99	1 gram	385	500 mg
IV				End of infusion	220	1 gram		
Cefotetan		3–4.6	Prolonged					
IM				1–3	71	1 gram		
					91	2 grams		
IV				End of infusion	158	1 gram	1700	1 gram
					237	2 grams	3500	2 grams
Cefoxitin		0.7–1.1#	13–20					
IV				End of infusion	110	1 gram		
					244	2 grams		
Cefprozil	90–95	1.3**	5–6					
Oral				1.5–1.7	6.1	250 mg	700	250 mg
					10.5	500 mg	1000	500 mg
					18.3	1 gram	2900	1 gram
Ceftibuten		2–2.6††	7–22					
Oral				1.7–3††	10††	200 mg††		
					15	400 mg		
					23	800 mg		
Cefuroxime		1.2–1.9‡‡	3–17					
Oral suspension				2.7–3.6	3.3	10 mg/kg		
					5.1	15 mg/kg		
					7	20 mg/kg		
Tablet	After food§§ (52–68)			2.2–3	2	125 mg		
					4	250 mg		
	Fasting (37)				7	500 mg		
					13.6	1 gram		
IM				0.75	27	750 mg	1300	750 mg
IV				End of infusion	50	750 mg	1150	750 mg
					100	1.5 grams	2500	1.5 grams
Third generation								
Cefdinir		1.7	3–9					
Oral capsule	16–21			3	1.6	300 mg		
					2.9	600 mg		
Oral suspension	25			1.8–2.2	2.3	7 mg/kg		
					3.9	14 mg/kg		
Cefditoren		1.6						
Tablets				1.5 to 3 hours	1.8 mcg per mL	200 mg		
Cefixime	40–50	3–4	6.4–11.5					
Oral				2–6	1.3	100 mg	73	100 mg
					3.5–4.4	400 mg	164	400 mg
Cefoperazone		1.6–2.4##	2.1##					
IM				1–2	65–75	1 gram	1000	2 grams
					97	2 grams		
IV				End of infusion	153	1 gram	> 2200	2 grams
					252	2 grams		
					340	3 grams		
					506	4 grams		

Table 1. Pharmacology/Pharmacokinetics *(continued)*

Drug	Bioavailability (%)	Half-life (hr): Normal renal function	Half-life (hr): Impaired renal function	Time to peak serum concentration (hr)	Peak serum concentration after dose: mcg/mL	Peak serum concentration after dose: Dose	Peak urine concentration after dose: mcg/mL	Peak urine concentration after dose: Dose
Cefotaxime	90–95	1	2.6–3					
IM				0.5	12	500 mg		
					21	1 gram		
IV					39	500 mg		
					102	1 gram		
					214	2 grams		
Cefpodoxime	50§§	2.1–2.8	3.5–9.8					
Oral				2–3	1.4	100 mg		
					2.3	200 mg		
					3.9	400 mg		
Ceftazidime		1.4–2	13					
IM				1	17	500 mg	2100	500 mg
					39	1 gram		
IV				End of infusion	42	500 mg	12,100	2 grams
					69	1 gram		
					170	2 grams		
Ceftizoxime		1.4–1.7	30					
IM				1	14	500 mg		
					39	1 gram		
IV				End of infusion	60	1 gram	> 6000	1 gram
					132	2 grams		
					220	3 grams		
Ceftriaxone								
IM		5.8–8.7	12–24	2–3	38	500 mg	425	500 mg
					76	1 gram	628	1 gram
IV		4.3–4.6***		End of infusion	82	500 mg	526	500 mg
					151	1 gram	995	1 gram
					257	2 grams	2692	2 grams
Fourth generation								
Cefepime	100	2	14					
IM				1–2	14	500 mg		
					30	1 gram		
					57	2 grams		
IV				End of infusion	18	250 mg		
					39	500 mg		
					82	1 gram		
					164	2 grams		

*The half-life of cefazolin in neonates less than 1 week old is 4.5 to 5 hours.
†The half-life of cephalothin in neonates less than 1 week old is 1.5 to 2 hours.
‡Delayed in presence of food.
§ With food. Peak serum concentration is decreased when administered under fasting conditions.
#The half-life of cefoxitin is 5.6 hours in neonates 0 to 7 days of age; 2.5 hours in neonates 7 days to 1 month of age; and 1.7 hours in infants 1 to 3 months of age.
**In children, the half-life of cefprozil is 1.8 to 2.1 hours.
††In children, the half-life of ceftibuten is 1.4 to 2.6 hours; the time to peak serum concentration is 2 hours; and the peak serum concentration is 13 mcg/mL after a dose of 9 mg/kg. In geriatric patients, the peak serum concentration is 17 mcg/mL after a dose of 200 mg.
‡‡In neonates, the half-life of cefuroxime can be three to five times longer than it is in adults.
§§Bioavailability is increased when this medication is administered with food.
##In adults, not significantly different from normal values during hemodialysis; 2.8 to 4.2 hours between hemodialysis periods; 3 to 7 hours with impaired hepatic function and/or biliary obstruction. In pediatric patients, 6 to 10 hours in low-birth-weight neonates; 4 to 6 hours in infants approximately 1 month of age; 2.2 hours in infants and children 2 months to 11 years of age.
***The half-life of ceftriaxone in pediatric patients with meningitis after a 50- or 75-mg-per-kg dose.

Table 2. Pharmacology/Pharmacokinetics*

Drug	Protein binding (%)	Hepatic and renal biotransformation (%)	Renal excretion (% unchanged/hr)	Vol_D (L/kg)	Removal by dialysis: HD	Removal by dialysis: PD
First generation						
Cefadroxil	Low (15–20)	No	93/24 (GF; TS)	0.31	Yes	
Cefazolin	High (85)	No	60–89/6; 70-86/24 (GF; TS)	0.12	Moderate	No

Table 2. Pharmacology/Pharmacokinetics *(continued)**

Drug	Protein binding (%)	Hepatic and renal biotransformation (%)	Renal excretion (% unchanged/hr)	Vol_D (L/kg)	Removal by dialysis HD	PD
Cephalexin	Low (10–15)	No	80/6; 90/8 (TS; GF)	0.26	Moderate	Yes
Cephalothin	Moderate (70)	Yes; 20–30	60–70/6 (30 as metabolite/6) (TS)	0.26	Moderate	
Cephapirin	Moderate (44–50)	Yes; 40	70/6 (TS; GF; TR)	0.13	Slight	
Cephradine	Very low to low (8–17)	No	60–90/6 (TS)	0.25	Signif	Yes
Second generation						
Cefaclor	Low (25)	No	60–85/8	0.35	Moderate	Yes
Cefamandole	High (70–80)	No	65–85/8 (GF; TS)	0.16	Moderate	Slight
Cefonicid	Very high (> 90)	No	99/24	0.11	Slight	
Cefotetan	High to very high (78–91)	No	50–80/24	0.19	Slight	NS
Cefoxitin	High (70–80)	Slight; 0.2–5 (inactive metabolite)	85/6 (GF; TS)	0.16	Moderate	NS
Cefprozil	Moderate (36–45)	No	60–70/8	0.17–0.23	Moderate	
Ceftibuten	High (65–77)		95/24	0.21†	Yes	
Cefuroxime	Low to moderate (33–50)			0.82	Moderate	
Oral		No; prodrug rapidly hydrolyzed to cefuroxime	50/12 (GF; TS)§			
IM, IV			90/6; 96/24			
Third generation						
Cefdinir	High (60–70)	No	12–18/ 1.7	0.35‡		
Cefditoren	High (88)	Pivoxil salt hydrolyzed to active cefditoren		9.3 L	30%	
Cefixime	High (65)	No	16/24	0.11	NS	No
Cefoperazone	High to very high (82–93)	No	20–30/12§ (GF)	0.14–2	Slight	
Cefotaxime	Low to moderate (30–50)	Yes; 30–50 (active and inactive metabolites)	50–60/6 (15–25 as active metabolite) (GF)	0.25–0.39	Moderate	NS
Cefpodoxime	Low to moderate (21–40)	No; prodrug de-esterified to cefpodoxime	29–33/12 40/24	0.7–1.15	Moderate	
Ceftazidime	Very low to low (5–17)	No	80–90/24 (GF)	0.21–0.28	Yes	Yes
Ceftizoxime	Low (30)	No	70–100/24	0.35–0.4	Moderate	
Ceftriaxone	High to very high (83–96)		33–67/24	0.12–0.14#	No	No
Fourth generation						
Cefepime	Low (20)	Yes; 15	80–85/12 (G/F)	0.25**	Yes	Slight

*Abbreviations: GF = glomerular filtration; HD = hemodialysis; PD = peritoneal dialysis; TR = tubular reabsorption; TS = tubular secretion; NS = not significant; Signif = significant.

†In pediatric patients 6 months to 12 years of age, the Vol_D = 0.5 L/kg.

‡In pediatric patients 6 months to 12 years, the Vol_D=0.67 L/kg.

§75% excreted unchanged in bile; 15 to 30% (range: 10 to 36%) excreted unchanged in urine within 6 to 12 hours, primarily by glomerular filtration; up to 90% or more excreted in urine in patients with severe hepatic function impairment or biliary obstruction.

#In pediatric patients, the Vol_D = 0.3 L/kg.

**In pediatric patients 2 months to 16 years of age, the Vol_D = 0.33 L/kg.

CEPHALOTHIN—See *Cephalosporins (Systemic)*

CEPHAPIRIN—See *Cephalosporins (Systemic)*

CEPHRADINE—See *Cephalosporins (Systemic)*

CERIVASTATIN—See *HMG-CoA Reductase Inhibitors (Systemic)*

CETIRIZINE—See *Antihistamines (Systemic)*

CETIRIZINE AND PSEUDOEPHEDRINE Systemic

VA CLASSIFICATION (Primary): RE501

Commonly used brand name(s): *Zyrtec-D 12 Hour*.

NOTE: The *Citirizine and Pseudoephedrine (Systemic)* monograph is maintained on the *USP DI* electronic database. A copy of the most recent revision of the complete monograph can be accessed on the *USP DI* Updates Online website. See the front cover of book for details on accessing the site. The information that follows is selectively abstracted from the complete monograph and is provided to facilitate drug use review and patient counseling.

Note: For a listing of dosage forms and brand names by country availability, see *Dosage Forms* section(s).

Category

Antihistaminic, H_1-receptor-decongestant.

Indications

Accepted

Rhinitis, seasonal allergic (treatment) or

Rhinitis, perennial allergic (treatment)—Cetirizine and pseudoephedrine combination is indicated for symptomatic relief of seasonal or perennial allergic rhinitis in adults and children 12 years of age and older when both the antihistaminic and decongestant effects are desired.

Patient Consultation

As an aid to patient consultation, refer to *Advice for the Patient, Cetirizine and Pseudoephedrine (Systemic)*

In providing consultation, consider emphasizing the following selected information (» = major clinical significance):

Before using this medication

» Conditions affecting use, especially:

Hypersensitivity to cetirizine, hydroxyzine, pseudoephedrine or other sympathomimetic amines

Pregnancy—Studies in animals have shown that cetirizine and pseudoephedrine causes skeletal malformities and variants.

Breast-feeding—Cetirizine and pseudoephedrine are distributed into breast milk. Its use in nursing mothers is not recommended.

Use in children—Safety and efficacy have not been established in children up to 12 years of age.

Other medications, especially alcohol or CNS depression-producing medications, digitalis glycosides, and monoamine oxidase inhibitors

Other medical problems, especially narrow-angle glaucoma, urinary retention, hepatic impairment, renal impairment, severe coronary artery disease, severe hypertension, or increased intraocular pressure

Proper use of this medication

Proper administration technique for extended-release tablets

Swallowing tablet whole; not breaking, crushing, or chewing before swallowing

» Proper dosing

Missed dose: Taking as soon as possible; not taking if almost time for next scheduled dose; not doubling doses

Proper storage

Precautions while using this medication

» Avoiding use of alcohol or other CNS depressants including tricyclic antidepressants.

» Caution if dizziness or drowsiness occurs; not driving, using machines, or doing anything else that requires alertness while taking cetirizine and pseudoephedrine combination and for 24 hours after discontinuing it

Possible dryness of mouth; using sugarless candy or gum, ice or saliva substitute for relief; checking with physician or dentist if dry mouth continues for more than 2 weeks

» Taking last dose of medicine for each day a few hours before bedtime to avoid insomnia

Side/adverse effects

Signs of potential side effects, especially anaphylaxis, cholestasis, glomerulonephritis, hemolytic anemia, hepatitis, severe hypotension, orofacial dyskinesia, stillbirth, or thrombocytopenia

Oral Dosage Forms

CETIRIZINE HYDROCHLORIDE AND PSEUDOEPHEDRINE HYDROCHLORIDE EXTENDED-RELEASE TABLETS

Usual adult and adolescent dose

Seasonal or perennial allergic rhinitis (treatment)—

Oral, one tablet (5 mg cetirizine and 120 mg pseudoephedrine) two times a day.

Note: In renally impaired patients (creatinine clearance 11 to 31 mL per min), patients on hemodialysis (creatine clearance less than 7 mL per min) and in hepatically impaired patients, a dose of one tablet once a day is recommended.

Usual pediatric dose

Seasonal or perennial allergic rhinitis (treatment)—

Children younger than 12 years of age: Use is not recommended; the dosage limits of pseudoephedrine are exceeded in the extended-release formulation.

Children 12 years of age and over: See *Usual adult and adolescent dose*.

Usual geriatric dose

See *Usual adult and adolescent dose*.

Note: In general, dosing in the elderly patient should be cautious, reflecting the greater frequency of decreased hepatic, renal or cardiac function. The elderly are more likely to have adverse reactions to sympathomimetic amines.

Strength(s) usually available

U.S.—

5 mg of cetirizine hydrochloride and 120 mg of pseudoephedrine hydrochloride (Rx) [*Zyrtec-D 12 Hour* (The bilayer tablet enables the cetirizine component to be immediately released and the pseudoephedrine component to be extended released; colloidal silicon dioxide; croscarmellose sodium; hydroxypropyl methylcellulose; lactose monohydrate; magnesium stearate; microcrystalline cellulose)].

Auxiliary labeling

- May cause drowsiness. Be careful while driving or operating machinery.
- Avoid alcoholic beverages.
- Swallow tablet whole. Do not crush, break, or chew.

Revised: 01/24/2002
Developed: 10/23/2001

CETUXIMAB Systemic†

VA CLASSIFICATION (Primary): AN900

Commonly used brand name(s): *Erbitux*.

Note: For a listing of dosage forms and brand names by country availability, see *Dosage Forms* section(s).

†Not commercially available in Canada.

Category

Antineoplastic; Monoclonal antibody.

Indications

Accepted

Carcinoma, colorectal (treatment)—Cetuximab, used in combination with irinotecan, is indicated for the treatment of EGFR-expressing, metastatic colorectal carcinoma in patients who are refractory to irinotecan-based chemotherapy. Cetuximab, used as a monotherapy, is also indicated for the treatment of EGFR-expressing, metastatic colorectal carcinoma in patients who are intolerant to irinotecan-based chemotherapy.

Carcinoma, head and neck (treatment)—Cetuximab, in combination with radiation therapy, is indicated for the treatment of locally or regionally advanced squamous cell carcinoma of the head and neck.

Carcinoma, head and neck, recurrent or metastatic (treatment)—Cetuximab as a single agent is indicated for the treatment of patients with recurrent or metastatic squamous cell carcinoma of the head and neck for whom prior platinum-based therapy has failed.

Pharmacology/Pharmacokinetics

Physicochemical characteristics

Source—Recombinant, human/mouse chimeric monoclonal antibody produced in mammalian (murine myeloma) cell culture.

Molecular weight—Cetuximab: approximately 152 kilodaltons.

pH—7.0 to 7.4

Mechanism of action/Effect

Over expression of the epidermal growth factor receptor (EGFR) has been detected in many human cancers including those of the colon and rectum. Cetuximab specifically binds to EGFR blocking phosphorylation and activation of receptor-associated kinases, resulting in inhibition of cell growth, induction of apoptosis, and decreased matrix metalloproteinase and vascular endothelial growth factor production. Cetuximab inhibits growth and survival of tumor cells that over-express the EGFR.

Absorption

The area under the concentration time curve (AUC) increased in a greater than dose proportional manner as the dose increased from 20 to 400 mg/m^2.

Distribution

Volume of distribution (Vol_D)—2 to 3 L/m^2

Half-life

Elimination—After the third dose; 114 hours (range 75–188)

Peak serum concentration

Following 400 mg/m^2 IV dose: 184 μg/mL (range: 92–327 μg/mL)

Following 250 mg/m^2 IV dose: 140 μg/mL (range: 120–170 μg/mL)

Following 400 mg/m^2 initial dose/250 mg/m^2 weekly dose: 168 to 235 μg/mL.

Precautions to Consider

Carcinogenicity/Mutagenicity

Long term carcinogenicity studies in animals have not been done. No mutagenic or clastogenic potential was observed in the Salmonella-Escherichia coli (Ames) assay or in the *in-vivo* rat micronucleus test.

Pregnancy/Reproduction

Fertility—In a 39 week toxicity study in cynomolgus monkeys given doses of 0.4 to 4 times the human dose (based on total body surface area) results showed a tendency for impairment of menstrual cycling in female monkeys. The findings included higher incidences of irregularity or absence of cycles in comparison to control animals. There were no marked differences in serum testosterone levels, sperm counts, viability and motility of sperm in male monkeys treated with cetuximab compared to control monkeys. It is not known if cetuximab can impair fertility in humans.

Pregnancy—Adequate and well controlled studies in humans have not been done. However, human IgG1 is known to cross the placental barrier; therefore cetuximab has the potential to be transmitted from the mother to the fetus. EGFR has been implicated in the control of prenatal development and may be essential for the normal organogenesis, proliferation, and differentiation in the developing embryo. It is not known whether cetuximab can cause fetal harm when administered to a pregnant woman.

FDA Pregnancy Category C

Breast-feeding

It is not known whether cetuximab is distributed into human breast milk. However, human IgG1 is distributed into human milk, although the potential for absorption and consequent harm to the infant is unknown. It is recommended that women treated with cetuximab not breast-feed for 60 days following the last dose of cetuximab

Pediatrics

Safety and efficacy in pediatric patients have not been established.

Geriatrics

Appropriate studies performed to date have not demonstrated age-specific problems that would limit the usefulness of cetuximab in the elderly.

Pharmacogenetics

In a population pharmacokinetic analysis female patients were found to have had a 25% lower intrinsic clearance of cetuximab than male patients.

Laboratory value alterations

The following have been selected on the basis of their potential clinical significance (possible effect in parentheses where appropriate)—not necessarily inclusive (» = major clinical significance).

» EGFR expression
(assessment should be performed by laboratories with demonstrated proficiency in the specific technology utilized; improper assay performance, deviation from specific assay instructions, or failure to include appropriate controls for assay verification can lead to unreliable results)

» Calcium, serum or
» Magnesium, serum or
» Potassium, serum
(values may be decreased; approximately 50% of patients receiving cetuximab experienced hypomagnesemia; onset of electrolyte abnormalities may occur from days to months after initiation of cetuximab; electrolyte repletion may be necessary in some cases)

Medical considerations/Contraindications

The medical considerations/contraindications included have been selected on the basis of their potential clinical significance (reasons given in parentheses where appropriate)—not necessarily inclusive (» = major clinical significance).

Risk-benefit should be considered when the following medical problems exist:

» Hypersensitivity to cetuximab, murine proteins, or any component of the product
(caution should be used when administering cetuximab)

» Fibrotic lung disease, pre-existing, or
(administration of cetuximab may exacerbate this disease)

» Radiation therapy
(incidence and severity of cutaneous reactions with combined modality therapy may be additive)

Patient monitoring

The following may be especially important in patient monitoring (other tests may be warranted in some patients, depending on condition; » = major clinical significance):

» Electrolytes
(magnesium, calcium and potassium should be monitored periodically during cetuximab administration and for about 8 weeks after completion of cetuximab therapy)

Inflammation, development of or
Infection, development of
(patients developing dermatologic toxicities should be monitored for the development of inflammatory or infectious sequelae; may require a dose modification, in the case of severe acneform rash, or treatment with topical and/or oral antibiotics; topical corticosteroids are not recommended)

» Infusion reaction
(following the cetuximab infusion, a 1-hour observation period is recommended; in patients who experience infusion reactions, a longer observation period may be required)

Pulmonary symptoms, acute onset or worsening
(cetuximab should be interrupted for a prompt investigation, if interstitial lung disease is confirmed cetuximab should be discontinued and the patient treated appropriately)

Side/Adverse Effects

The following side/adverse effects have been selected on the basis of their potential clinical significance (possible signs and symptoms in parentheses where appropriate)—not necessarily inclusive:

Immunogenicity—development of non-neutralizing antibodies occurred in approximately 5% of the patients during clinical studies. These antibodies did not impact the safety or antitumor activity of cetuximab.

Infusion Reactions—severe infusion reactions occurred with the administration of cetuximab in approximately 3% of patients, rarely with fatal outcome (<1 in 1000). Approximately 90% of severe infusion reactions were associated with the first infusion. Severe infusion reactions are characterized by rapid onset of airway obstruction (bronchospasm, stridor, hoarseness), urticaria, and hypotension and require immediate interruption of the cetuximab infusion and permanent discontinuation from further treatment.

Those indicating need for medical attention

Incidence more frequent

Acneform rash (blemishes on the skin, pimples); ***anemia*** (pale skin; troubled breathing with exertion; unusual bleeding or bruising; unusual tiredness or weakness); ***dyspnea*** (shortness of breath; difficult or labored breathing; tightness in chest; wheezing); ***fever; infection*** (fever or chills; cough or hoarseness; lower back or side pain; painful or difficult urination); ***infusion reaction*** (dizziness; fever or chills; facial swelling; headache; nausea or vomiting; shortness of breath; skin rash, weakness); ***peripheral edema*** (bloating or swelling of face, arms, hands, lower legs, or feet; rapid weight gain; tingling of hands or feet, unusual weight gain or loss); ***skin drying and fissuring, severe*** (severe dry skin; deep cracks, grooves or lines in skin)

Incidence less frequent

Dehydration (confusion; decreased urination; dizziness; dry mouth; fainting; increase in heart rate; lightheadedness; rapid breathing; sunken eyes; thirst; unusual tiredness or weakness; wrinkled skin); ***kidney failure; leukopenia*** (black, tarry stools; chest pain; chills; cough; fever; painful or difficult urination; shortness of breath; sore throat; sores, ulcers, or white spots on lips or in mouth; swollen glands; unusual bleeding or bruising; unusual tiredness or weakness); ***pulmonary embolism*** (anxiety; chest pain; cough; fainting; fast heartbeat; sudden shortness of breath or troubled breathing; dizziness or lightheadedness); ***sepsis*** (chills; confusion; dizziness; lightheadedness; fainting fast heartbeat; fever; rapid, shallow breathing)

Incidence rare

Interstitial lung disease (cough; difficult breathing; fever; shortness of breath)

Those indicating need for medical attention only if they continue or are bothersome

Incidence more frequent

Abdominal pain (stomach pain); ***alopecia*** (hair loss, thinning of hair); ***anorexia*** (loss of appetite, weight loss); ***asthenia*** (lack or loss of strength); ***back pain; conjunctivitis*** (redness, pain, swelling of eye, eyelid, or inner lining of eyelid burning; dry or itching eyes; discharge; excessive tearing); ***cough increased; constipation*** (difficulty having a bowel movement (stool)); ***depression*** (discouragement; feeling sad or empty; irritability; lack of appetite; loss of interest or pleasure; tiredness; trouble concentrating; trouble sleeping); ***diarrhea; dyspepsia*** (acid or sour stomach; belching; heartburn; indigestion; stomach discomfort upset or pain); ***headache; insomnia*** (sleeplessness; trouble sleeping; unable to sleep); ***nail disorder*** (discoloration and swelling of fingernails or toenails); ***nausea; pain; pruritus*** (itching skin); ***stomatitis*** (swelling or inflammation of the mouth); ***vomiting; weight loss***

Overdose

For more information on the management of overdose or unintentional ingestion, **contact a poison control center** (see *Poison Control Center Listing*).

Treatment of overdose

Supportive care—

There is no known specific antidote to cetuximab. Treatment is generally symptomatic and supportive.

Patients in whom intentional overdose is confirmed or suspected should be referred for psychiatric consultation.

Patient Consultation

As an aid to patient consultation, refer to *Advice for the Patient, Cetuximab (Systemic)*.

In providing consultation, consider emphasizing the following selected information (» = major clinical significance):

Before using this medication

» Conditions affecting use, especially:

Hypersensitivity to cetuximab, murine proteins or any of its ingredients

Pregnancy—Human IgG_1 crossed the placenta; therefore, cetuximab has the potential to be transmitted from the mother to the developing fetus.Risk-benefit should be considered during pregnancy

Breast-feeding—Not recommended for 60 days following the last dose of cetuximab because of the risk of absorption and consequent harm to the infant

Pharmacogenetics—Female patients were found to have had a 25% lower intrinsic clearance of cetuximab than male patients.

Other medical problems, especially fibrotic lung disease, pre-existing or radiation therapy

Proper use of this medication

» Proper injection technique

» Proper dosing

Missed dose: Discuss with physician

» Proper storage

Precautions while using this medication

» Importance of observation period after each cetuximab treatment.

» Importance of keeping all appointments with your doctor to monitor the effectiveness and the side effects of this medicine.

» Importance of use of sunscreen, and hat and limiting sun exposure while receiving cetuximab.

Side/adverse effects

Signs of potential side effects, especially acneform rash, anemia, dehydration, dyspnea, fever, infection, infusion reaction, kidney failure, interstitial lung disease, leukopenia, peripheral edema, pulmonary embolism, sepsis or severe skin drying and fissuring

General Dosing Information

Cetuximab is recommended for administration by intravenous infusion only with a maximum infusion rate of 5 mL per minute. Rapid intravenous (push or bolus) administration is not recommended.

It is recommended that patients wear sunscreen and hats and limit sun exposure while receiving cetuximab as sunlight can exacerbate any skin reactions that may occur.

Treatment of adverse effects

It is recommended that medications for hypersensitivity reactions (e.g., epinephrine, intravenous antihistamines, bronchodilators, corticosteroids) and oxygen be readily available for each administration of cetuximab.

Premedication with an H_1 antagonist (e.g., 50 mg of intravenous diphenhydramine) may attenuate the hypersensitivity reaction and should be considered before each dose of cetuximab.

If the patient experiences a mild or moderate infusion reaction, the infusion rate should be permanently reduced by 50%.

If the patient experiences a severe infusion reaction, cetuximab should be immediately and permanently discontinued and patients should then receive appropriate medical care until the complete resolution of all signs and symptoms.

A 1–hour observation period of the patient is recommended following the cetuximab infusion.

Parenteral Dosage Forms

CETUXIMAB FOR INJECTION

Usual adult dose

Carcinoma, colorectal—

Single therapy or concomitant therapy with irinotecan—

Intravenous infusion, 400 mg/m² as an initial loading dose administered as a 120–minute IV infusion, then a weekly maintenance dose of 250 mg/m² infused over 60 minutes.

Carcinoma, head and neck (treatment)—

Intravenous infusion (maximum infusion rate of 5 mL per minute), 400 mg/m² as an initial loading dose administered as a 120–minute IV infusion one week prior to initiation of a course of radiation therapy, then a weekly maintenance dose of 250 mg/m² infused over 60 minutes for the duration of radiation therapy (6 to 7 weeks).

Carcinoma, head and neck, recurrent or metastatic (treatment)—

Intravenous infusion (maximum infusion rate of 5 mL per minute), 400 mg/m² as an initial loading dose followed by a weekly maintenance dose of 250 mg/m² until disease progression or unacceptable toxicity.

Carcinoma, colorectal or

Carcinoma, head and neck—

Patients with dermatologic toxicity occurrences (severe acneform rash NCI CTC Grades 3 or 4)—

- First occurrence: Delay infusion 1 to 2 weeks, if improvement continue at 250 mg/m²; if no improvement discontinue therapy.
- Second occurrence: Delay infusion 1 to 2 weeks, if improvement continue at 200 mg/m²; if no improvement discontinue therapy.
- Third occurrence: Delay infusion 1 to 2 weeks, if improvement continue at 150 mg/m²; if no improvement discontinue therapy.
- Fourth occurrence: Discontinue therapy

Note: Cetuximab is not recommended in severe radiation dermatitis.

Usual pediatric dose
Safety and efficacy have not been established.

Usual geriatric dose
See *Usual adult dose.*

Strength(s) usually available
U.S.—

100 mg of cetuximab per 50-mL vial of sterile, preservative-free injectable liquid (Rx) [*Erbitux* (sodium chloride; sodium phosphate dibasic heptahydrate; sodium phosphate monobasic monohydrate; water for injection)].

Packaging and storage
Store between 2 and 8 °C (36 and 46 °F). DO NOT FREEZE.

Preparation of dosage form
Do not shake or dilute contents of manufacturer supplied vial.

Infusion pump—

Each single use vial of cetuximab contains 50 mL of 2 mg/mL solution. The cetuximab solution should be clear and colorless and may contain a small amount of visible white particulate. Draw up the volume from the vial using a sterile syringe attached to an appropriate needle (a vented spike or other appropriate transfer device may be used) and fill into a sterile evacuated container or bag such as glass containers, polyolefin bags, DEHP plasticized PVC bags, or PVC bags. Repeat until the calculated volume has been put into the container. Use a new needle for each vial. Cetuximab must be administered through a low protein binding 0.22 micrometer in-line filter. Affix the infusion line and prime it with cetuximab before starting the infusion. The maximum infusion rate should not exceed 5 mL/min. To flush the line at the end of infusion use 0.9% saline solution. Discard any unused portions of the cetuximab vials. See the manufacturer's package insert for instructions.

Syringe pump—

Each single use vial of cetuximab contains 50 mL of 2 mg/mL solution. The cetuximab solution should be clear and colorless and may contain a small amount of visible white particulate. Draw up the volume from the vial using a sterile syringe attached to an appropriate needle and place the syringe into the syringe driver of a syringe pump and set the rate. Administered through a low protein binding 0.22 micrometer in-line filter rated for syringe pump use. Affix the infusion line and prime it with cetuximab before starting the infusion. Repeat until the calculated volume has been infused. Use a new needle and filter for each vial. The maximum infusion rate should not exceed 5 mL/min. To flush the line at the end of infusion use 0.9% saline solution. Discard any unused portions of the cetuximab vials. See the manufacturer's package insert for instructions.

Cetuximab should be piggybacked to the patient's infusion line.

Stability
Preparations of cetuximab in infusion containers are stable for up to 12 hours at 2 to 8 °C (36 to 46°F) and up to 8 hours at controlled room temperature (20 to 25 °C; 68 to 77 °F).

Revised: 05/10/2006
Developed: 04/05/2004

CEVIMELINE Systemic†

USA: Cevimeline hydrochloride
INN: Cevimeline
VA CLASSIFICATION (Primary): AU300
Commonly used brand name(s): *Evoxac.*

Note: For a listing of dosage forms and brand names by country availability, see *Dosage Forms* section(s).

†Not commercially available in Canada.

Category
Cholinergic enhancer.

Indications

General Considerations
Cevimeline is a cholinergic agonist with an affinity for muscarinic receptors. Muscarinic receptor activation has been shown to increase secretory activity of exocrine glands such as the salivary and sweat glands and increase tone of the smooth muscle in the gastrointestinal and urinary tracts.

Accepted
Xerostomia in Sjögren's syndrome (treatment)—Cevimeline is indicated for the treatment of symptoms of dry mouth commonly associated with Sjögren's syndrome.

Acceptance not established
The safety and efficacy of cevimeline for the treatment of dementia of *Alzheimer's disease* has not been established.

Pharmacology/Pharmacokinetics

Physicochemical characteristics
Molecular weight—244.79.

Solubility—Freely soluble in alcohol and chloroform; very soluble in water, and virtually insoluble in ether.

pH—Of a 1% solution, 4.6 to 5.6.

Mechanism of action/Effect
Cholinergic agonist, systemic—Cholinergic agonists such as cevimeline act directly on muscarinic receptors of effector cells to mimic the effects of acetylcholine. Stimulation of muscarinic receptors can increase secretion of exocrine glands such as salivary glands.

Other actions/effects
An increase in the smooth muscle tone of the gastrointestinal and urinary tracts is also observed after cholinergic agonist stimulation.

Absorption
Rapidly absorbed, fasting. Both the rate and extent of absorption are decreased when administered concomitantly with food.

Distribution
Volume of distribution (Vol_D)—6 liters/kilogram.

Protein binding
Low (less than 20%), to human plasma proteins.

Biotransformation
Hepatic, by isozymes CYP2D6 and CYP3A3/4. Approximately 44.5% of the dose is converted to the cis and trans-sulfoxides, while 22.3% is converted into the glucuronic acid conjugate and 4% as the N-oxide of cevimeline. Approximately 8% of the trans-sulfoxide is further metabolized into its corresponding glucuronic acid conjugate.

Half-life
Elimination—approximately 5 hours.

Time to peak concentration
Oral—1.53 hours, fasting state; 2.86 hours when administered after a meal

Elimination
Urine—97%
Feces—0.5%

Precautions to Consider

Carcinogenicity/Tumorigenicity
Lifetime carcinogenicity studies in CD-1 mice and F-344 rats revealed a significant increase in the incidence of uterine adenocarcinomas in female rats receiving cevimeline100 mg/kg/day.

Mutagenicity
Cevimeline was neither mutagenic nor clastogenic when studied in a series of assays that included an Ames test, a mammalian cell *in vitro* chromosomal aberration study, a mouse lymphoma study in L5178Y cells, and an ICR mouse *in vivo* micronucleus assay.

Pregnancy/Reproduction
Fertility—Reproductive performance and fertility were not affected in male Sprague-Dawley rats by the administration of cevimeline at doses of up to 45 mg per kg of body weight (mg/kg) a day (approximately 5 times the maximum recommended human dose for a 60 kg human). Female Sprague-Dawley rats exhibited a significantly smaller number of implantations after receiving cevimeline at doses of up to 45 mg/kg/day, prior to and during mating and through the seventh day of gestation.

Pregnancy—Adequate and well-controlled studies in pregnant women have not been done.

FDA Pregnancy Category C.

Breast-feeding
It is not known whether cevimeline is distributed into human breast milk. However, the potential for serious adverse reactions in nursing infants requires that a decision be made whether to discontinue the medication or discontinue nursing, based upon the anticipated clinical benefit to the mother.

Pediatrics
Appropriate studies on the relationship of age to the effects of cevimeline have not been performed in the pediatric population. Safety and effectiveness have not been established.

Geriatrics
No information is available on the relationship of age to the effects of cevimeline in geriatric patients. However, elderly patients are more likely to have age-related impairments in renal, hepatic, and cardiac functions, which may require additional caution in patients receiving cevimeline

Drug interactions and/or related problems
The following drug interactions and/or related problems have been selected on the basis of their potential clinical significance (possible mechanism in parentheses where appropriate)—not necessarily inclusive (» = major clinical significance):

Note: Combinations containing any of the following medications, depending on the amount present, may also interact with this medication.

» Anticholinergics
(cevimeline may interfere with the desired effects of concomitantly administered anticholinergic medications)

» Beta-adrenergic blocking agents, systemic
(cardiac conduction disturbances may occur after coadministration of cevimeline with beta-adrenergic blocking agents)

» Cholinergic agonists
(medications with parasympathetic effects can exert an additive effect when coadministered with cevimeline)

CYP2D6 and CYP3A3/4 inhibitors
(cevimeline metabolism is inhibited by medications known to be CYP2D6 and CYP3A3/4 isoenzyme inhibitors, and may lead to elevated plasma concentrations of cevimeline)

Medical considerations/Contraindications
The medical considerations/contraindications included have been selected on the basis of their potential clinical significance (reasons given in parentheses where appropriate)—not necessarily inclusive (» = major clinical significance).

Except under special circumstances, this medication should not be used when the following medical problem exists:

» Asthma, uncontrolled

» Known hypersensitivity to cevimeline

» Ophthalmic conditions in which miosis is undesirable
(e.g., in narrow-angle [angle-closure] glaucoma, and in acute iritis. Decreased visual acuity caused by blurring of vision and impairment of depth perception has occurred, especially in low light conditions, following the use of muscarinic ophthalmic formulations)

Risk-benefit should be considered when the following medical problems exist:

» Cardiovascular disease
(cevimeline is potentially capable of altering cardiac conduction as well as heart rate. Patients with significant cardiovascular disease may be unable to tolerate cevimeline-induced changes in hemodynamics and cardiac rhythm)

Cholelithiasis
(an increase in gallbladder or biliary smooth muscle contractility may precipitate biliary obstruction, cholecystitis, or cholangitis)

Nephrolithiasis
(an increase in ureteral smooth muscle tone may precipitate renal colic or ureteral reflux)

» Pulmonary disease
(cevimeline is potentially capable of increasing bronchiole smooth muscle contraction, airway resistance, and airway secretion production)

Side/Adverse Effects
The following side/adverse effects have been selected on the basis of their potential clinical significance (possible signs and symptoms in parentheses where appropriate)—not necessarily inclusive:

Those indicating need for medical attention
Incidence less frequent

Abscess; allergic reaction (itching; difficulty breathing; fast heartbeat); ***cystitis*** (bloody or cloudy urine; burning or painful urination); ***eye infection*** (eye pain or; redness or; blurred vision); ***erythematous rash ; fungal infection*** (itching in genital or other skin areas; scaling of skin); ***hypertonia*** (stiffness of muscles; tense muscles); ***increased serum amylase ; moniliasis*** (skin rash; cracks in skin; soreness or redness of skin); ***otitis media*** (earache; ringing or buzzing in ears); ***peripheral edema*** (swelling of hands, ankles, feet, or lower legs); ***pneumonia*** (chest pain; cough; shortness of breath); ***salivary gland enlargement*** (swelling on side of face and jaw); ***sialoadenenitis*** (swollen, tender, or painful swelling on side of face and jaw); ***ulcerative stomatatis*** (sores, ulcers, or white spots on tongue, lips, or inside of mouth); ***urinary tract infection*** (lower back pain; bloody or cloudy urine; difficult, burning, or painful urination); ***vaginitis*** (itching of vagina or genital area); ***vertigo*** (feeling of constant movement of self or surroundings; dizziness or light-headedness); ***xerophthalmia*** (dry or itching eyes; redness or pain in eye)

Incidence rare

Aggravated allergy; chest pain, precordial or substernal; choking; mouth edema (swelling of the gums and tongue); ***syncope*** (fainting or light-headedness when getting up from a lying or a sitting position)

Those indicating need for medical attention only if they continue or are bothersome
Incidence more frequent

Excessive sweating; nausea ; rhinitis (runny or stuffy nose)

Incidence less frequent

Abdominal pain; abnormal vision (change in vision); ***allergy; anemia*** (unusual bleeding or bruising; unusual tiredness or weakness); ***anorexia*** (loss of appetite; weight loss); ***arthralgia*** (pain, swelling, or redness of joints; muscle pain or stiffness); ***bronchitis*** (cough, mucus-producing; shortness of breath; tightness in chest); ***conjunctivitis*** (burning, dry or itching feeling in eye; redness, pain, and swelling of eye, eyelid, or inner lining of eye); ***constipation; depression*** (mood or mental changes); ***dry mouth; earache; edema*** (rapid weight gain; bloating or swelling of face, hands, feet, or lower legs); ***epistaxis*** (bloody nose); ***eructation*** (belching); ***eye abnormality or pain; excessive salivation; fatigue; fever; gastroesophageal reflux*** (heartburn; vomiting); ***hiccups; hot flushes*** (feelings of warmth in face, neck, arms, and occasionally, chest); ***hypoesthesia*** (decreased touch sensation); ***insomnia*** (sleeplessness; trouble in sleeping); ***injury; influenza-like symptoms*** (chills; cough; diarrhea; fever); ***leg cramps; migraine headache; myalgia*** (muscle aches or pains); ***pain; palpitations*** (fast, irregular, pounding, or racing heartbeat or pulse); ***pruritus*** (itching skin); ***postoperative pain; salivary gland pain*** (pain on side of face and jaw); ***skeletal pain*** (bone or joint pain); ***skin disorder; tooth disorder; tooth pain; tremor*** (trembling or shaking of hands or feet); ***vomiting***

Incidence rare

Abnormal crying; facial edema (swelling or puffiness of face); ***hematoma*** (deep, dark, purple bruise); ***malaise*** (unusual tiredness or weakness); ***temperature sensation changes; weight decrease or increase***

Overdose
For specific information on the agents used in the management of cevimeline toxicity or overdose, see

- *Atropine* in *Anticholinergics/Antispasmodics (Systemic)* monograph; and/or
- *Epinephrine* in *Sympathomimetic Agents—Cardiovascular Use (Parenteral-Systemic)*

For more information on the management of overdose or unintentional ingestion, **contact a poison control center** (see *Poison Control Center Listing*).

Clinical effects of overdose
The following effects have been selected on the basis of their potential clinical significance (possible signs and symptoms in parentheses where appropriate)—not necessarily inclusive:

Acute and Chronic

Atrioventricular block (chest pain; dizziness; fainting; slow heartbeat); ***bradycardia*** (slow or irregular heartbeat; light-headedness); ***cardiac arrhythmia*** (dizziness; fast, slow, or irregular heartbeat); ***diarrhea; gastrointestinal spasm*** (stomach cramps or pain); ***headache; hypertension*** (headache; pounding in the ears; slow or fast heartbeat); ***hypotension*** (dizziness, faintness, or light-headedness when getting up from a lying or sitting position); ***lacrimation*** (tearing of the eyes); ***mental confusion; nausea; respiratory distress*** (difficult or labored breathing; shortness of breath); ***shock*** (cold, clammy skin; decreased blood pressure; fast, weak pulse); ***sweating; tachycardia*** (fast, pounding, or irregular heartbeat or pulse; palpitations; fainting); ***tremors*** (shaking or trembling of hands or feet); ***visual disturbance*** (blurring or loss of vision; disturbed color perception); ***vomiting***

Treatment of overdose
Note: It is not known whether cevimeline is dialyzable

Specific treatment—
Treatment of signs and symptoms of cevimeline toxicity should occur in a manner consistent with that indicated for other muscarinic, cholinergic agonists

If medically indicated, atropine, an anti-cholinergic agent, may be of value as an antidote for emergency use.
If medically indicated, epinephrine may also be of value in the presence of severe cardiovascular depression or bronchoconstriction.

Supportive care—
General supportive measures should be initiated
Patients in whom intentional overdose is confirmed or suspected should be referred for psychiatric consultation.

Patient Consultation

As an aid to patient consultation, refer to *Advice for the Patient, Cevimeline (Systemic).*

In providing consultation, consider emphasizing the following selected information (» = major clinical significance):

Before using this medication

» Conditions affecting use, especially:
Hypersensitivity to cevimeline
Carcinogenicity/Tumorigenicity—Shown to be carcinogenic and tumorigenic in animal studies
Breast-feeding—Although not known whether cevimeline is distributed into breast milk, it is not recommended because of risk of serious side effects
Use in children—Appropriate studies on the relationship of age to the effects of cevimeline have not been performed in the pediatric population. Safety and effectiveness have not been established
Other medications, especially anticholinergic agents; beta-adrenergic blocking agents; and cholinergic agonists.
Other medical problems, especially asthma, uncontrolled; cardiovascular disease; ophthalmic conditions such as acute iritis and narrow-angle glaucoma; pulmonary disease other than asthma

Proper use of this medication

» Proper dosing
Missed dose: Taking as soon as possible; not taking if almost time for next dose; not doubling doses
» Proper storage

Precautions while using this medication

» Caution if driving a car at night or using machinery in low-lighting conditions (cevimeline may cause visual disturbance, especially at night)

Side/adverse effects

Signs of potential side effects, especially abscess, allergic reaction, chest pain (precordial or substernal), choking, cystitis, eye infection, erythematous rash, hypertonia, increased serum amylase, moniliasis, mouth edema, otitis media, peripheral edema, pneumonia, salivary gland enlargement, sialoadenitis, syncope, ulcerative stomatitis, urinary tract infection, vaginitis, vertigo, or xerophthalmia

General Dosing Information

For oral dosing forms: Cevimeline may cause visual disturbances, especially at night, that could impair the ability to drive safely.

Diet/Nutrition

Excessive perspiration can occur when using cevimeline, and may cause dehydration. In the event that this occurs, patients should drink extra water and consult with their physician.

For treatment of adverse effects

The signs and symptoms of cevimeline toxicity are usually characterized by an accentuation of its cholinergic effects. General supportive measures are indicated for the management of the signs and symptoms of toxicity. Atropine, an anticholinergic agent, may be of use if medically indicated by symptom severity. Epinephrine may also be of value for the reversal of profound cardiovascular depression

Oral Dosage Forms

CEVIMELINE HYDROCHLORIDE CAPSULES

Usual adult dose

Xerostomia in Sjögren's syndrome (treatment)—
Oral, 30 mg three times a day.

Usual adult prescribing limits

90 mg per day.

Usual pediatric dose

Infants and children—
Safety and efficacy have not been established.

Strength(s) usually available

U.S.—
30 mg (Rx) [*Evoxac* (lactose monohydrate; hydroxypropyl cellulose; magnesium stearate)].

Packaging and storage

Store between 15 and 30 °C (59 and 86 °F), in a tight container.

Auxiliary labeling

- Swallow capsule whole. Do not break or chew.
- May caused blurred vision.

Developed: 05/25/2000

CHLORAMBUCIL Systemic

VA CLASSIFICATION (Primary/Secondary): AN100/IM403

Commonly used brand name(s): *Leukeran.*

Note: For a listing of dosage forms and brand names by country availability, see *Dosage Forms* section(s).

Category

Antineoplastic; immunosuppressant.

Indications

Note: Bracketed information in the *Indications* section refers to uses that are not included in U.S. product labeling.

Accepted

Leukemia, chronic lymphocytic (treatment)—Chlorambucil is indicated for palliative treatment of chronic lymphocytic leukemia.

Lymphomas, Hodgkin's (treatment) or
Lymphomas, non-Hodgkin's (treatment)—Chlorambucil is indicated for palliative treatment of Hodgkin's disease and other malignant lymphomas including lymphosarcoma and giant follicular lymphoma.

[Carcinoma, ovarian, epithelial (treatment)][1]—Chlorambucil is indicated for the treatment of epithelial ovarian carcinoma.

[Lymphomas, cutaneous T-cell (treatment)][1]—Chlorambucil is indicated for the treatment of cutaneous T-cell lymphomas.

[Tumors, trophoblastic, gestational (treatment)][1]—Chlorambucil is indicated for the treatment of trophoblastic gestational tumors.

[Waldenström's macroglobulinemia (treatment)][1]—Chlorambucil is indicated for the treatment of Waldenström's macroglobulinemia.

[Leukemia, hairy cell (treatment)][1]—Chlorambucil is indicated for the treatment of hairy cell leukemia.

[Nephrotic syndrome (treatment)][1]—Chlorambucil has been used as an immunosuppressant, in combination with prednisone, in the treatment of steroid-resistant or frequently relapsing steroid-sensitive minimal-change nephrotic syndrome in children and adults, although there are significant risks associated with its use. The most common dose-limiting short-term toxicity is bone marrow depression. Because of potential long-term toxicity (male sterility, leukemia), use of chlorambucil is recommended only for patients unresponsive to or seriously intolerant of steroid treatment.

[Histiocytosis X (treatment)][1]—Chlorambucil is indicated as reasonable medical therapy at some point in the management of Histiocytosis X (Letterer-Siwe disease).

Extreme caution is recommended in use of chlorambucil for non-neoplastic conditions because of potential carcinogenicity with long-term use of this agent.

[1]Not included in Canadian product labeling.

Pharmacology/Pharmacokinetics

Physicochemical characteristics

Molecular weight—304.22.
pKa—5.8.

Mechanism of action/Effect

Chlorambucil is a bifunctional alkylating agent of the nitrogen mustard type. Chlorambucil is cell cycle-phase nonspecific, although it is also cytotoxic to nonproliferating cells. Activity occurs as a result of formation of an unstable ethylenimmonium ion, which alkylates or binds with many intracellular molecular structures, including nucleic acids. Its cytotoxic action is primarily due to cross-linking of strands of DNA, which inhibits nucleic acid synthesis.

Other actions/effects
Also has immunosuppressant activity.

Absorption
Rapidly and completely absorbed from the gastrointestinal tract.

Protein binding
Very high (99%), specifically to albumin.

Biotransformation
Hepatic, extensive and rapid. The primary metabolite, phenylacetic acid mustard (an aminophenyl acetic acid derivative), is active. Also undergoes spontaneous degradation, forming monohydroxy and dihydroxy derivatives.

Half-life
Chlorambucil—Approximately 1.5 hours.
Aminophenyl acetic acid derivative metabolite—2.4 hours.

Time to peak plasma concentration
1 hour.

Elimination
Renal, less than 1% as chlorambucil or phenylacetic acid mustard.
In dialysis—Not dialyzable.

Precautions to Consider

Cross-sensitivity and/or related problems
Patients sensitive to other alkylating agents (i.e., those who experience skin rash) may also be sensitive to chlorambucil.

Carcinogenicity
Secondary malignancies are potential delayed effects of many antineoplastic agents, although it is not clear whether the effect is related to their mutagenic or immunosuppressive action. The effect of dose and duration of therapy is also unknown, although risk seems to increase with long-term use. Although information is limited, available data seem to indicate that the carcinogenic risk is greatest with the alkylating agents.

Chlorambucil has been shown to be carcinogenic in miceand in humans. There are many reports of acute leukemia occurring in patients treated with chlorambucil for both malignant and nonmalignant diseases, often in combination with radiation or other chemotherapy. Risk appears to be related to cumulative dose and duration of therapy, but a threshold cumulative dose has not been defined.

Mutagenicity
Chlorambucil has been shown to cause chromatid or chromosome damage in humans.

Pregnancy/Reproduction
Fertility—Gonadal suppression, resulting in amenorrhea or azoospermia, may occur in patients taking antineoplastic therapy, especially with the alkylating agents. In general, these effects appear to be related to dose and length of therapy and may be irreversible. Prediction of the degree of testicular or ovarian function impairment is complicated by the common use of combinations of several antineoplastics, which makes it difficult to assess the effects of individual agents.

However, there have been numerous reports of prolonged or permanent azoospermia and permanent sterility with long-term use of chlorambucil, especially in prepubertal and pubertal males. Amenorrhea has been reported in pubertal and adult females; autopsy studies of ovaries from women treated with combination therapy including chlorambucil have shown varying degrees of fibrosis, vasculitis, and depletion of primordial follicles. Infertility has been observed when chlorambucil was employed in the therapy of malignant and non-malignant diseases.

Pregnancy—Adequate and well-controlled studies in humans have not been done. Although several successful pregnancies have been reported with chlorambucil use, two cases of an infant with an absent kidney and ureter have also been reported.

First trimester: It is usually recommended that use of antineoplastics, especially combination chemotherapy, be avoided whenever possible, especially during the first trimester. Although information is limited because of the relatively few instances of antineoplastic administration during pregnancy, the mutagenic, teratogenic, and carcinogenic potential of these medications must be considered.

Other hazards to the fetus include adverse reactions seen in adults.

In general, use of a contraceptive is recommended during cytotoxic drug therapy.

In rats, urogenital malformations including absence of a kidney have been reported.

FDA Pregnancy Category D.

Breast-feeding
Although very little information is available regarding distribution of antineoplastic agents into breast milk, breast-feeding is not recommended during chemotherapy because of the risks to the infant (adverse effects, mutagenicity, carcinogenicity). It is not known whether chlorambucil is distributed into breast milk.

Pediatrics
Appropriate studies performed to date generally have not demonstrated pediatrics-specific problems that would limit the usefulness of chlorambucil in children. However, children taking chlorambucil for nephrotic syndrome are reported to have an increased risk of seizures.

Geriatrics
No information is available on the relationship of age to the effects of chlorambucil in geriatric patients.

Dental
The bone marrow depressant effects of chlorambucil may result in an increased incidence of microbial infection, delayed healing, and gingival bleeding. Dental work, whenever possible, should be completed prior to initiation of therapy or deferred until blood counts have returned to normal. Patients should be instructed in proper oral hygiene during treatment, including caution in use of regular toothbrushes, dental floss, and toothpicks.

Chlorambucil may also infrequently cause stomatitis, which is associated with considerable discomfort.

Drug interactions and/or related problems
The following drug interactions and/or related problems have been selected on the basis of their potential clinical significance (possible mechanism in parentheses where appropriate)—not necessarily inclusive (» = major clinical significance):

Note: Combinations containing any of the following medications, depending on the amount present, may also interact with this medication.

Allopurinol or
Colchicine or
» Probenecid or
» Sulfinpyrazone
(chlorambucil may raise the concentration of blood uric acid; dosage adjustment of antigout agents may be necessary to control hyperuricemia and gout; allopurinol may be preferred to prevent or reverse chlorambucil-induced hyperuricemia because of risk of uric acid nephropathy with uricosuric antigout agents)

Antidepressants, tricyclic or
Bupropion or
Clozapine or
Haloperidol or
Loxapine or
Maprotiline or
Molindone or
Monoamine oxidase (MAO) inhibitors, including furazolidone and procarbazine or
Phenothiazines or
Pimozide or
Thioxanthenes
(these medications may lower the seizure threshold and increase the risk of chlorambucil-induced seizures)

Blood dyscrasia-causing medications (see *Appendix II*)
(leukopenic and/or thrombocytopenic effects of chlorambucil may be increased with concurrent or recent therapy if these medications cause the same effects; dosage adjustment of chlorambucil, if necessary, should be based on blood counts)

» Bone marrow depressants, other (see *Appendix II*) or
» Radiation therapy
(additive bone marrow depression may occur; dosage reduction may be required when two or more bone marrow depressants, including radiation, are used concurrently or consecutively)

» Immunosuppressants, other, such as:
Azathioprine or
Corticosteroids, glucocorticoid or
Corticotropin (ACTH) or
Cyclophosphamide or
Cyclosporine or
Cytarabine or
Mercaptopurine or
Muromonab-CD3 or
Tacrolimus
(concurrent use with chlorambucil may increase the risk of infection and development of neoplasms)

Vaccines, killed virus
(because normal defense mechanisms may be suppressed by chlorambucil therapy, the patient's antibody response to the vaccine may be decreased. The interval between discontinuation of medications that cause immunosuppression and restoration of the patient's ability to respond to the vaccine depends on the intensity and type of immunosuppression-causing medication used, the underlying disease, and other factors; estimates vary from 3 months to 1 year)

» Vaccines, live virus
(because normal defense mechanisms may be suppressed by chlorambucil therapy, concurrent use with a live virus vaccine may potentiate the replication of the vaccine virus, may increase the side/adverse effects of the vaccine virus, and/or may decrease the patient's antibody response to the vaccine; immunization of these patients should be undertaken only with extreme caution after careful review of the patient's hematologic status and only with the knowledge and consent of the physician managing the chlorambucil therapy. The interval between discontinuation of medications that cause immunosuppression and restoration of the patient's ability to respond to the vaccine depends on the intensity and type of immunosuppression-causing medication used, the underlying disease, and other factors; estimates vary from 3 months to 1 year. Patients with leukemia in remission should not receive live virus vaccine until at least 3 months after their last chemotherapy. In addition, immunization with oral poliovirus vaccine should be postponed in persons in close contact with the patient, especially family members)

Laboratory value alterations

The following have been selected on the basis of their potential clinical significance (possible effect in parentheses where appropriate)—not necessarily inclusive (» = major clinical significance).

With physiology/laboratory test values
Alkaline phosphatase and
Aspartate aminotransferase (AST [SGOT])
(values may rarely be increased, indicating hepatotoxicity)

Uric acid
(concentrations in blood and urine may be increased)

Medical considerations/Contraindications

The medical considerations/contraindications included have been selected on the basis of their potential clinical significance (reasons given in parentheses where appropriate)—not necessarily inclusive (» = major clinical significance).

Except under special circumstances, this medicine should not be used when the following medical problems exist:

» Hypersensitivity to chlorambucil and to other alkylating agents
» Prior resistance to chlorambucil

Risk-benefit should be considered when the following medical problems exist:

» Bone marrow depression
» Chickenpox, existing or recent (including recent exposure) or
» Herpes zoster
(risk of severe generalized disease)

Gout, history of or
Urate renal stones, history of
(risk of hyperuricemia)

Head trauma or
Seizure disorder, history of
(increased risk of seizures)

» Infection
» Tumor cell infiltration of bone marrow
» Caution should be used also in patients who have had previous cytotoxic drug therapy or radiation therapy.

Patient monitoring

The following are especially important in patient monitoring (other tests may be warranted in some patients, depending on condition; » = major clinical significance):

Alanine aminotransferase (ALT [SGPT]) values and
Alkaline phosphatase values and
Aspartate aminotransferase (AST [SGOT]) values and
Lactate dehydrogenase (LDH) values
(recommended prior to initiation of therapy and at frequent intervals during therapy; frequency varies according to clinical state, agent, dose, and other agents being used concurrently)

» Hematocrit or hemoglobin and
» Leukocyte count, total and, if appropriate, differential and
» Platelet count
(determinations recommended prior to initiation of therapy and at periodic intervals during therapy; frequency varies according to clinical state, agent, dose, and other agents being used concurrently)

Uric acid concentrations, serum
(recommended prior to initiation of therapy and at periodic intervals during therapy; frequency varies according to clinical state, agent, dose, and other agents being used concurrently)

Side/Adverse Effects

Note: Many "side effects" of antineoplastic therapy are unavoidable and represent the medication's pharmacologic action. Some of these (for example, leukopenia and thrombocytopenia) are actually used as parameters to aid in individual dosage titration.

The following side/adverse effects have been selected on the basis of their potential clinical significance (possible signs and symptoms in parentheses where appropriate)—not necessarily inclusive:

Those indicating need for medical attention

Incidence more frequent—dose-related

Lymphopenia, leukopenia, neutropenia, immunosuppression, or infection (fever or chills; cough or hoarseness; lower back or side pain; painful or difficult urination)—usually asymptomatic; ***thrombocytopenia*** (unusual bleeding or bruising; black, tarry stools; blood in urine or stools; pinpoint red spots on skin)—usually asymptomatic

Note: With a short course of therapy, *leukopenia* and *thrombocytopenia* may not occur until the third week of treatment and usually persist for 1 to 2 weeks (or sometimes up to 3 to 4 weeks) after withdrawal of chlorambucil. The neutrophil count may continue to decrease for up to 10 days after the last dose. After a single high dose of chlorambucil, the nadir of the leukocyte and platelet counts occurs after 7 to 14 days, with recovery in 2 to 3 weeks.

In general, short intermittent courses are thought to cause less risk of serious bone marrow depression than continuous therapy, by allowing bone marrow regeneration between courses. Excessive doses or prolonged therapy (a total dose of 6.5 mg per kg of body weight [mg/kg] in a single course) may result in pancytopenia and irreversible bone marrow damage.

Incidence less frequent

Allergic reaction (skin rash); ***angioneurotic edema*** (large, swollen hives; itching); ***hyperuricemia or uric acid nephropathy*** (joint pain; lower back or side pain; swelling of feet or lower legs); ***stomatitis*** (sores in mouth and on lips); ***urticaria*** (itching; hives)

Note: *Skin rash* has been reported to progress rarely to erythema multiforme, toxic epidermal necrolysis, and Stevens-Johnson syndrome.

Note: Urticaria and angioneurotic edema have been reported following initial or subsequent dosing.

Hyperuricemia or uric acid nephropathy occurs most commonly during initial treatment of patients with leukemia or lymphoma, as a result of rapid cell breakdown that leads to elevated serum uric acid concentrations.

Stomatitis may be associated with neutropenia.

Incidence rare

Drug fever; hepatotoxicity, hepatic necrosis, or cirrhosis (yellow eyes or skin); ***myoclonia*** (muscle twitching or jerking; rhythmic movement of muscles); ***neurotoxicity*** (agitation; confusion; hallucinations; seizures; severe weakness or paralysis; tremors; trouble in walking); ***pulmonary fibrosis*** (cough; shortness of breath)—occurs after long-term use; ***skin reactions, severe, including erythema multiforme, epidermal necrolysis, and Stevens-Johnson syndrome*** (blisters on skin; severe skin rash; sores in mouth; fever may also be associated with Stevens-Johnson syndrome)

Note: Rare, focal and/or generalized seizures have been reported in both children and adults at therapeutic daily doses, and in pulse dosing regimens and acute overdose. However, the risk may be increased in children with nephrotic syndrome (seizures may occur 6 to 90 days after initiation of treatment) and in patients receiving high pulse doses. *Neurotoxicity* is usually reversible on withdrawal of chlorambucil.

Pulmonary fibrosis is usually reversible after chlorambucil is withdrawn, but fatalities have been reported.

Those indicating need for medical attention only if they continue or are bothersome

Incidence less frequent or rare

Changes in menstrual period; dermatitis (itching of skin); ***nausea and vomiting***

Note: *Nausea and vomiting* are associated with single oral doses of 20 mg or more, usually last less than 24 hours, and become less frequent with continued therapy; may persist up to 7 days after a single high dose.

Those indicating need for medical attention if they occur after medication is discontinued

Bone marrow damage, possibly irreversible (fever or chills; cough or hoarseness; lower back or side pain; painful or difficult urination; unusual bleeding or bruising; black, tarry stools; blood in urine or stools; pinpoint red spots on skin) ***pulmonary toxicity*** (cough; shortness of breath)

Overdose

For more information on the management of overdose or unintentional ingestion, **contact a Poison Control Center** (see *Poison Control Center Listing*).

Clinical effects of overdose

The following effects have been selected on the basis of their potential clinical significance (possible signs and symptoms in parentheses where appropriate)—not necessarily inclusive:

Symptoms of overdose, in order of frequency

Pancytopenia, reversible (fever or chills; cough or hoarseness; lower back or side pain; painful or difficult urination; unusual bleeding or bruising; black, tarry stools; blood in urine or stools; pinpoint red spots on skin); ***neurotoxicity, including ataxia*** (trouble in walking); ***agitation; and seizures***

Treatment of overdose

To enhance elimination—Immediate evacuation of the stomach.

Monitoring—Monitoring of blood counts at least three times a week for at least 3 weeks or until bone marrow function has recovered.

Supportive care—Supportive, symptomatic treatment. Patients in whom intentional overdose is confirmed or suspected should be referred for psychiatric consultation.

Patient Consultation

As an aid to patient consultation, refer to *Advice for the Patient, Chlorambucil (Systemic)*.

In providing consultation, consider emphasizing the following selected information (» = major clinical significance):

Before using this medication

» Conditions affecting use, especially:
- Hypersensitivity to chlorambucil or other alkylating agents
- Pregnancy—Use not recommended because of mutagenic, teratogenic, and carcinogenic potential; advisability of using contraception; telling physician immediately if pregnancy is suspected
- Breast-feeding—Not recommended because of risk of serious side effects
- Other medications, especially probenecid, sulfinpyrazone, other bone marrow depressants, other immunosuppressants, or previous cytotoxic drug or radiation therapy
- Other medical problems, especially prior resistance to chlorambucil, bone marrow depression, chickenpox, herpes zoster, or infection.

Proper use of this medication

» Importance of not taking more or less medication than the amount prescribed

Caution in taking combination therapy; taking each medication at the right time

Importance of ample fluid intake and subsequent increase in urine output to aid in excretion of uric acid

» Possible nausea and vomiting; importance of continuing medication despite stomach upset

Checking with physician if vomiting occurs shortly after dose is taken

» Proper dosing

Missed dose: If dosing schedule is—
- Once a day: Taking as soon as possible if remembered same day; if not remembered until next day, skipping missed dose and taking next regularly scheduled dose
- Several times a day: Taking as soon as possible; however, if almost time for next dose, not taking missed dose; not doubling doses

» Proper storage

Precautions while using this medication

» Importance of close monitoring by the physician

» Avoiding immunizations unless approved by physician; other persons in patient's household should avoid immunizations with oral poliovirus vaccine; avoiding persons who have taken oral poliovirus vaccine or wearing a protective mask that covers nose and mouth

Caution if bone marrow depression occurs:

» Avoiding exposure to persons with infections, especially during periods of low blood counts; checking with physician immediately if fever or chills, cough or hoarseness, lower back or side pain, or painful or difficult urination occurs

» Checking with physician immediately if unusual bleeding or bruising; black, tarry stools; blood in urine or stools; or pinpoint red spots on skin occur
- Caution in use of regular toothbrush, dental floss, or toothpick; physician, dentist, or nurse may suggest alternatives; checking with physician before having dental work done
- Not touching eyes or inside of nose unless hands washed immediately before
- Using caution to avoid accidental cuts with use of sharp objects such as safety razor or fingernail or toenail cutters
- Avoiding contact sports or other situations where bruising or injury might occur

Side/adverse effects

May cause adverse effects such as blood problems and cancer

Signs of potential side effects, especially angioneurotic edema, lymphopenia, leukopenia, myoclonia, neutropenia, immunosuppression, infection, thrombocytopenia, allergic reaction, hyperuricemia, uric acid nephropathy, stomatitis, drug fever, hepatotoxicity, hepatic necrosis, cirrhosis, neurotoxicity, pulmonary fibrosis, urticaria, and severe skin reactions

Physician or nurse can help in dealing with side effects

General Dosing Information

Patients receiving chlorambucil should be under supervision of a physician experienced in use of alkylating agents.

A variety of dosage schedules and regimens of chlorambucil, alone or in combination with other antitumor agents, are used. The prescriber may consult the medical literature as well as the manufacturer's literature in choosing a specific dosage.

Dosage must be adjusted to meet the individual requirements of each patient, based on clinical response and degree of bone marrow depression.

Development of uric acid nephropathy in patients with leukemia or lymphoma may be prevented by adequate oral hydration and, in some cases, administration of allopurinol. Alkalinization of urine may be necessary if serum uric acid concentrations are elevated.

It is recommended that chlorambucil be withdrawn if signs of pulmonary toxicity or a severe skin reaction occurs.

Because of the risk of enhanced bone marrow toxicity, use of chlorambucil is not recommended within 4 to 6 weeks of radiation therapy or chemotherapy with drugs that depress bone marrow function.

Because the decrease in neutrophil count may continue for 10 days after the last dose of chlorambucil, caution is necessary as the total dose approaches 6.5 mg per kg of body weight (mg/kg) because of the risk of pancytopenia.

If the white blood cell count (particularly granulocyte count) falls suddenly, a reduction in dosage or withdrawal of therapy plus continued monitoring is required until leukocyte and platelet levels become adequate. Persistence of low neutrophil and platelet counts or presence of peripheral lymphocytosis may indicate bone marrow infiltration; if that is confirmed by bone marrow examination, the daily dosage of chlorambucil should not exceed 100 mcg (0.1 mg) per kg of body weight.

Special precautions are recommended in patients who develop thrombocytopenia as a result of administration of chlorambucil. These may include extreme care in performing invasive procedures; regular inspection of intravenous sites, skin (including perirectal area), and mucous membrane surfaces for signs of bleeding or bruising; limiting frequency of venipuncture and avoiding intramuscular injections; testing urine, emesis, stool, and secretions for occult blood; care in use of regular toothbrushes, dental floss, toothpicks, safety razors, and fingernail and toenail cutters; avoiding constipation; and using caution to prevent falls and other injuries. Such patients should avoid alcohol and aspirin intake because of the risk of gastrointestinal bleeding. Platelet transfusions may be required.

Patients who develop leukopenia should be observed carefully for signs of infection. Antibiotic support may be required. In neutropenic patients who develop fever, broad-spectrum antibiotic coverage should be initiated empirically, pending bacterial cultures and appropriate diagnostic tests.

Combination chemotherapy

Although chlorambucil is usually used alone, it may be used in combination with other agents in various regimens. As a result, incidence and/or severity of side effects may be altered and different dosages (usually reduced) may be used. For example, chlorambucil is part of the

following chemotherapeutic combination (a commonly used acronym is in parentheses):
—chlorambucil and prednisone (CHL + PRED).

For specific dosages and schedules, consult the literature. For information regarding each agent, consult the individual monographs.

Oral Dosage Forms

Note: Bracketed uses in the *Dosage Forms* section refer to categories of use and/or indications that are not included in U.S. product labeling.

CHLORAMBUCIL TABLETS USP

Usual adult dose

Leukemia, chronic lymphocytic or
Lymphomas, Hodgkin's or
Lymphomas, non-Hodgkin's—

Initiation or short course: Oral, 100 to 200 mcg (0.1 to 0.2 mg) per kg of body weight a day or 3 to 6 mg per square meter of body surface area, usually 4 to 10 mg, a day, as a single dose or in divided doses, for three to six weeks.

Note: An intermittent, biweekly, or once-monthly pulse course of therapy may produce less hematologic toxicity; an initial dose of 400 mcg (0.4 mg) per kg of body weight or 12 mg per square meter of body surface area is increased by 100 mcg (0.1 mg) per kg of body weight or 3 mg per square meter of body surface area until an effective or toxic dose is reached, then adjusted as necessary.

[Nephrotic syndrome][1]—

Oral, 100 to 200 mcg (0.1 to 0.2 mg) per kg of body weight per day, in a single dose, for eight to twelve weeks.

Note: The maximum recommended cumulative dose is 14 mg per kg of body weight or a maximum duration of treatment of 12 weeks; some clinicians recommend a maximum cumulative dose of 8.2 mg per kg of body weight or a maximum of 6 weeks of treatment.

[Histiocytosis X][1]—

Studies have shown that adults have benefited from treatment with oral chlorambucil, at a dosage of 5 mg per squared meter of body surface area per day, for a treatment duration determined by patient response.

Usual adult prescribing limits

Presence of lymphocytic infiltration of bone marrow or hypoplastic bone marrow—Up to 100 mcg (0.1 mg) per kg of body weight per day.

Usual pediatric dose

Leukemia, chronic lymphocytic or
Lymphomas, Hodgkin's or
Lymphomas, non-Hodgkin's—

Oral, 100 to 200 mcg (0.1 to 0.2 mg) per kg of body weight or 4.5 mg per square meter of body surface area a day, as a single dose or in divided daily doses.

[Nephrotic syndrome][1]—

See *Usual adult dose*.

[Histiocytosis X][1]—

Studies have shown that children older than 1 month of age have benefited from treatment with oral chlorambucil, at a dosage of 5 mg per squared meter of body surface area per day, for a treatment duration determined by patient response.

Strength(s) usually available

U.S.—

2 mg (Rx) [*Leukeran* (lactose; sucrose)].

Canada—

2 mg (Rx) [*Leukeran*].

Packaging and storage

Store in a refrigerator, 2 °C to 8 °C (36 to 46 °F)

[1]Not included in Canadian product labeling.

Revised: 01/08/2003
Developed: 09/02/1999

CHLORDIAZEPOXIDE—See *Benzodiazepines (Systemic)*

CHLOROPROCAINE—See *Anesthetics (Parenteral-Local)*

CHLOROTHIAZIDE—See *Diuretics, Thiazide (Systemic)*

CHLORPHENESIN—See *Skeletal Muscle Relaxants (Systemic)*

CHLORPHENIRAMINE—See *Antihistamines (Systemic)*

CHLORPROMAZINE—See *Phenothiazines (Systemic)*

CHLORPROPAMIDE—See *Antidiabetic Agents, Sulfonylurea (Systemic)*

CHLORPROTHIXENE—See *Thioxanthenes (Systemic)*

CHLORTETRACYCLINE—See *Tetracyclines (Ophthalmic), Tetracyclines (Topical)*

CHLORTHALIDONE—See *Diuretics, Thiazide (Systemic)*

CHLORZOXAZONE—See *Skeletal Muscle Relaxants (Systemic)*

CHOLESTYRAMINE Oral-Local

VA CLASSIFICATION (Primary/Secondary): CV359/AD400; DE890; GA208; GU900

Commonly used brand name(s): *Questran; Questran Light.*

Note: For a listing of dosage forms and brand names by country availability, see *Dosage Forms* section(s).

Category

Antihyperlipidemic; antipruritic (cholestasis); antidiarrheal (postoperative colonic bile acids); antidote (anion-exchange resin); antihyperoxaluric.

Indications

Note: Bracketed information in the *Indications* section refers to uses that are not included in U.S. product labeling.

Accepted

Hyperlipidemia (treatment)—Cholestyramine is indicated for use in patients with primary hypercholesterolemia (type IIa hyperlipidemia) and a significant risk of coronary artery disease who have not responded to diet or other measures alone. Cholestyramine reduces plasma total cholesterol and low density lipoprotein (LDL) concentrations, but causes no change or a slight increase in serum triglyceride concentrations, and so is not useful in patients with elevated triglyceride concentrations alone. Its use is limited in other types of hyperlipidemia (including type IIb) because it may cause further elevation of triglycerides.

Studies have suggested that control of elevated cholesterol and triglycerides may not lessen the danger of cardiovascular disease and mortality, although incidence of nonfatal myocardial infarctions may be decreased.

For additional information on initial therapeutic guidelines related to the treatment of hyperlipidemia, see *Appendix III*.

Cholestyramine is indicated to reduce the risks of atherosclerotic heart disease and myocardial infarctions.

Pruritus, associated with partial biliary obstruction (treatment)—Cholestyramine is indicated for the relief of pruritus associated with partial biliary obstruction (including primary biliary cirrhosis and various other forms of bile stasis). It is not useful in patients with complete biliary obstruction or with pruritus due to other causes.

[Diarrhea, due to bile acids (treatment)]—Cholestyramine has also been used to treat diarrhea caused by increased bile acids in the colon after surgery, although the risk of steatorrhea is increased.

[Hyperoxaluria (treatment)][1]—Cholestyramine is also being used in the treatment of hyperoxaluria.

[Cholestyramine has been used in the treatment of digitalis glycoside overdose; however, it generally has been replaced by other agents such as digoxin immune fab.]

---

[1]Not included in Canadian product labeling.

Pharmacology/Pharmacokinetics

Physicochemical characteristics
Cholestyramine is an anion-exchange resin

Mechanism of action/Effect
Cholestyramine binds with bile acids in the intestine, preventing their reabsorption and producing an insoluble complex, which is excreted in the feces.

Antihyperlipidemic—
Cholestyramine binds with bile acids in the intestine, causing an increase in hepatic synthesis of bile acids from cholesterol. This depletion of hepatic cholesterol increases hepatic low-density lipoprotein (LDL) receptor activity, which removes LDL cholesterol from the plasma. Cholestyramine may also increase hepatic very low-density lipoprotein (VLDL) production, thereby increasing the plasma concentration of triglycerides, especially in patients with hypertriglyceridemia.

Antipruritic (cholestasis)—
Reduction of serum bile acids and subsequent reduction of excess bile acids, which are deposited in dermal tissue, may lead to reduced pruritus.

Antidiarrheal (postoperative colonic bile acids)—
Cholestyramine binds with and removes bile acids.

Antidote (anion-exchange resin)—
Because it is an anion-exchange resin, cholestyramine is capable of binding negatively charged medications as well as some others, causing a decreased effect or shortened half-life.

Absorption
Not absorbed from the gastrointestinal tract.

Onset of action
Reduction of plasma cholesterol concentrations—Generally reduced within 1 to 2 weeks after initiation of cholestyramine therapy, but may continue to fall for up to 1 year. In some patients, after the initial decrease, serum cholesterol concentrations return to or exceed baseline levels with continued therapy.

Relief of pruritus associated with biliary stasis—Usually occurs within 1 to 3 weeks after initiation of therapy.

Relief of diarrhea associated with bile acids—Within 24 hours.

Duration of action
Reduction of plasma cholesterol concentrations—After withdrawal of cholestyramine, cholesterol concentrations return to baseline in about 2 to 4 weeks.

Relief of pruritus associated with biliary stasis—Pruritus returns within 1 to 2 weeks when the medication is withdrawn.

Precautions to Consider

Tumorigenicity
Cholestyramine was found to increase the incidence of intestinal tumors in rats receiving potent carcinogens.

Pregnancy/Reproduction
Pregnancy—Problems in humans have not been documented. Cholestyramine is almost totally unabsorbed after oral administration; however, adverse effects on the fetus may potentially occur because of impaired maternal absorption of vitamins and nutrients.

Breast-feeding
Problems in humans have not been documented. Cholestyramine is almost totally unabsorbed after oral administration. However, the possible impaired maternal vitamin and nutrient absorption may have an effect on nursing infants.

Pediatrics
Several studies performed to date have not demonstrated pediatrics-specific problems that would limit the usefulness of cholestyramine in children. However, experience with cholestyramine in children younger than 10 years of age is limited. Therefore, caution is recommended since cholesterol is required for normal development.

Geriatrics
Appropriate studies on the relationship of age to the effects of cholestyramine have not been performed in the geriatric population. However, patients over 60 years of age may be more likely to experience gastrointestinal side effects, as well as adverse nutritional effects.

Drug interactions and/or related problems
The following drug interactions and/or related problems have been selected on the basis of their potential clinical significance (possible mechanism in parentheses where appropriate)—not necessarily inclusive (» = major clinical significance):

Note: Combinations containing any of the following medications, depending on the amount present, may also interact with this medication.

» Anticoagulants, coumarin- or indandione-derivative
(concurrent use may significantly increase the anticoagulant effect as a result of depletion of vitamin K, but cholestyramine may also bind with oral anticoagulants in the gastrointestinal tract and reduce their effects; administration at least 6 hours before cholestyramine and adjustment of anticoagulant dosage based on frequent prothrombin-time determinations are recommended)

Chenodiol or
Ursodiol
(effect may be decreased when chenodiol or ursodiol is used concurrently with cholestyramine, which binds these medications and decreases their absorption and also tends to increase cholesterol saturation of bile)

» Digitalis glycosides, especially digitoxin
(cholestyramine may reduce the half-life of these medications by decreasing intestinal reabsorption and enterohepatic circulation; caution is recommended, especially when cholestyramine is withdrawn from a patient who was stabilized on the digitalis glycoside while receiving cholestyramine, because of the potential for serious toxicity; some clinicians recommend administration of cholestyramine approximately 8 hours after the digitalis glycoside)

» Diuretics, thiazide, oral or
» Penicillin G, oral or
» Phenylbutazone or
» Propranolol, oral or
» Tetracyclines, oral
(concurrent use with cholestyramine may result in binding of these medications, thus decreasing their absorption; an interval of several hours between administration of cholestyramine and any of these medications is recommended)

Folic acid
(concurrent use with cholestyramine may interfere with absorption of folic acid; folic acid supplementation recommended in patients receiving cholestyramine for prolonged periods)

» Thyroid hormones, including dextrothyroxine
(concurrent use with cholestyramine may decrease the effects of thyroid hormones by binding and delaying or preventing absorption; an interval of 4 to 5 hours between administration of the two medications and regular monitoring of thyroid function tests are recommended)

» Vancomycin, oral
(cholestyramine has been shown to bind oral vancomycin significantly when used concurrently, resulting in decreased stool concentrations and marked reduction in antibacterial activity of vancomycin; concurrent use is not recommended; patients should be advised to take oral vancomycin and cholestyramine several hours apart)

Vitamins, fat-soluble
(cholestyramine may interfere with absorption of fat-soluble vitamins as a result of its interference with fat absorption; supplemental vitamins A and D in water-miscible or parenteral form are recommended in patients receiving cholestyramine for prolonged periods; supplemental vitamin K may be required in some patients who develop bleeding tendencies)

Medications, other
(cholestyramine may delay or reduce absorption of other medications administered concurrently because of its anion-binding activity; administration of other medications 1 to 2 hours before or 4 to 6 hours after cholestyramine is recommended, although absorption of some medications is impaired even then; caution is recommended when cholestyramine is withdrawn because of the risk of toxicity when suddenly increased absorption of the other medication leads to higher serum concentrations)

Laboratory value alterations
The following have been selected on the basis of their potential clinical significance (possible effect in parentheses where appropriate)—not necessarily inclusive (» = major clinical significance).

With physiology/laboratory test values
Alkaline phosphatase values and

Aspartate aminotransferase (AST [SGOT]) values and
Chloride concentrations, serum and
Phosphorus concentrations, serum
(may be increased)

Calcium
(serum concentrations may be decreased due to impaired absorption; may lead to osteoporosis, especially in patients with biliary cirrhosis who already have impaired calcium absorption)

Potassium and
Sodium
(serum concentrations may be decreased)

Prothrombin time (PT)
(may be prolonged)

Schilling test for absorption of vitamin B_{12}
(test may be falsely abnormal due to drug binding with intrinsic factor, which prevents the formation of an intrinsic factor-vitamin B_{12} complex needed for absorption)

Medical considerations/Contraindications

The medical considerations/contraindications included have been selected on the basis of their potential clinical significance (reasons given in parentheses where appropriate)—not necessarily inclusive (» = major clinical significance).

Risk-benefit should be considered when the following medical problems exist:

Bleeding disorders or
Gallstones or
Gastrointestinal function impairment or
Hypothyroidism or
Malabsorption states, especially steatorrhea or
Peptic ulcer
(these conditions may be exacerbated)

» Complete biliary obstruction or complete atresia
(no bile acids in gastrointestinal tract for cholestyramine to bind)

» Constipation
(risk of fecal impaction)

Coronary artery disease and
Hemorrhoids
(exacerbation of these conditions may occur because of the risks associated with severe constipation)

» Phenylketonuria
(sensitivity to phenylalanine in aspartame, which is included in sugar-free preparation)

Renal function impairment
(increased risk of development of hyperchloremic acidosis)

Sensitivity to cholestyramine

Patient monitoring

The following may be especially important in patient monitoring (other tests may be warranted in some patients, depending on condition; » = major clinical significance):

Calcium concentrations, serum
(recommended periodically because of decreased absorption of calcium associated with chronic use of cholestyramine)

Cholesterol concentrations, serum and
Triglyceride concentrations, serum
(determinations recommended prior to initiation of therapy of hyperlipidemia and at periodic intervals during therapy to confirm efficacy and determine that a positive response is maintained)

Prothrombin-time (PT) determinations
(recommended periodically because vitamin K deficiency associated with chronic use of cholestyramine may increase bleeding tendency)

Side/Adverse Effects

Note: Side effects are more likely to occur with high doses and in patients over 60 years of age.
Less frequently, osteoporosis has been reported as a result of chronic long-term cholestyramine use.

The following side/adverse effects have been selected on the basis of their potential clinical significance (possible signs and symptoms in parentheses where appropriate)—not necessarily inclusive:

Those indicating need for medical attention

Incidence more frequent
Constipation—usually mild and transient, but may be severe and lead to fecal impaction

Incidence rare
Gallstones or pancreatitis (severe stomach pain with nausea and vomiting); ***gastrointestinal bleeding or peptic ulcer*** (black, tarry stools); ***steatorrhea or malabsorption syndrome*** (sudden loss of weight)

Those indicating need for medical attention only if they continue or are bothersome

Incidence more frequent
Heartburn or indigestion; nausea or vomiting; stomach pain

Incidence less frequent
Belching; bloating; diarrhea; dizziness; headache

Patient Consultation

As an aid to patient consultation, refer to *Advice for the Patient, Cholestyramine (Oral).*

In providing consultation, consider emphasizing the following selected information (» = major clinical significance):

Before using this medication

» Conditions affecting use, especially:
Sensitivity to cholestyramine
Use in children—Caution with use in children less than 10 years of age since cholesterol is required for normal development
Use in the elderly—Increased incidence of gastrointestinal side effects and potentially adverse nutritional effects in patients over 60 years of age
Other oral medications, especially anticoagulants, digitalis glycosides, thiazide diuretics, penicillin G, phenylbutazone, propranolol, tetracyclines, thyroid hormones, or vancomycin
Other medical problems, especially complete biliary obstruction or complete atresia, constipation, or phenylketonuria

Proper use of this medication

» Importance of not taking more or less medication than the amount prescribed

» Proper dosing
Missed dose: Taking as soon as possible; not taking if almost time for next dose; not doubling doses

» Proper storage

» Importance of mixing with fluids before taking; instructions for measuring and mixing—Placing in 2 ounces of any beverage and stirring vigorously, then adding 2 to 4 ounces of beverage and shaking vigorously (does not dissolve); rinsing glass and drinking to make sure all medication is taken; may also be mixed with milk in cereals, thin soups, or pulpy fruits

For use as an antihyperlipidemic
» Diet as preferred therapy; importance of following prescribed diet
This medication does not cure the condition but rather helps control it

Precautions while using this medication

» Importance of close monitoring by the physician

» Not taking any other medication unless discussed with physician

For use as an antihyperlipidemic:
» Checking with physician before discontinuing medication; blood lipid concentrations may increase significantly

Side/adverse effects

Signs of potential side effects, especially constipation, gallstones, pancreatitis, gastrointestinal bleeding, peptic ulcer, and steatorrhea or malabsorption syndrome

General Dosing Information

To prevent accidental inhalation or esophageal distress with the dry form, it is recommended that cholestyramine for suspension be mixed with at least 120 to 180 mL of water or other fluids before being ingested. It may also be taken in soups or with cereals or pulpy fruits.

Reduction in cholestyramine dosage or withdrawal of the medication may be necessary in some patients if constipation occurs or worsens, to prevent impaction. Administration of a laxative or stool softener or increased fluid intake may be helpful.

For use as an antihyperlipidemic

If a paradoxical increase in plasma cholesterol concentrations occurs, it is recommended that cholestyramine therapy be withdrawn.

If response is inadequate after 1 to 3 months of treatment, cholestyramine therapy should be withdrawn, except in the case of xanthoma tuberosum, which may require up to 1 year of treatment as long as reduction in size and/or number of xanthomata occurs.

For use as an antipruritic

Dosage may be reduced when relief of pruritus occurs.

Oral Dosage Forms

Note: Bracketed uses in the *Dosage Forms* section refer to categories of use and/or indications that are not included in U.S. product labeling.

CHOLESTYRAMINE FOR ORAL SUSPENSION USP

Usual adult and adolescent dose

Antihyperlipidemic; or
Antipruritic (cholestasis); or
[Antidiarrheal, postoperative colonic bile acids]—
Initial: Oral, 4 grams (anhydrous cholestyramine) one or two times a day before meals, adjusted according to response.
Maintenance: Oral, 8 to 24 grams (anhydrous cholestyramine) a day, in two to six divided doses.

Note: A single daily dose or two divided daily doses are equally effective, but up to six divided daily doses may be administered and may be more convenient for the patient, especially with the larger doses.

Usual adult prescribing limits

Antihyperlipidemic—24 grams (anhydrous cholestyramine) a day.
Antipruritic (cholestasis)—Up to 16 grams (anhydrous cholestyramine) a day.

Usual pediatric dose

Antihyperlipidemic—
Initial: Oral, 4 grams (anhydrous cholestyramine) a day, in two divided doses.
Maintenance: Oral, 8 to 24 grams (anhydrous cholestyramine) a day, in two or more divided doses.

Strength(s) usually available

U.S.—
5 grams (4 grams of anhydrous cholestyramine) per packet or level scoop (Rx) [*Questran Light* (aspartame; phenylalanine 16.8 mg per 5-gram dose)].
9 grams (4 grams of anhydrous cholestyramine) per packet or level scoop (Rx) [*Questran* (sucrose)].

Canada—
5 grams (4 grams of anhydrous cholestyramine) per packet or level scoop (Rx) [*Questran Light* (aspartame; phenylalanine 16.8 mg per 5-gram dose)].
9 grams (4 grams of anhydrous cholestyramine) per packet or level scoop (Rx) [*Questran*].

Packaging and storage

Store below 40 °C (104 °F), preferably between 15 and 30 °C (59 and 86 °F), unless otherwise specified by manufacturer. Store in a tight container.

Preparation of dosage form

Cholestyramine is prepared for administration by placing the measured powder in 2 ounces of any beverage and stirring vigorously. An additional 2 to 4 ounces of beverage should then be added, again shaking vigorously (does not dissolve). After the patient drinks the suspension, the glass should be rinsed with more liquid to make sure all the medication is taken. Cholestyramine may also be mixed with milk in hot or regular breakfast cereals, in thin soups (tomato or chicken noodle), or in pulpy fruits such as pineapple, pears, peaches, or fruit cocktail.

Stability

Variations in color do not reflect changes in potency of the product.

Auxiliary labeling

- Take mixed in cold water or juice.

Selected Bibliography

The Expert Panel. Report of the National Cholesterol Education Program Expert Panel on Detection, Evaluation, and Treatment of High Blood Cholesterol in Adults. Arch Intern Med 1988; 148: 36-69.
NIH Consensus Conference. Lowering blood cholesterol to prevent heart disease. JAMA 1985; 253: 2080-6.
Knodel LC, Talbert RL. Adverse effects of hypolipidaemic drugs. Med Toxicol 1987; 2: 10-32.

Revised: 08/13/1998

CHOLINE SALICYLATE—See *Salicylates (Systemic)*

CHORIONIC GONADOTROPIN
Systemic

VA CLASSIFICATION (Primary/Secondary): HS106/DX900; HS900

Note: Controlled substance classification
U.S.: Schedule IV (controlled substance in some states in the U.S.)

Commonly used brand name(s): *Chorex; Novarel; Pregnyl; Profasi; Profasi HP.*

Another commonly used name is human chorionic gonadotropin (hCG).

Note: For a listing of dosage forms and brand names by country availability, see *Dosage Forms* section(s).

Category

Gonadotropin; cryptorchidism therapy adjunct; infertility therapy adjunct; diagnostic aid (hypogonadism).

Indications

Note: Bracketed information in the *Indications* section refers to uses that are not included in U.S. product labeling.

Accepted

[Cryptorchidism (diagnosis)][1] or
Cryptorchidism (treatment)—Chorionic gonadotropin is indicated both as a diagnostic trial and for treatment of prepubertal cryptorchidism not due to anatomical obstruction. Treatment with chorionic gonadotropin usually begins at 4 to 9 years of age. If no signs of improvement occur during the initial course, surgery is indicated.

Infertility, male (treatment)—Chorionic gonadotropin is indicated, alone or in combination with menotropins or clomiphene, for treatment of male hypogonadism due to pituitary deficiency. Males who have been hypogonadotropic for prolonged periods may require treatment with testosterone instead.

Infertility, female (treatment)—Chorionic gonadotropin is indicated in conjunction with menotropins, urofollitropin, or in some cases, clomiphene, to stimulate ovulation. In general, use of chorionic gonadotropin with menotropins or urofollitropin is the treatment of choice for induction of ovulation in patients who do not respond to clomiphene.

Reproductive technologies, assisted—Chorionic gonadotropin is indicated, in conjunction with menotropins or urofollitropin, to stimulate the development and maturation of multiple oocytes in ovulatory patients who are attempting to conceive by means of assisted reproductive technologies, such as gamete intrafallopian transfer (GIFT) or *in vitro* fertilization (IVF).

[Hypogonadism, male (diagnosis)][1]—Chorionic gonadotropin is also used to test the ability of the testes to respond to gonadotropin stimulation in males with delayed puberty.

[Corpus luteum insufficiency (treatment)][1]—Chorionic gonadotropin is used to treat corpus luteum dysfunction. Treatment should begin in the cycle of conception and not after the first missed menses. It is continued until hormone production is taken over by the placenta after 7 to 10 weeks of gestation.

Unaccepted

Chorionic gonadotropin has not been found effective and is not indicated for weight reduction.

[1]Not included in Canadian product labeling.

Pharmacology/Pharmacokinetics

Physicochemical characteristics

Source—Produced by the placenta; extracted from urine of pregnant women.

Mechanism of action/Effect

The action of chorionic gonadotropin is almost identical to that of pituitary luteinizing hormone (LH). It is generally used as a substitute for LH.

Prepubertal cryptorchidism—
Stimulates androgen production by the testes, which may stimulate descent of the testes. The effect is usually permanent but may be temporary. In use as a diagnostic trial, chorionic gonadotropin administration should stimulate increased serum testosterone concentrations.

Hypogonadotropic hypogonadism—
Stimulates androgen production by the testes, which leads to the development of male secondary sexual characteristics.

For induction of ovulation and assisted reproductive technologies (ART)—
Clomiphene, menotropins, or urofollitropin prepare the ovarian follicle for ovulation. The combination of follicle-stimulating hormone (FSH) and LH stimulates follicular growth and maturation. Chorionic gonadotropin, whose actions are nearly identical to those of LH, is administered following administration of clomiphene, menotropins, or urofollitropin to mimic the naturally occurring surge of LH that triggers ovulation.

Diagnostic aid (hypogonadism)—
Should stimulate increased production of testosterone.

Corpus luteum insufficiency—
Promotes maintenance of the corpus luteum; stimulates ovarian production of progesterone.

Half-life

Biphasic, 11 and 23 hours (serum).

Time to peak effect

Females—Ovulation usually occurs within 32 to 36 hours after administration of chorionic gonadotropin.

Elimination

Renal, unchanged; 10 to 12% within 24 hours.

Precautions to Consider

Carcinogenicity/Mutagenicity

Adequate and well-controlled studies in humans have not been done. In otherwise healthy men receiving human chorionic gonadotropin for secondary infertility, there have been sporadic reports of testicular tumors. A small number of infertile women who have been treated with fertility drugs have developed ovarian cancer. A causal relationship between the use of human chorionic gonadotropin and cancer in males or females has not been established.

Pregnancy/Reproduction

Fertility—Use of chorionic gonadotropin in conjunction with menotropins or urofollitropin to induce ovulation is associated with a high incidence of multiple gestations and multiple births. As a result, this may increase the risk of neonatal prematurity, as well as other complications associated with multiple gestations.

Pregnancy—Adequate and well-controlled studies in humans have not been done. Alterations in sex ratio and defects of forelimbs and central nervous system have been reported in mice given combined gonadotropin and chorionic gonadotropin therapy in dosages to induce superovulation.

Ovarian hyperstimulation syndrome (OHS), which may occur during chorionic gonadotropin therapy, may be more common, more severe, and protracted in patients who conceive.

FDA Pregnancy Category X (Profasi®)

FDA Pregnancy Category C (Novarel™)

Breast-feeding

It is not known if human chorionic gonadotropin is distributed into human milk. However caution should be used when administering to a nursing woman.

Pediatrics

Safety and effectiveness in children younger than 4 years of age have not been established.

Solvent may contain benzyl alcohol, which is not for use in newborns.

Precocious puberty has been reported in males treated with chorionic gonadotropin for cryptorchidism. Generally, therapy is withdrawn and the use of chorionic gonadotropin re-evaluated if signs of precocious puberty appear. Also, prolonged or high doses of chorionic gonadotropin may cause abnormally rapid advancement of skeletal maturation and lead to premature epiphyseal fusion. This could result in reduced final adult height.

Geriatrics

No information is available on the relationship of age to the effects of human chorionic gonadotropin in geriatric patients.

Laboratory value alterations

The following have been selected on the basis of their potential clinical significance (possible effect in parentheses where appropriate)—not necessarily inclusive (» = major clinical significance).

With diagnostic test results

Immunologic assay for endogenous chorionic gonadotropin
(pregnancy test should be performed at least 10 days or longer after administration of chorionic gonadotropin to avoid false-positive result; the laboratory should be notified of patients on human chorionic gonadotropin if gonadotropin levels are requested)

With physiology/laboratory test values

17-Hydroxycorticosteroids and
17-Ketosteroids
(urine concentrations may be increased)

Medical considerations/Contraindications

The medical considerations/contraindications included have been selected on the basis of their potential clinical significance (reasons given in parentheses where appropriate)—not necessarily inclusive (» = major clinical significance).

Except under special circumstances, this medication should not be used when the following medical problems exist:

» Hypersensitivity to chorionic gonadotropin or other gonadotropins

For treatment of cryptorchidism

» Precocious puberty

For induction of ovulation

» Abnormal vaginal bleeding, undiagnosed
(may indicate the presence of endometrial hyperplasia or carcinoma, which may be exacerbated by ovulation-induced increases in estrogen serum concentrations; other possible endocrinopathies should also be ruled out)

» Fibroid tumors of the uterus or

» Ovarian cyst or enlargement not associated with polycystic ovarian disease
(risk of further enlargement)

» Thrombophlebitis, active
(increased risk of arterial thromboembolism due to elevations in serum estrogen concentrations)

For males only

» Prostatic carcinoma or other androgen-dependent neoplasm
(may be exacerbated by hCG-induced increases in testosterone serum concentrations)

Risk-benefit should be considered when the following medical problems exist:

Asthma or
Cardiac disease or
Epilepsy or
Migraine or
Renal disease
(human chorionic gonadotropin should be used with caution in patients with these conditions because they may be exacerbated by androgen-induced fluid retention)

For induction of ovulation

» Polycystic ovarian disease
(an exaggerated response to hCG may occur; lower dosage may be required)

Patient monitoring

The following may be especially important in patient monitoring (other tests may be warranted in some patients, depending on condition; » = major clinical significance):

For induction of ovulation

» Estradiol
(measurement of serum concentrations is recommended as needed, continuing through the day of chorionic gonadotropin administration; recommended to determine optimal dose and to lessen the risk of ovarian hyperstimulation)

» Ultrasound examination
(recommended prior to chorionic gonadotropin therapy to provide information on the number and size of mature follicles, to follow follicular development, and to lessen the risk of ovarian hyperstimulation syndrome and multiple gestation)

Daily basal body temperature
(can be used in ovulation induction to determine if ovulation has occurred; if basal body temperature following a treatment cycle is biphasic and is not followed by menses, a pregnancy test is recommended)

Progesterone
(measurement of serum concentrations can be performed after therapy to detect luteinized ovarian follicles)

For treatment of male infertility (hypogonadism)

Testosterone
(measurement of baseline serum concentrations recommended before and after chorionic gonadotropin administration to rule out other causes and evaluate success of treatment; should increase after chorionic gonadotropin therapy)

Sperm count and determinations of sperm motility
(to evaluate success of treatment)

For diagnosis of male hypogonadism (delayed puberty)

Testosterone
(measurement of baseline and post-treatment serum concentrations recommended prior to and 1 day following the course; should double if testes are normal)

Side/Adverse Effects

Note: Use of chorionic gonadotropin in conjunction with other ovulation-inducing agents is associated with an increased risk of thromboembolic events, possibly due to increased serum estrogen concentrations.

The following side/adverse effects have been selected on the basis of their potential clinical significance (possible signs and symptoms in parentheses where appropriate)—not necessarily inclusive:

Those indicating need for medical attention

Incidence more frequent

For induction of ovulation only

Ovarian cysts or mild to moderate, uncomplicated ovarian enlargement (mild bloating, stomach or pelvic pain)

Note: Symptoms of *ovarian cysts or enlargement* are usually mild to moderate and abate within 2 or 3 weeks.

Incidence less frequent or rare

For induction of ovulation only

Severe ovarian hyperstimulation syndrome (severe abdominal or stomach pain; feeling of indigestion; moderate to severe bloating; decreased amount of urine; continuing or severe nausea, vomiting, or diarrhea; severe pelvic pain; rapid weight gain; shortness of breath; swelling of lower legs); ***peripheral edema*** (swelling of feet or lower legs; rapid weight gain)

Note: *Ovarian hyperstimulation syndrome (OHS)* may occur in patients treated with hCG for ovulation induction. OHS may often occur 7 to 10 days after ovulation or completion of therapy. OHS is usually avoided or short-lived in patients for whom chorionic gonadotropin is withheld. OHS differs from uncomplicated ovarian enlargement and can rapidly progress to cause serious medical problems. With OHS, a marked increase in vascular permeability results in rapid accumulation of fluid in the peritoneal, pleural, and pericardial cavities (third-spacing of fluids). Medical complications ultimately arising from this increased vascular permeability may include hypovolemia, hemoconcentration, electrolyte imbalance, ascites, hemoperitoneum, pleural effusions, hydrothorax, acute pulmonary distress, and thromboembolic events. OHS is more common, more severe, and protracted in patients who conceive.

Incidence less frequent

In treatment of cryptorchidism only

Precocious puberty (acne; enlargement of penis or testes; growth of pubic hair; rapid increase in height)—generally requires discontinuance of chorionic gonadotropin and re-evaluation

Incidence not determined—Observed during clinical practice; estimates of frequency cannot be determined

Arterial thromboembolism (pain in chest, groin, or legs, especially the calves; difficulty breathing; severe, sudden headache; slurred speech; sudden, unexplained shortness of breath; sudden loss of coordination; sudden, severe weakness or numbness in arm or leg; vision changes); ***hypersensitivity reactions including; angioedema*** (large, hive-like swelling on face, eyelids, lips, tongue, throat, hands, legs, feet, sex organs); ***dyspnea*** (shortness of breath; difficult or labored breathing; tightness in chest; wheezing); ***erythema*** (flushing; redness of skin; unusually warm skin); ***shortness of breath; skin rash; urticaria*** (hives or welts; itching; redness of skin; skin rash)

Those indicating need for medical attention only if they continue or are bothersome

Incidence less frequent

Enlargement of breasts; headache; irritability; mental depression (discouragement; feeling sad or empty; irritability; lack of appetite; loss of interest or pleasure; tiredness; trouble concentrating; trouble sleeping); ***pain at injection site; tiredness***

Patient Consultation

As an aid to patient consultation, refer to *Advice for the Patient, Chorionic Gonadotropin (Systemic).*

In providing consultation, consider emphasizing the following selected information (» = major clinical significance):

Before using this medication

» Conditions affecting use, especially:

Hypersensitivity to chorionic gonadotropin

Pregnancy—FDA Pregnancy Category X (Profasi®)

FDA Pregnancy Category C (Novarel™)

Breast-feeding—It is not known if human chorionic gonadotropin is distributed into human milk.

Use in children—Safety and effectiveness in children younger than 4 years of age have not been established. Use of chorionic gonadotropin for treatment of cryptorchidism has resulted in precocious puberty.

Use in the elderly—No information is available on the relationship of age to the effects of human chorionic gonadotropin in geriatric patients.

Other medical problems, especially:

For induction of ovulation—Abnormal vaginal bleeding, uterine fibroids, ovarian cyst or enlargement, polycystic ovarian disease, or thrombophlebitis

For treatment of male hypogonadism—Precocious puberty, prostatic carcinoma or other androgen-dependent neoplasm

Proper use of this medication

» Proper dosing

Precautions while using this medication

» Importance of close monitoring by physician

» May take a long time to work; importance of continuing treatment

For induction of ovulation:

» Importance of following physician's instructions for recording of basal body temperature and timing of intercourse, when recommended by physician

Side/adverse effects

Signs of potential side effects, especially arterial thromboembolism, hypersensitivity reactions, peripheral edema, ovarian enlargement, cysts, or hyperstimulation syndrome (for ovulation induction), and precocious puberty (for treatment of cryptorchidism)

General Dosing Information

Patients receiving chorionic gonadotropin should be under supervision of a physician experienced in the treatment of gynecologic or endocrine disorders.

For induction of ovulation

Dosage varies considerably and must be adjusted to meet the individual requirements of each patient, on the basis of clinical response.

Conception should be attempted within 48 hours of ovulation. It is recommended that the couple have intercourse or insemination performed daily or every other day beginning the day after chorionic gonadotropin is administered until ovulation is thought to have occurred.

If ovulation does not occur after any cycle of therapy, the therapeutic regimen employed should be re-evaluated. After 3 cycles of non-ovulatory menses, the appropriateness of continuing the use of chorionic gonadotropin for ovulation induction should be reconsidered.

For corpus luteum insufficiency

Treatment must begin in the cycle of conception and not after the first missed menses.

Administration of chorionic gonadotropin should continue until hormone production is taken over by the placenta after 7 to 10 weeks gestation.

For treatment of adverse effects

Ovarian enlargement or ovarian cyst formation

- Discontinuing therapy until ovarian size has returned to baseline. Chorionic gonadotropin should also be withheld for that cycle.
- Prohibiting intercourse until ovarian size has returned to baseline to prevent cyst rupture.
- Reducing dosage in next course of therapy.

Ovarian hyperstimulation syndrome (OHS)

Acute phase

- Discontinuing therapy. Chorionic gonadotropin should also be withheld for that cycle.
- Prohibiting intercourse until ovarian size has returned to baseline to prevent cyst rupture.
- Most cases of OHS will spontaneously resolve when menses begins. In selected cases, hospitalization of the patient with bed rest may be necessary.
- Utilizing therapy to prevent hemoconcentration and minimize risk of thromboembolism and renal injury.
- Correcting (cautiously) electrolyte imbalance while maintaining acceptable intravascular volume; in the acute phase, intravascular volume deficit cannot be completely corrected without increasing third space fluid volume.
- Monitoring fluid intake and output, body weight, hematocrit, serum and urine electrolytes, urine specific gravity, blood urea nitrogen (BUN), creatinine, and abdominal girth daily or as often as required.
- Monitoring serum potassium concentrations for development of hyperkalemia.
- Limiting performance of pelvic examinations since they may result in rupture of ovarian cysts and hemoperitoneum.
- Administering intravenous fluids, electrolytes, and human serum albumin, as needed to maintain adequate urine output and to avoid hemoconcentration.
- Administering analgesics as needed.
- Avoiding diuretic use since it reduces intravascular volume further.

- Removing ascitic, pleural, or pericardial fluid *only* if it is imperative for relief of symptoms such as respiratory distress or cardiac tamponade; to do so may increase risk of injury to the ovary.
- In patients who require surgery to control bleeding from ovarian cyst rupture, employing surgical measures that also maximally conserve ovarian tissue.

Intermediate phase
- Once patient is stabilized, minimizing third spacing of fluids by cautiously replacing potassium, sodium, and fluids as required, based on monitoring of serum electrolyte concentrations.
- Avoiding diuretic use.

Resolution phase
- The third space fluid shifts to intravascular compartment, resulting in decreased hematocrit value and increased urinary output.
- Peripheral and/or pulmonary edema may result if third space fluid volume mobilized exceeds renal output.
- Administering diuretics when required, to manage pulmonary edema.

Parenteral Dosage Forms

Note: Bracketed uses in the *Dosage Forms* section refer to categories of use and/or indications that are not included in U.S. product labeling.

CHORIONIC GONADOTROPIN FOR INJECTION USP

Usual adult dose

Hypogonadotropic hypogonadism in males—

Intramuscular, 1000 to 4000 Units two to three times a week for several weeks to months; may be continued indefinitely as long as a response occurs.

For induction of spermatogenesis in infertility, treatment is usually continued for 6 months or longer. If sperm counts are still not adequate (>5 million per mL), menotropins or urofollitropin may be added to the regimen. It may be necessary to continue a combined regimen for up to 12 additional months.

[Corpus luteum insufficiency][1]—

Intramuscular, 1500 Units (average; dosage will vary depending upon patient) every other day from the day of ovulation until the time of expected menses or confirmed pregnancy. After pregnancy is confirmed, this dose may be continued for up to 10 weeks gestation.

Induction of ovulation or
Assisted reproductive technologies—

Intramuscular, 5000 to 10,000 Units one day following the last dose of menotropins or urofollitropin or five to nine days following the last dose of clomiphene.

Note: If the ovaries are abnormally enlarged or the serum estradiol concentration is excessively elevated on the last day of menotropins or urofollitropin therapy, chorionic gonadotropin should not be given for that cycle.

Dosage varies considerably and must be adjusted to meet the individual requirements of each patient, on the basis of clinical response.

Usual pediatric dose

Prepubertal cryptorchidism—

Intramuscular, 1000 to 5000 Units two to three times a week for a maximum of 10 doses, discontinuing when the desired response is achieved.

Note: Treatment with more than 10 doses is not recommended if progressive descent does not occur.

Several dosage schedules have been used; dosage will vary depending on the degree of sexual development already present.

[Diagnostic aid (hypogonadism) in males][1]—

Intramuscular, 2000 Units once a day for three days.

Strength(s) usually available

U.S.—

5000 Units (Rx) [*Chorex;* GENERIC].

10,000 Units (Rx) [*Chorex; Novarel* (benzyl alcohol); *Pregnyl* (benzyl alcohol); *Profasi* (benzyl alcohol); GENERIC].

Canada—

10,000 Units (Rx) [*Pregnyl* (benzyl alcohol); *Profasi HP* (benzyl alcohol)].

Packaging and storage

Store between 15 and 30 °C (59 and 86 °F), unless otherwise specified by manufacturer.

Preparation of dosage form

Using standard aseptic technique, add 1 to 10 mL of diluent provided to each vial, depending upon manufacturer labeling.

Stability

Reconstituted solution is stable in the refrigerator for 30 days or 60 days; unless otherwise specified by manufacturer

[1]Not included in Canadian product labeling.

Revised: 01/21/2004

CHROMIC CHLORIDE—See *Chromium Supplements (Systemic)*

CHROMIUM—See *Chromium Supplements (Systemic)*

CICLOPIROX Topical

VA CLASSIFICATION (Primary): DE102

Commonly used brand name(s): *Loprox; Penlac Nail Lacquer.*

Note: For a listing of dosage forms and brand names by country availability, see *Dosage Forms* section(s).

Category

Antifungal (topical)

Note: Ciclopirox is a broad-spectrum antifungal, which has an antifungal spectrum similar to that of the imidazoles.

Indications

Note: Bracketed information in the *Indications* section refers to uses that are not included in U.S. product labeling.

Accepted

Candidiasis, cutaneous (treatment)—Ciclopirox is indicated as a primary agent in the topical treatment of cutaneous candidiasis (moniliasis) caused by *Candida albicans (Monilia albicans).*

Tinea corporis (treatment)
Tinea cruris (treatment) or
Tinea pedis (treatment)—Ciclopirox cream or lotion is indicated as a primary agent in the topical treatment of tinea corporis (ringworm of the body), tinea cruris (ringworm of the groin; jock itch), or tinea pedis (ringworm of the foot; athlete's foot) caused by *Trichophyton rubrum, T. mentagrophytes, Epidermophyton floccosum (Acrothesium floccosum),* and *Microsporum canis.* Ciclopirox gel is indicated as a primary agent in the topical treatment of tinea pedis or tinea corporis caused by *Trichophyton rubrum, Trichophyton mentagrophytes, or Epidermophyton floccosum.*

Tinea versicolor (treatment)—Ciclopirox is indicated as a primary agent in the topical treatment of tinea versicolor (pityriasis versicolor; "sun fungus") caused by *Pityrosporon orbiculare (Malassezia furfur).*

Seborrheic dermatitis (treatment)—Ciclopirox gel and shampoo are indicated for the topical treatment of seborrheic dermatitis of the scalp.

Onychomycosis (treatment)—Ciclopirox topical solution is indicated as a primary agent in the topical treatment of mild to moderate onychomycosis of the nails (without lunula involvement) caused by *Trichophyton rubrum.*

Not all species or strains of a particular organism may be susceptible to ciclopirox.

Pharmacology/Pharmacokinetics

Physicochemical characteristics

Molecular weight—
Ciclopirox: 207.27.
Ciclopirox olamine: 268.36.

pH—Ciclopirox cream and lotion have a pH of 7.

Mechanism of action/Effect

Exact mechanism unknown; fungicidal *in vitro* against *Trichophyton rubrum, T. mentagrophytes, Epidermophyton floccosum (Acrothesium floccosum), Microsporum canis, Candida albicans (Monilia albicans), Malassezia furfur (Pityrosporum spp.), P. ovale,* and *P. orbiculare;* may inhibit transport of certain essential substrates into fungal cells; may also interfere with the synthesis of proteins, RNA, and DNA in growing fungal cells; alterations in cell permeability, osmotic fragility, and endogenous respiration are affected only at high concentrations of ciclopirox.

Absorption

1% Solution in polyethylene glycol 400—Rapid, but minimal; 1.3% of dose absorbed following topical application to 750 cm ^{2} of skin on the back, followed by occlusion for 6 hours.

0.77% Cream—In penetration studies of human cadaveric skin from the back, 0.8 to 1.6% of the dose was present in the stratum corneum 1.5 to 6 hours following application. In addition, the levels in the dermis were still 10 to 15 times the minimum inhibitory concentrations (MICs).

0.77% Lotion—Penetration studies have indicated that the penetration of the cream and the lotion are equivalent.

Ciclopirox olamine also penetrates into hair and through the epidermis and hair follicles into sebaceous glands and dermis.

8% Solution—Mean absorption of ciclopirox after application to nails of all twenty digits and adjacent 5 millimeters of skin once daily for 6 months in patients with dermatophytic onychomycoses was $<$ 5 % of the applied dose.

Protein binding

Very high (94-97%).

Biotransformation

The main metabolic pathway of absorbed ciclopirox is glucuronidation.

Half-life

1% Solution in polyethylene glycol 400—1.7 hours.

Elimination

1% Solution in polyethylene glycol 400—
- Renal: Absorbed portion rapidly and almost completely excreted in urine; only 0.01% of dose remains in urine 2 days following topical application.
- Fecal: Negligible.

1% Shampoo—
- Renal: Less than 0.5% of administered dose

Precautions to Consider

Carcinogenicity/Tumorigenicity

A study in female mice given cutaneous doses of ciclopirox twice a week for 50 weeks, followed by a six-month drug-free period, has shown that ciclopirox is not carcinogenic or tumorigenic at the application site.

Mutagenicity

Several studies have shown that ciclopirox is not mutagenic.

Pregnancy/Reproduction

Fertility—Studies in mice, rats, rabbits, and monkeys given ciclopirox by various routes at doses of 10 or more times the topical human dose have not shown that ciclopirox causes impaired fertility.

Pregnancy—Ciclopirox should be used during pregnancy only if clearly needed.

Adequate and well-controlled studies in humans have not been done.

Studies in rats have shown that ciclopirox crosses the placenta in very small amounts. Studies in mice, rats, rabbits, and monkeys given ciclopirox by various routes at doses of 10 or more times the topical human dose have not shown that ciclopirox causes adverse effects in the fetus.

FDA Pregnancy Category B.

Breast-feeding

It is not known whether ciclopirox is distributed into breast milk. However, problems in humans have not been documented. Because many drugs are distributed in human milk, caution should be exercised when ciclopirox is administered to a nursing woman.

Pediatrics

Cream and lotion—Appropriate studies on the relationship of age to the effects of ciclopirox lotion and cream have not been performed in infants and children up to 10 years of age.

Gel and shampoo—Although seborrheic dermatitis may appear at puberty, no clinical studies have been done with ciclopirox gel or shampoo in patients younger than 16 years of age.

Solution (8%)—Appropriate studies on the relationship of age to the effects of ciclopirox solution have not been performed in children up to 18 years of age.

Geriatrics

Appropriate studies on the relationship of age to the effects of ciclopirox have not been performed in the geriatric population. However, no geriatrics-specific problems have been documented to date, but greater sensitivity to adverse effects in some older individuals cannot be ruled out.

Medical considerations/Contraindications

The medical considerations/contraindications included have been selected on the basis of their potential clinical significance (reasons given in parentheses where appropriate)—not necessarily inclusive (» = major clinical significance).

Except under special circumstances, this medication should not be used when the following medical problem exists:

» Hypersensitivity to ciclopirox or any of its components

Side/Adverse Effects

The following side/adverse effects have been selected on the basis of their potential clinical significance (possible signs and symptoms in parentheses where appropriate)—not necessarily inclusive:

Those indicating need for medical attention

Incidence less frequent—in patients treated with ciclopirox shampoo
- ***Ventricular tachycardia*** (fainting; fast, pounding, or irregular heartbeat or pulse; palpitations)

Incidence rare
- ***Local irritation*** (burning, itching, redness, swelling, or other signs of irritation not present before therapy)

Those indicating need for medical attention only if thy continue or are bothersome

Incidence less frequent—in patients treated with ciclopirox shampoo
- ***Headache; pruritus*** (itching skin or scalp); ***rash; seborrhea*** (dandruff; oily skin); ***skin disorder***

Patient Consultation

As an aid to patient consultation, refer to *Advice for the Patient, Ciclopirox (Topical)*.

In providing consultation, consider emphasizing the following selected information (» = major clinical significance):

Before using this medication

» Conditions affecting use, especially:
- Hypersensitivity to ciclopirox or any of its components

Proper use of this medication

Applying sufficient medication to cover affected and surrounding areas, and rubbing in gently

Applying shampoo to hair and scalp and following doctor's instructions for proper use

Proper administration technique for topical solution

» Avoiding contact with the eyes and mucous membranes

» Not applying occlusive dressing over this medication unless directed to do so by physician

» Compliance with full course of therapy; fungal infections may require prolonged therapy

» Proper dosing

Missed dose: Applying as soon as possible; not applying if almost time for next dose

» Proper storage

Precautions while using this medication

Checking with physician if no improvement within 2 to 4 weeks

» Avoiding contact with eyes and mucous membranes; rinsing thoroughly with water if contact occurs

» Informing physician if area of application shows signs of increased irritation (redness, itching, burning, blistering, swelling, or oozing) indicative of possible allergic reaction.

Importance of using medication for full treatment time even though symptoms may have improved

Not using this medication for any disorder other than that for which it is prescribed

» Using hygienic measures to cure infection and prevent reinfection:

For tinea cruris:
- Avoiding underwear that is tight-fitting or made from synthetic materials; wearing loose-fitting cotton underwear instead
- Using a bland, absorbent powder or an antifungal powder on the skin; using the powder between administration times for ciclopirox

For tinea pedis:
- Carefully drying feet, especially between toes, after bathing
- Avoiding socks made from wool or synthetic materials; wearing clean, cotton socks and changing them daily or more often if feet perspire excessively
- Wearing sandals or well-ventilated shoes
- Using a bland, absorbent powder or an antifungal powder between toes, on feet, and in socks and shoes liberally once or twice daily; using the powder between administration times for ciclopirox

Side/adverse effects

Signs of potential side effects, especially local irritation or ventricular tachycardia (in patients treated with ciclopirox shampoo)

General Dosing Information

Use of topical antifungals may lead to skin sensitization, resulting in hypersensitivity reactions with subsequent topical use of the medication.

To reduce the possibility of recurrence, *Candida* infections, tinea cruris, tinea corporis, and tinea versicolor should be treated for at least 2 weeks to 1 month; tinea pedis should be treated for at least 1 month or longer. If no improvement is observed after 4 weeks while using the cream, lotion, gel, or shampoo, the diagnosis may need to be redetermined.

When this medication is used in the treatment of candidiasis, occlusive dressings should be avoided, since they provide conditions that favor growth of yeast and release of its irritating endotoxin.

When using the ciclopirox cream, lotion, or gel, the medication should be gently massaged into the affected and surrounding skin or scalp areas. Clinical improvement with relief of pruritus and other symptoms usually occurs within the first week of treatment. Patients with tinea versicolor usually exhibit clinical and mycological clearing after two weeks of treatment. Patients with seborrheic dermatitis of the scalp usually show clinical improvement within the first week, and continuing resolution of signs and symptoms through the fourth week of treatment.

When using ciclopirox shampoo for seborrheic dermatitis, medicated shampoo should be applied to wet hair and lathered into scalp and hair. Shampoo should remain on hair and scalp for 3 minutes and rinsed off. Treatment should be repeated twice per week for 4 weeks, with a minimum of 3 days between applications.

When using the ciclopirox topical solution, apply evenly with applicator brush. When possible, nail lacquer should be also be applied to the underside of the nail and to the skin beneath it. Allow the solution to dry, which should take approximately 30 seconds. Loose nail material should be filed down and trimmed as required every 7 days after the solution is removed with alcohol. Daily applications should be made over the previous coat and removed with alcohol every 7 days. This cycle should be repeated throughout the duration of therapy. Removal of the unattached, infected nail, trimming of the onycholytic nail, and filing of excess horny material should be performed by a health care professional, as frequently as monthly. A completely clear or almost clear toenail may not be achieved with use of this medication.

There is no relevant clinical experience with patients who have a history of immunosuppression (e.g., extensive, persistent, or unusual distribution of dermatomycoses, recent or recurring herpes zoster, or persistent herpes simplex), who are immunocompromised (e.g., HIV-infected patients and transplant patients), or who have a diabetic neuropathy.

Sensitivity reaction

If a reaction suggesting sensitivity or irritation should occur with use of ciclopirox, treatment should be discontinued and appropriate therapy instituted.

Topical Dosage Forms

CICLOPIROX OLAMINE CREAM USP

Usual adult and adolescent dose

Antifungal—

Topical, to the skin and surrounding areas, two times a day, morning and evening.

Usual pediatric dose

Antifungal—

Infants and children up to 10 years of age: Safety and efficacy have not been established.

Children 10 years of age and over: See *Usual adult and adolescent dose.*

Strength(s) usually available

U.S.—

0.77% (Rx) [*Loprox*].

Canada—

1% (Rx) [*Loprox*].

Packaging and storage

Store between 15 and 30 °C (59 and 86 °F).

Auxiliary labeling

- For external use only.
- Continue medicine for full time of treatment.

CICLOPIROX OLAMINE LOTION

Usual adult and adolescent dose

See *Ciclopirox Olamine Cream USP.*

Usual pediatric dose

See *Ciclopirox Olamine Cream USP.*

Strength(s) usually available

U.S.—

0.77% (Rx) [*Loprox*].

Canada—

1% (Rx) [*Loprox*].

Packaging and storage

Store between 15 and 30 °C (59 and 86 °F). Protect from freezing.

Auxiliary labeling

- Shake well.
- For external use only.
- Continue medicine for full time of treatment.

CICLOPIROX GEL

Usual adult and adolescent dose

Antifungal—

Topical, to the skin and surrounding areas, two times a day, morning and evening, immediately after cleaning or washing the areas to be treated.

For seborrheic dermatitis of scalp—

Topical, to affected scalp areas, two times a day, morning and evening.

Usual pediatric dose

Children up to 16 years of age—Safety and efficacy have not been established

Strength(s) usually available

U.S.—

0.77% (Rx) [*Loprox*].

Packaging and storage

Store between 15 and 30 °C (59 and 86 °F). Protect from freezing.

Auxiliary labeling

- For external use only.
- Continue medicine for full time of treatment.

CICLOPIROX SHAMPOO

Usual adult dose

Seborrheic dermatitis of the scalp (treatment)—

Topical, 5 mL to the scalp (10 mL for long hair) twice per week for 4 weeks, with a minimum of 3 days between applications.

Usual pediatric dose

Safety and efficacy have not been established in patients less than 16 years of age.

Usual geriatric dose

See *Usual adult dose.*

Strength(s) usually available

U.S.—

1% [*Loprox* (purified water; sodium laureth sulfate; disodium laureth sulfosuccinate; sodium chloride; laureth-2)].

Packaging and storage

Store between 15 and 30°C (59 and 86 °F).

Auxiliary labeling

- Keep out of reach of children
- External use only
- Avoid contact in or around eyes
- You should use this medication exactly as prescribed. Do not skip or discontinue unless directed.

Additional information

Once opened, shampoo may be used for up to 8 weeks.
Ciclopirox shampoo is not for ophthalmic, oral, or intravaginal use.
If contact with eyes occurs, rinse thoroughly with water.

CICLOPIROX TOPICAL SOLUTION

Usual adult dose

Antifungal—

Topical, to all affected nails and under the surface nail plate when it is free of the nail bed, once daily preferably at bedtime, or eight hours before washing. Apply with applicator brush. Patients should file away loose nail material and trim nails as required every 7 days after the solution is removed with alcohol. Daily applications should be made over the previous coat and removed with alcohol every 7 days. This cycle should be repeated throughout the duration of therapy.

Usual pediatric dose

Safety and efficacy have not been established.

Strength(s) usually available

U.S.—

8% (Rx) [*Penlac Nail Lacquer*].

Packaging and storage

Store between 15 and 30 °C (59 and 86 °F). Protect from light and from freezing.

Auxiliary labeling

- For external use only.
- Continue medicine for full time of treatment.
- Protect from light.
- Flammable—Keep away from heat and flame.

Revised: 11/02/2004

CIDOFOVIR Systemic†

VA CLASSIFICATION (Primary): AM890

Commonly used brand name(s): *Vistide*.

Note: For a listing of dosage forms and brand names by country availability, see *Dosage Forms* section(s).

†Not commercially available in Canada.

Category

Antiviral (systemic).

Indications

General Considerations

All cidofovir-resistant cytomegalovirus (CMV) isolates have been found to be resistant to ganciclovir, but remained susceptible to foscarnet.

Accepted

Cytomegalovirus retinitis (treatment)—Cidofovir is indicated, in combination with probenecid, for the treatment of cytomegalovirus (CMV) retinitis in patients with acquired immunodeficiency syndrome. Safety and efficacy have not been established for the treatment of CMV disease in non-HIV infected people, other CMV infections, or congenital or neonatal CMV disease.

Acceptance not established

There are insufficient data regarding efficacy and dosing to accept the use of cidofovir for the *treatment of systemic adenovirus infections in post-transplantation patients*.

Pharmacology/Pharmacokinetics

Physicochemical characteristics

Molecular weight—
- Cidofovir: 315.22.
- Cidofovir anhydrous: 279.19.

Mechanism of action/Effect

Cidofovir diphosphate, the active intracellular metabolite of cidofovir, suppresses cytomegalovirus (CMV) replication by selectively inhibiting viral DNA polymerase. Cidofovir diphosphate inhibits herpesvirus polymerases at concentrations that are 8- to 600-fold lower than those needed to inhibit the human cellular polymerases alpha, beta, and gamma. Reduction in the rate of viral DNA synthesis is due to incorporation of cidofovir into the growing viral DNA chain.

Distribution

Volume of distribution is 537 mL per kg (mL/kg) without concurrent probenecid administration and 410 mL/kg with concurrent probenecid administration.

Concentrations of cidofovir were undetectable 15 minutes after the end of a 1-hour infusion in one patient who had a corresponding serum concentration of 8.7 mcg per mL (mcg/mL).

Protein binding

Low (less than 6%).

Time to peak concentration

End of infusion.

Peak serum concentration

With concurrent probenecid administration—
- 3 mg per kg of body weight (mg/kg): 9.8 mcg/mL.
- 5 mg/kg: 19.6 mcg/mL.

Without concurrent probenecid administration—
- 3 mg/kg: 7.3 mcg/mL.
- 5 mg/kg: 11.5 mcg/mL.

Elimination

Renal (without concurrent probenecid administration)—Approximately 80 to 100% of an administered cidofovir dose was recovered unchanged in the urine within 24 hours.

Renal (with concurrent probenecid administration)—Approximately 70 to 85% of an administered cidofovir dose was recovered unchanged in the urine within 24 hours. The renal clearance of cidofovir was reduced to that of creatinine clearance, suggesting that probenecid blocks active renal tubular secretion of cidofovir.

In dialysis—The effect of hemodialysis on the pharmacokinetics of cidofovir is not known.

Precautions to Consider

Carcinogenicity

Cidofovir should be considered a carcinogen in rats and a potential carcinogen in humans.

Chronic, two-year carcinogenicity studies in rats and mice have not been done. However, a 26-week toxicology study was done in rats evaluating once weekly subscapular subcutaneous injections of cidofovir. The study was terminated at 19 weeks because palpable mammary adenocarcinomas were detected in females after only six doses. These masses developed at doses as low as 0.6 mg per kg (mg/kg) per week, which is equivalent to 0.04 times the human systemic exposure at the recommended cidofovir dose based on area under the plasma concentration-time curve (AUC) comparisons.

There was also a significant increase in mammary adenocarcinomas in female rats and a significant incidence of Zymbal's gland carcinomas in male and female rats administered 15 mg/kg of cidofovir once weekly; this was not seen at the 0.6 or 3 mg/kg doses. The 15 mg/kg dose is equivalent to 1.1 times the human systemic exposure at the recommended dose of cidofovir, based on AUC.

Tumorigenicity

No tumors were detected in cynomologus monkeys who received intravenous cidofovir, alone and in conjunction with concomitant oral probenecid, once a week for 52 weeks. This dose is equivalent to approximately 0.7 times the human systemic exposure. However, due to the small number of animals and the short duration of treatment, this study was not designed as a carcinogenicity study.

Mutagenicity

There was no mutagenic response observed in microbial mutagenicity assays involving *Salmonella typhimurium* (Ames) and *Escherichia coli* in the presence and absence of metabolic activation. There was an increase in micronucleated polychromatic erythrocytes *in vivo* seen in mice receiving ≥ 2000 mg/kg, a dose approximately 65-times higher than the maximum recommended clincial dose of cidofovir, based on body surface area estimations. Cidofovir induced chromosomal aberrations in human peripheral blood lymphocytes *in vitro* without metabolic activation. At the four doses tested, the percentage of damaged metaphases and the number of aberrations per cell increased in a concentration-dependent manner.

Pregnancy/Reproduction

Fertility—Cidofovir was shown to cause inhibition of spermatogenesis in rats and monkeys. However, there were no reported adverse effects on fertility or reproduction in male rats administered once-weekly intravenous injections for thirteen consecutive weeks at doses up to 15 mg/kg per week; this is equivalent to 1.1 times the recommended human dose based on AUC comparisons. Female rats dosed intravenously at 1.2 mg/kg per week (equivalent to 0.09 times the recommended human dose based on AUC) or higher for up to six weeks prior to mating, and for two weeks after mating, had decreased litter size and live births per litter, as well as an increased incidence of early resorptions per litter. Peri- and postnatal development studies in which female rats were administered subcutaneous cidofovir at doses up to 1 mg/kg per day from day 7 of gestation through day 21 postpartum (approximately five weeks) resulted in no adverse effects on viability, growth, behavior, sexual maturation, or reproductive capacity in the offspring.

Pregnancy—Adequate and well-controlled studies in humans have not been done. Cidofovir should be administered only if the potential benefit justifies the potential risk to the fetus.

Cidofovir was found to be embryotoxic (reduced fetal body weight) in rats administered 1.5 mg/kg per day and in rabbits given 1 mg/kg per day during the period of organogenesis; these doses were also maternotoxic. There was also an increased incidence of fetal external soft tissue and skeletal anomalies, such as meningocele, short snout, and short maxillary bones, seen in rabbits administered 1 mg/kg per day, which was also maternally toxic. The no-observable-effect levels for embryotoxicity in rats (0.5 mg/kg per day) and in rabbits (0.25 mg/kg per day) were approximately 0.04 and 0.05 times the human maintenance dose, respectively, based on AUC.

FDA Pregnancy Category C.

Breast-feeding

It is not known whether cidofovir is distributed into breast milk. However, it is recommended that HIV-infected women not breast-feed their infants to avoid postnatal transmission of HIV to a child who may not be infected.

Pediatrics

No information is available on the relationship of age to the effects of cidofovir in pediatric patients. Safety and efficacy have not been established. However, cidofovir should be used with caution in children with HIV infection because of the potential risk of long-term carcinogenicity and reproductive toxicity.

Geriatrics

No studies have been done assessing the safety and efficacy of cidofovir in patients over the age of 60. However, elderly patients are more likely to have age-related renal function impairment, which may require adjustment of dosage in patients receiving cidofovir.

Drug interactions and/or related problems

The following drug interactions and/or related problems have been selected on the basis of their potential clinical significance (possible mechanism in parentheses where appropriate)—not necessarily inclusive (» = major clinical significance):

Note: Combinations containing any of the following medications, depending on the amount present, may also interact with this medication.

» Nephrotoxic medications (see *Appendix II*)
(because cidofovir has been reported to be associated with severe renal function impairment, concurrent use with other nephrotoxic medications, such as aminoglycosides, amphotericin B, foscarnet, nonsteroidal anti-inflammatory drugs, and pentamidine, may increase the risk of nephrotoxicity and is contraindicated; it is recommended that patients undergo at least a 7-day washout period before receiving cidofovir)

» Probenecid
(probenecid must be administered concurrently with cidofovir; probenecid is known to interact with the metabolism or renal tubular excretion of many medications, such as acetaminophen, acyclovir, aminosalicylic acid, angiotensin-converting enzyme inhibitors, barbiturates, benzodiazepines, bumetanide, clofibrate, famotidine, furosemide, methotrexate, nonsteroidal anti-inflammatory agents, theophylline, and zidovudine; these medications should be used with caution when used concurrently with probenecid)

Zidovudine
(concurrent use with cidofovir, without probenecid, showed no evidence of an effect on the pharmacokinetics of zidovudine)

Laboratory value alterations

The following have been selected on the basis of their potential clinical significance (possible effect in parentheses where appropriate)—not necessarily inclusive (» = major clinical significance).

With physiology/laboratory test values
Creatinine, serum and
Protein, urine
(may be increased)
Bicarbonate, serum and
Neutrophils
(may be decreased)

Medical considerations/Contraindications

The medical considerations/contraindications included have been selected on the basis of their potential clinical significance (reasons given in parentheses where appropriate)—not necessarily inclusive (» = major clinical significance).

Except under special circumstances, this medication should not be used when the following medical problem exists:

» Hypersensitivity to cidofovir or probenecid

Risk-benefit should be considered when the following medical problem exists:

» Renal function impairment
(because cidofovir has been reported to be associated with severe renal function impairment, cidofovir is contraindicated in patients with a serum creatinine > 1.5 mL per dL, a creatinine clearance ≤ 55 mL per minute [0.92 mL per second], or a urine protein ≥ 100 mg per dL [equivalent to ≥ 2+ proteinuria])

Patient monitoring

The following may be especially important in patient monitoring (other tests may be warranted in some patients, depending on condition; » = major clinical significance):

» Creatinine, serum and
» Protein, urine and
» White blood cell count with differential
(because cidofovir has been reported to cause severe renal function impairment and cause neutropenia, these laboratory parameters should be monitored prior to each dose of cidofovir)

» Intraocular pressure
» Visual acuity
(because cidofovir can cause ocular hypotony, especially in patients with preexisting diabetes, intraocular pressure and visual acuity should be monitored periodically)

Side/Adverse Effects

Note: Nephrotoxicity, the major dose-limiting toxicity of cidofovir therapy, was manifested as > 1+ proteinuria, serum creatinine concentration ≥ 0.4 mg per dL, or a decrease in creatinine clearance to ≤ 55 mL per min (0.92 mL per second) in 53% of patients receiving a maintenance dose of 5 mg per kg of body weight every other week. Proteinuria may be an early indicator of cidofovir-related nephrotoxicity and continued administration may lead to additional proximal tubular cell injury, resulting in glycosuria, decreases in serum phosphate, uric acid, and bicarbonate, and elevations in serum creatinine. Patients with these side effects and meeting a criteria of Fanconi's syndrome have been reported. There have also been reports of severe renal function impairment associated with cidofovir use. To help reduce the risk of nephrotoxicity, patients must be pre-hydrated with at least 1 liter of 0.9% sodium chloride solution and probenecid must be administered at proper times. Dosage adjustment or discontinuation is necessary when changes in renal function occur during therapy.

Neutropenia (≤ 500 cells/mm^3) occurred in 20% of patients receiving the 5 mg per kg of body weight maintenance dose in clinical trials. Granulocyte colony stimulating factor was used in 34% of patients.

Ocular hypotony (≥ 50% change from baseline) was reported in 5 of 42 patients receiving the 5 mg per kg of body weight maintenance dose in clinical studies. Hypotony was reported in one patient with concomitant diabetes mellitus; the risk of ocular hypotony may be increased in patients with pre-existing diabetes.

Two percent of study patients were diagnosed with Fanconi's syndrome, manifested by multiple abnormalities of proximal tubule function. Decreases in serum bicarbonate to ≤ 16 milliequivalents per liter associated with evidence of renal tubular damage occurred in approximately 9% of patients.

The following side/adverse effects have been selected on the basis of their potential clinical significance (possible signs and symptoms in parentheses where appropriate)—not necessarily inclusive:

Those indicating need for medical attention

Incidence more frequent
Nephrotoxicity (decreased urination; increased thirst and urination); ***neutropenia*** (fever, chills, or sore throat)

Incidence less frequent
Fever

Incidence rare
Ocular hypotony (decreased vision or any change in vision)

Those indicating need for medical attention only if they continue or are bothersome

Incidence more frequent
Gastrointestinal effects (diarrhea; loss of appetite; nausea; vomiting); ***headache***

Incidence less frequent
Asthenia (generalized weakness; loss of strength)

Overdose

Overdosage with cidofovir has not been reported. However, probenecid may reduce potential nephrotoxicity through reduction of active tubular secretion. Hemodialysis and hydration may reduce plasma cidofovir concentrations.

For more information on the management of overdose or unintentional ingestion, **contact a Poison Control Center** (see *Poison Control Center Listing*).

Patient Consultation

As an aid to patient consultation, refer to *Advice for the Patient, Cidofovir (Systemic)*.

In providing consultation, consider emphasizing the following selected information (» = major clinical significance)

Before using this medication

» Conditions affecting use, especially:
Hypersensitivity to cidofovir or probenecid
Carcinogenicity—Cidofovir is a carcinogen in animals and should be considered a potential carcinogen in humans

Pregnancy—Cidofovir was embryotoxic and maternotoxic in animals; cidofovir should be administered only if the potential benefit justifies the potential risk to the fetus.

Breast-feeding—It is not known whether cidofovir is distributed into breast milk; however, it is recommended that HIV-infected women not breast-feed their infants to avoid postnatal transmission of HIV to a child who may not be infected.

Use in children—Safety and efficacy have not been established; however, cidofovir should be used with caution in HIV-infected children because of the potential risk of long-term carcinogenicity and reproductive toxicity.

Other medications, especially nephrotoxic medications and probenecid

Other medical problems, especially renal function impairment

Proper use of this medication

» Importance of receiving medication for full course of therapy and on a regular schedule

» Proper dosing

Precautions while using this medication

» Regular visits to physician to check blood counts

» Regular visits to ophthalmologist to examine eyes since progression of retinitis and visual loss may occur during cidofovir therapy

Side/adverse effects

Signs of potential side effects, especially, nephrotoxicity, neutropenia, fever, and ocular hypotony

General Dosing Information

Cidofovir must not be administered by intraocular injection. Direct injection may result in significant decreases in intraocular pressure and vision impairment.

Because cidofovir has been reported to be associated with severe renal function impairment, the recommended dosage, frequency, or infusion rate must not be exceeded. Cidofovir must be diluted in 100 mL of 0.9% sodium chloride injection prior to administration. Probenecid and intravenous sodium chloride prehydration must be administered with each cidofovir infusion to minimize potential nephrotoxicity. The dose of cidofovir must be reduced or discontinued if changes in renal function occur during therapy. Serum creatinine and urine protein must be monitored within 48 hours prior to each dose of cidofovir.

The dose of cidofovir must be reduced or discontinued if changes in renal function occur during therapy. For increases in serum creatinine of 0.3 to 0.4 mg per dL (mg/dL) above baseline, the dose of cidofovir must be reduced from 5 mg per kg (mg/kg) to 3 mg/kg. Cidofovir must be discontinued for an increase in serum creatinine of 0.5 mg/dL above baseline or development of 3+ proteinuria. Patients with 2+ proteinuria should be observed carefully; dose reduction or temporary discontinuation of treatment should be considered.

Two grams of probenecid should be administered 3 hours prior to each dose of cidofovir and 1 gram should be administered 2 and 8 hours after the completion of the 1-hour infusion (total 4 grams).

Each dose of cidofovir should be administered with 1 liter of 0.9% sodium chloride injection, infused over 1 to 2 hours immediately before the cidofovir infusion. If the patient can tolerate the fluid load, a second liter of 0.9% sodium chloride injection should be started either at the beginning of the cidofovir infusion or immediately afterwards, over a 1- to 3-hour period.

Ingestion of food before each dose of probenecid may reduce nausea and vomiting associated with probenecid administration. Administration of an antiemetic may also reduce the potential for nausea.

Safety considerations for handling this medication

Due to the mutagenic potential of cidofovir, use of appropriate safety equipment is recommended for the preparation, administration, and disposal of cidofovir. The National Institutes of Health recommends that cidofovir be prepared in a Class II laminar flow biological safety cabinet and that personnel preparing this medication wear surgical gloves and a closed-front surgical-type gown with knit cuffs. If cidofovir contacts the skin, membranes should be washed and flushed thoroughly with water. Excess cidofovir and materials used in the admixture and administration procedures should be placed in a leak-proof, puncture-proof container. High temperature incineration is the recommended method of disposal.

Parenteral Dosage Forms

CIDOFOVIR INJECTION

Usual adult dose

Antiviral—

Induction: Intravenous infusion, 5 mg per kg of body weight, administered continuously over one hour, once a week for two consecutive weeks. Probenecid must be administered with each dose of cidofovir. Two grams of probenecid should be administered three hours prior to each dose of cidofovir and 1 gram should be administered two and eight hours after the completion of the one-hour infusion (total 4 grams).

Maintenance: Intravenous infusion, 5 mg per kg of body weight, administered continuously over one hour, once every two weeks. Probenecid must be administered with each dose of cidofovir. Two grams of probenecid should be administered three hours prior to each dose of cidofovir and 1 gram should be administered two and eight hours after the completion of the one-hour infusion (total 4 grams).

Note: Cidofovir has not been studied in patients with pre-existing renal function impairment. The most appropriate dose of cidofovir for patients with a serum creatinine $>$ 1.5 mg per mL or a creatinine clearance $\leq$ 55 mL per min (mL/min) is not known. However, the following doses (in mg per kg of body weight) are recommended when the benefits of cidofovir exceed the potential risks:

Creatinine clearance (mL/min)	Induction (once weekly for 2 weeks)	Maintenance (once every 2 weeks)
41–55	2 mg per kg	2 mg per kg
30–40	1.5 mg per kg	1.5 mg per kg
20–29	1 mg per kg	1 mg per kg
$\leq$ 19	0.5 mg per kg	0.5 mg per kg

Usual pediatric dose

Safety and efficacy have not been established.

Strength(s) usually available

U.S.—

375 mg per 5 mL (Rx) [*Vistide*].

Packaging and storage

Store at room temperature between 20 and 25 °C (68 and 77 °F).

Preparation of dosage form

The vial should be visually inspected for particulate matter and discoloration prior to administration and discarded if particulate matter or discoloration is observed.

The appropriate volume of cidofovir should be extracted from the vial and the dose transferred to an infusion bag containing 100 mL of 0.9% sodium chloride solution. The entire volume should be infused into the patient at a constant rate over a 1-hour period. It is recommended that a standard infusion pump be used for administration.

Stability

It is recommended that cidofovir admixtures be administered within 24 hours of preparation and that refrigeration or freezer storage not be used to extend this 24-hour limit.

If admixtures are not intended for immediate use, they may be refrigerated (between 2 and 8 °C [36 and 46 °F]) for no more than 24 hours. Refrigerated admixtures should be allowed to equilibrate to room temperature prior to use.

Incompatibilities

Compatibility with Ringer's solution, Lactated Ringer's solution, or bacteriostatic infusion fluids has not been evaluated.

The chemical stability of cidofovir admixtures was determined in polyvinyl chloride composition and ethylene/propylene copolymer composition commercial infusion bags, and in glass bottles.

Note

Great care should be taken to prevent exposure of the skin to cidofovir. The use of gloves is recommended. Any cidofovir that comes in contact with the skin should be washed off thoroughly with soap and water.

Revised: 02/10/2004

CILAZAPRIL—See *Angiotensin-converting Enzyme (ACE) Inhibitors (Systemic)*

CILOSTAZOL Systemic†

VA CLASSIFICATION (Primary/Secondary): BL117/ CV900

Commonly used brand name(s): *Pletal*.

Note: For a listing of dosage forms and brand names by country availability, see *Dosage Forms* section(s).

†Not commercially available in Canada.

Category

Platelet aggregation inhibitor; vasodilator.

Indications

Accepted

Vascular disease, peripheral (treatment)—Cilostazol is indicated to provide symptomatic relief of intermittent claudication as indicated by an increase in the maximal walking distance of patients.

Pharmacology/Pharmacokinetics

Physicochemical characteristics

Chemical Group—a quinolinone derivative

Molecular weight—369.47.

Solubility—Slightly soluble in methanol and ethanol; practically insoluble in water, 0.1 N hydrochloric acid, and 0.1 N sodium hydroxide.

Chemical Name—6-[4-(1-cyclohexyl-1*H*-tetrazol-5-yl)butoxy]-3,4-dihydro-2(1*H*)-quinolinone

Molecular Formula—$C_{20}H_{27}N_5O_2$

Mechanism of action/Effect

Cilostazol and its active metabolites inhibit phosphodiesterase activity and suppress degradation of cyclic adenosine monophosphate (cAMP) resulting in an increase in cAMP in platelets and blood vessels. It reversibly inhibits platelet aggregation induced by various stimuli, including thrombin, adenosine diphosphate (ADP), collagen, arachidonic acid, epinephrine, and shear stress. Cilostazol produces non-homogenous vasodilation, with greater dilation in femoral beds than in vertebral, carotic, or superior mesenteric arteries, but without effect in renal arteries.

Other actions/effects

In one clinical study, plasma triglycerides were reduced by 15% and HDL-cholesterol was increased by approximately 10% after 12 weeks of treatment with cilostazol.

Cardiovascular function is also affected by cilostazol. In animal studies, cilostazol increased heart rate, myocardial contractile force, coronary blood flow, ventricular automaticity, left ventricular contractility and atrioventricular conduction. In humans, dose-proportional heart rate increased were observed at therapeutic doses. Non-dose-related increases in ventricular premature beats and transient ventricular tachycardia were observed in high numbers of cilostazol-treated patients than in those treated with placebo.

Absorption

Cilostazol is absorbed after oral administration. Absorption is increased after a high fat meal: peak concentration (C_{max}) is increased by approximately 90% and the area under the curve (AUC) is increased by 25%.

Protein binding

Very high (95% to 98%), predominantly to albumin.

Biotransformation

Hepatic metabolism of cilostazol is extensive via the cytochrome P-450 enzymes, primarily CYP3A4 and, to a lesser extent, CYP2C19.

Elimination—

11 to 13 hours.

Onset of action

Multiple doses—2 to 4 weeks.

Elimination

Renal (as metabolites)—74%

Feces—20%

In dialysis—Cilostazol is not removed by hemodialysis or peritoneal dialysis due to its high protein binding.

Precautions to Consider

Cross-sensitivity and/or related problems

Carcinogenicity

No evidence of carcinogenic potential was exhibited in animal studies with doses up to 500 mg/kg/day in rats and 1000 mg/kg/day in mice administered for up to 104 weeks. Based on systemic exposure, the maximum doses in mice and rates were less than human exposure at the maximum recommended human dose (MRHD).

Mutagenicity

Although a significant increase in chromosomal aberrations was associated with cilostazol in the *in vitro* Chinese Hamster Ovary Cell assay, negative results were reported in the following assays: bacterial gene mutation, bacterial DNA repair, mammalian cell gene mutation, and mouse *in vivo* bone marrow chromosomal aberration.

Pregnancy/Reproduction

Fertility—Cilostazol had no effect on the fertility of reproductive performance of male and female rats at doses of up to 1000 mg/kg/day. In comparison to systemic exposure (AUC) to unbound cilostazol in humans, this dose was less than 1.5 times the maximum recommended human dose (MHRD) in male rats, and approximately 5 times the MRHD in female rats.

Pregnancy—Adequate and well-controlled studies in humans have not been done.

In developmental toxicity studies in rats, decreased fetal weights and increased in the incidence rates of developmental abnormalities of the skeletal, cardiovascular, and renal systems (which consisted of 14th rib and retarded ossification; ventricular septal, aortic arch and subclavian artery anomalies; and dilation of the renal pelvis) was associated with oral administration of cilostazol at 5 times the MRHD. Increased in the incidence rates of retarded ossification and ventricular septal defect were also reported in rats given doses of 150 mg/kg/day, which is 5 times the MRHD on a systemic exposure basis. When this dose was given to rats during late pregnancy and lactation, decreased birth weights and stillbirths occurred with greater frequency.

Increased incidence of retardation of ossification of the sternum was reported in rabbits given doses as low as 150 mg/kg/day.

FDA Pregnancy Category C

Breast-feeding

It it not known whether cilostazol is distributed into human breast milk. Cilostazol was distributed into the milk of lactating rats. Because of the potential for serious adverse effects in nursing infants, a decision should be made to either stop breast-feeding or discontinue taking cilostazol.

Pediatrics

No information is available on the relationship of age to the effects of cilostazol in pediatric patients. Safety and efficacy have not been established.

Geriatrics

No age-related effects on the absorption, distribution, metabolism or elimination of cilostazol and its metabolites have been identified in elderly patients (over 65 years of age).

Drug interactions and/or related problems

The following drug interactions and/or related problems have been selected on the basis of their potential clinical significance (possible mechanism in parentheses where appropriate)—not necessarily inclusive (» = major clinical significance):

Pharmacokinetic interactions may occur as a result of the effects of other drugs on cilostazol metabolism by cytochrome P-450 isoenzymes CYP3A4 or CYP2C19; CYP3A4 does not appear to be inhibited by cilostazol. Pharmacodynamic interactions may occur with other drugs that inhibit platelet function.

Note: Combinations containing any of the following medications, depending on the amount present, may also interact with this medication.

Antiplatelet agents
(caution is advised)

Aspirin
(short-term concurrent administration with cilostazol increased ADP-induced inhibition of platelet aggregation by 23% to 35%, compared to aspirin alone; no clinically significant impact on prothrombin time (PT), activated partial thromboplastin time (aPTT) or bleeding time compared to aspirin alone; long-term effects of co-administration are unknown)

Clopidogrel
(although it can not be determined whether there was an additive effect on bleeding times with concomitant use, caution is advised for checking bleeding times during coadministration)

» Cytochrome P-450 inhibitors, such as:
Fluoxetine or
Fluvoxamine or
Itraconazole or
Ketoconazole or
Miconazole or
Nefazodone or
Sertraline
(strong inhibitors of cytochrome P-450 isoenzyme CYP3A4; although not investigated, it is anticipated that these drugs would exert a more significant effect on cilostazol plasma concentrations (increased cilostazol level) than that seen with erythromycin; dosage adjustment is recommended for ketoconazole and itraconazole when used concurrently with cilostazol)

» Diltiazem
(cilostazol plasma concentrations are increased by diltiazem, a moderate CYP3A4 inhibitor)

» Erythromycin or
Other macrolide antibiotics
(erythromycin decreases the metabolism of cilostazol through inhibition of the CYP3A4 isoenzyme; similar effects are expected from other macrolide antibiotics; dosage adjustment is recommended)

» Omeprazole
(although concurrent use with omeprazole did not significantly affect the metabolism of cilostazol, systemic exposure to cilostazol was increased by 69%; dosage adjustment of cilostazol is recommended)

Smoking, tobacco
(systemic cilostazol exposure is decreased by approximately 20% in association with tobacco smoking)

Laboratory value alterations

The following have been selected on the basis of their potential clinical significance (possible effect in parentheses where appropriate)—not necessarily inclusive (» = major clinical significance).

Blood glucose or
Blood uric acid
(may be increased)

Platelet count and
White blood cell count
(may be decreased)

Blood urea nitrogen (BUN)
(may be increased)

Medical considerations/Contraindications

The medical considerations/contraindications included have been selected on the basis of their potential clinical significance (reasons given in parentheses where appropriate)—not necessarily inclusive (» = major clinical significance).

Except under special circumstances this medication should not be used when the following medical problems exist:

» Active pathologic bleeding such as
Bleeding peptic ulcer or
Intracranial bleeding or
» Hemostatic disorders
(contraindicated; rare cases of thrombocytopenia or leukopenia progressing to agranulocytosis when cilostazol was not immediately discontinued; agranulocytosis was reversible upon cilostazol discontinuation)

» Congestive heart failure of any severity
(patients with class III to IV congestive heart failure have exhibited decreased survival when used with drugs that inhibit phosphodiesterase III)

» Hypersensitivity to cilostazol or other product components, known or suspected

Risk-benefit should be considered when the following medical problem exists:

Hepatic impairment, moderate or severe
(has not been studied in clinical trials; special caution is advised)

Renal function impairment, severe
(special caution is advised when used in patients with estimated creatinine clearance <25 mL/min; dialysis patients have not been studied but unlikely that cilostazol can be removed efficiently by dialysis because of its high protein binding; mild to moderate renal insufficiency has little effect on cilostazol pharmacology)

Thrombocytopenia
(caution is advised)

Side/Adverse Effects

The following side/adverse effects have been selected on the basis of their potential clinical significance (possible signs and symptoms in parentheses where appropriate)—not necessarily inclusive:

Those indicating need for medical attention

Incidence more frequent

Infection (fever); ***tachycardia*** (fast heartbeat)

Incidence less frequent

Atrial fibrillation (fast or irregular heartbeat); ***edema of the tongue*** (swelling of the tongue); ***epistaxis*** (nosebleeds); ***gastrointestinal effects, including duodenal ulcer or peptic ulcer*** (stomach pain, cramping, or burning, severe; bloody or black, tarry stools; vomiting of blood or material that looks like coffee grounds; nausea, heartburn and/or indigestion, severe and continuing); ***hemorrhage, various*** (abnormal bleeding)—(rectal, eye, gum, retinal, retroperitoneal, esophageal, vaginal); ***neck rigidity*** (stiff neck); ***purpura*** (bruises and/or red spots on the skin); ***syncope*** (fainting)

Incidence not determined—Observed during clinical practice; estimates of frequency cannot be determined

Abnormal liver function tests (lab results that show problems with the liver); ***agranulocytosis*** (cough or hoarseness; fever with or without chills; general feeling of tiredness or weakness; lower back or side pain; painful or difficult urination; sore throat; sores, ulcers, or white spots on lips or in mouth; unusual bleeding or bruising); ***bleeding tendency; cerebral hemorrhage*** (blurred vision; headache sudden and severe; inability to speak; seizures; slurred speech; temporary blindness; weakness in arm and/or leg on one side of the body, sudden and severe); ***cerebrovascular accident*** (blurred vision; headache sudden and severe; inability to speak; seizures; slurred speech; temporary blindness; weakness in arm and/or leg on one side of the body, sudden and severe); ***chest pain; extradural hematoma*** (loss of consciousness; headache; drowsiness; confusion; weakness of part of body); ***gastrointestinal hemorrhage*** (black, tarry stools; bloody stools; vomiting of blood or material that looks like coffee grounds); ***granulocytopenia*** (fever; chills; cough; sore throat; ulcers, sores, or white spots in mouth; shortness of breath; unusual tiredness or weakness); ***hepatic dysfunction*** (dark urine; light-colored stools; loss of appetite; nausea and vomiting; unusual tiredness; yellow eyes or skin; fever with or without chills; stomach pain); ***interstitial pneumonia*** (cough; difficult breathing; fever; shortness of breath); ***intracranial hemorrhage*** (confusion; headache, sudden and severe; weakness; nausea and vomiting); ***jaundice*** (chills; clay-colored stools; dark urine; dizziness; fever; headache; itching; loss of appetite; nausea; abdominal or stomach pain; area rash; unpleasant breath odor; unusual tiredness or weakness; vomiting of blood; yellow eyes or skin); ***leukopenia*** (black, tarry stools; chest pain; chills; cough; fever; painful or difficult urination; shortness of breath; sore throat; sores, ulcers, or white spots on lips or in mouth; swollen glands; unusual bleeding or bruising; unusual tiredness or weakness); ***pulmonary hemorrhage*** (coughing up blood; shortness of breath); ***skin drug eruption*** (hives; skin rash; itching of skin; itching of eyes; wheezing); ***Stevens-Johnson syndrome*** (blistering, peeling, loosening of skin; chills; cough; diarrhea; itching; joint or muscle pain; red irritated eyes; red skin lesions, often with a purple center; sore throat; sores, ulcers, or white spots in mouth or on lips; unusual tiredness or weakness); ***subdural hematoma*** (blurred vision; irregular heartbeat; nausea and vomiting; severe headache); ***thrombocytopenia*** (black, tarry stools; bleeding gums; blood in urine or stools; pinpoint red spots on skin; unusual bleeding or bruising)

Those indicating need for medical attention only if they continue or are bothersome

Incidence more frequent

Abdominal pain (stomach pain); ***back pain; diarrhea; dizziness; dyspepsia*** (heartburn); ***flatulence*** (gas); ***headache; increased cough; myalgia*** (pain or stiffness in muscles); ***nausea; palpitations*** (pounding heartbeat); ***peripheral edema*** (swelling of arms or legs); ***pharyngitis*** (sore throat); ***rhinitis*** (runny or stuffy nose); ***vertigo*** (dizziness)

Incidence less frequent

Arthralgia (pain or stiffness in joints); ***bone pain; colitis*** (stomach pain, cramping, or discomfort; bloody stools; diarrhea); ***esophagitis*** (burning feeling in throat or chest; difficulty in swallowing); ***fever with or without chills; gastritis*** (burning feeling in chest or stomach; indigestion; tenderness in stomach area); ***generalized edema*** (swelling of face, fingers, and/or lower legs); ***postural hypotension*** (lightheadedness or dizziness when getting up from a lying or sitting position); ***sinusitis*** (headache; runny or stuffy nose); ***tinnitus*** (ringing or buzzing in the ears); ***urticaria*** (hives)

Incidence not determined—Observed during clinical practice; estimates of frequency cannot be determined

Hot flushes; pain; pruritus (itching skin); ***subcutaneous hemorrhage*** (bruising)

Overdose

For more information on the management of overdose or unintentional ingestion, *contact a Poison Control Center* (see *Poison Control Center Listing*).

Clinical effects of overdose

The following effects have been selected on the basis of their potential clinical significance (possible signs and symptoms in parentheses where appropriate)—not necessarily inclusive:

Acute effects

Cardiac arrhythmias (fast or irregular heartbeat); ***diarrhea; headache, severe; hypotension*** (dizziness or lightheadedness when getting up from a lying or sitting position); ***tachycardia*** (fast heartbeat)

Treatment of overdose

To enhance elimination—Hemodialysis or peritoneal dialysis are unlikely to be of value because of the high degree of protein binding of cilostazol.

Supportive care—Symptomatic and supportive treatment. Patients in whom intentional overdose is confirmed or suspected should be referred for psychiatric consultation.

Patient Consultation

As an aid to patient consultation, refer to *Advice for the Patient, Cilostazol (Systemic).*

In providing consultation, consider emphasizing the following selected information (» = major clinical significance):

Before using this medication

» Conditions affecting use, especially:
- Hypersensitivity to cilostazol or other product components
- Breast-feeding—Breast-feeding is not recommended because of possible unwanted effects in nursing infants
- Other medications, especially cytochrome P-450 inhibitors, diltiazem, erythromycin or other macrolide antibiotics, or omeprazole
- Other medical problems, especially active pathologic bleeding, congestive heart failure, or hemostatic disorders

Proper use of this medication

To increase compliance, taking medication at the same time each day

» Proper dosing

Missed dose: Taking as soon as possible; not taking if almost time for next dose; not doubling doses

» Proper storage

Precautions while using this medication

Checking with physician before discontinuing medication

Avoiding smoking

Avoiding consumption of grapefruit juice

Side/adverse effects

Signs of potential side effects, especially infection, tachycardia, atrial fibrillation, edema of the tongue, epistaxis, gastrointestinal effects, hemorrhage, neck rigidity, purpura, and syncope

Signs of potential side effects observed during clinical practice, especially abnormal liver function tests, agranulocytosis, bleeding tendency, cerebral hemorrhage, cerebrovascular accident, chest pain, extradural hematoma, gastrointestinal hemorrhage, granulocytopenia, hepatic dysfunction, interstitial pneumonia, intracranial hemorrhage, jaundice, leukopenia, pulmonary hemorrhage, skin drug eruption, Stevens-Johnson syndrome, subdural hematoma, or thrombocytopenia

General Dosing Information

Reduction or discontinuation of cilostazol does not appear to result in rebound (platelet hyperaggregability).

Patients may respond as early as 2 to 4 weeks after the initiation of therapy, but treatment for up to 12 weeks may be needed before a beneficial effect is experienced.

Diet/Nutrition

Cilostazol should be administered at least half an hour before or two hours after breakfast and dinner.

Patients receiving cilostazol should avoid consuming grapefruit juice.

Oral Dosage Forms

CILOSTAZOL TABLETS

Usual adult dose

Peripheral vascular disease (symptomatic treatment of intermittent claudication)—

Oral, 100 milligrams two times a day, on an empty stomach

Note: A dose of 50 milligrams two times a day should be considered for patients who are coadministered medication that inhibit the cytochrome P-450 isoenzymes, as ketoconazole, itraconazole, erythromycin, diltiazem, or omeprazole.

Usual pediatric dose

Safety and efficacy have not been established

Strength(s) usually available

U.S.—

50 mg (Rx) [*Pletal* (triangular)].

100 mg [*Pletal* (round)].

Packaging and storage

Store at 25°C (77°F) or between 15 and 30°C (59 to 86°F).

Auxiliary labeling

- Avoid certain foods as directed.
- Take on an empty stomach.

Revised: 04/19/2006
Developed: 11/04/1999

CIMETIDINE—See *Histamine H_2-receptor Antagonists (Systemic)*

CINACALCET Systemic†

VA CLASSIFICATION (Primary): HS600

Commonly used brand name(s): *Sensipar.*

Note: For a listing of dosage forms and brand names by country availability, see *Dosage Forms* section(s).

†Not commercially available in Canada.

Category

Calcimimetic.

Indications

Accepted

Hypercalcemia (treatment)—Cinacalcet is indicated for the treatment of hypercalcemia in patients with parathyroid carcinoma.

Secondary hyperparathyroidism (treatment)—Cinacalcet is indicated for the treatment of secondary hyperparathyroidism in patients with chronic kidney disease on dialysis.

Acceptance not established

In chronic kidney disease [CKD] patients with secondary hyperparathyroidism and not on dialysis, the long-term safety and efficacy of cinacalcet have not been established. Exploratory investigation indicates that CKD patients not on dialysis have an increased risk for hypocalcemia compared to CKD patients on dialysis, which may be due to lower baseline calcium levels.

Pharmacology/Pharmacokinetics

Physicochemical characteristics

Molecular weight—
Cinacalcet: 357.4.
Cinacalcet hydrochloride: 393.9.

Solubility—Soluble in methanol or 95% ethanol; slightly soluble in water.

Mechanism of action/Effect

Secondary hyperparathyroidism [HPT] in patients with chronic kidney disease [CKD] is a progressive disease, associated with increases in parathyroid hormone [PTH] levels and derangements in calcium and phosphorus metabolism. Increased PTH stimulates osteoclastic activity resulting in cortical bone resorption and marrow fibrosis. The goals of treatment of secondary hyperparathyroidism are to lower levels of PTH, calcium, and phosphorus in the blood, in order to prevent progressive bone disease and the systemic consequences of disordered mineral metabolism. In CKD patients on dialysis with uncontrolled secondary HPT, reductions in PTH are associated with a favorable impact on bone-specific alkaline phosphatase [BALP], bone turnover and bone fibrosis.

The calcium-sensing receptor on the surface of the chief cell of the parathyroid gland is the principal regulator of PTH secretion. Cinacalcet directly lowers PTH levels by increasing the sensitivity of the calcium-sensing receptor to extracellular calcium. The reduction in PTH is associated with a concomitant decrease in serum calcium levels

Absorption

Area under the curve (AUC) when administered with a high fat meal—increased 68% compared to a fasting state

AUC when administered with a low fat meal—increased 50% compared to a fasting state

AUC increases proportionally over the dose range of 30 to 180 mg once daily

AUC in patients with moderate hepatic impairment—2.4 times higher than normal patients

AUC in patients with severe hepatic impairment—4.2 times higher than normal patients

Distribution
Volume of distribution (Vol_D)—approximately 1000 liters; high indicating extensive distribution

Protein binding
Very high (93 to 97%) to plasma protein(s)

Biotransformation
Rapidly and extensively metabolized hepatically by multiple enzymes, primarily CYP3A4, CYP2D6, and CYP1A2 via oxidative N-dealkylation to hydrocinnamic acid and hydroxy-hydrocinnamic acid which are further metabolized via β-oxidation and glycine conjugations; the oxidative N-dealkylation process also generates metabolites that contain the naphthalene ring; and oxidation of the naphthalene ring on the parent drug to form dihydrodiols which are further conjugated with glucuronic acid

The hydrocinnamic acid metabolite was shown to be inactive at concentrations up to 10 microM in a cell-based assay measuring calcium-receptor activation. The glucuronide conjugates formed after oxidation were shown to have a potency approximately 0.003 times that of cinacalcet in a cell-based assay measuring a calcimimetic response.

Half-life
Terminal—30 to 40 hours

Mean half-life in patients with moderate and severe hepatic impairment—prolonged by 33% and 70%, respectively

Time to peak concentration
Approximately 2 to 6 hours

Time to steady-state concentration
Within 7 days

Peak plasma concentration:
C_{max} when administered with a high fat meal—increased 82% compared to a fasting state

C_{max} when administered with a low fat meal—increased 65% compared to a fasting state

Increases proportionally over the dose range of 30 to 180 mg once daily

Elimination
Renal—80% of dose as metabolites

Fecal—15% of dose as metabolites

Precautions to Consider

Carcinogenicity
In mice and rat studies with cinacalcet exposures of up to 2 times those resulting with a human oral dose of 180 mg per day based on AUC comparison, no increased incidence of tumors was observed.

Mutagenicity
Cinacalcet was not genotoxic in the Ames bacterial mutagenicity assay or in the Chinese Hamster Ovary (CHO) cell HGPRT forward mutation assay and CHO cell chromosomal aberration assay, with and without metabolic activation or in the in vivo mouse micronucleus assay.

Pregnancy/Reproduction
Fertility—No effects were observed in male or female rat fertility with exposures up to 3 times those resulting with a human oral dose of 180 mg per day based on AUC comparison when given to female rats beginning two weeks before mating and continuing through gestation day 7 and when given to male rats 4 weeks prior to mating, during mating (three weeks) and 2 weeks post-mating. However, at 75 mg per kg of body weight per day, there were slight adverse effects of slight decreases in body weight and food consumption in male and female rats.

Pregnancy—Cinacalcet should be used during pregnancy only if the potential benefit justifies the potential risk to the fetus. There are no adequate and well-controlled studies in pregnant women. However studies in animals have shown that cinacalcet can cause low birth weights.

In pregnant female rats, decreased fetal body weights were observed at all doses (less than one to four times a human oral dose of 180 mg per day based on AUC comparison in conjunction with maternal toxicity [decreased food consumption and baby weight gain]). In pregnant rats given doses with exposures less than with a human therapeutic dose of 180 mg per day based on AUC comparison, no adverse fetal or pup (post-weaning) effects were observed. Higher doses with exposures two to three times a human oral dose of 180 mg per day based on AUC comparisons were accompanied by maternal signs of hypocalcemia (periparturient mortality and early postnatal pup loss), and reductions in postnatal maternal and pup body weight gain.

In pregnant female rabbits given oral doses with exposures less than with a human oral dose of 180 mg per day based on AUC comparisons, no fetal adverse effects were observed. Reductions in maternal food consumption and body weight gain were seen at doses of 12 and 25 mg per kg of body weight per day. Cinacalcet has been shown to cross the placental barrier in rabbits.

FDA Pregnancy Category C

Breast-feeding
It is not known whether cinacalcet is distributed into human breast milk. Rat studies have shown that cinacalcet is distributed into the milk with a high milk-to-plasma ratio. Because cinacalcet has been shown to be distributed into rat breast milk and because of the potential for clinically significant adverse reactions in infants, a decision should be made whether to discontinue nursing or to discontinue the drug, taking into account the importance of the drug to the lactating woman.

Pediatrics
Safety and efficacy of cinacalcet in pediatric patients has not been established.

Geriatrics
Appropriate studies performed to date have not demonstrated geriatrics-specific problems that would limit the usefulness of cinacalcet in the elderly. No differences in safety and efficacy were observed in patients greater or less than 65 years of age. Age does not alter the pharmacokinetics of cinacalcet. No dosage adjustment is required for geriatric patients.

Drug interactions and/or related problems
The following drug interactions and/or related problems have been selected on the basis of their potential clinical significance (possible mechanism in parentheses where appropriate)—not necessarily inclusive (» = major clinical significance):

Note: Combinations containing any of the following medications, depending on the amount present, may also interact with this medication.

» Amitriptyline
(concurrent administration increased amitriptyline and nortriptyline [active metabolite] exposure by about 20% in CYP2D6 extensive metabolizers)

» Drugs metabolized by CYP2D6 including:
Flecainide or
Thioridazine or
Tricyclic antidepressants (most) or
Vinblastine
(dosage adjustment of these drugs may be required with concomitant use)

» Strong CYP3A4 inhibitors such as
Erythromycin or
Itraconazole or
Ketoconazole
(increase in cinacalcet AUC and C_{max} of 2.3 and 2.2 times, respectively, with concomitant use of ketoconazole and cinacalcet; dose adjustment of cinacalcet may be required and iPTH and serum calcium levels should be closely monitored if patient initiates or discontinues therapy with a strong CYP3A4 inhibitor)

Laboratory value alterations
The following have been selected on the basis of their potential clinical significance (possible effect in parentheses where appropriate)—not necessarily inclusive (» = major clinical significance).

With physiology/laboratory test values
» Calcium, serum or
» Intact parathyroid hormone (iPTH), serumor
» Phosphorous, serum
(values may be lowered)
(reduction in iPTH levels correlated with cinacalcet concentrations in chronic kidney disease (CKD) patients; the nadir in iPTH level occurs approximately 2 to 6 hours post dose corresponding with the C_{max} of cinacalcet; after steady state is reached, serum calcium concentrations remain constant over the dosing interval in CKD patients)

Testosterone, serum
(often below normal range in male patients with end-stage renal disease; significance of these testosterone level reductions unknown)

Medical considerations/Contraindications
The medical considerations/contraindications included have been selected on the basis of their potential clinical significance (reasons given in parentheses where appropriate)—not necessarily inclusive (» = major clinical significance).

Except under special circumstances, this medication should not be used when the following medical problem exists:
» Hypersensitivity to cinacalcet or any component of the product

Risk-benefit should be considered when the following medical problems exist:

Hepatic impairment, moderate and severe
(should be monitored throughout treatment; cinacalcet exposure assessed by AUC values 2.4 and 4.2 times higher in patients with moderate and severe hepatic impairment, respectively, compared to normal)

» Seizure disorder, history of
(cinacalcet lowers serum calcium; because seizure threshold is lowered by significant reductions in serum calcium, these patients should be closely monitored for serum calcium)

Patient monitoring

The following may be especially important in patient monitoring (other tests may be warranted in some patients, depending on condition; » = major clinical significance):

» Calcium, serum and
» Phosphorus, serum
(should be measured within one week after initiation or dose adjustment of cinacalcet and approximately monthly after maintenance dose is established in patients with chronic kidney disease on dialysis with secondary hyperparathyroidism and every two months in patients with parathyroid carcinoma)

» Hypocalcemia
(because cinacalcet lowers serum calcium, patients should be monitored for signs of hypocalcemia including paresthesias, myalgias, cramping, tetany and convulsion)

» Intact parathyroid hormone (iPTH), serum
(should be measured one to four weeks after initiation or dose adjustment of cinacalcet and every one to three months after maintenance dose has been established; if iPTH levels are suppressed below 100 pg per mL, adynamic bone disease may develop; dose should be reduced and/or vitamin D sterols should be reduced or therapy discontinued if iPTH levels decrease below recommended target range of 150 to 300 pg per mL)

Side/Adverse Effects

The following side/adverse effects have been selected on the basis of their potential clinical significance (possible signs and symptoms in parentheses where appropriate)—not necessarily inclusive:

Those indicating need for medical attention

Incidence more frequent

Chest pain, non-cardiac; hypertension (blurred vision, dizziness, nervousness, headache, pounding in the ears, slow or fast heartbeat)

Incidence less frequent

Access infection (fever or chills, cough or hoarseness, lower back or side pain, painful or difficult urination); ***seizures*** (convulsions, muscle spasm or jerking of all extremities, sudden loss of consciousness, loss of bladder control)

Frequency unknown

Adynamic bone disease (low bone turnover); ***hypocalcemia*** (abdominal cramps; confusion; convulsions; difficulty in breathing; irregular heartbeats; mood or mental changes; muscle cramps in hands, arms, feet, legs, or face; numbness and tingling around the mouth, fingertips, or feet; shortness of breath; tremor)

Those indicating need for medical attention only if they continue or are bothersome

Incidence more frequent

Anorexia (loss of appetite, weight loss); ***asthenia*** (lack or loss of strength); ***diarrhea; dizziness; myalgia*** (joint pain, swollen joints, muscle aching or cramping, muscle pains or stiffness, difficulty in moving); ***nausea; vomiting***

Overdose

For more information on the management of overdose or unintentional ingestion, **contact a poison control center** (see *Poison Control Center Listing*).

Clinical effects of overdose

The following effects have been selected on the basis of their potential clinical significance (possible signs and symptoms in parentheses where appropriate)—not necessarily inclusive:

Hypocalcemia (abdominal cramps; confusion; convulsions; difficulty in breathing; irregular heartbeats; mood or mental changes; muscle cramps in hands, arms, feet, legs, or face; numbness and tingling around the mouth, fingertips, or feet; shortness of breath; tremor)

Treatment of overdose

Treatment is generally symptomatic and supportive including:

Monitoring—
Monitoring for signs and symptoms of hypocalcemia

Supportive care—
Taking appropriate measures to correct serum calcium levels
Hemodialysis is not an effective treatment for overdosage of cinacalcet
Patients in whom intentional overdose is confirmed or suspected should be referred for psychiatric consultation.

Patient Consultation

As an aid to patient consultation, refer to *Advice for the Patient, Cinacalcet (Systemic)*.

In providing consultation, consider emphasizing the following selected information (» = major clinical significance):

Before using this medication

» Conditions affecting use, especially:
Pregnancy—Risk-benefit should be established for use in pregnancy
Breast-feeding—Because of the potential for adverse reactions in infants, a decision should be made whether to discontinue nursing or to discontinue the drug, taking into account the importance of the drug to the lactating woman
Other medications, especially amitriptyline, drugs metabolized by CYP2D6, or strong CYP3A4 inhibitors
Other medical problems, especially history of seizure disorder or hypersensitivity to cinacalcet or any of it components

Proper use of this medication

» Importance of dosage being individualized for each patient
» Taking tablet whole and not dividing it
» Taking tablet with food or shortly after a meal
» Proper dosing
Missed dose: Taking as soon as possible; not taking if almost time for next scheduled dose; not doubling doses
» Proper storage

Precautions while using this medication

» Importance of contacting physician immediately if signs and symptoms of hypocalcemia occur
» Importance of patient being monitored frequently for decreased levels of calcium, iPTH, and phosphorus
» Notifying physician if patient has history of seizure disorder

Side/adverse effects

Signs of potential side effects, especially non-cardiac chest pain, hypertension, access infection, adynamic bone disease, or hypocalcemia

General Dosing Information

Diet/Nutrition

Cinacalcet should be taken with food or shortly after a meal. Food increases absorption.

For treatment of adverse effects

If symptoms of hypocalcemia occur or serum calcium level is in the range from 7.5 to 8.4 mg per dL—calcium-containing phosphate binders and/or vitamin D sterols can be used to raise serum calcium.

If symptoms of hypocalcemia persist or serum calcium levels falls below 7.5 mg per dL and vitamin D cannot be increased—should withhold cinacalcet administration until serum calcium levels reach 8 mg per dL and/or symptoms of hypocalcemia have resolved. Treatment should be reinitiated using the next lowest dose of cinacalcet.

Oral Dosage Forms

CINACALCET HYDROCHLORIDE TABLETS

Usual adult dose

Hypercalcemia associated with parathyroid carcinoma (treatment)—
Oral, initially 30 mg twice daily
Then, should be titrated every 2 to 4 weeks through sequential doses of 30 mg twice daily, 60 mg twice daily, 90 mg twice daily, and 90 mg three or four times daily as necessary to normalize serum calcium levels

Secondary hyperparathyroidism (treatment)—
Oral, initially 30 mg once daily.
Then, should be titrated no more frequently than every 2 to 4 weeks through sequential doses of 60, 90, 120, and 180 mg once daily to target iPTH consistent with the NKF-K/DOQI recommendation for chronic kidney disease (CKD) patients on dialysis of 150 to 300 pg per mL

Note: Cinacalcet can be used alone or in combination with vitamin D sterols and/or phosphate binders for treatment of secondary hyperparathyroidism.

Note: Dosage must be individualized.

Note: Dosage adjustments for patients with renal or hepatic impairment are not required.

Usual pediatric dose
Safety and efficacy have not been established.

Usual geriatric dose
See *Usual adult dose*.

Strength(s) usually available
U.S.—

30 mg base (Rx) [*Sensipar* (film-coated; pregelatinized starch; microcrystalline cellulose; povidone; crospovidone; colloidal silicon dioxide; magnesium stearate; Opadry II green; Opadry clear; carnauba wax; Opacode black ink)].

60 mg base (Rx) [*Sensipar* (film-coated; pregelatinized starch; microcrystalline cellulose; povidone; crospovidone; colloidal silicon dioxide; magnesium stearate; Opadry II green; Opadry clear; carnauba wax; Opacode black ink)].

90 mg base (Rx) [*Sensipar* (film-coated; pregelatinized starch; microcrystalline cellulose; povidone; crospovidone; colloidal silicon dioxide; magnesium stearate; Opadry II green; Opadry clear; carnauba wax; Opacode black ink)].

Packaging and storage
Store at 25 °C (77 °F) excursions permitted to 15 and 30 °C (59 and 86 °F).

Auxiliary labeling
- Swallow whole. Do not crush or chew.
- Take with food or shortly after a meal.

Revised: 11/02/2004
Developed: 04/08/2004

CIPROFLOXACIN—See *Fluoroquinolones (Systemic)*

CIPROFLOXACIN Ophthalmic

VA CLASSIFICATION (Primary): OP201

Commonly used brand name(s): *Ciloxan*.

Note: For a listing of dosage forms and brand names by country availability, see *Dosage Forms* section(s).

Category
Antibacterial (ophthalmic).

Indications

Accepted
Corneal ulcers, bacterial (treatment)—Ophthalmic ciprofloxacin solution and [ophthalmic ciprofloxacin ointment] are indicated in the treatment of corneal ulcers caused by susceptible strains of bacteria, including *Pseudomonas aeruginosa*, *Serratia marcescens*, *Staphylococcus aureus*, *Staphylococcus epidermidis*, *Streptococcus pneumoniae*, and *Streptococcus (Viridans Group)*.

Conjunctivitis, bacterial (treatment)—Ophthalmic ciprofloxacin ointment and solution are indicated in the treatment of conjunctivitis caused by *Haeomophilus influenzae*, *Staphylococcus aureus*, *Staphylococcus epidermidis*, *Streptococcus pneumoniae*, and *Streptococcus (Viridans Group)*.

Note: Not all species or strains of a particular organism may be susceptible to ciprofloxacin. Streptococcal species are often less susceptible.

Pharmacology/Pharmacokinetics

Physicochemical characteristics
Chemical Group—Fluoroquinolone.
Molecular weight—385.82.

Mechanism of action/Effect
Ciprofloxacin's bactericidal action results from interference with the enzyme DNA gyrase, which is needed for the synthesis of bacterial DNA.

Absorption
During the patient's waking hours, ciprofloxacin was administered in each eye every 2 hours for 2 days followed by every 4 hours for an additional 5 days. The maximum reported plasma concentration of ciprofloxacin was less than 5 nanograms per mL. The mean concentration was usually less than 2.5 nanograms per mL.

Precautions to Consider

Cross-sensitivity and/or related problems
Patients sensitive to other quinolones, such as cinoxacin, nalidixic acid, norfloxacin, or ofloxacin, may be sensitive to this medication also.

Carcinogenicity
Rats and mice administered ciprofloxacin orally for up to 2 years did not show carcinogenic effects.

Mutagenicity
Ciprofloxacin was not found to be mutagenic in the following *in vitro* tests: *Salmonella* /Microsome test, *E. coli* DNA Repair assay, Chinese Hamster V_{79} Cell HGPRT test, Syrian Hamster Embryo Cell Transformation assay, *Saccharomyces cerevisiae* Point Mutation assay, and *Saccharomyces cerevisiae* Mitotic Crossover and Gene Conversion assay. In addition, ciprofloxacin was not found to be mutagenic in the following *in vivo* tests: Rat Hepatocyte DNA Repair assay, Micronucleus test (mice), and Dominant Lethal test (mice). However, ciprofloxacin was found to be mutagenic in the *in vitro* Mouse Lymphoma Cell Forward Mutation assay and the *in vitro* Rat Hepatocyte DNA Repair assay.

Pregnancy/Reproduction
Fertility—Studies performed in rats and mice administered ciprofloxacin in oral doses up to 6 times the usual daily human oral dose revealed no evidence of impaired fertility.

Pregnancy—Adequate and well-controlled studies in humans have not been done. However, problems in humans have not been documented.

Reproduction studies performed in rats and mice administered ciprofloxacin in oral doses up to 6 times the usual daily human oral dose revealed no evidence of harm to the fetus. In rabbits, ciprofloxacin, like most antimicrobial agents, when administered in oral doses of 30 and 100 mg per kg of body weight (mg/kg) per day produced gastrointestinal disturbances resulting in maternal weight loss and an increased incidence of abortion. However, no teratogenicity was observed at either dose. Ciprofloxacin administered intravenously in doses of up to 20 mg/kg, produced no maternal toxicity, embryotoxicity, or teratogenicity.

FDA Pregnancy Category C.

Breast-feeding
It is not known whether ophthalmic ciprofloxacin is distributed into breast milk. However, oral ciprofloxacin was shown to be distributed into breast milk after a single 500 mg dose.

Pediatrics
Appropriate studies on the relationship of age to the effects of ciprofloxacin have not been performed in children up to 2 years of age for the ophthalmic ointment dosage form and 1 year of age for the ophthalmic solution dosage form. Safety and efficacy have not been established.

Although ciprofloxacin and other quinolones cause arthropathy in immature Beagle dogs after oral administration, ophthalmic ciprofloxacin administered to immature animals did not cause any arthropathy. In addition, there is no evidence that the ophthalmic dosage form has any effect on the weight bearing joints.

Geriatrics
No information is available on the relationship of age to the effects of ciprofloxacin in geriatric patients.

Medical considerations/Contraindications
The medical considerations/contraindications included have been selected on the basis of their potential clinical significance (reasons given in parentheses where appropriate)—not necessarily inclusive (» = major clinical significance).

Risk-benefit should be considered when the following medical problem exists:
Sensitivity to ciprofloxacin

Side/Adverse Effects

Note: In corneal ulcer studies, frequent administration of ophthalmic ciprofloxacin resulted in white crystalline precipitates in the eyes of 17% of patients using the ophthalmic solution and 13% of patients using the ophthalmic ointment. This precipitate did not prevent the continued use of the medication and did not adversely affect treatment outcome.

The following side/adverse effects have been selected on the basis of their potential clinical significance (possible signs and symptoms in parentheses where appropriate)—not necessarily inclusive:

Those indicating need for medical attention
Incidence rare

Allergic reaction, such as skin rash, hives, or itching; blurred vision; corneal infiltrates; corneal staining; decreased vision; epi-

theliopathy; or keratopathy (blurred vision or other change in vision); ***dermatitis*** (skin rash); ***eye pain or irritation; keratitis*** (severe irritation or redness of eye); ***nausea***

Those indicating need for medical attention only if they continue or are bothersome

Incidence more frequent

Burning or other discomfort of the eye; crusting or crystals in corner of eye

Incidence less frequent

Bad taste following instillation; foreign body sensation (feeling of something in eye); ***hyperemia, conjunctival*** (redness of the lining of the eyelids); ***itching of eye***

Rare

Dryness of eye; lid edema (swelling of eyelid); ***photophobia*** (increased sensitivity of eyes to light); ***tearing of eye***

Overdose

For more information on the management of overdose or unintentional ingestion, **contact a Poison Control Center** (see *Poison Control Center Listing*).

Treatment of overdose

A topical overdose of ciprofloxacin ophthalmic solution may be flushed from the eye(s) with warm tap water.

Patient Consultation

As an aid to patient consultation, refer to *Advice for the Patient, Ciprofloxacin (Ophthalmic)*.

In providing consultation, consider emphasizing the following selected information (» = major clinical significance):

Before using this medication

» Conditions affecting use, especially:
Sensitivity to ciprofloxacin or other quinolones
Breast-feeding—Oral ciprofloxacin is distributed into breast milk; it is not known whether ophthalmic ciprofloxacin is distributed into breast milk.
Use in children—Safety and efficacy have not been established in children up to 2 years of age for the ophthalmic ointment and 1 year of age for the ophthalmic solution.

Proper use of this medication

Proper administration technique
» Compliance with full course of therapy
» Proper dosing
Missed dose: Applying as soon as possible; not applying if almost time for next dose
» Proper storage

Precautions while using this medication

Checking with physician if no improvement within a few days
Possible photophobic reactions; wearing sunglasses and avoiding prolonged exposure to bright light

Side/adverse effects

Signs of potential side effects, especially allergic reaction, blurred vision, corneal infiltrates, corneal staining, decreased vision, epitheliopathy, keratopathy, dermatitis, eye pain or irritation, keratitis, or nausea

General Dosing Information

Ciprofloxacin ophthalmic solution is not for injection into the eye.

Although some manufacturers recommend doses of 2 drops of ophthalmic solutions at appropriate intervals, the conjunctival sac usually holds less than 1 drop.

If hypersensitivity develops, therapy with ophthalmic ciprofloxacin should be discontinued.

For treatment of adverse effects

Recommended treatment includes

• For mild hypersensitivity reaction—Administering antihistamines and, if necessary, glucocorticoids.

• For severe hypersensitivity or anaphylactic reaction—Administering epinephrine. Antihistamines and/or glucocorticoids may also be administered as required.

Ophthalmic Dosage Forms

Note: The dosing and strengths of the dosage forms available are expressed in terms of ciprofloxacin base.

CIPROFLOXACIN HYDROCHLORIDE OPHTHALMIC OINTMENT

Usual adult and adolescent dose

Bacterial conjunctivitis—
Topical, to the conjunctiva, ½-inch (1.25 cm) strip of ointment in each eye three times a day for two days, then two times a day for the next five days.

[Corneal ulcers]—
Topical, to the conjunctiva, ½-inch (1.25 cm) strip of ointment in the affected eye every 1 or 2 hours around the clock for the first two days, then every 4 hours for up to twelve days. If corneal re-epithelialization has not occurred after twelve days of treatment, treatment may be continued.

Usual pediatric dose

Bacterial conjunctivitis—
Infants and children up to 2 years of age: Safety and efficacy have not been established.
Children over 2 years of age: See *Usual adult and adolescent dose.*

[Corneal ulcers]—
Infants and children up to 12 years of age: Safety and efficacy have not been established.
Children over 12 years of age: See *Usual adult and adolescent dose.*

Strength(s) usually available

U.S.—
3.33 mg (3 mg base) per gram (Rx) [*Ciloxan*].

Canada—
3.5 mg (3 mg base) per gram (Rx) [*Ciloxan*].

Packaging and storage

Store between 2 and 25 °C (36 and 77 °F), unless otherwise specified by manufacturer.

Auxiliary labeling

• For the eye.
• Continue medicine for full time of treatment.

CIPROFLOXACIN HYDROCHLORIDE OPHTHALMIC SOLUTION USP

Usual adult and adolescent dose

Bacterial conjunctivitis—
Topical, to the conjunctiva, 1 drop in each eye every two hours, while patient is awake, for two days, then 1 drop every four hours, while patient is awake, for the next five days.

Corneal ulcers—
Topical, to the conjunctiva, 2 drops in the affected eye every fifteen minutes for six hours, then 2 drops every thirty minutes, while patient is awake, for the rest of day one; 2 drops every hour, while patient is awake, on day two; and 2 drops every four hours, while patient is awake, on days three through fourteen. If corneal re-epithelialization has not occurred after fourteen days of treatment, treatment may be continued.

Note: During the initial 24 to 48 hours, additional doses may be necessary during the night in some cases.

Usual pediatric dose

Bacterial conjunctivitis—
Infants and children up to 1 year of age: Safety and efficacy have not been established.
Children over 1 year of age: See *Usual adult and adolescent dose.*

Corneal ulcers—
In the U.S.—
Infants and children up to 1 year of age: Safety and efficacy have not been established.
Children over 1 year of age: See *Usual adult and adolescent dose.*
In Canada—
Infants and children up to 12 years of age: Safety and efficacy have not been established.
Children over 12 years of age: See *Usual adult and adolescent dose.*

Strength(s) usually available

U.S.—
3.5 mg (3 mg base) per mL (Rx) [*Ciloxan* (benzalkonium chloride 0.006%)].

Canada—
3.5 mg (3 mg base) per mL (Rx) [*Ciloxan* (benzalkonium chloride 0.006%)].

Packaging and storage

Store below 40 °C (104 °F), preferably between 15 and 30 °C (59 and 86 °F), unless otherwise specified by manufacturer. Store in a tight container. Protect from light.

Auxiliary labeling

- For the eye.
- Continue medicine for full time of treatment.

Selected Bibliography

Yolton DP. New antibacterial drugs for topical ophthalmic use. Optom Clin 1992; 2(4): 59-72.

Revised: 06/14/1999

CIPROFLOXACIN AND DEXAMETHASONE Otic†

VA CLASSIFICATION (Primary): OT250

Commonly used brand name(s): *Ciprodex*.

Note: For a listing of dosage forms and brand names by country availability, see *Dosage Forms* section(s).

†Not commercially available in Canada.

Category

Antibacterial-corticosteroid (otic).

Indications

General Considerations

Ciprofloxacin has been shown to be active against most isolates of the following microorganisms, both *in vitro* and clinically in otic infections.

Aerobic and facultative gram-positive microorganisms:

—*Staphylococcus aureus*
—*Streptococcus pneumoniae*

Aerobic and facultative gram-negative microorganisms:

—*Haemophilus influenzae*
—*Moraxella catarrhalis*
—*Pseudomonas aeruginosa*

Accepted

Acute Otitis Media (treatment)—Ciprofloxacin and dexamethasone combination is indicated for the treatment of Acute Otitis Media infections in pediatric patients (age 6 months and older) with tympanostomy tubes due to *Staphylococcus aureus, Streptococcus pneumoniae, Haemophilus influenzae, Moraxella catarrhalis,* and *Pseudomonas aeruginosa.*

Acute Otitis Externa (treatment)—Ciprofloxacin and dexamethasone combination is indicated for the treatment of Acute Otitis Externa infections in pediatric patients (age 6 months and older), adult and elderly patients due to *Staphylococcus aureus* and *Pseudomonas aeruginosa.*

Pharmacology/Pharmacokinetics

Physicochemical characteristics

Chemical Group—
Ciprofloxacin: fluoroquinolone
Dexamethasone: anti-inflammatory corticosteroid

Mechanism of action/Effect

Ciprofloxacin has *in vitro* activity against a wide range of gram-positive and gram-negative microorganisms. The bactericidal action of ciprofloxacin results from the interference with the enzyme, DNA gyrase, which is needed for the synthesis of bacterial DNA.

Dexamethasone has been added to aid in the resolution of the inflammatory response accompanying bacterial infection (such as otorrhea in pediatric patients with AOM tympanostomy tubes).

Absorption

Following a single bilateral 4 drop (total dose = 0.28 mL, 0.84 mg ciprofloxacin, 0.28 mg dexamethasone) topical otic dose of ciprofloxacin and dexamethasone combination to pediatric patients after tympanostomy tube insertion, measurable plasma concentrations of ciprofloxacin and dexamethasone were observed at 6 hours following administration in 2 of 9 patients and 5 of 9 patients, respectively.

Time to peak concentration

Ciprofloxacin and Dexamethasone: Peak plasma concentrations were observed within 15 minutes and 2 hours post dose application.

Peak plasma concentration:

Ciprofloxacin: 0.543 ng/mL to 3.45 ng/mL; mean 1.39 ± 0.88 ng/mL
Dexamethasone: 0.135 ng/mL to 5.1 ng/mL; mean 1.14 ± 1.54 ng/mL

Precautions to Consider

Cross-sensitivity and/or related problems

Patients allergic to one fluoroquinolone or other chemically related quinolone derivative may be allergic to other fluoroquinolones.

Carcinogenicity/Tumorigenicity/Mutagenicity

Long-term carcinogenicity studies in mice and rats have been completed for ciprofloxacin. After daily oral doses of 750 mg/kg (mice) and 250 mg/kg (rats) were administered for up to 2 years, there was no evidence that ciprofloxacin had any carcinogenic or tumorigenic effects in these species. No long term studies of ciprofloxacin and dexamethasone have been performed to evaluate carcinogenic potential.

Eight *in vitro* mutagenicity tests have been conducted with ciprofloxacin. The tests that were conducted were: *Salmonella*/Microsome Test (Negative), *E. coli* DNA Repair Assay (Negative), Mouse Lymphoma Cell Forward Mutation Assay (Positive), Chinese Hamster V_{79} Cell HGPRT Test (Negative), Syrian Hamster Embryo Cell Transformation Assay (Negative), *Saccharomyces cerevisiae* Point Mutation Assay (Negative), *Saccharomyces cerevisiae* Mitotic Crossover and Gene Conversion Assay (Negative), Rat Hepatocyte DNA Repair Assay (Positive). Two of the eight tests were positive. The results of these three *in vivo* test systems gave negative results. Rat Hepatocyte DNA Repair Assay, Micronucleus Test (Mice), and Dominant Lethal Test (Mice).

Long term studies have not been performed to evaluate the carcinogenic potential of topical otic dexamethasone. Dexamethasone has been tested for *in vitro* and *in vivo* genotoxic potential and has shown to be positive in the following assays; chromosomal aberrations, sister-chromatid exchange in human lymphocytes and micronuclei and sister-chromatid exchanges in mouse bone marrow. However, the Ames/Salmonella assay, both with and without S9 mix, did not show any increase in His+ revertants.

Pregnancy/Reproduction

Fertility—Fertility studies performed in rats at oral doses of ciprofloxacin up to 100 mg/kg/day revealed no evidence of impairment. This would be over 100 times the maximum recommended clinical dose of ototopical ciprofloxacin based on body surface area, assuming total absorption of ciprofloxacin from the ear of a patient treated with ciprofloxacin and dexamethasone otic twice per day according to label directions.

The effects of dexamethasone on fertility has not been investigated following topical otic administration. However, the lowest toxic dose of dexamethasone identified following topical dermal application was 1.802 mg/kg in a 26-week study in male rats and resulted in changes to the testes, epididymis, sperm duct, prostate, seminal vesicle, Cowper's gland and accessory glands. The relevance of this study for short term topical otic use is unknown.

Pregnancy—No adequate and well controlled studies have been performed in pregnant women. Caution should be exercised when ciprofloxacin and dexamethasone combination is used by a pregnant woman.

Animal reproduction studies have not been conducted with ciprofloxacin and dexamethasone combination.

Reproduction studies have been performed in rats and mice using oral doses of up to 100 mg/kg and IV doses up to 30 mg/kg and have revealed no evidence of harm to the fetus as a result of ciprofloxacin. In rabbits, ciprofloxacin (30 and 100 mg/kg orally) produced gastrointestinal disturbances resulting in maternal weight loss and an increased incidence of abortion, but no teratogenicity was observed at either dose. After intravenous administration of doses up to 20 mg/kg, no maternal toxicity was produced in the rabbit, and no embryotoxicity or teratogenicity was observed.

Corticosteroids are generally teratogenic in laboratory animals when administered systemically at relatively low dosage levels. The more potent corticosteroids have been shown to be teratogenic after dermal application in laboratory animals.

FDA Pregnancy Category C

Breast-feeding

It is not known whether topical otic administration of ciprofloxacin or dexamethasone could result in sufficient systemic absorption to produce detectable quantities in human milk. Because of the potential for unwanted effects in nursing infants, a decision should be made whether to discontinue nursing or to discontinue the drug, taking into account the importance of the drug to the mother.

Ciprofloxacin and corticosteroids, as a class, appear in milk following oral administration. Dexamethasone in breast milk could suppress growth, interfere with endogenous corticosteroid production, or cause other untoward effects.

Pediatrics
Appropriate studies on the relationship of age to the effects of ciprofloxacin and dexamethasone combination have been performed in pediatric patients aged 6 months and older. Although no data are available on patients less than age 6 months, there are no known safety concerns or differences in the disease process in this population that would preclude use of this product.

No clinically relevant changes in hearing function were observed in 69 pediatric patients (age 4 to 12 years) treated with ciprofloxacin and dexamethasone combination and tested for audiometric parameters.

Geriatrics
Appropriate studies on the relationship of age to the effects of ciprofloxacin and dexamethasone combination have not been performed in the geriatric population. However, geriatrics specific problems have not been documented to date.

Drug interactions and/or related problems
The following drug interactions and/or related problems have been selected on the basis of their potential clinical significance (possible mechanism in parentheses where appropriate)—not necessarily inclusive (» = major clinical significance):

Specific drug interaction studies have not been conducted with ciprofloxacin and dexamethasone combination.

Medical considerations/Contraindications
The medical considerations/contraindications included have been selected on the basis of their potential clinical significance (reasons given in parentheses where appropriate)—not necessarily inclusive (» = major clinical significance).

Except under special circumstances, this medication should not be used when the following medical problem exists:

» Hypersensitivity to ciprofloxacin, to other quinolones, or to any of the components in this medication.

» Viral infections of the external ear canal
(Using this medicine is contraindicated in patients with viral infections of the external ear canal, including herpes simplex infections.)

Patient monitoring
The following may be especially important in patient monitoring (other tests may be warranted in some patients, depending on condition; » = major clinical significance):

» Skin rash and/ or
Hypersensitivity signs
(This medication should be discontinued immediately at the appearance of a skin rash or any other sign of Hypersensitivity)

Side/Adverse Effects
The following side/adverse effects have been selected on the basis of their potential clinical significance (possible signs and symptoms in parentheses where appropriate)—not necessarily inclusive:

Those indicating need for medical attention only if they continue or are bothersome
Incidence less frequent
Ear discomfort; ear pain; ear pruritus (itching skin on the ear)

Incidence rare
Ear congestion; ear debris; ear precipitate (residue); erythema (redness of skin); ***irritability; superimposed ear infection; taste perversion*** (bitter, sour or unusual taste in mouth)

Overdose
For more information on the management of overdose or unintentional ingestion, **contact a poison control center** (see *Poison Control Center Listing*).

Treatment is symptomatic and supportive.

There is no specific information regarding overdose of ciprofloxacin and dexamethasone used in combination.

Patient Consultation
As an aid to patient consultation, refer to *Advice for the Patient, Ciprofloxacin and Dexamethasone (Otic)*.

In providing consultation, consider emphasizing the following selected information (» = major clinical significance):

Before using this medication
» Conditions affecting use, especially:
Hypersensitivity to ciprofloxacin, to other quinolones, or to any of the components in this medication
Pregnancy—Not recommended for use during pregnancy
Breast-feeding—Not recommended for use while breast feeding
Use in children—Approved for use in pediatric patients 6 months of age and older.
Specific drug interaction studies have not been conducted with ciprofloxacin and dexamethasone combination.
Other medical problems such as viral ear infections of the external ear canal.

Proper use of this medication
» Proper dosing
Missed dose: Taking as soon as possible; not taking if almost time for next scheduled dose; not doubling doses
Proper storage
Proper administration technique
Avoid contaminating tip with material from the ear, fingers or other sources
Hold the bottle in your hand for one to two minutes before using in the ear to avoid dizziness from cold liquid.
Shake well immediately before use.
Protect from light
Compliance with therapy
Importance of keeping ear clean and dry; avoiding swimming if needed.
Discard unused portion after therapy is completed
Using only for otic administration; not approved for use in the eye

Precautions while using this medication
If infection is not improved within one week consult your doctor

» If rash or allergic reaction occurs, discontinue use immediately and contact doctor

General Dosing Information
For otic dosing forms:
Acute otitis media administration:
- The suspension should be warmed by holding the bottle in the hand for one or two minutes to avoid dizziness, which may result from the instillation of a cold solution.
- The patient should lie with the affected ear upward, and the drops should be instilled in the ear canal through the tympanostomy tube.
- The tragus (a small projection in front of the external opening of the ear) should be pumped 5 times by pushing inward to facilitate the penetration of the drops into the middle ear.
- This position should be maintained for 60 seconds.
- Repeat, if necessary, for the opposite ear.
- Discard unused portion after therapy is completed.

Acute otitis externa administration:
- The solution should be warmed by holding the bottle in the hand for one or two minutes to avoid dizziness, which may result from the instillation of a cold solution.
- The patient should lie with the affected ear upward, and the drops should be instilled.
- This position should be maintained for 60 seconds.
- Repeat, if necessary, for the opposite ear.
- Discard unused portion after therapy is completed.

This medicine is for otic use only. It is not approved for ophthalmic use.

As with other antibacterial preparations, use of this product may result in overgrowth of nonsusceptible organisms, including yeast and fungi. If the infection is not improved after one week of treatment, cultures should be obtained to guide further treatment. If otorrhea persists after a full course of therapy, or if two or more episodes of otorrhea occur within six months, further evaluation is recommended to exclude an underlying condition such as cholesteatoma, foreign body, or a tumor.

The systemic administration of quinolones, including ciprofloxacin at doses much higher than given or absorbed by the otic route, has led to lesions or erosions of the cartilage in weight-bearing joints and other signs of arthropathy in immature animals of various species.

Guinea pigs dosed in the middle ear with ciprofloxacin and dexamethasone combination for one month exhibited no drug-related structural or functional changes of the cochlear hair cells and no lesions in the ossicles. It was also shown to lack dermal sensitizing potential in the guinea pig when tested according to the method of Buehler. No signs of local irritation were found when ciprofloxacin and dexamethasone combination was applied topically in the rabbit eye.

Ciprofloxacin and dexamethasone combination should be discontinued at the first appearance of a skin rash or any other sign of hypersensitivity. Serious and occasionally fatal hypersensitivity (anaphylactic) reactions, some following the first dose, have been reported in patients receiving systemic quinolones. Serious acute hypersensitivity reactions may require immediate emergency medical treatment.

It is important that the infected ear(s) remain clean and dry. When bathing, avoid getting the infected ear(s) wet. Avoid swimming unless the doctor has instructed otherwise.

Otic Dosage Forms

CIPROFLOXACIN HYDROCHLORIDE AND DEXAMETHASONE OTIC SUSPENSION

Usual adult dose

Acute Otitis Externa—

Topical, to the ear canal, four drops instilled into the affected ear twice daily for seven days.

Usual pediatric dose

Acute Otitis Externa—

Topical, to the ear canal through tympanostomy tube, four drops instilled into the affected ear twice daily for seven days.

Acute Otitis Media—

Topical, to the ear canal, four drops instilled into the affected ear twice daily for seven days.

Usual geriatric dose

See *Usual adult dose.*

Strength(s) usually available

U.S.—

0.3% ciprofloxacin (3 mg base per mL) and 0.1% dexamethasone (1 mg per mL) (Rx) [*Ciprodex* (benzalkonium chloride; acetic acid; boric acid; hydroxyethyl cellulose; edetate disodium; purified water; sodium acetate; sodium chloride; tyloxapol)].

Canada—

Not commercially available.

Packaging and storage

Store between 15 to 30°C (59 to 86°F), Avoid freezing. Protect from light.

Auxiliary labeling

- For the ear
- Shake well
- Do not touch or contaminate the tip of the container
- Protect from light
- Discard unused portion after therapy is completed
- Not for injection

Developed: 06/22/2004

CISPLATIN Systemic

VA CLASSIFICATION (Primary): AN900

Commonly used brand name(s): *Platinol; Platinol-AQ.*

Note: For a listing of dosage forms and brand names by country availability, see *Dosage Forms* section(s).

Category

Antineoplastic.

Indications

Note: Bracketed information in the *Indications* section refers to uses that are not included in U.S. product labeling.

Accepted

Carcinoma, bladder (treatment)—Cisplatin is indicated as a single agent for treatment of transitional cell cancer of the bladder that is no longer amenable to local treatments such as surgery and/or radiotherapy.

Carcinoma, ovarian (treatment)—Cisplatin is indicated in combination with other chemotherapeutic agents for treatment of metastatic ovarian tumors in patients who have already received appropriate surgical and/or radiotherapeutic procedures. It is indicated, as a single agent, as secondary therapy of metastatic ovarian tumors refractory to standard chemotherapy that did not include cisplatin.

Cisplatin is indicated, in combination with paclitaxel, for the [treatment of fallopian tube and peritoneal carcinomas, of ovarian origin][1].

Carcinoma, testicular (treatment)—Cisplatin is indicated in combination with other chemotherapeutic agents for treatment of metastatic testicular tumors in patients who have already received appropriate surgical and/or radiotherapeutic procedures.

[Carcinoma, adrenocortical (treatment)][1]
[Carcinoma, breast (treatment)][1]
[Carcinoma, cervical (treatment)][1]
[Carcinoma, endometrial (treatment)][1]
[Carcinoma, esophageal (treatment)][1]
[Carcinoma, gastric (treatment)][1]
[Carcinoma, lung, non-small cell (treatment)][1]
[Carcinoma, lung, small cell (treatment)][1]
[Neuroblastoma (treatment)][1]
[Carcinoma, head and neck (treatment)][1]
[Carcinoma, hepatocellular, primary (treatment)][1]
[Carcinoma, thyroid (treatment)][1] or
[Thymoma (treatment)][1]—Cisplatin is indicated for treatment of adrenocortical carcinoma (Evidence rating: IIID), breast carcinoma, cervical carcinoma, endometrial carcinoma, esophageal carcinoma, gastric carcinoma, non-small cell lung carcinoma, small cell lung carcinoma, neuroblastoma in children, squamous cell carcinoma of the head and neck, primary hepatocellular carcinoma (Evidence rating: IA), thyroid carcinoma (Evidence rating: IIA), and thymoma.

[Carcinoma, anal (treatment)][1]—Cisplatin is indicated for treatment of anal carcinoma (Evidence rating: IIID).

[Carcinoma, biliary tract (treatment)][1] or
[Carcinoma, vulvar (treatment)][1]—Cisplatin, in combination therapy, is reasonable medical therapy at some point in the management of biliary tract carcinoma (Evidence rating: IIID) and vulvar carcinoma (Evidence rating: IIID).

[Carcinoma, prostatic (treatment)][1] or
[Retinoblastoma (treatment)][1]—Cisplatin is reasonable medical therapy at some point in the management of prostatic carcinoma (Evidence rating: IA) and retinoblastoma (Evidence rating: IIID).

[Carcinoma, skin (treatment)][1]—Cisplatin is indicated for the first- or second-line treatment of squamous cell skin carcinoma.

[Carcinoma, unknown primary site (treatment)][1]—Cisplatin is indicated for the treatment of carcinoma of unknown primary site (CUPS), when used in combination with other agents (e.g., bleomycin, docetaxel, etoposide, 5–fluorouracil). Some USP medical experts are hesitant about the neurotoxicity and nephrotoxicity associated with cisplatin, making it less attractive than carboplatin and suggest using individual case factors (e.g., metastatic sites, disease factors, patient characteristics, etc.) when considering an appropriate treatment.

[Melanoma, malignant (treatment)][1]—Cisplatin is indicated for treatment of malignant melanoma.

[Lymphoma, Hodgkin's (treatment)][1] or
[Lymphoma, non-Hodgkin's (treatment)][1]—Cisplatin is indicated for treatment of Hodgkin's and non-Hodgkin's lymphomas.

[Hepatoblastoma (treatment)][1]
[Tumors, germ cell, ovarian (treatment)][1]
[Tumors, germ cell (treatment)][1]
[Tumors, trophoblastic, gestational (treatment)][1] or
[Wilms' tumor (treatment)][1]—Cisplatin is indicated for treatment of hepatoblastoma in children, ovarian germ cell tumors, germ cell tumors in children, gestational trophoblastic tumors, and Wilms' tumors in children.

[Osteosarcoma (treatment)][1]—Cisplatin is indicated for treatment of osteosarcoma in children.

[Sarcoma, soft tissue (treatment)][1]—Cisplatin is indicated, in combination with other chemotherapeutic agents, for treatment of soft tissue sarcomas (Evidence rating: IA).

[Kaposi's sarcoma, acquired immunodeficiency syndrome (AIDS)-associated (treatment)][1]—Cisplatin is indicated for treatment of AIDS-associated Kaposi's sarcoma.

Unaccepted

There is evidence establishing that cisplatin is ineffective in the treatment of uterine sarcomas.

[1]Not included in Canadian product labeling.

Pharmacology/Pharmacokinetics

Physicochemical characteristics

Molecular weight—300.06.

Mechanism of action/Effect

Cisplatin resembles an alkylating agent. Although the exact mechanism of action is unknown, action is thought to be similar to that of the bifunctional alkylating agents, that is, possible cross-linking and interference with the function of DNA and a small effect on RNA. It is cell cycle phase–nonspecific. Stimulation of the host immune system is also possible.

Distribution

Does not readily cross the blood-brain barrier.

Protein binding
Metabolites—Very high (more than 90%) during excretory (beta) phase.

Biotransformation
By rapid nonenzymatic conversion to inactive metabolites.

Half-life
Alpha phase—
25 to 49 minutes.
Beta phase (in hours)—
Normal: 58 to 73.
Anuric: Up to 240.

Duration of action
Inhibition of DNA persists for several days following administration.

Elimination
Renal (27 to 43% after 5 days); platinum may be detected in tissues for 4 months or more after administration.
In dialysis—Cisplatin is removable by dialysis, but only within 3 hours after administration.

Precautions to Consider

Carcinogenicity
Secondary malignancies are potential delayed effects of many antineoplastic agents, although it is not clear whether the effect is related to their mutagenic or immunosuppressive action. The effect of dose and duration of therapy is also unknown, although risk seems to increase with long-term use. Although information is limited, available data seem to indicate that the carcinogenic risk is greatest with the alkylating agents.
Development of acute leukemia has been reported to occur rarely in patients treated with cisplatin, usually in combination with other leukemogenic agents.
In studies of 50 BD IX rats administered intraperitoneal doses of cisplatin at 1 mg per kg of body weight (mg/kg) three times per week for 3 weeks, 33 animals died within 455 days after the first application. Thirteen of the deaths were related to malignancies (12 cases of leukemias and 1 of fibrosarcoma).

Mutagenicity
Cisplatin is mutagenic in bacteria and has been shown to cause chromosome aberrations in animal cells in tissue culture.

Pregnancy/Reproduction
Fertility—Gonadal suppression, resulting in amenorrhea or azoospermia, may occur in patients taking antineoplastic therapy, especially with the alkylating agents. In general, these effects appear to be related to the dose and length of therapy and may be irreversible. Prediction of the degree of testicular or ovarian function impairment is complicated by the common use of combinations of several antineoplastics, which makes it difficult to assess the effects of individual agents.
Pregnancy—Cisplatin may be toxic to the fetal urogenital tract.
First trimester: It is usually recommended that use of antineoplastics, especially combination chemotherapy, be avoided whenever possible, especially during the first trimester. Although information is limited because of the relatively few instances of antineoplastic administration during pregnancy, the mutagenic, teratogenic, and carcinogenic potential of these medications must be considered.
Other hazards to the fetus include adverse reactions seen in adults.
In general, use of a contraceptive is recommended during cytotoxic drug therapy.
Cisplatin is embryotoxic and teratogenic in mice.
FDA Pregnancy Category D.

Breast-feeding
Although very little information is available regarding distribution of antineoplastic agents into breast milk, breast-feeding is not recommended during chemotherapy because of the risks to the infant (adverse effects, mutagenicity, carcinogenicity).

Pediatrics
Ototoxic effects of cisplatin may be more severe in children.

Geriatrics
No information is available on the relationship of age to the effects of cisplatin in geriatric patients. However, elderly patients are more likely to have age-related renal function impairment, which may require reduction of dosage in patients receiving cisplatin.

Dental
The bone marrow depressant effects of cisplatin may result in an increased incidence of microbial infection, delayed healing, and gingival bleeding. Dental work, whenever possible, should be completed prior to initiation of therapy or deferred until blood counts have returned to normal. Patients should be instructed in proper oral hygiene during treatment, including caution in use of regular toothbrushes, dental floss, and toothpicks.
Cisplatin may also rarely cause stomatitis associated with considerable discomfort.

Drug interactions and/or related problems
The following drug interactions and/or related problems have been selected on the basis of their potential clinical significance (possible mechanism in parentheses where appropriate)—not necessarily inclusive (» = major clinical significance):

Note: Combinations containing any of the following medications, depending on the amount present, may also interact with this medication.

Allopurinol or
Colchicine or
» Probenecid or
» Sulfinpyrazone
(cisplatin may raise the concentration of blood uric acid; dosage adjustment of antigout agents may be necessary to control hyperuricemia and gout; allopurinol may be preferred to prevent or reverse cisplatin-induced hyperuricemia because of risk of uric acid nephropathy with uricosuric antigout agents)

Antihistamines or
Buclizine or
Cyclizine or
Loxapine or
Meclizine or
Phenothiazines or
Thioxanthenes or
Trimethobenzamide
(concurrent use with cisplatin may mask the symptoms of ototoxicity, such as tinnitus, dizziness, or vertigo)

Bleomycin
(cisplatin-induced renal function impairment may result in bleomycin toxicity even at low doses; caution is recommended because of the frequent combination of these two agents)

Blood dyscrasia-causing medications (see *Appendix II*)
(leukopenic and/or thrombocytopenic effects of cisplatin may be increased with concurrent or recent therapy if these medications cause the same effects; dosage adjustment of cisplatin, if necessary, should be based on blood counts)

» Bone marrow depressants, other (see *Appendix II*) or
Radiation therapy
(concurrent use may increase the total effects of these medications and radiation therapy; dosage reduction is recommended)

» Nephrotoxic medications, other (see *Appendix II*) or
» Ototoxic medications, other (see *Appendix II*)
(concurrent and/or sequential administration should be avoided since the potential for ototoxicity and nephrotoxicity may be increased, especially in the presence of renal function impairment)

Vaccines, killed virus
(because normal defense mechanisms may be suppressed by cisplatin therapy, the patient's antibody response to the vaccine may be decreased. The interval between discontinuation of medications that cause immunosuppression and restoration of the patient's ability to respond to the vaccine depends on the intensity and type of immunosuppression-causing medication used, the underlying disease, and other factors; estimates vary from 3 months to 1 year)

» Vaccines, live virus
(because normal defense mechanisms may be suppressed by cisplatin therapy, concurrent use with a live virus vaccine may potentiate the replication of the vaccine virus, may increase the side/adverse effects of the vaccine virus, and/or may decrease the patient's antibody response to the vaccine; immunization of these patients should be undertaken only with extreme caution after careful review of the patient's hematologic status and only with the knowledge and consent of the physician managing the cisplatin therapy. The interval between discontinuation of medications that cause immunosuppression and restoration of the patient's ability to respond to the vaccine depends on the intensity and type of immunosuppression-causing medication used, the underlying disease, and other factors; estimates vary from 3 months to 1 year. In addition, immunization with oral poliovirus vaccine should be postponed in persons in close contact with the patient, especially family members)

Laboratory value alterations

The following have been selected on the basis of their potential clinical significance (possible effect in parentheses where appropriate)—not necessarily inclusive (» = major clinical significance).

With physiology/laboratory test values

Aspartate aminotransferase (AST [SGOT]), serum
(values may be increased transiently)

Bilirubin, serum
(concentrations may be increased transiently)

Blood urea nitrogen (BUN) and
Creatinine, serum and
Uric acid, serum
(concentrations may be increased, indicating nephrotoxicity)

Calcium, serum and
Creatinine clearance and
Magnesium, serum and
Phosphate, serum and
Potassium, serum and
Sodium, serum
(may be decreased, probably as a result of renal toxicity; rarely, tetany associated with hypocalcemia and hypomagnesemia has occurred)

Coombs' test
(positive results, associated with hemolytic anemia, have been reported)

Medical considerations/Contraindications

The medical considerations/contraindications included have been selected on the basis of their potential clinical significance (reasons given in parentheses where appropriate)—not necessarily inclusive (» = major clinical significance).

Risk-benefit should be considered when the following medical problems exist:

» Bone marrow depression

» Chickenpox, existing or recent (including recent exposure) or
» Herpes zoster
(risk of severe generalized disease)

Gout, history of or
Urate renal stones, history of
(risk of hyperuricemia)

» Hearing impairment

» Infection

» Renal function impairment
(reduced excretion; a lower dosage of cisplatin is recommended)

Sensitivity to cisplatin

» Caution should be used also in patients who have had previous cytotoxic drug therapy or radiation therapy.

Patient monitoring

The following are especially important in patient monitoring (other tests may be warranted in some patients, depending on condition; » = major clinical significance):

» Audiometric testing and
» Neurologic function studies
(determinations recommended prior to initiation of therapy and at periodic intervals during therapy)

Blood urea nitrogen (BUN) and
» Creatinine clearance and
Creatinine, serum
(determinations recommended prior to initiation of therapy and before each course of cisplatin to detect renal toxicity)

Calcium, serum and
Magnesium, serum and
Phosphate, serum and
Potassium, serum
(determinations recommended at periodic intervals during therapy)

» Hematocrit or hemoglobin and
» Leukocyte count, total and, if appropriate, differential and
» Platelet count
(determinations recommended prior to initiation of therapy and at periodic intervals during therapy; frequency varies according to clinical state, agent, dose, and other agents being used concurrently)

Uric acid, serum
(determinations recommended prior to initiation of therapy and at periodic intervals during therapy; frequency varies according to clinical state, agent, dose, and other agents being used concurrently)

Side/Adverse Effects

Note: Many "side effects" of antineoplastic therapy are unavoidable and represent the medication's pharmacologic action. Some of these (for example, leukopenia and thrombocytopenia) are actually used as parameters to aid in individual dosage titration.

Side effects are more pronounced at doses of cisplatin greater than 50 mg per square meter of body surface area.

Vascular toxicities have been reported rarely when cisplatin is given in combination with other antineoplastic agents, although it is unknown whether the toxicity is related to cisplatin administration or to other factors. Vascular toxicities reported include myocardial infarction, cerebrovascular accident, thrombotic microangiopathy, cerebral arteritis, and Raynaud's phenomenon.

The following side/adverse effects have been selected on the basis of their potential clinical significance (possible signs and symptoms in parentheses where appropriate)—not necessarily inclusive:

Those indicating need for medical attention

Incidence more frequent—severity increases with repeated doses

Anemia secondary to myelosuppression (unusual tiredness or weakness)—usually asymptomatic; ***leukopenia*** (fever or chills; cough or hoarseness; lower back or side pain; painful or difficult urination)—usually asymptomatic; ***nephrotoxicity, hyperuricemia, or uric acid nephropathy*** (joint pain; lower back or side pain; swelling of feet or lower legs); ***neurotoxicity*** (loss of reflexes; loss of taste; numbness or tingling in fingers or toes; seizures; trouble in walking; rarely, muscle cramps); ***ototoxicity*** (loss of balance; ringing in ears; trouble in hearing); ***thrombocytopenia*** (unusual bleeding or bruising; black, tarry stools; blood in urine or stools; pinpoint red spots on skin)—usually asymptomatic

Note: *Myelosuppression (leukopenia, thrombocytopenia, anemia)* is more pronounced at higher doses. Nadir of leukocyte and platelet counts occurs after 18 to 23 days and counts usually recover by 39 days after a dose.

Cisplatin frequently causes *nephrotoxicity* in the form of acute renal dysfunction, which may be detected initially only by means of renal function tests. Laboratory abnormalities occur during the second week after a dose. Nephrotoxicity is dose-related and cumulative; it is usually reversible, but may become irreversible at high doses or with repeated treatments, and is occasionally fatal.

Hypocalcemia and hypomagnesemia may occur due to *nephrotoxicity.* Rarely, tetany associated with hypocalcemia may occur, and tremors or seizures may occur as a result of hypomagnesemia.

With *hyperuricemia,* peak uric acid concentrations occur 3 to 5 days after a dose.

Neurotoxicity, usually characterized by peripheral neuropathies, may occur after a single dose or prolonged therapy (4 to 7 months) and may be severe and irreversible. Signs and symptoms of neuropathy usually develop during treatment, but may rarely begin 3 to 8 weeks after the last dose, and may progress even after withdrawal of cisplatin. Muscle cramps (localized, painful, involuntary skeletal contractions of sudden onset and short duration) have been reported, usually in patients receiving a relatively high cumulative dose of cisplatin and in a relatively advanced symptomatic stage of peripheral neuropathy. Lhermitte's sign, dorsal column myelopathy, and autonomic neuropathy have also been reported.

Ototoxicity may be more severe in children and may not be reversible. Ototoxicity may also occur more frequently and may be more severe in patients of any age who have received prior cranial radiotherapy. Ototoxicity is cumulative; hearing loss usually occurs first with high frequencies (above speech tones) and may be unilateral or bilateral.

Incidence less frequent

Anaphylactic reaction, occurring within a few minutes after administration (dizziness or fainting; fast heartbeat; swelling of face; wheezing); ***extravasation*** (pain or redness at site of injection)

Note: *Extravasation* may rarely produce local soft tissue toxicity, the severity of which is related to the concentration of the solution. Infusion of solutions containing cisplatin in a concentration greater than 500 mcg (0.5 mg) per mL may result in tissue cellulitis, fibrosis, and necrosis.

Incidence rare

Hemolytic anemia (unusual tiredness or weakness)—usually asymptomatic; ***optic neuritis, papilledema, or cerebral blindness*** (blurred vision; change in ability to see colors, especially blue or yellow); ***stomatitis*** (sores in mouth and on lips); ***syndrome of inappropriate antidiuretic hormone (SIADH) secretion*** (dizziness, confusion, or agitation; unusual tiredness or weakness)

Note: A Coombs'-positive *hemolytic anemia* has also been reported.

Optic neuritis, papilledema, or cerebral blindness is usually reversible after withdrawal of cisplatin. Fundoscopic examination usually finds only irregular retinal pigmentation of the macular area.

Those indicating need for medical attention only if they continue or are bothersome

Incidence more frequent—occurs in most patients

Nausea and vomiting, severe

Note: *Nausea and vomiting* usually begin 1 to 4 hours after a dose, and vomiting may persist for 24 hours. Nausea and anorexia may persist for up to 1 week. Serotonin antagonists (e.g., ondansetron), high-dose intravenous metoclopramide, or corticosteroids have been found to be useful in preventing severe nausea and vomiting; however, severe nausea and vomiting may require discontinuation of cisplatin.

Incidence less frequent

Loss of appetite

Those indicating need for medical attention if they occur after medication is discontinued

Myelosuppression (black, tarry stools; blood in urine or stools; cough or hoarseness; fever or chills; lower back or side pain; painful or difficult urination; pinpoint red spots on skin; unusual bleeding or bruising) ***nephrotoxicity*** (decrease in urination; swelling of feet or lower legs) ***neurotoxicity*** (loss of reflexes; loss of taste; numbness or tingling in fingers or toes; seizures; trouble in walking) ***ototoxicity*** (loss of balance; ringing in ears; trouble in hearing)

Patient Consultation

As an aid to patient consultation, refer to *Advice for the Patient, Cisplatin (Systemic)*.

In providing consultation, consider emphasizing the following selected information (» = major clinical significance):

Before using this medication

» Conditions affecting use, especially:

Sensitivity to cisplatin

Pregnancy—Use not recommended because of mutagenic, teratogenic, and carcinogenic potential; advisability of using a contraceptive; telling physician immediately if pregnancy is suspected

Breast-feeding—Not recommended because of serious side effects

Use in children—Ototoxicity may be more severe

Other medications, especially probenecid, sulfinpyrazone, other bone marrow depressants, other nephrotoxic medications, other ototoxic medications, live virus vaccines, or previous cytotoxic drug therapy or radiation therapy

Other medical problems, especially chickenpox, herpes zoster, hearing impairment, infection, or renal function impairment

Proper use of this medication

Caution if taking combination therapy; taking each medication at the right time

Importance of ample fluid intake and subsequent increase in urine output to aid in excretion of uric acid

Frequency of severe nausea and vomiting; importance of continuing medication despite stomach upset

» Proper dosing

Precautions while using this medication

» Importance of close monitoring by the physician

» Avoiding immunizations unless approved by physician; other persons in patient's household should avoid immunizations with oral poliovirus vaccine; avoiding persons who have taken oral poliovirus vaccine or wearing a protective mask that covers nose and mouth

Caution if bone marrow depression occurs:

» Avoiding exposure to persons with infections, especially during periods of low blood counts; checking with physician immediately if fever or chills, cough or hoarseness, lower back or side pain, or painful or difficult urination occurs

» Checking with physician immediately if unusual bleeding or bruising; black, tarry stools; blood in urine or stools; or pinpoint red spots on skin occur

Caution in use of regular toothbrush, dental floss, or toothpick; physician, dentist, or nurse may suggest alternatives; checking with physician before having dental work done

Not touching eyes or inside of nose unless hands washed immediately before

Using caution to avoid accidental cuts with use of sharp objects such as safety razor or fingernail or toenail cutters

Avoiding contact sports or other situations where bruising or injury could occur

» Possibility of local tissue injury and scarring if infiltration of intravenous solution occurs; telling doctor or nurse right away about redness, pain, or swelling at injection site

Side/adverse effects

Importance of discussing possible effects, including cancer, with physician

Signs of potential side effects, especially anemia, leukopenia, nephrotoxicity, hyperuricemia, uric acid nephropathy, neurotoxicity, ototoxicity, thrombocytopenia, anaphylactic reaction, extravasation, hemolytic anemia, optic neuritis, papilledema, cerebral blindness, stomatitis, and SIADH secretion

Physician or nurse can help in dealing with side effects

General Dosing Information

It is recommended that cisplatin be administered to patients in an appropriate setting under supervision of a physician or nurse experienced in cancer chemotherapy. It is also recommended that equipment and medications (including epinephrine, oxygen, antihistamines, and intravenous corticosteroids) necessary for treatment of a possible anaphylactic reaction be readily available at each administration of cisplatin.

A variety of dosage schedules and regimens of cisplatin, alone or in combination with other antitumor agents, are used. The prescriber may consult the medical literature as well as the manufacturer's literature in choosing a specific dosage.

It is recommended that cisplatin be administered with vigorous parenteral infusion to increase hydration; this is intended to maintain urine output and reduce nephrotoxicity and ototoxicity, although it will not prevent them.

Vigorous pretreatment intravenous hydration, followed by adequate hydration and urinary output for 24 hours, are recommended. Mannitol or furosemide may also be used to produce acute diuresis, provided that salt and water depletion are avoided.

Cisplatin has also been administered as a continuous intravenous infusion over periods ranging from 24 hours to 5 days; this method of administration appears to reduce nausea and vomiting but not nephrotoxicity or ototoxicity. It is very important that orders for the total dose to be given over the entire course of the infusion *not* be misinterpreted as a daily dose, because of the risk of fatal overdose.

Development of uric acid nephropathy may be prevented by adequate oral hydration and, in some cases, administration of allopurinol. Alkalinization of urine may be necessary if serum uric acid concentrations are elevated.

It is recommended that courses of cisplatin be administered no more frequently than every 3 to 4 weeks, to reduce the risk of cumulative nephrotoxicity.

Subsequent doses of cisplatin must not be given before renal function approaches normal (measured by BUN, creatinine clearance, and serum creatinine). Administration of subsequent doses of cisplatin also is not recommended before platelet levels return to at least 100,000 per cubic millimeter and leukocyte levels to at least 4000 per cubic millimeter, or before auditory acuity is confirmed to be within normal limits.

Therapy with cisplatin should be discontinued at the first sign of significant neurotoxicity, which may be irreversible.

Special precautions are recommended in patients who develop thrombocytopenia as a result of administration of cisplatin. These may include extreme care in performing invasive procedures; regular inspection of intravenous sites, skin (including perirectal area), and mucous membrane surfaces for signs of bleeding or bruising; limiting frequency of venipuncture and avoiding intramuscular injections; testing urine, emesis, stool, and secretions for occult blood; care in use of regular toothbrushes, dental floss, toothpicks, safety razors, and fingernail and toenail cutters; avoiding constipation; and using caution to prevent falls and other injuries. Such patients should avoid alcohol and aspirin intake because of the risk of gastrointestinal bleeding. Platelet transfusions may be required.

Patients who develop leukopenia should be observed carefully for signs of infection. Antibiotic support may be required. In neutropenic patients who develop fever, broad-spectrum antibiotic coverage should be initiated empirically, pending bacterial cultures and appropriate diagnostic tests.

Safety considerations for handling this medication

There is limited but increasing evidence and concern that personnel involved in preparation and administration of parenteral antineoplastics may be at some risk because of the potential mutagenicity, teratogenicity, and/or carcinogenicity of these agents, although the actual risk is unknown. USP advisory panels recommend cautious handling both in preparation and disposal of antineoplastic agents. Precautions that have been suggested include:

- Use of a biological containment cabinet during reconstitution and dilution of parenteral medications and wearing of disposable surgical gloves and masks.
- Use of proper technique to prevent contamination of the medication, work area, and operator during transfer between containers (including proper training of personnel in this technique).
- Cautious and proper disposal of needles, syringes, vials, ampuls, and unused medication.

A number of medical centers have developed detailed guidelines for handling of antineoplastic agents.

Combination chemotherapy

Cisplatin may be used in combination with other agents in various regimens. As a result, incidence and/or severity of side effects may be altered and different dosages (usually reduced) may be used. For example, cisplatin is part of the following chemotherapeutic combination (some commonly used acronyms are in parentheses):

—cyclophosphamide, doxorubicin, and cisplatin (CISCA or CAP).

For specific dosages and schedules, consult the literature. For information regarding each agent, consult the individual monographs.

Parenteral Dosage Forms

Note: Bracketed uses in the *Dosage Forms* section refer to categories of use and/or indications that are not included in U.S. product labeling.

CISPLATIN INJECTION

Usual adult and adolescent dose

Metastatic testicular tumors—

Intravenous, 20 mg per square meter of body surface area a day for five days per twenty-one–day cycle.

Metastatic ovarian tumors—

Intravenous, 75 to 100 mg per square meter of body surface area once every four weeks (day 1), in combination with 600 mg of cyclophosphamide per square meter of body surface area intravenously every four weeks on day 1 (administered sequentially), or

Intravenous, 100 mg per square meter of body surface area once every four weeks (as a single agent), or

Intravenous, 75 mg per square meter of body surface area once every three weeks, given in combination with 135 mg of paclitaxel (given over twenty-four hours) per square meter of body surface area every three weeks, for six courses.

For the treatment of [fallopian tube and peritoneal carcinomas of ovarian origin][1], patients have also benefited from intravenous doses of cisplatin 50 to 75 mg/m^2, in combination with paclitaxel 135 to 175 mg/m^2 (by 3–hour infusion), every 21 to 28 days. Duration of paclitaxel infusion may be increased to 24 hours, depending on toxicity.

Advanced bladder cancer—

Intravenous, 50 to 70 mg per square meter of body surface area every three to four weeks (as a single agent). The lower end of the dosage range is recommended in patients heavily pretreated with radiation or chemotherapy.

[Carcinoma, adrenocortical (treatment)][1] or
[Carcinoma, breast (treatment)][1] or
[Carcinoma, cervical (treatment)][1] or
[Carcinoma, endometrial (treatment)][1] or
[Carcinoma, esophageal (treatment)][1] or
[Carcinoma, gastric (treatment)][1] or
[Carcinoma, lung, non-small cell (treatment)][1] or
[Carcinoma, lung, small cell (treatment)][1] or
[Neuroblastoma (treatment)][1] or
[Carcinoma, prostatic (treatment)][1] or
[Carcinoma, head and neck (treatment)][1] or
[Carcinoma, hepatocellular, primary (treatment)][1] or
[Carcinoma, thyroid (treatment)][1] or
[Thymoma (treatment)][1] or
[Carcinoma, anal (treatment)][1] or
[Carcinoma, biliary tract (treatment)][1] or
[Carcinoma, vulvar (treatment)][1] or
[Retinoblastoma (treatment)][1] or
[Melanoma, malignant (treatment)][1] or
[Lymphoma, Hodgkin's (treatment)][1] or
[Lymphoma, non-Hodgkin's (treatment)][1] or
[Hepatoblastoma (treatment)][1] or
[Tumors, germ cell, ovarian (treatment)][1] or
[Tumors, germ cell (treatment)][1] or
[Tumors, trophoblastic, gestational (treatment)][1] or
[Wilms' tumor (treatment)][1] or
[Osteosarcoma (treatment)][1] or
[Sarcoma, soft tissue (treatment)][1] or
[Kaposi's sarcoma, acquired immunodeficiency syndrome (AIDS)-associated (treatment)][1]—

Consult medical literature and manufacturer's literature for specific dosage.

[Carcinoma, unknown primary site][1]—

Patients have benefited from intravenous doses of 60–80 mg/m^2 on day 1 or 20 mg/m^2/day on days 1 to 5, of a 21-day treatment cycle, for 4 to 8 cycles, in conjunction with other agents (e.g., bleomycin, docetaxel, etoposide, 5–fluorouracil).

Usual adult prescribing limits

Total dose for a single *course* of cisplatin (whether given as a single daily infusion or as a continuous infusion over several days, to be repeated every three to four weeks) should not exceed 120 mg per square meter of body surface area. Administration of higher doses in a single course may lead to potentially fatal overdose. Exceptions should be made, and care of these patients should be handled, only by medical professionals who fully understand and are prepared to deal with the potential toxicities of such dosing.

Usual pediatric dose

See *Usual adult and adolescent dose.*

Strength(s) usually available

U.S.—

1 mg per mL (50-, and 100-mL vials) (Rx) [*Platinol-AQ* (sodium chloride 9 mg per mL)].

Canada—

500 mcg (0.5 mg) per mL (20-, 50-, and 100-mL vials) (Rx) [*Platinol-AQ* (sodium chloride 9 mg per mL); GENERIC].

1 mg per mL (10-, 50-, and 100-mL vials) [*Platinol-AQ* (sodium chloride 9 mg per mL)].

Packaging and storage

Store between 15 and 25 °C (59 and 77 °F), unless otherwise specified by manufacturer. Do not refrigerate.

Stability

Caution—A black platinum precipitate will form if cisplatin comes in contact with aluminum.

Solution remaining in amber vial following initial entry is stable for 28 days protected from light or for 7 days under fluorescent room light.

Incompatibilities

Do not use needles, intravenous sets, or equipment containing aluminum for administration since cisplatin is incompatible with aluminum.

Note

No more than 120 mg per square meter of body surface area per course (with each course separated by three to four weeks) should be dispensed without verbal or written confirmation by the prescribing physician. To reduce the risk of fatal overdose, no more than the amount for one course should be dispensed at one time.

CISPLATIN FOR INJECTION USP

Usual adult and adolescent dose

See *Cisplatin Injection.*

Usual adult prescribing limits

See *Cisplatin Injection.*

Usual pediatric dose

See *Cisplatin Injection.*

Strength(s) usually available

U.S.—

Not commercially available.

Canada—

10 mg (Rx) [*Platinol*].

50 mg (Rx) [*Platinol*].

Packaging and storage

Store below 40 °C (104 °F), preferably between 15 and 30 °C (59 and 86 °F), unless otherwise specified by manufacturer. Protect from light.

Preparation of dosage form

Cisplatin for injection is reconstituted for intravenous use by adding 10 or 50 mL of sterile water for injection to the 10-mg or 50-mg vial, respectively, producing a clear, colorless solution containing 1 mg of cisplatin per mL. It is recommended that 5% dextrose injection in 0.3 or 0.45% sodium chloride injection be used if further dilution for administration by intravenous solution is required, in order to ensure stability.

Stability

Reconstituted solutions of cisplatin are stable for 20 hours at 27 °C (80 °F). Solution removed from the amber vial should be protected from light if it is not to be used within 6 hours.

Incompatibilities

Do not use needles, intravenous sets, or equipment containing aluminum for administration since cisplatin is incompatible with aluminum.

Caution

A precipitate will form if reconstituted solutions are refrigerated.

A black platinum precipitate will form if cisplatin comes in contact with aluminum.

Note

No more than 120 mg per square meter of body surface area per course (with each course separated by three to four weeks) should be dispensed without verbal or written confirmation by the prescribing physician. To reduce the risk of fatal overdose, no more than the amount for one course should be dispensed at one time.

[1]Not included in Canadian product labeling.

Revised: 12/12/2002

CITALOPRAM Systemic

VA CLASSIFICATION (Primary): CN603

Commonly used brand name(s): *Celexa*.

Note: For a listing of dosage forms and brand names by country availability, see *Dosage Forms* section(s).

Category

Antidepressant.

Indications

Accepted

Depressive disorder, major (treatment)—Citalopram is indicated for the treatment of depression. Maintenance of antidepressant response for 24 weeks following 6 to 8 weeks of acute treatment was demonstrated in two placebo-controlled trials of outpatients whose diagnosis corresponded most closely to the DSM-III or DSM-III-R category of major depressive disorder. Treatment of acute depressive episodes typically requires 6 to 12 months of antidepressant therapy, and patients with recurrent or chronic depression may require long-term treatment.

Note: A major depressive episode (DSM-IV) implies a prominent and relatively persistent (nearly every day for at least 2 weeks) depressed or dysphoric mood that usually interferes with daily function and includes at least five of the following nine symptoms: depressed mood, loss of interest in usual activities, significant change in weight and/or appetite, insomnia or hypersomnia, psychomotor agitation or retardation, increased fatigue, feelings of guilt or worthlessness, slowed thinking or impaired concentration, a suicide attempt or suicidal ideation

Acceptance not established

Citalopram has been used for the treatment of Obsessive-Compulsive Disorder (OCD), but more experience is needed to determine the risks and benefits of using citalopram for this indication.

The antidepressant action of citalopram in hospitalized depressed patients has not been adequately studied.

Pharmacology/Pharmacokinetics

Physicochemical characteristics

Chemical Group—Citalopram is a racemic, bicyclic phthalane derivative, chemically unrelated to other selective serotonin reuptake inhibitors.

Molecular weight—

Citalopram base: 324.4.

Citalopram hydrobromide: 405.35.

Solubility—Citalopram hydrobromide is sparingly soluble in water and soluble in ethanol.

Mechanism of action/Effect

The antidepressant effect of citalopram is presumed to be linked to specific serotonin (5-hydroxytryptamine [5-HT]) reuptake inhibition. Citalopram, primarily through its (S)-enantiomer, blocks 5-HT reuptake, leading to potentiation of serotonergic activity in the central nervous system. Neuronal uptake of norepinephrine and dopamine is minimally affected. Citalopram has little or no affinity for serotonin 5-HT_{1A} or 5-HT_{2A}; dopamine D_1 or D_2; adrenergic $alpha_1$, $alpha_2$, or beta; histamine H_1; gamma aminobutyric acid (GABA); muscarinic cholinergic; or benzodiazepine receptors.

Other actions/effects

One of the metabolites of citalopram, didemethylcitalopram (DDCT), was found to cause QT interval prolongation in beagle dogs at plasma concentrations many times higher than those seen in humans receiving citalopram at the maximum recommended human dose (MRHD). However, it is not known whether an individual patient might achieve higher-than-usual DDCT concentrations. The significance of this finding to humans is unknown.

Absorption

Absolute bioavailability of an oral dose of citalopram as compared to an intravenous dose is about 80% and is not affected by food.

Distribution

Vol_D—About 12 liters per kg of body weight (L/kg); range, 9 to 17 L/kg. Citalopram is distributed into human breast milk.

Protein binding

High (approximately 80%) to plasma proteins.

Biotransformation

Hepatic metabolism, primarily involving the cytochrome P450 3A4 (CYP3A4) and 2C19 (CYP2C19) isoenzymes and to a small extent, the cytochrome P450 2D6 (CYP2D6) isoenzyme, produces several metabolites. These metabolites inhibit the reuptake of serotonin with less potency and are present in the plasma at lower concentrations than the parent compound. Therefore, they are not thought to add significantly to the antidepressant effects of citalopram.

Half-life

Elimination—Terminal half-life is about 35 to 37 hours.

Onset of action

1 to 4 weeks.

Time to peak concentration

About 4 hours (range, 1 to 6 hours).

Time to steady-state concentration

About 1 week with once-a-day dosing.

Plasma concentration

Citalopram exhibits linear pharmacokinetics in a dosage range of 10 to 60 mg/day, and steady-state plasma concentrations are expected to be about 2.5 times single-dose plasma concentrations. The parent compound is the predominant form in plasma.

Elimination

Systemic clearance of citalopram was 330 mL per minute (mL/min), with approximately 20% due to renal clearance, after intravenous administration. About 10% to 12% of the administered dose was recovered in the urine unchanged.

Oral clearance of citalopram was reduced by 37% and 17% in patients with hepatic function impairment and mild to moderate renal function impairment, respectively.

Precautions to Consider

Carcinogenicity

An increased incidence of small intestine carcinomas was found in rats receiving citalopram doses equal to approximately 1.3 and 4 times the maximum recommended human dose (MRHD) on a mg per square meter of body surface area (mg/m^2) basis for 24 months. No evidence of carcinogenicity was seen in mice receiving citalopram doses equal to up to 20 times the MRHD on a mg/m^2 basis.

Mutagenicity

Citalopram was mutagenic in two of five bacterial strains in the *in vitro* bacterial reverse mutation assay (Ames test) without metabolic activation and was clastogenic in the *in vitro* Chinese hamster lung cell assay for chromosomal aberrations with and without metabolic activation. Citalopram was not mutagenic in the *in vitro* mammalian forward gene mutation assay in mouse lymphoma cells or in a coupled *in vitro/in vivo* unscheduled DNA synthesis assay in rat liver. Citalopram was not clastogenic in two *in vivo* mouse micronucleus assays or in the *in vitro* chromosomal aberration assay in human lymphocytes.

Pregnancy/Reproduction

Fertility—Male and female rats administered citalopram orally prior to and throughout mating and gestation showed decreased mating activity. Also, at doses of five times the MRHD on a mg/m^2 basis and greater, fertility was decreased, and at doses of eight times the MRHD on a mg/m^2 basis, gestation was prolonged.

Pregnancy—Adequate and well-controlled studies have not been done in humans. Citalopram should be used during pregnancy only if the potential benefit justifies the potential risk to the fetus.

When exposed to citalopram and other selective serotonin reuptake inhibitors (SSRIs) or selective norepinephrine reuptake inhibitors (SNRIs) late in the third trimester, neonates have developed complications requiring prolonged hospitalization, respiratory support, and tube feeding and these can arise immediately upon delivery. Features consistent with a direct toxic effect of SSRIs and SNRIs or a drug discontinuation syndrome including respiratory distress, cyanosis, apnea, seizures, temperature instability, feeding difficulty, vomiting, hypoglycemia, hypotonia, hypertonia, hyperreflexia, tremor, jitteriness, irritability, and constant crying have been reported. In some cases, it should be noted that the clinical picture is consistent with serotonin syndrome. When treating a pregnant woman with citalopram during the third trimester, the physician should carefully consider the potential risks and benefits of treatment.

Administration of citalopram to pregnant rats during the period of organogenesis at a dosage of approximately 18 times the MRHD on a mg/m^2 basis resulted in decreased fetal growth and survival, fetal abnormalities, including cardiovascular and skeletal defects, and maternal toxicity. No adverse developmental effects were seen in the offspring of rats and rabbits administered citalopram at dosages of up to approximately nine and five times, respectively, the MRHD on a mg/m^2 basis. Administration of citalopram to pregnant rats from late gestation through weaning at a dosage of approximately five times the MRHD on a mg/m^2 basis or throughout gestation and early lactation at a dosage of approximately four times the MRHD on a mg/m^2 basis resulted in increased offspring mortality during the first 4 days after birth and persistent offspring growth retardation.

FDA Pregnancy Category C.

Labor and delivery—The effect of citalopram on labor and delivery in humans is unknown.

Breast-feeding

Citalopram is distributed into human breast milk. Excessive somnolence, decreased feeding, and weight loss have been reported in two nursing infants whose mothers were taking citalopram. When one of the mothers discontinued citalopram, the infant recovered completely. The decision whether to continue or discontinue either nursing or citalopram therapy should take into account risk-benefit for the infant and nursing mother.

Pediatrics

No information is available on the relationship of age to the effects of citalopram in pediatric patients. Safety and efficacy have not been established.

The Food and Drug Administration [FDA] has reviewed reports of the occurrence of suicidality (both suicidal ideation and suicide attempts) in clinical trials for various antidepressant drugs including citalopram in pediatric patients with major depressive disorder [MDD]. There have been no reports of completed suicides in these clinical trials. However, FDA emphasizes that citalopram must be used with caution in treating pediatric MDD.

Geriatrics

No differences in safety or efficacy were seen between elderly and younger subjects in studies that included geriatric patients, but greater sensitivity of some older individuals cannot be ruled out. Area under the plasma concentration-time curve (AUC) and half-life of citalopram are increased in elderly patients. The recommended dosage for elderly patients is lower than that for younger patients.

Drug interactions and/or related problems

The following drug interactions and/or related problems have been selected on the basis of their potential clinical significance (possible mechanism in parentheses where appropriate)—not necessarily inclusive (» = major clinical significance):

Note: *In vitro* studies indicate that the primary isoenzymes involved in citalopram metabolism are cytochrome P450 3A4 (CYP3A4) and 2C19 (CYP2C19). Interactions with medications that inhibit CYP3A4, such as ketoconazole, itraconazole, fluconazole, and macrolide antibiotics, or with medications that inhibit CYP2C19, such as omeprazole, should be considered.

Combinations containing any of the following medications, depending on the amount present, may also interact with this medication.

Alcohol
(although studies indicate that the cognitive and motor effects of alcohol are not potentiated by citalopram, concurrent use is not recommended)

Antidepressants, tricyclic (TCAs)
(in subjects taking 40 mg per day of citalopram, the plasma concentration of desipramine, the active metabolite of imipramine, was increased by 50% after administration of a single 100-mg dose of imipramine; there was no effect on imipramine or citalopram concentration)

Aspirin or
Nonsteroidal anti-inflammatory drugs (NSAIDs) or
Other drugs affecting coagulation
(concurrent use may potentiate risk of abnormal bleeding; patients should be cautioned)

Carbamazepine
(although a short-term pharmacokinetic study showed no changes in plasma concentrations of carbamazepine or citalopram during concurrent use, the long-term enzyme-inducing effect of carbamazepine could lead to increased clearance of citalopram)

Central nervous system (CNS) drugs
(caution should be used given the primary CNS effects of citalopram)

Cimetidine
(AUC and maximum plasma concentration of citalopram were increased by 41% to 43% and 39%, respectively, by concomitant cimetidine use)

Ketoconazole
(decrease in C_{max} and AUC of ketoconazole; loss of efficacy may occur)

» Linezolid
(serotonin syndrome has been reported in two patients concomitantly receiving linezolid which is a reversible non-selective MAOI)

Lithium
(caution should be exercised with concomitant use because lithium may enhance the serotonergic effects of citalopram; plasma lithium levels should be monitored with appropriate adjustment to the lithium dose)

Metoprolol
(plasma concentrations of metoprolol were increased twofold by concomitant citalopram use; however, no clinically significant effects on heart rate or blood pressure were seen)

» Monoamine oxidase (MAO) inhibitors, including furazolidone, procarbazine, and selegiline
(serious and sometimes fatal reactions have occurred in patients receiving a serotonin reuptake inhibitor with an MAO inhibitor; reactions have included hyperthermia, rigidity, myoclonus, autonomic instability with rapid fluctuation of vital signs, and mental status changes including extreme agitation progressing to delirium and coma; some cases presented with features resembling neuroleptic malignant syndrome [NMS]; concurrent use of an MAO inhibitor and citalopram is **contraindicated;** at least 14 days should elapse between discontinuation of one medication [MAO inhibitor or citalopram] and the initiation of the other)

» Serotonergics or other medications or substances with serotonergic activity (see *Appendix II*)
(increased risk of developing the serotonin syndrome, a rare but potentially fatal hyperserotonergic state that may occur in patients receiving serotonergic medications such as citalopram, usually in combination; symptoms typically occur shortly [hours to days] after the addition of a serotonergic agent to a regimen that includes other serotonin-enhancing drugs or after an increase in dosage of a serotonergic agent; symptoms include agitation, diaphoresis, diarrhea, fever, hyperreflexia, incoordination, mental status changes [confusion, hypomania], myoclonus, shivering, or tremor)

Sumatriptan
(postmarketing reports describe patients with weakness, hyperreflexia, and incoordination following use of a selective serotonin reuptake inhibitor (SSRI) and sumatriptan; if concomitant use is clinically warranted; appropriate observation of the patient is advisable)

Warfarin
(although citalopram did not alter warfarin pharmacokinetics in one study, prothrombin time was increased by 5%)

Medical considerations/Contraindications

The medical considerations/contraindications included have been selected on the basis of their potential clinical significance (reasons given in parentheses where appropriate)—not necessarily inclusive (» = major clinical significance).

Except under special circumstances, this medication should not be used when the following medical problems exist:

» Hypersensitivity to citalopram or any of the inactive ingredients

Risk-benefit should be considered when the following medical problems exist:

Diabetic patients
(rare occurrences of hypoglycemia have been reported in diabetic patients receiving citalopram)

Drug abuse or dependence, or history of
(patients with a history of drug abuse should be observed closely for signs of misuse or abuse, as with any new central nervous system [CNS] agent)

» Heart disease (unstable) or
» Myocardial infarction (recent history of)
(use of citalopram has not been systematically evaluated in patients with these conditions)

» Hepatic function impairment
(citalopram clearance is reduced; cautious dosage titration and a lower maximum dosage are recommended)

Mania or hypomania, history of
(should be used with caution in these patients; condition may be re-activated)

Renal function impairment, severe
(although citalopram clearance was reduced to a clinically insignificant extent in patients with mild to moderate renal function impairment, there is no experience in patients with severe impairment; caution is recommended in these patients)

Seizure disorders, history of
(as with all antidepressants, citalopram should be introduced with caution in patients with a history of seizures)

Patient monitoring

The following may be especially important in patient monitoring (other tests may be warranted in some patients, depending on condition; » = major clinical significance):

Careful supervision of depressed patients including those with:
Abnormal behaviors (i.e., agitation, panic attacks, hostility) or
Clinical worsening of their depression or
Suicidal ideation and behavior (suicidality)
(recommended especially during early treatment phase before peak effectiveness of citalopram is achieved or at the time of increases or decreases in dose; prescribing the smallest number of tablets necessary for good patient management is recommended to decrease the risk of overdose; consideration should be given to changing the therapeutic regimen, including possibly discontinuing the medicine, in patients whose depression is persistently worse or whose emergent suicidality or other symptoms are severe, abrupt in onset, or were not part of the patient's presenting symptoms)

Patients with pre-existing slow heart rates
(citalopram has caused small but statistically significant reductions in heart rate)

Reevaluation of the long-term usefulness of the drug
(periodic evaluations are recommended to assess the long-term usefulness of citalopram for the individual patient)

Symptoms associated with discontinuation
(patients should be monitored for symptoms upon discontinuation; a gradual reduction in dose rather than abrupt cessation is recommended whenever possible; previously prescribed dose may be considered if intolerable symptoms occur following a decrease in the dose or upon discontinuation of treatment)

Side/Adverse Effects

The following side/adverse effects have been selected on the basis of their potential clinical significance (possible signs and symptoms in parentheses where appropriate)—not necessarily inclusive:

Those indicating need for medical attention

Incidence more frequent

Sexual dysfunction, including abnormal ejaculation; anorgasmia; decreased libido; or impotence (decrease in sexual ability or desire)

Note: *Abnormal ejaculation*, especially ejaculatory delay, is the most frequent form of sexual dysfunction associated with citalopram use. *Impotence* may be dose-related.

Incidence less frequent

Abnormal accommodation (blurred vision); ***agitation; amnesia*** (loss of memory); ***apathy*** (lack of emotion); ***confusion; dyspnea*** (trouble in breathing); ***fever; menstrual changes; polyuria*** (increase in frequency of urination or amount of urine produced); ***skin rash or itching***

Incidence rare

Abnormal bleeding or thrombocytopenia (nose bleed; purple or red spots on skin; bleeding gums); ***bradycardia*** (slow or irregular heartbeat [less than 50 beats per minute]); ***breast tenderness or enlargement; or galactorrhea*** (unusual secretion of milk)—in females; ***cardiac arrhythmia*** (dizziness or fainting; irregular heartbeat); ***epidermal necrolysis*** (redness, tenderness, itching, burning, or peeling of skin; red or irritated eyes; sore throat, fever, and chills); ***extrapyramidal effects*** (unusual or sudden body or facial movements or postures); ***hypoglycemia*** (anxiety; behavior change similar to drunkenness; difficulty in concentrating; increased hunger; nervousness; shakiness); ***hyponatremia*** (confusion; drowsiness; dryness of mouth; increased thirst; lack of energy; seizures); ***micturition disturbances*** (trouble in holding or releasing urine; painful urination); ***mood or mental changes, including aggressive reaction; delusions; depersonalization; emotional lability; euphoria; hallucinations; mania or hypomania; panic reaction; paranoid reaction; or psychosis; serotonin syndrome*** (agitation; confusion; diarrhea; fever; overactive reflexes; poor coordination; restlessness; shivering; sweating; talking or acting with excitement you cannot control; trembling or shaking; twitching); ***syndrome of inappropriate antidiuretic hormone secretion (SIADH)*** (agitation; coma; confusion; decreased urine output; depression; dizziness; headache; hostility; irritability; lethargy; muscle twitching; nausea; rapid weight gain; seizures; stupor; swelling of face, ankles, or hands; unusual tiredness or weakness)

Note: The *serotonin syndrome* is more likely to occur after an increase in dosage. Cardiac arrhythmias, coma, disseminated intravascular coagulation, hypertension or hypotension, renal failure, respiratory failure, seizures, and severe hyperthermia have been reported effects of the syndrome.

Incidence not determined—Observed during clinical practice; estimates of frequency cannot be determined.

Acute renal failure (agitation; coma; confusion; decreased urine output; depression; dizziness; headache; hostility; irritability; lethargy; muscle twitching; nausea; rapid weight gain; seizures; stupor; swelling of face, ankles, or hands; unusual tiredness or weakness); ***angioedema*** (large, hive-like swelling on face, eyelids, lips, tongue or throat); ***allergic reaction; anaphylaxis*** (cough; difficulty swallowing; dizziness; fast heartbeat; hives; itching, puffiness or swelling of the eyelids or around the eyes, face, lips or tongue; shortness of breath; skin rash; tightness in chest; unusual tiredness or weakness; wheezing); ***chest pain; choreoathetosis*** (restlessness or agitation; uncontrolled jerking or twisting movements); ***delirium*** (unusual excitement, nervousness, or restlessness; hallucinations; confusion as to time, place, or person; holding false beliefs that cannot be changed by fact); ***dyskinesia*** (twitching, twisting, uncontrolled repetitive movements of tongue, lips, face, arms, or legs); ***erythema multiforme*** (blistering, peeling, loosening of skin; chills; cough); ***gastrointestinal hemorrhage*** (black, tarry stools; bloody stools; vomiting of blood or material that looks like coffee grounds); ***grand mal convulsions*** (total body jerking; loss of bladder control; loss of consciousness); ***hemolytic anemia*** (back, leg, or stomach pains; bleeding gums; chills; dark urine; difficulty breathing; fatigue; fever; general body swelling; headache; loss of appetite; nausea or vomiting; nosebleeds; pale skin; sore throat; yellowing of the eyes or skin); ***hepatic necrosis*** (abdominal or stomach pain; black, tarry stools); ***myoclonus*** (muscle twitching or jerking; rhythmic movement of muscles); ***neuroleptic malignant syndrome*** (difficult or fast breathing; drooling; fast heartbeat; impaired consciousness, ranging from confusion to coma;); ***pancreatitis*** (bloating; constipation; darkened urine; indigestion); ***priapism*** (penile erections, frequent or continuing); ***prolactinemia*** (swelling of breasts or unusual milk production); ***QT prolonged*** (irregular heartbeat; recurrent fainting); ***rhabdomyolysis*** (dark-colored urine; fever; muscle cramps or spasms; muscle pain or stiffness; unusual tiredness or weakness); ***spontaneous abortion; thrombocytopenia; thrombosis*** (tenderness, pain, swelling, warmth, skin discoloration, and prominent superficial veins over affected area); ***torsades de pointes*** (fast, irregular heartbeat); ***ventricular arrhythmia*** (fast, slow or irregular heartbeat); ***withdrawal syndrome***

Those indicating need for medical attention only if they continue or are bothersome

Incidence more frequent

Drowsiness; dryness of mouth; insomnia (trouble in sleeping); ***nausea; somnolence*** (sleepiness or unusual drowsiness)

Note: *Drowsiness* and *insomnia* may be dose-related.

Incidence less frequent

Abdominal pain; anorexia (loss of appetite); ***anxiety; arthralgia or myalgia*** (pain in muscles or joints); ***asthenia or fatigue*** (unusual tiredness or weakness); ***diarrhea; dyspepsia*** (heartburn); ***flatulence*** (gas); ***hypotension or postural hypotension*** (dizziness or fainting)—especially when getting up from a lying or sitting position; ***increased salivation*** (watering of mouth); ***increased sweating; increased yawning; migraine*** (headache, severe and throbbing); ***paresthesia*** (tingling, burning, or prickly feelings on skin); ***rhinitis or sinusitis*** (headache; stuffy or runny nose); ***taste perversion*** (change in sense of taste); ***tooth grinding; tremor*** (trembling or shaking); ***unusual increase or decrease in weight; upper respiratory tract infection*** (ear congestion; nasal congestion; chills, cough, fever, sneezing, or sore throat; body aches or pain; headache; loss of voice; runny nose; unusual tiredness or weakness; difficulty in breathing); ***vomiting***

Note: *Fatigue, increased sweating,* and *increased yawning* may be dose-related.

Incidence not determined—Observed during clinical practice; estimates of frequency cannot be determined

Akathisia (inability to sit still; need to keep moving; restlessness); ***ecchymosis*** (bruising; large, flat, blue or purplish patches in the skin); ***nystagmus*** (uncontrolled eye movements)

Those indicating the need for medical attention if they occur after medication is discontinued

Incidence unknown

Agitation (anxiety; nervousness; restlessness; irritability; dry mouth; shortness of breath; hyperventilation; trouble sleeping; irregular heartbeats; shaking); ***anxiety; confusion*** (mood or mental changes); ***dysphoric mood*** (feeling unwell or unhappy); ***dizziness; emotional lability*** (crying; depersonalization; dysphoria; euphoria; mental depression; paranoia; quick to react or overreact emotionally; rapidly changing moods); ***headache; hypomania; insomnia*** (sleeplessness; trouble sleeping; unable to sleep); ***irritability; lethargy*** (unusual drowsiness, dullness, tiredness, weakness or feeling of sluggishness); ***nervousness; paresthesias*** (burning, crawling, itching, numbness, prickling, "pins and needles", or tingling feelings); ***tremor*** (trembling or shaking)

Note: *Discontinuation symptoms* have been reported very rarely following citalopram use. This rarity is believed to be due to the intermediate half-life of citalopram, which provides self-tapering, and to the selectivity of citalopram for serotonin reuptake inhibition (lack of noradrenergic effects). Tapering citalopram at discontinuation generally is not required.

Overdose

For specific information on the agents used in the management of citalopram overdose, see *Charcoal, Activated (Oral-Local)* monograph.

For more information on the management of overdose or unintentional ingestion, **contact a Poison Control Center** (see *Poison Control Center Listing*).

Clinical effects of overdose

Note: There have been reports of death after overdoses with citalopram alone, at doses of 2800 mg and 3920 mg, with no co-ingested substances. However, patients have survived overdoses of up to 6000 mg.

The following effects have been selected on the basis of their potential clinical significance (possible signs and symptoms in parentheses where appropriate)—not necessarily inclusive:

Acute

More frequent

Dizziness; drowsiness; nausea; sinus tachycardia (fast heartbeat); ***somnolence*** (sleepiness or unusual d rowsiness); ***sweating; tremor*** (trembling or shaking); ***vomiting***

Rare

Amnesia (loss of memory); ***confusion; convulsions; coma; cyanosis;*** (bluish colored skin or lips); ***ECG changes, including nodal rhythm; QT$_c$ prolongation;*** *torsades de pointes;* ***ventricular arrhythmia*** (dizziness or fainting; fast, slow, or irregular heartbeat); ***hyperventilation*** (deep or fast breathing with dizziness); ***rhabdomyolysis*** (general feeling of discomfort or illness; muscle pain; weakness)

Treatment of overdose

Treatment is essentially symptomatic and supportive.

To decrease absorption—Considering gastric lavage or administration of activated charcoal.

Monitoring—Monitoring cardiac and vital signs.

Supportive care—Establishing and maintaining airway. Patients in whom intentional overdose is confirmed or suspected should be referred for psychiatric consultation.

Note: Because of citalopram's large volume of distribution, forced diuresis, dialysis, hemoperfusion, and exchange transfusions are not likely to be of benefit in the treatment of overdose.

Patient Consultation

As an aid to patient consultation, refer to *Advice for the Patient, Citalopram (Systemic).*

In providing consultation, consider emphasizing the following selected information (» = major clinical significance):

Before using this medication

» Conditions affecting use, especially:

Hypersensitivity to citalopram or any of its components

Pregnancy—Should be used during pregnancy only if the potential benefit justifies the potential risk

Complications including prolonged hospitalization, respiratory support and tube feeding in neonates exposed to citalopram and other SSRIs late in the third trimester; physician should carefully consider potential risks and benefits when treating a pregnant woman in her third trimester

Breast-feeding—Distributed into breast milk; drowsiness, decreased feeding, weight loss reported in two nursing infants; decision whether to continue citalopram therapy should take into account risk-benefit for infant and nursing mother

Use in children—Because of Food and Drug Administration [FDA] reports of the occurrence of suicidality in clinical trials for various antidepressant drugs in pediatric patients with major depressive disorder [MDD], citalopram must be used with caution in treating pediatric patients for MDD.

Use in the elderly—Clearance is reduced; lower dosage recommended

Contraindicated medications—Monoamine oxidase (MAO) inhibitors

Other medications, especially linezolid, serotonergics or other medications or substances with serotonergic activity

Other medical problems, especially recent history of myocardial infarction, unstable heart disease, hypersensitivity to citalopram or any of its components or hepatic function impairment

Proper use of this medication

» Compliance with therapy; not taking more medication than prescribed

Taking with or without food, as directed by physician

» Four weeks of therapy may be required before antidepressant effects are seen; importance of continuing citalopram after symptoms are relieved

» Medication should not be abruptly discontinued by the patient

» Proper dosing

Missed dose: Discussing with physician what to do about any missed doses since some patients take citalopram in the morning and other patients take citalopram in the evening

» Proper storage

Precautions while using this medication

Regular visits to physician to check progress of therapy

» Not taking citalopram with or within 14 days of taking an MAO inhibitor; not taking an MAO inhibitor within 14 days of taking citalopram

Avoiding use of alcoholic beverages

Possible drowsiness, impairment of judgment, thinking, or motor skills; caution when driving or doing jobs requiring alertness or coordination until effects of medication are known

Side/adverse effects

Signs of potential side effects, especially sexual dysfunction, abnormal accommodation, agitation, amnesia, apathy, confusion, dyspnea, fever, menstrual changes, polyuria, skin rash or itching, upper respiratory tract infection, abnormal bleeding or thrombocytopenia, breast tenderness or enlargement or galactorrhea (in females), cardiac arrhythmia (including bradycardia), epidermal necrolysis, extrapyramidal effects, hypoglycemia, hyponatremia, micturition disturbances, mood or mental changes, serotonin syndrome, or syndrome of inappropriate antidiuretic hormone secretion (SIADH)

Signs of potential side effects observed during clinical practice, especially acute renal failure, angioedema, allergic reaction, anaphylaxis, chest pain, choreoathetosis, delirium, dyskinesia, erythema multiforme, gastrointestinal hemorrhage, grand mal convulsions, hemolytic anemia, hepatic necrosis, myoclonus, neuroleptic malignant syndrome, pancreatitis, priapism, prolactinemia, QT prolonged, rhabdomyolysis, spontaneous abortion, thrombocytopenia, thrombosis, torsades de pointes, ventricular arrhythmia, or withdrawal syndrome.

General Dosing Information

Potentially suicidal patients should not have immediate access to large quantities of citalopram since they may continue to exhibit suicidal tendencies until significant improvement occurs. Providing the patient with the smallest total amount of medication consistent with good patient management is recommended to decrease the risk of overdose.

Activation of hypomania or mania has been reported in patients treated with citalopram.

At least 14 days should elapse between discontinuation of an MAOI and initiation of citalopram therapy. Similarly, at least 14 days should be allowed after stopping citalopram before starting an MAOI.

Patients should be advised to continue citalopram therapy as directed even if improvement is noted in 1 to 4 weeks.

It is not known whether the maintenance dose of citalopram is identical to the dose needed to induce remission. If adverse reactions are bothersome, a decrease in dose to 20 mg per day can be considered.

Patients should be monitored for discontinuation symptoms when ceasing treatment. A gradual reduction in dose rather than abrupt cessation is recommended whenever possible. If intolerable symptoms occur following a decrease in dose or upon discontinuation of treatment, then resuming the previously prescribed dose may be considered. Subsequently, the physician may continue decreasing the dose but at a more gradual rate.

Diet/Nutrition

Citalopram may be taken with or without food, on a full or empty stomach.

Bioequivalence information

The table and oral solution dosage forms of citalopram hydrobromide are bioequivalent.

For treatment of adverse effects

Serotonin syndrome—The serotonin syndrome usually resolves shortly after discontinuation of serotonergic medications. Treatment is essentially symptomatic and supportive. However, the nonspecific serotonergic receptor antagonists cyproheptadine and methysergide have been reported to be of some use in shortening the duration of the serotonin syndrome.

Oral Dosage Forms

Note: The available dosage form contains citalopram hydrobromide, but dosage and strength are expressed in terms of the base.

CITALOPRAM HYDROBROMIDE TABLETS

Usual adult dose

Antidepressant—

Oral, initially 20 mg (base) per day as a single dose in the morning or evening (with or without food). Dosage may be increased by 20 mg per day at intervals of at least one week. Generally, the dosage is increased to 40 mg per day; however, some patients may require a dosage of 60 mg per day.

Note: A dose-response study found no advantage of 60 mg per day over 40 mg per day. Therefore, a dosage of 60 mg per day is not ordinarily recommended.

For patients with hepatic function impairment, a dosage of 20 mg per day is recommended, with only nonresponsive patients being titrated to 30 or 40 mg per day.

Usual adult prescribing limits

60 mg (base) per day.

Usual pediatric dose

Antidepressant—

Safety and efficacy have not been established.

Usual geriatric dose

Antidepressant—

Oral, 20 mg (base) per day as a single dose in the morning or evening. Dosage may be increased to 40 mg per day in nonresponding patients. Some elderly patients may respond to 10 mg per day.

Usual geriatric prescribing limits

40 mg (base) per day.

Strength(s) usually available

U.S.—

10 mg (base) (Rx) [*Celexa* (copolyvidone; corn starch; crosscarmellose sodium; glycerin; lactose monohydrate; magnesium stearate; hypromellose; microcrystalline cellulose; polyethylene glycol; titanium dioxide; iron oxides)].

20 mg (base) (Rx) [*Celexa* (scored; copolyvidone; corn starch; croscarmellose sodium; glycerin; lactose monohydrate; magnesium stearate; hypromellose; microcrystalline cellulose; polyethylene glycol; titanium dioxide; iron oxides)].

40 mg (base) (Rx) [*Celexa* (scored; copolyvidone; corn starch; croscarmellose sodium; glycerin; lactose monohydrate; magnesium stearate; hypromellose; microcrystalline cellulose; polyethylene glycol)].

Canada—

20 mg (base) (Rx) [*Celexa* (scored; copolyvidone; cornstarch; croscarmellose sodium; glycerin; lactose monohydrate; magnesium stearate; methylhydroxypropyl cellulose; microcrystalline cellulose; polyethylene glycol; titanium dioxide)].

40 mg (base) (Rx) [*Celexa* (scored; copolyvidone; cornstarch; croscarmellose sodium; glycerin; lactose monohydrate; magnesium stearate; methylhydroxypropyl cellulose; microcrystalline cellulose; polyethylene glycol; titanium dioxide)].

Packaging and storage

Store at 25 °C (77 °F), with excursions permitted between 15 and 30 °C (59 and 86 °F), unless otherwise specified by manufacturer.

Auxiliary labeling

- Avoid alcohol while on this medication.
- May cause drowsiness. Use care when driving or operating machinery. Use caution until you are familiar with its effects.
- Ask your doctor or pharmacist before using nonprescription drugs.
- You should take this medication exactly as prescribed. Do not skip or discontinue unless directed.

CITALOPRAM HYDROBROMIDE ORAL SOLUTION

Usual adult dose

See *Citalopram Hydrobromide Tablets*.

Usual adult prescribing limits

See *Citalopram Hydrobromide Tablets*.

Usual pediatric dose

Antidepressant—

Safety and efficacy have not been established.

Usual geriatric dose

See *Citalopram Hydrobromide Tablets*

Usual geriatric prescribing limits:

See *Citalopram Hydrobromide Tablets*

Strength(s) usually available

U.S.—

2 mg per mL (Rx) [*Celexa* (sorbitol; purified water; methylparaben; natural peppermint flavor; propylene glycol; propylparaben)].

Canada—

Not commercially available.

Packaging and storage

Store at 25 °C (77 °F); excursions permitted between 15 and 30 °C (59 and 86 °F).

Auxiliary labeling

- Avoid alcohol while on this medication
- May cause drowsiness. Use care when driving or operating machinery. Use caution until you are familiar with its effects.
- Ask your doctor or pharmacist before using nonprescription drugs.
- You should take this medication exactly as prescribed. Do not skip or discontinue unless directed.

Revised: 01/05/2005
Developed: 09/02/1998

CLARITHROMYCIN Systemic

VA CLASSIFICATION (Primary/Secondary): AM200/AM900

Commonly used brand name(s): *Biaxin*; *Biaxin XL*.

Note: For a listing of dosage forms and brand names by country availability, see *Dosage Forms* section(s).

Category

Antibacterial (systemic); antimycobacterial.

Indications

Note: Bracketed information in the *Indications* section refers to uses that are not included in U.S. product labeling.

General Considerations

Clarithromycin is a macrolide antibiotic with *in vitro* activity against many gram-positive and gram-negative aerobic and anaerobic organisms. The minimum inhibitory concentrations (MICs) of clarithromycin are generally twofold to fourfold lower than those of erythromycin against gram-positive bacteria, such as methicillin-sensitive *Staphylococcus aureus* and most *Streptococcus* species. However, sensitivities vary and *S. aureus* strains that are resistant to erythromycin, methicillin, or oxacillin also have been found to be resistant to clarithromycin. Clarithromycin is bactericidal against *Streptococcus pyogenes* and *Streptococcus pneumoniae;* however, *Streptococcus* strains resistant to one macrolide antibiotic have demonstrated cross resistance to other macrolide antibiotics.

The activity of erythromycin is twice that of clarithromycin against *Haemophilus influenzae;* however, clarithromycin's active metabolite, 14-hydroxyclarithromycin, is as active as erythromycin. When clarithromycin and 14-hydroxyclarithromycin are combined, their MIC is twofold to fourfold lower than that of erythromycin, suggesting additive or synergistic *in vitro* activity against *H. influenzae.*

Clarithromycin displays *in vitro* activity against *Mycobacterium avium* complex (MAC), being eightfold to thirty-twofold more active than erythromycin. High intracellular concentrations are achieved with clarithromycin, and it has been found to be effective against MAC in human macrophages. Clarithromycin may act synergistically with other agents used to treat MAC. It is also very active against many different species of mycobacteria. *In vitro* and *in vivo* activity against *Mycobacterium leprae* has been demonstrated, and there has been good clinical response to the treatment of cutaneous disease, including disseminated disease, caused by *Mycobacterium chelonae.* However, clarithromycin has not been found to have *in vitro* activity against *Mycobacterium tuberculosis.*

Clarithromycin has been found to have greater *in vitro* activity than erythromycin against *Legionella pneumophila, Moraxella (Branhamella) catarrhalis, Chlamydia trachomatis,* and *Ureaplasma urealyticum.* Its activity is variable and similar to that of erythromycin against *Neisseria gonorrhoeae,* anaerobic gram-positive cocci, and *Bacteroides* species. Clarithromycin also has good *in vitro* activity against *Helicobacter pylori* and has been clinically effective, when combined with amoxicillin and lansoprazole, or omeprazole in the treatment of duodenal ulcers.

Accepted

Bronchitis, chronic (treatment)—Clarithromycin is indicated in the treatment of acute bacterial exacerbations of chronic bronchitis due to *H. influenzae, H. parainfluenzae*[1] *M. catarrhalis,* or *S. pneumoniae*

Otitis media (treatment) or
Sinusitis, acute maxillary (treatment)—Clarithromycin is indicated in the treatment of bacterial exacerbations of otitis media, or acute maxillary sinusitis due to *H. influenzae, M. catarrhalis,* or *S. pneumoniae.*

Mycobacterium avium complex (MAC) disease, disseminated (prophylaxis)—Clarithromycin is indicated for the prevention of disseminated MAC disease in patients with advanced human immunodeficiency virus (HIV) infection.

Mycobacterium avium complex (MAC) disease, disseminated (treatment adjunct)—Clarithromycin is indicated, in combination with other antimycobacterials, in the treatment of disseminated MAC disease due to *M. avium* or *Mycobacterium intracellulare.*

Acquired resistance of *M. avium* complex to clarithromycin has been found to develop when clarithromycin is used as monotherapy. Clarithromycin should be used in combination with other antimycobacterials to prevent the development of resistance.

Pharyngitis (treatment) or
Tonsillitis (treatment)—Clarithromycin is indicated in the treatment of pharyngitis or tonsillitis due to *S. pyogenes.*

The usual drug of choice in the treatment of streptococcal infections and the prophylaxis of rheumatic fever is penicillin. Clarithromycin is generally effective in the eradication of *S. pyogenes* from the nasopharynx. However, data establishing the efficacy of clarithromycin in the subsequent prevention of rheumatic fever are not available at present.

Pneumonia, community-acquired (treatment)—Clarithromycin is indicated in the treatment of community-acquired pneumonia due to *Chlamydia pneumoniae,* or [TWAR], *Haemophilus influenzae*[1], *Mycoplasma pneumoniae,* or *Streptococcus pneumoniae.* Additionally the extended release formulation of clarithromycin is effective against *Haemophilus parainfluenzae*[1] and *Moraxella catarrhalis*[1].

Skin and soft tissue infections (treatment)—Clarithromycin is indicated in the treatment of uncomplicated skin and soft tissue infections due to susceptible strains of *S. aureus* or *S. pyogenes.* However, clarithromycin should not be used as first-line treatment where resistance may occur.

Ulcer, duodenal, *Helicobacter pylori*–associated (treatment adjunct)—Clarithromycin is indicated in dual therapy, in combination with omeprazole or as part of triple therapy with amoxicillin and lansoprazole[1] or amoxicillin and omeprazole for the treatment of duodenal ulcer associated with *H. pylori* infection.

[Legionnaires' disease (treatment)][1]—Clarithromycin is indicated in the treatment of Legionnaires' disease caused by *L. pneumophila* (Evidence rating: III).

Unaccepted

The efficacy and safety of the extended release formulation of clarithromycin in the prophylaxis and treatment of *Mycobacterium avium* complex (MAC) disease, pharyngitis and tonsillitis due to *S. pyogenes,* duodenal ulcer, due to *Helicobacter pylori* and uncomplicated skin and skin structure due to *S. aureus* or *S. pyogenes* has not been established. See *Clarithromycin Extended Release Tablets* for the specific approved indications for this dosage form.

[1]Not included in Canadian product labeling.

Pharmacology/Pharmacokinetics

Physicochemical characteristics

Molecular weight—747.96.

Mechanism of action/Effect

Clarithromycin binds to the 50S ribosomal subunit of the 70S ribosome of susceptible organisms, thereby inhibiting bacterial RNA-dependent protein synthesis.

Absorption

Tablets and oral suspension: Well absorbed from the gastrointestinal tract; stable in gastric acid; food delays the rate, but not the extent, of absorption; bioavailability is approximately 55% in healthy volunteers. In adults, the bioavailability of the oral suspension was similar to that of the tablets.

Extended-release tablets: Extended absorption from the gastrointestinal tract; provide lower and later steady-state peak plasma concentrations but equivalent AUCs to immediate-release tablets. The extent of formation of 14-hydroxyclarithromycin is not affected by food; however, the clarithromycin AUC is approximately 30% lower when associated with fasting conditions.

Distribution

Widely distributed into tissues and fluids; high concentrations found in nasal mucosa, tonsils, and lungs; concentrations in tissues are higher than those in serum because of high intracellular concentrations; readily enters leukocytes and macrophages.

Vol_D—243 to 266 liters.

Protein binding

High (65 to 75%).

Biotransformation

Hepatically metabolized via three main pathways, demethylation, hydroxylation, and hydrolysis, to eight metabolites. One metabolite, 14-hydroxyclarithromycin, has *in vitro* antimicrobial activity comparable to that of clarithromycin and may act synergistically with clarithromycin against *Haemophilus influenzae.* Saturation of metabolism involves the demethylation and hydroxylation pathways, and accounts for an increase in serum half-life.

Half-life

Clarithromycin:
- 250 mg every 12 hours—3 to 4 hours.
- 500 mg every 12 hours—5 to 7 hours.

14-Hydroxyclarithromycin:
- 250 mg every 12 hours—5 to 6 hours.
- 500 mg every 12 hours—Approximately 7 hours.

Normal renal function—
Clarithromycin: Approximately 22 hours.
- 14-Hydroxyclarithromycin: Approximately 47 hours.

Renal function impairment (creatinine clearance of < 30 mL per minute [0.5 mL per second])—

Time to peak concentration

2 to 3 hours.

Peak serum concentration

Clarithromycin (at steady state):
- 250 mg (suspension) every 12 hours—Approximately 2 mcg/mL.
- 250 mg (tablet) every 12 hours—Approximately 1 mcg/mL.
- 500 mg (tablet) every 12 hours—2 to 3 mcg/mL.
- 500 mg (extended-release tablet) every 24 hours—Approximately 1 to 2 mcg/mL.
- Two 500 mg (extended-release tablets) every 24 hours—Approximately 2 to 3 mcg/mL.

14-Hydroxyclarithromycin (at steady state):
- 250 mg (suspension) every 12 hours—Approximately 0.7 mcg/mL.
- 250 mg (tablet) every 12 hours—Approximately 0.6 mcg/mL.
- 500 mg (tablet) every 12 hours—Up to 1 mcg/mL.
- 500 mg (extended-release tablet) every 24 hours—Approximately 0.6 mcg/mL.
- Two 500 mg (extended-release tablets) every 24 hours—Approximately 0.8 mcg/mL.

Adults—
Clarithromycin (at steady state):
- 7.5 mg per kg of body weight (mg/kg) (suspension) every 12 hours—3 to 7 mcg/mL.
- 15 mg/kg (suspension) every 12 hours—6 to 15 mcg/mL.

14-Hydroxyclarithromycin (at steady state):
- 7.5 mg/kg (suspension) every 12 hours—1 to 2 mcg/mL.

Children—

Elimination

Renal—Approximately 20 and 30% of the dose of 250- and 500-mg tablets, respectively, given twice a day, is excreted in the urine as unchanged drug. Approximately 40% of the dose of 250-mg suspension given twice a day is excreted in the urine as clarithromycin. 14-Hydroxyclarithromycin accounts for 10 and 15% of the dose excreted in the urine after doses of 250 and 500 mg, respectively, given twice a day.

Fecal—Approximately 4% of a 250-mg dose is excreted in the feces.

Precautions to Consider

Cross-sensitivity and/or related problems

Patients who are hypersensitive to erythromycin or other macrolides may also be hypersensitive to clarithromycin.

Carcinogenicity/Mutagenicity

Long-term studies in animals have not been performed to evaluate the carcinogenic potential of clarithromycin.

Clarithromycin was not found to be mutagenic in the *Salmonella* /mammalian microsome tests, the bacterial induced mutation frequency test, the rat hepatocyte DNA synthesis assay, the mouse lymphoma assay, the mouse dominant lethal assay, or the mouse micronucleus test. However, the *in vitro* chromosome aberration test was weakly positive in one test and negative in another. The Ames test was negative when performed on clarithromycin metabolites.

Pregnancy/Reproduction

Fertility—Adequate and well-controlled studies in humans have not been done.

Studies in male and female rats given 160 mg per kg of body weight (mg/kg) per day (plasma concentrations equivalent to approximately two times the human serum concentrations) showed no adverse effects on the estrous cycle, fertility, parturition, or the number and viability of offspring.

Pregnancy—Adequate and well-controlled studies in humans have not been done. Clarithromycin should not be used in pregnant women except in clinical circumstances where no alternative therapy is appropriate. If pregnancy occurs while taking this drug, the patient should be apprised of the potential hazard to the fetus.

Monkeys administered oral doses of 150 mg/kg per day (plasma concentrations equivalent to three times the human serum concentrations) had embryonic loss, which was attributed to marked maternal toxicity at this dose. *In utero* fetal loss occurred in rabbits given intravenous doses of 33 mg per square meter of body surface area (mg/m^2), which is equivalent to 17 times less than the maximum recommended human daily dose.

Clarithromycin was not found to be teratogenic in four rat studies (three with oral doses and one with intravenous doses of up to 160 mg/kg per day administered during the period of major organogenesis) or in two rabbit studies (at oral doses of up to 125 mg/kg per day or intravenous doses of 30 mg/kg per day administered during gestation days 6 through 18). Two additional studies in a different rat strain demonstrated a low incidence of cardiovascular anomalies at oral doses of 150 mg/kg per day administered during gestation days 6 to 15. Cleft palate was seen at doses of 500 mg/kg per day. Fetal growth retardation was seen in monkeys given an oral dose of 70 mg/kg per day, which produced plasma concentrations that were equivalent to two times the human serum concentrations.

FDA Pregnancy Category C.

Breast-feeding

It is not known whether clarithromycin is distributed into human milk. Other drugs of this class are distributed into human milk. Because many drugs are distributed into human milk, caution should be exercised when clarithromycin is administered to a nursing woman.

Clarithromycin is distributed in the milk of lactating animals. Preweaned rats, exposed indirectly via consumption of milk from female rats treated with 150 mg per kg of body weight per day for 3 weeks, were not adversely affected, despite data indicating higher drug levels in milk than in plasma.

Pediatrics

Appropriate studies on the relationship of age to the effects of clarithromycin have not been performed in children up to 6 months of age. Safety and efficacy have not been established. The safety of clarithromycin has not been studied in MAC patients under the age of 20 months.

Geriatrics

One study performed in healthy elderly subjects found increased peak steady-state concentrations of clarithromycin and 14-hydroxyclarithromycin; this was thought to be due to an age-related decrease in renal function. There was no increase in side effects in elderly patients compared with younger subjects. Elderly patients with severe renal function impairment may require a decrease in dose.

Drug interactions and/or related problems

The following drug interactions and/or related problems have been selected on the basis of their potential clinical significance (possible mechanism in parentheses where appropriate)—not necessarily inclusive (» = major clinical significance):

Note: Combinations containing any of the following medications, depending on the amount present, may also interact with this medication.

» Astemizole
(QTc-interval prolongation and torsades de pointes have been reported with concurrent use of astemizole and erythromycin; since clarithromycin is also metabolized by the cytochrome P450 enzyme system, concurrent use of clarithromycin and astemizole is **contraindicated**)

Anticoagulants, coumarin- or indanedione-derivative or
» Warfarin
(concurrent administration with clarithromycin has been shown to potentiate the effects of warfarin; prothrombin time should be monitored closely in patients receiving oral anticoagulants and clarithromycin concurrently)

» Carbamazepine or
Other medications metabolized by the cytochrome P450 enzyme system
(concurrent administration with clarithromycin has been shown to significantly increase the plasma concentrations of carbamazepine and other medications metabolized by the cytochrome P450 enzyme system; serum concentrations of carbamazepine and these other medications should be monitored)

» Cisapride or
» Pimozide or
» Terfenadine
(concurrent administration with clarithromycin has resulted in cardiac arrhythmias, including QTc-interval prolongation, ventricular tachycardia, ventricular fibrillation, and torsades de pointes; fatalities have also occurred; the most likely cause is the inhibition of hepatic metabolism of these medications by clarithromycin; concurrent use is **contraindicated**)

» Colchicine
(postmarketing reports of cochicine toxicity with concomitant use, especially in the elderly, some of which occurred in patients with renal insufficiency)

» Digoxin
(concurrent administration with clarithromycin has been shown to increase serum digoxin concentrations; monitoring of digoxin serum concentrations is recommended in patients receiving digoxin and clarithromycin concurrently)

» Dihydroergotamine or
» Ergotamine
(postmarketing reports indicate acute ergot toxicity characterized by vasospasm and ischemia of the extremities and other tissues including the CNS associated with coadministration; concomitant use is **contraindicated**)

» Disopyramide or
» Quinidine
(postmarketing reports of torsades de pointes with concomitant use; electrocardiograms should be monitored for QTc prolongation and serum concentrations of these medications should also be monitored during coadministration)

HMG-CoA reductase inhibitors such as
Lovastatin or
Simvastatin
(clarithromycin has been reported to increase concentrations of HMG-CoA reductase inhibitors; rare reports of rhabdomyolysis with concomitant use)

» Omeprazole
(concomitant use increased omeprazole C_{max}, AUC, and $T_{1/2}$ by 30%, 89%, and 34%, respectively; gastric pH value was 5.2 when omeprazole was administered alone compared with 5.7 when administered concomitantly with clarithromycin)

» Rifabutin or
» Rifampin
(concurrent use with clarithromycin causes a decrease in the serum concentration of clarithromycin by > 50%)

» Sildenafil
(erythromycin reported to increase sildenafil AUC; similar interaction may occur with clarithromycin, so reduction of sildenafil dosage should be considered with concomitant use)

» Theophylline
(concurrent administration with clarithromycin has been shown to increase the area under the plasma concentration-time curve [AUC] of theophylline by 17%; monitoring of theophylline serum concentrations is recommended in patients receiving high doses of theophylline or in patients with theophylline serum concentrations in the upper therapeutic range)

Triazolobenziodidiazepines such as
Alprazolam or
Triazolam or
Related benzodiazepines such as
Midazolam
(erythromycin reported to decrease triazolam and midazolam clearance and thus, may increase pharmacologic effect of these benzodiazepines; postmarketing reports of drug interactions and CNS effects such as somnolence and confusion with the concomitant use of clarithromycin and triazolam)

» Zidovudine
(concurrent administration with clarithromycin causes a decrease in the steady-state concentration of zidovudine; doses of clarithromycin and zidovudine should be taken at least 4 hours apart)

Laboratory value alterations

The following have been selected on the basis of their potential clinical significance (possible effect in parentheses where appropriate)—not necessarily inclusive (» = major clinical significance).

With physiology/laboratory test values

Alanine aminotransferase (ALT [SGPT]) or
Alkaline phosphatase (ALP) or
Aspartate aminotransferase (AST [SGOT]) or
Bilirubin, total, or
Gamma-glutamyl transpeptidase (GGT) or
Lactate dehydrogenase (LDH) or
(serum values may be elevated)

Blood urea nitrogen (BUN) or
Serum creatinine
(concentration may be elevated)

Prothrombin time
(may be elevated)

White blood cell (WBC) count
(may be decreased)

Medical considerations/Contraindications

The medical considerations/contraindications included have been selected on the basis of their potential clinical significance (reasons given in parentheses where appropriate)—not necessarily inclusive (» = major clinical significance).

Except under special circumstances, this medication should not be used when the following medical problem exists:

» Hypersensitivity to clarithromycin, erythromycin, or any of the macrolide antibiotics

Risk-benefit should be considered when the following medical problems exist:

» Renal function impairment, severe
(the elimination of clarithromycin is reduced in patients with renal function impairment, especially those with a creatinine clearance of < 30 mL/min [0.5 mL/second] with or without coexisting hepatic function impairment; the dose of clarithromycin should be halved, or the dosing interval doubled, in patients with a creatinine clearance of < 30 mL/min [0.5 mL/second])
(liver function impairment alters the pharmacokinetics of clarithromycin by decreasing the amount of metabolites formed and increasing the renal clearance of the parent drug; however, steady-state concentrations in patients with mild to severe hepatic function impairment do not differ from those in patients with normal hepatic function, unless there is also concurrent severe renal function impairment; no dosage adjustment is necessary in patients with hepatic function impairment if renal function is normal)

Patient monitoring

The following may be especially important in patient monitoring (other tests may be warranted in some patients, depending on condition; » = major clinical significance):

» Pseudomembranous colitis
(monitor patient for development of diarrhea subsequent to clarithromycin therapy)

Side/Adverse Effects

The following side/adverse effects have been selected on the basis of their potential clinical significance (possible signs and symptoms in parentheses where appropriate)—not necessarily inclusive:

Those indicating need for medical attention

Incidence less frequent

Infection (fever or chills; cough or hoarseness; lower back or side pain; painful or difficult urination)

Incidence rare

Hepatotoxicity (fever; nausea and vomiting; yellow eyes or skin); ***hypersensitivity reaction*** (skin rash and itching); ***pseudomembranous colitis*** (abdominal or stomach cramps and pain, severe; abdominal tenderness; diarrhea, watery and severe, which may also be bloody; fever); ***thrombocytopenia*** (unusual bleeding and bruising)

Incidence not determined—Observed during clinical practice, estimates of frequency can not be determined

Allergic reaction (cough; difficulty swallowing; dizziness; fast heartbeat; hives; itching; puffiness or swelling of the eyelids or around the eyes, face, lips or tongue; shortness of breath; skin rash; tightness in chest; unusual tiredness or weakness; wheezing)—ranging in severity; ***cholestatic hepatitis*** (abdominal or stomach pain; chills; clay-colored stools; dark urine; diarrhea; dizziness; fever; headache; itching; loss of appetite; nausea; rash; unpleasant breath odor; unusual tiredness or weakness; vomiting of blood; yellow eyes or skin); ***depersonalization*** (feeling of unreality; sense of detachment from self or body); ***disorientation*** (confusion about identity, place, and time); ***glossitis*** (redness, swelling, or soreness of tongue); ***hallucinations*** (seeing, hearing, or feeling things that are not there); ***hepatic dysfunction*** (dark urine; light-colored stools; loss of appetite; nausea and vomiting; unusual tiredness; yellow eyes or skin; fever with or without chills; stomach pain); ***hepatic failure***—disease state may be a contributing factor; ***hepatocellular hepatitis; hypoglycemia*** (anxiety; blurred vision; chills; cold sweats; coma; confusion; cool pale skin; depression; dizziness; fast heartbeat; headache; increased hunger; nausea; nervousness; nightmares; seizures; shakiness; slurred speech; unusual tiredness or weakness)—some of which occurred with patients taking oral hypoglycemic agents or insulin; ***leukopenia*** (black, tarry stools; chest pain; chills; cough; fever; painful or difficult urination; shortness of breath; sore throat; sores, ulcers, or white spots on lips or in mouth; swollen glands; unusual bleeding or bruising; unusual tiredness or weakness); ***neutropenia*** (chills; cough; fever; sore throat; sores, ulcers, or white spots on lips or in mouth; swollen glands); ***psychosis*** (feeling that others can hear your thoughts; feeling that others are watching you or controlling your behavior; feeling, seeing, or hearing things that are not there; severe mood or mental changes; unusual behavior); ***QT prolongation*** (irregular heartbeat; recurrent fainting); ***Stevens-Johnson syndrome*** (blistering, peeling, loosening of skin; chills; cough; diarrhea; itching; joint or muscle pain; red irritated eyes; red skin lesions, often with a purple center; sore throat; sores, ulcers, or white spots in mouth or on lips; unusual tiredness or weakness); ***torsade de pointes*** (chest pain or discomfort; irregular or slow heart rate; fainting; shortness of breath; sudden death); ***toxic epidermal necrolysis*** (blistering, peeling, loosening of skin; chills; cough; diarrhea; itching; joint or muscle pain; red irritated eyes; red skin lesions, often with a purple center; sore throat; sores, ulcers, or white spots in mouth or on lips; unusual tiredness or weakness); ***ventricular arrhythmias*** (fainting; fast, pounding, or irregular heartbeat or pulse; palpitations); ***ventricular tachycardia*** (fainting; fast, pounding, or irregular heartbeat or pulse; palpitations)

Those indicating need for medical attention only if they continue or are bothersome

Incidence less frequent

Abnormal sensation of taste—3%; ***dyspepsia*** (acid or sour stomach; belching; heartburn; indigestion; stomach discomfort, upset, or pain); ***flatulence*** (bloated, full feeling; excess air or gas in stomach or intestines; passing gas); ***gastrointestinal disturbances*** (abdominal discomfort or pain; diarrhea; nausea; vomiting)—2 to 3%; ***headache***—2%

Incidence not determined—Observed during clinical practice, estimates of frequency can not be determined

Alterations of sense of smell; anorexia (loss of appetite; weight loss); ***anxiety*** (fear; nervousness); ***behavioral changes*** (anxiety; mental depression; mood changes; nervousness); ***confusional states*** (mood or mental changes); ***dizziness; hearing loss***—usually reversible and occurring chiefly in elderly women; ***insomnia*** (sleeplessness; trouble sleeping; unable to sleep); ***manic behavior; nightmares; oral moniliasis*** (sore mouth or tongue; white patches in mouth and/or on tongue); ***skin eruptions, mild; stomatitis*** (swelling or inflammation of the mouth); ***taste loss; tinnitus*** (continuing ringing or buzzing or other unexplained noise in ears; hearing loss); ***tongue discoloration; tooth discoloration; tremors*** (trembling or shaking of hands or feet; shakiness in legs, arms, hands, feet); ***vertigo*** (dizziness or lightheadedness; feeling of constant movement of self or surroundings; sensation of spinning); ***vomiting***

Patient Consultation

As an aid to patient consultation, refer to *Advice for the Patient, Clarithromycin (Systemic).*

In providing consultation, consider emphasizing the following selected information (» = major clinical significance):

Before using this medication

» Conditions affecting use, especially:

Hypersensitivity to clarithromycin, erythromycin, or other macrolide antibiotics

Pregnancy—Should not be used in pregnant women except where no alternative therapy is appropriate; if pregnancy occurs while taking clarithromycin, patient should be apprised of potential hazard to the fetus

Breast-feeding—Passes into breast milk; caution should be exercised when administering clarithromycin to a nursing woman

Use in children—Safety and efficacy not established in children up to 6 months of age; safety of clarithromycin not studied in MAC patients under 20 months of age

Contraindicated medications—Astemizole, cisapride, dihydroergotamine, ergotamine, pimozide, and terfenadine

Other medications, especially carbamazepine, colchicine, digoxin, disopyramide, omeprazole, quinidine, rifabutin, rifampin, sildenafil, theophylline, warfarin, and zidovudine

Other medical problems, especially severe renal function impairment

Proper use of this medication

Immediate release tablets and oral suspension: May be taken with food or milk or on an empty stomach

» Extended-release tablets: Should be taken with food

Separating from doses of zidovudine by at least 4 hours

» Compliance with full course of therapy

Proper administration technique for oral liquids

» Proper dosing

Missed dose: Taking as soon as possible; not taking if almost time for next dose; not doubling doses

» Proper storage especially do not refrigerate oral suspension

Precautions while using this medication

» Not taking with cisapride or pimozide

Checking with physician if no improvement within a few days

Side/adverse effects

Signs of potential side effects, especially hepatotoxicity, hypersensitivity reaction, or infection pseudomembranous colitisthrombocytopenia,

Signs of potential side effects observed during clinical practice, especially allergic reaction, cholestatic hepatitis, depersonalization, disorientation, glossitis, hallucinations, hepatic dysfunction, hepatic failure, hepatocellular hepatitis, hypoglycemia, leukopenia, neutropenia, psychosis, QT prolongation, Stevens-Johnson syndrome, torsade de pointes, toxic epidermal necrolysis, ventricular arrhythmias, or ventricular tachycardia

General Dosing Information

Clarithromycin tablets and suspension may be taken with meals or milk or on an empty stomach.

Extended release clarithromycin tablets should be taken with food.

For treatment of adverse effects

Treatment of pseudomembranous colitisMild cases—Usually respond to discontinuation of the drug alone

Moderate to severe cases—Consideration should be given to management with fluids and electrolytes, protein supplementation, and treatment with an antibacterial drug clinically effective against *Clostridium difficile* colitis.

Oral Dosage Forms

CLARITHROMYCIN EXTENDED-RELEASE TABLETS

Usual adult and adolescent dose

Bronchitis, chronic (treatment) bacterial exacerbations due to *H. influenzae, H. parainfluenzae, M. catarrhalis,* or *S. pneumoniae*[1]—

Oral, 1000 mg once a day for seven days.

Pneumonia, community-acquired (treatment) due to *H. influenzae, H. parainfluenzae, M. catarrhalis*[1], *S. pneumoniae, C. pneumoniae,* or *M. pneumoniae*—

Oral, 1000 mg once a day for seven days.

Sinusitis, acute maxillary[1]—

Oral, 1000 mg once a day for fourteen days.

Note: The efficacy and safety of clarithromycin in extended-release form in treating other infections for which other formulations of clarithromycin are approved have not been established.

Usual pediatric dose

This product is not suitable for young children. See *Clarithromycin for Oral Suspension.*

Strength(s) usually available

U.S.—

500 mg (Rx) [*Biaxin XL* (cellulosic polymers; D & C yellow No. 10; lactose monohydrate; magnesium stearate; propylene glycol; sorbic acid; sorbitan monooleate; talc; titanium dioxide; vanillin)].

Canada—

Not commercially available.

Packaging and storage

Store 20 to 25°C (68 to 77°F), excursions permitted between 15 and 30 °C (59 and 86 °F), USP controlled room temperature.

Auxiliary labeling

- Take with food

CLARITHROMYCIN FOR ORAL SUSPENSION

Usual adult and adolescent dose

Bronchitis, chronic (treatment) bacterial exacerbations due to *Haemophilus influenzae*—

Oral, 500 mg every twelve hours for seven to fourteen days.

Bronchitis, chronic (treatment) bacterial exacerbations due to *Haemophilus parainfluenzae*[1]—

Oral, 500 mg every twelve hours for seven days.

Bronchitis, chronic (treatment) bacterial exacerbations due to *M. catarrhalis,* or *S pneumoniae* or;

Skin and soft tissue infections, uncomplicated—

Oral, 250 mg every twelve hours for seven to fourteen days.

Note: Canadian product information lists the dose for bronchitis as 250 to 500 mg every twelve hours for seven to fourteen days.

*Mycobacterium avium*complex disease, disseminated (prophylaxis)—

Oral, 500 mg two times a day.

Mycobacterium avium complex disease, disseminated (treatment adjunct)—

Oral, 500 mg two times a day in combination with other antimycobacterial agents; clarithromycin therapy should continue for life if clinical and mycobacterial improvements are observed.

Pharyngitis, streptococcal (treatment) or

Tonsillitis (treatment)—

Oral, 250 mg every twelve hours for ten days.

Pneumonia, community-acquired (treatment) due to *C pneumoniae, M. pneumoniae,* or *S pneumoniae,*—

Oral, 250 mg every twelve hours for seven to fourteen days

Pneumonia, community-acquired (treatment) due to *H. influenzae*[1]—

Oral, 250 mg every twelve hours for seven days.

Pneumonia, community-acquired (treatment) due to *H. parainfluenzae,* or *M. catarrhalis*[1]—

See *Clarithromycin Extended Release Tablets*

Sinusitis, acute maxillary (treatment)—

Oral, 500 mg every twelve hours for fourteen days.

Ulcer, duodenal, (treatment adjunct) *Helicobacter pylori*–associated (Triple therapy-treatment adjunct with amoxicillin and lansoprazole)[1]—

Oral, 500 mg in combination with amoxicillin 1000 mg and lansoprazole 30 mg every twelve hours for ten to fourteen days.

Ulcer, duodenal, (treatment adjunct) *Helicobacter pylori*–associated (Triple therapy-with amoxicillin and omeprazole or amoxicillin and lansoprazole[1])—

Oral, 500 mg in combination with amoxicillin 1000 mg and omeprazole 20 mg every twelve hours for ten days

Oral, 500 mg in combination with amoxicillin 1000 mg and lansoprazole 30 mg every twelve hours for ten or fourteen days.

Note: In patients with an ulcer present at the time of initiation of therapy, an additional 18 days of omeprazole 20 mg once daily is recommended for ulcer healing and symptom relief.

Ulcer, duodenal, *H. pylori*–associated (Dual therapy-treatment adjunct with omeprazole)—

Oral, 500 mg three times a day in combination with omeprazole 40 mg once a day for fourteen days, followed by omeprazole alone 20 mg once a day for fourteen days.

Ulcer, duodenal, *H. pylori*-associated (Dual therapy-treatment adjunct with ranitidine bismuth citrate)—

Oral, 500 mg two times a day every 12 hours or three times a day every 8 hours in combination with ranitidine bismuth citrate 400 mg twice a day every 12 hours for fourteen days. An additional 14 days of 400 mg twice daily is recommended for ulcer healing and symptom relief.

Note: Clarithromycin and ranitidine bismuth citrate combination therapy is not recommended in patients with creatinine clearance less than 25 mL per minute.

Note: The dose of clarithromycin should be adjusted in patients with severe renal function impairment (creatinine clearance [CrCl] < 30 mL/min [0.5 mL/sec]). The following dosing guidelines are suggested:

Dose for CrCl of > 30 mL/min (0.5 mL/sec)	Adjusted dose for CrCl of < 30 mL/min (0.5 mL/sec)
500 mg two times a day	500 mg loading dose, then 250 mg two times a day
250 mg two times a day	250 mg once a day

Dosage should not be continued beyond fourteen days in patients with severe renal function impairment.

Usual pediatric dose

Otitis media, acute; or
Pharyngitis, streptococcal; or
Pneumonia, community-acquired (treatment) due to *C. pneumoniae*, *M. pneumoniae*, or *S pneumoniae*,
Sinusitis, acute maxillary or
Skin and soft tissue infections; or
Tonsillitis—

Oral, 7.5 mg per kg of body weight every twelve hours for ten days.

Mycobacterium avium complex disease, disseminated (prophylaxis)[1]—

Oral, 7.5 mg per kg of body weight, up to 500 mg, two times a day.

Mycobacterium avium complex disease, disseminated (treatment adjunct)—

Oral, 7.5 mg per kg of body weight, up to 500 mg, two times a day in combination with other antimycobacterial agents; clarithromycin therapy should continue for life if clinical and mycobacterial improvements are observed.

Note: The dose of clarithromycin should be halved, or the dosing interval doubled, in pediatric patients with severe renal function impairment (CrCl < 30 mL per minute [0.5 mL per second]), with or without coexisting hepatic function impairment.

Usual pediatric prescribing limits

1000 mg per day.

Strength(s) usually available

U.S.—

125 mg per 5 mL (when reconstituted according to manufacturer's instructions) (available in 50- and 100-mL bottles) (Rx) [*Biaxin* (sucrose)].

250 mg per 5 mL (when reconstituted according to manufacturer's instructions) (available in 50- and 100-mL bottles) (Rx) [*Biaxin* (sucrose)].

Canada—

125 mg per 5 mL (when reconstituted according to manufacturer's instructions) (available in 55-, 105-, and 150-mL bottles) (Rx) [*Biaxin* (saccharine; sodium chloride; sucrose)].

Packaging and storage

Store between 15 and 30 °C (59 and 86 °F) in a well-closed container. Protect from light.

Preparation of dosage form

Add the total volume of water indicated below, in two portions, shaking well after each addition.

Country available	Clarithromycin concentration after reconstitution	Total amount of water to be added	Total volume after reconstitution
U.S.	125 mg/5 mL	27 mL	50 mL
	125 mg/5 mL	55 mL	100 mL
	250 mg/5 mL	27 mL	50 mL
	250 mg/5 mL	55 mL	100 mL
Canada	125 mg/5 mL	29 mL	55 mL
	125 mg/5 mL	56 mL	105 mL
	125 mg/5 mL	80 mL	150 mL

Stability

After reconstitution, suspension retains its potency for 14 days. Do not refrigerate.

Auxiliary labeling

- Shake well.
- Do not refrigerate.
- Continue for full time of treatment.
- Beyond-use date.

Note

When dispensing, include a calibrated liquid-measuring device.

CLARITHROMYCIN TABLETS

Usual adult and adolescent dose

See *Clarithromycin for Oral Suspension*.

Usual pediatric dose

This product may not be suitable for young children. See *Clarithromycin for Oral Suspension*.

Strength(s) usually available

U.S.—

250 mg (Rx) [*Biaxin*].
500 mg (Rx) [*Biaxin*].

Canada—

250 mg (Rx) [*Biaxin*].
500 mg (Rx) [*Biaxin*].

Packaging and storage

Store below 40 °C (104 °F), preferably between 15 and 30 °C (59 and 86 °F), unless otherwise specified by manufacturer. Protect from light. Preserve in tight containers.

Auxiliary labeling

- Continue medicine for full time of treatment.

[1]Not included in Canadian product labeling.

Selected Bibliography

Piscitelli SC, Danziger LH, Rodvold KA. Clarithromycin and azithromycin: new macrolide antibiotics. Clin Pharm 1992; 11: 137-52.

Peters DH, Clissold SP. Clarithromycin. Drugs 1992; 44(1): 117-64.

Revised: 01/06/2006

CLEMASTINE—See *Antihistamines (Systemic)*

CLIDINIUM—See *Anticholinergics/Antispasmodics (Systemic)*

CLINDAMYCIN Systemic

VA CLASSIFICATION (Primary/Secondary): AM300/AP101

Commonly used brand name(s): *Cleocin; Cleocin Pediatric; Dalacin C; Dalacin C Flavored Granules; Dalacin C Phosphate.*

Note: For a listing of dosage forms and brand names by country availability, see *Dosage Forms* section(s).

Category

Antibacterial (systemic); antiprotozoal.

Indications

Note: Bracketed information in the *Indications* section refers to uses that are not included in U.S. product labeling.

Accepted

Bone and joint infections (treatment)—Parenteral clindamycin is indicated in the adjunctive surgical treatment of chronic bone and joint infections, and acute hematogenous osteomyelitis caused by staphylococci.

Pelvic infections, female (treatment)—Clindamycin is indicated in the treatment of female pelvic infections, including endometritis, nongonococcal tubo-ovarian abscess, pelvic cellulitis, and postsurgical vaginal cuff infections caused by anaerobes.

Intra-abdominal infections (treatment)—Clindamycin is indicated in the treatment of intra-abdominal infections (such as peritonitis and abscesses) caused by anaerobes.

Pneumonia, anaerobic (treatment)
Pneumonia, pneumococcal (treatment)
Pneumonia, staphylococcal (treatment) or
Pneumonia, streptococcal (treatment)—Clindamycin is indicated as a primary agent in the treatment of pneumonia, including serious respira-

tory tract infections (such as empyema, pneumonitis, and lung abscess) caused by anaerobes. Clindamycin is indicated as a secondary agent in the treatment of pneumonia caused by susceptible strains of pneumococci, staphylococci, and streptococci.

Septicemia, bacterial (treatment)—Oral and parenteral clindamycin are indicated in the treatment of septicemia caused by anaerobes. In addition, parenteral clindamycin is indicated in the treatment of septicemia caused by streptococci and staphylococci.

Skin and soft tissue infections (treatment)—Clindamycin is indicated in the treatment of serious skin and soft tissue infections caused by anaerobes, streptococci, and staphylococci.

[Actinomycosis (treatment)][1]—Clindamycin is used in the treatment of actinomycosis.

[Babesiosis (treatment)][1]—Clindamycin is used concurrently with quinine in the treatment of severe babesiosis caused by *Babesia microti*.

[Erysipelas (treatment)][1]—Clindamycin is used in the treatment of erysipelas.

[Malaria (treatment)][1]—Clindamycin is used in combination with quinine in the treatment of chloroquine-resistant malaria caused by *Plasmodium falciparum* in patients for whom standard therapy is contraindicated (e.g., children, pregnant women, sulfa allergy).

[Otitis media, chronic suppurative (treatment)][1]—Clindamycin is used in the treatment of chronic suppurative otitis media.

[Pneumonia, *Pneumocystis carinii* (treatment)][1]—Clindamycin is used in combination with primaquine in the treatment of *Pneumocystis carinii* pneumonia (PCP) in patients unresponsive or intolerant to standard therapy.

[Sinusitis (treatment)][1]—Clindamycin is used in the treatment of sinusitis.

[Toxoplasmosis, central nervous system (CNS) (treatment)][1]—Clindamycin is used in combination with pyrimethamine in the treatment of CNS toxoplasmosis in patients who are unresponsive or intolerant to standard therapy.

Not all species or strains of a particular organism may be susceptible to clindamycin.

Unaccepted

Clindamycin is not indicated in the treatment of meningitis since it penetrates poorly into cerebrospinal fluid (CSF), even in the presence of inflamed meninges.

[1]Not included in Canadian product labeling.

Pharmacology/Pharmacokinetics

Physicochemical characteristics

Molecular weight—
- Clindamycin hydrochloride: 461.44.
- Clindamycin palmitate hydrochloride: 699.86.
- Clindamycin phosphate: 504.96.

Mechanism of action/Effect

Antibacterial (systemic)—The lincomycins inhibit protein synthesis in susceptible bacteria by binding to the 50 S subunits of bacterial ribosomes and preventing peptide bond formation. They are usually considered bacteriostatic, but may be bactericidal in high concentrations or when used against highly susceptible organisms.

Absorption

Rapidly absorbed from the gastrointestinal tract following oral administration; not inactivated by gastric acid. Approximately 90% absorbed orally in fasting state; absorption unaffected by food.

Distribution

Widely and rapidly distributed to most fluids and tissues, except cerebrospinal fluid (CSF); high concentrations in bone, bile, and urine. Readily crosses the placenta. Also excreted in breast milk.

Vol_D—
- Adults: Approximately 0.66 liter per kg.
- Children: Approximately 0.86 liter per kg.

Protein binding

Very high (92–94%).

Biotransformation

Hepatic; some metabolites may possess antibacterial activity. Clindamycin palmitate and clindamycin phosphate are inactive; they are rapidly hydrolyzed *in vivo* to active clindamycin.

Half-life

Normal renal function—
- Adults: 2.4 to 3.0 hours.
- Infants and children: 2.5 to 3.4 hours.
- Premature infants: 6.3 to 8.6 hours.

End-stage renal failure or severe hepatic impairment—
- Slightly increased (3 to 5 hours in adults).

Time to peak serum concentration

Oral—0.75 to 1 hour.

Intramuscular—1 hour (children); 3 hours (adults).

Intravenous—End of infusion.

Peak serum concentration

Adults (steady-state)—
- 300 mg intravenously over 10 minutes every 8 hours: Approximately 7 mcg/mL.
- 600 mg intravenously over 20 minutes every 8 hours: Approximately 10 mcg/mL.
- 900 mg intravenously over 30 minutes every 12 hours: Approximately 11 mcg/mL.
- 1200 mg intravenously over 45 minutes every 12 hours: Approximately 14 mcg/mL.
- 300 mg intramuscularly every 8 hours: Approximately 6 mcg/mL.
- 600 mg intramuscularly every 12 hours: Approximately 9 mcg/mL.

Children (first dose)—
- 5 to 7 mg per kg of body weight (mg/kg) intravenously over 1 hour: Approximately 10 mcg/mL.
- 3 to 5 mg/kg intramuscularly: Approximately 4 mcg/mL.
- 5 to 7 mg/kg intramuscularly: Approximately 8 mcg/mL.

Elimination

Approximately 10% of a total dose is eliminated in the urine and 3.6% in the feces as active drug. The remainder is excreted as inactive metabolites.

Dialysis—Not removed from the blood by hemodialysis or peritoneal dialysis.

Precautions to Consider

Cross-sensitivity and/or related problems

Patients hypersensitive to lincomycin may be hypersensitive to clindamycin also. There is also a report of a possible cross-sensitivity between clindamycin and doxorubicin.

Pregnancy/Reproduction

Pregnancy—Clindamycin crosses the placenta and may be concentrated in the fetal liver. However, problems in humans have not been documented.

Breast-feeding

Clindamycin is excreted in breast milk. However, problems in humans have not been documented.

Pediatrics

Clindamycin should be used with caution in infants up to 1 month of age. Clindamycin phosphate injection contains benzyl alcohol, which has been associated with a fatal gasping syndrome in infants.

Geriatrics

No information is available on the relationship of age to the effects of clindamycin in geriatric patients.

Drug interactions and/or related problems

The following drug interactions and/or related problems have been selected on the basis of their potential clinical significance (possible mechanism in parentheses where appropriate)—not necessarily inclusive (» = major clinical significance):

Note: Combinations containing any of the following medications, depending on the amount present, may also interact with this medication.

» Anesthetics, hydrocarbon inhalation or

» Neuromuscular blocking agents

(concurrent use of these medications with clindamycin, if necessary, should be carefully monitored since neuromuscular blockade may be enhanced, resulting in skeletal muscle weakness and respiratory depression or paralysis [apnea]; caution is also recommended when these medications are used concurrently with clindamycin during surgery or in the postoperative period; treatment with anticholinesterase agents or calcium salts may help reverse the blockade)

» Antidiarrheals, adsorbent

(concurrent use of kaolin- or attapulgite-containing antidiarrheals with oral clindamycin may significantly delay the absorption of oral clindamycin; concurrent use should be avoided or patients should be advised to take adsorbent antidiarrheals not less than 2 hours before or 3 to 4 hours after oral lincomycins)

Antimyasthenics

(concurrent use of medications with neuromuscular blocking action may antagonize the effect of antimyasthenics on skeletal muscle; temporary dosage adjustments of antimyasthenics may be necessary to control symptoms of myasthenia gravis during and following concurrent use)

» Chloramphenicol or

» Erythromycins
(may displace clindamycin from or prevent its binding to 50 S subunits of bacterial ribosomes, thus antagonizing clindamycin's effects; concurrent use is not recommended)

Opioid (narcotic) analgesics
(respiratory depressant effects of drugs with neuromuscular blocking activity may be additive to central respiratory depressant effects of opioid analgesics, possibly leading to increased or prolonged respiratory depression or paralysis [apnea]; caution and careful monitoring of the patient are recommended)

Laboratory value alterations

The following have been selected on the basis of their potential clinical significance (possible effect in parentheses where appropriate)—not necessarily inclusive (» = major clinical significance).

With diagnostic test results
Alanine aminotransferase (ALT [SGPT]), serum and
Alkaline phosphatase, serum and
Aspartate aminotransferase (ALT [SGOT]), serum
(concentrations may be increased)

Medical considerations/Contraindications

The medical considerations/contraindications included have been selected on the basis of their potential clinical significance (reasons given in parentheses where appropriate)—not necessarily inclusive (» = major clinical significance).

Risk-benefit should be considered when the following medical problems exist:

» Gastrointestinal disease, history of, especially ulcerative colitis, regional enteritis, or antibiotic-associated colitis
(clindamycin may cause pseudomembranous colitis)

» Hepatic function impairment, severe
(the half-life of clindamycin is prolonged in patients with severe hepatic function impairment; this may require an adjustment in dosage)

Hypersensitivity to lincomycins or doxorubicin

Renal function impairment, severe
(patients with impaired renal function do not generally require a reduction in dose unless the impairment is severe; however, patients receiving clindamycin with very severe renal impairment and/or very severe hepatic impairment accompanied by severe metabolic abnormalities may require a reduction in dosage)

Patient monitoring

The following may be especially important in patient monitoring (other tests may be warranted in some patients, depending on condition; » = major clinical significance):

For antibiotic-associated pseudomembranous colitis (AAPMC)
Colonoscopy and/or
Proctosigmoidoscopy
(proctosigmoidoscopy and/or colonoscopy may be required in selected, severely ill patients with persistent symptoms of AAPMC to document the presence of pseudomembranes; it is no longer recommended as a routine monitoring parameter)

Stool examinations
(cytotoxin assays of stool samples for the presence of *Clostridium difficile* and its cytotoxin, neutralizable by *C. sordellii* antitoxin, may be required prior to treatment in patients with AAPMC to document the presence of *C. difficile* and/or its cytotoxin; however, *C. difficile* and its cytotoxin may persist following treatment with oral vancomycin despite clinical improvement; follow-up cytotoxin assays are generally not recommended with complete clinical improvement)

Side/Adverse Effects

The following side/adverse effects have been selected on the basis of their potential clinical significance (possible signs and symptoms in parentheses where appropriate)—not necessarily inclusive:

Those indicating need for medical attention

Incidence more frequent
Pseudomembranous colitis (severe abdominal or stomach cramps and pain; abdominal tenderness; diarrhea, watery and severe, which may also be bloody; fever)

Incidence less frequent
Hypersensitivity (skin rash, redness, and itching); ***neutropenia*** (sore throat and fever); ***thrombocytopenia*** (unusual bleeding or bruising)

Those indicating need for medical attention only if they continue or are bothersome

Incidence more frequent
Gastrointestinal disturbances (abdominal pain; diarrhea; nausea and vomiting)

Incidence less frequent
Fungal overgrowth (itching of rectal or genital areas)

Those indicating possible pseudomembranous colitis and the need for medical attention if they occur after medication is discontinued

Severe abdominal or stomach cramps and pain; abdominal tenderness; watery and severe diarrhea, which may also be bloody; fever

Patient Consultation

As an aid to patient consultation, refer to *Advice for the Patient, Clindamycin (Systemic)*.

In providing consultation, consider emphasizing the following selected information (» = major clinical significance):

Before using this medication

» Conditions affecting use, especially:
Hypersensitivity to clindamycin, lincomycin, or doxorubicin
Pregnancy—Clindamycin crosses the placenta
Breast-feeding—Clindamycin is excreted in breast milk
Use in children—Clindamycin should be used cautiously in infants up to 1 month of age; clindamycin injection contains benzyl alcohol, which has been associated with a fatal gasping syndrome in infants
Other medications, especially hydrocarbon inhalation anesthetics, neuromuscular blocking agents, adsorbent antidiarrheals, chloramphenicol, or erythromycins
Other medical problems, especially a history of gastrointestinal disease, particularly ulcerative colitis, or severe hepatic function impairment

Proper use of this medication

» Taking clindamycin capsules with a full glass of water or with meals to avoid esophageal ulceration

Proper administration technique for clindamycin oral solution; not using after expiration date

» Compliance with full course of therapy, especially in streptococcal infections

» Importance of not missing doses and taking at evenly spaced times

» Proper dosing
Missed dose: Taking as soon as possible; not taking if almost time for next dose; not doubling doses

» Proper storage

Precautions while using this medication

Regular visits to physician to check progress

Checking with physician if no improvement within a few days

» For severe diarrhea, checking with physician before taking any antidiarrheals; for mild diarrhea, taking attapulgite-containing antidiarrheals at least 2 hours before or 3 to 4 hours after taking oral clindamycin; other antidiarrheals may worsen or prolong the diarrhea; checking with physician or pharmacist if mild diarrhea continues or worsens

Caution if surgery with general anesthesia is required

Side/adverse effects

Signs of potential side effects, especially pseudomembranous colitis, hypersensitivity, neutropenia, and thrombocytopenia

General Dosing Information

Therapy should be continued for at least 10 days in group A beta-hemolytic streptococcal infections to help prevent the occurrence of acute rheumatic fever.

For oral dosage forms only:

- The capsule dosage form should be taken with food or a full glass (240 mL) of water to avoid esophageal irritation.

For treatment of adverse effects

For antibiotic-associated pseudomembranous colitis (AAPMC)—

- Some patients may develop antibiotic-associated pseudomembranous colitis (AAPMC), caused by *Clostridium difficile* toxin, during or following administration of lincomycins. Mild cases may respond to discontinuation of the drug alone. Moderate to severe cases may require fluid, electrolyte, and protein replacement.
- In cases not responding to the above measures or in more severe cases, oral doses of metronidazole, bacitracin, cholestyramine, or vancomycin may be used. Oral vancomycin is effective in doses of 125 to 500 mg every 6 hours for 5 to 10 days. The dose of metronidazole is 250 to 500 mg every 8 hours; cholestyramine, 4 grams four times a day; and bacitracin, 25,000 units, orally, four times a day. Recurrences may be treated with a second course of these medications.
- Cholestyramine and colestipol resins have been shown to bind *C. difficile* toxin *in vitro*. If cholestyramine or colestipol resin is administered in conjunction with oral vancomycin, the medications should be

administered several hours apart since the resins have been shown to bind oral vancomycin also.
• In addition, antibiotic-associated pseudomembranous colitis may result in severe watery diarrhea, which may occur during therapy or up to several weeks after therapy is discontinued. If diarrhea occurs, administration of antiperistaltic antidiarrheals (e.g., opiates, diphenoxylate and atropine combination, loperamide) is not recommended since they may delay the removal of toxins from the colon, thereby prolonging and/or worsening the condition.

Oral Dosage Forms

Note: Bracketed uses in the *Dosage Forms* section refer to categories of use and/or indications that are not included in U.S. product labeling.

CLINDAMYCIN HYDROCHLORIDE CAPSULES USP

Usual adult and adolescent dose

Antibacterial—
Oral, 150 to 300 mg (base) every six hours.

[Malaria (treatment)][1]—
Oral, 900 mg (base) three times a day for three days.

[Pneumonia, *Pneumocystis carinii* (treatment)][1]—
Oral, 1200 to 1800 mg (base) per day in divided doses in combination with 15 to 30 mg of primaquine daily.

[Toxoplasmosis, central nervous system (CNS) (treatment)][1]—
Oral, 1200 to 2400 mg (base) per day in divided doses in combination with 50 to 100 mg of pyrimethamine daily.

Usual pediatric dose

Antibacterial—
Infants up to 1 month of age: Dosage must be individualized by physician. Use with caution.
Infants 1 month of age and over: Oral, 2 to 5 mg (base) per kg of body weight every six hours; or 2.7 to 6.7 mg per kg of body weight every eight hours.
Note: In children weighing 10 kg or less, the minimum recommended dose is 37.5 mg every eight hours.

[Malaria (treatment)][1]—
Oral, 6.7 to 13.3 mg per kg of body weight three times a day for three days.

Strength(s) usually available

U.S.—
75 mg (base) (Rx) [*Cleocin* (tartrazine); GENERIC].
150 mg (base) (Rx) [*Cleocin* (tartrazine); GENERIC].
300 mg (base) (Rx) [*Cleocin* (tartrazine)].

Canada—
150 mg (base) (Rx) [*Dalacin C*].
300 mg (base) (Rx) [*Dalacin C*].

Packaging and storage

Store below 40 °C (104 °F), preferably between 15 and 30 °C (59 and 86 °F), unless otherwise specified by manufacturer. Store in a tight container.

Auxiliary labeling

• Take with food or water.
• Continue medicine for full time of treatment.

CLINDAMYCIN PALMITATE HYDROCHLORIDE FOR ORAL SOLUTION USP

Usual adult and adolescent dose

See *Clindamycin Hydrochloride Capsules USP*.

Usual pediatric dose

See *Clindamycin Hydrochloride Capsules USP*.

Strength(s) usually available

U.S.—
75 mg per 5 mL (base) (when reconstituted according to manufacturer's instructions) (Rx) [*Cleocin Pediatric* (sucrose)].

Canada—
75 mg per 5 mL (base) (when reconstituted according to manufacturer's instructions) (Rx) [*Dalacin C Flavored Granules*].

Packaging and storage

Prior to reconstitution, store below 40 °C (104 °F), preferably between 15 and 30 °C (59 and 86 °F), unless otherwise specified by manufacturer. Store in a tight container. Do not refrigerate the reconstituted solution since it may thicken and be difficult to pour when chilled.

Stability

After reconstitution, solutions retain their potency for 14 days at room temperature.

Auxiliary labeling

• Do not refrigerate.
• Shake well.
• Continue medicine for full time of treatment.
• Beyond-use date.

Note

When dispensing, include a calibrated liquid-measuring device.

Parenteral Dosage Forms

Note: Bracketed uses in the *Dosage Forms* section refer to categories of use and/or indications that are not included in U.S. product labeling.

CLINDAMYCIN PHOSPHATE INJECTION USP

Usual adult and adolescent dose

Antibacterial—
Intramuscular or intravenous, 300 to 600 mg (base) every six to eight hours; or 900 mg every eight hours.

[Babesiosis (treatment)][1]—
Intravenous, 300 to 600 mg clindamycin (base) four times a day with concurrent oral administration of 650 mg of quinine, three or four times a day for seven to ten days.

[Pneumonia, *Pneumocystis carinii* (treatment)][1]—
Intravenous, 2400 to 2700 mg (base) per day in divided doses in combination with 15 to 30 mg of primaquine daily.

[Toxoplasmosis, central nervous system (CNS) (treatment)][1]—
Intravenous, 1200 to 4800 mg (base) per day in divided doses in combination with 50 to 100 mg of pyrimethamine daily.

Usual adult prescribing limits

Up to 2.7 grams (base) daily.

Note: Doses up to 4.8 grams daily have been used. However, some medical experts recommend a maximum dose of 2.7 grams daily.

Usual pediatric dose

Antibacterial—
Infants up to 1 month of age: Intramuscular or intravenous, 3.75 to 5 mg (base) per kg of body weight every six hours; or 5 to 6.7 mg per kg of body weight every eight hours.
Infants 1 month of age and over: Intramuscular or intravenous, 3.75 to 10 mg (base) per kg of body weight or 87.5 to 112.5 mg per square meter of body surface every six hours; or 5 to 13.3 mg per kg of body weight or 116.7 to 150 mg per square meter of body surface every eight hours.

Note: In children, regardless of body weight, the minimum recommended dose is 300 mg (base) daily for severe infections.
Bone infection—Intramuscular or intravenous, 7.5 mg per kg of body weight every six hours.

[Babesiosis (treatment)][1]—
Dosage has not been established; however, based on one case report in an infant, the suggested dose is: Intravenous or intramuscular, 20 mg per kg of body weight per day of clindamycin with concurrent oral administration of 25 mg per kg of body weight per day of quinine for seven to ten days.

Strength(s) usually available

U.S.—
300 mg (base) in 2 mL (Rx) [*Cleocin* (benzyl alcohol 9.45 mg); GENERIC].
600 mg (base) in 4 mL (Rx) [*Cleocin* (benzyl alcohol 9.45 mg); GENERIC].
900 mg (base) in 6 mL (Rx) [*Cleocin* (benzyl alcohol 9.45 mg); GENERIC].
9000 mg (base) in 60 mL (Rx) [GENERIC].

Canada—
300 mg (base) in 2 mL (Rx) [*Dalacin C Phosphate* (benzyl alcohol)].
600 mg (base) in 4 mL (Rx) [*Dalacin C Phosphate* (benzyl alcohol)].
900 mg (base) in 6 mL (Rx) [*Dalacin C Phosphate* (benzyl alcohol)].

Packaging and storage

Store below 40 °C (104 °F), preferably between 15 and 30 °C (59 and 86 °F), unless otherwise specified by manufacturer. Protect from freezing.

Preparation of dosage form

To prepare initial dilution for intravenous use, each dose must be diluted as follows (it must not be administered undiluted as a bolus):

Dose (mg)	Diluent (mL)	Duration of administration (min)
300	50	10
600	100	20
900	100	30

Caution: Products containing benzyl alcohol are not recommended for use in neonates. A fatal toxic syndrome consisting of metabolic acidosis, CNS depression, respiratory problems, renal failure, hypotension, and possibly seizures and intracranial hemorrhages has been associated with this use.

Stability

Clindamycin phosphate retains its potency for 24 hours at room temperature in intravenous infusions containing sodium chloride, dextrose, potassium, vitamin B complex, cephalothin, kanamycin, gentamicin, penicillin, or carbenicillin.

Incompatibilities

Clindamycin phosphate is physically incompatible with ampicillin, phenytoin sodium, barbiturates, aminophylline, calcium gluconate, and magnesium sulfate.

Additional information

Clindamycin phosphate may also be administered as a single rapid infusion (initial dose) followed by continuous intravenous infusion as follows:

Clindamycin serum concentrations (desired maintenance—mcg/mL)	Infusion rate and duration (initial)		Infusion rate (continuous—mg/min)
	Rate (mg/min)	Duration (min)	
> 4	10	30	0.75
> 5	15	30	1
> 6	20	30	1.25

[1]Not included in Canadian product labeling.

Revised: 08/14/1998

CLINDAMYCIN Topical

VA CLASSIFICATION (Primary/Secondary): DE752/DE101

Commonly used brand name(s): *Cleocin T Gel; Cleocin T Lotion; Cleocin T Topical Solution; Clinda-Derm; Dalacin T Topical Solution; Evoclin.*

Note: For a listing of dosage forms and brand names by country availability, see *Dosage Forms* section(s).

Category

Antiacne agent (topical); antibacterial (topical).

Indications

Note: Bracketed information in the *Indications* section refers to uses that are not included in U.S. product labeling.

Accepted

Acne vulgaris(treatment)—Topical clindamycin is indicated in the treatment of acne vulgaris. It may be effective in grades II and III acne, which are characterized by inflammatory lesions such as papules and pustules. Topical antibacterials are not generally considered to be as effective as systemic antibacterials in the treatment of acne, especially more severe inflammatory acne. However, some studies have shown that clindamycin phosphate topical solution may be as effective as low-dose tetracycline for moderate cases of inflammatory acne.

[Skin infections, bacterial, minor (treatment)][1]—Topical clindamycin is used in the topical treatment of erythrasma caused by *Corynebacterium minutissimum*, rosacea, periorificial facial dermatitis, folliculitis, stasis, chronic lymphedema, and familial pemphigus.

[Ulcer, dermal (treatment)][1]—Clindamycin phosphate topical solution is used in the treatment of dermal ulcers.

Not all species or strains of a particular organism may be susceptible to clindamycin.

Unaccepted

Topical clindamycin is not effective in the treatment of deep cystic lesions or noninflammatory lesions.

[1]Not included in Canadian product labeling.

Pharmacology/Pharmacokinetics

Physicochemical characteristics

Molecular weight—504.96.

Mechanism of action/Effect

Antiacne agent (topical)—Probably due to its antibacterial activity. Topical clindamycin is thought to reduce free fatty acid concentrations on the skin and to suppress the growth of *Propionibacterium acnes (Corynebacterium acnes)*, an anaerobe found in sebaceous glands and follicles. *P. acnes* produces proteases, hyaluronidases, lipases, and chemotactic factors, all of which can produce inflammatory components or inflammation directly.

Absorption

Approximately 1.7% absorbed through the skin following topical application of the solution every 12 hours for 4 days to approximately 300 cm^2 of skin surface.

Mean comedonal extract concentration

597 mcg per gram after 4 weeks of topical application.

Biotransformation

Clindamycin phosphate is inactive *in vitro*, but is rapidly hydrolyzed *in vivo* by tissue phosphatases to active clindamycin.

Peak serum concentration

<1 to 6 nanograms per mL following topical application of the solution every 12 hours for 4 days.

Urine concentration

<1 to 53 nanograms per mL following topical application of the solution every 12 hours for 4 days.

Elimination

Renal—0.15 to 0.25% of cumulative dose excreted in urine following topical application of the solution every 12 hours.

Precautions to Consider

Cross-sensitivity and/or related problems

Patients sensitive to one lincomycin may be sensitive to other lincomycins also.

Carcinogenicity

No significant increase in tumors was noted in a carcinogenicity study applying 1% clindamycin phosphate **gel** daily approximately 3 and 15 times higher than the human dose to mice for two years. Median time to tumor onset was shortened in a study in hairless mice when tumors were induced by exposure to simulated sunlight and 1% clindamycin phosphate **gel**.

Mutagenicity

Rat micronucleus test and an Ames Salmonella reversion test for genotoxicity were negative.

Pregnancy/Reproduction

Fertility—Studies in rats and mice receiving subcutaneous and oral doses of clindamycin ranging from 100 to 600 mg per kg per day have not shown that clindamycin causes impaired fertility.

Pregnancy—Adequate and well-controlled studies in humans have not been done.

Studies in rats and mice receiving subcutaneous and oral doses of clindamycin ranging from 100 to 600 mg per kg per day have not shown that clindamycin causes adverse effects on the fetus.

FDA Pregnancy Category B.

Breast-feeding

It is not known whether topical clindamycin is distributed into breast milk. Since systemically administered clindamycin is distributed into breast milk, topical clindamycin may be also. However, clindamycin is unlikely to be distributed into breast milk in significant amounts following topical administration, since the total daily dose is small and only approximately 1.7% of the dose is absorbed through the skin.

A decision should be made whether to discontinue nursing or to discontinue the drug, taking into account the importance of the drug to the mother.

Pediatrics

Appropriate studies on the relationship of age to the effects of topical clindamycin have not been performed in children up to 12 years of age. Safety and efficacy have not been established.

Geriatrics

No information is available on the relationship of age to the effects of topical clindamycin in geriatric patients.

Drug interactions and/or related problems

The following drug interactions and/or related problems have been selected on the basis of their potential clinical significance (possible mechanism in parentheses where appropriate)—not necessarily inclusive (» = major clinical significance):

Note: Combinations containing any of the following medications, depending on the amount present, may also interact with this medication.

Abrasive or medicated soaps or cleansers or
Acne preparations or preparations containing a peeling agent, such as:
Resorcinol
Salicylic acid
Sulfur, or

Alcohol-containing preparations, topical, such as:
After-shave lotions
Astringents
Perfumed toiletries
Shaving creams or lotions, or
Cosmetics or soaps with a strong drying effect or
Isotretinoin or
Medicated cosmetics or "cover-ups"
(concurrent use with clindamycin phosphate topical solution may cause a cumulative irritant or drying effect, especially with the application of peeling, desquamating, or abrasive agents, resulting in excessive irritation of the skin)

Neuromuscular blocking agents
(clindamycin may enhance the action of other neuromuscular blocking agents)

Medical considerations/Contraindications

The medical considerations/contraindications included have been selected on the basis of their potential clinical significance (reasons given in parentheses where appropriate)—not necessarily inclusive (» = major clinical significance).

Except under special circumstances, this medication should not be used when the following medical problem exists:

» Antibiotic-associated colitis, ulcerative colitis, or regional enteritis, history of

» Hypersensitivity to clindamycin or lincomycin

Risk-benefit should be considered when the following medical problems exist:

Atopic reactions, history of

Patient monitoring

The following may be especially important in patient monitoring (other tests may be warranted in some patients, depending on condition; » = major clinical significance):

Endoscopy, large bowel
(if severe diarrhea not controlled by administration of vancomycin occurs and persists during therapy, large bowel endoscopy may be required as an aid in the diagnosis of pseudomembranous colitis)

Side/Adverse Effects

The following side/adverse effects have been selected on the basis of their potential clinical significance (possible signs and symptoms in parentheses where appropriate)—not necessarily inclusive:

Those indicating need for medical attention

Incidence less frequent

Contact dermatitis or hypersensitivity (skin rash, itching, redness, swelling, or other sign of irritation not present before therapy)

Incidence rare

Pseudomembranous colitis (abdominal or stomach cramps, pain, and bloating, severe; diarrhea, watery and severe, which may also be bloody; fever; increased thirst; nausea or vomiting; unusual tiredness or weakness; weight loss, unusual)

Those indicating need for medical attention only if they continue or are bothersome

Incidence more frequent

Dryness, scaliness, or peeling of skin—for the topical solution

Incidence less frequent

Gastrointestinal disturbances (abdominal pain; mild diarrhea); ***headache***—for the topical foam; ***irritation, sensitization or oiliness of skin; stinging or burning feeling of skin***—for the topical solution

Those indicating possible pseudomembranous colitis and the need for medical attention if they occur after medication is discontinued

Abdominal or stomach cramps, pain, and bloating, severe; diarrhea, watery and severe, which may also be bloody; fever; increased thirst; nausea or vomiting; unusual tiredness or weakness; weight loss, unusual

Patient Consultation

As an aid to patient consultation, refer to *Advice for the Patient, Clindamycin (Topical).*

In providing consultation, consider emphasizing the following selected information (» = major clinical significance):

Before using this medication

» Conditions affecting use, especially:
Hypersensitivity to clindamycin or lincomycin

Pregnancy—Adequate and well-controlled studies in humans have not been done. Studies in animals have not shown that clindamycin causes adverse effects in the fetus.

Breast-feeding—May be distributed into breast milk in small quantities since systemic clindamycin is distributed into breast milk

Other medical problems, especially a history of antibiotic-associated colitis, ulcerative colitis, or regional enteritis

Proper use of this medication

Before applying, washing affected areas with warm water and soap, rinsing, and patting dry

» Importance of applying medication to entire affected area

Avoiding too frequent washing of affected areas

» Compliance with full course of therapy, which may take months or longer

» Proper dosing

Missed dose: Applying as soon as possible; not applying if almost time for next dose

» Proper storage

For topical foam only

Do not dispense topical foam directly onto your hands or face. Dispense the amount of topical foam needed to cover the affected areas directly into the cap or onto a cool surface.

If the can seems warm or the foam seems runny, run the can under cold water.

Pick up small amounts of topical foam with your fingertips and gently massage into the affected areas until the foam disappears.

» Avoiding contact with eyes. Rinse eyes thoroughly with water if contact occurs.

Throw away any of the unused medicine that you dispensed out of the can.

For topical solution only

Waiting 30 minutes after washing or shaving before applying

» Not using near heat, near open flame, or while smoking

Proper administration technique for applicator-tip bottle:

» Avoiding contact with eyes, nose, mouth, or other mucous membranes

Not using more often than prescribed

For topical suspension only

» Shaking well before using

Precautions while using this medication

Checking with physician or pharmacist if no improvement within about 6 weeks

Applying other medications at different times

Checking with physician if treated skin becomes excessively dry (for topical solution only)

» For severe diarrhea, checking with physician before taking any antidiarrheals; for mild diarrhea, taking attapulgite-containing, but not other, antidiarrheals; checking with physician or pharmacist if mild diarrhea continues or worsens

Using only "water-base" cosmetics; not applying too heavily or too often

Side/adverse effects

Signs of potential side effects, especially hypersensitivity reactions and pseudomembranous colitis

General Dosing Information

Use of topical antibacterials may lead to skin sensitization, resulting in hypersensitivity reactions with subsequent topical or systemic use of the medication.

In the treatment of acne with topical clindamycin, noticeable improvement is usually seen after about 6 weeks in most patients. However, 8 to 12 weeks of treatment may be required before maximum benefit is seen.

For treatment of adverse effects

Some patients may develop antibiotic-associated pseudomembranous colitis (AAPMC), caused by *Clostridium difficile* toxin, during or following administration of topical clindamycin. Mild cases may respond to discontinuation of the drug alone. Moderate to severe cases may require fluid, electrolyte, and protein replacement.

In cases not responding to the above measures or in more severe cases, oral vancomycin, oral bacitracin, or oral metronidazole may be used. Oral vancomycin is effective in doses of 125 to 500 mg every 6 hours for 7 to 10 days. Recurrences may be treated with a second course of these medications.

Cholestyramine and colestipol resins have been shown to bind *C. difficile* toxin *in vitro*. If cholestyramine or colestipol resin is administered in conjunction with oral vancomycin, the medications should be administered several hours apart since the resins have been shown to bind oral vancomycin also.

In addition, AAPMC may result in severe watery diarrhea, which may occur during antibiotic therapy or up to several weeks after therapy is discontinued. If diarrhea occurs, administration of antiperistaltic antidiarrheals (e.g., opiates, diphenoxylate and atropine combination, loperamide) is *not* recommended since they may delay the removal of toxins from the colon, thereby prolonging and/or worsening the condition.

Topical Dosage Forms

CLINDAMYCIN PHOSPHATE TOPICAL FOAM USP

Usual adult and adolescent dose

Antiacne agent (topical)—
Topical, to the skin, a thin film applied once a day to the affected areas.

Usual pediatric dose

Children up to 12 years of age—Safety and efficacy have not been established.

Strength(s) usually available

U.S.—
1% (base) (Rx) [*Evoclin* (cetyl alcohol; dehydrated alcohol [ethanol 58%]; polysorbate 60; potassium hydroxide; propylene glycol; purified water; stearyl alcohol; pressurized with a hydrocarbon [propane/butane] propellant)].

Canada—
Not commercially available.

Packaging and storage

Store at controlled room temperature 20 to 25 °C (68 to 77 °F).

Auxiliary labeling

- Continue medicine for full time of treatment.
- External use only.
- Flammable - keep away from heat and flame.
- Keep out of reach of children.

Caution

Flammable. Avoid fire, flame or smoking during and immediately following application.

CLINDAMYCIN PHOSPHATE GEL USP

Usual adult and adolescent dose

Antiacne agent (topical)—
Topical, to the skin, a thin film applied two times a day to the affected areas.

Usual pediatric dose

Children up to 12 years of age—Safety and efficacy have not been established.

Strength(s) usually available

U.S.—
1% (base) (Rx) [*Cleocin T Gel* (methylparaben; propylene glycol; sodium hydroxide)].

Canada—
Not commercially available.

Packaging and storage

Store below 40 °C (104 °F), preferably between 15 and 30 °C (59 and 86 °F), unless otherwise specified by manufacturer. Store in a tight container. Protect from freezing.

Auxiliary labeling

- For external use only.
- Continue medicine for full time of treatment.

Additional information

Clindamycin phosphate gel is an aqueous, nonalcoholic, nondrying formulation.

CLINDAMYCIN PHOSPHATE TOPICAL SOLUTION USP

Usual adult and adolescent dose

Antiacne agent (topical)—
Topical, to the skin, two times a day to the affected areas.

Note: Solutions have been used one to four times a day.

Usual pediatric dose

See *Clindamycin Phosphate Gel USP*.

Strength(s) usually available

U.S.—
1% (base) (Rx) [*Cleocin T Topical Solution; Clinda-Derm* (isopropyl alcohol 50%; propylene glycol); GENERIC].

Canada—
1% (base) (Rx) [*Dalacin T Topical Solution* (isopropyl alcohol 50%; propylene glycol)].

Packaging and storage

Store below 40 °C (104 °F), preferably between 15 and 30 °C (59 and 86 °F), unless otherwise specified by manufacturer. Store in a tight container. Protect from freezing.

Auxiliary labeling

- For external use only.
- Continue medicine for full time of treatment.
- Keep container tightly closed.
- Flammable—Keep away from heat and flame.

CLINDAMYCIN PHOSPHATE TOPICAL SUSPENSION USP

Usual adult and adolescent dose

Antiacne agent (topical)—
See *Clindamycin Phosphate Topical Solution USP.*

Usual pediatric dose

See *Clindamycin Phosphate Topical Solution USP.*

Strength(s) usually available

U.S.—
1% (base) (Rx) [*Cleocin T Lotion* (cetostearyl alcohol 2.5%; isostearyl alcohol 2.5%)].

Canada—
Not commercially available.

Packaging and storage

Store below 40 °C (104 °F), preferably between 15 and 30 °C (59 and 86 °F), unless otherwise specified by manufacturer. Store in a tight container. Protect from freezing.

Auxiliary labeling

- Shake well.
- For external use only.
- Continue medicine for full time of treatment.

Revised: 01/21/2005

CLINDAMYCIN Vaginal

VA CLASSIFICATION (Primary): GU309

Commonly used brand name(s): *Cleocin; Clindesse; Dalacin.*

Note: For a listing of dosage forms and brand names by country availability, see *Dosage Forms* section(s).

Category

Anti-infective (vaginal).

Indications

Accepted

Vaginosis, bacterial (treatment)—Vaginal clindamycin is indicated in the local treatment of bacterial vaginosis (previously known as *Haemophilus* vaginitis, *Gardnerella* vaginitis, nonspecific vaginitis, *Corynebacterium* vaginitis, or anaerobic vaginosis).

In addition to its use in nonpregnant patients, vaginal clindamycin is indicated for use during the second and third trimesters of pregnancy. However, in a controlled clinical trial, no difference was found between vaginal clindamycin and placebo in reducing the risk of adverse pregnancy outcomes, such as premature rupture of the membranes, preterm labor, or preterm delivery. The best results are achieved when high-risk pregnant patients are screened early in the second trimester and asymptomatic high-risk and symptomatic low-risk patients are treated with oral metronidazole or oral clindamycin. Although some experts prefer the use of systemic therapy for low-risk pregnant patients to treat possible subclinical upper gential tract infections, vaginal metronidazole may be used in low-risk pregnant patients as an alternative therapy.

Not all species or strains of a particular organism may be susceptible to clindamycin.

Unaccepted

Vaginal clindamycin is not effective in the treatment of vulvovaginitis caused by *Trichomonas vaginalis, Chlamydia trachomatis, Neisseria gonorrhoeae, Candida albicans*, or *Herpes simplex* virus.

Pharmacology/Pharmacokinetics

Physicochemical characteristics

Molecular weight—Clindamycin phosphate: 504.97.

Mechanism of action/Effect
Clindamycin phosphate is hydrolyzed *in vivo* to clindamycin, which inhibits protein synthesis in susceptible bacteria by binding to the 50 S subunits of bacterial ribosomes and prevents peptide bond formation.

Absorption
Approximately 2 to 8% of the administered dose (100 mg) is absorbed systemically; little or no systemic accumulation has been produced with multiple dosing.

Biotransformation
Inactive clindamycin phosphate undergoes rapid hydrolysis *in vivo* to active clindamycin.

Half-life
Systemic—1.5 to 2.6 hours.

Time to peak concentration
Approximately 16 hours (range, 8 to 24 hours).

Peak serum concentration
Steady state—Approximately 16 mcg/L (0.032 micromoles/L).

Precautions to Consider

Cross-sensitivity and/or related problems
Patients hypersensitive to lincomycin may be hypersensitive to clindamycin also.

Carcinogenicity/Tumorigenicity
Long-term studies in animals have not been done.

Mutagenicity
No evidence of mutagenicity was found in tests, including the Ames test and a rat micronucleus test.

Pregnancy/Reproduction
Fertility—No evidence of adverse effects on fertility was found in rats when they were treated with oral doses of 300 mg per kg of body weight (mg/kg) a day (31 times the human exposure based on mg per square meter [mg/m^2] of body surface area).

Pregnancy—Systemic clindamycin crosses the placenta; up to 8% of vaginal clindamycin is systemically absorbed.

Well-controlled clinical trials using vaginal clindamycin during the second and third trimesters showed no adverse effects in the fetus; there is inadequate information on its use during the first trimester. For single-dose vaginal clindamycin, there are no adequate and well-controlled studies in pregnant women. Vaginal clindamycin should be used during pregnancy only if clearly needed.

Although vaginal clindamycin is effective in treating bacterial vaginosis in pregnant and nonpregnant women, it frequently causes cervicitis or vaginitis with or without candidiasis, especially in pregnant patients. Pregnant patients were not re-treated in clinical trials even though bacterial vaginosis returned in about 50% of patients several weeks after initial treatment. In general, best results for treatment and pregnancy outcomes are associated with treatment early in the second trimester. The incidence of bacterial vaginosis appears to lessen by an unknown mechanism as pregnancy continues into the third trimester.

Reproduction studies in animals in which high systemic doses of clindamycin were used showed no evidence of fetal malformations, except one small study in which the fetuses of treated mice developed cleft palates. This result has not been duplicated in other animals or other mouse strains.

FDA Pregnancy Category B.

Breast-feeding
Systemic clindamycin is distributed into breast milk. Problems in humans have not been documented. It is not known if vaginally administered clindamycin phosphate is distributed into breast milk. Because of potential for serious adverse reactions in nursing infants from clindamycin phosphate, a decision should be made whether to discontinue nursing or to discontinue the drug, taking into account the importance of the drug to the mother.

Pediatrics
No information is available on the relationship of age to the effects of vaginal clindamycin in pediatric patients. Safety and efficacy have not been established in pre-menarchal females. However, safety and efficacy of single-dose vaginal clindamycin have been established in post-menarchal females based on extrapolation of clinical trial data from adult women.

Geriatrics
No information is available on the relationship of age to the effects of clindamycin in geriatric patients.

Drug interactions and/or related problems
The following drug interactions and/or related problems have been selected on the basis of their potential clinical significance (possible mechanism in parentheses where appropriate)—not necessarily inclusive (» = major clinical significance):

Neuromuscular blocking agents
(should be used with caution; clindamycin has been shown to have neuromuscular blocking properties that may enhance action of other neuromuscular blocking agents)

Medical considerations/Contraindications
The medical considerations/contraindications included have been selected on the basis of their potential clinical significance (reasons given in parentheses where appropriate)—not necessarily inclusive (» = major clinical significance).

Except under special circumstances, this medication should not be used when the following medical problem exists:

» "Antibiotic-associated" colitis, history of, or
» Regional enteritis, history of, or
» Ulcerative colitis, history of
» Hypersensitivity to clindamycin, lincomycin, or any of the components of the product

Patient monitoring
The following may be especially important in patient monitoring (other tests may be warranted in some patients, depending on condition; » = major clinical significance):

Pseudomembranous colitis
(although there is minimal systemic absorption of vaginal clindamycin from the vagina, it is important to consider pseudomembranous colitis if patient presents with diarrhea; onset of symptoms may occur during or after antimicrobial treatment)

Side/Adverse Effects

Note: The side effects listed below are those reported in studies with vaginal clindamycin administration. Systemic side effects may occur since up to 8% of the vaginal dose is absorbed systemically. Pseudomembranous colitis has occurred rarely with topical use of clindamycin but has not been reported with vaginal administration.

The following side/adverse effects have been selected on the basis of their potential clinical significance (possible signs and symptoms in parentheses where appropriate)—not necessarily inclusive:

Those indicating need for medical attention
Incidence more frequent
Cervicitis, vaginitis, or vulvovaginal pruritus, primarily due to Candida albicans (itching of the vagina or genital area; pain during sexual intercourse; thick, white vaginal discharge with no odor or with a mild odor)—incidence of 33% for pregnant patients and 16% for nonpregnant patients

Incidence less frequent
CNS effects (dizziness; headache); ***gastrointestinal disturbances*** (diarrhea; nausea or vomiting; stomach pain or cramps)

Incidence rare
Hypersensitivity (burning, itching, redness, skin rash, swelling, or other signs of skin irritation not present before therapy)

Those indicating possible need for medical attention if they occur after medication is discontinued
Cervicitis, vaginitis, or vulvovaginal pruritus, primarily due to Candida albicans (itching of the vagina or genital area; pain during sexual intercourse; thick, white vaginal discharge with no odor or with a mild odor)

Patient Consultation
As an aid to patient consultation, refer to *Advice for the Patient, Clindamycin (Vaginal).*

In providing consultation, consider emphasizing the following selected information (» = major clinical significance):

Before using this medication
» Conditions affecting use, especially:
Hypersensitivity to clindamycin or lincomycin or any component of the product
Pregnancy—Systemic clindamycin crosses the placenta; up to 8% of vaginal clindamycin is systemically absorbed; should be used during pregnancy only if clearly needed
Breast-feeding—Systemically administered clindamycin is distributed into breast milk. It is not known if vaginal clindamycin also is distributed into breast milk; risk-benefit should be considered
Other medical problems, especially history of gastrointestinal disease (particularly ulcerative colitis, regional enteritis, or antibiotic-associated colitis)

Proper use of this medication
Washing hands immediately before and after vaginal administration

Avoiding getting medication into the eyes; washing eyes out immediately with large amounts of cool tap water if medication does get into eyes; checking with physician if eyes continue to be painful

Reading patient directions carefully before use

Proper administration technique: Following directions regarding the filling of the applicator, insertion technique, and discarding the applicator after each use

» Compliance with full course of therapy, even during menstruation

» Not missing doses; using at evenly spaced times

» Proper dosing

Missed dose: Inserting as soon as possible; not inserting if almost time for next dose

» Proper storage

Precautions while using this medication

Checking with physician if no improvement within a few days

Follow-up visit to physician after treatment for bacterial vaginosis to ensure that infection has been properly treated

Caution if dizziness occurs

Importance of contacting physician if diarrhea occurs during of after treatment with clindamycin

Protecting clothing because of possible soiling with vaginal clindamycin; avoiding use of tampons

» Using hygienic measures to help cure infection and prevent reinfection, e.g., wearing freshly washed cotton panties instead of synthetic panties

» Sexual abstinence is recommended during treatment to prevent a dilution of the dose, which may result in reduced efficacy of the medication and a relapse of the infection

» Not using latex contraceptives for up to 72 hours after vaginal clindamycin treatment, as oils in the clindamycin weaken latex products and may affect their efficacy

Side/adverse effects

Signs of potential side effects, especially cervicitis, vaginitis, or vulvovaginal pruritus, due to *Candida albicans;* CNS effects; gastrointestinal disturbances; and hypersensitivity

General Dosing Information

Use of vaginal latex or rubber products, such as condoms, cervical caps, or diaphragms, is not recommended for up to 72 hours after completion of vaginal clindamycin treatment. Vaginal clindamycin cream contains mineral oil that can weaken or damage these products and reduce their efficacy.

Concurrent treatment of the male partner is generally unnecessary when treating bacterial vaginosis.

Vaginal applicators should be used with caution after the sixth month of pregnancy.

For treatment of pseudomembranous colitis

Therapeutic measures should be implemented including:

- If mild case of pseudomembranous colitis, discontinuation of clindamycin is usually effective.
- If moderate to severe case, consideration should be given to management with fluids and electrolytes, protein supplementation, and treatment with an antibacterial drug effective against *Clostridium difficile* colitis.

Vaginal Dosage Form

CLINDAMYCIN PHOSPHATE VAGINAL CREAM USP

Usual adult and adolescent dose

Anti-infective (vaginal)—

For nonpregnant females: Intravaginal, 100 mg (one applicatorful) into vagina once a day, preferably at bedtime, for three or seven consecutive days.

For pregnant females (second or third trimesters): Intravaginal, 100 mg (one applicatorful) into vagina once a day, preferably at bedtime, for seven consecutive days.

For single-dose prefilled applicator: Intravaginal, recommended dose of 100 mg (a single applicatorful) once at anytime of the day. This is one complete course of therapy.

Usual pediatric dose

Safety and efficacy have not been established.

Strength(s) usually available

U.S.—

2% (Rx) [*Cleocin* (benzyl alcohol; cetostearyl alcohol; mineral oil)].

2% (Rx) [*Clindesse* (single-dose applicator; edetate disodium; glycerol monoisosterate; lecithin; methylparaben; microcrystalline wax; mineral oil; polyglyceryl-3-oleate; propylparaben; purified water; silicon dioxide; sorbitol solution)].

Canada—

2% (Rx) [*Dalacin* (benzyl alcohol; cetostearyl alcohol; mineral oil)].

Packaging and storage

Store below 40 °C (104 °F), preferably between 15 and 30 °C (59 and 86 °F), unless otherwise specified by manufacturer. Store in well-closed containers.

Auxiliary labeling

- May cause dizziness.
- Continue medicine for full time of treatment.
- For vaginal use only.

Note

Include patient package insert (PPI) when dispensing.

Selected Bibliography

Joesoef MR, Hillier SL, Wiknjosastro G, et al. Intravaginal clindamycin treatment for bacterial vaginosis: effects on preterm delivery and low birth weight. Am J Obstet Gynecol 1995; 173(5): 1527-31.

Product Information: Clindesse, clindamycin phosphate. Ther-Rx Corporation, St. Louis, Mo, (PI revised 11/2004) reviewed 12/2004.

Revised: 01/06/2005

CLOBAZAM—See *Benzodiazepines (Systemic)*

CLOBETASOL—See *Corticosteroids (Topical)*

CLOBETASONE—See *Corticosteroids (Topical)*

CLOCORTOLONE—See *Corticosteroids (Topical)*

CLOFARABINE Systemic†

VA CLASSIFICATION (Primary): AN300

Commonly used brand name(s): *Clolar.*

Note: For a listing of dosage forms and brand names by country availability, see *Dosage Forms* section(s).

†Not commercially available in Canada.

Category

Antineoplastic.

Indications

Note: Bracketed information in the *Indications* section refers to uses that are not included in U.S. product labeling.

Accepted

Leukemia, acute lymphoblastic (treatment)—Clofarabine is indicated for the treatment of pediatric patients 1 to 21 years old with relapsed or refractory acute lymphoblastic leukemia after at least two prior regimens. This use is based on the induction of complete responses.

Randomized trials demonstrating increased survival or other clinical benefit have not been conducted.

Pharmacology/Pharmacokinetics

Physicochemical characteristics

Source—Clofarabine is a purine nucleoside anti-metabolite.

Molecular weight—Clofarabine: 303.68.

pH—4.5 to 7.5

Mechanism of action/Effect

Clofarabine inhibits DNA synthesis by decreasing cellular deoxynucleotide triphosphate pools through and inhibitory action on ribonucleotide reductase, and by terminating DNA chain elongation and inhibiting repair through incorporation into the DNA chain by competitive inhibition of DNA polymerases. The affinity of clofarabine triphosphate for these enzymes is similar to or greater than that of deoxyadenosine triphosphate. In preclinical models, clofarabine has demonstrated the ability to inhibit DNA repair by incorporation into the DNA chain during the repair process. Clofarabine 5'-triphosphate also disrupts the integrity of mitochondrial membrane, leading to the release of the pro-apoptotic mitochondrial proteins, cytochrome C and apoptosis-inducing factor, leading to programmed cell death.

Clofarabine is cytotoxic to rapidly proliferating and quiescent cancer cell types *in vitro*.

Distribution
Volume of distribution (Vol_D)—Steady state: 172 L/m².

Protein binding
Moderate (47%) to plasma protein, predominantly to albumin.

Biotransformation
Clofarabine is sequentially metabolized intracellularly to the 5'-monophosphate metabolite by deoxycytidine kinase and mono- and diphosphokinases to the active 5'-triphosphate metabolite.

Half-life
Terminal—estimated to be 5.2 hours.

Elimination
Urine: 49 to 60% of the dose (unchanged), based on 24-hour urine collections.

Non-renal elimination remains unknown.

Clearance: 28.8 L/h/m².

Precautions to Consider

Carcinogenicity
Clofarabine has not been tested for carcinogenic potential.

Mutagenicity
Clofarabine was clastogenic in the *in vitro* mammalian cell chromosome aberration assay and in the *in vivo* rat micronucleus assay. However, it did not show evidence of mutagenic activity in the bacterial mutation assay (Ames test).

Pregnancy/Reproduction
Fertility—The effects on human fertility are unknown.

Studies done in mice, rats, and dogs have demonstrated dose-related adverse effects on male reproductive organs. Seminiferous tubule and testicular degeneration and atrophy were reported in male mice given IP doses of clofarabine at 3 mg/kg/day. Studies done in male rats given IV doses of clofarabine at 25 mg/kg/day for 6 months had bilateral degeneration of the seminiferous epithelium with retained spermatids and atrophy of interstitial cells. In a 6-month dog study, cell degeneration of the epididymis and degeneration of the seminiferous epithelium in the testes were observed at doses 0.375 mg/kg/day (approximately 14% of the clinical recommended dose on a mg/m² basis).

Studies done in female mice given clofarabine doses at 75 mg/kg/day revealed ovarian atrophy or degeneration and uterine mucosal apoptosis.

Pregnancy—Clofarabine may cause fetal harm when administered to a pregnant woman. Adequate and well controlled studies in humans have not been done. Women of child bearing potential should be advised to avoid becoming pregnant while receiving treatment with clofarabine. If clofarabine is used during pregnancy or if the patient becomes pregnant while taking this drug, the patient should be apprised of the potential hazard to the fetus.

Studies done with clofarabine in rats and rabbits revealed teratogenic effects. Rats given doses at 54 mg/m_2/day (approximately equivalent to the recommended clinical dose on a mg/m² basis), and in rabbits given 12 mg/m_2/day, showed developmental toxicity (reduced fetal body weight and increased post-implantation loss) and increased incidences of malformations and variations (gross external, soft tissue, skeletal and retarded ossification).

FDA Pregnancy Category D

Breast-feeding
It is not known whether clofarabine is distributed into human milk. Because of the potential for tumorigenicity shown for clofarabine in animal studies and the potential for serious adverse reactions, women treated with clofarabine should not breast-feed.

Pediatrics
Clofarabine is indicated for the treatment of pediatric patients 1 to 21 years old. Appropriate studies performed to date have not demonstrated pediatrics-specific problems that would limit the usefulness of clofarabine in children.

Geriatrics
Safety and efficacy of clofarabine in adult and geriatric patients have not been established.

Pharmacogenetics
No apparent differences in the pharmacokinetics were observed between males and females.

Drug interactions and/or related problems
The following drug interactions and/or related problems have been selected on the basis of their potential clinical significance (possible mechanism in parentheses where appropriate)—not necessarily inclusive (» = major clinical significance):

Note: Combinations containing any of the following medications, depending on the amount present, may also interact with this medication.

» Hepatotoxic medications, other (See *Appendix II*)
(should be avoided during clofarabine treatment)

Medications known to affect blood pressure or cardiac function
(closely monitor during clofarabine administration)

» Nephrotoxic medications, other (see *Appendix II*)
(should be avoided during the 5 days of clofarabine administration; clofarabine is primarily excreted by the kidneys)

Laboratory value alterations
The following have been selected on the basis of their potential clinical significance (possible effect in parentheses where appropriate)—not necessarily inclusive (» = major clinical significance).

With physiology/laboratory test values

Alanine aminotransferase (ALT [SGPT]) values, serum or
Aspartate aminotransferase (AST [SGOT]) values, serum
(levels may be elevated, predominatively occurring within 1 week of clofarabine administration and returning to baseline or less than grade 2 within several days)

Bilirubin
(levels may be elevated)

Medical considerations/Contraindications
The medical considerations/contraindications included have been selected on the basis of their potential clinical significance (reasons given in parentheses where appropriate)—not necessarily inclusive (» = major clinical significance).

Except under special circumstances, this medication should not be used when the following medical problem exists:

» Hypersensitivity to clofarabine

Risk-benefit should be considered when the following medical problems exist:

» Hepatic function impairment or
» Renal dysfunction
(use only with greatest caution; assess prior to and during treatment with clofarabine because clofarabine is predominately excreted renally and the liver is a target organ for clofarabine toxicity)

Patient monitoring
The following may be especially important in patient monitoring (other tests may be warranted in some patients, depending on condition; » = major clinical significance):

» Blood pressure and
» Respiratory status
(closely monitor during clofarabine infusion)

Complete blood counts and
Platelet counts
(obtain at regular intervals during clofarabine therapy and more frequently in patients who develop cytopenias)

» Cytokine release, signs and symptoms of
(close monitoring for signs and symptoms of capillary leak syndrome; immediately discontinue clofarabine administration if they occur and provide appropriate supportive measures; after patient is stabilized and organ function has returned to baseline, retreatment can be considered at a lower dose)

Hepatic function and
Renal function
(monitor frequently during 5 day treatment with clofarabine)

Side/Adverse Effects
The following side/adverse effects have been selected on the basis of their potential clinical significance (possible signs and symptoms in parentheses where appropriate)—not necessarily inclusive:

Those indicating need for medical attention
Incidence more frequent

Anemia (pale skin; troubled breathing with exertion; unusual bleeding or bruising; unusual tiredness or weakness); ***bacteremia*** (rapid breathing; chills; fever; abdominal pain; nausea; diarrhea); ***cellulitis*** (itching pain; redness; swelling; tenderness; warmth on skin); ***dyspnea*** (shortness of breath; difficult or labored breathing; tightness in chest; wheezing); ***febrile neutropenia*** (black, tarry stools; chills; cough; fever; lower back or side pain; painful or difficult urination; pale skin; shortness of breath; sore throat; ulcers, sores, or white spots in mouth; unusual bleeding or bruising; unusual tiredness or weakness); ***hematuria*** (blood in urine); ***herpes simplex*** (burning or stinging of skin; painful cold sores or blisters on lips, nose, eyes, or genitals); ***hyperbilirubinemia*** (yellow eyes or skin); ***hypertension*** (blurred vision; dizziness; nervousness; headache; pounding in the ears; slow or fast heartbeat); ***hypotension*** (blurred vision; confusion; dizziness, faintness, or lightheadedness when getting up from a lying or sitting position suddenly; sweating; unusual tiredness or weakness); ***infection*** (fever or chill; cough or hoarseness; lower back or side pain; painful or difficult urination); ***jaundice*** (chills; clay-colored stools; dark urine; dizziness; fever; headache; itching; loss of appetite; nausea; abdominal or stomach pain; area rash; unpleasant breath odor; unusual tiredness or weakness; vomiting of blood; yellow eyes or skin); ***left ventricular systolic dysfunction*** (chest pain; decreased urine output; dilated neck veins; extreme fatigue; irregular breathing; irregular heartbeat; shortness of breath; swelling of face, fingers, feet, or lower legs; tightness in chest; troubled breathing; weight gain; wheezing); ***leukopenia*** (black, tarry stools; chest pain; chills; cough; fever; painful or difficult urination; shortness of breath; sore throat; sores, ulcers, or white spots on lips or in mouth; swollen glands; unusual bleeding or bruising; unusual tiredness or weakness); ***neutropenia*** (black, tarry, stools; chills; cough; fever; lower back or side pain; painful or difficult urination; pale skin; shortness of breath; sore throat; ulcers, sores, or white spots in mouth; unusual bleeding or bruising; unusual tiredness or weakness); ***oral candidiasis*** (sore mouth or tongue; white patches in mouth and/or on tongue); ***pleural effusion*** (chest pain; shortness of breath); ***pneumonia*** (chest pain; cough; fever or chills; sneezing; shortness of breath; sore throat; troubled breathing; tightness in chest; wheezing); ***respiratory distress*** (shortness of breath; troubled breathing; tightness in chest, or wheezing); ***sepsis*** (chills; confusion; dizziness; lightheadedness; fainting; fast heartbeat; fever; rapid, shallow breathing); ***Staphylococcal infection; tachycardia*** (fast, pounding, or irregular heartbeat or pulse); ***thrombocytopenia*** (black, tarry stools; bleeding gums; blood in urine or stools; pinpoint red spots on skin; unusual bleeding or bruising); ***transfusion reaction*** (dizziness; fever or chills; facial swelling; headache; nausea or vomiting; shortness of breath; skin rash; weakness)

Incidence unknown

Capillary leak syndrome (cloudy urine; decrease or increase in amount of urine; fainting or lightheadedness; nausea; stomach pain; swelling of hands, ankles, feet, or lower legs)

Those indicating need for medical attention only if they continue or are bothersome

Incidence more frequent

Abdominal pain (stomach pain); ***anorexia*** (loss of appetite; weight loss); ***anxiety*** (fear; nervousness); ***appetite decreased; arthralgia*** (pain in joints; muscle pain or stiffness; difficulty in moving); ***back pain; constipation*** (difficulty having a bowel movement (stool)); ***contusion; cough; creatinine, elevated; dermatitis*** (blistering, crusting, irritation, itching, or reddening of skin; cracked, dry, scaly skin; swelling); ***depression*** (discouragement; feeling sad or empty; irritability; lack of appetite; loss of interest or pleasure; tiredness; trouble concentrating; trouble sleeping); ***diarrhea; dizziness; dry skin; edema*** (swelling); ***epistaxis*** (bloody nose); ***erythema*** (flushing, redness of skin; unusually warm skin); ***fatigue*** (unusual tiredness or weakness); ***flushing*** (feeling of warmth redness of the face, neck, arms and occasionally, upper chest); ***gingival bleeding*** (bleeding gums); ***headache; hepatomegaly*** (right upper abdominal pain and fullness); ***injection site pain; irritability; lethargy*** (unusual drowsiness; dullness, tiredness, weakness or feeling of sluggishness); ***mucosal inflammation*** (cracked lips; diarrhea; difficulty in swallowing; sores, ulcers, or white spots on lips, tongue, or inside mouth); ***myalgia*** (joint pain; swollen joints; muscle aching or cramping; muscle pains or stiffness; difficulty in moving); ***nausea; pain; pain in limb; palmar-plantar erythrodysesthesia*** (redness, swelling pain of skin; scaling of skin on hands and feet; tingling of hands and feet; ulceration of skin); ***petechia*** (small red or purple spots on skin); ***pruritus*** (itching skin); ***pyrexia*** (fever); ***rigors*** (feeling unusually cold; shivering); ***somnolence*** (sleepiness or unusual drowsiness); ***sore throat; tremor*** (trembling or shaking of hands or feet; shakiness in legs, arms, hands, feet); ***vomiting; weight decreased***

Overdose

For more information on the management of overdose or unintentional ingestion, **contact a poison control center** (see *Poison Control Center Listing*).

Clinical effects of overdose

The following effects have been selected on the basis of their potential clinical significance (possible signs and symptoms in parentheses where appropriate)—not necessarily inclusive:

Hyperbilirubinemia (yellow eyes or skin); ***maculopapular rash*** (rash with flat lesions or small raised lesions on the skin); ***vomiting***

Treatment of overdose

There is no known specific antidote to clofarabine. Treatment is generally symptomatic and supportive.

Patients in whom intentional overdose is confirmed or suspected should be referred for psychiatric consultation.

Patient Consultation

As an aid to patient consultation, refer to *Advice for the Patient, Clofarabine (Systemic)*.

In providing consultation, consider emphasizing the following selected information (» = major clinical significance):

Before using this medication

» Conditions affecting use, especially:

Hypersensitivity to clofarabine

Pregnancy—Use is not recommended; women of childbearing age should be advised to avoid pregnancy during treatment

Breast-feeding—Women treated with clofarabine should not breast-feed because of the potential for serious adverse effects in nursing infants

Use in children—Clofarabine is indicated for the treatment of pediatric patients 1 to 21 years old. Appropriate studies performed to date have not demonstrated pediatrics-specific problems that would limit the usefulness of clofarabine in children.

Use in the elderly—Safety and efficacy of clofarabine in adult and geriatric patients have not been established.

Other medications, especially hepatotoxic and nephrotoxic medications

Other medical problems, especially hepatic function impairment or renal dysfunction

Proper use of this medication

» Proper dosing

» Proper storage

Precautions while using this medication

» Importance of taking appropriate measures to avoid dehydration

» The importance of seeking medical advice if symptoms of dizziness, lightheadedness, fainting spells, or decreased urine output occur.

» Importance of advising all patients to use effective contraceptive measures to prevent pregnancy.

Side/adverse effects

Signs of potential side effects, especially anemia, bacteremia, capillary leak syndrome, cellulitis, dyspnea, febrile neutropenia, hematuria, herpes simplex, hyperbilirubinemia, hypertension, hypotension, infection, jaundice, left ventricular systolic dysfunction, leukopenia, neutropenia, oral candidiasis, pleural effusion, pneumonia, respiratory distress, sepsis, staphylococcal infection, tachycardia, thrombocytopenia, or transfusion reaction

General Dosing Information

Clofarabine should be administered under the supervision of a qualified physician experienced in the use of antineoplastic therapy.

Patients should be given continual IV fluids throughout the 5 days of clofarabine administration to reduce the effects of tumor lysis and other adverse events.

Renal and hepatic function should be closely monitored during the 5 days of clofarabine administration.

Because patients receiving clofarabine may experience vomiting and diarrhea, they should be advised on appropriate measures to avoid dehydration.

The use of prophylactic steroids (e.g., 100 mg/m^2 hydrocortisone on days 1 through 3) may benefit in the prevention of signs or symptoms of SIRS or capillary leak.

Because clofarabine results in a rapid reduction of peripheral leukemia cells, it is important that patients undergoing treatment be evaluated and monitored for signs and symptoms of tumor lysis syndrome as well as signs and symptoms of cytokine release.

For treatment of adverse effects

Clofarabine administration should be stopped if development of hypotension for any reason occurs during the 5 day treatment period. However, if hypotension is transient and resolves without pharmacological intervention, treatment can be reinstituted at a lower dose.

If early signs or symptoms of SIRS or capillary leak should occur, immediate discontinuation of clofarabine and provision of appropriate measures is recommended.

If substantial increases in creatinine or bilirubin should occur, immediate discontinuation of clofarabine is advised until the patient is stable and organ function has returned to baseline. When the patient is stable, clofarabine may be reinstituted at a lower dose.

If hyperuricemia is expected, allopurinol should be administered.

Parenteral Dosage Forms

CLOFARABINE INJECTION

Usual adult dose

Clofarabine is not indicated for use in adult patients

Usual pediatric dose

Leukemia, acute lymphoblastic (treatment)—

Intravenous, 52 mg/m²administered by infusion over 2 hours for 5 consecutive days. Treatment cycles are repeated approximately every 2 to 6 weeks, following recovery or return to baseline organ function.

Usual geriatric dose

See *Usual adult dose.*

Strength(s) usually available

U.S.—

20 mg of clofarabine per 20-mL vial in unbuffered normal saline solution (Rx) [*Clolar*].

Packaging and storage

Store at 25 °C (77 °F), excursions permitted to 15 to 30 °C (59 to 86 °F).

Preparation of dosage form

Prior to intravenous infusion, clofarabine should be filtered through a 0.2 micro meter syringe filter and then diluted with 5% dextrose injection, USP or 0.9% sodium chloride injection, USP. The solution should be clear and practically colorless, free from foreign matter. The resulting admixture may be stored at room temperature, but must be used within 24 hours of preparation. Clofarabine contains no preservatives.

Incompatibilities

To prevent drug incompatibilities, no other medications should be administered through the same intravenous line.

Auxiliary labeling

- May cause dizziness.

Developed: 05/11/2005

CLOMIPHENE Systemic

INN: Clomifene

JAN: Clomifene citrate

VA CLASSIFICATION (Primary/Secondary): HS106/DX900; HS900

Commonly used brand name(s): *Clomid; Milophene; Serophene.*

Note: For a listing of dosage forms and brand names by country availability, see *Dosage Forms* section(s).

Category

Antiestrogen; infertility therapy adjunct; diagnostic aid (ovarian function; hypothalamic-pituitary-gonadal axis function).

Indications

Note: Bracketed information in the *Indications* section refers to uses that are not included in U.S. product labeling.

Accepted

Infertility, female (treatment)—Clomiphene is indicated in the treatment of anovulation or oligo-ovulation in patients desiring pregnancy, whose sexual partners have adequate sperm, and who have potentially functional hypothalamic-hypophyseal-ovarian systems and adequate endogenous estrogen.

[Corpus luteum insufficiency (treatment)][1]—Clomiphene may be used to treat corpus luteum dysfunction.

[Hypothalamic-pituitary-gonadal axis function, in males (diagnosis)][1]—Clomiphene is used to detect abnormalities of the hypothalamic-pituitary-gonadal axis in males.

[Infertility, male (treatment)][1]—Clomiphene is used to treat infertility in males with oligospermia.

[Ovarian function studies][1]—Clomiphene is sometimes given as a test dose to aid in predicting whether an ovulatory response might occur.

[1]Not included in Canadian product labeling.

Pharmacology/Pharmacokinetics

Physicochemical characteristics

Source—Synthetic; nonsteroidal geometric isomer (30 to 50% is cis-clomiphene zuclomiphene and the remainder is trans-enclomiphene).

Molecular weight—598.10.

Mechanism of action/Effect

Clomiphene has mainly antiestrogenic effects and some estrogenic effects. The mechanism in stimulating ovulation is unknown but is believed to be related to its antiestrogenic properties. By clomiphene competing with estrogen for binding sites at the hypothalamic level, the gonadotropins, follicle-stimulating hormone (FSH) and luteinizing hormone (LH), secretion is increased, which results in ovarian follicle maturation, followed by the preovulatory LH surge, ovulation, and the subsequent development of the corpus luteum. Usefulness in male infertility is also likely related to the increases in FSH and LH secretion.

Absorption

Readily absorbed from gastrointestinal tract; undergoes enterohepatic recycling, especially with cis-zuclomiphene.

Biotransformation

Hepatic.

Half-life

Plasma—5 to 7 days.

Time to peak effect

Ovulation usually occurs 4 to 10 days (average 7 days) after the last day of treatment; this period of time may vary by patient and by cycle. In rare cases, ovulation may occur as late as 14 days after the last day of treatment.

Elimination

Biliary/fecal—Up to 42% of the oral dose; can be detectable in feces for up to 6 weeks.

Renal—Up to 8% of the oral dose.

Precautions to Consider

Carcinogenicity/Tumorigenicity/Mutagenicity

Long-term carcinogenicity or mutagenicity studies have not been done. Studies are ongoing to determine the additional risk, if any, of developing ovarian cancer in women taking fertility medication beyond that contributed by infertility. Although a causal relationship between hyperstimulation of the ovaries and ovarian cancer has not been established, a correlation does exist for certain risk factors, including ovarian cancer, nulliparity, and increasing age. In addition, prolonged use of clomiphene may contribute to the risk of a borderline or invasive ovarian tumor, which should be considered whenever ovarian cysts do not regress with clomiphene therapy. Two cases of bilateral female breast carcinoma and one case of testicular carcinoma have occurred during clomiphene therapy.

Pregnancy/Reproduction

Fertility—Clomiphene may cause a decrease in quantity or change in quality of cervical mucus, which may interfere with sperm function, fertilization, and, subsequently, the occurrence of pregnancy.

Pregnancy—Clomiphene is not recommended during pregnancy. Controlled studies in humans have not been done. However, there have been reports of congenital malformations and fetal death occurring with clomiphene administration in humans. In clinical use, the cumulative rate of congenital abnormalities associated with ovulation induction therapy does not appear to be greater than that reported in the general population for spontaneous pregnancy. However, because a direct causal relationship has not been established, careful monitoring of the patient is recommended to prevent inadvertent administration of clomiphene during pregnancy.

Use of clomiphene is associated with an increased incidence of multiple pregnancies and, therefore, possible premature deliveries, as well as ectopic and heterotopic pregnancy. The incidence of reported multiple pregnancies was 7.98% (6.9% twins, 0.5% triplets, 0.3% quadruplets, and 0.1% quintuplets) with about an 83.3% survival rate, or a lower rate (73%) when including stillbirths, spontaneous abortions, or neonatal deaths. The ratio of monozygotic twins to dizygotic twins is 1 to 5.

Studies in rats and rabbits have shown clomiphene to be teratogenic. The observed malformations were similar to those produced by *in utero* exposure to diethylstilbestrol and may include vaginal adenosis and other defects in the vaginal, uterine, and Fallopian tube structures.

FDA Pregnancy Category X.

Breast-feeding

It is not known whether clomiphene is distributed into breast milk. However, clomiphene suppresses lactation.

Laboratory value alterations

The following have been selected on the basis of their potential clinical significance (possible effect in parentheses where appropriate)—not necessarily inclusive (» = major clinical significance).

With physiology/laboratory test values
- Desmosterol (only with long-term use, possibly indicating interference with cholesterol synthesis) and
- Sex hormone-binding globulin and
- Transcortin
  - (plasma concentrations may be increased)

Medical considerations/Contraindications

The medical considerations/contraindications included have been selected on the basis of their potential clinical significance (reasons given in parentheses where appropriate)—not necessarily inclusive (» = major clinical significance).

Except under special circumstances, this medication should not be used when the following medical problems exist:

» Hepatic function impairment, active
  (potential for reduced clearance of clomiphene, leading to higher plasma concentrations or hepatoxicity)

» Mental depression
  (may be exacerbated)

» Ovarian cyst, not associated with polycystic ovary syndrome or
» Ovarian enlargement, not associated with polycystic ovary syndrome
  (risk of further enlargement)

» Thrombophlebitis, active
  (increased risk of thrombophlebitis in susceptible individuals can be caused by elevated estradiol levels associated with ovulation induction by clomiphene)

Risk-benefit should be considered when the following medical problems exist:

» Abnormal vaginal bleeding, undiagnosed
  (careful evaluation recommended; neoplastic lesions should be ruled out)

» Endometriosis
  (implants may be aggravated by elevated estradiol levels associated with ovulation induction)

» Fibroid tumors of the uterus
  (risk of further enlargement)

» Hepatic function impairment, history of
  (potential for reduced clearance of clomiphene, leading to higher plasma concentrations or hepatoxicity)

» Polycystic ovary syndrome or
Sensitivity to pituitary gonadotropins
  (patient may have an exaggerated response to clomiphene; lower dose or shorter duration of therapy may be necessary)

Sensitivity to clomiphene

Patient monitoring

The following may be especially important in patient monitoring (other tests may be warranted in some patients, depending on condition; » = major clinical significance):

Immunologic assay for human chorionic gonadotropin (HCG)
  (recommended for detection of pregnancy if menses does not occur before start of next course of clomiphene; should be measured 10 days or later after exogenous HCG is administered)

Liver function tests
  (recommended in some patients prior to initiation of therapy with clomiphene, especially in patients with risk factors increasing their susceptibility to hepatic dysfunction)

Ophthalmologic, including slit-lamp, examination
  (recommended if treatment with clomiphene is continued for more than 1 year or if visual disturbances occur)

» Urinary luteinizing hormone surge testing
  (may be used as adjunctive therapy to predict ovulation)

Side/Adverse Effects

Note: At the recommended dosage, adverse effects usually are rare. Incidence and severity of adverse effects tend to be related to dose and duration of treatment and are usually reversible after clomiphene therapy is discontinued. Doses over 100 mg a day for five days have been associated with a higher incidence of side effects; patients receiving these doses should be carefully monitored.

Rare reports of ovarian cancer have been associated with fertility medications but a causal relationship has not been determined partly because it is not possible to predict beyond the risk that infertility brings to developing ovarian cancer.

The following side/adverse effects have been selected on the basis of their clinical significance (possible signs and symptoms in parentheses where appropriate)—not necessarily inclusive:

Those indicating need for medical attention

Incidence more frequent—>5%

Ovarian cyst formation; ovarian enlargement; premenstrual syndrome; uterine fibroid enlargement (abdominal bloating; stomach pain; pelvic pain)

Note: Maximum *ovarian enlargement* occurs several days after clomiphene therapy is discontinued.

A patient's report of *abdominal pain* during clomiphene therapy indicates the need for immediate pelvic examination. If ovarian enlargement or cyst formation has occurred, it is recommended that clomiphene therapy be withdrawn until the ovaries have returned to pretreatment size, usually within a few days or weeks. Dosage and duration of the next course of clomiphene should be reduced.

Incidence less frequent or rare

Hepatotoxicity (yellow eyes or skin); ***vision changes, especially after-images*** (persistence of visual images); ***blurred vision***—especially with larger doses; ***diplopia*** (double vision); ***floaters*** (spots in visual field caused by protein deposits in the vitreous fluid of the eye); ***phosphenes*** (seeing flashes of light); ***photophobia*** (increased sensitivity of eyes to light); ***scotoma*** (area of decreased vision in visual field surrounded by normal or less-diminished vision)

Note: If the patient receiving clomiphene experiences any *visual disturbances*, it is recommended that clomiphene therapy be withdrawn and a complete ophthalmologic examination performed. Ocular side effects usually disappear within a few days or weeks after the last dose of clomiphene.

Those indicating need for medical attention only if they continue or are bothersome

Incidence more frequent—10%

Hot flashes

Incidence less frequent or rare—1 to 2%

Breast discomfort in women; gynecomastia in men (enlargement of breasts); ***dizziness or lightheadedness; headache; menorrhagia*** (increased amount of menstrual bleeding at regular monthly periods); ***mental depression; nausea or vomiting; nervousness; restlessness; spotting*** (light uterine bleeding between regular menstrual periods); ***tiredness; trouble in sleeping***

Patient Consultation

As an aid to patient consultation, refer to *Advice for the Patient, Clomiphene (Systemic).*

In providing consultation, consider emphasizing the following selected information (» = major clinical significance):

Before using this medication

» Conditions affecting use, especially:
- Sensitivity to clomiphene
- Pregnancy—Use during pregnancy is not recommended since animal studies have shown teratogenicity
- Breast-feeding—Suppresses lactation
- Other medical problems, especially hepatic function impairment, mental depression, ovarian cyst, ovarian enlargement, thrombophlebitis, undiagnosed abnormal vaginal bleeding, endometriosis, uterine fibroids, and polycystic ovary syndrome

Proper use of this medication

» Compliance with therapy; clarification of schedule; taking at same time every day to aid in remembering each dose

» Proper dosing

Missed dose: Taking as soon as possible; doubling dose if not remembered until time of next dose; checking with physician if more than one dose missed

» Proper storage

Precautions while using this medication

» Importance of close monitoring by physician

» Importance of following physician's instructions for timing of intercourse

» Telling physician immediately if pregnancy is suspected; importance of not taking medication while pregnant

» Caution when driving or doing jobs requiring alertness because of visual disturbances, dizziness, or lightheadedness

Side/adverse effects

Signs of potential side effects, especially ovarian cyst formation, ovarian enlargement, uterine fibroid enlargement, premenstrual syndrome, hepatotoxicity, or vision changes

General Dosing Information

Patients receiving clomiphene should be under supervision of a physician experienced in the treatment of gynecologic or endocrine disorders.

Patients who have been hypoestrogenic for prolonged periods may require pretreatment with estrogen to provide a more normal endometrium for ovum implantation. Estrogen therapy should be discontinued immediately before initiation of clomiphene therapy.

Properly timed coitus in relation to ovulation is important and may be predicted from ovulation test kits (the preferred method) or other appropriate tests for ovulation such as taking basal body temperature. Couples should be advised to have frequent intercourse at or around the time that ovulation is anticipated. Ovulation generally occurs 7 days (average) after the last dose of clomiphene (range is 5 to 10 days).

In some patients, a single injection of 5000 to 10,000 USP Units of human chorionic gonadotropin (HCG) given 5 to 9 days after the last dose of clomiphene to simulate the midcycle LH surge that results in ovulation may increase the efficacy of clomiphene.

If ovulation does not occur after 3 to 4 cycles of clomiphene therapy at the maximum dose, or if pregnancy does not result after a treatment interval of 3 to 6 months with documented ovulation, or if ovulatory menses does not occur, further treatment with clomiphene is not recommended and the diagnosis should be re-evaluated.

Oral Dosage Forms

CLOMIPHENE CITRATE TABLETS USP

Usual adult dose

Female infertility—

Oral, 50 mg a day for five days, starting on the fifth day of the menstrual cycle if bleeding occurs or at any time if the patient has had no recent uterine bleeding. If ovulation without conception occurs, this cycle is repeated until conception or for three or four cycles. A smaller dose or shorter duration may be necessary for individuals unusually sensitive to clomiphene, such as women with polycystic ovary syndrome. If ovulation does not occur, the dose is increased to 75 to 100 mg a day for five days (the next course beginning as early as thirty days after the previous course), repeated if ovulation without conception occurs. Rarely, patients require up to 250 mg a day to induce ovulation.

Note: A physical exam prior to the first and each subsequent treatment is needed to exclude pregnancy, ovarian enlargement, or ovarian cysts (not due to polycystic ovary syndrome) and to ensure normal liver function and no abnormal uterine bleeding before next course of clomiphene may be initiated.

Strength(s) usually available

U.S.—

50 mg (Rx) [*Clomid* (scored; lactose; sucrose); *Milophene* (scored; lactose; sucrose); *Serophene* (scored); GENERIC].

Canada—

50 mg (Rx) [*Clomid* (scored; sucrose; lactose); *Serophene*].

Packaging and storage

Store below 40 °C (104 °F), preferably between 15 and 30 °C (59 and 86 °F), unless otherwise specified by manufacturer. Store in a well-closed container. Protect from light.

Revised: 08/08/1995

CLOMIPRAMINE—See *Antidepressants, Tricyclic (Systemic)*

CLONAZEPAM—See *Benzodiazepines (Systemic)*

CLONIDINE Parenteral-Local†

VA CLASSIFICATION (Primary): CN103

Commonly used brand name(s): *Duraclon*.

Note: For a listing of dosage forms and brand names by country availability, see *Dosage Forms* section(s).

†Not commercially available in Canada.

Category

Analgesic.

Indications

Accepted

Pain, cancer (treatment adjunct)—Clonidine is indicated in combination with opiates for the treatment of severe pain in cancer patients that is not adequately relieved by opioid analgesics alone. Epidural clonidine is likely to be more effective in relieving neuropathic pain, characterized as electrical, burning, or shooting in nature, that is localized to a dermatomal or peripheral nerve distribution area, rather than in relieving pain that is diffuse, poorly localized, or visceral in origin.

[Shivering, post-operative (prophylaxis and treatment)][1]—Clonidine is indicated for the prevention and treatment of post-operative shivering.

[1]Not included in Canadian product labeling.

Pharmacology/Pharmacokinetics

Physicochemical characteristics

Chemical Group—Imidazoline derivative.

Molecular weight—266.56.

Mechanism of action/Effect

Clonidine, administered epidurally, is thought to produce analgesia by preventing pain-signal transmission to the brain at presynaptic and post-junctional alpha$_2$-adrenoceptors in the spinal cord. Analgesia occurs in body regions innervated by the spinal segments where clonidine concentrates. Clonidine-associated analgesia is dose-dependent and is not antagonized by opiate antagonists.

Other actions/effects

Clonidine decreases sympathetic outflow to the heart, kidneys, and peripheral vasculature, resulting in decreased peripheral resistance, renal vascular resistance, heart rate, and blood pressure.

Distribution

Clonidine is highly lipid soluble and is distributed into extravascular sites, including the central nervous system (CNS).

Volume of distribution (Vol$_D$)—2.1 ± 0.4 liters per kg (L/kg).

Protein binding

Low (20 to 40%, *in vitro*), primarily to albumin.

Biotransformation

Clonidine is metabolized through minor pathways. The major metabolite, *p*-hydroxyclonidine, is present in concentrations less than 10% of those of unchanged clonidine in urine.

Half-life

Elimination from plasma—

22 ± 15 hours. Half-life may be prolonged by up to 41 hours in patients with renal function impairment.

Time to peak plasma concentration

19 ± 27 minutes.

Elimination

Renal—72%, of which 40 to 50% is unchanged clonidine.

In dialysis—

Only 5% of clonidine body stores was removed in subjects undergoing hemodialysis. Therefore, it is not necessary to administer supplemental clonidine to patients undergoing routine hemodialysis.

Precautions to Consider

Carcinogenicity

Clonidine was not found to be carcinogenic in a study in rats given a dietary admixture of clonidine at a dose representing five to eight times the 50 mcg per kg (mcg/kg) maximum recommended human daily dose (MRHDD) for [the treatment of] hypertension, based on body surface area.

Mutagenicity

Clonidine was not found to be mutagenic in the Ames mutagenicity test.

Pregnancy/Reproduction

Fertility—No effect on fertility was found in studies in male or female rats given oral doses of clonidine of up to 150 mcg/kg. This dose represents approximately 0.5 times the MRHDD. In a separate study, fertility appeared to be affected in female rats given oral doses of 500 to 2000 mcg/kg. These doses represent two to seven times the MRHDD.

Pregnancy—Clondine crosses the placenta and reaches concentrations in umbilical cord plasma equal to those in maternal plasma. Concentrations in amniotic fluid may be four times those found in serum. Adequate and well-controlled studies have not been done in pregnant women during early gestation when organ formation occurs. Clonidine use during pregnancy is not recommended unless the potential benefits outweigh the potential risks to the fetus.

Teratogenic or embryotoxic potential was not found in reproduction studies in rabbits given clonidine in doses of up to approximately the MRHDD. A study in female rats given doses at one third the MRHDD for 2 months prior to mating resulted in an increase in resorptions. However, an increase in resorptions did not occur when female rats were given clonidine in the same doses or doses of up to 0.5 times the MRHDD on days 6 to 15 of gestation. An increase in resorptions was observed during a study in rats and mice given clonidine doses equivalent to seven times the MRHDD on days 1 to 14 of gestation.

FDA Pregnancy Category C.

Labor—Studies using epidural clonidine during labor have not shown any apparent adverse effects in the infant at the time of delivery, although hemodynamic effects in the infant on the days following delivery were not monitored. Adequate and well-controlled trials to evaluate dosing, safety, and effectiveness of epidural clonidine in obstetrics have not been done. The use of clonidine as an analgesic during labor and delivery is not recommended, essentially because maternal perfusion of the placenta is dependent on blood pressure.

Breast-feeding
Clonidine is distributed into human breast milk, reaching concentrations that are approximately twice those found in maternal plasma. Clonidine is not recommended for use in nursing mothers because of the potential for severe adverse reactions in the infant.

Pediatrics
No specific information is available on the relationship of age to the effects of epidurally administered clonidine in pediatric patients. Safety and efficacy have been established only in patients old enough to tolerate placement and management of an epidural catheter. Clonidine should be used in pediatric patients only for severe intractable pain associated with malignancy that is unresponsive to epidural or spinal opiates or other analgesic techniques.

Geriatrics
No information is available on the relationship of age to the effects of clonidine in geriatric patients.

Pharmacogenetics
Women have a lower mean plasma clearance rate, longer mean plasma half-life, and higher mean peak concentration of clonidine in both plasma and cerebro-spinal fluid (CSF) than do men.

Hypotension as a side effect of epidural clonidine was observed more frequently in women.

Surgical
Epidural clonidine has been reported to cause a marked hypotensive response when used for intra- or postoperative analgesia.

Drug interactions and/or related problems
The following drug interactions and/or related problems have been selected on the basis of their potential clinical significance (possible mechanism in parentheses where appropriate)—not necessarily inclusive (» = major clinical significance):

Note: Combinations containing any of the following medications, depending on the amount present, may also interact with this medication.

Alcohol or
Barbiturates or
Other CNS depression-producing medications (see *Appendix II*), including
  Analgesics, narcotic
  (concurrent use may cause CNS depressive effects and potentiation of hypotensive effects of clonidine)

Anesthetics, local, epidural
(concurrent use with clonidine may prolong the duration of effects of these drugs, including both sensory and motor blockade effects)

Antidepressants, tricyclic
(effects on clonidine's analgesic effects are unknown, but tricyclic antidepressants may antagonize the hypotensive effects of clonidine)

» Beta-adrenergic blocking agents
(concurrent use may cause potentiation of the hypertensive response seen with clonidine withdrawal and may exacerbate bradycardia and atrioventricular [AV] block)

Fluphenazine
(acute delirium was reported in one patient using oral clonidine concurrently; the symptoms resolved upon withdrawal of clonidine and recurred upon rechallenge)

Medications affecting sinus node function or AV nodal conduction, such as:
Digitalis glycosides
Calcium channel blocking agents
(concurrent use may exacerbate bradycardia and atrioventricular [AV] block)

Medical considerations/Contraindications
The medical considerations/contraindications included have been selected on the basis of their potential clinical significance (reasons given in parentheses where appropriate)—not necessarily inclusive (» = major clinical significance).

Except under special circumstances, this medication should not be used when the following medical problems exist:

» Allergic reaction to clonidine, history of or
» Sensitization to clonidine, history of

» Anticoagulant therapy or
» Hemorrhagic diathesis
(because of the potential for hemorrhage into the spinal epidural space, epidural administration should not be used in these settings)

» Infection present at the injection site
(increased risk of development of meningitis or epidural abscess)

Risk-benefit should be considered when the following medical problems exist:

Cardiovascular disease, severe or
Hemodynamic instability, such as:
Bradycardia or
Hypotension
(increased risk of severe hypotension, further worsening these conditions; clonidine may also mask the increase in heart rate associated with hypovolemia)

Obstetrical pain or
Perioperative pain or
Postpartum pain
(clonidine administration is associated with hypotension and/or bradycardia, which may not be tolerated by these patients)

Renal function impairment
(elimination half-life may be prolonged; dosage adjustment may be necessary)

Patient monitoring
The following may be especially important in patient monitoring (other tests may be warranted in some patients, depending on condition; » = major clinical significance):

» Blood pressure determinations
» Body temperature
» Heart rate determinations
» Respiratory rate
(frequent monitoring recommended, especially during the first few days of therapy)

Side/Adverse Effects
Note: Epidural clonidine may rarely cause atrioventricular (AV) block greater than first degree and may also mask the increase in heart rate associated with hypovolemia.

The following side/adverse effects may be related to administration of either clonidine or morphine and have been selected on the basis of their potential clinical significance (possible signs and symptoms in parentheses where appropriate)—not necessarily inclusive:

Those indicating need for medical attention
Incidence more frequent

Bradycardia (slow heart rate); ***hypotension*** (dizziness, lightheadedness, or fainting)

Note: In a study of cancer patients administered epidural clonidine at 30 mcg per hour (mcg/hr) in addition to epidural morphine, the incidence of *hypotension* was 45%. Hypotension occurred most often within the first 4 days after initiation of epidural clonidine, but also occurred throughout the duration of the study. Hypotension occurred more commonly in women, in patients with higher serum clonidine concentrations, and in patients with lower than average body weight. More pronounced hypotension may occur when clonidine is infused into the upper thoracic spinal segments. Severe hypotension may occur even with prior intravenous fluid treatment.

Incidence less frequent

Chest pain; fever; hallucinations (seeing, feeling, or hearing things that are not there); ***hypoventilation*** (extremely shallow or slow breathing); ***mental depression; sedation; tachycardia*** (fast heartbeat); ***vomiting***

Note: *Fever* occurring in a patient receiving clonidine therapy may be associated with catheter-related infection such as meningitis and/or epidural abscess. Catheter-related infections occur in 5 to 20% of patients, depending on the kind of catheter used, catheter placement technique, quality of catheter care, and duration of catheter placement.

Clonidine activates alpha-adrenoreceptors in the brain stem and may cause *sedation*. High doses of clonidine may cause sedation and *hypoventilation*, although tolerance to these effects may develop with long-term administration. Bolus doses that are significantly larger than the infusion rate recommended for treating cancer pain have been associated with these effects.

Mental depression has been associated with administration of oral or transdermal clonidine. Depression occurs commonly in cancer patients and may be potentiated by clonidine therapy. Patients should be monitored for signs and symptoms of depression, especially patients with a known history of affective disorders.

Those indicating need for medical attention only if they continue or are bothersome

Incidence more frequent

Anxiety and/or confusion; dizziness; dryness of mouth; nausea; somnolence (sleepiness)

Incidence less frequent

Asthenia (weakness); ***constipation; sweating, unusual; tinnitus*** (ringing, noises, or buzzing in the ear)

Those indicating possible rebound hypertension and/or the need for medical attention if they occur after medication is abruptly discontinued

Agitation; headache; nervousness; and/or tremor, accompanied or followed by a rapid rise in blood pressure

Note: The *abrupt withdrawal* of clonidine in some patients has resulted in the above symptoms. These symptoms may be more likely to occur after administration of higher doses of clonidine or with concurrent use of beta-adrenergic blocking agents. Rarely, hypertensive encephalopathy, cerebrovascular accidents, and death have occurred after abrupt withdrawal of clonidine. Patients with a history of hypertension and/or other cardiovascular conditions may be particularly susceptible to the symptoms of abrupt clonidine withdrawal. In clinical trials, 4 of 38 patients receiving 720 mcg of epidural clonidine per day experienced rebound hypertension following abrupt withdrawal of clonidine; one of these 4 patients subsequently experienced a cerebrovascular accident.

Overdose

For specific information on the agents used in the management of clonidine overdose, see:

- *Atropine* in *Anticholinergics/Antispasmodics (Systemic)* monograph; and/or
- *Diazoxide (Parenteral-Systemic)* monograph; and/or
- *Furosemide* in *Diuretics, Loop (Systemic)* monograph; and/or
- Vasopressor agents, including
- *Ephedrine* in *Sympathomimetic Agents—Cardiovascular Use (Parenteral-Systemic)* monograph; and/or
- *Naloxone (Systemic)* monograph; and/or
- *Phentolamine (Systemic)* monograph.

For more information on the management of overdose or unintentional ingestion, **contact a Poison Control Center** (see *Poison Control Center Listing*).

Clinical effects of overdose

The following effects have been selected on the basis of their potential clinical significance (possible signs and symptoms in parentheses where appropriate)—not necessarily inclusive:

Acute and/or chronic

Bradycardia (slow heart rate); ***decreased or absent reflexes; drowsiness; hallucinations; hypertension; hypotension; hypothermia; irritability; miosis*** (blurred vision); ***respiratory depression***

Note: *Hypertension* may develop early and may be followed by *hypotension* and the above clinical effects.

Large oral overdoses

Apnea (cessation in breathing); ***cardiac conduction defects or arrhythmias, reversible; coma; seizures***

Treatment of overdose

Treatment is symptomatic and supportive.

Specific treatment—

For bradycardia—Atropine.

For hypotension—Intravenous fluids and/or vasopressor agents, such as ephedrine.

For hypertension—Intravenous furosemide, diazoxide, or alpha-adrenergic blocking agents, such as phentolamine. Use of tolazoline has shown inconsistent results and is not recommended as first-line therapy.

For respiratory depression, hypotension, and/or coma—Naloxone.

Monitoring—

The administration of naloxone occasionally has resulted in paradoxical hypertension; blood pressure should be monitored.

Supportive care—

Patients in whom intentional overdose is confirmed and suspected should be referred for psychiatric consultation.

Patient Consultation

As an aid to patient consultation, refer to *Advice for the Patient, Clonidine (Injection)*.

In providing consultation, consider emphasizing the following selected information (» = major clinical significance):

Before using this medication

» Conditions affecting use, especially:

History of allergic reaction or sensitization to clonidine

Pregnancy—Clonidine crosses the placenta; not recommended for use during pregnancy

Breast-feeding—Clonidine is distributed into breast milk; not recommended for use in nursing mothers

Use in children—Safety and efficacy have not been established; should be used only for severe intractable pain due to malignancy unresponsive to opiates or other analgesic techniques

Pharmacogenetics—In women, plasma clearance rate may be lower and plasma half-life may be longer; peak concentration in plasma and cerebrospinal fluid (CSF) may be higher; hypotension may occur more frequently

Surgical—Epidural clonidine has been reported to cause a marked hypotensive response when used for intra- or post-operative analgesia

Other medications, especially beta-adrenergic blocking agents

Other medical problems, especially anticoagulant therapy, hemorrhagic diathesis, infection present at the injection site

Proper use of this medication

Proper administration of epidural clonidine

» Proper dosing

Missed dose: Notifying physician immediately if clonidine administration is interrupted for any reason

» Proper storage

Precautions while using this medication

Not discontinuing therapy without consultation with and supervision by physician because of the possibility of serious adverse effects occurring with abrupt withdrawal

Caution when driving or doing other things requiring alertness because of possible sedation and hypotensive effects of clonidine

Getting up slowly from a lying or sitting position to prevent dizziness or faintness from hypotension

Caution in use of alcohol or other CNS depressants because of additional sedation or hypotensive effects

Side/adverse effects

Signs of potential side effects, especially bradycardia, hypotension, chest pain, fever, hallucinations, hypoventilation, mental depression, sedation, tachycardia, and vomiting

General Dosing Information

Abrupt withdrawal of clonidine has resulted in serious adverse effects in some patients. To discontinue epidural clonidine therapy, the dose should be reduced gradually over 2 to 4 days to avoid withdrawal symptoms. In patients concurrently receiving a beta-adrenergic blocking agent, the beta-blocking agent should be discontinued several days before the epidural clonidine is gradually discontinued.

The epidural administration of clonidine above the C4 dermatome is contraindicated because of the lack of adequate safety data supporting this use. Inadvertent administration of clonidine intrathecally has not been associated with a significant increase in adverse events, although there is a lack of adequate data supporting safety and efficacy.

Familiarization with the continuous epidural infusion device and monitoring or inspecting the device and catheter tubing for obstruction or dislodgment are necessary in order to reduce the risk of inadvertent abrupt withdrawal of epidural clonidine.

In patients with renal function impairment, the dosage should be adjusted according to the degree of impairment; careful monitoring is recommended.

For treatment of adverse effects
Recommended treatment consists of the following:
- Symptomatic bradycardia may be treated with atropine.
- Hypotension may be treated with intravenous fluids and, if necessary, parenteral ephedrine.

For treatment of withdrawal symptoms—
Recommended treatment consists of the following:
- Hypertension following discontinuation of epidural clonidine may be treated by administration of clonidine or by intravenous phentolamine.

For specific information on phentolamine, see *Phentolamine (Systemic)* monograph.

Parenteral Dosage Forms

CLONIDINE HYDROCHLORIDE INJECTION

Usual adult dose
Analgesic—
Initially, by continuous epidural infusion, 30 mcg per hour. The dosage is titrated to the degree of pain relief and occurrence of adverse effects; patients should be closely monitored for the first few days to assess their response.

[Shivering, post-operative][1]—
Intravenous bolus, 75 to 150 micrograms.

Usual adult prescribing limits
Experience is limited with infusion rates above 40 mcg per hr.

Usual pediatric dose
Analgesic—
Initially, by continuous epidural infusion, 0.5 mcg per kg per hour, adjusted based on the clinical response.

Note: Safety and efficacy of epidural clonidine have been established only in pediatric patients who are old enough to tolerate placement and management of an epidural catheter.

Strength(s) usually available
U.S.—
100 mcg per mL (Rx) [*Duraclon* (individually packaged 10 mL vials; preservative-free)].
500 mcg per mL (Rx) [*Duraclon* (individually packaged 10 mL vials; preservative-free)].

Packaging and storage
Store at controlled room temperature, between 15 and 30 °C (59 and 86 °F). Discard unused portion.

Preparation of dosage form
The 500 mcg/mL (0.5 mg/mL) strength product must be diluted in 0.9% Sodium Chloride for Injection USP to a final concentration of 100 mcg/mL prior to use.

Auxiliary labeling
- Do not take other medicines without your doctor's advice.
- Avoid alcoholic beverages.

[1]Not included in Canadian product labeling.

Revised: 10/02/2003
Developed: 11/04/1997

CLONIDINE Systemic

VA CLASSIFICATION (Primary/Secondary):
Oral—CV409/DX900; CN105; CN900
Transdermal—CV409

Commonly used brand name(s): *Catapres; Catapres-TTS-1; Catapres-TTS-2; Catapres-TTS-3; Dixarit.*

Note: For a listing of dosage forms and brand names by country availability, see *Dosage Forms* section(s).

Category
Antihypertensive—Clonidine Hydrochloride Tablets; Clonidine Transdermal Systems.
Menopausal syndrome therapy adjunct—Clonidine Hydrochloride Tablets.
Vascular headache prophylactic—Clonidine Hydrochloride Tablets.
Antidysmenorrheal—Clonidine Hydrochloride Tablets.
Opioid withdrawal syndrome suppressant—Clonidine Hydrochloride Tablets

Indications
Note: Bracketed information in the *Indications* section refers to uses that are not included in U.S. product labeling.

Accepted
Hypertension (treatment)—Oral and transdermal dosage forms of clonidine are indicated in the treatment of hypertension. It may be used alone or concomitantly with other antihypertensive agents. Because it causes only mild postural hypotension, clonidine may be useful as a substitute for guanethidine or other adrenergic blockers in patients who cannot tolerate these agents because of severe orthostatic hypotension.

[Oral clonidine is also used in the urgent treatment of hypertensive emergencies.][1]

For additional information on initial therapeutic guidelines related to the treatment of hypertension, see *Appendix III*.

[Pheochromocytoma (diagnosis)][1]—A clonidine suppression test is used in the diagnosis of pheochromocytoma.

[Headache, vascular (prophylaxis)][1]—Clonidine has been used orally in the prevention of migraine.

[Dysmenorrhea (treatment)][1] or
[Menopause, vasomotor symptoms of (treatment)]—Clonidine is used orally as an adjunct in the treatment of dysmenorrhea and menopausal flushing.

[Opioid (narcotic) abstinence syndrome (treatment)][1]—Clonidine is used to control symptoms and aid in rapid detoxification in the treatment of opioid withdrawal.

[Nicotine dependence (treatment adjunct)][1]—Clonidine is used as an adjunct in the treatment of nicotine withdrawal.

[Gilles de la Tourette's syndrome (treatment)][1]—Clonidine is used in the treatment of Gilles de la Tourette's syndrome.

[1]Not included in Canadian product labeling.

Pharmacology/Pharmacokinetics

Physicochemical characteristics
Molecular weight—
Clonidine: 230.1.
Clonidine hydrochloride: 266.56.

Mechanism of action/Effect
Alpha-adrenergic agonist; also has some alpha-adrenergic antagonist effects.

Antihypertensive—
Thought to be due to central alpha$_2$-adrenergic stimulation, which results in a decreased sympathetic outflow to the heart, kidneys, and peripheral vasculature; this results in decreased peripheral vascular resistance, decreased systolic and diastolic blood pressure, and decreased heart rate.

Vascular headache prophylactic—
May block central vasomotor reflexes.

Dysmenorrhea therapy adjunct; or menopausal syndrome therapy adjunct—
Unknown, although may act as peripheral vascular stabilizer to reduce menopausal flushing.

Opioid withdrawal syndrome suppressant—
May be result of alpha-adrenergic inhibiting activity in areas of the brain such as the locus ceruleus.

Other actions/effects
Stimulates the release of growth hormone acutely, but not chronically.

Absorption
Oral—Well absorbed following oral administration. Bioavailability following chronic administration is approximately 65%.
Transdermal—Greatest from the chest and upper arm, and least from the thigh. Absorbed through the skin at a constant rate.

Protein binding
Low to moderate (20 to 40%).

Biotransformation
Hepatic (about 50% of the absorbed dose).

Half-life
Normal renal function—Range, 12 to 16 hours.
Renal function impairment—Up to 41 hours.

Onset of action
Antihypertensive—
Oral—30 to 60 minutes.
Transdermal—2 to 3 days.

Time to peak plasma concentration
Oral—3 to 5 hours.
Transdermal—2 to 3 days.

Time for peak effect
Antihypertensive—Oral: 2 to 4 hours.

Duration of action
Antihypertensive—
Oral—
Up to 8 hours (24 to 36 hours in some patients).
Transdermal—
About 7 days with the system in place; about 8 hours after removal.

Elimination
Renal—40 to 60% (as unchanged drug) in 24 hours.
Biliary/fecal—20% (probably via enterohepatic circulation).
In dialysis—Very little (maximum 5%) removable by hemodialysis.

Precautions to Consider

Cross-sensitivity and/or related problems
Patients sensitive to ophthalmic apraclonidine may be sensitive to clonidine.

Patients sensitive to topical clonidine transdermal system may also be sensitive to oral clonidine hydrochloride.

Carcinogenicity
Studies in rats at doses 32 to 46 times the maximum recommended human dose for 132 weeks found no evidence of carcinogenicity.

Pregnancy/Reproduction
Fertility—Studies in male and female rats at doses up to three times the maximum recommended human dose found no impairment of fertility. However, fertility was affected in female rats given 10 to 40 times the maximum recommended human dose.

Pregnancy—Adequate and well-controlled studies in humans have not been done.

Studies in rats at doses as low as one-third the maximum recommended human dose given for 2 months prior to mating found an increased incidence of resorptions; this effect did not occur at doses of one-third to three times the maximum recommended human dose given on days 6 to 15 of gestation. Increased resorptions also occurred in rats and mice given doses up to 40 times the maximum recommended human dose on days 1 to 14 of gestation. No teratogenicity or embryotoxicity was observed in rabbits given up to three times the maximum recommended human dose.

FDA Pregnancy Category C.

Breast-feeding
Clonidine is distributed into breast milk. However, problems in humans have not been documented. Caution is recommended if clonidine is used in nursing mothers.

Pediatrics
Appropriate studies on the relationship of age to the effects of clonidine have not been performed in the pediatric population. However, there are numerous reports describing accidental clonidine overdose in the pediatric population. These reports seem to indicate that neonates, infants, and children are especially sensitive to the effects of clonidine. Caution is recommended.

Geriatrics
The elderly may be more sensitive than younger adults to clonidine's hypotensive effects. In addition, elderly patients are more likely to have age-related renal function impairment, which may require reduction of dosage in patients receiving clonidine.

Dental
Use of clonidine may decrease or inhibit salivary flow, thus contributing to the development of caries, periodontal disease, oral candidiasis, and discomfort.

Drug interactions and/or related problems
The following drug interactions and/or related problems have been selected on the basis of their potential clinical significance (possible mechanism in parentheses where appropriate)—not necessarily inclusive (» = major clinical significance):

Note: Combinations containing any of the following medications, depending on the amount present, may also interact with this medication.

Alcohol or
Central nervous system (CNS) depression-producing medications (see *Appendix II*)
(concurrent use may enhance the CNS-depressant effects of either these medications or clonidine)

» Antidepressants, tricyclic, or
Appetite suppressants, with the exception of fenfluramine
(concurrent use may decrease the hypotensive effects of clonidine)

Anti-inflammatory drugs, nonsteroidal (NSAIDs), especially indomethacin
(NSAIDs may reduce the antihypertensive effects of clonidine, possibly by inhibiting renal prostaglandin synthesis and/or causing sodium and fluid retention; the patient should be monitored carefully to confirm that the desired effect is being obtained)

» Beta-adrenergic blocking agents, systemic
(discontinuation of clonidine therapy during concurrent use of beta-adrenergic blocking agents may increase the risk of clonidine-withdrawal hypertensive crisis; ideally, beta-adrenergic blocking agents should be discontinued several days before clonidine is discontinued; blood pressure control may also be impaired when the two are combined)

Fenfluramine
(concurrent use may increase the hypotensive effects of clonidine)

Hypotension-producing medications, other (see *Appendix II*), with the exception of systemic beta-adrenergic blocking agents and tricyclic antidepressants
(concurrent use may potentiate antihypertensive effects; although some antihypertensive and/or diuretic combinations are frequently used for therapeutic advantage, dosage adjustments may be necessary during concurrent use)

Sympathomimetic agents
(concurrent use may reduce the antihypertensive effects of clonidine; the patient should be carefully monitored to confirm that the desired effect is being obtained)

Laboratory value alterations
The following have been selected on the basis of their potential clinical significance (possible effect in parentheses where appropriate)—not necessarily inclusive (» = major clinical significance).

With physiology/laboratory test values
Catecholamine concentrations, urinary, and
Vanillylmandelic acid (VMA) excretion, urinary
(may be decreased, but may increase on abrupt withdrawal)

Direct antiglobulin (Coombs') tests
(may produce weakly positive results)

Growth hormone concentrations, plasma
(may be increased transiently because of stimulation of growth hormone release, but are not elevated chronically with long-term use of clonidine)

Medical considerations/Contraindications
The medical considerations/contraindications included have been selected on the basis of their potential clinical significance (reasons given in parentheses where appropriate)—not necessarily inclusive (» = major clinical significance).

Risk-benefit should be considered when the following medical problems exist:

Atrioventricular (AV) node function impairment
(vagal effect of clonidine may exacerbate condition)

Cerebrovascular disease or
Coronary insufficiency or
Myocardial infarction, recent
(lowered blood pressure may decrease perfusion and worsen ischemia)

Mental depression, history of or
Raynaud's syndrome
(may be exacerbated by clonidine)

Renal function impairment, chronic
(reduces the elimination of clonidine and may increase the risk of toxicity; dosage reduction may be necessary)

Sensitivity to clonidine

Sinus node function impairment
(function may be further impaired)

Thromboangiitis obliterans

For transdermal dosage form only (in addition to above)
Polyarteritis nodosa or
Scleroderma or
Systemic lupus erythematosus (SLE)
(absorption may be decreased; placement of patches on affected areas should be avoided)

Skin irritation or abrasion
(absorption may be increased; placement of patches on irritated or abraded areas should be avoided)

Patient monitoring

The following may be especially important in patient monitoring (other tests may be warranted in some patients, depending on condition; » = major clinical significance):

» Blood pressure measurements
(recommended at periodic intervals in patients being treated for hypertension; selected patients may be taught to monitor their blood pressure at home and report the results at regular physician visits)

Side/Adverse Effects

Note: Incidence and severity of adverse systemic effects may be reduced with the transdermal dosage form, possibly because this form of administration maintains lower peak blood concentrations than occur with oral administration and decreases fluctuation in blood concentration.

Administration of clonidine for 6 months or longer to albino rats has resulted in a dose-related increase in the incidence and severity of spontaneously occurring retinal degeneration. These effects have not been observed in humans.

The following side/adverse effects have been selected on the basis of their potential clinical significance (possible signs and symptoms in parentheses where appropriate)—not necessarily inclusive:

Those indicating need for medical attention

Incidence more frequent—about 15 to 20%, with transdermal systems only

Itching or redness of skin

Note: Patients who develop either a localized or an extended allergic reaction to the transdermal system may also experience a generalized allergic skin rash if oral clonidine is substituted.

Incidence less frequent

Mental depression; sodium and water retention or edema (swelling of feet and lower legs)

Incidence rare

Raynaud's phenomenon (paleness or cold feeling in fingertips and toes); ***vivid dreams or nightmares***

Those indicating need for medical attention only if they continue or are bothersome

Incidence more frequent

Constipation—about 10%; ***dizziness***—about 16% with oral use; ***drowsiness***—about 33% with oral use; ***dryness of mouth***—about 40% with oral use; ***unusual tiredness or weakness***—about 10%

Incidence less frequent—1 to 5%

Anorexia (loss of appetite); ***darkening of skin***—with transdermal systems only; ***decreased sexual ability; dry, itching, or burning eyes; orthostatic hypotension*** (dizziness, lightheadedness, or fainting, especially when getting up from a lying or sitting position); ***nausea or vomiting; nervousness***

Those indicating possible rebound hypertension and need for medical attention if they occur after medication is abruptly discontinued

Angina (chest pain); ***anxiety or tenseness; headache; increased salivation; nausea; nervousness; palpitations*** (pounding heartbeat); ***restlessness; shaking or trembling of hands and fingers; stomach cramps; sweating; tachycardia*** (fast heartbeat); ***trouble in sleeping; vomiting***

Note: *Rebound hypertension* may occur but is symptomatic in only 5 to 20% of patients. It is more likely to occur after abrupt withdrawal of clonidine in patients who had been receiving doses exceeding 1.2 mg per day or if clonidine therapy is discontinued before or at the same time as concurrent beta-adrenergic blocking agent therapy.

Overdose

For more information on the management of overdose or unintentional ingestion, **contact a Poison Control Center** (see *Poison Control Center Listing*).

Clinical effects of overdose

The following effects have been selected on the basis of their potential clinical significance (possible signs and symptoms in parentheses where appropriate)—not necessarily inclusive:

Apnea or respiratory depression (difficulty in breathing); ***bradycardia*** (slow heartbeat); ***hypotension*** (dizziness or faintness); ***hypothermia*** (feeling cold); ***lethargy*** (unusual tiredness or weakness, extreme); ***miosis*** (pinpoint pupils of eyes)

Note: Overdose may result in hypertension, especially in pediatric patients.

Toxicity may occur with ingestion of 100 mcg (0.1 mg) in children.

Treatment of overdose

Specific treatment—

Recommended treatment for clonidine overdose is usually symptomatic and supportive and may include use of intravenous fluids.

For significant bradycardia: Atropine.

For hypotension: Dopamine infusion.

For hypertension: Intravenous furosemide, diazoxide, phentolamine, or nitroprusside.

Tolazoline infusion if necessary.

Patient Consultation

As an aid to patient consultation, refer to *Advice for the Patient, Clonidine (Systemic)*.

In providing consultation, consider emphasizing the following selected information (» = major clinical significance):

Before using this medication

» Conditions affecting use, especially:
Hypersensitivity to clonidine or to ophthalmic apraclonidine
Pregnancy—Increased resorptions in rats and mice
Breast-feeding—Distributed into human breast milk
Use in children—Caution recommended in children because accidental overdoses have been reported
Use in the elderly—Hypotensive effects may be more likely
Other medications, especially tricyclic antidepressants or beta-adrenergic blocking agents

Proper use of this medication

Proper administration of the transdermal dosage form:
» Compliance with therapy; reading patient instructions carefully
Not trimming or cutting patch
Applying to clean, dry skin area on upper arm or torso; area should be free of hair, scars, cuts, or irritation
Should remain in place even during showering, bathing, or swimming; applying adhesive overlay to loose systems; replacing systems that have loosened excessively or fallen off
Alternating application sites
Folding used patches in half with adhesive sides together; disposing of patch carefully, out of reach of children
Taking or applying medication at the same time(s) each day or week to maintain the therapeutic effect
» Proper dosing
Missed dose: Taking or using as soon as possible; checking with physician if miss two or more oral doses in a row or if are late in changing the transdermal system by 3 or more days; possible severe reaction if stopped abruptly
» Proper storage

For use as an antihypertensive
Possible need for control of weight and diet, especially sodium intake
» Patient may not experience symptoms of hypertension; importance of taking medication even if feeling well
» Does not cure, but helps control hypertension; possible need for lifelong therapy; serious consequences of untreated hypertension

Precautions while using this medication

Regular visits to physician to check progress
» Checking with physician before discontinuing medication; gradual dosage reduction may be necessary to avoid serious rebound hypertension
» Having enough medication on hand to get through weekends, holidays, and vacations; possibly carrying second prescription for emergency use
» Caution in taking alcohol or other CNS depressants
» Caution when driving or doing things requiring alertness, because of possible drowsiness
» Caution if any kind of surgery or emergency treatment is required
Caution when getting up suddenly from a lying or sitting position
Caution in using alcohol, while standing for long periods or exercising, and during hot weather, because of enhanced orthostatic hypotensive effects
Possible dryness of mouth; using sugarless candy or gum, ice, or saliva substitute for relief; checking with physician or dentist if dry mouth continues for more than 2 weeks

For use as an antihypertensive:

» Not taking other medications, especially nonprescription sympathomimetic agents, unless discussed with physician

Side/adverse effects

Signs of potential side effects, especially itching or redness of skin (transdermal), mental depression, sodium and water retention, edema, Raynaud's phenomenon, vivid dreams or nightmares, and withdrawal reaction

General Dosing Information

With continued use, apparent tolerance to the antihypertensive effects of clonidine may develop as a result of fluid retention and expanded plasma volume. Concurrent administration of a diuretic may decrease this likelihood and will enhance the antihypertensive effects of clonidine. Other antihypertensives have also been used concurrently with clonidine. If combination therapy is indicated, individual titration is required to ensure the lowest possible therapeutic dose of each drug.

The abrupt interruption of clonidine therapy, including several consecutive missed doses, may result in rebound hypertension, which may be severe (acute post-treatment syndrome), or, in rare cases, overshoot hypertension, occurring within 12 to 48 hours of discontinuing therapy and lasting several days. Some patients may experience associated symptoms such as nervousness, agitation, and headache. At cessation of therapy, dosage should be gradually reduced (in the case of the transdermal system, by reducing patch strength and, if necessary, administering oral clonidine) over a 2- to 4-day period. Alternative therapy should be considered for unreliable or noncompliant patients. An excessive rise in blood pressure may be treated by resumption of oral clonidine therapy or by intravenous administration of diazoxide or an alpha-adrenergic blocking agent.

It is recommended that this medication be discontinued if mental depression occurs.

For oral dosage form only

It is recommended that the last daily dose be taken at bedtime to ensure overnight control of blood pressure and reduce daytime drowsiness.

If clonidine therapy must be interrupted for surgery, it is recommended that the last dose be given no later than 4 to 6 hours prior to surgery, that parenteral hypotensive medication be administered throughout the procedure, and that clonidine therapy be reinstituted as soon as possible afterwards.

Clonidine has been used investigationally for rapid detoxification in the treatment of opioid withdrawal. One protocol used consists of a test dose of 5 to 6 mcg (0.005 to 0.006 mg) of clonidine hydrochloride per kg of body weight on the first day. Patients showing a positive response then receive 17 mcg (0.017 mg) of clonidine hydrochloride per kg of body weight in divided daily doses for 9 or 10 days (adjusted to avoid hypotension and oversedation), followed by a reduction to 50% of the dose on Days 11, 12, and 13, and no medication on Day 14. Dosage must be individualized according to each patient's tolerance.

For transdermal dosage form only

Because the onset of action of transdermal clonidine is 2 to 3 days, when a patient is being switched from oral to transdermal therapy, the dose of oral clonidine should be gradually reduced over 2 to 3 days after transdermal therapy is begun, to avoid a withdrawal reaction.

Application should preferably be made at the same time of day each week to areas of clean, dry, hairless skin on the upper arm or torso. Skin areas with extensive scarring, calluses, or irritation should be avoided. Application sites should be alternated to avoid causing skin irritation.

The transdermal units *should not* be cut or trimmed in an attempt to adjust dosage.

If the transdermal system begins to loosen, the adhesive overlay provided by the manufacturer should be applied over the unit to hold it in place. A new dosage unit should be applied if the first becomes overly loosened or falls off.

If local skin irritation occurs before the system has been in place for 7 days, the system may be removed and a new one placed on a different site. If contact sensitization persists, withdrawal of transdermal therapy may be necessary.

Oral Dosage Forms

Note: Bracketed uses in the *Dosage Forms* section refer to categories of use and/or indications that are not included in U.S. product labeling.

CLONIDINE HYDROCHLORIDE TABLETS USP

Usual adult and adolescent dose

Antihypertensive—

Initial: Oral, 100 mcg (0.1 mg) two times a day, the dosage being increased by 100 mcg (0.1 mg) per day at weekly intervals if necessary for control of blood pressure.

Maintenance: Oral, 200 to 600 mcg (0.2 to 0.6 mg) per day, in divided doses.

Severe hypertension in the urgent but not emergency situation (loading dose): Oral, 200 mcg (0.2 mg), followed by 100 mcg (0.1 mg) every hour until diastolic blood pressure is controlled or a total of 800 mcg (0.8 mg) has been given; the patient is then controlled on a normal maintenance dose.

[Vascular headache prophylactic][1]—

Oral, 25 mcg (0.025 mg) two to four times a day up to 50 mcg (0.05 mg) three times a day.

[Antidysmenorrheal][1]—

Severe dysmenorrhea: Oral, 25 mcg (0.025 mg) two times a day for fourteen days before and during menses.

[Menopausal syndrome therapy adjunct]—

Oral, 25 to 75 mcg (0.025 to 0.075 mg) two times a day.

Note: Geriatric patients may be more sensitive to the effects of the usual adult dose and may benefit from a lower initial dose.

Usual adult and adolescent prescribing limit

Antihypertensive—2.4 mg daily.

Usual pediatric dose

Children under 12 years of age—Safety and efficacy have not been established.

Strength(s) usually available

U.S.—

Note: Not commercially available in 25-mcg (0.025-mg) strength used for indications other than hypertension; extemporaneous compounding required.

100 mcg (0.1 mg) (Rx) [*Catapres* (scored; lactose); GENERIC (may be scored; may contain lactose)].

200 mcg (0.2 mg) (Rx) [*Catapres* (scored; lactose); GENERIC (may be scored; may contain lactose)].

300 mcg (0.3 mg) (Rx) [*Catapres* (scored; lactose); GENERIC (may be scored; may contain lactose)].

Canada—

25 mcg (0.025 mg) (Rx) [*Dixarit* (lactose)].

100 mcg (0.1 mg) (Rx) [*Catapres* (scored; lactose)].

200 mcg (0.2 mg) (Rx) [*Catapres* (scored; lactose)].

Note: 100 mcg of the hydrochloride salt is equivalent to 87 mcg of the free base.

Packaging and storage

Store between 15 and 30 °C (59 and 86 °F), unless otherwise specified by manufacturer. Store in a well-closed container.

Auxiliary labeling

- Avoid alcoholic beverages.
- For control of blood pressure. Do not stop unless directed by a physician.
- Do not miss doses.
- Do not take other medicines without your doctor's advice.
- Dry mouth may occur when taking this medication.

Note

Check refill frequency to determine compliance in hypertensive patients.

Topical Dosage Forms

CLONIDINE TRANSDERMAL SYSTEM

Usual adult dose

Antihypertensive—

Topical, to the intact skin, 1 transdermal dosage system, beginning with the system delivering 100 mcg (0.1 mg) per day, once a week. Dosage adjustments may be made every one or two weeks by changing to the next larger dosage system or a combination of systems.

Usual pediatric dose

Children under 12 years of age—Safety and efficacy have not been established.

Strength(s) usually available

U.S.—

Note: All systems are designed to release a constant, controlled dose of clonidine. The actual dose delivered will be as labeled and as intended, but less than the total content of each system.

2.5 mg (delivering 100 mcg [0.1 mg] per day) (Rx) [*Catapres-TTS-1*].
5.0 mg (delivering 200 mcg [0.2 mg] per day) (Rx) [*Catapres-TTS-2*].
7.5 mg (delivering 300 mcg [0.3 mg] per day) (Rx) [*Catapres-TTS-3*].

Canada—
Not commercially available.

Packaging and storage
Store below 30 °C (86 °F), unless otherwise specified by manufacturer.

Auxiliary labeling
- Avoid alcoholic beverages.
- For external use only.
- Do not miss doses.
- Do not take other medicines without your doctor's advice.

Note
Include patient instructions when dispensing.

Check refill frequency to determine compliance in hypertensive patients.

[1]Not included in Canadian product labeling.

Selected Bibliography
Transdermal clonidine for hypertension. Med Lett Drugs Ther 1985 Nov 8; 27: 95-6.

The fifth report of the Joint National Committee on Detection, Evaluation, and Treatment of High Blood Pressure (JNC V). Arch Intern Med 1993; 153(2): 154-83.

Revised: 11/17/2004

CLONIDINE AND CHLORTHALIDONE Systemic

VA CLASSIFICATION (Primary): CV409

Commonly used brand name(s): *Combipres*.

NOTE: The *Clonidine and Chlorthalidone (Systemic)* monograph is maintained on the *USP DI* electronic data base. A copy of the most recent revision of the complete monograph can be accessed on the *USP DI* Updates Online website. See the front cover of book for details on accessing the site.

For information on the specific components of this combination, see the *USP DI* monographs for *Clonidine (Systemic)* and *Diuretics, Thiazide (Systemic)*.

The information that follows is selectively abstracted from the complete monograph and is provided to facilitate drug use review and patient counseling.

Note: For a listing of dosage forms and brand names by country availability, see *Dosage Forms* section(s).

Category
Antihypertensive.

Indications

Accepted
Hypertension (treatment)—The combination of clonidine and chlorthalidone is indicated for treatment of hypertension.

Fixed-dosage combinations are generally not recommended for initial therapy and are useful for subsequent therapy only when the proportion of the component agents corresponds to the dose of the individual agents, as determined by titration.

For additional information on initial therapeutic guidelines related to the treatment of hypertension, see *Appendix III*.

Patient Consultation
As an aid to patient consultation, refer to *Advice for the Patient, Clonidine and Chlorthalidone (Systemic)*.

In providing consultation, consider emphasizing the following selected information (» = major clinical significance):

Before using this medication
» Conditions affecting use, especially:
- Sensitivity to clonidine (oral or topical dosage form) or to ophthalmic apraclonidine, or to sulfonamide-type medications.
- Pregnancy—Chlorthalidone: Risk of jaundice, thrombocytopenia, hypokalemia in infant
- Breast-feeding—Distributed into breast milk; may suppress lactation
- Use in children—Caution recommended in children because accidental overdoses have been reported
- Use in the elderly—Hypotensive and hypokalemic effects may be more likely
- Other medications, especially tricyclic antidepressants, beta-adrenergic blocking agents, cholestyramine, colestipol, digitalis glycosides, or lithium
- Other medical problems, especially severe renal function impairment

Proper use of this medication
Diuretic effects of the medication and timing of doses to minimize inconvenience of diuresis

Possible need for control of weight and diet, especially sodium intake

» Patient may not experience symptoms of hypertension; importance of taking medication even if feeling well

» Does not cure, but helps control hypertension; possible need for lifelong therapy; serious consequences of untreated hypertension

Compliance with therapy; taking medication at the same time each day to maintain the therapeutic effect

» Proper dosing

Missed dose: Taking as soon as remembered; checking with physician if two or more doses in a row are missed

» Proper storage

Precautions while using this medication
Making regular visits to physician to check progress

» Checking with physician before discontinuing medication; gradual dosage reduction may be necessary to avoid serious rebound hypertension

» Having enough medication on hand to get through weekends, holidays, and vacations; possibly carrying second prescription for emergency use

» Caution if any kind of surgery or emergency treatment is required

» Not taking other medications, especially nonprescription sympathomimetic agents, unless discussed with physician

» Caution in taking alcohol or other CNS depressants

» Caution when driving or doing things requiring alertness, because of possible drowsiness

Caution when getting up suddenly from a lying or sitting position

Caution in using alcohol, while standing for long periods or exercising, and during hot weather because of enhanced orthostatic hypotensive effects

» Possibility of hypokalemia; possible need for additional potassium in diet; not changing diet without first checking with physician

To prevent dehydration, checking with physician if severe nausea, vomiting, or diarrhea occurs and continues

Patients with diabetes may increase blood sugar levels

Possible photosensitivity; avoiding unprotected exposure to sun; using protective clothing and sun block product; avoiding use of sunlamp, tanning bed, or tanning booth

Possible dryness of mouth; using sugarless candy or gum, ice, or saliva substitute for relief; checking with physician or dentist if dry mouth continues for more than 2 weeks

Side/adverse effects
Signs of potential side effects, especially electrolyte imbalance, mental depression, sodium and water retention or edema, agranulocytosis, allergic reaction, cholecystitis or pancreatitis, hyperuricemia or gout, hepatic function impairment, Raynaud's phenomenon, thrombocytopenia, and vivid dreams or nightmares

Oral Dosage Forms

CLONIDINE HYDROCHLORIDE AND CHLORTHALIDONE TABLETS USP

Usual adult dose
Oral, 1 tablet one or two times a day, for a minimum of 0.1 mg clonidine and 15 mg chlorthalidone daily, to a maximum of 0.6 mg clonidine and 30 mg chlorthalidone daily.

Note: Geriatric patients may be more sensitive to the effects of the usual adult dose.

Usual pediatric dose
Safety and efficacy have not been established.

Strength(s) usually available
U.S.—
100 mcg (0.1 mg) clonidine hydrochloride and 15 mg chlorthalidone (Rx) [*Combipres* (scored; lactose); GENERIC].
200 mcg (0.2 mg) clonidine hydrochloride and 15 mg chlorthalidone (Rx) [*Combipres* (scored; lactose); GENERIC].
300 mcg (0.3 mg) clonidine hydrochloride and 15 mg chlorthalidone (Rx) [*Combipres* (scored; lactose); GENERIC].
Canada—
Not commercially available.

Note: 100 mcg of clonidine hydrochloride is equivalent to 87 mcg of the free base.

Auxiliary labeling
- Avoid alcoholic beverages.
- Do not miss doses.
- Do not take other medicines without your doctor's advice.

Revised: 06/08/1999

CLOPIDOGREL Systemic

VA CLASSIFICATION (Primary): BL117

Commonly used brand name(s): *Plavix*.

Note: For a listing of dosage forms and brand names by country availability, see *Dosage Forms* section(s).

Category

Antithrombotic; platelet aggregation inhibitor.

Indications

Accepted

Myocardial infarction (prophylaxis) or
Stroke, thromboembolic (prophylaxis) or
Vascular death (prophylaxis)—Clopidogrel is indicated for reducing the risk of atherosclerotic events (myocardial infarction, stroke, and vascular death) in patients with atherosclerosis documented by recent myocardial infarction, recent stroke, or established peripheral arterial disease.

Pharmacology/Pharmacokinetics

Physicochemical characteristics

Molecular weight—419.9.
Solubility—Practically insoluble in water at neutral pH, but freely soluble at pH 1; freely soluble in methanol, sparingly soluble in methylene chloride, and practically insoluble in ethyl ether.

Mechanism of action/Effect

Clopidogrel is an inhibitor of platelet aggregation; doses of 75 mg per day inhibit platelet aggregation by 40 to 60% at steady state, which occurs within 3 to 7 days.

Clopidogrel inhibits adenosine diphosphate (ADP) binding to its platelet receptor and subsequent ADP-mediated activation of the glycoprotein GPIIb/IIIa complex, thus inhibiting platelet aggregation. Because clopidogrel irreversibly modifies the ADP receptor, platelets are affected for the remainder of their lifespan. An active metabolite, not yet isolated, is responsible for the medication's activity. Platelet aggregation induced by agonists other than ADP is also inhibited by blocking the amplification of platelet activation by released ADP. Clopidogrel does not inhibit phosphodiesterase activity.

Absorption

Rapid, at least 50%. Bioavailability has not been found to be affected by food.

Protein binding

Very high, for clopidogrel and its main circulating metabolite (98% and 94%, respectively). Binding is nonsaturable *in vitro* up to a concentration of 100 micrograms per mL.

Biotransformation

Hepatic, extensive and rapid, by hydrolysis to the main circulating metabolite, a carboxylic acid derivative, which accounts for approximately 85% of the circulating drug-related compounds. A glucuronic acid derivative of the carboxylic acid derivative has also been found in plasma and urine. Neither the parent compound nor the carboxylic acid derivative has a platelet inhibiting effect.

Half-life

Elimination—
Carboxylic acid derivative: 8 hours (after single and multiple doses).

Note: Covalent binding to platelets has accounted for 2% of radiolabeled clopidogrel with a half-life of 11 days.

Onset of action

Dose-dependent inhibition of platelet aggregation—
After a single oral dose: 2 hours.
After repeated doses of 75 mg: On the first day.

Time to peak concentration

Plasma—Approximately 1 hour for the carboxylic acid derivative.

Peak plasma concentration

Approximately 3 mg per liter (carboxylic acid derivative) after repeated doses of 75 mg. Pharmacokinetics of the main circulating metabolite are linear (increased in proportion to dose) in a dose range of 50 to 150 mg.

Time to peak effect

Steady-state inhibition of platelet aggregation with repeated doses of 75 mg per day usually occurs between day 3 and day 7.

Duration of action

Platelet aggregation and bleeding time gradually return to baseline levels within about 5 days after treatment is withdrawn.

Elimination

Renal, approximately 50%, five days after dosing with radiolabeled clopidogrel.

Fecal, approximately 46%, five days after dosing with radiolabeled clopidogrel

Pharmacogenetics

No significant differences in clopidogrel pharmacokinetics or pharmacodynamics were observed between male and female subjects.

Pharmacokinetic differences in different race populations have not been studied.

Precautions to Consider

Tumorigenicity

Studies in mice and rats for 78 and 104 weeks, respectively, at doses of up to 77 mg per kg of body weight (mg/kg) per day (producing plasma exposures more than 25 times those in humans at the recommended daily dose of 75 mg) found no evidence of tumorigenicity.

Mutagenicity

Clopidogrel was not found to be genotoxic in four *in vitro* tests (Ames test, DNA-repair test in rat hepatocytes, gene mutation assay in Chinese hamster fibroblasts, and metaphase chromosome analysis of human lymphocytes) or in one *in vivo* test (micronucleus test by oral route in mice).

Pregnancy/Reproduction

Fertility—Studies in rats and rabbits at doses of up to 500 and 300 mg/kg per day (65 and 78 times the recommended daily human dose on a mg per square meter of body surface area [mg/m^2] basis), respectively, found no evidence of impaired fertility. Studies in male and female rats at oral doses of up to 400 mg/kg per day (52 times the recommended human dose on a mg/m^2 basis) also found no evidence of impaired fertility.

Pregnancy—Adequate and well-controlled studies in humans have not been done.

Studies in rats and rabbits at doses of up to 500 and 300 mg/kg per day (65 and 78 times the recommended daily human dose on a mg/m^2 basis), respectively, found no evidence of fetotoxicity.

Consideration of risk-benefit is recommended before using clopidogrel during pregnancy.

FDA Pregnancy Category B.

Breast-feeding

It is not known whether clopidogrel is distributed into human breast milk. Clopidogrel and/or its metabolites are distributed into the milk of lactating rats. Consideration of risk-benefit is recommended in making decisions about using clopidogrel in breast-feeding women or continuing breast-feeding in women taking clopidogrel.

Pediatrics

Appropriate studies on the relationship of age to the effects of clopidogrel have not been performed in the pediatric population. Safety and efficacy have not been established.

Geriatrics

Plasma concentrations of the main circulating metabolite have been found to be significantly higher in elderly individuals (≥ 75 years of age) than in young healthy volunteers, but these higher concentrations have not been found to be associated with differences in platelet aggregation and bleeding time. No dosage adjustment is recommended for elderly patients.

Dental

Because of the risk of increased surgical blood loss, it is recommended that clopidogrel be discontinued 7 days prior to elective dental surgery if an antiplatelet effect is not desired.

Surgical

Because of the risk of increased surgical blood loss, it is recommended that clopidogrel be discontinued 7 days prior to elective surgery if an antiplatelet effect is not desired.

Drug interactions and/or related problems

The following drug interactions and/or related problems have been selected on the basis of their potential clinical significance (possible mechanism in parentheses where appropriate)—not necessarily inclusive (» = major clinical significance):

» Aspirin or
» Nonsteroidal anti-inflammatory drugs (NSAIDs)
(concurrent use of clopidogrel with these agents may increase the risk of gastrointestinal bleeding)

(aspirin has not been found to modify the clopidogrel-mediated inhibiton of ADP-induced platelet aggregation, nor has it been found to increase the prolongation of bleeding time induced by clopidogrel; however, clopidogrel potentiated the effect of aspirin on collagen-induced platelet aggregation)

Fluvastatin or
Nonsteroidal anti-inflammatory drugs (NSAIDs) or
Phenytoin or
Tamoxifen or
Tolbutamide or
Torsemide or
Warfarin
(because clopidogrel inhibits hepatic cytochrome P450 enzyme activity at high concentrations *in vitro*, a possibility exists that it could interfere with the metabolism of these medications; caution is recommended)

Heparin or
Warfarin
(safety of concurrent use has not been established; caution is recommended)

Laboratory value alterations

The following have been selected on the basis of their potential clinical significance (possible effect in parentheses where appropriate)—not necessarily inclusive (» = major clinical significance).

With physiology/laboratory test values

Bilirubin, serum concentrations and
Hepatic enzymes, serum values
(may be increased)

Cholesterol, total
(serum concentrations may be increased)

Neutrophil count and
Platelet count
(may be decreased)

Nonprotein nitrogen (NPN)
(serum concentrations may be increased)

Uric acid
(serum concentrations may be increased)

Medical considerations/Contraindications

The medical considerations/contraindications included have been selected on the basis of their potential clinical significance (reasons given in parentheses where appropriate)—not necessarily inclusive (» = major clinical significance).

Except under special circumstances, this medication should not be used when the following medical problems exist:

» Bleeding, active, such as:
Intracranial hemorrhage
Peptic ulcer
(risk of severe bleeding)

Risk-benefit should be considered when the following medical problems exist:

» Any condition in which there is a significant risk of bleeding, such as:
Gastrointestinal ulceration
Surgery
Trauma

Hepatic function impairment
(caution is recommended; experience is limited in patients with severe hepatic function impairment, who may have bleeding diatheses)

Sensitivity to clopidogrel

Side/Adverse Effects

The following side/adverse effects have been selected on the basis of their potential clinical significance (possible signs and symptoms in parentheses where appropriate)—not necessarily inclusive:

Those indicating need for medical attention

Incidence more frequent (≥ 5%)

Chest pain—incidence 8.3%; ***pain, generalized***—incidence 6.4%; ***purpura*** (red or purple spots on skin, varying in size from pinpoint to large bruises)—incidence 5.3%; ***upper respiratory infection*** (cough; runny nose; sneezing; sore throat)—incidence 8.7%

Incidence less frequent (1 to < 5%)

Atrial fibrillation; or palpitations (irregular heartbeat); ***bronchitis*** (cough; shortness of breath)—incidence 3.7%; ***dyspnea*** (shortness of breath)—incidence 4.5%; ***edema*** (swelling of feet or lower legs)—incidence 4.1%; ***epistaxis*** (nosebleed)—incidence 2.9%; ***gastrointestinal hemorrhage*** (vomiting of blood or material that looks like coffee grounds)—incidence 2%; ***gout*** (joint pain); ***hypertension***—incidence 4.3%; ***syncope*** (fainting); ***urinary tract infection*** (frequent urination; painful or difficult urination)

Note: Incidence of *gastrointestinal hemorrhage* is increased in patients receiving aspirin. Approximately 0.7% of patients receiving clopidogrel have experienced gastrointestinal hemorrhage severe enough to require hospitalization.

Incidence rare (< 1%)

Intracranial hemorrhage (headache, sudden severe; weakness, sudden)—incidence 0.4%; ***neutropenia, including agranulocytosis*** (fever, chills, sore throat, other signs of infection; ulcers, sores, or white spots in mouth); ***peptic, gastric, or duodenal ulcer*** (stomach pain, severe)—incidence 0.7%; ***skin reactions, severe*** (blistering, flaking, or peeling of skin)—incidence 0.7%; ***thrombocytopenia*** (unusual bleeding or bruising; black, tarry stools; blood in urine or stools; pinpoint red spots on skin)—usually asymptomatic

Those indicating need for medical attention only if they continue or are bothersome

Incidence more frequent (≥ 5%)

Abdominal or stomach pain—incidence 5.6%; ***arthralgia*** (joint pain)—incidence 6.3%; ***back pain***—incidence 5.8%; ***dizziness***—incidence 6.2%; ***dyspepsia*** (heartburn)—incidence 5.2%; ***flu-like symptoms*** (aching muscles; fever and chills; general feeling of discomfort or illness; headache)—incidence 7.5%; ***headache***—incidence 7.6%

Incidence less frequent (< 5%)

Anxiety; asthenia (weakness); ***constipation; cough***—incidence 3.1%; ***diarrhea***—incidence 4.5%; ***fatigue*** (unusual tiredness)—incidence 3.3%; ***hypoesthesia or paresthesia*** (numbness or tingling); ***insomnia*** (trouble in sleeping); ***itching***—incidence 3.3%; ***leg cramps; mental depression***—incidence 3.6%; ***nausea***—incidence 3.4%; ***rhinitis*** (runny nose)—incidence 4.2%; ***skin rash***—incidence 4.2%; ***vomiting***

Overdose

For more information on the management of overdose or unintentional ingestion, **contact a Poison Control Center** (see *Poison Control Center Listing*).

Clinical effects of overdose

No adverse effects have been reported after ingestion of up to fourteen 75-mg tablets; bleeding time after six 75-mg tablets was prolonged by about the same amount as with the usual therapeutic dose of one 75-mg tablet.

The lethal single oral dose in mice and rats was 1500 or 2000 mg per kg of body weight (mg/kg) and in baboons was 3000 mg/kg. Symptoms of acute toxicity included vomiting (in baboons), prostration, difficult breathing, and gastrointestinal hemorrhage in all species.

Treatment of overdose

If quick reversal of pharmacologic effects is required, platelet transfusions may be useful.

Patient Consultation

In providing consultation, consider emphasizing the following selected information (» = major clinical significance):

Before using this medication

» Conditions affecting use, especially:
Sensitivity to clopidogrel
Dental—Risk of increased blood loss during dental procedures
Surgical—Risk of increased blood loss during surgical procedures
Other medications, especially aspirin or nonsteroidal anti-inflammatory drugs (NSAIDs)
Other medical problems, especially bleeding, including bleeding from a stomach ulcer

Proper use of this medication

Compliance with prescribed treatment regimen
» Proper dosing
Missed dose: Taking as soon as possible; not taking if almost time for next dose; not doubling doses
» Proper storage

Precautions while using this medication

» Need to inform all health care providers of use of medicine
» Caution if any kind of surgery (including dental surgery) is required
» Notifying physician immediately if signs and symptoms of bleeding occur

Side/adverse effects

Signs of potential side effects, especially chest pain, generalized pain, purpura, upper respiratory infection, atrial fibrillation or palpitations, bronchitis, edema, epistaxis, gastrointestinal hemorrhage, gout, hypertension, syncope, urinary tract infection, intracranial hemorrhage, neutropenia, agranulocytosis, gastrointestinal ulcers, severe skin reactions, thrombocytopenia

General Dosing Information

It is recommended that clopidogrel be discontinued 7 days prior to elective surgery because of the risk of increased blood loss.

Diet/Nutrition

Clopidogrel tablets may be taken with or without food.

Oral Dosage Forms

CLOPIDOGREL BISULFATE TABLETS

Note: Strength and dosage are expressed in terms of base.

Usual adult dose

Antithrombotic—
Oral, 75 mg (base) once a day.

Usual pediatric dose

Safety and efficacy have not been established.

Usual geriatric dose

See *Usual adult dose.*

Strength(s) usually available

U.S.—
75 mg (base) (Rx) [*Plavix* (lactose)].

Packaging and storage

Store between 15 and 30 °C (59 and 86 °F), preferably at 25 °C (77 °F).

Developed: 05/22/1998

CLORAZEPATE—See *Benzodiazepines (Systemic)*

CLOTRIMAZOLE—See *Antifungals, Azole (Vaginal)*

CLOTRIMAZOLE Oral-Local†

VA CLASSIFICATION (Primary): AM700

Commonly used brand name(s): *Mycelex Troches.*

Note: For a listing of dosage forms and brand names by country availability, see *Dosage Forms* section(s).

†Not commercially available in Canada.

Category

Antifungal (oral-local)

Note: Clotrimazole is a broad-spectrum antifungal.

Indications

Accepted

Candidiasis, oropharyngeal (treatment)—Oral clotrimazole is indicated as a primary agent in nonimmunosuppressed and immunosuppressed patients in the local treatment of oropharyngeal candidiasis (thrush) caused by *Candida* species.

Candidiasis, oropharyngeal (prophylaxis)—Oral clotrimazole is indicated as a primary agent in immunosuppressed patients in the local prophylaxis of oropharyngeal candidiasis caused by *Candida* species.

Not all species or strains of a particular organism may be susceptible to clotrimazole.

Unaccepted

Clotrimazole lozenges are not indicated in the treatment of systemic mycoses.

Pharmacology/Pharmacokinetics

Physicochemical characteristics

Molecular weight—344.85.

Mechanism of action/Effect

Fungistatic; may be fungicidal, depending on concentration; inhibits biosynthesis of ergosterol or other sterols, damaging the fungal cell wall membrane and altering its permeability; as a result, loss of essential intracellular elements may occur; also inhibits biosynthesis of triglycerides and phospholipids by fungi; in addition, inhibits oxidative and peroxidative enzyme activity, resulting in intracellular buildup of toxic concentrations of hydrogen peroxide, which may contribute to deterioration of subcellular organelles and cellular necrosis. In *Candida albicans*, inhibits transformation of blastospores into invasive mycelial form.

Other actions/effects

Also has some antibacterial activity.

Absorption

Poorly and erratically absorbed, even when swallowed.

Binding

Apparently bound to oral mucosa from which it is slowly released.

Biotransformation

When swallowed, absorbed clotrimazole is metabolized in the liver to inactive compounds; induces hepatic microsomal enzyme activity, resulting in acceleration of its own catabolism.

Saliva concentration

Sufficient to inhibit most species of *Candida* present in saliva (5.2 to 15 mcg per mL after dissolution of troche).

Duration of action

Up to 3 hours.

Elimination

Fecal.

Precautions to Consider

Carcinogenicity

An 18-month study in rats has not shown any carcinogenic effects.

Pregnancy/Reproduction

Pregnancy—Adequate and well-controlled studies in humans have not been done.

Studies in rats and mice, given mg-per-kg doses 100 times the usual adult human dose, have shown that clotrimazole is embryotoxic. In addition, clotrimazole, given orally to mice in doses 120 times the usual human dose, has been shown to cause impairment of mating, decreased number of viable young, and decreased survival to weaning. No effects were seen at doses 60 times the usual human dose. When given to rats at doses 50 times the usual human dose, clotrimazole caused a slight decrease in the number of pups per litter and decreased pup viability. However, no teratogenic effects were seen in mice, rabbits, or rats given doses up to 200, 180, and 100 times the usual human dose, respectively.

FDA Pregnancy Category C.

Breast-feeding

It is not known whether clotrimazole is distributed into breast milk; however, clotrimazole is poorly and erratically absorbed, even when swallowed.

Pediatrics
Use of clotrimazole troches is not recommended in infants and children up to 3 years of age since this age group may not be capable of using the lozenge safely. No pediatrics-specific problems have been documented to date in children over 3 years old.

Geriatrics
Appropriate studies on the relationship of age to the effects of clotrimazole have not been performed in the geriatric population. However, no geriatrics-specific problems have been documented to date.

Laboratory value alterations
The following have been selected on the basis of their potential clinical significance (possible effect in parentheses where appropriate)—not necessarily inclusive (» = major clinical significance).

With physiology/laboratory test values
Aspartate aminotransferase (AST [SGOT]), serum
(concentration may be minimally increased in up to 15% of patients)

Medical considerations/Contraindications
The medical considerations/contraindications included have been selected on the basis of their potential clinical significance (reasons given in parentheses where appropriate)—not necessarily inclusive (» = major clinical significance).

Risk-benefit should be considered when the following medical problem exists:
Hepatic impairment
(periodic assessment of hepatic function may be appropriate in patients with hepatic impairment)
Hypersensitivity to clotrimazole

Patient monitoring
The following may be especially important in patient monitoring (other tests may be warranted in some patients, depending on condition; » = major clinical significance):
Hepatic function determinations
(periodic assessment of hepatic function may be appropriate, particularly in patients with pre-existing hepatic impairment)

Side/Adverse Effects
The following side/adverse effects have been selected on the basis of their potential clinical significance (possible signs and symptoms in parentheses where appropriate)—not necessarily inclusive:

Those indicating need for medical attention only if they continue or are bothersome
Incidence more frequent
Gastrointestinal disturbance (abdominal or stomach cramping or pain; diarrhea)—when medication is swallowed; ***nausea or vomiting; pruritus*** (itching); ***unpleasant mouth sensations***

Patient Consultation
As an aid to patient consultation, refer to *Advice for the Patient, Clotrimazole (Oral).*

In providing consultation, consider emphasizing the following selected information (» = major clinical significance):

Before using this medication
» Conditions affecting use, especially:
Hypersensitivity to clotrimazole
Use in children—Use is not recommended in children up to 3 years of age

Proper use of this medication
Proper administration technique:
Holding lozenge in mouth and allowing it to dissolve slowly and completely
Swallowing saliva during this time
» Not chewing or swallowing lozenge whole
» Not giving to infants or children under 3 years of age
» Compliance with full course of therapy; fungal infections may require prolonged therapy
» Proper dosing
Missed dose: Using as soon as possible; not using if almost time for next dose
» Proper storage

Precautions while using this medication
Checking with physician if no improvement within 1 week

General Dosing Information
To provide prolonged oral contact with the medication and to achieve maximum effect, clotrimazole lozenges should be held in the mouth and allowed to dissolve slowly (and completely) over a 15- to 30-minute period. Saliva should be swallowed during this time. Clotrimazole lozenges should not be chewed or swallowed whole.

Since only limited data are available on the safety and efficacy of clotrimazole lozenges during prolonged administration, short-term administration is recommended whenever possible. However, clotrimazole lozenges have been used daily for approximately 3 months in renal transplant patients without apparent ill effects.

Oral Dosage Forms

CLOTRIMAZOLE LOZENGES

Usual adult and adolescent dose
Antifungal—
Treatment: Oral, as a lozenge dissolved slowly and completely in the mouth, 10 mg five times a day for fourteen days or longer, especially in immunosuppressed patients.
Prophylaxis: Oral, as a lozenge dissolved slowly and completely in the mouth, 10 mg three times a day in immunosuppressed patients.

Usual pediatric dose
Antifungal—
Infants and children up to 3 years of age: Use is not recommended in infants and children up to 3 years of age since this age group may not be capable of using the lozenge safely.
Children 3 years of age and over: See *Usual adult and adolescent dose.*

Strength(s) usually available
U.S.—
10 mg (Rx) [*Mycelex Troches* (dextrose; microcrystalline cellulose; povidone; magnesium stearate)].
Canada—
Not commercially available.

Packaging and storage
Store below 30 °C (86 °F), in a tight container, unless otherwise specified by manufacturer.

Auxiliary labeling
- Dissolve slowly in mouth.
- Continue medicine for full time of treatment.

Revised: 10/31/1999

CLOTRIMAZOLE Topical

VA CLASSIFICATION (Primary): DE102

Commonly used brand name(s): *Canesten Cream; Canesten Solution; Canesten Solution with Atomizer; Clotrimaderm Cream; Lotrimin AF Cream; Lotrimin AF Lotion; Lotrimin AF Solution; Lotrimin Cream; Lotrimin Lotion; Lotrimin Solution; Mycelex Cream; Mycelex Solution; Myclo Cream; Myclo Solution; Myclo Spray Solution; Neo-Zol Cream.*

Note: For a listing of dosage forms and brand names by country availability, see *Dosage Forms* section(s).

Category
Antifungal (topical).

Indications
Note: Bracketed information in the *Indications* section refers to uses that are not included in U.S. product labeling.

Accepted
Candidiasis, cutaneous (treatment)—Topical clotrimazole is indicated in the treatment of cutaneous candidiasis (moniliasis) caused by *Candida albicans (Monilia albicans).*

Tinea corporis (treatment)
Tinea cruris (treatment) or
Tinea pedis (treatment)—Topical clotrimazole is indicated in the treatment of tinea corporis (ringworm of the body), tinea cruris (ringworm of the groin; jock itch), and tinea pedis (ringworm of the foot; athlete's foot) caused by *Trichophyton rubrum, T. mentagrophytes, Epidermophyton floccosum (Acrothesium floccosum),* and *Microsporum canis.*

Tinea versicolor (treatment)—Topical clotrimazole is indicated in the treatment of tinea versicolor (pityriasis versicolor; "sun fungus") caused by *Pityrosporon orbiculare (Malassezia furfur).*

[Paronychia (treatment)][1]

[Tinea barbae (treatment)][1] or
[Tinea capitis (treatment)][1]—Topical clotrimazole is used in the treatment of paronychia, tinea barbae, and tinea capitis.

Not all species or strains of a particular organism may be susceptible to clotrimazole.

[1]Not included in Canadian product labeling.

Pharmacology/Pharmacokinetics

Physicochemical characteristics
Molecular weight—344.84.

Mechanism of action/Effect
Fungistatic; may be fungicidal, depending on concentration; inhibits biosynthesis of ergosterol or other sterols, damaging the fungal cell wall membrane and altering its permeability; as a result, loss of essential intracellular elements may occur; also inhibits biosynthesis of triglycerides and phospholipids by fungi; in addition, inhibits oxidative and peroxidative enzyme activity, resulting in intracellular buildup of toxic concentrations of hydrogen peroxide, which may contribute to deterioration of subcellular organelles and cellular necrosis. In *Candida albicans*, inhibits transformation of blastospores into invasive mycelial form.

Absorption
Dermal penetration; minimal systemic absorption.

Precautions to Consider

Carcinogenicity
Studies in rats given oral doses of clotrimazole for 18 months have not shown that clotrimazole is carcinogenic.

Mutagenicity
Studies in Chinese hamsters given clotrimazole in five oral doses of 100 mg per kg of body weight (mg/kg) prior to testing have shown no mutagenic effects in the spermatophore chromosomes.

Pregnancy/Reproduction
Fertility—Clotrimazole caused impairment of mating in studies in mice and rats given oral doses of 50 to 120 mg per kg (mg/kg).

Pregnancy—Adequate and well-controlled studies in humans have not been done during the first trimester. Studies in humans given intravaginal clotrimazole during the second and third trimesters have not shown that clotrimazole causes adverse effects on the fetus.

Studies in rats given intravaginal doses of up to 100 mg/kg have not shown that clotrimazole causes adverse effects on the fetus. However, clotrimazole caused embryotoxicity, decreased litter size and number of viable young, and decreased pup survival to weaning in studies in mice and rats given oral doses of 50 to 120 mg/kg. Clotrimazole was not shown to be teratogenic in studies in mice, rabbits, and rats given oral doses of up to 200, 180, and 100 mg/kg, respectively.

FDA Pregnancy Category B.

Breast-feeding
It is not known whether clotrimazole, applied topically, is distributed into breast milk. However, problems in humans have not been documented.

Pediatrics
Appropriate studies performed to date have not demonstrated pediatrics-specific problems that would limit the usefulness of topical clotrimazole in children.

Geriatrics
Appropriate studies on the relationship of age to the effects of topical clotrimazole have not been performed in the geriatric population. However, no geriatrics-specific problems have been documented to date.

Medical considerations/Contraindications
The medical considerations/contraindications included have been selected on the basis of their potential clinical significance (reasons given in parentheses where appropriate)—not necessarily inclusive (» = major clinical significance).

Risk-benefit should be considered when the following medical problem exists:

Sensitivity to clotrimazole

Side/Adverse Effects
The following side/adverse effects have been selected on the basis of their potential clinical significance (possible signs and symptoms in parentheses where appropriate)—not necessarily inclusive:

Those indicating need for medical attention
Hypersensitivity (skin rash, hives, blistering, burning, itching, peeling, redness, stinging, swelling, or other sign of skin irritation not present before therapy)

Patient Consultation
As an aid to patient consultation, refer to *Advice for the Patient, Clotrimazole (Topical)*.

In providing consultation, consider emphasizing the following selected information (» = major clinical significance):

Before using this medication
» Conditions affecting use, especially:
  Sensitivity to clotrimazole

Proper use of this medication
Proper administration technique
» Avoiding contact with the eyes
» Not applying occlusive dressing over this medication unless directed to do so by physician
» Compliance with full course of therapy
» Proper dosing
Missed dose: Applying as soon as possible; not applying if almost time for next dose
» Proper storage

Precautions while using this medication
Checking with physician if no improvement within 4 weeks

Side/adverse effects
Signs of potential side effects, especially hypersensitivity reactions

General Dosing Information
Use of topical antifungals may lead to skin sensitization, resulting in hypersensitivity reactions with subsequent topical use of the medication.

Improvement of condition, with relief of pruritus, usually occurs within the first week of therapy.

When this medication is used in the treatment of candidiasis, occlusive dressings should be avoided since they provide conditions that favor growth of yeast and release of its irritating endotoxin.

Topical Dosage Forms

CLOTRIMAZOLE CREAM USP

Usual adult and adolescent dose
Antifungal (topical)—
Topical, to the affected area of skin and surrounding areas, two times a day, morning and evening.

Usual pediatric dose
Antifungal (topical)—
See *Usual adult and adolescent dose*.

Strength(s) usually available
U.S.—
1% (10 mg per gram) (Rx/OTC) [*Lotrimin AF Cream* (benzyl alcohol 1%); *Lotrimin Cream* (benzyl alcohol 1%); *Mycelex Cream* (benzyl alcohol 1%); GENERIC].

Canada—
1% (10 mg per gram) (Rx) [*Canesten Cream* (benzyl alcohol 1%); *Clotrimaderm Cream* (benzyl alcohol 1%); *Myclo Cream*; *Neo-Zol Cream*].

Packaging and storage
Store between 2 and 30 °C (36 and 86 °F). Store in a collapsible tube or in a tight container. Protect from freezing.

Auxiliary labeling
- For external use only.
- Continue medicine for full time of treatment.

CLOTRIMAZOLE LOTION USP

Usual adult and adolescent dose
Antifungal (topical)—
See *Clotrimazole Cream USP*.

Usual pediatric dose
Antifungal (topical)—
See *Clotrimazole Cream USP*.

Strength(s) usually available

U.S.—

1% (10 mg per gram) (Rx/OTC) [*Lotrimin AF Lotion* (benzyl alcohol; ceteryl alcohol); *Lotrimin Lotion* (benzyl alcohol; ceteryl alcohol)].

Canada—

Not commercially available.

Packaging and storage

Store between 2 and 30 °C (36 and 86 °F). Store in a tight container. Protect from freezing.

Auxiliary labeling

- Shake well.
- For external use only.
- Continue medicine for full time of treatment.

CLOTRIMAZOLE TOPICAL SOLUTION USP

Usual adult and adolescent dose

Antifungal (topical)—

See *Clotrimazole Cream USP*.

Usual pediatric dose

Antifungal (topical)—

See *Clotrimazole Cream USP*.

Strength(s) usually available

U.S.—

1% (10 mg per mL) (Rx/OTC) [*Lotrimin AF Solution* (polyethylene glycol); *Lotrimin Solution* (polyethylene glycol); *Mycelex Solution* (polyethylene glycol)].

Canada—

1% (10 mg per mL) (Rx) [*Canesten Solution* (isopropyl alcohol); *Canesten Solution with Atomizer* (isopropyl alcohol); *Myclo Solution* (isopropyl alcohol); *Myclo Spray Solution* (isopropyl alcohol)].

Packaging and storage

Store between 2 and 30 °C (36 and 86 °F). Store in a tight container. Protect from freezing.

Auxiliary labeling

- For external use only.
- Keep container tightly closed.
- Continue medicine for full time of treatment.

Revised: 03/29/1994

CLOTRIMAZOLE AND BETAMETHASONE Topical

VA CLASSIFICATION (Primary): DE250

Commonly used brand name(s): *Lotriderm; Lotrisone.*

NOTE: The *Clotrimazole and Betamethasone (Topical)* monograph is maintained on the *USP DI* electronic data base. A copy of the most recent revision of the complete monograph can be accessed on the *USP DI* Updates Online website. See the front cover of book for details on accessing the site.

For information on the specific components of this combination, see the *USP DI* monographs for *Clotrimazole (Topical)* and *Corticosteroids (Topical).*

The information that follows is selectively abstracted from the complete monograph and is provided to facilitate drug use review and patient counseling.

Note: For a listing of dosage forms and brand names by country availability, see *Dosage Forms* section(s).

Category

Antifungal-corticosteroid (topical)

Note: Clotrimazole is a broad-spectrum antifungal agent.

Indications

Note: Bracketed information in the *Indications* section refers to uses that are not included in U.S. product labeling.

Accepted

Tinea corporis (treatment)

Tinea cruris (treatment) or

Tinea pedis (treatment)—Clotrimazole and betamethasone dipropionate combination is indicated [as a secondary agent] in the topical treatment of tinea corporis (ringworm of the body), tinea cruris (jock itch; ringworm of the groin), and tinea pedis (athlete's foot; ringworm of the foot), [accompanied by inflammation], caused by *Epidermophyton floccosum (Acrothesium floccosum), Microsporum canis, Trichophyton rubrum,* and *Trichophyton mentagrophytes.*

The use of clotrimazole and betamethasone dipropionate combination has been shown to provide greater benefit than either clotrimazole or betamethasone dipropionate alone [during the first few days of treatment or for as long as inflammation persists, except on the palms of the hands and soles of the feet. After this time, USP medical experts recommend the use of plain clotrimazole or other topical antifungal agents].

[Candidiasis, cutaneous (treatment)][1]—Clotrimazole and betamethasone dipropionate combination is used as a secondary agent in the topical treatment of cutaneous candidiasis (moniliasis), accompanied by inflammation, caused by *Candida albicans (Monilia albicans).*

Not all species or strains of a particular organism may be susceptible to clotrimazole.

Unaccepted

Since corticosteroids may cause thinning of the skin and telangiectasia when used on the face or in intertriginous areas (e.g., axilla, genitals, perineum, groin, between the toes), clotrimazole and betamethasone dipropionate combination is not recommended for use in these areas for longer than a few days.

Clotrimazole is not effective against bacteria, protozoa, or viruses.

[1]Not included in Canadian product labeling.

Patient Consultation

As an aid to patient consultation, refer to *Advice for the Patient, Clotrimazole and Betamethasone (Topical).*

In providing consultation, consider emphasizing the following selected information (» = major clinical significance):

Before using this medication

» Conditions affecting use, especially:

Allergies to imidazoles or corticosteroids

Pregnancy—Not recommended in pregnancy because of possibility of teratogenicity, especially when used on extensive surface areas, in large amounts, or for prolonged periods of time

Breast-feeding—May cause systemic effects, such as growth suppression, in infants

Use in children—May cause HPA axis suppression, Cushing's syndrome, intracranial hypertension, or growth suppression

Other medical problems, especially eczema vaccinatum, herpes simplex, tubercular infections of the skin, vaccinia, varicella, or other viral infections of the skin

Proper use of this medication

Before applying, washing affected area with soap and water, and drying thoroughly

» Not for ophthalmic use

To use

» Checking with physician before using medication on other skin problems

Applying a thin layer of medication to affected area(s) and surrounding skin; rubbing in gently and thoroughly

» Not applying occlusive dressing over this medication unless directed to do so by physician; wearing loose-fitting clothing when using on inguinal area; avoiding tight-fitting diapers and plastic pants on diaper area of children

» Compliance with full course of therapy; not using more often or for longer than directed by physician; excessive use on thin skin areas may result in skin atrophy and stretch marks

» Proper dosing

Missed dose: Applying as soon as possible; not applying if almost time for next dose

» Proper storage

Precautions while using this medication

Checking with physician if no improvement is observed within 1 week for tinea corporis or tinea cruris and 2 weeks for tinea pedis; redness and itching should improve within 3 to 5 days

Using hygienic measures to help cure infection and to help prevent reinfection:

For tinea pedis:

Carefully drying feet, especially between toes, after bathing

Not wearing socks made from wool or synthetic materials; wearing clean, cotton socks and changing them daily or more often if feet perspire excessively

Wearing well-ventilated shoes or sandals

Using a bland, absorbent powder or an antifungal powder liberally between toes, on feet, and in socks and shoes once or twice daily; using the powder after cream has been applied and has disappeared into the skin; not using the powder as sole therapy for your fungal infection

For tinea cruris:

Carefully drying inguinal area after bathing

Not wearing underwear that is tight-fitting or made from synthetic materials; wearing loose-fitting cotton underwear instead

Using a bland, absorbent powder or an antifungal powder liberally once or twice daily; using the powder after cream has been applied and has disappeared into the skin; not using the powder as sole therapy for your fungal infection

For tinea corporis:

Carefully drying the body after bathing

Avoiding excess heat and humidity if possible; keeping moisture from accumulating on affected areas of the body

Wearing well-ventilated clothing

Using a bland, absorbent powder or an antifungal powder liberally once or twice daily; using the powder after cream has been applied and has disappeared into the skin; not using the powder as sole therapy for your fungal infection

» Patients with diabetes: Betamethasone may rarely cause hyperglycemia and glucosuria, especially with severe diabetes and use of large amounts; checking with physician before changing diet or dosage of antidiabetic medication

Side/adverse effects

Signs of potential side effects, especially hypersensitivity; stinging; urticaria; paresthesia; rash; secondary infection; swelling; and long-term effects, including acne or oily skin; allergic contact dermatitis; folliculitis; hypopigmentation; increased hair growth on face and body; increased hair loss on scalp; perioral dermatitis; reddish purple lines on arms, face, legs, trunk, or groin; skin atrophy; and skin maceration

Topical Dosage Forms

CLOTRIMAZOLE AND BETAMETHASONE DIPROPIONATE CREAM USP

Usual adult and adolescent dose

Tinea corporis; or
Tinea cruris—

Topical, to the affected skin and surrounding area(s), two times a day, morning and evening for 2 weeks.

Tinea pedis—

Topical, to the affected skin and surrounding area(s), two times a day, morning and evening for 4 weeks.

Usual pediatric dose

Infants and children up to 12 years of age—Safety and efficacy have not been established.

Children 12 years of age and over—See *Usual adult and adolescent dose.*

Strength(s) usually available

U.S.—

1% of clotrimazole and 0.05% of betamethasone (base) (Rx) [*Lotrisone* (purified water; mineral oil; white petrolatum; cetearyl alcohol; ceteareth-30; propylene glycol; sodium phosphate monobasic; phosphoric acid; benzyl alcohol)].

Canada—

1% of clotrimazole and 0.05% of betamethasone (base) (Rx) [*Lotriderm* (purified water; mineral oil; white petrolatum; cetearyl alcohol; ceteareth-30; propylene glycol; sodium phosphate monobasic; phosphoric acid; benzyl alcohol)].

Auxiliary labeling

- For external use only.
- Continue medication for full time of treatment.
- Do not use in the eyes.

Revised: 06/14/1999

CLOXACILLIN—See *Penicillins (Systemic)*

CLOZAPINE Systemic

VA CLASSIFICATION (Primary): CN709

Commonly used brand name(s): *Clozaril.*

Note: In the U.S. and Canada, clozapine is available only through pharmacies that agree to participate with physicians in a program to monitor patients' blood tests; a supply of medication sufficient to continue therapy until the next scheduled blood test may be dispensed if the results of the blood tests are within acceptable parameters.

Note: For a listing of dosage forms and brand names by country availability, see *Dosage Forms* section(s).

Category

Antipsychotic

Note: Clozapine is an atypical antipsychotic.

Indications

Accepted

Schizophrenia (treatment)—Clozapine is indicated only in the management of severely ill schizophrenic patients who have failed to respond to other neuroleptic agents or who cannot tolerate the adverse effects produced by those agents. Clozapine may produce a significant improvement in both the positive and negative symptoms of schizophrenia.

Because of the significant risk of agranulocytosis and seizures associated with clozapine use, the patient should be given adequate trials with at least two different standard antipsychotic medications before clozapine therapy is initiated.

Unaccepted

Clozapine is not approved for the treatment of behavioral symptoms in elderly patients with dementia.

Pharmacology/Pharmacokinetics

Physicochemical characteristics

Chemical Group—Tricyclic dibenzodiazepine derivative.
Molecular weight—326.83.
Solubility—Very slightly soluble in water.

Mechanism of action/Effect

The mechanism by which clozapine exerts its antipsychotic effect has not been defined. In some studies, clozapine has shown more dopamine blocking activity in the limbic region of the brain than in the neostriatum, but its potency is low in all regions.. These properties may account for the low extrapyramidal side effect profile of clozapine. Clozapine interferes weakly with the binding of dopamine at D_1, D_2, D_3, and D_5 receptors, and moderately at D_4 receptors. At alpha-adrenergic, cholinergic, histaminergic, and serotonergic receptors, clozapine acts as an antagonist. It is unclear whether a combination of these effects accounts for clozapine's superiorefficacy. Clozapine has little or no effect on serum prolactin concentrations, because it does not bind potently to D_2receptors on mammotrophic cells of the anterior pituitary, under tonic control by the tuberoinfundibular dopamine tract.

Other actions/effects

Clozapine may cause significant bone marrow suppression, which can lead to agranulocytosis. Deaths have occurred. The development of agranulocytosis has not been linked clearly to any patient characteristics and cannot be predicted reliably by either dose or duration of treatment. However, the greatest incidences have been seen during the first 6 months of clozapine use, in patients older than 50 years of age, and in patients of Jewish descent.

Electroencephalographic (EEG) studies show that clozapine increases delta and theta activity and slows dominant alpha frequencies. Sharp wave activity and spike and wave complexes may also develop. In some patients, the proportion of time spent in rapid eye movement (REM) sleep increases greatly and the REM sleep latency decreases greatly. Also, dose-related seizures are associated with clozapine use at a cumulative incidence at 1 year of approximately 5% in patients receiving 600 to 900 mg per day. Seizure incidence in patients receiving less than 300 mg per day of clozapine is about 1 to 2%.

Clozapine has potent anticholinergic effects.

Absorption

Rapid and nearly complete. However, first-pass metabolism results in an absolute bioavailability of 50 to 60%. Food does not affect the systemic bioavailability of clozapine.

Distribution

Rapid and extensive; crosses the blood-brain barrier.

Protein binding

Very high (95%).

Biotransformation

Extensive hepatic metabolism to metabolites with limited or no activity.

The cytochrome P450 1A2 (CYP1A2) isoenzyme is the primary isoenzyme involved in clozapine metabolism. CYP2D6 is involved in clozapine metabolism to a lesser extent.

Half-life

Elimination—

8 hours (range, 4 to 12 hours) after a single 75-mg dose; 12 hours (range, 4 to 66 hours) after reaching steady-state dosing of 100 mg twice a day.

Time to peak concentration

Average, 2.5 hours (range, 1 to 6 hours). Steady-state concentrations are attained in 8 to 10 days.

Peak serum concentration

Steady-state peak and minimum plasma concentrations of clozapine average 319 nanograms per mL (range, 102 to 771 nanograms per mL) and 122 nanograms per mL (range, 41 to 343 nanograms per mL), respectively, at a dosage of 100 mg two times a day. At steady-state, administration of 37.5 mg, 75 mg, and 100 mg of clozapine two times a day produced linearly dose-proportional changes in the area under the plasma concentration-time curve and in the peak and minimum plasma concentrations of clozapine.

Duration of action

4 to 12 hours.

Elimination

Renal—

Approximately 50% of an administered dose, only trace amounts as unchanged clozapine.

Fecal—

Approximately 30% of an administered dose, only trace amounts as unchanged clozapine.

Precautions to Consider

Carcinogenicity

Long-term studies in mice and rats given clozapine in doses approximately seven times the typical human dose on a mg per kg of body weight (mg/kg) basis demonstrated no potential carcinogenicity.

Tumorigenicity

Animal studies have shown no abnormalities.

Mutagenicity

Clozapine was not found to be genotoxic or mutagenic when assayed in appropriate bacterial and mammalian tests.

Pregnancy/Reproduction

Pregnancy—Clozapine crosses the placenta. Adequate and well-controlled studies in humans have not been done.

Studies in animals have not shown that clozapine causes adverse effects on the fetus.

FDA Pregnancy Category B.

Breast-feeding

Animal studies have suggested that clozapine may be distributed into breast milk. Clozapine may cause sedation, decreased suckling, restlessness or irritability, seizures, and cardiovascular instability in the nursing infant.

Pediatrics

Appropriate studies on the relationship of age to the effects of clozapine have not been performed in children up to 16 years of age. Safety and efficacy have not been established.

Geriatrics

No information is available on the relationship of age to the effects of clozapine in geriatric patients. However, the elderly may be at greater risk for orthostatic hypotension, and for anticholinergic side effects such as confusion and excitement. Also, elderly males are more likely to have age-related prostatic hypertrophy, which requires caution in the use of clozapine.

According to an FDA Public Health Advisory, clozapine is not approved for the treatment of behavioral symptoms in elderly patients with dementia. Clinical studies of clozapine and other atypical antipsychotic drugs for treatment of behavioral symptoms in the elderly with dementia have shown a higher death rate associated with their use compared to patients receiving a placebo. Causes of death varied, but most seemed to be either heart-related (i.e., heart failure or sudden death) or from infections (i.e., pneumonia).

Pharmacogenetics

A disproportionate number of U.S. cases of agranulocytosis occurred in patients of Jewish background compared to the overall proportion of such patients exposed during domestic development of clozapine.

Dental

Although hypersalivation occurs as a frequent consequence of clozapine administration, peripheral anticholinergic effects of clozapine may decrease or inhibit salivary flow, thus contributing to the development of caries, periodontal disease, oral candidiasis, and discomfort.

The leukopenic and thrombocytopenic effects of clozapine may result in an increased incidence of microbial infection, delayed healing, and gingival bleeding. If leukopenia or thrombocytopenia occurs, dental work should be deferred until blood counts have returned to normal, and patients should be instructed in proper oral hygiene, including caution in the use of regular toothbrushes, dental floss, and toothpicks.

Drug interactions and/or related problems

The following drug interactions and/or related problems have been selected on the basis of their potential clinical significance (possible mechanism in parentheses where appropriate)—not necessarily inclusive (» = major clinical significance):

Note: Clozapine metabolism is mediated mainly by cytochrome P450 1A2 (CYP1A2) and to a lesser extent by CYP2D6. Interactions with other medications that are metabolized by these isoenzymes (e.g., encainide, flecainide, propafenone) or that induce or inhibit (e.g., quinidine) the cytochrome P450 enzymes, in addition to those listed below, should be considered. Dosage adjustments of either clozapine or the other medication may be required.

Combinations containing any of the following medications, depending on the amount present, may also interact with this medication.

» Alcohol or
» Central nervous system (CNS) depression-producing medications, other (see *Appendix II*)
(concurrent use with clozapine may increase the severity and frequency of CNS depressant effects)

Anticholinergics, other (see *Appendix II*)
(concurrent use with clozapine may potentiate the anticholinergic effects of these medications)

» Bone marrow depressants, other (see *Appendix II*)
(concurrent use with clozapine may potentiate the myelosuppressive effects of these medications)

Carbamazepine or
Phenytoin or
Smoking tobacco
(concurrent use may decrease the plasma concentrations of clozapine, reducing the effectiveness of a given clozapine dose; discontinuation may increase the plasma concentrations of clozapine)

Cimetidine or
Ciprofloxacin or
Erythromycin
(clozapine plasma concentrations may be increased, increasing the risk of developing adverse effects)

Highly protein-bound medications, other, such as:
Digitoxin or
Warfarin
(concurrent use with clozapine may result in increased serum concentrations of these medications; also, clozapine may be displaced from its binding sites by these medications)

» Hypotension-producing medications, other (see *Appendix II*), especially
Benzodiazepines or
Psychotropic medications, other
(concurrent use with clozapine may cause additive hypotensive effects; epinephrine should not be used in the treatment of clozapine-induced hypotension because of a possible reverse epinephrine effect)
(very rarely, circulatory collapse, respiratory arrest, and cardiac arrest have accompanied orthostatic hypotension in patients receiving clozapine alone or with benzodiazepines or other psychotropic medications; although drug interaction has not been established as the mechanism for these events, clozapine should be introduced with caution in patients receiving other psychotropic medications)

» Lithium
(concurrent use with clozapine may increase the risk of seizures, confusional states, neuroleptic malignant syndrome, and dyskinesias)

» Selective serotonin reuptake inhibitors (SSRIs)
(three-foldelevations in clozapine serum concentrations have been reported during concurrent use with fluvoxamine; lesser elevations have been reported during concurrent use with other SSRIs [fluoxetine, paroxetine, sertraline]; patients should be monitored closely, and a reduced clozapine dosage should be considered)

Medical considerations/Contraindications

The medical considerations/contraindications included have been selected on the basis of their potential clinical significance (reasons given in parentheses where appropriate)—not necessarily inclusive (» = major clinical significance).

Except under special circumstances, this medication should not be used when the following medical problems exist:

Agranulocytosis, history of
Blood dyscrasias, or history of
Bone marrow depression
» CNS depression, severe
Epilepsy
Granulocytopenia, severe
» Myeloproliferative disorders, specifically:
Paralytic ileus
(may be potentiated)
Hypersensitivity to clozapine

Risk-benefit should be considered when the following medical problems exist:

Cardiovascular disorders
(increased risk of blood pressure alterations and arrhythmias)
» Glaucoma, narrow-angle, predisposition to or
» Intestinal motility impairment or
» Prostatic hypertrophy
(conditions may be exacerbated by the potent anticholinergic effects of clozapine)

Hepatic function impairment
(metabolism of clozapine may be altered; also, hepatitis has been reported with clozapine use in patients with normal hepatic function and in patients with impaired hepatic function)

Renal function impairment
(excretion of clozapine may be altered)

» Seizure disorders, or history of
(risk of seizures may be increased)

Patient monitoring

The following may be especially important in patient monitoring (other tests may be warranted in some patients, depending on condition; » = major clinical significance):

» Because of the risk of myocarditis, the patient should be instructed to report immediately any unexplained fatigue, dyspnea, tachypnea, fever, chest pain, palpitations, tachycardia or other signs or symptoms of heart failure. Myocarditis should be considered in patients who present with electrocardiographic findings such as ST-T wave abnormalities or arrhythmias. Patients who present with tachycardia during the first month of therapy should be closely monitored for other signs of myocarditis. Clozapine therapy should be promptly discontinued if myocarditis is suspected. Patients with clozapine-related myocarditis should not be rechallenged with clozapine.

» White blood cell (WBC) and differential counts
(a baseline white blood cell count and absolute neutrophil count are required before start of clozapine therapy; and every week for the first 6 months; if acceptable WBC counts [≥3500 per mm^3] and counts and ANC can be monitored every 2 weeks for the next 6 months; if acceptable WBC counts and ANC have been maintained during the second 6 months of continuous therapy, WBC count and ANC can be monitored every 4 weeks; when clozapine therapy is discontinued for any reason, WBC counts and ANC must be monitored weekly for a minimum of 4 weeks from the day of discontinuation of until the WBC ≥ 3500 per mm^3 and ANC ≥ 2000 per mm^3; any occurrence of leukopenia and/or granulocytopenia or substantial drop in WBC count or ANC, either as a single drop or a cumulative drop within 3 weeks, results in an increase in the frequency of WBC and ANC monitoring; see manufacturer's guidelines for details.)

Side/Adverse Effects

The following side/adverse effects have been selected on the basis of their potential clinical significance (possible signs and symptoms in parentheses where appropriate)—not necessarily inclusive:

Those indicating need for medical attention

Incidence more frequent

Cardiovascular effects, specifically tachycardia (fast or irregular heartbeat); ***hypotension*** (low blood pressure); ***or orthostatic hypotension*** (dizziness or fainting)—especially when getting up from a lying or sitting position; ***fever***

Incidence less frequent

Agitation (unusual anxiety, nervousness, or irritability); ***akathisia*** (restlessness or need to keep moving); ***confusion; difficulty in accommodation*** (blurred vision); ***electrocardiogram (ECG) changes; hypertension*** (dizziness; severe or continuing headaches; increase in blood pressure); ***syncope*** (fainting)

Incidence rare

Blood dyscrasias, specifically agranulocytosis (chills; fever; sore throat; unusual tiredness or weakness); ***eosinophilia*** (fever); ***granulocytopenia*** (chills; fever; sore throat; sores, ulcers, or white spots on lips or in mouth; unusual tiredness or weakness); ***leukopenia*** (chills; fever; sore throat); ***or thrombocytopenia*** (unusual bleeding or bruising); ***deep-vein thrombosis*** (swelling or pain in leg); ***or pulmonary embolism*** (chest pain; cough; fainting; fast heartbeat; sudden shortness of breath); ***extrapyramidal effects, specifically akinesia or hypokinesia*** (absence of or decrease in movement); ***rigidity*** (severe muscle stiffness); ***or tremor*** (trembling or shaking)—less frequent; ***hepatitis*** (dark urine; decreased appetite; nausea; vomiting; yellow eyes or skin); ***hyperglycemia*** (increased appetite; increased thirst; increased urination; weakness); ***impotence*** (decreased sexual ability); ***insomnia or disturbed sleep*** (trouble in sleeping); ***mental depression; myocarditis*** (chest pain or discomfort; fast heartbeat; fever and chills; troubled breathing;)—post-marketing data suggest that clozapine is associated with an increased risk of fatal myocarditis, especially during, but not limited to, the first month of therapy. In patients in whom myocarditis is suspected, clozapine treatment should be promptly discontinued.; ***neuroleptic malignant syndrome (NMS)*** (convulsions; difficult or fast breathing; fast heartbeat or irregular pulse; fever; high or low [irregular] blood pressure; increased sweating; loss of bladder control; severe muscle stiffness; unusually pale skin; unusual tiredness or weakness); ***seizures; tardive dyskinesia*** (lip smacking or puckering; puffing of cheeks; rapid or worm-like movements of tongue; uncontrolled chewing movements; uncontrolled movements of arms and legs); ***trouble in urinating***

Note: Liver function tests should be performed immediately in any patient who develops signs or symptoms of *hepatitis* during treatment with clozapine. If test values are significantly elevated or if the patient shows signs of jaundice, clozapine should be discontinued.

Several cases of *NMS* have occurred in patients receiving clozapine alone or concomitantly with lithium or other CNS-active agents.

For *seizures*, a dose-dependent relationship has been suggested, with *seizures* occurring in 1 to 2% of patients receiving low doses (< 300 mg per day), in 3 to 4% of patients receiving moderate doses (300 to 599 mg per day), and in 5% of patients receiving high doses (≥ 600 mg per day) of clozapine. Patients with a history of epilepsy or other predisposing factors may be at greater risk of developing seizures.

Although no confirmed cases of *tardive dyskinesia* have been attributed to clozapine, the possibility of occurrence cannot be ruled out. The smallest dose and shortest duration of treatment should be used, with periodic reassessment of need for clozapine treatment.

Those indicating need for medical attention only if they continue or are bothersome

Incidence more frequent

Constipation; dizziness or lightheadedness; drowsiness; headache; hypersalivation (increased watering of mouth); ***nausea or vomiting; unusual weight gain***

Note: *Salivation* may be profuse, very fluid, and especially prevalent during sleep. It has been suggested by the manufacturer that this effect may be ameliorated in some cases by a reduction of clozapine dosage or by use of a peripherally acting anticholinergic medication; however, caution should be used since additive anticholinergic effects may lead to toxicity in some patients.

Incidence less frequent

Abdominal discomfort or heartburn; dryness of mouth; hyperhidrosis (increased sweating)

Overdose

For specific information on the agents used in the management of clozapine overdose, see:

*Charcoal, Activated (Oral-Local)*monograph;
Dihydroergotamine in *Vascular Headache Suppressants, Ergot Derivative-containing (Systemic)* monograph;
Norepinephrine in *Sympathomimetic Agents—Cardiovascular Use (Parenteral-Systemic)* monograph; and/or
Physostigmine (Systemic) monograph.

For more information on the management of overdose or unintentional ingestion, **contact a Poison Control Center** (see *Poison Control Center Listing).*

Clinical effects of overdose

The following effects have been selected on the basis of their potential clinical significance (possible signs and symptoms in parentheses where appropriate)—not necessarily inclusive:

Cardiac arrhythmias or tachycardia (fast, slow, or irregular heartbeat); ***delirium*** (unusual excitement, nervousness, or restlessness; hallucinations); ***drowsiness, severe or coma; hypersalivation*** (increased watering of the mouth); ***hypotension*** (dizziness or fainting); ***respiratory depression or failure*** (slow, irregular, or troubled breathing); ***seizures***

Note: Aspiration pneumonia has also been reported.

Deaths have occurred, generally at clozapine doses > 2500 mg. However, overdoses as low as 400 mg in adults and 50 to 200 mg in young children have resulted in coma. Patients have recovered from doses > 4000 mg.

Treatment of overdose

There is no specific antidote for clozapine. Treatment of overdose is symptomatic and supportive.

To decrease absorption—Initiation of gastric lavage or administration of activated charcoal within 6 hours of ingestion, if possible. Administration of activated charcoal, which may be used with sorbitol, may be as effective as or more effective than induction of emesis or gastric lavage.

Specific treatment—Considering use of physostigmine, dihydroergotamine, angiotensin, or norepinephrine to counteract anticholinergic symptoms. *Not* using epinephrine or derivatives in treatment of hypotension. *Not* using quinidine or procainamide in treatment of cardiac arrhythmias.

Monitoring—Monitoring of cardiac and vital signs; continued monitoring of patient for several days because of risk of delayed effects.

Supportive care—Establishment and maintenance of a patent airway, ensuring adequate oxygenation and ventilation. Patients in whom intentional overdose is confirmed or suspected should be referred for psychiatric consultation.

Note: Forced diuresis, dialysis, hemoperfusion, and exchange transfusions are not likely to be of benefit due to clozapine's high degree of protein binding.

Patient Consultation

As an aid to patient consultation, refer to *Advice for the Patient, Clozapine (Systemic).*

In providing consultation, consider emphasizing the following selected information (» = major clinical significance):

Before using this medication

» Conditions affecting use, especially:
- Pregnancy—Crosses the placenta
- Breast-feeding—May cause sedation, decreased suckling, and restlessness or irritability in nursing infant
- Use in children—Greater risk of orthostatic hypotension and anticholinergic side effects in these patients; not approved for the treatment of behavioral disorders in elderly patients with dementia; associated with a higher death rate
- Dental—Clozapine-induced blood dyscrasias may result in infections, delayed healing, and bleeding; dry mouth may cause caries and candidiasis; hypersalivation occurs frequently
- Other medications, especially alcohol, other CNS depression-producing medications, other bone marrow depressants, other hypotension-producing medications, lithium, or selective serotonin reuptake inhibitors
- Other medical problems, especially severe CNS depression, myeloproliferative disorders, predisposition to narrow-angle glaucoma, intestinal motility impairment, prostatic hypertrophy, and seizure disorders

Proper use of this medication

» Compliance with therapy; not taking more or less medication than prescribed

» Importance of caregivers contacting doctor and not giving this medicine for treatment of behavioral problems in elderly patients with dementia

» Proper dosing

Missed dose: Taking as soon as possible; not taking if almost time for next dose; not doubling doses; not taking if clozapine has not been taken in 2 or more days but contacting physician for instructions

» Proper storage

Precautions while using this medication

» Regular visits to physician to check progress of therapy and to laboratory for blood tests required to continue treatment

» Contacting physician for instruction before resuming clozapine use if clozapine has not been taken for ≥ 2 days

Checking with physician before discontinuing medication; gradual dosage reduction may be needed

Avoiding use of alcoholic beverages or other CNS depressants during therapy

» Immediately reporting to physician any lethargy, weakness, fever, sore throat, or other sign or symptom of infection that occurs during clozapine treatment because of the risk of blood dyscrasias

» Immediately reporting to physician any unexplained fatigue, dyspnea, tachypnea, fever, chest pain, palpitations, or other signs or symptoms of heart failure that occur during clozapine treatment because of the risk of myocarditis

Possible drowsiness, blurred vision, or seizures; not driving, swimming, climbing, operating machinery, or doing other things that require alertness or accurate vision

Possible orthostatic hypotension; caution when getting up from a lying or sitting position

Possible dryness of mouth; using sugarless gum or candy, ice, or saliva substitute for relief; checking with physician or dentist if dryness of mouth continues for more than 2 weeks

Side/adverse effects

Signs of potential side effects, especially cardiovascular effects, fever, agitation, akathisia, confusion, difficulty in accommodation, ECG changes, hypertension, syncope, blood dyscrasias, deep-vein thrombosis or pulmonary embolism, extrapyramidal effects, hepatitis, hyperglycemia, impotence, insomnia or disturbed sleep, mental depression, or myocarditis, neuroleptic malignant syndrome, seizures, tardive dyskinesia, or trouble in urinating

General Dosing Information

Clozapine dosage must be individualized by cautious titration from the lower dosage range. A divided dosing schedule should be used, the need for clozapine periodically reassessed, and the patient maintained at the lowest possible dosage level. Cautious titration and divided doses are necessary to minimize the risks of hypotension, seizure, and sedation.

Because of the risk of blood dyscrasias, the patient should be instructed to report immediately any lethargy, weakness, fever, sore throat, or other sign or symptom of infection that occurs during clozapine treatment.

Because of the continuing risks of seizure and agranulocytosis, a patient who does not show acceptable clinical benefit should not receive extended clozapine therapy.

If clozapine is to be discontinued, the dosage should be tapered gradually over 1 to 2 weeks if possible. However, if abrupt termination is necessary, the patient should be monitored for recurrence of psychotic symptoms, as rapid decompensation has occurred after sudden withdrawal.

Caution should be exercised in restarting clozapine. The mechanisms by which clozapine's adverse effects occur are unknown. The possibility exists that agranulocytosis will be more likely and more severe when clozapine is restarted in a patient who has previously received clozapine if, for example, an immune-mediated mechanism is involved. Any patient whose white blood cell (WBC) count falls below 2000 per mm^3 or whose absolute neutrophil count falls below 1000 per mm^3 should *not* be restarted on clozapine.

For treatment of adverse effects

Neuroleptic malignant syndrome (NMS)—

Treatment is essentially symptomatic and supportive and may include the following:

- *Discontinuing clozapine immediately.*
- Hyperthermia—Administering antipyretics (aspirin or acetaminophen); using cooling blanket.
- Dehydration—Restoring fluids and electrolytes.
- Cardiovascular instability—Monitoring blood pressure and cardiac rhythm closely. Use of sodium nitroprusside may allow vasodilation with subsequent heat loss from the skin in patients with less dominant muscle rigidity.
- Hypoxia—Administering oxygen; considering airway insertion and assisted ventilation.

• Muscle rigidity—Administering dantrolene sodium (100 to 300 mg a day orally in divided doses; or 1.25 to 1.5 mg per kg of body weight [mg/kg], intravenously); or administering amantadine (100 mg twice daily) or bromocriptine (5 mg three times a day) to restore central balance of dopamine and acetylcholine at the receptor site.

Tardive dyskinesia—
No known effective treatment. Although no confirmed cases of tardive dyskinesia have been attributed to clozapine, the dosage of clozapine should be lowered or medication discontinued at earliest signs of tardive dyskinesia to prevent irreversible effects.

Agranulocytosis—
If the WBC count falls below 2000 per mm^3 or the granulocyte count falls below 1000 per mm^3:

• Reduce the dose of clozapine and begin anticonvulsant therapy if necessary.
• *Discontinuing clozapine immediately.*
• Considering bone marrow aspiration to determine granulopoietic status.
• Placing patient in protective isolation with close observation if granulopoiesis is deficient.
• Monitoring WBC and differential counts daily until WBC > 3000 mm^3 and ANC > 1500 mm^3.
• Monitor WBC and differential twice weekly until WBC > 3500 per mm^3 and ANC > 2000 per mm^3
• Performing appropriate cultures and instituting appropriate antibiotic therapy if signs of infection occur.
• *Not* rechallenging patient with clozapine.

Oral Dosage Forms

CLOZAPINE TABLETS

Usual adult dose

Antipsychotic—
Oral, initially 12.5 mg (one half of a 25-mg tablet) one or two times a day, the dosage being increased in increments of 25 to 50 mg a day, if tolerated, to achieve a dose of 300 to 450 mg a day by the end of two weeks. Subsequent dosage increments should not exceed 100 mg one or two times a week. Usual therapeutic daily dose range is 100 to 900mg per day, given as a divided dose three times a day.
If reinitiating clozapine treatment two or more days since the last dose was taken, an initial dosage of 12.5 mg (one half of a 25-mg tablet) one or two times a day is recommended. However, titration to an effective dosage may proceed more rapidly than initial titration if the medication is well-tolerated. In any patient who experienced respiratory or cardiac arrest during initial dosing but who was then successfully titrated to a therapeutic dosage, titration of clozapine following reinitiation should proceed with great caution after an interruption in therapy of ≥ 24 hours duration.

The dosage and administration recommendations outlined above regarding the use of clozapine in patients with treatment-resistant schizophrenia should also be followed when treating patients with schizophrenia or schizoaffective disorder at risk for recurrent suicidal behavior.

Note: For malnourished patients, or those with hepatic, renal, or cardiovascular disease, dosage should be titrated more slowly than for other patients.

Usual adult prescribing limits

900 mg per day.

Usual pediatric dose

Children younger than 16 years of age—
Safety and efficacy have not been established.

Strength(s) usually available

U.S.—
25 mg (Rx) [*Clozaril* (scored; lactose); GENERIC (scored)].
100 mg (Rx) [*Clozaril* (scored; lactose); GENERIC (scored)].

Canada—
25 mg (Rx) [*Clozaril* (scored; lactose)].
100 mg (Rx) [*Clozaril* (scored; lactose)].

Packaging and storage

Store below 30 °C (86 °F), in a tight container, unless otherwise specified by manufacturer.

Auxiliary labeling

• Avoid alcoholic beverages.

Note

Clozapine may be dispensed only upon presentation of acceptable white blood cell (WBC) count results and only in a quantity sufficient to cover the time until the next scheduled blood test.

Revised: 04/26/2006

CODEINE—See *Opioid (Narcotic) Analgesics (Systemic)*

COLCHICINE Systemic

VA CLASSIFICATION (Primary): MS400

Note: For a listing of dosage forms and brand names by country availability, see *Dosage Forms* section(s).

Category

Anti-inflammatory; antigout agent; familial Mediterranean fever suppressant; calcium pyrophosphate deposition disease suppressant; amyloidosis suppressant.

Indications

Note: Bracketed information in the *Indications* section refers to uses that are not included in U.S. product labeling.

Note: The toxicity and narrow margin of safety of therapeutic doses of colchicine (e.g., doses required to relieve an acute attack of gout or calcium pyrophosphate deposition disease) must be carefully considered before treatment is initiated, especially when the medication is to be administered intravenously. However, long-term administration of prophylactic doses for chronic gout or other chronic conditions responsive to such treatment is relatively unlikely to cause serious toxicity in patients with normal renal and hepatic function.

Accepted

Gouty arthritis, chronic (treatment) or
Gouty arthritis, acute (prophylaxis and treatment)—Colchicine is indicated to reduce the frequency and severity of acute attacks of gouty arthritis in patients with chronic gout. Complete remission of such attacks may occur in some patients. Prophylactic administration of colchicine may be especially important during the first several months of treatment with an antihyperuricemic agent (allopurinol, probenecid, or sulfinpyrazone) because the frequency of acute attacks may be increased when such therapy is initiated.

Although colchicine is also indicated to relieve the pain and inflammation of acute attacks of gouty arthritis, it has generally been replaced by less toxic medications for this purpose. Nonsteroidal anti-inflammatory drugs (NSAIDs) or corticosteroids (preferably via intrasynovial injection) are recommended for relief of an acute attack. Therapeutic doses of colchicine should be reserved for patients in whom these other agents are contraindicated or ineffective.

Intravenous administration of colchicine may be considered for treatment of acute attacks of gouty arthritis when oral administration is ineffective, gastrointestinal side effects limit administration of effective oral doses, or an especially rapid response is needed. Although the risk of gastrointestinal toxicity is considerably lower with intravenous administration than with oral administration, the risk of other forms of toxicity is very high, especially in patients with renal and/or hepatic function impairment; fatalities have been reported. It is recommended that the medication be administered intravenously with caution, in low doses, and only to carefully selected patients, if at all.

[Mediterranean fever, familial (prophylaxis and treatment)]—Colchicine is indicated to reduce the frequency and severity of acute attacks of familial Mediterranean fever (familial recurrent polyserositis). Complete remission of such attacks may occur in some patients.

Prophylactic use of colchicine prevents amyloidosis and amyloidosis-induced renal failure in patients with familial Mediterranean fever, including patients whose acute attacks are not suppressed by such treatment. Colchicine therapy must be started before nephrotic syndrome or uremia develops; initiation of treatment after either of these conditions is present will not prevent further deterioration of renal function. However, after renal transplantation, prophylactic colchicine prevents amyloid deposition and resultant tissue damage in the transplanted kidney. Prophylactic use of colchicine is therefore recommended for all patients with familial Mediterranean fever, even when frequent, severe attacks continue to occur despite colchicine administration.

Although colchicine may also be effective in aborting an acute attack of febrile polyserositis if taken at the earliest sign of an attack, it will not relieve or shorten a severe attack that is already in progress.

[Calcium pyrophosphate deposition disease, acute (prophylaxis and treatment)][1]—Colchicine is used for the symptomatic relief of acute attacks of calcium pyrophosphate deposition disease (chondrocalcinosis articularis; pseudogout; synovitis, crystal-induced). Intravenous administration of the medication is reported to be more consistently effective than oral administration for relief of an acute attack. However, the high risk of toxicity associated with intravenous administration of colchicine must be considered. Prophylactic use of oral colchicine may prevent repeat acute attacks.

[Arthritis, sarcoid (treatment)][1]—Colchicine is used to relieve acute arthritic symptoms associated with sarcoidosis.

[Amyloidosis (treatment)][1]—Colchicine is indicated to decrease amyloid deposition and resultant tissue damage in patients with primary amyloidosis or amyloidosis secondary to conditions such as psoriatic arthritis, ankylosing spondylitis, or familial Mediterranean fever. Colchicine has been used together with melphalan and prednisone for the treatment of primary amyloidosis.

[Behçet's syndrome (treatment)][1]—Colchicine is used in the treatment of patients with Behçet's syndrome. It relieves or prevents erythema nodosum and arthralgias and may also reduce the frequency or severity of oral and/or genital ulcerations in some patients. However, colchicine does not reduce the frequency or severity of ocular lesions associated with this disease or improve visual acuity in affected patients.

[Cirrhosis, biliary (treatment)][1]—Colchicine is used in the treatment of primary biliary cirrhosis. Biochemical indicators of disease activity (serum albumin, bilirubin, alkaline phosphatase, cholesterol, and aminotransferases) improve during treatment. Although colchicine may retard the development of fibrosis and hepatic failure in patients with biliary cirrhosis, it does not relieve symptoms, prevent or reverse histological changes characteristic of the disease, or decrease the need for hepatic transplantation. In a few studies colchicine-treated patients survived significantly longer than control patients. Colchicine may provide additional benefit when used concurrently with ursodiol for this indication. However, colchicine clearance is substantially reduced in patients with alcoholic cirrhosis. Caution and careful attention to dosage are recommended to prevent accumulation and toxicity if colchicine is administered to these patients.

[Pericarditis, recurrent (treatment)][1]—Limited data indicate that colchicine may be useful for preventing acute attacks of pericarditis that recur despite treatment with NSAIDs and/or corticosteroids. Colchicine has permitted withdrawal of corticosteroid therapy in some patients with this condition.

[1]Not included in Canadian product labeling.

Pharmacology/Pharmacokinetics

Physicochemical characteristics

Source—Colchicine is the active alkaloidal principle derived from various species of *Colchicum*.

Molecular weight—399.44.

pKa—1.7 and 12.4.

Mechanism of action/Effect

Anti-inflammatory and—

Antigout agent:

The precise mechanism of action has not been completely established. In patients with gout, colchicine apparently interrupts the cycle of monosodium urate crystal deposition in joint tissues and the resultant inflammatory response that initiates and sustains an acute attack. Colchicine decreases leukocyte chemotaxis and phagocytosis and inhibits the formation and release of a chemotactic glycoprotein that is produced during phagocytosis of urate crystals. Colchicine also inhibits urate crystal deposition, which is enhanced by a low pH in the tissues, probably by inhibiting oxidation of glucose and subsequent lactic acid production in leukocytes. Colchicine has no analgesic or antihyperuricemic activity.

Note: Colchicine inhibits microtubule assembly in various cells, including leukocytes, probably by binding to and interfering with polymerization of the microtubule subunit tubulin. Although some studies have found that this action probably does not contribute significantly to colchicine's antigout action, a recent *in vitro* study has shown that it may be at least partially involved.

Colchicine's effect on microtubule assembly and/or leukocyte function may be involved in the medication's efficacy in conditions other than gout. In patients with biliary cirrhosis, interference with microtubule formation may inhibit collagen production, thereby retarding the development of hepatic fibrosis. Colchicine may also increase degradation of collagenby stimulating production of collagenase. Also, colchicine corrects some of the abnormalities of lymphocyte and monocyte function that have been identified in patients with active biliary cirrhosis. In addition, colchicine has been found to reverse abnormalities in neutrophil activity that are present in patients with Behçet's disease, i.e., increased migration and reduced superoxide scavenging activity.

Familial Mediterranean fever suppressant and—

Amyloidosis suppressant:

The mechanism by which colchicine suppresses acute attacks of febrile polyserositis in patients with familial Mediterranean fever has not been determined, but it may differ from the mechanism responsible for suppression of amyloidosis in patients with this disease. Colchicine inhibits secretion of serum amyloid A in patients with familial Mediterranean fever. It has also been suggested that colchicine may interfere with polymerization of amyloid subunits into mature amyloid fibrils.

Other actions/effects

By inhibiting microtubule assembly, colchicine interferes with mitotic spindle formation, thereby arresting mitosis in metaphase.

Colchicine decreases body temperature, depresses the respiratory center, constricts blood vessels, and causes hypertension via central vasomotor stimulation.

Absorption

Colchicine is rapidly absorbed after oral administration, probably from the jejunum and ileum. However, the rate and extent of absorption are variable, depending on the tablet dissolution rate; variability in gastric emptying, intestinal motility, and pH at the absorption site; and the extent to which colchicine is bound to microtubules in gastrointestinal mucosal cells.

Distribution

Colchicine is rapidly distributed to peripheral leukocytes. Concentrations in these cells may exceed those in plasma. The medication can be detected in leukocytes for 9 to 10 days following administration of a single dose. Colchicine also concentrates in the kidneys, liver, and spleen. Accumulation in these tissues may lead to toxicity. Colchicine is distributed into breast milk; peak concentrations of 1.2 to 2.5 nanograms per mL ($<$ 0.001 micromole per liter) have been measured 40 to 50 minutes after administration of a 0.6-mg dose to a patient receiving long-term therapy with 0.6 mg twice a day.

Protein binding

In plasma—Low to moderate (30 to 50%).

Biotransformation

Probably hepatic. Although colchicine metabolites have not been identified in humans, metabolism by mammalian hepatic microsomes has been demonstrated *in vitro*.

Half-life

Distribution—3 to 5 minutes

Elimination—Approximately 1 hour in healthy subjects, although a study with an extended sampling time reported mean terminal elimination half-life values of approximately 9 to 10.5 hours. Other studies have reported half-life values of approximately 2 hours in patients with alcoholic cirrhosis and approximately 2.5 hours in patients with familial Mediterranean fever.

Onset of action

Acute gouty arthritis (following first dose)—

Intravenous: Within 6 to 12 hours

Oral: Within 12 hours

Time to peak concentration

Oral—0.5 to 2 hours

Time to peak effect

Acute gouty arthritis—

Relief of pain and inflammation: 24 to 48 hours following the first oral dose.

Relief of swelling: May require several days.

Elimination

Primarily biliary, with enterohepatic recirculation; 10 to 20% renal. Renal elimination may be increased in patients with hepatic disease. Because of the high degree of tissue uptake, only 10% of a single dose is eliminated within 24 hours; elimination of colchicine from the body may continue for 10 days or more after cessation of administration. Also, elimination is slower in patients with biliary disease; in one study mean clearance rates of 10.65 mL per minute per kg of body weight (mL/min/kg) and 4.22 mL/min/kg were measured in healthy control subjects and in patients with alcoholic cirrhosis, respectively.

In dialysis—Because of the high degree of tissue binding, colchicine is not dialyzable.

Precautions to Consider

Pregnancy/Reproduction

Fertility—Colchicine arrests cell division in animals and plants. Although colchicine has been reported to cause reversible azoospermia and fertility problems in male patients receiving long-term treatment with prophylactic doses, several studies in patients receiving such treatment have shown no significant reproductive difficulties, abnormalities in sperm counts, or alterations in testosterone, prolactin, luteinizing hormone, or follicle-stimulating hormone concentrations. Administration of colchicine does not increase, and may actually reduce, the risk of serious fertility problems in women with familial Mediterranean fever, who are subject to formation of fibrous adhesions, ovulatory disturbances, and, consequently, sterility.

Pregnancy—Controlled studies in pregnant women have not been done, but colchicine has been used prior to and throughout pregnancy by patients receiving long-term prophylaxis for familial Mediterranean fever. Although several miscarriages have been reported, the miscarriage rate in untreated women with this disease is high. A large majority of the pregnancies in female patients and wives of male patients receiving colchicine produced healthy, normal, full-term infants. However, a group of investigators reported 2 cases of trisomy 21 (in 91 pregnancies) and recommend that amniocentesis be performed when either parent is receiving colchicine.

Colchicine has been shown to be teratogenic in mice given doses of 0.5 mg per kg of body weight (mg/kg) or more, causing microtia, exencephaly, microphthalmia, anophthalmia, skeletal malformations, gastrochisis, abnormalities of the liver and stomach, dextrocardia, missing pulmonary lobe, and cleft palate. Colchicine has also produced fetotoxic and teratogenic effects in hamsters given 10 mg/kg. Administration to hamsters on Day 8 of pregnancy resulted in fatalities in 50% of the fetuses and congenital malformations including microphthalmia, anophthalmia, exencephaly, rib fusions and other skeletal anomalies, and umbilical hernias in a large number of the surviving fetuses. In other studies, colchicine was embryotoxic in rabbits and cattle, but not monkeys. Studies in rats produced contradictory results.

FDA Pregnancy Category D.

Breast-feeding

Colchicine is distributed into breast milk; peak concentrations of 1.2 to 2.5 nanograms per mL (< 0.001 micromole per liter) have been measured 40 to 50 minutes after administration of a 0.6-mg dose to a patient receiving long-term therapy with 0.6 mg twice a day. No adverse effects were apparent in the breast-fed infant during the first 6 months of life.

Pediatrics

For gouty arthritis—Appropriate studies on the relationship of age to the effects of colchicine have not been performed in the pediatric population (in whom gouty arthritis rarely if ever occurs). Safety and efficacy for this indication have not been established.

For familial Mediterranean fever—Studies in pediatric patients 3 years of age and older receiving long-term prophylactic treatment have not demonstrated pediatrics-specific problems that would limit the usefulness of colchicine for this indication in children.

Geriatrics

Geriatric patients, even those with normal renal and hepatic function, may be more susceptible to cumulative toxicity with colchicine. Also, elderly patients are more likely to have age-related renal function impairment, which increases the risk of myopathy and other toxic effects in patients receiving colchicine. Caution and careful attention to dosage are recommended.

Dental

The leukopenic and thrombocytopenic effects of colchicine may result in an increased incidence of microbial infection, delayed healing, and gingival bleeding. If leukopenia or thrombocytopenia occurs, dental work should be deferred until blood counts have returned to normal and patients should be instructed in proper oral hygiene, including caution in use of regular toothbrushes, dental floss, and toothpicks.

Drug interactions and/or related problems

The following drug interactions and/or related problems have been selected on the basis of their potential clinical significance (possible mechanism in parentheses where appropriate)—not necessarily inclusive (» = major clinical significance):

Note: Combinations containing any of the following medications, depending on the amount present, may also interact with this medication.

In addition to the interactions listed below, the possibility should be considered that colchicine, because of its potential for causing gastrointestinal hemorrhage, thrombocytopenia (with chronic use), and coagulation defects including disseminated intravascular coagulation (with an overdose), may cause increased risk to patients receiving other medications that may impair blood clotting or cause hemorrhage. Such medications may include anticoagulants (coumarin- or indandione-derivative) or other hypoprothrombinemia-inducing medications; heparin; thrombolytic agents; platelet aggregation inhibitors; other thrombocytopenia-inducing medications; and other medications having significant potential for causing gastrointestinal ulceration or hemorrhage.

Alcohol
(concurrent use with orally administered colchicine increases the risk of gastrointestinal toxicity, especially in alcoholics; also, alcohol increases blood uric acid concentrations and may decrease the efficacy of prophylactic gout therapy)

Anti-inflammatory drugs, nonsteroidal (NSAIDs), especially
» Phenylbutazone
(concurrent use of phenylbutazone with colchicine may increase the risk of leukopenia, thrombocytopenia, or bone marrow depression)
(concurrent use of any NSAID with colchicine may increase the risk of gastrointestinal ulceration or hemorrhage; also, NSAID-induced inhibition of platelet aggregation may increase the risk of bleeding in areas other than the gastrointestinal tract should colchicine-induced thrombocytopenia or clotting defects [with overdose] also occur)

Antineoplastic agents, rapidly cytolytic
(these medications may increase serum uric acid concentrations and decrease the efficacy of prophylactic gout therapy)

Blood dyscrasia-causing medications (See *Appendix II*)
(the leukopenic and/or thrombocytopenic effects of colchicine may be intensified with concurrent or recent therapy if these medications cause the same effects; blood counts should be monitored if concurrent or sequential use cannot be avoided)

» Bone marrow depressants, other (See *Appendix II*) or
Radiation therapy
(additive bone marrow depression may occur; dosage reductions may be required when 2 or more bone marrow depressants, including radiation, are used concurrently or consecutively)

Vitamin B_{12}
(absorption of this vitamin may be impaired by chronic administration or high doses of colchicine; requirement may be increased)

Laboratory value alterations

The following have been selected on the basis of their potential clinical significance (possible effect in parentheses where appropriate)—not necessarily inclusive (» = major clinical significance).

With diagnostic test results
Hemoglobin, in urine, or
Red blood cells (RBC), in urine
(colchicine may cause false-positive test results)

17-Hydroxycorticosteroid determinations, in urine
(interference may occur when the Reddy, Jenkins, and Thorn procedure is used)

With physiology/laboratory test values
Alkaline phosphatase, serum and
Aspartate aminotransferase (AST [SGOT]), serum
(values may be increased)

Platelet count
(may be decreased)

Medical considerations/Contraindications

The medical considerations/contraindications included have been selected on the basis of their potential clinical significance (reasons given in parentheses where appropriate)—not necessarily inclusive (» = major clinical significance).

Except under special circumstances, this medication should not be used when the following medical problems exist:

» Hepatic and renal disease, concurrent
(risk of toxicity is very high, especially with intravenous administration)

» Renal function impairment, severe
(high risk of myopathy and other forms of toxicity; use in patients with severe renal function impairment [i.e., creatinine clearance 10 mL per minute (0.17 mL per second) or less] is not recommended)

For intravenous administration only

» Hepatic function impairment, severe
(intravenous administration is not recommended because of the high risk of impaired elimination and resultant toxicity)

» Leukopenia
(may be exacerbated; intravenous administration is not recommended)

Risk-benefit should be considered when the following medical problems exist:

Alcoholism, active
(increased risk of gastrointestinal toxicity with oral administration; parenteral administration is preferred; however, it is recommended that hepatic and renal function, which may be impaired in alcoholics, be assessed prior to initiation of therapy in these patients)

» Blood dyscrasias
(may be exacerbated)

» Cardiac disorders or
» Hepatic function impairment or
» Renal function impairment
(increased risk of cumulative toxicity, with the risk increasing as the severity of impairment increases; colchicine should be given with caution, with the dose being reduced and/or the intervals between doses being increased; it has been recommended that half of the usual dose be administered to patients with creatinine clearances of 50 mL per minute [0.83 mL per second] or less)

» Gastrointestinal disorders
(the risk of colchicine-induced damage to gastrointestinal tissues may be increased; also, colchicine's gastrointestinal toxicity may be particularly hazardous to patients with these conditions)

Sensitivity to colchicine, history of

Caution is also advised in administration to geriatric or debilitated patients, who may be more susceptible to cumulative toxicity.

Patient monitoring

The following may be especially important in patient monitoring (other tests may be warranted in some patients, depending on condition; » = major clinical significance):

Complete blood counts
(recommended at periodic intervals during long-term treatment because bone marrow depression with agranulocytosis, thrombocytopenia, or aplastic anemia may occur)

Side/Adverse Effects

Note: There is no clear separation of nontoxic, toxic, and lethal doses of colchicine. Various sources report lethal doses ranging between 20 and 65 mg, although considerably lower doses may be fatal, especially in patients with renal and/or hepatic function impairment and with intravenous administration. Fatalities have occurred after ingestion of single doses as low as 7 mg or intravenous administration of cumulative doses of only 5 mg.

The following side/adverse effects have been selected on the basis of their potential clinical significance (possible signs and symptoms in parentheses where appropriate)—not necessarily inclusive:

Those indicating need for medical attention

Incidence rare

Hypersensitivity reactions including dermatoses (skin rash, hives); ***and angioedema*** (large, hive-like swellings on face, eyelids, mouth, lips, and/or tongue)

Note: *Skin rash* not associated with hypersensitivity may occur, especially with long-term treatment in patients with renal or hepatic function impairment.

With intravenous administration;

Cardiac arrhythmias—with too-rapid administration; ***localized reactions such as irritation, inflammation, or thrombophlebitis; median nerve neuritis in injected arm*** (pain; tenderness; feeling of burning, "crawling," or tingling in the skin over the affected nerve); ***necrosis of the skin and soft tissues*** (peeling of skin)—if extravasation occurs

With prolonged or long-term use

Bone marrow depression with agranulocytosis (fever with or without chills; sores, ulcers, or white spots on lips or in mouth; sore throat); ***aplastic anemia*** (unusual tiredness or weakness; headache; difficulty in breathing, exertional); ***and thrombocytopenia*** (usually asymptomatic; rarely, unusual bleeding or bruising; black, tarry stools; blood in urine or stools; pinpoint red spots on skin); ***myopathy*** (muscle weakness); ***neuropathy*** (mild numbness in fingers or toes)

Note: *Myopathy* is more likely to occur in patients with impaired renal or hepatic function who are receiving long-term treatment with prophylactic doses of colchicine. This condition is characterized by proximal muscle weakness, spontaneous activity in the electromyelogram, and elevated creatine kinase values. Because these findings are also present in patients with polymyositis, a muscle biopsy may be necessary to differentiate between the 2 conditions.

Those indicating need for medical attention only if they continue or are bothersome

Incidence more frequent (up to 80%) with therapeutic doses of oral colchicine; rare with intravenous administration

Gastrointestinal toxicity (diarrhea; nausea or vomiting; stomach pain)—early symptoms

Incidence less frequent

Loss of appetite

With long-term use or following recovery from severe toxicity

Loss of hair

Note: *Hair loss* may start to occur as soon as 2 to 3 weeks after initiation of long-term therapy; the risk is dose-dependent. Regrowth usually begins 3 to 12 weeks after discontinuation of the medication.

Overdose

For specific information on the agents used in the management of colchicine overdose, see:

- *Atropine* in *Anticholinergics/Antispasmodics (Systemic)* monograph;
- *Benzodiazepines (Systemic)* monograph;
- *Charcoal, Activated (Oral-Local)* monograph;
- *Opioid (Narcotic) Analgesics (Systemic)* monograph; and/or
- *Vitamin K (Systemic)* monograph.

For more information on the management of overdose or unintentional ingestion, **contact a Poison Control Center** (see *Poison Control Center Listing*).

Clinical effects of overdose

The following effects have been selected on the basis of their potential clinical significance (possible signs and symptoms in parentheses where appropriate)-not necessarily inclusive:

Acute

Acute—usually begins within 24 to 72 hours after an acute overdose

Fever—may be the first sign of this stage and may be associated with septicemia; ***cerebral edema; CNS toxicity*** (ascending paralysis of the CNS; convulsions; delirium); ***multiple organ failure caused by tissue damage; including bone marrow hypoplasia*** (agranulocytosis or leukopenia; thrombocytopenia and disseminated intravascular coagulation or other coagulation abnormalities); ***hepatocellular damage, possibly with necrosis; muscle damage, including rhabdomyolysis*** (myoglobinuria; severe muscle weakness or paralysis); ***or necrosis, possibly resulting in adult respiratory distress syndrome or other forms of respiratory distress*** (fast, shallow breathing); ***pulmonary edema, and hypoxia, and/or myocardial injury*** (ST segment elevation in electrocardiogram; decreased cardiac contractility, creatine kinase elevation, hemorrhages and microinfarctions in the myocardium); ***paralytic ileus ; renal damage*** (with hematuria; and oliguric renal failure)

Note: After a cumulative overdose has been administered intravenously, symptoms associated with *bone marrow depression* may be the first indications of toxicity. In some patients, *disseminated intravascular coagulation* may be the first hematologic sign of toxicity, with the most severe coagulopathy occurring about 25 hours following administration of a large overdose.

Fluid and electrolyte disturbances often occur in colchicine toxicity. *Hypovolemia* may lead to *hypokalemia, hyponatre-*

mia, and *metabolic acidosis.* Also, *hypocalcemia, hypokalemia, hypophosphatemia,* and/or *metabolic acidosis* may occur in association with *renal damage.*

Fatalities may result from *shock, respiratory or cardiac arrest,* or *rapidly progressive multiple organ failure.*

Chronic—may occur several hours after an acute overdose

Burning feeling in the throat or skin; gastrointestinal toxicity (burning feeling in the stomach; severe abdominal pain; diarrhea; nausea, and/or vomiting); ***sloughing of the gastrointestinal mucosa and/or; hemorrhagic gastroenteritis*** (bloody diarrhea)—with oral ingestion only; ***vascular damage***

Note: Early *gastrointestinal symptoms* generally do not occur in overdosage caused by intravenous administration.

Vascular damage may lead to *fluid extravasation* which, together with fluid losses caused by severe *diarrhea* and *vomiting,* may cause profound dehydration, hypotension, and shock. Also, *septicemia* secondary to severe intestinal damage may result in *septic shock.*

Chronic—generally begins about 10 days after an acute overdose;

Alopecia (hair loss)—reversible; ***rebound leukocytosis; stomatitis*** (sores, ulcers, or white spots on lips or in mouth)

Treatment of overdose

For early signs of overdose (gastrointestinal symptoms)—

Immediate discontinuation of colchicine administration (when used for short-term relief of an acute attack) or reducing the dose (when used prophylactically).

Specific treatment—Use of morphine or atropine for stomach pain.

Use of an opioid or other antidiarrheal agents for diarrhea.

For irritation caused by extravasation: Applying heat or cold to the affected area and administering analgesics.

For severe overdose—

To decrease absorption—May include removing unabsorbed medication (if taken orally) via gastric lavage and/or administration of activated charcoal. Because of colchicine's extensive biliary elimination and enterohepatic recirculation, repeated doses of activated charcoal are recommended to bind absorbed colchicine that re-enters the intestinal tract, which interrupts enterohepatic recirculation and hastens elimination.

To enhance elimination—Due to colchicine's high degree of uptake and binding in various tissues, forced diuresis, peritoneal dialysis, hemodialysis, charcoal hemoperfusion, or exchange transfusion cannot be expected to remove significant quantities of the medication from the body.

Specific treatment—

For treatment of convulsions caused by overdose:

Administering an anticonvulsant. A benzodiazepine, such as diazepam, may be administered. Since intravenously administered benzodiazepines may cause respiratory and circulatory depression, especially when administered rapidly, and respiratory distress and shock are also potential consequences of colchicine overdose, medications and equipment needed for support of respiration and for resuscitation must be immediately available.

For bone marrow suppression and resultant coagulation defects:

Vitamin K_1, fresh frozen plasma, platelets, and/or red blood cells may be administered as needed.

Note: One patient with colchicine induced aplastic anemia has been successfully treated with a single 300–mg subcutaneous dose of granulocyte colony-stimulating factor

For fever, leukopenia, and or sepsis:

Use of broad-spectrum antibiotics.

Monitoring—May include monitoring hemodynamic, cardiac, and respiratory status and blood electrolytes. Prolonged observation is recommended because the most severe toxic effects generally do not appear until 24 hours or more after ingestion of an acute overdose.

Supportive care—

May include correcting dehydration via fluid replacement and instituting other measures to prevent or treat shock, including administration of a vasopressor, if necessary.

Correcting electrolyte imbalances and metabolic acidosis.

For respiratory distress, securing and maintaining a patent airway, administering oxygen, and instituting assisted or controlled respiration as needed. Endotracheal intubation may be required.

Patient Consultation

As an aid to patient consultation, refer to *Advice for the Patient, Colchicine (Systemic).*

In providing consultation, consider emphasizing the following selected information (» = major clinical significance):

Before using this medication

» Conditions affecting use, especially:
- Sensitivity to colchicine
- Use in the elderly—Increased susceptibility to cumulative toxicity
- Other medications, especially other bone marrow depressants or radiation therapy
- Other medical problems, especially blood dyscrasias, severe cardiac disorders, gastrointestinal disorders, renal function impairment, or hepatic function impairment

Proper use of this medication

» Importance of not taking more medication than prescribed

For prophylactic use
- Compliance with therapy
- Not using additional colchicine to relieve an acute gout attack that occurs during prophylactic therapy, unless otherwise directed by physician; using alternative treatment as prescribed

For intermittent use to relieve acute attack
- Starting medication at earliest sign of attack
- » Stopping medication when pain is relieved; at first sign of diarrhea, nausea or vomiting, or stomach pain; or when maximum dosage is reached (even if symptoms are not relieved)
- Noting total quantity of colchicine taken before gastrointestinal symptoms occur and, in subsequent attacks, stopping treatment before this cumulative dose has been reached
- » Not taking additional colchicine for 3 days after using therapeutic oral doses to relieve an acute attack or for 7 days after receiving intravenous colchicine

» Continuing other gout medication (if applicable) while taking colchicine

» Proper dosing

Missed dose: If on fixed-dosage chronic therapy—Taking as soon as possible; not taking if almost time for next dose; not doubling doses

» Proper storage

Precautions while using this medication

Regular visits to physician to check progress and possibly to be tested for adverse effects during long-term therapy

» Possibility that large quantities of alcohol may increase the risk of gastrointestinal toxicity; also, alcohol may increase uric acid concentrations and thereby decrease the effectiveness of medication when used for gout

Not discontinuing prophylactic treatment without first consulting physician if acute attacks continue to occur

Side/adverse effects

» Checking with physician if diarrhea, nausea, vomiting, or stomach pain occurs and continues for more than 3 hours after medication is discontinued

» Checking with physician immediately if symptoms of angioedema, bone marrow depression, or overdose occur

Signs and symptoms of other potential side effects, especially skin rash or hives, localized reactions to extravasation after intravenous administration, myopathy, and neuropathy

General Dosing Information

Colchicine's toxicity and narrow margin of safety must be considered before therapeutic doses of the medication are administered, especially intravenously. Fatalities have occurred after ingestion of single doses as low as 7 mg or intravenous administration of cumulative doses of 5 mg.

If colchicine is used to relieve an acute attack of gout or to abort an acute attack of familial Mediterranean fever, therapy should be instituted at the first sign of the attack. Delay in starting treatment reduces the medication's effectiveness.

A reduction in the size of individual doses, an increase in the interval between doses, or a reduction in the total daily dosage may be necessary in patients with renal or hepatic function impairment. Specifically, it is recommended that dosage be reduced by half (for prophylactic use, limited to no more than 600 mcg [0.6 mg] per day, orally) if the patient's creatinine clearance is 50 mL per minute (0.83 mL per second) or less and that the medication not be used at all if the patient's creatinine clearance is 10 mL per minute (0.17 mL per second) or less.

Oral administration of colchicine is preferable for prophylactic treatment of recurrent or chronic gout; intravenous administration should be reserved for patients who are temporarily unable to take medications orally.

The risk of colchicine-induced toxicity depends on the total dose given over a period of time, as well as on the size of single doses, especially with intravenous administration. The following measures are recommended to reduce the risk of cumulative toxicity:

When therapeutic doses of colchicine are given for relief of an acute attack, **the oral and intravenous routes of administration should not be used concurrently or sequentially. Additional colchicine should not be administered for at least 3 days after a course of oral treatment or for at least 7 days (21 days for geriatric patients) after a course of intravenous treatment.**

Patients who are receiving prophylactic doses of colchicine should not increase the dose to therapeutic levels if an acute attack of gout occurs. An alternative agent (e.g., a nonsteroidal anti-inflammatory drug [NSAID] or a corticosteroid, preferably via intrasynovial injection) should be used instead of additional colchicine.

Maximum dosage should be reduced if intravenous administration of colchicine cannot be avoided in geriatric patients and/or patients who are receiving prophylactic doses of colchicine.

Desensitization has been successfully accomplished in several patients with familial Mediterranean fever who were unable to tolerate prophylactic doses of colchicine. The regimen used in a patient in whom adverse effects occurred with 1 mg per day of colchicine consisted of administering 1 mcg (0.001 mg) diluted in sodium chloride solution on the first day, doubling the dose each day until the tenth day, when 500 mcg (0.5 mg) was given, then increasing the dose to 750 mcg (0.75 mg) per day after 3 months and to 1 mg per day after another 3 months.

For oral dosage forms only

Treatment with therapeutic doses of colchicine should be discontinued immediately, even if symptoms of the acute attack have not been relieved, when gastrointestinal symptoms (abdominal pain, diarrhea, nausea, or vomiting) occur. The patient should be instructed to note the total dose taken prior to the appearance of these symptoms and, during subsequent attacks, to discontinue treatment before this cumulative dose has been reached.

A reduction in prophylactic dosage is recommended if weakness, loss of appetite, nausea, vomiting, or diarrhea occurs.

For parenteral dosage forms only

Colchicine must be given intravenously because severe local irritation occurs if it is administered subcutaneously or intramuscularly. Also, care must be taken to ensure that the needle is properly positioned in the vein and to avoid extravasation because local irritation, inflammation, thrombophlebitis, and sloughing of the skin and subcutaneous tissues may occur.

It is recommended that the injection be diluted with 10 to 20 mL of 0.9% sodium chloride injection prior to administration. Alternatively, the medication may be injected into a large vein via an established intravenous line through which 0.9% sodium chloride injection is being infused.

The intravenous injection should be administered slowly, over a period of at least 2 to 5 minutes. Some clinicians recommend administering an intravenous dose over a period of 10 minutes.

Gastrointestinal symptoms occur rarely with intravenous administration and therefore cannot be used as an indicator of impending toxicity or guide to dosage. **The total dose administered and the duration of treatment should be limited and the patient carefully monitored**.

Nutrition

Colchicine impairs absorption of vitamin B_{12} from the terminal ileum. Patients receiving long-term treatment may require supplementation with this vitamin.

Oral Dosage Forms

Note: Bracketed uses in the *Dosage Forms* section refer to categories of use and/or indications that are not included in U.S. product labeling.

COLCHICINE TABLETS USP

Usual adult dose

Antigout agent and
[Calcium pyrophosphate deposition disease suppressant][1]—
Prophylactic—
Oral, 500 or 600 mcg (0.5 or 0.6 mg) once a day, initially. If necessary, dosage may be increased to 500 or 600 mcg (0.5 or 0.6 mg) two or, rarely, three times a day. However, in mild cases, administration of a single dose one to four times a week may be sufficient.

In patients with gout who are undergoing surgery—Oral, 500 or 600 mcg (0.5 or 0.6 mg) three times a day for three days before and three days after surgery.

Therapeutic (relief of acute attack)—
Oral, 1 or 2 tablets (500 or 600 mcg [0.5 or 0.6 mg] each), or a single 1-mg tablet, initially; then 500 or 600 mcg (0.5 or 0.6 mg) every one or two hours or 1 to 1.2 mg every two hours until pain is relieved; nausea, vomiting, or diarrhea occurs; or the maximum dose of 6 mg has been taken.

[Familial Mediterranean fever suppressant and]
[Amyloidosis suppressant][1]—
Prophylactic—
Oral, 500 or 600 mcg (0.5 or 0.6 mg) a day, initially. Dosage may be increased, if necessary and tolerated, up to a maximum of 2 mg a day in divided doses.

Note: Patients with familial Mediterranean fever who continue to experience frequent, severe acute attacks at a prophylactic dose of 2 mg a day are not likely to obtain relief with higher doses. However, prophylactic colchicine has been shown to prevent amyloidosis in these patients and therefore should not be discontinued.

Therapeutic (suppression of acute attack)—
Oral, 600 mcg (0.6 mg) every hour for four doses, then every two hours for two additional doses on the first day; followed by 1.2 mg every twelve hours for two additional days. Administration may be discontinued at any time during this three-day regimen if it is apparent that the attack has been suppressed.

[Anti-inflammatory, in Behçet's disease][1]
Oral, 1 to 1.8 mg a day in two or three divided doses.

[Anti-inflammatory, in biliary cirrhosis][1]—
Oral, 1 or 1.2 mg a day in two divided doses.

[Anti-inflammatory, in recurrent pericarditis][1]—
Oral, 1 mg a day in two divided doses. After a beneficial response has been attained, some patients may be maintained on 500 mcg (0.5 mg) a day.

Usual adult prescribing limits

Antigout agent—
Prophylactic—
Patients with renal function impairment (creatinine clearance between 10 and 50 mL per minute [0.17 and 0.83 mL per second])—600 mcg (0.6 mg) once a day.

Therapeutic (relief of acute attacks)—
Patients with normal hepatic and renal function—6 mg.
Patients with renal function impairment (creatinine clearance between 10 and 50 mL per minute [0.17 and 0.83 mL per second])—3 mg.

Usual pediatric dose

[Familial Mediterranean fever suppressant]—
Children younger than 5 years of age: Oral, 500 mcg (0.5 mg) once a day.
Children 5 years of age and older: Oral, 500 mcg (0.5 mg) two times a day.
Other indications—Safety and efficacy have not been established.

Note: Dosage adjustment may be required as the child grows. One study found that children who were younger than 5 years of age when treatment was initiated often required an increase in dosage (to two 500–mcg [0.5–mg] doses a day) at about 7 years of age, and that children who were older than 5 years of age when treatment was initiated often required an increase in dosage (to three 500–mcg [0.5–mg] doses a day) at about 12.5 years of age.

Strength(s) usually available

U.S.—
500 mcg (0.5 mg) (Rx) [GENERIC].
600 mcg (0.6 mg) (Rx) [GENERIC].

Canada—
600 mcg (0.6 mg) (Rx) [GENERIC].
1 mg (Rx) [GENERIC].

Packaging and storage

Store below 40 °C (104 °F), preferably between 15 and 30 °C (59 and 86 °F). Store in a well-closed, light-resistant container.

Parenteral Dosage Forms

Note: Bracketed uses in the *Dosage Forms* section refer to categories of use and/or indications that are not included in U.S. product labeling.

COLCHICINE INJECTION USP

Usual adult dose

Antigout agent and

[Calcium pyrophosphate deposition disease suppressant][1]—

Prophylactic—

Intravenous, 500 mcg (0.5 mg) to 1 mg one or two times a day. Some clinicians recommend that single and total daily intravenous doses should be no larger than one-half of the doses recommended for oral administration if the intravenous route cannot be avoided.

Therapeutic (relief of acute attack)—

Intravenous, 2 mg initially, then 500 mcg (0.5 mg) every six hours or 1 mg every six to twelve hours until the desired response is obtained or a maximum of 4 mg has been administered. However, some clinicians recommend administering an initial dose not higher than 1 mg, followed by 500 mcg (0.5 mg) one or two times a day. Other clinicians recommend that single and cumulative intravenous doses should be no larger than one-half of the doses recommended for oral administration

Note: Administration of one-half of the above prophylactic and therapeutic doses is recommended for patients with renal function impairment (creatinine clearance between 10 and 50 mL per minute [0.17 and 0.83 mL per second]).

Usual adult prescribing limits

The cumulative dose administered over twenty-four hours or more is not to exceed—

For nongeriatric patients with normal renal and hepatic function: 4 mg. **After this quantity of colchicine has been administered, additional colchicine should not be administered by any route for at least seven days.**

For nongeriatric patients with renal function impairment (creatinine clearance between 10 and 50 mL per minute [0.17 and 0.83 mL per second]): 2 mg.

For geriatric patients: 2 mg. **After this quantity of colchicine has been administered, additional colchicine should not be administered by any route for at least twenty-one days.**

Note: It is recommended that patients who have been receiving oral prophylactic therapy receive total doses even lower than those recommended above. Specifically, a maximum dose of 1 or 2 mg is recommended for nongeriatric adults with normal hepatic and renal function.

Usual pediatric dose

Safety and efficacy have not been established.

Strength(s) usually available

U.S.—

1 mg per 2-mL ampul (500 mcg [0.5 mg] per mL) (Rx) [GENERIC].

Canada—

Not commercially available.

Packaging and storage

Store below 40 °C (104 °F), preferably between 15 and 30 °C (59 and 86 °F), unless otherwise specified by manufacturer. Protect from freezing. Protect from light.

Preparation of dosage form

To reduce the risk of sclerosis and other local reactions, it is recommended that the contents of 1 ampul (2 mL) be diluted to at least 10 to 20 mL with 0.9% sodium chloride injection. However, any solution that becomes turbid upon dilution should not be injected.

Incompatibilities

It is recommended that colchicine injection **not** be diluted with or injected into intravenous tubing containing 5% dextrose injection, solutions containing a bacteriostatic agent, or any other fluid that might change the pH of the colchicine solution, because precipitation may occur.

[1]Not included in Canadian product labeling.

Selected Bibliography

Levy M, Spino M, Read SE. Colchicine: a state-of-the-art review. Pharmacotherapy 1991; 11: 196-211.

Star VL, Hochberg MC. Prevention and management of gout. Drugs 1993; 45: 212-22.

Zemer D, Livneh A, Danon YL, Pras M, Sohar E. Long-term colchicine treatment in children with familial Mediterranean fever. Arthritis Rheum 1991; 34: 973-7.

Henderson A, Emmerson BT, Bailey NL, Pond SM. Colchicine overdose in 6 patients. Prospects for prevention and therapy. Drug Invest 1993; 6: 114-7.

Revised: 01/31/1994

COLESTIPOL Oral-Local

VA CLASSIFICATION (Primary/Secondary): CV359/DE890; GA208

Commonly used brand name(s): *Colestid*.

Note: For a listing of dosage forms and brand names by country availability, see *Dosage Forms* section(s).

Category

Antihyperlipidemic; antipruritic (cholestasis); antidiarrheal (postoperative colonic bile acids).

Indications

Note: Bracketed information in the *Indications* section refers to uses that are not included in U.S. product labeling.

Accepted

Hyperlipidemia (treatment)—Colestipol is indicated for use as an adjunct only in patients with primary hypercholesterolemia (type IIa hyperlipidemia) and a significant risk of coronary artery disease who have not responded to diet or other measures alone. Colestipol reduces plasma cholesterol concentrations but causes no change or a slight increase in serum triglyceride concentrations, and so is not useful in patients with elevated triglyceride concentrations alone. Its use is limited in other types of hyperlipidemia (including type IIb) because it may cause further elevation of triglycerides.

Studies have suggested that control of elevated cholesterol and triglycerides may not lessen the danger of cardiovascular disease and mortality, although incidence of nonfatal myocardial infarctions may be decreased.

For additional information on initial therapeutic guidelines related to the treatment of hyperlipidemia, see *Appendix III*.

[Pruritus, associated with partial biliary obstruction (treatment)][1]—Colestipol is also used for the relief of pruritus associated with partial biliary obstruction (including primary biliary cirrhosis and various other forms of bile stasis). It is not useful in patients with complete biliary obstruction or with pruritus due to other causes.

[Diarrhea, due to bile acids (treatment)][1]—Colestipol may also be used to treat diarrhea caused by increased bile acids in the colon after surgery, although the risk of steatorrhea is increased.

[Colestipol has been used in the treatment of digitalis glycoside overdose and hyperoxaluria; however, it generally has been replaced by more effective agents.][1]

[1]Not included in Canadian product labeling.

Pharmacology/Pharmacokinetics

Physicochemical characteristics

Colestipol is an anion-exchange resin.

Mechanism of action/Effect

Colestipol binds with bile acids in the intestine, preventing their reabsorption and producing an insoluble complex, which is excreted in the feces.

Antihyperlipidemic—

Colestipol binds with bile acids in the intestine, causing an increase in hepatic synthesis of bile acids from cholesterol. This depletion of hepatic cholesterol increases hepatic low-density lipoprotein (LDL) receptor activity, which removes LDL cholesterol from the plasma. Colestipol may also increase hepatic very low-density lipoprotein (VLDL) production, thereby increasing plasma concentration of triglycerides, especially in patients with hypertriglyceridemia.

Antipruritic (cholestasis)—

Reduction of serum bile acids and subsequent reduction of excess bile acids, which are deposited in dermal tissue, may lead to reduced pruritus.

Antidiarrheal (postoperative colonic bile acids)—

Colestipol binds with and removes bile acids.

Other actions/effects

Because it is an anion-exchange resin, colestipol is capable of binding negatively charged medications as well as some others, causing a decreased effect or shortened half-life.

Absorption

Not absorbed from the gastrointestinal tract.

Onset of action
Plasma cholesterol concentrations are generally reduced within 24 to 48 hours after initiation of colestipol therapy.

Time to peak effect
Within 1 month. In some patients, after the initial decrease, serum cholesterol concentrations return to or exceed baseline levels with continued therapy.

Duration of action
After withdrawal of colestipol, cholesterol concentrations return to baseline in about 1 month.

Precautions to Consider

Tumorigenicity/Mutagenicity
In rats given colestipol for 18 months, no evidence of drug-related intestinal tumor formation was found. Colestipol was not mutagenic in the Ames assay.

Pregnancy/Reproduction
Pregnancy—Studies have not been done in humans. Because colestipol is almost totally unabsorbed after oral administration, adverse effects on the fetus may potentially occur because of impaired maternal absorption of vitamins and nutrients.
Studies have not been done in animals.

Breast-feeding
Problems in humans have not been documented.

Pediatrics
Appropriate studies on the relationship of age to the effects of colestipol have not been performed in the pediatric population. However, use in children under 2 years of age is not recommended since cholesterol is required for normal development.

Geriatrics
Appropriate studies on the relationship of age to the effects of colestipol have not been performed in the geriatric population. However, patients over 60 years of age may be more likely to experience gastrointestinal side effects, as well as adverse nutritional effects.

Drug interactions and/or related problems
The following drug interactions and/or related problems have been selected on the basis of their potential clinical significance (possible mechanism in parentheses where appropriate)—not necessarily inclusive (» = major clinical significance):

Note: Combinations containing any of the following medications, depending on the amount present, may also interact with this medication.

» Anticoagulants, coumarin- or indandione-derivative
(concurrent use may significantly increase the anticoagulant effect as a result of depletion of vitamin K, but colestipol may also bind with oral anticoagulants in the gastrointestinal tract and reduce their effects; administration at least 6 hours before colestipol and adjustment of anticoagulant dosage based on frequent prothrombin-time determinations are recommended)

Chenodiol or
Ursodiol
(effect may be decreased when chenodiol or ursodiol is used concurrently with colestipol, which binds the medication and decreases its absorption and also tends to increase cholesterol saturation of bile)

» Digitalis glycosides
(colestipol may reduce the half-life of these medications by decreasing intestinal reabsorption and enterohepatic circulation; caution is recommended, especially when colestipol is withdrawn from a patient who was stabilized on the digitalis glycoside while receiving colestipol, because of the potential for serious toxicity; some clinicians recommend administration of colestipol approximately 8 hours after the digitalis glycoside)

» Diuretics, thiazide, oral or
» Penicillin G, oral or
» Propranolol, oral or
» Tetracyclines, oral
(concurrent administration with colestipol has been found to impair absorption of these medications; an interval of several hours between administration of colestipol and any of these medications is recommended; effects on absorption of other beta-blockers has not been determined)

» Thyroid hormones, including dextrothyroxine
(concurrent use with colestipol may decrease the effects of thyroid hormones by binding and delaying or preventing absorption; an interval of 4 to 5 hours between administration of the 2 medications and regular monitoring of thyroid function tests are recommended)

» Vancomycin, oral
(colestipol has been shown to bind oral vancomycin significantly when used concurrently, resulting in decreased stool concentrations and marked reduction in antibacterial activity of vancomycin; concurrent use is not recommended; patients should be advised to take oral vancomycin and colestipol several hours apart)

Vitamins, fat-soluble
(colestipol may interfere with absorption of fat-soluble vitamins as a result of its interference with fat absorption; supplemental vitamin A and D in water-miscible or parenteral form are recommended in patients receiving colestipol for prolonged periods; supplemental vitamin K may be required in some patients who develop bleeding tendencies)

Medications, other
(colestipol may delay or reduce absorption of other medications administered concurrently because of its anion-binding activity; administration of other medications 1 to 2 hours before or 4 hours after colestipol is recommended, although absorption of some medications is impaired even then; caution is recommended when colestipol is withdrawn because of the risk of toxicity when suddenly increased absorption of the other medication leads to higher serum concentrations)

Laboratory value alterations
The following have been selected on the basis of their potential clinical significance (possible effect in parentheses where appropriate)—not necessarily inclusive (» = major clinical significance).

With physiology/laboratory test values
Alkaline phosphatase and
Aspartate aminotransferase (AST [SGOT]), serum and
Chloride, serum and
Phosphorus, serum
(concentrations may be increased)

Potassium and
Sodium
(serum concentrations may be decreased)

Prothrombin time (PT)
(may be prolonged)

Medical considerations/Contraindications
The medical considerations/contraindications included have been selected on the basis of their potential clinical significance (reasons given in parentheses where appropriate)—not necessarily inclusive (» = major clinical significance).

Except under special circumstances, this medication should not be used when the following medical problem exists:

» Primary biliary cirrhosis
(may further raise the cholesterol concentration)

Risk-benefit should be considered when the following medical problems exist:

Bleeding disorders and
Gallstones and
Gastrointestinal dysfunction and
Hypothyroidism and
Malabsorption states, especially steatorrhea and
Peptic ulcer
(these conditions may be exacerbated)

» Complete biliary obstruction or complete atresia
(no bile acids in gastrointestinal tract for colestipol to bind)

» Constipation
(risk of fecal impaction)

Coronary artery disease and
Hemorrhoids
(because of the risks associated with severe constipation)

Renal function impairment
(increased risk of development of hyperchloremic acidosis)

Sensitivity to colestipol

Patient monitoring
The following may be especially important in patient monitoring (other tests may be warranted in some patients, depending on condition; » = major clinical significance):

Cholesterol and
Triglyceride
(serum concentration determinations recommended prior to initiation of therapy for hyperlipidemia and every 2 months after stabilization to confirm efficacy and determine that a positive response is maintained)

Prothrombin-time (PT) determinations
(recommended periodically because vitamin K deficiency associated with chronic use of colestipol may increase bleeding tendency)

Side/Adverse Effects

The following side/adverse effects have been selected on the basis of their potential clinical significance (possible signs and symptoms in parentheses where appropriate)—not necessarily inclusive:

Those indicating need for medical attention

Incidence more frequent—about 10%

Constipation—usually mild and transient, but may be severe and lead to fecal impaction

Incidence rare

Gallstones (severe stomach pain with nausea and vomiting); ***gastrointestinal bleeding or peptic ulcer*** (black, tarry stools); ***steatorrhea or malabsorption syndrome, especially with doses greater than 30 grams a day*** (sudden loss of weight)

Those indicating need for medical attention only if they continue or are bothersome

Incidence less frequent

Belching; bloating; diarrhea; dizziness; headache; nausea or vomiting; stomach pain

Patient Consultation

As an aid to patient consultation, refer to *Advice for the Patient, Colestipol (Oral).*

In providing consultation, consider emphasizing the following selected information (» = major clinical significance):

Before using this medication

Diet as preferred therapy; importance of following prescribed diet
This medication does not cure the condition but rather helps control it
» Conditions affecting use, especially:
Sensitivity to colestipol
Use in children—Not recommended in children under 2 years of age since cholesterol is required for normal development
Use in the elderly—Increased incidence of gastrointestinal side effects and adverse nutritional effects in patients over 60 years of age
Other medications, especially anticoagulants, digitalis glycosides, oral penicillin G, oral tetracyclines, oral propranolol, thyroid hormones, thiazide diuretics, or oral vancomycin
Other medical problems, especially primary biliary cirrhosis, complete biliary obstruction or complete atresia, or constipation

Proper use of this medication

» Importance of not taking more or less medication than the amount prescribed
» Compliance with prescribed diet
» Importance of mixing with fluids before taking; instructions for mixing: Stirring until completely mixed (does not dissolve); rinsing glass and drinking to make sure all medication is taken; may also be mixed with milk in cereals, thin soups, or pulpy fruits
» Proper dosing
Missed dose: Taking as soon as possible; not taking if almost time for next dose; not doubling doses
» Proper storage

Precautions while using this medication

» Importance of close monitoring by the physician
» Checking with physician before discontinuing medication; blood lipid concentrations may increase significantly
» Not taking any other medication unless discussed with physician

Side/adverse effects

Signs of potential side effects, especially constipation, gallstones, gastrointestinal bleeding, peptic ulcer, and steatorrhea or malabsorption syndrome

General Dosing Information

To prevent accidental inhalation or esophageal distress with the dry form, it is recommended that colestipol be mixed with at least 90 mL of water or other fluids (i.e., carbonated beverages, flavored drinks, juices, or milk) before being ingested. It may also be taken in soups or with cereals or pulpy fruits.

Reduction in colestipol dosage or withdrawal of the medication may be necessary in some patients if constipation occurs or worsens, to prevent impaction. Administration of a laxative or stool softener or increased fluid intake may be helpful.

For use as an antihyperlipidemic

If a paradoxical increase in plasma cholesterol levels occurs, it is recommended that colestipol therapy be withdrawn.

If response is inadequate after 3 months of treatment, colestipol therapy should be withdrawn, except in the case of xanthoma tuberosum, which may require up to 1 year of treatment as long as reduction in size and/or number of xanthomata occurs.

Oral Dosage Forms

COLESTIPOL HYDROCHLORIDE FOR ORAL SUSPENSION USP

Usual adult dose

Antihyperlipidemic—
Oral, 15 to 30 grams a day before meals in two to four divided doses.

Note: Colestipol has been used to treat digitalis glycoside toxicity at an oral dose of 10 grams, followed by 5 grams every six to eight hours.

Usual pediatric dose

Safety and efficacy have not been established.

Strength(s) usually available

U.S.—
5 grams per packet or level scoop (Rx) [*Colestid*].

Canada—
5 grams per packet or level scoop (Rx) [*Colestid*].

Packaging and storage

Store below 40 °C (104 °F), preferably between 15 and 30 °C (59 and 86 °F), unless otherwise specified by manufacturer. Store in a tight container.

Preparation of dosage form

Colestipol is prepared for administration by adding the measured powder to the liquid and stirring to mix thoroughly (does not dissolve). After the patient drinks the suspension, the glass should be rinsed with more liquid to make sure all the medication is taken. Colestipol may also be mixed with milk in hot or regular breakfast cereals, in thin soups (tomato or chicken noodle), or with pulpy fruits such as pineapples, pears, peaches, or fruit cocktail.

Auxiliary labeling

- Take mixed in cold water or juice.

Selected Bibliography

The Expert Panel. Report of the national cholesterol education program expert panel on detection, evaluation and treatment of high blood cholesterol in adults. Arch Intern Med 1988; 148: 36-69.

NIH Consensus Conference. Lowering blood cholesterol to prevent heart disease. JAMA 1985 Apr 12; 253: 2080-6.

Knodel LC, Talbert RL. Adverse effects of hypolipidaemic drugs. Med Toxicol 1987; 2: 10-32.

Revised: 08/12/1998

COLONY STIMULATING FACTORS Systemic

This monograph includes information on the following: 1) Filgrastim; 2) Sargramostim†.

VA CLASSIFICATION (Primary): BL400

Commonly used brand name(s): *Leukine*[2]; *Neupogen*[1].

Other commonly used names for filgrastim are: Granulocyte colony stimulating factor, recombinant, rG-CSF, recombinant methionyl human granulocyte colony stimulating factor, and r-met HuG-CSF. Other commonly used names for sargramostim are: Granulocyte-macrophage colony stimulating factor, recombinant, recombinant human granulocyte-macrophage colony stimulating factor, rGM-CSF, and rHu GM-CSF.

Note: For a listing of dosage forms and brand names by country availability, see *Dosage Forms* section(s).

†Not commercially available in Canada.

Category

Hematopoietic stimulant; antineutropenic.

Indications

Note: Bracketed information in the *Indications* section refers to uses that are not included in U.S. product labeling.

Accepted

Neutropenia, chemotherapy-related (treatment)—Filgrastim (rG-CSF) and [sargramostim (rGM-CSF)] are indicated to decrease the incidence of infection, as manifested by febrile neutropenia, in patients with non-myeloid malignancies receiving myelosuppressive anticancer drugs associated with a significant incidence of severe neutropenia with fever.

Filgrastim is indicated in adult and [pediatric] cancer patients receiving myelosuppressive chemotherapy.

Sargramostim is indicated for decreasing the duration of neutropenia after the completion of acute myelocytic leukemia (AML) induction chemotherapy in older adult patients (55 years of age and older).

Filgrastim is indicated for decreasing the duration of neutropenia and fever after the completion of AML induction or consolidation chemotherapy in adult patients.

Note: Caution is recommended in patients with myeloid malignancies such as AML because of the potential of colony stimulating factors to stimulate leukemic blasts. Filgrastim and sargramostim are not recommended for administration before or with chemotherapy in patients with AML. Criteria to define patients at increased risk (e.g., those with refractory anemia with excess blasts [RAEB] or refractory anemia with excess blasts in transformation [RAEBT], or cytogenetic abnormality) have been proposed but not established.

The theoretical risk that use of increased doses of chemotherapy permitted by administration of colony stimulating factors may result in an increase in other hematologic or nonhematologic toxicities not affected by colony stimulating factors has not been adequately studied, but caution is recommended.

Myeloid engraftment following bone marrow transplantation, promotion of (treatment adjunct)—Filgrastim is indicated for acceleration of myeloid recovery in patients undergoing autologous or allogeneic BMT following myeloablative chemotherapy for non-myeloid malignancies. [Filgrastim] and sargramostim are indicated for acceleration of myeloid recovery in patients with non-Hodgkin's lymphomas, acute lymphoblastic leukemia, and Hodgkin's disease undergoing autologous bone marrow transplantation (BMT). Sargramostim is indicated for acceleration of myeloid recovery in patients undergoing [autologous] or allogeneic BMT following myeloablative chemotherapy for non-myeloid malignancies. [Filgrastim] and sargramostim are indicated for acceleration of myeloid recovery in patients undergoing allogeneic BMT following myeloablative chemotherapy for myeloid malignancies.

Myeloid engraftment following bone marrow transplantation, failure or delay of (treatment)—[Filgrastim][1] and sargramostim are indicated for prolonging survival in patients who have undergone allogeneic or autologous BMT in whom engraftment is delayed or has failed, in the presence or absence of infection.

Note: Filgrastim and sargramostim are effective in patients receiving unpurged bone marrow or bone marrow purged with monoclonal (e.g., anti-B lymphocyte) antibodies; however, *in vitro* marrow purging with chemical agents may significantly reduce the number of responsive hematopoietic progenitors and prevent a response. The bone marrow purging process should preserve more than 1.2 $\times 10^4$ progenitors per kg of body weight.

The effect may also be limited in patients who received extensive radiotherapy to hematopoietic sites for treatment of primary disease in the abdomen or chest or who have been exposed to multiple myelotoxic agents (alkylating agents, anthracycline antibiotics, and antimetabolites) before autologous BMT.

Peripheral progenitor cell yield, enhancement of (treatment adjunct)—Filgrastimand sargramostim are indicated as adjuncts to enhance peripheral progenitor cell yield in autologous hematopoietic stem cell transplantation. However, the yield (quantity and quality) of peripheral progenitor cells is dependent on the extent of prior chemotherapy.

Myeloid engraftment following hematopoietic stem cell transplantation, promotion of (treatment adjunct)—[Filgrastim]and sargramostim are indicated for acceleration of myeloid recovery in patients who have undergone hematopoietic stem cell transplantation following myeloablative chemotherapy.

[Myeloid engraftment following hematopoietic stem cell transplantation, failure or delay of (treatment)]—Sargramostim is indicated for prolonging survival in patients who have undergone autologous or allogeneic hematopoietic stem cell transplantation in whom engraftment is delayed or has failed, in the presence or absence of infection.

[Neutropenia, AIDS-associated (treatment)]—Filgrastim and sargramostim are indicated to treat acquired immunodeficiency syndrome (AIDS) patients with neutropenia caused by the disease itself or infection with opportunistic organisms (such as cytomegalovirus), or antiretroviral agents (zidovudine, ganciclovir).

The effects of colony stimulating factors on infections, hospitalization, or survival have not been established.

Because there is some evidence that sargramostim (but not filgrastim) may increase human immunodeficiency virus (HIV) replication, it is recommended that sargramostim be given only in combination with an antiretroviral agent.

Ganciclovir is toxic to stem cells. If neutrophil counts decrease despite use of colony stimulating factor, dose reduction or withdrawal of ganciclovir is recommended.

[Myelodysplastic syndromes (treatment)]—Filgrastim[1] and sargramostim are indicated to enhance neutrophil function in patients with myelodysplastic syndromes and a history of infection.

Note: Caution is necessary because of the risk that colony stimulating factors may precipitate transformation of myelodysplastic syndromes into acute myelocytic leukemia. Assessment of risk is complicated by the fact that progression to acute leukemia may occur in the natural course of the disease.

Colony stimulating factors do not have a consistent effect on erythrocytes or platelets in these conditions.

Neutropenia, severe chronic (treatment)—Filgrastimand [sargramostim] are indicated for treatment of severe chronic neutropenia, including congenital neutropenia (Kostmann's syndrome), idiopathic neutropenia, and cyclic neutropenia.

[Neutropenia, drug-induced (treatment)]—Filgrastim[1] and sargramostim are indicated for treatment of drug-induced neutropenia.

Acceptance not established

Use of sargramostim, as a single-agent or in combination therapy, for the treatment of melanoma has not been established.

[1]Not included in Canadian product labeling.

Pharmacology/Pharmacokinetics

Physicochemical characteristics

Source—

Filgrastim (rG-CSF): Synthetic. A protein chain of 175 amino acids produced by a recombinant DNA process involving genetically engineered *Escherichia coli* (the human granulocyte colony stimulating factor gene has been inserted into the bacteria). The protein has an amino acid sequence identical to the sequence in naturally occurring human granulocyte colony stimulating factor (G-CSF), predicted from human DNA sequence analysis, except for the addition of an *N*-terminal methionine necessary for expression in *E. coli*. In addition, unlike G-CSF isolated from a human cell, filgrastim is non-glycosylated. Purification is done by conventional means; prior to final purification, filgrastim is allowed to oxidize to its native state and final purity is achieved by sequential passage over a series of chromatography columns; the product is then formulated in an acetate buffer with mannitol and Tween 80.

Sargramostim (rGM-CSF): Synthetic. The commercially available form is a glycoprotein chain of 127 amino acids, characterized by three primary molecular species, produced by a recombinant DNA process involving a yeast (*S. cerevisiae*) expression system. The amino acid sequence differs from that of natural human granulocyte-macrophage colony stimulating factor (GM-CSF) by a substitution of leucine at position 23, and the carbohydrate moiety may be different. Sargramostim produced in a yeast system is glycosylated; rGM-CSF produced in other systems may not be.

Chemical Group—Related to naturally occurring colony stimulating factors, which are hormone-like glycoprotein growth factors also known as cytokines.

Molecular weight—

Filgrastim: 18,800 daltons.

Sargramostim: Contains three primary molecular species with molecular masses of 19,500, 16,800, and 15,500 daltons.

Mechanism of action/Effect

In general, endogenous colony stimulating factors act on hematopoietic cells by binding to specific cell surface receptors and stimulating proliferation (clonal expansion), differentiation, and some end-cell functional activation. The recombinant colony stimulating factors have the same biological activity as the endogenous hormones. The actions of these growth factors promote differentiation of myeloid progenitor cells into granulocytes and monocytes; other pathways produce erythrocytes and platelets.

Filgrastim is a class II hematopoietic growth factor. It acts on progenitor cells capable of forming only one differentiated cell type—the neutrophil granulocyte; it is said to be lineage-specific. Sargramostim, a class I hematopoietic growth factor, stimulates formation of granulocytes (neutrophils, eosinophils) and macrophages and is therefore non-lineage specific.

Administration of colony stimulating factor to patients whose bone marrow has been depleted by myelotoxic agents or diseases such as acquired immunodeficiency syndrome (AIDS) results in an increased number of circulating hematopoietic progenitor cells. Filgrastim acts only on mature progenitor cells that are already committed to one pathway, the granulocyte pathway, and therefore increases only neutrophil concentrations. Sargramostim acts on progenitor cells at an earlier stage of development and can promote more than one lineage; it promotes formation of granulocyte, macrophage, and mixed granulocyte-macrophage colonies, resulting in increased concentrations of eosinophils and monocytes as well. Neither has a consistent effect on red cell or platelet counts.

Other actions/effects

Colony stimulating factors may have a proliferative effect on myeloid and erythroid leukemic cells. Sargramostim has been reported in some studies to increase replication of human immunodeficiency virus. Sargramostim has been reported to reduce low-density lipoprotein (LDL) concentrations in blood, with a variable effect on high-density lipoproteins (HDL); it has also been reported to transiently decrease cholesterol concentrations. Filgrastim has been reported to decrease serum cholesterol with variable changes in triglycerides; these changes return to normal or near baseline within 1 or 2 weeks after it is withdrawn.

Absorption

Filgrastim or sargramostim—Detected in serum within 5 minutes after subcutaneous administration.

Half-life

Distribution—
- Sargramostim:
  - Intravenous (2-hour infusion)—
    - 12 to 17 minutes.

Elimination—
- Filgrastim:
  - Approximately 3.5 hours.
- Sargramostim:
  - Intravenous (2-hour infusion)—Approximately 1 hour.
  - Subcutaneous—Approximately 3 hours.

Onset of action

Filgrastim—Decrease in circulating neutrophils occurs within the first 5 minutes of intravenous administration; after 4 hours, counts begin to rise, with an initial peak within 24 hours.

Sargramostim—Decrease in circulating neutrophils, eosinophils, and monocytes occurs, with a nadir at 30 minutes, and rebound to baseline or above by 2 hours. In addition, there is an apparent biphasic response over time; an initial plateau in leukocyte counts occurs after 3 to 7 days, which is followed by another increase and another plateau.

Time to peak concentration

Filgrastim—After subcutaneous administration: 2 to 8 hours.

Sargramostim—After subcutaneous administration: 2 hours.

Time to peak effect

Varies according to chemotherapy regimen, underlying disease and prior treatment history, and dose of colony stimulating factor.

Precautions to Consider

Cross-sensitivity and/or related problems

Patients hypersensitive to *Escherichia coli*-derived proteins may also be hypersensitive to filgrastim (rG-CSF).

Patients hypersensitive to yeast-derived products may also be hypersensitive to sargramostim (rGM-CSF).

Carcinogenicity

Studies have not been done.

Mutagenicity

Filgrastim did not induce bacterial gene mutations in either the presence or absence of a drug-metabolizing enzyme system.

Pregnancy/Reproduction

Fertility—

Filgrastim—

No effect has been observed on the fertility of male or female rats or on gestation at doses up to 500 mcg per kg of body weight (mcg/kg).

Sargramostim—

Studies in animals have not been donedue to species specificity of the human protein.

Pregnancy—Adequate and well-controlled studies in humans have not been done. Colony stimulating factors should be used during pregnancy only if the potential benefit justifies the potential risk to the fetus.

Filgrastim—

In pregnant rabbits, adverse effects have been observed at doses of 2 to 10 times the human dose. Studies in rabbits at doses of 80 mcg/kg per day found increased abortion and embryolethality. Studies in rabbits at doses of 80 mcg/kg per day during the period of organogenesis found increased fetal resorption, genitourinary bleeding, developmental abnormalities, and decreased body weight, live births, and food consumption; external abnormalities were not observed in the fetuses. Studies in rats at daily intravenous doses up to 575 mcg/kg per day during the period of organogenesis found no associated lethal, teratogenic, or behavioral effects on fetuses.

FDA Pregnancy Category C.

Sargramostim—

Studies in animals have not been done due to species specificity of the human protein.

FDA Pregnancy Category C.

Breast-feeding

It is not known whether filgrastim or sargramostim is distributed into human breast milk. However, problems in humans have not been documented. Because many drugs are distributed into human milk, caution should be exercised if a colony stimulating factor is administered to a nursing woman.

Pediatrics

Appropriate studies on the relationship of age to the effects of colony stimulating factors have not been performed in the pediatric population. Trials conducted in infants and children showed no differences in pharmacokinetics compared with results of studies in adults.

Although filgrastim is not approved by regulatory agencies in the U.S. for use in pediatric patients, there are some limited data available regarding its use in pediatric patients receiving filgrastim for severe chronic neutropenia. Pediatric patients 4 months to 17 years of age receiving filgrastim for about 18 months did not experience alterations in growth and development, sexual maturation, or endocrine function. Filgrastim was well-tolerated in pediatric patients receiving it for chemotherapy-related neutropenia. One of twelve pediatric patients experienced palpable splenomegaly and another experienced musculoskeletal pain. The safety and efficacy in neonates and patients with autoimmune neutropenia of infancy have not been established. In Canada, clinical data, in pediatric patients with neutropenia resulting from myelosuppressive chemotherapy, indicate that safety of filgrastim is similar in both adults and children receiving cytotoxic chemotherapy.

Although sargramostim is not approved by regulatory agencies for use in pediatric patients, there are some limited data available regarding its use in this population. Pediatric patients 4 months to 18 years of age have received sargramostim intravenously in doses of 60 to 1000 mcg per square meter of body surface area or subcutaneously in doses of 4 to 1500 mcg per square meter of body surface area. Pediatric patients receiving intravenously administered sargramostim 250 mcg per square meter of body surface area experienced side effects similar in type and frequency to those occurring in adult patients.

Sargramostim liquid injection contains benzyl alcohol. Administration of excessive amounts of benzyl alcohol to neonates has been associated with neurological and other complications.

Geriatrics

Appropriate studies on the relationship of age to the effects of colony stimulating factors have not been performed in the geriatric population. However, studies commonly include older patients, and geriatrics-specific problems that would limit the usefulness of these medications in the elderly are not expected.

Drug interactions and/or related problems

The following drug interactions and/or related problems have been selected on the basis of their potential clinical significance (possible mechanism in parentheses where appropriate)—not necessarily inclusive (» = major clinical significance):

» Chemotherapy or
» Cytotoxic chemotherapy or
» Radiation therapy

(filgrastim should not be administered in the period 24 hours before through 24 hours after cytotoxic chemotherapy administration; use of filgrastim in patients receiving chemotherapy associated with delayed myelosuppression has not been established; concurrent use of filgrastim with chemotherapy and radiation therapy should be avoided)

Lithium
(should be used with caution; concurrent use with filgrastim may potentiate release of neutrophils)

Laboratory value alterations

The following have been selected on the basis of their potential clinical significance (possible effect in parentheses where appropriate)—not necessarily inclusive (» = major clinical significance).

With physiology/laboratory test values

For filgrastim and sargramostim

Blood pressure
(transient decreases occur uncommonly; hypotension has been associated with a rare "first-dose reaction" to sargramostim)

For filgrastim only (in addition to the above)

Alkaline phosphatase, leukocyte (LAP scores) and serum values and
Lactic dehydrogenase (LDH), serum values and
Uric acid, serum concentrations
(commonly increased in patients receiving filgrastim; the increases coincide with the rise in neutrophil counts. Concentrations return to normal within 1 or 2 weeks after withdrawal of filgrastim)

For sargramostim only (in addition to the above)

Albumin, serum
(decreases have been reported during sargramostim therapy; possibly related to capillary leak syndrome)
Bilirubin, serum concentrations and
Creatinine, serum concentrations and
Hepatic enzymes, serum values
(reportedly increased by sargramostim in some patients with renal or hepatic function impairment)

Medical considerations/Contraindications

The medical considerations/contraindications included have been selected on the basis of their potential clinical significance (reasons given in parentheses where appropriate)—not necessarily inclusive (» = major clinical significance).

Except under special circumstances, this medication should not be used when the following medical problem exists:

» Hypersensitivity to the colony stimulating factor prescribed or any component of the product, to any other colony stimulating factor, or to E. coli-derived proteins

Risk-benefit should be considered when the following medical problems exist:

For filgrastim and sargramostim

Autoimmune disease, history of, e.g., autoimmune thrombocytopenia
or
Inflammatory conditions, e.g., vasculitis
(may be exacerbated)
Cardiovascular disease, pre-existing
(supraventricular arrhythmia has been reported occasionally in patients receiving sargramostim, especially in patients with a history of cardiac arrhythmia; myocardial infarction and arrhythmias have been reported with filgrastim)
» Excessive leukemic myeloid blasts in the bone marrow or peripheral blood (10% or more)
(growth of leukemic blasts may be stimulated by colony stimulating factors, especially at high doses)
Sepsis
(theoretical potential of adult respiratory distress syndrome as a result of possible influx of neutrophils at the site of inflammation)

For filgrastim only (in addition to the above)

Chronic myeloid leukemia (CML) or
Myelodysplasia
(safety of filgrastim has not been established; the possibility that filgrastim can act as a growth factor for any tumor type can not be excluded)
» Sickle cell disease
(severe sickle cell crises, some resulting in death, have been associated with filgrastim use in patients with sickle cell disease; only physicians qualified by specialized training in the treatment of these patients should prescribe filgrastim after careful consideration of the potential risks and benefits)

For sargramostim only (in addition to the above)

Congestive heart failure or
Fluid retention, pre-existing (including peripheral edema, capillary leak syndrome, pleural and/or pericardial effusion) or
Pulmonary infiltrates
(sargramostim may aggravate fluid retention)
Hepatic function impairment or
Renal function impairment
(elevation of serum creatinine or bilirubin and hepatic enzymes by sargramostim has been reported; monitoring of function is recommended at least biweekly during treatment)
Pulmonary disease, including hypoxia
(caution is recommended because sargramostim causes sequestration of granulocytes in the pulmonary circulation; dyspnea has been reported)
» Hypersensitivity to yeast-derived proteins

Patient monitoring

The following may be especially important in patient monitoring (other tests may be warranted in some patients, depending on condition; » = major clinical significance):

For filgrastim and sargramostim

Cardiac monitoring
(recommended in patients with pre-existing cardiac conditions)
» Complete blood count (CBC) with differential (including examination for the presence of blast cells) and
Platelet counts
(recommended twice weekly during treatment to monitor the neutrophil count to assess the hematopoietic response and avoid excessive leukocytosis; recommended prior to chemotherapy; recommended at least 3 times per week after bone marrow transplantation)
Hepatic function and/or
Renal function
(monitoring recommended at least biweekly in patients with hepatic and/or renal function impairment)

For filgrastim only (in addition to the above)

Adult respiratory distress syndrome (ARDS)
(neutropenic patients with sepsis receiving filgrastim who develop fever, lung infiltrates, or respiratory distress should be evaluated for ARDS; if ARDS occurs, therapy should be discontinued or withheld until resolution and patients should receive appropriate medical management for this condition)

For sargramostim only (in addition to the above)

Body weight and
Hydration status
(recommended during treatment with sargramostim)

Side/Adverse Effects

Note: There are relatively few side/adverse effects directly associated with colony stimulating factor administration alone. Most side/adverse effects reported are due to the underlying malignancy or cytotoxic therapy. Neutropenic effects caused by cytotoxic therapy (fever, infection, mucositis) are decreased in frequency when a colony stimulating factor is used. Only those side/adverse effects specifically caused by colony stimulating factor are listed below.

Development of antibodies to filgrastim (rG-CSF) has not been detected during treatment in 500 patients for up to almost 2 years and no blunting or diminishing of response has occurred. Neutralizing antibodies have been detected in 5 of 165 patients (3%) treated with sargramostim (rGM-CSF); because all 5 had impaired hematopoiesis prior to treatment, assessment of the effect of antibody development on normal hematopoiesis was not possible.

The following side/adverse effects have been selected on the basis of their potential clinical significance (possible signs and symptoms in parentheses where appropriate)—not necessarily inclusive:

Those indicating need for medical attention

For filgrastim

Incidence less frequent

Excessive leukocytosis—usually asymptomatic; ***redness or pain at site of subcutaneous injection***

Incidence rare;

Allergic or anaphylactic reaction (wheezing); ***splenomegaly***—usually asymptomatic; ***supraventricular arrhythmia, transient*** (rapid or irregular heartbeat); ***Sweet's syndrome*** (fever; sores on skin); ***vasculitis*** (sores on skin)

Note: *Splenomegaly* has been reported in patients receiving filgrastim for cyclic neutropenia. Subclinical splenomegaly occurs in approximately one third of patients and clinical splenomegaly in about 3% of patients receiving chronic treatment with filgrastim.

Rare cases of splenic rupture have been reported following the administration of filgrastim in both healthy donors and patients. Some of these cases were fatal. Individuals receiving filgrastim who report left upper abdominal and/or shoulder tip pain should be evaluated for an enlarged spleen or splenic rupture.

Adult respiratory distress syndrome (ARDS) with symptoms of shortness of breath, tightness in chest. troubled breathing, and wheezing, has been reported in neutropenic patients with sepsis receiving filgrastim, and is postulated to be secondary to an influx of neutrophils to sites of inflammation in the lungs. In the event that ARDS occurs, filgrastim should be discontinued until resolution and patients should receive appropriate medical management for this condition.

Sweet's syndrome (also known as acute febrile neutrophilic dermatosis) appears to coincide with the increase in neutrophils.

For sargramostim

Incidence less frequent

Capillary leak syndrome, including fluid retention, peripheral edema, or pleural and/or pericardial effusion (swelling of feet or lower legs; sudden weight gain; shortness of breath); ***fever; excessive leukocytosis***—usually asymptomatic; ***redness or pain at site of subcutaneous injection; shortness of breath***

Note: *Capillary leak syndrome* is dose-related and dose-limiting; pleural and/or pericardial effusion usually occurs at doses above 32 mcg per kg of body weight per day. Fluid retention occurs at usual doses.

Fever is usually mild and dose-related. It occurs in about 50% of patients. It is not related to leukopenia, but may complicate assessment of fever associated with neutropenia. Fever resolves on withdrawal of sargramostim or administration of antipyretics such as acetaminophen.

Shortness of breath may be the result of sequestration of granulocytes in the pulmonary circulation. An adult respiratory distress syndrome has been reported.

Incidence rare

Allergic or anaphylactic reaction (wheezing); ***pericarditis*** (chest pain; shortness of breath); ***supraventricular arrhythmia, transient*** (rapid or irregular heartbeat); ***thrombophlebitis***—may occur during continuous infusion into small veins; ***thromboses around tip of venous catheter; vasculitis*** (sores on skin)

Note: *Pericarditis* is a dose-limiting effect.

Development of *thromboses* is a dose-limiting effect.

Those indicating need for medical attention only if they continue or are bothersome

For filgrastim and sargramostim

Incidence more frequent

Arthralgias or myalgias (pain in joints or muscles); ***medullary bone pain*** (pain in lower back or pelvis; pain in arms or legs); ***mild to moderate headache; skin rash or itching***

Note: *Arthralgias or myalgias* seem to occur when granulocyte counts are returning to normal. Pain usually occurs in the lower extremities.

Bone pain is usually mild to moderate and is alleviated by analgesics. It occurs in 20 to 50% of patients and is dose-related. It disappears within hours after withdrawal of colony stimulating factor, but usually resolves even with continued treatment. Bone pain is probably secondary to bone marrow expansion; it occurs over the 1- to 3-day period before myeloid recovery and the rise in peripheral blood neutrophils. It originates from sites containing bone marrow, including the sternum, spine, pelvis, and long bones.

Skin rash is usually generalized and mild.

For sargramostim only (in addition to the above)

Incidence less frequent or rare;

First-dose reaction, with flushing, hypotension, and syncope (flushing of face; dizziness or faintness); ***weakness***

Note: The *first-dose reaction* does not recur with the first dose of each course, although it may occur with the first dose of more than one course. The first-dose reaction has been described more consistently with bacterially-derived GM-CSF (molgramostim; not commercially available), and included tachycardia, musculoskeletal pain, and dyspnea.

Overdose

There are no data on massive overdoses of filgrastim or sargramostim. However, sargramostim was administered to four patients at dosages sixteen times the recommended dose for 7 to 18 days in an uncontrolled study.

For more information on the management of overdose or unintentional ingestion, **contact a Poison Control Center** (see *Poison Control Center Listing*).

Clinical effects of overdose

The following effects have been selected on the basis of their potential clinical significance (possible signs and symptoms in parentheses where appropriate)—not necessarily inclusive:

Acute and chronic

Chills; dyspnea (shortness of breath); ***excessive leukocytosis***—usually asymptomatic; ***fever; headache; malaise*** (general feeling of bodily discomfort); ***nausea; skin rash; tachycardia*** (rapid heartbeat)

Treatment of overdose

Treatment of sargramostim overdose—

Specific treatment: Sargramostim should be discontinued.

Monitoring: Respiratory status and white blood cell counts should be monitored.

Patients in whom intentional overdose is confirmed or suspected should be referred for psychiatric consultation.

Patient Consultation

As an aid to patient consultation, refer to *Advice for the Patient, Colony Stimulating Factors (Systemic).*

In providing consultation, consider emphasizing the following selected information (» = major clinical significance):

Before using this medication

» Conditions affecting use, especially:

Hypersensitivity to the colony stimulating factor prescribed or any of its components, to any other colony stimulating factor, or to E. coli-derived proteins

Pregnancy—Risk benefit should be considered

Breast-feeding—Caution should be exercised

Use in children—Filgrastim—Safety and efficacy not established in neonates and patients with autoimmune neutropenia of infancy

Sargramostim—Solution for injection may contain benzyl alcohol; use in neonates should be avoided due to neurologic and other complications

Other medications, especially cytotoxic chemotherapy, chemotherapy, or radiation therapy

Other medical problems, especially sickle cell disease (for filgrastim)

Proper use of this medication

For subcutaneous use

» Compliance with therapy

» Reading patient directions carefully with regard to
- Preparation of the injection
- Use of disposable syringes
- Proper administration technique
- Stability of the injection

» Proper dosing

Missed dose: Checking with physician

» Proper storage

Precautions while using this medication

» Importance of close monitoring by physician

» Telling physician right away if signs or symptoms of infection (fever, chills) occur

» Reporting left upper abdominal and/or shoulder tip pain to the physician immediately. These could be symptoms of an enlarged spleen or splenic rupture.

» Checking with doctor if shortness of breath, tightness in chest. troubled breathing, or wheezing occur; these could be symptoms of adult respiratory distress syndrome (ARDS)

Possibility of mild bone pain as bone marrow begins to recover; usually relieved by mild analgesics; checking with physician if severe

Side/adverse effects

Signs of potential side effects, especially

For filgrastim—Redness or pain at site of subcutaneous injection, allergic or anaphylactic reaction, arrhythmias, Sweet's syndrome and other dermatoses, and splenic rupture

(For sargramostim—Fluid retention, peripheral edema, pleural and/or pericardial effusion, fever, redness or pain at site of subcutaneous injection, shortness of breath, allergic or anaphylactic reaction, arrhythmias, pericarditis, and Sweet's syndrome and other dermatoses)

General Dosing Information

Patients receiving colony stimulating factor should be under supervision of a physician experienced in cytokine and/or cancer chemotherapy.

It is recommended that appropriate precautions be taken in the event that an allergic reaction occurs. If a serious allergic or anaphylactic reaction occurs, colony stimulating factor should be immediately discontinued and appropriate therapy initiated.

It is recommended that colony stimulating factor be discontinued when the absolute neutrophil count (ANC) reaches or exceeds 10,000 per cubic millimeter after the ANC nadir has occurred, to avoid excessive leukocytosis.

Colony stimulating factor should not be administered within 24 hours before or after administration of the last dose of chemotherapy or within 12 hours before or after radiotherapy, because of potential sensitivity of rapidly dividing hematopoietic progenitor cells to cytotoxic chemotherapy or radiologic therapies.

FILGRASTIM

Summary of Differences

Pharmacology/pharmacokinetics: Mechanism of action—Lineage-specific; stimulates production of neutrophil granulocytes.

Laboratory value alterations: Alkaline phosphatase, lactic dehydrogenase, uric acid.

Medical considerations/contraindications: Hypersensitivity to *Escherichia coli* derived proteins.

Side/adverse effects: Causes splenomegaly with chronic use, Sweet's syndrome; development of antibodies not reported.

Additional Dosing Information

Filgrastim may be administered subcutaneously (by rapid injection or as a continuous 24-hour infusion) or intravenously (as a short 30-minute or continuous 24-hour infusion). *Intravenous administration should be by infusion over at least 30 minutes*, because there is a decrease in efficacy when filgrastim is administered by rapid intravenous injection; in addition, it is preferable not to flush the intravenous line after administration is complete.

A variety of dosage schedules are used, depending on the indication and the individual patient, for indications not included in the official labeling. The prescriber may consult the medical literature in choosing a specific dosage.

The chemotherapy-induced nadir usually occurs 2 or 3 days earlier during cycles in which filgrastim is administered.

Bone pain usually responds to treatment with non-narcotic analgesics; infrequently, it may be severe enough to require narcotic analgesics.

Parenteral Dosage Forms

Note: Bracketed information in the *Dosage Forms* section refers to uses that are not included in U.S. product labeling.

FILGRASTIM INJECTION

Usual adult dose

Neutropenia, chemotherapy-related—

Intravenous or subcutaneous, 5 mcg (0.005 mg) per kg of body weight once a day via continuous intravenous (IV) infusion or subcutaneous (SC) infusion *or* given by short-duration IV infusion (15 to 30 minutes) or SC bolus injection, beginning no earlier than twenty-four hours after administration of the last dose of cytotoxic chemotherapy and not during the period twenty-four hours before the administration of chemotherapy. This is continued for up to two weeks, until the absolute neutrophil count (ANC) reaches ten thousand per cubic millimeter following the nadir; in patients receiving dose-intensified chemotherapy, filgrastim should be continued until two consecutive ANC's of at least ten thousand per cubic millimeter are documented. Dosage may be increased, if necessary, in increments of 5 mcg (0.005 mg) per kg of body weight for each chemotherapy cycle.

Myeloid engraftment following bone marrow transplantation, promotion of—

Intravenous infusion (over four or twenty-four hours) or by continuous subcutaneous infusion (over twenty-four hours), 10 mcg (0.01 mg) per kg of body weight a day for twenty-one days beginning not less than twenty-four hours after bone marrow infusion, and not less than twenty-four hours after the last dose of chemotherapy. When the ANC reaches one thousand per cubic millimeter for three consecutive days, the dose of filgrastim may be lowered to 5 mcg (0.005 mg) per kg of body weight a day. If the ANC exceeds one thousand per cubic millimeter for three more additional days, filgrastim may be discontinued. If the ANC subsequently falls below one thousand per cubic millimeter, filgrastim may be resumed at 5 mcg (0.005 mg) per kg of body weight a day. If ANC decreases to less than one thousand per cubic millimeter at any time while the patient is receiving 5 mcg (0.005 mg) per kg of body weight a day, the dose may be increased to 10 mcg (0.01 mg) per kg of body weight a day.

[Myeloid engraftment following bone marrow transplantation, failure or delay of (treatment)][1]—

Intravenous or subcutaneous, 5 mcg (0.005 mg) per kg of body weight a day for fourteen days; course of therapy may be repeated after seven days if engraftment has not occurred. If engraftment has not occurred within seven days after the second fourteen-day course of therapy, a course of 10 mcg (0.01 mg) per kg of body weight a day for fourteen days may be tried.

[Myeloid engraftment following hematopoietic stem cell transplantation, promotion of]—

Subcutaneous, continuous or intermittent injection, or intravenous infusion, 5 mcg (0.005 mg) per kg of body weight a day.

Peripheral progenitor cell yield, enhancement of—

Subcutaneous, continuous or intermittent injection, 10 mcg (0.01 mg) per kg of body weight a day for at least four days prior to the first leukapheresis, and continuing until the last leukapheresis.

Note: The optimal schedule of filgrastim administration and leukapheresis has not been established. The administration of filgrastim for six or seven days, with leukapheresis on days five, six, and seven, was found to be effective in clinical trials.

[Neutropenia, AIDS-associated]—

Subcutaneously, 1 mcg (0.001 mg) per kg of body weight a day or 300 mcg (0.003 mg) three times per week until a normal neutrophil count is reached and maintained (ANC ≥ two thousand per cubic millimeter). Dose adjustments may be needed based on subsequent ANC monitoring.

Neutropenia, severe chronic—

Congenital neutropenia—

Subcutaneous, 6 mcg (0.006 mg) per kg of body weight two times a day.

Idiopathic or cyclic neutropenia—

Subcutaneous, 5 mcg (0.005 mg) per kg of body weight a day.

Note: The dose should be adjusted based on the clinical condition of the patient and the ANC. In some clinical trials, the target ANC was fifteen hundred per cubic millimeter.

Note: The calculated dose may be rounded off, within reason, to the nearest vial size (300 or 480 mcg) to reduce wastage.

Usual adult prescribing limits

Not defined. Patients have received doses as high as 115 mcg (0.115 mg) per kg of body weight a day without toxic effects.

Usual pediatric dose

[Neutropenia, chemotherapy-related]—

Subcutaneous, 5 mcg per kg of body weight once a day.

Strength(s) usually available

U.S.—

300 mcg (0.3 mg) per mL (300 mcg per 1-mL vial or 480 mcg per 1.6-mL vial) (Rx) [*Neupogen* (acetate 0.59 mg per mL; mannitol 50 mg per mL; 0.004% of Tween 80; sodium 0.035 mg per mL)].

Canada—

300 mcg (0.3 mg) per mL (300 mcg per 1-mL vial or 480 mcg per 1.6-mL vial) (Rx) [*Neupogen* (acetate 0.59 mg per mL; 0.004% of Tween 80; sodium 0.035 mg per mL)].

Note: The specific activity is $1 \pm 0.6 \times 10^8$ Units per mg as measured by a cell mitogenesis assay.

Packaging and storage

Store between 2 and 8 °C (36 and 46 °F), unless otherwise specified by manufacturer. Protect from freezing. Avoid shaking.

Preparation of dosage form

Filgrastim injection may be diluted for administration by intravenous infusion in 5% dextrose injection to produce a concentration greater than or equal to 15 mcg of filgrastim per mL, but not recommended for a final dilution concentration less than 5 mcg of filgrastim per mL. If the final concentration is to be between 5 and 15 mcg per mL, addition of human albumin to the dextrose injection before addition of filgrastim injection is necessary to prevent adsorption to the components of the drug delivery system. The concentration of human albumin in the final solution should be 0.2% (2 mg per mL); this can be achieved with 2 mL of 5% human albumin in 50 mL of 5% dextrose injection.

Stability

Filgrastim injection contains no preservative. Before use, filgrastim injection may be allowed to reach room temperature for a maximum of 6 hours; after that period of time, the vial should be discarded.

Incompatibilities

Filgrastim injection is not compatible with sodium chloride-containing solutions, as product may precipitate.

Auxiliary labeling

- Do not shake.

[1]Not included in Canadian product labeling.

SARGRAMOSTIM

Summary of Differences

Pharmacology/pharmacokinetics: Mechanism of action—Non-lineage specific; stimulates production of granulocytes, macrophages, and eosinophils.

Laboratory value alterations: Serum albumin, bilirubin, serum creatinine, hepatic enzymes.

Medical considerations/contraindications: Congestive heart failure, hepatic or renal function impairment, pulmonary disease.

Patient monitoring: Body weight, hydration status.

Side/adverse effects: Causes capillary leak syndrome and fluid retention, fever, shortness of breath, pericarditis, thrombophlebitis, thromboses, first-dose reaction, and weakness.

Additional Dosing Information

Sargramostim is administered as an intravenous infusion via a central venous line. An in-line membrane filter should not be used. Sargramostim also may be administered subcutaneously.

A variety of dosage schedules are used, depending on the indication and the individual patient, for indications not included in the official labeling. The prescriber may consult the medical literature in choosing a specific dosage.

Systemic adverse effects (bone pain, fever, asthenia, etc.) are usually prevented or reversed by administration of analgesics and antipyretics such as acetaminophen.

Fluid retention is reversible on withdrawal or dose reduction, with or without diuretic treatment.

If dyspnea occurs during sargramostim administration, the rate of administration should be reduced by half. The standard dosing schedule may be used, with careful monitoring, for subsequent infusions. If dyspnea persists following infusion rate reduction, the infusion should be discontinued.

If the absolute neutrophil count (ANC) exceeds 20,000 or the platelet count exceeds 500,000, sargramostim treatment should be discontinued or the dose reduced by half. Excessive blood counts usually return to normal or baseline levels within 3 to 7 days following withdrawal of sargramostim.

If progression of the underlying neoplastic disease (non-Hodgkin's lymphoma, acute lymphocytic leukemia, Hodgkin's disease) occurs during sargramostim therapy, it is recommended that sargramostim be discontinued.

If blast cells appear, it is recommended that sargramostim be discontinued.

Parenteral Dosage Forms

Note: Bracketed information in the *Dosage Forms* section refers to uses that are not included in U.S. product labeling.

SARGRAMOSTIM FOR INJECTION

Usual adult dose

Myeloid engraftment following bone marrow transplantation, promotion of—
Intravenous infusion (over two hours) or subcutaneous, 250 mcg (0.25 mg) per square meter of body surface area a day for twenty-one days beginning two to four hours after allogeneic or autologous bone marrow infusion, and not less than twenty-four hours after the last dose of chemotherapy or radiotherapy and continued until an absolute neutrophil count (ANC) of fifteen hundred per cubic millimeter is achieved and maintained for three consecutive days.

Myeloid engraftment following hematopoietic stem cell transplantation, promotion of—
Intravenous infusion (continuous) or subcutaneous, 250 mcg (0.25 mg) per square meter of body surface area a day through the period of peripheral blood progenitor cell (PBPC) collection, then immediately following infusion of progenitor cells and continued until an ANC of fifteen hundred per cubic millimeter is achieved and maintained for three consecutive days.

Myeloid engraftment following bone marrow transplantation, failure or delay of—
Intravenous infusion (over two hours) or subcutaneous, 250 mcg (0.25 mg) per square meter of body surface area a day for fourteen days; course of therapy may be repeated after seven days if engraftment has not occurred. If engraftment has not occurred within seven days after the second fourteen-day course of therapy, a course of 500 mcg (0.5 mg) per square meter of body surface area a day for fourteen days may be tried.

Neutropenia, chemotherapy-related, in older adult patients (55 years of age and older) with acute myelocytic leukemia (AML)—
Intravenous infusion (over four hours) or subcutaneous, 250 mcg (0.25 mg) per square meter of body surface area a day beginning approximately on day eleven (or four days after completion of induction chemotherapy) if the bone marrow is hypoplastic with fewer than five percent blasts on day ten.

[Neutropenia, chemotherapy-related]—
Intravenous infusion (over two hours) or subcutaneous, 250 mcg (0.25 mg) per square meter of body surface area a day beginning no earlier than twenty-four hours after administration of the last dose of cytotoxic chemotherapy. This is continued for up to two weeks, until the ANC reaches ten thousand per cubic millimeter following the nadir; in patients receiving dose-intensified chemotherapy, sargramostim should be continued until two consecutive ANC's of at least ten thousand per cubic millimeter are documented. Dosage may be increased, if necessary, in an increment of 250 mcg (0.25 mg) per square meter of body surface area, up to 500 mcg (0.5 mg) per square meter of body surface area.

Peripheral progenitor cell yield, enhancement of—
Intravenous infusion (continuous) or subcutaneous, 250 mcg (0.25 mg) per square meter of body surface area a day through the period of peripheral blood progenitor cell (PBPC) collection, then immediately following infusion of progenitor cells and continued until an ANC of fifteen hundred per cubic millimeter is achieved and maintained for three consecutive days.

Note: The calculated dose may be rounded off, within reason, to the nearest vial size (250 or 500 mcg) to reduce wastage.

Usual pediatric dose

Dosage has not been established.

Strength(s) usually available

U.S.—
250 mcg (0.25 mg) (Rx) [*Leukine* (lyophilized; mannitol 40 mg; sucrose 10 mg; tromethamine 1.2 mg)].
500 mcg (0.5 mg) (Rx) [*Leukine* (lyophilized; mannitol 40 mg; sucrose 10 mg; tromethamine 1.2 mg)].

Canada—
Not commercially available.

Note: The specific activity is approximately 5×10^7 colony forming units per mg in a normal human bone marrow colony formation assay.

Packaging and storage

Store between 2 and 8 °C (36 and 46 °F), unless otherwise specified by manufacturer. Protect reconstituted solution from freezing. Avoid shaking solution.

Preparation of dosage form

Lyophilized sargramostim for injection is reconstituted by adding 1 mL of sterile water for injection (without preservative) to the vial containing 250 or 500 mcg, producing a clear, colorless solution containing 250 or 500 mcg of sargramostim per mL, respectively. To avoid foaming during dissolution, the diluent should be directed at the side of the vial and the contents swirled gently; excessive or vigorous agitation should be avoided; the vial should not be shaken.

The reconstituted solution is diluted further for administration by intravenous infusion with 0.9% sodium chloride injection. If the final concentration of sargramostim is to be less than 10 mcg per mL, addition of human albumin to the saline before addition of sargramostim solution is necessary to prevent adsorption to the components of the drug delivery system. The concentration of human albumin in the final solution should be 0.1% (1 mg per mL); this can be achieved with 1 mL of 5% human albumin in 50 mL of 0.9% sodium chloride injection.

Stability

Because lyophilized sargramostim contains no antibacterial preservative, solutions reconstituted with sterile water for injection (without preservative) should be used within 6 hours and any unused portion should be discarded. Lyophilized sargramostim reconstituted with bacteriostatic water for injection may be stored for 20 days between 2 and 8 °C (36 and 46 °F).

Auxiliary labeling

- Do not shake.

SARGRAMOSTIM INJECTION

Usual adult dose

See *Sargramostim for Injection.*

Usual pediatric dose

Dosage has not been established.

Strength(s) usually available

U.S.—

500 mcg (0.5 mg) per mL (Rx) [*Leukine* (benzyl alcohol 1.1%; mannitol 40 mg; sucrose 10 mg; tromethamine 1.2 mg)].

Canada—

Not commercially available.

Packaging and storage

Store between 2 and 8 °C (36 and 46 °F), unless otherwise specified by manufacturer. Protect reconstituted solution from freezing.

Preparation of dosage form

Sargramostim injection for administration by intravenous infusion is diluted with 0.9% sodium chloride injection. The solution should not be shaken. If the final concentration of sargramostim is to be less than 10 mcg per mL, it is necessary to add human albumin to the saline before addition of sargramostim solution in order to prevent adsorption of sargramostim onto the components of the drug delivery system. The concentration of human albumin in the final solution should be 0.1% (1 mg per mL); this can be achieved with 1 mL of 5% human albumin in 50 mL of 0.9% sodium chloride injection.

Stability

After the vial has been entered, undiluted sargramostim injection may be stored for 20 days between 2 and 8 °C (36 and 46 °F). Unopened vials of sargramostim injection are stable for 14 days when stored at 30 °C (86 °F). After dilution with 0.9% sodium chloride injection in polyvinyl chloride bags to final concentrations of sargramostim of 2.5 mcg per mL (mcg/mL), 8 mcg/mL, or 12 mcg/mL, sargramostim injection may be stored for 48 hours between 2 and 8 °C (36 and 46 °F) or 25 °C (77 °F).

Auxiliary labeling

- Do not shake.

Revised: 03/25/2005

CONJUGATED ESTROGENS AND MEDROXYPROGESTERONE FOR OVARIAN HORMONE THERAPY (OHT) Systemic

Note: For information pertaining to the use of only estrogens or progestins, see *Estrogens (Systemic)* or *Progestins (Systemic).*

This monograph includes information on the following: 1) Conjugated Estrogens, and Conjugated Estrogens and Medroxyprogesterone†; 2) Conjugated Estrogens and Medroxyprogesterone.

VA CLASSIFICATION (Primary/Secondary):

Conjugated Estrogens—HS102/MS900

Conjugated Estrogens and Medroxyprogesterone Acetate—HS105/MS900

Commonly used brand name(s): *Premphase*[1]; *Premplus*[2]; *Prempro*[2].

Note: For a listing of dosage forms and brand names by country availability, see *Dosage Forms* section(s).

†Not commercially available in Canada.

Category

Estrogen-progestin; osteoporosis prophylactic; ovarian hormone therapy agent.

Indications

General Considerations

Estrogen deficiency in women without a uterus is best treated with unopposed estrogen therapy; combined estrogen-progestin therapy is not needed.

Accepted

Menopause, vasomotor symptoms of (treatment) or
Vaginitis, atrophic (treatment) or
Vulvar atrophy (treatment)—Conjugated estrogens and medroxyprogesterone tablets are indicated to treat symptoms of estrogen deficiency, including vasomotor symptoms of menopause, atrophic vaginitis, and vulvar atrophy. The progestin component, medroxyprogesterone acetate, is given only to modify estrogen's effect on the uterus, significantly reducing the incidence of endometrial hyperplasia.

Osteoporosis, postmenopausal (prophylaxis)—Conjugated estrogens and medroxyprogesterone are indicated to prevent osteoporosis due to estrogen deficiency in postmenopausal women who have a uterus. Proper diet, calcium supplementation, and physical activity also help lower the risk of osteoporosis. Although in one study estrogen reduced the rate of bone loss when it was given 6 years after the onset of menopause, the greatest benefit is achieved when treatment is initiated at menopause. Patient selection must be individualized according to the risks and benefits, and periodically re-evaluated for discontinuation when long-term treatment is prescribed. Although studies show that progestins positively influence bone density in postmenopausal women, a progestin is given mainly to oppose the effects of estrogen on the uterus; adding a progestin to increase bone mass is not warranted.

Unaccepted

Although a few studies show that estrogens have some effect on neurotransmitters and may improve memory and cognitive function, estrogen and progestin therapy is not indicated or effective in the treatment of clinical depression.

Estrogens and progestins should not be used for the prevention of cardiovascular disease.

Pharmacology/Pharmacokinetics

Physicochemical characteristics

Source—Conjugated estrogens are a mixture of many estrogenic substances found in equine urine; the complete profile of the mixture is not known. The primary estrogens are considered to be sodium estrone sulfate and sodium equilin sulfate. Other estrogens defined as concomitant components are the sodium sulfated conjugates of 17-alpha-dihydroequilin, 17-alpha-estradiol, and 17-beta-dihydroequilin.

Chemical Group—Estrogen: Conjugated estrogens.Progestin: Medroxyprogesterone acetate.

Molecular weight—Medroxyprogesterone acetate: 386.53.

Mechanism of action/Effect

Estrogen-progestin—

Both hormones diffuse into the nucleus of cells and bind to DNA via the receptor proteins; and, either a transcription process begins—messenger RNA (mRNA) increases, resulting in subsequent protein synthesis—or a transrepression process occurs. Transrepression occurs if transcription is not properly stimulated, resulting in no gene expression or protein synthesis. According to the cell's genetic makeup, the two hormones can affect different target tissues or dissimilarly affect the same responsive tissue. Depending on the target tissue, an increased concentration of a hormone can enhance, impede, or even negate its own effect (negative feedback mechanisms) or influence the effect of other hormones (either via receptor downregulation or upregulation). The magnitude of estrogen's effect and its influence with different hormones depends on the endogenous estrogen concentration, product formulation, and type and dose of exogenous estrogen administered. For example, medroxyprogesterone reduces the number of estrogen receptors in the uterus and reduces estrogen's effect on DNA. In the absence of the estrogen effect, protein synthesis decreases and endometrial proliferation is decreased or stopped, depending on the estrogen and progestin doses.

Ovarian hormone therapy agent—

Tissues especially responsive to estrogens include female urogenital organs, breasts, hypothalamus, and pituitary; breast and uterine tissues are especially responsive to progestins. Estrogens maintain tone and elasticity of the urogenital structures, improving tissue function. Women taking physiologic doses of estrogen during menopause experience less urinary urgency or stress incontinence, burning on urination, irritation or inflammation of the vagina or vulva, and vaginal dryness. Use of continuous or cyclic progestin with estrogen lessens hyperplastic changes of the endometrium either by inducing menstrual-like periods to slough off endometrial lining or by producing endometrial atrophy. Amenorrhea occurs over time. In addition, estrogens in physiologic doses given to postmenopausal women restore their vasomotor stability with fewer hot flushes.

Osteoporosis prophylactic—

Although the exact mechanism of this action is not known, it is thought that use of estrogens slows down the rate of bone loss by nearly restoring equilibrium between bone loss and bone formation, potentially reducing the risk of fractures. Estrogen's effect on bone loss depends on the dose and the initial bone mass density, and is independent of patient age or the route of estrogen administration. In the short term, a new, lower rate of bone loss is established within 24 months with significant gain in the first 12 months, regardless of whether a patient is 1 or 10 years past menopause. Women of heavy and light body weights gain similar amounts of bone, more so in the spine than in the hip. With discontinuation of estrogen therapy, the rate of bone mass loss returns to the rate usually observed in the immediate postmenopausal period; the rate of loss is greater in women of lighter weight than in heavier women.

Beginning estrogen therapy early in menopause and continuing for at least 7 years imparts some long-term protection against accelerated bone loss, but investigators of the Framingham study suggest that 7 to 10 years of estrogen use may not be enough to protect women 75 years of age or older from fractures. When estrogen was used for 10 years or more in the Framingham study, women younger than 75 years of age had a 44% reduction in the risk of hip fracture at the femoral neck and 52% risk reduction at the trochanter.

Other actions/effects

Estrogens help develop and maintain the female reproductive system and secondary sex characteristics. Estrogens may enhance mood and cognitive function by increasing serotonin and free tryptophan levels in the brain, and by modifying estrogen receptors in the pituitary, hypothalamus, limbic forebrain, and cerebral cortex. Estrogens, acting with other hormones and cytokines, stimulate the growth and development of breast tissue and skeleton formation, and are integral to the physiology of puberty, menstruation, ovulatory cycles, and pregnancy.

Estrogens prevent vessel constriction when challenged through a direct vessel wall effect and, to a lesser extent, improve the lipoprotein cholesterol profile; both effects are significant for cardioprotection and reduction of arteriosclerosis. Concomitant progestin therapy can diminish the magnitude of improvement induced by estrogens in the lipoprotein cholesterol profile.

Locally, progestins relax the uterine smooth muscle, decrease the immune response, and cause sodium and water retention.

Absorption

Conjugated estrogens and medroxyprogesterone—Well absorbed.

The following changes in absorption occur when conjugated estrogens and medroxyprogesterone are taken with a high-fat meal:

Continuous cycle (0.625 mg of conjugated estrogens and 2.5 mg of medroxyprogesterone):

Estrone—Peak plasma concentration (C_{max}) decreased by 34%;

Equilin—C_{max} not affected; and

Medroxyprogesterone acetate—C_{max} doubled, resulting in a 30% increase in the plasma concentration-time curve (AUC).

Phasic cycle (0.625 mg of conjugated estrogens continuously, and 14 days of 5 mg of medroxyprogesterone):

Estrone—C_{max} decreased by 18%;

Equilin—C_{max} increased by 38%; and

Medroxyprogesterone acetate—C_{max} doubled, resulting in a 20% increase in AUC.

Protein binding

Conjugated estrogens and medroxyprogesterone acetate—Moderate to high (50 to 80%). Conjugated estrogens bind mainly to albumin, and unconjugated estrogens bind to both albumin and sex hormone-binding globulin (SHBG). Medroxyprogesterone binds mainly to albumin or to other plasma proteins, but not to SHBG.

Biotransformation

Primarily hepatic.

Half-life

Apparent terminal-phase half-life—Conjugated estrogens: 10 to 24 hours. Medroxyprogesterone: 38 to 46 hours.

Time to peak concentration

Conjugated or unconjugated estrogens—4 to 10 hours.

Medroxyprogesterone—Within 2 to 4 hours.

Elimination

Conjugated estrogens—

Renal: Major route, as acidic ionized conjugates.

Fecal: Minimal; reabsorbed from intestines and returned through portal venous system.

Medroxyprogesterone—

Renal: Minor route; excreted mainly as glucuronide conjugates, with some sulfate metabolites.

Fecal: Major route; excreted as hydroxylated and conjugated metabolites.

Precautions to Consider

Carcinogenicity/Tumorigenicity

Estrogens may increase the incidence of breast cancer in some postmenopausal women. Long-term studies are still needed to fully characterize potential risk. The majority of data available does not seem to support a significant increase in risk for patients using physiologic doses. The Women's Health Initiative (WHI) trial reported an increased risk of breast cancer in women who took estrogen plus progestin for a mean follow-up of 5.6 years. Patients using estrogens in either high doses or low doses for a prolonged period, especially longer than 10 years, potentially may have greater risk. Some studies suggest but do not prove that the risk doubles for patients with an individual risk factor (such as early menarche, late menopause, or nulliparity) or familial risk (such as patients whose mother or sister have had breast cancer). Short-term use of estrogens during menopause for treatment of menopausal symptoms does not appear to increase risk, and no additional risk has been attributed to adding a progestin to the therapy. Regular breast examinations or mammography will help detect any developing abnormality.

Estrogen plus progestin may increase the incidence of ovarian cancer in some postmenopausal women. The relative risk and absolute risk of ovarian cancer for estrogen plus progestin versus placebo was 1.58 (95% confidence interval 0.77 to 3.24; not statistically significant) and 4.2 versus 2.7 cases per 10,000 women-years in the estrogen plus progestin substudy of the WHI trial. The use of estrogen-only products for 10 or more years has been associated with an increased risk of ovarian cancer in some epidemiologic studies.

Studies show a lower incidence of endometrial hyperplasia and, potentially, endometrial cancer when patients take a progestin for a minimum of 10 to 14 days a month along with an estrogen cycle. One study reported an incidence of less than 1% for continuous or cyclic regimens of conjugated estrogens and medroxyprogesterone after 1 year of use. When nonusers were compared to users of an estrogen-only cycle, no risk of endometrial hyperplasia was shown for the first year of use. When unopposed estrogens were taken for a prolonged period or at higher than physiologic doses, risk increased 2- to 12-fold. Furthermore, the risk increased as high as 24-fold when estrogen alone was used for 5 years or longer. Although the magnitude of risk decreases substantially within 6 months after unopposed oral estrogen therapy is discontinued, some risk can continue for 8 to 15 years.

In certain animal species, long-term, continuous administration of estrogens increases the frequency of cancers of the breast, cervix, liver, pancreas, testes, uterus, and vagina. Results of animal studies may not apply to humans because of the general hormonal differences of sex steroids among species.

In a two-year oral study of medroxyprogesterone acetate (MPA) in which female rats were exposed to dosages of up to 5000 mcg/kg/day in thier diets (50 times higher—based on AUC values—than the level observed experimentally in women taking 10 mg of MPA), a dose-related increase in pancreatic islet cell tumors (adenomas and carcinomas) occurred. Pancreatic tumor incidence was increased at 1000 and 5000 mcg/kg/day, but not at 2000 mcg/kg/day.

A decreased incidence of spontaneous mammary gland tumors was observed in all three MPA-treated groups, compared to controls, in the two-year rat study. The mechanism for the decreased incidence of mammary gland tumors observed in MPA-treated rats may be linked to the significant decrease in serum prolactin concentration observed in rats.

Beagle dogs treated with MPA developed mammary nodules, some of which were malignant. Although nodules occasionally appeared in control animals, they were intermittent in nature, whereas the nodules in the drug-treated animals were larger, more numerous, persistent, and there were some breast malignancies with metastases. It is known that progestins stimulate the synthesis and release of growth hormone in dogs. The growth hormone, along with the progestogen, stimulates mammary growth and tumors. In contrast, growth hormone in humans is not increased, nor does growth hormone have any significant mammotrophic role. No pancreatic tumors occurred in dogs.

Mutagenicity

There was no mutagenic response in the Ames and micronucleus tests for medroxyprogesterone.

Pregnancy/Reproduction

Pregnancy—Use of a combination of conjugated estrogens and medroxyprogesterone is not recommended during pregnancy. Pregnancy occurs rarely in menopausal women because of the natural change in their hormone milieu; on the rare chance of occurrence, a fetus surviving to term is unlikely. Conjugated estrogens and medroxyprogesterone do not demonstrate teratogenic effects, although medroxyprogesterone can lessen intrauterine fetal growth. Although the association is questionable, a few cases of polysyndactyly in the infants occurred when the mother used parenteral medroxyprogesterone in the first trimester. Other progestins produced hypospadias in male infants, and virilized the external genitalia in female infants.

FDA Pregnancy Category X.

Breast-feeding

Conjugated estrogens and medroxyprogesterone are distributed into breast milk. Estrogen administration to nursing mothers has been shown to decrease the quality and quantity of the breast milk. This combination is not recommended for use by nursing mothers.

Pediatrics

Conjugated estrogens and medroxyprogesterone are not indicated in children.

Geriatrics

Appropriate studies on the relationship of age to the effects of conjugated estrogens and medroxyprogesterone have not been performed in the geriatric population. There have not been sufficient numbers of geriatric patients involved in studies to determine whether those over 65 years of age differ from younger subjects in their response to conjugated estrogens and medroxyprogesterone

In the PREMPRO substudy of the Women's Health Initiative Study, there was a higher incidence of stroke and invasive breast cancer in women 75 years and over compared to younger subjects.

In the Women's Health Initiative Memory Study, there was a two-fold increase in the risk of developing probable dementia in women 65 years of age and older receiving conjugated equine estrogen 0.625 mg and medroxyprogesterone acetate 2.5 mg compared to the placebo group.

Surgical

If possible, estrogens should be discontinued at least 4 to 6 weeks before surgery of the type associated with an increased risk of thromboembolism, or during periods of prolonged immobilization.

Drug interactions and/or related problems

The following drug interactions and/or related problems have been selected on the basis of their potential clinical significance (possible mechanism in parentheses where appropriate)—not necessarily inclusive (» = major clinical significance):

Note: Combinations containing any of the following medications, depending on the amount present, may also interact with this medication.

Antidiabetic or antihypertensive agents, antihyperlipidemics, or antifibrinolytics may need a dosage adjustment if adding or deleting estrogens or progestins causes slight changes in the patient's underlying condition.

» Aminoglutethimide
(may significantly lower the serum concentrations of oral medroxyprogesterone by an undetermined mechanism; it has been suggested that aminoglutethimide may decrease the intestinal absorption of medroxyprogesterone)
(although not considered clinically significant, aminoglutethimide inhibits estrogen production from androgens in peripheral tissues by blocking the aromatase enzyme; it may also enhance metabolism of estrone sulfate)

» Barbiturates, especially phenobarbital or
» Carbamazepine or
» Hydantoins, especially phenytoin or
Rifabutin or
» Rifampin or
» St. John's Wort (Hypericum perforatum)-containing products
(hepatic enzyme-inducing properties of these drugs may reduce the activity of conjugated estrogens or medroxyprogesterone; rifabutin appears to be a less potent enzyme inducer of the hepatic cytochrome P450 system than rifampin)
(drug interaction data are not available for rifabutin, but because its structure is similar to that of rifampin, similar precautions may be warranted)

Calcium supplements
(concurrent use with estrogens may increase calcium absorption and exacerbate nephrolithiasis in susceptible individuals; this action can be used to therapeutic advantage to increase bone mass)

Clarithromycin or
Erythromycin or
Grapefruit juice or
Itraconazole or
Ketoconazole or
Ritonavir
(hepatic enzyme-inhibiting properties of these drugs may increase the plasma concentrations of estrogens and may result in adverse effects)

Corticosteroids, glucocorticoid
(concurrent use with estrogens may alter the metabolism and protein binding of the glucocorticoids, leading to decreased clearance, increased elimination half-life, and increased therapeutic and toxic effects of the glucocorticoids; glucocorticoid dosage adjustment may be required during and following concurrent use)

Corticotropin (long-term therapeutic use)
(concurrent use with estrogens may potentiate the anti-inflammatory effects of endogenous cortisol induced by corticotropin)

» Cyclosporine
(estrogens have been reported to inhibit cyclosporine metabolism and thereby increase plasma concentrations of cyclosporine, possibly increasing the risk of hepatotoxicity and nephrotoxicity; concurrent use is recommended only with great caution and frequent monitoring of blood cyclosporine concentrations and hepatic and renal function)

» Hepatotoxic medications, especially dantrolene and isoniazid (see *Appendix II*)
(concurrent use of these medications with estrogens may increase the risk of hepatotoxicity; fatal hepatitis has occurred)

Medications associated with pancreatitis, especially
Didanosine or
Lamivudine or
Zalcitabine
(estrogens should be used with caution with medications that cause pancreatitis, especially if patient has pre-existing risk factors, such as high triglyceride concentrations; however, physiologic doses of estrogen would not be expected to induce pancreatitis)

Progestins
(there are possible risks that may be associated with the use of progestins with estrogens compared to estrogen-only regimens. These include a possible increased risk of breast cancer, adverse effects on lipoprotein metabolism [e.g., lowering HDL, raising LDL] and impairment of glucose tolerance.)

Smoking, tobacco
(smoking increases the metabolism of estrogens and can result in a decreased estrogenic effect)
(smokers have an increased risk of coronary heart disease and are more likely to experience myocardial infarction and angina pectoris. Although data are unavailable for menopausal or postmenopausal patients who smoke tobacco, it is unlikely that the use of physiologic doses of estrogen in these patients increases risk. Smokers do have an increased risk of hip fractures, and estrogens provide some degree of protection)

Tamoxifen
(estrogens may interfere with tamoxifen's effect)

Laboratory value alterations

The following have been selected on the basis of their potential clinical significance (possible effect in parentheses where appropriate)—not necessarily inclusive (» = major clinical significance).

Note: When submitting specimens, the laboratory should be informed that the patient is receiving hormone replacement therapy. The results of laboratory determinations for the tests listed here should not be considered reliable unless hormone replacement therapy has been discontinued for two to four weeks.

With diagnostic test results

Fasting blood sugar (FBS) and
Glucose tolerance test
(impaired glucose tolerance)

Metyrapone stimulation test
(response is lower than expected)

With physiology/laboratory test values

Anti-factor Xa or
Antithrombin III, plasma or
Antithrombin III activity
(may be decreased)

Calcium, serum
(concentrations may be increased, especially for immobilized patients or patients with breast cancer or bone metastases)

Cholesterol, total, serum and
Folic acid, serum and
Lipoprotein (a), plasma and

Lipoprotein cholesterol, low-density (LDLC), serum
(concentrations may be decreased)
(lower total cholesterol occurs because cyclic doses of 5 mg or continuous doses of 2.5 or 5 mg medroxyprogesterone attenuate most of the favorable increase in the HDLC component produced from a continuously administered dose of 0.625 mg conjugated estrogens)

Coagulation factors, plasma, such as Factors II, VII antigen, VIII coagulant activity, IX, X, XII VII-X complex, II-VII-X complex, and beta-thromboglobulin and
Fibrinogen, plasma and fibrinogen activity and
Plasminogen antigen and activity, plasma and
Platelet count, whole blood
(may be increased)
(in one large clinical trial, patients taking either the continuous or phasic regimens of conjugated estrogen and medroxyprogesterone increased the plasminogen activity by 14% and the Factor X concentrations by 13% over their baseline values. In this same study, the magnitude of increase in the Factor VII concentration was 20% for the continuous regimen as compared with 8% for the cyclical regimen)

Insulin, serum or plasma and
Glucose, 2-hour postprandial, serum or plasma
(minimal effect on glucose metabolism and unlikely to influence heart disease risk. While the fasting serum insulin and glucose show little or change, the 2-hour serum glucose may be slightly increased and the insulin concentration may be slightly decreased)

Lipoprotein cholesterol, high-density (HDLC), serum and
Triglycerides (TG), serum
(concentrations are increased)
(5-mg doses of the cyclic or continuous doses of 2.5 or 5 mg medroxyprogesterone attenuated much of the favorable increase of the HDLC component induced by 0.625 mg conjugated estrogens)
(triglycerides are increased with the use of continuous doses of 2.5 or 5 mg medroxyprogesterone with 0.625 mg conjugated estrogens, but the increase is approximately half as great as that produced from use of 0.625 mg conjugated estrogens alone)

Liver profile test, serum
(values may be increased; if abnormal, liver tests may be repeated 4 to 6 months after medication is discontinued)

Plasma binding globulins, such as
Corticotropin-binding globulin (CBG), serum
Sex hormone-binding globulin (SHBG), serum
Thyroid-binding globulin (TBG), serum

Plasma proteins, other than plasma binding globulins, such as
Alpha$_1$-antitrypsin, serum
Angiotensinogen/renin substrate
Ceruloplasmin, serum
(concentrations may be increased from baseline; compensatory mechanisms keep the free serum concentrations of cortisol, sex steroids, and thyroid hormones unchanged)

Prothrombin time (PT), plasma and
Partial thromboplastin time (PTT), plasma and
Platelet aggregation time, plasma
(time to coagulation may be shortened)

Triiodothyronine T_3, total, serum and
Triiodothyronine T_3 uptake test, serum
(values for the T_3 uptake test may be decreased because of an increase in thyroid-binding globulin [TBG]; free T_3, thyroxine [T_4], and thyroid-stimulating hormone [TSH] concentrations remain unaltered and patient remains euthyroid even though the amount of total bound thyroid hormone may be increased)

Medical considerations/Contraindications

The medical considerations/contraindications included have been selected on the basis of their potential clinical significance (reasons given in parentheses where appropriate)—not necessarily inclusive (» = major clinical significance).

Except under special circumstances, these medications should not be used when the following medical problems exist:

» Deep vein thrombosis, active or history of, or
» Pulmonary Embolism, active or history of
(use is contraindicated)

» Endometrial hyperplasia
(use is contraindicated;)

» Genital or uterine bleeding, abnormal or undiagnosed
(use of estrogens or progestins may delay diagnosis; on occurrence, estrogen should be discontinued until clinical evaluation is completed. Condition may worsen if cause of abnormal uterine bleeding is endometrial hyperplasia or uterine cancer)

» Hepatic dysfunction or disease, especially of the obstructive type or
» Hepatic function impairment, severe, including benign or malignant liver tumors
(use is contraindicated; condition may worsen with use of oral estrogen or progestin. Hepatic function impairment may decrease estrogen or progestin metabolism and delay their elimination; medication should be discontinued)

» Hypercalcemia, associated with bone metastases or breast cancer or
» Neoplasia, breast, known, suspected or history of or
» Neoplasia, estrogen-dependent, known, history of, or suspected
(use is contraindicated in patients with known, suspected, or history of cancer of the breast)
(oral conjugated estrogens may promote tumor growth or interfere with the action of antiestrogen treatment regimens; when these conditions are present, estrogen medication should be discontinued)
(estrogens can elevate calcium levels by altering calcium and phosphorus metabolism and can result in severe hypercalcemia or aggravate the hypercalcemia associated with breast cancer or bone metastases; if hypercalcemia occurs, use of the drug should be stopped and appropriate measures taken to reduce the serum calcium level)

» Hypersensitivity to estrogens, progestins, or any of the ingredients in the combination product
(use is contraindicated)

» Thromboembolic disease, arterial, active or recent (within the past year)
Myocardial infarction
Stroke
(estrogen and progestins combined therapy should not used; estrogens should be discontinued if thromboembolic events occur)

Risk-benefit should be considered when the following medical problems exist:

Asthma or
Cardiac insufficiency, significant or
Epilepsy or
Hypertension or
Migraine headaches or
Renal impairment, severe
(rarely, the fluid retention caused by estrogens and progestins may aggravate these conditions)

Diabetes mellitus
(minimal risk of altered carbohydrate metabolism; however, some postmenopausal patients, with or without diabetes mellitus, who are taking conjugated estrogens and medroxyprogesterone in physiologic doses may experience a slight decrease in the glucose tolerance by an unknown mechanism, as shown by an increased 2-hour postprandial blood glucose concentration test)

Endometriosis
(endometrial implants may be aggravated by use of estrogens)

Gallbladder disease, or history of, especially gallstones
(a 2- to 4-fold increase in the risk of gallbladder disease requiring surgery in postmenopausal women has been reported)

Hypocalcemia
(estrogens should be used with caution in individuals with severe hypocalcemia)

Hypothyroidism
(estrogens lead to increased thyroid binding globulin [TBG] levels; patients dependent upon thyroid hormone replacement therapy who are also receiving estrogens may need to increase the dose of their thyroid replacement therapy)

Jaundice, cholestatic, history of, or
Jaundice, or history of during pregnancy or
Porphyria, hepatic—acute, intermittent, or variegate or
(impaired hepatic function may decrease the metabolism of conjugated estrogens and medroxyprogesterone and cause these conditions to worsen or recur; caution should be exercised and in the case of recurrence, medication should be discontinued.)

Hyperlipoproteinemia, familial or
» Hypertriglyceridemia, pre-existing or
Pancreatitis
(medroxyprogesterone, by lowering the beneficial effect of estrogens in decreasing LDLC and increasing HDLC levels, can rarely aggravate hyperlipidemia; estrogens at the premenopausal level can substantially increase serum triglycerides, which may lead to pancreatitis, especially in patients with familial defects in lipoprotein metabolism)

Leiomyomas, uterine
(may increase in size during estrogen therapy)

Thromboembolic disorders, including cerebrovascular disease, pulmonary embolism, and retinal thrombosis, history of or

Thrombophlebitis, history of
(may be exacerbated; hypercoagulability information for postmenopausal women with these conditions is not available. Estrogens and progestins have been used cautiously in women with predisposing risk factors but the medication should be discontinued if thromboembolic events occur)

» Visual abnormalities
(retinal visual thrombosis has been reported, discontinue medication if there is a sudden partial or complete loss of vision, or a sudden onset of proptosis, diplopia or migraine. If examination reveals papilledema or retinal vascular lesions, estrogens should be discontinued.)

Patient monitoring

The following may be especially important in patient monitoring (other tests may be warranted in some patients, depending on condition; » = major clinical significance):

Blood pressure determinations and
Physical examinations
(annual monitoring; special attention given to abdomen, breasts, and pelvic organs, including counseling patient about periodic self-examination of breasts. During treatment of vasomotor symptoms of menopause and vulvar or vaginal atrophy, patient should be evaluated every 3 to 6 months to determine whether continued use of therapy is appropriate)
(generally, blood pressure remains the same or decreases with physiologic doses of estrogen and continuous 2.5- or cyclic 5-mg doses of medroxyprogesterone; idiosyncratic increases in blood pressure have occurred. A large clinical trial showed that 2 to 4% of postmenopausal women had transient increases in systolic blood pressure of 40 mm Hg and transient increases in diastolic blood pressure of 20 mm Hg)

Endometrial evaluation
(routine or baseline evaluation is not needed for women with an intact uterus who use combination estrogens and progestins unless unexpected uterine bleeding problems occur. An endometrial evaluation should be considered if unexpected withdrawal bleeding occurs during Days 5 to 15 when a progestin is given on Days 1 to 10 for cyclic estrogen-progestin therapy; or, for continuous estrogen-progestin therapy, if bleeding is heavier than a normal period, lasts longer than 10 days at a time, or occurs more often than monthly. Also, an endometrial evaluation should be considered if endometrial atrophy does not occur within 10 months after initiation of treatment with continuous estrogen-progestin therapy)
(transvaginal sonography is commonly used for endometrial monitoring. Endometrial biopsy may be needed instead, if irregular uterine bleeding persists after the first year of continuous therapy; if uterine bleeding is refractory to an increase in the progestin dose; if irregular bleeding occurs after a period of amenorrhea; or if transvaginal sonography shows an endometrial thickness of greater than 4 millimeters)

Hepatic function determinations and
Lipid profile determinations
(recommended annually or as determined by physician, especially if hepatic disease exists or is suspected)

Mammography or
Papanicolaou (Pap) test
(recommended annually or as determined by physician; especially important for those patients on long-term estrogen therapy)
(sensitivity or specificity of mammography is decreased during estrogen use due to detection problems caused by estrogen-induced breast tissue growth, especially if the postmenopausal breast is fibrous. Ordering mammography during the week of no hormone use or after cessation of therapy may help recognize false-positive or false-negative mammograms)

Thyroid function
(patients who are dependent upon thyroid replacement therapy and who are also receiving estrogens should have their thyroid function monitored to maintain their free thyroid hormone levels in an acceptable range)

Side/Adverse Effects

Note: The risk of any serious adverse effect is minimal for healthy women using low doses of estrogen and progestins. Even women who have special risk factors successfully use estrogens and progestins.

Estrogen/progestin therapy has been associated with an increased risk of cardiovascular events such as myocardial infarction and stroke, as well as venous thrombosis and pulmonary embolism (venous thromboembolism or VTE). Should any of these occur or be suspected, estrogen/progestin therapy should be stopped immediately.

Embolic cerebrovascular events have been reported in women receiving postmenopausal estrogens.

Estrogen/progestin therapy in postmenopausal women has been associated with an increased risk of breast cancer. All postmenopausal women should receive yearly breast exams, perform monthly self-examinations, and have mammography exams based on patient age and risk factors.

The reported endometrial cancer risk among unopposed estrogen users is about 2- to 12-fold greater than in non-users, and appears dependent upon duration of treatment and on estrogen dose. Close clinical surveillance of all women taking estrogens/progestins is important. Adequate diagnostic measures, including endometrial sampling when indicated, should be undertaken to rule out malignancy in all cases of persistent or recurring vaginal bleeding.

The following side/adverse effects have been selected on the basis of their potential clinical significance (possible signs and symptoms in parentheses where appropriate)—not necessarily inclusive:

Those indicating need for medical attention

Incidence more frequent

Amenorrhea (absence of menstrual periods)—usually occurring within 10 months; ***changes in uterine bleeding pattern, including abnormal timing or amount of flow for withdrawal bleeding, breakthrough bleeding or spotting***—effects tapering off within 6 months; ***vaginitis*** (itching of the vagina or genital area; pain during sexual intercourse; thick, white vaginal discharge with no odor or with a mild odor); ***vulvovaginal candidiasis*** (vaginal itching or irritation; thick, white vaginal discharge)

Note: *Withdrawal bleeding* or menstrual-like bleeding frequently will occur when patients who have a uterus are placed on cyclic estrogen-progestin therapy. Any unusual uterine bleeding persisting longer than 3 to 6 months should be investigated. With continuous estrogen-progestin therapy, withdrawal bleeding is eliminated, and endometrial atrophy and *amenorrhea* are produced in most patients after 2 to 3 months and, in the remaining patients, after 7 to 13 months. Amenorrhea is highly desired by many women and not considered to be an adverse effect.

Incidence less frequent

Breast tumors (breast lumps; discharge from breast); ***chest pain; hypertension*** (blurred vision; dizziness; nervousness; headache; pounding in the ears; slow or fast heartbeat); ***skin rash; uterine spasm*** (severe cramping of the uterus); ***vaginal hemorrhage*** (heavy nonmenstrual vaginal bleeding)

Incidence rare

Endometrial hyperplasia (change in vaginal discharge; pain or feeling of pressure in pelvis; vaginal bleeding); ***gallbladder obstruction, hepatitis, or pancreatitis*** (yellow eyes or skin; pain or tenderness in stomach, side, or abdomen)

Incidence not determined

Endometrial cancer (change in vaginal discharge; pain or feeling of pressure in pelvis; vaginal bleeding); ***ovarian cancer*** (acid or sour stomach; belching; backache; full or bloated feeling or pressure in the stomach; heartburn; indigestion; loss of appetite; stomach discomfort, upset or pain; swelling of abdominal or stomach area); ***uterine leiomyomata, increase in size*** (abdominal bloating; pelvic pain; stomach pain)

Those indicating need for medical attention only if they continue or are bothersome

Incidence more frequent

Abdominal pain or cramping; arthralgia (joint pain); ***asthenia*** (lack or loss of strength); ***back pain; breast enlargement, pain, or tenderness; diarrhea; dizziness; dyspepsia*** (stomach discomfort following meals); ***dysmenorrhea*** (painful menstrual periods); ***flatulence*** (passing of gas); ***flu syndrome*** (chills; cough; diarrhea; fever; general feeling of discomfort or illness; headache; joint pain; loss of appetite; muscle aches and pains; nausea; runny nose; shivering; sore throat; sweating; trouble sleeping; unusual tiredness or weakness; vomiting); ***headaches including migraine headaches; infection*** (fever or chills; cough or hoarseness; lower back or side pain; painful or difficult urination); ***leukorrhea*** (increase in amount of clear vaginal discharge); ***mental depression; nausea; pain; pelvic pain; pharyngitis*** (body aches or pain; congestion; cough; dryness or soreness of throat; fever; hoarseness; runny nose; tender, swollen glands in neck; trouble in swallowing; voice changes); ***pruritus*** (itching); ***rhinitis*** (stuffy nose; runny nose; sneezing); ***sinusitis*** (pain or tenderness around eyes and cheekbones; fever; stuffy or runny nose; headache; cough; shortness of breath or troubled breathing; tightness of chest or wheezing); ***unusual tiredness; vasodilation*** (feeling of warmth or heat; flushing or redness of skin, especially on face and neck; headache; feeling faint, dizzy, or light-headedness; sweating)

Incidence less frequent

Acne; cervix disorder; emotional lability (crying; depersonalization; dysphoria; euphoria; mental depression; paranoia; quick to react or overreact emotionally; rapidly changing moods); ***hypertonia*** (tense muscles); ***increase in libido*** (increase in sexual desire); ***insomnia*** (sleeplessness; trouble sleeping; unable to sleep); ***leg cramps; nervousness; peripheral edema*** (bloating or swelling of face, ankles, or feet; unusual weight gain or loss); ***weight gain***

Incidence rare

CNS disturbances, such as mood changes; trouble in sleeping; vomiting

Incidence not determined

Cervical erosion (light vaginal bleeding between periods and after intercourse); ***cervical secretion, change in amount*** (change in amount of vaginal discharge; bloody vaginal discharge); ***cystitis-like syndrome*** (bloody or cloudy urine; difficult, burning, or painful urination; frequent urge to urinate); ***premenstrual-like syndrome*** (abdominal bloating and cramping; headache; pelvic pain)

Patient Consultation

As an aid to patient consultation, refer to *Advice for the Patient, Conjugated Estrogens and Medroxyprogesterone For Ovarian Hormone Therapy (OHT) (Systemic)*.

In providing consultation, consider emphasizing the following selected information (» = major clinical significance):

Before using this medication

» Conditions affecting use, especially:

Hypersensitivity to estrogens or progestins

Carcinogenicity—The use of estrogens and progestins by postmenopausal women may increase the risk of breast cancer, endometrial cancer (among unopposed estrogen users), and ovarian cancer. It is important to have regular examinations by a health professional to detect these serious problems early.

Pregnancy—Although not usually a concern for perimenopausal patients, conjugated estrogens and medroxyprogesterone are not recommended during pregnancy because of associated congenital abnormalities; physician should be informed immediately if pregnancy is suspected

Breast-feeding—Although not usually a concern for perimenopausal patients, conjugated estrogens and medroxyprogesterone are not recommended because estrogens and progestins are distributed into breast milk

Other medications, especially aminoglutethimide, barbiturates, carbamazepine, cyclosporine, hydantoins, hepatotoxic medications, rifampin, or St. John's wort-containing products

Other medical problems, especially abnormal or undiagnosed genital or uterine bleeding; breast cancer; deep vein thrombosis; endometrial hyperplasia; estrogen-dependent neoplasia (known or suspected); hypercalcemia due to bone metastases or breast cancer; hepatic dysfunction or disease, especially of the obstructive type; hepatic function impairment (severe); hypertriglyceridemia; pulmonary embolism; arterial thromboembolic disease (active or recent); or visual abnormalities

Proper use of this medication

Reading patient directions

» Importance of not taking more or less medication than the amount prescribed or for longer time than needed

» If taking combination therapy, taking each medication at the right time

» Taking with food if nausea occurs, especially for first few weeks after treatment initiation

» Proper dosing

Missed dose: Taking as soon as possible; not taking if almost time for next dose; not doubling doses

» Proper storage

Precautions while using this medication

» Regular visits to physician once every year, or more often, as determined by physician

» Checking breast by self-examination regularly and having clinical examination and mammography as required by physician; reporting unusual breast lumps or discharge

» Understanding that menstrual bleeding may begin again but, with continuous therapy, will stop by 10 months

» Understanding that intermenstrual vaginal bleeding will occur for the first 3 months; importance of not stopping medicine; checking with doctor immediately if uterine bleeding is unusual or continuous, missed period occurs, or pregnancy is suspected

If scheduled for laboratory tests, telling physician about taking estrogens or progestins; certain blood tests and tissue biopsies are affected

Importance of discontinuing estrogens at least 4 to 6 weeks before surgery of the type associated with an increased risk of thromboembolism, or during periods of prolonged immobilization

Side/adverse effects

Signs of potential side effects, especially amenorrhea; changes in uterine bleeding; vaginitis; vulvovaginal candidiasis; breast tumors; chest pain; hypertension; skin rash; uterine spasm; vaginal hemorrhage; endometrial hyperplasia; gallbladder obstruction, hepatitis, or pancreatitis; endometrial cancer; ovarian cancer; or increase in size of uterine leiomyomata (fibroid)

General Dosing Information

It is recommended that the patient package insert (PPI) be given to patients.

Use of the continuous regimen for both conjugated estrogen and medroxyprogesterone is a good choice for women who do not want to resume menses. If spotting or uterine bleeding occurs during the first 6 months, a higher dose of progestin may be used for a short time until endometrial atrophy occurs.

Decisions to treat menopausal symptoms with hormones for a limited time (1 to 5 years) or to use hormones to prevent diseases in postmenopausal women for a longer period of time (10 to 20 years) or a lifetime should be made separately.

Counseling asymptomatic postmenopausal women about the benefits and risks of using long-term estrogen and progestin hormone replacement therapy to prevent osteoporosis and coronary heart disease and to increase life expectancy is complex. Risk estimates are based on observational studies; the true estimates for long-term risk and benefit await controlled clinical trials. Women should understand that the benefits and risks of preventive hormone therapy depend on their risk status, and that women at higher risk for developing osteoporosis or coronary heart disease can derive the greatest benefit.

For women with a uterus, adding a progestin to estrogen therapy may benefit postmenopausal women at risk for osteoporosis and slightly increase the risk of breast cancer over that of nonusers.

During treatment of vasomotor symptoms of menopause or vulvar and vaginal atrophy, patient should be evaluated every 3 to 6 months to determine whether continued use of estrogens is appropriate.

Diet/Nutrition

Estrogen therapy may cause nausea, especially in the morning. Although this nausea is primarily of central origin, eating solid food often provides some relief.

CONJUGATED ESTROGENS, AND CONJUGATED ESTROGENS AND MEDROXYPROGESTERONE

Oral Dosage Forms

CONJUGATED ESTROGENS TABLETS USP CONJUGATED ESTROGENS AND MEDROXYPROGESTERONE ACETATE TABLETS USP

Usual adult dose

Menopause, vasomotor symptoms of or
Osteoporosis, postmenopausal, prophylaxis or
Vaginitis, atrophic or
Vulvar atrophy—

Oral, one tablet containing 0.625 mg conjugated estrogens a day on Days 1 through 14. Then one tablet containing 0.625 mg conjugated estrogens and 5 mg medroxyprogesterone a day is taken on Days 15 through 28. Repeat cycle.

Note: Other regimens may differ but also may be appropriate.

Strength(s) usually available

U.S.—

Note: *Premphase* contains twenty-eight tablets: fourteen tablets of Conjugated Estrogens Tablets USP 0.625 mg inscribed with the brand name *Premarin*, and fourteen tablets containing two hormones, conjugated estrogens 0.625 mg and medroxyprogesterone acetate 5 mg, inscribed with the brand name *Premphase*.

0.625 mg of conjugated estrogens, and 0.625 mg of conjugated estrogens and 5 mg of medroxyprogesterone acetate (Rx) [*Premphase*].

Canada—

Note: Not commercially available.

Packaging and storage

Store at controlled room temperature 20 to 25°C (68 to 77°F); excursions permitted between 15 to 30°C (59 to 86°F)

Note

Include mandatory patient package insert (PPI) when dispensing.

CONJUGATED ESTROGENS AND MEDROXYPROGESTERONE

Oral Dosage Forms

CONJUGATED ESTROGENS AND MEDROXYPROGESTERONE ACETATE TABLETS

Usual adult dose

Menopause, vasomotor symptoms of or
Osteoporosis, postmenopausal, prophylaxis or
Vaginitis, atrophic or
Vulvar atrophy—

Oral, one tablet containing 0.3 mg conjugated estrogens and 1.5 mg medroxyprogesterone once a day for a continuous (nonphasic) regimen. Dosage may be adjusted based on individual patient response. Dose may be increased in patients who continue to have undesired uterine bleeding or spotting, after appropriate evaluation. Treatment should be periodically reassessed by the health-care provider to ensure that treatment is necessary and the lowest effective dose is used.

Strength(s) usually available

U.S.—

Note: Available in dispenser containing 28 tablets.

0.3 mg of conjugated estrogens and 1.5 mg of medroxyprogesterone acetate (Rx) [*Prempro*].

0.45 mg of conjugated estrogens and 1.5 mg of medroxyprogesterone acetate (Rx) [*Prempro*].

0.625 mg of conjugated estrogens and 2.5 mg of medroxyprogesterone acetate (Rx) [*Prempro*].

0.625 mg of conjugated estrogens and 5 mg of medroxyprogesterone acetate (Rx) [*Prempro*].

Canada—

Not commercially available.

Packaging and storage

Store at controlled room temperature 20 to 25°C (68 to 77°F).

Note

Include mandatory patient package insert (PPI) when dispensing.

CONJUGATED ESTROGENS TABLETS MEDROXYPROGESTERONE ACETATE TABLETS USP

Usual adult dose

Menopause, vasomotor symptoms of or
Osteoporosis, postmenopausal, prophylaxis or
Valvar atrophy—

Oral, one tablet containing conjugated estrogens and one tablet containing medroxyprogesterone acetate once a day for a continuous (nonphasic) regimen. Repeat cycle.

Strength(s) usually available

U.S.—

Not commercially available.

Canada—

0.625 mg of conjugated estrogens, and 2.5 mg medroxyprogesterone acetate (Rx) [*Premplus*].

Note: *Premplus* contains two blister cards in a carton containing fifty-six tablets: each card contains fourteen tablets containing 0.625 mg of conjugated estrogens inscribed with the brand name *Premarin*, and fourteen tablets containing 2.5 mg medroxyprogesterone acetate, scored and debossed with two opposing "C"s

0.625 mg of conjugated estrogens, and 5 mg medroxyprogesterone acetate (Rx) [*Premplus*].

Note: *Premplus* contains two blister cards in a carton containing fifty-six tablets: each card contains fourteen tablets containing 0.625 mg of conjugated estrogens inscribed with the brand name *Premarin*, and fourteen tablets containing 5 mg medroxyprogesterone acetate, scored and debossed with two opposing "C"s

Packaging and storage

Store at 15 to 25°C (59 and 77°F)

Auxiliary labeling

- Keep out of the reach of children

Selected Bibliography

Product Information: Prempro™ and Premphase®, conjugated estrogens/medroxyprogesterone acetate tablets. Ayerst Laboratories, Philadelphia, PA (PI Revised 06/2003) PI Reviewed 12/2003

Product Monograph: Premplus™ and Premplus Cycle™, conjugated estrogens/medroxyprogesterone acetate tablets. Wyeth-Ayerst Canada, Inc, Montreal, CA (PI Revised 10/2000) PI Reviewed 12/2003

Revised: 06/25/2004

COPPER GLUCONATE—See *Copper Supplements (Systemic)*

CORTICOSTEROIDS Inhalation-Local

This monograph includes information on the following: 1) Beclomethasone; 2) Budesonide; 3) Flunisolide; 4) Triamcinolone.

Note: See also individual monograph, *Fluticasone (Inhalation-Local)*.

INN: Beclomethasone—Beclometasone

JAN: Beclomethasone—Beclometasone dipropionate

VA CLASSIFICATION (Primary/Secondary): RE110/RE190

Commonly used brand name(s): *AeroBid*[3]; *AeroBid-M*[3]; *Azmacort*[4]; *Beclodisk*[1]; *Becloforte*[1]; *Beclovent*[1]; *Beclovent Rotacaps*[1]; *Bronalide*[3]; *Pulmicort Nebuamp*[2]; *Pulmicort Respules*[2]; *Pulmicort Turbuhaler*[2]; *QVAR*[1]; *Vanceril*[1]; *Vanceril 84 mcg Double Strength*[1].

Other commonly used names for beclomethasone are beclomethasone dipropionate, beclometasone, and beclometasone dipropionate.

Note: For a listing of dosage forms and brand names by country availability, see *Dosage Forms* section(s).

Category

Anti-inflammatory (inhalation); antiasthmatic.

Indications

Note: Bracketed information in the *Indications* section refers to uses that are not included in U.S. product labeling.

Accepted

Asthma, bronchial, chronic (treatment)—Beclomethasone, budesonide, flunisolide, and triamcinolone are indicated as primary maintenance treatment in patients with persistent symptoms of chronic bronchial asthma. Treatment with inhaled corticosteroids is indicated in asthmatic patients whose conditions require anti-inflammatory treatment and in patients dependent on oral corticosteroids who may benefit from a gradual withdrawal from oral corticosteroids to decrease the likelihood of side effects. Regular, continuous use of inhaled corticosteroids controls chronic airway inflammation, decreases airway hyperresponsiveness, prevents asthma symptoms, reduces the frequency of asthma exacerbations, and reduces hospital admissions for asthma. Clinical studies have also reported that regular use with inhaled corticosteroids is associated with decreased mortality. Inhaled corticosteroids are effective in all types of asthma and in patients of all ages.

Initiation of therapy with daily doses of inhaled corticosteroids shortly after a diagnosis of chronic asthma (even if mild) may prevent irreversible structural changes in the airways resulting from uncontrolled inflammation, may decrease progression of severe disease, and may reduce the need for administration of systemic corticosteroids.

Information comparing dose-related systemic effects or the ratios of local to systemic activity of beclomethasone, budesonide, flunisolide, and triamcinolone is limited. However, since conclusive evidence is lacking and further studies are needed, the concept of individualized dose titration in each patient to identify the lowest effective dose of an inhaled corticosteroid to achieve and maintain the desired clinical control of asthma seems prudent.

Because of the potent anti-inflammatory effects of inhaled corticosteroids and the potential morbidity and mortality associated with theophylline treatment, inhaled corticosteroids in conventional low doses are preferred to theophylline as first-line therapy for chronic asthma.

Guidelines for the treatment of asthma:

Children aged 5 years and younger—Preferred treatment for mild asthma (more than 2 symptoms per week but less than 1 symptom per day) is a low-dose inhaled corticosteroid. Alternative treatment may consist of cromolyn or a leukotriene receptor antagonist. Preferred treatment with moderate asthma (greater than 1 symptom per night) is a low-dose inhaled corticosteroid and long-acting inhaled beta-adrenergic bronchodilator. Alternative treatment may consist of a low-dose inhaled corticosteroid and either a leukotriene receptor antagonist or theophylline. Preferred treatment with severe asthma (continual symptoms throughout the day) is a high-dose inhaled corticosteroid and a long-acting inhaled beta-adrenergic bronchodilator.

Children older than 5 years of age—Preferred treatment for mild asthma (more than 2 symptoms per week but less than 1 symptom per day) is a low-dose inhaled corticosteroid. Alternative treatment may consist of cromolyn, a leukotriene receptor antagonist, nedocromil, or theophylline. Preferred treatment with moderate asthma (greater than 1 symptom per night) is a low-to-medium dose inhaled corticosteroid and a long-acting inhaled beta-adrenergic bronchodilator. Alternative treatment may consist of a low-dose inhaled corticosteroid and either a leukotriene receptor antagonist or theophylline. Preferred treatment with severe asthma (continual symptoms throughout the day) is a high-dose inhaled corticosteroid and a long-acting inhaled beta-adrenergic bronchodilator.

Budesonide dry-powder inhalers are indicated for use in [children 3 months to 6 years of age][1] and older.Budesonide inhalation suspension is indicated for the maintenance treatment of asthma and as prophylactic therapy in children 12 months to 8 years of age.

[Croup (treatment)][1]—Budesonide is indicated for the treatment of croup in children. Studies have indicated that treatment with budesonide may increase the rate of discharge from the hospital emergency department and shorten hospitalization.

Acceptance not established

Use in children younger than 3 months of age for the treatment of asthma has not been established.

There is not enough medical literature or clinical experience to recommend the use of systemic corticosteroids for the treatment of *respiratory syncytial virus bronchiolitis*

Unaccepted

Corticosteroid inhalation therapy does not relieve acute bronchospasm and is not indicated for the primary treatment of status asthmaticus or other acute asthmatic episodes requiring more intensive or rapid treatment measures.Oral corticosteroids are more effective than inhaled corticosteroids for the treatment of acute asthmatic episodes.

Corticosteroid inhalation therapy is not indicated in the treatment of nonasthmatic bronchitis.

Dexamethasone inhalation is not recommended for use in asthma because it has demonstrated a significantly higher incidence of systemic effects with no additional benefit over other inhaled corticosteroids. The high ratio of systemic glucocorticoid activity to local anti-inflammatory activity of inhaled dexamethasone may be due to its greater water solubility and longer metabolic half-life after absorption relative to the other inhaled corticosteroids.

[1]Not included in Canadian product labeling.

Pharmacology/Pharmacokinetics

Physicochemical characteristics

Molecular weight—

Beclomethasone dipropionate: 521.05.
Budesonide: 430.54.
Flunisolide: 443.52.
Triamcinolone acetonide: 434.5.

Mechanism of action/Effect

In the treatment of chronic bronchial asthma, orally inhaled corticosteroids have many probable sites of action. The net effect is to reduce the chronic inflammation in asthmatic airways.

The potent anti-inflammatory action may be due to an inhibition of the secretion of growth factors, endothelial activating and other cytokines from lymphocytes, eosinophils, macrophages, fibroblasts, and mast cells. The results are decreased influx of inflammatory cells into the bronchial walls, due in part to inhibition of expression of adhesion molecules on the endothelium and in the tissue. Decreased activation and survival of eosinophils in the lung tissue and a reduction in numbers of mast cells are further effects.

Corticosteroids may inhibit release of mediators from basophils and enzymes from macrophages. There is decreased permeability through vasoconstriction and direct inhibition of endothelial cell contraction.

Beta-adrenergic-receptor numbers may be increased, which results in an enhanced response to beta-adrenergic bronchodilators and reduced down-regulation of beta-receptors after prolonged beta-agonist exposure.

Inhaled corticosteroids also inhibit mucus secretion in airways, possibly by a direct action on submucosal gland cells and an indirect inhibitory effect caused by the reduction in inflammatory mediators that stimulate mucus secretion. The amount and viscosity of sputum are reduced.

The effect of inhaled corticosteroids on bronchial asthma is to block the late inflammatory response to inhaled allergens and reduce over time the response to nonspecific triggers such as exercise. Bronchial wall inflammation and edema are reduced, sputum production is diminished, and the airways become less hyperresponsive to direct and indirect challenges.

Absorption

Beclomethasone, budesonide, and flunisolide are rapidly absorbed from the lungs and gastrointestinal tract. Triamcinolone is absorbed more slowly.

Without the use of a spacer, approximately 10 to 25% of an inhaled corticosteroid dose is deposited in the airways; the remainder is deposited in the mouth and throat, and swallowed. A greater percentage of the inhaled dose may reach the respiratory tract with the use of a spacer device. The Budesonide powder for inhalation does not require the use of a spacer device.The budesonide inhalation suspension requires the use of a jet nebulizer device. In asthmatic children 4 to 6 years of age, the total absolute bioavailability (i.e. lung and oral) is approximately 6% of the labeled dose, delivered via jet nebulizer.

Volume of distribution (Vol_D)

—Budesonide inhalation suspension: 3 liters per kilogram of body weight (L/kg) in children 4 to 6 years of age; approximately the same as in healthy adults.

Biotransformation

For beclomethasone dipropionate—

Rapidly transformed in the lungs to beclomethasone monopropionate, an active metabolite, which is significantly more potent topically than beclomethasone dipropionate.

For budesonide, flunisolide, and triamcinolone acetonide—

Absorbed unchanged. Those portions of each drug absorbed through the lungs or absorbed after being swallowed are rapidly and extensively transformed to inactive metabolites in the liver.

Half-life

For budesonide—120 to 180 minutes (plasma).
For flunisolide—90 to 120 minutes (plasma).
For triamcinolone—88 minutes (plasma).

Note: The plasma half-life of the inhaled corticosteroids does not correspond well with the biologic half-life.

Onset of action

Improvement in the control of asthma symptoms following inhalation of budesonide suspension can occur within 2 to 8 days of beginning treatment.

Maximum improvement in pulmonary function and symptoms may take up to 4 to 6weeks, while reduction in airway hyperresponsiveness occurs gradually over a period of weeks to months.Response depends on disease severity and the daily dose of the inhaled corticosteroid. Some patients fail to normalize their airway hyperresponsiveness despite years of treatment.

Time to peak concentration

The peak plasma concentration of inhaled budesonide suspension occurred 10 to 30 minutes after start of nebulization.

Elimination

Fecal and renal.

Precautions to Consider

Carcinogenicity

Studies in animals showed no evidence of carcinogenicity for beclomethasone or triamcinolone. Studies in mice and rats on oral flunisolide showed an increase in pulmonary adenomas in mice but not in rats.

Female rats showed an increased incidence of mammary adenocarcinoma. Studies of budesonide in mice showed no evidence of carcinogenesis. However, studies in rats showed an increase in gliomas in male rats at higher doses. No changes were found in female rats at higher doses or in male and female rats at lower doses. Two additional studies on male rats with budesonide at higher doses did not show an increase in glioma incidence but an increased incidence in hepatocellular tumors occurred.

Mutagenicity

Studies with budesonide have been performed using six different test systems: Ames Salmonella/microsome plate test, mouse micronucleus test, mouse lymphoma test, chromosome aberration test in human lymphocytes, sex-linked recessive lethal test in Drosophila melanogaster, and DNA repair analysis in rat hepatocyte culture. Budesonide was not found to be mutagenic. There have been no mutagenesis studies carried out with triamcinolone.

Pregnancy/Reproduction

Fertility—In animal studies performed in rats and dogs, some impairment of fertility was seen for beclomethasone, budesonide, and flunisolide at high doses. When lower doses were evaluated, no impairment of fertility was noted. Triamcinolone showed no evidence of impaired fertility in animal studies.

Pregnancy—Chronic administration of systemic corticosteroids to pregnant women has shown decreased birth weights and a slight increase in the incidence of premature deliveries.

The use of conventional doses of inhaled corticosteroids by pregnant asthmatic women has not been reported to be associated with an increased incidence of congenital abnormalities in the newborn. Inhaled corticosteroids may be used during pregnancy when clinically necessary, since poorly controlled asthma and loss of pulmonary function and hypoxia present a greater risk to the mother and may cause fetal hypoxia. If inhaled corticosteroids are effective before pregnancy, it is advisable to continue regular maintenance dosing during pregnancy.

In animal studies, decreases in fetal survival and weight have been demonstrated with systemic corticosteroids. All of the inhaled corticosteroids have been shown to be teratogenic in animal studies. Rodents appear to be more susceptible to the teratogenic effects of glucocorticoids than humans.

Beclomethasone is the preferred inhaled corticosteroid during pregnancy in the U.S. because of more extensive clinical experience with its use than with flunisolide or triamcinolone.

Beclomethasone; Budesonide inhalation suspension; Flunisolide; Triamcinolone —FDA Pregnancy Category C.

Budesonide inhalation powder—FDA Pregnancy Category B

Postpartum—

Infants whose mothers were treated with substantial doses of inhaled corticosteroids during pregnancy should be monitored for signs of hypoadrenalism.

Breast-feeding

It is not known whether inhaled corticosteroids are distributed into breast milk. However, problems in humans have not been documented. Although systemic corticosteroids are distributed into breast milk, it is unlikely that inhaled corticosteroids would reach significant quantities in maternal serum, and the concentration in breast milk would probably be of minor clinical significance.

Pediatrics

Orally inhaled corticosteroids are valuable and highly effective therapies in the management of asthma in pediatric patients. The Food and Drug Administration (FDA) and its advisory committees consider these products to be safe and effective in children when used according to their labeling guidelines. Clinical studies have shown that inhaled corticosteroids may cause a reduction in growth velocity in pediatric patients. In these studies (over a period of about 1 year), the mean reduction in growth velocity was approximately one centimeter (cm) per year (range 0.3 to 1.8 cm). This reduction appears to be related to the dose and the duration of exposure to the inhaled corticosteroid. This effect was observed in the absence of laboratory evidence of hypothalamic-pituitary-adrenal (HPA) axis suppression, which suggests that growth velocity is a more sensitive indicator of systemic corticosteroid exposure in pediatric patients than are some commonly used tests of HPA axis function.

However, recent clinical trials have reported that while there is a slowing of growth velocity during the first 12 months of therapy, children treated with inhaled corticosteroids attain their predicted adult height at maturity.Studies comparing inhaled corticosteroid use in asthma to placebo have found no significant difference in adult height. Conflicting data comparing the adult height in children who were asthmatic and nonasthmatics exists. Some data indicates that asthmatic children, regardless of treatment, attained a lower adult height than nonasthmatic children. Other data indicates that attained adult height of patients with asthma is not different from adult height in nonasthmatics patients, regardless of treatment with inhaled corticosteroids.

In general, it is recommended that the growth of pediatric patients receiving orally inhaled corticosteroids should be monitored routinely, for example, via stadiometry.The potential effects on growth velocity of prolonged treatment with inhaled corticosteroids should be weighed against the clinical benefits obtained and the availability of safe and effective noncorticosteroid treatment alternatives. To minimize the systemic effects of orally inhaled corticosteroids, the dose should be titrated to the lowest effective dose for the patient.

Use of prolonged, high daily doses of inhaled corticosteroids may cause a reduction in secretion of endogenous cortisol, although there have been no reports of clinically significant adrenal insufficiency in children treated with inhaled corticosteroids only. However, monitoring for the possibility of some suppression of the hypothalamic-pituitary-adrenal axis may be advisable in children receiving prolonged treatment.

Using a spacer device with beclomethasone, flunisolide, and triamcinolone (budesonide can not be used with a spacer device), rinsing the mouth after inhalations, using the lowest possible doses, and reducing doses after favorable responses have been obtained appear to minimize the risk of adverse systemic and local side effects. A spacer device may enhance inhalation techniques and thus improve intrapulmonary delivery of inhaled corticosteroids and increase compliance in pediatric patients.

Children who are taking systemic corticosteroids in immunosuppressant doses may be more susceptible to infectious diseases, especially chickenpox and measles. Chickenpox and measles may be more serious or possibly fatal in children on immunosuppressant doses of corticosteroids. Although it is highly unlikely that inhaled corticosteroids in usual doses would be associated with an increased risk of serious infection, some precautions are advisable for children who are taking larger than usual doses of inhaled corticosteroids and who have not had these diseases. Particular care should be taken to avoid exposure to chickenpox and measles and to immunize at an early age against infectious diseases for which there are vaccines, such as measles. If the child is exposed to chickenpox, preventative treatment with varicella zoster immune globulin (VZIG) may be appropriate. If the child is exposed to measles, pooled intramuscular immunoglobulin (IG) for prophylaxis may be indicated. Treatment with antiviral medications may be used if chickenpox should develop.

Geriatrics

Appropriate studies on the relationship of age to the effects of inhaled corticosteroids have not been performed in the geriatric population. However, in studies that have included patients over 65 years of age, geriatrics-specific problems that would limit the usefulness of this medication in the elderly have not been documented.

Drug interactions and/or related problems

Significant drug interactions are unlikely to occur with usual doses of inhaled corticosteroids. Although there are no defined drug interactions with inhaled corticosteroids, if these medications are used in high doses for a long time and systemic absorption occurs, some of the interactions seen with systemic corticosteroids have a potential to occur. (See *Corticosteroids—Glucocorticoid Effects [Systemic]*.)

Laboratory value alterations

The following have been selected on the basis of their potential clinical significance (possible effect in parentheses where appropriate)—not necessarily inclusive (» = major clinical significance).

With physiology/laboratory test values

Note: The following values may be affected with chronic use of larger-than-recommended doses of inhalation corticosteroids.

Adrenal function and

Hypothalamic-pituitary-adrenal (HPA) axis function as assessed by 24-hour urinary free cortisol, morning serum cortisol concentration, or short tetracosactrin cortisol test
(may be decreased if significant absorption of inhaled corticosteroid occurs, especially in children)

Glucose, blood or urine
(high-dose therapy may be associated with an increase in fasting insulin, peak glucose, and insulin to glucose ratios after glucose tolerance tests)

Hematologic status
(neutrophils and total white blood cell count may be increased; eosinophils and lymphocytes may be decreased; clinical relevance of these systemic effects may be insignificant)

Osteocalcin, serum
(may be decreased in children and adults taking inhaled corticosteroids; however, decrease may also be seen in asthma patients not taking corticosteroids)

Medical considerations/Contraindications

The medical considerations/contraindications included have been selected on the basis of their potential clinical significance (reasons given in parentheses where appropriate)—not necessarily inclusive (» = major clinical significance).

Risk-benefit should be considered when the following medical problems exist:

Cirrhosis
(may cause the effects of the corticosteroids to be enhanced)

Glaucoma
(may increase intraocular pressure)

Hypothyroidism
(may cause the effects of the corticosteroids to be enhanced)

Infections, untreated systemic, including bacterial, fungal, parasitic, or viral
(use with caution, if at all; however, if the infection is an upper respiratory viral infection, the patient should continue therapy with the inhaled corticosteroid. In patients who have a history of asthma control deteriorating quickly during viral respiratory infection, prompt treatment with a short course of systemic corticosteroids should be considered)

Osteoporosis
(may be exacerbated in postmenopausal women taking high doses over a prolonged time and not receiving an estrogen supplement. The daily dose of corticosteroid should be adjusted to the minimum required to maintain good control of asthma symptoms and estrogen replacement therapy may be considered)
(clinical studies have shown that cumulative inhaled corticosteroid doses have an inverse relationship with bone-mineral density at the lumbar spine and proximal femur)

Tuberculosis
(may be reactivated during prolonged inhaled corticosteroid therapy unless chemoprophylaxis is administered concurrently; asthmatic patients with a positive Mantoux test who are using inhaled corticosteroids should be carefully monitored for manifestation or reactivation, especially in countries with a high incidence of tuberculosis; inhaled corticosteroids should be avoided or used with great caution in patients with drug-resistant pulmonary tuberculosis or atypical tuberculosis)

Patient monitoring

The following may be especially important in patient monitoring (other tests may be warranted in some patients, depending on condition; » = major clinical significance):

Adrenal function assessment
(may be advisable periodically during, and for several months following, transfer of a patient from systemic to inhalation corticosteroid therapy)
(may be advisable every year during treatment in both children and adults if dosing guidelines are exceeded, especially if systemic corticosteroids are used concurrently or prior to inhaled corticosteroids)

Growth and development in children
(careful monitoring of growth, for example via stadiometry, is recommended periodically during therapy with inhaled corticosteroids)

Inhalation technique
(frequent assessment of inhalation technique and patient education on the importance of continuous prophylactic treatment with inhaled corticosteroids is recommended to ensure compliance, enhance delivery of medication to lungs, and reduce local and systemic side effects)

Intraocular pressure
(periodic assessment is advisable in patients, such as the elderly, who may be at risk for glaucoma; patients who have glaucoma should be monitored prior to initiating treatment with inhaled corticosteroids and at appropriate intervals)

Pulmonary function assessment
(periodic assessment is advisable during, and for several months following, transfer of a patient from systemic to inhalation corticosteroid therapy; frequent pulmonary function monitoring may be necessary in some patients for as long as 4 to 8 months after discontinuation of oral corticosteroids; daily outpatient peak expiratory flow rate [PEFR] measurements are useful in following the course of asthma and the patient's response to therapy)

Signs of systemic absorption
(patients on high doses of inhaled corticosteroids should be assessed periodically for signs of increased bruising, weight gain, cushingoid features, acneform lesions, and cataracts)

Side/Adverse Effects

Note: Some clinically important cases of growth suppression have been reported for orally inhaled corticosteroids. See also *Pediatrics* section.

Use of corticosteroids in immunosuppressant doses is associated with a higher risk of infection, with the potential for those infections to be of a more serious nature. Care should be taken in adults and children to avoid exposure to viral infections, especially chickenpox and measles, if the patient has not already had the disease or been immunized against it. Infections such as ear, eye, flu-like, sinus, urinary tract, viral, and yeast infections have occurred in a small number of patients on inhaled corticosteroids. Transfer of patients from systemic to inhalation corticosteroid therapy may unmask allergic conditions which were previously suppressed, such as conjunctivitis, eczema, and rhinitis, due to a lower level of systemic corticosteroids.

Pulmonary infiltrates with eosinophilia have occurred in patients receiving inhaled corticosteroids. While this effect probably occurs as a result of withdrawal of the systemic corticosteroid, a causative role of the inhaled corticosteroids or their vehicles cannot be ruled out.

Those indicating need for medical attention

Incidence less frequent

Bruising; chest pain; cystitis (burning or pain while urinating; blood in urine; frequent urge to urinate); ***edema*** (swelling of face, fingers, ankles, feet, or lower legs; weight gain); ***fatigue*** (unusual tiredness or weakness); ***itching, rash, or hives; malaise*** (general feeling of discomfort or illness); ***oropharyngeal candidiasis or thrush*** (creamy white, curd-like patches in mouth or throat; pain when eating or swallowing); ***palpitations or tachycardia*** (irregular or fast heartbeat); ***sinus problems; stomach or abdominal pain; vertigo*** (dizziness; sense of constant movement of self or surroundings); ***weight gain***

Incidence rare

Adrenal insufficiency (unusual tiredness or weakness; feeling faint; loss of appetite; nausea or vomiting; diarrhea; increased skin pigmentation); ***bronchospasm*** (shortness of breath; troubled breathing; tightness in chest; wheezing); ***cataracts*** (blurred vision or other changes in vision); ***esophageal candidiasis*** (pain or burning in chest); ***fever; gastroenteritis*** (diarrhea; nausea; stomach pain); ***growth inhibition***—in children; ***hypercorticism*** (increased fat deposits in face, neck, and trunk); ***hyperglycemia*** (frequent urination; unusual thirst); ***hypersensitivity reactions, such as angioedema*** (swelling of face, lips or eyelids); ***bronchospasm*** (severe wheezing or troubled breathing); ***rash; or urticaria*** (hives); ***hypertension*** (high blood pressure); ***loss of smell or taste; menstrual disturbances*** (menstrual changes); ***numbness; pneumonia; psychological disturbances, such as aggressive reactions, anxiety, behavioral changes, depression, psychosis, and restlessness*** (mood or mental changes); ***rectal hemorrhage*** (bleeding from rectum or bloody stools); ***syncope*** (fainting)

Note: If use of this medication causes *bronchospasm*, the medication should be immediately discontinued and replaced with an alternative therapy.

Those occurring principally during long-term use indicating need for medical attention

Osteoporosis (pain in back, ribs, arms, or legs)

Those indicating need for medical attention only if they continue or are bothersome

Incidence more frequent

Cold-like symptoms; cough; dry mouth or throat; headache; laryngitis, pharyngitis, or dysphonia (sore throat, hoarseness, or voice changes); ***throat irritation***

Incidence less frequent

Constipation or diarrhea; insomnia (trouble in sleeping); ***nausea or vomiting; unpleasant taste***

Incidence rare

Epistaxis (nosebleeds)

Overdose

Clinical effects of overdose

The following effects have been selected on the basis of their potential clinical significance (possible signs and symptoms in parentheses where appropriate)—not necessarily inclusive:

Acute

Suppression of hypothalamic-pituitary-adrenal (HPA) function—the potential for toxicity is low

Chronic
Adrenal suppression and hypercorticism

Treatment of overdose

For acute overdose, no emergency action is required. Inhaled corticosteroid therapy should be continued at recommended doses to control asthma. HPA function should return to normal range within one or two days.

For chronic overdose, treatment consists of decreasing the dose of the inhaled corticosteroid and then returning to the inhaled corticosteroid therapy slowly.

Patient Consultation

As an aid to patient consultation, refer to *Advice for the Patient, Corticosteroids (Inhalation).*

In providing consultation, consider emphasizing the following selected information (» = major clinical significance):

Before using this medication

» Conditions affecting use, especially:
Sensitivity to corticosteroids
Use in children—Use of inhaled corticosteroids may result in decreased growth velocity and reduced cortisol secretion; monitoring of growth and development and adrenal function is important. Except for budesonide powder for inhalation, the use of a spacer is necessary for better compliance and improved airway delivery. Budesonide inhalation suspension should be administered via jet nebulizer connected to an air compressor. Ultrasonic nebulizers are not recommended. Exposure to chickenpox or measles should be avoided

Proper use of this medication

» Not using to relieve acute asthma attack; continuing use even if using other medication for asthma attack
» Importance of not using more medication than the amount prescribed
» Compliance with therapy by using every day in regularly spaced doses; patients who are not taking systemic corticosteroids when inhalation therapy started may require up to 4 to 6 weeks for initial improvement and several months for full benefits
Gargling and rinsing mouth with water after each dose; not swallowing rinse water
» Reading patient instructions carefully; checking frequently with health care professional for proper use of inhaler nebulizer
» Proper dosing
Missed dose: Using as soon as possible; using any remaining doses for that day at regularly spaced intervals
Checking with pharmacist to determine availability of refills for aerosol inhalers; saving inhaler if refills available
» Proper storage
The canister should be stored at room temperature for best results. The dose delivered may be decreased if the canister is cold.

For beclomethasone, flunisolide, or triamcinolone inhalation aerosol dosage form
Testing or priming the inhaler before using first time
Proper administration technique
Proper administration technique with use of spacer device
Proper cleaning procedure for inhaler

For beclomethasone capsule for inhalation dosage form
» Not swallowing capsules; medication not effective if swallowed
Proper loading technique for inhaler
Proper administration technique
Proper cleaning procedure for inhaler

For beclomethasone powder for inhalation dosage form
Proper loading technique for inhaler
Proper administration technique
Proper cleaning procedure for inhaler

For budesonide powder for inhalation dosage form
Proper loading technique for inhaler
Prime inhaler before initial use
Proper administration technique

For budesonide suspension for inhalation dosage form
Using in a power-operated nebulizer with an adequate flow rate and equipped with face mask or mouthpiece
Preparation of medication for use in nebulizer
Proper administration technique
Proper cleaning procedure for nebulizer

Precautions while using this medication

» Checking with physician if:
Unusual physical stress occurs, such as surgery, injury, or infections
Exposure to the chickenpox or measles occurs
Asthma attack is not responsive to bronchodilator
Any sign indicating possible mouth, throat, or lung infection occurs
Symptoms do not improve or condition becomes worse
Carrying medical identification card stating that supplemental systemic corticosteroid therapy may be required in emergency situations, periods of unusual stress, or acute asthma attack
» Caution if any kind of surgery or emergency treatment is required; informing physician or dentist in charge that inhalation corticosteroid is being used
Avoid spraying in eyes

For patients receiving systemic corticosteroid therapy:
» Importance of not discontinuing systemic corticosteroid therapy without physician's advice; carefully reducing dose or discontinuing treatment if so directed
» Importance of regular visits to physician during time that systemic corticosteroid therapy is being withdrawn; obtaining physicians instructions to follow if severe asthma attack occurs, medical or surgical treatment is needed, or symptoms of corticosteroid withdrawal occur

Side/adverse effects

Signs of potential side effects, especially bruising; chest pain; cystitis; dysphonia; edema; fatigue; itching, rash, or hives; malaise; oropharyngeal candidiasis or thrush; palpitations or tachycardia; sinus problems; stomach or abdominal pain; vertigo; weight gain; adrenal insufficiency; bronchospasm; cataracts; esophageal candidiasis; fever; gastroenteritis; growth inhibition; hypercorticism; hyperglycemia; hypersensitivity reactions such as angioedema, bronchospasm, rash, or urticaria; hypertension; menstrual disturbances; numbness; pneumonia; psychological disturbances such as, aggressive reactions, anxiety, behavioral changes, depression, psychosis, and restlessness; rectal hemorrhage; syncope; and osteoporosis

General Dosing Information

Pharmacologic doses of inhaled corticosteroids should be carefully titrated to minimum effective doses to control asthma symptoms and prevent systemic effects. This is especially important for pediatric patients. See also *Pediatrics* section.

Gargling and rinsing the mouth with water after each dose are recommended to help prevent hoarseness, throat irritation, and oral candidiasis; the rinse water should not be swallowed. Rinsing the mouth without swallowing can also significantly reduce the amount of inhaled corticosteroid absorbed from the gastrointestinal tract.

The use of a spacer device with a metered dose inhaler may decrease the incidence of some adverse effects, especially oropharyngeal candidiasis and dysphonia. By reducing the need for proper coordination of timing of inhalation with activation of the inhaler and reducing the velocity and mean diameter of the aerosol particles, a spacer reduces the amount of medication deposited in the upper airways and increases the amount deposited in the lower respiratory tract. This enhances the local efficacy of the inhaled corticosteroid without significantly increasing systemic activity. Budesonide powder for inhalation can not be used with a spacer device.

Some patients may require relatively high doses of inhaled corticosteroids to prevent severe asthma relapse. For this purpose, the highly concentrated beclomethasone aerosol inhalation product available outside the U.S. facilitates the clinical use of high doses. The risk of local side effects, such as thrush and oropharyngeal candidiasis, may be minimized by twice-daily dosing and the use of a spacer device. However, these measures do not eliminate the risk of systemic side effects associated with prolonged use of high doses.

Patients whose asthma is controlled by their usual dose of inhaled corticosteroids may require temporary emergency use of systemic corticosteroids if their asthma control is rapidly deteriorating. The use of peak flow monitoring at home once or twice daily will provide objective information to the patient and the physician when this is necessary.

A short-acting inhaled bronchodilator is necessary to provide relief for the acute symptoms of asthma, such as bronchospasm.

Patients who use bronchodilators should administer the bronchodilator prior to the inhaled corticosteroid to enhance penetration of the corticosteroid into the bronchial tree. The inhaled bronchodilator should be used several minutes before the inhaled corticosteroid to allow time for bronchodilation and to reduce the potential for toxicity from fluorocarbon propellants of the inhaled corticosteroid.

If inhaled corticosteroid therapy requires discontinuation, the dosing regimen should be tapered off gradually and not stopped abruptly.

It is recommended that the 250-mcg-per-metered-spray product of beclomethasone be used only when the total daily dose is between 500 mcg and 1000 mcg.

For patients also receiving systemic corticosteroid therapy

Caution is required when transferring patients from systemic corticosteroids to inhaled corticosteroids. Deaths due to severe asthma relapse or possibly adrenal insufficiency have occurred in asthmatic patients during and after the transfer.

When transferring a patient from systemic corticosteroid therapy to inhaled corticosteroid therapy, the patient's asthmatic condition should be relatively stable. When initiating the transfer, the patient should add the inhaled corticosteroid to existing systemic therapy. After a week to ten days of concurrent therapy, the systemic agent should be withdrawn gradually by reducing the daily or alternate-daily dose. The reductions should be made at intervals of 1 to 2 weeks, depending on how well the patient responds to the withdrawal. *A slow rate of withdrawal is strongly urged.* As a rule, the reductions should not exceed 2.5 mg of prednisone or its equivalent at one time.

Some patients may not be able to discontinue use of systemic corticosteroids. A minimal oral maintenance dose may be required along with the inhaled corticosteroid.

Continued monitoring of the patient for signs of adrenal insufficiency is recommended following complete withdrawal of systemic corticosteroid therapy. Recovery of adrenal function may require up to 12 months in some patients, depending on the dosage and duration of systemic therapy.

During the period of hypothalamic-pituitary-adrenal (HPA) function recovery, the patient may show signs of adrenal insufficiency when exposed to stressors, such as trauma, surgery, or infections, especially gastroenteritis or other conditions which involve a loss of electrolytes over a short period of time. While the inhaled corticosteroid may control the symptoms of asthma during these episodes, it does not supply a sufficient amount of systemic corticosteroids to cope with these emergencies. Therefore, patients who have had systemic corticosteroid therapy withdrawn recently should be instructed to resume large doses of systemic corticosteroid for these periods of stress, or for an acute asthma attack, and to contact their physician for further instruction.

Severe asthma relapse may occur upon withdrawal of the systemic corticosteroid. Reinstitution of systemic therapy may be required if a severe asthma attack occurs. Frequent pulmonary function monitoring (peak expiratory flow rate measurements) may be needed for some patients for as long as 4 to 8 months after discontinuation of the systemic corticosteroid.

A syndrome of pseudo-rheumatism (consisting of joint or muscle pain, joint swelling, peripheral edema, lethargy, anorexia, and nausea) may occur when systemic corticosteroid is withdrawn. This syndrome can be avoided or minimized if the dosage of systemic corticosteroids is reduced slowly, using an alternate-day regimen. If the syndrome occurs, the symptoms may be alleviated by treatment with acetaminophen or nonsteroidal anti-inflammatory drugs (NSAIDs) in asthmatic patients who are not sensitive to NSAIDs. Resumption of systemic corticosteroid therapy may not be required.

For treatment of adverse effects

For laryngeal or pharyngeal candidiasis—Recommended treatment includes:
- Administration of an oral or systemic antifungal medication.
- Change in frequency of inhaled corticosteroid dosing from four to two times a day without decreasing the total daily dose. This may allow recovery and clearing of thrush or prevent its occurrence while maintaining therapeutic efficacy.
- Discontinuation of the inhaled corticosteroid is rarely necessary.

BECLOMETHASONE

Inhalation Dosage Forms

BECLOMETHASONE DIPROPIONATE INHALATION AEROSOL

Usual adult and adolescent dose

Antiasthmatic—

For the 42- or 50-mcg-per-metered-spray products—

Oral inhalation, 2 inhalations (84 or 100 mcg) three or four times a day. Alternatively, a dosage of 4 inhalations two times a day has been shown to be effective for some patients.

For severe asthma: Oral inhalation, initially, 12 to 16 inhalations a day. Dosage should then be decreased according to the patient's response.

For the 84-mcg-per-metered-spray product—

Oral inhalation, 2 inhalations (168 mcg) two times a day.

For severe asthma: Oral inhalation, initially, 6 to 8 inhalations a day. Dosage should then be decreased according to the patient's response.

Usual adult and adolescent prescribing limits

For the 42- or 50-mcg-per-metered-spray products—20 inhalations (840 or 1000 mcg) per day.

For the 84-mcg-per-metered-spray product—10 inhalations (840 mcg) per day.

Usual pediatric dose

Antiasthmatic—

Children up to 6 years of age—

Dosage has not been established.

Children 6 to 12 years of age—

For the 42- or 50-mcg-per-metered-spray products:

Oral inhalation, 1 or 2 inhalations three or four times a day. Alternatively, a dosage of 4 inhalations two times a day has been shown to be effective for some patients.

For the 84-mcg-per-metered-spray product:

Oral inhalation, 2 inhalations two times a day.

Children older than 12 years of age—

See *Usual adult and adolescent dose*.

Note: The 250-mcg-per-metered-spray product is not recommended for children up to 16 years of age.

Usual pediatric prescribing limits

For the 42- or 50-mcg-per-metered-spray products—10 inhalations (420 or 500 mcg per day.

For the 84-mcg-per-metered-spray product—5 inhalations (420 mcg) per day.

Strength(s) usually available

U.S.—

Note: The 84-mcg-per-metered spray must be primed by spraying twice into the air before the initial use and when the product has not been used for more than 7 days.

Each 6.7 gram canister contains medication for 80 inhalations.
Each 16.8 gram canister contains medication for about 200 inhalations.

42 mcg (0.042 mg) per metered spray (Rx) [*Beclovent; Vanceril*].
84 mcg (0.084 mg) per metered spray (Rx) [*Vanceril 84 mcg Double Strength* (chlorofluorocarbons)].

Canada—

Note: The 50-mcg-per-metered-spray product is available in two sizes that contain medication for 80 or 200 inhalations per canister.

The 250-mcg-per-metered-spray product is available in two sizes that contain medication for 80 or 200 inhalations per canister.

50 mcg (0.05 mg) per metered spray (Rx) [*Beclovent; Vanceril*].
250 mcg (0.25 mg) per metered spray (Rx) [*Becloforte*].

Packaging and storage

Store between 15° and 30° C (59° and 86° F). If medication is not used within this range of temperature, the dose may not be accurate.

Auxiliary labeling

- Shake well before using.
- For oral inhalation only.
- Store away from heat and direct sunlight.

Note

Include patient instructions when dispensing.

Demonstrate administration technique.

Additional information

In Canada, metered dose inhalers are labeled according to the amount of beclomethasone delivered at the valve; in the U.S., metered dose inhalers are labeled according to the amount of beclomethasone delivered at the mouthpiece or actuator. Thus, 50 mcg of beclomethasone delivered at the valve is equivalent to 42 mcg delivered at the mouthpiece.

These products contains dichlorodifluoromethane and trichloromonofluoromethane, substances that harm public health and the environment by destroying ozone in the upper atmosphere.

BECLOMETHASONE DIPROPIONATE HFA INHALATION AEROSOL

Usual adult and adolescent dose

Antiasthmatic—

For the 40-mcg-per-metered-spray product—

For patients who have previously used bronchodilators alone—

Oral inhalation, 1 (40 mcg) or 2 (80 mcg) inhalations twice daily.

For patients who have previously used inhaled corticosteroids—
Oral inhalation, 1 (40 mcg) to 4 (160 mcg) inhalations twice daily.

For the 50-mcg-per-metered-spray product—
Mild asthma—Oral inhalation, 1 (50 mcg) or 2 (100 mcg) inhalations twice daily.
Moderate asthma—Oral inhalation 2 (100 mcg) to 5 (250 mcg) inhalations twice daily.

For the 80-mcg-per-metered-spray product—
For patients who have previously used bronchodilators alone—
Oral inhalation, 1 inhalation (80 mcg) two times a day.
For patients who have previously used inhaled corticosteroids—
Oral inhalation, 1 or 2 inhalations (80 or 160 mcg) two times a day.

For the 100-mcg-per-metered-spray product—
Severe asthma—Oral inhalation, 3 (300 mcg) or 4 (400 mcg) inhalations twice daily.

Note: The prescribing information in Canada includes a suggested conversion of doses for patients switching from CFC-beclomethasone dipropionate (CFC-BDP) to HFA-beclomethasone dipropionate (HFA-BDP).
For patients using 200 mcg per day of CFC-BDP, use 100 mcg per day of HFA-BDP.
For patients using 400 to 500 mcg per day of CFC-BDP, use 200 mcg per day of HFA-BDP.
For patients using 600 to 750 mcg per day of CFC-BDP, use 300 mcg per day of HFA-BDP.
For patients using 800 to 1000 mcg per day of CFC-BDP, use 400 mcg per day of HFA-BDP.

Usual adult and adolescent prescribing limits

For the 40 mcg-per-metered-spray product—16 inhalations (640 mcg) per day.
For the 50 mcg-per-metered-spray product—10 inhalations (500 mcg) per day.
For the 80-mcg-per-metered-spray product—8 inhalations (640 mcg) per day.
For the 100 mcg-per-metered-spray product—8 inhalations (800 mcg) per day.

Usual pediatric dose

Antiasthmatic—
Children up to 5 years of age: Dosage has not been established.
Children 5 to 11 years of age: Oral inhalation, 1 (40 mcg) inhalation twice daily.
Children older than 12 years of age: See *Usual adult and adolescent dose.*

Usual pediatric prescribing limits

For the 40 mcg-per-metered-spray product—2 inhalations (80 mcg) per day.

Strength(s) usually available

U.S.—
Note: The 40-mcg-per-metered spray and 80-mcg-per-metered spray must be primed by spraying twice into the air (avoid eyes and face) before the initial use and when the product has not been used for more than 10 days. Each 7.3 gram canister contains medication for 100 inhalations
40 mcg (0.04 mg) per metered spray (Rx) [*QVAR*].
80 mcg (0.08 mg) per metered spray (Rx) [*QVAR* (tetrafluoroethane; ethanol)].

Canada—
Note: The 50-mcg-per-metered-spray product is available in two sizes that contain medication for 100 (6.5 grams) and 200 (12.4 grams) inhalations per canister.
The 100-mcg-per-metered-spray product is available in two sizes that contain medication for 100 (6.5 grams) and 200 (12.4 grams) inhalations per canister.
50 mcg (0.05 mg) per metered spray (Rx) [*QVAR; QVAR*].
100 mcg (0.1 mg) per metered spray (Rx) [*QVAR*].

Packaging and storage

Store between 25° C (77° F). Excursions permitted between 15° and 30° C (59° and 86° F). If medication is not used within this range of temperature, the dose may not be accurate.

Auxiliary labeling

- For oral inhalation only.
- Store away from heat and direct sunlight.
- Store the canister on the concave end with the plastic actuator on top
- Exposure to temperatures above 49° C (120° F) may cause bursting.

Note

Include patient instructions when dispensing.

Shaking the canister prior to administration is not necessary for this aerosol solution formulation.

Demonstrate administration technique.

Additional information

In Canada, metered dose inhalers are labeled according to the amount of beclomethasone delivered at the valve; in the U.S., metered dose inhalers are labeled according to the amount of beclomethasone delivered at the mouthpiece or actuator. Thus, 50 mcg of beclomethasone dipropionate delivered at the valve is equivalent to 40 mcg delivered at the mouthpiece and 100 mcg of beclomethasone dipropionate delivered at the valve is equivalent to 80 mcg delivered at the mouthpiece.

While the beclomethasone dipropionate HFA was developed for use without a spacer device being necessary, the AeroChamber® is a suitable device for use with beclomethasone dipropionate HFA metered dose inhaler to maintain the extrafine particle fraction.

BECLOMETHASONE DIPROPIONATE FOR INHALATION (CAPSULES)

Usual adult dose

Antiasthmatic—
Oral inhalation, 200 mcg (0.2 mg) three or four times a day. Dosage should then be decreased according to patient response; many patients may be maintained on 400 mcg (0.4 mg) a day.

Usual adult prescribing limits

1000 mcg (1 mg) per day.

Usual pediatric dose

Antiasthmatic—
Children up to 6 years of age: Dosage has not been established.
Children 6 to 14 years of age: Oral inhalation, 100 mcg (0.1 mg) two to four times a day. Dosage should then be decreased according to patient response.
Children over 14 years of age: See *Usual adult dose.*

Usual pediatric prescribing limits

500 mcg (0.5 mg) per day.

Strength(s) usually available

U.S.—
Not commercially available.

Canada—
100 mcg (0.1 mg) per capsule (Rx) [*Beclovent Rotacaps* (lactose)].
200 mcg (0.2 mg) per capsule (Rx) [*Beclovent Rotacaps* (lactose)].

Packaging and storage

Store below 30 °C (86 °F) and in a dry place.

Auxiliary labeling

- Do not swallow capsule.

Note

Include patient instructions when dispensing.

Demonstrate administration technique.

Use of beclomethasone for oral inhalation (capsules) requires a special device that separates the capsule into halves and releases the medication.

Each capsule should be inserted into the device only immediately prior to use. If this instruction is not followed, the delivery of the medicine may be affected.

BECLOMETHASONE DIPROPIONATE FOR INHALATION (POWDER)

Usual adult dose

See *Beclomethasone Dipropionate for Inhalation (Capsules).*

Usual adult prescribing limits

1000 mcg (1 mg) per day.

Usual pediatric dose

See *Beclomethasone Dipropionate for Inhalation (Capsules).*

Usual pediatric prescribing limits

500 mcg (0.5 mg) per day.

Strength(s) usually available

U.S.—
Not commercially available.

Canada—
100 mcg (0.1 mg) per blister (Rx) [*Beclodisk*].
200 mcg (0.2 mg) per blister (Rx) [*Beclodisk*].

Packaging and storage

Store below 30 °C (86 °F), in a well-closed container, unless otherwise specified by manufacturer.

Note

Include patient instructions when dispensing.

Demonstrate administration technique.

Use of beclomethasone for oral inhalation (powder) requires a special device that penetrates the blister and releases the medication.

BUDESONIDE

Inhalation Dosage Forms

Note: Bracketed information in the *Dosage Forms* section refer to categories of use and/or indications that are not included in U.S. product labeling.

BUDESONIDE POWDER FOR INHALATION

Usual adult dose

Antiasthmatic—

Previous asthma therapy consisting of bronchodilators alone—

Oral inhalation, 1 to 2 inhalations (200 to 400 mcg) two times a day.

Previous asthma therapy including inhaled corticosteroids—

Oral inhalation, 1 to 2 inhalations (200 to 400 mcg) two times a day. Dosage may be increased as needed and as tolerated to a maximum of 4 inhalations (800 mcg) two times a day.

Note: Once-daily dosing with 200 mcg or 400 mcg may be considered in patients with mild to moderate asthma who are well controlled on inhaled corticosteroids. This dose may be administered once daily either in the morning or in the evening. If the asthma symptoms are not controlled adequately with the once-daily treatment, the total daily dose should be increased and/or administered as a divided dose.

Previous asthma therapy including systemic corticosteroids—

Oral inhalation, 2 to 4 inhalations (400 to 800 mcg) two times a day.

Usual adult prescribing limits

1600 mcg a day for patients previously treated with inhaled or systemic corticosteroids or 800 mcg a day for patients previously treated with bronchodilators alone.

Usual pediatric dose

Antiasthmatic—

Children up to 6 years of age—

Use is not recommended. However, studies have shown that [children 3 months to 6 years of age][1] have benefited from inhaled budesonide, at a dosage of 1 to 2 inhalations (200 to 400 mcg) daily, with a spacer (i.e., Nebuhaler, Inhaler), after which the dosage is adjusted as needed and as tolerated, to a maximum of 2 inhalations (400 mcg) daily.

Children 6 years of age and older—

Oral inhalation, 1 inhalation (200 mcg) two times a day. Dosage may be increased as needed and as tolerated to a maximum of 2 inhalations (400 mcg) two times a day.

Note: Once-daily dosing with 200 mcg or 400 mcg may be considered in patients with mild to moderate asthma who are well controlled on inhaled corticosteroids. This dose may be administered once daily either in the morning or in the evening. If the asthma symptoms are not controlled adequately with the once-daily treatment, the total daily dose should be increased and/or administered as a divided dose.

Usual pediatric prescribing limits

800 mcg a day.

Strength(s) usually available

U.S.—

Note: Product is an inhalation-driven, multi-dose, dry powder inhaler.

200 mcg (0.2 mg) (Rx) [*Pulmicort Turbuhaler*].

Canada—

100 mcg (0.1 mg) (Rx) [*Pulmicort Turbuhaler*].
200 mcg (0.2 mg) (Rx) [*Pulmicort Turbuhaler*].
400 mcg (0.4 mg) (Rx) [*Pulmicort Turbuhaler*].

Packaging and storage

Store between 20 and 25 °C (68 and 77 °F). Protect from light.

Auxiliary labeling

- For oral inhalation only.

BUDESONIDE SUSPENSION FOR INHALATION

Usual adult and adolescent dose

[Antiasthmatic]—

Initial: Oral inhalation, 1 to 2 mg, diluted with sterile sodium chloride inhalation solution, if necessary, to a volume of two to four mL, and administered via nebulization over a period of ten to fifteen minutes two times a day.

Note: For severe asthma, dosage may be increased according to patient response.

Maintenance: After the desired clinical effect has been obtained, the maintenance dose should be reduced gradually to the smallest dose necessary for control of symptoms.

Usual pediatric dose

Antiasthmatic—

Children 12 months to 8 years of age: Previous Therapy: Bronchodilators alone—0.5 mg total daily dose via jet nebulizer, either as a single dose or twice daily in divided doses.

Previous Therapy: Inhaled Corticosteroids—0.5 mg total daily dose via jet nebulizer, either as a single dose or twice daily in divided doses.

Previous Therapy: Oral Corticosteroids—1 mg total daily dose via jet nebulizer, either as a single 1 mg dose or twice daily in divided doses of 0.5 mg.

Children up to 12 months of age: Dosage has not been established.

Note: In Canada, children 3 months to 12 years of age: Initial—Oral inhalation, 250 mcg (0.25 mg) to 1 mg, diluted with sterile sodium chloride inhalation solution, if necessary, to a volume of two to four mL, and administered via nebulization over a period of ten to fifteen minutes two times a day. Maintenance—After the desired clinical effect has been obtained, the maintenance dose should be reduced gradually to the smallest dose necessary for control of symptoms. Dosage has not been established for children younger than 3 months of age.

[Croup][1]—

Oral inhalation, 2 mg administered via nebulization over a period of ten to fifteen minutes.

Strength(s) usually available

U.S.—

125 mcg (0.125 mg) per mL (250 mcg per 2-mL ampul) (Rx) [*Pulmicort Respules* (disodium edetate; sodium chloride; sodium citrate; citric acid; polysorbate 80; water for injection)].

250 mcg (0.25 mg) per mL (500 mcg per 2-mL ampul) (Rx) [*Pulmicort Respules* (disodium edetate; sodium chloride; sodium citrate; citric acid; polysorbate 80; water for injection)].

Canada—

125 mcg (0.125 mg) per mL (250 mcg per 2-mL ampul) (Rx) [*Pulmicort Nebuamp*].

250 mcg (0.25 mg) per mL (500 mcg per 2-mL ampul) (Rx) [*Pulmicort Nebuamp*].

500 mcg (0.5 mg) per mL (1000 mcg per 2-mL ampul) (Rx) [*Pulmicort Nebuamp*].

Packaging and storage

Store between 5 and 30 °C (41 and 86 °F) in an upright position, unless otherwise specified by manufacturer. Protect from freezing. Protect from light.

Stability

Ampuls in an opened envelope should be stored in the envelope, protected from light, and used within 2 weeks.

Any opened ampul must be used promptly.

Note: For Canadian products, any unused suspension remaining in an opened ampul may be stored for later use as long as it is protected from light and is used within 12 hours after the ampul was opened. The entire contents of an ampul must be used within 12 hours after it is first opened. Ampuls in an opened envelope should be used within 3 months.

Auxiliary labeling

- For oral inhalation only.
- Shake gently before using.
- Do not freeze.

Note

When dispensing, include patient instructions for preparation of solution.

Additional information

For nebulization of budesonide inhalation suspension, a gas flow (oxygen or compressed air) of 6 to 10 liters per minute should be used. Nebulizers with either a facemask or mouthpiece have been used. Ultrasonic nebulizers are not recommended.

[1]Not included in Canadian product labeling.

FLUNISOLIDE

Inhalation Dosage Forms

FLUNISOLIDE INHALATION AEROSOL

Usual adult and adolescent dose

Antiasthmatic—

Oral inhalation, 500 mcg (0.5 mg—2 metered sprays) two times a day, morning and evening.

Usual adult prescribing limits

Oral inhalation, 2 mg per day (4 metered sprays twice a day). At the 2-mg-per-day dosage, the patient should be monitored at appropriate intervals for HPA suppression.

Usual pediatric dose

Antiasthmatic—

Children up to 6 years of age: Dosage has not been established.

Children 6 years of age and older: See *Usual adult and adolescent dose*.

Note: Doses higher than 1 mg per day have not been studied in children 4 to 15 years of age. In Canada the pediatric dosing is established for children 4 years of age and older.

Strength(s) usually available

U.S.—

250 mcg (0.25 mg) per metered spray (Rx) [*AeroBid; AeroBid-M* (menthol)].

Canada—

250 mcg (0.25 mg) per metered spray (Rx) [*Bronalide*].

Note: Each canister delivers at least 100 inhalations.

Packaging and storage

Store below 49 °C (120 °F), preferably between 15 and 30 °C (59 and 86 °F), unless otherwise specified by manufacturer.

Auxiliary labeling

- Shake well before using.
- For oral inhalation only.

Note

Include patient instructions when dispensing.

Demonstrate administration technique.

Additional information

These products contain dichlorodifluoromethane, trichloromonofluoromethane, and dichlorotetrafluoroethane, substances that harm public health and the environment by destroying ozone in the upper atmosphere.

TRIAMCINOLONE

Inhalation Dosage Forms

TRIAMCINOLONE ACETONIDE INHALATION AEROSOL

Usual adult and adolescent dose

Antiasthmatic—

Initial: Oral inhalation, 200 mcg (0.2 mg—2 metered sprays) three or four times a day, or four inhalations twice a day. For severe asthma: Oral inhalation, 1.2 to 1.6 mg (12 to 16 metered sprays) a day.

Maintenance: Dosage to be decreased according to patient response; maintenance may be achieved in some patients by administering the total daily dose in two divided doses.

Usual adult prescribing limits

1.6 mg (16 metered sprays) per day.

Usual pediatric dose

Antiasthmatic—

Children up to 6 years of age: Dosage has not been established.

Children 6 to 12 years of age: Oral inhalation, 100 to 200 mcg (0.1 to 0.2 mg—1 or 2 metered sprays) three or four times a day, or 200 to 400 mcg (2 or 4 metered sprays) twice a day. Dosage must be adjusted according to patient response.

Usual pediatric prescribing limits

1.2 mg (12 metered sprays) per day.

Strength(s) usually available

U.S.—

100 mcg (0.1 mg) per metered spray (Rx) [*Azmacort* (alcohol 1%)].

Canada—

200 mcg (0.2 mg) per metered spray (Rx) [*Azmacort* (alcohol 1%)].

Note: In Canada, metered dose inhalers are labeled according to the amount of medication delivered at the valve; in the U.S., metered dose inhalers are labeled according to the amount of medication delivered from the mouthpiece or actuator. Thus, 200 mcg of triamcinolone delivered at the valve is equivalent to 100 mcg delivered at the mouthpiece.

Each 60 gram canister delivers at least 240 inhalations. Canister should not be used after 240 inhalations. After 240 actuations, the dose may not be accurate.

Packaging and storage

Store at temperatures below 49 °C (120 °F), preferably between 15 and 30 °C (59 and 86 °F), unless otherwise specified by manufacturer.

Auxiliary labeling

- Shake well before using.
- For oral inhalation only.

Note

Include patient instructions when dispensing.

Demonstrate administration technique.

Additional information

Each actuation releases approximately 200 mcg of triamcinolone acetonide, of which approximately 100 mcg are delivered from the unit.

This product contains dichlorodifluoromethane, a substance that harms public health and the environment by destroying ozone in the upper atmosphere.

Revised: 06/03/2003

CORTICOSTEROIDS Nasal

This monograph includes information on the following: 1) Beclomethasone; 2) Budesonide; 3) Dexamethasone†; 4) Flunisolide; 5) Fluticasone; 6) Mometasone; 7) Triamcinolone.

INN: Beclomethasone—Beclometasone

VA CLASSIFICATION (Primary): NT201

Commonly used brand name(s): *Beconase*[1]; *Beconase AQ*[1]; *Dexacort Turbinaire*[3]; *Flonase*[5]; *Nasacort*[7]; *Nasacort AQ*[7]; *Nasalide*[4]; *Nasarel*[4]; *Nasonex*[6]; *Rhinalar*[4]; *Rhinocort*[2]; *Rhinocort Aqua*[2]; *Rhinocort Turbuhaler*[2]; *Vancenase*[1]; *Vancenase AQ 84 mcg*[1]; *Vancenase pockethaler*[1].

Note: For a listing of dosage forms and brand names by country availability, see *Dosage Forms* section(s).

†Not commercially available in Canada.

Category

Anti-inflammatory (steroidal), nasal; corticosteroid (nasal).

Indications

Note: Bracketed information in the *Indications* section refers to uses that are not included in U.S. product labeling.

Accepted

Rhinitis, perennial allergic (treatment)

Rhinitis, seasonal allergic (treatment) or

[Rhinitis, seasonal (prophylaxis) or]

[Rhinitis, vasomotor nonallergic (treatment)]—Nasal corticosteroids are indicated in the treatment of seasonal or perennial allergic or vasomotor nonallergic rhinitis in patients who have exhibited significant side effects from, or have exhibited poor response to, other therapies, such as antihistamines and decongestants. Antihistamines and decongestants are generally considered primary therapies for these disorders. However, some clinicians consider nasal corticosteroids primary therapy for perennial or seasonal rhinitis because they are more effective if prophylaxis is started two to four weeks prior to exposure to allergens. Nasal budesonide is indicated for use in [children 4 to 6 years of age][1] and older.

[Nasal corticosteroids are used in some patients for prophylaxis of seasonal rhinitis. This form of therapy is generally reserved for patients who have consistently demonstrated a need for nasal corticosteroids to control seasonal rhinitis symptoms. Antihistamines and decongestants are considered primary therapies for this disorder.]

Dexamethasone nasal aerosol is less frequently used because its use results in a significantly higher incidence of systemic adverse effects with no additional benefit over other nasal corticosteroids.

Allergic disorders, nasal (treatment)
Inflammatory conditions, noninfectious, nasal (treatment) or
Polyps, nasal (treatment)—Nasal corticosteroids are indicated in the treatment of allergic or inflammatory nasal conditions and nasal polyps.

Polyps, nasal, postsurgical recurrence of (prophylaxis)—Beclomethasone is indicated [and budesonide nasal solution, dexamethasone, flunisolide, and triamcinolone are used] to prevent recurrence of nasal polyps following their surgical removal and sufficient mucosal healing.

[Rhinitis, vasomotor (treatment)]—Budesonide is used in the treatment of vasomotor rhinitis in patients who are unresponsive to conventional therapy. Antihistamines are generally considered the primary therapy for this disorder.

Acceptance not established

Use of nasal budesonide in children younger than 4 years of age for the treatment of seasonal and perennial rhinitis has not been established.

[1]Not included in Canadian product labeling.

Pharmacology/Pharmacokinetics

Physicochemical characteristics

Molecular weight—
Beclomethasone dipropionate: 521.05.
Beclomethasone dipropionate monohydrate: 539.06.
Budesonide: 430.54.
Dexamethasone sodium phosphate: 516.41.
Flunisolide: 443.52.
Fluticasone propionate: 500.58.
Mometasone furoate: 521.44.
Triamcinolone acetonide: 434.51.

Mechanism of action/Effect

In the treatment of nasal symptoms, the primary action of nasally applied corticosteroids is anti-inflammatory. Nasal corticosteroids inhibit the IgE- and mast cell-mediated early-phase allergic reaction. They also inhibit the migration of inflammatory cells into the nasal tissue (the late-phase or late-onset allergic reaction), which may play a significant role in the pathology of chronic rhinitis.

During the late-phase allergic reaction, eosinophils, neutrophils, basophils, and mononuclear cells produce inflammatory mediators, which cause a reappearance of nasal symptoms.

Absorption

Beclomethasone dipropionate—Rapidly absorbed from the nasal mucosa; and from the gastrointestinal tract.
Budesonide—Very little is absorbed from the nasal mucosa; 20% reaches the systemic circulation.
Dexamethasone sodium phosphate—Rapidly and extensively absorbed from the nasal mucosa; readily absorbed from the gastrointestinal mucosa.
Flunisolide—50% of dose is absorbed from the nasal mucosa.
Fluticasone—Less than 2% from the nasal mucosa.
Mometasone—Rapid and extensive absorption from esophagus, trachea, nasal passages and mouth after intranasal dose.
Triamcinolone—Slow from the nasal mucosa.

Distribution

A portion of the drug administered nasally is swallowed.

Protein binding

Beclomethasone—87%, to albumin and transcortin.
Budesonide—88%, to albumin.
Dexamethasone sodium phosphate—High (65–90%) to albumin and transcortin.
Flunisolide—Moderate, to albumin and transcortin.
Fluticasone—91%, to albumin; not significantly bound to transcortin.

Biotransformation

Beclomethasone—Hepatic to free beclomethasone and other inactive metabolites. The portion of the dose that is swallowed and absorbed from the gastrointestinal tract undergoes extensive first-pass metabolism to inactive compounds. Initially hydrolyzed to beclomethasone-17-propionate by fecal esterases.
Budesonide—Rapid; hepatic to 16–alpha-hydroxyprednisolone and 6–beta-hydroxybudesonide
Flunisolide—Rapid; hepatic to a less active 6-beta-hydroxy metabolite and to glucuronide and sulfate conjugates. The portion of the dose that is swallowed and absorbed from the gastrointestinal tract undergoes extensive first-pass metabolism to inactive compounds.
Fluticasone—Hepatic to an active 17–beta-carboxylic acid derivative; only 0.02% renal.
Triamcinolone acetonide—Hepatic to 3 less active metabolites, 6-beta-hydroxytriamcinolone acetonide, 21-carboxytriamcinolone acetonide, and 21-carboxy-6-beta-hydroxytriamcinolone acetonide.

Half-life

Beclomethasone dipropionate—
15 hours (plasma).
Budesonide—
Approximately 2 hours (plasma).
Dexamethasone sodium phosphate—
190 minutes (plasma).
Flunisolide—
1 to 2 hours (plasma).
Fluticasone—
3 hours.
Triamcinolone acetonide—
Intravenous: Approximately 90 minutes (plasma).
Intranasal: Apparent half-life is 4 hours (plasma) (range, 1 to 7 hours); however, this value probably reflects lingering absorption; 3.1 hours with aqueous (AQ) formulation.

Onset of action

Beclomethasone and flunisolide—Usually 3 to 7 days; however, may rarely be as long as 2 to 3 weeks in some patients.
Budesonide—As early as 24 hours; usually 2 to 3 days.
Fluticasone—As early as 12 hours; usually 2 to 3 days.
Triamcinolone acetonide—As early as 12 hours; usually 4 to 7 days.

Time to peak concentration

Budesonide—
Oral, approximately 3 hours.
Inhalation, within 1 hour.
Flunisolide—
10 to 30 minutes.
Triamcinolone acetonide—
Average of 3.4 hours (range, 0.5 to 8 hours).

Peak plasma concentration

Flunisolide—0.4 to 1.0 nanogram per mL.

Triamcinolone acetonide—Less than 1 nanogram per mL.

Time to maximum benefit

Beclomethasone and flunisolide—Up to 3 weeks in some patients.

Budesonide—Usually 3 to 7 days, but up to 3 weeks in some patients.

Fluticasone—usually 4 to 7 days.

Triamcinolone acetonide—Usually 4 to 7 days.

Elimination

Beclomethasone—Fecal; renal, 12 to 15%.
Budesonide—Renal, 67%; feces 33%.
Dexamethasone sodium phosphate—Renal.
Flunisolide—Renal, 50% (65 to 75% primary metabolite); fecal, 50%.
Fluticasone—Renal, less than 5% as metabolite; fecal, remaining dose as parent drug and metabolites.

Precautions to Consider

Cross-sensitivity and/or related problems

Patients intolerant of benzalkonium chloride, disodium edetate, oleic acid or phenylethanol may be intolerant of some nasal corticosteroid preparations, since they may contain these substances as preservatives.
Beclomethasone dipropionate, dexamethasone, budesonide, and triamcinolone aerosols also contain fluorocarbon propellants; beclomethasone dipropionate monohydrate, budesonide, flunisolide, fluticasone propionate, mometasone furoate and triamcinolone solution, suspension and powder dosage forms contain no fluorocarbon propellants.
Flunisolide solution contains propylene glycol and polyethylene glycols.

Carcinogenicity

Beclomethasone—No evidence of carcinogenicity was demonstrated in rats receiving beclomethasone for 95 weeks (13 weeks by inhalation and 82 weeks orally).
Budesonide—No evidence of carcinogenic effect was found in mice and rats given oral doses of up to 200 mcg/kg/day for 91 weeks. An increase in incidence of gliomas and hepatocellular tumors were observed in a 104-week study in male rats given doses of 50 mcg/kg/day orally. No such changes were seen in male rats at doses of 10 and 25 mcg/kg/day or at any dose in female rats.
Flunisolide—In long-term studies, flunisolide given orally caused an increase in the incidence of benign pulmonary adenomas in mice but not in rats. Also, as reported for other corticosteroids, flunisolide

caused an increased incidence of mammary adenocarcinoma in female rats receiving the highest oral doses.

Fluticasone—Tumorigenic potential was found in mice given oral doses of up to 1000 mcg/kg (20 times the maximum recommended daily (MRD) intranasal dose in adults and 10 times the MRD in children) for 78 weeks and in rats given inhalation doses up to 57 mcg/kg (2 times MRD intranasal dose in adults and equal to the MRD intranasal dose in children), for 104 weeks.

Mometasone—No evidence of carcinogenicity was found in rats when given an inhalation dose of 67 mcg per kg body weight (mcg/kg) (approximately 3 times the MRD intranasal dose in adult humans on a mcg/m^2 basis). No evidence of an increase in tumors was found in mice given an inhalation dose of 160 mcg/kg (approximately 4 times the MRD intranasal dose in adult humans on a mcg/m^2 basis).

Triamcinolone—No evidence of carcinogenicity was demonstrated in a 2-year study on male and female rats administered oral doses of 1 mcg per kg of body weight (mcg/kg) a day and male and female mice administered oral doses of 3 mcg/kg a day.

Mutagenicity

Beclomethasone—Studies on mutagenicity have not been done.

Budesonide—No mutagenicity or clastogenic properties was found in any tests.

Fluticasone—No gene mutation induction was found in prokaryotic or eukaryotic cells *in vitro*.

Triamcinolone—Studies on mutagenicity have not been done.

Pregnancy/Reproduction

Fertility—*Beclomethasone:* Female dogs administered beclomethasone orally showed impaired fertility (inhibition of the estrous cycle). However, this effect was not observed following administration of the medication via inhalation.

Dexamethasone: Dexamethasone may increase or decrease spermatozoa count or motility in some patients.

Flunisolide: Studies in female rats showed some evidence of impaired fertility.

Fluticasone—No evidence of impairment of fertility was observed in studies of rats given subcutaneous doses of up to 50 mcg/kg (2 times the MRD intranasal dose in adult humans on a mcg/m^2 basis).

Mometasone—No impairment in fertility was observed in rats administered subcutaneous doses of 15 mcg/kg (approximately 3/4 the MRD intranasal dose in adult humans on a mcg/m^2 basis).

Triamcinolone: Male and female rats administered triamcinolone acetonide orally at doses of up to 15 mcg/kg per day (maternally toxic doses are 2.5 to 15 mcg/kg per day) exhibited no evidence of impaired fertility.

Pregnancy—Corticosteroids cross the placenta. Adequate and well-controlled studies in humans have not been done with beclomethasone, budesonide, dexamethasone, flunisolidefluticasone, mometasoneor triamcinolone nasal formulations. Use during pregnancy should be considered only if the benefit to the mother outweighs the potential risk to the fetus, especially during the first trimester.

Studies in animals have shown that corticosteroids are embryotoxic, fetotoxic, and/or teratogenic. However, teratogenic effects have not been confirmed in humans receiving systemic corticosteroids.

Infants born to mothers who have received substantial doses of corticosteroids during pregnancy should be carefully observed for signs of hypoadrenalism (anorexia, hypotension, weakness and weight loss).

Beclomethasone—

In one study of orally inhaled beclomethasone in humans, beclomethasone did not cause teratogenic or other adverse effects.

Studies in mice and rabbits have shown that beclomethasone administered subcutaneously at 10 times the MRD adult human dose causes increased fetal resorptions and birth defects, including cleft palate, agnathia, microstomia, absence of tongue, delayed ossification, and partial agenesis of the thymus. No teratogenic effects were observed in rats given an inhalation dose of 10 times the MRD adult human dose or an oral dose of 1000 times the MRD adult human dose.

FDA Pregnancy Category C.

Budesonide—

Studies in rats, mice, and rabbits have shown that subcutaneously administered budesonide causes fetal malformations, primarily skeletal defects, decrease in pup weight, piloerection, decrease in peri- and post-natal viability.

FDA Pregnancy Category C.

Dexamethasone—

Adequate and well-controlled studies in humans have not been done with dexamethasone nasal aerosol.

Flunisolide—

Adequate and well-controlled studies in humans have not been done.

Studies in rabbits and rats have shown that systemically administered flunisolide causes teratogenic and fetotoxic effects.

FDA Pregnancy Category C.

Fluticasone—

Studies on mice and rats given subcutaneous doses of 45 and 100 mcg/kg, respectively, (equal to and 4 times, respectively, the MRD intranasal dose in adult humans on a mcg/m^2 basis) revealed fetal toxicity including embryonic growth retardation, omphalocele, cleft palate and retarded cranial ossifications.

Studies on rabbits given a subcutaneous dose of 4 mcg/kg (less than the MRD in adult humans on a mcg/m^2 basis), revealed decrease in fetal weight and cleft palate. No teratogenic effects were reported at oral doses of up to 300 mcg/kg (25 times the MRD intranasal dose in adult humans on a mcg/m^2 basis). Fluticasone crossed the placenta following oral administration of 1000 mcg/kg given to rats and 300 mcg/kg given to rabbits (approximately 4 and 25 times the MRD intranasal dose in adult humans on a mcg/m^2 basis).

FDA Pregnancy Category C.

Mometasone—

Reproductive studies in rats administered subcutaneous doses of 15 mcg/kg (approximately 3/4 the MRD intranasal dose in adult humans on a mcg/m^2 basis), experienced prolonged gestation and labor, reduced offspring survival and reduced maternal weight gain.

Studies in mice given subcutaneous doses of 60 and 180 mcg/kg (approximately 2 and 4 times, respectively, the MRD intranasal dose in adult humans on a mcg/m^2 basis) experienced cleft palate, reduced fetal body weight, delayed ossification and reduced maternal weight gain. Offspring survival was reduced in the 180 mcg/kg dosage group. Studies in mice given a subcutaneous dose of 20 mcg/kg (approximately 1/2 of the MRD intranasal dose in adults on a mcg/m^2 basis) showed no teratogenic effects.

Rabbits given a dermal dose of 150 mcg/kg (approximately 14 times the MRD intranasal dose in adult humans on a mcg/m^2 basis) experienced flexed front paws, reduced maternal weight gain, reduced fetal weight and delayed ossification.

Rats given a dermal dose of 600 mcg/kg and 1200 mcg/kg (approximately 30 and 60 times the MRD intranasal dose in adult humans on a mcg/m^2 basis), experienced reduced maternal weight gain and passed on umbilical hernia, cleft palate, microphthalmia, reduced maternal weight gain, and delayed ossification to their rat pups.

FDA Pregnancy Category C.

Triamcinolone—

A few female rats administered oral doses of 8 mcg/kg per day exhibited dystocia and prolonged delivery and at oral doses of 5 mcg/kg per day exhibited an increase in fetal resorptions, stillbirths, decrease in pup body weight and survival.

Studies in rats and rabbits administered systemic doses of 20 to 80 mcg/kg per day have shown teratogenic effects, including a low incidence of cleft palate and/or internal hydrocephaly and axial skeletal defects. Studies in non-human primates administered systemic doses of 500 mcg/kg per day have shown teratogenic effects, including CNS and cranial malformations. Administration of triamcinolone nasal aerosol to pregnant rats and rabbits resulted in embryotoxic and fetotoxic effects that were comparable to those produced by administration by other routes.

FDA Pregnancy Category C.

Breast-feeding

Distribution of significant quantities of corticosteroids into breast milk may suppress growth, interfere with endogenous corticosteroid production, or cause other adverse effects in the nursing infant.

Beclomethasone, budesonide, flunisolide, fluticasone, and triamcinolone—It is not known whether beclomethasone, budesonide, flunisolide, fluticasone, or triamcinolone is distributed into breast milk. However, systemic corticosteroids are distributed into breast milk, and caution should be exercised when administering corticosteroids to nursing women. Use of corticosteroids while breast-feeding should be considered only if the benefit to the mother outweighs the potential risk to the infant.

Dexamethasone—It is distributed into breast milk. Nursing while receiving pharmacologic doses of dexamethasone is not recommended.

Mometasone—Plasma concentrations are not measurable in breast milk following the administration of the MRD intranasal adult human dose; thus fetal or breast milk exposure is expected to be negligible and toxicity low. Use of mometasone while breast-feeding should be considered if the benefit to the mother outweighs the risk to the infant.

Pediatrics

Significant suppression of growth has not been well documented with the use of usual doses of nasal beclomethasone and flunisolide. If significant systemic absorption of nasal corticosteroids occurs in pediatric patients, adrenal suppression and growth suppression may result. Prolonged or high-dose therapy with these medications during pregnancy, especially dexamethasone, requires careful attention to dosage and close monitoring of growth and development of the infant.

Geriatrics

Appropriate studies with nasal corticosteroids have not been performed in the geriatric population. However, geriatrics-specific problems that would limit the usefulness of this medication in the elderly are not expected.

Drug interactions and/or related problems

The following drug interactions and/or related problems have been selected on the basis of their potential clinical significance (possible mechanism in parentheses where appropriate)—not necessarily inclusive (» = major clinical significance):

Ephedrine or
Phenobarbital or
Rifampin
(induction of hepatic microsomal enzyme activity, by ephedrine, phenobarbital and rifampin, may result in increased metabolism, decreased serum concentration, decreased elimination half-life of dexamethasone and may warrant an increase in dexamethasone dosage.)

Laboratory value alterations

The following have been selected on the basis of their potential clinical significance (possible effect in parentheses where appropriate)—not necessarily inclusive (» = major clinical significance).

With diagnostic test results

For dexamethasone

Nitroblue tetrazolium test for bacterial infection
(dexamethasone may produce false-negative results)

With physiology/laboratory test values

Adrenal function as assessed by corticotropin (ACTH) stimulation or measurement of plasma cortisol and
Hypothalamic-pituitary-adrenal (HPA) axis function
(may be decreased if significant absorption occurs, especially in children; most likely with dexamethasone)

Glucose concentration, blood and urine
(may be increased if significant absorption occurs because of intrinsic hyperglycemic activity of glucocorticoids; most likely with dexamethasone)

Hematologic status
(should be monitored during long-term therapy)

Medical considerations/Contraindications

The medical considerations/contraindications included have been selected on the basis of their potential clinical significance (reasons given in parentheses where appropriate)—not necessarily inclusive (» = major clinical significance).

Risk-benefit should be considered when the following medical problems exist:

Amebiasis, latent or active
(dexamethasone or other corticosteroids may activate latent amebiasis)

Asthma
(may exacerbate symptoms)

Diabetes mellitus
(dexamethasone may decrease carbohydrate tolerance and use may warrant an increase in insulin dosage)

Glaucoma
(may increase intraocular pressure)

Hepatic function impairment

Hypothyroidism

» Left ventricular free wall rupture or
» Myocardial infarction, recent
(concurrent use with dexamethasone may exacerbate these conditions)

» Infections, fungal, bacterial, or systemic viral or
» Ocular herpes simplex
(corticosteroids may mask infection)

Nasal septal ulcers, recent or
Nasal surgery, recent or
Nasal trauma, recent
(corticosteroids inhibit wound healing)

» Tuberculosis, latent or active, of respiratory tract

» Hypersensitivity to corticosteroids

Patient monitoring

The following may be especially important in patient monitoring (other tests may be warranted in some patients, depending on condition; » = major clinical significance):

Adrenal function assessment
(assessment of HPA axis function may be advisable at periodic intervals in patients receiving long-term nasal corticosteroid therapy; important in patients receiving usual doses of dexamethasone or greater-than-recommended doses of beclomethasone, budesonide, flunisolide, fluticasone, mometasone or triamcinolone)

» Otolaryngologic examination
(should be performed in patients on long-term therapy to monitor nasal mucosa and nasal passages for infection, nasal septal perforation, nasal membrane ulceration, or other histologic changes.)

Side/Adverse Effects

Note: The risk of systemic effects is minimal with usual doses of nasal beclomethasone and flunisolide. Side effects from usual doses of beclomethasone are generally limited to local effects.

Systemic effects including hypothalamic-pituitary-adrenal (HPA) axis suppression may occur with usual doses of nasal dexamethasone greater-than-recommended doses of beclomethasone, budesonide flunisolide, fluticasone or triamcinolone. (Doses of 440 mcg of triamcinolone acetonide administered daily for 42 days did not measurably affect adrenal response to a 6-hour cosyntropin test.) If the patient is particularly sensitive or has recently used systemic corticosteroids prior to using nasal corticosteroids, the patient may also be predisposed to hypercorticism (blurred vision, bone fractures, excess facial hair growth in females, fullness or rounding of face, neck, and trunk, hypertension, increased thirst and urination, impotence in males, lack of menstrual periods, muscle wasting or weakness).

The following side/adverse effects have been selected on the basis of their potential clinical significance (possible signs and symptoms in parentheses where appropriate)—not necessarily inclusive:

Those indicating need for medical attention

Incidence more frequent

For beclomethasone

Headache—incidence 34%

For triamcinolone;

Headache—incidence 18%

Incidence less frequent

For all nasal corticosteroids

Crusting inside nose or epistaxis (bloody mucus or unexplained nosebleeds)—especially if spray is improperly aimed toward nasal septum, rather than onto the turbinates; ***sore throat; ulceration of nasal mucosa*** (sores inside nose)

For dexamethasone

Allergic reaction or bronchial asthma (shortness of breath, troubled breathing, tightness in chest, hives, or wheezing); ***cataracts, glaucoma, optic nerve damage, or secondary ocular fungal or viral infection*** (blindness; blurred vision; discharge or redness of the eye; eye pain); ***headache***

For fluticasone

Allergic reaction or bronchial asthma (shortness of breath, troubled breathing, tightness in chest, hives, or wheezing); ***cough; headache; nausea or vomiting***

For beclomethasone (monohydrate), budesonide, dexamethasone, and flunisolide

Cough; dizziness or light-headedness; hoarseness—not reported for budesonide; ***lethargy*** (unusual tiredness or weakness); ***loss of sense of taste or smell***—reported for dexamethasone and flunisolide; ***nausea or vomiting; rhinorrhea, continuing*** (runny nose); ***stuffy nose, continuing; watery eyes, continuing***—not reported for budesonide; ***stomach pains***—not reported for budesonide

For mometasone

Headache

Incidence rare

For all nasal corticosteroids

Nasal candidiasis (white patches inside nose); ***nasal septal perforation*** (bloody mucus or unexplained nosebleeds); ***ocular hy***

pertension (eye pain; nausea; vomiting; gradual loss of vision); ***pharyngeal candidiasis*** (white patches in throat)

For beclomethasone

Cataracts, conjunctivitis, or glaucoma (blindness; blurred vision; discharge or redness in the eye, eyelid, or inner lining of the eyelid; eye pain); ***myalgia*** (muscle pain); ***hypersensitivity reaction, delayed or immediate*** (large hives; rash; shortness of breath or troubled breathing; swelling of eyelids, face, or lips); ***rhinitis, atrophic*** (bad smell; dry or stuffy nose; headache behind eye sockets); ***tinnitus*** (ringing in the ears); ***ulceration of nasal mucosa*** (sores inside nose); ***wheezing***

For budesonide

Dermatitis (rash); ***urticaria*** (hives)

For fluticasone

Abdominal pain (stomach pain); ***bronchitis*** (cough); ***diarrhea; dizziness; fever; flu-like symptoms; hypersensitivity reaction, delayed or immediate*** (large hives; rash; shortness of breath or troubled breathing; swelling of eyelids, face, or lips); ***ophthalmic changes*** (blindness; blurred vision; eye pain; dry and irritated eyes); ***runny nose***

For triamcinolone

Burning or stinging, continuing, after use of spray, irritation inside nose

Symptoms of chronic overdose

Acneiform lesions (acne); ***Cushing's syndrome*** (blurred vision, increased thirst, and increased urination; bone fractures; excess facial hair growth in females; fullness or rounding of the face, neck, and trunk; high blood pressure; impotence in males; muscle wasting and weakness); ***menstrual changes***

Those indicating need for medical attention only if they continue or are bothersome

Incidence more frequent

For all nasal corticosteroids

Burning, dryness, or other irritation inside the nose, mild and transient

For beclomethasone and flunisolide

Irritation of throat—possibly due to vehicle in nasal spray; ***sneezing attacks***—may be more common in children using beclomethasone aerosol or flunisolide spray

Incidence less frequent

For all nasal corticosteroids

Sneezing

For budesonide

Throat itching

For dexamethasone

Cardiovascular changes (heart attack, high blood pressure, or weak heart); ***dermatological changes*** (flushing; impaired wound healing; suppressed reaction to skin tests); ***endocrine changes*** (suppressed growth in children); ***fluid and electrolyte disturbances*** (dehydration or extreme thirst; water retention); ***gastrointestinal changes*** (lower abdominal or stomach pain and burning; stomach bloating); ***hiccups; increased appetite and weight gain; malaise*** (general unwell feeling); ***musculoskeletal changes*** (bone fractures; muscle wasting and weakness); ***neurological disturbances*** (headache; seizures); ***thromboembolism*** (tingling or swelling in hands, lower legs, or feet); ***urticaria*** (hives)

For triamcinolone; ***Sinus congestion*** (stuffy nose or headache); ***stuffy nose; throat discomfort***

Overdose

For more information on the management of overdose or unintentional ingestion, **contact a Poison Control Center** (see *Poison Control Center Listing*).

Treatment of overdose

For acute overdose—Adverse effects due to acute overdose are unlikely with the small quantities of corticosteroid contained in each canister.

For chronic overdose—If symptoms of chronic overdose (hypercorticism) occur, nasal corticosteroids should be discontinued slowly.

Patient Consultation

As an aid to patient consultation, refer to *Advice for the Patient, Corticosteroids (Nasal).*

In providing consultation, consider emphasizing the following selected information (» = major clinical significance):

Before using this medication

» Conditions affecting use, especially:

Intolerance or sensitivity to corticosteroids

Pregnancy—Risk-benefit must be considered, since systemic corticosteroids cross the placenta and have demonstrated embryotoxicity, fetotoxicity, and teratogenicity in animals; infants born to mothers who received substantial doses of corticosteroids during pregnancy should be observed for hypoadrenalism

Breast-feeding—Risk-benefit must be considered, since systemic corticosteroids are distributed into breast milk and have demonstrated embryotoxicity, fetotoxicity, and teratogenicity in animals; infants breast-fed by mothers who received substantial doses of corticosteroids while breast-feeding should be observed for hypoadrenalism

Use in children—Significant effect on growth by beclomethasone or flunisolide has not been documented; importance of monitoring growth and development with prolonged or high-dose therapy

Other medical problems, especially amebiasis, diabetes mellitus, fungal, bacterial, or systemic viral infections, glaucoma, hepatic function impairment, hypothyroidism, left ventricular free wall rupture, recent myocardial infarction, nasal ulcers, surgery, or trauma, ocular herpes simplex, or latent or active tuberculosis of respiratory tract

Proper use of this medication

» Proper administration technique; reading patient directions carefully before use

Blowing nose to clear nasal passages before administration; aiming spray away from nasal septum (aiming towards the inner corner of the eye)

» Compliance with therapy; may require up to 3 weeks for full benefit

» Importance of not using more medication than the amount prescribed, because of potential enhanced absorption and increased severity of side effects

» Checking with physician before using medication for other nasal problems

Saving special inhaler used for beclomethasone or dexamethasone; refills may be available

» Proper dosing

Missed dose: Using as soon as possible if remembered within an hour or so; if remembered later, not using at all; not doubling doses

» Proper storage; not storing budesonide powder in damp places, especially if cap has not been tightly screwed on; decreased efficacy if aerosol canister is cold; not puncturing, breaking, or burning aerosol container; discarding unused portion of beclomethasone solution or flunisolide solution 3 months after opening package

Precautions while using this medication

Regular visits to physician to check progress during prolonged therapy

» Avoiding immunizations while taking nasal corticosteroids, unless approved by physician, due to a possible neurological hazard and lack of antibody response

» Checking with physician if:

—signs of infection of nose, throat, or sinuses occur
—no improvement within 7 days (for dexamethasone)
—no improvement within 3 weeks for other nasal corticosteroids
—condition becomes worse

Side/adverse effects

Signs of potential side effects, especially acneiform lesions, allergic reaction or bronchial asthma, burning, stinging or irritation in nose after use of spray, cardiovascular changes, cough, crusting inside nose, Cushing's syndrome, dermatological changes, dizziness or light-headedness, endocrine changes, epistaxis, fluid or electrolyte disturbances, gastrointestinal changes, headache, hoarseness, hypersensitivity reaction, increased appetite and weight gain, lethargy, loss of sense of taste or smell, malaise, musculoskeletal changes, nasal candidiasis, nasal septal perforation, nausea or vomiting, ocular hypertension, pharyngeal candidiasis, rhinitis, rhinorrhea, sore throat, stomach pain, stuffy nose, thromboembolism, or urticaria

General Dosing Information

In patients with blocked nasal passages, a topical decongestant may be used just prior to use of the nasal corticosteroid. However, because prolonged use of topical nasal decongestants may cause congestive rebound, they should preferably be used for a maximum of 3 to 5 days. An oral decongestant is recommended for chronic nasal congestion.

The smallest dose of a nasal corticosteroid required to control symptoms should be used as a maintenance dose after the desired clinical response is achieved.

The dosage of other corticosteroids being administered concurrently by other routes of administration, including oral inhalation, should be taken into account when determining the usual adult prescribing limits of nasal corticosteroids.

BECLOMETHASONE

Summary of Differences

Indications: Betamethasone dipropionate monohydrate is indicated for the treatment of vasomotor nonallergic rhinitis.

Pharmacology/pharmacokinetics: See *Pharmacology/Pharmacokinetics*.

Precautions: Cross-sensitivity and/or related problems—Nasal suspension dosage form contains no fluorocarbon propellants.

Side/adverse effects: See *Side/Adverse Effects*.

Additional Dosing Information

Regular use is required to obtain full therapeutic benefit. Medication should be discontinued if improvement is not evident after 3 weeks.

See also *General Dosing Information*.

Nasal Dosage Forms

BECLOMETHASONE DIPROPIONATE NASAL AEROSOL

Usual adult and adolescent dose

Anti-inflammatory (steroidal), nasal—

Nasal, 42 or 50 mcg (0.042 or 0.05 mg) (1 metered spray) in each nostril two to four times a day (total daily dose, 168 to 400 mcg [0.168 to 0.4 mg]); then decrease the dose to amount needed to maintain effect.

Usual adult prescribing limits

Nasal, 1 mg per day.

Note: If orally inhaled beclomethasone is used concurrently, the combined total daily dose should not exceed 1 mg.

Usual pediatric dose

Anti-inflammatory (steroidal), nasal—

Children up to 6 years of age: Safety and efficacy have not been established.

Children 6 to 12 years of age: Nasal, 42 (0.042mg) (1 metered spray) in each nostril three times a day (total daily dose, 252 mcg [0.252 mg]).

Children 12 years of age and older (In Canada, children 6 years of age and older): See *Usual adult and adolescent dose*.

Usual pediatric prescribing limits

Nasal, 500 mcg (0.5 mg) per day. If orally inhaled beclomethasone is used concurrently, the combined total daily dose should not exceed 500 mcg (0.5 mg).

Strength(s) usually available

U.S.—

42 mcg (0.042 mg) per metered spray (Rx) [*Beconase* (fluorocarbons; oleic acid); *Vancenase* (fluorocarbons; oleic acid); *Vancenase pockethaler* (fluorocarbons; oleic acid)].

Canada—

50 mcg (0.05 mg) per metered spray (Rx) [*Beconase; Vancenase* (fluorocarbons; oleic acid); GENERIC].

Packaging and storage

Store between 2 and 30 °C (36 and 86 °F), unless otherwise specified by manufacturer.. Protect from moisture and unusual temperature changes.

Auxiliary labeling

- For the nose.
- Shake well.

Note

When dispensing, include patient instructions.

Explain administration technique.

BECLOMETHASONE DIPROPIONATE MONOHYDRATE NASAL SUSPENSION

Usual adult and adolescent dose

Anti-inflammatory (steroidal), nasal—

Nasal, 42 to 100 mcg (0.042 to 0.1 mg) (1 or 2 metered sprays) in each nostril one or two times a day (total daily dose, 168 to 400 mcg [0.168 to 0.4 mg]).

Usual adult prescribing limits

Nasal, 600 mcg (0.6 mg) (12 metered sprays) per day.

Note: If orally inhaled beclomethasone is used concurrently, the combined total daily dose should not exceed 1 mg.

Usual pediatric dose

Anti-inflammatory (steroidal), nasal—

Children up to 6 years of age: Safety and efficacy have not been established.

Children 6 years of age and older: See *Usual adult and adolescent dose*.

Usual pediatric prescribing limits

Nasal, 400 mcg (0.4 mg) (8 metered sprays) per day. If orally inhaled beclomethasone is used concurrently, the combined total daily dose should not exceed 500 mcg (0.5 mg).

Strength(s) usually available

U.S.—

42 mcg (0.042 mg) per metered spray (Rx) [*Beconase AQ* (benzalkonium chloride; carboxymethylcellulose sodium; dextrose; hydrochloric acid; microcrystalline cellulose; phenylethanol 0.25%; polysorbate 80)].

84 mcg (0.084 mg) per metered spray (Rx) [*Vancenase AQ 84 mcg* (benzalkonium chloride; carboxymethylcellulose sodium; dextrose; microcrystalline cellulose; phenylethyl alcohol; polysorbate 80)].

Canada—

50 mcg (0.05 mg) per metered spray: Not commercially available. (Rx).

Note: Withdrawn from the Canadian market in March 2000.

Packaging and storage

Store between 2 and 30 °C (36 and 86 °F), unless otherwise specified by manufacturer.

Auxiliary labeling

- For the nose.
- Shake well.

Note

When dispensing, include patient instructions.

Explain administration technique.

BUDESONIDE

Summary of Differences

Pharmacology/pharmacokinetics: See *Pharmacology/Pharmacokinetics*.

Precautions: Cross-sensitivity and/or other related problems—Nasal powder and suspension dosage forms contain no fluorocarbon propellants

Side/adverse effects: See *Side/Adverse Effects*.

Additional Dosing Information

Regular use is required to obtain full therapeutic benefit. Treatment should not be continued beyond 3 weeks in the absence of significant symptomatic improvement.

See also *General Dosing Information*.

Nasal Dosage Forms

Note: Bracketed information in the *Dosage Forms* section refer to categories of use and/or indications that are not included in U.S. product labeling.

BUDESONIDE NASAL POWDER

Usual adult and adolescent dose

Anti-inflammatory (steroidal), nasal—

Nasal inhalation, initially 200 mcg (0.2 mg) (2 metered inhalations) in each nostril once a day in the morning (total daily dose, 400 mcg [0.4 mg]), the dosage then being decreased to the lowest effective dose according to patient response.

Usual adult prescribing limits

Nasal inhalation, 800 mcg (0.8 mg) (8 metered inhalations) per day.

Usual pediatric dose

Anti-inflammatory (steroidal), nasal inhalation—

Children up to 6 years of age: Safety and efficacy have not been established.

Children 6 years of age and older: See *Usual adult and adolescent dose*.

Note: [Children 4 to 6 years of age][1] have benefited from 100 mcg (1 metered inhalation) to 200 mcg (2 metered inhalations) in each nostril daily, up to 400 mcg (4 metered inhalations total) daily, followed by a dosage adjusted to the lowest effective dose as determined by the child's response.

Usual pediatric prescribing limits
Nasal inhalation, 400 mcg (0.4 mg) (4 metered inhalations) per day.

Strength(s) usually available
U.S.—
Not commercially available.
Canada—
100 mcg (0.1 mg) per metered inhalation (Rx) [*Rhinocort Turbuhaler*].

Packaging and storage
Store below 40 °C (104 °F), preferably between 15 and 30 °C (59 and 86 °F), unless otherwise specified by manufacturer.

Auxiliary labeling
- For the nose.

Note
When dispensing, include patient instructions.

Explain administration technique.

BUDESONIDE NASAL SUSPENSION

Usual adult and adolescent dose
Anti-inflammatory (steroidal), nasal or—
Rhinitis—Initial: Nasal, 128 mcg (0.128 mg) (2 metered sprays) in each nostril once a day in the morning or 64 mcg (0.064 mg) (1 metered spray) in each nostril twice a day (total daily dose, 256 mcg [0.256 mg]).).
Polyps—Initial: Nasal, 64 mcg (0.064 mg) (1 metered spray) in each nostril twice a day (total daily dose, 256 mcg [0.256 mg]).

Usual adult prescribing limits
Nasal, 800 mcg (0.8 mg) per day.

Usual pediatric dose
Anti-inflammatory (steroidal), nasal—
Children up to 6 years of age: Safety and efficacy have not been established.
Children 6 years of age and older: See *Usual adult and adolescent dose*.
Note: [Children 4 to 6 years of age][1]have benefited from 100 mcg (1 metered inhalation) to 200 mcg (2 metered inhalations) in each nostril daily, up to 400 mcg (4 metered inhalations total) daily, followed by a dosage adjusted to the lowest effective dose as determined by the child's response.

Usual pediatric prescribing limits
Nasal, 400 mcg (0.4 mg) per day.

Strength(s) usually available
U.S.—
Not commercially available.
Canada—
64 mcg (0.64 mg) per metered spray (Rx) [*Rhinocort Aqua* (carboxymethylcellulose sodium; disodium edetate; glucose (anhydrous); hydrochloric acid; microcrystalline cellulose; potassium sorbate; purified water); GENERIC].

Packaging and storage
Store below 40 °C (104 °F), preferably between 15 and 30 °C (59 and 86 °F), unless otherwise specified by manufacturer. Protect from freezing.

Auxiliary labeling
- For the nose.
- Shake well.

Note
When dispensing, include patient instructions.

Explain administration technique.

BUDESONIDE NASAL AEROSOL

Usual adult and adolescent dose
Anti-Inflammatory (steroidal), nasal—
Initial: Nasal, 64 mcg (0.064 mg) (2 metered sprays) in each nostril twice a day or 128 mcg (0.128 mg) (4 metered sprays) in each nostril once a day (total daily dose, 256 mcg [0.256 mg]).

Usual pediatric dose
Anti-inflammatory (steroidal), nasal—
Children up to 6 years of age: Safety and efficacy have not been established.
Children 6 years of age and older: See *Usual adult and adolescent dose*.
Note: [Children 4 to 6 years of age][1]have benefited from 100 mcg (1 metered inhalation) to 200 mcg (2 metered inhalations) in each nostril daily, up to 400 mcg (4 metered inhalations total) daily, followed by a dosage adjusted to the lowest effective dose as determined by the child's response.

Strength(s) usually available
U.S.—
32 mcg (0.032 mg) per metered spray (Rx) [*Rhinocort* (fluorocarbons)].
Canada—
Not commercially available.

Packaging and storage
Store below 40°C (104°F), preferably between 15 and 30°C (59 and 86°F), unless otherwise specified by manufacturer.

Auxiliary labeling
- For the nose.
- Shake well.

[1]Not included in Canadian product labeling.

DEXAMETHASONE

Summary of Differences

Indications: Less frequently used to significantly increased incidence of adverse effects.
Pharmacology/pharmacokinetics: See *Pharmacology/Pharmacokinetics*.
Precautions: Altered carbohydrate tolerance.
Cross-sensitivity and/or related problems—Nasal aerosol contains fluorocarbon propellants.
Breast-feeding—Dexamethasone is distributed into breast milk. Use caution when administering to nursing women.
Laboratory value alterations—False-negative results may occur with nitroblue tetrazolium test for bacterial infections.
Other medications—Concurrent use with ephedrine, phenobarbital and rifampin may warrant an increase in dexamethasone dosage.
Other medical conditions—Increased health risk if recent myocardial infarction or left ventricular free wall rupture.
Side/adverse effects:
HPA axis suppression or other systemic corticosteroid effects may occur with usual nasal inhalation doses
See also *Side/Adverse Effects*.

Additional Dosing Information

When medication is to be discontinued, dosage usually should be reduced gradually according to the dose, frequency, and duration of therapy.

Patients whose conditions do not improve within 7 days should be reevaluated. Use of dexamethasone should be limited to a maximum of 2 weeks.

See also *General Dosing Information*.

Nasal Dosage Forms

DEXAMETHASONE SODIUM PHOSPHATE NASAL AEROSOL

Usual adult and adolescent dose
Anti-inflammatory (steroidal), nasal—
Nasal, 200 mcg (0.2 mg) (2 metered sprays) of dexamethasone phosphate in each nostril two or three times a day (total daily dose, 800 mcg [0.8 mg] to 1.2 mg or dexamethasone phosphate), the dosage then being decreased according to patient response.
Note: Some patients may be maintained on 100 mcg (0.1 mg) (1 metered spray) of dexamethasone phosphate in each nostril two times a day. Therapy should be discontinued as soon as possible. If symptoms recur, therapy may be reinstituted.

Usual adult prescribing limits
Nasal, 1.2 mg (12 metered sprays) of dexamethasone phosphate per day.

Usual pediatric dose
Anti-inflammatory (steroidal), nasal—
Children up to 6 years of age: Use is not recommended.
Children 6 to 12 years of age: Nasal, 100 or 200 mcg (0.1 to 0.2 mg) (1 or 2 metered sprays) of dexamethasone phosphate in each nostril two times a day (total daily dose, 400 to 800 [0.4 to 0.8 mg] of dexamethasone phosphate.

Usual pediatric prescribing limits
Nasal, 800 mcg (0.8 mg) (8 metered sprays) of dexamethasone phosphate per day.

Strength(s) usually available

U.S.—

100 mcg (0.1 mg) as phosphate per metered spray (Rx) [*Dexacort Turbinaire* (alcohol 2%; chlorofluorocarbons)].

Canada—

Not commercially available.

Packaging and storage

Store below 49 °C (120 °F), preferably between 15 and 30 °C (59 and 86 °F), unless otherwise specified by manufacturer. Protect from freezing.

Auxiliary labeling

- For the nose.
- Shake well.

Note: When dispensing, include patient instructions.

Explain administration technique.

FLUNISOLIDE

Summary of Differences

Pharmacology/pharmacokinetics: See *Pharmacology/Pharmacokinetics.*

Precautions: Cross-sensitivity and/or related problems—Nasal solution dosage form contains no fluorocarbon propellants.

Side/adverse effects: See *Side/Adverse Effects.*

Additional Dosing Information

Regular use is required to obtain full therapeutic benefit. Treatment should not be continued beyond 3 weeks in the absence of significant symptomatic improvement.

See also *General Dosing Information.*

Nasal Dosage Forms

FLUNISOLIDE NASAL SOLUTION USP

Usual adult dose

Anti-inflammatory (steroidal), nasal—

Initial: Nasal, 50 mcg (0.05 mg) (2 metered sprays) in each nostril two times a day (total daily dose, 200 mcg [0.2 mg]); if necessary, dosing frequency may be increased to three times a day (total daily dose, 300 mcg [0.3 mg]).

Maintenance: Nasal, as little as 25 mcg (0.025 mg) (1 metered spray) in each nostril once a day has been effective (total daily dose, 50 mcg [0.05 mg]).

Usual adult prescribing limits

Nasal, 400 mcg (0.4 mg) (16 metered sprays) per day.

Note: In Canada, adult prescribing limits are as follows: 300 mcg (0.3 mg) (12 metered sprays) per day.

Usual pediatric dose

Anti-inflammatory (steroidal), nasal—

Children up to 6 years of age—

Safety and efficacy have not been established.

Children 6 to 14 years of age—

Initial—Nasal, 25 mcg (0.025 mg) (1 metered spray) in each nostril three times a day; or 50 mcg (0.05 mg) (2 metered sprays) in each nostril two times a day; (total daily dose, 150 or 200 mcg [0.15 or 0.2 mg]).

Maintenance—Nasal, as little as 25 mcg (0.025 mg) (1 metered spray) in each nostril once a day has been effective (total daily dose, 50 mcg [0.05 mg]).

Children 14 years of age and older—

See *Usual adult dose.*

Usual pediatric prescribing limits

Nasal, 200 mcg (0.2 mg) (8 metered sprays) per day.

Note: In Canada, pediatric dosing limits are as follows: 150 mcg (0.15 mg) (6 metered sprays) per day.

Strength(s) usually available

U.S.—

25 mcg (0.025 mg) per metered spray (Rx) [*Nasalide* (benzalkonium chloride; butylated hydroxyanisole; citric acid; disodium edetate; hydrochloric acid; polyethylene glycol 3350; propylene glycol; purified water; sodium citrate; sodium hydroxide); *Nasarel* (benzalkonium chloride; butylated hydroxyanisole; citric acid; disodium edetate; hydrochloric acid; polyethylene glycol 400; polysorbate 20; propylene glycol; sodium citrate dihydrate; sodium hydroxide; sorbitol)].

Canada—

25 mcg (0.025 mg) per metered spray (Rx) [*Rhinalar* (benzalkonium chloride; citric acid; polyethylene glycol; propylene glycol; sodium citrate)].

Packaging and storage

Store between 15 and 30 °C (59 and 86 °F). Store in a tight container and in an upright position. Protect from light.

Auxiliary labeling

- For the nose.

Note

When dispensing, include patient instructions.

Explain administration technique.

FLUTICASONE

Summary of Differences

Pharmacology/pharmacokinetics: See *Pharmacology/Pharmacokinetics.*

Precautions: Cross-sensitivity and/or other related problems—Nasal suspension dosage form contains no fluorocarbon propellants.

Side/adverse effects: See also *Side/Adverse Effects.*

Additional Dosing Information

Regular use is required to obtain full therapeutic benefit. Treatment should not be continued beyond 3 weeks in the absence of significant symptomatic improvement.

See also *General Dosing Information.*

Nasal Dosage Forms

FLUTICASONE PROPIONATE NASAL SUSPENSION

Usual adult and adolescent dose

Anti-inflammatory (steroidal), nasal—

Nasal, initially 100 mcg (0.1 mg) (2 metered sprays) in each nostril once a day or 50 mcg (0.05 mg) (1 metered spray) in each nostril twice a day (total daily dose, 200 mcg [0.2 mg]), the dosage then being decreased, to 50 mcg (0.05 mg) (1 metered spray) in each nostril once a day, according to patient response.

Note: In Canada, the dose may be increased to 100 mcg (0.1 mg) (2 metered sprays) in each nostril every twelve hours (total daily dose, 400 mcg [0.4 mg]), if no response at the usual and adolescent dose.

Usual adult prescribing limits

Nasal, 0.2 mg (4 metered sprays) of fluticasone propionate per day.

Note: In Canada, the maximum adult and adolescent dose is 400 mcg (0.4 mg) (8 metered sprays) of fluticasone propionate per day.

Usual pediatric dose

Anti-inflammatory (steroidal), nasal—

Children up to 4 years of age: Use is not recommended.

Children 4 to 11 years of age: Nasal, 50 to 100 mcg (0.05 to 0.1 mg) (1 or 2 metered sprays) in each nostril once a day in the morning (total daily dose, 100 to 200 mcg [0.1 to 0.2 mg]).

Children 11 years of age and older: See *Usual adult and adolescent dose.*

Usual pediatric prescribing limits

Nasal, 200 mcg (0.2 mg) (4 metered sprays) of fluticasone propionate per day.

Strength(s) usually available

U.S.—

50 mcg (0.05 mg) per metered spray (Rx) [*Flonase* (benzalkonium chloride 0.02%; carboxymethylcellulose sodium; dextrose; microcrystalline cellulose; phenylethyl alcohol 0.25%; polysorbate 80)].

Canada—

50 mcg (0.05 mg) per metered spray (Rx) [*Flonase* (benzalkonium chloride; carboxymethylcellulose sodium; dextrose; microcrystalline cellulose; phenylethyl alcohol; polysorbate 80; purified water)].

Packaging and storage

Store between 4 and 30 °C (39 and 86 °F), unless otherwise specified by manufacturer.

Auxiliary labeling

- For the nose.
- Shake well.

Note
When dispensing, include patient instructions.

Explain administration technique.

MOMETASONE

Summary of Differences
Pharmacology/Pharmacokinetics: See *Pharmacology/Pharmacokinetics.*
Precautions: Cross-sensitivity and/or other related problems—Nasal suspension dosage form contains no fluorocarbon propellants.
Breast-feeding—Not measurable in breast milk.
Side/adverse effects: See *Side/Adverse Effects*

Additional Dosing Information
Regular use is required to obtain full therapeutic benefit. Treatment should not be continued beyond 3 weeks in the absence of significant symptomatic improvement.

See also *General Dosing Information.*

Nasal Dosage Forms
MOMETASONE FUROATE NASAL SUSPENSION

Usual adult and adolescent dose
Anti-inflammatory (steroidal), nasal—
Nasal, 100 mcg (0.1mg) (2 metered sprays) in each nostril once a day (total daily dose, 200 mcg [0.2 mg]), the dosage then being decreased to a maintenance dose of 50 mcg (0.05 mg) (1 metered spray) in each nostril once a day, according to patient response.

Note: For prophylaxis, start therapy two to four weeks prior to allergen exposure.

Usual pediatric dose
Anti-inflammatory (steroidal), nasal—
Children up to 12 years of age: Use not recommended.
Children 12 years of age and older: See *Usual adult and adolescent dose.*

Strength(s) usually available
U.S.—
50 mcg (0.05 mg) per metered spray (Rx) [*Nasonex* (benzalkonium chloride; carboxymethylcellulose sodium; citric acid; glycerin; microcrystalline cellulose; phenylethyl alcohol 0.25%; polysorbate 80; sodium citrate)].

Canada—
50 mcg (0.05 mg) per metered spray (Rx) [*Nasonex* (benzalkonium chloride; citric acid; dispersable cellulose BP65 cps; glycerol; phenylethyl alcohol; polysorbate 80; purified water; sodium citrate dihydrate)].

Packaging and storage
Store between 2 and 25°C (35.6 and 77°F), unless otherwise specified by manufacturer.

Auxiliary labeling
- For the nose.
- Shake well.

Note
When dispensing, include patient instructions.

TRIAMCINOLONE

Summary of Differences
Pharmacology/pharmacokinetics: See *Pharmacology/Pharmacokinetics.*
Precautions: Cross-sensitivity and/or other related problems—Nasal suspension dosage form contains no fluorocarbon propellants.
Side/adverse effects: See *Side/Adverse Effects.*

Additional Dosing Information
Regular use is required to obtain full therapeutic benefit. Treatment should not continue beyond 3 weeks in the absence of significant symptomatic improvement.

See also *General Dosing Information.*

Nasal Dosage Forms
TRIAMCINOLONE ACETONIDE NASAL AEROSOL

Usual adult and adolescent dose
Anti-inflammatory (steroidal), nasal—
Nasal, 110 mcg (0.11 mg) (2 metered sprays) in each nostril once a day (total daily dose, 220 mcg [0.22 mg]), the dosage then being decreased to a maintenance dose of 55 mcg (0.55 mg) (1 metered spray) in each nostril once a day (total daily dose, 110 mcg [0.11 mg]), according to patient response.

Note: In Canada, the literature also includes that for each 55 mcg (0.55 mg) metered spray (dose reaching nasal mucosa), 100 mcg (0.1 mg) of triamcinolone acetonide is released from the actuator.

Usual adult prescribing limits
Nasal, 440 mcg (0.44 mg) (8 metered sprays) per day.

Usual pediatric dose
Anti-inflammatory (steroidal), nasal—
Children up to 6 years of age (In Canada, children up to 12 years of age): Safety and efficacy have not been established.
Children 6 years of age and older (In Canada, children 12 years of age and older): See *Usual adult and adolescent dose.*

Usual pediatric prescribing limits
Nasal, 220 mcg (0.22 mg) (4 metered sprays per day.

Strength(s) usually available
U.S.—
55 mcg (0.055 mg) per metered spray (Rx) [*Nasacort* (dehydrated alcohol 0.7% w/w; fluorocarbons)].

Canada—
55 mcg (0.055 mg) per metered spray (Rx) [*Nasacort* (dehydrated alcohol 0.7% w/w; fluorocarbons)].

Packaging and storage
Store between 20 and 25°C (68 and 77°F), unless otherwise specified by manufacturer.

Auxiliary labeling
- For the nose.
- Shake well.

Note
When dispensing, include patient instructions.

Explain administration technique.

TRIAMCINOLONE NASAL SUSPENSION

Usual adult and adolescent dose
Anti-inflammatory (steroidal), nasal—
110 mcg (0.11 mg) (2 metered sprays) in each nostril once a day (total daily dose, 220 mcg [0.22 mg]), the dosage then being decreased to a maintenance dose of 55 mcg (0.055 mg) (1 metered spray) in each nostril once a day (total daily dose, 110 mcg [0.11 mg]), according to patient response

Usual adult prescribing limits
Nasal, 220 mcg (0.22 mg) (4 metered sprays) per day.

Usual pediatric dose
Anti-inflammatory (steroidal), nasal—
Children up to 6 years of age (In Canada, children up to 4 years of age): Use is not recommended.
Children 6 to 11 years of age (In Canada, children 4 to 11 years of age): Nasal, 55 mcg (0.055 mg) (1 metered spray) in each nostril once a day
Children 11 years of age and older: See *Usual adult and adolescent dose.*

Usual pediatric prescribing limits
Nasal, 220 mcg (0.22 mg) (4 metered sprays) per day

Strength(s) usually available
U.S.—
55 mcg (0.055 mg) per metered spray (Rx) [*Nasacort AQ* (carboxymethylcellulose sodium; dextrose; edetate disodium; hydrochloric acid; microcrystalline cellulose; polysorbate 80; sodium hydroxide)].

Canada—
55 mcg (0.055 mg) per metered spray (Rx) [*Nasacort AQ* (carboxymethylcellulose sodium; dextrose; edetate disodium; hydrochloric acid; microcrystalline cellulose; polysorbate 80; purified water; sodium hydroxide)].

Packaging and storage
Store between 15 and 30°C (59 and 86°F), unless otherwise specified by manufacturer.

Auxiliary labeling
- For the nose.
  Shake well.

Note
When dispensing, include patient instructions.

Revised: 6/27/2000

CORTICOSTEROIDS Ophthalmic

This monograph includes information on the following: 1) Betamethasone*; 2) Dexamethasone; 3) Fluorometholone; 4) Hydrocortisone*; 5) Medrysone; 6) Prednisolone.

VA CLASSIFICATION (Primary):

Betamethasone—OP301
Dexamethasone—OP301
Fluorometholone—OP301
Hydrocortisone—OP301
Medrysone—OP301
Prednisolone—OP301

Commonly used brand name(s): *AK-Dex[2]; AK-Pred[6]; AK-Tate[6]; Baldex[2]; Betnesol[1]; Cortamed[4]; Decadron[2]; Dexair[2]; Dexotic[2]; Diodex[2]; Econopred[6]; Econopred Plus[6]; Eflone[3]; FML Forte[3]; FML Liquifilm[3]; FML S.O.P[3]; Flarex[3]; Fluor-Op[3]; HMS Liquifilm[5]; I-Pred[6]; Inflamase Forte[6]; Inflamase Mild[6]; Lite Pred[6]; Maxidex[2]; Ocu-Dex[2]; Ocu-Pred[6]; Ocu-Pred Forte[6]; Ocu-Pred-A[6]; Ophtho-Tate[6]; PMS-Dexamethasone Sodium Phosphate[2]; Pred Forte[6]; Pred Mild[6]; Predair[6]; Predair A[6]; Predair Forte[6]; R.O.-Dexasone[2]; Spersadex[2]; Storz-Dexa[2]; Ultra Pred[6].*

Another commonly used name for hydrocortisone is cortisol.

Note: For a listing of dosage forms and brand names by country availability, see *Dosage Forms* section(s).

*Not commercially available in U.S.

Category

Corticosteroid (ophthalmic); anti-inflammatory (steroidal), ophthalmic.

Note: Ophthalmic dosage forms of betamethasone and hydrocortisone are not commercially available in the U.S.; therefore, there is no U.S. product labeling identifying approved indications.

Indications

Note: Bracketed information in the *Indications* section refers to uses that are not included in U.S. product labeling.

Accepted

Ophthalmic disorders (treatment)—Ophthalmic corticosteroids are indicated in the treatment of corticosteroid-responsive allergic and inflammatory conditions of the palpebral and bulbar conjunctiva, cornea, and anterior segment of the globe.

Fluorometholone (0.1%), medrysone, or prednisolone (0.12 or 0.125%) may be preferred for long-term treatment because they are least likely to increase intraocular pressure.

Very severe ocular disorders that do not respond to topical corticosteroid therapy may require treatment with systemic corticosteroids. In some cases, concurrent topical and systemic corticosteroid therapy may be utilized. See *Table 1*, page 910.

Unaccepted

Topical corticosteroids for ophthalmic use are not indicated in the treatment of degenerative ocular disorders. Also, if corticosteroid therapy is required for the treatment of disorders involving deep ocular structures, the medication should be administered systemically because topical application will not be effective.

Pharmacology/Pharmacokinetics

Physicochemical characteristics

Molecular weight—
- Betamethasone sodium phosphate: 516.41.
- Dexamethasone: 392.47.
- Dexamethasone sodium phosphate: 516.41.
- Fluorometholone: 376.47.
- Fluorometholone acetate: 418.51.
- Hydrocortisone acetate: 404.50.
- Medrysone: 344.49.
- Prednisolone acetate: 402.49.
- Prednisolone sodium phosphate: 484.39.

Mechanism of action/Effect

Corticosteroids diffuse across cell membranes and complex with specific cytoplasmic receptors. These complexes then enter the cell nucleus, bind to DNA, and stimulate transcription of mRNA and subsequent protein synthesis of enzymes ultimately responsible for anti-inflammatory effects of topical application of corticosteroids to the eye. In high concentrations, which may be achieved after topical application, corticosteroids may exert direct membrane effects. Corticosteroids decrease cellular and fibrinous exudation and tissue infiltration, inhibit fibroblastic and collagen-forming activity, retard epithelial regeneration, diminish postinflammatory neovascularization, and reduce toward normal levels the excessive permeability of inflamed capillaries.

Absorption

Absorbed into aqueous humor, cornea, iris, choroid, ciliary body, and retina. Systemic absorption occurs, but may be significant only at higher dosages or in extended pediatric therapy.

Precautions to Consider

Carcinogenicity/Mutagenicity

Dexamethasone—Long-term animal studies have not been conducted to evaluate the carcinogenicity of dexamethasone.

Fluorometholone, medrysone, and prednisolone—Studies in animals or humans have not been conducted to evaluate the carcinogenic or mutagenic potential of fluorometholone, medrysone, and prednisolone.

Pregnancy/Reproduction

Pregnancy—Problems in humans have not been documented; however, adequate and well-controlled studies with these agents have not been done.

Infants born to mothers who have received substantial doses of corticosteroids during pregnancy should be carefully observed for signs of hypoadrenalism.

Studies in rabbits have shown that corticosteroids produce fetal resorptions and multiple abnormalities, including those of the head, ears, limbs, and palate.

Dexamethasone, hydrocortisone, and prednisolone—
Studies in pregnant mice have shown that these medications, when applied to both eyes 5 times a day on Days 10–13 of gestation, caused a significant increase in fetal cleft palate.
Dexamethasone and prednisolone—FDA Pregnancy Category C.

Fluorometholone—
Studies in pregnant rabbits have shown that fluorometholone is teratogenic and embryocidal when applied to the eyes at various dosage levels on Days 6–18 of gestation.
FDA Pregnancy Category C.

Medrysone—
Studies in pregnant rabbits have indicated that medrysone (doses 10 and 30 times the human dose or higher) is embryocidal. Also, application to the eyes (2 drops 4 times a day on Days 6–18 of gestation) of pregnant rabbits caused an increase in early resorptions.
FDA Pregnancy Category C.

Breast-feeding

Problems in humans have not been documented.

Pediatrics

Corticosteroids should be used with caution in children 2 years of age or younger because the different dose/weight ratio for children increases the risk of adrenal suppression. This risk increases with the length of therapy, which, therefore, should be limited to the shortest possible time (preferably less than 5 days).

Geriatrics

Appropriate studies on the relationship of age to the effects of ophthalmic corticosteroids have not been performed in the geriatric population. However, no geriatrics-specific problems have been documented to date.

Drug interactions and/or related problems

The following drug interactions and/or related problems have been selected on the basis of their potential clinical significance (possible mechanism in parentheses where appropriate)—not necessarily inclusive (» = major clinical significance):

Note: Combinations containing any of the following medications, depending on the amount present, may also interact with this medication.

Antiglaucoma agents
(chronic or intensive use of ophthalmic corticosteroids may increase intraocular pressure and decrease the efficacy of antiglaucoma agents)

Anticholinergics, especially atropine and related compounds
(risk of intraocular hypertension may be increased with prolonged corticosteroid therapy; may be more likely to occur during use of cycloplegic/mydriatic agents in patients predisposed to acute angle closure)

Contact lenses
(risk of infection increased)

Medical considerations/Contraindications

The medical considerations/contraindications included have been selected on the basis of their potential clinical significance (reasons given in parentheses where appropriate)—not necessarily inclusive (» = major clinical significance).

Except under special circumstances, these medications should not be used when the following medical problems exist:

» Fungal diseases, ocular, or
» Herpes simplex keratitis, acute superficial, or
» Tuberculosis, ocular, active or history of, or
» Viral disease, acute, infectious
(corticosteroids decrease human resistance to bacterial, fungal, and viral infections; application may exacerbate existing infections and encourage the development of new or secondary infections)

Risk-benefit should be considered when the following medical problems exist:

» Cataracts
(may be exacerbated)

Diabetes mellitus
(patient may be predisposed toward increases in intraocular pressure and/or cataract formation)

Diseases causing thinning of the cornea or sclera
(use may result in perforation)

» Glaucoma, chronic, open-angle, or family history of
(may be precipitated or exacerbated)

» Infections of the cornea or conjunctiva, other
(risk of exacerbation or development of secondary infections)

Sensitivity to corticosteroids

Patient monitoring

The following may be especially important in patient monitoring (other tests may be warranted in some patients, depending on condition; » = major clinical significance):

Ophthalmologic examinations, especially tonometry and slit-lamp examination
(initial ophthalmologic examinations should be performed 2 to 3 weeks following onset of chronic therapy; subsequent examinations are performed at intervals as determined by patient status or risk factors)

Side/Adverse Effects

Note: Frequent or intensive use of ophthalmic corticosteroids may retard corneal healing.

Systemic absorption occurs, but may be significant only at higher dosages or in extended pediatric therapy. The different dose/weight ratio for children increases the risk of adrenal suppression.

The following side/adverse effects have been selected on the basis of their potential clinical significance (possible signs and symptoms in parentheses where appropriate)—not necessarily inclusive:

Those indicating need for medical attention

Incidence less frequent or rare

Corneal thinning and/or globe perforation (decreased vision; watering of the eyes); ***glaucoma; ocular hypertension; optic nerve damage; posterior subcapsular cataract; visual acuity and field defects*** (gradual blurring or loss of vision; eye pain; nausea; vomiting); ***secondary ocular infection***

Those indicating need for medical attention only if they continue or are bothersome

Incidence more frequent

Temporary mild blurred vision—may be expected to occur after use of ointments

Incidence less frequent or rare

Burning, stinging, redness, or watering of the eyes

Overdose

For more information on the management of overdose or unintentional ingestion, **contact a Poison Control Center** (see *Poison Control Center Listing*).

Treatment of overdose

Generally, acute oral overdose of ophthalmic corticosteroids does not result in serious adverse effects. Dilution with fluids is the mainstay of therapy.

Patient Consultation

As an aid to patient consultation, refer to *Advice for the Patient, Corticosteroids (Ophthalmic)*.

In providing consultation, consider emphasizing the following selected information (» = major clinical significance):

Before using this medication

» Conditions affecting use, especially:
Sensitivity to corticosteroids
Use in children—Cautious and short-term use recommended
Other medical problems, especially eye infections (other), cataracts, or glaucoma

Proper use of this medication

For contact lens wearers: Checking with ophthalmologist prior to use; contact lenses should not be worn during, and possibly for a time following, application of these medications because of an increased risk of infection

Shaking suspensions vigorously before applying

Proper administration technique

Preventing contamination: Not touching applicator tip to any surface and keeping container tightly closed

» Importance of not using more medication than the amount prescribed (especially in children)

» Checking with physician before using medication for future eye problems

» Proper dosing
Missed dose: Using as soon as possible; not using if almost time for next dose

» Proper storage

Precautions while using this medication

Need for ophthalmologic examinations during long-term therapy

Checking with physician if there is no improvement after 5 to 7 days of therapy or if condition worsens

Side/adverse effects

Signs of potential side effects, especially corneal thinning and/or globe perforation, glaucoma, ocular hypertension, optic nerve damage, posterior subcapsular cataract, visual acuity and field defects, or secondary ocular infection

General Dosing Information

The severity and location of ocular inflammation often requires dosage to be higher and/or more frequent than the usual adult dose initially, then gradually reduced to as little as necessary to maintain the therapeutic effect. If infections do not respond promptly, the ophthalmic corticosteroid should be discontinued until the infection has been controlled.

Increasing the frequency of administration is usually as effective as, or more effective than, using higher concentrations of the medication.

The duration of treatment may vary from a few days to several weeks or months in some cases, depending on the condition being treated. Daily or alternate-day therapy may be indicated for extended periods in certain situations, such as following penetrating keratoplasty.

Although ophthalmic corticosteroids should not be used longer than is medically necessary, it is recommended that treatment be continued after apparent response, with the dosage gradually tapered to avoid relapse.

At night, the ophthalmic ointment, where available, may be used as an adjunct to the ophthalmic solution or suspension to provide prolonged contact with the eye.

BETAMETHASONE

Ophthalmic Dosage Forms

BETAMETHASONE SODIUM PHOSPHATE OPHTHALMIC/OTIC SOLUTION

Note: The dosing and strengths of the dosage form available are expressed in terms of betamethasone base.

Usual adult and adolescent dose

Ophthalmic disorders (treatment)—
Topical, to the conjunctiva, 1 or 2 drops of a 0.1% (base) solution every one or two hours initially, with dosage gradually being decreased as inflammation subsides.

Usual pediatric dose

See *Usual adult and adolescent dose*.

Usual geriatric dose

See *Usual adult and adolescent dose*.

Strength(s) usually available
U.S.—
Not commercially available.
Canada—
0.1% (base) (Rx) [*Betnesol*].

Packaging and storage
Store below 40 °C (104 °F), preferably between 15 and 30 °C (59 and 86 °F), unless otherwise specified by manufacturer. Protect from freezing.

Auxiliary labeling
- For the eye.

Note
Dispense in original unopened container.

DEXAMETHASONE

Ophthalmic Dosage Forms

DEXAMETHASONE OPHTHALMIC OINTMENT

Usual adult and adolescent dose
Ophthalmic disorders (treatment)—
Topical, to the conjunctiva, a thin strip (approximately 1 cm) of a 0.1% ointment three or four times a day initially. After a favorable response is obtained, the number of applications per day may be gradually reduced prior to discontinuation.

Usual pediatric dose
See *Usual adult and adolescent dose.*

Usual geriatric dose
See *Usual adult and adolescent dose.*

Strength(s) usually available
U.S.—
Not commercially available.
Canada—
0.1% (Rx) [*Maxidex* (methylparaben; propylparaben)].

Packaging and storage
Store below 40 °C (104 °F), preferably between 15 and 30 °C (59 and 86 °F), unless otherwise specified by manufacturer. Store in a tight container. Protect from freezing.

Auxiliary labeling
- For the eye.

Note
Dispense in original unopened container.

DEXAMETHASONE OPHTHALMIC SUSPENSION USP

Usual adult and adolescent dose
Ophthalmic disorders (treatment)—
Topical, to the conjunctiva, 1 or 2 drops of a 0.1% suspension four to six times a day.

Note: In severe conditions, treatment may be initiated with 1 or 2 drops every hour, with dosage gradually being decreased as inflammation subsides.

Usual pediatric dose
See *Usual adult and adolescent dose.*

Usual geriatric dose
See *Usual adult and adolescent dose.*

Strength(s) usually available
U.S.—
0.1% (Rx) [*Maxidex;* GENERIC].
Canada—
0.1% (Rx) [*Maxidex* (benzalkonium chloride)].

Packaging and storage
Store below 40 °C (104 °F), preferably between 15 and 30 °C (59 and 86 °F), unless otherwise specified by manufacturer. Store in a tight container. Protect from freezing.

Auxiliary labeling
- For the eye.
- Shake well.

Note
Dispense in original unopened container.

DEXAMETHASONE SODIUM PHOSPHATE OPHTHALMIC OINTMENT USP

Note: The dosing and strengths of the dosage form available are expressed in terms of dexamethasone phosphate not dexamethasone sodium phosphate.

Usual adult and adolescent dose
Ophthalmic disorders (treatment)—
Topical, to the conjunctiva, a thin strip (approximately 1 cm) of a 0.05% (phosphate) ointment three or four times a day initially. After a favorable response is obtained, the number of applications per day may be gradually reduced prior to discontinuation.

Usual pediatric dose
See *Usual adult and adolescent dose.*

Usual geriatric dose
See *Usual adult and adolescent dose.*

Strength(s) usually available
U.S.—
0.05% (phosphate) (Rx) [*AK-Dex* (methylparaben, propylparaben); *Baldex* (methylparaben; propylparaben); *Decadron; Dexair* (methylparaben; propylparaben); *Maxidex; Ocu-Dex;* GENERIC].
Canada—
Not commercially available.

Packaging and storage
Store below 40 °C (104 °F), preferably between 15 and 30 °C (59 and 86 °F), unless otherwise specified by manufacturer. Protect from freezing.

Auxiliary labeling
- For the eye.

Note
Dispense in original unopened container.

DEXAMETHASONE SODIUM PHOSPHATE OPHTHALMIC SOLUTION USP

Note: The dosing and strengths of the dosage form available are expressed in terms of dexamethasone phosphate not dexamethasone sodium phosphate.

Usual adult and adolescent dose
Ophthalmic disorders (treatment)—
Topical, to the conjunctiva, 1 or 2 drops of a 0.1% (phosphate) solution up to six times a day.

Note: In severe conditions, treatment may be initiated with 1 or 2 drops every hour, with dosage gradually being decreased as inflammation subsides.

Usual pediatric dose
See *Usual adult and adolescent dose.*

Usual geriatric dose
See *Usual adult and adolescent dose.*

Strength(s) usually available
U.S.—
0.1% (phosphate) (Rx) [*AK-Dex* (benzalkonium chloride); *Baldex* (sodium bisulfite; benzalkonium chloride); *Decadron* (sodium bisulfite 0.1%; benzalkonium chloride); *Dexair* (sodium bisulfite 0.1%; benzalkonium chloride); *Dexotic; Ocu-Dex; Storz-Dexa;* GENERIC].
Canada—
0.1% (phosphate) (Rx) [*Decadron* (sodium bisulfite 0.1%; benzalkonium chloride); *Diodex* (disodium edetate; benzalkonium chloride); *PMS-Dexamethasone Sodium Phosphate; R.O.-Dexasone* (benzalkonium chloride); *Spersadex* (disodium edetate; benzalkonium chloride)].

Packaging and storage
Store below 40 °C (104 °F), preferably between 15 and 30 °C (59 and 86 °F), unless otherwise specified by manufacturer. Store in a tight, light-resistant container. Protect from freezing.

Auxiliary labeling
- For the eye.

Note
Dispense in original unopened container.

FLUOROMETHOLONE

Ophthalmic Dosage Forms

FLUOROMETHOLONE OPHTHALMIC OINTMENT

Usual adult and adolescent dose
Ophthalmic disorders (treatment)—
Topical, to the conjunctiva, a thin strip (approximately 1 cm) of a 0.1% ointment one to three times a day.

Note: In severe conditions, treatment may be initiated with application every four hours, with dosage gradually being decreased as inflammation subsides.

Usual pediatric dose
See *Usual adult and adolescent dose.*

Usual geriatric dose
See *Usual adult and adolescent dose.*

Strength(s) usually available
U.S.—
0.1% (Rx) [*FML S.O.P* (phenylmercuric acetate)].
Canada—
Not commercially available.

Packaging and storage
Store below 40 °C (104 °F), preferably between 15 and 30 °C (59 and 86 °F), unless otherwise specified by manufacturer. Protect from freezing.

Auxiliary labeling
- For the eye.

Note
Dispense in original unopened container.

FLUOROMETHOLONE OPHTHALMIC SUSPENSION USP

Usual adult and adolescent dose
Ophthalmic disorders (treatment)—
Topical, to the conjunctiva, 1 or 2 drops of a 0.1% or 0.25% suspension two to four times a day.

Note: In severe conditions, treatment may be initiated with 1 or 2 drops every hour, with dosage gradually being decreased as inflammation subsides.

Usual pediatric dose
See *Usual adult and adolescent dose.*

Usual geriatric dose
See *Usual adult and adolescent dose.*

Strength(s) usually available
U.S.—
0.1% (Rx) [*Fluor-Op* (benzalkonium chloride); *FML Liquifilm* (benzalkonium chloride)].
0.25% (Rx) [*FML Forte* (benzalkonium chloride)].
Canada—
0.1% (Rx) [*FML Liquifilm* (benzalkonium chloride)].
0.25% (Rx) [*FML Forte* (benzalkonium chloride)].

Packaging and storage
Store below 40 °C (104 °F), preferably between 15 and 30 °C (59 and 86 °F), unless otherwise specified by manufacturer. Store in a tight container. Protect from freezing.

Auxiliary labeling
- For the eye.
- Shake well.

Note
Dispense in original unopened container.

FLUOROMETHOLONE ACETATE OPHTHALMIC SUSPENSION

Usual adult and adolescent dose
Ophthalmic disorders (treatment)—
Topical, to the conjunctiva, 1 or 2 drops of a 0.1% suspension two to four times a day.

Note: In severe conditions, treatment may be initiated with 2 drops every two hours during the initial twenty-four to forty-eight hours. Dosage should be gradually decreased as inflammation subsides.

Usual pediatric dose
See *Usual adult and adolescent dose.*

Usual geriatric dose
See *Usual adult and adolescent dose.*

Strength(s) usually available
U.S.—
0.1% (Rx) [*Eflone; Flarex* (benzalkonium chloride)].
Canada—
0.1% (Rx) [*Flarex* (benzalkonium chloride)].

Packaging and storage
Store below 40 °C (104 °F), preferably between 15 and 30 °C (59 and 86 °F), unless otherwise specified by manufacturer. Protect from freezing.

Auxiliary labeling
- For the eye.
- Shake well.

HYDROCORTISONE

Ophthalmic Dosage Forms

HYDROCORTISONE ACETATE OPHTHALMIC OINTMENT USP

Usual adult and adolescent dose
Ophthalmic disorders (treatment)—
Topical, to the conjunctiva, a thin strip (approximately 1 cm) of a 2.5% ointment three or four times a day initially, with frequency of application gradually being decreased as inflammation subsides.

Usual pediatric dose
See *Usual adult and adolescent dose.*

Usual geriatric dose
See *Usual adult and adolescent dose.*

Strength(s) usually available
U.S.—
Not commercially available.
Canada—
2.5% (Rx) [*Cortamed*].

Packaging and storage
Store below 40 °C (104 °F), preferably between 15 and 30 °C (59 and 86 °F), unless otherwise specified by manufacturer. Protect from freezing.

Auxiliary labeling
- For the eye.

Note
Dispense in original unopened container.

MEDRYSONE

Ophthalmic Dosage Forms

MEDRYSONE OPHTHALMIC SUSPENSION USP

Usual adult and adolescent dose
Ophthalmic disorders (treatment)—
Topical, to the conjunctiva, 1 drop of a 1% suspension up to every four hours.

Usual pediatric dose
See *Usual adult and adolescent dose.*

Usual geriatric dose
See *Usual adult and adolescent dose.*

Strength(s) usually available
U.S.—
1% (Rx) [*HMS Liquifilm* (benzalkonium chloride)].
Canada—
1% (Rx) [*HMS Liquifilm* (benzalkonium chloride)].

Packaging and storage
Store below 40 °C (104 °F), preferably between 15 and 30 °C (59 and 86 °F), unless otherwise specified by manufacturer. Store in a tight, light-resistant container. Protect from freezing.

Auxiliary labeling
- For the eye.
- Shake well.

Note
Dispense in original unopened container.

PREDNISOLONE

Ophthalmic Dosage Forms

PREDNISOLONE ACETATE OPHTHALMIC SUSPENSION USP

Usual adult and adolescent dose
Ophthalmic disorders (treatment)—
Topical, to the conjunctiva, 1 or 2 drops of a 0.12 to 1% suspension two to four times a day.

Note: In severe conditions, treatment may be initiated with 1 or 2 drops every hour, with dosage gradually being decreased as inflammation subsides.

Usual pediatric dose
See *Usual adult and adolescent dose.*

Usual geriatric dose
See *Usual adult and adolescent dose.*

Strength(s) usually available
U.S.—

0.12% (Rx) [*Pred Mild* (sodium bisulfite; benzalkonium chloride)].

0.125% (Rx) [*Econopred* (benzalkonium chloride)].

1% (Rx) [*AK-Tate* (benzalkonium chloride); *Econopred Plus* (benzalkonium chloride); *Ocu-Pred-A; Predair A* (sodium bisulfite; benzalkonium chloride); *Pred Forte* (sodium bisulfite; benzalkonium chloride); *Ultra Pred;* GENERIC].

Canada—

0.12% (Rx) [*Pred Mild* (sodium bisulfite; benzalkonium chloride); GENERIC].

1% (Rx) [*AK-Tate* (sodium bisulfite); *Ophtho-Tate; Pred Forte* (sodium bisulfite; benzalkonium chloride); GENERIC].

Packaging and storage
Store between 8 and 24 °C (46 and 75 °F), unless otherwise specified by manufacturer. Store in a tight container. Protect from light. Protect from freezing.

Auxiliary labeling
- For the eye.
- Shake well.

Note
Dispense in original unopened container.

PREDNISOLONE SODIUM PHOSPHATE OPHTHALMIC SOLUTION USP

Usual adult and adolescent dose
Ophthalmic disorders (treatment)—

Topical, to the conjunctiva, 1 or 2 drops of a 0.125 or 1% solution up to six times a day.

Note: In severe conditions, treatment may be initiated with 1 or 2 drops every hour, with dosage gradually being decreased as inflammation subsides.

Usual pediatric dose
See *Usual adult and adolescent dose.*

Usual geriatric dose
See *Usual adult and adolescent dose.*

Strength(s) usually available
U.S.—

0.125% (Rx) [*AK-Pred* (sodium bisulfite; benzalkonium chloride); *Inflamase Mild* (benzalkonium chloride); *I-Pred* (sodium metabisulfite; benzalkonium chloride); *Lite Pred; Ocu-Pred; Predair* (sodium bisulfite; benzalkonium chloride); GENERIC].

1% (Rx) [*AK-Pred* (sodium bisulfite; benzalkonium chloride); *Inflamase Forte* (benzalkonium chloride); *I-Pred* (sodium metabisulfite; benzalkonium chloride); *Ocu-Pred Forte; Predair Forte* (sodium bisulfite; benzalkonium chloride); GENERIC].

Canada—

0.125% (Rx) [*Inflamase Mild* (benzalkonium chloride)].

1% (Rx) [*Inflamase Forte* (benzalkonium chloride)].

Packaging and storage
Store below 40 °C (104 °F), preferably between 15 and 30 °C (59 and 86 °F), unless otherwise specified by manufacturer. Store in a tight, light-resistant container. Protect from freezing.

Auxiliary labeling
- For the eye.

Note
Dispense in original unopened container.

Revised: 08/12/1998

Table 1. Indications*

Note: Bracketed information refers to uses that are not included in U.S. product labeling. Ophthalmic dosage forms of betamethasone and hydrocortisone are not commercially available in the U.S.; therefore, there is no U.S. product labeling identifying approved indications.

Legend: I=Betamethasone, II=Dexamethasone, III=Fluorometholone, IV=Hydrocortisone, V=Medrysone, VI=Prednisolone

	I	II	III	IV	V	VI
Indicated in the treatment of corticosteroid-responsive inflammatory conditions of the palpebral and bulbar conjunctiva, cornea, and anterior segment of the globe, such as:						
Allergic disorders, ophthalmic (treatment)	✓	✓	✓	✓		✓
Anterior segment disease, inflammatory (treatment)	✓	✓	✓	✓		✓
Conjunctivitis, allergic (treatment)	✓	✓	✓	✓	✓	✓
Corneal injuries (treatment)	✓	✓	✓	✓		✓
Cyclitis (treatment)	✓	✓	✓	✓		✓
Episcleritis (treatment)	✓	✓	✓	✓	✓	✓
Iridocyclitis (treatment)	✓	✓	✓	✓	[✓][1]	✓
Keratitis, herpes zoster (treatment)		✓	✓	✓	[✓][1]	✓
Keratitis not associated with herpes simplex or fungal infection (treatment)	✓	✓	✓	✓	[✓][1]	✓
Keratitis, punctate, superficial (treatment)	✓	✓	✓	✓	[✓][1]	✓
Keratitis, vernal (treatment)	✓	✓	✓	✓	[✓][1]	✓
Keratoconjunctivitis, allergic (treatment)	✓	✓	✓	✓	[✓][1]	✓
Keratoconjunctivitis, vernal (treatment)	✓	✓	✓	✓	✓	✓
Ocular infections, superficial (treatment adjunct)†	✓	✓	✓	✓	[✓][1]	✓
Ocular sensitivity to epinephrine (treatment)	✓	✓	✓	✓	✓	✓
Ophthalmia sympathetic (treatment)	✓	✓	✓	✓	[✓][1]	✓
Rosacea, ocular (treatment)	✓	✓	✓	✓	[✓][1]	✓

*Indications for specific agents may vary because of lack of specific testing and/or clinical-use data. Although all of these medications are used for all of the listed indications, medrysone may be less effective than the other ophthalmic corticosteroids for any condition other than conjunctivitis.

†Use in the treatment of ocular infection requires that the risk of corticosteroid-induced exacerbation of existing infection or development of secondary infections be weighed against the need for reducing inflammation and edema. [Appropriate anti-infective therapy should also be administered as required.]

[1]Not included in Canadian product labeling.

CORTICOSTEROIDS Otic

This monograph includes information on the following: 1) Betamethasone*; 2) Dexamethasone.

VA CLASSIFICATION (Primary): OT200

Note: Otic corticosteroid formulations are identical to the corresponding ophthalmic formulations listed in *Corticosteroids (Ophthalmic)*. However, only the specific brand name products listed below are labeled for otic use.

Commonly used brand name(s): *Betnesol*[1]; *Decadron*[2].

Note: For a listing of dosage forms and brand names by country availability, see *Dosage Forms* section(s).

*Not commercially available in U.S.

Category

Corticosteroid (otic); anti-inflammatory (steroidal), otic.

Indications

Note: Bracketed information in the *Indications* section refers to uses that are not included in U.S. product labeling.

Accepted

Otic corticosteroids are indicated in the treatment of corticosteroid-responsive inflammatory disorders of the external auditory meatus such as:

Otitis externa, allergic (treatment)
Otitis, infective (treatment adjunct)
[Lichen simplex chronicus, localized (treatment)]
[Otitis externa, eczematoid, chronic (treatment)] or
[Otitis externa, seborrheic (treatment)]—Dexamethasone and betamethasone are used in the treatment of these and other corticosteroid-responsive disorders of the external auditory meatus.

Use in the treatment of infective otitis requires that the risk of corticosteroid-induced exacerbation of existing infection or development of secondary infections be weighed against the need for reducing inflammation and edema. Appropriate anti-infective therapy should also be administered as required.

Dexamethasone is indicated in the treatment of lichen simplex chronicus of the external auditory meatus.

Pharmacology/Pharmacokinetics

Physicochemical characteristics

Molecular weight—
Betamethasone sodium phosphate: 516.41.
Dexamethasone sodium phosphate: 516.41.

Mechanism of action/Effect

Corticosteroids diffuse across cell membranes and complex with specific cytoplasmic receptors. These complexes then enter the cell nucleus, bind to DNA, and stimulate transcription of messenger RNA and subsequent protein synthesis of enzymes responsible for anti-inflammatory effects of otic corticosteroids. In the high concentrations that may be achieved after otic use, corticosteroids may exert direct membrane effects. Corticosteroids decrease cellular and fibrinous exudation and tissue infiltration, inhibit fibroblastic and collagen-forming activity, retard epithelial regeneration, diminish postinflammatory neovascularization, and reduce toward normal levels the excessive permeability of inflamed capillaries.

Precautions to Consider

Carcinogenicity/Mutagenicity

For dexamethasone—Long-term animal studies have not been conducted to evaluate the carcinogenicity of dexamethasone ophthalmic/otic solution.

Pregnancy/Reproduction

Adequate and well-controlled studies in humans have not been done. Corticosteroids should be used during pregnancy only if potential benefit to the mother outweighs potential risk to the fetus. Studies in mice and rabbits have shown that corticosteroids are teratogenic, following topical ophthalmic application in multiples of the therapeutic dose. In mice, corticosteroids produced fetal resorptions and cleft palate. In rabbits, corticosteroids produced fetal resorptions and multiple abnormalities involving the head, ears, limbs, palate, etc.

FDA Pregnancy Category C.

Breast-feeding

Corticosteroids are distributed into breast milk. Therefore, the potential benefit to the mother needs to be weighed against the potential risk to the infant.

Pediatrics

Appropriate studies on the relationship of age to the effects of otic corticosteroids have not been performed in the pediatric population. Infants born of mothers who have received substantial doses of corticosteroids during pregnancy should be observed for signs of hypoadrenalism (anorexia, hypotension, and weakness).

Geriatrics

Appropriate studies on the relationship of age to the effects of otic corticosteroids have not been performed in the geriatric population. However, geriatrics-specific problems that would limit the usefulness of these medications in the elderly are not expected.

Drug interactions and/or related problems

The following drug interactions and/or related problems have been selected on the basis of their potential clinical significance (possible mechanism in parentheses where appropriate)—not necessarily inclusive (» = major clinical significance):

Phenytoin
(induction of hepatic microsomal enzyme activity, by phenytoin, may result in increased metabolism, decreased serum concentrations, and reduced elimination half-lives of corticosteroids; an increase in the corticosteroid dosage may be warranted)

Medical considerations/Contraindications

The medical considerations/contraindications included have been selected on the basis of their potential clinical significance (reasons given in parentheses where appropriate)—not necessarily inclusive (» = major clinical significance).

Except under special circumstances, these medications should not be used when the following medical problems exist:

» Fungal diseases, aural or
» Tuberculosis, aural or
» Viral infection, acute
(corticosteroids decrease human resistance to bacterial, fungal, and viral infections; application may mask or exacerbate existing infections and encourage the development of new or secondary infections)
» Otitis media, chronic, history of or
» Perforation of eardrum membrane
(possibility of ototoxicity and ear damage)
» Sensitivity to corticosteroids
(sensitivity to inactive ingredients, such as sulfites, may cause anaphylaxis or asthmatic episodes)

Risk-benefit should be considered when the following medical problems exist:

Congestive heart failure or
Diabetes mellitus or
Epilepsy or
Glaucoma or
Hypertension
(concurrent use with otic corticosteroids may make condition worse)
Infections, ear, acute or
Infections, ear, chronic or
Otitis media, especially in children
(risk of exacerbation or development of secondary infections)
Osteoporosis
(increased risk of bone fractures)

Side/Adverse Effects

The following side/adverse effects have been selected on the basis of their potential clinical significance (possible signs and symptoms in parentheses where appropriate)—not necessarily inclusive:

Those indicating need for medical attention only if they continue or are bothersome

Incidence less frequent or rare

Bacterial keratitis (blurred vision); ***burning or stinging of the ear; Cushing's syndrome*** (excess hair growth in females; filling or rounding out of the face; high blood pressure; impotence in males; muscle wasting and weakness; bone fractures); ***dermatological changes*** (flushing; impaired wound healing; increased sweating; suppressed reaction to skin tests; thin, fragile skin); ***diabetes mellitus*** (decreased or blurred vision; frequent urination; increased thirst); ***endocrine disturbances*** (menstrual changes; anorexia, low blood pressure, weight loss or weakness; suppressed growth in children); ***fluid or electrolyte disturbances*** (high blood pressure; rapid weight gain; swelling of feet or lower legs); ***gastrointestinal changes*** (stomach bloating; continual stomach pain or burning, nausea or vomiting; black or tarry stools); ***hypokalemic syndrome*** (irregular heartbeat; muscle cramps or pain; unusual tiredness or weakness); ***musculoskeletal changes*** (muscle weakness; bone fractures); ***neurological changes*** (seizures; vertigo and headache); ***persistent fungal infections of the ear; muscle wasting; thromboembolism*** (breathing difficulties; chest pain; fainting; tingling in arms and lower legs or feet)

Patient Consultation

As an aid to patient consultation, refer to *Advice for the Patient, Corticosteroids (Otic)*.

In providing consultation, consider emphasizing the following selected information (» = major clinical significance):

Before using this medication

» Conditions affecting use, especially:

Sensitivity to corticosteroids

Pregnancy—No studies in humans have been done; animal studies have shown fetal abnormalities, cleft palate and abnormalities involving the head, ears, limbs, and palate

Breast-feeding—Otic corticosteroids are distributed into breast milk and may cause hypoadrenalism in infants; weigh potential benefit to mother against the risk to the infant

Use in children—Cautious use is recommended because of possible hypoadrenalism (anorexia, hypotension, and weakness)

Other medications, especially phenytoin

Other medical problems, especially fungal infections, chronic otitis media, perforated eardrum, sensitivity to corticosteroids, tuberculosis, or viral infections

Proper use of this medication

Proper administration technique

Preventing contamination: Not touching applicator tip to any surface and keeping container tightly closed

» Importance of not using more medication than the amount prescribed

» Checking with physician before using medication for future ear problems

» Proper dosing

Missed dose: Using as soon as possible; not using if almost time for next dose

» Proper storage

Precautions while using this medication

Checking with physician if no improvement after 5 to 7 days of therapy or if condition worsens

» Avoiding immunizations during corticosteroid therapy, unless approved by physician, due to possible neurological hazards and lack of antibody response

Side/adverse effects

Signs of potential side effects, especially bacterial keratitis; burning or stinging of the ear; Cushing's syndrome; dermatological changes; diabetes mellitus; endocrine disturbances; fluid or electrolyte disturbances; gastrointestinal changes; hypokalemic syndrome; musculoskeletal changes; neurological changes; persistent fungal infections of the ear; muscle wasting; thromboembolism

General Dosing Information

To allow optimum contact between the medication and affected surfaces of the ear canal, all cerumen and debris should be carefully removed by a physician or a trained assistant prior to initiation of therapy.

Otic solutions may be instilled directly into the ear canal or administered by use of a saturated gauze or cotton wick gently placed into the canal. The wick should be kept moist with additional solution and removed after 12 to 24 hours.

The duration of treatment may vary from a few days to several weeks or months in some cases, depending on the condition being treated. Daily or alternate-day therapy may be indicated for extended periods in certain situations.

Treatment should be continued after apparent response, with the dosage being gradually tapered to avoid relapse.

BETAMETHASONE

Otic Dosage Forms

BETAMETHASONE SODIUM PHOSPHATE OPHTHALMIC/OTIC SOLUTION

Usual adult and adolescent dose

Topical, to the ear canal, 2 or 3 drops of a 0.1% (base) solution every 2 or 3 hours initially, with dosage gradually being decreased as inflammation subsides.

Usual pediatric dose

See *Usual adult and adolescent dose*.

Usual geriatric dose

See *Usual adult and adolescent dose*.

Strength(s) usually available

U.S.—

Not commercially available.

Canada—

0.1% (base) (Rx) [*Betnesol*].

Packaging and storage

Store below 40 °C (104 °F), preferably between 15 and 30 °C (59 and 86 °F), unless otherwise specified by manufacturer. Protect from freezing.

Auxiliary labeling

- For the ear.

Note

Dispense in original unopened container.

DEXAMETHASONE

Otic Dosage Forms

DEXAMETHASONE SODIUM PHOSPHATE OPHTHALMIC SOLUTION (Otic use) USP

Usual adult and adolescent dose

Topical, to the ear canal, 3 or 4 drops of a 0.1% (phosphate) solution two or three times a day. After a favorable response is obtained, dosage may be gradually reduced if required to provide continuing control of symptoms prior to discontinuation.

Usual pediatric dose

See *Usual adult and adolescent dose*.

Usual geriatric dose

See *Usual adult and adolescent dose*.

Strength(s) usually available

U.S.—

0.1% (phosphate) (Rx) [*Decadron* (benzalkonium chloride 0.02%; creatinine; sodium bisulfite 0.1%; sodium borate; sodium citrate; disodium edetate; phenylethanol 0.25%; polysorbate 80); GENERIC].

Canada—

0.1% (phosphate) (Rx) [*Decadron* (sodium bisulfite 0.1%; benzalkonium chloride 0.02%; disodium edetate 0.05%; phenylethanol 0.25%)].

Packaging and storage

Store below 40 °C (104 °F), preferably between 15 and 30 °C (59 and 86 °F), unless otherwise specified by manufacturer. Store in a tight, light-resistant container. Protect from freezing.

Auxiliary labeling

- For the ear.

Note

Dispense in original unopened container.

Revised: 08/21/2000

CORTICOSTEROIDS Rectal

This monograph includes information on the following: 1) Betamethasone*; 2) Budesonide*; 3) Hydrocortisone; 4) Tixocortol*.

INN: Hydrocortisone—Cortisol

BAN: Hydrocortisone—Cortisol

JAN: Hydrocortisone—Cortisol

VA CLASSIFICATION (Primary):

Betamethasone—RS100

Budesonide—RS100

Hydrocortisone—RS100

Tixocortol—RS100

Commonly used brand name(s): *Anu-Med HC*[3]; *Anucort-HC*[3]; *Anuprep HC*[3]; *Anusol-HC*[3]; *Anutone-HC*[3]; *Anuzone-HC*[3]; *Betnesol*[1]; *Cort-Dome*[3]; *Cortenema*[3]; *Cortifoam*[3]; *Cortiment-10*[3]; *Cortiment-40*[3]; *Entocort*[2]; *Hemorrhoidal HC*[3]; *Hemril-HC Uniserts*[3]; *Hycort*[3]; *Proctocort*[3]; *Proctosol-HC*[3]; *Rectocort*[3]; *Rectosol-HC*[3]; *Rectovalone*[4].

Note: For a listing of dosage forms and brand names by country availability, see *Dosage Forms* section(s).

*Not commercially available in U.S.

Category

Corticosteroid (rectal); anti-inflammatory, steroidal (rectal).

Indications

Note: Bracketed information in the *Indications* section refers to uses that are not included in U.S. product labeling.

Accepted

Colitis, ulcerative (treatment)—Rectal corticosteroids are indicated to induce remission in acute exacerbations of mild to moderate ulcerative colitis, especially the distal forms including ulcerative proctitis, ulcerative proctosigmoiditis, and left-sided ulcerative colitis. They also are used as adjuncts to systemic corticosteroids or other pharmacological therapies in severe disease and in mild to moderate disease extending proximal to the reach of topical therapy. Hydrocortisone enema has proven useful in some cases of ulcerative colitis involving the transverse and ascending colons. Systemic effects, such as adrenal suppression, preclude the use of corticosteroids for long-term or maintenance therapy.

Cryptitis (treatment)
Hemorrhoids (treatment) or
Proctitis, factitial (treatment)—Hydrocortisone suppositories are indicated in the treatment of inflammatory rectal disorders including cryptitis, inflamed hemorrhoids, and proctitis caused by radiation (factitial).

Pruritus, anogenital (treatment)—Hydrocortisone rectal dosage forms are indicated for treatment of anogenital pruritus.

[Crohn's disease (treatment)]—Hydrocortisone enema is indicated as an adjunct in the treatment of Crohn's disease (regional enteritis) with left-sided involvement.

Pharmacology/Pharmacokinetics

Physicochemical characteristics

Molecular weight—
- Betamethasone sodium phosphate: 516.41.
- Budesonide: 430.54.
- Hydrocortisone: 362.47.
- Hydrocortisone acetate: 404.51.
- Tixocortol pivalate: 462.65.

Solubility—Hydrocortisone acetate: 1 mg per 100 mL in water.

pH—Hydrocortisone enema: Between 5.5 and 7.

Mechanism of action/Effect

Rectal corticosteroids appear to exert a local anti-inflammatory effect on the colonic mucosa. Corticosteroids decrease or prevent tissue responses to inflammatory processes, thereby reducing development of symptoms of inflammation without affecting the underlying cause. Corticosteroids inhibit accumulation of inflammatory cells including macrophages, monocytes, endothelial cells, fibroblasts, and lymphocytes at sites of inflammation, in part by induction of lipocortin, a protein that inhibits phospholipase A_2. As a result, there is a decrease in the production and release of cytokines, an inhibition of the synthesis of arachidonic acid-derived mediators of inflammation (leukotrienes and prostaglandins), and decreased extravasation of leukocytes to areas of injury. An immunosuppressant effect of corticosteroids also may contribute to the anti-inflammatory effect, possibly because both involve inhibition of specific functions of leukocytes.

Absorption

Betamethasone—There is some systemic absorption following administration of the enema.

Budesonide—Rapid and essentially complete within 3 hours following a 2-mg low viscosity enema in healthy volunteers. Systemic availability is 15 ± 12%.

Hydrocortisone—Partially absorbed following rectal administration. In ulcerative colitis patients, up to 50% may be absorbed.

Hydrocortisone acetate—In normal healthy subjects, approximately 26% of the dose is absorbed following rectal administration of a suppository. However, absorption across abraded or inflamed surfaces may be increased. Systemic absorption may be greater from the foam dosage form than from the enema, because the foam is not expelled.

Tixocortol—Rapidly and well absorbed following rectal administration.

Protein binding

Budesonide—High (88%); to plasma proteins.

Biotransformation

Budesonide—Extensive (approximately 90%) first-pass metabolism via oxidative and reductive pathways to major metabolites, 6 beta-hydroxybudesonide and 16 alpha-hydroxyprednisolone. Glucocorticoid activity of metabolites is less than 1% that of budesonide.

Tixocortol—In the blood and liver; transformed into inactive metabolites.

Half-life

Budesonide—Plasma: 2 to 3 hours.

Time to peak concentration

Budesonide—1.5 hours.
Tixocortol—20 minutes.

Peak plasma concentration

Budesonide—3 ± 2 nanomoles per L.

Elimination

Tixocortol—Urinary and fecal excretion generally are completed within 72 to 96 hours.

Precautions to Consider

Carcinogenicity

Long-term animal studies have not been conducted to determine the carcinogenicity of rectal corticosteroids.

Pregnancy/Reproduction

Fertility—

For betamethasone—

Motility and number of spermatozoa may be increased or decreased.

Pregnancy—

For corticosteroids—

Appropriate studies have not been done in humans. Corticosteroids should not be used extensively, in large amounts, or for prolonged periods in patients who are pregnant or planning to become pregnant.

For budesonide—

Budesonide crosses the placenta. High doses of budesonide administered subcutaneously produced fetal malformations (primarily skeletal defects) in rabbits, rats, and mice. However, the relevance of these findings to humans has not been established.

For hydrocortisone and hydrocortisone acetate—

In laboratory animals, low doses administered to gestating females have been associated with an increase in the incidence of fetal abnormalities.

FDA Pregnancy Category C (hydrocortisone acetate).

Breast-feeding

It is not known whether rectal corticosteroids are distributed into breast milk. Systemic corticosteroids are distributed into breast milk and may cause unwanted effects, such as growth suppression, in the infant. Rectal corticosteroids are not recommended for use by breast-feeding mothers.

Pediatrics

For corticosteroids—

Infants born to mothers who received corticosteroids during pregnancy should be monitored closely for signs of hypoadrenalism.

Growth and development should be carefully observed in infants and children. Growth suppression may be a complication of corticosteroid therapy or of ulcerative colitis. Alternate-day therapy may minimize this effect.

For budesonide and tixocortol—

Safety and efficacy have not been established.

Geriatrics

Appropriate studies on the relationship of age to the effects of rectal corticosteroids have not been performed in the geriatric population. However, geriatrics-specific problems that would limit the usefulness of these medications in the elderly are not expected.

Drug interactions and/or related problems

The following drug interactions and/or related problems have been selected on the basis of their potential clinical significance (possible mechanism in parentheses where appropriate)—not necessarily inclusive (» = major clinical significance):

Anti-inflammatory drugs, nonsteroidal (NSAIDs) or
Aspirin
(potential for gastrointestinal ulceration or hemorrhage)
(caution is recommended when aspirin is used concurrently with corticosteroids in patients with hypoprothrombinemia)

Phenytoin
(therapeutic effect of the corticosteroid may be decreased because of increased metabolism and decreased plasma concentration, which may result from phenytoin's induction of hepatic microsomal enzymes; an increase in corticosteroid dosage may be necessary)

» Vaccines, live virus, or other immunizations
(immunizations are not recommended because of the increased risk of neurological complications and the possibility of decreased or absent antibody response)

Laboratory value alterations

The following have been selected on the basis of their potential clinical significance (possible effect in parentheses where appropriate)—not necessarily inclusive (» = major clinical significance).

With diagnostic test values
Skin tests
(reactions may be suppressed)

With physiology/laboratory test values
Calcium, serum
(concentrations may be decreased)

Glucose
(because of the intrinsic hyperglycemic activity of corticosteroids, blood and urine concentrations may be increased if significant absorption of the corticosteroid occurs)

» Hypothalamic-pituitary-adrenal (HPA) axis function as assessed by:
Adrenocorticotropic hormone (ACTH, corticotropin) or
Cortisol, blood or
Cortisol, urine (24-hour) or
17-hydroxycorticosteroids, urine (24-hour)
(may be decreased)

(because budesonide is almost completely eliminated during first-pass metabolism, it has minimal systemic effect on HPA axis function at a therapeutic dose)

Osteocalcin, serum
(may be decreased; serum osteocalcin concentrations are correlated with bone turnover; however, the clinical significance of the effect of rectal corticosteroids on these concentrations is not known)

Medical considerations/Contraindications

The medical considerations/contraindications included have been selected on the basis of their potential clinical significance (reasons given in parentheses where appropriate)—not necessarily inclusive (» = major clinical significance).

Except under special circumstances, this medication should not be used when the following medical problems exist:

» Herpes simplex, ocular
(corneal perforation or ulceration may be more likely to develop with use of corticosteroids)

» Psychosis, acute
(may be aggravated)

» Tuberculosis, active, latent, or questionably healed
(may be exacerbated or reactivated; appropriate antitubercular chemotherapy or prophylaxis should be administered concurrently)

Risk-benefit should be considered when the following medical problems exist:

» Abscess, fecal or
» Anastomoses, intestinal, fresh or
» Diverticulitis or
» Fistulas, intestinal, extensive or
» Obstruction, intestinal or
» Perforation, intestinal or
» Peritonitis or
» Sinus tracts
(rectal corticosteroids should be used with caution to prevent local damage to the mucosa)
(signs and symptoms of perforation and peritonitis may be masked)

Cirrhosis or
Hypothyroidism
(effects of corticosteroids may be enhanced)

Coronary disease, acute or
Glomerulonephritis, acute or
Hypertension or
Hyperthyroidism or
Limited cardiac reserve or
Myasthenia gravis or
Renal function impairment or
Thrombophlebitis
(corticosteroids should be used with caution)

Diabetes mellitus
(loss of control of diabetes may occur due to possible elevations in blood glucose; manifestations of latent diabetes may be precipitated; an increase in the dose of insulin or oral antidiabetic medication may be needed)

Glaucoma
(intraocular pressure may be increased)

Ileocolostomy, postoperative
(corticosteroids may inhibit wound healing)

» Infection, local or systemic or
» Chickenpox or
» Measles
(signs of infection may be masked; new infection may develop; resistance and ability to localize infection may be decreased; if infection occurs during therapy, appropriate antimicrobial therapy should be instituted)

(chickenpox and measles may be more serious or even fatal in nonimmune children and adults using corticosteroids; prophylaxis with varicella zoster immune globulin may be indicated following exposure to chickenpox, and prophylaxis with immune globulin intravenous may be indicated following exposure to measles; if chickenpox develops, treatment with the appropriate antiviral agent should be considered)

Osteoporosis
(may be exacerbated)

Peptic ulcer, active or latent
(may cause hyperacidity)

Sensitivity to betamethasone, budesonide, hydrocortisone, or tixocortol

» Ulcerative disease, severe
(increased risk of perforation of the bowel wall; when surgery is imminent, it is hazardous to delay surgery while awaiting response to treatment)

Patient monitoring

The following may be especially important in patient monitoring (other tests may be warranted in some patients, depending on condition; » = major clinical significance):

» Adrenal function assessment, may include adrenocorticotropic hormone (ACTH) stimulation test, blood or urine cortisol concentrations, or urine 17-hydroxycorticosteroids concentration
(periodic monitoring may be advisable if therapy is prolonged)

Biopsy and
Endoscopy and
Sigmoidoscopy and
Stool examinations
(recommended to confirm the presence of colitis and rule out infectious causes and to determine dosage adjustment, duration of therapy, and rate of improvement)

(endoscopy is recommended to diagnose peptic ulcer when corticosteroid therapy is prolonged and accompanied by epigastric pain, hematemesis, melena, and/or nausea and vomiting)

Intraocular pressure
(should be measured when rectal corticosteroids are used in the presence of glaucoma)

Side/Adverse Effects

Note: The risk of systemic effects, including adrenal suppression, with the use of rectal corticosteroids, although less than with oral or systemic preparations, generally increases with increasing dosage and duration of therapy.

The risk of systemic effects following the use of conventional corticosteroids, such as betamethasone and hydrocortisone, is greater than the risk with budesonide or tixocortol. Although budesonide and tixocortol are well absorbed, tixocortol is rapidly transformed into an inactive metabolite and budesonide is almost completely eliminated during first-pass metabolism. As a result, the systemic effects of these two agents on adrenal and hypothalamic-pituitary-adrenal (HPA) axis function are minimal at therapeutic doses. However, a decrease in cortisol concentrations has been seen following rectal administration of a high dose (10 mg) of budesonide.

For several months to 1 year after discontinuation of prolonged corticosteroid therapy, acute adrenal insufficiency may be precipitated by periods of unusual stress. The risk of occurrence may be minimized by gradual dosage reduction, but if adrenal insufficiency occurs, it may require *re*instatement of corticosteroid therapy or an increase in dosage.

The following side/adverse effects have been selected on the basis of their potential clinical significance (possible signs and symptoms in parentheses where appropriate)—not necessarily inclusive:

Those indicating the need for medical attention

Incidence less frequent or rare

Allergic contact dermatitis (burning and itching of skin); ***chills; decreased glucose tolerance; diarrhea; fever; folliculitis*** (painful, red or itchy, pus-containing blisters in hair follicles); ***infection, secondary; rectal irritation*** (rectal bleeding, burning, dryness, itching, or pain not present before therapy); ***neuropathy*** (sensation of pins and needles; stabbing pain); ***psychic disturbances*** (depression; false sense of well-being; mood swings; personality changes); ***tenesmus*** (straining while passing stool)—with tixocortol only

Those occurring principally during prolonged use indicating need for medical attention

Acne; ***adrenal suppression; cataracts, posterior subcapsular*** (gradual blurring or loss of vision); ***Cushing's syndrome effects including backache; filling or rounding out of the face; hirsutism or hypertrichosis*** (unusual increase in hair growth, especially on the face); ***hunchback; hypertension; impotence*** (unusual decrease in sexual desire or ability in men); ***menstrual irregularities; muscle weakness; or striae*** (reddish purple lines on arms, face, legs, trunk, or groin); ***decreased resistance to infection; ecchymosis*** (nonelevated blue or purplish patch on the skin); ***fluid or sodium retention*** (rapid weight gain; swelling of feet or lower legs); ***glaucoma with possible damage to optic nerves*** (blurred vision or other change in vision; eye pain); ***growth suppression***—in children; ***hypokalemia*** (dryness of mouth; increased thirst; irregular heartbeat; mood or mental changes; muscle cramps or pain; nausea or vomiting; unusual tiredness or weakness; weak pulse); ***impaired wound healing; increased intracranial pressure*** (headache; insomnia; unusual tiredness or weakness); ***necrotizing angiitis*** (chills; coughing; coughing up blood; headache; loss of appetite; pain in joints or muscles; shortness of breath; skin rash; unusual tiredness; unusual weight loss); ***ocular infection, secondary, fungal or viral*** (blurred vision or other change in vision; eye pain; redness of eye; sensitivity of eye to light; tearing); ***osteopenia, osteoporosis, or bone fractures***; ***pancreatitis*** (abdominal pain; chills; nausea or vomiting); ***peptic ulcer*** (stomach pain); ***thrombophlebitis*** (pain or discomfort over vein)

Those indicating need for medical attention only if they continue or are bothersome

Incidence less frequent or rare

Dry, scaly skin; flatulence (passing of gas)—with budesonide only; ***headache; hypopigmentation*** (lightened skin color); ***increased sweating; increase in appetite; insomnia*** (trouble in sleeping); ***nausea; skin rash; thin, fragile skin; thinning hair on scalp; unusual weight gain; vertigo*** (dizziness; sensation of spinning)

Incidence rare—with tixocortol only

Anorexia (loss of appetite); ***unusual tiredness or weakness; unusual weight loss***

Overdose

For more information on the management of overdose or unintentional ingestion, **contact a Poison Control Center** (see *Poison Control Center Listing*).

Clinical effects of overdose

The following effects have been selected on the basis of their potential clinical significance (possible signs and symptoms in parentheses where appropriate)—not necessarily inclusive:

Chronic

Adrenal suppression; cataracts, posterior subcapsular; Cushing's syndrome; ***glaucoma; growth suppression***—in children; ***impaired wound healing; osteoporosis; pancreatitis; peptic ulcer; psychosis***

Treatment of overdose

Since there is no specific antidote available, treatment is symptomatic and supportive, and consists of discontinuing corticosteroid therapy. Acute overdose usually does not require tapering of the dosage. However, corticosteroids should be withdrawn gradually following prolonged use.

Patient Consultation

As an aid to patient consultation, refer to *Advice for the Patient, Corticosteroids (Rectal).*

In providing consultation, consider emphasizing the following selected information (» = major clinical significance):

Before using this medication

» Conditions affecting use, especially:
- Sensitivity to betamethasone, budesonide, hydrocortisone, or tixocortol
- Fertility—Motility and number of spermatozoa may be increased or decreased in men using betamethasone
- Pregnancy—High doses and long-term use are not recommended; budesonide crosses the placenta
- Breast-feeding—Not recommended for use by breast-feeding mothers
- Use in children—Infants born to mothers who received corticosteroids during pregnancy should be monitored for signs of hypoadrenalism; growth suppression also may occur
- Other medications, especially live virus vaccines or other immunizations
- Other medical problems, especially acute psychosis; chickenpox; diverticulitis; extensive intestinal fistulas; fecal abscess; fresh, intestinal anastamoses; intestinal obstruction or perforation; local or systemic infection; measles; ocular herpes simplex; peritonitis; severe ulcerative disease; sinus tracts; or tuberculosis

Proper use of this medication

» Regular visits to physician to check progress

Proper administration technique; reading patient directions carefully

» Importance of not using more medication than the amount prescribed

» Proper dosing

Missed dose: Using as soon as possible; not using if almost time for next dose

» Proper storage

Precautions while using this medication

» Checking with physician before discontinuing medication; gradual dosage reduction may be necessary

» Checking with physician if symptoms do not improve within 2 or 3 weeks or if condition becomes worse

» Checking with physician immediately if bleeding occurs

Staining of fabric may occur following use of suppositories

» Caution in receiving skin tests

» Caution if any kind of surgery or emergency treatment is required

» Caution if serious infections or injuries occur

» Avoiding exposure to chickenpox or measles (especially for children); telling physician right away if exposure occurs

» Caution in receiving vaccinations or other immunizations

For diabetic patients: May increase blood sugar concentrations

Side/adverse effects

Signs of potential side effects, especially allergic contact dermatitis, chills, decreased glucose tolerance, diarrhea, fever, folliculitis, secondary infection, rectal irritation, neuropathy, psychic disturbances, and tenesmus

Signs of potential side effects occurring principally during prolonged therapy, especially acne; adrenal suppression; posterior subcapsular cataracts; Cushing's syndrome effects; decreased resistance to infection; ecchymosis; fluid or sodium retention; glaucoma with possible damage to optic nerves; growth suppression (in children); hypokalemia; impaired wound healing; increased intracranial pressure; necrotizing angiitis; secondary ocular infection (fungal or viral); osteopenia, osteoporosis, or bone fractures; pancreatitis; peptic ulcer; and thrombophlebitis

General Dosing Information

A complete colorectal examination should be performed before rectal corticosteroid therapy commences to rule out serious pathology and to gauge the extent of the disease process.

If rectal corticosteroid therapy is to be successful in treating the disease, the medication must reach the diseased mucosa. Therefore, the choice of dosage form should be determined by the upper extent of the disease. The spread of the enema dosage form reaches the splenic flexure, whereas the spread of the foam and suppositories dosage forms is restricted to the rectum and sigmoid colon. Many patients prefer the foam to the enema because it allows ambulation immediately after application, interferes less with daily activities, and is easier to retain.

The enema should be retained for at least 1 to 3 hours, but it is preferable to retain it overnight. This may be facilitated by prior sedation and/or antidiarrheal medication, especially early in therapy when the urge to evacuate is the greatest.

Rectal corticosteroids for treatment of ulcerative colitis should be used in conjunction with rational dietary control, sedatives, antidiarrheal agents, antimicrobial therapy, and blood replacement, if necessary. However, anticholinergics, antidiarrheals, and antispasmodics should be used with caution because of the risk of inducing paralytic ileus or toxic megacolon.

The lowest possible dose of rectal corticosteroid should be used to control the condition under treatment. Also, corticosteroid therapy should be withdrawn gradually as soon as possible after a patient reaches remission. At that time, other agents may be used to maintain remission and/or to reduce the likelihood or frequency of relapse.

Satisfactory response to rectal corticosteroid therapy usually occurs within 1 or 2 weeks and is marked by a decrease in symptoms. However, symptomatic improvement (decreased diarrhea and bleeding, weight gain, improved appetite, reduced fever, and decreased leukocytosis) may be misleading and should not be the sole criterion for evaluating efficacy.

If there is no evidence of clinical or colorectal improvement within 2 or 3 weeks, or if the patient's condition worsens, rectal corticosteroid therapy should be discontinued.

In the presence of an infection, appropriate antimicrobial therapy should be instituted. If a favorable response does not occur promptly, the corticosteroid should be discontinued until the infection has been adequately controlled.

BETAMETHASONE

Summary of Differences

Pharmacology/pharmacokinetics: Some systemic absorption.

Precautions: Fertility—May increase or decrease motility and number of spermatozoa.

Side/adverse effects: Risk of systemic effects greater than with budesonide or tixocortol.

Rectal Dosage Forms

BETAMETHASONE SODIUM PHOSPHATE ENEMA

Usual adult dose

Colitis, ulcerative—

Rectal, 5 mg as a retention enema every night for two to four weeks.

Usual pediatric dose

Dosage has not been established.

Strength(s) usually available

U.S.—

Not commercially available.

Canada—

5 mg per 100 mL (Rx) [*Betnesol*].

Packaging and storage

Store below 40 °C (104 °F), preferably between 15 and 30 °C (59 and 86 °F), unless otherwise specified by manufacturer. Protect from freezing.

Auxiliary labeling

- For rectal use only.

Note

When dispensing, explain administration technique.

BUDESONIDE

Summary of Differences

Pharmacology/pharmacokinetics:

Biotransformation—Undergoes extensive first-pass metabolism.

Potency ranking—High.

Precautions:

Pregnancy—Crosses the placenta.

Side/adverse effects:

Minimal systemic effect on hypothalamic-pituitary-adrenal axis function at a therapeutic dose.

Rectal Dosage Forms

BUDESONIDE ENEMA

Usual adult dose

Colitis, ulcerative—

Rectal, 2 mg as a retention enema every night for four to eight weeks.

Usual pediatric dose

Safety and efficacy have not been established.

Usual geriatric dose

See *Usual adult dose*.

Strength(s) usually available

U.S.—

Not commercially available.

Canada—

2 mg per 100 mL (Rx) [*Entocort* (tablet 2.3 mg)].

Packaging and storage

Store between 15 and 30 °C (59 and 86 °F), unless otherwise specified by manufacturer.

Preparation of dosage form

For each dose, 1 tablet should be added to the enema bottle, then the bottle should be shaken vigorously for 10 seconds or until the tablet dissolves completely. The resulting 115-mL (15 mL is residual volume) suspension will be slightly yellowish in color, and should be used immediately.

Auxiliary labeling

- For rectal use only.

Note

When dispensing, explain administration technique.

HYDROCORTISONE

Summary of Differences

Indications: Also indicated in cryptitis, hemorrhoids, factitial proctitis, and anogenital pruritus; and used in left-sided Crohn's disease.

Pharmacology/pharmacokinetics: Potency ranking—Low (acetate and base).

Side/adverse effects: Risk of systemic effects is greater than with budesonide or tixocortol.

Rectal Dosage Forms

Note: Bracketed uses in the *Dosage Forms* section refer to categories of use and/or indications that are not included in U.S. product labeling.

HYDROCORTISONE ENEMA USP

Usual adult dose

Colitis, ulcerative—

Rectal, 100 mg as a retention enema at bedtime for two or three weeks or until there is clinical and proctologic remission. Refractory cases may require treatment for up to two to three months.

[Crohn's disease]—

Rectal, 100 mg as a retention enema at bedtime for two or three weeks.

Note: If it is necessary to continue therapy beyond three weeks, therapy should be discontinued gradually by reducing administration to every other night for two or three weeks.

Usual pediatric dose

Dosage has not been established.

Strength(s) usually available

U.S.—

100 mg per 60 mL (Rx) [*Cortenema;* GENERIC].

Canada—

100 mg per 60 mL (Rx) [*Cortenema; Hycort*].

Packaging and storage

Store between 15 and 30 °C (59 and 86 °F), unless otherwise specified by manufacturer. Store in a tight container. Protect from freezing and from light.

Auxiliary labeling

- For rectal use only.
- Shake well before use.

Note

When dispensing, explain administration technique.

HYDROCORTISONE ACETATE FOAM

Note: Each applicatorful delivers approximately 900 mg of foam containing approximately 90 mg of hydrocortisone acetate (80 mg of hydrocortisone base).

Usual adult dose

Colitis, ulcerative—

Rectal, 1 applicatorful one or two times a day for two or three weeks, then 1 applicatorful every second day.

Usual pediatric dose

Dosage has not been established.

Strength(s) usually available

U.S.—
10% (Rx) [*Cortifoam* (inert propellants isobutane and propane)].

Canada—
10% (Rx) [*Cortifoam*].

Packaging and storage

Store between 15 and 30 °C (59 and 86 °F), unless otherwise specified by manufacturer.

Auxiliary labeling

- For rectal use only.
- Shake well before use.

Note

When dispensing, explain administration technique.

HYDROCORTISONE ACETATE SUPPOSITORIES

Usual adult dose

Colitis, ulcerative—
Rectal, 25 or 30 mg in the morning and at night for two weeks. In more severe cases, 25 or 30 mg three times a day or 50 or 60 mg two times a day.

Proctitis, factitial—
Rectal, 25 or 30 mg in the morning and at night for six to eight weeks, according to response.

Cryptitis or
Hemorrhoids or
Pruritus, anogenital—
Rectal, 20 to 30 mg a day for three days; or 40 to 80 mg a day, as needed.

Usual pediatric dose

Dosage has not been established.

Strength(s) usually available

U.S.—
25 mg (Rx) [*Anucort-HC; Anu-Med HC; Anuprep HC; Anusol-HC; Anutone-HC; Anuzone-HC; Cort-Dome; Hemril-HC Uniserts; Hemorrhoidal HC; Proctosol-HC; Rectosol-HC;* GENERIC].
30 mg (Rx) [*Proctocort*].

Canada—
10 mg (Rx) [*Cortiment-10*].
10 mg (base) (Rx) [*Rectocort*].
40 mg (Rx) [*Cortiment-40*].

Packaging and storage

Store below 30 °C (86 °F), unless otherwise specified by manufacturer. Store in a well-closed container. Protect from freezing.

Auxiliary labeling

- For rectal use only.
- Store in a cool place.
- May be refrigerated.

Note

When dispensing, explain administration technique.

TIXOCORTOL

Rectal Dosage Forms

TIXOCORTOL PIVALATE ENEMA

Usual adult dose

Colitis, ulcerative—
Rectal, 250 mg as a retention enema at bedtime for twenty-one consecutive days. If there is no improvement after twenty-one days, an alternative method of treatment should be considered.

Usual pediatric dose

Safety and efficacy have not been established.

Strength(s) usually available

U.S.—
Not commercially available.

Canada—
250 mg per 100 mL (Rx) [*Rectovalone* (benzyl alcohol)].

Packaging and storage

Store below 40 °C (104 °F), preferably between 15 and 30 °C (59 and 86 °F), unless otherwise specified by manufacturer. Protect from freezing.

Auxiliary labeling

- For rectal use only.
- Shake well before use.

Note

When dispensing, explain administration technique.

Selected Bibliography

Kornbluth A, Sachar DB. Ulcerative colitis practice guidelines in adults. Am J Gastroenterol 1997; 92: 204-11.

Revised: 07/29/1998

CORTICOSTEROIDS Topical

This monograph includes information on the following: 1) Alclometasone†; 2) Amcinonide; 3) Beclomethasone*; 4) Betamethasone; 5) Clobetasol; 6) Clobetasone*; 7) Clocortolone†; 8) Desonide; 9) Desoximetasone; 10) Dexamethasone†; 11) Diflorasone; 12) Diflucortolone*; 13) Flumethasone*; 14) Fluocinolone; 15) Fluocinonide; 16) Flurandrenolide; 17) Fluticasone†; 18) Halcinonide; 19) Halobetasol†; 20) Hydrocortisone; 21) Mometasone; 22) Prednicarbate†; 23) Triamcinolone.

INN:
Beclomethasone—Beclometasone
Flumethasone—Flumetasone
Flurandrenolide—Fludroxycortide
Halobetasol—Ulobetasol
Hydrocortisone—Cortisol

BAN:
Desoximetasone—Desoxymethasone
Flurandrenolide—Flurandrenolone
Hydrocortisone—Cortisol

JAN:
Beclomethasone—Beclometasone
Flumethasone—Flumetasone
Flurandrenolide—Fluoxycortide
Hydrocortisone—Cortisol
Hydrocortisone buteprate—Hydrocortisone butyrate propionate

VA CLASSIFICATION (Primary):

Alclometasone
Topical—DE200
Amcinonide
Topical—DE200
Beclomethasone
Topical—DE200
Betamethasone
Topical—DE200
Clobetasol
Topical—DE200
Clobetasone
Topical—DE200
Clocortolone
Topical—DE200
Desonide
Topical—DE200
Desoximetasone
Topical—DE200
Dexamethasone
Topical—DE200
Diflorasone
Topical—DE200
Diflucortolone
Topical—DE200
Flumethasone
Topical—DE200
Fluocinolone
Topical—DE200
Fluocinonide
Topical—DE200
Flurandrenolide
Topical—DE200
Fluticasone
Topical—DE200
Halcinonide
Topical—DE200
Halobetasol
Topical—DE200
Hydrocortisone
Dental—OR900
Topical—DE200
Mometasone
Topical—DE200
Triamcinolone
Dental—OR900
Topical—DE200

Commonly used brand name(s): *9-1-1*[20]; *Aclovate*[1]; *Acticort 100*[20]; *Aeroseb-Dex*[10]; *Aeroseb-HC*[20]; *Ala-Cort*[20]; *Ala-Scalp HP*[20]; *Allercort*[20]; *Alphaderm*[20]; *Alphatrex*[4]; *Anusol-HC*[20]; *Aristocort*[23]; *Aristocort A*[23]; *Aristocort C*[23]; *Aristocort D*[23]; *Aristocort R*[23]; *Bactine*[20]; *Barriere-HC*[20]; *Beben*[4]; *Beta-HC*[20]; *Beta-Val*[4]; *Betacort Scalp Lotion*[4]; *Betaderm*[4]; *Betaderm Scalp Lotion*[4]; *Betatrex*[4]; *Betnovate*[4]; *Betnovate-½*[4]; *Bio-Syn*[14]; *CaldeCORT Anti-Itch*[20]; *CaldeCORT Light*[20]; *Carmol-HC*[20]; *Celestoderm-V*[4]; *Celestoderm-V/2*[4]; *Cetacort*[20]; *Cloderm*[7]; *Cordran*[16]; *Cordran SP*[16]; *Cormax*[5]; *Cort-Dome*[20]; *Cortacet*[20]; *Cortaid*[20]; *Cortate*[20]; *Cortef*[20]; *Cortef Feminine Itch*[20]; *Corticaine*[20]; *Corticreme*[20]; *Cortifair*[20]; *Cortoderm*[20]; *Cortril*[20]; *Cutivate*[17]; *Cyclocort*[2]; *Decaderm*[10]; *Decadron*[10]; *Decaspray*[10]; *Delacort*[20]; *Delta-Tritex*[23]; *Dermabet*[4]; *Dermacort*[20]; *Dermarest DriCort*[20]; *Dermatop*[22]; *DermiCort*[20]; *Dermovate*[5]; *Dermovate Scalp Lotion*[5]; *Dermtex HC*[20]; *DesOwen*[8]; *Diprolene*[4]; *Diprolene AF*[4]; *Diprosone*[4]; *Drenison*[16]; *Drenison-¼*[16]; *Ectosone Mild*[4]; *Ectosone Regular*[4]; *Ectosone Scalp Lotion*[4]; *Elocom*[21]; *Elocon*[21]; *Emo-Cort*[20]; *Emo-Cort Scalp Solution*[20]; *Epifoam*[20]; *Eumovate*[6]; *Florone*[11]; *Florone E*[11]; *Fluocet*[14]; *Fluocin*[15]; *Fluoderm*[14]; *Fluolar*[14]; *Fluonid*[14]; *Fluonide*[14]; *Flurosyn*[14]; *Flutex*[23]; *FoilleCort*[20]; *Gly-Cort*[20]; *Gynecort*[20]; *Gynecort 10*[20]; *Halog*[18]; *Halog-E*[18]; *Hi-Cor 1.0*[20]; *Hi-Cor 2.5*[20]; *Hyderm*[20]; *Hydro-Tex*[20]; *Hytone*[20]; *Kenac*[23]; *Kenalog*[23]; *Kenalog in Orabase*[23]; *Kenalog-H*[23]; *Kenonel*[23]; *LactiCare-HC*[20]; *Lanacort*[20]; *Lanacort 10*[20]; *Lemoderm*[20]; *Licon*[15]; *Lidemol*[15]; *Lidex*[15]; *Lidex-E*[15]; *Locacorten*[13]; *Locoid*[20]; *Luxíq*[4]; *Lyderm*[15]; *Maxiflor*[11]; *Maximum Strength Cortaid*[20]; *Maxivate*[4]; *Metaderm Mild*[4]; *Metaderm Regular*[4]; *MyCort*[20]; *Nerisone*[12]; *Nerisone Oily*[12]; *Novobetamet*[4]; *Novohydrocort*[20]; *Nutracort*[20]; *Occlucort*[4]; *Olux Foam*[5]; *Orabase-HCA*[20]; *Oracort*[23]; *Oralone*[23]; *Pandel*[20]; *Penecort*[20]; *Pentacort*[20]; *Pharma-Cort*[20]; *Prevex B*[4]; *Prevex HC*[20]; *Propaderm*[3]; *Psorcon*[11]; *Rederm*[20]; *Rhulicort*[20]; *S-T Cort*[20]; *Sarna HC 1.0%*[20]; *Sential*[20]; *Synacort*[20]; *Synalar*[14]; *Synalar-HP*[14]; *Synamol*[14]; *Synemol*[14]; *Teladar*[4]; *Temovate*[5]; *Temovate E*[5]; *Temovate Scalp Application*[5]; *Texacort*[20]; *Topicort*[9]; *Topicort LP*[9]; *Topicort Mild*[9]; *Topilene*[4]; *Topisone*[4]; *Topsyn*[15]; *Triacet*[23]; *Triaderm*[23]; *Trianide Mild*[23]; *Trianide Regular*[23]; *Triderm*[23]; *Tridesilon*[8]; *Ultravate*[19]; *Unicort*[20]; *Uticort*[4]; *Valisone*[4]; *Valisone Reduced Strength*[4]; *Valisone Scalp Lotion*[4]; *Valnac*[4]; *Vanos*[15]; *Westcort*[20].

Other commonly used names are:
Beclometasone [Beclomethasone]
Cortisol [Hydrocortisone]
Fludroxycortide [Flurandrenolide]
Flumetasone [Flumethasone]
Ulobetasol [Halobetasol]

Note: For a listing of dosage forms and brand names by country availability, see *Dosage Forms* section(s).

*Not commercially available in U.S.
†Not commercially available in Canada.

Category

Corticosteroid (topical); anti-inflammatory, steroidal (topical).

Indications

Note: Bracketed information in the *Indications* section refers to uses that are not included in U.S. product labeling.

General Considerations

Topical corticosteroids are indicated to provide symptomatic relief of inflammation and/or pruritus associated with acute and chronic corticosteroid-responsive disorders.

The location of the skin lesion to be treated should be considered in selecting a formulation. In areas with thinner skin, such as facial, eye, and intertriginous areas, low-potency corticosteroid preparations are preferred for long-term therapy. Low- to medium-potency products may be used on the ears, trunk, arms, legs, and scalp. Medium- to very high-potency formulations may be required for treatment of dermatologic disorders in areas with thicker skin, such as the palms and soles. Lotion, aerosol, and gel formulations are cosmetically better suited for hairy areas.

The type of lesion to be treated should also be considered in product selection. For dry, scaly, cracked, thickened, or hardened skin, ointments of medium potency are often used. Medium-potency lotions, aerosols, or creams are preferred in treating moister, weeping lesions or areas or in treating conditions with intense inflammation. High- to very high-potency ointments may be required to treat hyperkeratotic or thick skin lesions.

Accepted

Dermatitis, atopic, mild to moderate
Dermatitis, contact
Dermatitis, nummular, mild
Dermatitis, seborrheic, facial and intertriginous areas
Dermatitis, other forms of, mild to moderate
Dermatoses, inflammatory, other, mild to moderate
Intertrigo
Lichen planus, facial and intertriginous areas
Lupus erythematosus, discoid, facial and intertriginous areas
Polymorphous light eruption
Pruritus, anogenital
Pruritus senilis
Psoriasis, facial and intertriginous areas or
Xerosis, inflammatory phase—Topical corticosteroids of low to medium potency (see *Table 1, Pharmacology/Pharmacokinetics*) are indicated in the treatment of corticosteroid-responsive dermatologic disorders. Occlusive dressings also may be required for chronic or severe cases of lichen simplex chronicus, psoriasis, eczema, atopic dermatitis, or chronic hand eczema. The more potent topical corticosteroids and/or occlusive dressings may be required for conditions such as discoid lupus erythematosus, lichen planus, granuloma annulare, psoriatic plaques, and psoriasis affecting the palms, soles, elbows, or knees.

Alopecia areata
Dermatitis, atopic, moderate to severe
Dermatitis, exfoliative, generalized
Dermatitis, nummular, moderate to severe
Dermatitis, other forms of, moderate to severe
Dermatoses, inflammatory, other, moderate to severe
Granuloma annulare
Keloids, reduction of associated itching
Lichen planus
Lichen simplex chronicus
Lichen striatus
Lupus erythematosus, discoid and subacute cutaneous
Myxedema, pretibial
Necrobiosis lipoidica diabeticorum
Pemphigoid
Pemphigus
Pityriasis rosea
Psoriasis
Sarcoidosis or
Sunburn—Topical corticosteroids of medium to very high potency (see *Table 1, Pharmacology/Pharmacokinetics*) are indicated in the treatment of corticosteroid-responsive dermatologic disorders. Systemic therapy with, or intralesional injection of, a corticosteroid may be required for some of the disorders, as determined by the type and severity of the condition or inadequate response to topical therapy. Occlusive dressings also may be required for conditions such as discoid lupus erythematosus; bullous disorders; lichen planus; granuloma annulare; psoriatic plaques; and psoriasis affecting the palms, soles, elbows, or knees.

Oral lesions, inflammatory or ulcerative (treatment)—Hydrocortisone acetate and triamcinolone acetonide dental pastes are indicated for adjunctive treatment and temporary relief of symptoms associated with nonherpetic oral inflammatory and ulcerative lesions, including recurrent aphthous stomatitis. [Formulations of high potency gels and very high potency ointments also are used in the treatment of aphthous stomatitis.][1]

[These agents also are used to treat other gingival disorders, such as desquamative gingivitis and oral lichen planus when the diagnosis has been confirmed by biopsy testing. Gel formulations of high potency corticosteroids and dental triamcinolone are used in the treatment of lichen planus of the mucous membranes.][1]

[Other topical corticosteroids also are used to treat gingival disorders.][1]

[Phimosis][1]—Topical corticosteroids are indicated for the treatment of phimosis in boys.

Unaccepted

Medium to very high potency topical corticosteroids should not be used in the treatment of rosacea and perioral dermatitis and should not be used on the face, groin, or axillae. Although topical corticosteroids may initially reduce the burning and pustulation associated with rosacea, a severe rebound flare-up may occur upon discontinuance of the steroid.

Topical corticosteroids should not be used in the treatment of acne.

Topical corticosteroids are not indicated for routine gingivitis, which should be treated by the removal of local causative factors and an improvement in oral hygiene.

Alclometasone cream or ointment should not be used in the treatment of diaper dermatitis.

[1]Not included in Canadian product labeling.

Pharmacology/Pharmacokinetics

See *Table 1*, page 935.

Physicochemical characteristics

Molecular weight—
- Alclometasone dipropionate: 521.05.
- Amcinonide: 502.58.
- Beclomethasone dipropionate: 521.05.
- Betamethasone: 392.47.
- Betamethasone benzoate: 496.58.
- Betamethasone dipropionate: 504.6.
- Betamethasone sodium phosphate: 516.41.
- Betamethasone valerate: 476.59.
- Clobetasol propionate: 466.98.
- Clobetasone butyrate: 478.99.
- Clocortolone pivalate: 495.03.
- Desonide: 416.52.
- Desoximetasone: 376.47.
- Dexamethasone: 392.47.
- Dexamethasone sodium phosphate: 516.41.
- Diflorasone diacetate: 494.54.
- Diflucortolone valerate: 478.6.
- Flumethasone pivalate: 494.58.
- Fluocinolone acetonide: 452.5.
- Fluocinolone acetonide, dihydrate: 488.53.
- Fluocinonide: 494.54.
- Flurandrenolide: 436.52.
- Fluticasone propionate: 500.58.
- Halcinonide: 454.97.
- Halobetasol propionate: 484.97.
- Hydrocortisone: 362.47.
- Hydrocortisone acetate: 404.51.
- Hydrocortisone buteprate: 488.62.
- Hydrocortisone butyrate: 432.56.
- Hydrocortisone valerate: 446.59.
- Mometasone furoate: 521.44.
- Prednicarbate: 488.58.
- Triamcinolone acetonide: 434.51.

Mechanism of action/Effect

Corticosteroids diffuse across cell membranes and complex with specific cytoplasmic receptors. These complexes then enter the cell nucleus, bind to DNA (chromatin), and stimulate transcription of messenger RNA (mRNA) and subsequent protein synthesis of various inhibitory enzymes responsible for the anti-inflammatory effects of topical corticosteroids. These anti-inflammatory effects include inhibition of early processes such as edema, fibrin deposition, capillary dilatation, movement of phagocytes into the area, and phagocytic activities. Later processes, such as capillary production, collagen deposition, and keloid formation also are inhibited by corticosteroids. The overall actions of topical corticosteroids are catabolic.

Factors that increase the clinical efficacy and potential for adverse effects of topical corticosteroids include enhancement of pharmacologic activity of the compound by altering molecular structure, increasing stratum corneum penetration of the compound, and increasing bioavailability of the compound from the vehicle.

The pharmacologic activity of topical corticosteroids is increased by several changes in molecular structure. Addition of a 9-alpha-fluorine atom increases the anti-inflammatory glucocorticoid activity, but simultaneously increases undesired mineralocorticoid activity. Mineralocorticoid activity is diminished by addition of a 16-hydroxy or 16-methyl group. Substitution or masking of 16- or 17-hydroxy groups with longer side chains such as acetonide, propionate, or valerate increases lipophilicity and subsequently stratum corneum penetration.

Dental paste in dental dosage forms acts as an adhesive vehicle for application of corticosteroids to oral mucosa. The vehicle also reduces pain by serving as a protective covering.

Absorption

Absorbed systemically across the stratum corneum.

Stratum corneum penetration is primarily enhanced by increasing skin hydration and/or temperature, or by changes in molecular structure of the compound.

Hydrating the skin with occlusive dressings such as plastic wrap, a tight-fitting diaper or one covered with plastic pants, plastic tape, or dermatological patches can increase corticosteroid penetration by up to tenfold. Ointment bases inhibit evaporation of moisture from skin. Intertriginous areas (axillae and groin) are self-occluding. Intertriginous areas and the face also have inherently thinner skin, are more macerated and therefore, allow for increased absorption.

Absorption of topical corticosteroids has been greatly increased by altering the product vehicle or the drug substance itself. Vehicles containing substances that solubilize the corticosteroid enhance absorption. Increasing the concentration of the drug increases skin penetration but also may increase wastage of the drug. Decreasing drug particle size has been shown to increase topical bioavailability.

Increased percutaneous absorption of corticosteroids also occurs when the skin or mucosa is abraded or inflamed, when body temperature is elevated, with prolonged use, or with extensive use.

There is some systemic absorption of topical corticosteroids through the oral mucosa; absorption increases with increased potency and prolonged use.

Biotransformation

Primarily in skin; once absorbed systemically, in the liver. Corticosteroids that contain substituted 17-hydroxyl groups or that are fluorinated are resistant to local metabolism in the skin. Repeated application results in a cumulative depot effect in the skin, which may lead to a prolonged duration of action, increased side effects, and increased systemic absorption.

The following topical corticosteroids contain substituted 17-hydroxyl groups (S) and/or are fluorinated (F) compounds:
- Alclometasone dipropionate—S
- Amcinonide—S, F
- Beclomethasone dipropionate—S
- Betamethasone—F
- Betamethasone benzoate—S, F
- Betamethasone dipropionate—S, F
- Betamethasone valerate—S, F
- Clobetasol propionate—S, F
- Clobetasone butyrate—S, F
- Clocortolone pivalate—S, F
- Desonide—S
- Desoximetasone—S (17-hydrogen), F
- Dexamethasone—F
- Dexamethasone sodium phosphate—F
- Diflorasone diacetate—S, F
- Diflucortolone valerate—F
- Flumethasone pivalate—F
- Fluocinolone acetonide—S, F
- Fluocinonide—S, F
- Flurandrenolide—S, F
- Fluticasone propionate—S, F
- Halcinonide—S, F
- Halobetasol propionate—S, F
- Hydrocortisone butyrate—S
- Hydrocortisone valerate—S
- Mometasone furoate—S
- Triamcinolone acetonide—S, F

Precautions to Consider

Carcinogenicity

Long-term animal studies to determine the carcinogenicity of topical corticosteroids have not been done.

Mutagenicity

Betamethasone—Betamethasone was found to be genotoxic in the *in vitro* human peripheral blood lymphocyte chromosome aberration assay with metabolic activation and in the *in vivo* mouse bone marrow micronucleus assay.

Fluocinonide—Fluocinonide revealed no evidence of mutagenic or clastogenic potential based on the Ames test and an *in vitro* chromosomal aberration assay in human lymphocytes. However, fluocinonide was positive for clastogenic potential when tested in the *in vivo* mouse micronucleus assay.

Fluticasone—No mutagenicity was shown with fluticasone propionate in the Ames test, *Escherichia coli* fluctuation test, *Saccharomyces cerevisiae* gene conversion test, or Chinese hamster ovarian cell assay. Fluticasone was not clastogenic in mouse micronucleus or cultured human lymphocyte tests.

Halobetasol—Halobetasol propionate was not found to be genotoxic in the Ames/ *Salmonella* assay, sister chromatid exchange test in Chinese hamster somatic cells, chromosome aberration studies of germinal and somatic cells of rodents, and a mammalian spot test to determine point mutations. It was found to be mutagenic in a Chinese hamster micronucleus test, and in a mouse lymphoma gene mutation assay *in vitro*.

Hydrocortisone and *prednisolone*—Studies on mutagenicity with hydrocortisone and prednisolone yielded negative results.

Mometasone—No mutagenicity was shown with mometasone in the Ames test, mouse lymphoma assay, and a micronucleus test.

Pregnancy/Reproduction

Pregnancy—Topical corticosteroids, especially the more potent ones, should not be used extensively, in large amounts, or for protracted periods in pregnant patients or in patients who are planning to become pregnant.

Adequate and well-controlled studies in humans have not been done.

Studies in animals have shown that topical corticosteroids are systemically absorbed and may cause fetal abnormalities, especially when used in large amounts, with occlusive dressings, for prolonged periods of time, or if the more potent agents are used.

Betamethasone: A dose-related increase in fetal resorptions was observed in rabbits and mice given betamethasone dipropionate intramuscularly. This effect was not observed in rats. Teratogenic effects (umbilical hernia, cephalocele, cleft palate) were observed in rabbits when betamethasone dipropionate was administered intramuscularly.

Desoximetasone: In studies in mice, rats, and rabbits, desoximetasone has been shown to be teratogenic and embryotoxic with subcutaneous or dermal use.

Fluticasone: In studies in mice, fluticasone was found to be teratogenic (cleft palate) with subcutaneous usage of doses approximately 14 and 45 times the usual human topical dose.

Halobetasol: In studies in rats and rabbits, halobetasol propionate administered systemically was shown to be teratogenic at doses 3 to 33 times the usual human topical dose. Cleft palate was observed in both species. Omphalocele was seen in rats only. Halobetasol propionate was shown to be embryotoxic in rabbits but not in rats.

Hydrocortisone dental dosage form: Studies have not been done in animals.

FDA Pregnancy Category C.

Breast-feeding

It is not known whether topical corticosteroids are distributed into breast milk. However, problems in humans have not been documented.

Systemic corticosteroids are distributed into breast milk and may cause unwanted effects, such as growth suppression, in the infant.

Topical corticosteroids should not be applied to the breasts prior to nursing.

Pediatrics

Children and adolescents have a large skin surface area to body weight ratio and less developed, thinner skin, which may result in absorption of greater amounts of topical corticosteroids compared with older patients. Absorption also is greater in premature infants than in full term newborns, due to inadequate development of the stratum corneum.

Adrenal suppression, Cushing's syndrome, intracranial hypertension, and growth retardation due to the systemic absorption of topical corticosteroids have been documented in children. Therefore, special care must be exercised when these agents are used in children and growing adolescents, especially if factors that increase absorption are involved. It is recommended that only low-potency, unfluorinated topical corticosteroids that have a free 17-hydroxyl group be used in children or growing adolescents unless there is a demonstrated need for one of the other topical corticosteroids.

Generally, pediatric therapy continuing for longer than 2 weeks and consisting of doses in excess of one daily application (with medium- or high-potency corticosteroids) or two daily applications (with low-potency corticosteroids) should be evaluated carefully by the physician. This is especially important if medication is applied to more than 5 to 10% of the body surface or if an occlusive dressing is used. A tight-fitting diaper or one covered with plastic pants may constitute an occlusive dressing.

Geriatrics

Although appropriate studies with topical corticosteroids have not been performed in the geriatric population, geriatrics-specific problems are not expected to limit the usefulness of topical corticosteroids in the elderly. However, elderly patients may be more likely to have pre-existing skin atrophy secondary to aging. Purpura and skin lacerations that may raise the skin and subcutaneous tissue from deep fascia may be more likely to occur with the use of topical corticosteroids in geriatric patients. Therefore, topical corticosteroids should be used infrequently, for brief periods, or under close medical supervision in patients with evidence of pre-existing skin atrophy. Use of lower potency topical corticosteroids also may be necessary in some patients.

Laboratory value alterations

The following have been selected on the basis of their potential clinical significance (possible effect in parentheses where appropriate)—not necessarily inclusive (» = major clinical significance).

With physiology/laboratory test values

Eosinophil count, total
(may be decreased as plasma cortisol concentration is decreased)

Glucose
(because of the intrinsic hyperglycemic activity of corticosteroids, blood and urine concentrations may be increased if significant absorption of the corticosteroid occurs)

Hypothalamic-pituitary-adrenal (HPA) axis function as assessed by:
Adrenocorticotropic hormone (ACTH, corticotropin) or
Cortisol, blood or
Cortisol, urine (24-hour) or
17-hydroxycorticosteroids, urine (24-hour)
(may be decreased if significant absorption of the corticosteroid occurs, especially in children)

Medical considerations/Contraindications

The medical considerations/contraindications included have been selected on the basis of their potential clinical significance (reasons given in parentheses where appropriate)—not necessarily inclusive (» = major clinical significance).

Except under special circumstances, this medication should not be used when the following medical problems exists:

» Hypersensitivity to topical corticosteroid prescribed or any of its components or to any other corticosteroid

Risk-benefit should be considered when the following medical problems exist:

Infection at treatment site
(may be exacerbated if no appropriate antimicrobial agent is used concurrently)

Skin atrophy, pre-existing
(may be exacerbated due to atrophigenic properties of corticosteroids)

For use in the oral cavity

Herpes simplex at treatment site
(may be transmitted to other sites, including the eye)

With long-term use of more potent formulations or if substantial absorption occurs

Cataracts
(corticosteroids may promote progression of cataracts, especially with the use of high- to very high-potency products in periorbital area)

Diabetes mellitus
(loss of control of diabetes may occur due to possible elevations in blood glucose)

Glaucoma
(intraocular pressure may be increased, especially with the use of high- to very high-potency products in periorbital area)

Tuberculosis
(may be exacerbated or reactivated; appropriate antitubercular chemotherapy or prophylaxis should be administered concurrently)

Patient monitoring

The following may be especially important in patient monitoring (other tests may be warranted in some patients, depending on condition; » = major clinical significance):

Adrenal function assessment, may include blood or urine cortisol concentration or ACTH stimulation test
(periodic monitoring may be advisable during and following use if factors that increase percutaneous absorption are present and treatment is prolonged)

Side/Adverse Effects

Note: Generally, local or systemic adverse effects do not often occur with the use of low-potency topical corticosteroids. However, as with all topical corticosteroids, the incidence and severity of local or systemic side effects increase with factors that increase percutaneous absorption.

Percutaneous absorption of topical corticosteroids has resulted in systemic side effects such as hyperglycemia, glycosuria, and hypothalamic-pituitary-adrenal (HPA) axis suppression. HPA axis suppression has resulted from use of low doses of very high-potency products and from use of less potent topical steroid preparations when occlusive dressings or excessive quantities were used. In all cases of HPA axis suppression, the effect was reversible upon discontinuation of therapy.

The following side/adverse effects have been selected on the basis of their potential clinical significance (possible signs and symptoms in parentheses where appropriate)—not necessarily inclusive:

Those indicating the need for medical attention

Incidence less frequent or rare

Allergic contact dermatitis (burning and itching of skin; apparent chronic therapeutic failure)—also may be caused by vehicle ingredients; ***folliculitis, furunculosis, pustules, pyoderma, or vesiculation*** (painful, red or itchy, pus-containing blisters in hair follicles)—more frequent with occlusion or use of ointments in intertriginous areas; ***hyperesthesia*** (increased skin sensitivity); ***numbness in fingers; purpura*** (blood-containing blisters on skin); ***skin atrophy*** (thinning of skin with easy bruising, especially when used on facial or intertriginous areas); ***skin infection, secondary***—more frequent with occlusion; ***stripping of epidermal layer***—for tape dosage forms; ***telangiectasia*** (raised, dark red, wart-like spots on skin, especially when used on the face)

Incidence rare—with prolonged use or other factors that increase absorption

Acneiform eruptions (acne or oily skin, especially when used on the face); ***cataracts, posterior subcapsular*** (gradual blurring or loss of vision)—reported with use of systemic corticosteroids; caution is advised with use of high- and very high-potency topical corticosteroids in periorbital area; ***Cushing's syndrome*** (backache; filling or rounding out of the face; irritability; menstrual irregularities; mental depression; in men—unusual decrease in sexual desire or ability; unusual tiredness or weakness); ***dermatitis, perioral*** (irritation of skin around mouth); ***ecchymosis*** (unusual bruising); ***edema*** (increased blood pressure; rapid weight gain; swelling of feet or lower legs); ***gastric ulcer*** (loss of appetite; nausea; stomach bloating, burning, cramping, or pain; vomiting; weight loss); ***glaucoma, secondary*** (eye pain; gradual decrease in vision; nausea; vomiting)—with use of high- and very high-potency topical corticosteroids in periorbital area; ***hirsutism or hypertrichosis*** (unusual increase in hair growth, especially on the face); ***hypertension; hypokalemic syndrome*** (irregular heartbeat; loss of appetite; muscle cramps or pain; nausea; severe weakness of extremities and trunk; vomiting); ***hypopigmentation*** (lightened skin color); ***or other changes in skin pigmentation; infection, aggravation of***; ***miliaria rubra*** (burning and itching of skin with pinhead-sized red blisters); ***protein depletion*** (muscle weakness); ***skin laceration*** (tearing of skin); ***skin maceration*** (softening of skin); ***striae*** (reddish purple lines on arms, face, legs, trunk, or groin); ***subcutaneous tissue atrophy; unusual loss of hair***—especially on the scalp

Those indicating need for medical attention only if they continue or are bothersome

Incidence less frequent or rare

Burning, dryness, irritation, itching, or redness of skin, mild and transient; increased redness or scaling of skin lesions, mild and transient; skin rash, minor and transient

Those not indicating need for medical attention

Stinging, mild and temporary—when foam, gel, lotion, solution, or aerosol form of medication is applied

Overdose

For more information on the management of overdose or unintentional ingestion, **contact a Poison Control Center** (see *Poison Control Center Listing*).

Clinical effects of overdose

The following effects have been selected on the basis of their potential clinical significance (possible signs and symptoms in parentheses where appropriate)—not necessarily inclusive:

Chronic

Hypercorticism

Treatment of overdose

For chronic topical overdose—Since there is no specific antidote available, treatment is symptomatic, supportive, and consists of discontinuance of topical corticosteroid therapy. Gradual withdrawal of the preparation may be necessary.

For acute oral overdose—Since there is no specific antidote available and serious adverse effects are unlikely, treatment consists of dilution with fluids.

Patient Consultation

As an aid to patient consultation, refer to *Advice for the Patient, Corticosteroids (Dental)*. For alclometasone, clocortolone, desonide, dexamethasone, flumethasone, flurandrenolide (*Drenison-¼* only), hydrocortisone, and hydrocortisone acetate—*Corticosteroids—Low Potency (Topical)*. For amcinonide, beclomethasone, betamethasone, clobetasol, clobetasone, desoximetasone, diflorasone, diflucortolone, fluocinolone, fluocinonide, flurandrenolide (except *Drenison-¼*), fluticasone, halcinonide, halobetasol, hydrocortisone butyrate, hydrocortisone valerate, mometasone, and triamcinolone—*Corticosteroids—Medium to Very High Potency (Topical)*.

In providing consultation, consider emphasizing the following selected information (» = major clinical significance):

Before using this medication

» Conditions affecting use, especially:
- Hypersensitivity to topical corticosteroid prescribed or any of its components or to any other corticosteroid
- Pregnancy—Use restricted because of possible fetal abnormalities
- Breast-feeding—Should not be applied to the breasts prior to nursing
- Use in children—Adrenal suppression, Cushing's syndrome, intracranial hypertension, and growth retardation possible
- Use in the elderly—Caution recommended because purpura and skin lacerations may be more likely

Proper use of this medication

For all topical corticosteroids

Keeping away from eyes

» Not bandaging or otherwise wrapping the treated skin area unless directed to do so by physician

Proper use of occlusive dressing, if prescribed

Not using on face, groin, or axillae unless directed to do so by physician

For dental paste dosage forms

Applying with cotton applicator; pressing, not rubbing, paste on lesion

Applying at bedtime and after meals for maximum effect

For foam dosage form

Reading and following patient directions carefully

Not smoking while using; not using near an open flame

For aerosol dosage forms

Reading and following patient directions carefully

Avoiding breathing vapors of spray

Avoiding getting vapors of spray in eyes

Not smoking while using aerosols; not using aerosols near an open flame

For flurandrenolide tape

Reading and following patient directions carefully

» Importance of not using more medication than the amount prescribed or recommended on package

» Checking with physician before using medication for other dental or skin problems

» Proper dosing

Missed dose: Using as soon as possible; not using if almost time for next dose

» Proper storage

Precautions while using this medication

» Checking with physician or dentist if symptoms do not improve within 1 week or condition becomes worse

For topical dosage forms:

Not using tight-fitting diapers or plastic pants on a child if the diaper area is being treated with this medication

Side/adverse effects

Signs of potential side effects, especially allergic contact dermatitis; folliculitis, furunculosis, pustules, pyoderma, or vesiculation; hyperesthesia; numbness in fingers; purpura; skin atrophy; skin infection, secondary; stripping of epidermal layer (for tape dosage forms); and telangiectasia

(Signs of potential side effects occurring with prolonged use or other factors that increase absorption, especially acneiform eruptions; cataracts, posterior subcapsular; Cushing's syndrome; dermatitis, perioral; ecchymosis; edema; gastric ulcer; glaucoma, secondary; hirsutism or hypertrichosis; hypertension; hypokalemic syndrome; hypopigmentation or other changes in skin pigmentation; infection, aggravation of; miliaria rubra; protein depletion; skin laceration; skin maceration; striae; subcutaneous tissue atrophy; and unusual loss of hair)

Possible stinging when foam, gel, lotion, solution, or aerosol form of medication is applied

General Dosing Information

For topical dosage forms

To minimize the possibility of significant systemic absorption of corticosteroids during long term therapy, treatment may be interrupted periodically, small amounts of the preparation may be applied, or one area of the body may be treated at a time.

Occlusion, whether by oleaginous ointment, a thin film of polyethylene, dermatological patch, or tape, promotes increased hydration of the stratum corneum and increased absorption. Rarely, body temperature may be elevated if large areas are covered with an occlusive dressing; occlusive dressings should not be used if body temperature is elevated. Use of intermittent, rather than continuous, occlusion may decrease the risk of side effects. Generally, occlusive dressings should be changed every 24 hours or more frequently. Very high-potency topical corticosteroid formulations should not be used with occlusive dressings.

Rarely, gradual withdrawal of therapy or supplemental systemic corticosteroid therapy may be required to avoid symptoms of steroid withdrawal. Gradual withdrawal of therapy by decreasing the frequency of application or by using products of decreasing potency also may be necessary to avoid a rebound flare-up of certain conditions such as psoriasis. Tachyphylaxis also may result from continual usage.

Certain topical corticosteroids may be used as adjunctive therapy to antimicrobial agents for controlling inflammation, erythema, and pruritus associated with bacterial or fungal skin infections. If symptomatic relief is not noted within a few days to one week, the topical corticosteroid should be discontinued until the infection is controlled.

For dental dosage forms only

Applying the paste with a cotton applicator will help to eliminate any possible absorption from contact with the skin.

The paste should be pressed, not rubbed, on the lesion. Rubbing the paste on the lesion will result in a granular, gritty sensation and cause the medication to crumble. A smooth, slippery film forms after application.

If significant repair or regeneration of oral tissues has not occurred in 7 days, the etiology of the lesion should be reinvestigated.

For treatment of adverse effects

If hypothalamic-pituitary-adrenal (HPA) axis suppression occurs, the topical corticosteroid should be discontinued or substituted with a less potent preparation, or the frequency of application should be decreased. If adrenal suppression occurs upon discontinuation, it may be necessary to institute treatment with a systemic corticosteroid until adrenal function returns to normal.

If a local infection develops at the site of application, discontinue occlusive dressings (if used) and institute appropriate antimicrobial therapy. Until the infection is controlled, discontinuance of the topical corticosteroid may be necessary.

If irritation or sensitization occurs at the site of application, discontinue use of the topical corticosteroid and institute appropriate symptomatic treatment.

ALCLOMETASONE

Summary of Differences

Pharmacology/pharmacokinetics:
Substituted; non-fluorinated.
Potency ranking—Low.

Topical Dosage Forms

ALCLOMETASONE DIPROPIONATE CREAM USP

Usual adult and adolescent dose

Topical, to the skin, two or three times a day.

Note: Therapy should be discontinued and the diagnosis reassessed if no improvement is seen after two weeks.

Usual pediatric dose

Children up to 1 year of age: Use is not recommended.

Children 1 year of age or older: See *Usual adult and adolescent dose.*

Note: Alclometasone should not be applied to the diaper area if the child still requires diapers or plastic pants.

Strength(s) usually available

U.S.—
0.05% (Rx) [*Aclovate* (chlorocresol)].

Canada—
Not commercially available.

Packaging and storage

Store between 2 and 30 °C (36 and 86 °F), unless otherwise specified by manufacturer. Store in a collapsible tube or a tight container.

Auxiliary labeling

- For external use only.
- Do not use in or around the eye.

ALCLOMETASONE DIPROPIONATE OINTMENT USP

Usual adult and adolescent dose

See *Alclometasone Dipropionate Cream USP.*

Usual pediatric dose

Dosage has not been established.

Strength(s) usually available

U.S.—
0.05% (Rx) [*Aclovate*].

Canada—
Not commercially available.

Packaging and storage

Store between 2 and 30 °C (36 and 86 °F), unless otherwise specified by manufacturer. Store in a collapsible tube or a tight container.

Auxiliary labeling

- For external use only.
- Do not use in or around the eye.

AMCINONIDE

Summary of Differences

Pharmacology/pharmacokinetics:
Substituted; fluorinated.
Potency ranking—High.

Topical Dosage Forms

AMCINONIDE CREAM USP

Usual adult dose

Topical, to the skin, two or three times a day.

Usual pediatric dose

Topical, to the skin, once a day.

Strength(s) usually available

U.S.—
0.1% (Rx) [*Cyclocort* (benzyl alcohol 2%)].

Canada—
0.1% (Rx) [*Cyclocort* (benzyl alcohol 2%)].

Packaging and storage

Store between 15 and 30 °C (59 and 86 °F), unless otherwise specified by manufacturer. Store in a tight container. Protect from freezing.

Auxiliary labeling

- For external use only.
- Do not use in or around the eye.

AMCINONIDE LOTION

Usual adult dose

See *Amcinonide Cream USP.*

Usual pediatric dose

See *Amcinonide Cream USP.*

Strength(s) usually available

U.S.—
0.1% (Rx) [*Cyclocort* (benzyl alcohol 1%)].

Canada—
0.1% (Rx) [*Cyclocort* (benzyl alcohol 1%)].

Packaging and storage

Store between 15 and 30 °C (59 and 86 °F), in a well-closed container, unless otherwise specified by manufacturer. Protect from freezing.

Auxiliary labeling

- For external use only.
- Do not use in or around the eye.

AMCINONIDE OINTMENT USP

Usual adult dose

See *Amcinonide Cream USP.*

Usual pediatric dose

See *Amcinonide Cream USP.*

Strength(s) usually available

U.S.—
0.1% (Rx) [*Cyclocort* (benzyl alcohol 2%)].

Canada—
0.1% (Rx) [*Cyclocort* (benzyl alcohol 2%)].

Packaging and storage

Store between 15 and 30 °C (59 and 86 °F), unless otherwise specified by manufacturer. Store in a tight container. Protect from freezing.

Auxiliary labeling

- For external use only.
- Do not use in or around the eye.

BECLOMETHASONE

Summary of Differences

Pharmacology/pharmacokinetics:
Substituted; non-fluorinated.
Potency ranking—Medium.

Topical Dosage Forms

BECLOMETHASONE DIPROPIONATE CREAM

Note: Preferred dosage form for moist or weeping lesion surfaces.

Usual adult dose
Topical, to the skin, one to three times a day.

Usual pediatric dose
Children up to 1 year of age: Use is not recommended.
Children 1 year of age or older: Dosage has not been established.

Strength(s) usually available
U.S.—
Not commercially available.
Canada—
0.025% (Rx) [*Propaderm*].

Packaging and storage
Store below 40 °C (104 °F), preferably between 15 and 30 °C (59 and 86 °F), unless otherwise specified by manufacturer.

Auxiliary labeling
- For external use only.
- Do not use in or around the eye.

BECLOMETHASONE DIPROPIONATE LOTION

Note: Preferred dosage form for large or hairy areas, or areas where the skin folds.

Usual adult dose
See *Beclomethasone Dipropionate Cream.*

Usual pediatric dose
See *Beclomethasone Dipropionate Cream.*

Strength(s) usually available
U.S.—
Not commercially available.
Canada—
0.025% (Rx) [*Propaderm*].

Packaging and storage
Store below 40 °C (104 °F), preferably between 15 and 30 °C (59 and 86 °F), unless otherwise specified by manufacturer.

Auxiliary labeling
- For external use only.
- Do not use in or around the eye.

BETAMETHASONE

Summary of Differences

Pharmacology/pharmacokinetics:
Substituted (benzoate, dipropionate, valerate); fluorinated (base, benzoate, dipropionate, valerate).
Potency ranking—
Betamethasone benzoate, Medium.
Betamethasone dipropionate (except for *Diprolene* and *Diprolene AF* products), High.
Diprolene and *Diprolene AF* products, Very high.
Betamethasone valerate, Medium.

Topical Dosage Forms

BETAMETHASONE BENZOATE CREAM

Usual adult dose
Topical, to the skin, two to four times a day.

Usual pediatric dose
Topical, to the skin, once a day.

Strength(s) usually available
U.S.—
0.025% (Rx) [*Uticort*].

Packaging and storage
Store between 15 and 30 °C (59 and 86 °F), in a well-closed container, unless otherwise specified by manufacturer. Protect from freezing.

Auxiliary labeling
- For external use only.
- Do not use in or around the eye.

BETAMETHASONE BENZOATE GEL USP

Usual adult dose
See *Betamethasone Benzoate Cream.*

Usual pediatric dose
See *Betamethasone Benzoate Cream.*

Strength(s) usually available
U.S.—
0.025% (Rx) [*Uticort* (alcohol 13.8%)].
Canada—
0.025% (base) (Rx) [*Beben* (alcohol)].

Packaging and storage
Store below 40 °C (104 °F), preferably between 15 and 30 °C (59 and 86 °F), unless otherwise specified by manufacturer. Store in a tight container. Protect from freezing.

Auxiliary labeling
- For external use only.
- Do not use in or around the eye.

BETAMETHASONE BENZOATE LOTION

Usual adult dose
Betamethasone Benzoate Cream.

Usual pediatric dose
Betamethasone Benzoate Cream.

Strength(s) usually available
U.S.—
0.025% (Rx) [*Uticort* (butylparaben; propylparaben; methylparaben)].

Packaging and storage
Store below 40 °C (104 °F), preferably between 15 and 30 °C (59 and 86 °F), in a well-closed container, unless otherwise specified by manufacturer. Protect from freezing.

Auxiliary labeling
- For external use only.
- Do not use in or around the eye.
- Shake well.

BETAMETHASONE DIPROPIONATE CREAM (AUGMENTED)

Note: The dosing and strengths of betamethasone dipropionate cream (augmented) are expressed in terms of betamethasone base.

Usual adult dose
Topical, to the skin, one or two times a day. Augmented betamethasone dipropionate cream may be used for only a short duration of therapy and on small surface areas. Occlusive dressings should not be used.

Usual adult prescribing limits
45 grams per week.

Usual pediatric dose
Children up to 12 years of age: Use is not recommended.

Strength(s) usually available
U.S.—
0.05% (base) (Rx) [*Diprolene AF*].
Canada—
0.05% (base) (Rx) [*Diprolene*].

Packaging and storage
Store between 2 and 30 °C (36 and 86 °F), unless otherwise specified by manufacturer. Store in a tight container. Protect from freezing.

Auxiliary labeling
- For external use only.
- Do not use in or around the eye.

BETAMETHASONE DIPROPIONATE CREAM USP

Note: The dosing and strengths of betamethasone dipropionate cream are expressed in terms of betamethasone base.

Usual adult dose
Topical, to the skin, one or two times a day.

Usual pediatric dose
Topical, to the skin, once a day.

Strength(s) usually available
U.S.—
0.05% (base) (Rx) [*Alphatrex; Diprosone; Maxivate; Teladar;* GENERIC].

Canada—
0.05% (base) (Rx) [*Diprosone; Topilene; Topisone*].

Packaging and storage
Store below 40 °C (104 °F), preferably between 15 and 30 °C (59 and 86 °F), unless otherwise specified by manufacturer. Store in a collapsible tube or a tight container. Protect from freezing.

Auxiliary labeling
- For external use only.
- Do not use in or around the eye.

BETAMETHASONE DIPROPIONATE GEL
Note: The dosing and strengths of betamethasone dipropionate gel are expressed in terms of betamethasone base.

Usual adult dose
Topical, to the skin, one or two times a day. Betamethasone dipropionate gel may be used for only a short duration of therapy and on small surface areas. Occlusive dressings should not be used.

Usual pediatric dose
Children up to 12 years of age—Use is not recommended.

Strength(s) usually available
U.S.—
0.05% (base) (Rx) [*Diprolene*].
Canada—
Not commercially available.

Packaging and storage
Store below 40 °C (104 °F), preferably between 15 and 30 °C (59 and 86 °F), unless otherwise specified by manufacturer. Store in a tight container. Protect from freezing.

Auxiliary labeling
- For external use only.
- Do not use in or around the eye.

BETAMETHASONE DIPROPIONATE LOTION (AUGMENTED)
Note: The dosing and strengths of betamethasone dipropionate lotion (augmented) are expressed in terms of betamethasone base.

Usual adult dose
Topical, to the skin, two times a day. Augmented betamethasone dipropionate lotion may be used for only a short duration of therapy and on small surface areas. Occlusive dressings should not be used.

Usual pediatric dose
Children up to 12 years of age—Dosage has not been established.

Strength(s) usually available
U.S.—
0.05% (base) (Rx) [*Diprolene*].
Canada—
Not commercially available.

Packaging and storage
Store below 40 °C (104 °F), preferably between 15 and 30 °C (59 and 86 °F), unless otherwise specified by manufacturer. Store in a tight container. Protect from light. Protect from freezing.

Auxiliary labeling
- For external use only.
- Do not use in or around the eye.
- Shake well.

BETAMETHASONE DIPROPIONATE LOTION USP
Note: The dosing and strengths of betamethasone dipropionate lotion are expressed in terms of betamethasone base.

Usual adult dose
Topical, to the skin, two times a day.

Usual pediatric dose
Topical, to the skin, once a day.

Strength(s) usually available
U.S.—
0.05% (base) (Rx) [*Alphatrex; Diprosone; Maxivate;* GENERIC].
Canada—
0.05% (base) (Rx) [*Diprosone; Occlucort; Topisone*].

Packaging and storage
Store below 40 °C (104 °F), preferably between 15 and 30 °C (59 and 86 °F), unless otherwise specified by manufacturer. Store in a tight container. Protect from light. Protect from freezing.

Auxiliary labeling
- For external use only.
- Do not use in or around the eye.
- Shake well.

BETAMETHASONE DIPROPIONATE OINTMENT (AUGMENTED)
Note: The dosing and strengths of betamethasone dipropionate ointment (augmented) are expressed in terms of betamethasone base.

Usual adult dose
Topical, to the skin, one or two times a day. Augmented betamethasone dipropionate ointment may be used for only a short duration of therapy and on small surface areas. Occlusive dressings should not be used.

Usual pediatric dose
Children up to 12 years of age—Use is not recommended.

Strength(s) usually available
U.S.—
0.05% (base) (Rx) [*Diprolene*].
Canada—
0.05% (base) (Rx) [*Diprolene*].

Packaging and storage
Store below 40 °C (104 °F), preferably between 15 and 30 °C (59 and 86 °F), unless otherwise specified by manufacturer. Store in a well-closed container. Protect from freezing.

Auxiliary labeling
- For external use only.
- Do not use in or around the eye.

BETAMETHASONE DIPROPIONATE OINTMENT USP
Note: The dosing and strengths of betamethasone dipropionate ointment are expressed in terms of betamethasone base.

Usual adult dose
Topical, to the skin, one or two times a day.

Usual pediatric dose
Topical, to the skin, once a day.

Strength(s) usually available
U.S.—
0.05% (base) (Rx) [*Alphatrex; Diprosone; Maxivate;* GENERIC].
Canada—
0.05% (base) (Rx) [*Diprosone; Topilene; Topisone*].

Packaging and storage
Store below 40 °C (104 °F), preferably between 15 and 30 °C (59 and 86 °F), unless otherwise specified by manufacturer. Store in a collapsible tube or a well-closed container. Protect from freezing.

Auxiliary labeling
- For external use only.
- Do not use in or around the eye.

BETAMETHASONE DIPROPIONATE TOPICAL AEROSOL
Note: The dosing and strengths of betamethasone dipropionate topical aerosol are expressed in terms of betamethasone base.

Usual adult dose
Topical, to the skin, a three-second spray three times a day.

Usual pediatric dose
Topical, to the skin, once a day.

Strength(s) usually available
U.S.—
0.1% (base) (Rx) [*Diprosone* (isobutane; isopropyl alcohol 10%; propane)].
Canada—
Not commercially available.

Note: A three-second spray delivers the equivalent of 60 mcg of betamethasone.

Packaging and storage
Store below 40 °C (104 °F), preferably between 2 and 30 °C (36 and 86 °F), unless otherwise specified by manufacturer. Protect from freezing.

Auxiliary labeling
- For external use only.
- Do not use in or around the eye.

Note
Explain administration technique.

When dispensing, include patient instructions.

BETAMETHASONE VALERATE CREAM USP
Note: The dosing and strengths of betamethasone valerate cream are expressed in terms of betamethasone base.

Usual adult dose
Topical, to the skin, one to three times a day.

Usual pediatric dose
Corticosteroid—
Topical, to the skin, as a 0.01% (base) cream one or two times a day; or as a 0.1% cream once a day.
[Phimosis][1]—
Topical, to the skin, as a 0.05% cream two to four times a day; or as a 0.1% cream two times a day.

Strength(s) usually available
U.S.—
0.01% (base) (Rx) [*Valisone Reduced Strength*].
0.1% (base) (Rx) [*Betatrex; Beta-Val; Dermabet; Valisone; Valnac;* GENERIC].
Canada—
0.05% (base) (Rx) [*Betaderm; Betnovate-½; Celestoderm-V/2; Ectosone Mild; Metaderm Mild; Novobetamet; Prevex B*].
0.1% (base) (Rx) [*Betaderm; Betnovate; Celestoderm-V; Ectosone Regular; Metaderm Regular; Novobetamet*].

Packaging and storage
Store below 40 °C (104 °F), preferably between 15 and 30 °C (59 and 86 °F), unless otherwise specified by manufacturer. Store in a tight container. Protect from freezing.

Auxiliary labeling
- For external use only.
- Do not use in or around the eye.

BETAMETHASONE VALERATE FOAM

Usual adult dose
Topical, to the scalp, two times a day.

Usual pediatric dose
Safety and efficacy have not been established.

Strength(s) usually available
U.S.—
0.12% (Rx) [*Luxíq* (ethanol 60.4%)].
Canada—
Not commercially available.

Packaging and storage
Store between 20 and 25 °C (68 and 77 °F), unless otherwise specified by manufacturer.

Auxiliary labeling
- For external use only.
- Do not use in or around the eye.
- Flammable—Keep away from heat or flame.

BETAMETHASONE VALERATE LOTION USP

Note: The dosing and strengths of betamethasone valerate lotion are expressed in terms of betamethasone base.

Usual adult dose
Topical, to the skin, one or two times a day.

Usual pediatric dose
Topical, to the skin, once a day.

Strength(s) usually available
U.S.—
0.1% (base) (Rx) [*Betatrex; Beta-Val; Valisone;* GENERIC].
Canada—
0.05% (base) (Rx) [*Betnovate-½; Ectosone Mild*].
0.1% (base) (Rx) [*Betacort Scalp Lotion; Betaderm Scalp Lotion; Betnovate; Ectosone Regular; Ectosone Scalp Lotion; Valisone Scalp Lotion*].

Packaging and storage
Store between 15 and 30 °C (59 and 86 °F). Store in a tight, light-resistant container. Protect from freezing.

Auxiliary labeling
- For external use only.
- Do not use in or around the eye.
- Shake well.

BETAMETHASONE VALERATE OINTMENT USP

Note: The dosing and strengths of betamethasone valerate ointment are expressed in terms of betamethasone base.

Usual adult dose
See *Betamethasone Valerate Cream USP*.

Usual pediatric dose
See *Betamethasone Valerate Lotion USP*.

Strength(s) usually available
U.S.—
0.1% (base) (Rx) [*Betatrex; Beta-Val; Valisone; Valnac;* GENERIC].
Canada—
0.05% (base) (Rx) [*Betaderm; Betnovate-½; Celestoderm-V/2; Metaderm Mild*].
0.1% (base) (Rx) [*Betaderm; Betnovate; Celestoderm-V; Metaderm Regular*].

Packaging and storage
Store below 40 °C (104 °F), preferably between 15 and 30 °C (59 and 86 °F). Store in a tight container. Protect from freezing.

Auxiliary labeling
- For external use only.
- Do not use in or around the eye.

[1]Not included in Canadian product labeling.

CLOBETASOL

Summary of Differences

Pharmacology/pharmacokinetics:
Substituted; fluorinated.
Potency rating: Very high.

Topical Dosage Forms

CLOBETASOL PROPIONATE CREAM USP

Usual adult dose
Topical, to the skin, two or three times a day. Clobetasol propionate cream may be used for only a short duration of therapy and on small surface areas. Occlusive dressings should not be used.

Usual pediatric dose
Children up to 12 years of age—Use is not recommended.

Strength(s) usually available
U.S.—
0.05% (Rx) [*Temovate; Cormax; Temovate E*].
Canada—
0.05% (Rx) [*Dermovate*].

Packaging and storage
Store between 15 and 30 °C (59 and 86 °F). Store in a collapsible tube or tight container. Do not refrigerate. Protect from freezing.

Auxiliary labeling
- For external use only.
- Do not use in or around the eye.

CLOBETASOL PROPIONATE FOAM

Usual adult dose
Topical, apply on the affected areas of the scalp, twice daily. Clobetasol propionate foam may be used for only a short duration of therapy and on small surface areas. Occlusive dressings should not be used.

Usual adult prescribing limits
Amounts greater than 50 grams per week should not be exceeded, and treatment should not exceed two weeks.

Usual pediatric dose
Children up to 12 years of age—Safety and efficacy have not been established

Strength(s) usually available
U.S.—
0.05% (Rx) [*Olux Foam* (cetyl alcohol; ethanol; polysorbate 80; potassium citrate; propylene glycol; purified water; stearyl alcohol)].

Packaging and storage
Store between 20 to 25°C (68 and 77 °F). Keep out of reach of children. Contents under pressure. Do not puncture or incinerate container. Do not expose to temperatures above 49°C (120°F). Protect from direct sunlight.

Auxiliary labeling
- For external use only.
- Do not use in or around the eye.

Note
Explain administration technique.

When dispensing, include patient instructions.

CLOBETASOL PROPIONATE TOPICAL SOLUTION USP

Usual adult dose
Topical, to the scalp, two times a day. Clobetasol propionate topical solution may be used for only a short duration of therapy and on small surface areas. Occlusive dressings should not be used.

Usual pediatric dose
Children up to 12 years of age—Use is not recommended.

Strength(s) usually available
U.S.—
0.05% (Rx) [*Temovate Scalp Application* (isopropyl alcohol)].
Canada—
0.05% (Rx) [*Dermovate Scalp Lotion* (alcohol)].

Packaging and storage
Store below 40 °C (104 °F), preferably between 15 and 30 °C (59 and 86 °F), unless otherwise specified by manufacturer. Store in a tight container. Do not refrigerate. Protect from freezing.

Auxiliary labeling
- For external use only.
- Do not use in or around the eye.

CLOBETASOL PROPIONATE OINTMENT USP

Usual adult dose
Topical, to the skin, two or three times a day. Clobetasol propionate ointment may be used for only a short duration of therapy and on small surface areas. Occlusive dressings should not be used.

Usual pediatric dose
Children up to 12 years of age—Use is not recommended.

Strength(s) usually available
U.S.—
0.05% (Rx) [*Temovate*].
Canada—
0.05% (Rx) [*Dermovate*].

Packaging and storage
Store below 40 °C (104 °F), preferably between 15 and 30 °C (59 and 86 °F), unless otherwise specified by manufacturer. Store in a collapsible tube or tight container. Protect from freezing.

Auxiliary labeling
- For external use only.
- Do not use in or around the eye.

CLOBETASONE

Summary of Differences

Pharmacology/pharmacokinetics:
Substituted; fluorinated.
Potency rating—Medium.

Topical Dosage Forms

CLOBETASONE BUTYRATE CREAM

Usual adult dose
Topical, to the skin, two or three times a day.

Usual adult prescribing limits
100 grams per week.

Usual pediatric dose
Dosage has not been established.

Strength(s) usually available
U.S.—
Not commercially available.
Canada—
0.05% (Rx) [*Eumovate*].

Packaging and storage
Store below 40 °C (104 °F), preferably between 15 and 30 °C (59 and 86 °F), unless otherwise specified by manufacturer.

Auxiliary labeling
- For external use only.
- Do not use in or around the eye.

CLOBETASONE BUTYRATE OINTMENT

Usual adult dose
See *Clobetasone Butyrate Cream.*

Usual adult prescribing limits
See *Clobetasone Butyrate Cream.*

Usual pediatric dose
Dosage has not been established.

Strength(s) usually available
U.S.—
Not commercially available.
Canada—
0.05% (Rx) [*Eumovate*].

Packaging and storage
Store below 40 °C (104 °F), preferably between 15 and 30 °C (59 and 86 °F), unless otherwise specified by manufacturer.

Auxiliary labeling
- For external use only.
- Do not use in or around the eye.

CLOCORTOLONE

Summary of Differences

Pharmacology/pharmacokinetics:
Substituted; fluorinated.
Potency rating—Low.

Topical Dosage Forms

CLOCORTOLONE PIVALATE CREAM USP

Usual adult dose
Topical, to the skin, three times a day.

Usual pediatric dose
Dosage has not been established.

Strength(s) usually available
U.S.—
0.1% (Rx) [*Cloderm* (methylparaben; propylparaben)].
Canada—
Not commercially available.

Packaging and storage
Store below 40 °C (104 °F), preferably between 15 and 30 °C (59 and 86 °F), unless otherwise specified by manufacturer. Store in a tight, light-resistant container. Protect from freezing.

Auxiliary labeling
- For external use only.
- Do not use in or around the eye.

DESONIDE

Summary of Differences

Pharmacology/pharmacokinetics:
Substituted; non-fluorinated.
Potency rating—Low.

Topical Dosage Forms

DESONIDE CREAM

Usual adult dose
Topical, to the skin, two to four times a day.

Usual pediatric dose
Topical, to the skin, once a day.

Strength(s) usually available
U.S.—
0.05% (Rx) [*DesOwen; Tridesilon;* GENERIC].
Canada—
0.05% (Rx) [*Tridesilon*].

Packaging and storage
Store between 15 and 30 °C (59 and 86 °F), in a tight container, unless otherwise specified by manufacturer. Protect from freezing.

Auxiliary labeling
- For external use only.
- Do not use in or around the eye.

DESONIDE LOTION

Usual adult dose
See *Desonide Cream.*

Strength(s) usually available
U.S.—
0.05% (Rx) [*DesOwen*].
Canada—
Not commercially available.

Packaging and storage
Store between 15 and 30 °C (59 and 86 °F), in a tight container, unless otherwise specified by manufacturer. Protect from freezing.

Auxiliary labeling
- For external use only.
- Shake well before using.
- Do not use in or around the eye.

DESONIDE OINTMENT

Usual adult dose
See *Desonide Cream.*

Usual pediatric dose
See *Desonide Cream.*

Strength(s) usually available
U.S.—
0.05% (Rx) [*DesOwen; Tridesilon*].
Canada—
0.05% (Rx) [*Tridesilon*].

Packaging and storage
Store between 15 and 30 °C (59 and 86 °F), in a tight container, unless otherwise specified by manufacturer. Protect from freezing.

Auxiliary labeling
- For external use only.
- Do not use in or around the eye.

DESOXIMETASONE

Summary of Differences

Pharmacology/pharmacokinetics:
Substituted (17-H); fluorinated.
Potency rating—
High (except cream 0.05%).
Cream 0.05%, Medium.

Topical Dosage Forms

DESOXIMETASONE CREAM USP

Usual adult dose
Topical, to the skin, two times a day.

Usual pediatric dose
Topical, to the skin, once a day.

Strength(s) usually available
U.S.—
0.05% (Rx) [*Topicort LP;* GENERIC].
0.25% (Rx) [*Topicort;* GENERIC].
Canada—
0.05% (Rx) [*Topicort Mild*].
0.25% (Rx) [*Topicort*].

Packaging and storage
Store between 15 and 30 °C (59 and 86 °F), in a well-closed container, unless otherwise specified by manufacturer. Protect from freezing.

Auxiliary labeling
- For external use only.
- Do not use in or around the eye.

DESOXIMETASONE GEL USP

Usual adult dose
See *Desoximetasone Cream USP.*

Usual pediatric dose
See *Desoximetasone Cream USP.*

Strength(s) usually available
U.S.—
0.05% (Rx) [*Topicort* (alcohol 20%)].
Canada—
0.05% (Rx) [*Topicort* (alcohol)].

Packaging and storage
Store between 15 and 30 °C (59 and 86 °F), in well-closed container, unless otherwise specified by manufacturer. Protect from freezing.

Auxiliary labeling
- For external use only.
- Do not use in or around the eye.

DESOXIMETASONE OINTMENT USP

Usual adult dose
See *Desoximetasone Cream USP.*

Usual pediatric dose
See *Desoximetasone Cream USP.*

Strength(s) usually available
U.S.—
0.25% (Rx) [*Topicort*].
Canada—
Not commercially available.

Packaging and storage
Store between 15 and 30 °C (59 and 86 °F), in well-closed container, unless otherwise specified by manufacturer. Protect from freezing.

Auxiliary labeling
- For external use only.
- Do not use in or around the eye.

DEXAMETHASONE

Summary of Differences

Pharmacology/pharmacokinetics:
Unsubstituted; fluorinated.
Potency rating—Low.

Topical Dosage Forms

DEXAMETHASONE GEL USP

Usual adult dose
Topical, to the skin, three or four times a day.

Usual pediatric dose
Topical, to the skin, one or two times a day.

Strength(s) usually available
U.S.—
0.1% (Rx) [*Decaderm*].
Canada—
Not commercially available.

Packaging and storage
Store below 30 °C (86 °F), in a tight container. Protect from freezing.

Auxiliary labeling
- For external use only.
- Do not use in or around the eye.

DEXAMETHASONE TOPICAL AEROSOL (SOLUTION) USP

Usual adult dose
Topical, to the skin, two to four times a day.

Usual pediatric dose
Topical, to the skin, one or two times a day.

Strength(s) usually available
U.S.—
0.01% (Rx) [*Aeroseb-Dex* (alcohol 59%)].
0.04% (Rx) [*Decaspray*].

Note: Each one-second spray of 0.01% and 0.04% aerosols delivers 20 mcg and 75 mcg of dexamethasone, respectively.

Canada—
Not commercially available.

Packaging and storage
Store below 40 °C (104 °F). Protect from freezing.

Auxiliary labeling
- For external use only.
- Do not use in or around the eye.
- Shake gently.

Note
Explain administration technique.

When dispensing, include patient instructions.

This medication comes with a special applicator tube for use on the scalp.

DEXAMETHASONE SODIUM PHOSPHATE CREAM USP

Usual adult dose
See *Dexamethasone Gel USP.*

Usual pediatric dose
Topical, to the skin, once a day.

Strength(s) usually available
U.S.—
0.1% (phosphate) (Rx) [*Decadron* (methylparaben)].
Canada—
Not commercially available.

Packaging and storage
Store below 40 °C (104 °F), preferably between 15 and 30 °C (59 and 86 °F), unless otherwise specified by manufacturer. Store in a tight container. Protect from freezing.

Auxiliary labeling
- For external use only.
- Do not use in or around the eye.

DIFLORASONE

Summary of Differences
Pharmacology/pharmacokinetics:
Substituted; fluorinated.
Potency rating—
High (except *Psorcon* ointment).
Psorcon ointment, Very high.

Topical Dosage Forms
DIFLORASONE DIACETATE CREAM USP
Usual adult dose
Topical, to the skin, one to four times a day.

Note: Some patients may be maintained with once daily applications after the initial acute symptoms subside. Once daily dosage also may be used to taper therapy before discontinuance.

Usual pediatric dose
Topical, to the skin, once a day.

Strength(s) usually available
U.S.—
0.05% (Rx) [*Florone; Florone E; Maxiflor; Psorcon*].
Canada—
0.05% (Rx) [*Florone*].

Packaging and storage
Store between 15 and 30 °C (59 and 86 °F), in a well-closed container, unless otherwise specified by manufacturer. Protect from freezing.

Auxiliary labeling
- For external use only.
- Do not use in or around the eye.

DIFLORASONE DIACETATE OINTMENT USP
Usual adult dose
See *Diflorasone Diacetate Cream USP*.

Note: *Psorcon* may be used for only a short duration of therapy and on small surface areas. Occlusive dressings should not be used with *Psorcon*.

Usual pediatric dose
See *Diflorasone Diacetate Cream USP*.

Note: *Psorcon* should be used cautiously in patients up to 12 years of age.

Strength(s) usually available
U.S.—
0.05% (Rx) [*Florone; Maxiflor; Psorcon*].
Canada—
0.05% (Rx) [*Florone*].

Packaging and storage
Store between 15 and 30 °C (59 and 86 °F), in a well-closed container, unless otherwise specified by manufacturer. Protect from freezing.

Auxiliary labeling
- For external use only.
- Do not use in or around the eye.

DIFLUCORTOLONE

Summary of Differences
Pharmacology/pharmacokinetics:
Unsubstituted; fluorinated.
Potency rating—Medium.

Topical Dosage Forms
DIFLUCORTOLONE VALERATE CREAM
Usual adult dose
Topical, to the skin, one to three times a day.

Note: Some patients may be maintained with once daily applications after the initial acute symptoms subside. Once daily dosage may also be used to taper therapy before discontinuance.

Usual adult prescribing limits
100 grams per week.

Usual pediatric dose
Dosage has not been established.

Strength(s) usually available
U.S.—
Not commercially available.
Canada—
0.1% (Rx) [*Nerisone; Nerisone Oily*].

Packaging and storage
Store below 40 °C (104 °F), preferably between 15 and 30 °C (59 and 86 °F), unless otherwise specified by manufacturer.

Auxiliary labeling
- For external use only.
- Do not use in or around the eye.

DIFLUCORTOLONE VALERATE OINTMENT
Usual adult dose
See *Diflucortolone Valerate Cream.*

Usual adult prescribing limits
See *Diflucortolone Valerate Cream.*

Usual pediatric dose
Dosage has not been established.

Strength(s) usually available
U.S.—
Not commercially available.
Canada—
0.1% (Rx) [*Nerisone*].

Packaging and storage
Store below 40 °C (104 °F), preferably between 15 and 30 °C (59 and 86 °F), unless otherwise specified by manufacturer.

Auxiliary labeling
- For external use only.
- Do not use in or around the eye.

FLUMETHASONE

Summary of Differences
Pharmacology/pharmacokinetics:
Unsubstituted; fluorinated.
Potency rating—Low.

Topical Dosage Forms
FLUMETHASONE PIVALATE CREAM USP
Usual adult dose
Topical, to the skin, one to three times a day.

Usual pediatric dose
Topical, to the skin, once a day.

Strength(s) usually available
U.S.—
Not commercially available.
Canada—
0.03% (Rx) [*Locacorten* (methylparaben; propylparaben)].

Packaging and storage
Store below 40 °C (104 °F), preferably between 15 and 30 °C (59 and 86 °F), in a well-closed container, unless otherwise specified by manufacturer. Protect from freezing.

Auxiliary labeling
- For external use only.
- Do not use in or around the eye.

FLUMETHASONE PIVALATE OINTMENT
Usual adult dose
See *Flumethasone Pivalate Cream USP*.

Usual pediatric dose
See *Flumethasone Pivalate Cream USP*.

Strength(s) usually available
U.S.—
Not commercially available.
Canada—
0.03% (Rx) [*Locacorten* (methylparaben; propylparaben)].

Packaging and storage
Store below 40 °C (104 °F), preferably between 15 and 30 °C (59 and 86 °F), in a well-closed container, unless otherwise specified by manufacturer. Protect from freezing.

Auxiliary labeling
- For external use only.
- Do not use in or around the eye.

FLUOCINOLONE

Summary of Differences

Pharmacology/pharmacokinetics:
Substituted; fluorinated.
Potency rating—
Medium (except cream 0.2%).
Cream 0.2%, High.

Topical Dosage Forms

FLUOCINOLONE ACETONIDE CREAM USP

Usual adult dose
Topical, to the skin, two to four times a day.

Usual pediatric dose
Topical, to the skin, as a 0.01% cream one or two times a day; or as a 0.025 or 0.2% cream once a day.

Note: The 0.2% strength is not recommended for use in children up to 2 years of age, should not be used for long periods, and should not be used in quantities greater than 2 grams per day.

Strength(s) usually available
U.S.—
0.01% (Rx) [*Bio-Syn; Fluocet; Flurosyn; Synalar;* GENERIC].
0.025% (Rx) [*Bio-Syn; Fluocet; Flurosyn; Synalar; Synemol;* GENERIC].
0.2% (Rx) [*Synalar-HP*].
Canada—
0.01% (Rx) [*Fluoderm; Fluolar; Fluonide; Synalar; Synamol*].
0.025% (Rx) [*Fluoderm; Fluolar; Fluonide; Synalar; Synamol*].

Packaging and storage
Store below 40 °C (104 °F), preferably between 15 and 30 °C (59 and 86 °F), unless otherwise specified by manufacturer. Store in a tight container. Protect from freezing.

Auxiliary labeling
- For external use only.
- Do not use in or around the eye.

FLUOCINOLONE ACETONIDE OINTMENT USP

Usual adult dose
See *Fluocinolone Acetonide Cream USP*.

Usual pediatric dose
Topical, to the skin once a day.

Strength(s) usually available
U.S.—
0.025% (Rx) [*Flurosyn; Synalar*].
Canada—
0.01% (Rx) [*Fluoderm*].
0.025% (Rx) [*Fluoderm; Synalar*].

Packaging and storage
Store below 40 °C (104 °F), preferably between 15 and 30 °C (59 and 86 °F), unless otherwise specified by manufacturer. Store in a tight container. Protect from freezing.

Auxiliary labeling
- For external use only.
- Do not use in or around the eye.

FLUOCINOLONE ACETONIDE TOPICAL SOLUTION USP

Usual adult dose
See *Fluocinolone Acetonide Cream USP*.

Usual pediatric dose
Topical, to the skin one or two times a day.

Strength(s) usually available
U.S.—
0.01% (Rx) [*Fluonid; Synalar;* GENERIC].
Canada—
0.01% (Rx) [*Synalar*].

Packaging and storage
Store below 40 °C (104 °F), preferably between 15 and 30 °C (59 and 86 °F), unless otherwise specified by manufacturer. Store in a tight container. Protect from freezing.

Auxiliary labeling
- For external use only.
- Do not use in or around the eye.

FLUOCINONIDE

Summary of Differences

Pharmacology/pharmacokinetics:
Substituted; fluorinated.
Potency rating—High.

Topical Dosage Forms

FLUOCINONIDE CREAM USP

Usual adult dose
Topical 0.01% and 0.05%, to the skin, two to four times a day.
Topical 0.1%, to the skin once or twice daily as directed by your physician. Twice daily application has been shown to be more effective in achieving treatment success after 2 weeks of treatment.

Usual adult prescribing limits
Topical 0.1%: Treatment should be limited to 2 consecutive weeks and no more than 60 grams per week.

Usual pediatric dose
Topical 0.01% and 0.05%, to the skin, once a day.
Topical 0.1%: Use in patients less than 18 years of age is not recommended. Safety and efficacy have not been established.

Strength(s) usually available
U.S.—
0.05% (Rx) [*Fluocin; Licon; Lidex; Lidex-E;* GENERIC].
0.1% (Rx) [*Vanos* (propylene glycol; dimethyl isosorbide; glyceryl stearate; PEG-100 stearate; glyceryl monostearate; purified water; carbopol 980; diisopropanolamine; citric acid)].
Canada—
0.01% (Rx) [*Lidex*].
0.05% (Rx) [*Lidemol; Lidex; Lyderm*].

Packaging and storage
Store below 40 °C (104 °F), preferably between 15 and 30 °C (59 and 86 °F), unless otherwise specified by manufacturer. Store in a tight container. Protect from freezing.

Auxiliary labeling
- For external use only.
- Do not use in or around the eye.

FLUOCINONIDE GEL USP

Usual adult dose
See *Fluocinonide Cream USP*.

Usual pediatric dose
See *Fluocinonide Cream USP*.

Strength(s) usually available
U.S.—
0.05% (Rx) [*Lidex;* GENERIC].
Canada—
0.05% (Rx) [*Topsyn*].

Packaging and storage
Store below 40 °C (104 °F), preferably between 15 and 30 °C (59 and 86 °F), unless otherwise specified by manufacturer. Store in a tight container. Protect from freezing.

Auxiliary labeling
- For external use only.
- Do not use in or around the eye.

FLUOCINONIDE OINTMENT USP

Usual adult dose
See *Fluocinonide Cream USP*.

Usual pediatric dose
See *Fluocinonide Cream USP*.

Strength(s) usually available
U.S.—
0.05% (Rx) [*Lidex;* GENERIC].
Canada—
0.01% (Rx) [*Lidex*].
0.05% (Rx) [*Lidex*].

Packaging and storage
Store below 40 °C (104 °F), preferably between 15 and 30 °C (59 and 86 °F), unless otherwise specified by manufacturer. Store in a tight container. Protect from freezing.

Auxiliary labeling
- For external use only.
- Do not use in or around the eye.

FLUOCINONIDE TOPICAL SOLUTION USP

Usual adult dose
See *Fluocinonide Cream USP*.

Usual pediatric dose
See *Fluocinonide Cream USP*.

Strength(s) usually available
U.S.—
0.05% (Rx) [*Lidex* (alcohol 35%); GENERIC].
Canada—
0.05% (Rx) [*Lidex* (alcohol 35%)].

Packaging and storage
Store below 40 °C (104 °F), preferably between 15 and 30 °C (59 and 86 °F), unless otherwise specified by manufacturer. Store in a tight container. Protect from freezing.

Auxiliary labeling
- For external use only.
- Do not use in or around the eye.

FLURANDRENOLIDE

Summary of Differences

Pharmacology/pharmacokinetics:
Substituted; fluorinated.
Potency ranking—
Medium (except cream and ointment 0.0125%).
Cream and ointment 0.0125%, Low.

Topical Dosage Forms

FLURANDRENOLIDE CREAM USP

Usual adult dose
Topical, to the skin, two or three times a day.

Usual pediatric dose
Topical, to the skin, as a 0.025% cream one or two times a day; or as a 0.05% cream once a day.

Strength(s) usually available
U.S.—
0.025% (Rx) [*Cordran SP*].
0.05% (Rx) [*Cordran SP*].
Canada—
0.0125% (Rx) [*Drenison-¼*].
0.05% (Rx) [*Drenison*].

Packaging and storage
Store below 40 °C (104 °F), preferably between 15 and 30 °C (59 and 86 °F), unless otherwise specified by manufacturer. Store in a tight container. Protect from light. Protect from freezing.

Auxiliary labeling
- For external use only.
- Do not use in or around the eye.

FLURANDRENOLIDE LOTION USP

Usual adult dose
See *Flurandrenolide Cream USP*.

Usual pediatric dose
Topical, to the skin, once a day.

Strength(s) usually available
U.S.—
0.05% (Rx) [*Cordran;* GENERIC].
Canada—
Not commercially available.

Packaging and storage
Store below 40 °C (104 °F), preferably between 15 and 30 °C (59 and 86 °F). Store in a tight container. Protect from heat, light, and freezing.

Auxiliary labeling
- For external use only.
- Do not use in or around the eye.
- Shake well.

FLURANDRENOLIDE OINTMENT USP

Usual adult dose
See *Flurandrenolide Cream USP*.

Usual pediatric dose
Topical, to the skin, as a 0.025% ointment one or two times a day; or as a 0.05% ointment once a day.

Strength(s) usually available
U.S.—
0.025% (Rx) [*Cordran*].
0.05% (Rx) [*Cordran*].
Canada—
0.0125% (Rx) [*Drenison-¼*].
0.05% (Rx) [*Drenison*].

Packaging and storage
Store below 40 °C (104 °F), preferably between 15 and 30 °C (59 and 86 °F), unless otherwise specified by manufacturer. Store in a tight container. Protect from light. Protect from freezing.

Auxiliary labeling
- For external use only.
- Do not use in or around the eye.

FLURANDRENOLIDE TAPE USP

Usual adult dose
Topical, to the skin, as a tape containing 4 mcg of flurandrenolide per square centimeter, to be replaced every twelve to twenty-four hours.

Usual pediatric dose
Topical, to the skin, as a tape containing 4 mcg of flurandrenolide per square centimeter; to be replaced once a day.

Strength(s) usually available
U.S.—
4 mcg per square centimeter (Rx) [*Cordran*].
Canada—
4 mcg per square centimeter (Rx) [*Drenison*].

Packaging and storage
Store between 15 and 30 °C (59 and 86 °F).

Auxiliary labeling
- For external use only.

Note
Explain administration technique.

When dispensing, include patient instructions.

Additional information
Tape of flexible polyethylene film impregnated with flurandrenolide in the acrylic adhesive serves as an occlusive dressing, and should not be used in intertriginous areas or applied to lesions exuding serum.

FLUTICASONE

Summary of Differences

Pharmacology/pharmacokinetics:
Substituted; fluorinated.
Potency ranking—Medium.

Topical Dosage Forms

FLUTICASONE PROPIONATE CREAM

Usual adult dose
Atopic Dermatitis—
Topical, apply to affected skin once or twice daily.
Other corticosteroid-responsive dermatoses—
Topical, apply to affected skin twice daily.

Usual pediatric dose
Children 3 months of age and older: See *Usual adult dose*. Use should not continue beyond 4 weeks.
Children up to 3 months of age: Safety and efficacy have not been established.

Usual geriatric dose
See *Usual adult dose*.

Strength(s) usually available
U.S.—
0.05% (Rx) [*Cutivate* (propylene glycol; mineral oil; cetostearyl alcohol; Ceteth-20; isopropyl myristate; dibasic sodium phosphate; citric acid; purified water; imidurea)].
Canada—
Not commercially available.

Packaging and storage
Store between 2 and 30 °C (36 and 86 °F)

Auxiliary labeling
- For external use only.
- Do not use in or around the eye.

Note

Fluticasone propionate cream should not be used with occlusive dressings. Fluticasone propionate cream should not be applied in the diaper area, as diapers or plastic pants may constitute occlusive dressings.

FLUTICASONE PROPIONATE OINTMENT

Usual adult dose

Topical, apply to the skin twice daily.

Usual pediatric dose

Safety and efficacy have not been established.

Usual geriatric dose

See *Usual adult dose*.

Strength(s) usually available

U.S.—

0.005% (Rx) [*Cutivate* (propylene glycol; sorbitan sesquioleate; microcrystalline wax; liquid paraffin)].

Canada—

Not commercially available.

Packaging and storage

Store between 2 and 30 °C (36 and 86 °F)

Auxiliary labeling

- For external use only.
- Do not use in or around the eye.

HALCINONIDE

Summary of Differences

Pharmacology/pharmacokinetics:

Substituted; fluorinated.

Potency ranking—High.

Topical Dosage Forms

HALCINONIDE CREAM USP

Usual adult dose

Topical, to the skin, one to three times a day.

Usual pediatric dose

Topical, to the skin, once a day.

Strength(s) usually available

U.S.—

0.025% (Rx) [*Halog*].

0.1% (Rx) [*Halog; Halog-E*].

Canada—

0.1% (Rx) [*Halog*].

Packaging and storage

Store between 15 and 30 °C (59 and 86 °F), unless otherwise specified by manufacturer. Store in a well-closed container. Protect from freezing.

Auxiliary labeling

- For external use only.
- Do not use in or around the eye.

HALCINONIDE OINTMENT USP

Usual adult dose

Topical, to the skin, two or three times a day.

Usual pediatric dose

See *Halcinonide Cream USP*.

Strength(s) usually available

U.S.—

0.1% (Rx) [*Halog*].

Canada—

0.1% (Rx) [*Halog*].

Packaging and storage

Store below 40 °C (104 °F), preferably between 15 and 30 °C (59 and 86 °F), unless otherwise specified by manufacturer. Store in a well-closed container. Protect from freezing.

Auxiliary labeling

- For external use only.
- Do not use in or around the eye.

HALCINONIDE TOPICAL SOLUTION USP

Usual adult dose

See *Halcinonide Ointment USP*.

Usual pediatric dose

See *Halcinonide Cream USP*.

Strength(s) usually available

U.S.—

0.1% (Rx) [*Halog*].

Canada—

0.1% (Rx) [*Halog*].

Packaging and storage

Store below 40 °C (104 °F), preferably between 15 and 30 °C (59 and 86 °F), unless otherwise specified by manufacturer. Store in a well-closed container. Protect from freezing.

Auxiliary labeling

- For external use only.
- Do not use in or around the eye.

HALOBETASOL

Summary of Differences

Pharmacology/pharmacokinetics:

Substituted; fluorinated.

Potency ranking—Very high.

Topical Dosage Forms

HALOBETASOL PROPIONATE CREAM

Usual adult dose

Topical, to the skin, one or two times a day. Halobetasol propionate cream may be used for only a short duration of therapy and on small surface areas. Occlusive dressings should not be used.

Usual pediatric dose

Dosage has not been established.

Strength(s) usually available

U.S.—

0.05% (Rx) [*Ultravate*].

Canada—

Not commercially available.

Packaging and storage

Store below 40 °C (104 °F), preferably between 2 and 30 °C (36 and 86 °F), in a well-closed container, unless otherwise specified by manufacturer.

Auxiliary labeling

- For external use only.
- Do not use in or around the eye.

HALOBETASOL PROPIONATE OINTMENT

Usual adult dose

Topical, to the skin, one or two times a day. Halobetasol propionate ointment may be used for only a short duration of therapy and on small surface areas. Occlusive dressings should not be used.

Usual pediatric dose

Dosage has not been established.

Strength(s) usually available

U.S.—

0.05% (Rx) [*Ultravate*].

Canada—

Not commercially available.

Packaging and storage

Store below 40 °C (104 °F), preferably between 2 and 30 °C (36 and 86 °F), in a well-closed container, unless otherwise specified by manufacturer.

Auxiliary labeling

- For external use only.
- Do not use in or around the eye.

HYDROCORTISONE

Summary of Differences

Pharmacology/pharmacokinetics:

Substituted (butyrate, valerate); non-fluorinated.

Potency ranking—Low (acetate and base); Medium (butyrate and valerate).

Dental Dosage Forms

HYDROCORTISONE ACETATE DENTAL PASTE

Usual adult dose

Topical, to the oral mucous membranes, two or three times a day after meals and at bedtime.

Usual pediatric dose

Dosage has not been established.

Strength(s) usually available

U.S.—

0.5% (Rx) [*Orabase-HCA*].

Canada—

Not commercially available.

Packaging and storage

Store between 4 and 30 °C (39 and 86 °F), unless otherwise specified by manufacturer. Protect from light. Protect from freezing.

Auxiliary labeling

- For use in the mouth only.

Topical Dosage Forms

HYDROCORTISONE CREAM USP

Usual adult dose

Topical, to the skin, one to four times a day.

Usual pediatric dose

Children up to 2 years of age—Dosage has not been established.

Children 2 years of age or older—Topical, to the skin, as a 0.25% to 0.5% cream one to four times a day; or as a 1% cream one or two times a day.

Strength(s) usually available

U.S.—

0.25% (OTC) [*Cort-Dome*].

0.5% (OTC) [*Bactine; Cort-Dome; Cortifair; DermiCort; Dermtex HC; Hydro-Tex* (sodium bisulfite); *Hytone;* GENERIC].

1% (Rx) [*Ala-Cort; Allercort; Alphaderm; Cort-Dome; Cortifair; Dermacort; Hi-Cor 1.0; Hydro-Tex* (sodium bisulfite); *Hytone; Lemoderm; Nutracort; Penecort; Synacort;* GENERIC].

2.5% (Rx) [*Allercort; Anusol-HC; Hi-Cor 2.5; Hytone; Lemoderm; Penecort; Synacort;* GENERIC].

Canada—

0.5% (OTC) [*Cortate; Unicort*].

0.5% (Rx) [*Sential* (urea 4%)].

1% (Rx) [*Barriere-HC; Emo-Cort; Prevex HC; Unicort*].

2.5% (Rx) [*Emo-Cort*].

Packaging and storage

Store below 40 °C (104 °F), preferably between 15 and 30 °C (59 and 86 °F), unless otherwise specified by manufacturer. Store in a tight container. Protect from freezing.

Auxiliary labeling

- For external use only.
- Do not use in or around the eye.

HYDROCORTISONE LOTION USP

Usual adult dose

See *Hydrocortisone Cream USP*.

Usual pediatric dose

Children up to 2 years of age—Dosage has not been established.

Children 2 years of age or older—Topical, to the skin, as a 0.25% to 0.5% lotion, one to four times a day; or as a 1% lotion one or two times a day; or as a 2.5% lotion once a day.

Strength(s) usually available

U.S.—

0.25% (OTC) [*Cetacort; Cort-Dome*].

0.5% (OTC) [*Cetacort; Delacort; MyCort; S-T Cort;* GENERIC].

1% (Rx) [*Acticort 100; Ala-Cort; Allercort; Beta-HC; Cetacort; Dermacort; Gly-Cort; Hytone; LactiCare-HC; Lemoderm; Nutracort; Pentacort; Rederm;* GENERIC].

2% (Rx) [*Ala-Scalp HP*].

2.5% (Rx) [*Hytone; LactiCare-HC; Nutracort*].

Canada—

0.5% (OTC) [*Cortate; Emo-Cort*].

1% (Rx) [*Emo-Cort; Sarna HC 1.0%*].

2.5% (Rx) [*Emo-Cort*].

Packaging and storage

Store below 40 °C (104 °F), preferably between 15 and 30 °C (59 and 86 °F), unless otherwise specified by manufacturer. Store in a tight container. Protect from freezing.

Auxiliary labeling

- For external use only.
- Do not use in or around the eye.
- Shake well.

HYDROCORTISONE OINTMENT USP

Usual adult dose

See *Hydrocortisone Cream USP*.

Usual pediatric dose

Children up to 2 years of age—Dosage has not been established.

Children 2 years of age or older—Topical, to the skin, as a 0.5% ointment one to four times a day; or as a 1% ointment one or two times a day; or as a 2.5% ointment once a day.

Strength(s) usually available

U.S.—

0.5% (OTC) [GENERIC].

1% [*Allercort; Cortril; Hytone; Lemoderm;* GENERIC].

2.5% (Rx) [*Allercort; Hytone;* GENERIC].

Canada—

0.5% (OTC) [*Cortate*].

1% (Rx) [*Cortate; Cortef*].

Packaging and storage

Store below 40 °C (104 °F), preferably between 15 and 30 °C (59 and 86 °F), unless otherwise specified by manufacturer. Store in a well-closed container. Protect from freezing.

Auxiliary labeling

- For external use only.
- Do not use in or around the eye.

HYDROCORTISONE TOPICAL SOLUTION

Usual adult dose

See *Hydrocortisone Cream USP*.

Usual pediatric dose

Topical, to the skin one or two times a day.

Strength(s) usually available

U.S.—

0.5% (OTC) [*Aeroseb-HC* (alcohol 58%); *CaldeCORT Anti-Itch* (alcohol 89.5%); *Cortaid* (alcohol 46%; parabens); GENERIC].

1% (OTC) [*Maximum Strength Cortaid* (alcohol 55%; parabens)].

1% (Rx) [*Penecort* (alcohol 57%); *Texacort* (alcohol 33%)].

2.5% (Rx) [*Texacort* (alcohol 49%)].

Canada—

2.5% (Rx) [*Emo-Cort Scalp Solution* (alcohol)].

Packaging and storage

Store below 40 °C (104 °F), preferably between 15 and 30 °C (59 and 86 °F), in a well-closed container, unless otherwise specified by manufacturer. Protect from freezing.

Auxiliary labeling

- For external use only.
- Do not use in or around the eye.

HYDROCORTISONE ACETATE CREAM USP

Usual adult dose

Topical, to the skin, one to four times a day.

Usual pediatric dose

Children up to 2 years of age—Dosage has not been established.

Children 2 years of age and older—See *Usual adult dose*.

Strength(s) usually available

U.S.—

0.5% (OTC) [*Corticaine; FoilleCort; Gynecort; Lanacort; 9-1-1; Pharma-Cort;* GENERIC].

0.5% (base) (OTC) [*CaldeCORT Light; Cortaid; Cortef Feminine Itch;* GENERIC].

1% (OTC) [*Anusol-HC; Gynecort 10; Lanacort 10*].

1% (base) (OTC) [*Dermarest DriCort; Maximum Strength Cortaid*].

1% (Rx) [*Carmol-HC* (sodium bisulfite); GENERIC].

Canada—

0.1% (Rx) [*Corticreme*].

0.5% (OTC) [*Cortacet; Hyderm; Novohydrocort*].

1% (Rx) [*Corticreme; Hyderm; Novohydrocort*].

Packaging and storage

Store below 40 °C (104 °F), preferably between 15 and 30 °C (59 and 86 °F), unless otherwise specified by manufacturer. Store in a well-closed container. Protect from freezing.

Auxiliary labeling

- For external use only.
- Do not use in or around the eye.

HYDROCORTISONE ACETATE TOPICAL AEROSOL FOAM

Usual adult dose

See *Hydrocortisone Acetate Cream USP*.

Usual pediatric dose

Topical, to the skin, one or two times a day.

Strength(s) usually available

U.S.—

1% (Rx) [*Epifoam* (butane; methylparaben; propane; propylparaben)].

Canada—
Not commercially available.

Packaging and storage
Store below 49 °C (120 °F), unless otherwise specified by manufacturer.

Auxiliary labeling
- Shake well.
- For external use only.
- Do not use in or around the eye.

HYDROCORTISONE ACETATE LOTION USP

Usual adult dose
See *Hydrocortisone Acetate Cream USP*.

Usual pediatric dose
Children up to 2 years of age—Dosage has not been established.
Children 2 years of age or older—See *Usual adult dose*.

Strength(s) usually available
U.S.—
0.5% (base) (OTC) [*Cortaid; Rhulicort*].
Canada—
Not commercially available.

Packaging and storage
Store below 40 °C (104 °F), preferably between 15 and 30 °C (59 and 86 °F), unless otherwise specified by manufacturer. Store in a tight container. Protect from freezing.

Auxiliary labeling
- For external use only.
- Do not use in or around the eye.
- Shake well.

HYDROCORTISONE ACETATE OINTMENT USP

Usual adult dose
See *Hydrocortisone Acetate Cream USP*.

Usual pediatric dose
Children up to 2 years of age—Dosage has not been established.
Children 2 years of age or older—Topical, to the skin, as a 0.5% ointment one to four times a day; or as a 1% ointment one or two times a day; or as a 2.5% ointment once a day.

Strength(s) usually available
U.S.—
0.5% (OTC) [*Lanacort*].
0.5% (base) (OTC) [*Cortaid*].
1% (Rx) [GENERIC].
1% (base) (OTC) [*Maximum Strength Cortaid*].
Canada—
0.5% (OTC) [*Cortoderm; Novohydrocort*].
1% (Rx) [*Cortef; Cortoderm; Novohydrocort*].

Packaging and storage
Store below 40 °C (104 °F), preferably between 15 and 30 °C (59 and 86 °F), unless otherwise specified by manufacturer. Store in a well-closed container. Protect from freezing.

Auxiliary labeling
- For external use only.
- Do not use in or around the eye.

HYDROCORTISONE BUTYRATE CREAM USP

Usual adult dose
Topical, to the skin, two or three times a day.

Usual pediatric dose
Topical, to the skin, one or two times a day.

Strength(s) usually available
U.S.—
0.1% (Rx) [*Locoid* (methylparaben)].
Canada—
Not commercially available.

Packaging and storage
Store below 40 °C (104 °F), preferably between 15 and 30 °C (59 and 86 °F), unless otherwise specified by manufacturer. Store in a well-closed container. Protect from freezing.

Auxiliary labeling
- For external use only.
- Do not use in or around the eye.

HYDROCORTISONE BUTYRATE OINTMENT

Usual adult dose
See *Hydrocortisone Butyrate Cream USP*.

Usual pediatric dose
See *Hydrocortisone Butyrate Cream USP*.

Strength(s) usually available
U.S.—
0.1% (Rx) [*Locoid*].
Canada—
Not commercially available.

Packaging and storage
Store below 40 °C (104 °F), preferably between 15 and 30 °C (59 and 86 °F), unless otherwise specified by manufacturer. Protect from freezing.

Auxiliary labeling
- For external use only.
- Do not use in or around the eye.

HYDROCORTISONE BUTYRATE TOPICAL SOLUTION

Usual adult dose
See *Hydrocortisone Butyrate Cream USP*.

Usual pediatric dose
See *Hydrocortisone Butyrate Cream USP*.

Strength(s) usually available
U.S.—
0.1% (Rx) [*Locoid*].

Packaging and storage
Store between 5 and 25 °C (41 and 77 °F).

Auxiliary labeling
- For external use only.
- Do not use in or around the eye.

HYDROCORTISONE PROBUTATE CREAM

Usual adult dose
Topical, to the affected area once or twice daily.

Usual pediatric dose
Dosage has not been established.

Strength(s) usually available
U.S.—
0.1% (Rx) [*Pandel*].

HYDROCORTISONE VALERATE CREAM USP

Usual adult dose
Topical, to the skin, two or three times a day.

Usual pediatric dose
Topical, to the skin, once a day.

Strength(s) usually available
U.S.—
0.2% (Rx) [*Westcort*].
Canada—
0.2% (Rx) [*Westcort*].

Packaging and storage
Store below 25 °C (77 °F), unless otherwise specified by manufacturer. Store in a well-closed container. Protect from freezing.

Auxiliary labeling
- For external use only.
- Do not use in or around the eye.

HYDROCORTISONE VALERATE OINTMENT

Usual adult dose
See *Hydrocortisone Valerate Cream USP*.

Usual pediatric dose
See *Hydrocortisone Valerate Cream USP*.

Strength(s) usually available
U.S.—
0.2% (Rx) [*Westcort*].
Canada—
0.2% (Rx) [*Westcort*].

Packaging and storage
Store below 26 °C (78 °F), in a well-closed container, unless otherwise specified by manufacturer. Protect from freezing.

Auxiliary labeling
- For external use only.
- Do not use in or around the eye.

MOMETASONE

Summary of Differences

Pharmacology/pharmacokinetics:
Substituted; non-fluorinated.
Potency ranking—Medium.

Topical Dosage Forms

MOMETASONE FUROATE CREAM USP

Usual adult dose
Topical, to the skin, once a day.

Usual pediatric dose
Dosage has not been established.

Strength(s) usually available
U.S.—
0.1% (Rx) [*Elocon*].
Canada—
0.1% (Rx) [*Elocom*].

Packaging and storage
Store below 40 °C (104 °F), preferably between 2 and 30 °C (36 and 86 °F), unless otherwise specified by manufacturer. Store in a well-closed container.

Auxiliary labeling
- For external use only.
- Do not use in or around the eye.

MOMETASONE FUROATE LOTION

Usual adult dose
See *Mometasone Furoate Cream USP*.

Usual pediatric dose
Dosage has not been established.

Strength(s) usually available
U.S.—
0.1% (Rx) [*Elocon* (isopropyl alcohol 40%)].
Canada—
0.1% (Rx) [*Elocom*].

Packaging and storage
Store below 40 °C (104 °F), preferably between 2 and 30 °C (36 and 86 °F), in a well-closed container, unless otherwise specified by manufacturer.

Auxiliary labeling
- For external use only.
- Do not use in or around the eye.

MOMETASONE FUROATE OINTMENT USP

Usual adult dose
See *Mometasone Furoate Cream USP*.

Usual pediatric dose
Dosage has not been established.

Strength(s) usually available
U.S.—
0.1% (Rx) [*Elocon*].
Canada—
0.1% (Rx) [*Elocom*].

Packaging and storage
Store below 40 °C (104 °F), preferably between 2 and 30 °C (36 and 86 °F), unless otherwise specified by manufacturer. Store in a well-closed container.

Auxiliary labeling
- For external use only.
- Do not use in or around the eye.

PREDNICARBATE

Topical Dosage Form

PREDNICARBATE EMOLLIENT CREAM

Usual adult dose
Topical, to the affected area twice daily.

Usual pediatric dose
Topical, to the affected area twice daily for up to 3 weeks in patients 1 year of age or older.

Strength(s) usually available
U.S.—
0.1% (Rx) [*Dermatop*].

TRIAMCINOLONE

Summary of Differences

Pharmacology/pharmacokinetics:
Substituted; fluorinated.

Potency ranking—
Medium (except cream and ointment 0.5%).
Cream and ointment 0.5%, High.

Dental Dosage Forms

TRIAMCINOLONE ACETONIDE DENTAL PASTE USP

Usual adult dose
Topical, to the oral mucous membranes, two or three times a day after meals and at bedtime.

Usual pediatric dose
Dosage has not been established.

Strength(s) usually available
U.S.—
0.1% (Rx) [*Kenalog in Orabase; Oracort; Oralone;* GENERIC].
Canada—
0.1% (Rx) [*Kenalog in Orabase*].

Packaging and storage
Store below 40 °C (104 °F), preferably between 15 and 30 °C (59 and 86 °F), unless otherwise specified by manufacturer. Store in a tight container. Protect from freezing.

Auxiliary labeling
- For use in the mouth only.

Topical Dosage Forms

TRIAMCINOLONE ACETONIDE CREAM USP

Usual adult dose
Topical, to the skin, two to four times a day.

Usual pediatric dose
Topical, to the skin, as a 0.025% cream one or two times a day; or as a 0.1% or 0.5% cream once a day.

Strength(s) usually available
U.S.—
0.025% (Rx) [*Aristocort; Aristocort A; Flutex; Kenac; Kenalog; Kenonel; Triacet;* GENERIC].
0.1% (Rx) [*Aristocort; Aristocort A; Delta-Tritex; Flutex; Kenac; Kenalog; Kenalog-H; Kenonel; Triacet; Triderm;* GENERIC].
0.5% (Rx) [*Aristocort; Aristocort A; Flutex; Kenalog; Kenonel; Triacet;* GENERIC].
Canada—
0.025% (Rx) [*Aristocort D; Triaderm; Trianide Mild*].
0.1% (Rx) [*Aristocort R; Kenalog; Triaderm; Trianide Regular*].
0.5% (Rx) [*Aristocort C*].

Packaging and storage
Store below 40 °C (104 °F), preferably between 15 and 30 °C (59 and 86 °F), unless otherwise specified by manufacturer. Store in a tight container. Protect from freezing.

Auxiliary labeling
- For external use only.
- Do not use in or around the eye.

TRIAMCINOLONE ACETONIDE LOTION USP

Usual adult dose
See *Triamcinolone Acetonide Cream USP*.

Usual pediatric dose
Topical, to the skin, as a 0.025% lotion one or two times a day; or as a 0.1% lotion once a day.

Strength(s) usually available
U.S.—
0.025% (Rx) [*Kenalog*].
0.1% (Rx) [*Kenalog; Kenonel*].
Canada—
Not commercially available.

Packaging and storage
Store between 15 and 30 °C (59 and 86 °F), unless otherwise specified by manufacturer. Store in a tight container. Protect from freezing.

Auxiliary labeling
- For external use only.
- Do not use in or around the eye.
- Shake well

TRIAMCINOLONE ACETONIDE OINTMENT USP

Usual adult dose
See *Triamcinolone Acetonide Cream USP*.

Usual pediatric dose
Topical, to the skin, as a 0.025% ointment one or two times a day; or as a 0.1 or 0.5% ointment once a day.

Strength(s) usually available

U.S.—

0.025% (Rx) [*Flutex; Kenalog;* GENERIC].

0.1% (Rx) [*Aristocort; Aristocort A; Flutex; Kenac; Kenalog; Kenonel;* GENERIC].

0.5% (Rx) [*Aristocort; Flutex; Kenalog*].

Canada—

0.025% (Rx) [*Aristocort D; Triaderm*].

0.1% (Rx) [*Aristocort R; Kenalog; Triaderm*].

Packaging and storage

Store below 40 °C (104 °F), preferably between 15 and 30 °C (59 and 86 °F), unless otherwise specified by manufacturer. Store in a well-closed container. Protect from freezing.

Auxiliary labeling

- For external use only.
- Do not use in or around the eye.

TRIAMCINOLONE ACETONIDE TOPICAL AEROSOL USP

Usual adult dose

Topical, to the skin, three or four times a day.

Usual pediatric dose

Topical, to the skin, one or two times a day.

Strength(s) usually available

U.S.—

0.015% (Rx) [*Kenalog* (alcohol 10.3%)].

Note: A 2-second spray delivers 0.2 mg of triamcinolone acetonide. Product applied to skin contains approximately 0.2% triamcinolone acetonide.

Canada—

Not commercially available.

Packaging and storage

Store below 40 °C (104 °F), preferably between 15 and 30 °C (59 and 86 °F). Protect from freezing.

Auxiliary labeling

- For external use only.
- Do not use in or around the eye.

Note

Explain administration technique.

When dispensing, include patient instructions.

Revised: 03/25/2005

Table 1. Pharmacology/Pharmacokinetics

Note: The following table lists topical corticosteroid products available in the U.S. and/or Canada. A potency rank of Low, Medium, High, or Very High also is listed for each preparation.

Products with a Low potency ranking have a modest anti-inflammatory effect and are safest for chronic application. These products also are the safest products for use on the face and intertriginous areas, with occlusion, and in infants and young children.

Products with a Medium potency ranking are used in moderate inflammatory dermatoses. Examples of conditions for which these products are frequently used include chronic eczematous dermatoses such as hand eczema and atopic eczema. Medium potency preparations may be used on the face and intertriginous areas for a limited duration.

High potency preparations are used in more severe inflammatory dermatoses. Examples of conditions for which these products are frequently used include more severe eczematous dermatoses, lichen simplex chronicus, and psoriasis. They may be used for an intermediate duration, or for longer periods in areas with thickened skin due to chronic conditions. High potency preparations also may be used on the face and intertriginous areas but only for a short treatment duration.

Very High potency products are used primarily as an alternative to systemic corticosteroid therapy when local areas are involved. Examples of conditions for which Very High potency products are frequently used include thick, chronic lesions caused by psoriasis, lichen simplex chronicus, and discoid lupus erythematosus. There is a high likelihood of skin atrophy with the use of Very High potency preparations. They may be used for only a short duration of therapy and on small surface areas. Occlusive dressings should not be used with these products.

Generic drug name	Dosage Form(s)	Strength (%)	Potency Ranking
Alclometasone dipropionate			
	Cream	0.05	Low
	Ointment	0.05	Low
Amcinonide			
	Cream	0.1	High
	Lotion	0.1	High
	Ointment	0.1	High
Beclomethasone dipropionate			
	Cream	0.025	Medium
	Lotion	0.025	Medium
	Ointment	0.025	Medium
Betamethasone benzoate			
	Cream	0.025	Medium
	Gel	0.025	Medium
	Lotion	0.025	Medium
Betamethasone dipropionate			
	Cream		
	Diprolene AF	0.05	Very high
	Others	0.05	High
	Gel		
	Diprolene	0.05	Very high
	Lotion		
	Diprolene	0.05	Very high
	Others	0.05	High
	Ointment		
	Diprolene	0.05	Very high
	Others	0.05	High
	Topical aerosol	0.1	High

Generic drug name	Dosage Form(s)	Strength (%)	Potency Ranking
Betamethasone valerate			
	Cream	0.01	Medium
	Cream	0.05	Medium
	Cream	0.1	Medium
	Foam	0.12	Medium
	Lotion	0.05	Medium
	Lotion	0.1	Medium
	Ointment	0.05	Medium
	Ointment	0.1	Medium
Clobetasol propionate			
	Cream	0.05	Very high
	Ointment	0.05	Very high
	Solution	0.05	Very high
Clobetasone butyrate			
	Cream	0.05	Medium
	Ointment	0.05	Medium
Clocortolone pivalate			
	Cream	0.1	Low
Desonide			
	Cream	0.05	Low
	Lotion	0.05	Low
	Ointment	0.05	Low
Desoximetasone			
	Cream	0.05	Medium
	Cream	0.25	High
	Gel	0.05	High
	Ointment	0.25	High

Table 1. Pharmacology/Pharmacokinetics *(continued)*

Note: The following table lists topical corticosteroid products available in the U.S. and/or Canada. A potency rank of Low, Medium, High, or Very High also is listed for each preparation.

Products with a Low potency ranking have a modest anti-inflammatory effect and are safest for chronic application. These products also are the safest products for use on the face and intertriginous areas, with occlusion, and in infants and young children.

Products with a Medium potency ranking are used in moderate inflammatory dermatoses. Examples of conditions for which these products are frequently used include chronic eczematous dermatoses such as hand eczema and atopic eczema. Medium potency preparations may be used on the face and intertriginous areas for a limited duration.

High potency preparations are used in more severe inflammatory dermatoses. Examples of conditions for which these products are frequently used include more severe eczematous dermatoses, lichen simplex chronicus, and psoriasis. They may be used for an intermediate duration, or for longer periods in areas with thickened skin due to chronic conditions. High potency preparations also may be used on the face and intertriginous areas but only for a short treatment duration.

Very High potency products are used primarily as an alternative to systemic corticosteroid therapy when local areas are involved. Examples of conditions for which Very High potency products are frequently used include thick, chronic lesions caused by psoriasis, lichen simplex chronicus, and discoid lupus erythematosus. There is a high likelihood of skin atrophy with the use of Very High potency preparations. They may be used for only a short duration of therapy and on small surface areas. Occlusive dressings should not be used with these products.

Generic drug name	Dosage Form(s)	Strength (%)	Potency Ranking
Dexamethasone			
	Gel	0.1	Low
	Topical aerosol	0.01	Low
	Topical aerosol	0.04	Low
Dexamethasone sodium phosphate			
	Cream	0.1 (phosphate)	Low
Diflorasone diacetate			
	Cream	0.05	High
	Ointment		
	Psorcon	0.05	Very high
	Others	0.05	High
Diflucortolone valerate			
	Cream	0.1	Medium
	Ointment	0.1	Medium
Flumethasone pivalate			
	Cream	0.03	Low
	Ointment	0.03	Low
Fluocinolone acetonide			
	Cream	0.01	Medium
	Cream	0.025	Medium
	Cream	0.2	High
	Ointment	0.01	Medium
	Ointment	0.025	Medium
	Topical solution	0.01	Medium
Fluocinonide			
	Cream	0.01	High
	Cream	0.05	High
	Gel	0.05	High
	Ointment	0.01	High
	Ointment	0.05	High
	Topical solution	0.05	High
Flurandrenolide			
	Cream	0.0125	Low
	Cream	0.025	Medium
	Cream	0.05	Medium
	Lotion	0.05	Medium
	Ointment	0.0125	Low
	Ointment	0.025	Medium
	Ointment	0.05	Medium
	Tape	4 mcg/cm	Medium
Fluticasone propionate			
	Cream	0.05	Medium
	Ointment	0.005	Medium
Halcinonide			
	Cream	0.025	High
	Cream	0.1	High
	Ointment	0.1	High
	Topical solution	0.1	High

Generic drug name	Dosage Form(s)	Strength (%)	Potency Ranking
Halobetasol propionate			
	Cream	0.05	Very high
	Ointment	0.05	Very high
Hydrocortisone			
	Cream	0.25	Low
	Cream	0.5	Low
	Cream	1	Low
	Cream	2.5	Low
	Lotion	0.25	Low
	Lotion	0.5	Low
	Lotion	1	Low
	Lotion	2	Low
	Lotion	2.5	Low
	Ointment	0.5	Low
	Ointment	1	Low
	Ointment	2.5	Low
	Topical aerosol solution	0.5	Low
	Topical spray solution	0.5	Low
	Topical solution	1	Low
	Topical solution	2.5	Low
Hydrocortisone acetate			
	Cream	0.1	Low
	Cream	0.5	Low
	Cream	1	Low
	Lotion	0.5	Low
	Ointment	0.5	Low
	Ointment	1	Low
	Topical aerosol foam	1	Low
Hydrocortisone butyrate			
	Cream	0.1	Medium
	Ointment	0.1	Medium
Hydrocortisone valerate			
	Cream	0.2	Medium
	Ointment	0.2	Medium
Mometasone furoate			
	Cream	0.1	Medium
	Lotion	0.1	Medium
	Ointment	0.1	Medium
Triamcinolone acetonide			
	Cream	0.025	Medium
	Cream	0.1	Medium
	Cream	0.5	High
	Lotion	0.025	Medium
	Lotion	0.1	Medium
	Ointment	0.025	Medium
	Ointment	0.1	Medium
	Ointment	0.5	High
	Topical aerosol	0.015	Medium

CORTICOSTEROIDS AND ACETIC ACID Otic

VA CLASSIFICATION (Primary): OT250

Commonly used brand name(s): *Vosol HC*.

Another commonly used name for hydrocortisone is cortisol.

Note: For a listing of dosage forms and brand names by country availability, see *Dosage Forms* section(s).

Category

Corticosteroid-antiseptic (otic); anti-inflammatory (steroidal), otic.

Indications

Note: Bracketed information in the *Indications* section refers to uses that are not included in U.S. product labeling.

Accepted

Ear canal infections, external (treatment)—Corticosteroid and acetic acid combinations are indicated in the treatment of superficial external ear canal infections, caused by organisms susceptible to these medications, that are accompanied by inflammation.

[Ear canal infections, external (prophylaxis)]—Hydrocortisone and acetic acid combination is indicated in the prophylaxis of external ear canal infections.

[Otitis externa, eczematoid, chronic (prophylaxis and treatment)]—Hydrocortisone and acetic acid combination is indicated in the prophylaxis and treatment of chronic eczematoid otitis externa.

[Otitis externa, seborrheic (prophylaxis and treatment)]—Hydrocortisone and acetic acid combination is indicated in the prophylaxis and treatment of seborrheic otitis externa.

Pharmacology/Pharmacokinetics

Physicochemical characteristics

Molecular weight—

Acetic acid: 60.05.

Hydrocortisone: 362.47.

Mechanism of action/Effect

Corticosteroids—

Otic corticosteroids possess anti-inflammatory, anti-allergic, and antipruritic actions.

Corticosteroids diffuse across cell membranes and complex with specific cytoplasmic receptors. These complexes then enter the cell nucleus, bind to DNA, and stimulate transcription of messenger RNA (mRNA) and subsequent protein synthesis of enzymes ultimately responsible for anti-inflammatory effects of otic corticosteroids. In high concentrations, which may be achieved locally after topical application, corticosteroids may exert direct membrane effects. Corticosteroids decrease cellular and fibrinous exudation and tissue infiltration, inhibit fibroblastic and collagen-forming activity, retard epithelial regeneration, diminish postinflammatory neovascularization, and reduce toward normal levels the excessive permeability of inflamed capillaries.

Acetic acid—

Possesses antibacterial, astringent, and antifungal properties.

Precautions to Consider

Pregnancy/Reproduction

Pregnancy—Adequate and well-controlled studies in humans have not been done. Use should be avoided during pregnancy unless absolutely necessary. Studies in animals have shown that corticosteroids cause adverse effects in the fetus, at high systemic exposure levels.

FDA Pregnancy Category C.

Breast-feeding

Corticosteroids are distributed into breast milk. Minimal systemic absorption from otic application allows only a low amount of medication to pass into the milk. Possible benefits of corticosteroids to the mother must be weighed against the potential hazards for the infant.

Pediatrics

Infants born of mothers who received substantial dosages of corticosteroids during pregnancy should be observed for hypoadrenalism (weight loss, anorexia, weakness). Appropriate studies on the relationship of age to the effects of corticosteroids have not been performed in children up to 3 years of age. Safety and efficacy have not been established.

Geriatrics

Appropriate studies with these medications have not been performed in the geriatric population. However, geriatrics-specific problems that would limit the usefulness of these medications in the elderly are not expected.

Medical considerations/Contraindications

The medical considerations/contraindications included have been selected on the basis of their potential clinical significance (reasons given in parentheses where appropriate)—not necessarily inclusive (» = major clinical significance).

Risk-benefit should be considered when the following medical problems exist:

» Infection, aural, fungal or

» Infection, aural, acute untreated or

» Tuberculosis, aural or

Viral infection, acute, infectious (infectionsmay be exacerbated)

» Perforation of the ear drum membrane (possibility of ototoxicity)

Sensitivity to acetic acid

Sensitivity to corticosteroids

Side/Adverse Effects

The following side/adverse effects have been selected on the basis of their potential clinical significance (possible signs and symptoms in parentheses where appropriate)—not necessarily inclusive:

Those indicating need for medical attention only if they continue or are bothersome

Anorexia, weakness, weight loss—in children; stinging, itching, irritation, or burning in the ear

Patient Consultation

As an aid to patient consultation, refer to *Advice for the Patient, Corticosteroids and Acetic Acid (Otic)*.

In providing consultation, consider emphasizing the following selected information (» = major clinical significance):

Before using this medication

» Conditions affecting use, especially:

Sensitivity to acetic acid or corticosteroids

Other medical problems, especially other untreated ear infections or perforated ear drum

Proper use of this medication

Proper administration technique

Preventing contamination: Avoiding touching applicator tip to any surface; keeping container tightly closed

» Not washing dropper or applicator tip (to prevent dilution of medication with water)—applicable only to the hydrocortisone and acetic acid formulation; if necessary, wiping with clean tissue after use

Importance of not using more medication than the amount prescribed

» Checking with physician before using medication for future ear problems

» Proper dosing

Missed dose: Using as soon as possible; not using if almost time for next dose; do not stop treatment abruptly

» Proper storage

Precautions while using this medication

Checking with physician if no improvement within 5 to 7 days or if ear condition becomes worse

General Dosing Information

To allow optimum contact between the medication and infected surfaces of the ear canal, all cerumen and debris should be carefully removed by a physician or a trained assistant before initiation of therapy.

Otic solutions may be instilled directly into the ear canal or administered by use of a saturated gauze or cotton wick gently placed into the canal. The wick may be saturated with the solution prior to or after its insertion into the ear canal. The wick should be kept moist with the solution, 3 to 5 drops every four to six hours, then the wick may be removed after twenty-four hours. Continue dosing with 5 drops three to four times a day. Pediatric patients may only need 3 to 4 drops per dose due to a smaller ear canal.

The duration of treatment may vary from a few days to several weeks or months in some cases, depending on the condition being treated. Daily or alternate-day therapy may be indicated for extended periods in certain situations. In severe or persistent cases of external ear canal infections, more intensive anti-infective therapy may be required.

Treatment should be continued after apparent response, with the dosage being tapered gradually to avoid relapse.

Otic Dosage Forms

Note: Bracketed uses in the *Dosage Forms*section refer to categories of use and/or indications that are not included in U.S. product labeling.

HYDROCORTISONE AND ACETIC ACID OTIC SOLUTION USP

Usual adult and adolescent dose

[Prophylaxis]—

Topical, to each affected ear canal, 2 drops of solution in the morning and evening.

Treatment—

Topical, to the affected ear canal, 3 to 5 drops of the solution every four to six hours for twenty-four hours, then continue dosing with 5 drops three to four times daily.

Note: To promote continuous contact for initial twenty-four to forty-eight hours, a saturated wick may be inserted into the ear canal. The wick should be moistened with 3 to 5 drops of solution every four to six hours, then it may be removed after twenty-four hours.

Usual pediatric dose

Safety and efficacy in children up to 3 years of age have not been established. Due to a smaller ear canal, 3 to 4 drops may be a sufficient dose for children over 3 years of age.

Usual geriatric dose

See *Usual adult and adolescent dose.*

Strength(s) usually available

U.S.—

1% hydrocortisone and 2% acetic acid (Rx) [*Vosol HC* (benzethonium chloride 0.02%; citric acid 0.05%; propylene glycol diacetate 3%; sodium acetate 0.015%); GENERIC].

Canada—

1% hydrocortisone and 2% acetic acid (Rx) [*Vosol HC* (benzethonium chloride 0.02%; citric acid 0.05%; propylene glycol diacetate 3%; sodium acetate 0.015%)].

Packaging and storage

Store at room temperature, 20 to 25 °C (68 to 77 °F), unless otherwise specified by manufacturer. Store in a tight, light-resistant container. Protect from freezing.

Auxiliary labeling

- For the ear.
- Keep container tightly closed.

Revised: 07/17/2000

CORTICOSTEROIDS—GLUCOCORTICOID EFFECTS Systemic

This monograph includes information on the following: 1) Betamethasone; 2) Budesonide*; 3) Cortisone; 4) Dexamethasone; 5) Hydrocortisone; 6) Methylprednisolone; 7) Prednisolone; 8) Prednisone; 9) Triamcinolone.

INN: Hydrocortisone—Cortisol

BAN: Hydrocortisone—Cortisol

JAN:

Hydrocortisone—Cortisol
Prednisolone tebutate—Prednisolone butylacetate

VA CLASSIFICATION (Primary/Secondary):

Betamethasone—HS051/IM403
Budesonide—HS051
Cortisone—HS051/IM403
Dexamethasone—HS051/DX900; GA609; IM403
Hydrocortisone—HS051/GA609; IM403
Methylprednisolone—HS051/IM403
Prednisolone—HS051/IM403
Prednisone—HS051/GA609; IM403
Triamcinolone—HS051/IM403

Commonly used brand name(s): *A-Hydrocort*[5]; *A-MethaPred*[6]; *Acetocot*[9]; *A-hydroCort*[5]; *Amcort*[9]; *Apo-Prednisone*[8]; *Aristocort*[9]; *Aristocort Forte*[9]; *Aristocort Intralesional*[9]; *Aristopak*[9]; *Aristospan*[9]; *Articulose-50*[7]; *Articulose-L.A.*[9]; *Betnesol*[1]; *Celestone*[1]; *Celestone Phosphate*[1]; *Celestone Soluspan*[1]; *Cinalone 40*[9]; *Cinonide 40*[9]; *Clinacort*[9]; *Clinalog*[9]; *Cordrol*[8]; *Cortastat*[4]; *Cortastat 10*[4]; *Cortastat LA*[4]; *Cortef*[5]; *Cortisone Acetate-ICN*[3]; *Cortone*[3]; *Cortone Acetate*[3]; *Cotolone*[7]; *Decadron*[4]; *Decadron Phosphate*[4]; *Delta-Cortef*[7]; *Deltasone*[8]; *Depo-Medrol*[6]; *Deronil*[4]; *Dexamethasone Intensol*[4]; *Dexasone*[4]; *Dexasone L.A.*[4]; *Dexone LA*[4]; *Entocort*[2]; *Hexadrol Phosphate*[4]; *Hydrocortone*[5]; *Hydrocortone Acetate*[5]; *Hydrocortone Phosphate*[5]; *Ken-Jec 40*[9]; *Kenacort*[9]; *Kenacort Diacetate*[9]; *Kenaject-40*[9]; *Kenalog-10*[9]; *Kenalog-40*[9]; *Key-Pred*[7]; *Key-Pred SP*[7]; *Liquid Pred*[8]; *Medrol*[6]; *Meprolone*[6]; *Meticorten*[8]; *Nor-Pred T.B.A.*[7]; *Oradexon*[4]; *Orasone 1*[8]; *Orasone 10*[8]; *Orasone 20*[8]; *Orasone 5*[8]; *Orasone 50*[8]; *Pediapred*[7]; *Pred-Ject-50*[7]; *Pred-Pak 45*[8]; *Pred-Pak 79*[8]; *Predacort 50*[7]; *Predalone 50*[7]; *Predalone T.B.A.*[7]; *Predate S*[7]; *Predate TBA*[7]; *Predate-50*[7]; *Predcor-25*[7]; *Predcor-50*[7]; *Predcor-TBA*[7]; *Predicort-RP*[7]; *Predisone Intensol*[8]; *Prednicot*[8]; *Prelone*[7]; *Robalog*[9]; *Scheinpharm Triamcine-A*[9]; *Selestoject*[1]; *Solu-Cortef*[5]; *Solu-Medrol*[6]; *Solurex*[4]; *Solurex LA*[4]; *Sterapred*[8]; *Sterapred DS*[8]; *Tac-3*[9]; *Tramacort-D*[9]; *Tri-Kort*[9]; *Triam-A*[9]; *Triam-Forte*[9]; *Triamolone 40*[9]; *Triamonide 40*[9]; *Trilog*[9]; *Trilone*[9]; *Tristoject*[9]; *Winpred*[8].

Note: For a listing of dosage forms and brand names by country availability, see *Dosage Forms* section(s).

*Not commercially available in U.S.

Category

Corticosteroid—Betamethasone; Budesonide; Cortisone; Dexamethasone; Hydrocortisone; Methylprednisolone; Prednisolone; Prednisone; Triamcinolone.

Anti-inflammatory (steroidal)—Betamethasone; Budesonide; Cortisone; Dexamethasone; Hydrocortisone; Methylprednisolone; Prednisolone; Prednisone; Triamcinolone.

Diagnostic aid (Cushing's syndrome)—Dexamethasone.

Immunosuppressant—Betamethasone; Cortisone; Dexamethasone; Hydrocortisone; Methylprednisolone; Prednisolone; Prednisone; Triamcinolone.

Antiemetic, in cancer chemotherapy—Dexamethasone; Hydrocortisone; Prednisone.

Diagnostic aid (endogenous depression)—Dexamethasone

Indications

Accepted

Allergic disorders—Indicated for the treatment of severe or incapacitating allergic disorders intractable to adequate trials of conventional treatment:

Allergic reactions, drug-induced (treatment)

(Betamethasone (sodium phosphate and acetate injectable suspension, syrup, tablets); cortisone (acetate injectable suspension, tablets); dexamethasone (acetate injectable suspension, elixir, oral solution, sodium phosphate injection, tablets); hydrocortisone (cypionate oral suspension, sodium phosphate injection, sodium succinate for injection, tablets); methylprednisolone (acetate injectable suspension, sodium succinate for injection, tablets); prednisolone (sodium phosphate oral solution, syrup); prednisone (tablets); and triamcinolone (tablets).)

Anaphylactic or anaphylactoid reactions (treatment adjunct)

(Dexamethasone (sodium phosphate injection); hydrocortisone (sodium succinate for injection); and methylprednisolone (sodium succinate for injection) are indicated as adjunctive treatment in prolonged reactions (those not responding to other forms of treatment within 1 hour), reactions requiring cardiovascular or respiratory resuscitation, or situations in which there is a significant risk of relapse.)

(Epinephrine is the drug of choice for this indication.)

Angioedema (treatment adjunct)

(Betamethasone (tablets) is indicated as an adjunct in the treatment of angioedema. Treatment should be initiated with intramuscular or intravenous administration of a rapid-acting preparation.)

Edema, laryngeal, acute noninfectious (treatment adjunct)

(Betamethasone (sodium phosphate and acetate injectable suspension); cortisone (acetate injectable suspension, tablets); dexamethasone (sodium phosphate injection); hydrocortisone (sodium phosphate injection, sodium succinate for injection); and methylprednisolone (acetate injectable suspension, sodium succinate for injection) are indicated as adjuncts in the treatment of acute noninfectious laryngeal edema. Treatment should be initiated with intramuscular or intravenous administration of a rapid-acting preparation.)

(Epinephrine is the drug of choice for this indication.)

Rhinitis, allergic, perennial or seasonal, severe (treatment)

(Betamethasone (sodium phosphate and acetate injectable suspension, syrup, tablets); cortisone (acetate injectable suspension, tablets); dexamethasone (acetate injectable suspension, elixir, oral solution, sodium phosphate injection, tablets); hydrocortisone (cypionate oral suspension, sodium phosphate injection, sodium succinate for injection, tablets); methylprednisolone (acetate injectable suspension, sodium succinate for injection, tablets); prednisolone (sodium phosphate oral solution, syrup); prednisone (tablets); and triamcinolone (acetonide injectable suspension, tablets).)

Serum sickness (treatment)

(Betamethasone (sodium phosphate and acetate injectable suspension, syrup, tablets); cortisone (acetate injectable suspension, tablets); dexamethasone (acetate injectable suspension, elixir, oral solution, sodium phosphate injection, tablets); hydrocortisone (cypionate oral suspension, sodium phosphate injection, sodium succinate for injection, tablets); methylprednisolone (acetate injectable suspension, sodium succinate for injection, tablets); prednisolone (sodium phosphate oral solution, syrup); prednisone (tablets); and triamcinolone (tablets).)

Transfusion reactions, urticarial (treatment)

(Betamethasone (sodium phosphate and acetate injectable suspension); cortisone (acetate injectable suspension, tablets); dexamethasone (acetate injectable suspension, sodium phosphate injection); hydrocortisone (sodium phosphate injection, sodium succinate for injection); and methylprednisolone (acetate injectable suspension, sodium succinate for injection) are indicated in the treatment of urticarial transfusion reactions. Treatment should be initiated with intramuscular or intravenous administration of a rapid-acting preparation.)

Collagen disorders—Indicated during an acute exacerbation or as maintenance therapy:

Arteritis, giant cell (treatment)

(Methylprednisolone (tablets); and prednisone (tablets).)

Carditis, rheumatic [or nonrheumatic][1], acute (treatment)

(Betamethasone (sodium phosphate and acetate injectable suspension, syrup, tablets); cortisone (acetate injectable suspension, tablets); dexamethasone (acetate injectable suspension, elixir, oral solution, sodium phosphate injection, tablets); hydrocortisone (cypionate oral suspension, sodium phosphate injection, sodium succinate for injection, tablets); methylprednisolone (acetate injectable suspension, sodium succinate for injection, tablets); prednisolone (sodium phosphate oral solution, syrup); prednisone (oral solution, tablets); and triamcinolone (tablets).)

Dermatomyositis, systemic (polymyositis) (treatment)

(Cortisone (acetate injectable suspension, tablets); dexamethasone (tablets); hydrocortisone (cypionate oral suspension, sodium phosphate injection, sodium succinate for injection, tablets); methylprednisolone (acetate injectable suspension, sodium succinate for injection, tablets); prednisolone (sodium phosphate oral solution, syrup); and prednisone (tablets).)

Lupus erythematosus, systemic (treatment)

(Betamethasone (sodium phosphate and acetate injectable suspension, syrup, tablets); cortisone (acetate injectable suspension, tablets); dexamethasone (acetate injectable suspension, elixir, oral solution, sodium phosphate injection, tablets); hydrocortisone (cypionate oral suspension, sodium phosphate injection, sodium succinate for injection, tablets); methylprednisolone (acetate injectable suspension, sodium succinate for injection, tablets); prednisolone (sodium phosphate oral solution, syrup); prednisone (tablets); and triamcinolone (tablets).)

[Connective tissue disease, mixed (treatment)][1]
[Polyarteritis nodosa (treatment)][1]
[Polychondritis, relapsing (treatment)][1] and
[Vasculitis (treatment)][1]

(Betamethasone; cortisone; dexamethasone; hydrocortisone; methylprednisolone; prednisolone; prednisone; and triamcinolone.)

[Depression, mental, endogenous (diagnosis)][1]—Dexamethasone is indicated to diagnose endogenous depression and to evaluate the efficacy of treatment. Dexamethasone reduces plasma cortisol to a greater extent in control subjects than in hospitalized patients with diagnosed depression; values return toward those of control subjects as the patient responds to therapy. However, the dexamethasone suppression test is less sensitive in patients with mild to moderate depression. Also, many medications, medical problems, and other psychiatric disorders have been reported to interfere with the test results. The Health and Public Policy Committee of the American College of Physicians recommends that the dexamethasone suppression test not be used as a screening test for depression.

Dermatologic disorders:

Alopecia areata (treatment)

(Betamethasone (sodium phosphate and acetate injectable suspension); dexamethasone (acetate injectable suspension, sodium phosphate injection); hydrocortisone (acetate injectable suspension); methylprednisolone (acetate injectable suspension); and triamcinolone (acetonide injectable suspension).)

Dermatitis, atopic (treatment)

(Betamethasone (sodium phosphate and acetate injectable suspension, syrup, tablets); cortisone (acetate injectable suspension, tablets); dexamethasone (acetate injectable suspension, elixir, oral solution, sodium phosphate injection, tablets); hydrocortisone (cypionate oral suspension, sodium phosphate injection, sodium succinate for injection, tablets); methylprednisolone (acetate injectable suspension, sodium succinate for injection, tablets); prednisolone (sodium phosphate oral solution, syrup); prednisone (tablets); and triamcinolone (tablets).)

Dermatitis, contact (treatment)

(Betamethasone (sodium phosphate and acetate injectable suspension, syrup, tablets); cortisone (acetate injectable suspension, tablets); dexamethasone (acetate injectable suspension, elixir, oral solution, sodium phosphate injection, tablets); hydrocortisone (cypionate oral suspension, sodium phosphate injection, sodium succinate for injection, tablets); methylprednisolone (acetate injectable suspension, sodium succinate for injection, tablets); prednisolone (sodium phosphate oral solution, syrup); prednisone (tablets); and triamcinolone (tablets).)

Dermatitis, exfoliative (treatment)

(Betamethasone (sodium phosphate and acetate injectable suspension, syrup, tablets); cortisone (acetate injectable suspension, tablets); dexamethasone (acetate injectable suspension, elixir, oral solution, sodium phosphate injection, tablets); hydrocortisone (cypionate oral suspension, sodium phosphate injection, sodium succinate for injection, tablets); methylprednisolone (acetate injectable suspension, sodium succinate for injection, tablets); prednisolone (sodium phosphate oral solution, syrup); prednisone (tablets); and triamcinolone (tablets).)

Dermatitis herpetiformis, bullous (treatment)

(Betamethasone (sodium phosphate and acetate injectable suspension, syrup, tablets); cortisone (acetate injectable suspension, tablets); dexamethasone (acetate injectable suspension, elixir, oral solution, sodium phosphate injection, tablets); hydrocortisone (cypionate oral suspension, sodium phosphate injection, sodium succinate for injection, tablets); methylprednisolone (acetate injectable suspension, sodium succinate for injection, tablets); prednisolone (sodium phosphate oral solution, syrup); prednisone (tablets); and triamcinolone (tablets).)

Dermatitis, seborrheic, severe (treatment)

(Betamethasone (sodium phosphate and acetate injectable suspension, syrup, tablets); cortisone (acetate injectable suspension, tablets); dexamethasone (acetate injectable suspension, elixir, oral solution, sodium phosphate injection, tablets); hydrocortisone (cypionate oral suspension, sodium phosphate injection, sodium succinate for injection, tablets); methylprednisolone (acetate injectable suspension, sodium succinate for injection, tablets); prednisolone (sodium phosphate oral solution, syrup); prednisone (tablets); and triamcinolone (tablets).)

Dermatoses, inflammatory, severe (treatment)

(Betamethasone (tablets) and triamcinolone (acetonide injectable suspension, tablets).)

Erythema multiforme, severe (Stevens-Johnson syndrome) (treatment)

(Betamethasone (sodium phosphate and acetate injectable suspension, syrup, tablets); cortisone (acetate injectable suspension, tablets); dexamethasone (acetate injectable suspension, elixir, oral solution, sodium phosphate injection, tablets); hydrocortisone (cypionate oral suspension, sodium phosphate injection, sodium succinate for injection, tablets); methylprednisolone (acetate injectable suspension, sodium succinate for injection, tablets); prednisolone (sodium phosphate oral solution, syrup); prednisone (tablets); and triamcinolone (tablets).)

Granuloma annulare (treatment)

(Betamethasone (sodium phosphate and acetate injectable suspension); dexamethasone (acetate injectable suspension, sodium phosphate injection); hydrocortisone (acetate injectable suspension) methylprednisolone (acetate injectable suspension); and triamcinolone (acetonide injectable suspension).)

Keloids (treatment)

(Betamethasone (sodium phosphate and acetate injectable suspension); dexamethasone (acetate injectable suspension, sodium phosphate injection); hydrocortisone (acetate injectable suspension); methylprednisolone (acetate injectable suspension); and triamcinolone (acetonide injectable suspension).)

Lichen planus (treatment)

(Betamethasone (sodium phosphate and acetate injectable suspension); dexamethasone (acetate injectable suspension, sodium phosphate injection); hydrocortisone (acetate injectable suspension); methylprednisolone (acetate injectable suspension); and triamcinolone (acetonide injectable suspension).)

Lichen simplex chronicus (neurodermatitis) (treatment)

(Betamethasone (sodium phosphate and acetate injectable suspension); dexamethasone (acetate injectable suspension, sodium phosphate injection); hydrocortisone (acetate injectable suspension); methylprednisolone (acetate injectable suspension); and triamcinolone (acetonide injectable suspension).)

Lupus erythematosus, discoid (treatment)

(Betamethasone (sodium phosphate and acetate injectable suspension); dexamethasone (acetate injectable suspension, sodium phosphate injection); hydrocortisone (acetate injectable suspension); methylprednisolone (acetate injectable suspension); and triamcinolone (acetonide injectable suspension).)

Mycosis fungoides (treatment)

(Betamethasone (sodium phosphate and acetate injectable suspension, syrup, tablets); cortisone (acetate injectable suspension, tablets); dexamethasone (acetate injectable suspension, elixir, oral solution, sodium phosphate injection, tablets); hydrocortisone (cypionate oral suspension, sodium phosphate injection, sodium succinate for injection, tablets); methylprednisolone (acetate injectable suspension, sodium succinate for injection, tablets); prednisolone (sodium phosphate oral solution, syrup); prednisone (tablets); and triamcinolone (tablets).)

Necrobiosis lipoidica diabeticorum (treatment)

(Betamethasone (sodium phosphate and acetate injectable suspension); dexamethasone (acetate injectable suspension, sodium phosphate injection); hydrocortisone (acetate injectable suspension); methylprednisolone (acetate injectable suspension); and triamcinolone (acetonide injectable suspension).)

Pemphigus (treatment)

(Betamethasone (sodium phosphate and acetate injectable suspension, syrup, tablets); cortisone (acetate injectable suspension, tablets); dexamethasone (acetate injectable suspension, elixir, oral solution, sodium phosphate injection, tablets); hydrocortisone (cypionate oral suspension, sodium phosphate injection, sodium succinate for injection, tablets); methylprednisolone (acetate injectable suspension, sodium succinate for injection, tablets); prednisolone (sodium phosphate oral solution, syrup); prednisone (tablets); and triamcinolone (tablets).)

Psoriasis, severe (treatment)

(Betamethasone (sodium phosphate and acetate injectable suspension, syrup, tablets); cortisone (acetate injectable suspension, tablets); dexamethasone (acetate injectable suspension, elixir, oral solution, sodium phosphate injection, tablets); hydrocortisone (cypionate oral suspension, sodium phosphate injection, sodium succinate for injection, tablets); methylprednisolone (acetate injectable suspension, sodium succinate for injection, tablets); prednisolone (sodium phosphate oral solution, syrup); prednisone (tablets); and triamcinolone (tablets).)

Psoriatic plaques (treatment)

(Betamethasone (sodium phosphate and acetate injectable suspension); dexamethasone (acetate injectable suspension, sodium phosphate injection); hydrocortisone (acetate injectable suspension); methylprednisolone (acetate injectable suspension); and triamcinolone (acetonide injectable suspension).)

[Eczema, severe (treatment)]

(Betamethasone (tablets); cortisone[1]; dexamethasone[1]; hydrocortisone[1]; methylprednisolone[1]; prednisolone[1]; prednisone[1]; and triamcinolone[1].)

[Pemphigoid (treatment)][1]

(Betamethasone; cortisone; dexamethasone; hydrocortisone; methylprednisolone; prednisolone; prednisone; and triamcinolone.)

[Sarcoid, localized cutaneous (treatment)][1]

(Betamethasone; dexamethasone; hydrocortisone; methylprednisolone; prednisolone; and triamcinolone.)

Endocrine disorders:

Adrenocortical insufficiency, acute (treatment) and

Adrenocortical insufficiency, chronic primary (Addison's disease) (treatment)

(Betamethasone (sodium phosphate and acetate injectable suspension, syrup, tablets); cortisone (acetate injectable suspension, tablets); dexamethasone (elixir, oral solution, sodium phosphate injection, tablets); hydrocortisone (cypionate oral suspension, sodium phosphate injection, sodium succinate for injection, tablets); methylprednisolone (acetate injectable suspension, sodium succinate for injection, tablets); prednisolone (sodium phosphate oral solution, syrup); prednisone (tablets); and triamcinolone (tablets) are indicated in the treatment of adrenocortical insufficiency. However, hydrocortisone and cortisone are preferred as replacement therapy because of their significant mineralocorticoid activity. A rapid-acting preparation should be administered intramuscularly or intravenously initially. Administration of sodium (as dietary salt) and fluids also is required. In some patients, additional mineralocorticoid replacement also may be necessary. Rarely, a patient will have only a glucocorticoid deficiency and will not require mineralocorticoid or sodium supplementation.)

Adrenocortical insufficiency, secondary (treatment)

(Betamethasone (sodium phosphate and acetate injectable suspension, syrup, tablets); cortisone (acetate injectable suspension, tablets); dexamethasone (elixir, oral solution, sodium phosphate injection, tablets); hydrocortisone (cypionate oral suspension, sodium phosphate injection, sodium succinate for injection, tablets); methylprednisolone (acetate injectable suspension, sodium succinate for injection, tablets); prednisolone (sodium phosphate oral solution, syrup); prednisone (tablets); and triamcinolone (tablets) are indicated in the treatment of secondary adrenocortical insufficiency. Glucocorticoid replacement usually is sufficient. Mineralocorticoid replacement is not always required.)

Congenital adrenal hyperplasia (treatment)

(Betamethasone (sodium phosphate and acetate injectable suspension, syrup, tablets); cortisone (acetate injectable suspension, tablets); dexamethasone (acetate injectable suspension, elixir, oral solution, sodium phosphate injection, tablets); hydrocortisone (cypionate oral suspension, sodium phosphate injection, sodium succinate for injection, tablets); methylprednisolone (acetate injectable suspension, sodium succinate for injection, tablets); prednisolone (sodium phosphate oral solution, syrup); and prednisone (oral solution, tablets) are indicated to reduce the virilization caused by enzyme deficiency–induced adrenal androgen hypersecretion. Corticosteroid and supplemental therapy depend upon the enzyme deficiency involved and the form of disease present. In salt-losing forms, hydrocortisone or cortisone plus increased sodium intake may be preferred. However, additional mineralocorticoid supplementation may be required. In salt-retaining or hypertensive forms, a glucocorticoid having minimal mineralocorticoid activity is preferred. However, long-acting glucocorticoids are best avoided because of the increased risk of growth retardation and difficulty in dosage adjustment.)

Cushing's syndrome (diagnosis)

(Dexamethasone (elixir, oral solution, sodium phosphate injection, tablets) is indicated in the diagnosis of Cushing's syndrome and to distinguish Cushing's syndrome caused by excessive corticotropin secretion from that due to other causes.)

Hypercalcemia associated with neoplasms [or sarcoidosis][1] (treatment)

(Betamethasone (sodium phosphate and acetate injectable suspension, syrup, tablets); cortisone (acetate injectable suspension, tablets); dexamethasone (acetate injectable suspension, elixir, oral solution, sodium phosphate injection, tablets); hydrocortisone (cypionate oral suspension, sodium phosphate injection, sodium succinate for injection, tablets); methylprednisolone (sodium succinate for injection, tablets); prednisolone (sodium phosphate oral solution, syrup); prednisone (tablets); and triamcinolone (tablets).)

Thyroiditis, nonsuppurative (treatment)

(Betamethasone (sodium phosphate and acetate injectable suspension, syrup, tablets); cortisone (acetate injectable suspension, tablets); dexamethasone (acetate injectable suspension, elixir, oral solution, sodium phosphate injection, tablets); hydrocortisone (cypionate oral suspension, sodium phosphate injection, tablets); methylprednisolone (sodium succinate for injection, tablets); prednisolone (sodium phosphate oral solution, syrup); prednisone (tablets); and triamcinolone (tablets).)

Gastrointestinal disorders:

Colitis, ulcerative (treatment)

(Betamethasone (sodium phosphate and acetate injectable suspension, syrup, tablets); cortisone (acetate injectable suspension, tablets); dexamethasone (acetate injectable suspension, elixir, oral solution, sodium phosphate injection, tablets); hydrocortisone (cypionate oral suspension, sodium phosphate injection, sodium succinate for injection, tablets); methylprednisolone (acetate injectable suspension, sodium succinate for injection, tablets); prednisolone (sodium phosphate oral solution, syrup); prednisone (tablets); and triamcinolone (tablets) are indicated when systemic therapy is required during a critical period of the disease. Long-term use is not recommended.)

Crohn's disease (regional enteritis) (treatment)

(Betamethasone (sodium phosphate and acetate injectable suspension, syrup, tablets); cortisone (acetate injectable suspension, tablets); dexamethasone (acetate injectable suspension, elixir, oral solution, sodium phosphate injection, tablets); hydrocortisone (cypionate oral suspension, sodium phosphate injection, sodium succinate for injection, tablets); methylprednisolone (acetate injectable suspension, sodium succinate for injection, tablets); prednisolone (sodium phosphate oral solution, syrup); prednisone (tablets); and triamcinolone (tablets) are indicated when systemic therapy is required during a critical period of the disease. Long-term use is not recommended.)

(Budesonide (capsules) is indicated for the induction and maintenance of remission in patients with mild to moderate Crohn's disease affecting the ileum and/or the ascending colon.)

[Sprue, refractory (treatment)]
(Betamethasone (tablets).)

Hematologic disorders:

Anemia, hemolytic, acquired (autoimmune) (treatment)
(Betamethasone (sodium phosphate and acetate injectable suspension, syrup, tablets); cortisone (acetate injectable suspension, tablets); dexamethasone (acetate injectable suspension, elixir, oral solution, sodium phosphate injection, tablets); hydrocortisone (cypionate oral suspension, sodium phosphate injection, sodium succinate for injection, tablets); methylprednisolone (acetate injectable suspension, sodium succinate for injection, tablets); prednisolone (sodium phosphate oral solution, syrup); prednisone (tablets); and triamcinolone (tablets).)

Anemia, hypoplastic, congenital (erythroid) (treatment)
(Betamethasone (sodium phosphate and acetate injectable suspension, syrup, tablets); cortisone (acetate injectable suspension, tablets); dexamethasone (acetate injectable suspension, elixir, oral solution, sodium phosphate injection, tablets); hydrocortisone (cypionate oral suspension, sodium phosphate injection, sodium succinate for injection, tablets); methylprednisolone (acetate injectable suspension, sodium succinate for injection, tablets); prednisolone (sodium phosphate oral solution, syrup); prednisone (tablets); and triamcinolone (tablets).)

Anemia, red blood cell (erythroblastopenia) (treatment)
(Betamethasone (sodium phosphate and acetate injectable suspension, syrup, tablets); cortisone (acetate injectable suspension, tablets); dexamethasone (acetate injectable suspension, elixir, oral solution, sodium phosphate injection, tablets); hydrocortisone (cypionate oral suspension, sodium phosphate injection, sodium succinate for injection, tablets); methylprednisolone (acetate injectable suspension, sodium succinate for injection, tablets); prednisolone (sodium phosphate oral solution, syrup); prednisone (tablets); and triamcinolone (tablets).)

Thrombocytopenia, secondary, in adults (treatment)
(Betamethasone (sodium phosphate and acetate injectable suspension, syrup, tablets); cortisone (tablets); dexamethasone (acetate injectable suspension, elixir, oral solution, sodium phosphate injection, tablets); hydrocortisone (cypionate oral suspension, sodium phosphate injection, sodium succinate for injection, tablets); methylprednisolone (acetate injectable suspension, sodium succinate for injection, tablets); prednisolone (sodium phosphate oral solution, syrup); prednisone (tablets); and triamcinolone (tablets).)

Thrombocytopenic purpura, idiopathic, in adults (treatment)
(Betamethasone (syrup, tablets); cortisone (tablets); dexamethasone (elixir, oral solution, sodium phosphate injection, tablets); hydrocortisone (cypionate oral suspension, sodium phosphate injection, sodium succinate for injection, tablets); methylprednisolone (sodium succinate for injection, tablets); prednisolone (sodium phosphate oral solution, syrup); prednisone (tablets); and triamcinolone (tablets).)

[Hemolysis (treatment)][1]
(Betamethasone; cortisone; dexamethasone; hydrocortisone; methylprednisolone; prednisolone; prednisone; and triamcinolone.)

[Hepatic disease][1]—Use is controversial:
[Hepatitis, alcoholic, with encephalopathy (treatment)][1]
[Hepatitis, chronic, active (treatment)][1]
[Hepatitis, nonalcoholic, in women (treatment)][1] and
[Necrosis, hepatic, subacute (treatment)][1]
(Methylprednisolone; prednisolone; and prednisone.)

Inflammatory disorders, nonrheumatic—Indicated during an acute episode or exacerbation. Local injections are preferred when only a few joints or areas are involved:

Bursitis, acute or subacute (treatment)
(Betamethasone (sodium phosphate and acetate injectable suspension, syrup, tablets); cortisone (acetate injectable suspension, tablets); dexamethasone (acetate injectable suspension, elixir, oral solution, sodium phosphate injection, tablets); hydrocortisone (acetate injectable suspension, cypionate oral suspension, sodium phosphate injection, sodium succinate for injection, tablets); methylprednisolone (acetate injectable suspension, sodium succinate for injection, tablets); prednisolone (sodium phosphate oral solution, syrup); prednisone (tablets); and triamcinolone (acetonide injectable suspension, hexacetonide injectable suspension, tablets).)

Epicondylitis (treatment)
(Betamethasone (sodium phosphate and acetate injectable suspension, syrup, tablets); cortisone (acetate injectable suspension, tablets); dexamethasone (acetate injectable suspension, elixir, oral solution, sodium phosphate injection, tablets); hydrocortisone (acetate injectable suspension, cypionate oral suspension, sodium phosphate injection, sodium succinate for injection, tablets); methylprednisolone (acetate injectable suspension, sodium succinate for injection, tablets); prednisolone (sodium phosphate oral solution, syrup); prednisone (tablets); and triamcinolone (acetonide injectable suspension, hexacetonide injectable suspension, tablets).)

Tenosynovitis, acute nonspecific (treatment)
(Betamethasone (sodium phosphate and acetate injectable suspension, syrup, tablets); cortisone (acetate injectable suspension, tablets); dexamethasone (acetate injectable suspension, elixir, oral solution, sodium phosphate injection, tablets); hydrocortisone (acetate injectable suspension, cypionate oral suspension, sodium phosphate injection, sodium succinate for injection, tablets); methylprednisolone (acetate injectable suspension, sodium succinate for injection, tablets); prednisolone (sodium phosphate oral solution, syrup); prednisone (tablets); and triamcinolone (acetonide injectable suspension, hexacetonide injectable suspension, tablets).)

[Fibrositis (treatment)] and
[Myositis (treatment)]
(Betamethasone (sodium phosphate and acetate injectable suspension) and dexamethasone (sodium phosphate injection).)

[Nausea and vomiting, cancer chemotherapy-induced (prophylaxis)]—Dexamethasone (sodium phosphate injection, tablets); [hydrocortisone][1]; and [prednisone][1] are indicated to prevent nausea and vomiting induced by antineoplastic agents. The medication is administered prior to and following each course of chemotherapy. However, the advisability of administering a potent glucocorticoid to a cancer patient, unless indicated for palliation of the disease, has been questioned. Although an increased incidence of infection has not been reported in patients receiving such therapy, the possibility must be considered.

The combination of dexamethasone plus ondansetron has been shown to provide better emetic control over cisplatin-induced emesis than ondansetron alone.

Neoplastic disease—Indicated in conjunction with appropriate specific antineoplastic disease therapy for palliative management:

Leukemia, acute or chronic lymphocytic (treatment)
(Betamethasone (sodium phosphate and acetate injectable suspension, syrup, tablets); cortisone (acetate injectable suspension, tablets); dexamethasone (acetate injectable suspension, elixir, oral solution, sodium phosphate injection, tablets); hydrocortisone (cypionate oral suspension, sodium phosphate injection, sodium succinate for injection, tablets); methylprednisolone (acetate injectable suspension, sodium succinate for injection, tablets); prednisolone (sodium phosphate oral solution, syrup); prednisone (oral solution, tablets); and triamcinolone (tablets).)

Lymphomas, Hodgkin's or non-Hodgkin's (treatment)
(Betamethasone (sodium phosphate and acetate injectable suspension, syrup, tablets); cortisone (acetate injectable suspension, tablets); dexamethasone (acetate injectable suspension, elixir, oral solution, sodium phosphate injection, tablets); hydrocortisone (cypionate oral suspension, sodium phosphate injection, sodium succinate for injection, tablets); methylprednisolone (acetate injectable suspension, sodium succinate for injection, tablets); prednisolone (sodium phosphate oral solution, syrup); prednisone (tablets); and triamcinolone (tablets).)

Waldenström's macroglobulinemia (treatment)
(Prednisone.)

[Carcinoma, breast (treatment)][1]
[Carcinoma, prostatic (treatment)][1]
[Fever, due to malignancy (treatment adjunct)][1]
[Multiple myeloma (treatment)][1] and
[Tumors, brain, primary (treatment adjunct)][1]
(Betamethasone; cortisone; dexamethasone; hydrocortisone; methylprednisolone; prednisolone; prednisone; and triamcinolone.)

Nephrotic syndrome (treatment)—Betamethasone (sodium phosphate and acetate injectable suspension, syrup, tablets); cortisone (acetate injectable suspension, tablets); dexamethasone (acetate injectable suspension, elixir, oral solution, sodium phosphate injection, tablets); hydrocortisone (cypionate oral suspension, sodium phosphate injection, sodium succinate for injection, tablets); methylprednisolone (acetate injectable suspension, sodium succinate for injection, tablets); prednisolone (sodium phosphate oral solution, syrup); prednisone (oral solution, tablets); and triamcinolone (tablets) are indicated to induce diuresis or remission of proteinuria in idiopathic nephrotic syndrome (without uremia), and to improve renal function in patients with lupus erythematosus. In idiopathic nephrotic syndrome, long-term therapy may be required to prevent frequent relapses.

Neurologic disease:

Meningitis, tuberculous (treatment adjunct)

(Betamethasone (sodium phosphate and acetate injectable suspension, syrup, tablets); cortisone (acetate injectable suspension, tablets); dexamethasone (elixir, oral solution, sodium phosphate injection, tablets); hydrocortisone (cypionate oral suspension, sodium phosphate injection, sodium succinate for injection, tablets); methylprednisolone (acetate injectable suspension, sodium succinate for injection, tablets); prednisolone (sodium phosphate oral solution, syrup); prednisone (tablets); and triamcinolone (tablets) are indicated in patients with concurrent or impending subarachnoid block.)

(The corticosteroid should be administered concurrently with appropriate antituberculosis chemotherapy.)

Multiple sclerosis (treatment)

(Dexamethasone (tablets); hydrocortisone (tablets); methylprednisolone (acetate injectable suspension, sodium succinate for injection, tablets); prednisolone (sodium phosphate oral solution, syrup); prednisone (oral solution, tablets); and triamcinolone (tablets) are indicated in acute exacerbations of the disease.)

[Myasthenia gravis (treatment)][1]

(Betamethasone; cortisone; dexamethasone; hydrocortisone; methylprednisolone; prednisolone; prednisone; and triamcinolone are indicated for treatment of severe cases not controlled by antimyasthenic agents alone. Glucocorticoid therapy may be more effective following thymectomy and in patients having disease onset after 40 years of age. Long-term therapy may be required.)

Neurotrauma:

Edema, cerebral, especially when associated with primary or metastatic brain tumor, craniotomy, or head injury ([prophylaxis][1] and treatment)

Dexamethasone (elixir, oral solution, sodium phosphate injection, tablets); methylprednisolone (sodium succinate for injection); and [prednisone][1] are indicated to prevent neurosurgery-associated cerebral edema and to treat edema caused by glioblastomas or metastatic brain tumors. These medications may be less effective in treating edema caused by astrocytomas or meningiomas. Efficacy in closed head injury or ischemic brain edema has not been established. Because very high doses are required, only those glucocorticoids having little or no mineralocorticoid activity should be used.

[Ischemia, cerebral (treatment)][1]

(Dexamethasone.)

[Pseudotumor cerebri (treatment)][1]

(Dexamethasone.)

[Spinal cord injury, acute (treatment)]

(Methylprednisolone (sodium succinate for injection) is indicated in the treatment of spinal cord injury. A large study concluded that patients receiving high-dose methylprednisolone therapy within 8 hours of acute spinal cord injury recover more motor and sensory function, as compared with those receiving naloxone or placebo. However, methylprednisolone did not improve patient prognosis when it was administered more than 8 hours after the spinal cord injury.)

Ophthalmic disorders—Indicated in the treatment of severe acute or chronic allergic and inflammatory ophthalmic conditions:

Chorioretinitis (treatment)

(Betamethasone (sodium phosphate and acetate injectable suspension, syrup, tablets); cortisone (acetate injectable suspension, tablets); dexamethasone (acetate injectable suspension, elixir, oral solution, sodium phosphate injection, tablets); hydrocortisone (cypionate oral suspension, sodium phosphate injection, sodium succinate for injection, tablets); methylprednisolone (acetate injectable suspension, sodium succinate for injection, tablets); prednisolone (sodium phosphate oral solution, syrup); prednisone (tablets); and triamcinolone (tablets).)

Choroiditis, posterior, diffuse (treatment)

(Betamethasone (sodium phosphate and acetate injectable suspension, syrup, tablets); cortisone (acetate injectable suspension, tablets); dexamethasone (acetate injectable suspension, elixir, oral solution, sodium phosphate injection, tablets); hydrocortisone (cypionate oral suspension, sodium phosphate injection, sodium succinate for injection, tablets); methylprednisolone (sodium succinate for injection, tablets); prednisolone (sodium phosphate oral solution, syrup); prednisone (tablets); and triamcinolone (tablets).)

Conjunctivitis, allergic (not controlled topically) (treatment)

(Betamethasone (sodium phosphate and acetate injectable suspension, syrup, tablets); cortisone (acetate injectable suspension, tablets); dexamethasone (acetate injectable suspension, elixir, oral solution, sodium phosphate injection, tablets); hydrocortisone (cypionate oral suspension, sodium phosphate injection, sodium succinate for injection, tablets); methylprednisolone (acetate injectable suspension, sodium succinate for injection, tablets); prednisolone (sodium phosphate oral solution, syrup); prednisone (tablets); and triamcinolone (tablets).)

Herpes zoster ophthalmicus (treatment)

(Betamethasone (sodium phosphate and acetate injectable suspension, syrup, tablets); cortisone (acetate injectable suspension, tablets); dexamethasone (acetate injectable suspension, elixir, oral solution, sodium phosphate injection, tablets); hydrocortisone (cypionate oral suspension, sodium phosphate injection, sodium succinate for injection, tablets); methylprednisolone (acetate injectable suspension, sodium succinate for injection, tablets); prednisolone (sodium phosphate oral solution, syrup); prednisone (tablets); and triamcinolone (tablets).)

Inflammation, anterior segment (treatment)

(Betamethasone (sodium phosphate and acetate injectable suspension, syrup, tablets); cortisone (acetate injectable suspension, tablets); dexamethasone (acetate injectable suspension, elixir, oral solution, sodium phosphate injection, tablets); hydrocortisone (cypionate oral suspension, sodium phosphate injection, sodium succinate for injection, tablets); methylprednisolone (acetate injectable suspension, sodium succinate for injection, tablets); prednisolone (sodium phosphate oral solution, syrup); prednisone (tablets); and triamcinolone (tablets).)

Iridocyclitis (treatment)

(Betamethasone (sodium phosphate and acetate injectable suspension, syrup, tablets); cortisone (acetate injectable suspension, tablets); dexamethasone (acetate injectable suspension, elixir, oral solution, sodium phosphate injection, tablets); hydrocortisone (cypionate oral suspension, sodium phosphate injection, sodium succinate for injection, tablets); methylprednisolone (acetate injectable suspension, sodium succinate for injection, tablets); prednisolone (sodium phosphate oral solution, syrup); prednisone (tablets); and triamcinolone (tablets).)

Iritis (treatment)

(Betamethasone (sodium phosphate and acetate injectable suspension, syrup, tablets); cortisone (acetate injectable suspension, tablets); dexamethasone (acetate injectable suspension, elixir, oral solution, sodium phosphate injection, tablets); hydrocortisone (cypionate oral suspension, sodium phosphate injection, sodium succinate for injection, tablets); methylprednisolone (acetate injectable suspension, sodium succinate for injection, tablets); prednisolone (sodium phosphate oral solution, syrup); prednisone (tablets); and triamcinolone (tablets).)

Keratitis (not associated with herpes simplex or fungal infection) (treatment)

(Betamethasone (sodium phosphate and acetate injectable suspension, syrup, tablets); cortisone (acetate injectable suspension, tablets); dexamethasone (acetate injectable suspension, elixir, oral solution, sodium phosphate injection, tablets); hydrocortisone (cypionate oral suspension, sodium phosphate injection, sodium succinate for injection, tablets); methylprednisolone (acetate injectable suspension, sodium succinate for injection, tablets); prednisolone (sodium phosphate oral solution, syrup); prednisone (tablets); and triamcinolone (tablets).)

Neuritis, optic (treatment)

(Betamethasone (sodium phosphate and acetate injectable suspension, syrup, tablets); cortisone (acetate injectable suspension, tablets); dexamethasone (acetate injectable suspension, elixir, oral solution, sodium phosphate injection, tablets); hydrocortisone (cypionate oral suspension, sodium phosphate injection, sodium succinate for injection, tablets); methylprednisolone (acetate injectable suspension, sodium succinate for injection, tablets); prednisolone (sodium phosphate oral solution, syrup); prednisone (tablets); and triamcinolone (tablets).)

Ophthalmia, sympathetic (treatment)

(Betamethasone (sodium phosphate and acetate injectable suspension, syrup, tablets); cortisone (acetate injectable suspension, tablets); dexamethasone (acetate injectable suspension, elixir, oral solution, sodium phosphate injection, tablets); hydrocortisone (cypionate oral suspension, sodium phosphate injection, sodium succinate for injection, tablets); methylprednisolone (sodium succinate for injection, tablets); prednisolone (sodium phosphate oral solution, syrup); prednisone (tablets); and triamcinolone (tablets).)

Ulcers, allergic, corneal marginal (treatment)

(Betamethasone (sodium phosphate and acetate injectable suspension, syrup, tablets); cortisone (acetate injectable suspension, tablets); dexamethasone (acetate injectable suspension, elixir, oral solution, sodium phosphate injection, tablets); hydrocortisone (cypionate oral suspension, sodium phosphate injection, sodium succinate for injection, tablets); methylprednisolone (acetate injectable suspension, sodium succinate for injection, tablets); prednisolone (sodium phosphate oral solution, syrup); prednisone (tablets); and triamcinolone (tablets).)

Uveitis, posterior, diffuse (treatment)

(Betamethasone (sodium phosphate and acetate injectable suspension, syrup, tablets); cortisone (acetate injectable suspension, tablets); dexamethasone (acetate injectable suspension, elixir, oral solution, sodium phosphate injection, tablets); hydrocortisone (cypionate oral suspension, sodium phosphate injection, sodium succinate for injection, tablets); methylprednisolone (acetate injectable suspension, sodium succinate for injection, tablets); prednisolone (sodium phosphate oral solution, syrup); prednisone (tablets); and triamcinolone (tablets).)

[Neuritis, retrobulbar (treatment)]

(Betamethasone (tablets); and dexamethasone (sodium phosphate injection).)

Oral disorders—Indicated for treatment of oral lesions unresponsive to topical therapy. The presence of an oral herpetic lesion must be ruled out prior to initiation of glucocorticoid therapy:

[Gingivitis, desquamative (treatment)][1]

(Betamethasone; cortisone; dexamethasone; hydrocortisone; methylprednisolone; prednisolone; prednisone; and triamcinolone are indicated when the diagnosis is confirmed via immunofluorescent biopsy assay.)

[Inflammatory reactions, postoperative, dental (treatment)]

(Betamethasone (tablets).)

[Lesions, oral, associated with corticosteroid-responsive disorders, such as discoid lupus erythematosus; erythema multiforme, severe (Stevens-Johnson syndrome); lichen planus; pemphigoid; pemphigus; and systemic lupus erythematosus (treatment)][1] and

[Stomatitis, aphthous, recurrent (treatment)][1]

(Betamethasone; cortisone; dexamethasone; hydrocortisone; methylprednisolone; prednisolone; prednisone; and triamcinolone.)

[Pericarditis (treatment)][1]—Betamethasone; cortisone; dexamethasone; hydrocortisone; methylprednisolone; prednisolone; prednisone; and triamcinolone are indicated to relieve fever and inflammation.

[Polyps, nasal (treatment)][1]—Betamethasone; dexamethasone; methylprednisolone; prednisolone; prednisone; and triamcinolone.

Respiratory disorders—Indicated in the treatment [and prophylaxis][1] of respiratory disorders. Prophylactic uses include administration prior to or during extracorporeal circulation in heart surgery if the patient has a pre-existing pulmonary disorder, and administration prior to, during, and following oral, facial, or neck surgery to prevent edema that may threaten the airway:

Asthma, bronchial (treatment)

(Betamethasone (sodium phosphate and acetate injectable suspension, syrup, tablets); cortisone (acetate injectable suspension, tablets); dexamethasone (acetate injectable suspension, elixir, oral solution, sodium phosphate injection, tablets); hydrocortisone (cypionate oral suspension, sodium phosphate injection, sodium succinate for injection, tablets); methylprednisolone (acetate injectable suspension, sodium succinate for injection, tablets); prednisolone (sodium phosphate oral solution, syrup); prednisone (tablets); and triamcinolone (tablets).)

Berylliosis (treatment)

(Betamethasone (sodium phosphate and acetate injectable suspension, syrup, tablets); cortisone (acetate injectable suspension, tablets); dexamethasone (acetate injectable suspension, elixir, oral solution, sodium phosphate injection, tablets); hydrocortisone (cypionate oral suspension, sodium phosphate injection, sodium succinate for injection, tablets); methylprednisolone (acetate injectable suspension, sodium succinate for injection, tablets); prednisolone (sodium phosphate oral solution, syrup); prednisone (tablets); and triamcinolone (tablets).)

[Croup (treatment)][1]

(Dexamethasone is indicated for the treatment of croup in children. Studies have indicated that treatment with dexamethasone may increase the rate of discharge from the hospital emergency department and shorten hospitalization.)

Löeffler's syndrome (eosinophilic pneumonitis or hypereosinophilic syndrome) (treatment)

(Betamethasone (sodium phosphate and acetate injectable suspension, syrup, tablets); cortisone (acetate injectable suspension, tablets); dexamethasone (acetate injectable suspension, elixir, oral solution, sodium phosphate injection, tablets); hydrocortisone (cypionate oral suspension, sodium phosphate injection, sodium succinate for injection, tablets); methylprednisolone (acetate injectable suspension, sodium succinate for injection, tablets); prednisolone (sodium phosphate oral solution, syrup); prednisone (tablets); and triamcinolone (tablets).)

Pneumonitis, aspiration (treatment)

(Betamethasone (sodium phosphate and acetate injectable suspension, syrup, tablets); cortisone (acetate injectable suspension, tablets); dexamethasone (acetate injectable suspension, elixir, oral solution, sodium phosphate injection, tablets); hydrocortisone (cypionate oral suspension, sodium phosphate injection, sodium succinate for injection, tablets); methylprednisolone (acetate injectable suspension, sodium succinate for injection, tablets); prednisolone (sodium phosphate oral solution, syrup); prednisone (tablets); and triamcinolone (tablets).)

Sarcoidosis, symptomatic (treatment)

(Betamethasone (sodium phosphate and acetate injectable suspension, syrup, tablets); cortisone (acetate injectable suspension, tablets); dexamethasone (acetate injectable suspension, elixir, oral solution, sodium phosphate injection, tablets); hydrocortisone (cypionate oral suspension, sodium phosphate injection, sodium succinate for injection, tablets); methylprednisolone (acetate injectable suspension, sodium succinate for injection, tablets); prednisolone (sodium phosphate oral solution, syrup); prednisone (tablets); and triamcinolone (tablets).)

Tuberculosis, pulmonary, disseminated or fulminating (treatment adjunct)

(Betamethasone (sodium phosphate and acetate injectable suspension, syrup, tablets); cortisone (acetate injectable suspension, tablets); dexamethasone (elixir, oral solution, sodium phosphate injection, tablets); hydrocortisone (cypionate oral suspension, sodium phosphate injection, sodium succinate for injection, tablets); methylprednisolone (acetate injectable suspension, sodium succinate for injection, tablets); prednisolone (sodium phosphate oral solution, syrup); prednisone (oral solution, tablets); and triamcinolone (tablets) are indicated as adjuncts in the treatment of tuberculosis. The corticosteroid should be administered concurrently with appropriate antituberculosis chemotherapy.)

[Bronchitis, asthmatic, acute or chronic (treatment)][1] and

[Pulmonary disease, chronic obstructive (not controlled with theophylline and beta-adrenergic agonists) (treatment)]

(Betamethasone; cortisone; dexamethasone; hydrocortisone; methylprednisolone; prednisolone; prednisone; and triamcinolone.)

[Edema, pulmonary, noncardiogenic (protamine sensitivity–induced) (treatment)][1] and

[Hemangioma, airway-obstructing, in infants (treatment)][1]

(Betamethasone; cortisone; dexamethasone; hydrocortisone; methylprednisolone; prednisolone; prednisone; and triamcinolone are indicated in the treatment of noncardiogenic pulmonary edema and airway-obstructing hemangioma in infants. Treatment should be initiated with intramuscular or intravenous administration of a rapid-acting preparation.)

[Emphysema, pulmonary (treatment)]

(Betamethasone (tablets) and triamcinolone (tablets) are indicated in the treatment of pulmonary emphysema when bronchospasm or bronchial edema plays a significant role.)

[Fibrosis, idiopathic pulmonary (Hamman-Rich syndrome) (treatment)]

(Betamethasone (tablets) and triamcinolone (tablets).)

[Pneumonia, *Pneumocystis carinii*, associated with acquired immunodeficiency syndrome (AIDS) (treatment adjunct)][1]

(In a small number of studies, early use of corticosteroids (e.g., corticosteroid therapy begun within 24 to 72 hours of initial anti-pneumocystis therapy) as an adjunct to specific antipneumocystis therapy was shown to significantly reduce the risk of oxygenation deterioration, respiratory failure, and death in patients being treated for moderate-to-severe AIDS-associated pneumocystis pneumonia. The corticosteroids used in these studies were prednisone and intravenous methylprednisolone. No improvement in clinical outcome was shown in another study when adjunctive corticosteroid therapy was begun after the onset of respiratory failure and after the initiation of primary pneumocystis therapy. Therefore if adjunctive corticosteroid is used, it should be started at the initiation of primary therapy for pneumocystis pneumonia in adults and children older than 13 years of age who have documented or suspected human immunodeficiency virus (HIV) infection and documented or suspected pneumocystis pneumonia, accompanied by moderate-to-severe pulmonary dysfunction ($PaO_2 < 70$ mm Hg on room air or A-a gradient > 35 mm Hg). The diagnosis of HIV infection and pneumocystis pneumonia should be confirmed as soon as possible.)

[Respiratory distress syndrome, adult (treatment)][1]

(Dexamethasone is indicated in the treatment of respiratory distress syndrome in adults, especially those with post-traumatic pulmonary insufficiency or burns, and during or following massive blood transfusions. However, the benefit of such treatment has not been established.)

[Respiratory distress syndrome, neonatal (prophylaxis)]

(Betamethasone[1]; dexamethasone (sodium phosphate injection); and hydrocortisone[1] are indicated to reduce the incidence and severity of respiratory distress syndrome (hyaline membrane disease) in premature neonates. The medication is administered to the pregnant woman, preferably 24 to 48 hours prior to delivery, to allow time for it to produce an effect. Corticosteroids are not effective when delivery is imminent. If necessary, ritodrine may be administered to delay delivery. If delivery does not occur within several days to 1 week following corticosteroid administration, but the risk of premature delivery persists, administration of a second course of corticosteroid therapy may be necessary. Corticosteroids are not effective in the treatment of respiratory distress syndrome in the premature neonate.)

[Status asthmaticus (treatment)]

(Betamethasone (sodium phosphate and acetate injectable suspension, tablets); cortisone[1]; dexamethasone (sodium phosphate injection); hydrocortisone (sodium succinate for injection); methylprednisolone (sodium succinate for injection); prednisolone[1]; and triamcinolone[1] are indicated in the treatment of status asthmaticus. Treatment should be initiated with intramuscular or intravenous administration of a rapid-acting preparation.)

Rheumatic disorders—Indicated as adjunctive therapy during an acute episode or exacerbation. Local injections are preferred when only a few joints or areas are involved:

Ankylosing spondylitis (treatment)

(Betamethasone (sodium phosphate and acetate injectable suspension, syrup, tablets); cortisone (acetate injectable suspension, tablets); dexamethasone (acetate injectable suspension, elixir, oral solution, sodium phosphate injection, tablets); hydrocortisone (cypionate oral suspension, sodium phosphate injection, sodium succinate for injection, tablets); methylprednisolone (acetate injectable suspension, sodium succinate for injection, tablets); prednisolone (sodium phosphate oral solution, syrup); prednisone (tablets); and triamcinolone (tablets).)

Arthritis, gouty, acute (treatment)

(Betamethasone (sodium phosphate and acetate injectable suspension, syrup, tablets); cortisone (acetate injectable suspension, tablets); dexamethasone (acetate injectable suspension, elixir, oral solution, sodium phosphate injection, tablets); hydrocortisone (acetate injectable suspension, cypionate oral suspension, sodium phosphate injection, sodium succinate for injection, tablets); methylprednisolone (sodium succinate for injection, tablets); prednisolone (acetate injectable suspension, sodium phosphate oral solution, syrup); prednisone (tablets); and triamcinolone (acetonide injectable suspension, hexacetonide injectable suspension, tablets).)

Arthritis, psoriatic (treatment)

(Betamethasone (sodium phosphate and acetate injectable suspension, syrup, tablets); cortisone (acetate injectable suspension, tablets); dexamethasone (acetate injectable suspension, elixir, oral solution, sodium phosphate injection, tablets); hydrocortisone (cypionate oral suspension, sodium phosphate injection, sodium succinate for injection, tablets); methylprednisolone (acetate injectable suspension, sodium succinate for injection, tablets); prednisolone (sodium phosphate oral solution, syrup); prednisone (tablets); and triamcinolone (tablets).)

Arthritis, rheumatoid (including juvenile arthritis) (treatment)

(Betamethasone (sodium phosphate and acetate injectable suspension, syrup, tablets); cortisone (acetate injectable suspension, tablets); dexamethasone (acetate injectable suspension, elixir, oral solution, sodium phosphate injection, tablets); hydrocortisone (acetate injectable suspension, cypionate oral suspension, sodium phosphate injection, sodium succinate for injection, tablets); methylprednisolone (sodium succinate for injection, tablets); prednisolone (sodium phosphate oral solution, syrup); prednisone (tablets); and triamcinolone (acetonide injectable suspension, hexacetonide injectable suspension, tablets).)

([Long-term use is controversial. It is recommended that such treatment be reserved for patients not responsive to other measures, such as aspirin or other nonsteroidal anti-inflammatory drugs, rest, and physical therapy.][1])

Osteoarthritis, post-traumatic (treatment)

(Betamethasone (sodium phosphate and acetate injectable suspension, syrup, tablets); cortisone (acetate injectable suspension, tablets); dexamethasone (acetate injectable suspension, elixir, oral solution, sodium phosphate injection, tablets); hydrocortisone (acetate injectable suspension, cypionate oral suspension, sodium phosphate injection, sodium succinate for injection, tablets); methylprednisolone (acetate injectable suspension, sodium succinate for injection, tablets); prednisolone (sodium phosphate oral solution, syrup); prednisone (tablets); and triamcinolone (acetonide injectable suspension, hexacetonide injectable suspension).)

Polymyalgia rheumatica (treatment)

(Methylprednisolone (tablets); and prednisone (tablets).)

Synovitis of osteoarthritis (treatment)

(Betamethasone (sodium phosphate and acetate injectable suspension, syrup, tablets); cortisone (acetate injectable suspension, tablets); dexamethasone (acetate injectable suspension, elixir, oral solution, sodium phosphate injection, tablets); hydrocortisone (acetate injectable suspension, cypionate oral suspension, sodium phosphate injection, sodium succinate for injection, tablets); methylprednisolone (acetate injectable suspension, sodium succinate for injection, tablets); prednisolone (sodium phosphate oral solution, syrup); prednisone (tablets); and triamcinolone (acetonide injectable suspension, hexacetonide injectable suspension, tablets).)

[Calcium pyrophosphate deposition disease, acute (chondrocalcinosis articularis; pseudogout; synovitis, crystal-induced) (treatment)][1] and

[Reiter's disease (treatment)][1]

(Betamethasone; cortisone; dexamethasone; hydrocortisone; methylprednisolone; prednisolone; prednisone; and triamcinolone.)

[Rheumatic fever (treatment)]

(Betamethasone[1]; cortisone[1]; dexamethasone[1]; hydrocortisone[1]; methylprednisolone (sodium succinate for injection); prednisolone[1]; prednisone[1]; and triamcinolone (tablets) are indicated in the treatment of rheumatic fever, especially if carditis is present.)

Shock (treatment)—Betamethasone (sodium phosphate and acetate injectable suspension); cortisone (acetate injectable suspension, tablets); dexamethasone (sodium phosphate injection); hydrocortisone (sodium phosphate injection, sodium succinate for injection); and methylprednisolone (sodium succinate for injection) are indicated in the treatment of shock caused by adrenocortical insufficiency (Addisonian shock).

Corticosteroids also are indicated as adjuncts in the treatment of shock associated with anaphylactic or anaphylactoid reactions. Treatment should be initiated with intramuscular or intravenous administration of a rapid-acting preparation.

[Intravenous corticosteroids are being used as adjuncts in the treatment of septic shock. Such use is very controversial because efficacy has not been established and superimposition of new infections has been reported. Specifically, methylprednisolone has been shown to be ineffective and hazardous in the treatment of septic shock and is not recommended.]

[Transplant rejection, organ (prophylaxis and treatment)]—Betamethasone[1]; cortisone[1]; dexamethasone[1]; hydrocortisone[1]; methylprednisolone (sodium succinate for injection, tablets); prednisolone[1]; prednisone[1]; and triamcinolone[1] are indicated concurrently with other immunosuppressants such as azathioprine or cyclosporine to reduce the risk of rejection of transplanted organs.

[High doses of rapidly acting corticosteroids are indicated in the treatment of rejection reactions.][1]

Trichinosis (treatment)—Betamethasone (sodium phosphate and acetate injectable suspension, syrup, tablets); cortisone (acetate injectable suspension, tablets); dexamethasone (acetate injectable suspension, elixir, oral solution, sodium phosphate injection, tablets); hydrocortisone (cypionate oral suspension, sodium phosphate injection, sodium succinate for injection, tablets); methylprednisolone (acetate injectable suspension, sodium succinate for injection, tablets); prednisolone (sodium phosphate oral solution, syrup); prednisone (tablets); and triamcinolone (tablets) are indicated in the treatment of trichinosis with neurological or myocardial involvement.

Tumors, cystic, of an aponeurosis or tendon (ganglia) (treatment)—Dexamethasone (acetate injectable suspension, sodium phosphate injection); hydrocortisone (acetate injectable suspension); and methylprednisolone (acetate injectable suspension).

Acceptance not established

There is currently not enough medical literature or clinical experience to recommend the use of prednisone for the treatment of *edema associated with brain cancer*.

There is not enough medical literature or clinical experience to recommend the use of systemic corticosteroids for the treatment of *respiratory syncytial virus bronchiolitis*

[1]Not included in Canadian product labeling.

Pharmacology/Pharmacokinetics

See *Table 1*, page 963.
See *Table 2*, page 963.

Physicochemical characteristics

Molecular weight—
- Betamethasone—392.47
- Budesonide—430.54
- Cortisone acetate—402.49
- Dexamethasone—392.47
- Hydrocortisone—362.47
- Methylprednisolone—374.48
- Prednisolone—360.45 (anhydrous); 387.47 (sesquihydrate)
- Prednisone—358.44
- Triamcinolone—394.44

Mechanism of action/Effect

Corticosteroids diffuse across cell membranes and complex with specific cytoplasmic receptors. These complexes then enter the cell nucleus, bind to DNA, and stimulate transcription of messenger RNA (mRNA) and subsequent protein synthesis of various enzymes thought to be ultimately responsible for two categories of effects of systemic corticosteroids. However, these agents may suppress transcription of mRNA in some cells (e.g., lymphocytes).

For glucocorticoid effects—

Anti-inflammatory (steroidal)—Glucocorticoids decrease or prevent tissue responses to inflammatory processes, thereby reducing development of symptoms of inflammation without affecting the underlying cause. Glucocorticoids inhibit accumulation of inflammatory cells, including macrophages and leukocytes, at sites of inflammation. They also inhibit phagocytosis, lysosomal enzyme release, and synthesis and/or release of several chemical mediators of inflammation. Although the exact mechanisms are not completely understood, actions that may contribute significantly to these effects include blockade of the action of macrophage inhibitory factor (MIF), leading to inhibition of macrophage localization; reduction of dilatation and permeability of inflamed capillaries and reduction of leukocyte adherence to the capillary endothelium, leading to inhibition of both leukocyte migration and edema formation; and increased synthesis of lipomodulin (macrocortin), an inhibitor of phospholipase A_2–mediated arachidonic acid release from membrane phospholipids, with subsequent inhibition of the synthesis of arachidonic acid-derived mediators of inflammation (prostaglandins, thromboxanes, and leukotrienes). Immunosuppressant actions also may contribute significantly to the anti-inflammatory effect.

Immunosuppressant—Mechanisms of immunosuppressant action are not completely understood but may involve prevention or suppression of cell-mediated (delayed hypersensitivity) immune reactions as well as more specific actions affecting the immune response. Glucocorticoids reduce the concentration of thymus-dependent lymphocytes (T-lymphocytes), monocytes, and eosinophils. They also decrease binding of immunoglobulin to cell surface receptors and inhibit the synthesis and/or release of interleukins, thereby decreasing T-lymphocyte blastogenesis and reducing expansion of the primary immune response. Glucocorticoids also may decrease passage of immune complexes through basement membranes and decrease concentrations of complement components and immunoglobulins.

For mineralocorticoid effects—

Water and electrolyte balance: Sodium reabsorption, and potassium and hydrogen excretion, along with subsequent water retention, are mediated through an action of mineralocorticoids on the area of the renal distal tubule that facilitates sodium transport. Cation transport in other secretory cells is similarly affected. Excretion of water and electrolytes by the large intestine and by salivary and sweat glands also is altered, but to a lesser extent. Only cortisone and hydrocortisone have clinically useful mineralocorticoid activity.

For specific indications—

Congenital adrenal hyperplasia: Glucocorticoids inhibit corticotropin (adrenocorticotropic hormone [ACTH]) secretion, leading to suppression of adrenal hypersecretion of androgens responsible for the androgenism associated with various enzyme deficiencies.

Hypercalcemia: Glucocorticoids reduce plasma calcium concentration by decreasing gastrointestinal absorption of calcium, probably by interfering with intestinal calcium transport (by decreasing the effect of vitamin D), and increasing calcium excretion.

Respiratory distress syndrome prophylaxis: Glucocorticoids may induce enzymes that accelerate or increase production of lung surfactant by type 2 pneumonocytes.

Other actions/effects

Pharmacologic (supraphysiologic) doses of exogenous corticosteroids produce hypothalamic-pituitary-adrenal (HPA) axis suppression via a negative feedback mechanism, i.e., they inhibit pituitary ACTH secretion, thereby reducing ACTH-mediated production of corticosteroids and androgens in the adrenal cortex. The development of adrenocortical insufficiency and the time required for recovery of adrenal function depend primarily on the duration of corticosteroid therapy and, to a lesser extent, on dosage, timing, and frequency of administration, as well as on the potency and biologic (tissue) half-life of the specific agent. Adrenal insufficiency may occur in approximately 5 to 7 days with daily administration of doses equivalent to 20 to 30 mg of prednisone or in up to 30 days with lower doses. Following discontinuation of short-term (up to 5 days) high-dose use, adrenal recovery may occur within 1 week. Following prolonged high-dose use, complete recovery of adrenal function may require up to 1 year and, in some patients, may never occur.

Glucocorticoids stimulate protein catabolism and induce enzymes responsible for metabolism of amino acids. They decrease synthesis and increase degradation of protein in lymphoid tissue, connective tissue, muscle, and skin. With prolonged use, atrophy of these tissues may occur.

Glucocorticoids increase glucose availability by inducing hepatic enzymes involved in gluconeogenesis, stimulating protein catabolism (which increases hepatic concentrations of amino acids required for gluconeogenesis), and decreasing peripheral utilization of glucose. These actions lead to increased hepatic glycogen storage, increased blood glucose concentrations, and insulin resistance.

Glucocorticoids increase lipolysis and mobilize fatty acids from adipose tissues, leading to increased plasma fatty acid concentrations. With prolonged use, an abnormal redistribution of fat may occur.

Glucocorticoids decrease bone formation and increase bone resorption. They reduce plasma calcium concentration, leading to secondary hyperparathyroidism and subsequent stimulation of osteoclasts, and directly inhibit osteoblasts. These actions, together with a decrease in the protein matrix of bone secondary to increased protein catabolism, may lead to inhibition of bone growth in children and adolescents and the development of osteoporosis at any age.

Absorption

Oral—
- Rapidly and almost completely absorbed.

Parenteral—
- Intramuscular:
  - Freely soluble esters (sodium phosphate, sodium succinate)—Rapidly absorbed.
  - Poorly soluble derivatives (acetate, acetonide, diacetate, hexacetonide, tebutate)—Slowly but completely absorbed.
- Local:
  - Freely soluble esters—Less rapidly absorbed than with intramuscular injection.
  - Poorly soluble derivatives—Slowly but completely absorbed.

Biotransformation

Primarily hepatic (rapid); also renal and tissue; mostly to inactive metabolites. Cortisone and prednisone are inactive until metabolized to the active metabolites hydrocortisone and prednisolone, respectively. Fluorinated corticosteroids are metabolized more slowly than other members of the group.

Duration of action

Duration of action depends upon the route/site of administration, solubility of the dosage form, dose administered, and the condition being treated. Following oral or intravenous administration, the duration of action depends upon the biological (tissue) half-life. Following intramuscular administration, the duration of action depends upon the solubility of the dosage form as well as the biological (tissue) half-life. Following local injections, the duration of action depends upon the solubility of the dosage form and the specific route/site of administration.

Elimination

Primarily by renal excretion of inactive metabolites.

Precautions to Consider

Pregnancy/Reproduction

Fertility—Corticosteroids have been reported to increase or decrease the number or motility of spermatozoa. However, it is not known whether reproductive capacity in humans is adversely affected.

Pregnancy—
For corticosteroids—
Corticosteroids cross the placenta. Although adequate studies have not been done in humans, there is some evidence that pharmacologic doses of corticosteroids may increase the risk of placental insufficiency, decreased birthweight, or stillbirth. However, teratogenic effects in humans have not been confirmed.

Prenatal administration of betamethasone or dexamethasone to the pregnant woman to prevent respiratory distress syndrome in the premature neonate has not been shown to affect the child's growth or development adversely. Physiologic replacement doses of corticosteroids administered for treatment of maternal adrenal insufficiency also are unlikely to adversely affect the fetus or neonate.

Studies in animals have shown that corticosteroids increase the incidence of cleft palate, placental insufficiency, spontaneous abortions, and intrauterine growth retardation.

FDA Pregnancy Category C (Dexamethasone, Prednisolone).

For budesonide—
High doses of budesonide administered subcutaneously produced fetal malformations (primarily skeletal defects) in rabbits, rats, and mice. However, the relevance of these findings to humans has not been established.

Breast-feeding

For corticosteroids—Problems in humans have not been documented. Administration of physiologic doses or low pharmacologic doses (the equivalent or less of 25 mg of cortisone or 5 mg of prednisone per day) is not considered likely to affect the infant adversely. Less than 1% of the administered dose of prednisolone is distributed into breast milk. However, breast-feeding during the use of higher pharmacologic doses is not recommended because corticosteroids are distributed into breast milk and may cause unwanted effects, such as growth suppression and inhibition of endogenous steroid production, in the infant.

Pediatrics

Infants born to women who have received substantial doses of corticosteroids during pregnancy should be carefully observed for signs of hypoadrenalism and replacement therapy should be administered as required.

Because infections such as chickenpox or measles may be more serious (or even fatal) in children receiving immunosuppressant doses of corticosteroids, extra care to avoid exposure to these infections is recommended. Prophylactic therapy with varicella zoster immune globulin (VZIG) or immune globulin intravenous (IGIV) or intramuscular (IGIM), as appropriate, may be indicated in exposed patients. Therapy with an antiviral agent may be indicated if chickenpox develops.

Chronic use of corticosteroids may suppress growth and development of the pediatric or adolescent patient and should be undertaken with caution. Use of long-acting glucocorticoids (betamethasone and dexamethasone) or daily doses of any corticosteroid that are larger than replacement therapy doses are especially likely to inhibit growth and are not recommended for any form of chronic therapy. For long-term therapy, a short-acting agent (cortisone or hydrocortisone) or an intermediate-acting agent (methylprednisolone, prednisolone, prednisone, or triamcinolone) is recommended. Alternate-day therapy with an oral intermediate-acting corticosteroid may decrease growth retardation effects. Some clinicians recommend that only cortisone, hydrocortisone, or prednisone be used for long-term replacement therapy. Also, pediatric patients may be at increased risk of developing osteoporosis, avascular necrosis of the femoral heads, glaucoma, or cataracts during prolonged therapy. Children and adolescents receiving prolonged therapy should be closely monitored.

Pediatric dosage is determined more by the severity of the condition and the response of the patient than by age or body weight. Also, for treatment of adrenocortical insufficiency, pediatric dosage is preferably determined in terms of mg per square meter of body surface area. Determination of pediatric dosage in terms of mg per kg of body weight (mg/kg) increases the possibility of overdosage, especially in very young, short, or heavy children.

Geriatrics

Geriatric patients may be more likely to develop hypertension during corticosteroid therapy. Geriatric patients, especially postmenopausal women, also may be more likely to develop glucocorticoid-induced osteoporosis that appear to be dose related. Bone mineral density losses appear to be greatest early on in treatment course and may recover over time after steroid withdrawal or use of lower doses (i.e., prednisolone ≤5 mg per day). Higher doses have been associated with an increased relative risk of both vertebral and nonvertebral fractures even in the presence of higher bone density. Routine screening of geriatric patients should be performed to minimize these complications.

Dose selection for an elderly patient should be cautious, usually starting at the low end of the dosing range, reflecting the greater frequency of decreased hepatic, renal, or cardiac function, and of concomitant disease or other drug therapy. It may also be useful to monitor renal function.

Drug interactions and/or related problems

The following drug interactions and/or related problems have been selected on the basis of their potential clinical significance (possible mechanism in parentheses where appropriate)—not necessarily inclusive (» = major clinical significance):

See also *Laboratory value alterations*.

Note: Combinations containing any of the following medications, depending on the amount present, also may interact with this medication.

Interactions listed below involving alterations in serum potassium concentration and/or changes in sodium or fluid balance are especially likely to occur with corticosteroids having significant mineralocorticoid activity. However, these interactions also may occur with other corticosteroids, depending on dosage and patient predisposition.

Acetaminophen
(induction of hepatic enzymes by corticosteroids may increase the formation of a hepatotoxic acetaminophen metabolite, thereby increasing the risk of hepatotoxicity, when they are used concurrently with chronic or high-dose acetaminophen therapy)

Alcohol or
Anti-inflammatory drugs, nonsteroidal (NSAIDs)
(risk of gastrointestinal ulceration or hemorrhage may be increased when these substances are used concurrently with glucocorticoids; however, concurrent use of NSAIDs in the treatment of arthritis may provide additive therapeutic benefit and permit glucocorticoid dosage reduction)

» Aminoglutethimide
(aminoglutethimide suppresses adrenal function so that glucocorticoid supplementation may be required; however, aminoglutethimide accelerates the metabolism of dexamethasone so that the half-life of dexamethasone may be reduced twofold; hydrocortisone is recommended instead because its metabolism is not known to be altered by aminoglutethimide and because its mineralocorticoid activity also may be required)

» Amphotericin B, parenteral or
Carbonic anhydrase inhibitors
(concurrent use with corticosteroids may result in severe hypokalemia and should be undertaken with caution; serum potassium concentrations and cardiac function should be monitored during concurrent use)
(the use of hydrocortisone to control adverse reactions to amphotericin B has resulted in cases of cardiac enlargement and congestive heart failure)
(concurrent use of corticosteroids with acetazolamide sodium may increase the risk of hypernatremia and/or edema because corticosteroids cause sodium and fluid retention; the risk with corticosteroids may depend on the patient's sodium requirement as determined by the condition being treated)
(the possibility should be considered that concurrent chronic use of both carbonic anhydrase inhibitors and corticosteroids may increase the risk of hypocalcemia and osteoporosis because carbonic anhydrase inhibitors also increase calcium excretion)

Anabolic steroids or
Androgens
(concurrent use with glucocorticoids may increase the risk of edema; also, concurrent use may promote the development of severe acne)

» Antacids
(concurrent chronic use with prednisone or dexamethasone may decrease absorption of these glucocorticoids; efficacy may be decreased sufficiently to require dosage adjustment in patients receiving small doses, but probably not in those receiving large doses, of the corticosteroid)

» Antibiotics, macrolide
(reported to cause a significant decrease in corticosteroid clearance)

» Anticholinesterases
(concomitant use of corticosteroids and anticholinesterase agents may produce severe weakness in patients with myasthenia gravis;

anticholinesterase agents should be withdrawn at least 24 hours before initiating corticosteroid therapy)

Anticholinergics, especially atropine and related compounds
(concurrent long-term use with glucocorticoids may increase intraocular pressure)

Anticoagulants, coumarin- or indanedione-derivative or
Heparin or
Streptokinase or
Urokinase
(effects of coumarin or indanedione derivatives usually are decreased [but may be increased in some patients] when these medications are used concurrently with glucocorticoids; dosage adjustments based on prothrombin time determinations may be necessary during and after glucocorticoid therapy)

(the potential occurrence of gastrointestinal ulceration or hemorrhage during glucocorticoid therapy, and the effects of glucocorticoids on vascular integrity, may cause increased risk to patients receiving anticoagulant or thrombolytic therapy)

Antidepressants, tricyclic
(these medications do not relieve, and may exacerbate, corticosteroid-induced mental disturbances; they should not be used for treatment of these adverse effects)

» Antidiabetic agents, oral or
» Insulin
(glucocorticoids may increase blood glucose concentration; dosage adjustment of one or both agents may be necessary during concurrent use; dosage readjustment of the hypoglycemic agent also may be required when glucocorticoid therapy is discontinued)

Antithyroid agents or
Thyroid hormones
(changes in the thyroid status of the patient that may occur as a result of administration, changes in dosage, or discontinuation of thyroid hormones or antithyroid agents may necessitate adjustment of corticosteroid dosage because metabolic clearance of corticosteroids is decreased in hypothyroid patients and increased in hyperthyroid patients; dosage adjustment should be based on results of thyroid function tests)

Asparaginase
(glucocorticoids, especially prednisone, may increase the hyperglycemic effect of asparaginase and the risk of neuropathy and disturbances in erythropoiesis; the toxicity appears to be less pronounced when asparaginase is administered following, rather than before or with, these medications)

Carbamazepine or
Ephedrine or
Phenobarbital or
Phenytoin or
Rifampin
(concurrent use may increase the metabolic clearance of corticosteroids; corticosteroid dosage adjustment may be required during and following concurrent use)

(concomitant use of dexamethasone and phenytoin may result in alterations in seizure control; both increases and decreases in phenytoin levels have been reported in post-marketing experience)

Contraceptives, oral, estrogen-containing or
Estrogens
(estrogens may alter the metabolism and protein binding of glucocorticoids, leading to decreased clearance, increased elimination half-life, and increased therapeutic and toxic effects of the glucocorticoid; glucocorticoid dosage adjustment may be required during and following concurrent use)

» Cyclosporine
(seizures have been observed in patients receiving cyclosporine and high doses of methylprednisolone)

» Digitalis glycosides
(concurrent use with glucocorticoids may increase the possibility of arrhythmias or digitalis toxicity associated with hypokalemia)

» Diuretics
(natriuretic and diuretic effects of these medications may be decreased by sodium- and fluid-retaining actions of corticosteroids, and vice versa)

(concurrent use of potassium-depleting diuretics with corticosteroids may result in severe hypokalemia; monitoring of serum potassium concentration and cardiac function is recommended)

(effects of potassium-sparing diuretics and/or corticosteroids on serum potassium concentration may be decreased during concurrent use; monitoring of serum potassium concentration is recommended)

Folic acid
(requirements may be increased in patients receiving long-term corticosteroid therapy)

» Hepatic enzyme-inducing agents (see *Appendix II*)
(concurrent use may decrease the corticosteroid effect because of increased corticosteroid metabolism resulting from induction of hepatic microsomal enzymes)

» Hepatic enzyme-inhibiting agents (see *Appendix II*)
(concurrent use may increase the corticosteroid effect because of decreased corticosteroid metabolism resulting from inhibition of hepatic microsomal enzymes)

Hepatic enzyme substrates
(dexamethasone is a moderate inducer of CYP 3A4; coadministration with other drugs that are metabolized by CYP 3A4 may increase their clearance resulting in decreased plasma concentration of the substrate drug)

Immunosuppressant agents, other
(concurrent use with immunosuppressant doses of glucocorticoids may increase the risk of infection and possibly the development of lymphomas or other lymphoproliferative disorders; these neoplasms may be associated with Epstein-Barr virus infections; a few studies in organ transplant patients receiving immunosuppressant therapy indicate that progression of the neoplasm may be reversed after immunosuppressant dosage is decreased or therapy is discontinued)

Iophendylate or
Metrizamide
(concurrent intrathecal administration of metrizamide or iophendylate with intrathecal administration of glucocorticoids may increase the risk of arachnoiditis)

Isoniazid
(glucocorticoids, especially prednisolone, may increase hepatic metabolism and/or excretion of isoniazid, leading to decreased plasma concentration and effectiveness of isoniazid, especially in patients who are rapid acetylators; isoniazid dosage adjustment may be required during and following concurrent use)

» Ketoconazole
(may decrease the metabolism of certain corticosteroids by up to 60%; may result in increased risk of corticosteroid side effects; ketoconazole alone can inhibit adrenal corticosteroid synthesis and may cause adrenal insufficiency during corticosteroid withdrawal)

Mexiletine
(concurrent use with glucocorticoids may accelerate metabolism of mexiletine, leading to decreased mexiletine plasma concentration)

» Mitotane
(mitotane suppresses adrenocortical function; glucocorticoid supplementation usually is required during mitotane administration, but higher doses than those generally used for replacement therapy may be required because mitotane alters glucocorticoid metabolism)

Neuromuscular blocking agents, nondepolarizing
(hypokalemia induced by glucocorticoids may enhance the blockade of nondepolarizing neuromuscular blocking agents, possibly leading to increased or prolonged respiratory depression or paralysis [apnea]; serum potassium determinations may be necessary prior to administration of these agents)

(hydrocortisone and prednisone also have been reported to decrease the efficacy of pancuronium by an unknown mechanism; increased dosage of pancuronium or use of an alternate neuromuscular blocking agent may be necessary)

» Potassium supplements
(effects of these medications and/or corticosteroids on serum potassium concentration may be decreased when these medications are used concurrently; monitoring of serum potassium concentration is recommended)

» Ritodrine
(concurrent use may cause pulmonary edema in the pregnant woman; maternal death has been reported; both medications should be discontinued at the first sign of pulmonary edema)

Salicylates
(although concurrent use with glucocorticoids in the treatment of arthritis may provide additive therapeutic benefit and permit glucocorticoid dosage reduction, glucocorticoids may increase salicylate excretion and reduce salicylate plasma concentrations so

that the salicylate dosage requirement may be increased; salicylism may occur when glucocorticoid dosage is subsequently decreased or discontinued, especially in patients receiving large [antirheumatic] doses of salicylates; also, the risk of gastrointestinal ulceration or hemorrhage may be increased during concurrent use)

(caution is recommended when salicylates are used concurrently with corticosteroids in patients with hypoprothrombinemia)

» Sodium-containing medications or foods

(concurrent use with pharmacologic doses of glucocorticoids may result in edema and increased blood pressure, possibly to hypertensive levels)

(although patients receiving replacement doses of glucocorticoids may require sodium supplementation, adjustment of dietary sodium intake may be required when a medication having a high sodium content is administered concurrently)

» Somatrem or
» Somatropin

(inhibition of the growth response to somatrem or somatropin may occur with chronic therapeutic use of daily doses [per square meter of body surface area] in excess of:

	Oral	Parenteral
Betamethasone	300–450 mcg	150–225 mcg
Cortisone	12.5–18.8 mg	6.25–9.4 mg
Dexamethasone	375–563 mcg	187.5–281.5 mcg
Hydrocortisone	10–15 mg	5–7.5 mg
Methylprednisolone	2–3 mg	1–1.5 mg
Prednisolone	2.5–3.75 mg	1.25–1.88 mg
Prednisone	2.5–3.75 mg	
Triamcinolone	2–3 mg	1–1.5 mg

(It is recommended that these doses not be exceeded during somatrem or somatropin therapy; if larger doses are required, administration of somatrem or somatropin should be postponed)

Streptozocin

(concurrent use with glucocorticoids may increase the risk of hyperglycemia)

Thalidomide

(use with caution; toxic epidermal necrolysis has been reported with concomitant use)

Troleandomycin

(troleandomycin may decrease metabolism of methylprednisolone and possibly other glucocorticoids, leading to increased plasma concentration, elimination half-life, and therapeutic and toxic effects; glucocorticoid dosage adjustment may be required during and following concurrent use)

» Vaccines, live virus, or other immunizations

(administration of live virus vaccines to patients receiving pharmacologic [immunosuppressant] doses of glucocorticoids may potentiate replication of the vaccine virus, thereby increasing the risk of the patient's developing the viral disease, and/or decreasing the patient's antibody response to the vaccine and is not recommended; the patient's immunologic status should be evaluated prior to administration of a live virus vaccine; also, immunization with oral poliovirus vaccine should be postponed in persons in close contact with the patient, especially family members)

(other immunizations are not recommended in patients receiving pharmacologic [immunosuppressant] doses of glucocorticoids because of the increased risk of neurological complications and the possibility of decreased or absent antibody response)

(immunizations may be administered to patients receiving glucocorticoids via routes or in quantities that are not likely to cause immunosuppression, for example, those receiving local injections, short-term [less than 2 weeks] therapy, or physiologic doses)

Laboratory value alterations

The following have been selected on the basis of their potential clinical significance (possible effect in parentheses where appropriate)—not necessarily inclusive (» = major clinical significance).

With results of dexamethasone suppression tests

Due to other medications/foods

Alcohol (chronic abuse) or
Glutethimide or
Meprobamate or
Methaqualone or
Methyprylon

(may cause false-positive results in test for endogenous depression)

Benzodiazepines (high doses) or
Cyproheptadine (high doses) or
Glucocorticoid therapy, long-term or
Indomethacin

(may cause false-negative results in test for endogenous depression)

Ephedrine or
Estrogens (high doses) or
Hepatic enzyme-inducing agents (see *Appendix II*)

(may cause false-positive results in tests for Cushing's disease or endogenous depression)

Due to medical problems or conditions

Adrenal hyperfunction (Cushing's disease) or
Anorexia nervosa or malnutrition leading to extreme weight loss, recent or
Carcinoma, disseminated, with concurrent serious infection or
Cardiac failure or
Dehydration or
Diabetes mellitus, unstable or
Fever or
Hypertension or
Pregnancy or
Renal failure or
Temporal lobe disease

(may cause false-positive results in test for endogenous depression)

Adrenal insufficiency or
Hypopituitarism

(may cause false-negative results in test for endogenous depression)

Psychiatric disorders such as acute psychosis, mania, chronic schizophrenia, and primary degenerative dementia

(may interfere with results of test for endogenous depression)

With *other* diagnostic test results

Brain imaging using sodium pertechnetate Tc 99m, technetium Tc 99m gluceptate, or technetium Tc 99m pentetate

(uptake of these diagnostic aids into cerebral tumors may be decreased in patients receiving large doses of glucocorticoids because of glucocorticoid-induced reduction of peritumor edema)

Gonadorelin test for hypothalamic-pituitary-gonadal axis function

(glucocorticoids may alter the results of the gonadorelin test by affecting pituitary secretion of gonadotropins through a complicated feedback mechanism)

Nitroblue-tetrazolium test

(false-negative test results may occur)

Protirelin test for thyroid function

(physiologic doses of corticosteroids have no effect, but pharmacologic doses may reduce the thyroid-stimulating hormone [TSH] response to protirelin; however, withdrawal of corticosteroids in patients with known hypopituitarism is generally not recommended)

Skeletal imaging using technetium Tc 99m medronate, technetium Tc 99m oxidronate, or technetium Tc 99m pyrophosphate

(long-term use of glucocorticoids may induce bone calcium depletion, thus causing decreased bone uptake of these diagnostic aids)

Skin tests, including tuberculin and histoplasmin skin tests and patch tests for allergy

(reactions may be suppressed, especially with daily administration of large doses of corticosteroids)

Thyroid ^{123}I or ^{131}I uptake

(may be decreased)

With physiology/laboratory test values

Calcium, serum

(concentrations may be decreased)

Glucose, blood and urine

(concentrations may be increased because of intrinsic hyperglycemic activity)

» Hypothalamic-pituitary-adrenal (HPA) axis function as assessed by:

Adrenocorticotropic hormone (ACTH, corticotropin) or
Cortisol, blood or
Cortisol, urine or
17-Hydroxycorticosteroids, urine (17-OHCS) or
17-Ketosteroids, total, urine (17-KS)

(may be decreased with pharmacologic doses of glucocorticoids, especially in children)

Lipid profile

(concentrations may be increased)

Platelet count
(may be increased or decreased)
Polymorphonuclear leukocyte count
(may be increased)
Potassium, serum
(concentrations may be decreased because of increased potassium excretion, especially with agents having significant mineralocorticoid activity)
Sodium, blood
(concentrations may be increased because of sodium retention, especially with glucocorticoids having significant mineralocorticoid activity)
Uric acid, serum
(concentrations may be increased in patients with acute leukemia but may be decreased in other patients because of weak uricosuric effect)
White blood count
(may be decreased)

Medical considerations/Contraindications

The medical considerations/contraindications included have been selected on the basis of their potential clinical significance (reasons given in parentheses where appropriate)—not necessarily inclusive (» = major clinical significance).

See also *Laboratory value alterations.*

Note: The medical problems listed below apply only to pharmacologic (supraphysiologic) doses of glucocorticoids, unless otherwise stated.

Except under special circumstances, these medications should not be used when the following medical problems exist:

For intra-articular injection
» Arthroplasty of joint, prior
(increased risk of infection)
» Blood clotting disorders
(risk of intra- and extra-articular hemorrhage)
» Fracture, intra-articular
(healing may be retarded)
» Infection, periarticular, current or history of
(may be exacerbated or reactivated)
» Osteoporosis, juxta-articular, non-arthritic
(may be exacerbated)
» Unstable joint

For neonatal respiratory distress syndrome prophylaxis
» Amnionitis
» Bleeding, uterine
» Febrile illness or infection, especially tuberculosis, maternal or
» Herpes simplex type 2 infection, active, maternal or
» Keratitis, viral, maternal
(may be exacerbated; if corticosteroid administration is essential, appropriate antimicrobial therapy must be administered concurrently)
» Placental insufficiency
» Premature membrane rupture
(increased risk of maternal infection; the glucocorticoid should be administered immediately if this occurs, since the risk of infection increases with time)

Risk-benefit should be considered when the following medical problems exist:

For all indications
» Acquired immunodeficiency syndrome (AIDS) or
» Human immunodeficiency virus (HIV) infection
(although pharmacologic doses of corticosteroids can be effective in the treatment of certain HIV-related diseases, careful medical evaluation of the risks and benefits of this therapy must be done, due to the possible increased risk of severe uncontrollable infections and/or neoplasms; in one study in patients given tapering doses of intravenous methylprednisolone starting with 60 mg every 6 hours for 8 days as an adjunct to antipneumocystis therapy, an increase in frequency or severity of life-threatening opportunistic infections was observed; in a study of similar patients given tapering doses of prednisone starting at 40 mg two times a day for 21 days, no increase in the incidence of Kaposi's sarcoma or life-threatening opportunistic infections was observed, though the incidence of oral candidiasis and mucocutaneous herpes simplex infection did increase)
» Anastomoses, intestinal, recent
(corticosteroids should be used with caution)
» Cardiac disease or
» Congestive heart failure or
Hypertension or
» Renal function impairment or disease, severe
(edema may be hazardous, especially with agents having significant mineralocorticoid activity)

(patients undergoing dialysis may have increased risk of avascular necrosis with long-term corticosteroid use)
» Chickenpox, existing or recent (including recent exposure) or
» Measles, existing or recent (including recent exposure)
(risk of severe, potentially fatal, generalized disease; extra care to avoid exposure to these infections is recommended; prophylactic therapy with varicella zoster immune globulin [VZIG] or immune globulin intravenous [IGIV] or intramuscular [IGIM], as appropriate, may be indicated in exposed patients; therapy with an antiviral agent may be indicated if chickenpox develops)
Colitis, ulcerative, nonspecific, with possibility of impending perforation, abscess, or other infection or
Diverticulitis or
» Esophagitis, gastritis, or peptic ulcer, active or latent
(symptoms of progression or reactivation may be masked; hemorrhage and/or perforation may occur without warning)
» Diabetes mellitus or predisposition to
(may be exacerbated or activated)
» Fungal infections, systemic
(may be exacerbated; pharmacologic doses of corticosteroids should not be given unless the patient is concurrently receiving an antifungal agent)
Glaucoma, open-angle
(intraocular pressure may be increased)
Hepatic function impairment or disease
(increased risk of glucocorticoid toxicity, especially if hypoalbuminemia is present; possibility of impaired conversion of cortisone or prednisone to their active metabolites, although this effect may be offset by decreased protein binding or clearance and/or conversion in other tissues)
» Herpes simplex, ocular
(possible corneal perforation)
Herpetic lesions, oral
Hyperlipidemia
(concentrations of fatty acids or cholesterol may be increased)
Hypersensitivity to corticosteroids
Hyperthyroidism
(glucocorticoid effect may be impaired because of accelerated metabolism; this may be especially important with physiologic doses or low pharmacologic doses)
Hypoalbuminemia or conditions predisposing to, including hepatic cirrhosis or nephrotic syndrome
(increased risk of toxicity because reduced availability of albumin for glucocorticoid binding leads to increased serum concentration of unbound drug; reduction in initial dosage is recommended)
Hypothyroidism
(decreased metabolism of corticosteroid may result)
Infections, viral or bacterial, uncontrolled, local or systemic
(symptoms of infection may be masked; new infection may develop; resistance and ability to localize infection may be decreased; if infection occurs during therapy, appropriate antimicrobial therapy should be instituted)
» Myasthenia gravis
(muscle weakness may be increased initially, possibly leading to respiratory distress; the patient should be hospitalized, and respiratory support should be immediately available, when glucocorticoid therapy is initiated)
» Myocardial infarction, recent
(possible risk of left ventricular free wall rupture; extreme caution is recommended)
Osteoporosis
(may be exacerbated)
» Psychosis, acute
(may be aggravated)
Renal function impairment, mild to moderate, or stones
(fluid retention may exacerbate these conditions; increased risk of edema, especially with agents having mineralocorticoid activity)

(patients receiving dialysis may have increased risk of avascular necrosis with long-term corticosteroid use)
» *Strongyloides* infestation, confirmed or suspected
(corticosteroid-induced immunosuppression may lead to hyperinfection and dissemination with widespread larval migration, often accompanied by severe enterocolitis and potentially fatal gram-negative septicemia)
Systemic lupus erythematosus (SLE)
(cautious use is recommended because of an increased risk of aseptic necrosis)

» Tuberculosis, active, positive skin test, latent, or history of
(may be exacerbated or reactivated; appropriate antitubercular chemotherapy or prophylaxis should be administered concurrently)

Patient monitoring

The following may be especially important in patient monitoring (other tests may be warranted in some patients, depending on condition; » = major clinical significance):

Adrenal function assessment, may include adrenocorticotropic hormone (ACTH) stimulation test, blood or urine cortisol concentrations, urine 17-hydroxycorticosteroids concentration, or urine 17-ketosteroids concentration
(may be required during, and following withdrawal of high-dose or long-term [more than 3 weeks] therapy to assess adrenal function; complete recovery of adrenal function may require up to 1 year following prolonged use, especially with high doses; in some patients receiving prolonged, high-dose therapy, complete recovery may never occur)

Blood pressure
(may be required at periodic intervals for adults or children receiving therapy)

Bone mineral density (BMD)
(routine screening of geriatric patients including BMD and fracture prevention strategies with regular review of prednisolone indication to minimize complications and keep dose at lowest acceptable level)

Clinical evaluation
(adults and children should be carefully observed for the presence of infection, psychosocial disturbances, thromboembolism, peptic ulcers, and osteoporosis)

Electrolytes, serum and
Occult blood, stool
(may be required during long-term therapy)

Glucose concentrations, blood or urine or
Glucose tolerance test
(may be required for patients with diabetes mellitus or a predisposition to diabetes mellitus)

Growth and development determinations
(recommended in children and adolescents receiving prolonged therapy)

Ophthalmologic examinations
(may be required at periodic intervals for adults or children receiving therapy for more than 6 weeks to detect the presence of cataracts, glaucoma, increased intraocular pressure, or ocular infections)

Prothrombin time (PT)
(frequent monitoring recommended in patients receiving coumarin anticoagulants concurrently)

Side/Adverse Effects

Note: The risk of adverse effects with pharmacologic doses of corticosteroids generally increases with the duration of therapy and frequency of administration and, to a lesser extent, with dosage.

Chronic administration of physiologic replacement doses of corticosteroids rarely causes adverse effects.

Administration of glucocorticoids via local injection reduces the risk of systemic effects. The risk of both systemic and local adverse effects is still present to a degree, however, and increases with the frequency of injections.

Pharmacologic doses of glucocorticoids lower resistance to infection; the patient may be predisposed to systemic infections during, and for a time following, therapy. Increased susceptibility to infection may occur with short-term high-dose use ("pulse" therapy) as well as with more prolonged use. Also, symptoms of onset or progression of infections may be masked.

The following side/adverse effects have been selected on the basis of their potential clinical significance (possible signs and symptoms in parentheses where appropriate)—not necessarily inclusive:

Those indicating need for medical attention

Incidence less frequent

Diabetes mellitus (decreased or blurred vision; frequent urination; increased thirst)

Incidence rare

Burning, numbness, pain, or tingling at or near injection site; congestive heart failure—in susceptible individuals; ***generalized allergic reaction*** (skin rash or hives); ***local allergic reaction or infection at injection site*** (redness, swelling, pain, or other signs of infection or allergic reaction); ***psychic disturbances such as delirium*** (confusion; excitement; restlessness); ***disorientation; euphoria*** (false sense of well-being); ***hallucinations*** (seeing, hearing, or feeling things that are not there); ***manic-depressive episodes*** (sudden, wide mood swings); ***mental depression, or paranoia*** (mistaken feelings of self-importance or being mistreated); ***sudden blindness***

Note: *Psychic disturbances* are more likely to occur in patients with chronic debilitating illnesses that predispose them to psychic disturbances and in patients receiving higher daily dosages. Psychic disturbances may be related to dose rather than duration of therapy; symptoms may appear within a few days to 2 weeks after initiation of therapy and usually are associated with doses equivalent to 40 mg or more of prednisone per day. Additionally, euphoria or fear of relapse may lead to psychological dependence or abuse of corticosteroids.

Sudden blindness following injection into sites in the head or neck area, such as nasal turbinates or scalp, is due to possible entry of drug crystals into ocular blood vessels.

With intravenous administration

Anaphylaxis, generalized (hives; shortness of breath; swelling of face, nasal membranes, and eyelids; tightness in chest; troubled breathing; wheezing); ***cardiac arrythmias; flushing of face or cheeks; seizures***

Note: Rapid intravenous administration of high doses of corticosteroids has been reported to cause angioedema and/or *anaphylactic reactions, seizures,* and sudden death associated with *cardiac arrhythmias.* Monitoring of the electrocardiogram (ECG) is recommended. Equipment, medications, and trained personnel necessary for treating these complications should be immediately available.

Those occurring principally during long-term use indicating need for medical attention

Acne adrenal suppression; avascular necrosis (hip or shoulder pain); ***cataracts, posterior subcapsular*** (gradual blurring or loss of vision); ***Cushing's syndrome effects including filling or rounding out of the face; hirsutism*** (unusual increase in hair growth); ***hypertension; menstrual irregularities; muscle weakness; or striae*** (reddish purple lines on arms, face, legs, trunk, or groin); ***cutaneous or subcutaneous tissue atrophy*** (thin, shiny skin; pitting or depression of skin at injection site)—with frequent repository injections; ***ecchymosis*** (unusual bruising); ***fluid and sodium retention*** (rapid weight gain; swelling of feet or lower legs); ***glaucoma with possible damage to optic nerves*** (blurred vision or other change in vision; eye pain); ***growth suppression***—in children; ***hypokalemic syndrome*** (irregular heartbeat; muscle cramps or pain; unusual tiredness or weakness); ***impaired wound healing; increased intracranial pressure*** (headache; insomnia; papilledema; unusual tiredness or weakness); ***ocular infection, secondary, fungal or viral*** (blurred vision or other change in vision; eye pain; redness of eyes; sensitivity of eyes to light; tearing); ***osteoporosis or bone fractures*** (pain in back, ribs, arms, or legs)—includes vertebral compression and long bone pathologic fractures; ***pancreatitis*** (continuing abdominal or stomach pain or burning; nausea; vomiting); ***peptic ulceration or intestinal perforation*** (bloody or black, tarry stools; continuing abdominal or stomach pain or burning); ***scarring at injection site; steroid myopathy*** (muscle weakness); ***tendon rupture; thin, fragile skin***

Those indicating need for medical attention only if they continue or are bothersome

Incidence more frequent

Gastrointestinal irritation (nausea; vomiting); ***increased appetite; indigestion; nervousness or restlessness; trouble in sleeping; weight gain***

For triamcinolone

Loss of appetite

Incidence less frequent or rare

Changes in skin color or hypopigmentation (darkening or lightening of skin color); ***dizziness or lightheadedness; flushing of face or cheeks; headache; hiccups; increased joint pain***—following intra-articular injection; ***increased sweating***; ***nosebleeds***—following intranasal injection; ***vertigo*** (dizziness; sensation of spinning)

Note: *Hypopigmentation* is more likely at the injection site.

Flushing of face or cheeks may persist for 24 to 48 hours.

Increased joint pain may occur within a few hours postinjection and persist for up to 48 hours.

Those occurring principally after medication is discontinued, indicating a corticosteroid withdrawal syndrome and the need for medical attention

Withdrawal syndrome (abdominal or back pain; dizziness; fainting; frequent or continuing unexplained headaches; low-grade fever; muscle or joint pain; nausea; prolonged loss of appetite; rapid weight loss;

reappearance of disease symptoms; shortness of breath; unusual tiredness or weakness; vomiting)

Note: Too-rapid *withdrawal of therapy*, especially after prolonged use, may cause acute, possibly life-threatening, adrenal insufficiency and/or a withdrawal syndrome not related to hypothalamic-pituitary-adrenal (HPA) axis suppression.

Patient Consultation

As an aid to patient consultation, refer to *Advice for the Patient, Corticosteroids—Glucocorticoid Effects (Systemic)*.

In providing consultation, consider emphasizing the following selected information (» = major clinical significance):

Before using this medication

» Conditions affecting use, especially:

Hypersensitivity to corticosteroids

Pregnancy—Pharmacologic doses in animals show some evidence of increased risk of placental insufficiency, decreased birth weight, or stillbirths; other animal studies show increased incidence of cleft palate, placental insufficiency, spontaneous abortions, and intrauterine growth retardation

Breast-feeding—Breast-feeding is not recommended during use of higher pharmacologic doses

Use in children—Infants born to women who received corticosteroids during pregnancy should be monitored for signs of hypoadrenalism; close monitoring also is required during chronic therapy because suppression of growth and development may result; possible increased severity of chicken pox or measles in children receiving immunosuppressant doses; increased risk for developing osteoporosis, avascular necrosis of the femoral heads, glaucoma, or cataracts during prolonged therapy

Use in the elderly—Dose selection should be cautious; also increased risk for developing osteoporosis (especially in postmenopausal females) or hypertension

Other medications, especially aminoglutethimide; amphotericin B, parenteral; antacids; anticholinesterases; antidiabetic agents, oral; cyclosporine; digitalis glycosides; diuretics; hepatic enzyme-inducing agents; hepatic enzyme–inhibiting agents; insulin; ketoconazole; macrolide antibiotics; mitotane; potassium supplements; ritodrine; sodium-containing medications; somatrem; somatropin; or vaccines, live virus, or other immunizations

Other medical problems, especially

For all uses—Acquired immunodeficiency syndrome (AIDS); anastomoses, intestinal, recent; cardiac disease; chickenpox; congestive heart failure; diabetes mellitus; esophagitis, gastritis, or peptic ulcer; fungal infections, systemic; herpes simplex, ocular; human immunodeficiency virus (HIV) infection; measles; myasthenia gravis; myocardial infarction, recent; psychosis, acute; renal function impairment or disease; *Strongyloides* infestation; or tuberculosis

For intra-articular injection only—Arthroplasty of joint, blood clotting disorders, intra-articular fracture, osteoporosis, periarticular infection, or unstable joint

For neonatal respiratory distress syndrome prophylaxis only—Amnionitis, febrile illness or infection, herpes simplex type 2 infection, maternal viral keratitis, placental insufficiency, premature membrane rupture, or uterine bleeding

Proper use of this medication

For oral dosage forms

» Taking with food to minimize gastrointestinal irritation

Possibility that alcohol may enhance ulcerogenic effects of medication

For budesonide capsules (micronized)

Swallowing capsules whole without breaking, crushing, or chewing

» Importance of not using more medication than the amount prescribed

» Proper dosing

Missed dose: If dosing schedule is—

Every other day: Taking as soon as possible if remembered same morning; if remembered later, not taking until next morning, then skipping a day

Once a day: Taking as soon as possible; not taking if almost time for next dose; not doubling doses

Several times a day: Taking as soon as possible; doubling if time for next dose

» Proper storage

Precautions while using this medication

» Regular visits to physician to check progress during and following therapy

» Checking with physician before discontinuing medication; gradual dosage reduction may be necessary

Checking with physician if symptoms recur or worsen when dose decreased or therapy discontinued

For patients on long-term therapy:

» Possible need for sodium restriction or potassium supplementation

Possible need for calorie restriction

Possible need for increased protein intake

Possible need for ophthalmologic examinations

Carrying medical identification card indicating use of corticosteroids

» Caution in receiving skin tests

» Caution if any kind of surgery or emergency treatment is required

» Caution if serious infections or injuries occur

» Avoiding exposure to chickenpox or measles (especially for children); telling physician right away if exposure occurs

» Caution in receiving vaccinations or other immunizations or coming in contact with persons receiving oral poliovirus vaccine

For patients with diabetes: May increase blood glucose concentrations

For parenteral dosage forms:

Restricting use of joint following intra-articular injection

Checking with physician if redness or swelling occurs and continues or becomes worse following local injection

Side/adverse effects

Signs of potential side effects, especially diabetes mellitus; burning, numbness, pain, or tingling at or near injection site; congestive heart failure (in susceptible individuals); generalized allergic reaction; local allergic reaction or infection at injection site; psychic disturbances; sudden blindness; anaphylaxis, generalized; cardiac arrythmias; flushing of face or cheeks; seizures; acne; adrenal suppression; avascular necrosis; cataracts, posterior subcapsular; Cushing's syndrome effects; cutaneous or subcutaneous tissue atrophy; ecchymosis; fluid and sodium retention; glaucoma with possible damage to optic nerves; growth suppression (in children); hypokalemic syndrome; impaired wound healing; increased intracranial pressure; ocular infection, secondary, fungal or viral; osteoporosis or bone fractures; pancreatitis; peptic ulceration or intestinal perforation; scarring at injection site; steroid myopathy; tendon rupture; and thin, fragile skin

General Dosing Information

See *Table 3*, page 964.

For replacement therapy in chronic adrenocortical insufficiency states, corticosteroid therapy must be continued for the life of the patient. It is recommended that dosage of cortisone or hydrocortisone be timed to simulate endogenous corticosteroid secretion, with two thirds of the daily dose administered in the morning and one third in the evening. Other corticosteroids usually are given once a day.

For treatment of congenital adrenal hyperplasia, suppression of corticotropin secretion is required to decrease hypersecretion of adrenal androgens. This usually is achieved by administering one third of the daily dose of cortisone or hydrocortisone in the morning and two thirds in the evening or giving one third of the daily dose three times a day at evenly spaced intervals. Other corticosteroids usually are given once a day.

Except in severe conditions or emergency situations, it is recommended that therapy be instituted with low doses that are increased as necessary to provide the desired effect. For most conditions, administration in the lowest effective dose for the shortest time possible is recommended. Dosage requirements are variable and should be individualized according to the disease being treated and patient response rather than by age or body weight. Whenever possible, local administration is recommended in order to concentrate the medication at the affected site and reduce the risk of systemic effects. After a favorable response is obtained, the dosage should be decreased gradually to the lowest dose that will maintain an adequate clinical response.

Frequent monitoring of drug effect is required. Situations that may necessitate dosage adjustments include remissions or exacerbations of the disease process and the patient's response to the medication.

Clinically significant hypothalamic-pituitary-adrenal (HPA) axis suppression leading to adrenal insufficiency may occur more readily with multiple daily doses or evening administration than with single doses given every morning or every other morning. Administration of a single daily dose of a short- or intermediate-acting corticosteroid prior to 9 a.m. may reduce the risk of HPA axis suppression (because maximum endogenous corticosteroid secretion occurs in the morning) and is recommended for daily administration whenever possible. However, some disease conditions may require multiple daily doses.

Following discontinuation of short-term (up to 5 days) high-dose use, adrenal recovery may occur within 1 week. However, following prolonged high-dose administration, complete recovery of adrenal function may require up to 1 year. Following very prolonged suppression, complete recovery may never occur. During the recovery period, monitoring of adrenal function may be required to assess the patient's ability to respond to stress.

Patients with confirmed or suspected adrenal insufficiency, including those already receiving replacement therapy, require an increase in dosage or reinstitution of therapy prior to, during, and for a time following, exposure to emotional stress or physical stress such as severe infection, surgery (including dental surgery), or injury. Administration of sodium and/or a mineralocorticoid also may be required. Dosage and duration of such therapy are dependent on the severity of the stress.

When medication is to be discontinued, dosage should be reduced gradually. The rate at which dosage can be decreased and the time required for complete withdrawal of therapy are variable, depending on the specific agent used; dose, frequency, and route of administration; duration of therapy; condition being treated; and patient response.

For oral dosage forms only

If oral long-term use is required for disease therapy, an alternate-day regimen using an intermediate-acting corticosteroid is recommended to minimize HPA axis suppression and possibly other adverse effects. An intermediate-acting corticosteroid is one that suppresses HPA axis activity for 12 to 36 hours following a single dose. Administration of longer-acting corticosteroids on an alternate-day schedule does not reduce the risk of HPA axis suppression and is not recommended.

Alternate-day therapy utilizes a single dose administered every other morning, usually in a quantity equivalent to, or somewhat higher than, twice the usual or pre-established daily dose. The patient should have a normal or moderately responsive HPA axis.

If treatment has been initiated with daily administration, changes to alternate-day therapy should be made gradually, after the patient's condition has stabilized. However, for some diseases, such as childhood nephrotic syndrome, therapy may be initiated with alternate-day dosing.

Alternate-day therapy may not be effective in treating hematologic disorders, malignancies, ulcerative colitis, or severe conditions. Also, some patients, such as those with asthma or rheumatoid arthritis, may experience exacerbation of symptoms on the second day. Administration of (or increasing the dosage of) suitable supplemental therapy on the second day may provide sufficient symptomatic relief to permit alternate-day dosing in some patients.

For parenteral dosage forms only

For acute adrenocortical insufficiency, initiation of corticosteroid therapy by intravenous injection followed by slow intravenous infusion or intramuscular administration is recommended. Certain other acute conditions also may require initiation of therapy with intramuscular or intravenous administration of a rapidly acting formulation.

In severe or life-threatening conditions, single-dose or short-term intravenous administration of a very high dose ("pulse" therapy) may produce the required therapeutic response with a minimum risk of prolonged HPA axis suppression or other adverse effects. Such therapy has been recommended for treating conditions such as organ transplant rejection reactions, acute nephritis associated with systemic lupus erythematosus, vasculitis, adult respiratory distress syndrome, and shock. However, rapid intravenous administration of high doses of corticosteroids has been reported to cause potentially life-threatening side effects and appropriate precautions should be observed.

When the suspension dosage forms are administered intramuscularly, they should be injected deeply into the gluteal muscle to prevent local tissue atrophy. It is recommended that the deltoid muscle not be used because of a higher incidence of local atrophy. In addition, do not inject repeatedly into the same site.

A standard textbook should be consulted for specific techniques and procedures applicable to local injection of corticosteroids for various indications.

Following intra-articular injection, the injected joint should not be overused, even if pain is relieved, because of the increased risk of joint damage or deterioration. It is recommended that weight-bearing joints be rested for 24 to 48 hours postinjection.

Administration of a local anesthetic concurrently with intra-articular or soft tissue injection of a corticosteroid may reduce the pain of injection and provide immediate relief of symptoms. However, a postinjection flare of pain may occur when the local anesthetic effect subsides.

Dosages for local injections (e.g., intra-articular, intrabursal, intradermal, intralesional) are given as ranges only. The actual dosage depends upon the size of the joint or lesion and the severity of the condition being treated.

Diet/Nutrition

Administration of oral dosage forms with food may relieve the indigestion or mild gastrointestinal irritation that may occur.

Patients receiving prolonged therapy with pharmacologic doses of corticosteroids, especially those with significant mineralocorticoid activity, may require sodium restriction and/or potassium supplementation during therapy.

Because corticosteroids promote protein catabolism, increased protein intake may be necessary during prolonged therapy.

Administration of calcium and vitamin D and, if the patient's condition permits, exercise or physical therapy may reduce the risk of corticosteroid-induced osteoporosis during prolonged therapy. Co-administration of bisphosphonates has also been shown to retard the rate of bone loss in corticosteroid-treated males and postmenopausal females, and these agents are recommended in the prevention and treatment of corticosteroid-induced osteoporosis.

For treatment of adverse effects

Recommended treatment consists of the following:

• For gastrointestinal effects—Administration of antacids between meals may relieve indigestion or mild gastrointestinal irritation that may occur during parenteral, as well as oral, corticosteroid therapy. However, the efficacy of antacids or other antiulcer medications in preventing severe gastrointestinal problems, such as ulceration, hemorrhage, and/or bowel perforation, during corticosteroid therapy has not been established.

• For mental depression or psychoses—If possible, decrease corticosteroid dosage or discontinue therapy. A phenothiazine may be administered if necessary; lithium also has been recommended. Some patients may require electroconvulsive therapy if severe depression persists. Tricyclic antidepressants should not be used since they do not relieve, and may exacerbate, corticosteroid-induced mental disturbances. Prophylactic administration of an antipsychotic agent may be indicated if additional courses of corticosteroid therapy are required by a patient with a history of corticosteroid-induced psychosis.

• For withdrawal effects (non-HPA axis suppression)—Administration of aspirin or another nonsteroidal anti-inflammatory drug may alleviate some of the symptoms of this condition.

BETAMETHASONE

Summary of Differences

Precautions: Pediatrics—Not recommended for chronic use; especially likely to inhibit growth.

Oral Dosage Forms

BETAMETHASONE SYRUP USP

Usual adult and adolescent dose

Corticosteroid—

Oral, 0.6 to 7.2 mg a day as a single dose or in divided doses.

Usual pediatric dose

Adrenocortical insufficiency—

Oral, 0.018 mg per kg of body weight or 0.5 mg per square meter of body surface area a day in three divided doses.

Other indications—

Oral, 0.063 to 0.25 mg per kg of body weight or 1.88 to 7.5 mg per square meter of body surface area a day in three or four divided doses.

Strength(s) usually available

U.S.—

0.6 mg per 5 mL (Rx) [*Celestone* (alcohol <1%; sodium chloride; sorbitol; sugar)].

Canada—

Not commercially available.

Packaging and storage

Store between 2 and 30 °C (36 and 86 °F), protected from light. Store in a well-closed container. Protect from freezing.

BETAMETHASONE TABLETS USP

Usual adult and adolescent dose

See *Betamethasone Syrup USP*.

Usual pediatric dose

See *Betamethasone Syrup USP*.

Strength(s) usually available

U.S.—

0.6 mg (Rx) [*Celestone* (scored)].

Canada—

Not commercially available.

Packaging and storage
Store between 2 and 30 °C (36 and 86 °F) in a well-closed container.

Note: Protect the 21-tablet pack from excessive moisture.

BETAMETHASONE SODIUM PHOSPHATE EFFERVESCENT TABLETS

Usual adult and adolescent dose
Corticosteroid—
Oral, 0.25 to 1 mg three or four times a day.

Usual pediatric dose
See *Betamethasone Syrup USP*.

Strength(s) usually available
U.S.—
Not commercially available.
Canada—
0.5 mg (Rx) [*Betnesol* (scored)].

Packaging and storage
Store below 40 °C (104 °F), preferably between 15 and 30 °C (59 and 86 °F), in a well-closed container, unless otherwise specified by manufacturer. Protect from moisture.

Preparation of dosage form
Dissolve in water immediately prior to ingestion.

Note
When dispensing, explain dissolution requirement to patient.

BETAMETHASONE SODIUM PHOSPHATE EXTENDED-RELEASE TABLETS

Usual adult and adolescent dose
Corticosteroid—
Oral, 2 to 6 mg a day initially, then adjusted according to patient response.

Usual pediatric dose
See *Betamethasone Syrup USP*.

Strength(s) usually available
U.S.—
Not commercially available.
Canada—
Not commercially available.

Packaging and storage
Store below 40 °C (104 °F), preferably between 15 and 30 °C (59 and 86 °F), in a well-closed container, unless otherwise specified by manufacturer.

Parenteral Dosage Forms

BETAMETHASONE SODIUM PHOSPHATE INJECTION USP

Note: The dosing and strengths of the dosage forms available are expressed in terms of betamethasone base (not the sodium phosphate salt).

Usual adult and adolescent dose
Corticosteroid—
Intra-articular, intralesional, or soft-tissue injection, up to 9 mg (base), repeated as needed.
Intramuscular or intravenous, up to 9 mg a day.

Usual pediatric dose
Adrenocortical insufficiency—
Intramuscular, 0.018 mg (base) per kg of body weight or 0.5 mg per square meter of body surface area a day (in three divided doses) every third day; or 0.0058 to 0.0088 mg per kg of body weight or 0.17 to 0.25 mg per square meter of body surface area once a day.
Other indications—
Intramuscular, 0.021 to 0.13 mg per kg of body weight or 0.63 to 3.75 mg per square meter of body surface area every twelve to twenty-four hours.

Strength(s) usually available
U.S.—
3 mg (base) (4 mg sodium phosphate) per mL (Rx) [*Celestone Phosphate* (sodium bisulfite 3.2 mg); *Selestoject* (sodium bisulfite); GENERIC].
Canada—
Not commercially available.

Packaging and storage
Store below 40 °C (104 °F), preferably between 15 and 30 °C (59 and 86 °F), protected from light, unless otherwise specified by manufacturer. Protect from freezing.

BETAMETHASONE SODIUM PHOSPHATE AND BETAMETHASONE ACETATE INJECTABLE SUSPENSION USP

Usual adult and adolescent dose
Arthritis, gouty, acute or
Bursitis, acute or subacute or
Tenosynovitis, nonspecific acute—
Intrabursal or intramuscular, 1.5 to 6 mg, repeated every three to seven days, or as needed.
Arthritis, rheumatoid or
Osteoarthritis, post-traumatic—
Intra-articular, 1.5 to 12 mg, depending upon the size of the affected joint, repeated as needed.
Asthma, bronchial or
Rhinitis, allergic, perennial or seasonal—
Intramuscular, 6 to 12 mg once a week.
Dermatologic disorders—
Intradermal, 1.2 mg per square centimeter of affected skin every three to seven days.
Status asthmaticus or
Lupus erythematosis, disseminated—
Intramuscular, initially 12 mg.

Usual adult and adolescent prescribing limits
Dermatologic disorders—
6 mg per week.

Usual pediatric dose
Dosage has not been established.

Strength(s) usually available
U.S.—
6 mg (3 mg of betamethasone acetate and 3 mg of betamethasone base) per mL (Rx) [*Celestone Soluspan*].
Canada—
6 mg (3 mg of betamethasone acetate and 3 mg of betamethasone base) per mL (Rx) [*Celestone Soluspan*].

Packaging and storage
Store between 2 and 25 °C (36 and 77 °F), protected from light, unless otherwise specified by manufacturer. Protect from freezing.

Incompatibilities
This medication should *not* be mixed with parenteral-local anesthetic formulations containing parabens, phenol, or other such preservatives, because flocculation of the corticosteroid may occur. The required quantity of corticosteroid suspension should be drawn into the syringe first, then the local anesthetic added. *Do not introduce the local anesthetic directly into the multiple-dose vial.*

Auxiliary labeling
- Shake well.

Additional information
For administration of injections, see manufacturer's labeling.
Do not administer this medication intravenously.

BUDESONIDE

Oral Dosage Forms

BUDESONIDE EXTENDED-RELEASE CAPSULES (MICRONIZED)

Usual adult dose
Crohn's disease—
Active disease: Oral, 9 mg once a day in the morning before breakfast for up to eight weeks.
Maintenance of remission: Oral, 6 mg once a day in the morning before breakfast.

Usual pediatric dose
Safety and efficacy have not been established.

Usual geriatric dose
See *Usual adult dose*.

Strength(s) usually available
U.S.—
Not commercially available.
Canada—
3 mg (Rx) [*Entocort*].

Packaging and storage
Store between 15 and 30 °C (59 and 86 °F), unless otherwise specified by manufacturer. Store in a tight container.

Auxiliary labeling
Store in original container.

Note
Dispense in original container.

CORTISONE

Oral Dosage Forms

CORTISONE ACETATE TABLETS USP

Usual adult and adolescent dose
Corticosteroid—
Oral, 25 to 300 mg a day as a single dose or in divided doses.

Usual pediatric dose
Adrenocortical insufficiency—
Oral, 0.7 mg per kg of body weight or 20 to 25 mg per square meter of body surface area a day in divided doses.
Other indications—
Oral, 2.5 to 10 mg per kg of body weight or 75 to 300 mg per square meter of body surface area a day as a single dose or in divided doses.

Strength(s) usually available
U.S.—
5 mg (Rx) [GENERIC (scored; lactose)].
10 mg (Rx) [GENERIC (scored)].
25 mg (Rx) [*Cortone Acetate* (scored); GENERIC (scored)].
Canada—
5 mg (Rx) [*Cortone*].
25 mg (Rx) [*Cortisone Acetate-ICN* (scored); *Cortone* (scored); GENERIC].

Packaging and storage
Store between 15 and 30 °C (59 and 86 °F), unless otherwise specified by manufacturer. Store in a well-closed container. Protect from light.

Parenteral Dosage Forms

CORTISONE ACETATE INJECTABLE SUSPENSION USP

Usual adult and adolescent dose
Corticosteroid—
Intramuscular, 20 to 300 mg a day.

Usual pediatric dose
Adrenocortical insufficiency—
Intramuscular, 0.7 mg per kg of body weight or 37.5 mg per square meter of body surface area a day every third day; or 0.23 to 0.35 mg per kg of body weight or 12.5 mg per square meter of body surface area once a day.
Other indications—
Intramuscular, 0.83 to 5 mg per kg of body weight or 25 to 150 mg per square meter of body surface area every twelve to twenty-four hours.

Strength(s) usually available
U.S.—
25 mg per mL (Rx) [GENERIC].
50 mg per mL (Rx) [*Cortone Acetate* (benzyl alcohol 9 mg); GENERIC].
Canada—
50 mg per mL (Rx) [*Cortone* (benzyl alcohol)].

Packaging and storage
Store below 40 °C (104 °F), preferably between 15 and 30 °C (59 and 86 °F), unless otherwise specified by manufacturer. Protect from freezing.

Stability
Dilutions or admixtures of this medication with other products are not recommended because the state of suspension or the rate of absorption may be affected.
This medication is heat-sensitive and should not be autoclaved.

Auxiliary labeling
• Shake well.

Caution
Use of preparations containing benzyl alcohol is not recommended in neonates. A fatal toxic syndrome consisting of metabolic acidosis, central nervous system (CNS) depression, respiratory problems, renal failure, hypotension, and possibly seizures and intracranial hemorrhages has been associated with this use.

Additional information
Do not administer this medication intravenously.

DEXAMETHASONE

Summary of Differences

Category: Also, diagnostic aid (Cushing's syndrome and endogenous depression) and antiemetic (in cancer chemotherapy).
Precautions: Pediatrics—Not recommended for chronic use; especially likely to inhibit growth.

Oral Dosage Forms

Note: Bracketed uses in the *Dosage Forms* section refer to categories of use and/or indications that are not included in U.S. product labeling.

DEXAMETHASONE ELIXIR USP

Usual adult and adolescent dose
Corticosteroid—
Oral, 0.75 to 9 mg a day as a single dose or in divided doses.
[Dexamethasone suppression test][1]—
Test for Cushing's syndrome: Oral, 1 mg as a single dose at 11:00 p.m. or 0.5 mg every six hours for forty-eight hours.
Test to distinguish Cushing's syndrome due to pituitary ACTH excess from Cushing's syndrome due to other causes: Oral, 2 mg every six hours for forty-eight hours.
[Depression, mental, endogenous, diagnosis of][1]: Oral, 1 mg as a single dose at 11:00 p.m.
Edema, cerebral, associated with recurrent or inoperable brain tumor—
Oral, 2 mg two or three times a day, administered as maintenance therapy after cerebral edema has initially been controlled using parenteral dexamethasone sodium phosphate.

Usual pediatric dose
Adrenocortical insufficiency—
Oral, 0.023 mg per kg of body weight or 0.67 mg per square meter of body surface area a day in three divided doses.
Other indications—
Oral, 0.083 to 0.33 mg per kg of body weight or 2.5 to 10 mg per square meter of body surface area a day in three or four divided doses.

Strength(s) usually available
U.S.—
0.5 mg per 5 mL (Rx) [GENERIC].
Canada—
Not commercially available.

Packaging and storage
Store below 40 °C (104 °F), preferably between 15 and 30 °C (59 and 86 °F), unless otherwise specified by manufacturer. Store in a tight container. Protect from freezing.

Auxiliary labeling
• Keep container tightly closed.

DEXAMETHASONE ORAL SOLUTION USP

Usual adult and adolescent dose
See *Dexamethasone Elixir USP*.

Usual pediatric dose
See *Dexamethasone Elixir USP*.

Strength(s) usually available
U.S.—
0.5 mg per 5 mL (Rx) [GENERIC].
1 mg per mL (Rx) [*Dexamethasone Intensol* (alcohol 30%)].
Canada—
Not commercially available.

Packaging and storage
Store between 15 and 30 °C (59 and 86 °F), unless otherwise specified by manufacturer, in a tight container. Protect from freezing.

Preparation of dosage form
Dexamethasone Intensol should be mixed with water, juice, soft drink, applesauce, or pudding before administration.

Stability
Dexamethasone Intensol should be consumed immediately after it is mixed with a beverage or a semi-solid food. Any unused portion should be discarded.

DEXAMETHASONE TABLETS USP

Usual adult and adolescent dose
Corticosteroid or
Dexamethasone suppression test or
Edema, cerebral, associated with recurrent or inoperable brain tumor—
See *Dexamethasone Elixir USP*.

Allergic disorders—
Therapy should be initiated with dexamethasone sodium phosphate injection (see *Dexamethasone Sodium Phosphate Injection USP*). Then, beginning on the second day, oral, 3 mg in two divided doses for two days, 1.5 mg in two divided doses for one day, 0.75 mg for two days, and a follow-up visit on the eighth day.

Allergic disorders, severe or
Carditis, rheumatic [or nonrheumatic][1] or
Neoplastic disease or
Pemphigus, acute or
Lupus erythematosus, systemic, crisis of—
Oral, initially 4 to 10 mg a day in divided doses.

Congenital adrenal hyperplasia—
Oral, 0.5 to 1.5 mg a day.

Lupus erythematosus, systemic or
Pemphigus, chronic or
Sarcoidosis, symptomatic—
Oral, initially 2 to 4.5 mg a day.

Multiple sclerosis, acute exacerbation (treatment)—
Oral, initially 30 milligrams a day for one week, followed by 4 to 12 milligrams every other day for one month.

[Nausea and vomiting, cancer chemotherapy-induced]—
Therapy should be initiated with dexamethasone sodium phosphate injection (see *Dexamethasone Sodium Phosphate Injection USP*). Then, oral, 4 mg every four to six hours, or 8 mg every eight hours with the dosage being reduced gradually over two to three days. Duration of therapy should not exceed five days beyond administration of chemotherapy.

Usual pediatric dose

Congenital adrenal hyperplasia—
Oral, 0.5 to 1.5 mg a day.

Adrenocortical insufficiency or
Other indications—
See *Dexamethasone Elixir USP*.

[Croup][1]—
Oral, 0.15 to 0.6 mg per kg of body weight given once.

Strength(s) usually available

U.S.—
0.25 mg (Rx) [GENERIC].
0.5 mg (Rx) [*Decadron* (scored); GENERIC (scored)].
0.75 mg (Rx) [*Decadron* (scored); GENERIC (scored)].
1 mg (Rx) [GENERIC (scored)].
1.5 mg (Rx) [GENERIC (scored)].
2 mg (Rx) [GENERIC (scored)].
4 mg (Rx) [GENERIC (scored)].
6 mg (Rx) [GENERIC (scored)].

Canada—
0.5 mg (Rx) [*Decadron* (scored); *Deronil* (scored); *Dexasone* (scored)].
0.75 mg (Rx) [*Deronil* (scored); *Dexasone* (scored)].
4 mg (Rx) [*Decadron* (scored); *Deronil* (scored); *Dexasone* (scored); *Oradexon* (scored)].

Packaging and storage

Store between 20 and 25 °C (68 and 77 °F), unless otherwise specified by manufacturer.

Preparation of dosage form

Tablets should be crushed and dissolved in liquid prior to administration to pediatric patients.

Parenteral Dosage Forms

Note: Bracketed uses in the *Dosage Forms* section refer to categories of use and/or indications that are not included in U.S. product labeling.

DEXAMETHASONE ACETATE INJECTABLE SUSPENSION USP

Note: The dosing and strengths of the dosage forms available are expressed in terms of dexamethasone base (not the acetate salt).

Usual adult and adolescent dose

Corticosteroid—
Intra-articular or soft-tissue injection, 4 to 16 mg of dexamethasone (base), repeated at one- to three-week intervals, if necessary.
Intralesional, 0.8 to 1.6 mg per injection site, repeated as needed.
Intramuscular, 8 to 16 mg, repeated at one- to three-week intervals, if necessary.

Usual pediatric dose

Dosage has not been established.

[Croup][1]—
Intramuscular, 0.6 mg per kg of body weight as a single injection.

Strength(s) usually available

U.S.—
8 mg (base) per mL (Rx) [*Cortastat LA; Dexasone L.A.; Dexone LA* (sodium bisulfite; benzyl alcohol); *Solurex LA* (sodium bisulfite; benzyl alcohol); GENERIC].

Canada—
Not commercially available.

Packaging and storage

Store between 15 and 30 °C (59 and 86 °F), unless otherwise specified by manufacturer. Protect from freezing. Protect from light.

Stability

This medication is heat-sensitive and should not be autoclaved.

Auxiliary labeling

- Shake well.

Additional information

For administration of injections, see manufacturer's labeling.
Do not administer this medication intravenously.
The suspension containing the equivalent of 16 mg of dexamethasone per mL is not for intralesional use.

DEXAMETHASONE SODIUM PHOSPHATE INJECTION USP

Note: The dosing and strength of the dosage forms available are expressed in terms of dexamethasone phosphate.

Usual adult and adolescent dose

Corticosteroid—
Intra-articular, intralesional, or soft-tissue injection, 0.2 to 6 mg (dexamethasone phosphate), repeated at three-day to three-week intervals, if necessary.
Intramuscular or intravenous, 0.5 to 9 mg a day.

Edema, cerebral—
Initial: Intravenous, 10 mg, followed by 4 mg intramuscularly every six hours until symptoms subside. Dosage may be reduced after two to four days and gradually discontinued over a period of five to seven days, unless a brain tumor, which must be treated before dexamethasone can be discontinued, is present.
Maintenance (for recurrent or inoperable brain tumors): Intramuscular, 2 mg two or three times a day initially, then adjusted according to patient response.

Shock—
The following regimens have been utilized—
Intravenous, 20 mg as a single dose initially, followed by 3 mg per kg of body weight per twenty-four hours via continuous intravenous infusion, or
Intravenous, 2 to 6 mg per kg of body weight as a single injection, or
Intravenous, 40 mg as a single dose, administered every two to six hours as needed, or
Intravenous, 1 mg per kg of body weight as a single injection.

Note: Administration of high-dose therapy for shock should be discontinued after the patient's condition has stabilized and usually is continued for no longer than two to three days.

Allergic disorders—
Intramuscular, initially 4 or 8 mg as a single dose. Maintenance therapy should be continued with dexamethasone tablets (see *Dexamethasone Tablets USP*).

[Nausea and vomiting, cancer chemotherapy-induced]—
Intravenous, 8 to 20 mg administered over five to fifteen minutes beginning just prior to chemotherapy. Therapy should be continued with dexamethasone tablets (see *Dexamethasone Tablets USP*).

[Respiratory distress syndrome, neonatal (prophylaxis)]—
Intramuscular, 5 mg every twelve hours up to a total of four doses beginning seven days to twenty-four hours before the estimated delivery date.

Usual adult prescribing limits

80 mg daily.

Usual pediatric dose

Adrenocortical insufficiency—
Intramuscular, 0.023 mg (dexamethasone phosphate) per kg of body weight or 0.67 mg per square meter of body surface area a day (in three divided doses) every third day; or 0.0078 to 0.012 mg per kg of body weight or 0.23 to 0.34 mg per square meter of body surface area once a day.

Other indications—
Intramuscular, 0.028 to 0.17 mg per kg of body weight or 0.83 to 5 mg per square meter of body surface area every twelve to twenty-four hours.

[Croup][1]—
Intramuscular, 0.6 mg per kg of body weight as a single injection.

Strength(s) usually available

U.S.—

4 mg (phosphate) per mL (Rx) [*Cortastat; Dexasone; Solurex* (sodium bisulfite); GENERIC (sodium metabisulfite)].

10 mg (phosphate) per mL (Rx) [*Cortastat 10; Dexasone;* GENERIC (sodium metabisulfite; benzyl alcohol 9 mg)].

Canada—

4 mg (phosphate) per mL (Rx) [*Decadron Phosphate* (sodium bisulfite); *Hexadrol Phosphate* (benzyl alcohol 10 mg; sodium sulfite); GENERIC (sodium metabisulfite)].

10 mg (phosphate) per mL (Rx) [*Hexadrol Phosphate* (benzyl alcohol 10 mg; sodium sulfite); GENERIC (sodium metabisulfite)].

Packaging and storage

Store below 40 °C (104 °F), preferably between 15 and 30 °C (59 and 86 °F), unless otherwise specified by manufacturer. Protect from light. Protect from freezing.

Preparation of dosage form

Dexamethasone sodium phosphate injection may be admixed with dextrose injection or sodium chloride injection and administered via intravenous infusion.

For use in cancer chemotherapy-induced nausea and vomiting, 20 mg of dexamethasone sodium phosphate injection may be admixed with 8 mg of ondansetron hydrochloride injection in 50 mL of 5% dextrose injection.

Stability

This medication is heat-sensitive and should not be autoclaved.

When dexamethasone sodium phosphate injection is admixed with dextrose injection or sodium chloride injection, the solution must be used within 24 hours.

When dexamethasone sodium phosphate injection is admixed with ondansetron hydrochloride injection in 5% dextrose injection, the resulting solution is stable for up to two days when stored at room temperature or for up to 7 days when stored at a temperature between 2 and 8 °C (36 and 46 °F).

Caution

Use of preparations containing benzyl alcohol is not recommended in neonates. A fatal toxic syndrome consisting of metabolic acidosis, central nervous system (CNS) depression, respiratory problems, renal failure, hypotension, and possibly seizures and intracranial hemorrhages has been associated with this use.

Additional information

For administration of injections, see manufacturer's labeling.

Dosage forms containing 24 mg (dexamethasone phosphate) per mL are for intravenous use only.

---

[1]Not included in Canadian product labeling.

HYDROCORTISONE

Oral Dosage Forms

HYDROCORTISONE TABLETS USP

Usual adult and adolescent dose

Corticosteroid—

Oral, 20 to 240 mg a day as a single dose or in divided doses.

Multiple sclerosis, acute exacerbations of—

Oral, 800 mg a day for one week, followed by 320 mg every other day for one month.

Usual pediatric dose

Adrenocortical insufficiency—

Oral, 0.56 mg per kg of body weight or 15 to 20 mg per square meter of body surface area a day as a single dose or in divided doses.

Other indications—

Oral, 2 to 8 mg per kg of body weight or 60 to 240 mg per square meter of body surface area a day as a single dose or in divided doses.

Strength(s) usually available

U.S.—

5 mg (Rx) [*Cortef* (scored)].

10 mg (Rx) [*Cortef* (scored); *Hydrocortone* (scored); GENERIC].

20 mg (Rx) [*Cortef* (scored); GENERIC (scored)].

Canada—

10 mg (Rx) [*Cortef* (scored)].

20 mg (Rx) [*Cortef* (scored)].

Packaging and storage

Store between 15 and 30 °C (59 and 86 °F), unless otherwise specified by manufacturer. Store in a well-closed container.

HYDROCORTISONE CYPIONATE ORAL SUSPENSION

Note: The dosing and strength of the dosage forms available are expressed in terms of hydrocortisone base (not the cypionate salt).

Usual adult and adolescent dose

Corticosteroid—

Oral, 20 to 240 mg (base) a day as a single dose or in divided doses.

Usual pediatric dose

Adrenocortical insufficiency—

Oral, 0.56 mg (base) per kg of body weight or 15 to 20 mg per square meter of body surface area a day as a single dose or in divided doses.

Other indications—

Oral, 2 to 8 mg per kg of body weight or 60 to 240 mg per square meter of body surface area a day as a single dose or in divided doses.

Strength(s) usually available

U.S.—

10 mg (base) per 5 mL (Rx) [*Cortef*].

Canada—

Not commercially available.

Packaging and storage

Store between 20 and 25 °C (68 and 77 °F), unless otherwise specified by manufacturer. Store in a tight, light-resistant container. Protect from freezing.

Auxiliary labeling

- Shake well.

Parenteral Dosage Forms

HYDROCORTISONE INJECTABLE SUSPENSION USP

Usual adult and adolescent dose

Corticosteroid—

Intramuscular, 15 to 240 mg a day.

Usual pediatric dose

Adrenocortical insufficiency—

Intramuscular, 0.56 mg per kg of body weight or 30 to 37.5 mg per square meter of body surface area a day every third day; or 0.19 to 0.28 mg per kg of body weight or 10 to 12.5 mg per square meter of body surface area once a day.

Other indications—

Intramuscular, 0.67 to 4 mg per kg of body weight or 20 to 120 mg per square meter of body surface area every twelve to twenty-four hours.

Strength(s) usually available

U.S.—

25 mg per mL (Rx) [GENERIC].

50 mg per mL (Rx) [GENERIC].

Canada—

Not commercially available.

Packaging and storage

Store below 40 °C (104 °F), preferably between 15 and 30 °C (59 and 86 °F), unless otherwise specified by manufacturer. Protect from freezing.

Auxiliary labeling

- Shake well.

Additional information

Do not administer this medication intravenously.

HYDROCORTISONE ACETATE INJECTABLE SUSPENSION USP

Usual adult and adolescent dose

Corticosteroid—

Intra-articular, intralesional, or soft-tissue injection, 5 to 75 mg, repeated at two- to three-week intervals.

Note: Severe conditions may require doses at one-week intervals.

Usual pediatric dose

Dosage has not been established.

Strength(s) usually available

U.S.—

25 mg per mL (Rx) [GENERIC].

50 mg per mL (Rx) [*Hydrocortone Acetate* (benzyl alcohol 9 mg); GENERIC].

Canada—

Not commercially available.

Packaging and storage
Store below 40 °C (104 °F), preferably between 15 and 30 °C (59 and 86 °F), unless otherwise specified by manufacturer. Protect from freezing.

Stability
For concurrent use of a parenteral-local anesthetic, withdraw the required quantity of corticosteroid suspension into a syringe, then add the local anesthetic. *Do not introduce the local anesthetic directly into the multiple-dose vial.* Also, the mixture must be used immediately and any unused portion discarded.

This medication is heat-sensitive and should not be autoclaved.

Auxiliary labeling
- Shake well.

Caution
Use of preparations containing benzyl alcohol is not recommended in neonates. A fatal toxic syndrome consisting of metabolic acidosis, central nervous system (CNS) depression, respiratory problems, renal failure, hypotension, and possibly seizures and intracranial hemorrhages has been associated with this use.

Additional information
For administration of injections, see manufacturer's labeling.

Do not administer this medication intravenously.

HYDROCORTISONE SODIUM PHOSPHATE INJECTION USP

Note: The dosing and strength of the dosage form available is expressed in terms of hydrocortisone base (not the sodium phosphate salt).

Usual adult and adolescent dose
Corticosteroid—

Intramuscular, intravenous, or subcutaneous, 15 to 240 mg (base) a day in divided doses.

Usual pediatric dose
Adrenocortical insufficiency—

Intramuscular or intravenous, 0.19 to 0.28 mg (base) per kg of body weight or 10 to 12 mg per square meter of body surface area a day in three divided doses.

Other indications—

Intramuscular, 0.67 to 4 mg per kg of body weight or 20 to 120 mg per square meter of body surface area every twelve to twenty-four hours.

Strength(s) usually available
U.S.—

50 mg (base) per mL (Rx) [*Hydrocortone Phosphate* (sodium bisulfite 3.2 mg); GENERIC (Quad—sodium metabisulfite 2 mg)].

Canada—

Not commercially available.

Packaging and storage
Store below 40 °C (104 °F), preferably between 15 and 30 °C (59 and 86 °F), unless otherwise specified by manufacturer. Protect from freezing.

Preparation of dosage form
Hydrocortisone sodium phosphate injection may be admixed with dextrose injection or sodium chloride injection and administered via intravenous infusion.

Stability
This medication is heat-sensitive and should not be autoclaved.

When hydrocortisone sodium phosphate injection is admixed with dextrose injection or sodium chloride injection, the solution must be used within 24 hours.

Caution
Use of preparations containing benzyl alcohol is not recommended in neonates. A fatal toxic syndrome consisting of metabolic acidosis, central nervous system (CNS) depression, respiratory problems, renal failure, hypotension, and possibly seizures and intracranial hemorrhages has been associated with this use.

Additional information
For administration of injections, see manufacturer's labeling.

HYDROCORTISONE SODIUM SUCCINATE FOR INJECTION USP

Note: The dosing and strength of the dosage forms available are expressed in terms of hydrocortisone base (not the sodium succinate salt).

Usual adult and adolescent dose
Corticosteroid—

Intramuscular or intravenous, 100 to 500 mg (base); may be repeated every two to six hours, depending upon patient condition and response.

Note: Initial intravenous dosage should be administered over a period of thirty seconds (100-mg dose) to ten minutes (doses 500 mg or higher).

Maintenance dosage (if required) should be no less than 25 mg per day.

Usual pediatric dose
Adrenocortical insufficiency—

Intramuscular or intravenous, 0.19 to 0.28 mg (base) per kg of body weight or 10 to 12 mg per square meter of body surface area a day in three divided doses.

Other indications—

Intramuscular, 0.67 to 4 mg per kg of body weight or 20 to 120 mg per square meter of body surface area every twelve to twenty-four hours.

Strength(s) usually available
U.S.—

100 mg (base) (Rx) [*A-hydroCort* (benzyl alcohol 18 mg per 2 mL—Univial); *Solu-Cortef* (benzyl alcohol 18.1 mg per 2 mL—Act-O-Vial, Mix-O-Vial); GENERIC].

250 mg (base) (Rx) [*A-hydroCort* (benzyl alcohol 18 mg per 2 mL—Univial); *Solu-Cortef* (benzyl alcohol 16.4 mg per 2 mL—Act-O-Vial, Mix-O-Vial); GENERIC].

500 mg (base) (Rx) [*A-hydroCort* (benzyl alcohol 36 mg per 4 mL—Univial); *Solu-Cortef* (benzyl alcohol 33.4 mg per 4 mL—Act-O-Vial, Mix-O-Vial); GENERIC].

1 gram (base) (Rx) [*A-hydroCort* (benzyl alcohol 72 mg per 8 mL—Univial); *Solu-Cortef* (benzyl alcohol 66.9 mg per 8 mL—Act-O-Vial, Mix-O-Vial); GENERIC].

Canada—

100 mg (base) (Rx) [*A-Hydrocort* (benzyl alcohol 18 mg); *Solu-Cortef* (benzyl alcohol 18.1 mg)].

250 mg (base) (Rx) [*A-Hydrocort* (benzyl alcohol 18 mg); *Solu-Cortef* (benzyl alcohol 16.4 mg)].

500 mg (base) (Rx) [*A-Hydrocort* (benzyl alcohol 36 mg); *Solu-Cortef* (benzyl alcohol 33.4 mg)].

1 gram (base) (Rx) [*A-Hydrocort* (benzyl alcohol 72 mg); *Solu-Cortef* (benzyl alcohol 66.9 mg)].

Packaging and storage
Store between 15 and 30 °C (59 and 86 °F), unless otherwise specified by manufacturer.

Stability
Reconstituted solution should be used only if it is clear and should be discarded after 3 days.

After reconstitution, protect the solution from light.

Caution
Use of preparations containing benzyl alcohol is not recommended in neonates. A fatal toxic syndrome consisting of metabolic acidosis, central nervous system (CNS) depression, respiratory problems, renal failure, hypotension, and possibly seizures and intracranial hemorrhages has been associated with this use.

Additional information
For preparation and administration of injections, see manufacturer's labeling.

METHYLPREDNISOLONE

Oral Dosage Forms

METHYLPREDNISOLONE TABLETS USP

Usual adult and adolescent dose
Corticosteroid—

Oral, 4 to 48 mg a day as a single dose or in divided doses.

Multiple sclerosis, acute exacerbations of—

Oral, 160 mg a day for one week, followed by 64 mg every other day for one month.

Usual pediatric dose
Adrenocortical insufficiency—

Oral, 0.18 mg per kg of body weight or 3.33 mg per square meter of body surface area a day in three divided doses.

Other indications—

Oral, 0.42 to 1.67 mg per kg of body weight or 12.5 to 50 mg per square meter of body surface area a day in three or four divided doses.

Strength(s) usually available
U.S.—

2 mg (Rx) [*Medrol* (scored)].

4 mg (Rx) [*Medrol* (scored); *Meprolone;* GENERIC].

8 mg (Rx) [*Medrol* (scored)].

16 mg (Rx) [*Medrol* (scored); GENERIC].
24 mg (Rx) [*Medrol* (scored); GENERIC].
32 mg (Rx) [*Medrol* (scored); GENERIC].

Canada—
4 mg (Rx) [*Medrol* (scored)].
16 mg (Rx) [*Medrol* (scored)].

Packaging and storage
Store between 20 and 25 °C (68 and 77 °F), unless otherwise specified by manufacturer. Store in a tight container.

Parenteral Dosage Forms
Note: Bracketed uses in the *Dosage Forms* section refer to categories of use and/or indications that are not included in U.S. product labeling.

METHYLPREDNISOLONE ACETATE INJECTABLE SUSPENSION USP

Usual adult and adolescent dose
Corticosteroid—
Intra-articular, intralesional, or soft-tissue injection, 4 to 80 mg, repeated at one- to five-week intervals, if necessary.
Intramuscular, varies with condition being treated. The usual dose is 40 to 120 mg as a single dose, repeated at one-day intervals temporarily as a substitute for oral therapy, or maintenance doses at intervals of one to two weeks.

Congenital adrenal hyperplasia—
Intramuscular, 40 mg at two-week intervals.

Multiple sclerosis, acute exacerbations of—
Intramuscular, 160 mg a day for one week, followed by 64 mg every other day for one month.

Usual pediatric dose
Adrenocortical insufficiency—
Intramuscular, 0.12 mg per kg of body weight or 3.33 mg per square meter of body surface area a day (in three divided doses) every third day; or 0.039 to 0.059 mg per kg of body weight or 1.11 to 1.66 mg per square meter of body surface area once a day.

Other indications—
Intramuscular, 0.14 to 0.84 mg per kg of body weight or 4.16 to 25 mg per square meter of body surface area every twelve to twenty-four hours.

Strength(s) usually available
U.S.—
20 mg per mL (Rx) [*Depo-Medrol* (benzyl alcohol 9.3 mg)].
40 mg per mL (Rx) [*Depo-Medrol*].
80 mg per mL (Rx) [*Depo-Medrol*].

Canada—
20 mg per mL (Rx) [*Depo-Medrol* (benzyl alcohol)].
40 mg per mL (Rx) [*Depo-Medrol* (benzyl alcohol)].
80 mg per mL (Rx) [*Depo-Medrol* (benzyl alcohol)].

Packaging and storage
Store between 20 and 25 °C (68 and 77 °F), unless otherwise specified by manufacturer. Protect from freezing.

Preparation of dosage form
For preparation and administration of injections, see manufacturer's labeling.

Incompatibilities
It is recommended that this medication not be diluted or mixed with other solutions because of possible physical incompatibility.

Auxiliary labeling
• Shake well.

Caution
Use of preparations containing benzyl alcohol is not recommended in neonates. A fatal toxic syndrome consisting of metabolic acidosis, central nervous system (CNS) depression, respiratory problems, renal failure, hypotension, and possibly seizures and intracranial hemorrhages has been associated with this use.

Additional information
Do not administer this medication intrathecally or intravenously.

METHYLPREDNISOLONE SODIUM SUCCINATE FOR INJECTION USP
Note: The dosing and strength of the dosage form available is expressed in terms of methylprednisolone base (not the sodium succinate salt).

Usual adult and adolescent dose
Corticosteroid—
Intramuscular or intravenous, 10 to 40 mg (base), repeated as needed.

Colitis, ulcerative—
Intravenous, 40 to 120 mg three to seven times a week for two or more weeks.

High-dose ("pulse") therapy—
Intravenous, 30 mg per kg of body weight administered over at least thirty minutes. This dose may be repeated every four to six hours for forty-eight hours.

Multiple sclerosis, acute exacerbations of—
Intramuscular or intravenous, 160 mg a day for one week, followed by 64 mg every other day for one month.

[Pneumonia, *Pneumocystis carinii*, associated with AIDS, adjunctive treatment][1]—
Intravenous, 30 mg two times a day on days one through five, 30 mg once a day on days six through ten, and 15 mg once a day on days eleven through twenty-one.

[Spinal cord injury, acute]—
Intravenous, 30 mg per kg of body weight administered over fifteen minutes, followed after forty-five minutes by a continuous infusion of 5.4 mg per kg of body weight per hour, for twenty-three hours.

Note: Treatment should begin within eight hours of the injury.

Usual pediatric dose
Adrenocortical insufficiency—
Intramuscular, 0.18 mg (base) per kg of body weight or 3.33 mg per square meter of body surface area a day (in three divided doses) every third day; or 0.039 to 0.059 mg per kg of body weight or 1.11 to 1.66 mg per square meter of body surface area once a day.

[High-dose ("pulse") therapy][1]—
Intravenous, 30 (base) mg/kg (to a maximum of 1 gram) administered over thirty minutes to one hour once a day for three consecutive days.

[Pneumonia, *Pneumocystis carinii*, associated with AIDS, adjunctive treatment][1]—
Children up to 14 years of age: Dosage has not been established.
Children 14 years of age or older: See *Usual adult and adolescent dose*.

[Spinal cord injury, acute][1]—
Intravenous, 30 mg per kg of body weight administered over fifteen minutes, followed after forty-five minutes by a continuous infusion of 5.4 mg per kg of body weight per hour, for twenty-three hours.

Other indications—
Intramuscular, 0.14 to 0.84 mg per kg of body weight or 4.16 to 25 mg per square meter of body surface area every twelve to twenty-four hours.

Strength(s) usually available
U.S.—
40 mg (base) (Rx) [*Solu-Medrol* (benzyl alcohol 8.8 mg); GENERIC].
125 mg (base) (Rx) [*Solu-Medrol* (benzyl alcohol 17.6 mg); GENERIC].
500 mg (base) (Rx) [*A-MethaPred; Solu-Medrol* (benzyl alcohol 70.2 mg—vial with diluent; 33.7 mg—single-dose vial); GENERIC].
1 gram (base) (Rx) [*A-MethaPred; Solu-Medrol* (benzyl alcohol 66.8 mg—single-dose vial); GENERIC].
2 grams (base) (Rx) [*Solu-Medrol* (benzyl alcohol 273 mg—vial with diluent)].

Canada—
40 mg (base) (Rx) [*Solu-Medrol* (diluent—benzyl alcohol 8.8 mg)].
125 mg (base) (Rx) [*Solu-Medrol* (diluent—benzyl alcohol 17.6 mg)].
500 mg (base) (Rx) [*Solu-Medrol* (diluent—benzyl alcohol 33.7 mg)].
1 gram (base) (Rx) [*Solu-Medrol* (diluent—benzyl alcohol 66.8 mg)].

Packaging and storage
Store between 20 and 25 °C (68 and 77 °F), unless otherwise specified by manufacturer. Protect from light.

Preparation of dosage form
For preparation and administration of injections, see manufacturer's labeling.

Stability
Use reconstituted solution within 48 hours. Do not use if solution is cloudy or contains a precipitate.

Caution
Use of diluents or preparations containing benzyl alcohol is not recommended in neonates. A fatal toxic syndrome consisting of metabolic acidosis, central nervous system (CNS) depression, respiratory problems, renal failure, hypotension, and possibly seizures and intracranial hemorrhages has been associated with this use.

Additional information
When used intravenously, Methylprednisolone Sodium Succinate for Injection USP should be administered over a period of 1 to several minutes.

[1]Not included in Canadian product labeling.

PREDNISOLONE

Oral Dosage Forms

PREDNISOLONE SYRUP USP

Usual adult and adolescent dose

Corticosteroid—

Oral, 5 to 60 mg a day as a single dose or in divided doses.

Multiple sclerosis, acute exacerbations of—

Oral, 200 mg a day for one week, followed by 80 mg every other day for one month.

Usual adult prescribing limits

250 mg a day.

Usual pediatric dose

Adrenocortical insufficiency—

Oral, 0.14 mg per kg of body weight or 4 mg per square meter of body surface area a day in three divided doses.

Other indications—

Oral, 0.5 to 2 mg per kg of body weight or 15 to 60 mg per square meter of body surface area a day in three or four divided doses.

Strength(s) usually available

U.S.—

5 mg per 5 mL (Rx) [*Prelone* (alcohol ≤0.4%)].

15 mg per 5 mL (Rx) [*Prelone* (alcohol 5%); GENERIC].

Canada—

Not commercially available.

Packaging and storage

Store between 15 and 30 °C (59 and 86 °F), unless otherwise specified by manufacturer. Store in a tight container. Protect from light and from freezing.

Auxiliary labeling

- Do not refrigerate.

Note

Dispense with a calibrated measuring device.

PREDNISOLONE TABLETS USP

Usual adult and adolescent dose

See *Prednisolone Syrup USP*.

Usual adult prescribing limits

See *Prednisolone Syrup USP*.

Usual pediatric dose

See *Prednisolone Syrup USP*.

Strength(s) usually available

U.S.—

5 mg (Rx) [*Cotolone; Delta-Cortef* (scored); GENERIC].

Canada—

Not commercially available.

Packaging and storage

Store below 40 °C (104 °F), preferably between 15 and 30 °C (59 and 86 °F). Store in a well-closed container.

PREDNISOLONE SODIUM PHOSPHATE ORAL SOLUTION

Note: The dosing and strength of the dosage form available is expressed in terms of prednisolone base (not the sodium phosphate salt).

Usual adult and adolescent dose

Corticosteroid—

Oral, 5 to 60 mg (base) a day as a single dose or in divided doses.

Multiple sclerosis, acute exacerbations of—

Oral, 200 mg a day for one week, followed by 80 mg every other day for one month.

Note: Dosage requirements are variable and must be individualized on the basis of the disease under treatment and the response of the patient.

Usual adult prescribing limits

250 mg a day.

Usual pediatric dose

Adrenocortical insufficiency—

Oral, 0.14 mg (base) per kg of body weight or 4 mg per square meter of body surface area a day in three divided doses.

Asthma (treatment)—

Oral, 1 to 2 mg per kg of body weight per day in single or divided doses. It is further recommended that short course, or "burst" therapy, be continued until a child achieved a peak expiratory flow rate of 80% of personal best or symptoms resolve. This usually requires 3 to 10 days of treatment, although it can take longer. There is no evidence that tapering the dose after improvement will prevent a relapse.

Nephrotic syndrome (treatment)—

Oral, 60 mg per m^2 per day given in three divided doses for 4 weeks, followed by 4 weeks of single dose alternate-day therapy at 40 mg per m^2 per day

Other indications—

Oral, 0.5 to 2 mg per kg of body weight or 15 to 60 mg per square meter of body surface area a day in three or four divided doses.

Usual geriatric dose

See *Usual adult dose*

Strength(s) usually available

U.S.—

5 mg (base) per 5 mL (Rx) [*Pediapred* (sorbitol)].

Canada—

5 mg (base) per 5 mL (Rx) [*Pediapred* (sorbitol)].

Packaging and storage

Store between 15 and 30 °C (59 and 86 °F), unless otherwise specified by manufacturer. Protect from freezing.

Auxiliary labeling

- Keep container tightly closed.

Parenteral Dosage Forms

PREDNISOLONE ACETATE INJECTABLE SUSPENSION USP

Usual adult and adolescent dose

Corticosteroid—

Intra-articular, intralesional, or soft-tissue injection, 4 to 100 mg, repeated as needed.

Intramuscular, 4 to 60 mg a day.

Usual pediatric dose

Adrenocortical insufficiency—

Intramuscular, 0.14 mg per kg of body weight or 4 mg per square meter of body surface area a day (in three divided doses) every third day; or 0.046 to 0.07 mg per kg of body weight or 1.33 to 2 mg per square meter of body surface area once a day.

Other indications—

Intramuscular, 0.17 to 1 mg per kg of body weight or 5 to 30 mg per square meter of body surface area every twelve to twenty-four hours.

Strength(s) usually available

U.S.—

25 mg per mL (Rx) [*Cotolone; Key-Pred; Predcor-25;* GENERIC].

50 mg per mL (Rx) [*Articulose-50* (benzyl alcohol); *Cotolone; Key-Pred; Predacort 50; Pred-Ject-50; Predalone 50; Predate-50; Predcor-50;* GENERIC].

Canada—

Not commercially available.

Packaging and storage

Store below 40 °C (104 °F), preferably between 15 and 30 °C (59 and 86 °F), unless otherwise specified by manufacturer. Protect from freezing.

Auxiliary labeling

- Shake well.

Additional information

Do not administer this medication intravenously.

PREDNISOLONE ACETATE AND PREDNISOLONE SODIUM PHOSPHATE INJECTABLE SUSPENSION

Usual adult and adolescent dose

Corticosteroid—

Intra-articular, intramuscular, or intrasynovial, 20 to 80 mg of prednisolone acetate and 5 to 20 mg of prednisolone sodium phosphate, repeated at three-day to four-week intervals, if necessary.

Usual pediatric dose

Dosage has not been established.

Strength(s) usually available

U.S.—

80 mg of prednisolone acetate and 20 mg of prednisolone sodium phosphate per mL (Rx) [GENERIC].

Canada—

Not commercially available.

Packaging and storage

Store below 40 °C (104 °F), preferably between 15 and 30 °C (59 and 86 °F), unless otherwise specified by manufacturer. Protect from light. Protect from freezing.

Auxiliary labeling
- Shake well.

Additional information
Do not administer this medication intravenously.

PREDNISOLONE SODIUM PHOSPHATE INJECTION USP

Note: The dosing and strength of the dosage form available is expressed in terms of prednisolone phosphate.

Usual adult and adolescent dose
Corticosteroid—
Intra-articular, intralesional, or soft-tissue injection, 2 to 30 mg (prednisolone phosphate), repeated at three-day to three-week intervals, if necessary.
Intramuscular or intravenous, 4 to 60 mg a day.

Usual pediatric dose
Adrenocortical insufficiency—
Intramuscular, 0.14 mg (prednisolone phosphate) per kg of body weight or 4 mg per square meter of body surface area a day (in three divided doses) every third day; or 0.046 to 0.07 mg per kg of body weight or 1.33 to 2 mg per square meter of body surface area once a day.
Other indications—
Intramuscular, 0.17 to 1 mg per kg of body weight or 5 to 30 mg per square meter of body surface area every twelve to twenty-four hours.

Strength(s) usually available
U.S.—
20 mg (phosphate) per mL (Rx) [*Key-Pred SP* (sodium bisulfite); *Predate S; Predicort-RP* (sodium bisulfite); GENERIC].
Canada—
Not commercially available.

Packaging and storage
Store below 40 °C (104 °F), preferably between 15 and 30 °C (59 and 86 °F), unless otherwise specified by manufacturer. Protect from light. Protect from freezing.

Preparation of dosage form
For preparation and administration of injections, see manufacturer's labeling.

Stability
This medication is heat-sensitive and should not be autoclaved.

PREDNISOLONE TEBUTATE INJECTABLE SUSPENSION USP

Usual adult and adolescent dose
Corticosteroid—
Intra-articular, intralesional, or soft-tissue injection, 4 to 40 mg, repeated at two- to three-week intervals, if necessary.

Note: Severe conditions may require doses at one-week intervals.

Usual pediatric dose
Dosage has not been established.

Strength(s) usually available
U.S.—
20 mg per mL (Rx) [*Nor-Pred T.B.A.* (benzyl alcohol); *Predalone T.B.A.* (benzyl alcohol); *Predate TBA; Predcor-TBA* (benzyl alcohol)].
Canada—
Not commercially available.

Packaging and storage
Store below 40 °C (104 °F), preferably between 15 and 30 °C (59 and 86 °F), protected from light, unless otherwise specified by manufacturer. Protect from freezing.

Preparation of dosage form
For preparation and administration of injections, see manufacturer's labeling.

Stability
For concurrent use of a parenteral-local anesthetic, withdraw the required quantity of corticosteroid suspension into a syringe, then add the local anesthetic. *Do not introduce the local anesthetic directly into the multiple-dose vial.* Also, the mixture should be injected immediately and any unused portion discarded.
This medication is heat-sensitive and should not be autoclaved.

Auxiliary labeling
- Shake well.

Caution
Use of preparations containing benzyl alcohol is not recommended in neonates. A fatal toxic syndrome consisting of metabolic acidosis, central nervous system (CNS) depression, respiratory problems, renal failure, hypotension, and possibly seizures and intracranial hemorrhages has been associated with this use.

Additional information
Do not administer this medication intravenously.

PREDNISONE

Oral Dosage Forms

Note: Bracketed uses in the *Dosage Forms* section refer to categories of use and/or indications that are not included in U.S. product labeling.

PREDNISONE ORAL SOLUTION USP

Usual adult and adolescent dose
Corticosteroid—
Oral, 5 to 60 mg a day as a single dose or in divided doses.
Congenital adrenal hyperplasia—
Oral, 5 to 10 mg a day as a single dose.
Multiple sclerosis, acute exacerbations of—
Oral, 200 mg a day for one week, followed by 80 mg every other day for one month.
[Pneumonia, *Pneumocystis carinii*, associated with AIDS, adjunctive treatment][1]—
Oral, 40 mg two times a day on days one through five, 40 mg once a day on days six through ten, and 20 mg once a day on days eleven through twenty-one.

Usual adult prescribing limits
250 mg a day.

Usual pediatric dose
Carditis, rheumatic [or nonrheumatic][1], acute or
Leukemia or
Tumors—
Oral, 0.5 mg per kg of body weight or 15 mg per square meter of body surface area four times a day for two to three weeks; then 0.38 mg per kg of body weight or 11.25 mg per square meter of body surface area four times a day for four to six weeks.
Congenital adrenal hyperplasia—
Oral, 5 mg per square meter of body surface area a day in two divided doses.
Nephrotic syndrome—
Children up to 18 months of age: Dosage has not been established.
Children 18 months to 4 years of age: Oral, initially 7.5 to 10 mg four times a day.
Children 4 to 10 years of age: Oral, initially 15 mg four times a day.
Children 10 years of age or older: Oral, initially 20 mg four times a day.
Tuberculosis (with concurrent antitubercular therapy)—
Oral, 0.5 mg per kg of body weight or 15 mg per square meter of body surface area four times a day for two months.
[Pneumonia, *Pneumocystis carinii*, associated with AIDS, adjunctive treatment][1]—
Children up to 14 years of age: Dosage has not been established.
Children 14 years of age or older: See *Usual adult and adolescent dose.*

Strength(s) usually available
U.S.—
5 mg per 5 mL (Rx) [GENERIC (alcohol 5%)].
5 mg per mL (Rx) [*Predisone Intensol* (alcohol 30%)].
Canada—
Not commercially available.

Packaging and storage
Store below 40 °C (104 °F), preferably between 15 and 30 °C (59 and 86 °F), in a light-resistant container, unless otherwise specified by manufacturer. Store in a tight container. Protect from freezing.

PREDNISONE SYRUP USP

Usual adult and adolescent dose
See *Prednisone Oral Solution USP.*

Usual adult prescribing limits
See *Prednisone Oral Solution USP.*

Usual pediatric dose
See *Prednisone Oral Solution USP.*

Strength(s) usually available
U.S.—
5 mg per 5 mL (Rx) [*Liquid Pred* (alcohol 5%; saccharin; sorbitol)].
Canada—
Not commercially available.

Packaging and storage
Store below 40 °C (104 °F), preferably between 15 and 30 °C (59 and 86 °F), in a light-resistant container, unless otherwise specified by manufacturer. Store in a tight container. Protect from freezing.

PREDNISONE TABLETS USP

Usual adult and adolescent dose
See *Prednisone Oral Solution USP.*

Usual adult prescribing limits
See *Prednisone Oral Solution USP.*

Usual pediatric dose
See *Prednisone Oral Solution USP.*

Strength(s) usually available
U.S.—
- 1 mg (Rx) [*Meticorten; Orasone 1* (scored); GENERIC (scored)].
- 2.5 mg (Rx) [*Deltasone* (scored); GENERIC (scored)].
- 5 mg (Rx) [*Deltasone* (scored); *Orasone 5* (scored); *Prednicot; Pred-Pak 45; Pred-Pak 79; Sterapred;* GENERIC (scored)].
- 10 mg (Rx) [*Deltasone* (scored); *Orasone 10* (scored); *Prednicot; Sterapred DS* (scored); GENERIC (scored)].
- 20 mg (Rx) [*Cordrol; Deltasone* (scored); *Orasone 20* (scored); *Prednicot;* GENERIC (scored)].
- 50 mg (Rx) [*Deltasone* (scored); *Orasone 50* (scored); GENERIC (scored)].

Canada—
- 1 mg (Rx) [*Apo-Prednisone; Winpred*].
- 5 mg (Rx) [*Apo-Prednisone* (scored); *Deltasone* (scored); GENERIC (scored)].
- 50 mg (Rx) [*Apo-Prednisone* (scored); *Deltasone* (scored)].

Packaging and storage
Store between 20 and 25 °C (68 and 77 °F), unless otherwise specified by manufacturer. Store in a well-closed container.

---

[1]Not included in Canadian product labeling.

TRIAMCINOLONE

Oral Dosage Forms

Note: Bracketed uses in the *Dosage Forms* section refer to categories of use and/or indications that are not included in U.S. product labeling.

TRIAMCINOLONE TABLETS USP

Usual adult and adolescent dose
Allergic disorders—
- Oral, 8 to 16 mg a day to achieve control within twenty-four to forty-eight hours.

Arthritis, rheumatoid—
- Initial: Oral, 8 to 16 mg a day for two to seven days.
- Maintenance: Oral, 2 to 16 mg a day.

Bursitis, acute—
- Oral, initially 2 to 16 mg a day; dosage may then be adjusted based on patient response.

Dermatoses, inflammatory—
- Initial: Oral, 8 to 16 mg a day.
- Maintenance: Oral, 1 to 2 mg a day.

Lupus erythematosus, disseminated—
- Initial: Oral, 20 to 30 mg a day.
- Maintenance: Oral, 3 to 30 mg a day.

Neoplastic disease—
- Oral, initially 16 to 40 mg a day; dosage may then be adjusted based on patient response.

Nephrotic syndrome—
- Oral, 16 to 20 mg a day until diuresis occurs. Dosage should be gradually tapered and discontinued when remission occurs.

Rhinitis, allergic, perennial or seasonal, severe—
- Initial: Oral, 8 to 12 mg a day.
- Maintenance: Oral, 2 to 6 mg a day.

[Emphysema, pulmonary] or
[Fibrosis, idiopathic pulmonary (Hamman-Rich syndrome)]—
- Initial: Oral, 8 to 12 mg a day.
- Maintenance: 2 to 4 mg a day.

[Rheumatic fever]—
- Initial: Oral, 16 to 20 mg a day.
- Maintenance: Oral, 6 to 20 mg a day.

Other indications—
- Oral, initially 8 to 20 mg a day in three or four divided doses. When a satisfactory response is obtained, the dose should be reduced by decrements of 2 mg every two to three days until the lowest dose that maintains the desired effect is reached.

Usual pediatric dose
Adrenocortical insufficiency—
- Oral, 0.12 mg per kg of body weight or 3.3 mg per square meter of body surface area a day as a single dose or in divided doses.

Neoplastic disease—
- Oral, initially 1 to 2 mg per kg of body weight a day; dosage may then be adjusted based on patient response.

Other indications—
- Oral, 0.42 to 1.7 mg per kg of body weight or 12.5 to 50 mg per square meter of body surface area a day as a single dose or in divided doses.

Note: Some pediatric patients with neoplastic disease (acute leukemia) may require initial doses as high as 2 mg per kg of body weight per day.

Strength(s) usually available
U.S.—
- 1 mg (Rx) [*Aristocort* (scored)].
- 4 mg (Rx) [*Aristocort* (scored); *Aristopak; Kenacort;* GENERIC].
- 8 mg (Rx) [*Aristocort* (scored); *Kenacort* (scored; tartrazine)].
- 16 mg (Rx) [*Aristocort* (scored)].

Canada—
- 2 mg (Rx) [*Aristocort* (scored)].
- 4 mg (Rx) [*Aristocort* (scored); *Kenacort* (scored)].

Packaging and storage
Store below 40 °C (104 °F), preferably between 15 and 30 °C (59 and 86 °F). Store in a well-closed container.

TRIAMCINOLONE DIACETATE SYRUP USP

Note: The dosing and strength of the dosage forms available are expressed in terms of triamcinolone base (not the diacetate salt).

Usual adult and adolescent dose
Adrenocortical insufficiency—
- Oral, 4 to 12 mg (base) a day as a single dose or in divided doses.

Other indications—
- Oral, 4 to 48 mg a day as a single dose or in divided doses.

Note: After an initial response has been attained, this medication may be administered on an intermittent schedule. An example of this schedule is as follows: three or four days of medication followed by three medication-free days.

In some patients (e.g., those with systemic lupus erythematosus, acute rheumatic carditis, or certain hematologic disorders), initial doses as high as 60 mg per day may be required.

Usual pediatric dose
Adrenocortical insufficiency—
- Oral, 0.12 mg (base) per kg of body weight or 3.3 mg per square meter of body surface area a day as a single dose or in divided doses.

Other indications—
- Oral, 0.42 to 1.7 mg per kg of body weight or 12.5 to 50 mg per square meter of body surface area a day as a single dose or in divided doses.

Note: Some pediatric patients with neoplastic disease (acute leukemia) may require initial doses as high as 2 mg per kg of body weight per day.

Strength(s) usually available
U.S.—
- 2 mg (diacetate) per 5 mL (Rx) [*Aristocort*].
- 4.85 mg anhydrous diacetate (4 mg base) per 5 mL (Rx) [*Kenacort Diacetate*].

Canada—
- 2 mg (diacetate) per 5 mL (Rx) [*Aristocort*].

Packaging and storage
Store below 40 °C (104 °F), preferably between 15 and 30 °C (59 and 86 °F), unless otherwise specified by manufacturer. Store in a tight, light-resistant container. Protect from freezing.

Parenteral Dosage Forms

TRIAMCINOLONE ACETONIDE INJECTABLE SUSPENSION USP

Usual adult and adolescent dose
Corticosteroid—
- Intra-articular, intrabursal, or tendon-sheath injection, 2.5 to 15 mg. Dosage may then be adjusted to 10 to 80 mg a day, as necessary.
- Intradermal or intralesional, up to 1 mg per injection site, repeated at one-week or less frequent intervals, if necessary.
- Intramuscular, initially 2.5 to 60 mg a day. Dosage may then be adjusted to 20 to 80 mg a day, as necessary.

Rhinitis, allergic, perennial or seasonal—
- Intramuscular, 40 to 100 mg as a single dose.

Usual pediatric dose

Corticosteroid—

Children up to 6 years of age—

Use is not recommended.

Children 6 to 12 years of age—

Intra-articular, intrabursal, or tendon-sheath injection, 2.5 to 15 mg, repeated as needed.

Intramuscular, 40 mg, repeated at four-week intervals if necessary; or 0.03 to 0.2 mg per kg of body weight or 1 to 6.25 mg per square meter of body surface area, repeated at one- to seven-day intervals.

Strength(s) usually available

U.S.—

3 mg per mL (Rx) [*Tac-3*].

10 mg per mL (Rx) [*Kenalog-10* (benzyl alcohol 0.9%)].

40 mg per mL (Rx) [*Clinalog; Cinonide 40; Kenaject-40* (benzyl alcohol); *Kenalog-40* (benzyl alcohol 0.9%); *Ken-Jec 40; Robalog; Triam-A* (benzyl alcohol); *Triamonide 40* (benzyl alcohol); *Tri-Kort* (benzyl alcohol); *Trilog* (benzyl alcohol); GENERIC].

Canada—

10 mg per mL (Rx) [*Kenalog-10* (benzyl alcohol)].

40 mg per mL (Rx) [*Kenalog-40* (benzyl alcohol); *Scheinpharm Triamcine-A* (benzyl alcohol 0.9%)].

Packaging and storage

Store between 15 and 30 °C (59 and 86 °F), unless otherwise specified by manufacturer. Protect from light. Protect from freezing.

Preparation of dosage form

For preparation and administration of injections, see manufacturer's labeling.

Auxiliary labeling

- Shake well.

Caution

Use of preparations containing benzyl alcohol is not recommended in neonates. A fatal toxic syndrome consisting of metabolic acidosis, central nervous system (CNS) depression, respiratory problems, renal failure, hypotension, and possibly seizures and intracranial hemorrhages has been associated with this use.

Additional information

Do not administer this medication intravenously.

Do not administer the 10-mg-per-mL strength intramuscularly.

Do not administer the 40-mg-per-mL strength intradermally or intralesionally.

TRIAMCINOLONE DIACETATE INJECTABLE SUSPENSION USP

Usual adult and adolescent dose

Corticosteroid—

Intra-articular, intrasynovial, intralesional, sublesional, or soft-tissue injection, 3 to 48 mg, repeated at one- to eight-week intervals, if necessary.

Intramuscular, 40 mg once a week. Alternatively, a dose equal to four to seven times the predetermined oral daily dose may be administered as a single injection and repeated at four-day to four-week intervals as required.

Usual pediatric dose

Corticosteroid—

Children up to 6 years of age—Use is not recommended.

Children 6 to 12 years of age—Intramuscular, 40 mg once a week.

Strength(s) usually available

U.S.—

25 mg per mL (Rx) [*Aristocort* (benzyl alcohol 0.9%)].

40 mg per mL (Rx) [*Acetocot; Amcort* (benzyl alcohol); *Aristocort Forte* (benzyl alcohol 0.9%); *Articulose-L.A.* (benzyl alcohol); *Cinalone 40; Clinacort; Tramacort-D; Triam-Forte* (benzyl alcohol); *Triamolone 40* (benzyl alcohol); *Trilone; Tristoject* (benzyl alcohol); GENERIC].

Canada—

25 mg per mL (Rx) [*Aristocort Intralesional*].

40 mg per mL (Rx) [*Aristocort Forte;* GENERIC].

Packaging and storage

Store between 15 and 30 °C (59 and 86 °F), unless otherwise specified by manufacturer. Protect from freezing.

Preparation of dosage form

For preparation and administration of injections, see manufacturer's labeling.

Stability

Admixtures containing local anesthetics will retain their potency for one full week.

Incompatibilities

This medication should *not* be mixed with parenteral-local anesthetic formulations containing preservatives such as parabens or phenol because flocculation of the corticosteroid may occur.

Auxiliary labeling

- Shake well.

Caution

Use of preparations containing benzyl alcohol is not recommended in neonates. A fatal toxic syndrome consisting of metabolic acidosis, central nervous system (CNS) depression, respiratory problems, renal failure, hypotension, and possibly seizures and intracranial hemorrhages has been associated with this use.

Additional information

Do not administer this medication intravenously.

TRIAMCINOLONE HEXACETONIDE INJECTABLE SUSPENSION USP

Usual adult and adolescent dose

Corticosteroid—

Intra-articular, 2 to 20 mg, repeated at three- or four-week intervals, if necessary.

Intralesional or sublesional, up to 0.5 mg per square inch of affected skin, repeated as needed.

Usual pediatric dose

Dosage has not been established.

Strength(s) usually available

U.S.—

20 mg per mL (Rx) [*Aristospan* (benzyl alcohol 0.9%)].

Canada—

20 mg per mL (Rx) [*Aristospan* (benzyl alcohol 0.9%)].

Packaging and storage

Store between 15 and 30 °C (59 and 86 °F), unless otherwise specified by manufacturer. Protect from freezing.

Preparation of dosage form

For preparation and administration of injections, see manufacturer's labeling.

Stability

Admixtures containing local anesthetics will retain their potency for one full week.

Incompatibilities

This medication should *not* be mixed with parenteral-local anesthetic formulations containing parabens, phenol, or other such preservatives because flocculation of the corticosteroid may occur.

Auxiliary labeling

- Shake well.

Caution

Use of preparations containing benzyl alcohol is not recommended in neonates. A fatal toxic syndrome consisting of metabolic acidosis, central nervous system (CNS) depression, respiratory problems, renal failure, hypotension, and possibly seizures and intracranial hemorrhages has been associated with this use.

Additional information

Do not administer this medication intravenously.

The 5-mg-per-mL strength is recommended for intralesional and sublesional injections only.

The 20-mg-per-mL strength is recommended for intra-articular injection only.

Revised: 03/25/2005

Table 1. Pharmacology/Pharmacokinetics*

Drug and Route	Onset of Action	Peak Effect	Duration of Action
Betamethasone			
Oral		1–2 hr	3.25 days
Sodium phosphate			
IV	Rapid		
IM	Rapid		
Acetate/Sodium phosphate			
IM	1–3 hr		1 wk
IA, IS			1–2 wk
IL, ST			1 wk
Cortisone acetate			
Oral	Rapid	2 hr	1.25–1.5 days
IM	Slow	20–48 hr	
Dexamethasone			
Oral		1–2 hr	2.75 days
Acetate			
IM		8 hr	6 days
IA, ST, IL			1–3 wk
Sodium phosphate			
IV	Rapid		
IM	Rapid		
IA, IS, IL, ST			3 days–3 wk
Hydrocortisone			
Oral		1 hr	1.25–1.5 days
IM		4–8 hr	
Acetate			
IA, IS, IB, IL, ST		24–48 hr	3 days–4 wk
Cypionate			
Oral		1–2 hr	
Sodium phosphate			
IV	Rapid		
IM	Rapid	1 hr	
Sodium succinate			
IV	Rapid		
IM	Rapid	1 hr	Variable
Methylprednisolone			
Oral		1–2 hr	1.25–1.5 days
Acetate			
IM	Slow 6–48 hr	4–8 days	1–4 wk
IA, IL, ST	Very slow	7 days	1–5 wk
Sodium succinate			
IV	Rapid		
IM	Rapid		
Prednisolone			
Oral		1–2 hr	1.25–1.5 days
Acetate			
IM	Slow		
Acetate/Sodium phosphate			
IM			Up to 4 wk
IB, IS, IA, ST			3 days–4 wk
Sodium phosphate			
IV	Rapid	1 hr	
IM	Rapid	1 hr	
IA, IL, ST			3 days–3 wk
Tebutate			
IA, IL, ST	Slow 1–2 days		1–3 wk
Prednisone			
Oral		1–2 hr	1.25–1.5 days
Triamcinolone			
Oral		1–2 hr	2.25 days
Acetonide			
IM	Slow 24–48 hr		1–6 wk
IB, IA, IS, IL, ST			Several wk
Diacetate			
Oral		1–2 hr	
IM	Slow		4 days–4 wk
IL			1–2 wk
IA, IS, ST			1–8 wk
Hexacetonide			
IA, IL			3–4 wk

*Abbreviations: IA = intra-articular; IB = intrabursal; IL = intralesional; IM = intramuscular; IS = intrasynovial; ST = soft tissue.

Table 2. Pharmacology/Pharmacokinetics

	Relative Potency				Half-life (hr)	
	Glucocorticoid Dose (mg)*	Glucocorticoid Activity†	Mineralocorticoid Activity‡	Protein Binding§	Plasma	Biological (Tissue)
Corticosteroids						
Short-acting						
Cortisone	25	0.8	2+		0.5	8–12
Hydrocortisone	20	1	2+	Very high	1.5–2	8–12
Intermediate-acting						
Methylprednisolone	4	5	0#		>3.5	18–36
Prednisolone	5	4	1+	High	2.1–3.5	18–36
Prednisone	5	4	1+	High to very high	3.4–3.8	18–36
Triamcinolone	4	5	0#	High	2–>5	18–36
Long-acting						
Betamethasone	0.6	20–30	0#	High	3–5	36–54
Dexamethasone	0.5–0.75	20–30	0#	High	3–4.5	36–54

*Approximate; applies to oral or intravenous administration only.
†Anti-inflammatory, immunosuppressant, metabolic effects.
‡Sodium and water retention, potassium depletion.
§Hydrocortisone binds to transcortin (corticosteroid-binding globulin [CBG]) and to albumin. Prednisone, but not betamethasone, dexamethasone, or triamcinolone, also binds to CBG.
#Although these glucocorticoids are considered not to have significant mineralocorticoid activity, hypokalemia and/or sodium and fluid retention may occur, depending on dosage and patient predisposition.

Table 3. General Dosing Information*

Drug	Parenteral Routes of Administration†								
	Systemic			Local					
	IM	IV	SC	IA	IB	IL	IS	ST	[IT][1]
Betamethasone									
Sodium phosphate	✓	✓		✓		✓		✓	
Sodium phosphate/Acetate	✓			✓		✓	✓	✓	
Cortisone Acetate	✓								
Dexamethasone									
Acetate	✓			✓		✓		✓	
Sodium phosphate	✓	✓		✓		✓	✓	✓	
Hydrocortisone									
Sterile suspension	✓								
Acetate				✓	✓	✓	✓	✓	
Sodium phosphate	✓	✓	✓						
Sodium succinate	✓	✓							
Methylprednisolone									
Acetate	✓			✓		✓	✓	✓	
Sodium succinate	✓	✓							
Prednisolone									
Acetate	✓								
Acetate/Sodium phosphate	✓			✓	✓		✓	✓	
Sodium phosphate	✓	✓		✓		✓		✓	
Tebutate				✓		✓		✓	[✓][1]
Triamcinolone									
Acetonide	✓			✓	✓	✓			[✓][1]
Diacetate	✓			✓		✓	✓	✓	[✓][1]
Hexacetonide				✓		✓			[✓][1]

*Bracketed information refers to routes of administration that are not included in U.S. product labeling.

†Abbreviations: Systemic—IM = intramuscular; IV = intravenous; SC = subcutaneous. Local—IA = intra-articular; IB = intrabursal; IL = intralesional; IS = intrasynovial; ST = soft tissue; IT = intraturbinal.

1Not included in Canadian product labeling.

CORTICOTROPIN Systemic

VA CLASSIFICATION (Primary):

Corticotropin for Injection—DX900
Repository Corticotropin—CN400

Commonly used brand name(s): *H.P. Acthar Gel.*

Another commonly used name is ACTH.

Note: For a listing of dosage forms and brand names by country availability, see *Dosage Forms* section(s).

Category

Diagnostic aid (adrenocortical function)—Corticotropin for Injection USP.
Anticonvulsant (specific in infantile myoclonic seizures)—Repository Corticotropin Injection USP

Indications

Note: Bracketed information in the *Indications* section refers to uses that are not included in U.S. product labeling. Additionally, because corticotropin for injection is not commercially available in the U.S. or Canada, the use of brackets and the superscript 1 in this monograph reflects the lack of labeled (approved) indications for this medication.

Accepted

[Adrenocortical insufficiency (diagnosis)[1]]—Corticotropin for injection is indicated as an aid in diagnosing adrenocortical insufficiency; however, the synthetic fragment of corticotropin, cosyntropin, is the preferred diagnostic aid because it is less antigenic. Additionally, corticotropin is purified from animal pituitary glands and can contain significant amounts of vasopressin and other peptides, which are not found in cosyntropin.

[Seizures, myoclonic, infantile (treatment)][1]—Repository corticotropin is used in the treatment of infantile myoclonic seizures (infantile spasms), although there are only limited data suggesting that it has greater efficacy than do glucocorticoids.

Unaccepted

Corticotropin is no longer recommended for its anti-inflammatory and immunosuppressant properties. Although corticotropin is FDA-approved for the treatment of secondary adrenocortical insufficiency and many nonendocrine disorders that are responsive to glucocorticoid therapy, treatment with a corticosteroid is preferred.

[1]Not included in Canadian product labeling.

Pharmacology/Pharmacokinetics

Physicochemical characteristics

Hormone; obtained from porcine pituitary glands.

Mechanism of action/Effect

Diagnostic aid (adrenocortical function)—Corticotropin combines with a specific receptor on the adrenal cell plasma membrane. In patients with normal adrenocortical function, it stimulates the initial reaction involved in the synthesis of adrenal steroids (including cortisol, cortisone, weak androgenic substances, and a limited quantity of aldosterone) from cholesterol by increasing the quantity of cholesterol within the mitochondria. Corticotropin does *not* significantly increase serum cortisol concentrations in patients with primary adrenocortical insufficiency (Addison's disease).

Anticonvulsant (specific in infantile myoclonic seizures)—The mechanism of action of corticotropin in the treatment of infantile myoclonic seizures is unknown.

Other actions/effects

Corticotropin is not a corticosteroid. However, it shares many actions of the corticosteroids due to its ability to increase endogenous corticosteroid synthesis.

Absorption

Corticotropin is rapidly absorbed following intramuscular administration; the repository dosage form is slowly absorbed over approximately 8 to 16 hours.

Half-life
About 15 minutes following intravenous administration.

Time to peak effect
Peak plasma cortisol concentrations are usually achieved within 1 hour after intramuscular or rapid intravenous administration of corticotropin for injection.

Duration of action
Following intramuscular or rapid intravenous administration of corticotropin, peak plasma cortisol concentrations begin to decrease after 2 to 4 hours.

The effects of repository corticotropin may last up to 3 days.

Precautions to Consider

Cross-sensitivity and/or related problems
Patients allergic to proteins of porcine origin or cosyntropin may also be allergic to corticotropin.

Carcinogenicity
Adequate and well-controlled animal studies have not been done in animals; however, use in humans has not shown an increase in malignant disease.

Pregnancy/Reproduction
Fertility—Studies have not been done in humans or in animals.

Pregnancy—Adequate and well-controlled studies have not been done in humans.

Studies in animals have shown that corticotropin is embryocidal.

FDA Pregnancy Category C.

Breast-feeding
It is not known whether corticotropin is distributed into breast milk. However, problems in humans have not been documented.

Pediatrics
Appropriate studies performed to date using corticotropin have not demonstrated pediatrics-specific problems that would limit the usefulness of corticotropin in children. However, prolonged use of corticotropin in children will inhibit skeletal growth; therefore, close monitoring is recommended.

Geriatrics
Appropriate studies performed to date using corticotropin have not demonstrated geriatrics-specific problems that would limit the usefulness of corticotropin in the elderly.

Drug interactions and/or related problems
The following drug interactions and/or related problems have been selected on the basis of their potential clinical significance (possible mechanism in parentheses where appropriate)—not necessarily inclusive (» = major clinical significance):

Note: Combinations containing any of the following medications, depending on the amount present, may also interact with this medication.

Estrogens
(estrogen may cause abnormally high plasma cortisol concentrations before and after corticotropin administration; however, a normal incremental response to corticotropin still occurs)

» Immunizations
(during chronic therapy, patients should not be vaccinated against smallpox; extreme caution is recommended if other immunizations are to be given, because of the risk of neurological complications and lack of antibody response)

Verapamil
(limited data show that chronic administration of oral verapamil may blunt the effect of corticotropin, resulting in a false negative diagnostic test result)

Laboratory value alterations
The following have been selected on the basis of their potential clinical significance (possible effect in parentheses where appropriate)—not necessarily inclusive (» = major clinical significance).

With results of adrenocortical function testing

Due to other medications/foods

» Corticosteroids, glucocorticoid
(if competitive protein binding assays or immunoassays showing cross-reactivity with prednisone or cortisone are used, a high baseline cortisol concentration with no response to corticotropin may be seen in patients taking these medications)

Medical considerations/Contraindications
The medical considerations/contraindications included have been selected on the basis of their potential clinical significance (reasons given in parentheses where appropriate)—not necessarily inclusive (» = major clinical significance).

Except under special circumstances, this medication should not be used when the following medical problems exist:

» Infections, serious bacterial or viral, especially varicella
(possible immunosupression may lead to infectious complications with chronic use)

Risk-benefit should be considered when the following medical problems exist:

» Allergy to corticotropin, cosyntropin, or porcine derivatives
(risk of allergic reaction)

Patient monitoring
The following may be especially important in patient monitoring (other tests may be warranted in some patients, depending on condition; » = major clinical significance):

For treatment of infantile myoclonic seizures

» Blood pressure and
» Calcium, serum and
» Electroencephalogram, waking and sleeping and
» Electrolytes, serum and
» Glucose, urine and
» Phosphorus, serum and
» Urinalysis and
» Weight
(recommended at periodic intervals during therapy to assess therapeutic and/or adverse effects)
» Calcium, serum and
» Complete blood count and
» Electrolytes, serum and
» Endocrine profile and
» Glucose, serum, fasting and 2-hour postprandial and
» Phosphorus, serum, and
» Renal function tests and
» Urinalysis
(recommended prior to initiation of therapy; caution in using corticotropin is recommended if any of these tests are abnormal)

Side/Adverse Effects

Note: Except for rare allergic reactions, there are no side/adverse effects associated with the use of corticotropin as a diagnostic aid.

The following side/adverse effects have been selected on the basis of their potential clinical significance (possible signs and symptoms in parentheses where appropriate)—not necessarily inclusive:

Those indicating need for medical attention
Incidence less frequent—with chronic use only
Cerebral ventriculomegaly; congestive heart failure; hyperglycemia; hypertension; hypothalamic-pituitary suppression; metabolic abnormalities, such as; hypernatremia; hypokalemia; hypocalcemia; hypophosphatemia; sepsis

Incidence rare
Allergic reaction (dizziness; nausea and vomiting; shock; skin rash); ***worsening of seizures***—with chronic use only

Those indicating need for medical attention only if they continue or are bothersome
Incidence more frequent—with chronic use only
Irritability, extreme

Those not indicating need for medical attention
Incidence more frequent—with chronic use only
Cushingoid facies; cutaneous pigmentation; hirsutism; seborrheic dermatitis

General Dosing Information

Following administration of corticotropin as a diagnostic agent, adrenal insufficiency can be confirmed when a plasma, serum, or urinary free cortisol concentration does not increase above a baseline concentration.

During chronic therapy of infantile myoclonic seizures, patients should not be vaccinated against smallpox. Extreme caution is recommended if other immunizations are to be given, because of the risk of neurological complications and lack of antibody response.

For treatment of adverse effects
Recommended treatment for hypertension that may develop during treatment of infantile spasms consists of sodium restriction and diuretic therapy rather than discontinuation of corticotropin.

Parenteral Dosage Forms

Note: Bracketed uses in the *Dosage Forms* section refer to categories of use and/or indications that are not included in U.S. product labeling.

CORTICOTROPIN FOR INJECTION USP

Note: Because corticotropin for injection is not commercially available in the U.S. or Canada, the bracketed uses and the use of the superscript 1 in this section reflect the lack of labeled (approved) indications for this medication in these countries.

Usual adult and adolescent dose

[Adrenocortical insufficiency (diagnosis)[1]]—

Intravenous infusion, 10 to 25 Units in 500 mL of 5% dextrose in water, infused over an eight-hour period.

Usual pediatric dose

[Adrenocortical insufficiency (diagnosis)[1]]—

Use is not recommended. The synthetic fragment of corticotropin, cosyntropin, is the recommended diagnostic agent.

[Seizures, myoclonic, infantile (treatment)][1]—

Use is not recommended. Repository corticotropin injection USP is the preferred product.

Strength(s) usually available

U.S.—

Not commercially available.

Canada—

Not commercially available.

Packaging and storage

Prior to reconstitution, store between 15 and 30 °C (59 and 86 °F), unless otherwise specified by manufacturer.

Preparation of dosage form

Corticotropin for injection should be reconstituted with sterile water or sodium chloride for injection, so that the individual dose is contained in 1 to 2 mL of solution.

Stability

After reconstitution, solution should be used immediately.

REPOSITORY CORTICOTROPIN INJECTION USP

Usual adult and adolescent dose

Use is not recommended.

Usual pediatric dose

[Seizures, myoclonic, infantile (treatment)][1]—

Intramuscular, 20 to 40 Units per day or 80 Units every other day.

Note: The optimal dose of corticotropin for the treatment of infantile myoclonic seizures has not been established. Another recommended regimen for infantile myoclonic seizures is an initial dose of 150 Units per square meter of body surface area per day administered intramuscularly in two divided doses for one week, followed by 75 Units per square meter of body surface area per day for one week, then 75 Units per square meter of body surface area administered every other day for one week. Corticotropin dosage is then gradually tapered over the subsequent nine weeks.

The optimal duration of therapy is not known.

Dose should be tapered gradually when discontinuing corticotropin therapy.

Strength(s) usually available

U.S.—

80 USP Units per mL (Rx) [*H.P. Acthar Gel*].

Note: In the US, corticotropin gel is available through the National Organization of Rare Disorders, at 1–800–459–7599

Canada—

Not commercially available.

Packaging and storage

Store between 2 and 8 °C (36 and 46 °F), unless otherwise specified by manufacturer.

[1]Not included in Canadian product labeling.

Selected Bibliography

Snead OC. Other antiepileptic drugs: adrenocorticotropic hormone (ACTH). In: Levy R, Mattson R, Meldrum B, editors. Antiepileptic drugs. New York: Raven Press, 1995: 941-8.

Revised: 12/30/1999

CORTISONE—See *Corticosteroids—Glucocorticoid Effects (Systemic)*

COSYNTROPIN Systemic

INN: Tetracosactide; BAN: Tetracosactide

JAN: Tetracosactide acetate

VA CLASSIFICATION (Primary/Secondary): DX900/HS701

Commonly used brand name(s): *Cortrosyn*.

Note: For a listing of dosage forms and brand names by country availability, see *Dosage Forms* section(s).

Category

Diagnostic aid (adrenal-pituitary function).

Indications

Accepted

Adrenocortical insufficiency (diagnosis)—Cosyntropin is indicated as an aid for diagnosing adrenocortical insufficiency.

Cosyntropin is a synthetic subunit of corticotropin (adrenocorticotropic hormone; ACTH). Cosyntropin is preferable to ACTH for diagnosing primary adrenocortical insufficiency because it is less allergenic and may be tolerated by most patients who have had an allergic reaction to ACTH or those with a history of allergies.

Unaccepted

Cosyntropin is not indicated for the treatment of corticosteroid-responsive medical conditions.

Pharmacology/Pharmacokinetics

Physicochemical characteristics

Chemical Group—Synthetic polypeptide identical to the first 24 of the 39 amino acids of corticotropin (ACTH).

Molecular weight—2933.5.

Mechanism of action/Effect

Cosyntropin combines with a specific receptor in the adrenal cell plasma membrane and, in patients with normal adrenocortical function, stimulates the initial reaction involved in the synthesis of adrenal steroids (including cortisol, cortisone, weak androgenic substances, and a limited quantity of aldosterone) from cholesterol by increasing the quantity of the substrate within the mitochondria. Cosyntropin does not significantly increase plasma cortisol concentration in patients with primary or secondary adrenocortical insufficiency.

Cosyntropin has less immunogenic activity than ACTH because the amino acid sequence having most of the antigenic activity of ACTH, i.e., amino acids 25–39, is not present in cosyntropin.

Time to peak effect

The maximal increase in plasma cortisol concentration usually occurs approximately 45 to 60 minutes following intravenous or subcutaneous administration of cosyntropin.

Precautions to Consider

Cross-sensitivity and/or related problems

Although most patients allergic to corticotropin (ACTH) do not exhibit an allergy to cosyntropin, some of these patients may be allergic to cosyntropin also.

Carcinogenicity/Mutagenicity

Long-term animal studies have not been conducted to evaluate the carcinogenic or mutagenic potential of cosyntropin.

Pregnancy/Reproduction

Pregnancy—Studies have not been done in humans.

Studies have not been done in animals.

FDA Pregnancy Category C.

Breast-feeding

It is not known whether cosyntropin is distributed into breast milk. However, problems in humans have not been documented.

Pediatrics

Appropriate studies on the relationship of age to the effects of cosyntropin have not been performed in the pediatric population. However, no pediatrics-specific problems have been documented to date.

Geriatrics

No information is available on the relationship of age to the effects of cosyntropin in geriatric patients.

Drug interactions and/or related problems

The following drug interactions and/or related problems have been selected on the basis of their potential clinical significance (possible

mechanism in parentheses where appropriate)—not necessarily inclusive (» = major clinical significance):

Note: Combinations containing any of the following medications, depending on the amount present, may also interact with this medication.

Blood, whole or
Plasma
(cosyntropin may be inactivated by the enzymes present in blood and plasma)

Laboratory value alterations

The following have been selected on the basis of their potential clinical significance (possible effect in parentheses where appropriate)—not necessarily inclusive (» = major clinical significance).

With Results of *this* test

Due to other medications/foods

Corticosteroids, glucocorticoid effects, especially cortisone or hydrocortisone
(baseline plasma cortisol concentration may be elevated in patients receiving cortisone or hydrocortisone on the test day and may decrease during the test period; it is recommended that the pretest dose of cortisone or hydrocortisone be omitted on the test day)
(with the exception of dexamethasone, other glucocorticoids may interfere with plasma cortisol determinations if radioligand assay tests used are not specific for cortisol)

Estrogen
(baseline plasma cortisol concentration may be elevated in patients receiving estrogen on the test day)

Spironolactone
(because spironolactone metabolites also fluoresce, plasma cortisol concentrations following cosyntropin administration may be falsely elevated in patients receiving spironolactone when the fluorometric procedure is used but not when radioimmunoassay [RIA] or competitive protein-binding methods are used; it is recommended that the pretest dose of spironolactone be omitted on the test day)

Due to medical problems or conditions

Elevated plasma bilirubin concentrations or
Free hemoglobin in plasma, presence of
(falsely elevated plasma cortisol concentrations may occur when the fluorometric method is used)

Medical considerations/Contraindications

The medical considerations/contraindications included have been selected on the basis of their potential clinical significance (reasons given in parentheses where appropriate)—not necessarily inclusive (» = major clinical significance).

Risk-benefit should be considered when the following medical problems exist:

Allergic disorders or history of
(increased risk of allergic reactions)

Allergy to ACTH or cosyntropin

Patient monitoring

The following may be especially important in patient monitoring (other tests may be warranted in some patients, depending on condition; » = major clinical significance):

17-Hydroxycorticosteroids, urine
(recommended before and after therapy to measure adrenal response)

Cortisol, blood
(recommended before and at the end of the cosyntropin injection to measure adrenal response; measurement of blood cortisol is preferred to measurement of urinary 17-hydroxycorticosteroids because the latter does not always accurately reflect adrenal response to ACTH)

Side/Adverse Effects

The following side/adverse effects have been selected on the basis of their potential clinical significance (possible signs and symptoms in parentheses where appropriate)—not necessarily inclusive:

Those indicating need for medical attention

Incidence rare

Anaphylaxis, generalized (dizziness; hives; irritability; itching of skin; lightheadedness; seizures; skin rash; slow heartbeat; trouble in breathing; wheezing)

Those indicating need for medical attention only if they continue or are bothersome

Incidence less frequent or rare

Allergic reaction, mild (mild fever; nausea; vomiting); ***redness or pain at injection site***

General Dosing Information

A dose of 250 mcg (0.25 mg) of cosyntropin is equivalent to 25 USP Units of corticotropin.

When used as a diagnostic agent in the screening test for adrenocortical insufficiency, cosyntropin may be administered intramuscularly, subcutaneously, or by intravenous injection. If greater stimulation of the adrenal gland is needed, cosyntropin may be administered as an intravenous infusion.

The following criteria may be used as guidelines to determine if the patient has a normal response to cosyntropin. Some interlaboratory variation may occur.

- Morning control plasma cortisol concentration exceeds 5 mcg (0.005 mg) per 100 mL.
- Thirty-minute cortisol concentration shows an increase of at least 7 mcg (0.007 mg) per 100 mL above the control level.
- Thirty-minute cortisol concentration exceeds l8 mcg (0.018 mg) per 100 mL.

If a 60-minute test interval is used, a normal response to cosyntropin is shown by a plasma cortisol concentration that is approximately two times the baseline concentration.

Patients who fail to respond to a single-dose corticotropin stimulation test using a dose of 250 mcg (0.25 mg) of cosyntropin may be diagnosed as having primary or secondary adrenocortical insufficiency. Further studies with corticotropin are then indicated to determine which type of adrenocortical insufficiency exists.

Parenteral Dosage Forms

COSYNTROPIN FOR INJECTION

Usual adult and adolescent dose

Diagnostic aid—
Intramuscular or subcutaneous, 250 mcg (0.25 mg).
Intravenous, 250 mcg (0.25 mg), administered over a two-minute period.
Intravenous infusion, 250 mcg (0.25 mg), administered at a rate of 40 mcg (0.04 mg) per hour over a six-hour period.

Usual pediatric dose

Diagnostic aid—
Children up to 2 years of age: Intramuscular, 125 mcg (0.125 mg).
Children 2 years of age and older: See *Usual adult and adolescent dose.*

Strength(s) usually available

U.S.—
250 mcg (0.25 mg) per vial (Rx) [*Cortrosyn* (mannitol 10 mg)].

Canada—
250 mcg (0.25 mg) per vial (Rx) [*Cortrosyn* (glacial acetic acid; mannitol; sodium chloride)].

Packaging and storage

Prior to reconstitution, store between 15 and 30 °C (59 and 86 °F), unless otherwise specified by manufacturer.

Preparation of dosage form

One mL of diluent provided (0.9% sodium chloride injection) should be added to the vial containing 250 mcg (0.25 mg) of cosyntropin. The resultant solution contains 250 mcg (0.25 mg) of cosyntropin per mL.

For intravenous infusion, cosyntropin may be further diluted with 5% dextrose injection or 0.9% sodium chloride injection.

Stability

After reconstitution with 0.9% sodium chloride injection, 250 mcg (0.25 mg)-per-mL solutions are stable for 24 hours at room temperature or for 21 days when refrigerated at 2 to 8 °C (36 to 46 °F). After further dilution, solutions are stable for 12 hours at room temperature.

Revised: 04/16/1999

CROMOLYN Inhalation-Local

INN: Cromoglicic acid; BAN: Cromoglycic acid

JAN: Sodium cromoglicate

VA CLASSIFICATION (Primary/Secondary): RE110/RE160

Commonly used brand name(s): *Intal; Intal Inhaler; Intal Syncroner; Novo-cromolyn; PMS-Sodium Cromoglycate.*

Other commonly used names are cromoglicic acid, cromoglycic acid, sodium cromoglicate, and sodium cromoglycate.

Note: For a listing of dosage forms and brand names by country availability, see *Dosage Forms* section(s).

Category

Anti-inflammatory, nonsteroidal (inhalation); mast cell stabilizer; asthma prophylactic; antiallergic (inhalation).

Indications

Accepted

Asthma (prophylaxis)—Cromolyn inhalation is indicated as first-line anti-inflammatory medication, either alone or as an adjunct to bronchodilator therapy, for the prevention of airway inflammation and bronchoconstriction in patients with mild to moderate asthma who require daily therapy.

Bronchospasm (prophylaxis)—Cromolyn inhalation is indicated to prevent acute bronchospasm induced by exercise, or by exposure to allergens, cold, dry air, environmental pollutants, aspirin ingestion, or other known precipitating factors, whether exposure is episodic or continuous.

Unaccepted

Cromolyn inhalation is not indicated for the reversal or relief of acute asthma attacks, especially in status asthmaticus; cromolyn has no immediate bronchodilating activity.

Pharmacology/Pharmacokinetics

Physicochemical characteristics

Molecular weight—512.34.

Mechanism of action/Effect

The exact mechanism by which cromolyn prevents immediate-onset and delayed-onset asthmatic reactions to inhaled allergens or nonimmunological stimuli is not completely known. Cromolyn inhibits the release of mediators, such as histamine and leukotrienes, from mast cells. Prevention of mediator release is thought to result from indirect blockade of the entry of calcium ions into the cells. Cromolyn has also been shown to inhibit the movement of other inflammatory cells such as neutrophils, eosinophils, and monocytes. Additionally, cromolyn has been shown in animal studies to inhibit neuronal reflexes within the lung, prevent down-regulation of beta$_2$-adrenergic receptors on lymphocytes, and to inhibit bronchospasm caused by tachykinins.

Cromolyn has no intrinsic bronchodilator, glucocorticoid, or antihistaminic action.

Absorption

Following administration by inhalation, approximately 8% of the dose of cromolyn penetrates the lungs, from which it is readily absorbed into systemic circulation. The remainder is either exhaled or swallowed and excreted via the alimentary tract, with very little medication absorbed.

Onset of action

Cromolyn inhibits a decrease in forced expiratory volume in 1 second (FEV$_1$) when inhaled 1 minute before antigen challenge. When cromolyn is used as maintenance therapy, clinical improvement in symptoms and lung function usually occurs within 4 weeks of beginning treatment. However, in some patients improvement may occur almost immediately.

Duration of action

Protection against antigen or exercise challenge—Up to 2 hours.

Elimination

Unchanged, approximately equally divided between urine and bile.

Precautions to Consider

Carcinogenicity

Long-term studies in mice (12 months intraperitoneal treatment followed by 6 months observation), hamsters (12 months intraperitoneal treatment followed by 12 months observation), and rats (18 months subcutaneous treatment) showed that cromolyn has no neoplastic effect.

Mutagenicity

In various mutagenicity studies, there was no evidence of chromosomal damage or cytotoxicity.

Pregnancy/Reproduction

Fertility—In animal reproduction studies with cromolyn, there was no evidence of impaired fertility.

Pregnancy—Adequate and well-controlled studies in humans have not been done. Studies in animals have not shown that cromolyn causes adverse effects in the fetus.

Although extensive studies in humans have not been done, some limited data suggest that cromolyn is not associated with an increased incidence of fetal anomalies. Poorly controlled asthma and loss of pulmonary function present a greater risk to the mother and may result in placental hypoxemia and increased perinatal mortality, increased prematurity, and low birth weight.

Reproduction studies in mice, rats, and rabbits with cromolyn administered parenterally in doses of up to 338 times the human clinical dose showed no evidence of fetal malformations. Adverse fetal effects (increased resorptions and decreased fetal weight) were noted only with very high parenteral doses that produced maternal toxicity.

Studies in pregnant mice have shown that the addition of cromolyn (338 times the human dose) to isoproterenol (90 times the human dose) appears to increase the incidence of both resorptions and malformations.

FDA Pregnancy Category B.

Breast-feeding

It is not known whether cromolyn is distributed into human breast milk; however, problems have not been documented. Since cromolyn reaches very low concentrations in maternal serum, it would be expected to reach even lower, and probably undetectable, concentrations in breast milk.

In monkeys given intravenous cromolyn, concentrations in breast milk measured less than 0.001% of the administered dose.

Pediatrics

Appropriate studies on the relationship of age to the effects of cromolyn administered by metered dose inhaler in children younger than 5 years of age or as a nebulizer solution in children younger than 2 years of age have not been performed. Safety and efficacy have not been established.

Because of the possibility that adverse effects of this drug could become apparent only after many years of use, a benefit/risk consideration of the long-term use of cromolyn inhalation aerosol is particularly important in pediatric patients.

Geriatrics

Although appropriate studies on the relationship of age to the effects of cromolyn inhalation have not been performed in the geriatric population, no geriatrics-specific problems have been documented to date.

Laboratory value alterations

The following have been selected on the basis of their potential clinical significance (possible effect in parentheses where appropriate)—not necessarily inclusive (» = major clinical significance).

With diagnostic test results

Bronchial airway hyperreactivity assessment
(cromolyn alters bronchial airway hyperreactivity over time by its proposed anti-inflammatory effect; this may lead to a lessened response to methacholine challenge in some patients)

Medical considerations/Contraindications

The medical considerations/contraindications included have been selected on the basis of their potential clinical significance (reasons given in parentheses where appropriate)—not necessarily inclusive (» = major clinical significance).

Risk-benefit should be considered when the following medical problems exist:

Sensitivity to cromolyn

» Coronary artery disease or history of cardiac arrhythmias
(propellants in the metered-dose inhaler may worsen these conditions)

Side/Adverse Effects

Note: Adverse reactions to cromolyn sodium are uncommon. Angioedema, bronchospasm, cough, dizziness, dysuria and urinary frequency, headache, joint swelling and pain, lacrimation, laryngeal edema, nasal congestion, nausea, rash, swollen parotid glands, and urticaria attributed to cromolyn have been reported to occur in fewer than 1 in 10,000 patients. Anemia, exfoliative dermatitis, hemoptysis, hoarseness, myalgia, nephrosis, periarteritic vasculitis, pericarditis, peripheral neuritis, photodermatitis, polymyositis, pulmonary infiltrates with eosinophilia, and vertigo have been reported in fewer than 1 in 100,000 patients. In all cases the causal relationship is unclear. However, cromolyn should be discontinued if the patient develops eosinophilic pneumonia (pulmonary infiltrates with eosinophilia).

The following side/adverse effects have been selected on the basis of their potential clinical significance (possible signs and symptoms in parentheses where appropriate)—not necessarily inclusive:

Those indicating need for medical attention

Incidence more frequent

Bronchospasm, sometimes severe (increased wheezing; tightness in chest; or difficulty in breathing)—associated with a precipitous fall in pulmonary function (FEV$_1$)

Incidence rare

Anaphylactic reaction (difficulty in swallowing; hives; itching of skin; swelling of face, lips, or eyelids; increased wheezing or difficulty in breathing; low blood pressure)—reported in fewer than 1 in 100,000 patients

Those indicating need for medical attention only if they continue or are bothersome

Incidence more frequent

Bad taste in mouth—for metered dose inhaler; ***coughing or wheezing; nausea; throat irritation or dryness***

Patient Consultation

As an aid to patient consultation, refer to *Advice for the Patient, Cromolyn (Inhalation).*

In providing consultation, consider emphasizing the following selected information (» = major clinical significance):

Before using this medication

» Conditions affecting use, especially:
- Sensitivity to cromolyn
- Other medical problems, especially coronary artery disease or a history of cardiac arrhythmias

Proper use of this medication

» Helps prevent, but does not relieve, acute attacks of asthma or bronchospasm

» Importance of taking medication at regular intervals

» Importance of not using more medication than the amount prescribed

Reading patient instructions carefully before using

Checking periodically with health care professional for proper use of inhaler to prevent incorrect dosage

» Proper dosing

Missed dose: If used regularly, using as soon as possible; using any remaining doses for that day at regularly spaced intervals

» Proper storage

For inhalation aerosol dosage form

Keeping record of number of sprays used, if possible; not floating canister in water to test fullness

Testing or priming inhaler before using first time or if not used for a while

Discarding canister after labeled number of metered dose sprays has been used, even if canister does not appear completely empty

Proper administration technique

Proper administration technique with spacer device

Proper cleaning procedure for inhaler

For inhalation capsule dosage form

» Not swallowing capsules; medication not effective if swallowed

Using with Spinhaler or Halermatic inhaler

Proper loading technique for inhaler

Proper administration technique

Proper cleaning procedure for inhaler

For inhalation solution dosage form

Not using if solution cloudy or contains particles

Proper breaking of ampul

Using in a power-operated nebulizer with an adequate flow rate and equipped with face mask or mouthpiece; not using hand-squeezed bulb nebulizers

For patients on scheduled dosing regimen

» Compliance with therapy; may require up to 4 weeks for full benefit

Precautions while using this medication

» Checking with physician if symptoms do not improve within first 4 weeks; checking with physician immediately if condition becomes worse

» Importance of not discontinuing concurrent systemic corticosteroid or bronchodilator therapy without physician's advice

Possible throat irritation or dryness; gargling and rinsing mouth or taking drink of water after each dose to help prevent these effects

Side/adverse effects

Signs of potential side effects, especially bronchospasm or anaphylactic reaction

Cromolyn inhalation aerosol may cause an unpleasant taste

General Dosing Information

When cromolyn is introduced into the patient's therapeutic regimen after an acute episode, the episode must be under control, the airway clear, and the patient able to inhale adequately.

A decrease in the severity of clinical symptoms or the need for concomitant therapy is a sign of improvement that will be evident in the first 4 weeks of therapy if the patient responds to cromolyn therapy.

In asthmatic patients receiving systemic corticosteroids and/or bronchodilators prior to institution of cromolyn, the dosage of corticosteroid and/or bronchodilator should be maintained following initiation of cromolyn therapy. When a clinical response to cromolyn is evident, usually within 2 to 4 weeks, and if the asthma is under good control, an attempt should be made to decrease (taper) the dosage of the systemic corticosteroid and other concomitant medications such as bronchodilators. This decrease should be implemented gradually to avoid an exacerbation of asthma.

If cromolyn is withdrawn in cases in which its use has permitted a decrease in the maintenance dose of corticosteroids, continued close patient monitoring is essential since acute asthma exacerbation may occur, requiring immediate therapy and possible reintroduction of corticosteroids.

Patients with impaired hepatic or renal function may require a decrease in the recommended dosage of cromolyn. Consideration should be given to discontinuing the administration of cromolyn in these patients due to the extensive biliary and renal routes of excretion of this medication.

For inhalation solution dosage form only—Cromolyn solution should be administered from a power-operated nebulizer having an adequate flow rate (6 to 8 liters per minute) and equipped with a suitable face mask or mouthpiece. Hand-squeezed bulb nebulizers are not suitable for administration of cromolyn solution.

Inhalation Dosage Forms

CROMOLYN SODIUM INHALATION AEROSOL

Usual adult and adolescent dose

Asthma (prophylaxis)—

Oral inhalation, 2 inhalations (1.6 or 2 mg) four times a day at regular intervals of four to six hours.

Note: When the patient is stabilized on a maintenance regimen of 2 inhalations of cromolyn four times a day, the dosing frequency may be gradually reduced to three times a day, then to two times a day in some patients. However, if the patient's clinical condition deteriorates, an increase in cromolyn and/or the addition of concomitant medications may become necessary.

Bronchospasm (prophylaxis)—

Oral inhalation, 2 inhalations (1.6 or 2 mg) as a single dose administered at least ten to fifteen (but not more than sixty) minutes before exercise or exposure to any precipitating factor, such as allergens, cold, dry air, aspirin ingestion, or environmental pollutants.

Usual adult prescribing limits

16 puffs (12.8 or 16 mg) daily.

Usual pediatric dose

Children up to 5 years of age: Safety and efficacy have not been established.

Children 5 years of age and older: See *Usual adult and adolescent dose.*

Usual geriatric dose

See *Usual adult and adolescent dose.*

Strength(s) usually available

U.S.—

800 mcg (0.8 mg) per metered dose actuation (spray) (Rx) [*Intal*].

Canada—

1 mg per metered dose actuation (spray) (Rx) [*Intal Inhaler; Intal Syncroner*].

Note: *Intal Syncroner* differs from *Intal Inhaler* in the design of the mouthpiece only. The *Syncroner* is an elongated mouthpiece approximately 8 cm in length, with a portion of its upper surface cut away.

In Canada, metered dose inhalers are labeled according to the amount of cromolyn delivered at the valve; in the U.S., metered dose inhalers are labeled according to the amount of cromolyn delivered at the mouthpiece or actuator. Therefore, 1 mg of cromolyn delivered at the valve is equivalent to 800 mcg delivered at the mouthpiece.

Packaging and storage

Store between 15 and 30 °C (59 and 86 °F), unless otherwise specified by manufacturer. Protect from freezing.

Auxiliary labeling

- For oral inhalation only.
- Shake well before using.
- Contents under pressure.
- Avoid spraying in eyes.
- Store away from heat and direct sunlight.

Note
Include patient instructions when dispensing.

Demonstrate inhalation technique to patient when dispensing.

Additional information
U.S.—Each 8.1-gram aerosol canister delivers at least 112 metered dose actuations (sprays); each 14.2-gram canister delivers at least 200 metered dose actuations (sprays).
Canada—Each canister delivers either 112 or 200 metered dose actuations (sprays).

Note: The correct amount of medication per inhalation cannot be assured after the dispensation of the maximum recommended number of metered dose actuations (sprays). Therefore, a record should be kept of the number of sprays dispensed, and the canister should be discarded when the labeled maximum number of sprays has been used, even though the canister may not appear completely empty.

CROMOLYN SODIUM FOR INHALATION (CAPSULES) USP

Usual adult and adolescent dose
Asthma (prophylaxis)—
Oral inhalation, 20 mg (1 capsule) four times a day at regular intervals of four to six hours.

Note: When the patient is stabilized on a maintenance regimen of four times a day, the dosing frequency may be gradually reduced to three times a day, then to two times a day in some patients.

Bronchospasm (prophylaxis)—
Oral inhalation, 20 mg (1 capsule) as a single dose administered at least ten to fifteen (but not more than sixty) minutes before exercise or exposure to the precipitating factor.

Usual adult prescribing limits
160 mg (8 capsules) daily.

Usual pediatric dose
Children up to 2 years of age: Safety and efficacy have not been established.
Children 2 years of age and older: See *Usual adult and adolescent dose.*

Usual geriatric dose
See *Usual adult and adolescent dose.*

Strength(s) usually available
U.S.—
Not commercially available.
Canada—
20 mg per inhalation capsule (Rx) [*Intal*].

Packaging and storage
Store below 40 °C (104 °F), preferably between 15 and 30 °C (59 and 86 °F), unless otherwise specified by manufacturer. Store in a tightly closed container to exclude light and humidity.

Auxiliary labeling
- For inhalation only—Do not swallow capsules.

Note
Include patient instructions when dispensing.

Demonstrate administration technique to patient when dispensing.

Demonstration kits may be available.

CROMOLYN SODIUM INHALATION SOLUTION USP

Usual adult and adolescent dose
Asthma (prophylaxis)—
Oral inhalation, 20 mg four times a day at regular intervals of four to six hours.

Note: When the patient is stabilized on a maintenance regimen of four times a day, the dosing frequency may be gradually reduced to three times a day, then to two times a day in some patients.

Bronchospasm (prophylaxis)—
Oral inhalation, 20 mg as a single dose administered at least ten to fifteen (but not more than sixty) minutes before exercise or exposure to the precipitating factor.

Usual adult prescribing limits
160 mg daily.

Usual pediatric dose
Children up to 2 years of age: Safety and efficacy have not been established.
Children 2 years of age and older: See *Usual adult and adolescent dose.*

Usual geriatric dose
See *Usual adult and adolescent dose.*

Strength(s) usually available
U.S.—
20 mg per 2-mL ampul (Rx) [*Intal;* GENERIC].
Canada—
20 mg per 2-mL ampul (Rx) [*Intal; Novo-cromolyn; PMS-Sodium Cromoglycate*].

Packaging and storage
Store below 40 °C (104 °F), preferably between 15 and 30 °C (59 and 86 °F), unless otherwise specified by manufacturer. Protect from freezing. Protect from light and humidity.

Stability
Solution should not be used if it is cloudy or contains a precipitate.

Any solution remaining in the nebulizer should be discarded.

Cromolyn sodium inhalation solution has been shown to be physically and chemically compatible with acetylcysteine, albuterol, epinephrine, isoetharine, isoproterenol, metaproterenol, and terbutaline solutions for up to 60 minutes.

When combining cromolyn and ipratropium inhalation solutions, it is recommended that only a *preservative-free* ipratropium solution be used. Mixing cromolyn inhalation solution with an ipratropium inhalation solution containing the preservative benzalkonium chloride is not recommended because mixing results in cloudiness of the solution, which is due to complexation between cromolyn sodium and benzalkonium chloride, although no precipitation or significant decrease in the concentration of cromolyn or ipratropium occurs.

Cromolyn should not be mixed with bitolterol inhalation solution, since mixing results in cloudiness of the solution.

Auxiliary labeling
- For inhalation only.

Note
Include patient information when dispensing.

Demonstrate opening and emptying of ampul when dispensing.

Selected Bibliography

Murphy S. Cromolyn sodium: basic mechanisms and clinical usage. Pediatr Asthma Allergy Immunol 1988; 2: 237-54.

Murphy S, Kelly HW. Cromolyn sodium: a review of mechanisms and clinical use in asthma. DICP 1987; 21: 22-35.

Revised: 05/28/1999

CROMOLYN Nasal

VA CLASSIFICATION (Primary): NT900

Commonly used brand name(s): *Apo-Cromolyn; Children's Nasalcrom; Cromolyn Nasal Solution; Gen-Cromoglycate; Nasalcrom.*

Another commonly used name is sodium cromoglycate.

Note: For a listing of dosage forms and brand names by country availability, see *Dosage Forms* section(s).

Category

Mast cell stabilizer (nasal); antiallergic (nasal).

Indications

Accepted
Rhinitis, allergic (prophylaxis and treatment)—Cromolyn sodium nasal solution is indicated for the prophylaxis and treatment of the symptoms of perennial and seasonal allergic rhinitis.

Pharmacology/Pharmacokinetics

Physicochemical characteristics
Molecular weight—512.34.
pH—4.5 to 6.5.

Mechanism of action/Effect
Cromolyn is a mast cell stabilizer that inhibits the Type I immediate hypersensitivity reaction by preventing the antigen-stimulated release of histamine. Cromolyn also prevents the release of leukotrienes and inhibits eosinophil chemotaxis.

In vitro and *in vivo* animal studies have shown that cromolyn inhibits the degranulation of sensitized mast cells that occurs after exposure to specific antigens. Cromolyn inhibits the release of histamine and SRS-A (slow-reacting substance of anaphylaxis). Some *in vitro* studies have shown that cromolyn inhibits the degranulation of nonsensitized rat mast cells by phospholipase A and the subsequent release of chemical mediators.

Other actions/effects
Cromolyn has no intrinsic bronchodilator, antihistaminic, decongestant, or anti-inflammatory action.

Absorption
Poorly absorbed from the gastrointestinal tract. After instillation of cromolyn nasal solution, less than 7% of the total dose administered is absorbed.

Onset of therapeutic effect
Seasonal allergic rhinitis—Results are usually noticeable in less than 1 week.

Time to peak effect
Perennial allergic rhinitis—Results are usually noticeable in approximately 1 week; however, in some cases up to 2 to 4 weeks may be required.

Elimination
Nasal solution—The portion of the dose that is absorbed (7%) is rapidly excreted unchanged in the bile and urine; the remainder of the dose is expelled from the nose, or swallowed and excreted via the alimentary tract.

Precautions to Consider

Carcinogenicity
Long-term studies with cromolyn in mice (12 months of intraperitoneal treatment followed by 6 months of observation), hamsters (12 months of intraperitoneal treatment followed by 12 months of observation), and rats (18 months of subcutaneous treatment) did not show any neoplastic effect.

Mutagenicity
In various mutagenicity studies, there was no evidence of chromosomal damage or cytotoxicity.

Pregnancy/Reproduction
Fertility—Animal reproduction studies with cromolyn showed no evidence of impaired fertility.

Pregnancy—Adequate and well-controlled studies in humans have not been done.

Reproduction studies in mice, rats, and rabbits with cromolyn administered parenterally in doses up to 338 times the human clinical doses showed no evidence of fetal malformations. (Adverse fetal effects [increased resorptions and decreased fetal weight] were noted only at very high parenteral doses that produced maternal toxicity.)

FDA Pregnancy Category B.

Breast-feeding
It is not known whether cromolyn is distributed into breast milk; however, nasal cromolyn reaches very low concentrations in maternal serum. Caution should be exercised when cromolyn is administered to nursing women. Problems in humans have not been documented.

Pediatrics
Appropriate studies on the relationship of age to the effects of nasal cromolyn have not been performed in the U.S. in children up to 6 years of age (in Canada, up to 5 years of age). In older children, no pediatrics-specific problems have been documented to date.

Geriatrics
Appropriate studies on the relationship of age to the effects of nasal cromolyn have not been performed in the geriatric population. However, no geriatrics-specific problems have been documented to date.

Drug interactions and/or related problems
The following drug interactions and/or related problems have been selected on the basis of their potential clinical significance (possible mechanism in parentheses where appropriate)—not necessarily inclusive (» = major clinical significance):

Methacholine, for inhalation
(cromolyn may decrease slightly, but inconsistently, the response to methacholine challenge in the diagnosis of bronchial airway hyperreactivity; however, cromolyn generally does not cause false-negative tests)

Medical considerations/Contraindications
The medical considerations/contraindications included have been selected on the basis of their potential clinical significance (reasons given in parentheses where appropriate)—not necessarily inclusive (» = major clinical significance).

Risk-benefit should be considered when the following medical problems exist:

Polyps, nasal
(medication may not be effective if nasal passage obstruction exists; patients need to be observed during treatment)

Hepatic function impairment

Renal function impairment

Sensitivity to cromolyn

Side/Adverse Effects

Note: Eosinophilic pneumonia has been reported rarely with cromolyn nasal products.

Although not reported for cromolyn nasal solution, some side/adverse effects that have occurred with cromolyn formulations for inhalation include joint pain and swelling, and, reported rarely, exfoliative dermatitis, heart failure, nephrosis, periarteritic vasculitis, pericarditis, peripheral neuritis, photodermatitis, pneumonitis, polymyositis, and serum sickness.

The following side/adverse effects have been selected on the basis of their potential clinical significance (possible signs and symptoms in parentheses where appropriate)—not necessarily inclusive:

Those indicating need for medical attention
Incidence rare

Anaphylactic reaction (coughing; difficulty in swallowing; hives; itching of skin; swelling of face, lips, or eyelids; wheezing or difficulty in breathing); ***epistaxis*** (nosebleeds); ***skin rash***

Those indicating need for medical attention only if they continue or are bothersome
Incidence more frequent

Burning, stinging, or irritation inside of nose; erythema (flushing); ***increase in sneezing; urticaria*** (hives)

Incidence less frequent

Cough; headache; postnasal drip; unpleasant taste

Patient Consultation

As an aid to patient consultation, refer to *Advice for the Patient, Cromolyn (Nasal)*.

In providing consultation, consider emphasizing the following selected information (» = major clinical significance):

Before using this medication
» Conditions affecting use, especially:
Sensitivity to cromolyn
Use in children—Safety and efficacy have not been established in the U.S. in children up to 6 years of age (in Canada, up to 5 years of age)

Proper use of this medication
Preventing spread of infection: Not using bottle for more than 1 person
Reading patient directions carefully
Clearing nasal passages before use

For *cromolyn nasal solution:*
Using with a special spray device; wiping nosepiece with a clean tissue and replacing dust cap after use to keep unit clean
» Importance of not using more medication than the amount prescribed
» Using every day in regularly spaced doses in order for medication to work properly; results are usually noticeable in approximately 1 week; however in perennial allergic rhinitis, up to 4 weeks may be required for full benefit
» Proper dosing
Missed dose: Using as soon as possible; using any remaining doses for that day at regularly spaced intervals; not doubling doses
» Proper storage

Precautions while using this medication
» Checking with physician if symptoms do not improve or if condition becomes worse

Side/adverse effects
Signs of potential side effects, especially anaphylactic reaction, epistaxis, and skin rash

General Dosing Information

Prior to administration of cromolyn nasal solution, the nasal passages should be cleared. During administration, patient should inhale through the nose.

In the management of seasonal allergic rhinitis (pollinosis) and for the prevention of rhinitis caused by other types of specific airborne allergens, treatment with nasal cromolyn is more effective if started prior to exposure to the offending allergen. Therapy should be continued throughout the period of exposure (i.e., until the pollen season is over or until the patient is no longer exposed to the offending allergen).

In the management of perennial allergic rhinitis, improvement of condition may not become apparent for up to 2 to 4 weeks. Concurrent use of an antihistamine and/or a nasal decongestant may be necessary during this time; however, the need for these medications should decrease and these medications may be discontinued when the full effect of nasal cromolyn is achieved.

For use of cromolyn sodium nasal solution beyond 12 weeks, consult a physician.

Nasal Dosage Forms

CROMOLYN SODIUM NASAL SOLUTION USP

Usual adult and adolescent dose

Allergic rhinitis, perennial or seasonal (prophylaxis and treatment)—
Intranasal, 5.2 mg (1 spray) in each nostril three or four times a day at regular intervals. Dose may be increased to 1 spray in each nostril six times a day.

Note: The following dosage guidelines are used in Canada: Intranasal, 2.6 mg (1 spray) in each nostril six times per day. Dose may be reduced to 1 spray in each nostril every eight to twelve hours, once adequate response is obtained.

Usual adult prescribing limits

5.2 mg in each nostril(2.6 mg in each nostril [Canada]) six times a day.

Usual pediatric dose

Allergic rhinitis, perennial or seasonal (prophylaxis and treatment)—
Children up to 6 years of age (in Canada, up to 5 years of age): Safety and efficacy have not been established.
Children 6 years of age (in Canada, 5 years of age) and over: See *Usual adult and adolescent dose*.

Usual geriatric dose

See *Usual adult and adolescent dose*.

Strength(s) usually available

U.S.—
40 mg per mL (5.2 mg per metered spray) (OTC) [*Children's Nasalcrom* (benzalkonium chloride 0.01%; edetate disodium 0.01%); *Nasalcrom* (benzalkonium chloride 0.01%; edetate disodium 0.01%)].

Canada—
20 mg per mL (2.6 mg per metered spray) (Rx) [*Apo-Cromolyn* (benzalkonium chloride; edetate disodium; purified water; sodium hydroxide); *Cromolyn Nasal Solution; Gen-Cromoglycate* (benzalkonium chloride; disodium edetate; purified water); GENERIC].

Packaging and storage

Store below 40 °C (104 °F), preferably between 15 and 30 °C (59 and 86 °F), unless otherwise specified by manufacturer. Store in a tight, light-resistant container. Protect from freezing.

Auxiliary labeling

- For the nose.

Note

Include patient instructions when dispensing.

Explain administration technique.

Additional information

The nasal spray bottle containing 520 mg/13 mL delivers at least 100 sprays.

Revised: 06/04/1999

CROMOLYN Ophthalmic

INN: Cromoglicic acid; BAN: Cromoglycic acid

VA CLASSIFICATION (Primary): OP801

Commonly used brand name(s): *Crolom; Opticrom; Vistacrom.*

Another commonly used name is sodium cromoglycate.

Note: For a listing of dosage forms and brand names by country availability, see *Dosage Forms* section(s).

Category

Mast cell stabilizer (ophthalmic); antiallergic (ophthalmic).

Indications

Note: Bracketed information in the *Indications* section refers to uses that are not included in U.S. product labeling.

Accepted

[Conjunctivitis, seasonal allergic (treatment)]
Conjunctivitis, vernal (treatment)[1]
Keratitis, vernal (treatment)[1] or
Keratoconjunctivitis, vernal (treatment)—Cromolyn ophthalmic solution is indicated in the treatment of certain allergic ocular disorders, specifically, seasonal allergic conjunctivitis, vernal conjunctivitis, vernal keratitis, and vernal keratoconjunctivitis.

[1]Not included in Canadian product labeling.

Pharmacology/Pharmacokinetics

Physicochemical characteristics

Molecular weight—512.34.
pH—4.0 to 7.0.

Mechanism of action/Effect

Cromolyn is a mast cell stabilizer that inhibits the Type I immediate hypersensitivity reaction by preventing the antigen-stimulated release of histamine. Cromolyn also prevents the release of leukotrienes and inhibits eosinophil chemotaxis.

In vitro and *in vivo* animal studies have shown that cromolyn inhibits the degranulation of sensitized mast cells that occurs after exposure to specific antigens. Some *in vitro* studies have shown that cromolyn inhibits the degranulation of nonsensitized rat mast cells by phospholipase A and the subsequent release of chemical mediators. One study has shown that cromolyn does not inhibit the enzymatic action of released phospholipase A on its specific substrate.

Absorption

Poorly absorbed.

In normal individuals, approximately 0.03% of cromolyn is absorbed systemically following ophthalmic administration.

Studies in rabbits have shown that less than 0.07% of the administered dose is absorbed systemically following multiple doses. Also, trace amounts (less than 0.01%) of the administered dose penetrate into the aqueous humor, and clearance from this chamber is almost complete within 24 hours following discontinuation of treatment.

Onset of therapeutic effect

Usually within a few days.

Precautions to Consider

Carcinogenicity

Long-term studies in mice (12 months of intraperitoneal treatment followed by 6 months of observation), hamsters (12 months of intraperitoneal treatment followed by 12 months of observation), and rats (18 months of subcutaneous treatment) did not show any neoplastic effect associated with administration of cromolyn.

Mutagenicity

In various mutagenicity studies, there was no evidence of chromosomal damage or cytotoxicity.

Pregnancy/Reproduction

Fertility—In animal reproduction studies with cromolyn, there was no evidence of impaired fertility.

Pregnancy—Adequate and well-controlled studies in humans have not been done.

Reproduction studies in mice, rats, and rabbits with cromolyn administered parenterally in doses up to 338 times the human clinical doses showed no evidence of fetal malformations. Adverse fetal effects (increased resorptions and decreased fetal weight) were noted only at very high parenteral doses that produced maternal toxicity.

FDA Pregnancy Category B.

Breast-feeding

It is not known whether cromolyn is distributed into breast milk. However, problems in humans have not been documented. Since cromolyn reaches very low concentrations in maternal serum, it would be expected to reach even lower and probably undetectable concentrations in breast milk.

Pediatrics

Appropriate studies on the relationship of age to the effects of ophthalmic cromolyn have not been performed in children up to 4 years of age. Safety and efficacy have not been established. In older children, no pediatrics-specific problems have been documented to date.

Geriatrics
Appropriate studies on the relationship of age to the effects of cromolyn have not been performed in the geriatric population. However, geriatrics-specific problems that would limit the usefulness of this medication in the elderly are not expected.

Medical considerations/Contraindications
The medical considerations/contraindications included have been selected on the basis of their potential clinical significance (reasons given in parentheses where appropriate)—not necessarily inclusive (» = major clinical significance).

Risk-benefit should be considered when the following medical problem exists:
Sensitivity to cromolyn

Side/Adverse Effects
The following side/adverse effects have been selected on the basis of their potential clinical significance (possible signs and symptoms in parentheses where appropriate)—not necessarily inclusive:

Those indicating need for medical attention
Incidence rare
Chemosis (swelling of the membrane covering the white part of the eye); ***conjunctival injection*** (redness of the white part of the eye); ***styes, or other signs of eye irritation not present before therapy; contact dermatitis*** (rash or redness around the eyes)

Those indicating need for medical attention only if they continue or are bothersome
Incidence more frequent
Burning or stinging of eye, mild, temporary

Incidence less frequent or rare
Dryness or puffiness around the eye; watering or itching of eye, increased

Patient Consultation
As an aid to patient consultation, refer to *Advice for the Patient, Cromolyn (Ophthalmic)*.

In providing consultation, consider emphasizing the following selected information (» = major clinical significance):

Before using this medication
» Conditions affecting use, especially:
Sensitivity to cromolyn
Use in children—Safety and efficacy have not been established in children up to 4 years of age

Proper use of this medication
Proper administration technique; not touching applicator tip to any surface; keeping container tightly closed
» Importance of not using more medication than the amount prescribed
» Compliance with therapy; symptomatic response usually occurs within a few days
» Proper dosing
Missed dose: Using as soon as possible
» Proper storage

Precautions while using this medication
» Checking with physician if symptoms do not improve or if condition becomes worse

Side/adverse effects
Signs of potential side effects, especially chemosis, conjunctival injection, styes, or other signs of eye irritation not present before therapy; or contact dermatitis

General Dosing Information
Symptomatic response to therapy (decreased itching, redness, watering, and discharge) usually occurs within a few days; however, treatment may be required for up to 6 weeks.

Corticosteroids may be used concurrently with cromolyn, if required.

Although the manufacturer recommends that patients not wear soft contact lenses during treatment with cromolyn ophthalmic solution, medical experts do not believe this precaution is necessary unless the patient has corneal epithelial problems and the medication is to be used more often than once every 1 to 2 hours. No significant problems have been documented with ophthalmic solutions containing 0.03% or less of benzalkonium chloride as a preservative, and used as eyedrops in patients with no significant corneal surface problems.

Ophthalmic Dosage Forms
Note: Bracketed uses in the *Dosage Forms* section refer to categories of use and/or indications that are not included in U.S. product labeling.

CROMOLYN SODIUM OPHTHALMIC SOLUTION USP

Usual adult and adolescent dose
[Conjunctivitis, seasonal allergic]
Conjunctivitis, vernal[1]
Keratitis, vernal or[1]
Keratoconjunctivitis, vernal—
Topical, to the conjunctiva, 1 drop four to six times a day at regular intervals.

Usual adult prescribing limits
Up to 12.8 mg.

Usual pediatric dose
[Conjunctivitis, seasonal allergic]
Conjunctivitis, vernal[1]
Keratitis, vernal[1] or
Keratoconjunctivitis, vernal—
Children up to 4 years of age: Safety and efficacy have not been established.
Children 4 years of age and older: See *Usual adult and adolescent dose*.

Usual geriatric dose
See *Usual adult and adolescent dose*.

Strength(s) usually available
U.S.—
4% (Rx) [*Crolom* (benzalkonium chloride; edetate disodium; hydrochloric acid; sodium hydroxide)].

Canada—
2% (Rx) [*Opticrom* (benzalkonium chloride); *Vistacrom* (benzalkonium chloride 0.01%; edetate disodium)].

Note: One drop of cromolyn sodium ophthalmic solution 2% contains approximately 0.8 mg of cromolyn sodium; and one drop of cromolyn sodium ophthalmic solution 4% contains approximately 1.6 mg of cromolyn sodium.

Packaging and storage
Store below 40 °C (104 °F), preferably between 15 and 30 °C (59 and 86 °F), unless otherwise specified by manufacturer. Store in a tight, light-resistant container. Protect from freezing.

Auxiliary labeling
- For the eye.

[1]Not included in Canadian product labeling.

Revised: 07/10/1995

CUPRIC SULFATE—See *Copper Supplements (Systemic)*

CYANOCOBALAMIN—See *Vitamin B_{12} (Systemic)*

CYCLOBENZAPRINE Systemic

VA CLASSIFICATION (Primary): MS200

Commonly used brand name(s): *Flexeril*.

Note: For a listing of dosage forms and brand names by country availability, see *Dosage Forms* section(s).

Category
Skeletal muscle relaxant.

Indications
Note: Bracketed information in the *Indications* section refers to uses that are not included in U.S. product labeling.

Accepted
Spasm, skeletal muscle (treatment)—Cyclobenzaprine is indicated as an adjunct to other measures, such as rest and physical therapy, for the relief of muscle spasm associated with acute, painful musculoskeletal conditions. It is not effective in relieving muscle spasm or spasticity caused by central nervous system (CNS) disorders.

[Fibromyalgia syndrome][1]—Cyclobenzaprine is indicated in the treatment of fibromyalgia syndrome (fibrositis, fibrositis syndrome). It has been shown to decrease pain, reduce muscle tightness and the number of tender points, and improve sleep in patients with this condition.

[1]Not included in Canadian product labeling.

Pharmacology/Pharmacokinetics

Physicochemical characteristics

Molecular weight—311.86.
pKa—8.47 (25 °C).

Mechanism of action/Effect

The precise mechanism of action has not been fully determined. Cyclobenzaprine acts primarily at the brain stem to reduce tonic somatic motor activity influencing both gamma and alpha motoneurons. Actions at spinal cord sites may also be involved.

Other actions/effects

Cyclobenzaprine is structurally related to, and may have actions similar to, the tricyclic antidepressants. These possible effects include central and peripheral anticholinergic actions, a sedative effect, and an increase in heart rate.

Absorption

Well (but slowly) absorbed following oral administration.

Protein binding

Very high (93%), with plasma concentrations ranging from 0.1 to 1 mcg per mL (0.32 to 3.21 micromoles per L).

Biotransformation

Gastrointestinal and hepatic.

Half-life

1 to 3 days.

Onset of action

Within 1 hour.

Time to peak concentration

3 to 8 hours.

Peak serum concentration

15 to 25 nanograms per mL (0.048 to 0.08 micromoles per L) following a single 10-mg oral dose; subject to large interpatient variation.

Therapeutic plasma concentration

20 to 30 nanograms per mL (0.064 to 0.096 micromoles per L).

Time to peak effect

1 to 2 weeks.

Duration of action

Single dose—12 to 24 hours.

Elimination

Renal, primarily as conjugated metabolites (< 1% of a dose is excreted unchanged); 51% of a single 10-mg dose is excreted within 5 days. Cyclobenzaprine undergoes enterohepatic circulation. Some unchanged cyclobenzaprine is also eliminated via the bile and feces.

Precautions to Consider

Carcinogenicity

Cyclobenzaprine did not show evidence of carcinogenicity in an 81-week study in mice or a 105-week study in rats.

Mutagenicity

No evidence of mutagenicity occurred in male mice receiving up to 20 times the human dose of cyclobenzaprine.

Pregnancy/Reproduction

Fertility—No evidence of impaired fertility occurred in male or female rats receiving up to 10 times the human dose of cyclobenzaprine.

Pregnancy—Adequate and well-controlled studies in humans have not been done.

Studies in rats, mice, and rabbits have not shown that cyclobenzaprine has adverse effects in the fetus when given in doses up to 20 times the human dose.

FDA Pregnancy Category B.

Breast-feeding

Problems in humans have not been documented. It is not known whether cyclobenzaprine is distributed into breast milk; however, it is known that some of the structurally related tricyclic antidepressants are distributed into breast milk.

Pediatrics

No information is available on the relationship of age to the effects of cyclobenzaprine in pediatric patients. Safety and efficacy have not been established.

Adolescents

No information is available on the relationship of age to the effects of cyclobenzaprine in adolescents up to 15 years of age. Safety and efficacy have not been established.

Geriatrics

No information is available on the relationship of age to the effects of cyclobenzaprine in geriatric patients. However, it is known that geriatric patients exhibit increased sensitivity to other medications with anticholinergic activity and are more likely than younger adults to experience adverse reactions to the tricyclic antidepressants, which are structurally related to cyclobenzaprine.

Dental

The peripheral anticholinergic effects of cyclobenzaprine may inhibit salivary flow, thus contributing to the development of caries, periodontal disease, oral candidiasis, and discomfort.

Drug interactions and/or related problems

The following drug interactions and/or related problems have been selected on the basis of their potential clinical significance (possible mechanism in parentheses where appropriate)—not necessarily inclusive (» = major clinical significance):

Note: Combinations containing any of the following medications, depending on the amount present, may also interact with this medication.

In addition to the documented interactions listed below, the possibility should be considered that other interactions applying to tricyclic antidepressants may also apply to cyclobenzaprine because they are all chemically related.

» Alcohol or
» Antidepressants, tricyclic or
» CNS depression-producing medications, other (see *Appendix II*)
(concurrent use with cyclobenzaprine may result in additive CNS depressant effects; caution is recommended, and dosage of one or both agents should be reduced)

(concurrent use of a tricyclic antidepressant with cyclobenzaprine may also increase the risk of other side effects, such as anticholinergic effects and increased heart rate)

Antidyskinetics or
Anticholinergics or other medications with anticholinergic activity (see *Appendix II*)
(cyclobenzaprine may potentiate the anticholinergic actions of these medications; patients should be advised to report occurrence of gastrointestinal problems promptly, since paralytic ileus may occur)

Guanadrel or
Guanethidine
(cyclobenzaprine may decrease or block the antihypertensive effects of these medications)

» Monoamine oxidase (MAO) inhibitors, including furazolidone, procarbazine, and selegiline
(concurrent use with cyclobenzaprine is not recommended on an outpatient basis, as hyperpyretic crises, severe seizures, and death have resulted when MAO inhibitors were used concurrently with tricyclic antidepressants; a minimum of 14 days should elapse between discontinuance of MAO inhibitors and initiation of cyclobenzaprine therapy, unless the patient is hospitalized; a minimum of 5 to 7 days should elapse between discontinuance of cyclobenzaprine and initiation of MAO inhibitor therapy)

Medical considerations/Contraindications

The medical considerations/contraindications included have been selected on the basis of their potential clinical significance (reasons given in parentheses where appropriate)—not necessarily inclusive (» = major clinical significance).

Except under special circumstances, this medication should not be used when the following medical problems exist:

» Acute recovery phase of myocardial infarction or
» Cardiac arrhythmias or
» Congestive heart failure or
» Heart block or other conduction disturbances
(possible adverse cardiovascular effects)

» Hyperthyroidism
(increased risk of cardiac arrhythmias; also, tachycardia associated with hyperthyroidism may be exacerbated)

Risk-benefit should be considered when the following medical problems exist:

Glaucoma or predisposition to or

Urinary retention or history of
(cyclobenzaprine's anticholinergic effects may be detrimental to patients with these conditions)

Sensitivity to cyclobenzaprine

Side/Adverse Effects

The following side/adverse effects have been selected on the basis of their potential clinical significance (possible signs and symptoms in parentheses where appropriate)—not necessarily inclusive:

Those indicating need for medical attention

Incidence rare

Anaphylaxis (changes in facial skin color; skin rash, hives, and/or itching; fast or irregular breathing; puffiness or swelling of the eyelids or the area around the eyes; shortness of breath, troubled breathing, tightness in chest, and/or wheezing); ***angioedema*** (large, hive-like swellings on face, eyelids, mouth, lips, and/or tongue); ***anticholinergic effect*** (problems in urinating); ***CNS toxicity*** (abnormal thinking and dreaming; clumsiness or unsteadiness; severe confusion or disorientation; mental depression; ringing or buzzing in ears); ***dermatitis, allergic*** (skin rash, hives, or itching); ***hepatitis/cholestasis*** (yellow eyes or skin); ***syncope*** (fainting)

Note: *Mania* has also been reported in a few patients with pre-existing psychiatric illness.

Those indicating need for medical attention only if they continue or are bothersome

Incidence more frequent

Anticholinergic effects (dryness of mouth [7 to 27%]; blurred vision [<3%]); ***dizziness or lightheadedness***—3 to 11%; ***drowsiness***—16 to 39%

Note: *Dizziness, lightheadedness,* and *drowsiness* may be caused by cyclobenzaprine's anticholinergic, as well as its CNS, effects.

Incidence less frequent or rare (< 3%)

CNS effects (headache; confusion; excitement or nervousness; general feeling of discomfort or illness; numbness, tingling, pain, or weakness in hands or feet; muscle twitching; trembling; trouble in sleeping; unusual tiredness); ***constipation; frequent urination; gastrointestinal irritation*** (stomach cramps or pain; bloated feeling or gas; diarrhea; indigestion; nausea; vomiting); ***pounding heartbeat; problems in speaking; unpleasant taste or other taste changes; unusual muscle weakness***

Overdose

For specific information on the agents used in the management of cyclobenzaprine overdose, see:

Benzodiazepines (Systemic) monograph;
Charcoal, Activated (Oral-Local) monograph;
Neostigmine in *Antimyasthenics (Systemic)* monograph;
Physostigmine (Systemic) monograph;
Propranolol in *Beta-adrenergic Blocking Agents (Systemic)* monograph; and/or
Pyridostigmine in *Antimyasthenics (Systemic)* monograph.

For more information on the management of overdose or unintentional ingestion, **contact a Poison Control Center** (see *Poison Control Center Listing*).

Clinical effects of overdose

The following effects have been selected on the basis of their potential clinical significance (possible signs and symptoms in parentheses where appropriate)—not necessarily inclusive:

Acute and chronic

Cardiotoxicity (fast or irregular heartbeat; troubled breathing)—may include bundle branch block or other arrhythmias and congestive heart failure; ***CNS toxicity*** (severe confusion; delirium; convulsions; severe drowsiness; hallucinations; severe nervousness or restlessness); ***dry, hot, flushed skin***—a few cases of paradoxical diaphoresis have also been reported; ***increase or decrease in body temperature; unexplained muscle stiffness; vomiting***

Treatment of overdose

To decrease absorption—Emptying the stomach via induction of emesis, gastric lavage, or activated charcoal.

Monitoring—Taking an electrocardiogram (ECG) and monitoring cardiac function if any signs of dysrhythmia are evident.

Careful monitoring of the patient.

Specific treatment—

Use of physostigmine salicylate for severe or life-threatening anticholinergic effects. Repeating dose as required if life-threatening symptoms (e.g., arrhythmias, convulsions, coma) persist or recur. Because of its toxicity, physostigmine is recommended only in severe cases. See the package insert or *Physostigmine (Systemic)* monograph for specific dosing guidelines for use of this product.

Use of neostigmine, pyridostigmine, or propranolol for cardiac arrhythmias. See the package insert or *Neostigmine* or *Pyridostigmine* in *Antimyasthenics (Systemic)* monograph or *Propranolol* in *Beta-adrenergic Blocking Agents (Systemic)* monograph for specific dosing guidelines for use of this product.

Use of a short-acting digitalis preparation for cardiac failure should be considered. Close monitoring of cardiac function for at least 5 days is recommended. See the package insert or *Digitalis Glycosides (Systemic)* monograph for specific dosing guidelines for use of this product.

Use of an appropriate anticonvulsant for convulsions. Benzodiazepines are most often used. However, because intravenously administered benzodiazepines may cause respiratory and circulatory depression, especially when administered rapidly, medications and equipment needed for support of respiration and for resuscitation must be immediately available. See the package insert or *Benzodiazepines (Systemic)* monograph for specific dosing guidelines for use of this product.

Supportive—May include maintaining an open airway, maintaining adequate fluid intake, regulating body temperature, and treating circulatory shock, convulsions, and metabolic acidosis, if necessary. Patients in whom intentional overdose is known or suspected should be referred for psychiatric consultation.

Note: Dialysis is probably of no value in removing cyclobenzaprine from the body.

Patient Consultation

As an aid to patient consultation, refer to *Advice for the Patient, Cyclobenzaprine (Systemic).*

In providing consultation, consider emphasizing the following selected information (» = major clinical significance):

Before using this medication

» Conditions affecting use, especially:
Sensitivity to cyclobenzaprine
Other medications, especially other CNS depression-producing medications, monoamine oxidase inhibitors, and tricyclic antidepressants
Other medical problems, especially cardiac arrhythmias, congestive heart failure, heart block or other conduction disturbances, hyperthyroidism, and myocardial infarction (acute recovery phase)

Proper use of this medication

Not taking more medication than the amount prescribed, to minimize possibility of side effects

» Proper dosing

Missed dose: Taking if remembered within an hour; not taking if not remembered until later; not doubling doses

» Proper storage

Precautions while using this medication

» Avoiding alcohol or other CNS depressants unless prescribed or otherwise approved by physician

» Caution if blurred vision, drowsiness, or dizziness occurs

Possible dryness of mouth; using sugarless gum or candy, ice, or saliva substitute for relief; checking with physician or dentist if dry mouth continues for more than 2 weeks

Side/adverse effects

Signs and symptoms of potential side effects, especially anaphylaxis, angioedema, anticholinergic effects, CNS toxicity, allergic dermatitis, hepatitis, cholestasis, and syncope

General Dosing Information

It is recommended that cyclobenzaprine therapy for acute, painful musculoskeletal conditions be discontinued after 2 to 3 weeks, because evidence of its effectiveness for longer periods is not available. However, studies of the usefulness of cyclobenzaprine in fibromyalgia syndrome have indicated that the medication remains effective for at least 12 weeks.

Cyclobenzaprine is closely related to the tricyclic antidepressants and shares many of their adverse reactions and drug interactions.

Oral Dosage Forms

Note: Bracketed uses in the *Dosage Forms* section refer to categories of use and/or indications that are not included in U.S. product labeling.

CYCLOBENZAPRINE HYDROCHLORIDE TABLETS USP

Usual adult dose

Acute musculoskeletal conditions—Oral, 20 to 40 mg a day in two to four divided doses, usually 10 mg three times a day.

[Fibromyalgia syndrome][1]—Oral, 5 to 40 mg at bedtime.

Usual adult prescribing limits

Not to exceed 60 mg daily.

Usual pediatric and adolescent dose

Children up to 15 years of age—Dosage has not been established.

Patients 15 years of age and older—See *Usual adult dose.*

Strength(s) usually available

U.S.—
  10 mg (Rx) [*Flexeril;* GENERIC].

Canada—
  10 mg (Rx) [*Flexeril*].

Packaging and storage

Store below 40 °C (104 °F), preferably between 15 and 30 °C (59 and 86 °F). Store in a well-closed container.

Auxiliary labeling

- May cause drowsiness.
- Avoid alcoholic beverages.

[1]Not included in Canadian product labeling.

Selected Bibliography

Katz WA, Dube J. Cyclobenzaprine in the treatment of acute muscle spasm: review of a decade of clinical experience. Clin Ther 1988; 10: 216-28.

Revised: 06/03/1999

CYCLOPENTOLATE Ophthalmic

VA CLASSIFICATION (Primary): OP600

Commonly used brand name(s): *AK-Pentolate; Ak-Pentolate; Cyclogyl; Cylate; Diopentolate; Minims Cyclopentolate; Ocu-Pentolate; Pentolair.*

Note: For a listing of dosage forms and brand names by country availability, see *Dosage Forms* section(s).

Category

Cycloplegic; mydriatic.

Indications

Note: Bracketed information in the *Indications* section refers to uses that are not included in U.S. product labeling.

Accepted

Refraction, cycloplegic—Indicated for measurement of refractive errors; also indicated for cycloplegia in diagnostic procedures, such as ophthalmoscopy.

Mydriasis, in diagnostic procedures—Indicated for mydriasis in diagnostic procedures, such as ophthalmoscopy.

[Synechiae, posterior (prophylaxis)][1]—Cyclopentolate is used for prophylaxis of posterior synechiae.

[Uveitis (treatment)][1]—Used in inflammatory conditions of the iris and uveal tract when a shorter-acting mydriatic and cycloplegic is required.

[1]Not included in Canadian product labeling.

Pharmacology/Pharmacokinetics

Physicochemical characteristics

Molecular weight—327.85.

Mechanism of action/Effect

Cyclopentolate is an anticholinergic drug that blocks the responses of the sphincter muscle of the iris and the accommodative muscle of the ciliary body to stimulation by acetylcholine. Dilation of the pupil (mydriasis) and paralysis of accommodation (cycloplegia) result.

Onset of action

Rapid.

Time to peak effect

Cycloplegia—Within 25 to 75 minutes.

Mydriasis—Within 30 to 60 minutes.

Duration of action

Has a shorter duration of action than atropine.

Complete recovery of accommodation usually takes 6 to 24 hours.

Complete recovery from mydriasis in some persons may take several days.

Precautions to Consider

Pregnancy/Reproduction

Pregnancy—Cyclopentolate may be systemically absorbed.

Studies have not been done in humans.

Studies have not been done in animals.

FDA Pregnancy Category C.

Breast-feeding

It is not known whether cyclopentolate is distributed into breast milk; however, cyclopentolate may be systemically absorbed.

Pediatrics

An increased susceptibility to cyclopentolate and similar drugs (such as atropine) has been reported in infants and young children and in children with blond hair, blue eyes, Down's syndrome, spastic paralysis, or brain damage; therefore, cyclopentolate should be used with great caution in these patients. In addition, premature and small infants are especially prone to CNS and cardiopulmonary side effects from systemic absorption of cyclopentolate. Infants should be closely observed for at least 30 minutes following administration of cyclopentolate. Also, feeding intolerance may follow ophthalmic use of cyclopentolate in neonates. It is recommended that feeding be withheld for 4 hours following administration of this medication.

Geriatrics

Geriatric patients are more susceptible to the effects of cyclopentolate and similar drugs (such as atropine), thus increasing the potential for systemic side effects.

Also, cyclopentolate should be used with caution in the elderly because of possible undiagnosed predisposition to angle-closure glaucoma.

Drug interactions and/or related problems

The following drug interactions and/or related problems have been selected on the basis of their potential clinical significance (possible mechanism in parentheses where appropriate)—not necessarily inclusive (» = major clinical significance):

Note: Combinations containing any of the following medications, depending on the amount present, may also interact with this medication.

Antiglaucoma agents, cholinergic, long-acting, ophthalmic
  (cyclopentolate may antagonize the antiglaucoma and miotic actions of ophthalmic long-acting cholinergic antiglaucoma agents, such as demecarium, echothiophate, and isoflurophate)

Carbachol or
Pilocarpine
  (cyclopentolate may interfere with the antiglaucoma action of carbachol or pilocarpine; also, these medications counteract the mydriatic effect of cyclopentolate, the result of which may be used to therapeutic advantage)

Medical considerations/Contraindications

The medical considerations/contraindications included have been selected on the basis of their potential clinical significance (reasons given in parentheses where appropriate)—not necessarily inclusive (» = major clinical significance).

Risk-benefit should be considered when the following medical problems exist:

Brain damage, in children or
Down's syndrome (mongolism), in children and adults or
Spastic paralysis, in children
  (increased susceptibility to the effects of cyclopentolate)

» Glaucoma, angle-closure or predisposition to angle-closure

Sensitivity to cyclopentolate

Side/Adverse Effects

Note: An increased susceptibility to cyclopentolate and similar drugs (such as atropine) has been reported in infants, young children, children with blond hair or blue eyes, adults and children with Down's syndrome, children with brain damage or spastic paralysis, and the elderly. This susceptibility increases the potential for systemic side effects.

The following side/adverse effects have been selected on the basis of their potential clinical significance (possible signs and symptoms in parentheses where appropriate)—not necessarily inclusive:

Those indicating need for medical attention

Symptoms of systemic absorption

Ataxia (clumsiness or unsteadiness); ***behavioral disturbances; psychotic reactions*** (unusual behavior, such as disorientation to time or place, failure to recognize people, hyperactivity, or restlessness, especially in children using 2% cyclopentolate); ***confusion; diminished gastrointestinal mobility*** (constipation; full feeling or passing gas; stomach cramps or pain); ***fast or irregular heartbeat; fever; hallucinations; increased intraocular pressure; seizures; skin rash; slurred speech; swollen stomach***—in infants; ***thirst or dryness of mouth; unusual drowsiness; tiredness or weakness; urinary retention*** (passing urine less often); ***vasodilation*** (flushing or redness of face)

Those indicating need for medical attention only if they continue or are bothersome

Blepharoconjunctivitis; conjunctivitis; hyperemia; punctate keratitis; synechiae (eye irritation not present before therapy); ***blurred vision; burning of eye; photophobia*** (increased sensitivity of eyes to light)

Overdose

For specific information on the agents used in the management of ophthalmic cyclopentolate overdose, see:

- *Physostigmine (Systemic)* monograph.

For more information on the management of overdose or unintentional ingestion, **contact a Poison Control Center** (see *Poison Control Center Listing*).

Clinical effects of overdose

Note: Excessive dosage may result in exaggerated symptoms as noted in the *Side/Adverse Effects* section.

The following effects have been selected on the basis of their potential clinical significance (possible signs and symptoms in parentheses where appropriate)—not necessarily inclusive:

Acute

Coma; medullary paralysis

Note: In some cases, overdose has resulted in death.

Treatment of overdose

Cessation of ophthalmic cyclopentolate usually results in spontaneous recovery from adverse systemic effects; for severe toxicity, physostigmine is the antidote of choice.

For children—A dose of 0.5 mg of physostigmine should be slowly administered intravenously. If toxic symptoms persist and no cholinergic symptoms are produced, the dose should be repeated at 5-minute intervals up to a maximum of 2 mg.

For adolescents and adults—A dose of 2 mg of physostigmine should be slowly administered intravenously. A second dose of 1 to 2 mg may be given after 20 minutes if no reversal of toxic manifestations has occurred. Physostigmine may also be administered subcutaneously.

Patient Consultation

As an aid to patient consultation, refer to *Advice for the Patient, Cyclopentolate (Ophthalmic)*.

In providing consultation, consider emphasizing the following selected information (» = major clinical significance):

Before using this medication

» Conditions affecting use, especially:

Sensitivity to cyclopentolate

Use in children—Infants and young children and children with blond hair or blue eyes may be especially sensitive to the effects of cyclopentolate and similar drugs (such as atropine); this may increase the chance of side effects during treatment; premature and small infants are especially prone to CNS and cardiopulmonary side effects from systemic absorption; feeding intolerance may occur following administration in neonates; it is recommended that feeding be withheld for 4 hours following administration

Use in the elderly—Geriatric patients are more susceptible to the effects of cyclopentolate and similar drugs (such as atropine), thus increasing the potential for systemic side effects

Other medical problems, especially angle-closure glaucoma or predisposition to angle-closure

Proper use of this medication

Proper administration technique

» Importance of nasolacrimal pressure, especially in infants

Washing hands immediately after application to remove any medicine that may be on them; if applying medication to infants or children, washing their hands also, and not letting any medication get into their mouths

Preventing contamination: Not touching applicator tip to any surface; keeping container tightly closed

» Importance of not using more medication than the amount prescribed

» Proper dosing

Missed dose: Applying as soon as possible; if almost time for next dose, skipping missed dose and going back to regular dosing schedule; not doubling doses

» Proper storage

Precautions while using this medication

» Medication causes blurred vision; checking with physician if effect continues for longer than 36 hours after discontinuation of medication

» Medication causes increased sensitivity of the eyes to light; wearing sunglasses that block ultraviolet light to protect eyes; checking with physician if effect continues for longer than 36 hours after discontinuation of medication

Side/adverse effects

Signs of potential side effects, especially symptoms of systemic absorption, such as ataxia, behavioral disturbances or psychotic reactions, confusion, diminished gastrointestinal mobility, fast or irregular heartbeat, fever, hallucinations, increased intraocular pressure, seizures, skin rash, slurred speech, swollen stomach (in infants), thirst or dryness of mouth, unusual drowsiness, tiredness or weakness, urinary retention, and vasodilation.

General Dosing Information

Although some manufacturers recommend a dose of 2 drops of an ophthalmic solution at appropriate intervals, the conjunctival sac will usually hold only 1 drop.

More frequent instillation or use of a stronger solution may be required to produce adequate cycloplegia in eyes with brown or hazel irides than in eyes with blue irides.

An estimation of the depth of the angle of the anterior chamber should be made to avoid inducing angle-closure glaucoma.

To avoid excessive systemic absorption, patient should apply digital pressure to the lacrimal sac during and for 2 or 3 minutes following instillation of the solution. This is especially important in infants.

Ophthalmic Dosage Forms

Note: Bracketed uses in the *Dosage Forms* section refer to categories of use and/or indications that are not included in U.S. product labeling.

CYCLOPENTOLATE HYDROCHLORIDE OPHTHALMIC SOLUTION USP

Usual adult and adolescent dose

Cycloplegic refraction—

Topical, to the conjunctiva, 1 drop of a 0.5 to 2% solution, repeated once in five to ten minutes if necessary, with refraction scheduled for forty to fifty minutes afterward.

For ophthalmoscopy—

Topical, to the conjunctiva, 1 drop of a 0.5 to 2% solution, repeated once in five to ten minutes if necessary.

[Uveitis][1]—

Topical, to the conjunctiva, 1 drop of a 0.5 or 1% solution three or four times a day.

Usual pediatric dose

Cycloplegic refraction—

Premature and small infants: Topical, to the conjunctiva, 1 drop of a 0.5% solution, as a single dose.

Children: Topical, to the conjunctiva, 1 drop of a 0.5 to 2% solution, followed by 1 drop of a 0.5 or 1% solution after five to ten minutes if necessary, with refraction scheduled for forty to fifty minutes afterward.

For ophthalmoscopy—

Premature and small infants: Topical, to the conjunctiva, 1 drop of a 0.5% solution, as a single dose.

Children: Topical, to the conjunctiva, 1 drop of a 0.5 to 2% solution, followed by 1 drop of a 0.5 or 1% solution after five to ten minutes if necessary.

[Uveitis][1]—

Topical, to the conjunctiva, 1 drop of a 0.5 or 1% solution three or four times a day.

Note: In small infants, use of concentrations above 0.5% is not recommended.

Infants should be closely observed for signs of adverse reactions for at least 30 minutes following administration.

To minimize systemic absorption, application of nasolacrimal pressure for 2 or 3 minutes is recommended, especially in infants.

Strength(s) usually available

U.S.—

0.5% (Rx) [*Cyclogyl* (benzalkonium chloride 0.01%)].

1% (Rx) [*Ak-Pentolate* (benzalkonium chloride 0.01%); *Cyclogyl* (benzalkonium chloride 0.01%); *Cylate; Ocu-Pentolate; Pentolair;* GENERIC].

2% (Rx) [*AK-Pentolate; Cyclogyl* (benzalkonium chloride 0.01%)].

Canada—

0.5% (Rx) [*Ak-Pentolate* (benzalkonium chloride); *Minims Cyclopentolate*].

1% (Rx) [*Ak-Pentolate* (benzalkonium chloride); *Cyclogyl* (benzalkonium chloride); *Diopentolate* (benzalkonium chloride); *Minims Cyclopentolate*].

Packaging and storage

Store between 15 and 30 °C (59 and 86 °F). Store in a tight container.

Auxiliary labeling

- For the eye.
- Keep container tightly closed.

[1]Not included in Canadian product labeling.

Revised: 08/14/1998

CYCLOPHOSPHAMIDE Systemic

VA CLASSIFICATION (Primary/Secondary): AN100/DE801; IM403; MS103

Commonly used brand name(s): *Cytoxan; Neosar; Procytox.*

Note: For a listing of dosage forms and brand names by country availability, see *Dosage Forms* section(s).

Category

Antineoplastic; immunosuppressant.

Indications

Note: Bracketed information in the *Indications* section refers to uses that are not included in U.S. product labeling.

Accepted

Leukemia, acute lymphocytic (treatment) or
Leukemia, acute nonlymphocytic (treatment)—Cyclophosphamide is indicated for treatment of acute lymphoblastic (stem-cell) leukemia in children (including during remission to prolong the duration), and for treatment of acute nonlymphocytic leukemia.

Leukemia, chronic myelocytic (treatment) or
Leukemia, chronic lymphocytic (treatment)—Cyclophosphamide is indicated for treatment of chronic granulocytic leukemia (it is usually ineffective in acute blastic crisis) and chronic lymphocytic leukemia.

Carcinoma, ovarian, epithelial (treatment)
Carcinoma, breast (treatment)
Neuroblastoma (treatment)
Retinoblastoma (treatment)
[Carcinoma, lung, non-small cell (treatment)]
[Carcinoma, lung, small cell (treatment)]
[Carcinoma, cervical (treatment)][1]
[Carcinoma, endometrial (treatment)][1]
[Carcinoma, bladder (treatment)][1]
[Carcinoma, prostatic (treatment)][1]
[Carcinoma, testicular (treatment)][1]
[Wilms' tumor (treatment)][1] or
[Carcinoma, adrenocortical (treatment)][1]—Cyclophosphamide is indicated for treatment of adenocarcinoma of the ovary, breast carcinoma, neuroblastoma [in patients with disseminated disease], retinoblastoma, small cell and non-small cell lung carcinoma, cervical carcinoma, and for endometrial carcinoma, bladder carcinoma, prostatic carcinoma, testicular carcinoma, Wilms' tumor, and adrenocortical carcinoma (Evidence rating: IIID).

Lymphomas, Hodgkin's (treatment) or
Lymphomas, non-Hodgkin's (treatment)—Cyclophosphamide is indicated for treatment of Stage III and IV (Ann Arbor or Peter's Staging System) Hodgkin's disease and non-Hodgkin's lymphomas including nodular or diffuse lymphocytic lymphoma, mixed-cell type lymphoma, histiocytic lymphoma, Burkitt's lymphoma, and [lymphoblastic lymphosarcoma].

Multiple myeloma (treatment)—Cyclophosphamide is indicated for treatment of multiple myeloma.

Mycosis fungoides (treatment)—Cyclophosphamide is indicated for treatment of advanced mycosis fungoides.

Nephrotic syndrome (treatment)[1]—Cyclophosphamide is indicated as an immunosuppressant in the treatment of steroid-resistant or frequently relapsing steroid-sensitive biopsy-proven minimal-change nephrotic syndrome in children [and adults].

[Ewing's sarcoma (treatment)][1]
[Osteosarcoma, (treatment)][1] or
[Sarcomas, soft tissue (treatment)][1]—Cyclophosphamide is indicated for treatment of various sarcomas, including Ewing's sarcoma, osteosarcoma, and soft-tissue sarcomas.

[Tumors, germ cell, ovarian (treatment)][1]
[Tumors, brain, primary (treatment)][1] or
[Tumors, trophoblastic, gestational (treatment)][1]—Cyclophosphamide is indicated for treatment of germ cell ovarian, primary brain, and gestational trophoblastic tumors.

[Thymoma (treatment)][1]—Cyclophosphamide is indicated for treatment of thymoma.

[Histiocytosis X (treatment)][1]—Cyclophosphamide is indicated as first-line therapy, as a single agent or in combination with other chemotherapeutic agents, for treatment of Histiocytosis X (Letterer-Siwe disease) (Evidence rating: IIID).

[Waldenström's macroglobulinemia][1]—Cyclophosphamide is indicated for treatment of Waldenström's macroglobulinemia.

[Transplant rejection, organ (prophylaxis)][1]—Cyclophosphamide is used for its immunosuppressant activity, for prevention of rejection in homotransplantation.

[Arthritis, rheumatoid (treatment)][1]
[Wegener's granulomatosis (treatment)][1]
[Lupus erythematosus, systemic][1]
[Dermatomyositis, systemic (treatment)][1] or
[Multiple sclerosis (treatment)][1]—Cyclophosphamide is used as an immunosuppressant in the treatment of rheumatoid arthritis and other autoimmune diseases such as polymyositis (systemic dermatomyositis), multiple sclerosis, Wegener's granulomatosis, systemic lupus erythematosus (SLE), and other types of vasculitis.

Extreme caution is recommended in use of cyclophosphamide for nonneoplastic conditions because of potential carcinogenicity with long-term use of this agent.

[1]Not included in Canadian product labeling.

Pharmacology/Pharmacokinetics

Physicochemical characteristics

Molecular weight—279.1.

Mechanism of action/Effect

Cyclophosphamide is classed as an alkylating agent of the nitrogen mustard type. An activated form of cyclophosphamide, phosphoramide mustard, alkylates or binds with many intracellular molecular structures, including nucleic acids. Its cytotoxic action is primarily due to cross-linking of strands of DNA and RNA, as well as to inhibition of protein synthesis.

Other actions/effects

Cyclophosphamide is a potent immunosuppressant. It also causes marked and persistent inhibition of cholinesterase activity.

Absorption

Well absorbed after oral administration (bioavailability greater than 75%).

Distribution

Crosses blood-brain barrier to limited extent.

Protein binding

Very low (some active metabolites—greater than 60%).

Biotransformation

Hepatic (including initial activation and subsequent degradation).

Half-life

Unchanged drug—3 to 12 hours.

Time to peak concentration

Plasma—Metabolites: 2 to 3 hours after intravenous administration.

Elimination

Renal, 5 to 25% unchanged.

In dialysis—Cyclophosphamide is dialyzable.

Precautions to Consider

Carcinogenicity/Mutagenicity

Secondary malignancies are potential delayed effects of many antineoplastic agents, although it is not clear whether the effect is related to their mutagenic or immunosuppressive action. The effect of dose and duration of therapy is also unknown, although risk seems to increase with long-term use. Although information is limited, available data seem to indicate that the carcinogenic risk is greatest with the alkylating agents.

Cyclophosphamide is a potent carcinogen in animals. In humans, it has been associated with development of myeloproliferative and lymphoproliferative carcinomas as well as urinary bladder carcinoma (especially in patients who developed hemorrhagic cystitis while receiving cyclophosphamide) up to several years after administration. One case of carcinoma of the renal pelvis occurred in a patient who received long-term treatment with cyclophosphamide for cerebral vasculitis.

Pregnancy/Reproduction

Fertility—Gonadal suppression, resulting in amenorrhea or azoospermia, may occur in patients taking antineoplastic therapy, especially with the alkylating agents. In general, these effects appear to be related to dose and length of therapy and may be irreversible. Prediction of the degree of testicular or ovarian function impairment is complicated by the common use of combinations of several antineoplastics, which makes it difficult to assess the effects of individual agents.

However, there have been numerous reports of gonadal suppression with use of cyclophosphamide, which seems to depend on dose, duration, and state of gonadal function at the time of therapy; sterility may be irreversible in some patients.

Paternal use of cyclophosphamide prior to conception has been associated with cardiac and limb abnormalities in an infant.

Pregnancy—Cyclophosphamide crosses the placenta. Use in humans has resulted in both normal and malformed (missing fingers and/or toes, cardiac anomalies, hernias) newborns; risk seems to be less in the second and third trimesters. Low birth weight is also a risk with exposure of the fetus to antineoplastics.

First trimester: It is usually recommended that use of antineoplastics, especially combination chemotherapy, be avoided whenever possible, especially during the first trimester. Although information is limited because of the relatively few instances of antineoplastic administration during pregnancy, the mutagenic, teratogenic, and carcinogenic potential of these medications must be considered.

Other hazards to the fetus include adverse reactions seen in adults.

In general, use of a contraceptive is recommended during cytotoxic drug therapy.

Studies in animals have shown that cyclophosphamide is teratogenic in mice, rats, rabbits, and monkeys given 0.02, 0.08, 0.5, and 0.07 times the human dose, respectively.

FDA Pregnancy Category D.

Breast-feeding

Cyclophosphamide is distributed into breast milk. Breast-feeding is not recommended during chemotherapy because of the risks to the infant (adverse effects, mutagenicity, carcinogenicity).

Pediatrics

Appropriate studies performed to date have not demonstrated pediatrics-specific problems that would limit the usefulness of cyclophosphamide in children.

Prepubescent girls treated with cyclophosphamide usually develop secondary sexual characteristics normally, have regular menses, and subsequently conceive; however, ovarian fibrosis and apparent complete loss of germ cells after prolonged treatment in late prepubescence have been reported. Prepubescent boys treated with cyclophosphamide develop secondary sexual characteristics normally, but may have oligospermia or azoospermia, increased gonadotropin secretion, and some degree of testicular atrophy; azoospermia may be reversible, although possibly not for several years after the end of cyclophosphamide therapy.

Geriatrics

Although appropriate studies on the relationship of age to the effects of cyclophosphamide have not been performed in the geriatric population, geriatrics-specific problems are not expected to limit the usefulness of this medication in the elderly. However, elderly patients are more likely to have age-related renal function impairment, which may require caution in patients receiving cyclophosphamide.

Dental

The bone marrow depressant effects of cyclophosphamide may result in an increased incidence of microbial infection, delayed healing, and gingival bleeding. Dental work, whenever possible, should be completed prior to initiation of therapy or deferred until blood counts have returned to normal. Patients should be instructed in proper oral hygiene during treatment, including caution in use of regular toothbrushes, dental floss, and toothpicks.

Cyclophosphamide may also rarely cause stomatitis associated with considerable discomfort.

Drug interactions and/or related problems

The following drug interactions and/or related problems have been selected on the basis of their potential clinical significance (possible mechanism in parentheses where appropriate)—not necessarily inclusive (» = major clinical significance):

Note: Combinations containing any of the following medications, depending on the amount present, may also interact with this medication.

Allopurinol or
Colchicine or
» Probenecid or
» Sulfinpyrazone
(cyclophosphamide may raise the concentration of blood uric acid; dosage adjustment of antigout agents may be necessary to control hyperuricemia and gout; uricosuric antigout agents may increase risk of uric acid nephropathy)
(concurrent use with allopurinol may enhance the bone marrow toxicity of cyclophosphamide; if concurrent use is required, close observation for toxic effects should be considered)

Anticoagulants, oral
(cyclophosphamide may increase anticoagulant activity as a result of decreased hepatic synthesis of procoagulant factors and interference with platelet formation, but may also decrease anticoagulant activity by an unknown mechanism)

Blood dyscrasia-causing medications (see *Appendix II*)
(leukopenic and/or thrombocytopenic effects of cyclophosphamide may be increased with concurrent or recent therapy if these medications cause the same effects; dosage adjustment of cyclophosphamide, if necessary, should be based on blood counts)

» Bone marrow depressants, other (see *Appendix II*) or
» Radiation therapy
(additive bone marrow depression may occur; dosage reduction may be required when two or more bone marrow depressants, including radiation, are used concurrently or consecutively)

» Cocaine
(inhibition of cholinesterase activity by cyclophosphamide reduces or slows cocaine metabolism, thereby increasing and/or prolonging its effects and increasing the risk of toxicity)

» Cytarabine
(concurrent use of high-dose cytarabine with cyclophosphamide for bone marrow transplant preparation has been reported to result in an increase in cardiomyopathy with subsequent death)

Daunorubicin or
Doxorubicin
(concurrent use with cyclophosphamide may result in increased cardiotoxicity; it is recommended that the total dose of daunorubicin or doxorubicin not exceed 400 mg per square meter of body surface area)

Hepatic enzyme inducers (see *Appendix II*)
(these agents may induce microsomal metabolism to increase formation of alkylating metabolites of cyclophosphamide, thereby reducing the half-life and increasing the activity of cyclophosphamide)

» Immunosuppressants, other, such as:
Azathioprine or
Chlorambucil or
Corticosteroids, glucocorticoid or
Cyclosporine or
Mercaptopurine or
Muromonab-CD3
(concurrent use with cyclophosphamide may increase the risk of infection and development of neoplasms)

Lovastatin
(concurrent use in cardiac transplant patients may be associated with an increased risk of rhabdomyolysis and acute renal failure)

Succinylcholine
(cyclophosphamide may decrease plasma concentrations or activity of pseudocholinesterase, the enzyme that metabolizes succinylcholine, thereby enhancing the neuromuscular blockade of succinylcholine. Increased or prolonged respiratory depression or paralysis [apnea] may occur but is of minor clinical significance while the patient is being mechanically ventilated; however, caution and careful monitoring of the patient are recommended during and following concurrent or sequential use, especially if there is a possibility of incomplete reversal of neuromuscular blockade postoperatively)

Vaccines, killed virus
(because normal defense mechanisms may be suppressed by cyclophosphamide therapy, the patient's antibody response to the vaccine may be decreased. The interval between discontinuation of medications that cause immunosuppression and restoration of the patient's ability to respond to the vaccine depends on the intensity and type of immunosuppression-causing medication used, the underlying disease, and other factors; estimates vary from 3 months to 1 year)

» Vaccines, live virus
(because normal defense mechanisms may be suppressed by cyclophosphamide therapy, concurrent use with a live virus vaccine may potentiate the replication of the vaccine virus, may increase the side/adverse effects of the vaccine virus, and/or may decrease the patient's antibody response to the vaccine; immunization of these patients should be undertaken only with extreme caution after careful review of the patient's hematologic status and only with the knowledge and consent of the physician managing the cyclophosphamide therapy. The interval between discontinuation of medications that cause immunosuppression and restoration of the patient's ability to respond to the vaccine depends on the intensity and type of immunosuppression-causing medication used, the underlying disease, and other factors; estimates vary from 3 months to 1 year. Patients with leukemia in remission should not receive live virus vaccine until at least 3 months after their last chemotherapy. In addition, immunization with oral poliovirus vaccine should be postponed in persons in close contact with the patient, especially family members)

Laboratory value alterations

The following have been selected on the basis of their potential clinical significance (possible effect in parentheses where appropriate)—not necessarily inclusive (» = major clinical significance).

With diagnostic test results

Candida skin test and
Mumps skin test and
Trichophyton skin test and
Tuberculin PPD skin test
(positive reactions may be suppressed)

Papanicolaou (PAP) test
(false-positive results may be produced)

With physiology/laboratory test values

Pseudocholinesterase
(serum concentrations may be decreased)

Uric acid
(blood and urine concentrations may be increased)

Medical considerations/Contraindications

The medical considerations/contraindications included have been selected on the basis of their potential clinical significance (reasons given in parentheses where appropriate)—not necessarily inclusive (» = major clinical significance).

Risk-benefit should be considered when the following medical problems exist:

Adrenalectomy
(toxic effects of cyclophosphamide may be increased; dosage adjustment of both replacement steroids and cyclophosphamide may be necessary)

» Bone marrow depression

» Chickenpox, existing or recent (including recent exposure) or
» Herpes zoster
(risk of severe generalized disease)

Gout, history of or
Urate renal stones, history of
(risk of hyperuricemia)

» Hepatic function impairment
(effect of cyclophosphamide may be reduced because of its dependence on hepatic microsomal enzyme activation)

» Infection

» Renal function impairment
(reduced elimination; dosage reduction usually not necessary)

Sensitivity to cyclophosphamide

» Tumor cell infiltration of bone marrow
(a reduction by one-third to one-half in cyclophosphamide dosage for induction is recommended for patients with bone marrow depression due to tumor cell infiltration)

» Caution should be used also in patients who have had previous cytotoxic drug therapy or radiation therapy; a reduction by one-third to one-half in cyclophosphamide dosage for induction is recommended for patients with bone marrow depression due to cytotoxic or radiation therapy.

Patient monitoring

The following may be especially important in patient monitoring (other tests may be warranted in some patients, depending on condition; » = major clinical significance):

Alanine aminotransferase (ALT [SGPT]) values, serum and
Aspartate aminotransferase (AST [SGOT]) values, serum and
Bilirubin values, serum and
Lactate dehydrogenase (LDH) values, serum
(determinations recommended prior to initiation of therapy and at periodic intervals during therapy; frequency varies according to clinical state, agent, dose, and other agents being used concurrently)

Blood urea nitrogen (BUN) concentrations and
Creatinine concentrations, serum
(determinations recommended prior to initiation of therapy and at periodic intervals during therapy; frequency varies according to clinical state, agent, dose, and other agents being used concurrently)

» Examination of urine for microscopic hematuria
(recommended at periodic intervals during therapy, as well as for several hours following a large intravenous dose)

» Hematocrit or hemoglobin and
» Leukocyte count, total and, if appropriate, differential and
» Platelet count
(determinations recommended prior to initiation of therapy and at periodic intervals during therapy; frequency varies according to clinical state, agent, dose, and other agents being used concurrently)

Uric acid concentrations, serum
(determinations recommended prior to initiation of therapy and at periodic intervals during therapy; frequency varies according to clinical state, agent, dose, and other agents being used concurrently)

Urinary output and
Urinary specific gravity
(determinations recommended following high-dose intravenous administration to detect possible syndrome of inappropriate antidiuretic hormone [SIADH])

Side/Adverse Effects

Note: Many "side effects" of antineoplastic therapy are unavoidable and represent the medication's pharmacologic action. Some of these (for example, leukopenia and thrombocytopenia) are actually used as parameters to aid in individual dosage titration.

The following side/adverse effects have been selected on the basis of their potential clinical significance (possible signs and symptoms in parentheses where appropriate)—not necessarily inclusive:

Those indicating need for medical attention

Incidence more frequent

Amenorrhea (missing menstrual periods); ***leukopenia or infection*** (less frequently, fever or chills; cough or hoarseness; lower back or side pain; painful or difficult urination)—usually asymptomatic

Note: With *amenorrhea*, regular menses usually resume within a few months after the end of cyclophosphamide therapy.

A marked *leukopenia* usually occurs, with the nadir of the leukocyte count occurring 7 to 12 days after administration and recovery after 17 to 21 days.

With high-dose and/or long-term therapy

Cardiotoxicity, including acute myopericarditis (fast heartbeat; fever or chills; shortness of breath); ***condition resembling syndrome***

of inappropriate antidiuretic hormone (SIADH) (dizziness, confusion, or agitation; unusual tiredness or weakness); ***hemorrhagic cystitis*** (blood in urine; painful urination); ***hyperuricemia, uric acid nephropathy, nonhemorrhagic cystitis, or nephrotoxicity*** (joint pain; lower back or side pain; swelling of feet or lower legs); ***pneumonitis or interstitial pulmonary fibrosis*** (cough, shortness of breath)

Note: *Cardiotoxicity* is most severe with use of doses of 180 to 270 mg per kg of body weight (mg/kg) within 4 to 6 days.

A few cases of severe and sometimes fatal congestive heart failure have occurred within a few days after the first dose of a high-dose course of cyclophosphamide; histopathologic examination primarily revealed hemorrhagic myocarditis. Hemopericardium has occurred secondary to hemorrhagic myocarditis and myocardial necrosis. Pericarditis has been reported independent of any hemopericardium.

Hemorrhagic cystitis may occur within a few hours or be delayed several weeks; thought to be caused by metabolites of cyclophosphamide (chloroacetic acid, acrolein) excreted in the urine. Usually resolves a few days after withdrawal of cyclophosphamide, but may persist; may be fatal. Fibrosis of the urinary bladder, with or without cystitis, may also occur and may be extensive. Atypical urinary bladder epithelial cells may be found in urine. Hemorrhagic ureteritis and renal tubular necrosis, which usually resolve after withdrawal of cyclophosphamide, have also been reported.

Hyperuricemia with uric acid nephropathy occurs most commonly during initial treatment of patients with leukemia or lymphoma, as a result of rapid cell breakdown which leads to elevated serum uric acid concentrations.

Incidence less frequent

Anemia; thrombocytopenia (unusual bleeding or bruising; black, tarry stools; blood in urine or stools; pinpoint red spots on skin)—usually asymptomatic

Incidence rare

Anaphylactic reaction (sudden shortness of breath); ***hemorrhagic colitis*** (black, tarry stools); ***hepatitis*** (yellow eyes or skin); ***hyperglycemia*** (frequent urination; unusual thirst); ***redness, swelling, or pain at site of injection; stomatitis*** (sores in mouth and on lips)

Note: *Anaphylaxis* has resulted in death.

Those indicating need for medical attention only if they continue or are bothersome

Incidence more frequent

Darkening of skin and fingernails; loss of appetite; nausea or vomiting—especially with high oral doses

Incidence less frequent

Diarrhea or stomach pain; flushing or redness of face; headache; increased sweating; myxedema (swollen lips); ***skin rash, hives, or itching***

Those not indicating need for medical attention

Incidence more frequent

Loss of hair

Note: Normal hair growth usually returns after treatment has ended, although it may be slightly different in color or texture.

Those indicating the need for medical attention if they occur after medication is discontinued

Hemorrhagic cystitis (blood in urine)

Overdose

For more information on the management of overdose, **contact a Poison Control Center** (see *Poison Control Center Listing*).

Treatment of overdose

There is no specific antidote to cyclophosphamide. Supportive therapy is recommended.

Patient Consultation

As an aid to patient consultation, refer to *Advice for the Patient, Cyclophosphamide (Systemic)*.

In providing consultation, consider emphasizing the following selected information (» = major clinical significance):

Before using this medication

» Conditions affecting use, especially:
- Sensitivity to cyclophosphamide
- Pregnancy—Use not recommended because of mutagenic, teratogenic, and carcinogenic potential; advisability of using contraception; telling physician immediately if pregnancy is suspected
- Breast-feeding—Not recommended because of risk of serious side effects
- Other medications, especially cytotoxic drugs, cocaine, cytarabine, other bone marrow suppressants, other immunosuppressants, probenecid, radiation therapy, or sulfinpyrazone
- Other medical problems, especially chickenpox, herpes zoster, hepatic function impairment, other infections, renal function impairment, or tumor cell infiltration of bone marrow

Proper use of this medication

» Importance of not taking more or less medication than the amount prescribed

Caution in taking combination therapy; taking each medication at the right time

» Importance of ample fluid intake and subsequent increase in urine output, as well as frequent voiding (including at least once during night), to prevent hemorrhagic cystitis and aid in excretion of uric acid; following physician instructions for recommended fluid intake; some patients may require up to 3000 mL (3 quarts) per day

Usually best if taken in the morning to reduce risk of hemorrhagic cystitis; however, physician may recommend taking in small doses throughout day to lessen stomach upset; following physician's instructions for timing of doses

» Probability of nausea, vomiting, and loss of appetite; importance of continuing medication despite stomach upset; checking with physician before discontinuing medication

Checking with physician if vomiting occurs shortly after dose is taken

» Proper dosing

Missed dose: Not taking at all; not doubling doses; checking with physician

» Proper storage

Precautions while using this medication

» Importance of close monitoring by physician

» Avoiding immunizations unless approved by physician; other persons in patient's household should avoid immunizations with oral poliovirus vaccine; avoiding persons who have taken oral poliovirus vaccine or wearing a protective mask that covers nose and mouth

Caution if any kind of surgery, including dental surgery, or emergency treatment with general anesthesia is required within 10 days of treatment

Caution if bone marrow depression occurs:

» Avoiding exposure to persons with infections, especially during periods of low blood counts; checking with physician immediately if fever or chills, cough or hoarseness, lower back or side pain, or painful or difficult urination occurs

» Checking with physician immediately if unusual bleeding or bruising; black, tarry stools; blood in urine; or pinpoint red spots on skin occur

Caution in use of regular toothbrush, dental floss, or toothpick; physician, dentist, or nurse may suggest alternatives; checking with physician before having dental work done

Not touching eyes or inside of nose unless hands washed immediately before

Using caution to avoid accidental cuts with use of sharp objects such as safety razor or fingernail or toenail cutters

Avoiding contact sports or other situations where bruising or injury could occur

Caution if any laboratory tests required; possible interference with test results

Side/adverse effects

Signs of potential side effects, especially, amenorrhea, leukopenia, infection, cardiotoxicity, SIADH, hemorrhagic cystitis, hyperuricemia, uric acid nephropathy, nonhemorrhagic cystitis, nephrotoxicity, pneumonitis, interstitial pulmonary fibrosis, anemia, thrombocytopenia, anaphylactic reaction, hemorrhagic colitis, hepatitis, hyperglycemia, redness or swelling or pain at site of injection, and stomatitis

Physician or nurse can help in dealing with side effects

Possibility of hair loss; normal hair growth should return after treatment has ended; new hair may be slightly different in color or texture

General Dosing Information

Patients receiving cyclophosphamide should be under supervision of a physician experienced in cancer chemotherapy or immunosuppressive therapy.

A variety of dosage schedules and regimens of cyclophosphamide, alone or in combination with other antitumor agents, are used. The prescriber may consult the medical literature as well as the manufacturer's literature in choosing a specific dosage.

Dosage must be adjusted to meet the individual requirements of each patient, based on clinical response and appearance or severity of toxicity.

Development of uric acid nephropathy in patients with leukemia or lymphoma may be prevented by adequate oral hydration and, in some cases, administration of allopurinol. Alkalinization of urine may be necessary if serum uric acid concentrations are elevated.

To reduce the risk of hemorrhagic cystitis, adequate hydration is recommended prior to cyclophosphamide treatment and for at least 72 hours following treatment to ensure ample urine output. In addition, the patient should be encouraged to take cyclophosphamide in the morning so that the majority of the metabolites have been excreted by bedtime and to void frequently, to prevent prolonged contact of irritating metabolites with bladder mucosa.

Cyclophosphamide should be discontinued at the first sign of hemorrhagic cystitis. In severe cases, blood replacement may be necessary. Electrocautery diversion of urine flow, cryosurgery, and formaldehyde bladder instillations have been used. Resumption of therapy should be undertaken with caution since recurrence is common.

Initiation of planned maintenance antineoplastic therapy is recommended as soon as the leukocyte count returns to adequate levels following induction.

If marked leukopenia (particularly granulocytopenia) or thrombocytopenia occurs, cyclophosphamide therapy should be withdrawn until leukocyte and platelet counts return to satisfactory levels. Then therapy may be reinstituted, possibly at a lower dose.

In acute leukemia, cyclophosphamide may be administered despite the presence of thrombocytopenia and bleeding; cessation of bleeding and increase in platelet count have occurred in some cases during treatment and platelet transfusions are useful in others.

Special precautions are recommended in patients who develop thrombocytopenia as a result of administration of cyclophosphamide. These may include extreme care in performing invasive procedures; regular inspection of intravenous sites, skin (including perirectal area), and mucous membrane surfaces for signs of bleeding or bruising; limiting frequency of venipuncture and avoiding intramuscular injections; testing urine, emesis, stool, and secretions for occult blood; care in use of regular toothbrushes, dental floss, toothpicks, safety razors, and fingernail and toenail cutters; avoiding constipation; and using caution to prevent falls and other injuries. Such patients should avoid alcohol and aspirin intake because of the risk of gastrointestinal bleeding. Platelet transfusions may be required.

Patients who develop leukopenia should be observed carefully for signs of infection. Antibiotic support may be required. In neutropenic patients who develop fever, broad-spectrum antibiotic coverage should be initiated empirically, pending bacterial cultures and appropriate diagnostic tests.

For parenteral dosage forms only

Cyclophosphamide may be administered by intravenous push or infusion, intramuscularly, intraperitoneally, or intrapleurally.

Diet/Nutrition

Oral cyclophosphamide should usually be taken on an empty stomach; however, if stomach upset occurs, doses may be divided and given with meals.

Safety considerations for handling this medication

There is limited but increasing evidence and concern that personnel involved in preparation and administration of parenteral antineoplastics may be at some risk because of the potential mutagenicity, teratogenicity, and/or carcinogenicity of these agents, although the actual risk is unknown. USP advisory panels recommend cautious handling both in preparation and disposal of antineoplastic agents. Precautions that have been suggested include:

• Use of a biological containment cabinet during reconstitution and dilution of parenteral medications and wearing of disposable surgical gloves and masks.

• Use of proper technique to prevent contamination of the medication, work area, and operator during transfer between containers (including proper training of personnel in this technique).

• Cautious and proper disposal of needles, syringes, vials, ampuls, and unused medication.

A number of medical centers have developed detailed guidelines for handling of antineoplastic agents.

Combination chemotherapy

Cyclophosphamide may be used in combination with other agents in various regimens. As a result, incidence and/or severity of side effects may be altered and different dosages (usually reduced) may be used. For example, cyclophosphamide is part of the following chemotherapeutic combinations (some commonly used acronyms are in parentheses):

—carmustine, cyclophosphamide, vinblastine, procarbazine, and prednisone (BCVPP).
—cyclophosphamide, doxorubicin, and fluorouracil (CAF).
—cyclophosphamide, doxorubicin, methotrexate, and procarbazine (CAMP).
—cyclophosphamide, doxorubicin, and cisplatin (CAP).
—cyclophosphamide, doxorubicin, vincristine, and prednisone (CHOP).
—cyclophosphamide, doxorubicin, and cisplatin (CISCA).
—cyclophosphamide, methotrexate, and lomustine (CMC).
—cyclophosphamide, methotrexate, and fluorouracil (CMF).
—cyclophosphamide, methotrexate, fluorouracil, vincristine, and prednisone (CMFVP).
—cyclophosphamide, vincristine, and prednisone (COP or CVP).
—cyclophosphamide, vincristine, doxorubicin, and dacarbazine (CyVADIC).
—vincristine, dactinomycin, and cyclophosphamide (VAC).

For specific dosages and schedules, consult the literature. For information regarding each agent, consult the individual monographs.

Oral Dosage Forms

Note: Bracketed uses in the *Dosage Forms* section refer to categories of use and/or indications that are not included in U.S. product labeling.

CYCLOPHOSPHAMIDE ORAL SOLUTION

Note: In the U.S. and Canada, Cyclophosphamide Injection USP [*Cytoxan; Neosar; Procytox*] is the dosage form being used to prepare the oral solution dosage form.

Usual adult dose

Leukemia, acute lymphocytic or
Leukemia, acute nonlymphocytic or
Leukemia, chronic myelocytic or
Leukemia, chronic lymphocytic or
Carcinoma, ovarian, epithelial or
Carcinoma, breast or
Neuroblastoma or
Retinoblastoma or
[Carcinoma, lung, non-small cell] or
[Carcinoma, lung, small cell] or
[Carcinoma, endometrial][1] or
[Carcinoma, bladder][1] or
[Carcinoma, prostatic][1] or
Lymphomas, Hodgkin's or
Lymphomas, non-Hodgkin's or
Multiple myeloma or
Mycosis fungoides or
[Ewing's sarcoma][1] or
[Sarcomas, soft tissue][1] or
[Tumors, germ cell, ovarian][1]—
Oral, 1 to 5 mg per kg of body weight per day.

[Carcinoma, adrenocortical][1]—
Consult medical literature or manufacturer's literature for specific dosage.

[Rheumatoid arthritis][1]—
Oral, 1.5 to 2 mg per kg of body weight per day, the dosage being increased up to a maximum of 3 mg per kg of body weight per day.

[Wegener's granulomatosis][1]—
Oral, 1 to 2 mg per kg of body weight per day, administered in combination with prednisone.

Usual pediatric dose

Leukemia, acute lymphocytic or
Leukemia, acute nonlymphocytic or
Leukemia, chronic myelocytic or
Leukemia, chronic lymphocytic or
Neuroblastoma or
Retinoblastoma or
Lymphomas, Hodgkin's; or
Lymphomas, non-Hodgkin's—
Induction: Oral, 2 to 8 mg per kg of body weight or 60 to 250 mg per square meter of body surface area a day in divided doses for six or more days.
Maintenance: Oral, 2 to 5 mg per kg of body weight or 50 to 150 mg per square meter of body surface area twice a week.

Nephrotic syndrome—
Oral, 2.5 to 3 mg per kg of body weight per day.

[Histiocytosis X][1]—
Consult medical literature or manufacturer's literature for specific dosage.

[1]Strength(s) usually available

U.S.—
Dosage form not commercially available. Compounding required for prescriptions.
Canada—
Dosage form not commercially available. Compounding required for prescriptions.

Packaging and storage

Store between 2 and 8 °C (36 and 46 °F). Protect from freezing. Store in a tight container.

Preparation of dosage form

Cyclophosphamide oral solution may be prepared by dissolving Cyclophosphamide for Injection USP in Aromatic Elixir NF to a concentration of 1 to 5 mg of cyclophosphamide per mL.

Stability

Stable for up to 14 days when stored in a glass container in the refrigerator.

Auxiliary labeling

- For oral use.
- Take on an empty stomach.
- Drink plenty of water with this medicine.

CYCLOPHOSPHAMIDE TABLETS USP

Usual adult dose

Leukemia, acute lymphocytic or
Leukemia, acute nonlymphocytic or
Leukemia, chronic myelocytic or
Leukemia, chronic lymphocytic or
Carcinoma, ovarian, epithelial or
Carcinoma, breast or
Neuroblastoma or
Retinoblastoma or
[Carcinoma, lung, non-small cell] or
[Carcinoma, lung, small cell] or
[Carcinoma, endometrial][1] or
[Carcinoma, bladder][1] or
[Carcinoma, prostatic][1] or
Lymphomas, Hodgkin's or
Lymphomas, non-Hodgkin's or
Multiple myeloma or
Mycosis fungoides or
[Ewing's sarcoma][1] or
[Sarcomas, soft tissue][1] or
[Tumors, germ cell, ovarian][1]—
Oral, 1 to 5 mg per kg of body weight per day.
[Carcinoma, adrenocortical][1]—
Consult medical literature or manufacturer's literature for specific dosage.
[Rheumatoid arthritis][1]—
Oral, 1 to 2 mg per kg of body weight per day, the dose being adjusted on the basis of leukocyte counts.
[Wegener's granulomatosis][1]—
Oral, 1.5 to 2 mg per kg of body weight per day, the dosage being increased up to a maximum of 3 mg per kg of body weight per day.

Usual pediatric dose

Leukemia, acute lymphocytic or
Leukemia, acute nonlymphocytic or
Leukemia, chronic myelocytic or
Leukemia, chronic lymphocytic or
Neuroblastoma or
Retinoblastoma or
Lymphomas, Hodgkin's or
Lymphomas, non-Hodgkin's—
Induction: Oral, 2 to 8 mg per kg of body weight or 60 to 250 mg per square meter of body surface area a day in divided doses for six or more days.
Maintenance: Oral, 2 to 5 mg per kg of body weight or 50 to 150 mg per square meter of body surface area twice a week.
Nephrotic syndrome[1]—
Oral, 2.5 to 3 mg per kg of body weight per day.
[Histiocytosis X][1]—
Consult medical literature or manufacturer's literature for specific dosage.

Strength(s) usually available

U.S.—
25 mg (Rx) [*Cytoxan* (lactose)].
50 mg (Rx) [*Cytoxan* (lactose)].
Canada—
25 mg (Rx) [*Cytoxan; Procytox*].
50 mg (Rx) [*Cytoxan; Procytox*].

Packaging and storage

Store between 2 and 25 °C (36 and 77 °F). Store in a tight container.

Auxiliary labeling

- Take on an empty stomach.
- Drink plenty of water with this medicine.

Parenteral Dosage Forms

Note: Bracketed uses in the *Dosage Forms* section refer to categories of use and/or indications that are not included in U.S. product labeling.

CYCLOPHOSPHAMIDE FOR INJECTION USP

Usual adult dose

Leukemia, acute lymphocytic or
Leukemia, acute nonlymphocytic or
Leukemia, chronic myelocytic or
Leukemia, chronic lymphocytic or
Carcinoma, ovarian, epithelial or
Carcinoma, breast or
Neuroblastoma or
Retinoblastoma or
[Carcinoma, lung, non-small cell] or
[Carcinoma, lung, small cell] or
[Carcinoma, endometrial][1] or
[Carcinoma, bladder][1] or
[Carcinoma, prostatic][1] or
Lymphomas, Hodgkin's or
Lymphomas, non-Hodgkin's or
Multiple myeloma or
Mycosis fungoides or
[Ewing's sarcoma][1] or
[Sarcomas, soft tissue][1] or
[Tumors, germ cell, ovarian][1]—
Initial: Intravenous, 40 to 50 mg per kg of body weight in divided doses over a period of two to five days, or 10 to 15 mg per kg of body weight every seven to ten days, or 3 to 5 mg per kg of body weight two times a week, or 1.5 to 3 mg per kg of body weight a day.
[Carcinoma, adrenocortical][1]—
Consult medical literature or manufacturer's literature for specific dosage.

Usual adult prescribing limits

Much higher dosages have been used, depending on the condition being treated. Physicians should consult the medical literature in choosing a specific dosage.

Usual pediatric dose

Leukemia, acute lymphocytic or
Leukemia, acute nonlymphocytic or
Leukemia, chronic myelocytic or
Leukemia, chronic lymphocytic or
Neuroblastoma or
Retinoblastoma or
Lymphomas, Hodgkin's or
Lymphomas, non-Hodgkin's—
Induction: Intravenous, 2 to 8 mg per kg of body weight or 60 to 250 mg per square meter of body surface area a day in divided doses for six or more days (or total dose for seven days once a week).
Maintenance: Intravenous, 10 to 15 mg per kg of body weight every seven to ten days, or 30 mg per kg of body weight at three- to four-week intervals or when bone marrow recovery occurs.
[Histiocytosis X][1]—
Consult medical literature or manufacturer's literature for specific dosage.

Strength(s) usually available

U.S.—
Lyophilized:
100 mg (Rx) [*Cytoxan* (mannitol 75 mg)].
200 mg (Rx) [*Cytoxan* (mannitol 150 mg)].
500 mg (Rx) [*Cytoxan* (mannitol 375 mg)].
1 gram (Rx) [*Cytoxan* (mannitol 750 mg)].
2 grams (Rx) [*Cytoxan* (mannitol 1.5 grams)].
Nonlyophilized:
100 mg (Rx) [*Neosar* (sodium chloride 45 mg [1.9 mmol])].
200 mg (Rx) [*Neosar* (sodium chloride 90 mg [3.9 mmol])].
500 mg (Rx) [*Neosar* (sodium chloride 225 mg [9.7 mmol])].

1 gram (Rx) [*Neosar* (sodium chloride 450 mg [19.5 mmol])].
2 grams (Rx) [*Neosar* (sodium chloride 900 mg [39 mmol])].

Canada—

Lyophilized:

1 gram (Rx) [*Cytoxan* (mannitol 750 mg)].
2 grams (Rx) [*Cytoxan* (mannitol 1.5 grams)].

Nonlyophilized:

200 mg (Rx) [*Procytox* (sodium chloride 90 mg [3.9 mmol])].
500 mg (Rx) [*Procytox* (sodium chloride 225 mg [9.7 mmol])].
1 gram (Rx) [*Procytox* (sodium chloride 450 mg [19.5 mmol])].
2 gram (Rx) [*Procytox* (sodium chloride 900 mg [39 mmol])].

Packaging and storage

Store at a temperature not exceeding 25 °C (77 °F).

Preparation of dosage form

Nonlyophilized cyclophosphamide for injection may be prepared for parenteral use by adding 5 mL (100-mg vial), 10 mL (200-mg vial), 25 mL (500-mg vial), 50 mL (1-gram vial), or 100 mL (2-gram vial) of sterile water for injection or bacteriostatic water for injection (paraben-preserved only) to the vial and shaking to dissolve (may be difficult and take up to 6 minutes) to provide a solution containing 20 mg of cyclophosphamide per mL. The resulting solution may be added to 5% dextrose injection, 5% dextrose and 0.9% sodium chloride injection, 5% dextrose and Ringer's injection, lactated Ringer's injection, 0.45% sodium chloride injection, or sodium lactate injection for administration by intravenous infusion.

Lyophilized cyclophosphamide for injection may be prepared for parenteral use by adding 5 mL (100-mg vial), 10 mL (200-mg vial), 20 to 25 mL (500-mg vial), 50 mL (1-gram vial), or 80 to 100 mL (2-gram vial) of sterile water for injection or bacteriostatic water for injection (paraben-preserved only) to the vial and shaking to dissolve (takes about 45 seconds) to provide a solution containing 20 mg of cyclophosphamide per mL. The resulting solution may be added to 5% dextrose injection, 5% dextrose and 0.9% sodium chloride injection, 5% dextrose and Ringer's injection, lactated Ringer's injection, 0.45% sodium chloride injection, or sodium lactate injection for administration by intravenous infusion.

Caution: Use of diluents containing benzyl alcohol is not recommended for preparation of medications for use in neonates. A fatal toxic syndrome consisting of metabolic acidosis, central nervous system (CNS) depression, respiratory problems, renal failure, hypotension, and possibly seizures and intracranial hemorrhages has been associated with this use.

Stability

Reconstituted solutions of cyclophosphamide are stable for 24 hours at room temperature, or for 6 days if refrigerated. If bacteriostatic water for injection is not used for reconstitution, it is recommended that the solution be used promptly (preferably within 6 hours).

Note

Because cyclophosphamide for injection contains no preservative, caution in preparing and storing solutions is required to ensure sterility.

[1]Not included in Canadian product labeling.

Revised: 05/22/2002

CYCLOSPORINE Ophthalmic†

VA CLASSIFICATION (Primary): OP900

Commonly used brand name(s): *Restasis.*

Note: For a listing of dosage forms and brand names by country availability, see *Dosage Forms* section(s).

†Not commercially available in Canada.

Category

Immunosuppressant (ophthalmic).

Indications

Accepted

Keratoconjunctivitis sicca (treatment)—Cyclosporine is indicated to increase tear production in patients whose tear production is presumed to be suppressed due to ocular inflammation associated with keratoconjunctivitis sicca.

Pharmacology/Pharmacokinetics

Physicochemical characteristics

Molecular weight—Cyclosporine: 1202.6.
pH—6.5 to 8.0
Osmolality—230 to 320 mOsmol/kg

Mechanism of action/Effect

The exact mechanism of action is not known. Cyclosporine emulsion is thought to act as a partial immunomodulator in patients whose tear production is presumed to be suppressed due to ocular inflammation associated with keratoconjunctivitis sicca.

Other actions/effects

When administered systemically, cyclosporine is an immunosuppressive agent.

Absorption

Blood concentrations of cyclosporine, after topical administration of cyclosporine 0.05%, twice per day, for up to 12 months, were below the quantitation limit of 0.1 ng/mL.

Precautions to Consider

Carcinogenicity

Systemic carcinogenicity studies were carried out, in both mice and rats given oral doses of at least 1000 and 500 times greater (low-dose), respectively, than the daily human dose of 0.001 mg per kg of body weight per day delivered ophthalmically. In the 78-week oral mouse study, evidence of a statistically significant trend was found for lymphocytic lymphomas in females, and the incidences of hepatocellular carcinomas in mid-dose males significantly exceeded the control value. In the 24-month oral rat study, pancreatic islet cell adenomas significantly exceeded the control rate.

Mutagenicity

Cyclosporine has not been found mutagenic or genotoxic in the Ames Test, the V79-HGPRT Test, the micronucleus test in mice and Chinese hamsters, the chromosome-aberration test in Chinese hamster bone-marrow, the mouse dominant lethal assay, and the DNA-repair test in sperm from treated mice. A study analyzing sister chromatid exchange (SCE) induction by cyclosporine using human lymphocytes *in vitro* gave indication of a positive effect (i.e., induction of SCE).

Pregnancy/Reproduction

Fertility—No impairment in fertility was demonstrated in studies in male and female rats receiving oral doses of cyclosporine up to 15,000 times the human ophthalmic dose.

Pregnancy—Adequate and well controlled studies with cyclosporine ophthalmic emulsion in humans have not been done. It should be administered to a pregnant woman only if needed.

No evidence of teratogenicity was observed in rats or rabbits receiving oral doses of cyclosporine up to 300,000 times greater than the human ophthalmic dose. Adverse effects were seen in reproduction studies in rats and rabbits receiving oral doses toxic to dams. The adverse effects seen were prenatal and postnatal mortality and reduced fetal weight together with related fetal skeletal retardations. The doses given were 30,000 and 100,000 times greater than the daily human ophthalmic dose.

Offspring of rats receiving an oral dose of cyclosporine from Day 15 of pregnancy until Day 21 postpartum, at a maternal toxic level, exhibited an increase in postnatal mortality; this dose is 45,000 times greater than the daily human topical dose.

FDA Pregnancy Category C

Breast-feeding

Cyclosporine is known to be distributed into human breast milk following systemic administration but, distribution into human milk after topical treatment has not been investigated. Although blood concentrations are undetectable after topical administration of cyclosporine, caution should be exercised when administering this drug to a nursing woman.

Pediatrics

The safety and efficacy of cyclosporine ophthalmic emulsion have not been established in pediatric patients below the age of 16 years.

Geriatrics

No overall difference in safety or effectiveness has been observed between elderly and younger patients.

Medical considerations/Contraindications

The medical considerations/contraindications included have been selected on the basis of their potential clinical significance (reasons given in parentheses where appropriate)—not necessarily inclusive (» = major clinical significance).

Except under special circumstances, this medication should not be used when the following medical problems exist:

» Active ocular infections

» Hypersensitivity to cyclosporine or any of the ingredients in the formulation

Risk-benefit should be considered when the following medical problems exist:

Contact lenses, use of
(patients with decreased tear production should not wear contact lenses)

» Herpes keratitis, history of
(caution should be used; studies with cyclosporine in patients with a history of herpes keratitis have not been done)

Side/Adverse Effects

The following side/adverse effects have been selected on the basis of their potential clinical significance (possible signs and symptoms in parentheses where appropriate)—not necessarily inclusive:

Those indicating need for medical attention only if they continue or are bothersome

Incidence more frequent

Ocular burning (burning or other discomfort of the eye)

Incidence less frequent

Conjunctival hyperemia (redness of the white part of eyes or inside of eyelids); ***discharge*** (clear or yellow fluid from eye; sticky or matted eyelashes); ***epiphora*** (watery eye); ***eye pain; foreign body sensation*** (feeling of having something in the eye); ***pruritus*** (itching skin); ***stinging; visual disturbance*** (blurred vision; difficulty reading; halos around lights)

Note: No increase in bacterial or fungal ocular infections was reported following the administration of cyclosporine ophthalmic emulsion.

Overdose

For more information on the management of overdose or unintentional ingestion, **contact a poison control center** (see *Poison Control Center Listing*).

Treatment of overdose

There is no known specific antidote to cyclosporine. Treatment is generally symptomatic and supportive.

Supportive care—
Patients in whom intentional overdose is confirmed or suspected should be referred for psychiatric consultation.

Patient Consultation

As an aid to patient consultation, refer to *Advice for the Patient, Cyclosporine (Ophthalmic)*.

In providing consultation, consider emphasizing the following selected information (» = major clinical significance):

Before using this medication

» Conditions affecting use, especially:
Pregnancy—Should be administered to a pregnant woman only if clearly needed.
FDA Pregnancy Category C
Breast-feeding—Caution should be exercised when administering this drug to a nursing woman.
Use in children—Safety and efficacy have not been established in pediatric patients below the age of 16 years.
Use in the elderly—No overall difference in safety or effectiveness has been observed between elderly and younger patients
Other medical problems, especially active ocular infections or hypersensitivity to cyclosporine or any of the other ingredients in the formulation.

Proper use of this medication

Cyclosporine should not be used while wearing contact lenses. If contact lenses are worn they should be removed prior to the use of the eye drops, and may be reinserted 15 minutes following the use of the eye drops.

Preventing contamination: Not touching applicator tip to any surface, or the eye.

Inverting the vial a few times to mix before using.

Discarding the vial and any unused contents immediately after use; vials are for single use only.

Cyclosporine eye drops can be used with artificial tears. Allow a 15-minute interval between the use of these eye medications.

» Proper dosing

Missed dose: Using as soon as possible; not using if almost time for next dose; using next dose at regularly scheduled time; not doubling doses

Proper storage

General Dosing Information

Cyclosporine should not be used while wearing contact lenses. If contact lenses are worn they should be removed prior to the administration of the emulsion, and may be reinserted 15 minutes following the administration of cyclosporine ophthalmic solution.

Cyclosporine ophthalmic emulsion can be used concomitantly with artifical tears, allowing 15 minute interval between products.

The vial should be inverted a few times before using, to obtain a uniform, white, opaque emulsion.

The tip of the vial should not touch the eye or any other surface, as this may contaminate the emulsion.

Increased tear production was not seen in patients currently taking topical anti-inflammatory drugs or using punctal plugs.

Ophthalmic Dosage Forms

CYCLOSPORINE OPHTHALMIC EMULSION

Usual adult dose

Keratoconjunctivitis sicca (treatment)—
Topical, to the conjunctiva, one drop twice a day in each eye approximately 12 hour apart.

Usual pediatric dose

Safety and efficacy have not been established in pediatric patients below the age of 16 years.

Usual geriatric dose

See *Usual adult dose*.

Strength(s) usually available

U.S.—
0.05% (Rx) [*Restasis* (preservative-free; glycerin; castor oil; polysorbate 80; carbomer 1342; purified water; sodium hydroxide to adjust the pH)].

Packaging and storage

Store between 15 and 25 °C (59 and 77 °F).

Auxiliary labeling

- For the eye
- Do not touch or contaminate the tip of the container
- Do not shake. Rotate the vial gently.
- For single dose only. Discard unused drug.
- Keep out of reach of children

Revised: 03/05/2004
Developed: 09/26/2003

CYCLOSPORINE Systemic

INN: Ciclosporin

VA CLASSIFICATION (Primary/Secondary): IM403/DE801; MS109

Commonly used brand name(s): *Neoral; Sandimmune; SangCya.*

Another commonly used name is cyclosporin A.

Note: For a listing of dosage forms and brand names by country availability, see *Dosage Forms* section(s).

Category

Immunosuppressant; antipsoriatic; antirheumatic.

Indications

Note: Bracketed information in the *Indications* section refers to uses that are not included in U.S. product labeling.

Accepted

Transplant rejection, organ (prophylaxis)—Cyclosporine is indicated, usually in combination with corticosteroids, for prevention of rejection of renal, hepatic, and cardiac transplants (allografts). [Cyclosporine is also indicated for prevention of rejection of heart-lung and pancreatic transplants.]

Transplant rejection, organ (treatment)—Cyclosporine is indicated for treatment of chronic rejection in patients previously treated with other immunosuppressants.

Arthritis, rheumatoid (treatment)—Cyclosporine is indicated for severe, active, rheumatoid arthritis failing to respond adequately to therapy with methotrexate alone.

Psoriasis, severe (treatment)—Cyclosporine is indicated for severe, recalcitrant, plaque-type psoriasis failing to respond to at least one systemic therapy or in patients unable to tolerate other systemic therapy.

[Graft-versus-host disease (prophylaxis)] or

[Graft-versus-host disease (treatment)]—Cyclosporine is indicated for prophylaxis and treatment of graft-versus-host disease after bone marrow transplantation.

[Nephrotic syndrome (treatment)]—Cyclosporine is indicated to induce and maintain remissions for steroid-dependent and steroid-resistant nephrotic syndrome due to glomerular diseases.

Acceptance not established

Data are insufficient to prove that cyclosporine is effective for treatment of generalized pustular or erythrodermic psoriasis.

Pharmacology/Pharmacokinetics

Physicochemical characteristics

Molecular weight—1202.64.

Mechanism of action/Effect

The exact mechanism of action is unknown but seems to be related to the inhibition of production and release of interleukin-2, which is a proliferative factor necessary for the induction of cytotoxic T lymphocytes in response to alloantigenic challenge, and which plays a major role in both cellular and humoral immune responses. Cyclosporine does not affect the nonspecific defense system of the host and does not cause significant myelosuppression.

Absorption

Variable and incomplete from gastrointestinal tract; bioavailability of *Sandimmune*® is about 30% but may increase with increasing dosage and duration of treatment. Absorption may be decreased after liver transplantation or in patients with liver disease or gastrointestinal function impairment (e.g., diarrhea, vomiting, ileus).

Cyclosporine modified capsules and oral solution (i.e., *Neoral*®) have increased bioavailability compared to the standard oral formulations of cyclosporine (i.e., *Sandimmune*®). However, the absorption is still variable and incomplete from the gastrointestinal tract; bioavailability may be less than 10% in some liver transplant patients, but may be as high as 89% in some kidney transplant patients. In studies in kidney transplant, liver transplant, psoriasis, and rheumatoid arthritis patients, the mean area under the serum concentration-versus-time curve (AUC) was 20 to 50% greater following administration of *Neoral*® compared to the AUC following administration of *Sandimmune*®.

Protein binding

Very high (90%), primarily to lipoproteins.

Biotransformation

Hepatic, extensive, primarily by cytochrome P450 3A enzymes. Cyclosporine is metabolized to a lesser extent in the gastrointestinal system and in the kidneys.

Half-life

Biphasic, variable—

Terminal:

Children—Approximately 7 hours (range, 7 to 19 hours).

Adults—Approximately 19 hours (range, 10 to 27 hours).

Time to peak concentration

Cyclosporine capsules and oral solution (*Sandimmune*®)—

Plasma or blood: 3.5 hours.

Cyclosporine modified capsules and oral solution (*Neoral*®)—

Blood: 1.5 to 2 hours.

Peak serum concentration

Plasma or blood—Whole blood concentrations may be 2 to 9 times higher than plasma concentrations.

Elimination

Biliary/fecal; renal, 6% (0.1% unchanged).

In dialysis—Not dialyzable.

Precautions to Consider

Cross-sensitivity and/or related problems

Patients sensitive to polyoxyethylated castor oil may be sensitive to the injectable dosage form also, since the injection contains a polyoxyethylated castor oil vehicle.

Carcinogenicity/Tumorigenicity

A 78-week study in mice at doses of 1, 4, and 16 mg per kg of body weight (mg/kg) a day found a statistically significant trend for lymphocytic lymphomas in females, and the incidence of hepatocellular carcinomas in mid-dose males significantly exceeded the control value. A 24-month study in rats at doses of 0.5, 2, and 8 mg/kg a day found that incidence of pancreatic islet cell adenomas significantly exceeded the control rate in the low dose level. The hepatocellular carcinomas and pancreatic islet cell adenomas were not dose-related. Published reports indicate that co-treatment of hairless mice with UV irradiation and cyclosporine or other immunosuppressive agents shorten the time to skin tumor formation compared to UV irradiation alone.

Lymphomas and skin malignancies have developed in humans treated with cyclosporine. The risk of these malignancies is related to the intensity and duration of immunosuppression. The incidence of malignancies is similar to that in patients receiving other (e.g., tacrolimus-based) regimens.

Psoriasis patients receiving cyclosporine are at increased risk of developing skin malignancies if they were treated previously with psoralen plus ultraviolet light A (PUVA), methotrexate, ultraviolet light B (UVB), coal tar, or radiation therapy. The risk of skin cancer is greatest with previous PUVA treatment.

Mutagenicity

No evidence of mutagenicity/genotoxicity was found in the Ames test, the V79-HGPRT test, the micronucleus test in mice and Chinese hamsters, the chromosome-aberration tests in Chinese hamster bone marrow, the mouse dominant lethal assay, and the DNA-repair test in sperm from treated mice. However, one study analyzing sister chromatid exchange (SCE) induction by cyclosporine using human lymphocytes *in vitro* gave indication of a positive effect (i.e., induction of SCE) at high concentrations in this system.

Pregnancy/Reproduction

Fertility—Studies in male and female rats found no evidence of impairment of fertility.

Pregnancy—Adequate and well-controlled studies in humans have not been done. Cyclosporine should be used during pregnancy only if the potential benefit justifies the potential risk to the fetus. In psoriasis patients, risk-benefit should be carefully weighed with serious consideration for discontinuation of cyclosporine.

Cyclosporine crosses the placenta.

In a retrospective study of 116 pregnancies of women who received cyclosporine during (and usually throughout) pregnancy, the only consistent patterns of abnormality were premature birth (gestational period of 28 to 36 weeks) and low birth weight for gestational age. Preterm delivery occurred in 47%. Seven malformations were reported in 5 viable infants and in 2 cases of fetal loss. Neonatal complications occurred in 27%. The exact relationship of cyclosporine to these effects has not been established.

Studies in rats and rabbits have shown that cyclosporine is embryotoxic and fetotoxic at doses 2 to 5 times the human dose. At toxic doses (30 mg/kg a day in rats and 100 mg/kg a day in rabbits), cyclosporine was embryotoxic and fetotoxic, as indicated by increased prenatal and postnatal mortality and reduced fetal weight together with related skeletal retardations. No embryolethal or teratogenic effects occurred at normal doses (up to 17 mg/kg a day in rats and up to 30 mg/kg a day in rabbits).

FDA Pregnancy Category C.

Breast-feeding

Cyclosporine is distributed into breast milk. Mothers taking cyclosporine should not breast-feed their babies, because of the potential risk of serious adverse effects (e.g., hypertension, nephrotoxicity, malignancy) in the infant.

Pediatrics

Appropriate studies performed to date in pediatric patients receiving cyclosporine for organ transplantation have not demonstrated pediatrics-specific problems that would limit the usefulness of cyclosporine in children. Cyclosporine has been used in pediatric patients 1 year of age and older receiving organ transplantations. Pediatric patients have increased clearance of cyclosporine as compared with adult patients. The safety and efficacy of cyclosporine to treat psoriasis and rheumatoid arthritis in pediatric patients have not been established.

Geriatrics

Geriatric patients were included in the clinical trials of cyclosporine to treat rheumatoid arthritis. Geriatric patients were more likely to experience hypertension and increases in serum creatinine concentrations than were younger adult patients.

Dental

Gingival hyperplasia, a common complication of cyclosporine therapy, usually starts as gingivitis or gum inflammation in the first month of treatment. The incidence is higher in children under 15 years of age than in adults. Gingival tissue changes are similar to those produced by phenytoin, although with less-mature collagen. Tissue overgrowth may be greater anteriorly than posteriorly, creating aesthetic and psychological problems for the young patient. A strict program of teeth cleaning by a professional combined with plaque control by the patient, if begun within 10 days of initiation of cyclosporine therapy, will minimize the growth rate and the severity of gingival enlargement. Periodontal surgery may be indicated and should be followed by careful plaque control to inhibit recurrence of gum enlargement.

The immunosuppressant effects of cyclosporine may result in an increased incidence of microbial infection and delayed healing. Dental work, whenever possible, should be completed prior to initiation of therapy with cyclosporine. Patients should be instructed in proper oral hygiene during treatment, including caution in use of regular toothbrushes, dental floss, and toothpicks.

Drug interactions and/or related problems

The following drug interactions and/or related problems have been selected on the basis of their potential clinical significance (possible mechanism in parentheses where appropriate)—not necessarily inclusive (» = major clinical significance):

Note: Combinations containing any of the following medications, depending on the amount present, may also interact with this medication.

» Allopurinol or
» Amiodarone or
» Androgens or
» Azithromycin or
» Bromocriptine or
» Cimetidine or
» Clarithromycin or
» Contraceptives or
» Danazol or
» Diltiazem or
» Erythromycin or
» Estrogens or
» Fluconazole or
» Human immunodeficiency virus (HIV) protease inhibitors or
» Imatinib or
» Itraconazole or
» Ketoconazole or
Metoclopramide or
Miconazole or
» Nefazodone or
» Nicardipine or
» Quinupristin/dalfopristin or
» Verapamil
(may increase blood concentrations of cyclosporine by inhibiting cytochrome P450 3A enzymes, and may increase the risk of hepatotoxicity and nephrotoxicity; because of its similarity to ketoconazole, miconazole may be expected to have the same effect; although concurrent use of HIV protease inhibitors and cyclosporine have not been studied, HIV protease inhibitors are known to inhibit cytochrome P450 3A enzymes; frequent monitoring of blood cyclosporine concentrations and hepatic and renal function may be needed if these drugs are used concurrently with cyclosporine; appropriate cyclosporine dosage adjustment are essential with concomitant use)

Amphotericin B or
Bezafibrate or
Ciprofloxacin or
Fenofibrate or
Gentamicin or
Melphalan or
Ranitidine or
Tacrolimus or
Tobramycin or
Trimethoprim with sulfamethoxazole or
Vancomycin
(concomitant use may potentiate renal dysfunction, particularly in the setting of dehydration)

» Anti-inflammatory drugs, nonsteroidal (NSAIDs) including
Azapropazon or
Diclofenac or
Naproxen or
Sulindac
(concomitant use, particularly in the setting of dehydration, may potentiate renal dysfunction; additive decreases in renal function associated with cyclosporine and both naproxen and sulindac use)
(clinical status and serum creatinine should be closely monitored with concomitant use in rheumatoid arthritis patients)
(although concomitant administration of diclofenac does not affect blood levels of cyclosporine, it has been associated with approximate doubling of diclofenac blood levels and reports of reversible decreases in renal function; diclofenac dose should be at lower end of therapeutic range)

» Atorvastatin or
» Fluvastatin or
» Lovastatin or
» Pravastatin or
» Simvastatin
(postmarketing cases of myotoxicity, including pain and weakness, myositis, and rhabdomyolysis with concomitant administration; dosage of these statins should be reduced according to label recommendations with concomitant use; statin therapy needs to be temporarily withheld or discontinued in patients with signs and symptoms of myopathy or those with risk factors predisposing to severe renal injury, including renal failure, secondary to rhabdomyolysis)

» Carbamazepine or
» Nafcillin or
» Octreotide or
» Orlistat or
» Phenobarbital or
» Phenytoin or
» Rifampin or
» St. John's Wort or
» Sulfinpyrazone or
» Terbinafine or
» Ticlopidine
(concomitant use decreases cyclosporine concentrations; monitoring of circulating cyclosporine concentrations and appropriate cyclosporine dosage adjustment are essential with concomitant use; serious drug interaction between cyclosporine and St. John's Wort has been reported to produce a marked reduction in cyclosporine blood concentrations resulting in subtherapeutic levels, rejections of transplanted organs, and graft loss)

» Coal tar or
» Methoxsalen or
» Radiation therapy or
» Trioxsalen
(patients with psoriasis receiving cyclosporine are at increased risk of developing skin malignancies if they were previously treated with a psoralen [e.g., methoxsalen or trioxsalen] plus ultraviolet light A [PUVA] or coal tar, or if they received previous radiation therapy)

» Colchicine or
» Digoxin
(cyclosporine may reduce digoxin and colchicine clearance; severe digitalis toxicity observed within days of starting cyclosporine in several patients taking digoxin; also reports on potential of cyclosporine to enhance toxic effects of colchicine such as myopathy and neuropathy, especially in patients with renal dysfunction; colchicine may potentiate renal dysfunction, particularly in the setting of dehydration; colchicine may increase cyclosporine concentrations with concomitant use; close clinical observation is required in order to enable early detection of toxic manifestations of digoxin or colchicine, followed by dosage reduction or withdrawal)

» Grapefruit or
» Grapefruit juice
(decreased metabolism of cyclosporine, resulting in increased blood concentrations of cyclosporine, may occur; there is an increased risk of toxicity with concurrent use)

Hepatic enzyme inducers (see *Appendix II*)
(may enhance metabolism of cyclosporine by induction of cytochrome P450 3A enzymes; dosage adjustment may be required)

Hyperkalemia-causing medications, such as:
Angiotensin-converting enzyme (ACE) inhibitors or
Angiotensin II receptor antagonists or
Beta-adrenergic blocking agents or
Digitalis glycosides, with acute overdose or
» Diuretics, potassium-sparing or
Heparin or
Penicillins, potassium-containing, with high doses or
Phosphates, potassium-containing or
Potassium citrate-containing medications or
Potassium iodide or

Potassium supplements or
Succinylcholine chloride
(concurrent administration with cyclosporine may result in hyperkalemia)

» Immunosuppressants, other, such as:
Azathioprine or
Chlorambucil or
Corticosteroids, glucocorticoid or
Cyclophosphamide or
Mercaptopurine or
Muromonab-CD3
(concurrent use with cyclosporine may increase the risk of infection and development of lymphoproliferative disorders)

Methotrexate
(in one study, concurrent administration of cyclosporine and methotrexate to patients to treat rheumatoid arthritis resulted in higher blood concentrations of methotrexate and lower blood concentrations of the primary metabolite of methotrexate than in patients receiving methotrexate alone; the clinical significance of this interaction is not known; patients with psoriasis receiving cyclosporine are at increased risk of developing skin malignancies if they were previously treated with methotrexate)

» Methylprednisolone
(seizures have been observed in patients receiving cyclosporine and high doses of methylprednisolone; methylprednisolone may increase cyclosporine concentrations)

Nephrotoxic medications (see *Appendix II*)
(concurrent use with cyclosporine may result in enhanced nephrotoxicity; dosage reduction or withdrawal of both medications may be necessary if renal impairment occurs)

Nifedipine
(increased risk of gingival hyperplasia)

Rifabutin
(known to increase metabolism of other drugs metabolized by the cytochrome P-450 system; interaction between rifabutin and cyclosporine has not been studied; care should be exercised with concomitant use)

» Sirolimus
(elevations in serum creatinine observed with concomitant use and often reversible with cyclosporine dose reduction; co-administration of cyclosporine significantly increases blood levels of sirolimus; to minimize increases in sirolimus blood concentrations; recommended that sirolimus be given 4 hours after cyclosporine administration)

Vaccines, killed virus
(because normal defense mechanisms may be suppressed by cyclosporine therapy, the patient's antibody response to the vaccine may be decreased. The interval between discontinuation of medications that cause immunosuppression and restoration of the patient's ability to respond to the vaccine depends on the intensity and type of immunosuppression-causing medication used, the underlying disease, and other factors; estimates vary from 3 months to 1 year)

» Vaccines, live virus
(because normal defense mechanisms may be suppressed by cyclosporine therapy, concurrent use with a live virus vaccine may potentiate the replication of the vaccine virus, may increase the side/adverse effects of the vaccine virus, and/or may decrease the patient's antibody response to the vaccine; immunization of these patients should be undertaken only after review of the patient's hematologic status and only with the knowledge and consent of the physician managing the cyclosporine therapy. The interval between discontinuation of medications that cause immunosuppression and restoration of the patient's ability to respond to the vaccine depends on the intensity and type of immunosuppression-causing medication used, the underlying disease, and other factors; estimates vary from 3 months to 1 year. Oral poliovirus vaccine should not be used in persons in close contact with the patient, especially family members)

Note: For additional information on cyclosporine drug interactions, please contact the Novartis Medical Affairs Department at 888-NOW-NOVA [888-669-6682].

Laboratory value alterations

The following have been selected on the basis of their potential clinical significance (possible effect in parentheses where appropriate)—not necessarily inclusive (» = major clinical significance).

With physiology/laboratory test values

Alanine aminotransferase (ALT [SGPT]) values, serum and
Alkaline phosphatase values, serum and
Amylase values, serum and
Aspartate aminotransferase (AST [SGOT]) values, serum and
Bilirubin concentrations, serum
(may be increased in association with hepatotoxicity)

Blood urea nitrogen (BUN) and
Creatinine, serum
(concentrations are commonly increased during first few days of cyclosporine therapy; does not necessarily indicate rejection in renal transplant patients)

Magnesium
(serum concentrations may be decreased; may be related to nephrotoxicity)

Potassium and
Uric acid
(serum concentrations may be increased)

Medical considerations/Contraindications

The medical considerations/contraindications included have been selected on the basis of their potential clinical significance (reasons given in parentheses where appropriate)—not necessarily inclusive (» = major clinical significance).

Except under special circumstances, this medication should not be used when the following medical problems exist:

» Abnormal renal function or
» Hypertension, uncontrolled
(rheumatoid arthritis and psoriasis patients with these conditions should not receive cyclosporine)

» Hypersensitivity to cyclosporine or to any of the ingredients of the formulation

» Malignancy, current or
» Premalignant skin lesions
(cyclosporine is associated with an increased susceptibility to malignancies)

Risk-benefit should be considered when the following medical problems exist:

» Chickenpox, existing or recent (including recent exposure) or
» Herpes zoster
(risk of severe generalized disease)

» Hepatic function impairment
(reduced biotransformation; reduced absorption; dosage reduction may be necessary)

Hyperkalemia

Hypertension
(cyclosporine may exacerbate hypertension)

» Infection

Malabsorption
(achieving therapeutic plasma concentrations of cyclosporine may be difficult)

Patient monitoring

The following may be especially important in patient monitoring (other tests may be warranted in some patients, depending on condition; » = major clinical significance):

Alanine aminotransferase (ALT [SGPT]) values, serum and
Alkaline phosphatase values, serum and
Amylase values, serum and
Aspartate aminotransferase (AST [SGOT]) values, serum and
Bilirubin concentrations, serum
(determinations recommended at periodic intervals to monitor hepatic function)

Blood pressure measurements
(recommended at periodic intervals to detect hypertension)
(blood pressure should be measured every 2 weeks for the first 2 months following the conversion from *Sandimmune®* to *Neoral®*)

» Blood urea nitrogen (BUN) concentrations and
» Creatinine concentrations, serum and
» Uric acid concentrations, serum
(determinations recommended at regular intervals to monitor renal function)
(serum creatinine concentrations should be measured every 2 weeks for the first 2 months following the conversion from *Sandimmune®* to *Neoral®*)

Cholesterol, serum
(values may be increased)

» Cyclosporine concentrations, plasma or blood, trough, by radioimmunoassay (RIA) or high pressure liquid chromatography (HPLC) (recommended for all patients, especially those receiving oral cyclosporine, because of erratic absorption, or for transplant patients to ensure that the patient is receiving an adequate but not toxic dose; because of extreme variability in results achieved depending on whether plasma or whole blood concentrations are measured, timing of samples, handling of samples, and choice of RIA or HPLC, determinations must be standardized within each individual medical center; trough blood concentrations usually are used to monitor therapy)

(when converting a transplant patient from cyclosporine capsules or cyclosporine oral solution [*Sandimmune*®] to cyclosporine modified capsules or cyclosporine modified oral solution [*Neoral*®], the trough blood concentration should be measured every 4 to 7 days during the conversion; if a patient is suspected of having poor absorption of *Sandimmune*®, the cyclosporine trough blood concentration should be monitored very frequently during the conversion because higher-than-expected trough blood concentrations are possible; the manufacturer recommends measuring the trough blood concentration daily until steady-state is reached for patients who required *Sandimmune*® doses exceeding 10 mg per kg of body weight a day)

» Dental examinations
(recommended at 3-month intervals for teeth cleaning and reinforcement of patient's careful plaque control for inhibition of gingival hyperplasia)

Magnesium concentrations, serum and
Potassium concentrations, serum
(determinations recommended at periodic intervals)

Note: *Neoral*® product labeling gives specific guidance for monitoring patients receiving *Neoral*® for treatment of psoriasis and rheumatoid arthritis. Patients receiving *Neoral*® for treatment of psoriasis should have two baseline serum creatinine measurements. Blood pressure, BUN, cholesterol, complete blood count (CBC), serum magnesium, serum potassium, and uric acid should be measured prior to beginning therapy with *Neoral*®. During the initial 3 months of therapy these parameters should be measured once every 2 weeks. After the first 3 months of therapy, these parameters should be measured once every month in stable patients. Patient condition or changes in dose may necessitate more frequent measurements.

Patients receiving *Neoral*® for treatment of rheumatoid arthritis should have two baseline blood pressure measurements and two baseline serum creatinine measurements. During the initial 3 months of therapy these parameters should be measured once every 2 weeks. After the first 3 months of therapy, these parameters should be measured once every month in stable patients. Addition of increased doses of nonsteroidal anti-inflammatory drug therapy to the regimen may necessitate additional monitoring of blood pressure and serum creatinine. Patients receiving methotrexate in addition to *Neoral*® should have CBC and liver function tests (LFT) monitored each month.

In patients receiving *Neoral*® for treatment of nephrotic syndrome, changes in renal function related to nephrotic syndrome may be difficult to distinguish from cyclosporine-induced renal dysfunction. Renal biopsy should be considered for patients with steroid-dependent minimal change nephropathy maintained on *Neoral*® for more than 1 year.

Side/Adverse Effects

Note: *Post-transplant lymphoproliferative disorders (PTLDs)*, including lymphomas and skin malignancies, have been reported in patients receiving cyclosporine; some have regressed when the medication was discontinued. *PTLD* results from the degree of immunosuppression, not specifically from the use of cyclosporine. Similarly, *infection* may occur in patients receiving cyclosporine. The occurrence of infections results from the degree of immunosuppression, not specifically from the use of cyclosporine.

Gingival hyperplasia, *hypertension*, *hirsutism*, *nephrotoxicity*, and *tremor* are the most significant adverse effects in transplant patients resulting from the use of cyclosporine.

Gastrointestinal disturbances, including *abdominal discomfort*, *dyspepsia*, and *nausea*, *headache*, *hirsutism*, *hypertension*, and *nephrotoxicity* are the most significant adverse effects resulting from the use of cyclosporine in patients with rheumatoid arthritis.

Gastrointestinal disturbances, *headache*, *hirsutism*, *hypertension*, *lethargy*, *muscle or joint pain*, *nephrotoxicity*, and *paresthesias* are the most significant adverse effects resulting from the use of cyclosporine in patients with psoriasis.

Gastrointestinal disturbances, *gingival hyperplasia*, *hirsutism*, *hypertension*, *nephrotoxicity*, *paresthesia*, and *tremor* are the most significant adverse effects resulting from the use of cyclosporine in patients with nephrotic syndrome.

The following side/adverse effects have been selected on the basis of their potential clinical significance (possible signs and symptoms in parentheses where appropriate)—not necessarily inclusive:

Those indicating need for medical attention

Incidence more frequent

Gingival hyperplasia (bleeding, tender, or enlarged gums); ***hypertension***—usually asymptomatic; ***nephrotoxicity***—usually asymptomatic

Note: *Gingival hyperplasia* is usually reversible within 6 months after withdrawal of cyclosporine.

Hypertension occurs commonly and may be acute, severe, and dose-related (usually associated with doses of 25 to 50 mg per kg of body weight [mg/kg] a day) or chronic and mild to moderate (usually associated with reduced renal function).

Nephrotoxicity has been reported in 25%, 37%, and 38% of kidney, liver, and heart transplantation patients receiving cyclosporine, respectively. Mild *nephrotoxicity* (presenting as an arrest in the fall of pre-operative elevations of blood urea nitrogen [BUN] and creatinine at a range of 35 to 45 mg per deciliter and 2 to 2.5 mg per deciliter, respectively) usually occurs 2 to 3 months after renal, cardiac, or hepatic transplantation and usually responds to dosage reduction. More overt toxicity, with rapidly rising BUN and creatinine concentrations, occurs early after transplantation and must be differentiated from rejection episodes; toxicity usually responds to dosage reduction. Up to 20% of renal transplant patients may have simultaneous nephrotoxicity and rejection.

A form of chronic progressive *nephrotoxicity*, characterized by serial deterioration in renal function and morphologic changes in the kidneys (interstitial fibrosis with tubular atrophy), may occur; reduction in a rising serum creatinine will fail to occur despite reduction in dose or withdrawal of cyclosporine in 5 to 15% of patients; in addition, toxic tubulopathy, peritubular capillary congestion, arteriolopathy, and a striped form of interstitial fibrosis with tubular atrophy may be present. Development of chronic *nephrotoxicity* may be related to high cumulative doses or persistently high circulating trough concentrations of cyclosporine. Effects may be irreversible.

Nephrotoxicity (interstitial fibrosis with tubular atrophy) has been reported in 21% of psoriasis patients receiving cyclosporine for an average period of 23 months, and in 10% of rheumatoid arthritis patients receiving cyclosporine for an average period of 19 months. *Nephrotoxicity* in these patients was established by biopsy. Most patients with *nephrotoxicity* were receiving daily doses in excess of 4 mg per kg of body weight.

Incidence less frequent

Hepatotoxicity—usually asymptomatic; usually seen as elevations of hepatic enzymes and bilirubin; ***hypomagnesemia***—usually asymptomatic; ***infection*** (fever or chills; frequent urge to urinate); ***seizures; vomiting***

Note: *Seizures* may be related to nephrotoxicity and hypomagnesemia.

Hepatotoxicity usually responds to dosage reduction.

Incidence rare

Anaphylaxis (flushing of face and neck; wheezing or shortness of breath)—with parenteral use; ***hemolytic-uremic syndrome; hyperkalemia*** (confusion; irregular heartbeat; numbness or tingling in hands, feet, or lips; shortness of breath or difficult breathing; unexplained nervousness; unusual tiredness or weakness; weakness or heaviness of legs); ***pancreatitis*** (severe stomach pain with nausea and vomiting); ***paresthesia*** (tingling); ***PTLD*** (fever; general feeling of discomfort and illness; weight loss); ***renal toxicity*** (blood in urine)

Note: *Anaphylaxis* occurs only with intravenous use and may be related to the vehicle. The reaction includes facial flushing, acute respiratory distress, blood pressure changes, and tachycardia. A fatality has been reported. Subsequent oral administration of cyclosporine in patients who have experienced an anaphylactic reaction to intravenous cyclosporine has not produced a reaction.

The *hemolytic-uremic syndrome* can occur in the absence of rejection but may result in graft failure. It is accompanied by avid platelet consumption within the graft. It usually responds, if detected early, to dosage reduction or withdrawal of cyclosporine.

Irregular heartbeat is usually the earliest clinical indication of *hyperkalemia* and is readily detected by electrocardiogram (ECG). *Hyperkalemia* sometimes may be associated with hyperchloremic metabolic acidosis.

Incidence not determined—Observed during clinical practice; estimates of frequency can not be determined

Encephalopathy (agitation; back pain; blurred vision; coma; confusion; dizziness; drowsiness; fever; hallucinations; headache; irritability; mood or mental changes; seizures; stiff neck; unusual tiredness or weakness; vomiting); ***optic disc edema*** (blurred vision)

Note: Predisposing factors such as hypertension, hypomagnesemia, hypocholesterolemia, high-dose corticosteroids, high cyclosporine blood concentrations, and graft-versus-host disease have been noted in many but not all of the reported encephalopathy cases. The changes in most cases have been reversible upon discontinuation of cyclosporine, and in some cases improvement was noted after dose reduction. Patients receiving liver transplant appeared to be more susceptible to encephalopathy than those receiving kidney transplant.

Optic disc edema including papilloedema, with possible visual impairment, secondary to benign intracranial hypertension is a rare manifestation of cyclosporine-induced neurotoxicity that occurs in transplant patients more frequently than in other indications.

Those indicating need for medical attention only if they continue or are bothersome

Incidence more frequent

Hirsutism (increase in hair growth); ***tremor*** (trembling and shaking of hands)—dose-related

Incidence less frequent

Acne or oily skin; gastrointestinal disturbances including abdominal discomfort, dyspepsia, and nausea; headache; leg cramps; lethargy

Overdose

For more information on the management of overdose or unintentional ingestion, **contact a Poison Control Center** (see *Poison Control Center Listing*).

Clinical effects of overdose

The following effects have been selected on the basis of their potential clinical significance (possible signs and symptoms in parentheses where appropriate)—not necessarily inclusive:

Acute

Flushing of face; gum soreness and bleeding; headache; hepatotoxicity (flu-like symptoms); ***hyperesthesia*** (tingling in the hands and feet); ***nephrotoxicity***—usually asymptomatic

Treatment of overdose

In general, treatment is symptomatic and supportive.

To decrease absorption—Forced emesis may be useful for up to 2 hours after oral ingestion of toxic doses of cyclosporine.

To enhance elimination—Cyclosporine is not removable by hemodialysis or charcoal hemoperfusion.

Specific treatment—Transient *hepatotoxicity* and *nephrotoxicity* usually respond to withdrawal of cyclosporine.

Patients in whom intentional overdose is confirmed or suspected should be referred for psychiatric consultation.

Patient Consultation

As an aid to patient consultation, refer to *Advice for the Patient, Cyclosporine (Systemic)*.

In providing consultation, consider emphasizing the following selected information (» = major clinical significance):

Before using this medication

» Conditions affecting use, especially:

Hypersensitivity to cyclosporine or to any of the ingredients of the formulation

Pregnancy—Crosses the placenta; causes birth defects or fetal death in animals; risk/benefit considerations

Breast-feeding—Distributed into breast milk; nursing women should not use cyclosporine because of risk of serious side effects

Dental—Dental work should be completed prior to initiation of therapy whenever possible

Other medications, especially allopurinol, amiodarone, androgens, atorvastatin, azithromycin, bromocriptine, carbamazepine, cimetidine, clarithromycin, coal tar, colchicine, contraceptives, danazol, digoxin, diltiazem, erythromycin, estrogens, fluconazole, fluvastatin, human immunodeficiency virus (HIV) protease inhibitors, imatinib, itraconazole, other immunosuppressants, ketoconazole, lovastatin, methoxsalen, methylprednisolone, nafcillin, nefazodone, nicardipine, nonsteroidal anti-inflammatory drugs (NSAIDs), octreotide, orlistat, potassium-sparing diuretics, phenobarbital, phenytoin, pravastatin, quinupristin/dalfopristin, radiation therapy, rifampin, simvastatin, sirolimus, St. John's Wort, sulfinpyrazone, terbinafine, ticlopidine, trioxsalen or verapamil

Other medical problems, especially abnormal renal function, chickenpox, current malignancy, hepatic function impairment, herpes zoster, infection, premalignant skin lesions, renal function impairment, or uncontrolled hypertension

Proper use of this medication

» Importance of not taking more or less medication than the amount prescribed

Getting into the habit of taking at the same time each day and in a consistent relation to the type and timing of the intake of food to help increase compliance and maintain steady blood concentrations; if cyclosporine causes stomach upset, checking with physician before changing relation between cyclosporine intake and type and timing of food intake

Not drinking grapefruit juice or eating grapefruit

Taking solution orally; special dropper to be used for accurate measuring

Mixing oral solution (*Sandimmune®*) with milk, chocolate milk, or orange juice and mixing modified oral solution (*Neoral®*) with apple juice or orange juice (preferably at room temperature) in a glass (not wax-lined or plastic disposable) container to improve palatability; stirring well and drinking immediately, then rinsing the glass with a small amount of additional liquid and drinking that also to make sure all medication is taken; wiping dropper dry but not rinsing with water (to prevent cloudiness)

» Checking with physician before discontinuing medication; possible need for lifelong therapy

» Proper dosing

Missed dose: Taking as soon as possible if remembered within 12 hours; not taking if almost time for next dose; not doubling doses

» Proper storage

Precautions while using this medication

» Importance of close monitoring by physician

» Avoiding immunizations unless approved by physician; other persons in patient's household should avoid immunizations with oral poliovirus vaccine; avoiding persons who have taken oral poliovirus vaccine or wearing a protective mask that covers nose and mouth

» Maintaining good dental hygiene and seeing dentist frequently for teeth cleaning to prevent tenderness, bleeding, and gum enlargement

Side/adverse effects

Importance of discussing possible effects, including cancer, with physician

Signs of potential side effects, especially gingival hyperplasia, hypertension, nephrotoxicity, hepatotoxicity, hypomagnesemia, infection, seizures, vomiting, anaphylaxis, hemolytic-uremic syndrome, hyperkalemia, pancreatitis, paresthesia, post-transplant lymphoproliferative disorders (PTLD), and renal toxicity

Signs of potential side effects observed during clinical practice, especially encephalopathy or optic disc edema

General Dosing Information

Patients receiving cyclosporine should be under the supervision of a physician experienced in immunosuppressive therapy.

If an infection develops, it must be treated promptly; reduction of dosage or withdrawal of cyclosporine may be necessary.

For parenteral dosage form

Because of the risk of anaphylaxis, it is recommended that the parenteral dosage form be used only in patients unable to take cyclosporine orally for prophylaxis and treatment of transplant rejection.

Cyclosporine usually should be administered by slow intravenous infusion over a period of 2 to 6 hours; however, it may be given over a period of up to 24 hours. Rapid intravenous administration may cause acute nephrotoxicity, as well as less serious side effects such as flushing and nausea.

It is recommended that patients receiving intravenous cyclosporine be under continuous observation for at least the first 30 minutes of the infusion and at frequent intervals after that. Equipment and medications (including epinephrine and oxygen) necessary for treatment of a possible anaphylactic reaction should be immediately available during each administration of cyclosporine.

For use in prophylaxis and treatment of transplant rejection

The dose of cyclosporine should be adjusted based on the clinical response of the patient, trough blood concentrations of the medicine, and the appearance or severity of toxicity.

If signs of allograft rejection occur, a larger dose may be necessary; other therapy should be considered if they persist.

Cyclosporine usually is used in conjunction with other immunosuppressants (e.g., corticosteroids and azathioprine).

Antiviral prophylaxis, i.e., with acyclovir, ganciclovir, and immune globulins, may be advisable for some patients receiving cyclosporine, especially cytomegalovirus (CMV) prophylaxis in patients who have not been exposed to CMV prior to transplantation and who receive a CMV-positive graft.

Vaccination schedules should be continued, except for live vaccines. Vaccinations against hepatitis A and B are recommended. Inactivated poliovirus vaccine should be used instead of oral poliovirus vaccine both for the patient and for people living in the same household as the patient. Vaccines given to immunosuppressed patients may not result in a protective antibody response. Protective antibody concentrations should be checked after the vaccine has been administered.

If a patient is exposed to measles, mumps, rubella, or varicella for the first time while receiving cyclosporine, the patient should receive prophylactic therapy with immune globulin, i.e., pooled human immune globulin or varicella immune globulin.

Newly transplanted patients usually receive adjunctive treatment with corticosteroids. The corticosteroids are tapered to target doses within a few months of transplantation. A typical dosage schedule may start with the equivalent of prednisone 2 mg/kg a day and taper to 0.15 mg/kg a day by 2 months following transplantation.

For use in treatment of rheumatoid arthritis

Salicylates, nonsteroidal anti-inflammatory drugs, and corticosteroids may be continued with cyclosporine.

There is little long-term data on the use of cyclosporine in the treatment of rheumatoid arthritis. Recurrence of disease activity is usually seen within 4 weeks after stopping cyclosporine.

For use in treatment of psoriasis

When cyclosporine is used to treat psoriasis, any skin lesions not typical for psoriatic plaque should be biopsied and assessed for malignant or premalignant status before beginning therapy with cyclosporine. Psoriasis patients receiving psoralen and ultraviolet light A (PUVA), ultraviolet light B (UVB), other radiation therapy, or other immunosuppressants should not receive cyclosporine because of the risk of excessive immunosuppression and malignancies.

Patients usually experience some improvement within 2 weeks of beginning cyclosporine, but satisfactory control may require 12 to 16 weeks of therapy with cyclosporine. After satisfactory control of psoriasis is achieved, the dose of cyclosporine should be decreased to the lowest dose needed to control the disease.

There is little experience with long-term treatment of psoriasis with cyclosporine, and continuous treatment longer than one year is not recommended. Relapse of psoriasis occurs in up to 75% of patients within 16 weeks of stopping treatment with cyclosporine.

Diet/Nutrition

The rate of absorption of oral cyclosporine is decreased in the presence of food, but the extent of absorption may or may not be affected, depending on the type of food ingested. Cyclosporine should be given consistently in relation to food.

Bioavailability of cyclosporine may be increased by ingestion of grapefruit or grapefruit juice, resulting in toxic blood concentrations of cyclosporine.

Cyclosporine oral solution (*Sandimmune*®) should be mixed with milk, chocolate milk, or orange juice to improve taste. Cyclosporine modified oral solution (*Neoral*®) should be mixed with apple juice or orange juice to improve taste. *Neoral*® should not be mixed with milk because the mixture may be unpalatable. Patients should avoid switching diluents frequently because the absorption may change with different diluents.

Bioequivalence information

Cyclosporine modified capsules and cyclosporine modified oral solution (*Neoral*®) are not bioequivalent to cyclosporine capsules and cyclosporine oral solution (*Sandimmune*®). For a given trough concentration, the mean area under the serum concentration-versus-time curve (AUC) is larger with *Neoral*® than it is with *Sandimmune*®. When converting from one product to another, frequent monitoring of cyclosporine blood concentrations and patient status are needed to monitor for organ rejection and/or cyclosporine toxicity.

When converting a transplant patient from cyclosporine capsules or cyclosporine oral solution (*Sandimmune*®) to cyclosporine modified capsules or cyclosporine modified oral solution (*Neoral*®), the same daily dose (i.e., a 1-to-1 dose conversion) of *Neoral*® should be started and adjusted based on trough blood concentration. The same target trough concentration should be used. The trough blood concentration should be measured once every 4 to 7 days during the conversion. If a patient is suspected of having poor absorption of *Sandimmune*®, the cyclosporine trough blood concentration should be monitored very frequently during the conversion because higher-than-expected trough blood concentrations are possible. The manufacturer recommends measuring the trough blood concentration daily until steady-state is reached for patients who required *Sandimmune*® doses exceeding 10 mg per kg of body weight a day. Blood pressure and serum creatinine should also be measured frequently (i.e., every 2 weeks) for the first 2 months following the conversion to *Neoral*®.

When converting a rheumatoid arthritis, psoriasis, or nephrotic syndrome patient from oral *Sandimmune*® to *Neoral*®, the initial dose of *Neoral*® should be 70% of the *Sandimmune*® dose (i.e., a 1-to-0.7 dose conversion). The dose should be adjusted based on the trough blood concentration and the clinical condition of the patient.

For treatment of adverse effects

Recommended treatment consists of the following:

Transplant patients

- Many adverse effects (e.g., gastrointestinal toxicity, hyperkalemia, hypomagnesemia, nephrotoxicity) may respond to a reduction in dose. If adverse effects do not respond to a reduction in dose, it may be advisable to convert the patient to a tacrolimus-based immunosuppressant regimen.

Nephrotic syndrome and rheumatoid arthritis patients

- The dose of cyclosporine should be decreased by 25 to 50% if a patient experiences hypertension, elevations in serum creatinine that are ≥ 30% above baseline, or other laboratory abnormalities. If this does not control the adverse effect, or if the adverse effect is severe, cyclosporine should be discontinued.

Psoriasis patients

- The dose of cyclosporine should be decreased by 25 to 50% if a patient experiences hypertension, elevations in serum creatinine that are ≥ 25% above baseline, or other laboratory abnormalities. If this does not control the adverse effect, or if the adverse effect is severe, cyclosporine should be discontinued.

Oral Dosage Forms

Note: Bracketed uses in the *Dosage Forms* section refer to categories of use and/or indications that are not included in U.S. product labeling.

CYCLOSPORINE CAPSULES USP

Usual adult and adolescent dose

Transplant rejection (prophylaxis) or
Transplant rejection (treatment)—

Initial: Oral, 12 to 15 mg per kg of body weight a day beginning four to twelve hours before surgery and continuing for one to two weeks postoperatively, then reduced, usually by 5% a week, to the maintenance dose.

Maintenance: Oral, 5 to 10 mg per kg of body weight a day.

Usual pediatric dose

See *Usual adult and adolescent dose*. Pediatric patients may require higher or more frequent dosing because of accelerated clearance.

Strength(s) usually available

U.S.—

25 mg (Rx) [*Sandimmune*].
50 mg (Rx) [*Sandimmune*].
100 mg (Rx) [*Sandimmune*].

Canada—

25 mg (Rx) [*Sandimmune*].
100 mg (Rx) [*Sandimmune*].

Packaging and storage

Store below 25 °C (77 °F), in a tight container, unless otherwise specified by manufacturer.

CYCLOSPORINE ORAL SOLUTION USP

Usual adult and adolescent dose

See *Cyclosporine Capsules USP*.

Usual pediatric dose
See *Cyclosporine Capsules USP*.

Strength(s) usually available
U.S.—
100 mg per mL (Rx) [*Sandimmune* (ethanol 100 mg per mL)].
Canada—
100 mg per mL (Rx) [*Sandimmune* (ethanol 100 mg per mL)].

Packaging and storage
Store below 30 °C (86 °F), unless otherwise specified by manufacturer. Store in a tight container. Do not refrigerate.

Stability
Contents of opened container must be used within 2 months.

Note
When dispensing, include a calibrated liquid measuring device provided by the manufacturer.

CYCLOSPORINE MODIFIED CAPSULES

Usual adult and adolescent dose
Transplant rejection (prophylaxis) or
Transplant rejection (treatment)—
See *Cyclosporine Capsules USP*.
Rheumatoid arthritis (treatment)—
Oral, 2.5 mg per kg of body weight a day, in two divided doses. If insufficient clinical benefit has been observed after eight weeks, the dose may be increased by 0.5 to 0.75 mg per kg of body weight a day. The dose may be increased again after four additional weeks of therapy to a maximum dose of 4 mg per kg of body weight a day. If no clinical benefit is evident after sixteen weeks of therapy, treatment with cyclosporine should be discontinued.
Psoriasis (treatment)—
Oral, 2.5 mg per kg of body weight a day, in two divided doses. If insufficient clinical benefit has been observed after four weeks the dose may be increased by 0.5 mg per kg of body weight a day. The dose may be increased again at two-week intervals to a maximum dose of 4 mg per kg of body weight a day. If no clinical benefit is evident after six weeks of treatment with 4 mg per kg of body weight a day, cyclosporine should be discontinued. After satisfactory control of psoriasis is achieved, the dose of cyclosporine should be decreased to the lowest dose needed to control the disease.
[Graft-versus-host disease (prophylaxis)]—
Oral, 12.5 mg per kg of body weight a day, in two divided doses. After three to six months of treatment, the cyclosporine dose should be tapered gradually to zero after one year following transplantation.
[Graft-versus-host disease (treatment)]—
Mild graft-versus-host disease occurring after discontinuation of cyclosporine may be treated by the re-introduction of low-dose *Neoral*®.
[Nephrotic syndrome (treatment)]—
Initial: Oral, 3.5 mg per kg of body weight a day, in two divided doses. If no clinical benefit is evident after three months of treatment, cyclosporine should be discontinued.
Maintenance: The dose should be adjusted based on efficacy, as measured by proteinuria, and side effects but should not exceed 5 mg per kg of body weight a day.

Usual pediatric dose
Transplant rejection (prophylaxis)—
See *Cyclosporine Capsules USP*.
[Nephrotic syndrome (treatment)]—
Initial: Oral, 4.2 mg per kg of body weight a day, in two divided doses. If no clinical benefit is evident after three months of treatment, cyclosporine should be discontinued.
Maintenance: The dose should be adjusted based on efficacy, as measured by proteinuria, and side effects but should not exceed 6 mg per kg of body weight a day.

Strength(s) usually available
U.S.—
25 mg (Rx) [*Neoral* (ethanol 95 mg per mL)].
100 mg (Rx) [*Neoral* (ethanol 95 mg per mL)].
Canada—
10 mg (Rx) [*Neoral*].
25 mg (Rx) [*Neoral*].
50 mg (Rx) [*Neoral*].
100 mg (Rx) [*Neoral*].

Packaging and storage
Store between 20 and 25 °C (68 and 77 °F). Store in a tight container. Do not refrigerate.

CYCLOSPORINE MODIFIED ORAL SOLUTION

Usual adult and adolescent dose
See *Cyclosporine Modified Capsules*.

Usual pediatric dose
See *Cyclosporine Modified Capsules*.

Strength(s) usually available
U.S.—
100 mg per mL (Rx) [*Neoral* (ethanol 95 mg per mL)].
100 mg per mL (Rx) [*SangCya* (ethanol 84 mg per mL)].
Canada—
100 mg per mL (Rx) [*Neoral* (ethanol 95 mg per mL)].

Packaging and storage
Store between 20 and 25 °C (68 and 77 °F). Store in a tight container. Do not refrigerate.
At temperatures below 68 °F (20 °C), the solution may gel. Light flocculation or the formation of a light sediment may also occur. There is no impact on product performance or dosing using the syringe provided. Allow to warm to room temperature 77 °F (25 °C) to reverse these changes.

Stability
Contents of opened container must be used within 2 months.

Note
When dispensing, include the calibrated liquid measuring device provided by the manufacturer.

Parenteral Dosage Forms

CYCLOSPORINE CONCENTRATE FOR INJECTION USP

Usual adult and adolescent dose
Transplant rejection (prophylaxis)—
Initial: Intravenous infusion, 2 to 6 mg per kg of body weight a day beginning four to twelve hours prior to surgery and continuing postoperatively until the patient can tolerate the oral solution.

Usual pediatric dose
See *Usual adult and adolescent dose*. Pediatric patients may require higher or more frequent dosing because of accelerated clearance.

Strength(s) usually available
U.S.—
50 mg per mL (Rx) [*Sandimmune* (polyoxyethylated castor oil 650 mg per mL; ethanol 278 mg per mL)].
Canada—
50 mg per mL (Rx) [*Sandimmune* (polyoxyethylated castor oil 650 mg per mL; ethanol 278 mg per mL)].

Packaging and storage
Store below 30 °C (86 °F), unless otherwise specified by manufacturer. Protect from freezing.

Preparation of dosage form
Cyclosporine Concentrate for Injection USP is prepared for intravenous administration by diluting each mL in 20 to 100 mL of 0.9% sodium chloride injection or 5% dextrose injection. Use of glass containers is recommended because of possible leaching of diethylhexylphthalate (DEHP) from polyvinyl chloride (PVC) bags into cyclosporine solutions.

Stability
Reconstituted solutions are stable for up to 24 hours in 5% dextrose injection and for 6 hours (in PVC containers) to 12 hours (in glass containers) in 0.9% sodium chloride injection. Significant amounts of cyclosporine are lost when it is administered through PVC tubing.

Selected Bibliography

Ptachcinski RJ, Burckart GJ, Venkataramanan R. Cyclosporine. Drug Intell Clin Pharm 1985; 19: 90-100.
Fahey JL, Sarna G, Gale RP, et al. UCLA Conference. Immune interventions in disease. Ann Intern Med 1987; 106: 257-74.
Scott JP, Higenbottam TW. Adverse reactions and interactions of cyclosporine. Med Toxicol Adverse Drug Exp 1988; 3: 107-27.

Revised: 10/06/2005

CYPROHEPTADINE—See *Antihistamines (Systemic)*

CYTARABINE Systemic

VA CLASSIFICATION (Primary): AN300

Commonly used brand name(s): *Cytosar; Cytosar-U.*

Other commonly used names are ara-C and cytosine arabinoside.

Note: For a listing of dosage forms and brand names by country availability, see *Dosage Forms* section(s).

Category

Antineoplastic.

Indications

Note: Bracketed information in the *Indications* section refers to uses that are not included in U.S. product labeling.

Accepted

Leukemia, acute nonlymphocytic (treatment)—Cytarabine is indicated, in combination with other antineoplastic agents, for treatment of acute nonlymphocytic leukemia in adults and children.

Leukemia, acute lymphocytic (treatment) or
Leukemia, chronic myelocytic (treatment)—Cytarabine is indicated for treatment of acute lymphocytic leukemia and chronic myelocytic leukemia (blast phase).

Leukemia, meningeal (prophylaxis and treatment)—Cytarabine is indicated for the prevention and treatment of meningeal leukemia (by intrathecal administration).

[Lymphomas, non-Hodgkin's (treatment)]
[Lymphomas, Hodgkin's (treatment)][1] or
[Myelodysplastic syndrome (treatment)][1]—Cytarabine is indicated for the treatment of non-Hodgkin's lymphomas in children, Hodgkin's lymphomas, and myelodysplastic syndrome.

[Carcinomatous meningitis (treatment)][1]—Cytarabine is indicated for treatment of carcinomatous meningitis (by intraventricular administration)(Evidence rating: IIID).

[1]Not included in Canadian product labeling.

Pharmacology/Pharmacokinetics

Physicochemical characteristics

Molecular weight—243.22.
pKa—4.2.
Solubility—Freely soluble in water; slightly soluble in alcohol and in chloroform.

Mechanism of action/Effect

Cytarabine is an antimetabolite. Cytarabine is cell cycle–specific for the S phase of cell division. Activity occurs as the result of activation to cytarabine triphosphate in the tissues and includes inhibition of DNA polymerase and incorporation of cytarabine into DNA and RNA.

Other actions/effects

Cytarabine is a potent immunosuppressant.

Distribution

Only moderate amounts of cytarabine cross the blood-brain barrier with rapid intravenous administration, although cerebrospinal concentrations of 40% of steady-state plasma concentrations are attained after continuous intravenous infusion.

Protein binding

Low (15%).

Biotransformation

Rapidly deaminated in blood and tissues, especially the liver, but minimally in the cerebrospinal fluid (CSF).

Half-life

Varies among individuals; may relate to cytotoxicity.
Alpha phase—10 minutes.
Beta phase—1 to 3 hours (about 2 hours after intrathecal administration).

Time to peak plasma concentration

Subcutaneous—20 to 60 minutes.

Elimination

Renal, less than 10% unchanged.

Precautions to Consider

Carcinogenicity

Secondary malignancies are potential delayed effects of many antineoplastic agents, although it is not clear whether the effect is related to their mutagenic or immunosuppressive action. The effects of dose and duration of therapy are also unknown, although risk seems to increase with long-term use.

Antimetabolites have been shown to be carcinogenic in animals and may be associated with an increased risk of development of secondary carcinomas in humans, although the risk appears to be less than with alkylating agents.

Mutagenicity

Cytarabine may cause chromosomal damage, including chromatoid breaks, in humans. Malignant transformation of rodent cells in culture has been reported.

Pregnancy/Reproduction

Fertility—Gonadal suppression, resulting in amenorrhea or azoospermia, may occur in patients taking antineoplastic therapy, especially with the alkylating agents. In general, these effects appear to be related to dose and length of therapy and may be irreversible. Prediction of the degree of testicular or ovarian function impairment is complicated by the common use of combinations of several antineoplastics, which makes it difficult to assess the effects of individual agents.

Cytarabine has been associated with reversible germ cell toxicity in humans.

Pregnancy—Studies in humans have not been done.

In humans, one case of trisomy, one case of extremity and ear deformities, one case of upper and lower distal limb defects, and one case of enlarged spleen have been reported in infants of mothers who received cytarabine. Other problems reported include pancytopenia; transient depression of leukocyte counts, hematocrit, or platelet counts; electrolyte abnormalities; transient eosinophilia; increased IgM concentrations and hyperpyrexia; fatal gastroenteritis; and prematurity and low birth weight. Several normal births have also been reported.

First trimester: It is usually recommended that use of antineoplastics, especially combination chemotherapy, be avoided whenever possible, especially during the first trimester. Although information is limited because of the relatively few instances of antineoplastic administration during pregnancy, the mutagenic, teratogenic, and carcinogenic potential of these medications must be considered.

Other hazards to the fetus include adverse reactions seen in adults.

In general, use of a contraceptive is recommended during cytotoxic drug therapy.

Cytarabine is teratogenic in some animal species.

FDA Pregnancy Category D.

Breast-feeding

Although very little information is available regarding distribution of antineoplastic agents into breast milk, breast-feeding is not recommended while cytarabine is being administered because of the risks to the infant (adverse effects, mutagenicity, carcinogenicity). It is not known whether cytarabine is distributed into breast milk.

Pediatrics

Appropriate studies on the relationship of age to the effects of cytarabine have not been performed in the pediatric population. However, pediatrics-specific problems that would limit the usefulness of this medication in children are not expected.

Geriatrics

Although appropriate studies on the relationship of age to the effects of cytarabine have not been performed in the geriatric population, geriatrics-specific problems that would limit the usefulness of this medication in the elderly are not expected. However, elderly patients are more likely to have age-related renal function impairment, which may require reduction of dosage in patients receiving cytarabine.

Dental

The bone marrow depressant effects of cytarabine may result in an increased incidence of microbial infection, delayed healing, and gingival bleeding. Dental work, whenever possible should be completed prior to initiation of therapy or deferred until blood counts have returned to normal. Patients should be instructed in proper oral hygiene during treatment, including caution in use of regular toothbrushes, dental floss, and toothpicks.

Cytarabine also commonly causes stomatitis associated with considerable discomfort.

Drug interactions and/or related problems

The following drug interactions and/or related problems have been selected on the basis of their potential clinical significance (possible

mechanism in parentheses where appropriate)—not necessarily inclusive (» = major clinical significance):

Note: Combinations containing any of the following medications, depending on the amount present, may also interact with this medication.

Allopurinol or
Colchicine or
» Probenecid or
» Sulfinpyrazone
(cytarabine may raise the concentration of blood uric acid; dosage adjustment of antigout agents may be necessary to control hyperuricemia and gout; allopurinol may be preferred to prevent or reverse cytarabine-induced hyperuricemia because of risk of uric acid nephropathy with uricosuric antigout agents)

Blood dyscrasia-causing medications (see *Appendix II*)
(leukopenic and/or thrombocytopenic effects of cytarabine may be increased with concurrent or recent therapy if these medications cause the same effects; dosage adjustment of cytarabine, if necessary, should be based on blood counts)

» Bone marrow depressants, other (see *Appendix II*) or
Radiation therapy
(additive bone marrow depression may occur; dosage reduction may be required when two or more bone marrow depressants, including radiation, are used concurrently or consecutively)

» Cyclophosphamide
(concurrent use with high-dose cytarabine therapy for bone marrow transplant preparation has been reported to result in an increase in cardiomyopathy with subsequent death; the cardiac toxicity may be schedule-dependent)

» Immunosuppressants, other, such as:
Azathioprine or
Chlorambucil or
Corticosteroids, glucocorticoid or
Cyclophosphamide or
Cyclosporine or
Mercaptopurine or
Muromonab CD-3 or
Tacrolimus
(concurrent use with cytarabine may increase the risk of infection)

Methotrexate
(administration of cytarabine 48 hours before or 10 minutes after initiation of methotrexate therapy may result in a synergistic cytotoxic effect; however, evidence is inconclusive and dosage adjustment based on routine hematologic monitoring is recommended)

Vaccines, killed virus
(because normal defense mechanisms may be suppressed by cytarabine therapy, the patient's antibody response to the vaccine may be decreased. The interval between discontinuation of medications that cause immunosuppression and restoration of the patient's ability to respond to the vaccine depends on the intensity and type of immunosuppression-causing medication used, the underlying disease, and other factors; estimates vary from 3 months to 1 year)

» Vaccines, live virus
(because normal defense mechanisms may be suppressed by cytarabine therapy, concurrent use with a live virus vaccine may potentiate the replication of the vaccine virus, may increase the side/adverse effects of the vaccine virus, and/or may decrease the patient's antibody response to the vaccine; immunization of these patients should be undertaken only with extreme caution after careful review of the patient's hematologic status and only with the knowledge and consent of the physician managing the cytarabine therapy. The interval between discontinuation of medications that cause immunosuppression and restoration of the patient's ability to respond to the vaccine depends on the intensity and type of immunosuppression-causing medication used, the underlying disease, and other factors; estimates vary from 3 months to 1 year. Patients with leukemia in remission should not receive live virus vaccine until at least 3 months after their last chemotherapy. In addition, immunization with oral poliovirus vaccine should be postponed in persons in close contact with the patient, especially family members)

Laboratory value alterations

The following have been selected on the basis of their potential clinical significance (possible effect in parentheses where appropriate)—not necessarily inclusive (» = major clinical significance).

With physiology/laboratory test values
Alkaline phosphatase values, serum and
Aspartate aminotransferase (AST [SGOT]) values, serum and
Bilirubin concentrations, serum
(may be increased, indicating possible hepatotoxicity)

Uric acid
(concentrations in blood and urine may be increased)

Medical considerations/Contraindications

The medical considerations/contraindications included have been selected on the basis of their potential clinical significance (reasons given in parentheses where appropriate)—not necessarily inclusive (» = major clinical significance).

Risk-benefit should be considered when the following medical problems exist:

» Bone marrow depression
(lower dosage may be necessary)

» Chickenpox, existing or recent (including recent exposure) or
» Herpes zoster
(risk of severe generalized disease)

Gout, history of or
Urate renal stones, history of
(risk of hyperuricemia)

» Hepatic function impairment
(reduced detoxification of cytarabine; lower dosage may be necessary)

» Infection

Renal function impairment
(reduced elimination; lower dosage may be necessary)

Sensitivity to cytarabine

» Tumor cell infiltration of the bone marrow

» Caution should be used also in patients who have had previous cytotoxic drug therapy or radiation therapy.

Patient monitoring

The following may be especially important in patient monitoring (other tests may be warranted in some patients, depending on condition; » = major clinical significance):

Alanine aminotransferase (ALT [SGPT]) values, serum and
Aspartate aminotransferase (AST [SGOT]) values, serum and
Bilirubin concentrations, serum and
Lactate dehydrogenase (LDH) values, serum
(recommended prior to initiation of therapy and at periodic intervals during therapy; frequency varies according to clinical state, agent, dose, and other agents being used concurrently)

» Bone marrow aspiration
(recommended at 2-week intervals until remission occurs)

» Hematocrit or hemoglobin and
Leukocyte count, total and, if appropriate, differential and
» Platelet count
(determinations recommended prior to initiation of therapy and at periodic intervals during therapy; frequency varies according to clinical state, agent, dose, and other agents being used concurrently)

Uric acid concentrations, serum
(recommended prior to initiation of therapy and at periodic intervals during therapy; frequency varies according to clinical state, agent, dose, and other agents being used concurrently)

Side/Adverse Effects

Note: Many "side effects" of antineoplastic therapy are unavoidable and represent the medication's pharmacologic action. Some of these (for example, leukopenia and thrombocytopenia) are actually used as parameters to aid in individual dosage titration.

Incidence of side effects (except nausea and vomiting) is higher with continuous intravenous administration than with rapid intravenous administration.

Intrathecal administration may result in systemic effects.

Acute pancreatitis has been reported in patients previously treated with asparaginase.

High-dose therapy has been associated with severe and potentially fatal toxicity, including reversible corneal toxicity and hemorrhagic conjunctivitis (which may be prevented or reduced by prophylactic administration of a local corticosteroid eye drop), cerebral dysfunction (confusion, tiredness, memory loss, seizures), cerebellar dysfunction (trouble in speaking, standing, or walking; tremors), gastrointestinal ulceration, peritonitis (including pneumatosis cystoides intestinalis leading to peritonitis), sepsis and liver abscess, pulmonary edema, hepatic damage with hyperbilirubinemia, bowel necrosis, necrotizing colitis, skin rash leading to desquamation, fatal cardiomyopathy, a potentially fatal syndrome of sudden respiratory distress progressing to pulmonary edema and cardiomegaly, and peripheral motor and sensory neuropathies.

The following side/adverse effects have been selected on the basis of their potential clinical significance (possible signs and symptoms in parentheses where appropriate)—not necessarily inclusive:

Those indicating need for medical attention

Incidence more frequent—occurring in 15 to 100% of patients

Leukopenia or infection (fever or chills; cough or hoarseness; lower back or side pain; painful or difficult urination)—usually asymptomatic; ***stomatitis*** (sores in mouth and on lips); ***thrombocytopenia*** (unusual bleeding or bruising; black, tarry stools; blood in urine or stools; pinpoint red spots on skin)—usually asymptomatic

Note: With *leukopenia*, leukocyte levels decline in two phases starting in the first 24 hours, with a nadir at days 7 to 9, a brief rise until the twelfth day, and a deeper fall with a nadir at days 15 to 24. Levels rise rapidly to baseline in the next 10 days.

With *thrombocytopenia*, platelet counts fall noticeably by 5 days following a dose, with the nadir at 12 to 15 days and a rise to baseline over the next 10 days.

Incidence less frequent—occurring in 10% or less of patients

Central nervous system (CNS) toxicity, cerebellar or cerebral (numbness or tingling in fingers, toes, or face; unusual tiredness)—more frequent with high-dose therapy; ***hyperuricemia or uric acid nephropathy*** (joint pain; lower back or side pain; swelling of feet or lower legs)

Note: *Hyperuricemia or uric acid nephropathy* occurs most commonly during initial treatment of leukemia or lymphoma, as a result of rapid cell breakdown, which leads to elevated serum uric acid concentrations.

Incidence rare—occurring in 2% or less of patients

Cellulitis or thrombophlebitis (pain at injection site); ***drug reaction or ara-C syndrome*** (bone or muscle pain; chest pain; fever; general feeling of discomfort or illness or weakness; reddened eyes; skin rash); ***esophagitis*** (difficulty in swallowing; heartburn); ***gastrointestinal hemorrhage*** (black, tarry stools); ***hepatotoxicity*** (yellow eyes or skin); ***megaloblastic anemia*** (fainting spells; irregular heartbeat; unusual tiredness; weakness); ***pulmonary edema or diffuse interstitial pneumonitis*** (cough; shortness of breath); ***urinary retention*** (decrease in urination)

Note: The *drug reaction or ara-C syndrome* usually occurs 6 to 12 hours after administration; it may be prevented by or respond to steroid treatment.

Those indicating need for medical attention only if they continue or are bothersome

Incidence more frequent—occurring in 15 to 100% of patients

Loss of appetite; nausea and vomiting

Note: *Nausea and vomiting* occur more frequently when large intravenous doses are administered quickly than when they are infused.

Incidence less frequent or rare—occurring in 10% or less of patients

Diarrhea; dizziness; headache, especially after intrathecal administration; itching of skin; skin freckling

Those not indicating need for medical attention

Incidence less frequent or rare

Alopecia (loss of hair)

Note: Complete *alopecia* is more frequent with high-dose therapy.

Those indicating the need for medical attention if they occur after medication is discontinued

Bone marrow depression (black, tarry stools; blood in urine or stools; cough or hoarseness; fever or chills; lower back or side pain; painful or difficult urination; pinpoint red spots on skin; unusual bleeding or bruising)

Patient Consultation

As an aid to patient consultation, refer to *Advice for the Patient, Cytarabine (Systemic)*.

In providing consultation, consider emphasizing the following selected information (» = major clinical significance):

Before using this medication

» Conditions affecting use, especially:
- Sensitivity to cytarabine
- Pregnancy—Use not recommended because of mutagenic, teratogenic, and carcinogenic potential; advisability of using contraception; telling physician immediately if pregnancy is suspected
- Breast-feeding—Not recommended because of risk of serious side effects
- Other medications, especially probenecid, sulfinpyrazone, other bone marrow depressants, other immunosuppressants, or other cytotoxic drug or radiation therapy
- Other medical problems, especially chickenpox, herpes zoster, hepatic function impairment, or infection

Proper use of this medication

Caution in taking combination therapy; taking each medication at the right time

Importance of ample fluid intake and subsequent increase in urine output to aid in excretion of uric acid

Frequency of nausea and vomiting; importance of continuing medication despite stomach upset

» Proper dosing

Precautions while using this medication

» Importance of close monitoring by the physician

» Avoiding immunizations unless approved by physician; other persons in patient's household should avoid immunizations with oral poliovirus vaccine; avoiding persons who have taken oral poliovirus vaccine or wearing a protective mask that covers nose and mouth

Caution if bone marrow depression occurs:

» Avoiding exposure to persons with infections, especially during periods of low blood counts; checking with physician immediately if fever or chills, cough or hoarseness, lower back or side pain, or painful or difficult urination occurs

» Checking with physician immediately if unusual bleeding or bruising; black, tarry stools; blood in urine or stools; or pinpoint red spots on skin occur

Caution in use of regular toothbrush, dental floss, or toothpick; physician, dentist, or nurse may suggest alternatives; checking with physician before having dental work done

Not touching eyes or inside of nose unless hands washed immediately before

Using caution to avoid accidental cuts with use of sharp objects such as safety razor or fingernail or toenail cutters

Avoiding contact sports or other situations where bruising or injury could occur

Side/adverse effects

May cause adverse effects such as blood problems; importance of discussing possible effects with physician

Signs of potential side effects, especially leukopenia, infection, stomatitis, thrombocytopenia, CNS toxicity, hyperuricemia, uric acid nephropathy, cellulitis, thrombophlebitis, drug reaction, ara-C syndrome, esophagitis, gastrointestinal hemorrhage, hepatotoxicity, megaloblastic anemia, pulmonary edema, diffuse interstitial pneumonitis, and urinary retention

Physician or nurse can help in dealing with side effects

Possibility of hair loss; normal hair growth should return after treatment has ended

General Dosing Information

It is recommended that for induction therapy cytarabine be administered in a hospital setting under supervision of a physician experienced in antimetabolite chemotherapy. Intrathecal therapy should be carried out only by a physician familiar with the regimen.

A variety of dosage schedules and regimens of cytarabine, alone or in combination with other antitumor agents, are used. The prescriber may consult the medical literature as well as the manufacturer's literature in choosing a specific dosage.

Dosage must be adjusted to meet the individual requirements of each patient, on the basis of clinical response and degree of bone marrow depression.

Patients generally tolerate higher doses with less hematologic depression when cytarabine is administered by rapid intravenous injection rather than by slow infusion, although nausea and vomiting may be more severe and may persist for several hours after the injection.

Development of uric acid nephropathy in patients with leukemia or lymphoma may be prevented by adequate oral hydration and, in some cases, administration of allopurinol. Alkalinization of urine may be necessary if serum uric acid concentrations are elevated.

It is recommended that an induction program be continued until either response or toxicity occurs, or until it becomes clear that the patient will not respond. Bone marrow improvement may require 7 to 64 days; treatment is stopped when the bone marrow becomes hypocellular and is resumed when it recovers.

If leukocyte counts fall below 1000 per cubic millimeter or platelet counts below 50,000 per cubic millimeter, cytarabine therapy may need to be withdrawn until definite signs of bone marrow recovery occur. The lowest leukocyte and platelet levels are usually reached after 12 to 24 drug-free days. Therapy should be resumed when appropriate leukocyte and platelet levels are reached; these levels may be lower than normal to avoid patient escape from control.

In acute leukemia, cytarabine may be administered despite the presence of thrombocytopenia and bleeding; cessation of bleeding and increase in platelet count have occurred in some cases during treatment and platelet transfusions are useful in others.

Special precautions are recommended in patients who develop thrombocytopenia as a result of administration of cytarabine. These may include extreme care in performing invasive procedures; regular inspection of intravenous sites, skin (including perirectal area), and mucous membrane surfaces for signs of bleeding or bruising; limiting frequency of venipuncture and avoiding intramuscular injections; testing urine, emesis, stool, and secretions for occult blood; care in use of regular toothbrushes, dental floss, toothpicks, safety razors, and fingernail and toenail cutters; avoiding constipation; and using caution to prevent falls and other injuries. Such patients should avoid alcohol and aspirin intake because of the risk of gastrointestinal bleeding. Platelet transfusions may be required.

Patients who develop leukopenia should be observed carefully for signs of infection. Antibiotic support may be required. In neutropenic patients who develop fever, broad-spectrum antibiotic coverage should be initiated empirically, pending bacterial cultures and appropriate diagnostic tests.

Safety considerations for handling this medication

There is limited but increasing evidence and concern that personnel involved in preparation and administration of parenteral antineoplastics may be at some risk because of the potential mutagenicity, teratogenicity, and/or carcinogenicity of these agents, although the actual risk is unknown. USP advisory panels recommend cautious handling both in preparation and disposal of antineoplastic agents. Precautions that have been suggested include:

- Use of a biological containment cabinet during reconstitution and dilution of parenteral medications and wearing of disposable surgical gloves and masks.
- Use of proper technique to prevent contamination of the medication, work area, and operator during transfer between containers (including proper training of personnel in this technique).
- Cautious and proper disposal of needles, syringes, vials, ampuls, and unused medication.

A number of medical centers have developed detailed guidelines for handling of antineoplastic agents.

Combination chemotherapy

Cytarabine is usually used in combination with other agents in various regimens. As a result, incidence and/or severity of side effects may be altered and different dosages (usually reduced) may be used.

Parenteral Dosage Forms

Note: Bracketed uses in the *Dosage Forms* section refer to categories of use and/or indications that are not included in U.S. product labeling.

CYTARABINE STERILE USP

Usual adult and adolescent dose

Acute nonlymphocytic leukemia—

Induction: Intravenous, 100 mg per square meter of body surface area (as a continuous infusion) on days one through seven or 100 mg per square meter of body surface area every twelve hours on days one through seven.

Note: High-dose cytarabine therapy has been used in selected patients with refractory acute leukemia or lymphomas. One commonly used regimen is 2 to 3 grams per square meter of body surface area intravenously (over one to three hours) every twelve hours for two to six days. High-dose cytarabine therapy should be used with extreme caution and only by clinicians familiar with the procedure.

Meningeal leukemia—

Intrathecal, 5 to 75 mg per square meter of body surface area at intervals ranging from once a day for four days to once every four days. A frequently used dosage is 30 mg per square meter of body surface area once every four days until cerebrospinal fluid (CSF) findings are normal, followed by one additional dose.

Acute lymphocytic leukemia or
Chronic myelocytic leukemia or
[Hodgkin's lymphomas][1] or
[Myelodysplastic syndrome][1] or
[Carcinomatous meningitis][1]—

Consult medical literature and manufacturer's literature for specific dosage.

Usual pediatric dose

[Non-Hodgkin's lymphomas]—

Consult medical literature and manufacturer's literature for specific dosage.

Antineoplastic, other—

See *Usual adult and adolescent dose.*

Note: Safety of use in infants has not been established.

Strength(s) usually available

U.S.—

100 mg (Rx) [*Cytosar-U;* GENERIC].
500 mg (Rx) [*Cytosar-U;* GENERIC].
1 gram (Rx) [*Cytosar-U*].
2 grams (Rx) [*Cytosar-U*].

Canada—

100 mg (Rx) [*Cytosar*].
500 mg (Rx) [*Cytosar*].
1 gram (Rx) [*Cytosar*].
2 grams (Rx) [*Cytosar*].

Packaging and storage

Store at controlled room temperature between 15 and 30 °C (59 and 86 °F).

Preparation of dosage form

Caution: Use of diluents containing benzyl alcohol is not recommended for preparation of medications for use in neonates. A fatal toxic syndrome consisting of metabolic acidosis, CNS depression, respiratory problems, renal failure, hypotension, and possibly seizures and intracranial hemorrhages has been associated with this use. Diluents containing benzyl alcohol should also be avoided in preparation of high-dose and intrathecal therapy.

Sterile Cytarabine USP is reconstituted for *intravenous* or *subcutaneous* (but *not intrathecal*) use by adding 5 mL of bacteriostatic water for injection (with benzyl alcohol) provided by the manufacturer to the 100-mg vial, producing a solution containing 20 mg of cytarabine per mL, or by adding 10 mL of bacteriostatic water for injection to the 500-mg vial, producing a solution containing 50 mg of cytarabine per mL.

Cytarabine solutions may be further diluted with water for injection, 5% dextrose injection, or 0.9% sodium chloride injection for administration by intravenous infusion.

Sterile Cytarabine USP is reconstituted for *intrathecal* use by adding 5 or 10 mL of an isotonic buffered diluent (without preservatives) such as Elliott's B solution, lactated Ringer's injection, or the patient's cerebrospinal fluid (CSF) to the 100- or 500-mg vial, respectively. The volume administered should correspond to an equal volume of CSF removed.

Stability

Reconstituted solutions are stable at room temperature for 48 hours. Solutions that develop a slight haze should be discarded. Infusion solutions containing up to 500 mcg (0.5 mg) of cytarabine per mL are stable at room temperature for 7 days. Solutions for intrathecal use should be used immediately after preparation.

[1]Not included in Canadian product labeling.

Selected Bibliography

DeVita VT, Hellman S, Rosenberg SA, editors. Cancer: principles and practice of oncology. 5th edition. Philadelphia: Lippincott-Raven; 1997.

Revised: 02/25/2004

CYTARABINE, LIPOSOMAL Intrathecal†

VA CLASSIFICATION (Primary): AN300

Commonly used brand name(s): *DepoCyt.*

Note: For a listing of dosage forms and brand names by country availability, see *Dosage Forms* section(s).

†Not commercially available in Canada.

Category

Antineoplastic.

Indications

Accepted

Meningitis, lymphomatous (treatment)—Liposomal cytarabine is indicated for the intrathecal treatment of lymphomatous meningitis.

Pharmacology/Pharmacokinetics

Physicochemical characteristics

Source—

Liposomal cytarabine is a suspension of cytarabine encapsulated within multivesicular lipid-based particles (liposomes) composed of a lipid bilayer of cholesterol, triolein, dioleoylphosphatidylcholine (DOPC), and dipalmitoylphosphatidylglycerol (DPPG).

Liposomal cytarabine is supplied as a sterile, white to off-white liposomal suspension.

Molecular weight—243.22.

Mechanism of action/Effect

Liposomal cytarabine is a sustained release, liposomal formulation of cytarabine formulated for direct administration into the cerebrospinal fluid (CSF). Cytarabine is an antimetabolite that is cell-cycle specific for the S-phase of cell division. Activity occurs as a result of intracellular activation to cytarabine-5'-triphosphate and includes inhibition of DNA polymerase and incorporation of cytarabine into DNA and RNA.

Other actions/effects

Cytarabine is a potent immunosuppressant.

Distribution

Following intrathecal administration, systemic exposure to cytarabine is negligible because of the slow rate of transfer of cytarabine from the CSF to plasma and a fast rate of conversion of cytarabine to inactive metabolite in plasma.

Biotransformation

The major metabolite of cytarabine is 1-beta-D-arabinofuranosyluracil (ara-U), an inactive compound formed rapidly after systemic administration of cytarabine. However, after intrathecal administration of liposomal cytarabine, conversion of cytarabine to the inactive form is negligible in the CSF.

Half-life

Terminal phase—100 to 263 hours.

Time to peak concentration

Cerebrospinal fluid— 5 hours.

Elimination

The clearance of cytarabine from the cerebrospinal fluid is similar to the cerebrospinal fluid bulk flow rate of 0.24 mL/minute.

Precautions to Consider

Cross-sensitivity and/or related problems

Liposomal cytarabine is not recommended in patients hypersensitive to cytarabine or to the liposomal components.

Carcinogenicity

Studies to evaluate the carcinogenic potential of liposomal cytarabine have not been performed.

Mutagenicity

The active ingredient, cytarabine, was found to be mutagenic in *in vitro* tests and clastogenic in *in vitro* (chromosomal aberrations and SCE assay in human leukocytes) and *in vivo* (chromosome aberrations and SCE assay in rodent bone marrow and the mouse micronucleus assay) test systems.

Cytarabine also caused the *in vitro* transformation of hamster embryo cells and rat H43 cells and was clastogenic to mouse meiotic cells (dose-dependent increase in sperm-head abnormalities and chromosomal aberrations).

Pregnancy/Reproduction

Fertility—Studies to evaluate the effects of liposomal cytarabine on fertility have not been performed.

Pregnancy—Adequate and well-controlled studies in humans have not been done. However, there is a potential for the active component, cytarabine, to cause fetal harm if systemic exposure occurs in a pregnant woman. In humans, major limb malformations in infants of mothers who had received intravenous cytarabine either alone or combined with other agents during the first trimester have been reported.

Studies in mice at intraperitoneal doses of ≥ 2 mg per kilogram of body weight (mg/kg) per day (about 0.2 times the recommended human dose on a mg per square meter of body surface area [mg/m^2] basis) found abnormalities of the skeleton, deformities of the appendages, cleft palate, and phocomelia. In rats, a single 20 mg/kg dose (about four times the recommended human dose on a mg/m^2 basis) resulted in deformed appendages. Doses of 50 mg/kg in rats (about 10 times the recommended human dose on a mg/m^2 basis) reduced pre- and postnatal brain size and permanently impaired learning ability. In mice, decreased fetal weight has occurred with doses of 0.5 mg/kg per day (about 0.05 times the recommended human dose on a mg/m^2 basis) and increased early and late resorptions with doses of 8 mg/kg per day (equal to the recommended human dose on a mg/m^2 basis).

Although the risk for fetal harm following intrathecal administration appears low, it is recommended that women of child-bearing potential being treated with liposomal cytarabine avoid becoming pregnant.

FDA Pregnancy Category D.

Breast-feeding

It is not known whether cytarabine is distributed into breast milk. Liposomal cytarabine is not recommended in nursing women because of the potential for serious adverse effects in nursing infants.

Pediatrics

Appropriate studies on the relationship of age to the effects of liposomal cytarabine have not been performed in the pediatric population. Safety and efficacy have not been established.

Geriatrics

No information is available on the relationship of age to the effects of liposomal cytarabine in geriatric patients.

Drug interactions and/or related problems

The following drug interactions and/or related problems have been selected on the basis of their potential clinical significance (possible mechanism in parentheses where appropriate)—not necessarily inclusive (» = major clinical significance):

Note: Combinations containing any of the following medications, depending on the amount present, may also interact with this medication.

Cytotoxic agents, other, intrathecal or systemic
(enhanced neurotoxicity has been known to occur with the co-administration of intrathecal cytotoxic agents)

Radiation therapy (cranial/spinal)
(increased risk of neurotoxicity may occur when intrathecal liposomal cytarabine is administered with cranial/spinal radiation)

Laboratory value alterations

The following have been selected on the basis of their potential clinical significance (possible effect in parentheses where appropriate)—not necessarily inclusive (» = major clinical significance).

With physiology/laboratory test values

Cerebrospinal fluid (CSF) protein and
White blood cells
(transient elevations may occur)

Diagnostic interference

The following drug interactions and/or related problems have been selected on the basis of their potential clinical significance (possible mechanism in parentheses where appropriate)—not necessarily inclusive (» = major clinical significance):

With *other* diagnostic test results

White blood cell count
(particles of liposomal cytarabine are similar in size and appearance to white blood cells; use care when interpreting cerebrospinal fluid [CSF] examinations)

Medical considerations/Contraindications

The medical considerations/contraindications included have been selected on the basis of their potential clinical significance (reasons given in parentheses where appropriate)—not necessarily inclusive (» = major clinical significance).

Except under special circumstances, this medication should not be used when the following medical problems exist:

» Active meningeal infection

» Hypersensitivity to cytarabine or to liposomal formulation or
(the use of this medication is contraindicated)

Risk-benefit should be considered when the following medical problems exist:

» Blockage to cerebrospinal fluid flow
(increased risk of neurotoxicity due to increased free cytarabine concentrations)

Patient monitoring

The following may be especially important in patient monitoring (other tests may be warranted in some patients, depending on condition; » = major clinical significance):

» Neurologic examinations
(recommended at regular intervals during therapy for monitoring development of neurotoxicity)

» Hematocrit or hemoglobin and

» Platelet count and

» Leukocyte count, total and, if appropriate, differential
(recommended at regular intervals during therapy)

Side/Adverse Effects

Note: Adverse effects associated with intrathecal administration of liposomal cytarabine are most likely to occur within five days of administration and may be associated with a single dose or with cumulative doses.

The following side/adverse effects have been selected on the basis of their potential clinical significance (possible signs and symptoms in parentheses where appropriate)—not necessarily inclusive:

Those indicating need for medical attention

Incidence more frequent

Chemical arachnoiditis (back pain; cerebrospinal fluid (CSF) pleocytosis; fever; headache; nausea; neck pain or rigidity; vomiting); ***confusion and somnolence*** (sleepiness); ***neurologic effects including asthenia*** (weakness)

Note: In an early study, chemical arachnoiditis was observed in 100% of cycles without dexamethasone prophylaxis; with concurrent administration of dexamethasone, chemical arachnoiditis was observed in 33% of cycles. Patients receiving liposomal cytarabine should be treated concurrently with dexamethasone to mitigate the symptoms of arachnoiditis.

Incidence less frequent

Neutropenia (lower back or side pain; fever or chills; cough or hoarseness; painful or difficult urination; sore throat); ***peripheral edema*** (swelling of fingers, hands, arms, lower legs, or feet); ***thrombocytopenia*** (unusual bleeding or bruising; black, tarry stools; blood in urine or stools; pinpoint red spots on skin)

Incidence rare

Anaphylactic reaction (fast or irregular breathing; puffiness or swelling around face; shortness of breath; sudden, severe decrease in blood pressure); ***anemia*** (unusual tiredness or weakness)

Those indicating need for medical attention only if they continue or are bothersome

Incidence less frequent

Constipation; urinary incontinence

Overdose

For more information on the management of overdose or unintentional ingestion, **contact a Poison Control Center** (see *Poison Control Center Listing*).

Clinical effects of overdose

The following effects have been selected on the basis of their potential clinical significance (possible signs and symptoms in parentheses where appropriate)—not necessarily inclusive:

Acute effects

There is no human experience with liposomal cytarabine; however, an overdose with liposomal cytarabine may be associated with severe chemical arachnoiditis and encephalopathy.

Treatment of overdose

Specific treatment—There is no known specific antidote for liposomal cytarabine. The exchange of cerebrospinal fluid with isotonic saline has been performed in a case of intrathecal overdose of free cytarabine. Supportive therapy is recommended.

Patient Consultation

As an aid to patient consultation, refer to.

In providing consultation, consider emphasizing the following selected information (» = major clinical significance):

Before using this medication

» Conditions affecting use, especially:
- Hypersensitivity to cytarabine or liposomal components
- Pregnancy—Use is not recommended because of embryotoxic, fetotoxic, and mutagenic potential; advisability of using contraception
- Breast-feeding—Not recommended because of potential serious adverse effects
- Other medications, especially concurrent intrathecal or systemic cytotoxic drug therapy or cranial/spinal radiation therapy
- Other medical problems, especially active meningeal infection or blockage to cerebrospinal fluid (CSF) flow

Proper use of this medication

» Frequency of nausea and vomiting; importance of continuing medication despite stomach upset

» Proper dosing

Precautions while using this medication

» Importance of close monitoring by the physician

Side/adverse effects

Signs of potential side effects, especially chemical arachnoiditis, confusion and somnolence, neurologic effects, neutropenia, peripheral edema, thrombocytopenia, anaphylactic reaction, and anemia

(Physician or nurse can help in dealing with side effects)

General Dosing Information

Liposomal cytarabine should be administered only under the supervision of a physician experienced in cancer chemotherapy. Adequate facilities and medications for diagnosis and treatment of complications should be readily available.

Liposomal cytarabine injection should not be mixed with other medications.

In-line filters must not be used in liposomal cytarabine administration.

Liposomal cytarabine is recommended for administration by intrathecal injection only (via intraventricular reservoir or direct injection into the lumbar sac). Liposomal cytarabine should be slowly injected over one to five minutes.

If liposomal cytarabine is administered by direct injection into the lumbar sac, it is recommended that the patient be advised to lie flat for one hour following injection.

The incidence and severity of chemical arachnoiditis is reduced by concurrent administration of dexamethasone. It is recommended that patients be treated with 4 mg dexamethasone (oral or intravenous) twice a day, for five days, starting on the day of liposomal cytarabine administration.

Safety considerations for handling this medication

The procedure for the preparation, handling, and disposal of liposomal cytarabine should be the same as that used with other antineoplastic agents.

Direct contact of skin or mucosa with liposomal cytarabine requires immediate washing with soap and water.

The use of disposable surgical gloves is recommended.

Intrathecal Dosage Forms

CYTARABINE LIPOSOME INJECTION

Usual adult dose

Meningitis, lymphomatous—

Induction: Intrathecal injection (intraventricular or lumbar puncture over one to five minutes), 50 mg every fourteen days for two doses (weeks 1 and 3).

Consolidation: Intrathecal injection (intraventricular or lumbar puncture over one to five minutes), 50 mg every fourteen days for three doses (weeks 5, 7, and 9) followed by one additional dose at week 13.

Maintenance: Intrathecal injection (intraventricular or lumbar puncture over one to five minutes), 50 mg every twenty-eight days for four doses (weeks 17, 21, 25, and 29).

Note: Dosage should be decreased to 25 mg for patients who develop drug-related neurotoxicity. If neurotoxicity persists, liposomal cytarabine therapy should be discontinued.

Strength(s) usually available

U.S.—

50 mg single-dose vial (Rx) [*DepoCyt* (cholesterol 4.1 mg/mL; triolein 1.2 mg/mL; dioleoylphosphatidylcholine 5.7 mg/mL; dipalmitoylphosphatidylglycerol 1 mg/mL)].

Canada—

Not commercially available.

Packaging and storage

Store between 2 and 8 °C (36 and 46 °F). Protect from freezing and aggressive agitation of vial.

Preparation of dosage form

Liposomal cytarabine should be allowed to warm to room temperature and the vial gently inverted or agitated prior to withdrawal from the vial. Avoid aggressive agitation of the vial. Further reconstitution or dilution of liposomal cytarabine is not required prior to administration.

Stability

Liposomal cytarabine contains no preservatives and should be used immediately after withdrawal from the vial. Unused portions of vials should be discarded. The drug can be used up to four hours after withdrawal from the vial.

Incompatibilities

Liposomal cytarabine should not be mixed with other medications.

Developed: 08/19/1999

DACARBAZINE Systemic

VA CLASSIFICATION (Primary): AN900

Commonly used brand name(s): *DTIC; DTIC-Dome.*

Note: For a listing of dosage forms and brand names by country availability, see *Dosage Forms* section(s).

Category

Antineoplastic.

Indications

Note: Bracketed information in the *Indications* section refers to uses that are not included in U.S. product labeling.

Accepted

Melanoma, malignant (treatment)—Dacarbazine is indicated for treatment of metastatic malignant melanoma.

Lymphomas, Hodgkin's (treatment)[1]—Dacarbazine is indicated for treatment of Hodgkin's disease as second-line therapy in combination with other effective agents.

[Sarcomas, soft tissue (treatment)][1]—Dacarbazine is used for treatment of some soft-tissue metastatic sarcomas.

[Carcinoma, islet cell (treatment)][1]—Dacarbazine is used for treatment of islet cell carcinoma.

[1]Not included in Canadian product labeling.

Pharmacology/Pharmacokinetics

Physicochemical characteristics

Molecular weight—182.19.

pKa—4.42.

Mechanism of action/Effect

Dacarbazine is thought to be an alkylating agent. Major action is believed to be alkylation; dacarbazine is cell cycle-phase-nonspecific. Dacarbazine may inhibit DNA and RNA synthesis via formation of carbonium ions. Some activity and toxicity may occur as the result of activation by hepatic enzymes.

Distribution

Crosses the blood-brain barrier only to a limited extent.

Protein binding

Very low.

Biotransformation

Hepatic, extensive.

Half-life

Normal—

Alpha phase: 19 minutes.

Beta phase: 5 hours.

Renal or hepatic function impairment—

Alpha phase: 55 minutes.

Beta phase: 7.2 hours.

Elimination

Renal; 40% of injected dose in 6 hours, one half of that unchanged.

Precautions to Consider

Carcinogenicity/Mutagenicity

Secondary malignancies are potential delayed effects of many antineoplastic agents, although it is not clear whether the effect is related to their mutagenic or immunosuppressive action. The effect of dose and duration of therapy is also unknown, although risk seems to increase with long-term use. Although information is limited, available data seem to indicate that the carcinogenic risk is greatest with the alkylating agents.

Dacarbazine is a potent carcinogen in animals. In rats, dacarbazine produced proliferative endocardial lesions, including fibrosarcomas and sarcomas; in mice, angiosarcomas of the spleen were induced.

Pregnancy/Reproduction

Fertility—Gonadal suppression, resulting in amenorrhea or azoospermia, may occur in patients taking antineoplastic therapy, especially with the alkylating agents. In general, these effects appear to be related to dose and length of therapy and may be irreversible. Prediction of the degree of testicular or ovarian function impairment is complicated by the common use of combinations of several antineoplastics, which makes it difficult to assess the effects of individual agents.

Pregnancy—Adequate and well-controlled studies in humans have not been done.

First trimester: It is usually recommended that use of antineoplastics, especially combination chemotherapy, be avoided whenever possible, especially during the first trimester. Although information is limited because of the relatively few instances of antineoplastic administration during pregnancy, the mutagenic, teratogenic, and carcinogenic potential of these medications must be considered.

Other hazards to the fetus include adverse reactions seen in adults.

In general, use of a contraceptive is recommended during cytotoxic drug therapy.

Studies in rats have shown that dacarbazine is teratogenic at doses 20 times the human daily dose given on day 12 of gestation. Administration of 10 times the human daily dose to male rats twice weekly for 9 weeks resulted in an increased incidence of fetal resorptions in female rats mated to them. Dacarbazine caused fetal skeletal anomalies in rabbits given seven times the human daily dose on days 6 to 15 of gestation.

FDA Pregnancy Category C.

Breast-feeding

Although very little information is available regarding distribution of antineoplastic agents into breast milk, breast-feeding is not recommended while dacarbazine is being administered because of the risks to the infant (adverse effects, mutagenicity, carcinogenicity). It is not known whether dacarbazine is distributed into breast milk.

Pediatrics

Appropriate studies on the relationship of age to the effects of dacarbazine have not been performed in the pediatric population.

Geriatrics

No information is available on the relationship of age to the effects of dacarbazine in geriatric patients. However, elderly patients are more likely to have age-related renal function impairment, which may require reduction of dosage in patients receiving dacarbazine.

Dental

The bone marrow depressant effects of dacarbazine may result in an increased incidence of microbial infection, delayed healing, and gingival bleeding. Dental work, whenever possible, should be completed prior to initiation of therapy or deferred until blood counts have returned to normal. Patients should be instructed in proper oral hygiene during treatment, including caution in use of regular toothbrushes, dental floss, and toothpicks.

Dacarbazine may also rarely cause stomatitis associated with considerable discomfort.

Drug interactions and/or related problems

The following drug interactions and/or related problems have been selected on the basis of their potential clinical significance (possible mechanism in parentheses where appropriate)—not necessarily inclusive (» = major clinical significance):

Note: Combinations containing any of the following medications, depending on the amount present, may also interact with this medication.

Allopurinol
(dacarbazine-induced inhibition of xanthine oxidase may cause additive hypouricemic effects when used concurrently with allopurinol)

Blood dyscrasia-causing medications (see *Appendix II*)
(leukopenic and/or thrombocytopenic effects of dacarbazine may be increased with concurrent or recent therapy if these medications cause the same effects; dosage adjustment of dacarbazine, if necessary, should be based on blood counts)

» Bone marrow depressants, other (see *Appendix II*) or
Radiation therapy
(additive bone marrow depression may occur; dosage reduction may be required when two or more bone marrow depressants, including radiation, are used concurrently or consecutively)

Hepatic enzyme inducers (see *Appendix II*)
(may enhance metabolism of dacarbazine by induction of hepatic microsomal enzymes; dosage adjustment may be necessary)

Vaccines, killed virus
(because normal defense mechanisms may be suppressed by dacarbazine therapy, the patient's antibody response to the vaccine may be decreased. The interval between discontinuation of medications that cause immunosuppression and restoration of the patient's ability to respond to the vaccine depends on the intensity and type of immunosuppression-causing medication used, the underlying disease, and other factors; estimates vary from 3 months to 1 year)

» Vaccines, live virus
(because normal defense mechanisms may be suppressed by dacarbazine therapy, concurrent use with a live virus vaccine may potentiate the replication of the vaccine virus, may increase the side/adverse effects of the vaccine virus, and/or may decrease the patient's antibody response to the vaccine; immunization of these patients should be undertaken only with extreme caution after careful review of the patient's hematologic status and only with the knowledge and consent of the physician managing the dacarbazine therapy. The interval between discontinuation of medications that cause immunosuppression and restoration of the patient's ability to respond to the vaccine depends on the intensity and type of immunosuppression-causing medication used, the underlying disease, and other factors; estimates vary from 3 months to 1 year. In addition, immunization with oral poliovirus vaccine should be postponed in persons in close contact with the patient, especially family members)

Laboratory value alterations

The following have been selected on the basis of their potential clinical significance (possible effect in parentheses where appropriate)—not necessarily inclusive (» = major clinical significance).

With physiology/laboratory test values
Alanine aminotransferase (ALT [SGPT]) and
Alkaline phosphatase and
Aspartate aminotransferase (AST [SGOT])
(serum values may be transiently increased; may indicate hepatotoxicity)
Blood urea nitrogen (BUN)
(concentrations may be transiently increased)

Medical considerations/Contraindications

The medical considerations/contraindications included have been selected on the basis of their potential clinical significance (reasons given in parentheses where appropriate)—not necessarily inclusive (» = major clinical significance).

Risk-benefit should be considered when the following medical problems exist:

» Bone marrow depression

» Chickenpox, existing or recent (including recent exposure) or
» Herpes zoster
(risk of severe generalized disease)

» Hepatic function impairment

» Infection

» Renal function impairment
(reduced elimination; dosage reduction may be required)

Sensitivity to dacarbazine

» Caution should be used also in patients who have had previous cytotoxic drug therapy or radiation therapy.

Patient monitoring

The following are especially important in patient monitoring (other tests may be warranted in some patients, depending on condition; » = major clinical significance):

Blood urea nitrogen (BUN) concentrations and
Creatinine concentrations, serum
(recommended prior to initiation of therapy and at periodic intervals during therapy; frequency varies according to clinical state, agent, dose, and other agents being used concurrently)

» Hematocrit or hemoglobin and
» Leukocyte count, total and, if appropriate, differential and
» Platelet count
(determinations recommended prior to initiation of therapy and at periodic intervals during therapy; frequency varies according to clinical state, agent, dose, and other agents being used concurrently)

Alanine aminotransferase (ALT [SGPT]) values, serum and
Aspartate aminotransferase (AST [SGOT]) values, serum and
Lactate dehydrogenase (LDH) values, serum
(recommended prior to initiation of therapy and at periodic intervals during therapy; frequency varies according to clinical state, agent, dose, and other agents being used concurrently)

Bilirubin concentrations, serum and
Uric acid concentrations, serum
(recommended prior to initiation of therapy and at periodic intervals during therapy; frequency varies according to clinical state, agent, dose, and other agents being used concurrently)

Side/Adverse Effects

Note: Many "side effects" of antineoplastic therapy are unavoidable and represent the medication's pharmacologic action. Some of these (for example, leukopenia and thrombocytopenia) are actually used as parameters to aid in individual dosage titration.

According to some investigators, photodegradation products of dacarbazine solution may be responsible for some of its adverse effects, including local toxicity (burning and vein pain), nausea and vomiting, and hepatotoxicity.

The following side/adverse effects have been selected on the basis of their potential clinical significance (possible signs and symptoms in parentheses where appropriate)—not necessarily inclusive:

Those indicating need for medical attention

Incidence more frequent

Anemia; extravasation and tissue damage or pain in injected vein (redness, swelling, or pain at site of injection); ***leukopenia*** (fever or chills; cough or hoarseness; lower back or side pain; painful or difficult urination)—usually asymptomatic; ***thrombocytopenia*** (unusual bleeding or bruising; black, tarry stools; blood in urine or stools; pinpoint red spots on skin)—usually asymptomatic

Note: The fall in leukocyte count usually begins within 16 to 20 days after administration, with the nadir at 21 to 25 days and recovery 3 to 5 days later. *Leukopenia* may be severe enough to be fatal.

The nadir usually occurs 16 days after administration, with recovery 3 to 5 days later. *Thrombocytopenia* may be severe enough to be fatal.

Incidence rare

Anaphylaxis (shortness of breath; swelling of face); ***hepatotoxicity, including hepatic vein thrombosis; and hepatocellular necrosis*** (fever; stomach pain; yellow eyes or skin); ***stomatitis*** (sores in mouth and on lips)

Note: *Hepatotoxicity* is uniformly fatal. It has been reported with use of dacarbazine alone and in combination with other agents.

Those indicating need for medical attention only if they continue or are bothersome

Incidence more frequent—greater than 90%

Loss of appetite; nausea and vomiting

Note: *Nausea and vomiting* may last for 1 to 12 hours after administration but usually lessen considerably within 1 to 2 days after treatment is started.

Incidence less frequent

Flushing of face; influenza-like syndrome (fever; feelings of uneasiness; joint or muscle pain); ***numbness of face***

Note: The *influenza-like syndrome* begins after 7 days and may last 1 to 3 weeks; it may occur with repeated treatments.

Those not indicating need for medical attention

Incidence less frequent

Loss of hair

Those indicating the need for medical attention if they occur after medication is discontinued

Bone marrow depression (black, tarry stools; blood in urine or stools; cough or hoarseness; fever or chills; lower back or side pain; painful or difficult urination; pinpoint red spots on skin; unusual bleeding or bruising)

Patient Consultation

As an aid to patient consultation, refer to *Advice for the Patient, Dacarbazine (Systemic).*

In providing consultation, consider emphasizing the following selected information (» = major clinical significance):

Before using this medication

» Conditions affecting use, especially:
Sensitivity to dacarbazine
Pregnancy—Use not recommended because of mutagenic, teratogenic, and carcinogenic potential; advisability of using contraception; telling physician immediately if pregnancy is suspected
Breast-feeding—Not recommended because of risk of serious side effects
Other medications, especially other bone marrow depressants or previous cytotoxic drug or radiation therapy

Other medical problems, especially chickenpox, herpes zoster, hepatic function impairment, infection, or renal function impairment

Proper use of this medication

Caution in taking combination therapy; taking each medication at the right time

Frequency of nausea, vomiting, and loss of appetite; importance of continuing medication despite stomach upset; should lessen after 1 or 2 days

» Proper dosing

Precautions while using this medication

» Importance of close monitoring by the physician

» Avoiding immunizations unless approved by physician; other persons in patient's household should avoid immunizations with oral poliovirus vaccine; avoiding persons who have taken oral poliovirus vaccine or wearing a protective mask that covers nose and mouth

Caution if bone marrow depression occurs:

» Avoiding exposure to persons with infections, especially during periods of low blood counts; checking with physician immediately if fever or chills, cough or hoarseness, lower back or side pain, or painful or difficult urination occurs

» Checking with physician immediately if unusual bleeding or bruising; black, tarry stools; blood in urine or stools; or pinpoint red spots on skin occur

Caution in use of regular toothbrush, dental floss, or toothpick; physician, dentist, or nurse may suggest alternatives; checking with physician before having dental work done

Not touching eyes or inside of nose unless hands are washed immediately before

Using caution to avoid accidental cuts with use of sharp objects such as safety razor or fingernail or toenail cutters

Avoiding contact sports or other situations where bruising or injury could occur

» Possibility of local tissue injury and scarring if infiltration of intravenous solution occurs; telling doctor or nurse right away about redness, pain, or swelling at injection site

Side/adverse effects

May cause adverse effects such as blood problems, loss of hair, and cancer; importance of discussing possible effects with physician

Signs of potential side effects, especially anemia, extravasation, pain in injected vein, leukopenia, thrombocytopenia, anaphylaxis, hepatotoxicity, and stomatitis

Physician or nurse can help in dealing with side effects

Possibility of hair loss; normal hair growth should return after treatment has ended

General Dosing Information

Patients receiving dacarbazine should be under supervision of a physician experienced in cancer chemotherapy.

A variety of dosage schedules and regimens of dacarbazine, alone or in combination with other antitumor agents, are used. The prescriber may consult the medical literature as well as the manufacturer's literature in choosing a specific dosage.

Dosage must be adjusted to meet the individual requirements of each patient, on the basis of clinical response and degree of bone marrow depression.

Dacarbazine may be administered into the tubing of a freely running intravenous solution over a 1- to 2-minute period, or by intravenous infusion over a 15- to 30-minute period. Administration by intravenous infusion may prevent pain along the injected vein.

Care should be taken to avoid extravasation of dacarbazine because of the risk of severe pain and tissue necrosis.

If extravasation of dacarbazine occurs during intravenous administration, as indicated by local burning or stinging, the injection and infusion should be stopped immediately and resumed, completing the dose, in another vein.

If marked leukopenia (particularly granulocytopenia) or thrombocytopenia occurs, dacarbazine should be discontinued until leukocyte and platelet counts return to satisfactory levels, usually within a week after the nadir.

Special precautions are recommended in patients who develop thrombocytopenia as a result of administration of dacarbazine. These may include extra care in performing invasive procedures, regular inspection of intravenous sites, skin (including perirectal area), and mucous membrane surfaces for signs of bleeding or bruising; limiting frequency of venipuncture and avoiding intramuscular injections; testing urine, emesis, stool, and secretions for occult blood; care in use of regular toothbrushes, dental floss, toothpicks, safety razors, and fingernail and toenail cutters; avoiding constipation; and using caution to prevent falls and other injuries. Such patients should avoid alcohol and aspirin intake because of the risk of gastrointestinal bleeding. Platelet transfusion may be required.

Patients who develop leukopenia should be observed carefully for signs of infection. Antibiotic support may be required. In neutropenic patients who develop fever, broad-spectrum antibiotic coverage should be initiated empirically, pending bacterial cultures and appropriate diagnostic tests.

Safety considerations for handling this medication

There is limited but increasing evidence and concern that personnel involved in preparation and administration of parenteral antineoplastics may be at some risk because of the potential mutagenicity, teratogenicity, and/or carcinogenicity of these agents, although the actual risk is unknown. USP advisory panels recommend cautious handling both in preparation and disposal of antineoplastic agents. Precautions that have been suggested include:

- Use of a biological containment cabinet during reconstitution and dilution of parenteral medications and wearing of disposable surgical gloves and masks.
- Use of proper technique to prevent contamination of the medication, work area, and operator during transfer between containers (including proper training of personnel in this technique).
- Cautious and proper disposal of needles, syringes, vials, ampuls, and unused medication.

A number of medical centers have developed detailed guidelines for handling of antineoplastic agents.

Combination chemotherapy

Dacarbazine may be used in combination with other agents in various regimens. As a result, incidence and/or severity of side effects may be altered and different dosages (usually reduced) may be used. For example, dacarbazine is part of the following chemotherapeutic combinations (some commonly used acronyms are in parentheses):

—doxorubicin, bleomycin, vinblastine, and dacarbazine (ABVD).

—cyclophosphamide, vincristine, doxorubicin, and dacarbazine (CY-VADIC).

For specific dosages and schedules, consult the literature. For information regarding each agent, consult the individual monographs.

Parenteral Dosage Forms

DACARBAZINE FOR INJECTION USP

Usual adult dose

Melanoma, malignant—

Intravenous, 2 to 4.5 mg per kg of body weight a day for ten days; may be repeated every twenty-eight days, or

Intravenous, up to 250 mg per square meter of body surface area a day for five days; may be repeated every twenty-one days.

Lymphomas, Hodgkin's[1]—

Intravenous, 150 mg per square meter of body surface area a day for five days, in combination with other agents; may be repeated every twenty-eight days, or

Intravenous, 375 mg per square meter of body surface area on day 1, in combination with other agents, repeated every fifteen days.

Note: Dacarbazine may be as effective at the lower dosage as at the higher dosage.

Dacarbazine has also been administered as a single daily dose of 850 mg per square meter of body surface area every twenty-one to forty-two days, with no apparent increase in hematologic toxicity, although extreme nausea and vomiting may occur.

Usual pediatric dose

Dosage has not been established.

Strength(s) usually available

U.S.—

100 mg (Rx) [*DTIC-Dome* (mannitol 37.5 mg); GENERIC (mannitol)].

200 mg (Rx) [*DTIC-Dome* (mannitol 75 mg); GENERIC (mannitol)].

Canada—

200 mg [*DTIC*].

Packaging and storage

Store below 40 °C (104 °F), preferably between 15 and 30 °C (59 and 86 °F), unless otherwise specified by the manufacturer. Protect from light.

Preparation of dosage form

Dacarbazine for Injection USP may be prepared for parenteral use by adding 9.9 mL (100-mg vial), 19.7 mL (200-mg vial), or 49.5 mL (500-

mg vial) of sterile water for injection to the vial, producing a colorless or clear yellow solution containing 10 mg of dacarbazine per mL.

Reconstituted solutions may be further diluted with up to 250 mL of 5% dextrose injection or 0.9% sodium chloride injection for administration by intravenous infusion.

Stability

Reconstituted solutions of dacarbazine are stable for up to 72 hours at 4 °C (39 °F) or for up to 8 hours at normal room conditions (temperature and light). Solutions further diluted for administration by intravenous infusion are stable for up to 24 hours at 4 °C (39 °F) or for up to 8 hours at normal room conditions (temperature and light). A change in color of the solution to pink indicates decomposition.

[1]Not included in Canadian product labeling.

Revised: 09/30/1997

DACLIZUMAB Systemic

VA CLASSIFICATION (Primary): IM403

Commonly used brand name(s): *Zenapax*.

Another commonly used name is dacliximab.

Note: For a listing of dosage forms and brand names by country availability, see *Dosage Forms* section(s).

Category

Immunosuppressant; monoclonal antibody.

Indications

General Considerations

The efficacy of daclizumab was demonstrated in two placebo-controlled, multicenter trials in which daclizumab was administered in conjunction with triple-therapy (cyclosporine, corticosteroids, and azathioprine) or double-therapy (cyclosporine and corticosteroids). The primary end point in the trials was the incidence of biopsy-proven acute rejection within the first 6 months following transplantation. The incidence of biopsy-proven acute rejection was lower in the daclizumab-treated group in both the triple-therapy ($P = 0.03$) and the double-therapy ($P = 0.001$) trials.

A secondary end point in the trials was the incidence of biopsy-proven acute rejection at 1 year following transplantation. Biopsy-proven rejection at 1 year was not significantly different between the placebo-treated group (38%) and the daclizumab-treated group (28%) in the triple-therapy regimen ($P = 0.09$). However, there was a significant difference in this end point in the double-therapy regimen (49% vs 28% incidence of biopsy-proven rejection in the placebo-treated and daclizumab-treated groups, respectively [$P < 0.001$]).

Another secondary end point in the trials was graft survival 1 year following transplantation. There was no significant difference in either the triple-therapy trial ($P = 0.08$) or the double-therapy trial ($P = 0.3$).

The trials also compared patient survival at 1 year following transplantation. Patient survival was not significantly different between the placebo-treated group (96%) and the daclizumab-treated group (98%) in the triple-therapy regimen ($P = 0.51$). However, there was a significant difference in this end point in the double-therapy regimen (94% vs 99% survival in the placebo-treated and daclizumab-treated groups, respectively [$P = 0.01$]).

The incidences of lymphoproliferative disorders and opportunistic infections were not increased in the daclizumab-treated patients in the trials. However, only 336 patients were treated with daclizumab in these trials. Additional experience with daclizumab is needed to evaluate its potential for causing lymphoproliferative disorders and opportunistic infections.

The long-term ability of the immune system to respond to antigens first encountered while being treated with daclizumab is not known.

Accepted

Transplant rejection, kidney (prophylaxis)—Daclizumab is indicated, in combination with cyclosporine and corticosteroids, for the prevention of acute rejection of transplanted kidneys.

Pharmacology/Pharmacokinetics

Physicochemical characteristics

Source—Composite of human (90%) and murine (10%) antibody sequences obtained through recombinant DNA technology.

Molecular weight—Approximately 144,000 daltons.

pH—Adjusted with hydrochloric acid or sodium hydroxide to approximately 6.9.

Mechanism of action/Effect

Daclizumab is an interleukin-2 (IL-2) receptor antagonist that binds to the alpha subunit of IL-2 receptor complex and inhibits IL-2 binding. By inhibiting IL-2 binding, IL-2–mediated activation of lymphocytes is prevented, and the response of the immune system to antigens is impaired.

Distribution

The volume of distribution (Vol_D) is approximately 0.074 L per kg of body weight (L/kg). The central and peripheral volumes of distribution are estimated to be about 0.031 and 0.0425 L/kg, respectively.

Half-life

Elimination—

11 to 38 days.

Peak serum concentration

The peak serum concentration in the five-dose course of treatment occurs after the fifth dose, and is estimated to be 32 ± 22 micrograms per milliliter (mcg/mL).

Therapeutic serum concentration

5 to 10 mcg/mL.

Precautions to Consider

Carcinogenicity

Studies have not been done to evaluate the carcinogenic potential of daclizumab. In the pre-approval trials of daclizumab, there was not an increased incidence of lymphoproliferative disorders in the daclizumab-treated patients. Long-term follow-up studies are not available in these patients. However, it is known that patients receiving immunosuppressive therapy are at increased risk for developing malignancies.

Mutagenicity

Daclizumab was not mutagenic in the Ames test or the V79 chromosomal aberration assay, with or without activation.

Pregnancy/Reproduction

Fertility—Adequate and well-controlled studies have not been done.

Pregnancy—Daclizumab crosses the placenta. Adequate and well-controlled studies have not been done in humans.

FDA Pregnancy Category C.

Breast-feeding

It is not known whether daclizumab is distributed into breast milk. The manufacturer recommends that patients receiving daclizumab discontinue breast-feeding.

Pediatrics

Appropriate studies on the relationship of age to the effects of daclizumab have not been performed in pediatric patients. Preliminary data from the use of daclizumab in 25 pediatric patients 11 months to 17 years of age suggest that pediatric patients receiving daclizumab may experience more hypertension and dehydration than adult patients. Although pediatric patients receiving the same weight-adjusted dose as adults (i.e., 1 milligram per kilogram of body weight [mg/kg]) had lower serum concentrations than did adult patients, the dose was sufficient to saturate the alpha subunit of the interleukin-2 (IL-2) receptor on lymphocytes.

Geriatrics

No information is available on the relationship of age to the effects of daclizumab in geriatric patients.

Dental

The immunosuppressive effects of daclizumab may result in an increased incidence of certain microbial infections and delayed healing. Dental work, whenever possible, should be completed prior to initiation of therapy and undertaken with caution during therapy. Patients should be instructed in proper oral hygiene.

Drug interactions and/or related problems

Note: In clinical trials, daclizumab was administered to patients receiving other immunosuppressants (antilymphocyte globulin, antithymocyte globulin, azathioprine, corticosteroids, cyclosporine, muromonab-CD3, mycophenolate mofetil, and tacrolimus) and anti-infectives (acyclovir and ganciclovir). No drug interactions have been evaluated or reported with daclizumab.

Laboratory value alterations

The following have been selected on the basis of their potential clinical significance (possible effect in parentheses where appropriate)—not necessarily inclusive (» = major clinical significance).

With physiology/laboratory test values
Glucose, blood
(concentration may be increased)

Medical considerations/Contraindications

The medical considerations/contraindications included have been selected on the basis of their potential clinical significance (reasons given in parentheses where appropriate)—not necessarily inclusive (» = major clinical significance).

Except under special circumstances, this medication should not be used when the following medical problem exists:

» Allergy to daclizumab, history of

Note: Anaphylactoid reactions have not been reported following administration of daclizumab. However, anaphylactoid reactions are possible following administration of proteins.

Risk-benefit should be considered when the following medical problems exist:

Diabetes mellitus
(risk of loss of blood glucose control)

Infection
(immunosuppression may exacerbate infection)

Malignancy, current or history of
(immunosuppression is associated with an increased incidence of some malignancies)

Patient monitoring

The following may be especially important in patient monitoring (other tests may be warranted in some patients, depending on condition; » = major clinical significance):

Blood pressure and
Heart rate and
Respiratory rate
(routine monitoring of vital signs is recommended while daclizumab is administered and for a short period of time following the infusion to monitor for anaphylactoid reaction)

Wound infection
(daclizumab may cause an increased risk of wound infection)

Note: Although the incidences of malignancies and systemic infection were not increased in the daclizumab-treated group in pre-approval clinical trials, patients receiving daclizumab should be monitored routinely for malignancy and systemic infection.

Side/Adverse Effects

Note: In clinical trials, the incidence of adverse effects in the daclizumab-treated group was similar to that in the placebo-treated group.

The following side/adverse effects have been selected on the basis of their potential clinical significance (possible signs and symptoms in parentheses where appropriate)—not necessarily inclusive:

Those indicating need for medical attention

Incidence less frequent

Chest pain; dyspnea (shortness of breath); ***fever; hypertension***—usually asymptomatic; ***hypotension*** (dizziness); ***nausea; peripheral edema*** (swelling of feet or lower legs); ***pulmonary edema*** (coughing; shortness of breath); ***tachycardia*** (rapid heartbeat); ***tremor*** (trembling or shaking of the hands or feet); ***vomiting; weakness; wound infection*** (red, tender, or oozing skin at incision)

Incidence rare

Hyperglycemia (frequent urination)

Those indicating need for medical attention only if they continue or are bothersome

Incidence less frequent

Arthralgia (joint pain); ***constipation; diarrhea; dizziness; dyspepsia*** (heartburn); ***headache; insomnia*** (trouble in sleeping); ***myalgia*** (muscle pain); ***slow wound healing***

Overdose

There is no clinical experience with overdose of daclizumab, and a maximum tolerated dose has not been established. Some bone marrow transplant recipients have received 1.5 mg per kg of body weight without any adverse effects.

Patient Consultation

As an aid to patient consultation, refer to *Advice for the Patient, Daclizumab—(Systemic).*

In providing consultation, consider emphasizing the following selected information (» = major clinical significance):

Before using this medication

» Conditions affecting use, especially:
Allergy to daclizumab
Carcinogenicity—Use of daclizumab may be associated with an increased risk of malignancy
Pregnancy—Daclizumab crosses the placenta
Breast-feeding—Use is not recommended
Use in children—Children receiving daclizumab may experience higher incidences of hypertension and dehydration than adult patients
Dental—Dental work should be completed prior to initiation of therapy whenever possible

Proper use of this medication

Proper dosing
Advisability of women of childbearing age using effective contraception before, during, and for several months after receiving daclizumab

Precautions while receiving this medication

» Importance of close monitoring by a physician

Side/adverse effects

Signs of potential side effects, especially chest pain, dyspnea, fever, hypertension, hypotension, nausea, peripheral edema, pulmonary edema, tachycardia, tremor, vomiting, weakness, wound infection and hyperglycemia

General Dosing Information

Daclizumab should be used only by physicians experienced in the management of organ transplant patients. Medications for the treatment of severe hypersensitivity reactions should be immediately available when daclizumab is administered.

Daclizumab must be diluted prior to administration.

Shaking of the vial or prepared solution of daclizumab may cause foaming and should be avoided.

No dosage adjustment is needed for administration to patients with renal function impairment. There are no data for administration to patients with hepatic function impairment.

There is no experience with treating patients with more than one course of therapy with daclizumab.

Parenteral Dosage Forms

DACLIZUMAB STERILE CONCENTRATE FOR INJECTION

Usual adult and adolescent dose

Transplant rejection, kidney (prophylaxis)—
Intravenous infusion over fifteen minutes, 1 mg per kg of body weight every fourteen days for five doses beginning no earlier than twenty-four hours prior to transplantation.

Usual pediatric dose

See *Usual adult and adolescent dose.*

Note: Although testing has not been completed in pediatric patients, preliminary data suggest that the same weight-adjusted dose used in adults is appropriate for pediatric patients.

Usual geriatric dose

See *Usual adult and adolescent dose.*

Strength(s) usually available

U.S.—
5 mg per mL (Rx) [*Zenapax* (sodium phosphate monobasic monohydrate 3.6 mg per mL; sodium phosphate dibasic heptahydrate 11 mg per mL; sodium chloride 4.6 mg per mL; polysorbate 80 0.2 mg per mL)].

Packaging and storage

Store between 2 and 8 °C (36 and 46 °F). Protect from light and freezing.

Preparation of dosage form

Daclizumab must be diluted prior to infusion. The dose may be diluted in 50 mL of 0.9% sodium chloride injection. When the diluted solution is mixed, the bag should be gently inverted. Care should be taken to avoid shaking vials and prepared solutions of daclizumab.

Stability

Daclizumab does not contain preservatives. Prepared solutions of daclizumab should be used within 4 hours. If refrigerated at 4 °C (39 °F), solutions should be used within 24 hours. The prepared solution should be inspected for particulate matter and clarity before administration to the patient, and should be discarded if particulate matter is present.

Incompatibilities

There are no data on the compatibility or incompatibility of other drugs or solutions with daclizumab. Until more data are available, other drugs should not be infused simultaneously through the same intravenous line.

Developed: 04/03/1998

DALTEPARIN Systemic

VA CLASSIFICATION (Primary): BL111

Commonly used brand name(s): *Fragmin*.

Another commonly used name is tedelparin.

Note: For a listing of dosage forms and brand names by country availability, see *Dosage Forms* section(s).

Category

Anticoagulant; antithrombotic

Note: Dalteparin is one of a group of substances known as low molecular weight heparins (LMWHs).

Indications

Note: Bracketed information in the *Indications* section refers to uses that are not included in U.S. product labeling.

General Considerations

The use of low molecular weight heparins (LMWHs) has several advantages compared to heparin. Improved bioavailability at low doses when administered subcutaneously, a longer plasma half-life, and a more predictable anticoagulant response allow for simpler dosing without laboratory monitoring. Studies in animals show that with doses of equivalent antithrombotic effect, LMWHs produce less bleeding than standard heparin. The clinical importance of this observation is uncertain, but may allow the use of higher anticoagulant doses of LMWHs, thereby improving efficacy without compromising safety. The potential advantage of reduced bleeding has been demonstrated in studies in patients receiving high doses for the treatment of venous thrombosis. However, in studies using prophylactic doses, no difference in bleeding has been demonstrated. This contrasting effect may be due to inappropriate dosage regimens in early studies, and the difficulty of measuring hemorrhagic tendencies in humans. LMWHs are associated with a lower incidence of heparin-induced thrombocytopenia, possibly due to reduced effects on platelet function and binding. These advantages must be weighed against the higher cost of the LMWHs, although the simpler dosing regimens used with LMWHs may allow home treatment in selected patients, thereby reducing overall costs and improving patient satisfaction.

Meta-analyses of randomized, controlled trials comparing various LMWHs to unfractionated heparin in the treatment of deep venous thrombosis (DVT) have shown a trend toward greater efficacy, fewer major hemorrhages, and reduced total mortality with the use of LMWHs.

Unfractionated heparin is routinely used during hemodialysis to prevent thrombosis in the extracorporeal system. However, increased risks of bleeding and, with long-term use, complications such as osteoporosis and altered lipid metabolism make it a less-than-ideal agent for this purpose. Dalteparin may have a lower risk of osteoporosis and a reduced stimulation of lipolytic activity, making it an advantageous alternative to heparin in this setting.

Accepted

Angina pectoris, unstable (treatment) and

Myocardial infarction, non–Q-wave (treatment)—Dalteparin is indicated for the treatment of unstable angina pectoris and non–Q-wave myocardial infarction for the prevention of ischemic complications in patients on concurrent aspirin therapy.

Thromboembolism, pulmonary (prophylaxis); and

Thrombosis, deep venous (prophylaxis)—Dalteparin is indicated for prevention of deep venous thrombosis (DVT), which may lead to pulmonary embolism, in patients undergoing abdominal or hip surgery who are at risk for thromboembolic complications.

Patients at risk include patients who are over 40 years of age, obese, undergoing surgery under general anesthesia lasting longer than 30 minutes, or patients who have additional risk factors such as malignancy or a history of DVT or pulmonary embolism.

Note: The use of LMWHs for the above indications has received grade A recommendations (supported by the highest level of evidence) from the Fourth American College of Chest Physicians (ACCP) Consensus Conference on Antithrombotic Therapy. The recommendations are based on the results of studies not only with dalteparin, but with other LMWHs also.

[Thrombosis, deep venous (treatment)]—Dalteparin is used in the treatment of DVT. It has been shown to be as safe and effective as unfractionated heparin when administered subcutaneously or by continuous intravenous infusion.

[Thrombosis of the extracorporeal system during hemodialysis (prophylaxis)]—Dalteparin, given as either a single intravenous injection prior to dialysis, or as a continuous intravenous infusion during dialysis, is used to prevent thrombosis in the extracorporeal system during hemodialysis.

Acceptance not established

Low molecular weight heparins have been used to *prevent venous thromboembolism in patients who have had an ischemic stroke* and have lower extremity weakness. Pooled data indicate that the incidence of leg DVT is 42% in these patients. Dalteparin has been shown to significantly reduce the incidence of DVT when compared with placebo in one small study. However, another placebo-controlled study failed to show a difference, although the dosing regimens used in the studies were not comparable. The Fourth ACCP Consensus Conference on Antithrombotic Therapy considers both low-dose unfractionated heparin and LMWH effective in this setting and gives the indication a grade A recommendation. The optimal prophylactic regimen for dalteparin has not yet been determined.

There have been reports of the use of dalteparin for other conditions, including:

- *long-term anticoagulant therapy following an acute DVT in patients unable to take oral anticoagulants*;
- *prevention of venous thromboembolism following an acute anterior wall myocardial infarction*;
- *maintaining femoropopliteal graft patency*;
- *an alternative to unfractionated heparin in patients with heparin-induced thrombocytopenia (HIT)*;
- *treatment of disseminated intravascular coagulation*; and
- *treatment of proliferative glomerulonephritis*

These reports were either case reports or single studies; therefore, the utility of dalteparin in these situations still requires confirmation with larger follow-up studies. It should be noted that LMWHs are not indicated for the treatment of HIT because of their potential cross-reactivity with heparin, but may have utility in patients who have a negative platelet aggregation test for the selected LMWH.

In addition, the Fourth ACCP Consensus Conference on Antithrombotic Therapy has stated that LMWHs may be used to prevent venous thromboembolism in patients undergoing *total knee replacement* (a grade A recommendation), patients with *acute spinal cord injury* (a grade B recommendation, supported by the second highest level of evidence), patients with *multiple trauma* (a grade C recommendation, supported by the lowest levels of evidence), and in *general medical* patients with clinical risk factors such as congestive heart failure and/or chest infections (a grade A recommendation). However, dalteparin has not been studied in any of these conditions, and its safety and efficacy for these uses are unknown. Until studies are available, use of dalteparin in these conditions can only be determined on a case-by-case basis.

Pharmacology/Pharmacokinetics

Physicochemical characteristics

Source—Obtained by nitrous acid depolymerization of sodium heparin from porcine intestinal mucosa.

Molecular weight—90% of the material is between 2000 and 9000 daltons (average 5000 daltons).

Mechanism of action/Effect

Dalteparin's antithrombotic properties are achieved by enhancing the inhibition of coagulation factor Xa and thrombin (factor IIa) by binding to antithrombin III (ATIII). Unlike heparin, however, dalteparin preferentially potentiates the inhibition of coagulation factor Xa. It is less able to inhibit thrombin because the inactivation of thrombin requires a minimum chain length of 18 saccharides; this chain length is found in only 25 to 50% of low molecular weight heparin molecules. While the ratio of anti-factor Xa activity to anti-factor IIa activity for heparin is 1:1, the ratio for dalteparin is 2.2:1. Dalteparin does not significantly affect clotting tests such as prothrombin time (PT), thrombin time (TT), or activated partial thromboplastin time (APTT).

Other actions/effects

Compared to heparin, dalteparin binds less to endothelial cells. Heparin's binding to these cells affects both lipid metabolism and platelet function. Dalteparin, therefore, produces no significant changes in platelet aggregation, fibrinolysis, platelet factor 4, or lipoprotein lipase.

Absorption
Approximately 90% bioavailable following subcutaneous injection, measured as anti-factor Xa activity.

Protein binding
Very low (< 10%). The much lower protein binding compared to heparin contributes to dalteparin's greater bioavailability and more predictable anticoagulant response.

Half-life
Elimination, apparent, based on anti-factor Xa activity—3 to 5 hours after subcutaneous administration; approximately 2 hours following intravenous injection. May be increased to approximately 6 to 7 hours in patients with impaired renal function.

Time to peak concentration
Approximately 4 hours following subcutaneous injection.

Peak serum concentration
Dose-related. After single subcutaneous doses of 2500, 5000, and 10,000 International Units (IU), peak concentrations of plasma anti-factor Xa activity were 0.19 ± 0.04, 0.41 ± 0.07, and 0.82 ± 0.10 IU/mL, respectively.

Therapeutic plasma concentration
As anti-factor Xa activity—0.2 to 1 IU/mL.

Elimination
Renal.

Precautions to Consider

Cross-sensitivity and/or related problems
Patients with known hypersensitivity to heparin or to pork products may be sensitive to dalteparin also.

Carcinogenicity
No long-term animal studies have been performed with dalteparin to determine its carcinogenic potential.

Mutagenicity
Dalteparin was not mutagenic in the *in vitro* Ames test, the mouse lymphoma cell forward mutation test, the human lymphocyte chromosomal aberration test, and the *in vivo* mouse micronucleus test.

Pregnancy/Reproduction
Fertility—In studies of rats, subcutaneous doses up to 1200 International Units per kg of body weight (IU/kg) did not affect fertility.

Pregnancy—Adequate and well-controlled studies in humans have not been done.

Heparin is considered to be the anticoagulant of choice during pregnancy since it does not cross the placenta. There is also evidence that dalteparin does not cross the placenta. The advantages of dalteparin over heparin during pregnancy include the potential for once-daily administration, a lower incidence of heparin-induced thrombocytopenia, and possibly a lower risk of heparin-induced osteoporosis. However, until adequate clinical studies comparing the use of dalteparin to heparin during pregnancy are performed, there is insufficient evidence to support the routine use of dalteparin.

Studies in pregnant rats and rabbits given intravenous doses of dalteparin up to 2400 IU/kg and 4800 IU/kg, respectively, showed no evidence of harm to the fetus.

FDA Pregnancy Category B.

Note: The 25,000-IU-per-mL multi-dose vial contains benzyl alcohol, which is not recommended for use during pregnancy since benzyl alcohol may cross the placenta.

Breast-feeding
It is not known whether dalteparin is distributed into breast milk. However, problems in humans have not been documented.

Pediatrics
No information is available on the relationship of age to the effects of dalteparin in pediatric patients. Safety and efficacy have not been established.

Note: The 25,000-IU-per-mL multi-dose vial contains benzyl alcohol, which is not recommended for use in neonates.

Geriatrics
Appropriate studies performed to date have not demonstrated geriatrics-specific problems that would limit the usefulness of dalteparin in the elderly.

Pharmacokinetic differences requiring dose reductions have not been noted in elderly subjects. Clinical studies performed in elderly patients have not shown an increase in bleeding.

Drug interactions and/or related problems
The following drug interactions and/or related problems have been selected on the basis of their potential clinical significance (possible mechanism in parentheses where appropriate)—not necessarily inclusive (» = major clinical significance):

Note: Combinations containing any of the following medications, depending on the amount present, may also interact with this medication.

In addition to the interactions listed below, the possibility should be considered that multiple effects leading to further impairment of blood clotting and/or increased risk of bleeding may occur if dalteparin is administered to a patient receiving any medication having a significant potential for causing hypoprothrombinemia, thrombocytopenia, or gastrointestinal ulceration or hemorrhage.

Anticoagulants, coumarin- or indandione-derivative, or
Platelet aggregation inhibitors (see *Appendix II*) such as:
» Anti-inflammatory drugs, nonsteroidal (NSAIDs)
» Aspirin
Dextran
» Ticlopidine
(increased risk of bleeding must be considered)

Thrombolytic agents, such as:
Alteplase (rt-PA)
Anistreplase (APSAC)
Streptokinase
Urokinase
(concurrent or sequential use may increase the risk of bleeding; however, unfractionated heparin is used concurrently with thrombolytic therapy in patients with acute myocardial infarction, and may be continued post-thrombolysis to prevent further thromboembolism; experience with the use of low molecular weight heparin in this setting is limited; careful monitoring of the patient is recommended if dalteparin is used under these circumstances)

Laboratory value alterations
The following have been selected on the basis of their potential clinical significance (possible effect in parentheses where appropriate)—not necessarily inclusive (» = major clinical significance).

With physiology/laboratory test values
Alanine aminotransferase (ALT [SGPT]) and
Aspartate aminotransferase (AST [SGOT])
(serum values may be increased during dalteparin therapy and are reversible; the usefulness of these enzymes in the differential diagnosis of myocardial infarction, pulmonary embolism, or liver disease may, therefore, be decreased)

Free fatty acids and
Triglycerides
(initially, plasma triglyceride concentrations may decrease, with a resulting increase in plasma free fatty acids, due to stimulation of lipolytic activity by release of lipoprotein lipase from tissue sites. However, release of lipoprotein lipase is not as pronounced as that seen with heparin. The subsequent increase in plasma triglyceride concentrations that is seen with long-term heparin use due to depletion of lipoprotein lipase has not been seen with dalteparin. Since the increase in triglyceride concentrations is a particular problem in uremic patients who require chronic hemodialysis and the long-term use of heparin, dalteparin may be advantageous in this population due to its reduced stimulation of lipolytic activity)

Medical considerations/Contraindications
The medical considerations/contraindications included have been selected on the basis of their potential clinical significance (reasons given in parentheses where appropriate)—not necessarily inclusive (» = major clinical significance).

Except under special circumstances, this medication should not be used when the following medical problems exist:
» Bleeding, major, active
(may be exacerbated)

» Hypertension, severe, uncontrolled
(increased risk of cerebral hemorrhage)

» Stroke, hemorrhagic or
» Stroke, ischemic, large
(increased risk of uncontrollable hemorrhage; cardioembolic strokes have a risk of secondary hemorrhagic transformation, with large infarcts [i.e., deficits involving the entire middle cerebral distribution] especially prone to worsening; some clinicians recommend waiting 7 days before initiating anticoagulant therapy in patients with large infarcts)

» Thrombocytopenia associated with positive *in vitro* tests for antiplatelet antibody in the presence of dalteparin or
» Thrombocytopenia, dalteparin- or heparin-induced, history of
(risk of recurrence)

Risk-benefit should be considered when the following medical problems exist:

Any medical procedure or condition in which the risk of bleeding or hemorrhage is present, such as:

» Anesthesia, epidural or spinal
(risk of epidural or spinal hematoma, which can result in long-term or permanent paralysis; this risk is increased with the use of indwelling epidural catheters or by the concomitant use of medications that affect hemostasis, such as nonsteroidal anti-inflammatory drugs, platelet inhibitors, or other anticoagulants; the risk also may be increased by traumatic or repeated epidural or spinal puncture. See *General Dosing Information* for guidelines regarding the use of regional anesthesia in patients receiving perioperative dalteparin.)

» Bleeding disorders, congenital or acquired
» Endocarditis, bacterial
» Hepatic function impairment, severe
» Platelet defects
» Renal function impairment, severe
» Retinopathy, diabetic or hypertensive
» Surgery, brain, ophthalmological, or spinal, recent
» Ulcers, other lesions, or recent bleeding of the gastrointestinal tract, active

Sensitivity to dalteparin or to heparin

Patient monitoring

The following may be especially important in patient monitoring (other tests may be warranted in some patients, depending on condition; » = major clinical significance):

Note: No special monitoring is needed when dalteparin is used prophylactically. Routine clotting assays such as activated partial thromboplastin time (APTT), prothrombin time (PT), or thrombin time (TT) are unsuitable for monitoring dalteparin's anticoagulant activity since dalteparin does not significantly affect these tests; increased doses intended to prolong the APTT could cause overdosing and bleeding. Prolongation of the APTT should only be used as a criterion of overdose.

» Anti-factor Xa activity
(monitoring of plasma anti-factor Xa activity is considered optional when dalteparin is used therapeutically, and is recommended in patients undergoing acute hemodialysis, with recommended plasma concentrations as follows:
- Treatment of deep venous thrombosis—
  Subcutaneous, > 0.3 International Units anti-factor Xa activity per mL (IU/mL) before injection and < 1.5 IU/mL 3 to 4 hours after injection;
  Intravenous, 0.5 to 1 IU/mL
- Acute hemodialysis—0.2 to 0.4 IU/mL)

Blood counts, complete (CBC), including:
Hematocrit
Hemoglobin
» Platelet count
(recommended prior to the initiation of therapy, then twice weekly for the duration of therapy to detect occult bleeding or any degree of thrombocytopenia)

Blood pressure measurement
(recommended periodically during therapy; an unexplained drop in blood pressure may signal occult bleeding)

» Neurologic status
(monitor for signs and symptoms of neurological impairment such as paresthesias, leg weakness, sensory loss, motor deficit, or bowel/bladder dysfunction, which may indicate a potential epidural or spinal hematoma; if neurologic compromise is noted, urgent intervention is necessary, including radiographic confirmation and decompressive laminectomy; good or partial recovery is more likely if surgery is performed within 8 hours of the development of paraplegia)

» Platelet aggregation test
(recommended prior to the initiation of therapy in patients who have congenital, or a history of drug-induced, thrombocytopenia or platelet defects; if the result is negative, dalteparin therapy may be instituted, with daily monitoring of the platelet count; however, if the result is positive, dalteparin should not be given)

Stool tests for occult blood
(should be performed at regular intervals during therapy)

Side/Adverse Effects

Note: The occurrence of hemorrhage may be increased with higher doses. Also, other risk factors may be associated with hemorrhage, including a serious concurrent illness, chronic heavy consumption of alcohol, use of platelet inhibiting drugs, renal failure, and female sex.

Osteoporosis is associated with the use of long-term, high-dose heparin. Dalteparin has been shown to have a weak osteopenic effect in dogs. However, the effect does not appear to be as great as that seen with heparin; therefore, the risk of heparin-induced osteoporosis may be lower with dalteparin.

The following side/adverse effects have been selected on the basis of their potential clinical significance (possible signs and symptoms in parentheses where appropriate)—not necessarily inclusive:

Those indicating need for medical attention

Incidence more frequent

Hematoma at injection site (deep, dark purple bruise, pain, or swelling at place of injection)

Incidence less frequent

Hemorrhage (bleeding gums; coughing up blood; difficulty in breathing or swallowing; dizziness; headache; increased menstrual flow or vaginal bleeding; nosebleeds; paralysis; prolonged bleeding from cuts; red or dark brown urine; red or black, tarry stools; shortness of breath; unexplained pain, swelling, or discomfort, especially in the chest, abdomen, joints, or muscles; unusual bruising; vomiting of blood or coffee ground-like material; weakness)

Incidence rare

Allergic reaction (fever; skin rash, hives, or itching); ***anaphylactoid reaction*** (bluish discoloration, flushing, or redness of skin; coughing; difficulty in swallowing; dizziness or feeling faint, severe; skin rash, hives [may include giant urticaria], or itching; swelling of eyelids, face, or lips; tightness in chest, troubled breathing, and/or wheezing); ***epidural or spinal hematoma*** (back pain; bowel/bladder dysfunction; leg weakness; numbness; paralysis; paresthesias)—back pain is not a typical presentation but some patients may experience this symptom; ***skin necrosis*** (blue-green to black skin discoloration; pain, redness, or sloughing of skin at place of injection); ***thrombocytopenia*** (bleeding from mucous membranes; rash consisting of pinpoint, purple-red spots, often beginning on the legs; unusual bruising)

Note: If an *epidural* or *spinal hematoma* is suspected, urgent intervention is necessary, including radiographic confirmation and decompressive laminectomy. Good or partial recovery is more likely if surgery is performed within 8 hours of the development of paraplegia.

The syndrome of *thrombocytopenia with thrombosis* is a well-known complication of unfractionated heparin therapy. Low molecular weight heparins (LMWHs) are associated with a lower incidence of heparin-induced thrombocytopenia. However, there have been case reports of this complication with LMWHs. Clinicians should be aware of the possible occurrence of thromboembolic events with the use of LMWHs, and should monitor the platelet count appropriately.

Those indicating need for medical attention only if they continue or are bothersome

Incidence less frequent

Pain at injection site

Overdose

For specific information on the agents used in the management of dalteparin overdose, see the *Protamine (Systemic)* monograph.

For more information on the management of overdose, **contact a Poison Control Center** (see *Poison Control Center Listing*).

Clinical effects of overdose

The following effects have been selected on the basis of their potential clinical significance (possible signs and symptoms in parentheses where appropriate)—not necessarily inclusive:

Acute effects

Bleeding complications or hemorrhage (bleeding gums; coughing up blood; difficulty in breathing or swallowing; dizziness; headache; increased menstrual flow or vaginal bleeding; nosebleeds; paralysis; prolonged bleeding from cuts; red or dark brown urine; red or black, tarry stools; shortness of breath; unexplained pain, swelling, or discomfort, especially in the chest, abdomen, joints, or muscles; unusual bruising; vomiting of blood or coffee ground-like material; weakness)

Treatment of overdose

Specific treatment—Administration of protamine, a heparin antagonist, is required. One mg of protamine sulfate (1% solution) per 100 anti-factor Xa International Units (IU) of dalteparin is given as a slow intravenous injection. If the activated partial thromboplastin time (APTT) measured 2 to 4 hours after the first injection remains prolonged, a second injection of 0.5 mg protamine sulfate per 100 anti-factor Xa IU of dalteparin may be administered. However, the APTT may remain more prolonged with dalteparin than with conventional heparin, despite the additional dosing of protamine. In all cases, the anti-factor Xa activity is only neutralized to about 25 to 50%.

Protamine sulfate should be administered with great care to avoid an overdose. Severe hypotensive and anaphylactoid reactions, possibly fatal, may occur with protamine sulfate. It should be administered only when resuscitation techniques and treatment of anaphylactic shock are readily available.

Patient Consultation

As an aid to patient consultation, refer to *Advice for the Patient, Dalteparin (Systemic)*.

In providing consultation, consider emphasizing the following selected information (» = major clinical significance):

Before using this medication

» Conditions affecting use, especially:

Sensitivity to dalteparin, heparin, or pork products

Other medications, especially platelet aggregation inhibitors, such as aspirin, nonsteroidal anti-inflammatory drugs, and ticlopidine

Other medical problems, especially bleeding, major, active; bleeding disorders; endocarditis, bacterial; hepatic function impairment, severe; hypertension, severe, uncontrolled; platelet defects; renal function impairment, severe; retinopathy, diabetic or hypertensive; stroke, hemorrhagic or ischemic; surgery, recent; thrombocytopenia; and ulcers, other lesions, or recent bleeding of the gastrointestinal tract

Proper use of this medication

» Proper injection technique

» Safe handling and disposal of syringe

» Proper dosing

Missed dose: Using as soon as possible; not using if almost time for next dose; not doubling doses

» Proper storage

Precautions while using this medication

» Need to inform all physicians and dentists that this medicine is being used

» Notifying physician immediately if signs and symptoms of bleeding or epidural/spinal hematoma occur

Side/adverse effects

Signs and symptoms of potential side effects, especially hematoma at injection site, hemorrhage, allergic reaction, anaphylactoid reaction, epidural/spinal hematoma, skin necrosis, and thrombocytopenia

General Dosing Information

Dalteparin cannot be used interchangeably (unit for unit) with unfractionated heparin or other low molecular weight heparins.

Dalteparin is administered by deep subcutaneous injection. It must not be injected intramuscularly.

Injection technique: The patient should be sitting or lying down during the injection. Injection sites include a U-shaped area around the navel, the upper outer side of the thigh, or the upper outer quadrant of the buttock. The site should be varied daily. When giving the injection around the navel or the thigh, a fold of skin must be lifted up with thumb and forefinger, and the entire length of the needle should be inserted at a 45- to 90-degree angle.

If a thromboembolic event occurs during dalteparin prophylaxis, dalteparin should be discontinued and appropriate therapy initiated.

Guidelines regarding the use of regional anesthesia in patients receiving perioperative dalteparin

Preoperative dalteparin—A single-dose spinal anesthetic may be the safest neuraxial technique. Needle placement should occur at least 10 to 12 hours after the last dose of dalteparin. Subsequent dosing should be delayed for at least 2 hours after needle placement. The presence of blood during needle placement may justify a delay in the start of postoperative prophylaxis.

Postoperative dalteparin—Patients may safely undergo single-dose and continuous catheter techniques. With a continuous technique, the epidural catheter should be left indwelling overnight and removed the following day, and the first dose of dalteparin should be given 2 hours after catheter removal. Postoperative prophylaxis in the presence of an indwelling catheter must be administered carefully and with close surveillance of the patient's neurologic status. An opioid and/or dilute local anesthetic solution is recommended in these patients to allow intermittent assessment of neurologic function.

The timing of catheter removal is extremely important. Removal should be delayed for at least 10 to 12 hours after a dose of dalteparin. Subsequent dosing should not occur for at least 2 hours following catheter removal.

Parenteral Dosage Forms

Note: Bracketed uses in the *Dosage Forms* section refer to categories of use and/or indications that are not included in U.S. product labeling.

DALTEPARIN SODIUM INJECTION

Usual adult dose

Angina pectoris, unstable (treatment) or
Myocardial infarction, non–Q-wave (treatment)—

Subcutaneous, 120 International Units (IU) per kg of body weight, but not more than 10,000 IU every 12 hours with concurrent aspirin (75 to 165 mg daily) until the patient is clinically stabilized. Concurrent aspirin therapy is recommended except when contraindicated.

Note: In clinical trials, the usual duration of treatment was 5 to 8 days.

Thromboembolism, pulmonary (prophylaxis) and
Thrombosis, deep venous (prophylaxis)—

Abdominal surgery associated with a risk of thromboembolic complications: Subcutaneous, 2500 IU initially, given one to two hours prior to abdominal surgery, then repeated once a day for five to ten days following surgery, until the patient is mobile.

Abdominal surgery associated with a high risk of thromboembolic complications, such as malignant disorder: Subcutaneous, 5000 IU given the evening before the operation, then repeated once a day every evening for five to ten days following surgery, until the patient is mobile. Alternatively, in patients with malignancy 2500 IU given one to two hours prior to surgery and again twelve hours later, followed by 5000 IU each morning for five to ten days following surgery, until the patient is mobile.

Hip replacement surgery: Subcutaneous

- Postoperative Start—2500 IU 4 to 8 hours after surgery, allow a minimum of 6 hours between this dose and the dose given on postoperative day 1. Adjust the timing of the dose on postoperative day 1 accordingly. Postoperative period dose is 5000 IU daily.
- Preoperative Start—Day of surgery: 2500 IU within 2 hours before surgery, allow a minimum of 6 hours between this dose and the dose given on postoperative day 1. Adjust the timing of the dose on postoperative day 1 accordingly. 2500 IU is administered 4 to 8 hours after surgery and 5000 IU is administered daily during the postoperative period.
- Preoperative Start—Evening before surgery: 5000 IU administered 10 to 14 hours before surgery. Allow approximately 24 hours between doses. 5000 IU is given 4 to 8 hours after surgery, and the postoperative dose is 5000 IU daily.

Note: Up to 14 days of treatment was well tolerated in controlled clinical trials, where the average duration of treatment was 5 to 10 days postoperatively.

[Thrombosis, deep venous (treatment)]—

Subcutaneous, 200 IU per kg of body weight once a day, or 100 IU per kg of body weight two times a day. Alternatively, it may be administered at a dose of 200 IU per kg of body weight given as a continuous intravenous infusion over twenty-four hours (i.e., 8.33 IU per kg of body weight per hour). Treatment may be guided by monitoring anti-factor Xa activity. Concomitant treatment with a vitamin K antagonist, such as warfarin, should begin at the same time, and dalteparin should be discontinued when the vitamin K antagonist reaches a full therapeutic effect, usually after five or six days of therapy.

[Thrombosis of the extracorporeal system during hemodialysis (prophylaxis)]—

Chronic renal failure in patients with no known bleeding risk—

Dialysis lasting up to four hours—Intravenous, 5000 IU, as a single injection into the arterial line at the start of dialysis; or dosed as for dialysis procedures of more than four hours" duration.

Dialysis lasting more than four hours—Intravenous loading dose, 30 to 40 IU per kg of body weight followed by a continuous intravenous infusion of 10 to 15 IU per kg of body weight per hour.

Acute renal failure in patients with a high bleeding risk—

Intravenous loading dose, 5 to 10 IU per kg of body weight, followed by a continuous intravenous infusion of 4 to 5 IU per kg of body weight per hour. Therapy should be guided by monitoring anti-factor Xa activity.

Usual pediatric dose

Safety and efficacy have not been established. A case report described the use of dalteparin in a neonate who developed a proximal deep vein thrombosis following balloon valvuloplasty for pulmonary stenosis. Dalteparin was administered subcutaneously at a dose of 100 IU per kg of body weight two times a day for two days, followed by 200 IU per kg of body weight once a day for twelve weeks (administered by the infant's mother at home). No problems were reported during treatment.

Note: The 10,000- and 25,000-IU-per-mL multi-dose vials contain benzyl alcohol, which is not recommended for use in neonates.

Strength(s) usually available

U.S.—

2500 anti-factor Xa IU (16 mg dalteparin sodium) per 0.2 mL (Rx) [*Fragmin* (in single unit-dose syringes)].

5000 anti-factor Xa IU (32 mg dalteparin sodium) per 0.2 mL (Rx) [*Fragmin* (in single unit-dose syringes)].

10,000 anti-factor Xa IU (64 mg dalteparin sodium) per mL (Rx) [*Fragmin* (in 9.5 mL multiple-dose vials; benzyl alcohol 14 mg per mL)].

Canada—

2500 anti-factor Xa IU (16 mg dalteparin sodium) per 0.2 mL (Rx) [*Fragmin* (in single unit-dose syringes)].

5000 anti-factor Xa IU (32 mg dalteparin sodium) per 0.2 mL (Rx) [*Fragmin* (in single unit-dose syringes)].

2500 anti-factor Xa IU (16 mg dalteparin sodium) per mL (Rx) [*Fragmin* (in 4-mL ampuls)].

10,000 anti-factor Xa IU (64 mg dalteparin sodium) per mL (Rx) [*Fragmin* (in 1-mL ampuls)].

25,000 anti-factor Xa IU (160 mg dalteparin sodium) per mL (Rx) [*Fragmin* (in 3.8-mL multi-dose vials; benzyl alcohol 14 mg per mL)].

Packaging and storage

Store at controlled room temperature, between 20 and 25 °C (68 and 77 °F).

Preparation of dosage form

For a continuous intravenous infusion, dalteparin may be diluted in 0.9% sodium chloride injection or 5% dextrose injection in glass or plastic containers. The recommended postdilution concentration is 20 IU per mL, which can be prepared by adding 2500 IU to 125 mL or 10,000 IU to 500 mL of solution. The solution should be used within 24 hours.

Stability

The 25,000-IU-per-mL multi-dose vial must be used within two weeks after initial penetration.

Incompatibilities

Dalteparin sodium injection should not be mixed with other injections or infusions unless compatibility has been established.

Additional information

The 10,000- and 25,000-IU-per-mL multi-dose vials contain benzyl alcohol, which is not recommended for use in neonates. A fatal syndrome consisting of metabolic acidosis, central nervous system depression, respiratory problems, renal failure, hypotension, and possibly seizures and intracranial hemorrhage has been associated with the administration of benzyl alcohol to neonates.

Selected Bibliography

Kakkar VV, Cohen AT, Edmonson RA, et al. Low molecular weight versus standard heparin for prevention of venous thromboembolism after major abdominal surgery. Lancet 1993; 341: 259-65.

Green D, Hirsh J, Heit J, et al. Low molecular weight heparin: a critical analysis of clinical trials. Pharmacol Rev 1994; 46: 89-109.

Dalen JE, Hirsh J, editors. Fourth ACCP Consensus Conference on Antithrombotic Therapy. Chest 1995; 108(Suppl): 225S-522S.

Revised: 12/18/2000
Developed: 01/06/1996

DANAPAROID Systemic

VA CLASSIFICATION (Primary): BL112

Another commonly used name is ORG 10172.

Note: For a listing of dosage forms and brand names by country availability, see *Dosage Forms* section(s).

Category

Antithrombotic

Note: Danaparoid has been categorized as one of a group of substances known as low molecular weight heparins (LMWHs), although it is technically a heparinoid.

Indications

Accepted

Thromboembolism, pulmonary (prophylaxis) and
Thrombosis, deep venous (prophylaxis)—Danaparoid is indicated for the prevention of postoperative deep venous thrombosis (DVT), which may lead to pulmonary embolism (PE), in patients undergoing elective hip replacement surgery.

Pharmacology/Pharmacokinetics

Physicochemical characteristics

Source—Isolated from porcine intestinal mucosa.

Composition—

Depolymerized mixture of low molecular weight sulfated glycosaminoglycans, consisting of approximately 84% heparan sulfate, approximately 12% dermatan sulfate, and approximately 4% chondroitin sulfates.

Molecular weight—Approximately 5500 daltons (average).

Mechanism of action/Effect

Danaparoid prevents fibrin formation in the coagulation pathway by inhibiting thrombin generation through the inhibition of coagulation factor Xa and thrombin (factor IIa). Unlike heparin, however, danaparoid preferentially potentiates the inhibition of coagulation factor Xa, with a ratio of anti-factor Xa activity to anti-factor IIa activity greater than 22:1. Danaparoid has little effect on clotting assays such as prothrombin time (PT), partial thromboplastin time (PTT), and bleeding time.

Other actions/effects

Danaparoid has only minor effects on platelet function, platelet aggregability, and fibrinolytic activity.

Absorption

Approximately 100% bioavailable following subcutaneous injection, measured as anti-factor Xa activity.

Half-life

Elimination—approximately 24 hours (average).

Time to peak concentration

Approximately 2 to 5 hours following subcutaneous injection.

Peak serum concentration

Dose-related. After single subcutaneous doses of 750, 1500, 2250, and 3250 anti-factor Xa units, peak concentrations of plasma anti-factor Xa activity were 102.4, 206.1, 283.9, and 403.4 microunits per mL, respectively.

Elimination

Renal. In patients with severely impaired renal function, the elimination half-life of plasma anti-factor Xa activity may be prolonged.

Precautions to Consider

Cross-sensitivity and/or related problems

Patients hypersensitive to heparin or to pork products may be sensitive to danaparoid also.

Carcinogenicity

No long-term animal studies have been performed with danaparoid to determine its carcinogenic potential.

Mutagenicity

Danaparoid was not mutagenic in the Ames test, the *in vitro* CHL/HGPRT forward gene mutation assay, the *in vitro* CHO cell chromosome aberration test, the *in vitro* HeLa cell unscheduled DNA synthesis (UDS) test or the *in vivo* mouse micronucleus test.

Pregnancy/Reproduction

Fertility—In studies in rats, intravenous doses of up to 1090 anti-factor Xa units per kg of body weight (units/kg) per day (up to 5.9 times the human subcutaneous dose on a body surface area basis) did not affect fertility or reproductive performance.

Pregnancy—Adequate and well-controlled studies in humans have not been done.

Studies in pregnant rats and rabbits given intravenous doses of danaparoid up to 1600 units/kg per day (up to 8.7 times the human dose on a body surface area basis) and up to 780 units/kg per day (up to 6 times the human dose on a body surface area basis), respectively, showed no evidence of harm to the fetus.

FDA Pregnancy Category B.

Breast-feeding

It is not known whether danaparoid is distributed into breast milk. However, problems in humans have not been documented.

Pediatrics

No information is available on the relationship of age to the effects of danaparoid in pediatric patients. Safety and efficacy have not been established.

Geriatrics

No information is available on the relationship of age to the effects of danaparoid in geriatric patients.

Drug interactions and/or related problems

The following drug interactions and/or related problems have been selected on the basis of their potential clinical significance (possible mechanism in parentheses where appropriate)—not necessarily inclusive (» = major clinical significance):

Note: Combinations containing any of the following medications, depending on the amount present, may also interact with this medication.

Anticoagulants, coumarin- or indandione-derivative or
Platelet aggregation inhibitors
(increased risk of bleeding must be considered; the results of the prothrombin time [PT] and *Thrombotest*™, used for monitoring oral anticoagulant activity, are unreliable within 5 hours following danaparoid administration)

Medical considerations/Contraindications

The medical considerations/contraindications included have been selected on the basis of their potential clinical significance (reasons given in parentheses where appropriate)—not necessarily inclusive (» = major clinical significance).

Except under special circumstances, this medication should not be used when the following medical problems exist:

» Bleeding, major, active
(may be exacerbated)

» Hypertension, severe, uncontrolled
(increased risk of cerebral hemorrhage)

» Stroke, hemorrhagic
(increased risk of uncontrollable hemorrhage)

Note: Danaparoid exhibits a low cross-reactivity with antiplatelet antibodies in individuals with Type II heparin-induced thrombocytopenia (HIT).

» Thrombocytopenia associated with positive *in vitro* tests for antiplatelet antibody in the presence of danaparoid
(risk of recurrence)

Risk-benefit should be considered when the following medical problems exist:

Any medical procedure or condition in which the risk of bleeding or hemorrhage is present, such as: (risk of epidural or spinal hematoma, which can result in long-term or permanent paralysis; this risk is increased with the use of indwelling epidural catheters or by the concomitant use of medications that affect hemostasis, such as nonsteroidal anti-inflammatory drugs, platelet inhibitors, or other anticoagulants; the risk may also be increased by traumatic or repeated epidural or spinal puncture)

» Anesthesia, epidural or spinal
» Blood dyscrasias, hemorrhagic, congenital or acquired
» Endocarditis, bacterial
» Renal function impairment, severe
» Stroke, nonhemorrhagic
» Surgery, especially brain, spinal, or ophthalmologic
» Ulceration, other lesions, or recent bleeding of the gastrointestinal tract, active

Sensitivity to danaparoid, heparin, pork products, or sulfites
(patients sensitive to sulfites may be sensitive to danaparoid injection because it contains sodium sulfite; sulfite sensitivity is seen more frequently in asthmatic than in nonasthmatic patients, and may result in allergic-type reactions, including anaphylactic symptoms and life-threatening or less severe asthmatic episodes)

Patient monitoring

The following may be especially important in patient monitoring (other tests may be warranted in some patients, depending on condition; » = major clinical significance):

Note: Since danaparoid has only a small effect on factor IIa activity, routine coagulation tests such as prothrombin time (PT), activated partial thromboplastin time (APTT), kaolin cephalin clotting time (KCCT), whole blood clotting time (WBCT), and thrombin time (TT) are unsuitable for monitoring danaparoid activity at recommended doses.

Patients with a serum creatinine ≥ 2 mg per deciliter should be carefully monitored, since danaparoid's activity may be prolonged in these patients.

» Blood counts, complete (CBC), including
Hematocrit
Platelet count
(recommended during treatment to detect occult bleeding or any degree of thrombocytopenia)

Blood pressure measurement
(recommended periodically during therapy; an unexplained drop in blood pressure may signal occult bleeding)

» Neurologic status
(frequent monitoring for signs and symptoms of neurological impairment is recommended; if neurologic compromise is noted, urgent treatment is necessary)

Stool tests for occult blood
(should be performed at regular intervals during therapy)

Side/Adverse Effects

The following side/adverse effects have been selected on the basis of their potential clinical significance (possible signs and symptoms in parentheses where appropriate)—not necessarily inclusive:

Note: No cases of *white clot syndrome* or *Type II thrombocytopenia* have been reported in clinical studies for the prophylaxis of deep venous thrombosis in patients receiving multiple doses of danaparoid for up to 14 days.

Those indicating need for medical attention

Incidence less frequent

Fever; hemorrhage (bleeding gums; coughing up blood; difficulty in breathing or swallowing; dizziness; headache; increased menstrual flow or vaginal bleeding; nosebleeds; paralysis; prolonged bleeding from cuts; red or dark brown urine; red or black, tarry stools; shortness of breath; unexplained pain, swelling, or discomfort, especially in the chest, abdomen, joints, or muscles; unusual bruising; vomiting of blood or coffee ground-like material; weakness)

Incidence rare

Epidural or spinal hematoma (back pain; bowel/bladder dysfunction; leg weakness; numbness; paralysis; paresthesias)—back pain is not a typical presentation but some patients may experience this symptom; ***skin rash***

Note: If an *epidural or spinal hematoma* is suspected, urgent intervention is necessary.

Those indicating need for medical attention only if they continue or are bothersome

Incidence more frequent

Pain at injection site

Incidence less frequent

Constipation; nausea

Overdose

For specific information on the agents used in the management of danaparoid overdose, see the *Protamine (Systemic)* monograph.

For more information on the management of overdose, **contact a Poison Control Center** (see *Poison Control Center Listing*).

Clinical effects of overdose

The following effects have been selected on the basis of their potential clinical significance (possible signs and symptoms in parentheses where appropriate)—not necessarily inclusive:

Acute

Bleeding complications, which may include blood in urine; bloody or black, tarry stools; bruising; coughing up blood; ecchymosis (large, non-elevated blue or purplish patches in the skin); ***hematoma; hypochromic anemia*** (fatigue; headache; irritability; lightheadedness); ***nosebleed; persistent bleeding or oozing from mucous membranes or surgical wound; shortness of breath; vomiting of blood or material that looks like coffee grounds***

Treatment of overdose

The effects of danaparoid on anti-factor Xa activity cannot be antagonized with any known agent at this time. Although protamine sulfate partially neutralizes the anti-factor Xa activity of danaparoid and can be safely coadministered, there is no evidence that protamine sulfate can reduce severe, nonsurgical bleeding during treatment with danaparoid.

Specific treatment—In the event of serious bleeding, danaparoid should be stopped and blood or blood product transfusions should be administered as needed.

Patient Consultation

As an aid to patient consultation, refer to *Advice for the Patient, Danaparoid (Systemic)*.

In providing consultation, consider emphasizing the following selected information (» = major clinical significance):

Before using this medication

» Conditions affecting use, especially:
  Sensitivity to danaparoid, heparin, pork products, or sulfites
  Other medical problems, especially bacterial endocarditis; bleeding; hemorrhagic blood dyscrasias; severe renal function impairment; severe, uncontrolled hypertension; stroke; surgery; thrombocytopenia; and ulcers or other lesions of the gastrointestinal tract

Proper use of this medication

» Proper dosing

Precautions while using this medication

» Need to inform all health care providers of use of medication

» Notifying physician immediately if signs and symptoms of bleeding or epidural/spinal hematoma occur

Side/adverse effects

Signs of potential side effects, especially fever, hemorrhage, epidural or spinal hematoma, and skin rash

General Dosing Information

The anti-factor Xa unit activity of danaparoid is not equivalent to that of heparin or low molecular weight heparins. Therefore, danaparoid cannot be used interchangeably (unit for unit) with unfractionated heparin or any low molecular weight heparin.

Danaparoid is administered by deep subcutaneous injection. **It must not be injected intramuscularly.**

Injection technique: The patient should be lying down during injection. A 25- to 26-gauge needle should be used to minimize tissue trauma. Administration should be alternated between the left and right anterolateral and left and right posterolateral abdominal wall. A fold of skin must be lifted up with thumb and forefinger, and the entire length of the needle should be inserted. The skin fold should be held throughout the injection and should not be pinched or rubbed afterwards.

Parenteral Dosage Forms

DANAPAROID SODIUM INJECTION

Usual adult dose

Thromboembolism, pulmonary (prophylaxis) and
Thrombosis, deep venous (prophylaxis)—
  Subcutaneous, 750 anti-factor Xa units two times a day, beginning one to four hours prior to hip replacement surgery, and then no sooner than two hours after surgery. Treatment should be continued until the risk of deep venous thrombosis has diminished, usually within seven to ten days, but may be continued for up to fourteen days.

Usual pediatric dose

Safety and efficacy have not been established.

Strength(s) usually available

U.S.—
  750 anti-factor Xa units per 0.6 mL (Rx) [*Orgaran* (in single unit-dose syringes; sodium sulfite 0.15% [to prevent discoloration])].
  750 anti-factor Xa units per 0.6 mL (Rx) [*Orgaran* (in 0.6-mL ampuls; sodium sulfite 0.15% [to prevent discoloration])].

Packaging and storage

Ampuls should be stored between 2 and 30 °C (36 and 86 °F). Syringes should be stored between 2 and 8 °C (36 and 46 °F). Protect from light.

Revised: 07/10/1998
Developed: 04/28/1997

DANAZOL Systemic

VA CLASSIFICATION (Primary/Secondary): HS109/IM900

Commonly used brand name(s): *Cyclomen; Danocrine.*

Note: For a listing of dosage forms and brand names by country availability, see *Dosage Forms* section(s).

Category

Gonadotropin inhibitor; angioedema (hereditary) prophylactic.

Indications

Note: Bracketed information in the *Indications* section refers to uses that are not included in U.S. product labeling.

Accepted

Endometriosis (treatment)—Danazol is indicated for the treatment of pain and/or infertility due to endometriosis.

Breast disease, fibrocystic (treatment)—Danazol is indicated for the treatment of fibrocystic breast disease in patients whose symptoms are not relieved by analgesics, the use of well-fitted bras, or other simple methods.

Angioedema, hereditary (prophylaxis)[1]—Danazol is indicated for the prophylactic treatment of hereditary angioedema (cutaneous, abdominal, and laryngeal) in males and females, including prior to surgery.

[Menorrhagia, primary (treatment)]—Danazol is indicated for short-term (up to 6 months) use in the treatment of severe primary menorrhagia at the time of expected menses in women with regular menstrual cycles. Secondary menorrhagia manifest as abnormalities of blood coagulation (e.g., thrombocytopenia, von Willebrand's disease), endocrine disorders (e.g., hypothyroidism), or organic pathology (e.g., fibroids, genital neoplasia, polyps) should be ruled out prior to initiation of therapy.

[Gynecomastia (treatment)][1] or
[Puberty, precocious (treatment)][1]—Danazol is indicated for the treatment of gynecomastia and precocious puberty in females.

[1]Not included in Canadian product labeling.

Pharmacology/Pharmacokinetics

Physicochemical characteristics

Chemical Group—Synthetic androgen.
Molecular weight—337.46.

Mechanism of action/Effect

Gonadotropin inhibitor—Danazol suppresses the pituitary-ovarian axis possibly by inhibiting the output of pituitary gonadotropins. Danazol also depresses the preovulatory surge in output of follicle-stimulating hormone (FSH) and luteinizing hormone (LH) and therefore reduces ovarian estrogen production. Danazol also may directly inhibit ovarian steroidogenesis, bind to androgen, progesterone, and glucocorticoid receptors, bind to sex-hormone-binding globulin and corticosteroid-binding globulin, and increase the metabolic clearance rate of progesterone.

Endometriosis—As a consequence of suppression of ovarian function, both normal and ectopic endometrial tissues become inactive and atrophic. As a result, anovulation and associated amenorrhea occur.

Fibrocystic breast disease—The exact mechanism of action is unknown, but may be related to suppressed estrogenic stimulation as a result of decreased ovarian production of estrogen. A direct effect on steroid receptor sites in breast tissue also is possible. Disappearance of nodularity, relief of pain and tenderness, and possibly changes in the menstrual pattern result.

Hereditary angioedema—Danazol corrects the underlying biochemical deficiency by increasing serum concentrations of the deficient C1 esterase inhibitor, resulting in increased serum concentrations of the C4 component of the complement system.

Other actions/effects

Danazol has weak androgenic effects and significantly decreases concentrations of immunoglobulins, IgA, IgG, and IgM, and also concentrations of phospholipids and IgG isotope autoantibodies in patients with endometriosis and associated elevations of autoantibodies.

Absorption

In studies in female volunteers, the mean time to peak concentration was delayed by food by approximately 30 minutes.

Biotransformation

Hepatic, to principal metabolites, ethisterone and 17-hydroxymethylethisterone.

Half-life

Elimination—Approximately 24 hours.

Onset of action

Endometriosis—Relief of dysmenorrhea and pelvic pain usually occurs within the first few weeks of therapy.

Fibrocystic breast disease—Relief of breast pain and tenderness usually begins within 1 month.

Peak serum concentration

Following a 100-mg dose twice a day—200 to 800 nanograms per mL.

Following a 200-mg dose twice a day for 14 days—250 nanograms to 2 mcg per mL.

Time to peak effect

Anovulation and amenorrhea—Usually occur after 6 to 8 weeks of therapy.

Fibrocystic breast disease—Breast pain and tenderness are usually eliminated after 2 to 3 months of therapy. Elimination of nodularity usually requires 4 to 6 months of uninterrupted therapy.

Duration of action

Anovulation and amenorrhea—Ovulation and cyclic bleeding usually return within 60 to 90 days after therapy is withdrawn.

Fibrocystic breast disease—Symptoms return to some degree within 1 year after therapy is withdrawn in 50% of patients.

Elimination

Renal.

Precautions to Consider

Carcinogenicity

Studies to determine the carcinogenic potential of danazol have not been performed.

Pregnancy/Reproduction

Pregnancy—**Danazol is contraindicated during pregnancy**. Exposure to danazol *in utero* may result in androgenic effects (ambiguous genitalia, clitoral hypertrophy, labial fusion of the external genitalia, urogenital sinus defect, vaginal atresia) in the female fetus.

Unless abstinence is the chosen method, it is recommended that the patient use a form of nonhormonal contraception to prevent pregnancy during therapy. In patients treated for fibrocystic breast disease, nonhormonal contraception should be continued after danazol therapy until a menstrual period that is normal in amount of flow and duration has occurred. If pregnancy occurs during therapy, danazol should be discontinued, and the patient should be made aware of the potential risk to the fetus.

Studies in pregnant rats administered danazol orally at doses of up to 250 mg per kg of body weight (mg/kg) per day (7 to 15 times the human dose) on days 6 through 15 of gestation did not show drug-induced embryotoxicity or teratogenicity or a difference in litter size, viability, or weight of offspring as compared with controls. However, studies in rabbits administered oral doses of 60 mg/kg per day (2 to 4 times the human dose) on days 6 through 18 of gestation showed inhibition in fetal development.

FDA Pregnancy Category X.

Breast-feeding

Nursing mothers should be advised to contact a physician before nursing infants. Use by nursing mothers is not recommended because of possible androgenic effects in the infant, such as precocious sexual development in males and virilization in females.

Pediatrics

Caution is recommended in children and growing adolescents who are being treated for hereditary angioedema, because of possible androgenic effects, such as precocious sexual development in males and virilization in females. Premature epiphyseal closure also may occur.

Geriatrics

No information is available on the relationship of age to the effects of danazol in geriatric patients.

Treatment of geriatric male patients with androgens may cause increased risk of prostatic hyperplasia or prostatic carcinoma.

Drug interactions and/or related problems

The following drug interactions and/or related problems have been selected on the basis of their potential clinical significance (possible mechanism in parentheses where appropriate)—not necessarily inclusive (» = major clinical significance):

» Anticoagulants, coumarin- or indanedione-derivative
(concurrent use with danazol may enhance effects of anticoagulants because of decreased hepatic synthesis of procoagulant factors, and may cause bleeding)

Antidiabetic agents, oral or
Insulin
(danazol may increase blood glucose concentrations and resistance to insulin due to changes in the metabolism of carbohydrates; dosage adjustment of the antidiabetic agent or insulin may be necessary)

Carbamazepine
(concurrent use may cause inhibition of carbamazepine metabolism, resulting in increased plasma concentrations and toxicity)

Cyclosporine or
» Tacrolimus
(danazol may increase plasma concentrations of cyclosporine and tacrolimus and may increase the risk of nephrotoxicity)

Glucagon
(danazol may increase the plasma concentrations of glucagon)

Laboratory value alterations

The following have been selected on the basis of their potential clinical significance (possible effect in parentheses where appropriate)—not necessarily inclusive (» = major clinical significance).

With diagnostic test results
Glucose tolerance test
(results may be impaired)

With physiology/laboratory test values
Alanine aminotransferase (ALT [SGPT]) or
Aspartate aminotransferase (AST [SGOT])
(values may be increased early in therapy and decreased toward baseline later in therapy; values generally return to baseline within one month following therapy)

Aldosase or
Creatine kinase (CK)
(concentrations may be increased in the presence of muscle toxicity or rhabdomyolysis)

Androstenedione, serum or
Dehydroepiandrosterone (DHEA) sulfate or
Testosterone, free and total
(concentrations may be abnormal)

Blood pressure
(may be increased as a result of volume expansion)

Cholic acid, serum or
Cholic acid-to-chenodeoxycholic acid, serum ratio
(fasting concentrations may be increased during therapy but generally return to baseline within one month following therapy)

Delta aminolevulinic acid (ALA), urine
(concentrations may be increased in response to induction of ALA dehydratase activity by danazol)

Glucose, blood or
Lipoproteins, low-density
(concentrations may be increased)

Lipoproteins, high-density
(concentrations may be decreased)

Prothrombin time
(may be prolonged in patients taking coumarin- or indanedione-derivative anticoagulants)

Thyroid function tests
(total serum thyroxine [T_4] may be decreased, and triiodothyroxine [T_3] uptake may be increased; however, free T_4 and thyroid-stimulating hormone [TSH] remain normal because of a concomitant decrease in thyroxine-binding globulin [TBG])

Medical considerations/Contraindications

The medical considerations/contraindications included have been selected on the basis of their potential clinical significance (reasons given in parentheses where appropriate)—not necessarily inclusive (» = major clinical significance).

Except under special circumstances, this medication should not be used when the following medical problems exist:

» Cardiac function impairment, severe
» Genital neoplasia
» Hepatic function impairment, severe
» Porphyria
(may be exacerbated)
» Renal function impairment, severe
» Thromboembolic disease or thrombosis, active or history of
» Tumor, androgen-dependent
» Vaginal bleeding, undiagnosed, abnormal

Risk-benefit should be considered when the following medical problems exist:

Cardiac function impairment or
Epilepsy or
Migraine headaches or
Renal function impairment
(may be aggravated by fluid retention induced by danazol)

Diabetes mellitus
(possible impairment of glucose tolerance)

Sensitivity to anabolic steroids, androgens, or danazol

Patient monitoring

The following may be especially important in patient monitoring (other tests may be warranted in some patients, depending on condition; » = major clinical significance):

Biopsy of cysts or

Mammography
(recommended prior to initiation of treatment for fibrocystic breast disease to rule out carcinoma; recommended during treatment if nodules persist or enlarge)

» Hepatic function determinations
(recommended at periodic intervals during therapy)

» Pregnancy test
(recommended immediately prior to treatment of endometriosis or fibrocystic breast disease, if treatment is not started during menstruation or if the patient has irregular menstrual cycles)

Semen analysis
(recommended every 3 to 4 months, especially in adolescents, to assess motility, viscosity, volume, and total count of spermatozoa)

Side/Adverse Effects

The following side/adverse effects have been selected on the basis of their potential clinical significance (possible signs and symptoms in parentheses where appropriate)—not necessarily inclusive:

Those indicating need for medical attention

Incidence more frequent

In females

Amenorrhea (stopping of menstrual periods); ***breakthrough bleeding*** (heavier, irregular vaginal bleeding between regular menses); ***decrease in breast size; irregular menstrual periods; spotting*** (lighter, irregular vaginal bleeding between regular menses); ***weight gain***

Note: *Amenorrhea* occurs in most patients treated for endometriosis. It also occurs in 50% of patients treated for fibrocystic breast disease with doses of 100 mg or more, although anovulation may not occur. Amenorrhea may be prolonged after danazol therapy is discontinued in any patient.

Breakthrough bleeding or *spotting* may occur in the first few months of therapy for endometriosis but does not necessarily indicate a lack of efficacy of the medication.

Irregular menstrual periods occur in 25% of patients treated for fibrocystic breast disease, although anovulation may not occur.

Incidence less frequent

In both females and males

Peripheral edema (rapid weight gain; swelling of feet or lower legs)—dose-related; ***rhabdomyolysis*** (dark-colored urine; muscle cramps or spasms; unusual tiredness or weakness); ***virilization*** (acne; oily hair; oily skin)—dose-related

Incidence rare

In both females and males

Adenoma, hepatocellular; bladder telangiectasia (blood in urine); ***bleeding gums; carpal tunnel syndrome*** (burning, numbness, pain, or tingling in all fingers except smallest finger); ***cataracts*** (gradual blurring or loss of vision); ***cholestatic jaundice***—has occurred during long-term treatment with other 17-alkylated androgens; ***discharge from nipple; eosinophilia*** (general feeling of illness; suddencoughing episodes); ***hepatic dysfunction*** (yellow eyes or skin)—with doses greater than 400 mg of danazol per day; ***intracranial hypertension, benign*** (decrease in vision; double vision; headache, severe; nausea; papilledema; vomiting); ***leukocytosis*** (chills; cough; eye pain; general feeling of illness; headache; sore throat; unusual tiredness); ***pancreatitis, acute*** (bloating and tenderness of abdomen; fast heartbeat; fever; nausea; pain in upper or middle abdomen, continuing, sudden, and severe; unusual tiredness; vomiting; yellow eyes or skin, transient); ***peliosis hepatis*** (dark-colored urine; fever; hives; light-colored stools; loss of appetite, continuing; nausea; purple- or red-colored spots on body or inside the mouth or nose; sore throat; vomiting)—has occurred during long-term treatment; ***polyneuritis, acute idiopathic*** (numbness; tingling sensation or weakness in both legs, moving upward to both arms, trunk, and face); ***skin rash; Stevens-Johnson syndrome*** (chest pain; cough; diarrhea; fever; general feeling of illness; joint pain; lesions on skin and inside the mouth or nose; muscle aches; sore throat; vomiting); ***thrombocytopenia*** (heavier menstrual periods; more frequent nosebleeds; unusual bruising or bleeding); ***thromboembolism or thrombotic and thrombophlebitic events including stroke*** (chest pain; complete or partial numbness or weakness on one side of body; cough; coughing up blood; difficulty in speaking; difficulty in swallowing; double vision; loss of muscle coordination; nausea; restlessness; shortness of breath; sweating; weakness)—may be life-threatening or fatal; ***or sagittal sinus thrombosis*** (extreme exhaustion; headache)

Note: *Hepatocellular adenoma* and *peliosis hepatis* may be asymptomatic until acute, potentially life-threatening intra-abdominal hemorrhage occurs.

If *benign intracranial hypertension* is suspected, the patient should be monitored for papilledema. If confirmed, danazol use should be immediately discontinued and the patient referred to a neurologist for further evaluation and care.

In females only;

Virilization (enlarged clitoris; hoarseness or deepening of voice; unnatural hair growth)—dose-related

Note: Danazol should be discontinued if symptoms of *virilization*, which may not be reversible, occur to prevent further progression.

In males only;

Abnormalities in semen viscosity and volume, and in sperm count and motility—may occur during long-term therapy; ***testicular atrophy*** (decrease in size of testicles)

Those indicating need for medical attention only if they continue or are bothersome

Incidence less frequent

In both females and males

Hypoestrogenemia (flushing or redness of skin; mood or mental changes; nervousness; sweating)

Incidence rare

In both females and males

Photosensitivity

In females only;

Vaginitis (burning, dryness, or itching of vagina; vaginal bleeding)—hypoestrogenic effect

Patient Consultation

As an aid to patient consultation, refer to *Advice for the Patient, Danazol (Systemic).*

In providing consultation, consider emphasizing the following selected information (» = major clinical significance):

Before using this medication

» Conditions affecting use, especially:
Sensitivity to anabolic steroids, androgens, or danazol
Pregnancy—Use is contraindicated during pregnancy because of possible androgenic effects in the female fetus
Breast-feeding—Use is usually not recommended, because of possible androgenic effects in the infant
Use in children—Caution is recommended because of possible androgenic effects
Other medications, especially coumarin- or indanedione-derivative anticoagulants or tacrolimus
Other medical problems, especially androgen-dependent tumor; genital neoplasia; porphyria; severe cardiac function impairment; severe hepatic function impairment; severe renal function impairment; thromboembolic disease or thrombosis, active or history of; or undiagnosed abnormal vaginal bleeding

Proper use of this medication

» Taking for full time of therapy
» Proper dosing
Missed dose: Taking as soon as possible; not taking if almost time for next dose; not doubling doses
» Proper storage

Precautions while using this medication

Regular visits to physician to check progress during therapy
» Discontinuing therapy if symptoms of virilization (which may not be reversible) occur
Patients with diabetes: May alter blood glucose concentrations
» Possible photosensitivity reactions: caution during exposure to sun or when using sunlamps, tanning booths or beds

For treatment of endometriosis or fibrocystic breast disease:
Possibility of amenorrhea or irregular menstrual periods; checking with physician if regular menstruation does not occur within 60 to 90 days after discontinuation of medication
Advisability of using nonhormonal forms of contraception during therapy; not using oral contraceptives
» Stopping medication and checking with physician if pregnancy is suspected

Side/adverse effects

Signs of potential side effects, especially:
In both females and males—Peripheral edema; rhabdomyolysis; virilization; adenoma, hepatocellular; bladder telangiectasia; bleeding gums; carpal tunnel syndrome; cataracts; cholestatic jaundice; discharge from nipple; eosinophilia; hepatic dysfunction; intracranial

hypertension, benign; leukocytosis; pancreatitis, acute; peliosis hepatis; polyneuritis, acute idiopathic; skin rash; Stevens-Johnson syndrome; thrombocytopenia; and thromboembolism or thrombotic and thrombophlebitic events

In females only—Decrease in breast size, irregular menstrual periods, weight gain, and virilization

In males only—Abnormalities in semen viscosity and volume, and in sperm count and motility and testicular atrophy

General Dosing Information

In the treatment of endometriosis and fibrocystic breast disease, it is recommended that therapy begin with the first day of the menstrual cycle after pregnancy has been ruled out.

Development of amenorrhea is usually evidence of a clinical response to danazol in the treatment of endometriosis, although spotting or bleeding from the atrophic endometrium can still occur.

In the treatment of endometriosis, therapy should be continued uninterrupted for 3 to 6 months, and may be continued for 9 months if necessary.

Dosage requirements for continuous treatment of hereditary angioedema should be individualized on the basis of the patient's clinical response.

It is recommended that danazol treatment be discontinued if symptoms of virilization (which may not be reversible) occur.

Oral Dosage Forms

DANAZOL CAPSULES USP

Usual adult and adolescent dose

Endometriosis—

Moderate to severe: Oral, 400 mg two times a day (beginning Day 1 of menstruation, if possible) for at least three to six months, and may be continued for nine months if necessary.

Mild: Oral, 100 to 200 mg two times a day (beginning Day 1 of menstruation, if possible) for at least three to six months, and may be continued for nine months if necessary.

Note: If symptoms recur after discontinuation of therapy, therapy may be reinstituted.

Fibrocystic breast disease—

Oral, 50 to 200 mg two times a day (beginning Day 1 of menstruation, if possible) for six months or until the symptoms completely disappear, whichever comes first.

Note: If symptoms recur within one year of discontinuation of therapy, therapy may be reinstituted.

Hereditary angioedema, prophylaxis of[1]—

Oral, initially 200 mg two or three times a day until the desired initial response is obtained; then the maintenance dosage is determined by decreasing the initial dosage by 50% or less at intervals of one to three months or longer, depending on the frequency of attacks prior to treatment.

Note: Daily dosage may be increased by up to 200 mg if the condition is not controlled at lower doses.

[Primary menorrhagia]—

Oral, 200 to 400 mg a day, in divided doses (beginning Day 1 of menstruation, if possible), for up to six months.

Note: If no improvement is seen after two or three cycles, therapy should be discontinued and the cause of the excess bleeding reassessed.

Usual adult prescribing limits

800 mg per day.

Usual pediatric dose

Dosage has not been established.

Strength(s) usually available

U.S.—

50 mg (Rx) [*Danocrine*; GENERIC].
100 mg (Rx) [*Danocrine*; GENERIC].
200 mg (Rx) [*Danocrine*; GENERIC].

Canada—

50 mg (Rx) [*Cyclomen*].
100 mg (Rx) [*Cyclomen*].
200 mg (Rx) [*Cyclomen*].

Packaging and storage

Store between 15 and 30 °C (59 and 86 °F), unless otherwise specified by manufacturer. Store in a well-closed container.

[1]Not included in Canadian product labeling.

Revised: 06/09/1999

DAPSONE Systemic

VA CLASSIFICATION (Primary/Secondary): AM900/AP101; AP109; AM700

Commonly used brand name(s): *Avlosulfon*.

Another commonly used name is DDS.

Note: For a listing of dosage forms and brand names by country availability, see *Dosage Forms* section(s).

Category

Antibacterial (antileprosy agent); dermatitis herpetiformis suppressant; antiprotozoal; antifungal.

Indications

Note: Bracketed information in the *Indications* section refers to uses that are not included in U.S. product labeling.

Accepted

Leprosy (treatment)—Dapsone is indicated in combination with other antileprosy agents in the treatment of all types of leprosy (Hansen's disease) caused by *Mycobacterium leprae*.

Dermatitis herpetiformis (treatment)—Dapsone is indicated in the treatment of dermatitis herpetiformis.

[Actinomycotic mycetoma (treatment)]—Dapsone is used in the treatment of actinomycotic mycetoma.

[Cicatricial pemphigoid (treatment)][1]—Dapsone is used in the treatment of desquamative gingival lesions caused by cicatricial pemphigoid.

[Dermatosis, subcorneal pustular (treatment)][1]—Dapsone is used in the treatment of subcorneal pustular dermatosis.

[Granuloma annulare (treatment)][1]—Dapsone is used in the treatment of granuloma annulare.

[Lupus erythematosus, systemic (treatment)][1]—Dapsone is used in the treatment of certain skin lesions of systemic lupus erythematosus, including bullous eruptions and urticarial vasculitis.

[Malaria (prophylaxis)][1]—Dapsone is used in combination with pyrimethamine as secondary agents in the prophylaxis of chloroquine-resistant malaria caused by *Plasmodium falciparum*. Dapsone is also used in combination with pyrimethamine and chloroquine in the prophylaxis of malaria caused by *Plasmodium vivax*.

[Pemphigoid (treatment)][1]—Dapsone is used in the treatment of pemphigoid lesions with oral manifestations.

[Pneumonia, *Pneumocystis carinii* (prophylaxis and treatment)][1]—Dapsone is used in combination with trimethoprim in the treatment of mild to moderate pneumonia caused by *Pneumocystis carinii* (PCP). No difference in efficacy was found in a study comparing the dapsone-trimethoprim combination with oral trimethoprim-sulfamethoxazole. However, studies have shown that dapsone alone appeared to have inferior efficacy for treatment of PCP.

Dapsone has also been used alone in the prophylaxis of PCP.

[Polychondritis, relapsing (treatment)][1]—Dapsone is used in the treatment of relapsing polychondritis.

[Pyoderma gangrenosum (treatment)][1]—Dapsone is used in the treatment of pyoderma gangrenosum.

[1]Not included in Canadian product labeling.

Pharmacology/Pharmacokinetics

Physicochemical characteristics

Molecular weight—248.30.

Mechanism of action/Effect

Antibacterial (antileprosy agent)—Dapsone, a sulfone, is bacteriostatic and probably acts by a mechanism similar to that of the sulfonamides, interfering with folate synthesis. Both have a similar range of antibacterial activity and are antagonized by para-aminobenzoic acid.

Dermatitis herpetiformis suppressant—Mechanism is unknown, but not due to dapsone's bacteriostatic effect. Dapsone may act as an enzyme inhibitor or oxidizing agent. In addition, it has numerous immunologic effects (e.g., immunosuppression), which most likely account for its suppression of dermatitis herpetiformis.

Absorption
Slowly absorbed from the gastrointestinal tract; absorption half-life of 1.1 hours. Overall bioavailability is 70 to 80%; may be less in patients with severe leprosy. An acidic environment is needed for optimal absorption.

Distribution
Well distributed throughout total body water and is found in all tissues, especially liver, muscle, kidneys, and skin. Saliva concentrations are 18 to 27% of corresponding plasma dapsone concentrations. Dapsone also crosses the placenta.

Vol_D—1.5 L per kg (1.9 L per kg when given with pyrimethamine).

Protein binding
Dapsone—Moderate to high (70–90%).

Monoacetyl dapsone (MADDS)—Very high (99%).

Biotransformation
Dapsone is acetylated by *N*-acetyltransferase in the liver to its major metabolite, monoacetyl dapsone (MADDS). MADDS is also deacetylated to dapsone; equilibrium is reached within a few hours. Patients may be divided into slow or fast acetylators. However, unlike with other medications, no relationship has been seen between acetylator type and side effects. There was also no significant difference between the 2 groups in plasma concentrations or pharmacokinetics; therapeutic response was the same in both groups.

Dapsone is also *N*-hydroxylated to dapsone hydroxylamine in the liver by the mixed oxidase system in the presence of oxygen and NADPH, and appears to be responsible for the drug's hematologic toxicity.

Both major metabolites have very low activity and do not contribute to the therapeutic effect of dapsone.

Half-life
10 to 50 hours (average, 30 hours) for both dapsone and MADDS.

Time to peak serum concentration
2 to 6 hours, but variable.

Peak serum concentration
50 mg (single dose)—0.6 to 0.7 mcg/mL.

100 mg (single dose)—1.7 to 1.9 mcg/mL.

100 mg (steady state)—3.1 to 3.3 mcg/mL.

Elimination
Renal—70 to 85% slowly excreted in the urine as dapsone and metabolites; 5 to 15% of dapsone dose excreted in urine by active tubular secretion, and the remainder excreted as metabolites. Metabolites are partly conjugated, primarily as glucuronides and sulfates.

Biliary—Enterohepatic circulation following biliary excretion of free drug also occurs. Because of this, dapsone may persist in the plasma for up to several weeks after therapy is discontinued.

Precautions to Consider

Cross-sensitivity and/or related problems
Patients allergic to dapsone may be allergic to sulfonamides, although this has not been clearly established.

Carcinogenicity/Tumorigenicity
Studies in male rats and female mice have shown that dapsone causes mesenchymal tumors of the spleen and peritoneum. Dapsone has been shown to cause thyroid carcinoma in female rats as well.

Mutagenicity
Dapsone has not been shown to be mutagenic in *Salmonella typhimurium* tester strains 1535, 1537, 1538, 98, or 100, when tested with or without microsomal activation.

Pregnancy/Reproduction
Pregnancy—Dapsone crosses the placenta. Adequate and well-controlled studies in humans and animals have not been done. However, other studies in humans have not shown that dapsone causes adverse effects on reproductive capacity or on the fetus. Dapsone has been recommended for maintenance therapy of pregnant leprosy and dermatitis herpetiformis patients.

FDA Pregnancy Category C.

Breast-feeding
Dapsone is distributed into breast milk. In one case report, the concentration of dapsone in breast milk was approximately 67% of the corresponding serum concentration. The serum dapsone concentration in the nursing infant reached 27% of the mother's serum concentration. In addition, dapsone could potentially cause hemolytic anemia in glucose-6-phosphate dehydrogenase (G6PD)–deficient neonates.

Pediatrics
Appropriate studies on the relationship of age to the effects of dapsone have not been performed in the pediatric population. However, no pediatrics-specific problems have been documented to date. Dapsone is generally not considered to have an effect on the later growth, development, and functional development of the child.

Geriatrics
No information is available on the relationship of age to the effects of dapsone in geriatric patients.

Drug interactions and/or related problems
The following drug interactions and/or related problems have been selected on the basis of their potential clinical significance (possible mechanism in parentheses where appropriate)—not necessarily inclusive (» = major clinical significance):

Note: Combinations containing any of the following medications, depending on the amount present, may also interact with this medication.

Aminobenzoates (PABA)
(concurrent use in the treatment of leprosy is not recommended since aminobenzoates may be absorbed by bacteria preferentially over sulfones, thereby antagonizing the bacteriostatic effect of sulfones; however, aminobenzoates do not antagonize the effect of dapsone in the treatment of dermatitis herpetiformis)

Blood dyscrasia-causing medications (See *Appendix II*)
(dapsone may, on rare occasions, cause an idiosyncratic agranulocytosis, aplastic anemia, or other blood dyscrasias; if concurrent use is required, close observation for myelotoxic effects should be considered)

» Didanosine (ddI)
(concurrent administration of dapsone with ddI may decrease the absorption of dapsone; ddI must be given with a buffer to neutralize stomach acidity in order to increase its absorption, and dapsone requires an acidic environment for optimal absorption; until studies are completed that confirm this interaction, dapsone should be administered at least 2 hours before or 2 hours after ddI is given)

» Hemolytics, other (See *Appendix II*)
(concurrent use with dapsone may increase the potential for toxic side effects)

Rifampin
(concurrent use may stimulate hepatic microsomal enzyme activity, resulting in as much as a 7- to 10-fold decrease in dapsone concentrations; however, dapsone dosage adjustments are not required during concurrent rifampin therapy for leprosy since dapsone concentrations are still higher than the MIC, although they may be required in the treatment of other diseases, such as PCP)

Trimethoprim
(concurrent use with dapsone may increase the plasma concentrations of both dapsone and trimethoprim, possibly due to an inhibition in dapsone metabolism, and/or competition for renal secretion between the 2 medications; increased serum dapsone concentrations may increase the frequency and severity of side effects, especially methemoglobinemia and hemolytic anemia)

Medical considerations/Contraindications
The medical considerations/contraindications included have been selected on the basis of their potential clinical significance (reasons given in parentheses where appropriate)—not necessarily inclusive (» = major clinical significance).

Risk-benefit should be considered when the following medical problems exist:

Allergy to dapsone or sulfonamides

» Anemia, severe or

» Glucose-6-phosphate dehydrogenase (G6PD) deficiency or

» Methemoglobin reductase deficiency
(hemolytic anemia may occur)

Hepatic function impairment
(dapsone may cause toxic hepatitis and cholestatic jaundice; alcoholic liver disease may decrease the plasma protein binding of dapsone, increasing the amount of circulating free drug)

Patient monitoring
The following may be especially important in patient monitoring (other tests may be warranted in some patients, depending on condition; » = major clinical significance):

» Alanine aminotransferase (ALT [SGPT]) and

» Aspartate aminotransferase (AST [SGOT])
(values should be determined prior to and periodically during treatment; dapsone should be discontinued if there is evidence of progressive hepatic damage)

Blood urea nitrogen and

Creatinine, serum
(determinations required periodically during treatment in patients with severely impaired renal function, who may also require a reduction in dose; dapsone should be discontinued in anuric patients)

» Complete blood counts (CBCs) and
» Platelet counts and
» Reticulocyte count
(required prior to treatment, followed by monthly counts for 1 to 3 months, and semi-annually thereafter; in patients with HIV infection, CBCs are recommended every 2 to 3 days for the first 2 to 3 weeks of therapy; if a significant reduction in leukocytes, platelets, or hematocrit occurs, or if there is an increase in the reticulocyte count, dapsone should be discontinued and the patient should be monitored closely)

Glucose-6-phosphate dehydrogenase (G6PD) concentration
(determination recommended in patients at high risk prior to treatment; if a deficiency is found, dapsone should be given with extreme caution since hemolytic effects may be exaggerated; dosage adjustments may be required)

Methemoglobin, serum
(level should be obtained in patients with cyanosis, lightheadedness, fatigue, headache, or shortness of breath; dapsone should be discontinued at a methemoglobin level of > 20%, and treatment with methylene blue should be considered in symptomatic patients with levels > 30%)

Side/Adverse Effects

Note: When dapsone is used in high doses, peripheral motor weakness may occur more frequently.

Fatalities have occurred due to agranulocytosis, aplastic anemia, and other blood dyscrasias. In addition, serious cutaneous reactions, such as exfoliative dermatitis, toxic erythema, erythema multiforme, toxic epidermal necrolysis, morbilliform and scarlatiniform reactions, and erythema nodosum may occur. Dapsone therapy should be promptly discontinued if new or toxic dermatologic reactions occur. However, leprosy reactional states do not require discontinuation of therapy.

A dose-related hemolysis is seen in all patients, with a slight decrease in hemoglobin and an increase in reticulocyte count. Patients with G6PD-deficiency or a decrease in activity in glutathione reductase are more susceptible to hemolysis. A low level of methemoglobinemia also occurs in all patients at recommended doses.

The following side/adverse effects have been selected on the basis of their potential clinical significance (possible signs and symptoms in parentheses where appropriate)—not necessarily inclusive:

Those indicating need for medical attention

Incidence more frequent

Hemolytic anemia (back, leg, or stomach pains; loss of appetite; pale skin; unusual tiredness or weakness; fever); ***hypersensitivity*** (skin rash); ***methemoglobinemia*** (cyanosis—bluish fingernails, lips, or skin; difficult breathing; unusual tiredness or weakness)

Incidence rare

Blood dyscrasias (fever and sore throat; unusual bleeding or bruising; unusual tiredness and weakness); ***exfoliative dermatitis*** (itching, dryness, redness, scaling, or peeling of the skin or loss of hair); ***hepatic damage*** (yellow eyes or skin); ***mood or other mental changes; peripheral neuritis*** (numbness, tingling, pain, burning, or weakness in hands or feet); ***"sulfone syndrome"*** (fever; malaise; exfoliative dermatitis; jaundice; lymphadenopathy; methemoglobinemia; anemia)—a hypersensitivity reaction that usually occurs after 6 to 8 weeks of therapy

Those indicating need for medical attention only if they continue or are bothersome

Incidence rare—usually dose-related

Central nervous system toxicity (headache; insomnia; nervousness); ***gastrointestinal disturbances*** (anorexia; nausea or vomiting)

Overdose

For more information on the management of overdose or unintentional ingestion, **contact a Poison Control Center** (see *Poison Control Center Listing*).

Treatment of overdose

Recommended treatment consists of the following:

To decrease absorption—

Performance of gastric lavage. Gastric emptying of dapsone may be delayed after an overdose, and tablet fragments have been found in stomach returns after lavage as late as 5 to 12 hours post-ingestion.

Administration of activated charcoal (30 grams), concurrently with a cathartic, every 6 hours for at least 48 to 72 hours. Repeated doses of activated charcoal reduce the half-life of dapsone and MADDS by approximately 50% to 12.7 hours.

Specific treatment—

In emergency situations, slow, intravenous administration of methylene blue, 1 to 2 mg per kg of body weight (mg/kg). Methylene blue should not be given to fully expressed G6PD-deficient patients. May be repeated if methemoglobin reaccumulates. A continuous infusion of methylene blue has also been used to prevent toxicity from accidental "over-bolusing" of methylene blue, and permit titration of the infusion to methemoglobin levels. A 0.05% solution in 0.9% sodium chloride is usually started at a rate of 0.1 mg/kg per hour.

Supportive care—Patients in whom intentional overdose is known or suspected should be referred for psychiatric consultation.

Patient Consultation

As an aid to patient consultation, refer to *Advice for the Patient, Dapsone (Systemic)*.

In providing consultation, consider emphasizing the following selected information (» = major clinical significance):

Before using this medication

» Conditions affecting use, especially:
Allergy to sulfonamides
Pregnancy—Dapsone crosses the placenta
Breast-feeding—Dapsone is distributed into breast milk; it may cause hemolytic anemia in G6PD-deficient neonates
Other medications, especially other hemolytics and didanosine
Other medical problems, especially severe anemia, G6PD deficiency, or methemoglobin reductase deficiency

Proper use of this medication

» Proper dosing
Missed dose: Taking as soon as possible; not taking if almost time for next dose; not doubling doses
» Proper storage

For leprosy
» Compliance with full course of therapy, which may take years
» Importance of not missing doses and taking at same time every day

For dermatitis herpetiformis
Possible need for gluten-free diet

For Pneumocystis carinii pneumonia
» Compliance with full course of therapy

Precautions while using this medication

Regular visits to physician to check progress

Checking with physician if no improvement within 2 to 3 months (leprosy), within 1 week (PCP), or within a few days (dermatitis herpetiformis)

Side/adverse effects

Signs of potential side effects, especially hemolytic anemia, blood dyscrasias, hypersensitivity reactions, methemoglobinemia, exfoliative dermatitis, peripheral neuropathy, hepatic damage, "sulfone syndrome", and mood and other mental changes

General Dosing Information

Since bacterial resistance may develop when dapsone is administered alone in the treatment of leprosy, for initial treatment, concurrent administration with rifampin is generally recommended. Clofazimine, ethionamide, or prothionamide (investigational) may be used in place of rifampin, but they are considered less effective.

Dapsone therapy should be discontinued promptly if new or toxic dermatologic reactions occur. However, leprosy reactional states do not require discontinuation of therapy. Large doses of corticosteroids should be given if severe "reversal" reactions (type 1) or neuritis occurs during treatment of leprosy.

Depending on the drug regimen used, therapy may have to be continued for 6 months to 3 years or more in indeterminate and tuberculoid leprosy, 2 to 10 years in borderline (dimorphous) leprosy, and 2 years to life in lepromatous leprosy.

In the treatment of dermatitis herpetiformis, a gluten-free diet for 6 months may allow a reduction in dose by approximately 50% or discontinuation of dapsone.

Oral Dosage Forms

Note: Bracketed uses in the *Dosage Forms* section refer to categories of use and/or indications that are not included in U.S. product labeling.

DAPSONE TABLETS USP

Usual adult and adolescent dose

Leprosy (Hansen's disease)—
Oral, in combination with one or more other antileprosy agents, 50 to 100 mg of dapsone once a day; or 1.4 mg per kg of body weight once a day.

Dermatitis herpetiformis suppressant—
Oral, initially 50 mg daily. Doses may be increased up to 300 mg daily if symptoms are not completely controlled. The dose should then be reduced to the lowest effective maintenance dose as soon as possible.

[Actinomycotic mycetoma]—
Oral, 100 mg twice a day for several months after clinical symptoms have disappeared.

[Dermatosis, subcorneal pustular][1]—
Oral, initially 100 mg once a day, increasing the dose by 50 mg every one to two weeks until remission occurs. The dose should then be gradually reduced to the lowest effective maintenance dose.

[Granuloma annulare][1]—
Oral, 100 mg once a day.

[Malaria (prophylaxis)][1]—
Oral, 100 mg of dapsone in combination with 12.5 mg of pyrimethamine once every seven days.

[Pneumonia, *Pneumocystis carinii*][1]—
Treatment: Oral, 100 mg of dapsone once a day in combination with 20 mg per kg of body weight per day of trimethoprim, for twenty-one days.
Prophylaxis: Oral, 50 to 100 mg once a day.

[Polychondritis, relapsing][1]—
Oral, 100 mg once or twice a day.

[Pyoderma gangrenosum][1]—
Oral, 50 to 100 mg once a day, in combination with other medications.

Usual adult prescribing limits

Leprosy (Hansen's disease)—
Up to 100 mg daily.

Dermatitis herpetiformis suppressant—
Up to 300 mg daily.

Polychondritis, relapsing[1]—
Up to 200 mg daily.

Usual pediatric dose

Leprosy (Hansen's disease)—
Oral, in combination with one or more other antileprosy agents, 1.4 mg of dapsone per kg of body weight once a day.

Dermatitis herpetiformis suppressant—
Oral, initially 2 mg per kg of body weight daily. Doses may be increased if symptoms are not completely controlled. The dose should then be reduced to the lowest effective maintenance dose as soon as possible.

[Pneumonia, *Pneumocystis carinii* (prophylaxis)][1]—
In children older than 1 month of age: Oral, 1 mg per kg of body weight, up to 100 mg daily.

Strength(s) usually available

U.S.—
25 mg (Rx) [GENERIC (may be scored)].
100 mg (Rx) [GENERIC (may be scored)].

Canada—
100 mg (Rx) [*Avlosulfon* (scored)].

Packaging and storage

Store below 40 °C (104 °F), preferably between 15 and 30 °C (59 and 86 °F), unless otherwise specified by manufacturer. Store in a well-closed, light-resistant container.

Auxiliary labeling

- Continue medicine for full time of treatment (for leprosy and PCP).

---

[1]Not included in Canadian product labeling.

Revised: 03/17/1994

DAPSONE Topical†

VA CLASSIFICATION (Primary): DE752

Commonly used brand name(s): *Aczone.*

Note: For a listing of dosage forms and brand names by country availability, see *Dosage Forms* section(s).

†Not commercially available in Canada.

Category

Antiacne agent.

Indications

Accepted

Acne vulgaris (treatment)—Dapsone is indicated for the topical treatment of acne vulgaris.

Pharmacology/Pharmacokinetics

Physicochemical characteristics

Molecular weight—Dapsone: 248.

Mechanism of action/Effect

The mechanism of action of dapsone gel in treating acne vulgaris is not known.

Absorption

In a pharmacokinetic study of dapsone gel 5% applied twice daily for 14 days (110 +/- 60 mg/day), the mean $AUC_{0-24\,h}$ was 415 +/- 224 ng h/mL; however, following a single 100 mg dose of oral dapsone the $AUC_{infinity}$ was 52,641 +/- 36,223 ng h/mL.

Precautions to Consider

Carcinogenicity

Studies done in female rats given oral dapsone for 92 weeks and male rats for 100 weeks at doses up to 15 mg/kg/day revealed no carcinogenic potential.

Dapsone did not induce carcinogenicity in mice administered topical doses of dapsone gel in concentrations of 3%, 5% and 10%.

Tumorigenicity

Dapsone gel 5% did not increase the rate of formation of ultra violet light-induced skin tumors when topically applied to hairless mice in a 12-month photocarcinogenicity study.

Mutagenicity

Dapsone was not mutagenic in a bacterial reverse mutation assay (Ames test) with *S. typhimurium* and *E. coli* with and without metabolic activation and was negative in a micronucleus assay with mice. However, dapsone increased both number and structural aberrations in a chromosome aberration assay in Chinese hamster ovary cells.

Pregnancy/Reproduction

Fertility—Fertility studies done in male rats given oral doses of dapsone 3 mg/kg/day or greater reduced sperm motility. Reduced numbers of embryo implantations and viable embryos in untreated females mated with treated males given doses of dapsone at 12 mg/kg/day were observed indicating impairment of fertility. Dapsone had no effect on male fertility at dosages of 2 mg/kg/day or less. Female rats given doses of dapsone 75 mg/kg/day for 15 days prior to mating and for 17 days thereafter, reduced the number of implantations, increased the mean early resorption rate, and reduced the mean liter size.

Dapsone orally administered to female rats at doses of 30 mg/kg/day from gestation day 7 through 27 days postpartum revealed maternal toxicity including decreased body weight and food consumption, and developmental effects including, increase in still born pups and decreased pup weight. No effects were observed on viability, physical development, behavior, learning ability, or reproductive function of surviving pups.

Pregnancy—Adequate and well controlled studies in pregnant women have not been done. Studies in animals have shown that dapsone causes adverse effects in the fetus. Dapsone gel 5% should be used during pregnancy only if the potential benefit justifies the potential risk to the fetus.

Embryocidal effects were observed in studies done in rats and rabbits given doses of dapsone at 75 mg/kg/day (approximately 800 and 500 times the systemic exposure observed in human females as a result of use of the maximum recommended topical dose, based on AUC comparisons).

FDA Pregnancy Category C

Breast-feeding

Dapsone is distributed into human milk; however, topical application is minimal relative to oral dapsone administration. Because of the potential for oral dapsone to cause adverse effects in nursing infants, a decision should be made whether to discontinue nursing or to discontinue dapsone, taking into account the importance of the drug to the mother.

Pediatrics

Safety and efficacy have not been established in pediatric patients under 12 years of age.

Geriatrics

Appropriate studies on the relationship of age to the effects of dapsone have not been performed in the geriatric population.

Pharmacogenetics

Female patients had greater percent reductions in lesions and greater success on the Global Acne Assessment Score than males.

Drug interactions and/or related problems

The following drug interactions and/or related problems have been selected on the basis of their potential clinical significance (possible mechanism in parentheses where appropriate)—not necessarily inclusive (» = major clinical significance):

Note: Combinations containing any of the following medications, depending on the amount present, may also interact with this medication.

Anticonvulsants or
Rifampin or
St. John's Wort
(may increase metabolite dapsone hydroxylamine which is associated with hemolysis)

Pyrimethamine
(may increase risk of hematologic reactions)

Trimethoprim/sulfamethoxazole
(levels of dapsone and its metabolites are increased; AUC_{0-12} of dapsone and N-acetyl-dapsone increase 40% and 20%)

Laboratory value alterations

The following have been selected on the basis of their potential clinical significance (possible effect in parentheses where appropriate)—not necessarily inclusive (» = major clinical significance).

» Hemoglobin
(may be decreased in patients with G6PD deficiency)

» Reticulocyte count
(may be increased in patients with G6PD deficiency)

Medical considerations/Contraindications

The medical considerations/contraindications included have been selected on the basis of their potential clinical significance (reasons given in parentheses where appropriate)—not necessarily inclusive (» = major clinical significance).

Except under special circumstances, this medication should not be used when the following medical problem exists:

» Hypersensitivity to dapsone or to any component of the formulation

Risk-benefit should be considered when the following medical problems exist:

» Anemia, history of or
» Hemoglobin M or
» Glucose-6-phosphate dehydrogenase (G6PD) deficiency or
» Methemoglobin reductase deficiency
(hemolysis may be exaggerated)

Patient monitoring

The following may be especially important in patient monitoring (other tests may be warranted in some patients, depending on condition; » = major clinical significance):

» Complete blood counts (CBCs) and
» Reticulocyte count
(required prior to treatment in patients who are G6PD deficient; routine follow-up should be implemented for patients at risk; if signs, symptoms or laboratory evidence of anemia develop during treatment, dapsone should be discontinued)

» Glucose 6-phosphate dehydrogenase level
(obtain in all patients prior to starting topical dapsone therapy)

Side/Adverse Effects

The following side/adverse effects have been selected on the basis of their potential clinical significance (possible signs and symptoms in parentheses where appropriate)—not necessarily inclusive:

Those indicating need for medical attention

Incidence unknown

Abdominal pain (stomach pain); ***pancreatitis*** (bloating; chills; constipation; darkened urine; fast heartbeat; fever; indigestion; loss of appetite; nausea; pains in stomach, side, or abdomen, possibly radiating to the back; vomiting; yellow eyes or skin); ***pharyngitis*** (body aches or pain; congestion; cough; dryness or soreness of throat; fever; hoarseness; runny nose; tender, swollen glands in neck; trouble in swallowing; voice changes); ***suicidal behavior*** (attempts at killing oneself); ***tonic and clonic muscle movements; vomiting, severe***

Reported in clinical trials

Depression (discouragement; feeling sad or empty; irritability; lack of appetite; loss of interest or pleasure; tiredness; trouble concentrating; trouble sleeping); ***psychosis*** (feeling that others can hear your thoughts; feeling that others are watching you or controlling your behavior; feeling, seeing, or hearing things that are not there; severe mood or mental changes; unusual behavior)

Those indicating need for medical attention only if they continue or are bothersome

Incidence more frequent

Dryness; erythema (flushing, redness of skin; unusually warm skin); ***oiliness/peeling***

Incidence less frequent

Burning; cough; headache; influenza (chills; cough; diarrhea; fever; general feeling of discomfort or illness; headache; joint pain; loss of appetite; muscle aches and pains; nausea; runny nose; shivering; sore throat; sweating; trouble sleeping; unusual tiredness or weakness; vomiting); ***joint sprain; nasopharyngitis*** (stuffy or runny nose; muscle aches; unusual tiredness or weakness; fever; sore throat; headache); ***pharyngitis*** (body aches or pain; congestion; cough; dryness or soreness of throat; fever; hoarseness; runny nose; tender, swollen glands in neck; trouble in swallowing; voice changes); ***pruritus*** (itching skin); ***pyrexia*** (fever); ***sinusitis*** (pain or tenderness around eyes and cheekbones; fever; stuffy or runny nose; headache; cough; shortness of breath or troubled breathing; tightness of chest or wheezing); ***upper respirator tract infection*** (ear congestion; nasal congestion; chills; cough; fever; sneezing, or sore throat; body aches or pain; headache; loss of voice; runny nose; unusual tiredness or weakness; difficulty in breathing)

Incidence unknown

Facial swelling

Overdose

For more information on the management of overdose or unintentional ingestion, **contact a poison control center** (see *Poison Control Center Listing*).

Treatment of overdose

There is no known specific antidote to dapsone gel 5%. Treatment is generally symptomatic and supportive.

Supportive care—

Dapsone gel is not for oral use. If oral ingestion occurs, medical advice should be sought.

Patients in whom intentional overdose is confirmed or suspected should be referred for psychiatric consultation.

Patient Consultation

As an aid to patient consultation, refer to *Advice for the Patient, Dapsone (Topical)*.

In providing consultation, consider emphasizing the following selected information (» = major clinical significance):

Before using this medication

» Conditions affecting use, especially:
Hypersensitivity to dapsone or to any of its components
Pregnancy—Not recommended for use during pregnancy
Breast-feeding—Dapsone is distributed into human milk. Because of the potential for oral dapsone to cause adverse effects in nursing infants, a decision should be made whether to discontinue nursing or to discontinue dapsone, taking into account the importance of the drug to the mother.
Use in children—Safety and efficacy have not been established in pediatric patients under 12 years of age
Other medical problems, especially anemia or history of, G6PD deficiency, hemoglobin M, or methemoglobin reductase deficiency

Proper use of this medication

» Proper administration technique
» Not using for any other disorder other than that for which it was prescribed
» Getting a proper laboratory evaluation prior to starting dapsone treatment
» Proper dosing
Missed dose: Applying as soon as possible; not applying if almost time for next dose
Proper storage

Precautions while using this medication

» Reporting any signs of adverse reactions to your physician
Reporting any history of anemia or an enzyme deficiency (such as G6PD)

Side/adverse effects

Signs of potential side effects, especially abdominal pain, pancreatitis, pharyngitis, suicidal behavior, tonic and clonic muscle movements, or vomiting, severe

General Dosing Information

Apply a pea-sized amount of dapsone gel after skin is gently washed and patted dry. Rub in gently and completely.

Wash hands after application of dapsone gel 5%.

If there is no improvement after 12 weeks of treatment, appropriateness should be reassessed.

Topical Dosage Forms

Note: Bracketed information in the *Indications* section refers to uses that are not included in U.S. product labeling.

DAPSONE GEL

Usual adult dose

Acne vulgaris—

Topical, a thin layer to the acne affected area(s) of skin twice daily.

Usual pediatric dose

Safety and efficacy in pediatric patients under 12 years of age have not been established.

Usual geriatric dose

See *Usual adult dose.*

Strength(s) usually available

U.S.—

5% (Rx) [*Aczone* (carbomer 980; diethylene glycol monoethyl ether, NF; methylparaben, NF; sodium hydroxide; purified water)].

Packaging and storage

Store at controlled room temperature 20 to 25 °C (68 to 76 °F), excursions permitted to 15 to 30 °C (59 to 86 °F). Protect from freezing. Protect from light. Store in the original carton after each use.

Auxiliary labeling

- Keep out of reach of children.

Developed: 09/13/2005

DAPTOMYCIN Systemic†

VA CLASSIFICATION (Primary): AM900

Commonly used brand name(s): *Cubicin*.

Note: For a listing of dosage forms and brand names by country availability, see *Dosage Forms* section(s).

†Not commercially available in Canada.

Category

Antibacterial (systemic).

Indications

General Considerations

Daptomycin is indicated for the treatment of bacteremia and complicated skin and skin structure infections caused by certain strains of gram-positive bacteria, including *Staphylococcus aureus (including methicillin-resistant strains)*, *Streptococcus pyogenes*, *Streptococcus agalactiae*, *Streptococcus dysgalactiae subsp equisimilis* and *Enterococcus faecalis (vancomycin-susceptible strains only)*. If documented or presumed pathogens include Gram-negative or anaerobic bacteria, combination therapy may be indicated.

To reduce the development of drug resistant bacteria and maintain the effectiveness of daptomycin it should be used only to treat or prevent infections that are proven or strongly suspected to be caused by susceptible bacteria. Therefore appropriate specimens should be obtained and examined in order to identify the causative pathogen and to determine their susceptibility to daptomycin.

Accepted

Bacteremia (treatment)—Daptomycin for injection is indicated for *Staphylococcus aureus* bloodstream infections (bacteremia), including those with right-sided infective endocarditis, caused by methicillin-susceptible and methicillin-resistant isolates.

Skin and skin-structure infections, complicated (treatment)—Daptomycin injection is indicated for the treatment of complicated skin and skin structure infections caused by susceptible strains of gram-positive bacteria.

Acceptance not established

The efficacy of daptomycin in patients with left-sided infective endocarditis due to *S. aureus* has not been demonstrated.

Daptomycin has not been studied in patients with prosthetic valve endocarditis or meningitis.

Unaccepted

Daptomycin is not indicated for the treatment of pneumonia.

Pharmacology/Pharmacokinetics

Physicochemical characteristics

Source—Daptomycin is a cyclic lipopeptide antibacterial agent derived from the fermentation of *Streptomyces roseosporus*.

Molecular weight—Daptomycin: 1620.67.

Mechanism of action/Effect

Daptomycin has a distinctive mechanism of action from other antibiotics, in which it binds to bacterial membrane causing rapid depolarization of membrane potential. The loss of membrane potential leads to inhibition of protein, DNA and RNA synthesis, which results in bacterial cell death.

Currently, there is no mechanism of resistance to daptomycin.

Distribution

Volume of distribution (Vol_D)—Steady state: approximately 0.09 L/kg.

Protein binding

Very high 92%; daptomycin is reversibly bound to human plasma proteins, primarily to serum albumin in a concentration independent manner

Biotransformation

Daptomycin does not inhibit or induce the activities of human cytochrome P450 isoforms. It is not know if daptomycin is a substrate of the cytochrome P450 system.

Daptomycin is metabolized and inactive metabolites have been detected in the urine. The site of metabolism has not been determined.

Half-life

Mean terminal elimination half-life in healthy volunteers on day 7, given intravenous daptomycin (4, 6, and 8 mg per kg) once daily (every 24 hr): 8.1 to 9 hours

Mean terminal elimination half-life in patients with varying degrees of renal function following a single 30-minute intravenous infusion of 4 mg per kg:

creatinine clearance > 80 mL per min: 9.39 hr
creatinine clearance 50 to 80 mL per min: 10.75 hr
creatinine clearance 30 to <50 mL per min: 14.7 hr
creatinine clearance <30 mL per min: 27.83 hr
creatinine clearance hemodialysis and CAPD: 29.81 hr

Time to steady state concentration:

Steady state concentrations are achieved by the third daily dose.

Mean peak plasma concentration:

57.8 mcg per mL—day 7 following an intravenous dose of 4 mg/kg once daily (every 24 hr)

98.6 mcg per mL—day 7 following an intravenous dose of 6 mg/kg once daily (every 24 hr)

133 mcg per mL—day 7 following an intravenous dose of 8 mg/kg once daily (every 24 hr)

Time to peak effect

30 to 60 minutes

Elimination

Renal excretion—approximately 78% of administered dose based on total radioactivity or 52% of administered based on microbiologically active concentrations.

Fecal excretion—5.7%

Mean total clearance in patients with varying degrees of renal function following a single 30-minute intravenous infusion of 4 mg per kg:

creatinine clearance > 80 mL per min: 10.9 mL per hr per kg
creatinine clearance 50 to 80 mL per min: 9.9 mL per hr per kg
creatinine clearance 30 to <50 mL per min: 8.5 mL per hr per kg
creatinine clearance <30 mL per min: 5.9 mL per hr per kg
creatinine clearance hemodialysis and CAPD: 3.7 mL per hr per kg

In hemodialysis, approximately 15% of daptomycin is recovered over 4 hours.

In peritoneal dialysis, approximately 11% of daptomycin is recovered over 48 hours.

Obesity—

Plasma clearance: increased 18% in moderately obese (body mass index 25 to 39.9 kg per m^2) subjects and 46% in extremely obese (body mass index ≥40 kg per m^2) subjects compared to controls matched for age, sex, and renal function.

Area under the concentration versus time curve (0 to ∞): increased 30% in moderately obese (body mass index 25 to 39.9 kg per m^2) subjects and 31% in extremely obese (body mass index ≥40 kg per m^2) subjects compared to controls matched for age, sex, and renal function.

These pharmacokinetic differences are likely due to differences in renal clearance of daptomycin in obese patients.

Precautions to Consider

Carcinogenicity

Long term carcinogenicity studies in animals have not been done.

Mutagenicity

Mutagenic nor clastogenic potential was found in genotoxicity tests including the Ames assay, a mammalian cell gene mutation assay, a test for chromosomal aberrations in Chinese hamster ovary cells, and *in vivo* micronucleus assay, an *in vitro* DNA repair assay, and an *in vivo* sister chromatid exchange assay in Chinese hamsters.

Pregnancy/Reproduction

Fertility—Daptomycin did not affect the fertility or reproductive ability of male or female rats given intravenous doses up to 150 mg/kg/day, approximately 9 times the human exposure based on AUCs.

Pregnancy—Adequate and well controlled studies in humans have not been done. Studies in animals have not shown that daptomycin causes adverse effects in the fetus. Because animal studies are not always predictive of human response, daptomycin should be used during pregnancy only if clearly needed.

Rats and rabbits given doses up to 75 mg/kg/day, 3 and 6 times the human dose revealed no evidence of harm to the fetus.

FDA Pregnancy Category B

Breast-feeding

It is not known if daptomycin is distributed into human milk. However caution should be used when administering to a nursing woman.

Pediatrics

Safety and efficacy of daptomycin in pediatric patients under the age of 18 years have not been established.

Geriatrics

In controlled clinical trials and phase 3 clinical studies, lower clinical success rates were seen in patients ≥ 65 years of age compared to those under 65 years of age. In addition, treatment-emergent adverse events are more common in patients ≥ 65 years of age than in patients under 65 years of age.

No dosage adjustment is necessary for elderly patients with normal (for age) renal function.

Pharmacogenetics

Gender—No clinically significant gender related differences in daptomycin have been been observed.

Obesity—Daptomycin dosage adjustment is not warranted in obese subjects with normal renal function.

Drug interactions and/or related problems

The following drug interactions and/or related problems have been selected on the basis of their potential clinical significance (possible mechanism in parentheses where appropriate)—not necessarily inclusive (» = major clinical significance):

Note: Combinations containing any of the following medications, depending on the amount present, may also interact with this medication.

Agents associated with rhabdomyolysis, such as
HMG-CoA reductase inhibitors
(concomitant use of simvastatin and daptomycin in healthy subjects was not associated with a increased risk of adverse events; however, caution is warranted due to the potential for additive adverse effects on skeletal muscle; consider temporarily suspending HMG-CoA reductase inhibitor therapy during treatment with daptomycin)

Tobramycin
(concomitant use of tobramycin and daptomycin [2 mg/kg] in healthy subjects had no significant effect on the pharmacokinetics of either drug; caution is warranted when therapeutic doses daptomycin are coadministered with tobramycin)

Warfarin
(concomitant use of warfarin and daptomycin in healthy subjects had no significant effect on the pharmacokinetics of either drug and did not significantly alter the International Normalized Ratio [INR]; patients should be monitored for the first several days after receiving concomitant therapy with daptomycin and warfarin)

Laboratory value alterations

The following have been selected on the basis of their potential clinical significance (possible effect in parentheses where appropriate)—not necessarily inclusive (» = major clinical significance).

Alkaline phosphatase, serum
(value was increased in 1% to 2% of patients during clinical studies)

» Creatine phosphokinase (CPK), serum
(value may increase; increases of CPK > 5 times the upper limit of normal [ULN], accompanied by muscle aches or weakness, are associated with myopathy, such as rhabdomyolysis; daptomycin should be discontinued if marked elevations of creatine phosphokinase occur)

Transaminases, serum
(abnormal liver function tests were observed in 3% of patients during clinical studies)

Medical considerations/Contraindications

The medical considerations/contraindications included have been selected on the basis of their potential clinical significance (reasons given in parentheses where appropriate)—not necessarily inclusive (» = major clinical significance).

Except under special circumstances, this medication should not be used when the following medical problem exists:

» Hypersensitivity to daptomycin

Risk-benefit should be considered when the following medical problems exist:

Hepatic impairment, severe
(use has not been sufficiently evaluated)

» Myopathy or
» Rhabdomyolysis or
» Creatinine phosphokinase (CPK), serum, marked elevation of
(daptomycin should be discontinued in patients with unexplained signs and symptoms of myopathy in conjunction with CPK elevation >1000 units per liter [5 times the upper limit of normal] or in asymptomatic patients with CPK elevation > 10 times the upper limit of normal; in addition, temporarily suspend any agents associated with rhabdomyolysis, such as HMG-CoA reductase inhibitors, in patients receiving daptomycin)

» Renal insufficiency, severe
(may require a dosage adjustment)

Patient monitoring

The following may be especially important in patient monitoring (other tests may be warranted in some patients, depending on condition; » = major clinical significance):

» Creatine phosphokinase (CPK), serum
(should be monitored weekly; and daptomycin should be discontinued if marked increases in CPK or if unexplained signs and symptoms of myopathy in conjunction with elevated CPK)

» Muscle pain, or
» Weakness
(should be monitored for development of muscle pain or weakness particularly of the distal extremities)

» Pseudomembranous colitis
(monitor patient for development of diarrhea subsequent to daptomycin therapy)

Repeat blood cultures
(for patients with continuing or relapsing *S. aureus* infection or poor clinical response; if culture is positive for *S. aureus*, MIC susceptibility testing of isolate should be performed using standard procedure and diagnostic evaluation to rule out sequestered foci of infection)

» Superinfection
(use of antibiotics may result in overgrowth of nonsusceptible organisms; careful observation is essential)

Side/Adverse Effects

The following side/adverse effects have been selected on the basis of their potential clinical significance (possible signs and symptoms in parentheses where appropriate)—not necessarily inclusive:

Note: Pseudomembranous colitis has been reported with nearly all antibacterial agents, including daptomycin, and may range in severity from mild to life-threatening. It is important to consider this diagnosis in patients who present with diarrhea subsequent to the administration of any antibacterial agents.

Those indicating need for medical attention

Incidence less frequent

Anemia (pale skin; troubled breathing with exertion; unusual bleeding or bruising; unusual tiredness or weakness); ***fungal infections*** (itching in genital or other skin areas scaling); ***hypertension*** (blurred vision; dizziness; nervousness; headache; pounding in the ears; slow or fast heartbeat); ***hypotension*** (blurred vision; confusion; dizziness, faintness, or lightheadedness when getting up from a lying or sitting position suddenly; sweating; unusual tiredness or weakness); ***renal failure*** (agitation; coma; confusion; decreased urine output; depression; dizziness; headache; hostility; irritability; lethargy; muscle twitching; nausea; rapid weight gain; seizures; stupor; swelling of face, ankles, or hands; unusual tiredness or weakness); ***urinary tract infections*** (bladder pain; bloody or cloudy urine; difficult, burning, or painful urination; frequent urge to urinate; lower back or side pain)

Incidence not determined

Pseudomembranous colitis (abdominal or stomach cramps; pain; bloating; abdominal tenderness; diarrhea, watery and severe, which may also be bloody; fever; increased thirst; nausea or vomiting; unusual tiredness or weakness; unusual weight loss)

Those indicating need for medical attention only if they continue or are bothersome

Incidence more frequent

Constipation (difficulty having a bowel movement (stool); ***diarrhea; headache; injection site reaction*** (bleeding, blistering, burning, coldness, discoloration of skin, feeling of pressure, hives, infection, inflammation, itching, lumps, numbness, pain, rash, redness, scarring, soreness, stinging, swelling, tenderness, tingling, ulceration, or warmth at site of injection); ***nausea***

Incidence less frequent

Dizziness; dyspnea (shortness of breath; difficult or labored breathing; tightness in chest wheezing); ***fever; insomnia*** (sleeplessness; trouble sleeping; unable to sleep); ***limb pain; pruritus*** (itching skin); ***skin rash; vomiting***

Incidence rare

Arthralgia (pain in joints; muscle pain or stiffness; difficulty in moving); ***dyspepsia*** (acid or sour stomach; belching; heartburn; indigestion; stomach discomfort upset or pain)

Overdose

For more information on the management of overdose or unintentional ingestion, **contact a poison control center** (see *Poison Control Center Listing*).

Treatment of overdose

To enhance elimination—

If necessary, daptomycin may be cleared from the body by hemodialysis and/or peritoneal dialysis.

Hemodialysis—approximately 15% of administered dose is recovered over 4 hours.

Peritoneal dialysis—approximately 11% of administered dose is recovered over 48 hours.

Supportive care—

Treatment should be symptomatic and supportive with maintenance of glomerular filtration.

Patients in whom intentional overdose is confirmed or suspected should be referred for psychiatric consultation.

Patient Consultation

As an aid to patient consultation, refer to *Advice for the Patient, Daptomycin (Systemic)*.

In providing consultation, consider emphasizing the following selected information (» = major clinical significance):

Before using this medication

» Conditions affecting use, especially:

Hypersensitivity to daptomycin

Pregnancy—Risk benefit considerations

Breast-feeding—Not known if distributed into human milk; caution should be exercised

Use in children—Safety and efficacy in pediatric patients under the age of 18 years not established.

Other medical problems, especially marked elevation of creatine phosphokinase serum levels, myopathy, renal insufficiency, or rhabdomyolysis

Proper use of this medication

» Importance of receiving medication for full course of therapy and on regular schedule

» Proper dosing

Missed dose: Taking as soon as possible; not taking if almost time for next scheduled dose; do not take more than one dose per day

Proper storage

Precautions while using this medicine

» Importance of repeat blood cultures for patients with persisting or returning *S. aureus* infection and performing MIC susceptibility testing and diagnostic evaluation to rule out sequestered foci of infection

Side/adverse effects

Signs of potential side effects, especially anemia, fungal infections, hypertension, hypotension, renal failure, urinary tract infections, or pseudomembranous colitis

General Dosing Information

For parenteral dosing forms:

Additives or other medicines should not be added to daptomycin single use vials or administered simultaneously through the same intravenous line.

If the same intravenous line is used for sequential infusion of different drugs, the line should be flushed with a compatible infusion solution before and after infusion with daptomycin.

For treatment of adverse effects

Pseudomembranous colitis—mild cases usually respond to drug discontinuation alone. In moderate to severe cases, consideration should be given to management with fluids and electrolytes, protein supplementation, and treatment with an antibacterial drug clinically effective against *Clostridium difficile*, which is one primary cause of antibiotic associated colitis. Other causes of colitis should also be considered.

Parenteral Dosage Forms

DAPTOMYCIN FOR INJECTION

Usual adult dose

Complicated skin and skin-structure infections—

Intravenous infusion, 4 mg per kg of body weight once every 24 hours for 7 to 14 days

Note: Dosage in adult patients with renal impairment:

• For creatinine clearance ≥ 30 mL per min: 4 mg per kg once every 24 hours

• For creatinine clearance <30 mL per min, including hemodialysis or CAPD: 4 mg per kg once every 48 hours; administer daptomycin following hemodialysis on hemodialysis days

Bacteremia—

Intravenous infusion, 6 mg per kg of body weight once every 24 hours for 2 to 6 weeks

Note: Dosage in adult patients with renal impairment:

• For creatinine clearance ≥ 30 mL per min: 6 mg per kg once every 24 hours

• For creatinine clearance <30 mL per min, including hemodialysis or CAPD: 6 mg per kg once every 48 hours; administer daptomycin following hemodialysis on hemodialysis days

Usual adult prescribing limits

Limited safety data for use longer than 28 days

Dose no more frequently than once daily

Usual pediatric dose

Safety and efficacy of daptomycin in pediatric patients under the age of 18 years have not been established.

Usual geriatric dose

See *Usual adult dose*.

Usual geriatric prescribing limits

See *Usual adult prescribing limits*

Strength(s) usually available

U.S.—

250 mg per vial (Rx) [*Cubicin* (sodium hydroxide)].

500 mg per vial (Rx) [*Cubicin* (sodium hydroxide)].

Packaging and storage

Store between 2 and 8 °C (36 and 46 °F); avoid excessive heat

Preparation of dosage form

Daptomycin vials are for single use only since daptomycin contains no perseverative or bacteriostatic agents. Aseptic technique must be used in preparation of final intravenous solution.

To prepare the initial dilution, daptomycin should be reconstituted with either 5 mL or 10 mL of 0.9% sodium chloride injection for 250 mg or 500 mg of daptomycin, respectively. Reconstituted daptomycin should be further diluted with 0.9% sodium chloride injection to be administered by intravenous infusion over a period of 30 minutes. See the manufacturer's package insert for instructions.

Inspect visually for particulate matter prior to administration

Stability

After reconstitution, solution is stable in the vial for 12 hours at room temperature or up to 48 hours after if stored under refrigeration. The diluted solution is also stable for 12 hours at room temperature and 48 hours if stored under refrigeration. The combined time (vial and infusion bag) should not exceed 12 hours at room temperature or 48 hours under refrigeration.

Incompatibilities
Daptomycin is not compatible with dextrose-containing diluents.

Revised: 07/20/2006
Developed: 01/21/2004

DARBEPOETIN ALFA Systemic

VA CLASSIFICATION (Primary): BL400
Commonly used brand name(s): *Aranesp.*

Note: For a listing of dosage forms and brand names by country availability, see *Dosage Forms* section(s).

Category
Antianemic.

Indications
Note: Bracketed information in the *Indications* section refers to uses that are not included in the U.S. product labeling.

Accepted
Anemia associated with chronic renal failure (treatment)—Darbepoetin alfa is indicated for the treatment of anemia associated with chronic renal failure, including patients on dialysis and patients not on dialysis.

Anemia associated with chemotherapy in cancer patients (treatment)[1]—Darbepoetin alfa is indicated for the treatment of anemia in adults with nonmyeloid malignancies in which the anemia is due to the effect of concomitantly administered chemotherapy.

[Anemia associated with malignancy (treatment)][1]—Darbepoetin alfa is indicated for the treatment of anemia associated with neoplastic diseases.

[1]Not included in Canadian product labeling.

Pharmacology/Pharmacokinetics

Physicochemical characteristics
Molecular weight—37,000 daltons.
pH—
Albumin solution: 6 ± 0.3.
Polysorbate solution: 6.2 ± 0.2.

Mechanism of action/Effect
Darbepoetin alfa is an erythropoiesis stimulating protein closely related to erythropoietin that is produced by recombinant DNA technology. Darbepoetin alfa is a 165-amino acid protein that differs from recombinant human erythropoietin in containing 5 N-linked oligosaccharide chains, whereas recombinant human erythropoietin contains 3.

Darbepoetin alfa stimulates erythropoiesis by the same mechanism as endogenous erythropoietin. A primary growth factor for erythroid development, erythropoietin is produced in the kidney and released into the bloodstream in response to hypoxia. In responding to hypoxia, erythropoietin interacts with progenitor stem cells to increase red blood cell production. Production of endogenous erythropoietin is impaired in patients with chronic renal failure (CRF), and erythropoietin deficiency is the primary cause of their anemia. Increased hemoglobin levels are not generally observed until 2 to 6 weeks after initiating treatment.

In patients with cancer receiving concomitant chemotherapy, the etiology of anemia is multifactorial.

Absorption
Bioavailability of darbepoetin alfa when given as a subcutaneous injection in chronic renal failure (CRF) patients is approximately 37% (range: 30% to 50%).

Bioavailability of darbepoetin when given as single SC dose in pediatric CRF patients (age 3 to 16 years) is 54% (range: 32% to 70%).

Terminal—
- CRF patients: Intravenous administration—21 hours
- CRF patients: Subcutaneous administration—49 hours (range: 27 to 89 hours)

Distribution
- CRF patients: Intravenous administration—1.4 hours

Following single IV or SC dose, half-life in pediatric CRF patients similar to those obtained in adult CRF patients.

Onset of action
Increased hemoglobin levels are not generally observed until 2 to 6 weeks after the initiation of treatment.

Time to peak concentration
CRF patients: Single subcutaneous dose—34 hours (range: 24 to 72 hours)
Cancer patients: Single subcutaneous dose—90 hours (range: 71 to 123 hours)

Peak serum concentration
C_{max} similar in pediatric CRF patients compared with adult CRF patients following single IV or SC dose.

Precautions to Consider

Carcinogenicity
The carcinogenic potential of darbepoetin alfa has not been evaluated in long-term animal studies.

Tumorigenicity
In toxicity studies of approximately 6 months duration in rats and dogs, no tumorigenic or unexpected mitogenic responses were observed in any tissue type.

Mutagenicity
Darbepoetin alfa was negative in the *in vitro* bacterial and CHO cell assays to detect mutagenicity and in the *in vivo* mouse micronucleus assay to detect clastogenicity.

Pregnancy/Reproduction
Fertility—When administered intravenously to male and female rats prior to and during mating, reproductive performance, fertility, and sperm assessment parameters were not affected at any doses evaluated (up to 10 mcg per kg per dose, administered 3 times weekly). An increase in postimplantation fetal loss was seen at doses equal to or greater than 0.5 mcg per kg per dose, administered 3 times weekly (3-fold higher than the recommended weekly starting human dose).

Pregnancy—Adequate and well-controlled studies in pregnant women have not been done. Darbepoetin alfa should be used during pregnancy only if the potential benefit justifies the potential risk to the fetus.

When darbepoetin alfa was administered intravenously to rats and rabbits during gestation, no evidence of a direct embryotoxic, fetotoxic, or teratogenic outcome was observed at doses up to 20 mcg per kg per day (40 fold higher than the recommended weekly starting dose). The only adverse effect observed was a slight reduction in fetal weight, which occurred at doses causing exaggerated pharmacological effects in the dams (1 mcg per kg per day and higher). No deleterious effects on uterine implantation were seen in either species. No significant placental transfer of darbepoetin alfa was observed in rats.

Intravenous injection of darbepoetin alfa to female rats every other day from day 6 of gestation through day 23 of lactation at doses of 2.5 mcg per kg per dose and higher resulted in offspring (F1 generation) with decreased body weights, which correlated with a low incidence of deaths, delayed eye opening and delayed preputial separation. No adverse effects were seen in the F2 offspring.

FDA Pregnancy Category C

Breast-feeding
It is not known whether darbepoetin alfa is distributed into human breast milk. Because many drugs are distributed into human breast milk, caution should be exercised when darbepoetin alfa is administered to a nursing woman.

Pediatrics
Pediatric chronic renal failure (CRF) patients—Safety and efficacy findings in a study of the conversion from epoetin alfa to darbepoetin alfa in pediatric patients over 1 year of age were similar to those found in adult conversion studies. Safety and efficacy in the conversion from another erythropoietin to darbepoetin alfa in pediatric CRF patients less than 1 year of age have not been established.

Pediatric cancer patients—No information is available on the relationship of age to the effects of darbepoetin alfa in the pediatric population. Safety and efficacy have not been established.

Geriatrics
Appropriate studies performed to date have not demonstrated geriatrics-specific problems that would limit the usefulness of darbepoetin alfa in the elderly. During clinical trials of chronic renal failure (CRF) patients receiving darbepoetin alfa, 42% of the patient population was age 65 and over and 15% were 75 and over. During clinical trials of cancer patients receiving darbepoetin alfa and concomitant chemotherapy, 45% were age 65 and over and 14% were 75 and over. No overall differences in safety and efficacy were observed between these patients and younger patients, but greater sensitivity of some older individuals cannot be ruled out.

Laboratory value alterations

The following have been selected on the basis of their potential clinical significance (possible effect in parentheses where appropriate)—not necessarily inclusive (» = major clinical significance).

With physiology/laboratory test values
Blood pressure
(may be increased, possibly to hypertensive levels)

Serum ferritin or
serum transferrin saturation
(may be decreased during administration of darbepoetin alfa.)

Medical considerations/Contraindications

The medical considerations/contraindications included have been selected on the basis of their potential clinical significance (reasons given in parentheses where appropriate)—not necessarily inclusive (» = major clinical significance).

Except under special circumstances, this medication should not be used when the following medical problems exist:

» Hypersensitivity to darbepoetin alfa or any of the excipients especially albumin

» Hypertension, uncontrolled
(may be exacerbated, especially during the early phase of treatment or when the hemoglobin is increasing; initiation of therapy should be delayed until blood pressure is adequately controlled)

» Red cell aplasia, pure
(darbepoetin alfa should not be administered to patients with pure red cell aplasia [PRCA] secondary to neutralizing antibodies to erythropoietin; patients should not be switched to another product as anti-erythropoietin antibodies cross-react with other erythropoietins)

Risk-benefit should be considered when the following medical problems exist:

Aluminum toxicity, severe or
Bone marrow fibrosis or
Folic acid deficiency or
Hemolysis or
Infection or
Inflammation or
Malignancy or
Occult blood loss or
Osteofibrosis cystica or
Vitamin B_{12} deficiency
(may cause failure of response to darbepoetin alfa therapy)

» Cardiovascular system abnormalities
(darbepoetin alfa may increase the risk of cardiovascular events in patients with CRF; the higher risk of cardiovascular events may be associated with higher hemoglobin and/or higher rates of rise of hemoglobin)

Hematologic disorders, such as:
Hemolytic anemia or
Porphyria or
Sickle cell anemia or
Thalassemia
(the safety and efficacy of darbepoetin alfa have not been established in patients with underlying hematologic diseases)

Hypertension, controlled
(blood pressure may rise during early stages of treatment with darbepoetin alfa requiring initiation or intensification of antihypertensive therapy.)

Patient monitoring

The following may be especially important in patient monitoring (other tests may be warranted in some patients, depending on condition; » = major clinical significance):

» Blood pressure determinations
(recommended prior to initiation of therapy and at frequent intervals during treatment; hypertensive encephalopathy and seizures have been observed in patients with CRF treated with darbepoetin alfa)

Fluid and electrolyte balance

» Hemoglobin
(After initiation of darbepoetin alfa therapy, the hemoglobin should be determined weekly until it has stabilized and the maintenance dose has been established. A recommended target level of 12 grams per dL should not be exceeded due to an increased incidence of thrombotic events and mortality in patients treated with erythropoietic agents and insufficient information to establish whether use of epoetic products have an adverse effect on time to tumor progression or progression-free survival; After a dose adjustment, the hemoglobin should be determined weekly for at least 4 weeks until it has been determined that the hemoglobin has stabilized in response to the dose change; hemoglobin should then be monitored at regular intervals. It is recommended that the dose of darbepoetin alfa be decreased if the hemoglobin increase exceeds 1 gram per dL in any 2 week period, because of the association of excessive rate of rise of hemoglobin with cardiovascular events)
(For hemoglobin-related dosage adjustment information based on the indication, see *Usual adult and adolescent dose* section; after the hematocrit has been stabilized in the target range [not to exceed 12 g/dL], the frequency of monitoring may be decreased)

» Iron status, including:
Serum ferritin and
Serum transferrin saturation
(evaluation recommended before and during treatment; supplemental iron therapy is recommended for all patients whose serum ferritin is below 100 mcg per L or whose serum transferrin saturation is below 20%)

» Neurologic status
(during the first several months of therapy, monitor patient for premonitory symptoms of seizures. In clinical trials seizures were reported in patients with chronic renal failure.While the relationship between seizures and the rate of rise of hemoglobin is uncertain, it is recommended that the dose of darbepoetin alfa be decreased if the hemoglobin increase exceeds 1 gram per dL in any 2 week period)

» Renal function
(due to a potential reduction in dialysis efficiency, close monitoring is recommended in patients with renal function impairment to determine the need for initiating or increasing dialysis, and additionally, predialysis patients may be more responsive to the effect of darbepoetin alfa administration.)

Side/Adverse Effects

Note: Products formulated with albumin carry an extremely remote risk for transmission of viral diseases, and theoretically, the Creutzfeldt-Jakob disease.

Note: There is a potential for immunogenicity with darbepoetin alfa administration. During clinical trials, high titer antibodies to darbepoetin alfa were not detected, but assay sensitivity may have been inadequate to reliably detect lower titers.

Note: In patients with cancer who received darbepoetin alfa, pulmonary emboli, thrombophlebitis and thrombosis occurred more frequently than in placebo controls. In a study with another erythropoietic product, epoetin alfa, treatment was associated with a higher rate of fatal thrombotic events in the first four months of the study and mortality at one year was higher for the epoetin alfa group. Until further information is available, the recommended target hemoglobin should not exceed 12 grams per dL in men or women.

Note: The possibility that darbepoetin alfa can act as a growth factor for any tumor type, particularly myeloid malignancies, has not been evaluated. In a study of head and neck cancer patients where epoetin beta was administered, locoregional progression-free survival was significantly shorter in patients receiving epoetin beta. Until further information is available, the recommended target hemoglobin should not exceed 12 grams per dL in men or women.

Note: There is a potential for immunogenicity with darbepoetin alfa administration.

Note: Cases of pure red cell aplasia (PRCA) and of severe anemia, with or without cytopenias, associated with neutralizing antibodies to erythropoietin have been reported in patients treated with darbepoetin alfa. This has been reported predominantly in patients with CRF receiving darbepoetin alfa by subcutaneous administration. Any patient who develops a sudden loss of response to darbepoetin accompanied by severe anemia and low reticulocyte count, should be evaluated for the etiology of loss of effect, including the presence of neutralizing antibodies to erythropoietin. If anti-erythropoetin antibody-associated anemia is suspected, darbepoetin and other erythropoietic proteins should be withheld. Amgen should be contacted at 1-800-77AMGEN to perform assays for binding and neutralizing antibodies. Darbepoetin should be permanently discontinued in patients with antibody-mediated anemia. Patients should not be switched to other erythropoietic proteins as antibodies may cross-react.

The following side/adverse effects have been selected on the basis of their potential clinical significance (possible signs and symptoms in parentheses where appropriate)—not necessarily inclusive:

Some of the side effects listed below are typically associated with chronic renal failure, or recognized complications of dialysis, and may not necessarily be attributable to darbepoetin alfa therapy.

Those indicating need for medical attention

Incidence more frequent

Abscess (accumulation of pus; swollen, red, tender area of infection; fever); ***angina pectoris*** (arm, back or jaw pain; chest pain or discomfort; chest tightness or heaviness; fast or irregular heartbeat; shortness of breath; sweating; nausea); ***bacteremia*** (rapid breathing; chills; fever; abdominal pain; nausea; diarrhea); ***bronchitis*** (cough producing mucus; difficulty breathing; shortness of breath; tightness in chest; wheezing); ***cardiac arrest*** (stopping of heart; unconsciousness); ***cardiac arrhythmias*** (dizziness; fainting; fast, slow, or irregular heartbeat; lightheadedness; pounding or rapid pulse); ***chest pain, unspecified; congestive heart failure*** (chest pain; decreased urine output; dilated neck veins; extreme fatigue; irregular breathing; irregular heartbeat; shortness of breath; swelling of face, fingers, feet, or lower legs; tightness in chest; troubled breathing; weight gain; wheezing); ***dyspnea*** (shortness of breath; difficult or labored breathing; tightness in chest; wheezing); ***edema, centralized*** (swelling)—disease state may be a contributing factor; ***edema, peripheral*** (swelling of hands, ankles, feet, or lower legs); ***fluid overload*** (decrease in amount of urine; noisy, rattling breathing; shortness of breath; swelling of fingers, hands, feet, or lower legs; troubled breathing at rest; weight gain); ***hemorrhage, access; hypertension*** (blurred vision; dizziness; headache; pounding in the ears; slow or fast heartbeat)—disease state may be a contributing factor; ***hypotension*** (blurred vision; confusion; dizziness, faintness, or lightheadedness when getting up from a lying or sitting position; sudden sweating; unusual tiredness or weakness); ***infection, access; peritonitis*** (abdominal or stomach pain; chills; nausea or vomiting); ***pneumonia*** (chest pain; cough; fever or chills; shortness of breath; troubled breathing; tightness in chest; wheezing); ***sepsis*** (chills; fever; fast heartbeat); ***thrombosis, vascular access- (including thrombophlebitis, thrombophlebitis deep, thrombosis venous, thrombosis venous deep, thromboembolism and thrombosis)*** (tenderness, pain, swelling, warmth, skin discoloration, and prominent superficial veins over affected area)—disease state may be a contributing factor.

Incidence less frequent

Convulsions (including grand mal and local convulsions) (seizures)—disease state may be a contributing factor; ***pulmonary embolism*** (anxiety; chest pain; cough; fainting; fast heartbeat; sudden shortness of breath or troubled breathing; dizziness or lightheadedness)—disease state may be a contributing factor; ***myocardial infarction, acute*** (chest pain or discomfort; pain or discomfort in arms, jaw, back or neck; shortness of breath; nausea; sweating; vomiting)—disease state may be a contributing factor; ***stroke*** (confusion; difficulty in speaking; slow speech; inability to speak; inability to move arms, legs, or facial muscles; double vision; headache); ***transient ischemic attack*** (confusion; numbness or tingling in face, arms or legs; trouble speaking, thinking or walking; headache)

Incidence rare

Allergic reaction (skin rash; and urticaria); ***pure red cell aplasia*** (fever and sore throat; pale skin; unusual bleeding or bruising; unusual tiredness or weakness)

Note: If a serious allergic or anaphylactic reaction occurs, darbepoetin alfa should be immediately and permanently discontinued

Those indicating need for medical attention only if they continue or are bothersome

Incidence more frequent

Abdominal pain; arthralgia (pain in joints; muscle pain or stiffness; difficulty in moving); ***asthenia*** (lack or loss of strength); ***back pain; constipation***—disease state may be a contributing factor; ***cough; dizziness; diarrhea; fatigue; fever; headache; influenza-like symptoms*** (chills; cough; diarrhea; fever; general feeling of discomfort or illness; headache; joint pain; loss of appetite; muscle aches and pains; nausea; runny nose; shivering; sore throat; sweating; trouble sleeping; unusual tiredness or weakness; vomiting); ***injection site pain; limb pain; myalgia*** (muscle ache or pain); ***nausea; pruritus*** (itching skin); ***rash***—disease state may be a contributing factor; ***upper respiratory infection*** (cough; fever; sneezing; or sore throat); ***vomiting***

Incidence less frequent

Dehydration (confusion; decreased urination; dizziness; dry mouth; fainting; increase in heart rate; lightheadedness; rapid breathing; sunken eyes; thirst; unusual tiredness or weakness; wrinkled skin)—disease state may be a contributing factor

Overdose

For more information on the management of overdose or unintentional ingestion, **contact a poison control center** (see *Poison Control Center Listing*)

Note: The maximum amount of darbepoetin alfa that can be safely administered in single or multiple doses has not been determined. Doses over 3 mcg per kg per week for up to 28 weeks have been administered to chronic renal failure (CRF) patients. Doses up to 8 mcg per kg per week and 15 mcg per kg every 3 weeks of up to 12 to 16 weeks have been administered to cancer patients.

Clinical effects of overdose

The following effects have been selected on the basis of their potential clinical significance (possible signs and symptoms in parentheses where appropriate)—not necessarily inclusive:

polycythemia

Treatment of overdose

For polycythemia—temporarily suspending therapy. In some patients, phlebotomy may be needed

Monitoring—

Monitor for excessive rise and rate of rise in hemoglobin

Supportive care—

Patients in whom intentional overdose is confirmed or suspected should be referred for psychiatric consultation.

Patient Consultation

As an aid to patient consultation, refer to *Advice for the Patient, Darbepoetin Alfa (Systemic)*.

In providing consultation, consider emphasizing the following selected information (» = major clinical significance):

Before using this medication

» Conditions affecting use, especially:

Hypersensitivity to darbepoetin alfa or any of the excipients especially albumin

Use in children—Chronic renal failure (CRF)—Safety and efficacy similar to those found in adult studies in conversion from another erythropoietin to darbepoetin alfa in patients ≥1 year of age

Cancer—Safety and efficacy not established

Other medical problems, especially cardiovascular system abnormalities, hypertension, uncontrolled, or pure red cell aplasia

Proper use of this medication

» Proper injection technique (if dispensed for home use)

» Safe handling and disposal of needles and syringes

» Proper dosing

Missed dose: Contacting physician for instructions if dose is missed.

Proper storage

Precautions while using this medication

» Importance of keeping medical and dialysis appointments

» Stressing importance of hemoglobin concentration monitoring

» Importance of compliance with antihypertensive regimen (medications and diet), if prescribed, and dietary restrictions pertinent to patients with chronic renal failure

» Importance of compliance with iron or other vitamin supplementation

Side/adverse effects

Signs of potential side effects, especially abscess, allergic reaction, angina pectoris, bacteremia, bronchitis, cardiac arrest, cardiac arrhythmias, unspecified chest pain, convulsions (including grand mal and local), congestive heart failure, dyspnea, centralized edema, peripheral edema, fluid overload, access hemorrhage, hypertension, hypotension, access infection, peritonitis, pneumonia, pure red cell aplasia, sepsis, vascular access thrombosis, acute myocardial infarction, pulmonary embolism, stroke, and transient ischemic attack

An increased incidence of *thrombotic events* and *tumor growth factor potential* have also been observed in studies of other erythropoietic agents. Until further information is available, recommended target hemoglobin should not exceed 12 grams per dL in men or women.

General Dosing Information

Due to individual variability, doses should be titrated to not exceed a target hemoglobin concentration of 12 grams per dL. For many patients, the appropriate maintenance dose will be lower than the starting dose.

Sufficient time should be allowed to determine a patient's responsiveness to a dosage of darbepoetin alfa before adjusting the dose. Because of the time required for erythropoiesis and the red cell half-life, an interval of 2 to 6 weeks may occur between the time of a dose adjustment and a significant change in hemoglobin.

Darbepoetin alfa may be administered either intravenously or subcutaneously for chronic renal failure (CRF) patients. And, it is administered subcutaneously only for cancer patients receiving concomitant chemotherapy.

For treatment of adverse effects

- For hypertension—Instituting or increasing administration of antihypertensive medications. In some patients, a decrease in darbepoetin alfa dosage or temporary withdrawal of therapy may be needed.

Parenteral Dosage Forms

Note: Bracketed uses in the *Dosage Forms* section refers to categories of use and/or indications that are not included in U.S. product labeling.

DARBEPOETIN ALFA INJECTION

Usual adult dose

Anemia associated with chronic renal failure—

Initial: Intravenous or subcutaneous, 0.45 mcg per kg of body weight once a week.

Note: Due to individual variability, doses should be titrated to not exceed a target hemoglobin concentration of 12 grams (g) per dL. For many patients, the appropriate maintenance dose will be lower than the starting dose.

Some patients have been treated successfully with a subcutaneous dose administered once every two weeks.

Increases in doses should not be made more than once a month. If the hemoglobin is increasing and approaching 12 gram per dL, the dose should be reduced by approximately 25%. If the hemoglobin continues to increase, doses should be temporarily withheld until the hemoglobin begins to decrease, at which point therapy should be reinitiated at a dose approximately 25% below the previous dose. If the hemoglobin increases by more than 1 gram per dL in a 2-week period, the dose should be decreased by approximately 25%.

If the increase in hemoglobin is less than 1 gram per dL over 4 weeks and iron stores are adequate, the dose of darbepoetin alfa may be increased by approximately 25% of the previous dose. Further increases may be made at 4 week intervals until the specified hemoglobin is obtained.

[Extended dosing for patients who do not require dialysis: Intravenous or subcutaneous, initially 0.75 mcg per kg of body weight once every two weeks. Once the target hemoglobin has been achieved with this regimen, darbepoetin alfa should be administered once monthly using twice the once every two week dose. The once-monthly dose should be titrated as necessary to maintain the target hemoglobin.][1]

Maintenance: Dosage should be adjusted for each patient to achieve and maintain a target hemoglobin not to exceed 12 gm per dL.

Note: Predialysis patients, in particular, may require a lower maintenance dose.

Conversion: Conversion from epoetin alfa to darbepoetin alfa should be estimated on the basis of the weekly epoetin alfa dose at the time of substitution. See *Epoetin Conversion Table* below. Doses should be titrated to maintain the target hemoglobin. Due to a longer serum half-life, darbepoetin alfa should be administered less frequently than epoetin alfa.

Darbepoetin alfa should be administered once a week if the patient was receiving epoetin alfa 2 to 3 times a week.

Darbepoetin alfa should be administered once every two weeks if the patient was receiving epoetin alfa once per week.

Note: The route of administration (IV or SC) should be maintained.

Previous weekly epoetin alfa dose (Units/week)	Weekly darbepoetin alfa dose (mcg/week)
<1,500	6.25
1,500–2,499	6.25
2,500–4,999	12.5
5,000–10,999	25
11,000–17,999	40
18,000–33,999	60
34,000–89,999	100
≥90,000	200

Anemia associated with chemotherapy in cancer patients[1]—

Subcutaneous, recommended starting dose of 2.25 mcg per kg of body weight once per week.

Subcutaneous, recommended starting dose of 500 mcg once every 3 weeks (Q3W).

[Subcutaneous, 3 to 5 mcg per kg body weight once every two weeks][1]

Note: For both FDA-approved dosing schedules, the dose should be adjusted for each patient to maintain a target hemoglobin not to exceed 12 g per dL. If the hemoglobin exceeds 13 g per dL, doses should be temporarily withheld until the hemoglobin falls to 12 g per dL. At this point, therapy should be reinitiated at a dose 40% below the previous dose. If the rate of hemoglobin increase is more than 1 g per dL per 2-week period or when the hemoglobin exceeds 11 g per dL, the dose should be reduced by 40% of the previous dose.

For patients receiving weekly administration, if there is less than a 1 g per dL increase in hemoglobin after 6 weeks of therapy, the dose of darbepoetin alfa should be increased up to 4.5 mcg per kg of body weight.

[Anemia associated with malignancy][1]—

Subcutaneous, 200 mcg once every two weeks.

Usual adult prescribing limits

Target hemoglobin should not exceed 12 gram per dL.

Usual pediatric dose

Anemia associated with chronic renal failure—

The use of darbepoetin alfa as the initial treatment has not been studied.

Conversion: Conversion from epoetin alfa to darbepoetin alfa should be estimated on the basis of the weekly epoetin alfa dose at the time of substitution. See the *Pediatric Epoetin Conversion Table* below. Doses should be titrated to maintain the target hemoglobin. Due to a longer serum half-life, darbepoetin alfa should be administered less frequently than epoetin alfa.

Darbepoetin alfa should be administered once a week if the patient was receiving epoetin alfa 2 to 3 times a week.

Darbepoetin alfa should be administered once every two weeks if the patient was receiving epoetin alfa once per week.

Note: The route of administration (IV or SC) should be maintained.

Previous weekly epoetin alfa dose (Units/week)	Weekly darbepoetin alfa dose (mcg/week)
<1,500	See text below
1,500–2,499	6.25
2,500–4,999	10
5,000–10,999	20
11,000–17,999	40
18,000–33,999	60
34,000–89,999	100
≥90,000	200

For pediatric patients receiving a weekly epoetin alfa dose of <1,500 units per week, the available data are insufficient to determine a darbepoetin alfa conversion dose.

Note: Due to individual variability, doses should be titrated to not exceed a target hemoglobin concentration of 12 grams (g) per dL. For many patients, the appropriate maintenance dose will be lower than the starting dose.

Some patients have been treated successfully with a subcutaneous dose administered once every two weeks.

Increases in doses should not be made more than once a month. If the hemoglobin is increasing and approaching 12 gram per dL, the dose should be reduced by approximately 25%. If the hemoglobin continues to increase, doses should be temporarily withheld until the hemoglobin begins to decrease, at which point therapy should be reinitiated at a dose approximately 25% below the previous dose. If the hemoglobin increases by more than 1 gram per dL in a 2-week period, the dose should be decreased by approximately 25%.

If the increase in hemoglobin is less than 1 gram per dL over 4 weeks and iron stores are adequate, the dose of darbepoetin alfa may be increased by approximately 25% of the previous dose. Further increases may be made at 4 week intervals until the specified hemoglobin is obtained.

Predialysis patients, in particular, may require a lower maintenance dose.

Anemia associated with chemotherapy in cancer patients[1]—

Safety and efficacy have not been established.

Usual geriatric dose
See *Usual adult dose.*

Usual geriatric prescribing limits
See *Usual adult prescribing limits.*

Strength(s) usually available
U.S.—

Albumin Solution:

25 mcg per 1 mL (Rx) [*Aranesp* (albumin human 2.5 mg; sodium phosphate monobasic monohydrate 2.23 mg; sodium phosphate dibasic anhydrous 0.53 mg; sodium chloride 8.18 mg; water for injection, USP)].

40 mcg per 1 mL (Rx) [*Aranesp* (albumin human 2.5 mg; sodium phosphate monobasic monohydrate 2.23 mg; sodium phosphate dibasic anhydrous 0.53 mg; sodium chloride 8.18 mg; water for injection, USP)].

60 mcg per 1 mL (Rx) [*Aranesp* (albumin human 2.5 mg; sodium phosphate monobasic monohydrate 2.23 mg; sodium phosphate dibasic anhydrous 0.53 mg; sodium chloride 8.18 mg; water for injection, USP)].

100 mcg per 1 mL (Rx) [*Aranesp* (albumin human 2.5 mg; sodium phosphate monobasic monohydrate 2.23 mg; sodium phosphate dibasic anhydrous 0.53 mg; sodium chloride 8.18 mg; water for injection, USP)].

150 mcg per 0.75 mL (Rx) [*Aranesp* (albumin human 1.875 mg; sodium phosphate monobasic monohydrate 1.67 mg; sodium phosphate dibasic anhydrous 0.40 mg; sodium chloride 6.14 mg; water for injection, USP)].

200 mcg per 1 mL (Rx) [*Aranesp* (albumin human 2.5 mg; sodium phosphate monobasic monohydrate 2.23 mg; sodium phosphate dibasic anhydrous 0.53 mg; sodium chloride 8.18 mg; water for injection, USP)].

300 mcg per 1 mL (Rx) [*Aranesp* (albumin human 2.5 mg; sodium phosphate monobasic monohydrate 2.23 mg; sodium phosphate dibasic anhydrous 0.53 mg; sodium chloride 8.18 mg; water for injection, USP)].

500 mcg per 1 mL (Rx) [*Aranesp* (albumin human 2.5 mg; sodium phosphate monobasic monohydrate 2.23 mg; sodium phosphate dibasic anhydrous 0.53 mg; sodium chloride 8.18 mg; water for injection, USP)].

Polysorbate Solution:

25 mcg per 1 mL (Rx) [*Aranesp* (0.05 mg polysorbate 80; sodium phosphate monobasic monohydrate 2.12 mg; sodium phosphate dibasic anhydrous 0.66 mg; sodium chloride 8.18 mg; water for injection, USP [to 1 mL])].

40 mcg per 1 mL (Rx) [*Aranesp* (0.05 mg polysorbate 80; sodium phosphate monobasic monohydrate 2.12 mg; sodium phosphate dibasic anhydrous 0.66 mg; sodium chloride 8.18 mg; water for injection, USP [to 1 mL])].

60 mcg per 1 mL (Rx) [*Aranesp* (0.05 mg polysorbate 80; sodium phosphate monobasic monohydrate 2.12 mg; sodium phosphate dibasic anhydrous 0.66 mg; sodium chloride 8.18 mg; water for injection, USP [to 1 mL])].

100 mcg per 1 mL (Rx) [*Aranesp* (0.05 mg polysorbate 80; sodium phosphate monobasic monohydrate 2.12 mg; sodium phosphate dibasic anhydrous 0.66 mg; sodium chloride 8.18 mg; water for injection, USP [to 1 mL])].

150 mcg per 0.75 mL (Rx) [*Aranesp* (0.05 mg polysorbate 80; sodium phosphate monobasic monohydrate 2.12 mg; sodium phosphate dibasic anhydrous 0.66 mg; sodium chloride 8.18 mg; water for injection, USP [to 1 mL])].

200 mcg per 1 mL (Rx) [*Aranesp* (0.05 mg polysorbate 80; sodium phosphate monobasic monohydrate 2.12 mg; sodium phosphate dibasic anhydrous 0.66 mg; sodium chloride 8.18 mg; water for injection, USP [to 1 mL])].

300 mcg per 1 mL (Rx) [*Aranesp* (0.05 mg polysorbate 80; sodium phosphate monobasic monohydrate 2.12 mg; sodium phosphate dibasic anhydrous 0.66 mg; sodium chloride 8.18 mg; water for injection, USP [to 1 mL])].

500 mcg per 1 mL (Rx) [*Aranesp* (0.05 mg polysorbate 80; sodium phosphate monobasic monohydrate 2.12 mg; sodium phosphate dibasic anhydrous 0.66 mg; sodium chloride 8.18 mg; water for injection, USP [to 1 mL])].

Canada—

Polysorbate Solution:

15 mcg per 1 mL (Rx) [*Aranesp* (polysorbate 80 0.05 mg; sodium phosphate monobasic monohydrate 2.12 mg; sodium phosphate dibasic anhydrous 0.66 mg; sodium chloride 8.18 mg; water for injection, USP)].

25 mcg per 1 mL (Rx) [*Aranesp* (polysorbate 80 0.05 mg; sodium phosphate monobasic monohydrate 2.12 mg; sodium phosphate dibasic anhydrous 0.66 mg; sodium chloride 8.18 mg; water for injection, USP)].

40 mcg per 1 mL (Rx) [*Aranesp* (polysorbate 80 0.05 mg; sodium phosphate monobasic monohydrate 2.12 mg; sodium phosphate dibasic anhydrous 0.66 mg; sodium chloride 8.18 mg; water for injection, USP)].

60 mcg per 1 mL (Rx) [*Aranesp* (polysorbate 80 0.05 mg; sodium phosphate monobasic monohydrate 2.12 mg; sodium phosphate dibasic anhydrous 0.66 mg; sodium chloride 8.18 mg; water for injection, USP)].

100 mcg per 1 mL (Rx) [*Aranesp* (polysorbate 80 0.05 mg; sodium phosphate monobasic monohydrate 2.12 mg; sodium phosphate dibasic anhydrous 0.66 mg; sodium chloride 8.18 mg; water for injection, USP)].

200 mcg per 1 mL (Rx) [*Aranesp* (polysorbate 80 0.05 mg; sodium phosphate monobasic monohydrate 2.12 mg; sodium phosphate dibasic anhydrous 0.66 mg; sodium chloride 8.18 mg; water for injection, USP)].

325 mcg per 1 mL (Rx) [*Aranesp* (polysorbate 80 0.05 mg; sodium phosphate monobasic monohydrate 2.12 mg; sodium phosphate dibasic anhydrous 0.66 mg; sodium chloride 8.18 mg; water for injection, USP)].

500 mcg per 1 mL (Rx) [*Aranesp* (polysorbate 80 0.05 mg; sodium phosphate monobasic monohydrate 2.12 mg; sodium phosphate dibasic anhydrous 0.66 mg; sodium chloride 8.18 mg; water for injection, USP)].

Packaging and storage
Store at 2 to 8°C (36 to 46°F). Protect from light. Protect from freezing.

Stability
Do not shake the vial of darbepoetin alfa, recombinant, injection. Shaking may denature the glycoprotein and render it biologically inactive.

Do not dilute darbepoetin alfa.

Because the single-dose injection contains no preservative, each vial should be used to administer one dose only. Any unused portion of the solution must be discarded. *Do not pool unused portions.*

Incompatibilities
It is recommended that darbepoetin alfa not be administered in conjunction with other drug solutions.

Auxiliary labeling
- Do not shake.

†Not included in Canadian product labeling.

Revised: 08/08/2006
Developed: 12/10/2001

DARIFENACIN Systemic†

VA CLASSIFICATION (Primary/Secondary): GU201/AU305

Commonly used brand name(s): *Enablex.*

Note: For a listing of dosage forms and brand names by country availability, see *Dosage Forms* section(s).

†Not commercially available in Canada.

Category
Antispasmodic (urinary).

Indications

Accepted
Bladder hyperactivity (treatment)—Darifenacin is indicated for the treatment of overactive bladder with symptoms of urinary incontinence, urgency, and urinary frequency.

Pharmacology/Pharmacokinetics

Physicochemical characteristics
Molecular weight—Darifenacin hydrobromide: 507.5.

Mechanism of action/Effect
Darifenacin is a competitive muscarinic receptor antagonist. It is an antagonist on the effects of muscarinic receptors in cholinergically mediated functions, including contractions of the urinary bladder smooth muscle and stimulation of salivary secretion.

Absorption
The mean oral bioavailability of darifenacin at steady state is 15% and 19% for 7.5-mg and 15-mg tablets. Food has no effect on the pharmacokinetics of darifenacin.

Distribution
Volume of distribution (Vol_D)—Steady state: 163 liters.

Protein binding
Very high (98%) to plasma proteins, primarily to alpha-1-acid glycoprotein.

Biotransformation
Darifenacin is extensively metabolized by the liver by cytochrome P450 enzymes CYP2D6 and CYP3A4. The main metabolic routes are monohydroxylation in the dihydrobenzofuran ring, dihydrobenzofuran ring opening, and N-dealkylation of the pyrrolidine nitrogen. Products of the hydroxylation and N-dealkylation are the major metabolites but are unlikely to contribute to the overall clinical effect of darifenacin.

Half-life
Elimination—approximately 13 to 19 hours following chronic dosing.

Time to peak plasma concentration:
Approximately 7 hours following multiple dosing and steady state plasma concentrations are achieved by the sixth day of dosing.

Peak plasma concentration:
For extensive metabolizers (EM) of CYP2D6: 2.01 ng/mL following a 7.5-mg dose and 5.76 ng/mL following a 15-mg dose.

For poor metabolizers (PM) of CYP2D6: 4.27 ng/mL following a 7.5-mg dose and 9.99 ng/mL following a 15-mg dose.

Elimination
Urine: 60%; 3% unchanged drug.
Fecal: 40%
Clearance: 40 L/h (EM) and 32 L/h (PM).

Precautions to Consider

Carcinogenicity
Carcinogenicity studies with darifenacin hydrobromide were done in mice and rats. No evidence of carcinogenicity was found in a 24-month study in mice given dietary doses up to 100 mg/kg/day (32 times the human exposure at the maximum recommended human dose [MRHD]), and in a 24-month rat study given doses up to 15 mg/kg/day, (12 times the AUC at MRHD in female rats and 8 times the AUC at MRHD in male rats).

Mutagenicity
Darifenacin hydrobromide was negative for mutagenicity in the bacterial mutation assays (Ames test) and the Chinese hamster ovary assay, and was not clastogenic in the human lymphocyte assay, and the *in vivo* mouse bone marrow cytogenetics assay.

Pregnancy/Reproduction
Fertility—Fertility studies done in rats given oral doses up to 50 mg/kg/day (78 times the AUC at MRHD) of darifenacin hydrobromide had no effect on fertility.

Pregnancy—Adequate and well controlled studies in humans have not been done. Studies in animals have shown that darifenacin can cause adverse effects in the fetus. Because animal reproduction studies are not always predictive of human response, darifenacin should be used during pregnancy only if the potential benefit justifies the potential risk to the fetus.

Studies done in rats and rabbits given doses of darifenacin at 50 and 30 mg/kg/day, respectively, produced no teratogenic effects. However, rats given doses of 50 mg/kg/day resulted in a delay in the ossification of the sacral and caudal vertebrae. Dystocia and slight developmental delays were observed in dams at 10 mg/kg/day. Increased post-implantation loss was seen in rabbits at the dose of 30 mg/kg but not at the dose of 10 mg/kg. In rabbits, dilated ureter and/or kidney pelvis was observed in offspring at 30 mg/kg/day dose and in one case at 10 mg/kg/day dose, along with urinary bladder dilation consistent with pharmacological action of darifenacin. No effect was seen at the 3 mg/kg/day dose.

FDA Pregnancy Category C

Breast-feeding
It is not known whether darifenacin is distributed into human milk. However, darifenacin is distributed into the milk of rats. Caution should be exercised before darifenacin is administered to a nursing woman.

Pediatrics
The safety and effectiveness of darifenacin in pediatric patients have not been established.

Geriatrics
Appropriate studies performed to date have not demonstrated geriatric-specific problems that would limit the usefulness of darifenacin in the elderly. However, studies indicate a trend for clearance to decrease with age (6% per decade relative to a median age of 44 years).

Pharmacogenetics
Darifenacin C_{max} and AUC at steady state were 57%-79% and 61%-73% higher in females than in males respectively.

A subset of individuals (approximately 7% Caucasians and 2% African Americans) are poor metabolizers of CYP2D6 drugs.

Drug interactions and/or related problems
The following drug interactions and/or related problems have been selected on the basis of their potential clinical significance (possible mechanism in parentheses where appropriate)—not necessarily inclusive (» = major clinical significance):

Note: Combinations containing any of the following medications, depending on the amount present, may also interact with this medication.

CYP2D6 inhibitors such as
Paroxetine
(darifenacin exposure has been shown to increase 33% when administered with CYP2D6 inhibitors)

» CYP2D6 substrates such as
Flecainide or
Imipramine or
Thioridazine or
Tricyclic antidepressants
(caution should be taken when concomitant administration of darifenacin and medications metabolized by CYP2D6)

» CYP3A4 inhibitors, potent such as
Clarithromycin or
Itraconazole or
Ketoconazole or
Nefazoxone or
Nelfinavir or
Ritonavir
(concomitant administration may increase C_{max} and AUC of darifenacin; daily darifenacin dose should not exceed 7.5 mg)

CYP3A4 substrates such as
Midazolam
(increased midazolam exposure by 17%)

CYP P450 inhibitors such as
Cimetidine
(concomitant administration may increase C_{max} and AUC of darifenacin)

Digoxin
(increased digoxin exposure 16%; routine therapeutic monitoring should be continued)

Other anticholinergic agents
(concomitant use with darifenacin may increase the frequency and or severity of dry mouth, constipation, blurred vision and other anticholinergic effects)

Warfarin
(monitoring of therapeutic prothrombin time should be continued)

Medical considerations/Contraindications
The medical considerations/contraindications included have been selected on the basis of their potential clinical significance (reasons given in parentheses where appropriate)—not necessarily inclusive (» = major clinical significance).

Except under special circumstances, this medication should not be used when the following medical problem exists:

» Hypersensitivity to darifenacin or any of its ingredients
» Gastric rentention or
» Narrow-angle glaucoma, uncontrolled or
» Urinary retention
(use is contraindicated in patients with these conditions or patients at risk for these conditions)

Risk-benefit should be considered when the following medical problems exist:

» Bladder outflow obstruction
(caution; risk of urinary retention)

Constipation, severe or
Decreased gastrointestinal motility or
Gastrointestinal obstructive disorders or
Myasthenia gravis, or
Ulcerative colitis
(administer with caution; risk of gastric retention)

» Hepatic function impairment, moderate
(administer with caution, not exceeding the 7.5-mg daily dose in patients with reduced hepatic function (Child-Pugh B))

» Hepatic function impairment, severe
(use is not recommended in patients with severe hepatic impairment (Child-Pugh C))

Narrow-angle glaucoma, controlled
(use with caution in patients being treated for narrow-angle glaucoma and only when the potential benefits outweigh the risk)

Side/Adverse Effects

The following side/adverse effects have been selected on the basis of their potential clinical significance (possible signs and symptoms in parentheses where appropriate)—not necessarily inclusive:

Those indicating need for medical attention

Reported during clinical trials
Urinary retention (decrease in urine volume; decrease in frequency of urination; difficulty in passing urine; [dribbling] painful urination)

Those indicating need for medical attention only if they continue or are bothersome

Incidence more frequent
Constipation (difficulty having a bowel movement (stool)); ***dry mouth; dyspepsia*** (acid or sour stomach; belching; heartburn; indigestion; stomach discomfort upset or pain)

Incidence less frequent
Abdominal pain (stomach pain); ***asthenia*** (lack or loss of strength); ***dizziness; dry eyes; nausea; urinary tract infection*** (bladder pain; bloody or cloudy urine; difficult, burning, or painful urination; frequent urge to urinate; lower back or side pain)

Incidence unknown
Abnormal vision (changes in vision); ***accidental injury; arthralgia*** (pain in joints; muscle pain or stiffness; difficulty in moving); ***back pain; bronchitis*** (cough producing mucus; difficulty breathing; shortness of breath; tightness in chest; wheezing); ***dry skin; flu syndrome*** (chills; cough; diarrhea; fever; general feeling of discomfort or illness; headache; joint pain; loss of appetite; muscle aches and pains); ***pain; hypertension*** (blurred vision; dizziness; nervousness headache; pounding in the ears; slow or fast heartbeat); ***peripheral edema*** (bloating or swelling of face, arms, hands, lower legs, or feet; rapid weight gain; tingling of hands or feet; unusual weight gain or loss); ***pharyngitis*** (body aches or pain; congestion; cough; dryness or soreness of throat; fever; hoarseness runny nose; tender, swollen glands in neck; trouble in swallowing; voice changes); ***pruritus*** (itching skin); ***rash; rhinitis*** (stuffy nose runny nose; sneezing); ***sinusitis*** (pain or tenderness around eyes and cheekbones; fever; stuffy or runny nose; headache; cough; shortness of breath or troubled breathing; tightness of chest or wheezing); ***urinary tract disorder; vaginitis*** (itching of the vagina or genital area; pain during sexual intercourse; thick, white vaginal discharge with no odor or with a mild odor); ***vomiting; weight gain***

Overdose

For more information on the management of overdose or unintentional ingestion, **contact a poison control center** (see *Poison Control Center Listing*).

Clinical effects of overdose

The following effects have been selected on the basis of their potential clinical significance (possible signs and symptoms in parentheses where appropriate)—not necessarily inclusive:

Abnormal vision (changes in vision)

Treatment of overdose

There is no known specific antidote to darifenacin. Treatment is generally symptomatic and supportive.

Monitoring—
Monitoring for cardiovascular function (ECG) is recommended.

Supportive care—
Patients in whom intentional overdose is confirmed or suspected should be referred for psychiatric consultation.

Patient Consultation

As an aid to patient consultation, refer to *Advice for the Patient, Darifenacin (Systemic)*.

In providing consultation, consider emphasizing the following selected information (» = major clinical significance):

Before using this medication

» Conditions affecting use, especially:
Hypersensitivity to darifenacin or any of its ingredients
Pregnancy—Should be used during pregnancy only if the potential benefit justifies the potential risk to the fetus.
Breast-feeding—Caution should be exercised before darifenacin is administered to a nursing woman.
Use in children—Safety and effectiveness of darifenacin in pediatric patients have not been established.
Other medications, especially CYP2D6 substrates such as flecainide, imipramine, thioridazine, tricyclic antidepressants; CYP3A4 inhibitors such as clarithromycin, itraconazole, ketoconazole, nefazoxone, nelfinavir, and ritonavir
Other medical problems, especially bladder outflow obstruction, gastric retention, hepatic function impairment (moderate or severe), narrow-angle glaucoma (uncontrolled), or urinary retention

Proper use of this medication

Taking darifenacin with liquids and swallowing the tablet whole.

» Proper dosing
Missed dose: If you miss a dose of this medicine, skipping the missed dose and going back to your regular dosing schedule; not doubling doses.

» Proper storage

Precautions while using this medication

» Caution during exercise or hot weather, overheating may result in heat exhaustion

» Caution if vision problems occur; caution while driving or doing dangerous activities

» Constipation; calling your doctor if you get severe stomach pain or become constipated for 3 or more days.

Possible dryness of mouth; checking with physician or dentist if dry mouth continues

Side/adverse effects

Signs of potential side effects, especially urinary retention

General Dosing Information

It is important to take the tablet with liquids and to swallow it whole, not chewed, divided, or crushed.

Darifenacin can be taken with or without food.

Oral Dosage Forms

Note: Bracketed information in the *Indications* section refers to uses that are not included in U.S. product labeling.

DARIFENACIN HYDROBROMIDE TABLETS

Usual adult dose

Urologic disorders, symptoms of—
Oral, one tablet (7.5 mg) once daily. Based on individual response the dose may be increased to 15 mg once daily, as early as two weeks after starting therapy.

Note: For patients with moderate hepatic impairment (Child Pugh B) or when administered with potent CYP3A4 inhibitors, the daily dose should not exceed 7.5 mg.

For patients with severe hepatic impairment (Child Pugh C), use is not recommended.

Usual pediatric dose

Safety and efficacy have not been established.

Usual geriatric dose

See *Usual adult dose*.

Strength(s) usually available

U.S.—
7.5 mg (Rx) [*Enablex* (dibasic calcium phosphate anhydrous; hydroxypropyl; hypromellose; lactose monohydrate; magnesium stearate; titanium dioxide; triacetin)].
15 mg (Rx) [*Enablex* (dibasic calcium phosphate anhydrous; hydroxypropyl; hypromellose; lactose monohydrate; magnesium stearate; titanium dioxide; triacetin; FD&C yellow No. 6 Aluminum Lake)].

Packaging and storage

Store at 25 °C (77 °F); excursions permitted to 15-30 °C (59 to 86 °F). Protect from light.

Auxiliary labeling

- May cause drowsiness. Be careful while driving or operating machinery. Use caution until you become familiar with its effects.
- May cause blurred vision
- Dry mouth may occur when taking this medicine
- Swallow whole. Do not crush or chew.

Developed: 04/12/2005

DAUNORUBICIN Systemic

VA CLASSIFICATION (Primary): AN200
Commonly used brand name(s): *Cerubidine*.

Note: For a listing of dosage forms and brand names by country availability, see *Dosage Forms* section(s).

Category

Antineoplastic.

Indications

Note: Bracketed information in the *Indications* section refers to uses that are not included in U.S. product labeling.

Accepted

Leukemia, acute lymphocytic (treatment) or
Leukemia, acute nonlymphocytic (treatment)—Daunorubicin is indicated, in combination with other antineoplastics, for treatment of acute lymphocytic leukemia and acute nonlymphocytic leukemia (acute myelocytic leukemia, acute monocytic leukemia[1], erythroleukemia[1]).

[Neuroblastoma (treatment)][1]—Daunorubicin is used for treatment of solid tumors of childhood, such as neuroblastoma.

[Lymphomas, non-Hodgkin's (treatment)]—Daunorubicin is used for treatment of non-Hodgkin's lymphomas such as lymphosarcoma and reticulum cell sarcomas.

[Ewing's sarcoma (treatment)]—Daunorubicin is used for treatment of Ewing's sarcoma.

[Wilms' tumor (treatment)]—Daunorubicin is used for treatment of Wilms' tumor.

[Leukemia, chronic myelocytic (treatment)]—Daunorubicin is used for treatment of chronic myelocytic (myelogenous) leukemia.

[1]Not included in Canadian product labeling.

Pharmacology/Pharmacokinetics

Physicochemical characteristics

Molecular weight—563.99.
pKa—10.3.

Mechanism of action/Effect

Daunorubicin is an anthracycline glycoside; it is classified as an antibiotic but is not used as an antimicrobial agent. Daunorubicin is most active in the S phase of cell division, but is not cycle phase–specific. Its exact mechanism of antineoplastic action is unknown but may involve binding to DNA by intercalation between base pairs and inhibition of DNA and RNA synthesis by template disordering and steric obstruction.

Other actions/effects

Also has immunosuppressant effects.

Distribution

Rapidly distributed throughout the body, especially to the kidneys, spleen, liver, and heart, as unchanged medication and metabolites. It does not cross the blood-brain barrier.

Biotransformation

Rapidly (within 1 hour) in the liver to produce an active metabolite, daunorubicinol. Further metabolism—Hepatic.

Half-life

Distribution—
45 minutes.
Elimination—
Daunorubicin: 18.5 hours.
Metabolites: 55 hours.
Daunorubicinol: 26.7 hours.

Elimination

In the urine, 25% in an active form; an estimated 40% is eliminated by biliary excretion.

Precautions to Consider

Carcinogenicity/Mutagenicity

Secondary malignancies are potential delayed effects of many antineoplastic agents, although it is not clear whether the effect is related to their mutagenic or immunosuppressive action. The effect of dose and duration of therapy is also unknown, although risk seems to increase with long-term use.

Daunorubicin subcutaneous injection causes fibrosarcomas at the injection site in mice; however, it did not cause a carcinogenic effect within 22 months of observation after oral or intraperitoneal administration in mice. Daunorubicin is potentially carcinogenic in humans.

Pregnancy/Reproduction

Fertility—Gonadal suppression, resulting in amenorrhea or azoospermia, may occur in patients taking antineoplastic therapy, especially with the alkylating agents. In general, these effects appear to be related to dose and length of therapy and may be irreversible. Prediction of the degree of testicular or ovarian function impairment is complicated by the common use of combinations of several antineoplastics, which makes it difficult to assess the effects of individual agents.

Daunorubicin causes testicular atrophy in male dogs.

Pregnancy—Adequate and well-controlled studies have not been done in humans.

First trimester: It is usually recommended that use of antineoplastics, especially combination chemotherapy, be avoided whenever possible, especially during the first trimester. Although information is limited because of the relatively few instances of antineoplastic administration during pregnancy, the mutagenic, teratogenic, and carcinogenic potential of these medications must be considered.

Other hazards to the fetus include adverse reactions seen in adults.

In general, use of a contraceptive is recommended during cytotoxic drug therapy.

Studies in rabbits found an increased incidence of fetal abnormalities (parieto-occipital cranioschisis, umbilical hernias, rachischisis) and abortions, and studies in mice showed decreases in fetal birth weight and postdelivery growth rate.

FDA Pregnancy Category D.

Breast-feeding

Although very little information is available regarding distribution of antineoplastic agents into breast milk, breast-feeding is not recommended while daunorubicin is being administered because of the risks to the infant (adverse effects, mutagenicity, carcinogenicity).

Pediatrics

Appropriate studies on the relationship of age to the effects of daunorubicin have not been performed in the pediatric population.

Geriatrics

Although appropriate studies on the relationship of age to the effects of daunorubicin have not been performed in the geriatric population, cardiotoxicity may be more frequent in the elderly. Caution should also used be in patients who have inadequate bone marrow reserves due to old age. In addition, elderly patients are more likely to have age-related renal function impairment, which may require reduction of dosage in patients receiving daunorubicin.

Dental

The bone marrow depressant effects of daunorubicin may result in an increased incidence of microbial infection, delayed healing, and gingival bleeding. Dental work, whenever possible, should be completed prior to initiation of therapy or deferred until blood counts have returned to normal. Patients should be instructed in proper oral hygiene during treatment, including caution in use of regular toothbrushes, dental floss, and toothpicks.

Daunorubicin also commonly causes stomatitis which may be associated with considerable discomfort.

Drug interactions and/or related problems

The following drug interactions and/or related problems have been selected on the basis of their potential clinical significance (possible mechanism in parentheses where appropriate)—not necessarily inclusive (» = major clinical significance):

Note: Combinations containing any of the following medications, depending on the amount present, may also interact with this medication.

Allopurinol or
Colchicine or
» Probenecid or
» Sulfinpyrazone
(daunorubicin may raise the concentration of blood uric acid; dosage adjustment of antigout agents may be necessary to control hyperuricemia and gout; allopurinol may be preferred to prevent or reverse daunorubicin-induced hyperuricemia because of risk of uric acid nephropathy with uricosuric antigout agents)

Blood dyscrasia-causing medications (see *Appendix II*)
(leukopenic and/or thrombocytopenic effects of daunorubicin may be increased with concurrent or recent therapy if these medications cause the same effects; dosage adjustment of daunorubicin, if necessary, should be based on blood counts)

» Bone marrow depressants, other (see *Appendix II*) or
Radiation therapy
(additive bone marrow depression may occur; dosage reduction may be required when two or more bone marrow depressants, including radiation, are used concurrently or consecutively)

Cyclophosphamide or
Radiation therapy to mediastinal area
(concurrent use may result in increased cardiotoxicity; it is recommended that the total dose of daunorubicin not exceed 400 mg per square meter of body surface)

Doxorubicin
(use of daunorubicin in a patient who has previously received doxorubicin increases the risk of cardiotoxicity; dosage adjustment is necessary. Daunorubicin should not be used in patients who have previously received complete cumulative doses of doxorubicin or daunorubicin; in patients who have previously received less than a complete cumulative dose of doxorubicin, the total cumulative dose of doxorubicin plus daunorubicin should not exceed 550 mg per square meter of body surface)

Hepatotoxic medications, other (see *Appendix II*)
(concurrent use may increase the risk of toxicity; for example, high-dose methotrexate may impair liver function and increase toxicity of subsequently administered daunorubicin)

Vaccines, killed virus
(because normal defense mechanisms may be suppressed by daunorubicin therapy, the patient's antibody response to the vaccine may be decreased. The interval between discontinuation of medications that cause immunosuppression and restoration of the patient's ability to respond to the vaccine depends on the intensity and type of immunosuppression-causing medication used, the underlying disease, and other factors; estimates vary from 3 months to 1 year)

» Vaccines, live virus
(because normal defense mechanisms may be suppressed by daunorubicin therapy, concurrent use with a live virus vaccine may potentiate the replication of the vaccine virus, may increase the side/adverse effects of the vaccine virus, and/or may decrease the patient's antibody response to the vaccine; immunization of these patients should be undertaken only with extreme caution after careful review of the patient's hematologic status and only with the knowledge and consent of the physician managing the daunorubicin therapy. The interval between discontinuation of medications that cause immunosuppression and restoration of the patient's ability to respond to the vaccine depends on the intensity and type of immunosuppression-causing medication used, the underlying disease, and other factors; estimates vary from 3 months to 1 year. Patients with leukemia in remission should not receive live virus vaccine until at least 3 months after their last chemotherapy. In addition, immunization with oral poliovirus vaccine should be postponed in persons in close contact with the patient, especially family members)

Laboratory value alterations

The following have been selected on the basis of their potential clinical significance (possible effect in parentheses where appropriate)—not necessarily inclusive (» = major clinical significance).

With physiology/laboratory test values
Alkaline phosphatase values, serum and
Aspartate aminotransferase (AST [SGOT]) values, serum and
Bilirubin concentrations, serum
(may be increased transiently)

Uric acid
(concentrations in blood and urine may be increased)

Medical considerations/Contraindications

The medical considerations/contraindications included have been selected on the basis of their potential clinical significance (reasons given in parentheses where appropriate)—not necessarily inclusive (» = major clinical significance).

Risk-benefit should be considered when the following medical problems exist:

» Bone marrow depression
» Chickenpox, existing or recent (including recent exposure) or
» Herpes zoster
(risk of severe generalized disease)

Gout, history of or
Urate renal stones, history of
(risk of hyperuricemia)

» Heart disease

» Hepatic function impairment
(reduction in dosage is recommended; three quarters of the normal dose is recommended in patients with serum bilirubin concentrations of 1.2 to 3 mg per 100 mL; one half of the normal dose is recommended in patients with serum bilirubin concentrations of greater than 3 mg per 100 mL)

» Infection

Renal function impairment
(reduced elimination; dosage reduction is recommended; one half of the normal dose is recommended in patients with serum creatinine concentrations of greater than 3 mg per 100 mL)

Sensitivity to daunorubicin

» Tumor cell infiltration of the bone marrow

» Caution should be used also in patients with inadequate bone marrow reserves due to previous cytotoxic drug or radiation therapy.

Patient monitoring

The following may be especially important in patient monitoring (other tests may be warranted in some patients, depending on condition; » = major clinical significance):

Alanine aminotransferase (ALT [SGPT]) values, serum and
Aspartate aminotransferase (AST [SGOT]) values, serum and
Bilirubin concentrations, serum and
Lactate dehydrogenase (LDH) values, serum
(recommended prior to initiation of therapy and at periodic intervals during therapy; frequency varies according to clinical state, agent, dose, and other agents being used concurrently)

» Chest x-ray and
» Echocardiography and
Electrocardiogram (ECG) studies and
» Radionuclide angiography determination of ejection fraction
(recommended prior to initiation of therapy and at periodic intervals during therapy)

» Hematocrit or hemoglobin and
» Leukocyte count, total and, if appropriate, differential and
» Platelet count
(determinations recommended prior to initiation of therapy and at periodic intervals during therapy; frequency varies according to clinical state, agent, dose, and other agents being used concurrently)

Uric acid concentrations, serum
(recommended prior to initiation of therapy and at periodic intervals during therapy; frequency varies according to clinical state, agent, dose, and other agents being used concurrently)

Side/Adverse Effects

Note: Many "side effects" of antineoplastic therapy are unavoidable and represent the medication's pharmacologic action. Some of these (for example, leukopenia and thrombocytopenia) are actually used as parameters to aid in individual dosage titration.

The following side/adverse effects have been selected on the basis of their potential clinical significance (possible signs and symptoms in parentheses where appropriate)—not necessarily inclusive:

Those indicating need for medical attention

Incidence more frequent

Esophagitis or stomatitis (sores in mouth and on lips); ***leukopenia or infection*** (fever or chills; cough or hoarseness; lower back or side pain; painful or difficult urination)—usually asymptomatic

Note: With *esophagitis* or *stomatitis*, sores in mouth and on lips occur 3 to 7 days after administration.

Leukopenia occurs in all patients. The nadir of the leukocyte count occurs 10 to 14 days after a dose. Recovery usually occurs within 21 days after a dose.

In addition to the risk of *infection*, febrile drug reactions may also occur during or immediately after administration.

Incidence less frequent

Cardiotoxicity in the form of congestive heart failure (irregular heartbeat; shortness of breath; swelling of feet and lower legs); ***cellulitis or tissue necrosis*** (pain at injection site)—caused by extravasation; ***gastrointestinal ulceration*** (stomach pain); ***hyperuricemia or uric acid nephropathy*** (joint pain; lower back or side pain); ***thrombocytopenia*** (unusual bleeding or bruising; black, tarry stools; blood in urine or stools; pinpoint red spots on skin)—usually asymptomatic

Note: Incidence of *cardiotoxicity* is more frequent in adults receiving a total cumulative dosage over 550 mg per square meter of body surface (450 mg per square meter of body surface in patients who have received previous chest irradiation), in the elderly, and in patients with a history of cardiac disease or mediastinal radiation.

Cardiotoxicity usually appears within 1 to 6 months after initiation of therapy. It may develop suddenly and may not be detected by routine ECG. It may be irreversible and fatal but responds to treatment if detected early.

Hyperuricemia or uric acid nephropathy occurs most commonly during initial treatment of patients with leukemia or lymphoma, as a result of rapid cell breakdown which leads to elevated serum uric acid concentrations.

Incidence rare

Allergic reaction (skin rash or itching); ***cardiotoxicity in the form of pericarditis-myocarditis***

Those indicating need for medical attention only if they continue or are bothersome

Incidence more frequent

Nausea and vomiting

Note: *Nausea and vomiting* are usually mild and transient, occurring soon after administration and lasting 24 to 48 hours.

Incidence less frequent or rare

Darkening or redness of skin—if patient has received previous radiation therapy; ***diarrhea***

Those not indicating need for medical attention

Incidence more frequent

Loss of hair; reddish urine

Note: *Loss of hair* occurs in most patients. Growth usually resumes 5 or more weeks after therapy is completed.

Reddish urine usually clears within 48 hours.

Those indicating the need for medical attention if they occur after medication is discontinued

Cardiotoxicity (irregular heartbeat; shortness of breath; swelling of feet and lower legs)

Patient Consultation

As an aid to patient consultation, refer to *Advice for the Patient, Daunorubicin (Systemic)*.

In providing consultation, consider emphasizing the following selected information (» = major clinical significance):

Before using this medication

» Conditions affecting use, especially:

Sensitivity to daunorubicin

Pregnancy—Use not recommended because of mutagenic, teratogenic, and carcinogenic potential; advisability of using a contraceptive; telling physician immediately if pregnancy is suspected

Breast-feeding—Not recommended because of risk of serious side effects

Use in the elderly—Increased risk of cardiotoxicity, bone marrow depression

Other medications, especially probenecid, sulfinpyrazone, other bone marrow depressants, or previous cytotoxic drug or radiation therapy

Other medical problems, especially chickenpox, herpes zoster, heart disease, hepatic function impairment, or infection

Proper use of this medication

Caution in taking combination therapy; taking each medication at the right time

Importance of ample fluid intake and subsequent increase in urine output to aid in excretion of uric acid

Frequency of nausea and vomiting; importance of continuing medication despite stomach upset

» Proper dosing

Precautions while using this medication

» Importance of close monitoring by the physician

» Avoiding immunizations unless approved by physician; other persons in patient's household should avoid immunizations with oral poliovirus vaccine; avoiding persons who have taken oral poliovirus vaccine or wearing a protective mask that covers nose and mouth

Caution if bone marrow depression occurs:

» Avoiding exposure to persons with infections, especially during periods of low blood counts; checking with physician immediately if fever or chills, cough or hoarseness, lower back or side pain, or painful or difficult urination occurs

» Checking with physician immediately if unusual bleeding or bruising; black, tarry stools; blood in urine or stools; or pinpoint red spots on skin occur

Caution in use of regular toothbrush, dental floss, or toothpick; physician, dentist, or nurse may suggest alternatives; checking with physician before having dental work done

Not touching eyes or inside of nose unless hands washed immediately before

Using caution to avoid accidental cuts with use of sharp objects such as safety razor or fingernail or toenail cutters

Avoiding contact sports or other situations where bruising or injury could occur

» Possibility of local tissue injury and scarring if infiltration of intravenous solution occurs; telling doctor or nurse right away about redness, pain, or swelling at injection site

Side/adverse effects

May cause adverse effects such as blood problems, loss of hair, heart problems, and cancer; importance of discussing possible effects with physician

Signs of potential side effects, especially esophagitis, stomatitis, leukopenia, infection, cardiotoxicity, cellulitis or tissue necrosis caused by extravasation, gastrointestinal ulceration, hyperuricemia, uric acid nephropathy, thrombocytopenia, and allergic reaction

Physician or nurse can help in dealing with side effects

Reddish urine may be alarming to patient although medically insignificant

Possibility of hair loss; normal hair growth should return after treatment has ended

General Dosing Information

Patients receiving daunorubicin should be under supervision of a physician experienced in cancer chemotherapy. It is recommended that the patient be hospitalized at least during initial treatment.

A variety of dosage schedules of daunorubicin, alone or in combination with other antitumor agents, are used. The prescriber may consult the medical literature as well as the manufacturer's literature in choosing a specific dosage.

Dosage must be adjusted to meet the individual requirements of each patient, on the basis of clinical response and appearance or severity of toxicity.

The desired dose of daunorubicin is withdrawn from the vial of reconstituted solution into a syringe containing 10 to 15 mL of 0.9% sodium chloride injection and then injected over 2 to 3 minutes into the tubing or side arm of a rapidly running intravenous infusion of 5% dextrose injection or 0.9% sodium chloride injection.

Care must be taken to avoid extravasation during intravenous administration. Facial flushing or erythematous streaking along the vein indicates overly rapid injection.

Administration by intravenous infusion is not recommended because of irritation to the vein and the risk of thrombophlebitis.

If extravasation of daunorubicin occurs during intravenous administration, as indicated by local burning or stinging, the injection and infusion should be stopped immediately and resumed, completing the dose, in another vein.

Because it will cause local tissue necrosis, daunorubicin must not be administered intramuscularly or subcutaneously.

Development of uric acid nephropathy in patients with leukemia or lymphoma may be prevented by adequate oral hydration and, in some cases, administration of allopurinol. Alkalinization of urine may be necessary if serum uric acid concentrations are elevated.

In general, it is recommended that a course of daunorubicin be administered no more frequently than every 21 days to allow the bone marrow to recover.

In acute leukemia, daunorubicin may be administered despite the presence of thrombocytopenia and bleeding; stoppage of bleeding and increase in platelet count have occurred during treatment in some cases and platelet transfusions are useful in others.

Special precautions are recommended in patients who develop thrombocytopenia as a result of administration of daunorubicin. These may include extreme care in performing invasive procedures; regular inspection of intravenous sites, skin (including perirectal area), and mucous membrane surfaces for signs of bleeding or bruising; limiting frequency of venipuncture and avoiding intramuscular injections; testing urine, emesis, stool, and secretions for occult blood; care in use of regular toothbrushes, dental floss, toothpicks, safety razors, and fingernail and toenail cutters; avoiding constipation; and using caution to prevent falls and other injuries. Such patients should avoid alcohol and aspirin intake because of the risk of gastrointestinal bleeding. Platelet transfusions may be required.

Patients who develop leukopenia should be observed carefully for signs of infection. Antibiotic support may be required. In neutropenic patients who develop fever, broad-spectrum antibiotic coverage should be initiated empirically, pending bacterial cultures and appropriate diagnostic tests.

Safety considerations for handling this medication

There is limited but increasing evidence and concern that personnel involved in preparation and administration of parenteral antineoplastics may be at some risk because of the potential mutagenicity, teratogenicity, and/or carcinogenicity of these agents, although the actual risk is unknown. USP advisory panels recommend cautious handling both in preparation and disposal of antineoplastic agents. Precautions that have been suggested include:

- Use of a biological containment cabinet during reconstitution and dilution of parenteral medications and wearing of disposable surgical gloves and masks.
- Use of proper technique to prevent contamination of the medication, work area, and operator during transfer between containers (including proper training of personnel in this technique).
- Cautious and proper disposal of needles, syringes, vials, ampuls, and unused medication.

A number of medical centers have developed detailed guidelines for handling of antineoplastic agents.

Combination chemotherapy

Daunorubicin may be used in combination with other agents in various regimens. As a result, incidence and/or severity of side effects may be altered and different dosages (usually reduced) may be used. For example, daunorubicin is part of the following chemotherapeutic combination:

—daunorubicin, vincristine, and prednisone.

For specific dosages and schedules, consult the literature. For information regarding each agent, consult the individual monographs.

Parenteral Dosage Forms

DAUNORUBICIN HYDROCHLORIDE FOR INJECTION USP

Note: The doses and strengths of the available dosage forms are expressed in terms of the daunorubicin base, not the hydrochloride salt.

Usual adult dose

Leukemia, acute lymphocytic—

Intravenous, 45 mg (base) per square meter of body surface on days 1, 2, and 3 of a thirty-two–day course in combination with vincristine, prednisone, and asparaginase.

Leukemia, acute nonlymphocytic—

Intravenous, 45 mg (base) per square meter of body surface on days 1, 2, and 3 of the first course and days 1 and 2 of the second course, in combination with cytarabine.

Usual adult prescribing limits

Up to a total lifetime dosage of 550 mg (base) per square meter of body surface, 450 mg per square meter of body surface in patients who have received previous chest irradiation (to reduce risk of cardiotoxicity).

Usual pediatric dose

Leukemia, acute lymphocytic—

Intravenous, 25 mg (base) per square meter of body surface once a week, in combination with vincristine and prednisone.

Note: In children less than 2 years of age or below 0.5 square meter of body surface, dosage should be calculated on the basis of mg per kg of body weight rather than body surface area.

Usual geriatric dose

For patients 60 years of age and older—

Leukemia, acute nonlymphocytic:

Intravenous, 30 mg (base) per square meter of body surface on days 1, 2, and 3 of the first course and days 1 and 2 of the second course, in combination with cytarabine.

Note: This dose is based on a single study and may not be appropriate if optimal supportive care is available.

Strength(s) usually available

U.S.—

20 mg (base) (21.4 mg as HCl) (Rx) [*Cerubidine* (mannitol 100 mg)].

Canada—

20 mg (base) (21.4 mg as HCl) (Rx) [*Cerubidine*].

Packaging and storage

Store below 40 °C (104 °F), preferably between 15 and 30 °C (59 and 86 °F), unless otherwise specified by manufacturer. Protect from light.

Preparation of dosage form

Daunorubicin for Injection USP is reconstituted for intravenous administration by adding 4 mL of sterile water for injection to the vial and shaking gently to dissolve, producing a solution containing 5 mg of daunorubicin (base) per mL.

Stability

Reconstituted solutions of daunorubicin are stable for 24 hours at room temperature or 48 hours between 2 and 8 °C (36 and 46 °F) when protected from light.

Note

Any daunorubicin powder or solution that comes in contact with the skin or mucosa should be washed off thoroughly with soap and water.

Selected Bibliography

DeVita VT, Hellman S, Rosenberg SA. Cancer principles and practice of oncology. 5th ed. Philadelphia: Lippincott-Raven Publishers; 1997.

Revised: 09/27/1997

DAUNORUBICIN, LIPOSOMAL Systemic†

VA CLASSIFICATION (Primary): AN200

Commonly used brand name(s): *DaunoXome*.

Note: For a listing of dosage forms and brand names by country availability, see *Dosage Forms* section(s).

†Not commercially available in Canada.

Category

Antineoplastic.

Indications

Accepted

Kaposi's sarcoma (KS), acquired immunodeficiency syndrome (AIDS)-associated (treatment)—Liposomal daunorubicin is indicated as a first-line cytotoxic therapy for advanced AIDS-associated KS. Liposomal daunorubicin is not recommended in patients with less than advanced AIDS-associated KS.

Note: The treatment of AIDS-associated KS is dependent on the extent and severity of the KS and the patient's clinical condition. For patients with minimal disease, local treatments such as excision, radiotherapy, or intralesional chemotherapy will be adequate. However, for those with severe cutaneous or systemic disease, systemic chemotherapy may be required. Patients with severe debilitation due to their general condition are best served by optimal palliative care.

Note: The USP medical experts chose to *not include* treatment for acute lymphoblastic leukemia, acute myelogenous leukemia, or multiple myeloma, as indications for liposomal daunorubicin. Currently, liposomal daunorubicin is appropriate for use in the treatment of acute lymphoblastic leukemia, acute myelogenous leukemia, and multiple myeloma, only in a clinical trial setting.

Pharmacology/Pharmacokinetics

Note: A human pharmacokinetics study has shown that the pharmacokinetics of liposomal daunorubicin are significantly different from those of conventional daunorubicin, which may account for both its reduced toxicity and its potentially enhanced activity. However, the pharmacokinetics of liposomal daunorubicin have not been evaluated in women, in a variety of ethnic groups, or in patients with renal and hepatic insufficiency.

Physicochemical characteristics

Source—Daunorubicin is an anthracycline antibiotic originally obtained from *Streptomyces peucetius.* Daunorubicin also may be isolated from *Streptomyces coeruleorubidus.* Liposomal daunorubicin is an aqueous solution of the citrate salt of daunorubicin encapsulated within lipid vesicles (liposomes) composed of a lipid bilayer of highly purified distearoylphosphatidylcholine (DSPC) and cholesterol in a 2:1 molar ratio.

Mechanism of action/Effect

Liposomal daunorubicin is a liposomal preparation of daunorubicin formulated to maximize the selectivity of daunorubicin for solid tumors *in situ.* While in the circulation, the liposomal formulation helps to protect the entrapped daunorubicin from chemical and enzymatic degradation, minimizes protein binding, and generally decreases uptake by normal (nonreticuloendothelial system) tissues. Once within the tumor environment, daunorubicin is released over time, enabling it to exert its antineoplastic activity.

The specific mechanism by which liposomal daunorubicin is able to deliver daunorubicin to solid tumors *in situ* is not known. However, it is believed to be a function of increased permeability of the tumor neovasculature to some particles in the size range of liposomal daunorubicin.

In animal studies, liposomal daunorubicin has demonstrated improved activity against solid tumors compared with that of conventional daunorubicin.

Distribution

Limited to vascular fluid.

Volume of distribution (Vol_D)—Steady-state: 6.4 liters following intravenous administration of 40 mg per square meter of body surface area (mg/m^2), over 30 to 60 minutes.

In animal studies, liposomal daunorubicin appeared to cross the blood-brain barrier and to accumulate selectively in solid tumor tissues to a greater extent than occurs with nonencapsulated daunorubicin.

Biotransformation

Daunorubicinol, the major active metabolite of daunorubicin, was detected at low concentrations in the plasma following intravenous administration of liposomal daunorubicin.

Half-life

Distribution—4.41 hours following intravenous administration of a 40 mg/m^2 dose over 30 to 60 minutes.

Elimination

Plasma clearance—17 mL per minute following intravenous administration of a 40 mg/m^2 dose over 30 to 60 minutes.

Precautions to Consider

Cross-sensitivity and/or related problems

Liposomal daunorubicin is not recommended in patients hypersensitive to daunorubicin or the liposomal components.

Carcinogenicity

Studies to evaluate the carcinogenic potential of liposomal daunorubicin have not been performed. However, the active ingredient, daunorubicin, was found to increase the incidence of mammary tumors in rats following a single dose of 12.5 mg per kg of body weight (mg/kg) (approximately two times the recommended human dose on a mg per square meter of body surface area [mg/m^2] basis).

Mutagenicity

Studies to evaluate the mutagenic potential of liposomal daunorubicin have not been performed. However, the active ingredient, daunorubicin, was mutagenic in *in vitro* tests (Ames test and V79 hamster cell assay) and clastogenic in *in vitro* (CCRF-CEM human lymphoblasts) and *in vivo* (SCE assay in mouse bone marrow) test systems.

Pregnancy/Reproduction

Fertility—Studies to evaluate the effects of liposomal daunorubicin on fertility have not been performed; however, the active ingredient, daunorubicin, caused testicular atrophy and total aplasia of spermatocytes in the seminiferous tubules in male dogs administered 0.25 mg/kg per day (approximately eight times the recommended human dose on a mg/m^2 basis).

Pregnancy—Adequate and well-controlled studies in humans have not been done. Furthermore, the pharmacokinetics of liposomal daunorubicin have not been evaluated in women.

In general, use of a contraceptive method is recommended during cytotoxic drug therapy.

Liposomal daunorubicin caused severe maternal toxicity and embryolethality in rats administered doses of 2 mg/kg per day (one third of the maximum recommended human dose) on days 6 through 15 of gestation. Studies in rats administered doses of 0.3 mg/kg per day (one twentieth of the maximum recommended human dose) on days 6 through 15 of gestation showed that liposomal daunorubicin caused embryotoxicity (increased embryofetal deaths, reduced numbers of litters, and reduced litter size) and caused fetal malformations (anophthalmia, microphthalmia, incomplete ossification).

FDA Pregnancy Category D.

Breast-feeding

It is not known whether liposomal daunorubicin is distributed into breast milk. However, breast-feeding is not recommended while liposomal daunorubicin is being administered because of the potential risk of adverse reactions in the infant.

Pediatrics

No information is available on the relationship of age to the effects of liposomal daunorubicin in pediatric patients. Safety and efficacy have not been established.

Geriatrics

No information is available on the relationship of age to the effects of liposomal daunorubicin in geriatric patients. However, elderly patients are more likely to have age-related renal function impairment, which may require caution in patients receiving liposomal daunorubicin. Safety and efficacy have not been established.

Dental

The leukopenic and thrombocytopenic effects of liposomal daunorubicin may result in an increased incidence of certain microbial infections of the mouth, delayed healing, and gingival bleeding. If leukopenia or thrombocytopenia occurs, dental work should be deferred until blood counts have returned to normal. Patients should be instructed in proper oral hygiene, including caution in use of regular toothbrushes, dental floss, and toothpicks.

Drug interactions and/or related problems

The following drug interactions and/or related problems have been selected on the basis of their potential clinical significance (possible mechanism in parentheses where appropriate)—not necessarily inclusive (» = major clinical significance):

Note: Combinations containing any of the following medications, depending on the amount present, may also interact with this medication.

Allopurinol or
Colchicine or
» Probenecid or
» Sulfinpyrazone
(liposomal daunorubicin may raise the concentration of blood uric acid; dosage adjustment of antigout agents may be necessary to control hyperuricemia and gout; allopurinol may be preferred to prevent or reverse liposomal daunorubicin–induced hyperuricemia because of risk of uric acid nephropathy with uricosuric antigout agents)

» Daunorubicin, prior use of or
» Doxorubicin, prior use of or
» Other anthracycline antineoplastics, prior use of
(use of liposomal daunorubicin in a patient who previously has received anthracenedione antineoplastic agents, daunorubicin, doxorubicin, or other anthracycline antineoplastics increases the risk for cardiotoxicity; dosage adjustment is necessary)

(prior anthracycline use is also significantly associated with short survival)

Blood dyscrasia-causing medications (see *Appendix II*)
(leukopenic and/or thrombocytopenic effects of liposomal daunorubicin may be increased with concurrent or recent therapy if these medications cause the same effects; dosage adjustment of liposomal daunorubicin, if necessary, should be based on blood counts)

» Bone marrow depressants, other (see *Appendix II*) or
Radiation therapy
(additive bone marrow depression may occur; dosage reduction may be required when two or more bone marrow depressants, including radiation, are used concurrently or consecutively)

Cyclophosphamide or
Radiation therapy to mediastinal area
(concurrent use may result in increased cardiotoxicity; it is recommended that the total dose of liposomal daunorubicin not exceed 400 mg/m^2)

Hepatotoxic medications, other (see *Appendix II*)
(concurrent use may increase the risk of toxicity; for example, high-dose methotrexate may impair liver function and increase toxicity of subsequently administered liposomal daunorubicin)

Vaccines, killed virus
(because normal defense mechanisms may be suppressed by liposomal daunorubicin therapy, the patient's antibody response to the vaccine may be decreased. The interval between discontinuation of medications that cause immunosuppression and restoration of the patient's ability to respond to the vaccine depends on the intensity and type of immunosuppression-causing medication used, the underlying disease, and other factors; estimates vary from 3 months to 1 year)

» Vaccines, live virus
(because normal defense mechanisms may be suppressed by liposomal daunorubicin therapy, concurrent use with a live virus vaccine may potentiate the replication of the vaccine virus, may increase the side/adverse effects of the vaccine virus, and/or may decrease the patient's antibody response to the vaccine; immunization of these patients should be undertaken only with extreme caution after careful review of the patient's hematologic status and only with the knowledge and consent of the physician managing the liposomal daunorubicin therapy. The interval between discontinuation of medications that cause immunosuppression and restoration of the patient's ability to respond to the vaccine depends on the intensity and type of immunosuppression-causing medication used, the underlying disease, and other factors; estimates vary from 3 months to 1 year. Patients with leukemia in remission should not receive live virus vaccine until at least 3 months after their last chemotherapy. In addition, immunization with oral poliovirus vaccine should be postponed in persons in close contact with the patient, especially family members)

Laboratory value alterations

The following have been selected on the basis of their potential clinical significance (possible effect in parentheses where appropriate)—not necessarily inclusive (» = major clinical significance).

With physiology/laboratory test values

» Cardiac function tests
(left ventricular ejection fraction may be decreased, possibly indicating cardiotoxicity)

Hematocrit or
Hemoglobin or
» Leukocyte counts or
Platelet counts
(may be decreased)

Medical considerations/Contraindications

The medical considerations/contraindications included have been selected on the basis of their potential clinical significance (reasons given in parentheses where appropriate)—not necessarily inclusive (» = major clinical significance).

Except under special circumstances, this medication should not be used when the following medical problem exists:

» Previous hypersensitivity reaction to liposomal daunorubicin or its components

Risk-benefit should be considered when the following medical problems exist:

» Bone marrow depression

» Cardiac disease, pre-existing
(may increase risk of cardiotoxicity; monitoring of cardiac function is recommended)

» Chickenpox, existing or recent (including recent exposure) or
» Herpes zoster
(risk of severe generalized disease)

» Granulocytopenia, severe
(treatment should be withheld if the absolute granulocyte count is lower than 750 cells per cubic millimeter)

» Hepatic function impairment
(excretion may be delayed; reduction in dosage is recommended; three fourths of the normal dose is recommended in patients with serum bilirubin concentrations of 1.2 to 3 mg per deciliter; one half of the normal dose is recommended in patients with serum bilirubin concentrations of greater than 3 mg per deciliter)

» Renal function impairment
(excretion may be delayed; reduction in dosage is recommended; one half of the normal dose is recommended in patients with serum creatinine concentrations greater than 3 mg per deciliter)

» Sensitivity to daunorubicin or to the liposomal components

» Tumor cell infiltration of the bone marrow

» Caution should be used also in patients with inadequate bone marrow reserves due to previous cytotoxic drug or radiation therapy

Patient monitoring

The following may be especially important in patient monitoring (other tests may be warranted in some patients, depending on condition; » = major clinical significance):

Alanine aminotransferase (ALT [SGPT]) values, serum and
Aspartate aminotransferase (AST [SGOT]) values, serum and
Bilirubin concentrations, serum and
Lactate dehydrogenase (LDH) values, serum
(recommended prior to initiation of therapy and at periodic intervals during therapy; frequently varies according to clinical state, agent, dose, and other agents being used concurrently)

» Cardiac function
(recommended prior to initiation of therapy and at periodic intervals during therapy)

» Hematocrit or hemoglobin and
» Leukocyte count, total and, if appropriate, differential and
» Platelet count
(determinations recommended prior to initiation of therapy and at periodic intervals during therapy; frequently varies according to clinical state, agent, dose, and other agents being used concurrently)

» Left ventricular ejection fraction
(determination recommended at total cumulative doses of 320 mg/m^2, 480 mg/m^2, and every 240 mg/m^2 thereafter)

» Observation for evidence of intercurrent or opportunistic infections

Side/Adverse Effects

The following side/adverse effects have been selected on the basis of their potential clinical significance (possible signs and symptoms in parentheses where appropriate)—not necessarily inclusive:

Those indicating need for medical attention

Incidence more frequent

Dyspnea (shortness of breath; troubled breathing)—less frequently, may be severe or associated with pulmonary infiltrations; ***neuropathy*** (weakness or numbness in arms or legs); ***neutropenia*** (cough or hoarseness; fever or chills; lower back or side pain; painful or difficult urination; sore throat)

Note: Clinical studies have demonstrated that *neutropenia* is the predominant hematologic toxicity following treatment with liposomal daunorubicin. In one study, 36% of patients experienced grade 3 neutropenia (< 1000 cells/mm^2), while 15% of patients experienced grade 4 neutropenia (< 500 cells/mm^2). Futhermore, patients receiving this medication may experience a higher frequency of opportunistic infections and neutropenic fevers. Acquired immunodeficiency syndrome (AIDS) patients are susceptible to a variety of opportunistic infections, and chemotherapy-associated bone marrow suppression may enhance this risk. It is possible that liposomal daunorubicin may interfere with monocyte-macrophage function, and thus increase susceptibility to opportunistic infections.

Incidence less frequent

Anemia (unusual tiredness or weakness); ***cardiotoxicity*** (irregular heartbeat; shortness of breath; swelling of the feet and lower legs); ***chest pain; edema*** (swelling of abdomen, face, fingers, hands, feet, or lower legs; weight gain); ***gastrointestinal hemorrhage*** (black, tarry stools; bloody stools; bloody vomit); ***hemoptysis*** (coughing up blood); ***hypertension***—usually asymptomatic; ***renal effects, including dysuria*** (painful or difficult urination); ***nocturia*** (unusual nighttime urination); ***or polyuria*** (producing large amounts of pale, dilute urine); ***stomatitis*** (sores in mouth and on lips); ***syncope*** (fainting); ***tachy-***

cardia (fast heartbeat); ***thrombocytopenia*** (black, tarry stools; unusual bleeding or bruising; blood in urine or stools; pinpoint red spots on skin)

Note: Cardiac function should be monitored regularly in patients receiving liposomal daunorubicin because of the potential risk for *cardiotoxicity* and congestive heart failure. Cardiac monitoring is advised especially in those patients who have received prior anthracycline therapy or who have pre-existing cardiac disease. Cardiotoxicity can occur with cumulative doses of greater than 300 mg per square meter of body surface area.

Those indicating need for medical attention only if they continue or are bothersome

Incidence more frequent

Abdominal pain; allergic reaction (chills; fever; skin rash or itching)—severe reactions occur less frequently; ***diarrhea; headache; infusion-related reaction*** (back pain; chest tightness; flushing)—usually mild to moderate in severity; ***nausea and vomiting***—severe reactions occur less frequently; ***rigors*** (feeling unusually cold; shivering)

Note: An *infusion-related reaction* may occur during the first 5 minutes of the infusion and may be related to the liposomal component of liposomal daunorubicin.

Incidence less frequent

Arthralgia or myalgia (pain in joints or muscles); ***conjunctivitis*** (dry, irritated, itching, or red eyes); ***constipation; dizziness; dry mouth; dysphagia*** (difficulty swallowing); ***eye pain; folliculitis*** (painful, red, hot, or irritated hair follicles); ***gingival bleeding*** (bleeding gums); ***hemorrhoids*** (bleeding after defecation; uncomfortable swelling around anus); ***injection site inflammation*** (red, hot, or irritated skin at site of injection; pain at site of injection; swelling or lump under skin at site of injection)—if extravasation occurs; ***insomnia*** (sleeplessness); ***somnolence*** (extreme feeling of sleepiness); ***tenesmus*** (frequent urge to defecate); ***tinnitus*** (ringing sound in ears); ***tooth caries*** (tooth pain); ***tremor*** (uncontrollable movement of body)

Note: Local tissue necrosis has not been observed when extravasation occurs.

Those not indicating need for medical attention

Incidence less frequent

Alopecia (loss of hair)

Note: *Alopecia*, a frequent side effect associated with anthracycline therapy, is usually mild to moderate in severity following liposomal daunorubicin therapy. In one study, alopecia occurred in only 8% of patients treated with liposomal daunorubicin.

Overdose

For specific information on the agents used in the management of liposomal doxorubicin overdose, see:

- *Filgrastim* and/or *Sargramostim* in *Colony Stimulating Factors (Systemic)* monograph.

For more information on the management of overdose, **contact a Poison Control Center** (see *Poison Control Center Listing*).

Clinical effects of overdose

The following effects have been selected on the basis of their potential clinical significance (possible signs and symptoms in parentheses where appropriate)—not necessarily inclusive:

Acute

Mucositis (sores in mouth and on lips); ***neutropenia*** (cough or hoarseness; fever or chills; lower back or side pain; painful or difficult urination; sore throat)—usually asymptomatic; ***thrombocytopenia*** (black, tarry stools; blood in urine or stools; pinpoint red spots on skin; unusual bleeding or bruising)—usually asymptomatic

Treatment of overdose

Treatment of leukopenia includes antibiotic therapy and administration of colony stimulating factors (filgrastim [rG-CSF] or sargramostim [rGM-CSF]).

Treatment of thrombocytopenia includes hospitalization of the patient and platelet transfusions.

Patient Consultation

As an aid to patient consultation, refer to *Advice for the Patient, Daunorubicin, Liposomal (Systemic)*.

In providing consultation, consider emphasizing the following selected information (» = major clinical significance):

Before using this medication

» Conditions affecting use, especially:

Hypersensitivity to daunorubicin or the liposomal component

Pregnancy—Use is not recommended because of embryotoxic and maternotoxic potential; advisability of using contraception

Breast-feeding—Use is not recommended because of the potential for serious adverse effects in nursing infants

Other medications, especially daunorubicin, doxorubicin, live virus vaccines, other anthracycline antineoplastics, other bone marrow depressants, previous cytotoxic drug or radiation therapy, probenecid or sulfinpyrazone

Other medical problems, especially bone marrow depression; cardiac disease, pre-existing; chickenpox; granulocytopenia, severe; hepatic function impairment; herpes zoster; renal function impairment; or tumor cell infiltration of bone marrow

Proper use of this medication

Caution in taking combination therapy; taking each medication at the right time

Importance of ample fluid intake and subsequent increase in urine output to aid in excretion of uric acid

Frequency of nausea and vomiting; importance of continuing medication despite stomach upset

» Proper dosing

Precautions while using this medication

» Importance of close monitoring by the physician

» Avoiding immunizations unless approved by the physician; other persons in patient's household should avoid immunizations with oral poliovirus vaccine; avoiding persons who have taken oral poliovirus vaccine, or wearing a protective mask that covers nose and mouth

Caution if bone marrow depression occurs:

» Avoiding exposure to persons with infections, especially during periods of low blood counts; checking with physician immediately if fever or chills, cough or hoarseness, lower back or side pain, or painful or difficult urination occurs

» Checking with physician immediately if unusual bleeding or bruising; black, tarry stools; blood in urine or stools; or pinpoint red spots on skin occur

Caution in use of regular toothbrush, dental floss, or toothpick; physician, dentist, or nurse may suggest alternatives; checking with physician before having dental work done

Not touching eyes or inside of nose unless hands washed immediately before

Using caution to avoid accidental cuts with use of sharp objects such as safety razor or fingernail or toenail cutters

Avoiding contact sports or other situations where bruising or injury could occur

» Possibility of local tissue injury and scarring if infiltration of intravenous solution occurs; telling doctor or nurse right away about redness, pain, or swelling at injection site

Side/adverse effects

May cause adverse effects such as blood problems, loss of hair, heart problems, and cancer

Signs of potential side effects, especially dyspnea; neuropathy; neutropenia; anemia; cardiotoxicity; chest pain; edema; gastrointestinal hemorrhage; hemoptysis; hypertension; renal effects, including dysuria, nocturia, or polyuria; stomatitis; syncope; tachycardia; and thrombocytopenia

Physician or nurse can help in dealing with side effects

Reddish urine for 1 to 2 days after administration may be alarming to patient although medically insignificant

Possibility of hair loss; normal hair growth should resume after treatment has ended

General Dosing Information

Patients receiving liposomal daunorubicin should be under supervision of a physician experienced in cancer chemotherapy.

Liposomal daunorubicin should be administered intravenously over a period of 60 minutes at a dose of 40 mg per square meter of body surface area (mg/m^2), with doses repeated every 2 weeks. Blood counts should be performed prior to each dose and therapy should be withheld if the absolute granulocyte count is less than 750 cells/mm^3.

Treatment with liposomal daunorubicin should be continued until there is evidence of progressive disease, or until other intercurrent complications of human immunodeficiency virus (HIV) disease preclude continuation of therapy.

Patients may experience an acute reaction following rapid infusion. The reaction usually consists of shortness of breath, facial flushing, back pain, fever, and chills. This reaction is related to the rate of infusion; slowing the infusion rate may eliminate this problem.

If the reaction persists after the infusion rate is decreased, the infusion should be discontinued. After discontinuation of the infusion, intravenous administration of diphenhydramine and hydrocortisone and oxygen administration via facial mask usually helps full recovery with no sequelae.

Dosage should be adjusted for patients with impaired renal function. A dose reduction of 50% is recommended if serum creatinine concentrations are > 3 mg per deciliter (mg/dL).

Dosage should be adjusted for patients with impaired hepatic function. A dose reduction of 25% is recommended if serum bilirubin concentrations are 1.2 to 3 mg/dL. A dose reduction of 50% is recommended if serum bilirubin concentrations are > 3 mg/dL.

Safety considerations for handling this medication

There is limited but increasing evidence and concern that personnel involved in preparation and administration of parenteral antineoplastic agents may be at some risk because of the potential mutagenicity, teratogenicity, and/or carcinogenicity of these agents, although the actual risk is unknown. USP advisory panels recommend cautious handling both in preparation and disposal of antineoplastic agents. Precautions that have been suggested include:

- Use of a biological containment cabinet during reconstitution and dilution of parenteral medications and wearing of disposable surgical gloves and masks.
- Use of proper technique to prevent contamination of the medication, work area, and operator during transfer between containers (including proper training of personnel in this technique).
- Cautious and proper disposal of needles, syringes, vials, ampuls, and unused medication.

A number of medical centers have developed detailed guidelines for handling of antineoplastic agents.

Parenteral Dosage Forms

Note: The dosing and strengths of the dosage forms available are expressed in terms of liposomal daunorubicin base (not the citrate salt).

DAUNORUBICIN, LIPOSOMAL INJECTION

Usual adult dose

AIDS-associated Kaposi's sarcoma—

Intravenous infusion (over sixty minutes), 40 mg (base) per square meter of body surface area, repeated every two weeks.

Note: Dosage should be adjusted for patients with impaired renal function. A dose reduction of 50% is recommended if serum creatinine concentrations are > 3 mg per deciliter (mg/dL).

Dosage should be adjusted for patients with impaired hepatic function. A dose reduction of 25% is recommended if serum bilirubin concentrations are 1.2 to 3 mg/dL. A dose reduction of 50% is recommended if serum bilirubin concentrations are > 3 mg/dL.

Usual pediatric dose

Safety and efficacy have not been established.

Usual geriatric dose

Safety and efficacy have not been established.

Strength(s) usually available

U.S.—

2 mg per mL (base) (25-mL, single-dose vial) (Rx) [*DaunoXome*].

Canada—

Not commercially available.

Packaging and storage

Store between 2 and 8 °C (36 and 46 °F). Do not freeze. Protect from light.

Preparation of dosage form

Liposomal daunorubicin should be diluted 1:1 with 5% dextrose injection before administration. Each vial of liposomal daunorubicin contains daunorubicin citrate equivalent to 50 mg daunorubicin base at a concentration of 2 mg per mL. The recommended concentration after dilution is 1 mg daunorubicin per mL.

Note: Aseptic techniques should be strictly observed when handling liposomal daunorubicin, since no preservatives or bacteriostatic agents are present in liposomal daunorubicin or in the materials recommended for dilution.

Stability

Diluted liposomal daunorubicin is stable for 6 hours when stored between 2 and 8 °C (36 and 46 °F).

Incompatibilities

Liposomal daunorubicin should be diluted only in 5% dextrose injection. Liposomal daunorubicin should not be mixed with other medications, other diluents, or bacteriostatic agents. Mixing liposomal daunorubicin with any other diluent may cause precipitation.

Note

Liposomal daunorubicin is a red, translucent dispersion. In-line filters should not be used because liposomal daunorubicin is not a clear solution.

Revised: 12/04/2001
Developed: 06/23/1998

DECONGESTANTS AND ANALGESICS Systemic

NOTE: The *Decongestants and Analgesics (Systemic)* monograph is maintained on the *USP DI* electronic data base. A copy of the most recent revision of the complete monograph can be accessed on the *USP DI* Updates Online website. See the front cover of book for details on accessing the site.

For information on the specific components of this combination, see the *USP DI* monographs for *Acetaminophen (Systemic), Anti-inflammatory Drugs, Nonsteroidal (Systemic), Caffeine (Systemic), Phenylpropanolamine (Systemic), Pseudoephedrine (Systemic), Salicylates (Systemic)*, and *Sympathomimetic Agents—Cardiovascular Use (Systemic)*.

The information that follows is selectively abstracted from the complete monograph and is provided to facilitate drug use review and patient counseling.

Note: Products containing phenylpropanolamine were removed from the U.S. and Canadian Markets in November 2000.

This monograph includes information on the following: 1) Phenylephrine and Acetaminophen; 2) Pseudoephedrine and Acetaminophen; 3) Pseudoephedrine and Ibuprofen.

VA CLASSIFICATION (Primary): RE599

Note: Other combinations containing decongestants in addition to other ingredients are found in

Antihistamines and Decongestants (Systemic), Antihistamines, Decongestants, and Analgesics (Systemic), Antihistamines, Decongestants, and Anticholinergics (Systemic), and *Cough/Cold Combinations (Systemic)*.

Commonly used brand name(s):.

Note: For a listing of dosage forms and brand names by country availability, see *Dosage Forms* section(s).

Category

Decongestant-analgesic.

Indications

Accepted

Congestion, nasal (treatment)
Congestion, sinus (treatment) and
Headache, sinus (treatment)—Decongestant and analgesic combinations are indicated for the temporary relief of nasal and sinus congestion and headache pain caused by sinusitis, common colds, allergy, and hay fever.

The therapeutic effectiveness of oral phenylephrine as a nasal decongestant has been questioned, especially at the usual oral dose.

Note: In November 2000, the Food and Drug Administration (FDA) issued a public health warning regarding phenylpropanolamine (PPA) due to the risk of hemorrhagic stroke. The FDA, supported by the final report of The Hemorrhagic Stroke Project (HSP), requested that manufacturers voluntarily discontinue marketing products that contain PPA and that consumers work with their healthcare providers to select alternative products.

Patient Consultation

Note: Products containing phenylpropanolamine were removed from the U.S. and Canadian Markets in November 2000.

As an aid to patient consultation, refer to *Advice for the Patient, Decongestants and Analgesics (Systemic)*.

In providing consultation, consider emphasizing the following selected information (» = major clinical significance):

Before using this medication

» Conditions affecting use, especially:

Sensitivity to other sympathomimetic amines, salicylates or other nonsteroidal anti-inflammatory drugs

Pregnancy—Concern with high doses and long-term therapy because of salicylate effects; use of aspirin-containing combinations not recommended during third trimester; use of ibuprofen-containing combinations during second half of pregnancy not recommended because of potential adverse effect on fetal blood flow

Breast-feeding—High risk for infants from sympathomimetic amines; also, concern with high doses and chronic use because of high salicylate intake by infant

Use in children—Increased sensitivity to vasopressor and psychiatric effects of sympathomimetic amines; also, increased susceptibility to toxic effects of salicylates, especially if fever and dehydration present; possible association between aspirin usage and Reyes syndrome

Use in adolescents—Possible association between aspirin usage and Reyes syndrome

Use in the elderly—Increased susceptibility to effects of sympathomimetic amines and toxic effects of salicylates; increased risk of toxicity with ibuprofen

Other medications, especially for high blood pressure or depression, CNS depressants or stimulants, and others that may interact with acetaminophen, ibuprofen, and/or salicylates depending on specific ingredients of combination

Other medical problems, especially hypertension (for all combinations); alcoholism or hepatitis (for acetaminophen-containing combinations); hemophilia or other bleeding problems (for aspirin-containing combinations); asthma, gastritis, or peptic ulcer (with salicylate-containing combinations); clotting defects, peptic ulcer or other gastrointestinal tract disease, or stomatitis (for ibuprofen-containing combinations)

Proper use of this medication

» Importance of not taking more medication than the amount recommended

» Proper dosing

Missed dose: If on scheduled dosing regimen—Taking as soon as possible; not taking if almost time for next dose; not doubling doses

» Proper storage

For salicylate-containing combinations

Taking with food or a full glass (240 mL) of water to minimize gastrointestinal irritation

» Not taking combinations containing aspirin if a strong vinegar-like odor is present

For ibuprofen-containing combinations

Taking with food or antacids (a magnesium- and aluminum-containing antacid may be preferred) to reduce gastrointestinal irritation; not lying down for 15 to 30 minutes after taking

Precautions while using this medication

Checking with physician if symptoms persist or become worse, or if high fever is present

» Caution if taking appetite suppressants

» Possible insomnia; taking the medication a few hours before bedtime

Need to inform physician or dentist of use of medication if any kind of surgery (including dental surgery or emergency treatment is required)

» Caution if other medications containing acetaminophen, aspirin, or other salicylates (including diflunisal) are used

» Avoiding use of alcoholic beverages while taking these medications; alcohol consumption may increase risk of ibuprofen- or salicylate-induced gastrointestinal toxicity and acetaminophen-induced liver toxicity

» Suspected overdose: Getting emergency help at once

Not taking products containing aspirin for 5 days prior to any kind of surgery, unless otherwise directed by physician

Diabetics: Aspirin present in some combination formulations may cause false urine sugar test results with prolonged use of 8 or more 325-mg (5-grain) doses per day

For ibuprofen-containing combinations:

» Caution if drowsiness or dizziness occurs

» Importance of immediately reporting to physician symptoms of edema, gastrointestinal bleeding or ulceration, cardiovascular events, unusual weight gain, or skin rash

Side/adverse effects

Signs of potential side effects, especially allergic reactions, anemia, cardiac effects, CNS stimulation, psychotic episodes, severe dizziness, severe nervousness or restlessness (for all combinations); blood dyscrasias, hepatitis, hepatotoxicity (for acetaminophen-containing); signs of gastrointestinal irritation or bleeding (for ibuprofen- or salicylate-containing); and cutaneous adverse effects, hepatitis, renal impairment (for ibuprofen-containing)

Oral Dosage Forms

DECONGESTANTS AND ANALGESICS

Note: Products containing phenylpropanolamine were removed from the U.S. and Canadian Markets in November 2000.

For Adult and Pediatric

Dose listing (refer to Table 1)—

See *Table 1*, page 1037.

Strength(s) usually available

U.S.—

See *Table 1. Oral Dosage Forms.*

Canada—

See *Table 1. Oral Dosage Forms.*

Revised: 08/04/2005

Table 1. Oral Dosage Forms

Note: Content per capsule, tablet, or 5 mL, unless otherwise stated.

Brand or generic name [availability]	Decongestants	Analgesics	Other content information as per product label	Usual adult and adolescent dose* (prn)	Usual pediatric dose (prn)	Packaging, storage, and auxiliary labeling
Actifed Sinus Daytime Tablets USP (OTC) [U.S.]	Pseudoephedrine HCl 30 mg	Acetaminophen 500 mg	Available in a dual package that also contains *Actifed Sinus Night-time Tablets*	2 tabs q 6 hr (max 8 total *Daytime* and *Night-time* tabs/day)	Not recommended	†
Actifed Sinus Daytime Caplets Tablets USP (OTC) [U.S.]	Pseudoephedrine HCl 30 mg	Acetaminophen 500 mg	Available in a dual package that also contains *Actifed Sinus Night-time Caplets*	2 tabs q 6 hr (max 8 total *Daytime* and *Night-time* tabs/day)	Not recommended	†
Advil Cold and Sinus Tablets USP (OTC) [U.S.]	Pseudoephedrine HCl 30 mg	Ibuprofen 200 mg		1–2 tabs q 4–6 hr (max 6 tabs/day)		†
Advil Cold and Sinus Caplets Tablets USP (OTC) [U.S./Canada]	Pseudoephedrine HCl 30 mg	Ibuprofen 200 mg		1–2 tabs q 4–6 hr (max 6 tabs/day)		†
Allerest No-Drowsiness Caplets Tablets USP (OTC) [U.S.]	Pseudoephedrine HCl 30 mg	Acetaminophen 325 mg		2 tabs q 4–6 hr (max 8 tabs daily)	6–12 yrs: 1 tab q 4–6 hr (max 4 tabs/day)	†
Coldrine Tablets USP (OTC) [U.S.]	Pseudoephedrine HCl 30 mg	Acetaminophen 325 mg	Sodium metabisulfate	2 tabs q 6 hr		†
Contac Allergy/Sinus Day Caplets Tablets USP (OTC) [U.S.]	Pseudoephedrine HCl 60 mg	Acetaminophen 650 mg	Available in a dual package that also contains *Contac Allergy/Sinus Night Caplets*	1 tab q 6 hr (max 4 tabs/day)		†
Dristan Cold Caplets Tablets USP (OTC) [U.S.]	Pseudoephedrine HCl 30 mg	Acetaminophen 500 mg		2 tabs q 4–6 hr (max 8 tabs/day)		†
Dristan N.D. Caplets Tablets USP (OTC) [Canada]	Pseudoephedrine HCl 30 mg	Acetaminophen 325 mg		2 tabs q 4 hr (max 8 tabs/day)	6–12 yrs: 1 tab q 4 hr (max 4 tabs/day)	†
Dristan N.D. Extra Strength Caplets Tablets USP (OTC) [Canada]	Pseudoephedrine HCl 30 mg	Acetaminophen 500 mg		1–2 tabs q 4–6 hr (max 8 tabs/day)		†
Dristan Sinus Caplets Tablets USP (OTC) [U.S.]	Pseudoephedrine HCl 30 mg	Ibuprofen 200 mg		1–2 tabs q 4–6 hr		†
Motrin IB Sinus Tablets USP (OTC) [U.S.]	Pseudoephedrine HCl 30 mg	Ibuprofen 200 mg		1–2 tabs q 4–6 hr (max 6 tabs/day)		†
Motrin IB Sinus Caplets Tablets USP (OTC) [U.S.]	Pseudoephedrine HCl 30 mg	Ibuprofen 200 mg		1–2 tabs q 4–6 hr (max 6 tabs/day)		†
Neo Citran Extra Strength Sinus for Oral Solution (OTC) [Canada]	Phenylephrine HCl 10 mg/pouch	Acetaminophen 650 mg/pouch	Vitamin C 50 mg/pouch	Contents of 1 pouch dissolved in 225 mL hot water		†
Ornex Maximum Strength Caplets Tablets USP (OTC) [U.S.]	Pseudoephedrine HCl 30 mg	Acetaminophen 500 mg		2 tabs q 4–6 hr (max 8 tabs/day)		†
PhenAPAP Without Drowsiness Tablets (OTC) [U.S.]	Pseudoephedrine HCl 30 mg	Acetaminophen 325 mg		2 tabs q 4 hr (max 8 tabs/day)		†
Sinarest No-Drowsiness Caplets Tablets USP (OTC) [U.S.]	Pseudoephedrine HCl 30 mg	Acetaminophen 325 mg		2 tabs q 4–6 hr (max 8 tabs/day)	6–12 yrs: 1 tab q 4–6 hr (max 4 tabs/day)	†

Table 1. Oral Dosage Forms *(continued)*

Note: Content per capsule, tablet, or 5 mL, unless otherwise stated.

Brand or generic name [availability]	Decongestants	Analgesics	Other content information as per product label	Usual adult and adolescent dose* (prn)	Usual pediatric dose (prn)	Packaging, storage, and auxiliary labeling
Sine-Aid Maximum Strength Tablets USP (OTC) [U.S.]	Pseudoephedrine HCl 30 mg	Acetaminophen 500 mg		2 tabs q 4–6 hr (max 8 tabs/ day)	Not recommended	†
Sine-Aid Maximum Strength Caplets Tablets USP (OTC) [U.S.]	Pseudoephedrine HCl 30 mg	Acetaminophen 500 mg		2 tabs q 4–6 hr (max 8 tabs/ day)	Not recommended	†
Sine-Off Maximum Strength No Drowsiness Formula Caplets Tablets USP (OTC) [U.S.]	Pseudoephedrine HCl 30 mg	Acetaminophen 500 mg		2 tabs q 6 hr (max 8 tabs/ day)		†
Sinus-Relief Tablets USP (OTC) [U.S.]	Pseudoephedrine HCl 30 mg	Acetaminophen 325 mg		2 tabs q 4 hr (max 8 tabs/day)		
Sinutab No Drowsiness Caplets Tablets USP (OTC) [Canada]	Pseudoephedrine HCl 30 mg	Acetaminophen 325 mg	Scored Tartrazine free	2 tabs q 4–6 hr (max 8 tabs/ day)	>6 yrs: 1 tab q 4–6 hr (max 4 tabs/ day)	†
Sinutab No Drowsiness Extra Strength Caplets Tablets USP (OTC) [Canada]	Pseudoephedrine HCl 30 mg	Acetaminophen 500 mg	Tartrazine free	1–2 tabs q 4–6 hr (max 8 tabs/ day)		†
Sinutab Sinus Maximum Strength Without Drowsiness Tablets USP (OTC) [U.S.]	Pseudoephedrine HCl 30 mg	Acetaminophen 500 mg		2 tabs q 6 hr (max 8 tabs/24 hr)		†
Sudafed Head Cold and Sinus Extra Strength Caplets Tablets USP (OTC) [Canada]	Pseudoephedrine HCl 60 mg	Acetaminophen 500 mg		1 tab q 4–6 hr (max 4 tabs/ day)		†
Sudafed Sinus Maximum Strength Without Drowsiness Tablets USP (OTC) [U.S.]	Pseudoephedrine HCl 30 mg	Acetaminophen 500 mg		2 tabs q 6 hr (max 8 tabs/day)	Not recommended	†
Sudafed Sinus Maximum Strength Without Drowsiness Caplets Tablets USP (OTC) [U.S.]	Pseudoephedrine HCl 30 mg	Acetaminophen 500 mg		2 tabs q 6 hr (max 8 tabs/day)	Not recommended	†
Tylenol Sinus Maximum Strength Tablets USP (OTC) [U.S.]	Pseudoephedrine HCl 30 mg	Acetaminophen 500 mg		2 tabs q 4–6 hr (max 8 tabs/ day)	Not recommended	†
Tylenol Sinus Maximum Strength Caplets Tablets USP (OTC) [U.S.]	Pseudoephedrine HCl 30 mg	Acetaminophen 500 mg		2 tabs q 4–6 hr (max 8 tabs/ day)	Not recommended	†
Tylenol Sinus Maximum Strength Gelcaps Capsules USP (OTC) [U.S.]	Pseudoephedrine HCl 30 mg	Acetaminophen 500 mg		2 caps q 4–6 hr (max 8 caps/day)	Not recommended	†
Tylenol Sinus Maximum Strength Geltabs Tablets USP (OTC) [U.S.]	Pseudoephedrine HCl 30 mg	Acetaminophen 500 mg		2 tabs q 4–6 hr (max 8 tabs/day)	Not recommended	†
Tylenol Sinus Medication Regular Strength Caplets Tablets USP (OTC) [Canada]	Pseudoephedrine HCl 30 mg	Acetaminophen 325 mg	Tartrazine free	1–2 tabs q 4–6 hr (max 8 tabs/day)		†
Tylenol Sinus Medication Extra Strength Caplets Tablets USP (OTC) [Canada]	Pseudoephedrine HCl 30 mg	Acetaminophen 500 mg	Tartrazine free	1–2 tabs q 4–6 hr (max 8 tabs/day)		†

*Geriatric patients may be more sensitive to the effects of usual adult dose
†Store below 40 °C (104 °F), preferably between 15 and 30 °C (59 and 86 °F), in a tight container, unless otherwise specified by manufacturer

DEHYDROCHOLIC ACID—See *Laxatives (Local)*

DELAVIRDINE Systemic

VA CLASSIFICATION (Primary): AM840

Commonly used brand name(s): *Rescriptor.*

Another commonly used name is DLV

Note: For a listing of dosage forms and brand names by country availability, see *Dosage Forms* section(s).

Category

Antiviral (systemic).

Indications

General Considerations

Delavirdine is a non-nucleoside reverse transcriptase inhibitor. Delavirdine used alone or in combination with other antiretroviral agents may confer cross-resistance to other non-nucleoside reverse transcriptase inhibitors. However, the potential for cross-resistance between delavirdine and nucleoside analog reverse transcriptase inhibitors is low because of the different sites of binding on the viral enzyme and distinct mechanisms of action. Also, the potential for cross-resistance between delavirdine and protease inhibitors is low because of the different enzyme targets involved.Non-nucleoside reverse transcriptase inhibitors (NNRTIs), when used alone or in combination, may confer cross-resistance to other non-nucleoside reverse transcriptase inhibitors.

Reduced sensitivity to delavirdine develops rapidly when it is administered as monotherapy.Delavirdine should always be administered in combination with other antiretroviral agents.

Accepted

Human immunodeficiency virus (HIV) infection (treatment)—Delavirdine is indicated in the treatment of human immunodeficiency virus type 1 (HIV-1) infection in combination with at least two other active antiretroviral agents when therapy is warranted.

Note: Health Canada has issued a conditional marketing authorization under the Notice of Compliance with Conditions policy to reflect the promising nature of the clinical evidence for this indication and the need for confirmatory studies to verify the clinical benefit. Patients should be advised of the conditional nature of the market authorization for this indication.

Pharmacology/Pharmacokinetics

Physicochemical characteristics

Source—Synthetic.

Chemical Group—Non-nucleoside reverse transcriptase inhibitor of the human immunodeficiency virus type 1 (HIV-1).

Molecular weight—Delavirdine mesylate: 552.68.

Solubility—Aqueous solubility of free base at 23 °C:

- 2942 micrograms per mL at pH 1.0
- 295 micrograms per mL at pH 2.0
- 0.81 micrograms per mL at pH 7.4

Mechanism of action/Effect

Delavirdine binds directly to HIV-1 reverse transcriptase and blocks RNA-dependent and DNA-dependent DNA polymerase activities. HIV-1 group 0, a group of highly divergent strains that are uncommon in North America, may not be inhibited by delavirdine. Human DNA polymerase activities are not affected.

Absorption

Delavirdine is rapidly absorbed following its oral administration. The bioavailability of delavirdine tablets is increased by approximately 20% when the medication is dissolved in water prior to administration.

Distribution

Delavirdine is distributed predominantly into blood plasma.

Protein binding

Very high (approximately 98%); primarily to albumin

Biotransformation

Delavirdine is extensively converted to several inactive metabolites, primarily by the enzyme cytochrome P450 3A (CYP3A). Delavirdine reduces the activity of CYP3A, thereby inhibiting the metabolism of delavirdine. Inhibition of CYP3A by delavirdine is reversible within 1 week after discontinuation of therapy.

Delavirdine may also be metabolized by CYP2D6.

The major metabolic pathways for delavirdine are *N*-desalkylation and pyridine hydroxylation.

Half-life

Elimination from plasma—Mean, 5.8 hours (range, 2 to 11 hours) following treatment with 400 mg three times a day. The apparent half-life increases with dose.

Time to peak plasma concentration

Approximately 1 hour.

Peak plasma concentration

Mean ± SD steady-state concentration in plasma, approximately 16.1 ± 9.2 mcg/mL (35 ± 20 micromoles per L [micromoles/L]) (range, 0.92 to 46 mcg/mL [2 to 100 micromoles/L]) following doses of 400 mg three times a day; systemic exposure as measured by the area under the plasma concentration-time curve (AUC) is 82.8 ± 46 mcg/mL (180 ± 100 micromoles/L) per hour (range, 2.3 to 236 mcg/mL [5 to 513 micromoles/L] per hour); trough concentration is 6.9 ± 4.6 mcg/mL (15 ± 10 micromoles/L) (range, 0.046 to 20.7 mcg/mL [0.1 to 45 micromoles/L]).

The median AUC in female patients is 31% higher than in male patients following doses of 400 mg every 8 hours.

Elimination

Fecal—44%, following multiple doses of 330 mg three times a day in healthy volunteers.

Renal—51%, following multiple doses of 330 mg three times a day in healthy volunteers. Less than 5% of the dose is recovered unchanged in urine.

Precautions to Consider

Carcinogenicity

Rats: Delavirdine was noncarcinogenic at maximally tolerated doses that produced exposures (AUC) up to 12 (male rates) and 9 (female rats) times human exposure at the recommended clinical dose.

Mice: Delavirdine produced significant increases in the incidence of hepatocellular adenoma/adenocarcinoma in both males and females, hepatocellular adenoma in females, and mesenchymal urinary bladder tumors in males. The systemic drug exposures (AUC) in male mice were 0.2- to 4-fold and in female mice 0.5- to 3-fold of those in humans at the recommended clinical dose. The relevance of urinary bladder and hepatocellular neoplasm in delavirdine-treated mice to humans is not know given the lack of genotoxic activity of delavirdine.

Mutagenicity

Delavirdine is not mutagenic *in vitro* in the Ames test, unscheduled DNA synthesis test, chromosome aberration assay in human lymphocytes, or mammalian cell mutation assay in Chinese hamster ovary cells, or *in vivo* in the mouse micronucleus assay.

Pregnancy/Reproduction

Fertility—Dosages of 20, 100, and 200 mg of delavirdine per kg of body weight (mg/kg) per day did not impair fertility in male or female rats.

Pregnancy—*An Antiretroviral Pregnancy Registry has been established to monitor the outcomes of pregnant women exposed to delavirdine. Physicians are encouraged by the manufacturer to register patients by calling (800) 258-4263.*

Adequate and well-controlled studies have not been done in humans. In premarketing clinical studies and post marketing experience, 9 pregnancies were reported. Ten infants were born, including one set of twins. Eight of the infants were born healthy. One infant was born HIV-positive with no congenital abnormalities detected. One infant was born at 34 to 35 weeks of gestation (prematurely) with a small muscular ventricular septal defect that spontaneously resolved. The patient received approximately six weeks of treatment with delavirdine and zidovudine early in the course of the pregnancy.

Delavirdine is teratogenic in rats. Dosages of 50, 100, and 200 mg/kg per day in pregnant rats during organogenesis caused ventricular septal defects. Exposure of rats to doses approximately five times higher than the expected human exposure resulted in marked maternal toxicity, embryotoxicity, fetal development delay, and reduced pup survival. Delavirdine also has been studied in rabbits. Dosages of 200 and 400 mg/kg per day in pregnant rabbits during organogenesis resulted in abortions, embryotoxicity, and maternal toxicity. The lowest dose of delavirdine that caused these toxic effects produced systemic exposures in pregnant rabbits approximately six times higher than that expected in humans at the recommended dose. Although malformations were not apparent at these dosages, only a limited number of fetuses were available for examination due to maternal and embryo death. The no-observed-adverse-effect dose in pregnant rabbits was 100 mg/kg per day, a dosage that exposed rabbits to a lower plasma concentration of delavirdine than would be expected in humans at the recommended clinical dose.

FDA Pregnancy Category C.

Breast-feeding

It is not known whether delavirdine is distributed into breast milk. However, breast-feeding is not recommended for HIV-infected mothers because of the potential for postnatal transmission of HIV to uninfected infants.

Delavirdine is distributed into milk in rats.

Pediatrics

Appropriate studies on the relationship of age to the effects of delavirdine have not been performed in children up to 16 years of age. Safety and efficacy have not been established.

Geriatrics

Although appropriate studies on the relationship of age to the effects of delavirdine have not been performed in the geriatric population, no geriatric-specific problems have been documented to date. However, elderly patients are more likely to have age-related hepatic impairment, renal impairment, cardiac function impairment and concomitant disease or other drug therapy, which may require caution or adjustment of dosage or dosing intervals in patients receiving delavirdine.

Drug interactions and/or related problems

The following drug interactions and/or related problems have been selected on the basis of their potential clinical significance (possible mechanism in parentheses where appropriate)—not necessarily inclusive (» = major clinical significance):

Note: Combinations containing any of the following medications, depending on the amount present, may also interact with this medication.

Delavirdine is an inhibitor of CYP450 3A isoform and other CYP isoforms to a lessor extent, including CYP2C9, CYP2D6, and CYP2C19.

Medications that are contraindicated or should not be co-administered with delavirdine

» Alprazolam or
» Carbamazepine or
» Cisapride or
» Dihydroergotamine or
» Ergonovine or
» Ergotamine or
» Lovastatin or
» Methylergonovine or
» Midazolam or
» Phenobarbital or
» Phenytoin or
» Pimozide or
» Rifabutin or
» Rifampin or
» Simvastatin or
» St. John's wort (hypericum perforatum) or
» Triazolam
(These medications should not be co-administered with delavirdine due to the expected magnitude of interaction and potential for serious adverse events)

Established drug interactions—alteration in dose or regimen is recommended

» Acid blockers including:
Cimetidine or
Famotidine or
Lansoprazole or
Nizatidine or
Omeprazole or
Ranitidine
(Concomitant use with delavirdine may result in reduced absorption of delavirdine; although the effect of these medications on delavirdine absorption have not been evaluated, chronic use of these medications with delavirdine is not recommended)

» Amphetamines
(Concomitant use with delavirdine may result in increased amphetamine concentrations; use with caution)

» Amprenavir
(Concomitant use with delavirdine may result in increased amprenavir concentrations; safety, efficacy, pharmacokinetics, and appropriate doses of this combination have not been established)

Antacids
(Concomitant use with delavirdine may result in decreased delavirdine concentrations; dosing of antacids and delavirdine should be separated by at least 1 hour)

» Antiarrhythmics such as:
Amiodarone or
Flecainide or
Lidocaine, systemic or
Propafenone or
Quinidine
(Concomitant use of delavirdine may result in increased concentrations of these antiarrhythmics; use with caution and monitor concentrations of antiarrhythmic medications, if available)

» Bepridil
(Concomitant use of delavirdine may result in increased bepridil exposure and the potential for life-threatening reactions such as cardiac arrhythmias; use with caution)

» Clarithromycin
(Concomitant use with delavirdine may result in increased clarithromycin concentrations; dosage reduction of clarithromycin is recommended for patients with renal impairment)

Dexamethasone
(Concomitant use of delavirdine may decrease delavirdine plasma concentrations; use with caution monitoring for delavirdine efficacy)

» Didanosine
(Concomitant use of delavirdine may result in decreased didanosine and delavirdine concentrations; dosing of didanosine buffered tablets and delavirdine should be separated by at least 1 hour)

» Dihydropyridine calcium channel blockers such as:
Amlodipine or
Diltiazem or
Felodipine or
Isradipine or
Nicardipine or
Nifedipine or
Nimodipine or
Nisoldipine or
Verapamil
(Concomitant use of delavirdine may result in increased dihydropyridine calcium channel blocker concentration; use with caution and monitor patient for calcium channel blocker toxicity)

Ethinyl estradiol-containing oral contraceptives
(Concomitant use of delavirdine may result in increased ethinyl estradiol concentrations; the clinical significance is unknown)

» HMG-CoA reductase inhibitors such as:
Atorvastatin or
Fluvastatin
(Concomitant use of delavirdine may result in increased HMG-CoA reductase inhibitor concentration; use lowest possible dose of atorvastatin or fluvastatin with careful monitoring or consider use of pravastatin with delavirdine)

» Immunosuppressants such as:
Cyclosporine or
Sirolimus [Rapamycin] or
Tacrolimus
(Concomitant use of delavirdine may result in increased immunosuppressant concentration; therapeutic concentration monitoring of immunosuppressant is recommended)

» Indinavir
(Concurrent use of delavirdine and indinavir may result in increased indinavir concentrations; dosage **reduction** of indinavir is recommended)

» Lopinavir/ritonavir combination therapy
(Concomitant use of delavirdine and lopinavir/ritonavir combination therapy may result in increased lopinavir and ritonavir concentrations; safety, efficacy, pharmacokinetics, and appropriate doses of this combination have not been established)

» Methadone
(Concurrent use of delavirdine may result in increased methadone concentrations; dosage **reduction** of methadone may be considered)

Nelfinavir
(Concomitant use of delavirdine may result in increased nelfinavir concentrations and decreased delavirdine concentrations; safety, efficacy, pharmacokinetics, and appropriate doses of this combination have not been established)

» Ritonavir
(Concomitant use of delavirdine may result in increased ritonavir concentrations; dosage and/or regimen reduction is recommended; safety, efficacy, pharmacokinetics, and appropriate doses of this combination have not been established)

» Saquinavir
(Concurrent use of delavirdine may result in increased saquinavir concentrations; dosage **reduction** of saquinavir soft gelatin capsules should be considered, however safety, efficacy, pharmacokinetics, and appropriate doses of this combination have not been established)

» Sildenafil
(Concurrent use of delavirdine may result in increased sildenafil concentrations; sildenafil should not exceed a maximum single dose of 25 mg in a 48-hour period in patients receiving concomitant delavirdine therapy)

» Warfarin
(Concurrent use of delavirdine may result in increased concentrations of warfarin; INR [international normalized ratio] monitoring is recommended)

Laboratory value alterations

The following have been selected on the basis of their potential clinical significance (possible effect in parentheses where appropriate)—not necessarily inclusive (» = major clinical significance).

With physiology/laboratory test values

Alanine aminotransferase (ALT [SGPT]) and
Aspartate aminotransferase (AST [SGOT])
(serum values may be increased)

Amylase
(may be increased)

Neutrophil count
(may be reduced)

Medical considerations/Contraindications

The medical considerations/contraindications included have been selected on the basis of their potential clinical significance (reasons given in parentheses where appropriate)—not necessarily inclusive (» = major clinical significance).

Risk-benefit should be considered when the following medical problem exists:

» Achlorhydria
(Delavirdine absorption may be reduced in patients with achlorhydria; delavirdine should be taken with an acidic beverage [e.g., orange or cranberry juice]; however, the effect of an acidic beverage on the absorption of delavirdine in patients with achlorhydria has not been studied)

» Hepatic function impairment
(delavirdine is metabolized primarily by the liver)

Side/Adverse Effects

Severe rash, including rare cases of erythema multiforme and Stevens-Johnson syndrome, has been reported in patients receiving delavirdine. Patients experiencing severe rash or rash accompanied by symptoms such as fever, blistering, oral lesions, conjunctivitis, swelling, and muscle or joint aches should discontinue delavirdine and contact their healthcare professional. Symptoms resolved after withdrawal of delavirdine.

The duration of rash, other than erythema multiforme or Stevens-Johnson, was less than two weeks and did not require dose reduction or discontinuation of delavirdine in most cases. The rash was distributed mainly on the upper body and proximal arms, with decreasing intensity of the lesions on the neck and face, and progressively less on the rest of the trunk and limbs.

The redistribution or accumulation of body fat, including central obesity, dorsocervical fat enlargement (buffalo hump), peripheral wasting, breast enlargement, and "cushingoid appearance" have been reported in patients on protease inhibitor therapy. A causal relationship between these events and use of protease inhibitors has not been confirmed.

The side/adverse effects listed below were observed when delavirdine was used in combination with other antiretrovirals.

The following side/adverse effects have been selected on the basis of their potential clinical significance (possible signs and symptoms in parentheses where appropriate)—not necessarily inclusive:

Those indicating need for medical attention

Incidence more frequent

Skin rash, severe, with itching

Incidence less frequent

Erythema multiforme or Stevens-Johnson syndrome (severe skin rash or skin rash accompanied by symptoms such as fever, blistering, oral lesions, conjunctivitis, swelling, muscle aches, or joint aches)

Incidence rare

Dyspnea (difficulty in breathing)

Incidence not determined—Observed during clinical practice; estimates of frequency cannot be determined

Acute kidney failure (agitation; coma; confusion; decreased urine output; depression; dizziness; headache; hostility; irritability; lethargy; muscle twitching; nausea; rapid weight gain; seizures; stupor; swelling of face, ankles, or hands; unusual tiredness or weakness); ***hemolytic anemia*** (back, leg, or stomach pains; bleeding gums; chills; dark urine; difficulty breathing; fatigue; fever; general body swelling; headache; loss of appetite; nausea or vomiting; nosebleeds; pale skin; sore throat; yellowing of the eyes or skin); ***hepatic failure*** (headache; stomach pain; continuing vomiting; dark-colored urine; general feeling of tiredness or weakness; light-colored stools yellow eyes or skin); ***rhabdomyolysis*** (dark-colored urine; fever; muscle cramps or spasms; muscle pain or stiffness; unusual tiredness or weakness)

Those indicating need for medical attention only if they continue or are bothersome

Incidence more frequent

Anxiety (fear; nervousness); ***asthenia*** (lack or loss of strength); ***bronchitis*** (cough producing mucus; difficulty breathing; shortness of breath; tightness in chest; wheezing); ***depressive symptoms*** (discouragement; feeling sad or empty; irritability; lack of appetite; loss of interest or pleasure; tiredness; trouble concentrating; trouble sleeping); ***diarrhea; fatigue*** (unusual tiredness or weakness); ***flu syndrome*** (chills; cough; diarrhea; fever; general feeling of discomfort or illness; headache; joint pain; loss of appetite; muscle aches and pains; nausea; runny nose; shivering; sore throat; sweating; trouble sleeping; unusual tiredness or weakness; vomiting); ***headache; nausea; pain, localized; sinusitis*** (pain or tenderness around eyes and cheekbones; fever stuffy or runny nose; headache; cough; shortness of breath or troubled breathing; tightness of chest or wheezing); ***upper respiratory infection*** (ear congestion; nasal congestion; chills; cough; fever; sneezing, or sore throat; body aches or pain; headache; loss of voice; runny nose; unusual tiredness or weakness; difficulty in breathing); ***vomiting***

Incidence less frequent

Abdominal pain, generalized; insomnia (sleeplessness; trouble sleeping; unable to sleep); ***pharyngitis*** (body aches or pain; congestion; cough; dryness or soreness of throat; fever; hoarseness; runny nose; tender, swollen glands in neck; trouble in swallowing; voice changes)

Overdose

For more information on the management of overdose or unintentional ingestion, **contact a Poison Control Center** (see *Poison Control Center Listing*).

There is limited human experience of acute overdose with delavirdine. However, doses of up to 850 mg three times a day for up to 6 months have been taken without serious medication-related events.

Treatment of overdose

To decrease absorption—Unabsorbed delavirdine should be removed by emesis or gastric lavage.

To enhance elimination—Dialysis is unlikely to result in significant removal of delavirdine since delavirdine is extensively metabolized by the liver and is highly protein bound.

Monitoring—Vital signs should be monitored.

Supportive care—Patients should receive supportive therapy. Patients in whom intentional overdose is confirmed or suspected should be referred for psychiatric consultation.

Patient Consultation

As an aid to patient consultation, refer to *Advice for the Patient, Delavirdine (Systemic)*.

In providing consultation, consider emphasizing the following selected information (» = major clinical significance):

Before using this medication

» Conditions affecting use, especially:

Hypersensitivity to delavirdine

Delavirdine was noncarcinogenic in rats at maximally tolerated doses. In mice, delavirdine produced significant increases in the incidence of hepatocellular adenoma/adenocarcinoma in both males and females.

Pregnancy—Adequate and well-controlled studies have not been done in humans. Delavirdine is teratogenic in rats.

FDA Pregnancy Category C

Breast-feeding—It is not known whether delavirdine is distributed into breast milk; however, breast-feeding is not recommended for HIV-infected mothers

Use in children—Safety and efficacy have not been established in children up to 16 years of age.

Use in the elderly—Elderly patients may have age-related hepatic impairment, renal impairment, cardiac function impairment and concomitant disease or other drug therapy which may require caution or adjustment of delavirdine dosage or dosing intervals.

Other medications, especially alprazolam, amiodarone, amlodipine, amphetamines, amprenavir, atorvastatin, bepridil, carbamazepine, cimetidine, cisapride, clarithromycin, cyclosporine, didanosine, dihydroergotamine, diltiazem, ergonovine, ergotamine, famotidine, felodipine, flecainide, fluvastatin, indinavir, isradipine, lansoprazole, lidocaine, lopinavir/ritonavir combination therapy, lovastatin, methadone, methylergonovine, midazolam, nicardipine, nifedipine, nimodipine, nisoldipine, nizatadine, omeprazole, phenobarbital, phenytoin, pimozide, propafenone, quinidine, ranitidine, rifabutin, rifampin, ritonavir, saquinavir, sildenafil, simvastatin, sirolimus, St. John's wort, tacrolimus, triazolam, verapamil, and warfarin.

Other medical problems, especially achlorhydria and hepatic function impairment

Proper use of this medication

» Find out about medications that should **NOT** be taken with delavirdine.

Taking with or without food

Taking tablets (100-mg or 200-mg tablets) whole or taking 100-mg tablet after dispersion in water

Not taking within 1 hour of antacids

For patients with achlorhydria, take with acidic beverage (e.g., orange or cranberry juice)

» Importance of not taking more medication than prescribed; importance of not discontinuing medication without checking with physician

» Compliance with full course of therapy

» Proper dosing

Missed dose: Taking as soon as possible; not taking if almost time for next dose; not doubling doses

» Proper storage

Precautions while using this medication

» Regular visits to physician to check progress

Side/adverse effects

Signs of potential side effects, especially severe skin rash with itching, blisters, conjunctivitis, fever, joint aches, muscle aches, oral lesions, swelling, dyspnea, acute kidney failure, hemolytic anemia, hepatic failure, or rhabdomyolysis.

General Dosing Information

Delavirdine should be used in combination with other antiretroviral agents.

Patients with achlorhydria should take delavirdine with an acidic beverage such as orange juice or cranberry juice.

Delavirdine should be taken at least 1 hour before or after taking antacids or didanosine.

For treatment of adverse effects

Recommended treatment consists of the following:

- Symptomatic relief of skin rash with diphenhydramine hydrochloride, hydroxyzine hydrochloride, and/or topical corticosteroids.

Oral Dosage Forms

DELAVIRDINE MESYLATE TABLETS

Usual adult dose

Human immunodeficiency virus (HIV) infection—

Oral, 400 mg (four 100-mg or two 200-mg tablets) three times a day in combination with other antiretroviral agents.

Note: 200-mg tablets are not available in Canada.

Concomitant Therapy

Atorvastatin or Fluvastatin: Oral, use lowest possible dose of atorvastatin or fluvastatin with careful monitoring.

Indinavir: Oral, dose reduction of indinavir to 600 mg three times a day when delavirdine and indinavir are coadministered.

Methadone: Oral, dose reduction of methadone may be needed when coadministered with delavirdine.

Sildenafil: Oral, maximum sildenafil dose 25 mg in 48 hours

Note: Renally impaired patients with concomitant clarithromycin administration: CL_{CR} 30 to 60 mL per minute clarithromycin dose should be reduced by 50%; $CL_{CR} < 30$ mL per minute clarithromycin dose should be reduced by 75%.

Usual pediatric dose

Safety and efficacy have not been established in children up to 16 years of age.

Usual geriatric dose

See *Usual adult dose.*

Note: Dose selection for elderly patients should be cautious due to the greater frequency of geriatric-specific problems.

Strength(s) usually available

U.S.—

100 mg (Rx) [*Rescriptor* (lactose; Opadry White YS-1-7000-E)].

200 mg (Rx) [*Rescriptor* (lactose; hydroxypropylmethylcellulose; Opadry White YS-1-18202; pharmaceutical ink black)].

Canada—

100 mg (Rx) [*Rescriptor* (lactose; hydroxypropyl methylcellulose; propylene glycol; titanium dioxide)].

Packaging and storage

Store between 20 and 25 °C (68 and 77 °F) in a tight container or according to the manufacturer's recommendation. Protect from high humidity.

Preparation of dosage form

Delavirdine tablets may be dispersed in water prior to consumption. To prepare a dispersion, four 100-mg tablets should be added to at least three ounces or 90 mL of water and allowed to stand for a few minutes. The mixture should then be stirred until a uniform dispersion occurs. This dispersion should be consumed promptly. The glass should be rinsed and the rinse swallowed to ensure that the entire dose is consumed.

Note: The 200-milligram tablets are not readily soluble in water and are approximately one third smaller in size.

Revised: 07/18/2003
Developed: 10/17/1997

DEMECARIUM—See *Antiglaucoma Agents, Cholinergic, Long-acting (Ophthalmic)*

DEMECLOCYCLINE—See *Tetracyclines (Systemic)*

DESERPIDINE—See *Rauwolfia Alkaloids (Systemic)*

DESIPRAMINE—See *Antidepressants, Tricyclic (Systemic)*

DESLORATADINE—See *Antihistamines (Systemic)*

DESLORATADINE Systemic

VA CLASSIFICATION (Primary): AH102

Commonly used brand name(s): *Aerius; Clarinex; Clarinex RediTabs.*

Note: For a listing of dosage forms and brand names by country availability, see *Dosage Forms* section(s).

Category

Antihistaminic (H_1-receptor).

Indications

Accepted

Rhinitis, allergic (treatment)—Desloratadine is indicated for the relief of the nasal and non-nasal symptoms of seasonal and perennial allergic rhinitis[1] in patients 2 years of age and older and 6 months of age and older, respectively.

Urticaria, idiopathic, chronic (treatment)—Desloratadine is indicated for the symptomatic relief of pruritus, reduction in the number of hives and size of hives, in patients with chronic idiopathic urticaria 6 months of age and older.

[1]Not included in Canadian product labeling.

Pharmacology/Pharmacokinetics

Physicochemical characteristics

Source—Metabolite of loratadine.

Chemical Group—Piperidine antihistamine

Molecular weight—310.8.

pKa—

Pyridine functional group: 4.2.

Piperidine functional group: 9.7.

Solubility—Slightly soluble in water; Very soluble in ethanol and propylene glycol.

Note: Canadian product information lists freely soluble in ethanol, methanol, methylene chloride, and octanol; very slightly soluble in water; soluble in 0.1N hydrochloric acid, and dimethyl sulfoxide; slightly soluble in pH 7.4 phosphate buffer; practically insoluble in 0.1N sodium hydroxide

Partition coefficient—

Note: Values expressed as log $K_{O/W}$.

n-octanol/0.1N HCl: -2.27
n-octanol/pH 3 buffer: -1.44
n-octanol/pH 6 buffer: 0.342
n-octanol/pH 7 buffer: 1.02
n-octanol/pH 8 buffer: 0.944

Mechanism of action/Effect
Desloratadine is a long-acting tricyclic histamine antagonist with selective H_1-receptor histamine antagonist activity. Receptor binding data indicates that at a concentration of 2-3 ng/mL (7 nanomolar), desloratadine shows significant interaction with the human histamine H_1-receptor. Desloratadine inhibited histamine release from human mast cells *in vitro* .

Absorption
The bioavailability of desloratadine is dose proportional over the range of 5 mg to 20 mg. Following 5 mg oral daily doses for 10 days, the AUC (area under the concentration-time curve) is 56.9 ng hr per mL.

In patients with mild or moderate renal impairment (creatine clearance of 34 to 69 mL per min per 1.73 m^2), AUC values increased by approximately 1.9-fold. In patients with severe renal impairment, (creatine clearance of 5 to 29 mL per min per 1.73 m^2) or who were hemodialysis dependent, AUC values increased by approximately 2.5-fold. Dosage adjustments are recommended.

In elderly patients over the age of 65, the AUC values were 20% greater than in younger subjects, but require no dosage adjustments.

In patients with mild (n=4), moderate (n=4) and severe (n=4) hepatic impairment had approximately 2.4-fold increase in AUC

Distribution
Desloratadine is distributed into breast milk.

Protein binding
Desloratadine: High (82 to 87%)—plasma protein
3-hydroxydesloratadine: High (85 to 89%)—plasma protein

Biotransformation
Desloratadine is extensively metabolized to 3-hydroxydesloratadine, an active metabolite, which is subsequently glucuronidated. The enzymes responsible for the metabolism have not been identified.

Note: Data from clinical trials indicate that a subset of the general patient population has a decreased ability to form 3-hydroxydesloratadine, and are slow metabolizers of desloratadine. In pharmacokinetic studies, approximately 7% of subjects were slow metabolizers of desloratadine (defined as a subject with an AUC ratio of 3-hydroxydesloratadine to desloratadine less than 0.1, or a subject with a desloratadine half-life exceeding 50 hours). The frequency of slow metabolizers is higher in African-Americans. The median exposure (AUC) to desloratadine in the slow metabolizers was approximately 6-fold greater than the subjects who are not slow metabolizers.

Half-life
Elimination—27 hours in healthy subjects; In patients 65 years of age and older, the mean elimination half-life was 33.7 hours.

Onset of action
Histamine skin wheal studies—within one hour.

Time to peak concentration
Following oral administration—approximately 3 hours.

Peak plasma concentration:
4 ng/mL—following a single 5 mg oral dose in normal healthy volunteers once daily for 10 days.

Note: In patients 65 years of age or older the mean C_{max} was 20% greater than in younger patients, but requires no changes in dosage.

In patients with mild or moderate renal impairment (creatine clearance of 34 to 69 mL per min per 1.73 m^2), median C_{max} values increased by approximately 1.2-fold. In patients with severe renal impairment, (creatine clearance of 5 to 29 mL per min per 1.73 m^2) or who were hemodialysis dependent, C_{max} values increased by approximately 1.7-fold. Dosage adjustments are recommended.

Duration of action
Histamine skin wheal studies—up to 24 hours.

Elimination
Fecal and Renal—

Approximately 87% of a ^{14}C-desloratadine dose was equally recovered in urine and feces.

Desloratadine and 3-hydroxydesloratadine were not removed by hemodialysis.

In patients with mild (n=4), moderate (n=4) and severe (n=4) hepatic impairment, the apparent oral clearance was 37%, 36%, and 28%, respectively, compared to healthy patients.

Precautions to Consider

Carcinogenicity
Note: The carcinogenic potential of desloratadine was assessed using loratadine studies.

In 18-month and 2 year studies in mice and rats, loratadine was administered in the diet at doses up to 40 mg/kg/day in mice and 25 mg/kg/day in rats. Male mice given 40 mg/kg/day of loratadine had a significantly higher incidence of hepatocellular tumors (combined adenomas and carcinomas) than concurrent controls. In rats, a significantly higher incidence of hepatocellular tumors (combined adenomas and carcinomas) was observed in males given 10 mg/kg/day and in males and females given 25 mg/kg/day. The estimated desloratadine and desloratadine metabolite exposures of rats given 10 mg/kg of loratadine were approximately 7 times the area under the curve in humans at the recommended daily oral dose.

Mutagenicity
Desloratadine showed no genotoxic potential in a reverse mutation assay (*Salmonella/E. coli* mammalian microsome bacterial mutagenicity assay) or in two assays for chromosomal aberrations (human peripheral blood lymphocyte clastogenicity assay and mouse bone marrow micronucleus assay).

Pregnancy/Reproduction
Fertility—At desloratadine doses up to 24 mg/kg/day, there was no effect on female fertility in rats. A male specific decrease in fertility, demonstrated by reduced female conception rates, decreased sperm numbers and motility, and histopathologic testicular changes, occurred at an oral desloratadine dose of 12 mg/kg in rats. Desloratadine had no effect on fertility in rats at an oral dose of 3 mg/kg/day.

Pregnancy—Adequate and well-controlled studies in humans have not been done

Desloratadine was not teratogenic in rats at doses up to 48 mg/kg/day or in rabbits at doses up to 60 mg/kg/day. In a separate study, an increase in pre-implantation loss and a decreased number of implantations and fetuses were noted in female rats at 24 mg/kg. Reduced body weight and slow righting reflex were reported in pups at doses of 9 mg/kg/day or greater. Desloratadine had no effect on pup development at an oral dose of 3 mg/kg/day.

FDA Pregnancy Category C

Breast-feeding
Desloratadine is distributed into breast milk.

Pediatrics
The effectiveness of desloratadine syrup in pediatric patients aged 6 months to 11 years is supported by evidence from adequate and well-controlled studies of desloratadine tablets in adults. Safety and efficacy of desloratadine tablets or syrup have not been demonstrated in pediatric patients less than 6 months of age. The desloratadine 2.5 mg orally disintegrating tablet has not been evaluated in pediatric patients. However, the bioequivalence of the desloratadine 5 mg orally disintegrating tablet was established in adults. In conjunction with the dose finding studies in pediatrics described, the pharmacokinetic data for desloratadine orally disintegrating tablets supports the use of the 2.5-mg dose strength in pediatric patients 6 to 11 years of age.

Geriatrics
Appropriate studies performed to date have not demonstrated geriatric-specific problems that would limit the usefulness of desloratadine in the elderly. However, elderly patients are more likely to have age-related impairment of hepatic or renal function which may require adjustment of dosage in patients receiving desloratadine.

In patients 65 years of age and older, peak plasma concentration and area under the curve values for desloratadine were 20% greater than in younger patients. The mean plasma elimination half-life was approximately 30% longer than in younger patients. This is not relevant clinically and no dosage adjustment is recommended. The oral total body clearance when normalized for body weight was similar between the two age groups.

Pharmacogenetics
Female patients treated for 14 days with desloratadine had peak plasma concentration and area under the curve values for desloratadine that were 10% and 3% higher, respectively, compared with male patients. The 3-hydroxydesloratadine peak plasma concentration and area under the curve values for desloratadine were increased by 45% and

48%, respectively, in females compared with males. This is not relevant clinically and no dosage adjustment is recommended.

African-American patients treated for 14 days with desloratadine had peak plasma concentration and area under the curve values for desloratadine that were 18% and 32% higher, respectively, in African-Americans compared with Caucasian patients. For 3-hydroxydesloratadine there was a corresponding 10% reduction in peak plasma concentration and area under the curve values in African-Americans compared to Caucasians. This is not relevant clinically and no dosage adjustment is recommended.

Medical considerations/Contraindications

The medical considerations/contraindications included have been selected on the basis of their potential clinical significance (reasons given in parentheses where appropriate)—not necessarily inclusive (» = major clinical significance).

Except under special circumstances, this medication should not be used when the following medical problem exists:

» Hypersensitivity to desloratadine or to any of its ingredients, or to loratadine

Risk-benefit should be considered when the following medical problems exist:

» Hepatic function impairment
(based upon increases in the values of bioavailability, mean elimination half-life and the area under the curve of desloratadine, dosage adjustment for patients with hepatic function impairment is recommended.)

Phenylketonuria (PKU)
(Desloratadine oral disintegrating tablets contains aspartame, which is metabolized to phenylalanine)

» Renal function impairment
(based upon increases in the values of the peak plasma concentration and the area under of the curve for desloratadine, dosage adjustment for patients with renal function impairment is recommended.)

Metabolism of desloratadine, impaired
(patients cannot be prospectively identified as slow metabolizers of desloratadine and may be more susceptible to dose-related adverse events.)

Patient monitoring

The following may be especially important in patient monitoring (other tests may be warranted in some patients, depending on condition; » = major clinical significance):

Liver enzymes including
Bilirubin
(elevated liver enzymes have been reported during post-marketing of desloratadine)

Side/Adverse Effects

The following side/adverse effects have been selected on the basis of their potential clinical significance (possible signs and symptoms in parentheses where appropriate)—not necessarily inclusive:

Those indicating need for medical attention

Incidence not determined—Observed during clinical practice, estimates of frequency cannot be determined

Anaphylaxis (cough; difficulty swallowing; dizziness; fast heartbeat; hives; itching; puffiness or swelling of the eyelids or around the eyes, face, lips or tongue; shortness of breath; skin rash; tightness in chest; unusual tiredness or weakness; wheezing); ***dyspnea*** (shortness of breath; difficult or labored breathing; tightness in chest; wheezing); ***edema*** (swelling); ***pruritus*** (itching skin); ***rash; tachycardia*** (fast, pounding, or irregular heartbeat or pulse); ***urticaria*** (hives or welts; itching; redness of skin; skin rash)

Those indicating need for medical attention only if they continue or are bothersome

Incidence more frequent

Headache; pharyngitis (body aches or pain; congestion; cough; dryness or soreness of throat; fever; hoarseness; runny nose; tender, swollen glands in neck; trouble in swallowing; voice changes)

Incidence less frequent

Dizziness; dry mouth; dysmenorrhea (difficult or painful menstruation); ***dyspepsia*** (acid or sour stomach; belching; heartburn; indigestion; stomach discomfort, upset or pain); ***fatigue*** (unusual tiredness or weakness); ***myalgia*** (joint pain; swollen joints; muscle aching or cramping; muscle pains or stiffness; difficulty in moving); ***somnolence*** (sleepiness or unusual drowsiness); ***nausea***

Overdose

For more information on the management of overdose or unintentional ingestion, **contact a poison control center** (see *Poison Control Center Listing*).

Clinical effects of overdose

The following effects have been selected on the basis of their potential clinical significance (possible signs and symptoms in parentheses where appropriate)—not necessarily inclusive:

Somnolence (sleepiness or unusual drowsiness)

Note: Single daily doses of 45 mg were given to normal male and female volunteers for 10 days. All ECGs obtained in this study were manually read in a blinded fashion by a cardiologist. In desloratadine-treated patients, there was an increase in mean heart rate of 9.2 bpm relative to placebo. The QT interval was corrected for heart (QT_c) by both the Bazett and Fridericia methods. Using the QT_c (Bazett) there was a mean increase of 8.1 msec in desloratadine-treated patients relative to placebo. Using QT_c (Fridericia) there was a mean increase of 0.4 msec in desloratadine-treated patients relative to placebo.

Lethality occurred in rats at oral doses of 250 mg/kg or greater (estimated desloratadine and desloratadine metabolite exposures were approximately 120 times the area under the curve in humans at the recommended daily oral dose). The oral median lethal dose in mice was 353 mg/kg (estimated desloratadine exposures were approximately 290 times the human daily oral dose on a mg/m^2 basis. No deaths occurred at oral doses up to 250 mg/kg in monkeys (estimated desloratadine exposures were approximately 810 times the human daily oral dose on a mg/m^2 basis).

Treatment of overdose

Note: Desloratadine and 3-hydroxydesloratadine are not eliminated by hemodialysis.

It is not known if desloratadine is eliminated by peritoneal dialysis.

Supportive care—
Treatment should be symptomatic and supportive
Patients in whom intentional overdose is confirmed or suspected should be referred for psychiatric consultation.

Patient Consultation

As an aid to patient consultation, refer to *Advice for the Patient, Desloratadine (Systemic)*.

In providing consultation, consider emphasizing the following selected information (» = major clinical significance):

Before using this medication

» Conditions affecting use, especially:
Hypersensitivity to desloratadine or any of its ingredients, or to loratadine.
Breast-feeding—Desloratadine is distributed into breast milk.
Use in children—Safety and efficacy of desloratadine tablets or syrup have not been demonstrated in pediatric patients less than 6 months of age. Pharmacokinetic data supports use of 2.5 mg desloratadine orally disintegrating tablets in pediatric patients 6 to 11 years of age.
Other medical problems, especially hepatic or renal function impairment.

Proper use of this medication

Proper administration of oral disintegrating tablets and syrup
Importance of taking medication exactly as prescribed and not skipping or discontinuing unless directed
» Proper dosing
Missed dose: Taking as soon as possible; not taking if almost time for next scheduled dose; not doubling doses
Proper storage

Precautions while using this medication

» Not prescribing oral disintegrating tablet to phenylketonuric patients; tablets contain phenylalanine

Side/adverse effects

Signs of potential side effects, especially anaphylaxis, dyspnea, edema, pruritus, rash, tachycardia or urticaria.

General Dosing Information

Desloratadine may be taken with or without food.

Desloratadine oral disintegrating tablets rapidly disintegrate on the tongue and do not require water to aid dissolution or swallowing.

Each oral disintegrating tablet contains 1.75 mg phenylalanine. This substance must be used with caution in patients with phenylketonuria.

Bioequivalence information

A single oral disintegrating tablet containing 5 mg of desloratadine is bioequivalent to a single 5 mg tablet and is bioequivalent to 10 mL of syrup containing 5 mg of desloratadine for both desloratadine and 3-hydroxydesloratadine.

Oral Dosage Forms

DESLORATADINE ORAL DISINTEGRATING TABLETS

Usual adult and adolescent dose

See *Desloratadine Tablets*

Usual pediatric dose

Rhinitis, allergic (treatment) and
Urticaria, idiopathic, chronic (treatment)—
Children 6 to 11 years of age—Oral, 2.5 mg once daily.

Usual geriatric dose

See *Desloratadine Tablets*

Strength(s) usually available

U.S.—
2.5 mg (Rx) [*Clarinex RediTabs* (orally disintegrating tablets; mannitol; microcrystalline cellulose; pregelatinized starch; sodium starch glycolate; magnesium stearate; butylated methacrylate; crospovidone; aspartame; citric acid; sodium bicarbonate; colloidal silicon dioxide; ferric oxide red; tutti frutti flavoring)].
5 mg (Rx) [*Clarinex RediTabs* (orally disintegrating tablets; mannitol; microcrystalline cellulose; pregelatinized starch; sodium starch glycolate; magnesium stearate; butylated methacrylate; crospovidone; aspartame; citric acid; sodium bicarbonate; colloidal silicon dioxide; ferric oxide red; tutti frutti flavoring)].

Packaging and storage

Store at 25 °C (77°F) excursions permitted between 15° and 30°C (59 and 86°F).

Auxiliary labeling

• You should take this medication exactly as prescribed. Do not skip or discontinue unless directed.

Caution

Phenylketonurics: Desloratadine oral disintegrating tablets contain phenylalanine 2.55 mg per 5-mg tablet and 1.28 mg per 2.5-mg tablet.

Additional information

Proper administration—Take tablet immediately after opening the blister. Place orally disintegrating tablet on the tongue. Tablet disintegration occurs rapidly. Administer with or without water.

DESLORATADINE SYRUP

Usual adult and adolescent dose

Rhinitis, allergic (treatment) and
Urticaria, idiopathic, chronic (treatment)—
Oral, 10 mL (5 mg) once daily.
Note: In patients with liver or renal impairment, the recommended starting dose is 5 mg every other day.

Usual pediatric dose

Rhinitis, allergic (treatment) and
Urticaria, idiopathic, chronic (treatment)—
Children 6 to 11 years of age—Oral, 5 mL (2.5 mg) once daily.
Children 12 months to 5 years of age—Oral, 2.5 mL (1.25 mg) once daily.
Children 6 to 11 months of age—Oral, 2 mL (1 mg) once daily.

Usual geriatric dose

See *Usual adult and adolescent dose.*

Strength(s) usually available

U.S.—
0.5 mg per mL (Rx) [*Clarinex* (propylene glycol; sorbitol solution; citric acid, anhydrous; sodium citrate dihydrate; sodium benzoate; disodium edetate; purified water; granulated sugar; natural and artificial flavor for bubble gum; FD&C Yellow #6 dye)].

Packaging and storage

Store at 25 °C (77°F) excursions permitted between 15° and 30°C (59 and 86°F). Protect from light.

Auxiliary labeling

• You should take this medication exactly as prescribed. Do not skip or discontinue unless directed.

Additional information

Proper administration—Desloratadine syrup should be administered at the age-appropriate dose with a commercially available measuring dropper or syringe that is calibrated to deliver 2 mL and 2.5 mL (½ teaspoon).

DESLORATADINE TABLETS

Usual adult and adolescent dose

Rhinitis, allergic (treatment)—
Oral, 5 mg once daily.
Urticaria, idiopathic, chronic (treatment)—
Oral, 5 mg once daily.
Note: In patients with liver or renal impairment, U.S. prescribing information recommends a starting dose of 5 mg every other day.

Usual pediatric dose

Safety and efficacy of desloratadine tablets have not been established in pediatric patients 12 years of age and younger.

Usual geriatric dose

See *Usual adult and adolescent dose.*

Strength(s) usually available

U.S.—
5 mg (Rx) [*Clarinex* (dibasic calcium phosphate dihydrate USP; microcrystalline cellulose NF; corn starch NF; talc USP; carnauba wax NF; white wax NF; lactose monohydrate; hydroxypropyl methylcellulose; titanium dioxide; polyethylene glycol; FD&C Blue # 2 Aluminum Lake)].
Canada—
5 mg (Rx) [*Aerius* (carnauba wax; microcrystalline cellulose; corn starch; dibasic calcium phosphate dihydrate; FD&C Blue # 2 Lake; hydroxypropyl methylcellulose; lactose monohydrate; polyethylene glycol; talc; titanium dioxide; white beeswax)].

Packaging and storage

Store between 2 and 25 °C (36 and 77 °F). Heat sensitive. Avoid exposure at or above 30 °C (86 °F). Protect from moisture.

Note: Canadian product information states to store between 15 and 30 °C.

Auxiliary labeling

• Do not use if you are breast-feeding. Contact your doctor or pharmacist.
• You should take this medication exactly as prescribed. Do not skip or discontinue unless directed.

Revised: 08/12/2005
Developed: 09/09/2002

DESLORATADINE AND PSEUDOEPHEDRINE Systemic†

VA CLASSIFICATION (Primary): RE501
Commonly used brand name(s): *Clarinex-D; Clarinex-D 12 Hour.*

Note: For a listing of dosage forms and brand names by country availability, see *Dosage Forms* section(s).

†Not commercially available in Canada.

Category

Antihistaminic (H_1-receptor)-decongestant.

Indications

Accepted

Rhinitis, seasonal allergic (treatment)—Desloratadine and pseudoephedrine combination is indicated for the relief of the nasal and non-nasal symptoms of seasonal allergic rhinitis, including nasal congestion, in patients 12 years of age and older. Desloratadine and pseudoephedrine combination should be administered when the antihistaminic properties of desloratadine and the nasal decongestant properties of pseudoephedrine are desired.

Pharmacology/Pharmacokinetics

Physicochemical characteristics

Chemical Group—Pseudoephedrine sulfate is an indirect sympathomimetic amine.
Molecular weight—Desloratadine: 310.8.

Solubility—
Desloratadine: Slightly soluble in water, but very soluble in ethanol and propylene glycol.
Pseudoephedrine sulfate: Very soluble in water, freely soluble in alcohol, and sparingly soluble in ether.

Mechanism of action/Effect
Desloratadine—Is a long-acting tricyclic histamine antagonist with selective H_1-receptor histamine antagonist activity.
Pseudoephedrine sulfate—Sympathomimetic amines exert a decongestant action on the nasal mucosa to relieve nasal congestion due to allergic rhinitis.

Absorption
Desloratadine—
AUC (0-24h) values under steady state conditions were 34.8 ng h/mL. Food and grapefruit juice had no effect on the bioavailability.
AUC (0-12h) values under steady state conditions were 1.7 ng/mL (16 ng h/mL).
Pseudoephedrine—
AUC (0-24h) values under steady state conditions were 523 ng/mL. Food had no effects.
AUC (0-12h) values under steady state conditions were 459 ng/mL (4658 ng h/mL).

Protein binding
Desloratadine—High (82 to 87%) to plasma protein.
3-hydroxydesloratadine—High (85 to 89%) to plasma protein.

Biotransformation
Desloratadine—
Extensively metabolized to active metabolite 3-hydroxydesloratadine, which is subsequently glucuronidated.
Pseudoephedrine—
Incompletely metabolized (less than 1%) in the liver by N-demethylation to an inactive metabolite.

Half-life
Desloratadine—
Elimination—24 hours (24 hour extended-release tablet); 27 hours (12 hour extended-release tablet).
Pseudoephedrine—
Elimination—dependent upon urinary pH, 3 to 6 hours when the urinary pH is 5, or 9 to 16 hours when the urinary pH is 8.

Time to peak plasma concentration
Desloratadine: Approximately 6 to 7 hours post dose.
Pseudoephedrine: 8 to 9 hours post dose.

Peak plasma concentration:
Desloratadine: Approximately 1.79 ng/mL following a single dose; 2.44 ng/mL on day 12 following oral administration once daily for 14 days.
Pseudoephedrine: 328 ng/mL; 523 ng/mL on day 10 following oral administration once daily for 14 days.

Elimination
Desloratadine—
Approximately 87% of a ^{14}C-desloratadine dose was equally distributed in urine and feces as metabolic products.
Pseudoephedrine hydrochloride—
Urine: 55 to 96% unchanged.

Precautions to Consider

Carcinogenicity
Animal studies with desloratadine and pseudoephedrine combination to evaluate the carcinogenic potential have not been done.
Loratadine—A carcinogenicity study, done in rats given oral doses of loratadine revealed a significantly higher incidence of hepatocellular tumors (combined adenomas and carcinomas) in males given 10 mg/kg/day and males and females given 25 mg/kg/day. The clinical significance of these findings during long-term use of desloratadine is not known.

Tumorigenicity
Tumorigenicity—
Desloratadine—
A 2-year study done in male and female mice given dietary doses of desloratadine at 16 mg/kg/day and 32 mg/kg/day did not show an increase in the incidence of any tumors.

Mutagenicity
Mutagenicity—
Desloratadine—
No evidence of genotoxic potential was observed in a reverse mutation assay with *Salmonella/E. Coli* or in two assays for chromosomal aberrations, including the human peripheral blood lymphocyte clastogenicity assay and the mouse bone marrow micronucleus assay.

Pregnancy/Reproduction
Fertility—
Desloratadine—
There was no effect on fertility in female rats given doses of desloratadine up to 24 mg/kg/day. However, a male specific decrease in fertility, was demonstrated by a reduced female conception rate, decreased sperm numbers and motility, and histopathologic testicular changes which occurred at an oral dose of 12 mg/kg. Desloratadine had no effect on fertility in rats at an oral dose of 3 mg/kg/day (approximately 8 times the AUC in humans at the recommended daily oral dose).

Pregnancy—There have been no reproductions studies done with the combination desloratadine and pseudoephedrine.
Desloratadine—
Adequate and well controlled studies in humans have not been done. Studies in animals have shown that desloratadine causes adverse effects in the fetus. Because animal reproduction studies are not always predictive of human response, desloratadine should be used during pregnancy only if clearly needed.
Increased pre-implantation loss and a decreased number of implantations and fetuses were observed in female rats given an oral dose at 24 mg/kg. Reduced body weight and slow righting reflex were reported in pups at doses of 9 mg/kg/day or greater. No effect on pup development was seen at an oral dose of 3 mg/kg/day (approximately 7 times the AUC in humans at the recommended daily oral dose).
Desloratadine was not teratogenic in rats at doses up to 48 mg/kg/day or in rabbits at doses up to 60 mg/kg/day

FDA Pregnancy Category C

Breast-feeding
Desloratadine is distributed into breast milk, therefore a decision should be made whether to discontinue nursing or to discontinue desloratadine and pseudoephedrine combination, taking into account the importance of the drug to the mother. Caution should be exercised when desloratadine and pseudoephedrine combination is administered to nursing women.

Pediatrics
Desloratadine and pseudoephedrine combination is not an appropriate formulation for use in pediatric patients under 12 years of age.

Geriatrics
Although appropriate studies on the relationship of age to the effects of desloratadine and pseudoephedrine combination have not been performed in the geriatric population, no geriatrics-specific problems have been documented to date. However, elderly patients are more likely to have age-related reactions to sympathomimetic amines due to decreased hepatic, renal, or cardiac function, and concomitant disease or other drug therapy, which may require caution in dosing.

Pharmacogenetics
There were no significant differences in the efficacy of desloratadine and pseudoephedrine combination across patients of different gender or race.

Drug interactions and/or related problems
The following drug interactions and/or related problems have been selected on the basis of their potential clinical significance (possible mechanism in parentheses where appropriate)—not necessarily inclusive (» = major clinical significance):

Note: Combinations containing any of the following medications, depending on the amount present, may also interact with this medication.

» Digitalis
(concomitant use with desloratadine and pseudoephedrine combination can increased ectopic pacemaker activity)

» Monoamine oxidase inhibitor (MAO)
(use is contraindicated in patients receiving MAO therapy or within 14 days of stopping such treatment)

Sympathomimetics amines such as
Beta-adrenergic blocking agents or
Mecamylamine or
Methyldopa or
Reserpine or
Veratum alkaloids
(antihypertensive effects may be reduced)

Medical considerations/Contraindications

The medical considerations/contraindications included have been selected on the basis of their potential clinical significance (reasons given in parentheses where appropriate)—not necessarily inclusive (» = major clinical significance).

Except under special circumstances, this medication should not be used when the following medical problem exists:

» Coronary artery disease, severe or
» Glaucoma, narrow angle or
» Hypertension, severe or
» Urinary retention
(use is contraindicated)
» Hypersensitivity to loratadine, adrenergic agents or to other drugs with similar chemical structures, desloratadine or pseudoephedrine, or to any of its ingredients

Risk-benefit should be considered when the following medical problems exist:

» Diabetes mellitus or
» Hypertension or
» Hyperthyroidism or
» Intraocular pressure, increased or
» Ischemic heart disease or
» Prostatic hypertrophy or
» Renal function impairment
(dosage adjustment is recommended; caution should be exercised when administering desloratadine and pseudoephedrine combination; use of 12-hour extended release tablets should generally be avoided in patients with renal impairment)
» Hepatic function impairment
(use should be avoided; a 2.4-fold increase in AUC was observed during clinical trials)

Side/Adverse Effects

The following side/adverse effects have been selected on the basis of their potential clinical significance (possible signs and symptoms in parentheses where appropriate)—not necessarily inclusive:

Those indicating need for medical attention

Observed during clinical practice

Elevated liver enzymes, including; bilirubin (chills; clay-colored stools; dark urine; dizziness; fever; headache; itching; loss of appetite; nausea; abdominal or stomach pain area; rash; unpleasant breath odor; unusual tiredness or weakness; vomiting of blood; yellow eyes or skin); ***hepatitis*** (dark urine; general tiredness and weakness; light-colored stools; nausea and vomiting; upper right abdominal pain; yellow eyes and skin); ***hypersensitivity reactions, including; anaphylaxis*** (cough; difficulty swallowing; dizziness; fast heartbeat; hives; itching; puffiness or swelling of the eyelids or around the eyes, face, lips or tongue; shortness of breath; skin rash; tightness in chest; unusual tiredness or weakness; wheezing); ***dyspnea*** (shortness of breath; difficult or labored breathing; tightness in chest; wheezing); ***edema*** (swelling); ***pruritus*** (itching skin); ***rash; urticaria*** (hives or welts; itching; redness of skin; skin rash); ***palpitations*** (irregular heartbeat); ***tachycardia*** (fast, pounding, or irregular heartbeat or pulse)

Those indicating need for medical attention only if they continue or are bothersome

Incidence more frequent

Dry mouth; headache; insomnia (sleeplessness; trouble sleeping; unable to sleep)

Incidence less frequent

Anorexia (loss of appetite; weight loss); ***dizziness; fatigue*** (unusual tiredness or weakness); ***hyperactivity*** (restlessness; trouble sitting still); ***nausea; nervousness; pharyngitis*** (body aches or pain; congestion; cough; dryness or soreness of throat; fever; hoarseness; runny nose; tender, swollen glands in neck; trouble in swallowing; voice changes); ***somnolence*** (sleepiness or unusual drowsiness)

Overdose

For more information on the management of overdose or unintentional ingestion, **contact a poison control center** (see *Poison Control Center Listing*).

Clinical effects of overdose

In large doses, sympathomimetics may give rise to giddiness, headache, nausea, vomiting, sweating, thirst, tachycardia, precordial pain, palpitations, difficulty in micturition, muscle weakness and tenseness, anxiety, restlessness, and insomnia. Many patients can present a toxic psychosis with delusions and hallucinations. Some may develop cardiac arrhythmias, circulatory collapse, convulsions, coma, and respiratory failure.

The following effects have been selected on the basis of their potential clinical significance (possible signs and symptoms in parentheses where appropriate)—not necessarily inclusive:

Increased heart rate; somnolence (sleepiness or unusual drowsiness)

Treatment of overdose

There is no known specific antidote to desloratadine and pseudoephedrine. Treatment is generally symptomatic and supportive

To decrease absorption—
Considering standard measures to remove any unabsorbed drug.

To enhance elimination—
Desloratadine and 3-hydroxydesloratadine are not eliminated by hemodialysis.

Supportive care—
Patients in whom intentional overdose is confirmed or suspected should be referred for psychiatric consultation.

Patient Consultation

As an aid to patient consultation, refer to *Advice for the Patient, Desloratadine and Pseudoephedrine (Systemic)*.

In providing consultation, consider emphasizing the following selected information (» = major clinical significance):

Before using this medication

» Conditions affecting use, especially:
Hypersensitivity to loratadine, adrenergic agents or to other drugs with similar chemical structures, desloratadine or pseudoephedrine, or to any of its ingredients
Pregnancy—Not recommended for use during pregnancy
Breast-feeding—Desloratadine is distributed into breast milk. Caution should be exercised when administering desloratadine and pseudoephedrine combination to nursing women.
Use in children—Desloratadine and pseudoephedrine combination is not an appropriate formulation for use in pediatric patients under 12 years of age.
Use in the elderly—Elderly patients may be more likely to have age-related reactions to sympathomimetic amines due to decreased hepatic, renal, or cardiac function, and concomitant disease or other drug therapy, which may require caution in dosing.
Other medications, especially digitalis, or monoamine oxidase inhibitors (MAOIs)
Other medical problems, especially diabetes mellitus, hepatic function impairment, hypertension, hyperthyroidism, increased intraocular pressure, ischemic heart disease, narrow angle glaucoma, prostatic hypertrophy, renal function impairment, severe coronary artery disease, or urinary retention.

Proper use of this medication

» Not taking over-the-counter antihistamines and decongestants while taking desloratadine and pseudoephedrine combination.
» Importance of not taking more medication or more often than recommended
» Swallowing the tablet whole, not breaking or chewing.
» Proper dosing
Missed dose: Taking as soon as possible; not taking if almost time for next scheduled dose; not doubling doses
Proper storage

Precautions while using this medication

Possible dryness of mouth; using sugarless gum or candy, ice, or saliva substitute for relief; checking with dentist if dry mouth continues for more than 2 weeks.

Side/adverse effects

Signs of potential side effects, especially elevated liver enzymes including bilirubin, or hepatitis; hypersensitivity reactions, including anaphylaxis, dyspnea, edema, pruritus, rash or urticaria; palpitations; or tachycardia.

General Dosing Information

Desloratadine and pseudoephedrine combination may be taken with or without food.

Bioequivalence information

Combination therapy was not bioequivalent to monotherapy (desloratadine 5 mg plus pseudoephedrine 240 mg). The systemic exposure to desloratadine and 3-hydroxydesloratadine was 15 to 20% lower from desloratadine and pseudoephedrine 24-hour extended release tablets than those from desloratadine 5 mg tablet.

Oral Dosage Forms

DESLORATADINE AND PSEUDOEPHEDRINE SULFATE EXTENDED RELEASE TABLETS 12 HOUR

Usual adult and adolescent dose

Congestion, nasal (treatment) or
Rhinorrhea (treatment)—

Oral, one tablet (2.5 mg desloratadine, 120 mg pseudoephedrine) twice daily, taken approximately 12 hour apart and with or without a meal

Note: For patients with hepatic impairment, use should generally be avoided.

For patients with renal impairment, use should generally be avoided.

Usual pediatric dose

Safety and efficacy for use in pediatric patients under 12 years of age have not been established.

Usual geriatric dose

See *Usual adult dose*.

Strength(s) usually available

U.S.—

2.5 mg desloratadine and 120 mg pseudoephedrine sulfate (Rx) [*Clarinex-D 12 Hour* (hypromellose; microcrystalline cellulose; povidone; silicon dioxide; magnesium stearate; corn starch; edetate disodium; citric acid anhydrous; stearic acid; FD&C Blue No. 2 aluminum lake dye)].

Packaging and storage

Store at 25 °C (77 °F), excursions permitted to 15° to 30°C (59° to 86°F). Avoid exposure at or above 30 °C (86 °F). Protect from excessive moisture.

Auxiliary labeling

- Swallow whole. Do not crush or chew.
- Protect from light.

DESLORATADINE AND PSEUDOEPHEDRINE SULFATE EXTENDED RELEASE TABLETS 24 HOUR

Usual adult and adolescent dose

Congestion, nasal (treatment) or
Rhinorrhea (treatment)—

Oral, one tablet (5 mg desloratadine, 240 mg pseudoephedrine) daily, taken with or without a meal

Note: For patients with renal impairment, a dose of one tablet every other day is recommended.

For patients with hepatic insufficiency, use should be avoided.

Usual pediatric dose

Safety and efficacy for use in pediatric patients under 12 years of age have not been established.

Usual geriatric dose

See *Usual adult dose.*

Strength(s) usually available

U.S.—

5 mg desloratadine and 240 mg pseudoephedrine sulfate (Rx) [*Clarinex-D* (Blue Lake Blend 50726; dibasic calcium phosphate dihydrate; ethylcellulose; hypromellose; ink; magnesium stearate NF; polyacrylate dispersion; polyethylene glycol NF; povidone; silicone dioxide NF; simethicone; talc)].

Packaging and storage

Store at 25 °C (77 °F), excursions permitted to 15° to 30°C (59° to 86°F)

Auxiliary labeling

- Swallow whole. Do not crush or chew.

Revised: 02/15/2006
Developed: 04/13/2005

DESMOPRESSIN Systemic

VA CLASSIFICATION (Primary/Secondary): HS702/CV900; BL116; DX900

Commonly used brand name(s): *DDAVP Injection; DDAVP Nasal Spray; DDAVP Rhinal Tube; DDAVP Rhinyle Nasal Solution; DDAVP Spray; DDAVP Tablets; Octostim; Stimate Nasal Spray.*

Note: For a listing of dosage forms and brand names by country availability, see *Dosage Forms* section(s).

Category

Antidiuretic (central diabetes insipidus)—Desmopressin Acetate Nasal Solution; Desmopressin Acetate Tablets; Desmopressin Acetate Injection.

Antidiuretic (primary nocturnal enuresis)—Desmopressin Acetate Nasal Solution; Desmopressin Acetate Tablets.

Antihemorrhagic—Desmopressin Acetate Nasal Solution (*Stimate* only); Desmopressin Acetate Injection.

Diagnostic aid—Desmopressin Acetate Injection

Indications

Note: Bracketed information in the *Indications* section refers to uses that are not included in U.S. product labeling.

Accepted

Diabetes insipidus, central (prophylaxis or treatment)—Desmopressin is indicated as antidiuretic replacement therapy in the management of central cranial diabetes insipidus and for management of the temporary polyuria and polydipsia following head trauma or surgery in the pituitary region.

Patients should be selected for desmopressin therapy based on the results of the water deprivation test, hypertonic saline infusion test, or response to antidiuretic hormone.

Enuresis, primary nocturnal (treatment)—Desmopressin is indicated for the management of primary nocturnal enuresis. It may be used alone or adjunctive to behavioral conditioning or other nonpharmacological intervention. It has been shown to be effective in some cases that are refractory to conventional therapies.

Hemophilia A (treatment) or
von Willebrand's disease (treatment)—Desmopressin injection and *Stimate* nasal solution are indicated for patients with mild hemophilia A or mild to moderate classic von Willebrand's disease (Type I), with factor VIII coagulant activity levels greater than 5%. It is useful when administered before surgery (according to the timeframe specified by the manufacturer) to maintain hemostasis. Desmopressin usually will stop the bleeding in these patients with episodes of spontaneous or trauma-induced hemarthroses, intramuscular hematomas, or mucosal bleeding.

[Uremia (treatment adjunct)]—Desmopressin injection is indicated to maintain hemostasis during surgical procedures and postoperatively in patients with uremia who are at increased risk of bleeding. Desmopressin should be administered to these patients prior to the procedure.

[Cushing's syndrome, adrenocorticotropic hormone (ACTH)–dependent (diagnosis)][1]—Desmopressin is indicated in the differential diagnosis of the cause of ACTH-dependent Cushing's syndrome. Desmopressin used in conjunction with corticotropin-releasing hormone (CRH) has a synergistic effect that allows the source of ACTH production, pituitary or ectopic, to be determined more accurately and produces results that are superior to those obtained when either peptide is used alone. (Evidence rating: I)

Unaccepted

Desmopressin is not indicated in the treatment of nephrogenic diabetes insipidus or polyuria associated with psychogenic diabetes insipidus, renal disease, hypokalemia, hypercalcemia, or the administration of demeclocycline or lithium.

Desmopressin is not indicated for patients with factor VIII concentrations of 5% or less (except in certain clinical situations with careful monitoring), or in patients who have factor VIII antibodies. Desmopressin is not indicated for treatment of severe classic von Willebrand's disease (Type I) or when there is evidence of an abnormal molecular form of von Willebrand antigen. In patients with Type IIB von Willebrand's disease, desmopressin may induce platelet aggregation and thrombocytopenia, and its use is not recommended.

[1]Not included in Canadian product labeling.

Pharmacology/Pharmacokinetics

Physicochemical characteristics

Source—Synthetic polypeptide structurally related to the posterior pituitary hormone arginine vasopressin (antidiuretic hormone)..

Molecular weight—Desmopressin acetate: 1183.34.

Mechanism of action/Effect

Antidiuretic—Increases water reabsorption in the kidney by increasing the cellular permeability of the collecting ducts and distal tubules, resulting in an increase in urine osmolality with a concurrent decrease in urine output.

Antihemorrhagic—Increases plasma concentrations of clotting factor VIII (antihemophilic factor) and von Willebrand's factor activity along with a possible direct effect on the blood vessel wall, causing increased platelet spreading and adhesion at sites of injury.

Diagnostic aid—Desmopressin and corticotropin-releasing hormone (CRH) stimulate release of adrenocorticotropic hormone (ACTH) and cortisol in patients with Cushing's disease, but rarely in patients with occult ectopic ACTH syndrome or in normal individuals. The mechanism by which desmopressin stimulates ACTH release is not completely understood. However, desmopressin is thought to function via G protein–coupled V_{1b} vasopressin receptors. The receptors are expressed in high concentrations in corticotroph adenoma and some ACTH-secreting bronchial carcinoid cells and appear to show a high level of sensitivity to desmopressin, perhaps as a result of up-regulation of the V_{1b} receptor in neuroendocrine tissue. It is believed that the lack of response seen in normal individuals is due to an insufficient number of V_{1b} receptors in normal pituitary corticotrophs. The CRH receptor also is present in corticotroph adenomas but far less commonly in bronchial carcinoid tumors. The synergistic effect demonstrated with the use of both desmopressin and CRH is thought to relate to a greater increase in the co-overexpression of CRH and V_{1b} receptors in corticotroph adenomas than in ACTH-secreting ectopic tumors.

Other actions/effects

Much less pressor activity than vasopressin and less action on visceral smooth muscle.

Absorption

10 to 20% from nasal mucosa. An intravenous dose of desmopressin possesses antidiuretic activity approximately 10 times that of the same nasal desmopressin dose.

Biotransformation

Renal.

Half-life

Intranasal or intravenous—
- Fast phase: 7.8 minutes.
- Slow phase: 75.5 minutes.
- Terminal half-life—normal healthy patient: 3 hours; patient with severe renal impairment: 9 hours

Oral—
- 1.5 to 2.5 hours.

Onset of action

Antidiuretic—Intranasal or oral: Within 1 hour.

Antihemorrhagic—Increased factor VIII activity and von Willebrand factor concentrations: Intravenous—15 to 30 minutes.

Time to peak plasma concentration

Intranasal—1.5 hours.

Oral—0.9 hour.

Time to peak effect

Antidiuretic—
- Intranasal: 1 to 5 hours.
- Oral: 4 to 7 hours.

Antihemorrhagic—
- Increased factor VIII activity and von Willebrand factor concentrations:
  - Intravenous—30 to 60 minutes.

Duration of action

Antidiuretic—
- Intranasal:
  - Variable, 8 to 20 hours; long duration of action is due to the medication's rate of absorption from nasal mucosa, persistence in plasma, and effect on renal tubules. Effect ends abruptly, over a period of 60 to 90 minutes.
- Oral:
  - Following a 0.1- to 0.2-mg dose—Up to 8 hours.
  - Following a 0.4-mg dose—Up to 12 hours.

Antihemorrhagic—
- Mild hemophilia A: Intravenous—4 to 24 hours.
- von Willebrand's disease: Intravenous—Approximately 3 hours.

Elimination

Mainly renal

Precautions to Consider

Carcinogenicity/Mutagenicity

Studies have not been done in either animals or humans.

Pregnancy/Reproduction

Fertility—Studies with desmopressin have not been performed to evaluate effects on fertility.

Pregnancy—Controlled studies have not been done in humans. Because animal reproduction studies are not always predictive of human response, this drug should be used during pregnancy only if clearly needed.

Clinical use of desmopressin in pregnant women has been reported, with no adverse effects in the fetus. Desmopressin does not appear to have uterotonic activity.

Studies in rats and rabbits at doses of 0.05 to 10 mcg per kg of body weight (mcg/kg) (approximately 0.1 time and up to 38 times, respectively, the maximum human systemic exposure, based on mg per square meter of body surface area [mg/m^2]) per day have not shown that desmopressin causes adverse effects in the fetus.

Several publications are available for use of desmopressin acetate in the management of diabetes insipidus during pregnancy. These publications have included anecdotal reports of congenital anomalies and low birth weight babies. However, causality has not been established and one study showed a low statistical power. Antidiuretic doses of desmopressin acetate have no uterotonic action and the physician will have to weigh the therapeutic advantages against possible risks in each case.

FDA Pregnancy Category B.

Breast-feeding

In one study conducted in postpartum women, desmopressin was distributed into breast milk in minimal amounts, following a 10-mcg intranasal dose. However, problems in humans have not been documented. Because many drugs are distributed into human breast milk, caution should be exercised when desmopressin is administered to a nursing woman.

Pediatrics

Nasal spray—For primary nocturnal enuresis: Short-term (4 to 8 weeks) administration has been shown to be safe and modestly effective in pediatric patients aged 6 years or older. Adequately controlled studies have not been conducted beyond 4 to 8 weeks. The dose should be individually adjusted to achieve the best results.

For central cranial diabetes insipidus: Use in infants and children requires careful fluid intake restriction to prevent possible hyponatremia and water intoxication. Dose must be individually adjusted with attention in the very young to the danger of an extreme decrease in plasma osmolality with resulting convulsions.

Injection—Hemophilia A or von Willebrand's: Should not be used in infants less than three months of age

For central cranial diabetes insipidus: Safety and efficacy in pediatric patients under 12 years of age have not been established.

Tablets—For primary nocturnal enuresis: Safety for up to 6 months has been established in pediatric patients 6 years of age and older. No increase in the frequency or severity of adverse reactions or decrease in efficacy was seen with an increased dose or duration. Dose should be individually adjusted to achieve the best results.

For central cranial diabetes insipidus: Safety for up to 44 months has been established in pediatric patients 4 years of age and older. Dose must be individually adjusted with attention in the very young to the danger of an extreme decrease in plasma osmolality with resulting convulsions. Use of desmopressin tablets in pediatric patients requires careful fluid intake restrictions to prevent possible hyponatremia and water intoxication.

Geriatrics

Although appropriate studies have not been performed in the geriatric population, caution and careful restriction of fluid intake are recommended with use of desmopressin in the elderly because of the increased risk of hyponatremia and water intoxication. Rarely, an extreme decrease in plasma osmolality may cause seizures that lead to coma.

In general, dose selection should be cautious, usually starting at the low end of the dosing range, reflecting the greater frequency of decreased hepatic, renal, or cardiac function, and of concomitant disease or drug therapy. Because desmopressin is known to be substantially excreted by the kidney, the risk of toxic reactions to this drug may be greater in patients with impaired renal function. Because elderly patients are more likely to have decreased renal function, care should be taken in dose selection, and it may be useful to monitor renal function.

Drug interactions and/or related problems

The following drug interactions and/or related problems have been selected on the basis of their potential clinical significance (possible mechanism in parentheses where appropriate)—not necessarily inclusive (» = major clinical significance):

Note: Combinations containing any of the following medications, depending on the amount present, may also interact with this medication.

Carbamazepine or
Chlorpropamide or
Clofibrate
(may potentiate the antidiuretic effect of desmopressin when used concurrently)

Demeclocycline or

Lithium or
Norepinephrine
(may decrease the antidiuretic effect of desmopressin when used concurrently)

Medical considerations/Contraindications

The medical considerations/contraindications included have been selected on the basis of their potential clinical significance (reasons given in parentheses where appropriate)—not necessarily inclusive (» = major clinical significance).

Except under special circumstances, this medication should not be used when the following medical problems exist:

» Hypersensitivity to desmopressin acetate or to any of the components of the product

» Renal impairment, moderate to severe
(should not be used if creatinine clearance is below 50 mL per minute)

Risk-benefit should be considered when the following medical problems exist:

Coronary artery disease or
Headache, vascular, predisposition to or
Hypertensive cardiovascular disease
(desmopressin may produce a slight increase in blood pressure or a transient decrease in blood pressure with a compensatory increase in heart rate)

Cystic fibrosis or
Dehydration
(risk of hyponatremia may be increased)

Thrombosis, predisposition to
(rarely, myocardial infarction and strokes have been reported to occur following the use of desmopressin in patients predisposed to thrombus formation; although it is not known whether these events were related to the use of desmopressin, caution is recommended in the use of desmopressin in this patient population)

For intranasal dosage form only (in addition to those listed above)

Allergic rhinitis or
Nasal congestion or edema or
Upper respiratory infection
(nasal absorption of desmopressin may be erratic)

Impaired consciousness or
Nasal packing or
Postoperative state or
Surgery, cranial
(intranasal delivery may be inappropriate)

Patient monitoring

The following may be especially important in patient monitoring (other tests may be warranted in some patients, depending on condition; » = major clinical significance):

For use as an antidiuretic

Electrolytes
(measurement of serum concentrations is recommended if therapy for primary nocturnal enuresis is continued beyond 7 days or as determined by physician)

Urine osmolality and/or
Urine volume
(determinations recommended at appropriate intervals to monitor response and aid in dosage adjustment; in some cases, plasma osmolality determinations may be necessary)

For use in hemophilia A or von Willebrand's disease

Activated partial thromboplastin time (APTT) and
Bleeding time and
Coagulation factor assay and
von Willebrand factor antigen (factor VIII–related antigen) and
von Willebrand factor assay (ristocetin cofactor)
(determinations recommended after initial administration and at appropriate intervals to monitor response)
(if factor VIII coagulant activity, as determined prior to administration of desmopressin, is present at less than 5% of normal, the efficacy of desmopressin may be uncertain)

For injection dosage form

Blood pressure and
Pulse rate
(recommended during intravenous infusion)

Fluid intake and
Fluid output
(close monitoring recommended to prevent water intoxication and hyponatremia)

Side/Adverse Effects

Note: Rarely, thrombotic events (myocardial infarction and strokes) have been reported to occur following the use of desmopressin in patients predisposed to thrombus formation. Although it is not known whether these events were related to the use of desmopressin, caution is recommended in the use of desmopressin in this patient population.

The following side/adverse effects have been selected on the basis of their potential clinical significance (possible signs and symptoms in parentheses where appropriate)—not necessarily inclusive:

Those indicating need for medical attention

Incidence rare—dose-related
Hypertension, slight; hyponatremia or water intoxication (coma; confusion; continuing headache; decreased urination; drowsiness; rapid weight gain; seizures); ***hypotension, transient; tachycardia*** (fast heartbeat)

Incidence rare
Allergic reaction, severe (chills; fever; shortness of breath, tightness in chest, trouble in breathing, or wheezing; skin rash, hives, or itching)

Those indicating need for medical attention only if they continue or are bothersome

Incidence less frequent or rare—dose-related
Abdominal or stomach cramps; flushing or redness of skin; pain in vulva

With high doses
Headache; nausea

With intranasal use
Epistaxis (nosebleed); ***runny or stuffy nose; upper respiratory infection*** (cough; fever; runny or stuffy nose; sneezing; sore throat)

With intravenous use
Pain, redness, or swelling at site of injection

Overdose

For specific information on the agent used in the management of desmopressin overdose, see *Furosemide* in *Diuretics, Loop (Systemic)* monograph.

For more information on the management of overdose or unintentional ingestion, **contact a Poison Control Center** (see *Poison Control Center Listing*).

Treatment of overdose

Treatment of overdose consists of reduction of dosage or withdrawal of the medication. Fluid intake should be restricted to less than urine output to allow plasma sodium concentration to return to normal gradually. This usually occurs within a few days. If fluid overload is severe, furosemide, along with intravenous hypertonic saline or oral salt, should be administered.

Patient Consultation

As an aid to patient consultation, refer to *Advice for the Patient, Desmopressin (Systemic)*.

In providing consultation, consider emphasizing the following selected information (» = major clinical significance):

Before using this medication

» Conditions affecting use, especially:
Hypersensitivity to desmopressin acetate or any components of the product
Pregnancy—Should be used during pregnancy only if clearly needed
Breast-feeding—Distributed into breast milk in minimal amounts; caution should be exercised
Use in children—Not recommended for use for any indication in infants younger than 3 months of age; increased risk of hyponatremia and water intoxication
Use in the elderly—Increased risk of hyponatremia and water intoxication; possible increased likelihood of renal impairment; dose selection should be cautious
Other medical problems, especially moderate or severe renal impairment

Proper use of this medication

» Importance of not using more medication than the amount prescribed

For intranasal use only

Reading patient instructions carefully before using

» Not using the nasal spray beyond the labeled number of sprays, because accuracy of dose delivered cannot be assured

» Proper dosing
  Missed dose: If dosing schedule is—
    Once a day: Using as soon as possible if remembered same day; if not remembered until next day, not using at all and not doubling dose, but going back to regular schedule
    More than once a day: Using as soon as possible; not using at all if almost time for next dose; not doubling doses

» Proper storage

Side/adverse effects

Signs of potential side effects, especially slight hypertension, hyponatremia or water intoxication, transient hypotension, tachycardia, and severe allergic reaction

General Dosing Information

Fluid intake should be adjusted to decrease the potential for water intoxication and hyponatremia, especially in very young or geriatric patients. Rarely, an extreme decrease in plasma osmolality may cause seizures that lead to coma.

Tolerance may develop with long-term (longer than 6 months) intranasal use or tachyphylaxis may occur when intravenous doses are administered more frequently than every 24 to 48 hours. This effect appears to be caused by the local inactivation of the peptide rather than by the development of binding antibodies.

For use in central diabetes insipidus

Initially, therapy should be directed to control nocturia.

The dosage of desmopressin should be adjusted according to the diurnal pattern of response, with the morning and evening doses being adjusted separately.

Response to therapy can be measured by the volume and frequency of urination and an adequate duration of sleep.

For use in primary nocturnal enuresis

Fluid intake should be restricted a few hours before administration of desmopressin.

For intranasal dosage forms

Desmopressin is administered intranasally as a spray or through a flexible, calibrated catheter known as a rhinal (or rhinyle) tube.

Because the nasal spray delivery unit cannot deliver less than 10 mcg, patients requiring smaller doses must use the rhinal tube delivery system.

The nasal spray delivery unit should not be used beyond the labeled number of sprays; if it is, the accuracy of the dose delivered cannot be assured.

Nasal Dosage Forms

Note: The antidiuretic activity of 10 mcg of desmopressin acetate nasal solution is equivalent to 40 International Units (IU).

DESMOPRESSIN ACETATE NASAL SOLUTION

Usual adult and adolescent dose

Central diabetes insipidus—
  Intranasal, 10 to 40 mcg per day, as a single dose or in two or three divided doses per day. Most adults require 0.2 mL daily in two divided doses
  Note: In one quarter to one third of patients, adequate control is maintained with a single daily dose; however, in some patients, three doses per day are necessary.

Primary nocturnal enuresis—
  Initial: Intranasal, 10 mcg into each nostril at bedtime (total dose per day of 20 mcg).
  Maintenance: Dosage is adjusted according to patient response; total dose per day may range from 10 to 40 mcg.

Antihemorrhagic (*Stimate* only)—
  Intranasal, 150 mcg into each nostril. The dose may be repeated based upon laboratory test parameters and the condition of the patient.
  Note: Patients who weigh less than 50 kg may require only a single 150-mcg dose.

Usual pediatric dose

Central diabetes insipidus—
  Children up to 3 months of age—
    Dosage has not been established.
  Children 3 months to 12 years of age—
    Intranasal, 0.05 to 0.3 mL daily either as a single dose or divided into two doses.
    Note: In one quarter to one third of patients, adequate control is maintained with a single daily dose of desmopressin administered intranasally.

Primary nocturnal enuresis—
  Children up to 6 years of age—
    Dosage has not been established.
  Children 6 years of age or older—
    See *Usual adult and adolescent dose*.
    Note: Because the nasal spray delivery unit cannot deliver less than 10 mcg, patients requiring smaller doses must use the rhinal tube delivery system.

Usual geriatric dose

Dose selection should be cautious starting at the lower end of the dosing range. See *Usual adult and adolescent dose*.

Strength(s) usually available

U.S.—
  10 mcg per 0.1 mL metered spray (0.01%) (Rx) [*DDAVP Nasal Spray* (7.5 mg/mL sodium chloride; 1.7 mg/mL citric acid monohydrate; 3.0 mg/mL disodium phosphate dihydrate; 0.2 mg/mL benzalkonium chloride solution [50%]); GENERIC].
  100 mcg per mL (0.01%) (Rx) [*DDAVP Rhinal Tube* (7.5 mg/mL sodium chloride; 1.7 mg/mL citric acid monohydrate; 3.0 mg/mL disodium phosphate dihydrate; 0.2 mg/mL benzalkonium chloride solution [50%]); GENERIC].
  150 mcg per 0.1 mL metered spray (0.15%) (Rx) [*Stimate Nasal Spray*].

Canada—
  10 mcg per 0.1 mL metered spray (0.01%) (Rx) [*DDAVP Spray*].
  100 mcg per mL (0.01%) (Rx) [*DDAVP Rhinyle Nasal Solution*].

Packaging and storage

Store *Stimate Nasal Spray* and the nasal solution for use with a rhinal tube at a temperature between 2 and 8 °C (36 and 46 °F). *DDAVP Nasal Spray* should be stored at room temperature between 20 and 25 °C (5968 and 77 °F) in an upright position Protect all products from freezing.

Auxiliary labeling

- For the nose
- Keep out of reach of children

Note

Include patient instructions when dispensing.

Oral Dosage Forms

DESMOPRESSIN ACETATE TABLETS

Usual adult and adolescent dose

Central diabetes insipidus—
  Initial: Oral, 0.05 mg two times a day.
  Maintenance: Dosage is adjusted according to patient response; total dose may range from 0.1 to 0.8 mg per day in divided doses.
  Note: Patients previously on intranasal therapy may begin oral therapy twelve hours after the last intranasal dose.

Primary nocturnal enuresis[1]—
  Initial: Oral, 0.2 mg once a day at bedtime.
  Maintenance: Dosage is adjusted according to patient response, and total dose may be up to 0.6 mg per day.
  Note: Patients previously on intranasal therapy may begin oral therapy twenty-four hours after the last intranasal dose.

Usual adult and adolescent prescribing limits

1.2 mg per day.

Usual pediatric dose

Central diabetes insipidus—
  See *Usual adult and adolescent dose*.

Primary nocturnal enuresis—
  Children up to 6 years of age: Dosage has not been established.
  Children 6 years of age or older: See *Usual adult and adolescent dose*.

Usual geriatric dose

Dose selection should be cautious starting at the lower end of the dosing range. See *Usual adult and adolescent dose*.

Strength(s) usually available

U.S.—
  0.1 mg (Rx) [*DDAVP Tablets* (scored; lactose; magnesium stearate; potato starch; povidone)].
  0.2 mg (Rx) [*DDAVP Tablets* (scored; lactose; magnesium stearate; potato starch; povidone)].

Canada—
0.1 mg (Rx) [*DDAVP Tablets* (lactose; magnesium stearate; potato starch; povidone)].
0.2 mg (Rx) [*DDAVP Tablets* (lactose; magnesium stearate; potato starch; povidone)].

Packaging and storage
Store between 20 and 25 °C (68 and 77 °F), unless otherwise specified by manufacturer. Protect from excessive heat and light.

Auxiliary labeling
- Keep out of reach of children

Parenteral Dosage Forms

Note: Bracketed uses in the *Dosage Forms* section refer to categories of use and/or indications that are not included in U.S. product labeling.

The antidiuretic activity of 1 mcg of desmopressin acetate injection is equivalent to 4 International Units (IU).

DESMOPRESSIN ACETATE INJECTION

Usual adult and adolescent dose
Antidiuretic—
Intramuscular, intravenous (direct), or subcutaneous, 2 to 4 mcg per day or 0.025 mcg per kg of body weight, usually in two divided doses in the morning and evening.
Antihemorrhagic—
Intravenous infusion, 0.3 mcg per kg of body weight diluted in 50 mL of 0.9% sodium chloride injection and infused slowly over fifteen to thirty minutes. The dose may be repeated based upon laboratory test parameters and the condition of the patient.
[Diagnostic aid][1]—
Intravenous, 10 mcg.
Note: Desmopressin should be administered with 100 mcg of corticotropin-releasing hormone (CRH; corticorelin).

Usual pediatric dose
Antidiuretic—
Intramuscular, intravenous (direct), or subcutaneous, 0.4 mcg or 0.025 mcg per kg of body weight once a day.
Antihemorrhagic—
Children up to 113 months of age—
Use is not recommended.
Children 113 months of age or older—
For children weighing 10 kg or less—Intravenous infusion, 0.3 mcg per kg of body weight diluted in 10 mL of 0.9% sodium chloride injection and infused slowly over fifteen to thirty minutes. The dose may be repeated based upon laboratory test parameters and the condition of the patient.
For children weighing more than 10 kg—See *Usual adult and adolescent dose*.
[Diagnostic aid][1]—
See *Usual adult and adolescent dose*.

Usual geriatric dose
Dose selection should be cautious starting at the lower end of the dosing range. See *Usual adult and adolescent dose*.

Strength(s) usually available
U.S.—
4 mcg per mL (Rx) [*DDAVP Injection* (9.0 mg sodium chloride; hydrochloric acid to adjust pH to 4; chlorobutanol 5 mg/mL as a preservative [10-mL multiple-dose vial only]); GENERIC].
15 mcg per mL (Rx) [*DDAVP Injection*].
Canada—
4 mcg per mL (Rx) [*DDAVP Injection*].
15 mcg per mL (Rx) [*Octostim*].

Packaging and storage
Store between 2 and 8 °C (36 and 46 °F), unless otherwise specified by manufacturer. Protect from freezing and light.

[1]Not included in Canadian product labeling.

Selected Bibliography

Miller K, Klauber GT. Desmopressin acetate in children with primary nocturnal enuresis. Clin Ther 1990; 12(4): 357-66.
Aledort LM. Treatment of von Willebrand's disease [review]. Mayo Clin Proc 1991; 66: 841-6.
Blevins LS Jr, Wand GS. Diabetes insipidus [review]. Crit Care Med 1992; 20(1): 69-79.
Salva KM, Kim HC, Nahum K, et al. DDAVP in the treatment of bleeding disorders. Pharmacother 1988; 8(2): 94-9.

Revised: 12/01/2005

DESONIDE—See *Corticosteroids (Topical)*

DESOXIMETASONE—See *Corticosteroids (Topical)*

DEXAMETHASONE—See *Corticosteroids—Glucocorticoid Effects (Systemic), Corticosteroids (Nasal), Corticosteroids (Ophthalmic), Corticosteroids (Otic), Corticosteroids (Topical)*

DEXCHLORPHENIRAMINE—See *Antihistamines (Systemic)*

DEXMETHYLPHENIDATE Systemic†

VA CLASSIFICATION (Primary): CN802
Note: Controlled substance classification
U.S.: Schedule II
Commonly used brand name(s): *Focalin; Focalin XR*.
Other commonly used names are: D-methylphenidate and Ritadex.
Note: For a listing of dosage forms and brand names by country availability, see *Dosage Forms* section(s).

†Not commercially available in Canada.

Category
CNS stimulant.

Indications

Accepted
Attention-deficit hyperactivity disorder (treatment)—Dexmethylphenidate is indicated for the treatment of attention deficit hyperactivity disorder [ADHD] in patients aged six years and older. Dexmethylphenidate is an integral part of a total treatment program for ADHD that may include other measures (psychological, educational, and social) for some patients with this syndrome.

Unaccepted
Dexmethylphenidate is *not* recommended for use in patients who exhibit symptoms secondary to environmental factors and/or other primary psychiatric disorders, including psychosis, for the treatment of severe depression, or for the prevention or treatment of normal fatigue states.

Note: When remedial measures (i.e., appropriate educational placement and psychosocial intervention) are insufficient, the physician's assessment of the patient's symptoms must be taken into account in deciding to prescribe dexmethylphenidate.

Pharmacology/Pharmacokinetics

Physicochemical characteristics
Molecular weight—269.77.
Solubility—Freely soluble in water and in methanol; soluble in alcohol; slightly soluble in chloroform and in acetone.

Mechanism of action/Effect
Central nervous system (CNS) stimulant—Although the therapeutic mode of action of dexmethylphenidate in attention deficit hyperactivity disorder [ADHD] is not known, it is thought to block the reuptake of norepinephrine and dopamine into the presynaptic neuron and increase the release of these monoamines in the extraneuronal space.

Absorption
Readily absorbed following oral administration
Following single and repeated twice daily dosing in children with ADHD, no differences in the pharmacokinetics of dexmethylphenidate were noted indicating no significant drug accumulation.

Distribution
Following oral administration of dexmethylphenidate, plasma dexmethylphenidate concentrations in children decline exponentially.

Biotransformation
Dexmethylphenidate is metabolized by de-esterification primarily to ritalinic acid which has little to no pharmacologic activity.

Half-life
Elimination half-life—
Approximately 2.2 hours (mean)

Time to peak concentration
Plasma concentration fasted state—
For tablets and time to first peak (t_{max1}) for extended-release capsules:
t_{max} 1.5 hours in adults
Extended-release time to the second peak (t_{max2}): about 6.5 hours
Note: The mean time to the interpeak minimum is slightly shorter and time to the second peak is slightly longer for dexmethylphenidate extended-release (ER) capsules given once daily compared with tablets given in two doses 4 hours apart. However the ranges observed are greater for the ER capsules.

Plasma concentration non-fasted state—
t_{max} 2.9 hours in adults (following a high fat meal)

Peak serum concentration
C_{max} and $AUC_{0\text{-}inf}$ of dexmethylphenidate were proportional to dose given.

Note: the C_{max} and $AUC_{0\text{-}inf}$ were comparable in both the fasted and non-fasted states.

Plasma dexmethylphenidate levels were comparable to plasma levels following single *dl-threo*-methylphenidate HCl doses given as capsules in twice the total mg amount (equimolar to dexmethylphenidate doses).

Dexmethylphenidate ER capsules given once daily exhibits a lower second peak concentration (C_{max2}, higher interpeak minimum concentrations (C_{minip}, and less peak and trough fluctuations than dexmethylphenidate tablets given in two doses four hours apart. This is due to an earlier onset and more prolonged absorption from the delayed-release beads.

The AUC after administration of dexmethylphenidate ER given once daily is equivalent to the same total dose of dexmethylphenidate tablets given in tow doses 4 hours apart. The variability in C_{max}, C_{min}, an AUC is similar between the extended-release and immediate-release with approximately a three-fold range in each.

Elimination
Renal—
After oral dosing 90% recovered in urine. Ritalinic acid, the main metabolite was approximately 80% of the dose

Precautions to Consider

Cross-sensitivity and/or related problems
Dexmethylphenidate is contraindicated in patients known to be hypersensitive to methylphenidate, dexmethylphenidate or other components of the product.

Carcinogenicity/Tumorigenicity
Lifetime carcinogenicity studies have not been carried out with dexmethylphenidate.

A lifetime carcinogenicity study with racemic methylphenidate was carried out on a mouse strain (B6C3F1) that is sensitive to the development of hepatic tumors. Racemic methylphenidate at a dose of 60 mg per kg of body weight per day, caused an increase in hepatocellular adenomas. In males only, an increase in hepatoblastomas, which are relatively rare rodent malignant tumors, was observed. There was no increase in total malignant hepatic tumors. The significance of these results to humans is unknown. In another study, a transgenic mouse strain (p53+/−) which is sensitive to genotoxic carcinogens was given racemic methylphenidate. There was no evidence of carcinogenicity.

In rats (F344), a study using a high dose (45 mg per kg of body weight per day) of racemic methylphenidate was given and it did not cause any increase in tumors.

Mutagenicity
Dexmethylphenidate was not found to be mutagenic in the *in vitro* Ames reverse mutation assay, the *in vitro* mouse lymphoma cell forward mutation assay, or the *in vivo*mouse bone marrow micronucleus test.

Racemic methylphenidate was also not found to be mutagenic in the *in vitro* Ames reverse mutation assay, the *in vitro* mouse lymphoma cell forward mutation assay, or the *in vivo*mouse bone marrow micronucleus test. However, in an *in vitro* assay of racemic methylphenidate in cultures Chinese Hamster Ovary (CHO) cells, sister chromatid exchanges and chromosomes aberrations were increased which is indicative of a weak clastogenic response.

Pregnancy/Reproduction
Fertility—No information is available on the effects of dexmethylphenidate on fertility.

Racemic methylphenidate did not impair fertility in male or female mice that were given doses of up to 160 mg per kg of body weight per day in an 18-week continuous breeding study.

Pregnancy—Adequate and well-controlled studies in pregnant women have not been conducted. Dexmethylphenidate should be used during pregnancy only if the potential benefit outweighs the potential risk to the fetus.

In studies of rats and rabbits, dexmethylphenidate was given orally at doses of up to 20 and 100 mg per kg of body weight per day, respectively, during organogenesis. Dexmethylphenidate plasma levels (AUCs) in pregnant rats and rabbits were approximately 5 and 1 times, respectively, higher than those in adults given the maximum recommended human dose of 20 mg per day at the highest doses tested. No evidence of teratogenicity was found in either the rat or rabbit study. Delayed fetal skeletal development was observed in rats at the highest dose level. At doses of 20 mg per kg of body weight per day administered to rats throughout pregnancy and lactation, a decreased postweaning body weight gain was observed in male offspring at the highest dose, but no other postnatal development effects were observed. Racemic methylphenidate has also been shown to have no teratogenic effects in rabbits at doses of 200 mg per kg of body weight per day throughout organogenesis.

FDA Pregnancy Category C

Breast-feeding
It is not known whether dexmethylphenidate is distributed into breast milk. Because many drugs are distributed into human milk, caution should be exercised if dexmethylphenidate is administered to a nursing woman.

Pediatrics
Children may experience a more frequent occurrence of loss of appetite, abdominal pain, weight loss (during prolonged therapy), insomnia and tachycardia. For more information see *Side and adverse effects.*

The safety and efficacy of dexmethylphenidate in children less than 6 years of age have not been established. Long-term effects have not been well established.

Geriatrics
No information is available on the relationship of age to the effects of dexmethylphenidate in geriatric patients.

Pharmacogenetics
In a single dose study conducted in adults, the mean dexmethylphenidate $AUC_{0\text{-}inf}$ values (adjusted for body weight) following single 2 x 10 mg doses of dexmethylphenidate were 25% to 35% higher in adult female volunteers (n=6) compared to male volunteers (n=9). Both t_{max} and $t_{1/2}$ were comparable for males and females.

Ethnic variations in pharmacokinetics could not be detected with the use of dexmethylphenidate.

Drug interactions and/or related problems
The following drug interactions and/or related problems have been selected on the basis of their potential clinical significance (possible mechanism in parentheses where appropriate)—not necessarily inclusive (» = major clinical significance):

Note: Combinations containing any of the following medications, depending on the amount present, may also interact with this medication.

» Acid suppressants or
» Antacids
(effects of gastrointestinal pH alterations on dexmethylphenidate absorption from extended-release [ER] formulation have not been studied; since modified release characteristics of dexmethylphenidate ER capsules are pH dependent, coadministration of antacids or acid suppressants could alter release of dexmethylphenidate)

» Anticonvulsants including phenobarbital, phenytoin, primidone or
» Coumarin anticoagulants or
» Selective serotonin reuptake inhibitors (SSRIs) or
» Tricyclic antidepressants
(concurrent use with methylphenidate inhibit metabolism; downward dose adjustments and monitoring of plasma drug concentration or coagulation times may be necessary especially when initiating or discontinuing concomitant methylphenidate)

Antihypertensive drugs
(methylphenidate may decrease the effectiveness of drugs used to treat hypertension)

» Clonidine or other centrally acting alpha-2 agonists
(serious adverse events have been reported; causality has not been established; the safety of using methylphenidate in combination with clonidine has not been evaluated)

» Monoamine oxidase inhibitors
(contraindicated during treatment and within a minimum of 14 days following discontinuation; hypertensive crises may result)

» Pressor agents
(methylphenidate may decrease the effectiveness of hypertension drugs; caution recommended during concurrent use because of possible effects on blood pressure)

Medical considerations/Contraindications

The medical considerations/contraindications included have been selected on the basis of their potential clinical significance (reasons given in parentheses where appropriate)—not necessarily inclusive (» = major clinical significance).

Except under special circumstances, this medication should not be used when the following medical problem exists:

» Agitation, marked or
» Anxiety, marked or
» Tension, marked
(symptoms may be aggravated; use is contraindicated)

» Depression, severe
(dexmethylphenidate should not be used to treat severe depression)

» Glaucoma or
» Motor tics or
» Tourette's syndrome, family history or diagnosis
(Use is contraindicated)

» Hypersensitivity to methylphenidate, dexmethylphenidate, or any components of this product

» Seizures, history of, or
» EEG abnormalities, prior
(may lower the convulsive threshold in patients with history of seizures, patients with prior EEG abnormalities and no history of seizures, and in rare cases, in the absence of a history of seizures and no prior EEG evidence of seizures; discontinue in the presence of seizures)

Risk-benefit should be considered when the following medical problems exist:

» Alcohol or drug abuse or dependence, history of
(use cautiously; chronic abusive use may lead to tolerance and psychological dependence with varying degrees of abnormal behavior; occurrence of frank psychotic episodes, especially with parenteral abuse. Caution required during drug withdrawal from abusive use since severe depression may occur. Withdrawal following chronic therapeutic use may unmask symptoms of underlying disorder and may require follow up)

Growth suppression, long-term
(has been reported with the long-term use of stimulants in children)

Heart failure or
Hypertension or
Hyperthyroidism or
Myocardial infarction, recent
(may increase blood pressure or heart rate)

Psychosis
(may exacerbate behavior disturbance and thought disorder symptoms)

Patient monitoring

The following may be especially important in patient monitoring (other tests may be warranted in some patients, depending on condition; » = major clinical significance):

» Blood pressure and
» Heart rate
(recommended monitoring at periodic intervals during therapy, especially for patients with hypertension)

» Complete blood cell (CBC), differential, and platelet counts
(advised at periodic intervals for patients during prolonged therapy)

» Monitoring of growth, both height and weight gain
(recommended during long-term therapy; treatment should be interrupted in patients who are not growing or gaining weight as expected)

» Re-evaluation of the long-term usefulness of the drug
(interruption of therapy at periodic intervals is recommended to assess the patient's functioning without therapy; the effectiveness for long term use (more than 6 weeks) has not been systematically evaluated in controlled trials)

Side/Adverse Effects

For information pertaining to the side and adverse effects of other methylphenidate products, see the *Methylphenidate (Systemic)* monograph

The following side/adverse effects have been selected on the basis of their potential clinical significance (possible signs and symptoms in parentheses where appropriate)—not necessarily inclusive:

Note: Children may experience a more frequent occurrence of loss of appetite, abdominal pain, weight loss (during prolonged therapy), insomnia and tachycardia.

Those indicating need for medical attention

More frequent
Anxiety (fear, nervousness)

Incidence less frequent
Tachycardia (fast, pounding, or irregular heartbeat or pulse)

Incidence rare
Visual disturbance (blurred vision; change in near or distance vision; difficulty in focusing eyes)

Frequency unknown
Seizures (convulsions, muscle spasm or jerking of all extremities, sudden loss of consciousness)

Those indicating need for medical attention only if they continue or are bothersome

Incidence more frequent
Abdominal pain (stomach pain); ***anorexia*** (loss of appetite, weight loss); ***dry mouth; dyspepsia*** (acid or sour stomach; belching; heartburn; indigestion; stomach discomfort, upset, or pain); ***headache; nausea; pharyngolaryngeal pain*** (throat pain)

Incidence less frequent
Fever; insomnia (sleeplessness; trouble sleeping; unable to sleep); ***twitching***—motor or vocal tics

Overdose

For more information on the management of overdose or unintentional ingestion, **contact a poison control center** (see *Poison Control Center Listing*).

Clinical effects of overdose

The following effects have been selected on the basis of their potential clinical significance (possible signs and symptoms in parentheses where appropriate)—not necessarily inclusive:

Acute
Agitation (anxiety, nervousness, restlessness, irritability, dry mouth, shortness of breath, hyperventilation, trouble sleeping, irregular heartbeats, shaking); ***cardiac arrhythmias*** (chest pain or discomfort, dizziness; fainting; fast, slow, or irregular heartbeat; lightheadedness; pounding or rapid pulse); ***coma*** (change in consciousness, loss of consciousness); ***confusion*** (mood or mental changes); ***convulsions*** (seizures); ***delirium*** (unusual excitement; nervousness or restlessness; hallucinations; confusion as to time, place, or person; holding false beliefs that cannot be changed by fact); ***dryness of mucous membranes; euphoria*** (false or unusual sense of well-being); ***flushing*** (feeling of warmth; redness of the face, neck, arms and occasionally, upper chest); ***hallucinations*** (seeing, hearing, or feeling things that are not there); ***headache*** (pain in one or more areas of the head); ***hyperpyrexia*** (fever); ***hyperreflexia*** (overactive reflexes); ***hypertension*** (blurred vision; dizziness; nervousness; headache; pounding in the ears; slow or fast heartbeat); ***muscle twitching; palpitations*** (fast, irregular, pounding, or racing heartbeat or pulse); ***mydriasis*** (bigger, dilated, or enlarged pupils [black part of eye]; increased sensitivity of eyes to light); ***sweating; tachycardia*** (fast, pounding, or irregular heartbeat or pulse); ***tremors*** (shakiness); ***vomiting***

Treatment of overdose

To decrease absorption—
Administering activated charcoal and a cathartic
Evacuating stomach contents by gastric lavage (control agitation and seizures if present and protect airway before performing gastric lavage)

Specific treatment—
Using external cooling procedures for hyperpyrexia

Note: With dexmethylphenidate extended-release capsules, keeping in mind that there is a prolonged release of dexmethylphenidate.

Supportive care—
Protecting patient against self-injury and external stimuli that would aggravate overstimulated condition
Maintaining adequate circulation and respiratory exchange
Patients in whom intentional overdose is confirmed or suspected should be referred for psychiatric consultation.

Note: Efficacy of peritoneal dialysis for dexmethylphenidate overdose has not been established.

Patient Consultation

As an aid to patient consultation, refer to *Advice for the Patient, Dexmethylphenidate (Systemic).*

In providing consultation, consider emphasizing the following selected information (» = major clinical significance):

Before using this medication

» Conditions affecting use, especially:
Hypersensitivity to dexmethylphenidate or methylphenidate or to any component of the product.
Pregnancy—Risk/benefit considerations
Breast-feeding—Caution should be exercised
Use in children—More frequent occurrence of loss of appetite, abdominal pain, weight loss (during prolonged therapy), insomnia and tachycardia in children; safety and efficacy not established in children less than 6 years of age
Other medications, especially acid suppressants, antacids, anticonvulsants, clonidine or other centrally acting alpha-2 agonists, coumarin anticoagulants, monoamine oxidase inhibitors, pressor agents, selective serotonin reuptake inhibitors, or tricyclic antidepressants
Other medical problems, especially agitation, anxiety, or tension, history of or current alcohol or drug abuse or dependence, history or diagnosis of Tourette's syndrome, history of or current EEG abnormalities, glaucoma, motor tics, severe depression, seizures

Proper use of this medication

» Importance of not using more medication than the amount prescribed. Call doctor immediately if more than the amount of dexmethylphenidate prescribed is taken.
» Swallowing extended-release capsule whole or following proper dosing instructions for taking with applesauce; not dividing, crushing or chewing
» Monitoring patient for blood pressure, CBC, differential and platelet counts, effectiveness of long term therapy, growth rates both height and weight, and heart rate
» Proper dosing
Missed dose: Taking as soon as possible; not taking if within 4 hours of next scheduled dose for tablets and within 24 hours for extended-release capsules; not doubling doses
Proper storage

Precautions while using this medication

» Regular visits to physician periodically to monitor progress and reevaluate long-term usefulness of the drug
Possible dizziness, drowsiness, or vision disturbances; not driving, riding a bicycle, operating machinery, or doing anything that could be dangerous until effects of medication are known
» Suspected dependence or abuse, consulting physician

Side/adverse effects

Signs of potential side effects, especially anxiety, seizures, tachycardia and visual disturbances

General Dosing Information

Dexmethylphenidate extended-release capsules should be taken in the morning.

Diet/Nutrition

May be given at the same time as food or with no food.

Bioequivalence information

Patients currently taking dexmethylphenidate tablets may be switched to the same daily dose of dexmethylphenidate extended-release capsules.

Treatment of side and adverse effects

If paradoxical aggravation of symptoms or other adverse events occur, the dosage should be reduced, or, if necessary, the drug should be discontinued. After appropriate dosage adjustment over a one month period, the drug should be discontinued if improvement is not observed.

Oral Dosage Forms

DEXMETHYLPHENIDATE HYDROCHLORIDE EXTENDED-RELEASE CAPSULES

Usual adult and adolescent dose

Attention deficit hyperactivity disorder [ADHD]—
Patients not currently taking dexmethylphenidate, racemic methylphenidate, or currently taking other stimulants other than methylphenidate—
Oral, initially 10 mg once daily in the morning
Dosage may be adjusted in 10 mg increments to a maximum of 20 mg per day at approximately weekly intervals.
Patients currently using methylphenidate—
Oral, initially half the total daily dose of racemic methylphenidate the patient is currently using

Usual adult prescribing limits

20 mg per day

Usual pediatric dose

For attention deficit hyperactivity disorder—
Children under 6 years of age: Safety and efficacy have not been established.
Patients not currently taking dexmethylphenidate, racemic methylphenidate, or currently taking other stimulants other than methylphenidate—
Oral, initially 5 mg once daily in the morning
Dosage may be adjusted in 5 mg increments to a maximum of 20 mg per day at approximately weekly intervals.
Patients currently using methylphenidate—
Oral, initially half the total daily dose of racemic methyiphenidate the patient is currently using

Usual pediatric prescribing limits

See *Usual adult prescribing limits.*

Strength(s) usually available

U.S.—
5 mg (Rx) [*Focalin XR* (ammonio methacrylate copolymer; FD&C Blue #2; gelatin; ink Tan SW-8010; methacrylic acid copolymer; polyethylene glycol; sugar spheres; talc; titanium dioxide; triethyl citrate)].
10 mg (Rx) [*Focalin XR* (ammonio methacrylate copolymer; FDA/E172 Yellow Iron Oxide; gelatin; ink Tan SW-8010; methacrylic acid copolymer; polyethylene glycol; sugar spheres; talc; titanium dioxide; triethyl citrate)].
20 mg (Rx) [*Focalin XR* (ammonio methacrylate copolymer; gelatin; ink Tan SW-8010; methacrylic acid copolymer; polyethylene glycol; sugar spheres; talc; titanium dioxide; triethyl citrate)].

Packaging and storage

Store at 25°C (77°F) excursions permitted between 15 and 30 °C (59 and 86 °F), in a tight container.

Preparation of dosage form

For those who cannot swallow capsules whole—Capsules may be carefully opened and the beads sprinkled over a spoonful of applesauce. The mixture of drug and applesauce should be consumed immediately in its entirety. The drug and applesauce mixture should not be stored for future use.

Auxiliary labeling

- May cause drowsiness
- Swallow whole. Do not crush or chew.
- Keep out of reach of children

Note: Schedule II controlled substance in the U.S.

DEXMETHYLPHENIDATE HYDROCHLORIDE TABLETS

Usual adult and adolescent dose

Attention deficit hyperactivity disorder [ADHD]—
Patients not currently taking racemic methylphenidate or currently taking other stimulants other than methylphenidate—
Oral, initially 2.5 mg twice daily, at least four hours apart
Dosage may be adjusted in 2.5 to 5 mg increments to a maximum of 20 mg per day (10 mg twice daily) at approximately weekly intervals.
Patients currently using methylphenidate—
Oral, initially half the dose of racemic methylphenidate the patient is currently using, at least four hours apart
Dosage may be adjusted to a maximum of 20 mg per day (10 mg twice daily) at approximately weekly intervals.

Usual adult prescribing limits

20 mg per day

Usual pediatric dose

For attention deficit hyperactivity disorder—
 Children under 6 years of age: Safety and efficacy have not been established.
 Children between the ages of 6 to 12 years: See *Usual adult and adolescent dose*

Usual pediatric prescribing limits

See *Usual adult prescribing limits.*

Strength(s) usually available

U.S.—
 2.5 mg (Rx) [*Focalin* (FD&C Blue No. 1 #5516 aluminum lake, lactose monohydrate, magnesium stearate, microcrystalline cellulose, pregelatinized starch, sodium starch glycolate)].
 5 mg (Rx) [*Focalin* (D&C Yellow Lake No. 10, lactose monohydrate, magnesium stearate, microcrystalline cellulose, pregelatinized starch, sodium starch glycolate)].
 10 mg (Rx) [*Focalin* (lactose monohydrate, magnesium stearate, microcrystalline cellulose, pregelatinized starch, sodium starch glycolate)].

Packaging and storage

Store at 25°C (77°F) excursions permitted between 15 and 30 °C (59 and 86 °F), in a tight container. Protect from light and moisture.

Auxiliary labeling

- May cause drowsiness.

Note: Controlled substance in the U.S.

Revised: 07/13/2005
Developed: 11/21/2002

DEXRAZOXANE Systemic

VA CLASSIFICATION (Primary): AN700

Commonly used brand name(s): *Zinecard.*

Note: For a listing of dosage forms and brand names by country availability, see *Dosage Forms* section(s).

Category

Chelating agent.

Indications

Accepted

Cardiomyopathy (prophylaxis)—Dexrazoxane is indicated for reducing the incidence and severity of cardiomyopathy associated with the administration of doxorubicin in women with metastatic breast cancer who have received a cumulative doxorubicin dose of 300 mg per square meter of body surface (mg/m²) and who would benefit from continued therapy with doxorubicin.

Dexrazoxane is not indicated for use at the time of initiation of doxorubicin therapy. Concurrent use of dexrazoxane with the initiation of fluorouracil, doxorubicin, and cyclophosphamide (FAC) therapy is not recommended because of possible interference with the antitumor efficacy of the regimen.

Pharmacology/Pharmacokinetics

Physicochemical characteristics

Molecular weight—268.28.
pKa—2.1.

Mechanism of action/Effect

The mechanism of action of dexrazoxane's cardioprotective activity is not fully understood. Dexrazoxane is a cyclic derivative of ethylenediamine tetra-acetic acid (EDTA) that readily penetrates cell membranes. Laboratory studies suggest that dexrazoxane is converted intracellularly to a ring-opened chelating agent that interferes with iron-mediated free radical generation thought to be responsible, in part, for anthracycline-induced cardiomyopathy. Dexrazoxane does not affect the pharmacokinetics of doxorubicin.

Distribution

Following a rapid distributive phase (0.2 to 0.3 hours), dexrazoxane reaches post-distributive equilibrium within 2 to 4 hours, primarily in total body water.

Volume of distribution—Steady-state: 25 liters per square meter of body surface.

Protein binding

Not bound to plasma proteins.

Biotransformation

Metabolic products include the unchanged drug, a diacid-diamide cleavage product, and two monoacid-monoamide ring products of unknown concentrations.

Half-life

Elimination—2.5 hours.

Peak concentration

Plasma—After administration of a dose of 500 mg per square meter of body surface (mg/m²): 36.5 mcg per mL.

Elimination

Renal—42%.
In dialysis—It is not known whether dexrazoxane is removable by dialysis. However, because a significant dose fraction (greater than 0.4) of unchanged drug is retained in the plasma pool, minimal tissue partitioning or binding occurs, and systemic drug availability in the unbound form is greater than 90%, it is possible that dexrazoxane is removable by conventional peritoneal dialysis or hemodialysis.

Precautions to Consider

Carcinogenicity

Carcinogenicity studies have not been done in animals or humans.

Mutagenicity

Dexrazoxane was not mutagenic in the Ames test but was found to be clastogenic to human lymphocytes *in vitro* and to mouse bone marrow erythrocytes *in vivo* (micronucleus test).

Pregnancy/Reproduction

Fertility—Dexrazoxane produced testicular atrophy in rats and dogs at doses as low as 30 mg per kg of body weight (mg/kg) weekly for 6 weeks (1/3 the human dose on a mg per square meter of body surface [mg/m²] basis) and 20 mg/kg weekly for 13 weeks (approximately equal to the human dose on a mg/m² basis), respectively.

Pregnancy—Adequate and well-controlled studies in humans have not been done.
Studies in pregnant rats, at doses of 2 mg/kg (1/40 the human dose on a mg/m² basis) given daily during the period of organogenesis, found dexrazoxane to be maternotoxic; dexrazoxane was embryotoxic and teratogenic at doses of 8 mg/kg (1/10 the human dose on a mg/m² basis) and also impaired fertility at maturity in both males and females. Teratogenic effects in rats included imperforate anus, microphthalmia, and anophthalmia. Studies in pregnant rabbits, at doses of 5 mg/kg (1/10 the human dose on a mg/m² basis), found dexrazoxane to be maternotoxic; dexrazoxane was embryotoxic and teratogenic at doses of 20 mg/kg (1/2 the human dose on a mg/m² basis). Teratogenic effects in rabbits included several skeletal malformations such as short tail, rib and thoracic malformations, and soft tissue variations including subcutaneous, eye, and cardiac hemorrhagic areas, as well as agenesis of the gallbladder and of the intermediate lobe of the lung.

FDA Pregnancy Category C.

Breast-feeding

It is not known whether dexrazoxane is distributed into breast milk.

Pediatrics

No information is available on the relationship of age to the effects of dexrazoxane in pediatric patients. Safety and efficacy have not been established.

Geriatrics

No information is available on the relationship of age to the effects of dexrazoxane in geriatric patients.

Drug interactions and/or related problems

The following drug interactions and/or related problems have been selected on the basis of their potential clinical significance (possible mechanism in parentheses where appropriate)—not necessarily inclusive (» = major clinical significance):

Note: Combinations containing any of the following medications, depending on the amount present, may also interact with this medicine.

» Bone marrow depressants (See *Appendix II*)
 (enhanced bone marrow depression may occur)

Patient monitoring

The following may be especially important in patient monitoring (other tests may be warranted in some patients, depending on condition; » = major clinical significance):

» Cardiac function tests
(recommended at periodic intervals because dexrazoxane reduces, but does not eliminate, the risk of doxorubicin cardiotoxicity, especially in patients who have already received a cumulative doxorubicin dose of 300 mg/m²)

» Complete blood count (CBC)
(frequent determinations are recommended because of the risk of increased bone marrow depression with concurrent use of cytotoxic medications)

Side/Adverse Effects

Note: Most adverse experiences encountered with the administration of dexrazoxane are probably the result of the FAC (fluorouracil, doxorubicin, and cyclophosphamide) chemotherapy regimen, with the exception of pain at the injection site.

Severity of leukopenia and thrombocytopenia at nadir with the FAC regimen was greater in patients receiving dexrazoxane, but recovery was similar with or without dexrazoxane.

The following side/adverse effects have been selected on the basis of their potential clinical significance (possible signs and symptoms in parentheses where appropriate)—not necessarily inclusive:

Those indicating need for medical attention

Incidence less frequent

Pain at injection site

Patient Consultation

As an aid to patient consultation, refer to *Advice for the Patient, Dexrazoxane (Systemic).*

Before using this medication

» Conditions affecting use, especially:
Pregnancy—Teratogenic effects in animals
Breast-feeding—Not recommended
Other medications, especially bone marrow depressants

Proper use of this medication

» Proper dosing

Side/adverse effects

Signs of potential side effects, especially pain at injection site

General Dosing Information

Dexrazoxane solution should be given by slow intravenous injection or rapid-drip intravenous infusion from a bag. The intravenous injection of doxorubicin should be administered within 30 minutes after the beginning of the infusion of dexrazoxane. Doxorubicin should not be administered prior to dexrazoxane.

Safety considerations for handling this medication

It is suggested that dexrazoxane be handled with the same caution as antineoplastic agents.

There is limited but increasing evidence and concern that personnel involved in preparation and administration of parenteral antineoplastics may be at some risk because of the potential mutagenicity, teratogenicity, and/or carcinogenicity of these agents, although the actual risk is unknown. USP advisory panels recommend cautious handling both in preparation and disposal of antineoplastic agents. Precautions that have been suggested include:

• Use of a biological containment cabinet during reconstitution and dilution of parenteral medications and wearing of disposable surgical gloves and masks.

• Use of proper technique to prevent contamination of the medication, work area, and operator during transfer between containers (including proper training of personnel in this technique).

• Cautious and proper disposal of needles, syringes, vials, ampuls, and unused medication.

A number of medical centers have developed detailed guidelines for handling of antineoplastic agents.

Parenteral Dosage Forms

DEXRAZOXANE FOR INJECTION

Note: Dexrazoxane for injection contains dexrazoxane hydrochloride, but strength and dosage are expressed in terms of dexrazoxane.

Usual adult dose

Cardiomyopathy—
Intravenous, in a dosage ratio of 10 parts dexrazoxane to 1 part doxorubicin (10:1), or 500 mg of dexrazoxane per square meter of body surface (mg/m²) for every 50 mg/m² of doxorubicin, repeated every three weeks, providing recovery has occurred.

Note: Patients with moderate to severe renal dysfunction (creatinine clearance values < 40 mL per min), the recommended dosage ratio of dexrazoxane:doxorubicin is 5:1, or 250 mg per m² dexrazoxane: 50 mg per m² doxorubicin.

Note: Administer solution by slow intravenous injection or by rapid-drip intravenous infusion from a bag. Doxorubicin should be administered within thirty minutes after the *beginning* of the dexrazoxane infusion.

Usual pediatric dose

Safety and efficacy have not been established.

Strength(s) usually available

U.S.—
250 mg (base) (single-dose vial) (Rx) [*Zinecard*].
500 mg (base) (single-dose vial) (Rx) [*Zinecard*].

Packaging and storage

Store at controlled room temperature between 15 and 30 °C (59 and 86 °F). Store reconstituted solution up to six hours at controlled room temperature or under refrigeration between 2 and 8 °C (36 and 46 °F).

Preparation of dosage form

Dexrazoxane for injection is prepared for intravenous administration by adding 25 or 50 mL of 0.167 molar (M/6) sodium lactate injection (provided by the manufacturer) to the 250- or 500-mg vial, respectively, to produce a solution containing 10 mg per mL (mg/mL).

The reconstituted solution may be further diluted with either 0.9% sodium chloride injection or 5% dextrose injection to a concentration ranging from 1.3 to 5.0 mg/mL in intravenous infusion bags.

Stability

After reconstitution or further dilution, dexrazoxane solution is stable for 6 hours at controlled room temperature (between 15 and 30 °C [59 and 86 °F]) or under refrigeration (between 2 and 8 °C [36 and 46 °F]). Any unused solution should be discarded.

Incompatibilities

Dexrazoxane should not be mixed with other medications.

Auxiliary labeling

• Discard unused solution.

Note

If accidental contamination of the skin or mucosae with dexrazoxane occurs, the area should be immediately and thoroughly washed with soap and water.

Revised: 02/01/2006
Developed: 09/28/1995

DEXTROAMPHETAMINE—See *Amphetamines (Systemic)*

DEXTROMETHORPHAN Systemic

VA CLASSIFICATION (Primary): RE302

Commonly used brand name(s): *Balminil DM; Balminil DM Children; Benylin Adult Formula Cough Suppressant; Benylin DM; Benylin DM 12 Hour; Benylin DM For Children 12 Hour; Benylin DM for children; Benylin Pediatric Cough Suppressant; Broncho-Grippol-DM; Calmylin #1; Cough-X; Creo-Terpin; Delsym; Delsym Cough Formula; Diabe-TUSS DM Syrup; Hold DM; Koffex DM; Novahistex DM; Novahistine DM; Pertussin CS Children's Strength; Pertussin DM Extra Strength; Robitussin Maximum Strength Cough Suppressant; Robitussin Pediatric; Robitussin Pediatric Cough Suppressant; Sucrets 4 Hour Cough Suppressant; Triaminic DM Long Lasting For Children; Trocal; Vicks 44 Cough Relief.*

Note: For a listing of dosage forms and brand names by country availability, see *Dosage Forms* section(s).

Category

Antitussive.

Indications

Accepted

Cough (treatment)—Dextromethorphan is indicated for the temporary symptomatic relief of nonproductive cough due to minor throat and bronchial irritation occurring with colds or inhaled irritants.

Pharmacology/Pharmacokinetics

Mechanism of action/Effect
Suppresses the cough reflex by a direct action on the cough center in the medulla of the brain.

Biotransformation
Hepatic. Rapidly and extensively metabolized to dextrorphan (active metabolite).

Onset of action
Usually within one-half hour, after 10- to 20-mg doses every 4 hours or 30 mg every 6 to 8 hours.

Duration of action
Up to 6 hours.

Note: The extended-release oral polistirex suspension delivers dextromethorphan from an ion-exchange complex over a period of 9 to 12 hours. One 60-mg dose of polistirex dextromethorphan delivers a plasma concentration similar to two 30-mg doses of dextromethorphan hydrobromide given every 6 hours.

Elimination
Primarily renal (excreted as unchanged dextromethorphan and demethylated metabolites, including dextrorphan).

Precautions to Consider

Pregnancy/Reproduction
Pregnancy—Adequate and well-controlled studies in humans have not been done.

Breast-feeding
It is not known whether dextromethorphan is distributed into breast milk. However, problems in humans have not been documented.

Pediatrics
Appropriate studies on the relationship of age to the effects of dextromethorphan have not been performed in the pediatric population. However, no pediatrics-specific problems have been documented to date.

Geriatrics
No information is available on the relationship of age to the effects of dextromethorphan in geriatric patients.

Drug interactions and/or related problems
The following drug interactions and/or related problems have been selected on the basis of their potential clinical significance (possible mechanism in parentheses where appropriate)—not necessarily inclusive (» = major clinical significance):

Note: Combinations containing any of the following medications, depending on the amount present, may also interact with this medication.

» Central nervous system (CNS) depression-producing medications, including psychiatric, emotional, and Parkinson's disease medications, other (see *Appendix II*)
(concurrent use may potentiate the CNS depressant effects of these medications or dextromethorphan)

» Monoamine oxidase (MAO) inhibitors, including furazolidone, phenelzine, procarbazine, selegiline, and tranylcypromine
(concurrent use with dextromethorphan, and also use of monoamine oxidase inhibitors within 2 to 3 weeks of dextromethorphan, may cause adrenergic crisis, collapse, coma, dizziness, excitation, hypertension, hyperpyrexia, intracerebral bleeding, lethargy, nausea, psychotic behavior, spasms, and tremors)

» Amiodarone or
» Fluoxetine or
» Quinidine
(inhibition of the cytochrome P4502D6 enzyme system by amiodarone, fluoxetine, or quinidine may cause a decrease in the hepatic metabolism of dextromethorphan, which may result in increased dextromethorphan serum concentrations; higher concentrations of dextromethorphan have been associated with an increased incidence of side effects)

» Smoking tobacco
(inhibition of cough reflex by dextromethorphan may lead to retention of secretions)

Medical considerations/Contraindications
The medical considerations/contraindications included have been selected on the basis of their potential clinical significance (reasons given in parentheses where appropriate)—not necessarily inclusive (» = major clinical significance).

Risk-benefit should be considered when the following medical problems exist:
» Asthma
(dextromethorphan may impair expectoration and thus increase airway resistance)

» Bronchitis, chronic or
» Cough, productive or
» Emphysema
(inhibition of cough reflex by dextromethorphan may lead to retention of secretions)

» Diabetes
(some dextromethorphan products contain sugar and may impair blood glucose control)

Hepatic function impairment
(metabolism of dextromethorphan may be impaired)

Respiratory depression
(dextromethorphan may make this condition worse)

Sensitivity to dextromethorphan, other ingredients, such as procaine, butacaine, benzocaine, or other "caine" anesthetics, or other inactive ingredients
(may result in adverse effects such as insomnia, dizziness, weakness, tremors, and arrhythmias)

Side/Adverse Effects

Note: Toxic psychosis (hyperactivity, visual and auditory hallucinations) has been reported after ingestion of 300 mg or more of dextromethorphan.

Respiratory depression has been reported to occur with very high doses.

Dextromethorphan abuse and dependence may occur rarely, especially following prolonged use of high doses.

The following side/adverse effects have been selected on the basis of their potential clinical significance (possible signs and symptoms in parentheses where appropriate)—not necessarily inclusive:

Those indicating need for medical attention only if they continue or are bothersome
Incidence less frequent or rare
Confusion; constipation; headache; mild dizziness; ***mild drowsiness***; ***nausea or vomiting; stomach pain***

Overdose
For more information on the management of overdose or unintentional ingestion, **contact a Poison Control Center** (see *Poison Control Center Listing*).

Clinical effects of overdose
The following effects have been selected on the basis of their potential clinical significance (possible signs and symptoms in parentheses where appropriate—not necessarily inclusive:
Symptoms of overdose
Ataxia (shakiness and unsteady walk); ***blurred vision; coma; confusion; drowsiness or dizziness; respiratory depression*** (slowed breathing); ***severe nausea or vomiting; severe unusual excitement, nervousness, restlessness, or irritability; urinary retention*** (difficulty in urination)

Treatment of overdose
Treatment is symptomatic and is directed toward the affected body systems. Gastric lavage, assisted respiration, vital sign monitoring, and intravenous (i.v.) naloxone are some of the possible prescribed treatments.

Patient Consultation
As an aid to patient consultation, refer to *Advice for the Patient, Dextromethorphan (Systemic)*.

In providing consultation, consider emphasizing the following selected information (» = major clinical significance):

Before using this medication
» Conditions affecting use, especially:
Sensitivity to dextromethorphan or other ingredients
Other medications, especially other CNS depressants, MAO inhibitors, amiodarone, fluoxetine, quinidine, and smoking tobacco
Other medical problems, especially asthma, chronic bronchitis, productive cough, emphysema, diabetes, hepatic function impairment, and respiratory depression

Proper use of this medication
» Importance of not using more medication than the amount prescribed because of habit-forming potential

» Proper dosing
  Missed dose: If on a scheduled dosing regimen—Taking as soon as possible; not taking if almost time for next dose; not doubling doses
» Proper storage

Precautions while using this medication

Checking with physician if cough persists after medication has been used for 7 days; if sore throat persists for more than 2 days; if high fever, skin rash, or continuing headache is present with cough; or if asthma or high blood pressure is present

Using lozenges with caution to prevent choking

Oral Dosage Forms

DEXTROMETHORPHAN HYDROBROMIDE LOZENGES

Usual adult and adolescent dose

Antitussive—
  Oral, 5 to 15 mg every two to four hours, as needed.

Usual adult prescribing limits

Up to to 90 mg per day.

Usual pediatric dose

Antitussive—
  Children up to 2 years of age: Dosage must be individualized by physician.
  Children 2 to 6 years of age: Oral, 5 mg every four hours, as needed.
  Children 6 to 12 years of age: Oral, 5 to 15 mg every two to six hours, as needed.
  Children 12 years of age and older: See *Usual adult and adolescent dose.*

Note: Administration of a specific product to a pediatric patient depends upon the ability to achieve suitable dosage for the age of the child.

Usual pediatric prescribing limits

Children 2 to 6 years of age: 30 mg per day.
Children 6 to 12 years of age: 60 mg per day.

Usual geriatric dose

See *Usual adult and adolescent dose.*

Strength(s) usually available

U.S.—
  5 mg (OTC) [*Cough-X* (benzocaine 2 mg; corn syrup; menthol; sucrose); *Hold DM* (corn syrup; sucrose)].
  7.5 mg (OTC) [*Trocal*].
  15 mg (OTC) [*Sucrets 4 Hour Cough Suppressant* (corn syrup; menthol; sucrose)].

Canada—
  Not commercially available.

Packaging and storage

Store below 40 °C (104 °F), preferably between 15 and 30 °C (59 and 86 °F), in a well-closed container, unless otherwise specified by manufacturer.
Protect from moisture.

DEXTROMETHORPHAN HYDROBROMIDE SYRUP USP

Usual adult and adolescent dose

Antitussive—
  Oral, 30 mg every six to eight hours, as needed.

Usual adult prescribing limits

Up to 120 mg per day.

Usual pediatric dose

Antitussive—
  Children up to 2 years of age: Dosage must be individualized by physician.
  Children 2 to 6 years of age: Oral, 3.5 mg every four hours or 7.5 mg every six to eight hours.
  Children 6 to 12 years of age: Oral, 7 mg every four hours or 15 mg every six to eight hours.
  Children 12 years of age and older: See *Usual adult and adolescent dose.*

Note: Dosage must be individualized for children up to 6 years of age, for dextromethorphan syrups containing alcohol.

Usual pediatric prescribing limits

Children 2 to 6 years of age: Up to 30 mg per day.
Children 6 to 12 years of age: Up to 60 mg per day.

Usual geriatric dose

See *Usual adult and adolescent dose.*

Strength(s) usually available

U.S.—
  3.5 mg per 5 mL (OTC) [*Pertussin CS Children's Strength* (alcohol-free; sucrose)].
  7.5 mg per 5 mL (OTC) [*Benylin Pediatric Cough Suppressant* (alcohol-free; sugar-free); *Robitussin Pediatric Cough Suppressant* (alcohol-free; sugar-free)].
  10 mg per 15 mL (OTC) [*Creo-Terpin* (alcohol 25%)].
  15 mg per 5 mL (OTC) [*Benylin Adult Formula Cough Suppressant* (alcohol-free; sugar-free); *Diabe-TUSS DM Syrup* (alcohol-free; sugar-free); *Pertussin DM Extra Strength* (alcohol 4%; sugar); *Robitussin Maximum Strength Cough Suppressant* (alcohol 1.4%; glucose; high fructose corn syrup); GENERIC].
  30 mg per 15 ml (OTC) [*Vicks 44 Cough Relief* (alcohol; high fructose corn syrup)].

Canada—
  7.5 mg per 5 mL (OTC) [*Balminil DM Children* (alcohol-free); *Benylin DM for children* (alcohol-free; sucrose-free); *Novahistine DM* (alcohol-free; glucose); *Robitussin Pediatric* (alcohol-free; sugar-free)].
  15 mg per 5 mL (OTC) [*Balminil DM* (alcohol-free; sucrose or sucrose-free); *Benylin DM* (alcohol-free; artificial sweetener; sucrose-free); *Broncho-Grippol-DM* (alcohol-free; sugar-free); *Calmylin #1* (alcohol-free; natural honey flavoring); *Koffex DM* (alcohol-free; sucrose or sucrose-free); *Novahistex DM* (alcohol-free; glucose)].

Packaging and storage

Store between 15 and 30 °C (59 and 86 °F), unless otherwise specified by manufacturer. Store in a tight, light-resistant container. Protect from freezing.

DEXTROMETHORPHAN POLISTIREX EXTENDED-RELEASE ORAL SUSPENSION

Usual adult and adolescent dose

Antitussive—
  Oral, 60 mg every twelve hours, as needed.

Usual adult prescribing limits

Up to 120 mg per day.

Usual pediatric dose

Antitussive—
  Children up to 2 years of age: Dosage must be individualized by physician.
  Children 2 to 6 years of age: Oral, 15 mg every twelve hours, as needed.
  Children 6 to 12 years of age: Oral, 30 mg every twelve hours, as needed.
  Children 12 years of age and older: See *Usual adult and adolescent dose.*

Usual pediatric prescribing limits

Children 2 to 6 years of age: Up to 30 mg per day.
Children 6 to 12 years of age: Up to 60 mg per day.

Usual geriatric dose

See *Usual adult and adolescent dose*

Strength(s) usually available

U.S.—
  30 mg (equivalent of dextromethorphan hydrobromide) per 5 mL (OTC) [*Delsym Cough Formula* (alcohol-free; high fructose corn syrup; sucrose)].

Canada—
  15 mg (equivalent of dextromethorphan hydrobromide) per 5 ml (OTC) [*Benylin DM For Children 12 Hour* (alcohol-free; sucralose; sucrose-free)].
  30 mg (equivalent of dextromethorphan hydrobromide) per 5 mL (OTC) [*Benylin DM 12 Hour* (alcohol-free; sucralose; sucrose-free); *Delsym* (alcohol-free; corn syrup; granulated sugar); *Triaminic DM Long Lasting For Children* (alcohol-free; corn syrup; sugar)].

Packaging and storage

Store below 40 °C (104 °F), preferably between 15 and 30 °C (59 and 86 °F), in a well-closed container, unless otherwise specified by manufacturer. Protect from freezing.

Auxiliary labeling

• Shake well.

Selected Bibliography

Irwin RS, Curley FJ, Bennett FM. Appropriate use of antitussives and protussives. Drugs 1993; 46(1): 80-91.

Segal S, et al. Use of codeine- and dextromethorphan-containing cough syrups in pediatrics. Pediatrics 1978; 62(1): 118-22.

Revised: 06/11/1999

DEXTROSE AND ELECTROLYTES—See *Carbohydrates and Electrolytes (Systemic)*

DIATRIZOATE MEGLUMINE—See *Diatrizoates (Local), Diatrizoates (Systemic)*

DIATRIZOATE MEGLUMINE AND DIATRIZOATE SODIUM (SYSTEMIC)—See *Diatrizoates (Systemic)*

DIATRIZOATE SODIUM—See *Diatrizoates (Local), Diatrizoates (Systemic)*

DIAZEPAM—See *Benzodiazepines (Systemic)*

DIBUCAINE—See *Anesthetics (Mucosal-Local), Anesthetics (Topical)*

DICHLORPHENAMIDE—See *Carbonic Anhydrase Inhibitors (Systemic)*

DICLOFENAC—See *Anti-inflammatory Drugs, Nonsteroidal (Ophthalmic), Anti-inflammatory Drugs, Nonsteroidal (Systemic)*

DICLOFENAC Topical

VA CLASSIFICATION (Primary): DE600

Commonly used brand name(s): *Solaraze*.

Note: For a listing of dosage forms and brand names by country availability, see *Dosage Forms* section(s).

Category

Antineoplastic (topical).

Indications

Accepted

Actinic keratoses (treatment)—Topical diclofenac is indicated for treatment of actinic keratoses

Pharmacology/Pharmacokinetics

Physicochemical characteristics

Chemical Group—Phenylacetic acid derivative, nonsteroidal anti-inflammatory drug (NSAID).

Molecular weight—Diclofenac sodium: 318.13.

Mechanism of action/Effect

The mechanism by which diclofenac affects actinic keratoses is unknown.

Other actions/effects

Like other nonsteroidal anti-inflammatory drugs (NSAIDs), diclofenac inhibits the actions of prostaglandins.

Absorption

Approximately 10% of the diclofenac dose was absorbed systemically following topical application four times daily for seven days.

Distribution

Volume of distribution (Vol_D) is 550 mL per kg following oral administration of diclofenac.

Protein binding

Very high (99%).

Biotransformation

The metabolism of topically administered diclofenac, thought to be similar to that following oral administration, likely results in several phenolic metabolites, two of which are biologically active. Following topical administration, however, diclofenac and its metabolites are present in the plasma in amounts too small to allow quantification of specific metabolites.

Terminal, plasma

Following oral administration:

Diclofenac—1 to 2 hours

Metabolites—1 to 3 hours

Time to peak concentration

4.5 ± 8 hours following topical application.

Peak plasma concentration:

4 ± 5 nanograms per milliliter following topical application

Elimination

Diclofenac and its metabolites are excreted mainly in the urine after oral dosing.

Precautions to Consider

Carcinogenicity

Following 2 years of oral treatment with diclofenac, neither mice nor rats displayed any carcinogenic effects. Male mice received 0.3 mg per kilogram of body weight (mg/kg) per day (25% of the estimated systemic human exposure, based on body surface area and assuming 10% bioavailability following topical application) while female mice received 1 mg/kg per day (83% of the estimated systemic human exposure). Rats received up to 2 mg/kg per day (3 times the estimated systemic human exposure).

A photococarcinogenicity study with up to 0.035% diclofenac gel was conducted in hairless mice at topical doses up to 2.8 mg/kg per day. Median tumor onset was earlier in the 0.035% group.

Mutagenicity

Diclofenac was not genotoxic in *in vitro* point mutation assays in mammalian mouse lymphoma cells and Ames microbial test systems, or when tested in mammalian *in vivo* assays including dominant lethal and male germinal epithelial chromosomal studies in mice, and nucleus anomaly and chromosomal aberration studies in Chinese hamsters. It was also negative in the transformation assay utilizing BALB/3T3 mouse embryo cells.

Pregnancy/Reproduction

Fertility—There was no evidence of impaired fertility in rats that received 4 mg of oral diclofenac sodium per kilogram of body weight per day (7 times the estimated systemic human exposure).

Pregnancy—Adequate and well controlled studies have not been conducted in humans. Like other nonsteroidal anti-inflammatory drugs (NSAIDs), diclofenac may cause adverse effects on the fetal cardiovascular system, including premature closure of the ductus arteriosus; use of diclofenac should be avoided in late pregnancy.

Studies in which rodents received oral diclofenac doses equivalent to 15–30 times the estimated systemic human exposure have not shown any teratogenic effects on the fetus despite the induction of maternal toxicity. However, in rats, maternally toxic doses were associated with dystocia, prolonged gestation, reduced fetal weights and growth, and reduced fetal survival.

FDA Pregnancy Category B.

Labor and delivery—The effects of diclofenac on labor and delivery are unknown. As with other NSAIDs, however, diclofenac may inhibit uterine contractions and delay parturition.

Breast-feeding

It is unknown whether diclofenac is distributed into human breast milk. Breast-feeding is not recommended due to the possibility of serious adverse effects in nursing infants.

Pediatrics

No information is available on the relationship of age to the effects of topical diclofenac in pediatric patients. Safety and efficacy have not been established.

Geriatrics

No geriatrics-related problems have been documented in studies done to date that included elderly patients.

Drug interactions and/or related problems

The following drug interactions and/or related problems have been selected on the basis of their potential clinical significance (possible

mechanism in parentheses where appropriate)—not necessarily inclusive (» = major clinical significance):

Nonsteroidal anti-inflammatory drugs (NSAIDs), other
(potential for increased adverse effects)

Laboratory value alterations

The following have been selected on the basis of their potential clinical significance (possible effect in parentheses where appropriate)—not necessarily inclusive (» = major clinical significance).

With physiology/laboratory test values

Alanine aminotransferase (ALT[SGPT]), and
Aspartate aminotransferase (AST[SGOT], and
(values may be increased during therapy)

Blood glucose, serum and
Cholesterol, serum and
Creatine kinase, serum and
Creatinine, serum
(concentrations may be increased)

Medical considerations/Contraindications

The medical considerations/contraindications included have been selected on the basis of their potential clinical significance (reasons given in parentheses where appropriate)—not necessarily inclusive (» = major clinical significance).

Risk-benefit should be considered when the following medical problems exist:

» Allergic reactions, severe, or
» Aspirin triad
(risk of severe allergic reaction due to cross-sensitivity)

Gastrointestinal ulceration, active, or bleeding
(condition may be exacerbated)

Hepatic impairment, severe
Renal impairment, severe
(decreases in metabolism and excretion may result in increased adverse effects)

Hypersensitivity to diclofenac, benzyl alcohol, polyethylene glycol monomethyl ether 350 and/or hyaluronate

Side/Adverse Effects

Note: As with other nonsteroidal anti-inflammatory drugs (NSAIDs), anaphylactoid reactions may occur in patients without prior exposure to diclofenac. Diclofenac should be administered with caution to patients with the aspirin triad. Typically, the aspirin triad occurs in asthmatic patients who experience rhinitis with or without nasal polyps, or who exhibit severe and potentially fatal bronchospasm after taking aspirin or other NSAIDs.

Patients should be made aware of the signs and symptoms of dermal adverse reactions and the possibility of irritant or allergic contact dermatitis. If severe dermal reactions occur, use of diclofenac may need to be interrupted until the reactions subside.

The following side/adverse effects have been selected on the basis of their potential clinical significance (possible signs and symptoms in parentheses where appropriate)—not necessarily inclusive:

Those indicating need for medical attention

Incidence more frequent

Application site reactions, including contact dermatitis (skin rash); ***pain; paresthesia*** (tingling or burning sensation); ***skin rash; flu-like syndrome*** (fever, with or without chills; body ache; headache)

Incidence less frequent

Application site reactions, including; edema (swelling); ***hyperesthesia*** (increased skin sensitivity); ***photosensitivity reaction*** (skin changes after exposure to sun, including skin rash, itching, redness, or pain); ***asthma*** (shortness of breath; troubled breathing; tightness in chest; wheezing); ***conjunctivitis*** (dry, itching, or burning eyes; redness or swelling of eyes; increased sensitivity of eyes to light); ***contact dermatitis*** (skin rash)—not limited to application site; ***dyspnea*** (shortness of breath); ***eye pain; hematuria*** (blood in the urine); ***hypertension*** (high blood pressure); ***hypokinesia*** (decrease in body movement); ***infection; migraines or other headaches; pharyngitis*** (sore throat; fever); ***pneumonia*** (cough; shortness of breath; troubled breathing; fever; tightness in chest; wheezing); ***sinusitis*** (pain or tenderness around eyes and cheekbones; fever; headache; nasal congestion); ***skin ulcers*** (sores on skin)—not limited to application site

Those indicating need for medical attention only if they continue or are bothersome

Incidence more frequent

Application site reactions, including; dry skin; exfoliation (scaling); ***pruritus*** (itching)—not limited to application site

Incidence less frequent

Abdominal pain; application site reactions including; acne; alopecia (loss or thinning of hair); ***arthralgia*** (joint pain); ***arthrosis*** (joint pain); ***asthenia*** (lack or loss of strength); ***back pain; chest pain; diarrhea; dry skin***—not limited to application site; ***dyspepsia*** (belching; heartburn; indigestion; stomach upset or pain); ***eye pain; myalgia*** (muscle pain); ***neck pain; rhinitis*** (runny nose); ***skin ulcers*** (sores on skin)—not limited to application site

Overdose

For more information on the management of overdose or unintentional ingestion, **contact a poison control center** (see *Poison Control Center Listing*).

An overdose of topical diclofenac gel is extremely unlikely due to the low systemic absorption of this dosage form. Oral ingestion of topical diclofenac sodium gel resulting in significant systemic side effects, although not reported to have occurred to date, may be treated as follows:.

Treatment of overdose

To decrease absorption—

Induction of emesis and/or gastric lavage should be initiated.

Oral administration of activated charcoal may help reduce absorption.

To enhance elimination—

Forced diuresis theoretically may increase urinary excretion

Note: The use of dialysis or hemoperfusion to enhance elimination of highly protein-bound diclofenac is unproven.

Specific treatment—

Symptomatic treatment for potential complications (such as renal failure, seizures, gastrointestinal irritation, and respiratory depression) may be given.

Supportive care—

Patients in whom intentional overdose is confirmed or suspected should be referred for psychiatric consultation.

Patient Consultation

As an aid to patient consultation, refer to *Advice for the Patient, Diclofenac (topical)*.

In providing consultation, consider emphasizing the following selected information (» = major clinical significance):

Before using this medication

» Conditions affecting use, especially:

Pregnancy—Use in late pregnancy not recommended due to risk of adverse effects on fetal cardiovascular system

Breast-feeding—Not recommended due to risk of adverse effects in nursing infant

Other medications, especially other NSAIDs

Other medical problems, especially gastrointestinal ulceration or bleeding and severe renal or hepatic impairments

Proper use of this medication

» Proper dosing
» Avoiding contact with eyes
» Not applying to areas with open skin wounds, infections, or exfoliative dermatitis

Missed dose: Applying as soon as possible; not applying if almost time for next scheduled dose; not doubling amount used

» Proper storage

Precautions while using this medication

» Importance of close monitoring by physician
» Possible photosensitivity reactions; avoiding direct sunlight; avoiding use of sunlamp, tanning bed, or tanning booth

Side/adverse effects

Signs of potential side effects, especially application site reactions, flu-like syndrome, asthma, conjunctivitis, contact dermatitis, dyspnea, eye pain, hematuria, hypertension, hypokinesia, infection, migraines or other headaches, pharyngitis, pneumonia, sinusitis, and skin ulcers

General Dosing Information

Diclofenac topical gel should be smoothed on gently, in an amount that will adequately cover the lesion site. Adequate coverage of a 5 cm^2 lesion is generally provided by 0.5 grams of gel.

The usual duration of treatment with diclofenac gel is 60 to 90 days. Complete healing or optimal therapeutic effect may not be evident for up to 30 days after cessation of treatment. Lesions that do not respond should be re-evaluated and management reconsidered.

Patients should be aware of the signs and symptoms of dermal adverse reactions and the possibility of irritant or allergic contact dermatitis. If severe dermal reactions occur, use of diclofenac may need to be interrupted until the reactions subside.

Topical Dosage Forms

DICLOFENAC SODIUM GEL

Usual adult dose

Actinic keratoses—

Topical, to the skin, twice a day in a sufficient amount to cover the lesions.

Usual pediatric dose

Safety and efficacy have not been established.

Usual geriatric dose

See *Usual adult dose*.

Strength(s) usually available

U.S.—

3%. (Rx) [*Solaraze* (benzyl alcohol; hyaluronate sodium; polyethylene glycol monomethyl ether; purified water)].

Packaging and storage

Store between 15 and 30 °C (59 and 86 °F), in a tight container. Protect from heat. Avoid freezing.

Auxiliary labeling

- Avoid direct sunlight.

Developed: 12/06/2000

DICLOFENAC AND MISOPROSTOL Systemic

VA CLASSIFICATION (Primary): MS109

Commonly used brand name(s): *Arthrotec 50; Arthrotec 75*.

NOTE: The *Diclofenac and Misoprostol (Systemic)* monograph is maintained on the *USP DI* electronic data base. A copy of the most recent revision of the complete monograph can be accessed on the *USP DI* Updates Online website. See the front cover of book for details on accessing the site.

For information on the specific components of this combination, see the *USP DI* monographs for *Diclofenac (Topical)*, and *Misoprostol (Systemic)*.

The information that follows is selectively abstracted from the complete monograph and is provided to facilitate drug use review and patient counseling.

Note: For a listing of dosage forms and brand names by country availability, see *Dosage Forms* section(s).

Category

Antirheumatic (nonsteroidal anti-inflammatory).

Indications

Accepted

Arthritis, rheumatoid (treatment) or

Osteoarthritis (treatment)—Diclofenac and misoprostol combination is indicated for treatment of the signs and symptoms of rheumatoid arthritis and osteoarthritis in patients at high risk of developing nonsteroidal anti-inflammatory drug (NSAID)–induced gastric and duodenal ulcers.

Patient Consultation

As an aid to patient consultation, refer to *Advice for the Patient, Diclofenac and Misoprostol (Systemic)*.

In providing consultation, consider emphasizing the following selected information (» = major clinical significance):

Before using this medication

» Conditions affecting use, especially:

Sensitivity to diclofenac or misoprostol

Allergies to aspirin or any other nonsteroidal anti-inflammatory drugs (NSAIDs), or other prostaglandins or prostaglandin analogs

Pregnancy—Use of diclofenac and misoprostol combination is contraindicated during pregnancy; patients of childbearing potential must take measures to assure they are not pregnant prior to therapy and to prevent pregnancy during therapy

Breast-feeding—Diclofenac is distributed into breast milk

Increased risk of toxicity

Other medications, especially anticoagulants, coumarin- or indandione-derivative, corticosteroids, aspirin, cyclosporine, digitalis glycosides, lithium, methotrexate, potassium-sparing diuretics

Other medical problems, especially allergic reaction (severe), aspirin-induced nasal polyps associated with bronchospasm, coagulation disorders, gastrointestinal bleeding or history of, hepatic function impairment, peptic ulcer disease or history of, platelet disorders, renal disease (severe) or history of, or renal function impairment

Proper use of this medication

» Not taking more medication than prescribed

Not taking with magnesium-containing antacids

Not chewing, crushing, or dissolving tablets

Not giving medication to another person

Taking with or after meals

» Proper dosing

Missed dose: Taking as soon as possible; not taking if almost time for next dose; not doubling doses

» Proper storage

Precautions while using this medication

» Stopping medication and checking with physician immediately if pregnancy is suspected

Consulting physician if diarrhea develops and continues for more than a week

Regular visits to physician during prolonged therapy

» Possibility of gastrointestinal ulceration or bleeding

» Possibility that alcohol may increase the risk of ulceration

Not taking NSAIDs, including ketorolac, concurrently, and not taking acetaminophen or aspirin or other salicylates for more than a few days while receiving diclofenac and misoprostol combination, unless concurrent use is prescribed by, and patient remains under the care of, a physician or dentist

Side/adverse effects

Signs of potential side effects, especially cardiovascular effects, central nervous system effects, fluid retention, gastrointestinal bleeding, gastrointestinal ulceration, hematologic effects, hepatic effects, intestinal perforation, mood or mental changes, pancreatitis, rectal bleeding, renal effects, seizures, Steven-Johnson syndrome, anaphylaxis or anaphylactoid reactions

Oral Dosage Forms

DICLOFENAC AND MISOPROSTOL TABLETS

Usual adult dose

Osteoarthritis—

Oral, 50 mg of diclofenac and 200 mcg of misoprostol three times a day.

Rheumatoid arthritis—

Oral, 50 mg of diclofenac and 200 mcg of misoprostol three to four times a day.

Rheumatoid arthritis and osteoarthritis (for patients who experience intolerance)—

Oral, 50 mg of diclofenac and 200 mcg of misoprostol two times a day or 75 mg of diclofenac and 200 mcg of misoprostol two times a day.

Note: Dosage may also be individualized using separate products of diclofenac and misoprostol. Thereafter, the patient may be changed to the appropriate diclofenac and misoprostol combination dose. If clinically indicated, misoprostol may be used with diclofenac and misoprostol combination to optimize the misoprostol drug regimen.

Usual adult prescribing limits

In osteoarthritis—150 mg of diclofenac and 800 mcg of misoprostol.

In rheumatoid arthritis—225 mg of diclofenac and 800 mcg of misoprostol.

Usual pediatric dose

Safety and efficacy have not been established in persons younger than 18 years of age.

Usual geriatric dose

See *Usual adult dose*.

Strength(s) usually available

U.S.—

50 mg of diclofenac and 200 micrograms of misoprostol (Rx) [*Arthrotec 50* (colloidal silicon dioxide; corn starch; crospovidone; hydrogenated castor oil; hydroxypropyl methylcellulose; lactose; mag-

nesium stearate; methacrylic acid copolymer; micro-crystalline cellulose; povidone (polyvidone) K-30; sodium hydroxide; talc; triethyl citrate)].

75 mg of diclofenac and 200 micrograms of misoprostol (Rx) [*Arthrotec 75* (colloidal silicon dioxide; corn starch; crospovidone; hydrogenated castor oil; hydroxypropyl methylcellulose; lactose; magnesium stearate; methacrylic acid copolymer; micro-crystalline cellulose; povidone (polyvidone) K-30; sodium hydroxide; talc; triethyl citrate)].

Canada—

50 mg of diclofenac and 200 micrograms of misoprostol (Rx) [*Arthrotec 50* (castor oil; cellulose; cellulose acetate phthalate; colloidal silicon dioxide; corn starch; crospovidone; diethyl phthalate; hydroxypropyl methylcellulose; lactose; magnesium stearate; methacrylic acid copolymer; povidone; talc)].

75 mg of diclofenac and 200 micrograms of misoprostol (Rx) [*Arthrotec 75* (castor oil; cellulose; colloidal silicon dioxide; corn starch; crospovidone; hydrogenated castor oil; hydroxypropyl methylcellulose; lactose; magnesium stearate; methacrylic acid copolymer; povidone; sodium hydroxide; talc; triethyl citrate)].

Auxiliary labeling

- Avoid alcoholic beverages.
- Take with food.
- Do not take this medication if you are pregnant.

Revised: 04/20/2000
Developed: 05/27/1998

DICLOXACILLIN—See *Penicillins (Systemic)*

DICUMAROL—See *Anticoagulants (Systemic)*

DICYCLOMINE—See *Anticholinergics/Antispasmodics (Systemic)*

DIDANOSINE Systemic

VA CLASSIFICATION (Primary): AM840

Commonly used brand name(s): *Videx; Videx EC.*

Other commonly used names are ddI and 2,3-dideoxyinosine.

Note: For a listing of dosage forms and brand names by country availability, see *Dosage Forms* section(s).

Category

Antiviral (systemic).

Indications

Note: Bracketed information in the *Indications* section refers to uses that are not included in U.S. product labeling.

Accepted

Human immunodeficiency virus (HIV) infection, advanced (treatment) or Immunodeficiency syndrome, acquired (AIDS) (treatment)—Didanosine in combination with other antiretroviral agents is indicated for the treatment of HIV–1 infection. Additionally, didanosine is indicated in the treatment of adults and children over 6 months of age with advanced HIV infection who are intolerant of zidovudine therapy or who have demonstrated significant clinical or immunologic deterioration during zidovudine therapy; didanosine is also indicated in the treatment of adults with advanced HIV infection who have received prior zidovudine therapy.[Didanosine is also used in combination with zidovudine.][1]

[1]Not included in Canadian product labeling.

Pharmacology/Pharmacokinetics

Physicochemical characteristics

Molecular weight—236.2.

Mechanism of action/Effect

Didanosine (ddI) is metabolized intracellularly by a series of cellular enzymes to its active moiety, 2,3–dideoxyadenosine-5-triphosphate (ddA-TP), which inhibits HIV DNA polymerase (reverse transcriptase). HIV replication is suppressed by chain termination, competitive inhibition of reverse transcriptase, or both. The intracellular half-life of ddA-TP is greater than 12 hours.

Absorption

Didanosine is acid labile; all oral formulations contain or are compounded with buffering agents to increase the gastric pH; this results in a decreased breakdown of didanosine and a subsequent increase in absorption. All formulations should be taken on an empty stomach. Administration of didanosine tablets up to 30 minutes before a meal did not result in any significant changes in bioavailability.Administration within 5 minutes of a meal decreases the peak plasma concentration (C_{max}) and mean area under the plasma concentration versus time curve (AUC) by approximately 50%. Administration of didanosine tablets up to 2 hours after a meal decreases the C_{max} and the AUC by approximately 55%. If didanosine delayed-release capsules (enteric-coated beadlets) are given with food, the C_{max} and the AUC are reduced by approximately 46% and 19%, respectively, as compared to the fasting state. Although the C_{max} of didanosine delayed-release capsules (enteric-coated beadlets) is decreased approximately 40% relative to didanosine buffered tablets, the AUC is equivalent for both didanosine formulations.If didanosine is not buffered in the stomach, it forms 2,3–dideoxyribose and hypoxanthine, a precursor of uric acid.

Bioavailability was extremely variable in both adults and children after ingestion of a lyophilized formulation similar to the pediatric product for oral solution.—

Adults—Approximately 33% after a single dose and approximately 37% after 4 weeks of therapy in adults receiving 7 mg per kg of body weight (mg/kg) or less.

Children (7 months to 19 years of age)—Average 19 to 42% (range, 2 to 89%).

The chewable/dispersible buffered tablets were found to be 20 to 25% more bioavailable than the buffered powder for oral solution when studied in 18 asymptomatic HIV-seropositive adults.

Distribution

Crosses blood-brain barrier and distributes into the cerebrospinal fluid (CSF)—

Adults: Approximately 19 to 21% of the simultaneous plasma concentration 1 hour after an intravenous dose.

Children (8 months to 18 years of age): In one study, didanosine distribution into the CSF of 7 children was approximately 46% (range, 12 to 85%) of the simultaneous plasma concentration 1.5 to 3.5 hours after a single dose; however, studies done in rhesus monkeys showed poor CSF penetration, and another study done in children found that didanosine was not detectable in 17 of 20 CSF samples, and penetration into the CSF was limited.

Vol_D—

Adults: Average 0.7 to 1 L per kg.

Children (8 months to 18 years of age): Approximately 35.6 L per square meter of body surface (L/m^2) [range, 18.4 to 60.7 L/m^2].

Protein binding

Low (<5%).

Biotransformation

Rapidly metabolized intracellularly to its active moiety, 2,3–dideoxyadenosine-5-triphosphate (ddA-TP). However, the metabolism of didanosine has not been fully evaluated in humans. Extensive metabolism occurred in dogs administered oral, radiolabeled didanosine; identified urinary metabolites include allantoin, which accounted for approximately 61% of the dose, hypoxanthine, xanthine, and uric acid.

Half-life

Adults—Approximately 1.5 hours (range, 0.8 to 2.7 hours).

Children (8 months to 18 years of age)—Approximately 0.8 hour (range, 0.5 to 1.2 hours).

Severe renal failure—Approximately 4.5 hours.

Intracellular half-life of ddA-TP is 8 to 24 hours *in vitro* .

Time to peak concentration

0.5 to 1 hour.

2 hours (delayed-release capsules).

Peak serum concentration

Adults—

Approximately 1.6 mcg per mL (range, 0.6 to 2.9 mcg per mL) after a single 375-mg dose of buffered powder for oral solution.

Approximately 1.6 mcg per mL (range, 0.5 to 2.6 mcg per mL) after a single 300-mg dose of the buffered chewable/dispersible tablet.

Children (8 months to 18 years of age)—

Steady state values after oral administration of 80, 120, and 180 mg per square meter of body surface were 0.8, 1.4, and 1.7 mcg per mL, respectively.

Elimination
Renal clearance by glomerular filtration and active tubular secretion makes up approximately 50% of the total body clearance; urinary recovery was approximately 20% (range, 3 to 31%) after a single oral dose in adults and approximately 17% (range, 5 to 30%) at steady state in children. No accumulation was evident in either adults or children.

Dialysis—A 4-hour hemodialysis session reduces the serum didanosine concentration by approximately 20%.

Precautions to Consider

Carcinogenicity
Lifetime carcinogenicity studies in mice and rats induced no significant increase in neoplastic lesions. Mice and rats were given maximally tolerated doses for 22 and 24 months, respectively.

Mutagenicity
No evidence of mutagenicity was observed in the Ames *Salmonella* mutagenicity assay or in rat and mouse *in vivo* micronucleus assays. Didanosine was positive in the following genetic toxicology assays: the *Escherichia coli* tester strain WP2 uvrA bacterial mutagenicity assay; the L5178Y/TK± mouse lymphoma mammalian cell gene mutation assay; the *in vitro* chromosome aberrations assay in cultured human peripheral lymphocytes; the *in vitro* chromosome aberrations assay in Chinese Hamster Lung cells; and the BALB/c 3T3 *in vitro* transformation assay.

Pregnancy/Reproduction
Fertility—No evidence of impaired fertility has been found in rats and rabbits receiving 12 and 14.2 times the estimated human dose of didanosine, based on plasma levels.

Pregnancy—Fatal lactic acidosis has been reported in pregnant women who received the combination of didanosine and stavudine with other antiretroviral agents. It is unclear if pregnancy augments the risk of lactic acidosis/hepatic steatosis syndrome reported in non-pregnant individuals receiving nucleoside analogues. The combination of didanosine and stavudine should be used with caution during pregnancy and is recommended only if the potential benefit clearly outweighs the potential risk.

Didanosine crosses the placenta. However, studies in humans have not been done. Unlike zidovudine, it is not known whether didanosine reduces perinatal transmission of HIV infection.

No evidence of harm to the fetus has been found in rats and rabbits receiving 12 and 14.2 times the estimated human dose of didanosine, based on plasma levels. At approximately 12 times the estimated human dose, didanosine was slightly toxic to female rats and their pups during mid and late lactation. The rats showed reduced body weight gains and food intake, but the physical and functional development of the offspring was not impaired and there were no major changes in the F2 generation.

FDA Pregnancy Category B.

Breast-feeding
It is not known whether didanosine is distributed into human breast milk.

There have been case reports of HIV being transmitted from an infected mother to her nursing infant through breast milk. Therefore, breast-feeding is not recommended in HIV-infected mothers where safe infant formula is available and affordable.

Pediatrics
Data in children over 3 months of age with symptomatic HIV infection suggest that didanosine is well tolerated and may produce an improvement in neuropsychological function, immunological function, p24 antigen levels, and weight gain. However, these data are preliminary. As with adults, the major serious side effect to date in children has been pancreatitis, which usually occurred at doses above 300 mg per square meter of body surface (mg/m^2) per day. Retinal depigmentation has been reported in approximately 7% of children treated with didanosine, especially at doses above 300 mg/m^2 per day.

Geriatrics
No information is available on the relationship of age to the effects of didanosine in geriatric patients. However, elderly patients are more likely to have an age-related decrease in renal function, which may require a reduction in dose.

Drug interactions and/or related problems
The following drug interactions and/or related problems have been selected on the basis of their potential clinical significance (possible mechanism in parentheses where appropriate)—not necessarily inclusive (» = major clinical significance):

Note: Combinations containing any of the following medications, depending on the amount present, may also interact with this medication.

» Alcohol or
» Asparaginase or
» Azathioprine or
» Estrogens or
» Furosemide or
» Methyldopa or
» Nitrofurantoin or
» Pentamidine, intravenous or
» Sulfonamides or
» Sulindac or
» Tetracyclines or
» Thiazide diuretics or
» Valproic acid or
Other drugs associated with pancreatitis
(medications associated with the development of pancreatitis should be avoided during didanosine therapy or, if concurrent use is necessary, used with caution since didanosine may cause pancreatitis, which, on rare occasion, has been fatal)

» Allopurinol
(not recommended for concurrent use with didanosine; allopurinol may increase the plasma AUC of didanosine 2–4 fold)

» Chloramphenicol or
» Cisplatin or
» Dapsone or
» Ethambutol or
» Ethionamide or
» Hydralazine or
» Isoniazid or
» Lithium or
» Metronidazole or
» Nitrofurantoin or
» Nitrous oxide or
» Phenytoin or
» Stavudine or
» Vincristine or
» Zalcitabine or
Other drugs associated with peripheral neuropathy
(since didanosine has been shown to cause peripheral neuropathy, medications associated with the development of neuropathy should be avoided during didanosine therapy or, if concurrent use is necessary, used with caution)

» Dapsone or
» Itraconazole or
» Ketoconazole
(concurrent administration of dapsone with didanosine may decrease the absorption of dapsone; didanosine is combined with a buffer to neutralize stomach acidity in order to increase its absorption, while dapsone requires an acidic environment for optimal absorption; dapsone and any other medications that also depend on the gastric acidity for optimal absorption, such as itraconazole and ketoconazole, should be administered at least 2 hours before or 2 hours after didanosine is given)

» Delavirdine or
» Indinavir
(concurrent administration of these medications with didanosine may decrease their absorption; these medications should be given 1 hour before didanosine is given)

» Fluoroquinolone antibiotics, such as ciprofloxacin, enoxacin, lomefloxacin, norfloxacin, and ofloxacin or
» Tetracyclines
(concurrent administration of the didanosine chewable/dispersible tablets or pediatric powder for oral solution with fluoroquinolone antibiotics or tetracyclines may cause a decrease in the plasma concentrations of these antibiotics; these 2 didanosine products contain magnesium- and aluminum-containing antacids, which will reduce the absorption of these antibiotics by chelation; fluoroquinolone antibiotics and tetracyclines should be administered at least 2 hours before or 6 hours after didanosine chewable/dispersible tablets or pediatric powder for oral solution is given; buffered didanosine powder for oral solution contains a citrate-phosphate buffer, which will not interact with the fluoroquinolone antibiotics or tetracyclines)

» Ganciclovir
(concurrent administration of didanosine with oral ganciclovir may increase plasma didanosine levels by as much as 111%)

Laboratory value alterations
The following have been selected on the basis of their potential clinical significance (possible effect in parentheses where appropriate)—not necessarily inclusive (» = major clinical significance).

With physiology/laboratory test values
Alanine aminotransferase (ALT [SGPT]) and
Alkaline phosphatase and
Aspartate aminotransferase (AST [SGOT]) and
Bilirubin, serum
(values may be increased to greater than 5 times the upper normal limit; the incidence of laboratory abnormalities occurs more frequently in patients with abnormal baseline values)

» Amylase, serum and
Lipase, serum and
Triglycerides, serum
(values may be increased)

Red blood cell counts and
White blood cell counts
(values may be decreased)

Platelet count
(values may be decreased)

Potassium, serum
(concentrations may be decreased; decrease may be secondary to diarrhea from the buffer rather than to didanosine itself)

» Uric acid, serum
(didanosine may cause an asymptomatic increase in uric acid concentrations; may be dose-related; uric acid levels fall with hydration and/or a decrease in dose)

Medical considerations/Contraindications

The medical considerations/contraindications included have been selected on the basis of their potential clinical significance (reasons given in parentheses where appropriate)—not necessarily inclusive (» = major clinical significance).

Risk-benefit should be considered when the following medical problems exist:

» Alcoholism, active or
» Hypertriglyceridemia, or history of or
» Pancreatitis, or history of
(didanosine has caused pancreatitis, which, on rare occasion, has been fatal; patients who have pancreatitis or a history of pancreatitis, or are at risk for pancreatitis should either not take didanosine or should take it with extreme caution)

» Conditions requiring sodium-restriction, such as cardiac failure, cirrhosis of the liver or severe hepatic disease, peripheral or pulmonary edema, hypernatremia, hypertension, renal function impairment, or toxemia of pregnancy
(each 2-tablet dose of didanosine chewable/dispersible tablets contains 529 mg of sodium, and each single-dose packet of buffered didanosine powder for oral solution contains 1380 mg of sodium)

Gouty arthritis
(didanosine may cause an increase in uric acid levels, especially in patients who already have an abnormally high baseline before the didanosine therapy is initiated)

Hepatic function impairment
(patients with hepatic function impairment may be at increased risk of toxicity due to altered metabolism; this may require a reduction in dose)

Phenylketonuria
(didanosine chewable/dispersible buffered tablets contain up to 73 mg of phenylalanine per 2-tablet dose, depending on the strength used)

» Peripheral neuropathy
(didanosine may cause peripheral neuropathy, which may require a reduction in dose)

Renal function impairment
(patients with renal function impairment may be at increased risk of toxicity due to decreased clearance through the kidneys, especially patients with a serum creatinine concentration of > 1.5 mg/dL or a creatinine clearance of < 60 mL/min; this may require a reduction in dose; also, each didanosine chewable/dispersible tablet contains 15.7 mEq of magnesium hydroxide, which may lead to a magnesium overload in patients with severe renal disease, especially after prolonged dosing)

Patient monitoring

The following may be especially important in patient monitoring (other tests may be warranted in some patients, depending on condition; » = major clinical significance):

» Amylase, serum and
» Lipase, serum and
Triglycerides, serum
(didanosine administration has been associated with pancreatitis; patients should be monitored for laboratory changes consistent with pancreatitis, such as elevated amylase, lipase, and triglyceride concentrations; didanosine should be discontinued if amylase concentration is elevated by 1.5 to 2 times normal limits and/or the patient has symptoms consistent with pancreatitis)

» Ophthalmologic examinations
(dilated ophthalmoscopy should be performed in children every 3 to 6 months, or if there is a change in vision, to monitor for the development and progression of retinal depigmentation; the lesions appear initially in the midperiphery of the fundus; therefore, central vision is not immediately threatened. If retinal lesions are observed, the patient should be re-examined monthly to assess progression; treatment with didanosine may need to be discontinued)

Potassium, serum
(serum potassium should be monitored regularly since hypokalemia has been associated with didanosine administration; however, this may be secondary to diarrhea from the buffer)

Uric acid, serum
(serum uric acid concentrations should be monitored regularly since didanosine may cause an asymptomatic hyperuricemia due to the catabolism of the drug; hyperuricemia occurs more frequently in patients who begin therapy with an abnormal baseline uric acid concentration)

Side/Adverse Effects

Note: Fatal lactic acidosis has been reported in pregnant women who received the combination of didanosine and stavudine with other antiretroviral agents. The combination of didanosine and stavudine should be used with caution during pregnancy and is recommended only if the potential benefit clearly outweighs the potential risk.

Health care providers caring for HIV-infected pregnant women receiving didanosine should be alert for early diagnosis of lactic acidosis/hepatic steatosis syndrome.

Some side effects, such as pancreatitis, peripheral neuropathy, hepatotoxicity, myalgias, hematologic abnormalities, and elevations in uric acid, may be seen with severe HIV disease; therefore, differentiation between the side effects of didanosine therapy and the complications of HIV disease may be difficult.

The incidence of pancreatitis associated with didanosine administration was 5 to 13% in adults in phase I studies, a controlled trial, and the expanded access program, and approximately 6% in children; the fatality rate of pancreatitis in adults was approximately 0.35%. An increased risk has been found to be associated with higher doses in both adults and children (≥ 12.5 mg/kg per day in adults, ≥ 300 mg/m² per day in children); other risk factors include a history of pancreatitis, renal function impairment (without a dose adjustment), alcoholism, a very low CD4 count, and elevated triglycerides. Pancreatitis usually resolves when didanosine is discontinued.

Peripheral neuropathy also appears to be related to higher daily doses. It has occurred more frequently in adults (34% of patients receiving ≤ 12.5 mg/kg per day in phase I trials and 13 to 14% in a controlled trial) than in children (3%), and usually resolves over time, but may persist.

Hematologic abnormalities, such as anemia (hemoglobin < 8.0 grams/dL), granulocytopenia (< 1000/microliter), leukopenia (< 2000/microliter), and thrombocytopenia (< 50,000/microliter) have occurred in 5% or less of patients who started therapy with normal baseline values; however, if the patient began didanosine therapy with abnormal baseline values, the incidence of anemia, granulocytopenia, leukopenia, and thrombocytopenia was 0%, 56%, 37%, and 25%, respectively, in adults, and 27%, 62%, 36%, and 67%, respectively, in children.

Peripheral atrophy of the retinal pigment epithelium has occurred in 3 children receiving high doses of didanosine (> 300 mg/m² per day) and one child receiving a lower dose. The lesions are described as mottling and atrophy of retinal-pigment epithelium, and later become well circumscribed with hyperpigmented borders in the midperiphery of the fundus. Central visual acuity is not affected. The lesions appear to progress with continued didanosine therapy. When the drug is discontinued, the lesions remain with no progression.

The following side/adverse effects have been selected on the basis of their potential clinical significance (possible signs and symptoms in parentheses where appropriate)—not necessarily inclusive:

Those indicating need for medical attention

Incidence more frequent

Peripheral neuropathy (tingling, burning, numbness, and pain in hands or feet)

Incidence less frequent

Pancreatitis (abdominal pain; nausea and vomiting); ***pneumonia***

Incidence rare

Cardiomyopathy (shortness of breath; swelling of feet or lower legs); ***hematologic toxicity, specifically anemia, granulocytopenia or leukopenia, or thrombocytopenia*** (unusual tiredness and weakness; fever, chills, or sore throat; unusual bleeding or bruising); ***hepatitis*** (yellow skin and eyes); ***hypersensitivity*** (fever and chills; skin rash and itching); ***retinal depigmentation; sarcoma; seizures*** (convulsions)

Those indicating need for medical attention only if they continue or are bothersome

Incidence more frequent

CNS toxicity (anxiety; headache; irritability; insomnia; restlessness); ***dryness of mouth; gastrointestinal disturbances*** (abdominal pain; nausea; diarrhea); ***rash***

Note: Diarrhea occurs frequently and may be related to the buffering agent; if the diarrhea becomes severe, the patient may require medical attention.

Overdose

For more information on the management of overdose or unintentional ingestion, **contact a poison control center** (see *Poison Control Center Listing*).

In phase 1 studies, didanosine administered at 10 times the currently recommended dose caused the following toxicities: pancreatitis, peripheral neuropathy, diarrhea, hyperuricemia, and hepatic dysfunction.

Clinical effects of overdose

The following effects have been selected on the basis of their potential clinical significance (possible signs and symptoms in parentheses where appropriate)—not necessarily inclusive:

Diarrhea (increased bowel movements; loose stools); ***hepatic dysfunction*** (dark urine; light-colored stools; loss of appetite; nausea and vomiting; unusual tiredness; yellow eyes or skin; fever with or without chills; stomach pain); ***hyperuricemia*** (joint pain; side, lower back, or stomach pain; swelling of feet or lower legs); ***pancreatitis*** (bloating; chills; constipation; darkened urine; fast heartbeat; fever; indigestion; loss of appetite; nausea; pains in stomach, side, or abdomen, possibly radiating to the back; vomiting; yellow eyes or skin); ***peripheral neuropathy*** (burning, numbness, tingling, or painful sensations; weakness in arms, hands, legs, or feet)

Treatment of overdose

To enhance elimination—

Didanosine is not dialyzable by peritoneal dialysis, although there is some clearance by hemodialysis. The fractional removal of didanosine during an average hemodialysis session of 3–4 hours is approximately 20–35% of the amount present in the body at the start of dialysis.

Specific treatment—

There is no known specific antidote to didanosine. Treatment is generally symptomatic and supportive.

Supportive care—

Patients in whom intentional overdose is confirmed or suspected should be referred for psychiatric consultation.

Patient Consultation

As an aid to patient consultation, refer to *Advice for the Patient, Didanosine (Systemic)*.

In providing consultation, consider emphasizing the following selected information (» = major clinical significance):

Before using this medication

» Conditions affecting use, especially:

Pregnancy—Fatal lactic acidosis has been reported in pregnant women who received the combination of didanosine and stavudine with other antiretroviral agents. The combination of didanosine and stavudine should be used with caution during pregnancy and is recommended only if the potential benefit clearly outweighs the potential risk.

Breast-feeding—It is not known whether didanosine is distributed into human breast milk. There have been case reports of HIV being transmitted from an infected mother to her nursing infant through breast milk. Therefore, breast-feeding is not recommended in HIV-infected mothers where safe infant formula is available and affordable.

Use in children—May cause retinal depigmentation, which is more likely to occur in children receiving doses above 300 mg/m^2 per day

Other medications, especially allopurinol, other drugs associated with pancreatitis and peripheral neuropathy, dapsone or medications that require an acidic environment for absorption, delavirdine, ganciclovir, indinavir, tetracyclines or fluoroquinolone antibiotics

Other medical problems, especially alcoholism, hypertriglyceridemia, pancreatitis or a history of pancreatitis, conditions requiring sodium-restriction, or peripheral neuropathy

Proper use of this medication

» Importance of not taking more medication than prescribed; importance of not discontinuing medication without checking with physician; discontinuing medication and calling physician at first signs and symptoms of pancreatitis

» Importance of not missing doses and of taking at evenly spaced times

» Proper administration:

For capsules, delayed-release

Swallowing the capsule intact

For oral solution, buffered powder

Preparing by opening the packet and dissolving its contents in 1/2 glass (4 ounces) of water. The powder should not be mixed with fruit juice or other acid-containing liquid.

Stirring the mixture for approximately 2 to 3 minutes until the powder is completely dissolved

Swallowing the entire solution immediately

For oral suspension, pediatric powder

Using a specially marked measuring spoon or other device to measure each dose accurately

For tablets, buffered—chewable and for oral suspension

Patients older than 1 year of age must take 2 tablets at each dose to provide adequate buffering and to prevent gastric acid degradation of didanosine.

Children under 1 year of age should receive a 1-tablet dose. The recommended dose for children is based on body surface area and, for adults, on body weight.

Thoroughly chewing, manually crushing, or dispersing in at least 1 ounce of water prior to consumption. Because the tablets are hard, they may be difficult to chew for some patients; manually crushing or dispersing the tablets may be preferable. To disperse tablets, 2 tablets should be added to at least 1 ounce of drinking water. The mixture should be stirred until a uniform dispersion forms and consumed immediately. For additional flavoring, dispersion may be diluted with 1 ounce of clear apple juice.

» Proper dosing

Missed dose: Taking as soon as possible; not taking if almost time for next dose; not doubling doses

» Proper storage

Precautions while using this medication

» Regular visits to physician for blood tests

» Importance of not taking other medications concurrently without checking with physician

» Using a condom to help prevent transmission of the AIDS virus to others; not sharing needles or injectable equipment with anyone

Side/adverse effects

Signs of potential side effects, especially peripheral neuropathy, pancreatitis, pneumonia, cardiomyopathy, hematologic toxicities, hepatitis, hypersensitivity, retinal depigmentation, sarcoma, and seizures

General Dosing Information

Two tablets must be taken at each dose by patients older than 1 year of age to provide adequate buffering and to prevent gastric acid degradation of didanosine. Children under 1 year of age should receive a 1-tablet dose. The recommended dose for children is based on body surface area and, for adults, on body weight.

The preferred dosing frequency of didanosine is twice daily because there is more evidence to support the effectiveness of this dosing regimen. Once-daily dosing with didanosine delayed-release capsules (enteric-coated beadlets) should be considered only for adult patients whose management requires once-daily administration of didanosine (or alternative didanosine formulation).

Due to the need for adequate buffering, the 200-mg strength tablet should only be used as a component of a once-daily regimen.

To reduce the risk of gastrointestinal side effects, patients should take no more than four tablets at each dose.

Didanosine delayed-release capsules are protected against degradation by stomach acid by the use of an enteric coating on the beadlets in the capsule and should be swallowed intact.

It is recommended that patients on hemodialysis receive their dose of didanosine after dialysis.

For patients requiring Continuous Ambulatory Peritoneal Dialysis (CAPD) or hemodialysis, it is recommended that one fourth of the total daily dose of didanosine be given once a day. It is not necessary to give a supplemental dose of didanosine after hemodialysis.

Diet/Nutrition

All didanosine formulations should be taken on an empty stomach, at least 30 minutes before or 2 hours after eating. Administration with food (up to 2 hours after eating) decreases absorption by approximately 46 to 55%, depending on the specific didanosine formulation.

Patients on sodium-restricted diets should be made aware that each 2-tablet dose of didanosine tablets contains 529 mg (23 mEq) of sodium, and each single-dose packet of buffered didanosine for oral solution contains 1380 mg (60 mEq) of sodium.

Patients with phenylketonuria should be made aware that each 2-tablet dose of didanosine (chewable, dispersible buffered) tablets contains up to 73 mg of phenylalanine, depending on the strength of tablets used.

Bioequivalence information

Didanosine tablets are 20 to 25% more bioavailable than the buffered powder for oral solution. Because of this, the dose of the tablets is correspondingly lower and the dosing of the 2 products cannot be interchanged.

Oral Dosage Forms

DIDANOSINE DELAYED-RELEASE CAPSULES

Usual adult and adolescent dose

Antiviral—
- Patients with normal renal function:—
  - Patients weighing up to 60 kg—Oral, 250 mg once a day.
  - Patients weighing 60 kg or more—Oral, 400 mg once a day.
- Patients with renal function impairment:—
  - Patients weighing up to 60 kg:
    - Creatinine clearance greater than or equal to 60 mL per minute: Oral, 250 mg once a day.
    - Creatinine clearance 10 to 59 mL per minute: Oral, 125 mg once a day.
    - Creatinine clearance less than 10 mL per minute: Use of Didanosine Delayed-release Capsules is not recommended. An alternative dosage form should be used.
  - Patients weighing 60 kg or more—
    - Creatinine clearance greater than or equal to 60 mL per minute: Oral, 400 mg once a day.
    - Creatinine clearance 30 to 59 mL per minute: Oral, 200 mg once a day.
    - Creatinine clearance up to 29 mL per minute: Oral, 125 mg once a day.

Usual pediatric dose

This product is usually not prescribed for small children. See *Didanosine for Oral Suspension (Pediatric Powder)* or *Didanosine Tablets (Buffered—Chewable and for Oral Suspension)*.

Strength(s) usually available

U.S.—
- 125 mg (Rx) [*Videx EC* (carboxymethylcellulose sodium 12; diethyl phthalate; methacrylic acid copolymer; sodium hydroxide; sodium starch glycolate; talc)].
- 200 mg (Rx) [*Videx EC* (carboxymethylcellulose sodium 12; diethyl phthalate; methacrylic acid copolymer; sodium hydroxide; sodium starch glycolate; talc)].
- 250 mg (Rx) [*Videx EC* (carboxymethylcellulose sodium 12; diethyl phthalate; methacrylic acid copolymer; sodium hydroxide; sodium starch glycolate; talc)].
- 400 mg (Rx) [*Videx EC* (carboxymethylcellulose sodium 12; diethyl phthalate; methacrylic acid copolymer; sodium hydroxide; sodium starch glycolate; talc)].

Canada—
- Not commercially available.

Packaging and storage

Store below 40 °C (104 °F), preferably between 15 and 30 °C (59 and 86 °F), in a tight container.

Auxiliary labeling

- Continue medicine for full time of treatment.
- Swallow capsules whole and intact.
- Take on an empty stomach.

DIDANOSINE FOR ORAL SOLUTION (BUFFERED POWDER)

Usual adult and adolescent dose

Antiviral—
- Patients with normal renal function:—
  - Patients weighing up to 60 kg—Oral, 167 mg every twelve hours.
  - Patients weighing 60 kg or more—Oral, 250 mg every twelve hours.
- Patients with renal function impairment:—
  - Patients weighing up to 60 kg:
    - Creatinine clearance greater than or equal to 60 mL per minute: Oral, 167 mg every twelve hours.
    - Creatinine clearance 30 to 59 mL per minute: Oral, 100 mg every twelve hours.
    - Creatinine clearance up to 29 mL per minute: Oral, 100 mg once a day.
  - Patients weighing 60 kg or more:
    - Creatinine clearance greater than or equal to 60 mL per minute: Oral, 250 mg every twelve hours.
    - Creatinine clearance 30 to 59 mL per minute: Oral, 100 mg every twelve hours.
    - Creatinine clearance 10 to 29 mL per minute: Oral, 167 mg once a day.
    - Creatinine clearance less than 10 mL per minute: Oral, 100 mg once a day.

Usual pediatric dose

This product is not usually prescribed for small children. See *Didanosine for Oral Suspension (Pediatric Powder)* or *Didanosine Tablets (Buffered—Chewable and for Oral Suspension)*.

Strength(s) usually available

U.S.—
- 100 mg per packet (Rx) [*Videx* (citrate-phosphate buffer; sodium 1380 mg; sucrose)].
- 167 mg per packet (Rx) [*Videx* (citrate-phosphate buffer; sodium 1380 mg; sucrose)].
- 250 mg per packet (Rx) [*Videx* (citrate-phosphate buffer; sodium 1380 mg; sucrose)].

Canada—
- Not commercially available.

Packaging and storage

Store below 40 °C (104 °F), preferably between 15 and 30 °C (59 and 86 °F), unless otherwise specified by manufacturer.

Stability

After preparation, the solution may be stored at room temperature for up to 4 hours.

Incompatibilities

Didanosine is unstable in acidic solutions and should not be mixed with fruit juice or other acid-containing liquid.

Auxiliary labeling

- Dissolve contents of packet in one-half glass (4 ounces) of water.
- Continue medicine for full time of treatment.
- Take on empty stomach.

DIDANOSINE FOR ORAL SUSPENSION (PEDIATRIC POWDER)

Usual adult and adolescent dose

This product is usually not used by adults and adolescents. See *Didanosine for Oral Solution (Buffered Powder)* and *Didanosine Tablets (Buffered—Chewable and for Oral Suspension)*.

Usual pediatric dose

Antiviral—
- Oral, 120 mg per square meter of body surface area every twelve hours.

Note: A decrease in dose or an increase in dosing interval should be considered in patients with renal function impairment. However, specific guidelines for dosage adjustment have not been established.

Strength(s) usually available

U.S.—
- 2 grams per 200 mL (when reconstituted according to manufacturer's instructions) (Rx) [*Videx* (aluminum hydroxide; magnesium hydroxide; simethicone)].

4 grams per 400 mL (when reconstituted according to manufacturer's instructions) (Rx) [*Videx* (aluminum hydroxide; magnesium hydroxide; simethicone)].

Canada—

2 grams per 200 mL (when reconstituted according to manufacturer's instructions) (Rx) [*Videx* (aluminum hydroxide; magnesium hydroxide)].

4 grams per 400 mL (when reconstituted according to manufacturer's instructions) (Rx) [*Videx* (aluminum hydroxide; magnesium hydroxide)].

Packaging and storage

Prior to reconstitution, store below 40 °C (104 °F), preferably between 15 and 30 °C (59 and 86 °F), unless otherwise specified by manufacturer.

Preparation of dosage form

Didanosine pediatric powder must initially be diluted by adding 100 mL or 200 mL of purified water to the 2-gram or 4-gram bottle of powder, respectively. This produces an initial concentration of 20 mg per mL. This solution must be further diluted as follows: One part of the 20 mg per mL solution should be mixed immediately with one part of an aluminum- and magnesium-containing antacid (e.g., Mylanta Double Strength Liquid [formerly Mylanta II], Extra Strength Maalox Plus Suspension, or Maalox TC Suspension). This provides a final dispensing concentration of 10 mg per mL.

For home use, the solution should be dispensed in an appropriately sized, flint-glass or plastic (HDPE, PET, or PETG) bottle with a child-resistant closure.

Stability

After reconstitution, the solution may be stored up to 30 days in the refrigerator (2 to 8 °C [36 to 46 °F]). Unused portion should be discarded after 30 days.

Auxiliary labeling

- Refrigerate.
- Shake well.
- Continue medicine for full time of treatment.
- Beyond-use date.
- Take on empty stomach.

Note

When dispensing, include a calibrated liquid-measuring device.

DIDANOSINE TABLETS (BUFFERED—CHEWABLE AND FOR ORAL SUSPENSION)

Usual adult and adolescent dose

Antiviral—

Patients with normal renal function:—

Patients weighing up to 60 kg—Oral, 125 mg every twelve hoursor 250 mg once a day.

Patients weighing 60 kg or more—Oral, 200 mg every twelve hours or 400 mg once a day.

Patients with renal function impairment:—

Patients weighing up to 60 kg:

Creatinine clearance greater than or equal to 60 mL per minute: Oral, 125 mg every twelve hours or 250 mg once a day.

Creatinine clearance 30 to 59 mL per minute: Oral, 75 mg every twelve hours or 150 mg once a day.

Creatinine clearance 10 to 29 mL per minute: Oral, 100 mg once a day.

Creatinine clearance less than 10 mL per minute: Oral 75 mg once a day.

Patients weighing 60 kg or more:

Creatinine clearance greater than or equal to 60 mL per minute: Oral, 200 mg every twelve hours or 400 mg once a day.

Creatinine clearance 30 to 59 mL per minute: Oral, 100 mg every twelve hours or 200 mg once a day.

Creatinine clearance 10 to 29 mL per minute: Oral, 150 mg once a day.

Creatinine clearance less than 10 mL per minute: Oral, 100 mg once a day.

Usual pediatric dose

Antiviral—

See *Didanosine for Oral Suspension (Pediatric Powder)*.

Strength(s) usually available

U.S.—

25 mg (Rx) [*Videx* (calcium carbonate; magnesium hydroxide; aspartame [phenylalanine 36.5 mg]; sorbitol; mandarin orange flavor; polyplasdone; microcrystalline cellulose; magnesium stearate; sodium 264.5 mg)].

50 mg (Rx) [*Videx* (calcium carbonate; magnesium hydroxide; aspartame [phenylalanine 36.5 mg]; sorbitol; mandarin orange flavor; polyplasdone; microcrystalline cellulose; magnesium stearate; sodium 264.5 mg)].

100 mg (Rx) [*Videx* (calcium carbonate; magnesium hydroxide; aspartame [phenylalanine 36.5 mg]; sorbitol; mandarin orange flavor; polyplasdone; microcrystalline cellulose; magnesium stearate; sodium 264.5 mg)].

150 mg (Rx) [*Videx* (calcium carbonate; magnesium hydroxide; aspartame [phenylalanine 36.5 mg]; sorbitol; mandarin orange flavor; polyplasdone; microcrystalline cellulose; magnesium stearate; sodium 264.5 mg)].

200 mg (Rx) [*Videx* (calcium carbonate; magnesium hydroxide; aspartame [phenylalanine 36.5 mg]; sorbitol; mandarin orange flavor; polyplasdone; microcrystalline cellulose; magnesium stearate; sodium 264.5 mg)].

Canada—

25 mg (Rx) [*Videx* (calcium carbonate; magnesium hydroxide; aspartame [phenylalanine 22.5 mg]; sorbitol; mandarin orange flavor; polyplasdone; microcrystalline cellulose; magnesium stearate; sodium 264.5 mg)].

50 mg (Rx) [*Videx* (calcium carbonate; magnesium hydroxide; aspartame [phenylalanine 22.5 mg]; sorbitol; mandarin orange flavor; polyplasdone; microcrystalline cellulose; magnesium stearate; sodium 264.5 mg)].

100 mg (Rx) [*Videx* (calcium carbonate; magnesium hydroxide; aspartame [phenylalanine 36.5 mg]; sorbitol; mandarin orange flavor; polyplasdone; microcrystalline cellulose; magnesium stearate; sodium 264.5 mg)].

150 mg (Rx) [*Videx* (calcium carbonate; magnesium hydroxide; aspartame [phenylalanine 36.5 mg]; sorbitol; mandarin orange flavor; polyplasdone; microcrystalline cellulose; magnesium stearate; sodium 264.5 mg)].

Packaging and storage

Store below 40 °C (104 °F), preferably between 15 and 30 °C (59 and 86 °F), unless otherwise specified by manufacturer.

Stability

If dispersed in water, the solution may be stored for up to 1 hour at room temperature.

Auxiliary labeling

- Continue medicine for full time of treatment.
- Do not swallow tablets whole.
- Take on empty stomach.

Revised: 02/23/2001
Developed: 06/22/1994

DIENESTROL—See *Estrogens (Vaginal)*

DIETHYLPROPION—See *Appetite Suppressants (Systemic)*

DIETHYLSTILBESTROL—See *Estrogens (Systemic)*

DIFLORASONE—See *Corticosteroids (Topical)*

DIFLUCORTOLONE—See *Corticosteroids (Topical)*

DIFLUNISAL—See *Anti-inflammatory Drugs, Nonsteroidal (Systemic)*

DIGITALIS GLYCOSIDES Systemic

This monograph includes information on the following: 1) Digitoxin*; 2) Digoxin.

VA CLASSIFICATION (Primary/Secondary): CV051/CV300; CV900

Commonly used brand name(s): *Digitaline*[1]; *Lanoxicaps*[2]; *Lanoxin*[2]; *Lanoxin Elixir Pediatric*[2]; *Lanoxin Injection*[2]; *Lanoxin Injection Pediatric*[2]; *Lanoxin Pediatric Elixir*[2]; *Lanoxin Pediatric Injection*[2]; *Novo-Digoxin*[2].

Note: For a listing of dosage forms and brand names by country availability, see *Dosage Forms* section(s).

*Not commercially available in U.S.

Category

Antiarrhythmic; cardiotonic.

Indications

Accepted

Arrhythmias, cardiac (prophylaxis and treatment)—Digitalis glycosides (digitalis) are indicated for the control of ventricular response rates in patients with chronic atrial fibrillation. Digitalis glycosides are also indicated for the control of paroxysmal atrioventricular (AV) nodal reentrant tachycardia; digitalis glycosides may convert paroxysmal AV nodal reentrant tachycardia to normal sinus rhythm.

Congestive heart failure (treatment)—Digitalis glycosides are indicated for the treatment of all degrees of congestive heart failure. Their positive inotropic action results in improved cardiac output and an improvement in the signs and symptoms of hemodynamic insufficiency such as dyspnea, edema, and/or venous congestion.

Although digoxin has been shown to improve symptoms of heart failure, it does not prolong life, as was determined in a large, randomized, double-blind trial known as the Digitalis Investigation Group (DIG) study. In this trial, the effect of digoxin on mortality and morbidity was evaluated in patients with heart failure. It was concluded that digoxin did not reduce overall mortality, but that it did reduce the rate of hospitalization for worsening heart failure.

Unaccepted

The use of digitalis glycosides in the treatment of obesity has been determined unwarranted and dangerous, since these drugs may cause potentially fatal arrhythmias or other adverse effects.

Pharmacology/Pharmacokinetics

Physicochemical characteristics

Molecular weight—
- Digitoxin: 764.96.
- Digoxin: 780.96.

Mechanism of action/Effect

Two major actions are produced by therapeutic doses of digitalis glycosides—

(1) Force and velocity of myocardial contraction are increased (positive inotropic effect). This effect is thought to result from inhibition of movement of sodium and potassium ions across myocardial cell membranes by complexing with adenosine triphosphatase. As a result, there is enhancement of calcium influx and an augmented release of free calcium ions within the myocardial cells to subsequently potentiate the activity of the contractile muscle fibers of the heart.

(2) A decrease in the conduction rate and increase in the effective refractory period of the atrioventricular (AV) node is due predominantly to an indirect effect resulting from enhancement of parasympathetic tone and possibly from a decrease in sympathetic tone (the occurrence of the latter effect is controversial).

Digitalis glycosides differ predominantly in their pharmacokinetic properties, as opposed to their pharmacodynamic properties.

Absorption

Digitoxin—Highly lipophilic; almost completely absorbed after oral administration.

Digoxin—Absorption occurs by passive diffusion in the proximal part of the small intestine. Bioavailability is 60 to 80% (tablets), 70 to 85% (oral elixir), or 90 to 100% (capsules). The rate, but not the extent, of oral absorption is reduced when the tablets are taken after meals.

Distribution

Digitoxin—Estimated volume of distribution (Vol_D): 0.61 liter per kg (L/kg) (range, 0.53 to 0.74 L/kg); however, estimates vary considerably.

Digoxin—Apparent Vol_D: 6 to 8 L/kg; digoxin concentrates in tissues, with a distribution space that correlates with lean body weight as opposed to total body weight. Digoxin is distributed into cerebrospinal fluid, although to a lesser degree than into other tissues.

Protein binding

Digitoxin—High (> 90%).

Digoxin—Low (approximately 30%).

Biotransformation

Digitoxin—Metabolism occurs in the liver and produces several metabolites. The only active metabolite is digoxin, which makes up a small fraction of the total metabolites of digitoxin.

Digoxin—Metabolism occurs partially in the stomach, but also may occur in the liver and, although only about 16% of a dose of digoxin is metabolized, several metabolites of digoxin and their metabolic pathways have been identified. The bis-digitoxoside and mono-digitoxoside metabolites are considered to be cardioactive. Other metabolites, such as digoxigenin, are considered to be less cardioactive than digoxin. In some patients (estimated to be approximately 10% of patients taking digoxin), other cardioinactive metabolites, such as dihydrodigoxin and dihydrodigoxigenin, may result from the metabolism of digoxin by intestinal bacteria. In these individuals, as much as 40% or more of an oral dose of digoxin may be converted to these inactive reduction products.

Half-life

Elimination—
- Digitoxin: 7 to 9 days.
- Digoxin: 36 to 48 hours; 3.5 to 5 days in patients with impaired renal function.

Time to peak concentration

Digitoxin—Approximately 1 hour (range, 0.5 to 4 hours).

Digoxin—1 to 3 hours.

Therapeutic serum concentration

Digitoxin—12 to 25 nanograms per mL (nanograms/mL).

Digoxin—0.8 to 2 nanograms/mL; however, interindividual variability can be substantial and a patient can show signs of toxicity even though serum concentrations are within this range. Infants and children may tolerate higher peak serum digoxin concentrations than do adults.

Elimination

Digitoxin—Primarily hepatic (biliary/fecal), but also renal. Elimination is independent of renal function.

Digoxin—Primarily renal (50 to 70% of an intravenous dose may be recovered unchanged in the urine), but also hepatic (biliary); digoxin may accumulate in patients with renal function impairment.

In dialysis—
- Digitoxin: Not expected to be removed by hemodialysis because digitoxin is extensively bound to plasma protein.
- Digoxin: Not effectively removed by dialysis or exchange transfusion because most of the drug is in the tissue instead of the blood.

Precautions to Consider

Carcinogenicity

Studies have not been done.

Pregnancy/Reproduction

Pregnancy—Appropriate and well-controlled studies have not been done in pregnant women. Use of digitalis glycosides in pregnant women is not recommended unless absolutely needed.

FDA Pregnancy Category C.

Postpartum—

Following delivery, and for up to 6 weeks thereafter, the maternal dosage often must be reduced to maintain acceptable serum concentrations.

Breast-feeding

Digoxin is distributed into breast milk, reaching concentrations similar to those in serum. Although the total amount received daily by the infant has been estimated to be less than the usual maintenance dose for an infant, caution should be used. It is not known whether digitoxin is distributed into breast milk.

Pediatrics

Digitalis glycosides are a major cause of poisoning in children. The tolerance of newborn infants to digitalis glycosides is variable, since their renal clearance of the medication is reduced. Premature and immature infants are especially sensitive. Dosage should be reduced and individualized according to the infant's degree of maturity, since renal clearance increases as the infant matures. Children older than l month of age generally require proportionally larger doses than adults on the basis of body weight or body surface area.

Geriatrics

Although appropriate studies on the relationship of age to the effects of digitalis glycosides have not been performed in the geriatric population, the majority of experience with digoxin is in this population. Elderly patients may be more likely to have age-related renal function impairment, which may significantly increase the elimination half-life of digoxin. Additionally, elderly patients may have a decreased volume of distribution of digitalis due to decreased muscle mass. These factors may contribute to digitalis toxicity in elderly patients.

Drug interactions and/or related problems

The following drug interactions and/or related problems have been selected on the basis of their potential clinical significance (possible

mechanism in parentheses where appropriate)—not necessarily inclusive (» = major clinical significance):

Note: Digitalis glycosides have a narrow therapeutic range and changes in digitalis pharmacokinetics and/or pharmacodynamics caused by a digitalis-drug interaction can result in toxicity or underdigitalization. The presence of or a change in an underlying disease state also can cause changes in digitalis pharmacokinetics and/or pharmacodynamics and may complicate or contribute to a digitalis-drug interaction. Although there are several consistent, well-known, digitalis-drug interactions, numerous studies, reports, opinions, and conclusions about digitalis-drug interactions disagree on the existence or clinical significance of a number of interactions. Because a risk of digitalis toxicity exists, and the clinical significance of an interaction may be variable and not necessarily predictable, it is important that the addition or withdrawal of a drug to or from a therapeutic regimen that includes digitalis be carefully evaluated in the context of the patient and the clinical situation.

Combinations containing any of the following medications, depending on the amount present, may also interact with this medication.

Albuterol
(concurrent use may decrease serum digoxin concentrations, possibly by redistributing digoxin to other tissues; albuterol may also decrease serum potassium concentrations, which may increase the risk of digoxin toxicity)

Alprazolam
(concurrent use may increase serum digoxin concentrations, possibly by decreasing the renal clearance of digoxin; although one small study performed in healthy volunteers concluded that alprazolam had no significant effect on digoxin clearance, contradictory evidence has been reported in patients [primarily elderly patients] receiving long-term digoxin therapy)

» Amiodarone
(increases in serum digoxin concentrations by as much as 100% have been reported with concurrent use. Although it is thought that amiodarone decreases renal and/or nonrenal clearance and/or the volume of distribution of digoxin, other contributing factors, such as amiodarone-induced displacement of digoxin from tissue binding sites, also may be involved. Amiodarone has a long elimination half-life [15 to 65 days or longer] and digoxin toxicity may not appear until several weeks after the addition of amiodarone or may persist long after discontinuation of amiodarone)

Antacids or
Antidiarrheal adsorbents (e.g., kaolin and pectin) or
Sulfasalazine
(concurrent use may decrease digoxin bioavailability by decreasing digoxin absorption. In the case of antidiarrheal adsorbents and sulfasalazine, the digoxin dose may be administered 8 hours before the interacting medication)

Antibiotics, oral, especially
Macrolide antibiotics, such as:
Clarithromycin or
Erythromycin or
Tetracycline
(concurrent use of some oral antibiotics may increase serum digoxin concentrations in patients who inactivate digoxin in the lower intestine by bacterial metabolism; in these individuals, altering the bowel flora with certain antibiotics may diminish digoxin conversion to inactive metabolites, resulting in increased serum digoxin concentration; the increase in serum digoxin concentration has been as much as twofold in some cases and correlates with the extent of bacterial inactivation. Although there are limited data, this interaction has been reported with oral use of clarithromycin, erythromycin, and tetracycline)

Anticancer medications (such as bleomycin, cyclophosphamide, cytarabine, doxorubicin, procarbazine, and vincristine) or
Radiation therapy
(concurrent use may decrease digoxin bioavailability by decreasing digoxin absorption; the reduced absorption that occurs during concurrent use with anticancer medications or radiation therapy may be due to temporary damage to the gastrointestinal mucosa and may continue for several days after treatment; in these patients, a dosage form with greater bioavailability, such as the capsule or solution, may help to minimize decreased bioavailability; digitoxin absorption does not appear to be affected by anticancer agents)

Atorvastatin
(concurrent use may increase digoxin serum concentrations; steady-state serum concentration increases of approximately 20% have been reported)

» Beta-adrenergic blocking agents, including
Atenolol
Carvedilol
Metoprolol and
Propranolol
(concurrent use with these agents may have additive effects on slowing atrioventricular [AV] nodal conduction; concurrent use with carvedilol in patients with hypertension increased the steady-state area under the plasma concentration-time curve [AUC] and trough concentrations of digoxin by 14% and 16%, respectively; monitoring of plasma digoxin concentrations is recommended)

Bran fiber, dietary
(it is uncertain whether concurrent administration of dietary bran fiber decreases digoxin bioavailability. In one small study, there was presumed to be a decrease in digoxin absorption when concurrent administration of digoxin with 5 grams of fiber resulted in a decrease in urinary excretion of digoxin. Another small study found no change in steady-state serum digoxin concentrations when digoxin was administered 15 to 30 minutes before administration of 11 grams of bran [as a bran muffin], with a second bran muffin administered several hours later)

» Calcium channel blocking agents, especially
Bepridil or
Diltiazem or
Nifedipine or
» Verapamil
(concurrent use with calcium channel blocking agents may have additive effects on AV nodal conduction, which could result in complete heart block; concurrent use also may increase serum digoxin concentrations by reducing digoxin renal clearance, possibly as a result of inhibition of active tubular secretion of digoxin; verapamil may increase serum digoxin concentrations by 30 to 200%; bepridil may increase serum digoxin concentrations by approximately 34%; some studies have reported no interaction with diltiazem while others have reported increases in serum digoxin concentrations of 20 to 60%; contradictory evidence of an interaction also exists for nifedipine, although serum digoxin increases of 15 to 50% have been reported; increases in serum digitoxin concentrations also have been reported with concurrent use of diltiazem and verapamil, although increases were less pronounced than with digoxin use and may be due to a reduction in extrarenal digitoxin clearance; serum digitalis concentrations and electrocardiogram [ECG] should be monitored and dosages adjusted accordingly)

Cholestyramine or
Colestipol
(colestipol and cholestyramine may delay and reduce the absorption of digoxin; the digoxin dose may be administered 8 hours before the interacting medication to minimize the interference with digoxin absorption)

Cyclosporine
(concurrent use has resulted in increases in serum digoxin concentrations, possibly as a result of decreased apparent volume of distribution and/or plasma clearance of digoxin)

Diphenoxylate or
Propantheline
(concurrent use may increase digoxin bioavailability; diphenoxylate and propantheline increase digoxin absorption by decreasing intestinal motility)

» Diuretics, potassium-depleting (such as bumetanide, ethacrynic acid, furosemide, indapamide, mannitol, or thiazides) or
Hypokalemia-causing medications, other (see *Appendix II*)
(decreases in serum potassium concentrations that can occur with these medications may increase the risk of digitalis toxicity; frequent serum potassium concentration determinations are recommended)

Flecainide
(concurrent use has increased serum digoxin concentrations, on average, by 24%; it also has been speculated that concurrent use may cause a slight additive increase in the PR interval)

Hepatic enzyme inducers (see *Appendix II*) such as:
Barbiturates or
Phenytoin or
Rifampin
(concurrent use may increase the metabolism of digitoxin; serum digitoxin concentrations have been reported to decrease by 50% in patients who received 180 mg of phenobarbital per day for 12 weeks; decreases in serum digoxin concentrations also have been reported with concurrent use of rifampin, although the mechanism for this interaction is not completely understood; serum digitalis

concentrations should be monitored and dosages adjusted accordingly)

Indomethacin

(concurrent use may increase digoxin serum concentrations, possibly by inhibiting the renal elimination of digoxin; two small studies that evaluated the interaction in healthy adult patients did not find a clinically significant interaction. Another small study found a significant increase [about 40% on average] in serum digoxin concentrations in adult heart failure patients treated with digoxin on a long-term basis. A small study in premature infants treated conventionally with indomethacin for patent ductus arteriosus [PDA] found an increase in serum digoxin concentrations of approximately 50% with concurrent use)

Itraconazole

(concurrent use may increase serum digoxin concentrations, possibly by decreasing renal elimination of digoxin; serum digoxin concentration increases of approximately 50% have been reported)

Metoclopramide

(concurrent use of metoclopramide may decrease digoxin absorption by increasing gastrointestinal motility; serum digoxin concentrations as determined by AUC have been reported to decrease by about 24%)

Neomycin, oral

(concurrent use decreases the rate and extent of absorption of digoxin. In a study in healthy volunteers, the extent of absorption of digoxin was decreased by as much as 51% after single doses of digoxin and neomycin. The absorption of digoxin also was decreased when the antibiotic was given 3 or 6 hours before the digoxin dose. The mechanism of this interaction has not been established, but it is recommended that digoxin be administered at least 8 hours before neomycin)

Omeprazole

(concurrent use with digoxin may increase digoxin absorption, possibly by altering gastric acidity; on average, C_{max} and AUC values have been reported to be about 10% higher with concurrent use)

» Propafenone

(concurrent use of propafenone with digoxin results in an increase in serum digoxin concentrations ranging from 35 to 85%, which appears to be unrelated to digoxin renal clearance but may be related to a decrease in the volume of distribution and nonrenal clearance of digoxin; careful monitoring of digoxin concentrations and dosage reduction of digoxin are recommended when propafenone is initiated)

» Quinidine or
Quinine

(concurrent use with quinidine has resulted in increased digoxin plasma concentrations, possibly due to an initial displacement of digoxin from quinidine binding sites, and a reduction in the renal and nonrenal clearance and volume of distribution of digoxin; the extent of the interaction is proportional to plasma quinidine concentrations and, on average, concurrent use results in 100% increases in serum digoxin concentrations, although increases of over 300% have been reported; concurrent use of quinidine with digitoxin has resulted in increases in serum digitoxin concentrations of 30 to 67%, the smaller increases possibly resulting from impairment of extrarenal clearance of digitoxin by quinidine; increases in serum digoxin concentrations also have been reported with concurrent use of quinine; serum digitalis concentrations should be monitored and dosage adjusted as indicated)

Spironolactone

(concurrent use with digoxin may increase serum digoxin concentrations, possibly by decreasing digoxin renal and nonrenal clearance and/or digoxin volume of distribution; it has been estimated that digoxin plasma concentrations may increase by one third with concurrent use)

Succinylcholine

(concurrent use may cause a sudden release of potassium from muscle cells, increasing the risk of arrhythmias in digitalized patients)

Sucralfate

(sucralfate was reported to reduce digoxin plasma concentrations by about 19%, presumably by reducing the bioavailability of digoxin. Sucralfate should not be taken within 2 hours of digoxin)

» Sympathomimetics

(concurrent use may increase the risk of cardiac arrhythmias)

Thyroid hormones

(patients with thyroid disease may have an altered sensitivity to digitalis: hyperthyroid patients may have a reduced response to digitalis and hypothyroid patients may have an increased risk of digitalis toxicity; use of thyroid hormones in a hypothyroid patient who has been digitalized may require an increase in the digitalis dose)

Laboratory value alterations

The following have been selected on the basis of their potential clinical significance (possible effect in parentheses where appropriate)—not necessarily inclusive (» = major clinical significance).

With diagnostic test results

Electrocardiogram (ECG)

(digitalis glycosides may produce false-positive ST-T changes during exercise testing)

Thallous chloride Tl 201

(in animal studies, concurrent use of digitalis glycosides decreased myocardial uptake of thallous chloride Tl 201; human data are not available)

Digoxin, serum

(false-positive increases in serum digoxin concentrations have occurred from the presence of a digoxin-like immunoreactive substance in patients with hepatic or renal function impairment, in pregnant women, in patients with hypertension, in infants and neonates, and in patients with chronic heart failure. In patients treated with digoxin-immune Fab antibody fragments, serum digoxin concentrations may increase 5 to 20 times as a result of inactive intravascular concentrations of Fab-bound digitalis complexes)

Medical considerations/Contraindications

The medical considerations/contraindications included have been selected on the basis of their potential clinical significance (reasons given in parentheses where appropriate)—not necessarily inclusive (» = major clinical significance).

Except under special circumstances, these medications should not be used when the following medical problems exist:

» Hypersensitivity to digoxin or digitoxin

» Ventricular fibrillation

Risk-benefit should be considered when the following medical problems exist:

» Cardiomyopathy, hypertrophic, with left ventricular outflow obstruction (idiopathic hypertrophic subaortic stenosis) or

» Cor pulmonale, acute or

» Heart failure associated with diastolic dysfunction, such as
Cardiomyopathy, restrictive, as associated with
Amyloid cardiomyopathy or
Pericarditis, constrictive

(these conditions may be particularly sensitive to the inotropic effects of digitalis or may worsen with digitalis administration)

» Atrioventricular (AV) accessory pathway accompanied by atrial flutter or fibrillation (Wolff-Parkinson-White syndrome)

(patients receiving intravenous digoxin have developed a rapid ventricular response or ventricular fibrillation as a result of an increase in antegrade conduction over the accessory pathway, bypassing the AV node. Digitalis should not be used in these patients unless accessory pathway conduction has been surgically blocked or pharmacologically depressed)

» AV block, without a functioning cardiac pacemaker or

» Sinus node dysfunction, without a functioning cardiac pacemaker

(because digitalis slows sinoatrial [SA] and AV conduction and prolongs the PR interval, administration of digitalis in patients with sinus node dysfunction can result in severe sinus bradycardia or SA block; similarly, administration of digitalis in patients with incomplete AV block can result in advanced or complete AV block)

Arteriovenous shunt or
Hypoxia or
Thyroid disease

(use of digitalis for the treatment of heart failure and/or atrial arrhythmias associated with these disease states may predispose the patient to toxicity once the primary disorder is corrected; patients with hypothyroidism may have reduced requirements for digitalis and, contrarily, patients with hyperthyroidism may be resistant to treatment with digitalis)

Electrical cardioversion

(conventionally, regardless of the serum concentration of digitalis, the dose of digitalis was reduced or withheld 1 to 2 days prior to cardioversion of atrial fibrillation because it was thought that the use of digitalis during electrical cardioversion would provoke ventricular arrhythmias. Although electrical cardioversion in patients with digitalis toxicity has been shown to provoke ventricular arrhythmias, a study in patients with clinically therapeutic digitalis serum concentrations [nontoxic concentrations] determined that these patients may safely undergo electrical cardioversion without reducing or withholding the dose of digitalis [and without the concurrent use of an antiarrhythmic agent]. It also should be taken into consideration that serum digitalis concentrations are not the only determining risk factor for development of ventricular arrhythmias postcardioversion. If digitalis toxicity is suspected, cardioversion should be postponed)

» Electrolyte disorders (resulting from dialysis, diarrhea, diuretics or other medications, malnutrition, prolonged vomiting, etc.), especially
» Hypercalcemia
» Hypocalcemia
» Hypokalemia and
» Hypomagnesemia
(hypokalemia and hypomagnesemia cause the myocardium to be sensitive to digoxin and toxicity may occur; hypercalcemia has an additive effect on the contractility and excitability of the heart and may increase the risk of digitalis toxicity; if intravenous calcium salts are administered rapidly to a digitalized patient, serious arrhythmias may occur; conversely, hypocalcemia can counteract the effects of digoxin on the heart)

Hepatic function impairment
(the dose of digitoxin may need to be reduced in these patients)

Myocardial infarction, acute
(the use of inotropic agents, such as digitalis, may increase myocardial oxygen demand and cause ischemia in some of these patients; digitalis should be used with caution in these patients)

» Renal function impairment
(because digoxin is eliminated predominantly by the kidneys, the elimination half-life of digoxin may be prolonged when renal function is impaired, increasing the time to reach a steady-state serum concentration; these patients may be more likely to experience digoxin toxicity and to have toxic effects of longer duration; the dose of digoxin should be reduced in these patients)

Patient monitoring

The following may be especially important in patient monitoring (other tests may be warranted in some patients, depending on condition; » = major clinical significance):

» Cardioglycoside, steady-state, trough serum concentrations
(it is recommended that concentrations be obtained at initiation of therapy and periodically thereafter, unless a change occurs in the patient's clinical status, in which case, more frequent monitoring may be necessary. Other factors that may indicate a need for monitoring are: a change in renal function, lack of a response to the digitalis glycoside, decompensated heart failure, addition of an interacting medication, suspected digoxin toxicity, or assessment of compliance. To allow adequate distribution of digoxin, sampling should be done just before the next scheduled dose or, if that is not possible, at least 6 to 8 hours after the last dose, regardless of the route of administration or formulation used; serum concentrations always should be interpreted in the overall clinical context and should not be used as a basis for changing the dosage. Furthermore, in patients with atrial fibrillation, serum concentrations are less important than the clinical response; if the heart rate is controlled and the patient is without signs of toxicity, serum concentrations should not be obtained nor the dosage changed. If a discrepancy exists between the reported serum concentration and the observed clinical response, the following reasons might be considered: analytical problems in the assay procedure, an inappropriate serum sampling time, administration of a digitalis glycoside other than what was prescribed, occurrence of a physiological condition that has altered the patient's sensitivity to digitalis, or an abnormal patient response to digitalis)

» Electrocardiogram (ECG) monitoring
(recommended at periodic intervals; if paroxysmal atrial tachycardias with atrioventricular (AV) block or ventricular tachycardia occurs, withholding the digitalis glycoside should be considered until serum digoxin concentration and electrolyte status are evaluated. Clinical judgment is essential since withholding of digitalis also may have adverse consequences)

» Electrolyte, especially potassium, calcium, and magnesium concentrations, serum
(recommended at periodic intervals, especially in patients also receiving diuretics, to detect possible electrolyte imbalance, which may increase the chance of digitalis toxicity, particularly with regard to arrhythmias, and may affect dosage requirements)

Hepatic function determinations and
Renal function determinations
(recommended at periodic intervals as appropriate)

Pulse (apical) check
(recommended at periodic intervals, especially in patients with atrial fibrillation or when a dosage change is made)

Side/Adverse Effects

Note: Digitalis side/adverse effects are dose-related and usually occur at doses higher than those needed for a therapeutic effect. Some patients may be particularly sensitive to some side/adverse effects of digitalis and may manifest symptoms of toxicity even though serum digitalis concentrations are within the therapeutic range. Physiological changes associated with aging, underlying illnesses, and concurrent use of other medications (diuretics) also can affect the occurrence of digitalis side/adverse effects and/or toxicity. Additionally, children may experience different side/adverse/toxic effects than adults.

The following side/adverse effects have been selected on the basis of their potential clinical significance (possible signs and symptoms in parentheses where appropriate)—not necessarily inclusive:

Those indicating need for medical attention

In adults

With therapeutic, high, or toxic doses

Cardiovascular effects, such as atrial tachycardia with block; atrioventricular (AV) dissociation; heart block, first-, second-, or third-degree; junctional (nodal) rhythm, accelerated; PR interval prolongation; ST segment depression; ventricular fibrillation; ventricular premature contractions, unifocal or multiform (especially bigeminy or trigeminy); and ventricular tachycardia (cardiovascular effects may be manifested as slow and/or irregular heartbeat, palpitations, or fainting); ***central nervous system (CNS) effects, such as anxiety; apathy*** (feeling of not caring); ***blurred or yellow vision; confusion; dizziness; hallucinations*** (seeing or hearing things that are not there); ***headache; mental depression; and weakness; gastrointestinal effects, such as abdominal pain; anorexia*** (loss of appetite); ***diarrhea; nausea; and vomiting***

Incidence rare

Skin rash; thrombocytopenia (may be seen as nosebleeds or bleeding gums)

With long-term use

Gynecomastia (enlargement of breast tissue in males)

In infants or children

With therapeutic, high, or toxic doses

Cardiovascular effects, especially atrial tachycardia (with or without block); conduction disturbances; junctional (nodal) tachycardia; sinus bradycardia; ventricular arrhythmias, or any other cardiac arrhythmia

Note: The earliest and most frequently encountered side effects that are associated with excessive dosing in infants and children are cardiac arrhythmias, especially *conduction disturbances* and supraventricular tachycardias (*atrial tachycardia [with or without block]* and *junctional [nodal] tachycardia*).

Incidence less frequent

CNS effects, such as anxiety; apathy; blurred or yellow vision; confusion; dizziness; hallucinations; headache; mental depression; weakness; gastrointestinal effects, such as anorexia; diarrhea; nausea; vomiting

Overdose

For specific information on the agents used in the management of digitalis glycoside toxicity or overdose, see:
- *Atropine* in *Anticholinergics/Antispasmodics (Systemic)* monograph; and/or
- *Digoxin Immune Fab (Ovine) (Systemic)* monograph; and/or
- *Potassium Supplements (Systemic)* monograph.

For more information on the management of overdose or unintentional ingestion, **contact a Poison Control Center** (see *Poison Control Center Listing*).

Clinical effects of overdose

The clinical effects of digitalis overdosage cannot be differentiated significantly from those of toxicity at therapeutic or high doses (see *Side/Adverse Effects* section), except in cases of massive overdose.

Clinical effects of massive overdose

The following effects have been selected on the basis of their potential clinical significance (possible signs and symptoms in parentheses where appropriate)—not necessarily inclusive:

Acute and/or chronic in adults

Bradyarrhythmias, progressive; cardiac arrest; heart block; ventricular fibrillation; ventricular tachycardia

Treatment of overdose

Note: Previous adjunctive treatments in the management of non-life-threatening digitalis intoxication, such as repetitive doses of activated charcoal, cholestyramine, and/or colestipol (presumably to interrupt the enterohepatic recycling of digoxin to enhance elimination), have not been shown to be clinically effective. Previous strategies for treatment of hyperkalemia (insulin, sodium bicarbonate, and/or sodium polystyrene sulfonate) and ventricular arrhythmias (antiarrhythmic agents such as amiodarone, bretylium, lidocaine, phenytoin, propranolol, verapamil, and other drugs) have been replaced by more clinically safe and effective treatment with Fab antibody fragments.

Subtle signs or symptoms of digitalis toxicity should be managed by a dosage reduction or withdrawal of digitalis or by identifying and correcting other factors that contribute to toxic effects (such as electrolyte disturbances or drug interactions). Asymptomatic bradycardia or atrioventricular (AV) block may require only temporary withdrawal of the drug and cardiac monitoring.

Specific treatment—
- For symptomatic sinus bradycardia or AV block: Atropine and/or digoxin immune Fab. Cardiac pacing has been associated with complications (traumatic thrombosis, infectious complications, and life-threatening arrhythmias associated with defects of pacing, or pacemaker insertion or adjustment) and is only recommended if digoxin immune Fab therapy is unsuccessful.
- For ventricular arrhythmias: Electrolyte disorders should be corrected (especially potassium and magnesium); administration of digoxin immune Fab.
- For hypokalemia: In cases of low or normal serum potassium concentrations, administration of potassium may help to antagonize the digitalis toxic effects; however, because severe digitalis intoxication can cause a redistribution of potassium from inside to outside the cell, resulting in hyperkalemia, administration of potassium may be dangerous in cases of massive overdose.
- For hyperkalemia: In cases of high serum potassium concentrations, further increases in serum potassium may result in complete AV block or cardiac arrest. If potassium concentrations exceed 5 mEq per L, digoxin immune Fab should be used.

For massive (acute) overdoses—
- To decrease absorption: Emesis generally is not recommended except prior to presentation at the hospital. Gastric lavage may be used only if ingestion occurred within 1 hour, but should not be used in patients who are obtunded or exhibit toxic symptoms. Emesis or gastric lavage also is not recommended in patients with underlying heart disease or arrhythmias because it may provoke arrhythmias by augmenting vagal tone.
- Also see *Specific treatment* above.

Monitoring—
- Constant electrocardiogram (ECG) monitoring is recommended to guide therapy and to monitor for potassium toxicity (T-wave peaking) during administration of potassium.

Supportive care—
- Patients in whom intentional overdose is confirmed or suspected should be referred for psychiatric consultation.

Patient Consultation

As an aid to patient consultation, refer to *Advice for the Patient, Digitalis Medicines (Systemic)*.

In providing consultation, consider emphasizing the following selected information (» = major clinical significance):

Before using this medication

» Conditions affecting use, especially:
- Hypersensitivity to digitoxin or digoxin
- Pregnancy—Digoxin crosses the placenta and should not be used in pregnant women unless absolutely needed; it is not known if digitoxin crosses the placenta
- Breast-feeding—Digoxin is distributed into breast milk; caution should be used. It is not known whether digitoxin is distributed into breast milk
- Use in children—Infant responses vary; careful dosage adjustment is required
- Use in the elderly—Elderly patients may be at greater risk of toxicity
- Other medications, especially amiodarone; beta-adrenergic blocking agents, including atenolol, carvedilol, metoprolol, and propranolol; calcium channel blocking agents, especially verapamil; potassium-depleting diuretics; propafenone; quinidine; or sympathomimetics
- Other medical problems, especially acute cor pulmonale; atrioventricular (AV) accessory pathway (Wolff-Parkinson-White syndrome) accompanied by atrial flutter or fibrillation; AV block, without a functioning cardiac pacemaker; electrolyte disorders; heart failure associated with diastolic dysfunction; hypertrophic cardiomyopathy with left ventricular outflow obstruction; renal function impairment; sinus node dysfunction, without a functioning cardiac pacemaker; or ventricular fibrillation

Proper use of this medication

» Compliance with therapy; taking exactly as directed, not taking more or less medication than the dosage prescribed; taking medication at the same time each day to maintain the therapeutic effect

Proper administration of elixir: Taking orally; special dropper to be used for accurate measuring

» Proper dosing

Missed dose: Taking as soon as remembered if within 12 hours of scheduled dose; not taking if remembered later; not doubling doses; checking with doctor if dose missed for 2 days or more

» Proper storage

Precautions while using this medication

Seeing the physician regularly to check progress

» Checking with physician before discontinuing medication

» Keeping medication out of reach of children

» Reporting to physician any nausea, vomiting, diarrhea, loss of appetite, irregular or slow pulse, palpitations, and/or fainting as possible signs of overdose; initial overdose signs may occur as gastrointestinal effects in adults and as cardiovascular effects in children

Carrying medical identification card

» Not taking other medications without consulting physician

Caution in using medications of similar appearance

Side/adverse effects

Signs of potential side effects and/or toxicity in adults, especially atrial tachycardia with block; AV dissociation; first-, second-, or third-degree heart block; accelerated junctional (nodal) rhythm; PR interval prolongation; ventricular fibrillation; unifocal or multiform (especially bigeminy or trigeminy) ventricular premature contractions; ventricular tachycardia; anxiety; apathy; blurred or yellow vision; confusion; dizziness; hallucinations; headache; mental depression; weakness; abdominal pain; anorexia; diarrhea; nausea; vomiting; skin rash; thrombocytopenia; and gynecomastia

(Signs of potential side effects and/or toxicity in infants and children, especially atrial tachycardia (with or without block); conduction disturbances; junctional (nodal) tachycardia; sinus bradycardia; ventricular arrhythmias, or any other cardiac arrhythmia; anxiety; apathy; blurred or yellow vision; confusion; dizziness; hallucinations; headache; mental depression; weakness; anorexia; diarrhea; nausea; and vomiting)

General Dosing Information

Recommended doses are averages only; each dose must be adjusted to meet the individual patient's requirements.

Reduction of digitalis glycoside dosage prior to cardioversion may be desirable; however, the benefit must be weighed against the risk of a rapid increase in ventricular response to atrial fibrillation if the digitalis glycoside is withheld 1 to 2 days prior to cardioversion. If digitalis glycoside toxicity is suspected, electrical cardioversion of arrhythmias should be delayed.

DIGITOXIN

Summary of Differences

Pharmacology/pharmacokinetics:
- Hepatically metabolized; renal excretion of inactive metabolites has little effect on digitoxin action.
- Protein binding—High.
- Half-life—7 to 9 days.

Precautions:
- Medical considerations/contraindications—Dosage reduction not necessary in renal function impairment; however, a dosage adjustment may be necessary in patients with hepatic function impairment.

Oral Dosage Forms

DIGITOXIN TABLETS USP

Usual adult dose

Arrhythmias, cardiac or
Congestive heart failure—
- Digitalization—
  - Rapid—Oral, 600 mcg (0.6 mg) initially, then 400 mcg (0.4 mg) after four to six hours and 200 mcg (0.2 mg) after another four- to six-hour period, followed by a daily maintenance dose as needed and tolerated, or
  - Slow—Oral, 200 mcg (0.2 mg) two times a day for four days, followed by a daily maintenance dose as needed and tolerated.

Maintenance—
Oral, 50 to 300 mcg (0.05 to 0.3 mg) once a day, the dosage being adjusted as needed and tolerated.

Note: Geriatric patients, debilitated patients, and patients using electronic cardiac pacemakers require careful dosage titration, as they may exhibit toxic responses at doses and serum concentrations generally tolerated by other patients.

Usual adult prescribing limits
Digitalization—A total of 1.6 mg over one or two days.

Usual pediatric dose
Prepared oral digitoxin dosage forms are limited and may not be suitable for small children.

Strength(s) usually available
U.S.—
Not commercially available.
Canada—
100 mcg (0.1 mg) (Rx) [*Digitaline*].

Packaging and storage
Store below 40 °C (104 °F), preferably between 15 and 30 °C (59 and 86 °F), unless otherwise specified by manufacturer. Store in a well-closed container.

Auxiliary labeling
- Keep out of reach of children.
- Do not take other medicines without advice from your doctor.

DIGOXIN

Summary of Differences

Pharmacology/pharmacokinetics:
Protein binding—Low.
Biotransformation—Minimal hepatic metabolism; excretion and half-life determined by renal function.
Half-life—36 to 48 hours.
Precautions:
Medical considerations/contraindications—Dosage reduction may be required in patients with renal function impairment.

Additional Dosing Information

Note: Patient response and sensitivity to digoxin can vary substantially and dosages may require considerable modification. Doses of digoxin should be based upon lean body weight and should be adjusted according to the patient's renal function (based on creatinine clearance), age, underlying illnesses, concurrent medications, and/or other factors that may alter the pharmacokinetics or pharmacodynamics of digoxin. A variety of equations, algorithms, dosing charts, nomograms, and recommendations exist for determining both the loading and maintenance doses of digoxin. The recommended dosages that appear in this text are based upon the manufacturer's product information. For dosing information in chart form, based on corrected creatinine clearance and lean body weight, see the manufacturer's product information.

Bioequivalence information
Bioavailability differences exist among dosage forms of digoxin. Changing therapy from one dosage form to another may require dosage adjustments.
Absolute bioavailability of digoxin is as follows: Tablets—60 to 80%; elixir—70 to 85%; liquid-filled capsules—90 to 100%; and intravenous injection—100%.
The following doses of digoxin are considered equivalent:

Intravenous injection or liquid capsule dosage (mcg)	Equivalent tablet or elixir dosage (mcg)
50	62.5
100	125
200	250
400	500

For digoxin tablets—
Variability in the bioavailability of digoxin tablets was recognized as a clinical problem in the early 1970s. These differences in bioavailability were reported among different brands of digoxin tablets as well as among different lots of digoxin tablets produced by the same manufacturer. In response to the problems of bio-inequivalence, official dissolution standards were established. Problems have not been reported following establishment of these standards. However, because bioavailability from any digoxin tablet is incomplete (≤ 80%), clinicians should consider this as a possible source of the problem when unexplained difficulty is encountered in the digitalization or maintenance therapy of patients with digoxin tablets.

Oral Dosage Forms

DIGOXIN CAPSULES

Note: Digoxin capsules (digoxin solution in capsules) have an absolute bioavailability close to that of the intravenous injection dosage form. However, the capsules have a greater bioavailability than the tablets or elixir because they are more completely absorbed. The recommended oral dose of digoxin capsules is 80% of that for the tablets or elixir. See *Bioequivalence information* section.

Usual adult dose
Congestive heart failure—
Digitalization—
Rapid digitalization is achieved by administering a loading dose based upon projected peak digoxin body stores (body stores of 8 to 12 mcg per kg of body weight in patients with heart failure and normal sinus rhythm; body stores of 6 to 10 mcg per kg of body weight for heart failure patients with renal insufficiency). Roughly one half the total loading dose is given as the first dose, with the remaining portion divided and administered every six to eight hours (e.g., 400 to 600 mcg [0.4 to 0.6 mg] initially, followed by 100 to 300 mcg [0.1 to 0.3 mg] administered every six to eight hours) until an appropriate clinical response is achieved. Before each additional dose is given, the patient's clinical response should be assessed carefully. If the patient's clinical response requires a change from the calculated loading dose of digoxin, calculation of the maintenance dose should be based upon the amount actually given. For a 70-kg patient to achieve peak body stores of 8 to 12 mcg per kg of body weight, the usual amount administered is 600 to 1000 mcg (0.6 to 1 mg).
Slow digitalization is achieved by beginning an appropriate maintenance dose (allowing digoxin body stores to accumulate slowly). Steady-state serum digoxin concentrations will be achieved in approximately five half-lives. Depending upon the patient's renal function, digitalization by this method will take between one and three weeks.
Maintenance—
Digoxin maintenance doses for estimated peak body stores of 10 mcg per kg of body weight generally have ranged from 50 to 350 mcg (0.05 to 0.35 mg), administered orally as one or two doses per day, the dosage titrated according to the patient's age, lean body weight, and renal function. In patients digitalized with a loading dose, the subsequent maintenance dose can be calculated as a percentage of the loading dose. Doses may be increased every two weeks according to clinical response.
Atrial fibrillation, chronic—
Doses should be titrated to the minimum dose that achieves the desired ventricular rate control without causing undesirable side effects.

Usual pediatric dose
Congestive heart failure—
Beyond the immediate newborn period, children generally require proportionally larger doses than adults on the basis of body weight or body surface area. Children older than 10 years of age require adult dosages in proportion to their body weight. Some researchers have suggested that infants and young children tolerate slightly higher serum digoxin concentrations than do adults. For digitalization and maintenance dosing of children younger than 2 years of age, see *Digoxin Elixir USP* or *Digoxin Injection USP*. The following digitalizing and maintenance doses are based on lean body weight for children with heart failure and normal renal function:
Digitalizing dose—
Digitalizing doses for the capsules are the same as intravenous digitalizing doses. The following total amounts should be *divided* into three or more doses, with the initial portion representing approximately one half the total, and the remaining doses administered every six to eight hours, with careful assessment of clinical response before each additional dose. If the patient's clinical response requires a change from the calculated loading dose of digoxin, the calculation of the maintenance dose should be based upon the amount actually given.

Children 2 to 5 years of age:
Oral, 25 to 35 mcg (0.025 to 0.035 mg) per kg of body weight.

Children 5 to 10 years of age:
Oral, 15 to 30 mcg (0.015 to 0.030 mg) per kg of body weight.

Children 10 years of age and older:
Oral, 8 to 12 mcg (0.008 to 0.012 mg) per kg of body weight.

Maintenance dose—

Note: Divided daily dosing is recommended for infants and children up to 10 years of age.

Children 2 years of age and older:
Oral, 25 to 35% of the oral or intravenous total digitalizing dose, based on desired clinical response.

Strength(s) usually available

U.S.

Note: Digoxin capsules consist of a stable digoxin solution enclosed in a soft gelatin capsule.

50 mcg (0.05 mg) (Rx) [*Lanoxicaps* (ethyl alcohol 8%)].
100 mcg (0.1 mg) (Rx) [*Lanoxicaps* (ethyl alcohol 8%)].
200 mcg (0.2 mg) (Rx) [*Lanoxicaps* (ethyl alcohol 8%)].

Canada—
Not commercially available.

Packaging and storage

Store between 15 and 25 °C (59 and 77 °F). Store in a tight container and protect from light.

Auxiliary labeling

- Keep out of reach of children.
- Keep container tightly closed.
- Do not take other medicines without advice from your doctor.

DIGOXIN ELIXIR USP

Note: Digoxin elixir and tablets are similar in bioavailability but are less bioavailable than the capsule or intravenous injection dosage forms. When switching from the intravenous injection dosage form to the less bioavailable oral elixir dosage form, the recommended dose of the oral elixir is 1.25 times the intravenous dose (e.g., 100 mcg of digoxin injection is considered equivalent to 125 mcg of the elixir). See *Bioequivalence information* section.

Usual adult dose

Congestive heart failure—
Digitalization—
See *Digoxin Tablets USP* section.

Maintenance—
See *Digoxin Tablets USP* section.

Atrial fibrillation, chronic—
See *Digoxin Tablets USP* section.

Usual pediatric dose

Congestive heart failure—
In newborns, digoxin renal clearance is diminished (especially in premature infants) and digoxin doses should be adjusted accordingly. Beyond the immediate newborn period, children generally require proportionally larger doses than do adults, on the basis of body weight or body surface area. Children older than 10 years of age require adult dosages in proportion to their body weight. Some researchers have suggested that infants and young children tolerate slightly higher serum digoxin concentrations than do adults. The following digitalizing and maintenance doses are based on lean body weight for children with heart failure and normal renal function:

Digitalization—
The following total amounts should be *divided* into three or more doses, with the initial portion representing approximately one half the total, and the remaining doses administered every six to eight hours, with careful assessment of clinical response before each additional dose. If the patient's clinical response requires a change from the calculated loading dose of digoxin, the calculation of the maintenance dose should be based upon the amount actually given.

Premature infants:
Oral, 20 to 30 mcg (0.02 to 0.03 mg) per kg of body weight.

Full-term infants:
Oral, 25 to 35 mcg (0.025 to 0.035 mg) per kg of body weight.

Infants 1 to 24 months of age:
Oral, 35 to 60 mcg (0.035 to 0.06 mg) per kg of body weight.

Children 2 to 5 years of age:
Oral, 30 to 40 mcg (0.03 to 0.04 mg) per kg of body weight.

Children 5 to 10 years of age:
Oral, 20 to 35 mcg (0.02 to 0.035 mg) per kg of body weight.

Children 10 years of age or older:
Oral, 10 to 15 mcg (0.01 to 0.015 mg) per kg of body weight.

Maintenance—

Note: Divided daily dosing is recommended for children up to 10 years of age.

Premature infants:
Oral, 20 to 30% of the total digitalizing dose providing the clinical response.

Full-term infants and older children:
Oral, 25 to 35% of the total digitalizing dose providing the clinical response.

Strength(s) usually available

U.S.—
50 mcg (0.05 mg) per mL (Rx) [*Lanoxin Elixir Pediatric* (alcohol 10%); GENERIC].

Canada—
50 mcg (0.05 mg) per mL (Rx) [*Lanoxin Pediatric Elixir* (alcohol 11.5%; tartrazine)].

Packaging and storage

Store between 15 and 25 °C (59 and 77 °F). Store in a tight container and protect from light.

Auxiliary labeling

- Keep out of reach of children.
- Keep container tightly closed.
- Do not take other medicines without advice from your doctor.

DIGOXIN TABLETS USP

Note: Variability in the bioavailability of digoxin tablets was recognized as a clinical problem in the early 1970s. These differences in bioavailability were reported among different brands of digoxin tablets as well as among different lots of digoxin tablets produced by the same manufacturer. In response to the problems of bio-inequivalence, official dissolution standards were established. Problems have not been reported following establishment of these standards. However, because bioavailability from any digoxin tablet is incomplete (≤ 80%), clinicians should consider this as a possible source of the problem when unexplained difficulty is encountered in the digitalization or maintenance therapy of patients with digoxin tablets.

Digoxin tablets are less bioavailable than digoxin injection; switching from the injection to the tablets for maintenance therapy will require a dosage adjustment. The recommended dose of the tablets is 1.25 times the intravenous dose (e.g., a 100-mcg dose of digoxin injection is considered equivalent to a 125-mcg tablet dose). See *Bioequivalence information* section.

Usual adult dose

Congestive heart failure—
Digitalization—
Rapid digitalization is achieved by administering a loading dose based upon projected peak digoxin body stores (e.g., body stores of 8 to 12 mcg per kg of body weight in patients with heart failure and normal sinus rhythm; 6 to 10 mcg per kg of body weight for patients with renal insufficiency): Oral, roughly one half the total loading dose given as the first dose, with the remaining portion divided and administered every six to eight hours (e.g., 500 to 750 mcg [0.5 to 0.75 mg] initially, followed by 125 to 375 mcg [0.125 to 0.375 mg] administered every six to eight hours) until an appropriate clinical response is achieved. Before each additional dose is given, the patient's clinical response should be assessed carefully. If the patient's clinical response requires a change from the calculated loading dose of digoxin, calculation of the maintenance dose should be based upon the amount actually given. For a 70-kg patient to achieve 8 to 12 mcg per kg of body weight peak body stores, the usual amount administered is 750 to 1250 mcg (0.75 to 1.25 mg).

Slow digitalization is achieved by beginning an appropriate maintenance dose (allowing digoxin body stores to accumulate slowly) and will be achieved in approximately five half-lives. Depending upon the patient's renal function, digitalization by this method will take between one and three weeks.

Maintenance—
Digoxin maintenance doses for estimated peak body stores of 10 mcg per kg of body weight generally have ranged from 62.5 to 500 mcg (0.0625 to 0.5 mg), administered orally as one or two doses per day, the dosage titrated according to the patient's

age, lean body weight, and renal function. In patients digitalized with a loading dose, the subsequent maintenance dose can be calculated as a percentage of the loading dose. Doses may be increased every two weeks according to clinical response. Therapy is generally initiated at the following doses:

For patients up to 70 years of age:

Oral, 250 mcg (0.25 mg) once a day.

For patients 70 years of age and older or with impaired renal function:

Oral, 125 mcg (0.125 mg) once a day.

For patients with marked impaired renal function:

Oral, 62.5 mcg (0.0625 mg) once a day.

Atrial fibrillation, chronic—

Doses should be titrated to the minimum dose that achieves the desired ventricular rate control without causing undesirable side effects.

Usual pediatric dose

Congestive heart failure—

Beyond the immediate newborn period, children generally require proportionally larger doses than adults on the basis of body weight or body surface area. Children older than 10 years of age require adult dosages in proportion to their body weight. Some researchers have suggested that infants and young children tolerate slightly higher serum digoxin concentrations than do adults. For digitalization dosing of infants and children, see *Digoxin Elixir USP* or *Digoxin Injection USP*. The following daily maintenance doses are based on average patient response for children with normal renal function. Divided daily dosing is recommended for children up to 10 years of age:

Maintenance—

Children 2 to 5 years of age:

Oral, 10 to 15 mcg (0.01 to 0.015 mg) per kg of body weight.

Children 5 to 10 years of age:

Oral, 7 to 10 mcg (0.007 to 0.01 mg) per kg of body weight.

Children 10 years of age and older:

Oral, 3 to 5 mcg (0.003 to 0.005 mg) per kg of body weight.

Strength(s) usually available

U.S.—

125 mcg (0.125 mg) (Rx) [*Lanoxin* (scored); GENERIC].

250 mcg (0.25 mg) (Rx) [*Lanoxin* (scored); GENERIC].

Canada—

62.5 mcg (0.0625 mg) (Rx) [*Lanoxin;* GENERIC].

125 mcg (0.125 mg) (Rx) [*Lanoxin* (scored); GENERIC].

250 mcg (0.25 mg) (Rx) [*Lanoxin* (scored); *Novo-Digoxin;* GENERIC].

Packaging and storage

Store between 15 and 25 °C (59 and 77 °F). Store in a tight container and protect from light.

Auxiliary labeling

- Keep out of reach of children.
- Do not take other medicines without advice from your doctor.

Caution

The small, white tablets of digoxin 0.25 mg have been confused by numerous patients with other, similar-looking medications such as furosemide, with resultant serious dosage accidents. To reduce this hazard, the dispenser may:

- check with the prescriber; suggest digoxin capsules be used instead of tablets.
- caution the patient about the potential hazard.
- apply auxiliary "Heart medicine" labels to digoxin tablet container.
- use containers of different size or appearance for similar-looking medications.
- suggest that patient not use tablets from both containers at same time.
- suggest that patient never transfer digoxin from original to other containers.
- suggest that patient use separate storage areas for medications that look alike.

Parenteral Dosage Forms

DIGOXIN INJECTION USP

Note: It is recommended that digoxin injection be administered intravenously, slowly, over a period of five minutes or longer. Rapid or bolus intravenous administration has been associated with systemic and coronary arteriolar constriction and is not recommended. Intramuscular administration of digoxin injection also is not recommended because it can cause severe pain at the injection site. If digoxin must be administered by the intramuscular route, it should be injected deep into the muscle, followed by massage. No more than 2 mL should be injected into a single site. Digoxin should not be mixed with other medications in the same container or simultaneously administered in the same intravenous line.

For equivalent doses for switching from the intravenous dosage form to the oral capsule, elixir, or tablet dosage forms, see *Bioequivalence information* section.

Usual adult dose

Congestive heart failure—

Rapid digitalization is achieved by administering a loading dose based upon projected peak digoxin body stores (e.g., body stores of 8 to 12 mcg per kg of body weight in patients with heart failure and normal sinus rhythm; 6 to 10 mcg per kg for patients with renal insufficiency). Roughly one half the total loading dose should be given intravenously as the first dose, with the remaining portion divided and administered every six to eight hours (e.g., 400 to 600 mcg [0.4 to 0.6 mg] initially, followed by 100 to 300 mcg [0.1 to 0.3 mg] administered every six to eight hours) until an appropriate clinical response is achieved. Before each additional dose is given, the patient's clinical response should be assessed carefully. If the patient's clinical response requires a change from the calculated loading dose of digoxin, calculation of the maintenance dose should be based upon the amount actually given. For a 70-kg patient to achieve 8 to 12 mcg per kg of body weight peak body stores, the usual amount administered is 600 to 1000 mcg (0.6 to 1 mg).

Slow digitalization is achieved by beginning an appropriate maintenance dose (allowing digoxin body stores to accumulate slowly) and will be achieved in approximately five half-lives. Depending upon the patient's renal function, digitalization by this method will take between one and three weeks.

Maintenance—

Digoxin injection maintenance doses required for estimated peak body stores of 10 mcg per kg of body weight generally have ranged from 75 mcg to 350 mcg (0.075 to 0.35 mg), administered once a day, the dose titrated according to the patient's age, lean body weight, and renal function. In patients digitalized with a loading dose, the subsequent maintenance dose can be calculated as a percentage of the loading dose. Doses may be increased every two weeks according to response.

Atrial fibrillation, chronic—

Doses should be titrated to the minimum dose that achieves the desired ventricular rate control without causing undesirable side effects.

Usual pediatric dose

Congestive heart failure—

In newborns, digoxin renal clearance is decreased (especially in premature infants) and digoxin doses should be adjusted accordingly. Beyond the immediate newborn period, children generally require proportionally larger doses than adults on the basis of body weight or body surface area. Children older than 10 years of age require adult dosages in proportion to their body weight. Some researchers have suggested that infants and young children tolerate slightly higher serum digoxin concentrations than do adults.

Digitalization—

The following total amounts *divided* into three or more doses, with the initial portion representing approximately one half the total, doses then being administered every four to eight hours, with careful assessment of clinical response before each additional dose. If the patient's clinical response requires a change from the calculated loading dose of digoxin, the calculation of the maintenance dose should be based upon the amount actually given.

Premature infants:

Intravenous, 15 to 25 mcg (0.015 to 0.025 mg) per kg of body weight.

Full-term infants:

Intravenous, 20 to 30 mcg (0.02 to 0.03 mg) per kg of body weight.

Infants 1 month to 2 years of age:

Intravenous, 30 to 50 mcg (0.03 to 0.05 mg) per kg of body weight.

Children 2 to 5 years of age:

Intravenous, 25 to 35 mcg (0.025 to 0.035 mg) per kg of body weight.

Children 5 to 10 years of age:

Intravenous, 15 to 30 mcg (0.015 to 0.03 mg) per kg of body weight.

Children 10 years of age and older:

Intravenous, 8 to 12 mcg (0.008 to 0.012 mg) per kg of body weight.

Maintenance (begun within twenty-four hours after digitalization)—
Premature infants:
Intravenous, 20 to 30% of the total digitalizing dose, divided and administered in two or three equal portions per day.

Full-term infants and older children:
Intravenous, 25 to 35% of the total digitalizing dose, divided and administered in two or three equal portions per day.

Strength(s) usually available
U.S.—
100 mcg (0.1 mg) per mL (Rx) [*Lanoxin Injection Pediatric* (alcohol 10%)].
250 mcg (0.25 mg) per mL (Rx) [*Lanoxin Injection* (alcohol 10%); GENERIC].

Canada—
50 mcg (0.05 mg) per mL (Rx) [*Lanoxin Pediatric Injection* (alcohol 10%); GENERIC].
250 mcg (0.25 mg) per mL (Rx) [*Lanoxin Injection* (alcohol 10%); GENERIC].

Packaging and storage
Store between 15 and 25 °C (59 and 77 °F). Protect from freezing and protect from light.

Preparation of dosage form
Digoxin Injection USP may be administered undiluted or may be diluted with a fourfold or greater volume (to reduce the risk of precipitation) of sterile water for injection, 0.9% sodium chloride injection, or 5% dextrose injection for intravenous administration.

Stability
Do not use if markedly discolored or if a precipitate is present. Immediate use of diluted Digoxin Injection USP is recommended.

Selected Bibliography
Epstein FH. Digitalis: mechanisms of action and clinical use. N Engl J Med 1988 Feb 11; 318: 358-65.

Revised: 03/15/1999

DIGITOXIN—See *Digitalis Glycosides (Systemic)*

DIGOXIN—See *Digitalis Glycosides (Systemic)*

DIGOXIN IMMUNE FAB (Ovine) Systemic

VA CLASSIFICATION (Primary): AD900

Commonly used brand name(s): *Digibind*.

Note: For a listing of dosage forms and brand names by country availability, see *Dosage Forms* section(s).

Category
Antidote, to digitalis glycoside toxicity.

Indications
Accepted
Toxicity, digitalis glycoside (treatment)—Digoxin immune Fab (ovine) is indicated for treatment of potentially life-threatening digoxin or digitoxin overdose (i.e., with severe arrhythmias or hyperkalemia).

Pharmacology/Pharmacokinetics
Physicochemical characteristics
Source—Produced by a process involving immunization of sheep with digoxin that has been coupled as a hapten to human serum albumin, to stimulate production of digoxin-specific antibodies. After papain digestion of the antibody, digoxin-specific antigen binding (Fab) fragments (molecular weight 46,200 daltons) are isolated and purified by affinity chromatography.

Molecular weight—46,200.

Mechanism of action/Effect
Preferentially binds molecules of digoxin or digitoxin, and the complex is then excreted by the kidneys. As free serum digoxin is removed, tissue-bound digoxin is also released into the serum to maintain the equilibrium and is bound and removed by digoxin immune Fab. The net result is a reduction in serum and tissue digoxin.

Half-life
15 to 20 hours.

Onset of action
Reduction of free active serum digoxin or digitoxin—Less than 1 minute.

Improvement in signs and symptoms of digitalis toxicity—15 to 30 minutes after administration (reversal of inotropic effect is usually slower than reversal of arrhythmias and hyperkalemia and may take several hours).

Elimination
Renal.

Precautions to Consider
Cross-sensitivity and/or related problems
Patients sensitive to sheep or any product of ovine origin may be sensitive to digoxin immune Fab (ovine) also.

Carcinogenicity
Studies have not been done in either animals or humans.

Pregnancy/Reproduction
Pregnancy—Studies have not been done in humans.

Studies have not been done in animals.

FDA Pregnancy Category C.

Breast-feeding
It is not known whether digoxin immune Fab (ovine) passes into breast milk. Problems in humans have not been documented.

Pediatrics
Studies performed to date have not demonstrated pediatrics-specific problems that would limit the usefulness of digoxin immune Fab (ovine) in children.

Geriatrics
No information is available on the relationship of age to the effects of digoxin immune Fab (ovine) in geriatric patients. However, elderly patients are more likely to have age-related renal function impairment, which may require caution in patients receiving this medication.

Laboratory value alterations
The following have been selected on the basis of their potential clinical significance (possible effect in parentheses where appropriate)—not necessarily inclusive (» = major clinical significance).

With diagnostic test results
Digitalis concentration determinations by immunoassay
(may be interfered with)

With physiology/laboratory test values
Digoxin or digitoxin concentrations, serum
(free active concentrations rapidly fall to undetectable levels)
(total serum concentrations rise suddenly after administration of Fab antibody but are almost totally bound to the Fab fragment and are inactive; these concentrations decline to undetectable levels several days later as Fab-digoxin complexes are excreted)

Potassium concentrations, serum
(may decrease rapidly from high concentrations associated with digitalis toxicity)

Medical considerations/Contraindications
The medical considerations/contraindications included have been selected on the basis of their potential clinical significance (reasons given in parentheses where appropriate)—not necessarily inclusive (» = major clinical significance).

Risk-benefit should be considered when the following medical problems exist:

Allergy, history of
(risk of allergic reaction to Fab antibody may be increased)

Renal function impairment
(elimination of Fab-digoxin complexes may be delayed since the complex is eliminated renally. In patients who are functionally anephric, glomerular filtration and renal excretion would not be expected to occur; instead, the complex may be eliminated by the reticuloendothelial system; because it is not clear whether reintoxication would result, prolonged monitoring for digitalis toxicity is recommended in these patients)

» Sensitivity to digoxin immune Fab (ovine)

Patient monitoring

The following may be especially important in patient monitoring (other tests may be warranted in some patients, depending on condition; » = major clinical significance):

Body temperature and
Electrocardiogram (ECG)
(monitoring recommended during treatment)

» Digoxin or digitoxin concentrations, serum
(recommended prior to administration of Fab antibody to aid in dosage calculation, but not useful for at least 5 to 7 days after Fab antibody treatment is begun because of interference by the antibody with the test)

» Potassium concentrations, serum
(recommended at frequent intervals during treatment; hypokalemia should be treated promptly)

Side/Adverse Effects

Allergic or febrile reactions to digoxin immune Fab (ovine) have been reported rarely. Patients previously treated with the product or allergic to ovine proteins appear to be especially at risk.

Side/adverse effects are related more to withdrawal of digitalis effects than to a direct effect of the antibody fragment. Low cardiac output, including congestive heart failure, may be exacerbated as a result of withdrawal of the inotropic effects of digitalis. Ventricular rate may increase as a result of withdrawal of digitalis being used for atrial fibrillation. Hypokalemia may occur as elevated serum potassium concentrations fall rapidly.

General Dosing Information

It is recommended that equipment and medications necessary for cardiopulmonary resuscitation be immediately available during administration of digoxin immune Fab (ovine). If necessary, in patients who respond poorly to withdrawal of digoxin's inotropic effect, other intravenous inotropes such as dopamine or dobutamine or cardiac load–reducing agents may be used. Caution is necessary in use of catecholamines because of the risk of aggravation of digitalis toxicity–associated arrhythmias.

Skin-testing for allergy to digoxin immune Fab (ovine) may be performed prior to administration in high-risk patients (i.e., those previously treated with the Fab antibody or with known allergy, especially to sheep proteins). One of two methods may be used:
- Intradermal test: Dilute 0.1 mL of the reconstituted solution (containing 9.5 mg of the Fab antibody per mL) in 9.9 mL of 0.9% sodium chloride injection to produce 10 mL of a solution containing 95 mcg (0.095 mg) per mL; then inject 0.1 mL (9.5 mcg or 0.0095 mg) intradermally. After 20 minutes, inspect the injection site for presence of an urticarial wheal surrounded by a zone of erythema.
- Scratch test: Dilute 0.1 mL of the reconstituted solution (containing 9.5 mg of the Fab antibody per mL) in 9.9 mL of 0.9% sodium chloride injection to produce 10 mL of a solution containing 95 mcg (0.095 mg) per mL; then place 1 drop of the solution on the skin and make a ¼-inch scratch through the drop with a sterile needle. After 20 minutes, inspect the site for presence of an urticarial wheal surrounded by a zone of erythema.
- If a positive skin test occurs, use of digoxin immune Fab (ovine) should be avoided unless absolutely necessary.
- If a systemic reaction occurs, measures to treat anaphylaxis should be used.

After reconstitution, digoxin immune Fab (ovine) is administered by intravenous infusion, through a 0.22-micron membrane filter, over 30 minutes. However, it may be given by rapid direct intravenous injection if cardiac arrest is imminent.

Redigitalization of the patient, if necessary, should be delayed until elimination of Fab fragments from the body is complete, usually after several days but may be up to a week or longer in patients with renal function impairment.

Parenteral Dosage Forms

DIGOXIN IMMUNE FAB (OVINE) FOR INJECTION

Usual adult and adolescent dose

Antidote, to digitalis glycoside toxicity—
Intravenous, in an amount equimolar to the amount of digoxin or digitoxin in the patient's body (total body load [TBL]). A dose of 38 mg of digoxin immune Fab (ovine) binds approximately 0.5 mg of digoxin or digitoxin.

Dosage may be calculated using one of the following formulas:

Table 1. Approximate dose of digoxin immune Fab (ovine) when amount of digoxin ingested is known.

Number of digoxin tablets or capsules ingested*	Dose of digoxin immune Fab (ovine)	
	mg	Number of 38-mg vials
25	380	10
50	760	20
75	1140	30
100	1520	40
150	2280	60
200	3040	80

*0.25-mg tablets with 80% bioavailability, or 0.2-mg capsules.

1) Based on dose of digoxin or digitoxin ingested—
For digoxin tablets, oral solution, or intramuscular injection:
Dose (mg) = (Dose ingested [mg] × 0.8)/0.5 × 38

For digitoxin tablets, digoxin capsules, or intravenous injection of digoxin or digitoxin:
Dose (mg) = [Dose ingested (mg)/0.5] × 38

Table 2. Approximate *adult and adolescent* dose *(number of 38-mg vials)* of digoxin immune Fab (ovine) when serum digoxin concentration (SDC) is known.

SDC (ng/mL)	Patient weight (kg)				
	40	60	70	80	100
1	0.5	0.5	1	1	1
2	1	1	2	2	2
4	2	3	3	3	4
8	3	5	6	7	8
12	5	7	9	10	12
16	7	10	11	13	16
20	8	12	14	16	20

2) Based on steady-state serum digoxin or digitoxin concentration (SDC)—
For digoxin:
Dose (mg) = (SDC [nanograms/mL] × body weight [kg])/100 × 38

For digitoxin:
Dose (mg) = (SDC [nanograms/mL] × body weight [kg])/1000 × 38

Table 2. Approximate *adult and adolescent* dose *(number of 38-mg vials)* of digoxin immune Fab (ovine) when serum digoxin concentration (SDC) is known.

Note: Dosage of digoxin immune Fab (ovine) is approximate, since total body digitalis load can be difficult to estimate. After the initial dose, need for and amount of additional dosing should be determined using clinical judgment.

If neither an estimated ingestion amount of digitalis nor the SDC is available, 760 mg of digoxin immune Fab (ovine) may be administered, which will be adequate to treat most life-threatening ingestions.

Usual pediatric dose

See *Usual adult and adolescent dose* (including Note).

Note: In small children, monitoring for volume overload is important.

For infants, who can have much smaller dosage requirements, it is recommended that digoxin immune Fab (ovine) be reconstituted as directed and administered with a tuberculin syringe. For very small doses, a reconstituted 38-mg vial can be diluted with 34 mL of 0.9% sodium chloride injection to produce a solution containing 1 mg per mL.

For approximate dose when amount of digoxin ingested is known, see *Usual adult and adolescent dose— Table 1*.

Table 3. Approximate *pediatric* dose *(mg)* of digoxin immune Fab (ovine) when serum digoxin concentration (SDC) is known.

SDC (ng/mL)	Patient weight (kg)				
	1	3	5	10	20
1	0.4	1	2	4	8
2	1	2	4	8	15
4	1.5	5	8	15	30
8	3	9	15	30	61
12	5	14	23	46	91
16	6	18	30	61	122
20	8	23	38	76	152

Strength(s) usually available

U.S.—
38 mg (Rx) [*Digibind* (preservative-free)].

Canada—
38 mg (Rx) [*Digibind* (preservative-free)].

Packaging and storage

Store between 2 and 8 °C (36 and 46 °F). Unreconstituted vials may be stored at up to 30 °C (86 °F) for up to 30 days.

Preparation of dosage form

Digoxin immune Fab (ovine) for injection is reconstituted for intravenous administration by dissolving 38 mg in 4 mL of sterile water for injection and mixing gently, to produce a solution containing 9.5 mg per mL. The resulting solution may be further diluted with 0.9% sodium chloride injection to a convenient volume for administration by intravenous infusion.

Stability

Reconstituted solution should be used immediately, but may be stored for up to 4 hours between 2 and 8 °C (36 and 46 °F).

Selected Bibliography

Stolshek BS, Osterhout SK, Dunham G. The role of digoxin-specific antibodies in the treatment of digitalis poisoning. Med Toxicol 1988; 3: 167-71.

Antman EM, Wenger TL, Butler VP, Haber E, Smith TW. Treatment of 150 cases of life-threatening digitalis intoxication with digoxin-specific Fab antibody fragments. Circulation 1990; 81: 1744-52.

Hickey AR, Wenger TL, Carpenter V, et al. Digoxin immune Fab therapy in the management of digitalis intoxication: safety and efficacy results of an observational study. J Am Coll Cardiol 1991; 17: 590-8.

Revised: 08/17/1995

DIHYDROERGOTAMINE—See *Vascular Headache Suppressants, Ergot Derivative–containing (Systemic)*

DIHYDROERGOTAMINE Nasal-Systemic

JAN: Dihydroergotamine Mesilate.

VA CLASSIFICATION (Primary): CN105

Note: For a listing of dosage forms and brand names by country availability, see *Dosage Forms* section(s).

Category

Antimigraine agent.

Indications

Accepted

Headache, migraine (treatment)—Intranasal dihydroergotamine is indicated to relieve (abort) acute migraine headaches (with or without aura).

Unaccepted

Intranasal dihydroergotamine is not recommended for treatment of basilar artery migraine or hemiplegic migraine.

Pharmacology/Pharmacokinetics

Physicochemical characteristics

Source—Synthetic.

Molecular weight—679.8.

Mechanism of action/Effect

Dihydroergotamine is an ergot derivative that interacts with several neurotransmitter receptors, including alpha-adrenergic, serotonergic (tryptaminergic), and dopaminergic receptors. The dihydroergotamine- induced decreases in the firing of serotonergic (5-hydroxytryptaminergic, 5-HT) neurons may be responsible for relief of migraine headache. Specifically, it is thought that agonist activity at the 5-HT_{1D} receptor subtype provides relief of acute headache. It has been proposed that constriction of cerebral blood vessels by the ergot derivative (resulting from alpha-adrenergic stimulation as well as from activity at 5-HT receptors) reduces the pulsation in cerebral arteries that may be responsible for the pain of migraine headaches. It has also been proposed that dihydroergotamine may relieve vascular headaches by decreasing the release of pro-inflammatory neuropeptide release.

Other actions/effects

Dihydroergotamine stimulates uterine smooth muscle.

Absorption

Following intranasal administration, the bioavailability of dihydroergotamine is 32%. The rate of absorption of intranasal dihydroergotamine demonstrates interpatient variability, which may be dependent on the administration technique.

Protein binding

Very high (93%).

Biotransformation

Hepatic; extensive. The principal metabolite, 8′-hydroxy-dihydroergotamine, is pharmacologically active. Following intranasal administration of dihydroergotamine, the metabolites represent 20 to 30% of the area under the plasma concentration-time curve (AUC).

Half-life

Approximately 10 hours.

Elimination

Primarily fecal (biliary). Following intranasal administration of dihydroergotamine, 2% of the dose is excreted in the urine.

Precautions to Consider

Carcinogenicity

Long-term studies in mice and rabbits are currently being done to evaluate the carcinogenic potential of dihydroergotamine.

Mutagenicity

Dihydroergotamine demonstrated no mutagenic effects in presence or absence of metabolic activation in the Ames test or the *in vitro* mammalian Chinese hamster gene mutation assays, or in the rat hepatocyte unscheduled DNA synthesis test assay. There was evidence of clastogenic activity in the V79 Chinese hamster cell assay with metabolic activation and the cultured human peripheral blood lymphocyte *in vitro* chromosomal aberration assays. However, there was no evidence of clastogenic activity in the *in vivo* mouse and hamster micronucleus tests.

Pregnancy/Reproduction

Fertility—There was no evidence of impairment of fertility in rats receiving doses of intranasal dihydroergotamine of up to 1.6 mg per kg of body weight (mg/kg) per day (area under the plasma concentration-time curve [AUC] exposure approximately 9 to 11 times the maximum recommended human dose [MRHD]).

Pregnancy—Adequate and well-controlled studies in humans have not been done. However, **use during pregnancy is contraindicated** because of intranasal dihydroergotamine's oxytocic activity, which may result in fetal harm. Therefore, if intranasal dihydroergotamine should be used by a pregnant woman, or if a woman becomes pregnant during treatment, she should be advised that this medication may harm the fetus.

An embryofetal developmental study during the organogenesis period in pregnant rabbits showed that intranasal dihydroergotamine doses of up to 0.16 mg per day or greater (AUC exposure approximately 0.4 to 1.2 times the exposure in humans receiving the MRHD) resulted in decreased fetal body weight and/or skeletal ossification. In rabbits receiving doses of intranasal dihydroergotamine of up to 3.6 mg per day during the organogenesis period (equivalent to maternal concentration of approximately 7 times the MRHD), a delay in skeletal ossification was observed in the fetuses. However, in rabbits receiving doses of up to 1.2 mg per day (equivalent to maternal concentrations of 2.5 times the MRHD), no delay in ossification was observed. In female rats receiving doses of intranasal dihydroergotamine of up to 0.16 mg per day or greater during pregnancy and lactation, decreased body weights and impaired reproductive function were observed in the offspring. Intranasal dihydroergotamine doses that produced developmental effects in these studies were below those that demonstrated evidence of any maternal toxicity. In addition, the prolonged vasoconstriction of the uterine vessels and/or increased myometrial tone resulted in a reduction in the uteroplacental blood flow, which is presumed to be the cause for dihydroergotamine-induced intrauterine growth retardation.

FDA Pregnancy Category X.

Breast-feeding

It is expected that intranasal dihydroergotamine would be distributed into human breast milk. However, there is currently no data on the concentration of dihydroergotamine distributed into human breast milk.

Ergot alkaloids are distributed into human breast milk and have the potential to cause adverse effects, such as vomiting, diarrhea, weak pulse, and unstable blood pressure. These medications may also inhibit lactation.

Due to intranasal dihydroergotamine's potential to cause serious adverse effects, use of this medicine is not recommended for nursing mothers.

Pediatrics
No information is available on the relationship of age to the effects of intranasal dihydroergotamine in pediatric patients. Safety and efficacy have not been established.

Geriatrics
No information is available on the relationship of age to the effects of intranasal dihydroergotamine in geriatric patients.

Drug interactions and/or related problems
The following drug interactions and/or related problems have been selected on the basis of their potential clinical significance (possible mechanism in parentheses where appropriate)—not necessarily inclusive (» = major clinical significance):

Note: Combinations containing any of the following medications, depending on the amount present, may also interact with this medication.

Antibiotics, macrolide, especially, such as:
Erythromycin
Troleandomycin
(these antibiotics may inhibit the metabolism of intranasal dihydroergotamine and increase the risk of vasospasm)

Beta-adrenergic blocking agents
(these medications may potentiate vasoconstriction)

» Ergot alkaloids, other or
» Vasoconstictors, systemic, other, such as:
Cocaine
Epinephrine, parenteral
Metaraminol
Methoxamine
Norepinephrine
Phenylephrine, parenteral
(concurrent use with intranasal dihydroergotamine may result in additive increases of blood pressure)

» 5-hydroxytryptamine agonists, such as:
Sumatriptan
(a delay of 24 hours between administration of sumatriptan and intranasal dihydroergotamine is recommended because of the possibility of additive and/or prolonged vasoconstriction)

Nicotine
(this medication may potentiate vasoconstriction)

Medical considerations/Contraindications
The medical considerations/contraindications included have been selected on the basis of their potential clinical significance (reasons given in parentheses where appropriate)—not necessarily inclusive (» = major clinical significance).

Except under special circumstances, this medication should not be used when the following medical problems exist:

» Coronary artery disease, especially:
Angina pectoris or
Myocardial infarction, history of or
Myocardial ischemia, silent, documented or
Prinzmetal's angina or
» Other conditions in which coronary vasoconstriction would be detrimental
(intranasal dihydroergotamine may cause coronary vasospasms)
» Hepatic function impairment, severe
» Hypertension, severe, uncontrolled
(may be exacerbated)
» Renal function impairment, severe
» Vascular surgery

Risk-benefit should be considered when the following medical problems exist:

Coronary artery disease, predisposition to
(intranasal dihydroergotamine may cause serious coronary adverse effects; patients in whom coronary artery disease is a possibility on the basis of age or the presence of other risk factors, such as diabetes, hypercholesterolemia, obesity, a strong family history of coronary artery disease, or tobacco smoking, should be evaluated for the presence of cardiovascular disease before intranasal dihydroergotamine is prescribed; even after a satisfactory evaluation, the advisability of administering the patient's first dose under medical supervision should be considered)

Hypersensitivity to ergot alkaloids
Hypertension, controlled
(may precipitate an increase in blood pressure)
» Sepsis

Patient monitoring
The following may be especially important in patient monitoring (other tests may be warranted in some patients, depending on condition; » = major clinical significance):

Electrocardiogram (ECG)
(monitoring is recommended for long-term intermittent users of intranasal dihydroergotamine)

Side/Adverse Effects
The following side/adverse effects have been selected on the basis of their potential clinical significance (possible signs and symptoms in parentheses where appropriate)—not necessarily inclusive:

Those indicating need for medical attention
Incidence less frequent or rare

Cardiovascular effects, including angina pectoris; arrythmias (irregular heartbeat); ***coronary vasospasm–induced*** (chest pain); ***myocardial infarction or ischemia*** (feeling of heaviness in chest; pain in back, chest, or left arm; shortness of breath or troubled breathing); ***peripheral ischemia*** (itching of skin; numbness and tingling of face, fingers, or toes; pain in arms legs, or lower back, especially pain in calves and/or heels upon exertion; pale, bluish-colored, or cold hands or feet; weak or absent pulses in legs); ***upper respiratory tract infection*** (cough, fever, sneezing, or sore throat)

Those indicating need for medical attention only if they continue or are bothersome
Incidence more frequent

Asthenia (unusual tiredness or weakness); ***diarrhea; dizziness; dry mouth; fatigue*** (unusual feeling of tiredness); ***hot flashes*** (sudden sweatings and feelings of warmth); ***irritation in the nose*** (burning or tingling sensation, dryness, soreness or pain in the nose; runny and/or stuffy nose; unexplained nosebleeds); ***increased sweating; muscle stiffness; nausea and/or vomiting; paresthesia*** (sensation of burning, warmth, heat, numbness, tightness, or tingling); ***pharyngitis*** (sore throat); ***sinusitis*** (runny or stuffy nose; headache); ***somnolence*** (sleepiness); ***taste perversion*** (change in sense of taste)

Note: *Irritation in the nose* was found to be mild to moderate. In most cases, the symptoms resolved within four hours of the administration of intranasal dihydroergotamine.

Incidence less frequent or rare

Anorexia (decreased appetite); ***bronchitis*** (congestion in chest; cough; difficult and/or painful breathing); ***central nervous system (CNS) effects, including anxiety; confusion; depression; euphoria*** (unusual feeling of well being); ***insomnia*** (trouble in sleeping); ***nervousness; cold, clammy skin; dyspepsia*** (heartburn); ***dysphagia*** (difficulty swallowing); ***dyspnea*** (shortness of breath); ***edema*** (swelling of face, fingers, feet or lower legs); ***ear pain; eye problems, including blurred vision; conjunctivitis*** (red or irritated eyes); ***eye pain; increased watering of the eyes; fever; hypotension*** (dizziness or lightheadedness when getting up from a lying or sitting position; sudden fainting); ***increased salivation*** (increased watering of the mouth); ***increased yawning; palpitations*** (pounding heartbeat); ***pruritus*** (itching of the skin); ***muscle weakness; petechia*** (pinpoint red spots on skin); ***skin rash; tinnitus*** (ringing or buzzing in the ears); ***stomach pain; tremors*** (trembling or shaking of hands or feet)

Overdose
For more information on the management of overdose or unintentional ingestion, **contact a Poison Control Center** (see *Poison Control Center Listing*).

Clinical effects of overdose
The following effects have been selected on the basis of their potential clinical significance (possible signs and symptoms in parentheses where appropriate)—not necessarily inclusive:

Acute and/or chronic

Confusion; convulsions; delirium; hypertension (dizziness; headaches, severe or continuing; increase in blood pressure); ***nausea and/or vomiting; numbness, tingling, and/or pain in the legs or arms; respiratory depression*** (shortness of breath); ***stomach pain***

Treatment of overdose
Specific treatment—

For peripheral vasospasm: Warmth should be applied to ischemic extremities. If necessary a vasodilator may be administered. Nursing measures designed to prevent tissue damage should be instituted.

Supportive care—

Patients in whom intentional overdose is confirmed or suspected should be referred for psychiatric consultation.

Patient Consultation
As an aid to patient consultation, refer to *Advice for the Patient, Dihydroergotamine (Nasal-Systemic)*.

In providing consultation, consider emphasizing the following selected information (» = major clinical significance):

Before using this medication

» Conditions affecting use, especially:
Hypersensitivity to ergot alkaloids
Pregnancy—Use of intranasal dihydroergotamine is contraindicated during pregnancy because of its potential oxytocic activity, which may result in fetal harm
Breast-feeding—Use of intranasal dihydroergotamine is not recommended for nursing mothers. Intranasal dihydroergotamine may be distributed into breast milk and cause adverse effects, such as vomiting, diarrhea, weak pulse, unstable blood pressure, seizures in the infant. Also, intranasal dihydroergotamine may inhibit lactation
Other medications, especially 5-hydroxytryptamine agonists and vasoconstrictors
Other medical problems, especially coronary artery disease, or other conditions that may be adversely affected by coronary artery constriction; hypertension, severe, uncontrolled

Proper use of this medication

» Proper administration technique; reading patient directions carefully before use
» Not administering if atypical headache symptoms are present; checking with physician instead
» Administering after onset of headache pain
Additional benefit may be obtained if the patient lies down in a quiet, dark room after administering medication
Using additional doses, if needed, for return of migraine headache after initial relief was obtained, provided that prescribed limits (quantity used and frequency of administration) are not exceeded
Compliance with prophylactic therapy, if prescribed
» Proper dosing
» Proper storage

Precautions while using this medication

Avoiding alcohol, which aggravates headache
Caution when driving or doing anything else requiring alertness because of possible drowsiness, dizziness, lightheadedness, impairment of physical or mental abilities

Side/adverse effects

Signs of potential side effects, especially cardiovascular effects, peripheral ischemia, or upper respiratory tract infection

Nasal Dosage Form

DIHYDROERGOTAMINE MESYLATE NASAL SOLUTION USP

Usual adult dose

Antimigraine agent—
Nasal, 0.5 mg (one spray) in each nostril. Followed by another 0.5 mg (one spray) dose in each nostril fifteen minutes later.

Usual adult prescribing limits

Nasal, 3 mg (6 sprays) per day; or 4 mg (8 sprays) per week.

Usual pediatric dose

Safety and efficacy have not been established in patients younger than 18 years of age.

Usual geriatric dose

See *Usual adult dose.*

Strength(s) usually available

U.S.—
0.5 mg per metered spray (Rx) [*Migranal* (caffeine; dextrose; carbon dioxide)].

Packaging and storage

Store below 25 °C (77 °F).

Developed: 07/08/1998

DIHYDROTACHYSTEROL—See *Vitamin D and Analogs (Systemic)*

DIHYDROXYALUMINUM AMINOACETATE—See *Antacids (Oral-Local)*

DIHYDROXYALUMINUM SODIUM CARBONATE—See *Antacids (Oral-Local)*

DILTIAZEM—See *Calcium Channel Blocking Agents (Systemic)*

DIMENHYDRINATE—See *Antihistamines (Systemic)*

DINOPROSTONE Cervical/Vaginal

Note: This monograph contains information on both the dinoprostone vaginal suppositories and the vaginal system (a suppository within a retrieval device). Each may be inappropriately referred to as dinoprostone vaginal insert in other types of information. It is important to avoid confusing the two dosage forms, since each has a different use and strength.

VA CLASSIFICATION (Primary/Secondary): HS200/GU600; GU900

Commonly used brand name(s): *Cervidil; Prepidil; Prostin E_2.*

Some other commonly used names are prostaglandin E_2 or PGE_2.

Note: For a listing of dosage forms and brand names by country availability, see *Dosage Forms* section(s).

Category

Prostaglandin; oxytocic; abortifacient; antihemorrhagic (postabortion uterine bleeding; postpartum uterine bleeding).

Indications

Note: Bracketed information in the *Indications* section refers to uses that are not included in U.S. product labeling.

Accepted

Abortion, elective—Dinoprostone vaginal suppositories are used for aborting midtrimester pregnancy (from the twelfth through the twentieth week of gestation as calculated from the first day of the last normal menstrual period).

Abortion, missed (treatment) or
Abortion, therapeutic—Dinoprostone vaginal suppositories are indicated for evacuation of the uterine contents in management of missed abortion or for therapeutic abortion in cases of intrauterine fetal death up to 28 weeks of gestational age as calculated from the first day of the last normal menstrual period. Dinoprostone vaginal gel or suppository is not approved for use as an abortifacient in cases of intrauterine fetal death at more than 28 weeks' gestation because it is associated with an increased risk of uterine rupture. Confirmation of intrauterine fetal death should be made prior to use of dinoprostone for missed abortion or intrauterine fetal death.

Cervical ripening—Prior to induction of labor when medically indicated, dinoprostone cervical gel or dinoprostone vaginal system is used to initiate or continue ripening an unfavorable cervix in pregnant patients at or near term. The vaginal system is removed when active labor begins. [Extemporaneously prepared dinoprostone gels have also been used in cervical ripening prior to induction of labor and prior to abortion procedures, such as vacuum curettage] .

[Hemorrhage, postpartum (treatment)] or
[Hemorrhage, postabortion (treatment)]—Dinoprostone vaginal suppositories are used to reduce blood loss and correct uterine atony postpartum and postabortion in patients unresponsive to conventional treatment such as oxytocin, ergonovine, or methylergonovine.

Hydatidiform mole, benign (treatment)—Although vacuum curettage is preferred, dinoprostone vaginal suppositories are indicated for evacuation of the uterine contents in the treatment of nonmetastatic benign hydatidiform mole.

Labor, induction of—Dinoprostone vaginal gel is used for induction of labor at or near term.

Unaccepted

Dinoprostone vaginal suppository is not indicated for use to terminate a pregnancy of greater than 28 weeks gestation or when a fetus *in utero* has reached a stage of viability. Also, the vaginal suppository or vaginal gel should not be used for cervical ripening.

Pharmacology/Pharmacokinetics

Physicochemical characteristics

Description—
Dinoprostone vaginal system: The system includes a flat suppository contained within a retrieval device (polyester pouch with string). The suppository in the vaginal system (polyethylene oxide and ure-

thane copolymer) measures 29 mm by 9.5 mm with a thickness of 0.8 mm.

Chemical Group—Dinoprostone is the naturally occurring prostaglandin E_2.

Molecular weight—352.47.

Mechanism of action/Effect

For uterine stimulation—

Dinoprostone appears to act directly on the myometrium, but this has not been completely established. It stimulates myometrial contractions in the gravid uterus that are similar to the contractions that occur in the term uterus during natural labor. These contractions are usually sufficient to cause abortion. Uterine response to prostaglandins increases gradually throughout pregnancy. Dinoprostone does not act directly on the fetoplacental unit and is not considered a fetocidal agent.

For cervical ripening—

Dinoprostone softens the cervix and facilitates cervical dilation and effacement. Dinoprostone stimulates collagenase secretion, and thus reduces the collagen network within the cervix. By favorably changing the cervical score, dinoprostone reduces the number of failed inductions or instrumental deliveries, shortens the induction-to-delivery interval, and reduces the amount of oxytocin that may be needed. The dose of dinoprostone used locally to ripen the cervix is lower than that used to stimulate the uterus. Although not prominent with low local doses, uterine stimulation may occur with the dinoprostone vaginal system or cervical gel.

Other actions/effects

Dinoprostone stimulates the smooth muscle of the gastrointestinal tract. It may also cause bronchodilation or bronchoconstriction and vasodilation. Dinoprostone can elevate body temperature due to its effect on hypothalamic thermoregulation.

Absorption

Dinoprostone vaginal system for cervical ripening—Absorbed at a rate of 0.3 mg per hour over 12 hours while the vaginal system is in place. Systemic effects are seen rarely, although the systemic contributions of dinoprostone and its metabolites are difficult to assess due to the prostaglandins endogenously produced during labor.

Protein binding

73%, to albumin.

Biotransformation

Rapid metabolism of dinoprostone occurs primarily in the local tissues; any systemic absorption of the medication is cleared mainly in the maternal lungs and, secondarily, at sites such as the liver and kidneys.

Half-life

Less than 5 minutes.

Onset of action

Uterine stimulation—Contractions begin within 10 minutes following insertion of a dinoprostone vaginal suppository.

Time to peak effect

Uterine stimulation—The mean abortion time with dinoprostone is about 17 hours (range, 12 to 24 hours).

Duration of action

Uterine stimulation—Contractions persist for 2 to 6 hours following insertion of a 20-mg dinoprostone vaginal suppository.

Cervical ripening—Continues, while in place, for up to 12 hours per dinoprostone vaginal system. On removal, action lasts 2 to 13 minutes.

Elimination

Primarily renal as metabolites, with a small amount excreted in the feces.

Precautions to Consider

Cross-sensitivity and/or related problems

Patients hypersensitive to oxytocin or other oxytocics may be hypersensitive to dinoprostone, even when it is used only for cervical ripening. Also, patients allergic to other prostaglandins, such as misoprostol, may be allergic to dinoprostone.

Carcinogenicity

Studies have not been done in animals or humans on the carcinogenicity of dinoprostone.

Mutagenicity

The micronucleus test, Ames assay, and unscheduled DNA synthesis assay revealed no evidence of mutagenicity with dinoprostone.

Pregnancy/Reproduction

Pregnancy—Any pregnancy termination that fails with dinoprostone should be completed by another method.

Proliferation of bone has been reported with clinical use of prostaglandin E_1 during prolonged therapy. There is no evidence to date that the short-term use of dinoprostone (prostaglandin E_2) causes proliferation of bone in the fetus and is unlikely since it is administered after the period of organogenesis.

Although animal studies with dinoprostone did not reveal teratogenic properties, dinoprostone has been shown to be embryotoxic in rats and rabbits. In animal studies, prostaglandins of the E and F series have caused proliferation of bone with high doses.

FDA Pregnancy Category C.

Labor and delivery—Use of high doses may result in excessive uterine tone, causing decreased uterine blood flow and fetal distress.

Drug interactions and/or related problems

The following drug interactions and/or related problems have been selected on the basis of their potential clinical significance (possible mechanism in parentheses where appropriate)—not necessarily inclusive (» = major clinical significance):

» Oxytocin or other oxytocics

(concurrent or sequential use with dinoprostone potentiates the effects of endogenous and exogenous oxytocin and can produce uterine hypertonus, uterine rupture, cervical laceration, or fetal distress, especially in the absence of adequate cervical dilation. Although oxytocin is used sequentially with dinoprostone for therapeutic advantage, a delay between administering oxytocin and dinoprostone is recommended: oxytocin may be administered 30 minutes after removal of the dinoprostone vaginal system, 6 to 12 hours after insertion of cervical gel or vaginal suppository, or 12 to 24 hours after insertion of vaginal gel. The patient should be continuously monitored)

(dinoprostone should not be used for cervical ripening or uterine stimulation if the patient is already receiving oxytocin or any other oxytocic agent)

Laboratory value alterations

The following have been selected on the basis of their potential clinical significance (possible effect in parentheses where appropriate)—not necessarily inclusive (» = major clinical significance).

With physiology/laboratory test values

Blood pressure, maternal or
Heart rate, maternal or fetal

(may be decreased or increased, especially with large doses; a decrease in diastolic blood pressure of greater than 20 mm of Hg has been reported in approximately 10% of patients receiving dinoprostone)

Body temperature

(a temperature increase of greater than 1.1 °C [2 °F] usually occurs within 15 to 45 minutes following insertion of suppository; this effect has not been seen with the doses of the cervical gel used for cervical ripening. Body temperature returns to normal within 2 to 6 hours after discontinuation of medication or removal of suppository from vagina)

Medical considerations/Contraindications

The medical considerations/contraindications included have been selected on the basis of their potential clinical significance (reasons given in parentheses where appropriate)—not necessarily inclusive (» = major clinical significance).

Except under special circumstances, this medication should not be used when the following medical problems exist:

» Allergy to dinoprostone or other prostaglandin E_2 analogs, such as misoprostol

» Conditions that contraindicate vaginal delivery or induction of labor, including

Actively contracting or hypertonic uterus or
Cephalopelvic disproportion, significant or
Fetal distress without imminent delivery or
Fetal malpresentation or
Multiparity greater than six, history of or
Pelvic inflammatory disease, acute or
Uterine or vaginal bleeding, unexplained

(induction of labor, vaginal delivery, or prolonged contractions are not generally recommended)

Risk-benefit should be considered when the following medical problems exist:

Anemia, or history of

(increased incidence of excessive uterine bleeding postabortion or postpartum with use of dinoprostone in doses that induce cervical ripening or stimulate the uterus)

Asthma, or history of

(increased risk of bronchoconstriction when dinoprostone is used in doses that induce uterine stimulation, including use in patients with a history of childhood asthma without adult asthma)

» Cardiac disease, active, including Eisenmenger complex (when dinoprostone is used in doses that stimulate the uterus, a decrease in blood pressure and bradycardia may result in cardiovascular collapse and angina pectoris)

Cardiovascular disease, history of or
Hypertension, or history of or
Hypotension, history of or
Preeclampsia
(condition may be aggravated by possible vasoconstriction or decreased blood pressure; two cases of myocardial infarction have occurred in patients with a history of cardiovascular disease with use of dinoprostone in doses that stimulate the uterus)

Cervical stenosis or
Uterine surgery, history of
(increased risk of uterine rupture with use of dinoprostone in doses that stimulate the uterus)

Cervicitis or
Endocervical lesions, infected or
Vaginitis, acute
(in some cases, medically induced cervical ripening may increase risk of cervical injury or chronic cervicitis)

Epilepsy, or history of
(rarely, when used in doses that stimulate the uterus, dinoprostone has been reported to cause seizures in patients with epilepsy whose seizures were poorly controlled prior to its use)

Glaucoma
(increases in intraocular pressure and miosis have been reported rarely during the use of prostaglandins; dinoprostone may have similar effects when used in doses that stimulate the uterus)

Hepatic disease, active or
Renal disease, active
(metabolism and elimination of dinoprostone may be impaired, resulting in prolonged half-life)

» Hypersensitivity to dinoprostone or other oxytocics, history of or
Hypertonus, uterine, history of
(excessive dosage, use of dinoprostone in doses that stimulate the uterus, or, to a lesser extent, sequential use of dinoprostone with oxytocin at doses that induce cervical ripening may cause uterine hypertonicity with spasm and tetanic contraction that can lead to posterior cervical perforations, cervical lacerations, uterine rupture, and hemorrhage)

Pulmonary disease, active
(use of dinoprostone in doses that stimulate the uterus may decrease pulmonary blood flow and increase pulmonary arterial pressure)

Patient monitoring

The following may be especially important in patient monitoring (other tests may be warranted in some patients, depending on condition; » = major clinical significance):

Blood pressure, maternal and
Contractions, frequency, duration, and force of and
Heart rate, fetal and maternal and
Temperature, maternal and
Uterine tone
(monitoring of these parameters is recommended at frequent intervals during abortion procedure or labor and delivery; well-hydrating patient with an electrolyte solution counteracts the decreased peripheral-resistance and induced vasodilatation)
(continuous monitoring of uterine activity and fetal state is especially recommended for patients with known history of hypertonic contractility or tetanic uterine contractions)
(maternal temperature increases of greater than 2° F (1.1° C) occurs in 50% of patients 15 to 45 minutes after vaginal suppository administration and normalizes within 2 to 6 hours after therapy is discontinued; differentiation between endometritis pyrexia and dinoprostone-induced pyrexia should be considered)

Vaginal examination
(recommended prior to each dose and after delivery or abortion to monitor cervical response and to check for signs of cervical trauma)

Side/Adverse Effects

The following side/adverse effects have been selected on the basis of their potential clinical significance (possible signs and symptoms in parentheses where appropriate)—not necessarily inclusive:

Those indicating need for medical attention

Incidence less frequent or rare

Anaphylaxis, generalized (swelling of face, inside the nose, and eyelids; hives; shortness of breath; trouble in breathing; tightness in chest; wheezing); ***bradycardia*** (slow heartbeat); ***bronchoconstriction*** (wheezing; troubled breathing; tightness in chest)—especially in asthmatics; ***increased uterine pain accompanying abortion***—correlates with efficacy; ***peripheral vasoconstriction*** (pale, cool, or blotchy skin on arms or legs; weak or absent pulse in arms or legs)—possibly severe; ***substernal pressure or pain*** (pressing or painful feeling in chest); ***tachycardia*** (fast heartbeat); ***uterine hypertonus*** (severe cramping of the uterus)

Note: If *uterine hypertonus* occurs with dinoprostone at any dose, fetal distress or uterine rupture can result. Uterine rupture has occurred with use of the cervical gel to cause cervical ripening.

Systemic effects of *bradycardia, bronchoconstriction, substernal pressure or pain*, and *tachycardia* are seen rarely when dinoprostone is used for cervical ripening.

Those indicating need for medical attention only if they continue or are bothersome

Incidence more frequent

Abdominal or stomach cramps; diarrhea—about 40% with use of 20-mg suppositories; 1% with use of cervical gel or vaginal system; ***fever, transient***—about 50% with use of 20-mg suppositories; 1% with use of cervical gel or vaginal system; ***nausea***—about 33% with use of 20-mg suppositories; 1% with use of cervical gel or vaginal system; ***vomiting***—about 67% with use of vaginal suppository or vaginal gel; 1% with use of cervical gel or vaginal system

Incidence less frequent—for vaginal suppositories or vaginal gel, about 10% with use of 20-mg suppositories

Chills or shivering; headache

Incidence rare—for vaginal suppositories or vaginal gel

Flushing; ileus, adynamic (constipation, tender or mildly bloated abdomen); ***vulvar edema***

Those indicating possible postabortion complications and the need for medical attention if they occur after medication is discontinued

Endometritis (continuing chills; shivering; continuing fever—usually on third day post-abortion; foul-smelling vaginal discharge; pain in lower abdomen); ***unusual increase in uterine bleeding***

Patient Consultation

As an aid to patient consultation, refer to *Advice for the Patient, Dinoprostone (Cervical/Vaginal)*.

In providing consultation, consider emphasizing the following selected information (» = major clinical significance):

Before using this medication

» Conditions affecting use, especially:
Allergies to dinoprostone or other prostaglandins or hypersensitivity to dinoprostone, oxytocin, or other oxytocics
Pregnancy—Any pregnancy termination that fails with dinoprostone should be completed by another method
Other medical problems, especially cardiac disease or conditions that contraindicate vaginal delivery or induction of labor

Proper use of this medication

» Remaining in supine position for 10 minutes following insertion of suppository, 10 to 30 minutes following application of cervical gel, 30 minutes following application of vaginal gel, and 2 hours following insertion of vaginal system

» Proper dosing

» Proper storage

Side/adverse effects

Signs of potential side effects, especially anaphylaxis, bradycardia, bronchoconstriction, increased uterine pain accompanying abortion, peripheral vasoconstriction, substernal pressure or pain, tachycardia, uterine hypertonus

(Fetal distress can result if maternal uterine hypertonus occurs at any dose of dinoprostone)

Signs of postabortion complications, such as endometritis or unusual increase in uterine bleeding, after medication has been discontinued

General Dosing Information

Patients receiving dinoprostone should be hospitalized and under the supervision of a physician experienced in its use.

Procedures for applying dinoprostone should be carefully followed. Amnionitis and intrauterine fetal sepsis have been associated with extra-amniotic intrauterine administration of dinoprostone.

When it is used in doses that stimulate the uterus, experts recommend that antiemetic and antidiarrheal medications be administered prior to or concurrently with dinoprostone to decrease the possibility of gastrointestinal side effects. Narcotic analgesics may be given for uterine pain.

In those patients with profuse vaginal bleeding or ruptured membranes, blood or fluid present in the cervix and vagina may cause expulsion of dinoprostone, thereby interfering with the absorption and efficacy of dinoprostone.

For cervical ripening

When using a water-miscible lubricant to aid the insertion of dinoprostone vaginal system, avoid applying excessive amounts; otherwise, premature release of dinoprostone can occur.

Avoid applying the dinoprostone cervical gel above the cervical os because of the greater possibility of causing uterine hyperstimulation. Select the proper catheter for cervical application of the cervical gel, depending on whether the cervix is effaced: use the 10-mm catheter with no effacement, and the 20-mm catheter with 50% effacement.

For uterine stimulation

Confirmation of intrauterine fetal death should be made prior to use of dinoprostone for missed abortion or intrauterine fetal death.

Dinoprostone is not feticidal and may result in delivery of a live fetus.

Safety considerations for handling this medication

Dinoprostone should be handled cautiously. Suggested precautions for handling, preparing, and disposing of dinoprostone include the following:

- Avoid skin contact with dinoprostone, washing hands immediately with soap and water after administration.
- Use proper technique to prevent contamination of the medication, work area, and operator during transfer to patient.
- Cautiously and properly dispose of catheters, vaginal retrieval system, and unused medication.

For treatment of adverse effects

Treatment is primarily symptomatic, conservative, and supportive and may include the following:

- Repositioning the patient and giving oxygen may be adequate to ease transient abnormal uterine contractions, especially if dinoprostone was used for cervical ripening. Removing the vaginal system reverses uterine hyperstimulation within 2 to 13 minutes without need for tocolytic therapy in most cases.
- Sponging or irrigation with sterile saline of upper vagina to remove residual dinoprostone or removing vaginal suppository or system to prevent further absorption.
- Using tocolytic therapy, such as ritodrine, terbutaline, or magnesium sulfate, to treat uterine hyperstimulation. Data on treating dinoprostone-induced adverse effects with prostaglandin antagonists are presently insufficient.

Cervical Dosage Forms

DINOPROSTONE CERVICAL GEL

Usual adult and adolescent dose

Cervical ripening—

Intracervical, 0.5 mg placed into the cervical canal, just below the internal cervical os, using the syringe and catheter provided. Patient should remain in supine position for at least fifteen to thirty minutes following administration. A need for an additional dose is determined by the physician and ensuing clinical events.

Usual adult prescribing limits

Cervical ripening—

Maximum cumulative dose is 1.5 mg (7.5 mL) in 24 hours.

Strength(s) usually available

U.S.—

0.5 mg per 2.5 mL (3 grams) prefilled single-use syringe (Rx) [*Prepidil*].

Canada—

0.5 mg per 2.5 mL (3 grams) prefilled single-use syringe (Rx) [*Prepidil*].

Note: Packaging contains two catheter tips (10 and 20 mm).

Packaging and storage

Store between 2 and 8° C (36 and 46° F).

Preparation of dosage form

Bring medication to room temperature just prior to administration. Do not force warming by use of external heat source, such as water bath or microwave oven.

Each application is for single use and unused contents should be discarded, including the small amount of gel remaining in the catheter.

Vaginal Dosage Forms

DINOPROSTONE VAGINAL GEL

Usual adult and adolescent dose

Induction of labor—

Intravaginal, 1 mg placed into the posterior fornix of the vaginal canal. The patient should remain in supine position for at least fifteen to thirty minutes after administration. A dose of 1 or 2 mg may be repeated once, six hours later, if needed.

Strength(s) usually available

U.S.—

Not commercially available.

Canada—

1 mg per 2.5 mL (3 grams) applicatorful (Rx) [*Prostin E_2*].
2 mg per 2.5 mL (3 grams) applicatorful (Rx) [*Prostin E_2*].

Packaging and storage

Store below 2 and 8 °C (36 and 46 °F).

Preparation of dosage form

Bring medication to room temperature just prior to administration. Do not force warming by use of external heat source, such as water bath or microwave oven.

DINOPROSTONE VAGINAL SUPPOSITORIES

Usual adult and adolescent dose

Abortifacient—

Intravaginal, 20 mg, repeated every three to five hours, adjusted according to patient response until abortion occurs. Patient should remain in supine position for at least ten minutes following insertion.

Usual adult prescribing limits

Abortifacient—

Maximum cumulative dose is 240 mg; continuous administration of dinoprostone for more than 2 days is not recommended.

Strength(s) usually available

U.S.—

20 mg (Rx) [*Prostin E_2*].

Canada—

Not commercially available.

Packaging and storage

Store below −20 °C (−4 °F), unless otherwise specified by manufacturer.

Preparation of dosage form

Bring medication to room temperature just prior to administration. Do not force warming by use of external heat source, such as water bath or microwave oven.

DINOPROSTONE VAGINAL SYSTEM

Note: This monograph contains information on both the dinoprostone vaginal suppositories and the vaginal system (a suppository within a retrieval device). Each may be inappropriately referred to as dinoprostone vaginal insert in other types of information. It is important to avoid confusing the two dosage forms, since each has a different use and strength.

Usual adult and adolescent dose

Cervical ripening—

Intravaginal, 10 mg (one system delivering 0.3 mg per hour) placed transversely into the posterior fornix of the vaginal canal and removed upon onset of active labor or twelve hours after insertion, whichever occurs first. The patient should remain in supine position for at least two hours after administration.

Note: A minimal amount of lubricant should be used to aid system insertion.

Strength(s) usually available

U.S.—

10 mg (Rx) [*Cervidil*].

Canada—

Not commercially available.

Packaging and storage

Store below 2 and 8 °C (36 and 46 °F), unless otherwise specified by manufacturer.

Preparation of dosage form

Warming is not necessary.

Selected Bibliography

Rayburn WF. Prostaglandin E2 gel for cervical ripening and induction of labor: a critical analysis. Am J Obstet Gynecol 1989; 160(3): 529-34.

Castadot RG. Pregnancy termination: techniques, risks, and complications and their management. Fertil Steril 1986; 45(1): 5-17.

Revised: 08/20/1997

DIPHENHYDRAMINE—See *Antihistamines (Systemic)*

DIPHENOXYLATE AND ATROPINE Systemic

VA CLASSIFICATION (Primary): GA208

Note: Controlled substance classification
U.S.: Schedule V
Canada: N

Commonly used brand name(s): *Lofene; Logen; Lomocot; Lomotil; Lonox; Vi-Atro.*

Note: For a listing of dosage forms and brand names by country availability, see *Dosage Forms* section(s).

Category

Antidiarrheal (antiperistaltic).

Indications

Note: The efficacy of any antidiarrheal medication for treatment of most cases of nonspecific diarrhea is questionable, especially in children. **Preferred treatment for acute, nonspecific diarrhea consists of fluid and electrolyte replacement, nutritional therapy, and, if possible, elimination of the underlying cause of the diarrhea.**

Accepted

Diarrhea (treatment adjunct)—Diphenoxylate and atropine combination is indicated in adults, as an adjunct to fluid and electrolyte therapy, in the symptomatic treatment of acute and chronic diarrhea.

Unaccepted

Diphenoxylate and atropine combination is not recommended for treatment of diarrhea in children.

Pharmacology/Pharmacokinetics

Physicochemical characteristics

Molecular weight—
Atropine sulfate: 694.84.
Diphenoxylate hydrochloride: 489.06.

Mechanism of action/Effect

Diphenoxylate—Probably acts both locally and centrally to reduce intestinal motility.

Atropine—Has anticholinergic activity. However, in this preparation atropine is included in doses below the therapeutic level in an attempt to prevent abuse by deliberate overdosage.

Duration of effect

3 to 4 hours.

Biotransformation

Diphenoxylate—Hepatic; the major metabolite difenoxin (diphenoxylic acid) has similar activity.

Half-life

Atropine—2.5 hours.
Diphenoxylate—2.5 hours.
Diphenoxylic acid—4.5 hours.

Onset of effect

45 to 60 minutes.

Elimination

Atropine—Renal; 30 to 50% excreted unchanged.
Diphenoxylate—Fecal/renal; less than 1% eliminated unchanged in urine.

Precautions to Consider

Pregnancy/Reproduction

Pregnancy—Adequate and well-controlled studies in humans have not been done.

Although studies in animals with diphenoxylate and atropine have not shown any evidence of teratogenicity, risk-benefit must be considered since a study in rats showed that maternal weight gain was reduced when diphenoxylate was given at doses of 20 mg per kg per day. Also, at the same dosage, fertility was decreased, and out of 27 matings only 4 rats conceived and bore 25 normal young. Studies in rabbits showed no embryotoxic, teratogenic, or contraceptive effects.

FDA Pregnancy Category C.

Breast-feeding

Problems in humans have not been documented. However, both diphenoxylate's metabolite, diphenoxylic acid, and atropine are distributed into breast milk.

Pediatrics

Diphenoxylate and atropine combination is not recommended for treatment of diarrhea in children. Recommended treatment consists of oral rehydration therapy to prevent loss of fluids and electrolytes, nutritional therapy, and, if possible, elimination of the underlying cause of the diarrhea.

Infants and young children are especially susceptible to the toxic effects of atropine.

Children may also be more susceptible to the respiratory depressant effects of diphenoxylate.

Geriatrics

No information is available on the relationship of age to the effects of diphenoxylate and atropine in geriatric patients. However, elderly patients may be more susceptible to the respiratory depressant effects of diphenoxylate, and to the mild anticholinergic effects and confusion caused by atropine.

In geriatric patients with diarrhea, caution is recommended because of the risk of fluid and electrolyte loss.

Drug interactions and/or related problems

The following drug interactions and/or related problems have been selected on the basis of their potential clinical significance (possible mechanism in parentheses where appropriate)—not necessarily inclusive (» = major clinical significance):

Note: Combinations containing any of the following medications, depending on the amount present, may also interact with this medication.

Addictive medications, other, especially central nervous system (CNS) depressants with habituating potential
(concurrent use with diphenoxylate may increase the risk of habituation; caution is recommended)

» Alcohol or
» CNS depression-producing medications, other (See *Appendix II*)
(concurrent use with diphenoxylate may increase the CNS depressant effects of either diphenoxylate or these medications; also, when tricyclic antidepressants are used concurrently with atropine, their anticholinergic effects may be intensified; dosage adjustment may be required)

» Anticholinergics or other medications with anticholinergic action (See *Appendix II*)
(these medications may enhance the effects of atropine during concurrent use; significant interaction is unlikely with usual doses of diphenoxylate and atropine combination, but may occur with its abuse)

» Monoamine oxidase (MAO) inhibitors, including furazolidone, procarbazine, and selegiline
(concurrent use with diphenoxylate may precipitate hypertensive crisis?O inhibitors may block detoxification of atropine, thus potentiating its action)

» Naltrexone
(administration of naltrexone to a patient physically dependent on opioid drugs, such as diphenoxylate, will precipitate withdrawal symptoms; symptoms may appear within 5 minutes of naltrexone administration, persist for up to 48 hours, and be difficult to reverse)
(naltrexone blocks the therapeutic effects of opioids, including the antidiarrheal effects; also, patients receiving naltrexone should be advised to use alternative antidiarrheals when necessary)

Opioid (narcotic) analgesics
(concurrent use with diphenoxylate may result in increased risk of severe constipation and additive CNS depressant effects)

Laboratory value alterations

The following have been selected on the basis of their potential clinical significance (possible effect in parentheses where appropriate)—not necessarily inclusive (» = major clinical significance).

With diagnostic test results

» Phenolsulfonphthalein (PSP) excretion test
(atropine utilizes the same tubular mechanism of excretion as PSP, resulting in decreased urinary excretion of PSP; concurrent

use of atropine is not recommended in patients receiving PSP excretion test)

With physiology/laboratory test values

Amylase, serum

(values may be increased as a result of spasm of the sphincter of Oddi)

Medical considerations/Contraindications

The medical considerations/contraindications included have been selected on the basis of their potential clinical significance (reasons given in parentheses where appropriate)—not necessarily inclusive (» = major clinical significance).

Except under special circumstances, this medication should not be used when the following medical problems exist:

» Colitis, severe

(patient may develop toxic megacolon)

» Diarrhea associated with pseudomembranous colitis resulting from treatment with broad-spectrum antibiotics

(inhibition of peristalsis may delay the removal of toxins from the colon, thereby prolonging and/or worsening the diarrhea)

Risk-benefit should be considered when the following medical problems exist:

Alcoholism, active or in remission, or

Drug abuse or dependence, history of

(diphenoxylate content may increase chances of drug abuse in patient already predisposed to dependence)

Cardiovascular instability

(possible increase in heart rate may be undesirable)

» Dehydration

(may predispose to delayed diphenoxylate intoxication; inhibition of peristalsis may result in fluid retention in colon and may further aggravate dehydration; discontinuation of medication and rehydration therapy is essential if signs or symptoms of dehydration, such as dryness of mouth, excessive thirst, wrinkled skin, decreased urination, and dizziness or light-headedness, are present; fluid loss may have serious consequences, such as circulatory collapse and renal failure)

Diarrhea caused by infectious organisms

(bacterial diarrhea may worsen due to the increased contact time between the mucosa and the penetrating microorganism; however, there is no evidence of this occurring in actual practice)

» Diarrhea caused by poisoning, until toxic material has been eliminated from gastrointestinal tract

Down's syndrome

(atropine may cause abnormal increase in pupillary dilation and acceleration of heart rate)

» Dysentery, acute, characterized by bloody stools and elevated temperature

(sole treatment with antiperistaltic antidiarrheals may be inadequate; antibiotic therapy may be required)

Gallbladder disease or gallstones

(diphenoxylate may cause biliary tract spasm)

» Gastrointestinal tract obstruction

(may result in pseudo-obstruction, or in dilation of the large or small bowel)

Glaucoma, angle-closure

(although unlikely with usual doses of this combination, atropine may precipitate an acute attack of angle-closure glaucoma)

» Hepatic function impairment or jaundice

(diphenoxylate may precipitate hepatic coma; it is recommended that dosage be reduced in patients with impaired hepatic function)

Hiatal hernia associated with reflux esophagitis

(although unlikely with usual doses of this combination, atropine may aggravate condition)

Hypertension

(although unlikely with usual doses of this combination, atropine may aggravate condition)

Hyperthyroidism

(characterized by tachycardia, which may be increased by atropine)

Hypothyroidism

(diphenoxylate may increase risk of respiratory depression)

Incontinence, overflow

(secondary to constipation, but often mistaken for diarrhea; use of diphenoxylate and atropine may worsen constipation and/or cause dilation or pseudo-obstruction of the colon)

Intestinal atony of the elderly or debilitated

(although unlikely with usual doses of this combination, use of atropine may result in obstruction)

Myasthenia gravis

(although unlikely with usual doses of this combination, atropine may aggravate condition because of inhibition of acetylcholine action)

Prostatic hypertrophy or

Urethral stricture, acute or

Urinary retention

(reduction in tone of urinary bladder may aggravate or lead to complete urinary retention)

Renal function impairment

(decreased elimination of atropine may increase the risk of side effects)

Respiratory disease or impairment

(increased risk of respiratory depression)

Sensitivity to atropine or diphenoxylate

Patient monitoring

The following may be especially important in patient monitoring (other tests may be warranted in some patients, depending on condition; » = major clinical significance):

» Hepatic function determinations

(recommended at periodic intervals during long-term therapy, especially for patients with hepatic function impairment)

Side/Adverse Effects

The following side/adverse effects have been selected on the basis of their potential clinical significance (possible signs and symptoms in parentheses where appropriate)—not necessarily inclusive:

Those indicating need for medical attention

Incidence less frequent or rare

Pancreatitis (abdominal pain, severe; back pain; fever; loss of appetite; nausea and vomiting); ***paralytic ileus or toxic megacolon*** (bloating; constipation; loss of appetite; severe stomach pain with nausea and vomiting)

Those indicating need for medical attention only if they continue, worsen, or are bothersome

Incidence less frequent or rare

Anticholinergic effects, mild (blurred vision; difficult urination; dryness of skin and mouth; fever); ***CNS depression*** (dizziness or lightheadedness; drowsiness; mental depression); ***confusion; headache; hyperthermia*** (flushing; increased body temperature; increased breathing rate; rapid heartbeat); ***numbness of hands or feet; skin rash or itching; swelling of the gums***

Note: Since atropine is present in a subtherapeutic dose, the appearance of these symptoms probably indicates overdosage.

Those indicating possible withdrawal and the need for medical attention if they occur after discontinuation of prolonged high-dose therapy

Incidence rare

Increased sweating; muscle cramps; nausea or vomiting; shivering or trembling; stomach cramps

Overdose

For specific information on the agents used in the management of diphenoxylate and atropine overdose, see:

- *Charcoal, Activated (Oral-Local)* monograph; and/or
- *Naloxone (Systemic)* monograph.

For more information on the management of overdose or unintentional ingestion, **contact a poison control center** (see *Poison Control Center Listing*).

Clinical effects of overdose

The following effects have been selected on the basis of their potential clinical significance (possible signs and symptoms in parentheses where appropriate)–not necessarily inclusive:

Anticholinergic effects, severe (continuing blurred vision or changes in near vision; fast heartbeat; severe drowsiness; severe dryness of mouth, nose, and throat; unusual warmth, dryness, and flushing of skin); ***coma; respiratory depression*** (severe shortness of breath or troubled breathing); ***unusual excitement, nervousness, restlessness, or irritability***

Note: *Respiratory depression* may occur as late as 12 to 30 hours after ingestion.

Possible symptoms of overdose

Anticholinergic effects, mild (blurred vision; difficult urination; dryness of skin and mouth; fever); ***CNS depression*** (dizziness or lightheadedness; drowsiness; mental depression); ***confusion; headache;***

numbness of hands or feet; skin rash or itching; swelling of the gums

Note: Since atropine is present in a subtherapeutic dose, the appearance of these symptoms probably indicates overdosage.

Treatment of overdose

Treatment of overdose with diphenoxylate and atropine is the same as treatment for meperidine or morphine overdosage and involves the following:

To decrease absorption—Induction of vomiting, or gastric lavage, if vomiting has not occurred; administration of a slurry of 100 grams of activated charcoal, after induction of vomiting or gastric lavage, in non-comatose patients.

Specific treatment—Intravenous administration of 0.4 mg (0.01 mg per kg of body weight in children) of narcotic antagonist naloxone, which may be repeated at 2- to 3-minute intervals, for respiratory depression.

Monitoring—Careful monitoring for 48 to 72 hours.

Supportive care—Support of respiration. Patients in whom intentional overdose is confirmed or suspected should be referred for psychiatric consultation.

Patient Consultation

As an aid to patient consultation, refer to *Advice for the Patient, Diphenoxylate and Atropine (Systemic)*.

In providing consultation, consider emphasizing the following selected information (» = major clinical significance):

Before using this medication

» Conditions affecting use, especially:
- Sensitivity to atropine or diphenoxylate
- Pregnancy—Studies in rats show decreased fertility and decreased maternal weight gain
- Breast-feeding—Diphenoxylate and atropine distributed into breast milk; potential for serious adverse effects in nursing infant
- Use in children—Not recommended for use in children; increased susceptibility to toxic effects of atropine and respiratory depressant effects of diphenoxylate; risk of dehydration
- Use in the elderly—Increased risk of respiratory depression, anticholinergic effects, and confusion; risk of dehydration
- Other medications, especially other anticholinergics, CNS depressants, MAO inhibitors, or naltrexone
- Other medical problems, especially acute dysentery; dehydration; diarrhea caused by antibiotics or poisoning; gastrointestinal tract obstruction; hepatic function impairment or jaundice; or severe colitis

Proper use of this medication

Taking with food or meals if gastric irritation occurs

» Importance of not taking more medication than the amount prescribed because of habit-forming potential

» Importance of maintaining adequate hydration and proper diet

» Proper dosing

Missed dose: If on a scheduled dosing regimen—Taking as soon as possible; not taking if almost time for next dose; not doubling doses

» Proper storage

For liquid dosage form

Proper administration technique: Measuring amount with dropper and taking by mouth

Precautions while using this medication

Regular visits to physician to check progress during prolonged therapy

» Consulting physician if diarrhea is not controlled within 48 hours and/or fever develops

» Avoiding use of alcohol or other CNS depressants during therapy

» Suspected overdose: Getting emergency help at once

Need to inform physician or dentist of use of medication if any kind of surgery (including dental surgery) or emergency treatment is required

» Caution if dizziness or drowsiness occurs

Side/adverse effects

Signs of potential side effects, especially paralytic ileus or toxic megacolon

General Dosing Information

Treatment with diphenoxylate and atropine should be continued for 24 to 48 hours before it is considered ineffective in acute diarrhea. If clinical improvement of chronic diarrhea after treatment with a maximum daily dose of 20 mg of diphenoxylate is not observed within 10 days, treatment should be discontinued.

Inhibition of peristalsis may produce fluid retention in the bowel, which may aggravate dehydration and depletion of electrolytes, and may also increase variability of response to the medication. If dehydration or electrolyte imbalance occurs, diphenoxylate and atropine therapy should be withheld until appropriate corrective therapy has begun.

To prevent development of toxic megacolon in patients with acute ulcerative colitis, treatment with diphenoxylate and atropine should be discontinued promptly if abdominal distention or other specific gastrointestinal symptoms such as anorexia, bloating, constipation, nausea, vomiting, or abdominal pain occur.

Prolonged use of larger than usual therapeutic doses may result in physical dependence.

Tolerance to the antidiarrheal effects of diphenoxylate and atropine may develop with prolonged use.

This medication may suppress respiration, especially in the elderly, the very ill, and patients with respiratory problems. Lower doses may be required for these patients.

Oral Dosage Forms

DIPHENOXYLATE HYDROCHLORIDE AND ATROPINE SULFATE ORAL SOLUTION USP

Usual adult and adolescent dose

Antidiarrheal (antiperistaltic)—

Initial: Oral, 5 mg of diphenoxylate hydrochloride and 50 mcg (0.05 mg) of atropine sulfate three or four times a day.

Maintenance: Oral, 5 mg of diphenoxylate hydrochloride and 50 mcg (0.05 mg) of atropine sulfate once a day, as needed.

Usual adult prescribing limits

20 mg per day.

Usual pediatric dose

Antidiarrheal (antiperistaltic)—

Children up to 12 years of age: Use is not recommended.

Children 12 years of age and older: See *Usual adult and adolescent dose*.

Usual geriatric dose

See *Usual adult and adolescent dose*.

Note: Geriatric patients may be more sensitive to the effects of the usual adult dose.

Strength(s) usually available

U.S.—

2.5 mg of diphenoxylate hydrochloride and 25 mcg (0.025 mg) of atropine sulfate, per 5 mL (Rx) [*Lomotil* (alcohol 15%); GENERIC].

Canada—

Not commercially available.

Packaging and storage

Store below 40 °C (104 °F), preferably between 15 and 30 °C (59 and 86 °F), unless otherwise specified by manufacturer. Store in a tight, light-resistant container. Protect from freezing.

Auxiliary labeling

- May cause drowsiness.
- Avoid alcoholic beverages.
- Keep out of reach of children.

Note

Controlled substance in the U.S.

DIPHENOXYLATE HYDROCHLORIDE AND ATROPINE SULFATE TABLETS USP

Usual adult and adolescent dose

See *Diphenoxylate Hydrochloride and Atropine Sulfate Oral Solution USP*.

Usual pediatric dose

Antidiarrheal (antiperistaltic)—

Children up to 12 years of age: Use is not recommended.

Children 12 years of age and older: See *Usual adult and adolescent dose*.

Usual geriatric dose

See *Usual adult and adolescent dose*.

Note: Geriatric patients may be more sensitive to the effects of the usual adult dose.

Strength(s) usually available

U.S.—

2.5 mg of diphenoxylate hydrochloride and 25 mcg (0.025 mg) of atropine sulfate (Rx) [*Lofene; Logen; Lomocot; Lomotil; Lonox; Vi-Atro;* GENERIC].

Canada—
2.5 mg of diphenoxylate hydrochloride and 25 mcg (0.025 mg) of atropine sulfate (Rx) [*Lomotil*].

Packaging and storage
Store below 40 °C (104 °F), preferably between 15 and 30 °C (59 and 86 °F), in a well-closed container, unless otherwise specified by manufacturer. Store in a light-resistant container.

Auxiliary labeling
- May cause drowsiness.
- Avoid alcoholic beverages.
- Keep out of reach of children.
- May be habit-forming.

Note
Controlled substance in the U.S. and Canada.

Selected Bibliography
Brownlee HJ, editor. Proceedings of a symposium: Management of acute nonspecific diarrhea. Am J Med 1990; 88(Suppl 6A).

Gaginella TS. Diarrhea: some new aspects of pharmacotherapy. Drug Intell Clin Pharm 1983; 17: 914-6.

Revised: 12/09/1999

DIPHTHERIA AND TETANUS TOXOIDS (DT)—See *Diphtheria and Tetanus Toxoids (Systemic)*

DIPHTHERIA AND TETANUS TOXOIDS Systemic

This monograph includes information on the following: 1) Diphtheria and Tetanus Toxoids for Pediatric Use (DT); 2) Tetanus and Diphtheria Toxoids for Adult Use (Td).

Note: There are some differences in terminology with respect to the use of the terms "primary" and "reinforcing" in some of the manufacturers" labeling used for this monograph. In this monograph, the term "primary immunizing series" will be used to denote the initial doses that are usually given 4 to 8 weeks apart as well as the "reinforcing" dose that is usually given 6 to 12 months thereafter. The dose usually given at 4 to 6 years of age and the doses given every 10 years will be called booster doses.

VA CLASSIFICATION (Primary): IM200

Commonly used brand name(s):.

Other commonly used names are: DT [Diphtheria and Tetanus Toxoids] Td [Tetanus and Diphtheria Toxoids]

Note: For a listing of dosage forms and brand names by country availability, see *Dosage Forms* section(s).

Category
Immunizing agent (active).

Indications
Accepted
Diphtheria and tetanus (prophylaxis)—Diphtheria and tetanus toxoid combination is indicated for immunization against diphtheria and tetanus.

Diphtheria and tetanus toxoids for pediatric use (DT) is indicated for immunization of infants and children 6 weeks up to 7 years of age who, because of a contraindication to pertussis vaccine, cannot receive diphtheria and tetanus toxoids and pertussis vaccine (DTP) combination. If there is no contraindication to pertussis vaccine, DTP is the vaccine of choice for this age group.

Tetanus and diphtheria toxoids for adult use (Td) is indicated for immunization of adults and children 7 years of age and older.

Pharmacology/Pharmacokinetics
Physicochemical characteristics
Source—Diphtheria toxoid is prepared by first cultivating a suitable strain of *Corynebacterium diphtheriae*. Tetanus toxoid is prepared by first cultivating a suitable strain of *Clostridium tetani*. The resulting toxins are detoxified with formaldehyde. The detoxified toxins (toxoids) are adsorbed onto an aluminum salt. This prolongs and enhances the antigenic properties by retarding the rate of absorption of the injected toxoid in the body.

Mechanism of action/Effect
Following intramuscular injection, diphtheria toxoid and tetanus toxoid induce the formation of diphtheria antitoxin and tetanus antitoxin, respectively.

Protective effect
Diphtheria antitoxin—
The protective level in serum is 0.01 unit per mL.

Tetanus antitoxin—
The protective level in serum is 0.01 unit per mL.

Time to protective effect
For diphtheria and tetanus toxoids for pediatric use (DT)—
In a study of 20 children under 1 year of age, protective levels of diphtheria and tetanus antitoxins were detected in 100% of the children after administration of 3 doses of DT. In addition, protective levels of diphtheria and tetanus antitoxins were detected in 100% of the children after administration of 2 doses of DT, but maternal antibody may have contributed to the total neutralizing antibody in some of these children.

For tetanus and diphtheria toxoids for adult use (Td)—
Response to primary immunization:
Diphtheria—In a study of 10 adults who had less than 0.001 unit per mL of diphtheria antitoxin in pre-immunization serum, protective levels of diphtheria antitoxin were detected in 50% of the adults after administration of 2 doses of Td, each containing 2 Lf units of diphtheria toxoid. In a similar study of 6 adults, protective levels of diphtheria antitoxin were detected in 100% of the adults after administration of 3 doses of Td.
Tetanus—In a study of 20 adults who had less than 0.0025 unit per mL of tetanus antitoxin in pre-immunization serum, protective levels of tetanus antitoxin were detected in 70% of the adults after administration of 2 doses, and in 100% of the adults after administration of 3 doses, of Td, each containing 2 Lf units of tetanus toxoid.
Response to booster doses:
Booster doses of Td given as long as 25 to 30 years after primary immunization series have produced rapid and significant increases in the levels of both tetanus and diphtheria antitoxins.
Diphtheria—In a study of 140 adolescent males, protective levels of diphtheria antitoxin were detected in 100% of the males after administration of a single booster dose of Td containing 1 Lf unit of diphtheria toxoid.
Tetanus—In a study of 36 adults, protective levels of tetanus antitoxin were detected in 100% of the adults after administration of a single booster dose of Td containing 1 Lf unit of tetanus toxoid.

Duration of protective effect
At least 10 years for both diphtheria toxoid and tetanus toxoid following a completed primary immunizing series of injections.

Precautions to Consider
Cross-sensitivity and/or related problems
Patients sensitive to diphtheria toxoid or tetanus toxoid may be sensitive to diphtheria and tetanus toxoids for pediatric use (DT) or tetanus and diphtheria toxoids for adult use (Td) also.

Carcinogenicity/Mutagenicity
Studies have not been done.

Pregnancy/Reproduction
Fertility—Studies have not been done.

Pregnancy—There is no evidence that diphtheria and tetanus toxoid combination is teratogenic.

For DT: Use of DT is not recommended in females of child-bearing age.

For Td: Unimmunized pregnant women should receive 2 properly spaced doses of Td before delivery, preferably during the last 2 trimesters. Incompletely immunized pregnant women should complete the primary immunizing series of Td. Those fully immunized more than 10 years ago should receive a booster dose of Td.

Studies have not been done in animals.

FDA Pregnancy Category C.

Breast-feeding
Diphtheria and tetanus toxoids have not been isolated from breast milk.

For DT—Use of DT is not recommended in females of child-bearing age.

For Td—There is no evidence that breast milk from women who have received Td is harmful to infants.

Pediatrics
For DT—
Infants up to 6 weeks of age: Use of DT is not recommended.

Infants and children up to 7 years of age: Pediatrics-specific problems that would limit the usefulness of DT in these children are not expected.

Children 7 years of age and older: Use of DT is not recommended in this age group.

For Td—

Infants and children up to 7 years of age: Use of Td is not recommended in this age group.

Children 7 years of age and older: Pediatrics-specific problems that would limit the usefulness of Td in these children are not expected.

Geriatrics

For DT—Use of DT is not recommended in this age group.

For Td—Although appropriate studies on the relationship of age to the effects of Td have not been performed in the geriatric population, geriatrics-specific problems are not expected to limit the usefulness of Td in the elderly. However, the immune response in the elderly may be slightly diminished.

Drug interactions and/or related problems

The following drug interactions and/or related problems have been selected on the basis of their potential clinical significance (possible mechanism in parentheses where appropriate)—not necessarily inclusive (» = major clinical significance):

Note: Combinations containing any of the following medications, depending on the amount present, may also interact with this medication.

Immunosuppressants or
Radiation therapy
(because normal defense mechanisms are suppressed, the patient's antibody response to DT or Td may be decreased during therapy and deferral of routine DT or Td administration may be considered. The precaution does not apply to corticosteroids used as replacement therapy, for short-term [less than 2 weeks] systemic therapy, or by other routes of administration that do not cause immunosuppression. Where possible, immunosuppressive therapy should be interrupted when immunization is required because of a tetanus-prone wound)

Medical considerations/Contraindications

The medical considerations/contraindications included have been selected on the basis of their potential clinical significance (reasons given in parentheses where appropriate)—not necessarily inclusive (» = major clinical significance).

Except under special circumstances, this medication should not be used when the following medical problems exist:

» Febrile illness or

» Infection, acute
(routine primary or booster immunization should not be administered until the acute symptoms of the patient's illness have abated; however, emergency tetanus prophylaxis for wounds should be administered as usual. A minor afebrile illness, such as an upper respiratory infection, usually does not preclude administration of DT or Td)

» Sensitivity to DT or Td

» Tetanus infection
(products containing tetanus toxoid should not be used to treat a tetanus infection; tetanus antitoxin, preferably tetanus immune globulin [TIG], should be used instead; after recovery, the primary immunizing series should be initiated or continued, since a tetanus infection does not confer immunity)

Risk-benefit should be considered when the following medical problem exists:

» Sensitivity to thimerosal

Side/Adverse Effects

Note: Although both the diphtheria toxoid and the tetanus toxoid components may evoke local and systemic allergic responses, it has been suggested that the tetanus toxoid component may be the more common cause.

If an Arthus-type hypersensitivity reaction or a fever over 39.4 °C (103 °F) occurs following a dose of diphtheria and tetanus toxoid combination, the patient usually has a very high serum tetanus antitoxin level and no additional doses of tetanus toxoid should be given for any reason, including wound management, more frequently than every 10 years.

Neurological reactions, such as convulsions, encephalopathy, and various mono- and polyneuropathies, have been reported following administration of preparations containing diphtheria toxoid and/or tetanus toxoid. Pallor, coldness, and hyporesponsiveness were reported in 1 child. In the differential diagnosis of polyradiculoneuropathies, previous administration of tetanus toxoid should be considered as a possible cause. If a neurologic reaction or a severe systemic allergic reaction occurs following a dose of diphtheria and tetanus toxoids for pediatric use (DT) or tetanus and diphtheria toxoids for adult use (Td), the person should not be further immunized with DT or Td.

Booster doses of tetanus toxoid administered more frequently than every 10 years have been reported to result in increased occurrence and severity of adverse reactions.

Generally, a history of hypersensitivity reactions other than anaphylaxis, such as delayed-type, cell-mediated allergic reaction (contact dermatitis), does not preclude immunization.

Sterile abscesses have been reported rarely following administration of DT or Td. These are thought to be caused by inadvertent subcutaneous injection of the aluminum adjuvant in the product.

Use of jet injectors, which deposit some toxoid in the subcutaneous tissue, has been associated with a higher frequency of local reactions than has intramuscular injection by needle.

The following side/adverse effects have been selected on the basis of their potential clinical significance (possible signs and symptoms in parentheses where appropriate)—not necessarily inclusive:

Those indicating need for medical attention

Incidence rare

For DT and Td

Anaphylactic reaction (difficulty in breathing or swallowing; hives; itching, especially of soles or palms; reddening of skin, especially around ears; swelling of eyes, face, or inside of nose; unusual tiredness or weakness, sudden and severe); ***arthralgias*** (joint aches or pain); ***neurologic reaction*** (confusion; excessive sleepiness; fever over 39.4 °C [103 °F]; headache, severe or continuing; seizures; unusual irritability; vomiting, severe or continuing); ***pruritus*** (itching); ***skin rash; urticaria*** (hives)

Additional side/adverse effects that may occur because of very high serum tetanus antitoxin levels and may indicate a need for medical attention

Incidence rare

Arthus-type reaction (swelling, blistering, pain, or other severe local reaction at injection site); ***fever over 39.4 °C (103 °F)***

Note: *Arthus-type reaction* and *fever over 39.4 °C* usually occur only in patients old enough to receive Td, i.e., persons old enough to have received multiple booster doses of a tetanus toxoid–containing product. An *Arthus-type reaction* generally starts within 2 to 8 hours after the injection and may be severe and extensive.

Those indicating need for medical attention only if they continue or are bothersome

Incidence more frequent

For DT and Td

Redness or hard lump at injection site—may persist for a few days

For DT only

Fever under 39.4 °C (103 °F); swelling, pain, or tenderness at injection site—may persist for a few days

Incidence less frequent

For DT and Td

Nodule (hard lump) at injection site; subcutaneous atrophy (dent or indentation) at injection site

Note: *Nodule (hard lump) at injection site* probably is caused by the aluminum content of the toxoids and may persist for a few weeks.

For DT only

Anorexia (loss of appetite); ***drowsiness; fretfulness; persistent crying; vomiting***

For Td only

Axillary lymphadenopathy (swelling of glands in armpit); ***chills; fever under 39.4 °C (103 °F); headache; hypotension*** (unusual tiredness or weakness); ***malaise*** (general feeling of discomfort or illness); ***muscle aches; tachycardia*** (fast heartbeat)

Patient Consultation

As an aid to patient consultation, refer to *Advice for the Patient, Diphtheria and Tetanus Toxoids (Systemic).*

In providing consultation, consider emphasizing the following selected information (» = major clinical significance):

Before receiving this vaccine

» Conditions affecting use, especially:
Sensitivity to diphtheria toxoid, tetanus toxoid, or thimerosal

Use in children—Not recommended for infants up to 6 weeks of age; only diphtheria and tetanus toxoids for pediatric use (DT) is recommended for infants and children 6 weeks to 7 years of age; only tetanus and diphtheria toxoids for adult use (Td) is recommended for children 7 years of age and older

Use in the elderly—Only tetanus and diphtheria toxoids for adult use (Td) is recommended; the immune response in the elderly may be slightly diminished

Other medical problems, especially acute infection, febrile illness, or tetanus infection

Proper use of this medication

» Proper dosing

Side/adverse effects

Notifying physician of any side effect that occurs after a dose of DT or Td, even if the side effect has gone away without treatment

Signs of potential side effects, especially anaphylactic reaction; arthralgias; neurologic reaction; pruritus; skin rash; urticaria; Arthus-type reaction; and fever over 39.4 °C (103 °F)

General Dosing Information

Diphtheria and tetanus toxoid combination is administered by deep intramuscular injection into the deltoid (for adults and older children) or into the area of the midlateral muscles (vastus lateralis) of the thigh (for infants and younger children). The same muscle site should not be used more than once during the course of the primary immunizing series. The vaccine should not be injected subcutaneously or intravenously.

Before each additional dose of diphtheria and tetanus toxoids for pediatric use (DT) or tetanus and diphtheria toxoids for adult use (Td), the health status of the patient should be assessed. In addition, information should be obtained regarding any symptom and/or sign of an adverse reaction that occurred after the previous dose.

Routine immunization of adults and children over 6 months of age should be deferred during an outbreak of poliomyelitis in the community, unless there is also an outbreak of diphtheria. In either case, emergency tetanus prophylaxis for wounds should be administered as usual.

Persons with impaired immune response may be immunized, but may have reduced antibody response to DT or Td. Persons infected with human immunodeficiency virus (HIV) may receive DT or Td whether they have asymptomatic or symptomatic HIV infection.

Diphtheria infection may not (and tetanus infection does not) confer immunity; therefore, initiation or completion of active immunization with DT or Td is indicated at the time of recovery from either of these infections.

Interruption of the recommended schedule for the primary immunizing series of DT or Td by a delay between doses does not interfere with the final immunity achieved and does not necessitate starting the series over again, regardless of the length of time that elapsed between doses.

Emergency tetanus prophylaxis of wounds

Patients who were unimmunized or inadequately immunized with a tetanus toxoid–containing product prior to a wound should complete their primary immunizing series as soon as possible.

For routine wound management in children under 7 years of age who have not received the primary immunizing series against tetanus, DT (or DTP, if appropriate) should be used instead of single-antigen tetanus toxoid. In addition, children whose wounds are considered to be prone to tetanus infection and who have had fewer than 3 doses (or an unknown number of doses) of a tetanus toxoid–containing product also should be administered tetanus antitoxin, preferably tetanus immune globulin (TIG). A separate syringe and site of administration should be used for DT and TIG.

The decision to administer Td for wound management with or without concomitant passive immunization using tetanus immune globulin (TIG) depends on the condition of the wound and the patient's immunization history. Examples of wounds that are not clean, minor wounds are: wounds contaminated with dirt, feces, soil, or saliva; puncture wounds; wounds caused by tearing; and wounds resulting from missiles, crushing, burns, or frostbite. Tetanus has rarely occurred in persons who have received a documented primary immunizing series of a tetanus toxoid–containing product. Persons who have received the primary immunizing series and whose wounds are minor and uncontaminated should receive a booster dose of a tetanus toxoid–containing product, such as Td, only if they have not received a tetanus toxoid booster dose within the past 10 years. Persons who have received the primary immunizing series and who have wounds that are not minor and uncontaminated should receive a booster dose of a tetanus toxoid–containing product, such as Td, only if they have not received a tetanus toxoid booster dose within the past 5 years. Persons who have not received the primary immunizing series against tetanus (or whose immunization history is unknown) should be immunized with a tetanus toxoid–containing product, such as Td. If persons who have not received the primary immunizing series against tetanus (or whose immunization history is unknown) have wounds that are considered to be prone to tetanus infection, tetanus antitoxin (preferably TIG) should be administered in addition to Td. A separate syringe and site of administration should be used for Td and TIG.

Emergency diphtheria prophylaxis

Immunization with diphtheria toxoid reduces the risk of developing diphtheria and lessens the severity of clinical illness. However, it does not eliminate *Corynebacterium diphtheriae* from the pharynx or the skin.

Household and other close contacts of persons with diphtheria infection who have received fewer than 3 doses of a diphtheria toxoid–containing product should receive an immediate dose of a diphtheria toxoid–containing product, such as DT or Td (according to their age requirement), and should complete the primary immunizing series according to schedule. Household and other close contacts who have received 3 or more doses of a diphtheria toxoid–containing product and who have not received an additional dose within 5 years should receive a booster dose of a diphtheria toxoid–containing product, such as DT or Td (according to their age requirement).

For treatment of adverse effects

Recommended treatment includes:

- For mild hypersensitivity reaction—Administering antihistamines and, if necessary, corticosteroids.
- For severe hypersensitivity or anaphylactic reaction—Administering epinephrine. Antihistamines or corticosteroids may also be administered as required.

DIPHTHERIA AND TETANUS TOXOIDS (DT)

Summary of Differences

Indications: Diphtheria and tetanus toxoids for pediatric use (DT) is indicated for immunization of infants and children 6 weeks up to 7 years of age.

Strength(s) usually available: DT contains 6.6 to 25 Lf units of diphtheria toxoid and 5 to 10 Lf units of tetanus toxoid, per dose.

Additional Dosing Information

Diphtheria toxoid of the strength used in DT is not recommended for adults and children 7 years of age and older, because of the increased risk of side/adverse effects associated with the use of higher doses of diphtheria toxoid in this age group.

It is recommended that infants and children up to 7 years of age receive diphtheria and tetanus toxoids as part of Diphtheria and Tetanus Toxoids and Pertussis Vaccine Adsorbed (DTP). In those cases in which the pertussis vaccine is contraindicated, it is recommended that DT be administered instead.

The primary immunizing series of DT consists of 4 doses (3 initial and 1 reinforcing) for children 6 weeks up to 1 year of age (in Canada, 2 months up to 7 years of age) or 3 doses (2 initial and 1 reinforcing) for children 1 to 7 years of age.

Preterm infants should be immunized according to their chronological age from birth.

DT can be administered concurrently with the following, using separate body sites and separate syringes (for parenterals), and the precautions that apply to each immunizing agent:

- Hepatitis B recombinant or plasma-derived vaccine.
- Polysaccharide vaccines, such as haemophilus b polysaccharide vaccine, haemophilus b conjugate vaccine, or pneumococcal polyvalent vaccine.
- Live virus vaccines, such as measles, mumps, and rubella (MMR) or oral polio vaccine (OPV).
- Inactivated poliovirus vaccine (IPV) or enhanced-potency inactivated vaccine (enhanced-potency IPV).

Parenteral Dosage Forms

DIPHTHERIA AND TETANUS TOXOIDS ADSORBED (DT) (FOR PEDIATRIC USE) USP

Note: DT is indicated for immunization of infants and children 6 weeks up to 7 years of age who cannot receive diphtheria and tetanus toxoids and pertussis vaccine (DTP) combination, because of a contraindication to pertussis vaccine. If there is no contraindication to pertussis vaccine, DTP is the vaccine of choice for this age group.

Usual adult and adolescent dose

Use is not recommended. Tetanus and diphtheria toxoids for adult use (Td) should be administered instead.

Usual pediatric dose

Diphtheria and tetanus (prophylaxis)—
Intramuscular, preferably into the deltoid or the midlateral muscles of the thigh.

U.S.—
Children 6 weeks to 1 year of age: 0.5 mL at four- to eight-week intervals for a total of three doses. A fourth dose of 0.5 mL is administered six to twelve months after the third dose. A booster (fifth) dose of 0.5 mL is usually administered at four through six years of age (i.e., preferably prior to school entry); however, if the fourth dose of the primary immunizing series was administered after the fourth birthday, a booster (fifth) dose is not necessary.
Children 1 to 7 years of age: 0.5 mL followed by 0.5 mL four to eight weeks later for a total of two doses. A third dose of 0.5 mL is administered six to twelve months after the second dose. A booster (fourth) dose of 0.5 mL is usually administered at four through six years of age (i.e., preferably prior to school entry); however, if the third dose of the primary immunizing series was administered after the fourth birthday, a booster (fourth) dose is not necessary.
Children 7 years of age and older: Use is not recommended. Td should be administered instead.

Canada—
Children 2 months to 7 years of age: 0.5 mL at eight-week intervals for a total of three doses. A fourth dose of 0.5 mL is administered twelve months after the third dose. A booster (fifth) dose of 0.5 mL is usually administered at four through six years of age (i.e., preferably prior to school entry); however, if the fourth dose of the primary immunizing series was administered after the fourth birthday, a booster (fifth) dose is not necessary.
Children 7 years of age and older: Use is not recommended. Td should be administered instead.

Strength(s) usually available

U.S.—
6.6 Lf units of diphtheria toxoid and 5 Lf units of tetanus toxoid per 0.5 mL dose (Rx) [GENERIC (may contain thimerosal)].
7.5 Lf units of diphtheria toxoid and 7.5 Lf units of tetanus toxoid per 0.5 mL dose (Rx) [GENERIC (may contain thimerosal)].
10 Lf units of diphtheria toxoid and 5 Lf units of tetanus toxoid per 0.5 mL dose (Rx) [GENERIC (may contain thimerosal)].
12.5 Lf units of diphtheria toxoid and 5 Lf units of tetanus toxoid per 0.5 mL dose (Rx) [GENERIC (may contain thimerosal)].
15 Lf units of diphtheria toxoid and 10 Lf units of tetanus toxoid per 0.5 mL dose (Rx) [GENERIC (may contain thimerosal)].

Canada—
25 Lf units of diphtheria toxoid and 5 Lf units of tetanus toxoid in each 0.5 mL dose (Rx) [GENERIC (may contain thimerosal)].

Note: Lf is the quantity of toxoid as assessed by flocculation.

Packaging and storage

Store between 2 and 8 °C (36 and 46 °F), unless otherwise specified by manufacturer. Store away from the freezer compartment. Protect from freezing.

Stability

Freezing destroys activity. The product should not be used if it has been exposed to freezing. In addition, the product should not be left out at room temperature (e.g., between patients).

Auxiliary labeling

- Shake the vial vigorously immediately before each dose is withdrawn in order to resuspend the contents.
- Protect from freezing.

TETANUS AND DIPHTHERIA TOXOIDS (Td)

Summary of Differences

Indications: Tetanus and diphtheria toxoids for adult use (Td) is indicated for immunization of adults and children 7 years of age and older.

Side/adverse effects: Arthus-type reaction and fever over 39.4 °C usually occur only in patients old enough to receive Td, i.e., persons old enough to have received multiple booster doses of a tetanus toxoid–containing product.

Strength(s) usually available: Td contains 2 Lf units of diphtheria toxoid and 2 to 10 Lf units of tetanus toxoid, per dose.

Additional Dosing Information

The concentration of diphtheria toxoid in Td, which is intended for use in persons 7 years of age and older, is lower than that of the concentration of diphtheria toxoid in diphtheria and tetanus toxoids for pediatric use (DT).

It is recommended that adults and children 7 years of age and older receive Td rather than the single-entity tetanus toxoid for the primary immunizing series, all booster doses, and active tetanus immunization in wound management. This is to help ensure protection against diphtheria infection, since a large proportion of adults is susceptible to diphtheria infection.

The primary immunizing series of Td consists of 3 doses (2 initial and 1 reinforcing) for adults and children 7 years of age and older.

Parenteral Dosage Forms

TETANUS AND DIPHTHERIA TOXOIDS ADSORBED FOR ADULT USE (Td) USP

Usual adult and adolescent dose

Diphtheria and tetanus (prophylaxis)—Intramuscular, preferably into the deltoid: 0.5 mL followed by 0.5 mL four to eight weeks later (in Canada, eight weeks later) for a total of two doses. A third dose of 0.5 mL is administered six to twelve months after the second dose. A booster dose of 0.5 mL is administered every ten years thereafter.

Note: If a booster dose of Td is administered less than ten years after the previous booster dose (e.g., as part of wound management or after exposure to diphtheria), the next booster dose should be administered ten years after the interim dose.

Usual pediatric dose

Diphtheria and tetanus (prophylaxis)—Intramuscular, preferably into the deltoid or the midlateral muscles of the thigh.—
Children up to 7 years of age—Use is not recommended. Diphtheria and tetanus toxoids for pediatric use (DT) should be administered instead.
Children 7 years of age and older—See *Usual adult and adolescent dose*.

Strength(s) usually available

U.S.—
2 Lf units of tetanus toxoid and 2 Lf units of diphtheria toxoid per 0.5 mL dose (Rx) [GENERIC (may contain thimerosal)].
5 Lf units of tetanus toxoid and 2 Lf units of diphtheria toxoid per 0.5 mL dose (Rx) [GENERIC (may contain thimerosal)].
10 Lf units of tetanus toxoid and 2 Lf units of diphtheria toxoid per 0.5 mL dose (Rx) [GENERIC (may contain thimerosal)].

Canada—
5 Lf units of tetanus toxoid and 2 Lf units of diphtheria toxoid per 0.5 mL dose (Rx) [GENERIC (may contain thimerosal)].

Note: Lf is the quantity of toxoid as assessed by flocculation.

Packaging and storage

Store between 2 and 8 °C (36 and 46 °F), unless otherwise specified by manufacturer. Store away from the freezer compartment. Protect from freezing.

Stability

Freezing destroys activity. The product should not be used if it has been exposed to freezing. In addition, the product should not be left out at room temperature (e.g., between patients).

Auxiliary labeling

- Shake the vial vigorously immediately before each dose is withdrawn in order to resuspend the contents.
- Protect from freezing.

Selected Bibliography

Centers for Disease Control and Prevention. Diphtheria, tetanus, and pertussis: recommendations for vaccine use and other preventive measures: recommendations of the Immunization Practices Advisory Committee (ACIP). MMWR 1991 Aug 8; 40(RR-10): 1-28.

Revised: 07/09/2003
Developed: 04/26/1995

DIPHTHERIA AND TETANUS TOXOIDS AND ACELLULAR PERTUSSIS ABSORBED AND HEPATITIS B (Recombinant) AND INACTIVATED POLIOVIRUS VACCINE COMBINED Systemic†

VA CLASSIFICATION (Primary): IM900

Commonly used brand name(s): *Pediarix*.

Another commonly used name is DTaP-HepB-IPV.

Note: For a listing of dosage forms and brand names by country availability, see *Dosage Forms* section(s).

†Not commercially available in Canada.

Category

Immunizing agent (active).

Indications

Accepted

Diphtheria, tetanus, pertussis, all known subtypes of hepatitis B virus, and poliomyelitis (prophylaxis)—DTaP-HepB-IPV is indicated for immunization of infants and children from 6 weeks of age up to the 7th birthday against diphtheria, tetanus, pertussis, hepatitis B, and poliomyelitis caused by poliovirus Types 1, 2, and 3 as a three dose primary series in infants born of HBsAg-negative mothers.

Acceptance not established

DTaP-HepB-IPV is not indicated for use as a booster dose following a 3–dose primary series of DTaP-HepB-IPV.

Pharmacology/Pharmacokinetics

Physicochemical characteristics

Source—

Diphtheria toxoid is produced by growing *Corynebacterium diphtheriae* in medium containing a bovine extract. Tetanus toxoid is produced by growing *Clostridium tetani* in medium derived from bovine casein. The resulting toxins are detoxified with formaldehyde, concentrated by ultrafiltration, purified, and adsorbed onto aluminum hydroxide.

The three acellular pertussis antigens (inactivated pertussis toxin (PT), filamentous hemagglutinin (FHA), and pertactin (69-kiloDalton outer membrane protein)) are isolated from *Bordetella pertussis*. The antigens are purified, detoxified using glutaraldehyde and formaldehyde, and adsorbed onto aluminum hydroxide.

Hepatitis B antigen (HbsAg) is produced by culturing genetically engineered *Saccharomyces cerevisiae* cells, which carry the surface antigen of the hepatitis B virus. The surface antigen is purified, residual thimerosal is removed, and adsorbed onto aluminum phosphate.

Inactivated poliovirus is produced from the three strains of poliovirus (Type 1,2, and 3) grown in monkey kidney cells in culture using calf serum and lactalbumin hydrolysate. Each viral suspension is purified and inactivated with formaldehyde. The three purified viral strains are then pooled to form a trivalent concentrate.

All antigens are then diluted and combined to produce the final formulated vaccine.

Mechanism of action/Effect

Diphtheria—Following intramuscular injection, diphtheria toxoid induces the formation of neutralizing antibodies to diphtheria toxin.

Tetanus—Following intramuscular injection, tetanus toxoid induces the formation of neutralizing antibodies to tetanus toxin.

Pertussis—Following intramuscular injection, acellular pertussis vaccine induces the formation of several antibodies thought to be clinically protective. The levels of antibody necessary for protection have not been determined.

Hepatitis B—Following intramuscular injection, antibody formation against HBsAg are recognized.

Inactivated Poliovirus Vaccine—Following intramuscular injection, IPV induces the production of neutralizing antibodies against each poliovirus serotype.

Other actions/effects

According to the Center for Disease Control (CDC), hepatitis B vaccine is recognized as the first anti-cancer vaccine because it can prevent primary liver cancer due to chronic hepatitis B infection. A clear link has been demonstrated between chronic hepatitis B infection and the occurrence of hepatocellular carcinoma.

Protective effect

Three doses of the vaccine are necessary in order to develop protection in pediatric patients 6 weeks up to 7 years of age.

Duration of protective effect

Diphtheria—Following immunization with diphtheria toxoid, protection persists for at least 10 years.

Tetanus—Following immunization it is thought that protection against tetanus toxoids persists for at least 10 years.

Peak serum concentration

Serum diphtheria antitoxin level of 0.01 IU per mL is the lowest level giving some degree of protection. Antitoxin levels of at least 0.1 IU per mL are generally regarded as protective.

Serum tetanus antitoxin level of 0.01 IU per mL is the minimum protective level. Antitoxin levels of ≥ 0.1 to 0.2 IU per mL are considered protective.

Antibodies ≥ 10 mIU per mL against HBsAg are recognized as protective against hepatitis B.

Precautions to Consider

Carcinogenicity/Mutagenicity

DTaP-HepB-IPV has not been evaluated for carcinogenic or mutagenic potential.

Pregnancy/Reproduction

Fertility—DTaP-HepB-IPV has not been evaluated for impairment of fertility.

Pregnancy—Adequate and well-controlled studies in humans have not been done.

DTaP-HepB-IPV is not indicated for use in women of child-bearing age. It is not known whether DTaP-HepB-IPV can cause fetal harm when administered to pregnant women or if DTaP-HepB-IPV can affect reproductive capability.

FDA Pregnancy Category C

Breast-feeding

It is not known whether DTaP-HepB-IPV is distributed into breast milk. However, DTaP-HepB-IPV is not indicated for use in persons 7 years of age and older.

Pediatrics

Safety and efficacy have not been established in children younger than 6 weeks of age and DTaP-HepB-IPV is not indicated for children over 7 years of age.

Geriatrics

DTaP-HepB-IPV is not indicated for use in adult populations.

Drug interactions and/or related problems

The following drug interactions and/or related problems have been selected on the basis of their potential clinical significance (possible mechanism in parentheses where appropriate)—not necessarily inclusive (» = major clinical significance):

Note: Combinations containing any of the following medications, depending on the amount present, may also interact with this medication.

» Anticoagulant therapy
(as with other intramuscular injections, this should not be administered to patients on anticoagulant therapy unless the potential benefit outweighs the risk)

Note: Although no specific data from studies under these conditions are available, if immunosuppressive therapy will be discontinued shortly, it would be reasonable to defer immunization until the patient has been off therapy for 3 months, otherwise the patient should be vaccinated while on therapy.

» Immunosuppressive therapies such as
Antimetabolites or
Alkylating agents or
Cytotoxic drugs or
Corticosteroids (used in greater than physiologic doses) or
Irradiation or

Immune globulin injection, recent
(an adequate immunological response may not be obtained)

Tetanus Immune Globulin or
Diphtheria Antitoxin
(these should be administered at a separate site with a separate needle and syringe)

Medical considerations/Contraindications

The medical considerations/contraindications included have been selected on the basis of their potential clinical significance (reasons given in parentheses where appropriate)—not necessarily inclusive (» = major clinical significance).

Except under special circumstances, this medication should not be used when the following medical problem exists:

» Anaphylaxis
(use of this vaccine is contraindicated after a serious allergic reaction temporally associated with a previous dose of this vaccine or with any components of this vaccine)

» Encephalopathy, including
Coma or
Decreased level of consciousness or
Prolonged seizures
(use is contraindicated in patients with these symptoms within 7 days of administration of a previous dose of a pertussis-containing vaccine that is not attributable to another identifiable cause)

» Hypersensitivity to any component of the vaccine including
Neomycin or
Polymyxin B or
Yeast
(use is contraindicated)

» Progressive neurologic disorder, including
Infantile spasms or
Progressive encephalopathy or
Uncontrolled epilepsy
(use is contraindicated in patients with these conditions until a treatment regimen has been established and the condition has been stabilized.)

Risk-benefit should be considered when the following medical problems exist:

Bleeding disorders, such as
Hemophilia or
Thrombocytopenia
(caution should be used and steps should be taken to avoid the risk of hematoma following the injection)

CNS disorders, stable
(a decision to administer a pertussis-containing vaccine to children with stable CNS disorders must be made by the physician on an individual basis, with consideration of all relevant factors and assessment of potential risks and benefits for that individual; guidelines for assessing such children have been issued by the Advisory Committee on Immunization Practices [ACIP] and the Committee on Infectious Diseases of the American Academy of Pediatrics (AAP))

» Guillain-Barre syndrome
(careful consideration of the potential benefits and possible risks of giving DTaP-HepB-IPV or any vaccine containing tetanus toxoid if this condition occurs within 6 weeks of receipt of prior vaccine containing tetanus toxoid)

» Immunodeficiency disorder
(an adequate immunological response may not be obtained)

» Moderate or severe illness, with or without fever
(vaccination should be deferred during the course of a moderate or severe illness, with or without a fever; should be vaccinated as soon as they have recovered from the acute phase of the illness)

» Previous adverse reaction to this vaccine or any of its components, such as
Collapse or shock-like state (hypotonic-hyporesponsive episode) within 48 hours or
Persistent, inconsolable crying lasting 3 hours or more, occurring within 48 hours or
Seizures with or without fever occurring within 3 days or
Temperature of ≥40.5°C (105°F) within 48 hours not due to another identifiable cause
(decision to give this or any other pertussis-containing vaccine should be based on careful consideration of the potential benefits and possible risks)

Seizures, higher risk
(for children at a higher risk for seizures an appropriate antipyretic may be administered at the time of vaccination with a vaccine containing an acellular pertussis component (including DTaP-HepB-IPV) and for the ensuing 24 hours according to the respective prescribing information recommended dosage to reduce the possibility of post-vaccination fever)

Side/Adverse Effects

Note: The adverse events listed in the following "Incidence not determined" sections are from a worldwide voluntary report with the use of Infanrix® (Diphtheria toxoid/pertussis vaccine, acellular/tetanus toxoid), and/or Engerix-B® (Hepatitis B Vaccine (Recombinant)). The components of these vaccines are present in Pediarix™ (diphtheria, tetanus, acellular pertussis, hepatitis B and inactivated poliovirus vaccine) and may produce similar adverse events.

Administration of Pediarix™ (diphtheria, tetanus, acellular pertussis hepatitis B and inactivated poliovirus vaccine) is associated with higher rates of fever relative to separately administered vaccines. The prevalence of fever was highest on the day of vaccination and the day following vaccination. More than 98% of episodes of fever resolved within the 4-day period following vaccination (i.e., the period including the day of vaccination and the next three days).

Reports of seizures have been received from a German safety study in patients receiving Pediarix™. The rate of seizures within 7 days after receiving the vaccine was 0.22 per 1000 doses (febrile seizures 0.07 per 1000 doses and afebrile seizures 0.14 per 1000 doses).

In clinical trials, 5 deaths were reported out of the 7,028 recipients of Pediarix™ and 1 death was reported out of the 1,764 recipients of comparator vaccines. Causes of death from patients receiving Pediarix™ included 2 cases of Sudden Infant Death Syndrome (SIDS) and one case of each of the following: convulsive disorder, congenital immunodeficiency with sepsis, and neuroblastoma. The rate of SIDS among recipients of Pediarix™ was 0.3 per 1000. One case of SIDS was reported in the comparator vaccine recipients.

Other reports of rare adverse events with the use of comparator vaccines that are components of Pediarix™ include, anaphylactic reaction, Arthus-type hypersensitivity reactions, brachial neuritis, and Guillain-Barre syndrome.

The following side/adverse effects have been selected on the basis of their potential clinical significance (possible signs and symptoms in parentheses where appropriate)—not necessarily inclusive:

Those indicating need for medical attention

Incidence not determined—Observed in clinical practice; estimates of frequency can not be determined

Anaphylactic reaction (cough; difficulty swallowing; dizziness; fast heartbeat; hives; itching, puffiness or swelling of the eyelids or around the eyes, face, lips or tongue; shortness of breath; skin rash; tightness in chest; unusual tiredness or weakness; wheezing); ***angioedema*** (large, hive-like swelling on face, eyelids, lips, tongue, throat, hands, legs, feet, sex organs); ***convulsions*** (seizures); ***cyanosis*** (bluish color of fingernails, lips, skin, palms, or nail beds); ***encephalopathy*** (agitation; back pain; blurred vision; coma; confusion; dizziness; drowsiness; fever; hallucinations; headache; irritability; mood or mental changes; seizures; stiff neck; unusual tiredness or weakness; vomiting); ***erythema*** (flushing, redness of skin; unusually warm skin); ***hypersensitivity*** (fast heartbeat; fever; hives; itching; irritation; hoarseness; joint pain; stiffness or swelling; rash; redness of skin; shortness of breath; swelling of eyelids, face, lips, hands, or feet; tightness in chest; troubled breathing or swallowing; wheezing); ***hypotonic-hyporesponsive episodes*** (collapse or shock-like state); ***idiopathic thrombocytopenic purpura*** (unusual bleeding or bruising; bloody nose; heavier menstrual periods; pinpoint red spots on skin; black, tarry stools; blood in urine; unusual tiredness or weakness; fever; skin rash); ***intussusception*** (diarrhea; pain or cramping in abdomen; nausea and vomiting); ***jaundice*** (chills; clay-colored stools; dark urine; dizziness; fever; headache; itching; loss of appetite; nausea; abdominal or stomach pain; area rash; unpleasant breath odor; unusual tiredness or weakness; vomiting of blood; yellow eyes or skin); ***Sudden Infant Death Syndrome (SIDS); thrombocytopenia*** (black, tarry stools; bleeding gums; blood in urine or stools; pinpoint red spots on skin; unusual bleeding or bruising)

Those indicating need for medical attention only if they continue or are bothersome

Incidence more frequent

Fever; fussiness; injection site reaction (Bleeding; blistering; burning; coldness; discoloration of skin; feeling of pressure; hives; infection; inflammation; itching; lumps; numbness; pain; rash; redness; scarring; soreness; stinging; swelling; tenderness; tingling; ulceration; warmth); ***loss of appetite; restlessness; sleeping more than usual; unusual cry***

Incidence not determined—Observed in clinical practice; estimates of frequency can not be determined

Abdominal pain; arthralgia (pain in joints; muscle pain or stiffness; difficulty in moving); ***asthenia*** (lack or loss of strength); ***cellulitis*** (itching, pain, redness, swelling, tenderness, warmth on skin); ***diarrhea; ear pain; edema*** (swelling); ***erythema multiforme*** (blistering, peeling, loosening of skin; chills; cough; diarrhea; fever; itching; joint or muscle pain; red irritated eyes; sore throat; sores, ulcers, or white spots in mouth or on lips; unusual tiredness or weakness); ***headache; hypotonia*** (unusual weak feeling; loss of strength or energy; muscle pain or weakness); ***irritability; lethargy***—unusual drowsiness; dullness, tiredness, weakness or feeling of sluggishness; ***limb swelling; loss of appetite; lymphadenopathy*** (swollen, painful, or tender lymph glands in neck, armpit, or groin); ***malaise; nausea; petechiae*** (small red or purple spots on skin); ***pruritus*** (itching skin); ***rash; respiratory tract infection*** (cough, fever, sneezing, sore throat); ***somnolence*** (sleepiness or unusual drowsiness); ***urticaria*** (hives or welts; itching; redness of skin; skin rash); ***vomiting***

Those not indicating need for medical attention

Incidence not determined—Observed in clinical practice; estimates of frequency can not be determined

Alopecia (hair loss; thinning of hair); ***pallor*** (paleness of skin)

Patient Consultation

As an aid to patient consultation, refer to *Diphtheria, Tetanus, Pertussis, Hepatitis B, Poliovirus Vaccine (Systemic)*.

In providing consultation, consider emphasizing the following selected information (» = major clinical significance):

Before receiving this vaccine

» Conditions affecting use, especially:

Sensitivity to any components of the vaccine and also neomycin, polymyxin B, and yeast

Use in children—Not using before 6 weeks of age or after 7 years of age

Other medications, especially anticoagulant therapy, immunosuppressive therapies such as antimetabolites, alkylating agents, cytotoxic drugs, corticosteroids, irradiation, or recent injection of immune globulin

Other medical problems, especially anaphylaxis, encephalopathy, including coma, decreased level of consciousness, prolonged seizures, Guillain-Barre syndrome, hypersensitivity to any component of the vaccine including neomycin, polymyxin B, or yeast, immunodeficiency disorder, moderate or severe illness, with or without fever, progressive encephalopathy, previous adverse reaction to this vaccine or any of its components, such as collapse or shock-like state, persistent, inconsolable crying lasting 3 hours or more, seizures with or without fever, or temperature of ≥40.5°C (105°F), progressive neurologic disorder, including infantile spasms, uncontrolled epilepsy, or stable CNS disorder

Proper use of this medication

» Proper dosing and adherence to vaccination schedule

Proper storage

Proper preparation of vaccine

Proper administration of vaccine

After receiving this vaccine

» Notifying physician or clinic of any side effect that occurs after receiving vaccination

Follow Up

Importance of following up when patient returns for next dose in series

Parents/Guardians should be given Vaccine Information Statements

Importance of calling VAERS if needed

Side/adverse effects

Signs of potential side effects, especially anaphylactic reaction, angioedema, convulsions, cyanosis, encephalopathy, erythema multiforme, hypersensitivity, hypotonic-hyporesponsive episodes, idiopathic thrombocytopenic purpura, intussusception, jaundice, Sudden Infant Death Syndrome (SIDS), thrombocytopenia

General Dosing Information

For parenteral dosing forms:

The vaccine should not be administered to any infant before 6 weeks of age. Only monovalent hepatitis B vaccine can be used for the birth dose.

Infants born of HBsAg-positive mothers should receive HBIG and monovalent Hepatitis B vaccine (recombinant) within 12 hours of birth at separate sites and should complete the Hepatitis B vaccination series according to a particular schedule. Infants born of mothers with unknown HBsAg status should receive HBIG and Hepatitis B vaccine (recombinant) within 12 hours of birth and should complete the Hepatitis B vaccination series according to a particular schedule. The administration of this vaccine for the completion of Hepatitis B vaccination series in infants who were born of HBsg positive mothers and who received monovalent Hepatitis B vaccine (recombinant) and HBIG has not been studied.

DTaP-HepB-IPV will not prevent hepatitis caused by other agents, such as hepatitis C, A, and E viruses, or other pathogens known to infect the liver. As hepatitis D (caused by the delta virus) does not occur in the absence of hepatitis B infection, hepatitis D will also be prevented by DTaP-HepB-IPV vaccination. Hepatitis B has a long incubation period. Vaccination with DTaP-HepB-IPV may not prevent hepatitis B infection in individuals who had an unrecognized hepatitis B infection at the time of vaccine administration.

When passive protection against tetanus or diphtheria is required, Tetanus Immune Globulin or Diphtheria Antitoxin, respectively, should be administered at separate sites.

The vial stopper is latex-free. The tip cap and the rubber plunger of the needless prefilled syringes contain dry natural latex rubber that may cause an allergic reaction in latex sensitive individuals.

Interchangeability of vaccines

- It is recommended that DTaP-HepB-IPV be given for all 3 doses because data are limited regarding the safety and efficacy of using acellular pertussis vaccines from different manufacturers for successive doses of the pertussis vaccination series. DTaP-HepB-IPV is not recommended for completion of the first three doses of the DTaP vaccination series initiated with a DTaP vaccine from a different manufacturer because no data are available regarding the safety and efficacy of using such a regimen.
- DTaP-HepB-IPV may be used to complete a hepatitis B vaccination series initiated with a licensed Hepatitis B Vaccine (recombinant) from a different manufacturer.
- DTaP-HepB-IPV may be used to complete the first 3 doses of the IPV vaccination series initiated with an IPV from a different manufacturer.

The use of reduced volume (fractional doses) is not recommended. The effect of such practices on the frequency of serious adverse events and on protection against disease has not been determined.

If any recommended dose of pertussis vaccine cannot be given, DT (for pediatric use), Hepatitis B (Recombinant), and inactivated poliovirus vaccines should be given as needed to complete the series.

Pre-term infants should be vaccinated according to their chronological age from birth.

Concomitant Vaccine Administration: In clinical trials, DTaP-HepB-IPV was routinely administered, at separate sites, concomitantly with Hib vaccine. Safety data are available following the first dose of DTaP-HepB-IPV, administered concomitantly, at separate sites, with Hib and pneumococcal conjugate vaccines. When concomitant administration of other vaccines is required they should be given with separate syringes and at different injection sites.

Before the injection of any biological, the physician should take all reasonable precautions to prevent allergic or other adverse reactions, including understanding the use of the biological concerned and the nature of the side effects and adverse reactions that may follow its use. Prior to immunization, the patient's current health status and medical history should be reviewed. The physician should review the patient's immunization history for possible vaccine sensitivity, previous vaccine related adverse reactions and the occurrence of any adverse-event related symptoms and/or signs, in order to determine the existence of any contraindication to immunization with DTaP-HepB-IPV and to allow assessment of benefits and risks. Epinephrine injection (1:1000) and other appropriate agents used for the control of immediate allergic reactions must be immediately available should an acute anaphylactic reaction occur.

As with any vaccine, DTaP-HepB-IPV may not protect 100% of the individuals receiving the vaccine, and it is not recommended for treatment of actual infections.

A separate sterile syringe and sterile disposable needle or sterile disposable unit should be used for each patient to prevent transmission of hepatitis or other infectious agents from one person to another. Needles should be disposed of properly and not be recapped. Special care should be taken to prevent injection into a blood vessel.

Information for vaccine recipients and parents or guardians:

- Parents or guardians should be informed of the potential risks and benefits of the vaccine, and the importance of completing the immunization series.
- When a child returns for the next dose in a series, it is important that the parent or guardian be questioned concerning occurrence of any symptoms and/or signs of an adverse reaction after a previous dose of the same vaccine. The physician should inform the parents/guardians about the potential for adverse events that have been temporally associated with administration of DTaP-HepB-IPV or other vaccines containing similar components. The parent/guardian accompanying the recipient should be told to report severe or unusual adverse events to the physician or clinic where the vaccine was administered.
- The parent/guardian should be given the Vaccine Information Statements, which are required by the National Childhood Vaccine Injury Act of 1986 to be given prior to immunization. These materials are available free of charge at the CDC website (www.cdc.gov/nip).

For treatment of adverse effects

The National Childhood Vaccine Injury Act requires that the manufacturer and lot number of the vaccine be recorded by the healthcare professional in the vaccine recipient's permanent medical record, along with the date of administration of the vaccine and the name, address, and title of the person administering the vaccine. The act further requires the healthcare provider to report to the U.S. Department of Health and Human Services via VAERS the occurrence following immunization of any event set forth in the Vaccine Injury Table including: Anaphylaxis or anaphylactic shock within 7 days, encephalopathy or encephalitis within 7 days, brachial neuritis within 28 days, or an acute complication or sequlae (including death) of an illness, disability, injury, or condition referred to above, or any events that would contraindicate further doses of vaccine. The VAERS toll-free number is 1–800–822–7967.

Parenteral Dosage Forms

DIPHTHERIA, TETANUS TOXOIDS, ACELLULAR PERTUSSIS ADSORBED, HEPATITIS B (RECOMBINANT) AND INACTIVATED POLIOVIRUS VACCINE

Usual adult dose

Use is not indicated for this age group

Usual pediatric dose

Immunizing agent—

Infants up to 6 weeks of age or children greater than 7 years of age: Use is not indicated

Children 6 weeks to 7 years of age: Intramuscular, 0.5 mL, preferably into the anterolateral aspect of the thigh or the deltoid muscle of the upper arm, at six- to eight-week intervals (preferably 8 weeks) for three doses.

Note: Interruption of the recommended schedule with a delay between doses should not interfere with the final immunity achieved by this vaccine. There is no need to start the series over again, regardless of the time elapsed between doses.

Children who have received a 3–dose primary series of DTaP-HepB-IPV should receive a fourth dose of IPV at 4 to 6 years of age and a fourth dose of DTaP vaccine at 15 to 18 months of age. Because the pertussis antigen components of Infanrix® are the same as those components in this vaccine (Pediarix™), these children should receive Infanrix® as their fourth dose of DTaP. However, data are insufficient to evaluate the safety of Infanrix® following three doses of DTaP-HepB-IPV (Pediarix™).

Children previously vaccinated with one or more doses of Hepatitis B Vaccine—

Infants born of HBsAg-negative mothers and who received a dose of hepatitis B vaccine at or shortly after birth: Intramuscular, administer 3 doses according to the recommended schedule. Safety and efficacy have not been established.

Note: There are no data to support the use of a 3–dose series of DTaP-HepB-IPV in infants who have previously received more than one dose of hepatitis B vaccine. DTaP-HepB-IPV may be used to complete a hepatitis B vaccination series in infants who have received one or more doses of Hepatitis B vaccine (recombinant) and who are also scheduled to receive other components of the DTaP-HepB-IPV vaccine.

Children previously vaccinated with Infanrix® (Diphtheria toxoid/pertussis vaccine, acellular/tetanus toxoid)—

Intramuscular, may be used to complete the first three doses of the DTaP and IPV series in infants who have received one or two doses of Infanrix® and are also scheduled to receive the other vaccine components of DTaP-HepB-IPV. Safety and efficacy have not been established.

Children previously vaccinated with one or more doses of IPV—

Intramuscular, may be used to complete the first three doses of the IPV series in infants who have received one or two doses of IPV and are also scheduled to receive the other vaccine components of DTaP-HepB-IPV. Safety and efficacy have not been established.

Usual geriatric dose

Use is not indicated for this age group.

Strength(s) usually available

U.S.—

25 Limit of flocculation (Lf) of diphtheria toxoid, 10 Lf of tetanus toxoid, 25 mcg protein of inactivated pertussis toxin (PT), 25 mcg of filamentous hemagglutinin (FHA), 8 mcg of pertactin, 10 mcg of HBsAg, 40 D-antigen units (DU) of Type 1 poliovirus, 8 DU of Type 2 poliovirus, and 32 DU of Type 3 poliovirus in each 0.5-mL dose. (Rx) [*Pediarix* (available in single-dose vials (0.5 mL) and disposable Tip-Lok® syringes; 2.5 mg of 2–phenoxyethanol; 4.5 mg of sodium chloride; aluminum adjuvant (not more than 0.85 mcg aluminum by assay); ≤ 100 mcg of residual formaldehyde; ≤ 100 mcg of polysorbate 80 (Tween 80))].

Canada—

Not commercially available

Packaging and storage

Store between 2 and 8 °C (36 and 46 °F). Do not freeze. Discard if the vaccine has been frozen. Do not use after expiration date on label.

Preparation of dosage form

Vaccine contains an adjuvant; shake vigorously to obtain a homogenous, turbid, white suspension. **Do not use if resuspension does not occur with vigorous shaking.** Inspect visually for particulate matter or discoloration prior to administration. After removal of dose, any remaining vaccine in the vial should be discarded. This vaccine should not be mixed with any other vaccine in the same syringe or vial.

Auxiliary labeling

- Shake well
- Do not freeze, discard if frozen

Note

The vaccine should not be given in the gluteal area or areas where there may be a major nerve trunk. Gluteal injections may result in suboptimal hepatitis B immune response. Do not administer subcutaneously or intravenously. After insertion of needle, aspirate to ensure the needle has not entered a blood vessel as special care should be taken to prevent injection into a blood vessel.

Revised: 3/19/2004
Developed: 10/31/2003

DIPHTHERIA AND TETANUS TOXOIDS AND PERTUSSIS VACCINE ADSORBED AND HAEMOPHILUS B CONJUGATE VACCINE (HBOC—DIPHTHERIA CRM$_{197}$ PROTEIN CONJUGATE)

—See *Diphtheria and Tetanus Toxoids and Pertussis Vaccine Adsorbed and Haemophilus B Conjugate Vaccine (Systemic)*

DIPHTHERIA AND TETANUS TOXOIDS AND PERTUSSIS VACCINE ADSORBED AND HAEMOPHILUS B CONJUGATE VACCINE (PRP-D—DIPHTHERIA TOXOID CONJUGATE)

—See *Diphtheria and Tetanus Toxoids and Pertussis Vaccine Adsorbed and Haemophilus B Conjugate Vaccine (Systemic)*

DIPHTHERIA AND TETANUS TOXOIDS AND PERTUSSIS VACCINE ADSORBED AND HAEMOPHILUS B CONJUGATE VACCINE Systemic

This monograph includes information on the following: 1) Diphtheria and tetanus toxoids combined with whole-cell pertussis vaccine and Haemophilus b conjugate vaccine (HbOC—diphtheria CRM_{197} protein conjugate); 2) Diphtheria and tetanus toxoids combined with whole-cell pertussis vaccine and Haemophilus b conjugate vaccine (PRP-D—diphtheria toxoid conjugate)*.

VA CLASSIFICATION (Primary): IM900

Commonly used brand name(s): *DPT-Hib*[2]; *Tetramune*[1].

Other commonly used names are:

DTP-HbOC [Diphtheria and tetanus toxoids combined with whole-cell pertussis vaccine and Haemophilus b conjugate vaccine (HbOC—diphtheria CRM_{197} protein conjugate)]

DTP-Hib [Diphtheria and tetanus toxoids combined with whole-cell pertussis vaccine and Haemophilus b conjugate vaccine (HbOC—diphtheria CRM_{197} protein conjugate)] or [Diphtheria and tetanus toxoids combined with whole-cell pertussis vaccine and Haemophilus b conjugate vaccine (PRP-D—diphtheria toxoid conjugate)]

DTP-PRP-D [Diphtheria and tetanus toxoids combined with whole-cell pertussis vaccine and Haemophilus b conjugate vaccine (PRP-D—diphtheria toxoid conjugate)]

Note: For a listing of dosage forms and brand names by country availability, see *Dosage Forms* section(s).

*Not commercially available in U.S.

Category

Immunizing agent (active).

Indications

Accepted

Diphtheria, tetanus, pertussis, and *Haemophilus influenzae* type b diseases (prophylaxis)—Diphtheria and tetanus toxoids and pertussis vaccine adsorbed and Haemophilus b conjugate vaccine combination (DTP-Hib) is indicated for immunization against the diseases caused by diphtheria, tetanus, pertussis, and *Haemophilus influenzae* type b organisms in infants and children up to 5 years of age when the schedules for immunization with the separate vaccines, diphtheria and tetanus toxoids and pertussis vaccine (DTP) and Haemophilus b conjugate vaccine (Hib), coincide.

Pharmacology/Pharmacokinetics

Physicochemical characteristics

Source—

Diphtheria and tetanus: Diphtheria toxoid is prepared from *Corynebacterium diphtheriae* toxin and tetanus toxoid is prepared from *Clostridium tetani* toxin. Both toxins are detoxified with formaldehyde. The toxoids are adsorbed onto aluminum phosphate.

Pertussis: Pertussis vaccine is prepared from *Bordetella pertussis* bacteria, which are inactivated with thimerosal.

Haemophilus b: Purified capsular polysaccharide, a polymer of ribose, ribitol, and phosphate (PRP), is derived from the bacterium *Haemophilus influenzae* type b. It is conjugated in one of the following ways.

For the diphtheria CRM_{197} protein conjugate: Oligosaccharides are derived from the polysaccharide and bound directly to CRM_{197} (a nontoxic variant of diphtheria toxin) by reductive amination.

For the diphtheria toxoid conjugate: The polysaccharide is conjugated to the diphtheria toxoid via a 6-carbon linker molecule.

Mechanism of action/Effect

Diphtheria—Following intramuscular injection, diphtheria toxoid induces the formation of diphtheria antitoxin.

Tetanus—Following intramuscular injection, tetanus toxoid induces the formation of tetanus antitoxin.

Pertussis—Following intramuscular injection, pertussis vaccine induces the formation of several antibodies thought to be clinically protective. The exact mechanism of protection is not known.

Haemophilus b—*Haemophilus influenzae* type b (Hib) bacteria are surrounded by polysaccharide capsules, which make these bacteria resistant to attack by white blood cells. The vaccine, which is derived from the purified polysaccharide from Hib cells, stimulates production of anticapsular antibodies and provides active immunity to the Hib bacteria. Whereas the nonconjugated polysaccharide vaccine predominantly stimulates B-cells to produce antibodies (known as being T-cell independent), Haemophilus b conjugate vaccine stimulates T-cells also. The additional stimulation of T-cells (known as being T-cell dependent) is particularly important in young children to ensure an adequate and persistent antibody response. Stimulation of T-cells also results in an anamnestic response to future doses of the conjugate or nonconjugate vaccine and to future natural exposure to Hib, resulting in elevated antibody titers.

Protective effect

Diphtheria—The protective titer of diphtheria antitoxin in serum is considered to be 0.01 unit per mL.

Tetanus—The protective titer of tetanus antitoxin in serum is considered to be 0.01 unit per mL.

Pertussis—The potency of the inactivated *B. pertussis* cells in the vaccine is assayed by comparison with the U.S. standard pertussis vaccine in the intracerebral mouse protection test. The protective efficacy of pertussis vaccines for humans has been shown to correlate with the measure of vaccine potency.

Haemophilus b—Antibody response to Haemophilus b conjugate vaccine is age related in children, with the immune response improving with increasing age. The titer of antibody from Haemophilus b conjugate vaccine required for protection against invasive disease has not been clearly established. However, in studies using Haemophilus b polysaccharide vaccine, a geometric mean titer (GMT) of 1 mcg per mL of serum 3 weeks after immunization correlated with protection and suggests long-term protection from invasive disease.

Duration of protective effect

Diphtheria—At least 10 years for diphtheria toxoid following a completed primary immunizing series of injections.

Tetanus—At least 10 years for tetanus toxoid following a completed primary immunizing series of injections.

Pertussis—Following a completed primary immunizing series of injections, immunity to pertussis usually persists throughout childhood, but is thought to decrease over time. Lifelong immunity is probably attained through subsequent mild pertussis infection.

Haemophilus b—The duration of immunity is unknown.

Precautions to Consider

Cross-sensitivity and/or related problems

Patients sensitive to diphtheria or tetanus toxoid, whole cell or acellular pertussis vaccine, Haemophilus b polysaccharide vaccine, or any type of Haemophilus b conjugate vaccine may be sensitive to diphtheria and tetanus toxoids and pertussis vaccine adsorbed and Haemophilus b conjugate vaccine combination (DTP-Hib) also.

Carcinogenicity/Mutagenicity

Studies have not been done.

Pregnancy/Reproduction

Fertility—Studies have not been done.

Pregnancy—Studies have not been done in humans. DTP-Hib is not recommended for use in persons 7 years of age or older.

Studies have not been done in animals.

FDA Pregnancy Category C.

Pediatrics

Safety and efficacy have not been established for children younger than 6 weeks of age for DTP-Hib (HbOC—diphtheria CRM_{197} protein conjugate) or younger than 18 months of age for DTP-Hib (PRP-D—diphtheria toxoid conjugate). DTP-Hib is not recommended for use in children 7 years of age or older. (The DTP component is not recommended for use in persons 7 years of age or older, because of the increased risk of side/adverse reactions; the Hib component is not recommended for use in persons 5 years of age or older, except for patients with certain chronic conditions associated with an increased risk of Hib disease.)

Immunization with DTP-Hib is *contraindicated* if a previous immunization with a DTP- or pertussis-containing vaccine was temporally related to an immediate anaphylactic reaction or encephalopathy occurring within 7 days after immunization. See also *General Dosing Information.*

Although the following events *were* considered contraindications in previous recommendations of the Advisory Committee of Immunization Practices (ACIP) of the Centers for Disease Control and Prevention (CDC), they are now considered *precautions*. Immunization with DTP-Hib should be carefully considered if a previous immunization with a DTP- or pertussis-containing vaccine was temporally related to fever of ≥ 40.5 °C (105 °F) occurring within 48 hours; hypotonic-hyporesponsive episode (collapse or shock-like state) occurring within 48 hours; persistent and inconsolable crying lasting 3 or more hours and occurring within 48 hours; or seizures with or without fever occurring within 3 days. See also *General Dosing Information.*

Drug interactions and/or related problems

The following drug interactions and/or related problems have been selected on the basis of their potential clinical significance (possible mechanism in parentheses where appropriate)—not necessarily inclusive (» = major clinical significance):

Note: Combinations containing any of the following medications, depending on the amount present, may also interact with this vaccine.

Immunosuppressive agents
Radiation therapy
(because normal defense mechanisms are suppressed by immunosuppressive agents or radiation treatment, the patient's antibody response to DTP-Hib may be decreased. If possible, children who are to undergo therapy with agents that cause immunosuppression, including treatment for Hodgkin's disease, should receive the vaccine at least 10 days, and preferably more than 14 days, before receiving the immunosuppressive agent; otherwise, it may be preferable to postpone the immunization until after the immunosuppressive therapy is completed. The interval between discontinuation of therapy that causes immunosuppression and the restoration of the patient's ability to respond to an active immunizing agent depends on the intensity and type of immunosuppressive therapy used, the underlying disease, and other factors; estimates vary from 3 months to 1 year. The precaution does not apply to corticosteroids used as replacement therapy, for short-term [less than 2 weeks] systemic therapy, or by other routes of administration that do not cause immunosuppression)

Laboratory value alterations

The following have been selected on the basis of their potential clinical significance (possible effect in parentheses where appropriate)—not necessarily inclusive (» = major clinical significance).

With diagnostic test results
Antigen detection tests
(there is a possibility that the conjugate vaccine may interfere with interpretation of antigen detection tests, such as latex agglutination and countercurrent immunoelectrophoresis, that are used for diagnosis of systemic Hib disease. For example, purified capsular polysaccharide [a polymer of ribose, ribitol, and phosphate (PRP)], which is associated with Haemophilus b vaccines, was detected in the urine of some persons for up to 7 days following immunization with an Haemophilus b vaccine conjugated with meningococcal protein [PRP-OMP])

Medical considerations/Contraindications

The medical considerations/contraindications included have been selected on the basis of their potential clinical significance (reasons given in parentheses where appropriate)—not necessarily inclusive (» = major clinical significance).

Except under special circumstances, this vaccine should not be used when the following medical problems exist:

» Central nervous system (CNS) disorders, evolving or changing, whether or not the disorder is associated with seizure activity
(there appears to be an increased risk of the appearance of manifestations of the underlying neurological disorder within 2 or 3 days after immunization. This may lead to confusion in interpretation of the neurological disorder. However, prolonged manifestations, increased progression, or exacerbation of the disorder has not been identified)

» Febrile illness or
» Infection, acute
(administration of DTP-Hib should be postponed until the acute symptoms of the patient's illness have abated to avoid confusing the symptoms of the illness with the side effects of the vaccine; however, minor illnesses, such as mild upper-respiratory infections with or without low-grade fever are not contraindications)

» Sensitivity to DTP-Hib

Risk-benefit should be considered when the following medical problems exist:

Neurological disease, suspected
(initiation of DTP, but not other childhood vaccines, should be delayed until there is clarification of the child's neurological status; however, the decision whether or not to commence immunization with DTP should be made by the child's first birthday. When making the decision, it should be recognized that neurologically disabled children may be at increased risk of pertussis because of their attendance at special schools or clinics where many of the other children attending may not be immunized. In addition, neurologically disabled children may be at increased risk from complications of pertussis)
(See also *General Dosing Information.*)

Seizures
(children who have had seizures prior to DTP administration, whether febrile or afebrile, appear to be more likely to have seizures following DTP immunization than children without such histories. However, current evidence indicates that seizures following DTP immunization do not cause permanent brain damage. A seizure occurring within 3 days of DTP immunization in a child with a history of seizures may be initiated by vaccine-induced fever in a child prone to febrile seizures, induced by the pertussis component, or unrelated to the vaccine. Therefore, it is prudent to delay DTP immunization in infants and children with a history of seizures until the child's status has been fully assessed and the condition has been stabilized. However, it should be noted that delaying DTP immunization until the second 6 months of life will increase the risk of febrile seizures among predisposed children. Children with a history of seizures should be given acetaminophen, 15 mg per kg of body weight (mg/kg), at the time of immunization and every 4 hours for the next 24 hours)
(See also *General Dosing Information.*)

Seizures or other CNS disorders, family history of
(children with a family history of seizures or other CNS disorders appear to be more likely to have seizures following DTP immunization than do children without such histories; however, these seizures are usually caused by fever. Acetaminophen, 15 mg/kg, should be given to these children at the time of immunization and every 4 hours for the next 24 hours)

Sensitivity to thimerosal

Side/Adverse Effects

Note: Children who have had seizures previously, whether febrile or afebrile, appear to be more likely to have seizures following a diphtheria and tetanus toxoids and pertussis vaccine (DTP)–containing immunization than children without such histories. However, current evidence indicates that seizures following a DTP-containing immunization do not cause permanent brain damage. See also *General Dosing Information.*

Fever that does not begin until 24 or more hours after immunization or persists for more than 24 hours after immunization should not be assumed to be due to a DTP-containing immunization.

The following side/adverse effects have been selected on the basis of their potential clinical significance (possible signs and symptoms in parentheses where appropriate)—not necessarily inclusive:

Those indicating need for medical attention

Incidence rare
Anaphylactic reaction (difficulty in breathing or swallowing; hives; itching, especially of soles or palms; reddening of skin, especially around ears; swelling of eyes, face, or inside of nose; unusual tiredness or weakness, sudden and severe); ***convulsions, with or without fever, occurring within 3 days; crying, persistent and inconsolable, occurring within 48 hours and lasting 3 or more hours; encephalopathy, occurring within 7 days*** (severe alterations in consciousness, with generalized or focal neurological signs; confusion; severe or continuing headache; unusual and continuing irritability; excessive sleepiness; severe or continuing vomiting); ***fever of 40.5 °C (105 °F) or more, occurring within 48 hours; hypotonic-hyporesponsive episode, occurring within 48 hours*** (collapse or shock-like state)

Those indicating need for medical attention only if they continue or are bothersome

Incidence more frequent
Drowsiness; erythema, swelling, or warm feeling at injection site (redness, swelling, or warm feeling at place of injection); ***fever up to 39 °C (102.2 °F)***—usually lasting up to, but no longer than, 48 hours; may be accompanied by fretfulness, drowsiness, vomiting, and anorexia; ***fretfulness; irritability; lump at injection site***—may be present for a few weeks after injection; ***pain or tenderness at injection site***

Incidence less frequent
Anorexia (loss of appetite); ***diarrhea; fever between 39 and 40 °C (102.2 and 104 °F)***—usually lasting up to, but no longer than, 48 hours; may be accompanied by fretfulness, drowsiness, vomiting, and anorexia; ***induration at injection site*** (hard lump)—may be present for a few days after injection; ***vomiting***

Incidence rare
Abscess, sterile (redness, swelling, tenderness, or pain at injection site); ***fever between 40 and 40.4 °C (104 and 104.8 °F)***—usually last-

ing up to, but no longer than, 48 hours; may be accompanied by fretfulness, drowsiness, vomiting, and anorexia; incidence 1 to 5%; ***lethargy*** (lack of interest; reduced physical activity); ***skin rash***

Patient Consultation

As an aid to patient consultation, refer to *Advice for the Patient, Diphtheria and Tetanus Toxoids and Pertussis Vaccine Adsorbed and Haemophilus b Conjugate Vaccine (Systemic).*

In providing consultation, consider emphasizing the following selected information (» = major clinical significance):

Before receiving this vaccine

» Conditions affecting use, especially:

Sensitivity to diphtheria or tetanus toxoid, whole cell or acellular pertussis vaccine, Haemophilus b polysaccharide vaccine, any type of Haemophilus b conjugate vaccine, or thimerosal

Use in children—Safety and efficacy have not been established for children younger than 6 weeks of age (administration usually begins at 2 months of age); not recommended for use in children 7 years of age or older

Other medical problems, especially acute infection; evolving or changing central nervous system (CNS) disorders, whether or not the disorder is associated with seizure activity; or febrile illness

Proper use of this medication

» Proper dosing

After receiving this vaccine

Possibly receiving acetaminophen at time of injection; possibly continuing acetaminophen every 4 hours for 24 hours following injection; checking with physician if there are questions

Possibility of vaccine interfering with laboratory tests that check for Hib disease; informing physician of recent DTP-Hib vaccination if treated for a severe infection within 2 weeks after administration

Side/adverse effects

Signs of potential side effects, especially anaphylactic reaction; convulsions, with or without fever, occurring within 3 days; crying, persistent and inconsolable, occurring within 48 hours and lasting 3 or more hours; encephalopathy, occurring within 7 days; fever of 40.5 °C (105 °F) or more, occurring within 48 hours; and hypotonic-hyporesponsive episode, occurring within 48 hours

General Dosing Information

Diphtheria and tetanus toxoids and pertussis vaccine adsorbed and Haemophilus b conjugate vaccine combination (DTP-Hib) is not recommended for use in persons 7 years of age or older. (The DTP component is not recommended for use in persons 7 years of age or older, because of the increased risk of side/adverse reactions; the Hib component is not recommended for use in persons 5 years of age or older, except for patients with certain chronic conditions associated with an increased risk of Hib disease.)

DTP-Hib vaccine may be administered concurrently with the following, using separate body sites and syringes for the parenterals, and the precautions that apply to each immunizing agent:

- Hepatitis B recombinant or plasma-derived vaccine.
- Influenza virus vaccine. In the past it was recommended that influenza virus vaccine and a pertussis-containing vaccine should not be administered within 3 days of one another. Since both influenza virus vaccine and pertussis vaccine may cause febrile reactions in young children, the time interval was recommended so that the cause of any adverse effect was clear. However, the American Academy of Pediatrics (AAP) now accepts concurrent administration of these vaccines.
- Measles, mumps, and rubella vaccine (MMR).
- Poliovirus vaccines (oral [OPV], inactivated [IPV], or enhanced-potency inactivated [enhanced-potency IPV]).

Preterm infants should be immunized according to their chronological age from birth.

Continued use of this vaccine is *contraindicated because of its DTP component,* according to the Advisory Committee Immunization Practices (ACIP), when the following medical problems occur:

- Anaphylactic reaction, immediate. Because of uncertainty as to which component of the vaccine may be responsible, it is recommended that no further immunization be carried out with any of the three antigens in DTP. Alternatively, because of the importance of tetanus immunization, such individuals should be referred to an allergist for evaluation and desensitized to tetanus toxoid if specific allergy can be demonstrated.
- Encephalopathy, not due to another identifiable cause. Encephalopathy is defined as an acute, severe CNS disorder occurring within 7 days following immunization and generally consisting of major alterations in consciousness, unresponsiveness, generalized or focal seizures that persist more than a few hours, and failure to recover within 24 hours. Even though causation by DTP cannot be established, subsequent doses of the pertussis component should not be given. In addition, it may be desirable to delay for a period of months so that the child's neurological status can clarify before continuing the immunization series with diphtheria and tetanus toxoids combination (DT) instead of DTP.

Although the following events *were* considered contraindications to continued use of pertussis vaccine, in previous ACIP recommendations, they are now considered *precautions.* There may be circumstances, such as a high incidence of pertussis in the community, in which the potential benefits outweigh possible risks, particularly since these events are not associated with permanent sequelae. Therefore, continued use of this vaccine should be *carefully considered because of its pertussis component* when the following medical problems occur:

- Fever ≥ 40.5 °C (105 °F) occurring within 48 hours and not due to other causes. This is considered a precaution because of the likelihood that fever following a subsequent dose of DTP vaccine also will be high. Because such febrile reactions are usually attributed to the pertussis component, the immunization series should be continued with DT.
- Hypotonic-hyporesponsive episode (collapse or shock-like state) occurring within 48 hours. Although these uncommon events have not been recognized to cause death or to induce permanent neurological sequelae, it is prudent to omit the pertussis component and continue the immunization series with DT.
- Persistent and inconsolable crying lasting 3 or more hours and occurring within 48 hours. Follow-up of infants who have cried inconsolably following DTP immunization has indicated that this reaction is without long-term sequelae and is not associated with other reactions of greater significance. Inconsolable crying occurs most frequently following the first dose of DTP. However, crying for longer than 30 minutes following a DTP injection can be a predictor of increased likelihood of persistent crying following subsequent doses. Children who react with persistent crying have had a higher rate of substantial local reactions than did children who had other DTP-associated reactions (including high fever, seizures, and hypotonic-hyporesponsive episodes), suggesting that prolonged crying was really a pain reaction.
- Seizures, with or without fever, occurring within 3 days. Short-lived seizures, with or without fever, have not been shown to cause permanent sequelae. Furthermore, the occurrence of prolonged febrile seizures (i.e., status epilepticus, defined as any seizure lasting longer than 30 minutes or recurrent seizures lasting a total of 30 minutes without the child fully regaining consciousness), irrespective of their cause, involving an otherwise normal child does not substantially increase the risk for subsequent febrile (brief or prolonged) or afebrile seizures. The risk is significantly increased only among those children who are neurologically abnormal before their episode of status epilepticus. Accordingly, although a seizure following DTP immunization previously has been considered a contraindication to further doses of the pertussis component, under certain circumstances subsequent doses may be indicated, particularly if the risk of pertussis in the community is high. If a child has a seizure following the first or second dose of DTP, it is desirable to delay subsequent doses until the child's neurologic status is better defined. By the child's first birthday, the presence of an underlying neurologic disorder has usually been determined. A decision should be made whether to continue with DTP instead of automatically switching to DT. Regardless of whether DTP or DT is chosen, acetaminophen, 15 mg per kg of body weight (mg/kg), should be given at the time of immunization and every 4 hours for the next 24 hours.

Continued use of this vaccine *should be carefully considered because of its DTP component* if a neurological event (e.g., seizure) occurs between doses of, but not temporally associated with, this vaccine. If the event occurs before the child's first birthday and the child has not received all 3 doses of the primary DTP series, further doses of DTP, but not other childhood vaccines, should be deferred until there is clarification of the child's neurological status; however, the decision whether or not to continue immunization with DTP should be made no later than the child's first birthday and should be based on the nature of the neurological event and the risk/benefit associated with the vaccine. If the event occurs after the child's first birthday, the child's neurological status should be evaluated to ensure that the disorder is stable before immunization with DTP is continued. See also *Medical considerations/Contraindications.*

Children with stable neurologic conditions, including well-controlled seizures, may be immunized with a DTP-containing vaccine. The occurrence of a single seizure that is not temporally associated with DTP does not contraindicate DTP immunization, particularly if the seizure can be explained. Parents of children with histories of seizures should be informed of the increased risk of postimmunization seizures. In addition, acetaminophen, 15 mg/kg, should be given at the time of immunization and every 4 hours for the next 24 hours to reduce the possibility of postimmunization fever. See also *Medical considerations/Contraindications*.

Immunization with a DTP-containing vaccine is recommended for children with certain neurologic problems, such as hydrocephalus (following placement of a shunt and if the child is without seizures) or neonatal hypocalcemic tetany, that have been corrected or have clearly subsided without residua.

Before each additional dose of DTP-Hib, the health status of the patient should be assessed. In addition, information should be obtained regarding any symptom or sign of an adverse reaction that occurred after the previous dose.

If tetanus immune globulin (TIG) or diphtheria antitoxin is being administered at the same time as DTP-Hib, separate body sites and separate syringes should be used.

For treatment of adverse effects

Recommended treatment includes:

- For mild hypersensitivity reaction—Administering antihistamines, and, if necessary, glucocorticoids.
- For severe hypersensitivity or anaphylactic reaction—Administering epinephrine. Antihistamines or glucocorticoids may also be administered as required.

DIPHTHERIA AND TETANUS TOXOIDS AND PERTUSSIS VACCINE ADSORBED AND HAEMOPHILUS B CONJUGATE VACCINE (HbOC—DIPHTHERIA CRM$_{197}$ PROTEIN CONJUGATE)

Parenteral Dosage Forms

DIPHTHERIA AND TETANUS TOXOIDS AND PERTUSSIS VACCINE ADSORBED AND HAEMOPHILUS B CONJUGATE VACCINE (HbOC—diphtheria CRM$_{197}$ protein conjugate) INJECTION

Note: Diphtheria and tetanus toxoids and pertussis vaccine adsorbed and Haemophilus b conjugate vaccine combination (DTP-Hib) may be used whenever the schedules for immunization with the separate vaccines, diphtheria and tetanus toxoids and pertussis vaccine (DTP) and Haemophilus b conjugate vaccine (Hib), coincide.

Usual adult and adolescent dose

Use is not recommended.

Usual pediatric dose

Active immunizing agent—

Intramuscular, 0.5 mL into the outer aspect of the upper arm (deltoid) or into the lateral mid thigh (vastus lateralis).

Children up to 2 months of age—Use is not recommended.

Children 2 to 6 months of age at the first dose—Three doses, at least two months apart. Then, a fourth dose at 12 to 18 months of age after at least a 6-month interval following the third dose.

Note: Alternatively, Hib vaccine and either acellular DTP (DTaP) or whole-cell DTP may be administered as separate injections for the fourth dose at 12 to 18 months of age. (DTaP is preferred for doses four and five of the five-dose DTP series in order to reduce the chance of side effects.)

Children 7 to 11 months of age at the first dose—Two doses, at least two months apart, followed by appropriate doses of DTP or Hib (or DTP-Hib, where use of the two vaccines coincides) to complete each vaccine's immunization schedule. (A child 7 to 11 months of age should receive a total of 3 doses of a product containing HbOC.)

Children 12 to 14 months of age at the first dose—One dose, followed by appropriate doses of DTP or Hib (or DTP-Hib, when use of the two vaccines coincides) to complete each vaccine's immunization schedule. (A child 12 to 14 months of age should receive a total of 2 doses of a product containing HbOC.)

Children 15 to 59 months of age at the first dose—One dose, followed by appropriate doses of DTP to complete the immunization schedule for DTP. (A child 15 to 59 months of age should receive a single dose of a product containing HbOC.)

Note: The above dosage schedules do not negate the necessity of any additional doses or boosters of DTP or Hib that are required.

The above doses assume that neither DTP nor Hib vaccine has been administered previously.

DTP-Hib vaccine may be used also to complete an immunization series already initiated with any Hib vaccine and/or any DTP vaccine in those instances where the two vaccine schedules coincide.

Although any Hib vaccine type (licensed for use in that particular age group) may be used where the individual vaccine is required, use of the same Hib vaccine type throughout a primary immunization series is preferable.

Strength(s) usually available

U.S.—

12.5 Lf of diphtheria toxoid, 5 Lf of tetanus toxoid, 4 protective units of pertussis vaccine, 10 mcg (0.01 mg) of purified Haemophilus b saccharide, and approximately 25 mcg (0.025 mg) of CRM$_{197}$ protein (a nontoxic variant of diphtheria toxin), per 0.5 mL dose. Each 0.5-mL dose contains not more than 850 mcg (0.85 mg) of aluminum (Rx) [*Tetramune* (thimerosal 1:10,000)].

Canada—

12.5 Lf of diphtheria toxoid, 5 Lf of tetanus toxoid, 4 protective units of pertussis vaccine, 10 mcg (0.01 mg) of purified Haemophilus b saccharide, and approximately 25 mcg (0.025 mg) of CRM$_{197}$ protein (a nontoxic variant of diphtheria toxin), per 0.5 mL dose. Each 0.5-mL dose contains not more than 850 mcg (0.85 mg) of aluminum (Rx) [*Tetramune* (thimerosal 1:10,000)].

Note: Lf is the quantity of toxoid as assessed by flocculation.

Packaging and storage

Store between 2 and 8 °C (36 and 46 °F), unless otherwise specified by manufacturer. Protect from freezing.

Preparation of dosage form

The product should be shaken well immediately before withdrawing each dose. The product should be discarded if clumps remain after vigorous agitation.

Stability

The vaccine should be refrigerated, but kept away from the freezer compartment. Vaccine that has been frozen should be discarded.

Auxiliary labeling

- Shake well.
- Do not freeze.

DIPHTHERIA AND TETANUS TOXOIDS AND PERTUSSIS VACCINE ADSORBED AND HAEMOPHILUS B CONJUGATE VACCINE (PRP-D—DIPHTHERIA TOXOID CONJUGATE)

Parenteral Dosage Forms

DIPHTHERIA AND TETANUS TOXOIDS AND PERTUSSIS VACCINE ADSORBED AND HAEMOPHILUS B CONJUGATE VACCINE (PRP-D—diphtheria toxoid conjugate) INJECTION

Usual adult and adolescent dose

Use is not recommended.

Usual pediatric dose

Active immunizing agent—

Intramuscular, 0.5 mL into the outer aspect of the upper arm (deltoid) or into the lateral mid thigh (vastus lateralis):

Children up to 18 months of age—Use is not recommended.

Children 18 to 59 months of age—DTP-Hib may be administered when the single dose of Hib coincides with the fourth or fifth scheduled dose of DTP.

Strength(s) usually available

U.S.—

Not commercially available.

Canada—

25 Lf of diphtheria toxoid, 5 Lf of tetanus toxoid, 4 to 12 protective units of pertussis vaccine, 25 mcg (0.025 mg) of purified Haemophilus b capsular polysaccharide, and 18 mcg (0.018 mg) of diphtheria toxoid protein, per 0.5 mL dose. Each 0.5-mL dose contains 1.5 mg of aluminum phosphate (Rx) [*DPT-Hib* (thimerosal 0.01%)].

Note: Lf is the quantity of toxoid as assessed by flocculation.

Packaging and storage

Store between 2 and 8 °C (36 and 46 °F), unless otherwise specified by manufacturer. Protect from freezing.

Preparation of dosage form

The product should be shaken well immediately before withdrawing each dose. The product should be discarded if clumps remain after vigorous agitation.

Stability

The vaccine should be refrigerated, but kept away from the freezer compartment. Vaccine that has been frozen should be discarded.

Auxiliary labeling

- Shake well.
- Do not freeze.

Selected Bibliography

Centers for Disease Control and Prevention. Recommendations for use of Haemophilus b conjugate vaccines and a combined diphtheria, tetanus, pertussis, and Haemophilus b vaccine. Recommendations of the Advisory Committee on Immunization Practices (ACIP). MMWR 1993 Sep 17; 42(RR-13): 1-15.

Centers for Disease Control and Prevention. Diphtheria, tetanus, and pertussis: recommendations for vaccine use and other preventive measures: recommendations of the Immunization Practices Advisory Committee (ACIP). MMWR 1991 Aug 8; 40(RR-10): 1-28.

Centers for Disease Control and Prevention. Haemophilus b conjugate vaccines for prevention of Haemophilus influenzae type b disease among infants and children two months of age and older: recommendation of the Immunization Practices Advisory Committee (ACIP). MMWR 1991 Jan 11: 40 (RR-1).

Developed: 11/27/1996

DIPYRIDAMOLE Systemic

VA CLASSIFICATION (Primary/Secondary): BL117/DX900

Commonly used brand name(s): *Apo-Dipyridamole FC; Apo-Dipyridamole SC; Novo-Dipiradol; Persantine.*

Note: For a listing of dosage forms and brand names by country availability, see *Dosage Forms* section(s).

Category

Platelet aggregation inhibitor; antithrombotic adjunct; diagnostic aid adjunct (ischemic heart disease); myocardial reinfarction prophylactic adjunct.

Indications

Note: Bracketed information in the *Indications* section refers to uses that are not included in U.S. product labeling.

Accepted

Platelet aggregation (prophylaxis)—Dipyridamole is indicated to inhibit platelet aggregation and correct shortened platelet survival time in the following:

Thromboembolism (prophylaxis adjunct)—Indicated, concurrently with a coumarin- or indanedione-derivative anticoagulant, to prevent postoperative thromboembolic complications associated with the placement of mechanical prosthetic heart valves. Use of dipyridamole for this purpose is optional, but is appropriate if an embolism occurs despite adequate anticoagulation. Also, it is recommended that dipyridamole be used whenever the anticoagulant must be administered in lower dosage than is usually recommended for this indication.

In three randomized controlled clinical trials involving 854 patients who had undergone surgical placement of a prosthetic heart valve, oral dipyridamole, in combination with warfarin, decreased the incidence of postoperative thromboembolic events by 62 to 91% (incidence 1.2 to 1.8%) compared to warfarin treatment alone. In three additional clinical trials involving 392 patients who received oral dipyridamole concurrently with a coumarin- or indanedione-derivative anticoagulant, the incidence of thromboembolic events ranged from 2.3 to 6.9%. In these trials, the oral anticoagulant was begun between 24 hours and 4 days postoperatively, and the dipyridamole was begun between 24 hours and 10 days postoperatively.

[A few studies have shown that platelet aggregation inhibitors, although not as consistently effective as an anticoagulant or an anticoagulant plus dipyridamole, may provide some protection against the development of thromboembolic complications in patients with mechanical prosthetic heart valves. Therefore, administration of dipyridamole together with aspirin may be considered if anticoagulant therapy is contraindicated for these patients.]

[The addition of dipyridamole to therapy with a coumarin- or indanedione-derivative anticoagulant may also be considered for patients with documented systemic embolism associated with mitral valve disease if an embolism recurs despite adequate anticoagulation.][1]

[Dipyridamole is also used, in conjunction with aspirin, to reduce the risk of thrombosis and/or occlusion of saphenous vein aortocoronary bypass grafts.][1]

[Dipyridamole is also used, in conjunction with aspirin, to reduce the risk of thromboembolism that may occur in conjunction with percutaneous transluminal coronary angioplasty. Use of these medications does not eliminate the need for administration of heparin during the procedure. Although the value of this regimen in preventing thromboembolism that may occur in conjunction with peripheral angioplasty has not been established via controlled trials, some clinicians recommend that dipyridamole and aspirin also be used, sequentially with heparin, in patients undergoing peripheral angioplasty.][1]

[Dipyridamole is also used, in conjunction with aspirin, to reduce the risk of thrombosis or occlusion of prosthetic or saphenous vein femoral popliteal bypass grafts.][1]

[Dipyridamole is also used, in conjunction with aspirin, in the treatment of lower extremity occlusive vascular disease. This combination of agents has been shown to be more effective than aspirin alone in improving claudication symptoms. Preliminary evidence also suggests that the combination of dipyridamole and aspirin may be more effective than aspirin alone in decreasing the formation of new and/or stenosing vascular lesions.][1]

[Myocardial reinfarction (prophylaxis adjunct)][1]—Used, concurrently with aspirin, to reduce the risk of reinfarction in patients recovering from myocardial infarction.

[Ischemic attacks, transient, in females and males (treatment)][1]—Used, concurrently with aspirin, to reduce the recurrence of transient ischemic attacks (TIAs) and the risk of stroke and death in patients who have had transient brain ischemia due to fibrin platelet emboli.

Note: Recent studies have shown that the combination of dipyridamole and aspirin for prophylaxis against myocardial reinfarction or treatment of TIAs is not more effective than aspirin used alone. It is recommended that such therapy be re-evaluated and that the use of aspirin alone be considered.

Myocardial perfusion imaging, radionuclide, adjunct and [Stress echocardiography adjunct]—Intravenous dipyridamole is indicated as an adjunct to thallous chloride, Tl 201, [and other radionuclides] in myocardial perfusion imaging, [and is also used in conjunction with two-dimensional echocardiography], for the diagnosis of perfusion deficits associated with coronary artery disease. Dipyridamole is used primarily as a substitute for exercise in patients who are unable to exercise sufficiently to provide the required level of myocardial stress or when exercise is otherwise not feasible. However, it is sometimes used in conjunction with low levels of exercise, such as isometric handgrip or submaximal treadmill exercise. Intravenous dipyridamole, like exercise, assists assessment via these studies of the risk of new or recurrent coronary events, such as myocardial infarction or ischemia by inducing coronary vasodilation. However, dipyridamole cannot provide the additional physiologic data, such as aerobic capacity, that is obtainable via exercise.

[Oral dipyridamole has also been used as an adjunct to myocardial perfusion imaging, but intravenous administration is preferred because the delayed and variable absorption of orally administered dipyridamole significantly prolongs the time required to perform the study. Also, the high doses used orally generally require prophylactic administration of intravenous aminophylline following the study to minimize the risk and/or severity of unwanted effects. In addition, dipyridamole's effects are more readily reversed by a single dose of intravenous aminophylline when dipyridamole has been administered intravenously than they are after high-dose oral administration.]

Unaccepted

The U.S. Food and Drug Administration (FDA) has classified dipyridamole as lacking substantial evidence of effectiveness for the long-term treatment of chronic angina pectoris. Dipyridamole has generally been replaced by more effective agents as an antianginal agent.

[1]Not included in Canadian product labeling.

Pharmacology/Pharmacokinetics

Physicochemical characteristics

Chemical Group—Dipyridamole is a 2,6-bis-(diethanolamino)-4,8-dipiperidinopyrimido-(5,4,- *d*) pyrimidine.

Molecular weight—504.64.

pKa—6.1.

Solubility—Soluble in dilute acids, in methanol, and in chloroform; practically insoluble in water.
Other characteristics—Lipophilic.

Mechanism of action/Effect
Dipyridamole lengthens abnormally shortened platelet survival time in a dose-dependent manner. Dipyridamole's mechanisms of action have not been fully elucidated, but may involve its ability to increase endogenous concentrations of adenosine, which is a coronary vasodilator and a platelet aggregation inhibitor, and of cyclic adenosine monophosphate (cAMP), which decreases platelet activation. Dipyridamole may increase concentrations of adenosine by inhibiting the activity of the enzyme adenosine deaminase, thereby decreasing adenosine metabolism, and by inhibiting adenosine uptake by erythrocytes and vascular endothelial cells. Adenosine stimulates adenylate cyclase activity, leading to increased cAMP synthesis and consequently to reduced platelet function. Also, dipyridamole may raise the intraplatelet cAMP concentration by increasing prostacyclin-induced stimulation of adenylate cyclase activity, which increases cAMP synthesis, and by inhibiting the enzyme phosphodiesterase, which decreases cAMP breakdown. Additionally, dipyridamole may inhibit the formation of thromboxane A_2, which is a potent stimulator of platelet activation.

Note: Dipyridamole does not affect prothrombin time when administered concurrently with coumarin- or indanedione-derivative anticoagulants.

Thromboembolism prophylaxis adjunct—Dipyridamole may act by inhibiting platelet aggregation, although studies of the medication's ability to reduce platelet function after oral administration of usual doses have yielded conflicting results. *In vitro*, high concentrations of dipyridamole are required to inhibit platelet function; the necessary concentrations may not be achieved *in vivo* with recommended doses. There is some evidence that the medication may be more effective in preventing platelet deposition on artificial surfaces (e.g., synthetic prosthetic heart valves) than on natural surfaces. Dipyridamole also restores toward normal the shortened platelet survival time that occurs in patients with thrombosis, prosthetic heart valves, vascular grafts, or vascular abnormalities. However, the relevance of this action to any antithrombotic effect of dipyridamole has not been established.

Diagnostic aid adjunct (ischemic heart disease)—Dipyridamole may preferentially dilate, and increase blood flow through, nondiseased coronary blood vessels, leading to a redistribution of blood flow away from significantly stenotic coronary vessels. This "coronary steal" effect increases the differential in perfusion, and consequently in radiopharmaceutical uptake, between regions of the myocardium supplied by normal coronary arteries and those supplied by stenotic vessels. Dipyridamole-induced changes in perfusion are similar to those produced by exercise stress.

Absorption
Oral—Slow and subject to interindividual variability; bioavailability varies from 27 to 66%.

Protein binding
Very high (91 to 99%); primarily to alpha$_1$-acid glycoprotein and, to a lesser extent, to albumin.

Biotransformation
Hepatic, to the glucuronic acid conjugate.

Half-life
Distribution—
- Intravenous: 5 minutes.
- Oral: About 40 minutes.

Redistribution—
- Intravenous: 53 minutes.

Elimination—
- Intravenous: 10 hours.
- Oral: 10 hours.

Time to peak plasma concentration
Oral—Usually about 75 minutes.
Intravenous—2 minutes following completion of a 4-minute infusion.

Peak plasma concentration
Oral—Dependent on dosage and subject to interindividual variability. Concentrations may be reduced when the medication is administered with food.
Single 25-mg dose: 0.5 mcg per mL (0.99 micromoles/L).
Single 75-mg dose: 1.6 mcg per mL (3.17 micromoles/L).
Chronic dosing with 75 mg 3 or 4 times a day: 1 to 2 mcg per mL (1.98 to 3.96 micromoles/L).

Intravenous—4.6 ± 1.3 mcg per mL (9.1 ± 2.57 micromoles/L).

Time to peak effect
Intravenous infusion of 0.56 mg per kg of body weight (mg/kg), infused over 4 minutes—The peak increase in coronary flow velocity occurs 3.8 to 8.7 (average, 6.5) minutes after the start of the infusion.

Elimination
Primarily biliary (up to 20% enterohepatic recirculation may occur).
Total body clearance (intravenous administration)—2.3 to 3.5 mL per minute per kg of body weight.

Precautions to Consider

Carcinogenicity
Studies in mice for 111 weeks and in rats for 128 to 142 weeks at doses of 8, 25, and 75 mg per kg of body weight (mg/kg) (1, 3.1, and 9.4 times the maximum recommended daily human dose [MRHD]) produced no significant carcinogenic effects.

Mutagenicity
Mutagenicity studies (cytogenic, microorganism, dominant lethal, and micronucleus tests) were negative.

Pregnancy/Reproduction
Fertility—Studies in male and female rats receiving oral doses of up to 60 times the MRHD revealed no evidence of impaired fertility. However, a significant reduction in the number of corpora lutea, with a consequent reduction in implantations and number of live fetuses, occurred with doses of up to 155 times the MRHD.

Pregnancy—Although adequate and well-controlled studies in humans have not been done, successful pregnancies have been reported in patients who received dipyridamole.

Studies in mice receiving doses of up to 125 mg/kg per day (15.6 times the MRHD) and in rabbits receiving oral doses of up to 40 mg/kg per day (5 times the MRHD) have not shown that dipyridamole causes adverse effects on the fetus.

FDA Pregnancy Category B.

Breast-feeding
Dipyridamole is distributed into human breast milk. However, problems in humans have not been documented.

Pediatrics
Appropriate studies on the relationship of age to the effects of dipyridamole have not been performed in children up to 12 years of age. Safety and efficacy have not been established for this age group.

Geriatrics
Studies of the efficacy of single doses of intravenous dipyridamole for myocardial perfusion imaging revealed no differences in the incidence of chest pain, ST segment depression, or severe ischemia in patients 70 years of age or older compared with patients younger than 70 years of age. Studies on the relationship of age to the effects of dipyridamole in geriatric patients receiving the medication as a platelet aggregation inhibitor have not been done. However, no geriatrics-specific problems have been documented to date with chronic oral administration of dipyridamole.

Drug interactions and/or related problems
The following drug interactions and/or related problems have been selected on the basis of their potential clinical significance (possible mechanism in parentheses where appropriate)—not necessarily inclusive (» = major clinical significance):

See also *Laboratory value alterations.*

Note: Combinations containing any of the following medications, depending on the amount present, may also interact with this medication.

Adenosine
(dipyridamole potentiates the effects of adenosine by inhibiting adenosine metabolism as well as its uptake by erythrocytes and vascular endothelial cells; a reduction of adenosine dosage may be needed)

» Heparin
(concurrent use with a platelet aggregation inhibitor such as dipyridamole may increase the risk of bleeding)

Anti-inflammatory drugs, nonsteroidal, (NSAIDs), especially
Indomethacin or
Pentoxifylline or
» Platelet aggregation inhibitors, other (see *Appendix II*) or
Salicylates, especially:
» Aspirin
(concurrent use of any of these medications with dipyridamole may increase the risk of bleeding because of additive inhibition of platelet aggregation; in addition, hypoprothrombinemia induced by large doses of salicylates, and the potential occurrence of gastrointestinal ulceration or hemorrhage during therapy with NSAIDs, salicylates [especially aspirin], or sulfinpyrazone, may cause increased risk to patients receiving dipyridamole)
(although aspirin and dipyridamole are commonly used concurrently to provide additional therapeutic benefit, the combination

has not been shown to be more effective than aspirin alone for prophylaxis against myocardial reinfarction or treatment of transient ischemic attacks)

(concurrent use of dipyridamole and indomethacin may increase both the risk and the severity of renal function impairment; in one short-term study in well-hydrated individuals with normal renal function, administration of a single dose of both agents produced an 80% reduction in diuresis and decreases in sodium excretion and glomerular filtration rate; the decrements were significantly greater than those occurring with either medication alone; although the risk of a significant effect on renal function with long-term therapy has not been determined, caution is recommended, especially for patients who may be at risk for such complications, e.g., dehydrated individuals or patients with pre-existing renal function impairment)

» Cefamandole or
» Cefoperazone or
» Cefotetan or
» Plicamycin or
» Valproic acid
(these medications may cause hypoprothrombinemia; in addition, plicamycin and valproic acid may inhibit platelet aggregation; concurrent use with dipyridamole may increase the risk of bleeding because of additive interferences with blood clotting)

» Thrombolytic agents, such as:
» Alteplase (tissue-type plasminogen activator, recombinant) or
» Anistreplase (anisoylated plasminogen-streptokinase activator complex) or
» Streptokinase or
» Urokinase
(dipyridamole-induced inhibition of platelet aggregation may increase the risk of severe bleeding in patients receiving thrombolytic therapy)

Laboratory value alterations

The following have been selected on the basis of their potential clinical significance (possible effect in parentheses where appropriate)—not necessarily inclusive (» = major clinical significance).

With results of dipyridamole-assisted myocardial perfusion studies

Due to other medications/foods

» Bronchodilators, xanthine-derivative or
» Caffeine
(these agents reverse the effects of dipyridamole on myocardial blood flow, thereby interfering with test results; dipyridamole-assisted myocardial perfusion studies should not be performed if therapy with a xanthine bronchodilator cannot be withheld for 36 hours prior to the test; also, patients should be instructed to avoid ingesting caffeine [from a dietary or medicinal source] for 8 to 12 hours prior to the test)

Medical considerations/Contraindications

The medical considerations/contraindications included have been selected on the basis of their potential clinical significance (reasons given in parentheses where appropriate)—not necessarily inclusive (» = major clinical significance).

Risk-benefit should be considered when the following medical problems exist:

» Angina pectoris, unstable or
Collateral blood vessels, presence of
(increased risk of myocardial ischemia due to a "coronary steal" phenomenon, which may lead to complications such as hypotension, ventricular arrhythmias, or cardiac arrest)

» Hypotension or propensity toward
(may be induced or aggravated by excessive doses, which may cause peripheral vasodilation)

Sensitivity to dipyridamole

For diagnostic use by intravenous injection only (in addition to those medical problems listed above)

» Asthma, current or history of
(increased risk of bronchospasm)

Patient monitoring

The following may be especially important in patient monitoring (other tests may be warranted in some patients, depending on condition; » = major clinical significance):

» Electrocardiogram and
» Vital signs, especially blood pressure
(monitoring recommended when large single doses of dipyridamole are used adjunctively for myocardial perfusion scanning, because of the risk of severe hypotension and myocardial ischemia, which may lead to ventricular arrhythmias and cardiac arrest; when dipyridamole is administered by intravenous infusion for this purpose, it is recommended that these parameters be monitored for at least 10 to 15 minutes following completion of the infusion)

Side/Adverse Effects

Note: In addition to the side/adverse effects listed below, asthenia, depersonalization, diaphoresis, dysgeusia, injection site reactions, intermittent claudication, leg cramping, pharyngitis, and pain in the back, breast, eyes, kidneys, muscles, or perineal area have also been reported, very rarely, following intravenous administration of dipyridamole for myocardial perfusion imaging.

The following side/adverse effects have been selected on the basis of their potential clinical significance (possible signs and symptoms in parentheses where appropriate)—not necessarily inclusive:

Those indicating need for medical attention

Incidence more frequent—with intravenous administration for diagnostic use

Angina pectoris or exacerbation of (chest pain)—incidence > 19%, rarely with oral administration; ***extrasystoles***—incidence 5.2%; ***ST-T segment changes***—incidence 7.5%

Note: *Angina pectoris* may be induced or exacerbated because of a "coronary steal" phenomenon. Its occurrence following administration of intravenous dipyridamole for diagnostic use is especially likely in patients with significant coronary artery disease, but does not always correlate with or predict the extent of disease. Intravenous dipyridamole has also induced chest pain in individuals without coronary artery disease. Although chest pain without other diagnostic evidence of coronary artery disease is a relatively nonspecific finding, myocardial infarction (incidence 0.1%) and cardiac arrest have occurred rarely.

Rarely, *angina pectoris* has also been reported with oral administration of conventional doses, usually at the beginning of therapy.

Incidence less frequent—with intravenous administration for diagnostic use

Allergic reaction (skin rash [incidence 2.3%]; itching); ***blood pressure lability*** (dizziness, sweating, or sudden, severe headache)—incidence 1.6%; ***dyspnea*** (difficult or labored breathing)—incidence 2.6%; ***hypertension***—incidence 1.5%; ***hypotension***—incidence 4.6%, also with oral administration at high doses; ***tachycardia*** (fast heartbeat)—incidence 3.2%

Incidence rare—with intravenous administration for diagnostic use

Allergic reaction, including bronchospasm, which may be severe (shortness of breath; troubled breathing; tightness in chest; wheezing); ***arrhythmias or electrocardiographic changes***—very rare; ***cardiomyopathy; cerebral ischemia, transient; cholelithiasis***—with oral administration; ***hypertonia*** (muscle stiffness); ***hyperventilation; hypoesthesia*** (decreased sensitivity to touch)—incidence 0.5%; ***larynx edema*** (tightness or swelling of neck)—with oral administration; ***liver dysfunction, including hepatitis*** (yellow eyes or skin)—with oral administration; ***migraine*** (headache, severe and throbbing); ***pleural pain*** (sharp pain in either or both sides of the chest); ***pulmonary edema***—reported in a patient with a history of pulmonary edema

Note: *Electrocardiographic changes* and/or *arrhythmias* may include ventricular fibrillation, ventricular tachycardia, bradycardia, atrial fibrillation, supraventricular tachycardia, atrioventricular block or other heart block, and syncope.

Those indicating need for medical attention only if they continue or are bothersome

Incidence more frequent

Abdominal discomfort or cramping—overall incidence 6.1% with chronic oral administration or with high doses; ***diarrhea; dizziness or lightheadedness***—incidence of dizziness 11.8% with intravenous administration for diagnostic use and 13.6% with chronic oral therapy; ***headache***—incidence 12.2% with intravenous administration for diagnostic use

Incidence less frequent

Flushing; headache—incidence 2.3% with chronic oral therapy; ***nausea***—incidence 4.6% with intravenous administration for diagnostic use; ***vomiting***—with high doses; ***weakness***

Incidence rare—with oral administration

Alopecia (hair loss); ***arthritis*** (joint pain and/or swelling); ***fatigue; malaise*** (general discomfort; unusual tiredness or weakness); ***myalgia*** (muscle pain); ***palpitation*** (fast or irregular heartbeat); ***rhinitis*** (runny nose; sneezing)

Patient Consultation

As an aid to patient consultation, refer to *Advice for the Patient, Dipyridamole—Therapeutic (Systemic),* and *Dipyridamole—Diagnostic (Systemic).*

In providing consultation, consider emphasizing the following selected information (» = major clinical significance):

Before using this medication

» Conditions affecting use, especially:
Sensitivity to dipyridamole
Other medications, especially heparin, other platelet aggregation inhibitors, plicamycin, those cephalosporins that may cause hypoprothrombinemia, thrombolytic agents, valproic acid, and, for myocardial perfusion studies, caffeine and xanthine bronchodilators
Other medical problems, especially angina pectoris (unstable), hypotension, and, for myocardial perfusion studies, asthma (or history of)

Proper use of this medication

» Importance of taking medication at evenly spaced times
Taking medication with water at least 1 hour before or 2 hours after meals for faster absorption; may be taken with meals or milk if gastrointestinal irritation occurs
» Proper dosing
Missed dose: Taking as soon as possible unless next scheduled dose is within 4 hours; returning to regular dosing schedule; not doubling doses
» Proper storage

Precautions while using this medication

Possibility that concurrent use with aspirin may increase the risk of bleeding
» Not taking aspirin concurrently unless specifically prescribed for concurrent use
» If taking aspirin concurrently, taking only the amount of aspirin prescribed; checking with physician about proper medication to use for relief of pain, fever
If taking aspirin concurrently, need for regular visits to physician to check progress during therapy
» Informing all physicians and dentists of use of dipyridamole and whether taking concurrently with an anticoagulant or aspirin
» Caution when getting up suddenly from lying or sitting position

Side/adverse effects

Signs of potential side effects, especially angina pectoris and, for diagnostic use, allergic reaction, blood pressure changes, bronchospasm, dyspnea, and migraine

General Dosing Information

For oral dosage form only

Dipyridamole should preferably be taken with a full glass (240 mL) of water on an empty stomach (either 1 hour before or 2 hours after meals) for faster absorption; however, it may be taken with or immediately after meals or with milk to lessen gastrointestinal irritation.

For intravenous administration as a diagnostic aid

Intravenous aminophylline and nitroglycerin should be immediately available for reversal of adverse effects such as chest pain, bronchospasm, or hypotension. Routine administration of aminophylline following administration of large doses of dipyridamole (70 mg intravenously) has been recommended to minimize the frequency of adverse effects. However, aminophylline should not be given until several (> 2) minutes after the radiopharmaceutical has been injected. Also, because cardiac arrest has occurred (rarely), personnel trained in cardiorespiratory resuscitation and all necessary medications and equipment for handling this emergency should be immediately available.

For parenteral administration only

Because small veins may be especially sensitive to the acidic pH of the dipyridamole injection, it is recommended that the medication be infused into an antecubital vein. Also, the injection should not be administered undiluted.

For treatment of adverse effects

Recommended treatment consists of the following:

• For angina pectoris, ventricular arrhythmias, or bronchospasm—Administering 50 to 250 mg of aminophylline by intravenous infusion at a rate of 50 to 100 mg over 30 to 60 seconds. If symptoms are relieved, continuing to monitor the patient and administering additional aminophylline if they recur. If chest pain persists, administering nitroglycerin. If angina continues, the possibility of myocardial infarction should be considered and appropriate diagnostic and treatment measures instituted as needed.

• Hypotension, severe—Placing the patient in a supine position, with the head tilted down if necessary, followed by administration of 50 to 250 mg of intravenous aminophylline. Intravenous fluids and/or a vasopressor may also be used if needed.

Oral Dosage Forms

Note: Bracketed uses in the *Dosage Forms* section refer to categories of use and/or indications that are not included in U.S. product labeling.

DIPYRIDAMOLE TABLETS USP

Usual adult dose

Prevention of thromboembolism after the placement of prosthetic heart valves—
Oral, 75 to 100 mg four times a day in combination with a coumarin- or indanedione-derivative anticoagulant.

Note: The combination of aspirin and an anticoagulant for this purpose is not recommended because of the increased risk of severe bleeding.

[Prevention of thromboembolism associated with prosthetic heart valves in patients for whom anticoagulants are contraindicated]—
Oral, 75 mg three or four times a day, in conjunction with 325 mg of aspirin a day.

[Prevention of recurrent systemic thromboembolism in patients with mitral valve disease][1]—
Oral, 225 to 400 mg a day, in conjunction with a coumarin- or indanedione-derivative anticoagulant.

[Prevention of thrombosis or occlusion of coronary bypass graft][1]—
Oral, 100 mg four times a day for two days prior to surgery; 100 mg one hour postoperatively; then 75 mg in combination with 325 mg of aspirin seven hours postoperatively (given via nasogastric tube); then 75 mg in combination with 325 mg of aspirin three times a day. Dipyridamole, but not aspirin, may be discontinued one week postoperatively.

[Myocardial reinfarction prophylactic]—
Oral, 75 mg three times a day in combination with 325 mg of aspirin a day.

Note: Optimum dosage of aspirin as a platelet aggregation inhibitor has not been established. Most studies have used doses ranging from 300 mg to 1.5 grams a day. However, there is evidence that doses as low as 160 mg every twenty-four hours or 325 mg every forty-eight hours may effectively inhibit platelet aggregation while minimizing the risk of aspirin-induced side effects. Therefore, lower doses of aspirin than those recommended above are sometimes used in antithrombotic regimens.

[Diagnostic aid adjunct]—
Oral, 300 to 400 mg as a single dose, administered approximately forty-five minutes prior to injection of the radiopharmaceutical. However, intravenous administration is preferred for this indication.

Usual pediatric dose

Safety and efficacy in children have not been established in children younger than 12 years of age.

Strength(s) usually available

U.S.—
25 mg (Rx) [*Persantine;* GENERIC].
50 mg (Rx) [*Persantine;* GENERIC].
75 mg (Rx) [*Persantine;* GENERIC].

Canada—
25 mg (Rx) [*Apo-Dipyridamole FC; Apo-Dipyridamole SC; Novo-Dipiradol; Persantine*].
50 mg (Rx) [*Apo-Dipyridamole FC; Apo-Dipyridamole SC; Novo-Dipiradol; Persantine*].
75 mg (Rx) [*Apo-Dipyridamole FC; Apo-Dipyridamole SC; Novo-Dipiradol; Persantine*].
100 mg (Rx) [*Persantine*].

Packaging and storage

Store between 15 and 30 °C (59 and 86 °F), unless otherwise specified by manufacturer. Store in a tight, light-resistant container.

Parenteral Dosage Forms

Note: Bracketed uses in the *Dosage Forms* section refer to categories of use and/or indications that are not included in U.S. product labeling.

DIPYRIDAMOLE INJECTION

Usual adult dose

Diagnostic aid adjunct—
Intravenous infusion, 570 mcg (0.57 mg) per kg of body weight, administered at a rate of 142 mcg (0.142 mg) per kg of body weight per minute for four minutes. The radiopharmaceutical is injected within five minutes after completion of the dipyridamole infusion.

[Platelet aggregation inhibitor]—
Intravenous infusion, 250 mg per day at a rate of 10 mg per hour.

Usual adult prescribing limits
Diagnostic aid adjunct—60 mg.
[Platelet aggregation inhibitor]—400 mg per day (lower when given in combination with aspirin).

Usual pediatric dose
Safety and efficacy in children have not been established.

Strength(s) usually available
U.S.—
5 mg per mL (2-mL and 10-mL ampuls) (Rx) [GENERIC].
Canada—
5 mg per mL (10-mL ampul) (Rx) [*Persantine*].

Packaging and storage
Store between 15 and 25 °C (59 and 77 °F), protected from direct light, unless otherwise specified by manufacturer. Protect from freezing.

Preparation of dosage form
Diagnostic aid adjunct—The required quantity of dipyridamole injection should be diluted in sufficient 0.45% sodium chloride injection, 0.9% sodium chloride injection, or 5% dextrose injection to yield a total volume of 20 to 50 mL.
[Platelet aggregation inhibitor]—250 mg of dipyridamole (50 mL of dipyridamole injection) should be added to 250 mL of 5% dextrose injection. The resultant solution contains 1 mg per mL. If doses higher than 250 mg per day are required, the concentration of dipyridamole in the infusion solution may be increased.

[1]Not included in Canadian product labeling.

Selected Bibliography

Iskandrian AS, Heo J, Askenase A, et al. Dipyridamole cardiac imaging. Am Heart J 1988; 115: 432-43.
Leppo JA. Dipyridamole-thallium imaging: the lazy man's stress test. J Nucl Med 1989; 30: 281-7.
FitzGerald GA. Medical intelligence. Dipyridamole. N Engl J Med 1987; 316: 1247-56.
Younis LT, Chaitman BR. Update on intravenous dipyridamole cardiac imaging in the assessment of ischemic heart disease. Clin Cardiol 1990; 13: 3-10.

Revised: 5/20/1999

DIPYRIDAMOLE AND ASPIRIN Systemic

USA: Dipyridamole and Aspirin
INN: none; BAN: Dipyridamole and Aspirin
JAN: Dipyridamole and Aspirin
VA CLASSIFICATION (Primary): BL117
Commonly used brand name(s): *Aggrenox*.
Other commonly used names are:
Aspirin—Acetylsalicylic acid ASA Salicylic acid acetate

NOTE: The *Dipyridamole and Aspirin (Systemic)* monograph is maintained on the *USP DI* electronic data base. A copy of the most recent revision of the complete monograph can be accessed on the *USP DI* Updates Online website. See the front cover of book for details on accessing the site.
For information on the specific components of this combination, see the *USP DI* monographs for *Dipyridamole (Systemic)*, and *Salicylates (Systemic)*.
The information that follows is selectively abstracted from the complete monograph and is provided to facilitate drug use review and patient counseling.

Note: For a listing of dosage forms and brand names by country availability, see *Dosage Forms* section(s).

Category
Platelet aggregation inhibitor.

Indications

Accepted
Stroke, thromboembolic, recurrent (prophylaxis)—Dipyridamole and aspirin is indicated to reduce the risk of stroke in patients who have had transient ischemia of the brain or completed ischemic stroke due to thrombosis.

Patient Consultation
As an aid to patient consultation, refer to *Advice for the Patient, Dipyridamole and Aspirin (Systemic)*.
In providing consultation, consider emphasizing the following selected information (» = major clinical significance):

Before using this medication
» Conditions affecting use, especially:
Sensitivity to nonsteroidal anti-inflammatory drugs (NSAIDs), aspirin, dipyridamole, or tartrazine dye
Pregnancy—Not recommended for use during the third trimester of pregnancy
Breast-feeding—Dipyridamole and aspirin are excreted in human breast milk in low concentrations, caution is recommended.
Use in children and adolescents—No information is available on the relationship of age to the effects of dipyridamole and aspirin in children and teenagers population. However, due to the risk of Reye's syndrome with the aspirin component, use of this product in the children and teenagers population is not recommended.
Other medications, especially anticoagulants such as heparin and warfarin, methotrexate, nonsteroidal anti-inflammatory drugs, and uricosuric agents such as probenecid and sulfinpyrazone.
Other medical problems, especially history of angioedema, anaphylaxis, bronchospasm or other severe sensitivity reaction induced by aspirin or other NSAIDs, asthma; rhinitis; nasal polyps associated with asthma that are induced or exacerbated by aspirin, severe hepatic or renal function impairment; coagulation abnormalities such as hypoprothrombinemia or vitamin K deficiency, severe coronary artery disease such as unstable angina pectoris or recent myocardial infarction, erosive gastritis or peptic ulcer, or hypotension.

Proper use of this medication
Swallowing capsule whole; not breaking, crushing, or chewing before swallowing
Do not lie down for 15 to 30 minutes after taking dipyridamole and aspirin combination. This will help to prevent irritation to your esophagus
» Proper dosing
Missed dose: Taking as soon as possible; not taking if almost time for next scheduled dose; not doubling doses
Proper storage

Precautions while using this medication
» Checking with prescribing physician about proper medication to use for relief of pain, fever, or arthritis
» Not discontinuing treatment for any reason without first consulting prescribing physician

Side/adverse effects
Signs of potential side effects, especially abdominal pain, vomiting, amnesia; anemia, gastrointestinal and rectal hemorrhage, melena, purpura, seizures; allergic reaction, arrhythmia, asthma, chest pain; cholelithiasis, jaundice, hematoma, hematuria, cerebral, intracranial or subarachnoid hemorrhage, hypotension, pruritus, urticaria, and tinnitus

Oral Dosage Forms

DIPYRIDAMOLE EXTENDED-RELEASE AND ASPIRIN CAPSULES

Usual adult dose
Stroke, thromboembolic, recurrent (prophylaxis)—
Oral, one capsule (200 mg extended-release dipyridamole and 25 mg aspirin) twice daily, one in the morning and one in the evening.

Usual pediatric dose
Use is not recommended.

Usual geriatric dose
See *Usual adult dose*.

Strength(s) usually available
U.S.—
200 mg extended-release dipyridamole and 25 mg aspirin (Rx) [*Aggrenox* (acacia; aluminum stearate; colloidal silicon dioxide; corn starch; dimethicone; hydroxypropyl methylcellulose; hydroxypropyl methylcellulose phthalate; lactose monohydrate; methacrylic acid copolymer; microcrystalline cellulose; povidone; stearic acid; sucrose; talc; tartaric acid; titanium dioxide; triacetin; red and yellow iron oxide)].
Canada—
200 mg extended-release dipyridamole and 25 mg aspirin (Rx) [*Aggrenox* (acacia; aluminum stearate; corn starch; dimethicone; gel-

atin; hydroxypropyl methylcellulose; hydroxypropyl methylcellulose phthalate; lactose monohydrate; methacrylic acid copolymer; microcrystalline cellulose; povidone; stearic acid; sucrose; talc; tartaric acid; titanium dioxide; triacetin; red and yellow iron oxide)].

Auxiliary labeling

- Swallow capsule whole; do not break, crush, or chew before swallowing

Revised: 02/21/2001
Developed: 05/02/2000

DISEASE-SPECIFIC ENTERAL NUTRITION FORMULAS

—See *Enteral Nutrition Formulas (Systemic)*

DISOPYRAMIDE Systemic

VA CLASSIFICATION (Primary): CV300

Commonly used brand name(s): *Norpace; Norpace CR; Rythmodan; Rythmodan-LA.*

Note: For a listing of dosage forms and brand names by country availability, see *Dosage Forms* section(s).

Category

Antiarrhythmic.

Indications

Note: Bracketed information in the *Indications* section refers to uses that are not included in U.S. product labeling.

Accepted

Arrhythmias, ventricular (treatment)—Disopyramide is indicated for the treatment of documented ventricular arrhythmias that, in the judgment of the physician, are considered to be life-threatening.

Note: Disopyramide is a class IA antiarrhythmic agent (Vaughan Williams classification) with some similarities in antiarrhythmic action to the class IC antiarrhythmic agents encainide and flecainide, and the class IA agent, moricizine. In a multicenter, randomized, placebo-controlled trial called the Cardiac Arrhythmias Suppression Trial (CAST), patients with prior myocardial infarction received either encainide, flecainide, or moricizine during an open-label titration phase and the same drug or a matching placebo for the remaining long-term phase of the trial. The objective of the trial was to determine if suppression of asymptomatic or mildly symptomatic ventricular arrhythmias would reduce the rate of death due to arrhythmia.

After a mean follow-up of 10 months, the encainide and flecainide arms of the study were terminated due to an excessive mortality or nonfatal cardiac arrest rate (7.7%), compared with that seen in patients assigned to a matching placebo (3%). The moricizine arm of the trial was continued in a second trial (CAST II), but this trial also was terminated early when an increase in mortality in the moricizine-treated patients occurred during the first 14-day period of the trial.

Scientists have speculated that the adverse results of the CAST trials may be attributed to proarrhythmic effects of the study drugs. Because these and previous studies with class I agents to suppress ventricular arrhythmias in patients after myocardial infarction have not resulted in a decrease in mortality, disopyramide is generally not recommended for treating less severe ventricular arrhythmias.

[Tachycardia, supraventricular (prophylaxis and treatment)][1]—Disopyramide is indicated for prophylaxis and treatment of supraventricular tachycardias, such as atrial fibrillation and atrial flutter.

[1]Not included in Canadian product labeling.

Pharmacology/Pharmacokinetics

Physicochemical characteristics

Molecular weight—Disopyramide phosphate: 437.47.
pKa—8.4.

Mechanism of action/Effect

Disopyramide, by blocking both sodium and potassium channels, depresses phase 0 depolarization and prolongs the duration of the action potential of normal cardiac cells in atrial and ventricular tissues; it has little direct effect on the atrioventricular (AV) node, but may enhance AV nodal conduction by an indirect vagolytic action. Disopyramide directly decreases the rate (slope) of phase 4 depolarization in cells with normal or augmented automaticity. In the presence of an accessory pathway, disopyramide increases the effective refractory period of the accessory pathway in both antegrade and retrograde directions. Electrocardiographically, disopyramide prolongs the QT interval and causes a widening of the QRS complex. In the Vaughan Williams classification of antiarrhythmics, disopyramide is considered to be a class IA agent.

Other actions/effects

Disopyramide has a potent depressant effect on myocardial contractility (negative inotropic effect). It also possesses strong anticholinergic activity and somewhat increases peripheral vascular resistance.

Absorption

Rapid and nearly complete.

Protein binding

Moderate (approximately 50% at therapeutic concentrations, but may range from 35 to 95%, depending largely on serum concentration).

Biotransformation

Hepatic; primary metabolite has antiarrhythmic and anticholinergic activity.

Elimination

Approximately 6.7 hours (range, 4 to 10 hours in healthy adults).
In patients with renal function impairment (creatinine clearance less than 40 mL per minute)—8 to 18 hours.

Time to peak concentration

Approximately 2 hours after oral administration of immediate-release disopyramide phosphate.
4.9 ± 1.4 hours after oral administration of controlled-release disopyramide phosphate.

Therapeutic serum concentration

Usual plasma levels range from 2 to 4 mcg per mL; however, because of variable protein binding and potential toxicity of free unbound drug, serum concentrations should not be used for dosage adjustment.

Elimination

Renal—Approximately 80% (about 50% unchanged and 30% metabolites).
Biliary—Approximately 15%.
In dialysis—Disopyramide is rapidly removed from general circulation during hemodialysis; dialysis patients may require additional dosage following dialysis and should remain under observation until condition is stabilized.

Precautions to Consider

Carcinogenicity

No evidence of carcinogenic potential was found in rats given oral disopyramide for 18 months at doses up to 30 times the usual human dose by weight.

Mutagenicity

The Ames test for mutagenic potential was negative.

Pregnancy/Reproduction

Fertility—No adverse effect on fertility was found in rats given disopyramide at doses up to 250 mg per kg of body weight (mg/kg) per day.

Pregnancy—Adequate and well-controlled studies in humans have not been done. However, disopyramide has been found in human fetal blood and has been reported to stimulate uterine contractions in pregnant women.

Administration of disopyramide to pregnant rats at doses 20 times the usual daily human dose by weight was associated with decreased numbers of implantation sites and decreased growth and survival of pups. Increased resorption rates were observed in rabbits given disopyramide 60 mg/kg per day.

FDA Pregnancy Category C.

Breast-feeding

Disopyramide is distributed into human breast milk at a concentration less than that in plasma.

Pediatrics

Studies performed to date have not demonstrated pediatrics-specific problems that would limit the usefulness of disopyramide in children.

Geriatrics

Although appropriate studies on the relationship of age to the effects of disopyramide have not been performed in the geriatric population, the elderly may exhibit increased sensitivity to the anticholinergic effects such as urinary retention and dry mouth. In addition, elderly patients are more likely to have age-related renal function impairment, which may require caution and reduction of dosage in patients receiving disopyramide.

Dental

The secondary anticholinergic effects of disopyramide may decrease or inhibit salivary flow, especially in middle-aged or elderly patients, thus contributing to the development of dental caries, periodontal disease, oral candidiasis, and discomfort.

Drug interactions and/or related problems

The following drug interactions and/or related problems have been selected on the basis of their potential clinical significance (possible mechanism in parentheses where appropriate)—not necessarily inclusive (» = major clinical significance):

Note: Combinations containing any of the following medications, depending on the amount present, may also interact with this medication.

» Antiarrhythmic agents, other, especially:
Amiodarone or
Diltiazem or
Encainide or
Flecainide or
Ibutilide or
Lidocaine or
Procainamide or
Propafenone or
Propranolol, sotalol, and other beta-adrenergic blocking agents or
Quinidine or
Tocainide or
Verapamil
(concurrent use with disopyramide may prolong cardiac conduction or produce serious negative inotropic effects, especially in patients with decompensated cardiac function or a history thereof; additionally, like disopyramide, amiodarone, ibutilide, procainamide, quinidine, and sotalol can prolong the QT interval, increasing the risk of cardiac arrhythmias; concurrent use should be avoided. Disopyramide should not be administered less than 48 hours before or 24 hours after verapamil; deaths have been reported. Rare instances of hypoglycemia have occurred with concurrent use of beta-adrenergic blocking agents)

Anticholinergics or other medications with anticholinergic activity (see *Appendix II*)
(anticholinergic effects may be additive when these medications are used concurrently with disopyramide)

Anticoagulants, coumarin- or indandione-derivative
(concurrent use of warfarin and disopyramide has been reported to increase or decrease the anticoagulant effect; although clinical significance has not been determined, caution is recommended)

Antidiabetic agents, oral or
Insulin
(hypoglycemic effects may be intensified in rare cases by the concurrent use of disopyramide; patients prone to hypoglycemia should be closely monitored)

» Erythromycin
(concurrent use may increase serum concentrations of disopyramide, possibly by interacting with disopyramide metabolism, which may result in excessive widening of the QRS complex and/or prolongation of the QT interval; additionally, erythromycin has a QT-interval–prolonging effect, which can be additive if administered with disopyramide; patients taking these medications concurrently should be monitored closely)

Hepatic enzyme inducers (see *Appendix II*), such as
Phenytoin or
Rifampin
(concurrent use may accelerate the metabolism of disopyramide and reduce its serum concentration)

Hypotension-producing medications, other (see *Appendix II*)
(concurrent use with disopyramide may increase the hypotensive effects)

» Medications that prolong the QT interval, such as
Antidepressants, tricyclic, such as
Amitriptyline
Clomipramine
Desipramine
Doxepin
Imipramine and
Nortriptyline or
Astemizole or
Bepridil or
Chloroquine or
Cisapride or
Diphenhydramine or
Fludrocortisone or
Halofantrine or
Haloperidol or
Indapamide or
Clarithromycin or
Maprotiline or
Pentamidine or
Phenothiazines, such as Chlorpromazine
Prochlorperazine and
Thioridazine or
Pimozide or
Risperidone or
Sparfloxacin or
Tamoxifen or
Thiothixene or
Trimethoprim and sulfamethoxazole combination
(concurrent use with disopyramide may have additive effects on prolongation of the QT interval, increasing the risk of cardiac arrhythmias)

Laboratory value alterations

The following have been selected on the basis of their potential clinical significance (possible effect in parentheses where appropriate)—not necessarily inclusive (» = major clinical significance).

With physiology/laboratory test values
Blood glucose concentrations
(may be decreased by an undetermined mechanism)

Medical considerations/Contraindications

The medical considerations/contraindications included have been selected on the basis of their potential clinical significance (reasons given in parentheses where appropriate)—not necessarily inclusive (» = major clinical significance).

Except under special circumstances, this medication should not be used when the following medical problems exist:

» Atrioventricular (AV) block, pre-existing second (particularly Type II) or third degree, without a pacemaker
(because disopyramide can reduce the firing or automaticity of latent or subsidiary pacemakers, disopyramide should not be used in patients with second- [particularly Type II] or third-degree AV block unless a pacemaker is in place)

» Cardiogenic shock
(because disopyramide can produce severe hypotension from its negative inotropic effects, it should not be used in these patients)

» Hypersensitivity to disopyramide

» QT interval prolongation, congenital
(effects on the QT interval may be additive)

Risk-benefit should be considered when the following medical problems exist:

Bladder neck obstruction
(anticholinergic activity of disopyramide may cause urinary retention)

» Cardiac conduction abnormalities, such as
Bundle branch block, or
Sick sinus syndrome, or
Wolff-Parkinson-White (WPW) syndrome
(because disopyramide has variable effects on cardiac conduction [see *Mechanism of action* section], it should be used with caution in patients with bundle branch block, sick sinus syndrome, or WPW syndrome)

» Cardiomyopathies or
» Congestive heart failure, uncompensated or poorly compensated or
» Hypotension
(due to its negative inotropic properties, disopyramide can worsen congestive heart failure or produce severe hypotension; patients with primary cardiomyopathy or inadequately compensated congestive heart failure may be at particular risk for hypotension; disopyramide should not be used in these patients unless the con-

gestive heart failure or hypotension is secondary to cardiac arrhythmia. If hypotension occurs or congestive heart failure worsens, disopyramide should be discontinued and the patient re-evaluated; rare cases of hypoglycemia have been reported in congestive heart failure patients treated with disopyramide)

» Diabetes mellitus
(rarely, disopyramide may significantly lower blood glucose levels)

» Electrolyte imbalance, including
Potassium and
Magnesium
(use of disopyramide in patients with electrolyte disturbances may potentiate the proarrhythmic effects of disopyramide)

» Glaucoma, closed-angle, history of
(anticholinergic activity of disopyramide may aggravate this condition; intraocular pressure should be measured before initiating disopyramide therapy in patients with glaucoma)

» Hepatic function impairment
(possible accumulation of disopyramide; dosage reduction may be required; rare cases of hypoglycemia have been reported with use of disopyramide in patients with hepatic function impairment)

Malnutrition, chronic
(rare cases of hypoglycemia have been reported in chronically malnourished patients treated with disopyramide)

» Myasthenia gravis
(anticholinergic effect of disopyramide may result in a myasthenic crisis)

» Prostatic enlargement
(possible urinary retention; may be exacerbated by anticholinergic effect)

» Renal function impairment
(accumulation of disopyramide because of reduced excretion; dosage reduction may be required; disopyramide extended-release capsules are not recommended for patients with severe renal insufficiency [creatinine clearance of 40 mL per minute (0.67 mL per second) or less]; rare cases of hypoglycemia have been reported with use of disopyramide in patients with renal function impairment)

Patient monitoring

The following may be especially important in patient monitoring (other tests may be warranted in some patients, depending on condition; » = major clinical significance):

Blood glucose concentrations
(recommended at periodic intervals in patients at risk of developing hypoglycemia, e.g., those with congestive heart failure, chronic malnutrition, or hepatic or renal function impairment, or those taking medications such as beta-blocking agents or using alcohol)

» Blood pressure determinations
(recommended at periodic intervals during therapy; if hypotension occurs and is not caused by an arrhythmia, disopyramide should be withdrawn and, if necessary, reinstituted at a lower dose only after adequate cardiac compensation is established)

» Electrocardiogram (ECG) monitoring
(recommended at periodic intervals during therapy; if significant QRS widening [> 25%] occurs, disopyramide should be withdrawn; if significant QT interval prolongation [> 25%] occurs, the patient requires dose monitoring and possible discontinuation of disopyramide)

Hepatic function and
Intraocularpressure and
Potassium concentrations, serum, and
Renal function
(determinations recommended prior to initiation of therapy and, if necessary, at periodic intervals during therapy)

Side/Adverse Effects

Note: Disopyramide may have a proarrhythmic effect. It can cause widening (> 25%) of the QRS complex, prolongation of the QT interval, and worsening of the arrhythmia, including *torsades de pointes*, ventricular tachycardia, and ventricular fibrillation. Patients who have experienced pathologic QT interval prolongation or who have potassium or magnesium electrolyte imbalance may be at risk for developing proarrhythmia.

The following side/adverse effects have been selected on the basis of their potential clinical significance (possible signs and symptoms in parentheses where appropriate)—not necessarily inclusive:

Those indicating need for medical attention

Incidence more frequent

Cardiovascular-associated symptoms, such as dizziness or feeling of faintness—incidence 22%; ***fatigue*** (unusual tiredness)—incidence 8%; ***palpitations*** (heartbeat sensations)—incidence 44%; ***shortness of breath***—incidence 9%; ***and syncope*** (fainting)—incidence 8%

Incidence less frequent

Cardiac conduction disturbances including atrioventricular (AV) block—see note above this section; ***chest pain; congestive heart failure, new or worsened*** (fast or slow heartbeat; shortness of breath; swelling of feet or lower legs; rapid weight gain); ***hypotension (with or without congestive heart failure)*** (dizziness, lightheadedness, or fainting); ***rash and/or itching***

Incidence rare

Agranulocytosis (sore throat and fever); ***cholestatic jaundice*** (yellow eyes or skin); ***fever; gynecomastia*** (enlargement of breasts in males); ***hypoglycemia*** (anxious feeling; chills; cold sweats; confusion; cool, pale skin; drowsiness; fast heartbeat; headache; hunger, excessive; nausea; nervousness; shakiness; unsteady walk; or unusual tiredness or weakness); ***mental depression; thrombocytopenia*** (may be seen as nosebleeds or bleeding gums)

Those indicating need for medical attention if they continue or are bothersome

Incidence more frequent

Anticholinergic effects (blurred vision; constipation; dry eyes, mouth, nose, or throat; urinary retention, frequency, or urgency)

Incidence less frequent

Anorexia (loss of appetite); ***bloating or stomach pain; diarrhea; headache; impotence; insomnia*** (trouble in sleeping); ***muscle weakness; nausea; nervousness***

Overdose

For specific information on the agents used in the management of disopyramide overdose, see the following monographs:
- *Charcoal, Activated (Oral-Local)* monograph;
- *Dopamine* and/or *Isoproterenol* in *Sympathomimetic Agents—Cardiovascular Use (Parenteral-Systemic)* monograph;
- *Magnesium Sulfate (Systemic)* monograph; and/or
- *Neostigmine* in *Antimyasthenics (Systemic)* monograph.

For more information on the management of overdose or unintentional ingestion, **contact a Poison Control Center** (see *Poison Control Center Listing*).

Clinical effects of overdose

The following effects have been selected on the basis of their potential clinical significance (possible signs and symptoms in parentheses where appropriate)—not necessarily inclusive:

Acute and/or chronic

Anticholinergic effects; apnea; asystole; bradycardia; cardiac arrhythmias; cardiac conduction disturbances, various types and degrees, such as excessive QRS complex and QT interval widening; congestive heart failure, worsening; hypotension; loss of consciousness; loss of spontaneous respiration; death

Treatment of overdose

Prompt treatment of disopyramide overdose is necessary, even in the absence of symptoms.

To decrease absorption—Treatment may include induction of emesis or gastric lavage (gastric lavage is not recommended unless it can be undertaken within 1 hour of ingestion) and/or administration of a cathartic followed by activated charcoal by mouth or by stomach tube.

To reduce disopyramide serum concentration—Hemodialysis or, preferably, hemoperfusion with charcoal may be used.

To enhance elimination—Measures to increase the glomerular filtration rate may reduce disopyramide toxicity in cases of impaired renal function, but altering the pH does not affect the disopyramide plasma half-life or the amount of disopyramide eliminated in the urine.

Specific treatment:

For anticholinergic effects—Neostigmine may be used.

For cardiovascular support—Treatment may include administration of isoproterenol, dopamine, and/or insertion of an intra-aortic balloon for counterpulsation.

For conduction system abnormalities—Endocardial pacing may be used if progressive AV block develops. For *torsades de pointes* ventricular tachycardia, endocardial pacing and intravenous magnesium sulfate may be used.

For respiratory support—Mechanically assisted ventilation may be used.

Monitoring—Electrocardiogram monitoring should be used.

Supportive care—Patients in whom intentional overdose is confirmed or suspected should be referred for psychiatric consultation.

Patient Consultation

As an aid to patient consultation, refer to *Advice for the Patient, Disopyramide (Systemic)*.

In providing consultation, consider emphasizing the following selected information (» = major clinical significance):

Before using this medication

» Conditions affecting use, especially:
  Hypersensitivity to disopyramide
  Pregnancy—May initiate uterine contractions
  Breast-feeding—Passes into breast milk
  Use in the elderly—Increased sensitivity to anticholinergic effects
  Other medications, especially other antiarrhythmic agents, erythromycin, or medications that prolong the QT interval
  Other medical problems, especially second- (particularly Type II) or third-degree atrioventricular (AV) block without a pacemaker; cardiogenic shock; cardiac conduction abnormalities, such as bundle branch block, sick sinus syndrome, or Wolff-Parkinson-White (WPW) syndrome; cardiomyopathies; congenital QT interval prolongation; uncompensated or poorly compensated congestive heart failure; diabetes mellitus; electrolyte imbalance, including potassium and magnesium; history of closed-angle glaucoma; hepatic function impairment; hypotension; myasthenia gravis; prostatic enlargement; or renal function impairment

Proper use of this medication

» Compliance with therapy; not taking more medication than directed
  Proper administration of extended-release capsules: Swallowing capsule whole, without breaking, crushing, or chewing
  Proper administration of extended-release tablets: Not crushing or chewing
» Importance of not missing doses and taking at evenly spaced intervals
» Proper dosing
  Missed dose: Taking as soon as possible, unless within 4 hours of next dose; not doubling doses
» Proper storage

Precautions while using this medication

» Seeing the physician regularly to check progress
» Checking with physician before stopping medication because of adverse cardiac effects with sudden withdrawal
» Caution when driving or doing things requiring alertness because of possible dizziness, lightheadedness, or fainting
» Notifying physician and taking sugar if symptoms of hypoglycemia occur
» Possible blurred vision; avoiding driving, using machines, or doing other things requiring clear vision if blurred vision occurs
  Possible dryness of eyes, mouth, and nose; using sugarless candy or gum, ice, or saliva substitute for relief of dry mouth; checking with physician or dentist if dry mouth continues for more than 2 weeks
» Caution during exercise or hot weather because of possible reduced sweating and impaired heat tolerance

Side/adverse effects

Signs of potential side effects, especially cardiovascular-associated symptoms, such as dizziness or feeling of faintness, fatigue, palpitations, shortness of breath, and syncope; cardiac conduction disturbances including atrioventricular (AV) block; chest pain; new or worsened congestive heart failure; hypotension (with or without congestive heart failure); rash and/or itching; agranulocytosis; cholestatic jaundice; fever; gynecomastia; hypoglycemia; mental depression; and thrombocytopenia

General Dosing Information

Disopyramide therapy should be initiated in a hospital. The dosage for each patient should be individualized based on response, tolerance, and body weight; dosage adjustments should be made gradually.

Because the use of disopyramide loading doses is not recommended, loading dose regimens do not appear in this text, but may be found in the manufacturer's product labeling. If a loading dose is used, the patient should be monitored closely for possible development of hypotension and/or congestive heart failure. Patients who are being transferred from other oral antiarrhythmic agents, such as quinidine or procainamide, should not receive a loading dose of disopyramide.

Patients in whom atrial flutter or fibrillation is present should be treated with an atrioventricular (AV) blocking drug, such as digoxin, prior to treatment with disopyramide in order to slow AV nodal conduction and prevent an increase in the ventricular rate.

Because of a risk of worsening heart function as a result of the negative inotropic effect of disopyramide, patients with a history of heart failure or who have compensated heart failure should undergo careful cardiac function monitoring and adequate digitalization prior to initiation of disopyramide therapy. If heart failure worsens or hypotension occurs, disopyramide should be discontinued and the patient re-evaluated.

Because disopyramide is removed by hemodialysis, additional dosage may be required following dialysis.

If first-degree atrioventricular (AV) block develops, the dosage of disopyramide should be reduced. If the block persists or worsens, a decision about whether to continue the medication should be made based on the risk of higher degrees of AV block occurring.

Oral Dosage Forms

Note: The dosing and strengths of the dosage forms available are expressed in terms of disopyramide base.

DISOPYRAMIDE CAPSULES

Usual adult dose
See *Disopyramide Phosphate Capsules USP*.

Usual adult prescribing limits
See *Disopyramide Phosphate Capsules USP*.

Usual pediatric dose
See *Disopyramide Phosphate Capsules USP*.

Strength(s) usually available
U.S.—
  Not commercially available.
Canada—
  100 mg (Rx) [*Rythmodan*].
  150 mg (Rx) [*Rythmodan*].

Packaging and storage
Store between 15 and 30 °C (59 and 86 °F), in a well-closed container, unless otherwise specified by manufacturer.

Auxiliary labeling
- May cause blurred vision.
- Do not take other medicines without advice from your doctor.

DISOPYRAMIDE PHOSPHATE CAPSULES USP

Usual adult dose
Antiarrhythmic—
  Oral, 400 to 800 mg (base) per day, administered in divided doses.
    For most adults, the recommended dosage is 600 mg (base) per day, given as 150 mg (base) every six hours. For patients with a body weight < 50 kg (110 pounds), the recommended dosage is 400 mg (base) per day, given as 100 mg (base) every six hours.
  For patients with cardiomyopathy or possible cardiac decompensation—
    Oral, initially, 100 mg (base) every six to eight hours. Subsequent dosage adjustments should be made gradually, with close patient monitoring for the possible development of hypotension and/or congestive heart failure.
  For patients with moderate renal function impairment (creatinine clearance > 40 mL per minute) or patients with hepatic function impairment—
    Oral, 100 mg (base) every six hours.
  For patients with severe renal function impairment (creatinine clearance ≤ 40 mL per minute)—
    Oral, 100 mg (base)
    For creatinine clearance of:
    30 to 40 mL/min—dose every 8 hours
    15 to 30 mL/min—dose every 12 hours
    less than 15 mL/min—dose every 24 hours.
  For transferring patients with normal renal function from either quinidine sulfate or procainamide therapy—

Disopyramide therapy should be started using the regular maintenance schedule, without a loading dose, six to twelve hours after the last dose of quinidine sulfate or three to six hours after the last dose of procainamide. Patients in whom withdrawal of quinidine sulfate or procainamide is likely to produce life-threatening arrhythmias should be carefully monitored.

Usual adult prescribing limits
800 mg (base) per day. A limited number of patients with severe refractory ventricular tachycardia have tolerated doses of up to 1600 mg (base) per day (400 mg every six hours), resulting in disopyramide plasma levels of up to 9 mcg per mL. If such treatment is warranted, patients must be hospitalized for close evaluation and continuous monitoring.

Usual pediatric dose
Note: Controlled clinical studies have not been conducted in pediatric patients and the following suggested dosages are based on published clinical experience. Disopyramide plasma levels and therapeutic response must be monitored closely and children should be hospitalized during the initial period of therapy to allow close monitoring until a maintenance dose is established.

Antiarrhythmic—
Oral, the following doses equally divided and administered every six hours (or at other individually appropriate intervals), starting at the lower end of the ranges provided.
Children up to 1 year of age—
10 to 30 mg (base) per kg of body weight per day.
Children 1 to 4 years of age—
10 to 20 mg (base) per kg of body weight per day.
Children 4 to 12 years of age—
10 to 15 mg (base) per kg of body weight per day.
Children 12 to 18 years of age—
6 to l5 mg (base) per kg of body weight per day.

Strength(s) usually available
U.S.—
100 mg (base) (Rx) [*Norpace;* GENERIC].
150 mg (base) (Rx) [*Norpace;* GENERIC].
Canada—
100 mg (base) (Rx) [GENERIC].
150 mg (base) (Rx) [GENERIC].

Packaging and storage
Store between 15 and 30 °C (59 and 86 °F), unless otherwise specified by manufacturer. Store in a well-closed container.

Preparation of dosage form
For patients who cannot take oral solids—Prepare a liquid suspension for oral use by adding the entire contents from the required number of l00-mg (base) regular Disopyramide Phosphate Capsules USP (do not use extended-release capsules) to an appropriate quantity of Cherry Syrup NF to make a suitable concentration of l to l0 mg per mL. Add accessory "Shake" and "Refrigerate" labels and dispense in amber glass bottles with childproof caps.

Stability
The extemporaneously prepared oral suspension of disopyramide is stable for 1 month when refrigerated.

Auxiliary labeling
- May cause blurred vision.
- Do not take other medicines without advice from your doctor.
- May cause blurred vision.
- Shake well.
- Refrigerate.
- Do not take other medicines without advice from your doctor.

For oral suspension—

DISOPYRAMIDE PHOSPHATE EXTENDED-RELEASE CAPSULES USP

Usual adult dose
Antiarrhythmic—
Oral, 400 to 800 mg (base) daily in divided doses. For most adults, the recommended dosage is 300 mg (base) every twelve hours (200 mg every twelve hours for patients with a body weight < 50 kg).

Note: Extended-release disopyramide is not recommended for initial therapy and should not be used in patients with cardiomyopathies or severe renal function impairment.

When transferring from the immediate-release oral dosage form, it is recommended that the first dose of the extended-release dosage form be given six hours after the last dose of the immediate-release dosage form. This method works well for most patients; however, for patients in whom breakthrough arrhythmias cannot be risked, the first extended-release dose of disopyramide may be combined with the last immediate-release dose in order to avoid a significant decrease in serum disopyramide concentrations.

When transferring patients with normal renal function from either quinidine sulfate or procainamide therapy to extended-release disopyramide, the extended-release dosage form of disopyramide should be started using the regular maintenance schedule, without a loading dose, six to twelve hours after the last dose of quinidine sulfate or three to six hours after the last dose of procainamide. For patients in whom withdrawal of quinidine sulfate or procainamide is likely to produce life-threatening arrhythmias, hospitalizing the patient should be considered.

Usual adult prescribing limits
800 mg (base) per day. A limited number of patients with severe refractory ventricular tachycardia have tolerated daily doses of up to 1600 mg (base) per day (400 mg every six hours), resulting in disopyramide plasma levels of up to 9 mcg per mL. If such treatment is warranted, patients must be hospitalized for close monitoring and evaluation.

Usual pediatric dose
Use is not recommended.

Strength(s) usually available
U.S.—
100 mg (base) (Rx) [*Norpace CR;* GENERIC].
150 mg (base) (Rx) [*Norpace CR;* GENERIC].
Canada—
Not commercially available.

Packaging and storage
Store between l5 and 30 °C (59 and 85 °F), unless otherwise specified by manufacturer. Store in a well-closed container.

Auxiliary labeling
- May cause blurred vision.
- Do not take other medicines without advice from your doctor.
- Swallow capsule whole.

DISOPYRAMIDE PHOSPHATE EXTENDED-RELEASE TABLETS

Usual adult dose
See *Disopyramide Phosphate Extended-release Capsules USP.*

Usual pediatric dose
Use is not recommended.

Strength(s) usually available
U.S.—
Not commercially available.
Canada—
150 mg (base) (Rx) [*Norpace CR; Rythmodan-LA* (scored)].

Packaging and storage
Store between 15 and 30 °C (59 and 86 °F), in a well-closed container, unless otherwise specified by manufacturer.

Auxiliary labeling
- May cause blurred vision.
- Swallow tablet whole.
- Do not take other medicines without advice from your doctor.

Selected Bibliography

Taylor EH, Pappas AA. Disopyramide: clinical indications, pharmacokinetics and laboratory assessment. Ann Clin Lab Sci 1986 Jul-Aug; 16(4): 289-95.

Siddoway LA, Woosley RL. Clinical pharmacokinetics of disopyramide. Clin Pharmacokinet 1986 May-Jun; 11(3): 214-22.

Revised: 03/19/1999

DISULFIRAM Systemic

VA CLASSIFICATION (Primary): AD100

Commonly used brand name(s): *Antabuse.*

Note: For a listing of dosage forms and brand names by country availability, see *Dosage Forms* section(s).

Category
Alcohol-abuse deterrent.

Indications

Accepted
Alcoholism (treatment)—Disulfiram is used to help maintain sobriety in the treatment of chronic alcoholism in conjunction with supportive and psychotherapeutic measures.

Pharmacology/Pharmacokinetics

Physicochemical characteristics
Molecular weight—296.52.

Mechanism of action/Effect
Produces irreversible inhibition of the enzyme responsible for oxidation of the ethanol metabolite acetaldehyde. The resultant accumulation of acetaldehyde may be responsible for most of the signs and symptoms occurring after ethanol ingestion in disulfiram-treated patients. The hypotensive response may be due to inhibition of norepinephrine synthesis by the major disulfiram metabolite diethyldithiocarbamate.

Absorption
Slow. 80 to 90% of an oral dose is absorbed.

Biotransformation
Hepatic.

Onset of action
A single dose of disulfiram will begin to affect ethanol metabolism within 1 to 2 hours.

Duration of action
Disulfiram-alcohol reactions may occur up to 14 days following last dose of disulfiram.

Elimination
Primarily renal, as metabolites. Some of the metabolites are also exhaled as carbon disulfide. Up to 20% of a dose may remain in the body for 1 week or longer. About 5 to 20% of a dose is eliminated unchanged in the feces.

Precautions to Consider

Cross-sensitivity and/or related problems
Patients sensitive to other thiuram derivatives (used in rubber, pesticides, or fungicides) may be sensitive to disulfiram also.

Pregnancy/Reproduction
Pregnancy—Adequate and well-controlled studies in humans have not been done. However, there have been a few reports of congenital defects in infants whose mothers received disulfiram during pregnancy. Further study is needed to determine the relationship between disulfiram and congenital malformations.

Disulfiram is reported to be embryotoxic in animals.

Breast-feeding
Problems in humans have not been documented.

Pediatrics
No information is available on the relationship of age to the effects of disulfiram in pediatric patients. Safety and efficacy have not been established.

Geriatrics
No information is available on the relationship of age to the effects of disulfiram in geriatric patients. However, elderly patients are more likely to have age-related renal function impairment, which may require caution in patients receiving this medication. In addition, elderly patients with cardiac or cerebrovascular disease may not tolerate the hypotension that accompanies the disulfiram-alcohol reaction as well as younger patients.

Drug interactions and/or related problems
The following drug interactions and/or related problems have been selected on the basis of their potential clinical significance (possible mechanism in parentheses where appropriate)—not necessarily inclusive (» = major clinical significance):

Note: Combinations containing any of the following medications, depending on the amount present, may also interact with this medication.

» Alcohol
(use of alcohol or alcohol-containing products within 14 days of disulfiram therapy will result in a disulfiram-alcohol reaction)

» Alfentanil
(chronic preoperative administration or perioperative use of hepatic enzyme inhibitors, such as disulfiram, may decrease plasma clearance and prolong the duration of action of alfentanil)

Amoxicillin and clavulanate combination or
Bacampicillin
(metabolism of bacampicillin produces low plasma concentrations of alcohol and acetaldehyde; although the risk of a disulfiram-alcohol interaction appears minimal, caution is recommended if concurrent use is unavoidable)
(a similar reaction is thought to occur with amoxicillin and clavulanate combination)

» Anticoagulants, coumarin- or indandione-derivative
(anticoagulant effect may be increased during concurrent use with disulfiram because of inhibition of the enzymatic metabolism of the anticoagulant; also, disulfiram may act directly in the liver to increase the hypoprothrombinemia-inducing activity of coumarin derivatives; anticoagulant dosage adjustments based on prothrombin time determinations may be necessary during and following concurrent use)

» Anticonvulsants, hydantoin, especially phenytoin
(concurrent use with disulfiram may increase the serum concentrations of hydantoins, possibly leading to hydantoin toxicity; hydantoin serum concentrations should be obtained prior to and during concurrent therapy with disulfiram and dosage adjustments made accordingly)

Antidepressants, tricyclic, especially amitriptyline
(concurrent use with disulfiram may cause transient delirium)

Ascorbic acid
(may interfere with the disulfiram-alcohol reaction, especially with chronic use or high doses of ascorbic acid; although controversial, this effect has been used beneficially by some clinicians in the management of disulfiram-alcohol reactions)

Central nervous system (CNS) depression-producing medications (See *Appendix II*)
(concurrent use may enhance the CNS depressant effects of either these medications or disulfiram)

Ethylene dibromide
(exposure to ethylene dibromide or its vapors concurrently with disulfiram treatment may result in a toxic reaction)

Hepatic enzyme inhibitors (See *Appendix II*)
(concurrent use of disulfiram with other hepatic enyzme inhibitors may potentiate the effect)

Hepatotoxic medication, other (See *Appendix II*)
(concurrent use of disulfiram with other hepatotoxic medications may increase the potential for hepatotoxicity)

» Isoniazid
(concurrent use may result in increased incidence of CNS effects, such as dizziness, incoordination, irritability, or insomnia; a reduction of dosage or discontinuation of disulfiram may be necessary)

» Metronidazole
(concurrent use with disulfiram may result in confusion and psychotic reactions because of combined toxicity; metronidazole is not recommended concurrently with, and for 2 weeks following, disulfiram)

Midazolam
(concurrent use may decrease first-pass metabolism and elimination of midazolam in the liver, probably by competitive inhibition at the cytochrome P-450 binding sites, thereby increasing steady-state plasma concentrations of midazolam)

Neurotoxic medications (See *Appendix II*)
(concurrent use of disulfiram with other neurotoxic medications may increase the potential for neurotoxicity)

» Organic solvents
(exposure to organic solvents, ingested or inhaled, which may contain alcohol, acetaldehyde, paraldehyde, or structural analogs, may result in a disulfiram-alcohol reaction)

» Paraldehyde
(concurrent use with disulfiram is not recommended, because inhibition of acetaldehyde dehydrogenase may occur, resulting in decreased metabolism of paraldehyde and increased blood concentrations of paraldehyde and acetaldehyde)

Laboratory value alterations

The following have been selected on the basis of their potential clinical significance (possible effect in parentheses where appropriate)—not necessarily inclusive (» = major clinical significance).

With physiology/laboratory test values
- Cholesterol concentrations, serum
  - (may be increased with doses of 500 mg a day)
- Vanillylmandelic acid (VMA) concentrations, urine
  - (may be decreased)

Medical considerations/Contraindications

The medical considerations/contraindications included have been selected on the basis of their potential clinical significance (reasons given in parentheses where appropriate)—not necessarily inclusive (» = major clinical significance).

Risk-benefit should be considered when the following medical problems exist:
- Allergic eczematous contact dermatitis
  - (may be exacerbated)
- Cardiovascular disorders
  - (disulfiram-alcohol reaction may exacerbate condition)
- Depression
  - (behavioral toxicity may be precipitated)
- Diabetes mellitus
  - (disulfiram-alcohol reaction may exacerbate condition)
- Epilepsy or other seizure disorder, or history of
  - (disulfiram-alcohol reaction may exacerbate condition)
- Hepatic function impairment or cirrhosis
  - (increased potential for hepatotoxicity)
- Hypothyroidism
  - (disulfiram-alcohol reaction may exacerbate condition)
- Psychoses
  - (behavioral toxicity may be precipitated)
- Pulmonary insufficiency, severe
  - (disulfiram-alcohol reaction may exacerbate condition)
- Renal function impairment
  - (disulfiram elimination may be inhibited)
- Sensitivity to disulfiram, rubber, pesticides, or fungicides

Patient monitoring

The following may be especially important in patient monitoring (other tests may be warranted in some patients, depending on condition; » = major clinical significance):
- Blood cell counts and
- Blood chemistry profiles
  - (recommended at 6-month intervals during therapy)
- Hepatic function determinations
  - (baseline studies are recommended, followed by transaminase tests after 10 to 14 days of therapy; additional liver function tests may also be required at periodic intervals during therapy)

Side/Adverse Effects

The following side/adverse effects have been selected on the basis of their potential clinical significance (possible signs and symptoms in parentheses where appropriate)—not necessarily inclusive:

Those indicating need for medical attention

Incidence less frequent

Neurotoxicity, including optic neuritis (eye pain or tenderness or any change in vision); ***peripheral neuritis or polyneuritis*** (numbness, pain, tingling, or weakness in hands or feet); ***psychotic reaction*** (mood or mental changes)

Note: *Neurotoxicity* is usually reversible if disulfiram is discontinued.

Incidence rare

Encephalopathy (mental changes); ***hepatitis*** (yellow eyes or skin; darkening of urine; light gray–colored stools; severe stomach pain)

Note: Fulminant hepatic necrosis occurs rarely. Although it cannot be predicted which patients will develop this potentially fatal hepatitis, published experience suggests that the chance of survival is markedly improved if disulfiram is stopped as soon as jaundice is detected. Careful clinical monitoring with discontinuation of disulfiram and laboratory (bilirubin and hepatic enzyme) determinations is recommended when hepatitis is suspected.

Those indicating need for medical attention only if they continue or are bothersome

Incidence more frequent

Drowsiness

Incidence less frequent or rare

Headache; impotence (decreased sexual ability in males); ***metallic or garlic-like taste in mouth; skin rash; unusual tiredness***

Patient Consultation

As an aid to patient consultation, refer to *Advice for the Patient, Disulfiram (Systemic)*.

In providing consultation, consider emphasizing the following selected information (» = major clinical significance):

Before using this medication

» Conditions affecting use, especially:
- Sensitivity to disulfiram, rubber, pesticides, or fungicides
- Other medications, especially alcohol; alfentanil; coumarin- or indandione-derivative anticoagulants; hydantoin anticonvulsants, especially phenytoin; isoniazid; metronidazole; organic solvents; or paraldehyde

Proper use of this medication

» Not taking this medication within 12 hours of using any alcohol-containing preparation or medication, or if the blood alcohol level is not zero

» Compliance with therapy

» Proper dosing

» Proper storage

Precautions while using this medication

» Not drinking or using any alcohol-containing products or medications while taking this medication and for 14 days after discontinuing this medication

Symptoms of disulfiram-alcohol reaction:
- Blurred vision
- Chest pain
- Confusion
- Dizziness or fainting
- Fast or pounding heartbeat
- Flushing or redness of face
- Increased sweating
- Nausea and vomiting
- Throbbing headache
- Troubled breathing
- Weakness, severe
- Rarely, seizures, heart attack, unconsciousness, or death if reaction is severe

Carrying medical identification card during therapy

Regular visits to physician to check progress during long-term therapy

» Checking all liquid medications for presence of alcohol

» Caution if drowsiness occurs

» Checking with physician before using other CNS depressants

Side/adverse effects

Signs of potential side effects, especially optic neuritis, peripheral neuritis, polyneuritis, or psychotic reaction

General Dosing Information

The patient should be made fully aware of the nature of this medicine and the disulfiram-alcohol reaction and its consequences.

Disulfiram should not be administered until the patient has abstained from alcohol for at least 12 hours and the blood alcohol level is zero.

The duration of the disulfiram-alcohol reaction is dependent upon the dose of disulfiram and on the quantity of alcohol ingested; it may persist from 30 minutes to several hours.

Reactions to alcohol may occur for up to 2 weeks following withdrawal of disulfiram therapy.

For treatment of disulfiram-alcohol reaction

In severe reactions, supportive measures to restore blood pressure and treat shock should be instituted. Other recommendations include:
- Administration of supplemental oxygen.
- Monitoring of serum potassium levels.
- Monitoring of ECG tracings.

Although controversial, administration of intravenous ascorbic acid or intravenous antihistamines has been advocated by some clinicians. Phenothiazines should not be used as they may exacerbate hypotension.

Oral Dosage Forms

DISULFIRAM TABLETS USP

Usual adult and adolescent dose

Alcohol-abuse deterrent—

Initial: Oral, up to 500 mg once a day for one or two weeks.

Maintenance: Oral, 125 to 500 mg (average of 250 mg) once a day.

Note: Some clinicians recommend the dose be administered at bedtime to reduce daytime drowsiness.

Usual pediatric dose

Safety and efficacy havenot been established.

Usual geriatric dose

See *Usual adult and adolescent dose.*

Note: Geriatric patients may be more sensitive to the effects of the usual adult dose.

Strength(s) usually available

U.S.—

250 mg (Rx) [*Antabuse* (scored); GENERIC].

500 mg (Rx) [*Antabuse* (scored); GENERIC].

Canada—

250 mg (Rx) [*Antabuse* (scored)].

500 mg (Rx) [*Antabuse* (scored)].

Packaging and storage

Store below 40 °C (104 °F), preferably between 15 and 30 °C (59 and 86 °F), in a tight, light-resistant container.

Note

Patient identification cards may be available from the manufacturer.

Selected Bibliography

Wright C, Moore RD. Disulfiram treatment of alcoholism. Am J Med 1990; 88: 647-55.

Revised: 07/20/1994

DIURETICS, LOOP Systemic

This monograph includes information on the following: 1) Bumetanide†; 2) Ethacrynic Acid; 3) Furosemide.

INN: Ethacrynic Acid—Etacrynic acid

JAN: Ethacrynic Acid—Etacrynic acid

VA CLASSIFICATION (Primary/Secondary): CV702/CV409; TN900

Commonly used brand name(s): *Apo-Furosemide*[3]; *Bumex*[1]; *Edecrin*[2]; *Furoside*[3]; *Lasix*[3]; *Lasix Special*[3]; *Myrosemide*[3]; *Novosemide*[3]; *Uritol*[3].

Note: For a listing of dosage forms and brand names by country availability, see *Dosage Forms* section(s).

†Not commercially available in Canada.

Category

Diagnostic aid adjunct (renal disease)—Furosemide.
Diuretic—Bumetanide; Ethacrynic Acid; Furosemide.
Antihypertensive—Bumetanide; Ethacrynic Acid; Furosemide.
Antihypercalcemic—Bumetanide; Ethacrynic Acid; Furosemide

Indications

Note: Bracketed information in the *Indications* section refers to uses that are not included in U.S. product labeling.

Accepted

Edema (treatment)—Bumetanide, ethacrynic acid, and furosemide are indicated in the treatment of edema associated with congestive heart failure, hepatic cirrhosis, and renal disease (including nephrotic syndrome).

Bumetanide, ethacrynic acid, and furosemide are indicated as adjuncts in the treatment of acute pulmonary edema.

Ethacrynic acid is indicated in the short-term management of ascites due to malignancy, idiopathic edema, and lymphedema; and in the short-term management of hospitalized pediatric patients with congenital heart disease or nephrotic syndrome.

Bumetanide, ethacrynic acid, and furosemide are especially useful in patients refractory to other diuretics or with existing acid-base disorders, congestive heart failure, or renal disease.

Hypertension (treatment)—[Bumetanide], [ethacrynic acid][1], and furosemide are indicated in the treatment of mild to moderate hypertension, usually in combination with other antihypertensive agents, and as adjuncts in the treatment of hypertensive crisis.

Bumetanide, ethacrynic acid, and furosemide are not considered to be primary agents in the treatment of essential hypertension. However, they may be indicated in combination with other antihypertensives in the treatment of hypertension associated with impaired renal function. In the stepped-care approach to antihypertensive treatment, bumetanide, ethacrynic acid, or furosemide may be substituted for a thiazide diuretic in patients with renal function impairment.

For additional information on initial therapeutic guidelines related to the treatment of hypertension, see *Appendix III.*

Hypercalcemia (treatment)—[Bumetanide], [ethacrynic acid][1], and [furosemide][1] are used in the treatment of hypercalcemia.

[Renography, adjunct][1] and
[Renal imaging, radionuclide, adjunct][1]—Furosemide augments radionuclide renography and renal scintigraphy by stimulating the flow of urine and thereby aiding in the differentiation of mechanical obstruction from nonobstructive dilatation in patients with hydroureteronephrosis.

Acceptance not established

Pharmacokinetic studies demonstrated efficacy in the use of bumetanide for the *treatment of edema in infant and pediatric patients.* However, data are insufficient to determine an optimal dose for safe and effective use in pediatric patients.

[1]Not included in Canadian product labeling.

Pharmacology/Pharmacokinetics

Physicochemical characteristics

Molecular weight—
Bumetanide: 364.42.
Ethacrynic acid: 303.14.
Furosemide: 330.74.

pKa—
Ethacrynic acid: 3.5.
Furosemide: 3.9.

Mechanism of action/Effect

Diuretic—Bumetanide, ethacrynic acid, and furosemide inhibit reabsorption of sodium and water in the ascending limb of the loop of Henle by interfering with the chloride binding site of the 1Na+, 1K+, 2Cl− cotransport system. Loop diuretics increase the rate of delivery of tubular fluid and electrolytes to the distal sites of hydrogen and potassium ion secretion, while plasma volume contraction increases aldosterone production. The increased delivery and high aldosterone levels promote sodium reabsorption at the distal tubules, thus increasing the loss of potassium and hydrogen ions. Bumetanide may have a small additional action on sodium reabsorption in the proximal tubule since phosphate reabsorption is reduced.

Antihypertensive—Diuretics lower blood pressure initially by reducing plasma and extracellular fluid volume; cardiac output also decreases. Eventually, cardiac output returns to normal with an accompanying decrease in peripheral resistance.

Antihypercalcemic—Loop diuretics increase the urinary excretion of calcium.

Absorption

Bumetanide—Almost completely absorbed from gastrointestinal tract. Absorption is probably reduced in patients with edematous bowel caused by congestive heart failure or nephrotic syndrome; parenteral administration may be preferable in these patients.

Furosemide—Approximately 60 to 70% of an oral dose of furosemide is absorbed. Food may slow the rate of absorption but does not appear to alter the bioavailability or diuretic effect. Absorption is reduced to 43 to 46% in patients with end-stage renal disease, and is probably reduced also in patients with edematous bowel caused by congestive heart failure or nephrotic syndrome; parenteral administration may be preferable in these patients.

Protein binding
Bumetanide—Very high (94 to 96%).
Ethacrynic acid—High.
Furosemide—Very high (91 to 97%; almost totally to albumin).

Biotransformation
Hepatic; metabolism of bumetanide is limited and produces inactive metabolites.

Half-life
Bumetanide—
1 to 1½ hours.
Furosemide—
Wide variation among individuals.
Normal:
½ to 1 hour.
Anuric:
75 to 155 minutes.
In patients with both renal and hepatic insufficiency, half-lives of 11 to 20 hours have been reported.
In neonates, reported half-lives are prolonged, probably due to low renal and hepatic clearance.

Onset of action
Diuretic—
Bumetanide:
Oral—30 to 60 minutes.
Intravenous—Within minutes.
Ethacrynic acid:
Oral—30 minutes.
Intravenous—5 minutes.
Furosemide:
Oral—20 to 60 minutes.
Intravenous—5 minutes.

Time to peak effect
Diuretic—
Bumetanide:
Oral—1 to 2 hours.
Intravenous—15 to 30 minutes.
Ethacrynic acid:
Oral—2 hours.
Intravenous—15 to 30 minutes.
Furosemide:
Oral—1 to 2 hours.
Intravenous—Within 30 minutes.

Note: The maximum antihypertensive effect may not occur until several days after initiation of loop diuretic therapy.

Duration of action
Diuretic—
Bumetanide:
Oral—4 hours with usual doses (1 to 2 mg); 4 to 6 hours with higher doses.
Intravenous—3.5 to 4 hours.
Ethacrynic acid:
Oral—6 to 8 hours.
Intravenous—2 hours.
Furosemide:
Oral—6 to 8 hours.
Intravenous—2 hours.

Elimination
Bumetanide—
Renal (81%; 45% unchanged); biliary/fecal (2%).
Ethacrynic acid—
Renal (67%); biliary/fecal (33%); 20% excreted unchanged.
Furosemide—
Renal (88%); biliary/fecal (12%).
In patients with severe renal impairment, renal clearance is reduced but overall plasma clearance may be unchanged because nonrenal clearance is increased. In patients with uremia, both renal and nonrenal clearance are reduced, and elimination is delayed.
In dialysis: Not dialyzable.

Precautions to Consider

Cross-sensitivity and/or related problems
Patients sensitive to sulfonamides (including thiazide diuretics) may be sensitive to bumetanide or furosemide also.

Carcinogenicity/Tumorigenicity
Bumetanide—One study in female rats given 60 mg per kg of body weight (mg/kg) of bumetanide for 18 months found an increase in mammary adenomas; repetition of the same study did not result in the same findings.
Ethacrynic acid—A 79-week study in rats at doses up to 45 times the human dose revealed no evidence of a tumorigenic effect.

Mutagenicity
Bumetanide—Studies with bumetanide in various strains of *Salmonella typhimurium* in the presence or absence of an *in vitro* metabolic activation system found no evidence of mutagenicity.
Furosemide—Mutagenicity studies have not been conducted.

Pregnancy/Reproduction
Pregnancy—Pregnant women should be advised to contact physician before taking this medication, since routine use of diuretics during normal pregnancy is inappropriate and exposes mother and fetus to unnecessary hazard. Diuretics do not prevent development of toxemia of pregnancy, and there is no satisfactory evidence that they are useful in the treatment of toxemia. Diuretics are indicated only in the treatment of edema due to pathologic causes or as a short course of treatment in patients with severe hypervolemia.

Bumetanide—
Adequate and well-controlled studies in humans have not been done.
Some studies in animals have shown that bumetanide may cause adverse effects on the fetus. Bumetanide has not been shown to be teratogenic in mice or hamsters; however, one study in rats showed moderate growth retardation and increased incidence of delayed ossification of sternebrae at doses 3400 times the maximum human therapeutic dose. These effects in the rat were associated with maternal weight reductions during dosing and were not observed at doses 1000 times the maximum human therapeutic dose. Delayed ossification of sternebrae was also noted in rabbits at doses 10 times the maximum human therapeutic dose. A slight embryocidal effect in rats and rabbits was evident at doses 3400 and 3.4 times the maximum human therapeutic dose, respectively. In rabbits, a dose-related decrease in litter size and an increase in resorption rate were noted at doses of 3.4 and 10 times the maximum human therapeutic dose.
FDA Pregnancy Category C.

Ethacrynic acid—
Adequate and well-controlled studies in humans have not been done.
Studies in mice and rabbits using doses up to 50 times the human dose have not shown evidence of external abnormalities of the fetus. In rats, a decrease in mean body weights of the fetuses was noted at doses 50 times the maximum human dose.
FDA Pregnancy Category B.

Furosemide—
Furosemide crosses the placenta. Studies in humans have not been done.
Studies in rabbits and mice have shown that furosemide causes an increased incidence of hydronephrosis in the fetus. In rabbits, unexplained maternal deaths and abortions have occurred at doses 2 to 8 times the maximum recommended human dose.
FDA Pregnancy Category C.

Breast-feeding
Furosemide is distributed into breast milk; it is not known whether bumetanide or ethacrynic acid is distributed into breast milk.

Pediatrics
Caution is required in neonates because of the prolonged half-life of furosemide. Usual pediatric doses may be used, but the dosing interval should be extended.

Geriatrics
Although appropriate studies on the relationship of age to the effects of loop diuretics have not been performed in the geriatric population, the elderly may be more sensitive to the hypotensive and electrolyte effects. In addition, elderly patients are at greater risk of developing circulatory collapse and thromboembolic episodes. Elderly patients are also more likely to have age-related renal function impairment, which may require adjustment of dosage or dosing interval in patients receiving loop diuretics.

Drug interactions and/or related problems
The following drug interactions and/or related problems have been selected on the basis of their potential clinical significance (possible

mechanism in parentheses where appropriate)—not necessarily inclusive (» = major clinical significance):

Note: Combinations containing any of the following medications, depending on the amount present, may also interact with this medication.

Alcohol or
Hypotension-producing medications, other (See *Appendix II*)
(hypotensive and/or diuretic effects may be potentiated when these medications are used concurrently with loop diuretics; although some antihypertensive and/or diuretic combinations are frequently used for therapeutic advantage, when used concurrently dosage adjustments may be necessary)

Amiodarone
(concurrent use of loop diuretics with amiodarone may lead to an increased risk of arrhythmias associated with hypokalemia)

» Amphotericin B, parenteral
(concurrent and/or sequential administration with loop diuretics should be avoided since the potential for ototoxicity and nephrotoxicity may be increased, especially in the presence of renal function impairment; in addition, concurrent use with loop diuretics may intensify electrolyte imbalance, particularly hypokalemia; frequent electrolyte determinations are recommended and potassium supplementation may be required)

Angiotensin-converting enzyme (ACE) inhibitors
(sudden and severe hypotension may occur within the first 1 to 5 hours after the initial dose of captopril, enalapril, or lisinopril, particularly in patients who are sodium- and volume-depleted as a result of diuretic therapy. Withdrawal of the diuretic or increase of salt intake approximately 1 week before start of captopril therapy or 2 to 3 days before start of benazepril, enalapril, fosinopril, lisinopril, quinapril, or ramipril therapy, or initiating ACE inhibitor therapy in lower doses, will minimize the reaction; this reaction does not usually recur with subsequent doses, although caution in increasing doses is recommended; diuretics may be reinstituted as necessary)
(risk of renal failure may be increased in patients who are sodium- and volume-depleted as a result of diuretic therapy)
(ACE inhibitors may reduce the secondary aldosteronism and hypokalemia caused by diuretics)

» Anticoagulants, coumarin- or indandione-derivative or
Heparin or
Streptokinase or
Urokinase
(anticoagulant effects may be decreased when these medications are used concurrently with loop diuretics, as a result of reduction of plasma volume leading to concentration of procoagulant factors in the blood; in addition, diuretic-induced improvement of hepatic congestion may lead to improved hepatic function, resulting in increased procoagulant factor synthesis; dosage adjustments may be necessary)
(anticoagulant effects may be potentiated when these medications are used concurrently with ethacrynic acid as a result of displacement of anticoagulant from protein-binding sites; dosage adjustments of the anticoagulant may be necessary during and after ethacrynic acid therapy or, alternatively, use of furosemide is recommended)
(gastrointestinal ulcerative or hemorrhagic potential of ethacrynic acid may increase the risk of hemorrhage in patients receiving anticoagulant or thrombolytic therapy; use of a different diuretic is recommended)

Antidiabetic agents, oral or
Insulin
(furosemide, and possibly bumetanide or ethacrynic acid, may rarely raise blood glucose concentrations or interfere with the hypoglycemic effects of these agents; for adult-onset diabetics, dosage adjustment of hypoglycemic medications may be necessary during and after therapy)

Anti-inflammatory drugs, nonsteroidal (NSAIDs), especially indomethacin
(may antagonize the natriuresis and increase in plasma renin activity [PRA] caused by loop diuretics; indomethacin, and possibly other NSAIDs with the exception of diflunisal, may also reduce the increase in urine volume caused by loop diuretics, possibly by inhibiting renal prostaglandin synthesis and/or by causing sodium and fluid retention)
(in addition, concurrent use of NSAIDs with a diuretic may increase the risk of renal failure secondary to a decrease in renal blood flow caused by inhibition of renal prostaglandin synthesis)
(in the premature neonate, administration of 1 mg/kg of furosemide immediately following indomethacin has been shown to prevent or reduce indomethacin-induced adverse renal effects without interfering with ductus arteriosus closure)

Digitalis glycosides
(concurrent use with loop diuretics may enhance the possibility of digitalis toxicity associated with hypokalemia and hypomagnesemia)

» Hypokalemia-causing medications, other (See *Appendix II*)
(risk of severe hypokalemia due to other hypokalemia-causing medications may be increased; monitoring of serum potassium concentrations and cardiac function and potassium supplementation may be required)

» Lithium
(concurrent use with loop diuretics may provoke lithium toxicity because of reduced renal clearance and is not recommended unless patient can be closely monitored)

» Nephrotoxic medications, other (See *Appendix II*) or
Ototoxic medications, other (See *Appendix II*)
(concurrent and/or sequential administration with loop diuretics should be avoided since the potential for ototoxicity and nephrotoxicity may be increased, especially in the presence of renal function impairment)

Neuromuscular blocking agents, nondepolarizing
(loop diuretics may induce hypokalemia, which may enhance the blockade of nondepolarizing neuromuscular blocking agents; serum potassium determinations may be necessary prior to administration of nondepolarizing neuromuscular blocking agents; careful postoperative monitoring of the patient may be necessary following concurrent or sequential use, especially if there is a possibility of incomplete reversal of neuromuscular blockade)

Sympathomimetics
(concurrent use may reduce the antihypertensive effects of the loop diuretics; the patient should be carefully monitored to confirm that the desired effect is being obtained)

For furosemide only (in addition to those listed above)
Chloral hydrate
(administration of chloral hydrate followed by intravenous furosemide may result in diaphoresis, hot flashes, and variable blood pressure, including hypertension due to a hypermetabolic state caused by displacement of thyroxine from its bound state)

Probenecid
(probenecid has been found to increase serum concentrations of furosemide by inhibiting active renal tubular secretion)

Laboratory value alterations

The following have been selected on the basis of their potential clinical significance (possible effect in parentheses where appropriate)—not necessarily inclusive (» = major clinical significance).

With physiology/laboratory test values
For bumetanide, ethacrynic acid, and furosemide
Blood glucose concentrations and
Urine glucose concentrations
(may be increased; ethacrynic acid increases blood glucose only rarely, especially in diabetics, prediabetics, or patients with compensated cirrhosis; in patients with uremia, large doses of ethacrynic acid may cause severe hypoglycemia; the effect of bumetanide is controversial and possibly variable)

Blood urea nitrogen (BUN) and
Uric acid, serum
(concentrations may be increased)

Calcium and
Chloride and
Magnesium and
Potassium and
Sodium
(serum concentrations may be decreased)

For bumetanide only (in addition to the above)
Phosphate
(urinary concentrations may be increased)

Medical considerations/Contraindications

The medical considerations/contraindications included have been selected on the basis of their potential clinical significance (reasons given in parentheses where appropriate)—not necessarily inclusive (» = major clinical significance).

Risk-benefit should be considered when the following medical problems exist:

For bumetanide, ethacrynic acid, and furosemide

» Anuria or
» Renal function impairment, severe
(impaired effectiveness and possible delayed excretion with increased risk of toxicity. Although bumetanide, ethacrynic acid, and furosemide are effective diuretics in patients with renal function impairment, reduced clearance may necessitate use of higher doses combined with more prolonged dosing intervals to prevent accumulation and reduce the risk of ototoxicity)
Diabetes mellitus
(loop diuretics cause impaired glucose tolerance)
Gout, history of or
Hyperuricemia
(loop diuretics may elevate serum uric acid concentrations)
Hearing function impairment
Hepatic function impairment, including cirrhosis and ascites
(risk of dehydration and electrolyte imbalance, which may precipitate hepatic coma and death; hospitalization during initiation of therapy is recommended)
Myocardial infarction, acute
(excessive diuresis should be avoided because of the danger of precipitating shock)
Pancreatitis, or history of
(pancreatitis has been reported with bumetanide, ethacrynic acid, and furosemide)
Sensitivity to loop diuretic prescribed
Caution is recommended also in patients who are at increased risk if hypokalemia occurs, including those taking digitalis and diuretics and those with:
Certain diarrheal states
Congestive heart failure
Hepatic cirrhosis and ascites
History of ventricular arrhythmias
Potassium-losing nephropathy
States of aldosterone excess with normal renal function

For ethacrynic acid and furosemide only (in addition to the above)

Lupus erythematosus, history of
(exacerbation or activation by ethacrynic acid and furosemide has been reported)

Patient monitoring

The following may be especially important in patient monitoring (other tests may be warranted in some patients, depending on condition; » = major clinical significance):

Blood pressure measurements
(recommended at periodic intervals in patients being treated for hypertension; selected patients may be taught to monitor their blood pressure at home and report the results at regular physician visits)

Blood urea nitrogen (BUN) and
Carbon dioxide (CO_2)
(determinations recommended at periodic intervals during therapy)

Electrolyte concentrations
(determinations recommended at periodic intervals, especially if patients are also taking cardiac glycosides or systemic steroids, or when severe hepatic cirrhosis is present)

Glucose, serum and
Hepatic function and
Renal function and
Uric acid, serum
(determinations recommended at periodic intervals)

Hearing examinations
(recommended at periodic intervals in patients receiving prolonged high-dose intravenous therapy)

Weight measurement
(recommended prior to initiation of therapy and at periodic intervals during therapy to monitor water loss)

Side/Adverse Effects

See *Table 1*, page 1119.

Patient Consultation

As an aid to patient consultation, refer to *Advice for the Patient, Diuretics, Loop (Systemic)*.

In providing consultation, consider emphasizing the following selected information (» = major clinical significance):

Before using this medication

» Conditions affecting use, especially:
Sensitivity to the loop diuretic prescribed, or to sulfonamides (for bumetanide and furosemide)
Pregnancy—Not recommended for routine use; reported to cause harmful effects, including birth defects, in animals
Breast-feeding—Furosemide distributed into breast milk
Use in the elderly—Elderly patients may be more sensitive to hypotensive and electrolyte effects, and may be at greater risk of developing circulatory collapse and thromboembolic episodes
Other medications, especially parenteral amphotericin B, oral anticoagulants, other hypokalemia-causing medications, lithium, or other nephrotoxic medications
Other medical problems, especially anuria or severe renal function impairment

Proper use of this medication

Diuretic effects of the medication and timing of doses to minimize inconvenience of diuresis
Compliance with therapy; taking medication at the same time(s) each day to maintain the therapeutic effect
Taking with food or milk to reduce gastrointestinal irritation
» Proper dosing
Missed dose: Taking as soon as possible; not taking if almost time for next dose; not doubling doses
» Proper storage

For use as an antihypertensive

Possible need for control of weight and diet, especially sodium intake
» Patient may not experience symptoms of hypertension; importance of taking medication even if feeling well
» Does not cure, but controls hypertension; possible need for lifelong therapy; serious consequences of untreated hypertension

For oral solution dosage form of furosemide (in addition to the above)

Taking orally, even if in dropper bottle; importance of accurate measurement

Precautions while using this medication

Making regular visits to physician to check progress
» Possibility of hypokalemia; possible need for additional potassium in diet; not changing diet without first checking with physician
To prevent dehydration, notifying physician if severe nausea, vomiting, or diarrhea occurs and continues
Caution if any kind of surgery (including dental surgery) is required
» Caution when getting up suddenly from a lying or sitting position
» Caution in using alcohol, while standing for long periods or exercising, and during hot weather because of enhanced orthostatic hypotensive effects
Diabetics: May increase blood sugar levels

For use as an antihypertensive:

» Not taking other medications, especially nonprescription sympathomimetics, unless discussed with physician

For furosemide (in addition to the above):

» Possible skin photosensitivity; avoiding unprotected exposure to sun; using protective clothing; using a sun block product that includes protection against both UVA-caused photosensitivity reactions and UVB-caused sunburn reactions; avoiding use of sunlamp, tanning bed, or tanning booth

Side/adverse effects

Signs of potential side effects, especially allergic reaction, blood in urine, electrolyte imbalance, gastrointestinal bleeding, gout, hepatic dysfunction, leukopenia, agranulocytosis, ototoxicity, pancreatitis, thrombocytopenia, and xanthopsia

General Dosing Information

Dosage must be adjusted to meet the individual requirements of each patient, on the basis of clinical response. The lowest effective dosage should be utilized to minimize potential fluid and electrolyte imbalance.

When loop diuretics are used to promote diuresis, intermittent dosage schedules may reduce the possibility of electrolyte imbalance or hyperuricemia resulting from therapy.

Concurrent administration of potassium supplements or potassium-sparing diuretics may be indicated in patients considered to be at higher risk for developing hypokalemia.

If a single daily dose is indicated, it is preferably taken on arising in order to minimize the effect of increased frequency of urination on sleep.

When bumetanide, ethacrynic acid, or furosemide is added to an antihypertensive regimen, the dose of other antihypertensive agents may have to be reduced in order to prevent an excessive drop in blood pressure.

It is recommended that bumetanide, ethacrynic acid, and furosemide be discontinued if oliguria persists for more than 24 hours at maximal dosage.

BUMETANIDE

Summary of Differences

Pharmacology/pharmacokinetics:

Mechanism of action/effect—May have additional action on proximal tubule.

Biotransformation and elimination—Excreted largely unchanged.

Side/adverse effects:

Muscle pain may occur with large doses. Chest pain, premature ejaculation, and difficulty in keeping an erection have also been reported.

Additional Dosing Information

See also *General Dosing Information.*

For parenteral dosage forms only

Intravenous administration is generally preferred over intramuscular administration.

Intravenous administration should be at a slow, controlled rate over a 2-minute period.

Oral Dosage Forms

Note: Bracketed uses in the *Dosage Forms* section refer to categories of use and/or indications that are not included in U.S. product labeling.

BUMETANIDE TABLETS USP

Usual adult dose

[Antihypertensive or]

Diuretic—

Oral, 500 mcg (0.5 mg) to 2 mg a day as a single daily dose. The dose may be increased, if necessary, by addition of a second or third daily dose with intervals of four to five hours between doses. An intermittent dosage schedule (administration on alternate days for three or four days, with one or two days in between) may also be used.

Note: Geriatric patients may be more sensitive to the effects of the usual adult dose.

Usual adult prescribing limits

10 mg a day.

Usual pediatric dose

Dosage has not been established.

Strength(s) usually available

U.S.—

500 mcg (0.5 mg) (Rx) [*Bumex* (lactose); GENERIC].
1 mg (Rx) [*Bumex* (lactose); GENERIC].
2 mg (Rx) [*Bumex* (lactose); GENERIC].

Canada—

Not commercially available.

Packaging and storage

Store below 40 °C (104 °F), preferably between 15 and 30 °C (59 and 86 °F), unless otherwise specified by manufacturer. Store in a tight, light-resistant container.

Auxiliary labeling

- Do not take other medicines without your doctor's advice.

Parenteral Dosage Forms

Note: Bracketed uses in the *Dosage Forms* section refer to categories of use and/or indications that are not included in U.S. product labeling.

BUMETANIDE INJECTION USP

Usual adult dose

[Antihypertensive or]

Diuretic—

Intravenous or intramuscular, 500 mcg (0.5 mg) to 1 mg, repeated at intervals of two to three hours, if necessary.

Usual adult prescribing limits

10 mg a day.

Usual pediatric dose

Dosage has not been established.

Strength(s) usually available

U.S.—

250 mcg (0.25 mg) per mL (Rx) [*Bumex* (benzyl alcohol 1%)].

Canada—

Not commercially available.

Packaging and storage

Store below 40 °C (104 °F), preferably between 15 and 30 °C (59 and 86 °F), unless otherwise specified by manufacturer. Protect from freezing. Protect from light.

Stability

Infusion solutions should be freshly prepared and used within a 24-hour period.

ETHACRYNIC ACID

Summary of Differences

Indications:

Also indicated for short-term management of ascites due to malignancy, idiopathic edema, and lymphedema, and for treatment of hypercalcemia.

Side/adverse effects:

Greatest risk of ototoxicity. Gastrointestinal bleeding and blood in urine may occur with parenteral use. Higher incidence of gastrointestinal upset. Confusion, loss of appetite, and nervousness were reported more often than with other loop diuretics.

Additional Dosing Information

See also *General Dosing Information.*

Concurrent administration of ammonium chloride or arginine chloride may be indicated in patients considered to be at higher risk of developing metabolic alkalosis as a result of the chloruretic effect.

Because of the profound effect of ethacrynic acid on sodium excretion, rigid dietary salt restriction is not necessary in most patients and may in fact increase the risk of adverse effects due to hyponatremia.

In patients with renal edema, administration of salt-poor albumin may be helpful in preventing reduced response to ethacrynic acid because of hypoproteinemia.

If severe, watery diarrhea occurs, it is recommended that ethacrynic acid be permanently withdrawn.

For parenteral dosage forms only

Intramuscular or subcutaneous administration is not recommended because of local pain and irritation.

Intravenous administration should be at a slow, controlled rate over a period of about 30 minutes.

If a second injection is required, use of a different injection site is recommended to prevent thrombophlebitis.

Oral Dosage Forms

ETHACRYNIC ACID ORAL SOLUTION

Usual adult dose

Diuretic—

Initial: Oral, 50 to 100 mg a day, in single or divided daily doses with increments of 25 to 50 mg a day as needed.

Maintenance: Oral, reduced to meet individual requirements once dry weight is achieved; usually 50 to 200 mg a day.

Note: Geriatric patients may be more sensitive to the effects of the usual adult dose.

Usual adult prescribing limits
400 mg a day.

Usual pediatric dose
Diuretic—
Initial: Oral, 25 mg a day, with increments of 25 mg a day as needed.
Maintenance: Oral, adjusted to meet individual requirements.

Note: Use in infants is not recommended.

Strength(s) usually available
U.S.—
Dosage form not commercially available in the U.S. Compounding required for prescriptions.
Canada—
Dosage form not commercially available in Canada. Compounding required for prescriptions.

Packaging and storage
Store at or below 24 °C (75 °F). Protect from freezing.

Preparation of dosage form
An oral liquid dosage form of ethacrynic acid has been prepared by dissolving ethacrynic acid powder in 10% alcohol in water, then bringing it to volume (to produce a solution containing 1 mg of ethacrynic acid per mL) with a 50% aqueous sorbitol solution (with added 0.005% methylparaben and 0.002% propylparaben as preservatives), and adjusting the pH to 7 with sodium hydroxide.

Stability
This product was found to be stable for several weeks when stored at 24 °C (75 °F).

Auxiliary labeling
- Take with meals or milk.
- Do not take other medicines without your doctor's advice.

Note
Check refill frequency to determine compliance in hypertensive patients.

ETHACRYNIC ACID TABLETS USP

Usual adult dose
See *Ethacrynic Acid Oral Solution*.

Usual adult prescribing limits
400 mg a day.

Usual pediatric dose
See *Ethacrynic Acid Oral Solution*.

Strength(s) usually available
U.S.—
25 mg (Rx) [*Edecrin* (lactose)].
50 mg (Rx) [*Edecrin* (lactose)].
Canada—
50 mg (Rx) [*Edecrin* (scored; lactose)].

Packaging and storage
Store below 40 °C (104 °F), preferably between 15 and 30 °C (59 and 86 °F), unless otherwise specified by manufacturer. Store in a well-closed container.

Auxiliary labeling
- Take with meals or milk.
- Do not take other medicines without your doctor's advice.

Note
Check refill frequency to determine compliance in hypertensive patients.

Parenteral Dosage Forms

ETHACRYNATE SODIUM FOR INJECTION USP

Usual adult dose
Diuretic—
Intravenous, 50 mg (base), or 500 mcg (0.5 mg) to 1 mg per kg of body weight; may be repeated in two to four hours if necessary, then every four to six hours if the patient is responsive. In some emergency situations, the injection may be repeated every hour.

Note: Geriatric patients may be more sensitive to the effects of the usual adult dose.

Usual adult prescribing limits
100 mg (base).

Usual pediatric dose
Diuretic—
Intravenous, 1 mg (base) per kg of body weight.

Strength(s) usually available
U.S.—
50 mg (base) (Rx) [*Edecrin* (mannitol 62.5 mg)].
Canada—
50 mg (base) (Rx) [*Edecrin* (mannitol 62.5 mg)].

Packaging and storage
Store below 40 °C (104 °F), preferably between 15 and 30 °C (59 and 86 °F), unless otherwise specified by manufacturer.

Preparation of dosage form
Infusion solutions can be prepared using 0.9% sodium chloride injection or 5% dextrose injection, after pH has been adjusted when necessary.

Stability
A hazy or opalescent solution may result from use of a diluent with a low pH (below 5); use of such a solution is not recommended.

Unused, reconstituted solution should be discarded after 24 hours at room temperature.

Incompatibilities
The solution is physically incompatible with whole blood or its derivatives.

FUROSEMIDE

Summary of Differences
Category:
Furosemide is used as a diagnostic aid adjunct in renal disease.
Precautions:
Breast-feeding—Distributed into breast milk.
Pediatrics—Prolonged half-life in neonates.
Drug interactions and/or related problems—Also interacts with chloral hydrate and probenecid.
Side/adverse effects:
Also causes xanthopsia and increased sensitivity of skin to sunlight.

Additional Dosing Information
See also *General Dosing Information*.

When furosemide is used as an antihypercalcemic, body fluid and sodium chloride should be replaced in order to maintain extracellular fluid volume and increase calcium excretion effectively.

For parenteral dosage forms only
Intravenous administration is generally preferred over intramuscular administration.

Intravenous administration should be at a slow, controlled rate over a 1- to 2-minute period.

If high-dose parenteral therapy is indicated, administration should be by controlled intravenous infusion at a rate not exceeding 4 mg per minute.

Oral Dosage Forms
Note: Bracketed uses in the *Dosage Forms* section refer to categories of use and/or indications that are not included in U.S. product labeling.

FUROSEMIDE ORAL SOLUTION

Usual adult dose
Diuretic—
Oral, initially 20 to 80 mg as a single dose, the dosage then being increased by an additional 20 to 40 mg at six- to eight-hour intervals, until the desired response is obtained. The maintenance dose as determined by titration is then given daily as a single dose or divided into two or three doses, given once a day every other day, or given once a day for two to four consecutive days out of each week.

Antihypertensive—

Oral, initially 40 mg two times a day, the dosage then being adjusted according to patient response.

[Antihypercalcemic][1]—

Oral, 120 mg a day as a single dose or divided into two or three doses.

Note: Geriatric patients may be more sensitive to the effects of the usual adult dose.

Usual adult prescribing limits
600 mg a day.

Note: In chronic renal failure, doses of up to 4 grams a day have been used.

Usual pediatric dose
Diuretic—

Oral, initially 2 mg per kg of body weight as a single dose, the dosage then being increased by an additional 1 to 2 mg per kg of body weight at six- to eight-hour intervals, until the desired response is obtained.

Note: Doses as large as 5 mg per kg of body weight may be required in some children with nephrotic syndrome.

Doses greater than 6 mg per kg of body weight are not recommended.

Dosing interval should be extended in neonates because of prolonged half-life.

Strength(s) usually available
U.S.—

8 mg per mL (Rx) [GENERIC].

10 mg per mL (Rx) [*Lasix* (alcohol 11.5%); *Myrosemide* (alcohol 11.5%); GENERIC].

Canada—

10 mg per mL (Rx) [*Lasix* (sugar-free)].

Packaging and storage
Store below 40 °C (104 °F), preferably between 15 and 30 °C (59 and 86 °F), in a well-closed container, unless otherwise specified by manufacturer. Protect from light. Protect from freezing.

Auxiliary labeling
- Take by mouth only (when dispensed with graduated dropper).
- Do not take other medicines without your doctor's advice.

Note
Do not dispense discolored solution.

When dispensing, include the manufacturer-provided graduated dropper or measuring spoon.

Explain administration technique when dispensed with graduated dropper.

Check refill frequency to determine compliance in hypertensive patients.

FUROSEMIDE TABLETS USP

Usual adult dose
See *Furosemide Oral Solution.*

Usual adult prescribing limits
600 mg a day.

Note: In chronic renal failure, doses of up to 4 grams a day have been used.

Usual pediatric dose
See *Furosemide Oral Solution.*

Strength(s) usually available
U.S.—

20 mg (Rx) [*Lasix;* GENERIC (may be scored)].

40 mg (Rx) [*Lasix* (scored); GENERIC (may be scored)].

80 mg (Rx) [*Lasix;* GENERIC (may be scored)].

Canada—

20 mg (Rx) [*Apo-Furosemide; Furoside* (scored); *Lasix; Novosemide* (scored); *Uritol* (scored)].

40 mg (Rx) [*Apo-Furosemide* (scored); *Furoside* (scored); *Lasix* (scored); *Novosemide* (scored); *Uritol* (scored)].

80 mg (Rx) [*Apo-Furosemide* (scored); *Novosemide* (scored); *Lasix* (scored)].

500 mg (Rx) [*Lasix Special* (scored)].

Packaging and storage
Store below 40 °C (104 °F), preferably between 15 and 30 °C (59 and 86 °F), unless otherwise specified by manufacturer. Store in a well-closed container. Protect from light.

Stability
Exposure to light may cause discoloration. Do not dispense discolored tablets.

Auxiliary labeling
- Do not take other medicines without your doctor's advice.

Note
Since variations in bioavailability have been found among brands, try to avoid switching brands when dispensing refills.

Check refill frequency to determine compliance in hypertensive patients.

Parenteral Dosage Forms

Note: Bracketed uses in the *Dosage Forms* section refer to categories of use and/or indications that are not included in U.S. product labeling.

FUROSEMIDE INJECTION USP

Usual adult dose
Diuretic—

Intramuscular or intravenous, initially 20 to 40 mg as a single dose, the dosage then being increased by an additional 20 mg at two-hour intervals until the desired response is obtained. The maintenance dose as determined by titration is then given one or two times a day.

Note: In acute pulmonary edema (not accompanied by hypertensive crisis), the usual initial dose is 40 mg intravenously, followed by 80 mg in one hour if a satisfactory response is not obtained.

Antihypertensive—

Hypertensive crisis in patients with normal renal function: Intravenous, 40 to 80 mg.

Hypertensive crisis accompanied by pulmonary edema or acute renal failure: Intravenous, 100 to 200 mg.

[Antihypercalcemic][1]—

Intramuscular or intravenous, 80 to 100 mg in severe cases, the dosage being repeated if necessary every one to two hours until the desired response is obtained. In less severe cases, smaller doses may be given every two to four hours.

[Diagnostic aid adjunct (renal disease)]—

Intravenous, 0.3 to 0.5 mg per kg of body weight to a maximum of 40 mg.

Note: Geriatric patients may be more sensitive to the effects of the usual adult dose.

Usual adult prescribing limits
Although controversial, doses of up to 6 grams a day administered by slow intravenous infusion have been used in acute renal failure by some clinicians.

Usual pediatric dose
Diuretic—

Intramuscular or intravenous, initially 1 mg per kg of body weight as a single dose, the dosage then being increased by an additional 1 mg per kg of body weight at two-hour intervals until the desired response is obtained.

[Antihypercalcemic][1]—

Intramuscular or intravenous, 25 to 50 mg, the dosage being repeated if necessary every four hours until the desired response is obtained.

Note: Doses greater than 6 mg per kg of body weight are not recommended.

Dosing interval should be extended in neonates because of prolonged half-life.

Strength(s) usually available
U.S.—

10 mg per mL (Rx) [*Lasix;* GENERIC].

Canada—

10 mg per mL (Rx) [*Lasix* (benzyl alcohol); *Lasix Special; Uritol;* GENERIC].

Packaging and storage

Store below 40 °C (104 °F), preferably between 15 and 30 °C (59 and 86 °F), unless otherwise specified by manufacturer. Protect from light. Protect from freezing.

Preparation of dosage form

Infusion solutions can be prepared using 0.9% sodium chloride injection, lactated Ringer's injection, or 5% dextrose injection, after pH has been adjusted when necessary.

Stability

Infusion solutions should be freshly prepared and used within a 24-hour period.

Incompatibilities

Furosemide Injection USP is a mildly buffered alkaline solution and should not be mixed with highly acidic solutions.

[1]Not included in Canadian product labeling.

Selected Bibliography

The fifth report of the Joint National Committee on Detection, Evaluation, and Treatment of High Blood Pressure (JNC V). Arch Intern Med 1993; 153(2): 154-83.

Revised: 08/08/2000

Table 1. Side/Adverse Effects*

Note: Nephrocalcinosis or nephrolithiasis may occur with furosemide administration if hypercalciuria is present.

Ethacrynic acid appears to be more likely to cause ototoxicity than bumetanide or furosemide and less likely to cause hyperglycemia than furosemide.

The following side/adverse effects have been selected on the basis of their potential clinical significance (possible signs and symptoms in parentheses where appropriate)—not necessarily inclusive:

Legend
I=Bumetanide
II=Ethacrynic acid
III =Furosemide

	I	II	III
Those indicating need for medical attention			
Allergic reaction (skin rash)	R	R	R
Blood in urine—associated with parenteral use	U	R	U
Electrolyte imbalance such as hyponatremia, hypochloremic alkalosis, and hypokalemia—occurs frequently, up to 10 to 15% of patients receiving ethacrynic acid (usually not symptomatic; symptoms include dry mouth, increased thirst, irregular heartbeat, mood or mental changes, muscle cramps or pain, nausea or vomiting, unusual tiredness or weakness, weak pulse)	L	L	L
Gastrointestinal bleeding (black, tarry stools)—associated with parenteral use	U	R	U
Gout (joint pain, lower back or side pain)	R	R	R
Hepatic dysfunction (yellow eyes or skin)	R	R	R
Leukopenia or agranulocytosis (fever or chills, cough or hoarseness, lower back or side pain, painful or difficult urination)	R	R	R
Ototoxicity—more frequent with renal function impairment and in rapid parenteral administration of large doses (ringing or buzzing in ears or any loss of hearing; usually transient, but permanent deafness has occurred, especially in patients receiving other ototoxic drugs)	R	L†	R
Pancreatitis (severe stomach pain with nausea and vomiting)	R	R	R
Thrombocytopenia (unusual bleeding or bruising; black, tarry stools; blood in urine or stools; pinpoint red spots on skin)	R	R	R
Xanthopsia (yellow vision)	U	U	[illegible]
Those indicating need for medical attention only if they continue or are bothersome			
Blurred vision	L	L	[illegible]
Chest pain	L	U	[illegible]
Confusion	U	L	[illegible]
Diarrhea	L	M†	[illegible]
Headache	L	L	[illegible]
Increased sensitivity of skin to sunlight	U	[illegible]	[illegible]
Local irritation (redness or pain at site of injection)	R	[illegible]	[illegible]
Loss of appetite	L	[illegible]	[illegible]
Nervousness	U	[illegible]	[illegible]
Orthostatic hypotension as a result of massive diuresis (dizziness or lightheadedness when getting up from a lying or sitting position)	M	[illegible]	[illegible]
Premature ejaculation ordifficulty in keeping an erection	[illegible]	[illegible]	[illegible]
Stomach cramps or pain	[illegible]	[illegible]	[illegible]

*Differences in frequency of occurrence may reflect either lack of clinical-use data or actual pharmacologic distinctions among ag[illegible] basic pharmacologic similarity suggests that side effects occurring with one may occur with the others). M = more frequent; L = les[illegible] U = unknown.

†Dose-related.

DIURETICS, POTASSIUM-SPARING Systemic

This monograph includes information on the following: 1) Amiloride; 2) Spironolactone; 3) Triamterene.

VA CLASSIFICATION (Primary/Secondary):

Amiloride—CV704/CV409; TN900
Spironolactone—CV704/CV409; TN900; HS900
Triamterene—CV704/CV409; TN900

Commonly used brand name(s): *Aldactone*[2]; *Dyrenium*[3]; *Midamor*[1]; *Novospiroton*[2].

Note: For a listing of dosage forms and brand names by country availability, see *Dosage Forms* section(s).

Category

Diuretic—Amiloride; Spironolactone; Triamterene.
Antihypertensive—Amiloride; Spironolactone; Triamterene.
Aldosterone antagonist—Spironolactone.
Diagnostic aid (primary hyperaldosteronism)—Spironolactone.
Antihypokalemic—Amiloride; Spironolactone; Triamterene

Indications

Note: Bracketed information in the *Indications* section refers to uses that are not included in U.S. product labeling.

Accepted

Edema (treatment)—Amiloride, spironolactone, and triamterene are indicated as adjuncts in the management of edematous states, especially when a potassium-sparing diuretic effect is desired. These may include congestive heart failure, hepatic cirrhosis, and nephrotic syndrome, which often involve secondary hyperaldosteronism, as well as idiopathic edema.

Hypertension (treatment adjunct)—Amiloride, spironolactone, and [triamterene][1] are indicated as adjuncts in the treatment of hypertension (for spironolactone, with or without accompanying hyperaldosteronism), especially when a potassium-sparing diuretic effect is desired.

For additional information on initial therapeutic guidelines related to the treatment of hypertension, see *Appendix III*.

Hyperaldosteronism, primary (diagnosis and treatment)—Spironolactone is indicated for diagnosis and short- or long-term management of primary hyperaldosteronism.

Hypokalemia (prophylaxis and treatment)—[Amiloride][1], spironolactone, and [triamterene][1] are indicated for prevention and treatment of hypokalemia in patients for whom other measures are inappropriate or inadequate.

[Congestive heart failure (treatment adjunct)][1]—Spironolactone may be used as adjunctive treatment for severe congestive heart failure to reduce morbidity and the risk of death.

[Polycystic ovary syndrome (treatment)][1]—Spironolactone is also used with some success in the treatment of polycystic ovary syndrome.

[Hirsutism, female (treatment)][1]—Spironolactone has been used in the treatment of female hirsutism.

[1]Not included in Canadian product labeling.

harmacology/Pharmacokinetics

ysicochemical characteristics

lecular weight—
Amiloride hydrochloride: 302.12.
Spironolactone: 416.57.
Triamterene: 253.27.

—
miloride: 8.7.
riamterene: 6.2.

anism of action/Effect

c or Antihypokalemic—Potassium-sparing diuretics interfere with dium reabsorption in the distal convoluted tubule, thereby promoting retion of sodium and water and retention of potassium. Amiloride triamterene have a direct inhibiting effect on the entry of sodium the cells, while spironolactone competitively inhibits the action of sterone.

rtensive—Diuretics lower blood pressure initially by reducing a and extracellular fluid volume; cardiac output also decreases. ually, the extracellular fluid volume and the cardiac output return mal with an accompanying decrease in peripheral resistance.

Aldosterone antagonist or Diagnostic aid (primary hyperaldosteronism)—Spironolactone is a competitive inhibitor of aldosterone; neither amiloride nor triamterene has this effect.

Hirsutism or Polycystic ovary syndrome—May be due to an antiandrogenic effect of spironolactone.

Absorption

Amiloride—Incompletely (15 to 20%) absorbed from gastrointestinal tract; rate, but not necessarily extent, of absorption is increased after 4 hours of fasting.

Spironolactone—Well absorbed following oral administration; bioavailability is greater than 90%. Absorption is enhanced by concomitant intake of food.

Triamterene—Rapidly but incompletely (30 to 70%) absorbed from the gastrointestinal tract.

Protein binding

Amiloride—Minimal.
Spironolactone and canrenone—Very high (more than 90%).
Triamterene—Moderate (67%).

Biotransformation

Amiloride—Not metabolized.
Spironolactone—Hepatic; approximately 25 to 30% converted to canrenone.
Triamterene—Hepatic.

Half-life

Amiloride—
6 to 9 hours.

Spironolactone—
Canrenone: 13 to 24 hours (average 19 hours) when administered once or twice daily; 9 to 16 hours (average 12.5 hours) when administered 4 times daily.

Triamterene—
Normal, 90 to 120 minutes; anuric, 10 hours. Some active metabolites have a normal half-life of up to 12 hours.
Terminal half-life: 5 to 7 hours.

Onset of action

Diuretic—
Amiloride: Single dose—Within 2 hours.
Triamterene: Single dose—2 to 4 hours.

Time to peak concentration

Amiloride—3 to 4 hours.
Triamterene—2 to 4 hours.

Time to peak effect

Diuretic—
Amiloride: Single dose—6 to 10 hours.
Spironolactone: Multiple doses—2 to 3 days.
Triamterene: Multiple doses—1 day to several days.

Duration of action

Diuretic—
Amiloride: Single dose—24 hours.
Spironolactone: Multiple doses—2 to 3 days.
Triamterene: Single dose—7 to 9 hours.

Elimination

Amiloride—Renal, 20 to 50% (unchanged); fecal, 40% (unchanged).
Spironolactone—Metabolites: Primary route, renal (less than 10% unchanged); secondary route, biliary/fecal.
Triamterene—Primary route, biliary/fecal; secondary route, renal.

Precautions to Consider

Carcinogenicity/Tumorigenicity

Amiloride—
One study in mice at doses up to 25 times the maximum daily human dose and another in male and female rats at doses up to 15 and 20 times the maximum daily human dose for 104 weeks showed no evidence of carcinogenicity or tumorigenicity.

Spironolactone—
Breast carcinoma has been reported in men and women taking this medication, but a direct causal relationship has not yet been established.

Spironolactone has been found to be tumorigenic in rats, mainly in endocrine organs and the liver.A statistically significant dose-related increase in benign adenomas of the thyroid and testes was found in male rats given spironolactone in doses up to 250 times the usual daily human dose of 2 mg per kg of body weight (mg/kg). In addition, a dose-related increase in proliferative liver changes was revealed in male rats. Hepatocytomegaly, hyperplastic nodules, and hepatocellular carcinoma were evident at the highest dosage level of 500 mg/kg. In female rats, a statistically significant increase in malignant mammary tumors was seen at the mid-dose level. There was also a statistically significant, but not dose-related, increase in benign uterine endometrial stromal polyps in female rats.

Triamterene—

Studies evaluating the carcinogenic potential of triamterene have not been done.

Mutagenicity

Amiloride—In Ames tests, no evidence of mutagenicity was found.

Pregnancy/Reproduction

Fertility—*Amiloride:* Studies in rats given amiloride at 20 times the expected maximum human daily dose revealed no evidence of fertility impairment. However, some toxicity in adult rats and rabbits and a decrease in rat pup growth and survival were seen at doses of 5 or more times the expected maximum daily human dose.

Pregnancy—Pregnant women should be advised to contact physician before taking these medications, since routine use of diuretics during normal pregnancy is inappropriate and exposes mother and fetus to unnecessary hazard. Diuretics do not prevent development of toxemia of pregnancy, and there is no satisfactory evidence that they are useful in the treatment of toxemia. Diuretics are indicated only in the treatment of edema due to pathologic causes or as a short course of treatment in patients with severe hypervolemia.

Amiloride—

Adequate and well-controlled studies in humans have not been done.

Amiloride crosses the placenta in modest amounts in rabbits and mice. However, teratogenicity studies in rabbits and mice given 20 and 25 times the maximum human dose, respectively, revealed no evidence of fetal harm.

FDA Pregnancy Category B.

Spironolactone—

Spironolactone may cross the placenta. However, problems in humans have not been documented.

Triamterene—

Adequate and well-controlled studies in humans have not been done.

Triamterene crosses the placenta and appears in the cord blood of ewes. Studies in rats given triamterene in doses up to 30 times the human dose have revealed no evidence of harm to the fetus.

FDA Pregnancy Category B.

Breast-feeding

Amiloride—It is not known whether amiloride is distributed into human breast milk. However, problems in humans have not been documented. Amiloride has been shown to be distributed into rat's milk.

Spironolactone—Problems in humans have not been documented. However, canrenone (an active metabolite of spironolactone) is distributed into breast milk.

Triamterene—It is not known whether triamterene is distributed into human breast milk. However, problems in humans have not been documented. Triamterene has been shown to be distributed into animal milk.

Pediatrics

Studies performed to date have not demonstrated pediatrics-specific problems that would limit the usefulness of potassium-sparing diuretics in children.

Geriatrics

Although appropriate studies on the relationship of age to the effects of potassium-sparing diuretics have not been performed in the geriatric population, the elderly may be at increased risk of developing hyperkalemia. In addition, elderly patients are more likely to have age-related renal function impairment, which may require caution in patients receiving potassium-sparing diuretics.

Drug interactions and/or related problems

The following drug interactions and/or related problems have been selected on the basis of their potential clinical significance (possible mechanism in parentheses where appropriate)—not necessarily inclusive (» = major clinical significance):

Note: Combinations containing any of the following medications, depending on the amount present, may also interact with this medication.

For all potassium-sparing diuretics

Allopurinol or
Colchicine or
Probenecid or
Sulfinpyrazone
(triamterene may raise the concentration of blood uric acid, but to a lesser extent than thiazide diuretics or ethacrynic acid or furosemide; dosage adjustment of antigout medications may be necessary to control hyperuricemia and gout)

» Anticoagulants, coumarin- or indandione-derivative or
» Heparin
(anticoagulant effects may be decreased when these medications are used concurrently with potassium-sparing diuretics, as a result of reduction of plasma volume leading to concentration of procoagulant factors in the blood; in addition, diuretic-induced improvement of hepatic congestion may lead to improved hepatic function, resulting in increased procoagulant factor synthesis; dosage adjustments may be necessary)

Anti-inflammatory drugs, nonsteroidal (NSAIDs), especially indomethacin
(may reduce the antihypertensive effects of the potassium-sparing diuretics; indomethacin may also reduce the natriuretic and diuretic effects of potassium-sparing diuretics, possibly because of renal prostaglandin synthesis inhibition and/or sodium and fluid retention; the patient should be carefully monitored to confirm that the desired effect is being obtained)
(concurrent use of NSAIDs with a diuretic may increase the risk of renal failure secondary to a decrease in renal blood flow caused by inhibition of renal prostaglandin synthesis)

» Angiotensin-converting enzyme (ACE) inhibitors or
Anti-inflammatory drugs, nonsteroidal (NSAIDs), especially indomethacin or
» Blood from blood bank (may contain up to 30 mEq [mmol] of potassium per liter of plasma or up to 65 mEq [mmol] per liter of whole blood when stored for more than 10 days) or
» Cyclosporine or
» Diuretics, potassium-sparing, other or
Heparin or
» Low-salt milk (may contain up to 60 mEq [mmol] of potassium per liter) or
» Potassium-containing medications or
» Potassium supplements or substances containing high levels of potassium or
Salt substitutes (most contain substantial amounts of potassium)
(concurrent administration with potassium-sparing diuretics tends to promote serum potassium accumulation; hyperkalemia may result, especially in patients with renal insufficiency)

Exchange resins, sodium cycle (such as sodium polystyrene sulfonate)
(whether administered orally or rectally, these medications reduce serum potassium levels by replacing potassium with sodium; fluid retention may occur in some patients because of the increased sodium intake)

Hypotension-producing medications, other (See *Appendix II*)
(antihypertensive and/or diuretic effects may be potentiated when these medications are used concurrently with potassium-sparing diuretics; although some antihypertensive and/or diuretic combinations are frequently used for therapeutic advantage, dosage adjustments may be necessary during concurrent use)

» Lithium
(concurrent use with potassium-sparing diuretics is not recommended, as they may provoke lithium toxicity by reducing renal clearance)

Sympathomimetics
(may reduce the antihypertensive effects of potassium-sparing diuretics; the patient should be carefully monitored to confirm that the desired effect is being obtained)

For spironolactone only (in addition to those listed for all potassium-sparing diuretics)

» Digoxin
(spironolactone may increase the half-life of digoxin; dosage reduction or increased dosing intervals of digoxin may be necessary and careful monitoring is recommended)

For triamterene only (in addition to those listed for all potassium-sparing diuretics)

Amantadine
(triamterene may reduce the renal clearance of amantadine, resulting in increased plasma concentrations and possible amantadine toxicity)

Folic acid
(triamterene may act as a folate antagonist by inhibiting dihydrofolate reductase; most significant with high doses and/or prolonged triamterene use; leucovorin calcium must be used instead of folic acid in patients receiving triamterene)

Laboratory value alterations

The following have been selected on the basis of their potential clinical significance (possible effect in parentheses where appropriate)—not necessarily inclusive (» = major clinical significance).

With diagnostic test results

For spironolactone only
Digoxin radioimmunoassays
(results may be falsely elevated)
Plasma cortisol concentration determination by Mattingly (fluorometric) assay
(concentration may be falsely increased; withdrawal of spironolactone 4 to 7 days prior to determinations, or substitution of Ertel, Peterson, or Norymberski method, is recommended)

For triamterene only
Fluorescent measurement of quinidine
(similar fluorescence spectra)

With physiology/laboratory test values
For amiloride, spironolactone, and triamterene
Blood urea nitrogen (BUN) concentrations (especially in patients with pre-existing renal impairment) and
Calcium excretion, urinary and
Creatinine concentrations, serum and
Magnesium concentrations, serum and
Plasma renin activity (PRA) and
Potassium concentrations, serum and
Uric acid concentrations, serum
(may be increased)
Sodium
(serum concentrations may be decreased)

Medical considerations/Contraindications

The medical considerations/contraindications included have been selected on the basis of their potential clinical significance (reasons given in parentheses where appropriate)—not necessarily inclusive (» = major clinical significance).

Except under special circumstances, this medication should not be used when the following medical problem exists:
» Hyperkalemia
(potassium-sparing diuretics may further increase serum potassium concentrations)

Risk-benefit should be considered when the following medical problems exist:
For amiloride, spironolactone, and triamterene
» Anuria or
» Renal function impairment
(potassium-sparing diuretics may aggravate electrolyte imbalance; risk of developing hyperkalemia is increased)
Diabetes mellitus, especially in patients with confirmed or suspected renal insufficiency or
» Diabetic nephropathy
(increased risk of hyperkalemia; potassium-sparing diuretic should be discontinued at least 3 days prior to a glucose tolerance test because of the risk of severe hyperkalemia)
» Hepatic function impairment
(increased sensitivity to electrolyte changes)
Hyponatremia
Metabolic or respiratory acidosis, predisposition to
(acidosis potentiates hyperkalemic effects of potassium-sparing diuretics; potassium-sparing diuretics may potentiate acidosis)
Sensitivity to the potassium-sparing diuretic prescribed
» Caution is also required in severely ill patients and those with relatively small urine volumes, who are at greater risk of developing hyperkalemia.

For spironolactone only (in addition to those listed above for all potassium-sparing diuretics)
Menstrual abnormalities or breast enlargement

For triamterene only (in addition to those listed above for all potassium-sparing diuretics)
Hyperuricemia or gout
Nephrolithiasis, history of
(increased risk of forming triamterene stones)

Patient monitoring

The following may be especially important in patient monitoring (other tests may be warranted in some patients, depending on condition; » = major clinical significance):

For amiloride, spironolactone, and triamterene
» Blood pressure measurements
(recommended at periodic intervals in patients being treated for hypertension; selected patients may be trained to perform blood pressure measurements at home and report the results at regular physician visits)
Blood urea nitrogen (BUN) determinations and/or
Creatinine concentrations, serum
(determinations recommended prior to initiation of therapy and at periodic intervals during therapy)
Electrocardiograms (ECG) and
» Electrolyte concentrations, serum, especially serum potassium determinations
(may be required at periodic intervals for patients on long-term therapy, especially if they are also taking systemic steroids, or when congestive heart failure or severe cirrhosis is present)

For triamterene only
Platelet count and
Total and differential leukocyte count
(recommended prior to initiation of therapy and at periodic intervals during therapy, especially in patients with impaired hepatic function)

Side/Adverse Effects

See *Table 1*, page 1125.

Overdose

For more information on the management of overdose or unintentional ingestion, **contact a Poison Control Center** (see *Poison Control Center Listing*).

Treatment of overdose

Overdose should be treated by immediate evacuation of the stomach followed by supportive, symptomatic treatment and monitoring of serum electrolyte concentrations and renal function.

Patient Consultation

As an aid to patient consultation, refer to *Advice for the Patient, Diuretics, Potassium-sparing (Systemic).*

In providing consultation, consider emphasizing the following selected information (» = major clinical significance):

Before using this medication

» Conditions affecting use, especially:
Sensitivity to the potassium-sparing diuretic prescribed
Pregnancy—Not recommended for routine use; triamterene crosses placenta; spironolactone may cross placenta
Breast-feeding—All potassium-sparing diuretics may be distributed into breast milk
Use in the elderly—Increased risk of hyperkalemia
Other medications, especially angiotensin-converting enzyme (ACE) inhibitors, cyclosporine, digoxin, other potassium-sparing diuretics, potassium-containing medications or supplements, or lithium
Other medical problems, especially diabetic nephropathy, hyperkalemia, renal function impairment or hepatic function impairment

Proper use of this medication

Diuretic effects of the medication and timing of doses to minimize inconvenience of diuresis
Getting into habit of taking at same time each day to help increase compliance
Taking with meals or milk to reduce gastrointestinal irritation
» Proper dosing
Missed dose: Taking as soon as possible; not taking if almost time for next dose; not doubling doses
» Proper storage

For use as an antihypertensive (amiloride and spironolactone only)
Possible need for control of weight and diet, especially sodium intake
» Patient may not experience symptoms of hypertension; importance of taking medication even if feeling well
» Does not cure, but helps control hypertension; possible need for lifelong therapy; checking with physician before discontinuing medication; serious consequences of untreated hypertension

Precautions while using this medication

Regular visits to physician to check progress
Avoiding excessive ingestion of foods high in potassium or use of salt substitutes or other potassium supplements
To prevent dehydration, checking with physician if severe nausea, vomiting, or diarrhea occurs and continues
Caution if any kind of surgery or emergency treatment is required
Caution if any laboratory tests required; possible interference with test results

For use as an antihypertensive (amiloride and spironolactone only):
» Not taking other medications, especially nonprescription sympathomimetics, unless discussed with physician

For triamterene only:
Possible photosensitivity; avoiding unprotected exposure to sun; using protective clothing and sun block product; avoiding use of sunlamp, tanning bed, or tanning booth

Side/adverse effects

Signs of potential side effects, especially agranulocytosis, allergic reaction, anaphylaxis, and hyperkalemia (for all potassium-sparing diuretics); megaloblastosis, nephrolithiasis, and thrombocytopenia (for triamterene)

For spironolactone only (in addition to the above)

Possibility of enlargement of breasts in males; usually reversible within several months

General Dosing Information

Dosage must be adjusted to meet the individual requirements of each patient, on the basis of clinical response. The lowest effective dose should be utilized to minimize potential electrolyte imbalance.

If a single daily dose is indicated, it is preferably taken on arising in order to minimize the effect of increased frequency of urination on sleep, although the diuretic effect of potassium-sparing diuretics alone is mild.

The normal adult concentration of plasma potassium is 3.5 to 5.0 mEq (mmol) per liter, with 4.5 mEq (mmol) often being used as a reference point. Potassium concentrations exceeding 6 mEq (mmol) per liter are dangerous because of possible initiation of cardiac arrhythmias. Normal potassium concentrations tend to be higher in neonates (7.7 mEq [mmol] per liter) than in adults.

Plasma potassium concentrations do not necessarily indicate the true body potassium concentration. A rise in serum pH may cause a decrease in serum potassium concentration and an increase in the intracellular potassium concentration.

It is recommended that potassium-sparing diuretic therapy be withdrawn if hyperkalemia occurs. If hyperkalemia is associated with ECG changes, prompt additional therapy with intravenous sodium bicarbonate, calcium gluconate, or calcium chloride; with oral or rectal sodium polystyrene sulfonate; or with parenteral glucose and insulin may be indicated. It is important to remember that severe hyperkalemia may occur suddenly and may not be preceded by any warning signs.

Recent evidence suggests that withdrawal of antihypertensive therapy prior to surgery is not necessary, but that the anesthesiologist must be aware of such therapy.

Diet/Nutrition

It is recommended that oral potassium-sparing diuretics be taken with or after meals to minimize stomach upset, and possibly also to enhance bioavailability.

AMILORIDE

Summary of Differences

Pharmacology/pharmacokinetics:

Protein binding—Minimal.

Biotransformation—None; excreted unchanged.

Duration of action—Diuretic: Single dose—24 hours.

Side/adverse effects:

No reported cases of agranulocytosis. Amiloride has been reported to cause constipation and muscle cramps.

Oral Dosage Forms

AMILORIDE HYDROCHLORIDE TABLETS USP

Usual adult dose

Diuretic or

Antihypertensive—

Oral, 5 to 10 mg per day as a single dose.

Note: Geriatric patients may be more sensitive to the effects of the usual adult dose.

Usual adult prescribing limits

Up to 20 mg per day.

Usual pediatric dose

Dosage has not been established.

Strength(s) usually available

U.S.—

5 mg (Rx) [*Midamor*].

Canada—

5 mg (Rx) [*Midamor*].

Packaging and storage

Store below 40 °C (104 °F), preferably between 15 and 30 °C (59 and 86 °F), unless otherwise specified by manufacturer. Store in a well-closed container.

Auxiliary labeling

- Take with meals or milk.
- Do not take other medicines without your doctor's advice.

Note

Check refill frequency to determine compliance in hypertensive patients.

SPIRONOLACTONE

Summary of Differences

Indications:

Diagnosis and treatment of primary hyperaldosteronism. Treatment of polycystic ovary syndrome and female hirsutism.

Pharmacology/pharmacokinetics:

Mechanism of action/effect—Aldosterone antagonist.

Protein binding—Very high (more than 90%).

Biotransformation—Hepatic, extensive, to active metabolite (canrenone).

Duration of action—Diuretic: Multiple doses—2 to 3 days.

Precautions:

Carcinogenicity—Tumorigenic in rats and possibly associated with breast carcinoma in humans.

Drug interactions and/or related problems—Use with digoxin may increase digoxin half-life.

Laboratory value alterations—May falsely increase plasma cortisol determinations by Mattingly (fluorometric) assay. May falsely elevate digoxin radioimmunoassays.

Medical considerations/contraindications—Menstrual abnormalities or breast enlargement.

Side/adverse effects:

Endocrine or antiandrogenic effects more common at doses exceeding 100 mg per day. May cause CNS effects and causes more frequent gastrointestinal irritation.

Additional Dosing Information

See also *General Dosing Information*.

To reduce delay in onset of effect, a loading dose of 2 to 3 times the daily dose may be administered on the first day of therapy.

When spironolactone is added to therapy with another diuretic or antihypertensive agent, it is recommended that the dosage of the other drug (especially ganglionic blocking agents) be reduced by at least 50% and then adjusted as required.

It is recommended that spironolactone be discontinued several days prior to adrenal vein catheterization for measurement of aldosterone concentrations, for the purpose of attempting lateralization in primary hyperaldosteronism, and for measurements of plasma renin activity.

When high doses of spironolactone are required for treatment of edema due to hepatic cirrhosis, drug dosage may be reduced prior to completion of diuresis to avoid dehydration and precipitation of hepatic coma, although dry weight may be achieved.

Oral Dosage Forms

Note: Bracketed uses in the *Dosage Forms* section refer to categories of use and/or indications that are not included in U.S. product labeling.

SPIRONOLACTONE TABLETS USP

Usual adult dose

Edema due to congestive heart failure, hepatic cirrhosis, or nephrotic syndrome—

Initial: Oral, 25 to 200 mg a day in two to four divided doses for at least five days, when used as monotherapy for diuresis.

Maintenance: Oral, adjusted to meet individual requirements.

Antihypertensive—

Initial: Oral, 50 to 100 mg a day as a single daily dose or in two to four divided doses for at least two weeks, followed by gradual dosage adjustment every two weeks as necessary up to 200 mg a day.

Maintenance: Oral, adjusted to meet individual requirements.

Primary hyperaldosteronism—

Maintenance: Oral, 100 to 400 mg per day in two to four divided daily doses prior to surgery; smaller doses may be used for long-term maintenance in patients unsuitable for surgery.

[Congestive heart failure treatment adjunct][1]—

Oral, 25 mg to 50 mg once daily.

[Polycystic ovary disease]—

Oral, 100 to 200 mg per day in two divided daily doses.

[Hirsutism, female]—

Oral, 100 mg two times a day.

Diagnostic aid (primary hyperaldosteronism)—
Long test: Oral, 400 mg per day in two to four divided daily doses for three to four weeks.
Short test: Oral, 400 mg per day in two to four divided daily doses for four days.
Antihypokalemic—
Diuretic-induced hypokalemia: Oral, 25 to 100 mg per day as a single daily dose or in two to four divided doses.

Note: Geriatric patients may be more sensitive to the effects of the usual adult dose.

Usual adult prescribing limits
Dose may be increased up to three times the initial dose or up to a maximum of 400 mg a day.

Usual pediatric dose
Edema
Ascites or
Hypertension—
Initial: Oral, 1 to 3 mg per kg of body weight or 30 to 90 mg per square meter of body surface a day as a single daily dose or in two to four divided doses, the dosage being readjusted after five days. Dosage may be increased up to three times the initial dose.

Strength(s) usually available
U.S.—
25 mg (Rx) [*Aldactone;* GENERIC (may be scored)].
50 mg (Rx) [*Aldactone* (scored)].
100 mg (Rx) [*Aldactone* (scored)].
Canada—
25 mg (Rx) [*Aldactone* (scored); *Novospiroton* (scored)].
100 mg (Rx) [*Aldactone* (scored); *Novospiroton* (scored)].

Packaging and storage
Store below 40 °C (104 °F), preferably between 15 and 30 °C (59 and 86 °F), unless otherwise specified by manufacturer. Store in a tight, light-resistant container.

Preparation of dosage form
For patients who cannot take oral solids—For small children or patients unable to swallow the tablets, Spironolactone Tablets USP may be crushed and dispensed as a suspension in Cherry Syrup NF. This suspension is stable in a refrigerator for 1 month.

Auxiliary labeling
- Take with meals or milk.
- Do not take other medicines without your doctor's advice.

Note
Check refill frequency to determine compliance in hypertensive patients.

[1]Not included in Canadian product labeling.

TRIAMTERENE

Summary of Differences

Pharmacology/pharmacokinetics:
Biotransformation—Hepatic.
Duration of action—Diuretic: Single dose—7 to 9 hours.
Precautions:
Drug interactions and/or related problems—Triamterene may increase blood uric acid and antagonize allopurinol, colchicine, probenecid, or sulfinpyrazone.
Laboratory value alterations—May interfere with fluorescent measurement of quinidine.
Medical considerations/contraindications—Hyperuricemia or gout; history of nephrolithiasis.
Side/adverse effects:
Nephrolithiasis; megaloblastosis; photosensitivity; thrombocytopenia. No decrease in sexual ability reported.

Additional Dosing Information

See also *General Dosing Information.*

Since triamterene is a weak folic acid antagonist, it may contribute to development of megaloblastosis in patients who have depleted folic acid stores (e.g., in pregnancy, hepatic cirrhosis).

When triamterene is combined with another diuretic, it is recommended that the initial dosage of each be reduced and then adjusted as required.

Oral Dosage Forms

TRIAMTERENE CAPSULES USP

Usual adult dose
Diuretic—
Initial: Oral, 100 mg twice daily when used alone as monotherapy.
Maintenance: Oral, adjusted to meet individual requirements.

Note: Geriatric patients may be more sensitive to the effects of the usual adult dose.

Usual adult prescribing limits
Up to 300 mg daily.

Usual pediatric dose
Diuretic—
Initial: Oral, 2 to 4 mg per kg of body weight or 120 mg per square meter of body surface a day or on alternate days in divided doses.
Maintenance: Oral, increased to 6 mg per kg of body weight a day according to individual requirements up to a maximum of 300 mg a day in divided doses.

Strength(s) usually available
U.S.—
50 mg (Rx) [*Dyrenium* (lactose)].
100 mg (Rx) [*Dyrenium* (lactose)].
Canada—
Not commercially available.

Packaging and storage
Store below 40 °C (104 °F), preferably between 15 and 30 °C (59 and 86 °F), unless otherwise specified by manufacturer. Store in a tight, light-resistant container.

Auxiliary labeling
- Take with meals or milk.
- Avoid overexposure to sun or use of sunlamp.
- Do not take other medicines without your doctor's advice.

TRIAMTERENE TABLETS

Usual adult dose
Diuretic—
Initial: Oral, 25 to 100 mg a day.
Maintenance: Oral, adjusted to meet individual requirements.

Note: Geriatric patients may be more sensitive to the effects of the usual adult dose.

Usual adult prescribing limits
Up to 300 mg daily.

Usual pediatric dose
Diuretic—
Initial: Oral, 2 to 4 mg per kg of body weight or 120 mg per square meter of body surface a day or on alternate days in divided doses.
Maintenance: Oral, increased to 6 mg per kg of body weight a day according to individual requirements up to a maximum of 300 mg a day in divided doses.

Strength(s) usually available
U.S.—
Not commercially available.
Canada—
50 mg (Rx) [*Dyrenium*].
100 mg (Rx) [*Dyrenium* (scored)].

Packaging and storage
Store below 40 °C (104 °F), preferably between 15 and 30 °C (59 and 86 °F), unless otherwise specified by manufacturer. Store in a tight, light-resistant container.

Auxiliary labeling
- Take with meals or milk.
- Avoid overexposure to sun or use of sunlamp.
- Do not take other medicines without your doctor's advice.

Selected Bibliography

The fifth report of the Joint National Committee on Detection, Evaluation, and Treatment of High Blood Pressure (JNC V). Arch Intern Med 1993; 153(2): 154-83.

Revised: 04/26/2000

Table 1. Side/Adverse Effects*

The following side/adverse effects have been selected on the basis of their potential clinical significance (possible signs and symptoms in parentheses where appropriate)—not necessarily inclusive:

Legend:
I = Amiloride
II = Spironolactone
III = Triamterene

Side/Adverse effect	I	II	III
Those indicating need for medical attention			
Agranulocytosis (fever or chills, cough or hoarseness, lower back or side pain, painful or difficult urination)	U	R	R
Allergic reaction or anaphylaxis (shortness of breath, skin rash or itching)	R	R	R
Hyperkalemia (confusion; irregular heartbeat; nervousness; numbness or tingling in hands, feet, or lips; shortness of breath or difficult breathing; unusual tiredness or weakness; weakness or heaviness of legs) Note: *Irregular heartbeat* is usually the earliest clinical indication of hyperkalemia and is readily detected by electrocardiogram (ECG).	M†	M†	M†
Megaloblastosis or overdose (burning, inflamed, or bright red tongue or cracked corners of mouth; weakness)	U	U	R
Nephrolithiasis (severe lower back or side pain)	U	U	R
Thrombocytopenia (unusual bleeding or bruising; black, tarry stools; blood in urine or stools; pinpoint red spots on skin)	U	U	R
Those indicating need for medical attention only if they continue or are bothersome			
Antiandrogenic or endocrine effect (breast tenderness in females, deepening of voice in females, enlargement of breasts in males, inability to have or keep an erection, increased hair growth in females, irregular menstrual periods, sweating) Note: *Gynecomastia* occurs frequently after several months of treatment at doses of spironolactone greater than 100 mg per day and rarely may persist even after spironolactone is discontinued.	U	L‡	U
Central nervous system (CNS) effect (clumsiness)	U	L‡	U
CNS effect (headache)	L	L‡	L
Constipation	L	U	U
Decreased sexual ability	L	L	U
Dizziness	L	L	L
Gastrointestinal irritation (nausea or vomiting, stomach cramps and diarrhea)	L	M	L
Hyponatremia (drowsiness, dryness of mouth, increased thirst, lack of energy)	L	L	L
Increased sensitivity of skin to sunlight	U	U	L
Muscle cramps	L	U	U

*Differences in frequency of occurrence may reflect either lack of clinical-use data or actual pharmacologic distinctions among agents. M = more frequent; L = less frequent; R = rare; U = unknown.

†Signs and symptoms of hyperkalemia may occur even when potassium-sparing diuretics are combined with thiazide diuretics. Hyperkalemia occurs in approximately 10% of patients when amiloride is used alone and may occur in up to 26% of patients receiving spironolactone even when combined with thiazide diuretics.

‡Incidence related to dose and/or duration of therapy.

DIURETICS, POTASSIUM-SPARING, AND HYDROCHLOROTHIAZIDE Systemic

This monograph includes information on the following: 1) Amiloride and Hydrochlorothiazide; 2) Spironolactone and Hydrochlorothiazide; 3) Triamterene and Hydrochlorothiazide.

VA CLASSIFICATION (Primary/Secondary): CV704/CV408; TN900

Commonly used brand name(s): *Aldactazide*[2]; *Apo-Triazide*[3]; *Dyazide*[3]; *Maxzide*[3]; *Moduret*[1]; *Moduretic*[1]; *Novo-Spirozine*[2]; *Novo-Triamzide*[3]; *Spirozide*[2].

Another commonly used name is Co-triamterzide [Triamterene and Hydrochlorothiazide]

NOTE: The *Diuretics, Potassium-sparing, and Hydrochlorothiazide (Systemic)* monograph is maintained on the *USP DI* electronic data base. A copy of the most recent revision of the complete monograph can be accessed on the *USP DI* Updates Online website. See the front cover of book for details on accessing the site.

For information on the specific components of this combination, see the *USP DI* monographs for *Diuretics, Potassium-sparing (Systemic)* and *Diuretics, Thiazide (Systemic)*.

The information that follows is selectively abstracted from the complete monograph and is provided to facilitate drug use review and patient counseling.

Note: For a listing of dosage forms and brand names by country availability, see *Dosage Forms* section(s).

Category

Antihypertensive; antihypokalemic; diuretic.

Indications

Accepted

Edema (treatment)—These combinations are indicated as adjuncts in the management of edematous states such as congestive heart failure, hepatic cirrhosis, and nephrotic syndrome, as well as in corticosteroid- and estrogen-induced edema and idiopathic edema.

Hypertension (treatment)—Spironolactone and hydrochlorothiazide, triamterene and hydrochlorothiazide, and amiloride and hydrochlorothiazide[1] are also indicated in the treatment of hypertension, especially when a potassium-sparing diuretic effect is desired.

Fixed-dosage combinations are generally not recommended in initial therapy and are useful in subsequent therapy only when the proportion of the component agents corresponds to the dose of the individual agents, as determined by titration.

For additional information on initial therapeutic guidelines related to the treatment of hypertension, see *Appendix III*.

Hypokalemia (treatment)[1]—Amiloride and hydrochlorothiazide, triamterene and hydrochlorothiazide, and spironolactone and hydrochlorothiazide combinations are also indicated for treatment of diuretic-induced hypokalemia in hypertensive patients in whom other measures are inappropriate or inadequate.

[1]Not included in Canadian product labeling.

Patient Consultation

As an aid to patient consultation, refer to *Advice for the Patient, Diuretics, Potassium-sparing, and Hydrochlorothiazide (Systemic)*.

In providing consultation, consider emphasizing the following selected information (» = major clinical significance):

Before using this medication

» Conditions affecting use, especially:
Sensitivity to the potassium-sparing diuretic prescribed, hydrochlorothiazide or other thiazide diuretics, other sulfonamide-type medications, bumetanide, furosemide, or carbonic anhydrase inhibitors
Pregnancy—Diuretics not recommended for routine use
Breast-feeding—Hydrochlorothiazide distributed into breast milk; spironolactone may be distributed into breast milk
Use in the elderly—Elderly patients may be more sensitive to hypotensive and electrolyte-depleting effects
Other medications, especially angiotensin-converting enzyme inhibitors, cholestyramine, colestipol, coumarin or indandione anticoagulants, cyclosporine, digitalis glycosides, heparin, lithium, low-salt milk, other potassium-sparing diuretics, potassium-containing medications or supplements, or stored blood from a blood bank
Other medical problems, especially, diabetic nephropathy, hepatic function impairment, renal function impairment or anuria

Proper use of this medication

Diuretic effects of the medication and timing of doses to minimize inconvenience of diuresis
Getting into habit of taking at same time each day to help increase compliance
Taking with meals or milk to reduce stomach upset
» Proper dosing
Missed dose: Taking as soon as possible; not taking if almost time for next dose; not doubling doses
» Proper storage

For use as an antihypertensive
Possible need for control of weight and diet, especially sodium intake
» Patient may not experience symptoms of hypertension; importance of taking medication even if feeling well
» Does not cure, but helps control hypertension; possible need for life-long therapy; checking with physician before discontinuing medication; serious consequences of untreated hypertension

Precautions while using this medication

Regular visits to physician to check progress
» Possibility of hypokalemia or hyperkalemia; possible need for monitoring potassium in diet; not changing diet without first checking with physician

To prevent dehydration, checking with physician if severe nausea, vomiting, or diarrhea occurs and continues

Diabetics: May increase blood sugar levels

Possible photosensitivity; avoiding too much sun; using protective clothing and sun block product; avoiding use of sunlamp, tanning bed, or tanning booth

Caution if any kind of surgery or emergency treatment is required

Caution if any laboratory tests required; possible interference with test results

For triamterene and hydrochlorothiazide combination:
Not changing brands of triamterene and hydrochlorothiazide combination without checking with physician

For use an an antihypertensive:
» Not taking other medications, especially nonprescription sympathomimetics, unless discussed with physician

Side/adverse effects

Signs of potential side effects, especially electrolyte imbalance, agranulocytosis, allergic reaction, cholecystitis or pancreatitis, gout or hyperuricemia, hepatic function impairment, thrombocytopenia, megaloblastosis (for triamterene)

For spironolactone
Possibility of enlargement of breasts in males and irregular menstrual periods in females; usually reversible within several months

AMILORIDE AND HYDROCHLOROTHIAZIDE

Summary of Differences

For amiloride:
Pharmacology/pharmacokinetics—
Biotransformation—None; excreted unchanged.
Onset of action—Diuretic: Single dose—Within 2 hours.
Duration of action—Diuretic: Single dose—24 hours.
Side/adverse effects—
Amiloride may cause constipation. Agranulocytosis has not been reported.

Oral Dosage Forms

AMILORIDE HYDROCHLORIDE AND HYDROCHLOROTHIAZIDE TABLETS USP

Usual adult dose

Diuretic or
Antihypertensive[1]—
Oral, 1 or 2 tablets a day.

Note: Geriatric patients may be more sensitive to the effects of the usual adult dose.

Usual pediatric dose

Dosage has not been established.

Strength(s) usually available

U.S.—
5 mg of amiloride hydrochloride and 50 mg of hydrochlorothiazide (Rx) [*Moduretic* (scored); GENERIC (may be scored)].

Canada—
5 mg of amiloride hydrochloride and 50 mg of hydrochlorothiazide (Rx) [*Moduret* (scored)].

Auxiliary labeling

- Take with meals or milk.
- Avoid overexposure to the sun or use of sunlamp.
- Do not take other medicines without your doctor's advice.

[1]Not included in Canadian product labeling.

SPIRONOLACTONE AND HYDROCHLOROTHIAZIDE

Summary of Differences

For spironolactone:
Pharmacology/pharmacokinetics—
Mechanism of action/effect—Aldosterone antagonist.
Protein-binding—Very high (more than 90%).
Biotransformation—Hepatic, extensive, to active metabolite (canrenone).
Duration of action—Diuretic: Multiple doses—2 to 3 days.
Precautions—
Carcinogenicity—Tumorigenic in rats and possibly associated with breast carcinoma in humans.
Drug interactions and/or related problems—May increase digoxin half-life.
Laboratory value alterations—May falsely increase plasma cortisol determinations by Mattingly (fluorometric) assay and may falsely elevate digoxin radioimmunoassays.
Medical considerations/contraindications—Menstrual abnormalities or breast enlargement.
Side/adverse effects—
Endocrine or antiandrogenic effects more common at doses exceeding 100 mg per day. May cause CNS effects and causes more frequent gastrointestinal irritation.

Additional Dosing Information

See also *General Dosing Information.*

When the spironolactone and hydrochlorothiazide combination is added to therapy with another diuretic or antihypertensive agent, it is recommended that the dosage of the other drug (especially ganglionic blocking agents) be reduced by at least 50% and then adjusted as required.

Oral Dosage Forms

SPIRONOLACTONE AND HYDROCHLOROTHIAZIDE TABLETS USP

Usual adult dose

Diuretic—Edema due to congestive heart failure, hepatic cirrhosis, or nephrotic syndrome:—
Maintenance—Oral, 1 to 4 tablets a day, taken as a single dose or in divided doses.

Antihypertensive—
Maintenance: Oral, 2 to 4 tablets a day in divided doses.

Note: Geriatric patients may be more sensitive to the effects of the usual adult dose.

Usual pediatric dose

Diuretic—
Maintenance: Oral, 1.65 to 3.3 mg of spironolactone and of hydrochlorothiazide per kg of body weight a day in divided doses.

Strength(s) usually available

U.S.—

25 mg of spironolactone and 25 mg of hydrochlorothiazide (Rx) [*Aldactazide; Spirozide;* GENERIC (may be scored)].

50 mg of spironolactone and 50 mg of hydrochlorothiazide (Rx) [*Aldactazide* (scored)].

Canada—

25 mg of spironolactone and 25 mg of hydrochlorothiazide (Rx) [*Aldactazide* (scored); *Novo-Spirozine* (scored)].

50 mg of spironolactone and 50 mg of hydrochlorothiazide (Rx) [*Aldactazide* (scored); *Novo-Spirozine* (scored)].

Auxiliary labeling

- Take with meals or milk.
- Avoid overexposure to the sun or use of sunlamp.
- Do not take other medicines without your doctor's advice.

TRIAMTERENE AND HYDROCHLOROTHIAZIDE

Summary of Differences

For triamterene:

Pharmacology/pharmacokinetics—

Biotransformation—Hepatic.

Onset of action—Diuretic: Single dose—Within 1 hour.

Duration of action—Diuretic: Single dose—7 to 9 hours.

Precautions—

Drug interactions and/or related problems—Use with allopurinol, colchicine, probenecid, or sulfinpyrazone may raise blood uric acid concentrations.

Laboratory value alterations—May interfere with fluorescent measurement of quinidine.

Medical considerations/contraindications—Hyperuricemia or gout; history of nephrolithiasis.

Side/adverse effects—

Nephrolithiasis; megaloblastosis. No decrease in sexual ability reported.

Additional Dosing Information

See also *General Dosing Information.*

Since triamterene is a weak folic acid antagonist, it may contribute to development of megaloblastosis in patients who have depleted folic acid stores (e.g., in pregnancy, hepatic cirrhosis).

Oral Dosage Forms

TRIAMTERENE AND HYDROCHLOROTHIAZIDE CAPSULES USP

Usual adult dose

Diuretic or

Antihypertensive—

Oral, 1 or 2 capsules once a day, as determined by individual titration with the component agents; some patients may be maintained on 1 capsule a day or every other day.

Note: Geriatric patients may be more sensitive to the effects of the usual adult dose.

Usual adult prescribing limits

Up to 4 capsules daily.

Usual pediatric dose

Dosage has not been established.

Strength(s) usually available

U.S.—

37.5 mg of triamterene and 25 mg of hydrochlorothiazide (Rx) [*Dyazide* (lactose)].

50 mg of triamterene and 25 mg of hydrochlorothiazide (Rx) [GENERIC].

75 mg of triamterene and 50 mg of hydrochlorothiazide (Rx) [GENERIC].

Canada—

Not commercially available.

Auxiliary labeling

- Take with meals or milk.
- Avoid overexposure to the sun or use of sunlamp.
- Do not take other medicines without your doctor's advice.

TRIAMTERENE AND HYDROCHLOROTHIAZIDE TABLETS USP

Usual adult dose

Antihypertensive or

Diuretic—

Maxzide—

Oral, 1 tablet per day, as determined by individual titration.

Apo-Triazide; Dyazide (Canada); *Novotriamzide*—

Oral, 1 or 2 tablets two times a day, as determined by individual titration with the component agents; some patients may be maintained on 1 tablet a day or every other day.

Note: Geriatric patients may be more sensitive to the effects of the usual adult dose.

Usual pediatric dose

Dosage has not been established.

Strength(s) usually available

U.S.—

37.5 mg of triamterene and 25 mg of hydrochlorothiazide (Rx) [*Maxzide* (scored)].

75 mg of triamterene and 50 mg of hydrochlorothiazide (Rx) [*Maxzide* (scored); GENERIC (may be scored; may contain lactose)].

Canada—

50 mg of triamterene and 25 mg of hydrochlorothiazide (Rx) [*Apo-Triazide* (scored); *Dyazide* (scored); *Novo-Triamzide* (scored)].

Auxiliary labeling

- Take with meals or milk.
- Avoid overexposure to the sun or use of sunlamp.
- Do not take other medicines without your doctor's advice.

Revised: 08/03/1994

DIURETICS, THIAZIDE Systemic

This monograph includes information on the following: 1) Bendroflumethiazide; 2) Chlorothiazide†; 3) Chlorthalidone; 4) Hydrochlorothiazide; 5) Hydroflumethiazide†; 6) Methyclothiazide; 7) Metolazone; 8) Polythiazide†; 9) Quinethazone†; 10) Trichlormethiazide†.

INN: Chlorthalidone—Chlortalidone

VA CLASSIFICATION (Primary/Secondary): CV701/CV409; GU900

Commonly used brand name(s): *Apo-Chlorthalidone*[3]; *Apo-Hydro*[4]; *Aquatensen*[6]; *Diucardin*[5]; *Diuchlor H*[4]; *Diulo*[7]; *Diuril*[2]; *Duretic*[6]; *Enduron*[6]; *Esidrix*[4]; *Hydro-D*[4]; *HydroDIURIL*[4]; *Hydro-chlor*[4]; *Hydromox*[9]; *Hygroton*[3]; *Metahydrin*[10]; *Microzide*[4]; *Mykrox*[7]; *Naqua*[10]; *Naturetin*[1]; *Neo-Codema*[4]; *Novo-Hydrazide*[4]; *Novo-Thalidone*[3]; *Oretic*[4]; *Renese*[8]; *Saluron*[5]; *Thalitone*[3]; *Trichlorex*[10]; *Uridon*[3]; *Urozide*[4]; *Zaroxolyn*[7].

Note: For a listing of dosage forms and brand names by country availability, see *Dosage Forms* section(s).

†Not commercially available in Canada.

Category

Diuretic; antihypertensive; antidiuretic (central and nephrogenic diabetes insipidus); antiurolithic (calcium calculi).

Indications

Note: Bracketed information in the *Indications* section refers to uses that are not included in U.S. product labeling.

Accepted

Edema (treatment)—Indications include edema associated with congestive heart failure, hepatic cirrhosis with ascites, corticosteroid and estrogen therapy, and some forms of renal function impairment including nephrotic syndrome, acute glomerulonephritis, and chronic renal failure. However, prompt metolazone tablets are not indicated for treatment of edema because a safe and effective diuretic dosage has not been established.

Hypertension (treatment)—Thiazide diuretics are indicated either alone or as adjunctive therapy in the treatment of hypertension.

For additional information on initial therapeutic guidelines related to the treatment of hypertension, see *Appendix III*.

[Diabetes insipidus, central or nephrogenic (treatment)][1]—Thiazide diuretics are used in the treatment of central and nephrogenic diabetes insipidus.

[Renal calculi, calcium (prophylaxis)][1]—Thiazide diuretics are also used for prevention of calcium-containing renal stones.

[1]Not included in Canadian product labeling.

Pharmacology/Pharmacokinetics

Note: Although they are not chemically the same, chlorthalidone, metolazone, and quinethazone have the same actions as the thiazide diuretics.

Physicochemical characteristics

Molecular weight—
- Bendroflumethiazide: 421.41.
- Chlorothiazide: 295.72.
- Chlorthalidone: 338.76.
- Hydrochlorothiazide: 297.73.
- Hydroflumethiazide: 331.28.
- Methyclothiazide: 360.23.
- Metolazone: 365.83.
- Polythiazide: 439.87.
- Quinethazone: 289.74.
- Trichlormethiazide: 380.65.

pKa—
- Bendroflumethiazide: 8.5.
- Chlorothiazide: 6.7 and 9.5.
- Chlorthalidone: 9.4.
- Hydrochlorothiazide: 7.9 and 9.2.
- Hydroflumethiazide: 8.9 and 10.7.
- Methyclothiazide: 9.4.
- Metolazone: 9.7.
- Quinethazone: 9.3 and 10.7.
- Trichlormethiazide: 8.6.

Mechanism of action/Effect

Diuretic—Thiazide diuretics increase urinary excretion of sodium and water by inhibiting sodium reabsorption in the early distal tubules. They increase the rate of delivery of tubular fluid and electrolytes to the distal sites of hydrogen and potassium ion secretion, while plasma volume contraction increases aldosterone production. The increased delivery and increase in aldosterone levels promote sodium reabsorption at the distal tubules, thus increasing the loss of potassium and hydrogen ions.

Antihypertensive—Diuretics lower blood pressure initially by reducing plasma and extracellular fluid volume; cardiac output also decreases. Eventually, cardiac output returns to normal. Thiazide diuretics decrease peripheral resistance by a direct peripheral effect on blood vessels.

Antidiuretic—The antidiuretic effect of thiazide diuretics is a result of mild sodium and water depletion leading to increased reabsorption of glomerular filtrate in the proximal renal tubule and reduced delivery of tubular fluid available for excretion.

Antiurolithic (calcium calculi)—Thiazide diuretics decrease urinary calcium excretion by a direct action on the distal tubule, which may prevent recurrence of calcium-containing renal calculi.

Absorption

Thiazide diuretics are absorbed relatively rapidly after oral administration.

Metolazone—The time to peak concentration is 8 hours for extended metolazone tablets and 2 to 4 hours for prompt metolazone tablets. In addition, prompt metolazone tablets have higher bioavailability.

Protein binding

Bendroflumethiazide—Very high (94%).
Chlorothiazide—Low to high (20 to 80%).
Chlorthalidone—High (75% [58% to albumin]); increased affinity to carbonic anhydrase in red blood cells.
Hydroflumethiazide—High (74%).
Metolazone—Very high (95%; 50 to 70% to red blood cells).
Polythiazide—High (84%).

Elimination

Unchanged; almost totally via the kidneys, with minute quantities in the bile; metolazone undergoes some enterohepatic recycling and slightly greater amounts are excreted in the bile.

Drug	Half-life (hr)	Diuretic Effect (hr)		
		Onset	Peak	Duration
Bendroflumethiazide	8.5	1–2	4	6–12
Chlorothiazide	1–2	2	4	6–12
Chlorthalidone	35 to 50	2	2	48–72
Hydrochlorothiazide	5.6–14.8	2	4	6–12
Hydroflumethiazide	17	1–2	3–4	18–24
Methyclothiazide		2	6	>24
Metolazone	14	1*	2*	12–24*
Polythiazide		2	6	24–48
Quinethazone		2	6	18–24
Trichlormethiazide		2	6	≤24

*Information on diuretic effect applies to extended metolazone tablets.

Note: In the absence of edema, negative sodium balance induced by thiazide diuretics lasts for 3 days to 4 weeks with chronic administration. Extracellular fluid volumes remain steady thereafter, although at a lower concentration and volume than before initiation of therapy.

The antihypertensive effects of the thiazide diuretics may be noted after 3 to 4 days of therapy, although up to 3 to 4 weeks may be required for optimal effect. Antihypertensive effects persist for up to 1 week after withdrawal of therapy.

Precautions to Consider

Cross-sensitivity and/or related problems

Patients sensitive to other sulfonamide-type medications, bumetanide, furosemide, or carbonic anhydrase inhibitors may be sensitive to this medication also.

Carcinogenicity/Mutagenicity

Bendroflumethiazide—Studies have not been done in either animals or humans.

Chlorothiazide—Carcinogenicity studies have not been done in either animals or humans. Chlorothiazide was not found to be mutagenic in the Ames microbial mutation test, dominant lethal assay, or a test in *Aspergillus nidulans.*

Hydrochlorothiazide—Carcinogenicity studies have not been done in either animals or humans. Hydrochlorothiazide was not found to be mutagenic *in vitro* in the Ames microbial mutation test or on examination of urine from patients who received hydrochlorothiazide; however, it did induce nondisjunction in *Aspergillus nidulans.*

Hydroflumethiazide—Studies have not been done in either animals or humans.

Methyclothiazide—Studies have not been done in either animals or humans.

Metolazone—Studies in mice and rats for 1½ to 2 years at doses of 2, 10, and 50 mg per kg of body weight (mg/kg) per day (100, 500, and 2500 times the maximum recommended human dose [MRHD]) found no evidence of carcinogenicity.

Trichlormethiazide—Studies have not been done in either animals or humans.

Pregnancy/Reproduction

Fertility—*Hydrochlorothiazide*: No adverse effects on fertility were found in rats given doses up to 2 times the maximum recommended human dose of hydrochlorothiazide.

Methyclothiazide: No adverse effects on fertility were found in rats given methyclothiazide in doses up to 4 mg per kg of body weight (mg/kg) per day (at least 20 times the maximum recommended human dose).

Metolazone: A study in which male rats were given metolazone at doses of 2, 10, and 50 mg/kg for 127 days prior to mating with untreated female rats revealed an increase in the number of resorption sites in dams mated with males given the 50 mg/kg dose. Furthermore, decreased fetal weight and reduced pregnancy rate were observed in dams mated with males from the 10 and 50 mg/kg groups. In mice, there was no evidence that metolazone alters reproductive capacity.

Pregnancy—Thiazide diuretics cross the placenta and appear in cord blood. Although studies in humans have not been done, thiazide diuretics can cause fetal harm when given to pregnant women. Fetal or neonatal jaundice has been reported.

Pregnant women should be advised to contact their physician before taking this medication, since routine use of diuretics during normal pregnancy is inappropriate and exposes mother and fetus to unnecessary hazard. Thiazide diuretics do not prevent development of toxemia of pregnancy, and there is no satisfactory evidence that they are useful in the treatment of toxemia. Thiazide diuretics are indicated only in the treatment of edema due to pathologic causes or as a short course of treatment in patients with severe hypervolemia. Possible hazards include fetal or neonatal jaundice, thrombocytopenia, or other adverse reactions seen in adults.

Studies in animals have not shown that thiazide diuretics cause adverse effects on the fetus at several times the human dose.

Bendroflumethiazide—

Adequate and well-controlled studies in humans and animals have not been done.

FDA Pregnancy Category C.

Chlorothiazide—

Adequate and well-controlled studies in humans have not been done.

Studies in rabbits, mice, and rats at doses up to 500 mg/kg per day (25 times the MRHD) have not shown that chlorothiazide causes adverse effects on the fetus.

FDA Pregnancy Category B.

Chlorthalidone—
Adequate and well-controlled studies in humans have not been done.
Studies in rats and rabbits at doses up to 420 times the human dose have not shown that chlorthalidone causes adverse effects on the fetus.
FDA Pregnancy Category B.

Hydrochlorothiazide—
Adequate and well-controlled studies in humans have not been done.
A study in rats at dosages up to 250 mg/kg per day (62.5 times the MRHD) has not shown that hydrochlorothiazide causes adverse effects on the fetus.
Studies in mice and rabbits with doses up to 100 mg/kg per day (50 times the maximum human dose) revealed no evidence of external abnormalities of the fetus.
FDA Pregnancy Category B.

Hydroflumethiazide—
Studies have not been done in humans.
Studies have not been done in animals.
FDA Pregnancy Category C.

Methyclothiazide—
Studies have not been done in humans.
Studies in rats and rabbits given methyclothiazide at doses up to 4 mg/kg per day have revealed no evidence of harm to the fetus.
FDA Pregnancy Category B.

Metolazone—
Adequate and well-controlled studies in humans have not been done.
Studies in mice, rabbits, and rats at doses up to 50 mg/kg per day (333 times the MRHD) have not shown that metolazone causes adverse effects on the fetus.
FDA Pregnancy Category B.

Trichlormethiazide—
Adequate and well-controlled studies in humans have not been done.
Studies in rats at doses 250 to 1250 times the recommended human daily dose have not shown that trichlormethiazide causes adverse effects on the fetus.
FDA Pregnancy Category C.

Breast-feeding
Thiazide diuretics are distributed into breast milk. The American Academy of Pediatrics recommends that nursing mothers avoid thiazide diuretics during the first month of lactation because of reports of suppression of lactation.

Pediatrics
Although appropriate studies on the relationship of age to the effects of thiazide diuretics have not been performed in the pediatric population, pediatrics-specific problems that would limit the usefulness of this medication in children are not expected. However, caution is required in jaundiced infants because of the risk of hyperbilirubinemia.

Geriatrics
Although appropriate studies on the relationship of age to the effects of thiazide diuretics have not been performed in the geriatric population, the elderly may be more sensitive to the hypotensive and electrolyte effects. In addition, elderly patients are more likely to have age-related renal function impairment, which may require caution in patients receiving thiazide diuretics.

Drug interactions and/or related problems
The following drug interactions and/or related problems have been selected on the basis of their potential clinical significance (possible mechanism in parentheses where appropriate)—not necessarily inclusive (» = major clinical significance):

Note: Combinations containing any of the following medications, depending on the amount present, may also interact with this medication.

Amantadine
(hydrochlorothiazide may reduce the renal clearance of amantadine, resulting in increased plasma concentrations and possible amantadine toxicity)

Amiodarone
(concurrent use of thiazide diuretics with amiodarone may lead to an increased risk of arrhythmias associated with hypokalemia)

Anticoagulants, coumarin- or indandione-derivative
(effects may be decreased when used concurrently with thiazide diuretics as a result of reduction of plasma volume leading to concentration of procoagulant factors in the blood; in addition, diuretic-induced improvement of hepatic congestion may lead to improved hepatic function resulting in increased procoagulant factor synthesis; dosage adjustments may be necessary)

Antidiabetic agents, oral or
Insulin
(thiazide diuretics may raise blood glucose concentrations; for adult-onset diabetics, dosage adjustment of hypoglycemic medications may be necessary during and after thiazide diuretic therapy; insulin requirements may be increased, decreased, or unchanged)

Anti-inflammatory drugs, nonsteroidal (NSAIDs), especially indomethacin
(may antagonize the natriuresis and increase in plasma renin activity [PRA] caused by thiazide diuretics; they may also reduce the antihypertensive effect and increase in urine volume caused by thiazide diuretics, possibly by inhibiting renal prostaglandin synthesis and/or by causing sodium and fluid retention; the patient should be carefully monitored to confirm that the desired effect is being obtained)
(in addition, concurrent use of NSAIDs with a diuretic may increase the risk of renal failure secondary to a decrease in renal blood flow caused by inhibition of renal prostaglandin synthesis)

Calcium-containing medications
(concurrent use of thiazide diuretics with large doses of calcium may result in hypercalcemia because of reduced calcium excretion)

» Cholestyramine or
» Colestipol
(may inhibit gastrointestinal absorption of the thiazide diuretics; administration of thiazide diuretics 1 hour before or 4 hours after cholestyramine or colestipol is recommended)

Diazoxide
(concurrent use with thiazide diuretics may enhance hyperglycemic effects; monitoring of blood glucose levels and/or dosage adjustment of one or both agents may be necessary)
(in addition, concurrent use with thiazide diuretics may enhance hyperuricemic and antihypertensive effects)

Diflunisal
(concurrent use of hydrochlorothiazide with diflunisal produces significantly increased plasma concentrations of hydrochlorothiazide; in addition, the hyperuricemic effect of hydrochlorothiazide is decreased)

» Digitalis glycosides
(concurrent use with thiazide diuretics may enhance the possibility of digitalis toxicity associated with hypokalemia or hypomagnesemia)

Dopamine
(concurrent use may increase the diuretic effect of either thiazide diuretics or dopamine, as a result of dopamine's direct effect on dopaminergic receptors to produce vasodilation of renal vasculature and increase renal blood flow; dopamine also has a direct natriuretic effect)

Hypokalemia-causing medications, other (see *Appendix II*)
(risk of severe hypokalemia due to other hypokalemia-causing medications may be increased; monitoring of serum potassium concentrations and cardiac function and potassium supplementation may be necessary)

Hypotension-producing medications, other (see *Appendix II*)
(antihypertensive and/or diuretic effects may be potentiated when these medications are used concurrently with thiazide diuretics; although some antihypertensive and/or diuretic combinations are frequently used for therapeutic advantage, when used concurrently dosage adjustments may be necessary)

» Lithium
(concurrent use with thiazide diuretics is not recommended, as they may provoke lithium toxicity because of reduced renal clearance; in addition, lithium has nephrotoxic effects)

Neuromuscular blocking agents, nondepolarizing
(thiazide diuretics may induce hypokalemia, which may enhance the blockade of nondepolarizing neuromuscular blocking agents; serum potassium determinations may be necessary prior to administration of nondepolarizing neuromuscular blocking agents; careful postoperative monitoring of the patient may be necessary following concurrent or sequential use, especially if there is a possibility of incomplete reversal of neuromuscular blockade)

Sympathomimetics
(may antagonize the antihypertensive effect of the thiazide diuretics; the patient should be carefully monitored to confirm that the desired effect is being obtained)

Laboratory value alterations

The following have been selected on the basis of their potential clinical significance (possible effect in parentheses where appropriate)—not necessarily inclusive (» = major clinical significance).

With diagnostic test results

Bentiromide
(administration of thiazide diuretics during a bentiromide test period will invalidate test results since thiazide diuretics are also metabolized to arylamines and will thus increase the percent of para-aminobenzoic acid [PABA] recovered; discontinuation of thiazide diuretics at least 3 days prior to the administration of bentiromide is recommended)

Phenolsulfonphthalein (PSP) excretion test
(bendroflumethiazide and trichlormethiazide may interfere with PSP excretion)

Phentolamine and tyramine tests
(bendroflumethiazide and trichlormethiazide may produce false negative results)

With physiology/laboratory test values

Bilirubin
(serum concentrations may be increased by displacement from albumin binding)

Calcium
(serum concentrations may be increased; thiazide diuretics should be discontinued before parathyroid function tests are carried out)

Cholesterol, low-density lipoprotein, and triglyceride and
Creatinine
(serum concentrations may be increased)

Glucose, blood and urine
(concentrations may be increased, usually only in patients with a predisposition to glucose intolerance)

Magnesium and
Potassium and
Sodium
(serum concentrations may be decreased; serum magnesium concentrations may increase in uremic patients; a fall in sodium can be life-threatening)

Protein-bound iodine (PBI)
(serum concentrations may be decreased)

Uric acid
(serum concentrations may be increased)

Urinary calcium concentrations
(may be decreased)

Medical considerations/Contraindications

The medical considerations/contraindications included have been selected on the basis of their potential clinical significance (reasons given in parentheses where appropriate)—not necessarily inclusive (» = major clinical significance).

Risk-benefit should be considered when the following medical problems exist:

» Anuria or severe renal function impairment
(ineffective; may precipitate azotemia; may produce cumulative effects)

Diabetes mellitus
(hypoglycemic medication requirements may be altered)

Gout, history of or
Hyperuricemia
(serum uric acid concentrations may be elevated)

Hepatic function impairment
(risk of dehydration which may precipitate hepatic coma and death; plasma half-life is unaltered)

Hypercalcemia or
Hypercholesterolemia or
Hypertriglyceridemia or
Hyponatremia
(conditions may be exacerbated; onset of hyponatremia can be sudden and life-threatening)

Lupus erythematosus, history of
(exacerbation or activation by thiazide diuretics has been reported)

Pancreatitis

Sensitivity to thiazide diuretics or other sulfonamide-derived medications

Sympathectomy
(antihypertensive effects may be enhanced)

» Caution is required also in jaundiced infants because of the risk of hyperbilirubinemia.

Patient monitoring

The following may be especially important in patient monitoring (other tests may be warranted in some patients, depending on condition; » = major clinical significance):

Blood glucose and
Blood urea nitrogen (BUN) and
Creatinine, serum and
Uric acid, serum
(determinations recommended prior to initiation of therapy and if clinical signs of a significant increase occur)

» Blood pressure measurements
(recommended at periodic intervals in patients being treated for hypertension; selected patients may be trained to perform blood pressure measurements at home and report the results at regular physician visits)

Cholesterol, serum and
Triglycerides, serum
(determinations recommended after 6 months of therapy and annually thereafter)

Electrolyte, serum, concentrations
(determinations may be required for patients on long-term therapy, especially if they are also taking cardiac glycosides or systemic steroids, or when severe cirrhosis is present)

Side/Adverse Effects

Note: Most side effects are dose-related.

The following side/adverse effects have been selected on the basis of their potential clinical significance (possible signs and symptoms in parentheses where appropriate)—not necessarily inclusive:

Those indicating need for medical attention

Incidence more frequent

Electrolyte imbalance such as hyponatremia (confusion; convulsions; decreased mentation; fatigue; irritability; muscle cramps); ***hypochloremic alkalosis, and hypokalemia*** (dryness of mouth; increased thirst; irregular heartbeat; mood or mental changes; muscle cramps or pain; nausea or vomiting; unusual tiredness or weakness; weak pulse)

Note: *Hyponatremia* as a complication is rare, but constitutes a medical emergency as onset may be rapid.

Incidence rare

Agranulocytosis (fever or chills; cough or hoarseness; lower back or side pain; painful or difficult urination); ***allergic reaction*** (skin rash or hives); ***cholecystitis or pancreatitis*** (severe stomach pain with nausea and vomiting); ***gout or hyperuricemia*** (joint pain, lower back or side pain); ***hepatic function impairment*** (yellow eyes or skin); ***thrombocytopenia*** (unusual bleeding or bruising; black, tarry stools; blood in urine or stools; pinpoint red spots on skin)

Those indicating need for medical attention only if they continue or are bothersome

Incidence less frequent

Anorexia (loss of appetite); ***decreased sexual ability; diarrhea; orthostatic hypotension*** (dizziness or lightheadedness when getting up from a lying or sitting position); ***photosensitivity*** (increased sensitivity of skin to sunlight); ***upset stomach***

Overdose

For more information on the management of overdose or unintentional ingestion, **contact a Poison Control Center** (see *Poison Control Center Listing*).

Treatment of overdose

Thiazide diuretic overdose should be treated by immediate evacuation of the stomach followed by supportive, symptomatic treatment and monitoring of serum electrolyte concentrations and renal function.

Patient Consultation

As an aid to patient consultation, refer to *Advice for the Patient, Diuretics, Thiazide (Systemic)*.

In providing consultation, consider emphasizing the following selected information (» = major clinical significance):

Before using this medication

» Conditions affecting use, especially:

Sensitivity to thiazide diuretics, other sulfonamide-type medications, bumetanide, furosemide, or carbonic anhydrase inhibitors

Pregnancy—Not recommended for routine use; may cause jaundice, thrombocytopenia, hypokalemia in infant

Breast-feeding—Distributed into breast milk; recommended that nursing mothers avoid thiazides during first month of breast-feeding because of reports of suppression of lactation
Use in children—Caution if giving to infants with jaundice
Use in the elderly—Elderly patients may be more sensitive to hypotensive and electrolyte effects
Other medications, especially cholestyramine, colestipol, digitalis glycosides, or lithium
Other medical problems, especially anuria or severe renal function impairment or infants with jaundice

Proper use of this medication
Diuretic effects of the medication and timing of doses to minimize inconvenience of diuresis (except in diabetes insipidus)
Compliance with therapy; taking medication at the same time each day to maintain the therapeutic effect
Proper administration of concentrated oral hydrochlorothiazide solution: Taking orally; special dropper to be used for accurate measuring
» Proper dosing
Missed dose: Taking as soon as possible; not taking if almost time for next dose; not doubling doses
» Proper storage
For use as an antihypertensive
Importance of diet; possible need for sodium restriction and/or weight reduction
» Patient may not experience symptoms of hypertension; importance of taking medication even if feeling well
» Does not cure, but helps control hypertension; possible need for lifelong therapy; checking with physician before discontinuing medication; serious consequences of untreated hypertension

Precautions while using this medication
Making regular visits to physician to check progress
» Possibility of hypokalemia; possible need for additional potassium in diet; not changing diet without first checking with physician
To prevent dehydration, checking with physician if severe nausea, vomiting, or diarrhea occurs and continues
Diabetics: May increase blood sugar levels
Possible photosensitivity; avoiding unprotected exposure to sun; using protective clothing and sun block product; avoiding use of sunlamp, tanning bed, or tanning booth
For use as an antihypertensive:
» Not taking other medications, especially nonprescription sympathomimetics, unless discussed with physician

Side/adverse effects
Signs of potential side effects, especially electrolyte imbalance, agranulocytosis, allergic reaction, cholecystitis, pancreatitis, hepatic function impairment, hyperuricemia, gout, and thrombocytopenia

General Dosing Information

The lowest effective dosage should be utilized to minimize potential electrolyte imbalance and the reflex increase in renin and aldosterone levels.

A single daily dose is preferably taken on arising in order to minimize the effect of increased frequency of urination on sleep. When used to promote diuresis, intermittent dosage schedules (drug-free days) may reduce the possibility of electrolyte imbalance or hyperuricemia resulting from therapy.

Concurrent administration of potassium supplements or potassium-sparing diuretics may be indicated in patients considered to be at higher risk for developing hypokalemia. Caution in administering potassium supplements is recommended, however, since loss of potassium is not clinically significant in most patients, and supplementation leads to a risk of development of hyperkalemia.

Recent evidence suggests that withdrawal of antihypertensive therapy prior to surgery is not necessary, but that the anesthesiologist must be aware of such therapy.

For hypertension
Low dose thiazide therapy has been found to be effective in the treatment of hypertension.

BENDROFLUMETHIAZIDE

Summary of Differences

Pharmacology/pharmacokinetics:
Protein binding—Very high.
Half-life—Normal: 8.5 hours.
Onset of action—Diuretic: 1 to 2 hours.
Time to peak effect—Diuretic: 4 hours.
Duration of action—Diuretic: 6 to 12 hours.
Laboratory value alterations:
May produce false-negative results in phentolamine, phenolsulfonphthalein, and tyramine tests.

Oral Dosage Forms

Note: Bracketed uses in the *Dosage Forms* section refer to categories of use and/or indications that are not included in U.S. product labeling.

BENDROFLUMETHIAZIDE TABLETS USP

Usual adult dose
Diuretic or
[Antidiuretic (central or nephrogenic diabetes insipidus)][1]—
Initial: Oral, 2.5 to 10 mg one or two times a day, once every other day, or once a day for three to five days a week.
Maintenance: Oral, 2.5 to 5 mg once a day, once every other day, or once a day for three to five days a week.
Antihypertensive—
Oral, 2.5 to 20 mg per day, as a single dose or in two divided daily doses, the dosage being adjusted according to response.
Note: Geriatric patients may be more sensitive to the effects of the usual adult dose.

Usual pediatric dose
Diuretic or
[Antidiuretic (central or nephrogenic diabetes insipidus)][1]—
Initial: Oral, up to 400 mcg (0.4 mg) per kg of body weight or 12 mg per square meter of body surface a day, as a single dose or in two divided daily doses.
Maintenance: Oral, 50 to 100 mcg (0.05 to 0.1 mg) per kg of body weight or 1.5 to 3 mg per square meter of body surface once a day.
Antihypertensive—
Oral, 50 to 400 mcg (0.05 to 0.4 mg) per kg of body weight or 1.5 to 12 mg per square meter of body surface per day, as a single dose or in two divided daily doses, the dosage being adjusted according to response.

Strength(s) usually available
U.S.—
5 mg (Rx) [*Naturetin* (scored; lactose)].
10 mg (Rx) [*Naturetin* (scored; lactose)].
Canada—
5 mg (Rx) [*Naturetin* (scored; tartrazine)].

Packaging and storage
Store below 40 °C (104 °F), preferably between 15 and 30 °C (59 and 86 °F), unless otherwise specified by manufacturer. Store in a tight container.

Auxiliary labeling
- Avoid overexposure to the sun or use of sunlamp.
- Do not take other medicines without your doctor's advice.

Note
Check refill frequency to determine compliance in hypertensive patients.

---

[1]Not included in Canadian product labeling.

CHLOROTHIAZIDE

Summary of Differences

Pharmacology/pharmacokinetics:
Protein binding—Low to high.
Half-life—Normal: 13 hours.
Onset of action—Diuretic: 2 hours.
Time to peak effect—Diuretic: 4 hours.
Duration of action—Diuretic: 6 to 12 hours.

Additional Dosing Information

See also *General Dosing Information.*
For parenteral dosage forms only
- Care must be taken to avoid extravasation during intravenous administration.
- Chlorothiazide should not be administered intramuscularly or subcutaneously.

Oral Dosage Forms

Note: Bracketed uses in the *Dosage Forms* section refer to categories of use and/or indications that are not included in U.S. product labeling.

CHLOROTHIAZIDE ORAL SUSPENSION USP

Usual adult dose

Diuretic or
[Antidiuretic (central or nephrogenic diabetes insipidus)]—
Oral, 250 mg every six to twelve hours.

Antihypertensive—
Oral, 250 mg to 1 gram per day, as a single dose or in divided daily doses, the dosage being adjusted according to response.

Note: Geriatric patients may be more sensitive to the effects of the usual adult dose.

Usual pediatric dose

Children up to 6 months of age—Oral, 10 to 30 mg per kg of body weight per day, as a single dose or in two divided daily doses, the dosage being adjusted according to response.

Children 6 months of age and over—Oral, 10 to 20 mg per kg of body weight per day, as a single dose or in two divided daily doses, the dosage being adjusted according to response.

Strength(s) usually available

U.S.—
50 mg per mL (Rx) [*Diuril* (alcohol 0.5%; glycerin; methylparaben 0.12%; sodium saccharin; sucrose)].

Canada—
Not commercially available.

Packaging and storage

Store below 40 °C (104 °F), preferably between 15 and 30 °C (59 and 86 °F), unless otherwise specified by manufacturer. Store in a tight container. Protect from freezing.

Auxiliary labeling

- Shake well.
- Avoid overexposure to the sun or use of sunlamp.
- Do not take other medicines without your doctor's advice.

Note

Check refill frequency to determine compliance in hypertensive patients.

CHLOROTHIAZIDE TABLETS USP

Usual adult dose

Diuretic or
[Antidiuretic (central or nephrogenic diabetes insipidus)]—
Oral, 250 mg every six to twelve hours.

Antihypertensive—
Oral, 250 mg to 1 gram per day, as a single dose or in divided daily doses, the dosage being adjusted according to response.

Note: Geriatric patients may be more sensitive to the effects of the usual adult dose.

Usual pediatric dose

Children up to 6 months of age—Oral, 10 to 30 mg per kg of body weight per day, as a single dose or in two divided daily doses, the dosage being adjusted according to response.

Children 6 months of age and over—Oral, 10 to 20 mg per kg of body weight per day, as a single dose or in two divided daily doses, the dosage being adjusted according to response.

Strength(s) usually available

U.S.—
250 mg (Rx) [*Diuril* (scored); GENERIC (may be scored)].
500 mg (Rx) [*Diuril* (scored); GENERIC (may be scored)].

Canada—
Not commercially available.

Packaging and storage

Store below 40 °C (104 °F), preferably between 15 and 30 °C (59 and 86 °F), in a well-closed container, unless otherwise specified by manufacturer.

Auxiliary labeling

- Avoid overexposure to the sun or use of sunlamp.
- Do not take other medicines without your doctor's advice.

Note

Check refill frequency to determine compliance in hypertensive patients.

Parenteral Dosage Forms

Note: Bracketed uses in the *Dosage Forms* section refer to categories of use and/or indications that are not included in U.S. product labeling.

CHLOROTHIAZIDE SODIUM FOR INJECTION USP

Usual adult dose

Diuretic or
[Antidiuretic (central or nephrogenic diabetes insipidus)]—
Intravenous, 250 mg (base) every six to twelve hours.

Antihypertensive—
Intravenous, 500 mg to 1 gram (base) of chlorothiazide a day, as a single dose or in two divided daily doses.

Note: Geriatric patients may be more sensitive to the effects of the usual adult dose.

Usual pediatric dose

Safety and efficacy have not been established.

Strength(s) usually available

U.S.—
500 mg (base) (Rx) [*Diuril* (mannitol 250 mg)].

Canada—
Not commercially available.

Packaging and storage

Store below 40 °C (104 °F), preferably between 15 and 30 °C (59 and 86 °F), unless otherwise specified by manufacturer.

Stability

Reconstituted solution may be stored at room temperature for 24 hours, after which it must be discarded.

Incompatibilities

Solutions of chlorothiazide are not compatible with whole blood or its derivatives.

Additional information

Chlorothiazide Sodium for Injection USP is reconstituted for intravenous administration by adding no less than 18 mL of sterile water for injection to the vial and shaking to dissolve, producing a solution containing 25 mg (base) per mL.

Reconstituted solutions may be further diluted with dextrose injection or 0.9% sodium chloride injection for administration by intravenous infusion.

CHLORTHALIDONE

Summary of Differences

Pharmacology/pharmacokinetics:
Although not chemically the same, chlorthalidone has the same actions as the thiazide diuretics.
Protein binding—Very high to carbonic anhydrase in red blood cells.
Half-life—Normal: 35 to 50 hours.
Onset of action—Diuretic: 2 hours.
Time to peak effect—Diuretic: 2 hours.
Duration of action—Diuretic: 48 to 72 hours.

Oral Dosage Forms

CHLORTHALIDONE TABLETS USP

Usual adult dose

Diuretic—
Oral, 25 to 100 mg once a day, or 100 to 200 mg once every other day, or once a day for three days a week.

Antihypertensive—
Oral, 25 to 100 mg once a day, the dosage being adjusted according to response.

Note: Geriatric patients may be more sensitive to the effects of the usual adult dose.

Usual pediatric dose

Oral, 2 mg per kg of body weight or 60 mg per square meter of body surface once a day for three days a week, the dosage being adjusted according to response.

Strength(s) usually available

U.S.—
25 mg (Rx) [*Hygroton; Thalitone;* GENERIC (may be scored)].
50 mg (Rx) [*Hygroton;* GENERIC (may be scored)].
100 mg (Rx) [*Hygroton* (scored); GENERIC (may be scored)].

Canada—
50 mg (Rx) [*Apo-Chlorthalidone* (scored); *Hygroton* (scored); *Novo-Thalidone* (scored); *Uridon* (scored)].
100 mg (Rx) [*Apo-Chlorthalidone* (scored); *Hygroton* (scored); *Novo-Thalidone* (scored); *Uridon* (scored)].

Packaging and storage

Store below 40 °C (104 °F), preferably between 15 and 30 °C (59 and 86 °F), unless otherwise specified by manufacturer. Store in a well-closed container.

Auxiliary labeling

- Avoid overexposure to the sun or use of sunlamp.
- Do not take other medicines without your doctor's advice.

Note
Check refill frequency to determine compliance in hypertensive patients.

HYDROCHLOROTHIAZIDE

Summary of Differences
Pharmacology/pharmacokinetics:
- Half-life—Normal: 15 hours.
- Onset of action—Diuretic: 2 hours.
- Time to peak effect—Diuretic: 4 hours.
- Duration of action—Diuretic: 6 to 12 hours.

Oral Dosage Forms
Note: Bracketed uses in the *Dosage Forms* section refer to categories of use and/or indications that are not included in U.S. product labeling.

HYDROCHLOROTHIAZIDE CAPSULES

Usual adult dose
Antihypertensive—
Oral, initially, 12.5 once a day, administered alone or in combination with other antihypertensive agents.

Note: This lower-dose product is recommended for patients in whom the development of hyperkalemia cannot be risked, including patients taking angiotensin-converting enzyme (ACE) inhibitors.

Note: Geriatric patients may be more sensitive to the effects of the usual adult dose.

Usual pediatric dose
See *Hydrochlorothiazide Oral Solution.*

Strength(s) usually available
U.S.—
12.5 mg (Rx) [*Microzide*].

Canada—
Not commercially available.

Packaging and storage
Store between 15 and 30 °C (59 and 86 °F). Store in a well-closed container. Protect from light, moisture, and freezing.

Auxiliary labeling
- Avoid overexposure to the sun or use of sunlamp.
- Do not take other medicines without your doctor's advice.

Note
Check refill frequency to determine compliance in hypertensive patients.

HYDROCHLOROTHIAZIDE ORAL SOLUTION

Usual adult dose
Diuretic or
[Antidiuretic (central or nephrogenic diabetes insipidus)]—
Oral, 25 to 100 mg one or two times a day, once every other day, or once a day for three to five days a week.

Antihypertensive—
Oral, 25 to 100 mg a day, as a single dose or in two divided daily doses, the dosage being adjusted according to response.

Note: Geriatric patients may be more sensitive to the effects of the usual adult dose.

Usual pediatric dose
Oral, 1 to 2 mg per kg of body weight or 30 to 60 mg per square meter of body surface per day, as a single dose or in two divided daily doses, the dosage being adjusted according to response.

Note: Infants under 6 months of age may receive up to 3 mg per kg of body weight per day.

Strength(s) usually available
U.S.—
10 mg per mL (Rx) [GENERIC].
100 mg per mL (Rx) [GENERIC].

Canada—
Not commercially available.

Packaging and storage
Store below 40 °C (104 °F), preferably between 15 and 30 °C (59 and 86 °F), in a well-closed container, unless otherwise specified by manufacturer. Protect from freezing.

Auxiliary labeling
- Avoid overexposure to the sun or use of sunlamp.
- Do not take other medicines without your doctor's advice.

Note
Check refill frequency to determine compliance in hypertensive patients.

Be careful not to confuse oral solution with concentrated oral solution.

Make sure patient understands how to measure dose of concentrated oral solution with calibrated dropper.

HYDROCHLOROTHIAZIDE TABLETS USP

Usual adult dose
Diuretic or
[Antidiuretic (central or nephrogenic diabetes insipidus)][1]—
Oral, 25 to 100 mg one or two times a day, once every other day, or once a day for three to five days a week.

Antihypertensive—
Oral, 25 to 100 mg a day, as a single dose or in two divided daily doses, the dosage being adjusted according to response.

Note: Geriatric patients may be more sensitive to the effects of the usual adult dose.

Usual pediatric dose
Oral, 1 to 2 mg per kg of body weight or 30 to 60 mg per square meter of body surface per day, as a single dose or in two divided daily doses, the dosage being adjusted according to response.

Note: Infants under 6 months of age may receive up to 3 mg per kg of body weight per day.

Strength(s) usually available
U.S.—
25 mg (Rx) [*Esidrix* (scored); *HydroDIURIL* (scored); *Oretic* (scored); GENERIC (scored)].
50 mg (Rx) [*Esidrix* (scored); *Hydro-chlor; Hydro-D; HydroDIURIL* (scored); *Oretic* (scored); GENERIC (scored)].
100 mg (Rx) [*Esidrix* (scored); *HydroDIURIL* (scored); GENERIC (scored)].

Canada—
25 mg (Rx) [*Apo-Hydro* (scored); *HydroDIURIL* (scored); *Neo-Codema* (scored); *Novo-Hydrazide* (scored); *Urozide* (scored)].
50 mg (Rx) [*Apo-Hydro* (scored); *Diuchlor H* (scored); *HydroDIURIL* (scored); *Neo-Codema* (scored); *Novo-Hydrazide* (scored); *Urozide* (scored)].
100 mg (Rx) [*Apo-Hydro* (scored); *HydroDIURIL* (scored); *Urozide* (scored)].

Packaging and storage
Store below 40 °C (104 °F), preferably between 15 and 30 °C (59 and 86 °F), unless otherwise specified by manufacturer. Store in a well-closed container.

Auxiliary labeling
- Avoid overexposure to the sun or use of sunlamp.
- Do not take other medicines without your doctor's advice.

Note
Check refill frequency to determine compliance in hypertensive patients.

[1]Not included in Canadian product labeling.

HYDROFLUMETHIAZIDE

Summary of Differences
Pharmacology/pharmacokinetics:
- Protein binding—High.
- Onset of action—Diuretic: 1 to 2 hours.
- Time to peak effect—Diuretic: 3 to 4 hours.
- Duration of action—Diuretic: 18 to 24 hours.

Oral Dosage Forms
Note: Bracketed uses in the *Dosage Forms* section refer to categories of use and/or indications that are not included in U.S. product labeling.

HYDROFLUMETHIAZIDE TABLETS USP

Usual adult dose
Diuretic or
[Antidiuretic (central or nephrogenic diabetes insipidus)]—
Oral, 25 to 100 mg one or two times a day, once every other day, or once a day for three to five days a week.

Antihypertensive—
Oral, 50 to 100 mg per day, as a single dose or in two divided daily doses, the dosage being adjusted according to response.

Note: Geriatric patients may be more sensitive to the effects of the usual adult dose.

Usual adult prescribing limits
Up to 200 mg per day in divided doses.

Usual pediatric dose
Oral, 1 mg per kg of body weight or 30 mg per square meter of body surface once a day, the dosage adjusted according to response.

Strength(s) usually available
U.S.—
50 mg (Rx) [*Diucardin* (scored); *Saluron* (scored); GENERIC (may be scored)].
Canada—
Not commercially available.

Packaging and storage
Store below 40 °C (104 °F), preferably between 15 and 30 °C (59 and 86 °F), unless otherwise specified by manufacturer. Store in a tight container.

Auxiliary labeling
- Avoid overexposure to the sun or use of sunlamp.
- Do not take other medicines without your doctor's advice.

Note
Check refill frequency to determine compliance in hypertensive patients.

METHYCLOTHIAZIDE

Summary of Differences

Pharmacology/pharmacokinetics:
Onset of action—Diuretic: 2 hours.
Time to peak effect—Diuretic: 6 hours.
Duration of action—Diuretic: More than 24 hours.

Oral Dosage Forms

Note: Bracketed uses in the *Dosage Forms* section refer to categories of use and/or indications that are not included in U.S. product labeling.

METHYCLOTHIAZIDE TABLETS USP

Usual adult dose
Diuretic or
[Antidiuretic (central or nephrogenic diabetes insipidus)][1]—
Oral, 2.5 to 10 mg once a day, once every other day, or once a day for three to five days a week.
Antihypertensive—
Oral, 2.5 to 5 mg once a day, the dosage being adjusted according to response.
Note: Doses beyond 5 mg once a day will usually not result in further lowering of blood pressure.

Note: Geriatric patients may be more sensitive to the effects of the usual adult dose.

Usual pediatric dose
Oral, 50 to 200 mcg (0.05 to 0.2 mg) per kg of body weight or 1.5 to 6 mg per square meter of body surface once a day, the dosage being adjusted according to response.

Strength(s) usually available
U.S.—
2.5 mg (Rx) [*Enduron;* GENERIC (may be scored)].
5 mg (Rx) [*Aquatensen; Enduron;* GENERIC (may be scored)].
Canada—
5 mg (Rx) [*Duretic*].

Packaging and storage
Store below 40 °C (104 °F), preferably between 15 and 30 °C (59 and 86 °F), unless otherwise specified by manufacturer. Store in a well-closed container.

Auxiliary labeling
- Avoid overexposure to the sun or use of sunlamp.
- Do not take other medicines without your doctor's advice.

Note
Check refill frequency to determine compliance in hypertensive patients.

[1]Not included in Canadian product labeling.

METOLAZONE

Summary of Differences

Pharmacology/pharmacokinetics:
Although not chemically the same, metolazone has actions similar to the thiazide diuretics.
Absorption—More rapid and more complete with prompt metolazone tablets than with extended metolazone tablets.
Protein binding—Very high (50 to 70% to red blood cells).
Half-life—Normal: 8 hours.
Onset of action—Diuretic: 1 hour.
Time to peak effect—Diuretic: 2 hours.
Duration of action—Diuretic: 12 to 24 hours.
Elimination—Metolazone undergoes some enterohepatic recycling, and slightly greater amounts are excreted in the bile.

Additional Dosing Information

Extended metolazone tablets and prompt metolazone tablets should not be substituted for one another because of significant differences in rate of absorption and bioavailability.

Absorption of metolazone after oral administration is reduced in patients with cardiac disease (65% in normal subjects as compared with 40% in cardiac disease patients).

Plasma clearance of metolazone is 20 mL per minute in patients with renal failure as compared with 110 mL per minute in healthy subjects.

Duration of diuretic effect is dose-related.

Metolazone may be more effective as a diuretic than other thiazides in patients with severe renal failure. Because of this, metolazone has been added to furosemide therapy in resistant patients; however, caution is necessary because of the risk of severe electrolyte imbalance.

Oral Dosage Forms

EXTENDED METOLAZONE TABLETS

Usual adult dose
Diuretic—
Oral, 5 to 20 mg once a day.
Antihypertensive—
Oral, 2.5 to 5 mg once a day, the dosage being adjusted according to response.
Note: Geriatric patients may be more sensitive to the effects of the usual adult dose.

Usual pediatric dose
Dosage has not been established.

Strength(s) usually available
U.S.—
2.5 mg (Rx) [*Diulo; Zaroxolyn*].
5 mg (Rx) [*Diulo; Zaroxolyn*].
10 mg (Rx) [*Diulo; Zaroxolyn*].
Canada—
2.5 mg (Rx) [*Zaroxolyn*].
5 mg (Rx) [*Zaroxolyn*].
10 mg (Rx) [*Zaroxolyn*].

Packaging and storage
Store below 40 °C (104 °F), preferably between 15 and 30 °C (59 and 86 °F), in a well-closed container, unless otherwise specified by manufacturer.

Auxiliary labeling
- Avoid overexposure to the sun or use of sunlamp.
- Do not take other medicines without your doctor's advice.

Note
Extended and prompt metolazone tablets are not bioequivalent. *One product should not be substituted for the other.* If patients are to be transferred from one to the other, retitration and appropriate changes in dosage may be necessary.

Check refill frequency to determine compliance in hypertensive patients.

PROMPT METOLAZONE TABLETS

Usual adult dose
Antihypertensive—
Initial: Oral, 500 mcg (0.5 mg) once a day, the dosage being adjusted according to response.
Maintenance: Oral, 500 mcg (0.5 mg) to 1 mg once a day.

Usual adult prescribing limits
Up to 1 mg per day.

Usual pediatric dose
Dosage has not been established.

Strength(s) usually available
U.S.—
500 mcg (0.5 mg) (Rx) [*Mykrox*].
Canada—
Not commercially available.

Packaging and storage
Store below 40 °C (104 °F), preferably between 15 and 30 °C (59 and 86 °F), in a well-closed container, unless otherwise specified by manufacturer.

Auxiliary labeling
- Avoid overexposure to the sun or use of sunlamp.
- Do not take other medicines without your doctor's advice.

Note
Extended and prompt metolazone tablets are not bioequivalent. *One product should not be substituted for the other.* If patients are to be transferred from one to the other, retitration and appropriate changes in dosage may be necessary.

Check refill frequency to determine compliance in hypertensive patients.

POLYTHIAZIDE

Summary of Differences
Pharmacology/pharmacokinetics:
Protein binding—High.
Onset of action—Diuretic: 2 hours.
Time to peak effect—Diuretic: 6 hours.
Duration of action—Diuretic: 24 to 48 hours.

Oral Dosage Forms
Note: Bracketed uses in the *Dosage Forms* section refer to categories of use and/or indications that are not included in U.S. product labeling.

POLYTHIAZIDE TABLETS USP

Usual adult dose
Diuretic or
[Antidiuretic (central or nephrogenic diabetes insipidus)]—
Oral, 1 to 4 mg once a day, once every other day, or once a day for three to five days a week.
Antihypertensive—
Oral, 2 to 4 mg once a day, the dosage being adjusted according to response.

Note: Geriatric patients may be more sensitive to the effects of the usual adult dose.

Usual pediatric dose
Oral, 20 to 80 mcg (0.02 to 0.08 mg) per kg of body weight or 500 mcg (0.5 mg) to 2.5 mg per square meter of body surface once a day, the dosage being adjusted according to response.

Strength(s) usually available
U.S.—
1 mg (Rx) [*Renese* (scored; lactose)].
2 mg (Rx) [*Renese* (scored; lactose)].
4 mg (Rx) [*Renese* (scored; lactose)].
Canada—
Not commercially available.

Packaging and storage
Store below 40 °C (104 °F), preferably between 15 and 30 °C (59 and 86 °F), unless otherwise specified by manufacturer. Store in a tight, light-resistant container.

Auxiliary labeling
- Avoid overexposure to the sun or use of sunlamp.
- Do not take other medicines without your doctor's advice.

Note
Check refill frequency to determine compliance in hypertensive patients.

QUINETHAZONE

Summary of Differences
Pharmacology/pharmacokinetics:
Although not chemically the same, quinethazone has the same actions as the thiazide diuretics.
Onset of action—Diuretic: 2 hours.
Time to peak effect—Diuretic: 6 hours.
Duration of action—Diuretic: 18 to 24 hours.

Oral Dosage Forms

QUINETHAZONE TABLETS USP

Usual adult dose
Diuretic or
Antihypertensive—
Oral, 50 to 200 mg per day, as a single dose or in two divided daily doses, adjusted according to response.

Note: Geriatric patients may be more sensitive to the effects of the usual adult dose.

Usual adult prescribing limits
Up to 200 mg daily in divided doses.

Usual pediatric dose
Dosage has not been established.

Strength(s) usually available
U.S.—
50 mg (Rx) [*Hydromox* (scored)].
Canada—
Not commercially available.

Packaging and storage
Store below 40 °C (104 °F), preferably between 15 and 30 °C (59 and 86 °F), unless otherwise specified by manufacturer. Store in a tight container.

Auxiliary labeling
- Avoid overexposure to the sun or use of sunlamp.
- Do not take other medicines without your doctor's advice.

Note
Check refill frequency to determine compliance in hypertensive patients.

TRICHLORMETHIAZIDE

Summary of Differences
Pharmacology/pharmacokinetics:
Onset of action—Diuretic: 2 hours.
Time to peak effect—Diuretic: 6 hours.
Duration of action—Diuretic: Up to 24 hours.
Laboratory value alterations:
May produce false-negative results in phentolamine, phenolsulfonphthalein, and tyramine tests.

Oral Dosage Forms
Note: Bracketed uses in the *Dosage Forms* section refer to categories of use and/or indications that are not included in U.S. product labeling.

TRICHLORMETHIAZIDE TABLETS USP

Usual adult dose
Diuretic or
[Antidiuretic (central or nephrogenic diabetes insipidus)]—
Oral, 1 to 4 mg once a day, once every other day, or once a day for three to five days a week.
Antihypertensive—
Oral, 2 to 4 mg once a day, the dosage being adjusted according to response.

Note: Geriatric patients may be more sensitive to the effects of the usual adult dose.

Usual pediatric dose
For children over 6 months of age—Oral, 70 mcg (0.07 mg) per kg of body weight or 2 mg per square meter of body surface per day, as a single dose or in two divided daily doses, the dosage being adjusted according to response.

Strength(s) usually available
U.S.—
2 mg (Rx) [*Metahydrin; Naqua* (scored); GENERIC].
4 mg (Rx) [*Metahydrin; Naqua* (scored); *Trichlorex;* GENERIC].
Canada—
Not commercially available.

Packaging and storage
Store below 40 °C (104 °F), preferably between 15 and 30 °C (59 and 86 °F), unless otherwise specified by manufacturer. Store in a tight container.

Auxiliary labeling
- Avoid overexposure to the sun or use of sunlamp.
- Do not take other medicines without your doctor's advice.

Note
Check refill frequency to determine compliance in hypertensive patients.

Selected Bibliography
The fifth report of the Joint National Committee on Detection, Evaluation, and Treatment of High Blood Pressure (JNC V). Arch Intern Med 1993; 153(2): 154-83.

Freis ED. The cardiovascular risks of thiazide diuretics. Clin Pharmacol Ther 1986 Mar; 39: 239-44.

Brater DC. Clinical use of thiazide diuretics. Hosp Form 1983; 18: 788-93.

Revised: 07/01/1998

DIVALPROEX—See *Valproic Acid (Systemic)*

DOBUTAMINE—See *Sympathomimetic Agents—Cardiovascular Use (Parenteral-Systemic)*

DOCETAXEL Systemic

VA CLASSIFICATION (Primary): AN900

Commonly used brand name(s): *Taxotere*.

Note: For a listing of dosage forms and brand names by country availability, see *Dosage Forms* section(s).

Category
Antineoplastic.

Indications
Note: Bracketed information in the *Indications* section refers to uses that are not included in U.S. product labeling.

Accepted
Carcinoma, breast (treatment)—Docetaxel is indicated for treatment of locally advanced or metastatic breast cancer after failure of first-line or subsequent chemotherapy. [Docetaxel is also accepted as first-line chemotherapy for locally advanced or metastatic breast cancer, based on reports of objective tumor response rates (mostly partial but some complete) in phase II clinical trials.][1]

Carcinoma, breast, node–positive (treatment adjunct)—Docetaxel in combination with doxorubicin and cyclophosphamide is indicated for the adjuvant treatment of patients with operable node-positive breast cancer.

Carcinomas, gastric (treatment)—Docetaxel in combination with cisplatin and fluorouracil is indicated for the treatment of patients with advanced gastric adenocarcinoma, including adenocarcinoma of the gastroesophageal junction, who have not received prior chemotherapy for advanced disease.

Carcinoma, lung, non-small cell (treatment)—Docetaxel is indicated for treatment of locally advanced or metastatic non-small cell lung carcinoma after platinum-based chemotherapy has failed. [It is also accepted as first-line treatment for non-small cell lung carcinoma, based on reports of objective tumor response rates in phase II clinical trials.][1] Docetaxel in combination with cisplatin is indicated for the treatment of patients with unresectable, locally advanced or metastatic non-small cell lung cancer who have not previously received chemotherapy for this condition.

Carcinoma, prostate (treatment)—Docetaxel in combination with prednisone is indicated for the treatment of patients with androgen independent (hormone refractory) metastatic prostate cancer

[Carcinomas, esophageal (treatment)][1]—Docetaxel is indicated, alone or in combination with other agents, for the treatment of advanced and/or metastatic esophageal carcinomas, including adenocarcinomas and squamous cell carcinomas.

[Carcinoma, lung, small cell (treatment)][1]—Docetaxel is accepted for treatment of small-cell lung carcinoma after first-line chemotherapy has failed, based on reports of objective tumor response rates in phase II clinical trials.

[Carcinoma, ovarian (treatment)][1]—Docetaxel is accepted for treatment of ovarian carcinoma after prior platinum-based therapy has failed, based on reports of objective tumor response rates in phase II clinical trials.

[Carcinoma, head and neck (treatment)][1]—Docetaxel is indicated, alone or in combination with other chemotherapeutic agents, as reasonable medical therapy at some point in the management of patients with advanced, recurrent, or metastatic head and neck carcinoma (Evidence rating: IIID).

[Carcinoma, bladder (treatment)][1]—Docetaxel is indicated, alone or in combination with other chemotherapeutic agents, as reasonable medical therapy at some point in the management of patients with bladder (urothelial) carcinoma.

Acceptance not established
Use of docetaxel for the treatment of pancreatic carcinoma has not been established, due to insufficient data supporting efficacy. Data is needed showing superiority of gemcitabine in combination with docetaxel vs. gemcitabine alone. Single-agent comparison data to gemcitabine or efficacy data in gemcitabine- or 5–FU-refractory population is needed.

Use of docetaxel for the treatment of malignant melanoma has not been established, due to insufficient data supporting efficacy as a single agent and an undefined role in combination chemotherapy.

[1]Not included in Canadian product labeling.

Pharmacology/Pharmacokinetics

Physicochemical characteristics
Source—Semisynthetic, starting with a precursor extracted from the needles of the European yew, *Taxus baccata*.

Chemical group—Docetaxel is a member of the taxoid family; chemically related to paclitaxel.

Molecular weight—861.94.

Solubility—Practically insoluble in water; highly lipophilic..

Mechanism of action/Effect
Docetaxel is an antimitotic agent. It binds to free tubulin, then promotes the polymerization of tubulin into stable microtubules and inhibits microtubule disassembly, resulting in blockade of cellular mitotic and interphase functions and, consequently, in inhibition of cell division. Unlike paclitaxel and other spindle poisons in clinical use, docetaxel does not alter the number of protofilaments in the bound microtubules.

The mechanisms by which resistance to docetaxel occurs are not completely understood. Studies have shown that docetaxel is active against several tumor cell lines overexpressing the multidrug resistance gene. Also, cross-resistance between docetaxel and paclitaxel does not occur consistently.

Other actions/effects
Several *in vitro* and *in vivo* studies have shown that docetaxel has only moderate immunosuppressive activity.

Distribution
Volume of distribution at steady-state—Mean, 113 liters (L).

In animal studies, docetaxel was widely distributed to all tissues and organs other than the brain, in which very low concentrations were attained.

Protein binding
Very high (97%), primarily to alpha$_1$-acid glycoprotein, albumin, and lipoproteins.

Biotransformation
Hepatic; extensively metabolized by cytochrome P450 subfamily 3A (CYP 3A) isoenzymes to one major and three minor metabolites.

Half-life
Dose-dependent. Doses of 70 mg per square meter of body surface area (mg/m^2) or higher produce a triphasic elimination profile. With lower doses, assay limitations precluded detection of the terminal elimination phase.

Alpha (distribution)—
4 minutes.

Beta—
36 minutes.

Gamma (terminal)—
11.1 hours. The prolonged terminal elimination half-life is caused, in part, by relatively slow efflux from the peripheral compartment.

Note: A preliminary study in pediatric patients receiving 55 mg/m^2 of docetaxel reported bi-exponential elimination and a terminal half-life of 2.4 ± 1.8 hours.

Peak serum concentration
2.57 to 3.67 mcg per mL (mcg/mL), with doses of 70 to 100 mg/m².

Note: The area under the docetaxel concentration-time curve (AUC) is 3.13 to 4.83 mcg/mL per hour with doses of 70 to 100 mg/m². Values may be increased in patients with hepatic function impairment.

Elimination
Primarily biliary/fecal. Following administration of radiolabeled docetaxel, fecal and urinary recovery over the next 7 days accounted for approximately 75% and 6%, respectively, of the administered radioactivity. Approximately 80% of the radioactivity that appeared in the feces was excreted during the first 2 days as one major and three minor metabolites; < 8% was unchanged docetaxel.

Total body clearance is approximately 21 L per hour per square meter of body surface area (L/hr/m²) and is not dose-dependent. Values are decreased by an average of 27 to 30%, but with substantial interpatient variability, in patients with hepatic function test abnormalities suggestive of mild to moderate hepatic function impairment.

Note: In a preliminary study in pediatric patients, total body clearance was approximately 9.3 L/hr/m².

Precautions to Consider

Cross-sensitivity and/or related problems
Patients hypersensitive to paclitaxel may be hypersensitive to docetaxel also.

Carcinogenicity
Carcinogenicity studies in animals have not been done.

Secondary malignancies are potential delayed effects of many antineoplastic agents, although it is not clear whether the effect is related to their mutagenic or immunosuppressive action. The effect of dose and duration of therapy is also unknown, although the risk seems to increase with long-term use. The risk of secondary malignancies developing after docetaxel therapy is not known.

Treatment-related acute myeloid leukemia is known to occur in patients treated with cyclophosphamide and/or anthracyclines for adjuvant breast cancer therapy.

Mutagenicity
Docetaxel was clastogenic in the *in vitro* chromosome aberration test in Chinese hamster ovary K_1 cells and in the *in vivo* mouse micronucleus test. No mutagenicity was observed in the Ames test or the Chinese hamster ovary/hypoxanthine-guanine phosphoribosyltransferase gene mutation assay.

Pregnancy/Reproduction
Fertility—Decrease in testicular weight, but no overt impairment of fertility, occurred in rats given multiple doses of up to 0.3 mg per kg of body weight (mg/kg) intravenously (approximately one-fiftieth the recommended human dose on a mg per square meter of body surface area [mg/m²] basis). Testicular atrophy or degeneration also occurred in a 10-cycle study (in which the medication was given intravenously at 21-day intervals for 6 months) in rats given 5 mg/kg and dogs given 0.375 mg/kg (approximately one-third and one-fifteenth the recommended human dose on a mg/m² basis, respectively). Similar effects also occurred in rats given lower doses at an increased frequency of administration.

Pregnancy—Adequate and well-controlled studies have not been done in humans.

It is usually recommended that use of antineoplastics, especially combination chemotherapy, be avoided whenever possible, especially during the first trimester. Although information is limited because of the relatively few instances of antineoplastic administration during pregnancy, the mutagenic, teratogenic, and carcinogenic potential of these medications must be considered.

Other hazards to the fetus include adverse reactions seen in adults.

In general, use of contraception is recommended during cytotoxic drug therapy.

Animal studies have shown that docetaxel is distributed to the fetus. Maternal toxicity resulting in embryo- and fetotoxicity occurred in rats given 0.3 mg/kg or more per day and in rabbits given 0.03 mg/kg or more per day (equivalent to or higher than one-fiftieth and one-three hundredth, respectively, the maximum recommended human dose on a mg/m² basis) during the period of organogenesis. Embryotoxic and fetotoxic effects were characterized by increased intrauterine deaths, increased resorptions, decreased fetal weights, and delayed fetal ossification. However, no teratogenicity was apparent in rats and rabbits given doses of 1.8 and 1.2 mg/kg per day, respectively.

FDA Pregnancy Category D.

Breast-feeding
Although very little information is available regarding distribution of antineoplastic agents into breast milk, breast-feeding is not recommended during chemotherapy because of the potential risks to the infant (adverse effects, mutagenicity, carcinogenicity). Due to these potential risks, mothers should discontinue nursing prior to taking docetaxel.

Pediatrics
Docetaxel has been studied in a limited number of children with refractory cancer. Dose-ranging studies have shown the maximum tolerated dose to be lower in pediatric patients (especially if treated with several prior courses of chemotherapy) than in adults, unless a colony-stimulating factor is used to reduce the occurrence of severe neutropenia. However, safety and efficacy in pediatric patients have not been established.

Geriatrics
A greater frequency of some adverse effects, including infections, has been observed in appropriate studies of docetaxel in combination with cisplatin and with carboplatin in patients greater than 65 years of age. Dose selection for an elderly patient should be cautious, reflecting the greater frequency of decreased hepatic, renal, or cardiac function and of concomitant disease or other drug therapy in elderly patients.

No information is available on the relationship of age to the effects of docetaxel in geriatric patients for combination use with doxorubicin and cyclophosphamide in the adjuvant treatment of breast cancer. Differences in safety and efficacy between elderly and younger patients were not determined.

Pharmacogenetics
A pharmacokinetic study showed no significant differences in total body clearance of docetaxel between Japanese patients and American or European patients.

Dental
Docetaxel commonly causes neutropenia, and, less commonly, thrombocytopenia, which may result in an increased incidence of microbial infection, delayed healing, and gingival bleeding. If severe neutropenia occurs, dental work should be deferred until blood counts have returned to normal. Also, patients should be instructed in proper oral hygiene, including caution in use of regular toothbrushes, dental floss, and toothpicks.

Docetaxel commonly causes stomatitis (ulceration of the lips, tongue, and oral cavity), which is usually mild but in some patients may be severe. There is some evidence that severe stomatitis tends to occur at the nadir of the neutrophil count and may contribute to the occurrence of neutropenic fever by providing an entry for pathogens into the body.

Drug interactions and/or related problems
The following drug interactions and/or related problems have been selected on the basis of their potential clinical significance (possible mechanism in parentheses where appropriate)—not necessarily inclusive (» = major clinical significance):

Note: Combinations containing any of the following medications, depending on the amount present, may also interact with this medication.

Blood dyscrasia-causing medications (see *Appendix II*)
(leukopenic and/or thrombocytopenic effects of docetaxel may be increased with concurrent or recent therapy if these medications cause the same effects; dosage adjustment of docetaxel, if necessary, should be based on blood counts)

» Bone marrow depressants, other (see *Appendix II*) or
Radiation therapy
(additive bone marrow depression may occur; dosage reduction may be required when two or more bone marrow depressants, including radiation, are used concurrently or consecutively)

» Enzyme inhibitors, hepatic, of the cytochrome P450 3A (CYP 3A) isoenzyme, such as:
Erythromycin
Ketoconazole
Midazolam
Orphenadrine
Testosterone
Troleandomycin
(caution in concurrent use is recommended because *in vitro* studies have shown that inhibitors of the CYP 3A isoenzyme [but not inhibitors of other cytochrome P450 isoenzymes] significantly inhibit docetaxel metabolism)

» Immunosuppressants, other, such as:
Azathioprine
Chlorambucil
Corticosteroids, glucocorticoid

Cyclophosphamide
Cyclosporine
Mercaptopurine
Muromonab CD-3
Tacrolimus
(concurrent use with docetaxel may increase the risk of infection)

Paclitaxel and
Other medications metabolized by the CYP 3A isoenzyme
(*in vitro* studies have shown that paclitaxel, which is partially metabolized by the CYP 3A isoenzyme, significantly inhibits docetaxel metabolism; also, docetaxel inhibits formation of the minor paclitaxel metabolite M4 via CYP 3A [but not formation of the major paclitaxel metabolite M5 via the cytochrome P450 2C isoenzyme]. The possibility should be considered that other medications that are metabolized by the CYP 3A isoenzyme may also alter docetaxel metabolism)

Vaccines, killed virus
(because normal defense mechanisms may be suppressed by docetaxel therapy, the patient's antibody response to the vaccine may be decreased. The interval between discontinuation of medications that cause immunosuppression and restoration of the patient's ability to respond to the vaccine depends on the intensity and type of immunosuppression-causing medication used, the underlying disease, and other factors; estimates vary from 3 months to 1 year)

» Vaccines, live virus
(because normal defense mechanisms may be suppressed by docetaxel therapy, concurrent use with a live virus vaccine may potentiate the replication of the vaccine virus, may increase the side/adverse effects of the vaccine virus, and/or may decrease the patient's antibody response to the vaccine; immunization of these patients should be undertaken only with extreme caution after careful review of the patient's hematologic status and only with the knowledge and consent of the physician managing the docetaxel therapy. The interval between discontinuation of medications that cause immunosuppression and restoration of the patient's ability to respond to the vaccine depends on the intensity and type of immunosuppression-causing medication used, the underlying disease, and other factors; estimates vary from 3 months to 1 year. In addition, immunization with oral poliovirus vaccine should be postponed in persons in close contact with the patient, especially family members)

Laboratory value alterations

The following have been selected on the basis of their potential clinical significance (possible effect in parentheses where appropriate)—not necessarily inclusive (» = major clinical significance).

With physiology/laboratory test values

Alanine aminotransferase (ALT [SGPT]) and
Alkaline phosphatase and
Aspartate aminotransferase (AST [SGOT]) and
Bilirubin concentrations, serum
(values may be increased; in clinical trials, bilirubin concentrations higher than the upper limit of normal, aminotransferase values > 1.5 times the upper limit of normal, alkaline phosphatase values > 2.5 times the upper limit of normal, and concomitant increases in aminotransferase and alkaline phosphatase values occurred in approximately 9%, 18%, 7.5%, and 4.5% of patients with normal pretreatment values, respectively. However, whether these changes were caused by docetaxel or the underlying disease has not been established)

Hematocrit/hemoglobin values and
Leukocyte, especially neutrophil, count and
Platelet count
(may be decreased; the neutrophil count usually reaches a nadir at a median of 8 days after a treatment and generally returns to pretreatment or near-pretreatment values within the next 1 or 2 weeks)

Medical considerations/Contraindications

The medical considerations/contraindications included have been selected on the basis of their potential clinical significance (reasons given in parentheses where appropriate)—not necessarily inclusive (» = major clinical significance).

Except under special circumstances, this medication should not be used when the following medical problem exists:

» Hepatic function impairment
(docetaxel clearance will be decreased, resulting in an increased risk of toxic effects, including severe stomatitis, dermatological reactions, and thrombocytopenia as well as severe neutropenia, febrile neutropenia, infections, and toxic death, even if dosage is decreased. Docetaxel is therefore not recommended for patients with hepatic function impairment, especially if bilirubin concentrations are elevated or when transaminase values are > 1.5 times the upper limit of normal and alkaline phosphatase values are > 2.5 times the upper limit of normal. If docetaxel is considered essential for a patient with mild hepatic function impairment, extreme caution and lower doses are recommended)

» Hypersensitivity reaction, severe, history of, to docetaxel, paclitaxel, or other medications formulated with polysorbate 80

Risk-benefit should be considered when the following medical problems exist:

Alcohol abuse or history of
(risk of severe neurotoxic reactions to docetaxel may be increased)

» Bone marrow depression
(will be exacerbated; treatment should be delayed until the neutrophil count recovers to > 1500 cells per cubic millimeter and the platelet count returns to > 100,000 cells per cubic millimeter)

» Chickenpox, existing or recent (including recent exposure) or
» Herpes zoster
(risk of severe, generalized disease)

Conditions that may predispose to pleural effusion, such as:
Chest radiotherapy, prior or
» Pleural effusion, pre-existing or
Pleural tumor or
Thoracotomy, prior
(increased risk of pleural effusion associated with docetaxel-induced fluid retention)

» Infection, pre-existing
(recovery may be impaired)

» Previous cytotoxic drug therapy
(associated with increased treatment-related mortality in locally advanced or metastatic non-small cell lung cancer patients)

Patient monitoring

The following may be especially important in patient monitoring (other tests may be warranted in some patients, depending on condition; » = major clinical significance):

» Alanine aminotransferase (ALT [SGPT]) values and
» Alkaline phosphatase values and
» Aspartate aminotransferase (AST [SGOT]) values and
» Total bilirubin concentrations, serum
(recommended prior to each treatment cycle; it is recommended that docetaxel not be given if abnormalities indicative of hepatic function impairment are present [e.g., bilirubin concentrations higher than the upper limit of normal or transaminase values > 1.5 times the upper limit of normal and alkaline phosphatase values > 2.5 times the upper limit of normal])

Hematocrit or hemoglobin and
» Leukocyte count, total and differential and
Platelet count
(determinations recommended prior to initiation of therapy and at frequent intervals during therapy; administration of docetaxel should be delayed if the neutrophil count is lower than 1500 cells per cubic millimeter and/or the platelet count is lower than 100,000 cells per cubic millimeter. If severe neutropenia [fewer than 500 cells per cubic millimeter] persists for 7 days or more, a reduction in dose is recommended for subsequent courses of therapy)

» Skin appearance and
» Vital signs
(should be monitored during, and for approximately 1 hour following, an infusion, especially during the first two treatment cycles, to detect signs of a severe hypersensitivity reaction, e.g., dyspnea, hypotension, generalized urticaria, or other signs of angioedema)

Side/Adverse Effects

Note: Many "side effects" of antineoplastic therapy are unavoidable and represent the medication's pharmacologic action. Some of these (for example, leukopenia and thrombocytopenia) are actually used as parameters to aid in individual dosage titration.

Bone marrow depression (primarily neutropenia) is the major dose-limiting toxicity.

Significant endocrine, hepatic, or renal toxicity clearly attributable to docetaxel has not been reported.

The following adverse events were reported in patients with prostate cancer being treated with combination docetaxel/prednisone therapy: anemia, neutropenia, thrombocytopenia, febrile neutropenia, infection, epistaxis, allergic reactions, fluid retention, weight gain, peripheral edema, neuropathy sensory, neuropathy motor, rash/desquamation, alopecia, nail changes, nausea, diarrhea, stomatitis/pharyngitis, taste disturbance, vomiting, anorexia, cough, dyspnea, cardiac left ventricular function, fatigue, myalgia, tearing, and arthralgia.

Note: The following adverse events were reported in patients being treated with combination docetaxel/doxorubicin/cyclophosphamide therapy in the adjuvant treatment of breast cancer (regardless of causality): anemia, neutropenia, fever in absence of infection, infection, thrombocytopenia, febrile neutropenia, neutropenic infection, hypersensitivity reactions, lymphedema, fluid retention (peripheral edema and weight gain), neuropathy sensory, neurocortical, neuropathy motor, neuro-cerebellar, syncope, alopecia, skin toxicity, nail disorders, nausea, stomatitis, vomiting, diarrhea, constipation, taste perversion, anorexia, abdominal pain, amenorrhea, cough, cardiac dysrhythmias, vasodilatation, hypotension, phlebitis, asthenia, myalgia, arthralgia, lacrimation disorder, conjunctivitis.

Gastrointestinal events reported with combination therapy include colitis, enteritis, and large intestine perforation. Cardiovascular events reported include dysrhythmia, hypotension, and congestive heart failure. One patient in each arm of the study died due to heart failure.

Treatment-related acute myeloid leukemia [AML] is known to occur in patients treated with anthracyclines and/or cyclophosphamide, including use in adjuvant therapy for breast cancer. AML occurs at a higher frequency when these agents are given in combination with radiation therapy. Risk of AML is comparable to risk observed for other anthracyclines/cyclophosphamide containing adjuvant breast chemotherapy regimens.

The following side/adverse effects have been selected on the basis of their potential clinical significance (possible signs and symptoms in parentheses where appropriate)—not necessarily inclusive:

Those indicating need for medical attention

Incidence more frequent (> 30%)

Anemia (unusual tiredness or weakness); ***fever***—not always associated with infection; ***fluid retention*** (more commonly, swelling of fingers, hands, feet, or lower legs; less commonly, swelling of abdomen or face; noisy, rattling breathing or troubled breathing while at rest; weight gain); ***leukopenia or neutropenia***—usually asymptomatic

Note: Although *anemia* occurs very frequently, severe anemia (hemoglobin < 8 grams per deciliter) is relatively infrequent in patients with normal hepatic function. However, the incidence of severe anemia is significantly increased in patients with mild to moderate hepatic function impairment.

Fluid retention usually begins in the lower extremities, but may become generalized and, less frequently, lead to pleural effusions, pericardial effusions, or ascites. Prophylactic corticosteroid administration decreases the incidence and severity of this complication and increases the median cumulative dose at which moderate or severe edema occurs (from 400 to 705 [mg/m^2]). However, even with recommended prophylaxis, docetaxel causes fluid retention in almost 50% of patients with normal hepatic function; moderate or severe fluid retention requiring medical treatment occurs in approximately 17% and 6%, respectively, of these patients. The incidence and severity of fluid retention are significantly higher in patients with hepatic function impairment. Fluid accumulation is due to increased capillary permeability rather than hypoalbuminemia or cardiac, hepatic, or renal damage. Fluid retention is slowly reversible after treatment is discontinued (median 29 [range, 0 to > 42] weeks to complete reversal).

Leukopenia and *neutropenia* occur in > 96% of patients receiving docetaxel; severe neutropenia (neutrophil count below 500 cells per cubic millimeter) is also very common. In most patients, the neutropenia is reversible, noncumulative, and short-lasting. The nadir of the neutrophil count usually occurs 8 days after an infusion. The median duration of severe neutropenia is 7 days, and neutrophil counts usually return to pretreatment or near-pretreatment values in 1 to 2 weeks. *Febrile neutropenia* (severe neutropenia with fever > 38 °C [100.4 °F] and infection requiring intravenous antibiotic therapy and/or hospitalization) occurs less frequently, and deaths due to sepsis are uncommon, in patients with normal hepatic function. Hepatic function impairment significantly increases the risk of severe neutropenia, febrile neutropenia, and septic deaths.

Incidence less frequent (5 to 29%)

Allergic reaction (cough; difficulty swallowing; dizziness; fast heartbeat; hives, itching, puffiness or swelling of the eyelids or around the eyes, face, lips or tongue; shortness of breath; skin rash; tightness in chest; unusual tiredness or weakness; wheezing); ***cardiac left ventricular function; cutaneous reaction, severe*** (red, scaly, swollen, or peeling areas of skin)—especially likely to occur on the hands and/or feet; ***dyspnea*** (shortness of breath; difficult or labored breathing; tightness in chest; wheezing); ***febrile neutropenia or other infection*** (fever with or without chills; cough or hoarseness; difficult or painful urination; lower back or side pain); ***hypersensitivity reaction, mild*** (back pain; flushing; skin rash or itching, localized; troubled breathing, mild); ***thrombocytopenia*** (rarely, unusual bleeding or bruising; black, tarry stools; blood in urine or stools; pinpoint red spots on skin)—usually asymptomatic

Note: *Infections* have also been reported in the absence of *febrile neutropenia* with single agent and combination dosing of docetaxel with doxorubicin and cyclophosphamide. Fever in the absence of infection has also been reported with combination docetaxel/doxorubicin/cyclophosphamide therapy.

Fatalities have occurred with docetaxel therapy at doses of 100 mg/m^2 (34 of 1435 patients with normal liver function and 6 of 55 patients with hepatic function impairment) and doses of 60 mg/m^2 (3 of 481 patients with normal liver function and 3 of 7 patients with hepatic function impairment). Most of the fatalities resulted from sepsis associated with *neutropenia*.

Hypersensitivity reactions are most likely to occur during the first two cycles of docetaxel treatment, generally within the first few minutes after the infusion is started. Signs and symptoms usually abate within 15 minutes after the infusion is stopped. After a mild reaction, treatment can usually be reinstituted without further difficulty. However, if a severe reaction (characterized by angioedema, hypotension, bronchospasm, and/or generalized erythema, urticaria, or skin rash) occurs, the infusion should be discontinued immediately and aggressive treatment instituted.

Incidence rare (< 5%)

Cardiovascular effects, including angina, unstable (chest pain); ***arrhythmia, such as sinus tachycardia, atrial flutter, or paroxysmal atrial tachycardia*** (fast or irregular heartbeat); ***heart failure*** (shortness of breath; swelling of face, fingers, feet, or lower legs); ***hypertension*** (increase in blood pressure; dizziness; headaches); ***and hypotension*** (dizziness; fainting)—usually asymptomatic; ***hypersensitivity reaction, severe*** (decrease in blood pressure, sudden and severe; shortness of breath, troubled breathing, tightness in chest, or wheezing; hives, skin rash, or redness, generalized)

Incidence not determined—Observed during clinical practice; estimates of frequency can not be determined

Acute pulmonary edema (chest pain; difficult, fast, noisy breathing, sometimes with wheezing; blue lips and fingernails; pale skin; increased sweating; coughing that sometimes produces a pink frothy sputum; shortness of breath; swelling in legs and ankles); ***acute respiratory distress syndrome*** (blue lips, fingernails, or skin; difficult or fast breathing); ***atrial fibrillation*** (fast or irregular heartbeat; dizziness; fainting); ***bleeding episode; chest pain; colitis*** (stomach cramps, tenderness, or pain; watery or bloody diarrhea; fever); ***deep vein thrombosis*** (pain, redness, or swelling in arm or leg); ***dyspnea*** (shortness of breath; difficult or labored breathing; tightness in chest; wheezing); ***ECG abnormalities; erythema multiforme*** (blistering, peeling, loosening of skin; chills; cough; diarrhea; fever; itching; joint or muscle pain; red irritated eyes; sore throat; sores, ulcers, or white spots in mouth or on lips; unusual tiredness or weakness); ***esophagitis*** (difficulty in swallowing; pain or burning in throat; chest pain; heartburn; vomiting; sores, ulcers, or white spots on lips or tongue or inside the mouth); ***gastrointestinal hemorrhage*** (black, tarry stools; bloody stools; vomiting of blood or material that looks like coffee grounds); ***gastrointestinal perforation*** (severe pain in abdomen; fever; nausea; vomiting); ***hepatitis*** (dark urine; general tiredness and weakness; light-colored stools; nausea and vomiting; upper right abdominal pain; yellow eyes and skin); ***ileus*** (abdominal pain; severe constipation; severe vomiting); ***interstitial pneumonia*** (cough; difficult breathing; fever; shortness of breath); ***intestinal obstruction*** (abdominal pain; severe constipation; nausea; vomiting); ***ischemic colitis*** (abdominal pain and tenderness; bloody stools; rectal bleeding); ***myocardial infarction*** (chest pain or discomfort; pain or discomfort in arms, jaw, back or neck; shortness of breath; nausea; sweating; vomiting); ***neutropenic enterocolitis*** (abdominal pain, cramping, or tenderness; diarrhea; vomitingl nausea; fever; chills; muscle pain); ***pulmonary embolism*** (anxiety; chest pain; cough; fainting; fast heartbeat; sudden shortness of breath or troubled breathing; dizziness or lightheadedness); ***pulmonary fibrosis*** (fever; troubled or quick, shallow breathing; unusual tiredness or weakness; loss of appetite and weight; chest discomfort); ***renal insufficiency*** (lower back/side pain; decreased frequency /amount of urine; bloody urine; increased thirst; loss of appetite; nausea; vomiting; unusual tiredness or weakness; swelling of face, fingers, lower legs; weight gain; troubled breathing; increased blood pressure); ***seizures*** (convulsions; muscle spasm or jerking of all extremities; sudden loss of consciousness; loss of bladder control); ***severe hand and foot syndrome*** (blistering, peeling, redness, and/or swelling of palms of hands or bottoms of feet; numbness, pain, tingling, or unusual sensations in palms of hands or bottoms of feet); ***Stevens-Johnson syndrome*** (blistering, peeling, loosening of skin; chills; cough; diarrhea; itching; joint or muscle pain; red irritated eyes; red skin lesions, often with a purple center; sore throat; sores, ulcers, or white spots in mouth or on lips; unusual tiredness or weakness); ***syncope*** (fainting); ***thrombophlebitis*** (changes in skin color; pain, tenderness, swelling of foot or leg); ***toxic epidermal necrolysis*** (blistering, peeling, loosening of skin; chills; cough; diarrhea; itching; joint or muscle pain; red irritated eyes; red skin lesions, often with a purple center; sore throat; sores, ulcers, or white spots in mouth or on lips; unusual tiredness or weakness); ***transient loss of consciousness; transient visual disturbances*** (blurred or loss of vision; disturbed color perception; night blindness; double vision; tunnel vision; halos around lights; overbright appearance of lights)—in association with hypersensitivity reaction

Those indicating need for medical attention only if they continue or are bothersome

Incidence more frequent (> 30%)

Cutaneous reaction, mild (skin rash or redness); ***diarrhea; nausea; neurologic effects, including asthenia*** (weakness); ***and paresthesias or dysesthesias*** (burning, numbness, tingling, or painful sensations); ***stomatitis*** (sores or ulcers on lips or tongue or inside the mouth)

Note: Rarely, *neurologic effects* may result in moderate to severe neuropathy, leading to decreased dexterity and/or disturbances in gait, usually after cumulative doses of 600 mg/m^2 have been given.

Severe *stomatitis* may contribute to the occurrence of febrile neutropenia by providing a portal for entry of pathogens into the body.

Incidence less frequent (5 to 29%)

Arthralgias or myalgias (pain in joints or muscles); ***cough; epistaxis*** (bloody nose); ***fatigue*** (unusual tiredness or weakness); ***headache; infusion site reactions*** (dry, red, hot, or irritated skin; pain; or swelling or lump under the skin at place of injection); ***nail disorder*** (discoloration of fingernails or toenails; rarely, loosening or loss of nails and pain); ***peripheral edema*** (swelling of hands, ankles, feet, or lower legs); ***pharyngitis*** (body aches or pain; congestion; cough; dryness or soreness of throat; fever; hoarseness; runny nose; tender, swollen glands in neck; trouble in swallowing; voice changes); ***vomiting***

Incidence not determined—Observed during clinical practice; estimates of frequency can not be determined

Abdominal pain (stomach pain); ***anorexia*** (loss of appetite; weight loss); ***confusion*** (mood or mental changes); ***conjunctivitis*** (redness, pain, swelling of eye, eyelid, or inner lining of eyelid; burning, dry or itching eyes; discharge; excessive tearing); ***constipation*** (difficulty having a bowel movement [stool]); ***dehydration*** (confusion; decreased urination; dizziness; dry mouth; fainting; increase in heart rate; lightheadedness; rapid breathing; sunken eyes; thirst; unusual tiredness or weakness; wrinkled skin); ***diffuse pain*** (pain all over body); ***duodenal ulcer*** (burning upper abdominal pain; loss of appetite; nausea; vomiting); ***excessive tearing; lacrimation with or without conjunctivitis*** (tearing of the eyes); ***radiation recall phenomenon*** (pain and redness of skin at place of earlier radiation treatment)

Those not indicating need for medical attention

Incidence more frequent

Alopecia (loss of hair)—occurs in 80% of patients, but is fully reversible after therapy has ended

Overdose

For more information on the management of overdose or unintentional ingestion, **contact a poison control center** (see *Poison Control Center Listing*).

Clinical effects of overdose

The following effects have been selected on the basis of their potential clinical significance (possible signs and symptoms in parentheses where appropriate)—not necessarily inclusive:

Acute and chronic

Bone marrow suppression, including anemia (unusual tiredness or weakness); ***leukopenia or neutropenia, with or without infection*** (fever with or without chills; cough or hoarseness; lower back or side pain; painful or difficult urination); ***and/or thrombocytopenia*** (black, tarry stools; blood in urine or stools; pinpoint red spots on skin; unusual bleeding or bruising); ***stomatitis*** (sores or ulcers on lips or tongue or inside the mouth); ***peripheral neuropathy*** (burning, numbness, tingling, or painful sensations; weakness in arms, hands, legs, or feet)

Treatment of overdose

It is recommended that the patient be hospitalized for close monitoring of vital functions and treatment of observed effects. Therapeutic G-CSF should be given as soon as possible after discovery of overdose. Other appropriate symptomatic measures should be taken, as needed. Severe bone marrow depression may require transfusion of required blood components. Febrile neutropenia should be treated empirically with broad-spectrum antibiotics, pending bacterial cultures and appropriate diagnostic tests.

Patient Consultation

As an aid to patient consultation, refer to *Advice for the Patient, Docetaxel (Systemic)*.

In providing consultation, consider emphasizing the following selected information (» = major clinical significance):

Before using this medication

» Conditions affecting use, especially:

Hypersensitivity to docetaxel, paclitaxel, or polysorbate 80

Pregnancy—Should not be used because of embryotoxic, fetotoxic, and carcinogenic potential; advisability of using contraception; informing physician immediately if pregnancy is suspected

Breast-feeding—Not recommended because of potential serious adverse effects

Use in the elderly—Dose selection for an elderly patient should be cautious, reflecting the greater frequency of decreased hepatic, renal, or cardiac function and of concomitant disease or other drug therapy in elderly patients.

Other medications, especially other bone marrow depressants, other immunosuppressants, inhibitors of the cytochrome P450 3A isoenzyme, such as erythromycin, ketoconazole, midazolam, orphenadrine, testosterone, and troleandomycin, and radiation therapy

Other medical problems, especially hepatic function impairment, history of severe hypersensitivity reaction to docetaxel, chickenpox, herpes zoster, infection, pleural effusion, or previous drug or radiation therapy

Proper use of this medication

Frequency of nausea and vomiting and/or neuropathy; importance of continuing treatment despite feeling ill

» Importance of compliance with peritreatment corticosteroid regimen

» Proper dosing

Precautions while using this medication

» Importance of close monitoring by the physician

» Avoiding immunizations unless approved by physician; other persons in patient's household should avoid immunizations with oral poliovirus vaccine; avoiding other persons who have taken oral poliovirus vaccine or wearing a protective mask that covers nose and mouth

Caution if bone marrow depression occurs:

» Avoiding exposure to persons with infections, especially during periods of low blood cell counts; checking with physician immediately if fever with or without chills, cough or hoarseness, lower back or side pain, or painful or difficult urination occurs

» Checking with physician immediately if unusual bleeding or bruising; black, tarry stools; blood in urine or stools; or pinpoint red spots on skin occur

Caution in use of regular toothbrush, dental floss, or toothpick; physician, dentist, or nurse may suggest alternatives; checking with physician before having dental work done

Not touching eyes or inside of nose unless hands washed immediately before

Using caution to avoid accidental cuts when using sharp objects such as safety razor or fingernail or toenail cutters

Avoiding contact sports or other situations where bruising or injury could occur

Side/adverse effects

May cause adverse effects such as blood problems; importance of discussing possible effects with physician

Signs of potential side effects, especially anemia, fever, fluid retention, severe cutaneous reactions, febrile neutropenia, thrombocytopenia, and cardiovascular effects

Signs of potential side effects observed during clinical practice, especially acute pulmonary edema, acute respiratory distress syndrome, atrial fibrillation, bleeding episode, chest pain, colitis, deep vein thrombosis, dyspnea, ECG abnormalities, erythema multiforme, esophagitis, gastrointestinal hemorrhage, gastrointestinal perforation, hepatitis, ileus, interstitial pneumonia, intestinal obstruction, ischemic colitis, myocardial infarction, neutropenic enterocolitis, pulmonary embolism, pulmonary fibrosis, renal insufficiency, seizures, severe hand and foot syndrome, Stevens-Johnson syndrome, syncope, thrombophlebitis, toxic epidermal necrolysis, transient loss of consciousness, and transient visual disturbances

» Possibility of hypersensitivity; notifying physician or nurse immediately if back pain, breathing problems, or itching occurs during infusion; physician or nurse will monitor for other signs of allergic reaction and be prepared to institute treatment

Some side effects may be asymptomatic, including anemia, leukopenia or neutropenia, thrombocytopenia, and cardiovascular effects

Side effects have been reported in patients taking docetaxel/prednisone therapy for prostate cancer, including: allergic reactions, anemia, cardiac left ventricular function, dyspnea, febrile neutropenia, infection, neuropathy, neutropenia, and thrombocytopenia

Side effects have been reported in patients taking docetaxel/doxorubicin/cyclophosphamide therapy for adjuvant breast cancer treatment including: allergic reactions, anemia, colitis, cardiac dysrhythmias, congestive heart failure, dyspnea, enteritis, febrile neutropenia, hypotension, infection, large intestine perforation, neuropathy, neutropenia, and thrombocytopenia

(Treatment-related acute myeloid leukemia also known to occur in patients treated with cyclophosphamide and/or anthracyclines for adjuvant breast cancer therapy.)

Physician or nurse can help in dealing with side effects

Probability of hair loss; regrowth should return after treatment has ended

General Dosing Information

Docetaxel should be administered only under the supervision of a physician experienced in cancer chemotherapy. Adequate facilities and medications for diagnosis and treatment of complications should be readily available.

Peritreatment administration of an oral corticosteroid is recommended to decrease the frequency and severity and delay the onset of docetaxel-induced fluid retention. Aggressive, early diuretic treatment may also be required.

Peritreatment administration of an oral corticosteroid, with or without antihistamines (both H_1- and H_2-receptor antagonists), also reduces the severity of docetaxel-induced hypersensitivity reactions and cutaneous toxicity. A commonly used regimen consists of 8 mg of dexamethasone orally two times a day for 5 days, beginning 1 day before the docetaxel infusion; the antihistamines, if used, are given intravenously 30 minutes prior to the start of the docetaxel infusion. A recent study has shown that administering 8 mg of dexamethasone orally two times a day for only 3 days, beginning 1 day before the docetaxel infusion, is as effective as the 5-day regimen in reducing the severity of hypersensitivity reactions and fluid retention and also decreases the occurrence of severe stomatitis and infection. Palmar-plantar erythrodysesthesias that occur despite prophylaxis may respond to administration of 50 mg three times a day of pyridoxine.

For hormone-refractory metastatic prostate cancer, the pretreatment regimen is oral dexamethasone 8 milligrams at 12 hours, 3 hours, and 1 hour before the docetaxel infusion.

Docetaxel is not highly emetogenic; routine prophylaxis with antiemetics is generally not required.

Docetaxel is administered by intravenous infusion. *Docetaxel for injection concentrate must be diluted before use.* The needle or catheter should be properly positioned to prevent leakage into surrounding tissue, which may result in irritation, local tissue necrosis, and thrombophlebitis. If extravasation occurs, the infusion should be stopped immediately and the remainder of the dose administered into another vein.

Mild hypersensitivity reactions (flushing, localized skin reactions, back pain, fever, chills, mild dyspnea) do not require interruption of docetaxel therapy. However, severe reactions (angioedema, hypotension requiring treatment, severe dyspnea, bronchospasm, or generalized rash, urticaria, or erythema) require immediate discontinuation of the infusion and aggressive treatment. It is generally recommended that docetaxel not be readministered to patients who experience a severe hypersensitivity reaction despite adequate premedication. However, in patients with objective tumor responses and without other options to docetaxel therapy, re-treatment may be attempted with extreme caution and aggressive premedication by experienced practitioners. It is recommended that a slower rate of infusion be used. One patient who experienced major hypersensitivity symptoms during the first two cycles of docetaxel therapy despite prophylaxis with a corticosteroid and a histamine H_1-blocking antagonist was able to continue treatment without further difficulty after cromolyn (400 mg four times a day, orally, starting immediately after the second cycle) was added to the prophylactic regimen.

A reduction in subsequent doses is recommended for patients who develop severe neutropenia (neutrophil count $<$ 500 cells per cubic millimeter) that persists for 7 days or more, febrile neutropenia, severe (grade 4) infection, severe peripheral neuropathy, or severe or cumulative cutaneous reactions.

In adjuvant treatment of operable node-positive breast cancer, prophylactic G-CSF may be used to reduce risk of hematological toxicities.

Patients who develop leukopenia should be observed carefully for signs and symptoms of infection. Antibiotic support may be required. In neutropenic patients who develop fever, broad-spectrum antibiotic coverage should be initiated empirically, pending bacterial cultures and appropriate diagnostic tests.

Special precautions are recommended for patients who develop thrombocytopenia as a result of docetaxel therapy. These may include extreme care in performing invasive procedures; regular inspection of intravenous sites, skin (including perirectal area), and mucous membrane surfaces for signs of bleeding or bruising; testing urine, emesis, stool, and secretions for occult blood; care in use of regular toothbrushes, dental floss, toothpicks, safety razors, and fingernail and toenail cutters; avoiding constipation; and using caution to prevent falls and other injuries. Such patients should avoid alcohol and aspirin intake because of the risk of gastrointestinal bleeding. Platelet transfusions may be required.

Safety considerations for handling this medication

There is limited but increasing evidence and concern that personnel involved in preparation and administration of parenteral antineoplastics may be at some risk because of the potential mutagenicity, teratogenicity, and/or carcinogenicity of these agents, although the actual risk is unknown. USP advisory panels recommend cautious handling both in preparation and disposal of antineoplastic agents. Precautions that have been suggested include:

Use of a biological containment cabinet during reconstitution and dilution of parenteral medications and wearing of disposable surgical gloves and masks.

Use of proper technique to prevent contamination of the medication, work area, and operator during transfer between containers (including proper training of personnel in this technique).

Cautious and proper disposal of needles, syringes, vials, ampuls, and unused medication.

A number of medical centers and organizations have developed detailed guidelines for handling of antineoplastic agents.

If docetaxel comes into contact with the skin, the skin should be washed immediately and thoroughly with soap and water. If the medication comes into contact with a mucous membrane, the area should be immediately and thoroughly flushed with water.

Parenteral Dosage Forms

Note: Bracketed uses in the Dosage Forms section refer to categories of use and/or indications that are not included in U.S. product labeling.

DOCETAXEL FOR INJECTION CONCENTRATE

Usual adult dose

Carcinoma, breast—

Intravenous infusion, 60 to 100 mg per square meter of body surface area, administered as a one-hour infusion every three weeks.

Note: If patients initially receiving a dose of 100 mg per square meter of body surface area experience febrile neutropenia, neutrophil count $<$ 500 cells per cubic millimeter for more than 1 week, or severe or cumulative cutaneous reactions, the dose of docetaxel should be reduced to 75 mg per square meter of body surface area. Further reduction to 55 mg per square meter of body surface area or discontinuation of therapy should be considered if these reactions continue. Conversely, patients initially receiving 60 mg per square meter of body surface area who do not manifest the reactions listed above or severe peripheral neuropathy may tolerate higher doses. Docetaxel therapy should be discontinued entirely if patients experience $\geq$ grade 3 peripheral neuropathy.

Carcinoma, breast, node–positive (treatment adjunct)—

Intravenous infusion, 75 mg per square meter of body surface area (mg/m^2), administered one hour after doxorubicin 50 mg/m^2 and cyclophosphamide 500 mg/m^2 every 3 weeks for 6 courses.

Note: Docetaxel in combination with doxorubicin and cyclophosphamide should be administered when the neutrophil count is ≥ 1500 cells per cubic millimeter. Patients who experience febrile neutropenia should receive G-CSF in all subsequent cycles. Docetaxel dose should be reduced to 60 mg/m² and patient should remain on G-CSF if febrile neutropenia reaction continues.

Patients who experience severe or cumulative cutaneous reactions or moderate neurosensory signs and/or symptoms during docetaxel therapy should have their dosage of docetaxel reduced from 75 to 60 mg/m². Treatment should be discontinued if patient continues to experience these reactions at 60 mg/m².

Carcinoma, gastric—

Intravenous infusion, 75 mg/m² administered as a one hour infusion, followed by cisplatin 75 mg/m², as a 1 to 3 hour intravenous infusion (both on day 1 only), followed by fluorouracil 750 mg/m² per day given as a 24-hour continuous intravenous infusion for 5 days, starting at the end of the cisplatin infusion. Treatment is repeated every three weeks.

Note: Patients must receive premedication with antiemetics and appropriate hydration for cisplatin administration. In the study, G-CSF was recommended during the second and/or subsequent cycles in case of febrile neutropenia, or documented infection with neutropenia, or neutropenia lasting more than 7 days.

If an episode of febrile neutropenia, prolonged neutropenia or neutropenic infections occurs despite G-CSF use, the docetaxel dose should be reduced from 75 to 60 mg/m². If subsequent episodes of complicated neutropenia occur, the docetaxel dose should be reduced from 60 to 45 mg/m².

In case of Grade 4 thrombocytopenia, the docetaxel dose should be reduced from 75 to 60 mg/m².

Patients should not be retreated with subsequent cycles of docetaxel until neutrophils recover to a level > 1500 cells/mm³ and platelets recover to a level > 100,000 cells/mm³. Discontinue treatment if these toxicities persist.

Recommended dose modifications for gastrointestinal toxicities in patients treated with docetaxel in combination with cisplatin and fluorouracil:

Toxicity	Dosage adjustment
Diarrhea grade 3	First episode: reduce 5-FU dose by 20% Second episode: then reduce docetaxel dose by 20%
Diarrhea grade 4	First episode: reduce docetaxel and 5-FU doses by 20% Second episode: discontinue treatment
Stomatitis grade 3	First episode: reduce 5-FU dose by 20% Second episode: stop 5-FU only, at all subsequent cycles. Third episode: reduce docetaxel dose by 20%
Stomatitis grade 4	First episode: stop 5-FU only, at all subsequent cycles. Second episode: reduce docetaxel dose by 20%

Liver dysfunction—In case of AST/ALT > 2.5 to ≤ 2.5 x UNL and AP < 2.5 x UNL, or AST/ALT > 1.5 to ≤ 5 x UNL and AP > 2.5 to ≤ 5 x UNL, docetaxel should be reduced by 20%. In case of AST/ALT > 5 x UNL and/or AP > 5 x UNL, docetaxel should be stopped.

The dose modifications for cisplatin and fluorouracil can be found in the manufacturer's prescribing information for docetaxel. The manufacturer's prescribing information for cisplatin and fluorouracil can also be consulted if more information is needed.

[Carcinoma, head and neck][1]—

Intravenous, 60 to 100 mg per square meter of body surface area administered as a one-hour infusion every three to four weeks, for an average of two to six cycles (maximum four to eight).

Note: Dose-limiting toxicities and the use of other chemotherapeutic agents (e.g., cisplatin and 5–fluorouracil) may warrant a dose reduction

Doses of 20 to 80 mg per square meter of body surface area administered as a one-hour intravenous infusion once every seven to seventeen days, for a maximum of six cycles or 25 to 90 mg per square meter of body surface area (with cisplatin, 5-fluorouracil, and with or without leucovorin), administered as one-hour intravenous infusion, once every four weeks, for a maximum of three cycles have been reported.

Carcinoma, lung, non-small cell—

Intravenous, 75 mg per square meter of body surface area, administered as a one-hour infusion every three weeks.

Note: A dose of 100 mg per square meter of body surface area in patients previously treated with chemotherapy was associated with increased hematologic toxicity, infection, and treatment-related mortality in randomized, controlled trials.

If patients initially receiving a dose of 75 mg per square meter of body surface area experience febrile neutropenia, neutrophil count < 500 cells per cubic millimeter for more than 1 week, severe or cumulative cutaneous reactions, or other grade 3 or 4 non-hematologic toxicities, docetaxel therapy should be withheld until the toxic reaction is resolved. Docetaxel therapy should then be resumed at a dose of 55 mg per square meter of body surface area. Docetaxel therapy should be discontinued entirely if patients experience ≥ grade 3 peripheral neuropathy.

[Carcinoma, esophageal][1]—

Patients have benefited from intravenous doses of 60 to 85 mg/m², by 1–hour infusion, every 21 to 28 days, in combination with other agents (e.g., gemcitabine, cisplatin, 5–fluorouracil, leucovorin) and radiation therapy. As single-agent therapy, patients have benefited from an intravenous dose of 100 mg/m², by 1–hour infusion, every 21 days.

[Carcinoma, lung, small cell or][1]
[Carcinoma, ovarian][1]—

Intravenous, 100 mg per square meter of body surface area, administered as a one-hour infusion every three weeks.

Carcinoma, prostate—

Intravenous, 75 mg per square meter of body surface area administered as a one-hour infusion once every three weeks, for an average of five to nine cycles. Prednisone 5 mg orally twice daily is administered continuously. Recommended premedication regimen is oral dexamethasone 8 mg, at 12 hours, 3 hours and 1 hour before the docetaxel infusion. Dose-limiting toxicities and the use of other chemotherapeutic agents (e.g., estramustine) may warrant a dose reduction. Other studies reported using doses of 20 to 40 mg per square meter of body surface area given by one-hour intravenous infusion once a week, for two weeks with a one-week rest or for six weeks with a two-week rest.

Note: For all indications, docetaxel administration should be delayed if the neutrophil count is lower than 1500 cells per cubic millimeter and/or the platelet count is lower than 100,000 cells per cubic millimeter.

A reduction in subsequent doses is recommended for patients who develop severe neutropenia (neutrophil count < 500 cells per cubic millimeter) that persists for 7 days or more, febrile neutropenia, severe (grade 4) infection, severe peripheral neuropathy, or severe or cumulative cutaneous reactions. Dosage in patients originally receiving 100 mg per square meter of body surface area should be decreased by 25%, to 75 mg per square meter of body surface area. If these complications persist or recur, dosage should be further decreased to 55 mg per square meter of body surface area or treatment discontinued.

Docetaxel is not recommended for patients with hepatic function impairment, especially moderate to severe impairment, because of the considerably higher risk of severe toxicity. If docetaxel is considered essential for a patient with mild hepatic function impairment, initial doses of 60 to 75 mg per square meter of body surface area should be used. However, the risk of severe toxicity and septic death will still be significantly higher than for patients with normal hepatic function.

Patients who originally receive 60 mg per square meter of body surface area and who do not develop severe neutropenia, cutaneous reactions, or peripheral neuropathy may tolerate higher doses.

[Carcinoma, bladder (treatment)][1]—

Patients have benefited from 1–hour intravenous infusions of 75 to 100 mg per square meter of body surface area, every 21 days, for up to 6 treatment cycles.

Usual pediatric dose

Safety and efficacy in pediatric patients below the age of 16 years have not been established.

Usual geriatric dose

See *Usual adult dose.*

Strength(s) usually available

U.S.—

Note: Product is packaged together with accompanying diluent (0.5 mL for the 20 mg per 0.5 mL vial; 2 mL for the 80 mg per 2 mL vial). The diluent contains 13% (w/w) ethanol. The vials contain overfills of docetaxel and diluent to allow for loss due to foaming, adhesion to vial walls, and dead space during initial dilution of the concentrate.

20 mg per 0.5 mL (single-dose vial) (Rx) [*Taxotere* (polysorbate 80 1040 mg per mL)].

80 mg per 2 mL (single-dose vial) (Rx) [*Taxotere* (polysorbate 80 1040 mg per mL)].

Canada—

Note: Product is packaged together with accompanying diluent (0.5 mL for the 20 mg per 0.5 mL vial; 2 mL for the 80 mg per 2 mL vial). The diluent contains 13% (w/w) ethanol. The vials contain overfills of docetaxel and diluent to allow for loss due to foaming, adhesion to vial walls, and dead space during initial dilution of the concentrate.

20 mg per 0.5 mL (single-dose vial) (Rx) [*Taxotere* (polysorbate 80 1040 mg per mL)].

80 mg per 2 mL (single-dose vial) (Rx) [*Taxotere* (polysorbate 80 1040 mg per mL)].

Packaging and storage

Store between 2 and 8 °C (36 and 46 °F). Protect from bright light.

Note: Docetaxel for injection concentrate is not adversely affected by freezing.

Preparation of dosage form

Docetaxel for injection concentrate must be diluted, using the following procedure—

To prepare premix solution—

Remove docetaxel and diluent from the refrigerator and allow to stand for approximately 5 minutes at room temperature. Using aseptic technique and a syringe, transfer the entire contents of the diluent vial to the vial containing docetaxel. Rotate the vial gently for approximately 15 seconds to assure complete mixture of the medication and diluent. The final concentration of docetaxel will be 10 mg per mL. Allow the solution to stand for a few minutes to allow any foam to dissipate. However, the foam need not dissipate completely before the preparation process is continued. Discard the premix solution if it is not clear or contains a precipitate.

To prepare the infusion—

Using aseptic technique and a calibrated syringe, transfer the required quantity of premix solution into a 250-mL infusion bag or bottle containing 5% dextrose injection or 0.9% sodium chloride injection to achieve a final concentration of 0.3 to 0.9 mg per mL. If a dose greater than 240 mg of docetaxel is required, a larger volume of vehicle should be used so that the concentration does not exceed 0.9 mg per mL. Thoroughly mix by manual rotation of the container. Discard the infusion if it is not clear or contains a precipitate.

Stability

The premix solution is stable for up to 8 hours at room temperature (15 to 25 °C [59 to 77 °F]) or in a refrigerator (2 to 8 °C [36 to 46 °F]). However, it is recommended that the solution be used as soon as possible after preparation.

Incompatibilities

Contact of undiluted docetaxel with plasticized polyvinyl equipment is not recommended because such contact may cause leaching of the plasticizer, di-2-ethylhexyl phthalate (DEHP). It is recommended that glass bottles or polypropylene or polyolefin plastic products be used for preparation and storage of the infusion, and that the infusion be administered through polyethylene-lined administration sets.

Auxiliary labeling

- Must be diluted prior to administration.

[1]Not included in Canadian product labeling.

Selected Bibliography

Hudis CA, Seidman AD, Crown JPA, et al. Phase II and pharmacologic study of docetaxel as initial chemotherapy for metastatic breast cancer. J Clin Oncol 1996; 14: 58-65.

Pronk LC, Stoter G, Verweij J. Docetaxel (Taxotere): single agent activity, development of combination treatment, and reducing side effects. Cancer Treatment Reviews 1995; 21: 463-78.

van Oosterom AT, Schriivers D. Docetaxel (Taxotere), a review of preclinical and clinical experience. Part II: clinical experience. Anti-Cancer Drugs 1995; 6: 356-68.

Revised: 04/28/2006
Developed: 09/17/1997

DOCOSANOL Topical

VA CLASSIFICATION (Primary): DE103

Commonly used brand name(s): *Abreva.*

Note: For a listing of dosage forms and brand names by country availability, see *Dosage Forms* section(s).

Category

Antiviral (topical).

Indications

General Considerations

Docosanol produces its effect by modifying the host cell rather than acting directly on the virus. Therefore, it is very unlikely that HSV strains develop any type of resistance to the antiviral effects of docosanol.

Docosanol exhibits antiviral activity *in vitro* against many lipid–enveloped viruses, including: HSV–1, HSV–2, VZV, CMV, HHV–6, RSV, influenza A, and HIV–1. HSV–1 and HSV–2 have been shown to be susceptible to antiviral activity *in vivo.*

Accepted

Oral-facial herpes simplex (treatment)—Topical docosanol is indicated in the treatment of recurrent oral-facial herpes simplex (fever blisters or cold sores) in adults.

Pharmacology/Pharmacokinetics

Physicochemical characteristics

Molecular weight—326.61

Mechanism of action/Effect

Docosanol reduces viral replication and activity by effectively inhibiting the fusion between the plasma membrane and the herpes simplex virus envelope.

Absorption

Absorption of docosanol has been shown to be minimal under conditions reflecting normal clinical use. Of 209 plasma samples taken from ten subjects 24 hours after a multi-day test, only one had a docosanol level above the quantitation limits (10 nanograms per mL).

Precautions to Consider

Carcinogenicity

Carcinogenicity tests were not conducted with docosanol. However, carcinogenic effects are unlikely because the body is unable to absorb large quantities of docosanol and demonstrates a high rate of docosanol elimination.

Mutagenicity

No increases in gene mutation were seen in adequate studies done on *Salmonella typhimurium* and Chinese hamster V79 cells.

Pregnancy/Reproduction

Fertility—No adverse effects on fertility were seen when rats and rabbits were dosed with either 1000 mg/kg/day or 2000 mg/kg/day, (2500 to 5000 times the expected human dose, respectively). Furthermore, rabbits did not exhibit any adverse effects on fertility following vaginal administration of docosanol.

Pregnancy—Adequate and well controlled studies have not been conducted in humans. Studies in which animals were administered several thousand times the recommended human dosage of docosanol have not shown that docosanol causes any adverse effects on the fetus.

FDA Pregnancy Category B

Breast-feeding

It is not known whether docosanol is distributed into breast milk. However, problems in humans have not been documented.

Pediatrics

Safety and efficacy have not been established.

Adolescents

Appropriate studies on the relationship of age to the effects of docosanol have not been performed in the adolescent population. However, adolescent–specific problems that would limit the usefulness of this medicine in teenagers are not expected.

Geriatrics

Appropriate studies performed to date have not demonstrated geriatrics–specific problems that would limit the usefulness of docosanol in the elderly.

Medical considerations/Contraindications

The medical considerations/contraindications included have been selected on the basis of their potential clinical significance (reasons given in parentheses where appropriate)—not necessarily inclusive (» = major clinical significance).

Except under special circumstances, this medication should not be used when the following medical problem exists:
Hypersensitivity to topical docosanol

Side/Adverse Effects

The following side/adverse effects have been selected on the basis of their potential clinical significance (possible signs and symptoms in parentheses where appropriate)—not necessarily inclusive:

Those indicating need for medical attention only if they continue or are bothersome

Incidence more frequent
Headache

Incidence less frequent
Application site reaction (burning, itching, redness, skin rash, swelling, or soreness at site of application)

Incidence rare
Skin manifestations, including: acne; dry skin; pruritus (itching); ***rash***

Overdose

For more information on the management of overdose or unintentional ingestion, **contact a poison control center** (see *Poison Control Center Listing*).

Treatment of overdose

Due to limited transcutaneous absorption and poor oral absorption of docosanol, the potential for an adverse reaction related to an overdose is extremely low.Treatment is essentially symptomatic and supportive.

Patients in whom intentional overdose is confirmed or suspected should be referred for psychiatric consultation.

Patient Consultation

As an aid to patient consultation, refer to *Advice for the Patient, Docosanol (Topical)*.

In providing consultation, consider emphasizing the following selected information (» = major clinical significance):

Before using this medication

» Conditions affecting use, especially:
Hypersensitivity to docosanol

Proper use of this medication

Reading patient information about herpes simplex infections
» Avoiding contact with eyes or genitalia
» Using medication as soon as possible after signs and symptoms of herpes begin to appear
» Proper administration technique

To use
Applying medication to affected areas; rubbing in gently and completely.

» Proper dosing
Proper storage

General Dosing Information

Topical docosanol is for oral-facial herpes only; it should not be used in the eyes or on the genitalia.

Therapy should be initiated as soon as possible following the onset of signs and symptoms of herpes infection.

Topical Dosage Forms

DOCOSANOL CREAM

Usual adult and adolescent dose

Antiviral—
Topical, to the affected area, five times a day until the lesion is healed. Apply a sufficient quantity to cover all lesions adequately. The cream should be rubbed in gently and completely.

Usual pediatric dose

Antiviral—
Children up to 12 years of age: Safety and efficacy have not been established.
Children 12 years of age and over: See *Usual adult and adolescent dose*.

Usual geriatric dose

See *Usual adult and adolescent dose*.

Strength(s) usually available

U.S.—
10% (0.1 gram per gram) (OTC) [*Abreva* (benzyl alcohol NF; light mineral oil NF; propylene glycol USP; purified water USP; sucrose distearate; sucrose stearate)].

Packaging and storage

Store at or below 25 °C (77 °F). Protect from freezing.

Auxiliary labeling

- For external use only.
- Do not use near the eyes.
- Continue with medicine until lesion is healed.

Revised: 12/22/2000

DOCUSATE—See *Laxatives (Local)*

DOFETILIDE Systemic

VA CLASSIFICATION (Primary): CV300

Commonly used brand name(s): *Tikosyn*.

Note: For a listing of dosage forms and brand names by country availability, see *Dosage Forms* section(s).

Category

Antiarrhythmic.

Indications

Accepted

Arrhythmias, atrial (treatment)—Dofetilide is indicated for the conversion of atrial fibrillation/atrial flutter to normal sinus rhythm. Dofetilide is also indicated for the maintenance of normal sinus rhythm in patients with highly symptomatic atrial fibrillation/atrial flutter of greater than one week's duration, who have been converted to normal sinus rhythm.

Note: Dofetilide is arrhythmogenic and therefore should be reserved for patients in whom atrial fibrillation/atrial flutter is highly symptomatic.

Unaccepted

Dofetilide has not demonstrated efficacy for the treatment of paroxysmal atrial fibrillation.

Pharmacology/Pharmacokinetics

Physicochemical characteristics

Molecular weight—441.6.
Solubility—
Very slightly soluble in water and propan−2−ol.
Soluble in 0.1M aqueous sodium hydroxide, acetone and aqueous 0.1M hydrochloric acid.

Mechanism of action/Effect

Dofetilide prolongs cardiac action potential duration and effective refractory periodwithout affecting conduction velocity. Dofetilide selectively blocks the cardiac delayed rectifier potassium current (I_K), specifically, the rapid component of the current (I_{kr}). At clinically relevant concentrations, dofetilide has no effect on sodium channels (associated with Class I effect), adrenergic alpha-receptors, or adrenergic beta−receptors. In the Vaughan Williams classification of antiarrhythmics, dofetilide is considered to be a pure Class III agent.

Absorption

Greater than 90%. Oral bioavailability is not affected by food or antacids.

Distribution

Volume of distribution (Vol_D)—3 L/kg

Protein binding

High (60% to 70%).

Biotransformation

Metabolites are formed by N−dealkylation and N−oxidation and to a small extent by the cytochrome P450 3A4. There are no quantifiable metabolites circulating in plasma, but 5 metabolites have been identified in urine. Dofetilide is not an inhibitor of the cytochrome P450 isoenzymes including CYP3A4.

Half-life

10 hours; prolonged in patients with impaired renal function.

Time to peak concentration

2 to 3 hours when dofetilide is taken in the fasted state.

Peak serum concentration

Mean peak serum levels of 0.5, 1.3, 2.3, and 2.7 ng/mL have been reported after oral doses of 2, 5, 7.5, and 10 mcg/kg, respectively, in healthy subjects.

Time to peak effect

2 hours with oral doses of 0.5 mg in healthy subjects, the maximal increase in the QT_c interval was 12% (from 396 to 445 milliseconds) and occurred in 2 hours.

Duration of action

4 hours after a single 0.5 mg dose of dofetilide significant increases in the QT_c interval have persisted.

Elimination

Renal—Approximately 80% of a single dose is excreted in urine (approximately 80% unchanged and 20% as inactive or minimally active metabolites). Renal elimination involves both glomerular filtration and active tubular secretion (via the cation transport system, a process that can be inhibited by cimetidine and ketoconazole). In volunteers with varying degrees of renal impairment and patients with arrhythmias, the clearance of dofetilide decreases with decreasing creatinine clearance.

Hemodialysis—lack of data

Precautions to Consider

Carcinogenicity and mutagenicity

Genotoxic effects, with or without metabolic activation, was not demonstrated in bacterial mutation assay and tests of cytogenetic aberrations *in vivo* in mouse bone marrow and *in vitro* in human lymphocytes.

Tumorigenicity

A two year study did not demonstrate an increased incidence of tumors in rats and mice treated with dofetilide in the diet compared with controls. The highest dofetilide dose administered for 24 months was 10 mg per kg a day in rats and 20 mg per kg a day in mice, which would be expected to provide mean dofetilide $AUCs_{(0-24\ hr)}$ 26 and 10 times, respectively, the maximum likely human AUC.

Pregnancy/Reproduction

Fertility—Male and female rat studies demonstrated no effect on mating or fertility when dofetilide was administered at doses as high as 1 mg per kg a day (which would be expected to provide a mean dofetilide $AUC_{(0-24\ hr)}$ about 3 times the maximum likely human AUC). Increased incidences of testicular atrophy and epididymal oligospermia and a reduction in testicular weight were, however, observed in other studies in rats. Reduced testicular weight and increased incidence of testicular atrophy were also consistent findings in dogs and mice. The no effect doses for these findings in chronic administration studies in these 3 species (3, 0.1, and 6 mg per kg a day) were associated with mean dofetilide AUCs that were about 4, 1.3 and 3 times the maximum likely human AUC, respectively.

Pregnancy—Adequate and well-controlled studies in humans have not been done. Studies in rats and mice have shown that dofetilide adversely affects *in utero* growth and survival when orally administered during organogenesis at doses of 2 or more mg per kg a day. The "no observed adverse effect dose" was 0.5 mg per kg a day which is expected to provide mean dofetilide $AUCs_{(0-24\ hr)}$ equal to the maximum likely human AUC and about half the likely human AUC in the rat and mouse, respectively.

FDA Pregnancy Category C.

Breast-feeding

It is not known whether dofetilide is distributed into breast milk. However, problems in humans have not been documented. Breast-feeding during dofetilide therapy is not recommended.

Pediatrics

Appropriate studies on the relationship of age to the effects of dofetilide have not been performed in the pediatric population in children up to 18 years of age. Safety and efficacy have not been established.

Geriatrics

Appropriate studies performed to date have not demonstrated geriatrics–specific problems that would limit the usefulness of dofetilide in the elderly. However, elderly patients are more likely to have age–related renal function impairment, which may require a dose reduction in patients receiving dofetilide.

Pharmacogenetics

Female patients constituted 32% of the patients in the placebo-controlled trials of dofetilide. Dofetilide was associated with a greater risk of torsades de pointes in female patients than in male patients. During the dofetilide clinical development program, females were 3 times more likely to experience torsade de pointes than males. In contrast, females receiving dofetilide were no more likely to experience other ventricular arrhythmias than patients receiving placebo. Although no study specifically investigated this risk, in post-hoc analyses, no increased mortality was observed in females receiving dofetilide compared with females on placebo.

Drug interactions and/or related problems

The following drug interactions and/or related problems have been selected on the basis of their potential clinical significance (possible mechanism in parentheses where appropriate)—not necessarily inclusive (» = major clinical significance):

Note: Combinations containing any of the following medications, depending on the amount present, may also interact with this medication.

» Antiarrhythmic agents, Class I and Class III, especially
Amiodarone
» Bepridil
» Cisapride
» Macrolides, oral
» Phenothiazines, especially
» Prochlorperazine
» Tricyclic antidepressants
(not recommended due to the possibility of prolonged QT interval when used concomitantly with dofetilide; Class I or Class III antiarrhythmic agents should be withheld for at least three half–lives prior to dosing with dofetilide; the exception is amiodarone; dofetilide should be withheld until plasma levels of amiodarone are below 0.3 mcg/mL or until amiodarone has been discontinued for at least 3 months)

Drugs eliminated by the renal cation transport system, such as
Amiloride
Metformin
Triamterene
(should be used cautiously because of the potential to increase dofetilide concentrations; a washout period of at least 2 days for dofetilide is recommended prior to initiating potentially interacting drugs)

Inhibitors of the renal cation transport system, especially
» Cimetidine
» Ketoconazole
» Megestrol
» Trimethoprim, alone or in combination with sulfamethoxazole
» Verapamil
(it is recommended these agents not be administered concomitantly with dofetilide; may cause substantial increases in dofetilide concentrations possibly resulting in serious ventricular arrhythmias, primarily torsade de pointes; cimetidine 400 mg twice a day co-administered with dofetilide 500 mcg twice a day for 7 days has been shown to increase dofetilide plasma concentrations by 58%; cimetidine 100 mg twice a day co-administered with dofetilide 500 mcg single dose resulted in a 13% increase in dofetilide plasma concentrations; if a patient requires dofetilide and anti-ulcer therapy, it is recommended that omeprazole, ranitidine, or antacids, such as aluminum and magnesium hydroxides, be used as alternatives to cimetidine, as these agents have no effect on the pharmacokinetic profile of dofetilide; ketoconazole 400 mg daily co-administered with dofetilide 500 mcg twice a day for 7 days has been shown to increase dofetilide C_{max} by 53% in males and 97% in females, and AUC by 41% in males and 69% in females; trimethoprim 160 mg in combination with 800 mg sulfamethoxazole co-administered twice daily with dofetilide 500 mcg twice daily for 4 days has been shown to increase dofetilide AUC by 93% and C_{max} by 103%; co-administration of dofetilide with verapamil resulted in increases in dofetilide peak plasma concentrations of 42%, although overall exposure to dofetilide was not significantly increased; the concomitant administration of verapamil with dofetilide was associated with a higher occurrence of torsade de pointes)

Diuretics, potassium-depleting
(increased risk for torsade de pointes if the patient has hypokalemia or hypomagnesemia.)

Cytochrome P450 3A4 inhibitors such as
Azole antifungal agents
Cannabinoids
Diltiazem
Grapefruit juice
Nefazodone
Norfloxacin

Protease inhibitors
Quinine
Serotonin reuptake inhibitors
Zafirlukast
(use cautiously because of the potential to increase dofetilide concentrations; a washout period of at least 2 days for dofetilide is recommended prior to initiating potentially interacting drugs)

Digoxin
(studies in healthy volunteers have shown that dofetilide does not affect the pharmacokinetics of digoxin. In patients, the concomitant administration of digoxin with dofetilide was associated with a higher occurrence of torsade de pointes. It is not clear whether this represents an interaction with dofetilide or the presence of more severe structural heart disease in patients on digoxin; structural heart disease is a known risk factor for arrhythmia. No increase in mortality was observed in patients taking digoxin as concomitant medication)

» Hydrochlorothiazide, alone or in combination with triamterene
(use is contraindicated)

Medical considerations/Contraindications

The medical considerations/contraindications included have been selected on the basis of their potential clinical significance (reasons given in parentheses where appropriate)—not necessarily inclusive (» = major clinical significance).

Except under special circumstances, this medication should not be used when the following medical problem exists:

» Hypersensitivity to dofetilide

» Long QT syndromes, congenital or acquired
(use of dofetilide not recommended in patients with a baseline QT or $QT_c > 440$ millisecond (msec) [500 msec in patients with ventricular conduction abnormalities])

» Renal impairment, severe
(use of dofetilide not recommended in patients with a calculated creatinine clearance of < 20 mL/min)

Risk-benefit should be considered when the following medical problems exist:

Cardiac conduction disturbances
(safety not established in patients with sick sinus syndrome or with 2nd or 3rd degree heart block without a pacemaker)

Hepatic impairment, severe
(safety has not been established)

» Hypokalemia or
» Hypomagnesemia
(increased risk of torsade de pointes; normalize potassium levels prior to initiating and during dofetilide administration)

» Renal impairment
(potential for increased dofetilide concentrations with decreasing creatinine clearance; dosage adjustment based on creatinine clearance is recommended)

Patient monitoring

The following may be especially important in patient monitoring (other tests may be warranted in some patients, depending on condition; » = major clinical significance):

» Creatinine, serum
(recommended prior to first dose of dofetilide and every three months thereafter)

» Electrocardiogram (ECG)
(a minimum of three days monitoring in a facility with personnel trained in the management of serious ventricular arrhythmias is required upon initiation of dofetilide, or a minimum of 12 hours after electrical or pharmacological conversion to normal sinus rhythm, whichever is greater; reevaluate every three months; discontinue dofetilide if the QT_c exceeds 500 milliseconds (msec) [550 msec in patients with ventricular conduction abnormalities])

Electrolytes, especially potassium and magnesium concentrations, serum
(it is recommended that potassium levels be normalized prior to initiating and during dofetilide administration)

Side/Adverse Effects

The following side/adverse effects have been selected on the basis of their potential clinical significance (possible signs and symptoms in parentheses where appropriate)—not necessarily inclusive:

Those indicating need for medical attention

Incidence more frequent

Ventricular arrhythmias and ventricular tachycardia including torsade de pointes (dizziness; fainting; fast or irregular heartbeat)—torsade de pointes is dose related

Incidence less frequent

Angioedema (swelling of the arms, face, legs, lips, tongue, and/or throat); ***atrioventricular block*** (chest pain; dizziness; fainting; pounding, slow heartbeat; troubled breathing; unusual tiredness or weakness); ***bradycardia*** (slow heartbeat); ***cerebral ischemia or cerebrovascular accident*** (sudden numbness or tingling of the hands, feet, or face; paralysis; confusion; weakness; slurred speech); ***chest pain; edema*** (swelling of face, fingers, ankles, feet, or lower legs; weight gain); ***facial or flaccid paralysis; heart arrest or myocardial infarct*** (crushing chest pain; unexplained shortness of breath); ***liver damage*** (yellow eyes or skin); ***paresthesia*** (numbness or tingling of hands, feet, or face); ***syncope*** (fainting); ***ventricular fibrillation*** (fainting; fast, slow, or irregular heartbeat; shortness of breath; unusual tiredness or weakness)

Incidence rare

Bundle branch block; heart block (slow or irregular heartbeat)

Those indicating need for medical attention only if they continue or are bothersome

Incidence less frequent

Abdominal or stomach pain; accidental injury; back pain; diarrhea; dizziness; dyspnea (shortness of breath); ***flu syndrome*** (chills; cough; diarrhea; fever; general feeling of discomfort or illness; headache; joint pain; loss of appetite; muscle aches and pains; nausea; runny nose; shivering; sore throat; sweating; trouble sleeping; unusual tiredness or weakness; vomiting); ***headache or migraine; increased cough; insomnia*** (trouble sleeping); ***nausea; rash; respiratory tract infection*** (cough; fever; sneezing; sore throat; flu-like symptoms)

Overdose

For more information on the management of overdose or unintentional ingestion, **contact a poison control center** (see *Poison Control Center Listing*).

Clinical effects of overdose

Note: The most prominent manifestation of overdosage is likely to be excessive prolongation of the QT interval.

The following effects have been selected on the basis of their potential clinical significance (possible signs and symptoms in parentheses where appropriate)—not necessarily inclusive:

Acute

cardiac arrest and ventricular fibrillation (fainting; fast, slow, or irregular heartbeat; shortness of breath; unusual tiredness or weakness)—occurring 2 hours in a patient who received two 500 mcg doses one hour apart

Treatment of overdose

To decrease absorption—
Charcoal slurry—useful only if given within 15 minutes of dofetilide.

Specific treatment—
There is no specific antidote for dofetilide.
- Isoproterenol infusion with or without cardiac pacing—treatment of torsade de pointes or overdose. See the package insert or
- *Sympathomimetic agents–Cardiovascular use (Parenteral-Systemic)* for specific dosing guidelines for use of this product.
- Magnesium sulfate, intravenous—management of torsade de pointes. See the package insert or
- *Magnesium sulfate (Systemic)* for specific dosing guidelines for use of this product.

Monitoring—
Cardiac monitoring including electrocardiogram. Continue monitoring until the QT interval returns to normal levels.

Supportive care—
Symptomatic and supportive.
Patients in whom intentional overdose is confirmed or suspected should be referred for psychiatric consultation.

Patient Consultation

As an aid to patient consultation, refer to *Advice for the Patient, Dofetilide (Systemic)*.

In providing consultation, consider emphasizing the following selected information (» = major clinical significance)

Before using this medication

» Conditions affecting use, especially:
Hypersensitivity to dofetilide
Pregnancy—Animal studies have shown that dofetilide adversely affects growth and survival *in utero*
Breast-feeding—Use is not recommended
Use in children—Safety and efficacy not established in children less than 18 years old.

Other medications, especially class I and III antiarrhythmics, bepridil, cimetidine, cisapride, hydrochlorothiazide/triamterene, ketoconazole, oral macrolides, megestrol, phenothiazines, prochlorperazine, tricyclic antidepressants, trimethoprim alone or in combination with sulfamethoxazole, and verapamil.

Other medical problems, especially congenital or acquired long QT syndromes, renal impairment, hypokalemia, or hypomagnesemia.

Proper use of this medication

» Reading patient package insert carefully

» Proper dosing

Missed dose: Skipping the missed dose and going back to regular dosing schedule; not doubling doses.

» Taking at the same time every day.

» Proper storage

Precautions while using this medication

» Regular visits to physician at least every 3 months to check progress.

Not taking other medicines unless discussed with physician, especially nonprescription medicines.

Side/adverse effects

Signs of potential side effects, especially ventricular arrhythmias and ventricular tachycardia including torsade de pointes, angioedema, atrioventricular block, bradycardia, cerebral ischemia or cerebrovascular accident, chest pain, edema, facial or flaccid paralysis, heart arrest or myocardial infarct, liver damage, paresthesia, syncope, ventricular fibrillation, bundle branch block, and heart block.

General Dosing Information

A switch from Class I or other Class III antiarrhythmic therapy requires a wash-out of a minimum of 3 plasma half-lives prior to initiating dofetilide. Amiodarone is the exception, in which case amiodarone plasma levels should be below 0.3 mcg/mL or until amiodarone has been discontinued for at least three months prior to initiating dofetilide.

A minimum of 3 days in a facility that can provide calculations of creatinine clearance, continuous electrocardiographic monitoring, and cardiac resuscitation is recommended for patients initiated and re-initiated on dofetilide. This precaution minimizes the risk of induced arrhythmia.

A wash-out of at least two days for dofetilide is required prior to initiating other potentially interacting drug(s).

Anticoagulation according to usual medical practice prior to and following cardioversion is recommended in patients with atrial fibrillation.

Sufficient supply of dofetilide should be provided to patients at the time of discharge from an in-patient setting to allow uninterrupted dosing in the out-patient setting until their prescription is filled.

Dofetilide is distributed only to those hospitals and other appropriate institutions determined to have received applicable dosing and treatment initiation education programs. Pharmacies dispense dofetilide only to hospitals and physicians on a list which verifies completion of one of the education programs.

Oral Dosage Forms

DOFETILIDE CAPSULE

Usual adult dose

Arrhythmias, atrial (treatment)—

Calculated Creatinine Clearance	First Oral Dose	Maintenance Dose is based on QT_c 2 to 3 hours After First Dose: QT_c increase is less than or equal to 15% compared to baseline	Maintenance Dose is based on QT_c 2 to 3 hours After First Dose: QT_c has increased by greater than 15% compared to the baseline or the QT_c is greater than 500 msec (550 msec in patients with ventricular conduction abnormalities)
greater than 60 mL/min	500 mcg	500 mcg twice daily*	250 mcg twice daily*
40 to 60 mL/min	250 mcg	250 mcg twice daily*	125 mcg twice daily*
20 to less than 40 mL/min	125 mcg	125 mcg twice daily*	125 mcg once daily*

Note: Dofetilide is contraindicated in patients with a QT_c greater than 440 msec (500 msec in patients with ventricular conduction abnormalities) or calculated creatinine clearance less than 20 mL/min

*If after the second dose the QT_c is greater than 500 msec (550 msec in patients with ventricular conduction abnormalities), then dofetilide should be discontinued.

Usual adult prescribing limits

500 mcg twice daily in patients with a calculated creatinine clearance greater than 60 mL/min; doses greater than 500 mcg twice daily have been associated with an increased incidence of torsade de pointes.

Usual pediatric dose

Safety and efficacy not established in children younger than 18 years of age.

Usual geriatric dose

See *Usual adult dose*

Strength(s) usually available

U.S.—

125 mcg (0.125 mg) (Rx) [*Tikosyn*].

250 mcg (0.25 mg) (Rx) [*Tikosyn*].

500 mcg (0.5 mg) (Rx) [*Tikosyn*].

Packaging and storage

Store at controlled room temperature, 15° to 30° C (59° to 86° F). Store in a tight container, unless otherwise specified by manufacturer. Protect from moisture and humidity.

Revised: 06/23/2004
Developed: 03/16/2000

DOLASETRON Systemic

VA CLASSIFICATION (Primary): GA605

Commonly used brand name(s): *Anzemet*.

Note: For a listing of dosage forms and brand names by country availability, see *Dosage Forms* section(s).

Category

Antiemetic.

Indications

Accepted

Nausea and vomiting, cancer chemotherapy-induced (prophylaxis)—Dolasetron injection is indicated for the prevention of nausea and vomiting associated with initial and repeat courses of emetogenic cancer chemotherapy, including high-dose cisplatin. Dolasetron tablets are indicated for the prevention of nausea and vomiting associated with moderately-emetogenic cancer chemotherapy, including initial and repeat courses.

Nausea and vomiting, postoperative (prophylaxis)—Dolasetron injection and tablets are indicated for the prevention of postoperative nausea and/or vomiting. Routine prophylaxis is not recommended when there is little risk of nausea and/or vomiting developing postoperatively, except in patients in whom nausea and/or vomiting must be avoided.

Nausea and vomiting, postoperative (treatment)—Dolasetron injection is indicated for the treatment of postoperative nausea and/or vomiting.

Pharmacology/Pharmacokinetics

Physicochemical characteristics

Molecular weight—438.5.

pH—Reconstituted solution: 3.2 to 3.8.

Solubility—Freely soluble in water and propylene glycol; slightly soluble in ethanol; slightly soluble in normal saline.

Mechanism of action/Effect

Dolasetron, and its active metabolite hydrodolasetron, are highly specific and selective antagonists of serotonin subtype 3 (5-HT_3) receptors. 5-HT_3 receptors are present peripherally on vagal nerve terminals and centrally in the area postrema of the brain. Chemotherapeutic medications appear to precipitate release of serotonin from the enterochromaffin cells of the small intestine, which then activates 5-HT_3 receptors on vagal efferents to initiate the vomiting reflex.

Dolasetron has not been shown to have activity at other known serotonin receptors, and has low affinity for dopamine receptors.

Other actions/effects

Dolasetron causes dose-related acute, and usually reversible, electrocardiogram (ECG) changes including QRS widening and PR, QT_c, and JT prolongation; QT_c prolongation is caused primarily by QRS widening. Dolasetron seems to prolong both depolarization and, to a lesser extent, repolarization time, and its active metabolites may block sodium channels.

Multiple daily doses of dolasetron have not been found to slow colonic transit time. Plasma prolactin concentrations are unaffected by dolasetron.

Pharmacokinetics

Note: The pharmacokinetics of dolasetron tablets have not been studied in the pediatric population. Data provided in the following sections are based on dolasetron injection administered orally to children.

Absorption

Orally-administered dolasetron is well absorbed, but the parent drug is rarely detected in plasma due to rapid and complete metabolism to hydrodolasetron.

The apparent absolute bioavailability of oral dolasetron is approximately 75%. Food does not affect the bioavailability of dolasetron taken by mouth.

Orally-administered dolasetron intravenous solution and tablets are bioequivalent.

Distribution

Dolasetron—Radiolabeled dolasetron was not found to be distributed extensively to blood cells.

Hydrodolasetron—Mean apparent volume of distribution is 5.8 liters per kg of body weight (L/kg).

Protein binding

High (69 to 77%). Binding to alpha$_1$-acid glycoprotein is approximately 50%.

Biotransformation

Hepatic, complete, mainly to the active metabolite hydrodolasetron (by means of the ubiquitous enzyme, carbonyl reductase). Further hydroxylation is mediated by cytochrome P450 CYP2D6 and further *N*-oxidation by both CYP3A and flavin monooxygenase.

Half-life

Elimination—

Following oral administration:

Hydrodolasetron—8.1 hours (mean).

Note: The apparent clearance of hydrodolasetron in adults is 13.4 mL per minute per kg of body weight (mL/min/kg). In one study, the apparent clearance of hydrodolasetron in children aged 2 to 12 years receiving dolasetron doses of 1.2 mg per kg of body weight (mg/kg) was approximately 1.6- to 3.4-fold higher than in adults. In a study of pediatric and adolescent cancer patients receiving 0.6, 1.2, or 1.8 mg of dolasetron, mean apparent clearances were 3 times greater for children and 1.8 times greater for adolescents than clearances observed in healthy adults receiving similar doses.

Apparent oral clearance decreases 42% in patients with severe hepatic impairment, and 44% in patients with severe renal impairment. No dosage adjustments appear necessary for these patients.

The pharmacokinetics of hydrodolasetron are linear, and similar in men and women.

Following intravenous injection:

Dolasetron—Less than 10 minutes after intravenous administration.

Hydrodolasetron—7.3 hours.

Note: The apparent clearance of hydrodolasetron is 9.4 mL/min/kg. In one study of children 2 to 11 years of age who received a single 1.2 mg/kg intravenous dose of dolasetron, mean apparent clearance was 40% greater than in healthy adults receiving the same dose. The terminal half-life in these children was 36% shorter than in healthy adults receiving the same dose. The apparent clearance of hydrodolasetron in pediatric and adolescent cancer patients was 1.4- to 2-fold higher than in adult cancer patients.

Following intravenous administration, apparent clearance of hydrodolasetron was unchanged in patients with severe hepatic impairment, and decreased 47% in patients with severe renal impairment. No dosage adjustments appear necessary for these patients.

The pharmacokinetics of hydrodolasetron are linear and independent of infusion rate.

Time to peak concentration

Hydrodolasetron—

Following oral administration: Approximately 1 hour.

Following intravenous injection: 0.6 hour.

Peak plasma concentration

In a study of children aged 3 to 17 years, maximum plasma concentrations were 0.6 to 0.7 times those observed in healthy adults receiving similar dosages.

Elimination

Hydrodolasetron—

Renal, 67% (53% unchanged and, to a lesser extent, as hydroxylated glucuronides and *N*-oxide metabolites).

Fecal, 33%, as metabolites.

In dialysis—

It is not known if dolasetron is removable by hemodialysis or peritoneal dialysis.

Precautions to Consider

Carcinogenicity

A study in male mice at oral doses of 75, 150, or 300 mg per kg of body weight per day (mg/kg/day) (225, 450, or 900 mg per square meter of body surface area (mg/m^2) per day, respectively; 3.4, 6.8, and 13.5 times the recommended human intravenous dose of 66.6 mg/m^2 or 3, 6, and 12 times the recommended human oral dose of 74 mg/m^2, respectively, for a 50-kg person of average height [1.46 square meters of body surface area]) found a statistically significant ($p < 0.001$) increase in the incidence of combined hepatocellular adenomas and carcinomas at doses of 150 mg/kg/day and above. No increased incidence of hepatic tumors was found at the dose of 75 mg/kg/day in male mice or at doses of up to 300 mg/kg/day in female mice.

Tumorigenicity

A 24-month study in Sprague-Dawley rats at oral doses of up to 150 mg/kg/day (900 mg/m^2; 13.5 times the recommended intravenous dose or 12 times the recommended oral human dose, based on body surface area) in males and up to 300 mg/kg/day (1800 mg/m^2; 27 times the recommended intravenous dose or 24 times the recommended oral human dose, based on body surface area) in females found no evidence of tumorigenicity.

Mutagenicity

Dolasetron was not found to be genotoxic in the Ames test, the rat lymphocyte chromosomal aberration test, the Chinese hamster ovary (CHO) cell (HGPRT) forward mutation test, the rat hepatocyte unscheduled DNA synthesis (UDS) test, and the mouse micronucleus test.

Pregnancy/Reproduction

Fertility—Studies in female rats at oral doses of up to 100 mg per kg of body weight per day (mg/kg/day) (600 mg/m^2 per day; 9 times the recommended human dose based on body surface area) and in male rats at oral doses of up to 400 mg/kg/day (2400 mg/m^2 per day; 36 times the recommended human dose based on body surface area) found no effect on fertility or reproductive performance.

Pregnancy—Adequate and well-controlled studies in humans have not been done.

Studies in pregnant rats at intravenous doses of up to 60 mg/kg/day (5.4 times the recommended human dose based on body surface area) or oral doses of up to 100 mg/kg/day (8 times the recommended human dose based on body surface area) and pregnant rabbits at intravenous doses of up to 20 mg/kg/day (3.2 times the recommended human dose based on body surface area) or oral doses of up to 100 mg/kg/day (16 times the recommended human dose based on body surface area) found no evidence of teratogenicity.

It is recommended that dolasetron be used during pregnancy only if clearly needed, since animal reproductive studies may not be predictive of human response.

FDA Pregnancy Category B.

Breast-feeding

It is not known whether dolasetron is distributed into human breast milk. However, risk-benefit should be considered before administering dolasetron to a nursing woman.

Pediatrics

Safety and efficacy studies have not been performed in pediatric patients. However, in four open-label, noncomparative pharmacokinetic studies, a total of 108 pediatric patients (between the ages of 2 and 17 years of age) being treated with emetogenic chemotherapy or undergoing surgery with general anesthesia received intravenous dolasetron doses of 0.6, 1.2, 1.8, or 2.4 mg/kg or oral doses of 0.6, 1.2, or 1.8 mg/kg. Overall, dolasetron was well-tolerated. Efficacy in pediatric patients receiving chemotherapy appeared to be consistent with that in adults; there is no efficacy information with regard to postoperative nausea and vomiting. Studies have not been performed in children younger than 2 years of age.

It is expected that the oral tablets of dolasetron will be as safe and effective as dolasetron injection given orally.

Geriatrics
Efficacy for prevention of nausea and vomiting appears to be the same in geriatric patients as in younger age groups. No dosage adjustment is recommended.

Drug interactions and/or related problems
The following drug interactions and/or related problems have been selected on the basis of their potential clinical significance (possible mechanism in parentheses where appropriate)—not necessarily inclusive (» = major clinical significance):

Note: Combinations containing any of the following medications, depending on the amount present, may also interact with this medication.

Atenolol
(concurrent use of intravenous dolasetron and atenolol has been found to result in a 27% decrease in clearance of hydrodolasetron)

Cimetidine
(concurrent use of cimetidine, which is a nonselective cytochrome P450 enzyme inhibitor, with dolasetron for 7 days has been found to result in a 24% increase in hydrodolasetron blood concentrations)

» Drugs causing QT_c interval prolongation
(caution is recommended)

Rifampin
(concurrent use of rifampin, which is a potent cytochrome P450 enzyme inducer, with dolasetron has been found to result in a 28% decrease in hydrodolasetron blood concentrations)

Laboratory value alterations
The following have been selected on the basis of their potential clinical significance (possible effect in parentheses where appropriate)—not necessarily inclusive (» = major clinical significance).

With physiology/laboratory test values

Alanine aminotransferase (ALT [SGPT]), serum and
Aspartate aminotransferase (AST [SGOT]), serum
(values may be increased; increases reportedly are transient and unrelated to dose or duration of therapy)

Electrocardiogram (ECG)
(dolasetron produces a number of ECG changes, including QRS widening and PR, QT_c, and JT prolongation; the magnitude of the effect is dose-related; the effect tends to disappear as blood concentrations decline but may persist for 24 hours or longer)

Medical considerations/Contraindications
The medical considerations/contraindications included have been selected on the basis of their potential clinical significance (reasons given in parentheses where appropriate)—not necessarily inclusive (» = major clinical significance).

Risk-benefit should be considered when the following medical problems exist:

» Conditions associated with a risk of development of prolongation of cardiac conduction intervals (especially QT_c), including:
Antiarrhythmic therapy or therapy with other drugs that may cause QT interval prolongation
Congenital QT syndrome
Cumulative high-dose anthracycline therapy
Diuretic treatment with the potential for inducing electrolyte abnormalities
Hypokalemia
Hypomagnesemia
(caution is recommended)

» Sensitivity to dolasetron

Side/Adverse Effects
The following side/adverse effects have been selected on the basis of their potential clinical significance (possible signs and symptoms in parentheses where appropriate)—not necessarily inclusive:

Those indicating need for medical attention
Incidence less frequent

Hypertension or hypotension (asymptomatic)

Incidence rare

Anaphylactic reaction (skin rash; hives, and/or itching; troubled breathing); ***bradycardia or palpitations*** (slow or irregular heartbeat); ***bronchospasm*** (troubled breathing); ***chest pain; edema*** (swelling of face; swelling of feet or lower legs); ***hematuria*** (blood in urine); ***oliguria*** (decrease in amount of urine); ***pain; pancreatitis*** (severe stomach pain with nausea and vomiting); ***tachycardia*** (fast heartbeat); ***urinary retention*** (painful urination or trouble in urinating)

Note: *Bradycardia* may be associated with electrocardiogram (ECG) changes including QRS widening and PR, QT_c, and JT prolongation.

Those indicating need for medical attention only if they continue or are bothersome
Incidence more frequent

Diarrhea; headache

Incidence less frequent

Abdominal or stomach pain; dizziness or lightheadedness; fatigue (unusual tiredness); ***fever or chills***

Overdose
For more information on the management of overdose or unintentional ingestion, **contact a Poison Control Center** (see *Poison Control Center Listing*).

Clinical effects of overdose
The following effects have been selected on the basis of their potential clinical significance (possible signs and symptoms in parentheses where appropriate)—not necessarily inclusive:

Acute

ECG effects, including QRS widening and PR and QT_c prolongation

Note: Doses of up to 5 mg per kg of body weight (mg/kg) intravenously or 400 mg orally have been administered safely to both healthy volunteers and cancer patients.

One patient, a 59-year-old male melanoma patient who developed severe hypotension and dizziness 40 minutes after receiving a dose of 13 mg/kg for 15 minutes, was treated by infusion of a plasma expander, dopamine, and atropine and recovered completely within several hours.

A 7-year-old boy who received an oral dose of 6 mg/kg before surgery developed no symptoms and required no treatment.

Treatment of overdose
If a patient exhibits signs of second-degree or higher atrioventricular (AV) conduction block following a suspected overdose of dolasetron, cardiac telemetry monitoring is recommended.

There is no known specific antidote for dolasetron. Supportive therapy is recommended.

Patient Consultation
In providing consultation, consider emphasizing the following selected information (» = major clinical significance):

Before using this medication
» Conditions affecting use, especially:
Sensitivity to dolasetron
Other medications, especially medications causing QT_c interval prolongation
Other medical problems, especially conditions associated with a risk of prolonged cardiac conduction intervals

Proper use of this medication
» Proper dosing

Side/adverse effects
Signs of potential side effects, especially hypertension or hypotension, anaphylactic reaction, bradycardia or palpitations, bronchospasm, chest pain, edema, hematuria, oliguria, pain, pancreatitis, tachycardia, and urinary retention

General Dosing Information
For oral dosage forms only
For children unable to swallow the tablet form of dolasetron, an oral solution may be prepared using dolasetron injection diluted in apple or apple-grape juice.

For parenteral dosage forms only
Dolasetron injection may be administered intravenously at a rate of up to 100 mg per thirty seconds, or may be diluted in a compatible intravenous solution to 50 mL and infused over a period of up to fifteen minutes.

Oral Dosage Forms
DOLASETRON MESYLATE TABLETS
Usual adult dose
Nausea and vomiting, cancer chemotherapy-induced (prophylaxis)—
Oral, 100 mg given within one hour before chemotherapy

Nausea and vomiting, postoperative (prophylaxis)—
Oral, 100 mg given within two hours before surgery.

Usual pediatric dose

Nausea and vomiting, cancer chemotherapy-induced (prophylaxis)—

Children 2 to 16 years of age: Oral, 1.8 mg per kg of body weight, up to a maximum of 100 mg, given within one hour before chemotherapy.

Children up to 2 years of age: Safety and efficacy have not been established.

Nausea and vomiting, postoperative (prophylaxis)—

Children 2 to 16 years of age: Oral, 1.2 mg per kg of body weight, up to a maximum of 100 mg, given within two hours before surgery.

Children up to 2 years of age: Safety and efficacy have not been established.

Usual pediatric prescribing limits

100 mg.

Usual geriatric dose

See *Usual adult dose*.

Strength(s) usually available

U.S.—

50 mg (Rx) [*Anzemet* (carnauba wax; croscarmellose sodium; hydroxypropyl methylcellulose; lactose; magnesium stearate; polyethylene glycol; polysorbate 80; pregelatinized starch; synthetic red iron oxide; titanium dioxide; white wax)].

100 mg (Rx) [*Anzemet* (carnauba wax; croscarmellose sodium; hydroxypropyl methylcellulose; lactose; magnesium stearate; polyethylene glycol; polysorbate 80; pregelatinized starch; synthetic red iron oxide; titanium dioxide; white wax)].

Packaging and storage

Store between 20 and 25 °C (68 and 77 °F). Protect from light.

Parenteral Dosage Forms

DOLASETRON MESYLATE INJECTION

Usual adult dose

Nausea and vomiting, cancer chemotherapy-induced (prophylaxis)—

Intravenous, 1.8 mg per kg of body weight as a single dose approximately thirty minutes before chemotherapy or

Intravenous, 100 mg as a single dose approximately thirty minutes before chemotherapy.

Nausea and vomiting, postoperative (prophylaxis)—

Intravenous, 12.5 mg as a single dose approximately fifteen minutes before the cessation of anesthesia.

Nausea and vomiting, postoperative (treatment)—

Intravenous, 12.5 mg as a single dose as soon as nausea or vomiting presents.

Note: Dolasetron mesylate injection may be administered intravenously at a rate of up to 100 mg per thirty seconds, or may be diluted in a compatible intravenous solution to 50 mL and infused over a period of up to fifteen minutes.

Usual pediatric dose

Nausea and vomiting, cancer chemotherapy-induced (prophylaxis)—

Children 2 to 16 years of age: Intravenous, 1.8 mg per kg of body weight as a single dose approximately thirty minutes before chemotherapy, to a maximum of 100 mg per dose.

Note: Dolasetron mesylate injection also may be administered orally, diluted in apple or apple-grape juice, at a dose of 1.8 mg per kg of body weight (up to a maximum of 100 mg) given within one hour before chemotherapy.

Children up to 2 years of age: Safety and efficacy have not been established.

Nausea and vomiting, postoperative (prophylaxis)—

Children 2 to 16 years of age: Intravenous, 0.35 mg per kg of body weight as a single dose approximately fifteen minutes before the cessation of anesthesia, to a maximum of 12.5 mg per dose.

Note: Dolasetron mesylate injection also may be administered orally, diluted in apple or apple-grape juice, at a dose of 1.2 mg per kg of body weight (up to a maximum of 100 mg) given within two hours before surgery.

Children up to 2 years of age: Safety and efficacy have not been established.

Nausea and vomiting, postoperative (treatment)—

Children 2 to 16 years of age: Intravenous, 0.35 mg per kg of body weight as a single dose as soon as nausea or vomiting presents, to a maximum of 12.5 mg per dose.

Children up to 2 years of age: Safety and efficacy have not been established.

Note: Dolasetron mesylate injection may be administered intravenously at a rate of up to 100 mg per thirty seconds, or may be diluted in a compatible intravenous solution to 50 mL and infused over a period of up to fifteen minutes.

Usual pediatric prescribing limits

100 mg.

Usual geriatric dose

See *Usual adult dose*.

Strength(s) usually available

U.S.—

20 mg per mL (Rx) [*Anzemet* (mannitol 38.2 mg per mL; acetate buffer)].

Packaging and storage

Store between 20 and 25 °C (68 and 77 °F). Protect from light.

Preparation of dosage form

Dolasetron mesylate injection may be diluted in 0.9% sodium chloride injection, 5% dextrose injection, 5% dextrose and 0.45% sodium chloride injection, 5% dextrose and Lactated Ringer's injection, Lactated Ringer's injection, or 10% mannitol injection for administration by intravenous infusion.

Dolasetron mesylate injection may be mixed in apple or apple-grape juice for oral administration to pediatric patients.

Stability

Because the intravenous solutions recommended for administration by intravenous infusion do not contain preservatives, it is recommended that diluted dolasetron mesylate injection not be used after 24 hours (48 hours if refrigerated).

The solution of dolasetron mesylate in apple or apple-grape juice may be kept for up to 2 hours at room temperature before use.

Incompatibilities

Dolasetron mesylate injection should not be mixed with other medications. The intravenous infusion line should be flushed both before and after administration.

Developed: 03/25/1998

DONEPEZIL Systemic

VA CLASSIFICATION (Primary): CN900

Commonly used brand name(s): *Aricept; Aricept ODT*.

Another commonly used name is E2020.

Note: For a listing of dosage forms and brand names by country availability, see *Dosage Forms* section(s).

Category

Dementia symptoms treatment adjunct.

Indications

Accepted

Dementia, Alzheimer's type, mild to moderate (treatment)—Donepezil is indicated for the treatment of mild to moderate dementia of the Alzheimer's type. There is no evidence that donepezil alters the underlying process that results in dementia, and the effectiveness of donepezil may be decreased as the disease progresses.

Pharmacology/Pharmacokinetics

Physicochemical characteristics

Chemical Group—Piperidine derivative.

Molecular weight—

Donepezil: 379.50.

Donepezil hydrochloride: 415.96.

Mechanism of action/Effect

Donepezil is a specific noncompetitive reversible inhibitor of acetylcholinesterase (AChE), and appears to exert its therapeutic effect by enhancing cholinergic function. By inhibiting the hydrolysis of acetylcholine by AChE, donepezil increases acetylcholine concentrations, thus enhancing cholinergic function. As the dementia progresses, fewer cholinergic neurons are thought to remain functionally intact, and the effects of donepezil may be lessened.

Donepezil exhibits a relatively high degree of selectivity for neuronal AChE; at relevant clinical doses, it has only weak inhibitory effects on butyrylcholinesterase (pseudocholinesterase), an enzyme that is widely distributed in plasma and peripheral tissues. Animal studies have shown that donepezil exhibits tissue selectivity; it significantly inhibits AChE in the brain but causes little inhibition of AChE in smooth, striated, or cardiac muscle.

Donepezil's inhibition of AChE in red blood cells corresponds closely to its effect at synapses in the central nervous system (CNS). AChE inhibition in red blood cells has been used as an indicator of the clinical effectiveness of donepezil in Alzheimer's disease patients.

Absorption
Well absorbed, with a relative oral bioavailability of 100%. The rate and extent of absorption are not influenced by food intake or the time of administration.

Distribution
Steady-state volume of distribution (Vol_D) is 12 liters per kg of body weight (L/kg).

Protein binding
Very high (approximately 96%, mainly to albumins [about 75%] and alpha$_1$-acid glycoprotein [about 21%] over the concentration range of 2 to 1000 nanograms per mL). This binding is not clinically significant at relevant plasma concentrations.

Biotransformation
Extensive. Donepezil undergoes first pass metabolism to four major metabolites, two of which are known to be active, and a number of minor metabolites. Donepezil is metabolized by cytochrome P450 isoenzymes CYP2D6 and CYP3A4, and undergoes glucuronidation. The rate of metabolism is slow and does not appear to be saturable. Following administration of radiolabeled donepezil, plasma radioactivity was present primarily as intact donepezil (53%) and as 6-*O*-desmethyl donepezil (11%); this metabolite has been reported to inhibit acetylcholinesterase to the same extent as donepezil does *in vitro* and was found in plasma at concentrations equal to about 20% of donepezil.

In a study of 10 patients with stable alcoholic cirrhosis, the clearance of a single dose of donepezil was decreased by 20% relative to that in 10 healthy age- and sex-matched subjects. With the exception of peak plasma concentrations, there were no statistically significant differences in the pharmacokinetics of donepezil between the groups, and dosage modifications in patients with hepatic function impairment should not be required.

Half-life
Elimination—
About 70 hours.

Time to peak concentration
3 to 4 hours.

Time to steady-state concentration
Pharmacokinetics are linear over a dose range of 1 to 10 mg given once a day. Following multiple-dose administration, donepezil accumulates in plasma by fourfold to sevenfold, and steady-state is reached within 15 days. The mean plasma concentration of donepezil at steady-state is 14.2 nanograms per mL.

Elimination
Renal, biliary. Following administration of radiolabeled donepezil, total radioactivity recovered over a period of 10 days was approximately 57% in urine (17% as unchanged drug) and 15% in feces (1% as unchanged drug); 28% remained unrecovered.

In one study of pairs of age- and sex-matched subjects, the clearance of donepezil in eleven patients with moderate to severe renal function impairment was not found to differ from the clearance in eleven healthy volunteers.

Precautions to Consider

Cross-sensitivity and/or related problems
Patients sensitive to other piperidine derivatives may be sensitive to donepezil also. Piperidine derivatives include: rifabutin, methylphenidate, biperiden hydrochloride, trihexyphenidyl hydrochloride, bupivacaine hydrochloride, and paroxetine hydrochloride.

Carcinogenicity
No evidence of a carcinogenic potential was observed in an 88-week study of mice that received approximately 63 times the maximum recommended human dose of donepezil, or in a 104-week study in rats that received approximately 24 times the maximum recommended human dose of donepezil.

Mutagenicity
Donepezil was not mutagenic in the Ames reverse mutation assay in bacteria or in a mouse lymphoma forward mutation assay *in vitro* . In the chromosome aberration test in cultures of Chinese hamster lung (CHL) cells, some clastogenic effects were observed. Donepezil was not clastogenic in the *in vivo* mouse micronucleus test and was not genotoxic in an evaluation of unscheduled DNA synthesis in primary hepatocyte cultures prepared from rats.

Pregnancy/Reproduction
Fertility—Donepezil demonstrated no effect on fertility in rats given doses approximately eight times the maximum recommended human dose on a mg per square meter of body surface area (mg/m^2) basis.

Pregnancy—Adequate and well-controlled studies have not been done in humans. Donepezil should be used during pregnancy only if potential benefit justifies potential risk to the fetus.

Studies in pregnant rats and rabbits at doses approximately 13 and 16 times, respectively, the maximum recommended human dose on a mg/m^2 basis showed no evidence of teratogenic potential. However, in a study of pregnant rats that received approximately eight times the maximum recommended human dose on a mg/m^2 basis from day 17 of gestation through day 20 postpartum, a slight increase in stillbirths and a slight decrease in pup survival through day 4 postpartum were observed.

FDA Pregnancy Category C.

Breast-feeding
It is not known whether donepezil is distributed into breast milk. Donepezil has no indication for use in nursing mothers.

Pediatrics
Appropriate studies on the relationship of age to the effects of donepezil have not been performed in the pediatric population. Safety and efficacy have not been established in any illness occurring in children.

Geriatrics
Mean plasma donepezil concentrations measured during therapeutic monitoring of elderly patients with Alzheimer's disease were comparable to those observed in young healthy volunteers. Although the plasma half-life and the time to peak plasma concentration (t_{max}) were longer in the elderly than in young healthy volunteers, the area under the plasma-concentration-time curve (AUC), peak plasma concentration (C_{max}), and oral clearance did not differ between the two groups; differences probably were due to the increased volume of distribution at steady-state. In general, modification of donepezil doses in the elderly is not necessary.

The incidence of nausea, diarrhea, vomiting, insomnia, fatigue, and anorexia increases with increasing age. Caution is advised regarding use of donepezil in low-body-weight elderly patients, especially those ≥ 85 years of age, due to the potential for significant weight loss.

Pharmacogenetics
No specific pharmacokinetic study was conducted to investigate the effects of gender and race on the disposition of donepezil. However, retrospective pharmacokinetic analysis suggests that gender and race (Japanese and caucasian) do not affect the clearance of donepezil.

Surgical
Because donepezil is a cholinesterase inhibitor, it is likely to exaggerate succinylcholine-type muscle relaxation during anesthesia.

Drug interactions and/or related problems
The following drug interactions and/or related problems have been selected on the basis of their potential clinical significance (possible mechanism in parentheses where appropriate)—not necessarily inclusive (» = major clinical significance):

Note: *In vitro* studies of donepezil and other highly protein-bound medications have shown no displacement of or by digoxin, furosemide, or warfarin. Other *in vitro* studies indicate little probability that donepezil interferes with the clearance of other drugs metabolized by CYP3A4 isoenzymes (e.g., cisapride, terfenadine) or by CYP2D6 isoenzymes (e.g., imipramine). It is not known if donepezil has any potential for enzyme induction.

Formal pharmacokinetic studies showed no significant effects of donepezil on the pharmacokinetics of cimetidine, digoxin, theophylline, or warfarin. Similarly, metabolism of donepezil is not significantly affected by concurrent administration of cimetidine or digoxin.

Combinations containing any of the following medications, depending on the amount present, may also interact with this medication.

Anticholinergics (see *Appendix II*)
(cholinesterase inhibitors such as donepezil have the potential to interfere with the activity of these medications)

Anti-inflammatory drugs, nonsteroidal (NSAIDs)
(donepezil may increase gastric acid secretion due to increased cholinergic activity; patients should be monitored for symptoms of active or occult gastrointestinal bleeding)

Carbamazepine or
Dexamethasone or
Phenobarbital or
Phenytoin or

Rifampin
(these medications may induce the isoenzymes CYP2D6 and CYP3A4, thus increasing the rate of elimination of donepezil)

Cholinergic agonists (e.g., bethanechol) or
Neuromuscular blocking agents metabolized by plasma cholinesterase (e.g., succinylcholine, mivacurium)
(a synergistic effect may be expected with concurrent use of these medications and donepezil)

Ketoconazole
(as an inhibitor of the CYP3A4 isoenzyme, ketoconazole has been shown to inhibit the metabolism of donepezil *in vitro;* inhibition of metabolism is unlikely to produce an increase in adverse effects or a change in the effects of donepezil due to the low plasma concentrations of active metabolites and their inability to cross the blood–brain barrier)

Quinidine
(as an inhibitor of the CYP2D6 isoenzyme, quinidine has been shown to inhibit the metabolism of donepezil *in vitro;* clinical significance is not known)

Medical considerations/Contraindications

The medical considerations/contraindications included have been selected on the basis of their potential clinical significance (reasons given in parentheses where appropriate)—not necessarily inclusive (» = major clinical significance).

Except under special circumstances, this medication should not be used when the following medical problem exists:

» Hypersensitivity to donepezil or to piperidine derivatives

Risk-benefit should be considered when the following medical problems exist:

Asthma, history of or
Chronic obstructive pulmonary disease
(cholinomimetic actions of cholinesterase inhibitors may aggravate the condition)

» Cardiovascular conditions, such as:
Sick sinus syndrome
Supraventricular conduction problems
Unexplained syncopal episodes
(cholinesterase inhibitors such as donepezil may have vagotonic effects on heart rate [e.g., bradycardia]; syncopal episodes have been reported)

Hepatic function impairment
(metabolism of donepezil may be impaired)

» Peptic ulcer disease, or history of
(cholinesterase inhibitors may increase gastric acid secretion due to increased cholinergic activity; condition may be exacerbated)

Seizures, history of
(cholinomimetics are believed to have the potential to cause generalized seizures; however, seizure activity also may be a manifestation of the Alzheimer's disease state)

Urinary tract obstruction
(cholinomimetics may cause bladder outflow obstruction)

Side/Adverse Effects

Note: Adverse effects are generally mild to moderate, and transient in nature; they may occur most often during dose initiation or escalation. The frequency of common adverse effects may be affected by the rate of dosage titration.

The incidence of nausea, diarrhea, vomiting, insomnia, fatigue, and anorexia increases with increasing dose and with increasing age. Also, adverse effects occur more commonly in patients who are ≥ 85 years of age, female, or of low body weight.

The following side/adverse effects have been selected on the basis of their potential clinical significance (possible signs and symptoms in parentheses where appropriate)—not necessarily inclusive:

Those indicating need for medical attention

Incidence more frequent

Anorexia (loss of appetite); ***diarrhea; fatigue*** (unusual tiredness or weakness); ***insomnia*** (trouble in sleeping); ***muscle cramps; nausea; vomiting***

Incidence less frequent

Abnormal dreams; arthritis (joint pain, stiffness, or swelling); ***constipation; dizziness; ecchymosis*** (unusual bleeding or bruising); ***frequent urination; headache; mental depression; pain; somnolence*** (drowsiness); ***syncope*** (fainting); ***weight loss***

Incidence rare

Aphasia (problems with speech); ***ataxia*** (clumsiness or unsteadiness); ***atrial fibrillation*** (irregular heartbeat; dizziness; fainting); ***bloating; blurred vision; bronchitis*** (cough; shortness of breath; tightness in chest; wheezing); ***cataract; chest or epigastric pain*** (pain in chest, upper stomach, or throat); ***dehydration*** (confusion; decrease in urination; dizziness; dryness of mouth; increase in heart rate and breathing; low blood pressure; severe thirst; sunken eyes; unusual tiredness or weakness; wrinkled skin); ***diaphoresis*** (increased sweating); ***dyspnea*** (troubled breathing); ***eye irritation; fecal incontinence*** (loss of bowel control); ***gastrointestinal bleeding*** (black, tarry stools); ***hot flashes; hypertension or hypotension*** (high or low blood pressure); ***increased libido*** (increase in sexual desire or performance); ***mood or mental changes, including abnormal crying, aggression, agitation, delusions, irritability, nervousness, or restlessness; nocturia*** (increased urge to urinate during the night); ***paresthesia*** (burning, prickling, or tingling sensations); ***pharyngitis*** (sore throat); ***pruritus*** (itching); ***tremor; upper respiratory infection*** (chills; cough; fever; nasal congestion; runny nose; sneezing; sore throat); ***urinary incontinence*** (loss of bladder control); ***urinary tract infection*** (bloody or cloudy urine; difficult or painful urination; frequent urge to urinate); ***urticaria*** (hives); ***vasodilation*** (flushing of skin); ***vertigo***

Incidence not known

Cholecystitis (indigestion; stomach pain; severe nausea; vomiting); ***convulsions*** (seizures); ***hallucinations*** (seeing, hearing, or feeling things that are not there); ***heart block (all types)*** (chest pain or discomfort; fainting; shortness of breath; slow or irregular heartbeat; sweating); ***hemolytic anemia*** (back, leg, or stomach pains; bleeding gums; chills; dark urine; difficulty breathing; fatigue; fever; general body swelling; headache; loss of appetite; nausea or vomiting; nosebleeds; pale skin; sore throat; yellowing of the eyes or skin); ***hepatitis*** (dark urine; general tiredness and weakness; light-colored stools; nausea and vomiting; upper right abdominal pain; yellow eyes and skin); ***hyponatremia*** (coma; confusion; convulsions; decreased urine output; dizziness; fast or irregular heartbeat; headache; increased thirst; muscle pain or cramps; nausea or vomiting; shortness of breath; swelling of face, ankles, or hands; unusual tiredness or weakness); ***neuroleptic malignant syndrome*** (convulsions; difficulty in breathing; fast heartbeat; high fever; high or low blood pressure; increased sweating; loss of bladder control; severe muscle stiffness; unusually pale skin; tiredness); ***pancreatitis*** (bloating; chills; constipation; darkened urine; fast heartbeat; fever; indigestion; loss of appetite; nausea; pains in stomach, side, or abdomen, possibly radiating to the back; vomiting; yellow eyes or skin); ***rash***

Those indicating need for medical attention only if they continue or are bothersome

Incidence not known

Abdominal pain (stomach pain); ***confusion*** (mood or mental changes)

Overdose

For specific information on the agents used in the management of donepezil overdose, see *Atropine* in the *Anticholinergics/Antispasmodics (Systemic)* monograph.

For more information on the management of overdose or unintentional ingestion, **contact a Poison Control Center** (see *Poison Control Center Listing*).

Clinical effects of overdose

The following effects have been selected on the basis of their potential clinical significance (possible signs and symptoms in parentheses where appropriate)—not necessarily inclusive:

Overdosage with cholinesterase inhibitors may result in cholinergic crisis characterized by:

Bradycardia (slow heartbeat); ***hypotension*** (low blood pressure); ***muscle weakness, increasing***—may result in death if respiratory muscles are involved; ***nausea, severe; respiratory depression*** (troubled breathing); ***salivation, increased*** (increased watering of mouth); ***seizures; sweating, increased; vomiting, severe***

Treatment of overdose

To enhance elimination—It is not known whether donepezil and/or its metabolites can be removed by hemodialysis, peritoneal dialysis, or hemofiltration.

Specific treatment—Tertiary anticholinergics such as atropine may be used as antidotes. Intravenous atropine sulfate titrated to effect is recommended; initially, an intravenous dose of 1 to 2 mg is given, with subsequent doses based upon clinical response. Atypical responses in blood pressure and heart rate have been reported with other cholinomimetics when coadministered with quaternary anticholinergics such as glycopyrrolate.

Supportive care—General supportive measures should be utilized. Patients in whom intentional overdose is confirmed or suspected should be referred for psychiatric consultation.

Patient Consultation

As an aid to patient consultation, refer to *Advice for the Patient, Donepezil (Systemic).*

In providing consultation, consider emphasizing the following selected information (» = major clinical significance):

Before using this medication

» Conditions affecting use, especially:
- Hypersensitivity to donepezil or other piperidine derivatives
- Pregnancy—Risk-benefit should be considered
- Breast-feeding—Has no indication for use in nursing mothers
- Other medical problems, especially cardiovascular conditions and peptic ulcer disease
- Surgical—A synergistic effect occurs when donepezil is used concurrently with neuromuscular blocking agents metabolized by plasma cholinesterase (e.g., succinylcholine)

Proper use of this medication

» Taking medication exactly as directed; not taking more medication than the amount prescribed because of increased risk of adverse effects

Taking donepezil at bedtime

Proper administration for liquid dosage form: Shaking well; using an accurate measuring device, such as a specially marked measuring spoon, a plastic syringe, or a small graduated cup

Proper handling/administration of the oral disintegrating tablets

» Proper dosing

Missed dose: Skipping the missed dose and returning to regular dosing schedule; not doubling doses

» Proper storage

Precautions while using this medication

» Importance of keeping regular appointments with physician

» Caution if any kind of surgery or emergency treatment is required; informing physician or dentist in charge that donepezil is being taken

» Caution if dizziness, drowsiness, or clumsiness or unsteadiness occurs

» Suspected overdose—Getting emergency help at once

Side/adverse effects

Signs of potential side effects, especially anorexia, diarrhea, fatigue, insomnia, muscle cramps, nausea, vomiting, abnormal dreams, arthritis, constipation, dizziness, ecchymosis, frequent urination, headache, mental depression, pain, somnolence, syncope, weight loss, aphasia, ataxia, atrial fibrillation, bloating, blurred vision, bronchitis, cataract, chest or epigastric pain, dehydration, diaphoresis, dyspnea, eye irritation, fecal incontinence, gastrointestinal bleeding, hot flashes, hypertension or hypotension, increased libido, mood or mental changes, nocturia, paresthesia, pruritus, tremor, upper respiratory infection, urinary incontinence, urinary tract infection, urticaria, vasodilation, and vertigo

Signs of potential side effects observed during clinical practice, especially cholecystitis, convulsions, hallucinations, heart block (all types), hemolytic anemia, hepatitis, hyponatremia, neuroleptic malignant syndrome, pancreatitis, or rash

General Dosing Information

Donepezil should be taken in the evening, just prior to retiring. However, if insomnia is a problem, this medication may be taken during the day. Donepezil may be taken with or without food.

In a population of cognitively-impaired persons such as Alzheimer's disease patients, safe use of donepezil (and all other medications) may require supervision.

Diet/Nutrition

Donepezil can be taken with or without food.

Bioequivalence information

Both donepezil orally disintegrating tablets and oral solution are bioequivalent to donepezil tablets.

Oral Dosage Forms

DONEPEZIL HYDROCHLORIDE ORAL DISINTEGRATING TABLETS

Note: Patients should allow the oral disintegrating tablets to dissolve on the tongue and follow with water.

Usual adult dose
See *Donepezil Hydrochloride Tablets.*

Usual adult limits
See *Donepezil Hydrochloride Tablets.*

Usual pediatric dose
See *Donepezil Hydrochloride Tablets.*

Usual geriatric dose
See *Donepezil Hydrochloride Tablets.*

Strength(s) usually available
U.S.—
- 5 mg (Rx) [*Aricept ODT* (Orally disintegrating tablets; carrageenan; mannitol; colloidal silicon dioxide; polyvinyl alcohol)].
- 10 mg (Rx) [*Aricept ODT* (Orally disintegrating tablets; carrageenan; mannitol; colloidal silicon dioxide; polyvinyl alcohol; yellow ferric oxide)].

Packaging and storage
Store at controlled room temperature 15 to 30 °C (59 to 86 °F).

DONEPEZIL HYDROCHLORIDE ORAL SOLUTION

Usual adult dose
See *Donepezil Hydrochloride Tablets.*

Usual adult limits
See *Donepezil Hydrochloride Tablets.*

Usual pediatric dose
See *Donepezil Hydrochloride Tablets.*

Usual geriatric dose
See *Donepezil Hydrochloride Tablets.*

Strength(s) usually available
U.S.—
- 1 mg per mL (Rx) [*Aricept* (sorbitol solution 70%; povidone K-30; citric acid anhydrous; sodium citrate dihydrate; sodium benzoate; methylparaben; propylene glycol; sodium metabisulfite; purified water; strawberry flavor)].

Additional information
Use a specially marked measuring spoon, a plastic syringe, or a small marked measuring cup to measure each dose accurately.

DONEPEZIL HYDROCHLORIDE TABLETS

Usual adult dose
Alzheimer's dementia—
Oral, initially 5 mg once a day, taken in the evening just prior to retiring. Although a higher dose of 10 mg did not provide a statistically significant greater clinical benefit than the 5-mg dose, a daily dose of 10 mg may provide additional benefit for some patients. However, the 10-mg dose is likely to be associated with a higher incidence of cholinergic side effects than the 5-mg dose. If a trial of the 10-mg dose is desired, dosage should not be increased until patients have been on a daily dose of 5 mg for four to six weeks because steady-state is not achieved for fifteen days and because the rate of adverse effects may be influenced by the rate of dose escalation.

Usual adult dosing limits
10 mg a day.

Usual pediatric dose
Safety and efficacy have not been established.

Usual geriatric dose
See *Usual adult dose.*

Note: In elderly women of low body weight, the dose should not exceed 5 mg a day.

Strength(s) usually available
U.S.—
- 5 mg (Rx) [*Aricept* (film-coated; lactose monohydrate)].
- 10 mg (Rx) [*Aricept* (film-coated; lactose monohydrate)].

Canada—
- 5 mg (Rx) [*Aricept* (film-coated; lactose monohydrate)].
- 10 mg (Rx) [*Aricept* (film-coated; lactose monohydrate)].

Packaging and storage
Store between 15 and 30 °C (59 and 86 °F).

Auxiliary labeling
- May cause dizziness.
- May cause drowsiness.

Revised: 01/07/2005
Developed: 06/11/1999

DOPAMINE—See *Sympathomimetic Agents—Cardiovascular Use (Parenteral-Systemic)*

DORNASE ALFA Inhalation-Local

VA CLASSIFICATION (Primary): RE900

Commonly used brand name(s): *Pulmozyme*.

Other commonly used names are: recombinant human deoxyribonuclease I (rhDNase) and DNase I.

Note: For a listing of dosage forms and brand names by country availability, see *Dosage Forms* section(s).

Category

Cystic fibrosis therapy adjunct.

Indications

Accepted

Cystic fibrosis (treatment adjunct)—Dornase alfa is indicated in the management of cystic fibrosis patients to improve pulmonary function when it is administered daily and in conjunction with standard therapies. Also, in patients with a forced vital capacity (FVC) greater than 40% of predicted value, daily administration of dornase alfa has been shown to reduce the frequency of respiratory infections requiring parenteral antibiotics.

No studies have been performed with dornase alfa for longer than 12 months.

Pharmacology/Pharmacokinetics

Physicochemical characteristics

Source—Produced by genetically engineered Chinese hamster ovary cells containing deoxyribonucleic acid (DNA) encoding for deoxyribonuclease (DNase).

Chemical Group—A purified glycoprotein containing 260 amino acids in primary sequence identical to that of the native human enzyme, DNase.

Molecular weight—29,250.18 daltons.

Mechanism of action/Effect

The bronchial secretions of cystic fibrosis patients contain high levels of extracellular, polyanionic DNA, which is released by disintegrating inflammatory cells, especially polymorphonuclear neutrophils, present after lung infections. The excess DNA causes the already abnormal sputum to thicken. The viscous, dehydrated mucus is difficult to expectorate, obstructs airways, and contributes to reduced lung volumes and expiratory flow rates. The accumulation of purulent secretions in the airways provides a continuing growth medium for bacteria, causing chronic pulmonary infections, which are the major cause of morbidity and mortality in patients with cystic fibrosis.

In vitro studies have shown that DNase, an enzyme normally produced in small quantities in the pancreas and salivary glands, reduces the viscoelasticity of sputum in patients with cystic fibrosis by breaking the long extracellular DNA molecules into smaller fragments.

Onset of action

Significant improvement in lung function—Within 3 to 8 days.

Reduction in respiratory tract infections—Up to several months.

Duration of action

Lung function gradually returns to baseline after the drug is discontinued. In one study, 12 to 14% of patients treated with dornase alfa had a forced expiratory volume in one second (FEV_1) 15% above baseline 32 days after therapy was discontinued, as compared with 6% of placebo-treated patients. In another study, the time to baseline was shorter; the mean improvement in FEV_1 was 7.5% in the patients treated with dornase alfa and 2.2% for the placebo-treated patients 4 days after the last dose.

Precautions to Consider

Carcinogenicity

Studies conducted over the lifetime of rats at doses of up to 246 mcg per kg (mcg/kg) of body weight per day, showed no carcinogenic effect. No increase in the development of benign or malignant neoplasms was seen, and no unusual tumor types appeared.

Mutagenicity

Ames tests using six different strains of bacteria at concentrations of up to 5000 mcg per plate, a cytogenetic assay using human peripheral blood lymphocytes at concentrations of up to 2000 mcg per plate, and a mouse lymphoma assay at concentrations of up to 1000 mcg per plate, with and without metabolic activation, showed no evidence of mutagenic potential.

A micronucleus assay in bone marrow cells of mice, conducted after administration of a bolus intravenous dose of 10 mg per kg of body weight (mg/kg) of dornase alfa on two consecutive days, showed no evidence of chromosomal damage.

Pregnancy/Reproduction

Fertility—Studies in rats and rabbits given intravenous doses of dornase alfa of up to 10 mg/kg per day (more than 600 times the exposure expected following the recommended human dose) showed no evidence of impairment of fertility in males or females.

Pregnancy—Adequate and well-controlled studies in humans have not been done.

Studies in rats and rabbits given intravenous doses of up to 10 mg/kg per day (more than 600 times the exposure expected following the recommended human dose) showed no evidence of harm or effects on development of the fetus.

FDA Pregnancy Category B.

Breast-feeding

It is not known whether dornase alfa is distributed into the breast milk of humans; however, little or no measurable concentrations of dornase alfa are expected in human breast milk after long-term administration of recommended doses.

Small amounts of dornase alfa were detected in the milk of monkeys after administration of an intravenous bolus of 100 mg/kg followed by a 6-hour infusion at a dosage of 80 mg/kg per hour.

Pediatrics

Dornase alfa should be used in patients younger than 5 years of age only if there is potential for improved pulmonary function or for decreasing the risk of respiratory infections, due to limited clinical experience in this population. The safety of dornase alfa was studied over a 2-week period in two groups, children 3 months to 5 years of age, and children 5 to 10 years of age. The PARI BABY reusable nebulizer with its tight-fitting face mask was used for patients unable to inhale and exhale orally throughout the entire treatment. Incidence of cough, rhinitis, and skin rash was slightly higher for the younger group.

Geriatrics

Clinical trials were conducted and did not include sufficient numbers of patients older than 65 years of age as cystic fibrosis is primarily a disease of pediatrics and young adults. However, no geriatric specific problems have been documented to date.

Drug interactions and/or related problems

Possible drug interactions with dornase alfa have not been studied. However, the medication has been used safely and effectively in conjunction with other medications commonly given orally, parenterally, or via inhalation to patients with cystic fibrosis, including analgesics, antibiotics, bronchodilators, corticosteroids, enzymes, and vitamins.

Medical considerations/Contraindications

The medical considerations/contraindications included have been selected on the basis of their potential clinical significance (reasons given in parentheses where appropriate)—not necessarily inclusive (» = major clinical significance).

Risk-benefit should be considered when the following medical problem exists:

Sensitivity to dornase alfa or Chinese hamster ovary cell products

Side/Adverse Effects

The following side/adverse effects have been selected on the basis of their potential clinical significance (possible signs and symptoms in parentheses where appropriate)—not necessarily inclusive:

Those indicating need for medical attention

Incidence rare

Allergic reactions including; urticaria (hives or welts; itching; redness of skin; skin rash)—mild to moderate, transient; ***and/or skin rash***

Those indicating need for medical attention only if they continue or are bothersome

Incidence more frequent

Chest pain or discomfort; hoarseness; sore throat

Incidence less frequent

Conjunctivitis (redness, itching, pain, swelling, or other irritation of eyes); ***decrease in forced vital capacity (FVC)***—≥ 10% decrease as compared with predicted value; ***dyspepsia*** (upset stomach); ***dyspnea*** (difficulty breathing); ***fever; rhinitis*** (runny or stuffy nose)

Patient Consultation

As an aid to patient consultation, refer to *Advice for the Patient, Dornase Alfa (Inhalation)*.

In providing consultation, consider emphasizing the following selected information (» = major clinical significance):

Before using this medication

» Conditions affecting use, especially:
 Sensitivity to dornase alfa

Proper use of this medication

Reading patient instructions carefully

» Not using ampul that has been previously opened; checking ampule for leaks; not using medication if out of date

» Not using if medication is cloudy or discolored

» Using only with power-operated nebulizer and compressor recommended by manufacturer of medication

» Importance of knowing how to use the medication in the nebulizer; using only with the mouthpiece provided with the nebulizer; not using a face mask unless needed

» Compliance with therapy; using at same time every day; some improvement may occur within 1 week; some patients may require weeks to months for full benefits

» Importance of continuing other cystic fibrosis medications as before; not mixing any other medication with dornase alfa in nebulizer; using other medications, such as inhalation bronchodilators, before or after dornase alfa treatment

Preparation of nebulizer for use

Preparation of medication for use in nebulizer; method of opening ampul and emptying ampul contents into nebulizer cup; using all medication in ampul

Proper administration technique

Proper care of nebulizer and compressor after use

» Proper dosing

Missed dose: Taking missed dose as soon as possible; if almost time for next dose, skipping missed dose and going back to regular dosing schedule

» Proper storage: Keeping ampuls in refrigerator in foil pouches at all times; not freezing; not leaving out of refrigerator for more than a total of 24 hours

Precautions while using this medication

» Checking with physician if condition becomes worse

Side/adverse effects

Signs of potential side effects, especially allergic reactions (urticaria and/or skin rash), chest pain or discomfort, hoarseness, sore throat, conjunctivitis, decrease in forced vital capacity, dyspepsia, dyspnea, fever, or rhinitis

General Dosing Information

Dornase alfa inhalation solution is administered by nebulization. The only nebulizers and compressors that should be used are the Hudson T Up-draft II disposable jet nebulizer with the Pulmo-Aide compressor, the Marquest Acorn II disposable jet nebulizer with the Pulmo-Aide compressor, the reusable PARI LC Jet+ nebulizer with the PARI PRONEB compressor, and the reusable Durable Sidestream jet nebulizer with the MOBILAIRE or the Porta-Neb compressors. The reusable PARI BABY nebulizer with its tight-fitting face mask may be used in patients who are unable to inhale and exhale orally throughout the entire nebulization period. The PARI BABY nebulizer should be used with the PARI PRONEB compressor. Safety and efficacy have not been studied with other systems. Therefore, battery-operated systems and ultrasonic nebulizers are not recommended for dornase alfa administration.

Patients who use the Durable Sidestream jet nebulizer with the MOBILEAIRE compressor should turn the compressor control knob fully to the right and then turn on the compressor. At this setting, the needle on the pressure gauge should vibrate between 35 and 45 pounds per square inch, which is the highest pressure output.

A mouthpiece is provided with each nebulizer. A face mask is not recommended, except in certain pediatric patients who are unable to use a mouthpiece, because it may reduce delivery of the medication to the lungs.

Wash hands thoroughly before assembling the nebulizer and adding the medication. The surface used for assembling the nebulizer also must be clean. The nebulizer and its parts must be kept clean at all times, according to the manufacturer's directions.

Squeeze each ampule prior to use to check for leaks.

Dornase alfa solution should not be mixed or diluted with any other medication in the nebulizer cup because of possible physicochemical incompatibilities. However, other concurrently used medications, such as inhaled bronchodilators, may be administered before or after dornase alfa treatment.

Inhalation Dosage Forms

DORNASE ALFA INHALATION SOLUTION

Usual adult and adolescent dose

Cystic fibrosis therapy adjunct—
 Oral inhalation, 2.5 mg per day via nebulization, the dosage being increased to 2.5 mg two times a day if necessary.

Usual pediatric dose

Cystic fibrosis therapy adjunct—
 Children up to 3 months of age: Safety and efficacy have not been established.
 Children 3 months to 5 years of age: Oral inhalation, 2.5 mg per day via nebulization.
 Children 5 years of age and over: See *Usual adult and adolescent dose*.

Strength(s) usually available

U.S.—
 1 mg per mL (2.5-mL single-use ampul) (Rx) [*Pulmozyme*].

Canada—
 1 mg per mL (2.5-mL single-use ampul) (Rx) [*Pulmozyme*].

Packaging and storage

Store between 2 and 8 °C (36 and 46 °F). Protect from light.

Stability

Ampul should be discarded if contents are cloudy or discolored.

Unopened ampuls should not be exposed to temperatures over 30 °C (86 °F) for longer than 24 hours.

Opened ampul must be used at once or discarded.

Incompatibilities

Dornase alfa solution should not be mixed or diluted with any other medication in the nebulizer cup due to possible physicochemical incompatibilities.

Auxiliary labeling

• For oral inhalation only.

Selected Bibliography

Bryson HM, Sorkin EM. Dornase alfa, a review of its pharmacological properties and therapeutic potential in cystic fibrosis. Drugs 1994; 48: 894-906.

Witt DM, Anderson L. Dornase alfa: a new option in the management of cystic fibrosis. Pharmacotherapy 1996; 16: 40-8.

Revised: 05/06/2002

DORZOLAMIDE Ophthalmic†

VA CLASSIFICATION (Primary): OP112

Commonly used brand name(s): *Trusopt*.

Note: For a listing of dosage forms and brand names by country availability, see *Dosage Forms* section(s).

†Not commercially available in Canada.

Category

Antiglaucoma agent (ophthalmic).

Indications

Accepted

Glaucoma, open-angle (treatment) or
Hypertension, ocular (treatment)—Dorzolamide is indicated in the treatment of elevated intraocular pressure in patients with ocular hypertension or open-angle glaucoma.

Pharmacology/Pharmacokinetics

Physicochemical characteristics

Chemical Group—Sulfonamide.

Molecular weight—360.91.

pH—Dorzolamide hydrochloride ophthalmic solution: Approximately 5.6.

Mechanism of action/Effect

Dorzolamide is a sulfonamide and a carbonic anhydrase inhibitor. Carbonic anhydrase is an enzyme found in many tissues of the body, including the eye. Carbonic anhydrase catalyzes the reversible reaction involving the hydration of carbon dioxide and the dehydration of carbonic acid. In humans, carbonic anhydrase exists as a number of isoenzymes, the most active of which is carbonic anhydrase II. Carbonic anhydrase II is found primarily in red blood cells, but it also appears in other tissues.

Antiglaucoma agent—Dorzolamide inhibits human carbonic anhydrase II. Inhibition of carbonic anhydrase in the ciliary processes of the eye decreases aqueous humor secretion, presumably by slowing the formation of bicarbonate ions, with subsequent reduction in sodium and fluid transport. The result is a reduction in intraocular pressure. In clinical studies of up to 1 year in duration in patients with glaucoma or ocular hypertension who had baseline intraocular pressure (IOP) of ≥ 23 mm of mercury (mm Hg), dorzolamide had an IOP-lowering effect of approximately 3 to 5 mm Hg throughout the day.

Other actions/effects

When dorzolamide was administered orally in doses of 2 mg twice a day for up to 20 weeks to 8 healthy volunteers, inhibition of both carbonic anhydrase II activity and total carbonic anhydrase activity was less than the degree of inhibition considered to be necessary for a pharmacological effect on renal function and respiration in healthy persons. (The oral dose of 2 mg twice a day closely approximates the amount of medication delivered systemically by ophthalmic administration of 2% dorzolamide 3 times a day.)

Absorption

Dorzolamide is systemically absorbed when applied to the eye. In a study designed to simulate systemic absorption during long-term ophthalmic administration, 8 healthy subjects were given 2 mg of oral dorzolamide twice a day for up to 20 weeks. (The oral dose of 2 mg twice a day closely approximates the amount of medication delivered systemically by ophthalmic administration of 2% dorzolamide 3 times a day.) Steady state was reached within 8 weeks.

Distribution

During chronic dosing, dorzolamide accumulates in red blood cells by binding to carbonic anhydrase II. The *N*-desethyl metabolite also accumulates in red blood cells by binding primarily to carbonic anhydrase I. Plasma concentrations of dorzolamide and the *N*-desethyl metabolite are generally below the minimum assay limit of 15 nanomoles.

Protein binding

Moderate (approximately 33%).

Biotransformation

The only metabolite is the active *N*-desethyl derivative, which inhibits carbonic anhydrase II to a lesser extent than does dorzolamide. The *N*-desethyl metabolite also inhibits carbonic anhydrase I.

Half-life

After therapy is discontinued, dorzolamide washes out of red blood cells in a nonlinear fashion, resulting in a rapid initial decline in blood concentration, followed by a slower elimination phase having a half-life of about 4 months.

Time to peak effect

Approximately 2 hours.

Elimination

Primarily renal, as unchanged dorzolamide and the *N*-desethyl metabolite.

Precautions to Consider

Cross-sensitivity and/or related problems

Patients sensitive to other carbonic anhydrase inhibitors or other sulfonamides, including furosemide, thiazide diuretics, and oral antidiabetic agents, may be sensitive to dorzolamide also.

Tumorigenicity

In a 21-month study in female and male mice, dorzolamide administered orally in doses of up to 75 mg per kg of body weight (mg/kg) a day (greater than 900 times the recommended human ophthalmic dose) did not result in any treatment-related tumors. In addition, no changes in bladder urothelium were seen in dogs given dorzolamide orally for 1 year at a dose of 2 mg/kg a day (25 times the recommended human ophthalmic dose) or monkeys given dorzolamide topically to the eye for 1 year at a dose of 0.4 mg/kg a day (greater than 5 times the recommended human ophthalmic dose). However, in a 2-year study in male and female Sprague-Dawley rats, dorzolamide administered orally at the highest dose of 20 mg/kg a day (250 times the recommended human ophthalmic dose) produced urinary bladder papillomas in the male rats. Papillomas were not seen in the rats that received the lower oral doses, equivalent to approximately 12 times the recommended human ophthalmic dose. The increased incidence of urinary bladder papillomas seen in the male rats given the highest dose of dorzolamide is also seen in rats given other medications of the carbonic anhydrase inhibitor class. Rats are particularly prone to develop papillomas in response to foreign bodies, compounds causing crystalluria, or diverse sodium salts.

Mutagenicity

The *in vivo* (mouse) cytogenetic assay, *in vitro* chromosomal aberration assay, alkaline elution assay, V-79 assay, and Ames test were negative for mutagenic potential.

Pregnancy/Reproduction

Fertility—There were no adverse effects on the reproductive capacity of either male or female rats given oral doses of dorzolamide of up to 188 or 94 times, respectively, the recommended human ophthalmic dose.

Pregnancy—Adequate and well-controlled studies in humans have not been done.

Developmental toxicity studies in rabbits given dorzolamide orally in doses ≥ 2.5 mg/kg a day (31 times the recommended human ophthalmic dose) revealed malformations of the vertebral bodies of the fetuses. Administration of dorzolamide at these doses also caused metabolic acidosis with reduction in body weight gain in dams and decreased weight in fetuses. No treatment-related fetal malformations were seen in rabbits given dorzolamide at a dose of 1 mg/kg a day (13 times the recommended human ophthalmic dose). In addition, there were no treatment-related fetal malformations in developmental toxicity studies in rats given dorzolamide orally at doses of up to 10 mg/kg a day (125 times the recommended human ophthalmic dose).

FDA Pregnancy Category C.

Breast-feeding

It is not known whether ophthalmic dorzolamide is distributed into breast milk. However, since there is the potential for serious adverse reactions with systemically absorbed carbonic anhydrase inhibitors, including ophthalmic dorzolamide, a decision should be made whether to discontinue breast-feeding or discontinue the medication.

In a study in lactating rats, dorzolamide administered orally at a dose of 7.5 mg/kg a day (94 times the recommended human ophthalmic dose) caused a reduction in body weight gain of 5 to 7% in the pups. In addition, a slight delay in postnatal development (incisor eruption, vaginal canalization, and eye opening) secondary to lower fetal body weight was noted.

Pediatrics

Safety and IOP-lowering effects of dorzolamide have been demonstrated in pediatric patients in a 3-month, multi-center, double masked, active-treatment-controlled trial.

Geriatrics

In clinical studies, 44 and 10% of the total number of patients were 65 and 75 years of age and over, respectively, and no overall differences in effectiveness or safety were observed between these patients and younger patients. Geriatrics-specific problems that would limit the usefulness of this medication in the elderly are not expected.

Drug interactions and/or related problems

The following drug interactions and/or related problems have been selected on the basis of their potential clinical significance (possible mechanism in parentheses where appropriate)—not necessarily inclusive (» = major clinical significance):

Note: Combinations containing any of the following medications, depending on the amount present, may also interact with this medication.

Amphetamines or
Mecamylamine or
Quinidine
(when amphetamines, mecamylamine, or quinidine are used concurrently with systemic carbonic anhydrase inhibitors, especially acetazolamide, therapeutic and/or side effects may be enhanced or prolonged as a result of decreased elimination caused by alkalinization of urine. A study has shown that ophthalmic dorzolamide does not cause alkalinization of urine when administered in normal therapeutic doses (see *Pharmacology, Other actions/effects*); nonetheless, medical experts suggest that dosage adjustments of amphetamines or quinidine may be needed when ophthalmic dorzolamide therapy is initiated or discontinued. In addition, some medical experts suggest that concurrent use with mecamylamine is not recommended, whereas other medical experts suggest that dosage adjustments of mecamylamine may be needed when ophthalmic dorzolamide therapy is initiated or discontinued)

Carbonic anhydrase inhibitors, oral
(potential for an additive effect on the known systemic effects of carbonic anhydrase inhibition; concomitant administration not recommended)

» Silver preparations, ophthalmic, such as silver nitrate
(topical sulfonamides are incompatible with silver salts; since ophthalmic dorzolamide is a sulfonamide, concurrent use with ophthalmic silver preparations is not recommended)

Medical considerations/Contraindications

The medical considerations/contraindications included have been selected on the basis of their potential clinical significance (reasons given in parentheses where appropriate)—not necessarily inclusive (» = major clinical significance).

Except under special circumstances, this medication should not be used when the following medical problem exists:

» Hypersensitivity to dorzolamide or any component of the product

Risk-benefit should be considered when the following medical problems exist:

Acute angle-closure glaucoma
(dorzolamide has not been studied in these patients; management of patients with acute angle-closure glaucoma requires therapeutic interventions in addition to ocular hypotensive agents)

Hepatic function impairment
(dorzolamide has not been studied in patients with hepatic impairment; caution should be used if the medication is used in these patients, since dorzolamide is metabolized by the liver)

» Renal calculi or history of
(may be exacerbated or induced during therapy)

Renal function impairment, severe
(dorzolamide and its metabolite are excreted primarily by the kidney; use of dorzolamide is not recommended in patients with a creatinine clearance of less than 30 mL per minute)

Side/Adverse Effects

Note: Since dorzolamide is a sulfonamide, the same types of adverse reactions that may occur with other sulfonamides may occur with dorzolamide also. With other sulfonamides, fatalities have occurred rarely because of severe reactions, including Stevens-Johnson syndrome, toxic epidermal necrolysis, fulminant hepatic necrosis, agranulocytosis, aplastic anemia, and other blood dyscrasias. If signs of serious reaction or hypersensitivity occur, *use of dorzolamide should be discontinued.*

In clinical studies, local ocular adverse effects, primarily conjunctivitis and eyelid reactions, were reported with chronic administration of dorzolamide. Many of these reactions had the clinical appearance and course of an allergic-type reaction that resolved upon discontinuation of the medication. If local ocular adverse effects such as conjunctivitis and eyelid reactions occur, *use of dorzolamide should be discontinued and the patient evaluated* before a decision is made whether to restart the medication.

Although acid-base and electrolyte disturbances were not reported in the clinical trials of dorzolamide, they have been reported with use of oral carbonic anhydrase inhibitors and have, in some instances, resulted in drug interactions (e.g., toxicity associated with high-dose salicylate therapy).

Carbonic anhydrase activity has been observed in the cytoplasm and around the plasma membranes of the corneal endothelium. However, the effect of continued administration of dorzolamide on the corneal endothelium has not been evaluated fully.

The following side/adverse effects have been selected on the basis of their potential clinical significance (possible signs and symptoms in parentheses where appropriate)—not necessarily inclusive:

Those indicating need for medical attention

Incidence more frequent

Allergic reaction, ocular (itching, redness, swelling, or other sign of eye or eyelid irritation)—incidence 10%

Incidence less frequent

Conjunctivitis (redness, pain, swelling of eye, eyelid, or inner lining of eyelid; burning, dry or itching eyes; discharge; excessive tearing)

Incidence rare

Iridocyclitis (eye pain, tearing, and blurred vision); ***skin rash; urolithiasis*** (blood in urine; nausea or vomiting; pain in side, back, or abdomen)

Incidence not determined—Observed during clinical practice, estimates of frequency can not be determined

Angioedema (large, hive-like swelling on face, eyelids, lips, tongue, throat, hands, legs, feet, sex organs); ***bronchospasm*** (cough; difficulty breathing; noisy breathing; shortness of breath; tightness in chest; wheezing); ***choroidal detachment following filtration surgery*** (change in vision; flashes of light; floaters in vision); ***dyspnea*** (shortness of breath; difficult or labored breathing; tightness in chest; wheezing); ***pruritus*** (itching skin); ***urticaria*** (hives or welts; itching; redness of skin; skin rash)

Those indicating need for medical attention only if they continue or are bothersome

Incidence more frequent

Bitter taste—incidence approximately 25%; ***burning, stinging, or discomfort when medicine is applied***—incidence 33%; ***superficial punctate keratitis*** (feeling of something in eye; sensitivity of eyes to light)—incidence 10 to 15%

Incidence less frequent

Asthenia (unusual tiredness or weakness)—infrequently; ***blurred vision***—incidence 1 to 5%; ***dryness of eyes***—incidence 1 to 5%; ***eye redness; eyelid reactions; fatigue*** (unusual tiredness or weakness)—infrequently; ***headache***—infrequently; ***nausea***—infrequently; ***photophobia*** (sensitivity of eye to light)—incidence 1 to 5%; ***tearing***—incidence 1 to 5%

Incidence not determined—Observed during clinical practice, estimates of frequency can not be determined

Contact dermatitis (blistering, burning, crusting, dryness, flaking of skin; itching; scaling; severe redness, soreness, swelling of skin); ***dizziness; dry mouth; epistaxis*** (bloody nose); ***eyelid crusting; ocular pain*** (eye pain); ***paresthesia*** (burning, crawling, itching, numbness, prickling, "pins and needles", or tingling feelings); ***throat irritation; transient myopia*** (blurred vision; change in distance vision; difficulty in focusing eyes)

Patient Consultation

As an aid to patient consultation, refer to *Advice for the Patient, Dorzolamide (Ophthalmic)*

In providing consultation, consider emphasizing the following selected information (» = major clinical significance):

Before using this medication

» Conditions affecting use, especially:

Hypersensitivity to dorzolamide or any component, other carbonic anhydrase inhibitors, or other sulfonamides

Pregnancy—One study in animals has shown maternal toxicity and fetal birth defects at very high doses

Breast-feeding—Carbonic anhydrase inhibitors (including ophthalmic dorzolamide) have the potential for serious adverse reactions; a decision should be made whether to discontinue breast-feeding or discontinue the medication

Use in children—Safety and IOP-lowering effects of dorzolamide have been demonstrated in pediatric patients in a 3-month trial.

Other medications, especially ophthalmic silver preparations such as silver nitrate

Other medical problems, especially renal calculi or history of

Proper use of this medication

Proper administration technique for ophthalmic solution

Washing hands immediately after application to remove any medicine that may be on the hand to prevent possible contamination of the applicator tip after application

Preventing contamination: Not touching applicator tip to any surface; keeping container tightly closed

» Importance of using medication only as directed

Waiting 10 minutes between the use of 2 different ophthalmic preparations to prevent "washing out" of the first one

» Proper dosing

Missed dose: Using as soon as possible; not using if almost time for next dose; not doubling doses

» Proper storage

Precautions while using this medication

Regular visits to physician to check progress during therapy

Checking with physician if signs of ocular allergic reaction, such as itching, redness, swelling, or other sign of eye or eyelid irritation, occur

» Caution if blurred vision occurs temporarily; checking with physician if blurred vision continues, since it may be sign of adverse effect

Possible sensitivity of eyes to sunlight or bright light; wearing sunglasses and avoiding exposure to bright light; checking with physician if discomfort continues

Side/adverse effects

Signs of potential side effects, especially ocular allergic reaction, conjunctivitis, iridocyclitis, skin rash, and urolithiasis

Signs of potential side effects observed during clinical practice, especially angioedema, bronchospasm, choroidal detachment following filtration surgery, dyspnea, pruritis, and urticaria

General Dosing Information

The efficacy of dorzolamide administered less frequently than 3 times a day (whether alone or in combination with other products) has not been established.

Because of the preservative, benzalkonium chloride, the manufacturer recommends that patients not wear soft contact lenses during treatment with dorzolamide ophthalmic solution. However, medical experts do not believe this precaution is necessary unless the patient has corneal epithelial problems and the medication is to be used more often than once every 1 to 2 hours. No significant problems have been documented with the use of ophthalmic solutions containing 0.03% or less of benzalkonium chloride as a preservative in patients with no significant corneal surface problems.

Dorzolamide may be used concurrently with other medications instilled in the eye to lower intraocular pressure. However, the medications should be administered at least 10 minutes apart.

There have been reports of bacterial keratitis associated with the use of multiple dose containers of topical ophthalmic products. These containers had been inadvertently contaminated by patients who, in most cases, had a concurrent corneal disease or a disruption of the ocular epithelial surface.

Ophthalmic Dosage Forms

DORZOLAMIDE HYDROCHLORIDE OPHTHALMIC SOLUTION

Usual adult and adolescent dose

Antiglaucoma agent (ophthalmic)—

Topical to the conjunctiva, 1 drop three times a day.

Usual pediatric dose

See *Usual adult dose*

Usual geriatric dose

See *Usual adult dose*

Strength(s) usually available

U.S.—

2% (20 mg base) (22.3 mg as the hydrochloride) (Rx) [*Trusopt* (benzalkonium chloride 0.0075%; hydroxyethyl cellulose; mannitol; sodium citrate dihydrate; sodium hydroxide; water for injection)].

Canada—

Not commercially available.

Packaging and storage

Store between 15 and 30 °C (59 and 86 °F), unless otherwise specified by manufacturer. Protect from light and freezing.

Auxiliary labeling

- For the eye.
- Do not touch or contaminate the tip of the container.

Selected Bibliography

Serle JB. Pharmacological advances in the treatment of glaucoma. Drugs Aging 1994 Sep; 5(3): 156-70.

Wilkerson M, Cyrlin M, Lippa EA, et al. Four-week safety and efficacy study of dorzolamide, a novel, active topical carbonic anhydrase inhibitor. Arch Ophthalmol 1993 Oct; 111(10): 1343-50.

Revised: 07/20/2004
Developed: 01/31/1996

DORZOLAMIDE AND TIMOLOL Ophthalmic

VA CLASSIFICATION (Primary): OP117

Commonly used brand name(s): *Cosopt*.

Note: For a listing of dosage forms and brand names by country availability, see *Dosage Forms* section(s).

Category

Antiglaucoma agent (ophthalmic).

Indications

Accepted

Glaucoma, open-angle (treatment) or

Hypertension, ocular (treatment)—Dorzolamide and timolol combination is indicated for the treatment of elevated intraocular pressure (IOP) in patients with open-angle glaucoma or ocular hypertension who are insufficiently responsive to beta-adrenergic blocking agents (failed to achieve target IOP after multiple measurements over time).

Pharmacology/Pharmacokinetics

Physicochemical characteristics

Chemical Group—Dorzolamide is a sulfonamide and a carbonic anhydrase inhibitor.Timolol is a beta-adrenergic blocking agent.

Molecular weight—

Dorzolamide hydrochloride: 360.91.

Timolol maleate: 432.5.

Mechanism of action/Effect

Both dorzolamide and timolol reduce elevated intraocular pressure, whether or not it is associated with glaucoma, by decreasing aqueous humor secretion.

Dorzolamide inhibits human carbonic anhydrase II (CA-II). Inhibition of carbonic anhydrase in the ciliary processes of the eye decreases aqueous humor secretion, presumably by slowing the formation of bicarbonate ions, with subsequent reduction in sodium and fluid transport.

Timolol is a beta-1 and beta-2 (nonselective) adrenergic blocking agent. Timolol does not have significant intrinsic sympathomimetic, direct myocardial depressant, or membrane-stabilizing (local anesthetic) activity.

The combined effect of dorzolamide and timolol administered twice a day results in additional intraocular pressure reduction compared to either component administered alone twice a day; however, the reduction is not as much as when 2% dorzolamide (administered three times a day) and 0.5% timolol (administered twice a day) are administered concomitantly as single agents.

Other actions/effects

When dorzolamide was administered orally in doses of 2 mg twice a day for up to 20 weeks in eight healthy volunteers, inhibition of both CA-II activity and total carbonic anhydrase activity was less than the degree of inhibition considered to be necessary for a pharmacologic effect on renal function and respiration in healthy persons. (The oral dose of 2 mg twice a day closely approximates the amount of medication delivered systemically by ophthalmic administration of 2% dorzolamide three times a day.)

Absorption

Dorzolamide—

Dorzolamide is systemically absorbed when applied to the eye. In a study designed to simulate systemic exposure during long-term ophthalmic administration, eight healthy subjects were given 2 mg of oral dorzolamide twice a day for up to 20 weeks. (The oral dose of 2 mg twice a day closely approximates the amount of medication delivered systemically by ophthalmic administration of 2% dorzolamide three times a day.) Steady state was reached within 8 weeks.

In a study designed to assess the potential for systemic carbonic anhydrase inhibition following ophthalmic administration, dorzolamide was found to accumulate in red blood cells (RBCs) during chronic dosing as a result of binding to CA-II. The *N*-desethyl metabolite inhibits CA-II less potently than does dorzolamide, but the metabolite also inhibits carbonic anhydrase I (CA-I). The metabolite also accumulates in RBCs, where it binds primarily to CA-I.

Plasma concentrations of both dorzolamide and its metabolite are generally below the assay limit of quantitation (15 nanomolar).

Timolol—

Timolol is systemically absorbed with ophthalmic administration. In a study in six subjects, administration of a 0.5% ophthalmic solution of timolol maleate twice a day produced a peak mean plasma concentration of 0.46 nanogram per mL following the morning dose.

Protein binding

Dorzolamide—Moderate (approximately 33%).

Biotransformation

Dorzolamide—The only metabolite, *N*-desethyldorzolamide, inhibits both CA-II (to a lesser extent than the parent drug) and CA-I.

Half-life

Elimination—

Dorzolamide: About 4 months (following an initial rapid decline in drug concentration, as a result of nonlinear washout from red blood cells).

Elimination

Dorzolamide—Renal, primarily unchanged (the metabolite is also eliminated renally).

In dialysis—

Timolol is not readily removable by dialysis.

Precautions to Consider

Cross-sensitivity and/or related problems

Patients sensitive to carbonic anhydrase inhibitors, other sulfonamides, or beta-adrenergic blocking agents may be sensitive to ophthalmic dorzolamide and timolol combination.

Carcinogenicity

Dorzolamide—

A 2-year study in male and female Sprague-Dawley rats found urinary bladder papillomas in male rats in the dosage group given the highest oral doses of 20 mg per kg of body weight (mg/kg) per day of dorzolamide hydrochloride (250 times the recommended human ophthalmic dose). Oral doses equivalent to approximately 12 times the recommended human ophthalmic dose did not produce papillomas. The increase in urinary bladder papillomas at high doses in male rats is a class effect of carbonic anhydrase inhibitors in rats, which are particularly prone to developing papillomas in response to foreign bodies, compounds causing crystalluria, and diverse sodium salts.

A 21-month study in female and male mice given oral doses of up to 75 mg/kg per day of dorzolamide hydrochloride (approximately 900 times the recommended human ophthalmic dose) did not find any treatment-related tumors.

In a 1-year study, no changes in bladder urothelium were found in dogs given oral doses of 2 mg/kg per day of dorzolamide hydrochloride (25 times the recommended human ophthalmic dose) or in monkeys given ophthalmic doses of 0.4 mg/kg per day of dorzolamide hydrochloride (approximately 5 times the recommended human ophthalmic dose).

Timolol—

A 2-year study in rats found a statistically significant increase in the incidence of adrenal pheochromocytomas in male rats given oral doses of 300 mg/kg per day of timolol maleate (approximately 42,000 times the systemic exposure following the maximum recommended human ophthalmic dose), but not in rats given oral doses equivalent to approximately 14,000 times the maximum recommended human ophthalmic dose.

A lifetime study of timolol maleate in mice found a statistically significant increase in the incidence of benign and malignant pulmonary tumors, benign uterine polyps, and mammary adenocarcinomas in female mice given oral doses of 500 mg/kg per day (approximately 71,000 times the systemic exposure following the maximum recommended human ophthalmic dose), but not in female mice given oral doses of 5 or 50 mg/kg per day (approximately 700 or 7000 times, respectively, the systemic exposure following the maximum recommended human ophthalmic dose). In a subsequent study in female mice, in which postmortem examinations were limited to the uterus and the lungs, a statistically significant increase in the incidence of pulmonary tumors also was observed at 500 mg/kg per day.

The increase in the incidence of mammary adenocarcinomas in female mice was associated with elevations in serum prolactin concentration. These elevations occurred in female mice given the 500 mg/kg per day dose but not those given the 5 or 50 mg/kg per day dose. Other agents that elevate serum prolactin in rodents have also been associated with increases in mammary adenocarcinomas. However, no correlation between serum prolactin concentration and mammary tumors has been established in humans. Studies in humans administered oral doses of up to 60 mg of timolol maleate (the maximum recommend human oral dose) found no clinically meaningful changes in serum prolactin.

Mutagenicity

Dorzolamide was not found to be mutagenic in the *in vivo* (mouse) cytogenetic assay, the *in vitro* chromosomal aberration assay, the alkaline elution assay, the V-79 assay, and the Ames test.

Timolol was not found to be mutagenic when tested *in vivo* (mouse) in the micronucleus test and cytogenetic assay (at doses of up to 800 mg/kg) and *in vitro* in a neoplastic cell transformation assay (up to 100 mcg per mL). In the Ames test, the highest concentrations of timolol (5000 or 10,000 mcg per plate) were associated with statistically significant elevations of revertants observed with tester strain TA100 (in seven replicate assays), but not in the remaining three strains. In the assays with tester strain TA100, no consistent dose-response relationship was observed, and the ratio of test to control revertants did not reach 2. (A ratio of 2 is usually considered the criterion for a positive Ames test.)

Pregnancy/Reproduction

Fertility—Reproduction and fertility studies in rats given either dorzolamide hydrochloride or timolol maleate (in doses of approximately 100 times the systemic exposure following the maximum recommended human ophthalmic dose) demonstrated no adverse affect on male or female fertility.

Pregnancy—Adequate and well-controlled studies in humans have not been done. Consideration of risk-benefit is recommended before using ophthalmic dorzolamide and timolol combination during pregnancy.

Dorzolamide: No treatment-related malformations were seen at oral doses of 1 mg/kg per day (13 times the recommended human ophthalmic dose). However, studies in rabbits given oral doses of dorzolamide hydrochloride of ≥ 2.5 mg/kg per day (31 times the recommended human ophthalmic dose) found malformations of the vertebral bodies. These doses also caused metabolic acidosis with decreased body weight gain in dams and decreased fetal weights.

Timolol: Studies in mice, rats, and rabbits given oral doses of timolol maleate of up to 50 mg/kg per day (7000 times the systemic exposure following the maximum recommended human ophthalmic dose) found no evidence of teratogenicity. Although delayed ossification was seen at this dose in fetal rats, there were no adverse effects on postnatal development of offspring. Studies in mice given doses (route of administration not specified) of timolol maleate of 1000 mg/kg per day (142,000 times the systemic exposure following the maximum recommended human ophthalmic dose) found maternotoxicity and an increased number of fetal resorptions. Studies in rabbits given doses (route of administration not specified) of timolol maleate of 14,000 times the systemic exposure following the maximum recommended human ophthalmic dose also found an increased number of fetal resorptions, but without apparent maternal toxicity.

FDA Pregnancy Category C.

Breast-feeding

Dorzolamide—It is not known whether dorzolamide is distributed into human breast milk.

Timolol—Timolol maleate has been detected in human breast milk following both oral and ophthalmic administration. Because of the potential for serious adverse effects in nursing infants, risk-benefit should be considered before breast-feeding during treatment with ophthalmic timolol.

Pediatrics

Safety and efficacy of dorzolamide hydrochloride ophthalmic solution and timolol maleate ophthalmic solution have been established when administered individually in pediatric patients aged 2 years and older. Use of these drug products in these children is supported by evidence from adequate and well-controlled studies in children and adults. Safety and efficacy in pediatric patients below the age of 2 years have not been established.

Geriatrics

No information is available on the relationship of age to the effects of dorzolamide and timolol combination in geriatric patients.

Surgical

The necessity or desirability of withdrawal of beta-adrenergic blocking agents prior to major surgery is controversial. Beta-adrenergic receptor blockade impairs the ability of the heart to respond to beta-adrenergically mediated reflex stimuli, which may augment the risk of general anesthesia in surgical procedures. In some patients receiving beta-adrenergic blocking agents, protracted severe hypotension during anesthesia has been reported, as well as difficulty in restarting and maintaining the heartbeat. For these reasons, some authorities recommend gradual withdrawal of beta-adrenergic blocking agents in patients undergoing elective surgery.

If necessary during surgery, the effects of beta-adrenergic blocking agents may be reversed by sufficient doses of adrenergic agonists.

Drug interactions and/or related problems

The following drug interactions and/or related problems have been selected on the basis of their potential clinical significance (possible mechanism in parentheses where appropriate)—not necessarily inclusive (» = major clinical significance):

Note: Combinations containing any of the following medications, depending on the amount present, may also interact with this medication.

» Beta-adrenergic blocking agents, systemic
(possibility of additive systemic and ophthalmic effects; concurrent use of two beta-adrenergic blocking agents is not recommended)

» Calcium channel blocking agents, oral or intravenous
(caution is advised with concurrent use of systemic or ophthalmic beta-adrenergic blocking agents because of possible atrioventricular [AV] conduction disturbances, left ventricular failure, and hypotension; in patients with impaired cardiac function, concurrent use should be avoided)

» Carbonic anhydrase inhibitors, systemic
(possibility of additive systemic effects with concurrent use of dorzolamide; concurrent administration of ophthalmic dorzolamide and timolol combination is not recommended)

» Catecholamine-depleting medications, such as reserpine
(concurrent use of beta-adrenergic blocking agents may lead to the possibility of additive effects and the production of hypotension and/or marked bradycardia, which may lead to vertigo, syncope, or postural hypotension; close observation of patients is recommended)

Clonidine
(oral beta-adrenergic blocking medications may exacerbate the rebound hypertension which can follow clonidine withdrawal; no reports of exacerbation of rebound hypertension with ophthalmic timolol maleate)

» Digitalis
(concurrent use of beta-adrenergic blocking agents with digitalis and calcium antagonists may have additive effects on prolonging AV conduction time)

» Quinidine
(potentiated systemic beta-blockade [e.g., decreased heart rate] has been reported during concurrent treatment with quinidine and timolol, possibly because of inhibition by quinidine on timolol metabolism via the cytochrome P450 enzyme CYP2D6)

Salicylates, high doses
(acid-base and electrolyte disturbances have been reported with oral carbonic anhydrase inhibitors, which may lead to toxicity with high doses of salicylates; although this effect has not been reported in clinical trials with dorzolamide and timolol ophthalmic solution, caution is recommended)

Medical considerations/Contraindications

The medical considerations/contraindications included have been selected on the basis of their potential clinical significance (reasons given in parentheses where appropriate)—not necessarily inclusive (» = major clinical significance).

Except under special circumstances, this medication should not be used when the following medical problems exist:

» Asthma, bronchial, or history of or
» Chronic obstructive pulmonary disease, severe
(timolol maleate administration [both systemic and ophthalmic] has been associated with severe respiratory reactions, including death due to bronchospasm in patients with asthma)

» Cardiac failure, overt or
» Cardiogenic shock or
» Heart block, 2nd or 3rd degree atrioventricular (AV) or
» Sinus bradycardia
(sympathetic stimulation may be essential for support of the circulation in individuals with diminished myocardial contractility, and its inhibition by beta-adrenergic receptor blockade may precipitate more severe failure)

» Hypersensitivity to dorzolamide or timolol or any component of the product

Risk-benefit should be considered when the following medical problems exist:

» Anaphylactic reactions, severe, history of (to a variety of allergens) or
» Atopy, history of (to a variety of allergens)
(when these patients are treated with beta-adrenergic blocking agents, they may be more reactive to repeated accidental, diagnostic, or therapeutic challenge with such allergens; in addition, they may be unresponsive to the usual doses of epinephrine used to treat anaphylactic reactions)

» Bronchospastic disease, or history of (other than bronchial asthma, or history of) or
» Chronic obstructive pulmonary disease, mild or moderate, e.g.,
Bronchitis, chronic
Emphysema
(use of ophthalmic dorzolamide and timolol combination is not recommended)

» Diabetes mellitus, especially labile diabetes or
» Hypoglycemia
(beta-adrenergic blocking agents may mask the signs and symptoms of acute hypoglycemia; caution is recommended in patients subject to spontaneous hypoglycemia or in diabetic patients [particularly those with labile diabetes] receiving insulin or oral hypoglycemic agents)

Hepatic function impairment
(studies have not been done; however, caution is recommended)

» Hyperthyroidism
(beta-adrenergic blocking agents may mask certain clinical signs, such as tachycardia, of hyperthyroidism; patients suspected of developing thyrotoxicosis should be managed carefully to avoid abrupt withdrawal of beta-adrenergic blocking agents that might precipitate a thyroid storm)

Myasthenia gravis
(beta-adrenergic blocking agents have been reported to potentiate muscle weakness consistent with certain myasthenic symptoms [e.g., diplopia, ptosis, generalized weakness]; timolol has been reported rarely to increase muscle weakness in some patients with myasthenia gravis or myasthenic symptoms)

» Renal function impairment, severe (creatinine clearance < 30 mL per minute)
(although studies have not been done, use is not recommended, because dorzolamide and its metabolite are eliminated primarily via the kidneys)

Patient monitoring

The following may be especially important in patient monitoring (other tests may be warranted in some patients, depending on condition; » = major clinical significance):

» Signs/symptoms of cardiac failure
(at the first sign or symptom of cardiac failure, dorzolamide/timolol should be discontinued; in some cases, continued depression of the myocardium with beta-blocking agents over a period of time can lead to cardiac failure in patients without a history of cardiac failure)

Side/Adverse Effects

Note: In clinical studies, local ocular adverse effects, primarily conjunctivitis and lid reactions, were reported with chronic administration of ophthalmic dorzolamide and timolol combination. Many of these reactions had the clinical appearance and course of an allergic-type reaction that resolved upon discontinuation of drug therapy. If such reactions are observed, ophthalmic dorzolamide and timolol combination should be discontinued and the patient evaluated before considering restarting the medication.

Choroidal detachment after filtration procedures has been reported with administration of aqueous suppressant therapy (e.g., timolol).

The side/adverse effects listed below have been reported for ophthalmic dorzolamide and timolol combination. In addition, other adverse effects reported with the individual ophthalmic agents are a possibility, as well as adverse effects reported with any of the systemic beta-adrenergic blocking agents.

For more information on possible side effects, see the side and adverse effects sections of *Beta-adrenergic Blocking Agents* and/or *Dorzolamide (Ophthalmic)*.

Because ophthalmic dorzolamide and timolol are absorbed systemically, the same types of adverse reactions that may occur with other sulfonamides or beta-adrenergic blocking agents may occur with this combination also. Timolol maleate administration (both systemic and ophthalmic) has been associated with severe respiratory reactions and cardiac reactions, including death due to bronchospasm in patients with asthma, as well as rare instances of death in association with cardiac failure. Even in patients without a history of cardiac failure, continued depression of the myocardium with beta-adrenergic blocking agents over a period of time can, in some cases, lead to cardiac failure. At the first sign or symptom of cardiac failure, ophthalmic dorzolamide and timolol combination should be discontinued. With sulfonamides, rare fatalities have occurred because of severe reactions, such as Stevens-Johnson syndrome, toxic epidermal necrolysis, fulminant hepatic necrosis, agranulocytosis, aplastic anemia, and other blood dyscrasias. Sensitization may recur when a sulfonamide is readministered, regardless of the route of administration. It is recommended that ophthalmic dorzolamide and timolol combination be discontinued if signs of a serious adverse reaction or hypersensitivity occur.

The following side/adverse effects have been selected on the basis of their potential clinical significance (possible signs and symptoms in parentheses where appropriate)—not necessarily inclusive:

Those indicating need for medical attention

Incidence more frequent—5 to 15%
Conjunctival hyperemia (redness of eye and lining of eyelid); ***itching of the eye; superficial punctate keratitis*** (feeling of something in eye; sensitivity of eyes to light)

Incidence less frequent—1 to 5%
Back, abdominal, or stomach pain; blepharitis (redness, swelling or itching of eyelid); ***bronchitis*** (coughing, shortness of breath, tightness in chest, or wheezing); ***cloudy vision; corneal staining; cortical lens opacity; lens nucleus coloration; lens opacity; nuclear lens opacity; post-subcapsular cataract; or visual field defect***

(blurred vision or other change in vision); ***conjunctival discharge*** (discharge from eye); ***conjunctival follicles*** (redness and tiny bumps on lining of eyelid); ***conjunctivitis or conjunctival edema or injection*** (swelling and/or redness of eye and lining of eyelid); ***corneal erosion*** (eye irritation or redness); ***cough; dizziness; eye discharge; eye or eyelid pain or discomfort; eyelid edema or erythema*** (swelling or redness of eyelid); ***foreign body sensation*** (feeling of something in eye); ***glaucomatous cupping; hypertension*** (increased blood pressure); ***urinary tract infection*** (increased frequency of urination; painful urination); ***vitreous detachment*** (seeing flashes or sparks of light; seeing floating spots before the eyes)

Incidence rare—Less than 1%

Bradycardia (slow heartbeat); ***cardiac failure*** (chest pain; shortness of breath or troubled breathing); ***cerebral vascular accident*** (headache or weakness, severe and sudden); ***chest pain; diarrhea; dyspnea*** (shortness of breath or troubled breathing); ***heart block*** (chest pain or discomfort; fainting; shortness of breath; slow or irregular heartbeat; sweating); ***hypotension*** (unusual tiredness or weakness; dizziness, lightheadedness, or fainting); ***iridocyclitis*** (eye redness or pain, tearing, or blurred vision); ***mental depression; myocardial infarction*** (chest pain, severe); ***paresthesia*** (pain, numbness, tingling, or burning feeling in hands or feet); ***respiratory failure*** (blue lips, fingernails, or skin; difficult or troubled breathing; irregular, fast or slow, or shallow breathing; shortness of breath); ***skin rash; urolithiasis*** (blood in urine; nausea or vomiting; pain in side, back, or abdomen)

Note: Continued depression of the myocardium by beta-adrenergic blocking agents over a period of time, even in patients without a history of cardiac failure, can lead to *cardiac failure* in some cases.

Those indicating need for medical attention only if they continue or are bothersome

Incidence more frequent

Blurred vision—frequency: 5 to 15%; ***burning or stinging of the eye, transient upon administration of medication***—frequency: up to 30%; ***taste perversion*** (bitter, sour, or unusual taste)—frequency: up to 30%

Incidence less frequent—1 to 5%

Dryness of eyes; dyspepsia (indigestion or upset stomach); ***eyelid exudate/scales*** (crusting or scales on eyelid); ***headache; influenza-like symptoms*** (flu-like symptoms); ***nausea; pharyngitis*** (sore throat); ***sinusitis*** (stuffy or runny nose); ***tearing of eye; upper respiratory infection-like symptoms*** (cold-like symptoms)

Overdose

For more information on the management of overdose or unintentional ingestion, **contact a Poison Control Center** (see *Poison Control Center Listing*).

Clinical effects of overdose

No human data are available regarding overdose with ophthalmic dorzolamide and timolol combination. Symptoms consistent with an overdose of a systemic beta-adrenergic blocking agent or carbonic anhydrase inhibitor may occur, including electrolyte imbalance, acidosis, dizziness, headache, shortness of breath, bradycardia, bronchospasm, cardiac arrest, and possible central nervous system effects.

Treatment of overdose

Timolol does not dialyze readily.

Monitoring of serum electrolyte concentrations (especially potassium) and blood pH levels is recommended.

Patient Consultation

As an aid to patient consultation, refer to *Advice for the Patient, Dorzolamide and Timolol (Ophthalmic)*.

In providing consultation, consider emphasizing the following selected information (» = major clinical significance):

Before using this medication

» Conditions affecting use, especially:

Hypersensitivity to dorzolamide or timolol or any component of the product

Pregnancy—Risk-benefit considerations

Breast-feeding—Risk-benefit considerations

Use in children—Safety/efficacy not established in children less than 2 years of age

Other medications, especially beta-adrenergic blocking agents; calcium channel blocking agents; carbonic anhydrase inhibitors; catecholamine-depleting medications, such as reserpine; digitalis; or quinidine

Other medical problems, especially anaphylactic reactions, severe, history of (to a variety of allergens); asthma, bronchial, or history of; atopy, history of (to a variety of allergens); bronchospastic disease, or history of; cardiac failure, overt; cardiogenic shock; chronic obstructive pulmonary disease; diabetes mellitus, especially labile diabetes; heart block, 2nd or 3rd degree atrioventricular (AV); hepatic function impairment; hyperthyroidism; hypoglycemia; myasthenia gravis; renal function impairment, severe; or sinus bradycardia

Proper use of this medication

Proper administration technique for ophthalmic solution

» Preventing contamination: Not touching applicator tip to any surface; keeping container tightly closed; serious damage to the eye and possible loss of vision may result from using contaminated eye drops

» Importance of not using more medication than the amount prescribed

Waiting 10 minutes between the use of two different ophthalmic preparations to prevent "washing out" of the first one

» Proper dosing

Missed dose: Using as soon as remembered; not using if almost time for next dose; not doubling doses

» Proper storage

Precautions while using this medication

Regular visits to physician to check eye pressure during therapy

» Stopping medication and checking with physician if signs of ocular allergic reaction, such as itching, redness, swelling, or other sign of eye or eyelid irritation, occur

» Caution if any kind of surgery (including dental surgery) or emergency treatment is required

» Checking with physician if a concurrent ocular condition (e.g., trauma or infection) occurs; a fresh bottle of medication may be needed to assure sterility

» Diabetic patients: May mask some signs of hypoglycemia

Soft contact lens users: Preservative (benzalkonium chloride) in product may be absorbed by soft contact lenses; removing soft contact lenses prior to instilling medication; waiting at least 15 minutes after instilling medication before inserting lenses

Side/adverse effects

Signs of potential side effects, especially conjunctival hyperemia; itching of the eye; superficial punctate keratitis; back, abdominal, or stomach pain; blepharitis; bronchitis; cloudy vision; corneal staining; cortical lens opacity; lens nucleus coloration; lens opacity; nuclear lens opacity; post-subcapsular cataract; visual field defect; conjunctival discharge; conjunctivitis or conjunctival edema or injection; conjunctival follicles; corneal erosion; cough; dizziness; eye discharge; eye or eyelid pain or discomfort; eyelid edema or erythema; foreign body sensation; glaucomatous cupping; hypertension; urinary tract infection; vitreous detachment; bradycardia; cardiac failure; cerebral vascular accident; chest pain; diarrhea; dyspnea; heart block, hypotension; iridocyclitis; mental depression; myocardial infarction; paresthesia; respiratory failure, skin rash; or urolithiasis

General Dosing Information

It is recommended that ophthalmic dorzolamide and timolol combination be discontinued at the first sign or symptom of cardiac failure or if signs of serious adverse reactions or hypersensitivity occur.

In clinical studies, local ocular adverse effects, primarily conjunctivitis and lid reactions, were reported with chronic administration of ophthalmic dorzolamide and timolol combination. Many of these reactions had the clinical appearance and course of an allergic-type reaction that resolved upon discontinuation of drug therapy. If such reactions are observed, ophthalmic dorzolamide and timolol combination should be discontinued and the patient evaluated before considering restarting the medication.

Because of the preservative benzalkonium chloride, the manufacturer recommends that patients remove soft contact lenses before instillation of dorzolamide and timolol combination ophthalmic solution. Lenses may be reinserted 15 minutes after instillation.

If more than one ophthalmic medication is being used, the medications should be administered at least 10 minutes apart to prevent the second medication from washing out the first one.

Ophthalmic Dosage Forms

DORZOLAMIDE HYDROCHLORIDE AND TIMOLOL MALEATE OPHTHALMIC SOLUTION

Note: Strength is expressed in terms of dorzolamide and timolol base.

Usual adult dose

Antiglaucoma agent (ophthalmic)—

Topical, to the conjunctiva, 1 drop in the affected eye(s) two times a day.

Usual pediatric dose

Antiglaucoma agent (ophthalmic)—
Safety and efficacy have not been established.

Strength(s) usually available

U.S.—

20 mg dorzolamide (base; 22.26 mg as the hydrochloride) and 5 mg timolol (base; 6.83 mg as the maleate) per mL (Rx) [*Cosopt* (benzalkonium chloride 0.0075%; sodium citrate; hydroxyethyl cellulose; sodium hydroxide; mannitol)].

Packaging and storage

Store between 15 and 30 °C (59 and 86 °F). Protect from light.

Auxiliary labeling

- For the eye.
- Do not touch or contaminate the tip of the container

Revised: 04/12/2005

DOXAZOSIN Systemic

VA CLASSIFICATION (Primary/Secondary): CV150/CV409; GU900

Commonly used brand name(s): *Cardura; Cardura XL; Cardura–1; Cardura–2; Cardura–4.*

Note: For a listing of dosage forms and brand names by country availability, see *Dosage Forms* section(s).

Category

Antihypertensive—Doxazosin Mesylate Tablets.

Benign prostatic hyperplasia therapy agent—Doxazosin Mesylate Tablets

Indications

Accepted

Hypertension (treatment)—Doxazosin is indicated in the treatment of hypertension.

For additional information on initial therapeutic guidelines related to the treatment of hypertension, see *Appendix III.*

Benign prostatic hyperplasia (treatment)—Doxazosin is indicated for the treatment of both the urinary outflow obstruction and the obstructive and irritative symptoms associated with benign prostatic hyperplasia (BPH). Obstructive symptoms are hesitation, intermittency, dribbling, weak urinary stream, and incomplete emptying of the bladder; while irritative symptoms include nocturia, daytime frequency, urgency, and burning. Doxazosin may be used in normotensive or hypertensive patients. In normotensive patients with BPH, doxazosin does not appear to significantly lower blood pressure. In hypertensive patients with BPH, both conditions are effectively treated with doxazosin. The long-term effects of doxazosin on the incidence of acute urinary obstruction or other complications of BPH or on the need for surgery have not yet been determined.

Unaccepted

The extended-release tablet formulation of doxazosin is not indicated for the treatment of hypertension.

Pharmacology/Pharmacokinetics

Physicochemical characteristics

Molecular weight—547.59.

Mechanism of action/Effect

Doxazosin has a selective postsynaptic alpha$_1$-adrenergic blocking action, which is thought to account primarily for its effects.

Hypertension—

Blockade of alpha$_1$-adrenergic receptors by doxazosin results in peripheral vasodilation, which produces a fall in blood pressure because of decreased peripheral vascular resistance.

Benign prostatic hyperplasia—

Relaxation of smooth muscle in the bladder neck, prostate, and prostate capsule produced by alpha$_1$-adrenergic blockade results in a reduction in urethral resistance and pressure, bladder outlet resistance, and urinary symptoms.

Other actions/effects

Doxazosin slightly lowers the levels of total cholesterol, low-density lipoprotein (LDL) cholesterol, and triglycerides. In addition, doxazosin slightly increases high-density lipoprotein (HDL) cholesterol and the HDL/total cholesterol ratio. These lipid effects appear to be the result of doxazosin's effect on lipid metabolism (i.e., increasing LDL receptor activity, decreasing intracellular LDL cholesterol synthesis, decreasing synthesis and secretion of very low-density lipoprotein [VLDL] cholesterol, stimulation of lipoprotein lipase activity, and decreasing the rate of cholesterol absorption). However, the implications of these changes are unclear.

Absorption

Well-absorbed from gastrointestinal tract; bioavailability is about 65% for immediate-release doxazosin; 54% for 4-mg extended-release tablets; 59% for 8-mg extended-release tablets.

AUC for 4-mg extended-release doxazosin: 97.5 to 268.5

AUC for 8-mg extended-release doxazosin: 301.2 to 642.8

C_{max} and AUC were approximately 32% and 18% higher, respectively, after extended-release doxazosin was administered in the fed state compared with the fasted state.

Protein binding

Very high (98 to 99%).

Biotransformation

Metabolized extensively in the liver. Although several active and inactive metabolites have been identified (2-piperazinyl, 6′ and 7′-hydroxy, 6′ and 7′-*O*-desmethyl, and 2-amino), there is no evidence that they are present in substantial amounts.

Half-life

For immediate-release tablet formulation: Elimination—19 to 22 hours; does not appear to be significantly influenced by age or mild to moderate renal impairment.

For extended-release tablet formulation: Elimination—15 to 19 hours

Onset of action

Hypertension—1 to 2 hours; there is a slight initial fall in blood pressure within the first hour, but the main hypotensive effect is apparent from 2 hours onwards.

Benign prostatic hyperplasia (BPH)—Within 1 to 2 weeks.

Time to peak concentration

For immediate-release tablets: 1.5 to 3.6 hours.

For extended-release tablets: 4.3 to 11.7 hours following 4-mg dose; 4.3 to 13.7 hours following 8-mg dose

Peak serum concentration

At steady state, there is a positive linear relationship between peak serum concentration and dose of doxazosin. Following an oral dose of 1 mg doxazosin, the standardized peak serum concentration was 9.6 mcg per L. Following an oral dose of 4-mg and 8-mg of extended-release doxazosin, C_{max} was 4.5 to 15.7 ng per mL and 13.7 to 37.9 ng per mL, respectively.

Time to peak effect

Antihypertensive—Single dose: 2 to 6 hours.

Duration of action

Antihypertensive—Single dose: 24 hours.

Elimination

Fecal—Unchanged drug, about 5%; metabolites, 63 to 65%.

Renal—9%.

In dialysis—Doxazosin is not removed by hemodialysis.

Precautions to Consider

Cross-sensitivity and/or related problems

Patients sensitive to other quinazolines (prazosin, terazosin) may also be sensitive to doxazosin.

Carcinogenicity

In one 24-month chronic dietary administration study in rats, doxazosin (given at a dose equivalent to 150 times the maximum recommended human dose) produced no evidence of carcinogenicity. In another similarly conducted study done in mice, up to 18 months of dietary administration produced no evidence of carcinogenicity. The latter study, however, did not use a maximally tolerated dose of doxazosin.

Mutagenicity

Doxazosin was not mutagenic in the *in vitro* bacterial Ames assays, the chromosomal aberration assay in human lymphocytes, or the mouse lymphoma assay. Doxazosin was not clastogenic in the *in vivo* mouse micronucleus assay.

Pregnancy/Reproduction

Fertility—Studies in rats given oral doses of 20 mg per kg of body weight (mg/kg) per day (equivalent to about 75 times the maximum recommended human dose) have shown that doxazosin reduces fertility in male rats. The effect was reversible after 2 weeks of discontinuation of treatment.

Pregnancy—Adequate and well-controlled studies in humans have not been done. Because animal reproduction studies are not always predictive of human response, doxazosin should be used during pregnancy only if clearly needed.

Studies in rabbits and rats given daily oral doses of 40 and 20 mg/kg, respectively, have shown no evidence of harm to the fetus. The rabbit study, however, did not use a maximally tolerated dose of doxazosin. Reduced fetal survival was associated with a dosage regimen of 82 mg/kg in rabbits. Following oral administration of labeled doxazosin to pregnant rats, radioactivity was found to cross the placenta.

Studies in perinatal and postnatal rats given 40 or 50 mg/kg per day of doxazosin revealed evidence of delayed postnatal development manifested by slower body weight gain and slightly later appearance of anatomical features and reflexes.

Extended-release doxazosin is not indicated for use in women.

FDA Pregnancy Category C.

Breast-feeding

It is not known whether doxazosin is distributed into breast milk. Problems in humans have not been documented. However, in rats given a single oral dose of 1 mg/kg, doxazosin accumulated in the milk of lactating rats with a maximum concentration about 20 times greater than the maternal plasma concentration. Use of doxazosin in nursing mothers is not recommended.

Extended-release doxazosin is not indicated for use in women.

Pediatrics

No information is available on the relationship of age to the effects of doxazosin in pediatric patients. Safety and efficacy have not been established.

Geriatrics

A study performed in approximately 2000 hypertensive patients older than 65 years of age did not demonstrate geriatrics-specific problems that would limit the usefulness of doxazosin in the elderly. However, the hypotensive effect of doxazosin may be more pronounced in elderly hypertensive individuals, and lower daily maintenance doses may be required.

Experience with use of doxazosin in elderly patients with benign prostatic hyperplasia (BPH) has shown that the safety profile of doxazosin is similar to that in younger patients.

Drug interactions and/or related problems

The following drug interactions and/or related problems have been selected on the basis of their potential clinical significance (possible mechanism in parentheses where appropriate)—not necessarily inclusive (» = major clinical significance):

Note: Combinations containing any of the following medications, depending on the amount present, may also interact with this medication.

Anti-inflammatory drugs, nonsteroidal (NSAIDs), especially indomethacin
(antihypertensive effects of doxazosin may be reduced when the medication is used concurrently with these agents; indomethacin, and possibly other NSAIDs, may antagonize the antihypertensive effect by inhibiting renal prostaglandin synthesis and/or by causing sodium and fluid retention; the patient should be carefully monitored to confirm that the desired effect is being obtained)

Cimetidine
(concurrent use may slightly increase the serum concentration of doxazosin; however, the clinical significance of this increase is not known)

Hypotension-producing medications, other (See *Appendix II*)
(antihypertensive effects may be potentiated when these medications are used concurrently with doxazosin; although some antihypertensive and/or diuretic combinations are frequently used to therapeutic advantage, dosage adjustments are necessary during concurrent use)

Sympathomimetics
(antihypertensive effects of doxazosin may be reduced when it is used concurrently with these agents; the patient should be carefully monitored to confirm that the desired effect is being obtained)

(concurrent use of doxazosin antagonizes the peripheral vasoconstriction produced by high doses of dopamine)

(concurrent use of doxazosin may decrease the pressor response to ephedrine)

(concurrent use of doxazosin may block the alpha-adrenergic effects of epinephrine, possibly resulting in severe hypotension and tachycardia)

(concurrent use of doxazosin usually decreases, but does not reverse or completely block, the pressor effect of metaraminol)

(prior administration of doxazosin may decrease the pressor effect and shorten the duration of action of methoxamine and phenylephrine)

Medical considerations/Contraindications

The medical considerations/contraindications included have been selected on the basis of their potential clinical significance (reasons given in parentheses where appropriate)—not necessarily inclusive (» = major clinical significance).

Except under special circumstances, this medication should not be used when the following medical problem exists:

» Hypersensitivity to doxazosin or any of its components or to other quinazolines (e.g., prazosin, terazosin)

Risk-benefit should be considered when the following medical problems exist:

Coronary insufficiency
(if symptoms of angina pectoris should newly appear or worsen, doxazosin should be discontinued; patients with congestive heart failure, angina pectoris, or acute myocardial infarction within the last 6 months were excluded from clinical studies)

Gastrointestinal narrowing (pathologic or iatrogenic), severe preexisting
(caution should be used when administering to patients with this condition; rare reports of obstructive symptoms in patients with known strictures in association with another drug in the extended-release formulation; markedly increased GI retention times can increase systemic exposure to doxazosin and potentially increase adverse reactions)

Hepatic function impairment
(caution should be used in patients with mild or moderately impaired hepatic function; this condition may increase exposure to doxazosin; use in patients with severe hepatic impairment is not recommended)

Hypotension, symptomatic
(care should be taken when doxazosin extended-release is administered to these patients; potential for syncope after initial dose or after an increase in dosage strength)

Prostate cancer
(prostate cancer causes many of the same symptoms associated with BPH and the two conditions frequently co-exist; therefore, prostate cancer should be ruled out prior to commencing doxazosin therapy)

Renal function impairment
(small incidence of increased risk of first-dose orthostatic hypotensive reaction and prolonged hypotensive effect)

Patient monitoring

The following may be especially important in patient monitoring (other tests may be warranted in some patients, depending on condition; » = major clinical significance):

» Blood pressure measurements
(recommended at 2 to 6 hours postdose following first dose and with each dosage increase, since postural effects are most likely to occur during this time; dosage to be increased as necessary and tolerated based on individual standing blood pressures taken at 2 to 6 hours and 24 hours postdose)

Side/Adverse Effects

Note: A "first-dose orthostatic hypotensive reaction" sometimes occurs with the initial dose of doxazosin, especially when the patient is in the upright position. Syncope or other postural symptoms such as dizziness may occur. Subsequent occurrence with dosage increases is also possible. Incidence appears to be dose-related; thus it is important that therapy be initiated with the 1-mg dose. Patients who are volume-depleted or sodium-restricted may be more sensitive to the orthostatic hypotensive effects of doxazosin, and the effect may be exaggerated after exercise.

Hypotensive side effects are more likely to occur in geriatric patients.

The following side/adverse effects have been selected on the basis of their potential clinical significance (possible signs and symptoms in parentheses where appropriate)—not necessarily inclusive:

Those indicating need for medical attention

Incidence more frequent

Dizziness; vertigo (dizziness or lightheadedness)

Incidence less frequent

Arrhythmias (irregular heartbeat); ***dyspnea*** (shortness of breath); ***hypotension*** (blurred vision; confusion; dizziness, faintness, or lightheadedness when getting up from a lying or sitting position suddenly; sweating; unusual tiredness or weakness); ***orthostatic hypotension*** (dizziness or lightheadedness when getting up from a lying or sitting position; sudden fainting); ***palpitations*** (pounding heartbeat); ***periph-***

eral edema (swelling of feet or lower legs); ***tachycardia*** (fast heartbeat)

Incidence rare

Priapism (painful or prolonged erection of the penis); ***syncope*** (fainting)

Incidence not determined—Observed during clinical practice; estimates of frequency can not be determined

Abnormal liver function tests (lab results that show problems with liver); ***bradycardia*** (chest pain or discomfort; lightheadedness, dizziness or fainting; shortness of breath; slow or irregular heartbeat; unusual tiredness); ***bronchospasm aggravated*** (cough; difficulty breathing; noisy breathing; shortness of breath; tightness in chest; wheezing); ***cerebrovascular accidents*** (blurred vision; headache, sudden and severe; inability to speak; seizures; slurred speech; temporary blindness; weakness in arm and/or leg on one side of the body, sudden and severe); ***hematuria*** (blood in urine); ***hepatitis*** (dark urine; general tiredness and weakness; light-colored stools; nausea and vomiting; upper right abdominal pain; yellow eyes and skin); ***hepatitis cholestatic*** (abdominal or stomach pain; chills; clay-colored stools; dark urine; diarrhea; dizziness; fever; headache; itching; loss of appetite; nausea; rash; unpleasant breath odor; unusual tiredness or weakness; vomiting of blood; yellow eyes or skin); ***jaundice*** (chills; clay-colored stools; dark urine; dizziness; fever; headache; itching; loss of appetite; nausea; abdominal or stomach pain; area rash; unpleasant breath odor; unusual tiredness or weakness; vomiting of blood; yellow eyes or skin); ***leukopenia*** (black, tarry stools; chest pain; chills; cough; fever; painful or difficult urination; shortness of breath; sore throat; sores, ulcers, or white spots on lips or in mouth; swollen glands; unusual bleeding or bruising; unusual tiredness or weakness); ***myocardial infarction*** (chest pain or discomfort; pain or discomfort in arms, jaw, back or neck; shortness of breath; nausea; sweating; vomiting); ***purpura*** (pinpoint red or purple spots on skin); ***thrombocytopenia*** (black, tarry stools; bleeding gums; blood in urine or stools; pinpoint red spots on skin; unusual bleeding or bruising)

Those indicating need for medical attention only if they continue or are bothersome

Incidence more frequent

Asthenia (lack or loss of strength); ***headache; unusual tiredness***

Incidence less frequent

Abdominal pain (stomach pain); ***back pain; dyspepsia*** (acid or sour stomach; belching; heartburn; indigestion; stomach discomfort, upset, or pain); ***myalgia*** (joint pain; swollen joints; muscle aching or cramping; muscle pains or stiffness; difficulty in moving); ***nausea; nervousness, restlessness, or unusual irritability; respiratory tract infection*** (cough; fever; sneezing; sore throat); ***rhinitis*** (runny nose); ***somnolence*** (sleepiness or unusual drowsiness); ***urinary tract infection*** (bladder pain; bloody or cloudy urine; difficult, burning, or painful urination; frequent urge to urinate; lower back or side pain)

Rare

Dysuria (difficult or painful urination; burning while urinating)

Incidence not determined—Observed during clinical practice; estimates of frequency can not be determined

Agitation (anxiety; nervousness; restlessness; irritability; dry mouth; shortness of breath; hyperventilation; trouble sleeping; irregular heartbeats; shaking); ***alopecia*** (hair loss; thinning of hair); ***anorexia*** (loss of appetite; weight loss); ***blurred vision; fatigue*** (unusual tiredness or weakness); ***gynecomastia*** (swelling of the breasts or breast soreness in both females and males); ***hot flushes*** (feeling of warmth; redness of the face, neck, arms and occasionally, upper chest); ***hypoesthesia*** (burning, crawling, itching, numbness, prickling, "pins and needles", or tingling feelings); ***malaise*** (general feeling of discomfort or illness; unusual tiredness or weakness); ***micturition disorder*** (trouble in holding or releasing urine; painful urination); ***micturition frequency*** (change in frequency of urination); ***muscle cramps or weakness; nervousness; nocturia*** (waking to urinate at night; increased urge to urinate during the night); ***paresthesia*** (burning, crawling, itching, numbness, prickling, "pins and needles", or tingling feelings); ***polyuria*** (frequent urination; increased volume of pale, dilute urine); ***urticaria*** (hives or welts; itching; redness of skin; skin rash); ***vomiting***

Overdose

For more information on the management of overdose or unintentional ingestion, **contact a Poison Control Center** (see *Poison Control Center Listing*).

Treatment of overdose

Because doxazosin is highly protein bound, dialysis would not be indicated.

Treatment of circulatory failure by placing the patient in the supine position and elevating the legs is most important; if shock is present, additional measures are necessary. Volume expanders may be used to treat shock, followed, if necessary, by administration of a vasopressor.

Symptomatic, supportive treatment and monitoring of fluid and electrolyte status.

Patient Consultation

As an aid to patient consultation, refer to *Advice for the Patient, Doxazosin (Systemic)*.

In providing consultation, consider emphasizing the following selected information (» = major clinical significance):

Before using this medication

» Conditions affecting use, especially:
- Hypersensitivity to doxazosin or any component of the product or to other quinazolines
- Pregnancy—Should be used during pregnancy only if clearly needed; extended-release form not indicated for use in women
- Breast-feeding—Use in nursing mothers not recommended; extended-release form not indicated for use in women
- Use in the elderly—Increased sensitivity to hypotensive effects

Proper use of this medication

Compliance with therapy; taking immediate-release doxazosin at the same time each day to maintain the therapeutic effect; taking extended-release doxazosin once daily in the morning with breakfast.

For extended-release tablets: Swallowing whole; not crushing or chewing

» Proper dosing

Missed dose: Taking as soon as possible; not taking if almost time for next dose; not doubling doses. If not taken for several days, calling doctor before restarting medication

» Proper storage

For use as an antihypertensive

Possible need for control of weight and diet, especially sodium intake

» Patient may not experience symptoms of hypertension; importance of taking medication even if feeling well

» Does not cure, but helps control hypertension; possible need for lifelong therapy; serious consequences of untreated hypertension

Extended-release doxazosin is not indicated for use as an antihypertensive.

For use in benign prostatic hyperplasia (BPH)

Relieves symptoms of BPH but does not change the size of the prostate; may not prevent the need for surgery in the future

May require 1 to 2 weeks of therapy before patient experiences improvement of symptoms

Precautions while using this medication

Making regular visits to physician to check progress, especially elderly patients

» Not taking other medications, especially nonprescription sympathomimetics, unless discussed with physician

» Caution if dizziness, lightheadedness, or sudden fainting occurs, especially after initial dose or following dosage increases; taking first dose at bedtime (for immediate-release doxazosin)

» Caution when getting up suddenly from a lying or sitting position

» Caution in using alcohol, while standing for long periods or exercising, and during hot weather, because of enhanced orthostatic hypotensive effects

» Possibility of drowsiness

» Caution when driving or doing anything else requiring alertness because of possible drowsiness, dizziness, or lightheadedness

» Possibility of priapism (painful erection of penis), though rare; must be brought to immediate medical attention

Side/adverse effects

Signs of potential side effects, especially dizziness, vertigo, arrhythmias, dyspnea, hypotension, orthostatic hypotension, palpitations, peripheral edema, tachycardia, priapism, and syncope.

Signs of potential side effects observed during clinical practice, especially abnormal liver function tests, bradycardia, bronchospasm (aggravated), cerebrovascular accidents, hematuria, hepatitis, hepatitis cholestatic, jaundice, leukopenia, myocardial infarction, purpura, and thrombocytopenia

General Dosing Information

For the immediate-release tablet dosage form—In order to minimize the "first-dose orthostatic hypotensive reaction," an initial dose of 1 mg is recommended, with gradual increases in dose every 2 weeks as needed. Administration of the initial dose and of the initial dose of each increment at bedtime is recommended.

If discontinuation occurs for several days or longer, the dose should restart using the initial dosing regimen.

If switching from the immediate-release tablet to the extended-release tablet form of doxazosin, therapy should be initiated with the lowest dose (4 mg once daily). Prior to starting therapy with extended-release doxazosin, the final evening dose of the regular tablet should not be taken.

Diet/Nutrition
Extended-release doxazosin should be administered with breakfast.

For use as an antihypertensive
Dosage of doxazosin should be adjusted to meet the individual requirements of each patient, on the basis of blood pressure response.

Doxazosin may be used alone or in combination with a thiazide diuretic or beta-adrenergic blocking agent, both of which reduce the tendency for sodium and water retention, although they also produce additive hypotension. If combination therapy is indicated, individual titration is required to ensure the lowest possible therapeutic dose of each medication.

Increases in dose beyond 4 mg increase the likelihood of excessive postural effects including syncope, postural dizziness or vertigo, and postural hypotension.

When a diuretic or another antihypertensive agent is added to doxazosin therapy, the dose of doxazosin may be reduced, followed by slow dosage titration of the combination. When doxazosin is added to existing diuretic or antihypertensive therapy, the dose of the other agent may be reduced and doxazosin started at a dose of 1 mg once a day.

For use in benign prostatic hyperplasia
Prior to initiation of doxazosin therapy, a number of clinical conditions can present with symptoms similar to those associated with BPH and should be ruled out. These conditions may be the presence of prostate carcinoma, stricture of urethra, stricture of bladder neck, urinary bladder stones, neurogenic bladder dysfunction secondary to diabetes, or Parkinson's disease.

Oral Dosage Forms

Note: The dosing and strengths of the dosage forms available are expressed in terms of doxazosin base (not the mesylate salt).

DOXAZOSIN MESYLATE TABLETS

Usual adult dose
Antihypertensive—
Initial: Oral, 1 mg (base) once a day.
Maintenance: Oral, the dosage being increased gradually to meet individual requirements; depending on periodic blood pressure measurements, dosage may be increased every two weeks, titrating upwards to 2, 4, 8, and 16 mg (base) once a day as needed and tolerated.

Note: Increases in dose beyond 4 mg (base) increase the likelihood of excessive postural effects including syncope, postural dizziness or vertigo, and postural hypotension.

Geriatric patients may be more sensitive to the effects of the usual adult dose.

Benign prostatic hyperplasia—
Initial: Oral, 1 mg (base) once a day, in the morning or in the evening.
Maintenance: Oral, 1 to 8 mg (base) once a day. Dosage increases made to 2 mg and afterwards to 4 mg and 8 mg once daily should be titrated at one- to two-week intervals.

Usual adult prescribing limits
16 mg once a day for hypertension.
8 mg once a day for BPH.

Usual pediatric dose
Safety and efficacy have not been established.

Strength(s) usually available
U.S.—
1 mg (base) (Rx) [*Cardura* (microcrystalline cellulose)].
2 mg (base) (Rx) [*Cardura* (microcrystalline cellulose)].
4 mg (base) (Rx) [*Cardura* (microcrystalline cellulose)].
8 mg (base) (Rx) [*Cardura* (microcrystalline cellulose)].

Canada—
1 mg (base) (Rx) [*Cardura–1*].
2 mg (base) (Rx) [*Cardura–2*].
4 mg (base) (Rx) [*Cardura–4*].

Packaging and storage
Store below 30 °C (86 °F), in a well-closed container, unless otherwise specified by manufacturer.

Auxiliary labeling
- Do not take other medicines without your doctor's advice.
- May cause dizziness.

Note
Check refill frequency to determine compliance in hypertensive patients.

DOXAZOSIN MESYLATE EXTENDED-RELEASE TABLETS

Usual adult dose
Benign prostatic hyperplasia (treatment)—
Initial: Oral, 4 mg (base) once daily administered with breakfast.
Dosage increases made up to 8 mg once daily should be titrated at three- to four-week intervals.

Note: If extended-release doxazosin administration is discontinued for several days, therapy should be restarted using the 4 mg once daily dose.

Usual adult prescribing limits
8 mg once daily

Usual pediatric dose
Safety and efficacy have not been established.

Strength(s) usually available
U.S.—
4 mg (base) (Rx) [*Cardura XL* (polyethylene oxide; sodium chloride; hypromellose; red ferric oxide; titanium dioxide; magnesium stearate; cellulose acetate; Macrogol®; pharmaceutical glaze; black iron oxide)].
8 mg (base) (Rx) [*Cardura XL* (polyethylene oxide; sodium chloride; hypromellose; red ferric oxide; titanium dioxide; magnesium stearate; cellulose acetate; Macrogol®; pharmaceutical glaze; black iron oxide)].

Packaging and storage
Store below 25 °C (77 °F); excursions permitted to 15 to 30 °C (59 to 86°F).

Auxiliary labeling
- Swallow whole. Do not crush or chew.
- Do not take other medicines without your doctor's advice.
- May cause dizziness.

Selected Bibliography

Cubeddu LX, Fuenmayor N, Caplan N, *et.al.* Clinical pharmacology of doxazosin in patients with essential hypertension. Clin Pharmacol Ther 1987; 41: 439-49.

Talseth T, Westlie L, Daae L. Doxazosin and atenolol as monotherapy in mild and moderate hypertension: a randomized, parallel study with a three year follow-up. Am Heart J 1991; 121: 280-5.

The fifth report of the Joint National Committee on Detection, Evaluation, and Treatment of High Blood Pressure. Arch Intern Med 1993; 153: 154-83.

Revised: 03/10/2005

DOXEPIN—See *Antidepressants, Tricyclic (Systemic)*

DOXERCALCIFEROL—See *Vitamin D and Analogs (Systemic)*

DOXORUBICIN Systemic

VA CLASSIFICATION (Primary): AN200

Commonly used brand name(s): *Adriamycin PFS; Adriamycin RDF; Rubex.*

Note: For a listing of dosage forms and brand names by country availability, see *Dosage Forms* section(s).

Category
Antineoplastic.

Indications
Note: Bracketed information in the *Indications* section refers to uses that are not included in U.S. product labeling.

Accepted
Leukemia, acute lymphocytic (treatment) or
Leukemia, acute nonlymphocytic (treatment)—Doxorubicin is indicated for treatment of acute lymphocytic (lymphoblastic) leukemia and acute nonlymphocytic (myeloblastic) leukemia.

Carcinoma, breast (treatment)
Carcinoma, gastric (treatment)
Carcinoma, lung, small cell (treatment)
Carcinoma, ovarian, epithelial (treatment)
Carcinoma, thyroid (treatment)
Neuroblastoma (treatment) or
Wilms' tumor (treatment)—Doxorubicin is indicated for treatment of breast carcinoma, gastric carcinoma, small cell lung carcinoma, epithelial ovarian carcinoma, thyroid carcinoma, neuroblastoma, and Wilms' tumor.

Carcinoma, bladder (treatment) or
[Carcinoma, bladder (prophylaxis)][1]—Doxorubicin is indicated for treatment of transitional bladder cell carcinoma. Doxorubicin may also be used intravesically, as a single agent (Evidence rating: IA), or intravenously, in combination with other chemotherapeutic agents (Evidence rating: IIID), for prophylaxis of bladder carcinoma.

[Leukemia, chronic lymphocytic (treatment)][1]—Doxorubicin is indicated for treatment of chronic lymphocytic leukemia.

[Carcinoma, cervical (treatment)]
[Carcinoma, endometrial (treatment)]
[Carcinoma, head and neck (treatment)]
[Carcinoma, hepatocellular, primary (treatment)][1]
[Carcinoma, lung, non-small cell (treatment)]
[Carcinoma, pancreatic (treatment)][1]
[Hepatoblastoma (treatment)][1]
[Thymoma (treatment)][1]
[Tumors, ovarian, germ cell (treatment)]or
[Tumors, trophoblastic, gestational (treatment)][1]—Doxorubicin is indicated for treatment of cervical carcinoma, endometrial carcinoma, squamous cell carcinoma of the head and neck, primary hepatocellular carcinoma, non-small cell lung carcinoma, pancreatic carcinoma, hepatoblastoma, thymoma, germ cell tumors of the ovary, and gestational trophoblastic tumors.

[Carcinoma, prostatic (treatment)][1]—Doxorubicin is indicated alone and in combination with other chemotherapeutic agents for treatment of prostate carcinoma (Evidence rating: IA).

Lymphoma, Hodgkin's (treatment) or
Lymphoma, non-Hodgkin's (treatment)—Doxorubicin is indicated for treatment of Hodgkin's and non-Hodgkin's lymphomas.

[Ewing's sarcoma (treatment)][1]
[Kaposi's sarcoma, acquired immunodeficiency syndrome (AIDS)-associated (treatment)][1]
Osteosarcoma (treatment) or
Sarcoma, soft tissue (treatment)—Doxorubicin is indicated for treatment of Ewing's sarcoma, AIDS-associated Kaposi's sarcoma, osteosarcoma, and soft tissue sarcoma.

[Multiple myeloma (treatment)][1]—Doxorubicin is indicated for treatment of multiple myeloma.

[Carcinoma, adrenocortical (treatment)][1] or
[Carcinoid tumors (treatment)][1]—Doxorubicin, alone or in combination with other chemotherapeutic agents, is considered reasonable medical therapy at some point in the management of a patient with adrenocortical carcinoma (Evidence rating: IIID) and carcinoid tumors (Evidence rating: IA).

[Carcinoma, esophageal (treatment)][1]—Doxorubicin, in combination with other chemotherapeutic agents, is considered reasonable medical therapy at some point in the management of a patient with advanced, inoperable esophageal carcinoma (Evidence rating: ID).

[Retinoblastoma (treatment)][1]—Doxorubicin is indicated, in combination with other chemotherapeutic agents, for first-line treatment of retinoblastoma (Evidence rating: IIID).

---

[1]Not included in Canadian product labeling.

Pharmacology/Pharmacokinetics

Physicochemical characteristics
Molecular weight—543.53.
Other characteristics—Unstable in solutions with a pH of less than 3 or greater than 7.

Mechanism of action/Effect
Doxorubicin is an anthracycline glycoside; it is classified as an antibiotic but is not used as an antimicrobial agent. Doxorubicin is cell cycle–specific for the S phase of cell division. Its exact mechanism of antineoplastic activity is unknown but may involve binding to DNA by intercalation between base pairs and inhibition of DNA and RNA synthesis by template disordering and steric obstruction. Other possible mechanisms of antineoplastic activity include binding to cell membrane lipids, thus altering a variety of cellular functions and interacting with topoisomerase II to form DNA-cleavable complexes.

Distribution
Vol_D—Steady state: > 20 to 30 L per kg, indicating extensive uptake into tissues.

Does not cross the blood-brain barrier.

Protein binding
High (74 to 76%); independent of plasma concentration of doxorubicin.

Biotransformation
Occurs rapidly (within 1 hour) in the liver to produce an active metabolite, doxorubicinol. Enzymatic reduction of doxorubicin by oxidases, reductases, and dehydrogenases results in the production of free radicals, which may contribute to cardiotoxicity.

Half-life
Distribution—
Approximately 5 minutes.
Elimination—
20 to 48 hours for doxorubicin and doxorubicinol.

Elimination
Biliary—
40% unchanged, over 5 days.
Renal—
5 to 12% of doxorubicin and metabolites appear in urine over 5 days.

Precautions to Consider

Carcinogenicity/Mutagenicity
Secondary malignancies are potential delayed effects of many antineoplastic agents, although it is not clear whether the effect is related to their mutagenic or immunosuppressive action. The effect of dose and duration of therapy is also unknown, although the risk seems to increase with long-term use. Although information is limited, available data seem to indicate that the carcinogenic risk is greatest with the alkylating agents.

Doxorubicin is carcinogenic in animals and is potentially carcinogenic in humans.

Pregnancy/Reproduction
Fertility—Gonadal suppression, resulting in amenorrhea or azoospermia, may occur in patients taking antineoplastic therapy, especially with the alkylating agents. In general, these effects appear to be related to dose and length of therapy and may be irreversible. Prediction of the degree of testicular or ovarian function impairment is complicated by the common use of combinations of several antineoplastics, which makes it difficult to assess the effects of individual agents.

Doxorubicin affects gonadal function but has a weaker effect on humans than that seen in experiments with mice.

Pregnancy—Some studies indicate that doxorubicin may cross the placenta in humans.

First trimester: It is usually recommended that use of antineoplastics, especially combination chemotherapy, be avoided whenever possible, especially during the first trimester. Although information is limited because of the relatively few instances of antineoplastic administration during pregnancy, the mutagenic, teratogenic, and carcinogenic potential of these medications must be considered.

Other hazards to the fetus include adverse reactions seen in adults.

In general, use of a contraceptive is recommended during cytotoxic drug therapy.

Doxorubicin is embryotoxic and teratogenic in rats and embryotoxic and abortifacient in rabbits.

Breast-feeding
Although very little information is available regarding distribution of antineoplastic agents into breast milk, breast-feeding is not recommended while doxorubicin is being administered because of the risks to the infant (adverse effects, mutagenicity, carcinogenicity).

Pediatrics
Although appropriate studies on the relationship of age to the effects of doxorubicin have not been performed in the pediatric population, cardiotoxicity may be more frequent in children up to 2 years of age.

Geriatrics
Although appropriate studies on the relationship of age to the effects of doxorubicin have not been performed in the geriatric population, cardiotoxicity may be more frequent in patients 70 years of age or older. Caution should also be used in patients who have inadequate bone marrow reserves due to old age.

Dental
The bone marrow depressant effects of doxorubicin may result in an increased incidence of microbial infection, delayed healing, and gingival bleeding. Dental work, whenever possible, should be completed prior to initiation of therapy or deferred until blood counts have returned to normal. Patients should be instructed in proper oral hygiene during

treatment, including caution in use of regular toothbrushes, dental floss, and toothpicks.

Doxorubicin also commonly causes stomatitis, which may be associated with considerable discomfort.

Drug interactions and/or related problems

The following drug interactions and/or related problems have been selected on the basis of their potential clinical significance (possible mechanism in parentheses where appropriate)—not necessarily inclusive (» = major clinical significance):

Note: Combinations containing any of the following medications, depending on the amount present, may also interact with this medication.

Allopurinol or
Colchicine or
» Probenecid or
» Sulfinpyrazone
(doxorubicin may raise the concentration of blood uric acid; dosage adjustment of antigout agents may be necessary to control hyperuricemia and gout; allopurinol may be preferred to prevent or reverse doxorubicin-induced hyperuricemia because of risk of uric acid nephropathy with uricosuric antigout agents)

Blood dyscrasia-causing medications (see *Appendix II*)
(leukopenic and/or thrombocytopenic effects of doxorubicin may be increased with concurrent or recent therapy if these medications cause the same effects; dosage adjustment of doxorubicin, if necessary, should be based on blood counts)

» Bone marrow depressants, other (see *Appendix II*) or
Radiation therapy
(additive bone marrow depression, including severe dermatitis and/or mucositis, may occur; dosage reduction may be required when two or more bone marrow depressants, including radiation, are used concurrently or consecutively)

Cyclophosphamide or
Dactinomycin or
Mitomycin or
Radiation therapy to mediastinal area
(concurrent use may result in increased cardiotoxicity; it is recommended that the total dose of doxorubicin not exceed 400 mg per square meter of body surface area)
(concurrent use of cyclophosphamide with doxorubicin may potentiate cyclophosphamide-induced hemorrhagic cystitis)

» Daunorubicin
(use of doxorubicin in a patient who has previously received daunorubicin increases the risk of cardiotoxicity; dosage adjustment is necessary. Doxorubicin should not be used in patients who have previously received complete cumulative doses of daunorubicin or doxorubicin)

Hepatotoxic medications (see *Appendix II*)
(concurrent use may increase the risk of toxicity; for example, high-dose methotrexate may impair liver function and increase toxicity of subsequently administered doxorubicin)

Streptozocin
(may prolong the half-life of doxorubicin when used concurrently; dosage reduction of doxorubicin is recommended)

Vaccines, killed virus
(because normal defense mechanisms may be suppressed by doxorubicin therapy, the patient's antibody response to the vaccine may be decreased. The interval between discontinuation of medications that cause immunosuppression and restoration of the patient's ability to respond to the vaccine depends on the intensity and type of immunosuppression-causing medication used, the underlying disease, and other factors; estimates vary from 3 months to 1 year)

» Vaccines, live virus
(because normal defense mechanisms may be suppressed by doxorubicin therapy, concurrent use with a live virus vaccine may potentiate the replication of the vaccine virus, may increase the side/adverse effects of the vaccine virus, and/or may decrease the patient's antibody response to the vaccine; immunization of these patients should be undertaken only with extreme caution after careful review of the patient's hematologic status and only with the knowledge and consent of the physician managing the doxorubicin therapy. The interval between discontinuation of medications that cause immunosuppression and restoration of the patient's ability to respond to the vaccine depends on the intensity and type of immunosuppression-causing medication used, the underlying disease, and other factors; estimates vary from 3 months to 1 year. Patients with leukemia in remission should not receive live virus vaccine until at least 3 months after their last chemotherapy. In addition, immunization with oral poliovirus vaccine should be postponed in persons in close contact with the patient, especially family members)

Laboratory value alterations

The following have been selected on the basis of their potential clinical significance (possible effect in parentheses where appropriate)—not necessarily inclusive (» = major clinical significance).

With physiology/laboratory test values

Electrocardiogram (ECG) changes, transient, including:
Arrhythmias
ST depression
T-wave flattening
(may last up to 2 weeks after a dose or course; withdrawal of doxorubicin is usually not necessary)

QRS reduction
(may be a sign of cardiomyopathy; withdrawal of doxorubicin should be considered)

Uric acid
(concentrations in blood and urine may be increased)

Medical considerations/Contraindications

The medical considerations/contraindications included have been selected on the basis of their potential clinical significance (reasons given in parentheses where appropriate)—not necessarily inclusive (» = major clinical significance).

Risk-benefit should be considered when the following medical problems exist:

» Bone marrow depression

» Chickenpox, existing or recent (including recent exposure) or
» Herpes zoster
(risk of severe generalized disease)

Gout, history of or
Urate renal stones, history of
(risk of hyperuricemia)

» Heart disease
(cardiotoxicity may occur at lower cumulative doses)

» Hepatic function impairment
(elimination may be decreased. Reduction in dosage is recommended; one half of the normal dose is recommended in patients with serum bilirubin concentrations of 1.2 to 3 mg per 100 mL; one quarter of the normal dose is recommended in patients with serum bilirubin concentrations of 3 to 5 mg per 100 mL)

Sensitivity to doxorubicin

» Tumor cell infiltration of the bone marrow

» Caution should be used also in patients with inadequate bone marrow reserves due to previous cytotoxic drug or radiation therapy.

Patient monitoring

The following are especially important in patient monitoring (other tests may be warranted in some patients, depending on condition; » = major clinical significance):

Alanine aminotransferase (ALT [SGPT]) values and
Alkaline phosphatase values and
Aspartate aminotransferase (AST [SGOT]) values and
Bilirubin concentrations, serum and
Lactate dehydrogenase (LDH) values
(recommended prior to initiation of therapy and at periodic intervals during therapy; frequency varies according to clinical state, agent, dose, and other agents being used concurrently)

Chest radiograph and
» Echocardiography and
Electrocardiogram (ECG) studies and
» Radionuclide angiography determination of ejection fraction
(recommended prior to initiation of therapy and at periodic intervals during therapy)

» Examination of patient's mouth for ulceration
(recommended before administration of each dose)

» Hematocrit or hemoglobin and
» Leukocyte count, total and, if appropriate, differential and
» Platelet count
(determinations recommended prior to initiation of therapy and at periodic intervals during therapy; frequency varies according to clinical state, agent, dose, and other agents being used concurrently)

Uric acid concentrations, serum
(recommended prior to initiation of therapy and at periodic intervals during therapy; frequency varies according to clinical state, agent, dose, and other agents being used concurrently)

Side/Adverse Effects

Note: Many "side effects" of antineoplastic therapy are unavoidable and represent the medication's pharmacologic action. Some of these (for example, leukopenia and thrombocytopenia) are actually used as parameters to aid in individual dosage titration.

A necrotizing colitis (cecal inflammation, bloody stools, severe and sometimes fatal infections) has been associated with a combination regimen of doxorubicin and cytarabine.

Excessively rapid intravenous administration may produce facial flushing.

The following side/adverse effects have been selected on the basis of their potential clinical significance (possible signs and symptoms in parentheses where appropriate)—not necessarily inclusive:

Those indicating need for medical attention

Incidence more frequent

Leukopenia or infection (fever or chills; cough or hoarseness; lower back or side pain; painful or difficult urination)—usually asymptomatic; ***stomatitis or esophagitis*** (sores in mouth and on lips)

Note: With *leukopenia*, the nadir of leukocyte count occurs 10 to 14 days after a dose. Recovery usually occurs within 21 days after a dose.

Stomatitis or esophagitis occurs 5 to 10 days after administration. It may be severe and lead to ulceration and the potential for severe infections. It is more severe with a dosage regimen of 3 successive days.

Incidence less frequent

Cardiotoxicity, usually in the form of congestive heart failure (shortness of breath; swelling of feet and lower legs; fast or irregular heartbeat); ***extravasation, cellulitis, or tissue necrosis*** (pain at injection site); ***gastrointestinal ulceration*** (stomach pain); ***hyperuricemia or uric acid nephropathy*** (joint pain; lower back or side pain); ***local reaction*** (red streaks along injected vein); ***phlebosclerosis*** (pain at injection site); ***postirradiation erythema, recall*** (darkening or redness of skin); ***thrombocytopenia*** (unusual bleeding or bruising; black, tarry stools; blood in urine or stools; pinpoint red spots on skin)—usually asymptomatic

Note: Incidence of *cardiotoxicity* is more frequent in patients receiving total dosages of over 550 mg per square meter of body surface area (400 mg per square meter of body surface area in patients who have previously received chest irradiation or medications increasing cardiotoxicity) and in patients with a history of cardiac disease or mediastinal radiation, and may be more frequent in children up to 2 years of age and in the elderly.

Cardiotoxicity usually appears within 1 to 6 months after initiation of therapy. Cardiomyopathy has been reported to be associated with persistent voltage reduction in the QRS wave, systolic interval prolongation, and reduction of ejection fraction. It may develop suddenly and may not be detected by routine ECG. It may be irreversible and fatal but responds to treatment if detected early.

Acute life-threatening arrhythmias have been reported during or within a few hours after administration.

Extravasation may also occur without accompanying stinging or burning and even if blood returns well on aspiration of the infusion needle.

Hyperuricemia or uric acid nephropathy occurs most commonly during initial treatment of patients with leukemia or lymphoma, as a result of rapid cell breakdown that leads to elevated serum uric acid concentrations.

A *local reaction* may indicate excessively rapid intravenous administration.

Phlebosclerosis occurs especially when small veins are used or a single vein is used repeatedly.

Recall postirradiation erythema occurs if patient has previously received radiation therapy; severe dermatitis and/or mucositis in the irradiated area may occur with concurrent use.

Incidence rare

Allergic reaction (skin rash or itching; fever; chills); ***anaphylaxis*** (wheezing)

Those indicating need for medical attention only if they continue or are bothersome

Incidence more frequent

Nausea and vomiting—may be severe

Incidence less frequent

Darkening of soles, palms, or nails—especially in children and black patients; ***diarrhea***

Those not indicating need for medical attention

Incidence more frequent

Loss of hair; reddish-colored urine

Note: *Loss of hair* is complete and reversible. It occurs in most cases.

Reddish-colored urine clears within 48 hours.

Those indicating the need for medical attention if they occur after medication is discontinued

Cardiotoxicity (fast or irregular heartbeat; shortness of breath; swelling of feet and lower legs)

Patient Consultation

As an aid to patient consultation, refer to Advice for the Patient, Doxorubicin (Systemic).

In providing consultation, consider emphasizing the following selected information (» = major clinical significance):

Before using this medication

» Conditions affecting use, especially:

Sensitivity to doxorubicin

Pregnancy—Use not recommended because of mutagenic, teratogenic, and carcinogenic potential; advisability of using contraception; telling physician immediately if pregnancy is suspected

Breast-feeding—Not recommended because of risk of serious side effects

Use in children—Cardiotoxicity more frequent in children up to 2 years of age

Use in the elderly—Cardiotoxicity may be more frequent in patients 70 years of age and over

Other medications, especially probenecid, sulfinpyrazone, other bone marrow depressants, daunorubicin, live virus vaccines, or previous cytotoxic drug or radiation therapy

Other medical problems, especially chickenpox, herpes zoster, heart disease, hepatic function impairment, or tumor cell infiltration of bone marrow

Proper use of this medication

Caution in taking combination therapy; taking each medication at the right time

Importance of ample fluid intake and subsequent increase in urine output to aid in excretion of uric acid

Frequency of nausea and vomiting; importance of continuing medication despite stomach upset

» Proper dosing

Precautions while using this medication

» Importance of close monitoring by the physician

» Avoiding immunizations unless approved by physician; other persons in patient's household should avoid immunizations with oral poliovirus vaccine; avoiding persons who have taken oral poliovirus vaccine, or wearing a protective mask that covers nose and mouth

Caution if bone marrow depression occurs:

» Avoiding exposure to persons with infections, especially during periods of low blood counts; checking with physician immediately if fever or chills, cough or hoarseness, lower back or side pain, or painful or difficult urination occurs

» Checking with physician immediately if unusual bleeding or bruising; black, tarry stools; blood in urine or stools; or pinpoint red spots on skin occur

Caution in use of regular toothbrush, dental floss, or toothpick; physician, dentist, or nurse may suggest alternatives; checking with physician before having dental work done

Not touching eyes or inside of nose unless hands washed immediately before

Using caution to avoid accidental cuts with use of sharp objects such as safety razor or fingernail or toenail cutters

Avoiding contact sports or other situations where bruising or injury could occur

» Possibility of local tissue injury and scarring if infiltration of intravenous solution occurs; telling doctor or nurse right away about redness, pain, or swelling at injection site

Side/adverse effects

May cause adverse effects such as blood problems, loss of hair, heart problems, and cancer

Signs of potential side effects, especially leukopenia, infection, stomatitis, esophagitis, cardiotoxicity, extravasation, cellulitis, tissue necrosis, gastrointestinal ulceration, hyperuricemia, uric acid nephropathy, local reaction, phlebosclerosis, recall of postirradiation erythema, thrombocytopenia, allergic reaction, and anaphylaxis

Physician or nurse can help in dealing with side effects

Reddish urine for 1 to 2 days after administration may be alarming to patient although medically insignificant

Possibility of hair loss; normal hair growth should resume after treatment has ended

General Dosing Information

Patients receiving doxorubicin should be under supervision of a physician experienced in cancer chemotherapy. It is recommended that the patient be hospitalized at least during initial treatment.

Doxorubicin should not be used in patients who have previously received the maximum acceptable cumulative doses of doxorubicin and/or daunorubicin.

A variety of dosage schedules of doxorubicin, alone or in combination with other antitumor agents, are used. The prescriber may consult the medical literature as well as the manufacturer's literature in choosing a specific dosage.

Dosage must be adjusted to meet the individual requirements of each patient, on the basis of clinical response and appearance or severity of toxicity.

Use of a weekly dosage of doxorubicin may be associated with a reduced risk of cardiotoxicity and hematologic toxicity.

It is recommended that doxorubicin be administered slowly into the tubing of a freely running intravenous infusion of 0.9% sodium chloride injection or 5% dextrose injection (over not less than 3 to 5 minutes). If possible, veins over joints or in extremities with compromised venous or lymphatic drainage should be avoided.

Care must be taken to avoid extravasation during intravenous administration because of the risk of severe ulceration and necrosis. Facial flushing indicates too-rapid injection.

If extravasation of doxorubicin occurs during intravenous administration, as indicated by local swelling at the tip of the needle and local burning or stinging (may also be painless), the injection and infusion should be stopped immediately and resumed, completing the dose, in another vein. Local infiltration of antidotes is not recommended. Use of ice packs and elevation of the extremity to reduce swelling are recommended. Surgical excision of the involved area may be necessary.

Because it will cause local tissue necrosis, doxorubicin must not be administered intramuscularly or subcutaneously.

Doxorubicin has also been administered intra-arterially and as a topical bladder instillation.

Development of uric acid nephropathy in patients with leukemia or lymphoma may be prevented by adequate oral hydration and, in some cases, administration of allopurinol. Alkalinization of urine may be necessary if serum uric acid concentrations are elevated.

In acute leukemia, doxorubicin may be administered despite the presence of thrombocytopenia and bleeding; stoppage of bleeding and increase in platelet count have occurred during treatment in some cases and platelet transfusions are useful in others.

Special precautions are recommended in patients who develop thrombocytopenia as a result of administration of doxorubicin. These may include extreme care in performing invasive procedures; regular inspection of intravenous sites, skin (including perirectal area), and mucous membrane surfaces for signs of bleeding or bruising; limiting frequency of venipuncture and avoiding intramuscular injections; testing urine, emesis, stool, and secretions for occult blood; care in the use of regular toothbrushes, dental floss, toothpicks, safety razors, and fingernail and toenail cutters; avoiding constipation; and using caution to prevent falls and other injuries. Such patients should avoid alcohol and aspirin intake because of the risk of gastrointestinal bleeding. Platelet transfusions may be required.

Patients who develop leukopenia should be observed carefully for signs of infection. Antibiotic support may be required. In neutropenic patients who develop fever, broad-spectrum antibiotic coverage should be initiated empirically, pending bacterial cultures and appropriate diagnostic tests.

Safety considerations for handling this medication

There is limited but increasing evidence and concern that personnel involved in preparation and administration of parenteral antineoplastic agents may be at some risk because of the potential mutagenicity, teratogenicity, and/or carcinogenicity of these agents, although the actual risk is unknown. USP advisory panels recommend cautious handling both in preparation and disposal of antineoplastic agents. Precautions that have been suggested include:

- Use of a biological containment cabinet during reconstitution and dilution of parenteral medications and wearing of disposable surgical gloves and masks.
- Use of proper technique to prevent contamination of the medication, work area, and operator during transfer between containers (including proper training of personnel in this technique).
- Cautious and proper disposal of needles, syringes, vials, ampuls, and unused medication.

A number of medical centers have developed detailed guidelines for handling of antineoplastic agents.

Combination chemotherapy

Doxorubicin may be used in combination with other agents in various regimens. As a result, incidence and/or severity of side effects may be altered and different dosages (usually reduced) may be used.

Parenteral Dosage Forms

Note: Bracketed uses in the *Dosage Forms* section refer to categories of use and/or indications that are not included in U.S. product labeling.

DOXORUBICIN HYDROCHLORIDE INJECTION USP

Usual adult dose

Leukemia, acute lymphocytic or
Leukemia, acute nonlymphocytic or
Carcinoma, bladder or
Carcinoma, breast or
Carcinoma, gastric or
Carcinoma, lung, small cell or
Carcinoma, ovarian, epithelial or
Carcinoma, thyroid or
Neuroblastoma or
Wilms" tumor or
[Carcinoma, cervical] or
[Carcinoma, endometrial] or
[Carcinoma, head and neck] or
[Carcinoma, lung, non-small cell] or
[Carcinoma, pancreatic][1] or
[Carcinoma, prostatic][1] or
[Tumors, ovarian, germ cell] or
Lymphoma, Hodgkin's or
Lymphoma, non-Hodgkin's or
Sarcoma, soft tissue or
Osteosarcoma or
[Ewing's sarcoma][1] or
[Multiple myeloma][1]—

Intravenous, 60 to 75 mg per square meter of body surface area, repeated every twenty-one days or

Intravenous, 25 to 30 mg per square meter of body surface area a day on two or three successive days, repeated every three to four weeks or

Intravenous, 20 mg per square meter of body surface area once a week.

When used in combination with other chemotherapy agents: Intravenous, 40 to 60 mg per square meter of body surface area, repeated every twenty-one to twenty-eight days.

[Carcinoma, bladder (prophylaxis)][1] or
[Leukemia, chronic lymphocytic][1] or
[Carcinoma, hepatocellular, primary][1] or
[Hepatoblastoma][1] or
[Thymoma][1] or
[Tumors, trophoblastic, gestational][1] or
[Kaposi's sarcoma, acquired immunodeficiency syndrome (AIDS)-associated][1] or
[Carcinoma, adrenocortical][1] or
[Carcinoid tumors][1] or
[Carcinoma, esophageal][1] or
[Retinoblastoma][1]—

Consult medical literature and manufacturer's literature for specific dosage.

Usual adult prescribing limits

The risk of developing congestive heart failure is estimated to be 1 to 2% at a total cumulative dosage of 300 mg per square meter of body surface area, 3 to 5% at a total cumulative dosage of 400 mg per square meter of body surface area, 5 to 8% at a total cumulative dosage of 450 mg per square meter of body surface area, and 6 to 20% at a total cumulative dosage of 500 mg per square meter of body surface area. This toxicity may develop at lower cumulative dosages in patients who have previously received chest irradiation, patients who have received medications increasing cardiotoxicity, or patients with pre-existing heart disease.

Usual pediatric dose

Intravenous, 30 mg per square meter of body surface area a day on three successive days every four weeks.

Strength(s) usually available

U.S.—

2 mg per mL (5-, 10-, 25-, and 37.5-mL single-dose vials, and 100-mL multidose vial) (Rx) [*Adriamycin PFS* (sodium chloride 0.9%); GENERIC (sodium chloride 0.9%)].

Canada—

2 mg per mL (5- and 25-mL single-dose vials, and 200-mL multidose vial) (Rx) [*Adriamycin PFS* (sodium chloride 0.9%)].

Packaging and storage

Store between 2 and 8 °C (36 and 46 °F). Protect from light.

Incompatibilities

Doxorubicin should not be mixed with heparin, dexamethasone, fluorouracil, hydrocortisone sodium succinate, aminophylline, or cephalothin, since a precipitate may form.

Caution

Caution in handling the 100- or 200-mL (200- or 400-mg) multiple-dose vial is recommended to prevent confusion with the single-dose vial and possible inadvertent overdose. For example, the manufacturer recommends that the multiple-dose vial be stored in the original carton until the contents are used.

Note

Great care should be taken to prevent exposure of the skin to doxorubicin. The use of gloves is recommended. Any doxorubicin solution that comes in contact with the skin or mucosa should be washed off thoroughly with soap and water.

DOXORUBICIN HYDROCHLORIDE FOR INJECTION USP

Usual adult dose

See *Doxorubicin Hydrochloride Injection USP*.

Usual adult prescribing limits

See *Doxorubicin Hydrochloride Injection USP*.

Usual pediatric dose

See *Doxorubicin Hydrochloride Injection USP*.

Strength(s) usually available

U.S.—

10 mg (single-dose vial) (Rx) [*Adriamycin RDF* (lactose 50 mg; methylparaben 1 mg); *Rubex* (lactose); GENERIC (may contain lactose 50 mg)].

20 mg (single-dose vial) (Rx) [*Adriamycin RDF* (lactose 100 mg; methylparaben 2 mg); GENERIC (may contain lactose 100 mg)].

50 mg (single-dose vial) (Rx) [*Adriamycin RDF* (lactose 250 mg; methylparaben 5 mg); *Rubex* (lactose 250 mg); GENERIC (may contain lactose 250 mg)].

100 mg (single-dose vial) (Rx) [*Rubex* (lactose 500 mg)].

150 mg (multidose vial) (Rx) [*Adriamycin RDF* (lactose 750 mg; methylparaben 15 mg)].

Canada—

10 mg (single-dose vial) (Rx) [*Adriamycin RDF* (lactose 50 mg; methylparaben 1 mg)].

20 mg (single-dose vial) (Rx) [*Adriamycin RDF* (lactose 100 mg; methylparaben 2 mg)].

50 mg (single-dose vial) (Rx) [*Adriamycin RDF* (lactose 250 mg; methylparaben 5 mg)].

150 mg (multidose vial) (Rx) [*Adriamycin RDF* (lactose 750 mg; methylparaben 15 mg)].

Packaging and storage

Store below 40 °C (104 °F), preferably between 15 and 30 °C (59 and 86 °F), unless otherwise specified by the manufacturer. Protect from light.

Preparation of dosage form

Doxorubicin Hydrochloride for Injection USP is reconstituted for intravenous administration by adding 5 mL (10-mg vial), 10 mL (20-mg vial), 25 mL (50-mg vial), 50 mL (100-mg vial), or 75 mL (150-mg vial) of 0.9% sodium chloride injection to the vial and shaking to dissolve, producing a solution containing 2 mg of doxorubicin hydrochloride per mL. Use of bacteriostatic diluents is not recommended. An appropriate volume of air should be withdrawn from the vial during reconstitution to avoid excessive pressure buildup.

Stability

Reconstituted solutions of *Adriamycin RDF* are stable for 7 days at room temperature and under normal room light (100-foot candles) or 15 days between 2 and 8 °C (36 and 46 °F) when protected from sunlight. Unused solution from single-dose vials or unused solution from the multiple-dose vial remaining beyond the recommended storage time should be discarded.

Reconstituted solutions of *Rubex* or generic doxorubicin are stable for 24 hours at room temperature or 48 hours between 2 and 8 °C (36 and 46 °F). The solution should be protected from light and any unused solution should be discarded.

Incompatibilities

Doxorubicin should not be mixed with heparin, dexamethasone, fluorouracil, hydrocortisone sodium succinate, aminophylline, or cephalothin, since a precipitate may form.

Note

Great care should be taken to prevent inhalation of particles of doxorubicin hydrochloride and exposure of the skin to it. The use of gloves is recommended. Any doxorubicin powder or solution that comes in contact with the skin or mucosa should be washed off thoroughly with soap and water.

[1]Not included in Canadian product labeling.

Revised: 06/15/1999

DOXORUBICIN, LIPOSOMAL Systemic

VA CLASSIFICATION (Primary): AN200

Commonly used brand name(s): *Caelyx; Doxil.*

Note: For a listing of dosage forms and brand names by country availability, see *Dosage Forms* section(s).

Category

Antineoplastic.

Indications

Note: Bracketed information in the *Indications* section refers to uses that are not included in U.S. product labeling.

Accepted

Kaposi's sarcoma (KS), acquired immunodeficiency syndrome (AIDS)-associated (treatment)—Liposomal doxorubicin is indicated for treatment of patients with AIDS-associated KS disease that has progressed in spite of prior combination chemotherapy or patients who are intolerant of such therapy.

Note: The treatment of AIDS-associated KS is dependent on the extent and severity of the KS and the patient's clinical condition. For patients with minimal disease, local treatments such as excision, radiotherapy, or intralesional chemotherapy may be adequate. However, for those with severe cutaneous or systemic disease, systemic chemotherapy may be required. Patients with severe debilitation due to their general condition are best served by optimal palliative care.

Carcinoma, ovarian (treatment)—Doxorubicin HCl liposome injection is indicated for the treatment of patients with ovarian cancer whose disease has progressed or recurred after platinum-based chemotherapy.

[Carcinoma, breast (treatment)][1]—Liposomal doxorubicin is indicated for first-line treatment or treatment at some point in the management of locally advanced and metastatic breast carcinoma.

[Multiple myeloma, in combination with vincristine and dexamethasone][1]—Data from published trials indicate that substitution of doxorubicin HCl with liposomal doxorubicin in combination with vincristine and dexamethasone for patients with multiple myeloma is active and well tolerated. Because the need for a 96-hour continuous infusion or daily injections for four days are eliminated, outpatient administration and patient convenience are achieved. Also, since liposomal doxorubicin is not a vesicant it can be administered via a peripheral line, eliminating the potential complications of central venous access.

[1]Not included in Canadian product labeling.

Pharmacology/Pharmacokinetics

Physicochemical characteristics

Source—Doxorubicin is isolated from *Streptomyces peucetius* var. *caesius*. Liposomal doxorubicin is doxorubicin encapsulated in long-circulating liposomes. Liposomes are microscopic vesicles, composed of a phospholipid bilayer, that are capable of encapsulating active drugs. Liposomal doxorubicin is supplied as a sterile, translucent, red liposomal dispersion.

Molecular weight—579.99 (as hydrochloride).

Mechanism of action/Effect

Doxorubicin is an anthracycline cytostatic antibiotic with activity against a variety of malignancies including Kaposi's sarcoma (KS). Liposomal doxorubicin has been shown to inhibit the growth of KS cells both *in vitro* and *in vivo*. KS spindle cell cultures are more sensitive to liposomal doxorubicin than are cultures of normal monocytes or normal endothelial or smooth muscle cells.

Tumor cell DNA fragmentation induced by doxorubicin is a result of topoisomerase II inhibition, which occurs when doxorubicin intercalates between DNA strands. The antitumor activity and toxicity of doxorubicin may also relate to the formation of intracellular oxygen free radicals, which are produced by reduction of the doxorubicin molecule. In addition, liposomal doxorubicin induces expression of monocyte chemoattractant protein-1, which results in intralesional recruitment of phagocytic cells in patients with KS.

The mechanism by which liposome encapsulation apparently enhances doxorubicin accumulation in lesions of acquired immunodeficiency syndrome (AIDS)-associated KS is not fully understood. However, polyethylene glycol (PEG)-containing liposomes of the same size and exhibiting approximately the same rate of plasma clearance as those used to encapsulate the doxorubicin, but containing entrapped colloidal gold designed to serve as a marker for following liposome distribution by light and electron microscopy, have been shown to enter solid colon tumors implanted in mice and KS-like lesions in human immunodeficiency virus (HIV)-transgenic mice.

Extravasation of liposomes also may occur by passage of the particles through endothelial cell gaps, which are reported to be present in certain solid tumors and which are known to be present in KS-like lesions. These processes may contribute to the enhanced accumulation of doxorubicin in lesions of AIDS-associated KS after administration of PEG-liposomal doxorubicin.

Once within the tumor, the active ingredient, doxorubicin, is presumably available to be released locally as the liposomes degrade and become permeable *in situ*.

Distribution

Limited to vascular fluid.

Vol_D—Steady-state: 2.7 to 2.8 liters per square meter of body surface area for doses of 20 and 10 mg per square meter of body surface area (mg/m^2), respectively.

Note: During circulation, at least 90% of liposomal doxorubicin remains encapsulated. This circulation is represented by a large area under the plasma concentration-time curve (AUC) of 277 and 590 mcg per mL (mcg/mL) per hour for doses of 10 and 20 mg/m^2, respectively. At a 50 mg/m^2 dose, the AUC is expected to be more than proportional when compared with the lower doses.

Protein binding

Protein binding of liposomal doxorubicin has not been determined; however, the active ingredient, doxorubicin, binds extensively to tissues (70%).

Biotransformation

The major metabolite of standard doxorubicin is doxorubicinol; after administration of 10 or 20 mg/m^2 of liposomal doxorubicin, doxorubicinol was detectable in plasma at very low levels (0.8 to 26.2 nanograms per mL). Metabolites of doxorubicin, including doxorubicinol and the sulfate and glucuronide conjugates of the 7-deoxyaglycones, were detected in small quantities in the urine.

Half-life

First phase—4.7 and 5.2 hours for doses of 10 and 20 mg/m^2, respectively.

Second phase—52.3 and 55 hours for doses of 10 and 20 mg/m^2, respectively.

Because the pharmacokinetics at a dose of 50 mg/m^2 are reported to be nonlinear, the elimination half-life is expected to be longer and the clearance lower at this dose compared with a 20 mg/m^2 dose.

Peak serum concentration

4.1 and 8.3 mcg/mL for doses of 10 and 20 mg/m^2, respectively.

Elimination

Renal—Total plasma clearance of liposomal doxorubicin is slower than total plasma clearance of standard doxorubicin, with a rate of 0.041 and 0.056 liters per hour per square meter of body surface area (L/h/m^2) for doses of 20 and 10 mg/m^2, respectively.

Renal elimination of PEG-liposomal doxorubicin is slower than elimination of the standard doxorubicin: 5.5% of an injected dose of liposomal doxorubicin was recovered in urine after 72 hours, compared with 11% of an injected dose of standard doxorubicin after only 24 hours.

Precautions to Consider

Cross-sensitivity and/or related problems

Patients hypersensitive to other doxorubicin formulations may be hypersensitive to liposomal doxorubicin also.

Carcinogenicity/Mutagenicity

Secondary acute myelogenous leukemia has been reported in patients treated with topoisomerase II inhibitors, including anthracyclines.

Studies to evaluate the carcinogenic potential of liposomal doxorubicin injection have not been performed; however, the active ingredient, doxorubicin, is carcinogenic and mutagenic in experimental models. The liposome component of liposomal doxorubicin demonstrated no mutagenic effects in the Ames test, mouse lymphoma assay, an *in vitro* chromosomal aberration assay, and an *in vivo* mammalian micronucleus assay.

Pregnancy/Reproduction

Fertility—Adequate and well-controlled studies in humans have not been done. However, fertility studies in mice have shown that liposomal doxorubicin causes ovarian and testicular degeneration at two times the 50 mg/m^2 human dose. Studies in dogs have shown that liposomal doxorubicin causes atrophy of the seminiferous tubules and diminished spermatogenesis at a dose one half the 50 mg/m^2 human dose. Studies in rats have shown that liposomal doxorubicin causes testicular degeneration at 3.3% of the 50 mg/m^2 human dose.

Pregnancy—Adequate and well-controlled studies in humans have not been done. Liposomal doxorubicin can cause fetal harm when administered to a pregnant woman. Women of childbearing age should be advised to avoid pregnancy during treatment. If pregnancy occurs within the first few months after treatment, the prolonged half-life of the drug must be considered.

In general, use of a contraceptive method is recommended during cytotoxic drug therapy.

Liposomal doxorubicin is embryotoxic in rats and embryotoxic and abortifacient in rabbits at doses about one-eighth the 50 mg per square meter human dose.

FDA Pregnancy Category D.

Breast-feeding

Breast-feeding is **contraindicated** while liposomal doxorubicin is being administered because of the potential risk of adverse reactions in the infant. Mothers should discontinue nursing prior to taking liposomal doxorubicin.It is not known whether liposomal doxorubicin is distributed into breast milk. However, many drugs, including anthracyclines, are distributed into human milk.

Pediatrics

Appropriate studies on the relationship of age to the effects of liposomal doxorubicin have not been performed in the pediatric population. Safety and efficacy have not been established. However, cardiotoxicity may occur frequently with the active ingredient, doxorubicin, in children up to 2 years of age.

Geriatrics

In clinical studies, 29% of the 373 ovarian cancer patients were 60 to 69 years of age, while 22.8% were 70 years of age and older. There were no overall differences observed between these patients and younger patients, but greater sensitivity of some older patients to the medication cannot be ruled out. The active ingredient, doxorubicin, may increase the risk of cardiotoxicity in patients 70 years of age or older. There is insufficient data to evaluate the comparative efficacy of liposomal doxorubicin according to age.

Dental

The leukopenic and thrombocytopenic effects of liposomal doxorubicin may result in an increased incidence of certain microbial infections of the mouth, delayed healing, and gingival bleeding. If leukopenia or thrombocytopenia occurs, dental work should be deferred until blood counts have returned to normal. Patients should be instructed in proper oral hygiene, including caution in use of regular toothbrushes, dental floss, and toothpicks.

Drug interactions and/or related problems

The following drug interactions and/or related problems have been selected on the basis of their potential clinical significance (possible mechanism in parentheses where appropriate)—not necessarily inclusive (» = major clinical significance):

Note: Combinations containing any of the following medications, depending on the amount present, may also interact with this medication.

» Anthracenedione antineoplastic agents, prior use of or
» Daunorubicin, prior use of or
» Doxorubicin, prior use of or
» Idarubicin, prior use of or
» Mitoxantrone, prior use of
(use of liposomal doxorubicin in a patient who previously has received anthracenedione antineoplastic agents, daunorubicin, doxorubicin, idarubicin, or mitoxantrone increases the risk of cardiotoxicity; dosage adjustment is necessary)

Blood dyscrasia-causing medications (see *Appendix II*)
(leukopenic and/or thrombocytopenic effects of liposomal doxorubicin may be increased with concurrent or recent therapy if these

medications cause the same effects; dosage adjustment of liposomal doxorubicin, if necessary, should be based on blood counts)

» Bone marrow depressants, other (see *Appendix II* (additive bone marrow depression, including severe dermatitis and/or mucositis, may occur; dosage reduction may be required when two or more bone marrow depressants are used concurrently or consecutively)

Cyclophosphamide or
Dactinomycin or
Mitomycin or
Radiation therapy to mediastinal area
(concurrent use may result in increased cardiotoxicity)
(concurrent use of cyclophosphamide with liposomal doxorubicin may potentiate cyclophosphamide-induced hemorrhagic cystitis)

Hepatotoxic medications (see *Appendix II*), including
6-Mercaptopurine
(concurrent use may increase the risk of toxicity; for example, high-dose methotrexate may impair liver function and increase toxicity of subsequently administered liposomal doxorubicin)

Vaccines, killed virus
(because normal defense mechanisms may be suppressed by liposomal doxorubicin therapy, the patient's antibody response to the vaccine may be decreased. The interval between discontinuation of medications that cause immunosuppression and restoration of the patient's ability to respond to the vaccine depends on the intensity and type of immunosuppression-causing medication used, the underlying disease, and other factors; estimates vary from 3 months to 1 year)

» Vaccines, live virus
(because normal defense mechanisms may be suppressed by liposomal doxorubicin therapy, concurrent use with a live virus vaccine may potentiate the replication of the vaccine virus, may increase the side/adverse effects of the vaccine virus, and/or may decrease the patient's antibody response to the vaccine; immunization of these patients should be undertaken only with extreme caution after careful review of the patient's hematologic status and only with the knowledge and consent of the physician managing the liposomal doxorubicin therapy. The interval between discontinuation of medications that cause immunosuppression and restoration of the patient's ability to respond to the vaccine depends on the intensity and type of immunosuppression-causing medication used, the underlying disease, and other factors; estimates vary from 3 months to 1 year. Patients with leukemia in remission should not receive live virus vaccine until at least 3 months after their last chemotherapy. In addition, immunization with oral poliovirus vaccine should be postponed in persons in close contact with the patient, especially family members)

Laboratory value alterations

The following have been selected on the basis of their potential clinical significance (possible effect in parentheses where appropriate)—not necessarily inclusive (» = major clinical significance).

With diagnostic test results
» Cardiac function tests
(echocardiography and radionuclide scans may be altered)

With physiology/laboratory test values
Alanine aminotransferase (ALT [SGPT]), serum
Alkaline phosphatase, serum or
Aspartate aminotransferase (AST [SGOT]), serum
(values may be increased)

Bilirubin, serum
(concentrations may be increased)

Blood urea nitrogen (BUN) or
Creatinine, serum
(values rarely may be increased)

Calcium, serum
(concentrations may be decreased)

Glucose, blood
(concentrations may be increased)

» Hemoglobin/hematocrit or
» Leukocyte counts or
» Platelet counts
(may be decreased)

Prothrombin time
(may be prolonged)

Medical considerations/Contraindications

The medical considerations/contraindications included have been selected on the basis of their potential clinical significance (reasons given in parentheses where appropriate)—not necessarily inclusive (» = major clinical significance).

Except under special circumstances, this medication should not be used when the following medical problem exists: :
» Hypersensitivity to doxorubicin or to liposomal doxorubicin or any of its components.

Risk-benefit should be considered when the following medical problems exist:
» Bone marrow depression
» Cardiovascular disease, history of
(may increase risk for cardiotoxicity)
» Chickenpox, existing or recent (including recent exposure) or
» Herpes zoster
(risk of severe generalized disease)
» Heart disease
(cardiotoxicity may occur at lower cumulative doses)
» Hepatic function impairment
(slowed excretion may occur. Reduction in dosage is recommended; one half of the normal dose is recommended in patients with serum bilirubin concentrations of 1.2 to 3 mg per 100 mL; one quarter of the normal dose is recommended in patients with serum bilirubin concentrations of greater than 3 mg per 100 mL)
Radiation therapy, prior
(recall of skin reaction due to prior radiotherapy has occurred with liposomal doxorubicin administration)
» Tumor cell infiltration of the bone marrow
» Caution should be used also in patients with inadequate bone marrow reserves due to previous cytotoxic drug or radiation therapy.

Patient monitoring

The following may be especially important in patient monitoring (other tests may be warranted in some patients, depending on condition; » = major clinical significance):

Alanine aminotransferase (ALT [SGPT]) values, serum and
Alkaline phosphatase values, serum and
Aspartate aminotransferase (AST [SGOT]) values, serum and
Bilirubin concentrations, serum
(recommended prior to initiation of therapy and at periodic intervals during therapy)

» Echocardiography and
Electrocardiogram (ECG) studies and
» Radionuclide angiography determination of ejection fraction
(recommended prior to initiation of therapy and at periodic intervals during therapy)

» Hematocrit or hemoglobin and
» Leukocyte count, total and, if appropriate, differential and
» Platelet count
(determinations recommended prior to initiation of therapy and at periodic intervals during therapy)

Side/Adverse Effects

Note: Clinical studies of liposomal doxorubicin to treat Kaposi's sarcoma (KS) were performed only in patients with acquired immunodeficiency syndrome (AIDS). Assessment of tolerability of liposomal doxorubicin is therefore complicated by underlying immune suppression and morbidity commonly present in these patients. Although liposomal doxorubicin was generally well tolerated, there was a strong likelihood that liposomal doxorubicin–related adverse effects would occur in the majority of the patients. In one study, 76% of patients reported at least one adverse effect that was probably or possibly related to liposomal doxorubicin and 30% of patients reported at least one severe adverse effect thought to be related to liposomal doxorubicin. However, the most common reason for termination of liposomal doxorubicin therapy in these studies was death from AIDS-related complications.

The following side/adverse effects have been selected on the basis of their potential clinical significance (possible signs and symptoms in parentheses where appropriate)—not necessarily inclusive:

Those indicating need for medical attention

Incidence more frequent

Anemia (unusual tiredness or weakness); ***asthenia*** (loss of strength and energy); ***fever; hand-foot syndrome*** (blistering, peeling, redness, and/or swelling of palms of hands or bottoms of feet; numbness, pain, tingling, or unusual sensations in palms of hands or bottoms of feet); ***infusion reactions*** (chills; facial swelling; headache; low blood pressure; shortness of breath); ***leukopenia*** (fever or chills; cough or hoarseness; lower back or side pain; painful or difficult urination); ***neutropenia*** (fever and sore throat)—usually asymptomatic; ***stomatitis***

(sores in mouth and on lips); ***thrombocytopenia*** (black, tarry stools; unusual bleeding or bruising; blood in urine or stools; pinpoint red spots on skin)—usually asymptomatic

Note: *Palmar-plantar erythrodysesthesia* or hand-food syndrome (HFS), characterized by ulceration, erythema, and desquamation on the hands and feet with pain and inflammation, occurs in some patients, most commonly after 6 to 8 weeks of treatment. At recommended dosages of liposomal doxorubicin, the incidence of all grades HFS toxicity was 37% and grades 3 and 4 HFS toxicity was 16% in patients with ovarian cancer. Although reactions may occasionally be severe and debilitating, they are more often mild, and most patients with the syndrome do not require dosage reduction or prolonged treatment delay. However, in severe cases, *palmar-plantar erythrodysesthesia* can be managed by withholding treatment until its resolution and by resuming therapy with longer intervals between doses and/or at a reduced dose.

Some patients may experience *infusion reactions* during the initial few minutes of the first infusion of liposomal doxorubicin. *Infusion reactions* will resolve upon cessation of infusion. However, these reactions often do not prevent further treatment with liposomal doxorubicin. Patients who do not experience *infusion reactions* during the first cycle of liposomal doxorubicin therapy are unlikely to react to subsequent cycles.

Neutropenia is the most common treatment-related side effect. In one study, 35% of enrolled patients had one or more episodes of grade 3 or 4 *neutropenia*. *Neutropenia* is manageable with the use of colony-stimulating factors. However, pre-existing immune system compromise complicates assessment of *neutropenia* and infectious events in patients with AIDS.

Incidence less frequent

Allergic reaction (chills; fever; skin rash or itching)

Incidence rare

Heart failure (chest pain; decreased urine output; dilated neck veins; extreme fatigue; irregular breathing; irregular heartbeat; shortness of breath; swelling of face, fingers, feet, or lower legs; tightness in chest; troubled breathing; weight gain; wheezing); ***jaundice*** (yellowing of eyes and skin)

Note: The risk of cardiac toxicity for patients treated with doxorubicin liposome injection was 11% at all cumulative anthracycline doses between 450 and 500 mg per square meter or between 500 and 550 mg per square meter in a clinical study in patients with advanced breast cancer.

For treatment of Kaposi's sarcoma patients (in addition to those listed above)

Incidence less frequent

Dyspnea (troubled breathing); ***pain at injection site; pneumonia*** (cough; fever; shortness of breath; troubled breathing; wheezing); ***postirradiation erythema, recall*** (darkening or redness of skin); ***tachycardia*** (fast or irregular heartbeat)

Incidence rare

Diabetes mellitus or hyperglycemia (blurred vision; flushed, dry skin; frequent urination; fruit-like breath odor; unusual thirst); ***optic neuritis*** (blurred vision; eye pain; loss of vision)

For treatment of refractory ovarian cancer patients (in addition to those listed above)

Incidence less frequent

Chest pain; edema (decreased urination; rapid weight gain; bloating or swelling of face, hands, lower legs, and/or feet); ***infection*** (fever or chills; cough or hoarseness; lower back or side pain; painful or difficult urination)

Incidence rare

Anaphylactoid reaction (cough; difficulty swallowing; hives; puffiness or swelling of the eyelids or around the eyes, face, lips or tongue; shortness of breath; tightness in chest; wheezing); ***pain at injection site***

Those indicating need for medical attention only if they continue or are bothersome

Incidence more frequent

Diarrhea; nausea; vomiting

Incidence less frequent

Back pain; dizziness; dysphagia (difficulty swallowing)

For treatment of Kaposi's sarcoma patients (in addition to those listed above)

Incidence more frequent

Oral moniliasis (creamy white, curd-like patches in mouth or throat; pain when eating or swallowing)

Incidence less frequent

Constipation; headache

For treatment of refractory ovarian cancer patients (in addition to those listed above)

Incidence more frequent

Abdominal pain; anorexia (loss of appetite); ***constipation; headache; mucous membrane disorder*** (changes in the lining of the mouth or nose); ***pain; paresthesia*** (tingling, burning, or prickly sensations); ***pharyngitis*** (sore throat); ***rash***

Incidence less frequent

Anxiety; conjunctivitis (redness, pain, swelling of eye, eyelid, or inner lining of eyelid; burning, dry or itching eyes; excessive tearing); ***dysphagia*** (difficulty swallowing); ***insomnia*** (trouble sleeping); ***myalgia*** (muscle aches); ***pruritus*** (itching skin); ***taste disturbance*** (change in taste; bad, unusual, or unpleasant [after] taste)

Incidence rare;

Ataxia (shakiness and unsteady walk; clumsiness, unsteadiness, trembling, or other problems with muscle control or coordination); ***flu-like syndrome*** (chills; cough; fever; general feeling of discomfort or illness; joint pain; nausea; shivering; sore throat; sweating; vomiting); ***leukorrhea*** (increased white vaginal discharge); ***parosmia*** (change in sense of smell); ***thinking abnormal***

Those not indicating need for medical attention

Incidence more frequent

Alopecia (loss of hair)

For treatment of refractory ovarian cancer patients (in addition to those listed above)

Incidence more frequent

Dry skin

Incidence less frequent

Skin discoloration (change in skin color); ***sweating***

Those indicating the need for medical attention if they occur after medication is discontinued

Cardiotoxicity (fast or irregular heartbeat; shortness of breath; swelling of feet and lower legs)

Overdose

For specific information on the agents used in the management of liposomal doxorubicin overdose, see:

- *Filgrastim* in *Colony Stimulating Factors (Systemic)* monograph; and/or
- *Sargramostim* in *Colony Stimulating Factors (Systemic)* monograph.

For more information on the management of overdose, **contact a poison control center** (see *Poison Control Center Listing*).

Clinical effects of overdose

The following effects have been selected on the basis of their potential clinical significance (possible signs and symptoms in parentheses where appropriate)—not necessarily inclusive:

Acute

Mucositis (sores in mouth and on lips); ***neutropenia*** (cough or hoarseness; fever or chills; lower back or side pain; painful or difficult urination)—usually asymptomatic; ***thrombocytopenia*** (black, tarry stools; unusual bleeding or bruising; blood in urine or stools; pinpoint red spots on skin)—usually asymptomatic

Treatment of overdose

Treatment of leukopenia includes antibiotic therapy and administration of colony stimulating factors (filgrastim [rG-CSF] or sargramostim [rGM-CSF]).

Treatment of overdose includes hospitalization of the patient, platelet and granulocyte transfusions, and symptomatic treatment of mucositis.

Patients in whom intentional overdose is confirmed or suspected should be referred for psychiatric consultation.

Patient Consultation

As an aid to patient consultation, refer to *Advice for the Patient, Doxorubicin, Liposomal (Systemic)*.

In providing consultation, consider emphasizing the following selected information (» = major clinical significance):

Before using this medication

» Conditions affecting use, especially:

Sensitivity to doxorubicin or liposomal component

Pregnancy—Use may cause fetal harm; women of childbearing age should be advised to avoid pregnancy during treatment

Breast-feeding—Use is contraindicated because of the potential for serious adverse effects in nursing infants

Use in children—Cardiotoxicity in children younger than 2 years old may occur frequently

Use in the elderly—Based on studies with the active ingredient, cardiotoxicity may be more frequent in patients 70 years of age and older

Other medications, especially anthracenedione antineoplastic agents, daunorubicin, doxorubicin, idarubicin, or mitoxantrone, live virus vaccines, other bone marrow depressants, or previous cytotoxic drug or radiation therapy

Other medical problems, especially bone marrow depression; cardiovascular disease, history of; chickenpox; heart disease; hepatic function impairment; herpes zoster; or tumor cell infiltration of bone marrow

Proper use of this medication

Caution in taking combination therapy; taking each medication at the right time

Importance of ample fluid intake and subsequent increase in urine output to aid in excretion of uric acid

Frequency of nausea and vomiting; importance of continuing medication despite stomach upset

» Proper dosing

Precautions while using this medication

» Importance of close monitoring by the physician

» Avoiding immunizations unless approved by the physician; other persons in patient's household should avoid immunizations with oral poliovirus vaccine; avoiding persons who have taken oral poliovirus vaccine, or wearing a protective mask that covers nose and mouth

Caution if bone marrow depression occurs:

» Avoiding exposure to persons with infections, especially during periods of low blood counts; checking with physician immediately if fever or chills, cough or hoarseness, lower back or side pain, or painful or difficult urination occurs

» Checking with physician immediately if unusual bleeding or bruising; black, tarry stools; blood in urine or stools; or pinpoint red spots on skin occur

Caution in use of regular toothbrush, dental floss, or toothpick; physician, dentist, or nurse may suggest alternatives; checking with physician before having dental work done

Not touching eyes or inside of nose unless hands washed immediately before

Using caution to avoid accidental cuts with use of sharp objects such as safety razor or fingernail or toenail cutters

Avoiding contact sports or other situations where bruising or injury could occur

» Telling doctor or nurse right away about redness, pain, or swelling at injection site

Side/adverse effects

May cause adverse effects such as blood problems, loss of hair, and heart problems

Signs of potential side effects, especially anemia; asthenia; fever; hand-foot syndrome; infusion reaction; leukopenia; neutropenia; stomatitis; thrombocytopenia; allergic reaction; heart failure; jaundice; cardiotoxicity; dyspnea; pain at injection site; pneumonia; postirradiation erythema, recall; tachycardia; diabetes mellitus or hyperglycemia; optic neuritis; chest pain; edema; infection; and anaphylactoid reaction

Physician or nurse can help in dealing with side effects

Reddish orange urine or other body fluids for 1 to 2 days after administration may be alarming to patient although medically insignificant

Possibility of hair loss; normal hair growth should resume after treatment has ended

General Dosing Information

Patients receiving liposomal doxorubicin should be under the supervision of a physician experienced in cancer chemotherapy.

In patients with acquired immunodeficiency syndrome (AIDS)-associated Kaposi's sarcoma (KS) it is not known whether the combination of liposomal doxorubicin with other antineoplastic agents will improve response rates or quality of life (QOL) compared with currently used combination regimens or liposomal doxorubicin monotherapy. However, because tumor cells are heterogeneous and the development of tumor resistance to a single antineoplastic agent is probable, combinations of cancer chemotherapy agents generally are preferred to monotherapy. Nevertheless, liposomal doxorubicin is one of the most active single agents studied so far in patients with AIDS-associated KS. Furthermore, liposomal doxorubicin 20 mg per square meter of body surface area (mg/m^2) administered at 2- or 3-week intervals seems to be more efficacious than the best available combination regimens.

The recommended dose of liposomal doxorubicin for patients with AIDS-associated KS is 20 mg/m^2 administered intravenously over a period of 30 minutes at 3-week intervals. However, in several studies, liposomal doxorubicin was administered at 2-week intervals. Doses as high as 40 mg/m^2 and treatment intervals of 1 week have been evaluated in patients with KS, but offer no clear advantages over 20 mg/m^2 administered every 2 or 3 weeks.

Liposomal doxorubicin should be used with caution in patients who have previously received complete cumulative doses of other anthracycline or anthracenedione agents.

Unlike extravasation of standard doxorubicin, which may result in severe local inflammation and tissue damage, extravasation of liposomal doxorubicin was associated with only transient, mild irritation at the infusion site. However, liposomal doxorubicin should be considered an irritant and precautions should be taken to avoid extravasation. If extravasation of liposomal doxorubicin occurs during intravenous administration, as indicated by local burning or stinging (may also be painless), the infusion should be stopped immediately, and resumed, completing the dose, in another vein. Application of ice packs to the site of extravasation for 30 minutes may be necessary to relieve symptoms.

Patients who develop thrombocytopenia may require platelet transfusions.

Patients who develop leukopenia should be observed carefully for signs of infection. Antibiotic support may be required. Use of colony stimulating factors may be necessary.

Acute infusion-related hypersensitivity reactions can occur in some patients during the first infusion of liposomal doxorubicin, usually within the first few minutes after the start of the infusion. These acute reactions do not appear to occur with subsequent doses of liposomal doxorubicin in patients who do not react to the first cycle. Reactions generally resolve within 1 day once the infusion is terminated. Slowing the infusion rate can sometimes eliminate this problem. Most patients who react to liposomal doxorubicin are able to tolerate further infusions without complication.

Liposomal doxorubicin should be administered at an initial rate of 1 milligram per minute (mg/min) to minimize the risk of infusion reactions.

The pharmacokinetics of liposomal doxorubicin have not been studied in patients with hepatic impairment. However, standard doxorubicin is known to be eliminated in large part by the liver. Therefore, dosage of liposomal doxorubicin should be reduced for patients with impaired hepatic function. A dose reduction of 50% is recommended if serum bilirubin concentrations are 1.2 to 3 mg per deciliter (mg/dL). A dose reduction of 75% is recommended if serum bilirubin concentrations are $>$ 3 mg/dL.

Dosage adjustment or discontinuation of therapy may be necessary for patients who experience stomatitis, bone marrow depression, or palmar-plantar erythrodysesthesia.

Rapid flushing of the infusion line should be avoided.

Safety considerations for handling this medication

There is limited but increasing evidence and concern that personnel involved in preparation and administration of parenteral antineoplastic agents may be at some risk because of the potential mutagenicity, teratogenicity, and/or carcinogenicity of these agents, although the actual risk is unknown. USP advisory panels recommend cautious handling both in preparation and disposal of antineoplastic agents. Precautions that have been suggested include:

- Use of a biological containment cabinet during reconstitution and dilution of parenteral medications and wearing of disposable surgical gloves and masks.
- Use of proper technique to prevent contamination of the medication, work area, and operator during transfer between containers (including proper training of personnel in this technique).
- Cautious and proper disposal of needles, syringes, vials, ampuls, and unused medication.

A number of medical centers have developed detailed guidelines for handling of antineoplastic agents.

Parenteral Dosage Forms

Note: Bracketed information in the *Dosage Forms* section refer to categories of use and/or indications that are not included in U.S. product labeling.

DOXORUBICIN, LIPOSOMAL INJECTION

Usual adult dose

Kaposi's sarcoma (KS), acquired immunodeficiency syndrome (AIDS)-associated—

Intravenous infusion (over thirty minutes), 20 mg per square meter of body surface area, repeated every three weeks, for as long as patient responds satisfactorily and tolerates treatment.

Note: Although AIDS-associated KS may respond to treatment with single or multiagent chemotherapy, disease recurrence is common because the underlying immunodeficiency is unremitting. Thus, multiple courses of therapy may be required to control the disease. This repeated use of cytotoxic chemotherapy in patients with AIDS can cause significant morbidity.

Carcinoma, ovarian (treatment)—

Intravenous infusion, 50 mg per square meter of body surface area, repeated every four weeks, for as long as the patient responds satisfactorily, shows no evidence of cardiotoxicity, and tolerates treatment (minimum of four courses). Initiate infusion at 1 mg/minute, and if no infusion-related reactions occur, the infusion rate may be increased to complete administration of the drug over one hour.

Note: The doses may be delayed or reduced to manage adverse events such as palmar-plantar erythrodysesthesia, stomatitis, or hematologic toxicity. Pretreatment with or concomitant use of antiemetics should be considered.

[Carcinoma, breast (treatment)][1]—

Patients have benefited from intravenous doses of 30 to 50 mg per square meter of body surface area, repeated every 2 to 4 weeks.

Note: **Dose Modification Guidelines**

Dose adjustments may result in a non-proportional greater change in plasma concentration and exposure to the drug due to the non-linear pharmacokinetics of liposomal doxorubicin at 50 mg per square meter.

Monitor patients carefully for toxicity. The dosing should be adjusted or delayed following the first appearance of a Grade 2 or higher adverse event, such as HFS, hematologic toxicities, and stomatitis.

Dose modification guidelines for Hand Foot Syndrome (HFS):

- **Grade 1 toxicity** (mild erythema, swelling, or desquamation not interfering with daily activities): **Redose unless the patient has experienced previous Grade 3 or 4 HFS**. If so, delay therapy up to 2 weeks and decrease the dose by 25%. Return to original dose interval.
- **Grade 2 toxicity** (erythema, desquamation, or swelling interfering with, but not precluding normal physical activities; small blisters or ulcerations less than 2 cm in diameter): **Delay dosing for up to 2 weeks or until resolved to Grade 0 to 1**. If after 2 weeks there is no resolution, liposomal doxorubicin should be discontinued. If resolved to Grade 0 to 1 within 2 weeks, and there was no prior Grade 3 to 4 HFS, continued treatment at previous dose and return to original dose interval. If patient experienced previous Grade 3 to 4 toxicity, continue treatment with a 25% dose reduction and return to the original dose interval.
- **Grade 3 toxicity** (blistering, ulceration, or swelling interfering with walking or normal daily activities; cannot wear regular clothing): **Delay dosing for up to 2 weeks or until resolved to Grade 0 to 1**. Decrease dose by 25% and return to the original dose interval. If after 2 weeks there is no resolution, liposomal doxorubicin should be discontinued.
- **Grade 4 toxicity** (diffuse or local process causing infectious complications, or a bed ridden state or hospitalization): **Delay dosing for up to 2 weeks or until resolved to Grade 0 to 1**. Decrease dose by 25% and return to the original dose interval. If after 2 weeks there is no resolution, liposomal doxorubicin should be discontinued.

Dose modification guidelines for hematological toxicity:

- **Grade 1 toxicity** (ANC: 1500 to 1900; Platelets: 75,000 to 150,000): Resume treatment with no dose reduction.
- **Grade 2 toxicity** (ANC: 1000 to <1500; Platelets: 50,000 to <75,000): Wait until ANC ≥1500 and platelets ≥75,000; redose with no dose reduction.
- **Grade 3 toxicity** (ANC: 500 to 999; Platelets: 25,000 to <50,000): Wait until ANC ≥1500 and platelets ≥75,000; redose with no dose reduction.
- **Grade 4 toxicity** (ANC: <500; Platelets: <25,000): Wait until ANC ≥1500 and platelets ≥75,000; redose at 25% dose reduction or continue full dose with cytokine support.

Dose modification guidelines for stomatitis:

- **Grade 1 toxicity** (painless ulcers, erythema, or mild soreness): **Redose unless the patient has experienced previous Grade 3 or 4 stomatitis**. If so, delay therapy up to 2 weeks and decrease the dose by 25%. Return to original dose interval.
- **Grade 2 toxicity** (painful erythema, edema, or ulcers, but can eat): **Delay dosing for up to 2 weeks or until resolved to Grade 0 to 1**. If after 2 weeks there is no resolution, liposomal doxorubicin should be discontinued. If resolved to Grade 0 to 1 within 2 weeks, and there was no prior Grade 3 to 4 stomatitis, continued treatment at previous dose and return to original dose interval. If patient experienced previous Grade 3 to 4 toxicity, continue treatment with a 25% dose reduction and return to the original dose interval.
- **Grade 3 toxicity** (painful erythema, edema, or ulcers, and cannot eat): **Delay dosing for up to 2 weeks or until resolved to Grade 0 to 1**. Decrease dose by 25% and return to the original dose interval. If after 2 weeks there is no resolution, liposomal doxorubicin should be discontinued.
- **Grade 4 toxicity** (requires parenteral or enteral support): **Delay dosing for up to 2 weeks or until resolved to Grade 0 to 1**. Decrease dose by 25% and return to the original dose interval. If after 2 weeks there is no resolution, liposomal doxorubicin should be discontinued.

Dose modification guidelines for patients with impaired hepatic function:

- Serum bilirubin, 1.2 to 3 mg per dL: give 1/2 the normal dose
- Serum bilirubin, >3 mg per dL: give 1/4 the normal dose

Usual pediatric dose

Safety and efficacy have not been established.

Strength(s) usually available

U.S.—

2 mg per mL (single-dose vial) (Rx) [*Doxil* (ammonium sulfate 2 mg; histidine; sucrose)].

Canada—

2 mg per mL (single-dose vial) (Rx) [*Caelyx* (ammonium sulfate 2 mg; histidine; sucrose)].

Packaging and storage

Store between 2 and 8 °C (36 and 46 °F), unless otherwise specified by manufacturer. Do not freeze for longer than 1 month.

Preparation of dosage form

Liposomal doxorubicin (up to a maximum of 90 mg) must be diluted in 250 mL of 5% dextrose injection for administration by intravenous infusion.Doses exceeding 90 mg should be diluted in 500 mL of 5% dextrose injection prior to administration by intravenous infusion.

Stability

Diluted liposomal doxorubicin is stable for 24 hours when stored between 2 and 8 °C (36 and 46 °F). Undiluted liposomal doxorubicin contains no preservatives or bacteriostatic agents. Aseptic techniques should be observed when handling liposomal doxorubicin.

Do not freeze for longer than 1 month. Long-term freezing may harm the liposomal component.

Incompatibilities

Liposomal doxorubicin should be diluted only in 5% dextrose injection. Liposomal doxorubicin should not be mixed with other medications, other diluents, or bacteriostatic agents. Mixing liposomal doxorubicin with any other diluent may cause precipitation.

Caution

Do not use if a precipitate is present.

Note

Liposomal doxorubicin is a red, translucent dispersion. In-line filters should not be used because liposomal doxorubicin is not a clear solution.

Great care should be taken to prevent exposure of the skin to liposomal doxorubicin. The use of gloves is recommended. Any liposomal doxorubicin solution that comes into contact with the skin or mucosa should be washed off thoroughly with soap and water.

---

[1]Not included in Canadian product labeling.

Revised: 08/01/2005
Developed: 06/30/1998

DOXYCYCLINE

—See *Tetracyclines (Systemic)*

DOXYCYCLINE Systemic†

VA CLASSIFICATION (Primary/Secondary): AM250/DE751

Commonly used brand name(s): *Doryx*; *Oracea*.

Note: For a listing of dosage forms and brand names by country availability, see *Dosage Forms* section(s).

†Not commercially available in Canada.

Category

Antiacne agent; antibiotic; antibacterial; antiprotozoal; antimalarial; antirosacea agent.

Indications

Note: Bracketed information in the *Indications* section refers to uses that are not included in U.S. product labeling.

General Considerations

To reduce the development of drug-resistant bacteria and maintain the effectiveness of doxycycline, it should be used only to treat or prevent infections that are proven or strongly suspected to be caused by susceptible bacteria. When culture and susceptibility information are available, they should be considered in selecting or modifying antibacterial therapy. In the absence of such data, local epidemiology and susceptibility patterns may contribute to the empirical selection of therapy.

Accepted

Acne, severe (treatment adjunct)—Doxycycline may be useful adjunctive therapy.

Actinomycosis (treatment) or
Gonorrhea (treatment) or
Infections caused by clostridrum species or
Listeriosis (treatment) or
Syphilis (treatment) or
Vincent's infection (treatment) or
Yaws (treatment)—Doxycycline is indicated in patients when penicillin is contraindicated as an alternative drug for the treatment of uncomplicated gonorrhea caused by *Neisseria gonorrhoeae*, syphilis caused by *Treponema pallidum*, yaws caused by *Treponema pertenue*, listeriosis due to *Listeria monocytogenes*, Vincent's infection caused by *Fusobacterium fusiforme* and actinomycosis caused by *Actinomyces israelii*, and infections caused by *Clostridum* species.

Amebiasis, intestinal (treatment adjunct)—Doxycycline may be an effective adjunct to amebicides.

Anthrax (treatment)—Doxycycline is indicated for the treatment of anthrax due to *Bacillus anthracis*, including inhalational anthrax (post-exposure): to reduce the incidence or progression of disease.

Bartonellosis (treatment) or
Brucellosis (treatment) or
Campylobacter fetus (treatment) or
Chancroid (treatment) or
Cholera (treatment) or
Granuloma inguinale (treatment) or
Plague (treatment) or
Tularemia (treatment)—Doxycycline is indicated for the treatment of infections caused by the following gram-negative microorganisms chancroid caused by *Haemophilus ducreyi*, plague due to *Yersinia pestis*, tularemia due to *Francisella tularensis*, cholera caused by *Vibrio cholerae*, campylobacter fetus infections caused by *Campylobacter fetus*, brucellosis due to *Brucella* species (in conjunction with streptomycin), bartonellosis due to *Bartonella bacilliformis* or granuloma inguinale caused by *Calymmatobacterium granulomatis*.

Chlamydial infections, endocervical, rectal and urethral (treatment)—Doxycycline is indicated for the treatment of uncomplicated urethral, endocervical, or rectal infections in adults caused by *Chlamydia trachomatis*.

Conjunctivitis, inclusion (treatment)—Doxycycline is indicated for the treatment of inclusion conjunctivitis caused by *Chlamydia trachomatis*.

Infections caused by gram-negative microorganisms (treatment)—Doxycycline is indicated for the treatment of infections caused by the following gram-negative microorganisms, when bacteriological testing indicates appropriate susceptibility to the drug: *Acinetobacter*, *Enterobacter aerogenes*, *Escherichia coli*, or *Shigella* species.

Infections caused by gram-positive microorganisms (treatment)—Doxycycline is indicated for the treatment of infections caused by the following gram-positive microorganism, *Streptococcus pneumoniae*.

Lymphogranuloma venereum (treatment)—Doxycycline is indicated in the treatment of lymphogranuloma venereum caused by *Chlamydia trachomatis*.

Malaria (prophylaxis)—Doxycycline is indicated in the prophylaxis of malaria due to *Plasmodium falciparum* in short-term travelers (<4 months) going to areas with chloroquine and/or pyrimethamine-sulfadoxine resistant strains.

Nongonococcal urethritis (treatment)—Doxycycline is indicated for the treatment of nongonococcal urethritis caused by *Ureaplasma urealyticum*.

Psittacosis (treatment)—Doxycycline is indicated in the treatment of psittacosis (ornithosis) caused by *Chlamydia psittaci*.

Q fever (treatment) or
Rickettsial pox (treatment) or
Rocky Mountain spotted fever (treatment) or
Typhus infections (treatment)—Doxycycline is indicated for the treatment of the following infections: Rocky Mountain spotted fever, typhus fever and the typhus group, Q fever, rickettsial pox, and tick fever caused by Rickettsiae.

Relapsing fever (treatment)—Doxycycline is indicated in the treatment of relapsing fever caused by *Borrelia recurrentis*.

Respiratory tract infections (treatment)—Doxycycline is indicated for the treatment of respiratory tract infections caused by *Haemophilus influenzae*, *Klebsiella* species, and *Mycoplasma pneumoniae*.

Rosacea (treatment)—Oracea™ brand doxycycline 40 mg (30 mg immediate release and 10 mg delayed release beads) capsules are indicated for the treatment of only inflammatory lesion (papules and pustules) of rosacea in adult patients.

Trachoma (treatment)—Doxycycline is indicated in the treatment of trachoma caused by *Chlamydia trachomatis*., although the infectious agent is not always eliminated as judged by immunofluorescence.

Urinary tract infections (treatment)—Doxycycline is indicated for the treatment of urinary tract infections caused by *Klebsiella* species.

Acceptance not established

Oracea™ brand doxycycline 40 mg (30 mg immediate release and 10 mg delayed release beads) capsules have not been evaluated for the treatment of the erythematous, telangioctatic, or ocular components of rosacea.

Efficacy of Oracea™ beyond 16 weeks and safety beyond 9 months have not been established.

Oracea™ brand doxycycline 40 mg (30 mg immediate release and 10 mg delayed release beads) capsules have not been evaluated in the treatment or prevention of infections. Oracea™ should not be used for treating bacterial infections, providing antibacterial prophylaxis, or reducing the number or eliminating micoorganisms associated with any bacterial disease.

Pharmacology/Pharmacokinetics

Physicochemical characteristics

Molecular weight—Doxycycline: 512.9.

Solubility—Soluble in water and solutions of alkali hydroxides and carbonates.

Mechanism of action/Effect

Tetracyclines are primarily bacteriostatic and are thought to exert their antimicrobial effect by the inhibition of protein synthesis, and have activity against a wide range of gram-positive and gram-negative organisms.

Absorption

Completely absorbed following oral administration.

$AUC_{0-\infty}$ is reduced 13% following single dose administration with a high fat meal.

Distribution

Animal studies indicate that tetracyclines cross the placenta and are found in fetal tissues.

Protein binding

Bound to plasma protein in varying degrees.

Biotransformation

Doxycycline will not degrade into an epianhydro form.

Half-life

Serum—(range 18-22 hours) in individuals with normal and severely impaired renal function.

Time to peak serum concentration

2 hours in normal adult volunteers.

Peak serum concentration:

2.6 mcg/mL following a 200 mg dose in normal adults.

Elimination

Kidney: 40% per 72 hours in patients with normal kidney function (creatinine clearance about 75 mL/min); 1-5% per 72 hours in patients with severe renal insufficiency (creatinine clearance below 10 mL/min).

Hemodialysis does not alter serum half-life.

Precautions to Consider

Carcinogenicity

Carcinogenicity studies have been done in Sprague-Dawley rats administered 20, 75 and 200 mg per kg of body weight per day for two years. An increased incidence of uterine polyps was observed in female rats at the 200 mg per kg of body weight per day dose that resulted in a systemic exposure to doxycycline approximately 12.2 times that observed in female humans. No impact was observed in male rats at any of the doses studied. Evidence of oncogenic activity was found in studies with related antibiotics, oxytetracycline (adrenal and pituitary tumors) and minocycline (thyroid tumors).

Mutagenicity

Doxycycline demonstrated no potential to cause genetic toxicity in an *in vitro* point mutation study with mammalian cells (CHO/HGPRT forward mutation assay) or in an *in vivo* micronucleus assay conducted in CD-1 mice. Data from an *in vitro* assay with CHO cells for potential to cause chromosomal aberrations suggest that doxycycline is a weak clastogen.

Pregnancy/Reproduction

Fertility—The effects of doxycycline on human fertility are unknown. In a Sprague-Dawley rat study, male and female rats administered oral doxycycline doses experienced adverse effects to fertility and reproductive performance including increased time for mating to occur, reduced sperm motility, velocity and concentration, abnormal sperm morphology, and increased pre- and post-implantation losses. Doxycycline induces reproductive toxicity at all dosages, even the lowest dose (50 mg per kg of body weight per day which is 3.6 times the MRHD) resulted in significant reductions in sperm velocity.

Pregnancy—Doxycycline can cause fetal harm to pregnant women. Doxycycline should not be used during pregnancy. If any tetracycline, including doxycycline, has been used during pregnancy or if the patient becomes pregnant while taking one of these drugs, the patient should be apprised of the potential hazard to the fetus. Tetracyclines cross the placenta; use is not recommended during the last half of pregnancy since tetracyclines may cause permanent staining of teeth, enamel hypoplasia, and inhibition of skeletal growth in the fetus.

Studies in animals indicate that tetracyclines cross the placenta and have toxic effects on the developing fetus (often related to retardation of skeletal development). Embryotoxicity has also been noted in animals treated during early pregnancy.

FDA Pregnancy Category D

Labor and delivery—The effect of tetracyclines on labor and delivery is unknown.

Breast-feeding

Tetracyclines are distributed into human milk. Because of the potential for serious adverse reactions in infants from doxycycline, it should not be used in mothers who breast-feed.

Pediatrics

Doxycycline should not be used in pediatric patients younger than 8 years of age, except for the treatment of anthrax, including inhalation anthrax (post-exposure), unless other drugs are not likely to be effective or are contraindicated.

The use of tetracycline class drugs during tooth development (last half of pregnancy, infancy and childhood to the age of 8 years) may cause permanent discoloration of the teeth. This reaction is more common during long-term use but has been observed during repeated during short-term courses. Enamel hypoplasia has also been reported.

Doxycycline has not been studied in children of any age with regard to safety or efficacy. Therefore, use in children is not recommended.

Geriatrics

No information is available on the relationship of age to the effects of doxycycline in geriatric patients. However, elderly patients are more likely to have age-related decreased hepatic, renal, or cardiac function, and a greater frequency of concomitant disease or other drug therapy which may require caution in dosing selection.

Drug interactions and/or related problems

The following drug interactions and/or related problems have been selected on the basis of their potential clinical significance (possible mechanism in parentheses where appropriate)—not necessarily inclusive (» = major clinical significance):

Note: Combinations containing any of the following medications, depending on the amount present, may also interact with this medication.

» Antacids containing
» Aluminum or
» Calcium or
» Iron or
» Magnesium
(absorption of tetracycline is impaired)

» Anticoagulant therapy
(tetracyclines have been shown to depress plasma prothrombin activity; a downward adjustment of anticoagulant therapy may be required)

Barbiturates or
Carbamazepine or
Phenytoin
(doxycycline half-life is decreased)

Bismuth subsalicylate
(absorption of tetracycline is impaired)

» Methoxyflurane
(fatal cases of renal toxicity have been reported with concurrent use)

» Oral contraceptives
(concurrent use with doxycycline may result in oral contraceptives being less effective)

» Penicillin
(doxycycline may interfere with the bactericidal action of penicillin; concomitant administration is not advised)

Laboratory value alterations

The following have been selected on the basis of their potential clinical significance (possible effect in parentheses where appropriate)—not necessarily inclusive (» = major clinical significance).

With diagnostic test results
Catecholamine determinations, urine
(may produce false elevations of urinary catecholamines because of interfering fluorescence)

With physiology/laboratory test values
BUN
(may be increased)

Medical considerations/Contraindications

The medical considerations/contraindications included have been selected on the basis of their potential clinical significance (reasons given in parentheses where appropriate)—not necessarily inclusive (» = major clinical significance).

Except under special circumstances, this medication should not be used when the following medical problem exists:

» Hypersensitivity to doxycycline or other tetracyclines

Risk-benefit should be considered when the following medical problems exist:

Candidiasis overgrowth, history of or predisposition to
(should be used with caution)

» Renal function impairment, significant
(may lead to excessive systemic accumulations of doxycycline and possible liver toxicity; lower than usual doses may be necessary and doxycycline serum levels determinations may be advisable)

Patient monitoring

The following may be especially important in patient monitoring (other tests may be warranted in some patients, depending on condition; » = major clinical significance):

Organ systems functions including
Hematopoietic and
Hepatic and
Renal
(periodic monitoring recommended during long-term therapy)

Dark-field examinations
(should be performed before treatment is started and blood serology repeated monthly for at least 4 months in patients with venereal disease and suspected coexistent syphilis)

Side/Adverse Effects

The following side/adverse effects have been selected on the basis of their potential clinical significance (possible signs and symptoms in parentheses where appropriate)—not necessarily inclusive:

Those indicating need for medical attention

Incidence not known

Anaphylactoid purpura (cough; difficulty swallowing; dizziness; fast heartbeat; hives, itching, puffiness or swelling of the eyelids or around the eyes, face, lips or tongue; shortness of breath; skin rash; tightness in chest; unusual tiredness or weakness; wheezing); ***anaphylaxis*** (cough; difficulty swallowing; dizziness; fast heartbeat; hives, itching, puffiness or swelling of the eyelids or around the eyes, face, lips or tongue; shortness of breath; skin rash; tightness in chest; unusual tiredness or weakness; wheezing); ***angioneurotic edema*** (large, hive-like swelling on face, eyelids, lips, tongue, throat, hands, legs, feet, sex organs); ***hepatotoxicity*** (abdominal pain or tenderness; clay colored stools; dark urine; decreased appetite; fever; headache; itching; loss of appetite; nausea and vomiting; skin rash; swelling of feet or lower legs; unusual tiredness or weakness; yellow eyes or skin); ***hypersensitivity reactions*** (abdominal or stomach pain; diarrhea; fever; joint or muscle pain; nausea; numbness or tingling of face, hands, or feet; redness and soreness of eyes; skin rash; shortness of breath; sores in mouth; swelling of feet or lower legs; vomiting); ***lupus erythematosus, exacerbated*** (fever; muscle pain; skin rash; sore throat); ***pseudomembranous colitis*** (abdominal or stomach cramps; pain; bloating; abdominal tenderness; diarrhea, watery and severe, which may also be bloody; fever; increased thirst; nausea or vomiting; unusual tiredness or weakness unusual weight loss); ***serum sickness*** (feeling of discomfort; fever; inflammation of joints; itching; muscle aches; rash; swollen lymph glands); ***urticaria*** (hives or welts; itching; redness of skin; skin rash)

Those indicating need for medical attention only if they continue or are bothersome

Incidence not known

Anorexia (loss of appetite; weight loss); ***bulging fontanels*** (bulging soft spot on head of an infant)—infants; ***diarrhea; discoloration of thyroid glands; dysphagia*** (difficulty swallowing); ***enterocolitis*** (fever; severe stomach pain; vomiting); ***eosinophilia*** (black, tarry stools; chest pain; chills; cough; fever; painful or difficult urination; shortness of breath; sore throat; sores, ulcers, or white spots on lips or in mouth; swollen glands; unusual bleeding or bruising; unusual tiredness or weakness); ***erythematous rashes*** (reddened skin; skin rash); ***esophageal ulceration*** (chest pain, discomfort, or burning; difficulty swallowing; pain with swallowing; vomiting blood); ***esophagitis*** (difficulty in swallowing; pain or burning in throat; chest pain; heartburn; vomiting; sores, ulcers, or white spots on lips or tongue or inside the mouth); ***exfoliative dermatitis*** (cracks in the skin; loss of heat from the body; red, swollen skin; scaly skin); ***glossitis*** (redness, swelling, or soreness of tongue); ***hemolytic anemia*** (back, leg, or stomach pains; bleeding gums; chills; dark urine; difficulty breathing; fatigue; fever; general body; swelling; headache; loss of appetite; nausea or vomiting; nosebleeds; pale skin; sore throat; yellowing of the eyes or skin); ***inflammatory lesions (with monilial overgrowth) in the anogenital region; intracranial hypertension, benign*** (decrease in vision; double vision; headache; severe nausea; blurred vision; change in ability to see colors, especially blue or yellow; vomiting)—adults; ***maculopapular rashes*** (rash with flat lesions or small raised lesions on the skin); ***nausea; neutropenia*** (black, tarry, stools; chills; cough; fever; lower back or side pain; painful or difficult urination; pale skin; shortness of breath; sore throat; ulcers, sores, or white spots in mouth; unusual bleeding or bruising; unusual tiredness or weakness); ***photosensitivity*** (increased sensitivity of skin to sunlight; itching; redness or other discoloration of skin; severe sunburn; skin rash); ***thrombocytopenia*** (black, tarry stools; bleeding gums; blood in urine or stools; pinpoint red spots on skin; unusual bleeding or bruising); ***vomiting***

Overdose

For more information on the management of overdose or unintentional ingestion, **contact a poison control center** (see *Poison Control Center Listing*).

Treatment of overdose

There is no known specific antidote to doxycycline. Treatment is generally symptomatic and supportive.

To enhance elimination—

Dialysis does not alter serum half-life, and would not be of benefit in treating overdosage.

Specific treatment—

Discontinuing doxycycline and treating symptomatically.

Instituting supportive measures.

Supportive care—

Patients in whom intentional overdose is confirmed or suspected should be referred for psychiatric consultation.

Patient Consultation

As an aid to patient consultation, refer to *Advice for the Patient, Doxycycline (Systemic)*.

In providing consultation, consider emphasizing the following selected information (» = major clinical significance):

Before using this medication

» Conditions affecting use, especially:

Hypersensitivity to doxycycline or other tetracyclines

Pregnancy—Should not be used during pregnancy because doxycycline crosses placenta and may cause adverse fetal effects

Breast-feeding—Should not be used in women who are breast-feeding due to potential for adverse effects

Use in children—Should not be used in pediatric patients younger than 8 years of age, except for treatment of anthrax, including inhalation anthrax (post-exposure), unless other drugs are not likely to be effective or are contraindicated

Safety and efficacy not established at any age; use in children NOT recommended

Use in the elderly—More likely to have age-related decreased hepatic, renal, or cardiac function, and a greater frequency of concomitant disease or other drug therapy which may require caution in dosing selection

Other medications, especially antacids containing aluminum, calcium, iron, or magnesium; anticoagulant therapy, methoxyflurane, oral contraceptives, or penicillin

Other medical problems, especially significant renal function impairment

Proper use of this medication

» Taking in the morning on an empty stomach at least one hour before or two hours after eating

» Not giving to children 8 years of age and younger

» Compliance with full course of therapy

» Drinking plenty of fluids to avoid esophageal irritation and ulceration

» Proper dosing

Missed dose: Taking as soon as possible; not taking if almost time for next scheduled dose; not doubling doses

Proper storage

Precautions while using this medication

» Avoiding extended exposure to sunlight or tanning beds while taking this drug; severe burns may result

» Using a second form of contraceptive if taking oral contraceptives

» Telling doctor immediately if stomach cramps, high fever, and bloody diarrhea occur

» Talking to doctor right away if fever, rash, joint pain, and tiredness are experienced

Side/adverse effects

Signs of potential side effects, especially anaphylactoid purpura, anaphylaxis, angioneurotic edema, hepatotoxicity, hypersensitivity reactions, lupus erythematosus exacerbated, pseudomembranous colitis, serum sickness, or urticaria.

General Dosing Information

Culture and susceptibility testing are recommended; many microorganisms have been shown to be resistant to doxycycline.

To reduce the development of drug-resistant bacteria, doxycycline should only be used to treat or prevent infections proven or strongly suspected to be caused by bacteria.

Oracea™ capsules should NOT be used to treat or prevent infections.

Doxycycline capsules should be administered with adequate amounts of fluid to wash down the capsule and reduce the risk of esophageal irritation and ulceration.

Patients should be advised that photosensitivity reactions can occur when exposed to direct sunlight or ultraviolet light while taking doxycycline.

Use of doxycycline may result in overgrowth of non-susceptible organisms.

Exceeding the recommended dosage may result in an increased incidence of side effects.

It is important to consider the diagnosis pseudomembranous colitis in patients who present diarrhea subsequent to administration of doxycycline.

Other surgical procedures including incision and drainage should be performed in conjunction with antibiotic therapy, when indicated.

Tetracyclines may cause an increase in BUN; however, studies to date indicate this does not occur with the use of doxycycline in patients with impaired renal function.

Treatment with antibacterial agents may alter the normal flora of the colon and permit overgrowth of clostridia.

All tetracycline drugs form a stable calcium complex in any bone-forming tissue; decrease in fibula growth rate has been observed in premature newborns given oral tetracyclines; however, the reaction was shown to be reversible upon discontinuation.

Bulging fontanels have been reported in infants receiving tetracycline drugs.

Benign intracranial hypertension has been reported in adults receiving tetracycline drugs.

Doxycycline offers substantial but not complete suppression of the asexual blood stages of *Plasmodium* strains.

Doxycycline does not suppress the *P. falciparum* sexual blood stage gametocytes; subjects may transmit infection to mosquitoes after completing the prophylactic regimen.

The therapeutic antibacterial serum activity will persist for 24 hours following recommended dosing.

Diet/Nutrition

Doxycycline capsules should be taken on an empty stomach, preferably at least one hour prior to or two hours after meals.

Treatment of adverse effects

Initiate therapeutic measures if pseudomembranous colitis is diagnosed. Mild cases usually respond to discontinuation of the drug alone, moderate and severe cases should be managed with fluids and electrolytes, protein supplementation, and treatment with an antibacterial drugs against *Clostridium difficile* colitis.

If superinfection occurs, doxycycline should be discontinued and appropriate therapy instituted.

If evidence of skin erythema, discontinue doxycycline treatment.

Oral Dosage Forms

Note: Bracketed information in the *Indications* section refers to uses that are not included in U.S. product labeling.

DOXYCYCLINE IMMEDIATE/DELAYED-RELEASE CAPSULES

Usual adult dose

Rosacea (treatment)—

Oral, 40 mg once daily in the morning on an empty stomach with an adequate amount of fluids.

Usual adult prescribing limits

Efficacy beyond 16 weeks and safety beyond 9 months have not been established.

Usual pediatric dose

Doxycycline should not be used in infants or children up to 8 years of age.

Safety and efficacy have not been established in children of any age. Therefore, use in children is not recommended.

Usual geriatric dose

See *Usual adult and adolescent dose.*

Strength(s) usually available

U.S.—

40 mg anhydrous doxycycline (Rx) [*Oracea* (30 mg immediate release and 10 mg delayed release beads; hypromellose; iron oxide red; iron oxide yellow; methacrylic acid copolymer; polyethylene glycol; Polysorbate 80; sugar spheres; talc; titanium dioxide; triethyl citrate)].

Packaging and storage

Store at controlled room temperature of 15° to 30°C (59° to 86°F), in a tight, light-resistant container.

Auxiliary labeling

- Continue medicine for full time of treatment.
- Avoid too much sun or use of sunlamp.
- Keep container tightly closed in a dry place.

DOXYCYCLINE HYCLATE

Usual adult and adolescent dose

Anthrax, inhalation (post exposure)—

Oral, 100 mg twice a day for 60 days.

Endocervical, rectal, or urethral infection, uncomplicated, caused by *Chlamydia trachomatis*—

Oral, 100 mg (base) two times a day for seven days.

Epididymo-orchitis caused by *N. gonorrhoeae* or *C. trachomatis*—

Oral, 100 mg (base) two times a day for at least ten days.

Gonococcal infections, uncomplicated (except anorectal infections in men)—

Oral, 100 mg (base) twice daily for seven days; or 300 mg initially, then 300 mg one hour later.

Malaria prophylaxis—

Oral, 100 mg (base) once a day. Prophylaxis should begin 1 to 2 days before travel to the malarious area and be continued daily during travel and for 4 weeks after the traveler leaves the malarious area.

Nongonococcal urethritis (NGU) caused by *C. trachomatis* and *U. urealyticum*—

Oral, 100 mg (base) two times a day for 7 days.

Syphilis (early), for penicillin-allergic patients—

Oral, 100 mg (base) two times a day for 2 weeks.

Syphilis (of > 1 year's duration), for penicillin-allergic patients—

Oral, 100 mg (base) two times a day for 4 weeks.

For all other infections—

Oral, 200 mg (100 mg every 12 hours) on the first day of treatment, followed by 100 mg per day administered as a single dose or as 50 mg every 12 hours; for more severe infections (particularly chronic infections of the urinary tract), 100 mg every 12 hours is recommended.

Note: For patients with streptococcal infections: Therapy should be continued for 10 days.

For patients with renal impairment: Studies to date have indicated that administration of doxycycline at the recommended doses does not lead to excessive accumulation of the antibiotic.

Usual pediatric dose

Anthrax, inhalation (post exposure)—

Children weighing less than 100 pounds (45 kg): Oral, 1 mg/lb (2.2 mg/kg) of body weight, twice daily for 60 days. Children 100 pounds or greater: See *Usual adult and adolescent dose*

Malaria prophylaxis—

Children greater than 8 years of age: Oral, 2 mg/kg given once daily up to the adult and adolescent dose.

For all other infections—

Children older than 8 years of age weighing less than 100 pounds: Oral, 2 mg per pound of body weight divided into two doses on the first day of treatment, followed by 1 mg per pound of body weight administered as a single daily dose or as divided into two doses on subsequent days; for more severe infections up to 2 mg per pound of body weight may be used; for children over 100 pounds: See *Usual adult and adolescent dose.*

Note: Tetracycline drugs should not be used in this age group, except for anthrax, including inhalation anthrax (post-exposure) unless other drugs are not likely to be effective or are contraindicated. The use of tetracycline class drugs during tooth development (last half of pregnancy, infancy and childhood to the age of 8 years) may cause permanent discoloration of the teeth (yellow-gray-brown). This reaction is more common during long-term use but has been observed during repeated short-term courses. Enamel hypoplasia has also been reported.

Usual geriatric dose

See *Usual adult and adolescent dose.*

Strength(s) usually available

U.S.—

100 mg (base) (Rx) [*Doryx* (anhydrous lactose; cellulosic polymer coating; corn starch; crospovidone; lactose monohydrate; magnesium stearate; microcrystalline cellulose; sodium chloride; sodium lauryl sulfate; talc)].

75 mg (base) [*Doryx* (anhydrous lactose; cellulosic polymer coating; corn starch; crospovidone; lactose monohydrate; magnesium stearate; microcrystalline; sodium chloride; sodium lauryl sulfate; talc)].

Packaging and storage

Store at 25 °C (77 °F), excursions permitted to 15° to 30°C (59° to 86°F), in a tight container. Protect from light.

Auxiliary labeling

- Continue medicine for full time of treatment.
- Avoid too much sun or use of sunlamp.
- Keep container tightly closed in a dry place.

Revised: 07/29/2006
Developed: 03/24/2006

DOXYLAMINE—See *Antihistamines (Systemic)*

DRONABINOL Systemic

VA CLASSIFICATION (Primary/Secondary): GA609/GA753

Note: Controlled substance classification

U.S.: Schedule III

Canada: N

Commonly used brand name(s): *Marinol*.

Another commonly used name is delta-9-tetrahydrocannabinol (THC).

Note: For a listing of dosage forms and brand names by country availability, see *Dosage Forms* section(s).

Category

Antiemetic; appetite stimulant.

Indications

Accepted

Nausea and vomiting, cancer chemotherapy-induced (prophylaxis)—Dronabinol is indicated in selected patients for the prevention of nausea and vomiting associated with emetogenic cancer chemotherapy when other antiemetic medications are not effective.

Anorexia, AIDS-associated (treatment)—Dronabinol is indicated for the treatment of anorexia associated with weight loss in patients with acquired immunodeficiency syndrome (AIDS).Tachyphylaxis and tolerance to some effects of dronabinol develop with chronic use; unlike cardiovascular and subjective adverse central nervous system (CNS) effects, the appetite stimulant effects of dronabinol have been sustained for up to 5 months in AIDS patients receiving doses ranging from 2.5 to 20 mg per day.

Pharmacology/Pharmacokinetics

Physicochemical characteristics

Chemical Group—A cannabinoid.

Molecular weight—314.47.

pKa—10.6.

Mechanism of action/Effect

The exact mechanism of action of dronabinol is not known. Cannabinoid receptors in neural tissues may mediate the effects of dronabinol and other cannabinoids. Animal studies with other cannabinoids suggest that dronabinol's antiemetic effects may be due to inhibition of the vomiting control mechanism in the medulla oblongata.

Other actions/effects

Central sympathomimetic activity may result in tachycardia and/or conjunctival injection. Dose-related reversible effects on appetite, mood, cognition, memory, and perception also occur, subject to great inter-patient variability.

Absorption

Although dronabinol is 90 to 95% absorbed after administration of single oral doses, only 10 to 20% reaches the systemic circulation, due to first-pass hepatic metabolism and high lipid solubility.

Distribution

Apparent volume of distribution is approximately 10 liters per kilogram (L/kg).

Distributed into human breast milk.

Protein binding

Very high (97%).

Biotransformation

Extensive first-pass hepatic metabolism, primarily by microsomal hydroxylation, yields both active and inactive metabolites. Dronabinol and its principal active metabolite, 11-OH-delta-9-THC, are present in approximately equal concentrations in plasma.

Half-life

Elimination—

Alpha phase: 4 hours.

Terminal (beta) phase: 25 to 36 hours.

Time to peak concentration

2 to 4 hours.

Duration of action

Psychoactive effects—4 to 6 hours.

Appetite stimulant effects—24 hours or longer.

Elimination

Primarily fecal (biliary); approximately 50% of an oral dose appears in the feces (less than 5% as unchanged drug) and 10 to 15% in the urine (either as unchanged drug or as metabolite) within 72 hours.

Following single dose administration, low levels of dronabinol metabolites are detectable in the urine and feces for more than 5 weeks.

Precautions to Consider

Cross-sensitivity and/or related problems

Patients sensitive to other marijuana products or sesame oil may be sensitive to this preparation also.

Carcinogenicity

Studies to evaluate the carcinogenic potential of dronabinol have not been performed.

Mutagenicity

Dronabinol was not shown to be mutagenic in an Ames test.

Pregnancy/Reproduction

Fertility—In a long-term study in rats at doses 0.3 to 1.5 times the maximum recommended human dose (MRHD) in cancer patients or 2 to 10 times the MRHD in AIDS patients, a decrease in seminal fluid volume, as well as reduced ventral prostate, seminal vesicle, and epididymal weights were reported. Decreases in spermatogenesis, number of developing germ cells, and number of Leydig cells in the testes were also observed. However, sperm count, mating success, and testosterone levels were not affected. The significance of these animal findings for use in humans is not known.

Pregnancy—Adequate and well-controlled studies in humans have not been done.

Reproduction studies in mice (at doses 0.2 to 5 times the MRHD in cancer patients and 1 to 30 times the MRHD in AIDS patients) and in rats (at doses 0.8 to 3 times the MRHD in cancer patients and 5 to 20 times the MRHD in AIDS patients) have revealed no evidence of teratogenicity. However, dose-dependent effects of dronabinol, including decreased maternal weight gain and number of viable pups, and increased fetal mortality and early resorptions were observed.

FDA Pregnancy Category C.

Breast-feeding

Use is not recommended since dronabinol is distributed into and concentrated in human breast milk and is absorbed by the nursing infant.

Pediatrics

No information is available on whether the risk of dronabinol-induced adverse effects is increased in children. However, because of this medication's psychoactive effects and potential for dependence, it should be used as an antiemetic with caution,after less toxic alternatives have been considered and found ineffective. Recommended doses should not be exceeded, and children should be carefully monitored during therapy.

Safety and efficacy of dronabinol for use in the treatment of AIDS-associated anorexia has not been established.

Geriatrics

Studies performed in a limited number of patients up to 82 years of age have not demonstrated geriatrics-specific problems that would limit the usefulness of dronabinol in the elderly. However, because of this medication's psychoactive effects and potential for dependence and withdrawal effects, therapy could be more troublesome in the elderly and should be used with caution, after less toxic alternatives have been considered and found ineffective. Recommended doses should not be exceeded, and the elderly patient should be carefully monitored during therapy.

Drug interactions and/or related problems

The following drug interactions and/or related problems have been selected on the basis of their potential clinical significance (possible mechanism in parentheses where appropriate)—not necessarily inclusive (» = major clinical significance):

Note: Combinations containing any of the following medications, depending on the amount present, may also interact with this medication.

Alcohol or

» Central nervous system (CNS) depression-producing medications, other (see *Appendix II*)
(concurrent use may potentiate the CNS-depressant effects of either these medications or dronabinol)

Anticholinergics (see *Appendix II*) or
Antihistamines
(additive or super-additive tachycardia may occur with concurrent use)

CNS stimulation-producing medications, other (see *Appendix II*), especially:
Amphetamines
Cocaine and
Sympathomimetic agents
(additive hypertension, tachycardia, and possible cardiotoxicity may occur with concurrent use)

Apomorphine
(prior administration of dronabinol may decrease the emetic response to apomorphine; also, concurrent use may potentiate the CNS-depressant effects of either apomorphine or dronabinol)

Medical considerations/Contraindications

The medical considerations/contraindications included have been selected on the basis of their potential clinical significance (reasons given in parentheses where appropriate)—not necessarily inclusive (» = major clinical significance).

Risk-benefit should be considered when the following medical problems exist:

» Bipolar disorder (manic or depressive states) or
» Psychosis
(symptoms may be exacerbated)

» Cardiac disorders
(dronabinol may cause cardiac effects, including occasional hypotension, hypertension, syncope, and tachycardia)

» Drug abuse or dependence, history of, including acute alcoholism
(increased risk of dronabinol abuse and dependence)

Hypersensitivity to dronabinol or sesame oil
Hypertension
(increase in sympathomimetic activity may exacerbate condition)

Patient monitoring

The following may be especially important in patient monitoring (other tests may be warranted in some patients, depending on condition; » = major clinical significance):

Blood pressure determinations and
Cardiac function monitoring
(recommended for early detection of tachycardia and changes in blood pressure, especially in patients with hypertension or cardiac disease)

Side/Adverse Effects

Note: Following abrupt withdrawal of dronabinol, an abstinence syndrome manifested by irritability, insomnia, and restlessness was observed within 12 hours in volunteers receiving dosages of 210 mg per day for 12 to 16 consecutive days; approximately 24 hours later, the withdrawal syndrome intensified with such symptoms as hot flashes, sweating, rhinorrhea, loose stools, hiccups, and anorexia. Withdrawal symptoms dissipated gradually over the next 48 hours. Electroencephalographic changes consistent with the hyperexcitation effects of drug withdrawal were recorded in patients after abrupt discontinuation.

Sleep disturbances, which continued for several weeks after discontinuation of high-dose dronabinol therapy, have been reported.

Although chronic abuse of cannabis has been associated with decreases in motivation, cognition, judgment, and perception, no such decrements in psychological, social, or neurological status have been associated with the administration of dronabinol for therapeutic purposes. In an open-label study in patients with AIDS who received dronabinol for up to 5 months, no abuse, diversion, or systematic change in personality or social functioning was observed, even in those patients with a history of drug abuse.

The following side/adverse effects have been selected on the basis of their potential clinical significance (possible signs and symptoms in parentheses where appropriate)—not necessarily inclusive:

Those indicating need for medical attention

Incidence less frequent

CNS effects (amnesia [memory loss]; changes in mood; confusion; delusions; feelings of unreality; hallucinations [seeing, hearing, or feeling things that are not there]; mental depression; nervousness or anxiety); ***palpitations*** (fast or pounding heartbeat); ***tachycardia*** (fast or pounding heartbeat)

Note: The above side/adverse effects may also be symptoms of overdose.

An initial *tachycardia* may be followed by normal sinus rhythm and then bradycardia. These effects may disappear when tolerance develops after continued use.

Those indicating need for medical attention only if they continue or are bothersome

Incidence more frequent

Ataxia (clumsiness or unsteadiness); ***dizziness; drowsiness; euphoria*** (false sense of well-being); ***nausea; trouble thinking; vomiting***

Incidence less frequent or rare

Asthenia (unusual tiredness or weakness); ***blurred vision or any changes in vision; dryness of mouth; flushing of face; orthostatic hypotension*** (feeling faint or lightheaded, especially when getting up from a lying or sitting position); ***restlessness***

Overdose

For specific information on the agents used in the management of dronabinol overdose, see:

- *Charcoal, Activated (Oral-Local)* monograph; and/or
- *Diazepam* in *Benzodiazepines (Systemic)* monograph.

For more information on the management of overdose or unintentional ingestion, **contact a Poison Control Center** (see *Poison Control Center Listing*).

Clinical effects of overdose

The following effects have been selected on the basis of their potential clinical significance (possible signs and symptoms in parentheses where appropriate)—not necessarily inclusive:

Mild intoxication

Heightened sensory awareness (change in your sense of smell, taste, sight, sound, or touch); ***altered time perception*** (change in how fast you think time is passing); ***drowsiness; dryness of mouth; euphoria*** (false sense of well-being); ***reddened conjunctiva*** (redness of eyes); ***tachycardia*** (fast or pounding heartbeat)

Moderate intoxication

Memory impairment (being forgetful); ***mood changes; reduced bowel motility*** (constipation); ***urinary retention*** (problems in urinating)

Severe intoxication

Decreased motor coordination; lethargy (unusual drowsiness or dullness; feeling sluggish); ***orthostatic hypotension; panic reaction; seizures; slurred speech***

Treatment of overdose

Overdose may occur either with therapeutic doses or with higher, nontherapeutic doses. Recommended treatment includes:

To decrease absorption—Gut decontamination, if ingestion is recent. Activated charcoal may be administered to unconscious patients (30 to 100 grams in adults, 1 to 2 grams per kilogram of body weight in infants) via a nasogastric tube; saline cathartic or sorbitol may be added to the first dose of charcoal.

Specific treatment—Treatment of hypertension or hypotension, if necessary. Hypotension usually responds to Trendelenburg position and administration of IV fluids. Pressors are rarely required. Benzodiazepines (5 to 10 mg of diazepam orally) may be used to treat extreme agitation. Patients with depressive, hallucinatory, or psychotic reactions should be placed in a quiet environment and offered reassurance.

Monitoring—Observation of patient in a quiet environment. Continuous blood pressure monitoring. Cardiac monitoring.

Supportive care—Supportive therapy. Patients in whom intentional overdose is confirmed or suspected should be referred for psychiatric consultation.

Patient Consultation

As an aid to patient consultation, refer to *Advice for the Patient, Dronabinol (Systemic)*.

In providing consultation, consider emphasizing the following selected information (» = major clinical significance):

Before using this medication

» Conditions affecting use, especially:
Hypersensitivity to marijuana products or sesame oil
Pregnancy—No studies in humans; increased risk of fetal mortality and resorptions in animal studies with doses many times the usual human dose
Breast-feeding—Not recommended; distributed into human breast milk
Use in children—Caution recommended because of psychoactive effects and potential for developing dependence and withdrawal effects
Use in the elderly—Caution recommended because of psychoactive effects and potential for developing dependence and withdrawal effects
Other medications, especially CNS depressants

Other medical problems, especially bipolar disorder, cardiac disorders, drug or alcohol abuse or dependence, or psychosis

Proper use of this medication

» Importance of not taking more medication than the amount prescribed because of danger of overdose

» Proper dosing

Missed dose: Taking as soon as possible; not taking if almost time for next dose; not doubling doses

» Proper storage

Precautions while using this medication

» Avoiding use of alcohol or other CNS depressants during therapy

» Caution if dizziness, drowsiness, lightheadedness, or false sense of well-being occurs

» Caution when getting up suddenly from a lying or sitting position

» Suspected overdose: Getting emergency help at once

Side/adverse effects

Signs of potential side effects, especially CNS effects, palpitations, and tachycardia

General Dosing Information

Because of the potential for abuse and risk of diversion, the amount of dronabinol dispensed should be limited to the amount necessary for the period between clinic visits.

Patients should remain under the supervision of a responsible adult during initial use of dronabinol and following dosage adjustments. Also, patients taking dronabinol should be advised of possible changes in mood and other adverse behavioral effects of the medication, so that occurrence of such effects will not be alarming.

Psychological and physical dependence may occur with high doses or chronic administration of dronabinol; an abstinence syndrome may be precipitated when dronabinol is discontinued (see *Side/Adverse effects*). However, this is very unlikely to occur with therapeutic doses and short-term use of dronabinol.

Oral Dosage Forms

DRONABINOL CAPSULES USP

Usual adult and adolescent dose

Antiemetic—

Oral, 5 mg per square meter of body surface area one to three hours prior to chemotherapy and every two to four hours following chemotherapy, for a total of four to six doses a day.

Note: The dose may be increased by increments of 2.5 mg per square meter of body surface area if the initial dose is ineffective and side effects are not significant. Caution should be exercised in dose escalation because the incidence of psychiatric symptoms increases significantly at maximum doses.

Appetite stimulant—

Oral, initially 2.5 mg two times a day, before lunch and supper. Patients unable to tolerate this dose may be given 2.5 mg a day, administered as a single dose in the evening or at bedtime.The dose may be increased, if clinically indicated and in the absence of significant adverse effects, to a maximum of 20 mg a day; however, the incidence of psychiatric symptoms increases significantly at maximum doses.

Usual adult prescribing limits

Antiemetic—

15 mg per square meter of body surface area per dose.

Appetite stimulant—

20 mg a day.

Usual pediatric dose

Antiemetic—

See *Usual adult and adolescent dose.*

Note: Caution is advised because of the psychoactive effects of dronabinol.

Appetite stimulant—

Safety and efficacy have not been established.

Usual geriatric dose

See *Usual adult and adolescent dose.*

Note: Caution is advised because of the psychoactive effects of dronabinol.

Strength(s) usually available

U.S.—

2.5 mg (Rx) [*Marinol* (sesame oil)].
5 mg (Rx) [*Marinol* (sesame oil)].
10 mg (Rx) [*Marinol* (sesame oil)].

Canada—

2.5 mg (Rx) [*Marinol* (sesame oil)].
5 mg (Rx) [*Marinol* (sesame oil)].
10 mg (Rx) [*Marinol* (sesame oil)].

Packaging and storage

Store between 8 and 15 °C (46 and 59 °F), in a well-closed container. Protect from freezing.

Auxiliary labeling

- Refrigerate.
- May cause drowsiness.
- Avoid alcoholic beverages.
- May be habit-forming.

Note

Controlled substance in the U.S. and Canada.

Revised: 01/06/2003

DROPERIDOL Systemic

VA CLASSIFICATION (Primary/Secondary): CN206/GA609; CN709

Commonly used brand name(s): *Inapsine*.

Note: For a listing of dosage forms and brand names by country availability, see *Dosage Forms* section(s).

Category

Anesthesia, adjunct; antiemetic; antipsychotic.

Indications

Note: Bracketed information in the *Indications* section refers to uses that are not included in U.S. product labeling.

General Considerations

Most of the adult patients included in published clinical trials of droperidol for prophylaxis of postoperative nausea and vomiting were women. Many of the trials involved gynecologic surgery. In these trials, droperidol was superior to placebo and usually equal to ondansetron in preventing postoperative nausea and vomiting. High-dose droperidol (i.e., 2.5 mg) was found to be superior to ondansetron (8 mg) in preventing postoperative nausea and vomiting in one trial; however, the patients receiving high-dose droperidol experienced increased sedation and delayed arousal compared to those receiving ondansetron. The degree to which these findings can be generalized to other types of surgery and male patients is not clear.

Most published trials in pediatric patients administered droperidol for prophylaxis of postoperative nausea and vomiting were placebo-controlled trials in strabismus surgery. Although droperidol was more effective than placebo, these studies did not establish the role of droperidol as compared to other antiemetic agents. In one trial in pediatric patients undergoing tonsillectomy, ondansetron was more effective than droperidol in preventing postoperative nausea and vomiting.

Although droperidol is not approved by the FDA to control severe agitation and combativeness, it can be used for this indication. Compared to haloperidol, droperidol is more sedating and controls agitation more quickly. Some, but not all, USP medical experts do not regard droperidol as first-line therapy for this indication.

Although droperidol has been used as an adjunctive agent in anesthesia, some USP medical experts do not regard droperidol as a first-line choice for use in anesthesia. When droperidol is used as an adjunctive agent in anesthesia, USP medical experts recommend lower doses than those indicated in the drug labeling.

Accepted

[Anesthesia, general, adjunct or]
[Anesthesia, local, adjunct]—Droperidol is indicated for use in anesthesia as premedication and for adjunctive use in the induction and maintenance of general and regional anesthesia. Droperidol combined with an opioid analgesic induces neuroleptanalgesia to produce tranquility and decrease anxiety and pain.

Nausea and vomiting (prophylaxis)—Droperidol is indicated to reduce the incidence of nausea and vomiting associated with surgical and diagnostic procedures.

Droperidol is effective in controlling postoperative nausea and vomiting in children undergoing strabismus repair.

Droperidol has been used as part of a regimen to control nausea and vomiting associated with emetogenic chemotherapy; however, droperidol is considered to be only moderately effective in preventing chemotherapy-associated nausea and vomiting.

[Sedation, conscious]—Droperidol is indicated to produce sedation without loss of consciousness in patients undergoing various diagnostic procedures.

[Psychotic disorder (treatment)][1]—Droperidol is indicated in the treatment of acute psychotic episodes manifested by severe agitation and combativeness (Evidence rating: I). In a comparative study with haloperidol, intramuscular administration of 5 mg of droperidol provided more rapid control of symptoms than an equal dose of haloperidol, without an increase in adverse effects.

Unaccepted

Droperidol has been used in the treatment of Meniere's disease, but it has been replaced by safer and more effective agents.

---

[1]Not included in Canadian product labeling.

Pharmacology/Pharmacokinetics

Physicochemical characteristics

Chemical Group—A butyrophenone neuroleptic, chemically related to haloperidol.

Molecular weight—379.44.

pH—Saturated solution at ambient temperature: 7.

Droperidol injection has lactic acid added to the formulation to adjust the pH to 3 to 3.8.

pKa—7.64.

Solubility—Practically insoluble in water; slightly soluble in methanol and ethanol.

Partition coefficient—The log-partition coefficient (n-octanol/aqueous buffer at pH 9.9) is 3.58.

Mechanism of action/Effect

The mechanism of action of droperidol is not known. It has been theorized that droperidol may bind postsynaptic gamma-aminobutyric acid (GABA) receptors. Binding of GABA receptors in the chemoreceptor trigger zone (CTZ) may be the mechanism by which droperidol produces an antiemetic effect. Droperidol may block dopaminergic receptors in the caudate nucleus and in the nucleus accumbens.

Other actions/effects

Droperidol selectively blocks postsynaptic alpha-adrenergic receptors. This action may cause vasodilation and hypotension.

Droperidol causes a dose-dependent prolongation of the QT interval and has been associated with cases of serious arrhythmias (e.g., torsades de pointes).

Absorption

Completely absorbed after intramuscular administration.

Distribution

Volume of distribution at steady state ($Vol_{D SS}$)—

Adults:

1.5 L per kg of body weight (L/kg).

Children:

0.58 L/kg.

Biotransformation

Extensively metabolized.

Half-life

Distribution—

Droperidol has biphasic distribution. The rapid distribution phase is 1.4 ± 0.5 minutes and the slower distribution phase is 14.3 ± 6.5 minutes.

Elimination—

Adults: 134 ± 13 minutes; may be increased in geriatric patients.

Children: 101.5 ± 26.4 minutes.

Onset of action

3 to 10 minutes.

Time to peak effect

Within 30 minutes of administration.

Duration of action

The duration of the sedative effects is 2 to 4 hours, although alteration of alertness may persist for up to 12 hours.

Elimination

Renal—

About 75% of intramuscularly administered droperidol is excreted in the urine; only 1% is excreted unchanged.

Biliary/fecal—

22% of intramuscularly administered droperidol is excreted in the feces; the high fraction of droperidol excreted in the feces suggests biliary excretion.

Precautions to Consider

Cross-sensitivity and/or related problems

Patients sensitive to other butyrophenones may be sensitive to droperidol also.

Carcinogenicity

Carcinogenicity studies have not been done with droperidol.

Mutagenicity

The micronucleus test in female rats revealed no mutagenicity after single doses of up to 160 mg per kg of body weight.

Pregnancy/Reproduction

Pregnancy—Droperidol has been used in pregnant patients to manage hyperemesis gravidarum. Compared to the control group, the mean birth weight and the incidence of premature birth were not different in the neonates born to droperidol-treated mothers. A similar number of congenital anomalies occurred in the two groups.

FDA Pregnancy Category C.

Labor and delivery—Droperidol has been used in patients undergoing cesarean section. Respiratory depression in the neonates has not been reported.

Breast-feeding

Droperidol is distributed into breast milk. Although problems in humans have not been documented, the manufacturer recommends breast-feeding be avoided in patients using droperidol.

Pediatrics

Although patients under 2 years of age have been included in some clinical trials, no information is available on the relationship of age to the effects of droperidol in these pediatric patients; safety and efficacy have not been established.

The comparative incidence of extrapyramidal effects from droperidol in pediatric patients as compared to adult patients is not known. However, pediatric patients are more likely than adult patients to experience extrapyramidal reactions after receiving haloperidol. It is expected that pediatric patients may be more likely than adult patients to experience extrapyramidal effects from droperidol also. Of the extrapyramidal effects, acute dystonic effects are more likely in pediatric patients.

Geriatrics

Geriatric patients may be more sensitive to the sedating effects of droperidol; in addition, geriatric patients may be more likely to experience hypotension and prolonged QT syndrome.

Drug interactions and/or related problems

The following drug interactions and/or related problems have been selected on the basis of their potential clinical significance (possible mechanism in parentheses where appropriate)—not necessarily inclusive (» = major clinical significance):

Note: Combinations containing any of the following medications, depending on the amount present, may also interact with this medication.

» Anesthetics, volatile or
» Benzodiazepines or
» Diuretics or
» Opiates, intravenous
(Prolonged QT syndrome may occur; initiate at a low dose and adjust upward with caution.)

Anesthetics, parenteral-local
(peripheral vasodilation and hypotension due to sympathetic blockade may occur)

Bromocriptine or
Levodopa
(dopamine agonists may be inhibited by droperidol)

Central nervous system (CNS) depression-producing medications (see *Appendix II*), including medications commonly used for anesthesia and analgesia
(additive CNS depression may occur; lower doses may be needed)

Epinephrine
(droperidol may antagonize the pressor effects of epinephrine, and may trigger a hypotensive episode)

Extrapyramidal reaction-causing medications, other (see *Appendix II*)
(may increase the frequency and severity of extrapyramidal effects)

Hypotension-producing medications (see *Appendix II*)
(orthostatic hypotension may occur; hypotension is especially likely if droperidol is used concurrently with drugs causing vasodilation)

Propofol
(droperidol may compete with propofol for binding sites in the chemoreceptor trigger zone; concurrent use of propofol and droperidol to control nausea and vomiting is less effective than using propofol alone)

Laboratory value alterations

The following have been selected on the basis of their potential clinical significance (possible effect in parentheses where appropriate)—not necessarily inclusive (» = major clinical significance).

With physiology/laboratory test values

» Electrocardiogram
(droperidol may cause prolongation of the QT interval and torsades de pointes.)

Prolactin, serum
(droperidol causes dose-dependent increase in serum prolactin)

Medical considerations/Contraindications

The medical considerations/contraindications included have been selected on the basis of their potential clinical significance (reasons given in parentheses where appropriate)—not necessarily inclusive (» = major clinical significance).

Except under special circumstances, this medication should not be used when the following medical problems exist:

Note: Due to its potential for serious proarrhythmic effects and death, droperidol should be reserved for treatment of patients who fail to show an acceptable response to other adequate treatments, either because of insufficient effectiveness or the inability to achieve an effective dose due to intolerable adverse effects from those drugs.

» Hypokalemia or
» Hypomagnesemia or
» QT interval prolongation, pre-existing
(risk of arrhythmia, rarely including sudden death, may be increased

Note: Cases of QT prolongation and/or torsades de pointes have been reported in patients receiving droperidol at doses at or below recommended doses. Some cases have occurred in patients with no known risk factors for QT prolongation and some cases have been fatal. Droperidol is contraindicated in patients with known or suspected QT prolongation, including patients with congenital long QT syndrome.)

» Hypersensitivity to droperidol
» Pheochromocytoma
(hypertension and tachycardia may occur)

Risk-benefit should be considered when the following medical problems exist:

» Alcoholism, acute or
» Bradycardia or
» Cardiac hypertrophy or
» Congestive heart failure or
» Elderly (over 65 years of age)
(risk of QT prolongation and torsades de pointes, rarely including sudden death, may be increased, even at doses at or below recommended doses.)

Cardiovascular function impairment or
Epilepsy or
Mental depression, severe or
» Parkinsonism
(may worsen condition)

Hepatic function impairment
(metabolism may be altered)

Hypovolemia
(risk of hypotension may be increased)

Patient monitoring

The following may be especially important in patient monitoring (other tests may be warranted in some patients, depending on condition; » = major clinical significance):

Blood pressure and
Body temperature and
Heart rate and
Respiratory and ventilatory status
(routine monitoring of vital signs is recommended)

» Electrocardiogram
(The manufacturer recommends that all patients should undergo a 12–lead electrocardiogram prior to administration of droperidol to determine if a prolonged corrected QT (QTc) interval is present. QTc intervals greater than 440 milliseconds for males or 450 milliseconds for females are prolonged. However, a consensus of USP experts disagree with the recommendation that all patients should undergo a 12–lead electrocardiogram prior to the administration of droperidol. Electrocardiogram monitoring should be performed prior to treatment and continued for two to three hours after completing treatment to monitor for arrhythmias.)

Motor functioning
(recommended to monitor for extrapyramidal effects)

Side/Adverse Effects

The following side/adverse effects have been selected on the basis of their potential clinical significance (possible signs and symptoms in parentheses where appropriate)—not necessarily inclusive:

Those indicating need for medical attention

Incidence less frequent

Akathisia (restlessness)—extrapyramidal reaction; ***anxiety***—extrapyramidal reaction; ***hypertension*** (high blood pressure)—asymptomatic

Note: *Hypertension* has occurred following the use of droperidol combined with an opioid analgesic (e.g., fentanyl) and may be due to surgical stimulation during light anesthesia.

Incidence rare

Dystonia (spasm of the muscles of the tongue, face, neck, and back)—extrapyramidal reaction; ***hyperpyrexia*** (fever)—may indicate neuroleptic malignant syndrome; ***oculogyric crisis*** (fixed upward position of eyeballs)—extrapyramidal reaction; ***QT syndrome, prolonged*** (irregular or slow heart rate; fainting; sudden death)

Those indicating need for medical attention only if they continue or are bothersome

Incidence more frequent

Hypotension (lightheadedness)—usually transient; ***excessive sedation*** (drowsiness); ***tachycardia*** (rapid heart rate)

Those indicating possible extrapyramidal reaction and the need for medical attention if they occur after medication is discontinued

Akathisia (restlessness); ***dystonia*** (spasm of the muscles of the tongue, face, neck, and back); ***oculogyric crisis*** (fixed upward position of eyeballs)

Note: *Dystonia* has been reported up to 30 hours after administration of a dose of droperidol.

Overdose

For specific information on the agents used in the management of droperidol overdose, see:

- *Benztropine* in *Antidyskinetics (Systemic)* monograph;
- *Diphenhydramine* in *Antihistamines (Systemic)* monograph; and/or
- *Phenylephrine* in *Sympathomimetic Agents—Cardiovascular Use (Parenteral-Systemic)* monograph.

For more information on the management of overdose or unintentional ingestion, **contact a Poison Control Center** (see *Poison Control Center Listing*).

Clinical effects of overdose

The following effects have been selected on the basis of their potential clinical significance (possible signs and symptoms in parentheses where appropriate)—not necessarily inclusive:

Acute and/or chronic

Akathisia (restlessness); ***dystonia*** (spasm of the muscles of the tongue, face, neck, and back); ***hypotension*** (dizziness); ***prolongation of QT interval***—usually asymptomatic; ***oculogyric crisis*** (fixed upward position of eyeballs); ***respiratory depression*** (slowed breathing)

Note: *Akathisia, dystonia,* and *oculogyric crisis* are effects that can occur with overdose of droperidol. However, these effects can also occur with usual therapeutic doses of droperidol.

Treatment of overdose

Discontinue droperidol.

Specific treatment—Extrapyramidal reactions (e.g., akathisia, dystonia, and oculogyric crisis) may be treated with anticholinergic agents such as benztropine or diphenhydramine.

Supportive care—A patent airway must be maintained, and respiration should be assisted or controlled if necessary. Oxygen should be administered. Blood pressure should be supported as needed. Phenylephrine may be needed to counteract the alpha-blocking effects of droperidol. In hypovolemic patients, administration of intravenous fluids may be required. Patients in whom intentional overdose is confirmed or suspected should be referred for psychiatric consultation.

Patient Consultation

As an aid to patient consultation, refer to *Advice for the Patient, Droperidol (Systemic).*

In providing consultation, consider emphasizing the following selected information (» = major clinical significance):

Before using this medication

» Conditions affecting use, especially:
Hypersensitivity to droperidol
Breast-feeding—Temporary discontinuation of breast-feeding is recommended in patients receiving droperidol, because droperidol is distributed into breast milk
Use in children—Children may be more likely than adult patients to experience extrapyramidal effects
Use in the elderly—Older patients may be more likely to experience drowsiness, hypotension and prolonged QT syndrome.
Other medical problems, especially acute alcoholism, bradycardia, cardiac hypertrophy, congestive heart failure, hypokalemia, hypomagnesemia, parkinsonism, pheochromocytoma or pre-existing QT interval prolongation

Proper use of this medication

» Proper dosing

Precautions after receiving this medication

Not driving or operating machinery for 24 hours after receiving droperidol
Not drinking alcohol or taking CNS depression-producing medications for about 24 hours after receiving droperidol

Side/adverse effects

Signs of potential side effects, especially akathisia, anxiety, hypertension, dystonia, hyperpyrexia, oculogyric crisis and prolonged QT syndrome.

General Dosing Information

Geriatric, debilitated, or critically ill patients are more likely to experience excessive sedation prolonged QT syndrome and hypotension from the use of droperidol. It is recommended that the initial dose be lower in these patients. Subsequent doses may be titrated based on the response to the initial dose.

Droperidol should not be administered as the sole agent for anesthesia induction for surgery.

Note: Dosage should be individualized. Some of the factors to be considered in determining the dose are age, body weight, physical status, underlying pathological condition, use of other drugs, type of anesthesia to be used and the surgical procedure involved.

Parenteral Dosage Forms

Note: Bracketed uses in the *Dosage Forms* section refer to categories of use and/or indications that are not included in U.S. product labeling.

DROPERIDOL INJECTION USP

Usual adult and adolescent dose

[Anesthesia, general, adjunct or]
[Anesthesia, local, adjunct]—
Premedication—
Intramuscular, 2.5 thirty to sixty minutes before surgery. The maximum recommended initial dose is 2.5 mg intramuscularly or slow intravenously. Additional 1.25 mg doses may be administered with caution to achieve the desired affect only if the potential benefit outweighs the potential risk. However, caution is indicated due to the potential for adverse psychotic effects.

Induction—
Intravenous or intramuscular, 1.25 mg per twenty to twenty-five pounds of body weight (0.1 to 0.14 mg [100 to 140 mcg] per kg of body weight). The maximum recommended initial dose is 2.5 mg intramuscularly or slow intravenously. Additional 1.25 mg doses may be administered with caution to achieve the desired affect only if the potential benefit outweighs the potential risk.

Maintenance—
Intravenous, 1.25 to 2.5 mg. When droperidol is used as an adjunct to regional anesthesia, 2.5 may be administered intramuscularly or intravenously if additional sedation is required. The maximum recommended initial dose is 2.5 mg intramuscularly or slow intravenously. Additional 1.25 mg doses may be administered with caution to achieve the desired affect only if the potential benefit outweighs the potential risk.

Nausea and vomiting, postoperative (prophylaxis)—
Intravenous, 7 to 20 mcg per kg of body weight. The maximum recommended initial dose is 2.5 mg intramuscularly or slow intravenously. Additional 1.25 mg doses may be administered with caution to achieve the desired affect only if the potential benefit outweighs the potential risk.

Sedation, conscious—
Intramuscular, 1.25 thirty to sixty minutes prior to a diagnostic procedure. The maximum recommended initial dose is 2.5 mg intramuscularly or slow intravenously. Additional 1.25 mg doses may be administered with caution to achieve the desired affect only if the potential benefit outweighs the potential risk.

[Psychotic disorder][1]—
Intramuscular or intravenous, 2.5 for acute agitation. The dose should be based on the size of the patient and the degree of agitation. The maximum recommended initial dose is 2.5 mg intramuscularly or slow intravenously. Additional 1.25 mg doses may be administered with caution to achieve the desired affect only if the potential benefit outweighs the potential risk.

Usual pediatric dose

[Anesthesia, general, adjunct or]
[Anesthesia, local, adjunct]—
Premedication—
Intramuscular or intravenous, 0.075 to 0.15 mg (75 to 150 mcg) per kg of body weight thirty to sixty minutes before surgery. For children 2 to 12 years of age, the maximum recommended initial dose is 0.1 mg per kg of body weight. Additional doses should be administered with caution and only if the potential benefit outweighs the potential risk.

Induction—
Intravenous, 0.075 to 0.15 mg (75 to 150 mcg) per kg of body weight. For children 2 to 12 years of age, the maximum recommended initial dose is 0.1 mg per kg of body weight. Additional doses should be administered with caution and only if the potential benefit outweighs the potential risk.

Nausea and vomiting, postoperative (prophylaxis)—
Intramuscular or intravenous, 0.02 to 0.075 mg (20 to 75 mcg) per kg of body weight. For children 2 to 12 years of age, the maximum recommended initial dose is 0.1 mg per kg of body weight. Additional doses should be administered with caution and only if the potential benefit outweighs the potential risk.

Usual geriatric dose

See *Usual adult and adolescent dose*. However, initial doses should be decreased for geriatric patients because geriatric patients are more likely to experience hypotension and excessive sedation after receiving droperidol.

Strength(s) usually available

U.S.—
Note: The 10-mL multidose vials available generically contain 1.8 mg of methylparaben and 0.2 mg of propylparaben per mL.

2.5 mg per mL (Rx) [*Inapsine;* GENERIC].

Canada—
2.5 mg per mL (Rx) [*Inapsine*].

Packaging and storage

Protect from light. Store between 15 and 30 °C (59 and 86 °F).

Preparation of dosage form

Droperidol may be diluted to a convenient volume with 5% dextrose injection, 0.9% sodium chloride injection, or lactated Ringer's injection.

[1]Not included in Canadian product labeling.

Selected Bibliography

Desilva P, Darvish A, McDonald S, et al. The efficacy of prophylactic ondansetron, droperidol, perphenazine, and metoclopramide in the prevention of nausea and vomiting after major gynecologic surgery. Anesth Analg 1995; 81: 139-43.

Resnick M, Burton B. Droperidol vs. haloperidol in the initial management of acutely agitated patients. J Clin Psychiatry 1984; 45: 298-9.

Antrobus J, Abbott P, Carr C, et al. Midazolam–droperidol premedication for cardiac surgery. A comparison with papaveretum and hyoscine. Anaesthesia 1991; 46: 407-9.

Revised: 01/29/2002
Developed: 05/21/1998

DROSPIRENONE AND ESTRADIOL Systemic†

VA CLASSIFICATION (Primary): HS105

Commonly used brand name(s): *Angeliq.*

Note: For a listing of dosage forms and brand names by country availability, see *Dosage Forms* section(s).

†Not commercially available in Canada.

Category

Estrogen-progestin; ovarian hormone therapy agent.

Indications

Accepted

Menopause, vasomotor symptoms of (treatment)—Drospirenone and estradiol combination is indicated in women who have a uterus for the treatment of moderate to severe vasomotor symptoms associated with menopause.

Vaginal atrophy (treatment)

Vulvar atrophy (treatment)—Drospirenone and estradiol combination is indicated in women who have a uterus for the treatment of moderate to severe symptoms of vulvar and vaginal atrophy associated with menopause. When prescribing solely for the treatment of symptoms of vulvar and vaginal atrophy, topical vaginal products should be considered.

Unaccepted

Estrogens with or without progestins should not be used for the prevention of cardiovascular disease or dementia.

Pharmacology/Pharmacokinetics

Physicochemical characteristics

Molecular weight—
Drospirenone—366.5.
Estradiol—272.39.

Mechanism of action/Effect

In postmenopausal women, estrone and the sulfate-conjugated form, estrone sulfate are the most abundant circulating estrogens. Estrogens bind to nuclear receptors in estrogen-responsive tissues. Circulating estrogens modulate the pituitary secretion of gonadotropins, luteinizing hormone (LH), and follicle stimulating hormone (FSH) through a negative feedback system. Drospirenone is a synthetic progestin and spironolactone analog with antimineralocorticoid activity. It has antiandrogenic activity, but no glucocorticoid, antiglucocorticoid, estrogenic, or androgenic activity. Progestins counter estrogenic effects by decreasing the number of nuclear estradiol receptors and suppressing epithelial DNA synthesis in endometrial tissue.

Absorption

Following administration of drospirenone/estradiol combination, relative bioavailability of drospirenone and estradiol is 102% and 107%, respectively, compared to a combination oral suspension.

Drospirenone—Absolute bioavailability of 76 to 85%

Bioavailability of both drugs is not affected by food intake.

Distribution

Drospirenone—Volume of distribution (Vol_D) is 4.2 L/kg

Estradiol—Widely distributed in the body and generally found in higher concentrations in the sex hormone target organs

Protein binding

Drospirenone—Very high (97%)

Estradiol—Very high, (sex hormone binding globulin [SHBG] 37% and albumin 61%)

Biotransformation

Drospirenone—Two main inactive metabolites

Estradiol—Estrone, estriol; sulfate conjugates, especially estrone sulfate in postmenopausal women

Half-life

Drospirenone—36 to 42 hours

Time to peak concentration

Drospirenone—One hour after drospirenone/estradiol administration

Estradiol—6 to 8 hours after drospirenone/estradiol administration

Peak plasma concentration:

Drospirenone—C_{max} is 18.3 ± 5.55 ng/mL

Estradiol—C_{max} is 43.8 ± 10 pg/mL

Estrone—C_{max} is 245 ± 50.6 pg/mL

Elimination

Drospirenone—Excretion nearly complete after 10 days and amounts slightly higher in feces than in urine; highly metabolized and only trace amounts of unchanged drospirenone; 38 to 47% of the metabolites in urine and 17 to 20% in the feces were glucuronide and sulfate conjugates

Estradiol—Urine, as estradiol, estrone, and estriol along with glucuronide and sulfate conjugates

Precautions to Consider

Carcinogenicity

Long-term continuous administration of estrogen, with and without progestin, in women with and without a uterus, has shown an increased risk of endometrial, breast, and ovarian cancer.

Long-term continuous administration of natural and synthetic estrogens in some animals increases the frequency of carcinomas of the breast, uterus, cervix, vagina, testis, and liver. In a 24-month study in mice given oral doses of drospirenone alone or drospirenone/ethinyl estradiol 0.24 to 10.3 times the exposure of women taking a 1-mg dose, there was an increase in carcinomas of the harderian gland in the group that received the high dose of drospirenone alone. In a similar study of rats given 2.3 and 51.2 times the exposure of women taking a 1-mg dose, there was an increased incidence of benign and total (benign and malignant) adrenal gland pheochrmocytomas in the group receiving the high dose of drospirenone.

Mutagenicity

Drospirenone was not mutagenic in a number of *in vitro* (Ames, Chinese Hamster Lung gene mutation and chromosomal damage in human lymphocytes) and *in vivo* (mouse micronucleus) genotoxicity tests. Drospirenone increased unscheduled DNA synthesis in rat hepatocytes and formed adducts with rodent liver DNA but not with human liver DNA.

Pregnancy/Reproduction

Pregnancy—Drospirenone/estradiol combination is **contraindicated** during pregnancy.

Breast-feeding

Caution should be exercised when drospirenone/estradiol is administered to a nursing woman. Estrogen administration to nursing mothers has been shown to decrease the quantity and quality of the milk. Detectable amounts of estrogens have been identified in the milk of mothers receiving this drug.

Following administration of an oral contraceptive containing drospirenone, about 0.02% of the drospirenone dose was distributed into the breast milk of the mother within 24 hours. This results in about a 3-mcg maximal daily dose of drospirenone in an infant.

Pediatrics

Drospirenone/estradiol is not indicated in children.

Geriatrics

Appropriate studies on the relationship of age to the effects of drospirenone/estradiol combination have not been performed in the geriatric population. However, the Women's Health Initiative Memory Study (WHIMS) reported increased risk of developing probable dementia in postmenopausal women ≥65 years of age during 5.2 years of conjugated estrogens alone treatment and during 4 years of oral conjugated estrogens plus medroxyprogesterone acetate treatment compared with placebo. Ninety percent of the cases of probably dementia occurred in the 54% of women who were older than 70 years of age.

Pharmacogenetics

No studies have been done to determine the effect of race on the pharmacokinetics of drospirenone/estradiol.

Surgical

Surgical—If possible, estrogens should be discontinued at least 4 to 6 weeks prior to surgery of the type associated with an increased risk of thromboembolism, or during periods of prolonged immobilization.

Drug interactions and/or related problems

The following drug interactions and/or related problems have been selected on the basis of their potential clinical significance (possible mechanism in parentheses where appropriate)—not necessarily inclusive (» = major clinical significance):

Note: Combinations containing any of the following medications, depending on the amount present, may also interact with this medication.

ACE inhibitors or
Angiotensin-II receptor antagonists or
Heparin or
NSAIDs or
Potassium supplements or
Potassium-sparing diuretics or
Other medications that can increase potassium
(use caution when prescribing drospirenone/estradiol; consider checking serum potassium levels during first treatment cycle in high-risk patients)

Laboratory value alterations

The following have been selected on the basis of their potential clinical significance (possible effect in parentheses where appropriate)—not necessarily inclusive (» = major clinical significance).

With diagnostic test results
- Glucose tolerance test
  - (may increase the glucose tolerance test results)
- Metapyrone test
  - (reduced response)
- Thyroid function tests, such as
  - Thyroxine (T_4) determinations
  - Triiodothyronine (T_3) determinations
  - (total thyroid hormone, T_4, or T_3 may be increased and values for the T_3 uptake test may be decreased because of an increase in thyroid-binding globulin [TBG]; free T_3 and thyroxine [T_4] concentrations remain unaltered)

With physiology/laboratory test values
- Alpha-1–antitrypsin and
- Angiotensinogen/renin substrate and
- Beta-thromboglobulin and
- Ceruloplasmin and
- Clotting factors II, VII, VIII, IX, X and XII and
- Corticosteroid binding globulin (CBG) and
- Fibrinogen and
- Lipoproteins, high density (HDL) and
- Plasminogen antigen and
- Platelets and
- Sex-hormone binding globulin (SHBG) and
- Triglycerides
  - (serum concentrations may be increased)
- Anti-factor Xa and
- Antithrombin III and
- Lipoproteins, low density (LDL)
  - (serum concentrations may be decreased)
- Partial thromboplastin time and
- Platelet aggregation time and
- Prothrombin time
  - (may be accelerated)

Medical considerations/Contraindications

The medical considerations/contraindications included have been selected on the basis of their potential clinical significance (reasons given in parentheses where appropriate)—not necessarily inclusive (» = major clinical significance).

Except under special circumstances, this medication should not be used when the following medical problem exists:

» Abnormal genital bleeding, undiagnosed, or
» Breast cancer, known, suspected, or history of, or
» Estrogen-dependent neoplasia, known or suspected

» Adrenal insufficiency or
» Liver dysfunction or disease or
» Renal insufficiency
(drospirenone has antialdosterone activity including potential for hyperkalemia in high-risk patients; drospirenone/estradiol **contraindicated** in patients with these conditions which predispose to hyperkalemia)

» Arterial thromboembolic disease, active or recent (within the past year):
Myocardial infarction or
Stroke or
» Deep vein thrombosis, active or history of, or
» Pulmonary embolism, active or history of

» Hypersensitivity to drospirenone, estradiol, or its ingredients

» Pregnancy, known or suspected
(no indication for drospirenone/estradiol in pregnancy; appears to be little/no increased risk of birth defects in children born to women who have used oral contraceptives with estrogens and progestins inadvertently during early pregnancy)

Risk-benefit should be considered when the following medical problems exist:

Asthma or
Diabetes mellitus or
Epilepsy or
Hepatic hemangiomas or
Lupus erythematosus, systemic, or
Migraine or
Porphyria
(estrogens should be used with caution; may cause exacerbation of these conditions)

Cardiac or renal dysfunction
(conditions which might be influenced by fluid retention warrant careful observation when patient is taking estrogen; estrogens may cause some degree of fluid retention)

Cardiovascular disease risk factors such as:
Diabetes mellitus or
Hypercholesterolemia or
Hypertension or
Obesity or
Tobacco use or
Venous thromboembolism (VTE) risk factors such as:
Obesity or
Personal or family history of VTE or
Systemic lupus erythematosus
(these risk factors should be managed appropriately)

» Cholestatic jaundice, history of, or
» Hepatic function impairment
(caution should be exercised and in case of recurrence, medication should be discontinued, in patients with history of cholestatic jaundice associated with past estrogen use or pregnancy; may be poorly metabolized in patients with hepatic function impairment; decreased drospirenone clearance in patients with moderate hepatic impairment)

Endometriosis
(may be exacerbated with estrogen administration)

» Hypertriglyceridemia, pre-existing
(estrogen therapy may be associated with plasma triglyceride elevations leading to pancreatitis and other complications)

Hypocalcemia, severe
(estrogens should be used with caution)

Hyponatremia, high risk for
(as an aldosterone antagonist, drospirenone may increase possibility of hyponatremia in high risk patients)

Hypothyroidism
(estrogens lead to increased thyroid binding globulin [TBG] levels; patients dependent upon thyroid hormone replacement therapy who are also receiving estrogens may need to increase the dose of their thyroid replacement therapy)

Patient monitoring

The following may be especially important in patient monitoring (other tests may be warranted in some patients, depending on condition; » = major clinical significance):

Blood pressure
(should be monitored at regular intervals with estrogen use; may be elevated due to idiosyncratic reactions of estrogens)

Endometrial biopsy
(should be considered periodically as necessary in patients with an intact uterus; patients with a uterus should be monitored for signs of endometrial cancer and malignancy should be ruled out in cases of persistent or abnormal vaginal bleeding; there is no evidence that natural estrogen use results in a different endometrial risk profile than synthetic estrogens of equivalent dose)

Side/Adverse Effects

The following side/adverse effects have been selected on the basis of their potential clinical significance (possible signs and symptoms in parentheses where appropriate)—not necessarily inclusive:

Those indicating need for medical attention

Incidence more frequent

Abdomen enlarged (swelling of abdominal or stomach area; full or bloated feeling; pressure in the stomach); ***breast pain; surgery; vaginal hemorrhage*** (heavy nonmenstrual vaginal bleeding)

Incidence less frequent

Endometrial disorder (change in vaginal discharge; pain or feeling of pressure in pelvis; vaginal bleeding); ***leukorrhea*** (increased clear or white vaginal discharge); ***peripheral edema*** (bloating or swelling of face, arms, hands, lower legs, or feet; rapid weight gain; tingling of hands or feet; unusual weight gain or loss)

Incidence unknown

Breast cancer (clear or bloody discharge from nipple; inverted nipple; dimpling of breast skin; lump in breast or under the arm; persistent crusting or scaling of nipple; redness or swelling of breast; sore on the skin of the breast that does not heal); ***dementia*** (poor insight and judgment; problems with memory or speech; trouble recognizing objects; trouble thinking and planning; trouble walking)—increased risk in postmenopausal women aged 65 to 79 years; ***diplopia*** (double vision; seeing double); ***endometrial hyperplasia or cancer*** (change in vaginal discharge; pain or feeling of pressure in pelvis; vaginal bleeding)—greater risk associated with prolonged use of estrogens; ***gallbladder disease*** (abdominal pain; nausea and vomiting); ***hypercalcemia*** (abdominal pain; confusion; constipation; depression; dry mouth; headache; incoherent speech; increased urination; loss of appetite; metallic taste; muscle weakness; nausea; thirst; unusual tiredness; vomiting; weight loss)—in patients with breast cancer and bone metastases; ***migraine*** (headache, severe and throbbing); ***myocardial infarction*** (chest pain or discomfort; pain or discomfort in arms, jaw, back or neck; shortness of breath; nausea; sweating; vomiting); ***pulmonary embolism*** (anxiety; chest pain; cough; fainting; fast heartbeat; sudden shortness of breath or troubled breathing; dizziness or lightheadedness); ***retinal vascular thrombosis*** (changes in vision; double vision; migraine headache; blurred vision; change in vision); ***stroke*** (confusion; difficulty in speaking; slow speech; inability to speak; inability to move arms, legs, or facial muscles; double vision; headache); ***venous thromboembolism (VTE)*** (chest pain; coughing up blood; numbness or weakness in your arm or leg, or on one side of your body; pain or redness in your lower leg (calf); sudden or severe headache; problems with vision, speech, or walking)

Those indicating need for medical attention only if they continue or are bothersome

Incidence more frequent

Abdominal pain (stomach pain); ***accidental injury; back pain; flu syndrome*** (chills; cough; diarrhea; fever; general feeling of discomfort or illness; headache; joint pain; loss of appetite; muscle aches and pains; nausea; runny nose; shivering; sore throat; sweating; trouble sleeping; unusual tiredness or weakness; vomiting); ***headache; pain in extremity*** (pain in arms or legs); ***sinusitis*** (pain or tenderness around eyes and cheekbones; fever; stuffy or runny nose; headache; cough; shortness of breath or troubled breathing; tightness of chest or wheezing); ***upper respiratory infection*** (ear congestion; nasal congestion; chills; cough, fever, sneezing, or sore throat; body aches or pain; headache; loss of voice; runny nose; unusual tiredness or weakness; difficulty in breathing)

Overdose

For more information on the management of overdose or unintentional ingestion, **contact a poison control center** (see *Poison Control Center Listing*).

Clinical effects of overdose

Serious ill effects have not been reported following acute ingestion of large doses of progestin/estrogen-containing oral contraceptives by young children.

The following effects have been selected on the basis of their potential clinical significance (possible signs and symptoms in parentheses where appropriate)—not necessarily inclusive:

Nausea; withdrawal bleeding—in females

Treatment of overdose

Monitoring serum concentrations of potassium and sodium since drospirenone has antimineralocorticosteroid properties

Patients in whom intentional overdose is confirmed or suspected should be referred for psychiatric consultation.

Patient Consultation

As an aid to patient consultation, refer to *Advice for the Patient, Drospirenone and Estradiol (Systemic)*.

In providing consultation, consider emphasizing the following selected information (» = major clinical significance):

Before using this medication

» Conditions affecting use, especially:
- Hypersensitivity to drospirenone, estradiol, or its ingredients
- Pregnancy—**Contraindicated** during pregnancy
- Breast-feeding—Caution should be exercised; estrogen shown to decrease quantity and quality of breast milk
- Use in children—Not indicated for use in children
- Use in the elderly—Women's Health Initiative Memory Study (WHIMS) reported increased risk of probably dementia in postmenopausal women ≥65 years of age
- Surgical—If possible, estrogens should be discontinued at least 4 to 6 weeks prior to any surgery associated with increased thromboembolism risk or during periods of prolonged immobilization.
- Other medical problems, especially abnormal genital bleeding (undiagnosed); adrenal insufficiency; arterial thromboembolic disease (active or recent); breast cancer (known, suspected, or history of); chronic jaundice (history of); deep vein thrombosis (active or history of); estrogen-dependent neoplasia (known or suspected); hepatic function impairment; hypertiglyceridemia (pre-existing); liver dysfunction or disease; pregnancy (known or suspected); pulmonary embolism (active or history of); or renal insufficiency

Proper use of this medication

» Reading patient package insert carefully
» Compliance with therapy
» Not using in women who have had their uterus removed
» Not using this medicine for the prevention of cardiovascular disease or dementia
» Using caution in prescribing this medicine to women who regularly take other medications that may increase potassium level
Swallowing tablet whole, not crushing or chewing
» Proper dosing
Missed dose: Calling doctor or pharmacist for instructions
» Proper storage

Precautions while using this medication

» Regular visits to physician every 3 to 6 months, or more often, as determined by physician to discuss whether continued treatment with drospirenone/estradiol is needed

» Checking breasts by self-examination regularly and having clinical examination and mammography as required by physician; reporting unusual breast lumps or discharge

» Checking with doctor immediately if vaginal bleeding occurs

If scheduled for laboratory tests, telling physician about taking estrogens; certain blood tests are affected

Telling physician about risk factors for cardiovascular disease such as hypertension, diabetes mellitus, tobacco use, hypercholesterolemia, and obesity

Side/adverse effects

Signs of potential side effects, especially abdomen enlarged, breast pain, surgery, vaginal hemorrhage, endometrial disorder, leukorrhea, peripheral edema, breast cancer, dementia, diplopia, endometrial hyperplasia or cancer, gallbladder disease, hypercalcemia, migraine, myocardial infarction, pulmonary embolism, retinal vascular thrombosis, stroke, or venous thromboembolism (VTE)

General Dosing Information

Women who are already using a product containing estrogen should stop taking that product before starting drospirenone/estradiol.

Estrogen use, alone or in combination with a progestin, should be limited to the lowest effective dose available and for the shortest duration consistent with treatment goals and risks for the individual woman.

The lowest effective dose of drospirenone/estradiol has not been determined.

Patients should be reevaluated periodically as clinically appropriate (e.g., 3-month or 6-month intervals) to determine the necessity of continued treatment.

Studies show that the addition of a progestin for 10 or more days of a cycle of estrogen treatment or daily with estrogen in a continuous regimen, have reported a lowered incidence of endometrial hyperplasia, a possible precursor to endometrial cancer, than would be induced by estrogen treatment alone. However, there is a possible increased risk of breast cancer associated with combination progestin/estrogen use compared to estrogen only regimens.

For treatment of adverse effects

Hypercalcemia—If hypercalcemia occurs, use of the drug should be stopped and appropriate measures taken to reduce the serum calcium level.

Retinal vascular thrombosis (e.g., sudden partial or complete loss of vision, sudden onset of proptosis, diplopia, or migraine)—Drospirenone/estradiol should be discontinued pending examination. If the examination reveals papilledema or retinal vascular lesions, the drug should be permanently discontinued.

Oral Dosage Forms

DROSPIRENONE AND ESTRADIOL TABLETS

Usual adult dose

Vasomotor symptoms of menopause (treatment)
Vaginal atrophy (treatment)
Vulvar atrophy (treatment)—
Oral, one tablet (0.5 mg drospirenone/1 mg estradiol) once daily.

Usual pediatric dose
Drospirenone/estradiol is not indicated for use in children.

Usual geriatric dose
See *Usual adult dose*.

Strength(s) usually available
U.S.—
0.5 mg drospirenone and 1 mg estradiol (Rx) [*Angeliq* (film-coated; lactose monohydrate; corn starch; modified starch; povidone 25000; magnesium stearate; hydroxypropylmethyl cellulose; macrogol 6000; talc; titanium dioxide; ferric oxide pigment)].

Packaging and storage
Store at 25 °C (77 °F); excursions permitted to 15 to 30 °C (59 to 86 °F).

Auxiliary labeling
- Swallow whole. Do not crush or chew.
- Please read patient leaflet information enclosed.

Developed: 04/11/2006

DROSPIRENONE AND ETHINYL ESTRADIOL Systemic

VA CLASSIFICATION (Primary): HS104

Commonly used brand name(s): *Yasmin*.

Note: For a listing of dosage forms and brand names by country availability, see *Dosage Forms* section(s).

Category
Contraceptive, systemic.

Indications
Accepted
Pregnancy, prevention of—Combination drospirenone-ethinyl estradiol oral contraceptive is indicated for the prevention of pregnancy.

Pharmacology/Pharmacokinetics
Physicochemical characteristics
Molecular weight—
Drospirenone—366.5.
Ethinyl estradiol—296.4.

Mechanism of action/Effect
Contraceptive, systemic—Drospirenone and ethinyl estradiol act to suppress gonadatropins. This is achieved through inhibition of ovulation and alterations to both the cervical mucus and the endometrium.

Absorption
Drospirenone and ethinyl estradiol combination—The absolute bioavailability of the drospirenone and ethinyl estradiol combination is unknown

Drospirenone—The absolute bioavailability of drospirenone is 76%

Ethinyl estradiol—The absolute bioavailability of ethinyl estradiol is 40%

Distribution
Oral contraceptives are widely distributed

Drospirenone—Volume of distribution (Vol_D) is 4 liters (L) per kilogram (kg).

Ethinyl estradiol—Volume of distribution (Vol_D) is 4–5 liters per kilogram.

Protein binding
Drospirenone—Binds to serum proteins (97%) other than sex hormone binding globulin and corticosteroid binding globulin

Ethinyl estradiol—Highly but non-specificaly bound to serum albumin.

Half-life
Drospirenone—30 hours

Ethinyl estradiol—24 hours

Elimination
Drospirenone—Excretion of drospirenone is nearly complete after 10 days and amounts excreted were slightly higher in feces compared to urine. It is highly metabolized and only trace amounts of unchanged drospirenone were excreted. 38 to 47% of the metabolites in urine were glucuronide and sulfate conjugates compared to 17 to 20% in feces.

Ethinyl estradiol—Ethinyl estradiol is not excreted unchanged. It is excreted in the urine and feces as glucuronide and sulfate conjugates and undergoes enterohepatic circulation

Precautions to Consider
Carcinogenicity
A 24 month oral carcinogenicity study in mice dosed with 10 mg per kg per day drospirenone alone or 1 + 0.01, 3 + 0.03 and 10 + 0.1 mg per kg per day of drospirenone and ethinyl estradiol (0.1 to 2 times the normal human exposure) found an increase in carcinomas of the harderian gland in the group that received the high dose of drospirenone alone. A similar study in rats given 10 mg per kg per day drospirenone alone or 0.3 + 0.003, 3 + 0.03 and 10 + 0.1 mg per kg per day drospirenone and ethinyl estradiol (0.8 to 10 times the normal human exposure) found an increased incidence of benign and total adrenal gland pheochromocytomas in the group receiving the high dose of drospirenone.

Mutagenicity
Drospirenone was not mutagenic in a number of *in vitro* (Ames, Chinese Hamster Lung gene mutation and chromosomal damage in human lymphocytes) and *in vivo* (mouse micronucleus) genotoxicity tests. Drospirenone increased unscheduled DNA synthesis in rat hepatocytes and formed adducts with rodent liver DNA but not with human liver DNA.

Pregnancy/Reproduction
Pregnancy—Drospirenone and ethinyl estradiol is not recommended for use during pregnancy and should be discontinued immediately if pregnancy is suspected. Studies in animals that it causes serious adverse effects on the fetus

Of the 14 pregnancies that occurred with drospirenone and ethinyl estradiol exposure *in utero*, one produced an infant with esophageal atresia. Animal studies have revealed various teratogenic effects. A study in pregnant rats given oral drospirenone doses of 5, 15, and 45 mg per kg per day (6 to 50 times the normal human exposure) resulted in fetuses with delayed ossification. A study in rabbits found an increase in fetal loss and retardation of fetal development following oral drospirenone doses of 1, 30, and 100 mg per kg per day (2 to 27 times the human exposure. An increase in feminization of male rat fetuses was seen when drospirenone and ethinyl estradiol was administered during late pregnancy at doses of 5, 15, and 45 mg per kg.

FDA Pregnancy Category X

Breast-feeding
Drospirenone and ethinyl estradiol is distributed into human breast milk and may cause adverse effects, jaundice and breast enlargement, on the child. The nursing mother should be advised not to use drospirenone and ethinyl estradiol until she has completely weaned her child.

Pediatrics
Use of drospirenone and ethinyl estradiol is not indicated in children that have not reached menarche.

Drug interactions and/or related problems
The following drug interactions and/or related problems have been selected on the basis of their potential clinical significance (possible mechanism in parentheses where appropriate)—not necessarily inclusive (» = major clinical significance):

Note: Combinations containing any of the following medications, depending on the amount present, may also interact with this medication.

Aldosterone antagonists or
» Angiotensin-converting enzyme (ACE) inhibitors or
Angiotensin-II receptor antagonists or
Anti-inflammatory drugs, nonsteroidal (NSAIDs) or
Diuretics, potassium-sparing or
Heparin
(concurrent use of these medications may increase serum potassium levels due to the antimineralocorticoid activity of drospirenone. Women receiving daily, long-term treatment for chronic conditions with these medications should have their serum potassium levels checked during the first treatment cycle)

Acetaminophen
(oral contraceptives may induce the conjugation of acetaminophen, resulting in decreased plasma concentrations of acetaminophen)

(concurrent use of acetaminophen with oral contraceptives may result in increased plasma concentrations of some synthetic estrogens, possibly by inhibition of conjugation)

Ascorbic acid
(concurrent use of ascorbic acid with oral contraceptives may result in increased plasma concentrations of some synthetic estrogens, possibly by inhibition of conjugation)

Atorvastatin
(coadministration with ethinyl estradiol resulted in an increased ethinyl estradiol AUC of 20%)

Ampicillin or
» Griseofulvin or
Tetracycline
(there have been rare case reports of reduced oral contraceptive effectiveness in women taking ampicillin, griseofulvin, or tetracycline, resulting in unplanned pregnancy. Although the association is very weak, patients, especially long-term users of antibiotic therapy, should be advised of this information and given the option of using an alternate or additional method of contraception while taking any of these antibiotics)

Clofibric acid or
Morphine or
Salicylic acid or
Temazepam
(concurrent use of oral contraceptives may result in increased clearance of clofibric acid, morphine, salicylic acid and temazepam)

» Cyclosporine or
Prednisolone or
» Theophylline
(concurrent use of these medications with combined oral contraceptives containing ethinyl estradiol may inhibit the metabolism of these medications, which results in increased plasma concentrations of cyclosporine, prednisone, and theophylline)

» Carbamazepine or
» Phenobarbital or
Phenylbutazone or
» Phenytoin or
» Rifampin or
St John's Wort
(concurrent use of these medications with oral contraceptives may increase ethinyl estradiol and some progestins metabolism, which could result in reduced contraceptive reliability and increased menstrual irregularities)

» Smoking, tobacco
(oral contraceptives are not recommended with heavy tobacco use because of an increased risk of serious cardiovascular side effects. Risk increases with increased tobacco usage and with age, especially in women over 35 years of age)

Laboratory value alterations

The following have been selected on the basis of their potential clinical significance (possible effect in parentheses where appropriate)—not necessarily inclusive (» = major clinical significance).

With diagnostic test results

Glucose tolerance test, oral
(glucose tolerance may be decreased, resulting in higher 2 hour oral glucose tolerance test results)

Thyroid function tests

Thyroxine (T_4) determinations
(estrogen-induced thyroid-binding globulin elevates the amount of T_4 that is protein bound)

Triiodothyronine (T_3) determinations
(T_3 resin uptake is decreased because estrogens increase serum thyroid-binding globulin [TBG])

With physiology/laboratory test values

Androstenedione or
Ceruloplasmin, serum or
Dehydroepiandrosterone sulfate (DHEA-S) or
Pregnenolone or
Sex hormone-binding globulin (SHBG), serum or
Testosterone or
Thyroid-binding globulin or
Transferrin or cortisol-binding globulin, serum
(oral contraceptives increase protein synthesis of SHBG, thyroid-binding globulin, transferrin, and ceruloplasmin. The serum concentrations of total sex steroidsand corticoids may also increase. The free thyroid concentration is unchanged, and thyroid function is unaltered. Response of the free non–protein-bound component may be variable)

Apolipoprotein A_1, A_2, or B or
Cholesterol, total or
Triglycerides
(in general, the net effect on lipoproteins is the result of the opposing actions of the estrogen and progestin and depends on the ratio between the two hormones. The estrogen component increases triglyceride, very low density lipoproteins (VLDL), and total cholesterol concentrations and decreases low density lipoproteins (LDL). The progestin component, if androgenic, decreases high density lipoproteins (HDL) and increases LDL. The low concentrations of the androgenic progestins in oral contraceptives have slight effect, which is of clinical significance only for some predisposed individuals. Sometimes, older women with higher serum concentrations of cholesterol may experience a reduction caused by a lowering of the serum LDL concentrations. Triglycerides are increased by all oral contraceptives because of the predominant estrogen effects. The increase in total cholesterol caused by desogestrel- and norgestimate-containing oral contraceptives is considered favorable because it is the net result of the increase in HDL_3-C (an estrogen effect) without an increase in HDL_2-C concentrations. The increase in HDL_2-C caused by other low-dose oral contraceptives is considered an androgenic effect of some of the 19−nortestosterone-derived progestins)

Clotting factors VII, VIII, IX, and X or
Prothrombin time or
Norepinephrine-induced platelet aggregability
(oral contraceptives increase levels of prothrombin, clotting factors VII,VIII, IX and X and norepinephrine-induced platelet aggregability)

Folate, serum
(serum folate levels may be decreased with oral contraceptive therapy)

Glucose, plasma or serum or
Insulin
(glucose intolerance has been reported in a significant percentage of oral contraceptives users. Progestogens increase insulin secretion and create insulin resistance; hyperinsulinism can occur in women using oral contraceptives containing greater than 75 micrograms of estrogens. Although fasting blood glucose is not affected in the nondiabetic woman, prediabetic and diabetic women should be carefully monitored while taking oral contraceptives)

High density lipoproteins (HDL), serum
(low-dose oral contraceptives show no change or a decrease in value of HDL; the estrogen component increases HDL and the progestin component, if androgenic, lowers HDL)

Low density lipoproteins (LDL), serum
(some progestins may elevate LDL levels and render control of hyperlipidemias more difficult)

Medical considerations/Contraindications

The medical considerations/contraindications included have been selected on the basis of their potential clinical significance (reasons given in parentheses where appropriate)—not necessarily inclusive (» = major clinical significance).

Except under special circumstances, this medication should not be used when the following medical problem exists:

Adrenal insufficiency or
Hepatic function impairment or
Renal insufficiency
(drospirenone and ethinyl estradiol should not be used in patients with conditions that predispose to hyperkalemia)

» Carcinoma, breast, known or suspected or
» Carcinoma, endometrium or
» Neoplasia, estrogen-dependent, known or suspected
(may worsen conditions; estrogen-containing oral contraceptives should be discontinued and nonhormonal contraceptives initiated, although sometimes progestin-only contraceptives are used for selected patients)

» Cardiac insufficiency
(oral contraceptives should not be used in patients with marginal cardiac reserve; fluid retention sometimes caused by estrogens may aggravate this condition)

» Cerebrovascular disease, active or history of or
» Coronary artery disease, active or history of
(the estrogen component of oral contraceptives has a protective effect against atherosclerosis. Any association with risk in these conditions has been related to thrombosis or interference with cholesterol-lipoprotein profile. Oral contraceptives should be discontinued or strictly avoided if any cardiovascular or cerebrovascular accidents occur; users should switch to nonhormonal contraception. If oral contraceptives are used in women at risk, special monitoring may be required)

Cholestatic jaundice of pregnancy or
Jaundice with prior pill use
(estrogens may increase risk of recurrence)

» Hepatic disease, cholestatic, active or

» Hepatic tumors, benign or malignant, or history of
(metabolism of estrogens may be impaired; also, estrogens may worsen the condition. Oral contraceptives should be discontinued and nonhormonal contraception initiated; for those women with active hepatic disease, oral contraceptive use may be resumed after liver function tests return to normal)

Pregnancy
(although studies have shown no increased risk of birth defects in women who have used oral contraceptives prior to pregnancy, and studies do not suggest a teratogenic effect of oral contraceptives when taken inadvertently during early pregnancy, oral contraceptives should be discontinued if pregnancy is confirmed and should not be used during pregnancy to treat threatened or habitual abortion or to induce withdrawal bleeding as a test for pregnancy)

» Thrombophlebitis, thrombosis, or thromboembolic disorders, active or history of
(oral contraceptives are not recommended for women with predisposing factors, especially those who smoke tobacco or who have an underlying abnormality of the coagulation system, that place them at special risk for thrombosis. Problems generally have not been associated with the low doses of hormones used for contraception for women not at risk for these conditions)
(cases of retinal thrombosis have been reported in association with the use of oral contraceptives. Oral contraceptives should be discontinued in patients with unexplained partial or complete loss of vision; onset of proptosis or diplopia; papilledema; or retinal vascular lesions)
(oral contraceptives should be started no earlier than 4 to 6 weeks after delivery because the immediate postpartum period is associated with an increased risk of thromboembolism)

» Uterine bleeding, abnormal or undiagnosed
(malignancy should be ruled out in cases of persistent or recurring abnormal uterine bleeding.)

Risk-benefit should be considered when the following medical problems exist:

Gallbladder disease, or history of, especially gallstones
(the overall risk is low and thought to be of minimal clinical importance; however, cautious use of oral contraceptives is recommended with known gallbladder disease)

Hypertension
(oral contraceptives have been shown to raise blood pressure in some normotensive women considered to be at high risk [although these women cannot be easily identified] or further raise blood pressure in hypertensive women)

» Hyperkalemia or
» Elevated serum potassium levels
(drospirenone posseses antimineralocorticoid activity, which can increase the potential for hyperkalemia in high-risk patients)

Mental depression, or history of
(the oral contraceptive should be discontinued if significant depression occurs, especially in women with a history of depression)

Migraine headaches
(since migraine headaches have been associated with an increased risk of stroke, discontinuation of oral contraceptives may be warranted if migraine headaches are recurring, persistent, or more severe with use of oral contraceptives, especially for those individuals predisposed to thrombosis)

Surgery, major
(concurrent oral contraceptive usage increases the relative risk of postoperative thromboembolism by two- to four-fold in predisposed women, especially for smokers of tobacco or for those women with a history of thromboembolism. When possible or if appropriate, oral contraceptives should be discontinued at least 4 weeks before and for 2 weeks after a major elective surgery)

Patient monitoring

The following may be especially important in patient monitoring (other tests may be warranted in some patients, depending on condition; » = major clinical significance):

Blood pressure determinations and
Hepatic function determinations and
Papanicolaou (Pap) test and
Physical examinations
(recommended as determined by physician. Special attention should be given to breast, liver, and pelvic area in the physical exam and patients should be encouraged to self-examine breasts monthly)
(special attention to rule out malignancy should be given to patients complaining of persistent or recurring uterine bleeding)

Glucose, serum and
Lipid profile, serum and
Lipoprotein profile, serum
(routine assessment is needed only for women at special risk, including women 35 years of age or older, women who have personal or strong family histories of heart disease, diabetes mellitus, or hypertension, or whose personal history includes gestational diabetes mellitus, xanthomatosis or obesity)

Side/Adverse Effects

The following side/adverse effects have been selected on the basis of their potential clinical significance (possible signs and symptoms in parentheses where appropriate)—not necessarily inclusive:

Those indicating need for immediate medical attention

Incidence rare

Cerebral hemorrhage (fever; sudden loss of consciousness); ***gallbladder disease; myocardial infarction*** (crushing chest pain; unexplained shortness of breath); ***pulmonary embolism*** (anxiety; burning pain in lower abdomen; chest pain; chills; convulsions; coughing; feeling of heat; feeling of warmth in lips and tongue; headache; nervousness; numbness of the fingertips; pain in lower back; pelvis, or stomach; ringing in the ears); ***thromboembolism or thrombosis*** (abdominal pain, sudden, severe, or continuing; coughing up blood; headache, severe or sudden; loss of coordination, sudden; pains in chest, groin, or leg, especially calf of leg; shortness of breath, sudden, unexplained; slurring of speech, sudden; vision changes, sudden; weakness, numbness, or pain in arm or leg, unexplained)—mainly exhibited in women having predisposing or pre-existing conditions, especially for those who smoke tobacco, but the event may be idiopathic; ***thrombophlebitis*** (bluish color; changes in skin color; pain; tenderness; swelling of foot or leg)

Those indicating need for medical attention

Incidence more frequent, especially during the first 3 months of oral contraceptive use

Changes in the menstrual bleeding pattern or intermenstrual bleeding, such as amenorrhea (complete stoppage of menstrual bleeding over several months); ***breakthrough bleeding*** (vaginal bleeding between regular menstrual periods, which may require the use of a pad or a tampon); ***scanty menses*** (very light menstrual bleeding); ***or spotting*** (light vaginal bleeding between regular menstrual periods)

Incidence less frequent

Headaches or migraines, worsening or increased frequency of; hypertension, worsening or exacerbation; vaginal candidiasis or vaginitis, sporadic or recurrent (vaginal discharge, thick, white, or curd-like, or vaginal itching or other irritation)

Incidence rare

Breast tumors (lumps in breast)—primarily in women having a predisposing or pre-existing condition; ***hepatic focal nodular hyperplasia, hepatitis, or hepatocellular carcinoma*** (pains in stomach, side, or abdomen, or yellow eyes or skin)—primarily in women having a predisposing or pre-existing condition, especially those who smoke tobacco; ***hepatic cell adenomas, benign*** (swelling, pain, or tenderness in upper abdominal area); ***mental depression, slight worsening***—in pre-existing conditions

Those indicating need for medical attention only if they continue or are bothersome

Incidence more frequent

Abdominal cramping or bloating; acne—usually less frequent after the first 3 months of use; ***breast pain, tenderness, or swelling; change in cervical erosion and secretion; change in corneal curvature; cholestatic jaundice; dizziness; infertility after discontinuation; intolerance to contact lenses; sodium and fluid retention*** (swelling of ankles and feet)

Incidence less frequent

Gain or loss of body or facial hair; libido changes (increase or decrease of interest in sexual intercourse); ***melasma*** (brown, blotchy spots on exposed skin); ***weight gain or loss***

Note: *Melasma* usually is temporary but can be permanent. Women having dark complexions, having a history of melasma during pregnancy, or having prolonged exposure to sunlight are most susceptible to developing melasma.

Overdose

Serious adverse effects generally do not occur with an acute overdosage. When children have accidently ingested a large amount of an oral contraceptive, more serious adverse effects also did not result. Withdrawal bleeding has occasionally occurred in young girls and does not require treatment.

For more information on the management of overdose or unintentional ingestion, **contact a poison control center** (see *Poison Control Center Listing*).

Clinical effects of overdose

The following effects have been selected on the basis of their potential clinical significance (possible signs and symptoms in parentheses where appropriate)—not necessarily inclusive:

Nausea or vomiting

Treatment of overdose

Specific treatment—Nausea or vomiting is treated for symptomatic relief.

Supportive care—Patients in whom intentional overdose is known or suspected should be referred for psychiatric consultation.

Monitoring—Serum concentrations of potassium and sodium, and evidence of metabolic acidosis, should be monitored

Patient Consultation

As an aid to patient consultation, refer to *Advice for the Patient, Drospirenone and Ethinyl Estradiol (Systemic)*.

In providing consultation, consider emphasizing the following selected information (» = major clinical significance):

Before using this medication

» Conditions affecting use, especially:
  Hypersensitivity to estrogens or progestins
  Pregnancy—Not recommended for use during pregnancy
  Breast-feeding—Oral contraceptives are distributed into breast milk
  Use in adolescents—Careful counseling may be required to increase compliance
  Other medications, especially angiotensin-converting enzyme (ACE) inhibitors, carbamazepine, cyclosporine, griseofulvin, phenobarbital, phenytoin, rifampin, theophylline, or tobacco smoking
  Other medical problems, especially carcinoma of the breast (known or suspected); carcinoma of the endometrium; cardiac insufficiency; cerebrovascular disease—especially if patient smokes cigarettes (active or history of); coronary artery disease; estrogen-dependent neoplasia (known or suspected); hepatic disease, cholestatic (active); hepatic tumors, benign or malignant (active or history of); hyperkalemia or elevated serum potassium levels; thrombophlebitis, thrombosis, or thromboembolic disorders (active or history of); or uterine bleeding (abnormal or undiagnosed)

Proper use of this medication

» Reading patient package insert carefully
  Using an additional method of birth control for the first 7 days; some clinicians may recommend that an additional method of birth control be used during the first cycle of oral contraceptive use
» Compliance with therapy; taking medication at the same time each day, at 24-hour intervals
  Keeping an extra 1-month supply available when possible
  Taking tablets in proper (color-coded) sequence
» Proper dosing
  Missed dose: Missing 1 yellow "active" tablet—Taking as soon as possible; taking the next tablet at the scheduled time even if it means taking two tablets in one day
  Missing 2 yellow "active" tablets in a row in the first or second week—Taking two tablets on the day you remember and two tablets the following day; continuing on regular dosing schedule and using another birth control method for 7 days after the last missed dose
  Missing 2 yellow "active" tablets in a row in the 3 week or
  Missing 3 or more yellow "active" tablets in a row (during the first 3 weeks)—
    Using Day-1 start: Starting a new cycle on the day you remember; discarding remaining doses for current cycle and using a second method of birth control, additionally, for 7 days after the last missed dose; contacting health care professional if two menstrual periods are missed
    Using Sunday start: Continuing on regular dosing schedule for current cycle until Sunday; on Sunday, throwing out remaining doses for current cycle and beginning a new cycle; using an additional method of birth control for 7 days after the last missed dose; contacting health care professional if two menstrual periods are missed
  Missing any of the last 7 white tablets is not important, but beginning new cycle on time is essential
  Proper storage

Precautions while using this medication

» Regular visits to physician at least every 6 to 12 months to check progress
  What to expect and do if vaginal bleeding occurs
  What to expect and do if a menstrual period is missed; contacting health professional if two menstrual periods are missed
» Stopping medication immediately and checking with physician if pregnancy is suspected
  If scheduled for laboratory tests, telling physician if taking birth control pills; certain blood tests may be affected by oral contraceptives
  Not refilling an old prescription for oral contraceptives without having a physical examination by physician, especially after a pregnancy

Side/adverse effects

Signs of potential side effects, especially cerebral hemorrhage; gallbladder disease; myocardial infarction; pulmonary embolism; thromboembolism or thrombosis; thrombophlebitis; changes in the menstrual bleeding pattern or intermenstrual bleeding; headaches or migraines; hypertension, worsening; vaginal candidiasis or vaginitis; breast tumors (usually for predisposed individuals); hepatic focal nodular hyperplasia, hepatitis, or hepatocellular carcinoma; hepatic cell adenomas, benign; slight worsening of mental depression

Cigarette smoking combined with oral contraceptive use causes increased risk of serious thromboembolic or hepatic side effects, especially for heavy smokers or women over age 35

General Dosing Information

For oral dosing forms:

Maximum contraceptive effect is obtained by taking doses at 24-hour intervals and beginning the new regimen on time. It is recommended to take drospirenone and ethinyl estradiol combination oral contraceptive at the same time each day, preferably after the evening meal or at bedtime.

To begin taking drospirenone and ethinyl estradiol combination oral contraceptive, the first tablet is taken either on Day 1 (first day of menstrual bleeding) of the menstrual cycle or the first Sunday following the start of menses. The treatment regimen consists of 21 tablets of a monophasic combined drospirenone and ethinyl estradiol in yellow color and 7 inert (nonhormonal) tablets in white color.

The patient should be advised to begin her next and all subsequent 28-day treatment cycles of drospirenone and ethinyl estradiol combination oral contraceptive on the same day of the week that she began her first treatment cycle, following the same schedule. A periodic pill-free *rest period* is not recommended. Patients should be informed to take their yellow tablets on the next day after ingestion of the last white tablet, regardless of whether or not a menstrual period has occurred or is still in progress.

Treatment with drospirenone and ethinyl estradiol combination oral contraceptive may be initiated 4 weeks postpartum in the nonlactating mother; the increased risk of thromboembolic disease associated with the postpartum period must be considered. The use of drospirenone and ethinyl estradiol combination oral contraceptive is not recommended in the nursing mother until she has completely weaned her child.

Oral Dosage Forms

DROSPIRENONE AND ETHINYL ESTRADIOL TABLETS

Usual Adult and Adolescent Dose

Contraceptive, systemic—
  Oral, 1 yellow active tablet a day for twenty-one consecutive days commencing on Day 1 of the menstrual cycle or on the first Sunday after the menstrual cycle begins followed by 1 white inert tablet a day on menstrual cycle days 22 through 28. The next round of treatment is begun on the eighth day after the last tablet of the previous cycle has been taken. Tablets should be taken at the same time each day, preferably after the evening meal or at bedtime.

Note: With a Sunday start schedule, the patient should take her first tablet on the first Sunday after the onset of menstruation. If the patients period begins on a Sunday, she should take her first tablet that same day.
  With a Day-1 start schedule, the patient should take her first tablet on Day 1 of the menstrual cycle.
  The last seven tablets of the twenty-eight day cycle contain no hormones. These seven companion tablets are a different color, white, from those containing hormones.

Strength(s) usually available

U.S.—

Note: Available in twenty-eight–day cycle which includes seven days of placebo tablets.

3 mg of drospirenone and 0.03 mg of ethinyl estradiol (Rx) [*Yasmin* (corn starch NF; ferric oxide pigment; hydroxylpropylmethyl cellulose USP; lactose monohydrate NF; macrogol 6000 NF; magnesium stearate NF; modified starch NF; povidone 25000 USP; talc USP; titanium dioxide USP; yellow NF)].

Packaging and storage

Store at 25 °C (77 °F); excursions permitted to 15-30° C (59-86° F) in a tight container.

Auxiliary labeling

- Avoid cigarettes.
- Avoid too much sun or use of sunlamp.

Note

Include mandatory patient package inserts (PPIs) (the brief summary of patient labeling and the detailed patient labeling) when dispensing.

Developed: 07/25/2001

DROTRECOGIN ALFA Systemic†

VA CLASSIFICATION (Primary): BL119

Commonly used brand name(s): *Xigris*.

Note: For a listing of dosage forms and brand names by country availability, see *Dosage Forms* section(s).

†Not commercially available in Canada.

Category

Antithrombotic.

Indications

Accepted

Sepsis, severe, reduction of mortality in—Drotrecogin alfa is indicated for the reduction of mortality in adult patients with severe sepsis (sepsis associated with acute organ dysfunction) who have a high risk of death, as determined by acute physiology and chronic health evaluation (APACHE) II scores.

Note: Acute organ dysfunction defined as one of the following: cardiovascular dysfunction (shock, hypotension, or the need for vasopressor support despite adequate fluid resuscitation); respiratory dysfunction (relative hypoxemia [PaO_2/FiO_2 ratio less than 250]); renal dysfunction (oliguria despite adequate fluid resuscitation); thrombocytopenia (platelet count less than 80,000 per mm^3 or 50% decrease from the highest value the previous 3 days); or metabolic acidosis with elevated lactic acid concentrations.

Acceptance not established

Efficacy has not been established for reducing the mortality of adult patients with severe sepsis and a lower risk of death.

Pharmacology/Pharmacokinetics

Physicochemical characteristics

Source—Drotrecogin alfa is a recombinant form of human Activated Protein C.

Molecular weight—Approximately 55 kilodaltons.

Mechanism of action/Effect

The specific mechanisms by which drotrecogin alfa exerts its effect on survival in patients with severe sepsis are not completely understood.

In patients with severe sepsis, drotrecogin alfa infusions produced dose dependent declines in D-dimer and IL-6. Compared to placebo, drotrecogin alfa treated patients experienced more rapid declines in D-dimer, PAI-1 levels, thrombin-antithrombin levels, prothrombin F1.2, IL-6, more rapid increases in protein C and antithrombin levels, and normalization of plasminogen.

Activated Protein C exerts an antithrombotic effect by proteolytic inactivation of Factors Va and VIIIa. *In vitro* Activated Protein C may exert an anti-inflammatory effect by inhibiting human tumor necrosis factor production by monocytes, by blocking leukocyte adhesion to selectins, and by limiting the thrombin-induced inflammatory responses within the microvascular endothelium. *In vitro* Activated Protein C has indirect profibrinolytic activity through its ability to inhibit plasminogen activator inhibitor-1 and limiting generation of activated thrombin-activatable-fibrinolysis-inhibitor.

Absorption

In patients with severe sepsis, steady-state concentrations (C_{ss}) are proportional to infusion rates of 12 to 30 micrograms per kg of body weight per hour.

Biotransformation

Drotrecogin alfa and endogenous Activated Protein C are inactivated by endogenous plasma protease inhibitors.

Time to steady-state concentration

2 hours.

Steady-state concentration

45 nanograms per mL.

Duration of action

2 hours post infusion—plasma concentrations fell below assay quantitation limit of 10 nanograms per mL.

Elimination

40 L per hr (range of 27 to 52 L per hr)—median clearance.

Precautions to Consider

Cross-sensitivity and/or related problems

Derived from an established human cell line, drotrecogin alfa has the potential for immunogenicity. The incidence of antibody development has not been adequately determined.

In clinical trials, two patients had a detectable antibody response, but the relationship of the clinical events to antibody formation is not clear.

Carcinogenicity

Long-term studies in animals to evaluate potential carcinogenicity of drotrecogin alfa have not been performed.

Mutagenicity

Drotrecogin alfa was not mutagenic in an *in vivo* micronucleus study in mice or in an *in vitro* chromosomal aberration study in human peripheral blood lymphocytes with or without rat liver metabolic activation.

Pregnancy/Reproduction

Fertility—The potential of drotrecogin alfa to impair fertility has not been evaluated in male or female animals.

Pregnancy—Studies have not been performed in humans

Drotrecogin alfa should be given to pregnant women only if clearly needed.

Studies have not been performed in animals.

FDA Pregnancy Category C.

Breast-feeding

It is not known whether drotrecogin alfa is distributed into breast milk or absorbed systemically after ingestion. Due to the potential for adverse effects to the nursing infant, a decision should be made whether to discontinue nursing or discontinue the medicine, taking into account the importance of the drug to the mother.

Pediatrics

Safety and efficacy have not been established in patients up to 18 years of age. The efficacy of drotrecogin alfa cannot be extrapolated to pediatric patients with severe sepsis.

Geriatrics

In clinical studies there was a greater reduction in mortality in patients with more severe physiologic disturbances, in patients with serious underlying disease predating sepsis, and in older patients.

Studies performed in approximately 910 patients 65 years of age or older have not demonstrated geriatrics-specific problems that would limit the usefulness of drotrecogin alfa in the elderly.

Drug interactions and/or related problems

The following drug interactions and/or related problems have been selected on the basis of their potential clinical significance (possible mechanism in parentheses where appropriate)—not necessarily inclusive (» = major clinical significance):

Note: Combinations containing any of the following medications, depending on the amount present, may also interact with this medication.

Drug interactions have not been studied in patients with severe sepsis.

» Anticoagulants, oral or

» Glycoprotein IIb/IIIa inhibitors

(the risk of bleeding must be weighed against the anticipated benefits when drotrecogin alfa is used within 7 days of these medications)

» Aspirin or

» Platelet inhibitors
(the risk of bleeding must be weighed against the anticipated benefits when drotrecogin alfa is used within 7 days of aspirin (more than 650 mg per day) or other platelet inhibitors)

» Heparin
(concurrent use of 15 units per kg of body weight per hour or greater has not been studied and may increase the risk of bleeding)

» Thrombolytic agents
(the risk of bleeding must be weighed against the anticipated benefits when drotrecogin alfa is used within 3 days of these medications)

Laboratory value alterations

The following have been selected on the basis of their potential clinical significance (possible effect in parentheses where appropriate)—not necessarily inclusive (» = major clinical significance).

With physiology/laboratory test values
APTT assay
(drotrecogin alfa may variably prolong the APTT (activated partial thromboplastin time). Present in plasma samples, it may interfere with one-stage coagulation assays based on the APTT (such as factor VIII, IX, and XI assays); this interaction may result in an apparent factor concentration that is lower than the true concentration)

Note: Drotrecogin alfa has minimal effect on the PT (prothrombin time) and does not interfere with one-stage factor assays such as factor II, V, VII, and X assays.

Medical considerations/Contraindications

The medical considerations/contraindications included have been selected on the basis of their potential clinical significance (reasons given in parentheses where appropriate)—not necessarily inclusive (» = major clinical significance).

Except under special circumstances, this medication should not be used when the following medical problem exists:

» Catheter, epidural, or
» Cerebral herniation, or
» Head trauma, severe or
» Internal bleeding, active, or
» Intracranial or intraspinal surgery, within 2 months, or
» Intracranial mass lesion, or
» Intracranial neoplasm, or
» Stroke, hemorrhagic, within 3 months, or
» Trauma, with increased risk of life-threatening bleeding
(drotrecogin alfa is contraindicated due to the increased risk of bleeding, which could be associated with a high risk of death or significant morbidity)

» Hypersensitivity to drotrecogin alfa or any component of the product
» Surgical procedure, invasive or with bleeding risk
(drotrecogin alfa should be discontinued 2 hours prior to surgery; after hemostasis has been established, reinitiation of therapy may be considered 12 hours after major invasive procedures or restarted immediately after uncomplicated less invasive procedures.)

Risk-benefit should be considered when the following medical problems exist:

Aneurysm, intracranial, or
Arteriovenous malformation, intracranial, or
Bleeding diathesis, or
Hepatic disease, chronic and severe, or
Platelet count less than 30,000 x 10^6 per L or
Prothrombin time-INR greater than 3.0 or
Other conditions in which bleeding constitutes a significant hazard
(may increase the risk of bleeding)

» Gastrointestinal bleeding
(the risk of bleeding must be weighed against the anticipated benefits when drotrecogin alfa is used within 6 weeks of this condition)

» Recent surgery or
» Single organ dysfunction
(careful consideration of risk benefit; study has shown higher mortality in these patients who were taking drotrecogin alfa compared to placebo group)

Side/Adverse Effects

The following side/adverse effects have been selected on the basis of their potential clinical significance (possible signs and symptoms in parentheses where appropriate)—not necessarily inclusive:

Those indicating need for medical attention

Incidence more frequent
Bleeding

Note: In clinical trials, 25% of treated patients experienced at least one *bleeding* event, mainly ecchymoses or gastrointestinal tract bleeding, during a 28-day study period. Serious bleeding, defined as any intracranial hemorrhage, any life-threatening bleed, any bleeding event requiring the administration of more than 3 units of packed red blood cells per day for 2 consecutive days, or any bleeding event assessed as a serious adverse event, occurred in 3.5% of treated patients.
If clinically important *bleeding* occurs, drotrecogin alfa should be immediately discontinued. After hemostasis has been established, reinstitution of therapy may be considered.

Overdose

For more information on the management of overdose or unintentional ingestion, **contact a poison control center** (see *Poison Control Center Listing*).

Clinical effects of overdose

In post-marketing experience, there have been a limited number of medication error reports of excessive rate of drotrecogin alfa infusion for short periods of time. No unexpected adverse events were observed during the overdose period. However, this information is insufficient to assess whether drotrecogin alfa overdose is associated with an increased hemorrhage risk beyond that observed with drotrecogin alfa administered at the recommended dose.

Treatment of overdose

Specific treatment—
There is no known antidote for drotrecogin alfa. In case of overdose, stop drotrecogin alfa infusion immediately.

Monitoring—
Patients experiencing an overdose should be monitored closely for hemorrhagic complications.

Patient Consultation

As an aid to patient consultation, refer to *Advice for the Patient, Drotrecogin Alfa (Systemic)*.

In providing consultation, consider emphasizing the following selected information (» = major clinical significance):

Before using this medication

» Conditions affecting use, especially:
Hypersensitivity to drotrecogin alfa or any component of the product
Other medications, especially aspirin, glycoprotein IIb/IIIa inhibitors, heparin, oral anticoagulants, platelet inhibitors, and thrombolytic agents.
Other medical problems, especially active internal bleeding, cerebral herniation, use of epidural catheter, gastrointestinal bleeding, hemorrhagic stroke, intracranial mass lesion or neoplasm, recent intracranial or intraspinal surgery, recent surgery, severe head trauma, single organ dysfunction, surgical procedure (invasive or with bleeding risk), or trauma with risk of bleeding.

Proper use of this medication

» Proper dosing

Precautions while using this medication

» Importance of following instructions of health care professional to prevent serious bleeding

Side/adverse effects

Signs of potential side effects, especially bleeding.

Parenteral Dosage Forms

DROTRECOGIN ALFA FOR INJECTION

Usual adult dose

Reduction of mortality in patients with severe sepsis at high risk of death—
Intravenous, 24 mcg per kg of body weight per hour for a total of 96 hours. Dosage adjustment based on clinical or laboratory parameters is not recommended.

Note: If the infusion is interrupted, drotrecogin alfa should be restarted at the 24 mcg per kg of body weight per hour infusion rate. Dose escalation or bolus doses are not recommended.

Usual pediatric dose

Reduction of mortality in patients with severe sepsis—
Safety and efficacy have not been established.

Usual geriatric dose

See *Usual adult dose*.

Strength(s) usually available

U.S.—

5-mg vial containing 5.3 mg of drotrecogin alfa (activated) (Rx) [*Xigris* (sodium chloride 40.3 mg; sodium citrate 10.9 mg; sucrose 31.8 mg)].

20-mg vial containing 20.8 mg of drotrecogin alfa (activated) [*Xigris* (sodium chloride 158.1 mg; sodium citrate 42.9 mg; sucrose 124.9 mg)].

Packaging and storage

Unreconstituted vials: Store in a refrigerator between 36 and 46° F (2 and 8° C). Protect from light. Retain in carton until time of use. Do not freeze. Do not use beyond the expiration date.

Reconstituted intravenous solution: May be stored at controlled room temperature between 59 and 86° F (15 and 30° C), but the infusion must be started within 3 hours.

Preparation of dosage form

Use appropriate aseptic technique during the preparation of drotrecogin alfa for intravenous administration.

Calculate the approximate amount of drotrecogin alfa needed based upon the patient's actual body weight and duration of this infusion period. The maximum duration of infusion form one preparation step is 12 hours. Multiple infusion periods will be needed to cover the entire 96-hour duration of administration.

mg of drotrecogin alfa= (patient weight, kg) x 24 mcg/kg/hr x (hours of infusion)/1000

Round the actual amount of drotrecogin alfa to be prepared to the nearest 5 mg increment to avoid discarding any reconstituted solution.

Determine the number of vials of drotrecogin alfa needed to make up this amount.

Reconstitute the 5-mg vial with 2.5 mL of Sterile Water for Injection, USP and the 20-mg vial with 10 mL of Sterile Water for Injection, USP. The resulting concentration of drotrecogin alfa is 2 mg per mL.

Do not invert or shake the vial. Gently swirl the vial until all of the powder is completely dissolved.

Withdraw the appropriate amount of reconstituted drotrecogin alfa and add to an infusion bag of sterile 0.9% Sodium Chloride Injection. When adding the reconstituted drotrecogin alfa into the infusion bag, direct the stream to the side of the bag to minimize the agitation of the solution. Gently invert the infusion bag to obtain a homogenous solution.

Do not transport the infusion bag between locations using mechanical delivery systems.

Inspect visually for particulate matter and discoloration prior to administration.

Drotrecogin alfa should be administered via a dedicated intravenous line or a dedicated lumen of a multilumen central venous catheter.

Intravenous infusion pump administration—The solution of reconstituted drotrecogin alfa is typically diluted into an infusion bag containing sterile 0.9% Sodium Chloride Injection to a final concentration between 100 and 200 micrograms per mL.

Syringe pump administration—The solution of reconstituted drotrecogin alfa is typically diluted with sterile 0.9% Sodium Chloride Injection to a final concentration between 100 and 1000 micrograms per mL. When administering at low concentrations (less than approximately 200 micrograms per mL) at low flow rates (less than approximately 5 mL per hour), the infusion set must be primed for approximately 15 minutes at a flow rate of approximately 5 mL per hour.

Stability

If the intravenous solution is not administered immediately, the solution may be stored refrigerated 2 to 8° C (36 and 46° F) for up to 12 hours. If the prepared solution is refrigerated prior to administration, the maximum time limit for use of the intravenous solution, including, preparation, refrigeration, and administration, is 24 hours.

Incompatibilities

No incompatibilities have been observed between drotrecogin alfa and glass infusion bottles or infusion bags and syringes made of polyvinylchloride, polyethylene, polypropylene, or polyolefin.

The only solutions that can be administered through the same line with drotrecogin alfa are 0.9% sodium chloride injection, Lactated Ringer's injection, dextrose injection, or dextrose and sodium chloride injection.

Revised: 04/14/2005
Developed: 06/30/2002

DULOXETINE Systemic†

VA CLASSIFICATION (Primary): CN603

Commonly used brand name(s): *Cymbalta*.

Note: For a listing of dosage forms and brand names by country availability, see *Dosage Forms* section(s).

†Not commercially available in Canada.

Category

Antidepressant; Antineuralgic.

Indications

Accepted

Depressive disorder, major (treatment)—Duloxetine is indicated for the treatment of major depressive disorder (MDD).

Pain, peripheral neuropathic, diabetic (treatment)—Duloxetine is indicated for the management of neuropathic pain associated with diabetic peripheral neuropathy.

Unaccepted

Duloxetine is not approved for use in treating bipolar depression.

Pharmacology/Pharmacokinetics

Physicochemical characteristics

Molecular weight—Duloxetine: 333.88.

Solubility—Slightly soluble in water.

Mechanism of action/Effect

The exact mechanism of action is unknown. However, the antidepressant and pain inhibitory actions are believed to be related to its potentiation of serotonergic and noradrenergic activity in the CNS. Duloxetine undergoes extensive metabolism but the major metabolites have not been shown to contribute to duloxetine pharmacologic activity.

Duloxetine does not inhibit monoamine oxidase (MAO) and has no significant affinity for dopaminergic, adrenergic, cholinergic, histaminergic, opioid, glutamate, and GABA receptors *in vitro* .

Absorption

Well absorbed following a 2-hour lag. Food does not affect the C_{max} but, delays the time to reach peak concentration from 6 to 10 hours and decreases the AUC by about 10%. There is also a 3-hour delay in absorption and a one-third increase in apparent clearance after an evening dose compared to a morning dose.

Distribution

Volume of distribution (Vol_D)—About 1640 L.

Protein binding

Very high (>90%), primarily to albumin and α_1-acid glycoprotein. Binding is not affected by renal or hepatic impairment.

Biotransformation

Duloxetine undergoes extensive metabolism via oxidation of the naphthyl ring followed by conjugation and further oxidation. Metabolites found in plasma include 4-hydroxy duloxetine glucuronide and 5-hydroxy, 6-methoxy duloxetine sulfate.

Half-life

Elimination—12 hours (range 8 to 17 hours).

Time to peak concentration

6 hours post dose.

Time to steady state:

Achieved after 3 days of dosing.

Elimination

Renal: 70% as metabolites, trace (<1% of the dose) unchanged.

Fecal: about 20%.

Precautions to Consider

Carcinogenicity

In a 2-year study done in mice given oral doses of duloxetine (11 times the maximum recommended human dose [MRHD 60 mg/day] on a mg/m² basis), there was an increase incidence of hepatocellular adenomas and carcinomas in females. There was not an increase in incidence of tumors in male mice given 8 times the MRHD. The no-effect dose was 4 times the MRHD.

Tumorigenicity

Studies done in rats given dietary doses of duloxetine (4 and 6 times the MRHD on a mg/m² basis), demonstrated no increase in incidence of tumors.

Mutagenicity

Duloxetine was not mutagenic in the bacterial reverse mutation assay (Ames test), and not clastogenic in an *in vivo* chromosomal aberration test in mouse bone marrow cells. Additionally, it was not genotoxic in an *in vitro* mammalian forward gene mutation assay in mouse lymphoma cells or in an *in vitro* unscheduled DNA assay in rat hepatocytes, and did not induce *in vivo* sister chromatid exchange assay in Chinese hamster bone marrow cells.

Pregnancy/Reproduction

Fertility—Duloxetine did not alter mating or fertility in male or female rats given oral doses (7 times the MRHD on a mg/m^2 basis) prior to and throughout mating.

Pregnancy—Duloxetine crosses the placenta. Adequate and well controlled studies in humans have not been done.

Studies in animals have shown duloxetine causes adverse effects on embryo/fetal and postnatal development.

Studies done in rats and rabbits given oral doses of duloxetine (7 times the MRHD on a mg/m^2 basis) during organogenesis showed no evidence of teratogenicity. However, fetal weights were decreased at this dose. The no effect dose for rats was 2 times the MRHD on a mg/m^2 basis and 3 times the MRHD on a mg/m^2 basis for rabbits. When pregnant rats were given oral doses of duloxetine (5 times the MRHD on a mg/m^2 basis) throughout gestation and lactation the survival rate to 1 day postpartum and birth weight were decreased. Behavior consistent with increased reactivity such as increased startle response and decreased habituation of locomotor activity were observed.

Non-teratogenic effects—When exposed to serotonin reuptake inhibitors (SSRIs) or selective norepinephrine reuptake inhibitors (SNRIs) late in the third trimester, neonates have developed complications requiring prolonged hospitalization, respiratory support, and tube feeding and these can arise immediately upon delivery. Features consistent with a direct toxic effect of SSRIs and SNRIs or a drug discontinuation syndrome including respiratory distress, cyanosis, apnea, seizures, temperature instability, feeding difficulty, vomiting, hypoglycemia, hypotonia, hypertonia, hyperreflexia, tremor, jitteriness, irritability, and constant crying have been reported. In some cases, it should be noted that the clinical picture is consistent with serotonin syndrome. When treating a pregnant woman with duloxetine during the third trimester, the physician should carefully consider the potential risks and benefits of treatment. The physician may consider tapering duloxetine in the third trimester.

FDA Pregnancy Category C

Labor and delivery—The effect of duloxetine in humans is unknown. Duloxetine should be used in labor and delivery only if the potential benefit justifies the potential risk to the fetus

Breast-feeding

It is not known whether duloxetine and/or its metabolites are distributed into breast milk. However, duloxetine and/or its metabolites are distributed into the milk of lactating rats. Duloxetine is not recommended for use while breast-feeding.

Pediatrics

Safety and efficacy in pediatric patients have not been established. Duloxetine is not approved for use in pediatric patients.

Antidepressants increase the risk of suicidal thinking and behavior (suicidality) in children and adolescents with major depressive disorder (MDD) and other psychiatric disorders. Anyone considering the use of duloxetine or any other antidepressant in a child or adolescent must balance this risk with the clinical need and families and caregivers should be advised of the need for close observation and communication with the prescriber.

Pooled analyses of short-term placebo controlled trials of nine antidepressant drugs in children and adolescents with MDD, obsessive compulsive disorder, or other psychiatric disorders have revealed a greater risk of adverse events representing suicidality during the first few months of treatment in those receiving antidepressants.

Geriatrics

Appropriate studies performed to date have not demonstrated geriatric-specific problems that would limit the usefulness of duloxetine in the elderly. However, greater sensitivity of some elderly cannot be ruled out.

Drug interactions and/or related problems

The following drug interactions and/or related problems have been selected on the basis of their potential clinical significance (possible mechanism in parentheses where appropriate)—not necessarily inclusive (» = major clinical significance):

Note: Combinations containing any of the following medications, depending on the amount present, may also interact with this medication.

Alcohol
(duloxetine and alcohol may interact to cause liver injury; use is not recommended in patients with substantial alcohol use)

» Antidepressants, tricyclic (TCAs) such as
Amitriptyline or
Imipramine or
Nortriptyline
(caution; TCA concentrations may need monitoring and the TCA dose reduced)

» Antiarrhythmics, type 1C such as
Flecainide or
Propafenone
(caution; concentration of antiarrhythmic may increase)

Cimetidine or
Fluvoxamine or
Quinolone antimicrobials such as
Ciprofloxacin or
Enoxacin
(co-administration with CYP1A2 inhibitors increase AUC over 5-fold, C_{max} about 2.5-fold, and $T_{1/2}$ 3-fold)

CNS acting drugs
(caution when taken in combination with other centrally acting drugs)

» CYP2D6 inhibitors, such as
Desipramine or
Fluoxetine or
Paroxetine or
Quinidine
(use with caution; concomitant use of duloxetine and other drugs metabolized by CYP2D6 may require lower doses of duloxetine or the other drug)

Drugs that affect gastric acidity
(duloxetine has an enteric coating and in extremely acidic conditions, the coating may undergo hydrolysis to form naphthol; drugs that raise GI pH may lead to an earlier duloxetine release)

Highly protein-bound drugs
(caution; duloxetine is highly bound to plasma proteins; concurrent use with other highly protein-bound drugs may cause increased concentrations, resulting in adverse events)

» Monoamine oxidase inhibitors (MAOIs)
(use is contraindicated within at least 14 days of discontinuing treatment with an MAOI and 5 days after stopping duloxetine before starting an MAOI; serious, sometimes fatal, reactions including hyperthermia, rigidity, myoclonus, autonomic instability with rapid fluctuations of vital signs, and mental changes that include extreme agitation progressing to delirium and coma have been reported)

» Phenothiazines
(caution; concentration of phenothiazines may increase)

» Thioridazine
(should not be co-administered; risk of serious ventricular arrythmias and sudden death associated with elevated levels of thioridazine)

Laboratory value alterations

The following have been selected on the basis of their potential clinical significance (possible effect in parentheses where appropriate)—not necessarily inclusive (» = major clinical significance).

With physiology/laboratory test values
Alanine aminotransferase (ALT [SGPT]), serum and
Aspartate aminotransferase (AST [SGOT]), serum and
Alkaline phosphatase and
Bilirubin, total and
Creatine phosphokinase (CPK)
(may increase in small amounts; evidence of a dose-response relationship for ALT and AST elevation)

Medical considerations/Contraindications

The medical considerations/contraindications included have been selected on the basis of their potential clinical significance (reasons given in parentheses where appropriate)—not necessarily inclusive (» = major clinical significance).

Except under special circumstances, this medication should not be used when the following medical problem exists:

» Hepatic insufficiency
(should not be administered to these patients due to the markedly increased exposure to duloxetine that occurs)

» Hypersensitivity to duloxetine or any of its inactive ingredients

» Narrow-angle glaucoma, uncontrolled
(contraindicated; increased risk of mydriasis)

» Renal function impairment, severe
(use is not recommended in patients with creatinine clearance <30 mL/min; increased plasma concentration of circulating metabolites)

Risk-benefit should be considered when the following medical problems exist:

Alcohol abuse or history of
(use of duloxetine not recommended in patients with substantial alcohol use; increased risk for liver injury)

» Bipolar disorder or risk of
(may increase likelihood of precipitation of a mixed/manic episode in these patients; prior to initiating duloxetine treatment, patient should be adequately screened to determine if they are at risk for bipolar disorder; such screening should include a detailed psychiatric history, including a family history of suicide, bipolar disorder, and depression.)

» Chronic liver disease
(should ordinarily not be prescribed to patients with evidence of chronic liver disease because of possibility of duloxetine aggravating pre-existing liver disease)

Diabetes mellitus
(may have small increases in fasting blood glucose)

Conditions that slow gastric emptying (i.e., some diabetics)
(caution is advised; may affect stability of enteric tablet coating)

Coronary artery disease, unstable or
Myocardial infarction, recent history of
(caution is advised; use in these patients not systematically evaluated)

» Hepatotoxicity
(increase risk of elevation of serum transaminase levels)

» Mania, history of
(caution; activation of hypomania or mania has been reported in depressed patients treated with duloxetine)

» Narrow-angle glaucoma, controlled
(caution; increase risk of mydriasis)

» Seizures, history of
(use with care)

Patient monitoring

The following may be especially important in patient monitoring (other tests may be warranted in some patients, depending on condition; » = major clinical significance):

» Careful supervision of patients including those with:
Abnormal behaviors (i.e., agitation, panic attacks, hostility) or
Clinical worsening of their depression or
Major depressive disorder or co-morbid depression in the setting of other psychiatric illness or
Suicidal ideation and behavior (suicidality)
(families and caregivers of patients being treated with duloxetine should be alerted to the need to monitor patients for the emergence of symptoms of depression or suicide, especially during early treatment phase or at the time of dose changes, either increase or decrease; prescribing the smallest number of capsules necessary for good patient management is recommended to decrease risk of overdose; consideration should be given to changing the therapeutic regimen, including possibly discontinuing the medicine, in patients whose depression is persistently worse or whose emergent suicidality or other symptoms are severe, abrupt in onset, or were not part of the patient's presenting symptoms)

Liver function
(reports of ALT and AST elevation of greater than 3 times and greater than 5 times the upper limit of normal, respectively; post-marketing report of transaminase elevation levels to more than twenty times the upper limit of normal)

Signs of misuse or abuse including
Development of tolerance or
Drug-seeking behavior or
Incrementation of dose
(as with any CNS active drug physicians should carefully observer patients for potential abuse, especially in patients with a history of drug abuse)

» Symptoms associated with discontinuation
(patients should be monitored for symptoms of dizziness, nausea, headache, paresthesia, vomiting, irritability and nightmare upon discontinuation; a gradual reduction in dose rather than abrupt cessation is recommended whenever possible; previously prescribed dose may be considered if intolerable symptoms occur following a decrease in the dose or upon discontinuation of treatment)

Vital sign changes including
Blood pressure and
Heart rate
(measure prior to beginning duloxetine treatment and periodically throughout treatment for increases)

Side/Adverse Effects

The following side/adverse effects have been selected on the basis of their potential clinical significance (possible signs and symptoms in parentheses where appropriate)—not necessarily inclusive:

Note: Duloxetine is in a class of drugs known to affect urethral resistance. If symptoms of urinary hesitation occur during treatment with duloxetine, consider possibility of drug-relatedness.

Those indicating need for medical attention

Incidence not determined—Observed during clinical practice; estimates of frequency cannot be determined

Anaphylactic reaction (cough; difficulty swallowing; dizziness; fast heartbeat; hives, itching, puffiness, or swelling of the eyelids or around the eyes, face, lips or tongue; shortness of breath; skin rash; tightness in chest; unusual tiredness or weakness; wheezing); ***angioneurotic edema*** (large, hive-like swelling on face, eyelids, lips, tongue, throat, hands, legs, feet, sex organs); ***glaucoma*** (blindness; blurred vision; decreased vision; eye pain; headache; nausea or vomiting; tearing); ***hepatitis*** (dark urine; general tiredness and weakness; light-colored stools; nausea and vomiting; upper right abdominal pain; yellow eyes and skin); ***hyponatremia*** (coma; confusion; convulsions; decreased urine output; dizziness; fast or irregular heartbeat; headache; increased thirst; muscle pain or cramps; nausea or vomiting; shortness of breath; swelling of face, ankles, or hands; unusual tiredness or weakness); ***jaundice*** (chills; clay-colored stools; dark urine; dizziness; fever; headache; itching; loss of appetite; nausea; abdominal or stomach pain; area rash; unpleasant breath odor; unusual tiredness or weakness; vomiting of blood; yellow eyes or skin); ***orthostatic hypotension*** (chills; cold sweats; confusion; dizziness, faintness, or lightheadedness when getting up from lying or sitting position)—especially at initiation of treatment; ***Stevens-Johnson syndrome*** (blistering, peeling, loosening of skin; chills; cough; diarrhea; itching; joint or muscle pain; red irritated eyes; red skin lesions, often with a purple center; sore throat; sores, ulcers, or white spots in mouth or on lips; unusual tiredness or weakness); ***syncope*** (fainting)—especially at initiation of treatment; ***urticaria*** (hives or welts; itching; redness of skin; skin rash)

Those indicating need for medical attention only if they continue or are bothersome

Incidence more frequent

Anorexia (loss of appetite; weight loss); ***asthenia*** (lack or loss of strength); ***appetite decreased; constipation*** (difficulty having a bowel movement (stool)); ***cough; diarrhea; dizziness; dry mouth; fatigue*** (unusual tiredness or weakness); ***headache; hyperhidrosis*** (excessive sweating); ***insomnia*** (sleeplessness; trouble sleeping; unable to sleep); ***nasopharyngitis*** (stuffy or runny nose; muscle aches; unusual tiredness or weakness; fever; sore throat; headache); ***nausea; pharyngolaryngeal pain*** (sore throat); ***pollakiuria*** (frequent urination); ***somnolence*** (sleepiness or unusual drowsiness); ***sweating increased; vomiting***

Incidence less frequent

Anxiety (fear; nervousness); ***dyspepsia*** (acid or sour stomach; belching; heartburn; indigestion; stomach discomfort upset or pain); ***ejaculation delayed*** (longer than usual time to ejaculation of semen); ***ejaculatory dysfunction*** (change or problem with discharge of semen); ***erectile dysfunction*** (inability to have or keep an erection); ***hot flushes*** (feeling of warmth redness of the face, neck, arms and occasionally, upper chest sudden sweating); ***libido decreased*** (loss in sexual ability, desire, drive, or performance; decreased interest in sexual intercourse; inability to have or keep an erection); ***loose stools; muscle cramp; myalgia*** (joint pain; swollen joints; muscle aching or cramping; muscle pains or stiffness; difficulty in moving); ***orgasm abnormal; pyrexia*** (fever); ***tremor*** (trembling or shaking of hands or feet; shakiness in legs, arms, hands, feet); ***vision blurred; weight decreased***

Overdose

For more information on the management of overdose or unintentional ingestion, **contact a poison control center** (see *Poison Control Center Listing*).

Clinical effects of overdose

The following effects have been selected on the basis of their potential clinical significance (possible signs and symptoms in parentheses where appropriate)—not necessarily inclusive:

Treatment of overdose

There is no known specific antidote to duloxetine. Treatment is generally symptomatic and supportive.

To decrease absorption—
Emptying the stomach with gastric lavage with a large-bore orogastric tube including appropriate airway protection may be indicated if performed soon after ingestion or in symptomatic patients.
To enhance elimination—
Administering activate charcoal slurry.
Forced diuresis, dialysis, hemoperfusion, and exchange transfusion are unlikely to be beneficial due to the large volume of distribution of duloxetine.
Monitoring—
Monitoring for cardiac rhythm and vital signs.
Extended monitoring for patients who have taken duloxetine and excessive quantities of a TCA.
Supportive care—
Assuring adequate airway, oxygenation, and ventilation.
Patients in whom intentional overdose is confirmed or suspected should be referred for psychiatric consultation.

Patient Consultation

As an aid to patient consultation, refer to *Advice for the Patient, Duloxetine (Systemic).*

In providing consultation, consider emphasizing the following selected information (» = major clinical significance):

Before using this medication

» Conditions affecting use, especially:
Hypersensitivity to duloxetine or any of its inactive ingredients
Pregnancy—Should be used during pregnancy only if the potential benefit justifies the potential risk to the fetus
Complications including prolonged hospitalization, respiratory support and tube feeding in neonates exposed to SSRIs and SNRIs late in the third trimester; physician should carefully consider potential risks and benefits when treating a pregnant woman in her third trimester
Breast-feeding—Not recommended while breast-feeding. Duloxetine is distributed into the milk of lactating rats.
Use in children—Safety and efficacy in pediatric patients have not been established. Although duloxetine is not approved for use in children, data suggests an excess of occurrence of suicidal ideation and suicide attempts in clinical trials for various antidepressant drugs, including duloxetine, in pediatric patients with major depressive disorder.
Use in the elderly—Elderly patients may have increased sensitivity.
Other medications, especially antiarrhythmics such as flecainide or propafenone; CYP2D6 substrate such as desipramine, fluoxetine, paroxetine or quinidine; monoamine oxidase inhibitors (MAOIs), phenothiazines, thioridazine, or tricyclic antidepressants such as amitriptyline, imipramine, or nortriptyline
Other medical problems, especially bipolar disorder or risk of, chronic liver disease, hepatic insufficiency, hepatotoxicity, mania, seizures or severe renal function impairment, uncontrolled narrow-angle glaucoma

Proper use of this medication

» Compliance with therapy; not taking more or less medicine than prescribed
» Swallowing the capsule whole, not chewing, crushing, or sprinkling the contents on food or mixing with liquids.
» Proper dosing
Missed dose: Taking as soon as possible; not taking if almost time for next scheduled dose; not doubling doses
» Proper storage

Precautions while using this medication

» Regular visits to physician to check progress of therapy
» Avoiding use of alcoholic beverages
» Not taking within at least 14 days of discontinuing treatment with an MAOI and 5 days after stopping duloxetine before starting an MAOI.
» Four weeks of therapy may be required before antidepressive effects are seen; importance of continuing therapy after symptoms are relieved.
» Checking with physician before discontinuing medication
» Importance of patient tapering off of the medication as directed by the physician
» For diabetic patients: possible change in blood sugar levels; discussing with physician
» Importance of patient or caregiver notifying physician immediately if any signs of abnormal behavior, worsening depression or suicidality occur
» Possible blurred vision, drowsiness, impairment of judgment, thinking, or motor skills; caution when driving or doing jobs requiring alertness until effects of medication are known
» Notifying physician right away if signs of hepatitis or liver injury occur

Side/adverse effects

Side effects observed during clinical practice, especially anaphylactic reaction, angioneurotic edema, glaucoma, hepatitis, hyponatremia, jaundice, orthostatic hypotension, Stevens-Johnson syndrome, syncope, or urticaria

General Dosing Information

Duloxetine should be swallowed whole, and not chewed or crushed, nor should the contents be sprinkled on food or mixed with liquid.

Doses of duloxetine higher than 60 mg show no evidence of additional significant benefit, and are less well tolerated.

Patients should be periodically reassessed to determine the need for continued treatment and the appropriate dose.

The effectiveness of duloxetine must be assessed individually in patients being treated for diabetic peripheral neuropathic pain as progression is highly variable and management of pain is empirical.

Abrupt discontinuation of duloxetine may result in discontinuation symptoms. Patients should be monitored for discontinuation symptoms, regardless of the indication for which duloxetine was prescribed. If intolerable symptoms occur following a decrease in dose or upon discontinuation of treatment, then resuming the previously prescribed dose may be considered. Subsequently the physician may continue decreasing the dose, but at a more gradual rate.

Oral Dosage Forms

DULOXETINE HYDROCHLORIDE CAPSULES

Usual adult dose

Antidepressant—
Oral, 40 mg/day (given as 20 mg twice a day) to 60 mg/day (given either once a day or as 30 mg twice a day) without regard to meals
Diabetic peripheral neuropathic pain—
Oral, 60 mg/day once daily, without regard to meals
Note: For patients with diabetes complicated by renal disease, a lower starting dose and gradual increase in dose should be considered.
For all indications, patients with end-stage renal disease (requiring dialysis) or in severe renal impairment (estimated creatinine clearance <30 mL/min), duloxetine is not recommended.
For all indications, it is recommended that duloxetine not be administered to patients with any hepatic insufficiency.

Usual pediatric dose

Safety and efficacy have not been established

Usual geriatric dose

See *Usual adult dose.*

Strength(s) usually available

U.S.—
20 mg (base) duloxetine (Rx) [*Cymbalta* (FD&C Blue No. 2; gelatin; hydroxypropyl methylcellulose acetate succinate; hypromellose; sodium lauryl sulfate; sucrose; sugar spheres; talc; titanium dioxide; triethyl citrate)].
30 mg (base) duloxetine [*Cymbalta* (FD&C Blue No. 2; gelatin; hydroxypropyl methylcellulose acetate succinate; hypromellose; sodium lauryl sulfate; sucrose; sugar spheres; talc; titanium dioxide; triethyl citrate)].
60 mg (base) duloxetine [*Cymbalta* (FD&C Blue No. 2; gelatin; hydroxypropyl methylcellulose acetate succinate; hypromellose; sodium lauryl sulfate; sucrose; sugar spheres; talc; titanium dioxide; triethyl citrate)].

Packaging and storage

Store at 25 °C (77 °F); excursions permitted to 15 to 30 °C.

Auxiliary labeling

- Swallow whole. Do not chew or crush.
- May cause drowsiness. Be careful while driving or operating machinery. Use caution until you become familiar with its effects.

Revised: 10/31/2005
Developed: 09/22/2004

DUTASTERIDE Systemic†

VA CLASSIFICATION (Primary): GU700

Commonly used brand name(s): *Avodart*.

Note: For a listing of dosage forms and brand names by country availability, see *Dosage Forms* section(s).

†Not commercially available in Canada.

Category

Benign prostatic hyperplasia therapy agent.

Indications

Accepted

Benign prostatic hyperplasia (treatment)—Dutasteride is indicated for the treatment of symptomatic benign prostatic hyperplasia (BPH) in men with an enlarged prostate to improve symptoms, reduce the risk of acute urinary retention, and to reduce the risk for the need for BPH related surgery.

Pharmacology/Pharmacokinetics

Physicochemical characteristics

Molecular weight—528.50.

Solubility—Soluble in ethanol (44 milligrams per milliliter), methanol (64 milligrams per milliliter) and polyethylene glycol 400 (3 milligrams per milliliter), but insoluble in water.

Mechanism of action/Effect

Dutasteride inhibits the conversion of testosterone to 5α-dihydrotestosterone (DHT). DHT is the androgen primarily responsible for the initial development and subsequent enlargement of the prostate gland. Testosterone is converted to DHT by the enzyme 5α-reductase, which exists as 2 isoforms, type 1 and type 2. Type 2 isoenzyme is primarily active in the reproductive tissue while type 1 isoenzyme is responsible for testosterone conversion in the skin and liver. Dutasteride is a competitive and specific inhibitor of both type 1 and type 2 5α-reductase isoenzymes, with which it forms a stable enzyme complex. Dissociation from this complex has been evaluated under *in vitro* and *in vivo* conditions and is extremely slow.

Absorption

Absolute bioavailability—approximately 60% following a single 0.5 milligram dose.

Distribution

Volume of distribution (Vol_D)—300 to 500 liters following single and repeat oral doses.

Semen dutasteride concentrations averaged 3.4 nanograms per milliliter at 12 months and achieve steady state concentrations at 6 months in healthy subjects receiving dutasteride 0.5 mg per day. On average, at 12 months, 11.5% of serum dutasteride concentrations partitioned into semen.

Protein binding

Very high—bound to plasma albumin (99%) and alpha-1 acid glycoprotein (96.6%).

Biotransformation

Dutasteride is extensively metabolized. In vitro studies show that dutasteride is metabolized by the CYP3A4 isoenzyme to 2 minor monohydroxylated metabolites. Dutasteride is not metabolized *in vitro* by human cytochrome P450 isoenzymes CYP1A2, CYP2C9, CYP2C19, and CYP2D6 at 2,000 nanograms per milliliter (50-fold greater than steady-state serum concentrations). In human serum, following dosing to steady state, unchanged dutasteride, 3 major metabolites (4'-hydroxydutasteride, 1,2-dihydrodutasteride, and 6-hydroxydutasteride), and 2 minor metabolites (6,4'-dihydroxydutasteride and 15-hydroxydutasteride), as assessed by mass spectrometric response, have been detected. The absolute stereochemistry of the hydroxyl additions in the 6 and 15 positions is not known. In vitro, the 4'-hydroxydutasteride and 1,2-dihydrodutasteride metabolites are much less potent than dutasteride against both isoforms of human 5AR. The activity of 6β-hydroxydutasteride is comparable to that of dutasteride.

Because dutasteride is extensively metabolized, exposure could be higher in hepatically impaired patients.

Half-life

Elimination, terminal—approximately 5 weeks at steady state.

In a study of healthy male patients ages 24 to 87, following a single 5 milligram dose, dutasteride half-life increased with age. Half-life increased approximately 170 hours in men 20 to 49 years of age, approximately 260 hours in men 50 to 69 years of age, and approximately 300 hours in men over 70 years of age. No overall differences in safety or efficacy were observed between these patients and younger patients, therefore, no dose adjustment is necessary in the elderly

Time to peak serum concentration:

Within 2 to 3 hours

Steady state serum concentration:

Following 0.5 milligrams per day for 1 year—average of 40 nanograms per milliliter. Following daily dosing, dutasteride serum concentration achieved 65% steady state after 1 month; approximately 90% after 3 months.

Note: Maximum serum concentrations decrease by 10% to 15% when administered with food.

Elimination

Mainly fecal; approximately 5% unchanged dutasteride and 40% as dutasteride-related metabolites.

Only trace amounts of unchanged dutasteride were found in urine (<1%)

Approximately 55% of the dose was unaccounted.

Due to a long half-life, serum concentrations remain detectable (> 0.1 nanogram per milliliter) for up to 4 to 6 months after discontinuation of treatment

Precautions to Consider

Cross-sensitivity and/or related problems

Patients sensitive to other 5α-reductase inhibitors may be sensitive to dutasteride.

Carcinogenicity

In a 2-year study in B6C3F1 mice at doses of 3, 35, 250, and 500 mg per kg of body weight per day for males and 3, 35, and 250 mg per kg of body weight per day for females, an increased incidence of benign hepatocellular adenomas was noted at 250 mg per kg per day (290-fold the expected clinical exposure to a 0.5 mg daily dose) in females only. Two of the three major human metabolites have been detected in mice. The exposure to these metabolites is either lower than in humans or is not known.

In a 2-year carcinogenicity study in Han Wistar rats at doses of 1.5, 7.5, and 53 mg per kg of body weight per day for males and 0.8, 6.3, and 15 mg per kg of body weight per day for females, there was an increase in Leydig cell adenomas in the testes at 53 mg per kg of body weight per day (135-fold the expected clinical exposure). An increased incidence of Leydig cell hyperplasia was present at 7.5 mg per kg of body weight per day (52-fold the expected clinical exposure) and 53 mg per kg of body weight per day in male rats. A positive correlation between proliferative changes in the Leydig cells and an increase in circulating luteinizing hormone levels has been demonstrated with 5α-reductase inhibitors and is consistent with an effect on the hypothalamic-pituitary-testicular axis following the 5α-reductase inhibition. At tumorigenic doses in rats, luteinizing hormones levels in rats were increased 167%. In this study, the major human metabolites were tested for carcinogenicity at approximately 1 to 3 times the expected clinical exposure.

Mutagenicity

Dutasteride was tested for genotoxicity in a bacterial mutagenesis assay (Ames test), a chromosomal aberration assay in CHO cells, and a micronucleus assay in rats. The results did not indicate any genotoxic potential of the parent drug. Two major human metabolites were also negative in either the Ames test or an abbreviated Ames test.

Pregnancy/Reproduction

Fertility—Treatment of sexually mature male rats with dutasteride at doses of 0.05, 10, 50, and 500 mg per kg of body weight per day (0.1 to 110-fold the expected clinical exposure of parent drug) for up to 31 weeks resulted in dose- and time-dependent decreases in fertility, reduced cauda epididymal (absolute) sperm counts but not sperm concentration (at 50 and 500 mg per kg per day), reduced weights of the epididymis, prostate and seminal vesicles, and microscopic changes in the male reproductive organs. The fertility effects were reversed by recovery week 6 at all doses, and sperm counts were normal at the end of a 14-week recovery period. The 5α-reductase-related changes consisted of cytoplasmic vacuolation of tubular epithelium in the epididymides and decreased cytoplasmic content of epithelium, consistent with decreased secretory activity in the prostate and seminal vesicles. The microscopic changes were no longer present at recovery week 14 in the low-dose group and were partly recovered in the remaining treatment groups. Low levels of dutasteride (0.6 to 17 ng per mL) were detected in the serum of untreated female rats mated to males dosed at 10, 50, or 500 mg per kg of body weight per day for 29 to 30 weeks.

In a fertility study in female rats, oral administration of dutasteride at doses of 0.05, 2.5, 12.5, and 30 mg per kg of body weight per day resulted in reduced litter size, increased embryo resorption and feminization of male fetuses (decreased anogenital distance) at doses of ≥ 2.5 mg per kg of body weight per day (2- to 10-fold the clinical exposure of parent drug in men). Fetal body weights were also reduced at ≥ 0.05 mg per kg of body weight per day (<0.02-fold the human exposure).

Pregnancy—Dutasteride is contraindicated for use in women.

Dutasteride is absorbed through the skin. Because of the potential risk to a male fetus, a woman who is pregnant or who may become pregnant should not handle dutasteride capsules because of the possibility of absorption of dutasteride and the potential risk of a fetal anomaly to a male fetus.

Adequate and well controlled studies in humans have not been done. The preclinical data suggests that the suppression of circulating levels of dihydrotestosterone may inhibit the development of the external genital organs in a male fetus carried by a woman exposed to dutasteride.

In an intravenous embryo-fetal development study in the rhesus monkey (12 per group), administration of dutasteride at 400, 780, 1,325, or 2,010 ng per day on gestation days 20 to 100 did not adversely affect development of male external genitalia. Reduction of fetal adrenal weights, reduction in fetal prostate weights, and increases in fetal ovarian and testis weights were observed in monkeys treated with the highest dose. Based on the highest measured semen concentration of dutasteride in treated men (14 ng per mL) these doses represent 0.8 to 16 times based on blood levels of parent drug (32 to 186 times based on a ng per kg of body weight daily dose) the potential maximum exposure of a 50-kg human female to 5 mL semen daily from a dutasteride-treated man, assuming 100% absorption. Dutasteride is highly bound to proteins in human serum (>96%), potentially reducing the amount of dutasteride available for vaginal absorption.

In an embryo-fetal development study in female rats, oral administration of dutasteride at doses of 0.05, 2.5, 12.5, and 30 mg per kg of body weight per day resulted in the feminization of male fetuses (decreased anogenital distance) and male offspring (nipple development, hypospadias, and distended preputial glands) at all doses (0.07- to 111-fold the expected male clinical exposure). An increase in stillborn pups was observed at 30 mg per kg of body weight per day, and reduced fetal body weight was observed at doses ≥ 2.5 mg per kg of body weight per day (15- to 111- fold the expected clinical exposure). Increased incidences of skeletal variations considered to be delays in ossification associated with reduced body weight were observed at doses of 12.5 and 30 mg per kg of body weight per day (56- to 111-fold the expected clinical exposure).

In an oral pre- and postnatal development study in rats, dutasteride doses of 0.05, 2.5, 12.5, or 30 mg per kg of body weight per day were administered. Unequivocal evidence of feminization of the genitalia (i.e., decreased anogenital distance, increased incidence of hypospadias, nipple development) of F1 generation male offspring occurred at doses ≥ 2.5 mg per kg of body weight per day (14- to 90-fold the expected clinical exposure in men). At a daily dose of 0.05 mg per kg of body weight per day (0.05-fold the expected clinical exposure), evidence of feminization was limited to a small, but statistically significant, decrease in anogenital distance. Doses of 2.5 to 30 mg per kg of body weight per day resulted in prolonged gestation in the parental females and a decrease in time to vaginal patency for female offspring and decrease prostate and seminal vesicle weights in male offspring. Effects on newborn startle response were noted at doses greater than or equal to 12.5 mg per kg of body weight per day. Increased stillbirths were noted at 30 mg per kg of body weight per day.

Feminization of male fetuses is an expected physiological consequence of inhibition of the conversion of testosterone to DHT by 5α-reductase inhibitors. These results are similar to observations in male infants with genetic 5α-reductase deficiency.

In the rabbit, embryo-fetal study doses of 30, 100, and 200 mg per kg (28- to 93- fold the expected clinical exposure in men) were administered orally on days 7 to 29 of pregnancy to encompass the late period of external genitalia development. Histological evaluation of the genital papilla of the fetuses revealed evidence of feminization of the male fetuses at all doses. A second embryo-fetal study in rabbits at doses of 0.05, 0.4, 3, and 30 mg per kg of body weight per day (0.3- to 53-fold the expected clinical exposure) also produced evidence of feminization of the genitalia in male fetuses at all doses.

It is not known whether rabbits or rhesus monkeys produce any of the major human metabolites.

FDA Pregnancy Category X

Breast-feeding

It is not known if dutasteride is distributed into breast milk. Dutasteride is contraindicated for use in women.

Pediatrics

Dutasteride is contraindicated for use in children. Safety and efficacy have not been established.

Geriatrics

Appropriate studies on the relationship of age to the effects of dutasteride have not been performed in the geriatric population. However clinical trials were conducted and geriatrics-specific problems that would limit the usefulness of this medication in elderly men are not expected.

Pharmacogenetics

Dutasteride is not indicated for use in women. The pharmacokinetics of dutasteride in women have not been studied.

The effects of race on dutasteride pharmacokinetics has not been studied.

Drug interactions and/or related problems

The following drug interactions and/or related problems have been selected on the basis of their potential clinical significance (possible mechanism in parentheses where appropriate)—not necessarily inclusive (» = major clinical significance):

Dutasteride does not inhibit the *in vitro* metabolism of model substrates for the major human cytochrome P450 isoenzymes (CYP1A2, CYP2C9, CYP2C19, CYP2D6, and CYP3A4) at concentrations of 1000 ng per mL (25 times greater than steady-state) in humans.

Note: Combinations containing any of the following medications, depending on the amount present, may also interact with this medication.

CYP3A4 and CYP3A5 inhibitors such as:
Cimetidine or
Ciprofloxacin or
Diltiazem or
Ketoconazole or
Troleandomycin or
Verapamil
(concomitant use may increase blood concentrations of dutasteride)

CYP3A4 inhibitors, potent such as:
Ritonavir
(dutasteride is metabolized by human cytochrome P450 isoenzyme CYP3A4; care should be taken when coadministering to patients who are taking potent, chronic CYP3A4 inhibitors)

Laboratory value alterations

The following have been selected on the basis of their potential clinical significance (possible effect in parentheses where appropriate)—not necessarily inclusive (» = major clinical significance).

With physiology/laboratory test values

PSA concentrations
(PSA levels generally decrease as the prostate volume decreases; 20% within first month of treatment, 50% decrease after 6 months of treatment; 50% decrease maintained for up to 2 years; may vary slightly in individual patients)

Testosterone concentrations
(median 17.9% increase from baseline adjusted mean of total testosterone at 8 weeks with dutasteride treatment)

Thyroid-stimulating hormone [TSH]
(median 12.4% increase from baseline adjusted mean of total TSH at 52 weeks with dutasteride treatment)

Medical considerations/Contraindications

The medical considerations/contraindications included have been selected on the basis of their potential clinical significance (reasons given in parentheses where appropriate)—not necessarily inclusive (» = major clinical significance).

Risk-benefit should be considered when the following medical problems exist:

Hepatic impairment
(dutasteride is extensively metabolized and exposure could be higher in hepatically impaired patients; caution should be used)

» Hypersensitivity to dutasteride, other 5α-reductase inhibitors, or to any component of the preparation

Large residual urinary volume or
Reduced urinary flow
(because of possible presence of obstructive uropathy, patients with these conditions may not be candidates for dutasteride therapy; lower urinary tract symptoms of BPH can be indicative of other urological diseases, including prostate cancer)

Patient monitoring

The following may be especially important in patient monitoring (other tests may be warranted in some patients, depending on condition; » = major clinical significance):

» Blood donation
(men treated with dutasteride should not donate blood while taking dutasteride and for at least 6 months after the last dose; deferral

is to prevent dutasteride exposure to a pregnant female transfusion recipient)

» Prostate cancer evaluations, such as:
  Digital rectal examinations
    (evaluations should be performed prior to initiation of therapy and periodically thereafter)
  PSA concentrations
    (a new baseline PSA should be established after 3 to 6 months of treatment and this value should be used for assessment; to interpret an isolated PSA in a patient treated 6 months or more, the PSA concentration should be doubled for comparison with normal values in untreated men)

» Urological diseases
  (patients should be assessed to rule out urological diseases prior to treatment; patients with large residual urinary volume and/or severely diminished urinary flow should be carefully monitored for obstructive uropathy)

Side/Adverse Effects

The following side/adverse effects have been selected on the basis of their potential clinical significance (possible signs and symptoms in parentheses where appropriate)—not necessarily inclusive:

Those indicating need for medical attention

Incidence not determined—Observed during clinical practice; estimates of frequency can not be determined

Allergic reaction (cough; difficulty swallowing; dizziness; fast heartbeat; hives; itching; puffiness or swelling of the eyelids or around the eyes, face, lips or tongue; shortness of breath; skin rash; tightness in chest; unusual tiredness or weakness; wheezing); ***edema, localized*** (swelling of face, fingers, feet, and/or lower legs); ***pruritus*** (itching skin); ***rash; urticaria*** (hives or welts; itching; redness of skin; skin rash)

Those indicating need for medical attention only if they continue or are bothersome

Incidence less frequent

Ejaculation disorder (decreased sexual performance or desire; abnormal ejaculation); ***gynecomastia*** (swelling of the breasts or breast soreness); ***impotence; libido, decreased*** (loss in sexual ability, desire, drive, or performance; decreased interest in sexual intercourse; inability to have or keep an erection)

Note: The incidence of most drug-related sexual adverse events (impotence, decreased libido and ejaculation disorder) decreased with duration of treatment. The incidence gynecomastia remained constant over the treatment period.

Ejaculate volume may be decreased in some patients. This decrease does not appear to interfere with normal sexual function.

Overdose

For more information on the management of overdose or unintentional ingestion, **contact a poison control center** (see *Poison Control Center Listing*).

Clinical effects of overdose

Single doses of up to 40 mg of dutasteride (80 times the therapeutic dose) for 7 days were administered in volunteer studies without significant safety concerns.

Daily doses of 5 mg of dutasteride (10 times the therapeutic dose) for 6 months were administered to 60 subjects with no additional adverse effects to those seen at therapeutic doses of 0.5 mg dutasteride.

Treatment of overdose

Supportive care—

There is no known specific antidote to dutasteride. Treatment is generally symptomatic and supportive, taking into consideration the long half-life of dutasteride.

Patients in whom intentional overdose is confirmed or suspected should be referred for psychiatric consultation.

Patient Consultation

As an aid to patient consultation, refer to *Advice for the Patient, Dutasteride (Systemic)*.

In providing consultation, consider emphasizing the following selected information (» = major clinical significance):

Before using this medication

» Conditions affecting use, especially:
  Increased incidence of benign hepatocellular adenomas in female mice and Leydig cell adenomas in the testes of male rats receiving high doses; positive correlation found in male rats between proliferative changes in the Leydig cells and an increase in circulating luteinizing hormone levels with 5α-reductase inhibitors; luteinizing hormone levels in rats were increased 167% at tumorigenic doses

  Pregnancy—Dutasteride is contraindicated for use in women; pregnant women should not use or handle capsules because of potential risk of abnormal external genitalia development in the male fetus

  FDA Pregnancy Category X

  Breast-feeding—Dutasteride is contraindicated for use in women

  Use in children—Contraindicated for use in children; safety and efficacy have not been established

Pharmacogenetics—Dutasteride is contraindicated for use in women

Other medical problems, especially hypersensitivity to dutasteride, other 5α-reductase inhibitors, or to any component of the preparation

Proper use of this medication

» Proper dosing

Missed dose: Taking as soon as possible; not taking if almost time for next dose; not doubling doses

Proper storage

Precautions while using this medication

» Importance of pregnant women or women who may become pregnant not handling capsules and washing contact area immediately with soap and water if contact is made with leaking capsules

Swallowing capsule whole, not chewing or crushing

May be taken with or without food.

Side/adverse effects

Amount of semen in ejaculate may be decreased in some patients. This decrease does not interfere with normal sexual function.

Signs of potential side effects observed during clinical practice, especially allergic reaction, localized edema, pruritus, rash, or urticaria

General Dosing Information

For oral dosing forms:

Dutasteride may be taken with or without food. The capsules should be swallowed whole.

Dutasteride is absorbed through the skin. Dutasteride should not be handled by women who are pregnant or who may become pregnant because of the potential for absorption of dutasteride and the subsequent potential risk to a developing male fetus. In addition, women should use caution whenever handling dutasteride capsules. If contact is made with leaking capsules, the contact area should be washed immediately with soap and water.

Men being treated with dutasteride should not donate blood until at least 6 months have passed following their last dose. The purpose of this deferred period is to prevent administration of dutasteride to a pregnant female transfusion recipient.

Oral Dosage Forms

DUTASTERIDE CAPSULES

Usual adult dose

Benign prostatic hyperplasia (treatment)—
  Oral, 0.5 mg once a day.

  Note: Dutasteride is contraindicated for use in women and children.

Usual geriatric dose

See *Usual adult dose*.

Strength(s) usually available

U.S.—

Note: Gelatin is from certified BSE-free bovine sources.

0.5 mg (Rx) [*Avodart* (mono-di-glycerides of caprylic/capric acid; butylated hydroxytoluene; gelatin; glycerin; ferric oxide)].

Packaging and storage

Store at 25 °C (77 °F), excursions permitted to 15 °C to 30 °C (59 °F to 86 °F).

Auxiliary labeling

- Swallow whole. Do not crush or chew.
- This medication may be taken with or without food.

Caution

Women who are pregnant or may be pregnant should not handle dutasteride capsules.

Revised: 12/13/2004
Developed: 09/16/2003

DYCLONINE—See *Anesthetics (Mucosal-Local)*

ECHOTHIOPHATE—See *Antiglaucoma Agents, Cholinergic, Long-acting (Ophthalmic)*

ECONAZOLE—See *Antifungals, Azole (Vaginal)*

ECONAZOLE Topical

VA CLASSIFICATION (Primary): DE102

Commonly used brand name(s): *Ecostatin cream; Spectazole cream.*

Note: For a listing of dosage forms and brand names by country availability, see *Dosage Forms* section(s).

Category

Antifungal (topical)

Note: Econazole is a broad-spectrum antifungal, which has an antifungal spectrum similar to that of miconazole.

Indications

Note: Bracketed information in the *Indications* section refers to uses that are not included in U.S. product labeling.

Accepted

Candidiasis, cutaneous (treatment)—Econazole is indicated as a primary agent in the topical treatment of cutaneous candidiasis (moniliasis) caused by *Candida (Monilia)* species.

Tinea corporis (treatment)
Tinea cruris (treatment) or
Tinea pedis (treatment)—Econazole is indicated as a primary agent in the topical treatment of tinea corporis (ringworm of the body), tinea cruris (ringworm of the groin; jock itch), or tinea pedis (ringworm of the foot; athlete's foot) caused by *Trichophyton rubrum, Trichophyton mentagrophytes, Trichophyton tonsurans, Microsporum canis, Microsporum audouini, Microsporum gypseum*, and *Epidermophyton floccosum (Acrothesium floccosum)*.

Tinea versicolor (treatment)—Econazole is indicated as a primary agent in the topical treatment of tinea versicolor (pityriasis versicolor; "sun fungus") caused by *Pityrosporon orbiculare (Malassezia furfur)*.

[Paronychia (treatment)][1]—Econazole is used in the topical treatment of paronychia caused by fungi.

[Tinea barbae (treatment)][1] or
[Tinea capitis (treatment)][1]—Econazole is used in combination with griseofulvin or systemic ketoconazole (for griseofulvin-resistant cases) in the treatment of tinea barbae and tinea capitis.

Not all species or strains of a particular organism may be susceptible to econazole.

Unaccepted

Econazole is not indicated for moderate to severe paronychia or onychomycosis.

[1]Not included in Canadian product labeling.

Pharmacology/Pharmacokinetics

Physicochemical characteristics

Chemical Group—Synthetic chlorinated imidazole derivative, structurally related to clotrimazole, ketoconazole, and miconazole.

Molecular weight—Econazole nitrate: 444.7.

Mechanism of action/Effect

Fungistatic; may be fungicidal, depending on concentration; inhibits biosynthesis of ergosterol or other sterols, damaging the fungal cell wall membrane and altering its permeability; as a result, loss of essential intracellular elements may occur; also inhibits biosynthesis of triglycerides and phospholipids by fungi; in addition, inhibits oxidative and peroxidative enzyme activity, resulting in intracellular buildup of toxic concentrations of hydrogen peroxide, which may contribute to deterioration of subcellular organelles and cellular necrosis.

Absorption

Minimal systemic absorption following topical application to normal skin.

Stratum corneum concentration

Far exceeded minimum inhibitory concentrations (MICs) for dermatophytes; inhibitory concentrations found in epidermis and as deep as middle region of dermis.

Elimination

Renal and fecal; < 1% of applied dose recovered in urine and feces.

Precautions to Consider

Carcinogenicity

Long-term studies in animals have not been done.

Pregnancy/Reproduction

Fertility—Studies in rats have shown that econazole given orally causes prolonged gestation. However, intravaginal administration of econazole nitrate in humans has not been shown to cause prolonged gestation or other adverse reproductive effects.

Pregnancy—Adequate and well-controlled studies in humans have not been done.

Segment I studies in rats have shown that econazole is fetotoxic or embryotoxic when given orally in doses 10 to 40 times the usual human dermal dose. Similar effects were seen in mice, rabbits, and/or rats in Segment II or Segment III studies when econazole was given orally in doses 80 or 40 times the usual human dermal dose, respectively. However, no teratogenic effects were seen in mice, rabbits, or rats when econazole was given orally.

FDA Pregnancy Category C.

Breast-feeding

It is not known whether econazole is distributed into human breast milk. Caution should be exercised when econazole nitrate is administered to a nursing woman. Econazole and/or its metabolites are distributed into the milk of rats following oral administration and were found in the nursing pups. Also, in lactating rats given large oral doses of econazole (40 or 80 times the usual human dermal dose), a decrease in the postpartum viability of pups and survival to weaning was seen.

Pediatrics

Appropriate studies on the relationship of age to the effects of econazole have not been performed in the pediatric population. However, pediatrics-specific problems that would limit the usefulness of this medicine in children are not expected.

Geriatrics

Appropriate studies on the relationship of age to the effects of econazole have not been performed in the geriatric population. However, geriatrics-specific problems that would limit the usefulness of this medicine in the elderly are not expected.

Medical considerations/Contraindications

The medical considerations/contraindications included have been selected on the basis of their potential clinical significance (reasons given in parentheses where appropriate)—not necessarily inclusive (» = major clinical significance).

Risk-benefit should be considered when the following medical problem exists:

Sensitivity to econazole

Side/Adverse Effects

The following side/adverse effects have been selected on the basis of their potential clinical significance (possible signs and symptoms in parentheses where appropriate)—not necessarily inclusive:

Those indicating need for medical attention

Incidence less frequent

Burning, itching, stinging, redness, or other signs of irritation not present before therapy

Incidence rare

Pruritic rash (skin rash with itching)

Patient Consultation

As an aid to patient consultation, refer to *Advice for the Patient, Econazole (Topical)*.

In providing consultation, consider emphasizing the following selected information (» = major clinical significance):

Before using this medication

» Conditions affecting use, especially:

Pregnancy—Fetotoxic and embryotoxic reactions were seen in rats, mice, and rabbits given large oral doses

Breast-feeding—It is not known if econazole nitrate is distributed into human breast milk; however, econazole was distributed into breast milk of rats given large oral doses

Proper use of this medication

Applying sufficient medication to cover affected and surrounding areas, and massaging in gently

» Avoiding contact with the eyes

» Not applying occlusive dressing over this medication unless directed to do so by physician
» Compliance with full course of therapy; fungal infections may require prolonged therapy
» Proper dosing
Missed dose: Applying as soon as possible; not applying if almost time for next dose
» Proper storage

Precautions while using this medication
Checking with physician if no improvement within 2 weeks or more, or if condition becomes worse

» Using hygienic measures to help cure infection or to help prevent reinfection
For tinea cruris:
Avoiding underwear that is tight-fitting or made from synthetic materials; wearing loose-fitting cotton underwear instead
Using a bland, absorbent powder or an antifungal powder on the skin; not using cream and powder concurrently
For tinea pedis:
Carefully drying feet, especially between toes, after bathing
Avoiding socks made from wool or synthetic materials; wearing clean, cotton socks and changing them daily or more often if feet perspire excessively
Wearing well-ventilated shoes or sandals
Using a bland, absorbent powder or an antifungal powder between toes, on feet, and in socks and shoes liberally once or twice daily; not using cream and powder concurrently

Side/adverse effects
Signs of potential side effects, especially burning, itching, stinging, redness, or other signs of irritation not present before therapy; or pruritic rash

General Dosing Information

Use of topical antifungals may lead to skin sensitization, resulting in hypersensitivity reactions with subsequent topical use of the medication.

To reduce the possibility of recurrence, *Candida* infections, tinea cruris, and tinea corporis should be treated for at least 2 weeks and tinea pedis should be treated for at least 1 month. (In Canada, the recommendations are 2 weeks of treatment for Candida infections and 1 month for dermatophyte infections.)

When this medication is used in the treatment of candidiasis, occlusive dressings should be avoided since they provide conditions that favor growth of yeast and release of its irritating endotoxin.

Topical Dosage Forms

ECONAZOLE NITRATE CREAM

Usual adult and adolescent dose
Candidiasis, cutaneous—
Topical, to the affected and surrounding skin areas, two times a day, morning and evening for two weeks.
Tinea corporis; or
Tinea cruris; or
Tinea versicolor—
Topical, to the affected and surrounding skin areas, one or two times a day for two to four weeks.
Tinea pedis—
Topical, to the affected and surrounding skin areas, one or two times a day for four weeks.

Usual pediatric dose
See *Usual adult and adolescent dose.*

Strength(s) usually available
U.S.—
1% (Rx) [*Spectazole cream* (benzoic acid; butylated hydroxyanisole; mineral oil; peglicol 5 oleate; pegoxol 7 stearate; purified water)].
Canada—
1% (Rx) [*Ecostatin cream* (benzoic acid; butylated hydroxyanisole; fragrance; mineral oil; palm oil; polyethylene glycol; polyethylene glycol stearate; water)].

Packaging and storage
Store below 30 °C (86 °F), preferably between 15 and 25 °C (59 and 77 °F), in a well-closed container, unless otherwise specified by manufacturer. Protect from freezing.

Auxiliary labeling
- For external use only.
- Continue medicine for full time of treatment.

Revised: 06/14/1999

EFALIZUMAB Systemic†

VA CLASSIFICATION (Primary/Secondary): DE801/IM403
Commonly used brand name(s): *Raptiva.*
Note: For a listing of dosage forms and brand names by country availability, see *Dosage Forms* section(s).

†Not commercially available in Canada.

Category

Antipsoriatic (systemic); Immunosuppressant.

Indications

Accepted
Psoriasis (treatment)—Efalizumab is indicated for the treatment of adults patients (18 years or older) with moderate to severe chronic plaque psoriasis who are candidates for systemic therapy or phototherapy.

Pharmacology/Pharmacokinetics

Physicochemical characteristics
Source—Recombinant humanized IgG1 kappa isotype monoclonal antibody produced in a Chinese Hamster Ovary (CHO) mammalian cell expression system.
Molecular weight—Efalizumab: 150 kilodaltons.
pH—6.2, after reconstitution

Mechanism of action/Effect
Efalizumab specifically binds to CD11a, the leukocyte function antigen-1 (LFA-1), and decreases cell surface expression of CD11a. Efalizumab inhibits the binding of LFA-1 to intercellular adhesion molecule-1 (ICAM-1) thereby inhibiting the adhesion of leukocytes to other cell types. The interaction between LFA-1 and ICAM-1 contributes to the initiation and maintenance of T lymphocytes, including activation, adhesion to endothelial cells, and migration to sites of inflammation including psoriatic skin. Lymphocyte activation and trafficking to skin play a role in the pathophysiology of chronic plaque psoriasis. In psoriatic, ICAM-1 cell surface expression is upregulated on endothelium and keratinocytes. CD11a is also expressed on the surface of B lymphocytes, monocytes, neutrophils, natural killer cells and other leukocytes. Therefore, the potential exists for efalizumab to affect the activation, adhesion, migration, and numbers of cells other than T lymphocytes.

Absorption
SC bioavailability—50%.

Time to steady state concentration:
Steady state—4 weeks

Peak serum concentration
12 mcg per mL

Elimination
Mean steady state clearance—24 mL per kg per day
Body weight was the most significant covariate affecting efalizumab clearance.

Precautions to Consider

Carcinogenicity
Long-term studies in animals to determine the carcinogenic potential of efalizumab have not been done.

Mutagenicity
Geneotoxicity studies have not been done.

Pregnancy/Reproduction
Fertility—Studies done in male and female mice given an antimouse CD11a antibody at doses up to 30 times the 1 mg/kg clinical dose revealed no evidence of adverse effects on mating, fertility, or reproduction parameters.

Pregnancy—*An Efalizumab Pregnancy Registry has been established to monitor the maternal-fetal outcomes of pregnant women exposed to efalizumab. Physicians are encouraged to register patients who be-*

come pregnant while taking efalizumab or (within 6 weeks of discontinuing efalizumab) in the efalizumab pregnancy registry.

Adequate and well controlled studies in humans have not been done.

Developmental toxicity studies in mice given an antimouse CD11a antibody at doses up to 30 times the clinical dose showed no evidence of maternal toxicity, embryotoxicity, or teratogenicity during organogenesis. There were also no adverse effects on behavioral, reproductive, or growth parameters in offspring of females treated with antimouse CD11a antibody during gestation and lactation. However, at 11 weeks of age the offspring of the treated females did show a reduction in antibody response, which was partially reversible by 25 weeks.

Since the effects of efalizumab on pregnant women and fetal development, including immune system development and because animal studies are not always predictive of human response, efalizumab should be given to a pregnant woman only if clearly needed.

FDA Pregnancy Category C

Breast-feeding

It is not know whether efalizumab is distributed into breast milk. However, efalizumab is distributed into the milk of lactating mice. The offspring of the exposed females exhibited a significant reduction in antibody response. Since maternal immunoglobulins are known to be present in the milk of lactating mothers and animal data suggests adverse effects in nursing infants, a decision should be made whether to discontinue nursing or to discontinue the use of efalizumab.

Pediatrics

Safety and efficacy have not been established.

Geriatrics

Although appropriate studies on the relationship of age to the effects of efalizumab have not been performed in the geriatric population, no geriatrics-specific problems have been documented to date. However, elderly patients in general are more likely to have a higher incidence of infections, which may require caution in elderly patients receiving efalizumab.

Pharmacogenetics

Efalizumab clearance was not significantly affected by race or gender.

Drug interactions and/or related problems

The following drug interactions and/or related problems have been selected on the basis of their potential clinical significance (possible mechanism in parentheses where appropriate)—not necessarily inclusive (» = major clinical significance):

Note: Combinations containing any of the following medications, depending on the amount present, may also interact with this medication.

» Immunosuppressive agents
(patients should not receive efalizumab concurrently with other immunosuppressive agents because of the possibility of increased risk of infection and malignancies)

» Phototherapy
(safety and efficacy of efalizumab and phototherapy have not been established)

» Vaccines
(acellular, live, or live-attenuated vaccines should not be administered during treatment with efalizumab)

Laboratory value alterations

The following have been selected on the basis of their potential clinical significance (possible effect in parentheses where appropriate)—not necessarily inclusive (» = major clinical significance).

With diagnostic test results
Alkaline phosphatase or
Liver function tests
(levels may be elevated)

Lymphocyte counts
(may increase due to the pharmacologic mechanism of action)

Medical considerations/Contraindications

The medical considerations/contraindications included have been selected on the basis of their potential clinical significance (reasons given in parentheses where appropriate)—not necessarily inclusive (» = major clinical significance).

Except under special circumstances, this medication should not be used when the following medical problem exists:

» Hypersensitivity to efalizumab or any of its components.

Risk-benefit should be considered when the following medical problems exist:

» Infection, clinically significant
(efalizumab is an immunosuppressive agent and has the potential to increase the risk of infection and reactivate latent, chronic infections; efalizumab should not be administered to patients with a clinically important infection; caution should be used in patients with chronic infections or history of recurrent infection; if patient develops a serious infection, medicine should be discontinued)

» Malignancies or history of
(caution should be exercised when considering use in patients with at high risk of malignancy or with a history of malignancy; if development of a malignancy should occur efalizumab should be discontinued)

» Thrombocytopenia
(efalizumab should be discontinued if thrombocytopenia develops)

Patient monitoring

The following may be especially important in patient monitoring (other tests may be warranted in some patients, depending on condition; » = major clinical significance):

» Infections, signs and symptoms
(patients should be monitored for signs and symptoms of an infection during and after a course of efalizumab therapy; new infections should be monitored closely; therapy should be discontinued if patient develops a serious infection)

Platelet counts
(recommended upon initiating treatment [e.g., monthly] and periodically [e.g., every 3 months] with continued treatment of efalizumab)

Psoriasis worsening including patients not responding to efalizumab
(should be closely observed following discontinuation; some patients required hospitalization and alternative antipsoriatic therapy)

» Thrombocytopenia, signs and symptoms of
(patients should be followed closely and platelet counts assessed during treatment with efalizumab)

Side/Adverse Effects

The following side/adverse effects have been selected on the basis of their potential clinical significance (possible signs and symptoms in parentheses where appropriate)—not necessarily inclusive:

Note: In patients evaluated for antibodies to efalizumab following efalizumab treatment, low-titer antibodies to efalizumab or other protein part of the efalizumab product were detected in 6.3% of patients.

Those indicating need for medical attention

Incidence less frequent

Hypersensitivity reaction (difficulty in breathing or swallowing; fast heartbeat; shortness of breath; skin itching; rash or redness; swelling of face, throat, or tongue); ***serious infection including; abscess*** (accumulation of pus; swollen, red, tender area of infection; fever); ***arthritis, septic*** (muscle or joint stiffness, tightness, or rigidity); ***aseptic meningitis*** (fever; headache; nausea; stiff neck or back; vomiting); ***bronchitis*** (cough producing mucus; difficulty breathing; shortness of breath; tightness in chest; wheezing); ***cellulitis*** (itching, pain, redness, swelling, tenderness, warmth on skin); ***gastroenteritis*** (abdominal or stomach pain; diarrhea; loss of appetite; nausea; weakness); ***Legionnaire's disease; pneumonia*** (chest pain; cough; fever or chills; sneezing; shortness of breath; sore throat; troubled breathing; tightness in chest; wheezing); ***sepsis*** (chest pain; cough; fever or chills; sneezing; shortness of breath; sore throat; troubled breathing; tightness in chest; wheezing); ***sinusitis*** (pain or tenderness around eyes and cheekbones; fever; stuffy or runny nose; headache; cough; shortness of breath or troubled breathing; tightness of chest or wheezing); ***vertebral osteomyelitis*** (increase bone pain in vertebrae)

Incidence rare

Bronchiolitis obliterans (coughing; wheezing; or shortness of breath); ***hepatitis, idiopathic*** (dark urine; general tiredness and weakness; light-colored stools; nausea and vomiting; upper right abdominal pain; yellow eyes and skin); ***inflammatory arthritis*** (pain, swelling, or redness in joints; muscle pain or stiffness; difficulty in moving); ***interstitial pneumonitis*** (cough; difficult breathing; fever; shortness of breath); ***malignancies*** (unusual lumps or skin changes); ***psoriasis worsening events including; erythrodermic*** (abnormal redness of the skin); ***guttate subtypes*** (small usually colored spots on skin); ***pustular*** (spots on your skin resembling a blister or pimple); ***hearing loss, sensorineural; sialadenitis*** (swollen salivary glands?); ***thrombocytopenia*** (black, tarry stools; bleeding gums; blood in urine or stools; pinpoint red spots on skin; unusual bleeding or bruising); ***transverse myelitis*** (back pain; sudden and severe muscle weakness, sudden and progressing)

Those indicating need for medical attention only if they continue or are bothersome

Incidence more frequent

Chills; fever; flu syndrome (chills; cough; diarrhea; fever; general feeling of discomfort or illness; headache; joint pain; loss of appetite; muscle aches and pains; nausea; runny nose; shivering; sore throat; sweating; trouble sleeping; unusual tiredness or weakness; vomiting); ***headache; myalgia*** (joint pain; swollen joints; muscle aching or cramping; muscle pains or stiffness; difficulty in moving); ***nausea***

Incidence less frequent

Acne (blemishes on the skin; pimples); ***arthralgia*** (pain in joints; muscle pain or stiffness; difficulty in moving); ***asthenia*** (lack or loss of strength); ***back pain; edema, peripheral*** (swelling of hands, ankles, feet, or lower legs); ***psoriasis, exacerbation of pre-existing***

Overdose

For more information on the management of overdose or unintentional ingestion, **contact a poison control center** (see *Poison Control Center Listing*).

Clinical effects of overdose

The following effects have been selected on the basis of their potential clinical significance (possible signs and symptoms in parentheses where appropriate)—not necessarily inclusive:

vomiting

Treatment of overdose

There is no known specific antidote to efalizumab. Treatment is generally symptomatic and supportive.

Monitoring—

Monitoring for 24 to 48 hours for acute signs or symptoms of adverse reactions or effects.

Supportive care—

Patients in whom intentional overdose is confirmed or suspected should be referred for psychiatric consultation.

Patient Consultation

As an aid to patient consultation, refer to *Advice for the Patient, Efalizumab (Systemic)*.

In providing consultation, consider emphasizing the following selected information (» = major clinical significance):

Before using this medication

» Conditions affecting use, especially:

Hypersensitivity to efalizumab or any of its components

Pregnancy—Efalizumab should be given to a pregnant woman only if clearly needed.

Breast-feeding—It is not known whether efalizumab is distributed into breast milk. However, efalizumab is distributed into the milk of lactating mice. Since animal data suggests adverse effects in nursing infants, a decision should be made whether to discontinue nursing or to discontinue the use of efalizumab.

Use in children—Safety and efficacy have not been established.

Use in the elderly—Elderly patients in general are more likely to have a higher incidence of infections.

Other medications, especially acellular, live and live-attenuated vaccines, immunosuppressive agents, or phototherapy

Other medical problems, especially clinically significant infection, malignancies or history of or thrombocytopenia

Proper use of this medication

» Proper dosing

Missed dose: If you miss a dose, contact your healthcare provider to find out when to take your next dose of efalizumab and what schedule to follow after that.

» Importance of proper reconstitution method

» Importance of proper administration

Proper storage

Precautions while using this medication

» Regular visits to physician to check lymphocyte counts

» Patients should be instructed to contact physician immediately if they have symptoms suggestive of an infection or malignancy

» Female patients should be instructed to contact physician if they become pregnant

Side/adverse effects

Signs of potential side effects, especially aseptic meningitis, bronchiolitis obliterans, idiopathic hepatitis, infection including, abscess, aseptic meningitis, bronchitis, cellulitis, gastroenteritis, Legionnaire's disease, pneumonia, sepsis, septic arthritis, sinusitis, and vertebral osteomyelitis; inflammatory arthritis, interstitial pneumonitis, malignancies, psoriasis worsening such as erythrodermic, guttate subtypes, and pustular; sensorineural hearing loss, sialadenitis, thrombocytopenia, or transverse myelitis

General Dosing Information

For parenteral dosing forms:

Efalizumab is intended for use under the guidance and supervision of a physician. If it has been determined appropriate, patients may self-inject after proper training in the preparation and injection technique, and with medical follow-up.

The reconstituted solution should be clear to pale yellow. Visually inspect the solution for particulate matter and discoloration prior to subcutaneous administration. The solution should not be used if discolored or if undissolved material remains. Do not reconstitute with other diluents.

Injection sites should be rotated. Sites for injection include thigh, abdomen, buttocks, or upper arm.

Following administration, discard any unused reconstituted efalizumab solution.

Parenteral Dosage Forms

EFALIZUMAB FOR INJECTION

Usual adult dose

Psoriasis—

Subcutaneous (SC), 0.7 mg/kg conditioning dose followed by weekly SC doses of 1 mg/kg.

Usual adult prescribing limits

Up to a single 200 mg dose.

Usual pediatric dose

Safety and efficacy have not been established

Usual geriatric dose

See *Usual adult dose*.

Usual geriatric prescribing limits

See *Usual adult prescribing limits*.

Strength(s) usually available

U.S.—

125 mg single-use vial (Rx) [*Raptiva* (L-histidine; L-histidine hydrochloride monohydrate; polysorbate 20; sterile water for injection (non USP); sucrose)].

Packaging and storage

Store between 2 and 8 °C (36 and 46 °F), in original carton. Protect from light.

Preparation of dosage form

Efalizumab should be administered using one of the sterile, disposable syringe and needles provided. Remove the cap from the pre-filled syringe containing sterile water for injection (non-USP) and attach the needle to the syringe. Remove the plastic cap protecting the rubber stopper of the efalizumab vial and wipe the top with one of the alcohol swabs provided. After cleaning with the alcohol swab, do not touch the top of the vial. To prepare the efalizumab solution, use the pre-filled diluent syringe and slowly inject the 1.3 mL of sterile water for injection (non-USP) into the vial. Swirl the vial gently to dissolve the product. DO NOT SHAKE. Shaking will cause the efalizumab solution to foam. Dissolution generally takes less than 5 minutes. Efalizumab is provided as a single-use vial and contains no antibacterial preservatives. Reconstitute immediately before use and use only once. The reconstituted solution should be clear to pale yellow and free of particulates. Inspect visually for particulate matter and discoloration prior to subcutaneous administration. If particulates or discolorations exist, do not use. Replace the needle on the syringe with a new needle. Insert the needle into the vial containing the efalizumab solution, invert the vial, and keeping the needle below the level of the liquid, withdraw the dose to be given into the syringe.

Stability

Following reconstitution, the product should be used immediately or stored at room temperature and used within 8 hours.

Incompatibilities

No other medications should be added to solutions containing efalizumab, and efalizumab should not be reconstituted with other diluents.

Auxiliary labeling

• This medication may lower your immune system's ability to fight off infection. Avoid contact with people with a contagious disease.
• Do not shake. Rotate vial gently.
• Please read patient information leaflet enclosed.

Developed: 10/13/2004

EFAVIRENZ Systemic

VA CLASSIFICATION (Primary): AM840

Commonly used brand name(s): *Sustiva.*

Another commonly use name is EFV

Note: For a listing of dosage forms and brand names by country availability, see *Dosage Forms* section(s).

Category

Antiviral (systemic).

Indications

General Considerations

The use of efavirenz for the treatment of human immunodeficiency virus type 1 (HIV-1) infection is based on analyses of plasma HIV-RNA levels and CD4 cell counts in controlled studies of up to 24 weeks duration. Results from controlled trials evaluating the long-term suppression of HIV-RNA with efavirenz have not yet been obtained.

When non-nucleoside reverse transcriptase inhibitors (NNRTIs) are administered as monotherapy, viral resistance occurs over a short period of time. Therefore, efavirenz should not be given as a single agent or added by itself to a failing regimen. Efavirenz should be initiated in combination with at least one new antiretroviral agent to which the patient has not been previously exposed.

Accepted

Human immunodeficiency virus (HIV) (treatment)—Efavirenz is indicated in combination with other antiretroviral agents for the treatment of human immunodeficiency virus type 1 (HIV-1) infection.

Pharmacology/Pharmacokinetics

Physicochemical characteristics

Molecular weight—315.68.

Solubility—Practically insoluble in water (< 10 mcg/mL).

Mechanism of action/Effect

Efavirenz is a non-nucleoside reverse transcriptase inhibitor (NNRTI) of human immunodeficiency virus type 1 (HIV-1). The action of efavirenz is through noncompetitive inhibition of HIV-1 reverse transcriptase. Efavirenz has no inhibitory effect on human immunodeficiency virus type 2 (HIV-2) reverse transcriptase or human cellular DNA polymerases alpha, beta, gamma, or delta.

Absorption

Dose-related increases in peak plasma concentration (C_{max}) and area under the curve (AUC) were seen for doses up to 1600 mg. The increases were less than proportional, suggesting diminished absorption at higher doses.

Meals of normal composition had no significant effect on the bioavailability of 100 mg of an investigational efavirenz formulation administered twice a day for 10 days with meals. The relative bioavailability of a single 1200 mg dose of an investigational efavirenz formulation in uninfected volunteers was increased by 50% (range 11 to 126%) following a high fat meal. Efavirenz may be taken with or without meals; however, it should not be taken with meals with a high fat content.

Distribution

In HIV-1 infected patients who received efavirenz 200 to 600 mg once a day for at least 1 month, cerebrospinal fluid concentrations ranged from 0.26 to 1.19% (mean 0.69%) of the corresponding plasma concentration. This proportion is approximately threefold higher than the non–protein-bound (free) fraction of efavirenz in plasma.

Protein binding

Very high (approximately 99.5 to 99.75%); primarily bound to albumin.

Biotransformation

Efavirenz is metabolized primarily by the hepatic cytochrome P450 system into hydroxylated, inactive metabolites. These metabolites undergo subsequent glucuronidation. *In vitro* studies suggest that CYP3A4 and CYP2B6 are the principal isoenzymes responsible for the metabolism of efavirenz. Efavirenz is an inducer of cytochrome P450 enzymes, resulting in the induction of its own metabolism. Ten days of therapy with 200 to 400 mg of efavirenz daily resulted in a lower-than-expected accumulation of medication (22 to 42% lower) and a shorter terminal half-life, 40 to 55 hours compared with the single-dose half-life of 52 to 76 hours.

Half-life

Elimination—

Terminal half-life:

Single dose—52 to 76 hours.

Multiple doses—40 to 55 hours.

Time to peak concentration

3 to 5 hours.

Peak serum concentration

12.9 ± 3.7 micromoles at steady state; 1.6 to 9.1 micromoles following single oral doses of 100 to 1600 mg.

Elimination

Renal; 14 to 34% of a radiolabeled dose of efavirenz was recovered in the urine, nearly all in the form of metabolites.

Fecal; 16 to 61% of a radiolabeled dose was recovered, primarily unchanged, in the feces.

Precautions to Consider

Carcinogenicity

Long-term carcinogenicity studies in mice and rat were carried out with efavirenz. Mice were dosed with up to 300 mg per kg of body weight per day for 2 years. Incidences of hepatocellular adenomas and carcinomas and pulmonary alveolar/bronchiolar adenomas were increased in females but not in males. In a rat studies with doses up to 100 mg per kg of body weight per day for 2 years, no increases in tumor incidence above background were observed. The systemic exposure (based on AUCs) in mice was approximately 1.7-fold that in humans receiving the 600-mg per day dose. The exposure in rats was lower than that in humans. The mechanism of the carcinogenic potential is unknown.

Mutagenicity

Efavirenz was not shown to be mutagenic or genotoxic in either *in vitro* or *in vivo* genotoxicity assays. The assays included bacterial mutation assays in *Salmonella typhimurium* and *Escherichia coli*, mammalian mutation assays in Chinese hamster ovary cells, chromosomal aberration assays in human peripheral blood lymphocytes or Chinese hamster ovary cells, and an *in vivo* mouse bone marrow micronucleus assay.

Pregnancy/Reproduction

Fertility—Efavirenz did not impair the mating or fertility of male or female rats. Sperm of male rats treated with efavirenz were not affected. The reproductive performance of offspring born to females given efavirenz was not affected. Rapid clearance of efavirenz occurs in rats. As a result, the systemic drug exposures achieved in these fertility studies were either equivalent to or below those achieved in humans on therapeutic doses of efavirenz.

Pregnancy—No adequate and well-controlled studies have been performed in pregnant women. Efavirenz should be used during pregnancy only if the potential benefit justifies the potential risk to the fetus, such as in pregnant women without other therapeutic options.

In animal studies, malformations have been observed in cynomolgus monkey fetuses whose mothers received doses of efavirenz throughout pregnancy (postcoital days 20 to 150) that resulted in plasma concentrations similar to those seen in humans at a 600 mg per day dose. The malformations occurred at a rate of 3 fetuses with malformations out of 20. The malformations included anencephaly and unilateral anophthalmia in one fetus, microophthalmia in another fetus, and cleft palate in a third fetus. Efavirenz crosses the placenta in cynomolgus monkeys and results in fetal blood concentrations that are similar to maternal blood concentrations. Efavirenz also has been shown to cross the placenta in both rats and rabbits, producing fetal blood concentrations similar to those of maternal concentrations. An increase in fetal resorptions was observed in rats at efavirenz doses that produced peak plasma concentrations and AUC values in rats equivalent to or lower than those achieved in humans at doses of 600 mg daily. No reproductive toxicities were seen when efavirenz was given to pregnant rabbits at doses that produced peak plasma concentrations that were similar to, and AUC values that were approximately half of, those achieved in humans at doses of 600 mg daily.

Efavirenz may cause fetal harm when administered during the first trimester to a pregnant woman. Pregnancy should be avoided in women receiving efavirenz. Two methods of birth control, a method of barrier contraception in combination with another method of contraception, such as an oral or other hormonal contraceptive, should be used to avoid pregnancy. Before initiating therapy with efavirenz, women of childbearing potential should undergo pregnancy testing. If this drug is used during the first trimester of pregnancy, or if the patient becomes pregnant while taking this drug, the patient should be apprised of the potential harm to the fetus.

An Antiretroviral Pregnancy Registry has been established to monitor the outcomes of pregnant women exposed to efavirenz. Physicians are encouraged by the manufacturer to register patients by calling (800) 258-4263.

As of July 2004, the Antiretroviral Pregnancy Registry has received prospective reports of 237 pregnancies exposed to efavirenz, most of which occurred in the first trimester (232 pregnancies). Birth defects occurred in 5 of 188 live births (first-trimester exposure) and 0 of 13 live births (second/third-trimester exposure). None of these prospectively reported defects were neural tube defects. However, there have been four retrospective reports of findings consistent with neural tube defects, including meningomyelocele, during first-trimester exposure. Although no causal relationship has been established, similar defects have been observed in preclinical studies of efavirenz.

FDA Pregnancy Category D

Breast-feeding

It is not known whether efavirenz is distributed into breast milk in humans. However, efavirenz is distributed into the milk of lactating rats. In addition, the Centers for Disease Control and Prevention recommends that HIV-infected mothers refrain from breast-feeding their infants to avoid risking postnatal transmission of HIV. Because of the potential for HIV transmission and the potential for serious adverse effects in nursing infants, mothers should be instructed not to breast-feed if they are receiving efavirenz.

Pediatrics

Safety and efficacy have not been established in children up to 3 years of age or those who weigh less than 13 kg. The types and severity of adverse reactions generally were similar to those of adults; however, children experienced a higher incidence of rash (40% of children compared with 28% of adults). In addition, the incidence of severe rash (Grade 3 or 4) was higher in children; 7% of children developed a severe rash compared with 0.7% of adults. The median time to onset of rash in children was 8 days. Prophylaxis with appropriate antihistamines prior to initiating therapy with efavirenz should be considered.

Geriatrics

No information is available on the relationship of age to the effects of efavirenz in geriatric patients. In general, dose selection should be caution, reflecting the greater frequency of decreased hepatic, renal, or cardiac function and of concomitant disease or other therapy.

Drug interactions and/or related problems

The following drug interactions and/or related problems have been selected on the basis of their potential clinical significance (possible mechanism in parentheses where appropriate)—not necessarily inclusive (» = major clinical significance):

Note: Combinations containing any of the following medications, depending on the amount present, may also interact with this medication.

Alcohol or
Psychoactive drugs
(concurrent use may have an additive effect on the central nervous system [CNS] effects of efavirenz)

» Amprenavir
(efavirenz may decrease the plasma concentrations of amprenavir; no specific dosage adjustment can be recommended until additional studies are conducted)

Anticonvulsants including
Carbamazepine
Phenobarbital
Phenytoin
(potential for anticonvulsant and/or efavirenz plasma levels reduction; periodic monitoring of anticonvulsant plasma levels should be conducted)

» Astemizole or
» Cisapride
(efavirenz may inhibit the metabolism of these medications through competition for the CYP3A4 isoenzyme, which may increase the potential for cardiac arrythmias; use is **contraindicated**)

Atazanavir
(efavirenz may decrease atazanavir concentration)

Clarithromycin
(efavirenz may decrease the plasma concentration of clarithromycin; consideration of alternatives to clarithromycin, such as azithromycin, is recommended since coadministration of azithromycin with efavirenz did not result in any clinically significant pharmacokinetic interactions; other macrolide antibiotics, such as erythromycin, have not been studied in combination with efavirenz)

» Ergot derivatives
(efavirenz may inhibit the metabolism of these medications, increasing the potential for respiratory depression; use is **contraindicated**)

Ethinyl estradiol
(plasma concentrations of this medication may be increased by efavirenz; the clinical significance is unknown; the addition of a reliable method of barrier contraception is recommended)

» Indinavir
(efavirenz may decrease plasma concentrations of indinavir through enzyme induction; it is recommended that the dose of indinavir be increased from 800 milligrams every 8 hours to 1000 milligrams every 8 hours when used concurrently with efavirenz)

Itraconazole or
Ketoconazole
(drug interaction studies have not been conducted; concomitant use has potential to decrease itraconazole and ketoconazole plasma concentrations)

Lopinavir/ritonavir combination
(efavirenz may decrease lopinavir concentration)

Medications metabolized by hepatic enzymes 2C9, 2C19, and 3A4
(concurrent use of efavirenz with medications primarily metabolized by the isoenzymes 2C9, 2C19, and 3A4 may result in altered plasma concentrations of the coadministered medication due to induction or inhibition of these enzymes by efavirenz)

Methadone
(coadministration in HIV patients with a history of injection drug use resulted in decreased methadone plasma levels and opiate withdrawal symptoms; patient monitoring for signs of withdrawal and methadone dose increases as required to alleviate withdrawal symptoms)

» Midazolam or
» Triazolam
(efavirenz may inhibit the metabolism of these medications through competition for the CYP3A4 isoenzyme, increasing the potential for prolonged sedation; use is **contraindicated**)

Non-nucleoside reverse transcriptase inhibitors (NNRTIs)
(no studies have been performed)

» Rifabutin
(plasma concentrations of rifabutin may be decreased by efavirenz; increasing the dose of rifabutin by at least 50% may be considered for concurrent administration; adjustment of efavirenz dosage is not necessary)

Rifampin
(concurrent use of rifampin may decrease efavirenz plasma concentrations; the clinical significance of decreased efavirenz concentrations is unknown; adjustment of efavirenz or rifampin dosage is not recommended)

» Ritonavir
(concurrent use of efavirenz with ritonavir may result in a higher frequency of adverse effects [dizziness, nausea, and paresthesia] and laboratory abnormalities [elevated liver enzymes]; monitoring of liver enzymes is recommended)

» Saquinavir
(plasma concentrations of saquinavir may be decreased by efavirenz; it should not be used as the sole protease inhibitor in combination with efavirenz)

Sertraline
(may decrease sertraline concentration; increases in sertraline dose should be guided by clinical response)

» St. John's wort
(concomitant use not recommended; coadministration is expected to substantially decrease efavirenz concentrations and may result in suboptimal levels of efavirenz and lead to loss of virologic response and possible resistance to efavirenz or other non-nucleoside reverse transcriptase inhibitors)

» Voriconazole
(concomitant administration **contraindicated** because efavirenz significantly decreases voriconazole plasma concentrations)

» Warfarin
(plasma concentrations and clinical effects may be either increased or decreased when the medication is used concurrently with efavirenz)

Laboratory value alterations

The following have been selected on the basis of their potential clinical significance (possible effect in parentheses where appropriate)—not necessarily inclusive (» = major clinical significance).

With diagnostic test results
Cannabinoid test
(although efavirenz does not bind to cannabinoid receptors, false positive urine cannabinoid test results have been reported in uninfected volunteers who received efavirenz; the false-positive test results have been observed only with the CEDIA DAU Multi-Level THC assay, used for screening, and were not observed with other cannabinoid assays, including those used for confirmation of positive results)

With physiology/laboratory test values
Alanine aminotransferase (ALT [SGPT]) or
Aspartate aminotransferase (AST [SGOT]) or
Gamma-glutamyl transferase (GGT)
(values may be increased)

Neutrophils
(values may be decreased)

Medical considerations/Contraindications

The medical considerations/contraindications included have been selected on the basis of their potential clinical significance (reasons given in parentheses where appropriate)—not necessarily inclusive (» = major clinical significance).

Except under special circumstances, this medication should not be used when the following medical problem exists:

» Hypersensitivity to efavirenz or any of its components

Risk-benefit should be considered when the following medical problems exist:

» Hepatic function impairment or
» Hepatitis B or C, confirmed or suspected history of
(caution is recommended because of the lack of experience with efavirenz in hepatic function impairment and the necessary metabolism of efavirenz by the cytochrome P450 system; liver enzymes should be monitored periodically)

Mental illness, history of or
Substance abuse, history of
(may increase occurrence of serious psychiatric symptoms that have been reported in patients receiving efavirenz)

» Seizures, history of
(caution must be taken; convulsions have been observed in patients receiving efavirenz)

Patient monitoring

The following may be especially important in patient monitoring (other tests may be warranted in some patients, depending on condition; » = major clinical significance):

Liver enzymes
(monitoring of liver enzymes is recommended in patients in whom a history of hepatitis B or C is confirmed or suspected and in patients treated with other medications associated with liver toxicity)

Lipids
(efavirenz may increase total cholesterol or serum triglycerides; clinical significance is not yet known)

Side/Adverse Effects

Note: Fifty-two percent of patients treated with efavirenz reported CNS or psychiatric symptoms. In 2.6% of patients these symptoms were severe and resulted in discontinuation of therapy with efavirenz. The CNS and psychiatric symptoms usually appear within the first or second day of treatment and generally resolve after 2 to 4 weeks of therapy.

Skin rashes usually appear as mild or moderate maculopapular skin eruptions that occur within the first 2 weeks of therapy with efavirenz.

Redistribution/accumulation of body fat including central obesity, dorsocervical fat enlargement (buffalo hump), peripheral wasting, facial wasting, breast enlargement, and "cushingoid appearance" have been observed in patients receiving antiretroviral therapy. The mechanism and long-term consequences are currently unknown and a causal relationship has not been established.

Immune reconstitution syndrome has been reported in patients treated with combination antiretroviral therapy, including efavirenz. During initial phase of combination treatment, patients whose immune system responds may develop an inflammatory response to indolent or residual opportunistic infections such as *Mycobacterium avium* infection, cytomegalovirus, *Pneumocystis carinii* pneumonia, or tuberculosis. This may require further evaluation and treatment

The side/adverse effects listed below were observed when efavirenz was used in combination with other antiretrovirals.

The following side/adverse effects have been selected on the basis of their potential clinical significance (possible signs and symptoms in parentheses where appropriate)—not necessarily inclusive:

Those indicating need for medical attention

Incidence more frequent
Depression; pruritus (itching); ***skin rash***—incidence 27% in adults, 40% in children

Incidence less frequent
Hematuria (blood in urine); ***increase in total cholesterol concentration***—asymptomatic; ***renal calculus*** (difficult or painful urination; pain in lower back and/or side)

Incidence rare
Abnormal vision (changes in vision); ***allergic reaction*** (skin rash or hives; fever; troubled breathing; tightness in chest; wheezing); ***asthma*** (cough; difficulty breathing; tightness in chest; wheezing); ***ataxia*** (clumsiness or unsteadiness); ***confusion; convulsions; depression, severe acute; diplopia*** (double vision); ***elevated liver enzymes***—asymptomatic; ***erythema multiforme*** (possible prodrome of chills, fever, sore throat, muscle aches or pains, or nausea or vomiting; sores, ulcers, or white spots in mouth or on lips; skin rash or sores, hives, or itching); ***fever; hepatitis*** (yellow eyes or skin; loss of appetite; unusual tiredness; weight loss; fever; skin rash or itching; nausea or vomiting; dark urine); ***impaired coordination*** (difficulty with coordination); ***migraine headache*** (headache, severe and throbbing); ***neuralgia*** (nerve pain); ***pancreatitis*** (abdominal pain; fever with or without chills; swelling and/or tenderness in upper abdominal or stomach area); ***paresthesia*** (tingling, burning, or prickling sensations); ***peripheral edema*** (swelling of hands, arms, feet, or legs; rapid weight gain); ***peripheral neuropathy*** (tingling, burning, numbness, or pain in the hands, arms, feet, or legs); ***psychological reactions, such as; delusions or inappropriate behavior***—primarily in patients with a history of mental illness or substance abuse (incidence 0.1 to 0.2%); ***hallucinations*** (seeing, hearing, or feeling things that are not there); ***psychosis*** (severe mood or mental changes); ***speech disorder; Stevens-Johnson syndrome; suicidal ideation or attempts*** (thoughts of suicide or attempts at suicide); ***syncope*** (fainting); ***tachycardia or palpitations*** (fast or pounding heartbeat); ***thrombophlebitis*** (pain, tenderness, bluish color, or swelling of leg or foot); ***skin rash, severe, associated with blistering, moist desquamation, or ulceration*** (blistering; open sores; ulcers)—incidence 1%; ***tremor; urticaria*** (hives); ***vertigo*** (sense of constant movement of self or surroundings)

Incidence not determined—Observed during clinical practice; estimates of frequency can not be determined
Aggressive reactions (attack, assault, force); ***dyspnea*** (shortness of breath; difficult or labored breathing; tightness in chest; wheezing); ***hepatic failure*** (headache; stomach pain; continuing vomiting; dark-colored urine; general feeling of tiredness or weakness; light-colored stools; yellow eyes or skin); ***mania*** (actions that are out of control; irritability; nervousness; talking, feeling, and acting with excitement); ***neurosis; paranoia*** (delusions of persecution, mistrust, suspiciousness, and/or combativeness); ***photoallergic dermatitis*** (early appearance of redness or swelling of the skin; late appearance of rash with or without weeping blisters that become crusted, especially in sun-exposed areas of skin, may extend to unexposed areas)

Those indicating need for medical attention only if they continue or are bothersome

Incidence more frequent
Diarrhea; dizziness; fatigue; headache; impaired concentration (poor concentration); ***increased sweating; insomnia*** (trouble in sleeping); ***nausea or vomiting; somnolence*** (drowsiness)

Incidence less frequent
Abdominal pain or dyspepsia (abdominal pain; heartburn; indigestion; stomach discomfort); ***abnormal dreams; anorexia*** (loss of appetite); ***flatulence*** (belching; excessive gas); ***hypoesthesia*** (abnormally decreased sensitivity, particularly to touch); ***nervousness***

Incidence rare
Agitation or anxiety; alopecia (loss of hair); ***amnesia*** (loss of memory); ***apathy*** (lack of feeling or emotion); ***arthralgia or myalgia*** (joint or muscle pain); ***asthenia*** (weakness); ***depersonalization*** (loss of sense of reality); ***dry mouth; eczema*** (skin rash); ***emotional lability*** (mood changes); ***euphoria*** (false sense of well-being); ***folliculitis*** (painful, red, hot, or irritated hair follicles); ***flushing; malaise*** (general feeling of discomfort); ***parosmia*** (change in sense of smell); ***skin exfoliation*** (flaking and falling off of skin); ***taste perversion*** (change in sense of taste); ***tinnitus*** (ringing in the ears)

Incidence not determined—Observed during clinical practice; estimates of frequency can not be determined
Constipation (difficulty having a bowel movement [stool]); ***gynecomastia*** (swelling of the breasts or breast soreness in both females

and males); ***hypertriglyceridemia*** (large amount of triglyceride in the blood); ***malabsorption; myopathy*** (muscular pain, tenderness, wasting or weakness); ***nail disorders*** (discoloration of fingernails or toenails); ***redistribution/accumulation of body fat; skin discoloration*** (change in color of treated skin)

Overdose

Some patients who accidentally took twice the recommended adult daily dose reported increased CNS symptoms. One patient experienced involuntary muscle contractions.

For more information on the management of overdose or unintentional ingestion, **contact a Poison Control Center** (see *Poison Control Center Listing*).

Treatment of overdose

There is no specific antidote for overdose of efavirenz. Treatment of overdose should consist of general supportive measures, including monitoring the patient's vital signs and clinical status.

To decrease absorption—Activated charcoal may be administered to aid the removal of unabsorbed efavirenz. Dialysis is not expected to significantly remove efavirenz from the blood since the drug is highly protein bound.

Supportive care—Patients in whom intentional overdose is confirmed or suspected should be referred for psychiatric consultation.

Patient Consultation

As an aid to patient consultation, refer to *Advice for the Patient, Efavirenz (Systemic)*.

In providing consultation, consider emphasizing the following selected information (» = major clinical significance):

Before using this medication

» Conditions affecting use, especially:

Hypersensitivity to efavirenz or any component of the product

Pregnancy—Should be used during pregnancy only if potential benefit justifies potential risk, such as in women with no other therapeutic options; if used during first trimester of if patient becomes pregnant while taking efavirenz, patient should be apprised of potential harm to the fetus

Breast-feeding—Because of potential for HIV transmission and serious adverse effects in nursing infants, mothers should be instructed NOT to breast-feed if they are receiving efavirenz.

Use in children—Children are at an increased risk for skin rash, which may be severe; the appearance of a rash should be reported to the physician as soon as possible

Use in the elderly—Dose selection should be cautious in elderly patients.

Other medications, especially amprenavir, astemizole, cisapride, ergot derivatives, indinavir, midazolam, rifabutin, ritonavir, saquinavir, St. John's wort, triazolam, voriconazole, or warfarin

Other medical problems, especially liver function impairment, history of hepatitis B or C, or history of seizures

Proper use of this medication

» Importance of not taking more medication than prescribed; importance of not discontinuing efavirenz without checking with physician

» Compliance with full course of therapy with efavirenz and with any other medications prescribed for HIV infection

» Importance of informing doctor of all medicines you are taking, prescription (Rx) and nonprescription (over-the-counter [OTC])

Taking efavirenz at bedtime on an empty stomach because food may increase the absorption of the medication and dosing at bedtime may make nervous system symptoms more tolerable.

Being aware that the CNS and psychiatric side effects are likely to decrease with continued therapy; dosing at bedtime, especially during the first 2 to 4 weeks of treatment, may make these side effects more tolerable

» Proper dosing

Missed dose: Taking as soon as possible; not taking if almost time for next dose; not doubling doses

» Proper storage

Precautions while using this medication

» Avoiding potentially hazardous tasks such as driving or operating machinery since efavirenz may cause dizziness, impaired concentration, and/or drowsiness

» Checking with physician before taking efavirenz with alcohol or other psychoactive medications since concurrent use may exacerbate the CNS effects

» Seeking medical attention immediately if serious psychiatric symptoms occur

» Being aware that efavirenz therapy does not reduce the risk of transmitting HIV to others through sexual contact or contamination through blood

» Using two methods of contraception, a reliable barrier method and an oral or other hormonal contraceptive, when the potential for pregnancy exists

» Advising patient to contact physician promptly if skin rash develops

Side/adverse effects

Signs of potential side effects, especially depression; pruritus; skin rash; hematuria; renal calculus; abnormal vision; allergic reaction; asthma; ataxia; confusion; convulsions; diplopia; erythema multiforme; fever; hepatitis; impaired coordination; migraine headache; neuralgia; pancreatitis; paresthesia; peripheral edema; peripheral neuropathy; psychological reactions, such as delusions, inappropriate behavior, hallucinations, or psychosis; speech disorder; Stevens-Johnson syndrome; suicidal ideation or attempts; syncope; tachycardia or palpitations; thrombophlebitis; tremor; urticaria; and vertigo

Signs of potential side effects observed during clinical practice, especially aggressive reactions, dyspnea, hepatic failure, mania, neurosis, paranoia, or photoallergic dermatitis

General Dosing Information

When non-nucleoside reverse transcriptase inhibitors (NNRTIs) are administered as monotherapy, viral resistance occurs over a short period of time. Therefore, efavirenz should not be given as a single agent or added solely to a failing regimen. Efavirenz should be initiated in combination with at least one new antiretroviral agent to which the patient has not previously been exposed.

Treatment with efavirenz may be reinitiated in patients whose therapy was interrupted by a skin rash. The use of appropriate antihistamines and/or corticosteroids is recommended when efavirenz is restarted.

Prophylaxis with antihistamines is recommended in children before initiating therapy with efavirenz due to the high incidence of skin rash, which may be severe, in this population.

Efavirenz should be taken at bedtime because this may make nervous system symptoms more tolerable.

Diet/Nutrition

It is recommended that efavirenz be taken on an empty stomach. Increased efavirenz concentrations observed following administration of efavirenz with food may lead to an increase in frequency of adverse events.

For treatment of adverse effects

Recommended treatment consists of the following:

- Discontinuation of efavirenz in patients who experience skin rash associated with blistering, desquamation, mucosal involvement, or fever. Treatment with antihistamines and/or corticosteroids may increase the tolerability of symptoms and shorten the time to resolution of the rash.

Oral Dosage Forms

EFAVIRENZ CAPSULES

Note: Efavirenz is indicated in combination with other antiretroviral medications and must not be taken as a single agent.

Usual adult and adolescent dose

Antiviral—

Oral, 600 mg once a day in combination with a protease inhibitor and/or nucleoside analogue reverse transcriptase inhibitors (NRTIs).

Concomitant therapy with atazanavir and ritonavir: Oral, efavirenz 600 mg with atazanavir 300 mg and ritonavir 100 mg (all once daily) in treatment-naive patients. Dose recommendations not established in treatment-experienced

Concomitant therapy with lopinavir/ritonavir combination: Oral, efavirenz 600 mg once daily with lopinavir/ritonavir 533/133 mg (4 capsules or 6.5 mL) twice daily with food.

Usual pediatric dose

Antiviral—

Children up to 3 years of age: Safety and efficacy have not been established.

Children 3 years of age and older (by weight):

10 to less than 15 kg—Oral, 200 mg once a day.
15 to less than 20 kg—Oral, 250 mg once a day.
20 to less than 25 kg—Oral, 300 mg once a day.
25 to less than 32.5 kg—Oral, 350 mg once a day.
32.5 to less than 40 kg—Oral, 400 mg once a day.
≥ 40 kg—See *Usual adult and adolescent dose*.

Usual geriatric dose
Antiviral—
See *Usual adult and adolescent dose.*

Strength(s) usually available
U.S.—
50 mg (Rx) [*Sustiva*].
100 mg (Rx) [*Sustiva*].
200 mg (Rx) [*Sustiva*].

Packaging and storage
Store at 25 °C (77 °F); brief deviations between 15 and 30 °C (59 and 86 °F) are allowed.

Auxiliary labeling
• This drug alone or with alcohol may cause drowsiness. Use care when driving or operating machinery.
• Take at bedtime.
• Tell your doctor about all medications you are taking; prescription and nonprescription

EFAVIRENZ TABLETS

Note: Efavirenz is indicated in combination with other antiretroviral medications and must not be taken as a single agent.

Usual adult and adolescent dose
See *Efavirenz Capsules.*

Usual pediatric dose
See *Efavirenz Capsules.*

Usual geriatric dose
See *Efavirenz Capsules.*

Strength(s) usually available
U.S.—
600 mg (Rx) [*Sustiva* (croscarmellose sodium; hydroxypropylcellulose; lactose monohydrate; magnesium stearate; microcrystalline cellulose; sodium lauryl sulfate; carnauba wax; Opadry yellow; Opadry clear; Opacode WB)].

Packaging and storage
Store at 25 °C (77 °F); excursions permitted to 15 to 30 °C (59 to 86 °F) are allowed.

Auxiliary labeling
• This drug alone or with alcohol may cause drowsiness. Use care when driving or operating machinery.
• Take at bedtime.
• Tell your doctor about all medications you are taking; prescription and nonprescription

Selected Bibliography

Product Information: Sustiva®, efavirenz. Bristol-Myers Squibb, Princeton, NJ, (PI revised 08/2004) reviewed 12/2004.

Revised: 06/07/2005
Developed: 12/14/1998

EFLORNITHINE Systemic†

VA CLASSIFICATION (Primary): AP109

Commonly used brand name(s): *Ornidyl.*

Other commonly used names are DFMO and alpha-difluoromethylornithine.

Note: For a listing of dosage forms and brand names by country availability, see *Dosage Forms* section(s).

†Not commercially available in Canada.

Category

Antiprotozoal (systemic).

Indications

Accepted

Trypanosomiasis, African (treatment)—Eflornithineis indicated in the treatment of the meningoencephalitic stage of *Trypanosoma brucei gambiense* infection (West African sleeping sickness).

Not all species or strains of a particular organism may be susceptible to eflornithine.

Pharmacology/Pharmacokinetics

Physicochemical characteristics
Molecular weight—236.65.

Mechanism of action/Effect
Eflornithine is an enzyme-activated, irreversible inhibitor of ornithine decarboxylase (ODC), the key enzyme in the conversion of ornithine to polyamines. Polyamines (putrescine, spermidine, and spermine) play an essential role in the growth, differentiation, and replication of cells by participating in nucleic acid and protein synthesis in protozoa, as well as in normal tissue and tumors in humans. Eflornithine's inhibition of ODC results in complete intracellular elimination of putrescine and a 60–75% reduction in spermidine, producing morphologic changes of trypanosomes in the bloodstream. Because the clearance of parasites from the bloodstream is slow, it is likely that eflornithine is cytostatic rather than cytolytic; in addition, animal studies have suggested that an intact immune response is probably necessary for complete elimination of the parasites from the bloodstream.

Absorption
Well absorbed after oral administration; bioavailability approximately 50%.

Distribution
Crosses the blood-brain barrier, with cerebrospinal fluid (CSF) concentrations reaching 6 to 51% of corresponding blood concentrations. One very small study found higher penetration into the CSF of patients with the most severe form of the disease, suggesting that penetration into the CSF may be related to the degree of CNS involvement.

Vol_D=0.30 to 0.43 L per kg.

Protein binding
No significant plasma protein binding.

Half-life
Normal renal function—Elimination: 3.2 to 3.6 hours.

Time to peak serum concentration:
End of infusion.

Mean peak serum concentration
196.6 to 317.9 mcg per mL after 100 mg per kg of body weight every 6 hours.

Elimination
Renal; approximately 80% excreted unchanged in the urine within 24 hours. The renal clearance of eflornithine approximates that of creatinine clearance.

Precautions to Consider

Carcinogenicity
Long-term studies in animals have not been performed to evaluate the carcinogenic potential of eflornithine.

Mutagenicity
Eflornithine did not induce mutagenic changes in *in vitro* studies using *Salmonella* and 2 strains of *Saccharomyces.*

Pregnancy/Reproduction
Fertility—Decreased spermatogenic effects and impaired fertility were found in rats and rabbits at doses equivalent to one-half the recommended human dose and in mice at approximately 2 times the human dose.

Pregnancy—Adequate and well-controlled studies in humans have not been done. Eflornithine should only be used during pregnancy if the potential benefit justifies the potential risk to the fetus. The meningoencephalitic stage of African trypanosomiasis has such a high mortality rate if left untreated that treatment with eflornithine may justify the potential risk to the fetus.

Eflornithine has been shown to be contragestational in rats, rabbits, and mice given doses of 0.5, 0.5, and 2 times the human dose, respectively. In postnatal studies, retarded development was reported in rat pups receiving doses slightly higher than the human dose.

FDA Pregnancy Category C.

Breast-feeding
It is not known whether eflornithine is distributed into breast milk. However, problems in humans have not been documented.

Pediatrics
No information is available on the relationship of age to the effects of eflornithine in pediatric patients. Safety and efficacy have not been established.

Geriatrics
No information is available on the relationship of age to the effects of eflornithine in geriatric patients.

Dental

The bone marrow–depressant effects of eflornithine may result in an increased incidence of microbial infection, delayed healing, and gingival bleeding.

Drug interactions and/or related problems

The following drug interactions and/or related problems have been selected on the basis of their potential clinical significance (possible mechanism in parentheses where appropriate)—not necessarily inclusive (» = major clinical significance):

Note: Combinations containing any of the following medications, depending on the amount present, may also interact with this medication.

» Bone marrow depressants, other (See *Appendix II*)
(concurrent use with eflornithine may increase the bone marrow–depressant effects of these medications and radiation therapy)

Ototoxic medications, other (See *Appendix II*)
(concurrent use of these medications with long-term eflornithine therapy may increase the potential for ototoxicity)

Medical considerations/Contraindications

The medical considerations/contraindications included have been selected on the basis of their potential clinical significance (reasons given in parentheses where appropriate)—not necessarily inclusive (» = major clinical significance).

Risk-benefit should be considered when the following medical problems exist:

Eighth-cranial-nerve impairment, pre-existing
(hearing loss has occurred in patients receiving long-term therapy with eflornithine for treatment of cancer and *Pneumocystis carinii* pneumonia [conditions in which efficacy of eflornithine has not been clearly demonstrated]; although treatment for African trypanosomiasis is relatively short, the risk of hearing loss may still exist)

» Hematologic abnormalities, pre-existing
(eflornithine may cause anemia, leukopenia, or thrombocytopenia, worsening any pre-existing hematologic abnormalities)

» Renal function impairment
(because eflornithine is excreted primarily through the kidneys and its renal clearance approximates that of the creatinine clearance, the dose of eflornithine may need to be reduced in patients with renal function impairment)

Patient monitoring

The following may be especially important in patient monitoring (other tests may be warranted in some patients, depending on condition; » = major clinical significance):

Audiograms, serial
(may be required prior to, periodically during, and following treatment, especially in patients with pre-existing eighth-cranial-nerve impairment or patients receiving long-term therapy)

» Complete blood counts (CBCs) and
» Platelet counts
(because eflornithine may cause anemia, leukopenia, and thrombocytopenia, a complete blood count and platelet count should be performed before treatment, 2 times a week during therapy, and then weekly, thereafter, until blood counts return to baseline)

Side/Adverse Effects

Note: Most side effects are transient and reversible by discontinuing the drug or decreasing the dose. Hematologic abnormalities occur frequently, ranging from 10–55%. These abnormalities are dose-related and usually reversible. Thrombocytopenia is thought to be due to a production defect rather than to peripheral destruction. Seizures were seen in approximately 8% of patients, but may be related to the disease state rather than the drug.

Reversible sensorineural hearing loss has occurred in 30–70% of patients receiving long-term therapy (more than 4–8 weeks of therapy or a total dose of >300 grams); high-frequency hearing is lost first, followed by middle- and low-frequency hearing. Because treatment for African trypanosomiasis is short-term, patients are unlikely to experience hearing loss.

The following side/adverse effects have been selected on the basis of their potential clinical significance (possible signs and symptoms in parentheses where appropriate)—not necessarily inclusive:

Those indicating need for medical attention

Incidence more frequent

Hematologic abnormalities, specifically anemia (unusual tiredness or weakness); ***leucopenia*** (sore throat and fever); ***or thrombocytopenia*** (unusual bleeding or bruising)

Incidence rare

Ototoxicity (sensorineural hearing loss); ***seizures***

Those indicating need for medical attention only if they continue or are bothersome

Incidence more frequent

Gastrointestinal disturbances (diarrhea; nausea; abdominal pain; vomiting)

Incidence rare

Alopecia (hair loss); ***headache***

Patient Consultation

As an aid to patient consultation, refer to *Advice for the Patient, Eflornithine (Systemic)*.

In providing consultation, consider emphasizing the following selected information (» = major clinical significance):

Before receiving this medication

» Conditions affecting use, especially:
Pregnancy—Because the meningoencephalitic stage of African trypanosomiasis has such a high mortality rate if left untreated, treatment with eflornithine justifies the potential risk to the fetus
Dental—The neutropenic and thrombocytopenic effects of eflornithine may result in an increased incidence of microbial infection, delayed healing, and gingival bleeding
Other medications, especially other bone marrow depressants
Other medical problems, especially hematologic disturbances or renal function impairment

Proper use of this medication

» Importance of receiving medication for full course of therapy and on a regular schedule
» Proper dosing

Precautions after receiving this medication

Regular visits to physician to check progress

Caution if bone marrow depression occurs:

» Checking with physician immediately if fever or chills occur or if you think you are getting an infection
» Checking with physician immediately if unusual bleeding or bruising; black, tarry stools; blood in urine or stools; or pinpoint red spots on skin occur
Caution in use of regular toothbrushes, dental floss, and toothpicks; physician, dentist, or nurse may suggest alternative methods for cleaning teeth and gums; checking with physician before having dental work done
Using caution to avoid accidental cuts with use of sharp objects such as a safety razor or fingernail or toenail cutters

Side/adverse effects

Signs of potential side effects, especially hematologic disturbances, ototoxicity, and seizures

General Dosing Information

Severe anemia, leukopenia or thrombocytopenia requires an interruption in therapy until there is evidence of bone marrow recovery.

Because eflornithine's excretion through the kidneys is approximately the same as creatinine clearance, patients with renal function impairment may need an adjustment in dosage, based on their creatinine clearance.

Parenteral Dosage Forms

EFLORNITHINE HYDROCHLORIDE CONCENTRATE FOR INJECTION

Usual adult and adolescent dose

Trypanosomiasis, African (treatment)—
Intravenous infusion, 100 mg per kg of body weight, infused over at least forty-five minutes, every six hours for fourteen days.

Usual pediatric dose

Safety and efficacy have not been established.

Strength(s) usually available

U.S.—
20,000 mg in 100 mL (Rx) [*Ornidyl*].

Canada—
Not commercially available.

Packaging and storage

Store below 30 °C (86 °F), unless otherwise specified by manufacturer. Protect from freezing and light.

Preparation of dosage form

Eflornithine hydrochloride concentrate for injection is hypertonic and must be diluted with sterile water for injection before infusion. To prepare initial dilution for intravenous infusion, withdraw the entire 100 mL from the vial and add 25 mL of eflornithine into each of 4 containers with 100 mL of sterile water for injection. This produces a concentration of 40 mg per mL (5000 mg in 125 mL).

Stability

After dilution with sterile water for injection, eflornithine must be used within 24 hours. Bags containing diluted eflornithine should be stored at 4 °C (39 °F) to minimize the risk of microbial proliferation.

Incompatibilities

Eflornithine hydrochloride for injection should not be administered intravenously with any other drugs.

Revised: 06/26/1995

ELETRIPTAN Systemic†

VA CLASSIFICATION (Primary): CN105

Commonly used brand name(s): *Relpax*.

Note: For a listing of dosage forms and brand names by country availability, see *Dosage Forms* section(s).

†Not commercially available in Canada.

Category

Antimigraine agent.

Indications

General Considerations

Eletriptan should only be prescribed for patients where a clear diagnosis of migraine has been established.

Accepted

Headache, migraine (treatment)—Eletriptan is indicated for the acute treatment of migraine with or without aura in adults.

Unaccepted

Eletriptan is not indicated for use in the management of hemiplegic or basilar migraine. Efficacy and safety of eletriptan have not been established for these conditions.

Eletriptan is not indicated for use in cluster headaches. Safety and effectiveness of eletriptan in this condition have not been established.

Eletriptan is not intended for the prophylactic therapy of migraine.

Pharmacology/Pharmacokinetics

Physicochemical characteristics

Source—Synthetic. Eletriptan is structurally related to serotonin (5-hydroxytryptamine, 5-HT).

Molecular weight—Eletriptan hydrobromide: 463.40.

Solubility—Eletriptan hydrobromide: Readily soluble in water.

Mechanism of action/Effect

Two different theories have been proposed to explain the efficacy of 5-HT receptor agonists in migraine. One theory suggests that activation of 5-HT_1 receptors located on intracranial blood vessels, including those on the arteriovenous, lead to vasoconstriction, which correlated with relief of migraine headaches. A second theory suggests that activation of 5-HT_1 receptors on sensory nerve endings, in the trigeminal system, result in the inhibition of pro-inflammatory neuropeptide release.

Eletriptan binding affinity to receptors:

- High affinity—5-HT_{1B}, 5-HT_{1D}, and 5-HT_{1F}
- Modest affinity—5-HT_{1A}, 5-HT_{1E}, 5-HT_{2B}, and 5-HT_7
- Little or no affinity—5-HT_{2A}, 5-HT_{2C}, 5-HT_3, 5-HT_4, 5-HT_{5A}, and 5-HT_6
- No significant binding affinity or pharmacologic activity—adrenergic $alpha_1$ or $alpha_2$, beta, dopaminergic D_1 or D_2, muscarinic, or opioid receptors.

Other actions/effects

Eletriptan has been shown to inhibit trigeminal nerve activity in the rat.

Absorption

Eletriptan is well absorbed after oral administration (absolute bioavailability about 50%). The AUC and C_{MAX} of eletriptan are increased by approximately 20 to 30% following oral administration with a high fat meal.

Distribution

Volume of distribution (Vol_D)—138 liters, following IV administration.

Eletriptan is distributed into human breast milk. In one study of eight women given a single dose of 80 mg the mean total amount of eletriptan in breast milk over 24 hours, was approximately 0.02% of the administered dose. The mean concentration in breast milk to maternal plasma ratio is 1:4.

Protein binding

High (approximately 85%)

Biotransformation

The N-demethylated metabolite of eletriptan is the only known active metabolite.

In vitro studies indicate that eletriptan is primarily metabolized by P-450 enzyme CYP3A4.

Eletriptan has little potential to inhibit CYP1A2, CYP2C9, CYP2E1, and CYP3A4 based on *in vitro* studies. Eletriptan has an effect on CYP2D6 at high concentrations, however this effect should not interfere with metabolism of other drugs when eletriptan is used at recommended doses.

There is no evidence suggesting eletriptan will induce drug metabolizing enzymes at clinical doses.

Half-life

Elimination—approximately 4 hours

Time to peak concentration

Oral—1.5 hours after administration to healthy patients and 2 hours after administration to patients with moderate to severe migraine.

Elimination

Mean renal clearance (CL_R)—approximately 3.9 liters per hour.

Nonrenal clearance—90% of the total clearance.

The effect of hemodialysis or peritoneal dialysis on the serum concentration of eletriptan is unknown.

Precautions to Consider

Carcinogenicity/Tumorigenicity

Lifetime carcinogenicity studies, up to 104 weeks, were carried out in mice and rats by oral administration of eletriptan. In rats, there was an increase of testicular interstitial cell adenomas, at the high dose of 75 mg per kg of body weight per day. This dose was approximately 6 times that of the human maximum recommended daily dose [MRDD] of 80 mg per kg of body weight. At a dose of 15 mg per kg of body weight per day, two times the human MRDD, there was no-effect.

In mice, the incidence of hepatocellular adenomas was increased at the high dose of 400 mg per kg of body weight per day. The exposure to the parent drug area under the plasma concentration time curve [AUC] at that dose was approximately 18 times that achieved in humans receiving the MRDD. And, the AUC at the no-effect dose of 90 mg per kg of body weight per day was approximately 7 times the human MRDD.

Mutagenicity

No evidence of mutagenicity was found in a variety of *in vitro* studies including the Ames reverse mutation test and the hypoxanthine-guanine phosphoribosyl transferase mutation test. Eletriptan was not clastogenic in two *in vivo* mouse micronucleus assays. In *in vitro* human lymphocyte clastogenicity test an increase of polyploidy was noted in the absence of metabolic activation, but not in the presence of metabolic activation.

Pregnancy/Reproduction

Fertility—In rat fertility studies in females, there was a prolongation of the estrous cycle at the 200 mg per kg of body weight per day dose due to an increase in duration of estrous. There were also dose related decreases in numbers of corpora lutea per dam, in all doses, resulting in a decreased number of implants and viable fetuses per dam. This suggest a partial inhibition of ovulation due to eletriptan. There was no effect on fertility of male rats.

Pregnancy—Adequate and well controlled studies in pregnant women have not been done.

In reproductive toxicity studies in rats and rabbits given oral doses of eletriptan, developmental toxicity included decreased fetal and pup weights and an increased incidence of fetal structural abnormalities. The doses given were 6 to 12 times greater than the MRDD of 80 mg in humans.

In two other studies, rats and rabbits were administered eletriptan during organogenesis at doses 12 times the MRDD on a mg per m^2 basis and in both cases fetal weights decreased. In rats this dose was maternally toxic and incidences of vertebral and sternebral variations increased, while in rabbits incidences of fused sternebral and vena cava deviations increased and maternal toxicity was not produced at any dose.

FDA Pregnancy Category C

Breast-feeding
Caution should be exercised when administering eletriptan to a nursing woman. Eletriptan is distributed into human breast milk. In one study of 8 women given a single dose of 80 mg, the mean total amount of eletriptan distributed into breast milk was 0.02% of the administered dose over 24 hours.

Pediatrics
Safety and efficacy have not been established in pediatric patients less than 18 years of age

Adolescents
The efficacy of eletriptan in patients 11 to 17 years of age, was not established in a randomized, placebo-controlled trial of 274 adolescents. Adverse effects were similar to those reported in clinical trials in adults. However, postmarketing experience with other triptans includes a limited number of reports that describe pediatric patients who have experienced clinically serious adverse events that are similar to those reported rarely in adults.

Geriatrics
Appropriate studies performed to date have not demonstrated geriatrics-problems that would limit the usefulness of eletriptan in the elderly. However, blood pressure was increased to a greater extent in older adults than in young adults. There was also a significant increased half-life from about 4.4 hours to 5.7 hours between older adults (65 to 93 years of age) and young adults (18 to 45 years of age).

Pharmacogenetics
In two clinical studies, there was no evidence indicating pharmacokinetic differences between Caucasian and non Caucasian patients. A comparison of pharmacokinetic studies in western countries and Japan indicated an approximate 35% reduction in exposure of eletriptan in Japanese male volunteers compared to western males.

The pharmacokinetics of eletriptan are unaffected by gender.

Drug interactions and/or related problems
The following drug interactions and/or related problems have been selected on the basis of their potential clinical significance (possible mechanism in parentheses where appropriate)—not necessarily inclusive (» = major clinical significance):

Eletriptan is metabolized by the CYP3A4 enzyme. Studies *in vitro* suggest that eletriptan has little potential to inhibit CYP1A2, CYP2C9, CYP2E1, and CYP3A4. Eletriptan has an effect on CYP2D6 at high concentrations, however this effect should not interfere with metabolism of other drugs when eletriptan is used at recommended doses.

There is no evidence suggesting eletriptan will induce drug metabolizing enzymes at clinical doses.

Note: Combinations containing any of the following medications, depending on the amount present, may also interact with this medication.

CYP3A4 inhibitors, such as:
Erythromycin or
Fluconazole or
Verapamil
(concomitant use of these medicines with eletriptan was associated with an increase in C_{MAX} and increase in the AUC of eletriptan)

» CYP3A4 inhibitors, potent, such as:
Clarithromycin or
Itraconazole or
Ketoconazole or
Nefazodone or
Nelfinavir or
Ritonavir or
Troleandomycin
(eletriptan should not be used within at least 72 hours of treatment with drugs that have demonstrated potent CYP3A4 inhibition or have this potent effect described in their labeling)

Propranolol
(concomitant us of propranolol and eletriptan was associated with an increase in the C_{MAX} and AUC of eletriptan; however, no increase in blood pressure was observed and no dosage adjustment appears to be necessary)

» 5-HT_1 agonist or
» Ergot-containing or ergot-type medication, such as:
Dihydroergotamine
Methysergide
(eletriptan should not be used within 24 hours of treatment with these medicines; concomitant use may cause serious cardiac events including acute myocardial infraction, life threatening disturbances of cardiac rhythm, or death)

Medical considerations/Contraindications
The medical considerations/contraindications included have been selected on the basis of their potential clinical significance (reasons given in parentheses where appropriate)—not necessarily inclusive (» = major clinical significance).

Except under special circumstances, this medication should not be used when the following medical problem exists:

» Cerebrovascular syndrome, including:
Strokes or
Transient ischemic attacks
(eletriptan should not be administered to patients with these conditions; cerebrovascular events, including some fatalities, have been reported in patients treated with 5-HT_1 agonists)

» Coronary artery disease, especially:
Angina pectoris or
Myocardial infarction, history of, or
Myocardial ischemia, silent, documented, or
Prinzmetal's angina or
Other conditions in which coronary vasoconstriction would be detrimental
(eletriptan should not be administered to patients with these conditions; cardiac events, including some fatalities, have been reported in patients treated with 5-HT_1 agonists)

» Hemiplegic migraine or
» Basilar migraine
(eletriptan should not be administered to patients with these conditions)

» Hepatic impairment; severe
(eletriptan should not be given to patients with severe hepatic impairment)

» Hypersensitivity to eletriptan or any of its inactive ingredients
» Hypertension, uncontrolled
(eletriptan should not be given to patients with uncontrolled hypertension)

» Peripheral vascular disease, including:
Ischemic bowel disease
Raynaud's syndrome
(eletriptan should not be given to patients with peripheral vascular disease; eletriptan may cause vasospastic reactions other than coronary artery vasospasm)

Risk-benefit should be considered when the following medical problems exist:

» Cerebrovascular event, increased risk of
(patients with migraine may be at increased risk of certain cerebrovascular events; caution is advised since a severe headache, a symptom of a cerebrovascular event, may be mistaken for a migraine; eletriptan should not be given to patients with cerebrovascular hemorrhage, stroke, or transient ischemic attack)

» Coronary artery disease (CAD), predisposition to
(5-HT_1 agonists have caused serious coronary adverse effects; patients in whom coronary artery disease is a possibility on the basis of age or the presence of other risk factors, such as diabetes, hypercholesterolemia, obesity, a strong family history of coronary artery disease, female gender with physiological or surgical menopause, male gender over 40 years of age, or tobacco smoking should be evaluated for the presence of cardiovascular disease before eletriptan is prescribed; even after a satisfactory evaluation, the advisability of administering the patient's first dose under medical supervision should be considered)

Hepatic impairment, mild or moderate
(increases in C_{MAX}, AUC, and half-life have been reported; no eletriptan dose adjustment is necessary)

Hypertension, controlled
(blood pressure elevation, including rare occurrences of hypertensive crisis, have been reported in patients treated with 5-HT_1 agonists; the effect on blood pressure is more pronounced in older adults or patients with renal impairment)

Renal impairment
(blood pressure elevation may occur)

Patient monitoring
The following may be especially important in patient monitoring (other tests may be warranted in some patients, depending on condition; » = major clinical significance):

Cardiovascular evaluation
(initial and periodic evaluations are recommended to rule out clinical evidence of cardiovascular disease; eletriptan should not be given to patients with ischemic heart disease or other significant underlying cardiovascular disease)

Electrocardiogram (ECG)
(recommended immediately following the first dose of eletriptan for patients with cardiovascular risk factors and a satisfactory cardiovascular evaluation)

Side/Adverse Effects

Note: Most adverse events reported in clinical trials were mild in intensity and were transient. The incidence of adverse events in controlled clinical trials was not affected by gender, age, race, or use of prophylactic medications, estrogen replacement therapy or oral contraceptives. Although extremely rare, cases of serious cardiac events such as coronary artery vasospasm, transient myocardial ischemia, myocardial infraction, ventricular tachycardia, and ventricular fibrillation have occurred following the use of 5-HT_1 agonists mostly in patients with risk factors predictive of coronary artery disease (CAD).

The following side/adverse effects have been selected on the basis of their potential clinical significance (possible signs and symptoms in parentheses where appropriate)—not necessarily inclusive:

Those indicating need for medical attention

Incidence less frequent

Chest pain or tightness; dysphagia (difficulty swallowing)

Those indicating need for medical attention only if they continue or are bothersome

Incidence more frequent

Asthenia (lack or loss of strength); ***dizziness; nausea; somnolence*** (sleepiness or unusual drowsiness)

Incidence less frequent

Abdominal discomfort (stomach soreness or discomfort); ***dry mouth; dyspepsia*** (acid or sour stomach; belching; heartburn; indigestion; stomach discomfort upset, or pain); ***flushing*** (feeling of warmth; redness of the face, neck, arms and occasionally, upper chest); ***headache; paresthesia*** (burning, crawling, itching, numbness, prickling, "pins and needles", or tingling feelings)

Overdose

For more information on the management of overdose or unintentional ingestion, **contact a poison control center** (see *Poison Control Center Listing*).

No significant overdoses have been reported in premarketing clinical trials. No significant adverse effects were reported in volunteers who received a single oral dose of 120 mg.

Clinical effects of overdose

Hypertension or other more serious cardiovascular symptoms could occur on overdose.

Treatment of overdose

There is no specific antidote to eletriptan. Treatment is generally symptomatic and supportive.

To enhance elimination—
The effect of hemodialysis or peritoneal dialysis on the serum concentration of eletriptan is unknown.

Monitoring—
Monitoring of patients after overdose should continue for at least 20 hours or longer should symptoms persist.

Supportive care—
Intensive care procedures recommended including establishing and maintaining a patent airway, ensuring adequate oxygenation and ventilation, and monitoring and support of the cardiovascular system.

Patients in whom intentional overdose is confirmed or suspected should be referred for psychiatric consultation.

Patient Consultation

As an aid to patient consultation, refer to *Advice for the Patient, Eletriptan (Systemic).*

In providing consultation, consider emphasizing the following selected information (» = major clinical significance):

Before using this medication

» Conditions affecting use, especially:
Hypersensitivity to eletriptan or any of its ingredients
Pregnancy—Eletriptan crosses the placenta in animals.
FDA Pregnancy Category C
Breast-feeding—Eletriptan is distributed into human breast milk. Caution should be used when administering to a nursing woman.
Use in children—Safety and efficacy of eletriptan have not been established in the pediatric population below the age of 18 years.
Other medications, especially potent CYP3A4 inhibitors, other 5-HT_1 agonists, ergot-containing medication, or ergot-type medication
Other medical problems, especially cerebrovascular syndrome; coronary artery disease or predisposition to; hemiplegic or basilar migraine, hepatic impairment (severe); hypersensitivity to eletriptan or any of its inactive ingredients, hypertension (uncontrolled); or peripheral vascular disease

Proper use of this medication

» Not administering if atypical headache symptoms are present; checking with physician instead

Administering after onset of headache pain

Additional benefit may be obtained if the patient lies down in a quiet, dark room after administering medication

» Not using additional doses if a first dose does not provide substantial relief; additional eletriptan is not likely to be effective in these circumstances; taking alternate medication as previously advised by physician, then checking with physician as soon as possible

» Taking an additional dose, if needed, for return of migraine after initial relief was obtained, provided that prescribed limits (quantity used and frequency of administration) are not exceeded

» Compliance with prophylactic therapy, if prescribed

» Proper dosing

Proper storage

Precautions while using this medication

» Call your doctor right away if you have severe chest pains or shortness of breath

Checking with physician if usual dose fails to relieve three consecutive headaches, or frequency and/or severity of headaches increases

Avoiding alcohol, which aggravates headache

» Caution when driving or doing anything else requiring alertness because of possible drowsiness, dizziness, lightheadedness, impairment of physical or mental abilities

Side/adverse effects

Signs of potential side effects, especially chest pain or tightness, or dysphagia.

General Dosing Information

For oral dosing forms:

Dosing decisions should be made on an individual basis because of varying responses to doses of eletriptan.

A repeat dose may be beneficial if the headache returns, but it should be taken at least 2 hours after the initial dose. However, controlled clinical trials have not shown a benefit of a second dose to treat the same attack.

The safety of treating an average of more than 3 headaches in a 30-day period has not been established

With prolonged usage of eletriptan there could be an accumulation in melanin-rich tissues, therefore patients should be aware of the possibility of long-term ophthalmologic effects.

Oral Dosage Forms

Note: Eletriptan tablets contain eletriptan hydrobromide. However, dosage and strength are expressed in terms of eletriptan base (not the hydrobromide salt).

ELETRIPTAN HYDROBROMIDE TABLETS

Usual adult dose

Antimigraine agent—
Oral, 20 or 40 mg (base) as a single dose. If necessary, an additional dose may be taken after 2 hours.

Note: Controlled trials have not adequately established the efficacy of a second dose of eletriptan if the initial dose is ineffective.
Eletriptan should not be given to patients with severe hepatic impairment. No dose adjustment is necessary with mild to moderate hepatic impairment.

Usual adult prescribing limits

Up to 40 mg (base) per dose and 80 mg (base) per day

Usual pediatric dose

Safety and efficacy in patients up to 18 years of age have not been established.

Usual geriatric dose

See *Usual adult dose.*

Usual geriatric prescribing limits
See *Usual adult prescribing limits.*

Strength(s) usually available
U.S.—

20 mg (base) (Rx) [*Relpax* (microcrystalline cellulose; lactose; croscarmellose sodium; magnesium stearate; titanium dioxide; hydroxypropyl methylcellulose; triacetin; FD&C Yellow No. 6 aluminum lake)].

40 mg (base) (Rx) [*Relpax* (microcrystalline cellulose; lactose; croscarmellose sodium; magnesium stearate; titanium dioxide; hydroxypropyl methylcellulose; triacetin; FD&C Yellow No. 6 aluminum lake)].

Canada—

Not commercially available.

Packaging and storage
Store at 25 °C (77 °F), excursions permitted to 15 to 30 °C (59 to 86 °F).

Auxiliary labeling
- May cause drowsiness. Be careful while driving or operating machinery. Use caution until you become familiar with its effects.
- Do not exceed prescribed dose.

Developed: 09/26/2003

EMEDASTINE Ophthalmic

VA CLASSIFICATION (Primary): OP801

Commonly used brand name(s): *Emadine.*

Note: For a listing of dosage forms and brand names by country availability, see *Dosage Forms* section(s).

Category
Antihistamine (H_1-receptor), ophthalmic; antiallergic, ophthalmic.

Indications

Accepted
Conjunctivitis, allergic (treatment)—Ophthalmic emedastine is indicated for temporary relief of the symptoms of allergic conjunctivitis.

Pharmacology/Pharmacokinetics

Physicochemical characteristics
Molecular weight—Emedastine difumarate: 534.57.

pH—Approximately 7.4.

Mechanism of action/Effect
Emedastine is a relatively selective histamine H_1-receptor antagonist according to *in vitro* studies. Topical ocular administration of emedastine produces concentration-dependent inhibition of histamine-stimulated vascular permeability in the conjunctiva. Emedastine does not affect adrenergic, dopamine, or serotonin receptors.

Absorption
Ophthalmic use of emedastine usually does not produce measurable plasma concentrations. A study in normal volunteers (10 subjects) who were administered emedastine 0.05% ophthalmic solution in each eye twice a day for 16 days found that plasma concentrations were generally below the quantitative limit of the assay (less than 0.3 nanogram per mL). Samples in which emedastine was quantifiable contained plasma concentrations ranging from 0.3 to 0.49 nanogram per mL.

Biotransformation
Two primary metabolites, 5- and 6-hydroxyemedastine, are found in the urine as both free and conjugated forms. Minor metabolites include the 5′-oxoanalogs of 5- and 6-hydroxyemedastine and the *N*-oxide.

Half-life
Elimination—3 or 4 hours.

Elimination
Renal, approximately 44% of an oral dose over 24 hours (3.6% unchanged).

Precautions to Consider

Carcinogenicity
No evidence of carcinogenicity was found in lifetime studies in mice and rats given dietary doses of emedastine that were more than 80,000 times and 26,000 times, respectively, the maximum recommended ocular human use level of 0.002 mg per kg of body weight (mg/kg) per day for a 50-kg adult.

Mutagenicity
Emedastine was not found to be mutagenic in *in vitro* tests, including a bacterial reverse mutation (Ames) test, a modification of the Ames test, a mammalian chromosome aberration test, a mammalian forward mutation test, and a mammalian DNA repair synthesis test, or in *in vivo* tests including a mammalian sister chromatid exchange test and a mouse micronucleus test.

Pregnancy/Reproduction
Fertility—Studies in rats given doses of emedastine that were 15,000 times the maximum recommended ocular human use level found no evidence of impairment of fertility or reproductive capacity.

Pregnancy—Adequate and well-controlled studies in humans have not been done.

Studies in rats and rabbits given doses of emedastine that were 15,000 times the maximum recommended ocular human use level found no evidence of teratogenicity, and the same dose produced no effect on perinatal or postnatal development in rats. However, studies in rats given doses of emedastine that were 70,000 times the maximum recommended ocular human use level found an increased incidence of external, visceral, and skeletal anomalies.

FDA Pregnancy Category B.

Breast-feeding
It is not known whether ophthalmic emedastine is absorbed in sufficient quantities to be distributed into human breast milk. However, emedastine has been detected in the milk of lactating rats following oral administration. Risk-benefit should be considered before use of ophthalmic emedastine during breast-feeding.

Pediatrics
Appropriate studies on the relationship of age to the effects of ophthalmic emedastine have not been performed in children up to 3 years of age. Safety and efficacy have not been established.

Geriatrics
No information is available on the relationship of age to the effects of ophthalmic emedastine in geriatric patients.

Medical considerations/Contraindications
The medical considerations/contraindications included have been selected on the basis of their potential clinical significance (reasons given in parentheses where appropriate)—not necessarily inclusive (» = major clinical significance).

Risk-benefit should be considered when the following medical problem exists:

» Sensitivity to emedastine

Side/Adverse Effects
The following side/adverse effects have been selected on the basis of their potential clinical significance (possible signs and symptoms in parentheses where appropriate)—not necessarily inclusive:

Those indicating need for medical attention
Incidence less frequent—Less than 5%

Abnormal dreams; asthenia (weakness); ***corneal infiltrates or staining*** (blurred vision or other change in vision); ***keratitis*** (eye redness, irritation, or pain); ***tearing, discomfort, or other eye irritation not present before therapy or becoming worse during therapy***

Those indicating need for medical attention only if they continue or are bothersome
Incidence more frequent

Headache—11%

Incidence less frequent—Less than 5%

Bad taste; burning or stinging of the eye; dermatitis (skin rash or itching); ***dry eye; foreign body sensation*** (feeling of something in the eye); ***hyperemia*** (redness of eye); ***pruritus*** (itching); ***rhinitis*** (stuffy or runny nose); ***sinusitis*** (headache or runny nose)

Patient Consultation
As an aid to patient consultation, refer to *Advice for the Patient, Emedastine (Ophthalmic).*

In providing consultation, consider emphasizing the following selected information (» = major clinical significance):

Before using this medication
» Conditions affecting use, especially:

Sensitivity to emedastine

Breast-feeding—Detected in the milk of lactating rats following oral administration of emedastine

Proper use of this medication

» Not wearing contact lenses if eyes are red; if eyes are not red, removing contact lenses prior to administration; waiting at least 10 minutes after administration before reinserting lenses

» Proper administration; not touching applicator tip to any surface; keeping container tightly closed

» Proper dosing

Missed dose: Using as soon as possible; not using if almost time for next dose; using next dose at regularly scheduled time

» Proper storage

Precautions while using this medication

» Checking with physician if symptoms do not improve or if condition worsens

Side/adverse effects

Signs of potential side effects, especially abnormal dreams; asthenia; corneal infiltrates or staining; keratitis; sinusitis; and tearing, discomfort, or other eye irritation not present before therapy or becoming worse during therapy

General Dosing Information

Emedastine contains benzalkonium chloride, which may be absorbed by contact lenses. The manufacturer does not recommend use of contact lenses if eyes are red. If eyes are not red, contact lenses should be removed prior to administration of emedastine and may be reinserted 10 minutes after administration.

Ophthalmic Dosage Forms

EMEDASTINE DIFUMARATE OPHTHALMIC SOLUTION

Note: The dosing and strength of the dosage form available are expressed in terms of emedastine base.

Usual adult and adolescent dose

Allergic conjunctivitis—

Topical, to the conjunctiva, 1 drop in each affected eye up to four times a day.

Usual pediatric dose

Allergic conjunctivitis—

Children younger than 3 years of age: Safety and efficacy have not been established.

Children 3 years of age and older: See *Usual adult and adolescent dose*.

Strength(s) usually available

U.S.—

0.05% (Rx) [*Emadine* (benzalkonium chloride 0.01%; tromethamine; sodium chloride; hydroxypropyl methylcellulose; hydrochloric acid/sodium hydroxide; purified water)].

Note: Each mL contains 0.884 mg emedastine difumarate, which is equivalent to 0.5 mg emedastine base.

Packaging and storage

Store between 4 and 30 °C (39 and 86 °F).

Auxiliary labeling

• For the eye.

Developed: 08/14/1998

EMTRICITABINE Systemic†

VA CLASSIFICATION (Primary): AM840

Commonly used brand name(s): *Emtriva*.

Note: For a listing of dosage forms and brand names by country availability, see *Dosage Forms* section(s).

†Not commercially available in Canada.

Category

Antiviral (Systemic).

Indications

General Considerations

This indication is based on analyses of plasma HIV-1 RNA levels and CD4 cell counts from controlled studies of 48 weeks duration in antiretroviral-naive and antiretroviral-treatment-experienced patients who were virologically suppressed on an HIV treatment regimen. HIV strains with mutation at codon position 184 on the RT gene are highly resistant to emtricitabine.

Emtricitabine-resistant isolates of HIV have been selected *in vitro*. Genotypic analysis of these isolates showed that the resistance was due to M1841V/I mutations in the HIV reverse transcriptase gene.

Cross-resistance among certain nucleoside analog reverse transcriptase inhibitors has been recognized. Emtricitabine-resistant isolates (M184V/I) were cross-resistant to lamivudine and zalcitabine but remained sensitive to abacavir, didanosine, stavudine, tenofovir, zidovudine and NNRTIs (delavirdine, efavirenz, and nevirapine). HIV-isolates containing the K65R mutation, selected *in vivo* by abacavir, didanosine, tenofovir, and zalcitabine, showed reduced susceptibility to inhibition by emtricitabine. Viruses with mutations conferring reduced susceptibility to stavudine and zidovudine or didanosine remained sensitive to emtricitabine. HIV-1 containing the K103N mutation associated with resistance to NNRTIs was susceptible to emtricitabine.

Accepted

Human immunodeficiency virus (HIV) infection (treatment)—Emtricitabine is indicated, in combination with other antiretroviral agents, for the treatment of HIV-1 infection in patients over three months of age.

In antiretroviral-treatment-experienced patients, the use of emtricitabine may be considered for adults with HIV strains that are expected to be susceptible to emtricitabine as assessed by genotypic or phenotypic testing.

Unaccepted

Emtricitabine is not indicated for the treatment of chronic hepatitis B virus (HBV) infection and the safety and efficacy of emtricitabine have not been established in patients co-infected with HBV and HIV.

Pharmacology/Pharmacokinetics

The multiple dose pharmacokinetics of emtricitabine are dose proportional over a dose range of 25 to 200 mg.

Physicochemical characteristics

Source—Synthetic.

Molecular weight—247.24.

pKa—2.65.

Solubility—112 mg per mL in water at 25°C.

Log P—0.43

Mechanism of action/Effect

Emtricitabine, a synthetic nucleoside analog of cytosine, is phosphorylated by cellular enzymes to form emtricitabine 5′-triphosphate. Emtricitabine 5′-triphosphate inhibits the activity of the HIV-1 reverse transcriptase by competing with the natural substrate deoxycytidine 5′-triphosphate and by being incorporated into nascent viral DNA which results in chain termination. Emtricitabine 5′-triphosphate is a weak inhibitor of mammalian DNA polymerase α, β, epsilon and mitochondrial DNA polymerase γ.

Absorption

Rapidly and extensively absorbed following oral administration

Bioavailability (mean)—93%

AUC—10.0 $\pm$ 3.1 hr μg per mL

Emtricitabine may be taken with or without food. Systemic exposure (AUC) was unaffected while C_{max} decreased by 29% when emtricitabine was administered with food (an approximately 1000 kcal high-fat meal).

Distribution

Plasma to blood concentration ratio (mean)— 1

Semen to plasma drug concentration (mean)— 4

Protein binding

Very low: < 4%; independent of concentration

Biotransformation

The biotransformation of emtricitabine includes oxidation of the thiol moiety to form the 3′-sulfoxide diastereomers (9% of the dose) and conjugation with glucuronic acid to form 2′-O-glucuronide (4% of the dose). No other metabolites were identified.

Emtricitabine is not metabolized by liver enzymes

Half-life

Plasma—10 hours

Time to peak concentration

1 to 2 hours post dose

Peak plasma concentration:

C_{max}—1.8 ±.07 μg per mL

Peak serum concentration

Steady state plasma trough concentration—0.09 μg per mL at 24 hours post dose

Elimination

The renal clearance is greater than the estimated creatinine clearance, suggesting elimination by both glomerular filtration and active tubular secretion. There may be competition for elimination with other compounds that are also renally eliminated.

Fecal: 14%

Urine: 86%

13% of the dose was recovered in the urine as three putative metabolites.

In dialysis, hemodialysis treatment removes approximately 30% of the emtricitabine dose over a 3 hour dialysis period starting within 1.5 hours of emtricitabine dosing (blood flow rate of 400 mL per min and a dialysate flow rate of 600 mL per min). It is not known whether emtricitabine can be removed by peritoneal dialysis.

Precautions to Consider

Carcinogenicity

In long-term carcinogenicity studies, no drug-related increases in tumor incidence were found in mice or rats at doses up to 750 mg per kg of body weight per day (26 times the human systemic exposure) or 600 mg per kg of body weight per day (31 times the human systemic exposure), respectively.

Mutagenicity

Emtricitabine was not genotoxic in the reverse mutation bacterial test (Ames test), mouse lymphoma or mouse micronucleus assays.

Pregnancy/Reproduction

Fertility—Emtricitabine did not affect fertility in male rats at approximately 140-fold or in male and female mice at approximately 60-fold higher exposures (AUC) than in humans given the recommended 200 mg daily dose. Fertility was normal in the offspring of mice exposed daily from before birth (in utero) through sexual maturity at daily exposures (AUC) of approximately 60-fold higher than human exposures at the recommended 200 mg daily dose.

Pregnancy—There are no adequate and well controlled studies in pregnant women. Because animal reproduction studies are not always predictive of human response, emtricitabine should be used during pregnancy only if clearly needed.

Studies in animals have shown that the incidence of fetal variations and malformations was not increased in embryofetal toxicity studies performed with emtricitabine in mice at exposures (AUC) approximately 60-fold higher and in rabbits at approximately 120-fold higher than human exposures at the recommended daily dose.

To monitor fetal outcomes of pregnant women exposed to emtricitabine, an antiretroviral pregnancy registry has been established. Healthcare providers are encouraged to register patients by calling 1-800-258-4263.

FDA Pregnancy Category B

Breast-feeding

It is not known whether emtricitabine is distributed into breast milk. Because of both the potential for HIV transmission and the potential for serious adverse reactions in nursing infants, mothers should be instructed not to breast feed if they are receiving emtricitabine.

The Centers for Disease Control and Prevention recommend that HIV-infected mothers not breast-feed their infants to avoid risking postnatal transmission of HIV.

Pediatrics

Safety and effectiveness in pediatric patients below the age of 3 months have not been established.

Geriatrics

Appropriate studies on the relationship of age to the effects of emtricitabine have not been performed in the geriatric population. Dose selection for the elderly patient should be cautious, keeping in mind the greater frequency of decreased hepatic, renal, or cardiac function, and of concomitant disease or other drug therapy.

Drug interactions and/or related problems

The following drug interactions and/or related problems have been selected on the basis of their potential clinical significance (possible mechanism in parentheses where appropriate)—not necessarily inclusive (» = major clinical significance):

There were no clinically significant drug interactions when emtricitabine was used in combination with famciclovir, indinavir, stavudine, and tenofovir disoproxil fumarate.

Laboratory value alterations

The following have been selected on the basis of their potential clinical significance (possible effect in parentheses where appropriate)—not necessarily inclusive (» = major clinical significance).

With physiology/laboratory test values

Alanine aminotransferase (ALT [SGPT])
Aspartate aminotransferase (AST [SGOT])
Bilirubin
Creatine kinase (CK)
Pancreatic amylase
Serum amylase
Serum lipase
Triglycerides
(values may be increased)

Neutrophils
(values may be decreased)

Serum glucose
(values may be decreased or increased)

Medical considerations/Contraindications

The medical considerations/contraindications included have been selected on the basis of their potential clinical significance (reasons given in parentheses where appropriate)—not necessarily inclusive (» = major clinical significance).

Except under special circumstances, this medication should not be used when the following medical problem exists:

» Hypersensitivity to emtricitabine or to any components of the product or to lamivudine

» Chronic hepatitis B virus (HBV) infection
(the safety and efficacy of emtricitabine have not been established in patients co-infected with HIV and HBV; exacerbations of hepatitis B have been reported in patients after the discontinuation of emtricitabine)
(in the presence of chronic HBV infection, there is an anticipated cross-resistance to lamivudine-resistant HBV strains)

Risk-benefit should be considered when the following medical problems exist:

» Renal impairment
(dosage reduction is recommended for patients with impaired renal function; emtricitabine is principally eliminated by the kidney)

Obesity or
Prolonged nucleoside exposure
(may be risk factors for lactic acidosis/severe hepatomegaly with steatosis; cases have been reported with the use of nucleoside analogues alone or in combination with other antiretrovirals; a majority of these cases have been in women and cases have been reported with no known risk factors)

Patient monitoring

The following may be especially important in patient monitoring (other tests may be warranted in some patients, depending on condition; » = major clinical significance):

» Chronic hepatitis B virus (HBV)
(all patients with HIV be should be tested for the presence of HBV before initiating antiretroviral therapy)
(co-infected patients [HIV and HBV] should be closely monitored with clinical and laboratory follow-up for at least several months after stopping treatment; exacerbation of hepatitis B has been reported after discontinuation of emtricitabine)

Immune reconstitution syndrome
(reported in patients treated with emtricitabine; during initial phase of combination antiretroviral treatment, patients whose immune system responds may develop inflammatory response to indolent or residual opportunistic infections [*Mycobacterium avium* infection, cytomegalovirus, *Pneumocystis jirovecii* pneumonia (PCP), or tuberculosis] which may necessitate further evaluation and treatment)

Lactic acidosis or
Hepatotoxicity, pronounced
(treatment should be immediately suspended in patients who develop clinical or laboratory findings suggestive of lactic acidosis or pronounced hepatotoxicity [which may include hepatomegaly and steatosis even in the absence of marked transaminase elevations])

Side/Adverse Effects

The redistribution or accumulation of body fat, including central obesity, dorsocervical fat enlargement (buffalo hump), peripheral wasting, facial wasting, breast enlargement, and “cushingoid appearance” have been observed in patients on antiretroviral therapy. The mechanism and long-term consequences of these events are unknown. A causal relationship has not been established.

Lactic acidosis and severe hepatomegaly with steatosis, including fatal cases, have been reported with the use of nucleoside analogues alone or in combination, including emtricitabine and other antiretrovirals. A majority of these cases have been in women. Obesity and prolonged nucleoside exposure may be risk factors. Treatment with emtricitabine should be suspended in any patient who develops clinical or laboratory findings suggestive of lactic acidosis or pronounced hepatotoxicity (which may include hepatomegaly and steatosis even in the absence of marked transaminase elevations).

Those indicating need for medical attention

Incidence unknown

Lactic acidosis (abdominal discomfort; decreased appetite; diarrhea; fast, shallow breathing; general feeling of discomfort; muscle pain or cramping; nausea; shortness of breath; sleepiness; unusual tiredness or weakness)

Those indicating need for medical attention only if they continue or are bothersome

Incidence more frequent

Asthenia (lack or loss of strength); ***cough; diarrhea; headache; nausea; rhinitis*** (stuffy nose; runny nose; sneezing)

Incidence less frequent

Abdominal pain; abnormal dreams; arthralgia (pain in joints; muscle pain or stiffness; difficulty in moving); ***depressive disorders; dizziness; dyspepsia*** (acid or sour stomach; belching; heartburn; indigestion; stomach discomfort, upset, or pain); ***insomnia*** (sleeplessness; trouble sleeping; unable to sleep); ***myalgia*** (joint pain; swollen joints; muscle aching or cramping; muscle pains or stiffness; difficulty in moving); ***neuritis*** (numbness or tingling of hands, feet, or face); ***paresthesia*** (burning, crawling, itching, numbness, prickling, "pins and needles", or tingling feelings); ***peripheral neuropathy*** (burning, numbness, tingling, or painful sensations; weakness in arms, hands, legs, or feet; unsteadiness or awkwardness); ***rash; skin discoloration; vomiting***

Overdose

For more information on the management of overdose or unintentional ingestion, **contact a poison control center** (see *Poison Control Center Listing*).

Treatment of overdose

There is no known antidote to emtricitabine. Limited clinical experience is available at doses higher than the therapeutic dose of emtricitabine. In one clinical pharmacology study, single doses of emtricitabine 1200 mg were administered to 11 patients. No serious adverse events were reported. The effects of higher doses are not known. If overdose occurs the patient should be monitored for signs of toxicity, and standard supportive treatment applied as necessary.

Hemodialysis treatment removes approximately 30% of the emtricitabine dose over a 3–hour dialysis period starting within 1.5 hours of emtricitabine dosing (blood flow rate of 400 mL per minute and a dialysate flow rate of 600 mL per minute). It is not known whether emtricitabine can be removed by peritoneal dialysis.

Patients in whom intentional overdose is confirmed or suspected should be referred for psychiatric consultation.

Patient Consultation

As an aid to patient consultation, refer to *Advice for the Patient, Emtricitabine (Systemic)*.

In providing consultation, consider emphasizing the following selected information (» = major clinical significance):

Before using this medication

» Conditions affecting use, especially:
- Hypersensitivity to emtricitabine or any components of this medicine or to lamivudine
- Pregnancy—Risk-benefit should be considered
- Breast-feeding—Not recommended because of the risk of postnatal transmission and potential side effects
- Use in children—Safety and efficacy below the age of 3 months not established
- Use in the elderly—Elderly patients may be more sensitive to the effects of emtricitabine; dose selection should be cautious
- Other medical problems, especially chronic hepatitis B virus infection; renal impairment

Proper use of this medication

» Proper dosing; importance of taking with combination therapy on a regular dosing schedule to avoid missing doses

Missed dose: Taking as soon as possible; not taking if almost time for next scheduled dose; not doubling doses

Importance of not taking more medication than prescribed; importance of not discontinuing medication without checking with physician; importance of not missing doses and of taking at evenly spaced times

Importance of refilling prescription in advance; medicine should not be stopped, even for a short time

Proper storage

Not sharing medication with others

Importance of telling physician about all other medicines or dietary supplements

Precautions while using this medication

» Importance of reading the patient information before using emtricitabine and each time the prescription is refilled

Regular visits to physician and the importance of staying under a doctor's care while taking emtricitabine

Being aware that emtricitabine therapy does not reduce the risk of transmitting HIV to others through sexual contact or contamination through blood

Importance of knowing what to do for lactic acidosis, hepatotoxicity, and hepatitis B exacerbations

General Dosing Information

For oral dosing forms:

Emtricitabine is not a cure for HIV infection and patients may continue to experience the illnesses associated with HIV infection, including opportunistic infections. Patients should remain under the care of a physician while using emtricitabine. The use of emtricitabine does not reduce the risk of transmission of HIV to others through sexual contact or blood contamination.

It is recommended that all patients with HIV be tested for the presence of chronic hepatitis B virus (HBV) before initiating antiretroviral therapy.

Diet/Nutrition

May be taken with or without food

Oral Dosage Forms

EMTRICITABINE CAPSULES

Usual adult dose

Human immunodeficiency virus (HIV) infection—
Oral, 200 mg taken once daily

Note: Dose adjustment in patients with renal impairment—The dosing interval of emtricitabine should be adjusted in patients with baseline creatinine clearance <50 mL per min. The safety and effectiveness of these dosing interval adjustment guidelines have not been clinically evaluated. Therefore, clinical response to treatment and renal function should be closely monitored in these patients.

Formulation	Creatinine Clearance ≥ 50 mL/min	Creatinine Clearance 30 to 49 mL/min	Creatinine Clearance 15 to 29 mL/min	Creatinine Clearance < 15 (including patients requiring hemodialysis)
Capsule (200 mg)	200 mg every 24 hours	200 mg every 48 hours	200 mg every 72 hours	200 mg every 96 hours

Usual pediatric dose

Human immunodeficiency virus (HIV) infection—

Children weighing more than 33 kg who can swallow an intact capsule: Oral, 200 mg once daily.

Children weighing less than 33 kg or who can not swallow an intact capsule: See Usual pediatric dose for the oral solution.

Note: Although there are insufficient data to recommend a specific emtricitabine dose adjustment for pediatric patients with renal impairment, a dose reduction and/or a dosing interval increase similar to adjustments for adults should be considered.

Usual geriatric dose

See *Usual adult dose*.

Strength(s) usually available

U.S.—
200 mg (Rx) [*Emtriva* (crospovidone; magnesium stearate; microcrystalline cellulose; povidone)].

Canada—
Not commercially available

Packaging and storage

Store at 25 °C (77 °F), excursions permitted to 15 to 30°C (59 to 86 °F).

Auxiliary labeling
- Keep out of reach of children.
- Do not use if you are breast-feeding. Contact your doctor or pharmacist.

EMTRICITABINE ORAL SOLUTION

Usual adult dose

Human immunodeficiency virus (HIV) infection—
Oral, 240 mg (24 mL) taken once daily

Note: Dose adjustment in patients with renal impairment—The dosing interval of emtricitabine should be adjusted in patients with baseline creatinine clearance <50 mL per min. The safety and effectiveness of these dosing interval adjustment guidelines have not been clinically evaluated. Therefore, clinical response to treatment and renal function should be closely monitored in these patients.

Formulation	Creatinine Clearance ≥ 50 mL/min	Creatinine Clearance 30 to 49 mL/min	Creatinine Clearance 15 to 29 mL/min	Creatinine Clearance < 15 (including patients requiring hemodialysis)
Oral solution (10 mg/mL)	240 mg (24 mL) every 24 hours	120 mg (12 mL) every 24 hours	80 mg (8 mL) every 24 hours	60 mg (6 mL) every 24 hours

Usual pediatric dose

Human immunodeficiency virus (HIV) infection—
Oral, 6 mg per kg of body weight once daily.

Note: Although there are insufficient data to recommend a specific emtricitabine dose adjustment for pediatric patients with renal impairment, a dose reduction and/or a dosing interval increase similar to adjustments for adults should be considered.

Usual pediatric prescribing limits

Up to a maximum of 240 mg (24 mL) once daily

Usual geriatric dose

See *Usual adult dose.*

Strength(s) usually available

U.S.—
10 mg per mL (Rx) [*Emtriva* (cotton candy flavor; FD&C yellow No. 6; edetate disodium; methylparaben [as a preservative]; propylparaben [as a preservative]; sodium phosphate [monobasic]; propylene glycol; water; xylitol [added as a sweetener]; sodium hydroxide may be used to adjust pH; hydrochloric acid may be used to adjust pH)].

Canada—
Not commercially available

Packaging and storage

Store refrigerated 2 to 8 °C (36 to 46 °F). Emtricitabine oral solution should be used within 3 months if stored by the patient at 25 °C (77 °F); excursions permitted to 15 to 30°C (59 to 86 °F).

Auxiliary labeling
- Keep out of reach of children.
- Do not use if you are breast-feeding. Contact your doctor or pharmacist.

Revised: 11/28/2005
Developed: 01/06/2004

EMTRICITABINE AND TENOFOVIR
Systemic†

VA CLASSIFICATION (Primary): AM840

Commonly used brand name(s): *Truvada.*

Note: For a listing of dosage forms and brand names by country availability, see *Dosage Forms* section(s).

†Not commercially available in Canada.

Category

Antiviral (systemic).

Indications

General Considerations

Antiviral activity—
Synergistic antiviral effects were observed in emtricitabine/tenofovir combination studies evaluating *in vitro* antiviral activity.

Emtricitabine: Synergistic additive antiviral effects were observed in drug combination studies of emtricitabine with nucleoside reverse transcriptase inhibitors, non-nucleoside reverse transcriptase inhibitors, and protease inhibitors. (Most of these drug combinations have not been studied in humans.) The IC_{50} values for emtricitabine were in the range of 0.0013 to 0.64 microM (0.0003 to 0.158 micrograms per mL). Emtricitabine displayed antiviral activity *in vitro* against HIV-1 clades A, B, C, D, E, F, and G (IC_{50} values ranged from 0.007 to 0.075 microM) and showed strain specific activity against HIV-2 (IC_{50} values ranged from 0.007 to 1.5 microM).

Tenofovir disoproxil fumarate: Synergistic additive antiviral effects were observed in drug combination studies of tenofovir with nucleoside reverse transcriptase inhibitors, non-nucleoside reverse transcriptase inhibitors, and protease inhibitors. (Most of these drug combinations have not been studied in humans.) The IC_{50} values (50% inhibitory concentration) for tenofovir were in the range of 0.04 to 8.5 microM. Tenofovir displayed antiviral activity *in vitro* against HIV-1 clades A, B, C, D, E, F, G, and O (IC_{50} values ranged from 0.5 to 2.2 microM).

Resistance—
HIV-1 isolates with reduced susceptibility to emtricitabine/tenofovir combination have been selected *in vitro* . Genotypic analysis of these isolates identified the M184I/V and/or K65R amino acid substitutions in the viral RT.

Emtricitabine: Emtricitabine-resistant isolates of HIV have been selected *in vitro* . Genotypic analysis of these isolates showed that reduced susceptibility to emtricitabine was associated with a mutation in the HIV RT gene at codon 184 which resulted in the M184V/I amino acid substitution. Emtricitabine-resistant isolates of HIV have been recovered from some patients treated with emtricitabine alone or in combination with other antiretroviral agents. Viral isolates from 37.5% treatment-naive patients with virologic failure showed a greater than 20-fold reduced susceptibility to emtricitabine due to M184V/I mutations.

Tenofovir disoproxil fumarate: HIV-1 isolates with reduced susceptibility to tenofovir have been selected in vitro. These viruses expressed a K65R mutation in RT and showed a 2- to 4-fold reduction in susceptibility to tenofovir. Tenofovir-resistant isolates of HIV have been recovered from some patients treated with tenofovir alone or in combination with other antiretroviral agents. Viral isolates from 24% treatment-naive patients with virologic failure to tenofovir, lamivudine and efavirenz at 48 weeks and from 4.6% treatment-experienced patients with virologic failure to tenofovir both showed a greater than 1.4-fold reduced susceptibility in vitro to tenofovir due to K65R mutations.

Cross-resistance—
Cross-resistance among certain nucleoside reverse transcriptase inhibitors (NRTIs) has been recognized. M184V/I and/or K65R substitutions selected *in vitro* by emtricitabine and tenofovir combinations are also observed in some HIV-1 isolates from subjects failing treatment with tenofovir in combination with either lamivudine or emtricitabine, and either abacavir or didanosine. Therefore, cross-resistance among these drugs may occur in patients whose virus has either or both of these amino acid substitutions.

Emtricitabine: M184V/I substitutions were cross-resistant to lamivudine and zalcitabine but retained susceptibility *in vitro* to didanosine, stavudine, tenofovir, zidovudine, delavirdine, efavirenz, and nevirapine. K65R substitutions selected *in vivo* by abacavir, didanosine, tenofovir, and zalcitabine, demonstrated reduced susceptibility to inhibition by emtricitabine. Viruses harboring mutations conferring reduced susceptibility to stavudine and zidovudine or didanosine remained sensitive to emtricitabine. K103N substitutions associated with NNRTI resistance was susceptible to emtricitabine.

Tenofovir disoproxil fumarate: HIV-1 isolates from patients with a mean of 3 zidovudine-associated RT amino acid substitutions showed a 3.1-fold decrease in susceptibility to tenofovir. Multinucleoside resistant HIV-1 with a T69S double insertion mutation also showed reduced susceptibility to tenofovir.

Accepted

Human immunodeficiency virus type 1 (HIV-1) infection (treatment)—Emtricitabine/tenofovir is indicated in combination with other antiretroviral agents (such as non-nucleoside reverse transcriptase inhibitors or protease inhibitors) for the treatment of HIV-1 infection in adults. Safety and efficacy studied using emtricitabine/tenofovir tablets or using single emtricitabine and single tenofovir in combination are ongoing.

Emtricitabine and tenofovir have each been studied as part of multidrug regimens. These drugs have been found to be safe and effective and support the use of emtricitabine/tenofovir in treatment of HIV-1 infection in treatment-naive adults. In treatment experienced patients, the use of emtricitabine/tenofovir should be guided by laboratory testing and treatment history.

There are no study results demonstrating the effect of emtricitabine and tenofovir combination on clinical progression of HIV-1.

Unaccepted
It is not recommended that emtricitabine and tenofovir combination be used as a component of a triple nucleoside regimen.

Pharmacology/Pharmacokinetics

Physicochemical characteristics
Molecular weight—
- Emtricitabine: 247.24.
- Tenofovir disoproxil fumarate: 635.52.

pKa—
- Emtricitabine: 2.65.
- Tenofovir disoproxil: 3.75.

Solubility—
- Emtricitabine: 112 mg per mL in water at 25 °C.
- Tenofovir disoproxil: 13.4 mg per mL in water at 25 °C.

Partition coefficient—
- Emtricitabine: −0.43
- Tenofovir disoproxil: 1.25

Mechanism of action/Effect
Emtricitabine: Emtricitabine, a synthetic nucleoside analog of cytidine, is phosphorylated by cellular enzymes to form emtricitabine 5′-triphosphate. Emtricitabine 5′-triphosphate inhibits the activity of the HIV-1 reverse transcriptase by competing with the natural substrate deoxycytidine 5′-triphosphate and by being incorporated into nascent viral DNA which results in chain termination. Emtricitabine 5′-triphosphate is a weak inhibitor of mammalian DNA polymerase alpha, beta, epsilon and mitochondrial DNA polymerase gamma.

Tenofovir disoproxil fumarate: Tenofovir disoproxil fumarate is an acyclic nucleoside phosphonate diester analog of adenosine monophosphate. Tenofovir disoproxil fumarate requires initial diester hydrolysis for conversion to tenofovir and subsequent phosphorylations by cellular enzymes to form tenofovir diphosphate. Tenofovir diphosphate inhibits the activity of HIV-1 reverse transcriptase by competing with the natural substrate deoxyadenosine 5'-triphosphate and, after incorporation into DNA, by DNA chain termination. Tenofovir diphosphate is a weak inhibitor of mammalian DNA polymerases alpha, beta, and mitochondrial DNA polymerase gamma.

Absorption
Emtricitabine—
- Rapid and extensive; oral bioavailability is 92%
- AUC—6.9 to 13.1 mcg hr per mL; unaffected by high fat or light meal

Tenofovir disoproxil fumarate—
- Oral bioavailability is 25%
- AUC—1.6 to 2.98 mcg hr per mL; mean increase of approximately 35% following a high fat or light meal

AUC of emtricitabine and tenofovir were increased in patients with creatinine clearance less than 50 mL per minute.

Protein binding
Emtricitabine: Very low, < 4%; independent of concentration
Tenofovir disoproxil fumarate: Very low, < 0.7%; independent of concentration

Biotransformation
Emtricitabine: 3′-sulfoxide diastereomers and their glucuronic acid conjugates
Emtricitabine is not significantly metabolized by liver enzymes

Half-life
Emtricitabine: approximately 10 hours
Tenofovir disoproxil fumarate: approximately 17 hours

Time to peak concentration
Emtricitabine: 1 to 2 hours
Tenofovir disoproxil fumarate: 0.6 to 1.4 hours; delayed by approximately 0.75 hour following a high fat or light meal

Peak plasma concentration
Emtricitabine: C_{max}—1.08 to 2.52 mcg per mL; unaffected by high fat or light meal
Tenofovir disoproxil fumarate: C_{max}—0.21 to 0.39 mcg per mL; mean increase of 15% following a high fat or light meal

C_{max} of emtricitabine and tenofovir were increased in patients with creatinine clearance less than 50 mL per minute.

Elimination
Emtricitabine: Urine—86%; glomerular filtration and active tubular secretion; 13% recovered as metabolites
Tenofovir disoproxil fumarate: Urine—approximately 70 to 80% of the intravenous dose; glomerular filtration and active tubular secretion

Precautions to Consider

Carcinogenicity
Emtricitabine—
Long-term carcinogenicity studies of emtricitabine in rats and mice are in progress.

Tenofovir disoproxil fumarate—
Liver adenomas were increased in female mice at exposures 16 times that in humans. The long-term carcinogenicity study was negative in rats at exposures up to 5 times that observed in humans at the therapeutic dose.

Mutagenicity
Emtricitabine—
Emtricitabine was not genotoxic in the reverse mutation bacterial test (Ames test), mouse lymphoma or mouse micronucleus assays.

Tenofovir disoproxil fumarate—
Tenofovir was mutagenic in the *in vitro* mouse lymphoma assay and negative in an *in vitro* bacterial mutagenicity test (Ames test). In an *in vivo* mouse micronucleus assay, tenofovir was negative when administered to male mice.

Pregnancy/Reproduction
Fertility—

Emtricitabine—
Emtricitabine did not affect fertility in male rats at approximately 140-fold or in male and female mice at approximately 60-fold higher exposures (AUC) than in humans given the recommended 200 mg daily dose. Fertility was normal in the offspring of mice exposed daily from before birth (in utero) through sexual maturity at daily exposures (AUC) of approximately 60-fold higher than human exposures at the recommended 200 mg daily dose.

Tenofovir disoproxil fumarate—
There were no effects on fertility, mating performance or early embryonic development when tenofovir was administered at doses equivalent to 10 times the human dose based on surface are comparisons to male rats for 28 days prior to mating and to female rats for 15 days prior to mating through day seven of gestation. There was, however, an alteration of the estrous cycle in female rats.

Pregnancy—There are no adequate and well controlled studies in pregnant women. Because animal reproduction studies are not always predictive of human response, emtricitabine/tenofovir disoproxil fumarate should be used during pregnancy only if clearly needed.

Emtricitabine—
Studies in animals have shown that the incidence of fetal variations and malformations was not increased in embryofetal toxicity studies performed with emtricitabine in mice at exposures (AUC) approximately 60-fold higher and in rabbits at approximately 120-fold higher than human exposures at the recommended daily dose.

Tenofovir disoproxil fumarate—
Studies have been done in rats and rabbits with administered doses up to 14 and 19 times, respectively, the human dose based on body surface area. There was no evidence of impaired fertility or harm to the fetus due to tenofovir.

FDA Pregnancy Category B

Note: An Antiretroviral Pregnancy Registry has been established to monitor fetal outcomes of pregnant women exposed to emtricitabine and tenofovir disoproxil fumarate combination. Healthcare providers are encouraged to register patients by calling (800) 258-4263.

Breast-feeding
Tenofovir is distributed into breast milk of rats. It is not known whether emtricitabine or tenofovir are distributed into human breast milk. Because of both the potential for HIV transmission and the potential for serious adverse reactions in nursing infants, mothers should be instructed not to breast-feed if they are receiving emtricitabine/tenofovir combination. **The Centers for Disease Control and Prevention recommend that HIV-infected mothers not breast-feed their infants to avoid risking postnatal transmission of HIV.**

Pediatrics
Safety and efficacy in pediatric patients less than 18 years of age have not been established.

Geriatrics

Appropriate studies on the relationship of age to the effects of emtricitabine or tenofovir have not been performed in the geriatric population. In general, dose selection should be cautious in elderly patients reflecting the greater frequency of decreased hepatic, renal or cardiac function, and of concomitant disease or other drug therapy.

Drug interactions and/or related problems

The following drug interactions and/or related problems have been selected on the basis of their potential clinical significance (possible mechanism in parentheses where appropriate)—not necessarily inclusive (» = major clinical significance):

Note: No drug interaction studies have been conducted using emtricitabine and tenofovir combination. There were no clinically significant drug interactions when emtricitabine was used in combination with famciclovir, indinavir, and stavudine.

Combinations containing any of the following medications, depending on the amount present, may also interact with this medication. The drug interactions described are based on studies conducted using the individual drugs.

Abacavir
(coadministration of abacavir and tenofovir resulted in increase of abacavir C_{max})

» Atazanavir and/or
» Lopinavir/ritonavir
(concurrent use of atazanavir and emtricitabine/tenofovir may result in increased concentrations of tenofovir and decreases in the AUC and C_{min} of atazanavir; recommended that atazanavir be administered with ritonavir; atazanavir without ritonavir should not be coadministered with emtricitabine/tenofovir)
(atazanavir and lopinavir/ritonavir have been shown to increase tenofovir concentrations; mechanism of interaction unknown; monitor patients for emtricitabine/tenofovir-associated adverse events and discontinue emtricitabine/tenofovir in patients who develop these adverse events)

» Didanosine
(tenofovir disoproxil fumarate coadministered with didanosine increased didanosine concentrations significantly which could potentiate didanosine-associated adverse events, including pancreatitis and neuropathy; concurrent use of didanosine and emtricitabine/tenofovir should be undertaken with caution; monitor patients closely for didanosine-associated adverse events and discontinue didanosine in patients who develop these adverse events; didanosine dose adjustments recommended with concurrent use)

» Emtricitabine or
» Tenofovir disoproxil fumarate
(emtricitabine and tenofovir disoproxil fumarate combination is a fixed-dose product; emtricitabine or tenofovir disoproxil fumarate should not be used with the combination product)

Indinavir
(concurrent administration of indinavir and tenofovir resulted in an increase of tenofovir C_{max} and a decrease in indinavir C_{max})

» Lamivudine or
» Products containing lamivudine
(should not be coadministered due to similarities between emtricitabine and lamivudine; also, lamivudine C_{max} decreases with tenofovir coadministration)

» Nephrotoxic medications, other (see *Appendix II*)
(emtricitabine/tenofovir should be avoided with concomitant or recent use)

Renally eliminated drugs, such as:
Acyclovir or
Adefovir dipivoxil or
Cidofovir or
Ganciclovir or
Valacyclovir or
Valganciclovir
(concurrent administration of emtricitabine and tenofovir with drugs that are primarily renally eliminated may increase serum concentrations of emtricitabine, tenofovir, or the concurrently administered drug due to competition for this elimination pathway)

Laboratory value alterations

The following have been selected on the basis of their potential clinical significance (possible effect in parentheses where appropriate)—not necessarily inclusive (» = major clinical significance).

With physiology/laboratory test results
Alanine aminotransferase (ALT [SGPT])
Aspartate aminotransferase (AST [SGOT])
Bilirubin
Blood urea nitrogen (BUN)
Creatine kinase (CK)
Pancreatic amylase
Serum amylase
Serum lipase
Triglycerides
(values may be increased)

Amino acids, urine or
Calcium, urine
(may be increased)

Creatinine, serum
(may be increased)

Glucose, serum
(values may be decreased or increased)

Glucose, urine
(concentration may be increased)

Neutrophil count
(may be decreased)

Phosphate, serum
(may be decreased)

Phosphate, urine
(may be increased)

Protein, urine
(may be increased)

Red blood cells (RBC), in urine
(may be increased)

Medical considerations/Contraindications

The medical considerations/contraindications included have been selected on the basis of their potential clinical significance (reasons given in parentheses where appropriate)—not necessarily inclusive (» = major clinical significance).

Except under special circumstances, this medication should not be used when the following medical problem exists:

» Hypersensitivity to emtricitabine, tenofovir, or any component of the product

Risk-benefit should be considered when the following medical problems exist:

Co-infection with
» Human immunodeficiency virus [HIV]
» Hepatitis B virus [HBV]
(emtricitabine/tenofovir is not indicated for chronic HBV treatment and safety and efficacy of emtricitabine and tenofovir have not been established in patients infected with both of these viruses; severe acute exacerbations of hepatitis B have also been reported after discontinuation of emtricitabine and tenofovir)

» Hepatic disease or
» Risk factors for hepatic disease or
» Obesity or
» Prolonged nucleoside exposure
(lactic acidosis and severe hepatomegaly with steatosis have been reported in patients with the use of nucleoside analogues alone or in combination; fatal cases have been reported; obesity and prolonged nucleoside exposure may be risk factors; majority of cases have been in women; treatment should be suspended in patients with evidence of lactic acidosis or pronounced hepatotoxicity which may include hepatomegaly and steatosis even in the absence of marked transaminase elevations)

» Renal dysfunction, history or risk of
» Renal impairment or
(patients with these conditions should be carefully monitored; should not be administered to patients with creatine clearance <30 mL per minute or patients requiring hemodialysis)

Patient monitoring

The following may be especially important in patient monitoring (other tests may be warranted in some patients, depending on condition; » = major clinical significance):

Bone monitoring
(should be considered for HIV infected patients who have a history of pathologic bone fracture or are at substantial risk for osteopenia; studies showed decrease from bone mineral density [BMD] baseline at the lumbar spine and hip with tenofovir use and clinical significance of these BMD changes unknown; toxicology studies in rats, dogs, and monkeys at exposures 6-fold or greater than those in humans caused bone toxicity [diagnosed as osteomalacia in monkeys appearing to be reversible upon dose reduction or discontinuation of tenofovir and reduced BMD in rats and dogs]; cal-

cium and vitamin D supplementation, although not studied, may be considered for HIV-associated osteopenia or osteoporosis; if bone abnormalities suspected, appropriate consultation should be obtained)

» Hepatic function
(should be monitored closely with both clinical and laboratory follow-up for at least several months in patients who discontinue emtricitabine/tenofovir and are co-infected with HIV and HBV; if appropriate, initiation of anti-hepatitis B therapy may be warranted)

» Hepatitis B virus
(all patients with HIV should be tested for the presence of hepatitis B virus (HBV) before initiating antiretroviral therapy; emtricitabine/tenofovir is not indicated for the treatment of chronic HBV infection and the safety and efficacy of emtricitabine/tenofovir have not been established in patients co-infected with HBV and HIV)

» Lactic acidosis or
» Hepatotoxicity, pronounced
(treatment should be immediately suspended in patients who develop clinical or laboratory findings suggestive of lactic acidosis or pronounced hepatotoxicity [which may include hepatomegaly and steatosis even in the absence of marked transaminase elevations])

Serum creatinine and
Serum phosphorous
(monitoring for signs of renal impairment should be considered in patients at risk or with a history of renal dysfunction)

Side/Adverse Effects

Lactic acidosis and severe hepatomegaly with steatosis, including fatal cases, have been reported with the use of nucleoside analogs alone or in combination with other antiretrovirals.

Although a causal relationship has not been established, redistribution and accumulation of body fat, including breast enlargement, central obesity, cushingoid appearance, dorsocervical fat enlargement (buffalo hump), facial wasting, and peripheral wasting, have been seen in patients receiving antiretroviral therapy. The mechanism and long-term consequences of these effects are not known.

It is not known if long-term (more than 1 year) use of emtricitabine/tenofovir causes bone abnormalities. It is recommended that appropriate consultation be obtained if bone abnormalities are suspected.

The following side/adverse effects have been selected on the basis of their potential clinical significance (possible signs and symptoms in parentheses where appropriate)—not necessarily inclusive:

Those indicating need for medical attention

Less frequent

Maculopapular rash (rash with flat lesions or small raised lesions on the skin); ***pruritus*** (itching skin); ***pustular rash*** (spots on your skin resembling a blister or pimple); ***urticaria*** (hives or welts; itching; redness of skin; skin rash); ***vesiculobullous rash*** (blisters under the skin)

Incidence rare

Chest pain; neuropathy (burning, tingling, numbness or pain in the hands, arms, feet, or legs; sensation of pins and needles; stabbing pain); ***paresthesia*** (burning, crawling, itching, numbness, prickling, "pins and needles", or tingling feelings); ***peripheral neuritis*** (burning, crawling, itching, numbness, painful, prickling, "pins and needles", or tingling feelings; burning of face or mouth; blindness or vision changes; clumsiness or unsteadiness; weakness in hands or feet); ***pneumonia*** (chest pain; cough; fever or chills; sneezing; shortness of breath; sore throat; troubled breathing; tightness in chest; wheezing)

Incidence is not determined—Observed during clinical practice; estimates of frequency can not be determined

Allergic reaction (cough; difficulty swallowing; dizziness; fast heartbeat; hives; itching; puffiness or swelling of the eyelids or around the eyes, face, lips or tongue; shortness of breath; skin rash; tightness in chest; unusual tiredness or weakness; wheezing); ***dyspnea*** (shortness of breath; difficult or labored breathing; tightness in chest; wheezing); ***Fanconi syndrome; hepatotoxicity, including lactic acidosis*** (abdominal discomfort; decreased appetite; diarrhea; fast, shallow breathing; general feeling of discomfort; muscle pain or cramping; nausea; shortness of breath; sleepiness; unusual tiredness or weakness); ***hypophosphatemia*** (bone pain; convulsions; loss of appetite; trouble breathing; unusual tiredness or weakness); ***pancreatitis*** (bloating; chills; constipation; darkened urine; fast heartbeat; fever; indigestion; loss of appetite; nausea; pains in stomach, side, or abdomen, possibly radiating to the back; vomiting; yellow eyes or skin); ***proximal tubulopathy*** (cloudy urine; increase in amount of urine; increased thirst); ***renal failure or insufficiency*** (lower back or side pain; decreased frequency or amount of urine; bloody urine; increased thirst; loss of appetite; nausea; vomiting; unusual tiredness or weakness; swelling of face, fingers, lower legs; weight gain; troubled breathing; increased blood pressure); ***renal failure, acute*** (agitation; coma; confusion; decreased urine output; depression; dizziness; headache; hostility; irritability; lethargy; muscle twitching; nausea; rapid weight gain; seizures; stupor; swelling of face, ankles, or hands; unusual tiredness or weakness); ***tubular necrosis, acute*** (bloody or cloudy urine; difficult or painful urination; sudden decrease in amount of urine)

Note: *Hepatotoxicity*, consisting of *lactic acidosis* and severe hepatomegaly with steatosis, has been reported with nucleoside therapy (including emtricitabine/tenofovir), alone or in combination. Fatalities have occurred. The majority of cases have occurred in women. Possible risk factors include obesity and prolonged nucleoside exposure, as well as other risk factors for liver disease, although cases have occurred in the absence of any known risk factors. Treatment with emtricitabine/tenofovir should be discontinued if clinical or laboratory findings suggestive of lactic acidosis or pronounced hepatotoxicity (possibly including hepatomegaly and steatosis, with or without marked transaminase elevations) occur.

Those indicating need for medical attention only if they continue or are bothersome

Incidence less frequent

Abdominal pain; anorexia (loss of appetite; weight loss); ***asthenia*** (lack or loss of strength); ***diarrhea; dizziness; flatulence*** (passing of gas); ***headache; nausea or vomiting***

Incidence rare

Abnormal dreams; arthralgia (pain in joints; muscle pain or stiffness; difficulty in moving); ***back pain; depressive disorder*** (discouragement; feeling sad or empty; irritability; lack of appetite; loss of interest or pleasure; tiredness; trouble concentrating; trouble sleeping); ***dyspepsia*** (acid or sour stomach; belching; heartburn; indigestion; stomach discomfort, upset, or pain); ***fever; increased cough; insomnia*** (sleeplessness; trouble sleeping; unable to sleep); ***myalgia*** (joint pain; swollen joints; muscle aching or cramping; muscle pains or stiffness; difficulty in moving); ***pain; rhinitis*** (stuffy nose; runny nose; sneezing); ***sweating; weight loss***

Overdose

For more information on the management of overdose or unintentional ingestion, **contact a poison control center** (see *Poison Control Center Listing*).

Clinical effects of overdose

Emtricitabine: Limited clinical experience is available at doses higher than the therapeutic dose of emtricitabine. In one clinical pharmacology study, single doses of emtricitabine 1200 mg were administered to 11 patients. No serious adverse events were reported.

Tenofovir: Limited clinical experience at doses higher than the therapeutic dose of 300 mg tenofovir disoproxil fumarate is available. In one study, 600 mg of tenofovir disoproxil fumarate was administered to 8 patients orally for 28 days. No severe adverse reactions were reported. The effects of higher doses are not known.

Treatment of overdose

To enhance elimination—

Emtricitabine: Hemodialysis treatment removes approximately 30% of the emtricitabine dose over a 3–hour dialysis period starting within 1.5 hours of emtricitabine dosing (blood flow rate of 400 mL per minute and a dialysate flow rate of 600 mL per minute). It is not known whether emtricitabine can be removed by peritoneal dialysis.

Tenofovir: Hemodialysis efficiently removes tenofovir with an extraction coefficient of approximately 54%. Following a 300-mg dose of tenofovir disoproxil fumarate, a four-hour hemodialysis session removed approximately 10% of the administered tenofovir dose.

Monitoring—

Monitor for evidence of toxicity.

Supportive care—

Treatment should be symptomatic and supportive.

Patients in whom intentional overdose is confirmed or suspected should be referred for psychiatric consultation.

Patient Consultation

As an aid to patient consultation, refer to *Advice for the Patient, Emtricitabine and Tenofovir (Systemic)*.

In providing consultation, consider emphasizing the following selected information (» = major clinical significance):

Before using this medication

» Conditions affecting use, especially:

Hypersensitivity to emtricitabine, tenofovir, or any other component of the product

Pregnancy—Risk-benefit should be considered
Breast-feeding—Not recommended because of the potential for postnatal transmission of HIV
Use in children—Safety and efficacy not established
Use in the elderly—Dose selection should be cautious
Other medications, especially atazanavir and/or lopinavir/ritonavir, didanosine, emtricitabine, lamivudine or products containing lamivudine, nephrotoxic agents, or tenofovir disoproxil fumarate,
Other medical problems, especially co-infection with HIV and HBV, hepatic disease, obesity, prolonged nucleoside exposure, risk factors for hepatic disease, renal dysfunction (history or risk of), or renal impairment

Proper use of this medication

» Proper dosing
Missed dose: Taking as soon as possible; not taking if almost time for next scheduled dose; not doubling doses
» Proper storage
Importance of not taking more medication than prescribed; importance of not discontinuing medication without checking with physician; importance of not missing doses and of taking at evenly spaced times
Importance of refilling prescription in advance; medicine should not be stopped, even for a short time
Not sharing medication with others
Importance of telling physician about all other medicines or dietary supplements

Precautions while using this medication

» Importance of reading the patient information before using emtricitabine/tenofovir and each time the prescription is refilled
» Regular visits to physician and the importance of staying under a doctor's care while taking emtricitabine/tenofovir
Being aware that emtricitabine/tenofovir therapy does not reduce the risk of transmitting HIV to others through sexual contact or contamination through blood
» Importance of knowing what to do for lactic acidosis, hepatotoxicity, and hepatitis B exacerbations

Side/adverse effects

Signs of potential side effects, especially maculopapular rash, pruritus, pustular rash, urticaria, vesiculobullous rash, chest pain, neuropathy, paresthesia, peripheral neuritis, or pneumonia
Signs of potential side effects observed during clinical practice, especially acute renal failure, acute tubular necrosis, allergic reaction, dyspnea, Fanconi syndrome, hepatotoxicity (including lactic acidosis), hypophosphatemia, pancreatitis, proximal tubulopathy, or renal failure or insufficiency

General Dosing Information

Emtricitabine/tenofovir is not a cure for HIV infection and patients may continue to experience the illnesses associated with HIV infection, including opportunistic infections. Patients should remain under the care of a physician while using emtricitabine/tenofovir. The use of emtricitabine/tenofovir does not reduce the risk of transmission of HIV to others through sexual contact or blood contamination.

Diet/Nutrition

Emtricitabine/tenofovir can be taken with or without food.

Bioequivalence information

One *Truvada* tablet (200 mg emtricitabine and 300 mg tenofovir disoproxil fumarate) was bioequivalent to one *Emtriva* capsule (200 mg emtricitabine) plus one *Viread* tablet (300 mg tenofovir disoproxil fumarate) following single-dose administration to fasting healthy subjects.

Oral Dosage Forms

EMTRICITABINE AND TENOFOVIR DISOPROXIL FUMARATE TABLETS

Usual adult dose

Human immunodeficiency virus (HIV-1) infection—
Oral, 200 mg of emtricitabine and 300 mg of tenofovir disoproxil fumarate once daily with or without food

Note: The dosing interval adjustment recommendation of emtricitabine/tenofovir disoproxil fumarate in patients with moderate to severe renal impairment is as follows:
- Creatinine clearance of 50 mL per minute or greater—No adjustment necessary
- Creatinine clearance of 30 to 49 mL per minute—Every 48 hours
- Creatinine clearance less than 30 mL per minute (including those requiring dialysis)—Should not receive emtricitabine/tenofovir disoproxil fumarate

Safety and efficacy of these dosing interval adjustment recommendations have not been clinically evaluated. Therefore, clinical response to treatment and renal function should be closely monitored in these patients.

Note: Dosing recommendations for didanosine when coadministered with emtricitabine and tenofovir combination:
- Patients weighing >60 kilograms: 250 mg didanosine
- Patients weighing <60 kilograms: Data are not available to recommend a didanosine dose adjustment.
- When coadministered, emtricitabine/tenofovir and the didanosine delayed-release capsule may be taken under fasted conditions or with a light meal (<400 kcal, 20% fat).
- Coadministration of emtricitabine/tenofovir and didanosine buffered tablet formulation should be under fasted conditions.

When coadministered with emtricitabine/tenofovir, it is recommended that atazanavir 300 mg is given with ritonavir 100 mg. *Atazanavir without ritonavir should not be coadministered with emtricitabine/tenofovir.*

Usual pediatric dose

Safety and effectiveness have not been established.

Usual geriatric dose

See *Usual adult dose*.

Strength(s) usually available

U.S.—
200 mg of emtricitabine and 300 mg of tenofovir disoproxil fumarate (equivalent to 245 mg of tenofovir disoproxil) (Rx) [*Truvada* (film-coated; croscarmellose sodium; lactose monohydrate; magnesium stearate; microcrystalline cellulose; pregelatinized starch [gluten free]; FD&C Blue #2 aluminum lake; hypromellose; titanium dioxide; triacetin)].

Packaging and storage

Store at 25 °C (77 °F), excursions permitted to 15 and 30 °C (59 and 86 °F), in a tight container.

Auxiliary labeling

- Keep in the original container. Close container tightly after use

Developed: 02/23/2005

ENALAPRIL—See *Angiotensin-converting Enzyme (ACE) Inhibitors (Systemic)*

ENALAPRIL AND FELODIPINE Systemic

VA CLASSIFICATION (Primary/Secondary): CV408/CV800; CV200

Commonly used brand name(s): *Lexxel*.

NOTE: The *Enalapril and Felodipine (Systemic)* monograph is maintained on the *USP DI* electronic data base. A copy of the most recent revision of the complete monograph can be accessed on the *USP DI* Updates Online website. See the front cover of book for details on accessing the site.

For information on the specific components of this combination, see the *USP DI* monographs for *Angiotensin-Converting Enzyme (ACE) Inhibitors (Systemic)*, and *Calcium Channel Blocking Agents (Systemic)*.

The information that follows is selectively abstracted from the complete monograph and is provided to facilitate drug use review and patient counseling.

Note: For a listing of dosage forms and brand names by country availability, see *Dosage Forms* section(s).

Category

Antihypertensive.

Indications

Accepted

Hypertension (treatment)—The combination of enalapril maleate and felodipine is indicated for the treatment of hypertension. It is not indicated as initial treatment for hypertension.

For additional information on initial therapeutic guidelines related to the treatment of hypertension, see *Appendix III.*

Patient Consultation

As an aid to patient consultation, refer to *Advice for the Patient, Enalapril and Felodipine (Systemic).*

In providing consultation, consider emphasizing the following selected information (» = major clinical significance):

Before using this medication

» Conditions affecting use, especially:
- Hypersensitivity to enalapril or felodipine or any component of the product
- Pregnancy—Can cause fetal and neonatal morbidity and mortality; not recommended for use during pregnancy
- Breast-feeding—Enalapril and enalaprilat are distributed into breast milk; potential for serious adverse reactions in the infant
- Pharmacogenetics—Black patients may have a lower than average response to enalapril and a higher incidence of ACE inhibitor-associated angioedema
- Dental—Mild gum swelling has been reported; good dental hygiene may decrease incidence and severity
- Surgical—Anesthesia with hypotension-producing agents may cause excessive hypotension
- Other medications, especially anticonvulsants such as carbamazepine, phenytoin, and phenobarbital; diuretics, potassium-containing salt substitutes, potassium-sparing diuretics, or potassium supplements
- Other medical problems, especially history of angioedema related to previous ACE inhibitor therapy, angioedema (hereditary or idiopathic), hypotension associated with congestive heart failure, renal artery stenosis, or renal function impairment

Proper use of this medication

» Compliance with therapy; taking medication at the same time each day to maintain the therapeutic effect

Swallowing tablets whole without dividing, crushing, or chewing

Importance of not taking tablets with grapefruit juice

» Proper dosing

Missed dose: Taking as soon as possible; not taking if almost time for next scheduled dose; not doubling doses

» Proper storage

Precautions while using this medication

Regular visits to physician to check progress

Notifying physician immediately if pregnancy is suspected because of possibility of fetal or neonatal injury and/or death

Not taking other medications, especially potassium supplements or salt substitutes that contain potassium, without consulting physician

Caution when driving or doing other things requiring alertness because of possible dizziness, lightheadedness, or fainting due to symptomatic hypotension

Notifying physician if lightheadedness or fainting occurs, especially during the first few days of therapy

Reporting any signs of infection (fever, sore throat, chills) to physician because of risk of neutropenia

Reporting any signs of facial or extremity swelling and/or difficulty in swallowing or breathing because of risk of angioedema

Checking with physician if severe nausea, vomiting, or diarrhea occurs and continues because of risk of dehydration, which may result in hypotension

Caution when exercising or during exposure to hot weather because of risk of dehydration, which may result in hypotension

Caution if any kind of surgery (including dental surgery) or emergency treatment is required

Side/adverse effects

Signs of potential side effects, especially peripheral edema, hypotension, angioedema, hepatotoxicity, hyperkalemia, neutropenia or agranulocytosis, and thrombocytopenia

Oral Dosage Forms

ENALAPRIL MALEATE AND FELODIPINE TABLETS

Usual adult dose

Antihypertensive—

Oral, initially 1 tablet daily, 5 mg enalapril and 5 mg felodipine extended-release. If blood pressure is not adequately controlled after one or two weeks, the dose may be increased to 2 tablets daily. The next increment is 4 tablets once daily of 5 mg enalapril and 2.5 mg felodipine extended-release. If blood pressure is still not controlled, a thiazide diuretic may be added.

Note: In patients with severe renal impairment, the recommended initial dose of enalapril is 2.5 mg.

Usual adult prescribing limits

20 mg enalapril and 10 mg felodipine in combination.

Usual pediatric dose

Antihypertensive—

Safety and efficacy have not been established.

Strength(s) usually available

U.S.—

5 mg enalapril and 2.5 mg felodipine extended-release (Rx) [*Lexxel* (film coated; lactose)].

5 mg enalapril and 5 mg felodipine extended-release (Rx) [*Lexxel* (film-coated)].

Auxiliary labeling

- Swallow whole. Do not crush or chew.
- Do not take other medicines without your doctor's advice.

Revised: 09/20/2004

ENALAPRILAT—See *Angiotensin-converting Enzyme (ACE) Inhibitors (Systemic)*

ENFLURANE—See *Anesthetics, Inhalation (Systemic)*

ENFUVIRTIDE Systemic†

VA CLASSIFICATION (Primary): AM890

Commonly used brand name(s): *Fuzeon.*

Another commonly used name is T-20.

Note: For a listing of dosage forms and brand names by country availability, see *Dosage Forms* section(s).

†Not commercially available in Canada.

Category

Antiviral (systemic).

Indications

General Considerations

HIV-1 isolates resistant to nucleoside analogue reverse transcriptase inhibitors (NRTI), non-nucleoside analogue reverse transcriptase inhibitors (NNRTI), and protease inhibitors (PI) were susceptible to enfuvirtide in cell cultures.

In clinical trials, HIV-1 isolates with reduced susceptibility to enfuvirtide have been recovered from subjects treated with enfuvirtide in combination with other antiretroviral agents. Posttreatment HIV-1 virus from 277 subjects exhibited decreases in susceptibility to enfuvirtide ranging from 0.4–fold to 6318–fold relative to their respective baseline virus and exhibited genotypic changes in gp41 HR1 domain amino acids 36 to 45. Substitutions in this region were observed with decreasing frequency at amino acid positions 38, 43, 36, 40, 42, and 45.

Accepted

Human immunodeficiency virus (HIV-1) infection (treatment)—Enfuvirtide is used in combination with other antiretroviral agents for the treatment of HIV-1 infection in treatment-experienced patients with evidence of HIV-1 replication despite ongoing antiretroviral therapy. Enfuvirtide must be paired with at least one other antiretroviral agent that is active *in vitro* according to HIV resistance tests and drug history.

This indication is based on analyses of plasma HIV-1 RNA levels and CD4 cell counts in controlled studies of 48 weeks' duration. Subjects enrolled were treatment-experienced adults, many of whom had advanced disease. There are no studies of enfuvirtide in antiretroviral-naive patients. There are no results from controlled trials evaluating the effect of enfuvirtide on clinical progression of HIV-1.

Pharmacology/Pharmacokinetics

Physicochemical characteristics

Note: The pharmacokinetic properties of enfuvirtide were evaluated in HIV-1 infected adult and pediatric patients.

Molecular weight—Enfuvirtide: 4492.

pH—9.0, reconstituted solution

Solubility—Negligible solubility in pure water; increased solubility in aqueous buffers (pH 7.5) to 85 to 142 g/100 mL.

Mechanism of action/Effect

Enfuvirtide interferes with the entry of HIV-1 into cells by inhibiting fusion of viral and cellular membranes. Enfuvirtide binds to the first heptad-repeat (HR1) in the gp41subunit of the viral envelope glycoprotein and prevents confirmational changes required for fusion of viral and cellular membranes.

Other actions/effects

Enfuvirtide was active *in vitro* against R5, X4, and dual topic viruses. Enfuvirtide has no activity against HIV-2.

Enfuvirtide exhibited additive to synergistic effects in cell culture assays when combined with individual members of various antiretroviral classes, including zidovudine, lamivudine, nelfinavir, indinavir, and efavirenz.

Absorption

Absolute bioavailability—84.3% ± 15.5%.

AUC—55.8 ± 12.1 μg/mL/hr.

$AUC_{0-12\ hr}$—48.7 ± 19.1 μg/mL/hr.

M3 metabolite AUC—2.4% to 15% of the enfuvirtide AUC.

Distribution

Volume of Distribution (Vol_D)—5.5 ± 1.1L.

Protein binding

92% bound to plasma proteins over a concentration range of 2 to 10 μg/mL; predominantly bound to albumin and somewhat bound to α-1 acid glycoprotein.

Biotransformation

As a peptide, enfuvirtide is expected to undergo catabolism to its constituent amino acids, with subsequent recycling of the amino acids in the body pool. *In vitro* studies with human microsomes and hepatocytes indicate that enfuvirtide undergoes hydrolysis to form a deaminated metabolite at the C-terminal phenylalanine residue, M3. The hydrolysis reaction is not NADPH dependent. The M3 metabolite is detected in human plasma following administration of enfuvirtide.

Half-life

Elimination—3.8 ± 0.6 h.

Time to peak concentration

T_{max}—4 hours (range: 4 to 8 hours).

Peak plasma concentration:

C_{max}—5.0 ± 1.7 μg/mL.

Elimination

Mean apparent clearance—

Enfuvirtide: 24.8 ± 4.1 mL/h/kg.

Enfuvirtide in combination with other antiretroviral agents: 30.6 ± 10.6 mL/h/kg.

Gender and Weight

Analysis of plasma concentration data from subjects in clinical trials indicated that the clearance of enfuvirtide is 20% lower in females than males after adjusting for body weight.

Enfuvirtide clearance decreases with decreased body weight irrespective of gender. Relative to clearance of a 70–kg male, a 40–kg male will have 20% lower clearance and a 110–kg male will have a 26% higher clearance. Relative to a 70–kg male, a 40–kg female will have 36% lower clearance and a 110–kg female will have the same clearance.

No dose adjustment is recommended for weight or gender.

Precautions to Consider

Carcinogenicity

No long-term carcinogenicity studies have been conducted.

Mutagenicity

Enfuvirtide was neither mutagenic nor clastogenic in a series of *in vivo* and *in vitro* assays including the Ames bacterial reverse mutation assay, a mammalian cell forward gene assay in AS52 Chinese Hamster ovary cells or an *in vivo* mouse micronucleus assay.

Pregnancy/Reproduction

Fertility—Enfuvirtide produced no adverse effects on fertility in male or female rats at doses up to 30 mg/kg/day administered by subcutaneous injection (1.6 times the maximum recommended adult human daily dose on a meter squared [m^2] basis).

Pregnancy—Adequate and well-controlled studies in pregnant women have not been done.

Reproduction studies performed in rats and rabbits at doses up to 27 times and 3.2 times the adult human dose on a m^2 basis, respectively, revealed no evidence of harm to the fetus from enfuvirtide. Because animal reproductive studies are not always predictive of human response, the drug should be used during pregnancy only if clearly needed.

To monitor fetal outcomes of pregnant women exposed to enfuvirtide and other antiretroviral drugs, an Antiretroviral Pregnancy Registry has been established. Physicians are encouraged to register patients by calling 1-800-258-4263.

FDA Pregnancy Category B

Breast-feeding

It is not known whether enfuvirtide is distributed into human breast milk. The Centers for Disease Control and Prevention recommends that HIV-infected mothers refrain from breast-feeding their infants to avoid risking postnatal transmission of HIV. Because of the potential for HIV transmission and the potential for serious adverse reactions in nursing infants, mothers should be instructed not to breast-feed if they are receiving enfuvirtide.

When radiolabeled ^{3}H-enfuvirtide was administered to lactating rats, radioactivity was present in the milk. It is not known if the radioactivity present in the milk is from enfuvirtide or from metabolites of enfuvirtide.

Pediatrics

Safety and efficacy have not been established in pediatric patients younger than 6 years of age. Limited efficacy data is available for pediatrics 6 years of age and older. Adverse events seen in pediatric patients during clinical trials were similar to those observed in adult patients.

Geriatrics

Appropriate studies on the relationship of age to the effects of enfuvirtide have not been performed in the geriatric population. However, no geriatrics-specific problems have been documented to date.

Laboratory value alterations

The following have been selected on the basis of their potential clinical significance (possible effect in parentheses where appropriate)—not necessarily inclusive (» = major clinical significance).

With diagnostic test results

HIV test

(use of enfuvirtide in non-HIV infected individuals may lead to a false positive HIV test with an ELISA assay; a confirmatory western blot test would be expected to be negative)

Alanine aminotransferase (ALT [SGPT]), serum and
Aspartase aminotransferase (AST [SGOT]), serum and
Amylase, serum and
Creatine phosphokinase and
Eosinophils and
Gamma glutamyl transferase (GGT) and
Hemoglobin and
Lipase and
Triglycerides

(enfuvirtide may lead to increased values in these tests)

Medical considerations/Contraindications

The medical considerations/contraindications included have been selected on the basis of their potential clinical significance (reasons given in parentheses where appropriate)—not necessarily inclusive (» = major clinical significance).

Except under special circumstances, this medication should not be used when the following medical problem exists:

Hypersensitivity to enfuvirtide or any of its components

Risk-benefit should be considered when the following medical problems exist:

Pneumonia risk factors, such as:
» CD4 cell count, low or
» Initial viral load, high or
» Intravenous drug use or
» Lung disease, history of, or
» Smoking, tobacco

(an increased rate of bacterial pneumonia was observed in clinical trials; it is unclear whether the increased incidence is related to enfuvirtide, use with caution in patients with underlying conditions that may predispose them to pneumonia)

Patient monitoring

The following may be especially important in patient monitoring (other tests may be warranted in some patients, depending on condition; » = major clinical significance):

» Pneumonia, signs and symptoms
(patients should be carefully monitored, especially if they have underlying conditions that may predispose them to pneumonia)

» Hypersensitivity reaction
(patients developing signs and symptoms of a hypersensitivity reaction should discontinue enfuvirtide and seek medical evaluation immediately; therapy should not be restarted following systemic signs and symptoms consistent with a hypersensitivity reaction)

Injection site reaction
(injection site reactions occur commonly and must be monitored for signs and symptoms of cellulitis or local infection; patients must be instructed as to when to contact their healthcare professional about these reactions)

Side/Adverse Effects

The following side/adverse effects have been selected on the basis of their potential clinical significance (possible signs and symptoms in parentheses where appropriate)—not necessarily inclusive:

The following side/adverse effects are for enfuvirtide plus a background regimen:

Hypersensitivity reactions have been associated with enfuvirtide therapy and may recur on re-challenge. Hypersensitivity reactions have included individually and in combination: rash, fever, nausea, vomiting, chills, rigors, hypotension and elevated serum liver transaminases. Primary immune complex reaction, respiratory distress, glomerulonephritis, and Guillain-Barre syndrome have been also reported in subjects receiving enfuvirtide and may be immune mediated. Patients developing signs and symptoms of a systemic hypersensitivity reaction should discontinue enfuvirtide and seek medical evaluation immediately. Patients who have developed systemic signs and symptoms consistent with a hypersensitivity reaction to enfuvirtide should not be restarted on enfuvirtide.

Local injection site reactions (ISR) were the most frequent adverse events associated with the use of enfuvirtide and occurs in almost all patients. The majority of ISRs were associated with mild to moderate pain at the injection site, erythema, induration, ecchymosis, pruritus, and the presence of nodules or cysts. The average duration of individual injection site reactions was between three and seven days in 41% of subjects and more than seven days in 24% of subjects. The number of injection site reactions per subject at any one time was between six to fourteen in 26% of subjects and more than fourteen injection site reactions in 1.3% of subjects. Infection at the injection site occurred in 1.7% of subjects.

Other adverse events that may be immune mediated and have been reported in subjects receiving enfuvirtide include primary immune complex reaction, respiratory distress, glomerulonephritis, and Guillain-Barre syndrome.

Those indicating need for medical attention

Incidence more frequent

Peripheral neuropathy (burning, numbness, tingling, or painful sensations or weakness in arms, hands, legs, or feet; unsteadiness; awkwardness); ***sinusitis*** (pain or tenderness around eyes and cheekbones; fever; stuffy or runny nose; headache; cough; shortness of breath or troubled breathing; tightness of chest; wheezing)

Incidence less frequent

Conjunctivitis (redness, pain, swelling of eye, eyelid, or inner lining of eyelid burning; dry or itching eyes; discharge; excessive tearing); ***infection at injection site*** (itching, pain, redness, swelling, tenderness, or warmth on skin at injection site); ***pancreatitis*** (bloating; chills; constipation; darkened urine; fast heartbeat; fever; indigestion; loss of appetite; nausea; pains in stomach, side, or abdomen, possibly radiating to the back; vomiting; yellow eyes or skin); ***skin papilloma*** (lump or growth on skin)

Incidence rare

Hypersensitivity reaction (difficulty in breathing or swallowing; fast heartbeat; shortness of breath; skin itching, rash, or redness; swelling of face, throat, or tongue)

Incidence unknown

Guillain-Barre syndrome (sudden numbness and weakness in the arms and legs; inability to move arms and legs); ***neutropenia*** (chills; cough; fever; lower back or side pain; painful or difficult urination; pale skin; shortness of breath; sore throat; ulcers, sores, or white spots in mouth; unusual tiredness or weakness); ***pneumonia*** (chest pain; cough; fever or chills; sneezing; shortness of breath; sore throat; troubled breathing; tightness in chest; wheezing); ***renal failure*** (lower back/side pain; decreased frequency/amount of urine; bloody urine; increased thirst; loss of appetite; nausea; vomiting; unusual tiredness or weakness; swelling of face, fingers, lower legs; weight gain; troubled breathing; increased blood pressure); ***thrombocytopenia*** (black, tarry stools; bleeding gums; blood in urine or stools; pinpoint red spots on skin; unusual bleeding or bruising); ***sixth nerve palsy***

Those indicating need for medical attention only if they continue or are bothersome

Incidence more frequent

Anorexia (loss of appetite; weight loss); ***anxiety*** (fear; nervousness); ***appetite decreased; asthenia*** (lack or loss of strength); ***cough; depression*** (discouragement; feeling sad or empty; irritability; lack of appetite; loss of interest or pleasure; tiredness; trouble concentrating; trouble sleeping); ***diarrhea; dry mouth; fatigue*** (unusual tiredness or weakness); ***herpes simplex*** (burning or stinging of skin; painful cold sores or blisters on lips, nose, eyes, or genitals); ***injection site reactions, including; ecchymosis*** (bruising; large, flat, blue or purplish patches in the skin); ***erythema*** (flushing; redness of skin; unusually warm skin); ***cysts*** (abnormal growth filled with fluid or semisolid material); ***induration*** (hard lump); ***nodules*** (small lumps under the skin); ***pain/discomfort; pruritus*** (itching skin); ***insomnia*** (sleeplessness; trouble sleeping; unable to sleep); ***myalgia*** (muscle pain); ***nausea; weight decreased***

Incidence less frequent

Abdominal pain, upper; constipation (difficulty having a bowel movement (stool)); ***folliculitis*** (burning, itching, and pain in hairy areas; pus at root of hair); ***influenza-like illness*** (chills; cough; diarrhea; fever; general feeling of discomfort or illness; headache; joint pain; loss of appetite; muscle aches and pains); ***lymphadenopathy*** (swollen, painful, or tender lymph glands in neck, armpit, or groin); ***taste disturbance*** (change in taste; bad, unusual or unpleasant (after) taste)

Overdose

For more information on the management of overdose or unintentional ingestion, **contact a poison control center** (see *Poison Control Center Listing*).

Treatment of overdose

There are no reports of human acute overdose with enfuvirtide. The highest dose administered to 12 subjects in a clinical trial was 180 mg as a single dose subcutaneously.

Supportive care—
There is no specific antidote for overdose with enfuvirtide. Treatment should consist of general supportive measures.
Patients in whom intentional overdose is confirmed or suspected should be referred for psychiatric consultation.

Patient Consultation

As an aid to patient consultation, refer to *Advice for the Patient, Enfuvirtide (Systemic).*

In providing consultation, consider emphasizing the following selected information (» = major clinical significance):

Before using this medication

» Conditions affecting use, especially:
Hypersensitivity to enfuvirtide or any of its components
Pregnancy—Risk-benefit should be considered; contact your healthcare provider if you become pregnan while taking this medication
Breast-feeding—Breast-feeding is not recommended due to the potential for postnatal transmission of the HIV-1 virus; it is unknown whether enfuvirtide is distributed into human breast milk
Other medical problems, especially pneumonia risk factors such as CD4 cell count; low, initial viral load; high, intravenous drug use, lung disease; history of, smoking tobacco; history of

Proper use of this medication

Reading patient package insert and patient instructions for proper injection technique; rotating injection sites

Checking with physician immediately if signs or symptoms of a hypersensitivity reaction (rash, fever, nausea and vomiting, chills, rigors, and/or hypotension) occur

» Checking with physician immediately if signs or symptoms suggestive of pneumonia (cough with fever, rapid breathing, shortness of breath) occur

» Knowing how to monitor injection site reactions and when to contact physician

» Proper administration technique

» Importance of proper reconstitution

» Proper training for patient in reconstitution and administration techniques
» Safe handling and disposal of needles and syringes
Importance of taking medication as prescribed; importance of not discontinuing medicine without checking with physician
» Proper dosing; Importance of taking enfuvirtide in combination with other antiretroviral medications
Missed dose: Taking as soon as possible; not taking if almost time for next scheduled dose; not doubling doses
Proper storage

Precautions while using this medication
Regular visits to physician
» Being aware that enfuvirtide therapy does not reduce the risk of transmitting HIV to others through sexual contact or contamination through blood
» This medication may cause dizziness. Avoid driving, using machines, or doing anything else that could be dangerous if you are not alert.

Side/adverse effects
Conjunctivitis, Guillain-Barre syndrome, hypersensitivity reaction, infection at injection site, neutropenia, peripheral neuropathy, pancreatitis, pneumonia, renal failure, sinusitis, sixth nerve palsy, skin papilloma, and thrombocytopenia

General Dosing Information

For parenteral dosing forms:

For more detailed injection instructions, see Fuzeon® *Injection Instructions*.

Each injection should be given at a site different than the preceding injection site, and only where there is no current injection site reaction from an earlier dose. Enfuvirtide should not be injected into moles, scar tissue, bruises, or the navel. The reconstituted solution should be injected subcutaneously in the upper arm, abdomen, or anterior thigh. A vial is suitable for single use only; unused portions must be discarded.

Before the solution is withdrawn for administration, the vial should be inspected visually to ensure that the contents are fully dissolved in solution, and that the solution is clear, colorless and without bubbles or particulate matter. If there is evidence of particulate matter the vial must not be used and should be returned to the pharmacy.

Enfuvirtide contains no preservatives. Once reconstituted, it should be injected immediately or kept refrigerated in the original vial until use. Reconstituted enfuvirtide must be used within 24 hours. The subsequent dose can be reconstituted in advance and must be stored in the refrigerator in the original vial and used within 24 hours. Refrigerated reconstituted solution should be brought to room temperature before injection and the vial should be inspected visually to ensure that the contents are fully dissolved in solution, and that the solution is clear, colorless and without bubbles or particulate matter.

• Patients should contact their healthcare provider for any questions regarding administration. Patients should be told not to reuse needles or syringes, and be instructed in safe disposal procedures including the use of a puncture-resistant container for disposal of used needles and syringes. Patients must be instructed on the safe disposal of full containers per local requirements. Caregivers who experience an accidental needlestick after patient injection should contact a healthcare provider immediately.

• Information about self-administration for patients may also be obtained by calling 1−877-438−9366 or at www.Fuzeon.com

• Patients should be informed that injection site reactions always occur. Patients must be familiar with the Fuzeon® *Injection Instructions* on how to appropriately inject enfuvirtide and how to carefully monitor for signs or symptoms of cellulitis or local infection. Patients should be taught to recognize the signs and symptoms of injection site reactions and instructed when to contact their healthcare provider about these reactions.

• Patients should be made aware that an increased rate of bacterial pneumonia was observed in subjects treated with enfuvirtide in Phase 3 clinical trials compared to the control arm. Patients should be advised to seek medical evaluation immediately if they develop signs or symptoms suggestive of pneumonia.

• Patients should be advised of the possibility of a hypersensitivity reaction. Patients should be advised to discontinue therapy and immediately seek medical evaluation if they develop signs/symptoms of hypersensitivity.

• Enfuvirtide is not a cure for HIV-1 infection and patients may continue to contract illnesses associated with HIV-1 infection. The long-term effects of enfuvirtide are unknown at this time and therapy has not been shown to reduce the risk of transmitting HIV-1 to others through sexual contact or blood contamination.

• Enfuvirtide must be taken as part of a combination antiretroviral regimen, including at least one other antiretroviral agent with *in vitro* activity. Use of enfuvirtide alone may lead to rapid development of virus resistant to enfuvirtide and possibly to other agents of the same class.

• Patients and caregivers must be instructed in the use of aseptic technique to avoid injection site infections. Appropriate training for reconstitution and self-injection must be given by a healthcare provider, including a careful review of the package insert and the Injection Instructions. The first injection should be performed under the supervision of an appropriately qualified healthcare provider. It is recommended that the patient and/or caregiver's understanding and use of aseptic self-injection techniques and procedures be periodically reevaluated.

• Patients should inform their healthcare provider if they are pregnant, plan to become pregnant or become pregnant while taking this medicine. Patients should inform their healthcare professional if they are breast-feeding.

• Patients should not change the dose or dosing schedule of enfuvirtide or any antiretroviral medication without consulting their healthcare provider. Patients should contact their healthcare provider immediately if they stop taking enfuvirtide or any other drug in their antiretroviral regimen.

• Patients should be advised that no studies have been conducted on the ability to drive or operate machinery while taking enfuvirtide. If patients experience dizziness they should be advised to talk to their healthcare provider before driving or operating machinery.

Information for Patients—
To assure safe and effective use the following information and instructions should be given to patients. Patients must be familiar with the Fuzeon® *Injection Instructions*.

Parenteral Dosage Forms

ENFUVIRTIDE FOR INJECTION

Usual adult dose
Human immunodeficiency virus (HIV) infection—
Subcutaneously, 90 mg (1 mL) injected twice daily into the upper arm, anterior thigh, or abdomen.

Usual pediatric dose
Human immunodeficiency virus (HIV) infection—
Children 6 to 16 years of age: Subcutaneously, 2 mg/kg injected twice daily into the upper arm, anterior thigh, or abdomen.
Weight should be monitored periodically and dose adjusted accordingly.
Children under 6 years of age: Safety and efficacy have not been established.

Weight Kilograms (kg)	Weight Pounds (lbs)	Dose per bid Injection (mg/dose)	Injection Volume (90 mg enfuvirtide per mL)
11.0 to 15.5	24 to 34	27	0.3 mL
15.6 to 20.0	>34 to 44	36	0.4 mL
20.1 to 24.5	>44 to 54	45	0.5 mL
24.6 to 29.0	>54 to 64	54	0.6 mL
29.1 to 33.5	>64 to 74	63	0.7 mL
33.6 to 38.0	>74 to 84	72	0.8 mL
38.1 to 42.5	>84 to 94	81	0.9 mL
≥42.6	>94	90	1.0 mL

Usual pediatric prescribing limits
90 mg twice daily.

Usual geriatric dose
See *Usual adult dose*.

Strength(s) usually available
U.S.—
90 mg per 1 mL (Rx) [*Fuzeon* (mannitol; sodium carbonate; sodium hydroxide; hydrochloric acid)].

Canada—
Not commercially available.

Packaging and storage
Store at 25 °C (77 °F), excursions permitted to 15 to 30°C (59 to 86°F). Reconstituted solution should be stored under refrigeration at 2 to 8°C (36 to 46°F) and used within 24 hours.

Preparation of dosage form
Enfuvirtide must only be reconstituted with 1.1 mL of Sterile Water for Injection. After adding sterile water, the vial should be gently tapped for 10 seconds and then gently rolled between the hands to avoid foaming and to ensure all particles of drug are in contact with the liquid and no drug remains on the vial wall. The vial should then be allowed

to stand until the powder goes completely into solution, which could take up to 45 minutes. Reconstitution time can be reduced by gently rolling the vial between the hands until the product is completely dissolved.

Stability

Reconstituted solution must be refrigerated and used within 24 hours.

Auxiliary labeling

- May cause dizziness.

Note

Enfuvirtide is used in combination with other antiretroviral agents.

Revised: 12/22/2004
Developed: 11/20/2003

ENOXACIN—See *Fluoroquinolones (Systemic)*

ENOXAPARIN Systemic

VA CLASSIFICATION (Primary): BL111

Commonly used brand name(s): *Lovenox; Lovenox HP.*

Note: For a listing of dosage forms and brand names by country availability, see *Dosage Forms* section(s).

Category

Antithrombotic

Note: Enoxaparin is one of a group of substances known as low molecular weight heparins (LMWHs).

Indications

Note: Bracketed information in the *Indications* section refers to uses that are not included in U.S. product labeling.

General Considerations

The use of low molecular weight heparins (LMWHs) has several advantages compared to heparin. Improved bioavailability at low doses when administered subcutaneously, a longer plasma half-life, and a more predictable anticoagulant response allow for simpler dosing without laboratory monitoring. Studies in animals show that with doses of equivalent antithrombotic effect, LMWHs produce less bleeding than standard heparin. The clinical importance of this observation is uncertain, but may allow the use of higher anticoagulant doses of LMWHs, thereby improving efficacy without compromising safety. The potential advantage of reduced bleeding has been demonstrated in studies in patients receiving high doses for the treatment of venous thrombosis. However, in studies using prophylactic doses, no difference in bleeding has been demonstrated. This contrasting effect may be due to inappropriate dosage regimens in early studies, and the difficulty of measuring hemorrhagic tendencies in humans. LMWHs are associated with a lower incidence of heparin-induced thrombocytopenia, possibly due to reduced effects on platelet function and binding. These advantages must be weighed against the higher cost of the LMWHs, although the simpler dosing regimens used with LMWHs may allow home treatment in selected patients, thereby reducing overall costs and improving patient satisfaction.

Accepted

Thromboembolism, pulmonary (prophylaxis); and

Thrombosis, deep venous (prophylaxis)—Enoxaparin is indicated to prevent deep venous thrombosis (DVT) and to reduce the risk of pulmonary embolism following hip or knee replacement surgery. In addition, following hip replacement surgery, enoxaparin is indicated for extended prophylaxis following hospitalization.[1]

Enoxaparin is also indicated to prevent DVT and reduce the risk of pulmonary embolism in patients undergoing abdominal surgery who are at increased risk of thromboembolic complications. Patients at risk include patients who are over 40 years of age, obese, undergoing surgery under general anesthesia lasting longer than 30 minutes, or patients who have additional risk factors such as malignancy or a history of DVT or pulmonary embolism.

Enoxaparin is indicated to prevent DVT in patients who are at risk for thromboembolic complications due to severely restricted mobility during acute illness.

[Enoxaparin has been shown to be as effective as unfractionated heparin in preventing deep venous thrombosis and is indicated following general surgical procedures, including gynecological, urological and colorectal surgery, that leave the patient immobilized.]

Thrombosis, deep venous (treatment)—Enoxaparin is indicated for the **inpatient treatment** of acute deep vein thrombosis **with and without pulmonary embolism**, and the **outpatient treatment** of acute deep vein thrombosis **without pulmonary embolism**, both when administered in conjunction with warfarin sodium.

Thrombosis, coronary arterial, acute (prophylaxis)[1]—Enoxaparin is indicated to prevent ischemic complications associated with unstable angina and non–Q-wave myocardial infarction, when concurrently administered with aspirin.

[Unstable angina and non-Q-wave myocardial infarction (treatment)]—Enoxaparin is indicated for the treatment of unstable angina and non-Q-wave myocardial infarction, concurrently with ASA

[1]Not included in Canadian product labeling.

Pharmacology/Pharmacokinetics

Physicochemical characteristics

Source—Obtained by alkaline depolymerization of heparin benzyl ester derived from porcine intestinal mucosa.

Molecular weight—3500 to 5500 daltons (average 4500 daltons).

pH—5.5 to 7.5

Specific activity—

Anti-factor Xa: 100 to 160 International Units (IU) per mg.

Anti-factor IIa: 20 to 40 IU per mg.

Mechanism of action/Effect

Enoxaparin, like unfractionated heparin, potentiates the actions of an endogenous inhibitor of blood coagulation, antithrombin III (heparin cofactor). Antithrombin III combines in a 1:1 molar ratio with activated serine proteases of the intrinsic and common coagulation pathways (primarily thrombin [factor IIa] and factor Xa, and, to a lesser extent, factors IXa, XIa, and XIIa) to form inactive complexes. Enoxaparin binds to antithrombin III, producing a conformational change in the cofactor molecule that results in significantly more rapid binding with and inactivation of the clotting factors than is achieved by the endogenous inhibitor alone.

Enoxaparin acts primarily by increasing antithrombin III–mediated inhibition of the formation and activity of factor Xa. This activity, in turn, reduces thrombin generation. These actions decrease thrombin-mediated events in coagulation, including the conversion of fibrinogen to fibrin, thereby inhibiting fibrin clot formation. Unlike unfractionated heparin, which has an anti-factor Xa (antithrombotic) to anti-factor IIa (anticoagulant) activity ratio of approximately 1 to 1, enoxaparin has an anti-factor Xa to anti-factor IIa activity ratio of approximately 3 to 1. Enoxaparin's higher ratio of antithrombotic to anticoagulant activity is thought to result in an antithrombotic effect equivalent to that of unfractionated heparin with a lower risk of bleeding. However, it has not been consistently demonstrated that the risk of bleeding is lower with enoxaparin than with unfractionated heparin. Enoxaparin also decreases inhibition of platelet function and disrupts vascular permeability to a lesser extent than does unfractionated heparin.

Other actions/effects

Enoxaparin has been shown to increase the plasma concentration of non-esterified fatty acids, without affecting plasma cholesterol, triglycerides, or phospholipids.

Absorption

Absorbed rapidly and almost completely following subcutaneous injection, with approximately 100% bioavailability based on anti-Factor Xa activity.

Distribution

The volume of distribution of anti-Factor Xa activity is about 4.3 liters..

Biotransformation

Hepatic; weakly metabolized by desulfation and depolymerization.

Half-life

Elimination, based on anti-factor Xa activity—4.5 hours after subcutaneous administration. May be prolonged in the presence of chronic, severe renal failure.

Time to peak effect

3 to 5 hours following subcutaneous injection.

Duration of action

Up to 24 hours following subcutaneous injection. Anti-Factor Xa activity persists in plasma approximately 12 hours following a 40 milligram SC, once a day dose.

Elimination

Primarily renal. After intravenously dosing with enoxaparin labeled with the gamma-emmiter, ^{99m}Tc, 40% of radioactivity and 8 to 20% of anti-

Factor Xa activity were recovered in urine in 24 hours. Total body clearance following an intravenous dose is approximately 26 milliliters per minute. Following a subcutaneous (SC) dose of enoxaparin, the apparent clearance (CL/F) is approximately 15 mL per minute. Apparent clearance is decreased approximately 30% in patients with chronic, severe renal failure.

Pharmacokinetic Profile

The following table represents the pharmacokinetic parameters after 5 days of 1.5 mg/kg SC, once daily dosing regimen of enoxaparin using 100 mg/mL or 200 mg/mL concentrations.

Pharmacokinetic Activity	Concentration (mg/mL)	Anti-Xa (IU/mL)	Anti-IIa (IU/mL)	Heptest	aPTT
A_{max} (IU/mL) or Δ sec	100	1.37 ± 0.23	0.23 ± 0.05	104.5 ±16.6	19.3 ±4.7
	200	1.45 0.22	0.26 0.05	110.9 ±17.1	22 ±6.7
t_{max} (h)	100	3.0	4.0	2.5	3.0
	200	3.5	4.5	3.3	3.0
AUC (h*IU/mL) or h*Δ sec	100	14.26 ± 2.93	1.54 ± 0.61	1321 ±219	
	200	15.43 ± 2.96	1.77 ± 0.67	1401 ±227	

*± SD at Day 5 and 90% confidence interval of the ratio

Precautions to Consider

Cross-sensitivity and/or related problems

Patients with a history of allergies, especially those who are allergic to heparin, or to pork or pork products, may be allergic to this medication also.

Carcinogenicity

The carcinogenic potential of enoxaparin has not been investigated.

Mutagenicity

No mutagenicity was demonstrated *in vitro*, in the Ames test, mouse lymphoma cell forward mutation test, or human lymphocyte chromosomal aberration test; or *in vivo*, in the rat bone marrow chromosomal aberration test.

No disruption of chromosomes was demonstrated *in vitro*, in rat bone marrow cells, or *in vivo*, in human peripheral lymphocytes.

Pregnancy/Reproduction

Pregnancy—The use of enoxaparin is not recommended for thromboprophylaxis in pregnant women with prosthetic heart valves. In a clinical study, 2 of 7 women with prosthetic heart valves given enoxaparin developed clots resulting in blockage of the valve leading to maternal and fetal death.

Adequate and well-controlled studies in humans have not been done; however, pregnant women receiving enoxaparin should be carefully monitored. Pregnant women and women of child-bearing potential should be apprised of the potential hazard to the fetus and the mother if enoxaparin is administered during pregnancy.

Note: In post marketing reports, there have been reports of fetal death and congenital anomalies in infants born to women who received enoxaparin during pregnancy including cerebral anomalies, limb anomalies, hypospadias, peripheral vascular malformation, fibrotic dysplasia, and cardiac defect. A causal relationship has not been established nor has the incidence been shown to be higher than in the general population.

Pregnant women are at increased risk for bleeding. Hemorrhage can occur at any site and may lead to death of mother and/or fetus.

No evidence of teratogenicity was found in studies in mice receiving 30 mg per kg of body weight per day or 211 mg per square meter of body surface area per day, or in rabbits receiving 410 mg per square meter of body surface area per day.

FDA Pregnancy Category B.

Breast-feeding

It is not known whether enoxaparin is distributed into breast milk.

Pediatrics

Appropriate studies on the relationship of age to the effects of enoxaparin have not been performed in the pediatric population. Safety and efficacy have not been established.

Geriatrics

Elderly patients, especially females, may be more susceptible than other patients to bleeding during enoxaparin therapy. The risk of associated bleeding and serious adverse events increases with age. Also, the time to peak concentration and the half-life of enoxaparin may be prolonged in elderly patients. Careful attention to dosing intervals and concomitant mediations (especially antiplatelet medications is advised. Monitoring of elderly patients with low body weight (< 45 kg) and those predisposed to decreased renal function should be considered.

Drug interactions and/or related problems

The following drug interactions and/or related problems have been selected on the basis of their potential clinical significance (possible mechanism in parentheses where appropriate)—not necessarily inclusive (» = major clinical significance):

Note: Combinations containing any of the following medications, depending on the amount present, may also interact with this medication.

In addition to the interactions listed below, the possibility should be considered that multiple effects leading to further impairment of blood clotting and/or increased risk of bleeding may occur if enoxaparin is administered to a patient receiving any medication having a significant potential for causing hypoprothrombinemia, thrombocytopenia, or gastrointestinal ulceration or hemorrhage.

Anticoagulants, coumarin- or indandione-derivative
(concurrent use may increase the risk of bleeding)

» Anti-inflammatory drugs, nonsteroidal (NSAIDs) including Epidural or spinal hematoma formation have occurred in ongoing safety surveillance since 1993 with concurrent use of enoxaparin and spinal/epidural anesthesia or receiving additional drugs affecting hemostasis such as NSAIDs; resulted in neurologic injury, including long term or permanent paralysis.
Ketorolac tromethamine

» Platelet aggregation inhibitors, other (see *Appendix II*), especially:
» Aspirin or
» Dipyridamole or
» Salicylates or
» Sulfinpyrazone or
» Ticlopidine
(inhibition of platelet function by these agents may increase the risk of bleeding)
(hypoprothrombinemia induced by large [antirheumatic] doses of aspirin, and the potential occurrence of gastrointestinal ulceration or hemorrhage during therapy with NSAIDs, aspirin, dipyridamole, salicylates, or sulfinpyrazone, also may increase the risk of bleeding in patients receiving enoxaparin If coadministration is essential, conduct close clinical and laboratory monitoring.)

Cefamandole or
Cefoperazone or
Cefotetan or
» Plicamycin or
» Valproic acid
(these medications may cause hypoprothrombinemia; in addition, plicamycin or valproic acid may inhibit platelet aggregation; concurrent use with enoxaparin may increase the risk of hemorrhage and is not recommended)

» Thrombolytic agents, such as:
» Alteplase (tissue-type plasminogen activator, recombinant) or
» Anistreplase (anisoylated plasminogen-streptokinase activator complex; APSAC)
» Streptokinase or
» Urokinase
(concurrent or sequential use with enoxaparin may increase the risk of bleeding complications)

Laboratory value alterations

The following have been selected on the basis of their potential clinical significance (possible effect in parentheses where appropriate)—not necessarily inclusive (» = major clinical significance).

With physiology/laboratory test values
Alanine aminotransferase (ALT [SGPT]) and
Alkaline phosphatase and
Aspartate aminotransferase (AST [SGOT])
(serum values may be increased)

Hemoglobin concentration and
Hematocrit value and
Red blood cell count
(values may be decreased)

Medical considerations/Contraindications

The medical considerations/contraindications included have been selected on the basis of their potential clinical significance (reasons given in parentheses where appropriate)—not necessarily inclusive (» = major clinical significance).

Except under special circumstances, this medication should not be used when the following medical problems exist:

» Abortion, threatened, or
» Aneurysm, cerebral or dissecting aorta, except in conjunction with corrective surgery, or
» Cerebrovascular hemorrhage, confirmed or suspected
(increased risk of uncontrollable hemorrhage)
» Hemorrhage, active uncontrollable
Hypersensitivity to enoxaparin, heparin, or to pork or pork products
Hypersensitivity to benzyl alcohol
(patients should not be treated with the multi-dose formulation of enoxaparin)
» Hypertension, severe uncontrolled
(increased risk of cerebral hemorrhage)
» Septic shock
» Thrombocytopenia, severe, enoxaparin- or heparin-induced, within past several months
(risk of recurrence, which may cause resistance to enoxaparin and new thromboembolic complications)

Risk-benefit should be considered when the following medical problems exist:

Any medical or dental procedure or condition in which the risk of bleeding or hemorrhage is present, such as: (risk of epidural or spinal hematoma, which can result in long-term or permanent paralysis; this risk is increased with the use of indwelling epidural catheters or by the concomitant use of medications that affect hemostasis, such as nonsteroidal anti-inflammatory drugs, platelet inhibitors, or other anticoagulants; the risk may also be increased by traumatic or repeated epidural or spinal puncture. See *General Dosing Information* for guidelines regarding the use of regional anesthesia in patients receiving perioperative enoxaparin.)
» Anesthesia, epidural or spinal
» Blood dyscrasias, hemorrhagic, especially thrombocytopenia, hemophilia, or von Willebrand disease; or other hemorrhagic tendency
» Childbirth, recent
Diabetes, severe
» Endocarditis, acute or subacute bacterial
Gastrointestinal ulceration, history of
Intrauterine contraceptive device, use of
» Neurosurgery, recent or contemplated
» Ophthalmic surgery, recent or contemplated
» Pericarditis or pericardial effusion
Radiation therapy, recent
Renal function impairment, mild to moderate
» Retinopathy, diabetic or hemorrhagic
» Spinal puncture, recent
» Trauma, severe, especially to the central nervous system (CNS)
Tuberculosis, active
» Ulceration or other lesions of the gastrointestinal, respiratory, or urinary tract, active
» Vasculitis, severe
» Wounds resulting in large open surfaces
Hepatic function impairment, mild to moderate
» Hepatic function impairment, severe
Hypertension, mild to moderate
(increased risk of cerebral hemorrhage)
Low-body weight
(women weighing less than 45 kg and men weighing less than 57 kg may experience increased exposure of enoxaparin; patients should be observed closely for signs and symptoms of bleeding)
Mechanical prosthetic heart valves
(although this condition has not been studied adequately, isolated instances of prosthetic heart valve thrombosis have been reported in patients with mechanical prosthetic heart valves; pregnant women with this condition may be at higher risk)
» Renal function impairment, severe
(may increase exposure of enoxaparin; patients should be monitored for signs and symptoms of bleeding; a dosage adjustment is recommended for those that have a creatinine clearance $\leq$ 30 mL per min)
» Prosthetic heart valves
(may lead to prosthetic heart valve thrombosis; pregnant women may be at greater risk; cases of maternal and fetal death have been reported)

Patient monitoring

The following may be especially important in patient monitoring (other tests may be warranted in some patients, depending on condition; » = major clinical significance):

Anti-Factor Xa levels
(frequent monitoring of peak and trough levels in pregnant women may be necessary; adjustment of dosage may be needed)
» Blood coagulation tests
(although enoxaparin, in therapeutic doses, does not alter activated partial thromboplastin time [APTT], prothrombin time [PT], or thrombin time test values, these tests should be performed prior to therapy to establish a baseline or control value; also recommended to identify pre-existing coagulation defects and aid in determining whether the patient is a suitable candidate for treatment)
Blood pressure measurement
Hemoglobin concentration and
Hematocrit value
(recommended periodically during therapy; an unexplained fall in the blood pressure or hematocrit may signal occult bleeding; bleeding should be considered major if the hemoglobin concentration is decreased by more than 2 grams per deciliter [20 grams per liter], or if a transfusion of 2 or more units of blood is required)
» Neurologic status
(monitor for signs and symptoms of neurologic impairment such as paresthesias, leg weakness, sensory loss, motor deficit, or bowel/bladder dysfunction indicating a potential epidural or spinal hematoma; if neurologic compromise is noted, urgent intervention is necessary, which includes radiographic confirmation and decompressive laminectomy; good or partial recovery is more likely if surgery is performed within 8 hours of the development of paraplegia)
» Platelet aggregation test
(recommended prior to initiation of therapy in patients who have developed thrombocytopenia following administration of unfractionated heparin; if the result is negative, enoxaparin therapy may be instituted, with daily monitoring of the platelet count; however, if the result is positive, enoxaparin should not be given)
» Platelet count
(recommended prior to initiation of therapy, then twice weekly for the duration of therapy to detect thrombocytopenia)
Stool tests for occult blood loss
(recommended periodically during therapy)

Side/Adverse Effects

Since 1993, there have been over 80 reports of epidural or spinal hematoma formation with concurrent use of enoxaparin injection and spinal/epidural anesthesia or spinal puncture. The majority of patients had a post-operative indwelling epidural catheter placed for analgesia or received additional drugs affecting hemostasis such as NSAIDs. Many of the epidural or spinal hematomas caused neurologic injury, including long-term or permanent paralysis. Because these events were reported voluntarily from a population of unknown size, estimates of frequency cannot be made.

The following side/adverse effects have been selected on the basis of their potential clinical significance (possible signs and symptoms in parentheses where appropriate)—not necessarily inclusive:

Those indicating need for medical attention

Note: Surgical procedure may be a contributing factor to the incidence of side effects.

Incidence more frequent

Anemia (pale skin; troubled breathing with exertion; unusual bleeding or bruising; unusual tiredness or weakness)—which may be severe; ***hemorrhage*** (bleeding gums; coughing up blood; difficulty in breathing or swallowing; dizziness; headache; increased menstrual flow or vaginal bleeding; nosebleeds; paralysis; prolonged bleeding from cuts; red or dark brown urine; red or black, tarry stools; shortness of breath)—which may be severe; ***edema, peripheral*** (swelling of ankles, feet, fingers); ***thrombocytopenia*** (black, tarry stools; bleeding gums; blood in urine or stools; moderate to severe pain or numbness in the arms, legs, hands, feet; pinpoint red spots on skin; unusual bleeding or bruising;)—which may cause gangrene

Incidence less frequent

Bleeding complications, which may include blood in urine; bloody or black, tarry stools; bruising; coughing up blood; ecchymosis (large, nonelevated blue or purplish patches in the skin); ***hematoma*** (collection of blood under the skin); ***hypochromic anemia*** (fatigue; headache; irritability; lightheadedness); ***nosebleed; persistent bleeding or oozing from mucous membranes or surgical***

wound; shortness of breath; vomiting of blood or material that looks like coffee grounds; ***confusion; dyspnea*** (shortness of breath; difficult or labored breathing; tightness in chest; wheezing); ***edema, central*** (swelling); ***hematuria*** (blood in urine; lower back pain; pain or burning while urinating); ***hemorrhage at injection site*** (uncontrolled bleeding at site of injection); ***organ infarction; pulmonary embolism*** (chest discomfort; convulsions; dizziness or lightheadedness when getting up from a lying or sitting position; shortness of breath or fast breathing); ***and stroke***—caused by excessive platelet aggregation

Incidence rare

Angioedema (swelling of the face, genitalia, larynx [voice box], mouth, or tongue); ***atrial fibrillation*** (fast or irregular heartbeat; dizziness; fainting); ***cardiovascular toxicity*** (chest pain; dizziness or lightheadedness when getting up from a lying or sitting position; fast or irregular heartbeat; shortness of breath; sudden fainting); ***epidural or spinal hematoma*** (back pain; bowel/bladder dysfunction; leg weakness; numbness; paralysis; paresthesias)—back pain is not a typical presentation but some patients may experience this symptom; ***heart failure; lung edema*** (chest pain; chills; cough; fever; general feeling of discomfort or illness; shortness of breath; thickening of bronchial secretions; troubled breathing); ***pneumonia*** (chest pain; cough; fever or chills; sneezing; shortness of breath; sore throat; troubled breathing; tightness in chest; wheezing); ***skin rash or hives***

Note: If an *epidural or spinal hematoma* is suspected, urgent intervention is necessary, which includes radiographic confirmation and decompressive laminectomy. Good or partial recovery is more likely if surgery is performed within 8 hours of the development of paraplegia.

Those indicating need for medical attention only if they continue or are bothersome

Incidence more frequent

Fever

Incidence less frequent or rare

Diarrhea; increased menstrual bleeding; irritation, pain, or redness at injection site; nausea; vomiting

Overdose

For specific information on the agents used in the management of enoxaparin overdose, see the *Protamine (Systemic)* monograph.

For more information on the management of overdose or unintentional ingestion, **contact a Poison Control Center** (see *Poison Control Center Listing*).

Clinical effects of overdose

The following effects have been selected on the basis of their potential clinical significance (possible signs and symptoms in parentheses where appropriate)—not necessarily inclusive:

Acute

Bleeding complications

Note: A single SC dose of 46.4 mg per kg enoxaparin was lethal to rats. The symptoms of acute toxicity in rats were ataxia, decreased motility, dyspnea, cyanosis, and coma.

Treatment of overdose

Specific treatment—Administration of protamine sulfate by slow intravenous injection. The dose of protamine sulfate should be equivalent, on a mg-per-mg basis, to the dose of enoxaparin. A second infusion of 0.5 mg protamine sulfate per 1 mg of enoxaparin may be administered if the aPTT measured 2 to 4 hours after the first infusion remains prolonged.An equivalent dose of protamine sulfate will neutralize the anti-factor IIa (anticoagulant) activity of enoxaparin, but will only neutralize approximately 60% of its anti-factor Xa (antithrombotic) activity. Care should be taken to avoid overdosage with protamine sulfate resulting in severe hypotensive and anaphylactoid reactions. For additional information see *Protamine (Systemic)*

Studies in animals indicate that protamine sulfate stops microvascular bleeding produced by very high concentrations of enoxaparin.

Patient Consultation

As an aid to patient consultation, refer to *Advice for the Patient, Enoxaparin (Systemic)*.

In providing consultation, consider emphasizing the following selected information (» = major clinical significance):

Before using this medication

» Conditions affecting use, especially:

Sensitivity to enoxaparin, heparin, benzyl alcohol, or to pork products

Pregnancy—Pregnant woman taking enoxaparin are at increased risk for hemorrhage. Hemorrhage can occur at any site and may lead to death of mother and/or fetus; not recommended for thromboprophylaxis in pregnant women with prosthetic heart valves.

Other medications, especially platelet aggregation inhibitors, hypoprothrombinemia-inducing medications, and thrombolytic agents

Other medical problems, especially threatened abortion; aneurysm; hemorrhage; hypersensitivity to enoxaparin, pork products, or benzyl alcohol; hypertension; septic shock; thrombocytopenia; hemorrhagic blood dyscrasias; recent childbirth; endocarditis; pericarditis or pericardial effusion; severe renal function impairment; diabetic or hemorrhagic retinopathy; spinal puncture, surgery, or other trauma; ulcers or other lesions of the gastrointestinal, respiratory, or urinary tract; severe vasculitis; wounds resulting in large open surfaces; severe hepatic function impairment, and prosthetic heart valves (especially in pregnant women)

Proper use of this medication

» Proper injection technique

» Safe handling and disposal of syringe

» Proper dosing

Missed dose: Using as soon as possible; not using if almost time for next dose; not doubling doses

» Proper storage

Precautions while using this medication

» Need to inform all physicians and dentists that this medicine is being used

» Notifying physician immediately if signs and symptoms of bleeding or epidural/spinal hematoma occur

Notifying physician immediately if pregnancy is suspected because of possible harm to the mother and/or fetus

Side/adverse effects

Signs and symptoms of potential side effects, including anemia, angioedema, atrial fibrillation, bleeding complications, cardiovascular toxicity, confusion, central or peripheral edema, dyspnea, epidural/spinal hematoma, heart failure, hematuria, hemorrhage, hemorrhage at injection site, lung edema, pneumonia, skin rash or hives, thrombocytopenia.

General Dosing Information

Enoxaparin is administered by deep subcutaneous (intrafat) injection into the abdominal fat layer; injection sites should be rotated. Enoxaparin must not be administered intramuscularly or intravenously.

The prefilled syringes are ready for use and no attempt should be made to expel air prior to giving the injection.

When using enoxaparin injection ampules, to assure withdrawal of the appropriate volume of drug, the use of a tuberculin syringe or equivalent is recommended.

A controlled, comparative study found that in non-dialyzed patients with severe renal impairment (mean creatinine clearance 11.4 mL per minute), the total clearance of enoxaparin was 1.9 times slower and the apparent half-lives of absorption and elimination were 1.7 times longer than in healthy subjects. Dosage modifications are therefore recommended in patients with severe renal impairment who are not receiving hemodialysis particularly when using high doses. However, dosage modifications are not required in dialysis patients.

Guidelines regarding the use of regional anesthesia in patients receiving perioperative enoxaparin

Preoperative enoxaparin—A single-dose spinal anesthetic may be the safest neuraxial technique. Needle placement should occur at least 10 to 12 hours after the last dose of enoxaparin. Subsequent dosing should be delayed for at least 2 hours after needle placement. The presence of blood during needle placement may justify a delay in the start of postoperative prophylaxis.

Postoperative enoxaparin—Patients may safely undergo single-dose and continuous catheter techniques. With a continuous technique, the epidural catheter should be left indwelling overnight and removed the following day, with the first dose of enoxaparin given 2 hours after catheter removal. Using postoperative prophylaxis in the presence of an indwelling catheter must be done carefully and with close surveillance of the patient's neurologic status. An opioid and/or dilute local anesthetic solution is recommended in these patients to allow intermittent assessment of neurologic function.

The timing of catheter removal is extremely important. Removal should be delayed for at least 10 to 12 hours after a dose of enoxaparin.

Subsequent dosing should not occur for at least 2 hours following catheter removal.

Parenteral Dosage Forms

ENOXAPARIN INJECTION

Usual adult dose

Thromboembolism, pulmonary (prophylaxis); and
Thrombosis, deep venous (prophylaxis)—
Hip or knee replacement surgery—
Subcutaneously, 30 mg every twelve hours for an average of seven to ten days. The initial dose should be given twelve to twenty-four hours postoperatively.
Alternatively, for hip replacement surgery, enoxaparin may be given subcutaneously, 40 mg once a day, with the initial dose given nine to fifteen hours prior to surgery. Following the initial phase of thromboprophylaxis for hip replacement surgery (either 30 mg every twelve hours or 40 mg once a day), continued prophylaxis at a dose of 40 mg once a day for three weeks is recommended. The usual duration is 7 to 10 days, but up to 14 days administration has been well tolerated in clinical trials. Those with severe renal impairment (creatinine clearance ≤ 30 mL per min) should receive 30 mg once daily.[1]

Abdominal, [and gynecological, urological, or colorectal] surgery—
Subcutaneously, 40 mg once a day for an average of seven to ten days. The initial dose should be given two hours prior to surgery. Up to twelve days administration has been well tolerated in clinical trials. Those with severe renal impairment (creatinine clearance ≤ 30 mL per min) should receive 30 mg once daily.

Thrombosis, deep venous (treatment)—
Inpatient treatment, with and without pulmonary embolism—
Subcutaneous, 1 mg per kg of body weight every twelve hours or 1.5 mg per kg of body weight once a day, administered the same time each day, for an average of seven days. Those with severe renal impairment (creatinine clearance ≤ 30 mL per min) should receive 1 mg per kg once daily.

Medical patients during acute illness—
Subcutaneous, 40 mg once a day for six to eleven days. Administration for up to fourteen days was well tolerated in one controlled clinical trial. Those with severe renal impairment (creatinine clearance ≤ 30 mL per min) should receive 30 mg once daily.

Outpatient treatment, without pulmonary embolism—
Subcutaneous, 1 mg per kg of body weight every twelve hours for an average of seven days. Those with severe renal impairment (creatinine clearance ≤ 30 mL per min) should receive 1 mg per kg once daily.

Note: In both inpatients and outpatients, warfarin sodium should be initiated as soon as appropriate and enoxaparin should be continued until the international normalized ratio (INR) has achieved a therapeutic level, usually 2.0 to 3.0. Therapy with enoxaparin should be at least five days; up to seventeen days have been well tolerated in clinical trials.

Thrombosis, coronary arterial, acute; associated with unstable angina or non–Q-wave myocardial infarction (prophylaxis)[1]—
Subcutaneous, 1 mg per kg of body weight every twelve hours in conjunction with oral aspirin therapy (100 to 325 mg once a day). Treatment should be prescribed for a minimum of two days, and continued until the patient is clinically stable (usual duration is two to eight days). Up to 12.5 days administration has been well tolerated in clinical trials.

Note: To minimize the risk of bleeding following vascular instrumentation during the treatment of unstable angina, adhere precisely to the recommended dosing intervals. The vascular access sheath for instrumentation should remain in place for six to eight hours following a dose of enoxaparin. Following sheath removal, the next scheduled dose of enoxaparin should be given no sooner than six to eight hours later. The site of the procedure should be observed for signs of bleeding or hematoma formation.

[Unstable angina and non-Q-wave myocardial infarction (treatment)]—
Subcutaneous, 1 mg per kg of body weight (100 IU per kg of body weight) every 12 hours. Concomitant therapy with ASA (100 to 325 mg once daily) is recommended. Treatment should be continued for a minimum of two days and continued until clinical stabilization has been achieved (two to eight days). The effect of the short-term treatment was sustained over a one-year period.

Usual adult prescribing limits

Thrombosis, deep venous (treatment)—
Inpatient treatment, with and without pulmonary embolism—
Subcutaneous, single daily dose should not exceed 18,000 IU.

[Unstable angina and non-Q-wave myocardial infarction (treatment)]—
Subcutaneous, maximum dose should not exceed 10,000 IU per 12 hours.

Usual pediatric dose

Safety and efficacy have not been established.

Usual geriatric dose

See *Usual adult dose.*

Note: Approximate anti-Factor Xa activity based on reference to the W.H.O. First International Low Molecular Weight Heparin Reference Standard.

Strength(s) usually available

U.S.—
30 mg in 0.3 mL of Water for Injection 100 mg per mL (3000 IU anti-Xa activity) (Rx) [*Lovenox* (prefilled syringes)].
40 mg in 0.4 mL of Water for Injection 100 mg per mL (4000 IU anti-Xa activity) (Rx) [*Lovenox* (prefilled syringes)].
60 mg in 0.6 mL of Water for Injection 100 mg per mL (6000 IU anti-Xa activity) (Rx) [*Lovenox* (graduated prefilled syringes)].
80 mg in 0.8 mL of Water for Injection 100 mg per mL (8000 IU anti-Xa activity) (Rx) [*Lovenox* (graduated prefilled syringes)].
100 mg in 1 mL of Water for Injection 100 mg per mL (10,000 IU anti-Xa activity) (Rx) [*Lovenox* (graduated prefilled syringes)].
120 mg in 0.8 mL of Water for Injection 150 mg per mL (12,000 IU anti-Xa activity) (Rx) [*Lovenox* (graduated prefilled syringes)].
150 mg in 1 mL of Water for Injection 150 mg per mL (15,000 IU anti-Xa activity) (Rx) [*Lovenox* (graduated prefilled syringes)].
300 mg in 3 mL of Water for Injection 300 mg per mL (30,000 IU anti-Xa activity) (Rx) [*Lovenox* (graduated prefilled syringes)].

Canada—
30 mg in 0.3 mL of Water for Injection (3000 IU anti-Xa activity) (Rx) [*Lovenox* (in single unit-dose syringes)].
40 mg in 0.4 mL of Water for Injection (4000 IU anti-Xa activity) (Rx) [*Lovenox* (in single unit-dose syringes)].
60 mg in 0.6 mL of Water for Injection (6000 IU anti-Xa activity) (Rx) [*Lovenox* (in single unit-dose syringes)].
80 mg in 0.8 mL of Water for Injection (8000 IU anti-Xa activity) (Rx) [*Lovenox* (in single unit-dose syringes)].
100 mg in 1 mL of Water for Injection (10,000 IU anti-Xa activity) (Rx) [*Lovenox* (in single unit-dose syringes)].
300 mg in 3 mL (10 mg per 0.1 mL) of Water for Injection(30,000 IU anti-Xa activity) (Rx) [*Lovenox* (in multiple-dose vials; benzyl alcohol 1.5% w/v)].
120 mg in 0.8 mL of Water for Injection (12,000 IU anti-Xa activity) (Rx) [*Lovenox HP* (in single unit-dose syringes)].
150 mg in 1 mL of Water for Injection (15,000 IU anti-Xa activity) (Rx) [*Lovenox HP* (in single unit-dose syringes)].

Packaging and storage

Store between 15 and 25 °C (59 and 77 °F), unless otherwise specified by manufacturer. Protect from freezing. Protect from heat

Stability

Because the injection contains no preservative, each syringe should be used to administer a single dose only.

Incompatibilities

Enoxaparin should not be admixed with intravenous fluids or other medications.

Additional information

The 300-mg-per-3-mL multi-dose vial contains benzyl alcohol, which is not recommended for use in neonates. A fatal syndrome consisting of metabolic acidosis, central nervous system depression, respiratory problems, renal failure, hypotension, and possibly seizures and intracranial hemorrhage has been associated with the administration of benzyl alcohol to neonates.

[1]Not included in Canadian product labeling.

Selected Bibliography

Food and Drug Administration. Q & A's: low molecular weight heparins/heparinoids and spinal/epidural anesthesia. 1998 May 6. Available from: URL: http://www.fda.gov/medwatch/safety/1998/lovq&a.htm.

Nader, Francois, M.D., Important Prescribing Information [from Dear Health Care Professional letter]. Retrieved 4/4/2002, from The World Wide Web: http://www.fda.gov/medwatch/SAFETY/2002/lovenox.htm

Revised: 2/1/2006
Developed: 11/22/1993

ENTACAPONE Systemic

VA CLASSIFICATION (Primary): CN500

Commonly used brand name(s): *Comtan*.

Note: For a listing of dosage forms and brand names by country availability, see *Dosage Forms* section(s).

Category

Antidyskinetic (COMT inhibitor).

Indications

Accepted

Parkinsonism (treatment adjunct)—Entacapone is indicated as an adjunct to levodopa/carbidopa to treat patients with idiopathic Parkinson's Disease who experience the signs and symptoms of end-of-dose "wearing-off".

Pharmacology/Pharmacokinetics

Physicochemical characteristics

Chemical Group—Catechol-*O*-methyltransferase (COMT) inhibitor
Molecular weight—305.29.

Mechanism of action/Effect

Entacapone is a selective and reversible inhibitor of catechol-*O*-methyltransferase (COMT). COMT, an enzyme with highest activity in the liver and kidney, is responsible for catalyzing levodopa. In the presence of a decarboxylase inhibitor (carbidopa), COMT becomes the major metabolizing enzyme for levodopa in the brain and periphery. Because of entacapone's inhibition of COMT, concomitant administration with levodopa leads to higher plasma levels of levodopa, resulting in more dopaminergic stimulation in the brain and lessening of the symptoms of Parkinson's disease. Increased dopaminergic stimulation in the brain, however, also leads to increased adverse effects of levodopa, and may require dosage adjustments.

Pharmacodynamics

Studies in healthy volunteers have shown that entacapone reversibly inhibits human erythrocyte catechol-*O*-methyltransferase (COMT) activity after oral administration. This inhibition has a linear correlation with dose, with maximum inhibition being 82% following a single 800-mg dose. Maximum inhibition of erythrocyte COMT averaged 65% following a single 200-mg dose; return to baseline levels occurred within 8 hours.

Pharmacokinetics

Entacapone pharmacokinetics are linear over the dose range of 5 to 800 mg, independent of levodopa/carbidopa administration.

Absorption

Bioavailability is 35%. The absorption is unaffected by food.

Distribution

Volume of distribution (Vol_D) is 20 L, indicative of minimal distribution into the tissues.

Protein binding

Very high (98%), predominately to serum albumin.

Biotransformation

Almost completely metabolized, predominately by isomerization to the *cis*-isomer, followed by direct glucuronidation of the parent and *cis*-isomer. The glucuronide conjugate is inactive.

Half-life

Elimination—Biphasic
—Beta-phase: 0.4 to 0.7 hours
—Gamma phase: 2.4 hours

Time to peak concentration

Approximately 1 hour.

Peak serum concentration

1.2 mcg/mL after a single 200 mg dose.

Elimination

Renal—Following administration of an oral dose of radiolabeled entacapone, 10% is excreted in the urine. Only 0.2% of a dose is found unchanged in the urine.

Biliary/Fecal—Following administration of an oral dose of radiolabeled entacapone, 90% is excreted in feces.

In dialysis—Because of the high degree of protein binding, entacapone is not likely to be significantly dialyzed.

Effect of entacapone on the pharmacokinetics of levodopa and its metabolites

When administered together with levodopa/carbidopa, entacapone increases the area under the plasma concentration-time curve (AUC) of levodopa by approximately 35%, and the elimination half-life of levodopa is prolonged from 1.3 to 2.4 hours. The average peak plasma concentration (C_{max}) and the time of its occurrence (T_{max}) generally are not affected. The onset of effect occurs after the first administration and is maintained during long-term therapy. Studies in Parkinson's disease patients indicate that the maximum effect occurs with a 200-mg dose of entacapone. When given with levodopa/carbidopa, entacapone markedly decreases plasma concentrations of the metabolite of levodopa in the brain and the periphery (3-methoxy-4-hydroxy-L-phenylalanine [3-OMD]) in a dose dependent manner.

Precautions to Consider

Carcinogenicity

A two year study demonstrated an increased incidence of renal tubular adenomas and carcinomas in male rats treated with doses 20 times higher than estimated plasma exposures of humans receiving maximum recommended daily dose (MRDD) of entacapone (MRDD= 1600mg). A high incidence of premature mortality in mice receiving 600 mg per kg of body weight (mg/kg) per day (2 times the MRDD for humans on a mg per square meter of body surface area [mg/m^2] basis) of entacapone prevented full evaluation of carcinogenic potential.

Mutagenicity

Mutagenicity and clastogenicity was evident in the *in vitro* mouse lymphoma/thymidine kinase assay in the presence and absence of metabolic activation, and clastogenicity was evident in cultured human lymphocytes in the presence of metabolic activation. Entacapone, either alone or in combination with levodopa/carbidopa, was not clastogenic in the *in vivo* mouse micronucleus test or mutagenic in the bacterial reverse mutation assay (Ames test).

Pregnancy/Reproduction

Fertility—Fertility and general reproductive performance was not impaired when rats. Delayed mating, but no fertility impairment, was evident in female rats treated with 700 mg/kg per day of entacapone.

Pregnancy—Adequate and well-controlled studies in humans have not been done.

Increased incidences of fetal variations were evident in litters from rats treated with 1000 mg/kg per day (34 times the estimated plasma exposure in humans receiving the maximum recommended daily dose (MRDD) of 1600 mg). Increased frequencies of abortions and late/total resorptions and decreased fetal weights were observed in the litters of rabbits treated with maternotoxic doses of 100 mg/kg per day (areas under the plasma concentration-time curve [AUCs] were 0.4 times those in humans receiving the MRDD) or greater. There was no evidence of teratogenicity in these studies.

An increased incidence of fetal eye anomalies (macrophthalmia, microphthalmia, anophthalmia) was observed in the litters of dams (female rats) treated with doses of 160 mg/kg per day (plasma AUCs 7 times those in humans receiving the MRDD) prior to mating and during early gestation. There was no evidence of developmental impairment in the offspring of female rats administered up to 700 mg/kg per day during the latter part of gestation and throughout lactation.

Although entacapone has not been shown to be teratogenic in animals, it is always given in conjunction with levodopa/carbidopa, which is known to cause visceral and skeletal malformations in the rabbit.

FDA Pregnancy Category C

Breast-feeding

It is not known if entacapone is distributed into breast milk. However, entacapone, is distributed into the milk of rats. Caution should be exercised when entacapone is administered to a nursing woman.

Pediatrics

No information is available on the relationship of age to the effects of entacapone in the pediatric population. Safety and efficacy have not been established. There is no identified potential use of entacapone in pediatric patients.

Geriatrics

No geriatrics-related problems have been documented in studies done to date that included elderly patients.

Drug interactions and/or related problems

The following drug interactions and/or related problems have been selected on the basis of their potential clinical significance (possible mechanism in parentheses where appropriate)—not necessarily inclusive (» = major clinical significance):

Note: *In vitro* studies have shown that entacapone inhibits the CYP enzyme 1A2, 2A6, 2C9, 2C19, 2D6, 2E1, and 3A only at concentrations greatly exceeding those achieved at therapeutic dosing levels. Also, no binding displacement between entacapone and other highly bound agents including warfarin, salicylic acid, phenylbutazone, and diazepam has been demonstrated *in vitro* .

Combinations containing any of the following medications, depending on the amount present, may also interact with this medication.

Drugs that interfere with biliary excretion, glucuronidation, and intestinal beta-glucuronidase, including
Ampicillin or
Chloramphenicol or
Cholestyramine or
Erythromycin or
Probenecid or
Rifamipicin
(potential for inhibition of entacapone excretion)

» Drugs metabolized by catechol-O-methyltransferase (COMT) including
» Apomorphine or
» Bitolterol or
» Dobutamine or
» Dopamine or
» Epinephrine or
» Isoetherine or
» Isoproterenol or
» Methyldopa or
» Norepinephrine
(may result in increased heart rates, possibly arrhythmias, and excessive changes in blood pressure when administered concurrently. Overall mean maximal changes in heart rate during isoproterenol and epinephrine infusions with a single 400 mg dose of entacapone were about 50% and 80%, respectively, higher than with placebo.)

Note: Entacapone may be taken with the selective MAO inhibitor selegiline.

» Monoamine oxidase inhibitors, non-selective including
» Phenelzine or
» Tranylcypromine
(potential for inhibition of the majority of pathways responsible for normal catecholamine metabolism.)

Laboratory value alterations

The following have been selected on the basis of their potential clinical significance (possible effect in parentheses where appropriate)—not necessarily inclusive (» = major clinical significance).

With physiology/laboratory test values
Iron, serum
(concentrations may be decreased due to chelation by entacapone; however, the impact on body stores of iron is unknown; in one controlled study, no changes in serum ferritin concentrations, hemoglobin levels, and incidence of anemia were demonstrated after one year of treatment with entacapone.)

Note: Levodopa is known to depress prolactin secretion and increase growth hormone concentrations. Concomitant administration of entacapone does not influence these effects of levodopa.

Medical considerations/Contraindications

The medical considerations/contraindications included have been selected on the basis of their potential clinical significance (reasons given in parentheses where appropriate)—not necessarily inclusive (» = major clinical significance).

Except under special circumstances, this medication should not be used when the following medical problem exists:

» Hypersensitivity to entacapone

Risk-benefit should be considered when the following medical problems exist:

Dyskinesia
(may be exacerbated due to entacapone increasing the dopaminergic side effects of levodopa; decreasing the dose of levodopa may ameliorate this side effect.)

» Hepatic function impairment
(potential for doubling of AUC and maximum concentration of entacapone.)

Hypotension or
Orthostatic hypotension or
Syncope
(may be exacerbated)

Side/Adverse Effects

Note: Entacapone enhances levodopa bioavailability and may increase the occurrence of orthostatic hypotension. Baseline treatment with dopamine agonists or selegiline did not appear to increase the likelihood of orthostatic hypotension for patients treated with entacapone. Syncope was also reported and generally occurred more frequently in patients who had a documented episode of hypotension.

Entacapone may potentiate the dopaminergic side effects of levodopa, and may cause or exacerbate preexisting dyskinesia. These effects may be ameliorated by reducing the concomitant levodopa dose, but many patients in the premarketing clinical trials continued to experience frequent dyskinesias despite reductions in the levodopa dose.

A symptom complex characterized by elevated temperature, muscular rigidity, altered consciousness, and elevated creatine kinase concentrations (CK), and resembling the neuroleptic malignant syndrome, have been reported with the abrupt withdrawal or lowering of the dose of entacapone. The role of entacapone in the pathogenesis of this symptom complex has not been established. This syndrome should be considered in the differential diagnosis for any patient treated with entacapone who develops a high fever or severe rigidity.

Cases of severe rhabdomyolysis have been reported with entacapone use. The role of entacapone in the pathogenesis of these cases is unclear. Severe prolonged motor activity, including dyskinesia, may be a contributing factor, or rhabdomyolysis may be a result of the symptom complex described above.

Fibrotic complications, including retroperitoneal fibrosis, pulmonary infiltrates, pleural effusion, and pleural thickening have been reported in some patients treated with ergot-derived dopaminergic medications. These complications may resolve upon discontinuation of the agent, but complete resolution does not always occur. Although these fibrotic effects are believed to be associated with the ergoline structure of these compounds, it is not known if non–ergot-derived medications that increase dopaminergic activity, such as entacapone, may produce similar adverse effects. During premarketing clinical trials with entacapone, four cases of pulmonary fibrosis were reported; three of these patients also were taking concomitant dopamine agonists pergolide and bromocriptine.

The following side/adverse effects have been selected on the basis of their potential clinical significance (possible signs and symptoms in parentheses where appropriate)—not necessarily inclusive:

Those indicating need for medical attention

Incidence more frequent

Dyskinesia (twitching; twisting; uncontrolled repetitive movements of tongue, lips, face, arms, or legs)—may cause or exacerbate preexisting dyskinesia; decreasing levodopa dose may ameliorate the dyskinesia; ***hallucinations*** (seeing, hearing, or feeling things that are not there); ***hyperkinesia*** (hyperactivity; increase in body movements); ***hypokinesia*** (absence of or decrease in body movements)

Incidence less frequent

Infection, bacterial (fever or chills; cough or hoarseness; lower back or side pain; painful or difficult urination)

Incidence rare

Confusion; hyperpyrexia (fever); ***pulmonary fibrosis*** (fever; cough; shortness of breath); ***rhabdomyolysis*** (muscle cramps; pain; stiffness; weakness; unusual tiredness)

Those indicating need for medical attention only if they continue or are bothersome

Incidence more frequent

Dizziness; fatigue; gastrointestinal effects including; abdominal pain; constipation; diarrhea; nausea—especially at the initiation of treatment

Note: Diarrhea typically presents within 4 to 12 weeks following initiation of therapy, but it may appear as early as the first week and as late as several months after starting entacapone therapy. Most cases are mild to moderate, but may be severe in a small percentage of patients. Diarrhea generally resolves upon discontinuation of entacapone.

Incidence less frequent

Agitation (anxiety; nervousness; restlessness; irritability; dry mouth; tremor); ***anxiety; asthenia*** (loss of strength or energy; muscle pain or weakness; unusual weak feeling); ***back pain; dyspnea*** (shortness of breath; difficult or labored breathing; tightness in chest; wheezing); ***gastrointestinal effects including; dry mouth; dyspepsia*** (acid or sour stomach; belching; heartburn; indigestion; stomach discomfort, upset or pain); ***flatulence*** (passing gas); ***gastritis*** (burning feeling in chest or stomach; tenderness in stomach area; stomach upset; indigestion); ***vomiting; purpura*** (small, red spots on skin; bruising); ***somnolence*** (sleepiness or unusual drowsiness); ***sweating increased; taste perversion*** (unusual or unpleasant (after) taste)

Those not indicating need for medical attention

Incidence more frequent

Urine discoloration (to brownish orange)

Overdose

For more information on the management of overdose or unintentional ingestion, **contact a poison control center** (see *Poison Control Center Listing*).

Human overdose data are lacking. COMT inhibition by entacapone is dose-dependent. In theory, a massive overdose of entacapone may produce a 100% inhibition of the COMT enzyme, thereby preventing metabolism of endogenous and exogenous catechols.

The highest daily dose of entacapone administered to humans was 2400 mg a day (400 mg six times daily for 14 days or 800 mg three times daily for 7 days). In these studies, the most frequently reported adverse effects were abdominal pain and loose stools.

Treatment of overdose

There is no known antidote to entacapone overdose. Treatment is essentially symptomatic and supportive, possibly including:

To decrease absorption—

An immediate gastric lavage.

To enhance elimination—

Repeated doses of charcoal over time. Hemodialysis and hemoperfusion are unlikely to be of benefit because entacapone is highly protein bound.

Monitoring—

Respiratory and circulatory systems should be monitored.

Supportive care—

Supportive measures as necessary.

Patients in whom intentional overdose is confirmed or suspected should be referred for psychiatric consultation.

Patient Consultation

As an aid to patient consultation, refer to *Advice for the Patient, Entacapone (Systemic)*.

In providing consultation, consider emphasizing the following selected information (» = major clinical significance):

Before using this medication

» Conditions affecting use, especially:

Hypersensitivity to entacapone

Pregnancy—Risk-benefit must be considered

Breast-feeding—Risk-benefit must be considered

Use in children—There is no identified potential use of entacapone in pediatric patients.

Other medications, especially apomorphine, bitolterol, epinephrine, isoproterenol, isoetherine, methyldopa, and monoamine oxidase inhibitors

Other medical problems, especially hepatic function impairment

Proper use of this medication

Always taking medication with levodopa/carbidopa; never alone.

» Compliance with therapy; taking medication only as directed; not stopping medication unless ordered by physician

» Proper dosing

Missed dose: Taking as soon as possible; not taking if almost time for next dose; not doubling doses

Proper storage

Precautions while using this medication

Regular visits to physician to check progress

Checking with physician before discontinuing medication; gradual dosage reduction may be needed

» Caution when getting up suddenly from lying or sitting position

Possible drowsiness or dizziness; caution when driving or doing jobs requiring alertness until effects of medication are known

Possible hallucinations

Possible exacerbation of dyskinesia

Medication may cause urine to turn brownish orange

Side/adverse effects

Signs of potential side effects, especially bacterial infection, confusion, dyskinesia, hallucination, hyperkinesia, hyperpyrexia, hypokinesia, pulmonary fibrosis, and rhabdomyolysis.

General Dosing Information

Always administer entacapone with levodopa/carbidopa. Entacapone has no antiparkinsonian effect of its own.

Before beginning treatment consider a decrease (by 25%) in the daily levodopa dose, especially if the dose of levodopa had been ≥ 800 mg a day, or if patients had moderate or severe dyskinesias before beginning treatment.

Entacapone can be combined with both the immediate and sustained release formulations of levodopa/carbidopa.

Because biliary excretion is the major route of elimination of entacapone, this medication should be administered with caution to patients with biliary obstruction.

Entacapone should not be discontinued abruptly because the possibility of symptoms resembling neuroleptic malignant syndrome such as elevated temperature, muscular rigidity, altered consciousness, and elevated creatine kinase may occur. Withdraw entacapone slowly with close monitoring of the patient and adjusting other dopaminergic treatments as needed.

Diet/Nutrition

Entacapone may be taken with or without food.

Oral Dosage Forms

ENTACAPONE TABLETS

Usual adult dose

Antidyskinetic—

Oral, 200 mg administered concomitantly with each levodopa/carbidopa dose, up to a maximum of 8 times a day.

Usual adult prescribing limits

Up to 1600 mg daily.

Usual pediatric dose

There is no identified potential use in pediatrics.

Usual geriatric dose

See *Usual adult dose*.

Usual geriatric prescribing limits

See *Usual adult prescribing limits*.

Strength(s) usually available

U.S.—

200 mg (Rx) [*Comtan* (microcrystalline cellulose; mannitol; croscarmellose sodium; hydrogenated vegetable oil; hydroxypropyl methylcellulose; polysorbate 80; glycerol 85%; sucrose; magnesium stearate; yellow iron oxide; red oxide; titanium dioxide)].

Packaging and storage

Store between at 25 °C (77 °F) excursions permitted to 15 °C to 30 °C (59 °C to 86 °C).

Auxiliary labeling

- May cause drowsiness.
- May discolor urine

Developed: 03/10/2000

ENTECAVIR Systemic†

VA CLASSIFICATION (Primary): AM810

Commonly used brand name(s): *Baraclude*.

Note: For a listing of dosage forms and brand names by country availability, see *Dosage Forms* section(s).

†Not commercially available in Canada.

Category

Antiviral (systemic).

Indications

Note: Bracketed information in the *Indications* section refers to uses that are not included in U.S. product labeling.

Accepted

Hepatitis B virus (HBV) infection, chronic (treatment)—Entecavir is indicated for the treatment of chronic hepatitis B virus infection in adults with evidence of active viral replication and either evidence of persistent elevations in serum aminotransferases (ALT or AST) or histologically active disease.

This indication is based on histologic, virologic, biochemical and serologic responses after one year of treatment in nucleoside-treatment-naive and lamivudine-resistant adult patients with HBeAg-positive or HBeAg-negative chronic HBV infection with compensated liver disease and on more limited data in adult patients with HIV/HBV co-infection who have received prior lamivudine therapy.

Pharmacology/Pharmacokinetics

Physicochemical characteristics

Molecular weight—Entecavir: 295.3.
Solubility—Slightly soluble in water.
pH (saturated solution)—7.9 at 25 °C ± 0.5 °C

Mechanism of action/Effect

Entecavir is a nucleoside analogue with activity against HBV polymerase. It is efficiently phosphorylated to the active triphosphate form, which competes with the natural substrate deoxyguanosine triphosphate and inhibits all three activities of the HBV polymerase (reverse transcriptase): 1) base priming, 2) reverse transcription of the negative strand from the pregenomic messenger RNA and 3) synthesis of the positive strand of HBV DNA. Entecavir triphosphate is a weak inhibitor of cellular DNA polymerases alpha, beta, and delta and mitochondrial DNA polymerase gamma with K_i values ranging from 18 to > 160 microM.

Absorption

The bioavailability of the tablet was 100% relative to the oral solution.

Oral administration of 0.5 mg of entecavir given with a standard high fat meal resulted in a delayed in absorption (1 to 1.5 hours fed vs. 0.75 hours fasted), a decrease in C_{max} of 44% to 46%, and a decrease in AUC of 18% to 20%.

Distribution

In excess of total body water; extensively distributed into tissues.

Protein binding

Low (13%) to serum protein.

Biotransformation

Following administration of ^{14}C-entecavir, no oxidative or acetylated metabolites were observed. Minor amounts of phase II metabolites (glucuronide and sulfate conjugates) were observed. Entecavir is not a substrate, inhibitor, or inducer of the cytochrome P450 enzyme system.

Half-life

Elimination—approximately 128 to 149 hours.
Accumulation—24 hours

Time to peak concentration

0.5 to 1.5 hours following oral administration.

Time to steady state

The area under the plasma concentration-time curve (AUC) at steady state was achieved after 6 to 10 days of once daily administration with approximately 2-fold accumulation.

Peak plasma concentration:

4.2 ng/mL for a 0.5-mg oral dose.
8.2 ng/mL for a 1-mg oral dose.

Elimination

Urinary—62% to 73% of the administered dose as unchanged drug. Renal clearance is independent of dose and ranges from 360 to 471 mL/min suggesting both glomerular filtration and net tubular secretion.

Precautions to Consider

Carcinogenicity

Entecavir was positive for carcinogenicity in long-term studies done with doses up to 42 (mice) and 35 (rats) times the highest recommended human dose of 1 mg/day. Lung adenomas were increased in male and female mice at exposures 3 and 40 times those in humans and, lung carcinomas were increased at exposures 40 times those in humans. Combined lung adenomas and carcinomas were increased in male mice at exposures 3 times and in female mice at exposures 40 times those in humans. Lung tumors in mice may be a species-specific event. Tumor development in mice was preceded by pneumocyte proliferation in the lung. Pneumocyte proliferation in the lung was not observed in rats, dogs, or monkeys. Hepatocellular carcinomas were increased in male mice and combined liver adenomas and carcinomas were also increased at exposures 42 times those in humans. Vascular tumors in female mice were increased at 40 times those in humans.

Hepatocellular adenomas were increased in female rats and combined liver adenomas and carcinomas were also increased at exposures 24 times those in humans. Brain gliomas were induced in both males and females at exposures 35 and 24 times those in humans. Skin fibromas were induced in females at exposures 4 times those in humans.

Mutagenicity

Entecavir was clastogenic to human lymphocyte cultures. Entecavir was not mutagenic in the Ames bacterial reverse mutation assay with *S. typhimurium* and *E. coli* in the presence or absence of metabolic activation, a mammalian-cell gene mutation assay, and a transformation assay with Syrian hamster embryo cells. Entecavir was also negative in an oral micronucleus study and an oral DNA repair study in rats.

Pregnancy/Reproduction

Fertility—No evidence of impaired fertility was seen in male or female rats at systemic exposures > 90 times those achieved in humans at the highest recommended dose of 1 mg/day. However, in rodent and dog toxicology studies, seminiferous tubular degeneration was observed at exposures ≥ 35 times those achieved in humans. No testicular changes were seen in monkeys.

Pregnancy—*A Pregnancy Registry has been established to monitor the maternal-fetal outcomes of pregnant women exposed to entecavir. Physicians are encouraged to register patients by calling (800) 258-4263.*

Adequate and well controlled studies in pregnant women have not been done. Studies in animals have shown that entecavir causes adverse effects in the fetus. Because animal reproduction studies are not always predictive of human response entecavir should be used during pregnancy only if clearly needed and after careful consideration of the risks and benefits.

Studies done in rats revealed maternal toxicity, embryo-fetal toxicity, lower fetal body weights, tail and vertebral malformations, reduced ossification, and extra lumbar vertebrae and ribs at exposures 3100 times those in humans. In rabbits, embryo-fetal toxicity, reduced ossification and an increased incidence of 13th rib were observed at exposures 883 times those in humans.

Studies in rats and rabbits given oral doses up to 200 and 16 mg/kg/day showed no embryotoxicity or maternal toxicity. In a peri-postnatal study, no adverse effects were seen in the offspring of rats given oral doses of entecavir with exposures >94 times those in humans.

FDA Pregnancy Category C

Labor and delivery—There are no studies in pregnant women and no data on the effect of entecavir on transmission of HBV from mother to infant. Therefore appropriate interventions should be used to prevent neonatal acquisition of HBV.

Breast-feeding

Entecavir is distributed into the milk of rats. It is not known whether entecavir is distributed into human milk. Mothers should be instructed not to breast-feed if they are taking entecavir.

Pediatrics

Safety and effectiveness of entecavir in pediatric patients below the age of 16 years have not been established.

Geriatrics

No information is available on the relationship of age to the effects of entecavir in geriatric patients. However, elderly patients are more likely to have age-related renal function impairment which may require caution in dosing selection and monitoring of renal function.

Pharmacogenetics

There are no significant racial differences in entecavir pharmacokinetics.

Drug interactions and/or related problems

The following drug interactions and/or related problems have been selected on the basis of their potential clinical significance (possible mechanism in parentheses where appropriate)—not necessarily inclusive (» = major clinical significance):

Note: Combinations containing any of the following medications, depending on the amount present, may also interact with this medication.

Drugs that compete for active tubular secretion or
Drugs that reduce renal function
(may increase serum concentrations of either entecavir or the coadministered drug)

Renally eliminated drugs
(patients should be monitored closely; the effects of concurrent administration of entecavir with other drugs that are renally eliminated or affect renal function have not been evaluated)

Laboratory value alterations
The following have been selected on the basis of their potential clinical significance (possible effect in parentheses where appropriate)—not necessarily inclusive (» = major clinical significance).

With physiology/laboratory test values
- Alanine aminotransferase (ALT [SGPT]) or
- Aspartate aminotransferase (AST [SGOT]) or
- Amylase or
- Bilirubin or
- Blood, urine or
- Glucose, blood or
- Glucose, urine or
- Lipase
  - (values may be increased)
- Albumin or
- Platelets
  - (values may be decreased)

Medical considerations/Contraindications
The medical considerations/contraindications included have been selected on the basis of their potential clinical significance (reasons given in parentheses where appropriate)—not necessarily inclusive (» = major clinical significance).

Except under special circumstances, this medication should not be used when the following medical problem exists:
» Hypersensitivity to entecavir or any components of the product

Risk-benefit should be considered when the following medical problems exist:
» Renal function impairment
(dosage adjustment is recommended for patients with a creatinine clearance <50 mL/min, including patients on hemodialysis or CAPD)

» Liver transplant recipients
(if entecavir treatment is determined to be necessary for a liver transplant recipient who has received or is receiving a immunosuppressant that may affect renal function, renal function must be carefully monitored both before and during treatment with entecavir)

Patient monitoring
The following may be especially important in patient monitoring (other tests may be warranted in some patients, depending on condition; » = major clinical significance):

» Hepatic function
(periodic monitoring of hepatic function is recommended during treatment; monitor closely with both clinical and laboratory follow-up for at least several months in patients who discontinue entecavir; if appropriate, initiation of anti-hepatitis B therapy may be warranted)

Side/Adverse Effects
The following side/adverse effects have been selected on the basis of their potential clinical significance (possible signs and symptoms in parentheses where appropriate)—not necessarily inclusive:

Those indicating need for medical attention
Incidence unknown

Hepatomegaly (right upper abdominal pain and fullness); ***lactic acidosis*** (abdominal discomfort; decreased appetite; diarrhea; fast, shallow breathing; general feeling of discomfort; muscle pain or cramping; nausea; shortness of breath; sleepiness; unusual tiredness or weakness)

Those indicating need for medical attention only if they continue or are bothersome
Incidence less frequent

Fatigue (unusual tiredness or weakness); ***headache***

Incidence rare

Diarrhea; dizziness; dyspepsia (acid or sour stomach; belching; heartburn; indigestion; stomach discomfort upset or pain); ***insomnia*** (sleeplessness; trouble sleeping; unable to sleep); ***nausea; somnolence*** (sleepiness or unusual drowsiness); ***vomiting***

Overdose
For more information on the management of overdose or unintentional ingestion, **contact a poison control center** (see *Poison Control Center Listing*).

Treatment of overdose
There is no known specific antidote to entecavir. Treatment is generally symptomatic and supportive.

To enhance elimination—
Hemodialysis removed approximately 13% of a single 1-mg dose of entecavir.

Monitoring—
Monitor for evidence of toxicity.

Supportive care—
Patients in whom intentional overdose is confirmed or suspected should be referred for psychiatric consultation.

Patient Consultation
As an aid to patient consultation, refer to *Advice for the Patient, Entecavir (Systemic)*.

In providing consultation, consider emphasizing the following selected information (» = major clinical significance):

Before using this medication
» Conditions affecting use, especially:
- Hypersensitivity to entecavir or any component of the product
- Entecavir was positive for carcinogenicity in long-term studies done in mice and rats
- Pregnancy—Entecavir should be used during pregnancy only if clearly needed and after careful consideration of the risks and benefits.
- Breast-feeding—Mothers should be instructed not to breast-feed if they are taking entecavir.
- Use in children—Safety and effectiveness of entecavir in pediatric patients below the age of 16 years have not been established.
- Use in the elderly—Elderly patients may have age-related renal function impairment which may require caution in dosing selection and monitoring of renal function.
- Other medications, especially drugs that compete for active tubular secretion, drugs that reduce renal function or renally eliminated drugs
- Other medical problems, especially liver transplant recipients or renal function impairment

Proper use of this medication
» Compliance with therapy; importance of not discontinuing medication without checking with physician.

» Importance of taking on an empty stomach.

» The importance of reading the patient information leaflet before starting entecavir treatment and each time you refill.

» Correctly measuring the oral solution and rinsing the dosing spoon with water after each use.

» Proper dosing
Missed dose: Taking as soon as possible; not taking if almost time for next scheduled dose; not doubling doses
Proper storage

Precautions while using this medication
» Regular visits to physician to check progress

» Consulting physician immediately if symptoms of lactic acidosis or severe hepatomegaly occur

» Informing patient that liver disease may worsen if treatment with entecavir is stopped

» Advising patient that treatment with entecavir has not been shown to decrease the chance of giving hepatitis B virus infection to others through sexual contact or blood contamination

Side/adverse effects
Signs of potential side effects, especially lactic acidosis or severe hepatomegaly.

General Dosing Information
Entecavir should be taken on an empty stomach (at least 2 hours after a meal and 2 hours before the next meal).

The optimal duration of treatment with entecavir in patients with chronic hepatitis B infection and the relationship between treatment and long-term outcomes such as cirrhosis and hepatocellular carcinoma are unknown.

Caution should be used upon discontinuation of entecavir therapy. Severe acute exacerbations of hepatitis B have been reported.

Oral Dosage Forms
Note: Bracketed information in the *Indications* section refers to uses that are not included in U.S. product labeling.

ENTECAVIR ORAL SOLUTION

Usual adult and adolescent dose

Hepatitis B virus (HBV) infection, chronic (treatment)—

Lamivudine naive; Oral, 0.5 mg once daily, administered on an empty stomach (at least 2 hours after a meal and 2 hour before the next meal).

Note: For adults and adolescents (≥16 years of age) with a history of hepatitis B viremia while receiving lamivudine or known lamivudine resistance mutations: 1 mg once daily.

The dosing interval of entecavir should be adjusted in patients with baseline creatinine clearance <50 mL per minute.
- Creatinine clearance ≥50 mL per min: oral, 0.5 mg once daily
- Creatinine clearance 30 to 49 mL per min: oral, 0.25 mg once daily
- Creatinine clearance 10 to 29 mL per min: oral, 0.15 mg once daily
- Creatinine clearance <10 mL per min: oral, 0.05 mg once daily
- Hemodialysis or CAPD patients: administer after hemodialysis

No dosage adjustment is recommended for patients with hepatic impairment.

Lamivudine resistant; Oral, 0.5 mg once daily, administered on an empty stomach (at least 2 hours after a meal and 2 hour before the next meal).

Note: The dosing interval of entecavir should be adjusted in lamivudine resistant patients with baseline creatinine clearance <50 mL per minute.
- Creatinine clearance ≥50 mL per min: oral, 1 mg once daily
- Creatinine clearance 30 to 49 mL per min: oral, 0.5 mg once daily
- Creatinine clearance 10 to 29 mL per min: oral, 0.3 mg once daily
- Creatinine clearance <10 mL per min: oral, 0.1 mg once daily
- Hemodialysis or CAPD patients: administer after hemodialysis

No dosage adjustment is recommended for patients with hepatic impairment.

Usual pediatric dose

Safety and efficacy in pediatric patients below 16 years of age have not been established.

Usual geriatric dose

See *Usual adult and adolescent dose.*

Strength(s) usually available

U.S.—

0.05 mg/mL (Rx) [*Baraclude* (citric acid; maltitol; methylparaben; orange flavor; sodium citrate)].

Packaging and storage

Store at 25 °C (77 °F); excursions permitted between 15° to 30 °C (59° to 86 °F); Protect form light.

Preparation of dosage form

Entecavir is a ready to use product; dilution or mixing with water or any other solvent or liquid is not recommended.

Entecavir oral solution contains 0.05 mg per milliliter. Therefore, 10 mL of the oral solution provides a 0.5-mg dose and 20 mL provides a 1-mg dose.

Auxiliary labeling

• You should take this medicine exactly as prescribed. Do not skip or discontinue unless directed.

ENTECAVIR TABLETS

Usual adult and adolescent dose

Hepatitis B virus (HBV) infection, chronic (treatment)—

Lamivudine naive; Oral, 0.5 mg once daily, administered on an empty stomach (at least 2 hours after a meal and 2 hour before the next meal).

Note: For adults and adolescents (≥16 years of age) with a history of hepatitis B viremia while receiving lamivudine or known lamivudine resistance mutations: 1 mg once daily.

The dosing interval of tenofovir should be adjusted in patients with baseline creatinine clearance <50 mL per minute.
- Creatinine clearance ≥50 mL per min: oral, 0.5 mg once daily
- Creatinine clearance 30 to 49 mL per min: oral, 0.25 mg once daily
- Creatinine clearance 10 to 29 mL per min: oral, 0.15 mg once daily
- Creatinine clearance <10 mL per min: oral, 0.05 mg once daily
- Hemodialysis or CAPD patients: administer after hemodialysis

No dosage adjustment is recommended for patients with hepatic impairment.

Lamivudine resistant; Oral, 0.5 mg once daily, administered on an empty stomach (at least 2 hours after a meal and 2 hour before the next meal).

Note: The dosing interval of entecavir should be adjusted in lamivudine resistant patients with baseline creatinine clearance <50 mL per minute.
- Creatinine clearance ≥50 mL per min: oral, 1 mg once daily
- Creatinine clearance 30 to 49 mL per min: oral, 0.5 mg once daily
- Creatinine clearance 10 to 29 mL per min: oral, 0.3 mg once daily
- Creatinine clearance <10 mL per min: oral, 0.1 mg once daily
- Hemodialysis or CAPD patients: administer after hemodialysis

No dosage adjustment is recommended for patients with hepatic impairment.

Usual pediatric dose

Safety and efficacy in pediatric patients below 16 years of age have not been established.

Usual geriatric dose

See *Usual adult and adolescent dose.*

Note: Dose selection for elderly patients should be cautious because of the possibility of age-related renal function impairment.

Strength(s) usually available

U.S.—

0.5 mg (Rx) [*Baraclude* (crospovidone; hypromellose; lactose monohydrate; magnesium stearate; microcrystalline cellulose; polyethylene glycol 400; polysorbate 80; povidone; titanium dioxide)].

1 mg (Rx) [*Baraclude* (crospovidone; hypromellose; iron oxide red; lactose monohydrate; magnesium stearate; microcrystalline cellulose; polyethylene glycol 400; povidone; titanium dioxide)].

Packaging and storage

Store at 25 °C (77 °F); excursions permitted between 15 to 30 °C (59 to 86 °F).

Auxiliary labeling

• You should take this medicine exactly as prescribed. Do not skip or discontinue unless directed.

Developed: 05/10/2005

EPHEDRINE—See *Bronchodilators, Adrenergic (Systemic), Sympathomimetic Agents—Cardiovascular Use (Parenteral-Systemic)*

EPINASTINE Ophthalmic†

VA CLASSIFICATION (Primary): OP801

Commonly used brand name(s): *Elestat.*

Note: For a listing of dosage forms and brand names by country availability, see *Dosage Forms* section(s).

†Not commercially available in Canada.

Category

Antihistaminic (H_1—receptor), ophthalmic; antiallergic, ophthalmic; mast cell stabilizer, ophthalmic.

Indications

Accepted

Conjunctivitis, allergic (treatment)—Epinastine ophthalmic solution is indicated for the prevention of itching associated with allergic conjunctivitis.

Pharmacology/Pharmacokinetics

Physicochemical characteristics

Molecular weight—Epinastine HCl 285.78.

Osmolality—250 to 310 mOsm/kg

Osmolality—250 to 310 mOsm/kg

Mechanism of action/Effect

Epinastine is a direct H_1-receptor antagonist and an inhibitor of the release of histamine from mast cells involved in the allergic response. Epinastine is selective for the H_1-receptor and also has an affinity for the histamine H_2-receptor, the α_1, α_2, and 5−HT_2-receptors.

Absorption

After ocular administration, systemic absorption of epinastine was relatively low.

Distribution

Epinastine does not cross the blood/brain barrier.

Protein binding

Moderate 64%, plasma protein

Biotransformation

Epinastine is mainly excreted unchanged; less than 10% is metabolized

Half-life

Elimination—about 12 hours

Onset of action

Ophthalmic administration—Within 3 to 5 minutes of administration.

Time to peak concentration

about two hours

Peak plasma concentration:

0.04 ± 0.014 ng/mL following one drop in each eye twice daily for seven days

Duration of action

Ophthalmic administration—Approximately 8 hours.

Elimination

Renal—about 55% following an intervenous dose; via active tubular secretion

Fecal—about 30% following an intervenous dose

Total systemic clearance: 56 L/hour

Precautions to Consider

Carcinogenicity/Mutagenicity

Studies in rats and mice have shown that epinastine is not carcinogenic. This conclusion was reached after 18 or 24 months of oral administration of epinastine, with doses up to 40 mg/kg. These doses represent the equivalent of approximately 30,000 times greater than the maximum daily recommended ocular human dose (MROHD).

Mutagenicity findings in newly synthesized batches of epinastine were negative as verified by the following genotoxic tests: Ames/Salmonella assay; *in vitro* chromosome aberration assay; *in vivo* clastogenicity studies including the mouse micronucleus assay; and chromosomal aberration assay in Chinese hamsters. Epinastine was also negative in the cell transformation assay using Syrian hamster embryo cells, V79/HGPRT mammalian cell point mutation assay and *in vivo/in vitro* unscheduled DNA synthesis assay in primary rat hepatocytes. Positive results were seen in earlier batches of epinastine in two *in vitro* chromosomal aberration studies conducted in the 1980s with human peripheral lymphocytes and with V79 cells, respectively.

Pregnancy/Reproduction

Fertility—Epinastine had no effect on fertility of male rats, but decreased fertility in female rats was observed at an oral dose up to approximately 90,000 times the MROHD.

Pregnancy—Adequate and well controlled studies in pregnant women have not been done. Studies in animals have shown that epinastine causes adverse effects in the fetus. Therefore epinastine should only be used during pregnancy if the potential benefit justifies the potential risk to the fetus.

Animal studies with rats showed maternal toxicity with no embryofetal effects at oral doses approximately 150,000 times the MROHD. However epinastine reduced pup body weight gain following oral doses approximately 90,000 times the MROHD. Total resorptions and abortion were observed in rabbits after oral doses approximately 55,000 times the MROHD. No drug-induced teratogenic effects were noted.

FDA Pregnancy Category C

Breast-feeding

Epinastine is distributed into the breast milk of rats. It is not known whether epinastine is distributed into human milk. Because many drugs are distributed into human milk caution should be exercised when epinastine is administered to a nursing woman.

Pediatrics

Safety and effectiveness in pediatric patients below the age of 3 years have not been established.

Geriatrics

Appropriate studies performed to date have not demonstrated geriatrics-specific problems that would limit usefulness of epinastine in the elderly.

Medical considerations/Contraindications

The medical considerations/contraindications included have been selected on the basis of their potential clinical significance (reasons given in parentheses where appropriate)—not necessarily inclusive (» = major clinical significance).

Except under special circumstances, this medication should not be used when the following medical problem exists:

» Hypersensitivity to epinastine or any of the other ingredients contained in the solution, such as benzalkonium chloride.

Risk-benefit should be considered when the following medical problems exist: :

Contact lens-related irritation
(epinastine should not be used to treat the symptoms of contact lens-related irritation)

Side/Adverse Effects

The following side/adverse effects have been selected on the basis of their potential clinical significance (possible signs and symptoms in parentheses where appropriate)—not necessarily inclusive:

Those indicating need for medical attention only if they continue or are bothersome

Incidence more frequent (approximately 10%)—some of these events were similar to the underlying disease being studied

Cold-like symptoms (runny nose; sore throat); ***respiratory infection*** (cough; fever; sneezing; sore throat)

Incidence less frequent (1% to 10%)—some of these events were similar to the underlying disease being studied

Burning eyes; folliculosis (redness, itching, pain, swelling, or other irritation of the eye); ***headache; hyperemia*** (increase in blood flow to an area of the body); ***increased cough; pharyngitis*** (body aches or pain; congestion; cough; dryness or soreness of throat; fever; hoarseness; runny nose; tender, swollen glands in neck; trouble in swallowing; voice changes); ***pruritus*** (itching skin); ***rhinitis*** (stuffy nose; runny nose; sneezing); ***sinusitis*** (pain or tenderness around eyes and cheekbones; fever; stuffy or runny nose; headache; cough; shortness of breath or troubled breathing; tightness of chest or wheezing)

Overdose

For more information on the management of overdose or unintentional ingestion, **contact a poison control center** (see *Poison Control Center Listing*).

Treatment of overdose

There is no known specific antidote to epinastine. Treatment is generally symptomatic and supportive.

Supportive care—
Patients in whom intentional overdose is confirmed or suspected should be referred for psychiatric consultation.

Patient Consultation

As an aid to patient consultation, refer to *Advice for the Patient, Epinastine (Ophthalmic)*.

In providing consultation, consider emphasizing the following selected information (» = major clinical significance):

Before using this medication

» Conditions affecting use, especially:
Hypersensitivity to epinastine or any of its ingredients, such as benzalkonium chloride.
Pregnancy—Should be administered to a pregnant woman only if clearly needed.
FDA Pregnancy Category C
Breast-feeding—Caution should be exercised when administering this drug to a nursing woman.
Use in children—Safety and efficacy have not been established in pediatric patients below the age of 3 years.
Use in the elderly—No overall difference in safety or effectiveness has been observed between elderly and younger patients

Proper use of this medication

» Importance of removing contact lenses prior to administration of medication; not using if eyes are red or irritated due to contact lenses

» Preventing contamination: Not touching applicator tip to any surface; keeping container tightly closed

» Proper dosing
Missed dose: Using as soon as possible; not using if almost time for next dose; using next dose at regularly scheduled time; not doubling doses

Proper storage

Precautions while using this medication

» Checking with physician if symptoms do not improve or if condition worsens

General Dosing Information

Epinastine is for topical ophthalmic use only and not for injection or oral use.

Patients should be advised not to wear contact lenses if their eye is red.

Epinastine should not be administered if eyes are red or irritated secondary to use of contact lenses.

Because the preservative, benzalkonium chloride, may be absorbed by contact lenses, it is recommended that they be removed prior to administration of epinastine. The lenses may be reinserted 10 minutes following administration of the medication.

The tip of the dispensing container should not touch the eye or any other surface, as this may contaminate the solution.

Serious damage to the eye and subsequent loss of vision may result from using contaminated solutions.

Treatment should be continued throughout the period of exposure, even when symptoms are absent.

Ophthalmic Dosage Forms

EPINASTINE HYDROCHLORIDE OPHTHALMIC SOLUTION

Usual adult and adolescent dose

Allergic conjunctivitis—

Topical to the conjunctiva, 1 drop in each eye twice a day.

Usual pediatric dose

Allergic conjunctivitis—

Children younger than 3 years of age: Safety and efficacy have not been established.

Children 3 years of age and older: See *Usual adult and adolescent dose*.

Usual geriatric dose

See *Usual adult and adolescent dose*.

Strength(s) usually available

U.S.—

0.5 mg (0.44 mg base) per mL (Rx) [*Elestat* (Benzalkonium chloride 0.01%; edetate disodium; hydrochloric acid; sodium chloride; sodium hydroxide; sodium phosphate monobasic; purified water)].

Packaging and storage

Store between 15 and 25 °C (59 and 77 °F), store in a tight container.

Auxiliary labeling

- For the eye
- Do not touch or contaminate the tip of the container
- Keep out of reach of children.

Developed: 02/19/2004

EPINEPHRINE—See *Bronchodilators, Adrenergic (Inhalation-Local), Bronchodilators, Adrenergic (Systemic), Sympathomimetic Agents—Cardiovascular Use (Parenteral-Systemic)*

EPINEPHRYL BORATE—See *Epinephrine (Ophthalmic)*

EPIRUBICIN Systemic

USA: Epirubicin hydrochloride

INN: Epirubicin; BAN: Epirubicin

VA CLASSIFICATION (Primary): AN200

Commonly used brand name(s): *Ellence; Pharmorubicin PFS*.

Note: For a listing of dosage forms and brand names by country availability, see *Dosage Forms* section(s).

Category

Antineoplastic adjunct.

Indications

Note: Bracketed information in the *Indications* section refers to uses that are not included in U.S. product labeling.

Accepted

Carcinoma, breast (treatment)—Epirubicin is indicated as an adjuvant therapy in patients withaxillary-node tumor involvement following resection[1], in primary breast cancer.

Epirubicin is also indicated, as a single agent and in combination therapy with other agents, for the treatment of [metastatic breast carcinoma].

[Carcinoma, esophageal (treatment adjunct)][1]—Epirubicin is indicated, in combination with other agents (e.g., cisplatin and fluorouracil [ECF regimen]), for the treatment of esophageal and esophagogastric junction carcinomas and adenocarcinomas.

[Carcinoma, gastric (treatment)]—Epirubicin is indicated, as a single agent and in combination therapy with other agents, for the treatment of locally unresectable and metastatic gastric carcinoma.

[Carcinoma, lung, non-small cell (treatment)] or
[Carcinoma, lung, small cell (treatment)]—Epirubicin is indicated, as a single agent and in combination therapy with other agents, for the treatment of advanced non-small cell lung carcinoma and limited and extensive small cell lung carcinoma.

[Carcinoma, ovarian (treatment)]—Epirubicin is indicated, as a single agent and in combination therapy with other agents, for the treatment of Stage III and IV (FIGO) ovarian carcinoma.

[Lymphomas, Hodgkin's (treatment)] or
[Lymphomas, non-Hodgkin's (treatment)]—Epirubicin is indicated, in combination therapy with other agents, for the treatment of Hodgkin's lymphomas. Epirubicin is also indicated, as a single agent and in combination therapy with other agents, for the treatment of non-Hodgkin's lymphomas.

[Sarcoma, soft tissue (treatment)][1]—Epirubicin is indicated, alone or in combination with other agents (e.g., ifosfamide, cisplatin) and/or surgery, for the treatment of soft tissue sarcomas, in place of doxorubicin.

Acceptance not established

Use of epirubicin for the treatment of pancreatic carcinomas has not been established.

[1]Not included in Canadian product labeling.

Pharmacology/Pharmacokinetics

Physicochemical characteristics

Chemical Group—Anthracycline

Molecular weight—579.95.

Mechanism of action/Effect

Epirubicin (4′-epidoxorubicin) is the 4′-epimer of doxorubicin and is a semi-synthetic derivative of daunorubicin. The exact mechanism of antineoplastic activity is unknown but epirubicin may produce a cytotoxic effect through intercalation with DNA, eventually inducing DNA cleavage by topoisomerase II. Epirubicin also inhibits DNA helicase activity, eventually interfering with DNA replication and transcription. Free radical production results in further cytotoxic activity.

Distribution

Volume of distribution (Vol_D)—Steady state: 21 to 27 L per kg, indicating extensive uptake into the tissues.

Epirubicin concentrates in red blood cells, resulting in a whole blood concentration of epirubicin that is two times greater than the plasma concentration.

Other anthracyclines are known to distribute into human breast milk but it is unknown if epirubicin does.

Protein binding

High (77%); predominantly to albumin.

Biotransformation

Hepatic, primarily, rapid; producing an active metabolite, epirubicinol, with one-tenth the activity of epirubicin. Enzymatic reduction, glucuronidation and hydrolysis produce 3 metabolites with no inherent activity.

Half-life

Elimination—

Triphasic manner with mean half-lives of alpha, beta, and gamma phases of about 3 minutes, 2.5 hours, and 33 hours, respectively.

Elimination

Biliary—

35% as drug or metabolite over 4 days.

Renal—

20% as drug or metabolite over 4 days.

Precautions to Consider

Carcinogenicity
Secondary acute myelogenous leukemia has been reported in patients treated with anthracycline cytotoxic agents. Risk of secondary leukemia increases with increasing doses of anthracyclines, when anthracyclines are used in combination with other DNA damaging agents or when other cytotoxic agents are given prior to anthracycline use. A cumulative risk of secondary acute myelogenous leukemia or myelodysplastic syndrome (AML/MDS) of about 0.27%, 0.46%, and 0.55% was reported at 3, 5, and 8 years, respectively, in an analysis of 7110 patients who received adjuvant treatment with epirubicin in controlled clinical trials as a component of polychemotherapy regimens for early breast cancer. In patients who received more than the maximum recommended cumulative dose of epirubicin (720 mg per m^2) or cyclophosphamide (6,300 mg per m^2), the cumulative probability of developing AML/MDS was found to be particularly increased.

In animals epirubicin is carcinogenic. The carcinogenic potential of epirubicin has not been conducted in conventional long-term animal studies.

Mutagenicity
Epirubicin was found to be mutagenic and clastogenic *in vitro* and clastogenic *in vivo*. Positive *in vitro* mutagenicity tests included those in bacteria (Ames test) either in the presence or absence of metabolic activation and mammalian cells (HGPRT assay in V79 Chinese hamster lung fibroblasts) in the absence of metabolic activation. Epirubicin was clastogenic in *in vivo* chromosome aberration in mouse bone marrow and *in vitro* chromosome aberrations in human lymphocytes both in the presence and absence of metabolic activation.

Pregnancy/Reproduction
Fertility—Uterine and testicular atrophy have occurred in study animals. When epirubicin 0.3 milligrams per kilogram (mg/kg) (0.015 times the maximum recommended human dose on a body surface area basis) was administered daily to male and female rats during the mating cycle, no pregnancies resulted. Epirubicin may be genotoxic to human sperm, therefore males being treated with epirubicin should use contraception. Epirubicin may induce irreversible amenorrhea in premenopausal women.

Pregnancy—No adequate and well-controlled studies have been done in pregnant women. Due to the potential hazard to the fetus, women of child-bearing potential should be advised against becoming pregnant. If the patient becomes pregnant while receiving epirubicin, the patient should be apprised of the potential hazard to the fetus.

Case reports: A 34-year-old woman experienced a spontaneous abortion after being removed from study due to pregnancy. She was randomized to FEC-50 for breast cancer metastatic to the liver. In another case report, a 34-year-old woman delivered a healthy baby at 35 weeks. She was diagnosed with breast cancer when 28 weeks pregnant. She was treated with cyclophosphamide and epirubicin every 3 weeks for 3 cycles. The last dose received was at 34 weeks of pregnancy.

Epirubicin crosses the placenta and has been shown to cause fetal harm in animals, including fetal growth retardation, internal and external physical malformations, and fetal death. Risk-benefit must be carefully considered when this medication is required in life-threatening situations or in serious diseases for which other medications cannot be used or are ineffective.

Intravenous epirubicin doses of 0.8 mg/kg per day (0.04 times the maximum single human dose on a body surface area basis) were embryotoxic in rats. Doses of 2 mg/kg per day (0.1 times the maximum single human dose on a body surface area basis) were embryotoxic and produced malformations in surviving fetal rats. Intravenous doses of up to 0.2 mg/kg per day (0.02 times the maximum recommended human dose on a body surface area basis) of epirubicin given to rats and rabbits late in pregnancy did not adversely affect the offspring.

FDA Pregnancy Category D

Breast-feeding
It is unknown if epirubicin is distributed into human milk. Because many drugs, including other anthracyclines, are excreted in human milk and because of the potential harm to nursing infants, nursing should be discontinued prior to epirubicin administration.

Pediatrics
Appropriate studies on the relationship of age to the effects of epirubicin have not been performed in the pediatric population. Safety and efficacy have not been established. Pediatric patients may be at a higher risk for anthracycline induced acute manifestations of cardiotoxicity and for chronic heart failure.

Geriatrics
Care should be taken in monitoring for toxicity in elderly women, who have a predicted 35% decrease in the plasma clearance of epirubicin.

Dental
The bone marrow depressant effects of epirubicin may result in an increased incidence of microbial infection, delayed healing, and gingival bleeding. If leukopenia or thrombocytopenia occurs, dental work should be deferred until blood counts have returned to normal, and patients should be instructed in proper oral hygiene, including caution in use of regular toothbrushes, dental floss, and toothpicks.

Epirubicin causes oral stomatitis, which can be severe and lead to painful mucosal ulcerations.

Drug interactions and/or related problems
The following drug interactions and/or related problems have been selected on the basis of their potential clinical significance (possible mechanism in parentheses where appropriate)—not necessarily inclusive (» = major clinical significance):

Note: Combinations containing any of the following medications, depending on the amount present, may also interact with this medication.

» Blood dyscrasia-causing medications (see *Appendix II*)
(leukopenic and/or thrombocytopenic effects of epirubicin may be increased with concurrent or recurrent therapy if these medications cause the same effects; dosage of epirubicin should be based on blood counts in these cases)

» Bone marrow depressants (see *Appendix II*) or
» Radiation therapy
(additive bone marrow depression may occur; dosage reduction may be required when two or more bone marrow depressants, including radiation, are used concurrently or consecutively)

» Cardioactive compounds
(medications that could cause heart failure (i.e., calcium channel blockers) may contribute to or precipitate cardiomyopathy; additional monitoring of cardiac function may be indicated)

» Cimetidine
(concomitant use of cimetidine increases the body concentration of epirubicin by reducing plasma clearance by as much as 30%; concurrent use of cimetidine and epirubicin is not recommended)

» Daunorubicin or
» Doxorubicin or
» Idarubicin or
» Mitoxantrone
(use of epirubicin in patients previously treated with maximum cumulative doses of anthracyclines may increase the risk of cardiotoxicity, gastrointestinal, hematological, and hepatic effects)

» Hepatotoxic medications (see *Appendix II*)
(concomitant use may increase the risk of toxicity; for example, high dose methotrexate may impair liver function and increase toxicity of subsequently administered epirubicin.)

» Radiation therapy to the pericardial or mediastinal region
(simultaneous use may result in increased cardiotoxicity)

Vaccines, killed virus
(because normal defense mechanisms may be suppressed by epirubicin therapy, the patient's antibody response to the vaccine may be decreased; the interval between discontinuation of medications that cause immunosuppression and restoration of the patient's ability to respond to the vaccine depends on the intensity and type of immunosuppression-causing medication used, the underlying disease, and other factors; estimates vary from 3 months to 1 year)

» Vaccines, live virus
(because normal defense mechanisms may be suppressed by epirubicin therapy, concurrent use with a live virus vaccine may potentiate the replication of the vaccine virus, may increase the side/adverse effects of the vaccine virus, and/or may decrease the patient's antibody response to the vaccine; immunization of these patients should be undertaken only with extreme caution after careful review of the patient's hematologic status and only with the knowledge and consent of the physician managing the epirubicin therapy; the interval between discontinuation of medications that cause immunosuppression and restoration of the patient's ability to respond to the vaccine depends on the intensity and type of immunosuppression-causing medication used, the underlying disease, and other factors; estimates vary from 3 months to 1 year; in addition, immunization with oral poliovirus vaccine should be postponed in persons in close contact with the patient, especially family members)

Laboratory value alterations

The following have been selected on the basis of their potential clinical significance (possible effect in parentheses where appropriate)—not necessarily inclusive (» = major clinical significance).

With physiology/laboratory test values

Electrocardiogram (ECG) changes, transient, including:
Arrythmias
Non-specific ST-T wave changes
Tachyarrhythmias
Atrioventricular block
Bundle-branch block
(withdrawal of epirubicin is not usually required)

Uric acid
(concentrations in blood and urine may increase secondary to increased purine catabolism)

Medical considerations/Contraindications

The medical considerations/contraindications included have been selected on the basis of their potential clinical significance (reasons given in parentheses where appropriate)—not necessarily inclusive (» = major clinical significance).

Except under special circumstances, this medication should not be used when the following medical problem exists:

» Allergic reaction to epirubicin, other anthracyclines or anthracenediones
» Baseline neutrophil count <1,500 cells per mL
» Myocardial infarction, recent, severe arrhythmias, or severe cardiac insufficiency
» Prior treatment to maximum cumulative doses with anthracycline chemotherapeutic agents
» Severe hepatic function impairment
(contributes to toxicity by decreasing metabolism and clearance of epirubicin by up to 30%)

Risk-benefit should be considered when the following medical problems exist:

» Bone marrow depression
(lower starting doses of 75 to 90 milligrams per square meter of body surface area are recommended for patients with pre-existing bone marrow depression)

» Infection, bacterial, viral, or fungal
(risk of severe generalized disease especially in the presence of recent or existing chickenpox and herpes zoster viruses)

» Heart disease
(cardiotoxicity may occur at lower doses)

» Hepatic function impairment
(elimination may be decreased; reduction in dosage is recommended; one half of the normal starting dose is recommended in patients with serum bilirubin concentrations of 1.2 to 3 milligrams per 100 mL or aspartate aminotransferase (AST [SGOT]) levels of 2 to 4 times the upper limit of normal; one quarter of the normal starting dose is recommended in patients with serum bilirubin concentrations of greater than 3 milligrams per 100 mL or AST [SGOT] levels of greater than 4 times the upper limit of normal)

» Caution should be used also in patients who have had previous cytotoxic drug therapy or radiation therapy.

Renal function impairment
(lower doses are recommended for patients with serum creatinine levels greater than 5 milligrams per 100 mL)

» Tumor cell infiltration of the bone marrow
» Caution should be used in patients with decreased bone marrow reserves secondary to prior chemotherapy or radiation therapy.

Patient monitoring

The following are especially important in patient monitoring (other tests may be warranted in some patients, depending on condition; » = major clinical significance):

» Alanine aminotransferase (ALT [SGPT]) values and
» Aspartate aminotransferase (AST [SGOT]) values and
» Total bilirubin concentrations, serum
(recommended prior to initiation of therapy and at periodic intervals during treatment; frequency varies according to clinical state, agent, dose, and other agents being used concurrently)

» Creatinine, serum
(recommended prior to initiation of therapy and at periodic intervals during treatment)

Chest radiograph and
» Echocardiography (ECHO) or
» Multi–gated radionuclide angiography (MUGA) and
Electrocardiogram (ECG) studies
(recommended prior to initiation of therapy and at periodic intervals during treatment to evaluate left ventricular ejection fraction and cardiac function; frequency should increase if patient has preexisting cardiac disease or shows signs of cardiotoxicity)

Absolute neutrophil counts and
Leukocyte counts and
Platelet counts and
Red blood cell counts
(recommended prior to initiation of therapy and at periodic intervals during treatment; frequency varies according to clinical state, agent, dose, and other agents being used concurrently)

Calcium phosphate concentration, serum and
Potassium concentration, serum and
Uric acid concentration, serum
(recommended immediately following initial chemotherapy administration)

Side/Adverse Effects

Note: Many "side effects" of antineoplastic therapy are unavoidable and represent the medication's pharmacologic action. Some of these (for example, leukopenia and thrombocytopenia) are actually used as parameters to aid in individual dosage titration.

Excessively rapid intravenous administration may produce facial flushing.

The following side/adverse effects have been selected on the basis of their potential clinical significance (possible signs and symptoms in parentheses where appropriate)—not necessarily inclusive:

Those indicating need for medical attention

Incidence more frequent (>50%)

Anemia, leukopenia, neutropenia, or infection (fever or chills; cough or hoarseness; lower back or side pain; painful or difficult urination)—usually asymptomatic; ***mucositis (mainly oral) stomatitis, less often esophagitis*** (pain or burning in mouth or throat; bleeding, redness, or ulcers in mouth or throat; sores in mouth and on lips)

Note: With *leukopenia*, the nadir of leukocyte count occurs 10 to 14 days after a dose. Recovery usually occurs within 21 days after a dose. *Stomatitis or esophagitis* progresses over a few days after administration. It may be severe and lead to ulceration and the potential for severe infections. Most patients recover 3 weeks after dosing.

Incidence less frequent (5–50%)

Conjunctivitis (redness or discharge of the eye, eyelid, or lining of the eyelid); ***local reaction*** (red streaks along injected vein); ***thrombocytopenia*** (unusual bleeding or bruising; black, tarry stools; blood in urine or stools; pinpoint red spots on skin)—usually asymptomatic

Note: *Extravasation* may also occur without accompanying stinging or burning and even if blood returns well on aspiration of the infusion needle.

A *local reaction* may indicate excessively rapid intravenous administration.

Phlebitis or thrombophlebitis occurs especially when small veins are used or a single vein is used repeatedly.

Recall postradiation erythema occurs if the patient has previously received radiation therapy; severe dermatitis and/or mucositis in the irradiated area may occur with concurrent use.

Incidence rare (<5%)

Allergic reaction (skin rash or itching; fever; chills); ***anaphylaxis*** (wheezing or difficulty breathing); ***cardiotoxicity, usually in the form of congestive heart failure*** (shortness of breath; swelling of abdomen, feet, and lower legs; fast or irregular heartbeat); ***extravasation, cellulitis, or tissue necrosis*** (pain at place of injection); ***hyperuricemia or uric acid nephropathy*** (joint pain; lower back or side pain); ***phlebitis or thrombophlebitis*** (pain, redness, or warmth at injection site); ***postirradiation erythema, recall*** (darkening or redness of skin at place of irradiation); ***secondary leukemia*** (bleeding; enlarged liver, lymph nodes, and spleen; infection); ***severe myelosuppression*** (fever; general tiredness or weakness; infection)

Note: Incidence of *cardiotoxicity* is greater in patients receiving total dosages of over 900 milligrams per square meter of body surface area, in patients with a history of cardiac disease or mediastinal/pericardial radiation, in patients taking other cardioactive drugs, and may be more frequent in children up to 2 years of age and in the elderly.

Cardiotoxicity usually appears toward the end of treatment or within 2 to 3 months after completion of treatment. Early onset is manifested by a fast, slow, or irregular heartbeat. Delayed onset is usually in the form of congestive heart failure and is dependent on dose accumulation. Cardiomyopathy has been reported to be associated with persistent voltage reduction in the QRS complex, systolic interval prolongation, and reduction of ejection fraction. It may develop suddenly and may not be detected by routine ECG. It may be irreversible and fatal but responds to treatment if detected early.

Acute life-threatening arrhythmias have been reported during or within a few hours after administration.

Those indicating need for medical attention only if they continue or are bothersome

Incidence more frequent (>50%)

Amenorrhea (lack of menstrual periods); ***Nausea and vomiting***—may be severe, causing dehydration and may require antiemetic prophylaxis

Incidence less frequent (5–50%)

Diarrhea—may lead to dehydration; ***hot flashes***

Incidence rare (< 5%)

Anorexia (loss of appetite; weight loss); ***darkening of soles, palms, or nails***

Those not indicating need for medical attention

Incidence more frequent

Loss of hair; reddish-colored urine

Note: *Loss of hair* is complete and reversible. It occurs in most cases and resolves 2 to 3 months after last dose.

Reddish-colored urine clears within 48 hours.

Those indicating the need for medical attention if they occur after medication is discontinued

Cardiotoxicity (fast or irregular heartbeat; shortness of breath; swelling of abdomen, feet, and lower legs)

Overdose

For more information on the management of overdose or unintentional ingestion, **contact a poison control center** (see *Poison Control Center Listing*).

Clinical effects of overdose

The following effects have been selected on the basis of their potential clinical significance (possible signs and symptoms in parentheses where appropriate)—not necessarily inclusive:

Bone marrow suppression; delayed congestive heart failure—manifested by ascites, gallop rhythm, hepatomegaly, pleural effusion, pulmonary edema, and tachycardia and affected by cumulative doses of epirubicin; ***Gastritis or gastrointestinal bleeding; grade 4 mucositis; Hematologic abnormalities***—symptoms of overdose are qualitatively similar to the known toxicities of epirubicin; ***hyperthermia; multiple organ failure (respiratory and renal)***—manifested by anuria, an increase in lactate dehydrogenase, and lactic acidosis

Treatment of overdose

Supportive care—(antibiotic therapy, blood transfusions, colony-stimulating factors, intensive care and platelet transfusions as necessary).

Monitor for congestive heart failure over time.

Patient Consultation

As an aid to patient consultation, refer to *Advice for the Patient, Epirubicin (Systemic)*.

In providing consultation, consider emphasizing the following selected information (» = major clinical significance):

Before using this medication

» Conditions affecting use, especially:

Hypersensitivity to epirubicin or other anthracyclines

Risk of secondary leukemia with increasing doses of anthracyclines, when anthracyclines are used in combination chemotherapy, or when cytotoxic agents are given prior to anthracycline use

Pregnancy—Use not recommended because of mutagenic, teratogenic, and carcinogenic potential; advisability of using contraception; telling physician immediately if pregnancy is suspected

Breast-feeding—Not recommended because of risk of serious side effects

Use in children—Cardiotoxicity more frequent in children up to 2 years of age

Use in the elderly—Cardiotoxicity may be more frequent in patients 70 years of age and over, especially in women.

Other medications, especially blood dyscrasia-causing medications, cardioactive compounds, cimetidine, daunorubicin, doxorubicin, hepatotoxic medications, idarubicin, mitoxantrone, other bone marrow depressants, previous cytotoxic drug or radiation therapy

Other medical problems, especially baseline neutrophil count < 1500 per mL, previous allergic reaction to epirubicin, other anthracyclines, or anthracenediones, prior treatment to maximum cumulative doses with anthracycline agents, recent myocardial infarction, severe arrhythmias, or severe cardiac insufficiency, bone marrow depression, bacterial, fungal, or viral infections, heart disease, hepatic function impairment, or tumor cell infiltration of bone marrow

Proper use of this medication

» Caution in taking combination therapy; taking each medication at the right time

Importance of ample fluid intake and subsequent increase in urine output to aid in excretion of uric acid

Frequency of nausea and vomiting; importance of continuing medication despite stomach upset

» Proper dosing

Precautions while using this medication

» Importance of close monitoring by the physician, especially blood counts, cardiac monitoring, and liver function tests

» Avoiding immunizations unless approved by physician; other persons in patient's household should avoid immunizations with oral poliovirus vaccine; avoiding persons who have taken oral poliovirus vaccine, or wearing a protective mask that covers nose and mouth

Caution if bone marrow depression occurs:

» Avoiding exposure to persons with infections, especially during periods of low blood counts; checking with physician immediately if fever or chills, cough or hoarseness, lower back or side pain, or painful or difficult urination occurs

» Checking with physician immediately if unusual bleeding or bruising; black, tarry stools; blood in urine or stools; or pinpoint red spots on skin occur

Caution in use of regular toothbrush, dental floss, or toothpick; physician, dentist, or nurse may suggest alternatives; checking with physician before having dental work done

Not touching eyes or inside of nose unless hands washed immediately before

Using caution to avoid accidental cuts with use of sharp objects such as safety razor or fingernail or toenail cutters

Avoiding contact sports or other situations where bruising or injury could occur

» Possibility of local tissue injury and scarring if infiltration of intravenous solution occurs; telling doctor or nurse right away about redness, pain, or swelling at injection site

Side/adverse effects

Signs of potential side effects, especially anemia, leukopenia, neutropenia, infection, mucositis, conjunctivitis, local reaction, thrombocytopenia, allergic reaction, anaphylaxis, cardiotoxicity, extravasation, cellulitis, tissue necrosis, hyperuricemia, uric acid nephropathy, phlebitis, thrombophlebitis, recall of postirradiation erythema, secondary leukemia, and severe myelosuppression

Physician or nurse can help in dealing with side effects

Reddish urine for 1 to 2 days after administration may be alarming to patient although medically insignificant

Possibility of hair loss; normal hair growth should resume after treatment has ended

General Dosing Information

Patients receiving epirubicin should be under supervision of a physician experienced in cancer chemotherapy. It is recommended that the patient be hospitalized at least during initial treatment.

Epirubicin should not be used in patients who have previously received the maximum acceptable cumulative doses of any anthracycline cytotoxic agents.

A variety of dosage schedules of epirubicin, in combination with other antitumor agents, are used. The prescriber should consult the medical literature as well as the manufacturer's literature in choosing a specific dosage.

Dosage must be adjusted to meet the individual requirements of each patient, on the basis of clinical response and appearance or severity of toxicity.

It is recommended that epirubicin be administered slowly into the tubing of a freely running intravenous infusion of 0.9% sodium chloride injection or 5% dextrose injection (over not less than 3 to 5 minutes). If possible, injection of epirubicin into small veins, veins over joints or in extremities with compromised venous or lymphatic drainage, or repeated injection into the same vein should be avoided. Epirubicin should not be administered as a direct push injection.

Care must be taken to avoid extravasation during intravenous administration because of the risk of severe ulceration and necrosis. Facial flushing indicates too-rapid injection.

If extravasation of epirubicin occurs during intravenous administration, as indicated by local swelling, burning or stinging (may also be painless), or erythematous streaking along the vein, the infusion should be stopped immediately and resumed, completing the dose, in another vein.

Because it will cause local tissue necrosis, epirubicin must not be administered intramuscularly or subcutaneously.

Development of hyperuricemia due to lysis of neoplastic cells (tumor lysis syndrome) may be prevented by adequate oral hydration and, in some cases, administration of allopurinol. Alkalinization of urine may be necessary if serum uric acid concentrations are elevated. Monitor serum uric acid, potassium, calcium phosphate, and creatinine beginning after first dose of epirubicin.

Special precautions are recommended in patients who develop thrombocytopenia as a result of administration of epirubicin. These may include extreme care in performing invasive procedures; regular inspection of intravenous sites, skin (including perirectal area), and mucous membrane surfaces for signs of bleeding or bruising; limiting frequency of venipuncture and avoiding intramuscular injections; testing urine, emesis, stool, and secretions for occult blood; care in the use of regular toothbrushes, dental floss, toothpicks, safety razors, and fingernail and toenail cutters; avoiding constipation; and using caution to prevent falls and other injuries. Such patients should avoid alcohol and aspirin intake because of the risk of gastrointestinal bleeding. Platelet transfusions may be required.

Patients who develop leukopenia should be observed carefully for signs of infection. Antibiotic support may be required. In neutropenic patients who develop fever, broad-spectrum antibiotic coverage should be initiated empirically, pending bacterial cultures and appropriate diagnostic tests. For patients at the maximum starting dose of epirubicin, prophylaxis with sulfamethoxazole-trimethoprim or a fluoroquinolone is recommended.

Safety considerations for handling this medication

There is limited but increasing evidence and concern that personnel involved in preparation and administration of parenteral antineoplastic agents may be at some risk because of the potential mutagenicity, teratogenicity, and/or carcinogenicity of these agents, although the actual risk is unknown. USP advisory panels recommend cautious handling both in preparation and disposal of antineoplastic agents. Precautions that have been suggested include:

- Use of a biological containment cabinet during reconstitution and dilution of parenteral medications and wearing of disposable surgical gloves, goggles, gowns, and masks.
- Pregnant personnel should not come in contact with antineoplastic medication containers or mixing supplies.
- Use of proper technique to prevent contamination of the medication, work area, and operator during transfer between containers (including proper training of personnel in this technique).
- Cautious and proper disposal of needles, syringes, vials, ampules, and unused medication.
- Use of proper technique in handling spills, including the use of dilute sodium hypochlorite solution (1% active chlorine) and water, and proper disposal of waste.

A number of medical centers have developed detailed guidelines for handling of antineoplastic agents.

Combination chemotherapy

Epirubicin may be used in combination with other agents in various regimens. As a result, incidence and/or severity of side effects may be altered and different dosages may be used.

Parenteral Dosage Forms

EPIRUBICIN HYDROCHLORIDE INJECTION

Usual adult dose

Carcinoma, breast—

When used in combination with other chemotherapy agents, for primary breast carcinoma: Intravenous, 100 to 120 milligrams per square meter of body surface area, given on Day 1 of cycle or divided into 2 doses and given on Day 1 and Day 8, repeated every twenty-one to twenty-eight days for six cycles.

Note: For primary breast carcinoma, the Canadian manufacturer states that epirubicin should be administered in combination with cyclophosphamide and fluorouracil (CEF-120 regimen): Intravenous, 60 mg/m^2 on Days 1 and 8, repeated every four weeks, for 6 cycles.

Note: For metastatic breast carcinoma, the Canadian manufacturer states epirubicin may be administered in combination with cyclophosphamide and fluorouracil (FEC regimen): Intravenous, 50 mg/m^2. As single-agent therapy: Intravenous, 75 to 90 mg/m^2, every three weeks. The dosage may be divided over 2 successive days. An alternative weekly dosage schedule of 12.5 to 25 mg/m^2 has been used, producing less clinical toxicity.

Note: In patients with severe hepatic impairment, reduction in dosage is recommended; one half of the normal starting dose is recommended in patients with serum bilirubin concentrations of 1.2 to 3 milligrams per 100 mL or aspartate aminotransferase (AST [SGOT]) levels of 2 to 4 times the upper limit of normal; one quarter of the normal starting dose is recommended in patients with serum bilirubin concentrations of greater than 3 milligrams per 100 mL or AST [SGOT] levels of greater than 4 times the upper limit of normal.

In patients with severe renal impairment, reduction in the starting dose is recommended if serum creatinine level is greater than 5 milligrams per 100 mL.

In patients with bone marrow depression or neoplastic bone marrow infiltration, a reduction in the starting dose to 75 to 90 milligrams per square meter of body surface area is recommended.

Note: If at anytime during therapy the following occurs: Platelets $< 50,000$ per mL, absolute neutrophil count (ANC) < 250 per mL, neutropenic fever, or grade 3/4 non-hematologic toxicity, it is recommended that the Day 1 dose of subsequent treatment cycles be reduced to 75%. Subsequent cycles of treatment should be postponed until platelets $\geq 100,000$ per mL, ANC ≥ 1500 per mL, and non-hematologic toxicity $\leq$ Grade 1.

If at anytime during divided dose therapy the following occurs: Platelets 75,000 to 100,000 per mL or ANC 1000 to 1499 per mL, it is recommended that the Day 8 dose be reduced to 75% of the Day 1 dose. If on Day 8 platelets $< 75,000$ per mL, ANC < 1000 per mL, or Grade 3/4 non-hematologic toxicity occurs, omit the Day 8 dose.

[Carcinoma, esophageal][1]—

As part of an ECF regimen, patients have benefited from intravenous doses of epirubicin 50 mg/m^2, on day 1 of a 21–day treatment cycle, in conjunction with cisplatin (day 1) and a continuous infusion of fluorouracil, for up to 8 cycles. Patients have also benefited from intravenous doses of epirubicin 50 to 60 mg/m^2, on day 1, or 20 mg/m^2, on days 1 to 3 of a 28–day treatment cycle, in conjunction with cisplatin and fluorouracil, for up to 6 cycles.

[Carcinoma, gastric]—

Combination Therapy—Intravenous, doses of 80 mg/m^2 can be used in combination with fluorouracil.

Single Agent—Intravenous, doses range from 75 to 100 mg/m^2

[Carcinoma, lung, small cell]—

Combination Therapy—Intravenous, doses range from 50 to 90 mg/m^2, in combination with cisplatin or ifosfamide, cyclophosphamide and vincristine (CEV regimen), cyclophosphamide and etoposide (CEVP-16 regimen), or cisplatin and etoposide.

Single Agent—Intravenous, 90 to 120 mg/m^2 administered every three weeks.

[Carcinoma, lung, non-small cell]—

Combination Therapy—Intravenous, doses range from 90 to 120 mg/m^2 administered day 1, every three to four weeks, in combination with etoposide, cisplatin, mitomycin, vindesine, and vinblastine.

Single agent—Intravenous, 120 to 150 mg/m^2 administered day 1, every three to four weeks.

[Carcinoma, ovarian]—

Combination Therapy—Intravenous, doses range from 50 to 90 mg/m^2, repeated at three to four week intervals, as second-line therapy, and in combination with cisplatin and cyclophosphamide when using as first-line therapy.

Single Agent—Intravenous, doses range from 50 to 90 mg/m^2, at three to four week intervals, as second-line therapy.

[Lymphomas, Hodgkin's]—

Combination Therapy—Intravenous, 35 mg/m^2 every two weeks or 70 mg/m^2 every three to four weeks (replacing doxorubicin in the ABVD regimen).

[Lymphomas, non-Hodgkin's]—

Combination Therapy—Intravenous, doses range from 60 to 75 mg/m^2 (replacing doxorubicin in the CHOP, CHOP-bleo, or BACAP regimens).

Single Agent—Intravenous, 75 to 90 mg/m^2, every three weeks.

[Sarcoma, soft tissue][1]—

Patients have benefited from intravenous doses of 45 to 60 mg/m²/day, for 2 to 3 days of a twenty-one to twenty-eight day treatment cycle. Doses of 150 to 180 mg/m², every twenty-one days, for up to 8 treatment cycles, has not been established as being more efficacious, but is more toxic. G-CSF support should be considered.

Usual adult prescribing limits

The risk of developing congestive heart failure is estimated to be 0.9% at a total cumulative dosage of 550 mg per square meter of body surface area, 1.6% at a total cumulative dosage of 700 mg per square meter of body surface area, and 3.3.% at a total cumulative dosage of 900 mg per square meter of body surface area. This toxicity may develop at lower cumulative dosages in patients who have previously received chest irradiation, patients who have received medications increasing cardiotoxicity, or patients with pre-existing heart disease.

Usual pediatric dose

Safety and efficacy have not been established.

Strength(s) usually available

U.S.—

2 mg per mL (25–and 100–mL single–use vials) (Rx) [*Ellence* (sodium chloride USP; water for injection USP)].

Canada—

2 mg per mL (5–and 25–mL vials) (Rx) [*Pharmorubicin PFS* (sodium chloride USP; water for injection USP; lactose-free)].

2 mg per mL (100–mL Pharmacy Bulk vial) (Rx) [*Pharmorubicin PFS* (sodium chloride USP; water for injection USP; lactose-free)].

Packaging and storage

Store between 2 and 8 °C (36 and 46 °F). Do not freeze. Protect from light.

Preparation of dosage form

Epirubicin is provided as a preservative-free, ready to use solution.

Dispensing from the Pharmacy Bulk Vial should be completed within 8 hours of initial entry, due to risk of bacterial contamination. Use of the Pharmacy Bulk Vial is restricted to hospitals with a recognized intravenous admixture program and is intended for single puncture, multiple dispensing, and for intravenous use only.

Stability

Epirubicin should be used within 24 hours of the first penetration of the rubber stopper and any unused solution should be discarded.

Avoid alkaline pH: causes hydrolysis of epirubicin.

Canadian manufacturer states that prepared syringes filled from the Pharmacy Bulk Vials are stable for 24 hours at room temperature or 48 hours under refrigeration. Any unused solution should be discarded.

Incompatibilities

Epirubicin should not be mixed with heparin or fluorouracil or other medications since a precipitate may form.

Canadian manufacturer states that epirubicin should not be mixed with any other drugs unless specific compatibility data is available.

Auxiliary labeling

- Refrigerate. Do not freeze.
- Protect from light.

---

[1]Not included in Canadian product labeling.

Revised: 08/15/2005
Developed: 11/02/1999

EPLERENONE Systemic†

VA CLASSIFICATION (Primary): CV409

Commonly used brand name(s): *INSPRA; Inspra.*

Note: For a listing of dosage forms and brand names by country availability, see *Dosage Forms* section(s).

†Not commercially available in Canada.

Category

Antihypertensive.

Indications

Accepted

Hypertension (treatment)—Eplerenone is indicated for the treatment of hypertension. It may be used alone or in combination with other antihypertensive agents.

For additional information on initial therapeutic guidelines related to the treatment of hypertension, see *Appendix III.*

Pharmacology/Pharmacokinetics

Physicochemical characteristics

Molecular weight—414.50.

Solubility—Slightly soluble in water; solubility is pH independent.

Partition coefficient—Octanol/water partition coefficient: approximately 7.1 at pH 7.0

Mechanism of action/Effect

Eplerenone binds to the mineralocorticoid receptor and blocks the binding of aldosterone, a component of the renin-angiotensin-aldosterone-system (RAAS). Aldosterone synthesis, which occurs primarily in the adrenal gland, is modulated by multiple factors, including angiotensin II and non-RAAS mediators such as adrenocorticotropic hormone (ACTH) and potassium. Aldosterone binds to mineralocorticoid receptors in both epithelial (e.g., kidney) and nonepithelial (e.g., heart, blood vessels, brain) tissues and increases blood pressure through induction of sodium resorption and possibly other mechanisms.

Eplerenone has been shown to produce sustained increases in plasma renin and serum aldosterone, consistent with the inhibition of the negative regulatory feedback of aldosterone on renin secretion. The resulting increased plasma renin activity and aldosterone circulating levels do not overcome the effect of eplerenone on blood pressure.

Eplerenone has relative selectivity in binding to recombinant human mineralocorticoid receptors compared to its binding to recombinant human glucocorticoid, progesterone, and androgen receptors.

Absorption

The area under the curve (AUC) is dose proportional over doses of 25 to 100 mg and less than proportional at doses above 100 mg. Absorption is not affected by food. The absolute bioavailability is unknown.

In elderly subjects the AUC was increased by 45%. In black patients the AUC was 26% lower.

Distribution

Volume of distribution (Vol_D): 43 to 90 L.

Protein binding

Moderate (50%); primarily bound to alpha 1–glycoproteins; does not preferentially bind to red blood cells.

Biotransformation

Eplerenone metabolism is primarily mediated via CYP3A4. No active metabolites have been identified in human plasma.

Half-life

Elimination—4 to 6 hours

Time to peak concentration

Steady state—within 2 days

Peak plasma concentration:

Peak plasma concentration: 1.5 hours after oral administration

Peak plasma concentration (C_{max}) is dose proportional over doses of 25 to 100 mg and less than proportional at doses above 100 mg.

The C_{max} was increased by 22% in elderly subjects at steady state and was 19% lower in black patients.

Time to peak effect

Maximal antihypertensive effects achieved within 4 weeks.

Elimination

Apparent plasma clearance: approximately 10 L per hour.

Less than 5% is recovered as unchanged drug in the urine and feces.

Renal: 67%

Fecal: 32%

In hemodialysis, eplerenone was not removed.

Precautions to Consider

Tumorigenicity

There was no drug-related tumor response in heterozygous P53 deficient mice. Increases in benign thyroid tumors were observed after 2 years in both male and female rats administered eplerenone. However, this appears to be rodent-specific and the effect has not been seen in humans.

Mutagenicity

Eplerenone was non-genotoxic in the following assays: *in vitro* bacterial mutagenesis, *in vitro* mammalian cell mutagenesis, *in vitro* chromosomal aberration, *in vivo* rat bone marrow micronucleus formation, and *in vivo/ex vivo* unscheduled DNA synthesis in rat liver.

Pregnancy/Reproduction

Fertility—Male rats treated with eplerenone at 1000 mg per kg per day for 10 weeks (17 times a human therapeutic dose) had decreased weights of seminal vesicles and epididymides and slightly decreased fertility.

Dose-related prostate atrophy was observed in dogs administered 15 mg per kilogram of body weight per day and higher (AUC 5 times that at the 100-mg per day human therapeutic dose). The prostate atrophy was reversible after daily treatment for 1 year. There was no decline in libido, sexual performance, or semen quality in the dogs with prostrate atrophy.

Pregnancy—Adequate and well controlled studies in humans have not been done. Eplerenone should be used during pregnancy only if the potential benefit justifies the potential risk to the fetus.

Studies in animals have not shown that eplerenone causes teratogenic effects in the fetus. However, decreased body weight in maternal rabbits and increased rabbit fetal resorptions and post-implantation loss were observed at the highest administered dosage (up to 32 [rats] and 31 [rabbits] times the human AUC for the 100-mg per day human therapeutic dose).

FDA Pregnancy Category B

Breast-feeding

It is unknown whether eplerenone is distributed into breast milk. However, preclinical data show that eplerenone and/or metabolites are present in rat breast milk. A decision should be made whether to discontinue nursing or discontinue the drug taking into account the importance of the drug to mother.

Pediatrics

Appropriate studies have not been performed on the relationship of age to the effects of eplerenone in the pediatric population. Safety and efficacy have not been established.

Geriatrics

Although appropriate studies on the relationship of age to the effects of eplerenone have not been performed in the geriatric population, geriatrics-specific problems are not expected to limit the usefulness of eplerenone in the elderly. However, elderly patients are more likely to have age-related renal function impairment or hepatic function impairment, which may require careful monitoring of the patient for adverse effects, especially hyperkalemia.

Geriatric patients show increases in C_{max} and AUC when compared to younger patients. No overall differences in safety or effectiveness were observed between geriatric patients and younger patients.

Pharmacogenetics

C_{max} and AUC appear to be lower in the black population.

Drug interactions and/or related problems

The following drug interactions and/or related problems have been selected on the basis of their potential clinical significance (possible mechanism in parentheses where appropriate)—not necessarily inclusive (» = major clinical significance):

Eplerenone is not an inhibitor of CYP1A2, CYP3A4, CYP2C19, CYP2C9, or CYP2D6.

Note: Combinations containing any of the following medications, depending on the amount present, may also interact with this medication.

Allopurinol or
Colchicine or
Probenecid or
Sulfinpyrazone
(may raise the concentration of blood uric acid; dosage adjustment of antigout medications may be necessary to control hyperuricemia and gout)

» Angiotensin-converting enzyme (ACE) inhibitors or
» Angiotensin II receptor antagonists
(monitor for increases in serum potassium; may lead to hyperkalemia)

CYP3A4 inducers such as:
St. Johns Wort
(may case a small decrease in eplerenone AUC)

» CYP3A4 inhibitors, less potent including:
» Erythromycin or
» Fluconazole or
» Saquinavir or
» Verapamil
(concomitant use of less potent inhibitors of CYP450 3A4 with eplerenone may result in increased concentrations of eplerenone; eplerenone dosage reduction is recommended while the patient is receiving less potent CYP450 3A4 inhibitors)

» CYP3A4 inhibitors, potent including:
» Itraconazole or
» Ketoconazole
(Concomitant use of potent inhibitors of CYP450 3A4 with eplerenone is contraindicated)

Grapefruit juice
(may cause a small increase in exposure)

Hypotension-producing medications, other (See *Appendix II*)
(antihypertensive and/or diuretic effects may be potentiated when these medications are used concurrently with eplerenone; although some antihypertensive and/or diuretic combinations are frequently used for therapeutic advantage, dosage adjustments may be necessary during concurrent use)

Lithium
(lithium toxicity has been reported in patients receiving lithium concomitantly with diuretics and ACE inhibitors; serum lithium concentrations should be monitored if eplerenone is administered concomitantly with lithium)

Nonsteroidal anti-inflammatory drugs (NSAIDs)
(administration of other potassium-sparing antihypertensives with NSAIDs has been shown to reduce the antihypertensive effects and might result in hyperkalemia in patients with impaired renal function; monitor patients to determine whether the desired effect on blood pressure is obtained)

» Potassium sparing diuretics including:
Amiloride or
Spironolactone or
Triamterene
(these medications should not be used concomitantly with eplerenone)

» Potassium supplements or
» Salt substitutes containing potassium
(these medications should not be used concomitantly with eplerenone)

Sympathomimetics
(may reduce the antihypertensive effects of eplerenone; the patient should be carefully monitored to confirm that the desired effect is being obtained)

Laboratory value alterations

The following have been selected on the basis of their potential clinical significance (possible effect in parentheses where appropriate)—not necessarily inclusive (» = major clinical significance).

With physiology/laboratory test values
Alanine aminotransferase (ALT[SGPT]), serum or
Blood urea nitrogen (BUN) or
Cholesterol, serum or
Creatinine, serum or
Gamma glutamyl transpeptidase (GGT) or
Potassium, serum or
Triglycerides, serum or
Uric acid
(may be increased; increases appear to be dose related)

Sodium, serum
(may be decreased; decreases appear to be dose related)

Medical considerations/Contraindications

The medical considerations/contraindications included have been selected on the basis of their potential clinical significance (reasons given in parentheses where appropriate)—not necessarily inclusive (» = major clinical significance).

Except under special circumstances, this medication should not be used when the following medical problem exists:

» Diabetes mellitus, Type II with microalbuminuria
(therapy is contraindicated; increased risk of developing persistent hyperkalemia)

» Potassium, serum high
(therapy is not recommended in those with serum potassium levels greater than 5.5 mEq per L; may result in serious sometimes fatal arrhythmias)

» Renal impairment, defined as
» Creatinine clearance, less than 50 mL per minute or
» Creatinine, serum greater than 2 mg per dL in males or 1.8 mg per dL in females
(therapy is contraindicated)

Risk-benefit should be considered when the following medical problems exist:

Hepatic impairment, mild to moderate
(C_{max} and AUC may be increased)

» Hepatic impairment, severe
(Safety and efficacy of eplerenone have not been established)

» Hypersensitivity to eplerenone

Patient monitoring

The following may be especially important in patient monitoring (other tests may be warranted in some patients, depending on condition; » = major clinical significance):

Blood pressure measurements
(recommended at periodic intervals in patients being treated for hypertension; selected patients may be trained to perform blood pressure measurements at home and report the results at regular physician visits)

» Potassium, serum
(periodic monitoring is recommended in patients at risk for the development of hyperkalemia, including patients receiving concomitant ACE inhibitors or angiotensin II receptor antagonists, until the effect of eplerenone is established; during clinical trials serum potassium levels were monitored every 2 weeks for the first 1 to 2 months and then monthly thereafter)

Side/Adverse Effects

The following side/adverse effects have been selected on the basis of their potential clinical significance (possible signs and symptoms in parentheses where appropriate)—not necessarily inclusive:

Those indicating need for medical attention

Incidence less frequent

Albuminuria (cloudy urine); ***hypercholesterolemia*** (large amount of cholesterol in the blood); ***hypertriglyceridemia*** (large amount of triglyceride in the blood)

Incidence unknown

Angina pectoris (arm, back or jaw pain; chest pain or discomfort; chest tightness or heaviness; fast or irregular heartbeat; shortness of breath; sweating; nausea); ***dizziness; headache; hyperkalemia*** (abdominal pain; confusion; irregular heartbeat; nausea or vomiting; nervousness; numbness or tingling in hands, feet, or lips; shortness of breath; difficult breathing; weakness or heaviness of legs); ***myocardial infarction*** (chest pain or discomfort; pain or discomfort in arms, jaw, back or neck; shortness of breath; nausea; sweating; vomiting)

Note: The most common reasons for discontinuation of eplerenone were headache, dizziness, angina pectoris/myocardial infarction, and increased GGT. Therapy was discontinued due to an adverse event in 3% of patients treated with eplerenone and 3% of patients given placebo.

Those indicating need for medical attention only if they continue or are bothersome

Incidence less frequent

Abdominal pain (stomach pain); ***abnormal vaginal bleeding; diarrhea; coughing; fatigue*** (unusual tiredness or weakness); ***gynecomastia*** (swelling of the breasts or breast soreness in both females and males); ***influenza-like symptoms*** (chills; cough; diarrhea; fever; general feeling of discomfort or illness; headache; joint pain; loss of appetite; muscle aches and pains); ***mastodynia*** (breast pain)

Overdose

For more information on the management of overdose or unintentional ingestion, **contact a poison control center** (see *Poison Control Center Listing*).

Clinical effects of overdose

The most likely manifestations of human overdosage would be hypotension or hyperkalemia

Treatment of overdose

To decrease absorption—
Eplerenone has been shown to bind extensively to charcoal

To enhance elimination—
Eplerenone cannot be removed by hemodialysis

Monitoring—
Monitor blood pressure, weight, and electrocardiogram
Patients should be monitored for fluid status and serum electrolytes (particularly sodium and potassium).

Supportive care—
Treatment should be symptomatic and supportive.
Patients in whom intentional overdose is confirmed or suspected should be referred for psychiatric consultation.

Patient Consultation

As an aid to patient consultation, refer to *Advice for the Patient, Eplerenone (Systemic).*

In providing consultation, consider emphasizing the following selected information (» = major clinical significance):

Before using this medication

» Conditions affecting use, especially:
Hypersensitivity to eplerenone.
Pregnancy—Should be used during pregnancy only if the potential benefit justifies the potential risk to the fetus.
FDA Pregnancy Category B
Breast-feeding—Decision should be made whether to discontinue nursing or discontinue eplerenone, taking into account the importance of the drug to the mother
Use in the elderly—Greater sensitivity to eplerenone in elderly patients cannot be ruled out.
Other medications, especially angiotensin converting enzyme inhibitors, angiotensin II receptor antagonists, CYP3A4 inhibitors especially ketoconazole and itraconazole, potassium sparing diuretics including amiloride, spironolactone, or triamterene, and potassium supplements.
Other medical problems, especially type II diabetes mellitus with microalbuminuria, elevated serum potassium concentrations, severe hepatic function impairment, and renal function impairment.

Proper use of this medication

» Proper dosing especially decreased dose with concomitant CYP3A4 inhibitors.
Proper storage

Precautions while using this medication

» Avoiding potassium supplements or salt substitutes containing potassium

Asking your doctor or pharmacist before taking amiloride, spironolactone, triamterene, ketoconazole, or itraconazole.

» May cause dizziness

Side/adverse effects

Signs of potential side effects, especially albuminuria, angina pectoris, dizziness, headache, hyperkalemia, hypercholesterolemia, hypertriglyceridemia, and myocardial infarction

General Dosing Information

Eplerenone may be used alone or in combination with other antihypertensive agents.

The full therapeutic effect of eplerenone is apparent within four weeks.

Diet/Nutrition

Patients should not use potassium supplements,or salt substitutes containing potassium without consulting their healthcare professional.

Oral Dosage Forms

EPLERENONE TABLETS

Usual adult dose

Antihypertensive—
Oral, initially 50 mg once daily. For patients with an inadequate blood pressure response to 50 mg once daily the dosage should be increased to 50 mg twice daily. The full therapeutic effect of eplerenone is apparent within 4 weeks

Note: For patients receiving weak CYP3A4 inhibitors, such as erythromycin, saquinavir, verapamil, and fluconazole, the starting dose should be reduced to 25 mg once daily.

Usual adult prescribing limits

Up to 100 mg daily.

Usual pediatric dose

Safety and efficacy have not been established.

Usual geriatric dose

See *Usual adult dose.*

Usual geriatric prescribing limits

See *Usual adult prescribing limits.*

Strength(s) usually available

U.S.—
25 mg (Rx) [*Inspra* (lactose; microcrystalline cellulose; croscarmellose sodium; hydroxypropyl methylcellulose; sodium lauryl sulfate; talc; magnesium stearate; titanium dioxide; polyethylene glycol; polysorbate 80; iron oxide yellow; iron oxide red)].
50 mg (Rx) [*Inspra* (lactose; microcrystalline cellulose; croscarmellose sodium; hydroxypropyl methylcellulose; sodium lauryl sulfate; talc; magnesium stearate; titanium dioxide; polyethylene glycol; polysorbate 80; iron oxide red)].

100 mg (Rx) [*INSPRA* (lactose; microcrystalline cellulose; croscarmellose sodium; hydroxypropyl methylcellulose; sodium lauryl sulfate; talc; magnesium stearate; titanium dioxide; polyethylene glycol; polysorbate 80; iron oxide red)].

Canada—

Not commercially available

Packaging and storage

Store at 25 °C (77 °F), excursions permitted to 15-30 °C (59-86 °F).

Auxiliary labeling

- May cause dizziness
- Do not use a salt substitute containing potassium

Developed: 04/10/2003

EPOETIN Systemic

VA CLASSIFICATION (Primary): BL400

Commonly used brand name(s): *Epogen; Eprex; Procrit.*

Other commonly used names are human erythropoietin, recombinant; EPO; and r-HuEPO.

Note: For a listing of dosage forms and brand names by country availability, see *Dosage Forms* section(s).

Category

Antianemic.

Indications

Note: Bracketed information in the *Indications* section refers to uses that are not included in U.S. product labeling.

Accepted

Anemia associated with chronic renal failure (treatment)—Epoetin is indicated for the treatment of anemia associated with chronic renal failure in adults and children. It is used for adults and children who do not require dialysis as well as adults and children receiving dialysis (continuous peritoneal dialysis, high-flux short-time hemodialysis, or conventional hemodialysis). However, in patients not receiving dialysis, use of epoetin should be limited to individuals having hemoglobin less than 10 g per dL.

Anemia, severe, associated with zidovudine therapy in human immunodeficiency virus (HIV) –infected patients (treatment)—Epoetin is indicated for the treatment of severe anemia associated with zidovudine therapy in HIV-infected adults and children. Epoetin is not indicated for the treatment of anemia in HIV-infected patients due to other factors.

Epoetin is effective in decreasing the transfusion requirement and increasing the red blood cell level of anemic, HIV-infected patients treated with zidovudine, when the endogenous serum erythropoietin level is ≤ 500 mUnits per mL and when patients are receiving a dose of zidovudine ≤ 4200 mg per week.

Anemia associated with chemotherapy in cancer patients (treatment)—Epoetin is indicated for the treatment of anemia in adults and children with nonmyeloid malignancies in which the anemia is due to the effect of concomitantly administered chemotherapy.

Epoetin is indicated to decrease the need for transfusions in patients who will be receiving concomitant chemotherapy for a minimum of 2 months. Epoetin is **not** indicated for the treatment of anemia in cancer patients due to other factors such as iron or folate deficiencies, hemolysis, or gastrointestinal bleeding, which should be managed appropriately.

Blood transfusions, allogeneic, in anemic surgery patients, reduction of—Epoetin is indicated for use in anemic patients (hemoglobin > 10 to ≤ 13 grams per dL) who are scheduled to undergo elective, noncardiac, nonvascular surgery, to reduce the need for allogeneic blood transfusions. It is indicated for patients who are at high risk for perioperative transfusions with significant, anticipated blood loss. Epoetin is not indicated for anemic patients who are willing to donate autologous blood.

The safety of the perioperative use of epoetin has been studied only in patients who are receiving anticoagulant prophylaxis.

[Anemia associated with frequent blood donation (prophylaxis)]—Epoetin is indicated to prevent anemia in patients who donate blood and to increase the capacity for donation (for future autologous transfusion) prior to elective surgery. The medication has been found to be effective in females, patients with low packed-cell volumes due to anemia or small body size, and patients requiring donation of 4 units or more of blood.

[Anemia associated with malignancy (treatment)]—Epoetin is indicated for treatment of chronic anemia associated with neoplastic diseases.

[Anemia associated with myelodysplastic syndromes (treatment)[1]—Epoetin is indicated for treatment of anemia associated with myelodysplastic syndromes in selected patients. (Evidence rating: IIID)

[Anemia associated with the management of hepatitis C (treatment)][1]—Epoetin is indicated for the treatment of anemia in patients with hepatitis C virus infection who are being treated with the combination of ribavirin and interferon alfa or ribavirin and peginterferon alfa.

[Anemia, in critically ill patients (treatment)][1]—Epoetin is indicated for the treatment of anemia in critically ill patients in hospital intensive care units. Epoetin therapy has been shown to increase hematocrit values and hemoglobin concentrations and to reduce the need for red blood cell transfusions in this patient population.

Note: Epoetin is not a substitute for blood transfusions, which may be required for the emergency treatment of severe anemia. However, with chronic use, epoetin reduces the need for repeated maintenance blood transfusions.

[1]Not included in Canadian product labeling.

Pharmacology/Pharmacokinetics

Physicochemical characteristics

Molecular weight—Epoetin alfa: 30,400 daltons.

Mechanism of action/Effect

Epoetin alfa is a glycoprotein, produced by recombinant DNA technology, that contains 165 amino acids in a sequence identical to that of endogenous human erythropoietin. Recombinant epoetin has the same biological activity as the endogenous hormone, which induces erythropoiesis by stimulating the division and differentiation of committed erythroid progenitor cells, including burst-forming units–erythroid, colony-forming units–erythroid, erythroblasts, and reticulocytes, in bone marrow. Erythropoietin also induces the release of reticulocytes from the bone marrow into the blood stream, where they mature into erythrocytes.

Endogenous erythropoietin is produced primarily in the kidney. The anemia associated with chronic renal failure is caused primarily by inadequate production of the hormone. Administration of epoetin corrects the erythropoietin deficiency in patients with chronic renal failure. Epoetin also stimulates red blood cell production in patients who do not have a documented erythropoietin deficiency, i.e., patients with normal or slightly elevated concentrations of endogenous erythropoietin. However, it may not be effective in patients who are anemic despite having significantly elevated concentrations of erythropoietin.

Other actions/effects

The increase in hematocrit induced by epoetin may increase blood viscosity and peripheral vascular resistance, leading to a rise in blood pressure. The medication does not appear to have a direct pressor effect.

Epoetin may correct the bleeding tendency associated with chronic renal failure, which may be caused partially by red blood cell deficiency. However, the medication may also increase the thrombotic tendency in some patients.

Correction of anemia by epoetin may result in an improved feeling of well-being; increased appetite; relief of anemia-induced fatigue, tachycardia, headache, weakness, or angina pectoris; increased exercise tolerance and physical activity; and improved sleep, sexual function, and cognitive function.

Administration of epoetin alfa apparently does not induce antibody formation, because antibodies have not been detected in the blood of patients treated with the recombinant hormone for up to 12 months.

Endogenous erythropoietin production may be suppressed by chronic administration of recombinant epoetin.

Half-life

Elimination—May average 4 to 13 hours following intravenous or subcutaneous administration. The elimination half-life is generally higher after the first few doses (> 7.5 hours) than after 2 or more weeks of treatment (6.2 hours after 7 doses; 4.6 hours after 24 doses).

Note: The pharmacokinetic profile of epoetin alfa in children and adolescents is similar to that of adults.

Onset of action

Increase in reticulocyte count (initial effect)—Within 7 to 10 days.

Increase in red cell count, hematocrit, hemoglobin—Clinically significant increases generally occur in 2 to 6 weeks. The rate and extent of the response are dependent on dosage and availability of iron stores. Over a 2-week period, administration of 50 Units per kg of body weight

3 times weekly increases the hematocrit by an average of 1.5 points, administration of 100 Units per kg of body weight 3 times weekly increases the hematocrit by an average of 2.5 points, and administration of 150 Units per kg of body weight 3 times weekly increases the hematocrit by an average of 3.5 points.

Time to peak concentration

Single intravenous dose—15 minutes.

Single subcutaneous dose—5 to 24 hours. Peak concentrations may be maintained for 12 to 16 hours, and detectable quantities are present for at least 24 hours, after administration.

Note: With repeated subcutaneous administration, peak concentrations are achieved and maintained over the same time periods as with single subcutaneous doses, but are substantially lower than those achieved by a single dose. However, the lower epoetin concentrations are sufficient for achieving, and even lower concentrations are sufficient for maintaining, the desired response.

Time to peak effect

Increase in hematocrit to target area—Dose dependent; usually within 2 months with administration of 100 or 150 Units per kg of body weight 3 times weekly.

Duration of action

The hematocrit may begin to decrease about 2 weeks after treatment has been discontinued.

Precautions to Consider

Carcinogenicity

The carcinogenic potential of epoetin alfa has not been investigated.

Mutagenicity

Epoetin alfa does not induce bacterial gene mutation (Ames test), chromosomal aberrations in mammalian cells, micronuclei in mice, or gene mutation at the HGPRT locus. Also, examination of the bone marrow of patients receiving epoetin for up to 8 weeks has revealed no evidence of karyotypic abnormalities or alteration in the sister chromatid exchange rate.

Pregnancy/Reproduction

Fertility—Administration of 100 or 500 Units per kg of body weight intravenously to male and female rats showed a trend toward slightly increased fetal wastage.

Pregnancy—Adequate and well-controlled studies in humans have not been done. However, administration of 500 Units per kg of body weight to female rats caused decreases in weight gain, delays in the appearance of abdominal hair, delayed eyelid opening, delayed ossification, and decreases in the number of caudal vertebrae in first-generation fetuses. Administration of up to 500 Units per kg of body weight to female rabbits from Day 6 to Day 18 of gestation produced no adverse effects.

FDA Pregnancy Category C.

Breast-feeding

It is not known whether epoetin alfa is excreted in human breast milk. However, in animal studies, administration of up to 500 Units per kg of body weight to female rats during lactation produced no adverse effects in the pups.

Pediatrics

Neonates: Safety and effectiveness has not been established in pediatric patients less than 1 month old.

Note: The multidose vials contain benzyl alcohol, which is not recommended for use in neonates.

Pediatric patients on dialysis: Epoetin alfa is indicated in infants 1 month to 2 years and children 2 years to 12 years for the treatment of anemia associated with chronic renal failure requiring dialysis. There was no increased risk to pediatric chronic renal failure patients on dialysis when compared to the safety profile of epoetin alfa in adult chronic renal failure patients.

Pediatric patients not requiring dialysis: Epoetin alfa has been used in 133 pediatric patients, ages 3 months to 20 years, with anemia associated with chronic renal failure not requiring dialysis. Reductions in transfusion requirements and dose-dependent increases in hematocrit and hemoglobin were observed.

Pediatric HIV-infected patients: Epoetin alfa has been used in 20 zidovudine-treated anemic HIV-infected pediatric patients, ages 8 months to 17 years. Decreases or elimination of blood transfusion requirements, increases in hemoglobin levels, and increases in reticulocyte counts were observed.

Pediatric cancer patients on chemotherapy: Epoetin alfa has been used in 64 anemic pediatric cancer patients, ages 6 months to 18 years. Decreases in transfusion requirements and increases in hemoglobin were observed.

Adolescents

Pediatric patients on dialysis: Epoetin alfa is indicated in adolescents 12 years to 16 years for the treatment of anemia associated with chronic renal failure requiring dialysis. There was no increased risk to pediatric chronic renal failure patients on dialysis when compared to the safety profile of epoetin alfa in adult chronic renal failure patients.

Geriatrics

No published geriatrics-specific information is available.

Drug interactions and/or related problems

The following drug interactions and/or related problems have been selected on the basis of their potential clinical significance (possible mechanism in parentheses where appropriate)—not necessarily inclusive (» = major clinical significance):

Note: Combinations containing any of the following medications, depending on the amount present, may also interact with this medication.

Antihypertensive agents
(epoetin may increase blood pressure, possibly to hypertensive levels, especially when the hematocrit is rising rapidly; more intensive antihypertensive therapy [increase in dosage, administration of additional and/or more potent medications] may be required to control blood pressure)

Heparin
(an increase in heparin dosage may be required in patients receiving hemodialysis, because epoetin-induced increases in red blood cell volume may lead to blood clotting in the dialyzer and/or vascular access [arteriovenous shunt])

Iron supplements
(iron requirement may be increased as existing iron stores are used for erythropoiesis; some clinicians recommend supplementation for all patients who are not overloaded with iron because of frequent blood transfusions; in some patients, oral iron supplementation may be insufficient and intravenous iron dextran may be required)

Laboratory value alterations

The following have been selected on the basis of their potential clinical significance (possible effect in parentheses where appropriate)—not necessarily inclusive (» = major clinical significance).

With physiology/laboratory test values

Bleeding time
(may be decreased; also, the prolonged bleeding time associated with chronic renal failure in some patients may be corrected during epoetin treatment)

Blood pressure
(may be increased, possibly to hypertensive levels in patients with *chronic renal failure*)

Blood urea nitrogen (BUN) and
Serum creatinine concentrations and
Serum phosphorus concentrations and
Serum potassium concentrations and
Serum sodium concentrations and
Serum uric acid concentrations
(may be increased; however, whether the increases reported in patients with chronic renal failure are caused by a direct effect of epoetin on the renal clearance of these substances or the efficacy of dialysis and/or by noncompliance with required dietary restrictions, which may occur when improvement of anemia increases the patient's appetite and feeling of well-being, has not been established)

Iron concentration and
Serum ferritin
(usually are decreased, unless the patient is receiving adequate iron supplementation; as iron stores are utilized for hemoglobin synthesis, functional iron deficiency may occur and lead to a decrease or loss of epoetin efficacy)

Platelet counts and
White blood cell counts
(may be increased, but usually remain within expected range)

Medical considerations/Contraindications

The medical considerations/contraindications included have been selected on the basis of their potential clinical significance (reasons given in parentheses where appropriate)—not necessarily inclusive (» = major clinical significance).

Except under special circumstances, this medication should not be used when the following medical problems exist:

» Hypersensitivity to human albumin or to mammalian cell–derived products
(risk of a serious allergic reaction to the albumin present in the commercial formulation or to the recombinant product itself)

» Hypertension, uncontrolled
(may be exacerbated, especially during the early phase of treatment or when the hematocrit is rising; a few cases of hypertensive encephalopathy and seizure have occurred in patients with poorly controlled blood pressure during epoetin therapy; initiation of therapy should be delayed until blood pressure is adequately controlled)

» Red cell aplasia, pure
(epoetin should not be administered to patients with pure red cell aplasia [PRCA] secondary to neutralizing antibodies to erythropoietin; patients should not be switched to another product as anti-erythropoietin antibodies cross-react with other erythropoietins)

Risk-benefit should be considered when the following medical problems exist:

Any condition that may decrease or delay the response to epoetin alfa, such as:
Aluminum intoxication
Folic acid deficiency
Hemolysis
Infection
Inflammation

» Cardiac problems including:
» Congestive heart failure
» Coronary artery bypass surgery, not hemodialysis patient
» Ischemic heart disease or
» Thrombosis, at risk for
(treatment may lead to increased risk for thrombotic events and mortality in patients with clinically evident cardiac disease or in patients at risk for thrombosis; the cause of this effect is unknown)

Iron deficiency
(virtually all patients will eventually require supplemental iron therapy)

Malignancy
(the possibility that epoetin can act as a growth factor for any tumor type, particularly myeloid malignancies, cannot be excluded)

Osteitis fibrosa cystica
Occult blood loss
Vitamin B_{12} deficiency

Cardiovascular system abnormalities caused by hypertension or
» Hypertension, previous, controlled
(increased risk of hypertension in *chronic renal failure patients*, which may lead to hypertensive encephalopathy)

Hematologic disorders, such as:
Hypercoagulable disorders
Myelodysplastic syndromes
Sickle cell anemia
Vascular disease
(caution and close monitoring are recommended because of an increased thrombotic tendency or other potential complications associated with increases in blood viscosity and peripheral vascular resistance that may occur as a result of epoetin-induced increases in hematocrit)
(the safety and efficacy of epoetin therapy in patients with hematologic disorders have not been determined; also, the presence of myelodysplastic disorders may slow or decrease the bone marrow response to the medication)

Porphyria
(may be exacerbated by epoetin therapy)

Seizure disorders, history of or
Seizures, at increased risk for
(seizures not associated with hypertensive encephalopathy have been reported during epoetin therapy in patients with *chronic renal failure*; although a causal association has not been established [in clinical studies, seizures occurred at the same rate in both epoetin-treated and placebo-treated patients with chronic renal failure], caution is recommended)

Patient monitoring

The following may be especially important in patient monitoring (other tests may be warranted in some patients, depending on condition; » = major clinical significance):

» Blood pressure determinations
(recommended at frequent intervals because epoetin may increase blood pressure, possibly to hypertensive levels; although the risk may be greatest in patients with pre-existing hypertension [even if optimally controlled at the time epoetin therapy is initiated], epoetin may also increase blood pressure in previously normotensive patients; control of blood pressure is essential because a few cases of hypertensive encephalopathy and seizure have occurred during epoetin therapy in patients with poorly controlled hypertension and because hypertension may be especially hazardous to patients with chronic renal failure, who are predisposed to cardiovascular complications including myocardial ischemia, myocardial infarction, heart failure, and/or stroke; initiation of or increase in antihypertensive therapy, reduction in dosage or temporary withdrawal of epoetin alfa, or even phlebotomy may be required to control hypertension)

Complete blood count with differentialand
Platelet count
(recommended periodically because increases in white blood cell and platelet counts have been reported, although the counts have generally remained within the normal range)

Fluid and electrolyte balance
(should be monitored closely, especially in patients with chronic renal failure not on dialysis; an improved sense of well-being may obscure the need to initiate dialysis in some patients)

» Hemoglobin
(should not exceed 12 g/dL in men or women)
(determinations recommended prior to initiation of therapy, then twice a week during therapy in chronic renal failure patients and once a week in HIV and cancer patients as a guide to efficacy and dosage of epoetin; because a too-rapid rise in hemoglobin may be associated with an increased risk of adverse effects in patients with chronic renal failure, it is recommended that epoetin dosage be reduced if the hemoglobin increase exceeds 1 g/dL in any 2-week period; for hemoglobin-related dosage adjustment information based on the indication, see *Usual adult and adolescent dose* section; after the hematocrit has been stabilized in the target range [10 to 12 g/dL], the frequency of monitoring may be decreased)
(after each dosage adjustment, determinations should be performed twice a week in chronic renal failure patients and once a week in HIV and cancer patients for at least 2 to 6 weeks, until the hematocrit has stabilized at the new level)

» Iron status, including:
Serum ferritin
Transferrin saturation
(determination recommended prior to initiation of therapy, because epoetin's efficacy is decreased when the available iron is insufficient to support erythropoiesis; serum ferritin should be at least 100 nanograms per mL, and transferrin saturation at least 20%, before therapy is initiated)
(monitoring recommended at regular intervals throughout therapy to determine whether iron supplementation should be initiated or increased, because incorporation of iron into hemoglobin may decrease iron stores to the point of functional iron deficiency, leading to a decrease or loss of epoetin efficacy)

Neurologic evaluation
(recommended periodically, especially during the first 90 days of therapy, to detect premonitory signs indicative of a risk of seizures; although a causal association between the rate of rise of hemoglobin and seizures is uncertain, it is recommended that the dose of epoetin be decreased if the hemoglobin increase exceeds 1 g/dL in any 2-week period)

» Renal function, including:
Blood urea nitrogen (BUN) and
Serum creatinine and
Serum phosphorous and
Serum potassium and
Serum sodium and
Serum uric acid
(close monitoring recommended in patients with renal function impairment to determine the need for initiating or increasing dialysis; however, whether the increases in concentrations of these substances that have been reported during epoetin therapy are caused by a direct effect of the hormone on renal function or the efficacy of dialysis and/or by noncompliance with dietary restrictions required by patients with chronic renal failure, which may occur when improvement of anemia produces increased appetite and feeling of well-being, has not been established)

Side/Adverse Effects

Note: Some of the side effects listed below are known sequelae of chronic renal failure; therefore, a causal association with epoetin therapy has not always been established.

Menses have resumed during treatment in some female patients. Therefore, the risk of pregnancy should be evaluated and an appropriate method of contraception instituted if necessary.

There is a potential for immunogenicity with epoetin administration. Pure red cell aplasia (PRCA) has been observed in patients treated with recombinant erythropoietins and has been reported predominantly in patients with chronic renal failure. Any patient with loss of response to epoetin should be evaluated for the etiology of loss of effect. Epoetin should be discontinued in any patient with evidence of pure red cell aplasia and should be evaluated for the presence of binding and neutralizing antibodies to epoetin, native erythropoietin, and any other recombinant erythropoietin administered to the patient. Amgen/Ortho Biotech Products should be contacted to assist in this evaluation.

Products formulated with albumin carry an extremely remote risk for transmission of viral diseases, and theoretically, the Creutzfeldt-Jakob disease.

The following side/adverse effects have been selected on the basis of their potential clinical significance (possible signs and symptoms in parentheses where appropriate)—not necessarily inclusive:

Those indicating need for medical attention

Incidence less frequent

Thrombotic events including: cerebrovascular accident (blurred vision; headache; sudden and severe inability to speak; seizures; slurred speech; temporary blindness; weakness in arm and/or leg on one side of the body, sudden and severe); ***myocardial infarction; non-fatal*** (chest pain or discomfort; pain or discomfort in arms, jaw, back or neck, shortness of breath; nausea; sweating; vomiting); ***pulmonary embolism*** (anxiety; chest pain; cough; fainting; fast heartbeat; sudden shortness of breath or troubled breathing; dizziness or lightheadedness); ***vascular access thrombosis*** (severe headaches of sudden onset, sudden loss of coordination; pains in chest, groin, or legs, especially calves of legs; sudden onset of shortness of breath for no apparent reason; sudden onset of slurred speech; sudden vision changes)

For treatment of anemia in chronic renal failure patients

Incidence more frequent

Chest pain; edema (swelling of face, fingers, ankles, feet, or lower legs; weight gain); ***headache***—may rarely indicate hypertensive encephalopathy; ***increased blood pressure***—may reach hypertensive levels and, rarely, lead to cerebral ischemia or to hypertensive encephalopathy (blurred vision or other change in vision, grand mal seizures, headache); ***polycythemia***—may lead to hyperviscosity resulting in increased peripheral vascular resistance, hypertension, and thrombotic complications, e.g., clotting of arteriovenous (AV) shunts and/or dialyzer, and, rarely, transient ischemic attacks or cerebrovascular accident or myocardial infarction

Incidence rare

Pure red cell aplasia (fever and sore throat; pale skin; unusual bleeding or bruising; unusual tiredness or weakness); ***skin rash or hives; thrombo-embolic events including; thrombophlebitis, migratory*** (changes in skin color; pain, tenderness, swelling of foot or leg); ***thrombosis, microvascular*** (tenderness, pain, swelling, warmth, skin discoloration, and prominent superficial veins over affected area); ***thrombosis, retinal artery*** (changes in vision; double vision; migraine headache; partial or complete loss of vision in eye)

For treatment of anemia in chronic renal failure requiring dialysis (in addition to those listed above)

Incidence more frequent

Fever; hyperkalemia; infection, dialysis access (redness or pain at the dialysis access site; fever)—in pediatric patients with chronic renal failure; ***shortness of breath; tachycardia*** (fast heartbeat); ***upper respiratory tract infection*** (cough, fever, sneezing, or sore throat)

For treatment of zidovudine-treated HIV-infected patients

Incidence more frequent

Fever; headache; shortness of breath; skin rash or hives

Incidence less frequent or rare; ***Seizures*** (convulsions)—may be related to underlying pathology

For treatment of cancer patients on chemotherapy

Incidence more frequent

Edema (swelling of face, fingers, ankles, feet, or lower legs; weight gain); ***fever; shortness of breath; upper respiratory tract infection*** (cough, fever, sneezing, or sore throat)

For treatment of surgical patients

Incidence more frequent

Deep venous thrombosis (swelling or pain in leg); ***edema*** (swelling of face, fingers, ankles, feet, or lower legs; weight gain); ***fever; headache; increased blood pressure; skin rash or hives; urinary tract infection*** (blood in urine; lower back pain; pain or burning while urinating)

Those indicating need for medical attention only if they continue or are bothersome

Incidence more frequent

Diarrhea; dizziness; nausea and vomiting

For treatment of anemia in chronic renal failure patients (in addition to those listed above)

Administration site reaction (itching or stinging at site of injection); ***asthenia*** (loss of strength or energy; muscle pain or weakness); ***fatigue*** (general feeling of tiredness and weakness); ***influenza-like syndrome, mild*** (bone or joint pain; muscle aches; chills; shivering; sweating)—may appear 1 to 2 hours after intravenous administration and persist for up to 12 hours

For treatment of anemia in chronic renal failure patients requiring dialysis(in addition to those listed above)

Constipation; cough; peritonitis (abdominal pain and swelling; fever; weight loss)—in children receiving peritoneal dialysis; ***pharyngitis*** (sore throat)

For treatment of zidovudine-treated HIV-infected patients

Administration site reaction (itching or stinging at site of injection); ***asthenia*** (loss of strength or energy; muscle pain or weakness); ***cough; congestion, respiratory; fatigue*** (general feeling of tiredness and weakness)

For treatment of cancer patients on chemotherapy

Asthenia (loss of strength or energy; muscle pain or weakness); ***fatigue*** (general feeling of tiredness and weakness); ***paresthesia*** (tingling, burning, or prickly sensation)

For treatment of surgical patients

Administration site reaction (itching or stinging at site of injection); ***anxiety; constipation; dyspepsia*** (stomach discomfort, upset, or pain; heartburn; belching; acid or sour stomach); ***insomnia*** (inability to sleep); ***skin pain***

Patient Consultation

As an aid to patient consultation, refer to *Advice for the Patient, Epoetin (Systemic).*

In providing consultation, consider emphasizing the following selected information (» = major clinical significance):

Before using this medication

» Conditions affecting use, especially:

Other medical problems, especially hypertension and a history of hypersensitivity to albumin or to mammalian cell–derived products, pure red cell aplasia, cardiac problems

Proper use of this medication

» Proper injection technique (if dispensed for home use)

» Proper dosing

Missed dose: Administering as soon as possible; not administering if almost time for next dose; not doubling doses

» Proper storage

Precautions while receiving this medication

Risk of seizures, especially during the first 90 days of treatment; avoiding activities that may be hazardous should a seizure occur

» Importance of keeping medical and dialysis appointments

» Importance of compliance with antihypertensive regimen (medications and diet), if prescribed, and dietary restrictions pertinent to patients with chronic renal failure

» Importance of compliance with iron or other vitamin supplementation

Side/adverse effects

Signs of potential side effects, especially chest pain, edema, headache, increased blood pressure, infection at site of dialysis access, polycythemia, skin rash or hives, migratory thrombophlebitis, microvascular thrombosis, retinal artery thrombosis, fever, hyperkalemia, shortness of breath, tachycardia, upper respiratory tract infection, seizures, deep venous thrombosis, and urinary tract infection

General Dosing Information

Epoetin alfa is administered intravenously or subcutaneously. In general, it is given intravenously to patients with an available intravenous access, i.e., patients receiving hemodialysis, and either intravenously or subcutaneously to other patients.

An increase in dosage may be required if aluminum intoxication, which is not uncommon in patients with chronic renal failure, is present.

Diet/Nutrition

Failure to achieve an adequate response to the medication, or loss of efficacy during therapy, may indicate a lack of sufficient iron to support erythropoiesis. Iron supplementation should be initiated or increased as needed. Also, folic acid and/or vitamin B_{12} deficiency may reduce or delay the response to the medication; supplementation with these nutrients may also be required.

Correction of anemia often results in increased appetite and a feeling of well-being, which, in turn, may lead to noncompliance with dietary restrictions (e.g., regulated protein, sodium, and potassium intake) that are necessary in patients with chronic renal failure. Noncompliance with such restrictions may require institution of, or an increase in, dialysis.

For treatment of adverse effects

Recommended treatment consists of the following

• For clotting of arteriovenous (AV) shunt and/or dialyzer—Clotting complications should be managed according to the dialysis center's policy and procedures. AV shunts may be cleared by use of a syringe with heparinized saline solution. If this is unsuccessful, a thrombolytic agent (streptokinase or urokinase) may be used, after allowing the effects of prior anticoagulation to diminish. Increasing heparin dosage helps prevent recurrent clotting complications.

• For hypertension—Instituting or increasing administration of antihypertensive medications. In some patients, a decrease in dosage or temporary withdrawal of epoetin and/or phlebotomy may be needed.

• For polycythemia—Decreasing the dosage of, or temporarily suspending therapy with, epoetin. In some patients, phlebotomy may be needed.

Parenteral Dosage Forms

Note: Bracketed information in the *Dosage Forms* section refers to categories of use and/or indications or dosages that are not included in U.S. product labeling.

EPOETIN ALFA, RECOMBINANT, INJECTION

Usual adult and adolescent dose

Anemia associated with chronic renal failure—

Initial: Intravenous or subcutaneous, 50 to 100 Units per kg of body weight three times a week.

Note: Some clinicians begin therapy with lower doses, e.g., 40 Units per kg of body weight three times a week.

Maintenance: Intravenous or subcutaneous, 12.5 to 525 Units per kg of body weight three times a week is the reported dose range in a multicenter trial in patients on hemodialysis to maintain their hematocrit in the suggested range. Epoetin doses of 75 to 150 Units per kg of body weight per week have been shown to maintain hematocrits of 36 to 38 percent for up to 6 months.

Note: Once-weekly subcutaneous administration of the entire week's dosage requirement may be sufficient to maintain some patients at the desired hematocrit range.

Dose adjustment:

• **Therapeutic goal:** The dosage of epoetin must be individualized to maintain the hemoglobin within the suggested target range, 10 to 12 g per dL. At the physician's discretion, the suggested target hemoglobin range may be expanded to achieve maximal patient benefit.

• **Dose reduction for hemoglobin approaching target range:** The dose of epoetin should be reduced as the hemoglobin approaches 12 g per dL. The dose should be reduced by approximately 25% if the hemoglobin is increasing and approaching 12 g per dL. The dose of epoetin should be temporarily withheld if the hemoglobin continues to increase. When the hemoglobin begins to decrease, epoetin therapy should be reinitiated at a dose approximately 25% below the previous dose.

• **Dose reduction for hemoglobin increases more than 1 g per dL in a 2-week period:** The dose of epoetin should be reduced by approximately 25% if the hemoglobin is increasing by more than 1 g per dL in any 2-week period.

• **Dose increase for inadequate response:**

—The dose may be increased if the increase in the hemoglobin is less than 1 g per dL over 4 weeks of therapy, iron stores are adequate, and hemoglobin is below the suggested target range. The dose may be increased by approximately 25% of the previous dose. Subsequent dose increases should be made at 4-week intervals until the specified hemoglobin is obtained.

—Iron stores should be re-evaluated if the hemoglobin remains below, or falls below, the suggested target range. Supplemental iron should be administered if transferrin saturation is less than 20%. Subsequent dose increases should not be made more frequently than once a month unless clinically indicated. The dose of epoetin may be increased if transferrin saturation is greater than 20%. The response time of hemoglobin to a dose increase can be 2 to 6 weeks.

• **Lack or loss of response:** Other etiologies should be considered and evaluated as clinically indicated if a patient fails to respond or fails to maintain a response.

Extended dosing: In adults there are four alternative off- label maintenance dosing regimens for patients already receiving epoetin alfa with a stable Hb level ≥ 11g/dL:

• [**Weekly dosing or:**][1]
—Subcutaneously, 10,000 Units weekly to maintain a target hemoglobin range defined as a mean Hb ≥ 11 g/dL.

• [**Every two weeks dosing or:**][1]
—Subcutaneously, 20,000 Units once every two weeks to maintain a target hemoglobin range defined as a mean Hb ≥ 11 g/dL.

• [**Every three weeks dosing or:**][1]
—Subcutaneously, 30,000 Units once every three weeks to maintain a target hemoglobin range defined as a mean Hb ≥ 11 g/dL.

• [**Every four weeks dosing:**][1]
—Subcutaneously, 40,000 Units once every four weeks to maintain a target hemoglobin range defined as a mean Hb ≥ 11 g/dL.

Anemia in zidovudine-treated HIV-infected patients—

Initial: Intravenous or subcutaneous, 100 Units per kg of body weight three times a week for eight weeks for patients with serum erythropoietin levels ≤ 500 milliUnits per mL and who are receiving a dose of zidovudine ≤ 4200 mg per week. Dosage may be increased if, after eight weeks of therapy, a satisfactory increase in hematocrit or reduction of transfusion requirements is not obtained. The dose can be increased by 50 to 100 Units per kg of body weight three times a week, with weekly monitoring of the hematocrit. Thereafter, the response should be evaluated every four to eight weeks, with the dose adjusted accordingly by 50 to 100 Units per kg of body weight three times a week. Patients who do not have a satisfactory response to a dose of 300 Units per kg of body weight three times a week are unlikely to respond to higher doses.

Note: Prior to beginning treatment with epoetin, it is recommended that the endogenous serum erythropoietin level be determined. Available evidence suggests that patients receiving zidovudine who have endogenous serum erythropoietin levels > 500 mUnits/mL are unlikely to respond to therapy with epoetin.

Maintenance: Dosage should be titrated to maintain the desired response and should be based on factors such as variations in zidovudine dose and the presence of intercurrent infectious or inflammatory episodes. Treatment should be discontinued if the hemoglobin exceeds 13 g per dL. When the hemoglobin drops to 12 g per dL, epoetin therapy may be reinitiated at a dose approximately 25% below the previous dose. The dose may be subsequently titrated to maintain the desired hemoglobin.

Anemia in cancer patients on chemotherapy—

In adults there are two epoetin dosing regimens:

• **Three times a week dosing or:**

—Initial: Subcutaneously, 150 Units per kg of body weight three times a week to achieve the suggested target hemoglobin range, 10 to 12 g per dL.

—Withhold dose: Temporarily discontinue epoetin when hemoglobin exceeds 13 g per dL. When hemoglobin falls to 12 g per dL, epoetin may be reinitiated at a dose 25% below the previous dose.

—Dose reduction: Reduce dose by 25% when hemoglobin approaches 12 g per dL or hemoglobin increases by more than 1 g per dL in any 2-week period.

—Increase dose: If response is not satisfactory (no reduction in transfusion requirements or no rise in hemoglobin after 8 weeks), increase dose to 300 Units per kg of body weight three times a week to achieve the suggested target hemoglobin range, 10 to 12 g per dL.

• **Weekly dosing:**

—Initial, Subcutaneously, 40,000 Units weekly to achieve the suggested target hemoglobin range, 10 to 12 g per dL.

—Withhold dose: Temporarily discontinue epoetin when hemoglobin exceeds 13 g per dL. When hemoglobin falls to 12 g per dL, epoetin may be reinitiated at a dose 25% below the previous dose.

—Dose reduction: Reduce dose by 25% when hemoglobin increases by more than 1 g per dL in any 2-week period.

—Increase dose: If after 4 weeks of therapy, the hemoglobin has not increased by 1 g per dL, in the absence of RBC transfusion, the epoetin dose should be increased to 60,000 Units weekly. If the patient has not responded after 4 weeks of additional therapy at 60,000 Units weekly, it is unlikely the patient will respond to higher doses of epoetin.

Note: Treatment of patients with grossly elevated serum erythropoietin levels (e.g., > 200 mUnits/mL) is not recommended.

Reduction of allogeneic blood transfusion in anemic surgery patients—

Subcutaneous, 300 Units per kg of body weight per day for ten days prior to surgery, on the day of surgery, and for four days after surgery. Alternatively, subcutaneous, 600 Units per kg of body weight once a week, twenty-one, fourteen, and seven days prior to surgery, and on the day of surgery.

Note: Prior to treatment with epoetin, it should be established that the patient's hemoglobin is > 10 and ≤ 13 grams per deciliter.

[Anemia associated with the management of hepatitis C][1]—
Subcutaneous, 40,000 Units once weekly.

[Anemia in critically ill patients][1]—
Subcutaneous, 40,000 Units once a week or 300 Units per kg of body weight every other day.

Usual adult prescribing limits

The dose should be adjusted for each patient to achieve and maintain a target hemoglobin not to exceed 12 g per dL.

Usual pediatric dose

Anemia associated with chronic renal failure requiring dialysis—
Children ages 1 month to 16 years: Initial, intravenous or subcutaneous, 50 Units per kg of body weight three times a week.
Maintenance: 49 to 447 Units per kg of body weight per week administered in divided doses three times a week or 24 to 323 Units per kg of body weight per week administered in divided doses two times a week to achieve the hematocrit in the target range of 30 to 36% in pediatric patients on hemodialysis or peritoneal dialysis in a multicenter trial.

Dose adjustment:

- **Therapeutic goal:** The dosage of epoetin must be individualized to maintain the hemoglobin within the suggested target range, 10 to 12 g per dL. At the physician's discretion, the suggested target hemoglobin range may be expanded to achieve maximal patient benefit.
- **Dose reduction for hemoglobin approaching target range:** The dose of epoetin should be reduced as the hemoglobin approaches 12 g per dL. The dose should be reduced by approximately 25% if the hemoglobin is increasing and approaching 12 g per dL. The dose of epoetin should be temporarily withheld if the hemoglobin continues to increase. When the hemoglobin begins to decrease, epoetin therapy should be reinitiated at a dose approximately 25% below the previous dose.
- **Dose reduction for hemoglobin increases more than 1 g per dL in a 2-week period:** The dose of epoetin should be reduced by approximately 25% if the hemoglobin is increasing by more than 1 g per dL in any 2-week period.
- **Dose increase for inadequate response:**

The dose may be increased if the increase in the hemoglobin is less than 1 g per dL over 4 weeks of therapy, iron stores are adequate, and hemoglobin is below the suggested target range. The dose may be increased by approximately 25% of the previous dose. Subsequent dose increases should be made at 4-week intervals until the specified hemoglobin is obtained.

Iron stores should be re-evaluated if the hemoglobin remains below, or falls below, the suggested target range. Supplemental iron should be administered if transferrin saturation is less than 20%. Subsequent dose increases should not be made more frequently than once a month unless clinically indicated. The dose of epoetin may be increased if transferrin saturation is greater than 20%. The response time of hemoglobin to a dose increase can be 2 to 6 weeks.

- **Lack or loss of response:** Other etiologies should be considered and evaluated as clinically indicated if a patient fails to respond or fails to maintain a response.

Anemia associated with chronic renal failure not requiring dialysis—
Children ages 3 months to 20 years: Doses of 50 to 250 Units per kg of body weight given intravenously or subcutaneously one to three times a week have been reported.

Anemia in zidovudine-treated HIV-infected children—
Children ages eight months to 17 years: Doses of 50 to 400 Units per kg of body weight given intravenously or subcutaneously two to three times a week have been reported.

Anemia in cancer patients on chemotherapy—
Children ages six months to 18 years: Doses of 25 to 300 Units per kg of body weight given intravenously or subcutaneously three to seven times a week have been reported.

Strength(s) usually available

U.S.—
In 1-mL single-dose vials:
2000 Units per mL (Rx) [*Epogen* (human albumin 2.5 mg); *Procrit* (human albumin 2.5 mg)].
3000 Units per mL (Rx) [*Epogen* (human albumin 2.5 mg); *Procrit* (human albumin 2.5 mg)].
4000 Units per mL (Rx) [*Epogen* (human albumin 2.5 mg); *Procrit* (human albumin 2.5 mg)].
10,000 Units per mL (Rx) [*Epogen* (human albumin 2.5 mg); *Procrit* (human albumin 2.5 mg)].
40,000 Units per mL (Rx) [*Epogen* (human albumin 2.5 mg); *Procrit* (human albumin 2.5 mg)].
In multi-dose vials:
10,000 Units per mL in 2-mL vials (Rx) [*Epogen* (human albumin 2.5 mg; benzyl alcohol 1%); *Procrit* (human albumin 2.5 mg; benzyl alcohol 1%)].
20,000 Units per mL in 1-mL vials (Rx) [*Epogen* (human albumin 2.5 mg; benzyl alcohol 1%); *Procrit* (human albumin 2.5 mg; benzyl alcohol 1%)].

Canada—
In 1-mL single-dose vials:
2000 International Units (IU) per mL (Rx) [*Eprex* (human albumin 2.5 mg)].
4000 IU per mL (Rx) [*Eprex* (human albumin 2.5 mg)].
10,000 IU per mL (Rx) [*Eprex* (human albumin 2.5 mg)].
In multi-dose vials:
20,000 IU per mL in 1-mL vials (Rx) [*Eprex* (human albumin 2.5 mg; benzyl alcohol 1%)].
In single-dose, pre-filled syringes:
1000 IU per 0.5 mL (Rx) [*Eprex*].
2000 IU per 0.5 mL (Rx) [*Eprex*].
3000 IU per 0.3 mL (Rx) [*Eprex*].
4000 IU per 0.4 mL (Rx) [*Eprex*].
10,000 IU per mL (Rx) [*Eprex*].

Packaging and storage

Store at 2 to 8 °C (36 to 46 °F), unless otherwise specified by manufacturer. Protect from freezing.

Stability

Do not shake the vial of epoetin alfa, recombinant, injection. Shaking may denature the glycoprotein and render it biologically inactive.

Because the single-dose injection contains no preservative, each vial should be used to administer one dose only. Any unused portion of the solution must be discarded.

The multi-dose vials should be discarded 21 days after initial entry.

Incompatibilities

It is recommended that epoetin alfa, recombinant, not be admixed with other medications.

Auxiliary labeling

- Refrigerate, do not freeze.
- Do not shake.

Additional information

The multi-dose vials contain benzyl alcohol, which is not recommended for use in neonates. A fatal syndrome consisting of metabolic acidosis, central nervous system depression, respiratory problems, renal failure, hypotension, and possibly seizures and intracranial hemorrhage has been associated with the administration of benzyl alcohol to neonates.

[1]Not included in Canadian product labeling.

Selected Bibliography

Provenzano R, Bhaduri S, Singh AK. Extended epoetin alfa dosing as maintenance treatment for the anemia of chronic kidney disease: the PROMPT study. Clin Nephrol 2005 Aug;64(2):113–23.

Revised: 10/21/2005

EPROSARTAN Systemic†

USA: Eprosartan

INN: Eprosartan; BAN: Eprosartan

VA CLASSIFICATION (Primary/Secondary): CV805/CV409

Commonly used brand name(s): *Teveten.*

Note: For a listing of dosage forms and brand names by country availability, see *Dosage Forms* section(s).

†Not commercially available in Canada.

Category

Antihypertensive; angiotensin II receptor antagonist.

Indications

Accepted

Hypertension (treatment)—Eprosartan is indicated for the treatment of hypertension. It may be used alone or in combination with other antihypertensives such as diuretics and calcium channel blockers.

For additional information on initial therapeutic guidelines related to the treatment of hypertension, see *Appendix III*.

Pharmacology/Pharmacokinetics

Physicochemical characteristics

Molecular weight—Eprosartan mesylate: 520.625.

Mechanism of action/Effect

Eprosartan is a non-biphenyl non-tetrazole nonpeptide angiotensin II antagonist that selectively blocks the binding of angiotensin II to the AT_1 receptors in tissues such as vascular smooth muscle and the adrenal gland. In the renin-angiotensin system, angiotensin I is converted by angiotensin-converting enzyme (ACE) to form angiotensin II. Angiotensin II stimulates the adrenal cortex to synthesize and secrete aldosterone, which decreases the excretion of sodium and increases the excretion of potassium. By blocking the binding of angiotensin II to the AT_1 receptors, eprosartan causes vasodilation and decreases the effects of aldosterone. The negative feedback regulation of angiotensin II on renin secretion also is inhibited, resulting in a rise in plasma renin concentrations and a consequent rise in angiotensin II plasma concentrations; however, these effects do not counteract the blood pressure-lowering effect that occurs.

Absorption

Absolute bioavailability is approximately 13% after a 300 mg oral dose of eprosartan. Food delays absorption and causes non-clinically significant variable changes (<25%) in peak plasma concentration (C_{max}) and area under the plasma concentration-time curve (AUC).

Distribution

Vol_D—308 liters.

Protein binding

Very high (approximately 98%), and is constant over the therapeutic dosage range concentrations.

Biotransformation

Eprosartan is primarily eliminated as unchanged compound. Less than 2% of an oral dose is excreted in the urine as a glucuronide.

Half-life

Elimination—

Approximately 5 to 9 hours.

Onset of action

Within 1 to 2 hours.

Time to peak concentration

1 to 2 hours after an oral dose on an empty stomach.

Time to peak effect

Maximal blood pressure response may take up to 2 to 3 weeks of treatment to achieve.

Elimination

Elimination of eprosartan is primarily as unchanged drug.

After oral administration—

Fecal (biliary)—Approximately 90%

Renal—Approximately 7%

After intravenous administration—

Fecal (biliary)—Approximately 61%

Renal—Approximately 37%

In dialysis—Eprosartan is poorly removed by hemodialysis (Cl_{HD} < 1 L/hr).

Precautions to Consider

Carcinogenicity

No evidence of carcinogenicity was found when eprosartan was given to rats or mice for up to 2 years in doses at 600 mg and 2000 mg/kg/day, respectively. These doses approximate 20% and 25 times, respectively, the human systemic exposure to 400 mg twice a day.

Mutagenicity

Eprosartan was not mutagenic *in vitro* in bacteria or mammalian cells (mouse lymphoma assay), and *in vivo* in mouse micronucleus assay. In human peripheral lymphocytes *in vitro* , with metabolic activation eprosartan mesylate was equivocal for clastogenicity and it was negative without metabolic activation. In this same assay, with metabolic activation eprosartan mesylate was positive for polyploidy and it was equivocal for polyploidy without metabolic activation.

Pregnancy/Reproduction

Fertility—Reproductive performance was not affected in male or female rats given eprosartan at doses up to 1000 mg/kg/day, which was equivalent to 0.6 times the human systemic exposure to eprosartan 400 mg twice a day.

Pregnancy—Medications that act directly on the renin-angiotensin system can cause fetal and neonatal morbidity and mortality when administered to pregnant women during the second and third trimesters. Eprosartan should be discontinued as soon as possible when pregnancy is detected, unless no alternative therapy can be used. In the latter instance, serial ultrasound examinations should be performed to assess the intra-amniotic environment. If oligohydramnios is observed, eprosartan should be discontinued unless it is considered lifesaving for the mother. Perinatal diagnostic tests, such as contraction-stress testing (CST), a nonstress test (NST), or biophysical profiling (BPP) may be appropriate during the applicable week of pregnancy.However, oligohydramnios may not appear until after the fetus has sustained irreversible damage.

Fetal exposure to drugs that act directly on the renin-angiotensin system during the second and third trimesters can cause hypotension, reversible or irreversible renal failure, anuria, neonatal skull hypoplasia, and death in the fetus or neonate. Maternal oligohydramnios, which may result from decreased fetal renal function, has been reported and is associated with fetal limb contractures, craniofacial deformation, and hypoplastic lung development. Other adverse effects that have been reported are prematurity, intrauterine growth retardation, and patent ductus arteriosus, although it is not clear how these effects are related to drug exposure. When limited to the first trimester, exposure to this medication does not appear to be associated with these adverse effects.

Infants exposed in utero to angiotensin II receptor antagonists should be observed closely for hypotension, oliguria, and hyperkalemia. Oliguria should be treated with support of blood pressure and renal perfusion. Dialysis or exchange transfusion may be necessary to reverse hypotension and/or substitute for disordered renal function.

Eprosartan was found to produce maternal and fetal toxicities (maternal and fetal mortality, low maternal body weight and food consumption, resorptions, abortions and litter loss) in pregnant rabbits at 10 mg/kg/day but not at 3 mg/kg/day (approximately 0.8 times the human systemic exposure to eprosartan 400 mg twice a day). Eprosartan did not have any adverse effects on *in utero* or postnatal development and maturation of offspring in pregnant rats at doses up to 1000 mg/kg/day (approximately 0.6 times the human systemic exposure to 400 mg twice a day).

FDA Pregnancy Category C (first trimester)

FDA Pregnancy Category D (second and third trimesters)

Breast-feeding

It is not known whether eprosartan is distributed into human breast milk; however, it is distributed into the milk of lactating animals. Because of the potential for adverse effects in the nursing infant, it is recommended that a decision should be made to discontinue breast-feeding or to discontinue eprosartan, taking into account the importance of the drug to the mother.

Pediatrics

No information is available on the relationship of age to the effect of eprosartan in pediatric patients. Safety and effectiveness in pediatric patients have not been established.

Geriatrics

In patients 65 and 75 years of age and older taking eprosartan (29% and 5% of patients in clinical trials, respectively), the reduction in diastolic and systolic blood pressure was slightly less than in younger patients. Adverse events were similar in younger and older patients.

Pharmacogenetics

No difference in the pharmacokinetics was found between genders and races.

Although there were insufficient black patients in the clinical studies, they are expected to have a smaller response to angiotensin converting enzyme (ACE) inhibitors and angiotensin II inhibitors than Caucasian populations.

Drug interactions and/or related problems

The following drug interactions and/or related problems have been selected on the basis of their potential clinical significance (possible mechanism in parentheses where appropriate)—not necessarily inclusive (» = major clinical significance):

Note: Combinations containing any of the following medications, depending on the amount present, may also interact with this medication.

Diuretics, potassium-sparing or

Potassium-containing medications or
Potassium supplements or substances containing high concentrations of potassium
(concurrent administration with eprosartan may result in hyperkalemia since reduction of aldosterone production induced by eprosartan may lead to elevation of serum potassium; determination of serum potassium concentrations is recommended if concurrent use of these agents is necessary)

Hypotension-producing medications (See *Appendix II*)
(concurrent use with eprosartan may produce additive hypotensive effects)

Laboratory value alterations

The following have been selected on the basis of their potential clinical significance (possible effect in parentheses where appropriate)—not necessarily inclusive (» = major clinical significance).

With physiology/laboratory test values

Blood urea nitrogen (BUN), and
creatinine
(minor elevation in BUN and creatinine occurred in 1.3% and 0.6% of patients taking eprosartan and 0.3% and 0.9% of patients taking placebo, respectively, in controlled clinical trials)

Hemoglobin
(0.1% of patients taking eprosartan had a greater than 20% decrease in hemoglobin as compared to none from those taking placebo during controlled clinical trials)

Liver function tests
(in clinical trials, minor elevation of liver enzymes, ALAT, ASAT, and alkaline phosphatase, occurred infrequently in patients taking eprosartan and the incidence was comparable to those taking placebo)

Potassium, serum
(0.9% of patients taking eprosartan and 0.3% of patients taking placebo in clinical studies had potassium values ≥ 5.6 mmol/L, and one patient was withdrawn from clinical trials because of hyperkalemia)

Thrombocytopenia
(in clinical studies, 0.3% of patients taking eprosartan had platelet counts of ≤ 100 x 10^9/L as compared to none in those taking placebo, and four patients were withdrawn because of thrombocytopenia)

Medical considerations/Contraindications

The medical considerations/contraindications included have been selected on the basis of their potential clinical significance (reasons given in parentheses where appropriate)—not necessarily inclusive (» = major clinical significance).

Except under special circumstances, this medication should not be used when the following medical problem exists:

» Hypersensitivity to eprosartan

Risk-benefit should be considered when the following medical problems exist:

» Congestive heart failure, severe
(therapy with angiotensin receptor-antagonists in these patients, who may be especially susceptible to changes in the renin-angiotensin-aldosterone system, has been associated with oliguria, azotemia, acute renal failure, and/or death)

Dehydration and
salt depletion
(patients with reduced salt or fluid volume may have an increased risk of symptomatic hypotension)

Renal artery stenosis, unilateral or bilateral
(increases in serum creatinine or blood urea nitrogen [BUN] have occurred in patients with unilateral or bilateral renal artery stenosis and treated with angiotensin-converting enzyme [ACE] inhibitors; similar effects have been reported with angiotensin II antagonists.)

Patient monitoring

The following may be especially important in patient monitoring (other tests may be warranted in some patients, depending on condition; » = major clinical significance):

» Blood pressure measurements
(periodic monitoring is necessary for titration of dose according to the patient's response)

Side/Adverse Effects

The following side/adverse effects have been selected on the basis of their potential clinical significance (possible signs and symptoms in parentheses where appropriate)—not necessarily inclusive:

Those indicating need for medical attention

Incidence less frequent

Upper respiratory infection (cough, fever, or sore throat); ***urinary tract infection*** (burning or painful urination or changes in urinary frequency)

Incidence rare

Angioedema (swollen lips, face, tongue, or limbs); ***hypotension or syncope*** (dizziness, light-headedness, or fainting)—usually seen in volume- or salt-depleted patients, such as those treated with diuretics, especially upon standing

Those indicating need for medical attention only if they continue or are bothersome

Incidence less frequent or rare

Abdominal pain; arthralgia (joint pain); ***fatigue*** (unusual tiredness); ***cough***

Overdose

For more information on the management of overdose or unintentional ingestion, **contact a poison control center** (see *Poison Control Center Listing*).

Clinical effects of overdose

Data regarding eprosartan overdose is limited. There was no fatality in rats and mice receiving oral doses of up to 3000 mg of eprosartan/kg and in dogs for doses up to 1000 mg/kg.

Treatment of overdose

Treatment should be symptomatic and supportive.

Supportive care—Patients in whom intentional overdose is confirmed or suspected should be referred for psychiatric consultation.

Patient Consultation

As an aid to patient consultation, refer to *Advice for the Patient, Eprosartan (Systemic)*.

In providing consultation, consider emphasizing the following selected information (» = major clinical significance):

Before using this medication

» Conditions affecting use, especially:
Hypersensitivity to eprosartan
Pregnancy—Fetal and neonatal hypotension, skull hypoplasia, renal failure, and death have been reported; eprosartan should be discontinued as soon as possible when pregnancy is detected
Breast-feeding—Eprosartan is distributed into the milk of lactating animals; due to the potential for serious adverse effects, breast-feeding should be discontinued
Use in the elderly—Decrease in blood pressure may be slightly less in older patients
Pharmacogenetics—Black patients may have a somewhat smaller therapeutic response
Other medical problems, especially severe congestive heart failure

Proper use of this medication

» Compliance with therapy; taking medication at the same time each day to maintain the antihypertensive effect

» Proper dosing
Missed dose: Taking as soon as possible; not taking if almost time for next scheduled dose; not doubling doses

» Proper storage

Precautions while using this medication

» Visiting the physician regularly to check progress

» Notifying physician immediately if pregnancy is suspected

Not taking other medications without consulting the physician

Caution when driving, using machines, or doing other things that may be dangerous if dizziness or light-headedness occurs from hypotension

To prevent dehydration and hypotension, checking with physician if severe nausea, vomiting, or diarrhea occurs and continues

Caution when exercising or during exposure to hot weather, because of the risk of dehydration and hypotension due to reduced fluid volume

Side/adverse effects

Signs of potential side effects, especially upper respiratory infection, urinary tract infection, angioedema, and hypotension or syncope.

General Dosing Information

Dosage must be adjusted, on the basis of clinical response, to meet the individual requirements of each patient. In most patients, maximal response is achieved in 2 to 3 weeks.

If the antihypertensive effect with once-a-day dosing at trough is inadequate, a twice-a-day dosing regimen using the same total daily dose or an increase in dose may provide a better response.

Volume and/or salt depletion should be corrected prior to administration of eprosartan to avoid symptomatic hypotension.

Eprosartan does not appear to have a rapid rebound effect with discontinuation of treatment.

Diet/Nutrition

Eprosartan may be taken with or without food.

For treatment of adverse effects

Recommended treatment consists of the following:

- Treatment of symptomatic hypotension involves placing the patient in a supine position and, if needed, administering normal saline intravenously.

Oral Dosage Forms

EPROSARTAN TABLETS

Usual adult dose

Antihypertensive—

Oral, initially 600 mg once daily, when used as monotherapy in patients who are not volume-depleted.

Eprosartan may be administered once or twice a day with total daily doses ranging from 400 mg to 800 mg. The maximal antihypertensive effect usually is attained in 2 to 3 weeks.

Note: If adequate blood pressure control is not achieved by eprosartan alone, other antihypertensive agents such as thiazide diuretics or calcium channel blockers may be added for an additive effect.

Usual adult prescribing limits

800 mg per day.

Usual pediatric dose

Safety and efficacy have not been established.

Strength(s) usually available

U.S.—

400 mg (Rx) [*Teveten* (lactose monohydrate; propylene glycol; pregelatinized starch)].

600 mg (Rx) [*Teveten* (lactose monohydrate; propylene glycol; pregelatinized starch)].

Packaging and storage

Store at room temperature between 20 and 25°C (68 and 77°F).

Auxiliary labeling

- Do not take other medicines without your doctor's advice.
- Do not take this medication if you are pregnant.

Developed: 12/16/1999

ERGOCALCIFEROL—See *Vitamin D and Analogs (Systemic)*

ERGOTAMINE—See *Vascular Headache Suppressants, Ergot Derivative–containing (Systemic)*

ERLOTINIB Systemic

VA CLASSIFICATION (Primary): AN300

Commonly used brand name(s): *Tarceva*.

Note: For a listing of dosage forms and brand names by country availability, see *Dosage Forms* section(s).

Category

Antineoplastic.

Indications

Note: Bracketed information in the *Indications* section refers to uses that are not included in U.S. product labeling.

Accepted

Carcinoma, lung, non-small cell (treatment)—Erlotinib is indicated for the treatment of patients with locally advanced or metastatic non-small cell lung cancer after failure of at least one prior chemotherapy regimen.

Carcinoma, pancreatic (first-line treatment)—Erlotinib in combination with gemcitabine is indicated for the first-line treatment of patients with locally advanced, unresectable or metastatic pancreatic cancer.

Unaccepted

Erlotinib is not recommended for concurrent administration with platinum-based chemotherapy (carboplatin and paclitaxel or gemcitabine and cisplatin) for first-line treatment of patients with locally advanced or metastatic non-small cell lung cancer.

Pharmacology/Pharmacokinetics

Physicochemical characteristics

Source—Erlotinib is a human epidermal growth factor receptor type 1/epidermal growth factor receptor (HER1/EGFR) tyrosine kinase inhibitor.

Molecular weight—Erlotinib Hydrochloride: 429.90.

pKa—5.42 at 25°C.

Solubility—Erlotinib hydrochloride is very slightly soluble in water, slightly soluble in methanol and practically insoluble in acetonitrile, acetone, ethyl acetate and hexane. Aqueous solubility of erlotinib hydrochloride is dependent on pH with increased solubility at a pH less than 5 due to prolongation of the secondary amine. Maximum solubility of approximately 0.4 mg/mL occurs at a pH of approximately 2.

Mechanism of action/Effect

The antitumor action of erlotinib has not been fully characterized. However, erlotinib inhibits the intracellular phosphorylation of tyrosine kinase associated with the epidermal growth factor receptor (EGFR), which is expressed on the surface of normal cells and cancer cells.

Absorption

Erlotinib is 60% absorbed following oral administration and its bioavailability is increased to almost 100% when given with food.

Distribution

Volume of distribution (Vol_D)—232 liters.

Protein binding

Very high (approximately 93%) to albumin and alpha-1 acid glycoprotein (AAG).

Biotransformation

Erlotinib is metabolized primarily by CYP3A4 and to a lesser extent by CYP1A2 and the extrahepatic isoform CYP1A1.

Half-life

Elimination—Approximately 36 hours.

Time to peak concentration

Peak plasma levels occur 4 hours after dosing.

Elimination

Feces: 83% (1% as intact parent)

Urine: 8% (0.3% as intact parent)

Clearance: Smokers had a 24% higher rate of erlotinib clearance.

Precautions to Consider

Carcinogenicity

Carcinogenicity studies with erlotinib have not been done.

Mutagenicity

Erlotinib was not found to be genotoxic in a series of *in vitro* tests including a bacterial mutation assay, the human lymphocyte chromosome aberration assay and mammalian cell mutation assay and in an *in vivo* mouse bone marrow micronucleus test.

Pregnancy/Reproduction

Fertility—Erlotinib did not impair fertility in either male or female rats.

Pregnancy—Adequate and well-controlled studies with erlotinib in pregnant women have not been done. Women of childbearing potential should be advised to avoid pregnancy while receiving erlotinib therapy. Adequate contraceptive methods should be used during therapy and for at least two weeks following completion of therapy.

Erlotinib crosses the placenta and has been shown to cause death in the fetus in animal studies. Risk benefit must be carefully considered when this medication is required in life-threatening situations or in serious diseases for which other medications cannot be used or are ineffective. If erlotinib therapy is used during pregnancy, the patient should be apprised of the potential hazard to the fetus or potential risk for loss of the pregnancy.

Studies done in rabbits given doses that result in plasma concentrations approximately 3 times those in humans have been shown to cause maternal toxicity associated with embryo/lethality and abortion. When given during organogenesis in doses equal to those in humans, there was no increased incidence of embryo/lethality and abortion in rabbits and rats. However, female rats given erlotinib at doses of 30 mg/m^2/day or 60 mg/m^2/day prior to mating and through the first week of pregnancy had an increase in early resorptions which resulted in a decrease in the number of live fetuses.

FDA Pregnancy Category D

Breast-feeding

It is not known whether erlotinib is distributed into breast milk. Because many drugs are distributed in human milk and because of the potential risks to the infant, women should be advised against breast-feeding while receiving erlotinib therapy.

Pediatrics

Safety and effectiveness of erlotinib in pediatric patients have not been established.

Geriatrics

Appropriate studies performed to date have not demonstrated geriatrics-specific problems that would limit the usefulness of erlotinib in the elderly.

Pharmacogenetics

No differences in the safety of erlotinib were seen between male and female or between Caucasian and Asian patients.

Drug interactions and/or related problems

The following drug interactions and/or related problems have been selected on the basis of their potential clinical significance (possible mechanism in parentheses where appropriate)—not necessarily inclusive (» = major clinical significance):

Note: Combinations containing any of the following medications, depending on the amount present, may also interact with this medication.

» CYP3A4 inducers, such as
» Carbamazepine or
» Phenobarbital or
» Phenytoin or
» Rifabutin or
» Rifampin or
» Rifapentin or
» St. John's Wort
(may decrease erlotinib AUC; alternative treatments lacking CYP3A4 inducing activity should be considered, if an alternative is unavailable an increased erlotinib dose should be considered; if erlotinib dose is upward adjusted the dose will need to be reduced upon discontinuation of the inducer)

» CYP3A4 inhibitors, potent such as
» Ketoconazole or
» Other CYP3A4 inhibitors, strong such as
» Atazanavir or
» Clarithromycin or
» Indinavir or
» Itraconazole or
» Nefazodone or
» Nelfinavir or
» Ritonavir or
» Saquinavir or
» Telithromycin or
» Troleandomycin or
» Voriconazole
(caution; may increase erlotinib AUC; reduction in dosage should be considered should severe adverse reactions occur)

NSAID
(concomitant use with erlotinib may increase risk of gastrointestinal bleeding)

» Warfarin
» Other coumarin-derivative anticoagulants
(gastrointestinal bleeding has been reported with concomitant administration of warfarin and erlotinib; monitor regularly for changes in prothrombin time or INR)

Laboratory value alterations

The following have been selected on the basis of their potential clinical significance (possible effect in parentheses where appropriate)—not necessarily inclusive (» = major clinical significance).

With physiology/laboratory test values
» Alanine aminotransferase (ALT) or
» Aspartate aminotransferase (AST) or
» Bilirubin
(levels may be elevated)

Medical considerations/Contraindications

The medical considerations/contraindications included have been selected on the basis of their potential clinical significance (reasons given in parentheses where appropriate)—not necessarily inclusive (» = major clinical significance).

Except under special circumstances, this medication should not be used when the following medical problem exists:

» Hypersensitivity to erlotinib or any of its components

Risk-benefit should be considered when the following medical problems exist:

» Hepatic function impairment
(erlotinib exposure may be increased; a dose reduction or interruption of erlotinib should be considered if changes in liver function are severe)

Patient monitoring

The following may be especially important in patient monitoring (other tests may be warranted in some patients, depending on condition; » = major clinical significance):

» Alanine aminotransferase (ALT) or
» Aspartate aminotransferase (AST) or
» Bilirubin
(periodic liver function testing should be considered; dose reduction or interruption of erlotinib should be considered if changes in liver function are severe)

» Prothrombin time (INR)
(patients concomitantly receiving warfarin or other coumarin-derivative anti coagulants should be monitored regularly for changes in prothrombin time or INR; INR elevations and bleeding including gastrointestinal bleeding have been reported)

Side/Adverse Effects

The following side/adverse effects have been selected on the basis of their potential clinical significance (possible signs and symptoms in parentheses where appropriate)—not necessarily inclusive:

Those indicating need for medical attention

Incidence more frequent

Cough; diarrhea, severe; dyspnea (shortness of breath; difficult or labored breathing; tightness in chest; wheezing); ***fever; neuropathy*** (burning, tingling, numbness or pain in the hands, arms, feet, or legs; sensation of pins and needles; stabbing pain); ***rash, severe***

Incidence rare

Cerebrovascular accident (blurred vision; headache sudden and severe; inability to speak; seizures; slurred speech; temporary blindness; weakness in arm and/or leg on one side of the body, sudden and severe); ***corneal ulceration*** (eye irritation or redness); ***gastrointestinal bleeding*** (bloody or black, tarry stools; vomiting of blood or material that looks like coffee grounds; severe stomach pain; constipation); ***interstitial lung disease*** (cough, difficult breathing, fever, shortness of breath); ***keratitis*** (eye redness, irritation, or pain); ***microangiopathic hemolytic anemia with thrombocytopenia*** (sudden weakness in arms or legs; sudden, severe chest pain); ***myocardial infarction/ischemia*** (chest pain or discomfort; pain or discomfort in arms, jaw, back or neck; shortness of breath; nausea; sweating; vomiting)

Those indicating need for medical attention only if they continue or are bothersome

Incidence more frequent

Abdominal pain (stomach pain); ***alopecia*** (hair loss; thinning of hair); ***anorexia*** (loss of appetite; weight loss); ***anxiety*** (fear; nervousness); ***bone pain; conjunctivitis*** (redness, pain, swelling of eye, eyelid, or inner lining of eyelid; burning, dry or itching eyes; discharge; excessive tearing); ***constipation*** (difficulty having a bowel movement [stool]); ***depression*** (discouragement; feeling sad or empty; irritability; lack of appetite; loss of interest or pleasure; tiredness; trouble concentrating; trouble sleeping); ***diarrhea, mild; dizziness; dry skin; dyspepsia*** (acid or sour stomach; belching; heartburn; indigestion; stomach discomfort, upset, or pain); ***edema*** (swelling); ***fatigue*** (unusual tiredness or weakness); ***flatulence*** (bloated full feeling; excess air or gas in stomach or intestines; passing gas); ***headache; infection*** (fever or chills; cough or hoarseness; lower back or side pain; painful or difficult urination); ***insomnia*** (sleeplessness; trouble sleeping; unable to sleep); ***keratoconjunctivitis sicca*** (dryness of the eye); ***myalgia*** (joint pain; swollen joints; muscle aching or cramping; muscle pains or stiffness; difficulty in moving); ***nausea; pruritus*** (itching skin); ***pyrexia*** (fever); ***rash, mild; rigors*** (feeling unusually cold; shivering); ***stomatitis*** (swelling or inflammation of the mouth); ***vomiting; weight decreased***

Overdose

For more information on the management of overdose or unintentional ingestion, **contact a poison control center** (see *Poison Control Center Listing*).

Clinical effects of overdose

The following effects have been selected on the basis of their potential clinical significance (possible signs and symptoms in parentheses where appropriate)—not necessarily inclusive:

Diarrhea; elevated liver transaminase; rash

Treatment of overdose

There is no known specific antidote to erlotinib. Treatment is generally symptomatic and supportive.

Supportive care—

Patients in whom intentional overdose is confirmed or suspected should be referred for psychiatric consultation.

Patient Consultation

As an aid to patient consultation, refer to *Advice for the Patient, Erlotinib (Systemic)*.

In providing consultation, consider emphasizing the following selected information (» = major clinical significance):

Before using this medication

» Conditions affecting use, especially:

Pregnancy—Not recommended for use during pregnancy; advisability of using contraception; telling physician immediately if pregnancy is suspected

Breast-feeding—Not recommended because of potential risks to the infant

Use in children—Safety and effectiveness of erlotinib in pediatric patients have not been established.

Other medications, especially CYP3A4 inducers, such as rifampin, rifabutin, rifapentin, phenytoin, carbamazepine, phenobarbital, St. John's Wort; CYP3A4 inhibitors such as ketoconazole, atazanavir, clarithromycin, indinavir, itraconazole, nefazodone, nelfinavir, ritonavir, saquinavir, telithromycin, troleandomycin, voriconazole, or warfarin or other coumarin anticoagulants

Other medical problems, especially hepatic function impairment

Proper use of this medication

» Taking at least one hour or at least two hours after the ingestion of food

» Proper dosing

Missed dose: Taking as soon as possible; not taking if almost time for next scheduled dose; not doubling doses

Proper storage

Precautions while using this medication

» Seeking prompt medical attention should severe or persistent diarrhea, nausea, anorexia, or vomiting occur

» Seeking prompt medical attention if onset or worsening of unexplained shortness of breath or cough occur

Contacting your physician if you develop eye irritations

Side/adverse effects

Signs of potential side effects, especially cerebrovascular accident, corneal ulcerations, gastrointestinal bleeding, interstitial lung disease including cough, dyspnea, or fever; keratitis, microangiopathic hemolytic anemia with thrombocytopenia, myocardial infarction/ischemia, neuropathy, severe diarrhea, or severe rash

General Dosing Information

Erlotinib treatment should continue until disease progression or unacceptable toxicity occurs.

Treatment of adverse effects

Erlotinib treatment should be interrupted if development of acute onset of new progressive pulmonary symptoms such as dyspnea, cough, or fever occur until after an evaluation for interstitial lung disease (ILD) has been done. If ILD is diagnosed erlotinib treatment should be discontinued and appropriate treatment be given.

If diarrhea develops it can usually be managed with loperamide, patients who are unresponsive to loperamide or who become dehydrated may require dosage reduction or temporary interruption of erlotinib therapy.

If patients develop severe skin reactions a dosage reduction or temporary interruption of erlotinib therapy may be required.

Oral Dosage Forms

Note: Bracketed information in the *Indications* section refers to uses that are not included in U.S. product labeling.

ERLOTINIB HYDROCHLORIDE TABLETS

Usual adult dose

Carcinoma, lung, non-small cell—

Oral, 150 mg daily, taken at least one hour before or two hour after ingestion of food.

Note: When dose reduction is necessary, erlotinib should be reduced in 50 mg decrements.

For patients pretreated with a CYP3A4 inducer, a dose of erlotinib greater than 150 mg should be considered.

Carcinoma, pancreatic—

Oral, 100 mg daily, taken at least one hour before or two hour after ingestion of food, in combination with gemcitabine.

For information on gemcitabine dosing, see *Gemcitabine (Systemic)*.

Note: When dose reduction is necessary, erlotinib should be reduced in 50 mg decrements.

For patients pretreated with a CYP3A4 inducer, a dose of erlotinib greater than 150 mg should be considered.

Usual pediatric dose

Safety and effectiveness in pediatric patients have not been established

Usual geriatric dose

See *Usual adult dose.*

Strength(s) usually available

U.S.—

25 mg (base) (Rx) [*Tarceva* (lactose monohydrate; hypromellose; hydroxypropyl cellulose; magnesium stearate; microcrystalline cellulose; sodium starch glycolate; sodium lauryl sulfate; titanium dioxide; FD&C yellow #6)].

100 mg (base) [*Tarceva* (lactose monohydrate; hypromellose; hydroxypropyl cellulose; magnesium stearate; microcrystalline cellulose; sodium starch glycolate; sodium lauryl sulfate; titanium dioxide)].

150 mg (base) [*Tarceva* (lactose monohydrate; hypromellose; hydroxypropyl cellulose; magnesium stearate; microcrystalline cellulose; sodium starch glycolate; sodium lauryl sulfate; titanium dioxide)].

Canada—

100 mg (base) [*Tarceva*].

150 mg (base) [*Tarceva*].

Packaging and storage

Store at 25 °C (77 °F); excursions permitted to 15° to 30°C (59° to 86°F).

Auxiliary labeling

- Take on an empty stomach - 1 hour before or 2 to 3 hours after eating.
- This medication could be harmful if you are pregnant or breast-feeding. Consult your pharmacist or doctor about using this medication if you are pregnant, plan to become pregnant, or if you are breast-feeding.
- Keep out of reach of children

Revised: 11/14/2005
Developed: 02/17/2005

ERTAPENEM Systemic†

VA CLASSIFICATION (Primary): AM119

Commonly used brand name(s): *Invanz*.

Note: For a listing of dosage forms and brand names by country availability, see *Dosage Forms* section(s).

†Not commercially available in Canada.

Category

Antibacterial (systemic).

Indications

General Considerations

To reduce the development of drug-resistant bacteria and maintain the effectiveness of ertapenem and other antibacterial drugs, ertapenem should be used only to treat or prevent infections that are proven or strongly suspected to be caused by bacteria.

Ertapenem has *in vitro* activity against gram-positive and gram-negative aerobic and anaerobic bacteria. The bactericidal activity results from the inhibition of cell wall synthesis and is mediated through ertapenem binding to penicillin binding proteins (PBPs). In *Escherichia coli* it has strong affinity towards PBPs, 1a, 1b, 2, 3, 4, and 5 with preference for

PBPs 2 and 3. Ertapenem is stable against hydrolysis by a variety of beta-lactamases, including penicillinases, cephalosporinases, and extended spectrum beta-lactamases, and it is hydrolyzed by metallo-beta-lactamases.

Ertapenem has been shown to be active against most strains of the following microorganisms *in vitro* and in clinical infections. It is active against the following aerobic gram-positive microorganisms: *Staphylococcus aureus* (methicillin susceptible strains only), *Streptococcus agalactiae, Streptococcus pneumoniae* (penicillin susceptible strains only), *Streptococcus pyogenes*. It should be noted that methicillin-resistant staphylococci and *Enterococcus* species are resistant to ertapenem. Ertapenem has been shown to be active against most strains of the following aerobic gram-negative microorganisms: *Escherichia coli, Haemophilus influenzae* (beta-lactamase negative strains only) *Klebsiella pneumoniae,* and *Moraxella catarrhalis*.

Ertapenem has been shown to be active against most strains of the following anaerobic microorganisms: *Bacteroides fragilis, Bacteroides distasonis, Bacteroides ovatus, Bacteroides thetaiotaomicron, Bacteroides uniformis, Clostridium clostridioforme, Eubacterium lentum, Peptostreptococcus* species, *Porphyromonas asaccharolytica*, and *Prevotella bivia*.

Accepted

Intra-abdominal infections, complicated (treatment)—Intravenous and intramuscular ertapenem is indicated for the treatment of complicated intra-abdominal infections due to *Escherichia coli, Clostridium clostridioforme, Eubacterium lentum, Peptostreptococcus*species, *Bacteroides fragilis, Bacteroides distasonis, Bacteroides ovatus, Bacteroides thetaiotaomicron* or *Bacteroides uniformis*.

Pelvic infections, acute, including postpartum endomyometritis, septic abortion, and post surgical gynecological infections (treatment)—Intravenous and intramuscular ertapenem is indicated for the treatment of acute pelvic infections, including postpartum endomyometritis, septic abortion, and post surgical gynecologic infections due to *Streptococcus agalactiae, Escherichia coli, Bacteroides fragilis, Porphyromonas asaccharolytica, Peptostreptococcus* species or *Prevotella bivia*.

Pneumonia, community-acquired (treatment)—Intravenous and intramuscular ertapenem is indicated for the treatment of community acquired pneumonia due to *Streptococcus pneumoniae* (penicillin susceptible strains only) including cases with concurrent bacteremia *Haemophilus influenzae* (beta-lactamase negative strains only) or *Moraxella catarrhalis*.

Skin and skin structure infections, complicated (treatment)—Intravenous and intramuscular ertapenem is indicated for the treatment of patients with complicated skin and skin structure infections, including diabetic foot infections without osteomyelitis due to *Staphylococcus aureus* (methicillin resistant isolates only), *Streptococcus agalactiae, Streptococcus pyogenes, Escherichia coli, Klebsiella pneumoniae, Proteus mirabilis, Bacteroides fragilis, Peptostreptococcus* species, *Porphyromonas asaccharolytica*, or *Prevotella bivia*.

Urinary tract infections, complicated, including pyelonephritis (treatment)—Intravenous and intramuscular ertapenem is indicated for the treatment of complicated urinary tract infections including pyelonephritis due to *Escherichia coli* including cases with concurrent bacteremia, or *Klebsiella pneumoniae*.

Unaccepted

Ertapenem has not been studied in diabetic foot infections with concomitant osteomyelitis.

Pharmacology/Pharmacokinetics

Physicochemical characteristics

Chemical Group—Carbapenem antibiotic—chemically similar to beta-lactam antibiotics

Molecular weight—497.50.

pH—Approximately 7.5 after reconstitution.

Solubility—Ertapenem is soluble in water and 0.9% sodium chloride solution, practically insoluble in ethanol, and insoluble in isopropyl acetate and tetrahydrofuran.

Mechanism of action/Effect

Bactericidal resulting from the inhibition of cell wall synthesis with antibacterial activity against gram-positive and gram-negative anaerobic and aerobic pathogens. Ertapenem exerts its inhibitory effects via affinity for penicillin-binding proteins (PBPs) 1a, 1b, 2, 3, 4, and 5 with preference for PBPs 2 and 5 in *Escherichia coli*. It is stable in the presence of a variety of beta-lactamases, including penicillinases and some cephalosporinases, and extended spectrum beta-lactamases.

Absorption

Bioavailability—Following intramuscular administration, ertapenem reconstituted with 1% lidocaine hydrochloride injection, USP (in sodium chloride without epinephrine) is almost completely absorbed with a mean bioavailability of 90%.

Distribution

Volume of distribution at steady state (V_{SS})—8.2 L

Breast milk—The concentration of ertapenem in the breast milk ranged from <0.13 (lower limit of quantitation) to 0.38 mcg per mL measured within 24 hours of the last dose of therapy in 5 lactating women with pelvic infections. The concentration of ertapenem in the breast milk was undetectable in 4 women and below the lower limit of quantitation in 1 woman by day 5 after discontinuation of therapy.

Skin blister fluid—The concentration of ertapenem in suction-induced skin blister fluid on the third day of 1 gram given intravenously once daily was 7, 12, 17, 24, 24, 21, and 8 mcg per mL at 0.5, 1, 2, 4, 8, 12, and 24 hours, respectively.

Protein binding

Ertapenem is highly bound to human plasma proteins, primarily albumin.

Concentration-dependent plasma protein binding—The protein binding of ertapenem decreases as plasma concentrations increase. At a plasma concentration of <100 mcg per mL, approximately 95% of ertapenem is protein bound. Protein binding of ertapenem decreases to approximately 85% at an approximate plasma concentration of 300 mcg per mL.

Biotransformation

The major metabolite is the inactive ring-opened derivative formed by hydrolysis of the β-lactam ring.

Ertapenem did not inhibit metabolism mediated by cytochrome p450 (CYP) isoforms 1A2, 2C9, 2C19, 2D6, 2E1, or 3A4 when evaluated by *in vitro* studies in human liver microsomes.

Half-life

Elimination—The mean plasma half-life is approximately 4 hours.

Time to peak concentration

2.3 hours following intramuscular injection

Plasma concentration:

There was no accumulation of ertapenem in healthy adults given repeat 1-gram doses of intravenous or intramuscular ertapenem.

Elimination

Renal—90% is excreted into the urine, with 38% as unchanged drug and 37% as the ring-opened metabolite

Fecal—10%

Clearance, plasma—1.8 L per hour

In dialysis—Approximately 30% of the dose was recovered in the dialysate in a study of 5 patients with end-stage renal insufficiency given a single 1 gram intravenous dose of ertapenem immediately before a 4 hour hemodialysis session.

Precautions to Consider

Cross-sensitivity and/or related problems

Patients allergic to other beta-lactam antibacterials (e.g., penicillins, cephalosporins, imipenem) may also be allergic to ertapenem.

Patients allergic to multiple allergens may also be allergic to ertapenem.

Caution should be exercised in individuals with a history of penicillin sensitivity because there have been reports of individuals with a penicillin hypersensitivity who have had severe hypersensitivity reactions when treated with other β-lactams. Before therapy is started with ertapenem, careful inquiry should be made concerning previous hypersensitivity reactions to penicillins, cephalosporins, other beta-lactam antibacterials, and other allergens.

Patients allergic to local anesthetics of the amide type may also be allergic to the intramuscular formulation of ertapenem which is reconstituted with lidocaine hydrochloride.

Carcinogenicity

No long term studies have been performed.

Mutagenicity

Ertapenem was neither mutagenic or genotoxic in the following *in vitro* assays: alkaline elution/rat hepatocyte assays, chromosomal aberration assay in Chinese hamster ovary cells, and TK6 human lymphoblastoid cell mutagenesis assay; and in the *in vivo* mouse micronucleus assay.

Pregnancy/Reproduction

Fertility—In mice and rats, IV doses of up to 700 mg per kg of body weight per day resulted in no effects on mating performance, fecundity, fertility, or embryonic survival.

Pregnancy—Adequate and well controlled studies in humans have not been done. Ertapenem should be used during pregnancy only if clearly needed.

Ertapenem crosses the placental barrier in rats.

Slight decreases in average fetal weights and associated decrease in the average number of ossified sacrocaudal vertebrae were observed in mice given IV doses of ertapenem up to 700 mg per kg of body weight per day. For mice, this dose is approximately 3 times the recommended human dose of 1 gram based on body surface area. For rats, this dose is approximately 1.2 times the human exposure at the recommended human dose of 1 gram based on plasma AUCs.

No evidence of developmental toxicity as assessed by external, visceral, and skeletal examination of the fetuses in a study in mice and rats given IV doses of ertapenem up to 700 mg per kg of body weight per day.

FDA Pregnancy Category B

Labor and delivery—Ertapenem has not been studied for use during labor and delivery.

Breast-feeding

Ertapenem is distributed in breast milk. Ertapenem should be administered to nursing mothers only when the expected benefit outweighs the risk.

The concentration of ertapenem in the breast milk ranged from <0.13 (lower limit of quantitation) to 0.38 mcg per mL measured within 24 hours of the last dose of therapy in 5 lactating women with pelvic infections. The concentration of ertapenem in the breast milk was undetectable in 4 women and below the lower limit of quantitation in 1 woman by day 5 after discontinuation of therapy.

Pediatrics

Appropriate studies performed to date have not demonstrated pediatrics-specific problems that would limit the usefulness of ertapenem in children 3 months to 17 years of age with complicated intra-abdominal infections, complicated skin and skin structure infections, community acquired pneumonia, complicated urinary tract infections, or acute pelvic infections. Ertapenem is not recommended in the treatment of meningitis in the pediatric population due to lack of sufficient CSF penetration. Ertapenem is not recommended in infants under 3 months of age as no data are available.

Geriatrics

Appropriate studies performed to date have not demonstrated geriatrics–specific problems that would limit the usefulness of ertapenem in the elderly. Dose selection should be done with caution. Elderly patients are more likely to have age related problems, such as decreased renal function.

For elderly patients with normal renal function for their age, no dosage adjustment is necessary.

The unbound and total AUC increased 67% and 37% in elderly adults compared to young adults in a study to evaluate the impact of age on the pharmacokinetics of ertapenem in 7 healthy male and 7 healthy female subjects ≥ 65 year of age.

Pharmacogenetics

No differences in pharmacokinetics of ertapenem could be attributed to the effect of gender in a study of 8 healthy male and 8 healthy female subjects.

Drug interactions and/or related problems

The following drug interactions and/or related problems have been selected on the basis of their potential clinical significance (possible mechanism in parentheses where appropriate)—not necessarily inclusive (» = major clinical significance):

Note: Combinations containing any of the following medications, depending on the amount present, may also interact with this medication.

» Probenecid
(renal clearance is reduced through competition with ertapenem for active tubular secretion; AUC increased by 25% based on total ertapenem concentrations; plasma and renal clearances decreased by 20% and 35%; half-life increased from 4.0 to 4.8 hours; due to the small extension to the half-life and increased risk of toxicity, coadministration is not recommended to prolong ertapenem serum and tissue concentrations)

Laboratory value alterations

The following have been selected on the basis of their potential clinical significance (possible effect in parentheses where appropriate)—not necessarily inclusive (» = major clinical significance).

With physiology/laboratory test values
Alanine aminotransferase (ALT [SGPT])
Alkaline phosphatase
Aspartate aminotransferase (AST [SGOT])
Bilirubin
Blood urea nitrogen
Creatinine, serum
Eosinophils
Glucose
Monocytes
Partial thromboplastin time (PTT)
Prothrombin time or
Sodium
(values may be increased)
Albumin
Bicarbonate
Hematocrit
Hemoglobin or
White blood count
(values may be decreased)
Platelet count
(value may be increased or decreased)
Epithelial cells
Red blood cells and or
White blood cells
(urine values may be increased)

Medical considerations/Contraindications

The medical considerations/contraindications included have been selected on the basis of their potential clinical significance (reasons given in parentheses where appropriate)—not necessarily inclusive (» = major clinical significance).

Except under special circumstances, this medication should not be used when the following medical problem exists:

» Hypersensitivity to ertapenem, any component of this product or to other drugs in the same class, or hypersensitivity to beta-lactams
» Hypersensitivity to local anesthetics of the amide type (intramuscular administration only)
(serious and occasionally fatal hypersensitivity [anaphylactic] reactions have been reported in patients receiving therapy with beta-lactams; these reactions are more likely to occur in individuals with a history of sensitivity to multiple allergens.)

Risk-benefit should be considered when the following medical problems exist:

» Gastrointestinal disease, active or a history of, especially diarrhea
(treatment with antibacterial agents may cause pseudomembranous colitis; severity can range from mild to life-threatening)
» CNS disorders, such as brain lesions or history of seizures and/or
» Impaired renal function
(increased chance of seizures; close adherence to correct dosage regimen is recommended)

Patient monitoring

The following may be especially important in patient monitoring (other tests may be warranted in some patients, depending on condition; » = major clinical significance):

Organ system function including
Hepatic function,
Hematopoietic function, and
Renal function
(periodic assessment is advised during prolonged therapy)

Patient evaluation
(prolonged use may result in overgrowth of non-susceptible organisms; repeated evaluation of patient's condition is recommended)

Side/Adverse Effects

The following side/adverse effects have been selected on the basis of their potential clinical significance (possible signs and symptoms in parentheses where appropriate)—not necessarily inclusive:

Those indicating need for medical attention

Incidence more frequent

Infused vein complication (bleeding; blistering; burning; coldness; discoloration of skin; feeling of pressure; hives; infection; inflammation; itching; lumps; numbness; pain; rash; redness; scarring; soreness; stinging; swelling; tenderness; tingling; ulceration; warmth)

Incidence less frequent

Phlebitis or thrombophlebitis (bluish color changes in skin color; pain, tenderness, swelling of foot or leg); ***tachycardia*** (fast, pounding, or irregular heartbeat or pulse)

Incidence rare

Allergic reaction (fainting or loss of consciousness; fast or irregular breathing; swelling of eyes or eyelids; trouble in breathing; tightness in chest; wheezing; skin rash; itching); ***pseudomembranous colitis*** (abdominal or stomach cramps; pain; bloating; abdominal tenderness; diarrhea, watery and severe, which may also be bloody; fever; increased thirst; nausea or vomiting; unusual tiredness or weakness; unusual weight loss); ***seizures*** (convulsions; muscle spasm or jerking of all extremities; sudden loss of consciousness; loss of bladder control)

Incidence not determined—Observed during clinical practice; estimates of frequency can not be determined

Anaphylaxis including anaphylactoid reactions (cough; difficulty swallowing; dizziness; fast heartbeat; hives; itching, puffiness or swelling of the eyelids or around the eyes, face, lips or tongue; shortness of breath; skin rash; tightness in chest; unusual tiredness or weakness; wheezing); ***hallucinations*** (seeing, hearing, or feeling things that are not there)

Those indicating need for medical attention only if they continue or are bothersome

Incidence more frequent

Altered mental status (agitation; confusion about identity, place, and time; mental depression; drowsiness; unusual tiredness); ***chest pain; diarrhea*** (loose or frequent bowel movements); ***fever; headache; nausea***

Incidence less frequent

Acid regurgitation (heartburn); ***anxiety*** (fear; nervousness); ***asthenia or fatigue*** (lack or loss of strength; unusual tiredness or weakness); ***constipation*** (difficulty having a bowel movement (stool)); ***cough; dizziness; dyspnea or respiratory distress*** (shortness of breath; difficult or labored breathing; tightness in chest; wheezing); ***dyspepsia*** (acid or sour stomach; belching; heartburn; indigestion; stomach discomfort, upset, or pain); ***edema*** (swelling); ***erythema*** (flushing; redness of skin; unusually warm skin); ***hypertension*** (blurred vision; dizziness; nervousness; headache; pounding in the ears; slow or fast heartbeat); ***hypotension*** (blurred vision; confusion; dizziness; faintness or lightheadedness when getting up from a lying or sitting position; sudden sweating; unusual tiredness or weakness); ***insomnia*** (sleeplessness; trouble sleeping; unable to sleep); ***leg pain; oral candidiasis*** (sore mouth or tongue; white patches in mouth and/or on tongue); ***pharyngitis*** (body aches or pain; congestion; cough; dryness or soreness of throat; fever; hoarseness; runny nose; tender, swollen glands in neck; trouble in swallowing; voice changes); ***pruritus*** (itching skin); ***rash; vaginitis*** (itching of the vagina or genital area; pain during sexual intercourse; thick, white vaginal discharge with no odor or with a mild odor); ***vomiting***

Those indicating the need for medical attention if they occur after medication is discontinued

Pseudomembranous colitis (abdominal or stomach cramps; pain; bloating; abdominal tenderness; diarrhea, watery and severe, which may also be bloody; fever; increased thirst; nausea or vomiting; unusual tiredness or weakness; unusual weight loss)

Overdose

No human cases of overdose have been reported. In healthy volunteers, intravenous administration of 2 grams of ertapenem over 30 minutes or 3 grams of ertapenem over 1 to 2 hours resulted in an increased incidence of nausea. Inadvertent administration of three 1 gram doses of ertapenem in a 24 hour period resulted in diarrhea and transient dizziness in one patient. In pediatric clinical studies, a single IV dose of 40 mg per kg of body weight up to a maximum of 2 grams did not result in toxicity.

For more information on the management of overdose or unintentional ingestion, **contact a poison control center** (see *Poison Control Center Listing*).

Treatment of overdose

There is no known specific antidote to ertapenem. Treatment is generally symptomatic and supportive, possibly including:

To enhance elimination—

Ertapenem can be removed by hemodialysis. The plasma clearance of the total fraction of ertapenem was increased 30% in subjects with end-stage renal insufficiency when hemodialysis (4-hour session) was performed immediately following administration. There is no specific information available on the use of hemodialysis to treat overdosage.

Supportive care—

In the event of an overdose ertapenem should be discontinued and general supportive treatment given until renal elimination takes place.

Patients in whom intentional overdose is confirmed or suspected should be referred for psychiatric consultation.

Patient Consultation

As an aid to patient consultation, refer to *Advice for the Patient, Ertapenem (Systemic)*.

In providing consultation, consider emphasizing the following selected information (» = major clinical significance):

Before using this medication

» Conditions affecting use, especially:

Hypersensitivity to ertapenem, beta-lactam antibacterials (e.g., cephalosporins, penicillins, imipenem), or history of hypersensitivity to multiple allergens.

Intramuscular—Hypersensitivity to local anesthetics of the amide type (e.g., lidocaine)

Pregnancy—Ertapenem crosses the placenta in rats. It should be used during pregnancy only if clearly needed

FDA Pregnancy Category B

Breast-feeding—Ertapenem is distributed into breast milk. Ertapenem should be administered to nursing mothers only when the expected benefit outweighs the risk.

Use in children—Safety and effectiveness established in infants and children 3 months to 17 years of age; not recommended for use in infants under 3 months of age or in the treatment of meningitis in pediatrics

Other medications, especially probenecid

Other medical problems, especially gastrointestinal disease (e.g., diarrhea), CNS disorders (e.g., brain lesions, history of seizures), or impaired renal function

Proper use of this medication

» Importance of using this medicine only to treat bacterial infections and not viral infections such as the common cold

» Importance of receiving medication for full course of therapy and on regular schedule.

» Proper dosing

» Proper storage

Precautions while using this medication

» Continuing anticonvulsant therapy in patients with a history of seizures

» For severe diarrhea, checking with physician before taking any antidiarrheals; for mild diarrhea, taking kaolin- or attapulgite-containing, but not other, antidiarrheals; checking with physician or pharmacist if mild diarrhea continues or worsens

Side/adverse effects

Signs of potential side effects, especially infused vein complication, phlebitis or thrombophlebitis, tachycardia, allergic reaction, pseudomembranous colitis, and seizures

Signs of potential side effects observed during clinical practice, especially anaphylaxis including anaphylactoid reactions and hallucinations

General Dosing Information

Lidocaine HCl is the diluent for intramuscular administration of ertapenem. Refer to the lidocaine prescribing information for lidocaine HCl.

When ertapenem is administered intravenously, the dose should be infused over a period of 30 minutes.

Intramuscular administration of ertapenem may be used as an alternative to intravenous administration of ertapenem in the treatment of those infections for which intramuscular therapy is appropriate.

Prescribing ertapenem in the absence of a proven or strongly suspected bacterial infection or a prophylactic indication is not likely to provide benefit to the patient and increases the risk of the development of drug-resistant bacteria.

For treatment of adverse effects

Anticonvulsants should be continued in the treatment of patients receiving ertapenem who have known seizure disorders. In patients who develop symptoms of CNS toxicity (e.g., focal tremors, myoclonus, or seizures) during treatment with ertapenem, the patient should be evaluated neurologically, placed on anticonvulsant therapy (e.g., phenytoin or benzodiazepines) if not already initiated, and the dosage of ertapenem should be reduced or the drug should be discontinued. In patients with impaired renal function, dosage adjustment is recommended.

If an allergic reaction to ertapenem occurs, the drug should be discontinued. Severe hypersensitivity reactions may require immediate emergency treatment with epinephrine, oxygen, intravenous steroids, airway management including intubation, or other emergency measures as indicated.

For antibiotic-associated pseudomembranous colitis (AAPMC)—

Some patients may develop AAPMC, caused by *Clostridium difficile* toxin, during or following administration of ertapenem. Mild cases may respond to discontinuation of the drug alone. Moderate to severe cases may require fluid, electrolyte, and protein replacement.

In cases not responding to the above measures or in more severe cases, treatment with an antibacterial medication effective against AAPMC may be necessary.

In addition, AAPMC may result in severe watery diarrhea which may occur during therapy or up to several weeks after therapy is discontinued. If diarrhea occurs, administration of antiperistaltic antidiarrheals is not recommended since they may delay the removal of toxins from the colon, thereby prolonging and/or worsening the diarrhea.

Parenteral Dosage Forms

ERTAPENEM SODIUM FOR INJECTION

Usual adult and adolescent dose

Intravenous, 1 gram infused over 30 minutes every 24 hours for up to 14 days.

Intramuscular, 1 gram every 24 hours for up to 7 days.

Intra-abdominal infections, complicated—
Intravenous or Intramuscular, 1 gram every 24 hours, for 5 to 14 days.

Pelvic infections, acute, including postpartum endomyometritis, septic abortion, and post surgical gynecological infections—
Intravenous or Intramuscular, 1 gram every 24 hours, for 3 to 10 days.

Pneumonia, community-acquired—
Intravenous or Intramuscular, 1 gram every 24 hours, for 10 to 14 days. Duration of treatment includes a possible switch to an appropriate oral therapy, after at least 3 days of parenteral therapy, once clinical improvement has been demonstrated.

Skin and skin structure infections, complicated—
Intravenous or Intramuscular, 1 gram every 24 hours, for 7 to 14 days.

Urinary tract infections, complicated, including pyelonephritis—
Intravenous or Intramuscular, 1 gram every 24 hours, for 10 to 14 days. Duration of treatment includes a possible switch to an appropriate oral therapy, after at least 3 days of parenteral therapy, once clinical improvement has been demonstrated.

Note: A dose of 500 mg every 24 hours is recommended for patients with advanced (creatinine clearance $\leq$ 30 mL per minute per 1.73 m^2) and end-stage renal insufficiency (creatinine clearance $\leq$ 10 mL per minute 1.73 m^2).

Patients on hemodialysis who are given the recommended dose of 500 mg within 6 hours prior to the start of hemodialysis should receive a supplementary dose of 150 mg following the hemodialysis session. If ertapenem is given at least 6 hours prior to the start of the hemodialysis session, no supplementary dose is needed.

Usual adult and adolescent prescribing limits

Intravenous or intramuscular, 500 mg to 1 gram every 24 hours for 3 to 14 days.

Usual pediatric dose

Safety and efficacy have not been established in children less than 3 months of age

The following doses are for patients 3 months to 12 years of age:

Intravenous, 15 mg per kg of body weight infused over 30 minutes every twice daily (not to exceed 1 gram per day) for up to 14 days.

Intramuscular, 15 mg per kg of body weight twice daily (not to exceed 1 gram per day) for up to 7 days.

Intra-abdominal infections, complicated—
Intravenous or Intramuscular, 15 mg per kg of body weight twice daily for 5 to 14 days.

Pelvic infections, acute, including postpartum endomyometritis, septic abortion, and post surgical gynecological infections—
Intravenous or Intramuscular, 15 mg per kg of body weight twice daily for 3 to 10 days.

Pneumonia, community-acquired—
Intravenous or Intramuscular, 15 mg per kg of body weight twice daily for 10 to 14 days. Duration of treatment includes a possible switch to an appropriate oral therapy, after at least 3 days of parenteral therapy, once clinical improvement has been demonstrated.

Skin and skin structure infections, complicated—
Intravenous or Intramuscular, 15 mg per kg of body weight twice daily for 7 to 14 days.

Urinary tract infections, complicated, including pyelonephritis—
Intravenous or Intramuscular, 15 mg per kg of body weight twice daily for 10 to 14 days. Duration of treatment includes a possible switch to an appropriate oral therapy, after at least 3 days of parenteral therapy, once clinical improvement has been demonstrated.

Usual pediatric limits

Daily dose should not exceed 1 gram.

Usual geriatric dose

Dose selection for the elderly should be cautious due to the greater frequency of geriatric specific problems, including decreased renal function.

Strength(s) usually available

U.S.—

Note: The sodium content is approximately 137 mg (approximately 6 mEq)

1 gram (base) (Rx) [*Invanz* (sodium bicarbonate; sodium hydroxide)].

Packaging and storage

Prior to reconstitution, do not store above 25°C (77 °F).

The reconstituted solution, immediately diluted in 0.9% Sodium Chloride Injection, may be stored at room temperature (25°C) and used within 6 hours or stored for 24 hours under refrigeration (5°C) and used within 4 hours after removal from refrigeration. Solution should not be frozen.

Preparation of dosage form

Intravenous administration: Ertapenem must be reconstituted and then diluted prior to administration.

• Reconstitute the contents of a 1 g vial of ertapenem with 10 mL of one of the following: Water for Injection, 0.9% Sodium Chloride Injection or Bacteriostatic Water for Injection

• For adult and adolescent patients 13 years of age and older—Shake well to dissolve and immediately transfer contents of the reconstituted vial to 50 mL of 0.9% Sodium Chloride Injection

• For infant and pediatric patients 3 months to 12 years of age—Shake well to dissolve and immediately withdraw a volume equal to 15 mg per kg of body weight (not to exceed 1 gram per day) and dilute in 0.9% Sodium Chloride Injection to a final concentration of 20 mg per mL or less.

• Complete the infusion within 6 hours of reconstitution

Intramuscular administration: Ertapenem must be reconstituted prior to administration.

• Reconstitute the contents of a 1 g vial of ertapenem with 3.2 mL of 1% lidocaine HCl injection (**without epinephrine**). Shake vial thoroughly to form solution

• For adult and adolescent patients 13 years of age and older—Immediately withdraw the contents of the vial and administer via deep intramuscular injection into a large muscle mass (such as the gluteal muscles or lateral part of the thigh).

• For infant and pediatric patients 3 months to 12 years of age—Immediately withdraw a volume equal to 15 mg per kg of body weight (not to exceed 1 gram per day) and administer by deep intramuscular injection into a large muscle mass (such as the gluteal muscles or lateral part of the thigh).

• The reconstituted intramuscular solution should be used within 1 hour of preparation.

Note: The reconstituted intramuscular solution should not be administered intravenously.

Incompatibilities

Ertapenem should not be mixed with diluents containing dextrose (α-D-Glucose), and should not be mixed or co-infused with other medications.

Auxiliary labeling

• You should take this medication exactly as prescribed. Do not skip or discontinue unless directed.

Revised: 04/13/2006
Developed: 12/11/2002

ERYTHROMYCIN Ophthalmic

VA CLASSIFICATION (Primary): OP201

Commonly used brand name(s): *Ilotycin*.

Note: For a listing of dosage forms and brand names by country availability, see *Dosage Forms* section(s).

Category

Antibacterial (ophthalmic).

Indications

Note: Bracketed information in the *Indications* section refers to uses that are not included in U.S. product labeling.

Accepted

Conjunctivitis, neonatal (prophylaxis)—Erythromycin is indicated in the topical prophylaxis of neonatal conjunctivitis caused by *Chlamydia trachomatis.*

Ocular infections (treatment)—Erythromycin is indicated in the topical treatment of superficial ocular infections of the conjunctiva and/or cornea caused by susceptible organisms.

Ophthalmia neonatorum (prophylaxis)—Erythromycin is indicated alone in the prophylaxis of ophthalmia neonatorum caused by *Neisseria gonorrhoeae* or *C. trachomatis.* However, in infants born to mothers who have clinically apparent gonorrhea, ophthalmic erythromycin is indicated concurrently with parenteral aqueous penicillin G.

[Blepharitis, bacterial (treatment)][1]
[Blepharoconjunctivitis (treatment)][1]
[Chlamydial infections (treatment)][1]
[Conjunctivitis, bacterial (treatment)][1]
[Keratitis, bacterial (treatment)][1]
[Keratoconjunctivitis, bacterial (treatment)][1]
[Meibomianitis (treatment)][1] or
[Trachoma (treatment)][1]—Erythromycin is used in the topical treatment of bacterial blepharitis, blepharoconjunctivitis, chlamydial infections, bacterial conjunctivitis, bacterial keratitis, bacterial keratoconjunctivitis, meibomianitis, and trachoma.

Not all species or strains of a particular organism may be susceptible to erythromycin.

[1]Not included in Canadian product labeling.

Pharmacology/Pharmacokinetics

Physicochemical characteristics

Molecular weight—733.94.
Family—Macrolide group of antibiotics.

Mechanism of action/Effect

Erythromycin is a bacteriostatic macrolide antibiotic. However, it may be bactericidal in high concentrations or when used against highly susceptible organisms. It is thought to penetrate the bacterial cell membrane and to reversibly bind to the 50 S subunit of bacterial ribosomes or near the "P" or donor site so that binding of tRNA (transfer RNA) to the donor site is blocked. Translocation of peptides from the "A" or acceptor site to the "P" or donor site is prevented, and subsequent protein synthesis is inhibited.

Erythromycin is effective only against actively dividing organisms.

Absorption

Topical application of the ophthalmic ointment to the eye may result in absorption into the cornea and aqueous humor.

Precautions to Consider

Cross-sensitivity and/or related problems

Patients intolerant of one erythromycin may be intolerant of other erythromycins also.

Tumorigenicity

Two-year studies of rats administered erythromycin orally showed no evidence of tumorigenicity.

Mutagenicity

Studies have not been done.

Pregnancy/Reproduction

Fertility—Studies of rats, mice, and rabbits given high doses of systemic erythromycin showed no evidence of impaired fertility

Pregnancy—Problems in humans have not been documented.

Studies of rats, mice, and rabbits given high doses of systemic erythromycin showed no evidence of harm to the fetus.

FDA Pregnancy Category B.

Breast-feeding

Problems in humans have not been documented.

Pediatrics

Appropriate studies on the relationship of age to the effects of this medicine have not been performed in the pediatric population. However, no pediatrics-specific problems have been documented to date.

Geriatrics

Appropriate studies on the relationship of age to the effects of this medicine have not been performed in the geriatric population. However, no geriatrics-specific problems have been documented to date.

Medical considerations/Contraindications

The medical considerations/contraindications included have been selected on the basis of their potential clinical significance (reasons given in parentheses where appropriate)—not necessarily inclusive (» = major clinical significance).

Risk-benefit should be considered when the following medical problem exists:

Intolerance to erythromycin or parabens

Side/Adverse Effects

The following side/adverse effects have been selected on the basis of their potential clinical significance (possible signs and symptoms in parentheses where appropriate)—not necessarily inclusive:

Those indicating need for medical attention

Incidence rare

Eye irritation not present before therapy

Patient Consultation

As an aid to patient consultation, refer to *Advice for the Patient, Erythromycin (Ophthalmic).*

In providing consultation, consider emphasizing the following selected information (» = major clinical significance):

Before using this medication

» Conditions affecting use, especially:
Allergy to this or any of the other erythromycins

Proper use of this medication

Proper administration technique for ophthalmic ointment
» Compliance with full course of therapy
» Proper dosing
Missed dose: Applying as soon as possible; not applying if almost time for next dose
» Proper storage

Precautions while using this medication

Checking with physician if no improvement within a few days
Blurred vision after application of ophthalmic ointments

Side/adverse effects

Signs of potential side effects, especially eye irritation not present before therapy

General Dosing Information

Use of topical antibacterials may lead to skin sensitization, resulting in hypersensitivity reactions with subsequent topical or systemic use of the medication.

In the prophylaxis of ophthalmia neonatorum, erythromycin ophthalmic ointment should not be flushed from the eye following administration. In addition, ophthalmic erythromycin is given concurrently with parenteral aqueous penicillin G in infants born to mothers who have clinically apparent gonorrhea.

Ophthalmic Dosage Forms

ERYTHROMYCIN OPHTHALMIC OINTMENT USP

Usual adult and adolescent dose

Ocular infections—
Topical, to the conjunctiva, a thin strip (approximately 1 cm) of ointment up to six times a day, depending on the severity of the infection.

Usual pediatric dose

Conjunctivitis, neonatal or
Ophthalmia neonatorum—
Topical, to each conjunctiva, a thin strip (approximately 0.5 to 1 cm) of ointment as a single dose following cesarean or vaginal delivery.

Ocular infections—
See *Usual adult and adolescent dose.*

Strength(s) usually available

U.S.—
0.5% (Rx) [*Ilotycin* (methylparaben, propylparaben); GENERIC].

Canada—
0.5% (Rx) [*Ilotycin;* GENERIC].

Packaging and storage

Store below 40 °C (104 °F), preferably between 15 and 30 °C (59 and 86 °F), unless otherwise specified by manufacturer. Protect from freezing.

Auxiliary labeling

- For the eye.
- Continue medicine for full time of treatment.

Revised: 11/28/1994

ERYTHROMYCIN Topical

VA CLASSIFICATION (Primary/Secondary): DE752/DE101

Commonly used brand name(s): *A/T/S; Akne-Mycin; ETS; Emgel; Ery-Derm; Ery-Sol; Erycette; Erygel; Erymax; Erythra-Derm; Sans-Acne; Staticin; T-Stat; Theramycin Z.*

Note: For a listing of dosage forms and brand names by country availability, see *Dosage Forms* section(s).

Category

Antiacne agent (topical)—Erythromycin Ointment; Erythromycin Pledgets; Erythromycin Topical Gel; Erythromycin Topical Solution.

Antibacterial (topical)—Erythromycin Ointment.

Indications

Note: Bracketed information in the *Indications* section refers to uses that are not included in U.S. product labeling.

Accepted

Acne vulgaris (treatment)—Topical erythromycin is indicated in the topical treatment of acne vulgaris. It may be effective in grades II and III acne, which are characterized by inflammatory lesions such as papules and pustules. Topical antibacterials are not generally considered to be as effective as systemic antibacterials in the treatment of acne, especially more severe inflammatory acne.

[Skin infections, bacterial, minor (prophylaxis)][1] or

[Skin infections, bacterial, minor (treatment)][1]—Erythromycin ointment is used in the topical prophylaxis and treatment of superficial pyogenic infections of the skin.

Unaccepted

Topical erythromycin is not effective in deep cystic lesions or in noninflammatory lesions.

[1]Not included in Canadian product labeling.

Pharmacology/Pharmacokinetics

Physicochemical characteristics

Molecular weight—733.94.

Mechanism of action/Effect

Antiacne agent (topical)—Probably due to its antibacterial activity. Topical erythromycin is thought to suppress the growth of *Propionibacterium acnes (Corynebacterium acnes)*, an anaerobe found in sebaceous glands and follicles. *P. acnes* produces proteases, hyaluronidases, lipases, and chemotactic factors, all of which can produce inflammatory components or inflammation directly.

Precautions to Consider

Cross-sensitivity and/or related problems

Patients sensitive to one erythromycin may be sensitive to other erythromycins also.

Carcinogenicity

For erythromycin pledgets; erythromycin topical gel; erythromycin topical solution—

Long-term studies in animals have not been done to evaluate carcinogenicity.

Mutagenicity

For erythromycin pledgets; erythromycin topical gel—

Long-term studies in animals have not been done to evaluate mutagenicity.

For erythromycin topical solution—

Erythromycin topical solution has not been shown to be mutagenic in the Ames Salmonella/Microsome Plate Test.

Pregnancy/Reproduction

Pregnancy—

For erythromycin pledgets—

Fertility; pregnancy:

Studies have not been done in humans or animals.

FDA Pregnancy Category C.

For erythromycin topical gel; erythromycin topical solution—

Fertility; pregnancy:

Erythromycin crosses the placenta, although fetal serum concentrations are generally low. Adequate and well-controlled studies in humans have not been done.

Studies in rats, fed erythromycin base in amounts up to 0.25% of their diet prior to and during mating, during gestation, and through weaning, have not shown that erythromycin causes adverse effects on the fetus. In addition, studies in rats and rabbits, given 1.5, 4, and 13 times the estimated human dose, have not shown that erythromycin causes impaired fertility or adverse effects on the fetus.

FDA Pregnancy Category B.

Breast-feeding

For erythromycin pledgets; erythromycin topical gel—

It is not known whether erythromycin, applied topically, is distributed into breast milk. Erythromycin, given systemically, is distributed into breast milk. However, problems in humans have not been documented.

Pediatrics

For erythromycin topical gel—

Appropriate studies on the relationship of age to the effects of this medicine have not been performed in the pediatric population.

For erythromycin topical solution—

Appropriate studies on the relationship of age to the effects of this medicine have not been performed in children up to 12 years of age.

Geriatrics

Appropriate studies on the relationship of age to the effects of this medicine have not been performed in the geriatric population. However, geriatrics-specific problems that would limit the usefulness of this medication in the elderly are not expected.

Drug interactions and/or related problems

The following drug interactions and/or related problems have been selected on the basis of their potential clinical significance (possible mechanism in parentheses where appropriate)—not necessarily inclusive (» = major clinical significance):

Note: Combinations containing any of the following medications, depending on the amount present, may also interact with this medication.

Abrasive or medicated soaps or cleansers or
Acne preparations or preparations containing a peeling agent, such as:
- Benzoyl peroxide
- Resorcinol
- Salicylic acid
- Sulfur
- Tretinoin or

Alcohol-containing preparations, topical, such as:
- After-shave lotions
- Astringents
- Perfumed toiletries
- Shaving creams or lotions or

Cosmetics or soaps with a strong drying effect or
Isotretinoin or
Medicated cosmetics or "cover-ups"
(concurrent use with erythromycin pledgets, topical gel, or topical solution may cause a cumulative irritant or drying effect, especially with the application of peeling, desquamating, or abrasive agents, resulting in excessive irritation of the skin)

Medical considerations/Contraindications

The medical considerations/contraindications included have been selected on the basis of their potential clinical significance (reasons given in parentheses where appropriate)—not necessarily inclusive (» = major clinical significance).

Risk-benefit should be considered when the following medical problem exists:

Sensitivity to erythromycin

Side/Adverse Effects

The following side/adverse effects have been selected on the basis of their potential clinical significance (possible signs and symptoms in parentheses where appropriate)—not necessarily inclusive:

Those indicating need for medical attention only if they continue or are bothersome

For ointment

Incidence less frequent

Peeling; redness

For pledgets, topical gel, and topical solution

Incidence more frequent

Dry or scaly skin; irritation; itching; stinging or burning feeling

Incidence less frequent

Peeling; redness

Patient Consultation

As an aid to patient consultation, refer to *Advice for the Patient, Erythromycin (Topical)*.

In providing consultation, consider emphasizing the following selected information (» = major clinical significance):

Before using this medication

» Conditions affecting use, especially:
Sensitivity to erythromycins
Pregnancy—Erythromycin crosses the placenta
Breast-feeding—Erythromycin enters breast-milk

Proper use of this medication

Proper administration technique
» Compliance with full course of therapy, which may take months or longer
» Proper dosing
Missed dose: Applying as soon as possible; not applying if almost time for next dose
» Proper storage

For pledgets, topical gel, and topical solution
» Not using near heat or open flame or while smoking
Not using medication more often than prescribed
Avoiding too frequent washing of affected areas
» Importance of applying medication to entire affected area
» Not using in eyes, nose, mouth, or on other mucous membranes

Precautions while using this medication

Checking with physician if no improvement in acne within 3 to 4 weeks; may take up to 8 to 12 weeks before full therapeutic benefit is seen

For pledgets, topical gel, and topical solution:
Waiting at least 1 hour before applying any other topical medication for acne
Possibility of stinging or burning after application
Checking with physician if treated skin becomes excessively dry
Proper use of cosmetics

General Dosing Information

For topical solution dosage form

If the treated area(s) become uncomfortable because of excessive dryness or irritation, the dosage of erythromycin topical solution may be reduced to once a day or less often until the symptoms have subsided.

In the treatment of acne with erythromycin topical solution, noticeable improvement may be seen in 3 to 4 weeks. However, 8 to 12 weeks of treatment may be required before maximum benefit is seen.

Topical Dosage Forms

ERYTHROMYCIN OINTMENT USP

Note: The composition of *Akne-Mycin* available in the U.S. is different from that of *Akne-Mycin* available in Europe.

Usual adult and adolescent dose

Acne vulgaris—
Topical, to the skin, two times a day, morning and evening.

Usual pediatric dose

See *Usual adult and adolescent dose.*

Strength(s) usually available

U.S.—
2% (Rx) [*Akne-Mycin*].

Canada—
Not commercially available.

Packaging and storage

Store preferably between 15 and 30 °C (59 and 86 °F). Store in a collapsible tube or in another tight container. Protect from freezing.

Auxiliary labeling

- For external use only.
- Continue medication for full time of treatment.

ERYTHROMYCIN PLEDGETS USP

Usual adult and adolescent dose

Acne vulgaris—
Topical, to the skin, two times a day.

Usual pediatric dose

See *Usual adult and adolescent dose.*

Strength(s) usually available

U.S.—
2% (Rx) [*Erycette* (alcohol 66%; propylene glycol); *T-Stat* (alcohol 71.2%; propylene glycol)].

Canada—
Not commercially available.

Note: Supplied as foil-covered pledgets (swabs) saturated with 2% erythromycin topical solution.

Packaging and storage

Store below 40 °C (104 °F), preferably between 15 and 30 °C (59 and 86 °F), unless otherwise specified by manufacturer. Store in a tight container.

Auxiliary labeling

- For external use only.
- Continue medication for full time of treatment.
- Flammable—Keep from heat and flame.

ERYTHROMYCIN TOPICAL GEL

Usual adult and adolescent dose

See *Erythromycin Ointment USP.*

Usual pediatric dose

Dosage has not been established.

Strength(s) usually available

U.S.—
2% (Rx) [*A/T/S* (alcohol 92%); *Emgel; Erygel* (alcohol 92%)].

Canada—
Not commercially available.

Packaging and storage

Store below 40 °C (104 °F), preferably between 15 and 30 °C (59 and 86 °F), unless otherwise specified by manufacturer. Protect from freezing.

Auxiliary labeling

- For external use only.
- Continue medication for full time of treatment.
- Flammable—Keep from heat and flame.

ERYTHROMYCIN TOPICAL SOLUTION USP

Usual adult and adolescent dose

See *Erythromycin Ointment USP.*

Usual pediatric dose

Infants and children up to 12 years of age—Dosage has not been established.

Children 12 years of age and over—See *Usual adult and adolescent dose.*

Strength(s) usually available

U.S.—
1.5% (Rx) [*Staticin* (alcohol 55%; propylene glycol); GENERIC].
2% (Rx) [*Akne-Mycin* (alcohol 66%; propylene glycol); *A/T/S* (alcohol 66%; propylene glycol); *EryDerm* (alcohol 77%; propylene glycol); *Erymax* (alcohol 66%; propylene glycol); *Ery-Sol; Erythra-Derm* (erythromycin base); *ETS* (alcohol 66%; propylene glycol); *Theramycin Z; T-Stat* (alcohol 71.2%; propylene glycol); GENERIC].

Canada—
1.5% (Rx) [*Staticin* (alcohol 55%)].
2% (Rx) [*Sans-Acne* (alcohol 44%)].

Packaging and storage

Store below 40 °C (104 °F), preferably between 15 and 30 °C (59 and 86 °F), unless otherwise specified by manufacturer. Store in a tight container.

Auxiliary labeling

- For external use only.
- Continue medication for full time of treatment.
- Keep container tightly closed.
- Flammable—Keep from heat and flame.

Note

Explain administration technique.

Revised: 09/18/2000

ERYTHROMYCIN AND BENZOYL PEROXIDE Topical

VA CLASSIFICATION (Primary): DE752

Commonly used brand name(s): *Benzamycin.*

NOTE: The *Erythromycin and Benzoyl Peroxide (Topical)* monograph is maintained on the *USP DI* electronic data base. A copy of the most recent revision of the complete monograph can be accessed on the *USP DI* Updates Online website. See the front cover of book for details on accessing the site.

For information on the specific components of this combination, see the *USP DI* monographs for *Benzoyl Peroxide (Topical)* and *Erythromycin (Topical)*.

The information that follows is selectively abstracted from the complete monograph and is provided to facilitate drug use review and patient counseling.

Note: For a listing of dosage forms and brand names by country availability, see *Dosage Forms* section(s).

Category

Antiacne agent (topical).

Indications

Note: Bracketed information in the *Indications* section refers to uses that are not included in U.S. product labeling.

Accepted

Acne vulgaris (treatment)—Erythromycin and benzoyl peroxide combination is indicated [as a primary agent] in the topical treatment of acne vulgaris. [It may be effective in grades II and III acne, which are characterized by inflammatory lesions such as papules and pustules.]

[Topical antibacterials are not generally considered to be as effective as systemic antibacterials in the treatment of acne, especially more severe inflammatory acne.]

Unaccepted

Topical erythromycin-containing preparations are not as effective in deep cystic lesions or in noninflammatory lesions.

Patient Consultation

As an aid to patient consultation, refer to *Advice for the Patient, Erythromycin and Benzoyl Peroxide (Topical)*.

In providing consultation, consider emphasizing the following selected information (» = major clinical significance):

Before using this medication

» Conditions affecting use, especially:
Sensitivity to erythromycins

Proper use of this medication

» Not applying medication to raw or irritated skin
Before applying, thoroughly washing affected area(s), rinsing well, and patting dry; after washing or shaving, waiting 30 minutes before applying medication
Avoiding too frequent washing of affected area(s)

To use

» Importance of not using more medication than the amount prescribed
After washing affected area(s), applying medication with fingertips; however, washing medication off hands afterward
» Importance of applying medication to entire affected area
» Not using in or around eyes, nose, or mouth, or on other mucous membranes
Not using medication after expiration date
» Compliance with full course of therapy, which may take months or longer
» Proper dosing
Missed dose: Applying as soon as possible; not applying if almost time for next dose
» Proper storage

Precautions while using this medication

Checking with physician if no improvement in acne within 3 to 4 weeks; may take up to 8 to 12 weeks before full therapeutic benefit is seen

Waiting at least 1 hour after applying the first medication before applying the second topical medication for acne

Possibility of mild stinging or burning of the skin after application; checking with physician if irritation continues; using medication less frequently

Checking with physician if treated skin becomes excessively dry

» Medication may bleach hair or colored fabrics

Using only "oil-free" cosmetics to avoid worsening acne

Side/adverse effects

Signs of potential side effects, especially allergic contact dermatitis, painful irritation of the skin, or skin rash

Topical Dosage Forms

ERYTHROMYCIN AND BENZOYL PEROXIDE TOPICAL GEL USP

Usual adult and adolescent dose

Acne vulgaris—
Topical, to the affected area(s), two times a day, morning and evening; or as directed by physician.

Usual pediatric dose

Acne vulgaris—
Infants and children up to 12 years of age: Dosage has not been established.
Children 12 years of age and over: See *Usual adult and adolescent dose*.

When reconstituted and mixed according to manufacturer's instructions

U.S.—

Note: Erythromycin and benzoyl peroxide topical gel is supplied in a package containing 20 grams of benzoyl peroxide gel and a plastic vial containing 800 mg of active erythromycin powder. After reconstitution and mixing, the combined weight is 23.3 grams.

3% of erythromycin and 5% of benzoyl peroxide (Rx) [*Benzamycin* (alcohol 22%; fragrance)].

Canada—
Not commercially available.

Preparation of dosage form

- Add 3 mL of ethyl alcohol (to the mark) to the vial containing the erythromycin powder.
- Shake the vial well to dissolve the erythromycin powder.
- Add the erythromycin-containing solution to the benzoyl peroxide gel. Stir the mixture until it is homogeneous in appearance (approximately 1 to 1½ minutes).

Prior to dispensing—

Auxiliary labeling

- Refrigerate.
- For external use only.
- Keep container tightly closed.
- Continue medication for full time of treatment.
- Beyond-use date.

Revised: 07/06/1994

ERYTHROMYCIN AND SULFISOXAZOLE Systemic

VA CLASSIFICATION (Primary): AM900

Commonly used brand name(s): *Eryzole; Pediazole*.

NOTE: The *Erythromycin and Sulfisoxazole (Systemic)* monograph is maintained on the *USP DI* electronic data base. A copy of the most recent revision of the complete monograph can be accessed on the *USP DI* Updates Online website. See the front cover of book for details on accessing the site.

For information on the specific components of this combination, see the *USP DI* monographs for *Erythromycins (Systemic)* and *Sulfonamides (Systemic)*.

The information that follows is selectively abstracted from the complete monograph and is provided to facilitate drug use review and patient counseling.

Note: For a listing of dosage forms and brand names by country availability, see *Dosage Forms* section(s).

Category

Antibacterial (systemic).

Indications

Note: Bracketed information in the *Indications* section refers to uses that are not included in U.S. product labeling.

Accepted

Otitis media, acute (treatment)—Erythromycin and sulfisoxazole combination is indicated in the treatment of acute otitis media caused by *Haemophilus influenzae*, [pneumococci, group A streptococci, and *Branhamella catarrhalis*] in children.

[Sinusitis (treatment)][1]—Erythromycin and sulfisoxazole combination is used in the treatment of acute sinusitis caused by *H. influenzae*, pneumococci, group A streptococci, and *B. catarrhalis* in children.

Not all species or strains of a particular organism may be susceptible to erythromycin and sulfisoxazole combination.

[1]Not included in Canadian product labeling.

Patient Consultation

As an aid to patient consultation, refer to *Advice for the Patient, Erythromycin and Sulfisoxazole (Systemic)*.

In providing consultation, consider emphasizing the following selected information (» = major clinical significance):

Before using this medication

» Conditions affecting use, especially:

Allergy to erythromycins or sulfonamides; patients allergic to furosemide, thiazide diuretics, sulfonylureas, or carbonic anhydrase inhibitors may also be allergic to this medication

Pregnancy—Erythromycin crosses the placenta; sulfisoxazole also crosses the placenta and should not be used at term because it may cause kernicterus in the infant; it has also been associated with cleft palates and skeletal defects in the offspring of mice and rats

Breast-feeding—Erythromycins are distributed into breast milk in concentrations that may exceed maternal serum concentrations; sulfisoxazole is also distributed into breast-milk and is not recommended in nursing women since sulfonamides may cause kernicterus in nursing infants

Use in children—Sulfonamides should not be used in children up to 2 months of age because they may cause kernicterus

Dental—Systemic erythromycins may cause oral candidiasis; the leukopenic and thrombocytopenic effects of sulfonamides may result in an increased incidence of certain microbial infections, delayed healing, and gingival bleeding

Other medications, especially alfentanil; astemizole; coumarin- or indanedione-derivative anticoagulants; hydantoin anticonvulsants; oral antidiabetic agents; carbamazepine; chloramphenicol; cyclosporine; other hemolytics; other hepatotoxic medications; clindamycin; lincomycin; methenamine; methotrexate; terfenadine; or xanthines, especially theophylline

Other medical problems, especially blood dyscrasias, a history of cardiac arrythmias or QT prolongation, glucose-6-phosphate dehydrogenase (G6PD) deficiency, hepatic function impairment, loss of hearing, megaloblastic anemia, porphyria, or renal function impairment

Proper use of this medication

» Maintaining adequate fluid intake; may be taken with food

» Not giving to infants under 2 months of age

Using specially marked measuring spoon or other device to measure dose

Proper administration technique for oral liquids; not using after expiration date

» Compliance with full course of therapy

» Importance of not missing doses, and taking at evenly spaced times

» Proper dosing

Missed dose: Taking as soon as possible; not taking if almost time for next dose; not doubling dose

» Proper storage

Precautions while using this medication

» Regular visits to physician to check blood counts, especially in long-term therapy

Checking with physician if no improvement within a few days

» Possible photosensitivity reactions

Using caution in use of regular toothbrushes, dental floss, and toothpicks; delaying dental work until blood counts have returned to normal; checking with physician or dentist concerning proper oral hygiene

Side/adverse effects

Signs of potential side effects, especially blood dyscrasias, cardiac toxicity, crystalluria, goiter, hematuria, hepatotoxicity, hypersensitivity reactions, interstitial nephritis, loss of hearing, Lyell's syndrome, pancreatitis, Stevens-Johnson syndrome, thyroid function disturbance, and tubular necrosis

Oral Dosage Forms

ERYTHROMYCIN ETHYLSUCCINATE AND SULFISOXAZOLE ACETYL FOR ORAL SUSPENSION USP

Usual adult and adolescent dose

Use is not indicated in adults.

Usual pediatric dose

Antibacterial—

Infants up to 2 months of age—

Use is contraindicated since sulfonamides may cause kernicterus in neonates.

Infants and children 2 months of age and over—

The dose can be calculated, based on either the equivalent of erythromycin or sulfisoxazole base, as follows:

Oral, 50 mg (erythromycin) per kg of body weight per day in three or four divided doses for ten days; or

Oral, 150 mg (sulfisoxazole) per kg of body weight per day in three or four divided doses for ten days.

Body Weight	Dose (Every 6 hours for ten days)
Less than 8 kg (Less than 18 lb)	Adjust dosage by body weight
8 kg (18 lb)	1/2 teaspoonful (2.5 mL)
16 kg (35 lb)	1 teaspoonful (5 mL)
24 kg (53 lb)	1 1/2 teaspoonfuls (7.5 mL)
Over 32 kg (over 70 lb)	2 teaspoonfuls (10 mL)

Note: The maximum dose for children should not exceed 6 grams (sulfisoxazole) daily.

Body Weight	Dose (Every 8 hours for ten days)
Less than 6 kg (Less than 13 lb)	Adjust dosage by body weight
6 kg (13 lb)	1/2 teaspoonful (2.5 mL)
12 kg (26 lb)	1 teaspoonful (5 mL)
18 kg (40 lb)	1 1/2 teaspoonfuls (7.5 mL)
24 kg (53 lb)	2 teaspoonfuls (10 mL)
Over 30 kg (over 66 lb)	2 1/2 teaspoonfuls (12.5 mL)

Note: The maximum dose for children should not exceed 6 grams (sulfisoxazole) daily.

The following dosage schedules can also be used—

Four-times-a-day dosing schedule:

Three-times-a-day dosing schedule:

Strength(s) usually available

U.S.—

200 mg of erythromycin and 600 mg of sulfisoxazole per 5 mL (when reconstituted according to manufacturer's instructions) (Rx) [*Eryzole; Pediazole* (sucrose); GENERIC].

Canada—

200 mg of erythromycin and 600 mg of sulfisoxazole per 5 mL (when reconstituted according to manufacturer's instructions) (Rx) [*Pediazole*].

Auxiliary labeling

- Refrigerate.
- Shake well.
- Take with water.
- Avoid too much sun or use of sunlamp.
- Continue medicine for full time of treatment.
- Beyond-use date.

Revised: 06/14/1999

ERYTHROMYCIN BASE—See *Erythromycin (Ophthalmic), Erythromycins (Systemic), Erythromycin (Topical)*

ERYTHROMYCIN ESTOLATE—See *Erythromycins (Systemic)*

ERYTHROMYCIN ETHYLSUCCINATE—See *Erythromycins (Systemic)*

ERYTHROMYCIN GLUCEPTATE—See *Erythromycins (Systemic)*

ERYTHROMYCIN LACTOBIONATE—See *Erythromycins (Systemic)*

ERYTHROMYCIN STEARATE—See *Erythromycins (Systemic)*

ERYTHROMYCINS Systemic

This monograph includes information on the following: 1) Erythromycin Base; 2) Erythromycin Estolate; 3) Erythromycin Ethylsuccinate; 4) Erythromycin Gluceptate; 5) Erythromycin Lactobionate; 6) Erythromycin Stearate.

BAN: Erythromycin ethylsuccinate—Erythromycin ethyl succinate

VA CLASSIFICATION (Primary/Secondary):

Erythromycin Base—AM200/DE751
Erythromycin Estolate—AM200/DE751
Erythromycin Ethylsuccinate—AM200/DE751
Erythromycin Gluceptate—AM200
Erythromycin Lactobionate—AM200
Erythromycin Stearate—AM200/DE751

Commonly used brand name(s): *Apo-Erythro*[1]; *Apo-Erythro E-C*[1]; *Apo-Erythro-ES*[3]; *Apo-Erythro-S*[6]; *E-Base*[1]; *E.E.S.*[3]; *E-Mycin*[1]; *ERYC*[1]; *ERYC-250*[1]; *ERYC-333*[1]; *EryPed*[3]; *Ery-Tab*[1]; *Erybid*[1]; *Erythro*[3]; *Erythrocin*[5]; *Erythrocot*[6]; *Erythromid*[1]; *Ilosone*[2]; *Ilotycin*[1]; *My-E*[6]; *Novo-Rythro*[3]; *Novo-rythro*[2]; *Novo-rythro Encap*[1]; *PCE*[1]; *Wintrocin*[6].

Note: For a listing of dosage forms and brand names by country availability, see *Dosage Forms* section(s).

Category

Antibacterial (systemic)—Erythromycin Base; Erythromycin Estolate; Erythromycin Ethylsuccinate; Erythromycin Gluceptate; Erythromycin Lactobionate; Erythromycin Stearate.

Antiacne agent—Erythromycin Base; Erythromycin Estolate; Erythromycin Ethylsuccinate; Erythromycin Stearate.

Bowel preparation (preoperative) adjunct—Erythromycin Base

Indications

Note: Bracketed information in the *Indications* section refers to uses that are not included in U.S. product labeling.

General Considerations

Erythromycin is a broad-spectrum antibiotic with activity against gram-positive and gram-negative bacteria, and other infectious agents, including *Chlamydia trachomatis*, mycoplasmas (*Mycoplasma pneumoniae* and *Ureaplasma urealyticum*), and spirochetes (*Treponema pallidum* and *Borrelia* species).

Erythromycin has good activity against *Streptococcus pneumoniae*, *S. pyogenes* (group A beta-hemolytic streptococci), and *Staphylococcus aureus*. Resistant strains of both streptococci have been encountered, especially in populations recently exposed to erythromycin. The incidence of resistance to group A streptococci has ranged from 1 to 18% in small studies to up to 60% in a population that had been widely treated with erythromycin for respiratory infections. Most strains of *S. aureus* are currently sensitive to erythromycin. However, the incidence of resistance is increasing. Resistance may develop to erythromycin alone, or may be the result of cross-resistance to other macrolides.

Erythromycin also has good activity against certain gram-negative bacteria, including *Legionella pneumophila*, *Campylobacter jejuni*, and *Bordetella pertussis*, and somewhat lower activity against *Haemophilus influenzae*. There is activity against some gram-negative anaerobes, but most strains of *Bacteroides fragilis* are resistant. Enterobacteriaceae are usually resistant.

Accepted

Bowel preparation, preoperative—Enteric-coated erythromycin base is indicated concurrently with oral-local neomycin as part of an adjunctive regimen for the suppression of normal bacterial flora in the preoperative preparation of the bowel.

Bronchitis, bacterial exacerbations (treatment)
Otitis media, acute (treatment) or
Sinusitis (treatment)—Erythromycins are indicated in the treatment of bacterial exacerbations of bronchitis and in the treatment of sinusitis caused by susceptible organisms. Erythromycins are indicated concurrently with sulfonamides in the treatment of acute otitis media caused by susceptible organisms.

Chlamydial infections, endocervical and urethral (treatment)—Erythromycins are indicated in the treatment of endocervical and urethral chlamydial infections caused by *Chlamydia trachomatis*. Erythromycins are recommended for the treatment of chlamydia in pregnant women. However, erythromycin estolate is contraindicated in pregnancy because of drug-related hepatotoxicity.

Conjunctivitis, chlamydial (treatment) or
Pneumonia, chlamydial (treatment)—Erythromycins are indicated in the treatment of conjunctivitis in newborns and pneumonia in infants caused by *Chlamydia trachomatis*. The efficacy of erythromycin treatment for these uses is approximately 80%; a second course of therapy may be required.

Diphtheria (prophylaxis and treatment)—Erythromycins are indicated as an adjunct to antitoxin, to prevent establishment of chronic carriers and to eradicate the organsim in carriers of diphtheria caused by *Corynebacterium diphtheriae*.

Endocarditis, bacterial (prophylaxis)—Erythromycins are indicated in the prophylaxis of bacterial endocarditis in penicillin-allergic patients who have congenital heart disease, rheumatic or other acquired valvular heart disease, prosthetic heart valves, previous bacterial endocarditis, hypertrophic cardiomyopathy, mitral valve prolapse with valvular regurgitation, and who undergo certain dental or surgical procedures.

Erythrasma (treatment)—Erythromycins are indicated in the treatment of erythrasma caused by *Corynebacterium minutissimum*.

Gonorrhea, endocervical (treatment) or
Gonorrhea, urethral (treatment)—Erythromycins are indicated in the treatment of gonorrhea caused by *Neisseria gonorrhoeae*; cephalosporins and fluoroquinolones are recommended for first-line treatment.

Legionnaires' disease (treatment)—Erythromycins are indicated in the treatment of Legionnaires' disease caused by *Legionella pneumophila*.

Listeriosis (treatment)—Erythromycins are indicated in the treatment of listeriosis caused by *Listeria monocytogenes*.

Pertussis (treatment)—Erythromycins are indicated in the treatment of pertussis (whooping cough) caused by *Bordetella pertussis*.

Pharyngitis, streptococcal (treatment)—Erythromycins are indicated in the treatment of pharyngitis caused by *Streptococcus pyogenes* (group A beta-hemolytic streptococci) in patients allergic to penicillin.

Pneumonia, mycoplasmal (treatment) or
Pneumonia, pneumococcal (treatment)—Erythromycins are indicated in the treatment of pneumonia caused by *Mycoplasma pneumoniae* and *Streptococcus pneumoniae*.

Rheumatic fever (prophylaxis)—Erythromycins are indicated as an alternative to penicillin in the long-term prophylaxis of rheumatic fever.

Skin and soft tissue infections (treatment)—Erythromycins are indicated in the treatment of skin and soft tissue infections, including burn wound infections, caused by *S. pyogenes* (group A beta-hemolytic streptococci).

Syphilis (treatment)—Erythromycins are indicated in the treatment of syphilis caused by *Treponema pallidum* in penicillin-allergic patients. However, erythromycin is less effective than other recommended regimens, and its use in pregnancy has failed to prevent congenital syphilis.

Urethritis, nongonococcal (treatment)—Erythromycins are indicated in the treatment of nongonococcal urethritis caused by *Chlamydia trachomatis* and *Ureaplasma urealyticum*.

[Acne vulgaris (treatment)]—Oral erythromycins are used in the treatment of acne vulgaris.

[Actinomycosis (treatment)][1];
[Anthrax (treatment)][1];
[Chancroid (treatment)][1];
[Lymphogranuloma venereum (treatment)][1]; or
[Relapsing fever (treatment)][1]—Erythromycins are used in the treatment of actinomycosis, anthrax, chancroid, lymphogranuloma venereum, and relapsing fever caused by *Borrelia* species.

[Enteritis, *Campylobacter* (treatment)][1]—Erythromycins are used in the treatment of enteritis caused by *Campylobacter jejuni*. Erythromycin therapy shortened the excretion of *C. jejuni* in the feces, but had no effect on the clinical course of the disease.

[Gastroparesis (treatment)][1]—Erythromycins are used in the treatment of gastroparesis, including severe diabetic gastroparesis, gastroparesis associated with progressive systemic sclerosis, and postvagotomy gastroparesis. Intravenous erythromycin appears to be more effective than oral erythromycin at increasing gastric emptying.

[Lyme disease (treatment)][1]—Erythromycins are used in the treatment of early stage Lyme disease in patients who are allergic to penicillin and in children under 9 years of age; however, erythromycins may be less effective than amoxicillin or doxycycline, possibly due to erratic absorption.

Not all species or strains of a particular organism may be susceptible to erythromycins.

---

[1]Not included in Canadian product labeling.

Pharmacology/Pharmacokinetics

Physicochemical characteristics

Molecular weight—
- Erythromycin base: 733.94.
- Erythromycin estolate: 1056.39.
- Erythromycin ethylsuccinate: 862.06.
- Erythromycin gluceptate: 960.12.
- Erythromycin lactobionate: 1092.23.
- Erythromycin stearate: 1018.42.

Mechanism of action/Effect

Antibacterial—Erythromycin is a bacteriostatic macrolide antibiotic. However, it may be bactericidal in high concentrations or when used against highly susceptible organisms. It is thought to penetrate the bacterial cell membrane and to reversibly bind to the 50 S subunit of bacterial ribosomes; it does not directly inhibit peptide formation, but rather inhibits the translocation of peptides from the acceptor site on the ribosome to the donor site, inhibiting subsequent protein synthesis. Erythromycin is effective only against actively dividing organisms.

Gastroparesis—Erythromycin is thought to bind to motilin receptors and to act as an agonist. Erythromycin administration accelerates gastric emptying by increasing the amplitude of antral contractions and improving antroduodenal coordination. The effect appears to be dose-related. In patients with diabetic gastroparesis, low intravenous doses (40 mg) induce phase 3 of the migrating motor complex in the antrum of the stomach; and higher doses (200 mg) elicit prolonged periods of strong antral contractions. Faster emptying from the proximal stomach contributes to more rapid gastric emptying.

Absorption

Bioavailability varies between 30 and 65%, depending on the salt. Erythromycin film-coated tablets (base and stearate) are subject to gastric acid inactivation and are best absorbed on an empty stomach. However, enteric-coated erythromycin base and erythromycin estolate are acid-stable and may be taken without regard to meals, and erythromycin ethylsuccinate is better absorbed when taken with meals.

Distribution

Widely distributed to most tissues and fluids, including middle ear exudate, prostatic fluid, and semen. Highest concentrations are found in the liver, bile, and spleen. Low concentrations are found in the cerebrospinal fluid (CSF); however, penetration into CSF increases with meningeal inflammation.

Vol_D—0.9 L per kg.

Protein binding

High (70 to 90%).

Biotransformation

Hepatic; > 90% is hepatically metabolized, partially to inactive metabolites; may accumulate in patients with severe hepatic disease.

Erythromycin estolate (lauryl sulfate salt of the propanoate ester)—Propanoate ester is partially hydrolyzed in the gastrointestinal tract, then hydrolyzed in the blood to produce 20 to 40% of the dose as base in the serum.

Erythromycin ethylsuccinate—Absorbed into the blood as the ethylsuccinate salt and hydrolyzed to erythromycin base in the gastrointestinal tract and in the blood to produce 56 to 69% of the dose as base in the serum. Also, despite the high rate of biotransformation of erythromycin ethylsuccinate to active base, the area-under-the-curve (AUC) of active base generated from the ethylsuccinate salt was 1.6 times lower than that generated from a comparable dose of erythromycin estolate.

Erythromycin stearate—Dissociated to erythromycin base in the duodenum.

Half-life

Normal renal function—1.4 to 2 hours.

Anuric patients—Approximately 5 hours.

Time to peak concentration

2 to 4 hours, depending on the specific product (see *Peak serum concentration*).

Peak serum concentration

Erythromycin base—
- Delayed-release capsules: Single dose of 250 mg—1.1 to 1.7 mcg per mL (mcg/mL) at 3 hours.
- Delayed-release tablets: Single dose of 250 mg—Approximately 0.9 mcg/mL at 4 hours.
- Delayed-release tablets: Multiple doses of 250 mg—Approximately 2.8 mcg/mL at 2 hours.

Erythromycin estolate—
- Single dose of 250 mg: Approximately 0.8 to 1.2 mcg/mL at 2 to 4 hours.

Erythromycin ethylsuccinate—
- Single dose of 400 mg: Approximately 0.8 mcg/mL at 1 hour.
- Multiple doses (400 mg twice a day), fasting: Approximately 1.4 mcg/mL.
- Multiple doses (400 mg twice a day), with food: Approximately 3 mcg/mL.

Erythromycin gluceptate—
- Single dose of 200 mg: 3 to 4 mcg/mL.

Erythromycin lactobionate—
- Single dose of 500 mg: Approximately 10 mcg/mL.

Erythromycin stearate—
- Single dose of 250 mg: Approximately 0.8 mcg/mL at 3 hours.

Elimination

Biliary; primarily excreted into the bile.

Renal, by glomerular filtration; 2 to 5% excreted unchanged following oral administration; 12 to 15% excreted unchanged following intravenous administration.

Erythromycins are not removed by hemodialysis or peritoneal dialysis.

Precautions to Consider

Cross-sensitivity and/or related problems

Patients intolerant of one erythromycin or other macrolides may be intolerant of other erythromycins also.

Tumorigenicity/Mutagenicity

Long-term (20 month) oral studies done in rats did not demonstrate erythromycin base to be tumorigenic. Mutagenicity studies have not been conducted.

Pregnancy/Reproduction

Fertility—Adequate and well-controlled studies in humans have not been done.

Studies in rats fed erythromycin base at concentrations up to 0.25% of their diet found no apparent effect on male or female fertility.

Pregnancy—Erythromycins cross the placenta, resulting in low fetal plasma concentrations (5 to 20% of maternal plasma concentrations). Erythromycin estolate has been associated with an increased risk of reversible, subclinical hepatotoxicity in approximately 10% of pregnant women; its use during pregnancy is not recommended. However, problems with other erythromycins have not been documented.

There was no evidence of teratogenicity or any other adverse effect on reproduction in female rats fed erythromycin base (up to 0.25% of their diet) prior to and during mating, during gestation, and through weaning of 2 successive litters.

FDA Pregnancy Category B.

Breast-feeding

Erythromycins are distributed into breast milk. However, problems in humans have not been documented.

Pediatrics

Studies performed to date have not demonstrated pediatrics-specific problems that would limit the usefulness of erythromycin in children.

Geriatrics

Studies performed to date have not demonstrated geriatrics-specific problems that would limit the usefulness of erythromycin in the elderly. However, elderly patients may be at increased risk of hearing loss if they also have decreased renal or hepatic function associated with aging and are receiving high doses of erythromycin.

Dental

Systemic erythromycins may lead to oral candidiasis in patients undergoing long-term therapy.

Drug interactions and/or related problems

The following drug interactions and/or related problems have been selected on the basis of their potential clinical significance (possible mechanism in parentheses where appropriate)—not necessarily inclusive (» = major clinical significance):

Note: Combinations containing any of the following medications, depending on the amount present, may also interact with this medication.

Alcohol
(concurrent use with intravenous erythromycin was found to increase the peak blood alcohol concentration by 40%; erythromycin is not known to affect alcohol metabolism directly, but is thought to be related to more rapid gastric emptying; less exposure to alcohol dehydrogenase in the gastric mucosa and slower small intestine transit time may also favor the increase of alcohol absorption; there may be less of an effect with oral erythromycin)

» Alfentanil
(chronic preoperative or perioperative use of erythromycins, which are hepatic enzyme inhibitors, may decrease the plasma clearance and prolong the duration of action of alfentanil)

» Astemizole or
» Terfenadine
(concurrent use of astemizole or terfenadine with erythromycins is contraindicated; concurrent use may increase the risk of cardiotoxicity, such as torsades de pointes and ventricular tachycardia, and death)

» Carbamazepine or
Valproic acid
(erythromycins may inhibit carbamazepine and valproic acid metabolism, resulting in increased anticonvulsant plasma concentrations and toxicity; it is recommended that erythromycins be used with caution if at all in patients receiving carbamazepine or valproic acid)

» Chloramphenicol or
» Lincomycins
(erythromycins may displace these medications from, or prevent them from binding to, 50 S subunits of bacterial ribosomes, thus antagonizing the effects of chloramphenicol and lincomycins; concurrent use is not recommended)

» Cyclosporine
(erythromycin has been reported to increase cyclosporine plasma concentrations and may increase the risk of nephrotoxicity)

Digoxin
(although no clinical cases of toxicity have been reported, concurrent use of oral antibiotics may increase serum digoxin concentrations in some individuals; in these individuals, alteration of the gut flora by antibiotics may diminish digoxin conversion to inactive metabolites, resulting in increased serum digoxin concentrations; although limited data are available, this interaction has been reported with oral use of erythromycins, neomycin, and tetracyclines)

Ergotamine
(erythromycin inhibits the metabolism of ergotamine and has been reported to increase the vasospasm associated with ergotamines)

» Hepatotoxic medications, other (see *Appendix II*)
(concurrent use of other hepatotoxic medications with erythromycins may increase the potential for hepatotoxicity)

Lovastatin
(concurrent use of lovastatin with erythromycin may increase the risk of rhabdomyolysis, which typically occurs after the completion of erythromycin therapy; this is thought to be due to erythromycin's inhibition of lovastatin metabolism, which increases lovastatin serum concentrations; simultaneous administration of erythromycin and lovastatin should be used with caution)

Midazolam or
Triazolam
(concurrent use with erythromycin may decrease the clearance of these medications, increasing the pharmacological effect of midazolam or triazolam)

Ototoxic medications, other (see *Appendix II*)
(concurrent use of other ototoxic medications with high-dose erythromycin in patients with renal function impairment may increase the potential for ototoxicity)

Penicillins
(since bacteriostatic drugs may interfere with the bactericidal effect of penicillins in the treatment of meningitis or in other situations where a rapid bactericidal effect is necessary, it is best to avoid concurrent therapy)

» Warfarin
(use of erythromycins in patients receiving chronic warfarin therapy may result in excessive prolongation of prothrombin time and increased risk of hemorrhage, especially in elderly patients, because of possible decreased warfarin metabolism and clearance; warfarin dosage adjustments may be necessary during and after therapy with erythromycins, and prothrombin times should be monitored closely)

» Xanthines, such as:
Aminophylline
Caffeine
Oxtriphylline
Theophylline
(concurrent use of the xanthines [except dyphylline] with erythromycins may decrease hepatic clearance of theophylline, resulting in increased serum theophylline concentrations and/or toxicity; this effect may be more likely to occur after 6 days of concurrent therapy because the magnitude of theophylline clearance reduction is proportional to the peak serum erythromycin concentrations; dosage adjustment of the xanthines may be necessary during and after therapy with erythromycins)

Laboratory value alterations

The following have been selected on the basis of their potential clinical significance (possible effect in parentheses where appropriate)—not necessarily inclusive (» = major clinical significance).

With diagnostic test results
Aspartate aminotransferase (AST [SGOT])
(use of erythromycin may interfere with AST [SGOT] determinations if azonefast violet B or diphenylhydrazine colorimetric tests are used)

Catecholamines, urinary
(erythromycin may produce false elevations of urinary catecholamines because of interference with the fluorometric determination)

With physiology/laboratory test values
Alanine aminotransferase (ALT [SGPT]) and
Alkaline phosphatase and
Aspartate aminotransferase (AST [SGOT]) and
Bilirubin, serum
(values may be increased by all erythromycins, but more commonly by erythromycin estolate)

Medical considerations/Contraindications

The medical considerations/contraindications included have been selected on the basis of their potential clinical significance (reasons given in parentheses where appropriate)—not necessarily inclusive (» = major clinical significance).

Risk-benefit should be considered when the following medical problems exist:

» Cardiac arrhythmias, history of, or QT prolongation
(patients with a history of cardiac arrhythmias or QT prolongation may be at risk for arrhythmias or torsades de pointes while receiving high doses of erythromycin)

» Hepatic function impairment, especially with erythromycin estolate
(erythromycins, especially erythromycin estolate, may be hepatotoxic on rare occasion)

Hypersensitivity to erythromycins

Loss of hearing
(patients with a history of hearing loss may be at increased risk of further hearing loss, especially if the patient has renal or hepatic function impairment, is elderly, and is receiving high doses of erythromycin)

Patient monitoring

The following may be especially important in patient monitoring (other tests may be warranted in some patients, depending on condition; » = major clinical significance):

Electrocardiogram
(monitoring of QT interval recommended, especially in patients receiving high doses of parenteral erythromycin)

» Hepatic function determinations
(may be required periodically if signs of hepatic dysfunction occur with any of the erythromycins; erythromycins should be discontinued promptly if signs of hepatic dysfunction occur)

Side/Adverse Effects

Note: Hepatotoxicity has been associated, rarely, with all erythromycin salts, but more frequently with erythromycin estolate. Reports suggest that a hypersensitivity mechanism may be involved. Symptoms include malaise, nausea, vomiting, abdominal cramps, skin rash, and fever. Jaundice may or may not be present. Liver function tests often indicate cholestasis. Symptoms typically appear within a few days to 1 or 2 weeks after the start of continuous therapy, and are reversible when erythromycin is discontinued. However, hepatotoxicity reappears promptly on readministration to sensitive patients.

Hearing loss is more likely to occur with administration of high doses ($\geq$ 4 grams per day) in patients with renal or hepatic disease and/or in elderly patients. It appears to be related to high peak plasma concentrations, usually exceeding 12 mcg per mL. Hearing loss is usually reversible, although irreversible deafness has occurred. It occurs from 36 hours to 8 days after treatment is started, and begins to recover within 1 to 14 days after erythromycin is discontinued.

The following side/adverse effects have been selected on the basis of their potential clinical significance (possible signs and symptoms in parentheses where appropriate)—not necessarily inclusive:

Those indicating need for medical attention

Incidence less frequent

Hepatotoxicity (fever; nausea; skin rash; stomach pain, severe; unusual tiredness or weakness; yellow eyes or skin; vomiting); ***hypersensitivity*** (skin rash, redness, or itching)

Incidence less frequent—parenteral erythromycins only

Inflammation or phlebitis at the injection site

Incidence rare

Cardiac toxicity, especially QT prolongation and torsades de pointes (irregular or slow heart rate; recurrent fainting; sudden death); ***loss of hearing, usually reversible; pancreatitis*** (severe abdominal pain, nausea, and vomiting)

Those indicating need for medical attention only if they continue or are bothersome

Incidence more frequent

Gastrointestinal disturbances (abdominal or stomach cramping and discomfort; diarrhea, nausea or vomiting)

Incidence less frequent

Oral candidiasis (sore mouth or tongue; white patches in mouth and/or on tongue); ***vaginal candidiasis*** (vaginal itching and discharge)

Overdose

For specific information on the agents used in the management of erythromycin overdose, see:

- *Epinephrine (Systemic)* monograph;
- *Corticosteroids (Inhalation-Local)* monograph; and/or
- *Antihistamines (Systemic)* monograph.

For more information on the management of overdose or unintentional ingestion, **contact a Poison Control Center** (see *Poison Control Center Listing*).

Treatment of overdose

Recommended treatment consists of the following:

To decrease absorption—Evacuating the stomach to eliminate unabsorbed drug.

Specific treatment—Administering epinephrine, corticosteroids, and antihistamines for allergic reactions.

Supportive care—Using supportive measures as needed. Patients in whom intentional overdose is known or suspected should be referred for psychiatic consultation.

Patient Consultation

As an aid to patient consultation, refer to *Advice for the Patient, Erythromycins (Systemic)*.

In providing consultation, consider emphasizing the following selected information (» = major clinical significance):

Before using this medication

» Conditions affecting use, especially:

Hypersensitivity to erythromycins or other macrolides

Pregnancy—Erythromycins cross the placenta; erythromycin estolate has been associated with an increased risk of reversible, subclinical hepatotoxicity in pregnant women

Breast-feeding—Erythromycins are distributed into breast milk

Dental—Oral candidiasis may occur with long-term therapy

Other medications, especially alfentanil, astemizole, carbamazepine, chloramphenicol, cyclosporine, other hepatotoxic medications, lincomycins, terfenadine, warfarin, and xanthines

Other medical problems, especially a history of cardiac arrhythmias or QT prolongation or hepatic function impairment

Proper use of this medication

Taking with a full glass of water, on an empty stomach; may be taken with food if stomach upset occurs

Proper administration technique for oral liquids and/or pediatric drops, chewable tablets, delayed-release capsules and tablets

Not using oral liquids and/or pediatric drops after expiration date

» Compliance with full course of therapy, especially in streptococcal infections

» Importance of not missing doses and taking at evenly spaced times

» Proper dosing

Missed dose: Taking as soon as possible; not taking if almost time for next dose; not doubling dose

» Proper storage

Precautions while using this medication

Checking with physician if no improvement within a few days

Side/adverse effects

Signs of potential side effects, especially, hepatotoxicity, hypersensitivity, inflammation or phlebitis at the injection site, cardiac toxicity, loss of hearing, or pancreatitis

General Dosing Information

Therapy should be continued for at least 10 days in group A beta-hemolytic streptococcal infections to help prevent the occurrence of acute rheumatic fever.

For oral dosage forms only

Doses greater than 1 gram per dose are not recommended with twice-a-day dosing.

Erythromycin film-coated tablets (base and stearate) are best absorbed on an empty stomach; however, if gastrointestinal irritation occurs, they may be taken with food. Enteric-coated erythromycin base and erythromycin estolate may be taken without regard to meals; and erythromycin ethylsuccinate is better absorbed when taken with meals.

ERYTHROMYCIN BASE

Oral Dosage Forms

Note: Bracketed uses in the *Dosage Forms* section refer to categories of use and/or indications that are not included in U.S. product labeling.

ERYTHROMYCIN DELAYED-RELEASE CAPSULES USP

Usual adult and adolescent dose

Antibacterial—

Oral, 250 mg (base) every six hours; 333 mg every eight hours; or 500 mg every twelve hours if twice-a-day dosage is desired.

Note: Acne vulgaris—Oral, 250 mg (base) every six hours; 333 mg every eight hours; or 500 mg every twelve hours for four weeks. This dose may be reduced to 333 to 500 mg once a day for a maintenance dose.

Bowel preparation (preoperative) adjunct—Oral, 1 gram (base) administered at nineteen hours, eighteen hours, and nine hours (total of 3 grams) before the start of surgery.

Chlamydial infections, endocervical and urethral—Oral, 333 mg (base) every eight hours, or 500 mg every six hours for seven days; or 250 mg every six hours for fourteen days. Erythromycin base may be used in pregnant women.

[Chancroid][1]—Oral, 500 mg (base) every six hours for seven days.

Endocarditis prophylaxis—Oral, 1 gram (base) two hours prior to the procedure, and 500 mg six hours after the initial dose.

[Enteritis, *Campylobacter*][1]—Oral, 250 mg (base) four times a day for five days.

[Gastroparesis][1]—Oral, 250 mg (base) taken thirty minutes before meals, three times a day.

Legionnaires' disease—Oral, 500 mg (base) to 1 gram every six hours.

[Lyme disease][1]—Oral, 250 mg (base) four times a day for ten to twenty-one days.

[Lymphogranuloma venereum][1]—Oral, 500 mg (base) every six hours for twenty-one days.

Pelvic inflammatory disease, caused by *Neisseria gonorrhoeae*—Oral, 250 mg (base) every six hours for seven days, after intravenous administration of erythromycin 500 mg every six hours for three days.

[Relapsing fever][1]—Oral, 10 mg (base) per kg of body weight every six hours for ten days.

Streptococcal prophylaxis—Continuous prophylaxis of streptococcal infections in patients with a history of rheumatic heart disease: Oral, 250 mg (base) every twelve hours.

Syphilis, primary—Oral, 30 to 40 grams (base) over a ten- to fifteen-day period.

Urethritis, nongonococcal, caused by *Ureaplasma urealyticum*—Oral, 500 mg (base) every six hours for seven days; or 250 mg every six hours for fourteen days.

Usual adult prescribing limits

Antibacterial—

Up to 4 grams (base) a day.

Usual pediatric dose

Antibacterial—

Oral, 7.5 to 12.5 mg (base) per kg of body weight every six hours; or 15 to 25 mg per kg of body weight every twelve hours.

Severe infections, 15 to 25 mg (base) per kg of body weight every six hours.

Note: Chlamydial infections, endocervical and urethral—

Children up to 45 kg of body weight: Oral, 10 mg (base) per kg of body weight every six hours for ten to fourteen days.

Children 45 kg of body weight and over but less than 8 years of age: See *Usual adult and adolescent dose.*

Conjunctivitis, chlamydial[1]—Oral, 12.5 mg (base) per kg of body weight every six hours for at least ten to fourteen days.

Diphtheria—Oral, 10 to 12.5 mg (base) per kg of body weight every six hours for fourteen days.

Endocarditis prophylaxis—Oral, 20 mg (base) per kg of body weight two hours prior to the procedure, and 10 mg per kg of body weight six hours after the initial dose.

[Enteritis, *Campylobacter*][1]—Oral, 10 mg (base) per kg of body weight every six hours for five days.

[Lyme disease][1]—Oral, 7.5 mg (base) per kg of body weight every six hours for ten to twenty-one days.

Pertussis—Oral, 10 to 12.5 mg (base) per kg of body weight every six hours for fourteen days.

Pneumonia, chlamydial[1]—Oral, 12.5 mg (base) per kg of body weight every six hours for two weeks.

[Relapsing fever][1]—Oral, 10 mg (base) per kg of body weight every six hours for ten days.

Streptococcal pharyngitis—Oral, 5 to 7.5 mg (base) per kg of body weight every six hours; or 10 to 15 mg per kg of body weight every twelve hours for at least ten days.

Strength(s) usually available

U.S.—

250 mg (base) (Rx) [*ERYC;* GENERIC].

Canada—

250 mg (base) (Rx) [*Apo-Erythro E-C; ERYC-250; Novo-rythro Encap*].

333 mg (base) (Rx) [*Apo-Erythro E-C; ERYC-333*].

Packaging and storage

Store below 40 °C (104 °F), preferably between 15 and 30 °C (59 and 86 °F), unless otherwise specified by manufacturer. Store in a tight container.

Auxiliary labeling

- Continue medicine for full time of treatment.
- Swallow capsules whole.

Note

Erythromycin delayed-release capsules contain enteric-coated pellets. The entire contents of a capsule may be sprinkled on applesauce, jelly, or ice cream immediately prior to ingestion. Subdividing the contents of the capsule is not recommended.

ERYTHROMYCIN TABLETS USP

Usual adult and adolescent dose

See *Erythromycin Delayed-release Capsules USP.*

Usual adult prescribing limits

See *Erythromycin Delayed-release Capsules USP.*

Usual pediatric dose

See *Erythromycin Delayed-release Capsules USP.*

Strength(s) usually available

U.S.—

250 mg (base) (Rx) [GENERIC].

500 mg (base) (Rx) [GENERIC].

Canada—

250 mg (base) (Rx) [*Apo-Erythro; Erythromid*].

Packaging and storage

Store below 40 °C (104 °F), preferably between 15 and 30 °C (59 and 86 °F), unless otherwise specified by manufacturer. Store in a tight container.

Auxiliary labeling

- Continue medicine for full time of treatment.

ERYTHROMYCIN DELAYED-RELEASE TABLETS USP

Usual adult and adolescent dose

See *Erythromycin Delayed-release Capsules USP.*

Note: Endocarditis prophylaxis—The manufacturer of E-Mycin recommends taking 1 gram three to four hours prior to the procedure because of the pharmacokinetics of their enteric-coated product.

Usual adult prescribing limits

See *Erythromycin Delayed-release Capsules USP.*

Usual pediatric dose

See *Erythromycin Delayed-release Capsules USP.*

Note: Endocarditis prophylaxis—The manufacturer of E-Mycin recommends taking 1 gram three to four hours prior to the procedure because of the pharmacokinetics of their enteric-coated product.

Strength(s) usually available

U.S.—

250 mg (base) (Rx) [*E-Mycin; Ery-Tab; Ilotycin;* GENERIC].

333 mg (base) (Rx) [*E-Base; E-Mycin; Ery-Tab; PCE;* GENERIC].

500 mg (base) (Rx) [*E-Base; Ery-Tab; PCE*].

Canada—

250 mg (base) (Rx) [*E-Mycin;* GENERIC].

333 mg (base) (Rx) [*PCE*].

500 mg (base) (Rx) [*Erybid*].

Packaging and storage

Store below 40 °C (104 °F), preferably between 15 and 30 °C (59 and 86 °F), unless otherwise specified by manufacturer. Store in a tight container.

Auxiliary labeling

- Continue medicine for full time of treatment.
- Swallow tablets whole.

[1]Not included in Canadian product labeling.

ERYTHROMYCIN ESTOLATE

Summary of Differences

Precautions:

Pregnancy—Associated with increased risk of reversible, subclinical hepatotoxicity.

Laboratory value alterations—Serum alkaline phosphatase, bilirubin, AST (SGOT), and ALT (SGPT) concentrations may be increased more frequently than with other erythromycins.

Side/adverse effects:

May also cause cholestatic jaundice less frequently (rare with other erythromycins).

Oral Dosage Forms

Note: Bracketed uses in the *Dosage Forms* section refer to categories of use and/or indications that are not included in U.S. product labeling.

Note: The dosing and strengths of the dosage forms available are expressed in terms of erythromycin base (not the estolate salt).

ERYTHROMYCIN ESTOLATE CAPSULES USP

Usual adult and adolescent dose

Antibacterial—

Oral, 250 mg (base) every six hours; or 500 mg every twelve hours if twice-a-day dosage is desired.

Note: Chlamydial infections, endocervical and urethral—Oral, 500 mg (base) every six hours for seven days; or 250 mg every six hours for fourteen days. Erythromycin estolate is not recommended for use in pregnant women.

Endocarditis prophylaxis—Oral, 1 gram (base) two hours prior to the procedure, and 500 mg six hours after the initial dose.

[Gastroparesis][1]—Oral, 250 mg (base) taken thirty minutes before meals, three times a day.

Legionnaires' disease—Oral, 500 mg (base) to 1 gram every six hours.

Streptococcal prophylaxis—Continuous prophylaxis of streptococcal infections in patients with a history of rheumatic heart disease: Oral, 250 mg (base) every twelve hours.

Syphilis, primary—Oral, 20 to 30 grams (base) over a ten-day period.

Usual adult prescribing limits
Antibacterial—
Up to 4 grams (base) daily.

Usual pediatric dose
Antibacterial—
Oral, 7.5 to 12.5 mg (base) per kg of body weight every six hours; or 15 to 25 mg per kg of body weight every twelve hours.
Severe infections, 15 to 25 mg (base) per kg of body weight every six hours.

Note: Conjunctivitis, chlamydial[1]—Oral, 12.5 mg (base) per kg of body weight every six hours for at least two weeks.

Diphtheria—Oral, 10 to 12.5 mg (base) per kg of body weight every six hours for fourteen days.

Endocarditis prophylaxis—Oral, 20 mg (base) per kg of body weight two hours prior to the procedure, and 10 mg per kg of body weight six hours after the initial dose.

Pertussis—Oral, 10 to 12.5 mg (base) per kg of body weight every six hours for fourteen days.

Pneumonia, chlamydial[1]—Oral, 12.5 mg (base) per kg of body weight every six hours for two weeks.

Streptococcal pharyngitis—Oral, 5 to 7.5 mg (base) per kg of body weight every six hours; or 10 to 15 mg per kg of body weight every twelve hours for at least ten days.

Strength(s) usually available
U.S.—
250 mg (base) (Rx) [*Ilosone;* GENERIC].
Canada—
250 mg (base) (Rx) [*Ilosone; Novo-rythro*].

Packaging and storage
Store below 40 °C (104 °F), preferably between 15 and 30 °C (59 and 86 °F), unless otherwise specified by manufacturer. Store in a tight container.

Auxiliary labeling
- Continue medicine for full time of treatment.

ERYTHROMYCIN ESTOLATE ORAL SUSPENSION USP

Usual adult and adolescent dose
See *Erythromycin Estolate Capsules USP*.

Usual adult prescribing limits
See *Erythromycin Estolate Capsules USP*.

Usual pediatric dose
See *Erythromycin Estolate Capsules USP*.

Strength(s) usually available
U.S.—
125 mg (base) per 5 mL (Rx) [*Ilosone* (methylparaben; propylparaben); GENERIC].
250 mg (base) per 5 mL (Rx) [*Ilosone* (methylparaben; propylparaben); GENERIC].
Canada—
125 mg (base) per 5 mL (Rx) [*Ilosone; Novo-rythro*].
250 mg (base) per 5 mL (Rx) [*Ilosone; Novo-rythro*].

Packaging and storage
Store between 2 and 8 °C (36 and 46 °F). Store in a tight container.

Auxiliary labeling
- Refrigerate.
- Shake well.
- Continue medicine for full time of treatment.
- Take by mouth only (pediatric drops).

Note
Explain administration technique for pediatric drops (100 mg per mL).
When dispensing, include a calibrated liquid-measuring device.

ERYTHROMYCIN ESTOLATE TABLETS USP

Usual adult and adolescent dose
See *Erythromycin Estolate Capsules USP*.

Usual adult prescribing limits
See *Erythromycin Estolate Capsules USP*.

Usual pediatric dose
See *Erythromycin Estolate Capsules USP*.

Strength(s) usually available
U.S.—
250 mg (base) (Rx) [GENERIC].
500 mg (base) (Rx) [*Ilosone*].
Canada—
500 mg (base) (Rx) [*Ilosone*].

Packaging and storage
Store below 40 °C (104 °F), preferably between 15 and 30 °C (59 and 86 °F), unless otherwise specified by manufacturer. Store in a tight container.

Auxiliary labeling
- Continue medicine for full time of treatment.

[1]Not included in Canadian product labeling.

ERYTHROMYCIN ETHYLSUCCINATE

Summary of Differences

1.6 grams of erythromycin ethylsuccinate produce approximately the same blood levels as 1 gram erythromycin base.
In pediatric patients, equivalent doses of erythromycin ethylsuccinate and erythromycin base produce comparable blood levels.

Oral Dosage Forms

Note: Bracketed uses in the *Dosage Forms* section refer to categories of use and/or indications that are not included in U.S. product labeling.

Note: The dosing and dosage forms available are expressed in terms of ethylsuccinate salt. 400 mg of erythromycin ethylsuccinate produces approximately the same blood levels as 250 mg erythromycin base.

ERYTHROMYCIN ETHYLSUCCINATE ORAL SUSPENSION USP

Usual adult and adolescent dose
Antibacterial—
Oral, 400 mg every six hours; or 800 mg every twelve hours if twice-a-day dosing is desired.

Note: Chlamydial infections, endocervical and urethral—Oral, 800 mg (base) every six hours for seven days, or 400 mg every six hours for fourteen days. Erythromycin ethylsuccinate may be used in pregnant women.

Endocarditis prophylaxis—Oral, 1.6 grams two hours prior to the procedure, and 800 mg six hours after the initial dose.

[Gastroparesis][1]—Oral, 400 mg taken thirty minutes before meals, three times a day.

Legionnaires' disease—Oral, 400 mg to 1 gram every six hours.

Streptococcal prophylaxis—Continuous prophylaxis of streptococcal infections in patients with a history of rheumatic heart disease: Oral, 400 mg every twelve hours.

Syphilis, primary—Oral, 48 to 64 grams (base) over a ten- to fifteen-day period.

Urethritis, nongonococcal, caused by *Ureaplasma urealyticum*—Oral, 800 mg every eight hours for seven days; or 400 mg every six hours for fourteen days.

Usual adult prescribing limits
Antibacterial—
Up to 4 grams daily.

Usual pediatric dose
Antibacterial—
Oral, 7.5 to 12.5 mg per kg of body weight every six hours; or 15 to 25 mg per kg of body weight every twelve hours.
Severe infections, 15 to 25 mg per kg body weight every six hours.

Note: Conjunctivitis, chlamydial[1]—Oral, 12.5 mg (base) per kg of body weight every six hours for ten to fourteen days.

Diphtheria—Oral, 10 to 12.5 mg (base) per kg of body weight every six hours for fourteen days.

Endocarditis prophylaxis—Oral, 20 mg per kg of body weight two hours prior to the procedure, and 10 mg per kg of body weight six hours after the initial dose.

[Enteritis, *Campylobacter*][1]—Oral, 10 mg (base) per kg of body weight every six hours for five days.

Pertussis—Oral, 10 to 12.5 mg per kg of body weight every six hours for fourteen days.

Pneumonia, chlamydial[1]—Oral, 12.5 mg (base) per kg of body weight every six hours for ten to fourteen days.

Strength(s) usually available
U.S.—
200 mg per 5 mL (Rx) [*E.E.S.* (methylparaben; propylparaben); *Erythro;* GENERIC].
400 mg per 5 mL (Rx) [*E.E.S.* (methylparaben; propylparaben); *Erythro;* GENERIC].
Canada—
Not commercially available.

Packaging and storage
Store between 2 and 8 °C (36 and 46 °F). Store in a tight container.
Note: After dispensing, suspensions do not require refrigeration if used within 14 days. Some manufacturers recommend storage in light-resistant containers to prevent discoloration.

Auxiliary labeling
- Shake well.
- Continue medicine for full time of treatment.
- Beyond-use date.

Note
When dispensing, include a calibrated liquid-measuring device.

ERYTHROMYCIN ETHYLSUCCINATE FOR ORAL SUSPENSION USP

Usual adult and adolescent dose
See *Erythromycin Ethylsuccinate Oral Suspension USP*.

Usual adult prescribing limits
See *Erythromycin Ethylsuccinate Oral Suspension USP*.

Usual pediatric dose
See *Erythromycin Ethylsuccinate Oral Suspension USP*.

Strength(s) usually available
U.S.—
200 mg per 5 mL (when reconstituted according to manufacturer's instructions) (Rx) [*E.E.S.; EryPed;* GENERIC].
400 mg per 5 mL (when reconstituted according to manufacturer's instructions) (Rx) [*EryPed;* GENERIC].
Canada—
100 mg per 5 mL (when reconstituted according to manufacturer's instructions) (Rx) [*Novo-Rythro*].
200 mg per 5 mL (when reconstituted according to manufacturer's instructions) (Rx) [*E.E.S.; Novo-Rythro*].
400 mg per 5 mL (when reconstituted according to manufacturer's instructions) (Rx) [*E.E.S.*].

Packaging and storage
Prior to reconstitution, store below 40 °C (104 °F), preferably between 15 and 30 °C (59 and 86 °F), unless otherwise specified by manufacturer. Store in a tight container.
Note: After reconstitution, depending on manufacturer or specific product, suspensions do not require refrigeration if used within 14 days.

Auxiliary labeling
- Shake well.
- Continue medicine for full time of treatment.
- Beyond-use date.
- Take by mouth only (pediatric drops).

Note
Explain administration technique for pediatric drops.
When dispensing, include a calibrated liquid-measuring device.

ERYTHROMYCIN ETHYLSUCCINATE TABLETS USP

Usual adult and adolescent dose
See *Erythromycin Ethylsuccinate Oral Suspension USP*.

Usual adult prescribing limits
See *Erythromycin Ethylsuccinate Oral Suspension USP*.

Usual pediatric dose
See *Erythromycin Ethylsuccinate Oral Suspension USP*.

Strength(s) usually available
U.S.—
400 mg (Rx) [*E.E.S.;* GENERIC].
Canada—
600 mg (Rx) [*Apo-Erythro-ES; E.E.S.*].

Packaging and storage
Store below 40 °C (104 °F), preferably beween 15 and 30 °C (59 and 86 °F), unless otherwise specified by manufacturer. Store in a tight container.

Auxiliary labeling
- Continue medicine for full time of treatment.

ERYTHROMYCIN ETHYLSUCCINATE TABLETS (CHEWABLE) USP

Usual adult and adolescent dose
See *Erythromycin Ethylsuccinate Oral Suspension USP*.

Usual adult prescribing limits
See *Erythromycin Ethylsuccinate Oral Suspension USP*.

Usual pediatric dose
See *Erythromycin Ethylsuccinate Oral Suspension USP*.

Strength(s) usually available
U.S.—
200 mg (Rx) [*EryPed*].
400 mg (Rx) [*Erythro*].
Canada—
200 mg (Rx) [*E.E.S.* (scored); *EryPed*].

Packaging and storage
Store below 40 °C (104 °F), preferably between 15 and 30 °C (59 and 86 °F), unless otherwise specified by manufacturer. Store in a tight container.

Auxiliary labeling
- Chew or crush tablets before swallowing.
- Continue medicine for full time of treatment.

---

[1]Not included in Canadian product labeling.

ERYTHROMYCIN GLUCEPTATE

Summary of Differences

Category: Indicated only as an antibacterial.

Parenteral Dosage Forms

Note: Bracketed uses in the *Dosage Forms* section refer to categories of use and/or indications that are not included in U.S. product labeling.

Note: The dosing and strengths of the dosage forms available are expressed in terms of erythromycin base (not the gluceptate salt).

ERYTHROMYCIN GLUCEPTATE STERILE USP

Usual adult and adolescent dose
Antibacterial—
Intravenous infusion, 250 to 500 mg (base) every six hours; or 3.75 to 5 mg per kg of body weight every six hours.
Note: [Gastroparesis][1]—Oral, 200 mg taken thirty minutes before meals, three times a day.
Legionnaires' disease—Intravenous infusion, 1 gram (base) every six hours.
Pelvic inflammatory disease, caused by *Neisseria gonorrhoeae*—Intravenous infusion, 500 mg (base) every six hours for three days, then oral administration of erythromycin 250 mg every six hours for seven days.

Usual adult prescribing limits
Up to 4 grams (base) daily.

Usual pediatric dose
Antibacterial—
Intravenous infusion, 3.75 to 5 mg (base) per kg of body weight every six hours.
Note: Diphtheria—Oral, 10 to 12.5 mg (base) per kg of body weight every six hours for fourteen days.

Strength(s) usually available
U.S.—
1 gram (base) (Rx) [*Ilotycin*].
Canada—
500 mg (base) (Rx) [*Ilotycin*].
1 gram (base) (Rx) [*Ilotycin*].

Packaging and storage
Prior to reconstitution, store below 40 °C (104 °F), preferably between 15 and 30 °C (59 and 86 °F), unless otherwise specified by manufacturer.

Preparation of dosage form
To prepare initial dilution, add at least 10 mL of sterile water for injection (without preservatives) to each 500-mg vial and at least 20 mL of diluent to each 1-gram vial.
After initial dilution, solution may be further diluted to a concentration of 1 gram per liter in 0.9% sodium chloride injection or 5% dextrose injection for slow, continuous infusion.

Stability
After reconstitution, initial dilutions (25 to 50 mg per mL) retain their potency for 7 days if refrigerated.

Additional information
Infusions with a pH below 5.5 tend to lose potency rapidly and should be administered completely within 4 hours after dilution.

If administration time is prolonged, infusions should be buffered to neutrality with a suitable buffer and administered completely within 24 hours after dilution.

If administered by intermittent infusion, dose may be diluted in 100 to 250 mL of 0.9% sodium chloride injection or 5% dextrose injection and administered slowly over a 20- to 60-minute period.

---

[1]Not included in Canadian product labeling.

ERYTHROMYCIN LACTOBIONATE

Summary of Differences
Category: Indicated only as an antibacterial.

Parenteral Dosage Forms
Note: Bracketed uses in the *Dosage Forms* section refer to categories of use and/or indications that are not included in U.S. product labeling.

Note: The dosing and strengths of the dosage forms available are expressed in terms of erythromcyin base (not the lactobionate salt).

ERYTHROMYCIN LACTOBIONATE FOR INJECTION USP

Usual adult and adolescent dose
Antibacterial—

Intravenous infusion, 250 to 500 mg (base) every six hours; or 3.75 to 5 mg per kg of body weight every six hours.

Note: [Gastroparesis][1]—Oral, 200 mg administered thirty minutes before meals, three times a day.

Legionnaires' disease—Intravenous infusion, 1 gram (base) every six hours.

Pelvic inflammatory disease, caused by *Neisseria gonorrhoeae*—Intravenous infusion, 500 mg (base) every six hours for three days, then oral administration of erythromycin 250 mg every six hours for seven days.

Usual adult prescribing limits
Up to 4 grams (base) daily.

Usual pediatric dose
Antibacterial—

Intravenous infusion, 3.75 to 5 mg (base) per kg of body weight every six hours. This product should be used with caution in neonates since it contains benzyl alcohol.

Note: Diphtheria—Oral, 10 to 12.5 mg (base) per kg of body weight every six hours for fourteen days.

Strength(s) usually available
U.S.—

500 mg (base) (Rx) [*Erythrocin* (may contain benzyl alcohol 90 mg per 500 mg vial); GENERIC].

1 gram (base) (Rx) [*Erythrocin* (may contain benzyl alcohol 180 mg per 1 gram vial); GENERIC].

Canada—

500 mg (base) (Rx) [*Erythrocin* (may contain benzyl alcohol 0.9% per vial)].

1 gram (base) (Rx) [*Erythrocin* (may contain benzyl alcohol 0.9% per vial)].

Packaging and storage
Prior to reconstitution, store below 40 °C (104 °F), preferably between 15 and 30 °C (59 and 86 °F), unless otherwise specified by manufacturer.

Preparation of dosage form
To prepare initial dilution, add 10 mL of sterile water for injection (without preservatives) to each 500-mg vial and 20 mL of diluent to each 1-gram vial.

After initial dilution, solution may be further diluted to a concentration of 1 to 5 mg per mL in 0.9% sodium chloride injection, lactated Ringer's injection, or other electrolyte solutions (see manufacturer's package insert) for slow, continuous infusion. Dextrose-containing solutions may also be used if suitably buffered by adding 1 mL of 4% sodium bicarbonate per 100 mL of solution.

For reconstitution of piggyback infusion bottles, see manufacturer's labeling for instructions.

Caution: Use of diluents containing benzyl alcohol is not recommended for preparation of medications for use in neonates. A fatal toxic syndrome consisting of metabolic acidosis, CNS depression, respiratory problems, renal failure, hypotension, and possibly seizures and intracranial hemorrhages has been associated with this use.

Stability
After reconstitution, initial dilutions (50 mg per mL) retain their potency for 14 days if refrigerated, or for 24 hours at room temperature.

Infusions prepared in piggyback infusion bottles retain their potency for 8 hours at room temperature, for 24 hours if refrigerated, or for 30 days if frozen.

Infusions prepared in the ADD-vantage system should not be stored.

Additional information
Acidic infusions are unstable and lose potency rapidly. A pH of at least 5.5 is recommended for final dilutions, which should be administered completely within 8 hours after dilution.

If administered by intermittent infusion, dose may be diluted to a maximum concentration of 5 mg per mL with specified diluent and administered slowly over a 20- to 60-minute period.

---

[1]Not included in Canadian product labeling.

ERYTHROMYCIN STEARATE

Oral Dosage Forms
Note: Bracketed uses in the *Dosage Forms* section refer to categories of use and/or indications that are not included in U.S. product labeling.

Note: The dosing and strengths of the dosage forms available are expressed in terms of erythromycin base (not the stearate salt).

ERYTHROMYCIN STEARATE ORAL SUSPENSION

Usual adult and adolescent dose
Antibacterial—

Oral, 250 mg (base) every six hours; or 500 mg every twelve hours if twice a day dosage is desired.

Note: Chlamydial infections, endocervical and urethral—Oral, 500 mg (base) every six hours for seven days; or 250 mg every six hours for fourteen days. Erythromycin stearate may be used in pregnant women.

Endocarditis prophylaxis—Oral, 1 gram (base) two hours prior to the procedure, and 500 mg six hours after the initial dose.

Legionnaires' disease—Oral, 500 mg (base) to 1 gram every six hours.

Pelvic inflammatory disease, caused by *Neisseria gonorrhoeae*—Oral, 250 mg (base) every six hours for seven days, after intravenous administration of erythromycin 500 mg (base) every six hours for three days.

Streptococcal prophylaxis—Continuous prophylaxis of streptococcal infections in patients with a history of rheumatic heart disease: Oral, 250 mg (base) every twelve hours.

Syphilis, primary—Oral, 30 to 40 grams (base) over a ten- to fifteen-day period.

[Gastroparesis][1]—Oral, 150 to 250 mg (base) taken thirty minutes before meals, three times a day.

Usual adult prescribing limits
Antibacterial—

Up to 4 grams (base) daily.

Usual pediatric dose
Antibacterial—

Oral, 7.5 to 12.5 mg (base) per kg of body weight every six hours; or 15 to 25 mg per kg of body weight every twelve hours.

Severe infections, 15 to 25 mg (base) per kg of body weight every six hours.

Note: Conjunctivitis, chlamydial[1]—Oral, 12.5 mg (base) per kg of body weight every six hours for at least two weeks.

Endocarditis prophylaxis—Oral, 20 mg (base) per kg of body weight two hours prior to the procedure, and 10 mg per kg of body weight six hours after the initial dose.

Pertussis—Oral, 10 to 12.5 mg (base) per kg of body weight every six hours for fourteen days.

Pneumonia, chlamydial[1]—Oral, 12.5 mg (base) per kg of body weight every six hours for two weeks.

Streptococcal pharyngitis—Oral, 5 to 7.5 mg (base) per kg of body weight every six hours; or 10 to 15 mg per kg of body weight every twelve hours for at least ten days.

Strength(s) usually available

U.S.—

Not commercially available.

Canada—

125 mg per 5 mL (base) (Rx) [*Erythrocin* (parabens); *Novo-rythro*].

250 mg per 5 mL (base) (Rx) [*Erythrocin* (parabens); *Novo-rythro*].

Packaging and storage

Prior to reconstitution, store below 40 °C (104 °F), preferably between 15 and 30 °C (59 and 86 °F), unless otherwise specified by manufacturer. Store in a tight container.

Auxiliary labeling

- Refrigerate.
- Shake well.
- Continue medicine for full time of treatment.
- Beyond-use date.

Note

When dispensing, include a calibrated liquid-measuring device.

ERYTHROMYCIN STEARATE TABLETS USP

Usual adult and adolescent dose

See *Erythromycin Stearate Oral Suspension*.

Usual adult prescribing limits

See *Erythromycin Stearate Oral Suspension*.

Usual pediatric dose

See *Erythromycin Stearate Oral Suspension*.

Strength(s) usually available

U.S.—

250 mg (base) (Rx) [*Erythrocin; Erythrocot; My-E; Wintrocin;* GENERIC].

500 mg (base) (Rx) [*Erythrocin;* GENERIC].

Canada—

250 mg (base) (Rx) [*Apo-Erythro-S; Erythrocin; Novo-rythro*].

500 mg (base) (Rx) [*Apo-Erythro-S; Erythrocin*].

Packaging and storage

Store below 40 °C (104 °F), preferably between 15 and 30 °C (59 and 86 °F), unless otherwise specified by manufacturer. Store in a tight container.

Note: Some manufacturers recommend storage in light-resistant containers to prevent discoloration.

Auxiliary labeling

- Continue medicine for full time of treatment.

[1]Not included in Canadian product labeling.

Revised: 08/14/1997

ESCITALOPRAM Systemic†

VA CLASSIFICATION (Primary/Secondary): CN603/CN304

Commonly used brand name(s): *Lexapro*.

Note: For a listing of dosage forms and brand names by country availability, see *Dosage Forms* section(s).

†Not commercially available in Canada.

Category

Antidepressant; Antianxiety agent.

Indications

Accepted

Depressive disorder, major (treatment)—Escitalopram is indicated for the treatment of major depressive disorder. In an 8-week controlled trial, outpatients given a 10 mg per day or 20 mg per day dose showed significantly greater mean improvement compared to placebo on the Montgomery Asberg Depression Rating Scale (MADRS). Longer-term efficacy of escitalopram in major depressive disorder has not been systematically evaluated.

Note: The efficacy of escitalopram in the treatment of major depressive disorder was established, in part, on the basis of extrapolation from the established effectiveness of racemic citalopram, of which escitalopram is the active isomer.

Generalized Anxiety Disorder (treatment)—Escitalopram is indicated for the treatment of Generalized Anxiety Disorder (GAD). Long-term efficacy of escitalopram in the treatment of GAD has not been systematically evaluated.

Unaccepted

Escitalopram is not approved for use in treating bipolar depression.

Pharmacology/Pharmacokinetics

Escitalopram is an enantiomer of citalopram, for pharmacology and pharmacokinetic information on citalopram refer to *Pharmacology and Pharmacokinetics, Citalopram (Systemic)*.

Physicochemical characteristics

Source—Escitalopram is a pure S-enantiomer of the racemic, bicyclic phthalane derivative citalopram.

Molecular weight—414.40.

Solubility—Escitalopram is freely soluble in methanol and dimethylsulfoxide (DMSO), sparingly soluble in water and in ethanol, slightly soluble in ethyl acetate, and insoluble in heptane.

Mechanism of action/Effect

Escitalopram is a selective serotonin reuptake inhibitor (SSRI). The mechanism of antidepressant action of escitalopram is presumed to be linked to potentiation of serotonergic activity in the central nervous system resulting from its inhibition of central nervous system neuronal reuptake of serotonin (5-HT). It is a highly selective SSRI with minimal effects on norephinephrine and dopamine neuronal reuptake.

In vitro studies show that escitalopram is at least 7 and 27 times more potent than S-DCT and S-DDCT, respectively, in the inhibition of serotonin reuptake, suggesting that the metabolites of escitalopram do not contribute significantly to the antidepressant actions of escitalopram. S-DCT and S-DDCT also have no or very low affinity for serotonergic ($5\text{-}HT_{1\text{-}7}$) or other receptors including alpha- and beta- adrenergic, dopamine ($D_{1\text{-}5}$), histamine ($H_{1\text{-}3}$), muscarinic ($M_{1\text{-}5}$) and benzodiazepine receptors. S-DCT and S-DDCT also do not bind to various ion channels including Na^+, K^+, Cl^- and Ca^{++} channels.

Absorption

Escitalopram absorption is not affected by food.

In elderly patients the area under the concentration curve (AUC) is increased by 50%.

The absolute bioavailability of escitalopram is about 80% relative to an intravenous dose.

Distribution

Volume of distribution (Vol_D)—about 12 L per kg.

Protein binding

Moderate (approximately 56%) to plasma protein

Biotransformation

Escitalopram is mainly metabolized via hepatic pathways to S-demethylcitalopram (S-DCT) and S-didemethylcitalopram (S-DDCT). Unchanged escitalopram is the predominant compound in plasma. At steady state, the concentration of the escitalopram metabolite S-DCT in plasma is approximately one-third that of escitalopram. The level of S-DDCT was not detectable in most subjects. *In vitro* studies using human liver microsomes indicated that CYP3A4 and CYP2C19 are the primary isozymes involved in the N-demethylation of escitalopram.

Half-life

Approximately 27 to 32 hours.

In the elderly patients the half-life increased by approximately 50%.

Due to a doubling of half life with citalopram in hepatically impaired patients, escitalopram half life is expected to be greater also.

Time to peak concentration

Following a single oral dose (20 milligram tablet) the mean T_{max} was 5 ± 1.5 hours.

Elimination

Oral clearance of escitalopram is 600 milliliters per minute, with approximately 7% of that due to renal clearance.

Following oral administration, the fraction of drug recovered in the urine as escitalopram and S-demethylcitalopram is approximately 8% and 10%, respectively.

Due to an oral clearance reduction of citalopram by 37% in patients with reduced hepatic function, escitalopram clearance can be anticipated to be reduced as well. Dosing adjustments are recommended.

Precautions to Consider

Cross-sensitivity and/or related problems

Escitalopram is contraindicated in patients known to be hypersensitive to citalopram, escitalopram or other components of the product.

Carcinogenicity

There was no evidence for carcinogenicity of racemic citalopram in mice receiving up to 240 mg per kg of body weight per day for 18 months. However, there was an increased incidence of small intestine carcinoma in rats receiving 8 or 24 mg per kg of body weight per day for 24 months. A no-effect dose for this finding was not established.

Mutagenicity

Racemic citalopram was mutagenic in two of five bacterial strains (Salmonella TA98 and TA1537) in the *in vitro* bacterial reverse mutation assay in the absence of metabolic activations and was clastogenic in the *in vitro* Chinese hamster lung cell assay for chromosomal aberrations in the presence and absence of metabolic activation. Racemic citalopram was not mutagenic in the *in vitro* mammalian forward gene mutation assay (HPRT) in mouse lymphoma cells or in a coupled *in vitro/in vivo* unscheduled DNA synthesis (UDS) assay in rat liver. It was also not clastogenic in the *in vitro* chromosomal aberration assay in human lymphocytes or in two *in vivo* mouse micronucleus assays.

Pregnancy/Reproduction

Fertility—Studies in male and female rats given oral racemic citalopram doses ranging from 32 to 72 mg per kg of body weight per day found fertility to be decreased at doses greater than or equal to 32 mg per kg of body weight per day and mating was decreased at all doses.

Pregnancy—Adequate and well-controlled studies in humans have not been done. Therefore, escitalopram should be used during pregnancy only if the potential benefit justifies the potential risk to the fetus.

Neonates exposed to escitalopram and or other SSRIs or SNRIs, late in the third trimester, have developed complications requiring prolonged hospitalization, respiratory support, and tube feeding. These complications may arise immediately upon delivery and are consistent with either a direct toxic effect or, possibly a drug discontinuation syndrome. Consider tapering the dose in the third trimester if the potential benefits outweigh risk of treatment during pregnancy.

In animal reproduction studies, racemic citalopram has been shown to have adverse effects on embryo/fetal and postnatal development, including teratogenic effects, when administered at doses greater than human therapeutic doses.

In a rat embryo/fetal development study, oral administration of escitalopram to pregnant animals during the period of organogenesis resulted in decreased fetal body weight and associated delays in ossification at doses approximately greater than or equal to 56 times the maximum recommended human dose [MRHD] of 20 mg per day on a mg/m^2 basis. Maternal toxicity was present at all dose levels and mild at 56 mg per kg of body weight per day. The developmental no effect dose of 56 mg per kg of body weight per day is approximately 28 times the MRHD on a mg/m^2 basis. No teratogenicity was observed at any of the doses tested as high as 75 times the MRHD on a mg/m^2 basis. In two rat embryo/fetal development studies, oral administration of racemic citalopram to pregnant animals during the period of organogenesis resulted in decreased embryo/fetal growth and survival, an increased incidence of fetal abnormalities including cardiovascular and skeletal defects, and maternal toxicity at the high dose of 112 mg per kg of body weight per day. The developmental no effect dose was 56 mg per kg of body weight per day. In a rabbit study, no adverse effects on embryo/fetal development were observed at doses of racemic citalopram of up to 16 mg per kg of body weight per day. Thus, teratogenic effects of racemic citalopram were observed at a maternally toxic dose in the rat and were not observed in the rabbit.

Administration of escitalopram to female rats during pregnancy and through weaning at oral doses ranging from 6 to 48 mg per kg of body weight resulted in a slightly increased offspring mortality, growth retardation, and maternal toxicity at 48 mg per kg of body weight per day which is approximately 24 times the MRHD on a mg/m^2 basis. Slightly increased offspring mortality was seen at 24 mg per kg of body weight per day. The no effect dose was 12 mg per kg of body weight per day which is approximately 6 times the MRHD on a mg/m^2 basis. Administration of racemic citalopram to female rats from late gestation through weaning at oral doses ranging from 4.8 to 32 mg per kg of body weight per day resulted in increased offspring mortality during the first four days after birth and persistent offspring growth retardation at the highest dose. The no effect dose was 12.8 mg per kg of body weight per day. Similar effects on offspring mortality and growth were seen when dams were treated throughout gestation and early lactation at doses greater than or equal to 24 mg per kg of body weight per day. A no effect dose was not determined in that study. Administration of racemic citalopram to male and female rats at oral doses ranging from 16 to 72 mg per kg of body weight per day resulted in an increase in gestation duration at 48 mg per kg of body weight per day.

FDA Pregnancy Category C

Labor and delivery—The effect of escitalopram on labor and delivery in humans is unknown

Breast-feeding

Racemic citalopram is distributed into human breast milk. Excessive somnolence, decreased feeding, and weight loss have been reported in association with breast feeding from a citalopram-treated mother. In one case, the infant was reported to recover completely upon discontinuation of citalopram by the mother. The second case provided no available follow up information. The decision whether to continue or discontinue either nursing or escitalopram therapy should take into account the risks of citalopram exposure for the infant and the benefits of treatment for the mother.

Pediatrics

Safety and efficacy have not been established.

Antidepressants increase the risk of suicidal thinking and behavior (suicidality) in children and adolescents with major depressive disorder (MDD) and other psychiatric disorders. Anyone considering the use of escitalopram or any other antidepressant in a child or adolescent must balance this risk with the clinical need.

Pooled analyses of short-term placebo controlled trials of nine antidepressant drugs in children and adolescents with MDD, obsessive compulsive disorder, or other psychiatric disorders have revealed a greater risk of adverse events representing suicidality during the first few months of treatment in those receiving antidepressants.

Geriatrics

Escitalopram AUC and half life were increased approximately 50% in elderly subjects ≥ 65 years of age as compared to younger subjects in clinical studies; decreased dosing is recommended for elderly patients.

The number of elderly patients 60 years of age or older who received escitalopram in controlled trials was insufficient to assess differences in safety and efficacy on the basis of age. In clinical studies of racemic citalopram, no overall differences in safety or effectiveness were observed between elderly patients and younger patients. However, greater sensitivity of some elderly individuals to effects of escitalopram cannot be ruled out.

Pharmacogenetics

In a multiple-dose study of escitalopram, there were no differences based on gender in AUC, C_{max}, and half life. No adjustment of dosage on the basis of gender is needed.

Drug interactions and/or related problems

The following drug interactions and/or related problems have been selected on the basis of their potential clinical significance (possible mechanism in parentheses where appropriate)—not necessarily inclusive (» = major clinical significance):

Note: Combinations containing any of the following medications, depending on the amount present, may also interact with this medication.

» Alcohol
(although studies indicate that racemic citalopram did not increase the cognitive and motor effects of alcohol, concurrent use is not recommended)

CYP2D6 metabolized drugs such as:
Tricyclic antidepressants
(*in vivo* studies suggest a modest CYP2D6 inhibitory effect for escitalopram; coadministration of escitalopram with the tricyclic antidepressant desipramine, a substrate for CYP2D6, resulted in increases of C_{max} and AUC of desipramine by 40% and 100%, respectively; caution is recommended in concurrent use of escitalopram and drugs metabolized by CYP2D6)

Carbamazepine
(due to the enzyme inducing properties of carbamazepine, a CYP3A4 substrate, the possibility that carbamazepine might increase the clearance of escitalopram should be considered with concurrent use)

Central nervous system (CNS) drugs
(caution should be used due to the primary CNS effects of escitalopram)

Cimetidine
(AUC and C_{max} of citalopram were increased by 43% and 39%, respectively, by concomitant cimetidine use; clinical significance is unknown)

» Citalopram
(since escitalopram is the active isomer of racemic citalopram, the two should not be co-administered)

Ketoconazole
(C_{max} and AUC of ketoconazole were decreased by 21% and 10%, respectively, by concomitant racemic citalopram use)

» Linezolid
(serotonin syndrome has been reported in patients concomitantly receiving linezolid [which is a reversible non-selective MAOI] and escitalopram)

Lithium
(because lithium may enhance the serotonergic effects of escitalopram, caution is recommended and plasma lithium levels should be monitored and adjusted)

Metoprolol
(C_{max} and AUC of metoprolol were increased by 50% and 82%, respectively, by concomitant escitalopram use; increased metoprolol plasma levels have been associated with decreased cardioselectivity, but no clinically significant effects on blood pressure or heart rate.)

» Monoamine oxidase inhibitors (MAOI's)
(concomitant use is contraindicated; serious and sometimes fatal reactions have occurred in patients receiving an SSRI with an MAOI; reactions have included hyperthermia, rigidity, myoclonus, autonomic instability with possible rapid fluctuations of vital signs, and mental status changes including extreme agitation progressing to delirium and coma; some cases presented with features resembling neuroleptic malignant syndrome; these reactions have also been reported in patients who have recently discontinued SSRI treatment and have been started on an MAOI; concurrent use of an MAOI and escitalopram is **contraindicated;** at least 14 days should be allowed between discontinuation of one drug, escitalopram or MAOI, and the initiation of the other)

NSAID's such as
Aspirin or
Other drugs that affect coagulation
(caution; risk of upper gastrointestinal bleeding associated with the concomitant use of escitalopram)

» Sumatriptan
(there have been rare postmarketing reports of patients with weakness, hyperreflexia and incoordination following the use of a selective serotonin reuptake inhibitor (SSRI) such as escitalopram and sumatriptan; appropriate observation of the patient is advised when concomitant treatment is clinically warranted)

Warfarin
(racemic citalopram did not affect the pharmacokinetics of warfarin; however, prothrombin time was increased by 5%, the clinical significance is unknown.)

Note: *In vitro* studies indicate that CYP3A4 and -2C19 are the primary enzymes involved in the metabolism of escitalopram. However, coadministration of ritonavir, a potent inhibitor of CYP3A4, with escitalopram did not significantly affect the pharmacokinetics of escitalopram. Because escitalopram is metabolized by multiple enzyme systems, inhibition of a single enzyme may not appreciably decrease escitalopram clearance.

Medical considerations/Contraindications

The medical considerations/contraindications included have been selected on the basis of their potential clinical significance (reasons given in parentheses where appropriate)—not necessarily inclusive (» = major clinical significance).

Except under special circumstances, this medication should not be used when the following medical problem exists:

Hypersensitivity to escitalopram or citalopram, parabens (oral solution only) or any of the inactive ingredients in escitalopram.

Risk-benefit should be considered when the following medical problems exist:

Altered metabolism or hemodynamic responses
(caution should be used in patients with diseases or conditions that produce altered metabolism or hemodynamic responses)

Drug abuse, history of
(patients with a history of drug abuse should be closely observed for signs of misuse or abuse such as development of tolerance, increased dose, and/or drug seeking behavior)

» Heart disease (unstable) or
» Myocardial infarction (recent history of)
(use of escitalopram has not been systematically evaluated in patients with these conditions)

» Hepatic impairment
(racemic citalopram clearance was decreased and plasma concentrations were increased; recommended dose of escitalopram in hepatically impaired patients is 10 mg per day)

» Mania or hypomania, history of
(condition may be activated by escitalopram; caution should be used in patients with history of mania or hypomania)

» Renal impairment, severe
(until adequate numbers of patients with severe renal impairment (creatinine clearance < 20 mL per min) have been evaluated during chronic treatment with escitalopram, it should be used with caution)

» Seizure disorder, history of
(escitalopram should be introduced with caution in patients with a history of seizure disorder)

Patient monitoring

The following may be especially important in patient monitoring (other tests may be warranted in some patients, depending on condition; » = major clinical significance):

Careful supervision of depressed patients including those with:
Abnormal behaviors (i.e., agitation, panic attacks, hostility) or
Clinical worsening of their depression or
Suicidal ideation and behavior (suicidality)
(recommended especially during early treatment phase before peak effectiveness of escitalopram is achieved or at the time of increases or decreases in dose; prescribing the smallest number of tablets necessary for good patient management is recommended to decrease the risk of overdose; consideration should be given to changing the therapeutic regimen, including possibly discontinuing the medicine, in patients whose depression is persistently worse or whose emergent suicidality or other symptoms are severe, abrupt in onset, or were not part of the patient's presenting symptoms)

Close supervision of patients with suicidal tendencies or severe symptoms with abrupt onset
(recommended especially during initial escitalopram therapy; good patient management practices with prescriptions for the smallest quantity of tablets)

Reevaluation of the long-term usefulness of the drug
(periodic evaluations are recommended to assess the usefulness of escitalopram for the individual patient; the longer-term efficacy has not been systematically evaluated in controlled trials)

Symptoms associated with discontinuation
(patients should be monitored for symptoms upon discontinuation; a gradual reduction in dose rather than abrupt cessation is recommended whenever possible.)

Side/Adverse Effects

The following side/adverse effects have been selected on the basis of their potential clinical significance (possible signs and symptoms in parentheses where appropriate)—not necessarily inclusive:

Those indicating need for medical attention

Incidence rare

Hyponatremia (coma; confusion; convulsions; decreased urine output; dizziness; fast or irregular heartbeat; headache; increased thirst; muscle pain or cramps; nausea or vomiting; shortness of breath; swelling of face, ankles, or hands; unusual tiredness or weakness)—or syndrome of inappropriate antidiuretic hormone secretion

Those indicating need for medical attention only if they continue or are bothersome

Incidence more frequent

Abnormal ejaculation (ejaculation delay); ***constipation; diarrhea; dizziness; dry mouth; fatigue*** (unusual tiredness or weakness); ***impotence; libido, decreased*** (loss in sexual ability, desire, drive, or performance; decreased interest in sexual intercourse; inability to have or keep an erection); ***increased sweating; indigestion*** (gas in stomach; heartburn; nausea; stomach pain); ***insomnia*** (sleeplessness; trouble sleeping; unable to sleep); ***nausea; somnolence*** (sleepiness or unusual drowsiness)

Note: The incidence of *constipation, diarrhea, dizziness, dry mouth, fatigue, increased sweating, indigestion, insomnia,* and *somnolence* may be dose-related.

Incidence less frequent

Abdominal pain; anorgasmic (not able to have an orgasm); ***appetite, decreased; influenza like symptoms*** (chills; cough; diarrhea; fever; general feeling of discomfort or illness; headache; joint pain; loss of appetite; muscle aches and pains; nausea; runny nose; shivering; sore throat; sweating; trouble sleeping; unusual tiredness or weakness; vomiting); ***rhinitis*** (stuffy nose; runny nose; sneezing); ***sinusitis*** (pain or tenderness around eyes and cheekbones; fever; stuffy or runny nose; headache; cough; shortness of breath or troubled breathing; tightness of chest or wheezing)

Occurrence upon discontinuation

Incidence less frequent

Abnormal ejaculation (ejaculation delay); ***nausea***

Overdose

For specific information on the agents used in the management of escitalopram overdose, see *Charcoal, Activated (Oral-Local)* monograph.

For more information on the management of overdose or unintentional ingestion, **contact a poison control center** (see *Poison Control Center Listing*).

Clinical effects of overdose

There have been three reports of escitalopram overdose involving doses of up to 600 mg. All three patients recovered and no symptoms associated with the overdoses were reported.

Note: Escitalopram effects of overdose were not reported. Because escitalopram is an racemic enantiomer of citalopram, the citalopram effects of overdose may be useful in evaluating escitalopram overdose. The following effects accompany citalopram overdose, alone or in combination with other drugs and/or alcohol: dizziness, sweating, nausea, vomiting, tremor, somnolence, sinus tachycardia, and convulsions. In more rare cases, observed symptoms include amnesia, confusion, coma, hyperventilation, cyanosis, rhabdomyolysis, and ECG changes (including QTc prolongation, nodal rhythm, ventricular arrhythmia, and one possible case of Torsades de pointes.)

Treatment of overdose

There are no specific antidotes for escitalopram. Treatment is essentially symptomatic and supportive.

To decrease absorption—
  Considering gastric evacuation by lavage and administration of activate charcoal

Monitoring—
  Cardiac and vital sign monitoring and careful observation are recommended

Supportive care—
  Establishing and maintaining an airway to ensure adequate ventilation and oxygenation
  Patients in whom intentional overdose is confirmed or suspected should be referred for psychiatric consultation.

Note: Due to the large volume of distribution of escitalopram, forced diuresis, dialysis, hemoperfusion, and exchange transfusion are unlikely to be of benefit.

Patient Consultation

As an aid to patient consultation, refer to *Advice for the Patient, Escitalopram (Systemic)*.

In providing consultation, consider emphasizing the following selected information (» = major clinical significance):

Before using this medication

» Conditions affecting use, especially:
  Sensitivity to escitalopram, citalopram, or parabens (oral solution only).
  Pregnancy—Should be used during pregnancy only if the potential benefit justifies the potential risk to the fetus.
  Breast-feeding—Racemic citalopram is distributed into human breast milk.
  Use in the elderly—Elderly patients may have greater sensitivity to the effects of escitalopram; decreased dosing
  Other medications, especially alcohol, citalopram, linezolid, monoamine oxidase inhibitors (MAOI's) or sumatriptan
  Other medical problems, especially hepatic impairment, history of mania or hypomania, history of seizure disorder, or severe renal impairment

Proper use of this medication

» Importance of continuing escitalopram even if improvement of symptoms is noticeable in the first 1 to 4 weeks
» Proper dosing
  Missed dose: Discussing with physician what to do about any missed doses
» Proper storage

Precautions while using this medication

» Not taking escitalopram with or within 14 days of taking a monoamine oxidase inhibitor (MAOI), not taking an MAOI within 14 days of taking escitalopram
  Avoiding use of alcoholic beverages
  Possible impaired judgement, thinking or motor skills; not driving, operating machinery, or doing anything that could be dangerous until effects of medication are known
» Contact your doctor right away if you develop unusual agitation, irritability, or thoughts of doing harm to yourself.
» Importance of not stopping this medicine suddenly. Contact your doctor about decreasing the dose of this medication gradually.

Side/adverse effects

Signs of potential side effects, especially hyponatremia or syndrome of inappropriate antidiuretic hormone secretion.

General Dosing Information

Patients who are at high risk for suicide attempts should be closely supervised and prescribed the smallest quantity of tablets consistent with good patient management, in order to reduce the risk of overdose.

Patients should be advised to continue escitalopram therapy as directed even though they may notice improvement of symptoms in one to four weeks.

Patients should be periodically reassessed to determine the need for maintenance treatment and the appropriate dose for such treatment.

Patients should be monitored for discontinuation symptoms when ceasing treatment. A gradual reduction in dose rather than abrupt termination is recommended. If intolerable symptoms occur following a decrease in dose or discontinuation of treatment, resuming the previously prescribed dose may be considered while subsequently the physician may continue to decrease the dose at a more gradual rate.

At least 14 days should be allowed between discontinuation of escitalopram or monoamine oxidase inhibitors (MAOI's), and the initiation of the other.

Diet/Nutrition

May be taken with or without food once daily in the morning or evening.

Bioequivalence information

The oral solution and the tablet dosage forms of escitalopram oxalate are bioequivalent.

Oral Dosage Forms

ESCITALOPRAM OXALATE ORAL SOLUTION

Usual adult dose

Antidepressant—
  Oral, initially 10 mg once daily. After a minimum of one week the dose may be increased to 20 mg once daily; however, a fixed dose trial of 10 mg and 20 mg doses of escitalopram failed to demonstrate a greater benefit of 20 mg over 10 mg.
  Note: For patients with hepatic impairment, the recommended dose is 10 mg once daily. For patients with mild or moderate renal impairment, no dosage adjustment is necessary.

Antianxiety agent—
  Oral, initially 10 mg once daily. After a minimum of one week the dose may be increased to 20 mg once daily.

Usual pediatric dose

Safety and efficacy have not been established

Usual geriatric dose

Antidepressant—
  Oral, 10 mg once daily recommended for most elderly patients.

Strength(s) usually available

U.S.—
  1 mg/mL (base) (Rx) [*Lexapro* (citric acid; glycerin; malic acid; methylparaben; natural peppermint flavor; propylene glycol; propylparaben; purified water; sodium citrate; sorbitol)].

Canada—
  Not commercially available.

Packaging and storage

Store at 25 °C (77 °F); excursions permitted between 15 and 30 °C (59 and 86 °F).

Auxiliary labeling

- May impair judgement, thinking, or motor skills. Be careful while driving or operating machinery. Use caution until you become familiar with its effects.
- Avoid alcoholic beverages

ESCITALOPRAM OXALATE TABLETS

Usual adult dose

Antidepressant—
  Oral, initially 10 mg once daily. After a minimum of one week the dose may be increased to 20 mg once daily; however, a fixed dose trial of 10 mg and 20 mg doses of escitalopram failed to demonstrate a greater benefit of 20 mg over 10 mg.
  Note: For patients with hepatic impairment, the recommended dose is 10 mg once daily. For patients with mild or moderate renal impairment, no dosage adjustment is necessary.

Antianxiety agent—
Oral, initially 10 mg once daily. After a minimum of one week the dose may be increased to 20 mg once daily.

Usual pediatric dose
Safety and efficacy have not been established

Usual geriatric dose
Antidepressant—
Oral, 10 mg once daily recommended for most elderly patients.

Strength(s) usually available
U.S.—
5 mg (base) (Rx) [*Lexapro* (croscarmellose sodium; colloidal silicon dioxide; hydroxypropyl methyl cellulose; magnesium stearate; microcrystalline cellulose; polyethylene glycol; talc; titanium dioxide)].
10 mg (base) (Rx) [*Lexapro* (scored; croscarmellose sodium; colloidal silicon dioxide; hydroxypropyl methyl cellulose; magnesium stearate; microcrystalline cellulose; polyethylene glycol; talc; titanium dioxide)].
20 mg (base) (Rx) [*Lexapro* (scored; croscarmellose sodium; colloidal silicon dioxide; hydroxypropyl methyl cellulose; magnesium stearate; microcrystalline cellulose; polyethylene glycol; talc; titanium dioxide)].

Canada—
Not commercially available.

Packaging and storage
Store at 25 °C (77 °F); excursions permitted between 15 and 30 °C (59 and 86 °F).

Auxiliary labeling
- May impair judgement, thinking, or motor skills. Be careful while driving or operating machinery. Use caution until you become familiar with its effects.
- Avoid alcoholic beverages

Revised: 01/24/2005
Developed: 01/21/2003

ESMOLOL Systemic†

VA CLASSIFICATION (Primary/Secondary): CV100/CV300

Commonly used brand name(s): *Brevibloc*.

Note: For a listing of dosage forms and brand names by country availability, see *Dosage Forms* section(s).

†Not commercially available in Canada.

Category

Antiadrenergic; antiarrhythmic.

Indications

Note: Bracketed information in the *Indications* section refers to uses that are not included in U.S. product labeling.

Accepted
Arrhythmias, cardiac (treatment)—Esmolol is indicated for rapid and short-term control of ventricular rate in patients with atrial fibrillation or atrial flutter in perioperative, postoperative, or other emergency situations. It is also indicated in noncompensatory sinus tachycardia judged by the physician to need intervention. [Esmolol is used for control of heart rate in patients with myocardial ischemia.] It is not recommended for use in chronic situations where transfer to another agent is anticipated.

Tachycardia, intraoperative and postoperative (treatment)—Esmolol is indicated for the treatment of refractory tachycardia that occurs during surgery, on emergence from anesthesia, and in the postoperative period. It is recommended for use only when other treatable causes of tachycardia, such as bleeding or hypovolemia, have been ruled out.

Hypertension, intraoperative and postoperative (treatment)—Esmolol is indicated for the treatment of refractory hypertension that occurs during surgery, on emergence from anesthesia, and in the postoperative period. Esmolol is not considered to be a first-line agent and should be reserved for situations in which agents known to be effective in treating the etiology of the hypertension have failed. It is not recommended for use in patients with hypertension secondary to the vasoconstriction associated with hypothermia.

Pharmacology/Pharmacokinetics

Physicochemical characteristics
Molecular weight—331.84.

Mechanism of action/Effect
Like other beta-blockers, esmolol blocks the agonistic effect of the sympathetic neurotransmitters by competing for receptor binding sites. Because it predominantly blocks the beta-1 receptors in cardiac tissue, it is said to be cardioselective. In general, so-called cardioselective beta-blockers are relatively cardioselective; at lower doses they block beta-1 receptors only but begin to block beta-2 receptors as the dose increases. At therapeutic dosages, esmolol does not have intrinsic sympathomimetic activity (ISA) or membrane-stabilizing (quinidine-like) activity.

Antiarrhythmic activity is due to blockade of adrenergic stimulation of cardiac pacemaker potentials. In the Vaughan Williams classification of antiarrhythmics, beta-blockers are considered to be class II agents.

Protein binding
Moderate (55%).

Biotransformation
Rapid hydrolysis by esterases in red blood cells to a free acid metabolite (with 1/1500 the activity of esmolol) and methanol.

Half-life
Esmolol—
Distribution: Approximately 2 minutes.
Elimination: Approximately 9 minutes.
Free acid metabolite—
Approximately 3.7 hours (increased up to tenfold in renal failure).

Time to steady-state blood concentration
With loading dose—Within 5 minutes.

Without loading dose—Approximately 30 minutes.

Note: Use of a loading dose expedites achievement of constant plasma drug concentrations, but true steady-state occurs at 30 minutes, with or without a loading dose.

Duration of action
10 to 20 minutes after infusion is discontinued.

Elimination
Renal, almost entirely as metabolite.

Precautions to Consider

Carcinogenicity/Mutagenicity
Studies have not been done in either animals or humans.

Pregnancy/Reproduction
Fertility—Studies have not been done in either animals or humans.

Pregnancy—Adequate and well-controlled studies in humans have not been done.

Studies in rats and rabbits at intravenous doses of up to 10 and 3 times the maximum human maintenance dose (MHMD), respectively, for 30 minutes daily showed no evidence of maternal toxicity, embryotoxicity, or teratogenicity. However, doses of approximately 30 and 8 times the MHMD in rats and rabbits, respectively, caused maternal toxicity, death, and increased fetal resorptions.

FDA Pregnancy Category C.

Breast-feeding
Although it is not known whether esmolol is distributed into human breast milk, problems have not been documented.

Pediatrics
Appropriate studies on the relationship of age to the effects of esmolol have not been performed in the pediatric population. However, limited experience with esmolol in the evaluation and management of pediatric tachyarrhythmias have not demonstrated pediatrics-specific problems that would limit the usefulness of esmolol in children.

Geriatrics
Although appropriate studies on the relationship of age to the effects of esmolol have not been performed in the geriatric population, the elderly may be less sensitive to some of the effects of beta-blockers. However, reduced metabolic and excretory capabilities in many elderly patients may lead to increased myocardial depression and require dosage reduction of beta-blockers. The net effect is uncertain; dosage adjustment should be based on clinical response.

Drug interactions and/or related problems
The following drug interactions and/or related problems have been selected on the basis of their potential clinical significance (possible

mechanism in parentheses where appropriate)—not necessarily inclusive (» = major clinical significance):

Note: Combinations containing any of the following medications, depending on the amount present, may also interact with this medication.

Because of esmolol's short duration of action and the short periods of time over which it is used, many of the drug interactions associated with other beta-blockers do not apply.

» Antidiabetic agents, sulfonylurea or
» Insulin
(esmolol may mask certain symptoms of developing hypoglycemia, such as increases in pulse rate and blood pressure)

Gallamine or
Metocurine or
Pancuronium or
Tubocurarine
(esmolol may potentiate and prolong the action of nondepolarizing neuromuscular blocking agents when used concurrently; careful postoperative monitoring of the patient may be necessary following concurrent or sequential use, especially if there is a possibility of incomplete reversal of neuromuscular blockade)

Hypotension-producing medications, other (See *Appendix II*)
(antihypertensive effects may be potentiated when these medications are used concurrently with esmolol; dosage adjustments should be based on blood pressure measurements)

» Monoamine oxidase (MAO) inhibitors, including furazolidone, procarbazine, and selegiline
(possible significant hypertension may theoretically occur up to 14 days following discontinuation of the MAO inhibitor; although sufficient clinical reports are lacking, concurrent use with esmolol is not recommended)

Phenytoin
(concurrent use of esmolol with intravenous phenytoin may produce additive cardiac depressant effects)

Reserpine
(concurrent use with esmolol may result in additive and possibly excessive beta-adrenergic blockade; close observation is recommended since bradycardia and hypotension may occur)

» Sympathomimetics
(concurrent use of esmolol with sympathomimetic amines having beta-adrenergic stimulant activity may result in mutual but short-lived inhibition of therapeutic effects)

» Xanthines, especially aminophylline or theophylline
(concurrent use with esmolol may result in mutual inhibition of therapeutic effects; in addition, concurrent use of beta-blockers with the xanthines [except dyphylline] may decrease theophylline clearance, especially in patients with increased theophylline clearance induced by smoking; concurrent use requires careful monitoring)

Medical considerations/Contraindications

The medical considerations/contraindications included have been selected on the basis of their potential clinical significance (reasons given in parentheses where appropriate)—not necessarily inclusive (» = major clinical significance).

Except under special circumstances, this medication should not be used when the following medical problems exist:

» Cardiac failure, overt or
» Cardiogenic shock or
» Heart block, 2nd- or 3rd-degree atrioventricular (AV) block or
» Sinus bradycardia (heart rate less than 45 beats per minute)
(risk of further myocardial depression; may be used with extreme caution in some patients with cardiac failure [e.g., high output failure associated with thyrotoxicosis])

Risk-benefit should be considered when the following medical problems exist:

» Allergy, history of or
» Asthma, bronchial or
» Emphysema or nonallergenic bronchitis
(esmolol may promote bronchospasm and block the bronchodilating effect of epinephrine; however, because esmolol is cardioselective and may be less likely to cause such effects than less cardioselective beta-blockers, it may be used with caution)

» Congestive heart failure
(risk of further depression of myocardial contractility)

» Diabetes mellitus
(all beta-blockers may mask tachycardia associated with hypoglycemia, but not dizziness and sweating)

Renal function impairment

Sensitivity to esmolol

Patient monitoring

The following may be especially important in patient monitoring (other tests may be warranted in some patients, depending on condition; » = major clinical significance):

» Blood pressure and
» Electrocardiogram (ECG) and
» Heart rate
(should be carefully monitored during intravenous administration)

Side/Adverse Effects

The following side/adverse effects have been selected on the basis of their potential clinical significance (possible signs and symptoms in parentheses where appropriate)—not necessarily inclusive:

Those indicating need for medical attention

Incidence less frequent

Confusion; redness or swelling at place of injection; reduced peripheral circulation (cold hands and feet)

Incidence rare

Bradycardia, especially less than 50 beats per minute; breathing difficulty and/or wheezing; chest pain; fainting; fever; mental depression

Those indicating need for medical attention only if they continue or are bothersome

Incidence more frequent

Hypotension (dizziness; sweating)—symptomatic in about 12% of patients, asymptomatic in about 25% of patients

Note: *Hypotension* can occur at any dose, but is dose-related.

Incidence less frequent

Anxiety or nervousness; drowsiness or tiredness; flushing or pale skin; headache; nausea or vomiting

Overdose

For specific information on the agents used in the management of esmolol overdose, see:

- *Atropine* in *Anticholinergics/Antispasmodics (Systemic)* monograph;
- *Bronchodilators, Theophylline (Systemic)* monograph;
- *Glucagon (Systemic)* monograph;
- *Isoproterenol* in *Bronchodilators, Adrenergic (Systemic)* monograph;
- *Lidocaine (Systemic)* monograph; and/or
- *Sympathomimetic Agents—Cardiovascular Use (Parenteral-Systemic)* monograph.

For more information on the management of overdose or unintentional ingestion, **contact a Poison Control Center** (see *Poison Control Center Listing*).

Clinical effects of overdose

The following effects have been selected on the basis of their potential clinical significance (possible signs and symptoms in parentheses where appropriate)—not necessarily inclusive:

Slow heartbeat; dizziness, severe, or fainting; drowsiness, severe; difficulty in breathing; bluish-colored fingernails or palms of hands; seizures

Treatment of overdose

In most cases, symptoms of esmolol overdose disappear quickly after esmolol is withdrawn.

Specific treatment—
Clinical reports are increasing for the successful use of glucagon to counteract the cardiovascular effects (bradycardia, hypotension) resulting from overdose with beta-blockers. An intravenous dose of 2 to 3 mg is administered over a period of 30 seconds and repeated if necessary, followed by an intravenous glucagon infusion at the rate of 5 mg per hour until the patient has been stabilized.

Supportive care—
Bradycardia—Atropine sulfate may be administered intravenously to correct severe bradycardia if the patient is hypotensive. If vagal blockade is unresponsive, atropine may be repeated or intravenous isoproterenol or dobutamine may be given cautiously. Intravenous epinephrine or a transvenous pacemaker may be necessary.

Premature ventricular contractions—Intravenous lidocaine or phenytoin (quinidine, procainamide, and disopyramide should be avoided since they may further depress myocardial function).

Cardiac failure—Provision of oxygen. Digitalization of patient and/or administration of diuretic.

Hypotension—Trendelenburg position and intravenous fluids (unless pulmonary edema is present). Intravenous administration of a vasopressor such as epinephrine, norepinephrine, dopamine, or dobutamine (some reports indicate epinephrine may be the agent of choice). Serial monitoring of blood pressure. Hypotension does not respond to beta-2 agonists. (See *Drug interactions and/or related problems* for precautions in use of sympathomimetic vasopressors.)

Bronchospasm—Administration of a beta-2 agonist such as isoproterenol and/or a theophylline derivative.

General Dosing Information

The 250-mg-per-mL strength of esmolol hydrochloride injection must be diluted before it is administered by intravenous infusion. Concentrations of greater than 10 mg of esmolol hydrochloride per mL may produce irritation. The 10-mg-per-mL strength may be given by direct infusion.

If a reaction occurs at the infusion site, the infusion should be stopped and resumed at another site. Use of butterfly needles for administration is not recommended.

To convert to other antiarrhythmic therapy after control has been achieved with esmolol

—30 minutes after administration of the first dose of the alternative agent, infusion rate of esmolol should be reduced by one-half, and

—after the second dose of the alternative agent, if a satisfactory response is maintained for 1 hour, esmolol should be discontinued.

For treatment of adverse effects

Hypotension is usually reversed within 30 minutes after dosage reduction or withdrawal of esmolol.

Dosage reduction or withdrawal of esmolol is recommended at the first sign of congestive heart failure.

Parenteral Dosage Forms

ESMOLOL HYDROCHLORIDE INJECTION

Usual adult dose

Antiarrhythmic—

Dosage is established by means of a series of loading and maintenance doses

Loading: Intravenous infusion, 500 mcg (0.5 mg) per kg of body weight per minute for one minute, followed by

Maintenance: Intravenous infusion, 50 mcg (0.05 mg) per kg of body weight per minute for four minutes.

If an adequate response is observed at the end of five minutes, the infusion dosage should be maintained with periodic adjustments as needed.

If an adequate response is not observed at the end of the five minutes, the sequence is repeated with an increment of 50 mcg (0.05 mg) per kg of body weight per minute in the maintenance dose

Loading: Intravenous infusion, 500 mcg (0.5 mg) per kg of body weight per minute for one minute, followed by

Maintenance: Intravenous infusion, 100 mcg (0.1 mg) per kg of body weight per minute for four minutes.

The sequence is repeated until an adequate response is obtained, with an increment of 50 mcg (0.05 mg) per kg of body weight per minute in the maintenance dose at each step. As the desired endpoint (defined by desired heart rate or undesirable decrease in blood pressure) is approached, the loading dose may be omitted and increments in the maintenance dose reduced to 25 mcg (0.025 mg) per kg of body weight per minute or less. If desired, the interval between titration steps may be increased from five to ten minutes. The established maintenance dose usually does not exceed 200 mcg (0.2 mg) per kg of body weight per minute and can be given for up to forty-eight hours.

Note: Because of the time required for titration, the above dosage regimen may not be optimal for intraoperative use.

Tachycardia, intraoperative or postoperative or
Hypertension, intraoperative or postoperative—

Initial: Intravenous, 250 to 500 mcg (0.25 to 0.5 mg) per kg of body weight over one minute.

Maintenance: Intravenous infusion, 50 mcg (0.05 mg) per kg of body weight per minute for four minutes.

If an adequate response is not observed, the sequence may be repeated, with an increment of 50 mcg (0.05 mg) per kg of body weight per minute in the maintenance dose

Initial: Intravenous, 250 to 500 mcg (0.25 to 0.5 mg) per kg of body weight over one minute.

Maintenance: Intravenous infusion, 100 mcg (0.1 mg) per kg of body weight per minute for four minutes.

The sequence may be repeated up to four times if needed, with an increment of 50 mcg (0.05 mg) per kg of body weight per minute in the maintenance dose at each step.

Usual adult prescribing limits

Maintenance—Up to 200 mcg (0.2 mg) per kg of body weight per minute (because of the risk of hypotension).

Usual pediatric dose

Arrhythmias, supraventricular—

Intravenous infusion, 50 mcg (0.05 mg) per kg of body weight per minute; dosage may be titrated upwards every ten minutes up to 300 mcg (0.3 mg) per kg of body weight per minute.

Hypertension, intraoperative and postoperative (treatment)—

Intravenous infusion, 100 to 500 mcg per kg of body weight per minute.

Strength(s) usually available

U.S.—

Note: The 10-mg-per-mL strength is prediluted and may be used for the loading dose.

Note: The 250-mg-per-mL strength must be diluted before use. It is not intended for direct intravenous injection.

10 mg per mL (100 mg per 10-mL single-dose vial) (Rx) [*Brevibloc*].

250 mg per mL (2500 mg per 10-mL ampul) (Rx) [*Brevibloc* (alcohol 25%)].

Canada—

Not commercially available.

Packaging and storage

Store below 40 °C (104 °F), preferably between 15 and 30 °C (59 and 86 °F), unless otherwise specified by manufacturer. Not adversely affected by freezing.

Preparation of dosage form

Esmolol hydrochloride injection (250-mg-per-mL strength) is prepared for administration by intravenous infusion by aseptically removing 20 mL from a 500-mL bottle of intravenous fluid (5% dextrose injection, 5% dextrose in Ringer's injection, 5% dextrose and 0.45% sodium chloride injection, 5% dextrose and 0.9% sodium chloride injection, lactated Ringer's injection, 0.45% sodium chloride injection, or 0.9% sodium chloride injection) and then adding 5 grams of esmolol hydrochloride injection to the bottle, producing a solution containing 10 mg of esmolol hydrochloride per mL.

Stability

Diluted solutions of esmolol hydrochloride are stable for at least 24 hours at room temperature.

Incompatibilities

Not compatible with 5% sodium bicarbonate injection.

Auxiliary labeling

For 250-mg-per-mL vial

- Must be diluted before administration.

Caution

Confusion caused by two significantly different concentrations of esmolol has resulted in massive overdoses, including several deaths. The incidents occurred when the 250-mg-per-mL ampul, which requires dilution prior to administration, was given undiluted. The 250-mg-per-mL ampul of esmolol must be diluted before administration. Caution should be utilized when dispensing, using, and storing this medication.

Selected Bibliography

Angaran DM, Schultz NJ, Tschida VH. Esmolol hydrochloride: an ultra-short-acting, beta-adrenergic blocking agent. Clin Pharm 1986 Apr; 5: 288-303.

Covinsky JO. Esmolol: a novel cardioselective, titratable, intravenous beta-blocker with ultrashort half-life. DICP, Ann Pharmacother 1987; 21: 316-21.

Murthy VS, Frishman WH. Controlled beta-receptor blockade with esmolol and flestolol. Pharmacother 1988; 8(3): 168-82.

Revised: 11/17/2004

ESOMEPRAZOLE Systemic

VA CLASSIFICATION (Primary): GA304

Note: For a listing of dosage forms and brand names by country availability, see *Dosage Forms* section(s).

Category

Gastric acid pump inhibitor; antiulcer agent.

Indications

Accepted

Gastroesophageal reflux disease [GERD] (prophylaxis and treatment)—Esomeprazole is indicated for the treatment of heartburn and other symptoms associated with gastroesophageal reflux disease (GERD). Esomeprazole is indicated for the short-term treatment of diagnostically confirmed erosive esophagitis (associated with GERD). Esomeprazole is also indicated to maintain symptom resolution and healing of erosive esophagitis.

Esomeprazole I.V. for injection is indicated for the short-term (up to 10 days) of GERD patients with a history of erosive esophagitis as an alternative to oral therapy in patients when therapy with esomeprazole delayed-release capsules is not possible or appropriate.

Ulcer, duodenal, *Helicobacter pylori*-associated (treatment adjunct)—Esomeprazole, in combination with clarithromycin and amoxicillin, is indicated for the treatment of patients with *H. pylori* infection and duodenal ulcer disease (active or history of within the past 5 years) to eradicate *H. pylori*. Eradication of *H. pylori* has been shown to reduce the risk of duodenal ulcer recurrence.

Ulcer, gastric, nonsteroidal anti-inflammatory drug–induced (prophylaxis)—Esomeprazole is indicated for the reduction in the occurrence of gastric ulcers associated with continuous NSAID therapy in patients at risk for developing gastric ulcers. Patients are considered to be at risk due to their age (60 years of age or older) and/or documented history of gastric ulcers.

Note: Symptomatic response to therapy with esomeprazole does not preclude the presence of gastric malignancy.

Pharmacology/Pharmacokinetics

Physicochemical characteristics

Chemical Group—

Substituted benzimidazole.

Esomeprazole is an enantiomer of omeprazole, specifically the S-isomer.

Molecular weight—Esomeprazole magnesium trihydrate: 767.2.

Mechanism of action/Effect

Esomeprazole is a proton pump inhibitor. It suppresses gastric acid secretion by specific inhibition of the H^+/K^+-ATPase in the gastric parietal cell. The S- and R- isomers are protonated and converted in the acidic compartment of the parietal cell forming the active inhibitor, the achiral sulphenamide. By acting specifically on the proton pump, esomeprazole blocks the final step in acid production, thus reducing gastric activity. This effect is dose related up to a daily dose of 20 to 40 mg and leads to inhibition of gastric acid secretion.

Other actions/effects

Esomeprazole magnesium, amoxicillin and clarithromycin triple therapy has demonstrated antimicrobial activity *in vitro* against most strains of *Helicobacter pylori*.

Absorption

After a single oral dose of 40-mg, the systemic bioavailability is 64%. With repeated once-daily dosing the bioavailability increases to 90%. The area under the plasma concentration time curve (AUC) is increased three-fold when the dose is increased from 20 to 40 mg, and the C_{max} also increases proportionally with increases in dose.

The AUC after administration of a single 40-mg dose of esomeprazole is decreased 33 to 53% after food intake compared to fasting conditions. Esomeprazole should be taken at least one hour before meals.

Distribution

Volume of Distribution (Vol_D)—

Steady state—16 L.

Protein binding

Very high (97%).

Biotransformation

Extensive hepatic metabolism by the cytochrome P450 (CYP) enzyme system. The metabolites lack any anti-secretory activity. Metabolism of esomeprazole is primarily dependent on the CYP2C19 isoenzyme, which forms the hydroxy and desmethyl metabolites. The remaining esomeprazole metabolism is dependent on the CYP3A4 isoenzyme, which forms the sulphone metabolite.

Following administration of equimolar doses the S- and R- isomers are metabolized differently by the liver, resulting in higher plasma levels of the S- rather than the R-isomer.

Half-life

Elimination—1 to 1.5 hours.

Time to peak concentration

1.6 hours.

Peak plasma concentration

After 5 days of 40 mg of esomeprazole once daily, the peak plasma concentration was 4.7 micromoles per L.

Note: The AUC and C_{max} values at steady-state were 25% and 18% higher, respectively, in elderly subjects as compared to younger subjects. However, dosage adjustments based on age are not deemed necessary.

The AUC and C_{max} values at steady-state were 13% higher in female subjects than in male subjects. However, dosage adjustments based on gender are not deemed necessary.

The AUC values at steady-state were 2 to 3 times higher in patients with severe hepatic function impairment than in patients with normal hepatic function; esomeprazole dosages should be reduced in these patients and should not exceed 20 mg a day.

Elimination

Renal—Approximately 80% (as inactive metabolites) of a oral dose is excreted in the urine. Less than 1% of the parent drug is excreted in the urine. The remainder is found as inactive metabolites in the feces.

Precautions to Consider

Carcinogenicity/Tumorigenicity/Mutagenicity

The carcinogenic potential of esomeprazole was assessed using omeprazole studies.

In two 2-year studies in rats, omeprazole, given in doses corresponding to 0.7 to 57 times the human dose of 20 mg a day (expressed on a body surface area basis), caused gastric enterochromaffin-like (ECL) cell hyperplasia and carcinoids in a dose-related manner in both male and female animals. Incidence was markedly higher in female rats, who had higher blood levels of omeprazole.

Esomeprazole was negative in the Ames mutation test, in the *in vivo* rat bone marrow cell chromosome aberration test, and in the *in vivo* mouse micronucleus test. Esomeprazole was positive in the *in vitro* human lymphocyte chromosome aberration test. Omeprazole was positive in the *in vitro* human lymphocyte chromosome aberration test, the *in vivo* mouse bone marrow cell chromosome aberration test and the *in vivo* mouse micronucleus test.

Pregnancy/Reproduction

Fertility—The potential effects of esomeprazole on fertility and reproduction were assessed using omeprazole studies. Omeprazole was given orally to rats in doses up to 138 mg/kg/day (56 times the human dose on a body surface area basis). Omeprazole was not found to be toxic or deleterious to the reproductive performance of parental animals.

Pregnancy—Adequate and well-controlled studies in humans have not been done. Esomeprazole should be used during pregnancy only if clearly needed.

Teratology studies have been done in rats given oral doses up to 280 mg/kg/day (about 57 times the human dose on a body surface area basis) and in rabbits at oral doses up to 86 mg/kg/day (about 35 times the human dose on a body surface area basis) and have revealed no evidence of impaired fertility or harm to the fetus as a result of esomeprazole.

FDA Pregnancy Category B

Breast-feeding

It is not known whether esomeprazole is distributed into human milk. However, omeprazole concentrations have been measured in the breast milk of a woman following oral administration of 20 mg. Because of the potential for serious unwanted effects in the nursing infant, risk-benefit must be considered.

Pediatrics

Appropriate studies on the relationship of age to the effects of esomeprazole have not been performed in the pediatric population. Safety and efficacy have not been established for indications other than GERD.

For short-term treatment of GERD—Safety and efficacy have not been established in children less than 12 years of age.

Adolescents

For short-term treatment of GERD—Safety and efficacy have been established in adolescents 12 to 17 years of age.

Geriatrics

No geriatrics-related problems have been documented in studies done to date that included elderly patients. However, greater sensitivity of some older individuals cannot be ruled out.

Pharmacogenetics

The CYP2C19 isoenzyme exhibits polymorphism in the metabolism of esomeprazole. 15 to 20% of Asians, and 3% of Caucasians, lack CYP2C19 and are termed poor metabolizers. At steady state, the ratio of AUC in poor metabolizers to AUC in the rest of the population (extensive metabolizers) is approximately 2.

Drug interactions and/or related problems

The following drug interactions and/or related problems have been selected on the basis of their potential clinical significance (possible mechanism in parentheses where appropriate)—not necessarily inclusive (» = major clinical significance):

Note: Only specific interactions between esomeprazole and other medications have been identified in this monograph. However, esomeprazole, by inhibiting gastric acid secretion, has the potential to affect the bioavailability of any medication for which absorption is pH-dependent. *In vitro* and *in vivo* studies have shown that esomeprazole is not likely to inhibit CYPs 1A2, 2A6, 2C9, 2D6, 2E1, and 3A4. No clinically relevant interactions with drugs metabolized by these CYP enzymes are expected to occur. Drug interaction studies have shown that esomeprazole does not have any clinically significant interactions with phenytoin, warfarin, quinidine, clarithromycin, or amoxicillin. Esomeprazole potentially may interfere with CYP2C19, its major metabolizing enzyme. Coadministration of esomeprazole 30 mg and diazepam, a CYP2C19 substrate, resulted in a 45% decrease in the clearance of diazepam. Increased plasma levels of diazepam were observed at twelve hours after dosing and beyond. Since diazepam plasma levels at that time were below the therapeutic interval, this interaction is judged unlikely to be clinically significant.

Amoxicillin or
Clarithromycin
(co-administration with esomeprazole may result in increased plasma levels of esomeprazole and 14–hydroxyclarithromycin)

Ketoconazole or
Iron salts or
Digoxin
(esomeprazole may interfere with the absorption of these agents as it increases gastrointestinal pH)

» Warfarin
(post-marketing reports of changes in prothrombin measures with concomitant therapy; monitoring for increases in INR and prothrombin time with concomitant use as these increases may lead to abnormal bleeding and even death)

Laboratory value alterations

The following have been selected on the basis of their potential clinical significance (possible effect in parentheses where appropriate)—not necessarily inclusive (» = major clinical significance).

With physiology/laboratory test values

Gastrin, serum
(mean fasting gastrin concentrations increase in a dose-related manner, reaching a plateau within two to three months of therapy; concentrations return to baseline within four weeks after discontinuation of esomeprazole therapy)

Medical considerations/Contraindications

The medical considerations/contraindications included have been selected on the basis of their potential clinical significance (reasons given in parentheses where appropriate)—not necessarily inclusive (» = major clinical significance).

Except under special circumstances, this medication should not be used when the following medical problem exists:

Hypersensitivity to any component of the formulation of esomeprazole, omeprazole, or to substituted benzimidazoles

Hepatic function impairment
(dosage reduction may be required)

Patient monitoring

The following may be especially important in patient monitoring (other tests may be warranted in some patients, depending on condition; » = major clinical significance):

International Normalized Ratio (INR) or
Prothrombin time
(monitor patients for increases when treated with proton pump inhibitors and warfarin concomitantly)

» Pseudomembranous colitis
(monitor patient for development of diarrhea subsequent to esomeprazole in combination with amoxicillin and clarithromycin)

Side/Adverse Effects

Note: Atrophic gastritis has been occasionally noted in the gastric corpus biopsies of patients treated long-term with omeprazole, of which esomeprazole is an enantiomer.

The following side/adverse effects have been selected on the basis of their potential clinical significance (possible signs and symptoms in parentheses where appropriate)—not necessarily inclusive:

Those indicating need for medical attention

Incidence not determined—Observed with postmarketing use of esomeprazole

Anaphylactic reaction (cough; difficulty swallowing; dizziness; fast heartbeat; hives; itching; puffiness or swelling of the eyelids or around the eyes, face, lips or tongue; shortness of breath; skin rash; tightness in chest; unusual tiredness or weakness; wheezing); ***dermatologic reactions including; erythema multiforme*** (blistering, peeling, loosening of skin; chills; cough; diarrhea; fever; itching; joint or muscle pain; red irritated eyes; sore throat; sores, ulcers, or white spots in mouth or on lips; unusual tiredness or weakness); ***Stevens-Johnson syndrome*** (blistering, peeling, loosening of skin; chills; cough; diarrhea; itching; joint or muscle pain; red irritated eyes; red skin lesions, often with a purple center; sore throat; sores, ulcers, or white spots in mouth or on lips; unusual tiredness or weakness); ***toxic epidermal necrolysis*** (blistering, peeling, loosening of skin; chills; cough; diarrhea; itching; joint or muscle pain; red irritated eyes; red skin lesions, often with a purple center; sore throat; sores, ulcers, or white spots in mouth or on lips; unusual tiredness or weakness); ***pancreatitis*** (bloating; chills; constipation; darkened urine; fast heartbeat; fever; indigestion; loss of appetite; nausea; pains in stomach, side, or abdomen, possibly radiating to the back; vomiting; yellow eyes or skin)

Those indicating need for medical attention only if they continue or are bothersome

Incidence more frequent

Dyspepsia (acid or sour stomach; belching; heartburn; indigestion; stomach discomfort, upset, or pain)

Incidence less frequent

Abdominal pain; application site reaction (burning, itching, redness, skin rash, swelling, or soreness at site)—with esomeprazole for injection; ***constipation; diarrhea; dizziness; dryness of mouth; flatulence*** (gas); ***headache; nausea; pruritus; respiratory infection*** (cough; fever; sneezing; sore throat); ***sinusitis*** (pain or tenderness around eyes and cheekbones; fever; stuffy or runny nose; headache; cough; shortness of breath or troubled breathing; tightness of chest or wheezing)

Overdose

For more information on the management of overdose or unintentional ingestion, **contact a poison control center** (see *Poison Control Center Listing*).

Clinical effects of overdose

The following effects have been selected on the basis of their potential clinical significance (possible signs and symptoms in parentheses where appropriate)—not necessarily inclusive.

Blurred vision; confusion (mood or mental changes); ***diaphoresis*** (increased sweating); ***drowsiness*** (sleepiness); ***dry mouth; flushing*** (feeling of warmth; redness of the face, neck, arms and occasionally, upper chest); ***headache; nausea; tachycardia*** (fast, pounding, or irregular heartbeat or pulse)

Treatment of overdose

There is no known specific antidote for esomeprazole. Treatment is essentially symptomatic and supportive.

To enhance elimination—Hemodialysis does not remove an appreciable fraction of the total quantity of esomeprazole or its metabolites due to extensive protein binding.

Patients in whom intentional overdose is confirmed or suspected should be referred for psychiatric consultation.

Patient Consultation

As an aid to patient consultation, refer to *Advice for the Patient, Esomeprazole (Systemic)*.

In providing consultation, consider emphasizing the following selected information (» = major clinical significance):

Before using this medication

» Conditions affecting use, especially:
 Hypersensitivity to esomeprazole, omeprazole, or substituted benzimidazoles
 Pregnancy—Should be used during pregnancy only if clearly needed
 Breast-feeding—May be distributed into breast milk; may cause potentially serious adverse effects in nursing infants
 Use in children—Safety and efficacy not established for indications other than GERD
 For short-term treatment of GERD—Safety and efficacy not established in children <12 years of age
 Use in adolescents—For short-term treatment of GERD—Safety and efficacy established in adolescents 12 to 17 years of age
 Use in the elderly—No overall differences in safety and efficacy observed between elderly and younger individuals; however, greater sensitivity of some older individuals cannot be ruled out
 Other medications, especially warfarin

Proper use of this medication

» Importance of taking at least 1 hour before a meal
» Swallowing capsule whole without crushing, breaking, or chewing; however, if patient cannot swallow whole, capsule may be opened and intact granules sprinkled on one tablespoon of applesauce that is not hot, or granules may be dispersed in water, apple or orange juice, or yogurt, and swallowed immediately; granules should not be chewed or crushed
» Compliance with therapy
» Switching from injectable to capsule form when directed by physician
» Proper dosing
 Missed dose: Taking as soon as possible; not taking if almost time for next dose; not doubling doses
» Proper storage

Precautions while using this medication

» Regular visits to physician to check progress
» Report any severe diarrhea during or following treatment with esomeprazole in combination with amoxicillin and clarithromycin

Side/adverse effects

Signs of potential side effects observed during clinical practice, especially anaphylactic reaction, dermatologic reactions, erythema multiforme, Stevens-Johnson syndrome, toxic epidermal necrolysis, or pancreatitis

General Dosing Information

Oral dosage forms

Since esomeprazole is acid-labile, it is administered as a capsule containing enteric-coated granules to prevent gastric decomposition and to increase bioavailability. Capsules should be swallowed whole, and not chewed or crushed. However, if the patient has difficulty swallowing capsules, the capsule may be opened and the intact granules may be sprinkled on one tablespoon of applesauce that is not hot, or the granules may be dispersed in tap water, orange or apple juice, or yogurt and swallowed immediately; granules should not be chewed or crushed.

For long-term maintenance of healing of erosive esophagitis or for the symptomatic relief of heartburn, using a dose of esomeprazole of 40 mg a day demonstrated no additional clinical benefit over using a dose of 20 mg a day in premarketing studies.

Parenteral dosage forms

Treatment with esomeprazole for injection should be discontinued as soon as the patient is able to resume treatment with esomeprazole delayed-release capsules.

Antacids may be used while taking esomeprazole.

Diet/Nutrition

Esomeprazole should be taken at least one hour before meals.

Treatment of side and adverse effects

Pseudomembranous colitis—mild cases usually respond to discontinuation of antibacterial drug (e.g. amoxicillin or clarithromycin) alone. In moderate to severe cases, consideration should be given to management with fluids and electrolytes, protein supplementation, and treatment with an antibacterial drug clinically effective against *Clostridium difficile*.

Oral Dosage Forms

ESOMEPRAZOLE MAGNESIUM DELAYED-RELEASE CAPSULES

Note: The dosing and dosage forms of esomeprazole magnesium are expressed in terms of esomeprazole base.

Usual adult dose

Gastroesophageal reflux disease (treatment)—
 Oral, 20 or 40 mg once a day for four to eight weeks.
 For patients who have not healed in the initial four to eight week treatment period, an additional four to eight week course of therapy with esomeprazole may be considered.
Maintenance of healed erosive esophagitis—
 Oral, 20 mg once a day.
Symptomatic gastroesophageal reflux disease (treatment)—
 Oral, 20 mg once a day for four weeks.
 For patients whose symptoms have not resolved completely after the four week treatment period, an additional four week course of therapy with esomeprazole may be considered.
Duodenal ulcer associated with *Helicobacter pylori* infection (treatment)—
 Oral, triple therapy regimen of esomeprazole 40 mg once a day taken in combination with clarithromycin 500 mg twice a day and amoxicillin 1000 mg twice a day, for 10 days.
 Patients who fail triple therapy will likely have clarithromycin resistant *H. pylori* isolates, and susceptibility testing should be done when possible. Alternative antimicrobial therapy should be instituted if appropriate.
Risk reduction of NSAID-associated gastric ulcer—
 Oral, 20 or 40 mg once daily for up to 6 months

Note: In patients with severe hepatic function impairment (Child Pugh Class C), dosing should not exceed 20 mg of esomeprazole a day.

Usual pediatric dose

Safety and efficacy have not been established for indications other than GERD.
Short-term treatment of GERD—
 Children 12 to 17 years of age: Oral, 20 or 40 mg once daily for up to 8 weeks.
 Children less than 12 years of age: Safety and efficacy not established.

Usual geriatric dose

See *Usual adult dose*.

Strength(s) usually available

U.S.—
 20 mg (Rx) [*Nexium* (glyceryl monostearate 40–50; hydroxypropyl cellulose; hydroxypropyl methylcellulose; magnesium stearate; methacrylic acid copolymer type C; polysorbate 80; sugar spheres; talc; triethyl citrate)].
 40 mg (Rx) [*Nexium* (glyceryl monostearate; hydroxypropyl methylcellulose; magnesium stearate; methacrylic acid copolymer type C; polysorbate 80; sugar spheres; talc; triethyl citrate)].
Canada—
 Not commercially available.

Packaging and storage

Store at 25 °C (77 °F), excursions permitted to 15 - 30 °C (59 - 86 °F). Keep container tightly closed. Dispense in a tight container if the product package is subdivided.

Preparation of dosage form

For patients who cannot take oral solids—
 One tablespoon of applesauce may be added to an empty bowl; the esomeprazole capsule may then be opened, and the pellets inside carefully emptied into the applesauce. The pellets should be mixed with the applesauce, and the mixture swallowed immediately. The applesauce should not be hot and should be soft enough to be swallowed without chewing. The pellets should not be chewed or crushed. The pellet/applesauce mixture should not be stored for future use.
 The pellets also have been shown *in vitro* to remain intact when exposed to tap water, orange juice, apple juice, and yogurt.

Auxiliary labeling

- Take at least one hour before meals.
- Swallow capsules whole.

Parenteral Dosage Forms

ESOMEPRAZOLE SODIUM FOR INJECTION

Note: The dosing and dosage forms of esomeprazole sodium are expressed in terms of esomeprazole base.

Usual adult dose
Gastroesophageal reflux disease (treatment)—
Intravenous, 20 or 40 mg once daily by injection (no less than 3 minutes) or infusion (10 to 30 minutes) for up to 10 days.

Note: In patients with severe hepatic function impairment (Child Pugh Class C), dosing should not exceed 20 mg of esomeprazole a day. No dosage adjustment is necessary in patients with mild to moderate hepatic impairment (Child Pugh Classes A and B).

In patients with renal insufficiency, no dosage adjustment is necessary.

Usual adult prescribing limits
Safety and efficacy for more than 10 days have not been demonstrated.

Usual pediatric dose
Safety and efficacy have not been established.

Usual geriatric dose
See *Usual adult dose.*

Strength(s) usually available
U.S.—
20 mg (Rx) [*Nexium I.V.* (edetate disodium 1.5 mg; sodium hydroxide)].
40 mg (Rx) [*Nexium I.V.* (edetate disodium 1.5 mg; sodium hydroxide)].
Canada—
Not commercially available.

Packaging and storage
Store at 25 °C (77 °F), excursions permitted to 15 to 30 °C (59 to 86 °F). Store in carton until time of use.

Preparation of dosage form
Intravenous injection over no less than 3 minutes—
The esomeprazole lyophilized powder should be reconstituted with 5 mL of 0.9% Sodium Chloride Injection. The 5-mL reconstituted solution should be withdrawn and administered as an intravenous injection over no less than 3 minutes.
The reconstituted solution should be stored at room temperature up to 30 °C (86 °F) and administered within 12 hours after reconstitution. No refrigeration is required.

Intravenous infusion over 10 to 30 minutes—
The esomeprazole lyophilized powder should be reconstituted with 5 mL of 0.9% Sodium Chloride Injection, Lactated Ringer's Injection, or 5% Dextrose Injection, and further diluted to a final volume of 50 mL. The solution (admixture) should be administered as an intravenous infusion over a period of 10 to 30 minutes.
The admixture should be stored at room temperature up to 30 °C (86 °F). No refrigeration is required.The admixture should be administered within the designated time period as follows:
0.9% Sodium Chloride Injection—12 hours
Lactate Ringer's Injection—12 hours
5% Dextrose Injection—6 hours

Stability
Esomeprazole for injection should not be administered concomitantly with any other medications through the same intravenous site and/or tubing. Both prior to and after administration with esomeprazole for injection, the intravenous line should always be flushed with 0.9% Sodium Chloride Injection, Lactated Ringer's Injection, or 5% Dextrose Injection.
This product should be inspected visually for particulate matter and discoloration prior to administration, whenever solution and container permit.

Auxiliary labeling
• Protect from light

Revised: 05/04/2006
Developed: 05/17/2001

ESTAZOLAM—See *Benzodiazepines (Systemic)*

ESTRADIOL—See *Estrogens (Systemic), Estrogens (Vaginal)*

ESTRAMUSTINE Systemic

VA CLASSIFICATION (Primary): AN900
Commonly used brand name(s): *Emcyt.*
Note: For a listing of dosage forms and brand names by country availability, see *Dosage Forms* section(s).

Category
Antineoplastic.

Indications
Accepted
Carcinoma, prostatic (treatment)—Estramustine is indicated for palliative treatment of metastatic, progressive, and/or [hormone-refractory][1] (Evidence rating: IA) carcinoma of the prostate gland.

[1]Not included in Canadian product labeling.

Pharmacology/Pharmacokinetics
Physicochemical characteristics
Molecular weight—Estramustine phosphate sodium: 582.36.

Mechanism of action/Effect
Exact mechanism of antineoplastic action is unknown. Structurally, estramustine is a phosphorylated combination of estradiol and mechlorethamine (nitrogen mustard). However, estramustine has very weak alkylating activity and may be effective in some patients refractory to estrogen therapy. Therefore, its antineoplastic activity may be due to the estrogen component, a direct effect of estramustine or one of its metabolites, other antimitotic activity, or a combination of effects. Prolonged use elevates total plasma estradiol concentrations to within ranges similar to those produced in prostatic carcinoma patients given conventional estradiol therapy. Estrogenic effects (changes in circulating concentrations of steroids and pituitary hormones) are also similar to those produced by estradiol. A suppressive effect on the hypothalamic-hypophyseal-gonadal axis with a resultant reduction in serum testosterone concentrations may also be involved. Estramustine is highly localized in prostatic tissue because of binding to an estramustine-specific protein.

Absorption
Well absorbed (up to 75%) from the gastrointestinal tract; impaired by milk, milk products, and other substances high in calcium.

Biotransformation
Rapidly dephosphorylated during absorption into peripheral circulation, then estramustine is oxidized and hydrolyzed to estromustine, with low levels of estradiol and estrone, and to mechlorethamine; metabolism is by conjugation in the liver.

Half-life
Multiphasic; 20 hours (terminal phase).

Elimination
Biliary/fecal; renal (minor). The metabolites derived from estramustine phosphate are excreted at a slower rate than the native agent.

Precautions to Consider
Cross-sensitivity and/or related problems
Patients sensitive to estradiol or mechlorethamine may be sensitive to estramustine also.

Carcinogenicity/Mutagenicity
Secondary malignancies are potential delayed effects of many antineoplastic agents, although it is not clear whether the effect is related to their mutagenic or immunosuppressive action. The effect of dose and duration of therapy is also unknown, although risk seems to increase with long-term use. Although information is limited, available data seem to indicate that the carcinogenic risk is greatest with the alkylating agents.
Studies with estramustine have not been done. Antimitotic agents have been associated with an increased risk of development of secondary carcinomas in humans. Long-term continuous administration of estrogens in some animals has been associated with an increased frequency of carcinomas of the breast and liver. Compounds structurally similar to estramustine are carcinogenic in mice.
Although estramustine was not found to be mutagenic in Ames tests, both estradiol and nitrogen mustard alone are mutagenic.

Pregnancy/Reproduction

Fertility—Gonadal suppression, resulting in azoospermia, has been reported in patients taking estramustine. These effects appear to be related to dose and length of therapy and may be irreversible. On the other hand, patients impotent from previous therapy may regain potency when taking estramustine.

Antimitotic agents have been reported to cause alterations in sperm cells that could result in mutagenicity and teratogenicity.

Pregnancy—Because of the possibility of mutagenic effects, patients or their partners should be advised to use contraceptive measures.

Geriatrics

Appropriate studies on the relationship of age to the effects of estramustine have not been performed in the geriatric population. However, elderly patients are more likely to have age-related renal function impairment and/or peripheral vascular disease, which may require caution in patients receiving estrogens.

Drug interactions and/or related problems

The following drug interactions and/or related problems have been selected on the basis of their potential clinical significance (possible mechanism in parentheses where appropriate)—not necessarily inclusive (» = major clinical significance):

Note: Combinations containing any of the following medications, depending on the amount present, may also interact with this medication.

Calcium-containing medications or
Calcium supplements
(calcium binds with estramustine in the gastrointestinal tract and forms an insoluble calcium phosphate salt, which is not absorbed; simultaneous administration should be avoided)

Corticosteroids, glucocorticoid
(concurrent use with estrogens may alter the metabolism and protein binding of the glucocorticoids, leading to decreased clearance, increased elimination half-life, and increased therapeutic and toxic effects of the glucocorticoids; glucocorticoid dosage adjustment may be required during and following concurrent use)

Corticotropin (chronic therapeutic use)
(concurrent use with estrogens may potentiate the anti-inflammatory effects of endogenous cortisol [adrenal secretion of endogenous cortisol is increased by corticotropin])

» Hepatotoxic medications (see *Appendix II*)
(concurrent use of these medications with estrogens may increase the risk of hepatotoxicity)

» Smoking, tobacco
(not recommended during estrogen therapy because of the increased risk of serious cardiovascular side effects, including cerebrovascular accident, transient ischemic attacks, thrombophlebitis, and pulmonary embolism; risk increases with increasing tobacco usage and with age)

Vaccines, killed virus
(because normal defense mechanisms may be suppressed by estramustine therapy, the patient's antibody response to the vaccine may be decreased. The interval between discontinuation of medications that cause immunosuppression and restoration of the patient's ability to respond to the vaccine depends on the intensity and type of immunosuppression-causing medication used, the underlying disease, and other factors; estimates vary from 3 months to 1 year)

Vaccines, live virus
(because normal defense mechanisms may be suppressed by estramustine therapy, concurrent use with a live virus vaccine may potentiate the replication of the vaccine virus, may increase the side/adverse effects of the vaccine virus, and/or may decrease the patient's antibody response to the vaccine; immunization of these patients should be undertaken only with extreme caution after careful review of the patient's hematologic status and only with the knowledge and consent of the physician managing the estramustine therapy. The interval between discontinuation of medications that cause immunosuppression and restoration of the patient's ability to respond to the vaccine depends on the intensity and type of immunosuppression-causing medication used, the underlying disease, and other factors; estimates vary from 3 months to 1 year. Immunization with oral poliovirus vaccine should be postponed in persons in close contact with the patient, especially family members)

Laboratory value alterations

The following have been selected on the basis of their potential clinical significance (possible effect in parentheses where appropriate)—not necessarily inclusive (» = major clinical significance).

With diagnostic test results

» Metyrapone test
(reduced response)

Norepinephrine-induced platelet aggregability
(may be increased)

Sulfobromophthalein (BSP) test
(increased BSP retention)

Thyroid function test
(protein-bound thyroxine [T_4] is increased; serum free T_4 concentrations may be unchanged or decreased; triiodothyronine [T_3] serum resin uptake is decreased, because estrogens increase serum thyroid-binding globulin [TBG]; serum T_3 may be increased)

With physiology/laboratory test values

Alanine aminotransferase (AST [SGOT]) values, and
Bilirubin concentrations, serum and
Lactate dehydrogenase (LDH) values
(may be increased)

Antithrombin 3 concentrations and
Folate concentrations, serum and
Pregnanediol excretion and
Pyridoxine concentrations
(may be decreased)

Ceruloplasmin and
Cortisol and
Glucose and
Phospholipids and
Prolactin and
Prothrombin and clotting factors VII, VIII, IX, and X and
Sodium and
Triglycerides
(serum concentrations may be increased)

Phosphate
(serum concentrations may be decreased)

Medical considerations/Contraindications

The medical considerations/contraindications included have been selected on the basis of their potential clinical significance (reasons given in parentheses where appropriate)—not necessarily inclusive (» = major clinical significance).

Note: Estramustine may be poorly metabolized in patients with impaired liver function and should be administered with caution in such patients. Estramustine also may influence the metabolism of calcium and phosphorus. Therefore, it should be used with caution in patients who have metabolic bone diseases that are associated with hypercalcemia and in patients with renal insufficiency.

Except under special circumstances, this medication should not be used when the following medical problems exist:

» Hypersensitivity to estramustine or
» Hypersensitivity to estradiol or
» Hypersensitivity to mechlorethamine
(estramustine is a molecule combining estradiol and normechlorethamine by a carbamate link. It should not be used if the patient is known to be hypersensitive to either estradiol or nitrogen mustard)

» Thromboembolic disorders, active, including recent myocardial infarction or stroke or
» Thrombophlebitis, active
(may be aggravated by estrogen component; an exception may be made when the actual tumor mass is the cause of the thromboembolic phenomenon)

Risk-benefit should be considered when the following medical problems exist:

Asthma or
Cardiac insufficiency or
Epilepsy or
Mental depression, or history of or
Migraine headaches or
Renal function impairment
(fluid retention sometimes caused by estrogen component may aggravate these conditions)

Bone disease, metabolic, associated with hypercalcemia or
Renal insufficiency
(estrogens influence metabolism of calcium and phosphorus)

Bone marrow depression, moderate to severe

Cerebrovascular disease or
Coronary artery disease or
» Thrombophlebitis, thrombosis, or thromboembolic disorders, history of, especially if associated with estrogen therapy
(risk of thromboembolic disorders caused by estrogens)

» Chickenpox, existing or recent (including recent exposure) or
» Herpes zoster
(risk of severe generalized disease)
Cholestatic jaundice, history of, including previous jaundice that occurred with estrogens or as a reaction to other medication
Diabetes mellitus
(glucose tolerance may be decreased)
Gallbladder disease, or history of, especially gallstones
Hepatic function impairment
(reduced metabolism and possible hepatotoxicity)
» Hypercalcemia associated with metastatic breast disease
» Peptic ulcer

Patient monitoring

The following are especially important in patient monitoring (other tests may be warranted in some patients, depending on condition (» = major clinical significance):

Acid phosphatase values, serum and/or
Alkaline phosphatase values, serum
(to assess response; elevated values should be reduced)
Blood counts, complete and
Platelet counts
(may be appropriate at periodic intervals, although leukopenia and thrombocytopenia are rare with estramustine)
Blood pressure and
Hepatic function
(determinations recommended at periodic intervals)
Calcium concentrations, serum and
Phosphate concentrations, serum
(recommended at periodic intervals, especially in patients with bone metastases)

Side/Adverse Effects

The following side/adverse effects have been selected on the basis of their potential clinical significance (possible signs and symptoms in parentheses where appropriate)—not necessarily inclusive:

Those indicating need for medical attention

Incidence more frequent
Sodium and fluid retention (swelling of feet or lower legs)

Incidence rare
Allergic reaction (skin rash or fever); ***anemia*** (unusual tiredness or weakness); ***leukopenia*** (fever or chills; cough or hoarseness; lower back or side pain; painful or difficult urination)—usually asymptomatic; ***thrombocytopenia*** (unusual bleeding or bruising; black, tarry stools; blood in urine or stools; pinpoint red spots on skin)—usually asymptomatic; ***thrombosis*** (severe or sudden headaches; sudden loss of coordination; pains in chest, groin, or leg, especially calf of leg; sudden and unexplained shortness of breath; sudden slurred speech; sudden vision changes; weakness or numbness in arm or leg)

Those indicating need for medical attention only if they continue or are bothersome

Incidence more frequent
Breast tenderness or enlargement—incidence 20 to 50%; ***decreased interest in sex***—occurs in most patients; ***diarrhea***—incidence 20 to 50%; ***nausea***—incidence 20 to 50%

Incidence less frequent
Trouble in sleeping; vomiting

Note: *Vomiting* is intolerable in approximately 8% of patients.

Overdose

For more information on the management of overdose or unintentional ingestion, **contact a Poison Control Center** (see *Poison Control Center Listing*).

Clinical effects of overdose

There has been no documented experience with estramustine overdose. However, it is reasonable to expect that such episodes may produce pronounced manifestations of the known adverse reactions.

Treatment of overdose

Treatment of overdose is symptomatic and supportive.

To decrease absorption—Removal of gastric contents by gastric lavage.

Monitoring—Monitoring of hematologic and hepatic parameters for at least 6 weeks.

Patient Consultation

As an aid to patient consultation, refer to *Advice for the Patient, Estramustine (Systemic).*

In providing consultation, consider emphasizing the following selected information (» = major clinical significance):

Before using this medication

» Conditions affecting use, especially:
Hypersensitivity to estramustine, estradiol, or mechlorethamine
Pregnancy—It is recommended that patients or their partners use contraceptive measures
Other medications, especially hepatotoxic medications
Other medical problems, especially chickenpox, herpes zoster, hypercalcemia, peptic ulcer, active or history of thromboembolic disorders (including recent myocardial infarction or stroke), or active or history of thrombophlebitis

Proper use of this medication

» Importance of not taking more or less medication than the amount prescribed
For best results, taking 1 hour before or 2 hours after meals or milk or milk products
» Frequently causes nausea and sometimes causes vomiting; checking with physician before discontinuing medication
Checking with physician if vomiting occurs shortly after dose is taken
» Proper dosing
Missed dose: Not taking at all; not doubling doses
» Proper storage

Precautions while using this medication

» Importance of close monitoring by physician
» Avoiding immunizations unless approved by physician; other persons in patient's household should avoid immunizations with oral poliovirus vaccine; avoiding persons who have taken oral poliovirus vaccine or wearing a protective mask that covers nose and mouth

Side/adverse effects

Signs of potential side effects, especially sodium and fluid retention, allergic reaction, anemia, leukopenia, thrombocytopenia, and thrombosis

General Dosing Information

Patients receiving estramustine should be under supervision of a physician experienced in cancer chemotherapy.

Patients should be treated for 30 to 90 days before the physician determines the possible benefits of continued therapy. Therapy should be continued as long as the response to estramustine is favorable. Some patients have been maintained on therapy for more than 3 years at doses ranging from 10 to 16 mg per kg of body weight (mg/kg) per day.

Nausea and vomiting sometimes responds to treatment with phenothiazines but may be severe enough to necessitate withdrawal of estramustine in some patients.

Diet/Nutrition

Patients should be instructed to take estramustine at least 1 hour before or 2 hours after meals. Estramustine should be swallowed with water. Milk, milk products, or calcium-rich foods or medications should not be taken simultaneously with estramustine.

Oral Dosage Forms

ESTRAMUSTINE PHOSPHATE SODIUM CAPSULES

Usual adult dose

Carcinoma, prostatic—
Oral, 600 mg (base) per square meter of body surface area per day in three divided doses (one hour before or two hours after meals) or 14 mg per kg of body weight (range 10 to 16 mg per kg) per day in three or four divided doses (one hour before or two hours after meals).

Strength(s) usually available

U.S.—
140 mg (base) (Rx) [*Emcyt*].
Canada—
140 mg (base) (Rx) [*Emcyt*].

Packaging and storage

Store between 2 and 8 °C (36 and 46 °F), in a tight container, unless otherwise specified by the manufacturer. Protect from light.

Auxiliary labeling

- Take 1 hour before or 2 hours after meals.
- Avoid milk or milk products.

Revised: 06/24/1998

ESTROGENS Systemic

This monograph includes information on the following: 1) Conjugated Estrogens; 2) Diethylstilbestrol; 3) Esterified Estrogens; 4) Estradiol; 5) Estrone†; 6) Estropipate; 7) Ethinyl Estradiol.

INN: Diethylstilbestrol diphosphate—Fosfestrol

BAN:
Diethylstilbestrol diphosphate—Fosfestrol
Diethylstilbestrol—Stilboestrol
Estradiol—Oestradiol
Estrone—Oestrone

JAN: Diethylstilbestrol diphosphate—Fosfestrol

VA CLASSIFICATION (Primary/Secondary):
Conjugated Estrogens—HS102/AN500; HS104; MS900
Diethylstilbestrol—HS102/AN500; HS104; MS900
Esterified Estrogens—HS102/AN500; MS900
Estradiol—HS102/AN500; MS900
Estrone—HS102/AN500
Estropipate—HS102/MS900
Ethinyl Estradiol—HS102/AN500; HS104; MS900

Commonly used brand name(s): *Alora*[4]; *C.E.S.*[1]; *Climara*[4]; *Clinagen LA 40*[4]; *Congest*[1]; *Delestrogen*[4]; *Depo-Estradiol*[4]; *Depogen*[4]; *Estinyl*[7]; *Estrace*[4]; *Estraderm*[4]; *Estradot*[4]; *Estragyn 5*[5]; *Estragyn LA 5*[4]; *Estrasorb*[4]; *Estro-A*[5]; *Estro-L.A.*[4]; *Kestrone-5*[5]; *Menaval-20*[4]; *Menest*[3]; *Neo-Estrone*[3]; *Ogen*[6]; *Ogen 1.25*[6]; *Ogen 2.5*[6]; *Ogen.625*[6]; *Ortho-Est 1.25*[6]; *Ortho-Est.625*[6]; *Premarin*[1]; *Premarin Intravenous*[1]; *Valergen-20*[4]; *Valergen-40*[4]; *Vivelle*[4]; *Vivelle-Dot*[4].

Other commonly used names are: DES [Diethylstilbestrol], Fosfestrol [Diethylstilbestrol diphosphate], Oestradiol [Estradiol], Oestrone [Estrone], Piperazine Estrone Sulfate [Estropipate], and Stilboestrol [Diethylstilbestrol].

Note: For a listing of dosage forms and brand names by country availability, see *Dosage Forms* section(s).

†Not commercially available in Canada.

Category

Estrogen (systemic)—Conjugated Estrogens; Diethylstilbestrol; Esterified Estrogens; Estradiol; Estrone; Estropipate; Ethinyl Estradiol.

Antineoplastic—Conjugated Estrogens Tablets; Diethylstilbestrol; Esterified Estrogens; Estradiol; Estradiol Valerate; Estrone; Ethinyl Estradiol.

Osteoporosis prophylactic—Conjugated Estrogens Tablets; Esterified Estrogens; Estradiol Tablets; Estradiol Transdermal System; Estropipate.

Ovarian hormone therapy agent—Conjugated Estrogens Tablets; Esterified Estrogens; Estradiol Tablets; Estradiol Transdermal System; Estropipate

Indications

Note: Bracketed information in the *Indications* section refers to uses that are not included in U.S. product labeling.

General Considerations

Estradiol transdermal system is indicated for use in women only.

Estrogen deficiency in women without a uterus is best treated with unopposed estrogen therapy; combined estrogen-progestin therapy is not needed.

Accepted

Bleeding, uterine, hormonal imbalance–induced (treatment)—Conjugated estrogens for injection and estrone are indicated in the treatment of abnormal uterine bleeding associated with a hypoplastic or atrophic endometrium without organic pathology. Continuous treatment with estrogen without a progestin may cause abnormal uterine bleeding with or without organic pathology.

Carcinoma, breast (treatment)—Conjugated estrogens tablets, esterified estrogens[1], estradiol tablets[1], and ethinyl estradiol are indicated for palliative treatment of metastatic breast carcinoma in selected men and postmenopausal or oophorectomized women.

Carcinoma, prostatic (treatment)—Conjugated estrogens tablets, diethylstilbestrol, esterified estrogens[1], estradiol tablets[1], estradiol valerate, estrone, and ethinyl estradiol are indicated for palliative treatment of advanced prostatic carcinoma.

Estrogen deficiency, due to ovariectomy (treatment) or
Hypogonadism, female (treatment) or
Ovarian failure, primary (treatment)—Conjugated estrogens tablets, esterified estrogens, estradiol tablets[1], matrix- or reservoir-type estradiol transdermal system, estrone, estropipate[1], and ethinyl estradiol[1] are indicated to replace estrogen in the treatment of female hypogonadism, primary ovarian failure, or ovariectomy. Estradiol cypionate and estradiol valerate[1] are indicated to replace estrogen in the treatment of female hypogonadism. Estradiol valerate also is indicated for the treatment of estrogen deficiency resulting from an ovariectomy or primary ovarian failure.

Menopause, vasomotor symptoms of (treatment) or
Vaginitis, atrophic (treatment) or
Vulvar atrophy (treatment)—Conjugated estrogens tablets, esterified estrogens, estradiol tablets, matrix- or reservoir-type estradiol transdermal system, estradiol valerate, estrone, and estropipate are indicated to replace estrogen in the treatment of atrophic vaginitis, vulvar atrophy (also called kraurosis vulvae), and moderate to severe vasomotor symptoms associated with menopause. Also, estradiol cypionate and ethinyl estradiol are indicated for treatment of moderate to severe vasomotor symptoms of menopause.

Osteoporosis, postmenopausal (prophylaxis)—Conjugated estrogens tablets, esterified estrogens[1], estradiol tablets, matrix- or reservoir-type estradiol transdermal system, and estropipate[1] are indicated in postmenopausal women to retard bone loss and estrogen deficiency–induced osteoporosis. Replacing estrogen can reduce the rate of bone loss and fractures in postmenopausal women. Proper diet, calcium supplementation, and physical activity should also be encouraged along with estrogen replacement therapy.

[Gender identity disorder, male-to-female transsexualism in patients]—Administration of various preparations of estrogen, with or without cyproterone acetate (a progestin with anti-androgen properties) was effective in producing female characteristics in male-to-female transsexual patients with gender identity disorder. Significant improvements have been reported in sexual function and many secondary sex characteristics. The Harry Benjamin International Gender Dysphoria Association recommends the use of estrogen as a standard of care in appropriate individuals.

[Osteoporosis, premenopausal, estrogen deficiency–induced (prophylaxis)][1]—Conjugated estrogens tablets, esterified estrogens, estradiol tablets, matrix- or reservoir-type estradiol transdermal systems, and estropipate also are used in premenopausal women who are estrogen-deficient to protect them against bone loss.

[Turner's syndrome (treatment)][1]—Ethinyl estradiol is used in the treatment of Turner's syndrome (gonadal dysgenesis).

Acceptance not established

Conjugated estrogens, diethylstilbestrol tablets, and ethinyl estradiol have been used as *emergency contraception* (also called intraception, morning-after treatment, or postcoital contraception). However, the combination oral contraceptive containing ethinyl estradiol with either norgestrel or levonorgestrel is more commonly prescribed for this indication. Although the failure rate for postcoital contraception is higher (2% versus 1%) for these oral estrogen-progestin contraceptives compared to these estrogens used alone, the oral contraceptives cause fewer and less severe side effects (such as nausea or vomiting) and have better patient compliance.

Unaccepted

The use of estrogens to reduce postpartum breast engorgement is not recommended. In many patients, postpartum breast engorgement is a benign, self-limited condition that may respond to breast support and mild analgesics, such as acetaminophen and ibuprofen. Evidence supporting the efficacy of estrogens for this indication is lacking. Therefore, the questionable benefits of administering the large doses of estrogens required for this indication are outweighed by the risk of increasing the incidence of puerperal thromboembolism.

Although a few studies show estrogens having some effect on brain neurotransmitters in improving memory and cognitive function, estrogens are not indicated or effective in treatment of clinical mental depression.

Estradiol valerate, ethinyl estradiol, and the matrix-type estradiol transdermal system are indicated to treat abnormal uterine bleeding due to a hormonal imbalance but are not recommended. These estrogens are considered obsolete for this use.

Although estradiol valerate and estrone are indicated for palliative treatment of breast carcinoma, both have a long duration of action, making discontinuation of the medication or management of hypercalcemia more difficult if hypercalcemia develops. These estrogens are not recommended. These estrogens are considered obsolete for this use.

There is no indication for estradiol transdermal system therapy during pregnancy or during the immediate postpartum period. And, an estradiol transdermal system is ineffective for the prevention or treatment of threatened or habitual abortion.

Estrogens should not be used for the prevention of cardiovascular disease.

---

[1]Not included in Canadian product labeling.

Pharmacology/Pharmacokinetics

Physicochemical characteristics

Physical description—

Two types of estradiol transdermal systems are available:

Drug-in-adhesive matrix on film (ethylene vinyl acetate and rubber) (matrix-type)—Three layers that include a polyester liner that must be removed before using, an adhesive matrix containing estradiol, and the back outermost layer, a flexible polyurethane protective film with epoxy resin.

Membrane-controlled drug reservoir (reservoir-type)—Five layers that include a protective liner to be removed before using, an adhesive layer, a membrane providing a slow release of estradiol, a drug reservoir containing the estradiol and alcohol gelled with hydroxypropyl cellulose, and the back outermost layer, a polyester protective film.

Patch size may differ for products among different manufacturers and among products of different strengths from the same manufacturer. Generally, the matrix-type transdermal system is smaller and thinner than the reservoir-type transdermal system.

Source—

Naturally occurring compounds include estradiol (E_2), conjugated estrogens (sodium estrone sulfate, sodium equilin sulfate, and others as found in equine urine), esterified estrogens (sodium sulfate esters of estrogenic substances, primarily estrone), and estrone (E_1).

Semisynthetic compounds include estradiol cypionate, estradiol valerate, estropipate, and ethinyl estradiol.

Synthetic compounds include diethylstilbestrol and diethylstilbestrol phosphate.

Molecular weight—

Diethylstilbestrol: 268.36.
Diethylstilbestrol diphosphate: 428.32.
Estradiol: 272.39.
Estradiol cypionate: 396.57.
Estradiol valerate: 356.51.
Estrone: 270.37.
Estropipate: 436.58.
Ethinyl estradiol: 296.41.

Mechanism of action/Effect

At the cellular level, estrogens increase the synthesis of DNA, RNA, and various proteins in target tissues. Pituitary mass is also increased. Estrogens reduce the release of gonadotropin-releasing hormone from the hypothalamus, leading to a reduction in release of follicle-stimulating hormone and luteinizing hormone from the pituitary.

For ovarian hormone therapy—

In healthy females, endogenous estrogens maintain genitourinary function and vasomotor stability. Replacing estrogens helps to alleviate or prevent symptoms caused by the decreased amounts of estrogens produced by the ovaries after natural or surgical menopause or other estrogen-deficiency states.

For prevention of postmenopausal osteoporosis—

During periods of estrogen deficiency, the rate of bone resorption by osteoclasts greatly exceeds the rate of bone formation by osteoblasts. Replacing estrogen prevents this accelerated bone loss by inhibiting bone resorption to a level where the near equilibrium between bone resorption and formation is restored. However, estrogens do not replace previously lost bone or significantly increase total bone mass.

For prostatic carcinoma—

Inhibition of pituitary secretion of luteinizing hormone and a possible minor, direct effect on the testis, resulting in decreased serum concentrations of testosterone.

Absorption

Conjugated estrogen tablets—well absorbed; released slowly over several hours

Transdermal—transported across intact skin into the systemic circulation

Distribution

To most tissues, especially breast, uterine, vaginal, hypothalamic, and pituitary tissues; high affinity for adipose tissue.

Protein binding

Moderate to high (50 to 80% to albumin and sex hormone-binding globulin).

Biotransformation

Primarily hepatic; some metabolism also occurs in muscle, kidneys, and gonads. The metabolic sites for all synthetic estrogens have not been completely determined, although some seem to undergo hepatic change.

Urinary metabolites for exogenous estrogens may include estradiol, estrone, estriol (major), and glucuronide and sulfate conjugates.

Transdermal—absence of first pass metabolism

Half-life

Estradiol transdermal systems:
Alora (mean serum)—1.75 hr
Climara—approximately 4 hours
Estradot (mean)—7.7 hours
Vivelle-Dot—5.9 to 7.7 hours
Estrogen, conjugated (mean total estrone)—15 hours
Estrogen, unconjugated (mean estrone)—28 hours

Elimination

Primarily renal excretion of metabolites, some fecal; undergo extensive enterohepatic recirculation. Prolonged in obese patients.

Precautions to Consider

Carcinogenicity

Independent studies have shown an increased risk of endometrial cancer in postmenopausal women placed on unopposed (without a progestin) estrogen therapy for prolonged periods. The risk of endometrial cancer in estrogen users, which appears to depend on duration of treatment and dose, was 5 to 10 times greater than in nonusers. However, studies have shown that administration of a progestin for at least 10 to 14 days of an estrogen cycle is associated with a lower incidence of endometrial hyperplasia and endometrial carcinoma than an estrogen-only cycle. There is no risk of endometrial cancer in patients who have undergone hysterectomies and, therefore, no documented need for concurrent progestin therapy.Use of natural estrogens has not been shown to result in a different endometrial risk profile than synthetic estrogens of equivalent estrogen dose.

Whether the use of systemic estrogens increases the incidence of breast cancer in some postmenopausal women is unresolved. Some large studies reported an increase in the relative risk for development of breast cancer for women taking high doses of estrogen or using estrogens for a prolonged period of time, especially longer than 10 years. The Women's Health Initiative (WHI) trial reported an increased risk of breast cancer in women who took estrogen plus progestin for a mean follow-up of 5.6 years.

Estrogen plus progestin may increase the incidence of ovarian cancer in some postmenopausal women. The relative risk and absolute risk of ovarian cancer for estrogen plus progestin versus placebo was 1.58 (95% confidence interval 0.77 to 3.24; not statistically significant) and 4.2 versus 2.7 cases per 10,000 women-years in the estrogen plus progestin substudy of the WHI trial. The use of estrogen-only products for 10 or more years has been associated with an increased risk of ovarian cancer in some epidemiologic studies.

In certain animal species, long-term, continuous administration of estrogens increases the frequency of cancers of the breast, cervix, liver, pancreas, testis, uterus, and vagina.

Estrogens have been reported to be associated with carcinoma of the male breast. Males treated with estrogens should have regular breast examinations.

Pregnancy/Reproduction

Pregnancy—Estrogens are contraindicated for use during pregnancy or during the immediate postpartum period. Studies suggest an association of congenital malformations with use of some estrogens during pregnancy.

Diethylstilbestrol: Daughters of women who took diethylstilbestrol (DES) during pregnancy have developed abnormalities of the reproductive tract and, in rare cases, cancer of the vagina and/or uterine cervix upon reaching childbearing age. In addition, sons of women who took DES during pregnancy have developed urogenital tract abnormalities. Patients who become pregnant while taking estrogens should be informed of the potential risks to the fetus.

FDA Pregnancy Category X.

Breast-feeding

Estrogens are distributed into breast milk. Use by breast-feeding women is not recommended with estrogen doses larger than those used in oral contraceptives. Estrogen administration to nursing mothers has been shown to decrease the quality and quantity of human breast milk.

Ethinyl estradiol—Traces of ethinyl estradiol are distributed into breast milk when estrogen is given in high doses as an antineoplastic agent. Also, use of oral contraceptives containing ethinyl estradiol during lactation has been associated with a decrease in milk production and in the milk protein and nitrogen content. However, the magnitude of these effects is small and probably of clinical significance only in malnourished mothers.

Pediatrics

Estrogens may accelerate epiphyseal closure. Therefore, estrogens should be used with caution in children and adolescents in whom bone growth is not complete.

Estrogen replacement therapy has been used for the induction of puberty in adolescents with some forms of pubertal delay. Safety and effectiveness in pediatric patients has otherwise not been established. Estrogen treatment of prepubertal girls also induces premature breast development and vaginal cornification, and may induce vaginal bleeding. In boys, estrogen treatment may modify the normal pubertal process and induce gynecomastia.

Geriatrics

Appropriate studies on the relationship of age to the effects of conjugated estrogens have not been performed in the geriatric population. There have not been sufficient numbers of geriatric patients involved in studies to determine whether those over 65 years of age differ from younger subjects in their response to conjugated estrogens.

In the PREMPRO substudy of the Women's Health Initiative Study, there was a higher incidence of stroke and invasive breast cancer in women 75 years and over compared to younger subjects.

In the Women's Health Initiative Memory Study, there was a two-fold increase in the risk of developing probable dementia in women 65 years of age and older receiving conjugated equine estrogen 0.625 mg and medroxyprogesterone acetate 2.5 mg compared to the placebo group. It is not known whether this finding applies to women taking estrogen-only therapy or to younger postmenopausal women.

Dental

Estrogens may predispose the patient to bleeding of the gingival tissues. In addition, gingival hyperplasia may occur during estrogen therapy, usually starting as gingivitis or gum inflammation. A strictly enforced program of teeth cleaning by a professional, combined with plaque control by the patient, will minimize growth rate and severity of gingival enlargement.

Surgical

If possible, estrogens should be discontinued at least 4 to 6 weeks before surgery of the type associated with an increased risk of thromboembolism, or during periods of prolonged immobilization.

Drug interactions and/or related problems

The following drug interactions and/or related problems have been selected on the basis of their potential clinical significance (possible mechanism in parentheses where appropriate)—not necessarily inclusive (» = major clinical significance):

Note: Combinations containing any of the following medications, depending on the amount present, may also interact with this medication.

Bromocriptine
(estrogens may interfere with the effects of bromocriptine; dosage adjustment may be needed)

Calcium supplements
(concurrent use with estrogens may increase calcium absorption and exacerbate nephrolithiasis in susceptible individuals; this can be used to therapeutic advantage to increase bone mass)

Corticosteroids, glucocorticoid
(concurrent use with estrogens may alter the metabolism and protein binding of the glucocorticoids, leading to decreased clearance, increased elimination half-life, and increased therapeutic and toxic effects of the glucocorticoids; glucocorticoid dosage adjustment may be required during and following concurrent use)

Corticotropin (chronic therapeutic use)
(concurrent use with estrogens may potentiate the anti-inflammatory effects of endogenous cortisol induced by corticotropin)

» Cyclosporine
(estrogens have been reported to inhibit cyclosporine metabolism and thereby increase plasma concentrations of cyclosporine, possibly increasing the risk of hepatotoxicity and nephrotoxicity; concurrent use is recommended only with great caution and frequent monitoring of blood cyclosporine concentrations and liver and renal function)

Cytochrome P450 3A4 (CYP3A4) inducers, such as
Carbamazepine or
Dexamethasone or
Meprobamate or
Phenobarbital or
Phenylbutazone or
Phenytoin or
Rifampin or
St. John's Wort preparations
(concurrent use may result in reduced plasma concentrations of estrogens, which could result in decreased therapeutic effects or changes in uterine bleeding profile; extent of interference with transdermally administered estrogen metabolism is not known)

Cytochrome P450 3A4 (CYP3A4) inhibitors, such as
Cimetidine or
Clarithromycin or
Erythromycin or
Grapefruit juice or
Itraconazole or
Ketoconazole or
Ritonavir
(concurrent use may increase plasma concentrations of estrogens, which could result in increased side effects)

» Hepatotoxic medications, especially dantrolene and isoniazid (see *Appendix II*)
(concurrent use of these medications with estrogens may increase the risk of hepatotoxicity and fatal hepatitis has occurred; risk may be further increased with use in females over 35 years of age, prolonged use, or use in patients with a history of liver disease)

Medications associated with pancreatitis, especially
Didanosine or
Lamivudine or
Zalcitabine
(estrogens should be used with caution with medications that cause pancreatitis, especially if the patient has pre-existing risk factors such as high triglyceride concentrations; however, physiologic doses of estrogen would not be expected to induce pancreatitis)

Progestins
(there are possible risks that may be associated with the use of progestins with estrogens compared to estrogen-alone regimens such as possible increased risk of breast cancer, adverse effects on lipoprotein metabolism, and impairment of glucose tolerance)

Smoking, tobacco
(data from studies on tobacco smoking and the use of high-dose estrogen oral contraceptives indicate that there is an increased risk of serious cardiovascular side effects, including cerebrovascular accident, transient ischemic attacks, thrombophlebitis, and pulmonary embolism; risk increases with increasing tobacco usage and with age, especially in women over 35 years of age; it is not known whether any elevation of risk occurs with tobacco smoking during the use of ovarian hormone therapy)
(metabolism of estrogens may also be increased by smoking, resulting in a decreased estrogenic effect)

Somatrem or
Somatropin
(in prepubertal patients, concurrent use of estrogens with somatrem or somatropin may accelerate epiphyseal maturation)

Tamoxifen
(concurrent use may interfere with therapeutic effect of tamoxifen)

Laboratory value alterations

The following have been selected on the basis of their potential clinical significance (possible effect in parentheses where appropriate)—not necessarily inclusive (» = major clinical significance).

Note: When submitting specimens, the laboratory should be informed that the patient is receiving estrogen therapy. The results of laboratory determinations for the tests listed here should not be considered reliable unless estrogen therapy has been discontinued for two to four months.

With diagnostic test results

Fasting blood sugar (FBS) and
Glucose tolerance test
(may be altered by large doses of estrogens)

Liver function test using sulfobromophthalein
(increase in sulfobromophthalein retention)

Metyrapone test
(reduced response)

Norepinephrine-induced platelet aggregability
(may be increased)

Thyroid function tests, such as
Thyroxine (T_4) determinations
Triiodothyronine (T_3) determinations
(values for the T_3 uptake test may be decreased because of an increase in thyroid-binding globulin [TBG]; free T_3, thyroxine

[T_4], and thyroid-stimulating hormone [TSH] concentrations remain unaltered and patient remains euthyroid, even though the total thyroid hormone may be increased)

(transdermally administered estradiol has no effect on TBG)

With physiology/laboratory test values

Anti-factor Xa or
Antithrombin III activity
(may be decreased)

Antithrombin III, serum and
Cholesterol, total, serum and
Folate, serum and
Lipoproteins, low density (LDL), serum and
Pregnanediol, urine and
Pyridoxine, serum
(concentrations may be decreased; however, transdermal estradiol may have little effect on lowering LDL, total serum cholesterol, or serum antithrombin III concentrations)

Binding proteins, such as
Corticosteroid binding globulin (CBG) or
Sex hormone binding globulin (SHBG)
(levels may be elevated; transdermally administered estradiol has no effect on CBG or SHBG)

Calcium
(increased serum concentrations, especially for immobilized patients or for patients with bone cancer or metastatic breast cancer)

Ceruloplasmin and
Cortisol and
Glucose—especially in diabetic or prediabetic patients taking larger doses of estrogens, and
Lipoproteins, high density (HDL) and
Phospholipids and
Prolactin and
Prothrombin and
Sodium and
Triglycerides
(serum concentrations may be increased. Transdermal estradiol may lower serum triglyceride concentrations and have little effect on increasing HDL or hepatic clotting factors)

Clotting factors such as:
II or
VII antigen or
VIII coagulant activity or
IX or
X or
XII or
VII-X complex or
II-VII-X complex or
Beta-thromboglobulin
(may be increased)

Fibrinogen levels and
Fibrinogen activity
(may be increased; transdermally administered estradiol has no effect on fibrinogen)

Plasma proteins, including
Alpha-1-antitrypsin or
Angiotensinogen/renin substrate
(may be increased)

Plasminogen antigen and
Plasminogen activity
(may be increased)

Platelet count
(may be increased)

Prothrombin time, or
Platelet aggregation time or
Thromboplastin time, partial
(may be accelerated)

Medical considerations/Contraindications

The medical considerations/contraindications included have been selected on the basis of their potential clinical significance (reasons given in parentheses where appropriate)—not necessarily inclusive (» = major clinical significance).

Except under special circumstances, this medication should not be used when the following medical problems exist:

» Endometrial hyperplasia
(use of estrogen is contraindicated)

» Genital or uterine bleeding, abnormal and undiagnosed
(use of estrogens may delay diagnosis; on occurrence, estrogen should be discontinued awaiting clinical evaluation. Condition may worsen if cause of abnormal uterine bleeding is endometrial hyperplasia or uterine cancer)

» Hepatic dysfunction or disease, especially of the obstructive type
(use of estrogen is contraindicated in these patients)

» Hypersensitivity to estrogen or any of its ingredients
(use is contraindicated)

» Neoplasia, estrogen-dependent, known or suspected
(estrogen use contraindicated; associated with increased risk especially with prolonged use)

» Porphyria
(use of estrogen is contraindicated)

» Visual abnormalities including
Diplopia, sudden onset or
Migraine, sudden onset or
Proptosis, sudden onset or
Vision loss, partial or complete
(discontinue medication pending examination if any of these conditions occur; if examination reveals papilledema or retinal vascular lesions estrogens should be stopped; retinal vascular thrombosis has been reported in patients receiving estrogens)

For all indications, except for the treatment of breast cancer or prostatic cancer

» Thrombophlebitis or thromboembolic disorders, active or recent (within last year)
Cerebral embolism or
Deep vein thrombosis, active or
Myocardial infarction or
Pulmonary embolism or
Retinal thrombosis or
Stroke
(use of estrogen is contraindicated; estrogens should be discontinued if thromboembolic events occur)

Risk-benefit should be considered when the following medical problems exist:

Asthma or
Epilepsy or
Cardiac or renal dysfunction or
Migraine
(conditions which might be influenced by fluid retention warrant careful observation when patient is taking estrogen; estrogens may cause some degree of fluid retention)

Diabetes mellitus, history of or predisposition to
(condition may be exacerbated and estrogens should be used with caution)

Endometriosis
(endometrial implants and endometriosis may be aggravated by use of estrogens; the addition of a progestin should be considered in women who have undergone hysterectomy but are known to have residual endometriosis.)

Gallbladder disease, or history of, especially gallstones
(conflicting evidence exists as to whether an increased risk of recurrence or exacerbation occurs secondary to oral estrogen use; a 2 to 4 fold increase in the risk of gallbladder disease requiring surgery in postmenopausal women receiving estrogens has been reported)

Hepatic hemangiomas or
Lupus erythematosus, systemic
(may be exacerbated by estrogens; use with caution)

» Hypercalcemia associated with bone metastases, breast cancer, metabolic bone disease, or renal insufficiency
(severe hypercalcemia may occur in patients with any of these conditions who are treated with estrogens; estrogens may aggravate breast cancer–induced hypercalcemia through alterations in the metabolism of calcium and phosphorus; appropriate monitoring is recommended)

Hyperlipoproteinemia, familial or
Hypertriglyceridemia or
Pancreatitis
(may cause these conditions to worsen or recur; estrogens given to achieve serum concentrations at the premenopausal level can rarely increase triglycerides to concentrations that result in pancreatitis, especially in patients with familial defects in lipoprotein metabolism; caution should be used, and in the case of recurrence, medication may need to be discontinued)

Hypothyroidism
(estrogens lead to increased thyroid binding globulin [TBG] levels; patients dependent upon thyroid hormone replacement therapy who are also receiving estrogens may need to increase the dose of their thyroid replacement therapy)

Hypocalcemia, severe
(should be used with caution)

Leiomyoma, uterine
(may increase in size during estrogen therapy)

Renal impairment, including
End stage renal disease (ESRD)
(conventional transdermal estradiol doses may be excessive for postmenopausal women with ESRD receiving maintenance hemodialysis)

For all indications, except for the treatment of breast cancer or prostatic cancer

» Thrombophlebitis, thrombosis, or thromboembolic disorders, estrogen-induced, history of
(resumption of estrogen therapy may result in recurrence. Hypercoagulability information for postmenopausal women taking ovarian hormone therapy is not available. Estrogens can be used cautiously in women with predisposing risk factors and should be discontinued if thromboembolic events occur)

For treatment of male breast cancer or prostatic cancer only (in addition to those conditions listed above)

Cerebrovascular disease or
Coronary artery disease or
Thrombophlebitis, active or
Thromboembolic disorders
(the large doses of estrogens used in males to treat breast and prostatic cancer have been associated with an increased risk of myocardial infarction, pulmonary embolism, and thrombophlebitis)

Patient monitoring

The following may be especially important in patient monitoring (other tests may be warranted in some patients, depending on condition; » = major clinical significance):

Blood glucose, serum and
Calcium, serum
(should be done initially and at least annually to assess response to treatment)

Blood pressure determinations
(blood pressure elevations that generally occur within a short time after initiation of therapy are due to a reversible effect on the renin-angiotensin system and have only been documented during the use of conjugated estrogens and high-dose combination oral contraceptives; hypertension occurring during the treatment of gonadal dysgenesis also may be a result of worsening of the disease state itself, and may not necessarily be attributable to estrogen therapy; blood pressure should be monitored at regular intervals)

Bone age determinations
(x-ray of hand and wrist recommended every 6 months for children and adolescents to determine rate of bone maturation and effects on epiphyseal centers)

Breast examinations
(should be performed routinely by patient and physician for early detection of possible breast cancer; teaching patient about periodic self-examination of breasts)

Endometrial biopsy
(should be considered periodically as necessary in patients with an intact uterus; patients with a uterus should be monitored for signs of endometrial cancer and malignancy should be ruled out in cases of persistent or abnormal vaginal bleeding; there is no risk of endometrial cancer in patients who have undergone a hysterectomy)

Fluid status
(estrogens may cause fluid retention; patients with conditions that might be influenced by fluid retention, such as cardiac or renal dysfunction, warrant careful observation)

Hepatic function determinations
(recommended at regular intervals, especially during therapy in patients who have or are suspected of having hepatic disease)

Lipid profile determinations, serum
(recommended annually in women who are receiving ovarian hormone therapy, especially if taking a progestin)

Mammogram
(every 12 months, or as determined by physician)
(sensitivity or specificity of mammography testing is decreased with concurrent use of estrogens due to detection problems caused by estrogen-induced breast tissue growth, especially if the postmenopausal breast is fibrous. Ordering mammography during week of no hormonal use or after cessation of therapy may help in recognizing false-positive or false-negative mammograms)

Papanicolaou (Pap) test and
Physical examinations
(every year or more frequently when so determined by physician, with special attention being given to abdomen, breast, and pelvic organs)

Thyroid function
(patients dependent on thyroid hormone replacement therapy who are also taking estrogens should have their thyroid function monitored to maintain free thyroid hormone levels in an acceptable range.)

Side/Adverse Effects

The following side/adverse effects have been selected on the basis of their potential clinical significance (possible signs and symptoms in parentheses where appropriate)—not necessarily inclusive:

Adverse reactions reported may include reactions with estrogen therapy and/or progestin therapy.

Estrogen and estrogen/progestin therapy have been associated with an increased risk of cardiovascular events such as myocardial infarction and stroke, as well as venous thrombosis and pulmonary embolism (venous thromboembolism or VTE). Should any of these occur or be suspected, estrogens should be discontinued immediately.

Embolic cerebrovascular events have been reported in women receiving postmenopausal estrogens.

Estrogens increase the risk of endometrial cancer. Close clinical surveillance of all women taking estrogens is important. Adequate diagnostic measures, including endometrial sampling when indicated, should be undertaken to rule out malignancy in all cases of persistent or recurring vaginal bleeding. The use of unopposed estrogens in women who have a uterus is associated with an increased risk of endometrial cancer.

Estrogen and estrogen/progestin therapy have been associated with an increased risk of breast cancer. All postmenopausal women should receive yearly breast exams, perform monthly self-examinations, and have mammography exams based on patient age and risk factors.

Those indicating need for medical attention

Incidence more frequent

Breast pain or tenderness—in females as well as in males treated for prostatic cancer; ***enlargement of breasts***—in females; ***gynecomastia*** (increased breast size)—in males treated for prostatic cancer; ***hypersensitivity reactions*** (fast heartbeat; fever; hives; itching; irritation; hoarseness; joint pain; stiffness or swelling; rash; redness of skin; shortness of breath; swelling of eyelids, face, lips, hands, or feet; tightness in chest; troubled breathing or swallowing; wheezing); ***peripheral edema*** (swelling of feet and lower legs; rapid weight gain)

Incidence less frequent or rare

Amenorrhea (stopping of menstrual bleeding); ***breakthrough bleeding*** (heavier vaginal bleeding between regular menses); ***menorrhagia*** (prolonged or heavier menses); ***or spotting*** (lighter vaginal bleeding between regular menses); ***breast tumors*** (breast lumps; discharge from breast); ***chest pain; gallbladder obstruction; hepatitis; or pancreatitis*** (pains in stomach, side, or abdomen; yellow eyes or skin); ***pleural infection*** (chest pain; cough; fever or chills; shortness of breath; troubled breathing); ***vaginal hemorrhage*** (heavy nonmenstrual vaginal bleeding)

Note: If persistent or recurring abnormal vaginal bleeding occurs, malignancy should be ruled out. However, *withdrawal bleeding* will frequently occur in patients placed on cyclic estrogen therapy with a progestin who have not undergone hysterectomy. Any unusual uterine bleeding persisting longer than 3 to 6 months should be investigated. With continuous estrogen-progestin therapy, withdrawal bleeding is eliminated, endometrial atrophy and amenorrhea are produced in most patients after 2 to 3 months and, in the remaining patients, after 7 to 13 months. Amenorrhea is highly desired by many women and not considered by them to be a true adverse effect.

For treatment of male breast cancer or prostatic cancer only (in addition to those listed above)

Thromboembolism or thrombus formation (severe or sudden headache; sudden loss of coordination; pains in chest, groin, or leg, especially calf; sudden and unexplained shortness of breath; sudden slurred speech; sudden vision changes; weakness or numbness in arm or leg)

Note: The use of large doses of estrogens (5 mg a day) in males to treat breast and prostate cancer has been associated with an increased risk of *myocardial infarction, pulmonary embolism,* and *thrombophlebitis.*

Incidence not determined—Observed during clinical practice, estimates of frequency can not be determined

Asthma, exacerbation of (cough; difficulty breathing; noisy breathing; shortness of breath; tightness in chest; wheezing); ***breast cancer*** (clear or bloody discharge from nipple; inverted nipple; dimpling of breast skin; lump in breast or under the arm; persistent crusting or scaling of nipple; redness or swelling of breast; sore on the skin of the breast that does not heal); ***cholestatic jaundice*** (abdominal or stomach pain; chills; clay-colored stools; dark urine; diarrhea; dizziness; fever; headache; itching; loss of appetite; nausea; rash; unpleasant breath odor; unusual tiredness or weakness; vomiting of blood; yellow eyes or skin); ***endometrial hyperplasia or endometrial cancer*** (change in vaginal discharge; pain or feeling of pressure in pelvis; vaginal bleeding); ***epilepsy, exacerbation of*** (convulsions; muscle spasm or jerking of all extremities; sudden loss of consciousness; loss of bladder control); ***erythema multiforme*** (blistering, peeling, loosening of skin; chills; cough; diarrhea; fever; itching; joint or muscle pain; red, irritated eyes; sore throat; sores, ulcers, or white spots in mouth or on lips; unusual tiredness or weakness); ***erythema nodosum*** (fever; pain in ankles or knees; painful, red lumps under the skin, mostly on the legs); ***fibrocystic breast changes*** (lumps in breasts; painful or tender cysts in the breasts); ***hemorrhagic eruption*** (pinpoint red or purple spots on skin); ***hepatic hemangioma, enlargement of*** (full feeling in upper abdomen; nausea; pain in upper abdomen)—usually asymptomatic; ***hypercalcemia*** (abdominal pain; confusion; constipation; depression; dry mouth; headache; incoherent speech; increased urination; loss of appetite; metallic taste; muscle weakness; nausea; thirst; unusual tiredness; vomiting; weight loss)—in patients with breast cancer and bone metastases; ***hypocalcemia*** (abdominal cramps; confusion; convulsions; difficulty in breathing; irregular heartbeats; mood or mental changes; muscle cramps in hands, arms, feet, legs, or face; numbness and tingling around the mouth, fingertips, or feet; shortness of breath; tremor); ***liver function, impaired, asymptomatic; lupus erythematosus, exacerbation of*** (fever; muscle pain; skin rash; sore throat); ***myocardial infarction or coronary thrombosis*** (chest pain or discomfort; pain or discomfort in arms, jaw, back or neck; shortness of breath; nausea; sweating; vomiting); ***neuritis*** (numbness or tingling of hands, feet, or face); ***neuro-ocular lesions including; optic neuritis or*** (blindness; blue-yellow color blindness; blurred vision; decreased vision; eye pain); ***retinal thrombosis*** (changes in vision; double vision; migraine headache; partial or complete loss of vision in eye); ***ovarian cancer*** (acid or sour stomach; belching; backache; full or bloated feeling or pressure in the stomach; heartburn; indigestion; loss of appetite; stomach discomfort, upset or pain; swelling of abdominal or stomach area); ***palpitations*** (irregular heartbeat); ***porphyria, aggravation of*** (darkening of urine; dark urine; fluid-filled skin blisters; itching of the skin; light-colored stools; sensitivity to the sun; skin thinness; yellow eyes or skin); ***pulmonary embolism*** (anxiety; chest pain; cough; fainting; fast heartbeat; sudden shortness of breath or troubled breathing; dizziness or lightheadedness); ***sodium retention*** (decrease in amount of urine; noisy, rattling breathing; shortness of breath; swelling of fingers, hands, feet, or lower legs; troubled breathing at rest; weight gain); ***stroke*** (confusion; difficulty in speaking; slow speech; inability to speak; inability to move arms, legs, or facial muscles; double vision; headache); ***thromboembolic disorders*** (severe headaches of sudden onset; sudden loss of coordination; pains in chest, groin, or legs, especially calves of legs; sudden onset of shortness of breath for no apparent reason; sudden onset of slurred speech; sudden vision changes); ***thrombophlebitis*** (changes in skin color; pain; tenderness; swelling of foot or leg); ***uterine leiomyomata, increase in size*** (abdominal bloating; stomach pain; pelvic pain); ***venous thrombosis*** (tenderness, pain, swelling; warmth; skin discoloration; prominent superficial veins over affected area)—deep or superficial

Those indicating need for medical attention only if they continue or are bothersome

Incidence more frequent

Abdominal pain, cramping or bloating; accidental injury; anorexia (loss of appetite); ***anxiety*** (fear; nervousness); ***asthenia*** (lack or loss of strength); ***back pain; bronchitis*** (cough producing mucus; difficulty breathing; shortness of breath; tightness in chest; wheezing); ***constipation*** (difficulty having a bowel movement (stool)); ***cyst*** (abnormal growth filled with fluid or semisolid material); ***depression*** (discouragement; feeling sad or empty; irritability; lack of appetite; loss of interest or pleasure; tiredness; trouble concentrating; trouble sleeping); ***dizziness, mild; dysmenorrhea*** (pain; cramps; heavy bleeding); ***dyspepsia*** (acid or sour stomach; belching; heartburn; indigestion; stomach discomfort upset or pain); ***flatulence*** (bloated full feeling; excess air or gas in stomach or intestines; passing gas); ***flu syndrome*** (chills; cough; diarrhea; fever; general feeling of discomfort or illness; headache; joint pain; loss of appetite; muscle aches and pains; nausea; runny nose; shivering; sore throat; sweating; trouble sleeping; unusual tiredness or weakness; vomiting); ***fluid retention or edema*** (decrease in amount of urine; noisy, rattling breathing; shortness of breath; swelling of fingers, hands, feet, or lower legs; troubled breathing at rest; weight gain); ***fungal infection*** (coating or white patches on tongue; itching of the rectal or genital areas; sore mouth or tongue); ***headache; hot flushes*** (feeling of warmth; redness of the face, neck, arms and occasionally, upper chest; sudden sweating); ***infection*** (fever or chills; cough or hoarseness; lower back or side pain; painful or difficult urination); ***insomnia*** (sleeplessness; trouble sleeping; unable to sleep); ***leukorrhea*** (increased clear or white vaginal discharge); ***migraine headaches*** (headache, severe and throbbing); ***nasopharyngitis*** (stuffy or runny nose; muscle aches; unusual tiredness or weakness; fever; sore throat; headache); ***nausea; neck pain; pain; pruritus*** (itching skin); ***pharyngitis*** (body aches or pain; congestion; cough; dryness or soreness of throat; fever; hoarseness; runny nose; tender, swollen glands in neck; trouble in swallowing; voice changes); ***rash; rhinitis*** (stuffy nose; runny nose; sneezing); ***sinus congestion*** (stuffy nose; headache); ***sinusitis*** (pain or tenderness around eyes and cheekbones; fever; stuffy or runny nose; headache; cough; shortness of breath or troubled breathing; tightness of chest or wheezing); ***skin irritation and redness***—with transdermal system; ***upper respiratory tract infection [URTI]*** (chest pain; chills; cough; ear congestion or pain; fever; head congestion; hoarseness or other voice changes; nasal congestion; runny nose); ***urinary tract infection*** (bladder pain; bloody or cloudy urine; difficult, burning, or painful urination; frequent urge to urinate; lower back or side pain); ***vaginitis*** (itching of the vagina or genital area; pain during sexual intercourse; thick, white vaginal discharge with no odor or with a mild odor); ***vaginosis, fungal*** (change in the color, amount, or odor of vaginal discharge); ***weight, increased***

Incidence less frequent

Acne (blemishes on the skin; pimples); ***bladder infection*** (blood in urine; burning with urination; fever; lower abdominal pain or pressure; painful, difficult, or frequent urination); ***candidal infection*** (itching of the vagina or outside genitals; pain during sexual intercourse; thick, white curd-like vaginal discharge without odor or with mild odor); ***cough, increased; diarrhea, mild; dyspareunia*** (painful sexual intercourse); ***dysuria*** (difficult or painful urination; burning while urinating); ***emotional disturbance*** (mood or mental changes); ***fatigue*** (unusual tiredness or weakness); ***gastroenteritis*** (abdominal or stomach pain; diarrhea; loss of appetite; nausea; weakness); ***herpes simplex infection*** (burning or stinging of skin; painful cold sores or blisters on lips, nose, eyes, or genitals); ***hirsutism*** (increased hair growth, especially on the face); ***hypertension*** (blurred vision; dizziness; nervousness; headache; pounding in the ears; slow or fast heartbeat); ***hypoesthesia*** (burning, crawling, itching, numbness, prickling, "pins and needles", or tingling feelings); ***intolerance to contact lenses; libido decrease*** (loss in sexual ability, desire, drive, or performance; decreased interest in sexual intercourse; inability to have or keep an erection)—in males; ***libido increase*** (increased in sexual ability, desire, drive, or performance; increased interest in sexual intercourse)—in females; ***muscle spasms or cramps; nasal congestion*** (stuffy nose); ***osteoarthritis*** (pain, swelling, or redness in joints; muscle pain or stiffness; difficulty in moving); ***tooth abscess*** (tooth or gum pain); ***vaginal discharge*** (white or brownish vaginal discharge); ***vomiting***—primarily of central origin; usually with high doses

Incidence not determined—Observed during clinical practice, estimates of frequency can not be determined

Appetite, changes in; blood sugar levels, increased or glucose tolerance, reduced (abdominal pain; blurred vision; dry mouth; fatigue; flushed, dry skin; fruit-like breath odor; increased hunger; increased thirst; increased urination; nausea; sweating; troubled breathing; unexplained weight loss; vomiting); ***cervical ectropion, change in*** (abnormal turning out of cervix); ***cervical secretion, change in*** (change in amount of vaginal discharge; bloody vaginal discharge); ***chloasma or melasma*** (patchy brown or dark brown discoloration of skin)—may persist when drug is discontinued; ***chorea*** (twitching, uncontrolled movements of tongue, lips, face, arms, or legs); ***cystitis*** (bloody or cloudy urine difficult; burning or painful urination; frequent urge to urinate); ***dementia*** (poor insight and judgment; problems with memory or speech; trouble recognizing objects; trouble thinking and planning; trouble walking); ***galactorrhea*** (unexpected or excess milk flow from breasts); ***irritability; leg cramps; nervousness; premenstrual like syndrome*** (abdominal bloating and cramping; headache; pelvic pain); ***steepening of corneal cur-***

vature (vision changes); ***triglycerides, increased*** (large amount of triglyceride in the blood); ***varicose veins, exacerbation of*** (dull ache or feeling of pressure or heaviness in legs; itching skin near damaged veins; swollen feet and ankles); ***visual disturbances*** (any change in vision); ***weight decrease***

Those not indicating need for medical attention

Incidence not determined—Observed during clinical practice, estimates of frequency can not be determined

Loss of scalp hair

Patient Consultation

As an aid to patient consultation, refer to *Advice for the Patient, Estrogens (Systemic)*.

In providing consultation, consider emphasizing the following selected information (» = major clinical significance):

Before using this medication

» Conditions affecting use, especially:

Hypersensitivity to estrogens

The use of estrogens and progestins by postmenopausal women may increase the risk of breast cancer, endometrial cancer (among unopposed estrogen users with intact uterus), and ovarian cancer. It is important to have regular examinations by a health professional to detect these serious problems early.

Pregnancy—Use of some estrogens may be associated with congenital abnormalities. Physician should be informed immediately if pregnancy is suspected Use is contraindicated in pregnant women

Breast-feeding—Use is not recommended because estrogens are distributed into breast milk and may have unpredictable effects

Use in children—Use in children or growing adolescents may slow or stop growth

Other medications, especially cyclosporine or hepatotoxic medications

Other medical problems, especially abnormal or undiagnosed genital or uterine bleeding; active thrombophlebitis or thromboembolic disorders; sudden onset of diplopia; endometrial hyperplasia; estrogen-dependent neoplasia; hepatic function or disease, especially of the obstructive type; history of estrogen-induced thrombophlebitis; hypercalcemia associated with bone cancer or metastatic breast cancer; sudden onset of migraine; myocardial infarction; porphyria; sudden onset of proptosis; stroke; thrombosis, or thromboembolic disorders; or partial or complete vision loss

Proper use of this medication

» Reading patient package insert carefully before you start estrogen therapy and each time you refill your prescription

» Compliance with therapy

For oral or parenteral dosage forms

Taking with or immediately after food to reduce nausea

For topical emulsion

Washing and drying hands thoroughly before and after application

Apply while you are sitting comfortably. Daily dose is 2 pouches, apply one pouch to each leg.

(Apply the entire contents of one pouch to clean, dry skin on thigh every morning. Rub the emulsion into the entire thigh and calf for 3 minutes until thoroughly absorbed.)

(Apply entire contents of the second pouch on the other thigh. Rub the emulsion into the entire thigh and calf for 3 minutes until thoroughly absorbed.)

(Rub any remaining emulsion on both hands on the buttocks.)

To avoid transfer to other individuals, allow the application areas to dry completely before covering with clothing.

For transdermal estradiol

Washing and drying hands thoroughly before and after application

Applying to clean, dry, nonoily, hairless, intact area of skin on the lower abdomen, hips below the waistline, or buttocks; not applying over cuts or irritation. The manufacturer of the 0.025-mg matrix transdermal system recommends applying its patch to the buttocks only, rotating the application site from left buttock to right buttock every 7 days

» Not applying to breasts; not applying to waistline or other areas where tight clothes may rub disk loose

Pressing the disk firmly in place with palm for about 10 seconds; making sure there is good contact, especially around edges

Reapplying disk if it comes loose, or discarding and applying a new one

Applying each patch to different area of skin on lower abdomen, hips below waistline, or buttocks so at least 1 week elapses before the area is used again to help prevent skin irritation

» Proper dosing

Missed dose: Taking or using as soon as possible; not using if almost time for next dose; not doubling doses

» Proper storage

Precautions while using this medication

» Regular visits to physician every year, or more often, as determined by physician

Possibility of dental problems, such as tenderness, swelling, or bleeding of gums; brushing and flossing teeth, massaging gums, and having dentist clean teeth regularly; checking with dentist if there are questions about care of teeth or gums or if tenderness, swelling, or bleeding of gums is noticed

» Checking breast by self-examination regularly and having clinical examination and mammography as required by physician; reporting unusual breast lumps or discharge

» Understanding that menstrual bleeding may begin again but, with continuous therapy, will stop by 10 months

» Understanding that intermenstrual uterine bleeding will occur for the first 3 months; importance of not stopping medicine; checking with doctor immediately if uterine bleeding is unusual or continuous, missed period occurs, or pregnancy is suspected

If scheduled for laboratory tests, telling physician about taking estrogens; certain blood tests and tissue biopsies are affected

Side/adverse effects

Withdrawal bleeding will occur in many postmenopausal patients with an intact uterus who are placed on cyclic estrogen therapy with a progestin

Signs of potential side effects, especially breast pain or tenderness, enlargement of breasts in females, gynecomastia in males treated for prostatic cancer, hypersensitivity reactions, peripheral edema, amenorrhea, breakthrough bleeding, menorrhagia, or spotting; breast tumors; chest pain; gallbladder obstruction, hepatitis, or pancreatitis; pleural infection; vaginal hemorrhage

Signs of potential side effects observed during clinical practice, especially exacerbation of asthma, breast cancer, cholestatic jaundice, endometrial cancer, endometrial hyperplasia, exacerbation of epilepsy, erythema multiforme, erythema nodosum, fibrocystic breast changes, hemorrhagic eruption, enlargement of hepatic hemangioma, hypercalcemia, hypocalcemia, asymptomatic impairment of liver function, exacerbation of lupus erythematosus, myocardial infarction or coronary thrombosis, neuritis, neuro-ocular lesions, optic neuritis, retinal thrombosis, ovarian cancer, palpitations, aggravation of porphyria, pulmonary embolism, sodium retention, stroke, thromboembolic disorders, thrombophlebitis, increase in size of uterine leiomyomata, venous thrombosis

General Dosing Information

It is recommended that the patient package insert be given to patients.

As a general rule, estrogen therapy should be administered at the lowest effective dosage. If prolonged therapy is necessary, the patient should be re-evaluated at least every year to determine the need for continued therapy.

A complete medical and family history should be taken prior to the initiation of any estrogen therapy. The pretreatment and periodic physical examinations should include special reference to blood pressure, breasts, abdomen, and pelvic organs, and should include a Papanicolaou smear. As a general rule, estrogen should not be prescribed for longer than one year without reexamining the patient.

With chronic administration of estrogens in patients with the uterus *in situ*, the concurrent use of a progestin for at least 10 to 14 days of the cycle should be considered. Administration of a progestin decreases the risk of occurrence of endometrial hyperplasia and endometrial carcinoma. There is no risk of endometrial hyperplasia or endometrial carcinoma in patients who do not have an intact uterus.

An estrogen may be administered for the entire period of estrogen deficiency. Estrogens may be administered on a cyclic or continuous regimen when used to treat estrogen deficiency states, for prevention of osteoporosis, and for prevention of atherosclerotic disease. Some patients are placed on a cyclic regimen consisting of 3 weeks of estrogen therapy, with a progestin concurrently administered (if indicated) for the first or last 10 to 14 days of the 3-week period. During the fourth and final week of the cycle, no medication is administered. Other physicians advocate the use of continuous estrogen dosing with continuous progestin administration.

Use of the continuous regimen for both conjugated estrogen and medroxyprogesterone is a good choice for women who do not want to resume menses. If spotting or uterine bleeding occurs during the first 6 months, a higher dose of progestin may be used for a short time until endometrial atrophy occurs.

For ovarian hormone therapy

Decisions to treat menopausal symptoms with hormones for a limited time (1 to 5 years) or to use hormones to prevent diseases in postmenopausal women for a longer period of time (10 to 20 years), or a lifetime, should be made separately.

Counseling asymptomatic postmenopausal women about the benefits and risks of using long-term ovarian hormone therapy to prevent osteoporosis and coronary heart disease and to increase life expectancy is complex. Risk estimates are based on observational studies; the true estimates for long-term risks and benefits await controlled clinical trials. Women should understand that the benefits and risks of preventive hormone therapy depend on their risk status, and that women at higher risk for developing osteoporosis or coronary heart disease can derive the greatest benefit.

For women with a uterus, adding a progestin for 10 or more days of a cycle of estrogen administration, or daily with estrogen in a continuous regimen, may lower the incidence of endometrial hyperplasia. Possible risks associated with the use of progestins with estrogens compared to estrogen-alone may include a possible increased risk of breast cancer, adverse effects on lipoprotein metabolism, or impairment of glucose metabolism. Careful selection of the progestin, its dose, and its regimen may be important in minimizing these adverse effects.

Diet/Nutrition

Estrogen therapy with either the oral or parenteral dosage form may cause nausea, especially in the morning. Although this nausea is primarily of central origin, eating solid food often provides some relief.

The mainstays of prevention and management of osteoporosis are adequate calcium and vitamin D intake, exercise, and when indicated, estrogen. Postmenopausal women absorb dietary calcium less efficiently than premenopausal women and require an average of 1500 mg per day of elemental calcium to remain in neutral calcium balance. The average calcium intake in the United States is 400 to 600 mg per day. Therefore, when not contraindicated, calcium supplementation may be helpful for women with suboptimal calcium intake. Vitamin D supplementation of 400 to 800 IU per day may also be required to ensure adequate daily intake in postmenopausal women. Weight-bearing exercise and nutrition may be important adjuncts to the prevention and management of osteoporosis. Immobilization and prolonged bed rest produce rapid bone loss, while weight-bearing exercise has been shown both to reduce bone loss and to increase bone mass. The optimal type and amount of physical activity that would prevent osteoporosis have not been established.

For parenteral dosage forms only

Intramuscular injections should be administered slowly and deeply into a large muscle area such as the upper outer quadrant of the buttock.

Rapid intravenous injections may cause perineal or vaginal burning.

A dry syringe and needle of at least 21 gauge should be used for the oil-vehicle preparations.

For estradiol transdermal dosage forms

In patients who are currently taking oral estrogen, treatment with an estradiol transdermal system can be initiated 1 week after withdrawal of oral therapy or sooner if symptoms reappear in less than 1 week..

The minimum dose that has been shown to be effective for the prevention of postmenopausal osteoporosis is the 0.025 mg per day estradiol transdermal system. Response to therapy can be assessed by biochemical markers and measurement of bone mineral density.

Transdermal estradiol generally is administered on a continuous regimen, with repeating cycles of 3 weeks on and 1 week off. In women with an intact uterus, administration of a progestin for at least 10 to 14 days of each month is recommended. For women who have had a hysterectomy, transdermal estradiol may be given continuously or cyclically without adding a progestin to the therapeutic regimen.

The adhesive side of the transdermal system should be placed on a clean, dry area of the skin on the trunk of the body. The lower abdomen is the preferred site, although the patch may be applied to the buttocks or sides of hip below the waist instead. However, the manufacturer of the 0.025-mg matrix transdermal system recommends applying its patch to the buttock site only, rotating the site of application between left and right buttocks. None of the transdermal systems should be applied to the breasts or waistline. The area selected should not be oily or irritated and the skin should not be broken. The application site should be rotated, and no site should be reused until 1 week has passed.

The system should be applied immediately after removal from the pouch and removal of the protective liner. It should not be stored unprotected. The system should be pressed firmly in place with the palm of the hand for about 10 seconds, making sure there is good contact, especially around the edges.

If a transdermal system loosens or falls off, it may be reapplied or a new system may be applied instead. In either case, the patient should continue with the original treatment schedule.

Swimming, bathing, or using a sauna while using an estradiol transdermal system has not been studied, and these activities may decrease the adhesion of the system and the delivery of estradiol. One manufacturer states contact with water while bathing, swimming or showering will not affect the patch.

Attempts to taper or discontinue estradiol transdermal system should be made at 3- to 6-month intervals.

For topical emulsion

Apply the entire contents of one pouch to clean, dry skin on each leg every morning. Rub the emulsion into the entire thigh and calf for 3 minutes until thoroughly absorbed. Rub any remaining emulsion on both hands on the buttocks.

To avoid transfer to other individuals, allow the application areas to dry completely before covering with clothing.

Both hands should be washed with soap and water to remove any residual estradiol when application to both legs is completed.

CONJUGATED ESTROGENS

Oral Dosage Forms

CONJUGATED ESTROGENS TABLETS USP

Usual adult dose

Atrophic vaginitis or
Menopausal (vasomotor) symptoms or
Vulvar atrophy—
Oral, 300 mcg (0.3 mg), cyclically or continuously. Subsequent dosage adjustment may be based on patient response.

Note: May be used in conjunction with vaginal dosage forms.

Breast carcinoma (inoperable and progressing in selected men and postmenopausal women)—
Oral, 10 mg three times a day for at least three months.

Estrogen deficiency, due to ovariectomy or
Primary ovarian failure—
Oral, 1.25 mg a day, cyclically. For maintenance, adjust estrogen dose to lowest level that provides control.

Note: In Canada, dosing may be continuous as required.

Female hypogonadism—
Oral, 0.3 to 0.625 mg daily, administered cyclically. For maintenance, adjust estrogen dose to the lowest level that provides control of symptoms and minimizes responsiveness of the endometrium.

Note: In Canada, dosing may be continuous as required.

Osteoporosis, postmenopausal (prophylaxis)—
Oral, 0.3 mg a day, cyclically or continuously as appropriate Subsequent dosage adjustment may be based on patient response.

Prostatic carcinoma (inoperable and progressing)—
Oral, 1.25 to 2.5 mg three times a day.

Strength(s) usually available

U.S.—
300 mcg (0.3 mg) (Rx) [*Premarin*].
450 mcg (0.45 mg) (Rx) [*Premarin*].
625 mcg (0.625 mg) (Rx) [*Premarin*].
900 mcg (0.9 mg) (Rx) [*Premarin*].
1250 mcg (1.25 mg) (Rx) [*Premarin*].

Canada—
300 mcg (0.3 mg) (Rx) [*C.E.S.; Congest; Premarin*].
625 mcg (0.625 mg) (Rx) [*C.E.S.; Congest; Premarin;* GENERIC].
900 mcg (0.9 mg) (Rx) [*C.E.S.; Congest; Premarin*].
1.25 mg (Rx) [*C.E.S.; Congest; Premarin;* GENERIC].

Packaging and storage

Store at room temperature (approximately 25°C) in a well-closed container.

Note

Include mandatory patient package insert (PPI) when dispensing.

Parenteral Dosage Forms

CONJUGATED ESTROGENS FOR INJECTION

Usual adult dose

Uterine bleeding, hormonal imbalance–induced—

Intramuscular or intravenous, 25 mg, repeated in six to twelve hours if needed.

Note: Intravenous administration is preferred because of the more rapid response obtained. To reduce the possibility of a flushing reaction, the medication should be administered slowly.

Strength(s) usually available

U.S.—

25 mg (Rx) [*Premarin Intravenous* (benzyl alcohol 2%—diluent)].

Canada—

25 mg (Rx) [*Premarin Intravenous*].

Packaging and storage

Prior to reconstitution, store between 2 and 8 °C (36 and 46 °F), unless otherwise specified by manufacturer.

Preparation of dosage form

With aseptic technique, at least 5 mL of air should be withdrawn from the container of dry powder. Then 5 mL of the sterile diluent provided should be added slowly against the side of the container. The vial should be agitated gently to dissolve the contents. Do not shake vigorously.

Stability

When stored between 2 and 8 °C (36 and 46 °F), the reconstituted solution retains potency for about 60 days. Do not use if solution has darkened or if a precipitate is present.

Incompatibilities

The prepared injection is compatible with normal saline, dextrose, and invert sugar solutions. It is *not* compatible with solutions having an acid pH, such as protein hydrolysate or ascorbic acid.

Note

Include mandatory patient package insert (PPI) if dispensed to patient.

DIETHYLSTILBESTROL

Oral Dosage Forms

DIETHYLSTILBESTROL TABLETS USP

Usual adult dose

Prostatic carcinoma (inoperable and progressing)—

Oral, 1 to 3 mg initially and increased as needed in advanced cases, with the dosage later reduced to 1 mg a day.

Note: Doses used to treat prostatic carcinoma have been found to have a maximal effect in maintenance doses of up to 1 mg a day. Higher doses do not appreciably increase the therapeutic results, but may increase the risk of cardiovascular embolism.

Strength(s) usually available

U.S.—

Not commercially available.

Canada—

Not commercially available.

Packaging and storage

Store below 40 °C (104 °F), preferably between 15 and 30 °C (59 and 86 °F), unless otherwise specified by manufacturer. Store in a well-closed container.

Note

Include patient package insert (PPI) when dispensing.

DIETHYLSTILBESTROL DIPHOSPHATE TABLETS

Usual adult dose

Prostatic carcinoma (inoperable and progressing)—

Oral, 50 to 166 mg three times a day; the dosage being increased gradually to 200 mg or more, three times a day as needed and tolerated.

Usual adult prescribing limits

Oral, 1 gram a day.

Strength(s) usually available

U.S.—

Not commercially available.

Canada—

Not commercially available.

Packaging and storage

Store below 40 °C (104 °F), preferably between 15 and 30 °C (59 and 86 °F), in a well-closed container, unless otherwise specified by manufacturer.

Note

Include mandatory patient package insert (PPI) when dispensing.

Parenteral Dosage Forms

DIETHYLSTILBESTROL DIPHOSPHATE INJECTION USP

Usual adult dose

Prostatic carcinoma (inoperable and progressing)—

Induction: Intravenous infusion, initially 500 mg in 250 mL of Sodium Chloride Injection USP or 5% Dextrose Injection USP administered at a rate of 1 mL per minute during the first ten to fifteen minutes; then the flow is adjusted to permit dose completion within one hour. The dosage is increased to 1 gram a day for the subsequent five or more days as needed for relief.

Maintenance: Intravenous infusion, 250 to 500 mg in 250 mL of Sodium Chloride Injection USP or 5% Dextrose Injection USP administered one or two times a week at the same rate as during induction.

Strength(s) usually available

U.S.—

Not commercially available.

Canada—

Not commercially available.

Packaging and storage

Store below 21 °C (70 °F), unless otherwise specified by manufacturer. Protect from freezing.

Note

Include mandatory patient package insert (PPI) if dispensed to patient.

ESTERIFIED ESTROGENS

Oral Dosage Forms

ESTERIFIED ESTROGENS TABLETS USP

Usual adult dose

Atrophic vaginitis or
Vulvar atrophy—

Oral, 300 mcg (0.3 mg) to 1.25 mg or more a day, cyclically or continuously as appropriate.

Note: May be used in conjunction with vaginal dosage forms.

Breast carcinoma (inoperable and progressing in selected men and postmenopausal women)[1]—

Oral, 10 mg three times a day for at least three months.

Estrogen deficiency, due to ovariectomy or
Primary ovarian failure—

Oral, 1.25 mg a day, cyclically or continuously. For maintenance, adjust estrogen dose to lowest level that provides control.

Female hypogonadism—

Oral, 2.5 to 7.5 mg a day, in divided doses, cyclically or continuously.

Menopausal (vasomotor) symptoms—

Oral, 625 mcg (0.625 mg) to 1.25 mg a day, cyclically or continuously as appropriate.

Osteoporosis, postmenopausal (prophylaxis)[1]—

Oral, 300 mcg (0.3 mg) to 1.25 mg a day, cyclically or continuously.

Prostatic carcinoma (inoperable and progressing)[1]—

Oral, 1.25 to 2.5 mg three times a day.

Strength(s) usually available

U.S.—

300 mcg (0.3 mg) (Rx) [*Menest*].
625 mcg (0.625 mg) (Rx) [*Menest*].
1.25 mg (Rx) [*Menest*].
2.5 mg (Rx) [*Menest*].

Canada—

300 mcg (0.3 mg) (Rx) [*Neo-Estrone*].
625 mcg (0.625 mg) (Rx) [*Neo-Estrone*].
1.25 mg (Rx) [*Neo-Estrone*].

Packaging and storage

Store below 40 °C (104 °F), preferably between 15 and 30 °C (59 and 86 °F), unless otherwise specified by manufacturer. Store in a well-closed container.

Note

Include mandatory patient package insert (PPI) when dispensing.

---

[1]Not included in Canadian product labeling.

ESTRADIOL

Oral Dosage Forms

ESTRADIOL TABLETS USP

Usual adult dose

Atrophic vaginitis or
Estrogen deficiency, due to ovariectomy[1] or
Female hypogonadism[1] or
Menopausal (vasomotor) symptoms or
Primary ovarian failure[1] or
Vulvar atrophy—
Oral, 500 mcg (0.5 mg) to 2 mg a day, cyclically or continuously as appropriate.

Breast carcinoma (inoperable and progressing in selected men and postmenopausal women)[1]—
Oral, 10 mg three times a day for at least three months.

Prostatic carcinoma (inoperable and progressing)[1]—
Oral, 1 to 2 mg three times a day.

Osteoporosis, postmenopausal (prophylaxis)—
Oral, 0.5 mg (500 mcg) a day, cyclically (twenty-three days on and five days off per month).

Strength(s) usually available

U.S.—
500 mcg (0.5 mg) (Rx) [*Estrace* (scored); GENERIC (scored)].
1 mg (Rx) [*Estrace* (scored); GENERIC (scored)].
2 mg (Rx) [*Estrace* (scored); GENERIC (scored)].

Canada—
Not commercially available.

Packaging and storage

Store below 40 °C (104 °F), preferably between 15 and 30 °C (59 and 86 °F), unless otherwise specified by manufacturer. Store in a tight, light-resistant container.

Note

Include mandatory patient package insert (PPI) when dispensing.

Parenteral Dosage Forms

ESTRADIOL CYPIONATE INJECTION USP

Usual adult dose

Female hypogonadism—
Intramuscular, 1.5 to 2 mg administered at monthly intervals.

Menopausal (vasomotor) symptoms—
Intramuscular, 1 to 5 mg once a week for three to four weeks, usually administered cyclically (three weeks on and one week off).

Strength(s) usually available

U.S.—
5 mg per mL (Rx) [*Depo-Estradiol* (chlorobutanol 5.4 mg; cottonseed oil); *Depogen* (chlorobutanol; cottonseed oil); *Estragyn LA 5; Estro-L.A.;* GENERIC].

Canada—
Not commercially available.

Packaging and storage

Store below 40 °C (104 °F), preferably between 15 and 30 °C (59 and 86 °F), in a light-resistant container, unless otherwise specified by manufacturer. Protect from freezing.

Note

Include mandatory patient package insert (PPI) if dispensed to patient.

ESTRADIOL VALERATE INJECTION USP

Usual adult dose

Atrophic vaginitis or
Estrogen deficiency, due to ovariectomy or
Female hypogonadism[1] or
Menopausal (vasomotor) symptoms or
Primary ovarian failure or
Vulvar atrophy—
Intramuscular, 10 to 20 mg repeated every four weeks as needed.

Prostatic carcinoma (inoperable and progressing)—
Intramuscular, 30 mg every one or two weeks, the dose being adjusted as needed.

Strength(s) usually available

U.S.—
10 mg per mL (Rx) [*Delestrogen* (chlorobutanol 5 mg; sesame oil); GENERIC].
20 mg per mL (Rx) [*Delestrogen* (benzyl alcohol; benzyl benzoate; castor oil); *Menaval-20; Valergen-20* (benzyl alcohol; benzyl benzoate; castor oil); GENERIC].
40 mg per mL (Rx) [*Clinagen LA 40; Delestrogen* (benzyl alcohol; benzyl benzoate; castor oil); *Valergen-40* (benzyl alcohol; benzyl benzoate; castor oil); GENERIC].

Canada—
10 mg per mL (Rx) [*Delestrogen* (chlorobutanol 0.5%; sesame oil)].

Packaging and storage

Store below 40 °C (104 °F), preferably between 15 and 30 °C (59 and 86 °F), unless otherwise specified by manufacturer. Store in a light-resistant container. Protect from freezing.

Note

Include mandatory patient package insert (PPI) if dispensed to patient.

Topical Dosage Forms

Note: Bracketed uses in the *Dosage Forms* section refer to categories of use and/or indications that are not included in U.S. product labeling.

ESTRADIOL TRANSDERMAL SYSTEM (Matrix-type)

Usual adult dose

Atrophic vaginitis or
Estrogen deficiency, due to ovariectomy or
Female hypogonadism or
Menopausal (vasomotor) symptoms or
Osteoporosis, postmenopausal (prophylaxis) or
Primary ovarian failure or
Vulvar atrophy—
Topical, to the skin, one transdermal system delivering 25 mcg to 50 mcg a day is worn continuously and replaced, depending on the product, every seven days or every three or four days (two times a week) for three weeks of a four-week cycle. No patch is worn for the fourth week of the cycle, although estrogen treatment may be continued uninterrupted for appropriate patients. After the first thirty days, the dosage may be adjusted and then reevaluated every three to six months for treatment continuance. If osteoporosis is established, a higher dose of 100 mcg may be used initially.

Strength(s) usually available

U.S.—
Once–weekly transdermal system:
25 mcg (0.025 mg) delivered per day (Rx) [*Climara*].
50 mcg (0.05 mg) delivered per day (Rx) [*Climara*].
75 mcg (0.075 mg) delivered per day (Rx) [*Climara*].
100 mcg (0.1 mg) delivered per day (Rx) [*Climara*].
Twice–weekly transdermal system:
25.0 mcg (0.025 mg) delivered per day (Rx) [*Alora; Vivelle; Vivelle-Dot*].
37.5 mcg (0.0375 mg) delivered per day (Rx) [*Vivelle; Vivelle-Dot*].
50 mcg (0.05 mg) delivered per day (Rx) [*Alora; Vivelle; Vivelle-Dot*].
75 mcg (0.075 mg) delivered per day (Rx) [*Alora; Vivelle; Vivelle-Dot*].
100 mcg (0.1 mg) delivered per day (Rx) [*Alora; Vivelle; Vivelle-Dot*].

Canada—
Twice-weekly transdermal system:
25 mcg (0.025 mg) delivered per day (Rx) [*Estradot*].
37.5 mcg (0.0375 mg) delivered per day (Rx) [*Estradot*].
50 mcg (0.05 mg) delivered per day (Rx) [*Vivelle; Estradot*].
75 mcg (0.075 mg) delivered per day (Rx) [*Estradot*].
100 mcg (0.1 mg) delivered per day (Rx) [*Estradot*].

Packaging and storage

Store between 15 and 30 °C (59 and 86 °F). Do not store above 86 °F (30 °C).Do not freeze.

Auxiliary labeling

- Do not store unpouched. Application must be immediately after removal from protective pouch.
- Keep out of the reach of children and pets before use and when disposing used patches.

Note

Include mandatory patient package insert (PPI) when dispensing.

ESTRADIOL TRANSDERMAL SYSTEM (Reservoir-type)

Usual adult dose

Atrophic vaginitis or
Estrogen deficiency, due to ovariectomy or
Female hypogonadism or
Menopausal (vasomotor) symptoms or
Osteoporosis, postmenopausal (prophylaxis) or
Primary ovarian failure or

Vulvar atrophy—

Topical, to the skin, one 50-mcg transdermal system delivering 50 mcg a day, worn continuously and replaced every three or four days (two times a week) for three weeks of a four-week cycle. No patch is worn for the fourth week of the cycle, although estrogen treatment may be continued uninterrupted for appropriate patients. After the first thirty days, the dosage may be adjusted and then re-evaluated every three to six months for treatment continuance. If osteoporosis is established, a higher dose of 100 mcg may be used initially.

Strength(s) usually available

U.S.—

Twice–weekly transdermal system:

50 mcg (0.05 mg) delivered per day (Rx) [*Estraderm*].

100 mcg (0.1 mg) delivered per day (Rx) [*Estraderm*].

Canada—

Twice–weekly transdermal system:

25 mcg (0.025 mg) delivered per day (Rx) [*Estraderm*].

50 mcg (0.05 mg) delivered per day (Rx) [*Estraderm*].

100 mcg (0.1 mg) delivered per day (Rx) [*Estraderm*].

Packaging and storage

Store below 30 °C (86 °F).

Note

Include mandatory patient package insert (PPI) when dispensing.

ESTRADIOL HEMIHYDRATE Encapsulated TOPICAL EMULSION USP

Usual adult dose

Menopausal (vasomotor) symptoms or—

Topical, to the skin, two 1.74-gram foil-laminated pouches delivering 50 mcg a day. Apply the entire contents of each pouch (one pouch per leg) to the thigh and calf of each leg. For each leg, rub the emulsion into the entire thigh and calf for three minutes until thoroughly absorbed. Rub any remaining emulsion on both hands on the buttocks.

Strength(s) usually available

U.S.—

4.35 mg per 1.74-gram pouch (Rx) [*Estrasorb* (soybean oil; water; polysorbate 80; ethanol)].

Packaging and storage

Store between 20 and 25 °C (68 and 77 °F); excursions permitted between 15 and 30 °C (59 and 86 °F)

Auxiliary labeling

- External use only

Note

Include mandatory patient package insert (PPI) when dispensing.

[1]Not included in Canadian product labeling.

ESTRONE

Parenteral Dosage Forms

ESTRONE INJECTABLE SUSPENSION USP

Usual adult dose

Atrophic vaginitis or

Menopausal (vasomotor) symptoms or

Vulvar atrophy—

Intramuscular, 100 to 500 mcg (0.1 to 0.5 mg) two or three times a week, cyclically or continuously as appropriate.

Estrogen deficiency, due to ovariectomy or

Female hypogonadism or

Primary ovarian failure—

Intramuscular, 100 mcg (0.1 mg) to 1 mg a week, administered as a single dose or in divided doses, cyclically or continuously. A few patients may need doses of up to 2 mg a week.

Prostatic carcinoma (inoperable and progressing)—

Intramuscular, 2 to 4 mg two or three times a week.

Uterine bleeding, abnormal (hormonal imbalance–induced)—

Intramuscular, 2 to 5 mg a day for several days.

Strength(s) usually available

U.S.—

2 mg estrone per mL (Rx) [GENERIC].

5 mg estrone per mL (Rx) [*Estragyn 5; Estro-A; Kestrone-5;* GENERIC].

Canada—

Not commercially available.

Packaging and storage

Store below 40 °C (104 °F), preferably between 15 and 30 °C (59 and 86 °F), unless otherwise specified by manufacturer. Protect from freezing.

Note

Include mandatory patient package insert (PPI) if dispensed to patient.

ESTROPIPATE

Oral Dosage Forms

ESTROPIPATE TABLETS USP

Usual adult dose

Atrophic vaginitis or

Menopausal (vasomotor) symptoms or

Vulvar atrophy—

Oral, 750 mcg (0.75 mg) to 6 mg of estropipate a day, cyclically.

Estrogen deficiency, due to ovariectomy[1] or

Primary ovarian failure[1]—

Oral, 1.5 to 9 mg of estropipate a day, cyclically or continuously. For maintenance, adjust dose to lowest level that provides control.

Female hypogonadism[1]—

Oral, 1.5 to 9 mg of estropipate a day, cyclically or continuously.

Osteoporosis, postmenopausal (prophylaxis)[1]—

Oral, 750 mcg (0.75 mg) a day for twenty-five days of a thirty-one–day cycle and continued cyclically.

Strength(s) usually available

U.S.—

750 mcg (0.75 mg) estropipate—equivalent to 625 mcg (0.625 mg) sodium estrone sulfate (Rx) [*Ogen.625* (scored); *Ortho-Est.625;* GENERIC].

1.5 mg estropipate—equivalent to 1.25 mg sodium estrone sulfate (Rx) [*Ogen 1.25* (scored); *Ortho-Est 1.25;* GENERIC].

3 mg estropipate—equivalent to 2.5 mg sodium estrone sulfate (Rx) [*Ogen 2.5* (scored); GENERIC].

Canada—

750 mcg (0.75 mg) estropipate—equivalent to 625 mcg (0.625 mg) sodium estrone sulfate (Rx) [*Ogen* (scored)].

1.5 mg estropipate—equivalent to 1.25 mg sodium estrone sulfate (Rx) [*Ogen* (scored)].

3 mg estropipate—equivalent to 2.5 mg sodium estrone sulfate (Rx) [*Ogen* (scored)].

Note: Estropipate previously was called piperazine estrone sulfate and the strengths were calculated as sodium estrone sulfate (0.625 mg, 1.25 mg, and 2.5 mg). Both strengths may appear on the manufacturer's labeling.

Packaging and storage

Store below 25 °C (77 °F), unless otherwise specified by manufacturer. Store in a well-closed container.

Note

Include mandatory patient package insert (PPI) when dispensing.

[1]Not included in Canadian product labeling.

ETHINYL ESTRADIOL

Oral Dosage Forms

ETHINYL ESTRADIOL TABLETS USP

Usual adult dose

Breast carcinoma (inoperable and progressing in selected men and postmenopausal women)—

Oral, 1 mg three times a day.

Estrogen deficiency, due to ovariectomy[1] or

Primary ovarian failure[1]—

Oral, 50 mcg (0.05 mg) three times a day for a few weeks, then reduced to 50 mcg (0.05 mg) once a day, cyclically or continuously.

Female hypogonadism[1]—

Oral, 50 mcg (0.05 mg) one to three times a day, cyclically or continuously, followed by a progestin during the last half of the menstrual cycle. This treatment cycle can be repeated for three to six months to establish a normal menses.

Menopausal (vasomotor) symptoms—

Oral, 20 to 50 mcg (0.02 to 0.05 mg) a day, cyclically or continuously.

Prostatic carcinoma (inoperable and progressing)—

Oral, 150 mcg (0.15 mg) to 3 mg a day.

Strength(s) usually available
U.S.—
20 mcg (0.02 mg) (Rx) [*Estinyl*].
Canada—
Not commercially available.

Packaging and storage
Store below 40 °C (104 °F), preferably between 15 and 30 °C (59 and 86 °F), unless otherwise specified by manufacturer. Store in a well-closed container.

Note
Include mandatory patient package insert (PPI) when dispensing.

[1]Not included in Canadian product labeling.

Selected Bibliography

Product Information: Alora®, estradiol transdermal system. Watson Pharma, Corona, CA (PI revised 06/2002) PI reviewed 08/2003.
Product Information: Climara®, estradiol transdermal system. Berlex Laboratories, Wayne, NJ (PI revised 06/2001) PI reviewed 08/2003.
Product Information: Estrasorb™, estradiol topical emulsion. Novavax, Inc., Columbia, MD (PI revised 10/2003) PI reviewed 12/2003.
Product Information: Ogen®, estropipate tablets. Pharmacia & Upjohn Company, Kalamazoo, MI (PI revised 08/2001) PI reviewed 12/2003.
Health Canada: Advisory on diethylstilbestrol (DES) and the risk of genital and obstetrical complication. March 18, 2003. Available at: http://www.hc-sc.gc.ca/hpb-dgps/therapeut/htmleng/adviss_tpd_bgtd_e.html
Product Information: Premarin®, conjugated estrogens tablets. Wyeth Pharmaceuticals, Inc., Philadelphia, PA, (PI revised 04/2004) PI reviewed 06/2004.
Product Information: Premarin® Intravenous, conjugated estrogens for injection. Wyeth Pharmaceuticals, Inc., Philadelphia, PA, (PI revised 04/2004) PI reviewed 06/2004.

Revised: 07/20/2006

ESTROGENS Vaginal

This monograph includes information on the following: 1) Conjugated Estrogens; 2) Dienestrol; 3) Estradiol; 4) Estrone*; 5) Estropipate†.

BAN:
Dienestrol—Dienoestrol
Estradiol—Oestradiol
Estrone—Oestrone

VA CLASSIFICATION (Primary/Secondary): GU500/HS102

Commonly used brand name(s): *Estrace*[3]; *Estring*[3]; *Oestrilin*[4]; *Premarin*[1].

Other commonly used names are Dienoestrol [Dienestrol], Oestradiol [Estradiol], Oestrone [Estrone], and Piperazine Estrone Sulfate [Estropipate].

Note: For a listing of dosage forms and brand names by country availability, see *Dosage Forms* section(s).

*Not commercially available in U.S.
†Not commercially available in Canada.

Category

Urogenital symptoms suppressant.

Indications

General Considerations

Vaginal estrogen doses that maintain the serum estradiol concentration in the postmenopausal range do not produce systemic effects of the hormone, such as suppression of *vasomotor symptoms of menopause* or protection against *cardiovascular disease* or *osteoporosis*, and they are not indicated for these uses. While sufficiently high serum estradiol concentrations can be produced from use of vaginal estrogens, use of oral or transdermal estrogen therapy may be preferred instead if systemic benefits are desired.

After menopause, serum estradiol concentrations are approximately 10 to 20 picograms per mL (pg/mL) (40 to 70 picomoles per L [pmol/L]) and serum estrone concentrations are approximately 30 to 70 pg/mL (110 to 260 pmol/L). If vaginal administration provides serum estrogen concentrations greater than these concentrations, systemic effects of estrogen should be considered and their potential side effects appropriately managed, such as adding a progestin to the treatment regimen to decrease estrogen-induced endometrial hyperplasia.

Women without a uterus are best treated with unopposed estrogen therapy; combined estrogen-progestin therapy is not needed.

Accepted

Urethritis, atrophic, postmenopausal (treatment)—Estradiol vaginal insert is indicated to treat atrophic urethritis in postmenopausal women who have symptoms of dysuria or urinary frequency, urgency, or incontinence.

Vaginitis, atrophic (treatment)—Conjugated estrogens, dienestrol, estradiol vaginal cream, [estradiol vaginal insert], and estropipate are indicated to treat symptoms of atrophic vaginitis due to estrogen deficiency that may include dyspareunia. Estradiol vaginal insert[1] and estrone are indicated to treat atrophic vaginitis in postmenopausal women only (also called senile vaginitis).

Vulvar atrophy—Conjugated estrogens, dienestrol, estradiol vaginal cream, [estradiol vaginal insert], estrone, and estropipate are indicated for treatment of symptomatic atrophic vulva due to estrogen deficiency, including kraurosis vulvae and pruritus vulvae.

Unaccepted

Although a few studies show that estrogens have some effect on neurotransmitters and may improve memory and cognitive function, estrogen is not indicated or effective in the treatment of clinical depression.

[1]Not included in Canadian product labeling.

Pharmacology/Pharmacokinetics

Physicochemical characteristics

Source—
Naturally occurring estrogens: Estradiol (E_2), estrone (E_1), and estriol (E_3) in humans.
Conjugated estrogens are a mixture of estrogenic metabolites found in equine urine; the complete profile is not known. The primary estrogens, sodium estrone sulfate and sodium equilin sulfate, make up 79.5 to 88% of the total mixture. Other estrogens defined by USP as concomitant components are the sodium sulfated conjugates of 17-alpha-dihydroequilin, 17-alpha-estradiol, and 17-beta-dihydroequilin.
Semi-synthetic estrogen: Estropipate (estrone sulfate piperazine compound).
Synthetic nonsteroidal estrogen: Dienestrol.

Molecular weight—
Dienestrol: 266.34.
Estradiol: 272.39.
Estrone: 270.37.
Estropipate: 436.58.

Mechanism of action/Effect

Estrogens—
Estrogens passively diffuse into target cells of responsive tissues, complex with the estrogen receptors, and enter the cell's nucleus to initiate or enhance gene transcription of protein synthesis after binding to DNA.
The magnitude of estrogen's effect and its influence upon different hormones depends on the endogenous estrogen concentration in the plasma, and the product formulation and type and dose of exogenous estrogen administered. A 2:1 ratio of serum estradiol to estrone normally found in premenopausal women can be achieved with intravaginal or transdermal use; this ratio is not achievable with oral use. Total estrogen serum concentrations is dose-dependent.

Urogenital symptoms suppressant—
After the menopause when ovarian follicles are absent, symptoms of estrogen deficiency begin when the serum estradiol concentration falls. Restoring the more potent estrogens, such as estradiol, or increasing the estrone concentration helps to lessen or stop symptoms of genital itching, vaginal dryness, dyspareunia, dysuria, urinary frequency, urgency, and urinary or stress incontinence. Clinical data show estrogens cause the vaginal and urethral environment to return to normal. As the vaginal pH falls below 5, normal flora recolonize, and the vaginal and urethral mucosa mature. The maturation of the mucosa is clinically apparent with the disappearance of parabasal cells and an increase in the number of intermediate and superficial epithelial cells.
Estrogens may act to increase the collagen content in the urethra and bladder base and cause growth of urethral epithelium. How intravaginal administration distributes estrogen to the urethral mucosa is not known, but it is likely due to an increased systemic concentration or is provided by local access to urogenital tissue through a venous plexus.
In most menopausal patients, vaginal estrogen doses that maintain the serum estradiol concentrations at postmenopausal levels pro-

duce mainly local vaginal effects without sufficiently stimulating the endometrium to resume menstrual-like cycles. For some patients, the dose may be sufficient to stimulate the endometrium; rarely, endometrial hyperplasia occurs. Also, at these low doses, vaginal estrogens do not significantly suppress the gonadotropins FSH or LH, lessen systemic menopausal symptoms, or diminish the rate of bone loss. Systemic effects must be considered and expected if serum estrogen concentrations increase beyond the postmenopausal range.

Other actions/effects

Estrogens help develop and maintain the female reproductive system, urogenital tissue tone and elasticity, and secondary sex characteristics. Estrogens, acting with other hormones and cytokines, stimulate the growth and development of breast tissue and skeleton formation, and are integral to the physiology of puberty, menstruation, ovulatory cycles, and pregnancy.

Absorption

Estrogens are well absorbed from the vagina, mucous membranes, subcutaneous fat, and gastrointestinal tract. Vaginal absorption is dependent on estrogen particle size, dose and type of estrogen, vehicle used, and status of the vaginal mucosa. Smaller-sized particles of estrogens (micronized) show rapid absorption while coarser particles absorb slowly over a longer period of time. Low doses of estrogen used several times a week or ultralow doses given continuously, such as with the estradiol vaginal insert, achieve mainly local effects, while daily vaginal dosing can produce high systemic concentrations and effects. Conjugated or sulfated estrogens and creams and suppositories provide longer effects. Atrophied mucosa exhibits more systemic absorption for 3 to 4 months until mucosa is revitalized by estrogens, after which less of the estrogen is absorbed systemically.

For conjugated estrogens—Conjugates of estrogens, largely estrone sulfate, are absorbed intravaginally but to a lesser extent than estradiol.

For estradiol vaginal insert: 8% (range 3 to 13%) of the daily release from the estradiol vaginal insert is absorbed systemically. After an initial 24-hour peak release of 50 mcg, 7.5 mcg is released every 24 hours for 90 days of continuous use. Maximum peak concentration is approximately 38% lower after 3 months, when the second vaginal insert is used and the vaginal mucosa is no longer atrophied.

Protein binding

Moderate to high (50 to 80%); to sex hormone-binding globulin and albumin.

Vaginal conjugated estrogens, by delivering supraphysiologic doses to the liver, are capable of inducing the synthesis of proteins, such as sex hormone-binding globulin, and sulfating estrogens to create a drug reservoir of estrogen. Except for conjugated estrogens, vaginally administered estrogens in appropriate doses can deliver physiologic doses of estrogen to the liver that do not induce production of hepatic proteins.

Biotransformation

Estrogens are metabolized primarily by hepatic and local target tissues such as skeletal muscles, the kidneys, and the gonads. Tissues dynamically metabolize and interconvert between estrogens—estrone and estradiol—as well as between their metabolites, such as unconjugated and conjugated estrogen sulfates, and unesterified and esterified estrogens. On a dose-to-dose basis, a higher ratio of estradiol to estrone serum concentrations can be achieved through use of vaginal or transdermal products as compared with oral products.

During hepatic metabolism estrogens are desulfated, resulfated, and oxidized to less active estrogens, to nonestrogenic substances that interact with catecholamine receptors in the CNS, and to conjugates of glucuronic acid that may be quickly eliminated.

Vaginal metabolism of estradiol is minimal; conjugated estrogens, however, are metabolized in the vaginal epithelia.

Half-life

For estradiol—20 minutes.

Time to peak concentration

For estradiol vaginal insert—Time to peak is 0.5 to 1 hour, declining to a constant release after 24 hours, reaching the steady-state serum concentration within 7 to 10 days.

Duration of action

For estradiol vaginal insert—3 months.

Elimination

Renal—Major route for excretion of acidic ionized conjugates, such as glucuronides and sulfates.

Fecal—Minimal; reabsorbed from intestines and recirculated through portal venous system.

Precautions to Consider

Note: Vaginally administered estrogen attains serum estradiol concentrations that are about 25 to 40% of that reached by the same dose given orally. Risk of endometrial proliferation should be considered with use of vaginal estrogen, even if systemic effects are not produced. If the serum estrone and estradiol concentrations increase beyond the postmenopausal range, systemic effects of the hormones should be considered with vaginal use.

Carcinogenicity

Risk of developing endometrial cancer for users of vaginal estrogens has not been determined, but is probably related to estrogen dose and duration of treatment. Developing endometrial cancer is less likely if the vaginal dose affects only the urogenital tissue, not the uterine lining, and is not greatly absorbed systemically. Low doses used intravaginally for prolonged periods of time may increase risk of endometrial hyperplasia and, although no cases have been reported, endometrial carcinoma. Use of natural estrogens has not been shown to result in a different endometrial risk profile than synthetic estrogens of equivalent estrogen dose.

The following data are based on use of oral estrogens. Estrogens may increase the incidence of breast cancer in some postmenopausal women. The Women's Health Initiative (WHI) trial reported an increased risk of breast cancer in women who took estrogen plus progestin for a mean follow-up of 5.6 years. Patients using estrogen in either high doses or low doses for a prolonged period of time, especially longer than 10 years, potentially may have greater risk. Short-term use of estrogens for treatment of menopausal symptoms does not appear to increase risk, and no additional risk has been attributed to adding a progestin to the therapy. Regular breast examinations or mammography will help detect any developing problems.

Estrogen plus progestin may increase the incidence of ovarian cancer in some postmenopausal women. The relative risk and absolute risk of ovarian cancer for estrogen plus progestin versus placebo was 1.58 (95% confidence interval 0.77 to 3.24; not statistically significant) and 4.2 versus 2.7 cases per 10,000 women-years in the estrogen plus progestin substudy of the WHI trial. The use of estrogen-only products for 10 or more years has been associated with an increased risk of ovarian cancer in some epidemiologic studies.

When nonusers were compared with users of an oral estrogen-only cycle, no risk of endometrial hyperplasia was shown for the first year of use. When oral estrogens were taken for a prolonged period of time or at higher-than-physiologic doses, the risk increased 2 to 12 times. Furthermore, the risk can be increased as much as 24 times when oral estrogens are used for 5 years or longer. Although the magnitude of the risk decreases substantially within 6 months after unopposed oral estrogen therapy is discontinued, some risk can continue for 8 to 15 years. Studies show a lower incidence of endometrial hyperplasia and, potentially, endometrial cancer when patients take a progestin for a minimum period of 10 to 14 days a month along with an estrogen cycle.

In certain animal species, long-term, continuous administration of systemic estrogens increases the frequency of cancers of the breast, cervix, liver, testes, uterus, and vagina. Results of animal studies may not apply to humans because of the general hormonal differences in sex steroids among species.

Pregnancy/Reproduction

Pregnancy—Estrogens are not recommended for use during pregnancy. This recommendation is based on studies showing an association of congenital malformations with use of oral diethylstilbestrol (DES). Patients who become pregnant while taking estrogens should be informed of the potential risks to the fetus. Pregnancy occurs rarely in menopausal women because of the natural change in their hormonal milieu; on the rare chance of its occurrence, a fetus surviving to term is unlikely.

FDA Pregnancy Category X.

Breast-feeding

Estrogens are distributed into breast milk. Use of estrogens by breast-feeding women is not recommended. The quantity and quality of breast milk has been shown to be decreased in nursing mothers receiving estrogen therapy.

Pediatrics

Estrogen therapy has been used for the induction of puberty in adolescents with some forms of pubertal delay. Safety and effectiveness have not otherwise been established.

Use of large and repeated doses of estrogen over an extended time period have been shown to accelerate epiphyseal closure. Periodic monitoring of bone maturation and effects on epiphyseal centers is recommended during estrogen administration.

Premature breast development and vaginal cornification and possible vaginal bleeding may occur from estrogen treatment of pre-pubertal girls. Estrogen treatment in boys may modify the normal pubertal process and induce gynecomastia.

Geriatrics

Appropriate studies on the relationship of age to the effects of conjugated estrogens have not been performed in the geriatric population. There have not been sufficient numbers of geriatric patients involved in studies to determine whether those over 65 years of age differ from younger subjects in their response to vaginal conjugated estrogens.

In the PREMPRO substudy of the Women's Health Initiative Study, there was a higher incidence of stroke and invasive breast cancer in women 75 years and over compared to younger subjects.

In the Women's Health Initiative Memory Study, there was a two-fold increase in the risk of developing probable dementia in women 65 years of age and older receiving conjugated equine estrogen 0.625 mg and medroxyprogesterone acetate 2.5 mg compared to the placebo group. It is not known whether this finding applies to women taking estrogen-only therapy or to younger postmenopausal women.

Laboratory value alterations

The following have been selected on the basis of their potential clinical significance (possible effect in parentheses where appropriate)—not necessarily inclusive (» = major clinical significance).

With diagnostic test results

- Fasting blood sugar (FBS) and
  Glucose tolerance test
  (impaired glucose tolerance)
- Metyrapone test
  (reduced response)
- Norepinephrine-induced platelet aggregability
  (may be increased)
- Thyroid function tests, such as
  Thyroxine (T_4) determinations
  Triiodothyronine (T_3) determinations
  (values for the T_3 uptake test may be decreased because of an increase in thyroid-binding globulin [TBG]; free T_3, thyroxine [T_4], and thyroid-stimulating hormone [TSH] concentrations remain unaltered and patient remains euthyroid, even though the total thyroid hormone may be increased)

With physiology/laboratory test values

- Anti-factor Xa or
  Antithrombin III activity
  (may be decreased)
- Antithrombin III, serum and
  Lipoproteins, low density (LDL), serum and
  (concentrations may be decreased)
- Binding proteins, such as:
  Corticosteroid binding globulin (CBG) or
  Sex hormone binding globulin (SHBG)
  (levels may be elevated)
- Calcium
  (estrogen use may result in severe hypercalcemia in patients with breast cancer and bone metastases)
- Clotting factors such as:
  II or
  VII antigen or
  VIII antigen or
  VIII coagulant activity or
  IX or
  X or
  XII or
  VII-X complex or
  II-VII-X complex or
  Beta-thromboglobulin
  (may be increased)
- Fibrinogen levels and
  Fibrinogen activity
  (may be increased)
- HDL and HDL_2 cholesterol subfraction or
  Triglyceride
  (values may be increased)
- Plasma proteins, such as:
  Alpha-1-antitrypsin or
  Angiotensinogen/renin substrate or
  Ceruloplasmin
  (values may be increased)
- Plasminogen antigen and
  Plasminogen activity
  (may be increased)
- Prothrombin time, or
  Platelet aggregation time or
  Thromboplastin time, partial
  (may be accelerated)

Medical considerations/Contraindications

The medical considerations/contraindications included have been selected on the basis of their potential clinical significance (reasons given in parentheses where appropriate)—not necessarily inclusive (» = major clinical significance).

Note: If vaginal doses increase the serum estradiol concentrations beyond the postmenopausal range, consider the precautions for systemic estrogens.

Except under special circumstances, this medication should not be used when the following medical problems exist:

- » Allergy to cream components, including parabens
- » Neoplasia, estrogen-dependent, known or suspected
  (may promote tumor growth or interfere with the action of antiestrogen treatment regimens for any systemically absorbeddose. Carefully chosen patients with these conditions have used low vaginal doses for treating urogenital conditions; however, estrogen use in these patients is still considered to introduce an unknown risk)
- » Genital or uterine bleeding, abnormal or undiagnosed
  (use of estrogens may delay diagnosis; on occurrence, estrogen should be discontinued until clinical evaluation is completed. Condition may worsen if cause of abnormal uterine bleeding is endometrial hyperplasia or endometrial cancer)
- Hepatic dysfunction or disease
  (use is contraindicated)
  (severe hepatic function impairment can decrease estrogen metabolism, especially when using conjugated estrogens. Carefully chosen patients with severe hepatic function impairment have used low vaginal doses of estrogens for treating urogenital conditions. Locally or vaginally administered estradiol and estrone have less effect on the liver than conjugated estrogens)
- Thromboembolic disorders, including:
  Deep vein thrombosis, active or history of
  Pulmonary embolism, active or history of
  Arterial thromboembolic disease, including:
  Stroke, active or recent (e.g., within past year)
  Myocardial infarction, active or recent (e.g., within past year)
  (use is contraindicated)

Risk-benefit should be considered when the following medical problems exist:

- Asthma or
  Epilepsy or
  Cardiac or renal dysfunction or
  Migraine
  (these conditions may be exacerbated with administration of estrogen therapy; caution is advised)
- Cervicitis or
  Vaginal infection or
  Vaginitis
  (use of vaginal estrogen may worsen these conditions or, for the estradiol vaginal insert, cause ulceration; on occurrence, discontinuing use of estrogen may not be necessary but the underlying irritation or infection should be treated as appropriate)
- Diabetes mellitus, history of or predisposition to
  (condition may be exacerbated and estrogens should be used with caution)
- Endometriosis or
  Leiomyomata, uterine
  (may be aggravated by use of estrogens)
- Gallbladder disease, or history of, especially gallstones
  (a 2- to 4-fold increase in the risk of gallbladder disease requiring surgery in postmenopausal women receiving estrogens has been reported)
- Hepatic hemangiomas or
  Lupus erythematosus, systemic
  (may be exacerbated by estrogens; use with caution)
- » Hypercalcemia
  (severe hypercalcemia may occur in patients with bone metastases, breast cancer, metabolic bone disease, or renal insufficiency who are treated with estrogens)
- Hyperlipoproteinemia, familial or

Hypertriglyceridemia or
Pancreatitis
(estrogen therapy may be associated with elevations of plasma triglycerides in patients with pre-existing hypertriglyceridemia; hypertriglyceridemia may lead to pancreatitis and other complications)

Hypocalcemia, severe
(should be used with caution)

Hypothyroidism
(estrogens lead to increased thyroid binding globulin [TBG] levels; patients dependent upon thyroid hormone replacement therapy who are also receiving estrogens may need to increase the dose of their thyroid replacement therapy)

Jaundice, cholestatic, history of, or
Jaundice, or history of during pregnancy or
(impaired hepatic function may decrease the metabolism of estrogens and cause these conditions to worsen or recur; caution should be exercised and in the case of recurrence, medication should be discontinued)

» Porphyria
(may be exacerbated by estrogens; use with caution)

Vaginal narrowing or
Vaginal prolapse or
Vaginal stenosis
(use of the estradiol vaginal insert may cause abdominal or back pain, vaginal irritation or ulceration, urinary incontinence, or frequent device expulsion in some of these patients)

» Visual abnormalities including
Diplopia, sudden onset or
Migraine, sudden onset or
Proptosis, sudden onset or
Vision loss, partial or complete
(discontinue medication pending examination if any of these conditions occur; if examination reveals papilledema or retinal vascular lesions estrogens should be stopped; retinal vascular thrombosis has been reported in patients receiving estrogens)

Patient monitoring

The following may be especially important in patient monitoring (other tests may be warranted in some patients, depending on condition; » = major clinical significance):

Blood pressure determinations
(substantial increases in blood pressure have been reported in a small number of patients receiving estrogen therapy; blood pressure should be monitored at regular intervals)

Breast examination and
Mammography and
Papanicolaou (Pap) test and
Physical examinations
(recommended annually or more often as determined by physician, with emphasis on examining blood pressure, breasts, abdomen, and pelvic organs, including a Papanicolaou [Pap] test; regular self-examination to detect breast problems should be done by patient)

Endometrial biopsy
(patients with a uterus should be monitored for signs of endometrial cancer, and malignancy should be ruled out in cases of persistent or recurring abnormal vaginal bleeding)

Fluid status
(estrogens may cause fluid retention; patients with conditions that might be influenced by fluid retention, such as cardiac or renal dysfunction, warrant careful observation)

Thyroid function
(patients dependent on thyroid hormone replacement therapy who are also taking estrogens should have their thyroid function monitored to maintain free thyroid hormone levels in an acceptable range)

Side/Adverse Effects

Note: The risk of any serious adverse effect is minimal for women using low doses of estrogen. Even women who have special risk factors successfully use estrogens.

Consider the side effects of systemic estrogens if serum estradiol concentrations increase beyond the postmenopausal range as shown by laboratory tests or evidence of patient complaints, especially complaints of uterine bleeding or breast tenderness. Risk of endometrial proliferation should be considered with use of vaginal estrogens, with or without systemic effects.

Estrogen and estrogen/progestin therapy has been associated with an increased risk of cardiovascular events such as myocardial infarction and stroke, as well as venous thrombosis and pulmonary embolism (venous thromboembolism or VTE). Should any of these occur or be suspected, estrogen/progestin therapy should be stopped immediately.

The following side/adverse effects have been selected on the basis of their potential clinical significance (possible signs and symptoms in parentheses where appropriate)—not necessarily inclusive:

Those indicating need for medical attention

Incidence less frequent

Breast pain or enlargement; headache; nausea; vulvovaginal candidiasis (itching of the vagina or genitals; thick, white vaginal discharge without odor or with a mild odor)—estrogens usually prevent; ***vulvovaginitis*** (itching, stinging, or redness of the genital area)—estrogens usually prevent

Note: *Vulvovaginal candidiasis* or *vulvovaginitis* occur more frequently in untreated postmenopausal patients, but since they are reported in up to 13% of vaginal estrogen users, infection or irritation should be evaluated and treated. Although estrogen is used in treating vulvovaginal irritation, *vulvovaginitis* may be caused by other ingredients in the vaginal formulation.

Breast pain, *headache*, or *nausea* can indicate systemic absorption, and may require reduction of dose or frequency if systemic absorption is not desired.

Incidence rare

Uterine bleeding or spotting, unusual or unexpected; vaginal discomfort, pain, or ulceration due to a foreign object (feeling of vaginal pressure; vaginal burning or pain)—with use of estradiol vaginal insert

Note: Any *unusual or unexpected uterine bleeding or spotting*, especially if persistent or recurrent, should be evaluated for endometrial hyperplasia or endometrial cancer. If workup is uneventful, then lowering patient's estrogen dose or frequency or adding a progestin for at least 10 to 14 days a month may be needed.

Those indicating need for medical attention only if they continue or are bothersome

Incidence less frequent

Abdominal or back pain; leukorrhea (clear vaginal discharge)—usually indicates therapeutic effect

Patient Consultation

As an aid to patient consultation, refer to *Advice for the Patient, Estrogens (Vaginal)*.

In providing consultation, consider emphasizing the following selected information (» = major clinical significance):

Before using this medication

» Conditions affecting use, especially:
Allergy to cream components, such as parabens
Carcinogenicity—For patients taking estrogens or progestins, risk of endometrial cancer for vaginal estrogen users is not fully understood or easily quantified, but thought to be less likely if doses are kept low enough to treat urogenital conditions locally; also, endometrial hyperplasia is less likely to occur
The use of estrogens and progestins by postmenopausal women may increase the risk of breast cancer, endometrial cancer (among unopposed estrogen users with intact uterus), and ovarian cancer. It is important to have regular examinations by a health professional to detect these serious problems early.
Pregnancy—Use of estrogens during pregnancy is not recommended because of reported congenital abnormalities caused by diethylstilbestrol (DES); although pregnancy is not usually a concern for perimenopausal patients, patient should inform physician immediately if pregnancy is suspected
Breast-feeding—Use is not recommended because estrogens are distributed into breast milk
Other medical problems, especially deep vein thrombosis, estrogen-dependent neoplasia (known or suspected) genital or uterine bleeding (abnormal or undiagnosed), liver disease/dysfunction, myocardial infarction, pulmonary embolism, or stroke

Proper use of this medication

» Reading patient package insert (PPI) carefully
Washing hands immediately before and after vaginal administration; avoiding contact with eyes; washing it out of eyes with water if medication accidentally gets into eyes

» Understanding directions of use and that full therapeutic effect may take 3 or 4 months to appear; checking with physician for changes in dose and not using medication longer than prescribed

Proper administration technique

For cream dosage form—Understanding the markings on applicator and how to withdraw the proper dose

For cream and suppository dosage form—Following directions regarding the filling of the applicator with medication; understanding the insertion technique; and, depending on the applicator type supplied by the product's packaging, either discarding the disposable applicators after each use or, if reusable, cleaning and drying applicators thoroughly after each use

For estradiol vaginal insert—Knowing how to place, reposition, or remove the vaginal insert in the upper part of vagina, and how to dispose of the old vaginal insert safely, especially avoiding flushing it down the toilet

» Compliance with therapy

» Proper dosing

Missed dose:

For weekly dosing of suppository or cream—Using as soon as possible within 1 or 2 days; however, not using if almost time for next dose; not doubling doses

For daily dosing of suppository or cream—Using missed dose within 12 hours. Not using missed dose if almost time for next dose; not doubling doses

» Proper storage

Precautions while using this medication

» Regular annual visits to physician, or more often, as determined by physician

» Checking breasts by self-examination regularly and having clinical examination and mammography as required by physician; reporting unusual breast lumps or discharge

» Stopping medication immediately and checking with physician if pregnancy is suspected

If scheduled for laboratory tests, telling physician about estrogen use; certain blood tests and tissue biopsies are affected

For all vaginal creams:

» Not using latex condoms for up to 72 hours after vaginal estrogen treatment because oils in the vaginal cream dosage form may weaken latex products

Using medication at bedtime to increase effectiveness; wearing sanitary napkin to protect clothing

Avoiding exposing male partner to estrogen vaginal cream through sexual intercourse; having sexual intercourse, when desired, prior to administering vaginal dose

For estradiol vaginal insert:

Not needing to remove for sexual intercourse unless desired

Washing the vaginal insert before reinsertion when expelled or if taken out for sexual intercourse

Replacing with new vaginal insert after 3 months

Side/adverse effects

Signs of potential side effects, especially breast pain or enlargement; headache; nausea; vulvovaginal candidiasis; vulvovaginitis; unusual or unexpected uterine bleeding or spotting; vaginal discomfort, pain, or ulceration due to a foreign object (for estradiol vaginal insert)

(Reporting to physician if vaginal use produces systemic estrogen side/adverse effects, such as uterine bleeding or breast tenderness; understanding that vaginal administration can produce systemic estrogen effects and, on their occurrence, may warrant a dosage reduction)

General Dosing Information

It is required that the patient package insert (PPI) be given to patients.

Generally, the lowest dose to control urogenital symptoms is used. The patient is often titrated over a 6-week period and re-evaluated at 3- to 6-month intervals to assess whether to continue her estrogen treatment or to make dosage or frequency adjustments.

Doses that maintain serum estradiol concentrations within the postmenopausal range will not cause endometrial stimulation or monthly uterine bleeding. While serum estradiol concentrations of 140 to 200 picomoles per liter (pmol/L) suppress vasomotor symptoms, these concentrations do not frequently occur when low maintenance doses of estrogen are applied or used vaginally 2 to 3 times a week. Concentrations below 70 pmol/L associated with atrophy of the endometrium are produced instead.

Postmenopausal patients should be counseled that they will not show an improved lipoprotein cholesterol profile or be protected against bone loss while their serum estradiol concentration remains in the postmenopausal range. Although sufficiently high serum estradiol concentrations can be produced from use of vaginal estrogens, use of oral, transdermal, or parenteral estrogen therapy may be preferred instead for these uses.

For vaginal creams

The cream vehicles for some vaginal estrogen products contain mineral oil or other lipid-based components that may adversely affect the performance of latex barrier devices, such as condoms, cervical caps, or diaphragms, to prevent pregnancy or sexually transmitted diseases.

Low doses given vaginally cause few systemic effects and, rarely, cause endometrial stimulation; concomitant progestin treatment for 10 to 14 days is recommended by some medical organizations for patients with a uterus and is especially important when uterine bleeding or systemic effects occur. Usually when 2 or 3 low maintenance doses a week are used intravaginally, cyclic treatment of 3 weeks on and 1 week off is sufficient to prevent endometrial proliferation without adding a progestin.

If oral estrogens are given for 10 to 14 days as a priming dose, then the initial dosage regimen for vaginal treatment is discontinued and the maintenance treatment regimen is initiated instead.

Patient counseling on withdrawing the proper dose into applicator is important, especially when transferring a patient to a different product. Applicator markings indicate the amount of cream in grams. Patients may confuse the dose (in mg) with the amount of cream to be applied (in grams).

For vaginal cream or suppository

To properly place vaginal cream or suppository, patient lies on back with knees drawn up and apart, gently inserting applicator into vagina, carefully releasing dose by pressing plunger downward to original position. Cleaning the applicator, if reusable, is accomplished by separating the plunger from the barrel and washing each separately with soap and water; never using boiling or hot water. Applicator unit is reassembled after each part dries thoroughly. A new disposable applicator can be used with each dose if one is contained in the packaging.

For estradiol vaginal insert

Systemic effects from a daily dose of 7.5 mcg of estradiol released over 24 hours are minimal, making concomitant progestin treatment unnecessary as use of the vaginal insert at this dose rarely causes endometrial stimulation. Use of the vaginal insert beyond ninety days does not result in an overdose, but rather an underdose, and increases the likelihood of vaginal infections or epithelial ulcers occurring due to lack of efficacy.

Insertion technique—Pinching or pressing the sides of the vaginal insert together, between forefinger and middle finger, into a smaller oval-shape allows placement into the upper third of the vagina, and can be managed by patient or physician. Patient can place vaginal insert while lying on her back with knees up or while standing with one foot raised on a chair. Although an exact placement in the vagina is not critical, any discomfort felt by the patient requires that the vaginal insert be moved higher by gently pushing the insert further into the vagina.

Removal technique—Removed by hooking a finger through the ring-shaped vaginal insert and gently pulling it out through the vagina.

Removal of the vaginal insert is not needed for sexual intercourse unless preferred by the patient; in one study, only 6 of approximately 182 postmenopausal patients (17%) removed the vaginal insert for sexual intercourse. Straining on defecation may cause the vaginal insert to move lower in the vagina or to be expelled accidentally from the vagina.

If the vaginal insert is removed by the patient or expelled accidentally, rinsing in lukewarm water is sufficient before replacing the vaginal insert back into the vagina.

CONJUGATED ESTROGENS

Summary of Differences

Indications: Atrophic vaginitis and vulvar atrophy.

Pharmacology/pharmacokinetics: Mixture of estrogenic metabolites, extracted from the urine of pregnant mares; highly sulfated. Vaginal conjugated estrogens provide longer duration of action and induce liver to increase proteins, such as SHBG, TBG, and renin substrate; metabolized by vaginal mucosa; absorbed slower than other estrogens.

Medical considerations/Contraindications—May exacerbate existing hepatic function impairment.

Vaginal Dosage Forms

CONJUGATED ESTROGENS VAGINAL CREAM

Usual adult dose
Atrophic vaginitis or
Vulvar atrophy—
Intravaginal or topical, 0.3 to 1.25 mg of conjugated estrogens (one-half to two grams of cream) daily or as directed by physician based on the lowest dose needed for three weeks, with no medication used in the fourth week; the schedule being repeated each month.

Usual geriatric dose
See *Usual adult dose.*

Strength(s) usually available
U.S.—
625 mcg (0.625 mg) per gram (Rx) [*Premarin* (benzyl alcohol; cetyl esters wax; cetyl alcohol; glycerin; glyceryl monostearate; methyl stearate; mineral oil; propylene glycol monostearate; sodium lauryl sulfate; white wax)].
Canada—
625 mcg (0.625 mg) per gram (Rx) [*Premarin* (cetyl alcohol; phenylethyl alcohol)].

Packaging and storage
Store below 40 °C (104 °F), preferably between 15 and 30 °C (59 and 86 °F), unless otherwise specified by manufacturer.

Auxiliary labeling
• For vaginal use only.

Note
Include mandatory patient package insert (PPI) when dispensing.

Additional information
Canadian brand of *Premarin* is gluten-, paraben-, sugar-, sulfite-, and tartazine-free.
Calibrated applicator measures in 0.5 gram increments up to 2 grams of cream.

DIENESTROL

Summary of Differences
Indications: Atrophic vaginitis and vulvar atrophy.
Pharmacology/pharmacokinetics: Source—Synthetic, nonsteroidal estrogen.

Vaginal Dosage Forms

DIENESTROL CREAM USP

Usual adult dose
Atrophic vaginitis or
Vulvar atrophy—
Initial: Intravaginal, 0.5 mg (one applicatorful) one or two times a day for one or two weeks, the dose then being reduced to either 0.25 or 0.5 mg (one-half or one applicatorful) a day for an additional one or two weeks.
Maintenance: Intravaginal, 0.5 mg (one applicatorful) one to three times a week for three weeks with no medication used in the fourth week after vaginal mucosa is no longer atrophied; this schedule being repeated each month.

Usual geriatric dose
See *Usual adult dose.*

Strength(s) usually available
U.S.—
0.01% (Rx) [GENERIC].
Canada—
Not commercially available.

Packaging and storage
Store below 40 °C (104 °F), preferably between 15 and 30 °C (59 and 86 °F), unless otherwise specified by manufacturer. Store in collapsible tubes or tight containers.

Auxiliary labeling
• For vaginal use only.

Note
Include mandatory patient package insert (PPI) when dispensing.

Additional information
Applicator is not calibrated.

ESTRADIOL

Summary of Differences
Indications: Atrophic vaginitis, vulvar atrophy, and atrophic postmenopausal urethritis.
Pharmacology/pharmacokinetics: Natural estrogen easily absorbed vaginally without metabolism by vaginal mucosa; does not induce hepatic protein synthesis.
Medical considerations/Contraindications—Does not exacerbate existing hepatic function impairment; vaginal insert is more likely to be expelled or cause problems for women with narrow vaginas, vaginal prolapse or vaginal stenosis; cream may exacerbate allergy to parabens.
Side/Adverse effects: Vaginal insert, as a foreign device, may cause vaginal discomfort, pain, or ulceration.

Vaginal Dosage Forms
Note: Bracketed uses in the *Dosage Forms* section refer to categories of use or indications that are not included in U.S. product labeling.

ESTRADIOL VAGINAL CREAM USP

Usual adult dose
Atrophic vaginitis or
Vulvar atrophy—
Initial: Intravaginal, 200 to 400 mcg of estradiol (two to four grams of cream) daily for one or two weeks, the dosage then being gradually reduced to one-half the initial dosage for one or two weeks.
Maintenance: Intravaginal, 100 mcg of estradiol (one gram of cream) one to three times a week for three weeks with no medication used in the fourth week after vaginal mucosa is no longer atrophied; this schedule being repeated each month.

Usual geriatric dose
See *Usual adult dose.*

Strength(s) usually available
U.S.—
0.01% (Rx) [*Estrace* (2208 4000 CPS; edetate disodium; glyceryl monostearate; hydroxypropyl methylcellulose; methylparaben; propylene glycol; sodium lauryl sulfate; stearyl alcohol; tertiary-butylhydroquinone; water; white ceresin wax)].
Canada—
Not commercially available.

Packaging and storage
Store below 40 °C (104 °F), preferably between 15 and 30 °C (59 and 86 °F), unless otherwise specified by manufacturer. Store in collapsible tubes or tight containers.

Auxiliary labeling
• For vaginal use only.

Note
Include mandatory patient package insert (PPI) when dispensing.

Additional information
Calibrated applicator measures 1 to 4 grams of cream in increments of 1 gram.

ESTRADIOL VAGINAL INSERT
Note: Also called estradiol vaginal ring.

Usual adult dose
[Atrophic vaginitis] or
Urethritis, atrophic, postmenopausal or
[Vulvar atrophy, postmenopausal]—
Intravaginal, 2 mg (one vaginal insert) releases 7.5 mcg from its ring-shape over twenty-four hours when worn continuously high in the upper third of the vagina and is replaced every ninety days.

Usual geriatric dose
See *Usual adult dose.*

Strength(s) usually available
U.S.—
2 mg delivering 7.5 mcg per 24 hours (Rx) [*Estring* (barium sulfate in device; silicone polymers in device)].
Canada—
2 mg delivering 7.5 mcg per 24 hours (Rx) [*Estring* (barium sulfate in device; silicone polymers in device)].

Packaging and storage
Store below 40 °C (104 °F), preferably between 15 and 30 °C (59 and 86 °F), unless otherwise specified by manufacturer.

Auxiliary labeling
• For vaginal use only.

Note

Include mandatory patient package insert (PPI) when dispensing.

ESTRONE

Summary of Differences

Indications: Atrophic vaginitis, postmenopausal, and vulvar atrophy.

Pharmacology/pharmacokinetics: Natural estrogen easily absorbed vaginally without metabolism by vaginal mucosa; does not induce hepatic proteins synthesis.

Medical considerations/Contraindications—Does not exacerbate existing hepatic function impairment; cream may exacerbate allergy to parabens.

Vaginal Dosage Forms

ESTRONE VAGINAL CREAM

Usual adult dose

Atrophic vaginitis, postmenopausal or
Vulvar atrophy—
Intravaginal, 2 to 4 mg of estrone (two to four grams of cream) daily or as directed by physician based on the lowest dose needed.

Usual geriatric dose

See *Usual adult dose.*

Strength(s) usually available

U.S.—
Not commercially available.
Canada—
1 mg per gram (Rx) [*Oestrilin* (methylparaben; mineral oil; propylparaben)].

Packaging and storage

Store below 40 °C (104 °F), preferably between 15 and 30 °C (59 and 86 °F), in a well-closed container, unless otherwise specified by manufacturer.

Auxiliary labeling

- For vaginal use only.

Note

Include mandatory patient package insert (PPI) when dispensing.

Additional information

Calibrated applicator measures 1 to 4 grams of cream in increments of 1 gram.

ESTRONE VAGINAL SUPPOSITORIES

Note: Also called cones.

Usual adult dose

Atrophic vaginitis, postmenopausal or
Vulvar atrophy—
Intravaginal, 250 to 500 mcg daily or as directed by physician based on the lowest dose needed.

Usual geriatric dose

See *Usual adult dose.*

Strength(s) usually available

U.S.—
Not commercially available.
Canada—
250 mcg (Rx) [*Oestrilin* (gelatin; glycerin)].

Packaging and storage

Store below 40 °C (104 °F), preferably between 15 and 30 °C (59 and 86 °F), in a well-closed container, unless otherwise specified by manufacturer.

Auxiliary labeling

- For vaginal use only.

Note

Include mandatory patient package insert (PPI) when dispensing.

ESTROPIPATE

Summary of Differences

Indications: Atrophic vaginitis and vulvar atrophy.

Pharmacology/pharmacokinetics: Semi-synthetic estrogen.

Medical considerations/Contraindications—Cream may exacerbate allergy to parabens.

Vaginal Dosage Forms

ESTROPIPATE VAGINAL CREAM USP

Note: Formerly called piperazine estrone sulfate.

Usual adult dose

Atrophic vaginitis or
Vulvar atrophy—
Intravaginal, 3 to 6 mg of estropipate (two to four grams of cream) daily for three weeks with no medication used the fourth week, the schedule being repeated each month.

Usual geriatric dose

See *Usual adult dose.*

Strength(s) usually available

U.S.—
Not commercially available.
Canada—
Not commercially available.

Packaging and storage

Store below 40 °C (104 °F), preferably between 15 and 30 °C (59 and 86 °F), unless otherwise specified by manufacturer.

Auxiliary labeling

- For vaginal use only.

Note

Include mandatory patient package insert (PPI) when dispensing.

Additional information

Calibrated applicator measures 1 to 4 grams of cream in increments of 1 gram.

Selected Bibliography

Product Information: Premarin®, conjugated estrogens vaginal cream. Wyeth Pharmaceuticals, Inc., Philadelphia, PA, (PI revised 04/2004) PI reviewed 07/2004.

Revised: 07/19/2004

ESTROGENS AND PROGESTINS (Ovarian Hormone Therapy) Systemic

This monograph includes information on the following: 1) 17 beta–Estradiol and Norgestimate; 2) Ethinyl Estradiol and Norethindrone Acetate; 3) Estradiol and norethindrone.

INN:
Ethinyl Estradiol—Ethinylestradiol
Norethindrone—Norethisterone

BAN:
Ethinyl estradiol—Ethinyloestradiol
Norethindrone—Norethisterone

JAN:
Ethinyl Estradiol—Ethinylestradiol
Norethindrone—Norethisterone

VA CLASSIFICATION (Primary): HS105

Commonly used brand name(s): *Activella[3]; Ortho-Prefest[1]; femhrt[2].*

Note: For a listing of dosage forms and brand names by country availability, see *Dosage Forms* section(s).

Category

Estrogen-progestin—17 beta-Estradiol and norgestimate tablets; Ethinyl estradiol and norethindrone tablets.

Ovarian hormone therapy agent—17 beta-Estradiol and norgestimate tablets; Ethinyl estradiol and norethindrone tablets.

Osteoporosis prophylactic—17 beta-Estradiol and norgestimate tablets; Ethinyl estradiol and norethindrone tablets

Indications

Accepted

Menopause, vasomotor symptoms of (treatment) or
Vaginal atrophy (treatment) or
Vulvar atrophy (treatment)—17 beta-Estradiol and norgestimate tablets and estradiol and norethindrone tablets are indicated in the treatment of vaginal or vulvar atrophy, and moderate to severe vasomotor symp-

toms associated with menopause. Ethinyl estradiol and norethindrone tablets are indicated in the treatment of moderate to severe vasomotor symptoms associated with menopause.

Osteoporosis, postmenopausal (prophylaxis)—17 beta-Estradiol and norgestimate tablets, ethinyl estradiol and norethindrone tablets, and estradiol and norethindrone tablets are indicated in postmenopausal women to retard bone loss and estrogen deficiency–induced osteoporosis. Replacing estrogen can reduce the rate of bone loss and fractures in postmenopausal women. Proper diet, elemental calcium supplementation, and weight bearing exercise should also be encouraged along with estrogen replacement.

Unaccepted

The use of estrogens and progestins to reduce postpartum breast engorgement is not recommended.

The use of estrogen and progestin combinations in hysterectomized women is not recommended.

Pharmacology/Pharmacokinetics

Physicochemical characteristics

Chemical Group—

Estrogens—
- 17 beta-estradiol
- Ethinyl estradiol
- Estradiol (E_2)

Progestins, 19-nortestosterone derivatives—
- Norethindrone acetate
- Norgestimate

Molecular weight—
- 17 beta-estradiol: 272.39.
- Ethinyl estradiol: 296.41.
- Estradiol (E_2): 281.4.
- Norethindrone acetate: 340.47.
- Norgestimate: 369.50.

Mechanism of action/Effect

At the cellular level, estrogens increase the synthesis of DNA, RNA, and various proteins in target tissues including the breasts and genitourinary structures.

For treatment of genitourinary atrophy and vasomotor symptoms—

In healthy females, estrogens maintain genitourinary function and vasomotor stability. By direct action, they cause growth and development of reproductive organs and help to maintain the tone and elasticity of the urogenital tract. Circulating estrogens regulate pituitary secretion of gonadotropins, luteinizing hormone (LH), and follicle stimulating hormone (FSH) via a negative feedback loop. Progestins counter estrogenic effects by decreasing the number of estrogen receptors, suppressing epithelial DNA synthesis in endometrial tissue, increasing local metabolism of estrogen to less active metabolites, and inducing gene products that blunt cellular responses to estrogen.

For prevention of postmenopausal osteoporosis—

During periods of estrogen deficiency, the rate of bone resorption by osteoclasts greatly exceeds the rate of bone formation by osteoblasts. Replacing estrogen prevents this accelerated bone loss by inhibiting bone resorption to a level where the near equilibrium between bone resorption and formation is restored. However, estrogens do not replace previously lost bone or significantly increase total bone mass.

Absorption

Both estrogen and progestin components are rapidly and well absorbed.

Ethinyl estradiol and norethindrone—Absolute bioavailability is 55% and 64%, respectively; both components undergo first-pass metabolism. Ethinyl estradiol may also undergo enterohepatic recirculation.

Distribution

Widely distributed throughout the body; concentrations generally higher in the sex hormone target organs

Ethinyl estradiol and norethindrone: Volume of distribution (Vol_D)—2 to 4 L per kg of body weight.

Protein binding

17 beta-estradiol and norgestimate—estradiol binds to albumin and sex hormone binding globulin (SHBG) while 17–deacetylnorgestimate (the primary active metabolite of norgestimate) binds with high affinity (99%) to serum proteins but not to SHBG.

Ethinyl estradiol and norethindrone—High (> 95%); ethinyl estradiol binds to albumin only, whereas norethindrone binds to both albumin and SHBG.

Estradiol and norethindrone—Very high (90% or more); estradiol binds to albumin (61%) and sex hormone binding globulin (SHBG) (37%) while norethindrone binds to albumin (61%) and SHBBG (36%) to a similar extent.

Biotransformation

In the liver, many estrogens are interconverted to various forms. Estrogens may be glucuronidated or sulfated via enterohepatic recirculation. These compounds are secreted into the intestines, then hydrolized and reabsorbed. Estradiol is reversibly converted to estrone; both compounds can be converted to estriol. Norgestimate is metabolized to 17–deacetylnorgestimate via first pass mechanisms in the gastrointestinal tract and liver.Norethindrone is reduced, then undergoes sulfate and glucuronide conjugation.

Elimination

17 beta-estradiol—16 hours
17–deacetylnorgestimate—37 hours
Ethinyl estradiol—24 hours
Estradiol—12 to 14 hours.
Norethindrone—8 to 13 hours

Time to peak concentration

17 beta-estradiol—7 hours
17–deacetylnorgestimate—2 hours
Ethinyl estradiol—1 to 2 hours
Estradiol—7 hours
Norethindrone—1 to 2 hours

Peak steady state concentration—

17 beta-estradiol—49.7 pg per mL

17–deacetylnorgestimate—643 pg per mL

Ethinyl estradiol—38.3 ng per mL

Estradiol—33 to 47% above levels following single dose administration (34.6 pg per mL)

Norethindrone—7.5 ng per mL

Elimination

Primarily renal, as metabolites, glucuronide and sulfate conjugates*me fecal.

Ethinyl estradiol—
- Renal: 22 to 58%.
- Fecal: 30 to 53%.
- Biliary: 26 to 43%.

Norethindrone—
- Renal: 37 to 87%, of which 3% is unchanged, and 40% is excreted as glucuronide and 15% as sulfate conjugates.
- Fecal: Up to 40%.

Norgestimate—
- Renal: 45 to 49%.
- Fecal: 16 to 49%.

Precautions to Consider

Carcinogenicity/Tumorigenicity

The risk of endometrial cancer in unopposed estrogen users, which appears to depend on duration of treatment and dose, is about 2 to 12 times greater than in nonusers. The risk increases to 15 to 24–fold when the duration of use increases to five to ten or more years, and persists for at least 8 to 15 years after discontinuation of therapy. Risk reduction occurs when estrogen therapy is opposed with progestins.

Whether the use of systemic estrogens increases the incidence of breast cancer in some postmenopausal women is unresolved. Some studies have reported relative risks of 1.3 to 2.0 for breast cancer in patients taking high doses and patients taking lower doses over long periods of time (e.g. greater than 10 years). Other studies have reported breast cancer rates similar to the background rate for women not on hormone replacement therapy. Progestin therapy appears to impart no benefits in terms of decreasing the risk of breast cancer development.

Continuous, long-term administration of estrogens in certain animal species resulted in increases in the incidence of carcinomas of the breast, cervix, liver, testis, uterus and vagina.

Pregnancy/Reproduction

Pregnancy—Estrogen/progestin combinations should be avoided during pregnancy. Risk-benefit must be carefully considered.

FDA Pregnancy Category X

Breast-feeding

Estrogens and progestins are distributed into breast milk. The effect of this on the nursing infant has not been determined. Decreases in milk quantity and quality have been observed in nursing mothers who took estrogens. Estrogens are not indicated for the prevention of postpartum breast engorgement.

Pediatrics

Estrogen/progestin combinations are not indicated for children.

Geriatrics

Appropriate studies on the relationship of age to the effects of estrogens and progestins have not been performed in the geriatric population.

Drug interactions and/or related problems

The following drug interactions and/or related problems have been selected on the basis of their potential clinical significance (possible mechanism in parentheses where appropriate)—not necessarily inclusive (» = major clinical significance):

Note: Combinations containing any of the following medications, depending on the amount present, may also interact with this medication.

Acetaminophen or
Ascorbic acid or
Atorvastatin
(plasma concentrations of ethinyl estradiol may be increased)

Acetaminophen or
Aspirin or
Clofibric acid or
Morphine or
Temazepam
(decreased plasma concentrations or increased clearance of these drugs may occur when given concomitantly with ethinyl estradiol)

Anticonvulsants, such as
Carbamazepine or
Phenobarbital or
Phenytoin
Rifampin
(plasma concentrations of ethinyl estradiol may be decreased)

» Cyclosporine or
Prednisolone or
Theophylline
(metabolism of these drugs may be inhibited by ethinyl estradiol; increased plasma concentrations have been reported)

Laboratory value alterations

The following have been selected on the basis of their potential clinical significance (possible effect in parentheses where appropriate)—not necessarily inclusive (» = major clinical significance).

With diagnostic test results

Glucose tolerance test
(may increase the glucose tolerance test results)

Metapyrone test
(reduced response)

Thyroid function tests, such as
Thyroxine (T_4) determinations
Triiodothyronine (T_3) determinations
(total thyroid hormone, T_4, or T_3 may be increased and values for the T_3 uptake test may be decreased because of an increase in thyroid-binding globulin [TBG]; free T_3 and thyroxine [T_4] concentrations remain unaltered)

With physiology/laboratory test values

Anti-factor Xa and
Antithrombin III and
Factor VII and
Folate
Lipoproteins, low density (LDL) and
Plasminogen activator inhibitor-1
(serum concentrations may be decreased)

Alpha-1–antitrypsin and
Angiotensinogen/renin substrate and
Ceruloplasmin and
Clotting factors II, VII, VIII, IX, X and XII and
Corticosteroid binding globulin (CBG) and
Fibrinogen and
Glucose—especially in diabetic or prediabetic patients taking larger doses of estrogens, and
Lipoproteins, high density (HDL) and
Plasminogen antigen and
Platelets and
Sex-hormone binding globulin (SHBG) and
Triglycerides
(serum concentrations may be increased)

» Calcium
(increased serum concentrations, especially for patients with bone cancer or metastatic breast cancer)

Partial thromboplastin time
Platelet aggregation time
Prothrombin time
(may be increased)

Medical considerations/Contraindications

The medical considerations/contraindications included have been selected on the basis of their potential clinical significance (reasons given in parentheses where appropriate)—not necessarily inclusive (» = major clinical significance).

Except under special circumstances, this medication should not be used when the following medical problems exist:

» Breast cancer, known or suspected
(possible promotion of tumor growth may occur)

» Genital or uterine bleeding, abnormal and undiagnosed

» Hepatic dysfunction or disease
(estrogens should not be used in women with these conditions)

» Hypersensitivity to estrogens, progestins, or any of the components of the product prescribed

» Neoplasia, estrogen-dependent, known or suspected
(possible promotion of tumor growth may occur)

» Pregnancy, known or suspected

» Thrombophlebitis or thromboembolic disorders, active or past history or

» Deep vein thrombosis, active or history of or

» Pulmonary embolism, active or history of
(estrogens should not be used in women with any of these conditions)

Risk-benefit should be considered when the following medical problems exist:

Asthma or
Diabetes mellitus or
Epilepsy or
Hepatic hemangiomas or
Lupus erythematosus, systemic or
Migraine or
Porphyria
(estrogens should be used with caution; may cause exacerbation of these conditions)

Cardiac or renal dysfunction
(conditions which might be influenced by fluid retention warrant careful observation when patient is taking estrogen; estrogens may cause some degree of fluid retention)

Endometriosis
(endometrial implants and endometriosis may be aggravated by use of estrogen alone therapy; the addition of a progestin should be considered in women who have undergone hysterectomy but are known to have residual endometriosis)

Gallbladder disease, or history of
Hepatic function impairment or
Cholestatic jaundice, history of
(estrogens may be poorly metabolized in patients with impaired hepatic function; patients with history of cholestatic jaundice associated with past estrogen use or with pregnancy, caution should be exercised; if case of recurrence, medication should be discontinued)

» Hypercalcemia associated with bone or metastatic breast cancer
(severe hypercalcemia may occur in patients with bone cancer or metastatic breast cancer who are treated with estrogens)

» Hyperlipoproteinemia, familial or
» Hypertriglyceridemia or
» Pancreatitis
(increased triglycerides may lead to or exacerbate pancreatitis in susceptible individuals)

Hypocalcemia, severe
(estrogens should be used with caution)

Hypothyroidism
(estrogens lead to increased thyroid binding globulin [TBG] levels; patients dependent upon thyroid hormone replacement therapy who are also receiving estrogens may need to increase the dose of their thyroid replacement therapy)

» Visual abnormalities including
Diplopia, sudden onset or
Migraine, sudden onset or
Proptosis, sudden onset or
Vision loss, partial or complete
(discontinue medication pending examination if any of these conditions occur; if examination reveals papilledema or retinal vascular lesions estrogens should be stopped; retinal vascular thrombosis has been reported in patients receiving estrogens)

Patient monitoring

The following may be especially important in patient monitoring (other tests may be warranted in some patients, depending on condition; » = major clinical significance):

Blood pressure determinations and
Breast examination or
Mammogram and
Papanicolaou (Pap) test and
Physical examinations
(recommended as determined by physician—generally every 12 months. Special attention should be given to breast, liver, and pelvic area in the physical examination and patient should be taught to perform periodic self-examination of breasts)

Endometrial biopsy
(should be considered periodically as necessary in patients with an intact uterus; patients with a uterus should be monitored for signs of endometrial cancer and malignancy should be ruled out in cases of persistent or abnormal vaginal bleeding; there is no risk of endometrial cancer in patients who have undergone a hysterectomy)

Hepatic function determinations
(recommended at regular intervals, especially during therapy in patients who have or are suspected of having hepatic disease)

Lipid profile, serum and
Lipoprotein profile, serum
(recommended in patients with familial defects of lipoprotein metabolism)

Side/Adverse Effects

The following side/adverse effects have been selected on the basis of their potential clinical significance (possible signs and symptoms in parentheses where appropriate)—not necessarily inclusive:

Those indicating need for medical attention

Incidence more frequent

Breast pain or tenderness; hypertension (dizziness or light-headedness; headache); ***peripheral edema*** (swelling of feet and lower legs; rapid weight gain); ***upper respiratory tract infection*** (cough, fever, sneezing, or sore throat); ***vaginal bleeding***

Incidence less frequent or rare

Breast tumors (breast lumps; discharge from nipple); ***endometrial hyperplasia*** (change in vaginal discharge; pain or feeling of pressure in pelvis; vaginal bleeding); ***gallbladder obstruction; liver dysfunction, or; pancreatitis*** (nausea and vomiting; pains in stomach, side, or abdomen; yellow eyes or skin); ***thrombus formation*** (severe or sudden headache; sudden loss of coordination; pains in chest, groin, or leg, especially calf; sudden and unexplained shortness of breath; sudden slurred speech; sudden vision changes; weakness or numbness in arm or leg)

Those indicating need for medical attention only if they continue or are bothersome

Incidence more frequent

Back pain; dizziness; fatigue (general feeling of tiredness); ***flatulence*** (bloating or gas); ***flu-like symptoms; headache; insomnia*** (sleeplessness); ***mental depression; muscle aches; nausea; vaginitis***

Overdose

For more information on the management of overdose or unintentional ingestion, **contact a poison control center** (see *Poison Control Center Listing*).

Clinical effects of overdose

No serious ill effects have been reported following acute ingestion of large doses of estrogen/progestin-containing oral contraceptives by young children. The following effects have been selected on the basis of their potential clinical significance (possible signs and symptoms in parentheses where appropriate)—not necessarily inclusive:

Nausea or vomiting; withdrawal bleeding

Treatment of overdose

Treatment of overdose is symptomatic.

Patients in whom intentional overdose is known or suspected should be referred for psychiatric consultation.

Patient Consultation

As an aid to patient consultation, refer to *Advice for the Patient, Estrogens and Progestins (Ovarian Hormone Therapy) (Systemic).*

In providing consultation, consider emphasizing the following selected information (» = major clinical significance)

Before using this medication

» Conditions affecting use, especially:
Hypersensitivity to estrogens or progestins or any component of the product prescribed
Carcinogenicity—Increased risk of endometrial cancer for patients with intact uteri placed on unopposed estrogen therapy; decreased risk occurs when used with a progestin; continuous, long-term estrogen use in animal studies increased frequency of cancers of the breast, cervix, and liver
Pregnancy—Not recommended for use during pregnancy
Breast-feeding—Estrogens and progestins are distributed into breast milk
Other medications, especially cyclosporine
Other medical problems, especially abnormal or undiagnosed genital or uterine bleeding; active thrombophlebitis or thromboembolic disorders; breast cancer, known or suspected; deep vein thrombosis (active or history of); estrogen-dependent neoplasia; hepatic dysfunction or disease; history of estrogen-induced thrombophlebitis, thrombosis, or thromboembolic disorders; hypercalcemia associated with bone cancer or metastatic breast cancer; hyperlipoproteinemia (familial); pancreatitis, pulmonary embolism (active or history of); or visual abnormalities

Proper use of this medication

» Reading patient package insert carefully
» Compliance with therapy
» Proper dosing
Missed dose: Taking or using as soon as possible; not using if almost time for next dose; not doubling doses
» Proper storage

Precautions while using this medication

» Regular visits to physician every year, or more often, as determined by physician
» Checking breast by self-examination regularly and having clinical examination and mammography as required by physician; reporting unusual breast lumps or discharge
» Understanding that menstrual bleeding may begin again; checking with doctor immediately if uterine bleeding is unusual or continuous
If scheduled for laboratory tests, telling physician about taking estrogens; certain blood tests are affected

Side/adverse effects

Irregular vaginal bleeding or spotting may occur in many postmenopausal patients with an intact uterus who are placed on continuous estrogen therapy with a progestin

Signs of potential side effects, especially breast pain or tenderness, enlargement of breasts in females, peripheral edema, amenorrhea, breakthrough bleeding, menorrhagia, or spotting; breast tumors; gallbladder obstruction, hepatitis, or pancreatitis

General Dosing Information

It is recommended that the patient package insert be given to patients.

In general, combination estrogen/progestin therapy should be administered at the lowest effective dosage. The recommended dose may not be the lowest effective dose for treatment of vulvar and vaginal atrophy or for the prevention of osteoporosis. Patients should be reevaluated at three- to six-month intervals to determine if treatment is still necessary for symptoms.

17 beta-estradiol and Norgestimate

Oral Dosage Forms

17 BETA-ESTRADIOL AND NORGESTIMATE TABLETS

Usual adult dose

Menopause, vasomotor symptoms of (treatment) or
Vaginal atrophy (treatment) or
Vulvar atrophy (treatment)—
Oral, 1 mg estradiol for three days followed by 1 mg of estradiol combined with 0.09 mg of norgestimate for three days. The regimen is repeated continuously without interruption.

Osteoporosis, postmenopausal (prophylaxis)—
Oral, 1 mg estradiol for three days followed by 1 mg of estradiol combined with 0.09 mg of norgestimate for three days. The regimen is repeated continuously without interruption.

Strength(s) usually available

U.S.—

Intermittent formulation:

1 mg estradiol (three days) followed by 1 mg estradiol and 0.09 mg norgestimate (three days) (Rx) [*Ortho-Prefest* (croscarmellose sodium; microcrystalline cellulose; magnesium stearate; ferric oxide red; lactose monohydrate)].

Note: Product is packaged as 30 tablets (15 of each type) encased in a blister card, with weekly schedule stickers which are to be placed on the card by the patient.

Packaging and storage

Store at 25 °C (77 °F); excursions permitted to 15–30 °C (59–86 °F)

Note

Include patient package inserts (PPIs) when dispensing.

Ethinyl Estradiol and Norethindrone

Oral Dosage Forms

ETHINYL ESTRADIOL AND NORETHINDRONE TABLETS

Usual adult dose

Menopause, vasomotor symptoms of (treatment)—

Oral, 2.5 mcg (0.025 mg) ethinyl estradiol and 0.5 mg norethindrone once daily.

Osteoporosis, postmenopausal (prophylaxis)—

Oral, 2.5 mcg (0.025 mg) ethinyl estradiol and 0.5 mg norethindrone once daily.

Note: The dose should be periodically reassessed for lowest effective dose and to determine if treatment is still necessary.

Strength(s) usually available

U.S.—

Continuous formulation:

2.5 mcg (0.025 mg) ethinyl estradiol and 5 mcg (0.5 mg) norethindrone (Rx) [*femhrt* (calcium stearate; lactose monohydrate; microcrystalline cellulose; cornstarch)].

5 mcg (0.05 mg) ethinyl estradiol and 1 mg norethindrone (Rx) [*femhrt* (calcium stearate; lactose monohydrate; microcrystalline cellulose; cornstarch)].

Packaging and storage

Store at 25 °C (77 °F); excursions permitted to 15–30 °C (59–86 °F)

Note

Include patient package inserts (PPIs) when dispensing.

Estradiol and Norethindrone

Oral Dosage Forms

ESTRADIOL (E_2) AND NORETHINDRONE TABLETS

Usual adult dose

Menopause, vasomotor symptoms of (treatment) or
Vaginal atrophy (treatment) or
Vulvular atrophy (treatment)—

Oral, 1 mg estradiol and 0.5 mg norethindrone once daily.

Osteoporosis, postmenopausal (prophylaxis)—

Oral, 1 mg estradiol and 0.5 mg norethindrone a day.

Strength(s) usually available

U.S.—

Continuous formulation:

1 mg estradiol and 0.5 mg norethindrone (Rx) [*Activella* (lactose monohydrate; cornstarch; copovidone; talc; magnesium stearate; hydroxypropylmethylcellulose; triacetin)].

Packaging and storage

Store in a dry place protected from light at 25 °C (77 °F); excursions permitted to 15–30 °C (59–86 °F)

Note

Include patient package inserts (PPIs) when dispensing.

Revised: 03/25/2005
Developed: 04/10/2000

ESTROGENS AND PROGESTINS ORAL CONTRACEPTIVES Systemic

This monograph includes information on the following: 1) Desogestrel and Ethinyl Estradiol; 2) Ethynodiol Diacetate and Ethinyl Estradiol; 3) Levonorgestrel and Ethinyl Estradiol; 4) Norethindrone Acetate and Ethinyl Estradiol; 5) Norethindrone and Ethinyl Estradiol; 6) Norethindrone and Mestranol; 7) Norgestimate and Ethinyl Estradiol; 8) Norgestrel and Ethinyl Estradiol.

Note: For information pertaining to the use of progestin-only contraceptives, see *Progestins (Systemic)*.

INN:

Ethinyl estradiol—Ethinylestradiol
Ethynodiol diacetate—Etynodiol
Norethindrone—Norethisterone

BAN:

Ethinyl estradiol—Ethinyloestradiol
Ethynodiol diacetate—Ethynodiol
Norethindrone—Norethisterone

JAN:

Ethinyl estradiol—Ethinylestradiol
Ethynodiol diacetate—Etynodiol acetate
Norethindrone—Norethisterone

VA CLASSIFICATION (Primary/Secondary): HS104/HS109

Commonly used brand name(s): *Alesse*[3]; *Brevicon*[5]; *Brevicon 0.5/35*[5]; *Brevicon 1/35*[5]; *Cyclen*[7]; *Cyclessa*[1]; *Demulen 1/35*[2]; *Demulen 1/50*[2]; *Demulen 30*[2]; *Demulen 50*[2]; *Desogen*[1]; *Estrostep*[4]; *Estrostep Fe*[4]; *Genora 0.5/35*[5]; *Genora 1/35*[5]; *Genora 1/50*[6]; *Intercon 0.5/35*[5]; *Intercon 1/35*[5]; *Intercon 1/50*[6]; *Jenest*[5]; *Levlen*[3]; *Levlite*[3]; *Levora 0.15/30*[3]; *Lo/Ovral*[8]; *Loestrin 1/20*[4]; *Loestrin 1.5/30*[4]; *Loestrin Fe 1/20*[4]; *Loestrin Fe 1.5/30*[4]; *Marvelon*[1]; *Min-Ovral*[3]; *Minestrin 1/20*[4]; *Mircette*[1]; *ModiCon*[5]; *N.E.E. 1/35*[5]; *N.E.E. 1/50*[5]; *Necon 0.5/35*[5]; *Necon 10/11*[5]; *Necon 1/35*[5]; *Necon 1/50*[6]; *Nelova 10/11*[5]; *Nelova 0.5/35E*[5]; *Nelova 1/35E*[5]; *Nelova 1/50M*[6]; *Nordette*[3]; *Norethin 1/35E*[5]; *Norethin 1/50M*[6]; *Norinyl 1+35*[5]; *Norinyl 1+50*[6]; *Norinyl 1/50*[6]; *Ortho 0.5/35*[5]; *Ortho 10/11*[5]; *Ortho 1/35*[5]; *Ortho 7/7/7*[5]; *Ortho Tri-Cyclen*[7]; *Ortho-Cept*[1]; *Ortho-Cyclen*[7]; *Ortho-Novum 10/11*[5]; *Ortho-Novum 1/35*[5]; *Ortho-Novum 1/50*[6]; *Ortho-Novum 7/7/7*[5]; *Ovcon-35*[5]; *Ovcon-50*[5]; *Ovral*[8]; *Select 1/35*[5]; *Synphasic*[5]; *Tri-Cyclen*[7]; *Tri-Levlen*[3]; *Tri-Norinyl*[5]; *Triphasil*[3]; *Triquilar*[3]; *Trivora*[3]; *Zovia 1/35E*[2]; *Zovia 1/50E*[2].

Other commonly used names are Ethinylestradiol and Ethinyloestradiol [Ethinyl estradiol]; Ethynodiol, Etynodiol, and Etynodiol acetate [Ethynodiol diacetate]; and Norethindrone [Norethisterone].

Note: For a listing of dosage forms and brand names by country availability, see *Dosage Forms* section(s).

Category

Contraceptive, systemic—Desogestrel and Ethinyl Estradiol; Ethynodiol Diacetate and Ethinyl Estradiol; Levonorgestrel and Ethinyl Estradiol; Norethindrone Acetate and Ethinyl Estradiol; Norethindrone and Ethinyl Estradiol; Norethindrone and Mestranol; Norgestimate and Ethinyl Estradiol; Norgestrel and Ethinyl Estradiol.

Antiacne agent, systemic—Norethindrone Acetate and Ethinyl Estradiol (Triphasic formulation only); Norgestimate and Ethinyl Estradiol (Triphasic formulation only).

Antiendometriotic agent—Desogestrel and Ethinyl Estradiol; Ethynodiol Diacetate and Ethinyl Estradiol; Levonorgestrel and Ethinyl Estradiol; Norethindrone Acetate and Ethinyl Estradiol; Norethindrone and Ethinyl Estradiol; Norethindrone and Mestranol; Norgestimate and Ethinyl Estradiol; Norgestrel and Ethinyl Estradiol.

Contraceptive, postcoital (systemic)—Levonorgestrel and Ethinyl Estradiol; Norgestrel and Ethinyl Estradiol.

Estrogen-progestin—Desogestrel and Ethinyl Estradiol; Ethynodiol Diacetate and Ethinyl Estradiol; Levonorgestrel and Ethinyl Estradiol; Norethindrone Acetate and Ethinyl Estradiol; Norethindrone and Ethinyl Estradiol; Norethindrone and Mestranol; Norgestimate and Ethinyl Estradiol; Norgestrel and Ethinyl Estradiol.

Gonadotropin inhibitor, female, noncontraceptive use—Desogestrel and Ethinyl Estradiol; Ethynodiol Diacetate and Ethinyl Estradiol; Levonorgestrel and Ethinyl Estradiol; Norethindrone Acetate and Ethinyl Estradiol; Norethindrone and Ethinyl Estradiol; Norethindrone and Mestranol; Norgestimate and Ethinyl Estradiol; Norgestrel and Ethinyl Estradiol

Indications

Note: Bracketed information in the *Indications* section refers to uses that are not included in U.S. product labeling.

Accepted

Pregnancy, prevention of—Combination estrogen-progestin oral contraceptives are indicated for the prevention of pregnancy. The lowest expected failure rate for women who use oral contraceptives consistently and correctly under clinical conditions is 0.1% in the first year of use; however, under nonclinical conditions the typical use is less perfect and typical failures may range from 0 to 6%. All regimens are considered equally effective for preventing pregnancy.

The following table presents the results of studies examining contraceptive failure rates calculated using the life-table method. The first column lists the contraceptive method used. The second column indicates the percentage of women experiencing an accidental pregnancy in the first year of use of a contraceptive method while using the method perfectly under clinical conditions. The range of failure rates in the clinical trials may be explained by interstudy variations in study design or patient population characteristics, such as motivation, fecundity, or socioeconomic factors (including education). The third column indicates contraceptive failure rates in the first year of contraceptive use under clinical conditions for typical couples who start using a method (not necessarily for the first time). Failure rates among adolescents may be higher due to poorer compliance than in other age groups.

Method used	*Failure rate range (over 12 months) in clinical studies (%)*	*Typical first year failure rate (%)*
None	78–94	85
Spermicides*	0.3–37	21
Periodic abstinence†	13–35	20
Withdrawal	7–22	19
Cervical cap with spermicide	6–27	18
Diaphragm with spermicide	2–23	18
Condom without spermicide	2–14	12
IUD		
Progesterone-releasing	1.9–2	2
Copper-T 200	3–3.6	
Copper-T 200Ag‡	0–1.2	
Copper-T 220C§	0.9–1.8	
Copper-T 380A	0.5–0.8	0.8
Copper-T 380S	0.9	
Oral contraceptive		3
Estrogen and progestin	0–6	
Progestin only	1–10	
Medroxyprogesterone injection (90-day)	0–0.3	0.3
Levonorgestrel (subdermal)		
Six implants	0–0.09	0.09
Two rods	0–0.2	0.3
Sterilization		
Female#	0–8	0.4
Male	0–0.5	0.15

*Spermicides studied include creams, foams, gels, jellies, and suppositories.

†Methods studied include calendar, ovulation method, and symptothermal (cervical mucus method supplemented by basal body temperature post-ovulation).

‡Life-table method rate is unavailable for Copper-T 200Ag and the Pearl method rate at 12 months was reported; these methods at 12 months are considered comparable.

§Copper-T 220C is manufactured with copper sleeves instead of copper wire; often used as a control in clinical studies.

#Methods studied include culdotomy laparoscopy, minilaparotomy, electrocoagulation, laparotomy, tubal diathermy and/or use of rings or clips.

[Contraception, emergency postcoital (prophylaxis)][1]—A combination of levonorgestrel or norgestrel with ethinyl estradiol is used as emergency contraception (also called intraception, morning-after treatment, or postcoital contraception) for postcoital birth control, after pregnancy has been ruled out. The dosing method using high doses of estrogen-progestin hormones is commonly called the Yuzpe method. Using oral contraceptives for emergency postcoital contraception is preferable to using ethinyl estradiol alone because, although the failure rate is higher (2% versus 1%) with oral contraceptives, they cause fewer and less severe side effects to occur. Treatment is initiated within the first 72 hours, preferably within the first 12 hours, after unprotected intercourse.

Acne vulgaris (treatment)[1]—The triphasic formulation of norgestimate and ethinyl estradiol and the triphasic formulation of norethindrone and ethinyl estradiol are indicated to treat moderate acne vulgaris in females, 15 years of age or older, who have no known contraindications to oral contraceptive therapy, desire oral contraception, have achieved menarche, plan to stay on it for at least 6 months, and are unresponsive to topical anti-acne medications.

[Amenorrhea (treatment)] or
[Dysfunctional uterine bleeding (DUB) (treatment)] or
[Dysmenorrhea (treatment)] or
[Hypermenorrhea (treatment)]—[Norethindrone and mestranol tablets (dose of 1/50)] are indicated [and other estrogen-progestin combinations and doses are used][1] as a hormonal treatment for hypoestrogenic or hyperandrogenic conditions, which may present as menstrual cycle abnormalities or unusual uterine bleeding, such as amenorrhea, dysfunctional uterine bleeding, or hypermenorrhea. When treating amenorrhea and hypermenorrhea, the abnormality should be diagnosed first and then treated appropriately; oral contraceptives have limited use for treating conditions not caused by a hypoestrogenic or hyperandrogenic state. Patients who require contraception as well as relief from primary dysmenorrhea may benefit from treatment with oral contraceptives. If contraception is not needed, prostaglandin-inhibiting medications, such as nonsteroidal anti-inflammatory drugs (NSAIDs), are used. If dysmenorrhea is not relieved by oral contraceptives or NSAIDs, endometriosis or another organic cause should be considered.

Endometriosis (prophylaxis and treatment)—[Norethindrone and mestranol tablets (dose of 1/50)] are indicated [and other estrogen-progestin combinations and doses are used][1] to reduce the size and growth of endometrial tissue.

[Hirsutism, female (treatment and treatment adjunct)][1] or
[Hyperandrogenism, ovarian (treatment and treatment adjunct)][1] or
[Polycystic ovary syndrome (treatment)][1]—When treating these conditions, the basic cause should be ascertained first, if possible, and treated accordingly. When contraception is needed as well, oral contraceptives are used to help suppress hypothalamic-pituitary function in luteinizing hormone–dependent hyperandrogenism in conditions such as polycystic ovary syndrome. Oral contraceptive treatment results in regularity of the menstrual cycle and lessening of hirsutism in these conditions.

Acceptance not established

Only limited data are available evaluating the use of oral contraceptives as adjunct agents to replace the estrogen component as *add-back therapy* when gonadotropin-releasing hormone agonists are used to suppress the hypothalamic-pituitary axis. Using oral contraceptives as the estrogen replacement may be especially useful in women needing contraception as well. By replacing estrogen, hypoestrogenic side effects caused by the gonadotropin-releasing hormone agonist, such as bone loss and the associated vasomotor symptoms, are reduced. Further studies are needed to evaluate the safety and efficacy of this use.

Oral contraceptives, which are effective in dysmenorrhea, have been used to reduce premenstrual pain associated with the *premenstrual syndrome* in some patients, but generally oral contraceptives are not considered useful for this indication.

Unaccepted

Administration of oral contraceptives to induce withdrawal bleeding should not be used as a test for pregnancy.

Oral contraceptives should not be used during pregnancy for the treatment of threatened or habitual abortion.

[1]Not included in Canadian product labeling.

Pharmacology/Pharmacokinetics

Physicochemical characteristics

Chemical Group—
Estrogens—
Ethinyl estradiol.
Mestranol.

Progestins, 19-nortestosterone derivatives—
Desogestrel.
Ethynodiol diacetate.
Levonorgestrel (levorotatory isomer).
Norethindrone.
Norethindrone acetate.
Norgestimate.
Norgestrel (racemic mixture).

Molecular weight—
- Desogestrel: 310.48.
- Ethinyl estradiol: 296.41.
- Ethynodiol diacetate: 384.52.
- Levonorgestrel: 312.45.
- Mestranol: 310.44.
- Norethindrone: 298.43.
- Norethindrone acetate: 340.47.
- Norgestimate: 369.51.
- Norgestrel: 312.45.

Mechanism of action/Effect

Estrogen-progestin—Estrogens increase the cellular synthesis of chromatin (DNA), RNA, and various proteins in responsive tissues, and progestins increase the synthesis of RNA by means of an interaction with DNA.

Contraceptive, systemic—The synergistic anti-ovulatory effect from the combined use of estrogen and progestin directly decreases the secretion of the gonadotropin-releasing hormone (GnRH) from the hypothalamus and is considered the main action. This negative feedback mechanism disrupts ovulation by interfering with the hypothalamus-pituitary-ovary axis and gonadotropin secretion from the pituitary. Specifically, the progestin component blunts or suppresses luteinizing hormone (LH) release and the LH surge, which is necessary for ovulation, and the estrogen component blunts or suppresses the follicle-stimulating hormone (FSH), which prevents the selection and maturation of the dominant follicle. Neither the estrogen nor the progestin hormone dose used in combination hormonal oral contraceptives alone would be able to suppress ovulation but together the estrogen and progestin hormones work synergistically to suppress ovulation successfully. Other contributing effects include delayed maturation of the endometrium, which prevents implantation of ova; and the development of viscous cervical mucus, which slows spermatic ingress. The effects on the endometrium and cervical mucus are considered the mechanisms of action for the estrogen-progestin oral contraceptives used for emergency contraception (intraception).

Antiendometriotic agent—Oral contraceptives can produce a pseudopregnant state (especially when used continuously) in which the uterine endometrium and ectopic endometriotic implants undergo decidual reaction, necrosis, and eventual atrophy. Sometimes endometriotic symptoms may increase before improvement is noted.

Gonadotropin inhibitor, female, noncontraceptive use—Suppressed ovarian steroidogenesis secondary to LH concentration reduction prevents ovarian cyst formation in functional ovarian cysts, corpus luteum cysts, or polycystic ovary syndrome. Although a decrease in occurrence of repetitively forming functional ovarian cysts is possible, treatment to either speed the resolution of existing ovarian cysts or to treat functional ovarian cysts secondary to ovulation induction has not been established. The likelihood of suppressing ovarian cyst formation is greatest with 50-mcg ethinyl estradiol–containing monophasic formulations but 35-mcg ethinyl estradiol–containing monophasic formulations are used effectively, also. Suppression is least likely with triphasic formulations. In addition to suppression of ovarian steroidogenesis, there is an increase in sex hormone-binding globulin, which binds testosterone and decreases the quantity of free hormone. This effectively reduces the androgenic symptoms of hirsutism, polycystic ovary syndrome, and hyperandrogenism. Desogestrel and norgestimate additionally improve acne or hirsutism conditions because of their high level of progestational effects and absence of androgenic effects. Other progestins having androgenic properties, such as levonorgestrel, norgestrel, or norethindrone, may or may not worsen acne or hirsutism, depending on the progestin-estrogen dose relationship.

Other actions/effects

The following noncontraceptive effects have been observed with the use of oral contraceptives: menstrual cycle regularity, fewer occurrences of iron-deficient anemia associated with heavy menses flow or pelvic inflammatory disease; and fewer ectopic pregnancies. Although low-dose oral contraceptives may have less effect, high-dose formulations (containing $\geq$ 50 mcg [0.05 mg] estrogen) used long-term have decreased the occurrence of benign breast disease, including fibroadenomas and fibrocystic breast disease. Also, oral contraceptives may protect against or delay development of benign or malignant endometrial and ovarian cancers, atherosclerosis, or rheumatoid arthritis (although some of these are still controversial).

Norgestrel and levonorgestrel have the most androgenic activity of all the progestins. Norethindrone and ethynodiol diacetate possess slight estrogenic activity, and norethindrone has some androgenic activity. Norgestimate and desogestrel have high progestational activity and are low in androgenicity.

Absorption

Both estrogen and progestin components are rapidly and well absorbed.

Ethinyl estradiol or
Mestranol—Relative bioavailability is 83% because these estrogens have both a first-pass effect and enterohepatic recirculation with similar blood concentrations achieved for both 50 mcg of mestranol-containing and 35 mcg of ethinyl estradiol–containing oral contraceptives.

Desogestrel—Desogestrel is primarily absorbed in the intestine as its active metabolite, etonogestrel, but because of a significant first-pass effect, the relative bioavailability of etonogestrel is 84%.

Ethynodiol diacetate or
Norethindrone or
Norethindrone acetate—Ethynodiol diacetate and norethindrone acetate are completely hydrolyzed by intestinal tissue to norethindrone, which is then absorbed. All of these progestins are rapidly and well absorbed but because of a first-pass effect, 53% bioavailability results.

Levonorgestrel or
Norgestimate or
Norgestrel—Intestinal absorption within 2 hours; completely bioavailable because these progestins do not exhibit a first-pass effect.

Distribution

Oral contraceptives are widely distributed.

Ethinyl estradiol—Distributed into the uterus (0.9%), blood (8.8%), adipose tissue (28.2%), and other tissues. Fifty mcg of ethinyl estradiol taken orally would yield a concentration of 10 nanograms/100 mL a day in breast milk, which is not considered clinically significant.

Desogestrel (with ethinyl estradiol administration)—Volume of distribution (Vol_D) is 143 $\pm$ 61 liters (L).

Norethindrone (with ethinyl estradiol)—Vol_D is approximately 236 $\pm$ 60 L.

Protein binding

Oral contraceptives differ in their ability to increase the concentration of sex hormone-binding globulin (SHBG) that is induced by estrogen because contraceptive progestins differ in their ability to suppress this estrogenic effect. Also, contraceptive progestins have different affinities for albumin and SHBG. Therefore, progestins binding to serum proteins differ relative to how the estrogen and the progestin together affect serum proteins. For instance, a progestin with greater affinity for albumin than SHBG but faced with greater serum concentration of SHBG induced by estrogen would result in greater binding of progestin to SHBG.

Ethinyl estradiol—High; specifically, ethinyl estradiol is 95% bound to albumin, but not to SHBG; ethinyl estradiol induces production of SHBG. Tissue-specific receptor proteins form complexes with estrogens in estrogen-responsive tissues.

Desogestrel (with ethinyl estradiol administration)—High; albumin (66 $\pm$ 12%), SHBG (31 $\pm$ 12%), unbound (2.5 $\pm$ 0.2%). Because desogestrel does not counteract the increase in SHBG caused by daily estrogen administration, nonlinear kinetics result; desogestrel binds to a threefold increase in SHBG, which is highest between the third and sixth months of treatment.

Levonorgestrel (with ethinyl estradiol administration)—High; proportion bound to albumin or SHBG varies by strength and phasic relationship of both levonorgestrel and estrogen. Specifically, 250 mcg levonorgestrel and 50 mcg ethinyl estradiol have decreased SHBG by 24%, 150 mcg levonorgestrel and 30 mcg ethinyl estradiol decreased SHBG by 10%, and triphasic formulations increased SHBG. Levonorgestrel's affinity for SHBG is greater than its affinity for albumin.

Norethindrone—Without use of estrogen, norethindrone binds 61% to albumin and 35.5% to SHBG while 3.5% is unbound. With use of ethinyl estradiol, an 80 to 100% increase in SHBG may be expected, which will increase the SHBG-bound proportion of norethindrone.

Biotransformation

Desogestrel—In Phase I hydroxylation, desogestrel, a prodrug, is metabolized in the intestinal tract and by hepatic first-pass metabolism to the biologically active metabolite etonogestrel and several inactive metabolites. The metabolism is completed in Phase II, resulting in polar conjugated glucuronide and sulfate metabolites.

Ethinyl estradiol or
Mestranol—Exhibits Phase I and Phase II metabolism. Seventy percent of the prodrug, mestranol, converts to ethinyl estradiol by demethylation. Estrogen metabolites, mainly conjugates, are hydroxylated by enzymes of intestinal bacteria then reabsorbed via enterohepatic recirculation.

Ethynodiol diacetate or
Norethindrone or

Norethindrone acetate—Hydrolysis of ethynodiol diacetate and norethindrone acetate to norethindrone occurs mainly in the intestines, but also in the liver. Norethindrone is metabolized to sulfate (predominately in plasma) and glucuronide conjugates, which may prolong activity if active metabolites are discovered. Also, it is postulated that the aromatization of norethindrone to ethinyl estradiol by tissues such as the liver, ovaries, and placenta may be of clinical significance.

Levonorgestrel or
Norgestrel—Metabolism of the inactive isomer L-(d)-norgestrel differs considerably from metabolism of the active isomer L-(l)-norgestrel; the latter is sulfated more rapidly than is the inactive isomer.

Norgestimate—Considered an incomplete prodrug for levonorgestrel; has biological activity, but 85% of activity is thought to be due to norgestrel acetate and, to a much lesser extent, norgestrel. Metabolized to active metabolites, levonorgestrel and 17-deactyl norgestimate (has activity similar to norgestimate), as well as to other hydroxy compounds.

Half-life

With ethinyl estradiol administration:

Desogestrel or
Levonorgestrel—Elimination, plasma: 8 to 13 hours.

Ethynodiol diacetate or
Norethindrone or
Norethindrone acetate—Elimination, plasma: 8 hours.

Norgestimate—Elimination, plasma: 30 to 71 hours for norgestimate; 17 to 30 hours for 17-deactyl norgestimate, a metabolite.

With desogestrel administration:

Ethinyl estradiol—Elimination, plasma: 26 hours.

With norgestimate administration:

Ethinyl estradiol—Elimination, plasma: 6 to 14 hours.

Elimination

Desogestrel—
Renal: 45%, of which 14 to 28% is unchanged, and 38 to 61% is excreted as glucuronide and 23 to 39% as sulfate conjugates.
Fecal: Up to 30%.

Ethinyl estradiol or
Mestranol—
Renal: 22 to 58%.
Fecal: 30 to 53%.
Biliary: 26 to 43%.

Ethynodiol diacetate or
Norethindrone acetate or
Norethindrone—
Renal: 37 to 87%, of which 3% is unchanged, and 40% is excreted as glucuronide and 15% as sulfate conjugates.
Fecal: Up to 40%.

Levonorgestrel or
Norgestrel—Renal, as inactive metabolites.

Norgestimate—
Renal: 45 to 49%.
Fecal: 16 to 49%.

Precautions to Consider

Carcinogenicity

Recent and current users of high-dose oral contraceptives (containing 50 mcg or more of estrogen) for at least 2 years have shown a progressive reduction of up to 40% in incidence of benign fibrocystic breast disease; it is unknown if low-dose oral contraceptives (containing less than 50 mcg of estrogen) have similar effects.

Use of oral contraceptives in women between 25 and 39 years of age does not increase the risk of developing breast cancer at 45 years of age or older. Whether oral contraceptives increase the risk of breast cancer in certain subgroups of women, such as women under 20 years of age using oral contraceptives for more than 4 years or women 46 to 54 years of age using oral contraceptives for more than 3 years, is unresolved. Some case-control studies have shown no association between oral contraceptive use and breast cancer in women under 20 years of age and a protective effect or no enhancement of risk in women 46 to 54 years of age. Because risk factors vary for women of different age groups, parity, environment, and age at first use, controlling for these and other confounding factors and establishing whether additional risk occurs is difficult. The magnitude of increased risk, if it exists at all, is considered very small, and does not warrant withholding the use of oral contraceptives in any subgroup of women (including those women having a family history of either breast cancer or benign breast disease, or women having a history of benign breast disease) or restricting use for young nulliparous women. Further analyses of risks associated with using low-dose oral contraceptives as compared to high-dose contraceptives and to characterize effects of duration of use are being evaluated.

If an oral contraceptive containing 50 mcg of estrogen is taken for at least 12 months, a 15-year protective effect against the development of endometrial cancer persists after the oral contraceptive treatment is discontinued. Similar effects for low-dose oral contraceptives are expected but an evaluation is needed.

High and low doses of monophasic oral contraceptives used continuously for at least 3 years have shown a protective effect against ovarian cancer, an effect that is fully developed in 6 years and may persist for at least 10 years; shorter-term use has not shown a protective effect. Similar short- and long-term effects are expected for low-dose bi- and triphasic oral contraceptives since they suppress ovulation, but further evaluation is needed.

Epidemiologic studies suggest that women taking oral contraceptives for 8 or more years have an increased risk of developing hepatocellular carcinoma as compared to women not taking oral contraceptives. However, these cancers are extremely rare and occur in less than one per million women using oral contraceptives long-term.

Risk for dysplasia and carcinoma of the cervix is increased with oral contraceptive use for more than 1 year. The risk of invasive cervical cancer could increase twofold after 5 years of use; the greatest risk is in women using oral contraceptives for longer than 10 years. A great portion of the risk is thought to be due to the number of sexual partners a woman has and the age at first coitus, a factor that may be different between users and never-users.

Tumorigenicity

Although benign and rare, liver cell adenomas, many of which regressed with the cessation of oral contraceptive use, have occurred in women using oral contraceptives for longer than 5 years. Liver cell adenomas should be suspected in patients having abdominal pain and tenderness, abdominal mass, or hypovolemic shock. These adenomas may rupture and may cause death through intra-abdominal hemorrhage.

Mutagenicity

It is generally believed that there is no increased risk of mutagenicity or teratogenicity, including any development of fetal sexual malformation, when oral contraceptives are inadvertently taken in early pregnancy. This information is based on a small number of case reports, and well-designed studies still are needed.

Pregnancy/Reproduction

Fertility—Delayed fertility has been shown to occur rarely in users of oral contraceptives, especially in nulliparous women. In one study, the rate of impaired fertility normalized by 48 and 72 months for two groups of nulliparous women (25 to 29 years of age and 30 to 34 years of age, respectively). Infertility rates have not been shown to increase.

Pregnancy—Studies have shown that combination oral contraceptives do not appear to increase the risk of birth defects when they are used before pregnancy. Studies have also shown that oral contraceptives, when taken inadvertently during early pregnancy, do not seem to have a teratogenic effect. However, oral contraceptives are not recommended for use during pregnancy and should be discontinued immediately if pregnancy is suspected.

Any patient who has missed two consecutive menstrual periods while taking oral contraceptives should discontinue their use; a nonhormonal contraceptive method should be used until pregnancy is ruled out. If the patient has not followed the dosing schedule, pregnancy should be ruled out after the first missed menstrual period.

When considering pregnancy, it is recommended that conception be delayed for 1 or 2 months after cessation of oral contraceptives or until after the first regular menses to accurately date the gestation period.

FDA Pregnancy Category X.

Postpartum or postabortion—Oral contraceptive use and the immediate postpartum period are both associated with an increased risk of thromboembolism occurrence. Therefore, to lessen any potential risk that may exist, oral contraceptives should be started no sooner than 2 weeks after delivery in women choosing to not breast-feed. Also, ovulation usually does not occur before this time and contraception is not needed. However, the chance of early ovulation is high following abortion but the risk of thromboembolic phenomena is not great. Therefore, some clinicians recommend that use of a low-dose oral contraceptive may begin immediately after a first-trimester or second-trimester abortion. Also, immediate use of an oral contraceptive is recommended following a second-trimester premature delivery or after a pregnancy of less than 12 weeks; however, for a pregnancy of 12 or more weeks, use of a low-dose oral contraceptive is recommended after 2 weeks.

Breast-feeding

Oral contraceptives are distributed into breast milk, and may diminish its quantity or quality or shorten the time of lactation, especially for those women who are only partially breast-feeding and have less physical stimulus for lactation. Use of oral contraceptives by nursing mothers in the early postpartum period is generally not recommended. When used by mothers who are exclusively breast-feeding, oral contraceptive therapy is recommended to begin after the third postpartum month or, if only partially or not breast-feeding, to begin in the third postpartum week. If contraception is needed prior to this, some clinicians begin low-dose oral contraceptives after lactation has been well-established.

Adolescents

One of the most accepted, frequently prescribed, and, when used regularly, effective contraceptive methods for adolescents is oral contraceptives. However, the pregnancy rate for adolescents using oral contraceptives is estimated at 6 to 12 per 100 woman years, which is higher than the pregnancy rate, 0.3 to 0.7 per 100 woman years, for all age groups of women.

Studies generally have shown that adolescents tend to be less compliant users of any type of contraceptive. Any psychosocial factors involved and discussion of preconceived thoughts on side effects, including weight gain, fluid retention, or breakthrough uterine bleeding, are important areas for patient counseling to help aid in this age group's compliance problem with using oral contraceptives.

Dental

Increased concentrations of progestins increase the normal oral flora growth rate, leading to an increase in inflammation of the gingival tissues and increased bleeding. A strictly enforced program of teeth cleaning by a professional, combined with plaque control by the patient, will minimize severity.

An increased incidence of local alveolar osteitis (dry socket) after dental extractions has been seen with the use of estrogen and progestin combination oral contraceptives. A direct correlation exists between the incidence of dry socket occurrence and increasing estrogen dose. Therefore, it is recommended that patients inform their dentist or oral surgeon that they are taking an estrogen and progestin contraceptive.

Drug interactions and/or related problems

The following drug interactions and/or related problems have been selected on the basis of their potential clinical significance (possible mechanism in parentheses where appropriate)—not necessarily inclusive (» = major clinical significance):

Note: Combinations containing any of the following medications, depending on the amount present, may also interact with this medication.

Acetaminophen or
Ascorbic acid
(may increase plasma ethinyl estradiol concentrations, possibly by inhibition of conjugation)

Amoxicillin or
Ampicillin or
Doxycycline or
Penicillin V or
Tetracycline
(there have been rare case reports of reduced oral contraceptive effectiveness in women taking amoxicillin, ampicillin, doxycycline, penicillin V, or tetracycline, resulting in unplanned pregnancy. This is thought to be due to a reduction in enterohepatic circulation of estrogens, which may cause a lower estrogen plasma concentration than expected. Although the association is very weak, patients, especially long-term users of antibiotic therapy, should be advised of this information and given the option of using an alternate or additional method of contraception while taking any of these antibiotics, especially if the duration of antibiotic therapy is greater than 2 weeks)

Anticoagulants, coumarin- or indandione-derivative
(concurrent use with oral contraceptives has modestly increased, and in some cases decreased, the effectiveness of anticoagulants; however, the mechanism is unknown and appropriate studies have not been done. Because estrogens increase hepatic synthesis of procoagulant factors and decrease antithrombin III, it is possible that adjustment of the anticoagulant dosage based on prothrombin time determinations may be needed)

Antidiabetic agents, sulfonylurea or
Insulin
(estrogen-containing oral contraceptives may cause glucose or insulin resistance in diabetic patients, resulting in a loss, probably slight, of metabolic control of plasma glucose concentration; unless the changes can be controlled with diet, this may necessitate an increased sulfonylurea or insulin dose and regular monitoring)

Atorvastatin
(coadministration of atorvastatin and certain oral contraceptives containing ethinyl estradiol increase AUC values for ethinyl estradiol by approximately 20%)

Benzodiazepines
(metabolism of those benzodiazepines, such as diazepam, alprazolam, and triazolam, that undergo oxidation may be inhibited, resulting in delayed elimination of diazepam and triazolam and an increased risk of adverse effect. Although the pharmacokinetics of alprazolam were not affected with long-term use, a study has shown a greater sensitivity to alprazolam and psychomotor impairment with single doses of alprazolam in long-term contraceptive users; pharmacokinetic factors were not believed to contribute to this effect. Metabolism of those benzodiazepines that undergo conjugation, such as oxazepam, lorazepam, and temazepam, is not impaired)
(reduction of oral contraceptive effectiveness has not been shown with concurrent use of benzodiazepines)

Caffeine
(oral contraceptives reduce or inhibit the hepatic metabolism of caffeine, thereby increasing the plasma concentration of caffeine up to 30 to 40%; patient may need to be counseled about the increased effects of caffeine if warranted)

Clofibrate
(concurrent use with oral contraceptives may lower the effectiveness of clofibrate)

» Corticosteroids, glucocorticoid
(concurrent use with estrogens may lower the metabolism of glucocorticoids, decrease the elimination of potent metabolites, decrease the protein binding of glucocorticoids, and increase the production of the protein-binding globulin, transcortin (also called cortisol-binding globulin). This leads to decreased clearance [approximately 30 to 50% for prednisolone] of the glucocorticoid free fraction, prolonged elimination half-life, and increased effects of the glucocorticoids; lower doses of the glucocorticoid are needed with concurrent use of estrogen-containing oral contraceptives)

» Cyclosporine
(a case report has shown that concurrent use with oral contraceptives increased the plasma concentration of cyclosporine, which may increase its effects; monitoring of plasma cyclosporine concentration and hepatic factors for toxicity, reducing cyclosporine dose, or changing to nonhormonal contraception may be required to minimize the risk of cyclosporine toxicity)

» Hepatic enzyme inducers (see *Appendix II*), especially:
Barbiturates
Carbamazepine
Griseofulvin
Phenytoin
Primidone
Rifabutin
Rifampin
(concurrent use of these medications with oral contraceptives may induce hepatic enzyme oral contraceptive metabolism, especially of the estrogen component, which could result in reduced contraceptive reliability and increased incidence of breakthrough bleeding. High interindividual variability in hepatic enzyme induction exists. Patients should be advised to use a high-dose estrogen-containing contraceptive if oral contraceptives are used, or an alternative or additional method of contraception during use of any of these medications, especially if breakthrough bleeding occurs)
(additionally, phenobarbital and phenytoin have been shown to increase sex hormone-binding globulin [SHBG], which may lower the amount of free progestin available for biological action and contribute to the lowered effectiveness of the oral contraceptive)

» Hepatotoxic medications, especially troleandomycin (see *Appendix II*)
(the estrogen component of oral contraceptives increases hepatic blood flow and size of the liver with increased vesiculation of the smooth and rough endoplasmic reticulum, which results in altered hepatic metabolism. It is possible that concurrent use of these medications with estrogens may increase the risk of hepatotoxicity; more frequent monitoring of hepatic function is needed)

» Ritonavir
(area under the plasma concentration-time curve [AUC] of estrogen is decreased by 40% during use of ritonavir; the estrogen dose of the oral contraceptive should be increased or an alternative form of birth control used with concurrent use of ritonavir)

» Smoking, tobacco
(polycyclic hydrocarbons in cigarette smoke are potent inducers of certain hepatic cytochrome P450 isoenzymes; the consequences of this effect on metabolism have not been fully explored but may influence the associated risks of using oral contraceptives and smoking concurrently. Although some studies showed inhibition of

metabolism of a metabolite of ethinyl estradiol, smoking did not affect the metabolism of ethinyl estradiol)

(oral contraceptives are not recommended with heavy tobacco use because of an increased risk of serious cardiovascular side effects, including cerebrovascular accident, transient ischemic attacks, thrombophlebitis, and pulmonary embolism. Risk increases with increased tobacco usage and with age, especially in women over 35 years of age. The mechanisms for these outcomes are still being explored. Some clinicians have used low-dose estrogen oral contraceptives in women who are light smokers or who use a nicotine patch)

St. John's Wort (hypericum perforatum)

(herbal products containing St. John's Wort [hypericum perforatum] may induce hepatic enzymes [cytochrome P450] and p-glycoprotein transporter and may reduce the effectiveness of oral contraceptives; this may also result in breakthrough bleeding)

Tamoxifen

(concurrent use with estrogens may interfere with the antiestrogenic therapeutic effect of tamoxifen)

» Theophylline

(although theophylline reduced the apparent clearance of ethinyl estradiol 30 to 35% in oral contraceptive users, clinical significance was not noted because of the wide interindividual variability in metabolism of the estrogen; however, reduction of the total plasma clearance of theophylline by 25 to 35% by oral contraceptives was considered clinically significant. These effects result in an increase in both the theophylline and ethinyl estradiol plasma concentration; a lower dose of the theophylline may be needed)

Tricyclic antidepressants

(inhibition of imipramine oxidation by oral contraceptives results in higher plasma concentrations of imipramine; imipramine dose may need to be adjusted)

(estrogen has facilitated the development of neuroleptic antipsychotic or tricyclic antidepressant medication–associated movement disorders, such as akathisia, but not tardive dyskinesia. It is not known if the low doses of estrogen used in oral contraceptives are also implicated in akathisia)

(rare cases of chorea have developed in women with chorea gravidarum using oral contraceptives, but oral contraceptives do not appear to create any additional risk in women not predisposed to develop chorea)

» Troglitazone

(troglitazone may induce drug metabolism by cytochrome P450 isoenzyme CYP3A4; ethinyl estradiol and norethindrone are substrates for this isoenzyme; therefore, caution is recommended when they are used concurrently with troglitazone)

(concurrent use may decrease the plasma concentrations of ethinyl estradiol and norethindrone by approximately 30%, resulting in a loss of efficacy)

Laboratory value alterations

The following have been selected on the basis of their potential clinical significance (possible effect in parentheses where appropriate)—not necessarily inclusive (» = major clinical significance).

With diagnostic test results

Aldosterone, serum or
Aldosterone, urine or
Renin, plasma

(the estrogen component decreases the plasma concentration of plasma renin but increases plasma renin activity; oral contraceptives should be discontinued at least 2 weeks, and preferably 4 weeks, before testing plasma renin activity)

Antipyrine test

(lower values result because oral contraceptives significantly reduce antipyrine metabolism, particularly the oxidative mechanism)

Corticotropin-releasing hormone stimulation test or
Metyrapone test

(corticotropin plasma levels were reduced approximately 25% overall in a study of women using triphasic oral contraceptives who had been given a morning corticotropin-releasing hormone [CRH] stimulation test; normal basal levels were unchanged. Reduced response also has been noted for the metyrapone test with other oral contraceptives)

Dexamethasone suppression test

(oral contraceptive users had a significantly higher plasma cortisol level pre- and post-dexamethasone testing; this effect caused by estrogen may persist for up to 1 month after oral contraceptive treatment ends)

Glucose tolerance test, oral

(significantly higher 2-hour oral glucose tolerance test results)

Norepinephrine-induced platelet aggregability

(may be increased)

Thyroid function tests

Thyroxine (T_4) determinations

(estrogen-induced thyroid-binding globulin elevates the amount of T_4 that is protein bound; this effect reverses in about 2 months after discontinuation of oral contraceptives; serum free T_4 concentrations are unchanged. Specifically, triphasic oral contraceptives containing 30 mcg of ethinyl estradiol have increased thyroid-binding globulin by about 20% and elevated total T_4 by 40%)

Triiodothyronine (T_3) determinations

(free T_3 and reverse T_3 are unchanged, but T_3 resin uptake is decreased because estrogens increase serum thyroid-binding globulin [TBG]; total T_3 radioimmunoassay [RIA] values are increased but proportionately less than total T_4 values)

With physiology/laboratory test values

Albumin or
Alkaline phosphatase

(levels were decreased in women taking norethindrone-ethinyl estradiol 1/35 throughout the 1-year treatment period in one study; these effects were not seen in the same study among women taking levonorgestrel-ethinyl estradiol 0.15/30)

Androstenedione or
Ceruloplasmin, serum or
Dehydroepiandrosterone sulfate (DHEA-S) or
Pregnenolone or
Sex hormone-binding globulin (SHBG), serum or
Testosterone or
Thyroid-binding globulin or
Transferrin or cortisol-binding globulin, serum

(oral contraceptives increase protein synthesis of SHBG, thyroid-binding globulin, transferrin, and ceruloplasmin. The serum concentrations of total sex steroids, copper, and cortisol may also increase. The free thyroid concentration is unchanged, and thyroid function is unaltered. Response of the free non-protein-bound component may be variable)

(oral contraceptives" net effect on SHBG is the result of the opposing actions of the estrogen and progestin. A dose-related response to progestins of greater androgenicity, such as norgestrel, has a greater suppressive effect on the estrogen-induced increases of SHBG than do those with low androgenic effect, such as desogestrel or norgestimate, which have little suppressive effect on estrogen-induced SHBG levels and can result in a three- to fourfold increase in SHBG. However, further elevations of SHBG, above some level that remains undetermined, do not appear to result in any further decrease in free testosterone. For instance, one study showed that an elevation of SHBG by 92% and 175% decreased free testosterone similarly [by 35%]. Ethinyl estradiol and norethindrone 1/35 and 1/50 increased SHBG levels by 183 to 390%; ethinyl estradiol and norgestrel increased SHBG by 12%. Testosterone levels are further changed by those progestins that have greater affinity for SHBG, such as levonorgestrel-containing oral contraceptives, that can displace testosterone from its SHBG binding site)

(also, norgestrel-, ethynodiol diacetate–, and norethindrone-containing oral contraceptives reduce circulating DHEA-S by 28%, androstenedione by 47%, and testosterone by 40%, including the precursor, pregnenolone, by causing a decrease in corticotropin stimulation or by direct effect on hepatic enzyme inhibition. The complexity of these factors causes a variable clinical effect among individuals taking oral contraceptives)

Antithrombin III

(may be decreased by most oral contraceptives, which contributes to decreased anticoagulant or increased fibrinolytic activity of oral contraceptives. A study showed that desogestrel increased fibrinolytic activity less than did a triphasic formulation of levonorgestrel but that there was significantly more activity in users of desogestrel than in nonusers. Although the increase in activity was generally within normal laboratory ranges, extreme values among individuals may need to be taken into consideration. Specifically, users of a triphasic formulation of levonorgestrel and ethinyl estradiol showed a slight increase in antithrombin III concentration at 12 weeks, followed by a decrease until the end of the 48-week study. In the same study, users of desogestrel and ethinyl estradiol showed a decreased concentration of antithrombin III at 24 weeks that returned to the normal range at 48 weeks)

Apolipoprotein A_1, A_2, or B or

Cholesterol, total or
Triglycerides
(in general, the net effect on lipoproteins is the result of the opposing actions of the estrogen and progestin and depends on the ratio between the two hormones. The estrogen component increases triglyceride, very low density lipoproteins (VLDL), and total cholesterol concentrations and decreases low density lipoproteins (LDL). The progestin component, if androgenic, decreases high density lipoproteins (HDL) and increases LDL. The low concentrations of the androgenic progestins in oral contraceptives have slight effect, which is of clinical significance only for some predisposed individuals. Sometimes, older women with higher serum concentrations of cholesterol may experience a reduction caused by a lowering of the serum LDL concentrations. Triglycerides are increased by all oral contraceptives because of the predominant estrogen effects. The increase in total cholesterol caused by desogestrel- and norgestimate-containing oral contraceptives is considered favorable because it is the net result of the increase in HDL_3-C (an estrogen effect) without an increase in HDL_2-C concentrations. The increase in HDL_2-C caused by other low-dose oral contraceptives is considered an androgenic effect of some of the 19–nortestosterone-derived progestins)

For monophasics
users of ethynodiol diacetate-ethinyl estradiol 1/35 showed the greatest increase in apolipoprotein A_1 and levonorgestrel-ethinyl estradiol 0.15/30 showed the smallest increase. Users of ethinyl estradiol-norgestrel have shown significant decrease in apolipoproteins A_1 and A_2

(in one study, norethindrone-ethinyl estradiol 1/35 increased triglycerides to levels that continued throughout a 1-year treatment period while levonorgestrel-ethinyl estradiol 0.15/30 caused no change in triglyceride levels over a 1-year treatment period. Total cholesterol levels were slightly decreased for norethindrone-ethinyl estradiol 1/35 but returned toward baseline within the 1-year treatment period. Levonorgestrel-ethinyl estradiol 0.15/30 slightly reduced total cholesterol levels at 3-month and 1-year treatment periods)

For triphasics
in a study comparing users of triphasic formulations with nonusers, levonorgestrel-ethinyl estradiol [7/7/7- and 9/5/7-day regimens] and norethindrone-ethinyl estradiol produced significant increases in plasma triglyceride [28 to 52%] and plasma apolipoprotein B levels [20 to 23%] in each treatment group at 6 months compared with levels in nonusers. In the contraceptive users, total plasma cholesterol concentrations increased 3 to 11% and plasma apolipoprotein A_1 concentrations increased 5 to 12%. The increases in the concentrations shown in a 12-month study remained within an acceptable clinical range. Another study of oral triphasics showed a significant decrease in total cholesterol in users during the first week of use, an effect associated with a decrease in LDL; the total serum cholesterol returned to baseline over the next 3 weeks

Aspartate aminotransferase (AST [SGOT]), serum or
Bilirubin, total, serum or
Urobilinogen, urine
(these values are decreased with oral contraceptives containing 50 mcg of ethinyl estradiol; the incidence of abnormal liver test values is lower for oral contraceptives containing 35 mcg of ethinyl estradiol or 50 mcg of mestranol. Total bilirubin, urinary urobilinogen, and serum AST were significantly decreased at 3 months for norethindrone-ethinyl estradiol 1/35, but returned to baseline at 12 months. Users of levonorgestrel-ethinyl estradiol 0.15/30 showed only slightly decreased concentrations that were not considered clinically significant)

Clotting factors VII, VIII, IX, and X or
Prothrombin time or
Thromboplastin time, partial
(oral contraceptives shorten partial thromboplastin and prothrombin time, but these results are neither consistent nor do they occur in all individuals. Activation of the segments of the intrinsic and extrinsic system of coagulation by oral contraceptives enhances, depending on the factor, either the fibrinolysis or procoagulation or affects both. If baseline values were increased, the increase was within normal laboratory ranges in most cases, and did not consistently alter bleeding or clotting time)

Cortisol, serum or urine
(the net effect of oral contraceptives on serum cortisol is the result of the opposing actions of the estrogen and progestin and depends on the ratio between the two hormones. Progestins, such as norethindrone, having glucocorticoid effects decrease corticotropin release and adrenal cortisol production. Estrogens augment corticotropin release by downregulating pituitary glucocorticoid receptors and increase adrenal cortisol responsiveness to corticotropin stimulation. This results in an increase in serum cortisol concentrations and a decrease in urinary cortisol clearance)

Glucose, plasma or serum or
Insulin
(reduced glucose tolerance and elevated fasting insulin and C-peptide values can occur with use of low-dose oral contraceptives during the first 12 months of use, returning to normal between 12 and 24 months of continued use. These changes from baseline were considered not to be of clinical significance in most prospective studies of low-dose oral contraceptives, as many values were still within the normal range. Levonorgestrel- or norgestrel-containing combinations caused the greatest insulin resistance, followed by combinations of desogestrel and low-dose norethindrone oral contraceptives. Levonorgestrel significantly increased second-phase pancreatic insulin production while desogestrel and norgestimate did not)

Growth hormone
(physiologic levels may increase during the first year)

High density lipoproteins (HDL), serum
(low-dose oral contraceptives show no change or a decrease in value of HDL; the estrogen component increases HDL and the progestin component, if androgenic, lowers HDL. If the progestin is nonandrogenic, HDL is not influenced. In studies clinically comparing oral contraceptives, formulations containing levonorgestrel and norgestrel had a greater adverse effect on lipids than did less androgenic formulations such as those containing ethynodiol diacetate, norethindrone, or norethindrone acetate. However, if levonorgestrel or norgestrel is given in low doses or if the total dose given is limited, such as in biphasic or triphasic formulations, these potent androgenic progestins exhibit only mild lipid changes similar to those of less potent androgenic progestins given in monophasic formulations. Nonandrogenic formulations, such as desogestrel and norgestimate, had little effect on lipid profile)

Low density lipoproteins (LDL), serum or
Very low density lipoproteins (VLDL), serum
(low-dose oral contraceptives show no change or an increase in value of LDL; the estrogen component decreases LDL and the progestin component, if androgenic, raises LDL. If the progestin is nonandrogenic, LDL is not influenced. In clinical studies comparing oral contraceptives, formulations containing levonorgestrel and norgestrel had a greater adverse effect on lipids than did less androgenic formulations, such as those containing ethynodiol diacetate, norethindrone, or norethindrone acetate. However, if levonorgestrel or norgestrel is given in low doses or if the total dose given is limited, such as in biphasic or triphasic formulations, these potent androgenic progestins exhibit only mild lipid changes similar to those of less potent androgenic progestins given in monophasic formulations. Nonandrogenic formulations, such as desogestrel and norgestimate, had little effect)

Oxytocin, serum
(mean basal oxytocin levels were higher in women on oral contraceptives)

Plasminogen activity
(activity is increased above normal laboratory reference values)

Medical considerations/Contraindications

The medical considerations/contraindications included have been selected on the basis of their potential clinical significance (reasons given in parentheses where appropriate)—not necessarily inclusive (» = major clinical significance).

Except under special circumstances, this medication should not be used when the following medical problems exist:

» Carcinoma, breast, known or suspected or
» Carcinoma, endometrium or
» Neoplasia, estrogen-dependent, known or suspected
(may worsen conditions; estrogen-containing oral contraceptives should be discontinued and nonhormonal contraceptives initiated, although sometimes progestin-only contraceptives are used for selected patients)

» Cardiac insufficiency
(oral contraceptives should not be used in patients with marginal cardiac reserve; fluid retention sometimes caused by estrogens may aggravate this condition)

» Cerebrovascular disease, active or history of or
» Coronary artery disease, active or history of
(the estrogen component of oral contraceptives has a protective effect against atherosclerosis. Any association with risk in these conditions has been related to thrombosis or interference with cholesterol-lipoprotein profile, such as with levonorgestrel, a proges-

tin, in doses greater than 150 to 250 mcg for those individuals predisposed to thrombosis. No correlation has been seen between coronary artery disease and use of low-dose oral contraceptives, including those formulated with levonorgestrel, in these women or in women who are not predisposed to these conditions. Oral contraceptives should be discontinued or strictly avoided if any cardiovascular or cerebrovascular accidents occur; users should switch to nonhormonal contraception. If oral contraceptives are used in women at risk, special monitoring may be required)

(the progestins norgestimate and desogestrel have minimal negative impact and may improve the cholesterol-lipoprotein profile, which is thought to additionally protect against cardiovascular disease along with the estrogen component of oral contraceptives)

» Hepatic disease, cholestatic, active or
» Hepatic tumors, benign or malignant, or history of
(metabolism of estrogens may be impaired; also, estrogens may worsen the condition. Oral contraceptives should be discontinued and nonhormonal contraception initiated; for those women with active hepatic disease, oral contraceptive use may be resumed after liver function tests return to normal)

» Jaundice, obstructive or history of during pregnancy or
» Jaundice with prior oral contraceptives use
(estrogens may increase risk of recurrence but low-dose contraceptives have not done so consistently; risk is higher shortly after hormone exposure; increased monitoring may be needed)

» Thrombophlebitis, thrombosis, or thromboembolic disorders, active or history of
(oral contraceptives are not recommended for women with predisposing factors, especially those who smoke tobacco or who have an underlying abnormality of the coagulation system, that place them at special risk for thrombosis. Although hormones can increase thrombin formation, the coagulation effect is offset by an increase in fibrolytic activity. Some women with coagulation disorders may successfully use oral contraceptives as evaluated by the physician if only a slight risk for a thrombogenic condition exists. Problems generally have not been associated with the low doses of hormones used for contraception for women not at risk for these conditions)

» Uterine bleeding, abnormal or undiagnosed
(malignancy should be ruled out in cases of persistent or recurring abnormal uterine bleeding; use of a progestin-containing oral contraceptive may delay diagnosis by masking underlying conditions, including cancer)

Risk-benefit should be considered when the following medical problems exist:

Breast cancer, strong family history of or
Breast disease, benign
(although studies have failed to conclusively prove that use of oral contraceptives causes any excess risk for developing breast disease in these women, caution and more frequent monitoring for potential problems may be warranted)

Chorea gravidarum
(oral contraceptives do not cause chorea gravidarum but rarely they have aggravated pre-existing conditions)

Diabetes mellitus
(use of oral contraceptives may slightly decrease glucose tolerance, slightly increase insulin release in patients with Type 2 diabetes mellitus, or produce a mild adverse effect on the cholesterol-lipoprotein profile. Depending on the oral contraceptive used, a change in the dose of the antidiabetic agent or more frequent monitoring for plasma glucose or lipid profile may be needed. If adverse metabolic effects cannot be controlled, the oral contraceptive should be discontinue)

(norethindrone-, ethynodiol diacetate-, norgestimate-, and desogestrel-containing oral contraceptives affect carbohydrate metabolism less than do levonorgestrel- or norgestrel-containing oral contraceptives; many clinicians recommend low-dose oral contraceptives, such as the triphasic oral contraceptives, for patients with diabetes mellitus)

(use of oral contraceptives in patients with Type 1 diabetes mellitus who are 35 years of age or older or in any patient having diabetes mellitus complications is generally not recommended because of the potential increased risk of thrombosis. Healthy patients up to 35 years of age who have diabetes mellitus have minimal risk for adverse effects from oral contraceptive use and usually do not need an adjustment in their insulin dose. They may require more frequent monitoring of the cholesterol-lipoprotein profile and serum glucose concentration)

Epilepsy
(oral contraceptives can be used effectively with this condition but their use may affect the pharmacokinetics of certain antiepileptic medications; dose changes for both medications and special monitoring may be needed)

Gallbladder disease, or history of, especially gallstones
(estrogens may alter the composition of gallbladder bile and can cause a rise in cholesterol saturation that may moderately accelerate the development of gallstones during the first 2 years of use in predisposed individuals. The overall risk is low and thought to be of minimal clinical importance; however, cautious use of oral contraceptives is recommended with known gallbladder disease)

» Hepatic function impairment
(metabolism of estrogens may be impaired, resulting in a worsening of the condition; therefore, oral contraceptives should be discontinued and nonhormonal contraception initiated with active disease; oral contraceptive use may be resumed after liver function tests return to normal. Oral contraceptives are not thought to aggravate cirrhosis or exacerbate previous hepatitis)

Hypertension
(low-dose monophasic oral contraceptives have been shown to raise blood pressure in some normotensive women considered to be at high risk [although these women cannot be easily identified] or further raise blood pressure in hypertensive women. Use of low-dose multiphasic contraceptives may be an appropriate choice for these women)

Immobilization, extended or
Surgery, major
(although controversial, many guidelines suggest that concurrent oral contraceptive usage increases the risk of postoperative thromboembolism in predisposed women, especially for smokers of tobacco or for those women with a history of thromboembolism. When possible or if appropriate, oral contraceptives should be discontinued at least 4 weeks before and for 2 weeks after an extended period of immobilization or scheduled major elective surgery. If not possible, prophylactic low-dose heparin therapy should be considered prior to surgery)

Mental depression, or history of
(may be aggravated; however, low-dose contraceptives are considered to have minimal effect on mental depression; the oral contraceptive should be discontinued if significant depression occurs, especially in women with a history of depression)

Migraine headaches
(since migraine headaches have been associated with an increased risk of stroke, discontinuation of oral contraceptives may be warranted if migraine headaches are recurring, persistent, or more severe with use of oral contraceptives, especially for those individuals predisposed to thrombosis)

Patient monitoring

The following may be especially important in patient monitoring (other tests may be warranted in some patients, depending on condition; » = major clinical significance):

Blood pressure determinations and
Hepatic function determinations and
Papanicolaou (Pap) test and
Physical examinations
(recommended as determined by physician—generally every 12 months for healthy women with no risk factors but every 6 months if needed when such risk factors exist, although breast and pelvic examinations are needed only annually. New oral contraceptive users should be reassessed at 3 months. Special attention should be given to breast, liver, and pelvic area in the physical exam and patients should be encouraged to self-examine breasts monthly)

(special attention to rule out malignancy should be given to patients complaining of persistent or recurring uterine bleeding)

Glucose, serum and
Lipid profile, serum and
Lipoprotein profile, serum
(routine assessment is needed only for women at special risk, including women 35 years of age or older, women who have personal or strong family histories of heart disease, diabetes mellitus, or hypertension, or whose personal history includes gestational diabetes mellitus, xanthomatosis, or obesity)

For perimenopausal women using oral contraceptives

Gonadotropin determination
(FSH levels should be measured annually after the age of 52 years to determine when menopause occurs; levels should be measured during the end of the placebo week)

Side/Adverse Effects

Note: The risk of any serious adverse effect is minimal for healthy women using low-dose oral contraceptives. Some women who are at special risk have successfully used low-dose oral contraceptives, although in others the use of oral contraceptives rarely will increase the incidence of life-threatening effects, such as benign hepatic adenomas, hepatocellular carcinoma, or thromboembolism or thromboembolic events such as deep vein thrombosis, cerebral or coronary ischemia and/or infarction, pulmonary embolism, or stroke. Pre-existing risk factors for these events include genetic predisposition (i.e., antiestrogen antibodies, activated protein C or antithrombin deficiencies or resistance, or genetic thrombotic disorder), hypertension, hyperlipidemia, obesity, diabetes, or smoking of cigarettes.

Low-dose oral contraceptives are recommended for most women throughout their reproductive years without need for discontinuance. Mortality rates in oral contraceptive users are lower than those that are associated with childbirth. This is true even for smokers 35 years and older and nonsmokers 40 years and older.

There is no evidence of an etiological relationship between oral contraceptive use and pituitary prolactinoma; however, the appearance of galactorrhea while on oral contraceptives merits investigation.

The following side/adverse effects have been selected on the basis of their potential clinical significance (possible signs and symptoms in parentheses where appropriate)—not necessarily inclusive:

Those indicating need for immediate medical attention

Incidence rare

Thromboembolism or thrombosis (abdominal pain, sudden, severe, or continuing; coughing up blood; headache, severe or sudden; loss of coordination, sudden; pains in chest, groin, or leg, especially calf of leg; shortness of breath, sudden, unexplained; slurring of speech, sudden; vision changes, sudden; weakness, numbness, or pain in arm or leg, unexplained)—mainly exhibited in women having predisposing or pre-existing conditions, especially for those who smoke tobacco, but the event may be idiopathic

Those indicating need for medical attention

Incidence more frequent, especially during the first 3 months of oral contraceptive use

Changes in the menstrual bleeding pattern or intermenstrual bleeding, such as amenorrhea (complete stoppage of menstrual bleeding over several months); ***absence of withdrawal bleeding*** (occasional stoppage of menses over nonconsecutive months); ***breakthrough bleeding*** (vaginal bleeding between regular menstrual periods, which may require the use of a pad or a tampon); ***metrorrhagia*** (prolonged bleeding); ***scanty menses*** (very light menstrual bleeding); ***or spotting*** (light vaginal bleeding between regular menstrual periods)

Note: Malignancy should be ruled out as the cause if persistent or recurring abnormal *uterine bleeding* occurs.

Up to 46% of women using oral contraceptives experience *changes in the intermenstrual uterine bleeding pattern*. These problems become less frequent with duration of use; women who use high-dose oral contraceptives or who are changing formulations have fewer uterine bleeding problems than do women who are new users. *Breakthrough bleeding* occurs in 6 to 12% of women; some may require a change to a higher formulation with progestin or a change to a monophasic oral contraceptive after 3 months. Intervention with therapeutic doses of estrogen and/or progestin may be necessary if breakthrough bleeding is heavy or further prolonged.

For women experiencing *changes in the menstrual bleeding pattern*, 6 to 12%, 6 to 10%, and less than 1% of women will experience *spotting*, *scanty menses*, or *metrorrhagia*, respectively. Up to 12% of women using norethindrone-containing oral contraceptives and less than 2% of women using desogestrel-, norgestimate-, or levonorgestrel-containing oral contraceptives will experience an *absence of withdrawal bleeding*. Early or mid-cycle spotting or absence of withdrawal bleeding may be seen with use of low doses of monophasic contraceptives and may not be an unexpected side effect but is a major reason for discontinuance. A change to a different formulation with a greater estrogen:progestin ratio or less progestin, such as multiphasic formulations, or temporary supplementation with an estrogen, may improve these adverse effects. Failure of oral contraceptives to induce *withdrawal uterine bleeding* may be caused by insufficient estrogen activity to induce endometrial development. A change to a different formulation with increased estrogen:progestin ratio may improve this effect.

Incidence less frequent

Glucose tolerance, mildly reduced (faintness; nausea; skin paleness; sweating)—usually for women with predisposing conditions; ***headaches or migraines, worsening or increased frequency of***—21%; ***hypertension, worsening or exacerbation; vaginal candidiasis or vaginitis, sporadic or recurrent*** (vaginal discharge, thick, white, or curd-like, or vaginal itching or other irritation)—10 to 16%

Note: Several studies have confirmed that 15 to 18% of oral contraceptive users will experience an increase, but not a clinically significant elevation, in blood pressure. Another study has observed that 4% of contraceptive users will develop *hypertension*, especially when either a history of hypertension in pregnancy or a family history of hypertension exists. Severe or *malignant hypertension* has been rarely seen.

Although one large cross-sectional study has shown a 43 to 61% increase in the area under the plasma concentration-time curve for glucose, past or current use of oral contraceptives does not increase risk for developing Type 2 diabetes mellitus; the increase is considered transitory and reversible with discontinuation. Oral contraceptive formulations vary in the degree to which they cause *reduced glucose tolerance*, which is usually mild, and may be of clinical importance only for a subset of women at particular risk. In separate studies, norgestimate- and desogestrel-containing oral contraceptives showed minimal impact on glucose tolerance.

Frequency and severity of *headaches or migraines* are reduced in some patients using oral contraceptives, but can be increased in others if they experience fluid retention. If headaches or migraines worsen considerably, discontinuation of oral contraceptives should be considered since this may be a prodomal symptom of stroke.

Withdrawal of oral contraceptives does not seem to affect the frequency of *recurrent vaginal candidiasis or vaginitis;* the increased risk may depend on other factors, such as lifestyle.

Incidence rare

Breast tumors (lumps in breast)—primarily in women having a predisposing or pre-existing condition; ***hepatic focal nodular hyperplasia, hepatitis, or hepatocellular carcinoma*** (pains in stomach, side, or abdomen, or yellow eyes or skin)—primarily in women having a predisposing or pre-existing condition, especially those who smoke tobacco; ***hepatic cell adenomas, benign*** (swelling, pain, or tenderness in upper abdominal area); ***mental depression, slight worsening***—in pre-existing conditions

Note: Association of increased incidence of *breast tumors* is controversial. One study of women 20 to 34 years of age who were long-term oral contraceptive users (10 or more years of use) or recent users (within 5 years of breast cancer diagnosis) found only 1 more case of invasive breast cancer per year among oral contraceptive users than in nonusers for every 100,000 women. It still has not been determined whether the risk of breast cancer increases for early users under 20 years of age or for long-term users.

Although very rare, *hepatic cell adenomas* should be considered in patients having abdominal pain and tenderness, abdominal mass, or hypovolemic shock; one third of patients are asymptomatic at diagnosis. Studies of developing countries that have a high incidence of primary liver cancer have not associated oral contraceptives with an increased risk; however, Western countries, with a low incidence of hepatic carcinoma, have shown a fivefold increase in incidence that persisted for 10 years or more in long-term (5 to 10 years) users of oral contraceptives after stopping treatment. Studies in the U.S., also a country with low incidence of hepatic carcinoma, have not confirmed this finding. Whether hepatic cell adenomas are premalignant is disputed. On occurrence, discontinuing the oral contraceptives is necessary and may result in spontaneous regression of the adenoma.

Mental depression has improved for many women with pre-existing conditions; otherwise, no effect with oral contraceptive use usually is noted but severe depression should be reported to and treatment continuance evaluated by a physician.

Those indicating need for medical attention only if they continue or are bothersome

Incidence more frequent

Abdominal cramping or bloating; acne—usually less frequent after the first 3 months of use; ***breast pain, tenderness, or swelling***—8.5

to 25%; ***dizziness***—10 to 14%; ***nausea or vomiting***—6 to 12%; ***sodium and fluid retention*** (swelling of ankles and feet); ***unusual tiredness or weakness***

Note: When compared with those patients using levonorgestrel, norgestrel, or norethindrone, patients using oral contraceptives containing desogestrel or norgestimate showed improvement in their condition of *acne. Nausea, vomiting, breast tenderness,* and *sodium and fluid retention* diminish after the first 2 or 3 months of oral contraceptive use.

Incidence less frequent

Gain or loss of body or facial hair; increased skin sensitivity to sun; libido changes (increase or decrease of interest in sexual intercourse); ***melasma*** (brown, blotchy spots on exposed skin); ***weight gain or loss***—1%

Note: *Melasma* usually is temporary but can be permanent. Women having dark complexions, having a history of melasma during pregnancy, or having prolonged exposure to sunlight are most susceptible to developing melasma.

Overdose

Serious adverse effects have not been reported following acute ingestion of large doses of oral contraceptives by young children. Overdosage may cause drowsiness, fatigue, nausea, or vomiting. In females, withdrawal bleeding may occur.

For more information on the management of overdose or unintentional ingestion, **contact a Poison Control Center** (see *Poison Control Center Listing*).

Clinical effects of overdose

The following effects have been selected on the basis of their potential clinical significance (possible signs and symptoms in parentheses where appropriate)—not necessarily inclusive:

Drowsiness or fatigue (sleepiness; unusual tiredness or weakness); ***nausea or vomiting; withdrawal bleeding*** (vaginal bleeding)

Treatment of overdose

Treatment, if necessary, is generally symptomatic and supportive. Gastric decontamination may be considered to prevent absorption, especially if soon after ingestion and if significant iron may have been ingested from an oral contraceptive containing iron.

Patients in whom intentional overdose is known or suspected should be referred for psychiatric consultation.

Patient Consultation

As an aid to patient consultation, refer to *Advice for the Patient, Estrogens and Progestins Oral Contraceptives (Systemic).*

Consider advising the patient on the following (» = major clinical significance):

Before using this medication

» Conditions affecting use, especially:
- Sensitivity to estrogens or progestins
- Pregnancy—Not recommended for use during pregnancy
- Breast-feeding—Oral contraceptives are distributed into breast milk
- Use in adolescents—Careful counseling may be required to increase compliance
- Dental—May increase possibility of bleeding of gingival tissues, gingival hyperplasia, or local alveolar osteitis (dry socket)
- Other medications, especially corticosteroids, cyclosporine, hepatic enzyme inducers, hepatotoxic medications (especially troleandomycin), ritonavir, theophylline, tobacco smoking, or troglitazone
- Other medical problems, especially carcinoma of the breast (known or suspected); carcinoma of the endometrium; cardiac insufficiency; cerebrovascular disease—especially if patient smokes cigarettes (active or history of); coronary artery disease; estrogen-dependent neoplasia (known or suspected); hepatic disease, cholestatic (active); hepatic function impairment; hepatic tumors, benign or malignant (active or history of); obstructive jaundice, or history of obstructive jaundice during pregnancy; jaundice with prior use of oral contraceptives, thrombophlebitis, thrombosis, or thromboembolic disorders (active or history of); or uterine bleeding (abnormal or undiagnosed)

Proper use of this medication

» Reading patient package insert carefully

Taking with or immediately after food to reduce nausea

Using an additional method of birth control for the first 7 days; some clinicians may recommend that an additional method of birth control be used during the first cycle of oral contraceptive use

» Compliance with therapy; taking medication at the same time each day, at 24-hour intervals

Keeping an extra 1-month supply available when possible

Taking tablets in proper (color-coded) sequence

» Proper dosing

- Missed doses for the monophasic, biphasic, or triphasic cycle—
  - Missing the first tablet of a new cycle—Taking as soon as possible; if not remembered until next day, taking two tablets; continuing on regular dosing schedule and using another birth control method for 7 days after the last missed dose
  - Missing 1 day—Taking as soon as possible; if not remembered until next day, taking 2 tablets; continuing on regular dosing schedule
  - Missing 2 days in a row in the first or second week—Taking two tablets a day for next 2 days, then continuing on regular dosing schedule; using additional method of birth control for remainder of cycle
  - Missing 2 days in a row in the third week or
  - Missing 3 days in a row—
    - Using Day-1 start: Discarding remaining doses for current cycle; beginning a new cycle following the recommended dosing schedule and using a second method of birth control, additionally, for 7 days after the last missed dose; contacting health care professional if two menstrual periods are missed
    - Using Sunday start: Continuing on regular dosing schedule for current cycle until Sunday; on Sunday, throwing out remaining doses for current cycle and beginning a new cycle; using an additional method of birth control for 7 days after the last missed dose; contacting health care professional if two menstrual periods are missed
- Missing any of the last seven tablets of a twenty-eight-day cycle is not important, but beginning new cycle on time is essential

» Proper storage

Precautions while using this medication

» Regular visits to physician at least every 6 to 12 months to check progress

» Caution if medical or dental surgery or emergency treatment is required—increased risk of thrombotic complications

» Using an additional method of birth control during each cycle in which the following medications are used: ampicillin, hepatic enzyme inducers, penicillin V, ritonavir, tetracyclines, or troglitazone

What to expect and do if vaginal bleeding occurs

What to expect and do if a menstrual period is missed; contacting health professional if two menstrual periods are missed

Possibility of dental problems, such as tenderness, swelling, or bleeding of gums; brushing and flossing teeth, massaging gums, and having dentist clean teeth regularly; checking with dentist if there are questions about care of teeth or gums or if tenderness, swelling, or bleeding of gums is noticed

Possibility of photosensitivity

» Stopping medication immediately and checking with physician if pregnancy is suspected

If scheduled for laboratory tests, telling physician if taking birth control pills; certain blood tests may be affected by oral contraceptives

Not refilling an old prescription for oral contraceptives without having a physical examination by physician, especially after a pregnancy

Side/adverse effects

Signs of potential side effects, especially thromboembolism or thrombosis; changes in the menstrual bleeding pattern or intermenstrual bleeding; headaches or migraines; hypertension, worsening; mildly reduced glucose tolerance (usually for predisposed individuals); vaginal candidiasis or vaginitis; breast tumors (usually for predisposed individuals); hepatic focal nodular hyperplasia, hepatitis, or hepatocellular carcinoma; hepatic cell adenomas, benign; slight worsening of mental depression

Cigarette smoking combined with oral contraceptive use causes increased risk of serious thromboembolic or hepatic side effects, especially for heavy smokers or women over age 35

General Dosing Information

The doses of estrogens and progestins used for contraception are much greater than those doses of estrogens and progestins used for hormone replacement therapy. Perimenopausal women should be tested for serum FSH levels annually for accurate dating of menopause; oral contraceptives should be discontinued and hormone replacement therapy started if or when appropriate.

Low doses of estrogen (doses containing 35 mcg or less of ethinyl estradiol or 50 mcg mestranol) are preferred to higher doses (equal to 50 mcg of ethinyl estradiol). Many side effects are related to the dominance of either the estrogen or progestin present in the preparation. By changing to preparations of differing component ratios, side effects can often be lessened or eliminated. In some instances low-dose estrogen formulations are not acceptable and the high-dose estrogen formulations should be used, such as when the effectiveness of oral contraceptives is compromised because of increased hepatic metabolism. This may occur when some anticonvulsant medications are used concurrently. All effects of long-term use of the lower-dose oral contraceptives have not been determined. Most long-term studies performed have been in patients using higher doses of estrogens and progestins than are used commonly at present.

Thirty-five mcg of ethinyl estradiol and 50 mcg of mestranol are considered to have equal therapeutic potency as the estrogen component for contraception. Norgestrel (d,l-norgestrel) is a racemic mixture of dextro- and levonorgestrel and has one-half the potency of levonorgestrel on a weight basis. Dextronorgestrel can be considered an inactive isomer.

The multiphasic formulations were developed to supply the lowest possible total hormone dose over a treatment cycle. Monophasic, biphasic, and triphasic regimens are considered equally effective for preventing pregnancy and choice may be unique to an individual's lifestyle, health risks, or other factors. The success of an oral contraceptive is also highly dependent on proper selection of the formulation for an individual, according to her menstrual cycle regularity, her ability to be compliant, and her tolerance for side effects. When possible, the lowest dose of hormones should be used to achieve these goals.

- The *monophasic regimen* provides constant doses of estrogen and progestin in 21 days.
- The *biphasic regimen* provides two different dose ratios of two phases of the estrogen:progestin in 21 days and includes a constant estrogen dose throughout the cycle with a progestin dose increase either at the 7th or the 10th day, depending on the product.
- The *triphasic regimen* provides four different dose ratios of three phases of estrogen:progestin in 21 days and includes:
  - —Variable doses of estrogen and progestin changing after the 6th and 10th days.
  - —A constant progestin dose throughout the cycle plus an increase in the estrogen dose after the 5th and 7th days.
  - —A constant estrogen dose throughout the cycle plus an increase in the progestin dose for only 9 days (8th through the 16th day).
  - —A constant estrogen dose throughout the cycle with an increase in the progestin dose every 7 days.

For routine contraception

To begin taking oral contraceptives, the first tablet is taken either on Day 1 (first day of menstrual bleeding) of the menstrual cycle or the first Sunday following the start of menses. Dosage schedules are arranged on a 21- or 28-day cycle to correspond with the 28 days of the menstrual cycle. The 21-day regimens provide 21 active tablets containing estrogen and progestin hormone therapy. The 28-day cycle adds 7 inactive (nonhormonal) tablets to the 21-day regimen for either 7 days of placebo tablets for ease of daily counting or 7 days of iron (ferrous fumarate) companion tablets to supplement the diet. To help the patient to comply with this schedule, most manufacturers integrate the schedule into a non-childproof dispensing container, which should be utilized whenever possible. Tablets containing different strengths of hormones are colored differently to help the patient differentiate between the tablet strengths; this is especially helpful for biphasic and triphasic formulations. Also, the active and inactive tablets are different colors. Patients should be informed of the necessity of taking different colored tablets in the proper sequence and not mixing tablets of different colors indiscriminately. Also, even if the hormone formulation is the same for two products of different manufacturers, tablet colors do not always correspond.

Maximum contraceptive effect is obtained by taking doses at 24-hour intervals and beginning the new regimen on time; this enhances patient compliance, also. When initiating oral contraceptive treatment, many clinicians instruct patients to use a nonhormonal backup method for 7 days if contraceptive therapy is started within the first 5 days of the menstrual cycle. Other clinicians counsel patients to use a nonhormonal backup method of contraception for the first month. Contraceptive effectiveness is continued when transferring patients between oral contraceptive formulations when initiated at the beginning of the menstrual cycle, with minimal side effects. Breakthrough bleeding or spotting may recur for several months when an oral contraceptive is started, but is usually less for those patients transferred between formulations than for initial users.

A periodic pill-free *rest period* is not recommended, since it appears to provide no therapeutic advantage and does not enhance the resumption of ovulatory cycles after cessation of oral contraceptive therapy. Such intervals may result in noncompliance with the substituted contraceptive and unwanted pregnancies.

For emergency postcoital contraception

Therapy is initiated as soon as possible or up to 72 hours after intercourse; repeated courses in a single cycle are not recommended as efficacy may be compromised.

The use of norgestrel or levonorgestrel and ethinyl estradiol tablets as a postcoital contraceptive (the *morning-after pill*) has been employed primarily in emergency situations, such as when possible contraceptive method failure is realized early or when any unprotected sexual intercourse is of concern to the patient. Effectiveness depends on the time interval between coitus and administration of the medication. A pregnancy test should be performed prior to administering medication. A patient requesting treatment should be fully informed of the risks involved, such as potential increased risk of blood clot formation because of the higher dosage of hormone required, although treatment is of short duration. Also, nausea and vomiting may result, increasing the possibility of contraceptive failure because of the difficulty of maintaining compliance.

For patients with endometriosis

Oral contraceptives can be given continuously or cyclically for 6 to 9 months to aid in ectopic implant atrophy. Low-dose estrogen preparations containing a high progestational progestin, such as desogestrel, are probably best for this. Endometriotic symptoms may increase before improvement is noted by patient.

For patients with hirsutisim

Treatment with oral contraceptives for 6 months to 1 year may be required before effects are apparent. Although hormones suppress new hair growth, normal androgen levels maintain hair that is already present.

Diet/Nutrition

Should be taken with food or milk to lessen gastrointestinal irritation if it occurs or tablets may be taken at bedtime.

DESOGESTREL AND ETHINYL ESTRADIOL

Summary of Differences

Pharmacology/pharmacokinetics—Desogestrel is a prodrug that is metabolized to a more active form, etonogestrel. Exhibits first-pass effect. Highly progestational and does not counteract the estrogen increase in sex hormone-binding globulin (SHBG) levels; highly bound to SHBG and albumin; low androgenicity.

Laboratory value alterations—Little effect on lipoproteins.

Medical considerations/contraindications—Desogestrel plus ethinyl estradiol increases glucose tolerance but does not affect 2-hour insulin release; has less effect on carbohydrate metabolism compared with other oral contraceptives.

Side/adverse effects—Absence of withdrawal menstrual bleeding is low; improves pre-existing acne.

Oral Dosage Forms

Note: Bracketed uses in the *Dosage Forms* section refer to categories of use and/or indications that are not included in U.S. product labeling.

DESOGESTREL AND ETHINYL ESTRADIOL TABLETS

Usual adult and adolescent dose

Contraceptive, systemic or
Estrogen-progestin or
[Antiendometriotic agent][1] or
[Gonadotropin inhibitor, female, noncontraceptive use][1]—

Twenty-one day cycle: Oral, 1 tablet a day for twenty-one days commencing on Day 1 of the menstrual cycle or on the first Sunday after the menstrual cycle begins; the next round of treatment is begun on the eighth day after the last tablet of the previous cycle has been taken.

Twenty-eight day cycle: Oral, 1 tablet a day for twenty-eight days commencing on Day 1 of the menstrual cycle, or on the first Sunday after the menstrual cycle begins; the next round of treatment is begun on the day after the last tablet of the previous cycle has been taken.

Note: With a Sunday start schedule, the patient should take her first tablet on the first Sunday after the onset of menstruation. If the patient's period begins on a Sunday, she should take her first tablet that same day.

With a Day-1 start schedule, the patient should take her first tablet on Day 1 of the menstrual cycle.

The last seven tablets of the twenty-eight day cycle contain no hormones. These seven companion tablets are a different color from those containing hormones.

Oral contraceptives may be given continuously or cyclically for endometriosis.

Strength(s) usually available

U.S.—

Monophasic formulation:

150 mcg (0.15 mg) of desogestrel and 30 mcg (0.03 mg) of ethinyl estradiol (Rx) [*Desogen; Ortho-Cept*].

Triphasic formulation:

100 mcg (0.100 mg) of desogestrel and 25 mcg (0.025 mg) of ethinyl estradiol (Rx) [*Cyclessa*].

125 mcg (0.125 mg) of desogestrel and 25 mcg (0.025 mg) of ethinyl estradiol (Rx) [*Cyclessa*].

150 mcg (0.150 mg) of desogestrel and 25 mcg (0.025 mg) of ethinyl estradiol (Rx) [*Cyclessa*].

Canada—

Monophasic formulation:

150 mcg (0.15 mg) of desogestrel and 30 mcg (0.03 mg) of ethinyl estradiol (Rx) [*Marvelon; Ortho-Cept*].

Note: *Marvelon* and *Ortho-Cept* are available in twenty-one or twenty-eight day cycles. The twenty-eight day cycle includes an additional seven days of placebo tablets.

Packaging and storage

Store below 40 °C (104 °F), preferably between 15 and 30 °C (59 and 86 °F), unless otherwise specified by manufacturer. Store in a well-closed container.

Auxiliary labeling

- Take with food.
- Avoid too much sun or use of sunlamp.

Note

Include mandatory patient package inserts (PPIs) (the brief summary of patient labeling and the detailed patient labeling) when dispensing.

Caution first-time users to use an additional form of birth control as directed by their physicians until maximum contraceptive protection begins.

DESOGESTREL AND ETHINYL ESTRADIOL TABLETS ETHINYL ESTRADIOL TABLETS USP

Usual adult and adolescent dose

Contraceptive, systemic or
Estrogen-progestin or
[Antiendometriotic agent][1] or
[Gonadotropin inhibitor, female, noncontraceptive use][1]—

See *Desogestrel and Ethinyl Estradiol Tablets*.

Strength(s) usually available

U.S.—

Monophasic formulation:

150 mcg (0.15 mg) of desogestrel and 20 mcg ethinyl estradiol (0.02 mg) (Rx) [*Mircette*].

Canada—

Not commercially available in Canada.

Note: Available in twenty-eight day cycles. The twenty-eight day cycle includes an additional seven days of tablets containing two placebo tablets for the first two days, then five tablets of 10 mcg (0.10 mg) of ethinyl estradiol. Similar to placebo tablets, the last seven days of a this twenty-eight day cycle need not be taken, even though it contains a low-dose of estrogen; contraceptive efficacy is not dependent on the low doses of estrogen given Days 24 through 28.

Packaging and storage

Store below 40 °C (104 °F), preferably between 15 and 30 °C (59 and 86 °F), unless otherwise specified by manufacturer. Store in a well-closed container.

Auxiliary labeling

- Take with food.
- Avoid too much sun or use of sunlamp.

Note

Include mandatory patient package inserts (PPIs) (the brief summary of patient labeling and the detailed patient labeling) when dispensing.

Caution first-time users to use an additional form of birth control as directed by their physicians until maximum contraceptive protection begins.

[1]Not included in Canadian product labeling.

ETHYNODIOL DIACETATE AND ETHINYL ESTRADIOL

Summary of Differences

Pharmacology/pharmacokinetics—Ethynodiol diacetate hydrolyzed to norethindrone; aromatization by tissues may be clinically significant. Greater affinity for albumin but significant SHBG binding occurs because of estrogen-induced SHBG levels. Exhibits first-pass effect. Slightly estrogenic.

Laboratory value alterations—Triglycerides increase; shows the greatest increase in apolipoprotein A_1 of all contraceptives.

Dosage forms—High estrogen dose formulation available.

Oral Dosage Forms

Note: Bracketed uses in the *Dosage Forms* section refer to categories of use and/or indications that are not included in U.S. product labeling.

ETHYNODIOL DIACETATE AND ETHINYL ESTRADIOL TABLETS USP

Usual adult and adolescent dose

Contraceptive, systemic or
Estrogen-progestin or
[Antiendometriotic agent][1] or
[Gonadotropin inhibitor, female, noncontraceptive use][1]—

Twenty-one day cycle: Oral, 1 tablet a day for twenty-one days commencing on Day 1 of the menstrual cycle or on the first Sunday after the menstrual cycle begins; the next round of treatment is begun on the eighth day after the last tablet of the previous cycle has been taken.

Twenty-eight day cycle: Oral, 1 tablet a day for twenty-eight days commencing on Day 1 of the menstrual cycle, or on the first Sunday after the menstrual cycle begins; the next round of treatment is begun on the day after the last tablet of the previous cycle has been taken.

Note: With a Sunday start schedule, the patient should take her first tablet on the first Sunday after the onset of menstruation. If the patient's period begins on a Sunday, she should take her first tablet that same day.

With a Day-1 start schedule, the patient should take her first tablet on Day 1 of the menstrual cycle.

The last seven tablets of the twenty-eight day cycle contain no hormones. These seven companion tablets are of a different color from those containing hormones.

Oral contraceptives may be given continuously or cyclically for endometriosis.

Strength(s) usually available

U.S.—

Monophasic formulation:

1 mg of ethynodiol diacetate and 35 mcg (0.035 mg) of ethinyl estradiol (Rx) [*Demulen 1/35; Zovia 1/35E*].

1 mg of ethynodiol diacetate and 50 mcg (0.05 mg) of ethinyl estradiol (Rx) [*Demulen 1/50; Zovia 1/50E*].

Canada—

Monophasic formulation:

1 mg of ethynodiol diacetate and 50 mcg (0.05 mg) of ethinyl estradiol (Rx) [*Demulen 50*].

2 mg of ethynodiol diacetate and 30 mcg (0.03 mg) of ethinyl estradiol (Rx) [*Demulen 30*].

Note: Available in twenty-one or twenty-eight day cycles. The twenty-eight day cycle includes an additional seven days of placebo tablets.

Packaging and storage

Store below 40 °C (104 °F), preferably between 15 and 30 °C (59 and 86 °F), unless otherwise specified by manufacturer. Store in a well-closed container.

Auxiliary labeling

- Take with food.
- Avoid too much sun or use of sunlamp.

Note

Include mandatory patient package inserts (PPIs) (the brief summary of patient labeling and the detailed patient labeling) when dispensing.

Caution first-time users to use additional form of birth control as directed by their physicians until maximum contraceptive protection begins.

[1]Not included in Canadian product labeling.

LEVONORGESTREL AND ETHINYL ESTRADIOL

Summary of Differences

Indications—Also used for emergency postcoital contraception.

Pharmacology/pharmacokinetics—Levonorgestrel is the active enantiomer of norgestrel. Proportion bound to SHBG depends on both estrogen and levonorgestrel dose; suppresses estrogen-induced increase of SHBG levels except when the triphasic formulation is used, which slightly increases SHBG levels. No first-pass effect. One of the most androgenic progestins; androgenic effects depend on both progestin and estrogen dose.

Laboratory value alterations—No change in triglycerides over 1 year; may slightly decrease or increase total cholesterol; negatively affected lipoprotein—increases LDL and lowers HDL; increases apolipoprotein A_1 the least of all contraceptives; can increase free testosterone by displacing it from SHBG.

Dosage forms—High estrogen dose formulation available.

Oral Dosage Forms

Note: Bracketed uses in the *Dosage Forms* section refer to categories of use and/or indications that are not included in U.S. product labeling.

LEVONORGESTREL AND ETHINYL ESTRADIOL TABLETS USP

Usual adult and adolescent dose

Contraceptive, systemic or
Estrogen-progestin or
[Antiendometriotic agent][1] or
[Gonadotropin inhibitor, female, noncontraceptive use][1]—

Twenty-one day cycle: Oral, 1 tablet a day for twenty-one days commencing on Day 1 of the menstrual cycle or on the first Sunday after the menstrual cycle begins; the next round of treatment is begun on the eighth day after the last tablet of the previous cycle has been taken.

Twenty-eight day cycle: Oral, 1 tablet a day for twenty-eight days commencing on Day 1 of the menstrual cycle, or on the first Sunday after the menstrual cycle begins; the next round of treatment is begun on the day after the last tablet of the previous cycle has been taken.

Note: With a Sunday start schedule, the patient should take her first tablet on the first Sunday after the onset of menstruation. If the patient's period begins on a Sunday, she should take her first tablet that same day.

With a Day-1 start schedule, the patient should take her first tablet on Day 1 of the menstrual cycle.

The last seven tablets of the twenty-eight day cycle contain no hormones. These seven companion tablets are a different color from those containing hormones.

Oral contraceptives may be given continuously or cyclically for endometriosis.

[Contraceptive, postcoital, systemic][1]—

Four tablets (150 mcg levonorgestrel and 30 mcg of ethinyl estradiol per tablet) taken as soon as possible after unprotected coitus, preferably within twelve hours but not longer than seventy-two hours later. Then, four more tablets are taken twelve hours after the first dose.

Note: Monophasic or only phase-three tablets of the triphasic oral contraceptives contain sufficient hormone doses for postcoital emergency contraception use.

Strength(s) usually available

U.S.—

Monophasic formulation:

100 mcg (0.1 mg) of levonorgestrel and 20 mcg (0.02 mg) of ethinyl estradiol (Rx) [*Alesse; Levlite*].

150 mcg (0.15 mg) of levonorgestrel and 30 mcg (0.03 mg) of ethinyl estradiol (Rx) [*Levlen; Levora 0.15/30; Nordette*].

Triphasic formulation:

Phase one (six days)—50 mcg (0.05 mg) of levonorgestrel and 30 mcg (0.03 mg) of ethinyl estradiol. **Phase two (five days)**—75 mcg (0.075 mg) of levonorgestrel and 40 mcg (0.04 mg) of ethinyl estradiol. **Phase three (ten days)**—125 mcg (0.125 mg) of levonorgestrel and 30 mcg (0.03 mg) of ethinyl estradiol. (Rx) [*Tri-Levlen; Triphasil; Trivora*].

Canada—

Monophasic formulation:

150 mcg (0.15 mg) of levonorgestrel and 30 mcg (0.03 mg) of ethinyl estradiol (Rx) [*Min-Ovral*].

Triphasic formulation:

Phase one (six days)—50 mcg (0.05 mg) of levonorgestrel and 30 mcg (0.03 mg) of ethinyl estradiol. **Phase two (five days)**—75 mcg (0.075 mg) of levonorgestrel and 40 mcg (0.04 mg) of ethinyl estradiol. **Phase three (ten days)**—125 mcg (0.125 mg) of levonorgestrel and 30 mcg (0.03 mg) of ethinyl estradiol. (Rx) [*Triphasil; Triquilar*].

Note: Available in twenty-one–or twenty-eight day cycles. The twenty-eight day cycle includes an additional seven days of placebo tablets.

Packaging and storage

Store below 40 °C (104 °F), preferably between 15 and 30 °C (59 and 86 °F), unless otherwise specified by manufacturer. Store in a well-closed container.

Auxiliary labeling

- Take with food.
- Avoid too much sun or use of sunlamp.

Note

Include mandatory patient package inserts (PPIs) (the brief summary of patient labeling and the detailed patient labeling) when dispensing.

Explain sequence of administration of triphasic cycle formula when dispensing, especially for twenty-eight day cycle (colored tablet sequence).

Caution first-time users to use an additional form of birth control as directed by their physicians until maximum contraceptive protection begins.

[1]Not included in Canadian product labeling.

NORETHINDRONE ACETATE AND ETHINYL ESTRADIOL

Summary of Differences

Pharmacology/pharmacokinetics—Proportion bound to SHBG depends on both estrogen and norethindrone dose; does not suppress estrogen-induced increase in SHBG levels. Norethindrone acetate metabolized to norethindrone, which exhibits no first-pass effect. Androgenic effect depends on both progestin and estrogen dose; androgenic effects less than those of levonorgestrel or norgestrel; possesses slight estrogenic activity.

Laboratory value alterations—Slightly increases total cholesterol; negatively affects lipoproteins—increases LDL and lowers HDL; increases apolipoprotein A_1.

Dosage forms—High estrogen dose formulation available.

Oral Dosage Forms

Note: Bracketed uses in the *Dosage Forms* section refer to categories of use and/or indications that are not included in U.S. product labeling.

NORETHINDRONE ACETATE AND ETHINYL ESTRADIOL TABLETS USP

Usual adult and adolescent dose

Contraceptive, systemic or
Estrogen-progestin or
[Antiendometriotic agent][1] or
[Gonadotropin inhibitor, female, noncontraceptive use][1]—

Twenty-one day cycle: Oral, 1 tablet a day for twenty-one days commencing on Day 1 of the menstrual cycle or on the first Sunday after the menstrual cycle begins; the next round of treatment is begun on the eighth day after the last tablet of the previous cycle has been taken.

Twenty-eight day cycle: Oral, 1 tablet a day for twenty-eight days commencing on Day 1 of the menstrual cycle, or on the first Sunday after the menstrual cycle begins; the next round of treatment is begun on the day after the last tablet of the previous cycle has been taken.

Note: With a Sunday start schedule, the patient should take her first tablet on the first Sunday after the onset of menstruation. If the patient's period begins on a Sunday, she should take her first tablet that same day.

With a Day-1 start schedule, the patient should take her first tablet on Day 1 of the menstrual cycle.

The last seven tablets of the twenty-eight day cycle contain no hormones. These seven companion tablets are a different color from those containing hormones.

Oral contraceptives may be given continuously or cyclically for endometriosis.

Acne vulgaris, systemic[1]—

Twenty-one day cycle (Triphasic formulation only):

Oral, 1 tablet a day for twenty-one days commencing on Day 1 of the menstrual cycle or on the first Sunday after the menstrual cycle begins; the next round of treatment is begun on the eighth day after the last tablet of the previous cycle has been taken.

Twenty-eight day cycle (Triphasic formulation only):

Oral, 1 tablet a day for twenty-eight days commencing on Day 1 of the menstrual cycle, or on the first Sunday after the menstrual cycle begins; the next round of treatment is begun on the day after the last tablet of the previous cycle has been taken.

Strength(s) usually available

U.S.—

Monophasic formulation:

1 mg of norethindrone acetate and 20 mcg (0.02 mg) of ethinyl estradiol (Rx) [*Loestrin 1/20*].

1.5 mg of norethindrone acetate and 30 mcg (0.03 mg) of ethinyl estradiol (Rx) [*Loestrin 1.5/30*].

Triphasic formulation:

Phase one (five days)—1 mg of norethindrone acetate and 20 mcg (0.02 mg) of ethinyl estradiol. **Phase two (seven days)**—1 mg of norethindrone acetate and 30 mcg (0.03 mg) of ethinyl estradiol. **Phase three (nine days)**—1 mg of norethindrone acetate and 35 mcg (0.035 mg) of ethinyl estradiol. (Rx) [*Estrostep*].

Canada—

Monophasic formulation:

1 mg of norethindrone acetate and 20 mcg (0.02 mg) of ethinyl estradiol (Rx) [*Minestrin 1/20*].

1.5 mg of norethindrone acetate and 30 mcg (0.03 mg) of ethinyl estradiol (Rx) [*Loestrin 1.5/30*].

Note: Available in twenty-one or twenty-eight day cycles. The twenty-eight day cycle includes an additional seven days of placebo tablets.

Packaging and storage

Store below 40 °C (104 °F), preferably between 15 and 30 °C (59 and 86 °F), unless otherwise specified by manufacturer. Store in a well-closed container.

Auxiliary labeling

- Take with food.
- Avoid too much sun or use of sunlamp.

Note

Include mandatory patient package inserts (PPIs) (the brief summary of patient labeling and the detailed patient labeling) when dispensing.

Caution first-time users to use an additional form of birth control as directed by their physicians until maximum contraceptive protection begins.

NORETHINDRONE ACETATE AND ETHINYL ESTRADIOL TABLETS USP FERROUS FUMARATE TABLETS USP

Usual adult and adolescent dose

Contraceptive, systemic or
Estrogen-progestin or
[Antiendometriotic agent][1] or
[Gonadotropin inhibitor, female, noncontraceptive use][1]—

See *Norethindrone Acetate and Ethinyl Estradiol Tablets USP*.

Acne vulgaris, systemic[1]—

Twenty-one day cycle (Triphasic formulation only):

Oral, 1 tablet a day for twenty-one days commencing on Day 1 of the menstrual cycle or on the first Sunday after the menstrual cycle begins; the next round of treatment is begun on the eighth day after the last tablet of the previous cycle has been taken.

Twenty-eight day cycle (Triphasic formulation only):

Oral, 1 tablet a day for twenty-eight days commencing on Day 1 of the menstrual cycle, or on the first Sunday after the menstrual cycle begins; the next round of treatment is begun on the day after the last tablet of the previous cycle has been taken.

Strength(s) usually available

U.S.—

Monophasic formulation:

1 mg of norethindrone acetate and 20 mcg (0.02 mg) of ethinyl estradiol (Rx) [*Loestrin Fe 1/20*].

1.5 mg of norethindrone acetate and 30 mcg (0.03 mg) of ethinyl estradiol (Rx) [*Loestrin Fe 1.5/30*].

Triphasic formulation:

Phase one (five days)—1 mg of norethindrone acetate and 20 mcg (0.02 mg) of ethinyl estradiol. **Phase two (seven days)**—1 mg of norethindrone acetate and 30 mcg (0.03 mg) of ethinyl estradiol. **Phase three (nine days)**—1 mg of norethindrone acetate and 35 mcg (0.035 mg) of ethinyl estradiol. (Rx) [*Estrostep Fe*].

Canada—

Not commercially available in Canada.

Note: Available in twenty-eight day cycles. The twenty-eight day cycle includes an additional seven days of tablets containing 75 mg ferrous fumarate each.

Packaging and storage

Store below 40 °C (104 °F), preferably between 15 and 30 °C (59 and 86 °F), unless otherwise specified by manufacturer. Store in a well-closed container.

Auxiliary labeling

- Take with food.
- Avoid too much sun or use of sunlamp.

Note

Include mandatory patient package inserts (PPIs) (the brief summary of patient labeling and the detailed patient labeling) when dispensing.

Caution first-time users to use an additional form of birth control as directed by their physicians until maximum contraceptive protection begins.

---

[1]Not included in Canadian product labeling.

NORETHINDRONE AND ETHINYL ESTRADIOL

Summary of Differences

Pharmacology/pharmacokinetics—Proportion bound to SHBG depends on both estrogen and norethindrone dose; does not suppress estrogen-induced increase in SHBG levels. Norethindrone exhibits no first-pass effect; less androgenic than levonorgestrel or norgestrel; its androgenic effect depends on both progestin and estrogen doses; slight estrogenic activity.

Laboratory value alterations—Triglycerides increase as with all oral contraceptives; slightly increases total cholesterol; negatively affects lipoproteins—increases LDL and lowers HDL; increases apolipoprotein A_1.

Dosage forms—High estrogen dose formulation available.

Oral Dosage Forms

Note: Bracketed uses in the *Dosage Forms* section refer to categories of use and/or indications that are not included in U.S. product labeling.

NORETHINDRONE AND ETHINYL ESTRADIOL TABLETS USP

Usual adult and adolescent dose

Contraceptive, systemic or
Estrogen-progestin or
[Antiendometriotic agent][1] or
[Gonadotropin inhibitor, female, noncontraceptive use][1]—

Twenty-one day cycle: Oral, 1 tablet a day for twenty-one days commencing on Day 1 of the menstrual cycle or on the first Sunday after the menstrual cycle begins; the next round of treatment is begun on the eighth day after the last tablet of the previous cycle has been taken.

Twenty-eight day cycle: Oral, 1 tablet a day for twenty-eight days commencing on Day 1 of the menstrual cycle, or on the first Sunday after the menstrual cycle begins; the next round of treatment is begun on the day after the last tablet of the previous cycle has been taken.

Note: With a Sunday start schedule, the patient should take her first tablet on the first Sunday after the onset of menstruation. If the patient's period begins on a Sunday, she should take her first tablet that same day.

With a Day-1 start schedule, the patient should take her first tablet on Day 1 of the menstrual cycle.

The last seven tablets of the twenty-eight day cycle contain no hormones. These seven companion tablets are a different color from those containing hormones.

Oral contraceptives may be given continuously or cyclically for endometriosis.

Strength(s) usually available

U.S.—

Monophasic formulation:

400 mcg (0.4 mg) of norethindrone and 35 mcg (0.035 mg) of ethinyl estradiol (Rx) [*Ovcon-35*].

500 mcg (0.5 mg) of norethindrone and 35 mcg (0.035 mg) of ethinyl estradiol (Rx) [*Brevicon; Genora 0.5/35; Intercon 0.5/35; ModiCon; Necon 0.5/35; Nelova 0.5/35E*].

1 mg of norethindrone and 35 mcg (0.035 mg) of ethinyl estradiol (Rx) [*Genora 1/35; Intercon 1/35; Necon 1/35; N.E.E. 1/35; Nelova 1/35E; Norethin 1/35E; Norinyl 1+35; Ortho-Novum 1/35*].

1 mg of norethindrone and 50 mcg (0.05 mg) of ethinyl estradiol (Rx) [*N.E.E. 1/50; Ovcon-50*].

Biphasic formulation, Option one:

Phase one (ten days): 500 mcg (0.5 mg) of norethindrone and 35 mcg (0.035 mg) of ethinyl estradiol. **Phase two (eleven days):** 1 mg of norethindrone and 35 mcg (0.035 mg) of ethinyl estradiol. (Rx) [*Necon 10/11; Nelova 10/11; Ortho-Novum 10/11*].

Biphasic formulation, Option two:

Phase one (seven days): 500 mcg (0.5 mg) of norethindrone and 35 mcg (0.035 mg) of ethinyl estradiol. **Phase two (fourteen days):** 1 mg norethindrone and 35 mcg (0.035 mg) of ethinyl estradiol. (Rx) [*Jenest*].

Triphasic formulation, Option one:

Phase one (seven days): 500 mcg (0.5 mg) of norethindrone and 35 mcg (0.035 mg) of ethinyl estradiol. **Phase two (nine days):** 1 mg of norethindrone and 35 mcg (0.035 mg) of ethinyl estradiol. **Phase three (five days):** 500 mcg (0.5 mg) of norethindrone and 35 mcg (0.035 mg) of ethinyl estradiol. (Rx) [*Tri-Norinyl*].

Triphasic formulation, Option two:

Phase one (seven days): 500 mcg (0.5 mg) of norethindrone and 35 mcg (0.035 mg) of ethinyl estradiol. **Phase two (seven days):** 750 mcg (0.75 mg) of norethindrone and 35 mcg (0.035 mg) of ethinyl estradiol. **Phase three (seven days):** 1 mg of norethindrone and 35 mcg (0.035 mg) of ethinyl estradiol. (Rx) [*Ortho-Novum 7/7/7*].

Canada—

Monophasic formulation:

500 mcg (0.5 mg) of norethindrone and 35 mcg (0.035 mg) of ethinyl estradiol (Rx) [*Brevicon 0.5/35; Ortho 0.5/35*].

1 mg of norethindrone and 35 mcg (0.035 mg) of ethinyl estradiol (Rx) [*Brevicon 1/35; Ortho 1/35; Select 1/35* (povidone)].

Biphasic formulation:

Phase one (ten days)—500 mcg (0.5 mg) of norethindrone and 35 mcg (0.035 mg) of ethinyl estradiol. **Phase two (eleven days)**—1 mg of norethindrone and 35 mcg (0.035 mg) of ethinyl estradiol. (Rx) [*Ortho 10/11; Synphasic*].

Triphasic formulation:

Phase one (seven days)—500 mcg (0.5 mg) of norethindrone and 35 mcg (0.035 mg) of ethinyl estradiol. **Phase two (seven days)**—750 mcg (0.75 mg) of norethindrone and 35 mcg (0.035 mg) of ethinyl estradiol. **Phase three (seven days)**—1 mg of norethindrone and 35 mcg (0.035 mg) of ethinyl estradiol. (Rx) [*Ortho 7/7/7*].

Note: Most products are available in twenty-one or twenty-eight day cycles. The twenty-eight day cycle includes an additional seven days of placebo tablets.

Packaging and storage

Store below 40 °C (104 °F), preferably between 15 and 30 °C (59 and 86 °F), unless otherwise specified by manufacturer. Store in a well-closed container.

Auxiliary labeling

- Take with food.
- Avoid too much sun or use of sunlamp.

Note

Include mandatory patient package inserts (PPIs) (the brief summary of patient labeling and the detailed patient labeling) when dispensing.

Explain sequence of administration of biphasic or triphasic cycle formula when dispensing, especially for twenty-eight day cycle (colored tablet sequence).

Caution first-time users to use an additional form of birth control as directed by their physicians until maximum contraceptive protection begins.

[1]Not included in Canadian product labeling.

NORETHINDRONE AND MESTRANOL

Summary of Differences

Pharmacology/pharmacokinetics—Proportion bound to SHBG depends on both estrogen and norethindrone dose; does not suppress estrogen-induced increase in SHBG levels. Norethindrone exhibits no first-pass effect. Mestranol is a prodrug metabolized to ethinyl estradiol at about 83% conversion rate; high first-pass effect and enterohepatic recirculation. Norethindrone is less androgenic than levonorgestrel or norgestrel; its androgenic effect depends on both progestin and estrogen doses; slight estrogenic activity.

Laboratory value alterations—Triglycerides increase as with all oral contraceptives; slightly increases total cholesterol; negatively affects lipoproteins—increases LDL and lowers HDL; increases apolipoprotein A_1.

Dosage forms—High estrogen dose formulation available.

Oral Dosage Forms

Note: Bracketed uses in the *Dosage Forms* section refer to categories of use and/or indications that are not included in U.S. product labeling.

NORETHINDRONE AND MESTRANOL TABLETS USP

Usual adult and adolescent dose

Contraceptive, systemic or
Estrogen-progestin or
[Antiendometriotic agent] or
[Gonadotropin inhibitor, female, noncontraceptive use][1]—

Twenty-one day cycle: Oral, 1 tablet a day for twenty-one days commencing on Day 1 of the menstrual cycle or on the first Sunday after the menstrual cycle begins; the next round of treatment is begun on the eighth day after the last tablet of the previous cycle has been taken.

Twenty-eight day cycle: Oral, 1 tablet a day for twenty-eight days commencing on Day 1 of the menstrual cycle, or on the first Sunday after the menstrual cycle begins; the next round of treatment is begun on the day after the last tablet of the previous cycle has been taken.

Note: With a Sunday start schedule, the patient should take her first tablet on the first Sunday after the onset of menstruation. If the patient's period begins on a Sunday, she should take her first tablet that same day.

With a Day-1 start schedule, the patient should take her first tablet on Day 1 of the menstrual cycle.

The last seven tablets of the twenty-eight day cycle contain no hormones. These seven companion tablets are a different color from those containing hormones.

Oral contraceptives may be given continuously or cyclically for endometriosis.

Strength(s) usually available

U.S.—

Monophasic formulation:

1 mg of norethindrone and 50 mcg (0.05 mg) of mestranol (Rx) [*Genora 1/50; Intercon 1/50; Necon 1/50; Nelova 1/50M; Norethin 1/50M; Norinyl 1+50; Ortho-Novum 1/50*].

Canada—

Monophasic formulation:

1 mg of norethindrone and 50 mcg (0.05 mg) of mestranol (Rx) [*Norinyl 1/50; Ortho-Novum 1/50*].

Note: Most products are available in twenty-one–or twenty-eight day cycles. The twenty-eight day cycle includes an additional seven days of placebo tablets.

Packaging and storage
Store below 40 °C (104 °F), preferably between 15 and 30 °C (59 and 86 °F), unless otherwise specified by manufacturer. Store in a well-closed container.

Auxiliary labeling
- Take with food.
- Avoid too much sun or use of sunlamp.

Note
Include mandatory patient package inserts (PPIs) (the brief summary of patient labeling and the detailed patient labeling) when dispensing.

Caution first-time users to use an additional form of birth control as directed by their physicians until maximum contraceptive protection begins.

[1]Not included in Canadian product labeling.

NORGESTIMATE AND ETHINYL ESTRADIOL

Summary of Differences
Pharmacology/pharmacokinetics—Norgestimate is an incomplete pro-drug, which is metabolized to other active forms, such as levonorgestrel, norgestrel acetate, and norgestrel. No first-pass effect. Highly progestational; does not counteract the estrogen increase in SHBG levels—highly bound to SHBG and albumin; low androgenicity.

Laboratory value alterations—Triglycerides increase but little effect on lipoproteins.

Medical considerations/contraindications—Norgestimate plus ethinyl estradiol increase glucose tolerance; do not affect 2-hour insulin release; had one of the smallest effects on both areas of carbohydrate metabolism compared with other oral contraceptives.

Side/adverse effects—Absence of withdrawal menstrual bleed was low with norgestimate and ethinyl estradiol formulation; improves pre-existing acne.

Oral Dosage Forms
Note: Bracketed uses in the *Dosage Forms* section refer to categories of use and/or indications that are not included in U.S. product labeling.

NORGESTIMATE AND ETHINYL ESTRADIOL TABLETS

Usual adult and adolescent dose
Contraceptive, systemic or
Estrogen-progestin or
[Antiendometriotic agent][1] or
[Gonadotropin inhibitor, female, noncontraceptive use][1]—

Twenty-one day cycle: Oral, 1 tablet a day for twenty-one days commencing on Day 1 of the menstrual cycle or on the first Sunday after the menstrual cycle begins; the next round of treatment is begun on the eighth day after the last tablet of the previous cycle has been taken.

Twenty-eight day cycle: Oral, 1 tablet a day for twenty-eight days commencing on Day 1 of the menstrual cycle, or on the first Sunday after the menstrual cycle begins; the next round of treatment is begun on the day after the last tablet of the previous cycle has been taken.

Acne vulgaris, systemic[1]—

Twenty-one day cycle (Triphasic formulation only):

For adults and adolescents 15 years of age and over—Oral, 1 tablet a day for twenty-one days commencing on Day 1 of the menstrual cycle or on the first Sunday after the menstrual cycle begins; the next round of treatment is begun on the eighth day after the last tablet of the previous cycle has been taken.

For adolescents up to 15 years of age—Safety and efficacy have not been established.

Twenty-eight day cycle (Triphasic formulation only):

For adults and adolescents 15 years of age and over—Oral, 1 tablet a day for twenty-eight days commencing on Day 1 of the menstrual cycle, or on the first Sunday after the menstrual cycle begins; the next round of treatment is begun on the day after the last tablet of the previous cycle has been taken.

For adolescents up to 15 years of age—Safety and efficacy have not been established.

Note: With a Sunday start schedule, the patient should take her first tablet on the first Sunday after the onset of menstruation. If the patient's period begins on a Sunday, she should take her first tablet that same day.

With a Day-1 start schedule, the patient should take her first tablet on Day 1 of the menstrual cycle.

The last seven tablets of the twenty-eight day cycle contain no hormones. These seven companion tablets are a different color from those containing hormones.

Oral contraceptives may be given continuously or cyclically for endometriosis.

Strength(s) usually available
U.S.—

Monophasic formulation:

250 mcg (0.25 mg) of norgestimate and 35 mcg (0.035 mg) of ethinyl estradiol (Rx) [*Ortho-Cyclen*].

Triphasic formulation:

Phase one (seven days)—180 mcg (0.18 mg) of norgestimate and 35 mcg (0.035 mg) of ethinyl estradiol. **Phase two (seven days)**—215 mcg (0.215 mg) of norgestimate and 35 mcg (0.035 mg) of ethinyl estradiol. **Phase three (seven days)**—250 mcg (0.25 mg) of norgestimate and 35 mcg (0.035 mg) of ethinyl estradiol. (Rx) [*Ortho Tri-Cyclen*].

Canada—

Monophasic formulation:

250 mcg (0.25 mg) of norgestimate and 35 mcg (0.035 mg) of ethinyl estradiol (Rx) [*Cyclen*].

Triphasic formulation:

Phase one (seven days)—180 mcg (0.18 mg) of norgestimate and 35 mcg (0.035 mg) of ethinyl estradiol. **Phase two (seven days)**—215 mcg (0.215 mg) of norgestimate and 35 mcg (0.035 mg) of ethinyl estradiol. **Phase three (seven days)**—250 mcg (0.25 mg) of norgestimate and 35 mcg (0.035 mg) of ethinyl estradiol. (Rx) [*Tri-Cyclen*].

Note: Available in twenty-one or twenty-eight day cycles. The twenty-eight day cycle includes an additional seven days of placebo tablets.

Packaging and storage
Store below 40 °C (104 °F), preferably between 15 and 30 °C (59 and 86 °F), unless otherwise specified by manufacturer. Store in a well-closed container.

Auxiliary labeling
- Take with food.
- Avoid too much sun or use of sunlamp.

Note
Include mandatory patient package inserts (PPIs) (the brief summary of patient labeling and the detailed patient labeling) when dispensing.

Explain sequence of administration of biphasic or triphasic cycle formula when dispensing, especially for twenty-eight day cycle (colored tablet sequence).

Caution first-time users to use an additional form of birth control as directed by their physicians until maximum contraceptive protection begins.

[1]Not included in Canadian product labeling.

NORGESTREL AND ETHINYL ESTRADIOL

Summary of Differences
Indications: Also used for emergency postcoital contraception.

Pharmacology/pharmacokinetics: Proportion bound to SHBG depends on both estrogen and norgestrel dose; suppressed estrogen-induced increase in SHBG levels in most contraceptive doses except for triphasic formulation which only slightly increased SHBG levels. No first-pass effect. Norgestrel is one of the most androgenic progestins; its androgenic effect depends on both progestin and estrogen doses.

Laboratory value alterations: No change of triglycerides over 1 year; may slightly decrease or increase total cholesterol; negatively affects lipoprotein—increases LDL and lowers HDL; increases apolipoprotein A_1 the least of all contraceptives; can increase free testosterone by displacing it from SHBG.

Dosage forms: High estrogen dose formulation available.

Oral Dosage Forms
Note: Bracketed uses in the *Dosage Forms* section refer to categories of use and/or indications that are not included in U.S. product labeling.

NORGESTREL AND ETHINYL ESTRADIOL TABLETS USP

Usual adult and adolescent dose
Contraceptive, systemic or
Estrogen-progestin or

[Antiendometriotic agent][1] or
[Gonadotropin inhibitor, female, noncontraceptive use][1]—
Twenty-one day cycle: Oral, 1 tablet a day for twenty-one days commencing on Day 1 of the menstrual cycle or on the first Sunday after the menstrual cycle begins; the next round of treatment is begun on the eighth day after the last tablet of the previous cycle has been taken.
Twenty-eight day cycle: Oral, 1 tablet a day for twenty-eight days commencing on Day 1 of the menstrual cycle, or on the first Sunday after the menstrual cycle begins; the next round of treatment is begun on the day after the last tablet of the previous cycle has been taken.

Note: With a Sunday start schedule, the patient should take her first tablet on the first Sunday after the onset of menstruation. If the patient's period begins on a Sunday, she should take her first tablet that same day.

With a Day-1 start schedule, the patient should take her first tablet on Day 1 of the menstrual cycle.

The last seven tablets of the twenty-eight day cycle contain no hormones. These seven companion tablets are a different color from those containing hormones.

Oral contraceptives may be given continuously or cyclically for endometriosis.

[Contraceptive, postcoital, systemic][1]—
Two tablets (500 mcg norgestrel and 50 mcg of ethinyl estradiol per tablet) or four tablets (300 mcg norgestrel and 30 mcg ethinyl estradiol per tablet) taken as soon as possible after unprotected coitus, preferably within twelve hours but not longer than seventy-two hours later. Then, repeat the dose twelve hours after the first dose.

Strength(s) usually available

U.S.—
Monophasic formulation:
300 mcg (0.3 mg) of norgestrel and 30 mcg (0.03 mg) of ethinyl estradiol (Rx) [*Lo/Ovral*].
500 mcg (0.5 mg) of norgestrel and 50 mcg (0.05 mg) of ethinyl estradiol (Rx) [*Ovral*].

Canada—
Monophasic formulation:
500 mcg (0.50 mg) of norgestrel and 50 mcg (0.05 mg) of ethinyl estradiol (Rx) [*Ovral*].

Note: Available in twenty-one–or twenty-eight day cycles. The twenty-eight day cycle includes an additional seven days of placebo tablets.

Packaging and storage

Store below 40 °C (104 °F), preferably between 15 and 30 °C (59 and 86 °F), unless otherwise specified by manufacturer. Store in a well-closed container.

Auxiliary labeling

- Take with food.
- Avoid too much sun or use of sunlamp.

Note

Include mandatory patient package inserts (PPIs) (the brief summary of patient labeling and the detailed patient labeling) when dispensing.
Caution first-time users to use an additional form of birth control as directed by their physicians until maximum contraceptive protection begins.

[1]Not included in Canadian product labeling.

Selected Bibliography

For norethindrone acetate and ethinyl estradiol

Goldzieher JW. Pharmacokinetics and metabolism of ethynyl estrogens. In: Goldzieher JW, editor. Pharmacology of the contraceptive steroids. New York: Raven Press; 1994. p. 127-51.

For norethindrone and ethinyl estradiol

Godsland IF, Crook D, Simpson R, et al. The effects of different formulations of oral contraceptive agents on lipid and carbohydrate metabolism. N Engl J Med 1990 Nov 15; 323(20): 1375-81.

For levonorgestrel and ethinyl estradiol

Godsland IF, Walton C, Felton C, et al. Insulin resistance, secretion, and metabolism in users of oral contraceptives. J Clin Endocrinol Metab 1992; 74(1): 64-70.

For ethynodiol diacetate and ethinyl estradiol

Burkman RT, Robinson CJ, Kruszone-Moran DA, et al. Lipid and lipoprotein changes associated with oral contraceptive use: a randomized clinical trial. Obstet Gynecol 1988 Jan; 71(1): 33-8.

General

Fraser IS. Contraceptive choice for women with 'risk factors.' Drug Saf 1993 Apr; 8(4): 271-9.

Speroff L, DeCherney A, The Advisory Board for the New Progestins. Evaluation of a new generation of oral contraceptives. Obstet Gynecol 1993 Jun; 81(6): 1034-47.

World Health Organization. Oral contraceptives and neoplasia. WHO Technical Report Series 1992; 817: 1-45.

For norgestrel and ethinyl estradiol

Ayangade O, Akinyemi A. A comparative study of Norinyl 1/35 versus Lo-Ovral in Ile-Ife, Nigeria. Int J Gynaecol Obstet 1989; 30: 165-70.

For norethindrone and mestranol

Policar M. Clinical experience with multiphasic oral contraceptives. J Reprod Med 1986; 31(9): 939-45.

For desogestrel and ethinyl estradiol

Burkman RT, editor. Desogestrel: a progestin for the 1990s. Am J Obstet Gynecol 1993 May; 168(3 Pt 2): 1009-52.

For norgestimate and ethinyl estradiol

McGuire JL, Phillips A, Hahn DW, et al. Pharmacologic and pharmacokinetic characteristics of norgestimate and its metabolites. Am J Obstet Gynecol 1990; 163(6 Pt 2): 2127-31.

Revised: 03/15/2004

ESTROGENS, CONJUGATED—See *Estrogens (Systemic), Estrogens (Vaginal)*

ESTROGENS, ESTERIFIED—See *Estrogens (Systemic)*

ESTRONE—See *Estrogens (Systemic), Estrogens (Vaginal)*

ESTROPIPATE—See *Estrogens (Systemic), Estrogens (Vaginal)*

ESZOPICLONE Systemic†

VA CLASSIFICATION (Primary): CN309
U.S.: Schedule IV controlled substance
Commonly used brand name(s): *Lunesta*.

Note: For a listing of dosage forms and brand names by country availability, see *Dosage Forms* section(s).

†Not commercially available in Canada.

Category

Sedative-hypnotic.

Indications

Accepted

Insomnia (treatment)—Eszopiclone is indicated for the treatment of insomnia.

Pharmacology/Pharmacokinetics

Physicochemical characteristics

Chemical Group—Pyrrolopyrazine derivative of the cyclopyrrolone class.
Molecular weight—Eszopiclone: 388.81.
Solubility—Eszopiclone is very slightly soluble in water, slightly soluble in ethanol, and soluble in phosphate buffer (pH 3.2).

Mechanism of action/Effect

The precise mechanism of action of eszopiclone as a hypnotic is unknown. Its pharmacologic effect is believed to result from its interaction with GABA-receptor complexes at binding domains located close to or allosterically coupled to benzodiazepine receptors.

Eszopiclone is a nonbenzodiazepine hypnotic with a chemical structure unrelated to pyrazolopyrimidines, imidazopyridines, benzodiazepines, barbiturates, or other drugs with known hypnotic properties.

Absorption
Rapidly absorbed following oral administration.

Protein binding
Moderate (52 to 59%).

Biotransformation
Extensively metabolized by CYP3A4 and CYP2E1 via oxidation and demethylation. The two primary metabolites are (S)-zopiclone-N-oxide (inactive) and (S)-N-demethylzopiclone which binds to GABA receptors with a lower potency than eszopiclone.

Half-life
Elimination: Approximately 6 hours

Onset of action
May be reduced if taken with or immediately after a high-fat or heavy meal.

Time to peak plasma concentration:
Approximately 1 hour following oral administration.

Elimination
Urine: Up to 75% as primary metabolites is expected: less than 10% as parent drug.

Precautions to Consider

Carcinogenicity
Carcinogenicity studies done in Sprague-Dawley rats given oral doses of racemic zopiclone at 100 mg/kg/day produced an increase in mammary gland adenocarcinomas in females and an increase in thyroid gland follicular cell adenomas and carcinomas in males. The increase in thyroid tumors is thought to be due to increased levels of TSH secondary to increased metabolism of circulating thyroid hormones; however, this is not relevant to humans.

Carcinogenicity studies done in B6C3F1 mice given oral doses of racemic zopiclone at 100 mg/kg/day produced pulmonary carcinomas and carcinomas plus adenomas in females and increases in skin fibromas and sarcomas in male. The skin tumors were due to lesions induced by aggressive behavior.

Tumorigenicity
Eszopiclone did not increase tumors in a p53 transgenic mouse bioassay at oral doses up to 300 mg/kg/day.

Mutagenicity
Eszopiclone was positive in the mouse lymphoma chromosomal aberration assay and produced an equivocal response in Chinese hamster ovary cell chromosomal aberration assay. However, no mutagenic or clastogenic potential was seen in the bacterial Ames gene mutation assay, an unscheduled DNA synthesis assay, or in an *in vivo* mouse bone marrow micronucleus assay.

The metabolite, (S)-N-desmethyl zopiclone, was positive in the Chinese hamster ovary cell and human lymphocyte chromosomal aberration assays. However, it was negative in the bacterial Ames gene mutation assay, an *in vitro* ^{32}P-postlabeling DNA adduct assay, and in an *in vivo* mouse bone marrow chromosomal aberration and micronucleus assay.

Pregnancy/Reproduction
Fertility—Fertility studies were done in male and female rats given oral doses of eszopiclone up to 45 mg/kg/day (males) from 4 weeks premating through mating and up to 180 mg/kg/day (females) from 2 weeks premating through day 7 of pregnancy. Fertility was decreased with no females becoming pregnant when both male and female rats were treated with the highest dose; the no effect dose in both sexes was 5 mg/kg/day (16 times the MRHD on a mg/m^2 basis). Other effects seen included increased preimplantation loss, abnormal estrus cycles, and decreases in sperm number and motility and increases in morphologically abnormal sperm.

Pregnancy—Adequate and well controlled studies in pregnant women have not been done. Eszopiclone should be used during pregnancy only if the potential benefit justifies the potential risk to the fetus.

Pregnant rats given eszopiclone at maternally toxic doses of 125 and 150 mg/kg/day during organogenesis showed slight reductions in fetal weight and developmental delay. When eszopiclone was administered throughout pregnancy and lactation at doses from 60 to 180 mg/kg/day, increases in post-implantation loss, decreased post-natal pup weights and survival, and increased pup startle response were seen at all doses. Eszopiclone had no other behavioral measures or reproductive function effects in the offspring.

FDA Pregnancy Category C

Labor and delivery—Eszopiclone has no established use in labor and delivery.

Breast-feeding
It is not known whether eszopiclone is distributed into human milk. Because many drugs are distributed in human milk, caution should be exercised when eszopiclone is administered to a nursing woman.

Pediatrics
Safety and effectiveness of eszopiclone in children below the age of 18 years have not been established.

Geriatrics
Appropriate studies performed to date have not demonstrated geriatrics-specific problems that would limit the usefulness of eszopiclone in the elderly. Because older adults had an increase of 41% in AUC and a slightly prolonged elimination of eszopiclone (half-life approximately 9 hours), elderly patients require a lower starting dose.

Pharmacogenetics
The pharmacokinetics of eszopiclone seem to appear similar among men and women and among all races.

Drug interactions and/or related problems
The following drug interactions and/or related problems have been selected on the basis of their potential clinical significance (possible mechanism in parentheses where appropriate)—not necessarily inclusive (» = major clinical significance):

Note: Combinations containing any of the following medications, depending on the amount present, may also interact with this medication.

» Alcohol or
» Anticonvulsants or
» Antihistamines or
» Other CNS-depressant agents, (See *Appendix II*) or
» Other psychotropic medications
(concurrent use with eszopiclone may produce additive CNS depressant effects, and a downward dose adjustment is recommended)

CYP3A4 inducers, potent such as
Rifampicin (also known as rifampin in the USA)
(may decrease eszopiclone exposure)

» CYP3A4 inhibitors, potent or strong such as
Clarithromycin or
Itraconazole or
Ketoconazole or
Nefazodone or
Nelfinavir or
Ritonavir or
Troleandomycin
(coadministration with ketoconazole resulted in a 2.2-fold increase in exposure to eszopiclone, other CYP3A4 inhibitors would be expected to behave similar; a downward dose adjustment is recommended)

Lorazepam
(coadministration with eszopiclone decreased C_{max} of both drugs by 22%)

Olanzapine
(coadministration with eszopiclone decreased DSST [Digital Symbol Substitution Test] scores)

Medical considerations/Contraindications
The medical considerations/contraindications included have been selected on the basis of their potential clinical significance (reasons given in parentheses where appropriate)—not necessarily inclusive (» = major clinical significance).

Except under special circumstances, this medication should not be used when the following medical problem exists:

» Depression, signs and symptoms of
(caution; suicidal tendencies may be present in such patients, and protective measures may be required; the smallest feasible dose should be prescribed)

» Hypersensitivity to eszopiclone or any of its ingredients

Risk-benefit should be considered when the following medical problems exist:

» Alcohol abuse, history of or
» Drug abuse, history of or
» Psychiatric disorders
(patients with these conditions have an increased risk of abuse and dependence and should be under careful surveillance when receiving eszopiclone or any other hypnotic)

Concomitant illness such as
Compromised respiratory function or

Diseases or conditions that affect metabolism or hemodynamic responses
(caution should be used when administering eszopiclone)

» Hepatic function impairment
(use with caution; eszopiclone exposure may be increased in patients with hepatic function impairment; patients with severe hepatic function impairment may require a reduced dose)

Side/Adverse Effects

The following side/adverse effects have been selected on the basis of their potential clinical significance (possible signs and symptoms in parentheses where appropriate)—not necessarily inclusive:

Those indicating need for medical attention only if they continue or are bothersome

Incidence more frequent

Dizziness; dry mouth; dyspepsia (acid or sour stomach; belching; heartburn; indigestion; stomach discomfort upset or pain); ***headache; infection*** (fever or chills; cough or hoarseness; lower back or side pain; painful or difficult urination); ***nausea; nervousness; pain; somnolence*** (sleepiness or unusual drowsiness); ***unpleasant taste***

Incidence less frequent

Abnormal dreams; accidental injury; anxiety (fear; nervousness); ***confusion*** (mood or mental changes); ***diarrhea; depression*** (discouragement, feeling sad or empty; irritability; lack of appetite; loss of interest or pleasure; tiredness; trouble concentrating; trouble sleeping); ***dysmenorrhea*** (pain, cramps, heavy bleeding)—females; ***gynecomastia*** (swelling of the breasts or breast soreness)—males; ***hallucinations*** (seeing, hearing, or feeling things that are not there); ***libido decreased*** (loss in sexual ability, desire, drive, or performance; decreased interest in sexual intercourse; inability to have or keep an erection); ***neuralgia*** (nerve pain); ***pruritus*** (itching skin); ***rash; urinary tract infection*** (bladder pain; bloody or cloudy urine; difficult, burning, or painful urination; frequent urge to urinate; lower back or side pain); ***viral infection*** (chills; cough or hoarseness; fever; cold flu-like symptoms); ***vomiting***

Incidence unknown

Amnesia (loss of memory; problems with memory)

Those indicating possible withdrawal reaction and/or need for medical attention only if they occur after medication is discontinued

Abnormal dreams; anxiety (fear; nervousness); ***nausea; upset stomach***

Overdose

For more information on the management of overdose or unintentional ingestion, **contact a poison control center** (see *Poison Control Center Listing*).

Clinical effects of overdose

The following effects have been selected on the basis of their potential clinical significance (possible signs and symptoms in parentheses where appropriate)—not necessarily inclusive:

In clinical trials with eszopiclone, one case of overdose with up to 36 mg of eszopiclone was reported in which the individual fully recovered.

Coma (change in consciousness; loss of consciousness); ***impaired consciousness*** (confusion; unconsciousness; very drowsy or sleepy); ***somnolence*** (sleepiness or unusual drowsiness)

Treatment of overdose

There is no known specific antidote to eszopiclone. Treatment is generally symptomatic and supportive.

To decrease absorption—
Emptying the stomach with immediate gastric lavage if appropriate.

To enhance elimination—
The usefulness of dialysis in the treatment of overdosage with eszopiclone has not been determined.

Monitoring—
Monitoring of respiration, pulse, blood pressure, and other appropriate vital signs.
Monitoring of hypotension and CNS depression, and appropriate treatment if necessary.

Supportive care—
General supportive measures should be employed.
Contacting a poison control center for up-to-date information on the management of hypnotic drug product overdosage.

Administration of intravenous fluids as needed.
Administering flumazenil may be useful.
Patients in whom intentional overdose is confirmed or suspected should be referred for psychiatric consultation.

Patient Consultation

As an aid to patient consultation, refer to *Advice for the Patient, Eszopiclone (Systemic)*.

In providing consultation, consider emphasizing the following selected information (» = major clinical significance):

Before using this medication

» Conditions affecting use, especially:
Hypersensitivity to eszopiclone or any of its ingredients
Pregnancy—Adequate and well controlled studies in pregnant women have not been done. Eszopiclone should be used during pregnancy only if the potential benefit justifies the potential risk to the fetus.
Breast-feeding—It is not known whether eszopiclone is distributed into human milk. Because many drugs are distributed in human milk, caution should be exercised when eszopiclone is administered to a nursing woman.
Use in children—Safety and effectiveness of eszopiclone in children below the age of 18 years have not been established.
Other medications, especially alcohol, anticonvulsants, antihistamines, other CNS depression-producing medications, other psychotropic medications, or potent CYP3A4 inhibitors
Other medical problems, especially alcohol or drug abuse (or history of), depression, hepatic function impairment, or psychiatric disorders

Proper use of this medication

» Not taking more eszopiclone than the amount prescribed due to potential for dependency

» Not increasing dose if medication becomes less effective over time; checking with physician

» Not using for longer than directed by your doctor

» The importance of swallowing the tablet whole, do not chew, crush or break the tablet.

» Proper dosing
Missed dose: Skipping missed dose; not doubling doses

» Proper storage

Precautions while using this medication

» Avoiding use of alcohol or other CNS depressants during therapy

» Caution if clumsiness or unsteadiness occurs, especially in the elderly

» Caution if dizziness or drowsiness occurs; not driving, using machines, or doing anything else that requires alertness until effects of eszopiclone are known

» Amnesia and hallucinations; avoiding by only taking eszopiclone when able to get a full night's sleep (8 hours) before the need to be active again, and not taking more medicine than prescribed

» Checking with physician if unusual or strange thoughts or behavior develops while taking eszopiclone

Checking with physician before discontinuing medication if therapy is prolonged; gradual dosage reduction may be necessary to avoid withdrawal symptoms

General Dosing Information

Treatment with eszopiclone should only be initiated after careful evaluation of the patient for manifestations of physical and/or psychiatric disorders.

Eszopiclone should only be ingested immediately prior to going to bed or after the patient has gone to bed and experienced difficulty falling asleep. Taking while still up may result in short-term memory impairment, hallucinations, impaired coordination, dizziness, and lightheadedness.

Worsening of insomnia or failure of insomnia to remit after 7 to 10 days of treatment may indicate primary psychiatric and/or medical illness that should be evaluated.

Patients may experience signs and symptoms associated with withdrawal from other CNS-depressant drugs following rapid dose decrease or abrupt discontinuation of eszopiclone.

The emergence of any new behavioral sign or symptom including aggressiveness and extroversion that seem out of character, bizarre behavior, agitation, halluncinations and depersonalization should be evaluated.

Oral Dosage Forms

ESZOPICLONE TABLETS

Usual adult dose

Insomnia (treatment)—
Oral, 2 mg immediately before bedtime; dosing may be initiated at or raised to 3 mg if clinically indicated. For sleep maintenance, 3 mg is more effective.

Note: For patients with severe hepatic impairment the starting dose should not exceed 1 mg.

For patients receiving concomitant therapy with potent CYP3A4 inhibitors the starting dose should not exceed 1 mg. If needed the dose can be raised to 2 mg.

For debilitated patients the starting dose should not exceed 1 mg.

Usual adult prescribing limits

Up to 3 mg daily

Usual pediatric dose

Safety and effectiveness of eszopiclone in children below the age of 18 years have not been established.

Usual geriatric dose

Insomnia (treatment)—

For difficulty falling asleep: Oral, 1 mg immediately before bedtime for older adults whose primary complaint is difficulty falling asleep; dosing may be raised to 2 mg if clinically indicated.

For difficulty staying asleep: Oral, 2 mg immediately before bedtime for older adults whose primary complaint is difficulty staying asleep.

Usual geriatric prescribing limits

Up to 2 mg daily.

Strength(s) usually available

U.S.—

1 mg (Rx) [*Lunesta* (calcium phosphate; colloidal silicon dioxide; croscarmellose sodium; hypromellose; lactose; magnesium stearate; microcrystalline cellulose; polyethylene glycol; titanium dioxide; triacetin; FD&C blue #2)].

2 mg (Rx) [*Lunesta* (calcium phosphate; colloidal silicon dioxide; croscarmellose sodium; hypromellose; lactose; magnesium stearate; microcrystalline cellulose; polyethylene glycol; titanium dioxide; triacetin)].

3 mg [*Lunesta* (calcium phosphate; colloidal silicon dioxide; croscarmellose sodium; hypromellose; lactose; magnesium stearate; microcrystalline cellulose; polyethylene glycol; titanium dioxide; triacetin; FD&C blue #2)].

Packaging and storage

Store at 25 °C (77 °F); excursions permitted to 15 °C to 30 °C (59 °F to 86 °F).

Auxiliary labeling

- May cause drowsiness. Be careful while driving or operating machinery. Use caution until you become familiar with its effects.
- Avoid alcoholic beverages.

Note

Controlled substance in the U.S., schedule IV.

Developed: 08/05/2005

ETANERCEPT Systemic

VA CLASSIFICATION (Primary): MS109

Commonly used brand name(s): *Enbrel*.

Note: For a listing of dosage forms and brand names by country availability, see *Dosage Forms* section(s).

Category

Antirheumatic (biologic response modifier).

Indications

Accepted

Ankylosing spondylitis (treatment)—Etanercept is indicated for reducing signs and symptoms in patients with ankylosing spondylitis.

Arthritis, rheumatoid (treatment)—Etanercept is indicated for reducing signs and symptoms, inducing major clinical response, inhibiting the progression of structural damage, and improving physical function in patients with moderately to severely active rheumatoid arthritis. Etanercept can be initiated in combination with methotrexate or used alone.

Arthritis, rheumatoid, juvenile (treatment)—Etanercept is indicated for reduction of signs and symptoms of moderately to severely active polyarticular-course juvenile rheumatoid arthritis in patients who have had an inadequate response to one or more DMARDs.

Psoriasis (treatment)—Etanercept is indicated for treatment of adult patients (18 years or older) with chronic moderate to severe plaque psoriasis who are candidates for systemic therapy or phototherapy.

Psoriatic arthritis (treatment)—Etanercept is indicated for reducing signs and symptoms, inhibiting the progression of structural damage of active arthritis, and improving physical function in patients with psoriatic arthritis. Etanercept can be used in combination with methotrexate in patients who do not respond adequately to methotrexate alone.

[Reactive arthritis (treatment)][1]—Etanercept is indicated for the treatment of reactive arthritis.

[Inflammatory bowel disease arthritis (treatment)][1]—Etanercept is indicated for the treatment of inflammatory bowel disease arthritis.

[1]Not included in Canadian product labeling.

Pharmacology/Pharmacokinetics

Physicochemical characteristics

Source—Etanercept is obtained from a Chinese hamster ovary (CHO) mammalian cell expression system via recombinant DNA technology.

Molecular weight—Approximately 150 kilodaltons.

Solubility—Freely soluble in water.

Mechanism of action/Effect

Tumor necrosis factor (TNF) is a naturally occurring cytokine that is involved with the inflammatory and immune responses. The biological activity of TNF is dependent on two distinct receptors for TNF, 55 kilodalton protein (p55) and 75 kilodalton protein (p75), that exist naturally as monomeric molecules on cell surfaces. Etanercept is a dimeric soluble form of the human 75 kilodalton tumor necrosis factor receptor (TNFR) that binds specifically to TNF and lymphotoxin alpha and inhibits TNF from binding with cell surface TNFR, thereby rendering TNF biologically inactive.

Etanercept also modulates biological responses that are induced or regulated by TNF, including expression of adhesion molecules responsible for leukocyte migration, serum levels of cytokines and metalloproteinase-3.

Antibodies to the TNF receptor portion or other protein components of the etanercept drug product, all non-neutralizing, were detected at least once in sera of 5% of adult rheumatoid arthritis patients.

Half-life

Following a single dose of etanercept 25 mg subcutaneous (SC) in 25 patients with rheumatoid arthritis: mean 102 +/- 30 hours.

Note: Preliminary data suggests that etanercept clearance may be reduced slightly in children 4 to 8 years of age.

Time to peak concentration

Approximately 72 hours (range, 48 to 96 hours).

Peak serum concentration

Following a 25-mg subcutaneous injection—1.2 mcg per mL (range, 0.6 to 1.5 mcg per mL).

After six months of twice weekly 25-mg doses:

Mean C_{max}: 2.4 ± 1 mcg per mL

Peak serum concentration: increased by two- to seven-fold

$AUC_{(0-72\ hour)}$: approximately four-fold increase (range 1- to 17-fold)

Elimination

Mean C_{max}, C_{min} and AUC are comparable in patients receiving 25 mg twice weekly and 50 mg once weekly. Mean clearance—160 ± 80 mL per hour

Precautions to Consider

Carcinogenicity

Long-term studies in animals have not been done to evaluate the carcinogenic potential of etanercept.

More cases of lymphoma have been observed among patients receiving the TNF blocker compared to control patients. Patients with rheumatoid arthritis or psoriasis, particularly those with highly active disease, may be at a higher risk for the development of lymphoma. The potential role of TNF-blocking therapy in the development of malignancies is not known.

Mutagenicity

No evidence of mutagenicity was seen in *in vitro* or *in vivo* testing.

Pregnancy/Reproduction

Fertility—Studies have not been done in either humans or animals.

Pregnancy—*A Pregnancy Registry has been established to monitor the outcomes of pregnant women exposed to etanercept. Physicians are encouraged by the manufacturer to register patients by calling (877) 311-8972.*

Adequate and well-controlled studies have not been done in humans.

Developmental studies in rats and rabbits given doses 60 to 100 times the maximum recommended human dose have not shown that etanercept causes adverse effects in the fetusBecause animal reproduction studies are not always predictive of human response, etanercept should be used during pregnancy only if clearly needed.

FDA Pregnancy Category B.

Breast-feeding

It is not known whether etanercept is distributed into the breast milk of humans and problems have not been documented. However, because etanercept may potentially cause serious adverse effects to the nursing infant, a decision should be made whether to discontinue nursing or to discontinue the drug.

Pediatrics

Safety in children younger than 4 years of age has not been established. A 3-month open-label study in children 4 to 17 years of age who were refractory to or intolerant of methotrexate and had moderately to severely active polyarticular course juvenile rheumatoid arthritis (JRA) demonstrated improvement following treatment with etanercept (0.4 mg per kg of body weight subcutaneously twice weekly; maximum dose of 25 mg). The side effect profile was similar to that in adults. However, adverse effects such as abdominal pain and vomiting occurred more frequently in the pediatric group. Preliminary pharmacokinetic data suggests that etanercept clearance may be reduced slightly in children 4 to 8 years of age.

Responses to immunizations have not been studied in pediatric patients receiving etanercept. However, it is recommended that JRA patients, if possible, be brought up to date with all immunizations prior to receiving etanercept.

The safety and effectiveness of etanercept in pediatric patients with plaque psoriasis have not been studied.

Geriatrics

Appropriate studies performed to date have not demonstrated geriatrics-specific problems that would limit the usefulness of etanercept in the elderly. However, dose selection for elderly patients should be cautious reflecting the higher incidence of infections in the elderly population in general.

Drug interactions and/or related problems

The following drug interactions and/or related problems have been selected on the basis of their potential clinical significance (possible mechanism in parentheses where appropriate)—not necessarily inclusive (» = major clinical significance):

» Anakinra
  (may lead to a higher incidence of serious infections and/or neutropenia; concurrent use is not recommended)

» Cyclophosphamide
  (concomitant use of etanercept and cyclophosphamide has been associated with a higher incidence of non-cutaneous solid malignancies; concurrent use is not recommended)

» Immunosuppressive agents
  (concomitant use of etanercept and immunosuppressive agents in patients with Wegener's granulomatosis is not recommended)

Sulfasalazine
  (concomitant use of etanercept and sulfasalazine may lead to a decrease in mean neutrophil counts)

» Vaccines, live virus
  (no data are available on the effects of vaccination or secondary transmission of infection by live vaccines in patients receiving etanercept therapy; concurrent use is not recommended)

Laboratory value alterations

The following have been selected on the basis of their potential clinical significance (possible effect in parentheses where appropriate)—not necessarily inclusive (» = major clinical significance).

With physiology/laboratory test values

Anti-double-stranded DNA antibodies or
Antinuclear antibodies [ANA]
  (may be newly positive in patients taking etanercept)

Liver transaminases
  (levels may be elevated)

Medical considerations/Contraindications

The medical considerations/contraindications included have been selected on the basis of their potential clinical significance (reasons given in parentheses where appropriate)—not necessarily inclusive (» = major clinical significance).

Except under special circumstances, this medication should not be used when the following medical problems exist:

» Immunodeficiency or
» Serious infections, including chronic or localized infections or
» Malignancies
  (etanercept may potentially suppress normal defense mechanisms against infections and malignancies)
  (if a patient develops a serious infection while receiving etanercept, use of etanercept should be discontinued; the safety and efficacy of etanercept in patients with chronic infections or immunosuppression have not been evaluated)
  (data from an etanercept clinical trial suggest that etanercept may increase mortality in patients with established sepsis; use of etanercept in sepsis patients is contraindicated)

» Hematologic abnormalities, history of
  (data from postmarketing trials suggests that etanercept may increase the risk of developing or exacerbating hematologic abnormalities such as aplastic anemia; consider discontinuation of therapy with etanercept in patients with confirmed significant hematologic abnormalities)

» Hypersensitivity to etanercept or any of its components or
» Sepsis
  (etanercept use contraindicated)

» Hypersensitivity to latex (natural rubber)
  (the needle cover of the prefilled syringe contains natural rubber [latex]; caution is advised in patients sensitive to latex)

Risk-benefit should be considered when the following medical problems exist:

» Demyelinating disorders, preexisting or recent–onset
  (data from postmarketing trials suggests that etanercept may increase the risk of exacerbating demyelinating disorders)

» Diabetes, advanced or poorly controlled
  (patients with these conditions may be at higher risk of developing infection)

Heart failure
  (use with caution and monitor patients carefully)

Lung disorder, history of
  (etanercept may worsen prior lung disorder)

» Recurring infections, history of
  (caution should be exercised when considering the use of etanercept)

» Seizure disorder, history of
  (caution is advised; new onset or exacerbation of seizure disorders have been observed in association with etanercept therapy)

» Wegener's granulomatosis
  (patients with this condition that are receiving immunosuppressive agents may be at greater risk of malignancies; use is not recommended)

Side/Adverse Effects

The following side/adverse effects have been selected on the basis of their potential clinical significance (possible signs and symptoms in parentheses where appropriate)—not necessarily inclusive:

Note: Among 4462 rheumatoid arthritis patients treated with etanercept in clinical trials for a mean of 27 months, 9 lymphomas were observed at a rate of 0.09 cases per 100 patient-years. This is 3-fold higher than the rate of lymphomas expected in the general population. The potential role of etanercept in the development of malignancies is not known. An increased rate of lymphoma up to several fold has been reported in the rheumatoid arthritis patient population, and may be further increased in patients with more severe disease activity. Sixty-seven malignancies other than lymphoma were observed, with the most common being colon, breast, lung, and prostate, which were similar in type and number to what would be expected in the general population.

Note: In the placebo-controlled portions of the psoriasis studies, 8 of 933 patients who received etanercept at any dose were diagnosed with malignancy compared to 1 of 414 patients who received placebo. Among the 1261 patients with psoriasis who received etanercept at any dose in the controlled and uncontrolled portions of the psoriasis studies (1062 patient-years), a total of 22 patients were diagnosed with 23 malignancies; 9 patients with non-cutaneous solid tumors, 12 patients with 13 non-melanoma skin cancers (8 basal, 5 squamous), and 1 patient with non-Hodgkin's lymphoma. Among the placebo treated patients (90 patient-years of observation) 1 patient was diagnosed with 2 squamous cell cancers. The size of the placebo group and limited duration of the controlled portions of studies precludes the ability to draw firm conclusions.

Note: Among 89 patients with Wegener's granulomatosis receiving etanercept in a randomized, placebo-controlled trial, 5 experienced a variety of non-cutaneous solid malignancies compared with none receiving placebo.

Note: Forty-three of 69 (62%) children experienced infection while receiving etanercept for juvenile rheumatoid arthritis. Most of these infections consisted of those most commonly seen in the pediatric population.In the double-blind controlled portion of the study, the rate and type of infections were similar in the etanercept and placebo treated juvenile rheumatoid arthritis groups.

Note: The impact of long-term treatment with etanercept on the development of autoimmune diseases is unknown. Rare adverse event reports have described patients with rheumatoid factor positive and/or erosive RA who have developed additional autoantibodies in conjunction with rash and other features suggesting a lupus-like syndrome which may resolve following withdrawal of etanercept. If a patient develops symptoms suggestive of a lupus-like syndrome following treatment with etanercept, treatment should be discontinued and the patient should be carefully evaluated.

Note: No new positive *ANA anti-double-stranded DNA antibodies* or other new autoimmune diseases have been seen in children with juvenile rheumatoid arthritis.

Note: Rare cases of tuberculosis [TB] have been observed in patients treated with TNF antagonists including etanercept.

Those indicating need for medical attention

Incidence more frequent

Infection (fever or chills); ***respiratory tract infections*** (cough; fever; sneezing; sore throat)

Incidence less frequent

Abdominal abscess (stomach discomfort and/or pain); ***allergic reaction*** (cough, difficulty swallowing, dizziness, fast heartbeat, hives, itching, puffiness or swelling of the eyelids or around the eyes, face, lips or tongue, shortness of breath, skin rash, tightness in chest, unusual tiredness or weakness, wheezing); ***arthritis, septic*** (muscle or joint stiffness, tightness, or rigidity); ***asthenia*** (lack or loss of strength); ***bronchitis*** (congestion in chest; cough); ***cellulitis*** (itching, pain, swelling, or redness on skin); ***foot abscess*** (itching, pain, redness, or swelling on the foot); ***leg ulcer*** (itching, pain, redness, or swelling on the leg, sore on leg); ***osteomyelitis*** (increase in bone pain); ***pneumonia*** (cough; fever; shortness of breath; sneezing; sore throat; tightness in chest or wheezing); ***pyelonephritis*** (chills; fever; frequent or painful urination; headache; stomach pain); ***sepsis*** (chills; fever; fast heartbeat); ***sinusitis, severe*** (pain or tenderness around eyes and cheekbones, fever, stuffy or runny nose, headache, cough, shortness of breath or troubled breathing, tightness of chest or wheezing); ***wound infection*** (red, tender, or oozing skin at incision)

Incidence rare

Varicella infection (skin rash on face, scalp, or stomach)

Incidence not determined—Observed during clinical practice, estimates of frequency can not be determined

Anemia (pale skin, troubled breathing, exertional); ***anemia, aplastic*** (chest pain, chills, cough, fever, headache, shortness of breath, sores, ulcers, or white spots on lips or in mouth, swollen or painful glands, tightness in chest, unusual bleeding or bruising, unusual tiredness or weakness, wheezing); ***angioedema*** (large, hive-like swelling on face, eyelids, lips, tongue, throat, hands, legs, feet, sex organs); ***appendicitis*** (stomach or lower abdominal pain; severe cramping; bloating; nausea; vomiting; fever); ***bursitis*** (pain and inflammation at the joints); ***central nervous system effects suggestive of multiple sclerosis, transverse myelitis, or other demyelinating conditions***; ***cerebral ischemia*** (confusion, headache, severe numbness, especially on one side of the face or body); ***chest pain; cholecystitis*** (severe stomach pain with nausea or vomiting); ***congestive heart failure, new-onset*** (chest pain, decreased urine output, dilated neck veins, extreme fatigue, irregular breathing, irregular heartbeat, shortness of breath, swelling of face, fingers, feet, or lower legs, tightness in chest, troubled breathing, weight gain, wheezing); ***cutaneous vasculitis*** (blisters on skin)—occurred in adult patients and in pediatric patients with juvenile rheumatoid arthritis; ***deep vein thrombosis*** (pain, redness, or swelling in arm or leg); ***depression*** (discouragement, feeling sad or empty, irritability, lack of appetite, loss of interest or pleasure, tiredness, trouble concentrating, trouble sleeping)—occurred in adult patients and in pediatric patients with juvenile rheumatoid arthritis; ***dyspnea*** (shortness of breath, difficult or labored breathing, tightness in chest, wheezing); ***fever; gastrointestinal hemorrhage*** (black, tarry stools bloody stools, vomiting of blood or material that looks like coffee grounds); ***hydrocephalus, normal pressure*** (confusion; drowsiness; headache); ***hypertension*** (dizziness; headache, severe or continuing); ***hypotension*** (light-headedness or fainting); ***interstitial lung disease*** (cough, difficult breathing, fever, shortness of breath); ***intestinal perforation*** (severe abdominal pain, cramping, burning, bloody, black, or tarry stools, trouble breathing, vomiting of material that looks like coffee grounds, severe and continuing nausea, heartburn and/or indigestion); ***kidney calculus*** (blood in urine; nausea and vomiting; pain in groin or genitals; sharp back pain just below ribs); ***lupus-like syndrome with manifestations including rash consistent with subacute or discoid lupus*** (fever or chills, general feeling of discomfort or illness or weakness); ***leukopenia*** (black, tarry stools; painful or difficult urination); ***lymphadenopathy*** (swollen, painful, or tender lymph glands in neck, armpit, or groin); ***lymphoma*** (swollen glands; weight loss; general feeling of illness; black, tarry stools; yellow skin and eyes); ***membranous glomerulonephropathy*** (cloudy or bloody urine; high blood pressure; swelling of face, feet or lower legs); ***myocardial infarction or ischemia*** (chest pain or discomfort, pain or discomfort in arms, jaw, back or neck, shortness of breath, nausea, sweating, vomiting); ***neutropenia*** (black, tarry, stools, chills, cough, fever, lower back or side pain, painful or difficult urination, pale skin, shortness of breath, sore throat, ulcers, sores, or white spots in mouth, unusual bleeding or bruising, unusual tiredness or weakness); ***optic neuritis*** (blindness, blue-yellow color blindness, blurred vision, decreased vision, eye pain); ***pancreatitis*** (bloating, chills, constipation, darkened urine, fast heartbeat, fever, indigestion, loss of appetite, nausea, pains in stomach, side, or abdomen, possibly radiating to the back, vomiting, yellow eyes or skin); ***pancytopenia*** (high fever; chills; unexplained bleeding or bruising; bloody, black, or tarry stools; pale skin; unusual tiredness or weakness; cough; shortness of breath; sores, ulcers, or white spots on lips or in mouth; swollen glands); ***polymyositis*** (fever, joint pain, muscle tenderness, weakness, or pain, skin rash unusual tiredness or weakness, weight loss); ***psoriasis*** (skin irritation or rash); ***pulmonary disease*** (shortness of breath); ***pulmonary embolism*** (anxiety, chest pain, cough, fainting, fast heartbeat, sudden shortness of breath or troubled breathing, dizziness or lightheadedness); ***seizures*** (convulsions, muscle spasm or jerking of all extremities, sudden loss of consciousness, loss of bladder control); ***streptococcal septic shock, group A*** (chills; confusion; dizziness; lightheadedness; fainting; fast heartbeat; fever; rapid, shallow breathing); ***stroke*** (confusion, difficulty in speaking, slow speech, inability to speak, inability to move arms, legs, or facial muscles, double vision, headache); ***thrombocytopenia*** (black, tarry stools; bleeding gums; blood in urine or stools; pinpoint red spots on skin; unusual bleeding or bruising); ***thrombophlebitis*** (changes in skin color, pain, tenderness, swelling of foot or leg); ***tuberculosis*** (chest pain; cough; coughing or spitting up blood; difficulty in breathing; sore throat; muscle aches; night sweats; sudden high fever or low-grade fever for months; unusual tiredness); ***urticaria*** (hives or welts, itching, redness of skin, skin rash); ***worsening of prior lung disorder*** (difficulty in breathing worsening)

Incidence not determined—Observed during clinical practice in pediatric patients with juvenile rheumatoid arthritis, estimates of frequency can not be determined

Abscess with bacteremia (accumulation of pus; swollen, red, tender area of infection; fever); ***coagulopathy*** (unusual bleeding or bruising); ***cutaneous ulcer*** (sores on the skin); ***diabetes mellitus, type 1*** (blurred vision, dry mouth, fatigue, flushed, dry skin, fruit-like breath odor, increased hunger, increased thirst, increased urination, loss of consciousness, nausea, stomach ache, sweating, troubled breathing, unexplained weight loss, vomiting); ***esophagitis*** (difficulty in swallowing; pain or burning in throat; chest pain; heartburn; vomiting; sores, ulcers, or white spots on lips or tongue or inside the mouth); ***gastritis*** (burning feeling in chest or stomach, tenderness in stomach area, stomach upset, indigestion); ***gastroenteritis*** (abdominal or stomach pain, diarrhea, loss of appetite, nausea, weakness); ***personality disorder*** (change in personality); ***tuberculous arthritis*** (pain, swelling, or redness in joints; muscle pain or stiffness; difficulty in moving); ***urinary tract infection*** (bladder pain, bloody or cloudy urine, difficult, burning, or painful urination, frequent urge to urinate, lower back or side pain)

Those indicating need for medical attention only if they continue or are bothersome

Incidence more frequent

Abdominal pain—more common in children; ***dizziness; headache***—more common in children; ***injection site reaction*** (bleeding or bruising; itching; pain; swelling; redness)—decrease in frequency with subsequent injection; ***nausea and vomiting***—more common in children; ***pharyngitis*** (pain or burning in throat); ***rhinitis*** (runny nose)

Incidence less frequent or rare

Alopecia (hair loss, thinning of hair); ***anorexia*** (loss of appetite); ***cough; cutaneous vasculitis*** (blisters on skin); ***diarrhea; dry eyes; dry mouth; dyspepsia*** (heartburn); ***fatigue*** (unusual tiredness or weakness); ***mouth ulcer*** (irritation or soreness of mouth); ***ocular in-***

flammation (itching, redness, or tearing of eye); ***pain, generalized; skin rash; subcutaneous nodules*** (bumps below the skin)

Incidence not determined—Observed during clinical practice, estimates of frequency can not be determined

Adenopathy (swollen glands); ***altered sense of taste; flu syndrome*** (chills, cough, diarrhea, fever, general feeling of discomfort or illness, headache, joint pain, loss of appetite, muscle aches and pains); ***paresthesia*** (burning, crawling, itching, numbness, prickling, "pins and needles", or tingling feelings); ***pruritus*** (itching skin); ***vasodilation (flushing)*** (feeling of warmth or heat; flushing or redness of skin, especially on face and neck; headache; feeling faint, dizzy, or light-headedness; sweating); ***weight gain***

Overdose

For more information on the management of overdose or unintentional ingestion, **contact a poison control center** (see *Poison Control Center Listing*).

Note: No evidence of dose-limiting toxicities was found during clinical trials of etanercept. No evidence of dose-limiting toxicity was observed in healthy volunteers administered single IV doses up to 60 mg per square meter of body surface area in an endotoxemia study.

Patients in whom intentional overdose is known or suspected should be referred for psychiatric consultation.

Patient Consultation

As an aid to patient consultation, refer to *Advice for the Patient, Etanercept (Systemic)*.

In providing consultation, consider emphasizing the following selected information (» = major clinical significance):

Before using this medication

» Conditions affecting use, especially:

More cases of lymphoma have been observed among patients receiving the TNF blocker (3 cases per 4,509 patients) compared to control (0 cases per 2,040 patients). The role of TNF-blocking therapy in the development of malignancies is not known.

Pregnancy—Etanercept should be used only if clearly needed

Breast-feeding—Etanercept may potentially cause serious adverse effects in the nursing infant

Use in the elderly—Dose selection for elderly patients should be cautious reflecting the higher incidence of infections in the elderly population in general.

Other medications, especially anakinra, cyclophosphamide, immunosupressive agents, or vaccines (live virus)

Other medical problems, especially demyelinating disorders; diabetes mellitus (uncontrolled); hematologic abnormalities; immunodeficiency; infections (serious); malignancies; seizure disorder; Wegener's granulomatosis or hypersensitivity to etanercept or any of its components

Proper use of this medication

» Reading patient directions carefully with regard to:

- Preparation of injection
- Use of disposable syringes
- Proper administration technique
- Stability of the injection

» Proper dosing

Missed dose: Using as soon as possible; not using if almost time for next dose; not doubling doses

» Proper storage

Precautions while using this medication

» Importance of close monitoring by physician, especially for infections

» Telling physician right away if signs or symptoms of infection (fever, chills) occur

» Avoiding immunizations unless approved by physician

Side/adverse effects

Signs of potential side effects, especially infection, respiratory tract infections, abdominal abscess, allergic reaction, appendicitis, arthritis (septic), asthenia, bronchitis, cellulitis, foot abscess, kidney calculus, leg ulcer, lymphadenopathy, lymphoma, osteomyelitis, optic neuritis, pneumonia, psoriasis, pyelonephritis, sepsis, severe sinusitis, or varicella infection

Signs of potential side effects observed in adult patients during clinical practice, especially anemia, aplastic anemia, angioedema, bursitis, central nervous system effects suggestive of multiple sclerosis, transverse myelitis or other demyelinating illnesses, cerebral ischemia, chest pain, cholecystitis, congestive heart failure (new-onset), cutaneous vasculitis, deep vein thrombosis, depression, dyspnea, fever, gastrointestinal hemorrhage, hydrocephalus (normal pressure), hypertension, hypotension, interstitial lung disease, intestinal perforation, lupus-like syndrome with manifestations including rash consistent with subacute or discoid lupus, leukopenia, membranous glomerulonephropathy, myocardial infarction, myocardial ischemia, neutropenia, optic neuritis, pancreatitis, pancytopenia, polymyositis, pulmonary disease, pulmonary embolism, seizures, stroke, thrombocytopenia, thrombophlebitis, tuberculosis, urticaria, or worsening of prior lung disorder

Signs of potential side effects observed in pediatric patients with juvenile rheumatoid arthritis during clinical practice, especially abscess with bacteremia, coagulopathy, cutaneous ulcer, diabetes mellitus (type 1), esophagitis, gastritis, gastroenteritis, personality disorder, tuberculous arthritis, or urinary tract infection

General Dosing Information

Patients who develop a new infection while undergoing treatment with etanercept should be monitored closely. Treatment should be discontinued in patients with serious infections or sepsis.

Treatment with etanercept should not be initiated in patients with active infections including chronic or localized infections. Physicians should exercise caution when considering the use of etanercept in patients with a history of recurring infections or with underlying conditions that may predispose patients to infections, such as advanced or poorly controlled diabetes.

Live vaccines should not be used in patients receiving etanercept treatment.

Prior to initiating etanercept therapy, it is recommended that juvenile rheumatoid arthritis [JRA] patients be brought up to date with all immunizations in agreement with current immunization guidelines, if possible.

Etanercept may be administered concurrently with analgesics, glucocorticoids, methotrexate, nonsteroidal anti-inflammatory drugs, or salicylates; however, concurrent administration of methotrexate in polyarticular juvenile rheumatoid arthritis has not been studied.

If the physician determines that it is appropriate, etanercept may be self-administered by the patient. However, patients should receive proper injection training and medical follow-up as necessary.

Injection sites should be rotated. New injections should be given at least one inch from an old site. Bruised, hard, red or tender skin should be avoided.

If a patient has a significant exposure to varicella virus, etanercept therapy should be temporarily discontinued and prophylactic treatment with Varicella Zoster Immune Globulin should be considered.

Parenteral Dosage Forms

ETANERCEPT FOR INJECTION

Usual adult dose

Ankylosing spondylitis (treatment)—

Subcutaneous, 50 mg weekly given as 25 mg at two separate injection sites either on the same day or 3 or 4 days apart.

Arthritis, rheumatoid—

Subcutaneous, 50 mg weekly given as 25 mg at two separate injection sites either on the same day or 3 or 4 days apart.

Psoriatic arthritis (treatment)—

Subcutaneous, 50 mg weekly given as 25 mg at two separate injection sites either on the same day or 3 or 4 days apart.

[Reactive arthritis (treatment)][1]—

Subcutaneous, 25 mg twice weekly.

[Inflammatory bowel disease arthritis (treatment)][1]—

Subcutaneous, 25 mg twice weekly.

Usual adult prescribing limits

50 mg weekly.

Usual pediatric dose

Arthritis, rheumatoid, juvenile—

Children 4 to 17 years of age—

Weight greater than 31 to 62 kg (68 to 136 pounds): Subcutaneous, 0.8 mg per kg of body weight, weekly given as 0.4 mg per kg of body weight at two separate injection sites either on the same day or 3 to 4 days apart

Weight equal to or less than 31 kg (68 pounds): Subcutaneous, 0.8 mg per kg of body weight once weekly

Children up to 4 years of age—

Safety and efficacy have not been established.

Note: The maximum dose that should be administered at a single injection site is 25 mg (1mL).

Usual pediatric prescribing limits
50 mg weekly.

Usual geriatric dose
See *Usual adult dose.*

Strength(s) usually available
U.S.—

25 mg (Rx) [*Enbrel* (mannitol 40 mg; sucrose 10 mg; tromethamine 1.2 mg)].

Note: Etanercept is packaged in a carton containing 4 dosing trays, each of which contains a single-use vial of drug, diluent syringe (1 mL sterile bacteriostatic water for injection, USP, containing 0.9% benzyl alcohol), one 27-gauge ½ inch needle, one vial adapter, one plunger and two alcohol swabs.

Packaging and storage
Store between 2 and 8 °C (36 and 46 °F). Protect from freezing.

Preparation of dosage form
Reconstitute 25 mg vial with 1 mL of Bacteriostatic Sterile Water for Injection (0.9% benzyl alcohol), USP. Inject diluent slowly. Some foaming will occur. To avoid excessive foaming, do not shake or vigorously agitate. The solution should be clear and colorless, without particulate matter. Do not filter.

Stability
Reconstituted solutions may be stored for up to 14 days if refrigerated at 2 to 8 °C (36 to 46 °F). Discard reconstituted solution after 14 days. The prepared solution should be inspected for particulate matter and discoloration before administration to the patient. The solution should not be used if discolored, cloudy, or if particulate matter remains.

Incompatibilities
Etanercept should not be combined with other medications.

Auxiliary labeling
- Do not freeze.
- Do not shake.

ETANERCEPT INJECTION

Usual adult dose
Ankylosing spondylitis (treatment) or
Arthritis, rheumatoid or
Psoriatic arthritis (treatment)—
Subcutaneous, 50 mg per week.

Psoriasis (treatment)—
Subcutaneous, 50 mg twice weekly administered 3 or 4 days apart for 3 months followed by a reduction to a maintenance dose of 50 mg per week.

Starting doses of etanercept 25 mg or 50 mg per week were also shown to be efficacious. The proportion of responders were related to etanercept dosage.

[Inflammatory bowel disease arthritis (treatment)][1]—
See *Etanercept for injection.*

[Reactive arthritis (treatment)][1]—
See *Etanercept for injection, usual adult dose.*

Usual adult prescribing limits
50 mg weekly.

Usual pediatric dose
Arthritis, rheumatoid, juvenile—
Children 4 to 17 years of age—
Weight equal to or greater than 63 kg (138 pounds): Subcutaneous, 50 mg per week
Weight equal to or less than 62 kg (136 pounds): See *Etanercept for injection, usual pediatric dose.*

Children up to 4 years of age—
Safety and efficacy have not been established.

Usual pediatric prescribing limits
50 mg per week

Usual geriatric dose
See *Etanercept for injection, usual adult dose*

Strength(s) usually available
U.S.—

50 mg per mL (Rx) [*Enbrel* (L-arginine hydrochloride 5.3 mg per mL; sodium chloride 5.8 mg per mL; sodium phosphate, dibasic, anhydrous 0.9 mg per mL; sodium phosphate, monobasic, monohydrate 2.6 mg per mL; sucrose 10 mg per mL)].

Note: Etanercept is packaged in a carton containing 4 prefilled syringes with 27-gauge ½ inch needle attached.

Packaging and storage
Store between 2 and 8 °C (36 and 46 °F). Protect from freezing.

Preparation of dosage form
Single-use prefilled syringe may be allowed to reach room temperature (approximately 15 to 30 minutes) before injection. Do not remove the needle shield while allowing the prefilled syringe to reach room temperature.

Incompatibilities
Etanercept should not be combined with other medications.

Auxiliary labeling
- Do not freeze.
- Do not shake.

---

[1]Not included in Canadian product labeling.

Revised: 11/01/2005
Developed: 06/03/1999

ETHACRYNIC ACID—See *Diuretics, Loop (Systemic)*

ETHAMBUTOL Systemic

VA CLASSIFICATION (Primary): AM500

Commonly used brand name(s): *Etibi; Myambutol.*

Note: For a listing of dosage forms and brand names by country availability, see *Dosage Forms* section(s).

Category
Antibacterial (antimycobacterial).

Indications
Note: Bracketed information in the *Indications* section refers to uses that are not included in U.S. product labeling.

General Considerations

Tuberculosis is a highly infectious life-threatening bacterial disease with 8 million new cases and 3 million deaths reported worldwide each year to the World Health Organization (WHO). The vast majority of these cases are in developing countries; however, tuberculosis also has emerged as an important public health problem in the U.S. in recent years after the decline in number of cases observed between 1950 and 1980.

The resurgence of tuberculosis in the U.S. has been complicated by an increase in the proportion of patients with strains resistant to antituberculosis medications. Outbreaks of multidrug-resistant tuberculosis have been documented in hospitals and prisons. Drug-resistant tuberculosis, particularly that caused by strains resistant to isoniazid and rifampin, is much harder to treat and often is fatal. Among acquired immunodeficiency syndrome (AIDS) patients infected with tuberculosis bacilli resistant to both rifampin and isoniazid, a case-fatality rate of 91% has been reported. Recent investigations of outbreaks of multidrug-resistant tuberculosis have found an extraordinarily high case-fatality rate, with the median time to mortality being reached between 4 and 16 weeks. In almost all instances, these outbreaks have involved patients with severe immunosuppression by infection with the human immunodeficiency virus (HIV).

Acquired drug resistance develops during treatment for drug-sensitive tuberculosis with regimens that are poorly conceived or poorly complied with, allowing the emergence of naturally occurring drug-resistant mutations. Resistant organisms from affected patients may subsequently infect other people who have not been infected with *M. tuberculosis* previously, resulting in primary drug resistance.

Resistance to antituberculosis agents can develop not only in the strain that caused the initial disease, but also as a result of reinfection with a new strain of *M. tuberculosis* that is drug-resistant. Reinfection with a new multidrug-resistant *M. tuberculosis* strain can occur during therapy for the original infection or after completion of therapy. Most recent data suggest that outcomes can be improved if patients promptly begin therapy with two or more drugs that have *in vitro* activity against the multidrug-resistant isolate.

HIV infection is the strongest risk factor yet identified for the development of active tuberculosis disease in persons infected with tuberculosis. In addition, persons with HIV infection are at an increased risk of tuberculosis resulting either from newly acquired disease or from reactivation of latent infections. Tuberculosis is a major clinical manifestation of immunodeficiency induced by HIV. In hospital-based retrospective studies, high rates of tuberculosis have been found among patients with AIDS. In communities where tuberculosis and HIV infection are common, the prevalence of HIV seropositivity among patients with tuberculosis is greatly increasing.

WHO has estimated that 5.6 million people worldwide and 80,000 people in the U.S. are infected with both HIV and tuberculosis. Persons dually infected with *M. tuberculosis* and HIV have a high risk of developing clinically active tuberculosis. One study of HIV-positive drug users with positive tuberculin skin test results found a rate of the development of active tuberculosis to be 8 cases per 100 person-years (8% yearly) as compared with the 10% lifetime risk (1 to 3% risk within the first year after skin test conversion) in the general population.

Persons who are known to be HIV-infected and who are contacts of patients with infectious tuberculosis should be carefully evaluated for evidence of tuberculosis. If there are no findings suggestive of current tuberculosis, preventive therapy with isoniazid should be given. Because HIV-infected contacts are not managed in the same way as those who are not HIV-infected, HIV testing is recommended if there are known or suspected risk factors for their acquiring HIV infection.

According to investigators at the National Institute of Allergy and Infectious Diseases (NIAID), levels of HIV in the bloodstream increase 5- to 160-fold in HIV-infected persons who develop active tuberculosis. Clinical and epidemiologic observations have demonstrated that HIV-infected individuals have an estimated 113-times higher risk and AIDS patients have a 170-times higher risk as compared with uninfected persons. Furthermore, the problem of drug resistance may worsen as the HIV epidemic spreads. Immunosuppressed patients with HIV infection who subsequently become infected with *M. tuberculosis* have an extraordinarily high risk of developing active tuberculosis within a short period of time.

In addition to the convincing evidence that HIV infection increases the risk and worsens the course of tuberculosis, there is increasing clinical evidence that coinfection with *M. tuberculosis* accelerates progression of disease caused by HIV infection. Understanding the interaction of these two pathogens is clinically important, given the high prevalence of patients coinfected with HIV and *M. tuberculosis* in both the U.S. and Africa; it is estimated that by the year 2000 about 500,000 deaths per year will occur in coinfected patients worldwide.

Persons with a positive tuberculin skin test and HIV infection, and persons with a positive tuberculin skin test and at risk of acquiring HIV infection with unknown HIV status should be considered for tuberculosis preventive therapy regardless of age. One study showed that isoniazid prophylaxis in HIV-infected, tuberculin-positive individuals not only decreased the incidence of tuberculosis disease, but also delayed the progression to AIDS and death.

Twelve months of preventive therapy is recommended for adults and children with HIV infection and other conditions associated with immunosuppression. Persons with HIV infection should receive at least 6 months of preventive therapy. The American Academy of Pediatrics recommends that children receive 9 months of therapy.

Tuberculosis control programs should ensure that drug susceptibility tests are performed on all initial isolates of *M. tuberculosis* and the results are reported promptly to the primary care provider and the local health department. Tuberculosis control programs should monitor local drug resistance rates to assess the effectiveness of local tuberculosis control efforts and to determine the appropriateness of the currently recommended initial tuberculosis treatment regimen for the area.

Relapse of rifampin-resistant tuberculosis has been reported in HIV-infected patients. Reinfection with new strains of *M. tuberculosis* has also been reported in these patients. Rifampin-resistant tuberculosis is a serious threat because responses to therapy are more difficult to achieve and require long courses of treatment. Therefore, careful follow-up of HIV-infected patients with treated tuberculosis is essential.

Multidrug-resistant tuberculosis also has been transmitted to persons without HIV infection in health care facilities. Together with the lack of effective agents for second-line treatment and methods of prophylaxis, the transmission of multidrug-resistant strains of *M. tuberculosis* may create a substantial reservoir of latently infected people and the potential for clinical multidrug-resistant tuberculosis for many years to come.

Several studies have documented a high prevalence of extrapulmonary disease in HIV-infected patients with clinical tuberculosis disease, particularly in conjunction with pulmonary manifestations. Cutaneous miliary tuberculosis, also known as *tuberculosis cutis miliaris disseminata*, was in the past a rare condition in adults, with only 24 cases reported in nearly a century. However, since the first reported case of cutaneous miliary tuberculosis in 1990 in a patient with AIDS, five additional cases have been reported in HIV-infected patients. Its appearance can be quite nondescript; therefore, a high level of suspicion must be maintained, particularly for patients with CD4+ cell counts of < 200 per cubic millimeter, in order to diagnose the condition and initiate therapy appropriately.

Accepted

Tuberculosis (treatment)—Ethambutol is indicated in combination with other antituberculosis medications in the treatment of all forms of tuberculosis, including tuberculous meningitis, caused by *Mycobacterium tuberculosis*.

[Mycobacterial infections, atypical (treatment)]—Ethambutol is used in the treatment of atypical mycobacterial infections, such as *Mycobacterium avium* complex (MAC).

No cross-resistance with other available antimycobacterial agents has been demonstrated.

Not all species or strains of a particular organism may be susceptible to ethambutol.

Pharmacology/Pharmacokinetics

Note: Preliminary data suggest that patients coinfected with the human immunodeficiency virus (HIV) and mycobacteria (*Mycobacterium tuberculosis* or *M. avium*) have altered pharmacokinetic profiles for antimycobacterial agents. In particular, malabsorption of these agents appears to occur frequently, and could seriously affect the efficacy of treatment.

Physicochemical characteristics

Molecular weight—277.24.

Mechanism of action/Effect

Ethambutol is a synthetic, bacteriostatic antitubercular agent. Its mechanism of action is not fully known. It diffuses into mycobacteria and appears to suppress multiplication by interfering with RNA synthesis. It is effective only against mycobacteria that are actively dividing.

Absorption

Rapidly absorbed (75 to 80%) from the gastrointestinal tract following oral administration.

Distribution

Widely distributed to most tissues and body fluids except cerebrospinal fluid (CSF). CSF concentrations are 10 to 50% of the corresponding serum concentrations.

Erythrocytes—

Equal to or double the plasma concentrations, which provide a depot effect for 24 hours.

Distributed into breast milk.

CSF—

Does not penetrate intact meninges, but 10 to 50% may penetrate the meninges of patients with tuberculous meningitis.

Vol_D—1.6 liters per kg.

Protein binding

Low (20 to 30%).

Biotransformation

Hepatic; up to 15% metabolized to inactive metabolites.

Half-life

Normal renal function—

3 to 4 hours.

Impaired renal function—

Up to 8 hours.

Time to peak concentration

2 to 4 hours.

Peak serum concentration

2 to 5 mcg per mL after a single oral dose of 25 mg per kg of body weight (mg/kg).

Elimination

Renal—

By glomerular filtration and tubular secretion; up to 80% excreted within 24 hours (at least 50% excreted unchanged and up to 15% as inactive metabolites).

Fecal—

20% excreted unchanged.

In dialysis—

Ethambutol is removed from the blood by hemodialysis and peritoneal dialysis.

Precautions to Consider

Pregnancy/Reproduction

Note: Tuberculosis in pregnancy should be managed in concert with an expert in the management of tuberculosis. Women who have only pulmonary tuberculosis are not likely to infect the fetus until after delivery, and congenital tuberculosis is extremely rare. *In utero* infections with tubercle bacilli, however, can occur after maternal bacillemia occurs at different stages in the course of tuberculosis. Miliary tuberculosis can seed the placenta and thereby gain access to the fetal circulation. In women with tuberculous endometritis, transmission of infection to the fetus can result from fetal aspiration of bacilli at the time of delivery. A third mode of transmission is through ingestion of infected amniotic fluid *in utero*.

If active disease is diagnosed during pregnancy, a 9-month regimen of isoniazid and rifampin, supplemented by an initial course of ethambutol if drug resistance is suspected, is recommended. Pyrazinamide usually is not given because of inadequate data regarding teratogenesis. Hence, a 9-month course of therapy is necessary for drug-susceptible disease. When isoniazid resistance is a possibility, isoniazid, ethambutol, and rifampin are recommended initially. One of these medications can be discontinued after 1 or 2 months, depending on results of susceptibility tests. If rifampin or isoniazid is discontinued, treatment is continued for a total of 18 months; if ethambutol is discontinued, treatment is continued for a total of 9 months. Prompt initiation of chemotherapy is mandatory to protect both the mother and fetus. If isoniazid or rifampin resistance is documented, an expert in the management of tuberculosis should be consulted.

Asymptomatic pregnant women with positive tuberculin skin tests and normal chest radiographs should receive preventive therapy with isoniazid for 9 months if they are HIV seropositive or have recently been in contact with an infectious person. For these individuals, preventive therapy should begin after the first trimester. In other circumstances in which none of these risk factors is present, although no harmful effects of isoniazid to the fetus have been observed, preventive therapy can be delayed until after delivery.

For all pregnant women receiving isoniazid, pyridoxine should be prescribed. Isoniazid, ethambutol, and rifampin appear to be relatively safe for the fetus. The benefit of ethambutol and rifampin for therapy of active disease in the mother outweighs the risk to the infant. Streptomycin and pyrazinamide should not be used unless they are essential to the control of the disease.

Pregnancy—Ethambutol crosses the placenta, resulting in fetal plasma concentrations that are approximately 30% of maternal plasma concentrations. However, problems in humans have not been documented.

Studies in mice given high doses of ethambutol have shown that this antimycobacterial causes a low incidence of cleft palate, exencephaly, and vertebral column abnormalities. In addition, studies in rats given high doses this medication have shown that ethambutol causes minor abnormalities of the cervical vertebrae. Studies in rabbits given high doses have shown that ethambutol may cause monophthalmia, limb reduction defects, hare lip, and cleft palate.

Breast-feeding

Ethambutol is distributed into breast milk in concentrations approximating maternal serum concentrations. However, problems in humans have not been documented.

Pediatrics

Note: If an infant is suspected of having congenital tuberculosis, a Mantoux tuberculin skin test, chest radiograph, lumbar puncture, and appropriate cultures should be performed promptly. Regardless of the skin test results, treatment of the infant should be initiated promptly with isoniazid, rifampin, pyrazinamide, and streptomycin or kanamycin. In addition, the mother should be evaluated for the presence of pulmonary or extrapulmonary (including uterine) tuberculosis. If the physical examination or chest radiograph support the diagnosis of tuberculosis, the patient should be treated with the same regimen as that used for tuberculous meningitis. The drug susceptibilities of the organism recovered from the mother and/or infant should be determined.

Possible isoniazid resistance should always be considered, particularly in children from population groups in which drug resistance is high, especially in foreign-born children from countries with a high prevalence of drug-resistant tuberculosis. For contacts who are likely to have been infected by an index case with isoniazid-resistant but rifampin-susceptible organisms, and in whom the consequences of the infection are likely to be severe (e.g., children up to 4 years of age), rifampin (10 mg per kg of body weight, maximum 600 mg, given daily in a single dose) should be given in addition to isoniazid (10 mg per kg, maximum 300 mg, given daily in a single dose) until susceptibility test results for the isolate from the index case are available. If the index case is known or proven to be excreting organisms resistant to isoniazid, then isoniazid should be discontinued and rifampin given for a total of 9 months. Isoniazid alone should be given if no proof of exposure to isoniazid-resistant organisms is found. Optimal therapy for children with tuberculosis infection caused by organisms resistant to isoniazid and rifampin is unknown. In deciding on therapy in this situation, consultation with an expert is advised.

Adjuvant treatment with corticosteroids in treating tuberculosis is controversial. Corticosteroids have been used for therapy in children with tuberculous meningitis to reduce vasculitis, inflammation, and, as a result, intracranial pressure. Data indicate that dexamethasone may lower mortality rates and lessen long-term neurologic impairment. The administration of corticosteroids should be considered in all children with tuberculous meningitis, and also may be considered in children with pleural and pericardial effusions (to hasten reabsorption of fluid), severe miliary disease (to mitigate alveolocapillary block), and endobronchial disease (to relieve obstruction and atelectasis). Corticosteroids should be given only when accompanied by appropriate antituberculosis therapy. Consultation with an expert in the treatment of tuberculosis should be obtained when corticosteroid therapy is considered.

Appropriate studies on the relationship of age to the effects of ethambutol have not been performed in children up to 13 years of age. Ethambutol is generally not recommended in children whose visual acuity cannot be monitored (younger than 6 years of age). However, ethambutol should be considered for all children with organisms resistant to other medications, and in whom susceptibility to ethambutol has been demonstrated or is likely.

Geriatrics

No information is available on the relationship of age to the effects of ethambutol in geriatric patients. However, elderly patients are more likely to have an age-related decrease in renal function, which may require an adjustment of dosage in patients receiving ethambutol.

Drug interactions and/or related problems

The following drug interactions and/or related problems have been selected on the basis of their potential clinical significance (possible mechanism in parentheses where appropriate)—not necessarily inclusive (» = major clinical significance):

Note: Combinations containing any of the following medications, depending on the amount present, may also interact with this medication.

Neurotoxic medications, other (see *Appendix II*)
(concurrent administration of ethambutol with other neurotoxic medications may increase the potential for neurotoxicity, such as optic and peripheral neuritis)

Laboratory value alterations

The following have been selected on the basis of their potential clinical significance (possible effect in parentheses where appropriate)—not necessarily inclusive (» = major clinical significance).

With physiology/laboratory test values

Uric acid, serum
(concentrations may be increased)

Medical considerations/Contraindications

The medical considerations/contraindications included have been selected on the basis of their potential clinical significance (reasons given in parentheses where appropriate)—not necessarily inclusive (» = major clinical significance).

Risk-benefit should be considered when the following medical problems exist:

Gouty arthritis, acute
(ethambutol may increase uric acid concentrations)

» Hypersensitivity to ethambutol

» Optic neuritis
(ethambutol may cause retrobulbar optic neuritis)

» Renal function impairment
(because ethambutol is excreted primarily through the kidneys, patients with renal function impairment may require a reduction in dosage)

Patient monitoring

The following may be especially important in patient monitoring (other tests may be warranted in some patients, depending on condition; » = major clinical significance):

Ophthalmologic examinations
(tests for visual fields and acuity and red-green discrimination may be required prior to and monthly during treatment, especially if treatment is prolonged or if dosage is greater than 15 mg per kg of body weight [mg/kg] daily)

Uric acid concentrations, serum
(may be required during treatment since elevated serum uric acid concentrations frequently occur, possibly precipitating acute gout)

Side/Adverse Effects

Note: Retrobulbar optic neuritis is thought to be dose-related, occurring most frequently with daily doses of 25 mg per kg of body weight (mg/kg) and after 2 months of therapy; however, optic neuritis has occurred after only a few days of treatment. Most cases are reversible after several weeks or months. Visual changes may be unilateral or bilateral; therefore, each eye must be tested separately and both eyes tested together.

The following side/adverse effects have been selected on the basis of their potential clinical significance (possible signs and symptoms in parentheses where appropriate)—not necessarily inclusive:

Those indicating need for medical attention

Incidence less frequent

Gouty arthritis, acute (chills; pain and swelling of joints, especially big toe, ankle, or knee; tense, hot skin over affected joints)

Incidence rare

Hypersensitivity (skin rash; fever; joint pain); ***peripheral neuritis*** (numbness, tingling, burning pain, or weakness in hands or feet); ***retrobulbar optic neuritis*** (blurred vision, eye pain, red-green color blindness, or any loss of vision)

Those indicating need for medical attention only if they continue or are bothersome

Incidence less frequent

Confusion; disorientation; gastrointestinal disturbances (abdominal pain; loss of appetite; nausea and vomiting); ***headache***

Patient Consultation

As an aid to patient consultation, refer to *Advice for the Patient, Ethambutol (Systemic).*

In providing consultation, consider emphasizing the following selected information (» = major clinical significance):

Before using this medication

» Conditions affecting use, especially:
Pregnancy—Ethambutol crosses the placenta. However, problems in humans have not been documented
Breast-feeding—Ethambutol is distributed into breast milk
Use in children—Appropriate studies have not been done in children up to 13 years of age. Ethambutol is generally not recommended in children whose visual acuity cannot be monitored (younger than 6 years of age)
Other medical problems, especially optic neuritis and renal function impairment

Proper use of this medication

Taking with food if gastrointestinal irritation occurs
» Compliance with full course of therapy, which may take months or years
» Proper dosing
Missed dose: Taking as soon as possible; not taking if almost time for next dose; not doubling doses
» Proper storage

Precautions while using this medication

Checking with physician if no improvement within 2 or 3 weeks
» Regular visits to physician to check progress; need to report promptly to physician signs of optic neuritis and prodromal signs of peripheral neuritis; need for ophthalmologic examinations if signs of optic neuritis occur
» Caution if blurred vision or loss of vision occurs

Side/adverse effects

Signs of potential side effects, especially acute gouty arthritis, hypersensitivity, peripheral neuritis, or retrobulbar optic neuritis

General Dosing Information

Ethambutol may be taken with food if gastrointestinal irritation occurs.

Since daily administration in divided doses may not result in therapeutic serum concentrations, ethambutol should be administered only in a single daily dose.

Since bacterial resistance may develop rapidly when ethambutol is administered alone, it should only be administered concurrently with other antituberculosis medications.

The duration of treatment with an antituberculosis regimen is at least 6 months, and may be continued for 2 years. Uncomplicated pulmonary tuberculosis is often successfully treated within 6 to 12 months. Several different treatment regimens are currently recommended.

The duration of antituberculosis therapy is based on the patient's clinical and radiographic responses, smear and culture results, and susceptibility studies of *Mycobacterium tuberculosis* isolates from the patient or the suspect source case. With directly observed therapy (DOT), clinical evaluation is an integral component of each visit for administration of medication. Careful monitoring of the clinical and bacteriologic responses to therapy on a monthly basis in sputum-positive patients is important.

If therapy is interrupted, the treatment schedule should be extended to a later completion date. Although guidelines cannot be provided for every situation, the following factors need to be considered in establishing a new date for completion:
- The length of interruption;
- The time during therapy (early or late) in which interruption occurred; and
- The patient's clinical, radiographic, and bacteriologic status before, during, and after interruption. Consultation with an expert is advised.

Therapy should be administered based on the following guidelines, published by the American Thoracic Society (ATS) and by the Centers for Disease Control and Prevention (CDC), and endorsed by the American Academy of Pediatrics (AAP).
- A 6-month regimen consisting of isoniazid, rifampin, and pyrazinamide given for 2 months followed by isoniazid and rifampin for 4 months is the preferred treatment for patients infected with fully susceptible organisms who adhere to the treatment course.
- Ethambutol (or streptomycin in children too young to be monitored for visual acuity) should be included in the initial regimen until the results of drug susceptibility studies are available, and unless there is little possibility of drug resistance (i.e., there is less than 4% primary resistance to isoniazid in the community, and the patient has had no previous treatment with antituberculosis medications, is not from a country with a high prevalence of drug resistance, and has no known exposure to a drug-resistant case).
- Alternatively, a 9-month regimen of isoniazid and rifampin is acceptable for persons who cannot or should not take pyrazinamide. Ethambutol (or streptomycin in children too young to be monitored for visual acuity) should also be included until the results of drug susceptibility studies are available, unless there is little possibility of drug resistance. If isoniazid resistance is demonstrated, rifampin and ethambutol should be continued for a minimum of 12 months.
- Consideration should be given to treating all patients with DOT. DOT programs have been demonstrated to increase adherence in patients receiving antituberculosis chemotherapy in both rural and urban settings.
- Multidrug-resistant tuberculosis (i.e., resistance to at least isoniazid and rifampin) presents difficult treatment problems. Treatment must be individualized and based on susceptibility studies. In such cases, consultation with an expert in tuberculosis is recommended.
- Children should be managed in essentially the same ways as adults, but doses of the medications must be adjusted appropriately and specific important differences between the management of adults and children addressed. However, optimal therapy of tuberculosis in children with HIV infection has not been established. The Committee on Infectious Diseases of the AAP recommends that therapy always should include at least three drugs initially, and should be continued for a minimum period of 9 months. Isoniazid, rifampin, and pyrazinamide with or without ethambutol or an aminoglycoside should be given for at least the first 2 months. A fourth drug may be needed for disseminated disease and whenever drug-resistant disease is suspected.
- Extrapulmonary tuberculosis should be managed according to the principles and with the drug regimens outlined for pulmonary tuberculosis, except in children who have miliary tuberculosis, bone/joint tuberculosis, or tuberculous meningitis. These children should receive a minimum of 12 months of therapy.

• A 4-month regimen of isoniazid and rifampin is acceptable therapy for adults who have active tuberculosis and who are sputum smear– and culture–negative, if there is little possibility of drug resistance.

Rifampin is an essential component of the currently recommended regimen for treating tuberculosis. This regimen is effective in treating HIV-infected patients with tuberculosis, and consists of isoniazid and rifampin for a minimum period of 6 months, plus pyrazinamide and either ethambutol or streptomycin for the first 2 months.

Because of the common association of tuberculosis with HIV infection, an increasing number of patients probably will be considered candidates for combined therapy with rifampin and protease inhibitors. Prompt initiation of appropriate pharmacologic therapy for patients with HIV infection who acquire tuberculosis is critical because tuberculosis may become rapidly fatal. The management of these patients is complex, requires an individualized approach, and should be undertaken only by or in consultation with an expert. In addition, all HIV-infected patients at risk for tuberculosis infection should be carefully evaluated and administered isoniazid preventive treatment if indicated, regardless of whether they are receiving protease inhibitor therapy.

For HIV-infected patients diagnosed with drug-susceptible tuberculosis and for whom protease inhibitor therapy is being considered but has not been initiated, the suggested management strategy is to complete tuberculosis treatment with a regimen containing rifampin before starting therapy with a protease inhibitor. The duration of antituberculosis regimen is at least 6 months, and therapy should be administered according to the guidelines developed by ATS and CDC, including the recommendation to carefully assess clinical and bacteriologic responses in patients coinfected with HIV and to prolong treatment if response is slow or suboptimal.

Health care or correctional institutions experiencing outbreaks of tuberculosis that are resistant to isoniazid and rifampin, or that are resuming therapy for a patient with a prior history of antitubercular therapy, may need to begin 5- or 6-drug regimens as initial therapy. These regimens should include the 4-drug regimen and at least 3 medications to which the suspected multidrug–resistant strain may be susceptible.

ATS, CDC, and AAP recommend preventive treatment of tuberculosis infection in the following patients:

• Preventive therapy with isoniazid given for 6 to 12 months is effective in decreasing the risk of future tuberculosis disease in adults and children with tuberculosis infection demonstrated by a positive tuberculin skin test reaction.

• Persons with a positive skin test and any of the following risk factors should be considered for preventive therapy regardless of age:

—Persons with HIV infection.

—Persons at risk for HIV infection with unknown HIV status.

—Close contacts of sputum-positive persons with newly diagnosed infectious tuberculosis.

—Newly infected persons (recent skin test convertors).

—Persons with medical conditions reported to increase the risk of tuberculosis (i.e., diabetes mellitus, corticosteroid therapy and other immunosuppressive therapy, intravenous drug users, hematologic and reticuloendothelial malignancies, end-stage renal disease, and clinical conditions associated with rapid weight loss or chronic malnutrition).

In some circumstances, persons with negative skin tests should be considered for preventive therapy. These include children who are close contacts of infectious tuberculosis cases and anergic HIV-infected adults at increased risk of tuberculosis, tuberculin-positive adults with abnormal chest radiographs showing fibrotic lesions probably representing old healed tuberculosis, adults with silicosis, and persons who are known to be HIV-infected and who are contacts of patients with infectious tuberculosis.

• In the absence of any of the above risk factors, persons up to 35 years of age with a positive skin test who are in the following high-incidence groups should be also considered for preventive therapy:

—Foreign-born persons from high-prevalence countries.

—Medically underserved low-income persons from high-prevalence populations (especially blacks, Hispanics, and Native Americans).

—Residents of facilities for long-term care (e.g., correctional institutions, nursing homes, and mental institutions).

• Twelve months of preventive therapy is recommended for adults and children with HIV infection and other conditions associated with immunosuppression. Persons without HIV infection should receive preventive therapy for at least 6 months.

• In persons younger than 35 years of age, routine monitoring for adverse effects of isoniazid should consist of a monthly symptom review. For persons 35 years of age and older, hepatic enzymes should be measured prior to starting isoniazid and monitored monthly throughout treatment, in addition to monthly symptom reviews.

• Persons who are presumed to be infected with isoniazid-resistant organisms should be treated with rifampin rather than with isoniazid.

• As with the treatment of active tuberculosis, the key to success of preventive treatment is patient adherence to the prescribed regimen. Although not evaluated in clinical studies, directly observed, twice-weekly preventive therapy may be appropriate for adults and children at risk, who cannot or will not reliably self-administer therapy.

Serum concentrations may be increased and half-life prolonged in patients with impaired renal function. Therefore, patients with impaired renal function may require a reduction in dose.

Most infants ≤ 12 months of age with tuberculosis are asymptomatic at the time of diagnosis, and the gastric aspirate cultures in these patients have a high yield for *M. tuberculosis*. When an infant is suspected of having tuberculosis, a thorough household investigation should be undertaken. A 6-month regimen of isoniazid and rifampin supplemented during the first 2 months by pyrazinamide has been found to be well-tolerated and effective in infants with pulmonary tuberculosis. Furthermore, twice-weekly DOT appears to be as effective as daily therapy, and is an essential alternative in patients for whom social issues prevent reliable daily therapy.

Physicians caring for children should be familiar with the clinical forms of the disease in infants to enable them to make an early diagnosis. Any child, especially one in a high-risk group or area, who has unexplained pneumonia, cervical adenitis, bone or joint infections, or aseptic meningitis should have a Mantoux tuberculin skin test performed, and a detailed epidemiologic history for tuberculosis should be obtained.

Management of a newborn infant whose mother, or other household contact, is suspected of having tuberculosis is based on individual considerations. If possible, separation of the mother, or contact, and infant should be minimized. The Committee on Infectious Diseases of the AAP offers the following recommendations in the management of the newborn infant whose mother, or any other household contact, has tuberculosis:

• *Mother, or any other household contact, with a positive tuberculin skin test reaction but no evidence of current disease:* Investigation of other members of the household or extended family to whom the infant may later be exposed is indicated. If no evidence of current disease is found in the mother or in members of the extended family, the infant should be tested with a Mantoux tuberculin skin test at 3 to 4 months of age. When the family members cannot be promptly tested, consideration should be given to administering isoniazid (10 mg per kg of body weight a day) to the infant until skin testing and other evaluation of the family members have excluded contact with a case of active tuberculosis. The infant does not need to be hospitalized during this time if adequate follow-up can be arranged, but adherence to medication administration should be closely monitored. The mother also should be considered for isoniazid therapy.

• *Mother with untreated (newly diagnosed) disease or disease that has been treated for 2 or more weeks and who is judged to be noncontagious at delivery:* Careful investigation of household members and extended family is mandatory. A chest radiograph and Mantoux tuberculin skin test should be performed on the infant at 3 to 4 months and at 6 months of age. Separation of the mother and infant is not necessary if adherence to treatment for the mother and infant is assured. The mother can breast-feed. The infant should receive isoniazid even if the tuberculin skin test and chest radiograph do not suggest clinical tuberculosis, since cell-mediated immunity of a degree sufficient to mount a significant reaction to tuberculin skin testing may develop as late as 6 months of age in an infant infected at birth. Isoniazid can be discontinued if the Mantoux skin test is negative at 3 to 4 months of age, the mother is adherent to treatment and has a satisfactory clinical response, and no other family members have infectious tuberculosis. The infant should be examined carefully at monthly intervals. If nonadherence is documented, the mother has an acid-fast bacillus (AFB)–positive sputum or smear, and supervision is impossible, the infant should be separated from the ill family member and Bacillus Calmette-Guérin (BCG) vaccine may be considered for the infant. However, the response to the vaccine in infants may be delayed and inadequate for prevention of tuberculosis.

• *Mother has current disease and is suspected of having been contagious at the time of delivery:* The mother and infant should be separated until the infant is receiving therapy or the mother is confirmed to be noncontagious. Otherwise, management is the same as when the disease is judged to be noncontagious to the infant at delivery.

• *Mother has hematogenously spread tuberculosis (e.g., meningitis, miliary disease, or bone involvement):* The infant should be evaluated for congenital tuberculosis. If clinical and radiographic findings do not support the diagnosis of congenital tuberculosis, the infant should be separated from the mother until she is judged to be noncontagious. The infant should be given isoniazid until 3 or 4 months of age, at which time the Mantoux skin test should be repeated. If the skin test is positive, isoniazid should be continued for a total of 12 months. If the skin test is negative and the chest radiograph is normal, isoniazid may be discontinued, depending on the status of the mother and whether there are other cases of infectious tuberculosis in the family. The infant should continue to be examined carefully at monthly intervals.

Oral Dosage Forms

Note: Bracketed uses in the *Dosage Forms* section refer to categories of use and/or indications that are not included in U.S. product labeling.

ETHAMBUTOL HYDROCHLORIDE TABLETS USP

Usual adult and adolescent dose

Tuberculosis—

In combination with other antituberculosis medications: Oral, 15 to 25 mg per kg of body weight once a day; or 50 mg per kg of body weight, up to 2.5 grams, two times a week; or 25 to 30 mg per kg of body weight, up to 2.5 grams, three times a week.

[Mycobacterial infections, atypical]—Oral, 15 to 25 mg per kg of body weight once a day.

Usual adult prescribing limits

Tuberculosis—

2.5 grams daily.

Usual pediatric dose

Children up to 13 years of age—Dosage has not been established. However, ethambutol should be considered for all children with organisms resistant to other medications, and in whom susceptibility to ethambutol has been demonstrated or is likely. Ethambutol is generally not recommended in children whose visual acuity cannot be monitored (younger than 6 years of age).

Children 13 years of age and over—See *Usual adult and adolescent dose*.

Strength(s) usually available

U.S.—

100 mg (Rx) [*Myambutol*].
400 mg (Rx) [*Myambutol* (scored)].

Canada—

100 mg (Rx) [*Etibi* (scored); *Myambutol*].
400 mg (Rx) [*Etibi* (scored); *Myambutol* (scored)].

Packaging and storage

Store below 40 °C (104 °F), preferably between 15 and 30 °C (59 and 86 °F), unless otherwise specified by manufacturer. Store in a well-closed container.

Auxiliary labeling

- Continue medicine for full time of treatment.

Selected Bibliography

The American Thoracic Society (ATS). Ad Hoc Committee on the Scientific Assembly on Microbology, Tuberculosis, and Pulmonary Infections. Treatment of tuberculosis and tuberculosis infection in adults and children. Clin Infect Dis 1995; 21: 9-27.

Revised: 08/29/1997

ETHINYL ESTRADIOL—See *Estrogens (Systemic)*

ETHOPROPAZINE—See *Antidyskinetics (Systemic)*

ETHOSUXIMIDE—See *Anticonvulsants, Succinimide (Systemic)*

ETHOTOIN—See *Anticonvulsants, Hydantoin (Systemic)*

ETIDOCAINE—See *Anesthetics (Parenteral-Local)*

ETIDRONATE Systemic

VA CLASSIFICATION (Primary/Secondary): HS303/HS302

Commonly used brand name(s): *Didronel*.

Another commonly used name is EHDP.

Note: For a listing of dosage forms and brand names by country availability, see *Dosage Forms* section(s).

Category

Bone resorption inhibitor; antihypercalcemic.

Indications

Accepted

Paget's disease of bone (treatment)—Oral etidronate is indicated for the treatment of symptomatic Paget's disease (osteitis deformans), characterized by abnormal and accelerated bone turnover in one or more bones. Signs and symptoms may include bone pain, deformity, and/or fractures; increased concentrations of serum alkaline phosphatase and/or urinary hydroxyproline; neurologic disorders associated with skull lesions and vertebral deformities; and elevated cardiac output and other vascular disorders associated with increased vascularity of bones.

Although studies have not been done on etidronate's effects in *asymptomatic* Paget's disease, treatment may be considered for such patients if extensive involvement of the skull or vertebral column might lead to neurologic damage; if extensive involvement of weight-bearing bones threatens their integrity; or if juxta-articular involvement threatens the integrity of adjacent joints.

Ossification, heterotopic (prophylaxis and treatment)—Oral etidronate is indicated for the prevention and treatment of heterotopic ossification (myositis ossificans—circumscripta, progressiva, or traumatica; ectopic calcification; periarticular ossification; or paraosteoarthropathy) following total hip replacement or caused by spinal cord injury. Heterotopic ossification is characterized by metaplastic osteogenesis, and may be accompanied by localized inflammation and pain, and elevated skin temperature or redness. Also, loss of joint function or reduction in range of motion may occur when tissues near joints are involved.

Hypercalcemia, associated with neoplasms (treatment adjunct)—Parenteral etidronate is indicated as adjunctive therapy for the treatment of hypercalcemia of malignancy that is inadequately managed by dietary changes and/or oral hydration alone. It is used in conjunction with adequate saline hydration and with "high ceiling" or loop diuretics, such as bumetanide, ethacrynic acid, and furosemide. Limited clinical study results show that oral etidronate may be used in some patients after the last dose of etidronate infusion to maintain clinically acceptable serum calcium concentrations and to prolong normocalcemia.

Unaccepted

Hypercalcemia caused by hyperparathyroidism, where increased tubular reabsorption of calcium may be a factor in the hypercalcemia, is refractory to parenteral etidronate.

Note: Oral etidronate is presently being used experimentally in the U.S. to treat osteoporosis in adults. A small increase in bone mineral density has been noted. Some studies with continuous dosing of etidronate have found abnormal mineralization of osteoid and microfractures that might potentially result in increased susceptibility to fractures, especially nonvertebral fractures. Further studies are needed to determine the safety profile and dosing information.

Pharmacology/Pharmacokinetics

Physicochemical characteristics

Molecular weight—249.99.

Mechanism of action/Effect

Although the exact mechanism is not completely understood, etidronate chemisorbs to calcium phosphate surfaces of calcium hydroxyapatite crystals and their amorphous precursors, and, *in vitro* , blocks the aggregation, growth, and mineralization of the crystals. A similar process is believed to be responsible *in vivo* for retarding the mineralization and growth of heterotopic ossification. This process may also be responsible for retarding bone resorption, and, secondarily, for retarding the accelerated rate of bone turnover in Paget's disease.

Paget's disease—Etidronate induces a reduction of bone resorption, which is accompanied by a reduction in the number of osteoclasts. Secondarily, coupled bone formation is reduced, which is associated with a reduction in the number of osteoblasts. New bone formed following the reduction in bone turnover is histologically more normal. Lamellar bone is formed, and the marrow becomes less vascular and fibrotic. Etidronate reduces serum alkaline phosphatase and urinary hydroxyproline concentrations, reduces radionuclide uptake at pagetic lesions, decreases elevated cardiac output by reducing bone vascularity, and reduces elevated skin temperature over pagetic lesions. The incidence of pagetic fractures may be reduced when etidronate is administered intermittently over a period of years.

Heterotopic ossification—Etidronate slows the progression of immature bone lesions, thus reducing the severity of the disease.

Hypercalcemia of malignancy—Bone resorption is increased in the presence of neoplastic tissue. Etidronate inhibits abnormal bone resorption and reduces the flow of calcium from the resorbing bone into the blood, effectively decreasing total and ionized serum calcium. When kidney function is adequate for the fluid load, hydration with saline increases urine output and the use of diuretics increases the rate of calcium excretion.

Duration of therapeutic effect

Paget's disease—Possibly up to a year or more after discontinuation of therapy.

Heterotopic ossification—Several months after discontinuation of therapy.

Hypercalcemia—Clinical studies indicate a median duration of normocalcemia of 11 days.

Absorption

Lower doses (5 mg per kg of body weight (mg/kg) a day)—1% (average).

Higher doses (10 to 20 mg per kg a day)—2.5 to 6% (average).

Distribution

Approximately half of absorbed dose is chemically adsorbed to bone, presumably upon hydroxyapatite crystals, in areas of elevated osteogenesis.

Biotransformation

None.

Half-life

Elimination—Approximately 50% of the absorbed/infused dose is eliminated from the body within 24 hours. The remainder is presumably chemisorbed to bone and slowly eliminated.

Plasma—5 to 7 hours.

Onset of action

Paget's disease—May be observed after 1 month of treatment; initially observed as a reduction in urinary hydroxyproline.

Hypercalcemia—Reductions in urinary calcium excretion, which accompany reductions in bone resorption, may become apparent after 24 hours.

Time to peak effect

Hypercalcemia—Decreases in serum calcium are maximal on the day following the third infusion, in most patients.

Elimination

Absorbed dose—50% excreted intact in the urine via the kidneys.

Unabsorbed dose—Intact in the feces.

Precautions to Consider

Carcinogenicity

Long-term studies in rats have shown no evidence of carcinogenicity.

Pregnancy/Reproduction

Pregnancy—

For oral etidronate—

Adequate and well-controlled studies in humans have not been done.

Studies in rats and rabbits administered oral doses up to 5 times the maximum human dose have shown no evidence of impaired fertility or harm to the fetus. However, studies in rats administered doses 22 times the maximum human dose of etidronate have shown a decrease in live fetuses.

FDA Pregnancy Category B.

For parenteral etidronate—

Reproductive studies have not been done in either animals or humans. Rats administered large parenteral doses showed skeletal malformations, which were attributed to the pharmacologic action of the drug

FDA Pregnancy Category C.

Breast-feeding

It is not known if etidronate is distributed into breast milk. However, problems in humans have not been documented.

Pediatrics

Appropriate studies have not been performed in the pediatric population. However, in children treated for heterotopic ossification or soft tissue calcifications at doses of 10 mg or more per kg of body weight a day for prolonged periods (approaching or exceeding a year), signs of a rachitic syndrome were infrequently reported. Epiphyseal radiologic changes associated with retarded mineralization of new osteoid and cartilage have been reversible upon discontinuation of etidronate.

Geriatrics

Appropriate studies have not been performed in the geriatric population. However, elderly patients may be more prone to overhydration when treated with parenteral etidronate in conjunction with hydration therapy. Careful monitoring of fluid and electrolyte status is recommended.

Dental

Osteonecrosis of the jaw (ONJ) has been reported in patients treated with bisphosphonates. Most cases have been in cancer patients undergoing dental procedures such as tooth extraction. For patients requiring dental procedures, there are no data available to suggest whether discontinuation of bisphosphonate treatment, prior to the procedure, reduces the risk of osteonecrosis of the jaw. Clinical judgment should guide the management plan of each patient based on individual benefit/risk assessment.

Drug interactions and/or related problems

The following drug interactions and/or related problems have been selected on the basis of their potential clinical significance (possible mechanism in parentheses where appropriate)—not necessarily inclusive (» = major clinical significance):

Note: Combinations containing any of the following medications, depending on the amount present, may also interact with this medication.

» Antacids containing calcium, magnesium, or aluminum or

» Foods containing large amounts of calcium, such as milk or other dairy products or

» Mineral supplements or other medications containing calcium, iron, magnesium, or aluminum

(concurrent use may prevent absorption of oral etidronate; patients should be advised to avoid using within 2 hours of etidronate)

Laboratory value alterations

The following have been selected on the basis of their potential clinical significance (possible effect in parentheses where appropriate)—not necessarily inclusive (» = major clinical significance).

With diagnostic test results

Technetium Tc 99m medronate or

Technetium Tc 99m oxidronate or

Technetium Tc 99m pyrophosphate

(etidronate may theoretically interfere with bone uptake of these diagnostic agents; clinical significance is unknown)

Medical considerations/Contraindications

The medical considerations/contraindications included have been selected on the basis of their potential clinical significance (reasons given in parentheses where appropriate)—not necessarily inclusive (» = major clinical significance).

Except under special circumstances, this medication should not be used when the following medical problem exists:

For hypercalcemia

» Renal function impairment when serum creatinine is 5 mg per dL or greater

(kidney function may be inadequate for the increased fluid load and the excretion of etidronate)

Risk-benefit should be considered when the following medical problems exist:

» Bone fractures, especially of long bones

(mineralization of osteoid laid down during the bone accretion process may be retarded because of the inhibition of hydroxyapatite crystal growth; delay or interruption of etidronate treatment for Paget's disease may be necessary until callus formation and calcification are evident)

» Cardiac failure

(overhydration should be avoided with use of parenteral etidronate in patients with cardiac failure)

» Enterocolitis

(risk of diarrhea is increased, particularly at higher doses)

Hyperphosphatemia
(high doses of oral etidronate may increase the tubular reabsorption of phosphate; occurs less frequently with parenteral therapy)

Hypocalcemia or
Hypovitaminosis D
(patients with restricted intake of calcium or vitamin D may be more sensitive to medications that affect calcium homeostasis)

» Renal function impairment when serum creatinine is 2.5 to 4.9 mg per dL
(excretion of etidronate may be reduced; reduction of dose may be necessary; in addition, renal function impairment may be exacerbated by etidronate infusion)

Sensitivity to etidronate

Patient monitoring

The following may be especially important in patient monitoring (other tests may be warranted in some patients, depending on condition; » = major clinical significance):

For Paget's disease and hypercalcemia

Renal function determinations, especially glomerular filtration rate (GFR) and/or blood urea nitrogen (BUN)
(recommended at periodic intervals during therapy; reduction in dosage in patients with impairment of renal function [GFR] should be considered and such patients closely monitored; occasional mild to moderate abnormalities in renal function [increases of serum creatinine >0.5 mg per dL and elevated BUN] may occur when etidronate infusion is given to patients with hypercalcemia; these increases are reversible or may remain stable without worsening after completion of the course of infusion)

For Paget's disease only

Pain relief, assessment of
(pain may be an indication of Paget's disease activity; however, in elderly patients, biochemical indices, periodically monitored during therapy, are more valuable)

» Serum alkaline phosphatase concentrations and
» Urine hydroxyproline concentrations
(determinations recommended every 3 to 6 months during therapy; decreases in urine hydroxyproline result from decreased collagen resorption following reduced osteoclastic activity and reduced bone resorption; decreases in alkaline phosphatase result from a secondary reduction in osteoblastic activity; reduction in both parameters are an indication of improvement; sustained decreases during drug-free period are evidence of remission; retreatment is started when biochemical indices re-elevate to 75% of pretreatment values or symptoms recur)

Serum phosphate concentrations
(determinations recommended prior to and 4 weeks after initiation of therapy; at higher doses [10 mg or more per kg of body weight per day], a rise of greater than 0.5 mg per deciliter over pretreatment is normal and without clinical consequence and is probably related to an alteration in renal tubular reabsorption of phosphate [normal values return within 2 to 4 weeks after discontinuation of etidronate]; a rise of 0.5 mg per deciliter or greater at lower doses [5 mg or less per kg of body weight per day] is uncommon and may indicate above average bioavailability; if such a rise is seen at the lower dose, the serum alkaline phosphatase and urinary hydroxyproline values should be examined for evidence that the drug is reducing bone turnover as expected; if there are no significant declines in these values, etidronate dosage should be reduced or the medication discontinued to avoid possible reduced mineralization of osteoid with no accompanying clinical benefit)

For hypercalcemia only

Serum albumin concentrations and
Serum calcium concentrations
(determinations recommended periodically during therapy; since serum proteins, especially albumin, may influence the ratio of free and bound calcium, corrected serum calcium values should be calculated by using an established algorithm; albumin-corrected serum calcium determinations may be useful when the signs and symptoms of hypercalcemia are inconsistent with unadjusted calcium values)

Side/Adverse Effects

The following side/adverse effects have been selected on the basis of their potential clinical significance (possible signs and symptoms in parentheses where appropriate)—not necessarily inclusive:

Those indicating need for medical attention

Incidence more frequent

Bone pain or tenderness, increased, continuing, or recurrent—in patients with Paget's disease

Note: Usually occurs over the site of pagetic lesions, but sometimes occurs at previously asymptomatic sites, beginning within 4 to 6 weeks of initiation of therapy; more common with doses of 5 mg per kg of body weight (mg/kg) or greater for more than six months. Pain may persist in some patients, even with continued therapy; usually subsides days to months after etidronate is discontinued.

Incidence less frequent

Osteomalacia (bone fractures, especially of the femur)

Note: Usually occur in patients taking doses higher than 20 mg/kg or continuous administration of etidronate for longer than 6 months. Microfractures may be due to decreased strength of active pagetic bone or may be caused by a mineralization defect accompanying etidronate therapy.

Incidence rare

Allergic reaction, specifically; angioedema (swelling of the extremities, face, lips, tongue, glottis, and/or larynx); ***skin rash or itching; urticaria*** (hives)

Incidence not determined—Observed during clinical practice; estimates of frequency can not be determined

Bone, joint, and/or muscle pain, severe and occasionally incapacitating—most patients had relief from symptoms after stopping etidronate; ***Osteonecrosis of the jaw [ONJ]*** (heavy jaw feeling; loosening of a tooth; pain, swelling, or numbness in the mouth or jaw)—most cases in cancer patients undergoing dental procedures, but some in patients with postmenopausal osteoporosis or other diagnoses

Those indicating need for medical attention only if they continue or are bothersome

Incidence more frequent—at higher doses

Diarrhea; nausea

Incidence less frequent—with parenteral dosage form

Loss of taste or metallic or altered taste

Patient Consultation

As an aid to patient consultation, refer to *Advice for the Patient, Etidronate (Systemic)*.

In providing consultation, consider emphasizing the following selected information (» = major clinical significance):

Before using this medication

» Conditions affecting use, especially:
Sensitivity to etidronate
Use in children—Children given adult dosages for nearly a year or more were reported to have signs of a rachitic syndrome that were reversible upon discontinuation of etidronate
Use in the elderly—Elderly patients may be more prone to overhydration when treated with parenteral etidronate in conjunction with hydration therapy
Dental—Increased risk of osteonecrosis of the jaw (ONJ) in cancer patients undergoing dental procedures; clinical judgment should guide individual management plan based on individual risk/benefit assessment
Other medications, especially antacids or mineral supplements
Other medical problems, especially renal function impairment, bone fractures, cardiac failure, or enterocolitis

Proper use of this medication

» Taking with water on an empty stomach, at least 2 hours before or after food (upon arising, midmorning, or at bedtime)
» Compliance with therapy; not taking more or less medication or for longer period of time than prescribed
Checking with physician before discontinuing medication; may require 1 to 3 months for symptomatic improvement
» Maintaining a well-balanced diet with adequate intake of calcium and vitamin D; not taking within 2 hours of milk or milk products, antacids, mineral supplements, or other medicines high in calcium, magnesium, iron, or aluminum
» Proper dosing
Missed dose: Taking as soon as possible; not taking if almost time for next dose; not doubling doses
» Proper storage

Precautions while using this medication

» Regular visits to physician to check progress even if between treatments

Checking with physician if nausea or diarrhea occurs and continues; dosage adjustment may be necessary

» Checking with physician if bone pain appears or worsens during treatment

» Assessing risk/benefit for dental surgery or other dental procedures if patient has risk factors for ONJ

Side/adverse effects

Signs of potential side effects, especially increased or continuing bone pain, fractures, or allergic reaction

Signs of potential side effects observed during clinical practice, especially bone, joint, and/or muscle pain (severe and occasionally incapacitating) or osteonecrosis of the jaw

General Dosing Information

See also *Patient monitoring.*

For Paget's disease

Symptomatic improvement as evidence of therapeutic response may not be seen for 1 to 3 months; dosage should not be prematurely increased or discontinued during that time.

Although etidronate is usually taken as a single dose, divided doses may be preferred if diarrhea or nausea occurs.

In patients with Paget's disease, retreatment should be initiated only after a medication-free period of at least 3 months and only if there is evidence of active disease or if the biochemical indices have become reelevated to 75% of pretreatment values or symptoms recur.

Analgesics may be required at any time if patient experiences bone pain.

In many patients with Paget's disease, the disease process may be suppressed for a year or more after discontinuing therapy.

Etidronate therapy in patients with total hip replacement does not promote loosening of the prosthesis or impede trochanteric reattachment.

The dosage of etidronate should be reduced when there is a decrease in the glomerular filtration rate

For hypercalcemia

Retreatment with parenteral etidronate for more than 3 days and the safety and effectiveness of more than 2 courses of therapy have not been studied.

The daily dose must be diluted in at least 250 mL of normal saline solution or 5% dextrose injection. More of the diluent may be used, if convenient. The diluted dose should be administered over a period of at least 2 hours.

Limited clinical studies suggest that oral administration of etidronate in some patients may be started on the day following the last dose of parenteral therapy. If serum calcium levels remain normal, treatment may be extended for up to 90 days. Normocalcemia may be defined as serum calcium concentrations usually within 8.5 to 10.5 mg per dL.

Diet/Nutrition

Etidronate should be taken with water on an empty stomach, at least 2 hours before or after food (e.g., upon arising, midmorning, or at bedtime) for maximum absorption.

A well-balanced diet with adequate intake of calcium and vitamin D should be maintained.

Foods containing large amounts of calcium, such as milk or other dairy products, mineral supplements, or other medicines high in calcium, magnesium, iron, or aluminum, may prevent absorption of etidronate and should not be taken within 2 hours of etidronate.

Oral Dosage Forms

ETIDRONATE DISODIUM TABLETS USP

Usual adult dose

Paget's disease of bone—

Oral, initially 5 mg per kg of body weight a day, usually as a single dose, for a period of time not to exceed six months; or 6 to 10 mg per kg of body weight a day, for a period of time not to exceed six months; or 11 to 20 mg per kg of body weight a day, for no longer than three months.

Note: Doses above 5 mg per kg of body weight are recommended only when lower doses are ineffective or there is an overriding requirement for suppression of increased bone turnover or when a more prompt reduction of elevated cardiac output is required.

The retreatment dose after a drug-free period remains the same as the initial dose for most patients.

Heterotopic ossification—

Patients with total hip replacement: Oral, 20 mg per kg of body weight a day for one month prior to and for three months after surgery.

Patients with spinal cord injury: Oral, initially 20 mg per kg of body weight a day for two weeks, beginning as soon as medically feasible after injury and preferably before evidence of heterotopic ossification, the dosage then being decreased to 10 mg per kg of body weight a day for an additional ten weeks.

Hypercalcemia—

Maintenance: Oral, 20 mg per kg of body weight a day for thirty days, up to a maximum of ninety days.

Usual adult prescribing limits

20 mg per kg of body weight a day.

Usual pediatric dose

Dosage has not been established.

Strength(s) usually available

U.S.—

200 mg (Rx) [*Didronel*].

400 mg (Rx) [*Didronel* (scored)].

Canada—

200 mg (Rx) [*Didronel*].

Packaging and storage

Store below 40 °C (104 °F), preferably between 15 and 30 °C (59 and 86 °F), unless otherwise specified by manufacturer. Store in a tight container.

Auxiliary labeling

- Take on an empty stomach.
- Do not take with milk or antacids.

Parenteral Dosage Forms

ETIDRONATEDISODIUM INJECTION

Note: Etidronate disodium injection is not commercially available in Canada.

Usual adult dose

Hypercalcemia—

Intravenous infusion, initially 7.5 mg per kg of body weight per day, administered over a period of at least two hours, for three consecutive days.

Note: Some patients may be treated for up to seven days, but the risk of hypocalcemia is increased after three days.

The retreatment dose after a seven-day drug-free interval remains the same as the initial dose for most patients.

Usual pediatric dose

Dosage has not been established.

Strength(s) usually available

U.S.—

50 mg per mL (Rx) [*Didronel*].

Packaging and storage

Store below 40 °C (104 °F), preferably between 15 and 30 °C (59 and 86 °F), unless otherwise specified by manufacturer. Protect from freezing.

Preparation of dosage form

Dilute the daily dose in at least 250 mL of 0.9% sodium chloride injection or 5% dextrose injection.

Stability

Diluted solution may be stored at controlled room temperature for at least 48 hours without loss of drug.

Revised: 04/26/2006

ETODOLAC—See *Anti-inflammatory Drugs, Nonsteroidal (Systemic)*

ETONOGESTREL AND ETHINYL ESTRADIOL Vaginal†

VA CLASSIFICATION (Primary): HS104

Commonly used brand name(s): *NuvaRing*.

Note: For a listing of dosage forms and brand names by country availability, see *Dosage Forms* section(s).

†Not commercially available in Canada.

Category

Contraceptive (vaginal).

Indications

Accepted

Pregnancy, prevention of—Etonogestrel and ethinyl estradiol vaginal ring is indicated for the prevention of pregnancy in women who elect to use this product as a method of contraception.

Pharmacology/Pharmacokinetics

Physicochemical characteristics

Molecular weight—
Etonogestrel: 324.46.
Ethinyl Estradiol: 296.40.

Mechanism of action/Effect

Contraceptive, vaginal—Combination hormonal contraceptives act by suppression of gonadotropins. The primary effect of this action is inhibition of ovulation. Other alterations include changes in the cervical mucus (which increases the difficulty of sperm entry into the uterus) and the endometrium (which reduce the likelihood of implantation).

Absorption

Both etonogestrel and ethinyl estradiol are rapidly absorbed.

Etonogrestrel and ethinyl estradiol—Bioavailability is approximately 100% and 55.6%, respectively, after vaginal administration.

Protein binding

Etonogestrel—approximately 32% bound to sex hormone binding globulin (SHBG) and approximately 66% bound to albumin in blood.

Ethinyl estradiol—high (approximately 98.5%), not specifically bound to serum albumin; induces an increase in serum concentrations of SHBG

Biotransformation

In vitro data shows that both etonogestrel and ethinyl estradiol are metabolized in liver microsomes by the cytochrome P450 3A4 isoenzyme. Ethinyl estradiol is primarily metabolized by aromatic hydroxylation, but a wide variety of hydroxylated and methylated metabolites are formed. These are present as free metabolites and as sulfate and glucuronide conjugates. The hydroxylated ethinyl estradiol metabolites have weak estrogenic activity. The biological activity of etonogestrel metabolites is unknown.

Half-life

Elimination—
Etonogestrel—29.3 hours
Ethinyl estradiol—44.7 hours

Time to peak concentration

Etonogestrel—200.3 hours
Ethinyl estradiol—59.3 hours

Peak serum concentration

Etonogestrel—1716 picograms per milliliter

Ethinyl estradiol—34.7 picograms per milliliter

Elimination

Etonogestrel and ethinyl estradiol—apparent clearance is 3.4 liters per hour and 34.8 liters per hour, respectively; primarily eliminated in urine, bile and feces.

Precautions to Consider

Carcinogenicity

In a 24-month carcinogenicity study in rats with subdermal implants releasing 10 and 20 μg etonogestrel per day, (approximately 0.3 and 0.6 times the systemic steady state exposure of women using the etonogestrel and ethinyl estradiol vaginal ring), no drug-related carcinogenic potential was observed.

Mutagenicity

Etonogestrel was not genotoxic in the *in-vitro* Ames/Salmonella reverse mutation assay, the chromosomal aberration assay in Chinese hamster ovary cells or in the *in-vivo* mouse micronucleus test.

Pregnancy/Reproduction

Fertility—Fertility returns after withdrawal of the etonogestrel and ethinyl estradiol vaginal ring treatment.

Pregnancy—Etonogestrel and ethinyl estradiol vaginal ring is not recommended during pregnancy.

Teratology studies have been performed in rats and rabbits, given oral doses up to 130 and 260 times the human etonogestrel and ethinyl estradiol dose (based on body surface area) and no evidence of harm to the fetus due to etonogestrel has been revealed.

FDA Pregnancy Category X

Postpartum—

Combination hormonal contraceptives should be started no earlier than four weeks after delivery in women who elect not to breast feed due to increased risk of thromboembolism.

Breast-feeding

The effects of etonogestrel and ethinyl estradiol on nursing mothers is unknown. Small amounts of contraceptive steroids have been identified in the milk of nursing mothers and adverse effects on the infant such as jaundice and breast enlargement have been reported. Contraceptive steroids given in the postpartum period may interfere with lactation by decreasing the quantity and quality of breast milk. It is recommended that nursing women use other forms of contraception until the child is weaned.

Pediatrics

The use of the etonogestrel and ethinyl estradiol vaginal ring before menarche is not indicated.

Adolescents

Safety and efficacy of the etonogestrel and ethinyl estradiol vaginal ring is expected to be the same for postpubertal adolescents under the age of 16, as for users 16 years of age and older.

Geriatrics

This product has not been studied in women over 65 years of age and is not indicated in this population.

Pharmacogenetics

No information is available for the effects of race on the ethinyl estradiol vaginal ring.

Surgical

Combination hormonal contraceptives should be discontinued at least four weeks prior to and for two weeks after elective surgery of a type associated with an increase in risk of thromboembolism and during prolonged immobilization.

Drug interactions and/or related problems

The following drug interactions and/or related problems have been selected on the basis of their potential clinical significance (possible mechanism in parentheses where appropriate)—not necessarily inclusive (» = major clinical significance):

Note: Combinations containing any of the following medications, depending on the amount present, may also interact with this medication.

Acetaminophen
(acetaminophen levels may be decreased; ethinyl estradiol levels may be increased)

Ascorbic acid
(may increase plasma ethinyl estradiol levels by inhibition of conjugation)

» Antibiotics, such as
Ampicillin or
Rifampin or
Tetracycline antibiotics
(may result in unintended pregnancy or breakthrough bleeding)

» Anticonvulsants, such as
Carbamazepine or
Felbamate or
Oxcarbazepine or
Phenytoin or
Topiramate
(may result in unintended pregnancy or breakthrough bleeding)

» Antifungals, such as
Griseofulvin
(may result in unintended pregnancy or breakthrough bleeding)

Atorvastatin
(increase AUC values for ethinyl estradiol by approximately 20%)

» Barbiturates
(may result in unintended pregnancy or breakthrough bleeding)

Clofibric acid or
Morphine or
Salicylic acid or
Temazepam
(concomitant administration with oral contraceptives has shown to increase clearance of these drugs)

» Cyclosporine or
» Prednisolone or
» Theophylline
(oral contraceptives may inhibit metabolism of certain compounds and thereby increase their plasma concentrations)

CYP3A4 inhibitors, such as
Itraconazole or
Ketoconazole
(may increase plasma hormone levels)

Miconazole, vaginal
(increases serum concentrations of etonogestrel and ethinyl estradiol)

» Phenylbutazone
(may result in unintended pregnancy or breakthrough bleeding)

» Protease inhibitors
(efficacy and safety of oral contraceptives may be affected; coadministration with oral combination hormonal contraceptives can have significant changes [increases and decreases] in the mean AUC of estrogen and progestin; refer to the label of the individual protease inhibitors for further drug-drug interaction information)

» Smoking, tobacco
(contraindicated, cigarette smoking increases the risk of serious cardiovascular side effects including myocardial infraction, this risk increases with age [35 years of age or older] and with heavy smoking [15 or more cigarettes per day])

» St. John's Wort
(may induce hepatic enzymes such as cytochrome P450 and p-glycoprotein transporter and reduce the effectiveness of oral contraceptive steroids which may also result in breakthrough bleeding)

Laboratory value alterations

The following have been selected on the basis of their potential clinical significance (possible effect in parentheses where appropriate)—not necessarily inclusive (» = major clinical significance).

With diagnostic test results

Glucose tolerance test
(tolerance may be decreased)

Norepinephrine-induced platelet aggregability
(may be increased)

Thyroid function test, such as
Thyroxine (T_4) determinations
Triiodothyronine (T_3) determinations
(values for the T_3 uptake test may be decreased because of an increase in thyroid-binding globulin [TBG]; free thyroxine [T_4] concentration remain unaltered, even though the total thyroid hormone may be increased)

With physiology/laboratory test values

Antithrombin III, serum and
Folate levels, serum
(concentrations may be decrease)

Binding proteins, such as
Sex hormone-binding globulins (SHBG)
(levels may be elevated)

Clotting factors VII, VIII, IX and X
(may be increased)

Prothrombin time
(may increase)

Triglycerides
(may be increased)

Medical considerations/Contraindications

The medical considerations/contraindications included have been selected on the basis of their potential clinical significance (reasons given in parentheses where appropriate)—not necessarily inclusive (» = major clinical significance).

Except under special circumstances, this medication should not be used when the following medical problem exists:

» Cerebral vascular disease (current or history of) or
» Cholestatic jaundice, of pregnancy or with prior hormonal contraceptive uses, or
» Coronary artery disease (current or history of) or
» Diabetes mellitus with vascular involvement or
» Genital bleeding, abnormal, undiagnosed or
» Headache with focal neurological symptoms or
» Hepatic disease (active) or
» Hepatic tumors (benign or malignant) or
» Hypertension, severe or
» Neoplasm, breast (known, suspected, or personal history of) or
» Neoplasm, endometrium (known or suspected) or
» Neoplasm, estrogen-dependent (know or suspected) or
» Surgery, major, with prolonged immobilization or
» Thrombophlebitis or thromboembolic disorders (current or history of) or
» Tobacco smoking, heavy (≥ 15 cigarettes per day, and especially in patients 35 years of age or older)
» Valvular heart disease with complications
(etonogestrel and ethinyl estradiol, combination hormonal contraceptive should not be used in women who currently have any of these conditions.)

» Hypersensitivity to any of the ingredients contained in the etonogestrel and ethinyl estradiol combination vaginal ring.

Risk-benefit should be considered when the following medical problems exist:

Amenorrhea, or
Oligomenorrhea
(some women may encounter these conditions after discontinuing the use of vaginal ring, especially if the condition was pre-existent)

Blood pressure, elevated
(increases in blood pressure have been reported in women taking oral contraceptives, this is more likely to occur in older users with continued use)

Conditions aggravated by fluid retention
(steroid hormones may cause some degree of fluid retention; caution and careful monitoring is advised)

» Coronary artery disease, patients with know risk factors such as
Diabetes mellitus or
Hypercholesterolemia or
Hypertension or
Obesity, morbid or
(increased risk of myocardial infarction has been associated with oral contraceptive use in patients with these underlying risk factors)

Depression, history of
(observe patient for signs of worsening depression; discontinue combination hormonal contraceptive if significant depression occurs)

Diabetes mellitus or
Prediabetic
(decrease in glucose tolerance may occur in some patients; prediabetic and diabetic women should be carefully observed while taking combination hormonal contraceptives)

Gallbladder disease
(combination hormonal contraceptives may worsen existing gallbladder disease, and may accelerate the development of this disease in previously asymptomatic women)

Genital bleeding, irregularities
(breakthrough bleeding or spotting may occur; if persistent or severe bleeding occur while using the vaginal ring an appropriate investigation should be instituted to rule out the possibility of organic pathology or pregnancy)

Hyperinsulinism
(some estrogens may create a state of hyperinsulinism)

Hyperlipidemias
(use with caution; patients should be followed closely since some progestogens may elevate LDL levels, decrease HDL levels, and may render control of hyperlipidemias more difficult)

Hypertension, history of, or
Hypertension-related diseases, or
Renal disease
(other methods of contraception should be considered; if patient elects to use the vaginal insert they should be monitored closely and if significant elevation of blood pressure occurs, vaginal insert should be discontinued)

Hypertriglyceridemia, persistent
(some women will have changes in serum triglycerides; persistent hypertriglyceridemia may occur)

Migraine or
Headache with a new pattern
(discontinue use if exacerbation of migraine or the development of headache which is recurrent, persistent, or severe occurs)

» Thromboembolic disorders, such as
Thromboembolic disease or
Thrombotic disease
(increased risk of these conditions has been associated with oral contraceptive use; should thrombophlebitis, pulmonary embolism, cerebrovascular disorders, or retinal thrombosis occur or be suspected, the combination hormonal contraceptive should be discontinued immediately)

» Tobacco smoking
(cigarette smoking increases the risk of serious cardiovascular side effects; risk increases with age [especially women over 35 years of age] and with heavy smoking [15 or more cigarettes per day])

Patient monitoring

The following may be especially important in patient monitoring (other tests may be warranted in some patients, depending on condition; » = major clinical significance):

Blood pressure
(women with a history of hypertension, hypertension-related diseases, or renal disease should be monitored closely)

Breast nodules
(monitor patients with particular care)

Contact lens tolerance or
Visual changes
(should be assessed by an ophthalmologist)

Emotional disorders such as
Depression, history of
(should be carefully observed)

» Fluid status
(careful monitoring in weight and for swelling of fingers and ankles in patients with conditions that may be aggravated by fluid retention)

» Physical examinations
(an annual medical evaluation with special reference to blood pressure, breasts, abdomen, pelvic organs and vagina [including cervical cytology])

Side/Adverse Effects

Note: Although not all of the following side/adverse effects have been reported during clinical trials with etonogestrel and ethinyl estradiol vaginal insert, the following have been associated with the use of oral combination hormonal contraceptives and have been selected on the basis of their potential clinical significance (possible signs and symptoms in parentheses where appropriate)—not necessarily inclusive:

Those indicating the need for medical attention
Incidence not determined
Arterial thromboembolism (severe headaches of sudden onset; sudden loss of coordination; pains in chest, groin, or legs, especially calves of legs; sudden onset of shortness of breath for no apparent reason; sudden onset of slurred speech; sudden vision changes); ***cerebral hemorrhage*** (blurred vision; headache sudden and severe; inability to speak; seizures; slurred speech; temporary blindness; weakness in arm and/or leg on one side of the body, sudden and severe); ***cerebral thrombosis*** (confusion; numbness of hands); ***gallbladder disease*** (abdominal fullness; gaseous abdominal pain; recurrent fever; yellow eyes or skin); ***hepatic adenomas or benign liver tumors*** (swelling, pain, or tenderness in upper abdominal area); ***hypertension*** (blurred vision; dizziness; nervousness; headache; pounding in the ears; slow or fast heartbeat); ***mesenteric thrombosis*** (abdominal pain usually after eating a meal; constipation; diarrhea; nausea; vomiting); ***myocardial infarction*** (chest pain or discomfort; pain or discomfort in arms, jaw, back or neck; shortness of breath; nausea; sweating; vomiting); ***pulmonary embolism*** (anxiety; chest pain, cough; fainting; fast heartbeat; sudden shortness of breath or troubled breathing; dizziness or lightheadedness); ***retinal thrombosis*** (decreased vision or other changes in vision); ***thrombophlebitis*** (changes in skin color; pain; tenderness; swelling of foot or leg); ***venous thrombosis*** (tenderness, pain, swelling; warmth; skin discoloration; prominent superficial veins over affected area)

Those indicating need for medical attention only if they continue or are bothersome
Incidence more frequent
Headache; leukorrhea (increased clear or white vaginal discharge); ***nausea; sinusitis*** (pain or tenderness around eyes and cheekbones; fever; stuffy or runny nose; headache; cough; shortness of breath or troubled breathing; tightness of chest or wheezing); ***upper respiratory infection*** (cough; sore throat); ***vaginitis*** (itching of the vagina or genital area; pain during sexual intercourse; thick, white vaginal discharge with no odor or with a mild odor); ***weight gain***

Incidence less frequent
Emotional lability (crying; depersonalization; dysphoria; euphoria; mental depression; paranoia; quick to react or overreact emotionally; rapidly changing moods)

Note: Some patients experienced device-related effects, including sensations of a foreign body, coital problems, and device expulsions.

Incidence not determined
Abdominal cramps (stomach cramps); ***amenorrhea*** (absent, missed, or irregular menstrual periods; stopping of menstrual bleeding); ***bloating*** (swollen); ***breakthrough bleeding*** (medium to heavy, irregular vaginal bleeding between regular monthly periods, which may require the use of a pad or a tampon); ***breast symptoms*** (pain, soreness, swelling, or discharge from the breast or breasts); ***cervical erosion*** (light vaginal bleeding between periods and after intercourse); ***cervical secretion*** (change in amount of vaginal discharge; bloody vaginal discharge); ***cholestatic jaundice*** (abdominal or stomach pain; chills; clay-colored stools; dark urine; diarrhea; dizziness; fever; headache; itching; loss of appetite; nausea; rash; unpleasant breath odor; unusual tiredness or weakness; vomiting of blood; yellow eyes or skin); ***contact lenses intolerance; corneal curvature, steepening of*** (vision changes); ***decreased lactation, postpartum*** (decreased amount or quality of milk); ***edema*** (swelling); ***infertility, temporary after discontinuation*** (trouble getting pregnant); ***melasma*** (brown, blotchy spots on exposed skin); ***menstrual disturbances*** (menstrual changes); ***mental depression*** (mild feeling of sadness or discouragement that come and go); ***migraine*** (headache, severe and throbbing); ***rash; spotting*** (light vaginal bleeding between regular menstrual periods); ***tolerance to carbohydrates, reduced*** (abdominal pain; blurred vision; dry mouth; fatigue; flushed, dry skin; fruit-like breath odor; increased hunger; increased thirst; increased urination; nausea; sweating; troubled breathing; unexplained weight loss; vomiting); ***vaginal candidiasis*** (itching of the vagina or outside genitals; pain during sexual intercourse; thick, white curd-like vaginal discharge without odor or with mild odor); ***vomiting; weight loss***

Overdose

For more information on the management of overdose or unintentional ingestion, **contact a poison control center** (see *Poison Control Center Listing*).

Clinical effects of overdose

The following effects have been selected on the basis of their potential clinical significance (possible signs and symptoms in parentheses where appropriate)—not necessarily inclusive:

Given the nature of the etonogestrel and ethinyl estradiol vaginal ring, overdose is unlikely; even if the ring is broken, it does not release a higher dose of hormones. However, overdose of combination hormonal contraceptives may cause:

Menstrual irregularities (menstrual changes); ***nausea; vaginal bleeding; vomiting***

Treatment of overdose

Supportive care—
There is no specific antidote for etonogestrel and ethinyl estradiol vaginal ring. Treatment is generally symptomatic and supportive.
Patients in whom intentional overdose is confirmed or suspected should be referred for psychiatric consultation.

Patient Consultation

As an aid to patient consultation, refer to *Advice for the Patient, Etonogestrel and Ethinyl Estradiol (Vaginal)*.

In providing consultation, consider emphasizing the following selected information (» = major clinical significance):

Before using this device

» Conditions affecting use, especially:

Hypersensitivity to estrogens, progestins, or any of the components of etonogestrel and ethinyl estradiol vaginal ring.

Pregnancy—Contraindicated during pregnancy

Breast-feeding—Contraceptive steroids have been identified in human breast milk and may cause adverse effects in the nursing infant

Other medications, especially ampicillin, barbiturates, carbamazepine, cyclosporine, felbamate, griseofulvin, itraconazole, ketoconazole, oxcarbazepine, phenylbutazone, phenytoin, prednisolone, protease inhibitors, rifampin, St John's Wort, tetracycline antibiotics, theophylline, topiramate, tobacco smoking

Other medical problems, cerebral vascular disease, cholestatic jaundice, coronary artery disease, diabetes mellitus with vascular involvement, undiagnosed abnormal genital bleeding, headache with focal neurological symptoms, active hepatic disease, hepatic tumors (benign or malignant), severe hypertension, breast neoplasm, endometrial neoplasm, other estrogen-dependent neoplasm, major surgery with prolonged immobilization, thrombophlebitis or thromboembolic disorders, heavy tobacco smoking, valvular heart disease with complications, or hypersensitivity

Proper use of this medication

» Reading a copy of the patient information brochure provided by the health care professional helps explain the possible side effects, risks, and warning signs of trouble with the vaginal insert.

» Proper dosing, including vaginal insert removal or replacement times

Missed dose: If this device is removed or expelled, re-insert the vaginal device as soon as possible (within three hours); patient must use additional contraception if the vaginal ring is not re-inserted within three hours

» Importance of ruling out pregnancy if there is a deviation from the recommended regimen

» Importance of using additional contraception in the event of a deviation from recommended regimen; additional contraception must be used until ring has been used continuously for seven days.

Proper insertion technique

» Importance of adherence to the recommended prescribed regimen

Proper storage

Precautions while using this device

» Regular annual visits to physician, or more often, as determined by physician

Reporting possible pregnancy, including ectopic pregnancy, to physician

» This product does not protect against HIV infection (AIDS) and other sexually transmitted diseases

Side/adverse effects

Signs of potential side effects that have been associated with use of oral combination hormonalcontraceptives especially arterial thromboembolism, cerebral hemorrhage, cerebral thrombosis, hepatic adenomas or benign liver tumors, hypertension, mesenteric thrombosis, myocardial infarction, pulmonary embolism, retinal thrombosis, thrombophlebitis, or venous thrombosis.

General Dosing Information

Note: The possibility of ovulation and conception prior to the first use of the etonogestrel and ethinyl estradiol vaginal ring should be considered.

Counting the first day of menstruation as "Day 1", etonogestrel and ethinyl estradiol vaginal ring should be inserted on or prior to day 5 of the menstruation cycle, counting the first day of menstruation as "Day 1" even if the women is not finished bleeding. During the first cycle an additional method of contraception such as male condoms or spermicide is recommended until after seven consecutive days of use. The ring is to remain in place continuously for three weeks. It is then removed for a one-week break, during which withdrawal bleeding usually occurs (2–3 days after removal of the ring). A new ring is inserted one week after the last ring was removed, on the same day of the week and at about the same time as the last ring was inserted in the previous cycle.

Like oral contraceptives, the etonogestrel and ethinyl estradiol vaginal ring is highly effective if used as recommended. In two large clinical trials of 13 cycles of etonogestrel and ethinyl estradiol vaginal ring use, pregnancy rates were between one and two per 100 women-years of use.

Etonogestrel and ethinyl estradiol vaginal ring does not protect against HIV infection (AIDS) and other sexually transmitted diseases.

The etonogestrel and ethinyl estradiol vaginal ring may not be suitable for women with conditions that make the vagina more susceptible to vaginal irritation or ulceration.

Insertion technique—The ring is to be compressed and inserted into the vagina, the exact position is not critical for its function. The user can place the ring while lying on her back, standing with one foot raised on a chair or while squatting.

Removal technique—Removed by hooking the index finger under the forward rim or by grasping the rim between the index and middle finger and pulling it out through the vagina. The used ring should be placed back into the sachet that it came in and discarded in a waste receptacle. The ring should not be flushed in the toilet.

Removal of the vaginal ring is not necessary before sexual intercourse. During intercourse some sexual partners may feel the vaginal ring in the vagina, however in clinical studies 90% of the couples did not find it to be a problem.

If the vaginal ring has been removed by the user or accidentally expelled during the three week use period, it should be rinsed with cool to luke warm water and re-inserted as soon as possible and within three hours. If the vaginal ring has been lost a new ring should be inserted and the regimen should continue without alteration.

If the vaginal ring has been out of the vagina for more than three hours, contraceptive effectiveness may be reduced and an additional method of contraception, such as a male condom must be used until the ring has been used continuously for seven days. If the ring free interval has been extended beyond one week, the possibility of pregnancy should be considered.

Switching from a combination oral contraceptive—The etonogestrel and ethinyl estradiol vaginal ring may be inserted anytime within seven days after the last combined oral contraceptive tablet and no later than the day that a new cycle of pills would have been started. No back-up contraception is needed.

Switching from a progestin only method—The vaginal ring should be inserted as follows: any day of the month when switching form a progestin only pill, without skipping any days between the last pill and the vaginal ring use; on the same day as contraceptive implant removal; on the same day as removal of progestin-containing IUD; or on the day when the next contraceptive injection would be due. In all cases additional methods of contraception such as a male condom should be used for the first seven days after insertion of the vaginal ring.

Following complete first trimester abortions—The patient may start using the vaginal ring within five days without the need to use an additional method of contraception. If the ring is not started within 5 days following a first-trimester abortion, the patient should follow the instructions for "No preceding hormonal contraceptive use in the past month."

Following delivery or second trimester abortions—The patient may start using the vaginal ring four weeks postpartum (if she elects not to breast feed) or four weeks after a second trimester abortion, however increased risk of thromboembolic disease must be considered.

For prolonged use—If the vaginal ring has been left in place for up to one week extra, it should be removed and a new ring inserted after the one-week ring-free interval. If the ring has been left in for longer than four weeks, pregnancy should be ruled out, however additional contraception, such as a male condom must be used until a new ring has been used continuously for seven days.

If a missed period occurs due to nonadherence of the prescribed regimen, pregnancy should be considered and the vaginal ring discontinued if pregnancy is confirmed.

If two consecutive periods have been missed, and the patient has adhered to the prescribed regimen, pregnancy should be ruled out.

Contraceptive failures may result in ectopic or intrauterine pregnancy.

Vaginal Dosage Form

ETONOGESTREL AND ETHINYL ESTRADIOL VAGINAL INSERT

Note: Also called etonogestrel and ethinyl estradiol vaginal ring.

Usual adult and adolescent dose

Contraceptive—

Intravaginal, one insert, duration of use is three weeks.

Strength(s) usually available

U.S.—

11.7 mg of etonogestrel delivering 0.12 mg per day and 2.7 mg of ethinyl estradiol delivering 0.015 mg per day (Rx) [*NuvaRing* (ethylene vinylacetate copolymers [28% and 9% vinylacetate]; magnesium stearate)].

Canada—
Not commercially available.

Packaging and storage

Prior to dispensing: Store refrigerated between 2 and 8 °C (36 and 46 °F)

After dispensing: Store at 25 °C (77 °F). Excursions permitted to 15 to 30 °C (59 to 86 °F). Protect from direct sunlight and temperatures above 30 °C (86 °F). Can be stored up to 4 months.

Auxiliary labeling

- Vaginal use only

Additional information

When the etonogestrel and ethinyl estradiol vaginal ring is dispensed to a user, an expiration date should be placed on the label. This date should not exceed either 4 months from the date of dispensing or the expiration date, whichever comes first.

Revised: 03/05/2004
Developed: 01/12/2004

ETOPOSIDE Systemic

VA CLASSIFICATION (Primary): AN900

Commonly used brand name(s): *Etopophos; Toposar; VePesid.*

Another commonly used name is VP-16.

Note: For a listing of dosage forms and brand names by country availability, see *Dosage Forms* section(s).

Category

Antineoplastic.

Indications

Note: Bracketed information in the *Indications* section refers to uses that are not included in U.S. product labeling.

Accepted

Tumors, germ cell, testicular (treatment)—Etoposide injection is indicated, in combination with other antineoplastics, for first-line treatment of testicular tumors (Evidence rating: IA).

Carcinoma, lung, small cell (treatment)—Etoposide is indicated in combination with other agents as first-line treatment of small cell lung carcinoma.

[Lymphomas, Hodgkin's (treatment)][1]
[Lymphomas, non-Hodgkin's (treatment)] or
[Leukemia, acute nonlymphocytic (treatment)][1]—Etoposide also is indicated, alone and in combination with other agents, for treatment of Hodgkin's and non-Hodgkin's lymphomas and acute nonlymphocytic (myelocytic) leukemia.

[Ewing's sarcoma (treatment)][1] or
[Kaposi's sarcoma, autoimmune deficiency syndrome (AIDS)-associated (treatment)][1]—Etoposide is indicated for treatment of Ewing's sarcoma and AIDS-associated Kaposi's sarcoma.

[Carcinoma, adrenocortical (treatment)][1]
[Carcinoma, gastric (treatment)][1]
[Hepatoblastoma (treatment)][1]
[Leukemia, acute lymphocytic (treatment)][1]
[Lymphomas, cutaneous T-cell (treatment)][1]
[Multiple myeloma (treatment)][1]
[Neuroblastoma (treatment)][1]
[Sarcomas, soft tissue (treatment)][1]
[Tumors, brain, primary (treatment)][1] or
[Tumors, trophoblastic, gestational (treatment)][1]—Etoposide is indicated, alone or in combination with other agents, for treatment of adrenocortical carcinoma, gastric carcinoma, hepatoblastoma, acute lymphocytic leukemia, cutaneous T-cell lymphomas, multiple myeloma, neuroblastoma, soft tissue sarcomas, primary brain tumors, and gestational trophoblastic tumors.

[Carcinoma, lung, non-small cell (treatment)]—Etoposide is indicated, alone or in combination with other agents, for treatment of non-small cell lung carcinoma.

[Carcinoma, endometrial (treatment)][1]—Etoposide is considered reasonable medical therapy at some point in the management of endometrial carcinoma (Evidence rating: IIID).

[Carcinoma, unknown primary site (treatment)][1]—Etoposide is indicated for the first-line treatment of carcinoma of unknown primary site (CUPS), as part of a combination regimen with paclitaxel and carboplatin. There was not a clear consensus by the USP medical experts. Some of the experts are hesitant about the use of this regimen and suggest that individual case factors (e.g. metastatic sites, disease factors, patient characteristics, etc.) be considered when choosing an appropriate treatment.

[Myelodysplastic syndromes (treatment)][1]—Etoposide may be used for salvage treatment, in combination with amifostine and topotecan, for the treatment of myelodysplastic syndromes (MDS). There was not a clear consensus by the USP medical experts. Some of the experts are hesitant about the use of amifostine and suggest that individual case factors (e.g., International Prognostic Scoring System [IPSS] risk group, patient characteristics, etc.) be considered when choosing an appropriate treatment.

[Retinoblastoma (treatment)][1]
[Thymoma (treatment)][1] or
[Wilms' tumor (treatment)][1]—Etoposide is considered reasonable medical therapy at some point in the management of retinoblastoma (Evidence rating: IIID), thymoma (Evidence rating: IIID), and Wilms' tumor (Evidence rating: IIID).

[Osteosarcoma (treatment)][1]—Etoposide is considered reasonable medical therapy at some point in the management of osteosarcoma (Evidence rating: IIID).

[Tumors, germ cell, ovarian (treatment)][1]—Etoposide is indicated, in combination with other antineoplastics, for first-line treatment of ovarian germ cell tumors (Evidence rating: IIID).

Acceptance not established

Use of etoposide for the treatment of hormone-refractory prostate cancer has not been established.

[1]Not included in Canadian product labeling.

Pharmacology/Pharmacokinetics

Physicochemical characteristics

Molecular weight—
Etoposide: 588.57.
Etoposide phosphate: 668.55.

Other characteristics—
Etoposide: Lipophilic.

Mechanism of action/Effect

The exact mechanism of etoposide's antineoplastic effect is unknown. Etoposide is a topoisomerase II inhibitor. It seems to act at the premitotic stage of cell division to inhibit DNA synthesis; it is cell cycle–dependent and phase-specific, with maximum effect on the S and G_2 phases of cell division.

Absorption

Variable, dose-dependent oral bioavailability; absorption decreases as the dose of etoposide increases; mean 50% (range, 25 to 75%).

Distribution

Low and variable into cerebrospinal fluid (CSF). Concentrations are higher in normal lung than in lung metastases, and are similar in primary tumors and normal tissues of the myometrium.

Protein binding

Very high (97%) *in vitro* . Etoposide binding ratio correlates directly with serum albumin in healthy individuals and cancer patients. The unbound fraction has been found to correlate significantly with bilirubin in a group of cancer patients. Phenylbutazone, sodium salicylate, and aspirin displace protein-bound etoposide *in vitro* .

Biotransformation

Hepatic.

Half-life

Terminal (biphasic)—7 hours (range, 3 to 12).

Elimination

Renal—44 to 60% (67% of that unchanged).
Fecal—Up to 16% (as unchanged drug and metabolites).
Biliary—6% or less.

Precautions to Consider

Carcinogenicity

Secondary malignancies are potential delayed effects of many antineoplastic agents, although it is not clear whether the effect is related to their mutagenic or immunosuppressive action. The effects of dose and duration of therapy are also unknown, although risk seems to increase with long-term use. Although information is limited, available data seem to indicate that the carcinogenic risk is greatest with the alkylating agents.

Acute leukemia (onset 2 to 3 years) has been reported in patients treated with topoisomerase II inhibitors such as etoposide.

Mutagenicity

Etoposide is mutagenic and genotoxic in mammalian cells. Etoposide caused aberrations in chromosome number and structure in embryonic murine cells and human hematopoietic cells, gene mutations in Chinese hamster ovary cells, and DNA damage by strand breakage and DNA-protein cross-links in mouse leukemia cells; it also caused a dose-related increase in sister chromatid exchanges in Chinese hamster ovary cells and was mutagenic in the Ames test.

Pregnancy/Reproduction

Fertility—Gonadal suppression, resulting in amenorrhea or azoospermia, may occur in patients receiving antineoplastic therapy, especially with the alkylating agents. In general, these effects appear to be related to dose and length of therapy and may be irreversible. Prediction of the degree of testicular or ovarian function impairment is complicated by the common use of combinations of several antineoplastics, which makes it difficult to assess the effects of individual agents.

Pregnancy—Adequate and well-controlled studies in humans have not been done.

First trimester: It is usually recommended that use of antineoplastics, especially combination chemotherapy, be avoided whenever possible, especially during the first trimester. Although information is limited because of the relatively few instances of antineoplastic administration during pregnancy, the mutagenic, teratogenic, and carcinogenic potential of these medications must be considered.

Other hazards to the fetus include adverse reactions seen in adults.

In general, use of a contraceptive is recommended during cytotoxic drug therapy.

Etoposide has been shown to be teratogenic and embryotoxic in mice and rats. Dose-related maternal toxicity, embryotoxicity, and teratogenicity (major skeletal abnormalities, exencephaly, encephalocele, and anophthalmia) have been reported with intravenous administration of 0.4 mg of etoposide per kg of body weight per day (mg/kg per day) (one twentieth of the recommended clinical dose based on body surface area) to rats during organogenesis; doses of 1.2 and 3.6 mg/kg per day (one seventh and one half of the recommended clinical dose, respectively, based on body surface area) caused 90% and 100% embryonic resorptions, respectively. Embryotoxicity and teratogenicity (cranial abnormalities, major skeletal abnormalities) also have been reported in mice following intraperitoneal administration of 1 mg/kg (one sixteenth of the recommended clinical dose based on body surface area) on day 6, 7, or 8 of gestation; intraperitoneal administration of 1.5 mg/kg (one tenth of the recommended clinical dose based on body surface area) on day 7 of gestation caused an increase in the incidences of intrauterine fetal death, fetal malformations, and decreased fetal weights. Risk-benefit must be carefully considered when this medication is required in life-threatening situations or in serious diseases for which other medications cannot be used or are ineffective.

FDA Pregnancy Category D.

Breast-feeding

Etoposide is distributed into breast milk. Breast-feeding is not recommended during chemotherapy because of the risks to the infant (adverse effects, mutagenicity, carcinogenicity).

Pediatrics

Appropriate studies on the relationship of age to the effects of etoposide have not been performed in the pediatric population. However, use of higher-than-recommended dosages of etoposide has been associated with a higher incidence of anaphylactic reactions in the pediatric population.

Geriatrics

No information is available on the relationship of age to the effects of etoposide in geriatric patients. However, elderly patients are more likely to have age-related renal function impairment, which may require adjustment of dosage in patients receiving etoposide.

Dental

The bone marrow depressant effects of etoposide may result in an increased incidence of microbial infection, delayed healing, and gingival bleeding. Dental work, whenever possible, should be completed prior to initiation of therapy or deferred until blood counts have returned to normal. Patients should be instructed in proper oral hygiene during treatment, including caution in use of regular toothbrushes, dental floss, and toothpicks.

Etoposide may also cause stomatitis, which may be associated with considerable discomfort.

Drug interactions and/or related problems

The following drug interactions and/or related problems have been selected on the basis of their potential clinical significance (possible mechanism in parentheses where appropriate)—not necessarily inclusive (» = major clinical significance):

Note: Combinations containing any of the following medications, depending on the amount present, may also interact with this medication.

Blood dyscrasia-causing medications (see *Appendix II*)
(leukopenic and/or thrombocytopenic effects of etoposide may be increased with concurrent or recent therapy if these medications cause the same effects; dosage adjustment of etoposide, if necessary, should be based on blood counts)

» Bone marrow depressants, other (see *Appendix II*) or
Radiation therapy
(additive bone marrow depression may occur; dosage reduction may be required when two or more bone marrow depressants, including radiation, are used concurrently or consecutively)

Vaccines, killed virus
(because normal defense mechanisms may be suppressed by etoposide therapy, the patient's antibody response to the vaccine may be decreased. The interval between discontinuation of medications that cause immunosuppression and restoration of the patient's ability to respond to the vaccine depends on the intensity and type of immunosuppression-causing medication used, the underlying disease, and other factors; estimates vary from 3 months to 1 year)

» Vaccines, live virus
(because normal defense mechanisms may be suppressed by etoposide therapy, concurrent use with a live virus vaccine may potentiate the replication of the vaccine virus, may increase the side/adverse effects of the vaccine virus, and/or may decrease the patients antibody response to the vaccine; immunization of these patients should be undertaken only with extreme caution after careful review of the patients hematologic status and only with the knowledge and consent of the physician managing the etoposide therapy. The interval between discontinuation of medications that cause immunosuppression and restoration of the patients ability to respond to the vaccine depends on the intensity and type of immunosuppression-causing medication used, the underlying disease, and other factors; estimates vary from 3 months to 1 year. Patients with leukemia in remission should not receive live virus vaccine until at least 3 months after their last chemotherapy. In addition, immunization with oral poliovirus vaccine should be postponed in persons in close contact with the patient, especially family members)

Medical considerations/Contraindications

The medical considerations/contraindications included have been selected on the basis of their potential clinical significance (reasons given in parentheses where appropriate)—not necessarily inclusive (» = major clinical significance).

Risk-benefit should be considered when the following medical problems exist:

» Bone marrow depression

» Chickenpox, existing or recent (including recent exposure) or
» Herpes zoster
(risk of severe generalized disease)

Hepatic function impairment
(reduced clearance)

» Infection

Renal function impairment
(reduced elimination; lower dosage may be necessary)

Sensitivity to etoposide

» Caution should be used also in patients who have had previous cytotoxic drug therapy or radiation therapy.

Patient monitoring

The following are especially important in patient monitoring (other tests may be warranted in some patients, depending on condition; » = major clinical significance):

» Examination of patients mouth for ulceration
(recommended prior to each dose)

» Hematocrit or hemoglobin and
» Leukocyte count, total and, if appropriate, differential and
» Platelet count
(determinations recommended prior to initiation of therapy and at periodic intervals during therapy; frequency varies according to clinical state, agent, dose, and other agents being used concurrently)

Albumin, serum
(low concentrations may be associated with increased risk of etoposide-related toxicities)

Side/Adverse Effects

Note: Many "side effects" of antineoplastic therapy are unavoidable and represent the medication's pharmacologic action. Some of these (for example, leukopenia and thrombocytopenia) actually are used as parameters to aid in individual dosage titration.

Hypotension may occur temporarily if etoposide is administered by intravenous infusion over a period of less than 30 minutes.

Use of higher-than-recommended doses has been associated with hepatic toxicity and metabolic acidosis.

The following side/adverse effects have been selected on the basis of their potential clinical significance (possible signs and symptoms in parentheses where appropriate)—not necessarily inclusive:

Those indicating need for medical attention

Incidence more frequent

Anemia (unusual tiredness or weakness); ***leukopenia*** (fever or chills; cough or hoarseness; lower back or side pain; painful or difficult urination)—usually asymptomatic; ***thrombocytopenia*** (unusual bleeding or bruising; black, tarry stools; blood in urine or stools; pinpoint red spots on skin)—usually asymptomatic

Note: With *leukopenia*, the nadir of the granulocyte count occurs 7 to 14 days after administration, and recovery is usually complete by the 20th day; cumulative myelosuppression has not been reported.

With *thrombocytopenia*, the nadir of the platelet count occurs 9 to 16 days after administration, and recovery is usually complete by the 20th day; cumulative myelosuppression has not been reported.

Incidence less frequent

Stomatitis (sores in mouth or on lips)

Incidence rare

Anaphylaxis (fast heartbeat; fever or chills; shortness of breath or wheezing; back pain; cough; loss of consciousness; sweating; swelling of face or tongue; tightness in throat); ***chemical phlebitis*** (pain at site of injection); ***neurotoxicity*** (difficulty in walking; numbness or tingling in fingers and toes; weakness); ***skin rash or itching***

Note: *Anaphylaxis* also is associated with hypotension; hypertension and flushing also have been reported; blood pressure usually returns to normal within a few hours after the intravenous infusion is discontinued. An apparent hypersensitivity-associated apnea has been reported rarely. Use of higher-than-recommended dosages of etoposide has been associated with a higher rate of anaphylaxis in pediatric patients. Rarely, anaphylaxis may be fatal.

At investigational doses, a generalized pruritic erythematous maculopapular *rash*, consistent with perivasculitis, has been reported.

Those indicating need for medical attention only if they continue or are bothersome

Incidence more frequent

Loss of appetite; nausea and vomiting

Incidence less frequent

Central nervous system (CNS) toxicity (unusual tiredness); ***diarrhea***

Those not indicating need for medical attention

Incidence more frequent

Alopecia (loss of hair)

Note: *Alopecia* sometimes progresses to total baldness; it is reversible.

Patient Consultation

As an aid to patient consultation, refer to *Advice for the Patient, Etoposide (Systemic)*.

In providing consultation, consider emphasizing the following selected information (» = major clinical significance):

Before using this medication

» Conditions affecting use, especially:
Sensitivity to etoposide
Pregnancy—Use not recommended because of mutagenic, teratogenic, and carcinogenic potential; advisability of using contraception; telling physician immediately if pregnancy is suspected
Breast-feeding—Not recommended because of risk of serious side effects
Use in children—Severe allergic reactions can occur if children receive higher-than-recommended doses
Other medications, especially other bone marrow depressants or previous cytotoxic drug or radiation therapy
Other medical problems, especially chickenpox, herpes zoster, or infection

Proper use of this medication

» Importance of not taking more or less medication than the amount prescribed
Caution in taking combination therapy; taking each medication at the right time
Frequency of nausea, vomiting, and loss of appetite; importance of continuing medication despite stomach upset
Checking with physician if vomiting occurs shortly after oral dose is taken
» Proper dosing
Missed dose: Not taking at all; not doubling doses
» Proper storage

Precautions while using this medication

» Importance of close monitoring by physician
» Avoiding immunizations unless approved by physician; other persons in patient's household should avoid immunizations with oral poliovirus vaccine; avoiding persons who have taken oral poliovirus vaccine or wearing a protective mask that covers nose and mouth

Caution if bone marrow depression occurs:
» Avoiding exposure to persons with infections, especially during periods of low blood counts; checking with physician immediately if fever or chills, cough or hoarseness, lower back or side pain, or painful or difficult urination occurs
» Checking with physician immediately if unusual bleeding or bruising; black, tarry stools; blood in urine or stools; or pinpoint red spots on skin occur
Caution in use of regular toothbrush, dental floss, or toothpick; physician, dentist, or nurse may suggest alternatives; checking with physician before having dental work done
Not touching eyes or inside of nose unless hands are washed immediately before
Using caution to avoid accidental cuts with use of sharp objects such as safety razor or fingernail or toenail cutters
Avoiding contact sports or other situations where bruising or injury could occur

Side/adverse effects

Importance of discussing possible effects, including cancer, with physician
Signs of potential side effects, especially anemia, leukopenia, thrombocytopenia, stomatitis, anaphylaxis, chemical phlebitis, neurotoxicity, and skin rash or itching
Physician or nurse can help in dealing with side effects
Possibility of hair loss; normal hair growth should resume after treatment has ended

General Dosing Information

Patients receiving etoposide should be under supervision of a physician experienced in cancer chemotherapy.

A variety of dosage schedules of etoposide, alone or in combination with other antitumor agents, are used. The prescriber may consult the medical literature as well as the manufacturer's literature in choosing a specific dosage.

Dosage must be adjusted to meet the individual requirements of each patient, based on clinical response and appearance of or severity of toxicity.

Frequency and duration of nausea and vomiting may be reduced in some patients by administration of antiemetics prior to dosing.

Special precautions are recommended in patients who develop thrombocytopenia as a result of administration of etoposide. These may include extreme care in performing invasive procedures; regular inspection of intravenous sites, skin (including perirectal area), and mucous membrane surfaces for signs of bleeding or bruising; limiting frequency of venipuncture and avoiding intramuscular injections; testing urine, emesis, stool, and secretions for occult blood; care in use of regular toothbrushes, dental floss, toothpicks, safety razors, and fingernail and toenail cutters; avoiding constipation; and using caution to prevent falls and other injuries. Such patients should avoid alcohol and aspirin intake because of the risk of gastrointestinal bleeding. Platelet transfusions may be required.

Patients who develop leukopenia should be observed carefully for signs of infection. Antibiotic support may be required. In neutropenic patients who develop fever, broad-spectrum antibiotic coverage should be initiated empirically, pending bacterial cultures and appropriate diagnostic tests.

It is recommended that the dosage of etoposide be reduced in patients with renal function impairment. A dose reduction of 25% is recommended if creatinine clearance is 15 to 50 mL per minute.

For parenteral dosage form only

It is recommended that etoposide injection be diluted prior to use, and that it be administered by slow intravenous infusion over a period of 30 to 60 minutes to prevent hypotension. Etoposide should not be administered by rapid intravenous injection or by any other route.

Etoposide phosphate may be administered intravenously over 5 to 210 minutes.

Safety considerations for handling this medication

There is limited but increasing evidence and concern that personnel involved in preparation and administration of parenteral antineoplastics may be at some risk because of the potential mutagenicity, teratogenicity, and/or carcinogenicity of these agents, although the actual risk is unknown. USP advisory panels recommend cautious handling both in preparation and disposal of antineoplastic agents. Precautions that have been suggested include:

- Use of a biological containment cabinet during reconstitution and dilution of parenteral medications and wearing of disposable surgical gloves and masks.
- Use of proper technique to prevent contamination of the medication, work area, and operator during transfer between containers (including proper training of personnel in this technique).
- Cautious and proper disposal of needles, syringes, vials, ampuls, and unused medication.

A number of medical centers have developed detailed guidelines for handling of antineoplastic agents.

Combination chemotherapy

Etoposide may be used in combination with other agents in various regimens. As a result, incidence and/or severity of side effects may be altered and different dosages (usually reduced) may be used. For example, etoposide is part of the following chemotherapeutic combinations (some commonly used acronyms are in parentheses):

—etoposide, cyclophosphamide, doxorubicin, and vincristine (CAVE).
—cyclophosphamide, doxorubicin, and etoposide (CAE).
—cisplatin, bleomycin, and etoposide (BEP).
—cisplatin and etoposide (EP).

For specific dosages and schedules, consult the literature. For information regarding each agent, consult the individual monograph.

For treatment of adverse effects

Hypotension may be treated by stopping the infusion, administering fluids and other supportive treatment, then resuming the infusion at a slower rate.

Anaphylaxis should be treated by stopping the infusion and administering pressor agents, corticosteroids, antihistamines, or volume expanders as necessary.

Oral Dosage Forms

Note: Bracketed information in the *Dosage Forms* section refer to categories of use and/or indications that are not included in U.S. product labeling.

ETOPOSIDE CAPSULES, USP

Note: The dosing and strengths of the dosage forms available are expressed in terms of etoposide base (not the phosphate salt).

Usual adult dose

Small cell lung carcinoma—
Oral, 70 mg (base) per square meter of body surface area (rounded to the nearest 50 mg) per day for four days to 100 mg per square meter of body surface area (rounded to the nearest 50 mg) per day for five days, repeated every three to four weeks.

[Carcinoma, unknown primary site][1]—
Patients have benefited from an oral daily dose of 50 mg alternating with 100 mg, on days 1 to 10 of a 21–day treatment cycle, combined with intravenous paclitaxel and carboplatin, for 4 to 8 cycles.

[Myelodysplastic syndromes][1]—
Consult medical literature and/or experts in the field of hematology/oncology for information on dosage.

Usual pediatric dose

Dosage has not been established.

Strength(s) usually available

U.S.—
50 mg (base) (Rx) [*VePesid*].
Canada—
50 mg (base) (Rx) [*VePesid*].

Packaging and storage

Store between 2 and 8 °C (36 and 46 °F), in a tight container. Protect from freezing.

Parenteral Dosage Forms

Note: Bracketed uses in the *Dosage Forms* section refer to categories of use and/or indications that are not included in U.S. product labeling.

ETOPOSIDE INJECTION

Usual adult dose

Germ cell testicular tumors—
Intravenous infusion, 50 to 100 mg (base) per square meter of body surface area per day on days 1 through 5 to 100 mg per square meter of body surface area on days 1, 3, and 5 of a regimen that is repeated every three to four weeks.

Small cell lung carcinoma—
Intravenous infusion, 35 mg (base) per square meter of body surface area per day for four days to 50 mg per square meter of body surface area per day for five days, repeated every three to four weeks.

[Lymphomas, Hodgkin's][1] or
[Lymphomas, non-Hodgkin's] or
[Lymphomas, cutaneous T-cell][1] or
[Leukemia, acute nonlymphocytic][1] or
[Leukemia, acute lymphocytic][1] or
[Multiple myeloma][1] or
[Ewing's sarcoma][1] or
[Kaposi's sarcoma, autoimmune deficiency syndrome (AIDS)-associated][1] or
[Sarcomas, soft tissue][1] or
[Osteosarcoma][1] or
[Carcinoma, adrenocortical][1] or
[Carcinoma, gastric][1] or
[Carcinoma, lung, non-small cell] or
[Carcinoma, endometrial][1] or
[Hepatoblastoma][1] or
[Neuroblastoma][1] or
[Retinoblastoma][1] or
[Thymoma][1] or
[Wilms' tumor][1] or
[Tumors, brain, primary][1] or
[Tumors, trophoblastic, gestational][1] or
[Tumors, germ cell, ovarian][1]—
Consult medical literature, and manufacturer's literature for specific dosage.

Usual pediatric dose

Dosage has not been established.

Strength(s) usually available

U.S.—
20 mg (base) per mL (Rx) [*VePesid* (citric acid 2 mg per mL; benzyl alcohol 30 mg per mL; polysorbate 80/tween 80, 80 mg per mL; polyethylene glycol 300, 650 mg per mL; alcohol 30.5% v/v); *Toposar* (citric acid 2 mg per mL; benzyl alcohol 30 mg per mL; polysorbate 80/tween 80, 80 mg per mL; polyethylene glycol 300, 650 mg per mL; alcohol 30.5% v/v); GENERIC].
Canada—
20 mg (base) per mL (Rx) [*VePesid* (benzyl alcohol 30 mg per mL; citric acid; polyethylene glycol 300; polysorbate 80; ethanol); GENERIC].

Packaging and storage

Store below 40 °C (104 °F), preferably between 15 and 30 °C (59 and 86 °F), unless otherwise specified by the manufacturer. Protect from freezing.

Preparation of dosage form

Etoposide injection may be diluted for administration by intravenous infusion in either 5% dextrose injection or 0.9% sodium chloride injection to produce a solution containing 200 to 400 mcg (0.2 to 0.4 mg) of etoposide per mL (precipitation may occur with concentrations greater than 400 mcg per mL).

Cracking and leaking of plastic containers made of ABS (a polymer composed of acrylonitrile, butadiene, and styrene) has been reported when used with undiluted (but not diluted) etoposide injection.

Stability

When diluted as recommended, 0.2 and 0.4 mg per mL solutions are stable for 96 and 24 hours, respectively, at 25 °C (77 °F) under normal room fluorescent light in glass or plastic containers.

Caution

Use of products containing benzyl alcohol is generally not recommended for preparation of medications for use in neonates. A fatal toxic syndrome consisting of metabolic acidosis, CNS depression, respiratory problems, renal failure, hypotension, and possibly seizures and intracranial hemorrhages has been associated with this use.

Use of products containing polysorbate 80 is generally not recommended for preparation of medications for use in premature infants. A life-threatening syndrome consisting of hepatic and renal failure, pulmonary deterioration, thrombocytopenia, and ascites has been associated with this use.

ETOPOSIDE PHOSPHATE FOR INJECTION

Note: The dosage and strength of the available dosage form are expressed in terms of etoposide base (not the phosphate salt).

Usual adult dose

Germ cell testicular tumors—
Intravenous infusion, 50 to 100 mg (base) per square meter of body surface area per day on days 1 through 5 to 100 mg per square meter of body surface area on days 1, 3, and 5 of a regimen that is repeated every three to four weeks.

Small cell lung carcinoma—
Intravenous infusion, 35 mg (base) per square meter of body surface area per day for four days to 50 mg per square meter of body surface area per day for five days, repeated every three to four weeks.

[Lymphomas, Hodgkin's][1] or
[Lymphomas, non-Hodgkin's] or
[Lymphomas, cutaneous T-cell][1] or
[Leukemia, acute nonlymphocytic][1] or
[Leukemia, acute lymphocytic][1] or
[Multiple myeloma][1] or
[Ewing's sarcoma][1] or
[Kaposi's sarcoma, autoimmune deficiency syndrome (AIDS)-associated][1] or
[Sarcomas, soft tissue][1] or
[Osteosarcoma][1] or
[Carcinoma, adrenocortical][1] or
[Carcinoma, gastric][1] or
[Carcinoma, lung, non-small cell] or
[Carcinoma, endometrial][1] or
[Hepatoblastoma][1] or
[Neuroblastoma][1] or
[Retinoblastoma][1] or
[Thymoma][1] or
[Wilms' tumor][1] or
[Tumors, brain, primary][1] or
[Tumors, trophoblastic, gestational][1] or
[Tumors, germ cell, ovarian][1]—
Consult medical literature, and manufacturer's literature for specific dosage.

Usual pediatric dose

Dosage has not been established.

Strength(s) usually available

U.S.—
100 mg (base) (Rx) [*Etopophos* (sodium citrate 32.7 mg; dextran 40, 300 mg)].

Canada—
Not commercially available.

Packaging and storage

Store between 2 and 8 °C (36 and 46 °F), unless otherwise specified by the manufacturer.

Preparation of dosage form

Etoposide phosphate for injection is reconstituted for intravenous use by the addition of 5 or 10 mL of either sterile water for injection, 5% dextrose injection, 0.9% sodium chloride injection, bacteriostatic water for injection with benzyl alcohol, or bacteriostatic sodium chloride for injection with benzyl alcohol, producing a solution containing 20 mg or 10 mg etoposide per mL (22.7 mg or 11.4 mg etoposide phosphate per mL), respectively. Following reconstitution, etoposide phosphate may be administered without further dilution, or it may be further diluted with 5% dextrose injection or 0.9% sodium chloride injection to a final concentration as low as 0.1 mg etoposide per mL.

Stability

When diluted as recommended, etoposide phosphate solution is stable for 24 hours at controlled room temperature (20 to 25 °C [68 to 77 °F]) or in a refrigerator (2 to 8 °C [36 to 46 °F]).

Caution

Use of products containing benzyl alcohol is generally not recommended for preparation of medications for use in neonates. A fatal toxic syndrome consisting of metabolic acidosis, CNS depression, respiratory problems, renal failure, hypotension, and possibly seizures and intracranial hemorrhages has been associated with this use.

[1]Not included in Canadian product labeling.

Revised: 02/25/2004

EXEMESTANE Systemic

VA CLASSIFICATION (Primary): AN500

Commonly used brand name(s): *Aromasin*.

Note: For a listing of dosage forms and brand names by country availability, see *Dosage Forms* section(s).

Category

Antineoplastic.

Indications

Accepted

Carcinoma, breast (treatment)—Exemestane is indicated in the treatment of advanced breast cancer in postmenopausal women whose disease has progressed following tamoxifen therapy.

Unaccepted

Use of exemestane in premenopausal women is not accepted.

Pharmacology/Pharmacokinetics

Physicochemical characteristics

Chemical Group—Steroidal aromatase inactivator, structurally related to the natural substrate androstenedione.

Molecular weight—296.41.

Mechanism of action/Effect

The principle source of circulating estrogen in postmenopausal women comes from conversion of androstenedione and testosterone (synthesized in the adrenals and ovaries) to estrone and estradiol via the aromatase enzyme. Exemestane acts as a false substrate for the aromatase enzyme, causing an irreversible inhibition. This inhibition results in estrogen deprivation to hormone dependent breast cancer cells.

Other actions/effects

Exemestane has no effect on other steroidogenic pathway enzymes. Exemestane has not been shown to affect cortisol or aldosterone secretion. At daily doses of 200 mg or greater, increases in testosterone and androstenedione levels were observed. Slight, non–dose-dependent increases in serum luteinizing hormone (LH) and follicle-stimulating hormone (FSH) were observed at low doses. A dose-dependent decrease in sex hormone binding globulin (SHBG) was observed at daily doses of 2.5 mg or greater.

Absorption

Rapidly absorbed after oral administration. The rate of absorption appears to be increased in postmenopausal women with breast cancer when compared with healthy postmenopausal subjects. Exemestane plasma levels increased by approximately 40% after a high-fat breakfast.

Distribution

Exemestane is extensively distributed into body tissues; distribution into blood cells is negligible.

Protein binding

Very high (90%); independent of the total plasma concentration. Primarily bound to albumin and α_1–acid glycoprotein

Biotransformation

Hepatic, extensive, principally by CYP 3A4 (oxidation)—Exemestane is oxidized and reduced to various secondary metabolites, none of which contributes substantially to the activity of the drug. The 17–dihydro metabolite binds to androgen receptors with an affinity 100 times greater than the parent compound, and may have androgenic activity.

Half-life
Mean terminal half-life is approximately 24 hours.

Time to peak concentration
1.2 hours in women with breast cancer; 2.9 hours in healthy postmenopausal controls

Time to peak effect
Maximal suppression of circulating estrogens occurs 2 to 3 days after a single 25 mg dose, and persists for 4 to 5 days.

Elimination
Fecal—
42%, over 7 days.
Renal—
42%, over 7 days; less than 1% of the oral dose appears in the urine as unchanged drug.

Precautions to Consider

Carcinogenicity/Tumorigenicity
Carcinogenicity studies in mice at doses between 50 and 450 mg per kg per day exemestane resulted in an incteased incidence of hepatocellular adenomas and/or carcinomas in both genders at the high dose level. Plasma AUC's at the high dose were 2575 ± 386 and 5667 ± 1833 ng hours per mL in males and females (approx. 34 and 75 fold the AUC in postmenopausal patients at the recommended clinical dose). An increased incidence of renal tubular adenomas was observed in male mice at the high dose of 450 mg per kg per day. Since the doses tested in mice did not achieve an MTD, neoplastic findings in organs other than liver and kidneys remain unknown.

A study in rats at the doses of 30 to 315 mg per kg per day exemestane for 92 weeks in males and 2 years in females. No evidence of carcinogenicity was seen in females treated with the highest dose. The male rat test was inconclusive and was terminated in the 92nd week.

Mutagenicity
Exemestane was not found to be mutagenic in the Ames test or in mammalian cells, nor did it increase unscheduled DNA synthesis in rat hepatocytes. Clastogenicity was observed in human lymphocytes *in vitro* , but not *in vivo* during the mouse micronucleus assay.

Pregnancy/Reproduction
Fertility—Ovarian changes, including hyperplasia and increased cyst ovarian formation, and decreases in the corpus luteum were seen in mice, rats, and dogs given doses ranging from three to 20 times the human dose on a mg per square meter of body surface area (mg/m^2) basis. Reduction in female fertility occurred when untreated female rats were mated with male rats given 500 mg per kg of body weight daily (mg/kg per day) (approximately 200 times the recommended human dose on a mg/m^2 basis) for 63 days before and during cohabitation. An increase in placental weight was observed at doses of 4 mg/kg per day (approximately 1.5 times the human dose on a mg/m^2 basis) for 14 days prior to mating through day 15 or 20 of gestation and resuming for the 21 days of lactation in female rats. Female fertility parameters, such as ovarian function, mating behavior, and conception rate, were not affected at doses up to 20 mg/kg per day (approximately 8 times the human dose on a mg/m^2 basis), but mean litter size was reduced.

Pregnancy—Human pregnancy studies have not been conducted. However, if a pregnant woman is exposed to the medication, she should be apprised of the possibility of fetal harm and/or loss of the pregnancy.

Radiolabeled exemestane crosses the placenta in rats. Maternal and fetal plasma concentrations of exemestane and metabolites were approximately equivalent following administration of 1 mg per kg (mg/kg) doses. Prolonged gestation and abnormal or difficult labor, increased resorption, reduction in the number of live fetuses, decreased fetal weight and retarded ossification were observed at doses ≥ 20 mg/kg per day. No malformations were noted when pregnant rats were given doses up to 810 mg/kg per day (approximately 320 times the recommended human dose on a mg/m^2 basis) during organogenesis, however, rabbits given 90 mg/kg per day (approximately 70 times the recommended human daily dose on a mg/m^2 basis) during organogenesis experienced a decrease in placental weight. At 270 mg/kg per day (approximately 210 times the recommended human dose on a mg/m^2 basis), abortion, increased resorption and reduced fetal body weight occurred in rats. No increases in the incidence of malformations were seen in rabbits given this dose.

FDA Pregnancy Category D

Breast-feeding
It is not known whether exemestane is distributed into human breast milk. Although very little information is available regarding distribution of antineoplastic agents into breast milk, breast-feeding is not recommended while exemestane is being administered because of the risks to the infant (adverse effects, mutagenicity, carcinogenicity). Exemestane distributes into rat milk within 15 minutes of oral administration of a 1 mg/kg single dose, with milk and plasma concentrations being approximately equivalent for 24 hours following the dose.

Pediatrics
No information is available on the relationship of age to the effects of exemestane in the pediatric population. Safety and efficacy have not been established.

Geriatrics
Appropriate studies performed to date have not demonstrated geriatrics-specific problems that would limit the usefulness of exemestane in the elderly population.

Drug interactions and/or related problems
The following drug interactions and/or related problems have been selected on the basis of their potential clinical significance (possible mechanism in parentheses where appropriate)—not necessarily inclusive (» = major clinical significance):

Note: Combinations containing any of the following medications, depending on the amount present, may also interact with this medication.

Cytochrome P450 3A4 enzyme inducers, such as:
Carbamazepine or
Phenobarbital or
Phenytoin or
Rifampin or
St. John's Wort
(may decrease exemestane plasma levels; dose modification of exemestane is recommended)

» Estrogens
(may interfere with the pharmacologic action of exemestane)

Laboratory value alterations
The following have been selected on the basis of their potential clinical significance (possible effect in parentheses where appropriate)—not necessarily inclusive (» = major clinical significance).

With physiology/laboratory test values
» Alanine aminotransferase (ALT [SGPT]) values, serum, and
» Alkaline phosphatase values, serum, and
» Aspartate aminotransferase (AST [SGOT]) values, serum, and
Gamma-glutamyltransferase (GGT) values, serum
(elevations up to >5 times upper limit of normal have been observed, mostly attributable to the presence of liver and/or bone metastases)

Lymphocyte count
(exemestane may experience Common Toxicity Criteria (CTC) grade 3 or 4 lymphocytopia)

Medical considerations/Contraindications
The medical considerations/contraindications included have been selected on the basis of their potential clinical significance (reasons given in parentheses where appropriate)—not necessarily inclusive (» = major clinical significance).

Risk-benefit should be considered when the following medical problems exist:
Hepatic function impairment or
Renal function impairment
(although increases in exemestane plasma concentrations have been observed in individuals with moderate or severe hepatic and renal impairment, no dosage adjustment is necessary; the safety of chronic dosing in patients with moderate or severe hepatic and renal impairment has not been studied)

» Hypersensitivity to exemestane

Patient monitoring
The following may be especially important in patient monitoring (other tests may be warranted in some patients, depending on condition; » = major clinical significance):

» Alanine aminotransferase (ALT [SGPT]) values, serum, and
» Alkaline phosphatase values, serum, and
» Aspartate aminotransferase (AST [SGOT]) values, serum, and
Gamma-glutamyltransferase (GGT) values, serum

White blood cell count with differential

Side/Adverse Effects

The following side/adverse effects have been selected on the basis of their potential clinical significance (possible signs and symptoms in parentheses where appropriate)—not necessarily inclusive:

Those indicating need for medical attention

Incidence more frequent

Dyspnea (shortness of breath; difficult or labored breathing; tightness in chest); ***edema*** (swelling of hands, ankles, feet, or lower legs); ***hypertension*** (increased blood pressure); ***lymphocytopenia*** (fever or chills; cough or hoarseness; lower back or side pain); ***mental depression***

Incidence less frequent

Bronchitis (cough; difficulty breathing; tightness in chest; wheezing or shortness of breath); ***chest pain; infection*** (fever or chills; cough or hoarseness; lower back or side pain; painful or difficult urination); ***lymphedema*** (swelling of legs, ankles and feet); ***pathological fracture*** (unexplained broken bone); ***sinusitis*** (headache); ***upper respiratory tract infection*** (cough; sore throat); ***urinary tract infection*** (difficult, burning, or painful urination; frequent urge to urinate)

Those indicating need for medical attention only if they continue or are bothersome

Incidence more frequent

Abdominal pain; anorexia (loss of appetite); ***anxiety; asthenia*** (tiredness or weakness); ***constipation; cough; dizziness; fatigue*** (general feeling of tiredness or weakness); ***headache; hot flashes; increased sweating; insomnia*** (trouble in sleeping); ***influenza-like symptoms*** (chills and fever; diarrhea; cough; general feeling of discomfort or illness); ***nausea and vomiting; pain***

Incidence less frequent

Alopecia (loss of hair); ***arthralgia*** (joint pain); ***back pain; bone pain; confusion; diarrhea; dyspepsia*** (stomach upset); ***Fever; hypoesthesia*** (decreased sense of touch); ***increased appetite; itching; paresthesia*** (burning, tingling or prickly sensations); ***pharyngitis*** (sore throat); ***rash; rhinitis*** (runny nose); ***weakness, generalized***

Overdose

For more information on the management of overdose or unintentional ingestion, **contact a poison control center** (see *Poison Control Center Listing*).

Clinical effects of overdose

The following effects have been selevted on the basis of their potential clinical significance (possible signs and symptoms in parentheses where appropriate)—not necessarily inclusive

Acute leukocytosis (chills; cough; eye pain; fever; general feeling of illness; headache; sore throat; unusual tiredness)

Treatment of overdose

There is no specific antidote for exemestane overdose. Treatment is essentially symptomatic and supportive.

Supportive care—General supportive care, including frequent monitoring of vital signs and close observation of the patient, is indicated. Patients in whom intentional overdose is confirmed or suspected should be referred for psychiatric consultation.

Patient Consultation

As an aid to patient consultation, refer to *Advice for the Patient, Exemestane (Systemic)*.

In providing consultation, consider emphasizing the following selected information (» = major clinical significance):

Before using this medication

» Conditions affecting use, especially:
- Sensitivity to exemestane
- Pregnancy—Use not recommended because of teratogenic potential; telling physician immediately if pregnancy is suspected
- Breast-feeding—Not recommended because of risk of serious side effects
- Other medications, especially estrogens

Proper use of this medication

» Importance of not taking more or less medication than the amount prescribed

Taking immediately after a meal

» Proper dosing

Missed dose: Taking as soon as possible; not taking if almost time for next dose; not doubling doses

» Proper storage

Precautions while using this medication

» Importance of close monitoring by the physician

Side/adverse effects

Signs of potential side effects, especially dyspnea, edema, hypertension, lymphocytopenia, mental depression, bronchitis, chest pain, infection, lymphedema, pathological fracture, sinusitis, upper respiratory tract infection, and urinary tract infection

General Dosing Information

Patients receiving exemestane should be under the supervision of a physician experienced in cancer chemotherapy.

Exemestane therapy should continue until progression of the disease occurs.

Exemestane has no effect on cortisol or aldosterone secretion; therefore, glucocorticoid or mineralocorticoid replacement therapy is not required.

Exemestane should be taken after a meal.

Oral Dosage Forms

EXEMESTANE TABLETS

Usual adult dose

Carcinoma, breast (treatment)—
- Oral, 25 mg once daily after a meal
- Oral, 50 mg once daily after a meal when taken with a potent CYP3A4 inducer such as rifampicin or phenytoin

Usual geriatric dose

See *Usual adult dose.*

Strength(s) usually available

U.S.—

25 mg (Rx) [*Aromasin* (mannitol; crospovidone; polysorbate 80; colloidal silicon dioxide; microcrystalline cellulose; sodium starch glycolate; magnesium stearate; simethicone; polyethylene glycol 6000; sucrose; magnesium carbonate; titanium dioxide; methylparaben; polyvinyl alcohol)].

Canada—

25 mg (Rx) [*Aromasin* (mannitol; crospovidone; polysorbate 80; hydroxypropyl methylcellulose; colloidal silicon dioxide; microcrystalline cellulose; sodium starch glycolate; magnesium stearate; simethicone; polyethylene glycol 6000; sucrose; magnesium carbonate; titanium dioxide; methyl-p-hydroxybenzoate; polyvinyl alcohol; cetyl esters wax; talc; carnauba wax; shellac; iron oxides)].

Packaging and storage

Store at 25 °C (77 °F); excursions permitted to 15 to 30 °C (59° to 86 °F). Store in a well-closed container, unless otherwise specified by manufacturer.

Auxiliary labeling

- Take immediately after a meal

Revised: 10/27/2004
Developed: 03/14/2000

EXENATIDE Systemic

VA CLASSIFICATION (Primary): HS509

Commonly used brand name(s): *Byetta*.

Note: For a listing of dosage forms and brand names by country availability, see *Dosage Forms* section(s).

Category

Antidiabetic agent.

Indications

Accepted

Diabetes, type 2 (treatment)—Exenatide is indicated as adjunctive therapy to improve glycemic control in patients with type 2 diabetes mellitus who are taking metformin, a sulfonylurea, or a combination of metformin and a sulfonylurea but who have not achieved adequate glycemic control.

Pharmacology/Pharmacokinetics

Physicochemical characteristics

Source—Exenatide is a 39 amino acid peptide amide. The amino acid sequence partially overlaps that of glucagon-like-peptide-1 (GLP-1).

Molecular weight—4186.6 Daltons.

pH—4.5

Mechanism of action/Effect

Exenatide is an incretin mimetic agent. Incretins (e.g., glucagon-like peptide-1 [GLP-1]) enhance glucose-dependent insulin secretion and exhibit other antihyperglycemic actions following their release into the circulation from the gut. Exenatide has been shown to bind and activate the known human GLP-1 receptor *in vitro*. Exenatide injection improves glycemic control in people with type 2 diabetes mellitus by several mechanisms:

- Improves pancreatic beta-cell responsiveness to glucose which leads to insulin release only in the presence of elevated glucose concentrations
- Restores first-phase insulin response
- Moderates glucagon secretion and lowers serum glucagon concentrations during periods of hyperglycemia
- Slows gastric emptying and reduces the rate at which meal-derived glucose appears in the circulation
- Reduces food intake

Absorption

Following subcutaneous administration of 10 mcg, area under the curve (AUC) was 1036 pg*h per mL

Distribution

Volume of Distribution (Vol_D): 28.3 L

Half-life

Elimination—2.4 hours

Time to peak concentration

2.1 hours

Peak plasma concentration

211 pg per mL

Elimination

Mean clearance: 9.1 L per hour

Kidney: predominantly eliminated by glomerular filtration with subsequent proteolytic degradation

In hemodialysis: mean clearance is reduced to 0.9 L per hour in patients with end-stage renal disease receiving dialysis

Precautions to Consider

Carcinogenicity

A 104 week- carcinogenicity study was conducted in male and female rats and mice at doses of 18, 70, or 250 mcg per kg per day administered by bolus subcutaneous injection. Benign thyroid C cell adenomas were observed in female rats at all exenatide doses, 5, 22 and 130 times the human exposure resulting from the maximum recommended dose (MRHD) of 20 mcg per kg per day, respectively, based on plasma area under the curve (AUC). No evidence of tumors was observed in mice given doses up to 250 mcg per kg per day, 95 times the MRHD, based on plasma AUC.

Mutagenicity

Exenatide was not mutagenic in the Ames bacterial mutagenicity assay or chromosomal aberration assay in Chinese hamster ovary cells and was negative in the *in vivo* mouse micronucleus assay.

Pregnancy/Reproduction

Fertility—Studies in male and female mice given up to 760 mcg per kg per day (390 times the MRHD) found no adverse effect on fertility.

Pregnancy—Adequate and well controlled studies in humans have not been done.

Reproduction studies in mice given exenatide doses of 3 times the MRHD showed reduced fetal and neonatal growth, and skeletal effects. Mice given exenatide doses ranging from 6 to 760 mcg per kg per day (3 to 390 times the MRHD) showed cleft palate (with some holes), irregular skeletal ossification of rib and skull bones, and neonatal deaths were observed. Rabbits given exenatide doses of 2 mcg per kg per day (12 times the MRHD) showed irregular skeletal effects.

FDA Pregnancy Category C

Breast-feeding

It is not known whether exenatide is distributed into breast milk. However, exenatide is distributed into the milk of lactating mice. Because exenatide has been shown to cause adverse effects in animals, a decision should be made whether to discontinue breast-feeding or discontinue the medication, taking into account the importance of exenatide to the mother.

Pediatrics

No information is available on the relationship of age to the effects of exenatide in the pediatric population. Safety and efficacy have not been established.

Geriatrics

Appropriate studies performed to date have not demonstrated geriatrics-specific problems that would limit the usefulness of exenatide in the elderly.

Pharmacogenetics

Population pharmacokinetic analysis suggests that gender, race (for Caucasian, Hispanic, and Black), and obesity have no significant effect on the pharmacokinetics of exenatide.

Drug interactions and/or related problems

The following drug interactions and/or related problems have been selected on the basis of their potential clinical significance (possible mechanism in parentheses where appropriate)—not necessarily inclusive (» = major clinical significance):

Note: Combinations containing any of the following medications, depending on the amount present, may also interact with this medication.

Acetaminophen
(concomitant use may decrease acetaminophen AUC and peak concentration and may increase the time to peak concentration of acetaminophen; AUC, peak concentration, and time to peak concentration were not changed significantly when acetaminophen was not given 1 hour before exenatide injection)

Digoxin
(may decrease the peak concentration and the time to peak concentration of oral digoxin)

Lisinopril
(may decrease the time to steady state peak concentration of lisinopril)

Lovastatin
(may decrease the peak concentration and the time to peak concentration of lovastatin)

Oral medications that require rapid gastrointestinal absorption or
Oral medications that are dependent on threshold concentrations
(exenatide may decrease the extent and rate of absorption of these drugs; drugs dependent on threshold concentrations should be taken 1 hour prior to exenatide administration)

Sulfonylurea
(when exenatide is added to sulfonylurea therapy, a reduction in the dose of sulfonylurea may be considered to reduce the risk of hypoglycemia)

Medical considerations/Contraindications

The medical considerations/contraindications included have been selected on the basis of their potential clinical significance (reasons given in parentheses where appropriate)—not necessarily inclusive (» = major clinical significance).

Except under special circumstances, this medication should not be used when the following medical problem exists:

» Diabetic ketoacidosis or
» Type 1 diabetes
(these conditions should be treated with insulin)
» Hypersensitivity to exenatide or any of its components

Risk-benefit should be considered when the following medical problems exist:

Gastrointestinal disease, severe
(may exacerbate conditions such as nausea, vomiting and diarrhea)

Hepatic insufficiency
(no pharmacokinetic study has been performed in patients with acute or chronic hepatic insufficiency)

» Renal disease, end-stage or
» Renal impairment, severe
(the mean clearance of exenatide may be greatly reduced in individuals with creatinine clearance of less than 30 mL per min; may lead to severe gastrointestinal side effects)

Patient monitoring

The following may be especially important in patient monitoring (other tests may be warranted in some patients, depending on condition; » = major clinical significance):

Blood glucose or
HbA_{1C}
(levels should be monitored periodically)

Side/Adverse Effects

Immunogenicity: Patients may develop anti-exenatide antibodies following treatment.

The following side/adverse effects have been selected on the basis of their potential clinical significance (possible signs and symptoms in parentheses where appropriate)—not necessarily inclusive:

Those indicating need for medical attention only if they continue or are bothersome

Incidence more frequent

Diarrhea; dizziness; dyspepsia (acid or sour stomach; belching; heartburn; indigestion; stomach discomfort upset or pain); ***feeling jittery; headache; nausea; vomiting***

Incidence less frequent

Appetite decreased; asthenia (lack or loss of strength); ***gastroesophageal reflux disease*** (heartburn; vomiting); ***hyperhidrosis*** (increased sweating)

Overdose

For more information on the management of overdose or unintentional ingestion, **contact a poison control center** (see *Poison Control Center Listing*).

Clinical effects of overdose

The following effects have been selected on the basis of their potential clinical significance (possible signs and symptoms in parentheses where appropriate)—not necessarily inclusive:

Hypoglycemia, severe (anxiety; blurred vision; chills; cold sweats; coma; confusion; cool pale skin; depression; dizziness; fast heartbeat; headache; increased hunger; nausea; nervousness; nightmares; seizures; shakiness; slurred speech; unusual tiredness or weakness); ***nausea, severe; rapidly declining blood glucose concentrations*** (anxiety; blurred vision; chills; cold sweats; coma; confusion; cool pale skin; depression; dizziness; fast heartbeat; headache; increased hunger; nausea; nervousness; nightmares; seizures; shakiness; slurred speech; unusual tiredness or weakness); ***vomiting, severe***

Treatment of overdose

Supportive care—

Appropriate supportive care should be based on the patient's clinical signs and symptoms.

Patients in whom intentional overdose is confirmed or suspected should be referred for psychiatric consultation.

Patient Consultation

As an aid to patient consultation, refer to *Advice for the Patient, Exenatide (Systemic)*.

In providing consultation, consider emphasizing the following selected information (» = major clinical significance):

Before using this medication

» Conditions affecting use, especially:

Pregnancy—Not recommended for use during pregnancy

Breast-feeding—Not recommended because risk of serious side effects.

Other medical problems, especially diabetic ketoacidosis, Type 1 diabetes, end-stage renal disease, or severe renal impairment

Proper use of this medication

» Proper dosing

Missed dose: Skip the missed dose; treatment regimen should be resumed as prescribed with the next scheduled dose.

» Proper storage

Precautions while using this medication

» Regular visits to physician to check progress

» *Carefully following special instructions of health care team:*

Discussing use of alcohol

Not taking other medications unless discussed with physician

Getting counseling for family members to help the patient with diabetes; also, special counseling for pregnancy planning and contraception

Making travel plans that include readiness for diabetic emergencies and eating meals at the usual times, even with changing time zones

» Preparing for and understanding what to do in case of diabetic emergency; carrying medical history and current medication list and wearing medical identification

» Recognizing what brings on symptoms of hypoglycemia, such as using other antidiabetic medication; delaying or missing a meal; exercising more than usual; drinking significant amounts of alcohol; or illness, including vomiting or diarrhea

» Recognizing symptoms of hypoglycemia: anxiety; behavior change similar to drunkenness; blurred vision; cold sweats; confusion; cool, pale skin; difficulty in concentrating; drowsiness; excessive hunger; fast heartbeat; headache; nausea; nervousness; nightmares; restless sleep; shakiness; slurred speech; or unusual tiredness or weakness

» Knowing what to do if symptoms of hypoglycemia occur, such as eating glucose tablets or gel, corn syrup, honey, or sugar cubes; drinking fruit juice, nondiet soft drink, or sugar dissolved in water; or injecting glucagon if symptoms are severe

» Recognizing what brings on symptoms of hyperglycemia, such as not taking enough or skipping a dose of antidiabetic medication, overeating or not following meal plan, having a fever or infection, or exercising less than usual

» Recognizing symptoms of hyperglycemia and ketoacidosis: blurred vision; drowsiness; dry mouth; flushed, dry skin; fruit-like breath odor; increased urination (frequency and volume); ketones in urine; loss of appetite; stomachache, nausea, or vomiting; tiredness; troubled breathing (rapid and deep); unconsciousness; and unusual thirst

» Knowing what to do if symptoms of hyperglycemia occur, such as checking blood glucose and contacting a member of the health care team

General Dosing Information

For subcutaneous dosing forms:

The patient should read the "Information for the Patient" insert and the Pen User Manual before starting therapy and review them each time the prescription is refilled.

The pen needles should not be shared.

Medication should be taken within one hour prior to morning and evening meals.

Parenteral Dosage Forms

EXENATIDE

Usual adult dose

Antidiabetic agent—

Subcutaneous to the thigh, abdomen or upper arm, 5 mcg twice daily at any time within the 60–minute period before the morning and evening meals. Dose may be increased to 10 mcg twice daily after one month.

Note: Renal impairment, mild to moderate: No dosage adjustment is required

Hepatic impairment: Because exenatide is cleared primarily by the kidney, hepatic dysfunction is not expected to affect blood concentrations; no pharmacokinetic study has been performed.

Concomitant sulfonylurea: When exenatide is added to sulfonylurea therapy, a reduction in the dose of sulfonylurea may be considered to reduce the risk of hypoglycemia.

Usual pediatric dose

Safety and efficacy have not been established.

Usual geriatric dose

See *Usual adult dose*.

Strength(s) usually available

U.S.—

5 mcg per dose, 250 mcg per mL exenatide (Rx) [*Byetta*™ (metacresol; mannitol; glacial acetic acid; sodium acetate trihydrate in water for injection)].

10 mcg per dose, 250 mcg per mL exenatide (Rx) [*Byetta*™ (metacresol; mannitol; glacial acetic acid; sodium acetate trihydrate in water for injection)].

Packaging and storage

Store refrigerated between 2 and 8 °C (36 and 46 °F). Protect from light. Do not freeze.

Note: The pen should be discarded 30 days after first use.

Do not use exenatide that has been frozen.

Preparation of dosage form

See the manufacturer's package insert for instructions.

Auxiliary labeling

- May cause drowsiness.
- Avoid alcoholic beverages.

Developed: 07/14/2005

EZETIMIBE Systemic†

VA CLASSIFICATION (Primary): CV359

Commonly used brand name(s): *Zetia*.

Note: For a listing of dosage forms and brand names by country availability, see *Dosage Forms* section(s).

†Not commercially available in Canada.

Category

Antihyperlipidemic.

Indications

Accepted

Hyperlipidemia (treatment)—Ezetimibe is indicated as an adjunct to diet for the reduction of elevated total-C, LDL-C, and Apo B in patients with primary hypercholesterolemia (heterozygous familial and non-familial).

Ezetimibe is indicated in combination with an HMG-CoA reductase inhibitor as adjunctive therapy to diet for the reduction of elevated total-C, LDL-C, and Apo B in patients with primary hypercholesterolemia (heterozygous familial and non-familial).

The combination of ezetimibe with atorvastatin or simvastatin is indicated as an adjunct to other lipid-lowering treatments (e.g., LDL aphresis) or if such treatments are unavailable for the reduction of elevated total-C and LDL-C in patients with homozygous familial hypercholesterolemia (HoFH).

For additional information on initial therapeutic guidelines related to the treatment of hyperlipidemia, see *Appendix III*.

Sitosterolemia (treatment)—Ezetimibe is indicated as adjunctive therapy to diet for the reduction of elevated sitosterol and campesterol levels in patients with homozygous familial sitosterolemia.

Pharmacology/Pharmacokinetics

Physicochemical characteristics

Molecular weight—409.4.

Solubility—Freely to very soluble in ethanol, methanol, acetone, and practically insoluble in water.

Mechanism of action/Effect

Ezetimibe reduces blood cholesterol by inhibiting absorption of cholesterol by the small intestine. Ezetimibe localizes and appears to act at the brush border of the small intestine and inhibits the absorption of cholesterol, leading to a decrease in the delivery of intestinal cholesterol to the liver. This causes a reduction of hepatic cholesterol stores and an increase in the clearance of cholesterol from the blood, this distinct mechanism is complementary to that of the HMG-CoA reductase inhibitors.

Absorption

Absorbed and extensively conjugated to a pharmacologically active phenolic glucuronide.

Variable bioavailability—coefficient of variation was 35% to 60% for AUC values based on inter-subject variability

Ezetimibe can be administered with or without food. Concomitant food administration (high-fat or non-fat meals) had no effect on the extent of absorption; the C_{max} value was increased by 38% with consumption of high-fat meals.

Protein binding

Very High (>90%); ezetimibe and ezetimibe-glucuronide are bound to human plasma proteins

Biotransformation

Rapidly metabolized to ezetimibe-glucuronide; ezetimibe and ezetimibe-glucuronide are 10 to 20% and 80 to 90% of the total drug in the plasma, respectively. Metabolized in the small intestine and liver via glucuronide conjugation (a phase II reaction). Minimal oxidative metabolism (a phase I reaction) has been observed.

Half-life

Ezetimibe and ezetimibe-glucuronide—22 hours for both

Time to peak concentration

Ezetimibe T_{max}: 4 to 12 hours

Ezetimibe-glucuronide T_{max}: 1 to 2 hours

Peak plasma concentration:

Ezetimibe C_{max}: 3.4 to 5.5 ng/mL

Ezetimibe-glucuronide C_{max}: 45 to 71 ng/mL

Elimination

Renal: 9%; ezetimibe-glucuronide was the major component

Fecal: 69%; ezetimibe was the major component

Precautions to Consider

Carcinogenicity/Tumorigenicity

In dietary carcinogenicity studies with ezetimibe in rats and mice, there were no statistically significant increases in tumor incidences in drug-treated rats or mice.

Mutagenicity

No evidence of mutagenicity was observed *in vitro* in an Ames test with *Salmonella typhimurium* and *Escherichia coli*. No evidence of clastogenicity was observed *in vitro* in a chromosomal aberration assay in human peripheral blood lymphocytes. In the *in vivo* mouse micronucleus test, there was no evidence of genotoxicity.

Pregnancy/Reproduction

Fertility—In oral fertility studies of ezetimibe in rats, there was no evidence of reproductive toxicity.

Pregnancy—Adequate and well-controlled studies in humans have not been done. Ezetimibe should be used during pregnancy only if the potential benefit justifies the risk to the fetus.

In oral embryo-fetal development studies of ezetimibe conducted in rats and rabbits during organogenesis, there was no evidence of embryolethal effects at the doses tested. In rats, increased incidences of common fetal skeletal findings were observed. In rabbits treated with ezetimibe, an increased incidence of extra thoracic ribs was observed. Ezetimibe crossed the placenta when pregnant rats and rabbits were give multiple oral doses.

FDA Pregnancy Category C

Note: All HMG-CoA reductase inhibitors are contraindicated in pregnant women. When ezetimibe is administered with an HMG-CoA reductase inhibitor in a woman of childbearing potential, refer to the pregnancy category and product labeling for the HMG-CoA reductase inhibitor.

Labor and delivery—The effects of ezetimibe on labor and delivery in pregnant women are unknown.

Breast-feeding

It is not known whether ezetimibe is distributed into human breast milk. Therefore, ezetimibe should not be used in nursing mothers unless the potential benefit justifies the potential risk to the infant. In rat studies, exposure to total ezetimibe in nursing pups was up to half of that observed in maternal plasma.

Note: All HMG-CoA reductase inhibitors are contraindicated in nursing women. When ezetimibe is administered with an HMG-CoA reductase inhibitor in a woman of childbearing potential, refer to the product labeling for the HMG-CoA reductase inhibitor.

Pediatrics

Treatment experience in the pediatric population is limited to 4 patients between 9 and 17 years of age in the sitosterolemia study and 5 patients between 11 and 17 years of age in the HoFH study. Treatment with ezetimibe in children less than 10 years of age is not recommended.

Geriatrics

The safety and effectiveness of ezetimibe were similar in patients 65 years of age and older and younger patients. However, greater sensitivity of some older individuals cannot be ruled out.

Pharmacogenetics

In a multiple dose study with ezetimibe given 10 mg once daily for 10 days, plasma concentrations for total ezetimibe were slightly higher (less than 20%) in women than in men.

Drug interactions and/or related problems

The following drug interactions and/or related problems have been selected on the basis of their potential clinical significance (possible mechanism in parentheses where appropriate)—not necessarily inclusive (» = major clinical significance):

Note: Combinations containing any of the following medications, depending on the amount present, may also interact with this medication.

Cholestyramine

(co-administration decreases the mean AUC of total ezetimibe approximately 55%; the incremental LDL-C reduction due to adding ezetimibe to cholestyramine may be reduced by this interaction)

Cyclosporine

(may increase risk of increased exposure to ezetimibe; exposure may be greater in patients with severe renal insufficiency; careful monitoring of patients taking both ezetimibe and cyclosporine is recommended)

Fenofibrate
(concomitant administration increases total ezetimibe concentrations approximately 1.5-fold)

Fibrates
(may increase cholesterol excretion leading to cholelithiasis; concurrent use with ezetimibe is not recommended until use in patients is studied)

Gemfibrozil
(concomitant administration increases total ezetimibe concentrations approximately 1.7-fold)

HMG-CoA reductase inhibitors
(concurrent administration with ezetimibe should be in accordance with the product labeling for that HMG-CoA reductase inhibitor)

Warfarin
(if ezetimibe is added to warfarin, the International Normalized Ratio [INR] should be appropriately monitored)

Laboratory value alterations

The following have been selected on the basis of their potential clinical significance (possible effect in parentheses where appropriate)—not necessarily inclusive (» = major clinical significance).

With physiology/laboratory test values
Creatine phosphokinase (CPK), serum
Liver transaminases
(may be elevated according to post-marketing experience)

Medical considerations/Contraindications

The medical considerations/contraindications included have been selected on the basis of their potential clinical significance (reasons given in parentheses where appropriate)—not necessarily inclusive (» = major clinical significance).

Except under special circumstances, this medication should not be used when the following medical problem exists:

» Hypersensitivity to ezetimibe or any of its components
» Liver disease, active or
» Unexplained persistent elevations in serum transaminases
(combination of ezetimibe and an HMG-CoA reductase inhibitor is contraindicated in patients with active liver disease)

Risk-benefit should be considered when the following medical problems exist:

» Hepatic insufficiency, moderate or severe
(ezetimibe is not recommended due to the unknown effects of the increased exposure to ezetimibe in patients with moderate or severe hepatic insufficiency)

Patient monitoring

The following may be especially important in patient monitoring (other tests may be warranted in some patients, depending on condition; » = major clinical significance):

» Liver function tests
(when ezetimibe is co-administered with an HMG-CoA reductase inhibitor, liver function tests should be performed at initiation of therapy and according to the recommendations of the HMG-CoA reductase inhibitor)

Side/Adverse Effects

The following side/adverse effects have been selected on the basis of their potential clinical significance (possible signs and symptoms in parentheses where appropriate)—not necessarily inclusive:

Those indicating need for medical attention

Incidence not determined—Observed during clinical practice, estimates of frequency cannot be determined

Cholecystitis (indigestion; stomach pain; severe nausea; vomiting); ***cholelithiasis*** (abdominal fullness; gaseous abdominal pain; recurrent fever; yellow eyes or skin); ***hepatitis*** (dark urine; general tiredness and weakness; light-colored stools; nausea and vomiting; upper right abdominal pain; yellow eyes and skin); ***hypersensitivity reactions, including angioedema and skin rash*** (large, hive-like swelling on face, eyelids, lips, tongue, throat, hands, legs, feet, sex organs; skin rash); ***myopathy*** (muscular pain, tenderness, wasting or weakness)—very rarely; ***pancreatitis*** (bloating; chills; constipation; darkened urine; fast heartbeat; fever; indigestion; loss of appetite; nausea; pains in stomach, side, or abdomen, possibly radiating to the back; vomiting; yellow eyes or skin); ***rhabdomyolysis*** (dark-colored urine; fever; muscle cramps or spasms; muscle pain or stiffness; unusual tiredness or weakness)—very rarely; ***thrombocytopenia*** (black, tarry stools; bleeding gums; blood in urine or stools; pinpoint red spots on skin; unusual bleeding or bruising)

Note: In post-marketing experience with ezetimibe, cases of myopathy and rhabdomyolysis have been reported regardless of causality. Most patients who developed rhabdomyolysis were taking an HMG-CoA reductase inhibitor prior to initiating ezetimibe. However, rhabdomyolysis has been reported very rarely with ezetimibe alone and very rarely with the addition of ezetimibe to agents known to be associated with increased risk of rhabdomyolysis such as fibrates. All patients starting ezetimibe therapy should be advised of the risk of myopathy and told to report promptly any unexplained muscle pain, tenderness, or weakness. The presence of these symptoms and a creatine phosphokinase (CPK) level greater than 10 times the ULN indicates myopathy.

Those indicating need for medical attention only if they continue or are bothersome

Incidence more frequent

Headache; myalgia (muscle pain); ***upper respiratory tract infection*** (headache; sore throat; runny nose; fever)

Incidence less frequent

Abdominal pain (stomach pain); ***arthralgia*** (pain in joints; muscle pain or stiffness; difficulty in moving); ***back pain; chest pain; coughing; diarrhea; dizziness; fatigue*** (unusual tiredness or weakness); ***pharyngitis*** (body aches or pain; congestion; cough; dryness or soreness of throat; fever; hoarseness; runny nose; tender, swollen glands in neck; trouble in swallowing; voice changes); ***sinusitis*** (pain or tenderness around eyes and cheekbones; fever; stuffy or runny nose; headache; cough; shortness of breath or troubled breathing; tightness of chest or wheezing); ***viral infection*** (chills; cough or hoarseness; fever; cold or flu-like symptoms)

Incidence not determined—Observed during clinical practice, estimates of frequency cannot be determined

Nausea

Overdose

In clinical studies, administration of ezetimibe, 50 mg per day to 15 healthy subjects for up to 14 days, or 40 mg per day to 18 patients with primary hypercholesterolemia for up to 56 days, was generally well tolerated. A few cases of ezetimibe overdosage have been reported. Most have not been associated with adverse reactions and reported adverse events have not been serious.

For more information on the management of overdose or unintentional ingestion, **contact a poison control center** (see *Poison Control Center Listing*).

Treatment of overdose

Treatment should be symptomatic and supportive.

Patients in whom intentional overdose is confirmed or suspected should be referred for psychiatric consultation.

Patient Consultation

As an aid to patient consultation, refer to *Advice for the Patient, Ezetimibe (Systemic)*.

In providing consultation, consider emphasizing the following selected information (» = major clinical significance):

Before using this medication

» Conditions affecting use, especially:
Hypersensitivity to ezetimibe or any of its components
Pregnancy—Should be used during pregnancy only if the potential benefit justifies the risk to the fetus
FDA Pregnancy Category C
Note: HMG-CoA reductase inhibitors contraindicated in pregnant women; co-administer ezetimibe with an HMG-CoA reductase inhibitor according to pregnancy category and product labeling for the HMG-CoA reductase inhibitor
Breast-feeding—Should not be used in nursing women unless potential benefit justifies potential risk to infant
Note: HMG-CoA reductase inhibitors contraindicated in nursing women; co-administer ezetimibe with an HMG-CoA reductase inhibitor according to product labeling for the HMG-CoA reductase inhibitor
Use in children—Not recommended for use in children less than 10 years of age
Other medical problems, especially active liver disease; moderate or severe hepatic insufficiency; or unexplained persistent elevations in serum transaminases

Proper use of this medication

Compliance with prescribed diet during treatment
May be taken with or without food
» Proper dosing
Missed dose: Take as soon as possible; do not take more than one dose each day
» Proper storage

Precautions while using this medication
Importance of regular visits to physician to check progress
Your doctor may do blood tests to check your liver before you start taking ezetimibe with a statin and during treatment
Consulting physician if patient is pregnant, plans to become pregnant, or if patient is breast-feeding
Taking all the medication prescribed unless otherwise directed
Telling your doctor about any prescription and non-prescription medications, including natural or herbal remedies, you are taking or plan to take.
Telling your doctor about unexplained muscle pain, muscle tenderness, or muscle weakness.

Side/adverse effects
Signs of potential side effects observed during clinical practice, especially cholecystitis; cholelithiasis; hepatitis; hypersensitivity reactions, including angioedema and skin rash; myopathy; pancreatitis; rhabdomyolysis; and thrombocytopenia

General Dosing Information

The patient should be placed on a standard cholesterol-lowering diet before receiving ezetimibe and should continue on this diet during treatment with ezetimibe.

Dosing of this drug should occur either at least 2 hours before or at least 4 hours after administration of a bile acid sequestrant.

Ezetimibe may be administered with an HMG-CoA reductase inhibitor for incremental effect. The daily dose of ezetimibe may be taken at the same time as the HMG-CoA reductase inhibitor, according to the dosing recommendations for the HMG-CoA reductase inhibitor.

This drug may be taken with or without food.

Myopathy
If myopathy (i.e., any unexplained muscle pain, tenderness or weakness, and/or a creatine phosphokinase [CPK] level > 10 times the ULN) is diagnosed or suspected, ezetimibe and any HMG-CoA reductase inhibitor or fibrate that the patient is taking concomitantly should be immediately discontinued.

Oral Dosage Forms

EZETIMIBE TABLETS

Usual adult and adolescent dose
Hyperlipidemia and
Sitosterolemia—
Oral, 10 mg once daily with or without food

Note: No dosage adjustment is necessary in patients with mild hepatic insufficiency or renal insufficiency.

Usual adult prescribing limits
See *Usual adult and adolescent dose.*

Usual pediatric dose
Use is not recommended in children less than 10 years of age. In children 10 to 18 years of age, see *Usual adult and adolescent dose*

Usual pediatric prescribing limits
For children 10 to 18 years of age, see *Usual adult and adolescent dose*

Usual geriatric dose
See *Usual adult and adolescent dose.*

Usual geriatric prescribing limits
See *Usual adult and adolescent dose*

Strength(s) usually available
U.S.—
10 mg (Rx) [*Zetia* (croscarmellose sodium; lactose monohydrate; magnesium stearate; microcrystalline cellulose; povidone; sodium lauryl sulfate)].
Canada—
Not commercially available

Packaging and storage
Store at 25° C (77 °F) with excursions permitted to 15 to 30 °C (59 and 86 °F). Protect from moisture.

Auxiliary labeling
• Consult your pharmacist or doctor about using this medication if you are pregnant, plan to become pregnant, or if you are breast-feeding.
• Take all of this medication unless otherwise directed.

Revised: 07/13/2005
Developed: 06/18/2003

EZETIMIBE AND SIMVASTATIN Systemic†

VA CLASSIFICATION (Primary): CV359

Commonly used brand name(s): *Vytorin.*

Note: For a listing of dosage forms and brand names by country availability, see *Dosage Forms* section(s).

†Not commercially available in Canada.

Category

Antihyperlipidemic.

Indications

Accepted
Hyperlipidemia (treatment)—Ezetimibe and simvastatin combination is indicated as an adjunct to diet for the reduction of elevated total-C, LDL-C, and Apo B, TG and non-HDL-C, and to increase HDL-C in patients with primary (heterozygous familial and non-familial) hypercholesterolemia or mixed hyperlipidemia.

The combination of ezetimibe and simvastatin is indicated as an adjunct to other lipid-lowering treatments (e.g., LDL aphresis) or, if such treatments are unavailable, for the reduction of elevated total-C and LDL-C in patients with homozygous familial hypercholesterolemia (HoFH).

For additional information on initial therapeutic guidelines related to the treatment of hyperlipidemia, see *Appendix III.*

Pharmacology/Pharmacokinetics

Physicochemical characteristics
Molecular weight—
Ezetimibe: 409.4.
Simvastatin: 418.57.
Solubility—
Ezetimibe is freely to very soluble in ethanol, methanol, and acetone and practically insoluble in water.
Simvastatin is practically insoluble in water, and freely soluble in chloroform, methanol and ethanol.

Mechanism of action/Effect
Ezetimibe—
Ezetimibe reduces blood cholesterol by inhibiting absorption of cholesterol by the small intestine. Ezetimibe localizes and appears to act at the brush border of the small intestine and inhibits the absorption of cholesterol, leading to a decrease in the delivery of intestinal cholesterol to the liver. This causes a reduction of hepatic cholesterol stores and an increase in the clearance of cholesterol from the blood. This distinct mechanism is complementary to that of the HMG-CoA reductase inhibitors.
Simvastatin—
Simvastatin reduces cholesterol by inhibiting the conversion of HMG-CoA to mevalonate. Simvastatin also reduces VLDL and TG and increases HDL-C.

Absorption
Ezetimibe—Absorbed and extensively conjugated to a pharmacologically active phenolic glucuronide. Ezetimibe can be administered with or without food. Concomitant food administration (high-fat or non-fat meals) had no effect on the extent of absorption; the C_{max} value was increased by 38% with consumption of high-fat meals.
Simvastatin—Not affected when administered immediately before a low-fat meal.

Distribution
Simvastatin—When radiolabeled simvastatin was administered to rats, simvastatin-derived radioactivity crossed the blood-brain barrier.

Protein binding
Ezetimibe—
Very high (> 90%); both ezetimibe and ezetimibe-glucuronide.
Simvastatin—
Very high (approximately 90%); both simvastatin and its β-hydroxy-acid metabolite.

Biotransformation
Ezetimibe—
Rapidly metabolized to ezetimibe-glucuronide; ezetimibe and ezetimibe-glucuronide are 10 to 20% and 80 to 90% of the total drug in the plasma, respectively. Metabolized in the small intestine and

liver via glucuronide conjugation. Minimal oxidative metabolism has been observed.

Simvastatin—

Simvastatin undergoes extensive first-pass extraction in the liver. It is then readily hydrolyzed to β-hydroxyacid, a potent inhibitor of HMG-CoA. Following base hydrolysis four major active metabolites present in plasma are the β-hydroxyacid of simvastatin, and its 6'-hydroxy, 6'-hydroxymethyl, and 6'-exomethylene derivatives.

Half-life

Elimination—Ezetimibe and ezetimibe-glucuronide: 22 hours for both.

Time to peak concentration

Ezetimibe—

Plasma concentration-time profiles exhibit multiple peaks, suggesting enterohepatic recycling.

Simvastatin—

Plasma concentrations peaked at 4 hours and declined rapidly to about 10% by 12 hours post dose.

Elimination

Ezetimibe—

Fecal: 78%; major component ezetimibe, 69% of the administered dose.

Urine: 11%, major component ezetimibe-glucuronide, 9% of the administered dose.

Simvastatin—

Fecal: 60%

Urine: 13%

Precautions to Consider

Carcinogenicity/Tumorigenicity

Ezetimibe—

In dietary carcinogenicity studies with ezetimibe in rats and mice given doses (20 times and >150 times the human dose at 10 mg daily), there were no statistically significant increases in tumor incidences in drug-treated rats or mice.

Simvastatin—

Seventy two week carcinogenicity studies done in mice given daily doses of simvastatin (25, 100 and 400 mg/kg body weight) resulted in higher plasma drug levels 1, 4, and 8 times the human plasma drug level following a 80-mg dose. Liver carcinomas were increased in high-dose females and mid- and high-dose males. Adenomas of the liver significantly increased in mid- to high-dose females. While drug treatment also significantly increased the incidence of lung adenomas in mid- and high-dose males and females. Adenomas of the Harderian gland (a gland in the eye of rodents) were also higher in high-dose mice than in controls. No evidence of a tumorigenic effect was observed at the 25 mg/kg/day dose.

Studies done in rats given 25 mg/kg/day (approximately 11 times higher than the 80 mg dose in humans) for two years showed a significant increase of thyroid follicular adenomas in female rats. Another 2 year carcinogenicity study done in rats given doses of 50 and 100 mg/kg/day produce hepatocellular adenomas and carcinomas (in female rats at both doses and in male rats at 100 mg/kg/day). Thyroid follicular cell adenomas were increased in male and females at both doses. The increased incidence of thyroid neoplasms appears to be consistent with findings from other HMG-CoA reductase inhibitors.

Mutagenicity

Ezetimibe—

No evidence of mutagenicity or clastogenicity was observed in the Ames test with Salmonella typhimurium and Escherichia coli or an *in-vitro* chromosomal aberration assay in human peripheral blood lymphocytes with or without metabolic activation. In addition, there was no evidence of genotoxicity observed in mice in the *in-vivo* mouse micronucleus test.

Simvastatin—

No evidence of mutagenicity was observed in a microbial mutagenicity (Ames) test with or without metabolic activation. In addition, there was no evidence of genotoxicity observed in an *in vitro* alkaline elution assay, a V-79 mammalian cell forward mutation study, an *in vitro* chromosome aberration study in CHO cells, or an *in vivo* chromosomal aberration assay in mouse bone marrow..

Pregnancy/Reproduction

Fertility—

Ezetimibe—

In rats given oral doses of ezetimibe there was no evidence of reproductive toxicity at doses 7 times the human exposure at 10 mg daily base on the $AUC_{0-24\ hr}$ for total ezetimibe.

Simvastatin—

Decreased fertility was seen in male rats given doses of 25 mg/kg body weight of simvastatin for 34 weeks. However this effect was not seen in a subsequent fertility study in which simvastatin was administered at the same dose level for 11 weeks (the entire cycle of spermatogenesis including epididymal maturation). No microscopic changes were observed in the testes of rats from either study. In rats given doses (22 times higher than those in humans taking 80 mg/day based on body surface area) seminiferous tubule degeneration (necrosis and loss of spermatogenic epithelium) was observed. In dogs drug-related testicular atrophy, decreased spermatogenesis, spermatocytic degeneration and giant cell formation at 10 mg/kg/day, (approximately 2 times the human exposure, based on AUC, at 80 mg/kg/day). However, the clinical significance of these findings is unclear.

Pregnancy—Ezetimibe and simvastatin combination is contraindicated in pregnancy.

Ezetimibe—

In oral embryo-fetal development studies of ezetimibe conducted in rats and rabbits during organogenesis, there was no evidence of embryolethal effects at the doses tested. In rats, increased incidences of common fetal skeletal findings were observed. In rabbits treated with ezetimibe, an increased incidence of extra thoracic ribs was observed. Ezetimibe crossed the placenta when pregnant rats and rabbits were give multiple oral doses.

Simvastatin—

Simvastatin was not found to be teratogenic in rats or rabbits at doses 3 times the human exposure based on mg/m² surface area. However, in another study with a structurally related HMG-CoA reductase inhibitor, skeletal malformations were observed in rats and mice.

Note: Rare reports of congenital anomalies, spontaneous abortion, and fetal death/still births have been received following intrauterine exposure to HMG-CoA reductase inhibitors. However the incidences of congenital anomalies did not exceed what would be expected in the normal population. The number of cases is adequate only to exclude a 3- to 4-fold increase in congenital anomalies over the background incidence.

FDA Pregnancy Category X

Labor and delivery—The effects of ezetimibe and simvastatin on labor and delivery in pregnant women are unknown.

Breast-feeding

It is not known whether ezetimibe and simvastatin are distributed into breast milk. Because a small amount of another drug in the same class as simvastatin is distributed in human milk and because of the potential for serious adverse reactions in nursing infants, women should not breast-feed.

In rat studies, exposure to ezetimibe in nursing pups was up to half of that observed in maternal plasma.

Pediatrics

Safety and effectiveness of ezetimibe and simvastatin in pediatric patients less then 10 years of age have not been established.

Adolescents

Ezetimibe—

The pharmacokinetics of ezetimibe in adolescents (10 to 18 years) have been shown to be similar to that in adults.

Simvastatin—

Studies done in adolescent boys and girls (10 to 17 years) with heterozygous familial hypercholesterolemia revealed an adverse experience similar to those treated with placebo. There was no detectable effect on growth or sexual maturation in adolescent boys or girls, or menstrual cycle length in girls. Doses greater than 40 mg have not been studied in this population.

Adolescent females should be counseled on appropriate contraceptive methods while on therapy with simvastatin.

Geriatrics

Appropriate studies performed to date have not demonstrated geriatric-specific problems that would limit the usefulness of ezetimibe and simvastatin in the elderly. However, greater sensitivity in some older people cannot be ruled out.

Ezetimibe given 10 mg once daily for 10 days, revealed plasma concentrations about 2-fold higher in older (≥ 65 years) healthy subjects compared to younger subjects.

Pharmacogenetics

When ezetimibe was given at doses of 10 mg daily for 10 days, women had slightly higher plasma concentration (<20%) than men.

Surgical

Ezetimibe and simvastatin therapy should be temporarily stopped a few days prior to elective major surgery and when any major medical or surgical condition supervenes.

Drug interactions and/or related problems

The following drug interactions and/or related problems have been selected on the basis of their potential clinical significance (possible mechanism in parentheses where appropriate)—not necessarily inclusive (» = major clinical significance):

Note: Combinations containing any of the following medications, depending on the amount present, may also interact with this medication.

» Alcohol, substantial use of
(caution when ezetimibe and simvastatin is used in patients with active liver disease or unexplained transaminase elevations)

» Amiodarone or
» Verapamil
(concomitant use with simvastatin, particularly at higher doses, increases risk of myopathy)

Cholestyramine
(concomitant administration decreases mean AUC of ezetimibe approximately 55%)

» Cyclosporine
(increased risk of myopathy/rhabdomyolysis; may increase risk of exposure to ezetimibe; exposure may be greater in patients with severe renal insufficiency; careful monitoring of patients taking both ezetimibe and cyclosporine is recommended; ezetimibe/simvastatin should not exceed 10/10 mg daily in patients receiving concomitant cyclosporine; risk benefit should be carefully weighed)

» CYP3A4 inhibitors, potent such as
» Clarithromycin or
» Erythromycin or
» Grapefruit juice, large quantities (>1 quart daily) or
» HIV protease inhibitors or
» Itraconazole or
» Ketoconazole or
» Nefazodone
(increased risk of myopathy/rhabdomyolysis; concomitant use should be avoided unless the benefits of combined therapy outweigh the risks; if treatment with itraconazole, ketoconazole or clarithromycin is unavoidable, therapy with ezetimibe and simvastatin should be suspended during the course of treatment)

» Danazol
(increased risk of myopathy/rhabdomyolysis, particularly at higher doses of ezetimibe/simvastatin; if used concomitantly with danazol, ezetimibe/simvastatin dose should not exceed 10/10 mg daily)

Digoxin
(concurrent administration may slightly increase plasma digoxin concentrations; patients should be monitored appropriately when ezetimibe and simvastatin therapy is initiated)

» Fibrates including:
» Fenofibrate or
» Gemfibrozil
(risk of myopathy is increased; safety and efficacy of ezetimibe with fibrates not established, so concomitant use should be avoided)
(concomitant administration with gemfibrozil increased total oral ezetimibe bioavailability by a factor of 1.7 and should be avoided unless benefit outweighs risk; although not recommended, if used concomitantly with gemfibrozil, ezetimibe/simvastatin dose should not exceed 10/10 mg daily)

» Niacin
(risk of myopathy is increased, especially when prescribing lipid-lowering doses of niacin ≥1 gram per day)

» Warfarin
(increased prothrombin time in healthy volunteers given warfarin and simvastatin concomitantly has been reported; prothrombin time should be monitored before and during therapy to ensure that no significant alteration in prothrombin time occurs.)

Laboratory value alterations

The following have been selected on the basis of their potential clinical significance (possible effect in parentheses where appropriate)—not necessarily inclusive (» = major clinical significance).

» Creatine kinase (CK)
(levels may be elevated)

Creatine phosphokinase
(post-marketing reports of elevated levels)

Transaminases, serum
(dose related increases have been noted)

Medical considerations/Contraindications

The medical considerations/contraindications included have been selected on the basis of their potential clinical significance (reasons given in parentheses where appropriate)—not necessarily inclusive (» = major clinical significance).

Except under special circumstances, this medication should not be used when the following medical problem exists:

» Hypersensitivity to ezetimibe or simvastatin or any of its components
» Liver disease, active or
» Unexplained persistent elevations in serum transaminases
(use is contraindicated)

Risk-benefit should be considered when the following medical problems exist:

» Complicated medical histories including:
» Diabetes mellitus, long-standing or
» Renal insufficiency
(patients with these conditions can develop rhabdomyolysis while on therapy with simvastatin)

» Hepatic insufficiency, moderate or severe
(ezetimibe is not recommended due to the unknown effects of the increased exposure to ezetimibe in patients with moderate [Child-Pugh score 7 to 9] or severe hepatic insufficiency [Child-Pugh score 10 to 15])

Medical condition, major or
Surgery, major
(therapy with ezetimibe and simvastatin should be temporarily stopped a few days prior to any major medical or surgical condition)

Patient monitoring

The following may be especially important in patient monitoring (other tests may be warranted in some patients, depending on condition; » = major clinical significance):

CK or
Muscle pain, tenderness or weakness, unexplained
(determinations should be considered in patients starting therapy or with patients whose dose is being increased)

» Liver function tests
(liver function tests should be performed at initiation of therapy and when clinically indicated thereafter; patients titered to the 10/80-mg dose should receive an additional test prior to titration, 3 months after titration and should be monitored periodically for the first year; patients with increased transaminase levels should receive a second evaluation to confirm the findings and be followed until the abnormality returns to normal; if increases in AST or ALT of 3 times the ULN or greater persist, withdrawal of therapy is recommended)

Side/Adverse Effects

The following side/adverse effects have been selected on the basis of their potential clinical significance (possible signs and symptoms in parentheses where appropriate)—not necessarily inclusive:

Those indicating need for medical attention

Incidence not determined—Observed during clinical practice, estimates of frequency can not be determined

Cholecystitis (indigestion; stomach pain; severe nausea; vomiting); ***cholelithiasis*** (abdominal fullness; gaseous abdominal pain; recurrent fever; yellow eyes or skin); ***hypersensitivity reaction including*** (fast heartbeat; fever; hives; itching; irritation; hoarseness; joint pain; stiffness or swelling; rash; redness of skin; shortness of breath; swelling of eyelids, face, lips, hands, or feet; tightness in chest; troubled breathing or swallowing; wheezing); ***angioedema*** (large, hive-like swelling on face, eyelids, lips, tongue, throat, hands, legs, feet, sex organs); ***rash; pancreatitis*** (bloating; chills; constipation; darkened urine; fast heartbeat; fever; indigestion; loss of appetite; nausea; pains in stomach, side, or abdomen, possibly radiating to the back; vomiting; yellow eyes or skin)

Those indicating need for medical attention only if they continue or are bothersome

Incidence less frequent

Extremity pain (pain in arms or legs); ***headache; influenza*** (chills; cough; diarrhea; fever; general feeling of discomfort or illness; headache; joint pain; loss of appetite; muscle aches and pains; nausea; runny nose; shivering; sore throat; sweating; trouble sleeping; unusual tiredness or weakness; vomiting); ***myalgia*** (joint pain; swollen joints; muscle aching or cramping; muscle pains or stiffness; difficulty in moving); ***upper respiratory tract infection*** (ear congestion; nasal congestion; chills; cough; fever; sneezing; sore throat; body aches or pain; headache; loss of voice; runny nose; unusual tiredness or weakness; difficulty in breathing)

Incidence not determined—Observed during clinical practice, estimates of frequency can not be determined

Nausea

Overdose

For more information on the management of overdose or unintentional ingestion, **contact a poison control center** (see *Poison Control Center Listing*).

Treatment of overdose

There is no known specific antidote to ezetimibe and simvastatin. Treatment is generally symptomatic and supportive.

To enhance elimination—

The dialyzability of simvastatin and its metabolites in humans is not known.

Supportive care—

Patients in whom intentional overdose is confirmed or suspected should be referred for psychiatric consultation.

Patient Consultation

As an aid to patient consultation, refer to *Advice for the Patient, Ezetimibe and Simvastatin (Systemic)*.

In providing consultation, consider emphasizing the following selected information (» = major clinical significance):

Before using this medication

» Conditions affecting use, especially:

Hypersensitivity to ezetimibe or simvastatin or any of its components

Pregnancy—HMG-CoA reductase inhibitors are contraindicated during pregnancy or in women planning to become pregnant.

Breast-feeding—HMG-CoA reductase inhibitors are contraindicated in nursing mothers.

Use in children—Not recommended for use in children less than 10 years of age

Use in adolescents—Careful counseling in adolescents females taking ezetimibe and simvastatin therapy on appropriate contraceptive methods

Other medications, especially alcohol, amiodarone, cyclosporine, potent CYP3A4 inhibitors such as clarithromycin, erythromycin, grapefruit juice, HIV protease inhibitors, itraconazole, ketoconazole, or nefazodone; danazol; fibrates including fenofibrate, or gemfibrozil; niacin, verapamil or warfarin

Other medical problems, especially active liver disease, complicated medical histories including diabetes mellitus, and renal insufficiency; moderate or severe hepatic insufficiency, or unexplained persistent elevations in serum transaminases

Proper use of this medication

Compliance with prescribed diet during treatment

May be taken with or without food

» Proper dosing

Missed dose: Taking as soon as possible; not taking more than one dose each day

» Proper storage

Precautions while using this medication

Regular visits to physician to check progress

Your doctor may do blood tests to check your liver before you start taking ezetimibe and simvastatin and during treatment

Consulting physician if patient is pregnant, plans to become pregnant, or if patient is breast-feeding

Taking all the medication prescribed unless otherwise directed

Telling your doctor about any prescription and non-prescription medications, including natural or herbal remedies, you are taking or plan to take

Importance of telling your doctor about unexplained muscle pain, muscle tenderness, or muscle weakness

Side/adverse effects

Signs of potential side effects, especially cholecystitis, cholelithiasis, hypersensitivity reactions, including angioedema and skin rash and pancreatitis

General Dosing Information

Prior to initiation of ezetimibe and simvastatin therapy, secondary causes for dyslipidemia (i.e., diabetes, hypothyroidism, obstructive liver disease, chronic renal failure, and drugs that increase LDL-C and decrease HDL-C), should be excluded or, if appropriate, treated.

The patient should be placed on a standard cholesterol-lowering diet before receiving ezetimibe and simvastatin and should continue on this diet during treatment with ezetimibe and simvastatin.

Dosing of ezetimibe and simvastatin combination should occur either at least 2 hours before or at least 4 hours after administration of a bile acid sequestrant.

At the time of hospitalization for an acute coronary event, lipid measures should be taken upon admission or within 24 hours to help guide the physician on initiation of LDL-lowering therapy.

Ezetimibe and simvastatin should be administered to women of childbearing age only when such women are highly unlikely to conceive.

Oral Dosage Forms

EZETIMIBE AND SIMVASTATIN TABLETS

Usual adult and adolescent dose

Hyperlipidemia—

Oral, 1 tablet individualized according to the baseline LDL-C level, the recommended goal of therapy, and the patient's response, taken as a single dose in the evening. May be taken with or without food.

Note: No dosage adjustment is necessary in patients with mild hepatic insufficiency or renal insufficiency.

Usual adult and adolescent prescribing limits

10 mg of ezetimibe and 80 mg of simvastatin per day

Note: Patients concomitantly receiving amiodarone or verapamil should not exceed 10/20 mg/day.

Note: Patients concomitantly receiving cyclosporine, danazol, or gemfibrozil should not exceed 10/10 mg/day.

Usual pediatric dose

Use is not recommended in children less than 10 years of age. In children 10 to 18 years of age, see *Usual adult and adolescent dose*

Usual pediatric prescribing limits

For children 10 to 18 years of age, see *Usual adult and adolescent dose*

Usual geriatric dose

See *Usual adult and adolescent dose*.

Usual geriatric prescribing limits

See *Usual adult and adolescent dose*

Strength(s) usually available

U.S.—

10 mg ezetimibe and 10 mg simvastatin (Rx) [*Vytorin* (off-white, 311; butylated hydroxyanisole NF; citric acid monohydrate USP; croscarmellose sodium NF; hydroxypropyl methylcellulose USP; lactose monohydrate NF; magnesium stearate NF; microcrystalline cellulose NF; propyl gallate NF)].

10 mg ezetimibe and 20 mg simvastatin (Rx) [*Vytorin* (off-white, 312; butylated hydroxyanisole NF; citric acid monohydrate USP; croscarmellose sodium NF; hydroxypropyl methylcellulose USP; lactose monohydrate NF; magnesium stearate NF; microcrystalline cellulose NF; propyl gallate NF)].

10 mg ezetimibe and 40 mg simvastatin (Rx) [*Vytorin* (off-white, 313; butylated hydroxyanisole NF; citric acid monohydrate USP; croscarmellose sodium NF; hydroxypropyl methylcellulose USP; lactose monohydrate NF; magnesium stearate NF; microcrystalline cellulose NF; propyl gallate NF)].

10 mg ezetimibe and 80 mg simvastatin (Rx) [*Vytorin* (off-white, 315; butylated hydroxyanisole NF; citric acid monohydrate USP; croscarmellose sodium NF; hydroxypropyl methylcellulose USP; lactose monohydrate NF; magnesium stearate NF; microcrystalline cellulose NF; propyl gallate NF)].

Packaging and storage

Store between 20 and 25 °C (68 and 77 °F), in a tight container.

Auxiliary labeling

- Ask your doctor or pharmacist before using non prescription drugs
- This medication could be harmful if you are pregnant or breast-feeding. Consult your pharmacist or doctor about using this medication if you are pregnant, or if you become pregnant, or if you are breast-feeding.

Revised: 05/10/2006
Developed: 12/06/2004

FAMCICLOVIR Systemic

VA CLASSIFICATION (Primary): AM820

Commonly used brand name(s): *Famvir.*

Note: For a listing of dosage forms and brand names by country availability, see *Dosage Forms* section(s).

Category

Antiviral (systemic).

Indications

Accepted

Herpes genitalis, recurrent episodes (suppression or treatment)—Famciclovir is indicated in the suppression or treatment of recurrent episodes of genital herpes. Treatment of recurrent episodes is most effective when started within 6 hours of the onset of symptoms or lesions.

Herpes simplex, HIV-associated (treatment)—Famciclovir is indicated in the treatment of recurrent mucocutaneous (orolabial and genital) herpes simplex infections in HIV-infected patients.

Herpes zoster (treatment)—Famciclovir is indicated in the treatment of herpes zoster infections (shingles) caused by varicella-zoster virus (VZV). Famciclovir has been found to decrease the duration of postherpetic neuralgia (defined as pain at or following healing) when compared to placebo (55 to 62 days versus 128 days, respectively). Famciclovir has also been found to be equivalent to acyclovir in decreasing the duration of acute pain. Therapy is most effective when started within 48 hours of the onset of rash.

Unaccepted

The efficacy of famciclovir has not been established in the treatment of initial episodes of genital herpes infection, ophthalmic zoster, disseminated zoster, or in immunocompromised patients with herpes zoster.

Pharmacology/Pharmacokinetics

Physicochemical characteristics

Molecular weight—321.3.

Mechanism of action/Effect

Famciclovir is a pro-drug; it is the diacetyl 6-deoxy analog of the active antiviral compound, penciclovir. Penciclovir is phosphorylated by viral thymidine kinase to penciclovir monophosphate, which is then converted to penciclovir triphosphate by cellular kinases. Penciclovir inhibits herpes viral DNA synthesis, and, therefore, replication. Penciclovir does not inhibit DNA synthesis in uninfected cells because it is phosphorylated only in herpes-infected cells.

Penciclovir has antiviral activity against herpes simplex virus type 1 (HSV-1), HSV-2, varicella-zoster virus (VZV), and Epstein-Barr virus. *In vitro* studies have shown that penciclovir triphosphate has greater intracellular stability in HSV-2–infected cells than does acyclovir triphosphate. Also, unlike acyclovir, the antiviral activity of penciclovir persists in the absence of extracellular drug.

Absorption

Famciclovir is absorbed in the upper intestine and rapidly converted in the intestinal wall to the active compound, penciclovir. The bioavailability of peniciclovir after oral administration of famciclovir is approximately 77%.

Famciclovir may be taken without regard to meals; although a decrease in the time to peak serum concentration and peak serum concentration of penciclovir was seen when famciclovir was taken with food or after a meal, there was no decrease in the extent of systemic availability.

Distribution

The steady-state volume of distribution of penciclovir is approximately 1 liter per kilogram (L/kg).

Protein binding

Low (20 to 25%).

Biotransformation

Famciclovir is deacetylated, and then oxidized to form the active agent, penciclovir. Little or no famciclovir is detected in the plasma or urine. Inactive metabolites include 6-deoxypenciclovir, monoacetylated penciclovir, and monoacetylated 6-deoxypenciclovir, all of which account for < 1.5% of the dose.

Half-life

Normal renal function—
2.1 to 3 hours.

Severe renal failure (creatinine clearance < 30 mL/min [0.33 mL/sec])—
10 to 13 hours.

Intracellular half-life of penciclovir triphosphate—
In HSV-1–infected cells—Approximately 10 hours.
In HSV-2–infected cells—Approximately 20 hours.
In VZV-infected cells—Approximately 7 hours.

Time to peak plasma concentration

0.7 to 0.9 hours.

Peak plasma concentration

3.3 to 4.2 mcg/mL [10.3 to 13.1 micromoles/L] after a single oral dose (fasting) of 500 mg.

Elimination

Renal (glomerular filtration and tubular secretion); 60 to 65% of an oral dose is recovered as penciclovir in the urine; 27% in the feces over 72 hours.

In dialysis—It is not known if hemodialysis removes penciclovir from the blood.

Precautions to Consider

Carcinogenicity

Dietary carcinogenicity studies of famciclovir were conducted in rats and mice at the doses listed below for approximately 1.5 years. A significant increase in the incidence of mammary adenocarcinoma was seen in female rats receiving 600 mg per kg (mg/kg) per day (1.5 times the human systemic exposure at 500 mg three times a day, based on the area under the plasma concentration-time curve [AUC] for penciclovir). Marginal increases in the incidence of subcutaneous tissue fibrosarcomas or squamous cell carcinomas of the skin were seen in female rats and male mice dosed at 600 mg/kg per day (0.4 times the human exposure, based on AUC for penciclovir). There was no increase in tumor incidence reported in male rats treated with doses of up to 240 mg/kg per day (0.9 times the human AUC), or in female mice treated with doses of up to 600 mg/kg per day (0.4 times the human AUC).

Mutagenicity

Famciclovir and penciclovir were negative in *in vitro* tests for gene mutations in bacteria (*S. typhimurium* and *E. coli*) and unscheduled DNA synthesis in mammalian HeLa 83 cells. Famciclovir was also negative in the L5178Y mouse lymphoma assay, the *in vivo* mouse micronucleus test, and rat dominant lethal study. Famciclovir induced increases in polyploidy in human lymphocytes *in vitro* in the absence of chromosomal damage.

Penciclovir was positive in the L5178Y mouse lymphoma assay for gene mutation/chromosomal aberrations, with and without metabolic activation. In human lymphocytes, penciclovir caused chromosomal aberrations in the absence of metabolic activation. Penciclovir caused an increased incidence of micronuclei in mouse bone marrow *in vivo* when administered intravenously at doses highly toxic to bone marrow, but not when administered orally.

Pregnancy/Reproduction

Fertility—Testicular toxicity was observed in rats, mice, and dogs following repeated administration of famciclovir or penciclovir. Testicular changes included atrophy of the seminiferous tubules, reduction in sperm count, and/or increased incidence of sperm with abnormal morphology or reduced motility. The degree of toxicity was related to dose and duration of exposure. In male rats, decreased fertility was observed after 10 weeks of dosing at 500 mg/kg per day (1.9 times the human AUC). Testicular toxicity was observed following chronic administration to mice (104 weeks) and dogs (26 weeks) at doses of 600 mg/kg per day (0.4 times the human AUC) and 150 mg/kg per day (107 times the human AUC), respectively.

Famciclovir had no effect on general reproductive performance or fertility in female rats at doses up to 1000 mg/kg per day (3.6 times the human AUC).

Pregnancy—No adequate and well-controlled studies have been done in pregnant women.

No adverse effects were observed on embryo-fetal development in rats and rabbits given oral famciclovir at doses of up to 1000 mg/kg per day (approximately 3.6 and 1.8 times the human exposure based on AUC, respectively), and intravenous doses of 360 mg/kg per day in rats (2 times the human exposure based on body surface area [BSA]) and 120 mg/kg per day in rabbits (1.5 times the human exposure based on BSA). Also, no adverse effects were observed after intravenous administration of penciclovir to rats given 80 mg/kg per day (0.4 times the human exposure based on BSA), and rabbits given 60 mg/kg per day (0.7 times the human exposure based on BSA). Physicians are encouraged to register patients in the Famvir® Pregnancy Registry maintained by SmithKline Beecham by calling (800)366–8900, ext.5231.

FDA Pregnancy Category B.

Breast-feeding

Following oral administration of famciclovir, it is not known whether penciclovir is distributed into breast milk.

However, it has been found to pass into the milk of lactating rats at concentrations higher than those seen in the plasma. Also, because of the tumorigenicity seen in rats, it is recommended that either breast-feeding or administration of famciclovir to the mother be discontinued.

Pediatrics

Safety and efficacy have not been established in children up to 18 years of age.

Geriatrics

Studies performed to date have not demonstrated geriatric-specific problems that would limit the usefulness of famciclovir in the elderly. However, elderly patients are more likely to have an age-related decrease in renal function, which may require an adjustment of famciclovir dosage or of dosing interval.

Drug interactions and/or related problems

The following drug interactions and/or related problems have been selected on the basis of their potential clinical significance (possible mechanism in parentheses where appropriate)—not necessarily inclusive (» = major clinical significance):

Note: Combinations containing any of the following medications, depending on the amount present, may also interact with this medication.

Probenecid
(probenecid may compete with penciclovir for active tubular secretion, resulting in increased plasma concentrations of penciclovir)

Medical considerations/Contraindications

The medical considerations/contraindications included have been selected on the basis of their potential clinical significance (reasons given in parentheses where appropriate)—not necessarily inclusive (» = major clinical significance).

Risk-benefit should be considered when the following medical problem exists:

» Renal function impairment
(because penciclovir is renally excreted, patients with renal function impairment may be at increased risk of toxicity; patients with a creatinine clearance of < 60 mL/min [1 mL/sec] require a reduction in dose)

Side/Adverse Effects

Note: No serious side effects have been noted to date with the administration of famciclovir.

Those indicating need for medical attention only if they continue or are bothersome

Incidence more frequent
Headache

Incidence less frequent
Dizziness; fatigue (unusual tiredness or weakness); ***gastrointestinal disturbances*** (diarrhea; nausea; vomiting)

Patient Consultation

As an aid to patient consultation, refer to *Advice for the Patient, Famciclovir (Systemic)*.

In providing consultation, consider» emphasizing the following selected information (» = major clinical significance):

Before using this medication

» Conditions affecting use, especially:
Breast-feeding—Because of the potential for tumorigenicity seen in rats, it is recommended that either breast-feeding or the use of famciclovir be discontinued
Use in children—Safety and efficacy have not been established in children up to 18 years of age
Other medical problems, especially renal function impairment

Proper use of this medication

Initiating use of famciclovir for herpes zoster at the earliest sign or symptom; it is most effective when started within 48 hours of the onset of rash
Initiating use of famciclovir for treatment of recurrent episodes of genital herpes at the earliest sign or symptom; it is most effective when started within 6 hours of the onset of symptoms or lesions
Famciclovir may be taken with meals
» Compliance with full course of therapy; not using more often or for longer than prescribed
» Proper dosing
Missed dose: Taking as soon as possible; not taking if almost time for next dose; not doubling doses
» Proper storage

Precautions while using this medication

Checking with physician if no improvement within a few days

Keeping affected areas as clean and dry as possible; wearing loose-fitting clothing to avoid irritation of lesions

General Dosing Information

Therapy should be initiated as soon as possible following the onset of signs and symptoms of varicella-zoster infection. Treatment was started within 72 hours of the onset of rash in clinical studies; however, famciclovir was found to be more useful if started within 48 hours.

For treatment of recurrent episodes of herpes genitalis, therapy should be initiated as soon as possible following the onset of signs and symptoms. Treatment was started within 6 hours of the onset of symptoms or lesions in clinical studies.

For treatment of recurrent mucocutaneous herpes simplex infections in HIV-infected patients, treatment was started within 48 hours of lesion onset in efficacy studies.

In clinical trials, the effect of famciclovir on the resolution of rash was most pronounced in patients over 50 years of age.

Famciclovir tablets may be taken with meals since absorption has not been shown to be significantly affected by food.

Oral Dosage Forms

FAMCICLOVIR TABLETS

Usual adult dose

Genital herpes, recurrent episodes (suppression)[1]—
Oral, 250 mg two times a day for up to one year.
Genital herpes, recurrent episodes (treatment)—
Oral, 125 mg two times a day for five days.
Herpes simplex, HIV-associated (treatment)—
Oral, 500 mg two times a day for seven days.
Herpes zoster (treatment)—
Oral, 500 mg every eight hours for seven days.

Note: Adults with impaired renal function may require a change in dosing as follows:

Indication	Creatinine clearance (mL/min)/(mL/sec)	Dosing regimen
Herpes zoster	≥ 60/1	500 mg every 8 hours
	40–59/0.67–0.98	500 mg every 12 hours
	20–39/0.33–0.65	500 mg every 24 hours
	< 20/0.33	250 mg every 24 hours
Treatment of recurrent genital herpes	≥ 40/0.67	125 mg every 12 hours
	20–39/0.33–0.65	125 mg every 24 hours
	< 20/0.33	125 mg every 24 hours
Treatment of recurrent mucocutaneous (orolabial and genital) herpes simplex in HIV-infected patients	≥ 40/0.67	500 mg every 12 hours
	20–39/0.33–0.65	500 mg every 24 hours
	< 20/0.33	250 mg every 24 hours
Suppression of recurrent genital herpes	≥ 40/0.67	250 mg every 12 hours
	20–39/0.33–0.65	125 mg every 12 hours
	< 20/0.33	125 mg every 24 hours
Hemodialysis patients	The recommended dose is 250 mg (herpes zoster or treatment of recurrent mucocutaneous (orolabial and genital) herpes simplex infections in HIV-infected patients) or 125 mg (treatment or suppression of recurrent genital herpes) administered after each dialysis session.	

Usual pediatric dose

Safety and efficacy have not been established for patients up to 18 years of age.

Strength(s) usually available

U.S.—
- 125 mg (Rx) [*Famvir* (lactose)].
- 250 mg (Rx) [*Famvir* (lactose)].
- 500 mg (Rx) [*Famvir* (lactose)].

Canada—
- 125 mg (Rx) [*Famvir* (lactose)].
- 250 mg (Rx) [*Famvir* (lactose)].
- 500 mg (Rx) [*Famvir* (lactose)].

Packaging and storage

Store between 15 and 30 °C (59 and 86 °F), in a well-closed container, unless otherwise specified by manufacturer.

Auxiliary labeling

- Continue medicine for full time of treatment.

[1]Not included in Canadian product labeling.

Revised: 04/04/2000
Developed: 11/28/1994

FAMOTIDINE—See *Histamine H_2-receptor Antagonists (Systemic)*

FELODIPINE—See *Calcium Channel Blocking Agents (Systemic)*

FENOFIBRATE Systemic

VA CLASSIFICATION (Primary): CV359

Commonly used brand name(s): *Antara*™; *LIPOFEN*; *Lipidil Micro*®; *Lipidil Supra*®; *Lofibra*™; *Tricor*; *Triglide*.

Note: For a listing of dosage forms and brand names by country availability, see *Dosage Forms* section(s).

Category

Antihyperlipidemic.

Indications

Accepted

Hypercholesterolemia (treatment)—Fenofibrate is indicated as an adjunct to diet to reduce elevated LDL-C, Total-C, Triglycerides and Apo B, and to increase HDL-C in adult patients with primary hypercholesterolemia or mixed dyslipidemia (Fredrickson Types IIa and IIb). Lipid-altering drugs should be used in addition to a diet restricted in saturated fat and cholesterol when response to diet and non-pharmacological intervention alone has been inadequate.

Hypertriglyceridemia (treatment)—Fenofibrate is indicated as an adjunct to diet for the treatment of adult patients with hypertriglyceridemia (Fredrickson Types IV and V hyperlipidemia) who have not responded adequately to diet and who are at risk of pancreatitis. A risk of pancreatitis is associated with a serum triglyceride concentration of over 2000 mg per dL and increases in very low-density lipoprotein (VLDL) cholesterol, as well as with fasting chylomicron (type V hyperlipidemia) concentrations. A total serum or plasma triglyceride concentration below 1000 mg per dL is not associated with a risk of pancreatitis. Fenofibrate therapy may be considered for those subjects with triglyceride concentrations between 1000 and 2000 mg per dL who have a history of pancreatitis or of recurrent abdominal pain typical of pancreatitis. Fenofibrate has not been adequately studied to decrease the risk of pancreatitis in patients with a type IV lipoprotein pattern, with triglyceride concentrations below 1000 mg per dL, who (through dietary indiscretion or alcohol consumption) convert to a type V lipoprotein pattern with large triglyceride concentrations accompanied by fasting chylomicronemia.

For additional information on initial therapeutic guidelines related to the treatment of hyperlipidemia, see *Appendix III*.

The effect of fenofibrate on coronary heart disease morbidity and mortality and noncardiovascular mortality has not been established. Because fenofibrate has chemical, pharmacologic, and clinical similarities to the other fibrate drugs, clofibrate and gemfibrozil, the adverse findings in four large randomized, placebo-controlled clinical studies with these drugs may also apply to fenofibrate. In one clofibrate study, there was no difference in mortality between the clofibrate-treated subjects and the placebo-treated subjects, but twice as many clofibrate-treated subjects developed cholelithiasis and cholecystitis requiring surgery. Another clofibrate study resulted in a 44% higher age-adjusted total mortality in the clofibrate-treated group than in a comparable placebo-treated group. The higher mortality rate was attributed to a 33% increase in noncardiovascular causes, including malignancy, postcholecystectomy complications, and pancreatitis. A third study with gemfibrozil resulted in a 22% higher total mortality, primarily due to a higher cancer mortality, in the gemfibrozil-treated group, while cancers (excluding basal cell carcinoma) were diagnosed in 2.5% of patients in both gemfibrozil- and placebo-treated patients. In a fourth study with gemfibrozil, cardiac deaths tended to be higher and gallbladder surgery and appendectomy were more frequent in the gemfibrozil-treated group than in the placebo-treated group.

Unaccepted

Fenofibrate is not indicated for the treatment of either primary or secondary hyperlipoproteinemia as a form of prevention to reduce the risk of developing coronary heart disease.

Pharmacology/Pharmacokinetics

Physicochemical characteristics

Molecular weight—360.83.

Solubility—Insoluble in water, soluble in ethanol, freely soluble in acetone and chloroform.

Mechanism of action/Effect

Fenofibrate is a lipid-regulating agent that has chemical, pharmacologic, and clinical similarities to the other fibrate drugs, clofibrate and gemfibrozil. Although the exact mechanism of action of fenofibrate is not completely understood, fenofibric acid, the active metabolite of fenofibrate, produces reductions in total cholesterol, LDL cholesterol, apolipoprotein B, total triglycerides and triglyceride rich lipoprotein (VLDL) in treated patients. Treatment with fenofibrate also results in increases in high density lipoprotein (HDL) and apoproteins apoAI and apoAII.

Fenofibric acid effects have been explained by the activation of perioxisome proliferator activated receptor alpha (PPARalpha). Through this mechanism, fenofibrate increases lipolysis and elimination of triglyceride-rich particles from plasma by activating lipoprotein lipase and reducing production of an inhibitor of lipoprotein lipase activity, apoprotein C-III. The fall in triglycerides produces an alteration in the composition and size of LDL from dense, small particles (possibly atherogenic), to buoyant, large particles. These larger particles are catabolized rapidly due to a greater affinity for cholesterol receptors. An increase in the synthesis of apoproteins A-I, A-II, and HDL-cholesterol also results by activation of PPARalpha.

Other actions/effects

Fenofibrate reduces serum uric acid concentrations in hyperuricemic and normal individuals by increasing the urinary excretion of uric acid.

Absorption

Fenofibrate is well absorbed from the gastrointestinal tract. Absorption of fenofibrate tablets is increased by approximately 35% when administered with food, as compared with that in the fasting state. Absorption of fenofibrate capsules is increased by approximately 58% and 25% under high-fat and low-fat fed conditions, respectively, compared with fasting conditions.

The extent of absorption (AUC) of fenofibric acid (the principal metabolite of fenofibrate) was 42% larger at steady state with multiple dose administration compared with single-dose administration.

The extent of absorption of fenofibrate capsules in terms of AUC value of fenofibric acid increased in a less than proportional manner while the rate of absorption in terms of C_{max} value of fenofibric acid increased proportionally related to dose.

Distribution

Volume of distribution (Vol_D)—30 L.

Protein binding

Very high (approximately 99% in normal and hyperlipidemic individuals).

Biotransformation

Fenofibrate undergoes rapid metabolism by esterase hydrolysis and is converted to the active metabolite, fenofibric acid. Fenofibric acid undergoes conjugation with glucuronic acid and is excreted in urine. A small amount of fenofibric acid undergoes reduction at the carbonyl moiety, resulting in a benzhydrol metabolite which is then conjugated with glucuronic acid and excreted in urine. *In vivo* metabolism data indicate that neither fenofibrate nor fenofibric acid undergo oxidative metabolism (e.g., cytochrome P450) to a significant effect.

Half-life

Elimination—

20 hours (between 10 and 35 hours).

Time to peak concentration

6 to 8 hours.

The rate of absorption of fenofibric acid was 73% greater after multiple-dose compared with single-dose administration.

Steady-state plasma levels

Steady-state plasma levels of fenofibric acid were achieved after 5 days of once daily dosing and demonstrated a mean 2.4-fold accumulation following multiple-dose administration. Steady-state plasma levels of fenofibrate demonstrated no accumulation.

Elimination

Renal—60%, primarily as fenofibric acid and fenofibric acid glucuronide

Fecal—25%.

In dialysis—

Hemodialysis is not expected to remove fenofibrate significantly because of its extensive binding to plasma proteins.

Precautions to Consider

Cross-sensitivity and/or related problems

Fenofibrate has chemical, pharmacological, and clinical similarities to the other fibrate agents, clofibrate and gemfibrozil.

Carcinogenicity

A 24-month study in rats, given fenofibrate doses of 10, 45, and 200 mg per kg of body weight (mg/kg), resulted in a significant increase in the incidence of liver carcinomas in both male and female rats given the 200-mg/kg dose. These doses represent 0.3, 1, and 6 times the maximum recommended human dose (MRHD) of fenofibrate, respectively, on a mg per square meter of body surface area (mg/m^2) basis. A significant increase in pancreatic carcinomas occurred in male rats given the 45- and 200-mg/kg doses of fenofibrate and increases in pancreatic adenomas and benign testicular interstitial cell tumors occurred in male rats given the 200-mg/kg fenofibrate dose. In a second 24-month study in a different strain of rats given fenofibrate in doses of 10 mg/kg and 60 mg/kg, significant increases in the incidence of pancreatic acinar adenomas occurred in both sexes and increases in interstitial cell tumors of the testes occurred in rats given the 60-mg/kg dose of fenofibrate. These doses represent 0.3 and 2 times the MRHD of fenofibrate, respectively, on a mg/m^2 basis.

A comparative carcinogenicity study was done in rats comparing three drugs: fenofibrate, given in doses of 10 mg/kg and 60 mg/kg or 0.3 and 2 times the MRHD of fenofibrate on a mg/m^2 basis; clofibrate, given in doses of 400 mg/kg or 2 times the MRHD of clofibrate on a mg/m^2 basis; and gemfibrozil, given in doses of 250 mg/kg or 2 times the MRHD of gemfibrozil on a mg/m^2 basis. An increased incidence of pancreatic acinar adenomas was observed in male and female rats given fenofibrate. An increase in hepatocellular carcinoma and pancreatic acinar adenomas occurred in male rats, and hepatic neoplastic nodules occurred in female rats given clofibrate; hepatic neoplastic nodules were increased in male and female rats given gemfibrozil, while an increase in testicular interstitial cell tumors occurred in male rats given all three drugs.

In a 21-month study in mice given fenofibrate in doses of 10, 45, and 200 mg/kg, significant increases in liver carcinoma occurred in both male and female mice given the 200-mg/kg dose of fenofibrate. These doses represent approximately 0.2, 0.7, and 3 times the MRHD of fenofibrate on a mg/m^2 basis, respectively. In a second 18-month study in mice given the same doses of fenofibrate, a significant increase in liver carcinoma in male mice and liver adenoma in female mice occurred when they were given the 200-mg/kg dose of fenofibrate.

Peroxisomal proliferation, as determined by electron microscopy studies, has occurred following administration of fenofibrate to rats. An adequate study to test for peroxisome proliferation in humans has not been done, but a comparison of liver biopsies before and after treatment of human subjects with other members of the fibrate class of medications has revealed changes in peroxisome morphology and numbers after treatment.

Mutagenicity

Fenofibrate was not found to be mutagenic in the Ames test and mouse lymphoma, chromosomal aberration, and unscheduled DNA synthesis tests.

Pregnancy/Reproduction

Pregnancy—Adequate and well-controlled studies in pregnant women have not been done. Fenofibrate should be used during pregnancy only if the potential benefit justifies the potential risk to the fetus. Fenofibrate has been shown to be embryocidal and teratogenic in rats given 7 to 10 times the MRHD of fenofibrate on a mg/m^2 basis, and embryocidal in rabbits given 9 times the MRHD of fenofibrate on a mg/m^2 basis.

A study in female rats given 9 times the MRHD of fenofibrate before and throughout gestation resulted in a delay of delivery in 100% of dams, a 60% increase in post implantation loss, a decrease in litter size, a decrease in birth weight, a 40% survival of pups at birth, a 4% survival of pups as neonates, a 0% survival of pups to weaning, and an increased occurrence of spina bifida. A study in female rats given 10 times the MRHD of fenofibrate on days 6 through 15 of gestation resulted in an increase in gross, visceral, and skeletal findings in fetuses, manifested as a domed head, hunched shoulders, a rounded body, an abnormal chest, kyphosis, stunted fetuses, elongated sternal ribs, malformed sternebrae, extra foramen in palatine, misshapen vertebrae, and supernumerary ribs.

A study in female rats given 7 times the MRHD of fenofibrate from day 15 of gestation through weaning resulted in a delay in delivery, a 40% decrease in live births, a 75% decrease in neonatal survival, and decreases in pup weight at birth, as well as on days 4 and 21 post partum. A study of fenofibrate in female rabbits resulted in abortions in 10% of dams given 9 times and 25% of dams given 18 times the MRHD of fenofibrate, and death of 7% of fetuses given 18 times the MRHD of fenofibrate.

FDA Pregnancy Category C.

Breast-feeding

Because of the potential for tumorigenicity as seen in animal studies, fenofibrate should not be used in women who are breast-feeding. A decision should be made whether to discontinue nursing or to discontinue fenofibrate.

Pediatrics

No information is available on the relationship of age to the effects of fenofibrate in pediatric patients. Safety and efficacy have not been established.

Geriatrics

Clearance of fenofibric acid following a single oral dose of fenofibrate in elderly volunteers, ages 77 through 87 years, was 1.2 L per hour (L/hr), compared to 1.1 L/hr in younger adults, indicating that a similar dosage regimen can be used in the elderly without resulting in an increase in accumulation of fenofibrate or its metabolites. Because elderly patients are more likely to have decreased renal function, care should be taken in dose selection.

Pharmacogenetics

Fenofibrate is not metabolized by enzymes known for exhibiting interethnic variability, therefore, interethnic pharmacokinetic differences are not expected. Pharmacokinetic differences have not been observed between male and female individuals administered fenofibrate.

Drug interactions and/or related problems

The following drug interactions and/or related problems have been selected on the basis of their potential clinical significance (possible mechanism in parentheses where appropriate)—not necessarily inclusive (» = major clinical significance):

Fenofibrate and fenofibric acid are mild-to-moderate inhibitors of cytochrome P450 isoform CYP2C9 at therapeutic concentrations. They are weak inhibitors of CYP2C19 and CYP2A6. They are not inhibitors of CYP3A4, CYP2D6, CYP2E1, or CYP1A2.

Note: Combinations containing any of the following medications, depending on the amount present, may also interact with this medication.

» Anticoagulants, oral

(concurrent use with fenofibrate may potentiate coumarin-type anticoagulants; prolongation of prothrombin time/INR has be observed; the dosage of the anticoagulant should be reduced to maintain the prothrombin time at the desired level in order to prevent bleeding complications)

Beta-adrenergic blocking medications or
Estrogens or
Estrogen-containing oral contraceptives or
Thiazide diuretic medications

(these medications have been associated with massive rises in plasma triglycerides, especially in patients with familial hypertriglyceridemia; discontinuation of the these medications may obviate the need for specific drug therapy of hypertriglyceridemia)

Bile acid sequestrants, such as:
Cholestyramine or
Colestipol

(concurrent use with these agents may bind fenofibrate; in order to avoid interfering with the absorption of fenofibrate, fenofibrate should be taken at least 1 hour before or 4 to 6 hours after taking a bile acid binding agent)

» Cyclosporine or

» Nephrotoxic medications, other such as: (see *Appendix II*)
(because fenofibrate is primarily eliminated by renal excretion and cyclosporine when used alone is potentially nephrotoxic, causing decreases in creatinine clearance and increases in serum creatinine concentrations, concurrent use of these agents may potentiate renal function deterioration; concurrent use of fenofibrate with immunosuppressants and other potentially nephrotoxic agents should be carefully considered, and the lowest effective dose should be used)

» HMG-CoA reductase inhibitors, such as:
Atorvastatin or
Fluvastatin or
Lovastatin or
Pravastatin or
Simvastatin
(although no data exists on the concurrent use of these agents with fenofibrate, concurrent use of gemfibrozil, another fibrate agent, with lovastatin has been associated with rhabdomyolysis, significantly increased creatine kinase [CK] concentrations, and myoglobinuria, resulting in a high percentage of acute renal failure cases; because the potential benefits of combined therapy do not outweigh the risks of severe myopathy, rhabdomyolysis, and acute renal failure, and because the use of fibrates alone, including fenofibrate, may occasionally be associated with myositis, myopathy, or rhabdomyolysis, their concurrent use with HMG-CoA reductase inhibitors is not recommended)

Insulin or
Sulfonylureas
(fibrates may potentiate the effects of these drugs, although there are no documented cases of hypoglycemia or hypoglycemic reactions associated with fenofibrate given concomitantly with insulin or sulfonylurea hypoglycemic medications)

MAO-inhibitors
(may increase the risk of hepatotoxicity)

Laboratory value alterations

The following have been selected on the basis of their potential clinical significance (possible effect in parentheses where appropriate)—not necessarily inclusive (» = major clinical significance).

With physiology/laboratory test values
Creatine kinase (CK), serum
(myopathy should be considered in patients with marked elevations of CK concentrations accompanied by diffuse myalgias, muscle tenderness or weakness)

Hematocrit and
Hemoglobin concentrations and
Leukocyte counts
(mild to moderate decreases in hemoglobin and hematocrit concentrations, and leukocyte counts have occurred; however, these values stabilize with continued use of fenofibrate)

Aspartate aminotransferase (AST [SGOT]), serum and/or
Alanine aminotransferase (ALT [SGPT]), serum
(in an 8-week dose-ranging study, increases in serum transaminase values to at least 3 times the upper limit of normal occurred in 13% of patients receiving fenofibrate in doses equivalent to 134 or 201 mg of fenofibrate per day and occurred in 0% of patients receiving doses equivalent to 33.5 or 67 mg per day, or placebo; in two U.S. placebo-controlled studies, serum transaminase values increased to > 3 times the upper limit of normal in 8 to 10% of patients taking fenofibrate in doses equivalent to 201 mg of fenofibrate per day; in controlled multiple-dose trials lasting 3 to 24 weeks, increases in serum transaminase values to > 3 times the upper limit of normal occurred in 28 of 442 patients [6.3%] taking fenofibrate in doses equivalent to 134 or 201 mg per day; in the latter trial, in the patients whose serum transaminase values were followed, values usually returned to normal limits either with continued treatment or after discontinuation of treatment; however, values remained above normal limits in 2 of the 28 patients [7.1%] at the end of follow-up of treatment)

Uric acid, serum
(concentrations may be decreased; fenofibrate reduces serum uric acid concentrations in hyperuricemic and normal individuals by increasing the urinary excretion of uric acid)

Medical considerations/Contraindications

The medical considerations/contraindications included have been selected on the basis of their potential clinical significance (reasons given in parentheses where appropriate)—not necessarily inclusive (» = major clinical significance).

Except under special circumstances, this medication should not be used when the following medical problems exist:

» Gallbladder disease, pre-existing
(use of fibrate agents, such as fenofibrate, has been associated with cholelithiasis and, therefore, is **contraindicated** in patients with pre-existing gallbladder disease)

» Hepatic function impairment, including primary biliary cirrhosis and unexplained persistent liver function abnormality
(use of fenofibrate has been associated with hepatotoxicity, which may further aggravate these conditions; use is **contraindicated**)

» Hypersensitivity to fenofibrate

» Renal function impairment, severe
(the rate of clearance of fenofibric acid may be significantly reduced in patients with severe renal function impairment [creatinine clearance < 50 mL per minute (mL/min)], resulting in the medication's accumulation during chronic dosing; use of fibrate agents, such as fenofibrate, has been associated with rhabdomyolysis in patients with impaired renal function; use is **contraindicated**)

Risk-benefit should be considered when the following medical problem exists:

Renal function impairment, moderate
(in patients having moderate renal function impairment [creatinine clearance of 50 to 90 mL/min], clearance and volume of distribution of fenofibric acid are increased when compared to healthy adults [2.1 L/hr and 95 L versus 1.1 L/hr and 30 L, respectively]; however, no modification of dosage is required in patients having moderate renal function impairment; use of fibrate agents, such as fenofibrate, has been associated with rhabdomyolysis in patients with impaired renal function)

Patient monitoring

The following may be especially important in patient monitoring (other tests may be warranted in some patients, depending on condition; » = major clinical significance):

Creatine kinase (CK), serum
(CK concentrations should be monitored in patients with symptoms of unexplained muscle pain, tenderness, or weakness, particularly if accompanied by malaise or fever; if marked CK concentrations occur, fenofibrate therapy should be discontinued)

Hematocrit and
Hemoglobin concentrations and
Leukocyte counts
(periodic monitoring of blood counts are recommended during the first 12 months of fenofibrate therapy)

» Hepatic function determinations, such as:
Alanine aminotransferase (ALT [SGPT]), serum and
Aspartate aminotransferase (AST [SGOT]), serum
(regular periodic monitoring should be performed [baseline, after 3 to 6 months, and yearly thereafter] for the duration of fenofibrate therapy; fenofibrate should be discontinued if serum transaminase values of > 3 times the upper limit of normal persist)

» Lipid concentrations, serum
(periodic monitoring should be done during initiation of therapy in order to establish the lowest effective dose of fenofibrate; fenofibrate should be discontinued in patients who do not have an adequate response after 2 months of treatment with the maximum recommended dose [160 mg per day])

Side/Adverse Effects

The effect of fenofibrate on coronary heart disease morbidity and mortality and non-cardiovascular mortality has not been established.

The following side/adverse effects have been selected on the basis of their potential clinical significance (possible signs and symptoms in parentheses where appropriate)—not necessarily inclusive:

Those indicating need for medical attention

Incidence less frequent

Influenza syndrome (chills, fever, muscle aches and pains, or nausea and/or vomiting); ***infections; pruritus*** (generalized itching); ***skin rash and/or urticaria*** (hives)

Note: In clinical trials, *skin rash* was the most frequent side effect, requiring discontinuation of fenofibrate treatment in 2% of patients. Acute hypersensitivity reactions, including severe skin rashes requiring patient hospitalization and treatment with steroids, have occurred very rarely during treatment with fenofibrate. *Urticaria* was seen in 1.25% versus 0% and rash in 2.82% versus 1.23% of fenofibrate-treated and placebo-treated patients, respectively, in controlled trials.

Incidence rare

Agranulocytosis (chills; fever; sore throat); ***alveolitis, allergic*** (cough; shortness of breath or troubled breathing); ***cholecystitis*** (abdominal pain, vague; indigestion, chronic; nausea); ***cholelithiasis***

(abdominal fullness, gaseous; abdominal pain, recurrent; fever; yellow eyes or skin); ***eczema; hepatotoxicity*** (abdominal fullness; dark urine; fever; general ill feeling; generalized itching; loss of appetite; unusual fatigue; yellow eyes or skin); ***musculoskeletal symptoms, such as myalgia*** (muscle pain); ***myasthenia*** (muscle weakness); ***myositis*** (inflammation or swelling of skeletal muscle); ***and/or rhabdomyolysis*** (fever; muscle cramps, pain, stiffness, or weakness; unusual tiredness); ***pancreatitis*** (abdominal pain and distention; fever; nausea; vomiting); ***thrombocytopenia*** (unusual bleeding or bruising)

Note: Rare cases of *agranulocytosis* and *thrombocytopenia* have been reported during postmarketing surveillance outside of the U.S.

Fenofibrate, like clofibrate and gemfibrozil, may increase cholesterol excretion into the bile, leading to *cholelithiasis.* A gallstone prevalence sub-study of a placebo-controlled trial with gemfibrozil revealed a trend toward a greater prevalence of gallstones in gemfibrozil-treated patients. If cholelithiasis is suspected, gallbladder studies should be performed and fenofibrate should be discontinued if gallstones are found.

Hepatotoxicity associated with fenofibrate therapy appears to be dose-related. Hepatocellular, chronic active, and cholestatic hepatitis have been reported after weeks to several years of exposure to fenofibrate. Rarely, cirrhosis has been reported in association with chronic active hepatitis.

Treatment with fibrate agents, such as fenofibrate, may occasionally be associated with *myositis. Rhabdomyolysis* has also been associated rarely with this class of agents, usually in patients with impaired renal function. Degradation of muscle occurs in rhabdomyolysis, resulting in the release of myoglobin into the urine, which can lead to acute renal failure. *Myopathy* and/or rhabdomyolysis should be considered in any patient with diffuse *myalgias*, muscle tenderness or weakness, and/or marked elevations of creatine kinase (CK) in serum. Patients receiving fenofibrate and complaining of muscle pain, tenderness, or weakness, especially if accompanied by malaise or fever, should have a prompt medical evaluation for myopathy, including serum CK determinations. If myopathy or myositis is suspected or diagnosed, or if serum CK concentrations are significantly elevated, fenofibrate therapy should be discontinued.

Pancreatitis has been reported in patients taking fenofibrate, gemfibrozil, and clofibrate and may be associated with a failure in fenofibrate efficacy or a blockage of the common bile duct by biliary tract stone or sludge formation.

Those indicating need for medical attention only if they continue or are bothersome

More frequent

Respiratory disorder (chest congestion, difficulty in breathing)

Incidence less frequent

Abdominal pain (stomach pain); ***asthenia*** (lack or loss of strength); ***back pain; diarrhea; dizziness; eye irritation; gastrointestinal symptoms, such as belching; constipation; flatulence*** (gas); ***headache; libido, decreased; nausea; photosensitivity*** (increased sensitivity of the skin to sunlight); ***rhinitis*** (stuffy nose)

Overdose

For more information on the management of overdose or unintentional ingestion, **contact a Poison Control Center** (see *Poison Control Center Listing*).

Treatment of overdose

Treatment should be symptomatic and supportive.

Specific treatment—Hemodialysis should not be considered in the treatment of fenofibrate overdosage because fenofibrate is extensively bound to plasma proteins.

If indicated, elimination of unabsorbed drug should be achieved by emesis or gastric lavage.

Precautions should be observed to maintain the airway.

Supportive care—Patients in whom intentional overdose is confirmed or suspected should be referred for psychiatric consultation.

Patient Consultation

As an aid to patient consultation, refer to *Advice for the Patient, Fenofibrate (Systemic).*

In providing consultation, consider emphasizing the following selected information (» = major clinical significance):

Before using this medication

» Conditions affecting use, especially:

Hypersensitivity to fenofibrate

Liver carcinomas and pancreatic acinar adenomas have occurred in rats given long-term, high doses of fenofibrate

Pregnancy—Not recommended during pregnancy unless potential benefit outweighs the risk

Breast-feeding—Not recommended in women who are breast-feeding

Use in the elderly—Dose selection should be cautious.

Other medications, especially oral anticoagulants, cyclosporine, or HMG-CoA reductase inhibitors

Other medical problems, especially pre-existing gallbladder disease; hepatic function impairment, including primary biliary cirrhosis and unexplained persistent liver function abnormality; or severe renal function impairment

Proper use of this medication

» Compliance with therapy; taking medication at the same time each day to maintain the therapeutic effect; not taking more or less medication than the amount prescribed

» Compliance with prescribed diet during treatment

Taking Lipofen™ and Lofibra™ with a meal to increase its bioavailability; Antara™, Tricor®, and Triglide™ can be given without regard to meals

» Proper dosing

Missed dose: Taking as soon as possible; not taking if almost time for next dose; not doubling doses

» Proper storage

Precautions while using this medication

» Regular visits to physician to check progress

» Notifying physician immediately if unexplained muscle pain, tenderness, or weakness occurs, especially if accompanied by unusual tiredness or fever

Notifying physician if pregnancy is suspected

Reporting any signs of infection (fever, sore throat, chills) to physician because of risk of agranulocytosis

Side/adverse effects

Signs of potential side effects, especially influenza-like syndrome; infections; pruritus; skin rash and/or urticaria; agranulocytosis; allergic alveolitis; cholecystitis; cholelithiasis; eczema; hepatotoxicity; musculoskeletal symptoms, such as myalgia, myasthenia, myositis, and/or rhabdomyolysis; pancreatitis; and thrombocytopenia

General Dosing Information

Prior to any drug therapy, an attempt should be made to treat hyperlipidemia with nondrug methods, such as dietary therapy specific for the type of lipoprotein abnormality, reduction of excess body weight, reduction of excess alcohol intake, and physical exercise. Secondary causes of hyperlipidemia, such as hypothyroidism or diabetes mellitus, should be ruled out or adequately treated. Treatment with estrogens, thiazide diuretics, and beta-adrenergic blocking agents may contribute to increases in plasma triglyceride levels, especially in individuals with familial hypertriglyceridemia. In such cases, the medication should be changed or discontinued if it is considered medically appropriate to do so. The use of lipid-lowering agents should be considered only when satisfactory results have not been obtained from using nondrug methods.

Diet/Nutrition

Patients should be placed on an appropriate triglyceride-lowering diet before receiving fenofibrate and should continue this diet during treatment with fenofibrate.

- Lipofen™ and Lofibra™ should be given with a meal to optimize the bioavailability of the medication.
- Antara™, Tricor®, and Triglide™ can be given without regard to meals.

Bioequivalence information

- Antara™ 130 mg capsule is equivalent to 200 mg fenofibrate capsule under low-fat fed conditions based on plasma concentrations of fenofibric acid after multiple dose administration.
- Lofibra™: 67 mg is bioequivalent to 100 mg non-micronized fenofibrate. Three 67-mg capsules are bioequivalent to a single 200 mg Lofibra™ capsule.
- Tricor® 145 mg capsule is equivalent to 200 mg fenofibrate capsule under low-fat fed conditions based on plasma concentrations of fenofibric acid. Three 48-mg capsules are equivalent to 200 mg fenofibrate capsule under low-fat fed conditions based on plasma concentrations of fenofibric acid.

Oral Dosage Forms

FENOFIBRATE CAPSULES (MICRONIZED)

Usual adult dose

Antihypercholestrolemic—
- Antara™: Oral, 130 mg per day.
- Lofibra™: Oral, 200 mg per day.

Antihypertriglyceridemic—
- Antara™: Oral, 43 to 130 mg per day.
- Lofibra™: Oral, 67 to 200 mg per day.

Dosage should be individualized according to patient response, and should be adjusted if necessary following repeat lipid determinations at 4 to 8 week intervals up to a maximum recommended dose per day.

Note: • Antara™: For patients with renal impairment, the recommended initial dose is 43 mg once daily. The dose can be increased only after evaluation of the effects on renal function and lipid levels at the initial dose.

• Lofibra™: For patients with renal impairment, the recommended initial dose is 67 mg once daily. The dose can be increased only after evaluation of the effects on renal function and lipid levels at the initial dose.

Usual adult prescribing limits
- Antara™: 130 mg per day.
- Lofibra™: Oral, 200 mg per day.

Usual pediatric dose

Safety and efficacy have not been established.

Usual geriatric dose

Antihyperlipidemic—
- Antara™: Oral, 43 mg per day. See *Usual adult dose.*
- Lofibra™: Oral, 67 mg per day. See *Usual adult dose.*

Strength(s) usually available

U.S.—

Note: Tricor® capsules are no longer being marketed. This formulation was replaced with a tablet formulation. According to the U.S. manufacturer, the bioavailability of fenofibrate was increased by changing the formulation from capsules to tablets.

43 mg (Rx) [*Antara*™ (black ink; dimethicone; D&C Yellow #10; hypromellose; Indigo carmine FD&C Blue No. 2; sodium lauryl sulfate; sugar spheres; simethicone; sulfur dioxide; talc; titanium dioxide; yellow iron oxide)].

67 mg (Rx) [*Lofibra*™ (croscarmellose sodium; crospovidone; lactose monohydrate; magnesium stearate; povidone; pregelatinized starch; sodium lauryl sulfate; talc; D&C Red No. 28; FD&C Blue No. 1; FD&C Red No. 40; titanium dioxide; gelatin); GENERIC].

87 mg (Rx) [*Antara*™ (black ink; dimethicone; D&C Yellow #10; hypromellose; Indigo carmine FD&C Blue No. 2; sodium lauryl sulfate; sugar spheres; simethicone; sulfur dioxide; talc; titanium dioxide; yellow iron oxide)].

130 mg (Rx) [*Antara*™ (black ink; dimethicone; D&C Yellow #10; hypromellose; Indigo carmine FD&C Blue No. 2; sodium lauryl sulfate; sugar spheres; simethicone; sulfur dioxide; talc; titanium dioxide; yellow iron oxide)].

134 mg (Rx) [*Lofibra*™ (croscarmellose sodium; crospovidone; lactose monohydrate; magnesium stearate; povidone; pregelatinized starch; sodium lauryl sulfate; talc; D&C Red No. 28; FD&C Blue No. 1; titanium dioxide; gelatin); GENERIC].

200 mg (Rx) [*Lofibra*™ (croscarmellose sodium; crospovidone; lactose monohydrate; magnesium stearate; povidone; pregelatinized starch; sodium lauryl sulfate; talc; FD&C Red No. 40; D&C Red No. 28; FDA/E172 yellow iron oxide; titanium dioxide; gelatin); GENERIC].

Canada—

67 mg (Rx) [*Lipidil Micro*® (lactose; magnesium stearate; pregelatinized starch; reticulated polyvinyl pyrrolidone; sodium laurylsulfate)].

200 mg (Rx) [*Lipidil Micro*® (lactose; magnesium stearate; pregelatinized starch; reticulated polyvinyl pyrrolidone; sodium laurylsulfate)].

Packaging and storage
- Antara™: Store at controlled room temperature, between 15 and 30 °C (59 and 86 °F).
- Lofibra™: Store at controlled room temperature, between 20 and 25 °C (68 and 77 °F). Protect from moisture. Keep out of the reach of children.

Auxiliary labeling
- Take with a meal.

FENOFIBRATE TABLETS

Usual adult dose

Antihypercholestrolemic—
- Tricor®: Oral, initially, 145 mg once daily.
- Triglide™: Oral, initially, 160 mg once daily.

Antihypertriglyceridemic—
- Tricor®: Oral, initially, 48 to 145 mg once daily. Dosage should be individualized according to patient response, and should be adjusted if necessary following repeat lipid determinations at 4 to 8 week intervals up to a maximum recommended dose of 145 mg per day.
- Triglide™: Oral, initially, 50 to 160 mg once daily. Dosage should be individualized according to patient response, and should be adjusted if necessary following repeat lipid determinations at 4 to 8 week intervals up to a maximum recommended dose of 160 mg per day.

Note: Tricor®: For patients with renal impairment, the recommended initial dose is 48 mg once daily. The dose can be increased only after evaluation of the effects on renal function and lipid levels at the initial dose.

Triglide™: For patients with renal impairment, the recommended initial dose is 50 mg once daily. The dose can be increased only after evaluation of the effects on renal function and lipid levels at the initial dose.

Usual adult prescribing limits

Tricor®: 145 mg per day.
Triglide™: 160 mg per day.

Usual pediatric dose

Safety and efficacy have not been established.

Usual geriatric dose
- Tricor®: Oral, initially 48 mg once daily.
- Triglide™: Oral, initially 50 mg once daily.

Strength(s) usually available

U.S.—

48 mg (Rx) [*Tricor* (crospovidone; docusate sodium; D&C Yellow No. 10 aluminum lake; FD&C Blue No. 2/indigo carmine aluminum lake; FD&C Yellow No. 6/sunset yellow FCF aluminum lake; hypromellose 2910 [3cps]; lactose monohydrate; magnesium stearate; polyvinyl alcohol; silicified microcrystalline cellulose; sodium lauryl sulfate; soybean lecithin; sucrose; talc; titanium dioxide; xanthan gum)].

50 mg (Rx) [*Triglide* (crospovidone; lactose monohydrate; mannitol; maltodextrin; carboxymethylcellulose sodium; egg lecithin; croscarmellose sodium; sodium lauryl sulfate; colloidal silicon dioxide; magnesium stearate; monobasic sodium phosphate)].

145 mg (Rx) [*Tricor* (crospovidone; docusate sodium; hypromellose 2910 [3cps]; lactose monohydrate; magnesium stearate; polyvinyl alcohol; silicified microcrystalline cellulose; sodium lauryl sulfate; soybean lecithin; sucrose; talc; titanium dioxide; xanthan gum)].

160 mg (Rx) [*Triglide* (crospovidone; lactose monohydrate; mannitol; maltodextrin; carboxymethylcellulose sodium; egg lecithin; croscarmellose sodium; sodium lauryl sulfate; colloidal silicon dioxide; magnesium stearate; monobasic sodium phosphate)].

Packaging and storage

Store at 25 °C (77 °F); excursions permitted between 15 and 30 °C (59 and 86 °F). Protect from moisture. Keep out of the reach of children.

Auxiliary labeling
- Keep out of reach of children.

FENOFIBRATE CAPSULES

Usual adult dose

Antihypercholestrolemic—

Oral, initially, 150 mg once daily.

Antihypertriglyceridemic—

Oral, initially, 50 to 150 mg once daily. Dosage should be individualized according to patient response, and should be adjusted if necessary following repeat lipid determination at 4 to 8 week intervals.

Note: For patients with renal impairment, the recommended initial dose is 50 mg once daily. The dose can be increased only after evaluation of the effects on renal function and lipid levels at this dose.

For patients with moderate renal impairment, no modification of dosage is required.

Usual adult prescribing limits

150 mg per day.

Usual pediatric dose

Safety and efficacy have not been established.

Usual geriatric dose
Antihypercholestrolemic or
Antihypertriglyceridemic—
Oral, initially, 50 mg once daily.

Strength(s) usually available
U.S.—
50 mg (Rx) [*LIPOFEN* (lauroyl macrogol glyceride type 1500; polyethylene glycol 20,00; polyethylene glycol 8000; hydroxypropylcellulose; sodium starch glycolate; gelatin; titanium dioxide; shellac; propylene glycol; may contain sodium hydroxide; may contain povidone; may contain red iron oxide; may contain black iron oxide; may contain FD&C Blue #1; may contain FD&C Blue #2; may contain FD&C Red #40; may contain D&C Yellow #10)].
100 mg (Rx) [*LIPOFEN* (lauroyl macrogol glyceride type 1500; polyethylene glycol 20,00; polyethylene glycol 8000; hydroxypropylcellulose; sodium starch glycolate; gelatin; titanium dioxide; shellac; propylene glycol; may contain sodium hydroxide; may contain povidone; may contain red iron oxide; may contain black iron oxide; may contain FD&C Blue #1; may contain FD&C Blue #2; may contain FD&C Red #40; may contain D&C Yellow #10)].
150 mg (Rx) [*LIPOFEN* (lauroyl macrogol glyceride type 1500; polyethylene glycol 20,00; polyethylene glycol 8000; hydroxypropylcellulose; sodium starch glycolate; gelatin; titanium dioxide; shellac; propylene glycol; may contain sodium hydroxide; may contain povidone; may contain red iron oxide; may contain black iron oxide; may contain FD&C Blue #1; may contain FD&C Blue #2; may contain FD&C Red #40; may contain D&C Yellow #10)].

Packaging and storage
Store at controlled room temperature, between 15 and 30 °C (59 and 86 °F). Protect from moisture and light.

Auxiliary labeling
- Take with a meal.

FENOFIBRATE TABLETS (MICROCOATED)

Usual adult dose
Antihypercholestrolemic—
Oral, initially, 160 mg once daily.
Antihypertriglyceridemic—
Oral, initially, 160 mg once daily.
Note: For patients with renal impairment (creatinine clearance between 20 and 100 mL/min), the recommended initial dose is 100 mg once daily. The dose can be increased only after evaluation of the tolerance and effects on the lipid parameters.

Usual adult prescribing limits
200 mg per day.

Usual pediatric dose
Safety and efficacy have not been established.

Usual geriatric dose
See *Usual adult dose*

Strength(s) usually available
U.S.—
Not commercially available as microcoated tablets
Canada—
100 mg (Rx) [*Lipidil Supra*® (povidone; lactose monohydrate; microcrystalline cellulose; crospovidone; colloidal silicon dioxide; sodium stearyl fumarate; sodium lauryl sulfate)].
160 mg (Rx) [*Lipidil Supra*® (povidone; lactose monohydrate; microcrystalline cellulose; crospovidone; colloidal silicon dioxide; sodium stearyl fumarate; sodium lauryl sulfate)].

Packaging and storage
Store at controlled room temperature, between 15 and 30 °C (59 and 86 °F). Protect from moisture.

Auxiliary labeling
- Take with a meal.

Revised: 05/17/2006
Developed: 05/18/1998

FENOPROFEN—See *Anti-inflammatory Drugs, Nonsteroidal (Systemic)*

FENOTEROL—See *Bronchodilators, Adrenergic (Inhalation-Local)*

FENTANYL—See *Fentanyl Derivatives (Systemic), Fentanyl (Transdermal-Systemic)*

FENTANYL Systemic

VA CLASSIFICATION (Primary): CN 101
Note: Controlled substance classification
U.S.: Schedule II
Commonly used brand name(s): *Actiq*.
Note: For a listing of dosage forms and brand names by country availability, see *Dosage Forms* section(s).

Category
Analgesic.

Indications

General Considerations
Transmucosal fentanyl should be used in opioid-tolerant patients only. Patients considered opioid-tolerant are those who are taking at least 60 mg of morphine per day, 50 mcg of transdermal fentanyl per hour, or an equivalent dose of another opioid analgesic for a week or longer.
Transmucosal fentanyl is intended to be used only in the care of cancer patients and only by oncologists and pain specialists who are knowledgeable of and skilled in the use of Schedule II opioids to treat cancer pain.

Accepted
Pain, chronic cancer (treatment)—Transmucosal fentanyl is indicated for the management of breakthrough cancer pain in adults with malignancies who are already receiving and who are tolerant to opioid therapy for their underlying persistent cancer pain.

Unaccepted
Transmucosal fentanyl is contraindicated in treatment of acute or postoperative pain. Use of this formulation for patients not taking chronic opiates may cause severe hypoventilation.

Pharmacology/Pharmacokinetics

Physicochemical characteristics
Source—Synthetic.
Chemical Group—Phenylpiperidine derivative.
Molecular weight—336.51.
pH—7.41.
pKa—7.3 and 8.41.
Partition coefficient—
816:1100.

Mechanism of action/Effect
Fentanyl produces its effects predominantly via agonist actions at the mu receptor.

Other actions/effects
Fentanyl, like other opioid analgesics, may cause respiratory depression. The risk of respiratory depression is less in patients receiving chronic opioid therapy who develop tolerance to respiratory depression and other opioid effects.
Fentanyl, like other opioid analgesics, increases the tone and decrease contractions of the smooth muscle of the gastrointestinal tract. While opioids generally increase the tone of urinary tract smooth muscle, the overall effect tends to vary.

Absorption
The absorption of the transmucosal dosage form is a combination of an initial rapid absorption from the buccal mucosa and a more prolonged absorption of swallowed fentanyl from the gastrointestinal tract. Both the blood fentanyl profile and the bioavailability of fentanyl will vary depending on the fraction of the dose that is absorbed through the oral mucosa and the fraction swallowed. Approximately 25% of the total dose of transmucosal fentanyl is rapidly absorbed from the buccal mucosa and becomes systemically available. The remaining 75% of the total dose is swallowed with the saliva and then is slowly absorbed from the gastrointestinal tract. About one-third of this amount (25% of the total dose) escapes hepatic and intestinal first-pass elimination and becomes systemically available. Lower peak concentrations and lower bioavailability may result if a unit dose is chewed and swallowed than when consumed as directed.

Distribution
Fentanyl is highly lipophilic. Fentanyl is distributed to the brain, heart, lungs, kidneys, and spleen followed by a slower redistribution to muscle and fat.

Protein binding
High (80 to 85%), primarily by alpha-1-acid glycoprotein, but both albumin and lipoproteins contribute.

Biotransformation
Primarily hepatic, via dealkylation and hydroxylation into inactive metabolites.

Half-life
Approximately 7 hours.

Time to peak concentration
Following administration of 200 mcg, 400 mcg, 800 mcg, 1600 mcg doses (based on consumption time of 15 minutes)—Within 20-40 (range, 20-480 minutes) minutes.

Elimination
Primarily hepatic; less than 7% and 1% of the dose is excreted as unchanged fentanyl in the urine and feces, respectively.

Precautions to Consider

Cross-sensitivity and/or related problems
Patients hypersensitive to fentanyl or its components may be hypersensitive to transmucosal fentanyl also.

Carcinogenicity
No carcinogenic studies have been conducted with fentanyl citrate.

Mutagenicity
No evidence of mutagenicity was demonstrated in the Ames test, the *in-vitro* mouse lymphoma mutagenesis assay, and the *in-vivo* micronucleus cytogenetic assay in the mouse.

Pregnancy/Reproduction
Fertility—Reproduction studies in rats revealed a significant decrease in the pregnancy rate of all experimental groups. This decrease was most pronounced in the high-dose group (1.25 mg per kg of body weight [mg/kg] subcutaneously) in which one of twenty animals became pregnant.

Fentanyl has been shown to impair fertility and to have embryocidal effects with an increase in resorptions in rats when given for a period of 12 to 21 days in doses of 30 mcg per kg of body weight (mcg/kg) intravenously or 160 mcg/kg subcutaneously.

Pregnancy—Adequate and well-controlled studies in humans with fentanyl have not been done.

No evidence of teratogenic effects has been observed after administration of fentanyl citrate to rats.

FDA Pregnancy Category C.

Labor and delivery—Use of transmucosal fentanyl to provide analgesia during labor and delivery is not recommended.

Breast-feeding
Fentanyl is distributed into human milk. Use of transmucosal fentanyl by nursing women is not recommended because of the possibility of sedation and/or respiratory depression in infants.

Pediatrics
Appropriate studies on the relationship of age to the effects of transmucosal fentanyl have not been performed in the pediatric population. Safety and efficacy have not been established. **Patients and their caregivers must be instructed that transmucosal fentanyl contains a medicine in an amount that can be fatal to a child.** Patients and their caregivers must be instructed to keep transmucosal fentanyl out of the reach of children and to discard open units properly in a secured container.

Geriatrics
No difference was noted in the safety profile of the patient group over 65 years of age as compared to younger patients in clinical trials, although the older population did titrate to a slightly lower dose. However, greater sensitivity to fentanyl in older individuals cannot be ruled out. Therefore, exercise caution in elderly patients to provide adequate efficacy while minimizing the risks.

Dental
Each oral transmucosal fentanyl unit contains approximately 2 grams of sugar as hydrated dextrates. Frequent consumption of this product may increase the risk of dental decay. Dry mouth associated with the use of opioid medications may add to this risk. Patients using oral transmucosal fentanyl should consult their dentist to ensure appropriate oral hygiene.

Drug interactions and/or related problems
The following drug interactions and/or related problems have been selected on the basis of their potential clinical significance (possible mechanism in parentheses where appropriate)—not necessarily inclusive (» = major clinical significance):

Note: Combinations containing any of the following medications, depending on the amount present, may also interact with this medication.

» Alcohol or
» CNS (central nervous system) depression-producing medications, other (see *Appendix II)* or
(concurrent use with transmucosal fentanyl may result in increased CNS depressant, respiratory depressant, and hypotensive effects; careful monitoring is recommended and dosage adjustment may be required)

Enzyme inhibitors, hepatic, cytochrome P450, such as:
» Erythromycin
» Itraconazole
» Ketoconazole
» Protease inhibitors such as:
» Ritonavir
(inhibitors of potent hepatic cytochrome P450 enzymes may increase the bioavailability and decrease the clearance of transmucosal fentanyl, thereby resulting in increased or prolonged opioid effects; patients should be monitored carefully and a dosage adjustment may be required)

» Monoamine oxidase (MAO) inhibitors, including furazolidone, procarbazine, and selegiline
(caution is recommended when any opioid analgesic is given to patients who have received an MAO inhibitor within 14 days because severe and unpredictable potentiation by MAO inhibitors has been reported with opioid analgesics)

Naloxone or
Nalmefene
(may precipitate withdrawal symptoms in physically dependent patients)

Opioid, other
(in addition to their potential for causing additive effects when used concurrently with fentanyl, opioids having partial mu-receptor activity [e.g., buprenorphine and dezocine] and some opioids having mixed agonist/antagonist activity [e.g., nalbuphine and pentazocine] have the potential to antagonize transmucosal fentanyl's therapeutic and adverse effects)

Medical considerations/Contraindications
The medical considerations/contraindications included have been selected on the basis of their potential clinical significance (reasons given in parentheses where appropriate)—not necessarily inclusive (» = major clinical significance).

Except under special circumstances, this medication should not be used when the following medical problem exists:

» Hypersensitivity to fentanyl or any of its components
» Respiratory depression, acute
(opioids may decrease respiratory drive in patients with this condition; transmucosal fentanyl should be titrated with caution in these patients)

Risk-benefit should be considered when the following medical problems exist:

» Respiratory impairment or disease, chronic
(opioids may decrease respiratory drive in patients with these conditions; transmucosal fentanyl should be titrated with caution in these patients)

» Bradyarrhythmias
(may be exacerbated)

» Diabetes mellitus
(each oral transmucosal fentanyl unit contains approximately 2 grams of sugar as hydrated dextrates)

Drug abuse or dependence, current or history of, including alcoholism
(patient predisposition to drug abuse)

Head injury or
Intracranial lesions
(risk of respiratory depression and further elevation of cerebrospinal fluid pressure, which may lead to complications such as impaired consciousness, is increased; also, transmucosal fentanyl may cause sedation and pupillary changes that may obscure the clinical course of patients with head injury)

Hepatic function impairment or

Renal function impairment
(potential for reduced clearance of fentanyl, leading to higher plasma concentrations)

Caution is also recommended in administration to elderly or very ill or debilitated patients, who may be more sensitive to the effects, especially the respiratory depressant effects, of opioid analgesics

Patient monitoring

The following may be especially important in patient monitoring (other tests may be warranted in some patients, depending on condition; » = major clinical significance):

Heart rate
» Respiratory rate
» Sedation, degree of
(should be monitored at periodic intervals, especially at the beginning of therapy and after increases in dosage)

Side/Adverse Effects

The following side/adverse effects have been selected on the basis of their potential clinical significance (possible signs and symptoms in parentheses where appropriate)—not necessarily inclusive:

Those indicating need for medical attention

Incidence more frequent

Central nervous system (CNS)-depression (dizziness, lightheadedness, feeling faint, unusual tiredness, or weakness); ***dyspnea*** (shortness of breath)

Incidence less frequent

CNS effects (abnormal thinking; anxiety; confusion; dizziness; drowsiness; false sense of well-being; nervousness; problems with coordination; weakness); ***hallucinations*** (seeing, hearing, or feeling things that are not there); ***urinary retention*** (decrease in urine volume; decrease in frequency of urination)

Incidence not determined—Observed during clinical practice, estimates of frequency can not be determined

Dental decay including; dental caries (tooth pain); ***tooth loss*** (trouble with teeth); ***gum line erosion*** (trouble with gums)

Those indicating need for medical attention only if they continue or are bothersome

Incidence more frequent

Constipation; dry mouth; nausea and/or vomiting

Those indicating possible need for medical attention if they occur after medication is discontinued

Diarrhea; nausea and/or vomiting; restlessness or irritability; speech disorder; stomach cramps; trouble in sleeping; weakness

Overdose

For specific information on the agents used in the management of fentanyl overdose, see:

- *Charcoal, Activated (Oral-Local)* monograph; and/or
- *Naloxone (Systemic)* monograph.

For more information on the management of overdose or unintentional ingestion, **contact a Poison Control Center** (see *Poison Control Center Listing*).

Clinical effects of overdose

The following effects have been selected on the basis of their potential clinical significance (possible signs and symptoms in parentheses where appropriate)—not necessarily inclusive:

Acute and/or chronic

Cold, clammy skin; convulsions; dizziness (severe), drowsiness, nervousness, restlessness, or weakness; hypotension (dizziness, lightheadedness, or feeling faint); ***miosis*** (pinpoint pupils of the eyes); ***slow or troubled breathing***

Treatment of overdose

General measures—Removing medicine, if still in mouth.

To decrease absorption—Emptying the stomach via gastric lavage.

To enhance elimination—Administering activated charcoal.

Specific treatment—For hypotension: Use of intravenous fluids and/or vasopressors and using other supportive measures as needed.

For hypoventilation: Verbal stimulation or waking the patient may be sufficient to increase the respiratory rate and provide adequate ventilation. Use of the opioid antagonist naloxone if necessary.

Supportive care—May include establishing adequate respiratory exchange through provision of a patent airway and institution of assisted or controlled respiration. Patients in whom intentional overdose is confirmed or suspected should be referred for psychiatric consultation.

Patient Consultation

As an aid to patient consultation, refer to *Advice for the Patient, Fentanyl (Systemic)*.

In providing consultation, consider emphasizing the following selected information; (» = major clinical significance):

Before using this medication

» Conditions affecting use, especially:
Hypersensitivity to fentanyl or its derivatives, or any of its components
Pregnancy—Use of transmucosal fentanyl is not recommended during labor and delivery
Breast-feeding—Opioid effects including sedation, respiratory depression, and physical dependence may occur in the nursing infant
Use in the elderly—May be more sensitive to the effects of transmucosal fentanyl
Dental—This product contains sugar and frequent consumption may increase the risk of dental decay. Patients should consult their dentist to ensure appropriate oral hygiene.
Other medications, especially alcohol, CNS depression producing medications, hepatic enzyme inhibitors, or MAO inhibitors
Other medical problems, especially acute or chronic pulmonary diseases, or bradyarrhythmias

Proper use of this medication

» Reading patient instructions carefully before using
» Keep medication in sealed pouch until ready to use. The foil package should be opened with scissors immediately prior to product use. Place the medicine in mouth between the cheek and lower gum, occasionally moving the medicine from one side to the other using the handle. The medicine should be sucked not chewed. Consume each dose of the medicine over a 15-minute period.
» Proper dosing
Missed dose: If on scheduled dosing, use as soon as possible; not using if almost time for next dose; not doubling doses
» Proper storage

Precautions while using this medication

» Transmucosal fentanyl contains a medicine in an amount which can be fatal to a child. Patients and their caregivers must be instructed to keep transmucosal fentanyl out of the reach of children and to discard open units
Regular consultations with health care professional during long-term therapy
» Avoiding use of alcoholic beverages or other CNS depressants during therapy, unless prescribed or otherwise approved by physician
» Caution if dizziness, drowsiness, lightheadedness, or false sense of well-being occurs; checking with health care professional if severe drowsiness persists for more than a few days
Getting up slowly from a lying or sitting position; lying down for a while may provide relief if patient becomes dizzy, lightheaded, or faint
Compliance with regimen for preventing severe constipation, if prescribed
» Informing physician or dentist of use of medication if any kind of surgery (including dental surgery) or emergency treatment is required
Not discontinuing medication abruptly after prolonged use; checking with physician instead, since gradual withdrawal may be needed to minimize risk of precipitating abstinence syndrome
» Suspected overdose: Getting emergency help at once
Regular visits with dentist to watch for tooth decay or other trouble with teeth or gums.

Side/adverse effects

Signs of potential side effects, especially CNS depression, dyspnea, CNS effects, hallucinations, urinary retention, or dental decay

General Dosing Information

Transmucosal fentanyl should be used in opioid-tolerant patients only. Patients considered opioid-tolerant are those who are taking at least 60 mg of morphine per day, 50 mcg of transdermal fentanyl per hour, or an equivalent dose of another opioid analgesic for a week or longer.

Transmucosal fentanyl may cause respiratory depression, especially in elderly, very ill, or debilitated patients and patients with preexisting respiratory problems. Lower doses may be required for these patients, at least initially.

Safety considerations for handling this medication

Patients must be advised to dispose of any units remaining from a prescription as soon as they are no longer needed. While all units should be disposed of immediately after use, partially consumed units represent a special risk because they are no longer protected by the child-resistant pouch, yet may contain enough medicine to be fatal to a child.

A temporary storage bottle is provided as part of the Actiq® Welcome Kit. This container is to be used by patients or their caregivers in the event that a partially consumed unit cannot be disposed of promptly (see manufacturer's patient leaflet for proper disposal information). If additional assistance is required, call 1-800-615-0187.

Oral Dosage Forms

TRANSMUCOSAL FENTANYL CITRATE LOZENGES

Note: Transmucosal fentanyl contains fentanyl citrate. However, dosage and strength are expressed in terms of fentanyl base.

Usual adult dose

Analgesic (opioid tolerant patients only)—

Transmucosal, 200 mcg (base), initially, with dosage then being adjusted according to the requirements of the individual patient. See manufacturer's prescribing information for recommended dose titration schedule.

Note: Each dose of transmucosal fentanyl should be consumed over a 15-minute period (30 minutes after start of the previous dose). Patients should not use any more than 2 units per episode of breakthrough pain. If signs of excessive opioid effects appear before the dose is consumed, the medicine should be removed from the patient's mouth immediately and future doses should be decreased.

Usual pediatric dose

Safety and efficacy in children younger than 16 years of age have not been established.

Usual geriatric dose

See *Usual adult dose.*

Strength(s) usually available

U.S.—

200 mcg (base) (Rx) [*Actiq* (hydrated dextrates; citric acid; dibasic sodium phosphate; artificial berry flavor; magnesium stearate; modified food starch; confectioner's sugar)].

400 mcg (base) (Rx) [*Actiq* (hydrated dextrates; citric acid; dibasic sodium phosphate; artificial berry flavor; magnesium stearate; modified food starch; confectioner's sugar)].

600 mcg (base) (Rx) [*Actiq* (hydrated dextrates; citric acid; dibasic sodium phosphate; artificial berry flavor; magnesium stearate; modified food starch; confectioner's sugar)].

800 mcg (base) (Rx) [*Actiq* (hydrated dextrates; citric acid; dibasic sodium phosphate; artificial berry flavor; magnesium stearate; modified food starch; confectioner's sugar)].

1200 mcg (base) (Rx) [*Actiq* (hydrated dextrates; citric acid; dibasic sodium phosphate; artificial berry flavor; magnesium stearate; modified food starch; confectioner's sugar)].

1600 mcg (base) (Rx) [*Actiq* (hydrated dextrates; citric acid; dibasic sodium phosphate; artificial berry flavor; magnesium stearate; modified food starch; confectioner's sugar)].

Packaging and storage

Store at 25° C (77 °F), preferably between 15 and 30 °C (59 and 86 °F), unless otherwise specified by manufacturer.

Auxiliary labeling

- May cause drowsiness.
- Avoid alcoholic beverages.
- May be habit-forming.

Revised: 11/29/2004
Developed: 06/14/1999

FENTANYL Transdermal-Systemic

VA CLASSIFICATION (Primary): CN101

Note: Controlled substance classification

U.S.: Schedule II

Canada: N

Commonly used brand name(s): *Duragesic; Ionsys.*

Note: For a listing of dosage forms and brand names by country availability, see *Dosage Forms* section(s).

Category

Analgesic.

Indications

General Considerations

Transdermal fentanyl should be prescribed, and its use monitored, only by persons knowledgeable in the continuous administration of potent opioid analgesics, in the care of patients requiring such treatment, and in the detection and management of hypoventilation.

Use of this formulation requires that the advantages of providing a continuous, prolonged analgesic effect via a noninvasive, non-oral route of administration outweigh the disadvantage of being unable to adjust dosage rapidly should analgesic requirements change or adverse effects occur.

Transdermal fentanyl should ONLY be used in patients who are already receiving opioid therapy, who have demonstrated opioid tolerance, and who require a total daily dose at least equivalent to 25 mcg per hour. Patients who are considered opioid-tolerant are those who have been taking, for a week or longer, at least 60 mg of morphine daily, or at least 30 mg of oral oxycodone daily, or at least 8 mg of oral hydromorphone daily or an equianalgesic dose of another opioid.

Iontophoretic transdermal fentanyl is NOT for home use. Therefore, it should not be used once a patient has been discharged from the hospital.

Accepted

Pain, acute postoperative (treatment)—Iontophoretic transdermal fentanyl is indicated for the short-term management of acute postoperative pain in adult patients requiring opioid analgesia during hospitalization.

Pain, chronic (treatment)—Transdermal fentanyl is indicated for management of persistent, moderate to severe chronic pain that:

- requires continuous, around-the-clock opioid administration for an extended period of time, and
- cannot be managed by other means such as non-steroidal analgesics, opioid combination products, or immediate-release opioids

Unaccepted

Transdermal fentanyl is contraindicated for treatment of acute pain (including postoperative pain). Use of this formulation for postoperative pain may cause severe hypoventilation; a few fatalities have been reported. Also, clinical trials have shown that application of transdermal fentanyl 2 hours prior to anesthesia does not eliminate the need for postoperative administration of a rapidly acting analgesic, especially in the first 12 to 24 hours after surgery. However, transdermal fentanyl need not be discontinued perioperatively if a patient being treated for chronic pain requires surgery.

This formulation is contraindicated for treatment of mild or intermittent pain that can be managed with less potent analgesics or with as-needed administration of short- or intermediate-acting opioid analgesics.

Pharmacology/Pharmacokinetics

Physicochemical characteristics

Source—Synthetic.

Chemical Group—Phenylpiperidine derivative; chemically related to meperidine.

Molecular weight—336.5.

pKa—8.4.

n-Octanol:water partition coefficient—860:1.

Note: Physicochemical characteristics that facilitate percutaneous absorption of a medication include high lipid solubility (as indicated by a high *n*-octanol:water partition coefficient) and relatively low molecular weight (< 1000 daltons). Lipophilic opioid analgesics such as fentanyl are well absorbed through intact skin; hydrophilic opioid analgesics (e.g., morphine, codeine, and hydromorphone) are not.

Mechanism of action/Effect

Opioid analgesics such as fentanyl bind with stereospecific receptors at many sites within the central nervous system (CNS) to alter processes affecting both the perception of and emotional response to pain. Although the precise sites and mechanisms of action have not been fully determined, alterations in the release of various neurotransmitters from afferent nerves sensitive to painful stimuli may be partially responsible for the analgesic effects.

Multiple subtypes of opioid receptors, each mediating various therapeutic and/or side effects of opioid analgesics, have been identified. The actions of an opioid analgesic may therefore depend on whether it acts as a full agonist or a partial agonist or is inactive at each type of receptor. Fentanyl probably produces its effects predominantly via agonist actions at the mu receptor.

On a weight basis, fentanyl is considerably more potent than morphine. Transdermal administration of fentanyl at a delivery rate of 100 mcg per hour (mcg/hr) is therapeutically equivalent to intramuscular administration of 60 mg of morphine, chronic oral administration of 180 mg of morphine, or intermittent oral administration of 360 mg of morphine per day in 6 divided doses administered at 4-hour intervals. This high potency permits a therapeutic dose to be applied to a relatively small skin area.

Other actions/effects

Fentanyl, like other opioid analgesics, may cause respiratory depression (characterized by decreases in respiratory rate, tidal volume, minute ventilation, and ventilatory response to carbon dioxide), increased biliary tone, increased smooth muscle tone in the urinary tract, decreased gastrointestinal motility, euphoria, miosis, hypotension, and bradycardia. However, unlike many other opioid analgesics, fentanyl does not cause clinically significant histamine release with therapeutic doses (as determined by intravenous administration of single doses of up to 50 mcg per kg of body weight [mcg/kg]).

Absorption

Following application of a transdermal system, some fentanyl is released relatively rapidly from the adhesive layer of the system. Most of the fentanyl is located in a reservoir layer within the system, from which it is released gradually at a rate controlled by a restrictive copolymer membrane located between the reservoir and adhesive layers. A very small quantity of alcohol present in the formulation enhances passage of the medication through both the rate-limiting restrictive membrane and the skin. Less than 0.2 mL of alcohol is released from a transdermal system. The rate at which fentanyl is delivered to the skin may vary across the 72-hour application time. The labeled strength of a transdermal system represents the average quantity of fentanyl delivered to the systemic circulation per hour across intact skin.

Absorption of fentanyl after application of a transdermal system is initially slow because a depot of fentanyl, from which the medication is subsequently absorbed into the systemic circulation, must first form in the upper skin layers. Absorption is subject to intra- as well as interindividual variability. The rate and/or extent of absorption may be altered by the temperature, state of hydration, and integrity of the skin at the application site. Also, absorption may depend on blood flow in the area of application, which may increase or decrease with the patient's level of activity. Despite these variables, the average quantity of fentanyl absorbed per hour into the systemic circulation of an individual patient is sufficiently consistent to permit dosage titration over extended periods of time.

Approximately 92% of the fentanyl contained in a transdermal system is absorbed into the systemic circulation over 72 hours (calculated value). In a multiple-dose study, absorption from the fifth consecutive transdermal system to be applied and kept in place for 72 hours was 47% complete after 24 hours, 88% complete after 48 hours, and 94% complete after 72 hours.

Absorption of fentanyl from the depot in the skin continues after removal of the transdermal system. When application sites are rotated, continued absorption prevents plasma concentrations from decreasing to subtherapeutic values while another depot is forming below the new application site. Failure to rotate application sites may lead to more rapid absorption and higher fentanyl concentrations, which may increase the risk of toxicity.

Distribution

Fentanyl is distributed to and accumulates in adipose tissue and skeletal muscle. The medication is slowly released from these tissues to the systemic circulation. Fentanyl readily crosses the blood/brain barrier. Alterations in pH may affect the medication's distribution between CNS tissues and plasma.

Volume of distribution (determined with intravenous administration to surgical patients)—6 (range, approximately 3 to 8) L per kg of body weight.

Protein binding

High (79 to 87%), primarily to albumin and lipoproteins; dependent on plasma pH.

Biotransformation

Fentanyl is metabolized primarily via human cytochrome P450 3A4 isoenzyme system. In humans, fentanyl is metabolized mostly by oxidative N-dealkylation to norfentanyl and other inactive metabolites.

Fentanyl delivered transdermally is not metabolized in the skin.

Half-life

Elimination—Transdermal—

Single application—17 (range, 13 to 22) hours

Multiple applications—21.9±8.9 hours, determined after 5 consecutive 72-hour applications.

Note: The prolonged elimination half-life with transdermal administration (relative to that with intravenous administration—about 3.6 hours) is due to prolonged continued absorption from the skin depot below the transdermal system.

Values may be greatly prolonged in geriatric patients. In a single-dose study the mean value for patients 78 to 88 years of age was 43.1±23.4 hours.

The half-life of transdermal fentanyl has not been assessed in patients with renal or hepatic function impairment.

Onset of action

Very slow (12 to 24 hours in most studies) because of delayed absorption following application of an initial transdermal dose.

Time to peak concentration

Single 72-hour application—Generally between 24 and 72 hours.

Multiple applications—Concentrations continue to increase during the first few 72-hour applications.

Peak serum concentration

Serum concentrations achieved with transdermal fentanyl have been studied primarily in clinical trials that investigated whether the formulation might be useful for postoperative pain control. In general, the studies found fentanyl concentrations to be proportional to the transdermal delivery rate in mcg per hour, subject to substantial interpatient variability, and significantly higher in geriatric patients than in younger adults. The concentrations produced were similar to those measured during continuous intravenous infusion of fentanyl at the same rate of administration, but took considerably longer to achieve. In many studies, measurable quantities of fentanyl were not present in serum within the first 2 hours after application of an initial transdermal system. Specific values determined during short-term use in postoperative patients are not likely to be relevant to prolonged use of this medication in chronic pain patients.

Steady-state concentrations

A multiple-dose study in which pharmacokinetics of fentanyl were assessed during 5 consecutive 72-hour applications of a system designed to deliver 100 mcg per hour reported mean trough concentrations of 0.91±0.55 nanograms/mL (0.0027±0.0016 micromoles/L) prior to, and mean maximum concentrations of 2.6±1.3 nanograms/mL (0.0077±0.0039 micromoles/L) during, application of the fifth dose. Steady-state concentrations are subject to substantial interpatient variability because of individual differences in skin permeability and clearance of fentanyl. Although several sequential 72-hour applications may be required to achieve steady-state, measurement of trough concentrations prior to application of each dose in the multiple-dose study suggested that steady-state concentrations are approached by the second dose.

Therapeutic concentrations

Generally 0.2 to 1.2 nanograms/mL (0.0006 to 0.0036 micromoles/L) in patients who are not tolerant to opioid analgesics. Required concentrations increase with the degree of tolerance to opioid analgesics. Fentanyl requirements are highly subject to intrapatient variability and dependent on the intensity of pain.

Effective concentrations were reached between 1.2 and 37.3 hours after application of a transdermal system in various postoperative pain studies. In 1 of these studies, concentrations decreased to subtherapeutic values between 2.3 and > 24.9 hours (mean, 16.1±7.1 hours) after the system was removed.

Duration of action

Individual transdermal systems are designed to release fentanyl over 72 hours. Analgesic effects may persist for several hours after a system is removed because of continued absorption. This provides relatively constant analgesia during the time required for an effective quantity of fentanyl to be absorbed from the next dose.

Elimination

Studies with intravenously administered fentanyl have shown that approximately 75% of a dose is eliminated in the urine (10% as unchanged fentanyl and the remainder as metabolites) and another 9% in the feces, mostly as metabolites. These studies also indicated that clearance rates are more variable and prolonged in patients with hepatic or renal function impairment than in patients with normal hepatic and renal function. Clearance rates for transdermally administered fentanyl have not been published.

Precautions to Consider

Cross-sensitivity and/or related problems

Patients hypersensitive to alfentanil or sufentanil may be hypersensitive to fentanyl also.

Carcinogenicity

Long-term studies with fentanyl have not been done.

Mutagenicity

No evidence of mutagenicity was demonstrated in the Ames test, primary rat hepatocyte unscheduled DNA synthesis assay, BALB/c-3T3 transformation test, and the human lymphocyte and CHO chromosomal aberration *in vitro* assays. In the mouse lymphoma assay, fentanyl concentrations more than 2000 times greater than those occurring with chronic systemic use were mutagenic only in the presence of metabolic activation.

Pregnancy/Reproduction

Fertility—In a male fertility study, male rats treated with fentanyl at doses up to 0.4 mg per kg of body weight per day (approximately 1.2 times the maximum available daily human dose on a mg per m^2 basis) for 28 days prior to mating with no treatment for female rats produced no effects on male fertility.

In a female fertility study, female rats treated with fentanyl at doses up to 0.4 mg per kg of body weight per day for 14 days prior to mating until day 16 of pregnancy with no treatment for male rats produced no effects on female fertility.

Intravenous administration of 0.3 times the human dose of fentanyl for 12 days impaired fertility in rats.

Pregnancy—Adequate and well-controlled studies with transdermal fentanyl have not been done in pregnant women. Fentanyl should be used during pregnancy only if the potential benefit justifies the potential risk to the fetus. Chronic use of other opioids by pregnant women has caused physical dependence in the fetus, leading to withdrawal symptoms (convulsions, irritability, excessive crying, tremors, hyperactive reflexes, fever, vomiting, diarrhea, sneezing, and yawning) in the neonate. Also, use of opioid analgesics shortly before or during labor may cause respiratory depression in the neonate.

Studies in rats have not shown that fentanyl is teratogenic.

In female rats treated with up to 0.4 mg per kg of body weight per day from day 6 of pregnancy through 3 weeks of lactation produced male and female pups with significantly decreased body weight and also decreased survival in pups at day 4. Both the middle and high doses of fentanyl in animals demonstrated delayed incisor eruption and eye opening and decreased locomotor activity at day 28 which recovered by day 50.

FDA Pregnancy Category C.

Labor and delivery—Use of transdermal fentanyl to provide analgesia during labor and delivery is not recommended.

Breast-feeding

Fentanyl is distributed into human breast milk. Nursing infants may ingest quantities of fentanyl sufficient to produce adverse effects typical of potent opioid analgesics, including sedation, respiratory depression, and physical dependence when the mother is receiving chronic, high-dose treatment. Use of transdermal fentanyl by nursing women is therefore not recommended.

Pediatrics

No information is available on the relationship of age to the effects of transdermal fentanyl in pediatric patients under 2 years of age. Safety and efficacy have been established in pediatric patients 2 years of age and older. Transdermal fentanyl should be administered to children only if they are opioid-tolerant and 2 years of age or older.

Iontophoretic transdermal systems—Safety and efficacy have not been adequately studied in pediatric patients under 18 years of age.

Note: Preliminary pediatric studies in which lower dose iontophoretic fentanyl was administered suggested that pediatric patients were more vulnerable to application site reactions which were more severe.

Geriatrics

No information is available on the relationship of age to the effects of transdermal fentanyl in geriatric patients with chronic pain. However, it is known that geriatric patients are generally more susceptible to the effects, especially the respiratory depressant effects, of opioid analgesics. Short-term pharmacokinetic studies with transdermal fentanyl have shown that the elimination half-life and serum concentrations are significantly higher in elderly individuals than in younger people. Also, in a study that utilized an investigational 24-hour transdermal system with a delivery rate of 50 mcg per hour, the systems were removed earlier than anticipated from all of the elderly subjects (planned application time 24 hours; mean time of removal 11.7 ± 4.9 hours), but none of the younger individuals, because of adverse effects. Caution and careful attention to dosage are recommended, especially if the patient is not tolerant to opioid analgesics.

Drug interactions and/or related problems

The following drug interactions and/or related problems have been selected on the basis of their potential clinical significance (possible mechanism in parentheses where appropriate)—not necessarily inclusive (» = major clinical significance):

Note: Combinations containing any of the following medications, depending on the amount present, may also interact with this medication.

» Alcohol or

» CNS depression-producing medications, other (See *Appendix II*)
(concurrent or sequential use with fentanyl may result in increased CNS depressant, respiratory depressant, and hypotensive effects; caution and careful titration of the dose of each agent are recommended)
(concurrent use of fentanyl with other CNS depressants that may cause habituation may increase the risk of habituation)

Anticholinergics or other medications with anticholinergic activity (See *Appendix II*)
(concurrent use with fentanyl may result in increased risk of severe constipation, which may lead to paralytic ileus, and/or urinary retention)

Antidiarrheals, antiperistaltic, such as:
Difenoxin and atropine
Diphenoxylate and atropine
Loperamide
Opium tincture
Paregoric
(repeated administration of any of these antidiarrheals with fentanyl, especially during chronic, high-dose fentanyl therapy, may increase the risk of severe constipation and CNS depression)

Antihypertensives, especially ganglionic blockers such as guanadrel, guanethidine, and mecamylamine or

Diuretics or

Hypotension-producing medications, other (see *Appendix II*)
(hypotensive effects of these medications may be potentiated when they are used concurrently with fentanyl; patients should be monitored for excessive fall in blood pressure)
(concurrent use of a beta-adrenergic blocking agent with fentanyl may also increase the risk of bradycardia)

» CYP3A4 Inducers, such as:
Carbamazepine,
Phenytoin or
Rifampin
(concurrent use of CYP3A4 inducers with fentanyl may cause increased clearance of fentanyl, resulting in decreased opioid effects)

» CYP3A4 Inhibitors, potent, such as:
Azole antifungal agents (e.g., ketoconazole or itraconazole),
Macrolide antibiotics (e.g., clarithromycin, troleandomycin, or erythromycin) or
Protease inhibitors (e.g., nelfinavir or ritonavir) or
Nefazodone
(concurrent use of CYP3A4 inhibitors with fentanyl may cause decreased clearance of fentanyl, resulting in increased or prolonged adverse effects and may cause potentially fatal respiratory depression; patients receiving fentanyl and a CYP3A4 inhibitor should be carefully monitored for an extended period of time and dosage adjustments should be made if warranted)

Hydroxyzine
(concurrent use with fentanyl may result in increased analgesia as well as increased CNS depressant and hypotensive effects)

Metoclopramide
(fentanyl may antagonize the effects of metoclopramide on gastrointestinal motility)

Monoamine oxidase (MAO) inhibitors, including furazolidone, procarbazine, and selegiline
(caution is recommended when any opioid analgesic is given to patients who have received an MAO inhibitor within 14 days because administration of meperidine to patients receiving MAO inhibitors has caused unpredictable, severe, and sometimes fatal reactions, including immediate excitation, sweating, rigidity, and severe hypertension, or, in some patients, hypotension, severe respiratory depression, coma, seizures, hyperpyrexia, and vascular collapse; although a few reports indicated that intravenous injections of fentanyl did not cause adverse reactions when ad-

ministered perioperatively to patients receiving MAO inhibitor therapy, administration of an intravenous test dose of fentanyl [to detect any possible interaction] may be advisable prior to initiation of transdermal therapy because the effects of transdermal fentanyl cannot be terminated rapidly)

Naloxone
(antagonizes the analgesic, CNS, and respiratory depressant effects of opioid analgesics; however, because naloxone may precipitate withdrawal symptoms in physically dependent patients, dosage of naloxone should be carefully titrated when it is used to treat opioid overdosage in dependent patients; also, because absorption of fentanyl from the depot that forms in the skin layers below the transdermal system continues after the system has been removed, prolonged infusion or repeated administration of naloxone may be required)

» Naltrexone
(fentanyl will be ineffective if administered to a patient receiving naltrexone, which blocks the therapeutic effects of opioid analgesics; administration of increased doses of an opioid analgesic to override naltrexone blockade of opioid receptors may result in increased and prolonged respiratory depression and/or circulatory collapse and is not recommended)
(administration of naltrexone to a patient who is physically dependent on fentanyl will precipitate withdrawal symptoms; symptoms may appear within 5 minutes of naltrexone administration, persist for up to 48 hours, and be very difficult to reverse)

Neuromuscular blocking agents and possibly other medications having some neuromuscular blocking activity
(respiratory suppressant effects of neuromuscular blockade may be additive to the central respiratory depressant effects of opioid analgesics; increased or prolonged respiratory depression [apnea] may occur but is of minor clinical significance if the patient is being ventilated mechanically; however, caution and careful monitoring of the patient are recommended during and following concurrent or sequential use, especially if there is a possibility of incomplete reversal of neuromuscular blockade)

» Opioid analgesics, other
(although most patients require supplemental administration of an analgesic with a rapid onset of action for pain relief during the interval between application of the first transdermal system and the onset of effective analgesia [24 hours or longer] and for relief of breakthrough pain, the risk of additive CNS and/or respiratory depression or other adverse effects must be considered, especially in patients who are not tolerant to opioid analgesics; use of long-acting opioid analgesics [or extended-release dosage forms of short-acting opioids] in conjunction with transdermal fentanyl may be especially hazardous and is not recommended)
(in addition to their potential for causing additive effects when used concurrently with fentanyl, opioids having partial mu-receptor activity [e.g., buprenorphine and dezocine] and some opioids having mixed agonist/antagonist activity [i.e., nalbuphine and pentazocine] have the potential to antagonize fentanyl's therapeutic and adverse effects; whether additive or antagonistic effects occur may depend on the dose of each medication as well as on the order in which the medications are given and the extent to which physical dependence has developed; administration of a partial mu-receptor agonist prior to an initial dose of fentanyl may reduce the therapeutic response to fentanyl, whereas administration of a partial mu-receptor agonist, nalbuphine, or pentazocine to a patient who is receiving fentanyl may antagonize fentanyl's effects to the extent of precipitating withdrawal symptoms in physically dependent patients)

Laboratory value alterations

The following have been selected on the basis of their potential clinical significance (possible effect in parentheses where appropriate)—not necessarily inclusive (» = major clinical significance).

With diagnostic test results

Gastric emptying studies
(opioid analgesics may delay gastric emptying, thereby invalidating test results)

Hepatobiliary imaging using a technetium Tc 99m–labeled iminodiacetic acid derivative
(delivery of the radiopharmaceutical to the small bowel may be slowed because of fentanyl-induced constriction of the sphincter of Oddi and increased biliary tract pressure; these actions result in delayed visualization, which may be falsely interpreted as indicating obstruction of the common bile duct)

With physiology/laboratory test values

Amylase, plasma and
Lipase, plasma
(enzyme values may be increased because fentanyl can cause contractions of the sphincter of Oddi and increased biliary tract pressure; the diagnostic utility of determinations of these enzymes may be compromised during, and for a time following discontinuation of, transdermal fentanyl therapy)

Cerebrospinal fluid pressure
(fentanyl may increase cerebrospinal fluid pressure; effect is secondary to respiratory depression–induced carbon dioxide retention)

Medical considerations/Contraindications

The medical considerations/contraindications included have been selected on the basis of their potential clinical significance (reasons given in parentheses where appropriate)—not necessarily inclusive (» = major clinical significance).

Except under special circumstances, this medication should not be used when the following medical problems exist:

» Bronchial asthma, acute or severe
(use is contraindicated because serious or life-threatening hypoventilation could occur)

» CAT scan or
» Cardioversion or
» Defrbrillation or
» MRI procedure or
» X-ray image
(iontophoretic transdermal patch should be removed to avoid damage to the system from the strong electromagnetic fields set up by these procedures)

» Coma or
» Head injury or
» Impaired consciousness or
» Increased intracranial pressure, pre-existing or
» Intracranial lesions
(should not be used in patients who may be particularly susceptible to the intracranial effects of CO_2 retention)

» Diarrhea associated with pseudomembranous colitis caused by cephalosporins, lincomycins (possibly including topical clindamycin), or penicillins or
» Diarrhea caused by poisoning, until toxic material has been eliminated from the gastrointestinal tract
(opioid analgesics may slow elimination of toxic material, thereby worsening and/or prolonging the diarrhea)

» Hypersensitivity to fentanyl or any components of the product

» Not opioid-tolerant
(use is contraindicated; fentanyl use in patients who are not opioid-tolerant may lead to fatal respiratory depression)

» Paralytic ileus, known or suspected
(use is contraindicated)

» Respiratory depression, acute
(may be exacerbated)

Risk-benefit should be considered when the following medical problems exist:

Abdominal conditions, acute
(diagnosis or clinical course may be obscured)

Allergic reaction to fentanyl, alfentanil, or sufentanil, or to the adhesives in the transdermal system
(risk of hypersensitivity reaction)

Biliary tract disease including
Acute pancreatitis
(should be used with caution because fentanyl may cause spasm of the spincter of Oddi)

Bradyarrhythmias
(may be exacerbated; should be administered with caution)

Brain tumors
(should be used with caution in these patients)

Drug abuse or dependence, current or history of, including alcoholism or
Emotional instability or
Mental illness (e.g., major depression) or
Suicidal ideation or attempts
(patient predisposition to drug abuse; possibility of adverse effects if patient uses nonprescribed CNS depressants concurrently with fentanyl)
(although this medication should not be withheld from known opioid addicts who require treatment for chronic pain, caution is recommended; addicts treated with fentanyl transdermal systems have been reported to increase the rate of fentanyl release by

disrupting the restrictive membrane and to remove fentanyl from the reservoir for rapid administration by other routes)

Fever

(temperature-dependent changes in fentanyl release from the transdermal system and increased skin permeability may result in a 33% increase in fentanyl plasma concentrations in patients with a fever of 40 °C [102 °F]; patients who develop a fever while a system is in place should be monitored for adverse effects and fentanyl dosage adjusted and/or treatment instituted as needed)

Gallbladder disease or gallstones

(fentanyl may cause biliary contraction and increased biliary tract pressure; biliary colic may be exacerbated rather than relieved)

Gastrointestinal tract surgery, current or recent

(alteration of gastrointestinal motility by fentanyl may be undesirable)

Hepatic disease or
Hepatic function impairment or
Renal function impairment

(should be used with caution in these patients; potential for reduced clearance of fentanyl, leading to higher plasma concentrations; pharmacokinetic studies on which recommendations regarding use of transdermal fentanyl could be based have not been done in patients with these conditions)

(fluid retention associated with renal function impairment may be exacerbated because fentanyl may also cause urinary retention)

High frequency hearing impairment

(iontophoretic transdermal system should be used with caution due to the error detection circuitry of the system using audible signals to alert patient of dose not being delivered when activated; tone should be demonstrated for patient who may be at risk of not being able to hear it)

Hypothyroidism

(risk of respiratory depression and prolonged CNS depression is greatly increased)

» Inflammatory bowel disease, severe

(risk of toxic megacolon, especially with prolonged use of fentanyl)

Prostatic hypertrophy or obstruction or
Urethral stricture or
Urinary tract surgery, current or recent

(patient predisposition to urinary retention)

» Pulmonary disease or
» Respiratory impairment or disease, chronic

(should be administered with caution in patients with medical conditions predisposing them to hypoventilation; opioids may decrease respiratory drive and increase airway resistance in patients with these conditions)

Caution is also recommended in administration to elderly or very ill or debilitated patients, who may be more sensitive to the effects, especially the respiratory depressant effects, of opioid analgesics.

Patient monitoring

The following may be especially important in patient monitoring (other tests may be warranted in some patients, depending on condition; » = major clinical significance):

Blood pressure and
Heart rate and
» Respiratory rate and
» Sedation, degree of

(should be monitored at periodic intervals, especially at the beginning of therapy and after increases in dosage; if the system is removed because of adverse effects, monitoring should continue for at least 24 hours because absorption of fentanyl continues, and serum concentrations decrease slowly, after the system is removed)

Side/Adverse Effects

Note: The frequencies of the adverse effects reported below were obtained in clinical studies in 510 patients (153 cancer patients, 56% of whom received treatment lasting from 30 days to more than a year, and 357 surgical patients who received the medication for 1 to 3 days), almost all of whom received supplemental doses of other opioid analgesic(s). The relative contribution of fentanyl, other opioid analgesic(s), the patient's underlying condition, and/or various surgical procedures to the occurrence of specific symptoms has not been established.

The risk of hypoventilation and of CNS adverse effects in opioid-naive individuals is increased when serum concentrations of fentanyl reach 2 nanograms per mL (nanograms/mL) (0.006 micromoles/liter [micromoles/L]) and more than 3 nanograms/mL (0.009 micromoles/L), respectively. The concentration at which toxicity occurs increases with increasing tolerance to the opioid analgesic.

In addition to the side/adverse effects listed below, a case of toxic delirium has been reported in an elderly patient receiving 125 mcg per hour of transdermal fentanyl together with other CNS depressants.

Physical dependence, with or without psychological dependence, may occur with chronic administration of fentanyl; an abstinence syndrome may occur when the medication is discontinued abruptly.

The following side/adverse effects have been selected on the basis of their potential clinical significance (possible signs and symptoms in parentheses where appropriate)—not necessarily inclusive:

Those indicating need for medical attention

Incidence more frequent (3 to 10%)

Apnea; CNS depression; difficult breathing; hypoventilation—respiratory rate < 8 breaths per minute, pCO_2 > 55 mm Hg; ***hallucinations*** (seeing, hearing, or feeling things that are not there); ***urinary retention*** (decreased frequency of urination; decrease in urine volume)

Note: The risk of *hypoventilation* is higher in nontolerant women than in men, in patients weighing less than 63 kg, in patients with pre-existing respiratory function impairment, and in patients receiving doses of 75 mcg per hour or higher.

Incidence less frequent (1 to 3%)

Chest pain; CNS effects (abnormal thinking; difficulty in speaking; fainting; problems with coordination or gait); ***paranoia*** (delusions of persecution, mistrust, suspiciousness, and/or combativeness)—frequency of CNS effects and paranoia symptoms is 1 to 3% in clinical studies; ***irregular heartbeat; localized skin reaction*** (redness, swelling, and/or bumps on the skin, with or without itching, at place of application); ***spitting blood***

Note: *Fainting* occurs more frequently in ambulatory than in recumbent patients and may be associated with postural hypotension. Localized reactions to the transdermal system are probably caused by the adhesive rather than by fentanyl. These reactions have been characterized as mild, transient (generally disappearing within 6 to 24 hours after removal of the transdermal system), and more typical of local irritation and occlusion than of allergic contact dermatitis. Generalized skin reactions also may occur; at least 1 case of diffuse, nonpruritic macular papules has been attributed to transdermal fentanyl therapy.

Incidence rare (less than 1%)

Abdominal distention (swelling of abdominal area); ***amblyopia*** (any change in vision); ***bladder pain; bradycardia*** (slow heartbeat); ***cessation of urination; CNS toxicity*** (inability to speak; depersonalization; stupor); ***dermatitis, exfoliative*** (fever with or without chills; red, thickened, orscaly skin; swollen and/or painful glands; unexplained bruising); ***fluid-filled blisters; frequent urge to urinate; respiratory problems, including asthma*** (noisy breathing; shortness of breath; troubled breathing; tightness in chest; wheezing)

Incidence not determined—Observed during clinical practice; estimates of frequency cannot be determined

Edema (decreased urination; rapid weight gain; bloating or swelling of face, hands, lower legs, and/or feet); ***tachycardia*** (fast, pounding, or irregular heartbeat or pulse)

Those indicating need for medical attention only if they continue or are bothersome

Incidence more frequent (each symptom 3% or higher)

CNS effects (anxiety; confusion; dizziness; drowsiness; false sense of well-being; nervousness; weakness); ***gastrointestinal effects*** (abdominal pain; constipation; diarrhea; indigestion; loss of appetite); ***headache; itching of skin; nausea; sweating; vomiting***

Note: *Nausea* and *vomiting* are more likely to occur in ambulatory than in recumbent patients. These effects may be induced by a direct effect on the chemoreceptor trigger zone in the CNS.

Incidence less frequent (1 to 3%)

Agitation (feeling anxious and restless); ***bloated feeling or gas; feeling of crawling, tingling, or burning of the skin; memory loss; unusual dreams***

Incidence not determined—Observed during clinical practice; estimates of frequency cannot be determined

Anorgasmia (not able to have an orgasm); ***blurred vision; decreased libido*** (loss in sexual ability, desire, drive, or performance; decreased interest in sexual intercourse; inability to have or keep an erection); ***ejaculatory difficulty; weight loss***

Those indicating possible withdrawal and the need for medical attention if they occur after medication is discontinued

Body aches; diarrhea; fast heartbeat; fever, runny nose, or sneezing; gooseflesh; increased sweating; increased yawning; loss of appetite; nausea or vomiting; nervousness, restlessness, or irritability; shivering or trembling; stomach cramps; trouble in sleeping; unusually large pupils; weakness

Note: Opioid withdrawal symptoms, such as nausea, vomiting, diarrhea, anxiety and shivering, are possible following a conversion or dose adjustment.

Overdose

For specific information on the agents used in the management of fentanyl overdose, see:

- *Atropine* in *Anticholinergics/Antispasmodics (Systemic)* monograph; and/or
- *Naloxone (Systemic)* monograph.

For more information on the management of overdose or unintentional ingestion, **contact a Poison Control Center** (see *Poison Control Listing*).

Clinical effects of overdose

Clinical effects of overdose

The following effects have been selected on the basis of their potential clinical significance (possible signs and symptoms in parentheses where appropriate)—not necessarily inclusive:

Acute and chronic

Cold, clammy skin; confusion; convulsions; severe dizziness, drowsiness, nervousness, restlessness, or weakness; low blood pressure; pinpoint pupils of eyes; slow heartbeat; slow or troubled breathing; unconsciousness

Treatment of overdose

General measures—Removing the transdermal system (if symptoms are judged sufficiently severe to warrant removal) and monitoring the patient, keeping in mind that fentanyl absorption continues and plasma concentrations decline slowly after the system has been removed. Prolonged monitoring may be needed.

Specific treatment—

For hypoventilation:

Verbal stimulation or waking the patient (if bradypnea occurs during sleep) may be sufficient to increase the respiratory rate and provide adequate ventilation.

Use of the opioid antagonist naloxone if necessary. However, usual doses of naloxone may reverse analgesia and precipitate withdrawal in opioid-dependent patients. Since naloxone's duration of action is considerably shorter than that of transdermal fentanyl, administration via continuous intravenous infusion at a rate titrated to the needs of the individual patient may be necessary.

For bradycardia: Use of atropine.

For hypotension: Use of intravenous fluids and/or vasopressors and using other supportive measures as needed.

Supportive care—May include establishing adequate respiratory exchange through provision of a patent airway and institution of assisted or controlled respiration.

Patient Consultation

As an aid to patient consultation, refer to *Advice for the Patient, Fentanyl (Transdermal-Systemic)*.

In providing consultation, consider emphasizing the following selected information (» = major clinical significance):

Before using this medication

» Conditions affecting use, especially:

Hypersensitivity to fentanyl, alfentanil, or sufentanil, or any components of the product

Pregnancy—Opioids cross the placenta; use by pregnant women may cause physical dependence in the fetus and withdrawal symptoms and/or respiratory depression in the neonate; should take into account risk/benefit considerations

Breast-feeding—Fentanyl is distributed into breast milk; opioid effects including sedation, respiratory depression, and physical dependence may occur in the infant if the mother is receiving chronic, high-dose therapy; not recommended for use in nursing women

Use in children—Safety not established in children under 2 years of age; should be administered to children only if they are opioid-tolerant and 2 years of age or older

Iontophoretic transdermal system—Safety and efficacy not established in children less than 18 years of age

Use in the elderly—Geriatric patients are more susceptible to the effects of opioids, especially respiratory depression; may need lower dose initiation

Other medications, especially alcohol or other CNS depressants (including other opioid analgesics), CYP3A inducers (such as carbamazepine, phenytoin or rifampin), CYP3A inhibitors (such as ketoconazole, itraconazole, clarithromycin, erythromycin, troleandomycin, nelfinavir, or ritonavir) and naltrexone

Other medical problems, especially acute or severe bronchial asthma, pulmonary disease, or other acute or chronic respiratory problems, CAT scan, cardioversion, defibrillation, MRI procedure, x-ray scan, coma, head injury, impaired consciousness, increased intracranial pressure (pre-existing), intracranial lesions, diarrhea caused by poisoning or antibiotic therapy, opioid intolerance, paralytic ileus (known or suspected), or severe inflammatory bowel disease

Proper use of this medication

» Reading patient instructions carefully before using

» Importance of healthcare personnel testing iontophoretic transdermal system prior to application

» Importance of patient understanding and following instructions for iontophoretic transdermal system

» Importance of using in opioid-tolerant patients ONLY

» Advising patients that fentanyl has a high potential for abuse; importance of adhering to prescribed doses

» Proper application technique

Keeping medication in sealed pouch until ready to apply

Using caution in handling; not touching adhesive surface with the hand; washing area with clear water if medication does touch the skin in an unintended location

Using care not to damage (puncture or tear) the surface of the transdermal system

Applying to clean, dry skin area of upper arm or torso that is free of oil, hair, scars, cuts, burns, or irritation; avoiding areas that have been irradiated

Clipping, not shaving, hair at application site, if necessary

If cleansing site prior to application, using only clear water (not soaps, lotions, or cleansers that contain oils, alcohol, or other agents) and allowing area to dry completely prior to application

Removing liner from adhesive layer, then pressing system in place with palm of hand for a minimum of 30 seconds; making sure that good contact is achieved, especially around the edges

If the patch does not stick well or loosens after application, tape the edges down with first aid tape

If the patch falls off after application, discard it and apply a new patch on a different skin site

If dose requires applying 2 or more systems, keeping them far enough apart so that the edges do not touch or overlap

Washing hands with clear water after applying or handling transdermal system

Removing system after 3 days; applying next system, if treatment is being continued, at new site, preferably on opposite side of the body; not reusing a site for at least 3 days

Disposing of used or unneeded systems by folding in half with adhesive layer inside the fold, then flushing down the toilet

» Not using more transdermal fentanyl than directed, even if medication appears ineffective; onset of action may require 24 hours or longer and several dosage adjustments may be required to achieve maximum effectiveness

» Taking "rescue" doses of short-acting opioid for first few days after initiation of therapy and for breakthrough pain, but not using more than prescribed because of danger of overdose

» Proper dosing

Missed dose: Applying as soon as possible

» Proper storage

Precautions while using this medication

Regular consultations with health care professional during long-term therapy

» Removing iontophoretic transdermal system before discharge from hospital

Not allowing others to activate fentanyl dose with iontophoretic transdermal system

» Telling nurse of any high frequency hearing impairment due to audible tones used to detect errors in dosing with iontophoretic transdermal system

» Checking with health care professional before increasing dose of transdermal fentanyl and/or "rescue" medication if treatment becomes less effective

» Avoiding use of alcoholic beverages or other CNS depressants during therapy, unless prescribed or otherwise approved by physician

» Caution if dizziness, drowsiness, lightheadedness, or false sense of well-being occurs; checking with health care professional if severe drowsiness persists for more than a few days

» Getting up slowly from a lying or sitting position; lying down for a while may provide relief if patient becomes dizzy, lightheaded, or faint

Caution that nausea or vomiting may occur, especially during first several days of treatment, and may be relieved by lying down; checking with health care professional if severe, since an antiemetic may be needed

» Compliance with regimen for preventing severe constipation, if prescribed

» Avoiding external sources of heat (e.g., heating pad, sunlamps, heated water beds, electric blankets, sunbathing, prolonged baths or showers in hot water) and checking with health care professional if fever occurs; absorption of fentanyl may be accelerated

» Importance of transdermal fentanyl being used only by the patient for whom it is prescribed; protecting fentanyl from theft or misuse

» *Removing fentanyl iontophoretic transdermal patches prior to an MRI procedure, cardioversion defibrillation, X-rays or CAT scans*

» Informing physician or dentist of use of medication if any kind of surgery (including dental surgery) or emergency treatment is required

System may be worn while bathing, showering, or swimming, but should not be rubbed vigorously because it may become loose or detached; discarding system and applying a new one in an alternate, dry location if this occurs

» Not discontinuing medication abruptly after prolonged use; checking with physician instead, since gradual withdrawal may be needed to minimize risk of precipitating abstinence syndrome

» To prevent accidental ingestion by children: Using caution when choosing the application site and monitoring the adhesion of the system closely

» If the patch comes off and accidentally sticks to the skin of another person: Importance of taking patch off immediately, washing the exposed area with water, and seeking medical attention for the accidentally exposed individual

» Suspected overdose: Getting emergency help at once

» Understanding proper disposal protocol

Side/adverse effects

Getting emergency help if symptoms of overdose occur, i.e., very slow (fewer than 8 breaths per minute) or troubled breathing, extreme drowsiness, convulsions, low blood pressure, or slow heartbeat

Other potential side effects, especially hallucinations or other CNS effects, urinary retention, chest pain, irregular heartbeat, localized skin reactions, skin rash or blisters, spitting blood, abdominal distention, amblyopia, bladder pain, bradycardia, exfoliative dermatitis, urinary frequency, edema and tachycardia

General Dosing Information

Transdermal fentanyl may cause respiratory depression, especially in elderly, very ill, or debilitated patients and patients with pre-existing respiratory problems. Lower doses may be required for these patients, at least initially. However, elderly patients may also be more sensitive to the analgesic effects of opioid analgesics, and lower doses may be sufficient to provide effective analgesia.

Since the peak fentanyl levels occur between 24 and 72 hours of treatment, prescribers should be aware that serious or life threatening hypoventilation may occur, even in opioid-tolerant patients, during the initial application period.

The iontophoretic transdermal system is for hospital use only. Medical personnel must remove the system prior to discharge from the hospital.

Only patients able to understand and follow instructions given to operate the iontophoretic transdermal system should use it. Only the patient should activate the system under the supervision and direction of healthcare professionals.

Before initiating dosing with the fentanyl iontophoretic transdermal system, patients should be titrated to an acceptable level of analgesia.

Dosage must be individualized. Pre-existing tolerance to opioid analgesics is the primary factor to be considered in determining the appropriate initial dose of transdermal fentanyl. The rate at which tolerance develops varies widely among individuals. For patients who have been receiving chronic therapy with another opioid analgesic, initial dosage of transdermal fentanyl should be based on the patient's daily opioid requirement.

The transdermal system should be kept in the protective packaging until it is used. It should be applied to a dry, flat, nonirritated, non-irradiated skin surface of the upper arm or torso. If necessary, hair at the application site may be clipped (but not shaved) prior to application. Also, if the site is cleansed prior to application, clear water should be used; soaps, oils, lotions, alcohol, or other agents that may irritate the skin or change its characteristics should be avoided. The system should be pressed firmly in place with the palm of the hand for about 30 seconds, making sure that contact is complete, especially around the edges.

Instructions for applying the iontophoretic transdermal system:

• Should be applied to intact, skin that is not irritated nor irradiated on the chest or upper outer arm.

• It should not be placed on abnormal skin sites, such as scars, burns, or tattoos.

• The application site should be clipped (not shaved) of any excessive hair before the system is applied.

• Wipe the site with a standard alcohol swab and allow the skin to dry completely.

• Do not used any soaps, oils, lotions or other agents that might irritate the skin or alter its absorption.

• The RN should write the time and date the system is applied to the patient on the sticker which is transferred to the transdermal system for the purpose of tracking the 24-hour time parameter for shift changes.

• Open the pouch with using scissors to cut along the dotted line.

• Remove and discard only the clear plastic liner covering the adhesive.

• Take care not to pull on the red tab while removing the clear plastic liner. The red tab is only to be used when separating the system for disposal.

• Press firmly in place with the sticky side down on the skin for at least 15 seconds and press around the outer edges to make sure the system sticks to the skin.

Because of the delayed onset of action after initial application of a fentanyl transdermal system, the adequacy of analgesia cannot be evaluated for 24 hours. A short-acting opioid analgesic must be administered as needed to relieve pain. If necessary, a higher dose may be applied for the second 72 hours, based on the quantity of supplemental opioid required during the second or third day of the first 72-hour application. Subsequent increases in dosage, if needed, should be made at 6-day intervals, with "rescue" doses continuing to be administered as needed until maximum analgesia has been attained. Some patients may require "rescue" dosing with a short-acting opioid analgesic for breakthrough pain throughout transdermal fentanyl therapy.

Some patients may not achieve adequate analgesia using a 72 hour dosing interval and may require systems to be applied every 48 hours. However, an increase in the fentanyl dose should be evaluated before reducing the dosing interval.

The fentanyl transdermal system should be removed after 72 hours. If treatment is being continued, a new system should be applied at a new site after the prior one has been removed.

The iontophoretic transdermal system should be removed after 24 hours or after 80 doses have been administered, whichever comes first. At this time, the system will become deactivated and the LED light will flash. If additional analgesia is required, a new system should be applied to a different skin site after removal and disposal of the previous system.

Concurrent administration of a nonopioid analgesic (such as aspirin or other salicylates, other nonsteroidal anti-inflammatory drugs, or acetaminophen) with opioid analgesics provides additive analgesia and may permit lower doses of the opioid analgesic to be utilized.

The overall treatment regimen for chronic pain patients who are receiving long-term opioid analgesic therapy includes management of common side effects such as sedation, nausea and vomiting, and constipation. An antiemetic may be needed, especially during the first few weeks of therapy. Also, measures to prevent constipation and decrease the risk of intestinal obstruction may be needed, such as administration of a laxative (a bowel stimulant and/or a stool softener), a high fluid intake, and an increase in dietary fiber. Appropriate medications and dosages must be determined according to the physical condition and the needs of the individual patient.

Increases in the dosage of transdermal fentanyl and/or "rescue" medications may be required as tolerance to the medication develops or increases and/or the intensity of pain increases. Tolerance to the respiratory depressant effects of an opioid analgesic develops concurrently with tolerance to its analgesic effects. Careful adjustment of dosage as required to provide adequate analgesia is not likely to increase the risk of respiratory depression. However, a reduction in dose may be needed to prevent respiratory depression, which may occur even at a previously well-tolerated opioid dose, if the intensity of pain decreases because of changes in the patient's condition or institution of other pain-relieving treatments.

Psychological and physical dependence may occur with chronic administration of an opioid analgesic; an abstinence syndrome may occur when the medication is discontinued. However, physical dependence in patients receiving prolonged therapy for severe chronic pain rarely leads to true addiction, i.e., a desire to continue taking the medication (for its euphoric effect) after it is no longer required for pain relief. **Fear of causing addiction should not result in failure to provide adequate pain relief,** although caution is advised if patient predisposition toward drug abuse is known or strongly suspected. Reducing the dose gradually prior to discontinuation may minimize the development of withdrawal symptoms following prolonged use.

If a patient is being changed from transdermal fentanyl to another opioid analgesic, the transdermal system should be removed and the new analgesic administered in a low dose that may be gradually increased according to the patient's report of pain until adequate analgesia is achieved. The fact that fentanyl concentrations decrease very slowly after removal of the system must be considered when selecting a starting dose of the new agent. Also, the oral morphine–to–transdermal fentanyl conversion ratios recommended by the manufacturer for determining initial doses of transdermal fentanyl for opioid-tolerant patients are very conservative. Using the reverse of these ratios to calculate an appropriate dose of a subsequently administered opioid could result in an overdose and is not recommended.

Safety considerations for handling this medication

The transdermal system is supplied in sealed systems that pose little risk of exposure to health care personnel. If any of the gel in the reservoir should contact the skin, the area should be flushed with copious quantities of water. Soap, alcohol, or other solvents may enhance penetration of fentanyl through the skin and should not be used.

The iontophoretic transdermal system should be disposed of by medical staff in accordance with state and federal regulations for controlled substances. The system should be removed carefully and only by the sides and top housing. To dispose of:

- Using gloves, pull the red tab to separate the bottom from the top housing.
- Fold the bottom hydrogel-containing housing in half with the sticky side facing in.
- Dispose of the folded over bottom housing which contains the residual fentanyl by flushing this part down the toilet. This step should be witnessed by a second health care provider.
- Dispose of top housing, containing electronics, according to hospital procedures for battery-containing waste.

Transdermal Dosage Forms

FENTANYL IONTOPHORETIC TRANSDERMAL SYSTEM

Usual adult dose

Acute postoperative pain—

Iontophoretically-delivered transdermal, delivers 40 micrograms (mcg) of fentanyl over a 10-minute period using a low electrical current and provides a maximum of six 10-minute doses per hour for 24 hours or delivers a maximum of 80 doses (3.2 milligrams), whichever occurs first.

Note: To discontinue fentanyl iontophoretic transdermal system and convert patients to another opioid or other analgesic—Remove the system and titrate the dose of the new analgesic, based upon the patient's report of pain, until adequate analgesia has been obtained. Using caution, due to the fact that serum fentanyl concentration will decrease, slowly following removal of the system.

Usual adult prescribing limits

Six 40-mcg doses per hour

Up to three consecutive systems used sequentially for a maximum of 72 hours of therapy

Usual pediatric dose

Safety and efficacy have not been studied in children less than 18 years of age.

Strength(s) usually available

U.S.—

10.8 mg fentanyl hydrochloride (Rx) [*Ionsys* (cetylpyridinium chloride; citric acid; polacrilin; polyvinyl alcohol; sodium citrate; sodium chloride; sodium hydroxide; purified water)].

Packaging and storage

Store at 25 °C (77 °F), excursions permitted to 15 to 30°C (59 to 86 °F).

Preparation of dosage form

Testing instructions—

Prior to dispensing while still in the sealed pouch, the pharmacist or pharmacy technician should:

- Hold the unopened foil pouch that contains the transdermal system
- The button side of transdermal patch is indicated on pouch label
- Run finger along the system until you feel the recessed button on one end
- Firmly press and release the button twice (double click) within 3 seconds
- Listen for a single beep, confirming that the system is functional and dispensable. If no tone is heard, the system is non-functional and should not be dispensed
- Hospital pharmacist should sign the front of pouch after performing functionality test. Sticker on the back is intended for use by the registered nurse.

Following the single beep based on the functionality test, a normally operating system will also beep for 15 seconds after 4 minutes. This indicates that it is not in contact with the skin. Therefore, a functional system is confirmed by a single beep and/or 15 seconds of beeps after pressing the button.

Note: No drug is delivered from the system unless the patch is applied to the skin. Therefore, 80 doses and 24 hours of use are still available after the functionality test is performed.

If neither the single button emits nor the 15 seconds of beeping after 4 minutes occurs, the system may be nonfunctional. It should not be opened or dispensed to the patient. See the Ionsys™ package insert for more information regarding product returns or troubleshooting.

Auxiliary labeling

- Only for in-hospital use

Caution

Fentanyl iontophoretic transdermal patches are intended for transdermal use (on intact skin) only. Inappropriate use of these patches leading to ingestion or contact with mucous membranes or unintended exposure to the fentanyl hydrogel could lead to the absorption of a potentially fatal dose of fentanyl. Therefore, the hydrogels should not come into contact with fingers or mouth.

If a hydrogel drug reservoir is touched accidentally, rinse the area thoroughly with water. Do not use soap, alcohol, or other solvents to remove the hydrogel as they may enhance the drug's ability to penetrate the skin.

Fentanyl iontophoretic transdermal patches contain metal parts and *must be removed before an MRI procedure, cardioversion, or defibrillation* to avoid damage to the system from the strong electromagnetic fields set up by these procedures. These patches *may also interfere with an X-ray image or CAT scan* due to the radio-opaque components. However, they will not interfere with other electromechanical devices like pacemakers or electrical monitoring equipment.

FENTANYL TRANSDERMAL SYSTEM

Note: The doses and strengths of the fentanyl transdermal system are expressed in terms of the delivery rate in mcg per hour.

Usual adult dose

Analgesic—

For chronic pain: Transdermal, the appropriate number of transdermal systems to be applied and kept in place for seventy-two hours.

For patients who are not opioid-tolerant—Not more than one transdermal system rated to deliver 25 mcg (0.025 mg) per hour, initially. Dosage may be increased gradually as needed and tolerated until an adequate response has been attained.

For opioid-tolerant patients—Initially, a quantity of fentanyl (in mcg per hour) equivalent to the patient's current twenty-four-hour oral morphine requirement, as follows:

Fentanyl (mcg/hr)	Morphine* (mg/24 hr) Oral
25	60–134
50	135–224
75	225–314
100	315–404
125	405–494
150	495–584
175	585–674
200	675–764
225	765–854
250	855–944
275	945–1034
300	1035–1124

Note: The oral morphine-to-transdermal fentanyl conversion ratios listed above are conservative; the need for an increase in dose should be anticipated. After 3 days, the initial dose may be increased based on the daily dose of supplemental opioid analgesics required by the patient during the second or third day of the initial application. Six days may be required to reach equilibrium after each increase in dose; therefore, the higher dose should be worn for two seventy-two-hour applications before further increases are made. Appropriate dosage increments, based on the daily dose of supplementary opioids, using the ratio of 45 mg per 24 hours of oral morphine to a 12.5 mcg per hour increase in fentanyl transdermal dose. If necessary, more than one transdermal system may be applied at a time.

A few patients may need replacement of the transdermal system(s) every forty-eight hours. Before the interval between applications is decreased, an attempt should be made to maintain the seventy-two-hour interval. Dosing intervals less than every seventy-two hours are not recommended in children and adolescents.

* A 10-mg intramuscular (IM) dose of morphine is therapeutically equivalent to 30 mg of chronically administered oral morphine or 60 mg of intermittently administered oral morphine. For patients who are receiving opioid analgesics other than morphine, the patient's twenty-four-hour opioid requirement should be determined, then converted to the equianalgesic oral morphine dose. The following quantities are equivalent to 30 mg of chronically administered oral morphine or 60 mg of intermittently administered oral morphine:

For buprenorphine—300 mcg (0.3 mg) IM.
For butorphanol—2 mg IM.
For codeine—200 mg orally; 130 mg IM.
For dezocine—10 mg IM.
For hydromorphone—7.5 mg orally; 1.5 mg IM.
For levorphanol—4 mg orally; 2 mg IM.
For meperidine—75 mg IM.
For methadone—20 mg orally; 10 mg IM.
For oxycodone—30 mg orally; 15 mg IM.
For oxymorphone—1 mg IM; 10 mg rectally.
For pentazocine—180 mg orally; 60 mg IM.

Note: This table should not be used to convert from fentanyl to other analgesic therapies. Use of the above table can overestimate the dosage of the new agent. Overdosage of the new analgesic agent is possible.

Usual pediatric dose

The safety of transdermal fentanyl has not been established in children under 2 years of age. Transdermal fentanyl should be administered to children only if they are opioid-tolerant and 2 years of age or older. Pediatric patients initiating therapy on a 25 mcg per hour fentanyl transdermal system should be receiving at least 60 mg oral morphine equivalents per day.

Usual geriatric dose

See *Usual adult dose*

Note: It is recommended that initial dosage not exceed 25 mcg (0.025 mg) per hour unless the patient has been receiving chronic therapy with more than 135 mg per day of oral morphine or an equivalent dose of another opioid analgesic.

Strength(s) usually available

U.S.—

12 mcg (0.012 mg) per hour (a total of 1.25 mg of fentanyl per 5 square centimeters [cm ^{2}]) (Rx) [*Duragesic*].

25 mcg (0.025 mg) per hour (a total of 2.5 mg of fentanyl per 10 square centimeters [cm ^{2}]) (Rx) [*Duragesic* (alcohol 0.1 mL)].

50 mcg (0.05 mg) per hour (a total of 5 mg of fentanyl per 20 cm ^{2}) (Rx) [*Duragesic* (alcohol 0.2 mL)].

75 mcg (0.075 mg) per hour (a total of 7.5 mg of fentanyl per 30 cm ^{2}) (Rx) [*Duragesic* (alcohol 0.3 mL)].

100 mcg (0.1 mg) per hour (a total of 10 mg of fentanyl per 40 cm ^{2}) (Rx) [*Duragesic* (alcohol 0.4 mL)].

Canada—

25 mcg (0.025 mg) per hour (a total of 2.5 mg of fentanyl per 10 cm ^{2}) (Rx) [*Duragesic* (alcohol 0.1 mL)].

50 mcg (0.05 mg) per hour (a total of 5 mg of fentanyl per 20 cm ^{2}) (Rx) [*Duragesic* (alcohol 0.2 mL)].

75 mcg (0.075 mg) per hour (a total of 7.5 mg of fentanyl per 30 cm ^{2}) (Rx) [*Duragesic* (alcohol 0.3 mL)].

100 mcg (0.1 mg) per hour (a total of 10 mg of fentanyl per 40 cm ^{2}) (Rx) [*Duragesic* (alcohol 0.4 mL)].

Packaging and storage

Store below 25 °C (77 °F), unless otherwise specified by manufacturer.

Auxiliary labeling

- May cause drowsiness.
- Avoid alcoholic beverages.
- Keep out of reach of children
- External use only
- May be habit-forming.
- Dispose properly by removing and folding sticky sides together. Discard away from children and pets.

Caution

Fentanyl transdermal patches are intended for transdermal use (on intact skin) only. Using damaged or cut fentanyl transdermal patches can lead to the rapid release of the content of the patch and absorption of a potentially fatal dose of fentanyl.

If the gel from the drug reservoir of a fentanyl transdermal patch accidentally contacts the skin, the area should be washed with copious amounts of water. Do not use soap, alcohol, or other solvents to remove the gel because they may enhance the drug's ability to penetrate the skin.

While using fentanyl transdermal systems, heat sources such as heating pads, electric blankets, heat lamps, saunas, hot tubs, heated waterbeds, long hot baths and sunbathing should all be avoided. There is a potential for temperature-dependent increases in fentanyl released from the system resulting in possible overdose and death.

Selected Bibliography

Calis KA, Kohler DR, Corso DM. Transdermally administered fentanyl for pain management. Clin Pharm 1992; 11: 22-36.

Yee LY, Lopez JR. Transdermal fentanyl. Ann Pharmacother 1992; 26: 1393-9.

Payne R. Transdermal fentanyl: Suggested recommendations for clinical use. J Pain Symptom Manage 1992; 7 No 3 (suppl): S40-S44.

Revised: 07/31/2006
Developed: 06/29/1994

FENTANYL DERIVATIVES Systemic

This monograph includes information on the following: 1) Alfentanil; 2) Fentanyl; 3) Sufentanil.

VA CLASSIFICATION (Primary/Secondary): CN101/CN206

Note: Controlled substance classification

U.S.: Schedule II

Canada: N

Commonly used brand name(s): *Alfenta*[1]; *Sublimaze*[2]; *Sufenta*[3].

Note: For a listing of dosage forms and brand names by country availability, see *Dosage Forms* section(s).

Category

Anesthesia adjunct (opioid analgesic)—Alfentanil; Fentanyl; Sufentanil.
Analgesic—Fentanyl; Sufentanil

Indications

Note: Bracketed information in the *Indications* section refers to uses that are not included in U.S. product labeling.

Accepted

Anesthesia, general or local adjunct—Fentanyl and its derivatives are indicated as opioid analgesic supplements to general anesthesia. During surgery, they are often used in conjunction with other agents, such as a combination of an ultrashort-acting barbiturate, a neuromuscular blocking agent, and an inhalation anesthetic (usually nitrous oxide), for the maintenance of "balanced" anesthesia.

Fentanyl and its derivatives are also indicated as primary agents for the induction of anesthesia in patients undergoing general surgery.

[Fentanyl][1] is indicated as an anesthetic agent during surgery in neonates.

Fentanyl and sufentanil are also indicated as primary agents for the maintenance of anesthesia in selected patients undergoing major surgery. In these cases, they are administered in high doses with 100% oxygen or nitrous oxide plus oxygen and a neuromuscular blocking agent.

Fentanyl [and sufentanil][1] are indicated to provide neuroleptanalgesia (in conjunction with a neuroleptic agent such as droperidol) or neuroleptanesthesia (in conjunction with a neuroleptic agent and nitrous oxide).

Alfentanil[1], fentanyl, [and sufentanil][1] are indicated as the analgesic supplements to regional or local anesthesia in a monitored anesthesia setting.

Fentanyl is approved by U.S. and Canadian regulatory agencies for use as presurgical medication. However, because of its short duration of action (following administration of single analgesic doses), fentanyl may be less desirable than longer-acting opioid analgesics for this purpose.

Pain, postoperative (treatment)—Fentanyl and [sufentanil] are indicated for prevention or relief of pain in the immediate postoperative period.

Pain, obstetrical (treatment)—Sufentanil is indicated for epidural administration, in combination with low-dose bupivacaine, for prevention or relief of the pain of labor and vaginal delivery.

[Sedation and analgesia][1]—Fentanyl is indicated to provide analgesia and/or sedation during mechanical ventilation in neonates.

Acceptance not established

Fentanyl has been studied for the facilitation of Broviac catheter placement and endotracheal intubation in neonates. However, there are insufficient data to establish its efficacy for these indications; therefore, further studies are warranted.

Unaccepted

Alfentanil has also been investigated for use as the primary agent, administered in conjunction with 100% oxygen and a neuromuscular blocking agent, for the maintenance of anesthesia in selected patients undergoing cardiovascular surgery. However, the patient must be heavily premedicated and continuous intravenous infusion of extremely high doses is required.

---

[1]Not included in Canadian product labeling.

Pharmacology/Pharmacokinetics

Physicochemical characteristics

Molecular weight—
- Alfentanil hydrochloride: 471.
- Fentanyl citrate: 528.61.
- Sufentanil citrate: 578.69.

pKa—
- Alfentanil: 6.5.
- Fentanyl: 8.43.
- Sufentanil: 8.01.

Partition coefficient—
Alfentanil hydrochloride: 130.
Fentanyl citrate: 816.
Sufentanil citrate: 1727.

Mechanism of action/Effect

Low to moderate doses of fentanyl and its derivatives produce analgesia. During surgery, analgesic actions provide dose-related protection against hemodynamic responses to surgical stress; however, patient responsiveness to the pharmacodynamic actions of these medications is highly variable. Although high doses of these medications produce loss of consciousness, the ability of opioid analgesics (when used alone) to induce a true anesthetic state has been questioned.

Opioid analgesics bind with stereospecific receptors at many sites within the central nervous system (CNS) to alter processes affecting both the perception of and emotional response to pain. Although the precise sites and mechanisms of action have not been fully determined, alterations in the release of various neurotransmitters from afferent nerves sensitive to painful stimuli may be partially responsible for the analgesic effects.

It has been proposed that there are multiple subtypes of opioid receptors, each mediating various therapeutic and/or side effects of opioid drugs. The actions of an opioid analgesic may therefore depend upon whether it acts as a full agonist or a partial agonist or is inactive at each type of receptor. Fentanyl and its derivatives probably produce their effects via agonist actions at the mu receptor.

Other actions/effects

Fentanyl and its derivatives may produce signs and symptoms common to opioid analgesics including respiratory depression (characterized by decreases in respiratory rate, tidal volume, minute ventilation, and ventilatory response to carbon dioxide), ureteral spasm, biliary spasm, decreased gastrointestinal motility, euphoria, miosis, hypotension, and bradycardia. However, unlike many other opioid analgesics, fentanyl and its derivatives have not been shown to cause histamine release (in doses used clinically).

Fentanyl and its derivatives, especially in moderate or high doses, may induce skeletal muscle rigidity.

Fentanyl and its derivatives may produce a dose-related decrease in certain hormonal responses during surgery, such as increased blood concentrations of circulating growth hormone, catecholamines, cortisol, antidiuretic hormone, and prolactin. However, alfentanil's effects on endocrine responses to surgical stimulation have not been fully evaluated. Also, in patients undergoing coronary bypass surgery, these agents may not suppress such endocrine responses, especially increased catecholamine concentrations, during the period of cardiopulmonary bypass.

Volume of distribution

Alfentanil—Usually 0.4 to 1 liter per kg of body weight but subject to interpatient variability; values ranging from 0.23 to 2.47 liters per kg of body weight have been reported. The volume of distribution may be increased during aortocoronary bypass or decreased in children, but is not altered by obesity or hepatic function impairment. However, the distribution volume of total alfentanil (but not of the unbound [free] fraction) may be increased in patients with renal failure.

Fentanyl—Usually 4 liters per kg of body weight, although values ranging from 3.1 to 7.8 liters per kg of body weight have been reported.

Sufentanil—1.08 to 2.78 liters per kg of body weight.

Note: Fentanyl and its derivatives readily cross the blood-brain barrier; however, because of alfentanil's lower degree of lipophilicity (and therefore lower degree of tissue binding) and its lower pKa, alfentanil reaches receptors in the brain significantly more rapidly than fentanyl.

Fentanyl and sufentanil are rapidly distributed to body tissues. The relatively poor blood flow to fatty tissues limits the rate of the medications' accumulation in these tissues. However, accumulation in body fat, as well as in other tissues, may occur with large or multiple doses or prolonged administration. Clearance of either of these agents from tissues may result in therapeutic blood concentrations being maintained following discontinuation of administration, leading to a prolonged duration of action.

Alfentanil is also rapidly distributed to body tissues. Although accumulation of alfentanil may occur with prolonged continuous infusion or with repeated administration of single doses and may lead to a prolonged duration of action, alfentanil's accumulation in body tissues is significantly less than that of fentanyl or sufentanil. Therefore, alfentanil's duration of action is less likely than that of fentanyl or sufentanil to be substantially prolonged by clearance from body tissues.

Protein binding

Alfentanil—About 92%; primarily to glycoproteins (especially alpha-1-acid glycoprotein [AAG]). Although independent of alfentanil plasma concentration or plasma pH, alfentanil protein binding is subject to interpatient variability and may be decreased in patients with alcoholic hepatic cirrhosis or renal failure and during cardiopulmonary bypass.

Fentanyl—80 to 89%, primarily to albumin and lipoproteins; dependent on plasma pH.

Sufentanil—92.5%, primarily to AAG; independent of sufentanil plasma concentration but highly dependent on plasma pH.

Biotransformation

Hepatic; sufentanil may also undergo some metabolism in the small intestine. Alfentanil, fentanyl, and sufentanil are oxidized by the cytochrome P450 3A4 isoenzyme. The rate of metabolism is dependent on total dosage, hepatic function, and factors affecting hepatic blood flow (possibly including certain surgical manipulations or, to a much lesser extent, concurrent use of a potent inhalation anesthetic). The rate of fentanyl or sufentanil metabolism is also dependent on the rate of its release from various body tissues. The rate of alfentanil metabolism is decreased in geriatric patients, obese patients, and patients with hepatic function impairment. In addition, genetic polymorphism has been suspected as a cause of unusually slow alfentanil metabolism in a few patients.

Half-life

Alfentanil—
- Triphasic (with a dose of 50 or 125 mcg per kg of body weight):
  - Distribution—0.4 to 3.1 minutes.
  - Redistribution—4.6 to 21.6 minutes.
  - Elimination—Generally 1 to 2.1 hours, although values well outside this range have been reported. The elimination half-life is not altered in patients with renal failure but may be decreased in children. Also, the elimination half-life is highly dependent on factors affecting the rate of metabolism. Increased values have been reported in patients with reduced hepatic function (up to 4.9 hours in asymptomatic patients with abnormal liver function test values and up to 5.8 hours in patients with active hepatic [alcoholic] cirrhosis), geriatric patients (about 2.3 hours), and obese patients (about 3 hours).

Fentanyl—
- Triphasic (with a dose of 6.4 mcg per kg of body weight):
  - Distribution—1.7 minutes.

Redistribution—13 minutes.
Elimination—3.6 hours; may be greatly prolonged during and following cardiopulmonary bypass and in geriatric patients. One study showed an average elimination half-life of 15.75 hours following administration of 10 mcg per kg of body weight to patients 60 years of age or older.

Sufentanil—
Triphasic (with a dose of 5 mcg per kg of body weight):
Distribution—1.4 minutes.
Redistribution—18 minutes.
Elimination—2.7 hours; may be greatly prolonged during and following cardiopulmonary bypass.

Onset of action

Alfentanil—
Analgesic effects (anesthesia adjunct doses):
Within 1 minute.
Time to loss of consciousness (induction doses):
Dependent on rate of administration; generally within 1 to 2 minutes.

Fentanyl—
Analgesic effects (anesthesia adjunct doses):
Intramuscular—7 to 15 minutes.
Intravenous—1 to 2 minutes.
Time to loss of consciousness (induction doses):
Dependent on rate of administration; 4 to 5 minutes when administered intravenously at a rate of 400 mcg per minute.

Sufentanil—
Analgesic effects:
Anesthesia adjunct doses—Within 1 minute.
Epidural use in obstetrics—Within 10 minutes.
Time to loss of consciousness (induction doses):
Dependent on rate of administration; 1 to 1.6 minutes when administered intravenously at a rate of 300 mcg per minute.

Note: The time to loss of consciousness with induction doses of these medications may be substantially decreased by premedication with a benzodiazepine.

Therapeutic plasma concentration

Requirements are highly subject to interpatient variability and dependent on the intensity of the surgical stimulus. With alfentanil, it has been shown that the highest plasma concentrations are required near the beginning of surgery (with intubation requiring higher concentrations than incision) and the lowest toward the end of surgery (i.e., during skin closure). Studies of therapeutic plasma concentrations of fentanyl or sufentanil required for different types of surgery, or at different times during a surgical procedure, have not been done.

For use of alfentanil as a supplement to inhalation (nitrous oxide/oxygen) anesthesia—
For superficial surgery: 100 to > 300 nanograms per mL.
For intra-abdominal surgery: 310 to > 400 nanograms per mL.

Time to peak effect

Alfentanil—
Single analgesic dose of up to 500 mcg:
Within 1.5 to 2 minutes (for both analgesia and respiratory depression).

Fentanyl—
Analgesic effects:
Intramuscular—20 to 30 minutes.
Intravenous—3 to 5 minutes.
Respiratory depressant effects:
5 to 15 minutes following administration of a single intravenous dose.

Duration of action

Alfentanil—
Analgesic effects (single dose of up to 500 mcg):
5 to 10 minutes.
Time to awakening (when used as a supplement to nitrous oxide/oxygen anesthesia):
Usually within 10 minutes following the end of surgery when administered either as single injections or as a variable-rate infusion that is discontinued approximately 15 minutes before the end of surgery.

Note: Alfentanil's duration of action may be decreased in children.

Fentanyl—
Analgesic effects (anesthesia adjunct doses):
Intramuscular—1 to 2 hours.
Intravenous—0.5 to 1 hour (single dose of up to 100 mcg).
Time to awakening (high doses):
0.7 to 3.5 hours following an average total dose of 122 mcg per kg of body weight.

Sufentanil—
Analgesic effects:
Anesthesia adjunct doses—5 minutes.
Epidural use in obstetrics—95 minutes (initial dose); 70 minutes (subsequent doses).
Time to awakening (high doses):
0.7 to 2.9 hours following an average total dose of 12.9 mcg per kg of body weight.

Note: The duration of action of fentanyl and its derivatives is dose-dependent. The effects of a low to moderate single dose of any of these medications are terminated rapidly because of redistribution.

With high or multiple doses or prolonged administration of fentanyl or sufentanil, the duration of action is prolonged because substantial plasma concentrations of these agents may be maintained during their clearance from tissue storage sites (although accumulation of sufentanil is less than that of fentanyl). Accumulation of alfentanil resulting in a prolonged duration of action may occur with prolonged continuous infusion or, to a lesser extent, with repeated administration of single injections during lengthy surgical procedures. However, because accumulation of alfentanil in body tissues is significantly less extensive than that of fentanyl or sufentanil, alfentanil's duration of action after multiple doses or prolonged continuous infusion is more highly dependent on total body clearance than on redistribution and subsequent removal from tissue storage sites. Therefore, alfentanil's duration of action may be affected to a greater extent than that of fentanyl or sufentanil by factors that tend to decrease the rate of metabolism (see *Biotransformation*).

When fentanyl or sufentanil is administered in high doses as the primary agent for maintenance of anesthesia, respiratory depression requiring continued mechanical ventilation may persist for many hours after the patient awakens.

Elimination

Alfentanil—Hepatic; only 0.2% of a dose is excreted in the urine as unchanged alfentanil. Inactive metabolites are also excreted in the urine. Approximately 81% of a dose is excreted within 24 hours.

Fentanyl—Primarily hepatic; 10 to 25% of a dose may be excreted in the urine as unchanged fentanyl. About 70% of a dose is excreted within 4 days.

Sufentanil—Via metabolism; about 2% of a dose is excreted in the urine as unchanged sufentanil. About 80% of a dose is excreted within 24 hours.

Precautions to Consider

Cross-sensitivity and/or related problems

Patients hypersensitive to fentanyl may be hypersensitive to the chemically related alfentanil or sufentanil also, and vice versa.

Carcinogenicity

Long-term animal studies of the carcinogenic potential of alfentanil have not been done.

Mutagenicity

Alfentanil—No evidence of mutagenicity was demonstrated in the Ames *Salmonella* metabolic activating test. Also, no mutagenicity was demonstrated in the micronucleus test in female rats or the dominant lethal assay in female and male mice with single intravenous doses of up to 20 mg per kg of body weight (mg/kg) (approximately 40 times the maximum recommended human dose).

Sufentanil—Sufentanil has not been shown to have mutagenic potential in the micronucleus test in female rats (with single intravenous doses of up to 80 mcg per kg) or in the Ames test.

Pregnancy/Reproduction

Pregnancy—
First trimester—
Alfentanil:
Although adequate and well-controlled studies in humans have not been done, one study demonstrated that alfentanil readily crosses the placenta. Studies in rats and rabbits have not shown that alfentanil is teratogenic. However, embryocidal effects (possibly related to maternal toxicity) occurred following administration of 2.5 times the maximum recommended human dose for 10 to more than 30 days.
FDA Pregnancy Category C.
Fentanyl:
Although studies on the teratogenic potential of fentanyl have not been done in either animals or humans, one study showed that fentanyl crosses the placenta when it is administered to the mother prior to cesarean section.
FDA Pregnancy Category C.

Sufentanil:

Although adequate and well-controlled studies in humans have not been done, studies in rats and rabbits have not shown that sufentanil is teratogenic. However, embryocidal effects (possibly related to maternal toxicity, decreased food consumption, and anoxia) occurred in rats and rabbits following administration of up to 2.5 times the maximum human dose for 10 to more than 30 days.

FDA Pregnancy Category C.

Labor and delivery—Drowsiness (but no other adverse effect) was observed in 4-hour-old neonates after administration of fentanyl to the mother prior to cesarean section. This effect was associated with a concentration of 0.8 nanogram (or more) of fentanyl per mL of cord blood. Drowsiness was not present 24 hours after birth.

Breast-feeding

Problems in humans have not been documented.

Alfentanil—

In one study, 0.88 nanogram of alfentanil per mL was measured in colostrum 4 hours following maternal administration of 60 mcg per kg of body weight. Measurable concentrations were not present 28 hours following administration.

Fentanyl and sufentanil—

It is not known whether fentanyl and sufentanil are distributed into breast milk.

Pediatrics

Neonates may be more susceptible to the effects, especially the respiratory depressant effects, of opioid analgesics. Caution is recommended if fentanyl is used as presurgical or postsurgical medication in these patients.

Neonates have been found to have low concentrations of alpha-1-acid glycoprotein, leading to a reduced protein-binding capacity for alfentanil and an increase in the quantity of the medication available to receptor sites. However, one study has demonstrated an increased alfentanil dosage requirement in neonates.

The elimination half-life and duration of action of alfentanil may be decreased in pediatric patients. More frequent administration of supplemental doses than is usually needed by adults may be required.

Muscle rigidity was observed in 20% of mechanically ventilated neonates who received alfentanil at the dose of 9 to 15 mcg per kg of body weight prior to treatment procedures. In some neonates, the rigidity caused difficulty with ventilation.

Geriatrics

Geriatric patients may be more susceptible to the effects, especially the respiratory depressant effects, of opioid analgesics. Also, elderly patients are more likely to have age-related renal function impairment, which may require caution in patients receiving alfentanil (because of decreased protein-binding, which increases the effects of alfentanil by increasing its concentration at receptor sites) or fentanyl (because excretion of fentanyl may be slowed). Lower initial and supplemental doses, a slower infusion rate, and/or a longer interval between doses than are usually recommended for younger adults may be required for these patients. However, geriatric patients may also be more sensitive to the therapeutic effects of opioid analgesics so that lower doses may be sufficient. In one study, possible increased brain sensitivity to alfentanil was demonstrated in geriatric patients (compared with healthy young adults) as shown by a 40% reduction in the dose required to produce delta waves in the electroencephalogram (EEG).

Many studies have indicated that clearance of opioid analgesics is significantly reduced in geriatric patients. Specifically, studies have shown that alfentanil clearance is reduced by approximately 30% (leading to a prolonged elimination half-life) in patients older than 65 years of age, and that the elimination half-life of fentanyl may be greatly prolonged (in one study, to 15.75 hours) because of reduced clearance in patients 60 years of age and older. Reduced clearance may lead to a risk of delayed postoperative recovery.

Drug interactions and/or related problems

The following drug interactions and/or related problems have been selected on the basis of their potential clinical significance (possible mechanism in parentheses where appropriate)—not necessarily inclusive (» = major clinical significance):

Note: Combinations containing any of the following medications, depending on the amount present, may also interact with this medication.

Anesthetics, peridural conduction or
Anesthetics, spinal
(alterations in respiration caused by high levels of spinal or peridural blockade may be additive to fentanyl derivative–induced alterations in respiratory rate and alveolar ventilation; also, the vagal effects of fentanyl derivatives may be more pronounced in patients with high levels of spinal or epidural anesthesia, possibly leading to bradycardia and/or hypotension)

Antihypertensives or
Diuretics or
Hypotension-producing medications, other (see *Appendix II)*
(hypotensive effects of these medications may be potentiated when they are used concurrently with a fentanyl derivative; patients should be monitored for excessive fall in blood pressure during and following concurrent use)

» Benzodiazepines
(premedication with a benzodiazepine such as diazepam, lorazepam, or midazolam may decrease the dose of a fentanyl derivative required for induction of anesthesia and decrease the time to loss of consciousness with induction doses; also, administration of a benzodiazepine prior to or during surgery may decrease the risk of patient recall of surgical events postoperatively; however, these potential benefits must be weighed against the potential risks of concurrent use, such as an increased risk of severe hypotension associated with decreases in systemic vascular resistance, increased risk of respiratory depression, and delayed recovery time, especially when the benzodiazepine is administered intravenously)

Beta-adrenergic blocking agents
(preoperative chronic use of systemic beta-adrenergic blocking agents may decrease the frequency and/or severity of hypertensive responses to surgery, especially during sternotomy and sternal spread in cardiac or coronary artery surgery; however, chronic preoperative use of systemic beta-adrenergic blocking agents or ophthalmic beta-adrenergic blocking agents [especially levobunolol or timolol] may also increase the risk of initial bradycardia following induction doses of a fentanyl derivative)

» Buprenorphine and other partial mu-receptor agonists
(use of buprenorphine as presurgical medication prior to opioid analgesic–assisted anesthesia should be undertaken with caution because this partial mu-receptor agonist has high affinity for, and dissociates slowly from, the mu receptor and may therefore decrease the therapeutic effects of a subsequently administered mu-receptor agonist)
(buprenorphine and other partial mu-receptor agonists have the potential to reverse respiratory depressant effects induced by high doses of other opioid analgesics [while providing adequate post-operative analgesia] or to cause additive respiratory depression, hypotension, and/or CNS depression if administered in conjunction with low doses of other opioids; although the effects of buprenorphine administered following alfentanil- or sufentanil-assisted anesthesia have not been determined, in one study, administration of 0.3 or 0.45 mg of buprenorphine intramuscularly every 6 hours following opioid-assisted anesthesia with total doses of 0.2 or 0.3 mg of fentanyl caused a higher incidence of hypotension, respiratory depression, and CNS depression than equianalgesic doses [10 or 15 mg] of morphine intramuscularly every 6 hours)

» Cimetidine or
» Erythromycin
(concurrent use of cimetidine or erythromycin with alfentanil can cause reduced clearance of alfentanil, can prolong recovery from alfentanil, and may increase the risk of respiratory depression; other inhibitors of cytochrome P450 3A4 enzymes have not been tested; however chronic preoperative administration or perioperative use of hepatic enzyme inhibitors may decrease plasma clearance and prolong the duration of action of alfentanil)

» CNS depression-producing medications, other, including those commonly used as preanesthetic medication or for induction, supplementation, or maintenance of anesthesia (see *Appendix II*)
(concurrent use with a fentanyl derivative may result in increased CNS depressant, respiratory depressant, and hypotensive effects; caution is recommended and the dosage of each agent should be carefully titrated)
(it is recommended that initial dosage of other opioid agonist analgesics used during recovery from fentanyl- or sufentanil-assisted anesthesia be decreased to as low as one fourth to one third of the usual recommended dose)
(dosage requirements of volatile inhalation anesthetics may be decreased by 30 to 50% for the first hour of maintenance following administration of anesthetic induction doses of alfentanil)

Monoamine oxidase (MAO) inhibitors
(caution is recommended when using a fentanyl derivative in patients who have received an MAO inhibitor within 14 days because concurrent use of MAO inhibitors with meperidine has resulted in unpredictable, severe, and sometimes fatal reactions, including

immediate excitation, sweating, rigidity, and severe hypertension, or, in some patients, hypotension, severe respiratory depression, coma, seizures, hyperpyrexia, and vascular collapse; the risk of a significant reaction with fentanyl-derivative opioid analgesics has been questioned because a few reports indicate that fentanyl caused no adverse reactions when administered to patients receiving MAO inhibitor therapy; however, there are reports in the medical literature of adverse reactions that might have resulted from an interaction between fentanyl and MAO inhibitors)

Nalbuphine or
Pentazocine
(these opioid agonist/antagonist analgesics may partially antagonize the analgesic, respiratory depressant, and CNS depressant effects of fentanyl derivatives; however, because of their agonist activity, concurrent use of these agents also has the potential to produce additive CNS, respiratory, and hypotensive effects; the extent to which antagonistic or additive effects will predominate may depend upon dosage of the fentanyl derivative, with antagonism being more likely with low to moderate doses)

Naloxone
(naloxone antagonizes the analgesic, hypotensive, CNS, and respiratory depressant effects of fentanyl derivatives; dosage of the antagonist should be carefully titrated when used to reverse the effects of opioid analgesics used during surgery in order to achieve the desired effect without interfering with control of postoperative pain or inducing other adverse effects)
(naloxone also reverses skeletal muscle rigidity induced by fentanyl derivatives)

» Naltrexone
(usual doses of opioid analgesics will be ineffective if administered to a patient receiving naltrexone, which blocks the therapeutic effects of opioid analgesics; if possible, alternative [nonopioid] medications should be used prior to, during, and following surgery, because administration of increased doses of opioids to override naltrexone blockade of opioid receptors may result in increased and more prolonged respiratory depression and/or circulatory collapse; naltrexone should be discontinued several days prior to elective surgery if administration of an opioid is unavoidable)

Neuromuscular blocking agents
(concurrent use with high doses of sufentanil may reduce the initial dosage requirements for a nondepolarizing neuromuscular blocking agent; it is recommended that a peripheral nerve stimulator be used to determine dosage)
(concurrent use of a neuromuscular blocking agent prevents or reverses muscle rigidity induced by fentanyl derivatives)
(a neuromuscular blocking agent having vagolytic activity such as pancuronium or gallamine may decrease the risk of fentanyl derivative–induced bradycardia or hypotension, especially in patients receiving chronic therapy with beta-adrenergic blocking agents and/or vasodilators for treatment of coronary artery disease; however, concurrent use may also increase the risk of tachycardia or hypertension in some patients)
(a nonvagolytic neuromuscular blocking agent such as succinylcholine will not decrease the risk of bradycardia or hypotension induced by a fentanyl derivative; however, in some patients, especially those with compromised cardiac function and/or those receiving a beta-adrenergic blocking agent preoperatively, concurrent use may increase the incidence and/or severity of these effects)
(respiratory depressant effects of neuromuscular blocking agents may be additive to respiratory depressant effects of fentanyl derivatives; although increased or prolonged respiratory depression or paralysis [apnea] may occur, clinical significance is minimal while the patient is being mechanically ventilated; however, patients should be carefully monitored during and following concurrent use, especially if there is a possibility of incomplete reversal of neuromuscular blockade postoperatively)

Nitrous oxide
(in addition to the increased CNS depressant, respiratory depressant, and hypotensive effects that may occur when a fentanyl derivative is used concurrently with any CNS depressant, concurrent use of nitrous oxide with high doses of these agents may decrease mean arterial pressure, heart rate, and cardiac output; these effects may be more pronounced in patients with poor left ventricular function)

Phenothiazines
(in addition to the increased CNS depressant, respiratory depressant, and hypotensive effects that may occur when a phenothiazine is used concurrently with an opioid analgesic, some phenothiazines increase, while others decrease, the effects of opioid analgesic supplements to anesthesia; however, the effect of various phenothiazines on fentanyl derivative–assisted anesthesia has not been determined)

Laboratory value alterations

The following have been selected on the basis of their potential clinical significance (possible effect in parentheses where appropriate)—not necessarily inclusive (» = major clinical significance).

With diagnostic test results
Gastric emptying studies
(opioid analgesics may delay gastric emptying, thereby invalidating test results)
Hepatobiliary imaging using technetium Tc 99m disofenin
(delivery of technetium Tc 99m disofenin to the small bowel may be prevented because of opioid analgesic-induced constriction of the sphincter of Oddi and increased biliary tract pressure; these actions result in delayed visualization and thus resemble obstruction of the common bile duct; contraction of the sphincter of Oddi has been demonstrated with alfentanil and fentanyl and, although not yet documented, should be considered a possibility with sufentanil also)
Plasma amylase determinations and
Plasma lipase determinations
(activity of these enzymes may be increased because alfentanil and fentanyl can cause contractions of the sphincter of Oddi and increased biliary tract pressure; the possibility should be considered that the diagnostic utility of determinations of these enzymes may be compromised for up to 24 hours after fentanyl administration or for several hours after alfentanil administration; although documentation is not yet available, the possibility exists that similar effects may occur with sufentanil)

With physiology/laboratory test values
Cerebrospinal fluid pressure
(opioid analgesics may increase cerebrospinal fluid pressure; effect is secondary to respiratory depression–induced carbon dioxide retention)

Medical considerations/Contraindications

The medical considerations/contraindications included have been selected on the basis of their potential clinical significance (reasons given in parentheses where appropriate)—not necessarily inclusive (» = major clinical significance).

Risk-benefit should be considered when the following medical problems exist:

For all indications
Allergic reaction to fentanyl or its derivatives, history of
Cardiac bradyarrhythmias
(may be induced or exacerbated)
Cardiac conditions leading to compromised cardiac reserve
(increased risk of severe bradycardia and/or undesirably large decreases in mean blood pressure, especially following rapid administration of induction doses of a fentanyl derivative)
Head injury or
Increased intracranial pressure, pre-existing or
Intracranial lesions
(risk of respiratory depression and further elevation of cerebrospinal fluid pressure is increased; also, opioid analgesic-induced sedation and pupillary changes may obscure clinical course of head injury)
» Hepatic function impairment or cirrhosis
(studies have demonstrated that alfentanil clearance rate is reduced, leading to increased elimination half-life and prolonged duration of action; although clearance of fentanyl or sufentanil may not be altered as greatly as that of alfentanil, caution is advised)
(alfentanil's effects may also be increased because of decreased protein-binding leading to increased concentration of medication at receptor sites; a reduction of alfentanil dosage may be required)
Hypothyroidism
(risk of respiratory depression and prolonged CNS depression is greatly increased; a reduction in dosage of the fentanyl derivative may be required)
Renal function impairment
(elimination of fentanyl [up to 25% of a dose is excreted unchanged in the urine] may be slowed)
(alfentanil's effects may be increased because of decreased protein-binding leading to increased concentration of medication at receptor sites; however, alfentanil's clearance rate and duration of action are not affected)
Respiratory impairment or pulmonary disease, pre-existing
(opioid analgesics may further decrease respiratory drive and increase airway resistance; although clinical significance is minimal

if the patient is being mechanically ventilated during surgery, respiratory support may be required with doses that usually permit spontaneous breathing)

Caution is also advised in elderly, very ill, or debilitated patients, who may be more sensitive to the effects, especially the respiratory depressant effects, of opioid analgesics.

For use of a fentanyl derivative for indications other than as a component of anesthesia

Abdominal conditions, acute
(diagnosis or clinical course may be obscured)

Gallbladder disease or gallstones
(opioid analgesics may cause biliary tract spasm)

Gastrointestinal tract surgery
(opioid analgesics may decrease gastrointestinal motility)

Prostatic hypertrophy or obstruction or
Urethral stricture or
Urinary tract surgery
(opioid analgesics may cause urinary retention)

» Respiratory impairment or pulmonary disease, pre-existing
(opioid analgesics may further decrease respiratory drive and increase airway resistance)

» Caution is also advised in elderly, very ill, or very young patients, who may be more sensitive to the effects, especially the respiratory depressant effects, of opioid analgesics.

Patient monitoring

The following may be especially important in patient monitoring (other tests may be warranted in some patients, depending on condition; » = major clinical significance):

Monitoring of vital signs, especially blood pressure and respiratory status
(required during and following administration; prolonged postoperative surveillance may be necessary following high or multiple doses or prolonged administration because of the risk of prolonged respiratory depression, especially after use of fentanyl or sufentanil; also, following high or multiple doses or prolonged administration of alfentanil or fentanyl, respiratory depression, respiratory arrest, bradycardia, asystole, arrhythmias, and hypotension have occurred or recurred following initial recovery)

Side/Adverse Effects

Note: *Fentanyl derivatives may cause rigidity in muscles of respiration in the chest and pharynx, which may lead to difficulty in establishing pulmonary ventilation. Rigidity* may occur more rapidly with alfentanil than with fentanyl or sufentanil. In addition, alfentanil may cause *rigidity of abdominal muscles*; *flexion of the fingers, wrists, and elbows*; *extension of the toes, ankles, knees, and hips*; *contraction of neck muscles; immobility of the head; and/or clenching of the jaw*. These effects are dose-dependent and must be anticipated with anesthetic induction doses. Abnormal eye movements (i.e., *disconjugate gaze*) have also been reported during induction with alfentanil. *Chest wall rigidity* has also been reported during emergence from fentanyl- or sufentanil-assisted anesthesia.

Delayed *respiratory depression*, *respiratory arrest*, *bradycardia*, *asystole*, *arrhythmias*, and *hypotension* have been reported to occur or recur following initial recovery from alfentanil- or fentanyl-assisted anesthesia and should be considered a possibility following sufentanil-assisted anesthesia also.

Like other opioid analgesics, fentanyl derivatives may cause physical dependence following prolonged use. It has been proposed that adverse effects (such as *tachycardia*, *hypertension*, *hyperpnea*, *hyperalgesia*, *nausea*, and *vomiting*) occurring (rarely) after naloxone is administered for reversal of opioid effects following lengthy surgical procedures may be manifestations of an induced abstinence syndrome in acutely dependent individuals. Alternatively, adverse effects occurring after administration of naloxone may be due to the abrupt reversal of analgesia in patients with significant acute postoperative pain.

In addition to the side effects listed below, *hypertension*, *tachycardia*, and *skeletal muscle movements* (not related to onset of rigidity) may occur during surgery. These effects may be indicative of a failure to suppress autonomic responses to surgical stimulation rather than a direct effect of the medication. The incidence and severity of these effects are lower with sufentanil than with alfentanil or fentanyl.

Although *not all* of the side/adverse effects listed below have been reported with all of the fentanyl derivatives, they have been reported with at least one of these medications and/or encountered during administration of other opioid analgesics. Therefore, they should be considered potential side effects of any of the fentanyl derivatives.

The following side/adverse effects have been selected on the basis of their potential clinical significance (possible signs and symptoms in parentheses where appropriate)—not necessarily inclusive:

Those indicating need for medical attention

Incidence more frequent

Bradycardia (dizziness, lightheadedness, or feeling faint); ***hypotension*** (dizziness, lightheadedness, or feeling faint)—most likely to occur shortly after administration; blood pressure may return to preadministration values with surgical stimulation; ***respiratory depression, intraoperative or postoperative***—may progress to apnea

Incidence less frequent

Cardiac arrhythmia (dizziness, lightheadedness, or feeling faint)—incidence 2% with alfentanil or fentanyl; < 1% with sufentanil; ***confusion, postoperative***—rare with alfentanil

Incidence rare

Bronchospasm, allergic (shortness of breath, trouble in breathing, tightness in chest, or wheezing)—not caused by histamine release; ***circulatory depression*** (dizziness)—may lead to cardiac arrest; ***dermatitis, allergic*** (skin rash, hives, and/or itching); ***laryngospasm*** (shortness of breath, trouble in breathing, tightness in chest, or wheezing)—may be a form of rigidity; ***mental depression, postoperative; paradoxical CNS excitation or delirium*** (unusual excitement); ***seizures*** (convulsions)—reported with fentanyl and sufentanil only

Those common to opioid analgesics (but not necessarily reported specifically with fentanyl derivatives) and indicating need for medical attention only if they continue or are bothersome

Incidence more frequent

Drowsiness, postoperative—less frequent with alfentanil; ***nausea or vomiting***—lower incidence reported with sufentanil than with alfentanil or fentanyl but highly variable; may depend on the specific surgical procedure performed, e.g., especially likely following gynecologic surgery

Incidence less frequent or rare

Biliary spasm (abdominal pain); ***blurred or double vision or other changes in vision; chills; constipation; ureteral spasm*** (decreased or difficult urination); ***urinary retention*** (difficult urination)

Overdose

For specific information on the agents used in the management of an overdose, see:

- *Atropine* in
- *Anticholinergics/Antispasmodics (Systemic)* monograph;
- *Naloxone (Systemic)* monograph;
- *Neuromuscular Blocking Agents (Systemic)* monograph; and/or
- *Sympathomimetic Agents—Cardiovascular Use (Parenteral-Systemic)* monograph.

For more information on the management of overdose or unintentional ingestion, **contact a Poison Control Center** (see *Poison Control Center Listing*).

Clinical effects of overdose

The following effects have been selected on the basis of their potential clinical significance (possible signs and symptoms in parentheses where appropriate)—not necessarily inclusive:

Acute

Bradycardia; circulatory depression; cold, clammy skin; dizziness, severe; drowsiness, severe; hypotension; nervousness or restlessness, severe; pinpoint pupils of eyes; respiratory depression; weakness, severe

Treatment of overdose

Specific treatment—

For bradycardia—Administering atropine. Alternatively, if a neuromuscular blocking agent is being used, administration of a neuromuscular blocking agent with vagolytic activity, such as pancuronium or gallamine, may antagonize fentanyl derivative–induced bradycardia.

For respiratory depression—During surgery, respiratory depression may be managed via endotracheal intubation and assisted or controlled respiration. If respiratory depression persists following surgery, prolonged mechanical ventilation may be required. Also, intravenous administration of the opioid antagonist naloxone may be required. Dosage of naloxone should be titrated to achieve the desired effect without interfering with control of postoperative pain or causing other adverse effects; hypertension and tachycardia, sometimes resulting in left ventricular failure and pulmonary edema, have occurred following naloxone administration in these circumstances (especially in cardiac patients). Initial doses as small as 0.5 mcg (0.0005 mg) of naloxone per kg of body weight have been recommended. Because the duration of respiratory depression may exceed the duration of action of a single intravenous dose of the antagonist, continued monitoring of the patient is mandatory so that additional antagonist may be administered as necessary. Continuous intravenous infusion of naloxone may provide continuing control of undesirable opioid effects.

For hypotension—Administration of appropriate parenteral fluid therapy is recommended. Repositioning of the patient to improve venous return to the heart should be considered when surgical conditions permit. If necessary, a vasopressor (during or following surgery) and/or naloxone (postoperatively only) may be administered.

For muscle rigidity—Administering a neuromuscular blocking agent and assisting respiration via controlled ventilation with oxygen. Alternatively, if muscle rigidity should occur upon emergence, naloxone may be administered.

Supportive care—

Other supportive measures should also be employed as needed. Patients in whom intentional overdose is confirmed or suspected should be referred for psychiatric consultation.

Patient Consultation

As an aid to patient consultation, refer to *Advice for the Patient, Narcotic Analgesics—For Surgery and Obstetrics (Systemic).*

In providing consultation, consider emphasizing the following selected information (» = major clinical significance):

Before receiving this medication

» Conditions affecting use, especially:
- Allergic reaction to fentanyl or its derivatives
- Pregnancy—Alfentanil and fentanyl cross the placenta
- Use in children—Increased sensitivity to the effects of opioid analgesics in neonates
- Use in the elderly—Increased sensitivity to the effects of opioid analgesics
- Other medications, epecially benzodiazepines, buprenorphine and other partial mu-receptor agonists, cimetidine, CNS depressants, erythromycin, naltrexone, and "street" drugs
- Other medical problems, especially hepatic function impairment or cirrhosis and pulmonary disease

Precautions after receiving this medication

To be followed for about 24 hours after receiving this medication as part of an outpatient regimen:

» Caution if dizziness, drowsiness, lightheadedness, or blurred vision occurs

» Avoiding use of alcohol or other CNS depressants unless specifically prescribed or otherwise approved by physician or dentist

Side/adverse effects

Signs and symptoms of potential side effects, especially bradycardia, hypotension, cardiac arrhythmias, confusion, bronchospasm, circulatory depression, allergic dermatitis, laryngospasm, mental depression, paradoxical excitement, seizures

General Dosing Information

Fentanyl derivatives should be administered only by personnel experienced in the use of intravenous anesthetics and in the management of the respiratory effects of opioid analgesics.

An opioid antagonist, resuscitative medications, intubation equipment, and oxygen should be readily available during and following administration of a fentanyl derivative. Careful monitoring of the patient's respiratory status is necessary during and following surgery. These medications suppress respiration, especially in elderly, very ill, or debilitated patients and those with respiratory problems. Postoperative respiratory depression may be prolonged or may recur following initial recovery, especially following use of moderate or high doses. Following administration of fentanyl or sufentanil, respiratory depression requiring mechanical ventilation may be greatly prolonged. Alfentanil-induced respiratory depression is of shorter duration than that induced by fentanyl or sufentanil. The peak respiratory depressant effect of fentanyl occurs 5 to 15 minutes after administration of a single intravenous dose and may persist longer than the analgesic effect.

Sufentanil is approximately 5 to 7 times more potent than fentanyl on a mcg-to-mcg (and mL-to-mL) basis. Administration of 100 mcg of fentanyl or 13 to 20 mcg of sufentanil produces analgesic effects equivalent to 10 mg of morphine. Alfentanil has been reported to be 3 to 10 times less potent than fentanyl on a mcg-to-mcg basis (as determined by dosage requirements). However, because of alfentanil's considerably smaller volume of distribution, much higher plasma concentrations are achieved with alfentanil than with equal doses of fentanyl; studies comparing plasma concentrations of fentanyl or alfentanil required to produce similar effects have indicated that fentanyl may be up to 75 times more potent than alfentanil. Also, interpatient variability in responsiveness to these medications and/or differences in analytic methodology may have contributed to the difficulty in determining relative potency.

The usual adult and pediatric doses stated below are intended as a guideline only. Dosage must be individualized on the basis of the age, weight, body size, and physical status of the patient; underlying pathology; other medications used concurrently, especially the type of anesthesia to be used; type and anticipated duration of the surgical procedure involved; and patient response. Also, for obese patients (more than 20% above ideal body weight), the dosage of alfentanil or sufentanil should be determined on the basis of lean body weight.

It is recommended that initial dosage be reduced in elderly or debilitated patients. The effects of the initial dose should be considered in determining supplemental doses. Lower doses may also be required in patients with chronic hepatic disease (especially for alfentanil) or hypothyroidism.

Fentanyl derivatives may cause rigidity of chest and abdominal muscles, which may interfere with pulmonary ventilation. Alfentanil may also cause rigidity in other muscles. The risk of muscle rigidity may be reduced if intravenous injections are administered slowly. A neuromuscular blocking agent compatible with the patient's condition may be administered prophylactically to prevent muscle rigidity or to induce muscle relaxation after rigidity occurs. Rigidity has also been reported upon emergence from fentanyl- or sufentanil-assisted anesthesia and should be considered a possibility upon emergence from alfentanil-assisted anesthesia.

It is recommended that intravenous injections of fentanyl or sufentanil be given slowly over a period of at least 1 to 2 minutes, especially if high doses are being administered. It is recommended that induction doses of alfentanil also be given slowly. Although the manufacturer's prescribing information recommends that induction doses of alfentanil be administered over a period of approximately 3 minutes, many investigators have administered induction doses within 90 seconds. Slow intravenous administration of these medications may reduce the incidence and/or severity of rigidity, bradycardia, and hypotension. Also, rapid intravenous administration of other opioid analgesics has caused anaphylactoid reactions, severe respiratory depression, hypotension, peripheral circulatory collapse, and cardiac arrest.

Premedication with a benzodiazepine may reduce induction dose requirements and decrease the time to loss of consciousness. In addition, administration of a benzodiazepine or other amnestic agent may help to prevent patient recall of intrasurgical events postoperatively. Patient recall of intrasurgical events despite the absence of autonomic or hormonal responses indicative of light or inadequate anesthesia has been reported following use of high-dose fentanyl with 100% oxygen and, although not reported to date, should be considered a possibility following use of high-dose sufentanil with 100% oxygen or following administration of alfentanil also. However, the fact that concurrent use of a benzodiazepine with a fentanyl derivative may increase the risk of hypotension, respiratory depression, or delayed recovery must be kept in mind. Alternatively, detection of signs of inadequate anesthesia may be facilitated if the neuromuscular blocking agent being used is administered in doses titrated to avoid complete paralysis.

Fentanyl derivatives, even in very high doses, may fail to suppress autonomic responses to surgical stimulation. Tachycardia and hypertension may occur and are more likely to respond rapidly to additional doses of alfentanil or sufentanil than to additional fentanyl. However, administration of a suitable antihypertensive agent may be required in some patients. In patients undergoing cardiac surgery, administration of a beta-adrenergic blocking agent with the presurgical medication (or continuation of previously instituted therapy with a beta-adrenergic blocking agent up to the time of surgery) may reduce or prevent these responses.

Like other opioid analgesics, fentanyl derivatives may cause physical dependence following prolonged use. Rarely, symptoms possibly indicating a type of withdrawal syndrome (e.g., tachycardia, hypertension, hyperpnea, hyperalgesia, nausea, and vomiting) may occur following administration of naloxone (especially in high doses) for reversal of opioid effects postoperatively. It has been proposed that adverse effects occurring after administration of naloxone for reversal of opioid effects following lengthy surgical procedures may be manifestations of an induced withdrawal syndrome in acutely dependent individuals. Alternatively, adverse effects occurring after administration of naloxone may be due to the abrupt reversal of analgesia in patients with significant acute postoperative pain.

For treatment of adverse effects

Recommended treatment may include
- For hypotension—Administration of appropriate parenteral fluid therapy is recommended. Repositioning of the patient to improve venous return to the heart should be considered when surgical condi-

tions permit. If necessary, a vasopressor (during or following surgery) and/or naloxone (postoperatively only) may be administered.

- For muscle rigidity—Administering a neuromuscular blocking agent and assisting respiration via controlled ventilation with oxygen. Alternatively, if muscle rigidity should occur upon emergence, naloxone may be administered.

Other supportive measures should also be employed as needed.

ALFENTANIL

Summary of Differences

Indications: See *Indications.*

Pharmacology/pharmacokinetics: See *Pharmacology/Pharmacokinetics.*

Pediatrics: Duration of action may be reduced in children. Muscle rigidity occurs more commonly in neonates receiving alfentanil than in older children or adults.

Drug interactions and/or related problems: Hepatic enzyme inhibitors may prolong duration of action.

Side/adverse effects: See *Side/Adverse Effects.*

Additional Dosing Information

See also *General Dosing Information.*

The anesthetic ED_{90} in unpremedicated patients (induction dose required to attenuate or abolish the response to placement of a nasopharyngeal airway in 90% of the patients) is approximately 169 to 182 mcg per kg of body weight (using a rapid induction); however, values ranging from 137 to 383 mcg per kg of body weight have been reported.

An initial loading dose of alfentanil is required to achieve therapeutic plasma concentrations rapidly. Administration of the induction or loading dose may be followed by continuous intravenous infusion of the medication and/or administration of supplemental single injections as required. Continuous intravenous infusion, with the rate of infusion adjusted according to the observed clinical effect, may reduce the total maintenance dosage requirement, decrease the risk of postoperative respiratory depression, and speed recovery time, and may be the preferred method of administration. If necessary, small single doses may be administered, in addition to or instead of increasing the infusion rate, as required to prevent or abolish responses to surgical stimuli or other signs of light or inadequate anesthesia.

Because alfentanil requirements are the lowest near the end of surgery, it is recommended that the maintenance infusion be discontinued 10 to 20 minutes before the end of surgery. If further administration of alfentanil is required after the infusion is discontinued, single injections of 7 to 15 mcg per kg of body weight may be given.

Because of alfentanil's short duration of action, postoperative pain requiring treatment may occur relatively early in the recovery period.

Parenteral Dosage Forms

ALFENTANIL HYDROCHLORIDE INJECTION

Note: Alfentanil injection contains alfentanil hydrochloride, but the dosing and strengths are expressed in terms of alfentanil base.

Usual adult dose

Anesthesia adjunct (opioid analgesic)—

Induction of anesthesia (for procedures lasting 45 minutes or longer)—

Intravenous, 130 to 245 mcg (0.13 to 0.245 mg) (base) per kg of body weight. Induction with alfentanil may be followed by administration of an inhalation anesthetic (with the required concentration of inhalation anesthetic generally being reduced by 30 to 50% during the first hour of maintenance) or by further administration of alfentanil in maintenance doses.

Maintenance of anesthesia (in conjunction with nitrous oxide and oxygen)—

Procedures lasting up to 30 minutes—Intravenous, 8 to 20 mcg (0.008 to 0.02 mg) (base) per kg of body weight as an initial loading dose, followed by administration of single doses of 3 to 5 mcg (0.003 to 0.005 mg) per kg of body weight as required or by continuous infusion at a rate of 0.5 to 1 mcg (0.0005 to 0.001 mg) per kg of body weight per minute.

Procedures lasting longer than 30 minutes—Intravenous, 20 to 75 mcg (0.02 to 0.075 mg) (base) per kg of body weight as an initial loading dose (if an agent other than alfentanil has been used for induction), followed by continuous infusion at a rate of 0.5 to 3 mcg (0.0005 to 0.003 mg) per kg of body weight per minute and/or by single injections of 5 to 15 mcg (0.005 to 0.015 mg) per kg of body weight as required. Following induction with alfentanil, infusion rate requirements may be reduced by 30 to 50% during the first hour of maintenance.

Note: For maintenance of anesthesia, continuous infusions of alfentanil are generally administered at an average rate of 0.5 to 1.5 mcg (0.0005 to 0.0015 mg) (base) per kg of body weight per minute. However, a variable rate of infusion is recommended, with the rate being increased in response to signs of light or inadequate anesthesia or decreased when signs of light or inadequate anesthesia have been absent for a suitable period of time.

Sedation, conscious—

Intravenous, 3 to 8 mcg (0.003 to 0.008 mg) (base) per kg of body weight as an initial loading dose, followed by administration of single doses of 3 to 5 mcg (0.003 to 0.005 mg) per kg of body weight as required.

Usual pediatric dose

[Anesthesia adjunct (opioid analgesic) for maintenance of anesthesia][1]—

Intravenous, 30 to 50 mcg (0.03 to 0.05 mg) (base) per kg of body weight as an initial loading dose, followed by supplemental single doses of 10 to 15 mcg (0.01 to 0.015 mg) per kg of body weight as required, or by continuous infusion at a rate of 0.5 to 1.5 mcg (0.0005 to 0.0015 mg) per kg of body weight per minute.

Note: Alfentanil's half-life and duration of action are decreased in children as compared with adults; therefore, more frequent supplemental dosing may be required.

Strength(s) usually available

U.S.—

Without preservative: 500 mcg (0.5 mg) (base) per mL (Rx) [*Alfenta*].

Canada—

Without preservative: 500 mcg (0.5 mg) (base) per mL (Rx) [*Alfenta*].

Packaging and storage

Store between 15 and 30 °C (59 and 86 °F), protected from light, unless otherwise specified by manufacturer. Protect from freezing.

Preparation of dosage form

Alfentanil hydrochloride injection may be diluted with 0.9% sodium chloride injection, 5% dextrose and sodium chloride injection (0.9% sodium chloride), 5% dextrose injection, or lactated Ringer's injection to a convenient concentration. As an example, 20 mL of alfentanil hydrochloride injection may be added to 230 mL of diluent to provide a solution containing 40 mcg (0.04 mg) of alfentanil per mL.

Stability

Alfentanil hydrochloride injection is stable when diluted to a concentration of 25 to 80 mcg of alfentanil base per mL using any of the solutions listed in

Preparation of dosage form above.

Note

Controlled substance in the U.S., Canada, and the U.K.

[1]Not included in Canadian product labeling.

FENTANYL

Summary of Differences

Indications: See *Indications.*

Pharmacology/pharmacokinetics: See *Pharmacology/Pharmacokinetics.*

Pediatrics: Neonates may be more susceptible to respiratory depressant effects, especially if used as presurgical or postsurgical medication.

Side/adverse effects: See *Side/Adverse Effects.*

Additional Dosing Information

See also *General Dosing Information.*

A reduction in dosage may be required in very young patients receiving fentanyl as presurgical or postsurgical medication.

Parenteral Dosage Forms

FENTANYL CITRATE INJECTION USP

Note: Fentanyl injection contains fentanyl citrate, but the dosing and strengths are expressed in terms of fentanyl base.

Usual adult dose

Anesthesia, general, adjunct—

For minor surgery—

Intravenous, 2 mcg (0.002 mg) (base) per kg of body weight.

For major surgery—

Moderate dose—Intravenous, 2 to 20 mcg (0.002 to 0.02 mg) (base) per kg of body weight.

High dose (for open-heart surgery or complicated neurological or orthopedic procedures requiring prolonged anesthesia and abolition of stress response)—Intravenous, 20 to 50 mcg (0.02 to 0.05 mg) (base) per kg of body weight.

Note: The total moderate or high dosage recommended during major surgery may be given as a single dose or in divided doses. The quantity of fentanyl given as an initial loading dose and as subsequent maintenance doses must be individualized, depending upon the anesthetic regimen being used, the type and anticipated duration of the surgical procedure involved, and the occurrence of signs of surgical stress or lightening of anesthesia during surgery. Although fentanyl may be administered intramuscularly during surgery, it is usually administered intravenously.

Anesthesia, local, adjunct—
Intravenous or intramuscular, 50 to 100 mcg (0.05 to 0.1 mg) (base).

Anesthesia, as primary agent in major surgery—
Intravenous, 50 to 100 mcg (0.05 to 0.1 mg) (base) per kg of body weight, to be administered with 100% oxygen or oxygen plus nitrous oxide and a neuromuscular blocking agent.

Note: Up to 150 mcg (0.l5 mg) (base) per kg of body weight may be required in some patients.

In order to provide both immediate and sustained effects throughout a prolonged surgical procedure, administration of an initial loading dose of fentanyl simultaneously with or followed by continuous intravenous infusion is recommended.

Presurgical medication—
Intramuscular, 50 to 100 mcg (0.05 to 0.1 mg) (base) thirty to sixty minutes prior to surgery.

Postoperative (in recovery room period)—
Intramuscular, 50 to 100 mcg (0.05 to 0.1 mg) (base); may be repeated in one or two hours as needed.

Usual pediatric dose

Anesthesia, as primary agent in major surgery—
[Neonates][1]: Intravenous, 10 to 30 mcg (base) per kg of body weight (mcg/kg).
Children 2 to 12 years of age: Intravenous, 2 to 3 mcg (0.002 to 0.003 mg) (base) per kg of body weight.

[Analgesia, during mechanical ventilation][1]—
Neonates: Intravenous, 1 to 3 mcg/kg (base) as a loading dose followed by 0.5 to 2 mcg/kg per hour and titrated to the requirements and response of the individual patient.

Strength(s) usually available

U.S.—
Without preservative: 50 mcg (0.05 mg) (base) per mL (Rx) [*Sublimaze;* GENERIC].

Canada—
Without preservative: 50 mcg (0.05 mg) (base) per mL (Rx) [GENERIC].

Packaging and storage

Store below 40 °C (104 °F), preferably between 15 and 30 °C (59 and 86 °F), unless otherwise specified by manufacturer. Protect from light. Protect from freezing.

Note

Controlled substance in the U.S., Canada, and the U.K.

[1]Not included in Canadian product labeling.

SUFENTANIL

Summary of Differences

Indications: See *Indications*.
Pharmacology/pharmacokinetics: See *Pharmacology/Pharmacokinetics*.
Drug interactions and/or related problems: See information on interaction with neuromuscular blocking agents in *Drug interactions and/or related problems* section for information that may not apply to alfentanil or fentanyl.
Side/adverse effects: See *Side/Adverse Effects*.

Parenteral Dosage Forms

SUFENTANIL CITRATE INJECTION USP

Note: Sufentanil injection contains sufentanil citrate, but the dosing and strengths are expressed in terms of sufentanil base.

Usual adult dose

Anesthesia, general, adjunct—
Low dose: Intravenous, 0.5 to 2 mcg (0.0005 to 0.002 mg) (base) per kg of body weight initially. Supplemental doses of 10 to 25 mcg (0.01 to 0.025 mg) may be administered as needed.
Moderate dose (for major surgical procedures requiring some attenuation of sympathetic response to surgical stimuli): Intravenous, 2 to 8 mcg (0.002 to 0.008 mg) (base) per kg of body weight initially. Supplemental doses of 10 to 50 mcg (0.01 to 0.05 mg) may be administered as needed.

Note: When administered with nitrous oxide and oxygen for procedures lasting up to eight hours, total doses of 1 mcg (0.001 mg) per kg of body weight per hour, or less, are recommended.

Anesthesia, as primary agent in major surgery—
Intravenous, 8 to 30 mcg (0.008 to 0.03 mg) (base) per kg of body weight initially, administered with 100% oxygen. Supplemental doses of 25 to 50 mcg (0.025 to 0.05 mg) may be administered as needed.

Note: In order to provide both immediate and sustained effects throughout a prolonged surgical procedure, administration of an initial loading dose of sufentanil simultaneously with or followed by continuous intravenous infusion is recommended.

[Pain, postoperative (treatment)]—
Epidural, 30 to 60 mcg (0.03 to 0.06 mg) (base) in 10 mL of 0.9% sodium chloride injection. Additional 25-mcg doses may be administered at intervals of not less than one hour.

Pain, obstetrical (treatment)—
Epidural, 10 to 15 mcg (0.01 to 0.015 mg) (base) in combination with 10 mL bupivacaine 0.0125%. Two additional doses may be administered at one hour intervals, if needed, to control pain.

Usual pediatric dose

Anesthesia, as primary agent in cardiovascular surgery—
Initial: Intravenous, 10 to 25 mcg (0.01 to 0.025 mg) (base) per kg of body weight, administered with 100% oxygen.
Maintenance: Intravenous, up to 25 to 50 mcg (0.025 to 0.05 mg) (base).

Strength(s) usually available

U.S.—
Without preservative: 50 mcg (0.05 mg) (base) per mL (Rx) [*Sufenta;* GENERIC].

Canada—
Without preservative: 50 mcg (0.05 mg) (base) per mL (Rx) [*Sufenta*].

Packaging and storage

Store below 40 °C (104 °F), preferably between 15 and 30 °C (59 and 86 °F), protected from light, unless otherwise specified by manufacturer. Protect from freezing.

Note

Controlled substance in both the U.S. and Canada.

Revised: 02/14/2001

FERROUS FUMARATE—See *Iron Supplements (Systemic)*

FERROUS GLUCONATE—See *Iron Supplements (Systemic)*

FERROUS SULFATE—See *Iron Supplements (Systemic)*

FEXOFENADINE—See *Antihistamines (Systemic)*

FEXOFENADINE Systemic

VA CLASSIFICATION (Primary): AH102
Commonly used brand name(s): *Allegra; Allegra 12 Hour; Allegra 24 Hour.*

Note: For a listing of dosage forms and brand names by country availability, see *Dosage Forms* section(s).

Category

Antihistaminic (H_1-receptor).

Indications

Accepted

Rhinitis, seasonal allergic (treatment)—Fexofenadine is indicated to relieve symptoms that are associated with seasonal allergic rhinitis in adults and children 6 years of age and older. Symptoms treated effectively were sneezing, rhinorrhea, itchy eyes, nose, and throat, and red, watery eyes.

Urticaria (treatment)—Fexofenadine is indicated for the treatment of uncomplicated skin manifestations of chronic idiopathic urticaria in adults and children 6 years of age and older. It significantly reduces pruritus and the number of wheals.

Pharmacology/Pharmacokinetics

Physicochemical characteristics

Chemical Group—Metabolite of terfenadine.

Molecular weight—538.13.

Solubility—Freely soluble in methanol and ethanol, slightly soluble in chloroform and water, and insoluble in hexane.

Mechanism of action/Effect

Fexofenadine is an antihistamine with selective peripheral H_1-receptor antagonist activity. It inhibits antigen-induced bronchospasm in sensitized guinea pigs and histamine release from peritoneal mast cells in rats.

Absorption

Rapid following oral administration. The bioavailabilities of fexofenadine capsule and tablet formulations are equivalent when administered in equal doses

Bioavailability of fexofenadine was shown to be reduced by 36% by fruit juices such as grapefruit and orange based on the results from three clinical studies including a population pharmacokinetic analysis. The same effects may be extrapolated to other fruit juices such as apple juice.

The pharmacokinetics of fexofenadine are linear for oral doses up to 240 mg a day (120 mg twice a day).

Distribution

Volume of distribution (V_d)—5.4 to 5.8 liters/kilogram

Tissue distribution studies in rats using radiolabeled fexofenadine show that it does not cross the blood-brain barrier.

Protein binding

High (60 to 70%)—predominantly to albumin and alpha$_1$-acid glycoprotein.

Biotransformation

About 5% of the total dose is metabolized; approximately 0.5 to 1.5% by cytochrome P450 3A4 isoenzyme metabolism and 3.5% transformed to a methyl ester metabolite by intestinal microflora.

Elimination

14.4 hours in healthy subjects; in patients with mild renal impairment (creatinine clearance of 41 to 80 mL per minute) and severe renal impairment (creatinine clearance of 11 to 40 mL per minute), the mean elimination half-life was 59% and 72% longer, respectively, than in healthy subjects. In patients on dialysis, half-life was 31% longer than in healthy subjects.

Onset of action

Within 1 hour, as determined by a reduction in rhinitis symptoms following administration of a single 60-mg dose to patients exposed to ragweed pollen and by human histamine skin wheal and flare studies following administration of single and twice-daily doses of 20 and 40 mg of fexofenadine.

Peak serum concentration

209 ng/mL—after a single 60-mg dose as an oral solution in healthy volunteers.

142 ng/mL—after a single 60–mg tablet in healthy volunteers.

494 ng/mL—after a single 180–mg oral tablet in healthy volunteers.

286 ng/mL—after 10 doses of 60-mg as an oral solution every 12 hours in healthy volunteers.

Time to peak effect

2 to 3 hours, as determined by human histamine skin wheal and flare studies following administration of single and twice-daily doses of 20 and 40 mg of fexofenadine.

Duration of action

Effect evident 12 hours after administration, as determined by clinical studies in patients with seasonal allergic rhinitis given a single 60-mg dose, and by human histamine skin wheal and flare studies in patients given single and twice-daily doses of 20 and 40 mg of fexofenadine.

Note: Tolerance to the antihistamine effect of fexofenadine was not demonstrated following 28 days of dosing.

Elimination

Renal—

Renal clearance: 3 to 4 L per hour; approximately 11% of a radioactive fexofenadine dose is excreted in the urine

Fecal—

Approximately 80% of a radioactive fexofenadine dose is excreted in the feces, however, it is unclear whether this represents unabsorbed drug or is the result of biliary excretion.

Precautions to Consider

Carcinogenicity

Fexofenadine showed no carcinogenic potential in 18- and 24-month studies in mice and rats given oral terfenadine doses of 50 and 150 mg per kg of body weight (mg/kg) per day, respectively. These doses resulted in area under the plasma concentration-time curve (AUC) values for fexofenadine of up to four times the human therapeutic value based on the recommended dosage.

Mutagenicity

Fexofenadine was not mutagenic in *in vitro* (Bacterial Reverse Mutation, CHO/HGPRT Forward Mutation, and Rat Lymphocyte Chromosomal Aberration assays) studies and *in vivo* (Mouse Bone Marrow Micronucleus assay) studies.

Pregnancy/Reproduction

Fertility—Dose-related reductions in implants and increases in postimplantation losses were seen in rats given oral doses of terfenadine ≥ 150 mg/kg. These doses resulted in AUC values for fexofenadine of ≥ three times the human therapeutic value based on the recommended dosage. In mice, fexofenadine hydrochloride produced no effect on male or female fertility at average dietary doses up to 4438 mg/kg (approximately 10 times the maximum recommended human daily oral dose).

Pregnancy—Adequate and well-controlled studies in humans have not been done. Fexofenadine should be used during pregnancy only if the potential benefit justifies the potential risk to the fetus.

Fexofenadine was not teratogenic in studies in which rats or rabbits were given oral doses of terfenadine of up to 300 mg/kg per day. These doses resulted in AUC values for fexofenadine of up to 4 and 37 times the human therapeutic value based on the recommended dosage, respectively. In mice, no adverse effects and no teratogenic effects during gestation were observed with fexofenadine at doses up to 3730 mg/kg (approximately 15 times the maximum recommended human daily oral dose).

In rats given oral doses of terfenadine ≥ 150 mg/kg, dose-related decreases in pup weight and survival were observed. These doses resulted in AUC values for fexofenadine of three or more times the human therapeutic value based on the recommended dosage, respectively.

FDA Pregnancy Category C.

Breast-feeding

It is not known whether fexofenadine is distributed into breast milk. Because many drugs are distributed into human milk, caution should be exercised when administering fexofenadine to a nursing woman.

Pediatrics

In clinical trials, 438 children 6 to 11 years of age were safely treated for seasonal allergic rhinitis with fexofenadine 30 mg twice daily, for up to 2 weeks. These studies have not demonstrated pediatrics-specific problems that would limit the usefulness of fexofenadine in children. However, the safety and efficacy of fexofenadine in children up to 6 years of age have not been established.

Geriatrics

Although appropriate studies on the relationship of age to the effects of fexofenadine have not been performed in the geriatric population, no geriatrics-specific problems have bee documented to date. However, elderly patients are more likely to have age-related renal function impairment which may require care in dose selection and monitoring of renal function.

Drug interactions and/or related problems

The following drug interactions and/or related problems have been selected on the basis of their potential clinical significance (possible mechanism in parentheses where appropriate)—not necessarily inclusive (» = major clinical significance):

Note: Combinations containing any of the following medications, depending on the amount present, may also interact with this medication.

» Antacids, aluminum and magnesium hydroxide-containing (administration of fexofenadine within 15 minutes of dosing with an aluminum and magnesium hydroxide-containing antacid has decreased the fexofenadine area under the time-concentration curve by 41% and C_{max} by 43%)

Erythromycin or

Ketoconazole
(concurrent administration with fexofenadine has been found to increase plasma fexofenadine concentrations; however, no differences in adverse effects or increased QT_c intervals were seen)

Medical considerations/Contraindications

The medical considerations/contraindications included have been selected on the basis of their potential clinical significance (reasons given in parentheses where appropriate)—not necessarily inclusive (» = major clinical significance).

Except under special circumstances, this medication should not be used when the following medical problem exists:

» Hypersensitivity to fexofenadine or any of its ingredients

Risk-benefit should be considered when the following medical problems exist:

» Renal function impairment
(based upon increases in the bioavailability and half-life of fexofenadine, once-daily administration is recommended initially in patients with impaired renal function)

Side/Adverse Effects

The following side/adverse effects have been selected on the basis of their potential clinical significance (possible signs and symptoms in parentheses where appropriate)—not necessarily inclusive:

Those indicating need for medical attention

Incidence rare—Observed during clinical practice
Anaphylaxis and hypersensitivity reactions (chest tightness; feeling of warmth redness of the face, neck, arms and occasionally, upper chest; large, hive-like swelling on face, eyelids, lips, tongue, throat, hands, legs, feet, sex organs; shortness of breath, difficult or labored breathing)

Those indicating need for medical attention only if they continue or are bothersome

Incidence less frequent—(≤ 2.5% but more common with fexofenadine than with placebo)
Back pain; coughing—observed in pediatric patients only; ***dizziness; drowsiness; dysmenorrhea*** (painful menstrual bleeding); ***dyspepsia*** (stomach upset); ***fatigue*** (unusual feeling of tiredness); ***fever***—observed in pediatric patients only; ***headache; myalgia*** (joint pain; swollen joints; muscle aching or cramping; muscle pains or stiffness; difficulty in moving); ***nasopharyngitis*** (stuffy or runny nose; muscle aches; unusual tiredness or weakness; fever; sore throat; headache); ***nausea; otitis media*** (earache; ringing or buzzing in ears)—observed in pediatric patients only; ***pain in extremity*** (pain in arms or legs); ***sinusitis*** (headache; pain or tenderness around eyes or cheekbones; runny or stuffy nose); ***upper respiratory tract infection*** (ear congestion; nasal congestion; chills; cough, fever, sneezing, or sore throat; body aches or pain; headache; loss of voice; runny nose; unusual tiredness or weakness; difficulty in breathing); ***viral infections such as cold, flu***

Incidence rare—Observed during clinical practice
Nervousness; rash—urticarial and pruritic; ***sleep disorders*** (sleeplessness; terrifying dreams; trouble sleeping)

Overdose

For more information on the management of overdose or unintentional ingestion, **contact a poison control center** (see *Poison Control Center Listing*).

Clinical effects of overdose

The following effects have been selected on the basis of their potential clinical significance (possible signs and symptoms in parentheses where appropriate)—not necessarily inclusive:
Dizziness; drowsiness; dry mouth

Treatment of overdose

To decrease absorption—consider standard measures to remove any unabsorbed drug.

Hemodialysis does not effectively remove fexofenadine from the blood (up to 1.7% removed).

There is no known antidote to fexofenadine. Treatment is generally symptomatic and supportive

Patients in whom intentional overdose is confirmed or suspected should be referred for psychiatric evaluation.

Patient Consultation

As an aid to patient consultation, refer to *Advice for the Patient, Fexofenadine (Systemic).*

In providing consultation, consider emphasizing the following selected information (» = major clinical significance):

Before using this medication

» Conditions affecting use, especially:
Hypersensitivity to fexofenadine or any of its ingredients
Other medications, especially aluminum and magnesium hydroxide-containing antacids
Other medical problems, especially renal function impairment

Proper use of this medication

» Importance of taking fexofenadine with water and NOT taking with any juices such as grape, orange, or apple juice.
» Waiting at least 15 minutes following administration of fexofenadine to take an antacid containing aluminum or magnesium hydroxide
» Proper dosing
Missed dose: If used regularly—using as soon as possible; using any remaining doses for that day at regularly spaced intervals; not doubling doses
» Proper storage

Side/adverse effects

Signs of potential side effects, especially anaphylaxis and hypersensitivity reactions

General Dosing Information

For oral dosing forms:

Fruit juices such as grapefruit, orange and apple may reduce the bioavailability and exposure of fexofenadine. This is based on the results from three clinical studies using histamine induced skin wheals and flared coupled with population pharmacokinetic analysis. The clinical significance of these observations is unknown. Therefore, to maximize the effects of fexofenadine, it is recommended that fexofenadine should be taken with water.

Bioequivalence information

The capsule and tablet formulations of fexofenadine are bioequivalent when administered at equal doses.

Oral Dosage Forms

FEXOFENADINE HYDROCHLORIDE CAPSULES

Usual adult and adolescent dose

Rhinitis, seasonal, allergic (treatment)—
Oral, 60 mg two times a day, or 180 mg once a day with water.
Urticaria (treatment)—
Oral, 60 mg two times a day or 180 mg one time a day with water.

Note: For patients with decreased renal function, an initial dose of 60 mg once a day is recommended.

Usual adult and adolescent prescribing limits

60 mg two times a day, or 180 mg once a day with water.

Usual pediatric dose

Rhinitis, seasonal, allergic (treatment)
Urticaria (treatment)—
Children 12 years of age and older: See *Usual adult and adolescent dose*
Children 6 to 11 years of age: Oral, 30 mg two times a day with water.
Children up to 6 years of age: Safety and efficacy have not been established.

Note: For pediatric patients with decreased renal function, an initial dose of 30 mg once a day is recommended

Usual pediatric prescribing limits

30 mg two times a day with water

Usual geriatric dose

Rhinitis, seasonal, allergic (treatment)
Urticaria (treatment)—
See *Usual adult and adolescent dose.*

Strength(s) usually available

U.S.—
60 mg (Rx) [*Allegra* (croscarmellose sodium; gelatin; lactose; microcrystalline cellulose; pregelatinized starch)].

Canada—
Not commercially available.

Packaging and storage

Store at controlled room temperature, between 20 and 25 °C (68 and 77 °F). Protect from moisture.

Auxiliary labeling

- May cause drowsiness
- Take with water. Do not take with milk, juice, or antacids.

FEXOFENADINE HYDROCHLORIDE TABLETS

Usual adult and adolescent dose

Rhinitis, seasonal, allergic (treatment)
Urticaria (treatment)—
See *Fexofenadine Hydrochloride Capsules*

Usual adult and adolescent prescribing limits

See *Fexofenadine Hydrochloride Capsules*

Usual pediatric dose

Rhinitis, seasonal, allergic (treatment)
Urticaria (treatment)—
See *Fexofenadine Hydrochloride Capsules*

Note: In Canada, not indicated for children younger than 12 years of age

Usual pediatric prescribing limits

See *Fexofenadine Hydrochloride Capsules*

Usual geriatric dose

Rhinitis, seasonal, allergic (treatment)
Urticaria (treatment)—
See *Usual adult and adolescent dose.*

Strength(s) usually available

U.S.—

30 mg (Rx) [*Allegra* (croscarmellose sodium; magnesium stearate; microcrystalline cellulose; pregelatinized starch)].

60 mg (Rx) [*Allegra* (croscarmellose sodium; magnesium stearate; microcrystalline cellulose; pregelatinized starch)].

180 mg (Rx) [*Allegra* (croscarmellose sodium; magnesium stearate; microcrystalline cellulose; pregelatinized starch)].

Canada—

60 mg (Rx) [*Allegra 12 Hour* (croscarmellose sodium; gelatin; hydroxypropyl methylcellulose; iron oxide; lactose; magnesium stearate; microcrystalline cellulose; povidone; polyethylene glycol; pregelatinized starch; silicon dioxide; starch; titanium dioxide)].

120 mg (Rx) [*Allegra 24 Hour*].

Packaging and storage

Store at controlled room temperature, between 20 and 25 °C (68 and 77 °F). Protect from moisture.

Auxiliary labeling

- May cause drowsiness
- Take with water. Do not take with milk, juice, or antacids.

Revised: 11/02/2005
Developed: 12/04/1996

FEXOFENADINE AND PSEUDOEPHEDRINE Systemic

VA CLASSIFICATION (Primary): RE501

Commonly used brand name(s): *Allegra-D; Allegra-D 24 Hour.*

NOTE: The *Fexofenadine and Pseudoephedrine (Systemic)* monograph is maintained on the *USP DI* electronic data base. A copy of the most recent revision of the complete monograph can be accessed on the *USP DI* Updates Online website. See the front cover of book for details on accessing the site.

For information on the specific components of this combination, see the *USP DI* monographs for *Fexofenadine (Systemic),* and *Pseudoephedrine (Systemic).*

The information that follows is selectively abstracted from the complete monograph and is provided to facilitate drug use review and patient counseling.

Note: For a listing of dosage forms and brand names by country availability, see *Dosage Forms* section(s).

Category

Antihistaminic (H_1-receptor)–decongestant.

Indications

Accepted

Rhinitis, seasonal allergic (treatment)—Fexofenadine and pseudoephedrine combination is indicated for symptomatic relief of seasonal allergic rhinitis (including sneezing; rhinorrhea; itchy nose, palate, and/or throat; itchy, watery, red eyes; and nasal congestion) in adults and children 12 years of age and older when both antihistaminic and decongestant effects are desired.

Patient Consultation

As an aid to patient consultation, refer to *Advice for the Patient, Fexofenadine and Pseudoephedrine (Systemic).*

In providing consultation, consider emphasizing the following selected information (» = major clinical significance):

Before using this medication

» Conditions affecting use, especially:

Hypersensitivity to fexofenadine, pseudoephedrine, adrenergic agents, or any component of the product

Pregnancy—In animal studies, terfenadine and pseudoephedrine caused reduced weight and delayed ossification in the offspring. Risk-benefit should be considered.

Breast-feeding—Pseudoephedrine is distributed into breast milk; risk-benefit should be considered

Use in the elderly—Older patients may be more sensitive to some of the effects of pseudoephedrine; and age-related decreases in hepatic, renal, or cardiac function are a possibility and may require a dosage reduction

Other medications, especially aluminum and magnesium containing antacids or monoamine oxidase (MAO) inhibitors

Other medical problems, especially severe coronary artery disease, severe hypertension, narrow-angle glaucoma, urinary retention, or renal function impairment

Proper use of this medication

Swallowing tablet whole; not breaking or chewing tablet

Taking medication on an empty stomach

Importance of taking medication with water and not taking with juice or antacids

» Proper dosing

Missed dose: Taking as soon as remembered; not taking if almost time for next dose; not doubling doses

Importance of not taking more than the prescribed dose or more frequently than recommended

» Proper storage

Side/adverse effects

Signs of potential side effects, especially dizziness, insomnia, nervousness, palpitations, or upper respiratory infection

Signs of potential side effects observed during clinical practice, especially anaphylaxis, angioedema, chest tightness, dyspnea, flushing, hypersensitivity reaction, pruritus, rash, or urticaria

Oral Dosage Forms

FEXOFENADINE HYDROCHLORIDE AND PSEUDOEPHEDRINE HYDROCHLORIDE EXTENDED-RELEASE TABLETS 12 HOUR

Usual adult and adolescent dose

Antihistaminic-decongestant—
Oral, 1 tablet twice a day.

Note: In patients with reduced renal function, a starting dose of 1 tablet once a day is recommended.

Usual pediatric dose

Antihistaminic-decongestant—
Children younger than 12 years of age—
Safety and efficacy have not been established
Children 12 years of age and over—
See *Usual adult and adolescent dose.*

Strength(s) usually available

U.S.—

Note: The fexofenadine hydrochloride is in immediate-release form and the pseudoephedrine is in extended-release form controlled by an insoluble wax matrix.

60 mg fexofenadine hydrochloride and 120 mg pseudoephedrine hydrochloride (Rx) [*Allegra-D*].

Auxiliary labeling

- Take on an empty stomach - 1 hour before or 2 hours after a meal. Take with a full glass of water.
- Take with water. Do not take with milk, juice or antacids.
- Swallow whole. Do not crush or chew.

FEXOFENADINE HYDROCHLORIDE AND PSEUDOEPHEDRINE HYDROCHLORIDE EXTENDED-RELEASE TABLETS 24 HOUR

Usual adult and adolescent dose

Antihistaminic-decongestant—
Oral, 1 tablet once daily

Note: In patients with renal insufficiency, 24-hour fexofenadine/pseudoephedrine should generally be avoided.

Usual pediatric dose

Safety and efficacy in children less than 12 years of age have not been established. And, doses of the individual components exceed recommended individual doses for pediatric patients less than 12 years of age.

Strength(s) usually available

U.S.—

180 mg fexofenadine hydrochloride and 240 mg pseudoephedrine hydrochloride (Rx) [*Allegra-D 24 Hour* (microcrystalline cellulose; sodium chloride; cellulose acetate; polyethylene glycol; opadry white; povidone; talc; hypromellose; croscarmellose sodium; copovidone; titanium dioxide; magnesium stearate; colloidal silicon dioxide; brilliant blue aluminum lake; acetone; isopropyl alcohol; methyl alcohol; methylene chloride; water; black ink)].

Note: The fexofenadine hydrochloride is in immediate-release form and the pseudoephedrine is in extended-release form controlled by an insoluble wax matrix.

Auxiliary labeling

- Take on an empty stomach - 1 hour before or 2 hours after a meal. Take with a full glass of water.
- Take with water. Do not take with milk, juice or antacids.
- Swallow whole. Do not crush or chew.

Revised: 01/06/2005
Developed: 08/12/1998

FIBER-CONTAINING ENTERAL NUTRITION FORMULAS

—See *Enteral Nutrition Formulas (Systemic)*

FILGRASTIM

—See *Colony Stimulating Factors (Systemic)*

FINASTERIDE Systemic

VA CLASSIFICATION (Primary): GU700/DE890

Commonly used brand name(s): *Propecia; Proscar.*

Note: For a listing of dosage forms and brand names by country availability, see *Dosage Forms* section(s).

Category

Benign prostatic hyperplasia therapy agent; hair growth stimulant, alopecia androgenetica (systemic).

Indications

Accepted

Note: **SEE THE *PREGNANCY/REPRODUCTION* SECTION OF *PRECAUTIONS TO CONSIDER* FOR RESTRICTIONS ON THE USE OF FINASTERIDE. WOMEN OF CHILDBEARING POTENTIAL SHOULD NOT USE OR HANDLE CRUSHED FINASTERIDE TABLETS BECAUSE OF A POTENTIAL RISK TO A MALE FETUS.**

Benign prostatic hyperplasia (treatment)—Finasteride is indicated for the treatment of symptomatic benign prostatic hyperplasia (BPH) in men with an enlarged prostate to improve symptoms, reduce the risk of acute urinary retention, and to reduce the risk for the need of surgery including the transurethral resection of the prostate (TURP) and prostatectomy.

In a four year study finasteride has been shown to reduce prostatic volume by an average of 17.9% in most treated patients compared with an increase of 14.7% in the placebo group.

One study comparing finasteride to terazosin for the treatment of BPH found that finasteride alone was no more effective than placebo, and that finasteride and terazosin given together were no more effective than terazosin alone. However, the patients receiving finasteride had, on average, smaller-volume prostates; a recent meta-analysis has determined that finasteride therapy is most useful in patients with large-volume prostates. Further studies are needed to assess the role of finasteride in the treatment of BPH.

Because finasteride causes only slight improvement in symptoms, it is probably less useful in patients with severe symptoms than in patients with mild to moderate symptoms.

Prior to initiation of finasteride therapy, infection, prostate cancer, stricture disease, hypotonic bladder, or other neurogenic disorders that might mimic BPH should be ruled out.

Alopecia androgenetica (treatment)—Finasteride is indicated for the treatment of alopecia androgenetica (also known as male-pattern baldness) in men only. Safety and efficacy were demonstrated in men between the ages of 18 to 41 with mild to moderate hair loss of the vertex and anterior midscalp area.

In a 96 week study investigating the effect of finasteride on hair weight and hair count, investigators concluded that finasteride increases hair weight to a larger extent than hair count. This data implies that factors other than the increase in the number of hairs contribute to the effect of finasteride, such as increases in growth rate and thickness of hairs.

Acceptance not established

Finasteride has been used for the treatment of hirsutism; however, because of potential risk to male fetuses, it should be used with caution, if at all, in women of childbearing years.

Finasteride has been used to treat prostate cancer; however, data are limited and results from ongoing trials are needed to define its role in this condition.

Efficacy of finasteride in the treatment of bitemporal hair recession has not been established.

Unaccepted

Finasteride is not useful in patients with obstructive uropathy accompanied by urinary retention.

Pharmacology/Pharmacokinetics

Physicochemical characteristics

Source—Synthetic.
Chemical Group—A 4-azasteroid compound.
Molecular weight—372.55.

Mechanism of action/Effect

Finasteride competitively and specifically inhibits 5-alpha-reductase, a type 2 isoenzyme that metabolizes testosterone to dihydrotestosterone (DHT) in the prostate gland, liver, and skin. Finasteride has no affinity for the androgen receptors and does not appear to affect the hypothalamic-pituitary-testicular axis.

Benign prostatic hyperplasia—Development of the prostate gland is dependent on DHT, which is a potent androgen. After administration of finasteride, 5-alpha–reduced steroid metabolites in blood and urine are decreased; serum DHT is reduced by approximately 70% with daily dosing. Concentrations of both DHT and prostate-specific antigen (PSA) are decreased in prostatic tissue, whereas intraprostatic testosterone concentrations are significantly increased.

Alopecia androgenetica—The scalps of men with alopecia androgenetica contain miniaturized hair follicles and increased amounts of DHT compared with the scalps of men with normal hair growth. Scalp and serum DHT concentrations decrease after administration of finasteride, thus disrupting the development of male-pattern balding. It is not known why a decrease in scalp and serum DHT disrupts the development of male-pattern balding.

Absorption

Finasteride is rapidly absorbed from the gastrointestinal tract. Mean bioavailability of a 5-mg tablet was 63% (range 34 to 108%) in a study in healthy male subjects. Mean bioavailability of a 1-mg tablet was 65% (range 26 to 70%) in a study in healthy male subjects. Bioavailability is not affected by food intake.

Distribution

Finasteride crosses the blood-brain barrier. It also is distributed into semen; however, the amount of finasteride in the semen of patients receiving 5 mg per day has no effect on circulating DHT concentrations in adults.

Volume of distribution (Vol_D)—Steady state: 76 L

Protein binding

Plasma—Very high (90%).

Biotransformation

Hepatic. The major metabolite isolated from urine is the monocarboxylic acid metabolite; the t-butyl side chain monohydroxylated metabolite has been isolated from plasma. These metabolites have no more than 20% of the 5-alpha-reductase inhibiting activity of finasteride.

Half-life

Mean 6 hours (range 3 to 16 hours) following a single 5-mg dose in healthy male subjects 45 to 60 years of age; approximately 8 hours in subjects 70 years of age or older. Mean 4.5 hours after multiple 1 mg doses in males 19 to 42

Time to peak concentration
Plasma—Ranged from 1.8 to 2.8 hours after administration of single doses of 5, 10, 20, 50, and 100 mg of finasteride and 1 to 2 hours after administration of multiple doses of 1 mg per day.

Peak serum concentration
Plasma—Ranged from 38.1 ± 7 to 835.5 ± 199.2 micrograms per L (mcg/L) after administration of single doses of 5, 10, 20, 50, and 100 mg of finasteride and 9.2 nanograms per mL (range 4.9 to 13.7 nanograms per mL) after administration of multiple doses of 1 mg per day. Slow accumulation occurs with multiple dosing; in one study, mean plasma concentrations were approximately 50% higher after 17 days of treatment than after the first dose, and mean trough concentrations in another study after 1 year were even higher. In one study, the mean area under the plasma concentration-time curve (AUC) (0 to 24 hours) after 17 days of administration was 15% higher in subjects 70 years of age or older.

Time to peak effect
Reduction in serum DHT concentration—8 hours after the first dose.

Duration of action
Single dose—Reduction in serum DHT concentration: 24 hours.

Multiple doses—DHT concentrations return to pretreatment levels within approximately 2 weeks after withdrawal of daily therapy. The prostate returns to pretreatment size in about 3 months.

Elimination
Fecal, 57% (range 51 to 64%), as metabolites; renal, 39% (range 32 to 46%), as metabolites. In renal function impairment, urinary excretion of metabolites is decreased, but fecal excretion of metabolites is increased; therefore, no dosage adjustment is necessary.

In dialysis—Unknown.

Precautions to Consider

Carcinogenicity
A 19-month study in CD-1 mice at a dose of 250 mg per kg of body weight (mg/kg) per day (228 times the human exposure of 5 mg and 1824 times the human exposure of 1 mg) found a statistically significant increase in incidence of testicular Leydig cell adenomas. An increase in the incidence of Leydig cell hyperplasia was observed in mice at a dose of 25 mg/kg per day (23 times the human exposure of 5 mg and 184 times the human exposure of 1 mg, estimated) and in rats at a dose ≥ 40 mg/kg per day (39 times the human exposure of 5 mg and 312 times the human exposure of 1 mg). A positive correlation between the proliferative changes in the Leydig cells and an increase in serum luteinizing hormone (LH) concentrations (two- to threefold higher than control) has been demonstrated in both rodent species treated with high doses of finasteride. No drug-related Leydig cell changes were seen in either rats or dogs treated for 1 year at doses of 20 mg/kg per day and 45 mg/kg per day (30 and 350 times, respectively, the human exposure of 5 mg and 240 and 2800 times, respectively, the human exposure of 1 mg) or in mice treated for 19 months at a dose of 2.5 mg/kg per day (2.3 times the human exposure of 5 mg and 18.4 times the human exposure of 1 mg, estimated).

Tumorigenicity
A 24-month study in Sprague-Dawley rats at doses up to 160 mg/kg per day in males and 320 mg/kg per day in females (producing 111 and 274 times, respectively, the systemic exposure observed in humans receiving the recommended human dose of 5 mg per day and 888 and 2192 times, respectively, the systemic exposure observed in humans receiving the recommended human dose of 1 mg per day) found no evidence of tumorigenicity.

Mutagenicity
No evidence of mutagenicity was found in an *in vitro* bacterial mutagenesis assay, a mammalian cell mutagenesis assay, or an *in vitro* alkaline elution assay. In an *in vitro* chromosome aberration assay, when Chinese hamster ovary cells were treated with high concentrations (450 to 550 micromoles, corresponding to 4000 to 5000 times the peak plasma concentrations in humans given a total dose of 5 mg and 18,000 to 22,000 times the peak plasma concentration in humans given a total dose of 1 mg) of finasteride, there was a slight increase in chromosome aberrations. In addition, the concentrations (450 to 550 micromoles) used in *in vitro* studies are not achievable in a biological system. In an *in vivo* chromosome aberration assay in mice, no treatment-related increase in chromosome aberration was observed at the maximum tolerated finasteride dose of 250 mg/kg per day (228 times the human exposure of 5 mg and 1824 times the human exposure of 1 mg) as determined in the carcinogenicity studies.

Pregnancy/Reproduction
Fertility—Volume of ejaculate may be decreased in some patients during therapy, but the decrease does not appear to interfere with normal sexual function.

No effect on fertility, sperm count, or ejaculation volume was found in sexually mature male rabbits treated with finasteride at doses of 80 mg/kg per day (543 times the human exposure of 5 mg and 4344 times the human exposure of 1 mg) for up to 12 weeks. No effects on fertility were found in sexually mature male rats treated with 80 mg/kg per day (61 times the human exposure of 5 mg and 488 times the human exposure of 1 mg) for 6 or 12 weeks. However, when treatment in male rats was continued for up to 24 or 30 weeks, there was an apparent decrease in fertility and fecundity and an associated significant decrease in the weights of the seminal vesicles and prostate, all of which were reversible within 6 weeks of withdrawal of finasteride. No drug-related effect on testes or on mating performance has been seen in rats or rabbits. The decrease in fertility in rats is secondary to an effect on accessory sex organs (prostate and seminal vesicles) that results in failure to form a seminal plug, which is essential for normal fertility in rats, but is not relevant in humans.

Pregnancy—Finasteride is not indicated for use in women.

Because of the ability of 5-alpha-reductase inhibitors to inhibit conversion of testosterone to dihydrotestosterone (DHT), finasteride administration to a pregnant woman may cause abnormalities of the external genitalia of a male fetus.

Because of the potential risk to a male fetus, a woman who is pregnant or who may become pregnant should not handle crushed finasteride or broken tablets. Finasteride tablets are coated and will prevent contact with the active ingredient during normal handling, provided that the tablets have not been broken or crushed.

Administration of finasteride to pregnant rats at doses ranging from 100 mcg per kg of body weight (mcg/kg) per day to 100 mg/kg per day (approximately 1 to 1000 times the recommended human dose of 5 mg and 5 to 5000 times the recommended human dose of 1 mg) produced dose-dependent development of hypospadias in 3.6 to 100% of male offspring. Pregnant rats given doses ≥ 30 mcg/kg per day (≥ three tenths of the recommended human dose of 5 mg and ≥ 1.5 times the recommended human dose of 1 mg) produced male offspring with decreased prostatic and seminal vesicular weights, delayed preputial separation, and transient nipple development; doses of ≥ 3 mcg/kg per day (≥ 3% of the recommended human dose of 5 mg and one fifth of the recommended human dose of 1 mg) produced decreased anogenital distance. All of these changes are expected pharmacologic effects of 5-alpha-reductase inhibitors and are similar to those reported in male infants with a genetic deficiency of 5-alpha-reductase. The critical period during which these effects can be induced in male rats has been defined as days 16 to 17 of gestation. No abnormalities were observed in female offspring exposed *in utero* to any dose of finasteride.

In reproduction studies using male rats treated with finasteride doses of 80 mg/kg per day (61 times the human exposure of 5 mg and 488 times the human exposure of 1 mg) and untreated female rats, no developmental abnormalities were observed in first filial generation (F_1) male or female offspring. Administration of 3 mg/kg per day (30 times the recommended human dose of 5 mg and 150 times the recommended human dose of 1 mg) during the late gestation and lactation period resulted in slightly decreased fertility in F_1 male offspring; no effects were seen in female offspring. In rabbit fetuses exposed to finasteride *in utero* from days 6 to 18 of gestation at doses up to 100 mg/kg per day (1000 times the recommended human dose of 5 mg and 5000 times the recommended human dose of 1 mg), no evidence of malformations was observed; however, effects on male genitalia would not be expected since the rabbits were not exposed during the critical period of urogenital system development.

The *in utero* effects of finasteride exposure during the period of embryonic and fetal development were evaluated in rhesus monkeys (gestation days 20 to 100), a species more predictive of human development than rats or rabbits. Intravenous administration of finasteride to pregnant monkeys at doses as high as 800 ng/day (at least 60 to 120 times the highest estimated exposure of pregnant women to finasteride from semen of men taking 5 mg/day) resulted in no abnormalities in male fetuses. In confirmation of the relevance of the rhesus model for human fetal development, oral administration of a dose of finasteride (2 mg/kg/day; 20 times the recommended human dose of 5 mg/kg/day or approximately 1–2 million times the highest estimated exposure to finasteride from semen of men taking 5 mg/kg/day) to pregnant monkeys resulted in external genitalia abnormalities in male fetuses. No other abnormalities were observed in male fetuses and no finasteride-related abnormalities were observed in female fetuses at any dose.

FDA Pregnancy Category X.

Breast-feeding
Finasteride is not indicated for use in women. It is not known whether finasteride is distributed into breast milk.

Pediatrics
Finasteride is not indicated for use in children. No information is available on the relationship of age to the effects of finasteride in pediatric patients.

Geriatrics
The elimination rate of finasteride is decreased in the elderly (70 years of age or older); however, no dosage adjustment is necessary.

Laboratory value alterations
The following have been selected on the basis of their potential clinical significance (possible effect in parentheses where appropriate)—not necessarily inclusive (» = major clinical significance).

With diagnostic test results
Prostate-specific antigen (PSA)
(serum concentrations are decreased by 50% by finasteride, even in the presence of prostatic cancer; the effect on usefulness of PSA determinations for prostatic cancer detection is unknown)
(PSA values should be doubled after treatment of 6 or more months. Any sustained increases in PSA levels while on finasteride should be carefully evaluated, including consideration of noncompliance to therapy.)
(Percent free PSA (free to total PSA ratio) is not significantly decreased by finasteride. The ratio of free to total PSA remains constant even under the influence of finasteride.)

With physiology/laboratory test values
Dihydrotestosterone (DHT)
(serum and prostatic concentrations are rapidly reduced)

Follicle-stimulating hormone (FSH) and
Luteinizing hormone (LH) and
Testosterone
(median circulating serum concentrations are increased by 10 to 20% but remain within the physiologic range; testosterone concentrations in prostatic tissue increase by up to tenfold)

Medical considerations/Contraindications
The medical considerations/contraindications included have been selected on the basis of their potential clinical significance (reasons given in parentheses where appropriate)—not necessarily inclusive (» = major clinical significance).

Risk-benefit should be considered when the following medical problems exist:
Hepatic function impairment
(metabolism of finasteride may be reduced)

Large residual urinary volume or
Reduced urinary flow
(because of possible presence of obstructive uropathy, patients with these conditions may not be candidates for finasteride therapy)

» Sensitivity to finasteride or to any component of the medication

Patient monitoring
The following may be especially important in patient monitoring (other tests may be warranted in some patients, depending on condition; » = major clinical significance):

For benign prostatic hyperplasia
» Digital rectal examination
(recommended prior to initiation of therapy and at periodic intervals during therapy, to detect possible prostate cancer)

Side/Adverse Effects
The following side/adverse effects have been selected on the basis of their potential clinical significance (possible signs and symptoms in parentheses where appropriate)—not necessarily inclusive:

Those indicating need for medical attention
Incidence less frequent
Gynecomastia (breast enlargement and tenderness); ***hypersensitivity reaction*** (skin rash; swelling of lips)

Note: *Gynecomastia* has been reported to develop from 14 days to 2.5 years after initiation of 5-mg finasteride therapy. Discontinuation of therapy has led to a partial or complete remission in most cases; however, a small percentage of patients have required mastectomy. In addition, gynecomastia has led to primary intraductal breast carcinoma in at least two patients receiving finasteride therapy. Cause and effect are not known at this time. In clinical trials, gynecomastia and *hypersensitivity reaction* events in patients receiving 1 mg of finasteride therapy were not different from subjects receiving placebo.

Those indicating need for medical attention only if they continue or are bothersome
Incidence less frequent or rare (< 4%)
Abdominal pain; back pain; decreased libido; decreased volume of ejaculate; diarrhea; dizziness; headache; impotence

Note: *Decreased libido, decreased volume of ejaculate,* and *impotence* usually resolve with continued treatment in over 60% of patients who report these side effects.

Incidence unknown—Observed during clinical practice; estimates of frequency can not be determined
Testicular pain

Patient Consultation
As an aid to patient consultation, refer to *Advice for the Patient, Finasteride (Systemic).*

In providing consultation, consider emphasizing the following selected information (» = major clinical significance):

Before using this medication
» Conditions affecting use, especially:
Sensitivity to finasteride or any component of the medication
Carcinogenicity—Increased incidence of testicular tumors in mice and rats receiving very high doses
Pregnancy—Pregnant women should not use or handle crushed tablets because of potential risk of abnormal external genitalia development in male fetuses
Breast-feeding—Not indicated for use in breast-feeding women

Proper use of this medication
Tablets may be crushed; however, pregnant women should not handle crushed tablets

For benign prostatic hyperplasia (BPH)
Getting into the habit of taking at same time each day to help increase compliance
» Does not cure, but helps control BPH; taking for at least 6 months for full effect; possible need for lifelong therapy; checking with physician before discontinuing medication
All patients with BPH should avoid drinking fluids, especially coffee or alcohol, in the evening, to reduce nocturia

For male-pattern balding
Taking for at least 3 months to see effect; improvement lasts only as long as treatment continues; new hair will be lost within one year of stopping treatment
» Proper dosing
Missed dose: Taking as soon as possible; not taking if almost time for next dose; not doubling doses
» Proper storage

Precautions while using this medication
» Women who are or who may become pregnant should not handle crushed tablets

Side/adverse effects
Signs of potential side effects, especially gynecomastia (more likely with 5 mg dose), hypersensitivity reaction (more likely with 5 mg dose), decreased libido, decreased volume of ejaculate, and impotence

General Dosing Information
Diet/Nutrition
Finasteride may be taken with or without food.

Oral Dosage Forms
FINASTERIDE TABLETS
Usual adult dose
Benign prostatic hyperplasia—
Oral, 5 mg once a day.

Note: At least six to twelve months of therapy may be required to assess clinical response.

Alopecia androgenetica—
Oral, 1 mg once a day.

Note: Three months of therapy may be required to assess response as a hair growth stimulant. Discontinuation of finasteride treatment leads to reversal of effects within one year.

Usual geriatric dose
See *Usual adult dose.*

Strength(s) usually available

U.S.—

1 mg (Rx) [*Propecia* (lactose)].

5 mg (Rx) [*Proscar* (lactose)].

Canada—

5 mg (Rx) [*Proscar*].

Packaging and storage

Store between 15° and 30 °C (59° and 86 °F), unless otherwise specified by the manufacturer. Store in a tight container. Protect from lightand moisture.

Selected Bibliography

Drugs for the treatment of benign prostatic hypertrophy: efficacy and safety criteria. Proceedings of meeting of the Endocrinology and Metabolic Drugs Advisory Committee, Center for Drug Evaluation and Research, Food and Drug Administration; 1992 Feb 3-4: Bethesda, MD.

Revised: 12/22/2004

FLAVOCOXID Systemic†

VA CLASSIFICATION (Primary): MS102

Commonly used brand name(s): *Limbrel*.

Note: For a listing of dosage forms and brand names by country availability, see *Dosage Forms* section(s).

†Not commercially available in Canada.

Category

Antirheumatic.

Indications

Accepted

Osteoarthritis (treatment)—Flavocoxid is indicated for the clinical dietary management of osteoarthritis (OA), including associated inflammation.

Unaccepted

Flavocoxid has not been investigated for use in the clinical dietary management of rheumatoid arthritis (RA), acute pain or primary dysmenorrhea.

Pharmacology/Pharmacokinetics

Physicochemical characteristics

Source—Flavocoxid consists of a proprietary blend of Free-B-Ring flavonoids and flavans from phytochemical food source materials which are Generally Recognized As Safe (GRAS). The primary flavonoid is derived from the source *Scutellaria baicalensis* and the primary flavin from the source *Acacia catechu*.

Molecular weight—

Primary Flavonoid (Baicalin): 446.37.

Primary Flavan (Catechin): 290.27.

Solubility—Flavocoxid is partially soluble in water and glycerol, soluble in ethanol, methanol, and acetonitrile. It is practically insoluble in hexane.

Mechanism of action/Effect

Flavocoxid is believed to inhibit prostaglandin synthesis, via the inhibition of cyclo-oxygenase (COX). In addition, flavocoxid has been observed to inhibit the inflammatory pathway of arachidonic acid metabolism, 5–lipoxygenase, which has been shown to reduce the production of leukotriene-B4, an agent that fosters white blood cell chemotaxis and the subsequent release of reactive oxygen species and pro-inflammatory cytokines. Reactive oxygen species (ROS) have been shown to play a role in the degradation of cartilage in osteoarthritis.

Flavocoxid may also act through an antioxidant mechanism by reduction of ROS including hydroxyl radical, superoxide anion radical and hydrogen peroxide.

Flavocoxid has been found to reduce pro-inflammatory cytokines interleukin-1–beta and tumor necrosis factor alpha.

Absorption

Co-ingestion of flavocoxid and food is believed to be safe, but may present modest absorption limitations.

Biotransformation

Flavocoxid is primarily metabolized via glucuronidation and sulfation, with little hepatic metabolism involving cytochrome P450 isoenzymes (CYP). Primary ingredient baicalin undergoes hydrolysis of the glucuronide moiety at the gut mucosal border and is absorbed as the aglycone, baicalein. Glucuronidation and sulfation of baicalein occurs intrahepatically.

Precautions to Consider

Pregnancy/Reproduction

Pregnancy—Adequate and well controlled studies have not been done. Flavocoxid is not recommended for pregnant women.

FDA Pregnancy Category: none reported.

Breast-feeding

It is not known whether flavocoxid is distributed into breast milk. Flavocoxid is not recommended for lactating patients.

Pediatrics

Safety and efficacy have not been established in patients under 18 years of age.

Geriatrics

No information is available on the relationship of age to the effects of flavocoxid in geriatrics.

Medical considerations/Contraindications

The medical considerations/contraindications included have been selected on the basis of their potential clinical significance (reasons given in parentheses where appropriate)—not necessarily inclusive (» = major clinical significance).

Except under special circumstances, this medication should not be used when the following medical problem exists:

» Hypersensitivity to flavocoxid or to any of its components.

Risk-benefit should be considered when the following medical problems exist:

» Stomach ulcers, history of
(use is not recommended.)

Side/Adverse Effects

The following side/adverse effects have been selected on the basis of their potential clinical significance (possible signs and symptoms in parentheses where appropriate)—not necessarily inclusive:

GI side effects such as bleeding, ulceration and stomach perforation can occur at any time, with or without symptoms with concomitant or previous use of NSAIDS or COX-2 inhibitors.

Those indicating need for medical attention only if they continue or are bothersome

Incidence more frequent

Fluid accumulation in the knee; hypertension (blurred vision; dizziness; nervousness; headache; pounding in the ears; slow or fast heartbeat); ***psoriasis*** (red, scaling, or crusted skin); ***varicose veins, increased*** (dull ache or feeling of pressure or heaviness in legs; itching skin near damaged veins; swollen feet and ankles)

Overdose

For more information on the management of overdose or unintentional ingestion, **contact a poison control center** (see *Poison Control Center Listing*).

Treatment of overdose

There are no known specific antidotes to flavocoxid. Treatment is generally symptomatic and supportive.

Supportive care—

Patients in whom intentional overdose is confirmed or suspected should be referred for psychiatric consultation.

Patient Consultation

As an aid to patient consultation, refer to *Advice for the Patient, Flavocoxid (Systemic)*.

In providing consultation, consider emphasizing the following selected information (» = major clinical significance):

Before using this medication

» Conditions affecting use, especially:

Hypersensitivity to flavocoxid or any of its ingredients

Pregnancy—Not recommended for use during pregnancy

Breast-feeding—Not recommended for lactating patients

Use in children—Safety and efficacy have not been established in patients under 18 years of age.

Other medical problems, especially history of stomach ulcers

Proper use of this medication

» Taking flavocoxid one hour before or after the consumption of food.

» Proper dosing

Missed dose: Taking as soon as possible; not taking if almost time for next scheduled dose; not doubling doses

» Proper storage

Precautions while using this medication
» Regular visits to physician to check progress

General Dosing Information

Flavocoxid is an ethical medical food offered exclusively by prescription and to be used only under physician supervision.

Flavocoxid is Generally Recognized As Safe (GRAS), however, specific studies in pediatric, geriatric, race, hepatic insufficiency, renal insufficiency, and immunological insufficiency patient populations have not been performed.

Flavocoxid cannot be substituted for the use of corticosteroids or to treat corticosteroid insufficiency.

Diet/Nutrition
Take flavocoxid one hour before or after the consumption of food.

Oral Dosage Forms

FLAVOCOXID CAPSULE

Usual adult dose
Osteoarthritis—
Oral, one capsule (250 mg), every 12 hours for a total of 500 mg daily, taken one hour before or after the consumption of food.

Usual adult prescribing limits
Up to 750 mg daily.

Usual pediatric dose
Safety and efficacy in pediatric patients under 18 years of age have not been established.

Usual geriatric dose
See *Usual adult dose.*

Usual geriatric prescribing limits
See *Usual adult prescribing limits.*

Strength(s) usually available
U.S.—
250 mg (Rx) [*Limbrel* (dextrose; FD&C Blue #1; FD&C Green #3; gelatin; magnesium stearate; maltodextrin NF; microcrystalline cellulose; starch oligosaccharides; titanium dioxide)].

Packaging and storage
Store between 15 and 30 °C (59 and 86 °F) USP controlled room temperature, Protect from light and moisture.

Auxiliary labeling
- Take on an empty stomach–1 hour before or 2 to 3 hours after eating.
- Protect from light.
- Do not freeze.

Note
Flavocoxid is an ethical medical food product to be used under physician supervision for the clinical dietary management of osteoarthritis (OA), including associated inflammation.

Developed: 10/06/2005

FLAVOXATE Systemic

VA CLASSIFICATION (Primary): GU201

Commonly used brand name(s): *Urispas.*

Note: For a listing of dosage forms and brand names by country availability, see *Dosage Forms* section(s).

Category

Antispasmodic (urinary tract).

Indications

Accepted
Urologic disorders, symptoms of (treatment); and
Irritative voiding, symptoms of (treatment)—Flavoxate is indicated for the symptomatic relief, but not the definitive treatment, of dysuria, urgency, nocturia, suprapubic pain, and frequency and incontinence associated with cystitis, prostatitis, urethritis, urethrocystitis, or urethrotrigonitis.

Pharmacology/Pharmacokinetics

Physicochemical characteristics
Molecular weight—427.93.

Mechanism of action/Effect
Exerts direct antispasmodic (relaxant) effect on smooth muscle, mainly of the urinary tract.

Other actions/effects
Also has weak antihistaminic, local anesthetic, and analgesic action. With high doses, flavoxate has weak anticholinergic properties.

Absorption
Well absorbed from gastrointestinal tract.

Elimination
Renal (10 to 30% eliminated within 6 hours; 57% eliminated in 24 hours)

Precautions to Consider

Pregnancy/Reproduction
Pregnancy—Adequate and well-controlled studies in pregnant women have not been done.

Reproduction studies in rats and rabbits at doses up to 34 times the recommended human dose have not shown that flavoxate causes impaired fertility or adverse effects on the fetus.

FDA Pregnancy Category B.

Breast-feeding
It is not known whether flavoxate is distributed in breast milk. Caution should be used when flavoxate is prescribed to nursing women because many medications are distributed into human milk.

Pediatrics
Appropriate studies on the relationship of age to the effects of flavoxate have not been performed in children younger than 12 years of age. Flavoxate is not recommended for this age group because safety and efficacy have not been established.

Geriatrics
Confusion is more likely to occur in geriatric patients taking flavoxate.

Dental
Prolonged use or use of large doses of flavoxate may decrease or inhibit salivary flow, thus contributing to the development of caries, periodontal disease, oral candidiasis, and discomfort.

Medical considerations/Contraindications
The medical considerations/contraindications included have been selected on the basis of their potential clinical significance (reasons given in parentheses where appropriate)—not necessarily inclusive (» = major clinical significance).

Risk-benefit should be considered when the following medical problems exist:

» Gastrointestinal tract obstructive disease as in achalasia and pyloroduodenal stenosis
(decrease in motility and tone may occur, resulting in obstruction and gastric retention)

Glaucoma, angle-closure
(mydriatic effect of flavoxate resulting in increased intraocular pressure may precipitate an acute attack of angle-closure glaucoma)

» Hemorrhage, gastrointestinal
(may exacerbate condition)

» Paralytic ileus
(may result in obstruction)

Sensitivity to flavoxate

» Uropathy, obstructive, such as bladder neck obstruction due to prostatic hypertrophy
(urinary retention may be precipitated)

Side/Adverse Effects

Note: Although weak, flavoxate's anticholinergic action should be taken into consideration when it is given to patients where the environmental temperature is high, since there is risk of a rapid increase in body temperature because of suppression of sweat gland activity.

The following side/adverse effects have been selected on the basis of their potential clinical significance (possible signs and symptoms in parentheses where appropriate)—not necessarily inclusive:

Those indicating need for medical attention
Incidence rare
Confusion—especially in the elderly; ***hypersensitivity*** (skin rash or hives); ***increased intraocular pressure*** (eye pain); ***leukopenia*** (sore throat and fever)

Those indicating need for medical attention only if they continue or are bothersome

Incidence more frequent

Drowsiness; dryness of mouth and throat

Incidence less frequent or rare

Constipation—more frequent with doses of 800 mg or above; ***difficult urination; difficulty concentrating; difficulty in eye accommodation*** (blurred vision); ***dizziness; fast heartbeat; headache; increased sweating; mydriatic effect*** (increased sensitivity of eyes to light); ***nausea or vomiting; nervousness; stomach pain; Urticaria and other dermatosis*** (hives)

Overdose

For specific information on the agents used in the management of flavoxate overdose, see:

Thiopental in Anesthetics, Barbiturate (Systemic) monograph;
Benzodiazepines (Systemic) monograph;
Charcoal, Activated (Oral-Local) monograph;
Chloral Hydrate (Systemic) monograph

For more information on the management of overdose or unintentional ingestion, **contact a Poison Control Center** (see *Poison Control Center Listing*).

Clinical effects of overdose

The following effects have been selected on the basis of their potential clinical significance (possible signs and symptoms in parenthesis where appropriate)—not necessarily inclusive:

Anticholinergic effects (clumsiness or unsteadiness; severe dizziness; severe drowsiness; fever; flushing or redness of face; hallucinations; shortness of breath or troubled breathing; unusual excitement; nervousness; restlessness; or irritability)

Treatment of overdose

Recommended treatment for overdose with flavoxate includes:

- To decrease absorption—Emesis or gastric lavage with 4% tannic acid solution or administration of an aqueous slurry of activated charcoal.
- Specific treatment—Administration of small doses of short-acting barbiturate (100 mg thiopental sodium) or benzodiazepines, or rectal infusion of 100 to 200 mL of a 2% solution of chloral hydrate, to control excitement. Artificial respiration with oxygen if needed for respiratory depression. Adequate hydration. Symptomatic treatment as necessary.
- Supportive care—Patients in whom intentional overdose is known or suspected should be referred for psychiatric consultation.

Patient Consultation

As an aid to patient consultation, refer to *Advice for the Patient, Flavoxate (Systemic)*.

In providing consultation, consider emphasizing the following selected information (» = major clinical significance):

Before using this medication

» Conditions affecting use, especially:
Sensitivity to flavoxate
Use in children—Flavoxate is not recommended for children younger than 12 years of age.
Use in the elderly—Confusion more likely
Dental—Possible development of dental problems because of decreased salivary flow
Other medical problems, especially gastrointestinal hemorrhage, paralytic ileus, or obstruction in gastrointestinal or urinary tract

Proper use of this medication

Taking medication on an empty stomach with water, or with food or milk to reduce gastric irritation
» Importance of not taking more medication than the amount prescribed
» Proper dosing
Missed dose: Taking as soon as possible; if almost time for next dose, not taking at all; not doubling doses
» Proper storage

Precautions while using this medication

Possible increased sensitivity of eyes to light
» Caution if drowsiness or blurred vision occurs
» Caution during exercise or hot weather; overheating may result in heat stroke
Possible dryness of mouth and throat; using sugarless gum or candy, ice, or saliva substitute for relief; checking with physician or dentist if dry mouth continues for more than 2 weeks

Side/adverse effects

Signs of potential side effects, especially hypersensitivity, confusion, increased intraocular pressure, and leukopenia

General Dosing Information

Flavoxate may be taken on an empty stomach with water; however, if gastric irritation occurs it may be taken with food or milk.

If urinary tract infection is present, appropriate antibacterial therapy should be administered.

Oral Dosage Forms

FLAVOXATE HYDROCHLORIDE TABLETS

Usual adult and adolescent dose

Urologic disorders or
Irritative voiding—
Oral, 100 to 200 mg three or four times a day, the dosage being adjusted as needed and tolerated.

Usual pediatric dose

Children up to 12 years of age–Use is not recommended because safety and efficacy have not been established.

Children 12 years of age and over–See *Usual adult and adolescent dose.*

Usual geriatric dose

See *Usual adult and adolescent dose.*

Strength(s) usually available

U.S.—
100 mg (Rx) [*Urispas*].

Canada—
200 mg (Rx) [*Urispas*].

Packaging and storage

Store below 40 °C (104 °F), preferably between 15 and 30 °C (59 and 86 °F), unless otherwise specified by manufacturer.

Auxiliary labeling

- May cause drowsiness or blurred vision.

Revised: 02/23/2000

FLOCTAFENINE—See *Anti-inflammatory Drugs, Nonsteroidal (Systemic)*

FLOXURIDINE Systemic†

VA CLASSIFICATION (Primary): AN300

Commonly used brand name(s): *FUDR*.

Note: For a listing of dosage forms and brand names by country availability, see *Dosage Forms* section(s).

†Not commercially available in Canada.

Category

Antineoplastic.

Indications

Note: Bracketed information in the *Indications* section refers to uses that are not included in U.S. product labeling.

Accepted

Carcinoma, colorectal (treatment)
Carcinoma, hepatic (treatment)
[Carcinoma, ovarian, epithelial (treatment)]or
[Carcinoma, renal (treatment)]—Floxuridine, given by continuous regional intra-arterial infusion, is indicated for palliative management of colorectal carcinoma metastatic to the liver that has not responded to other treatment. Floxuridine is most useful when the disease has not extended beyond an area capable of infusion via a single artery.

Floxuridine also is indicated for carcinoma of the ovary and kidney not responsive to other antimetabolites.

Pharmacology/Pharmacokinetics

Physicochemical characteristics

Molecular weight—246.20.

Mechanism of action/Effect

Floxuridine is an antimetabolite of the pyrimidine analog type. Floxuridine is considered to be cell cycle–specific for the S-phase of cell division. Activity occurs as the result of activation in the tissues, and includes inhibition of DNA and, as a result of action of the fluorouracil metabolite, RNA synthesis.

Distribution

Some crosses the blood-brain barrier; active metabolites are localized intracellularly.

Biotransformation

Hepatic and in tissues, extensive, to the monophosphate derivative and fluorouracil; after continuous intra-arterial infusion, conversion to the monophosphate derivative is enhanced; largely converted to fluorouracil after rapid intravenous or intra-arterial injection.

Elimination

Respiratory (as carbon dioxide), about 60%.

Renal, 10 to 13% (as unchanged drug and metabolites).

Precautions to Consider

Carcinogenicity

Secondary malignancies are potential delayed effects of many antineoplastic agents, although it is not clear whether the effect is related to their mutagenic or immunosuppressive action. The effect of dose and duration of therapy is also unknown, although risk seems to increase with long-term use. Although information is limited, available data seem to indicate that the carcinogenic risk is greatest with the alkylating agents.

Studies with floxuridine have not been done.

Antimetabolites have been shown to be carcinogenic in animals and may be associated with an increased risk of development of secondary carcinomas in humans, although the risk appears to be less than with alkylating agents.

Mutagenicity

Floxuridine produces oncogenic transformation of fibroblasts in cultured C3H/10T1/2 mouse embryo cells.

Floxuridine is mutagenic in human leukocytes *in vitro* and in the *Drosophila* test system.

Pregnancy/Reproduction

Fertility—Gonadal suppression, resulting in amenorrhea or azoospermia, may occur in patients taking antineoplastic therapy, especially with the alkylating agents. In general, these effects appear to be related to dose and length of therapy and may be irreversible. Prediction of the degree of testicular or ovarian function impairment is complicated by the common use of combinations of several antineoplastics, which makes it difficult to assess the effects of individual agents.

Studies with floxuridine have not been done. However, fluorouracil, which is a metabolite of floxuridine, has significant effects on fertility in animals.

Pregnancy—Adequate and well-controlled studies in humans have not been done.

First trimester: It is usually recommended that use of antineoplastics, especially combination chemotherapy, be avoided whenever possible, especially during the first trimester. Although information is limited because of the relatively few instances of antineoplastic administration during pregnancy, the mutagenic, teratogenic, and carcinogenic potential of these medications must be considered.

Other hazards to the fetus include adverse reactions seen in adults.

In general, use of a contraceptive is recommended during cytotoxic drug therapy.

Floxuridine is teratogenic in chick embryos, mice (at doses of 2.5 to 100 mg per kg of body weight [mg/kg]), and rats (at doses of 75 to 150 mg/kg); doses were 3.2 to 125 times, respectively, the recommended human therapeutic dose. Malformations included cleft palates, skeletal defects, and deformed appendages, paws, and tails.

FDA Pregnancy Category D.

Breast-feeding

It is not known whether floxuridine is distributed into breast milk. Although very little information is available regarding distribution of antineoplastic agents into breast milk, breast-feeding is not recommended during chemotherapy, because of the risks to the infant (adverse effects, mutagenicity, carcinogenicity).

Pediatrics

No information is available on the relationship of age to the effects of floxuridine in pediatric patients.

Geriatrics

Although appropriate studies on the relationship of age to the effects of floxuridine have not been performed in the geriatric population, geriatrics-specific problems are not expected to limit the usefulness of this medication in the elderly. However, elderly patients are more likely to have age-related renal function impairment, which may require reduction of dosage in patients receiving floxuridine.

Dental

The bone marrow depressant effects of floxuridine may result in an increased incidence of microbial infection, delayed healing, and gingival bleeding. Dental work, whenever possible, should be completed prior to initiation of therapy or deferred until blood counts have returned to normal. Patients should be instructed in proper oral hygiene during treatment, including caution in use of regular toothbrushes, dental floss, and toothpicks.

Floxuridine also commonly causes stomatitis, which may be associated with considerable discomfort.

Drug interactions and/or related problems

The following drug interactions and/or related problems have been selected on the basis of their potential clinical significance (possible mechanism in parentheses where appropriate)—not necessarily inclusive (» = major clinical significance):

Blood dyscrasia-causing medications (see *Appendix II*)
(leukopenic and/or thrombocytopenic effects of floxuridine may be increased with concurrent or recent therapy if these medications cause the same effects; dosage adjustment of floxuridine, if necessary, should be based on blood counts)

» Bone marrow depressants, other (see *Appendix II)* or
Radiation therapy
(additive bone marrow depression may occur; dosage reduction may be required when two or more bone marrow depressants, including radiation, are used concurrently or consecutively)

Vaccines, killed virus
(because normal defense mechanisms may be suppressed by floxuridine therapy, the patient's antibody response to the vaccine may be decreased. The interval between discontinuation of medications that cause immunosuppression and restoration of the patient's ability to respond to the vaccine depends on the intensity and type of immunosuppression-causing medication used, the underlying disease, and other factors; estimates vary from 3 months to 1 year)

» Vaccines, live virus
(because normal defense mechanisms may be suppressed by floxuridine therapy, concurrent use with a live virus vaccine may potentiate the replication of the vaccine virus, may increase the side/adverse effects of the vaccine virus, and/or may decrease the patient's antibody response to the vaccine; immunization of these patients should be undertaken only with extreme caution after careful review of the patient's hematologic status and only with the knowledge and consent of the physician managing the floxuridine therapy. The interval between discontinuation of medications that cause immunosuppression and restoration of the patient's ability to respond to the vaccine depends on the intensity and type of immunosuppression-causing medication used, the underlying disease, and other factors; estimates vary from 3 months to 1 year. Immunization with oral poliovirus vaccine should also be postponed in persons in close contact with the patient, especially family members)

Laboratory value alterations

The following have been selected on the basis of their potential clinical significance (possible effect in parentheses where appropriate)—not necessarily inclusive (» = major clinical significance).

With physiology/laboratory test values
Alanine aminotransferase (ALT [SGPT]) and
Alkaline phosphatase and
Aspartate aminotransferase (AST [SGOT]) and
Lactate dehydrogenase (LDH)
(serum values may be increased; possible chemical hepatitis or biliary sclerosis)

Bilirubin, serum
(concentrations may be increased)

Medical considerations/Contraindications

The medical considerations/contraindications included have been selected on the basis of their potential clinical significance (reasons given in parentheses where appropriate)—not necessarily inclusive (» = major clinical significance).

Risk-benefit should be considered when the following medical problems exist:

» Bone marrow depression

» Chickenpox, existing or recent (including recent exposure) or

» Herpes zoster
(risk of severe generalized disease)
» Hepatic function impairment
(reduced biotransformation; lower dosage is recommended)
» Hepatitis, history of
(increased risk of chemical hepatitis)
» Infection
» Renal function impairment
(reduced elimination; lower dosage is recommended)
Sensitivity to floxuridine
» Extreme caution should be used also in patients who have had previous cytotoxic drug therapy with alkylating agents or high-dose pelvic radiation therapy; a lower dosage is recommended.

Patient monitoring

The following are especially important in patient monitoring (other tests may be warranted in some patients, depending on condition; (» = major clinical significance):

Alanine aminotransferase (ALT [SGPT]) values, serum and
Aspartate aminotransferase (AST [SGOT]) values, serum and
Bilirubin concentrations, serum and
Lactate dehydrogenase (LDH) values, serum
(recommended prior to initiation of therapy and at periodic intervals during therapy; frequency varies according to clinical state, agent, dose, and other agents being used concurrently)
» Examination of patient's mouth for ulceration
(recommended before administration of each dose)
» Hematocrit or hemoglobin and
» Leukocyte count, total and, if appropriate, differential and
» Platelet count
(determinations recommended prior to initiation of therapy and at periodic intervals during therapy; frequency varies according to clinical state, agent, dose, and other agents being used concurrently)

Side/Adverse Effects

Note: Many "side effects" of antineoplastic therapy are unavoidable and represent the medication's pharmacologic action. Some of these (for example, leukopenia and thrombocytopenia) are actually used as parameters to aid in individual dosage titration.

Floxuridine is a highly toxic medication and serious toxic effects frequently occur. When floxuridine is administered intra-arterially, local reactions are more prominent than systemic reactions.

Because floxuridine is converted to fluorouracil, there is a possibility that some side/adverse effects associated with fluorouracil may also occur.

Adverse effects associated with prolonged use of an arterial catheter include arterial ischemia, thrombosis, bleeding at the catheter site, blocked catheters, leakage at the site, embolism, fibromyositis, infection at the catheter site, abscesses, thrombophlebitis, and perforation of the duodenum or stomach.

Floxuridine administered via hepatic artery infusion may cause a chemical hepatitis, characterized by elevated hepatic enzymes and nausea and vomiting. However, elevated hepatic enzymes may also be a sign of biliary sclerosis.

The following side/adverse effects have been selected on the basis of their potential clinical significance (possible signs and symptoms in parentheses where appropriate)—not necessarily inclusive:

Those indicating need for medical attention

Incidence more frequent

Aphthous stomatitis (sores in mouth and on lips); ***enteritis*** (diarrhea; stomach pain or cramps)

Incidence less frequent

Displaced hepatic artery catheter (heartburn; black tarry stools); ***esophagopharyngitis*** (heartburn); ***gastrointestinal ulceration or gastritis*** (black tarry stools); ***glossitis*** (swelling or soreness of tongue); ***nausea and vomiting; scaling or redness of hands or feet***—with prolonged infusion therapy

Incidence rare

Anemia (unusual tiredness or weakness); ***hepatotoxicity or intra- and extrahepatic biliary sclerosis or acalculus cholecystitis*** (yellow eyes or skin); ***leukopenia or infection*** (fever or chills; cough or hoarseness; lower back or side pain; painful or difficult urination)—usually asymptomatic; ***thrombocytopenia*** (unusual bleeding or bruising; black, tarry stools; blood in urine or stools; pinpoint red spots on skin)—usually asymptomatic; ***trouble in walking***

Those indicating need for medical attention only if they continue or are bothersome

Incidence less frequent or rare

Loss of appetite; skin rash or itching

Those not indicating need for medical attention

Incidence less frequent or rare

Thinning of hair

Patient Consultation

As an aid to patient consultation, refer to *Advice for the Patient, Floxuridine (Systemic).*

In providing consultation, consider emphasizing the following selected information (» = major clinical significance):

Before using this medication

» Conditions affecting use, especially:
Sensitivity to floxuridine
Pregnancy—Use not recommended because of mutagenic, teratogenic, and carcinogenic potential; advisability of using contraception; telling physician immediately if pregnancy is suspected
Breast-feeding—Not recommended because of risk of serious side effects
Other medications, especially other bone marrow depressants or previous cytotoxic drug or radiation therapy
Other medical problems, especially chickenpox, herpes zoster, hepatic function impairment, history of hepatitis, infection, or renal function impairment

Proper use of this medication

» Telling physician about nausea and vomiting, especially with stomach pain
» Proper dosing

Precautions while using this medication

» Importance of close monitoring by physician
» Avoiding immunizations unless approved by physician; other persons in patient's household should avoid immunizations with oral poliovirus vaccine; avoiding persons who have taken oral poliovirus vaccine or wearing a protective mask that covers nose and mouth

Side/adverse effects

May cause adverse effects such as blood problems, inflammation of gastrointestinal tract, chemical hepatitis, and cancer; importance of discussing possible effects with physician
Signs of potential side effects, especially aphthous stomatitis, enteritis, displaced hepatic artery catheter, esophagopharyngitis, gastrointestinal ulceration, gastritis, glossitis, nausea and vomiting, scaling or redness of hands or feet, anemia, hepatotoxicity, intra- and extrahepatic biliary sclerosis, acalculus cholecystitis, leukopenia, infection, thrombocytopenia, and trouble in walking
Physician or nurse can help in dealing with side effects
Possibility of thinning of hair; normal hair growth should return after treatment has ended

General Dosing Information

Patients receiving floxuridine should be under supervision of a physician experienced in antimetabolite chemotherapy and the technique of intra-arterial infusion.

Floxuridine is recommended mainly for intra-arterial use. Use of an appropriate infusion pump is recommended to ensure a uniform rate of infusion. In selected patients, a portable or implantable pump may be used.

Therapy with floxuridine is continued as long as a response occurs, which may vary from 1 week to several months (with appropriate rest periods). However, floxuridine is an extremely toxic medication; therapy should be discontinued promptly at the first sign of:
Diarrhea (five or more loose stools daily)
Esophagopharyngitis
Gastrointestinal ulceration and bleeding
Hemorrhage from any site
Leukopenia (particularly granulocytopenia), marked
Myocardial ischemia
Stomatitis
Thrombocytopenia, marked
Vomiting, intractable

Therapy may be reinitiated at a lower dosage when side effects have subsided.

Floxuridine should be withdrawn if signs of obstructive jaundice occur and reinstituted only after careful evaluation of the patient.

Special precautions are recommended in patients who develop thrombocytopenia as a result of administration of floxuridine. These may include extreme care in performing invasive procedures; regular inspection of intravenous sites, skin (including perirectal area), and mucous membrane surfaces for signs of bleeding or bruising; limiting frequency of venipuncture and avoiding intramuscular injections; testing urine, emesis, stool, and secretions for occult blood; care in use of regular toothbrushes, dental floss, toothpicks, safety razors, and fingernail and toenail cutters; avoiding constipation; and using caution to prevent falls and other injuries. Such patients should avoid alcohol and aspirin intake because of the risk of gastrointestinal bleeding. Platelet transfusions may be required.

Patients who develop leukopenia should be observed carefully for signs of infection. Antibiotic support may be required. In neutropenic patients who develop fever, broad-spectrum antibiotic coverage should be initiated empirically, pending bacterial cultures and appropriate diagnostic tests.

Safety considerations for handling this medication

There is limited but increasing evidence and concern that personnel involved in preparation and administration of parenteral antineoplastics may be at some risk because of the potential mutagenicity, teratogenicity, and/or carcinogenicity of these agents, although the actual risk is unknown. USP advisory panels recommend cautious handling both in preparation and disposal of antineoplastic agents. Precautions that have been suggested include:

- Use of a biological containment cabinet during reconstitution and dilution of parenteral medications and wearing of disposable surgical gloves and masks.
- Use of proper technique to prevent contamination of the medication, work area, and operator during transfer between containers (including proper training of personnel in this technique).
- Cautious and proper disposal of needles, syringes, vials, ampuls, and unused medication.

A number of medical centers have developed detailed guidelines for handling of antineoplastic agents.

Parenteral Dosage Forms

FLOXURIDINE STERILE USP

Usual adult dose

Carcinoma, colorectal or
Carcinoma, hepatic—
Intra-arterial, 100 to 600 mcg (0.1 to 0.6 mg) per kg of body weight per day continuously over twenty-four hours, continued until toxicity or a response occurs, usually for fourteen to twenty-one days, with a rest period of two weeks between courses.

Usual pediatric dose

Safety and efficacy have not been established.

Strength(s) usually available

U.S.—
500 mg (Rx) [*FUDR*; GENERIC].
Canada—
Not commercially available.

Packaging and storage

Store below 40 °C (104 °F), preferably between 15 and 30 °C (59 and 86 °F), unless otherwise specified by manufacturer. Protect from light.

Preparation of dosage form

Sterile Floxuridine USP is reconstituted for use by adding 5 mL of sterile water for injection to the vial; may be further diluted in 5% dextrose injection or 0.9% sodium chloride injection for administration by infusion.

Stability

Reconstituted solutions of floxuridine are stable at 2 to 8 °C (36 to 46 °F) for not more than 2 weeks.

Revised: 09/30/1997

FLUCLOXACILLIN—See *Penicillins (Systemic)*

FLUCONAZOLE—See *Antifungals, Azole (Systemic)*

FLUCYTOSINE Systemic

VA CLASSIFICATION (Primary): AM700
Other commonly used names are 5-fluorocytosine and 5-FC.
Note: For a listing of dosage forms and brand names by country availability, see *Dosage Forms* section(s).

Category

Antifungal (systemic).

Indications

Note: Bracketed information in the *Indications* section refers to uses that are not included in U.S. product labeling.

Accepted

Endocarditis, fungal (treatment)—Flucytosine is indicated in the treatment of endocarditis caused by *Candida* species.

Meningitis, fungal (treatment)—Flucytosine is indicated in the treatment of meningitis caused by *Cryptococcus* species.

Pneumonia, fungal (treatment)
Septicemia, fungal (treatment) or
Urinary tract infections, fungal (treatment)—Flucytosine is indicated in the treatment of pneumonia, septicemia, and urinary tract infections caused by *Candida* and *Cryptococcus* species.

Candidiasis (treatment)
[Chromomycosis (treatment)] or
Cryptococcosis (treatment)—Flucytosine is used in the treatment of disseminated candidiasis, chromomycosis, and cryptococcosis.

In the treatment of disseminated fungal disease, flucytosine is usually administered concurrently with parenteral amphotericin B because of rapid development of resistance when flucytosine is administered alone.

Not all species or strains of a particular organism may be susceptible to flucytosine.

Pharmacology/Pharmacokinetics

Physicochemical characteristics

Chemical Group—Fluorinated pyrimidine derivative; chemically related to fluorouracil and floxuridine
Molecular weight—129.09.

Mechanism of action/Effect

Flucytosine penetrates into fungal cells and is converted to fluorouracil, an antimetabolite. By interfering with purine and pyrimidine uptake and by deaminated to 5-fluorouracil (5-FU) and then converted to 5-fluorodeoxyuridylic acid monophosphate, a noncompetitive inhibitor of thymidylate synthetase which interferes with DNA synthesis., flucytosine interrupts nucleic acid and protein synthesis. The cells of the host do not convert large quantities of flucytosine to fluorouracil, accounting for the selective toxicity of the compound against fungi.

Absorption

Rapidly and well absorbed from the gastrointestinal tract.
Bioavailability—78 to 90%.

Distribution

Flucytosine is distributed widely throughout the body. The exact distribution in body fluids and organs is not known. However, cerebrospinal fluid (CSF) concentrations may range from about 60 to 90% of those achieved in the serum. Concentrations in the liver, kidneys, spleen, heart, and lungs appear to equal those in the serum.

Protein binding

Very low (2.9–4%).

Biotransformation

Flucytosine is not significantly metabolized.

Half-life

Elimination—2.5 to 6 hours in patients with normal renal function.
12 to 250 hours in patients with impaired renal function.

Time to peak serum concentration

1 to 2 hours.

Peak serum concentration

30 to 40 mcg/mL 2 to 4 hours after a 2-gram dose in adults.

Elimination

Renal; more than 90% excreted by glomerular filtration as unchanged drug.

Precautions to Consider

Carcinogenicity/Mutagenicity

Adequate studies in animals have not been performed to evaluate the carcinogenic potential of flucytosine. No mutagenicity was detected in Ames-type studies in the presence or absence of activating enzymes.

Pregnancy/Reproduction

Pregnancy—Flucytosine crosses the placenta. Problems in humans have not been documented.

However, studies in rats have shown that flucytosine, which is metabolized in rats to fluorouracil, is teratogenic.

FDA Pregnancy Category C.

Breast-feeding

It is not known whether flucytosine is excreted into breast milk. A decision should be made whether to discontinue nursing or to discontinue the drug, based on the importance of the drug to the mother.

Pediatrics

Appropriate studies on the relationship of age to the effects of flucytosine have not been performed in the pediatric population. However, no pediatrics-specific problems have been documented to date.

Geriatrics

No information is available on the relationship of age to the effects of flucytosine in geriatric patients. However, elderly patients are more likely to have an age-related decrease in renal function, which may require an adjustment of dosage in patients receiving flucytosine.

Dental

The bone marrow-depressant effects of flucytosine may result in an increased incidence of microbial infection, delayed healing, and gingival bleeding. Dental work, whenever possible, should be completed prior to initiation of therapy or deferred until blood counts have returned to normal. Patients should be instructed in proper oral hygiene during treatment, including caution in use of regular toothbrushes, dental floss, and toothpicks.

Drug interactions and/or related problems

The following drug interactions and/or related problems have been selected on the basis of their potential clinical significance (possible mechanism in parentheses where appropriate)—not necessarily inclusive (» = major clinical significance):

Note: Combinations containing any of the following medications, depending on the amount present, may also interact with this medication.

Amphotericin B, parenteral
(concurrent use of amphotericin B and flucytosine may have additive or slightly synergistic effects; amphotericin B-induced renal dysfunction may increase the bone marrow toxicity of flucytosine. However, 2-drug therapy may allow the total daily dose of amphotericin B to be lowered, decreasing its risk of nephrotoxicity)

Blood dyscrasia-causing medications (See *Appendix II*) or
» Bone marrow depressants, other, (See *Appendix II*) or
» Radiation therapy
(concurrent use with flucytosine may increase the bone marrow–depressant effects of these medications and radiation therapy; dosage reduction may be required)

Cytarabine
(cytarabine has been reported to antagonize the antifungal activity of flucytosine by competitive inhibition)

Glomerular filtration-reduction medication
(drugs that impair glomerular filtration may prolong the half-life of flucytosine)

Medical considerations/Contraindications

The medical considerations/contraindications included have been selected on the basis of their potential clinical significance (reasons given in parentheses where appropriate)—not necessarily inclusive (» = major clinical significance).

Except under special circumstances, this medication should not be used when the following medical problem exists:

» Allergy to flucytosine

Risk-benefit should be considered when the following medical problems exist:

» Bone marrow depression or
Hematologic disease
(flucytosine may cause bone marrow depression, resulting in anemia, leukopenia, and thrombocytopenia))

Hepatic function impairment
(flucytosine may cause jaundice or hepatic dysfunction, worsening any pre-existing hepatic function impairment)

» Renal function impairment
(because flucytosine is excreted renally, it is recommended that this medication be administered in a reduced dosage to patients with impaired renal function)

» Risk-benefit should be considered in patients who have had previous cytotoxic drug therapy or radiation therapy also.

Patient monitoring

The following may be especially important in patient monitoring (other tests may be warranted in some patients, depending on condition; » = major clinical significance):

» Alanine aminotransferase (ALT [SGPT]), serum and
» Alkaline phosphatase, serum and
» Aspartate aminotransferase (AST [SGOT]), serum and
» Bilirubin, serum
(concentrations are recommended prior to initiation of therapy and at frequent intervals during therapy)

» Blood urea nitrogen (BUN) and
» Creatinine, serum
(recommended prior to initiation of therapy and at periodic intervals during therapy since flucytosine may cause azotemia or an increase in these values; dosage must be reduced in renal function impairment)
(flucytosine may interfere with serum creatinine determinations that are measured by the Kodak Ektachem-700 analyzer, falsely elevating creatinine values; an analyzer that uses the Jaffe procedure should be used to measure serum creatinine)

Flucytosine concentrations, serum
(serum flucytosine concentrations are recommended in patients with renal function impairment [e.g., creatinine clearance <40 mL per min or 0.67 mL per sec], to assess the adequacy of renal excretion and to prevent flucytosine accumulation in the serum; side effects are more common with serum concentrations >100 mcg/mL)

» Hematocrit or hemoglobin and
» Leukocyte count, total and, if appropriate, differential and
» Platelet count
(determinations recommended prior to initiation of therapy and at periodic intervals during therapy; frequency varies according to clinical state, agent, dose, and other agents being used concurrently)

Potassium concentrations, serum
(because of hypokalemia, serum potassium concentration are recommended before and during therapy with flucytosine)

Side/Adverse Effects

The following side/adverse effects have been selected on the basis of their potential clinical significance (possible signs and symptoms in parentheses where appropriate)—not necessarily inclusive:

Those indicating need for medical attention

Incidence more frequent

Anemia (unusual tiredness or weakness); ***hepatitis or jaundice*** (yellow eyes or skin); ***hypersensitivity*** (skin rash, redness, or itching); ***leukopenia or*** (sore throat and fever); ***thrombocytopenia*** (unusual bleeding or bruising)—occur more frequently in patients whose blood levels exceed 100 to 125 micrograms/mL

Incidence less frequent

Confusion; hallucinations; photosensitivity (increased sensitivity of skin to sunlight)

Those indicating need for medical attention only if they continue or are bothersome

Incidence more frequent

Gastrointestinal disturbances (abdominal pain; diarrhea; loss of appetite; nausea; vomiting)—occur more frequently in patients whose blood levels exceed 100 to 125 micrograms/mL

Incidence less frequent

CNS effects (dizziness or lightheadedness; drowsiness; headache)

Overdose

For more information on the management of overdose or unintentional ingestion, **contact a poison control center** (see *Poison Control Center Listing*).

Clinical effects of overdose

Chronic—Prolonged serum concentration above 100 mcg/mL may be associated with an increase in the incidence of gastrointestinal (diarrhea, nausea, vomiting), hematologic (leukopenia, thrombocytopenia) and hepatic (hepatitis) adverse effects.

Treatment of overdose

Although there is not experience with acute overdosage of flucytosine, treatment may involve:

To decrease absorption—Gastric lavage or emesis are recommended.

To increase elimination—Adequate fluid intake, by the intravenous route if necessary and increase diuresis.

Hemodialysis rapidly reduces serum concentration of flucytosine in anuric patients and may be considered.

Monitoring—Hematologic parameters, liver and kidney function should be carefully monitored.

Supportive care—Patients in whom intentional overdose is confirmed or suspected should be referred for psychiatric consultation.

Patient Consultation

As an aid to patient consultation, refer to *Advice for the Patient, Flucytosine (Systemic).*

In providing consultation, consider emphasizing the following selected information (» = major clinical significance):

Before using this medication

» Conditions affecting use, especially:
- Allergy to flucytosine
- Pregnancy—Flucytosine crosses the placenta; studies in rats have shown this medication to be teratogenic
- Breast-feeding—It is not known whether flucytosine is distributed in the breast milk. However, flucytosine has the potential for serious adverse reactions in nursing infants, a decision should be made whether to discontinue nursing or to discontinue the drug.
- Dental—Bone marrow depression effects of flucytosine may result in an increased incidence of microbial infection, delayed healing, and gingival bleeding
- Other medication, especially bone marrow depressants or radiation therapy
- Other medical problems, especially bone marrow depression or renal function impairment
- Previous cytotoxic drug therapy or radiation therapy

Proper use of this medication

Taking multiple dosage units, prescribed as a single dose, over a period of 15 minutes to minimize nausea or vomiting

» Compliance with full course of therapy

» Proper dosing

Missed dose: Taking as soon as possible; not taking if almost time for next dose; not doubling doses

» Proper storage

Precautions while using this medication

Regular visits to physician to check progress during therapy

Using caution in use of regular toothbrushes, dental floss, and toothpicks; completing dental work prior to initiation of therapy or delaying it until blood counts have returned to normal; checking with physician or dentist concerning proper oral hygiene

» Possible photosensitivity reactions

» Caution if dizziness, lightheadedness, or drowsiness occurs

Side/adverse effects

Signs of potential side effects, especially anemia, confusion, hallucinations, hepatitis, hypersensitivity, jaundice, leukopenia, photosensitivity and thrombocytopenia

General Dosing Information

If multiple dosage units are prescribed as a single dose, administration may be spaced over a period of 15 minutes to prevent or reduce nausea or vomiting.

Since fungal resistance may develop rapidly when flucytosine is administered alone, it is usually administered concurrently with parenteral amphotericin B.

Dosing intervals may be adjusted according to creatinine clearance as follows:

Creatinine Clearance (mL/min)/(mL/sec)	Dosing Interval (hr)
>40/0.67	6
20–40/0.33–0.67	12
10–20/0.17–0.33	24
<10/0.17	>24

Oral Dosage Forms

FLUCYTOSINE CAPSULES USP

Usual adult and adolescent dose

Antifungal—

Oral, 12.5 to 37.5 mg per kg of body weight every six hours.

Note: Dosage should be reduced or dosage intervals lengthened in patients with renal impairment as shown in the table:

Creatinine clearance (mL/min)	Dose	Dosage interval
20–40	0.5 times the usual adult and adolescent dose	Usual dosage interval
10–20	0.25 times the usual adult and adolescent dose	Usual dosage interval
	See *Usual adult and adolescent dose*	Every 24 hours

Usual pediatric dose

Antifungal—

Oral, 12.5 to 37.5 mg per kg of body weight or 375 to 562.5 mg per square meter of body surface every six hours.

In neonates a dose of 20 to 40 mg/kg/dose orally every 6 hours has been recommended.

Strength(s) usually available

U.S.—

250 mg (Rx) [*Ancobon* (lactose; corn starch)].

500 mg (Rx) [*Ancobon* (lactose; corn starch)].

Canada—

500 mg (Rx) [*Ancotil*].

Packaging and storage

Store below 40 °C (104 °F), preferably between 15 and 30 °C (59 and 86 °F), unless otherwise specified by manufacturer. Store in a tight, light-resistant container.

Auxiliary labeling

- Continue medicine for full time of treatment.

Revised: 03/08/2000

FLUDARABINE Systemic

VA CLASSIFICATION (Primary): AN300

Commonly used brand name(s): *Fludara.*

Note: For a listing of dosage forms and brand names by country availability, see *Dosage Forms* section(s).

Category

Antineoplastic.

Indications

Accepted

Leukemia, chronic lymphocytic (treatment)—Fludarabine is indicated for treatment of patients with B-cell chronic lymphocytic leukemia (CLL) who have not responded to or whose disease has progressed during treatment with at least one standard alkylating agent–containing regimen.Fludarabine is also indicated for the [first-line treatment][1] of CLL.

[Lymphomas, non-Hodgkin's (treatment)]—Fludarabine is indicated for treatment of non-Hodgkin's lymphomas.

Note: In Canada, fludarabine is indicated for second-line therapy of low-grade non-Hodgkin's lymphoma, onlyafter other conventional therapies have failed.

[1]Not included in Canadian product labeling.

Pharmacology/Pharmacokinetics

Physicochemical characteristics

Chemical Group—Fludarabine is a fluorinated adenine analog (a fluorinated nucleotide analog of vidarabine [Ara-A], which differs from vidarabine in that it is resistant to deactivation by adenosine deaminase).

Molecular weight—365.22.

pKa—3.2 ± 0.1 and 5.8 ± 0.1.

pH—7.2 to 8.2 (after reconstitution).

Mechanism of action/Effect
Fludarabine is a purine antimetabolite. Activity occurs as the result of activation to 2-fluoro-ara-ATP and includes inhibition of DNA synthesis (primarily in the S-phase of cell division) by inhibition of ribonucleotide reductase and the DNA polymerases. It is also postulated that fludarabine interferes with RNA by decreased incorporation of uridine and leucine into RNA and protein, respectively. Fludarabine is also active against non-proliferating cells.

Other actions/effects
Fludarabine appears to have immunosuppressant activity by inhibiting lymphocytes.

Protein binding
Plasma protein binding— *in vitro* studies have shown protein binding of fludarabine is low.

Biotransformation
Rapidly dephosphorylated in serum to 2-fluoro-ara-A (9-beta-D-arabinofuranosyl-2-fluoroadenine) within minutes after intravenous infusion, then phosphorylated intracellularly by deoxycytidine kinase to the active triphosphate, 2-fluoro-ara-ATP, the principal active metabolite.

Half-life
2-Fluoro-ara-A—Triphasic: Terminal—Approximately 20 hours.

Onset of action
In two studies, the median time to response was 7 weeks (range, 1 to 68 weeks) and 21 weeks (range, 1 to 53 weeks).

Elimination
2-Fluoro-ara-A—Renal, approximately 40% to 60%.

The mean total body clearance for patients with normal renal function is 172 milliliters per minute. The mean total body clearance for patients with moderately impaired renal function is 124 milliliters per minute.

Precautions to Consider

Carcinogenicity
Secondary malignancies are potential delayed effects of many antineoplastic agents, although it is not clear whether the effect is related to their mutagenic or immunosuppressive action. The effect of dose and duration of therapy is also unknown, although risk seems to increase with long-term use. Although information is limited, available data seem to indicate that the carcinogenic risk is greatest with the alkylating agents.

Antimetabolites have been shown to be carcinogenic in animals and may be associated with an increased risk of development of secondary carcinomas in humans, although the risk appears to be less than with alkylating agents.

Studies with fludarabine in animals have not been done.

Mutagenicity
Fludarabine was not found to be mutagenic in several strains of *Salmonella typhimurium*, including TA-98, TA-100, TA-1535, and TA-1537. It was also nonmutagenic to Chinese hamster ovary (CHO) cells at the hypoxanthine-guanine-phosphoribosyltransferase (HGPRT) locus under both activated and nonactivated metabolic conditions. However, chromosomal aberrations were observed in an *in vitro* assay using CHO cells under metabolically activated conditions. It was also determined to cause increased sister chromatid exchanges in an *in vitro* sister chromatid exchange (SCE) assay under both metabolically activated and non-activated conditions. Fludarabine was clastogenic *in vivo* (mouse micronucleus assay) but was not mutagenic to germ cells (dominant lethal test in male mice).

Pregnancy/Reproduction
Fertility—Fertility effects in males and females have not been adequately evaluated.

Gonadal suppression, resulting in amenorrhea or azoospermia, may occur in patients taking antineoplastic therapy, especially with the alkylating agents. In general, these effects appear to be related to dose and length of therapy and may be irreversible. Prediction of the degree of testicular or ovarian function impairment is complicated by the common use of combinations of several antineoplastics, which makes it difficult to assess the effects of individual agents.

Dose-related adverse effects on the male reproductive system have been demonstrated in mice, rats, and dogs; effects consisted of a decrease in mean testicular weights in mice and rats with a trend toward decreased testicular weights in dogs, and degeneration and necrosis of spermatogenic epithelium of the testes in mice, rats, and dogs.

Pregnancy—Adequate and well-controlled studies in women have not been done.

Fludarabine should not be used during pregnancy. Women of child-bearing potential should be advised to avoid becoming pregnantand to inform the treating physician immediately should this occur.

It is recommended that females of child-bearing potential and males take contraceptive measures during fludarabine therapy, and for at least six months after the cessation of fludarabine therapy.

Studies in rats demonstrate a transfer of fludarabine and/or metabolites across the placental barrier.

First trimester: It is usually recommended that use of antineoplastics, especially combination chemotherapy, be avoided whenever possible, especially during the first trimester. Although information is limited because of the relatively few instances of antineoplastic administration during pregnancy, the mutagenic, teratogenic, and carcinogenic potential of these medications must be considered.

Other hazards to the fetus include adverse reactions seen in adults.

Studies in rats at intravenous doses of 0, 1, 10, or 30 mg per kg of body weight (mg/kg) per day on days 6 to 15 of gestation found an increased incidence of skeletal malformations. Studies in rabbits at doses of 5 and 8 mg/kg per day found dose-related teratogenic effects (external deformities and skeletal malformations).

FDA Pregnancy Category D.

Breast-feeding
It is not known whether fludarabine is distributed into human breast milk. However, breast-feeding is not recommended during treatment because of the potential risks to the infant. Discontinue breast-feeding or the drug, taking into account the importance of the drug to the mother.

Pediatrics
No information is available on the relationship of age to the effects of fludarabine in pediatric patients. Safety and efficacy have not been established.

Geriatrics
Although appropriate studies on the relationship of age to the effects of fludarabine have not been performed in the geriatric population, clinical trials have included elderly patients and geriatrics-specific problems that would limit the usefulness of this medication in the elderly are not expected. However, elderly patients are more likely to have age-related renal function impairment, which may require reduction of dosage in patients receiving fludarabine.

Dental
The bone marrow depressant effects of fludarabine may result in an increased incidence of microbial infection, delayed healing, and gingival bleeding. Dental work, whenever possible, should be completed prior to initiation of therapy or deferred until blood counts have returned to normal. Patients should be instructed in proper oral hygiene during treatment, including caution in use of regular toothbrushes, dental floss, and toothpicks.

Fludarabine also sometimes causes stomatitis associated with considerable discomfort.

Drug interactions and/or related problems
The following drug interactions and/or related problems have been selected on the basis of their potential clinical significance (possible mechanism in parentheses where appropriate)—not necessarily inclusive (» = major clinical significance):

Note: Combinations containing any of the following medications, depending on the amount present, may also interact with this medication.

Allopurinol or
Colchicine or
» Probenecid or
» Sulfinpyrazone
(fludarabine may raise the concentration of blood uric acid as part of a tumor lysis syndrome; dosage adjustment of antigout agents may be necessary to control hyperuricemia and gout; allopurinol may be preferred to prevent or reverse fludarabine-induced hyperuricemia because of risk of uric acid nephropathy with uricosuric antigout agents)

Blood dyscrasia-causing medications (see *Appendix II*)
(leukopenic and/or thrombocytopenic effects of fludarabine may be increased with concurrent or recent therapy if these medications cause the same effects; dosage adjustment of fludarabine, if necessary, should be based on blood counts)

» Bone marrow depressants, other (see *Appendix II*) or
Radiation therapy
(additive bone marrow depression may occur; dosage reduction may be required when two or more bone marrow depressants, including radiation, are used concurrently or consecutively)

Dipyridamole, and
Other inhibitors of adenosine uptake
(therapeutic efficacy of fludarabine may be reduced)

» Pentostatin
(concurrent use with fludarabine is not recommended because of a possible increased risk of fatal pulmonary toxicity)

Vaccines, killed virus
(because normal defense mechanisms may be suppressed by fludarabine therapy, the patient's antibody response to the vaccine may be decreased. The interval between discontinuation of medications that cause immunosuppression and restoration of the patient's ability to respond to the vaccine depends on the intensity and type of immunosuppression-causing medication used, the underlying disease, and other factors; estimates vary from 3 months to 1 year)

» Vaccines, live virus
(because normal defense mechanisms may be suppressed by fludarabine therapy, concurrent use with a live virus vaccine may potentiate the replication of the vaccine virus, may increase the side/adverse effects of the vaccine virus, and/or may decrease the patient's antibody response to the vaccine; immunization of these patients should be undertaken only with extreme caution after careful review of the patient's hematologic status and only with the knowledge and consent of the physician managing the fludarabine therapy. The interval between discontinuation of medications that cause immunosuppression and restoration of the patient's ability to respond to the vaccine depends on the intensity and type of immunosuppression-causing medication used, the underlying disease, and other factors; estimates vary from 3 months to 1 year. Patients with leukemia in remission should not receive live virus vaccine until at least 3 months after their last chemotherapy. In addition, immunization with oral poliovirus vaccine should be postponed in persons in close contact with the patient, especially family members)

Laboratory value alterations

The following have been selected on the basis of their potential clinical significance (possible effect in parentheses where appropriate)—not necessarily inclusive (» = major clinical significance).

With physiology/laboratory test values

Alkaline phosphatase and
Aspartate aminotransferase (AST [SGOT])
(serum values may rarely be increased)

Liver function, abnormal
(in clinical studies of 133 patients with CLL who received fludarabine, 3% had an abnormal liver function test)

Renal function, abnormal
(in clinical studies of 133 patients with CLL who received fludarabine, 1% had an abnormal renal function test)

Uric acid concentrations in blood and urine
(may be increased as part of a tumor lysis syndrome in patients with large tumor burdens)

Medical considerations/Contraindications

The medical considerations/contraindications included have been selected on the basis of their potential clinical significance (reasons given in parentheses where appropriate)—not necessarily inclusive (» = major clinical significance).

Risk-benefit should be considered when the following medical problems exist:

Autoimmune hemolytic anemia
(life threatening and sometimes fatal events have been reported with the use of fludarabine with or without this underlying condition)

» Bone marrow depression
(lower dosage may be necessary)

» Caution should be used also in patients who have had previous cytotoxic drug therapy or radiation therapy.

» Chickenpox, existing or recent (including recent exposure) or
» Herpes zoster
(risk of severe generalized disease)

Gout, history of or
Urate renal stones, history of
(risk of hyperuricemia as part of a tumor lysis syndrome in patients with large tumor burdens)

» Hypersensitivity to fludarabine or its components

Immunodeficiency

Infection

» Renal function impairment
(reduced elimination; dosage adjustment may be necessary)
(Fludarabine should not be administered to patients with severely impaired renal function (creatinine clearance less than 30 milliliters per minute per 1.73 square meters.)

Transfusion-associated graft-versus-host disease
(associated with the transfusion of non-irradiated blood in patients treated with fludarabine; patients who require blood transfusions and who are undergoing or have received fludarabine treatment should receive irradiated blood only.)

Patient monitoring

The following are especially important in patient monitoring (other tests may be warranted in some patients, depending on condition; » = major clinical significance):

» Hematocrit or hemoglobin and
» Leukocyte count, total and, if appropriate, differential and
» Platelet count
(determinations recommended prior to initiation of therapy and at periodic intervals during therapy; frequency varies according to clinical state, agent, dose, and other agents being used concurrently)

Uric acid concentrations, serum
(recommended prior to initiation of therapy and at periodic intervals during therapy in patients with large tumor burdens, because of the risk of tumor lysis syndrome; frequency varies according to clinical state, agent, dose, and other agents being used concurrently)

A number of clinical settings may predispose to increased toxicity from fludarabine. These include advanced age, renal insufficiency, and bone marrow impairment. Such patients should be monitored closely for excessive toxicity and the dose modified accordingly.

Side/Adverse Effects

Note: Many "side effects" of antineoplastic therapy are unavoidable and represent the medication's pharmacologic action. Some of these (for example, leukopenia and thrombocytopenia) are actually used as parameters to aid in individual dosage titration.

Dose-related bone marrow depression occurs in the majority of patients treated with fludarabine and may be severe and cumulative. Bone marrow fibrosis occurred in one patient.

High single doses (above 75 mg per square meter of body surface area) have been associated with severe, delayed, irreversible, and potentially fatal toxicity, including central nervous system (CNS) toxicity (cortical blindness, incontinence, seizure, continued deterioration of mental status, coma). Most patients experiencing neurotoxicity were found to have progressive CNS demyelination; leukoencephalopathy involving the subcortical white matter, optic nerves, and optic tract was found. High doses are also associated with severe thrombocytopenia and neutropenia.

The following side/adverse effects have been selected on the basis of their potential clinical significance (possible signs and symptoms in parentheses where appropriate)—not necessarily inclusive:

Those indicating need for medical attention

Incidence more frequent

Anemia (pale skin; troubled breathing with exertion; unusual bleeding or bruising; unusual tiredness or weakness)—usually asymptomatic; ***angina*** (arm, back or jaw pain; chest pain or discomfort; chest tightness or heaviness; fast or irregular heartbeat; shortness of breath; sweating; nausea); ***edema*** (swelling of face, fingers, feet, or legs); ***gastrointestinal bleed*** (bloody or black, tarry stools; vomiting of blood or material that looks like coffee grounds; severe stomach pain; constipation); ***hemoptysis*** (coughing or spitting up blood); ***leukopenia or infection*** (fever or chills; cough or hoarseness; lower back or side pain; painful or difficult urination)—usually asymptomatic; ***neutropenia*** (black, tarry, stools; chills; cough; fever; lower back or side pain; painful or difficult urination; pale skin; shortness of breath; sore throat; ulcers, sores, or white spots in mouth; unusual bleeding or bruising; unusual tiredness or weakness); ***pain; pneumonia*** (cough; fever; shortness of breath); ***pneumonitis, allergic*** (chest pain; chills; cough; fever; general feeling of discomfort or illness; shortness of breath; thickening of bronchial secretions; troubled breathing); ***thrombocytopenia*** (unusual bleeding or bruising; black, tarry stools; blood in urine or stools; pinpoint red spots on skin)—usually asymptomatic

Note: In *leukopenia*, the median time to nadir of granulocyte counts in a phase I study in solid tumor patients was 13 days (range, 3 to 25 days). Cumulative and severe myelosuppression may occur.

Infection may be caused by opportunistic organisms including herpes zoster, cytomegalovirus, *Pneumocystis carinii*, and *Candida*, among others. In a study in patients with chronic lymphocytic leukemia (CLL), immunodeficiency in the form of a marked and prolonged decrease in CD4+ and CD8+ T cells, associated with delayed severe infection, was reported after two courses of fludarabine in all 17 patients.

In *thrombocytopenia,* the median time to nadir of platelet counts in a phase I study in solid tumor patients was 16 days (range, 2 to 32 days). Cumulative and severe myelosuppression may occur.

Incidence less frequent

Aneurysm; arrhythmia (dizziness; fainting; fast, slow, or irregular heartbeat); ***cerebrovascular accident*** (blurred vision; headache; sudden and severe inability to speak; seizures; slurred speech; temporary blindness; weakness in arm and/or leg on one side of the body, sudden and severe); ***congestive heart failure*** (chest pain; decreased urine output; dilated neck veins; extreme fatigue; irregular breathing; irregular heartbeat; shortness of breath; swelling of face, fingers, feet, or lower legs; tightness in chest; troubled breathing; weight gain; wheezing); ***deep vein thrombosis*** (pain, redness, or swelling in arm or leg); ***hematuria*** (blood in urine); ***hemorrhage*** (bleeding gums; coughing up blood; difficulty in breathing or swallowing; dizziness; headache; increased menstrual flow or vaginal bleeding; nosebleeds; paralysis; prolonged bleeding from cuts; red or dark brown urine; red or black, tarry stools; shortness of breath); ***neurologic effects, including agitation or confusion; blurred vision; loss of hearing; peripheral neuropathy*** (numbness or tingling in fingers, toes, or face); ***or weakness; supraventricular tachycardia*** (fainting; fast, pounding, or irregular heartbeat, or pulse; palpitations); ***urinary hesitancy*** (difficult urination)

Incidence rare

Anaphylaxis (cough; difficulty swallowing; dizziness; fast heartbeat; hives; itching; puffiness or swelling of the eyelids or around the eyes, face, lips or tongue; shortness of breath; skin rash; tightness in chest; unusual tiredness or weakness; wheezing); ***Delayed severe neurologic effects*** (blindness; coma); ***hemolytic anemia*** (back, leg, or stomach pain; bleeding gums; chills; dark urine; difficulty breathing; fatigue; fever; general body swelling; headache; loss of appetite; nausea or vomiting; nosebleeds; pale skin; sore throat; yellowing of the eyes or skin; unusual tiredness or weakness); ***hemorrhagic cystitis*** (blood in urine; frequent urination; lower abdominal cramping; painful urination); ***hypoxia*** (confusion; dizziness; fast heartbeat; shortness of breath; weakness); ***liver failure*** (headache; stomach pain; continuing vomiting; dark-colored urine; general feeling of tiredness or weakness; light-colored stools; yellow eyes or skin); ***tumor lysis syndrome, including hyperuricemia; hyperphosphatemia; hypocalcemia; metabolic acidosis; hyperkalemia; hematuria; urate crystalluria; renal failure*** (blood in urine, lower back or side pain)

Note: Death may also occur as a result of *delayed neurologic effects.* This syndrome is rare in patients receiving fludarabine for chronic lymphocytic leukemia. However, it occurred commonly in patients treated for acute leukemia with high doses of fludarabine (approximately 4 times greater than the recommended dose); symptoms occurred 21 to 60 days following the last dose.

Hemolytic anemia has been reported after one or more cycles of fludarabine in patients with or without a history of autoimmune hemolytic anemia or a positive Coombs' test. Hospitalization and transfusion have been necessary in severe cases and a fatality has occurred.

Tumor lysis syndrome has been reported in chronic lymphocytic leukemia patients with large tumor burdens.

Severe central nervous system toxicity occurred rarely (coma and agitation) or uncommonly (confusion) in patients treated at doses in the range of the dose recommended for chronic lymphocytic leukemia (CLL) and low-grade non-Hodgkin's lymphoma (Lg-NHL).

Incidence not determined—Reporting in post-marketing surveillance; estimates of frequency cannot be determined.

Pancytopenia (high fever; chills; unexplained bleeding or bruising; bloody, black, or tarry stools; pale skin; unusual tiredness or weakness; cough; shortness of breath; sores, ulcers, or white spots on lips or in mouth; swollen glands); ***pulmonary toxicity, severe*** (cough or shortness of breath)

Those indicating need for medical attention only if they continue or are bothersome

Incidence more frequent

Anorexia (loss of appetite; weight loss); ***chills; cough; diaphoresis*** (increased sweating); ***diarrhea; dyspnea*** (shortness of breath; difficult or labored breathing; tightness in chest; wheezing); ***fatigue; fever; hyperglycemia*** (abdominal pain; blurred vision; dry mouth; fatigue; flushed, dry skin; fruit-like breath odor; increased hunger; increased thirst; increased urination; nausea; sweating; troubled breathing; unexplained weight loss; vomiting); ***infection, urinary*** (bladder pain; bloody or cloudy urine; difficult, burning, or painful urination; frequent urge to urinate; lower back or side pain); ***malaise*** (general feeling of discomfort or illness; unusual tiredness or weakness); ***myalgia*** (joint pain; swollen joints; muscle aching or cramping; muscle pains or stiffness; difficulty in moving); ***nausea or vomiting; pain; paresthesia*** (burning, crawling, itching, numbness, prickling, "pins and needles", or tingling feelings); ***pharyngitis*** (body aches or pain; congestion; cough; dryness or soreness of throat; fever; hoarseness; runny nose; tender, swollen glands in neck; trouble in swallowing; voice changes); ***skin rash; stomatitis*** (swelling or inflammation of the mouth); ***weakness***

Incidence less frequent

Arthralgia (difficulty in moving; muscle pain or stiffness; pain in joints); ***cholelithiasis*** (abdominal fullness; gaseous abdominal pain; recurrent fever; yellow eyes or skin); ***constipation; dehydration*** (confusion; decreased urination; dizziness; dry mouth; fainting; increase in heart rate; lightheadedness; rapid breathing; sunken eye; thirst; unusual tiredness or weakness; wrinkled skin); ***depression*** (discouragement; feeling sad or empty; irritability; lack of appetite; loss of interest or pleasure; tiredness; trouble concentrating; trouble sleeping); ***dysphagia*** (difficulty swallowing); ***dysuria*** (difficult or painful urination; burning while urinating); ***epistaxis*** (bloody nose); ***esophagitis*** (difficulty in swallowing; pain or burning in throat; chest pain; heartburn vomiting; sores, ulcers, or white spots on lips or tongue or inside the mouth); ***headache; mucositis*** (cracked lips; diarrhea; difficulty in swallowing; sores, ulcers, or white spots on lips, tongue, or inside mouth); ***osteoporosis*** (pain in back, ribs, arms, or legs; decrease in height); ***phlebitis*** (bluish color; changes in skin color; pain; tenderness; swelling of foot or leg); ***proteinuria*** (cloudy urine); ***pruritus*** (itching skin); ***seborrhea*** (dandruff; oily skin); ***sinusitis*** (pain or tenderness around eyes and cheekbones; fever; stuffy or runny nose; headache; cough; shortness of breath or troubled breathing; tightness of chest or wheezing); ***sleep disorder*** (difficulty in sleeping)

Incidence rare

bronchitis (cough producing mucus; difficulty breathing; shortness of breath; tightness in chest; wheezing)

Those not indicating need for medical attention

Incidence less frequent or rare

Loss of hair

Overdose

For more information on the management of overdose or unintentional ingestion, **contact a Poison Control Center** (see *Poison Control Center Listing*).

Clinical effects of overdose

High doses of fludarabine have been associated with an irreversible central nervous system toxicity characterized by delayed blindness, coma and death. High doses are also associated with severe thrombocytopenia and neutropenia due to bone marrow suppression.

Treatment of overdose

There is no known specific antidote to fludarabine.Treatment consists of withdrawal of fludarabine and supportive therapy.

Patient Consultation

As an aid to patient consultation, refer to *Advice for the Patient, Fludarabine (Systemic).*

In providing consultation, consider emphasizing the following selected information (» = major clinical significance):

Before using this medication

» Conditions affecting use, especially:

Hypersensitivity to fludarabine

Pregnancy—Use not recommended because of mutagenic, teratogenic, and carcinogenic potential; use of a contraceptive by women and men is recommended during fludarabine therapy and for at least six months after cessation of fludarabine therapy; telling physician immediately if pregnancy is suspected

Breast-feeding—Not recommended because of risk of serious side effects

Other medications, especially bone marrow depressants, cytotoxic drugs, live virus vaccines, pentostatin, probenecid, radiation therapy or sulfinpyrazone

Other medical problems, especially bone marrow depression, chickenpox, herpes zoster, or renal function impairment

Proper use of this medication

Possibility of nausea and vomiting; importance of continuing medication despite stomach upset

» Proper dosing

Precautions while using this medication

» Importance of close monitoring by the physician

» Avoiding immunizations unless approved by physician; other persons in patient's household should avoid immunizations with oral poliovirus vaccine; avoiding persons who have taken oral poliovirus vaccine or wearing a protective mask that covers nose and mouth

Caution if bone marrow depression occurs:

» Avoiding exposure to persons with infections, especially during periods of low blood counts; checking with physician immediately if fever or chills, cough or hoarseness, lower back or side pain, or painful or difficult urination occurs

» Checking with physician immediately if unusual bleeding or bruising; black, tarry stools; blood in urine or stools; or pinpoint red spots on skin occur

Caution in use of regular toothbrush, dental floss, or toothpick; physician, dentist, or nurse may suggest alternatives; checking with physician before having dental work done

Not touching eyes or inside of nose unless hands are washed immediately before

Using caution to avoid accidental cuts with use of sharp objects such as safety razor or fingernail or toenail cutters

Avoiding contact sports or other situations where bruising or injury could occur

Side/adverse effects

May cause adverse effects such as blood problems; importance of discussing possible effects with physician

Signs of potential side effects, especially anemia, angina, edema, gastrointestinal bleed, hemoptysis, leukopenia or infection, neutropenia, pain, pneumonia, allergic pneumonitis, thrombocytopenia, arrhythmia, cerebrovascular accident, congestive heart failure, deep vein thrombosis, hematuria, hemorrhage, neurologic effects, supraventricular tachycardia, anaphylaxis, delayed severe neurologic effects, hemolytic anemia, hemorrhagic cystitis, hypoxia, liver failure, tumor lysis syndrome, pancytopenia, severe pulmonary toxicity

Physician or nurse can help in dealing with side effects

Possibility of hair loss; normal hair growth should return after treatment has ended

General Dosing Information

Patients receiving fludarabine should be under supervision of a physician experienced in cancer chemotherapy.

A variety of dosage schedules and regimens of fludarabine, alone or in combination with other antitumor agents, are used. The prescriber may consult the medical literature as well as the manufacturer's literature in choosing a specific dosage.

Dosage must be adjusted to meet the individual requirements of each patient, on the basis of clinical response and degree of bone marrow depression.

If neurotoxicity occurs, consideration should be given to delaying or discontinuing fludarabine.

Development of uric acid nephropathy in patients with leukemia or lymphoma may be prevented by adequate oral hydration and, in some cases, administration of allopurinol. Alkalinization of urine may be necessary if serum uric acid concentrations are elevated.

Special precautions are recommended in patients who develop thrombocytopenia as a result of administration of fludarabine. These may include extreme care in performing invasive procedures; regular inspection of intravenous sites, skin (including perirectal area), and mucous membrane surfaces for signs of bleeding or bruising; limiting frequency of venipuncture and avoiding intramuscular injections; testing urine, emesis, stool, and secretions for occult blood; care in use of regular toothbrushes, dental floss, toothpicks, safety razors, and fingernail and toenail cutters; avoiding constipation; and using caution to prevent falls and other injuries. Such patients should avoid alcohol and aspirin intake because of the risk of gastrointestinal bleeding. Platelet transfusions may be required.

Patients who develop leukopenia should be observed carefully for signs of infection. Antibiotic support may be required. In neutropenic patients who develop fever, broad-spectrum antibiotic coverage should be initiated empirically, pending bacterial cultures and appropriate diagnostic tests.

In chronic lymphocytic leukemia (CLL) patients, it is recommended that three additional cycles of fludarabine be administered following the achievement of the maximal response and then the drug should be discontinued.

Safety considerations for handling this medication

There is limited but increasing evidence and concern that personnel involved in preparation and administration of parenteral antineoplastics may be at some risk because of the potential mutagenicity, teratogenicity, and/or carcinogenicity of these agents, although the actual risk is unknown. Pregnant personnel should not come in contact with antineoplastic medication containers or mixing supplies.USP advisory panels recommend cautious handling both in preparation and disposal of antineoplastic agents. Precautions that have been suggested include:

• Use of a biological containment cabinet during reconstitution and dilution of parenteral medications and wearing of disposable surgical gloves and masks.

• Use of proper technique to prevent contamination of the medication, work area, and operator during transfer between containers (including proper training of personnel in this technique).

• Cautious and proper disposal of needles, syringes, vials, ampuls, and unused medication.

A number of medical centers have developed detailed guidelines for handling of antineoplastic agents.

The manufacturer recommends use of latex gloves and safety glasses during handling and preparation of fludarabine to avoid exposure in case of breakage of the vial or other accidental spillage. If the solution contacts the skin or mucous membranes, they should be washed thoroughly with soap and water; eyes should be rinsed thoroughly with plain water. Exposure by inhalation or by direct contact of the skin or mucous membranes should be avoided.

Oral Dosage Forms

Note: Bracketed uses in the *Dosage Forms* section refer to categories of use and/or indications that are not included in U.S. product labeling.

FLUDARABINE PHOSPHATE TABLET

Usual adult dose

[Chronic lymphocytic leukemia]—

Oral, 40 milligrams per square meter of body surface, once daily for five consecutive days. Each five-day course of treatment should begin every twenty-eight days.

Note: Fludarabine tablets should be administered until the achievement of a maximal response (complete or partial remission, usually 6 cycles) and then discontinued.

Usual pediatric dose

Safety and efficacy have not been established.

Strength(s) usually available

U.S.—

Not commercially available.

Canada—

10 mg (Rx) [*Fludara* (microcystalline cellulose; lactose monohydrate; colloidal silicon dioxide; croscarmellose sodium; magnesium stearate; hydroxypropyl methylcellulose; talc; titanium dioxide; ferric oxide (red, yellow))].

Packaging and storage

Store between 15 and 30 °C (59 and 86 °F), unless otherwise specified by manufacturer.

Auxiliary labeling

May be taken with or without food.

Swallow whole with water. Do not crush or chew.

Keep out of reach of children.

Parenteral Dosage Forms

FLUDARABINE PHOSPHATE FOR INJECTION

Usual adult dose

Chronic lymphocytic leukemia or

[Non-Hodgkin's lymphoma]—

Intravenous (over approximately thirty minutes), 25 mg per square meter of body surface area per day for five consecutive days. Each five-day course of treatment should begin every twenty-eight days.

The optimal duration of treatment has not been clearly established. It is recommended that three additional cycles of fludarabine be administered following the achievement of a maximal response and then the drug should be discontinued.

Note: In Canada, it is recommended that fludarabine be administered until the achievement of a maximal response (complete or partial remission, usually 6 cycles) and then discontinued.

[Because several intravenous doses and regimens using fludarabine as first-line treatment of CLL are showing activity, no individual dose/regimen is listed here. Consult the medical literature and/or experts in the field of oncology for information on first-line dosage in CLL.][1]

Note: Dosage may be decreased or delayed based on evidence of hematologic or nonhematologic toxicity.

Patients with moderate renal function impairment (creatinine clearance 30 to 70 milliliters per minute per 1.73 square meters) should have a 20% dose reduction of fludarabine. Canadian information states that up to a 50% dose reduction in patients with renal function impairment (creatinine clearance 30 to 70 milliliters per minute per 1.73 square meters). Fludarabine should not be administered to patients with severely impaired renal function (creatinine clearance less than 30 milliliters per minute per 1.73 square meters).

Usual pediatric dose
Safety and efficacy have not been established.

Strength(s) usually available
U.S.—
50 mg (Rx) [*Fludara* (mannitol 50 mg; sodium hydroxide)].

Canada—
50 mg (Rx) [*Fludara* (mannitol 50 mg; sodium hydroxide)].

Packaging and storage
Store between 2 and 8 °C (36 and 46 °F), unless otherwise specified by manufacturer.

Preparation of dosage form
Fludarabine phosphate for injection is prepared for intravenous use by aseptically adding 2 mL of sterile water for injection to the 50-mg vial, producing a solution containing 25 mg of fludarabine phosphate per mL (the solid cake should fully dissolve within 15 seconds).

Parenteral drug products should be inspected visually for particulate matter and discoloration prior to administration.

Fludarabine phosphate solutions may be further diluted in 100 or 125 mL of 5% dextrose injection or 0.9% sodium chloride injection for administration by intravenous infusion.

Stability
Reconstituted solutions contain no preservative and should be used within 8 hours of reconstitution.

[1]Not included in Canadian product labeling.

Selected Bibliography

Hood MA, Finley RS. Fludarabine: a review. DICP Ann Pharmacother 1991 May; 25: 518-24.

Chun HG, Leyland-Jones B, Cheson BD. Fludarabine phosphate: a synthetic purine antimetabolite with significant activity against lymphoid malignancies. J Clin Oncol 1991 Jan; 9: 175-88.

Revised: 07/31/2003

FLUDROCORTISONE Systemic

VA CLASSIFICATION (Primary/Secondary): HS052/CV900; DX900

Commonly used brand name(s): *Florinef*.

Note: For a listing of dosage forms and brand names by country availability, see *Dosage Forms* section(s).

Category
Corticosteroid (mineralocorticoid); antihypotensive (idiopathic orthostatic); diagnostic aid (renal tubular acidosis).

Indications
Note: Bracketed information in the *Indications* section refers to uses that are not included in U.S. product labeling.

Accepted
Note: Because of its marked effect of sodium retention, the use of fludrocortisone acetate in the treatment of conditions other then those indicated herein is not advised

Adrenocortical insufficiency, chronic primary (treatment) or

Adrenocortical insufficiency, chronic secondary (treatment)—Fludrocortisone is indicated as partial replacement therapy in the treatment of adrenocortical insufficiency in Addison's disease.

Adrenogenital syndrome, congenital (treatment)—Fludrocortisone is indicated in salt-losing forms of adrenogenital syndrome.

[Hypotension, idiopathic orthostatic (treatment)][1]—Fludrocortisone is used in conjunction with increased sodium intake in the treatment of idiopathic orthostatic hypotension.

[Acidosis, in renal tubular disorders (diagnosis)][1]

[Acidosis, in renal tubular disorders (treatment)][1]—Fludrocortisone is used in the treatment of Type IV renal tubular acidosis associated with hyporeninemic hypoaldosteronism. Fludrocortisone is also used as an aid in diagnosing the cause of the condition. Effectiveness of fludrocortisone therapy indicates that the condition is caused by hyporeninemic hypoaldosteronism rather than by renal tubular transport dysfunction.

[1]Not included in Canadian product labeling.

Pharmacology/Pharmacokinetics

Physicochemical characteristics
Molecular weight—422.49.

Mechanism of action/Effect
Fludrocortisone acetate is an adrenal cortical steroid that has very high levels of mineralocorticoid activity and moderate levels of glucocorticoid activity. However, it is used only for its mineralocorticoid effects.

Mineralocorticoids act on the distal tubules to increase potassium excretion, hydrogen ion excretion, and sodium reabsorption and subsequent water retention. Cation transport in other secretory cells is similarly affected; excretion of water and electrolytes by the large intestine and by salivary and sweat glands is also altered, but to a lesser extent.

At the cellular level, corticosteroids diffuse across cell membranes and complex with specific cytoplasmic receptors. These complexes then enter the cell nucleus, bind to DNA (chromatin), and stimulate transcription of mRNA (messenger RNA) and subsequent protein synthesis of various enzymes thought to be ultimately responsible for the physiological effects of these hormones.

Protein binding
High.

Biotransformation
Hepatic, renal.

Half-life
≥3.5 hours (plasma); 18–36 hours (biological).

Duration of action
1–2 days.

Elimination
Renal, mostly as inactive metabolites.

Precautions to Consider

Carcinogenicity/Mutagenicity
Adequate animal studies have not been conducted on the carcinogenicity or mutagenicity of fludrocortisone.

Pregnancy/Reproduction
Pregnancy—Studies on use of fludrocortisone during pregnancy have not been done in humans.

Infants born to mothers who have received substantial doses of corticosteroids during pregnancy should be closely observed for signs of hypoadrenalism.

Adequate studies on use of fludrocortisone during pregnancy have not been done in animals. However, many corticosteroids have been shown to be teratogenic in laboratory animals at low doses. Teratogenicity of these agents in humans has not been demonstrated

FDA Pregnancy Category C.

Breast-feeding
Problems in humans have not been documented. However, corticosteroids are distributed into breast milk and may cause unwanted effects in the infant such as growth suppression and inhibition of endogenous steroid production.

Pediatrics
Although adequate and well-controlled studies have not been done in the pediatric population, corticosteroids may cause unwanted effects in children and growing adolescents, such as growth suppression and inhibition of endogenous steroid production.

Geriatrics
Appropriate studies have not been performed in the geriatric population. One published report described the use of fludrocortisone in the treatment of severe hyponatremia that occurred following head injury in 3 geriatric patients in whom syndrome of inappropriate antidiuretic hormone (SIADH) had been ruled out as the cause of the hyponatremia. Doses ranged from 0.1 to 0.4 mg of fludrocortisone per day.

Drug interactions and/or related problems
The following drug interactions and/or related problems have been selected on the basis of their potential clinical significance (possible mechanism in parentheses where appropriate)—not necessarily inclusive (» = major clinical significance):

Note: Combinations containing any of the following medications, depending on the amount present, may also interact with this medication.

Anabolic steroids
(enhanced tendency toward edema)

Anticoagulants, oral
(decreased prothrombin time response; monitor prothrombin levels; adjustment of anticoagulant dose may be required)

Antidiabetic drugs
(diminished antidiabetic effect; monitor for symptoms of hyperglycemia; increased antidiabetic dose may be necessary)

Aspirin
(increased ulcerogenic effect; decreased pharmacologic effect of aspirin; rarely salicylate toxicity may occur in patients who discontinue steroids after concurrent high-dose aspirin therapy; monitor salicylate levels or the therapeutic effect for which aspirin is given; adjustment in salicylate dose may be required)

» Digitalis glycosides
(risk of cardiac arrhythmias or digitalis toxicity associated with hypokalemia may be increased; serum potassium concentrations and cardiac function should be monitored; potassium supplements may be required)

Estrogen
(increased levels of corticosteroid-binding globulin, thereby increasing the bound (inactive) fraction; when estrogen therapy is initiated, an increase in corticosteroid dosage may be required)

» Hepatic enzyme inducers (See *Appendix II*)
(phenytoin and rifampin have been reported to increase 6-beta-hydroxylation of fludrocortisone, via induction of P-450 liver enzymes; fludrocortisone dosage increase may be required)

» Hypokalemia-causing medications (See *Appendix II*)
(risk of severe hypokalemia due to other hypokalemia-causing medications may be increased; monitoring of serum potassium concentrations and cardiac function and potassium supplementation may be required)

Lithium
(in one published case report, lithium antagonized the mineralocorticoid effects of fludrocortisone; increased fludrocortisone dose and dietary sodium supplementation were required during concurrent use)

» Sodium-containing medications or foods
(concurrent use with fludrocortisone in the treatment of Type IV renal tubular acidosis may result in hypernatremia, edema, and potentially severe increases in blood pressure; adjustment of sodium intake may be required)

Vaccines
(neurological complications and lack of antibody response)

Laboratory value alterations

The following have been selected on the basis of their potential clinical significance (possible effect in parentheses where appropriate)—not necessarily inclusive (» = major clinical significance).

With physiology/laboratory test values

Blood pressure
(may be increased)

Hematocrit percentage
(may be decreased due to increased blood volume)

Nitroblue tetrazolium test
(may show false-negative results)

Prothrombin time response
(may be decreased)

Potassium
(serum concentration may be decreased due to increased potassium excretion)

Sodium
(serum concentration may be increased due to sodium retention)

Medical considerations/Contraindications

The medical considerations/contraindications included have been selected on the basis of their potential clinical significance (reasons given in parentheses where appropriate)—not necessarily inclusive (» = major clinical significance).

Risk-benefit should be considered when the following medical problems exist:

» Cardiac disease or
» Congestive heart failure or
» Hypertension or
Peripheral edema or
» Renal function impairment, except when fludrocortisone is used to treat Type IV renal tubular acidosis
(sodium- and fluid-retaining effects detrimental to these patients)

Diverticulitis

Glomerulonephritis, acute

Hepatic function impairment or
Hypothyroidism
(clearance of fludrocortisone may be decreased)

Herpes simplex, ocular
(possible corneal perforation)

Hyperthyroidism
(clearance of fludrocortisone may be increased)

Hypoprothrombinemia
(use aspirin cautiously in conjunction with corticosteroids)

Intestinal anastomoses, fresh

Myasthenia gravis

Nephritis, chronic

Osteoporosis
(may be exacerbated by increased calcium excretion)

Peptic ulcer, active or latent

Sensitivity to fludrocortisone

Tuberculosis, active or latent
(suppression of immune system could cause overwhelming infection)

Ulcerative colitis, unspecific
(use corticosteroids with caution if there is a probability of impending perforation, abscess or other pyogenic infection)

Note: Canadian product information also lists the following medical conditions/contraindications for which risk-benefit should be considered if the medical problem exists: antibiotic resistant infections, convulsive disorders, Cushing's syndrome, diabetes mellitus, exanthema, metastatic carcinoma, thromboembolitic tendencies, thrombophlebitis, vaccinia and varicella

Patient monitoring

The following may be especially important in patient monitoring (other tests may be warranted in some patients, depending on condition; » = major clinical significance):

Blood pressure determinations and
Serum electrolyte concentrations
(recommended at onset of therapy and at periodic intervals during prolonged therapy)

Side/Adverse Effects

The following side/adverse effects have been selected on the basis of their potential clinical significance (possible signs and symptoms in parentheses where appropriate)—not necessarily inclusive:

Note: Most adverse reactions of fludrocortisone are caused by the drug's mineralocorticoid activity (retention of sodium and water). When fludrocortisone is used in the small dosages recommended, the glucocorticoid side effects are not usually a problem, however these effects should be kept in mind, particularly when fludrocortisone is used over a prolonged period of time or in conjunction with cortisone or a similar glucocorticoid.

Those indicating need for medical attention

Incidence less frequent or rare

Aggravating or masking of infections; anaphylaxis, generalized (cough; difficulty swallowing; hives; redness and itching of skin; redness of conjunctivae; shortness of breath; swelling of nasal membranes, face, and eyelids); ***aseptic necrosis of femoral and humeral heads*** (decreased range of motion; joint pain; walking with a limp); ***cardiac enlargement***—mineralocorticoid effect: see note above; ***congestive heart failure*** (chest pain; decreased urine output; dilated neck veins; extreme fatigue; irregular breathing; irregular heartbeat; shortness of breath; swelling of face, fingers, feet, or lower legs; tightness in chest; troubled breathing; weight gain; wheezing)—mineralocorticoid effect: see note above; ***convulsions; cushingoid state, development of*** (increased fat deposits on face, neck, and trunk); ***exophthalmos*** (eyeballs bulge out of eye sockets); ***facial erythema*** (redness of face); ***glaucoma*** (blindness; blurred vision; decreased vision; eye pain; headache; nausea or vomiting; tearing of eyes); ***glycosuria; growth suppression***—in children; ***hyperglycemia; hypertension*** (blurred vision; dizziness, severe or continuing; nervousnes headache; pounding in the ears; slow or fast heartbeat mineralocorticoid effect: see note above; ***hypokalemic syndrom*** regular heartbeat; loss of appetite; muscle cramps or pain; na severe weakness in arms, legs, or trunk; vomiting)—mineraloco effect: see note above; ***insulin requirements, increased*** (p taking insulin for diabetes may need to increase the amount th ***intracranial pressure with papilledema, increased***—usi treatment; ***intraocular pressure, increased; latent diabetes mellitus manifestations*** (blurred vision; dry mouth; fatigue; flushed, dry skin; fruit-like breath odor; increased hunger; increased thirst; increased urination; loss of consciousness; nausea; stomachache; sweating; troubled breathing; unexplained weight loss; vomiting); ***mental disturbances, severe*** (anxiety, confusion, agitation or combativeness, depression, hallucinations, expressed fear of impending death); ***necrotizing angiitis*** (chills; coughing; coughing up blood; headache; loss of appetite; pain in joints or muscles; shortness of breath; skin rash; unusual tiredness; unusual weight loss); ***negative nitrogen balance***—due to protein catabolism; ***oral hypoglycemic agents, increased requirements*** (patients taking oral hypoglycemic agents for diabetes may need to increase the amount they take); ***osteoporosis*** (back or rib pain; decrease in height); ***pancreatitis*** (bloating; chills; constipation; darkened urine; fast heartbeat; fever; indigestion; loss of appetite; nausea; pains in stomach, side, or abdomen, possibly radiating to the back; vomiting; yellow eyes or skin); ***pathologic fracture of long bones; peptic ulcer with possible perforation and hemorrhage*** (bloody or black, tarry stools; abdominal or stomach pain or burning); ***peripheral edema*** (rapid weight gain; swelling of feet or lower legs)—mineralocorticoid effect: see note above; ***posterior subcapsular cataracts; potassium loss***—mineralocorticoid effect: see note above; ***secondary adrenocortical and pituitary unresponsiveness***—particularly in times of stress; ***spontaneous fractures*** (fractures in arms or legs without any injury); ***subcutaneous fat atrophy; suppressed reactions to skin tests; syncopal episodes*** (fainting or lightheadedness when getting up from a lying or sitting position; unusually fast heartbeat palpitations); ***thrombophlebitis*** (changes in skin color; pain; tenderness; swelling of foot or leg); ***ulcerative esophagitis*** (chest pain; heartburn); ***vertebral compression fractures*** (fractures in the neck or back); ***wound healing, impaired*** (problems with would healing)

Those indicating need for medical attention only if they continue or are bothersome

Incidence less frequent or rare

abdominal distention (swelling of abdominal or stomach area; full or bloated feeling or pressure in the stomach); ***acneiform eruptions*** (acne, pimples); ***allergic skin rash; bruising; carbohydrate tolerance, decreased; dizziness; ecchymoses*** (bruising; large, flat, blue or purplish patches in the skin); ***headache, severe or continuing; hirsutism*** (unusual increase in hair growth); ***hives; hyperpigmentation of skin and nails*** (change in color of skin or nails); ***insomnia*** (sleeplessness; trouble sleeping; unable to sleep); ***loss of muscle mass; maculopapular rash*** (redness or discoloration of skin); ***menstrual irregularities*** (menstrual changes); ***muscle weakness; petechiae; purpura*** (small red or purple spots on skin); ***striae*** (reddish purple lines on arms, face, legs, trunk, or groin); ***steroid myopathy; sweating, increased; thin, fragile skin; urticaria*** (hives or welts; itching; redness of skin; skin rash)

Patient Consultation

As an aid to patient consultation, refer to *Advice for the Patient, Fludrocortisone (Systemic)*

In providing consultation, consider emphasizing the following selected information (» = major clinical significance):

Before using this medication

» Conditions affecting use, especially:
- Sensitivity to fludrocortisone
- Pregnancy—Infants born to mothers who received substantial doses of corticosteroids during pregnancy require close observation for signs of hypoadrenalism
- Use in children and growing adolescents—May cause growth suppression and inhibition of endogenous steroid production
- Breast-feeding—Corticosteroids are found in the breast milk of lactating women receiving systemic therapy with these agents. Caution should be exercised when fludrocortisone acetate is administered to a nursing woman
- Other medications, especially hypokalemia-causing medications, digitalis glycosides, hepatic enzyme inducers, or sodium-containing medications or food
- Other medical problems, especially cardiac disease, congestive heart failure, hypertension, or renal function impairment

Proper use of this medication

» Importance of not taking more medication than the amount prescribed

Missed dose: Taking as soon as possible; not taking if almost time for next dose; not doubling doses

» Proper dosing

» Proper storage

Precautions while using this medication

» Regular visits to physician to check progress during therapy

Carrying medical identification card during long-term therapy

Side/adverse effects

Signs of potential side effects, especially aggravating or masking of infections, generalized anaphylaxis, aseptic necrosis of femoral and humeral heads,cardiac enlargement, congestive heart failure, convulsions, development of cushingoid state, exophthalmos, facial erythema, glaucoma, glycosuria, growth suppression, hyperglycemia, hypertension hypokalemic syndrome,increased insulin requirements, increased intracranial pressure with papilledema, increased intraocular pressure, latent diabetes mellitus manifestations, severe mental disturbances, negative nitrogen balance, increased requirements for oral hypoglycemic agents, osteoporosis, pancreatitis, pathologic fracture of long bones, peptic ulcer with possible perforation and hemorrhage, peripheral edema, posterior subcapsular cataracts, potassium loss, secondary adrenocortical and pituitary unresponsiveness, spontaneous fractures, subcutaneous fat atrophy, suppressed reactions to skin tests, syncopal episodes, thrombophlebitis, ulcerative esophagitis, vertebral compression fractures, impaired wound healing

General Dosing Information

When used in the treatment of adrenocortical insufficiency or salt-losing forms of adrenogenital syndrome, fludrocortisone should be administered with appropriate glucocorticoid therapy such as 10 to 30 mg of hydrocortisone per day or 10 to 37.5 mg of cortisone per day. Sodium supplementation may also be necessary.

In the treatment of Type IV renal tubular acidosis, concurrent use of a diuretic may be necessary to decrease the risk of sodium and fluid retention, especially in patients with hypertension, congestive heart failure, or renal function impairment.

Use of glucocorticoids in immunosuppressant doses is associated with a higher risk of infection, with the potential for those infections to be of a more serious nature.

Care should be taken in adults and children to avoid exposure to viral infections, especially chickenpox and measles, if the patient has not already had the disease or been immunized against it. If exposed, therapy with varicella zoster immune globulin or pooled intravenous immunoglobulin may be a consideration.

Oral Dosage Forms

Note: Bracketed uses in the *Dosage Forms* section refer to categories of use and/or indications that are not included in U.S. product labeling.

FLUDROCORTISONE ACETATE TABLETS USP

Usual adult and adolescent dose

Adrenocortical insufficiency, chronic—
Oral, 100 mcg (0.1 mg) per day.

Note: Dose should be reduced to 50 mcg (0.05 mg) per day if transient hypertension occurs. Dosages of 100 mcg (0.1 mg) three times a week to 200 mcg (0.2 mg) once a day have been employed.

Adrenogenital syndrome, congenital—
Oral, 100 to 200 mcg (0.1 to 0.2 mg) per day.

[Antihypotensive, idiopathic orthostatic][1]—
Oral, 50 to 200 mcg (0.05 to 0.2 mg) per day.

Usual pediatric dose

Oral, 50 to 100 mcg (0.05 to 0.1 mg) per day.

Strength(s) usually available

U.S.—
100 mcg (0.1 mg) (Rx) [*Florinef* (scored; lactose)].

Canada—
100 mcg (0.1 mg) (Rx) [*Florinef* (scored; lactose)].

Packaging and storage

Store below 40 °C (104 °F), preferably between 15 and 30 °C (59 and 86 °F), unless otherwise specified by manufacturer. Store in a well-closed container.

[1]Not included in Canadian product labeling.

Revised: 02/22/2002

FLUMETHASONE—See *Corticosteroids (Topical)*

FLUNARIZINE—See *Calcium Channel Blocking Agents (Systemic)*

FLUNISOLIDE—See *Corticosteroids (Inhalation-Local), Corticosteroids (Nasal)*

FLUOCINOLONE—See *Corticosteroids (Topical)*

FLUOCINONIDE—See *Corticosteroids (Topical)*

FLUOROMETHOLONE—See *Corticosteroids (Ophthalmic)*

FLUOROQUINOLONES Systemic

This monograph includes information on the following: 1) Ciprofloxacin; 2) Enoxacin†; 3) Gatifloxacin†; 4) Levofloxacin; 5) Lomefloxacin†; 6) Moxifloxacin†; 7) Norfloxacin; 8) Ofloxacin; 9) Sparfloxacin†.

VA CLASSIFICATION (Primary): AM402

Commonly used brand name(s): *Avelox*[6]; *Avelox I.V.*[6]; *Cipro*[1]; *Cipro I.V.*[1]; *Cipro XL*[1]; *Cipro XR*[1]; *Floxin*[8]; *Floxin I.V.*[8]; *Levaquin*[4]; *Maxaquin*[5]; *Noroxin*[7]; *Penetrex*[2]; *Tequin*[3]; *Zagam*[9].

Note: For a listing of dosage forms and brand names by country availability, see *Dosage Forms* section(s).

*Not commercially available in U.S.
†Not commercially available in Canada.

Category

Antibacterial (systemic).

Indications

Note: Bracketed information in the *Indications* section refers to uses that are not included in U.S. product labeling.

General Considerations

Fluoroquinolones are broad-spectrum anti-infectives, active against a wide range of aerobic gram-positive and gram-negative organisms. They are active *in vitro* against most Enterobacteriaceae, including *Citrobacter diversus*, *Citrobacter freundii*, and *Citrobacter koseri; Enterobacter aerogenes* and *Enterobacter cloacae; Escherichia coli; Klebsiella oxytoca*, *Klebsiella ozaenae*, and *Klebsiella pneumoniae; Morganella morganii; Proteus mirabilis* and *Proteus vulgaris; Providencia alcalifaciens*, *Providencia rettgeri*, and *Providencia stuartii; Salmonella enteritidis* and *Salmonella typhi; Shigella boydii*, *Shigella dysenteriae*, *Shigella flexneri*, and *Shigella sonnei; Vibrio cholerae*, *Vibrio parahaemolyticus*, and *Vibrio vulnificus;* and *Yersinia enterocolitica.* All of the fluoroquinolones also have good *in vitro* activity against penicillin-resistant strains of *Neisseria gonorrhoeae*, beta-lactamase-producing strains of *Haemophilus influenzae* and *Moraxella (Branhamella) catarrhalis*, and some gram-negative bacilli that are resistant to other antimicrobial agents. Ciprofloxacin is the most active fluoroquinolone against *Pseudomonas aeruginosa*, although longitudinal studies have reported progressively decreasing susceptibility in Europe, North America, and South America. It is not generally effective against most strains of *Burkholderia (Pseudomonas) cepacia* or some strains of *Strenotrophomonas (Xanthomonas) maltophilia*. Ofloxacin's potency against *P. aeruginosa* is similar to that of norfloxacin, and greater than that of enoxacin or lomefloxacin.

Fluoroquinolones also have good *in vitro* activity against *Staphylococcus saprophyticus*, *Staphylococcus epidermidis*, and *Staphylococcus aureus*, including some methicillin-resistant (MRSA) strains. However, most methicillin-resistant strains also are resistant to fluoroquinolones. Any bacteria that are resistant to one fluoroquinolone also may be resistant to another. Streptococci, including *Streptococcus pneumoniae*, *Streptococcus pyogenes*, and *Enterococcus faecalis*, are all moderately susceptible to ofloxacin and ciprofloxacin *in vitro*. Sparfloxacin is more active *in vitro* against *S. pneumoniae* than is ciprofloxacin, and levofloxacin appears to be equal to or slightly more active than ciprofloxacin in this regard. Resistant strains of streptococci are often seen. The MIC_{90} values for these species, especially *E. faecalis*, are often equal to or greater than the susceptible breakpoint for ciprofloxacin and ofloxacin. Therapeutic failures have been reported in patients taking ciprofloxacin for the treatment of pneumococcal pneumonia. However, levofloxacin is highly effective against *S. pneumoniae* isolates, including penicillin-susceptible isolates and those with intermediate or high-level resistance to penicillin. Gatifloxacin and moxifloxacin are both effective *in vitro* against penicillin-resistant strains of *S. pneumoniae*.

Ciprofloxacin and ofloxacin have been found to have good *in vitro* activity against *Chlamydia trachomatis*, *Mycoplasma hominis*, *Mycoplasma pneumoniae*, and *Legionella pneumophila*. These two fluoroquinolones have moderate activity *in vitro* against *Mycobacterium tuberculosis*, but neither antimicrobial is indicated for tuberculosis. The susceptibility of *Mycobacterium avium-intracellulare*, however, is only fair to poor, and inhibition requires significantly higher drug concentrations.

Ciprofloxacin has been found to be active against *Bacillus anthracis*both in vitro and by use of serum levels as a surrogate marker.

The emergence of bacterial resistance to fluoroquinolones, and of cross-resistance within this class of antimicrobial agents, has become a significant clinical concern. Decreased susceptibility among Enterobacteriaceae, including *E. coli*, *K. pneumoniae*, and *Salmonella*, has been reported worldwide. Strains of *N. gonorrhoeae* with low-level resistance to fluoroquinolones have been isolated; strains with high-level resistance to ciprofloxacin have been documented, and treatment failures have been reported. Fluoroquinolone resistance also has been documented for *H. influenzae* in patients with recurrent respiratory tract infections, and for *S. epidermidis* in several cases of nosocomial infections. Use of fluoroquinolones in poultry may be at least partially responsible for the emergence of fluoroquinolone resistance in *Salmonella* and *Campylobacter*. Mechanisms underlying fluoroquinolone resistance may include plasmid transfer, chromosomal mutations in DNA gyrase (*gyrA*) or topoisomerase IV (*parC*), and/or antibiotic efflux. Prescribing quinolone antibacterial agents in the absence of a proven or strongly suspected bacterial infection or a prophylactic indication is unlikely to provide benefit to the patient and increases the risk of the development of drug-resistant bacteria. When culture and susceptibility information are available, they should be considered in selecting or modifying antibacterial therapy. In the absence of such data, local epidemiology and susceptibility patterns may contribute to the empiric selection of therapy.

Accepted

Anthrax, inhalational (treatment)[1]—Ciprofloxacin and levofloxacin are indicated to reduce the incidence or progression of the disease following exposure to aerosolized *Bacillus anthracis*

Bone and joint infections (treatment)—Ciprofloxacin is indicated in the treatment of bone and joint infections caused by susceptible organisms.

Bronchitis, bacterial exacerbations (treatment)—Ciprofloxacin, gatifloxacin, moxifloxacin, levofloxacin, lomefloxacin[1], ofloxacin, and sparfloxacin[1] are indicated in the treatment of bacterial exacerbations of chronic bronchitis caused by susceptible organisms.

Cervicitis, nongonococcal (treatment) or
Urethritis, nongonococcal (treatment)—Ofloxacin is indicated in the treatment of nongonococcal cervicitis or urethritis caused by *C. trachomatis.*

Diarrhea, infectious (treatment)—Ciprofloxacin is indicated in the treatment of infectious diarrhea caused by enterotoxigenic strains of *Campylobacter jejuni*, *E. coli*, *S. boydii*, *S. dysenteriae*, *S. flexneri*, or *S. sonnei.* Although ciprofloxacin is approved for the treatment of diarrhea caused by *Campylobacter*, use of fluoroquinolones is not generally recommended due to the high frequency with which single-step mutations occur in *Campylobacter*, which result in fluoroquinolone resistance.

[Norfloxacin is indicated in the treatment of acute diarrheal disease in patients with enterotoxigenic *E. coli* or *Shigella* infection, and in patients with severe enteritis. Norfloxacin is also effective in the treatment of symptoms due to *Salmonella* infection; however, treatment with norfloxacin appears to delay bacterial elimination. (Evidence rating: I)][1]

Gonorrhea, endocervical and urethral (treatment)—Ciprofloxacin, enoxacin[1], gatifloxacin, norfloxacin, and ofloxacin are indicated in the treatment of endocervical and urethral infections caused by *N. gonorrhoeae.* Ofloxacin is indicated also for mixed infections of the cervix or urethra caused by *C. trachomatis* and *N. gonorrhoeae*. Gatifloxacin is indicated for acute, uncomplicated rectal infection in women due to *N. gonorrhoeae.*

Intra-abdominal infections (treatment)—Ciprofloxacin, in combination with metronidazole, is indicated in the treatment of complicated intra-abdominal infections caused by *Bacteroides fragilis*, *E. coli*, *K. pneumoniae*, *P. mirabilis*, or *P. aeruginosa*.

Lower respiratory tract infections (treatment)—Ciprofloxacinand levofloxacin is indicated in the treatment of lower respiratory tract infections caused by susceptible organisms.

Neutropenia, febrile, empiric therapy (treatment)[1]—Parenteral ciprofloxacin, in combination with piperacillin, is indicated for empiric therapy in patients with febrile neutropenia.

Pelvic inflammatory disease (treatment)—Ofloxacin is indicated in the treatment of pelvic inflammatory disease, including severe infection, caused by *C. trachomatis* and/or *N. gonorrhoeae*.

If anaerobic microorganisms are suspected of contributing to the infection, appropriate therapy for anaerobic pathogens should also be administered.

Pneumonia, community-acquired (treatment)—gatifloxacin, moxifloxacin levofloxacin, ofloxacin, and sparfloxacin[1] are indicated in the treatment of community-acquired pneumonia caused by susceptible organisms.

Caution should be used in treating streptococcal and pneumococcal pneumonia with fluoroquinolones. Although they have been effective in limited trials, treatment failures have been reported; fluoroquinolones should not be considered the drugs of first choice in the treatment of presumed or confirmed pneumococcal pneumonia.

Pneumonia, nosocomial (treatment)—Parenteral ciprofloxacin is indicated in the treatment of nosocomial pneumonia.

Levofloxacin is indicated in the treatment of nosocomial pneumonia due to *Escherichia coli*, *Haemophilus influenza*, *Klebsiella pneumoniae*, *Pseudomonas aeruginosa*, *Serratia marcescens*, *Staphylococcus aureus* or *Streptococcus pneumoniae*.

Caution should be used in treating streptococcal and pneumococcal pneumonia with fluoroquinolones. Although they have been effective in limited trials, treatment failures have been reported; fluoroquinolones should not be considered the drugs of first choice in the treatment of presumed or confirmed pneumococcal pneumonia.

Prostatitis, bacterial (treatment)—Ciprofloxacin, levofloxacin, norfloxacin[1], and ofloxacin are indicated in the treatment of bacterial prostatitis caused by susceptible organisms.

Pyelonephritis (treatment)—Gatifloxacin and levofloxacin are indicated in the treatment of pyelonephritis caused by susceptible *E. coli*.

Ciprofloxacin is indicated for the treatment of pyelonephritis due to *E. coli* in pediatric patients from 1 to 17 years of age. Ciprofloxacin is not a drug of first choice in the pediatric population due to an increased incidence of adverse events compared to controls, including events related to joints and/or surrounding tissues.

Sinusitis, acute (treatment)—Ciprofloxacin[1]gatifloxacin, moxifloxacin, and levofloxacin are indicated in the treatment of acute sinusitis caused by *H. influenzae*, *M. catarrhalis*, or *S. pneumoniae*.

Skin and soft tissue infections (treatment)—Ciprofloxacin, levofloxacin, moxifloxacin and ofloxacin are indicated in the treatment of skin and soft tissue infections caused by susceptible organisms.

Typhoid fever (treatment)—Oral ciprofloxacin is indicated in the treatment of typhoid fever caused by susceptible strains of *S. typhi*.

Urinary tract infections, bacterial (prophylaxis)[1]—Lomefloxacin is indicated preoperatively for the prophylaxis of urinary tract infections in patients undergoing transurethral surgical procedures.

Urinary tract infections, bacterial (treatment)—Ciprofloxacin, enoxacin[1], gatifloxacinlevofloxacin, lomefloxacin[1], norfloxacin, and ofloxacin are indicated in the treatment of complicated and uncomplicated urinary tract infections, including cystitis, caused by susceptible organisms.

Ciprofloxacin is indicated for the treatment of complicated urinary tract infection due to *E. coli* in pediatric patients from 1 to 17 years of age. Ciprofloxacin is not a drug of first choice in the pediatric population due to an increased incidence of adverse events compared to controls, including events related to joints and/or surrounding tissues.

[Chancroid (treatment)][1]—Ciprofloxacin is indicated in the treatment of chancroid caused by *Haemophilus ducreyi*.

[Cystic fibrosis, pulmonary exacerbations (treatment)][1]—Ciprofloxacin, alone or in combination with other antibacterial agents, is indicated in patients with cystic fibrosis for the treatment of pulmonary exacerbations caused by susceptible *P. aeruginosa*.

Although studies have shown that ciprofloxacin decreases the number of viable *P. aeruginosa* organisms during treatment, the number of organisms returns to pretreatment levels within days of ciprofloxacin discontinuation. Some clinical studies report that treatment with ciprofloxacin for 14 to 21 days results in low to moderate levels of resistance; others report no change in ciprofloxacin susceptibility over the same period of treatment.

[Meningococcal carriers (treatment)]—Oral ciprofloxacin is indicated in the treatment of asymptomatic carriers of *Neisseria meningitidis* for the elimination of meningococci from the nasopharynx.

[Septicemia, bacterial (treatment)]—Parenteral ciprofloxacin is indicated in the treatment of septicemia caused by *E. coli* or *S. typhi*.

Not all species or strains of a particular organism may be susceptible to a particular fluoroquinolone.

Unaccepted

Fluoroquinolones have not been shown to be effective in the treatment of syphilis and have poor activity against most anaerobic bacteria (including *Bacteroides fragilis* and *Clostridium difficile*).

---

[1]Not included in Canadian product labeling.

Pharmacology/Pharmacokinetics

See *Table 1*, page 1429.

See *Table 2*, page 1429.

Physicochemical characteristics

Molecular weight—
- Ciprofloxacin: 331.35.
- Ciprofloxacin hydrochloride: 385.82.
- Enoxacin: 320.33.
- Gatifloxacin: 402.42.
- Levofloxacin: 370.38.
- Lomefloxacin: 351.36.
- Lomefloxacin hydrochloride: 387.82.
- Moxifloxacin: 437.9.
- Norfloxacin: 319.34.
- Ofloxacin: 361.38.
- Sparfloxacin: 392.41.

Mechanism of action/Effect

Bactericidal; fluoroquinolones act intracellularly by inhibiting topoisomerase II (DNA gyrase) and/or topoisomerase IV. Topoisomerases are essential bacterial enzymes that are critical catalysts in the duplication, transcription, and repair of bacterial DNA.

Distribution

Fluoroquinolones are widely distributed to most body fluids and tissues; high concentrations are attained in the kidneys, gallbladder, liver, lungs, gynecologic tissue, prostatic tissue, phagocytic cells, urine, sputum, and bile. Ciprofloxacin is also distributed to skin, fat, muscle, bone, and cartilage. The skin, fascia, and subcutaneous fat concentrations of ofloxacin are less than 50% of those found in the serum.

Ciprofloxacin and ofloxacin have been found to penetrate into the cerebrospinal fluid (CSF). CSF concentrations of ciprofloxacin reach 10% of the peak serum concentration with noninflamed meninges, and 30 to 50% with inflamed meninges. Ofloxacin penetrates into the CSF in both the presence and the absence of meningeal inflammation (range, 14 to 60%). The CSF distribution pattern of these agents has resulted in their bactericidal CSF titers ranging from inadequate to high, depending on the microorganism and its sensitivity to these antibiotics.

Precautions to Consider

Cross-sensitivity and/or related problems

Patients allergic to one fluoroquinolone or other chemically related quinolone derivatives (e.g., cinoxacin, nalidixic acid) may be allergic to other fluoroquinolones also.

Carcinogenicity/Tumorigenicity

Ciprofloxacin—Long-term carcinogenicity studies (up to 2 years) in rats and mice with oral ciprofloxacin have shown no evidence that ciprofloxacin had any carcinogenic or tumorigenic effects.

Enoxacin—Long-term studies to determine the carcinogenic potential of enoxacin in animals have not been conducted.

Gatifloxacin—Gatifloxacin given at doses up to 81 mg/kg/day in male and 90 mg/kg/day in female B6C3F1 mice (0.13 and 0.18 times the maximum recommended human dose (MRHD) based upon on daily systemic exposure) for 18 months showed no increases in neoplasms. In a 2-year study in Fischer 344 rats at a high dose of 100 mg/kg/day (approximately 0.74 times MRHD based upon daily systemic exposure), gatifloxacin significantly increased the incidence of large granular lymphocytes leukemia in males.

Levofloxacin—In a long-term study in rats, levofloxacin did not show carcinogenic or tumorigenic potential after daily dietary administration for 2 years. The highest dose was two times the recommended human dose based on body surface area, or 10 times the recommended human dose based on body weight.

Lomefloxacin—One study lasting up to 52 weeks showed that 92% of hairless (Skh-1) mice that were exposed to UVA light for 3.5 hours, five times every two weeks, and that had received lomefloxacin concurrently developed skin tumors within 16 weeks. These tumors were well-differentiated squamous cell carcinomas of the skin that were nonmetastatic and endophytic in character. Two thirds of these squamous cell carcinomas contained large keratinous inclusion masses and were thought to arise from the vestigial hair follicles in these hairless animals. In this study, mice treated with lomefloxacin alone did not develop skin or systemic tumors. The clinical significance of these findings to humans is not known.

Moxifloxacin—Long-term studies to determine the carcinogenic potential of moxifloxacin in animals has not been performed.

Norfloxacin—Studies lasting up to 96 weeks in rats given doses of eight to nine times the usual human dose have shown that norfloxacin causes no increase in neoplastic changes, compared with controls.

Ofloxacin—Long-term studies to determine the carcinogenic potential of ofloxacin in animals have not been conducted.

Sparfloxacin—Sparfloxacin was not carcinogenic in mice or rats administered 3.5 or 6.2 times, respectively, the maximum recommended human dose (MRHD) (400 mg per day), on a mg per square meter of body surface area (mg/m^2) basis, for 104 weeks. These doses correspond to plasma concentrations approximately equal to (in mice) and 2.2 times greater than (in rats) maximum human plasma concentrations.

Mutagenicity

Ciprofloxacin—*In vitro* mutagenicity studies have shown both positive and negative results. Negative results were obtained in the *Salmonella* microsome test, *Escherichia coli* DNA repair test, Chinese hamster V79 cell HGPRT test, Syrian hamster embryo cell transformation assay, *Saccharomyces cerevisiae* point mutation assay, and the *S. cerevisiae* mitotic crossover and gene conversion assay. Positive results were obtained in the mouse lymphoma cell forward mutation assay and the rat hepatocyte DNA repair assay. Although positive results were obtained in two of eight *in vitro* studies, negative results were obtained in the *in vivo* rat hepatocyte DNA repair assay, micronucleus test in mice, and the dominant lethal test in mice.

Enoxacin—Enoxacin did not induce point mutations in bacterial cells or mitotic gene conversion in yeast cells, with or without metabolic activation. Enoxacin did not induce sister chromatid exchanges or structural chromosomal aberrations in mammalian cells *in vitro*, with or without metabolic activation. Also, it did not induce chromosomal aberrations in mice. There was a minimal, dose-related, statistically significant increase in micronuclei at high doses of enoxacin in mice; however, the significance of these findings, in the absence of effects in other test systems, is not established.

Gatifloxacin—Gatifloxacin was not mutagenic in several strains of bacteria used in the Ames test; however, it was mutagenic to *Salmonella* strain TA102. Gatifloxacin was negative in *in vivo* oral and intravenous micronucleus tests in mice, oral cytogenetics test in rats, and oral DNA repair test in rats. Gatifloxacin was positive in *in vitro* gene-mutation assays in Chinese hamster V-79 cells and *in vivo* cytogenetics assays in Chinese hamster CHL/IU cells.

Levofloxacin—Levofloxacin was not mutagenic in the Ames test, CHO/HGPRT forward mutation assay, mouse micronucleus test, mouse dominant lethal assay, rat unscheduled DNA repair test, or the mouse sister chromatid exchange assay. It was positive in the *in vitro* chromosomal aberration (CHL cell line) and sister chromatid exchange (CHL/IU cell line) assays.

Lomefloxacin—One *in vitro* mutagenicity test (CHO/HGPRT assay) was weakly positive at concentrations of 226 mcg per mL (mcg/mL) and higher, and negative at concentrations of less than 226 mcg/mL. Mutagenicity tests were negative in two other *in vitro* tests (chromosomal aberrations in Chinese hamster ovary cells and in human lymphocytes). Two *in vivo* mouse micronucleus mutagenicity tests were also negative.

Moxifloxacin—Moxifloxacin was not mutagenic in the Ames *Salmonella* reversion assay and the CHO/HGPRT mammalian cell gene mutation assay. Moxifloxacin was clastogenic in the V79 chromosome aberration assay, but it did not induce unscheduled DNA synthesis in cultured rat hepatocytes. *In vivo* micronucleus test or dominant lethal test in mice did not show genotoxicity.

Norfloxacin—Studies in mice have shown that norfloxacin causes no mutagenic effects in the dominant lethal test. Studies in hamsters and rats given doses of 30 to 60 times the usual human dose have shown that norfloxacin causes no chromosomal aberrations. The Ames test, studies in Chinese hamster fibroblasts, and the V79 mammalian cell assay have shown that norfloxacin causes no mutagenic activity *in vitro*.

Ofloxacin—Ofloxacin was not found to be mutagenic in the Ames test, in *in vitro* and *in vivo* cytogenetic assays, in sister chromatid exchange (Chinese hamster and human cell lines) assays, in the unscheduled DNA repair test using human fibroblasts, in the mouse micronucleus assay, or in dominant lethal assays. However, ofloxacin was mutagenic in the unscheduled DNA repair test using rat hepatocytes and in the mouse lymphoma assay.

Sparfloxacin—Although sparfloxacin was not mutagenic in *Salmonella typhimurium* TA98, TA100, TA1535, or TA1537, in *E. coli* strain WP2 uvrA, or in Chinese hamster lung cells, it was mutagenic in *S. typhimurium* TA102, and it induced DNA repair in *E. coli*. Sparfloxacin induced chromosomal aberrations in Chinese hamster lung cells *in vitro* at cytotoxic concentrations; however, no increase in chromosomal aberrations or micronuclei in bone marrow cells was observed after sparfloxacin was administered orally to mice.

Pregnancy/Reproduction

Fertility—

Ciprofloxacin—

Adequate and well-controlled studies in humans have not been done. Studies in rats and mice given doses of up to six times the usual daily human dose have not shown that ciprofloxacin causes adverse effects on fertility.

Enoxacin—

No consistent effects on fertility and reproductive parameters were noted in female rats given oral doses of up to 1000 mg per kg of body weight (mg/kg) of enoxacin. Decreased spermatogenesis and subsequent impaired fertility were noted in male rats given oral doses of 1000 mg/kg.

Gatifloxacin—

Gatifloxacin did not adversely affect fertility or reproduction in rats at oral doses up to 200 mg/kg/day (approximately equivalent to the maximum human recommended dose (MHRD) based on systemic exposure).

Levofloxacin—

Levofloxacin had no effect on the fertility or reproductive performance of male or female rats at oral doses of up to 360 mg/kg (2124 mg/m^2) per day (corresponding to 18 and 3 times the MRHD based on body weight and body surface area, respectively), or at parenteral doses of up to 100 mg/kg (590 mg/m^2) per day (corresponding to 5 and 1 times the MRHD based on body weight and body surface area, respectively).

Lomefloxacin—

The fertility of male and female rats was not affected when lomefloxacin was administered at oral doses of up to eight times the recommended human dose on a mg/m^2 basis, or 34 times the recommended human dose on a mg/kg basis.

Moxifloxacin—

Moxifloxacin had not effect on fertility in male and female rats at oral doses up to 500 mg/kg/day (approximately 12 times the MRHD based on body surface area (mg/m^2). At 500 mg/kg, it had slight effects on sperm morphology (head-tail separation) in male rats and on the estrous cycle in female rats.

Norfloxacin—

Studies in male and female mice given oral doses of up to 30 times the usual human dose have not shown that norfloxacin causes adverse effects on fertility.

Sparfloxacin—

Sparfloxacin had no effect on the fertility or reproductive performance of male or female rats at oral doses of up to 15.4 times the MRHD (400 mg) on a mg/m^2 basis.

Pregnancy—

For all fluoroquinolones—

Adequate and well-controlled studies in humans have not been done. However, since fluoroquinolones have been shown to cause arthropathy in immature animals of a variety of species, their use is not recommended during pregnancy.

Ciprofloxacin—

Ciprofloxacin crosses the placenta.

Studies in rats and mice given doses of up to six times the usual daily human dose have not shown that ciprofloxacin causes adverse effects on the fetus. Studies in rabbits given oral doses of 30 and 100 mg/kg have shown that ciprofloxacin causes gastrointestinal disturbances, resulting in maternal weight loss and an increased incidence of abortion. However, these studies have not shown that ciprofloxacin is teratogenic at either dose. Studies using intravenous doses of up to 20 mg/kg have not shown that ciprofloxacin causes maternal toxicity, embryotoxicity, or teratogenic effects.

FDA Pregnancy Category C.

Enoxacin—

Rats and mice given oral enoxacin have shown no evidence of teratogenic potential. Intravenous infusion of enoxacin into pregnant rabbits at doses of 10 to 50 mg/kg caused dose-related maternal toxicity (venous irritation, weight loss, and reduced food intake). At 50 mg/kg, there were increased incidences of postimplantation loss and stunted growth of fetuses. The incidence of fetal malformations also was significantly increased at this dose in the presence of overt maternal and fetal toxicity.

FDA Pregnancy Category C.

Gatifloxacin—

Gatifloxacin was not teratogenic in rats or rabbits at oral doses up to 150 and 50 mg/kg, respectively (0.7 and 0.9 times the maximum human recommended dose (MHRD) based on systemic exposure). However, skeletal malformations were observed in rats at an oral dose of 200 mg/kg/day or intravenous dose of 60 mg/kg/day during organogenesis. Fetotoxicity was seen in rat fetuses at oral doses ≥ 150 mg/kg or intravenous doses ≥ 30 mg/kg daily during organogenesis, and in rats during late pregnancy and throughout lactation at oral doses of 200 mg/kg.

FDA Pregnancy Category C

Levofloxacin—

Levofloxacin was not teratogenic in rats at oral doses of up to 810 mg/kg (4779 mg/m^2) per day (corresponding to 82 and 14 times the MRHD based on body weight and body surface area, respectively), or at parenteral doses of up to 160 mg/kg (944 mg/m^2) per day (corresponding to 16 and 2.7 times the MRHD based on body weight and body surface area, respectively). Doses equivalent to 81 and 26 times the MRHD of levofloxacin (based on body weight and body surface area, respectively) caused decreased fetal body weight and increased fetal mortality in rats when administered orally at doses of 810 mg/kg (8910 mg/m^2) per day. No teratogenicity was observed when rabbits were given oral doses of up to 50 mg/kg (550 mg/m^2) per day (corresponding to 5 and 1.6 times the MRHD based on body weight and body surface area, respectively), or parenteral doses of up to 25 mg/kg (275 mg/m^2) per day (corresponding to 2.5 and 0.8 times the MRHD based on body weight and body surface area, respectively).

FDA Pregnancy Category C.

Lomefloxacin—

Reproduction studies done in rats given oral doses of up to 34 times the recommended human dose on a mg/kg basis reported no harm to the fetus. An increased incidence of fetal loss in monkeys has been observed at approximately 6 to 12 times the recommended human dose on a mg/kg basis. No teratogenicity has been observed in rats or monkeys at doses of up to 16 times the recommended human dose. In rabbits, maternal toxicity and associated fetal toxicity, decreased placental weight, and variations of the coccygeal vertebrae occurred at doses two times the recommended human dose on a mg/m^2 basis.

FDA Pregnancy Category C.

Moxifloxacin—

Moxifloxacin was not teratogenic in pregnant rats during organogenesis at oral doses up to 500 mg/kg/day (0.24 times the MRHD based on systemic exposure). Fetotoxicity such as decreased fetal body weights and slightly delayed fetal skeletal development were observed. There was also an increase in the incidence of rib and vertebral malformations. There was no evidence of teratogenicity when pregnant Cynomolgus monkeys were given oral doses up to 100 mg/kg/day (2.5 times the MRHD based on systemic exposure). There was an increase in incidence of smaller fetuses. At dose of 500 mg/kg/day in rats, slight increase in duration of pregnancy and prenatal loss, reduced pup birth weight, decreased neonatal survival, and treatment-related maternal mortality were observed.

FDA Pregnancy Category C

Norfloxacin—

The human umbilical cord serum concentration ranges from undetectable to 0.5 mg per mL (mg/mL) and the amniotic fluid concentration ranges from undetectable to 0.92 mg/mL following the administration of a single 200-mg dose of norfloxacin.

Studies in monkeys given doses of 10 times the MRHD (800 mg daily) have shown that norfloxacin causes embryonic loss. Peak plasma concentrations were two to three times those seen in humans. Studies in cynomolgus monkeys given doses of 150 mg/kg per day or more have shown that norfloxacin is embryocidal and causes slight maternal toxicity (vomiting and anorexia) as well. However, studies in rats, rabbits, mice, and monkeys given doses of 6 to 50 times the usual human dose have not shown that norfloxacin is teratogenic.

FDA Pregnancy Category C.

Ofloxacin—

Ofloxacin crosses the placenta. In one small study, umbilical cord serum concentrations reached 80 to 90% of maternal serum concentrations after mothers received 200-mg doses. Ofloxacin was also detected in the amniotic fluid from more than 50% of the mothers. Another small study found that ofloxacin concentrated in the amniotic fluid, reaching up to 35 to 257% of the simultaneous maternal serum concentration.

Studies in rats and rabbits given doses of up to 810 and 160 mg/kg per day, respectively, have not shown ofloxacin to be teratogenic. Studies in rats given doses of up to 360 mg/kg per day showed no adverse effect on late fetal development, labor, delivery, lactation, neonatal viability, or growth of the newborn. Doses equivalent to 50 and 10 times the MRHD were fetotoxic in rats (decreased fetal body weight) and rabbits (increased fetal mortality), respectively. Rats given 810 mg/kg per day, greater than 10 times the MRHD, were reported to produce offspring with minor skeletal variations.

FDA Pregnancy Category C.

Sparfloxacin—

Reproduction studies performed in rats, rabbits, and monkeys at oral doses of 6.2, 4.4, and 2.6 times the MRHD (on a mg/m^2 basis), respectively, did not show evidence of teratogenic effects. At these doses, sparfloxacin produced clear evidence of maternal toxicity in rabbits and in monkeys, and slight evidence of maternal toxicity in rats. When administered to pregnant rats at clearly defined maternally toxic doses, sparfloxacin induced a dose-dependent increase in the incidence of ventricular septal defects in fetuses. Among the three species tested, this effect was specific to the rat.

FDA Pregnancy Category C.

Breast-feeding

Ciprofloxacin, ofloxacin, and sparfloxacin are known to be distributed into human breast milk. The concentration of ofloxacin in breast milk is similar to that found in plasma. One small study found that ofloxacin was highly concentrated in breast milk, reaching 98% of the simultaneous maternal serum level within 2 hours of administration. It is not known whether enoxacin, gatifloxacin, levofloxacin, lomefloxacin, moxifloxacin, or norfloxacin is distributed into breast milk. However, based on data for ofloxacin, it is expected that levofloxacin is distributed into breast milk. Norfloxacin was not detected in breast milk following its administration in low (200-mg) doses to nursing mothers. However, other quinolone derivatives are distributed into human breast milk. Therefore, if an alternative antibiotic cannot be prescribed and a fluoroquinolone must be administered, breast-feeding is not recommended.

In immature animals, fluoroquinolones have been shown to cause permanent lesions of the cartilage of weight-bearing joints, as well as other signs of arthropathy. Moxifloxacin is distributed in the breast milk of lactating rats.

Pediatrics

For all fluoroquinolones—

With the exception of ciprofloxacin and levofloxacin when used post-exposure for inhalational anthrax on a clinical judgment of risk/benefit for individual patients, fluoroquinolones currently are not recommended for use in infants and children. Patients younger than 18 years of age usually have not been included in clinical trials because fluoroquinolones caused lameness in immature dogs due to permanent lesions of the cartilage of weight-bearing joints. Fluoroquinolones and other related quinolones have been reported to cause arthropathy in immature animals of various species; the effects vary with animal species and with quinolone dose and develop within days to weeks of the start of quinolone treatment. The mechanism by which quinolones produce this cartilage damage is unknown.

Fluoroquinolones have been used in neonates, infants, and children with serious infections that have not responded to other therapeutic regimens, or infections caused by multiple organisms resistant to other antibiotics. More than 2500 pediatric patients to date, most of whom have cystic fibrosis, a disease that has a significant background prevalence of arthralgia and arthritis, are reported to have undergone treatment with ciprofloxacin. The reported rate of musculoskeletal adverse events following ciprofloxacin administration in clinical trials was similar to that seen with placebo, and only 1 to 2% of these events were considered to be possibly or probably due to ciprofloxacin. Arthropathy was reversible in almost all of these patients without additional treatment or fluoroquinolone discontinuation. Additional studies in pediatric patients with multidrug-resistant typhoid fever also documented no evidence of acute or subclinical joint toxicity or of diminished height velocity over a 2-year follow-up period. Furthermore, postmortem examination of knee cartilage was normal in two juvenile patients who received oral ciprofloxacin for 9 to 10 months (and subsequently died secondary to complications of cystic fibrosis). There are case reports that document the reversibility of arthropathy only after discontinuation of ciprofloxacin. However, there has not been one report of irreversible damage to cartilage in a pediatric patient treated with fluoroquinolones.

In 1993, the International Society of Chemotherapy commission developed guidelines for use of fluoroquinolones in the pediatric population based on a review of international experience. The commission does not promote the use of fluoroquinolones in children; when effective and nonrestricted alternative therapies are available for infections in pediatric patients, these therapies should be used. However, the commission also stated that critical and cautious use of fluoroquinolone antibiotics in pediatric patients suffering from specific infections complicated by pathologic or special conditions is justified by experimental and clinical data when alternative safe therapy is not available. The recommendations conclude that the risks and benefits of fluoroquinolone use should be assessed and a determination made on an individual basis for each compassionate use.

Adolescents

For all fluoroquinolones—

With the exception of ciprofloxacin and levofloxacin when used post-exposure for inhalational anthrax on a clinical judgment of risk/benefit for individual patients, fluoroquinolones currently are not recommended for use in adolescents. Patients younger than 18 years of age usually have not been included in clinical trials because fluoroquinolones caused lameness in immature dogs due to permanent lesions of the cartilage of weight-bearing joints. One clinical report of 1219 adolescent patients (74 of whom had cystic fibrosis) who received ciprofloxacin at least once did not reveal any cases of newly diagnosed acute arthritis or joint toxicity that were likely to have been caused by the medication. In general, arthralgias have been reported primarily in adolescent females who received fluoroquinolones; these arthralgias were not severe, were transient, and disappeared with either a dosage reduction or discontinuation of the medication.

See also *Pediatrics*.

Geriatrics

Use in the elderly—

For all fluoroquinolones—

Studies performed to date have not demonstrated geriatrics-specific problems that would limit the usefulness of fluoroquinolones in the elderly. However, tendinitis or tendon rupture, central nervous system (CNS) effects (e.g., hallucinations), and other side effects may occur more frequently in the elderly. In addition, a possible increased risk of tendon rupture in elderly patients receiving concomitant corticosteroids has been observed with norfloxacin in clinical practice. Elderly patients also are more likely to have an age-related decrease in renal function, which may require an adjustment of dosage in patients receiving any of these medications.

In geriatric intravenous moxifloxacin trials in community acquired pneumonia, the following ECG abnormalities were reported: ST-T wave changes, QT prolongation, ventricular tachycardia, atrial flutter, atrial fibrillation, supraventricular tachycardia, ventricular extrasystoles, and arrhythmia. None of these abnormalities was associated with a fatal outcome and a majority of these patients completed a full-course of therapy.

Drug interactions and/or related problems

The following drug interactions and/or related problems have been selected on the basis of their potential clinical significance (possible mechanism in parentheses where appropriate)—not necessarily inclusive (» = major clinical significance):

Note: Combinations containing any of the following medications, depending on the amount present, may also interact with this medication.

Alkalizers, urinary, such as:
Carbonic anhydrase inhibitors
Citrates
Sodium bicarbonate
(urinary alkalizers may reduce the solubility of ciprofloxacin or norfloxacin in the urine; patients should be observed for signs of crystalluria and nephrotoxicity, although the incidence is rare)

» Aminophylline or
» Oxtriphylline or
» Theophylline
(concurrent use of aminophylline, oxtriphylline, or theophylline with ciprofloxacin or enoxacin significantly reduces the hepatic metabolism and clearance of theophylline, probably by competitive inhibition at its binding sites within the cytochrome P450 enzyme system; this may result in a prolonged theophylline elimination half-life, increased serum concentration, and increased risk of theophylline-related toxicity; enoxacin has the greatest effect on theophylline clearance and it is recommended that the dose of theophylline be decreased by 50% during concurrent use; ciprofloxacin may also increase the risk of toxicity, especially in patients with theophylline concentrations at the upper end of the therapeutic range; serum theophylline concentrations should be monitored and dosage adjustments may be required; norfloxacin and ofloxacin have a minor effect on theophylline clearance; one study with ofloxacin found an increase of approximately 10% in the theophylline serum concentration; however, other studies have found that ofloxacin has a negligible effect on theophylline metabolism; theophylline dosage adjustment is usually not necessary in patients receiving ofloxacin; monitoring of theophylline plasma levels should be considered and dosage of theophylline adjusted as required in patients receiving norfloxacin; theophylline clearance has not been found to be significantly altered by gatifloxacin, levofloxacin, lomefloxacin, or moxifloxacin)

» Amiodarone or
» Antidepressants, tricyclic or
» Astemizole or
» Bepredil or
» Cisapride or
» Disopyramide or
» Erythromycin or
» Pentamidine or
» Phenothiazines or
» Procainamide or
» Quinidine or
» Sotalol or
» Terfenadine or
» Other medications reported to prolong the QTc interval
(concurrent use of sparfloxacin with amiodarone and disopyramide has resulted in torsades de pointes; concurrent use of sparfloxacin with *any* medication reported to prolong the QTc interval or to produce torsades de pointes is **contraindicated**; concurrent use of gatifloxacin, levofloxacin, lomefloxacin, moxifloxacin, or norfloxacin with class IA (e.g., quinidine, procainamide) or class III (e.g., amiodarone, sotalol) antiarrhythmic agents should be avoided.)

» Antacids, aluminum, calcium, and/or magnesium-containing or
» Didanosine (Videx®) products including: or
chewable/buffered tablets or
pediatric powder for oral solution
» Ferrous sulfate or
Laxatives, magnesium-containing or
» Sucralfate or
Zinc
(antacids, ferrous sulfate, zinc, or sucralfate may reduce the absorption of fluoroquinolones by chelation, resulting in lower serum and urine concentrations; therefore, concurrent use is not recommended; because the bioavailability of enoxacin is decreased the most by concurrent administration of these medications, it is recommended that enoxacin be taken at least 2 hours before or 8 hours after taking any of these medications; ciprofloxacin should be taken at least 2 hours before or 6 hours after taking any of these medications; gatifloxacin should be taken 4 hours before taking iron, magnesium-containing antacids, and zinc; lomefloxacin should be taken at least 2 hours before or 4 hours after taking any of these medications; levofloxacin, norfloxacin, or ofloxacin should be taken at least 2 hours before or 2 hours after taking any of these medications; moxifloxacin should be taken at least 4 hours before and 8 hours after taking any of these medications; and sparfloxacin should be taken at least 4 hours before or 4 hours after taking any of these medications)

Anticonvulsants, hydantoin, especially:
» Phenytoin
(concurrent administration of ciprofloxacin with phenytoin has resulted in a 34 to 80% decrease in the plasma concentration of phenytoin; caution should be used when administering quinolones, especially ciprofloxacin, to patients stabilized on phenytoin; careful monitoring of phenytoin dosage after discontinuation of quinolones is highly recommended)

Antidiabetic agents, sulfonylurea, especially:
Glyburide or
Insulin
(concurrent use of ciprofloxacin, levofloxacin, or norfloxacin with glyburide or other antidiabetic agents has, on rare occasions, resulted in hypoglycemia; also, hyperglycemia and hypoglycemia have been reported in patients taking quinolone antibiotics and antidiabetic agents concurrently; since the mechanism is not understood, similar effects with other sulfonylurea antidiabetic agents may be expected when these medications are used with fluoroquinolones; careful monitoring of blood glucose concentrations is recommended when these medications are used concurrently; concurrent administration of moxifloxacin and glyburide did not result in clinically significant interaction)

Anti-inflammatory drugs, nonsteroidal (NSAIDs)
(fluoroquinolones, particularly enoxacin and norfloxacin, are competitive inhibitors of gamma-aminobutyric acid receptor binding, and some NSAIDs have been shown to enhance this effect; seizures have been reported in patients taking enoxacin and fenbufen concurrently; NSAIDs (excluding acetyl salicylic acid) in combination with very high doses of quinolones have been shown to provoke convulsions in preclinical studies)

Bismuth
(the bioavailability of enoxacin is decreased by approximately 25% when bismuth subsalicylate is administered concurrently or within 60 minutes of enoxacin administration; concurrent administration of these medications is not recommended)

» Caffeine or
Theobromine
(concurrent use of caffeine with enoxacin has been found to decrease the hepatic metabolism of caffeine, resulting in a dose-related increase in the half-life of caffeine of up to five times normal; ciprofloxacin and, to a lesser extent, norfloxacin also reduce the hepatic metabolism and clearance of caffeine, increasing its half-life and the risk of caffeine-related CNS stimulation; lomefloxacin and ofloxacin do not produce any significant change in caffeine metabolism)

Corticosteroids
(concomitant use with quinolones, including norfloxacin, may increase risk of rupturing shoulder, hand, Achilles tendons or other tendons that may require surgical repair or result in prolonged disability, especially in the elderly)

Cyclosporine
(concurrent use with ciprofloxacin or norfloxacin has been reported to elevate serum creatinine and serum cyclosporine concentrations; other studies have not found ciprofloxacin, enoxacin, or levofloxacin to alter the pharmacokinetics of cyclosporine; cyclosporine concentrations should be monitored when used concurrently with fluoroquinolones, and dosage adjustments may be required)

» Didanosine
(concurrent use of didanosine with ciprofloxacin, norfloxacin, or ofloxacin has been shown to reduce the absorption of these fluoroquinolones due to chelation of the fluoroquinolone by the aluminum and magnesium buffers in didanosine; didanosine should not be administered concurrently with any fluoroquinolone; also, didanosine should not be taken within 2 hours before or 2 hours after taking norfloxacin or ofloxacin; gatifloxacin should be taken 4 hours before didanosine; moxifloxacin should be taken at least 4 hours before and 8 hours after taking didanosine)

Digoxin
(enoxacin may raise serum digoxin concentrations in some patients; digoxin serum concentrations should be monitored; gatifloxacin and moxifloxacin did not have any clinically significant interaction with digoxin)

Nitrofurantoin
(concomitant use with norfloxacin not recommended since nitrofurantoin may antagonize antibacterial effect of norfloxacin in the urinary tract)

Probenecid
(concurrent use of probenecid decreases the renal tubular secretion of fluoroquinolones, resulting in decreased urinary excretion of the fluoroquinolone, prolonged elimination half-life, and increased risk of toxicity; this interaction is more significant with gatifloxacin and ofloxacin, which is excreted largely unchanged in the urine, and of less clinical significance with fluoroquinolones that have larger nonrenal elimination, such as ciprofloxacin and enoxacin; moxifloxacin did not have any clinically significant interaction with probenecid)

» Warfarin or
anticoagulants, oral
(quinolones may enhance the effects of oral anticoagulants, including warfarin; concurrent use of warfarin with ciprofloxacin, levofloxacin, or norfloxacin has been reported to increase the anticoagulant effect of warfarin, increasing the chance of bleeding; other studies have not found fluoroquinolones to alter the prothrombin time [PT] significantly; enoxacin decreases the clearance of R-warfarin, the less active isomer of racemic warfarin, but not the active S-isomer; changes in clotting time have not been observed when enoxacin, gatifloxacin, or moxifloxacin is administered concurrently with warfarin; however, it is recommended that the PT of patients receiving warfarin and fluoroquinolones concurrently be monitored carefully)

Laboratory value alterations

The following have been selected on the basis of their potential clinical significance (possible effect in parentheses where appropriate)—not necessarily inclusive (» = major clinical significance).

With diagnostic test results
Mycobacterium tuberculosis culture
(sparfloxacin may produce a false-negative culture result for *M. tuberculosis* by suppressing mycobacterial growth)

With physiology/laboratory test values
Alanine aminotransferase (ALT [SGPT]) and
Alkaline phosphatase and
Amylase and
Aspartate aminotransferase (AST [SGOT]) and
Creatine kinase (CK), serum and
Lactate dehydrogenase (LDH)
(serum values may be increased)

Electrocardiogram
(moxifloxacin and norfloxacin may prolong QT interval)

Prothrombin time
(International Normalized Ratio (INR) values may be increased with levofloxacin)

Medical considerations/Contraindications

The medical considerations/contraindications included have been selected on the basis of their potential clinical significance (reasons given in parentheses where appropriate)—not necessarily inclusive (» = major clinical significance).

Except under special circumstances, this medication should not be used when the following medical problems exist:

» Previous allergic reaction or hypersensitivity to fluoroquinolones or other chemically related quinolone derivatives

» Photosensitivity, history of
(moderate to severe phototoxic reactions have occurred in patients exposed to direct or indirect sunlight or to artificial ultraviolet light during or following sparfloxacin treatment; these reactions also have occurred in patients exposed to shaded or diffuse light, including exposure through glass or during cloudy weather; sparfloxacin is **contraindicated** in patients with a history of photosensitivity or those whose lifestyle or employment will not permit compliance with the required safety precautions)
(moderate to severe phototoxic reactions also have occurred in patients exposed to direct sunlight during or following treatment with enoxacin, levofloxacin, lomefloxacin, norfloxacin, or ofloxacin; treatment with these fluoroquinolones should be discontinued if phototoxic reactions occur)
(gatifloxacin and moxifloxacin does not show phototoxicity when compared to placebo, however patients should avoid exposure to excessive sunlight or artificial ultraviolet light (e.g. tanning beds))

» QTc-interval prolongation
(prolongation of the QTc interval has been observed in healthy volunteers receiving sparfloxacin lomefloxacin, or moxifloxacin; sparfloxacin is **contraindicated** and lomefloxacin and moxifloxacin are not recommended in patients with known QTc-interval prolongation)

» Tendinitis or tendon rupture, history of
(fluoroquinolones have been reported to cause tendinitis or tendon rupture during or after treatment; enoxacin and norfloxacin are **contraindicated** in patients with a history of tendinitis or tendon rupture; other fluoroquinolones are not recommended for patients with these problems)

Risk-benefit should be considered when the following medical problems exist:

» Bradycardia, significant
(levofloxacin may cause cardiac arrhythmias and prolongation of the QT interval in the presence of significant bradycardia; moxi-

floxacin should be used with caution; patients taking norfloxacin should be advised to inform their physicians of any personal or family history of bradycardia)

CNS disorders, including:

» Cerebral arteriosclerosis or
» Epilepsy or
» Other factors that predispose to seizures
(fluoroquinolones may cause CNS stimulation or toxicity; convulsions may occur within 3 to 4 days after the start of fluoroquinolone treatment and usually resolve with discontinuation of the fluoroquinolone; fluoroquinolones should be used with caution in patients with confirmed or suspected CNS disorders)

Diabetes mellitus
(levofloxacin has been reported to cause hyperglycemia and hypoglycemia, usually in diabetic patients who are taking oral hypoglycemic agents or insulin; diabetic patients should be monitored carefully)

Diarrhea
(pseudomembranous colitis diagnosis should be considered in these patients subsequent to the administration of antibacterial agents, including lomefloxacin and norfloxacin)

Glucose-6-phosphate dehydrogenase activity defects, actual or latent
(rare reports of hemolytic reactions in patients with this condition who take quinolone antibacterial agents)

Hepatic function impairment
(patients with severe hepatic function impairment, such as cirrhosis with ascites, may have decreased clearance of ofloxacin, resulting in an increase in peak serum concentration and elimination half-life; patients with *both* hepatic and renal function impairment may require a reduction in the dosage of ciprofloxacin; cirrhosis has not been found to decrease the nonrenal clearance of lomefloxacin)

» Hypokalemia, uncorrected
(gatifloxacin, levofloxacin, lomefloxacin, moxifloxacin, and norfloxacin may worsen QT prolongation in patients with uncorrected hypokalemia resulting in ventricular arrhythmias)

Myasthenia gravis
(may exacerbate the signs of myasthenia gravis and lead to life-threatening weakness of the respiratory muscles; caution should be exercised when using quinolones, including norfloxacin, in these patients)

Myocardial ischemia, acute
(moxifloxacin and norfloxacin should be used with caution)

» Proarrhythmias
(gatifloxacin, moxifloxacin, and sparfloxacin is not recommended for use in patients with ongoing proarrhythmias or cardiovascular conditions predisposing the patient to proarrhythmic conditions, including atrial fibrillation, congestive heart failure, hypokalemia, myocardial infarction, and significant bradycardia)

» Renal function impairment
(in general, fluoroquinolones primarily are excreted renally; it is recommended that patients with impaired renal function be administered reduced doses of fluoroquinolones)

Patient monitoring

The following may be especially important in patient monitoring (other tests may be warranted in some patients, depending on condition; » = major clinical significance):

Digoxin toxicity signs and symptoms
(gatifloxacin may increase digoxin serum concentrations, which should be determined in patients who showed signs of digoxin toxicity)

» Electrocardiogram (ECG)
(patients who are being treated concurrently with sparfloxacin or moxifloxacin and medications known to produce an increase in the QTc interval and/or torsades de pointes should receive appropriate cardiac monitoring)

Prothrombin time (PT)
(the PT of patients concurrently receiving fluoroquinolones and warfarin should be monitored closely)

Side/Adverse Effects

Note: The relative insolubility of ciprofloxacin and norfloxacin at an alkaline pH has resulted in crystalluria, usually when the urinary pH exceeds 7. Because normal urinary pH is acidic, approximately 5 to 6, crystalluria is very unlikely to occur unless the patient's urine has become alkalinized.

Seizures have been reported very rarely with ciprofloxacin therapy; however, the patients who did have seizures either had a previous seizure history, were alcoholic, or were taking ciprofloxacin concurrently with theophylline.

Prolongation of the QTc interval was observed in healthy volunteers receiving sparfloxacin, in some moxifloxacin patients, and rarely in lomefloxacin patients. The magnitude of QT prolongation may increase with increasing concentrations of moxifloxacin or increasing rates of intravenous infusion of moxifloxacin. QT prolongation may lead to an increased risk for ventricular arrhythmias including torsade de pointes.

Peripheral neuropathies have been associated with quinoline use. If symptoms of peripheral neuropathy including pain, burning, tingling, numbness and/or weakness develop, they should discontinue treatment and contact their physicians to prevent the development of an irreversible condition.

Phototoxic reactions have occurred in patients exposed to direct or indirect sunlight, or to artificial ultraviolet light, during or following sparfloxacin treatment; these reactions also have occurred in patients exposed to shaded or diffuse light, including exposure through glass or during cloudy weather. Phototoxic reactions have occurred with and without the use of sunscreens or sunblocks and have occurred after a single dose of sparfloxacin. Patients should avoid exposure to direct or indirect sunlight or artificial UV light during treatment and for 5 days following sparfloxacin treatment. Patients should discontinue sparfloxacin at the first sign or symptom of phototoxicity. Sparfloxacin is **contraindicated** in patients with a history of photosensitivity or those whose lifestyle or employment will not permit compliance with the required safety precautions. Patients who experience sparfloxacin-induced photosensitivity or phototoxicity should be treated within 2 weeks of the onset of symptoms to prevent development of lichenoid tissue reaction.

Shoulder, hand, Achilles and other tendon ruptures that required surgical repair or resulted in prolonged disability have been reported in patients receiving fluoroquinolones. Concomitant use of corticosteroids with fluoroquinolones may increase the risk of tendon disorders or ruptures. These injuries may require surgical repair or result in prolonged disability. It is recommended that fluoroquinolone treatment be discontinued at the first sign of tendon pain, inflammation, or rupture and that patients refrain from exercising until the diagnosis of tendinitis has been excluded. Tendon rupture can occur during or after therapy with quinolones.

The following side/adverse effects have been selected on the basis of their potential clinical significance (possible signs and symptoms in parentheses where appropriate)—not necessarily inclusive:

Those indicating need for medical attention

Incidence more frequent

QTc-interval prolongation (irregular or slow heart rate; recurrent fainting)—for sparfloxacin, less frequent for moxifloxacin, and rarely for lomefloxacin

Incidence less frequent

Chest pain; hypertension (blurred vision; dizziness; nervousness; headache; pounding in the ears; slow or fast heartbeat); ***peripheral edema*** (bloating or swelling of face, arms, hands, lower legs, or feet; rapid weight gain; tingling of hands or feet; unusual weight gain or loss); ***phototoxicity*** (blisters; sensation of skin burning; skin itching, rash, or redness; swelling)—more frequent for lomefloxacin and sparfloxacin

Incidence rare

Note: Frequency of incidence with moxifloxacin varies between $\geq 0.1\%$ and $\leq 3\%$

Amnesia (loss of memory; problems with memory); ***aphasia*** (problems with speech or speaking); ***Arthralgia*** (joint pain); ***asthenia*** (lack or loss of strength); ***asthma*** (cough; difficulty breathing; noisy breathing; shortness of breath; tightness in chest; wheezing); ***atrial fibrillation*** (fast or irregular heartbeat; dizziness; fainting); ***CNS stimulation*** (acute psychosis; agitation; confusion; hallucinations; tremors); ***cardiovascular reactions such as palpitation*** (fast or irregular heartbeat); ***vasodilation*** (dizziness; faintness; feeling of warmth or heat; flushing or redness of skin especially on face and neck; headache; light-headedness; sweating; weakness); ***or tachycardia*** (fainting; fast, pounding, or irregular heartbeat or pulse); ***convulsions*** (seizures); ***depersonalization*** (feeling of unreality; sense of detachment from self or body.); ***dysphagia*** (difficulty swallowing); ***dyspnea*** (shortness of breath; difficult or labored breathing; tightness in chest; wheezing); ***electrocardiogram (ECG), abnormal; eosinophilia; leukopenia*** (black, tarry stools; chest pain; chills; cough; fever; painful or difficult urination; shortness of breath; sore throat; sores, ulcers, or white spots on lips or in mouth); ***face edema*** (swelling or puffiness of face); ***glossitis*** (redness, swelling, or soreness of tongue); ***hematuria*** (blood in the urine); ***hepatotoxicity*** (dark or amber urine; loss of appetite; pale stools; stomach pain; unusual tiredness or weakness; yellow eyes or skin); ***hyperglycemia*** (abdominal pain; blurred vision; dry mouth; fatigue; flushed, dry skin; fruit-like breath odor; increased hunger; increased thirst; increased urination; nausea; sweating; troubled breathing; unexplained weight loss; vomiting); ***hyperlipidemia*** (large amount of fat in the blood); ***hypertonia*** (excessive muscle tone; muscle tension or tightness; muscle stiffness); ***hyperuricemia*** (joint pain, stiffness, or swelling; lower back, side, or stomach pain; swelling of feet or lower legs); ***hypesthesia*** (burning, crawling, itching, numbness, prickling, "pins and needles", or tingling feelings); ***injection site reaction*** (bleeding; blistering; burning; coldness; discoloration of skin; feeling of pressure; hives; infection; inflammation; itching; lumps; numbness; pain; rash; redness; scarring; soreness; stinging; swelling; tenderness; tingling; ulceration; warmth); ***hypersensitivity reactions*** (skin rash, itching, or redness; shortness of breath; swelling of face or neck; vasculitis); ***hypotension*** (blurred vision; confusion; dizziness, faintness, or lightheadedness when getting up from a lying or sitting position suddenly; sweating; unusual tiredness or weakness); ***incoordination; interstitial nephritis*** (bloody or cloudy urine; fever; skin rash; swelling of feet or lower legs); ***jaundice*** (chills; clay-colored stools; dark urine; dizziness; fever; headache; itching; loss of appetite; nausea; abdominal or stomach pain; area rash; unpleasant breath odor; unusual tiredness or weakness; vomiting of blood; yellow eyes or skin); ***maculopapular rash*** (rash with flat lesions or small raised lesions on the skin); ***phlebitis*** (pain at site of injection)—for intravenous ciprofloxacin and ofloxacin; occurred in 5% of patients receiving intravenous gatifloxacin; ***pseudomembranous colitis*** (abdominal or stomach cramps and pain, severe; abdominal tenderness; diarrhea, watery and severe, which may also be bloody; fever); ***Stevens-Johnson Syndrome*** (blistering, itching, loosening, peeling, or redness of skin; diarrhea,); ***stomatitis*** (swelling or inflammation of the mouth); ***superventricular tachycardia; ; ventricular tachycardia*** (fainting; fast, pounding, or irregular heartbeat or pulse; palpitations); ***thrombocythemia*** (pain, warmth, or burning in fingers, toes and legs; headache; dizziness; problems with vision or hearing); ***tendinitis or tendon rupture*** (pain in calves, radiating to heels; swelling of calves or lower legs); ***urticaria*** (hives or welts; itching; redness of skin; skin rash)

Incidence not determined and indicating the need for medical attention—Observed during clinical practice; estimates of frequency cannot be determined

Abnormal electroencephalogram (abnormal brain waves)—with levofloxacin; ***agranulocytosis*** (cough or hoarseness; fever with or without chills; general feeling of tiredness or weakness; lower back or side pain; painful or difficult urination; sore throat; sores, ulcers, or white spots on lips or in mouth; unusual bleeding or bruising)—with norfloxacin; ***allergic pneumonitis*** (difficult breathing)—with levofloxacin; ***anaphylactic reaction*** (cough; difficulty swallowing; dizziness fast heartbeat; hives; itching; puffiness or swelling of the eyelids or around the eyes, face, lips or tongue; shortness of)—with moxifloxacin and norfloxacin; ***anaphylactic shock*** (sharp drop in blood pressure; hives)—with levofloxacin and moxifloxacin; ***ataxia*** (shakiness and unsteady walk; unsteadiness, trembling, or other problems with muscle control or coordination); ***encephalopathy*** (blurred vision; coma; confusion; dizziness)—with levofloxacin; ***eosinophilia*** (black, tarry stools; sore throat; swollen glands; unusual bleeding or bruising)—with levofloxacin; ***erythema multiforme*** (blistering, peeling, loosening of skin; itching; joint or muscle pain)—with levofloxacin; ***Guillain-Barre*** (sudden numbness and weakness in the arms and legs; inability to move arms and legs)—with norfloxacin; ***hemolytic anemia*** (bleeding gums; dark urine; fatigue; general body swelling)—with levofloxacin; ***increased international normalized ratio/prothrombin time*** (increased bleeding time)—with levofloxacin; ***multi-system organ failure*** (failure of the heart, lungs, kidneys and/or liver)—with levofloxacin; ***peripheral neuropathy*** (burning, numbness, tingling, or painful sensations; weakness in arms, hands, legs, or feet, unsteadiness or awkwardness)—with ciprofloxacin, lomefloxacin, moxifloxacin, and norfloxacin; ***pseudomembranous colitis*** (abdominal or stomach cramps; pain; bloating; abdominal tenderness; diarrhea, watery and severe, which may also be bloody; fever; increased thirst; nausea or vomiting; unusual tiredness or weakness; unusual weight loss)—with moxifloxacin; ***torsades de pointes*** (fast heartbeat; prolonged QT interval); ***tendon rupture*** (bone pain; lower back or side pain; painful, swollen joints)

Those indicating need for medical attention only if they continue or are bothersome

Incidence more frequent

CNS toxicity (dizziness or lightheadedness; headache; nervousness; drowsiness; insomnia); ***gastrointestinal reactions*** (abdominal or stomach pain or discomfort, mild; diarrhea, mild; nausea or vomiting); ***vaginitis*** (vaginal pain and discharge)—most frequent for sparfloxacin and less frequent for moxifloxacin

Incidence less frequent or rare

Abdominal pain; allergic reaction (cough; difficulty swallowing; dizziness; fast heartbeat; hives; itching; puffiness or swelling of the eyelids or around the eyes, face, lips or tongue; shortness of breath); ***amblyopia*** (blurred vision; change in vision; impaired vision); ***anorexia*** (loss of appetite; weight loss); ***anxiety*** (fear; nervousness); ***arthritis*** (pain, swelling, or redness in joints; muscle pain or stiffness; difficulty in moving); ***back pain; change in sense of taste; constipation; depression; dizziness; dream, abnormal***—especially with gatifloxacin and rare with moxifloxacin; ***dry mouth; dyspepsia*** (acid or sour stomach; belching; heartburn; indigestion; stomach discomfort upset or pain); ***dysuria*** (difficulty in urination); ***emotional lability*** (crying; depersonalization; dysphoria; euphoria; mental depression; paranoia; quick to react or overreact emotionally; rapidly changing moods); ***flatulence*** (bloated full feeling; excess air or gas in stomach or intestines; passing gas); ***gastritis*** (burning feeling in chest or stomach; tenderness in stomach area; stomach upset; indigestion); ***headache***—more frequent for sparfloxacin; ***insomnia*** (sleeplessness; trouble sleeping; unable to sleep); ***leg pain; malaise*** (general feeling of discomfort or illness; unusual tiredness or weakness); ***moniliasis, oral*** (sore mouth or tongue; white patches in mouth and/or on tongue); ***moniliasis, vaginal*** (vaginal yeast infection); ***myalgia*** (muscle pain); ***nervousness; pain; paresthesia*** (burning, crawling, itching, numbness, prickling, "pins and needles", or tingling feelings); ***parosmia*** (change in sense of smell); ***pelvic pain; photosensitivity*** (increased sensitivity of skin to sunlight); ***pruritus*** (itching skin); ***purpuric rash*** (pinpoint red or purple spots on skin); ***pustular rash*** (spots on skin resembling a blister or pimple); ***sleep disorder*** (difficulty in sleeping); ***somnolence*** (sleepiness or unusual drowsiness); ***speech disorders*** (difficulty in speaking); ***sweating; taste; taste loss or perversion*** (change in taste; bad, unusual or unpleasant (after) taste); ***thinking, abnormal; tinnitus*** (continuing ringing or buzzing or other unexplained noise in ears; hearing loss); ***tongue discoloration; vertigo*** (dizziness or lightheadedness; feeling of constant movement of self or surroundings; sensation of spinning); ***vision, abnormal; vomiting***

Note: Some patients note a reduced incidence of nausea and taste perversion if the dose is administered in the evening.

Photosensitivity reactions generally appear within a few days of the start of fluoroquinolone treatment but can occur up to 3 weeks after its discontinuation. The reactions usually subside within 1 month of discontinuation.

Those indicating possible phototoxicity, pseudomembranous colitis, or tendinitis or tendon rupture and the need for medical attention if they occur after medication is discontinued

Abdominal or stomach cramps and pain, severe; abdominal tenderness; blisters; diarrhea, watery and severe, which may also be bloody; fever; pain in calves, radiating to heels; sensation of skin burning; skin rash, itching, or redness; swelling of calves or lower legs

Overdose

For more information on the management of overdose or unintentional ingestion, **contact a poison control center** (see *Poison Control Center Listing*).

Treatment of overdose

Since there is no specific antidote for overdose of fluoroquinolone antibiotics, treatment should be symptomatic and supportive and may include the following:

To decrease absorption—Induction of emesis or use of gastric lavage to empty the stomach; activated charcoal may be used with moxifloxacin.

Specific treatment—Patients with sparfloxacin overdose should avoid sun exposure for 5 days.

Monitoring—Electrocardiogram (ECG) monitoring for at least 24 hours after gatifloxacin, moxifloxacin, and sparfloxacin overdose is recommended, due to the possibility of prolongation of the QTc interval and other cardiac complications, including arrhythmias.

To enhance elimination—Gatifloxacin is not efficiently removed from the body by hemodialysis (about 14% recovered over 4 hours) or by chronic ambulatory peritoneal dialysis (about 11% recovered over 8 days).

Supportive care—Maintenance of adequate hydration. Patients in whom intentional overdose is confirmed or suspected should be referred for psychiatric consultation.

Patient Consultation

As an aid to patient consultation, refer to *Advice for the Patient, Fluoroquinolones (Systemic)*.

In providing consultation, consider emphasizing the following selected information (» = major clinical significance):

Before using this medication

» Conditions affecting use, especially:

Allergies to fluoroquinolones or other quinolone derivatives

Pregnancy—Fluoroquinolones are not recommended for use during pregnancy because they have been shown to cause arthropathy in immature animals

Breast-feeding—Not recommended since fluoroquinolones have been shown to cause arthropathy in immature animals

Use in children—With the exception of ciprofloxacin and levofloxacin on a risk/benefit basis for post-exposure inhalational anthrax, use of fluoroquinolones is not recommended in infants and children since these medications have been shown to cause arthropathy in immature animals.

Use in adolescents—With the exception of ciprofloxacin and levofloxacin on a risk/benefit basis for post-exposure inhalational anthrax, use of fluoroquinolones is not recommended in adolescents since these medications have been shown to cause arthropathy in immature animals.

Contraindicated medications—Amiodarone, astemizole, bepridil, cisapride, disopyramide, erythromycin, pentamidine, phenothiazines, procainamide, quinidine, sotalol, terfenadine, tricyclic antidepressants, or other medications reported to prolong the QTc interval (for sparfloxacin; should be avoided with other fluoroquinolones)

Other medications, especially aluminum, calcium, and/or magnesium-containing antacids, aminophylline, caffeine-containing products, didanosine, ferrous sulfate, oxtriphylline, phenytoin, sucralfate, theophylline, or warfarin

Gatifloxacin and moxifloxacin did not have any clinical significant drug interaction with theophylline or warfarin.

Other medical problems, especially allergy to quinolones; cerebral arteriosclerosis, bradycardia, epilepsy, or other factors that predispose to seizures; hepatic function failure; history of photosensitivity; history of tendinitis or tendon rupture; proarrhythmias; QTc-interval prolongation; renal function impairment, and uncorrected hypokalemia

Proper use of this medication

» Importance of using fluoroquinolones and other antibacterial medicine to treat bacterial infections only and not viral infections (e.g., common cold)

» Compliance with full course of therapy

» Not giving to infants, children, adolescents, or pregnant women; fluoroquinolones have been shown to cause arthropathy in immature animals

» Taking with full glass (240 mL) of water; maintaining adequate fluid intake

» For enoxacin, levofloxacin *oral solution*, or norfloxacin—Taking on an empty stomach (1 hour before or 2 hours after a meal)

» For ciprofloxacin, gatifloxacin, levofloxacin *tablets*, lomefloxacin, moxifloxacin, ofloxacin, or sparfloxacin—Taking with meals or on an empty stomach; sparfloxacin may also be taken with milk or caffeine-containing products; gatifloxacin may be taken with milk or calcium-containing antacids and supplements; ciprofloxacin should NOT be taken with dairy products or calcium-fortified juices alone, but may be taken with a meal that contains these products

» For ciprofloxacin and levofloxacin being taken for inhalation anthrax exposure—Importance of beginning medicine as soon as possible following suspected or confirmed exposure to anthrax

» Importance of not missing doses and taking at evenly spaced times

» Proper dosing

Missed dose: Taking as soon as possible; not taking if almost time for next dose; not doubling doses

» Proper storage

Precautions while using this medication

Checking with physician if no improvement of symptoms within a few days

» Avoiding concurrent use of antacids or sucralfate and fluoroquinolones; taking antacids, didanosine, or sucralfate at least 6 hours before or 2 hours after administration of ciprofloxacin; 4 hours after administration of gatifloxacin; 2 hours before or 2 hours after administration of levofloxacin, norfloxacin, or ofloxacin; 4 hours before or 2 hours after administration of lomefloxacin; 4 hours before or 4 hours after administration of sparfloxacin; 4 hours before or 8 hours after administration of moxifloxacin, and 8 hours before or 2 hours after administration of enoxacin

» Avoiding concurrent use of Class IA and Class III antiarrhythmic agents

» Avoiding taking caffeine-containing products (e.g., coffee, tea, chocolate, certain carbonated beverages) during treatment with enoxacin

Possible phototoxicity reactions (e.g., blistering or burning sensation of skin):

» Avoiding exposure to direct or indirect sunlight and to artificial ultraviolet light (e.g., sunlamps) during treatment and for 5 days after treatment

» Discontinuing medication at the first sign or symptom of phototoxicity, such as blistering; itching, rash, or redness of skin; sensation of skin burning; or swelling

» If phototoxicity has occurred, avoiding further sunlight and artificial light until the phototoxicity reaction has been resolved, or for 5 days, whichever is longer

» Possible photosensitivity reactions; discontinuing medicine at the first sign of skin rash or other allergic reaction; checking with physician to determine if further treatment is needed

» Caution if dizziness, lightheadedness, or drowsiness occurs

» Discontinuing medicine and notifying physician if pain, inflammation, or rupture of a tendon is experienced; resting and refraining from exercise until the diagnosis of tendinitis or tendon rupture has been excluded

» Discontinuing medicine and notifying physician if symptoms of peripheral neuropathies including pain, burning, tingling, numbness and/or weakness develop

» Discontinuing medicine and notifying physician if a diabetic patient has a hypoglycemic episode while being treated with a fluoroquinolone and insulin or an oral hypoglycemic agent

Side/adverse effects

Signs of potential side effects, especially abnormal electrocardiogram (ECG), amnesia, aphasia, arthralgia, asthenia, asthma, atrial fibrillation, CNS stimulation, cardiovascular reactions such as palpitation, vasodilation, and tachycardia, chest pain, convulsions, depersonalization, dysphagia, dyspnea, face edema, glossitis, hematuria, hepatotoxicity, hypesthesia, hyperglycemia, hyperlipidemia, hypersensitivity reactions, hypertension, hypertonia, hyperuricemia, hypotension, injection site reaction, interstitial nephritis, jaundice, leukopenia, maculopapular rash, peripheral edema, phlebitis, phototoxicity, QTc-interval prolongation, Stevens-Johnson syndrome, stomatitis, supraventricular tachycardia, thrombocythemia, ventricular tachycardia, tendinitis, or urticaria

Signs of potential side effects observed during clinical practice, especially abnormal electroencephalogram (EEG), agranulocytosis, allergic pneumonitis, anaphylactic reaction, anaphylactic shock, encephalopathy, eosinophilia, erythema multiforme, Guillain-Barre, hemolytic anemia, increased international normalized ratio/prothrombin time, multi-system organ failure, peripheral neuropathy, pseudomembranous colitis, torsade de pointes, or tendon rupture

General Dosing Information

Antibacterial drugs including quinolones should only be used to treat bacterial infections. They do not treat viral infections such as the common cold. When a quinolone is prescribed to treat a bacterial infection, patients should be told that although it is common to feel better early in the course of therapy, the medication should be taken exactly as directed. Skipping doses or not completing the full course of therapy may decrease the effectiveness of the immediate treatment and increase the likelihood that bacteria will develop resistance and will not be treatable by antibacterial drugs in the future.

Due to the risk of increase in magnitude of QT prolongation, the recommended dose of gatifloxacin, levofloxacin and moxifloxacin should not be exceeded. This is especially important in patients with risk factors such as significant bradycardia, acute myocardial ischemia, uncorrected hypoglycemia, and in patients receiving drugs that prolong QT interval.

Patients with impaired renal function may require a reduction in dosage based on creatinine clearance. Creatinine clearance (in mL per minute) may be calculated as follows:

Adult males—Creatinine clearance = [(140 − age) × (ideal body weight in kg)]/[72 × serum creatinine (in milligrams per dL)]

Adult females—Creatinine clearance = [(140 − age) × (ideal body weight in kg)]/[72 × serum creatinine (in milligrams per dL)] × 0.85

Creatinine clearance may also be calculated in SI units (as mL per second) as follows:

Adult males—Creatinine clearance = [(140 − age) × (ideal body weight in kg)]/[50 × serum creatinine (in micromoles per L)]

Adult females—Creatinine clearance = [(140 − age) × (ideal body weight in kg)]/[50 × serum creatinine (in micromoles per L)] × 0.85

Patients whose therapy is started with gatifloxacin or moxifloxacin injection may be switched to tablets or oral suspension without dosage adjustment.

*For inhalational anthrax (post exposure) treatment:*Drug administration should begin as soon as possible after suspected or confirmed exposure. This indication is based on a surrogate endpoint, ciprofloxacin serum concentrations achieved in humans. Total duration of ciprofloxacin administration (I.V. or oral) is 60 days.

Diet/Nutrition

Gatifloxacin can be administered without regard to food, including milk and dietary supplements containing calcium.

For treatment of adverse effects

• Some patients may develop antibiotic-associated pseudomembranous colitis (AAPMC), caused by *Clostridium difficile* toxin, during or after administration of a fluoroquinolone. Mild cases may respond to discontinuation of the medication alone. Moderate to severe cases may require fluid, electrolyte, and protein replacement.

• In cases not responding to the above measures or in more severe cases, oral doses of an antibacterial medication effective against *C. difficile* should be administered.

• In addition, AAPMC may result in severe watery diarrhea, which may occur during therapy or up to several weeks after therapy is discontinued. If diarrhea occurs, administration of antiperistaltic antidiarrheals (e.g., diphenoxylate and atropine combination, loperamide, opiates) is not recommended since they may delay the removal of toxins from the colon, thereby prolonging and/or worsening the condition.

For antibiotic-associated pseudomembranous colitis (AAPMC)—

• May require immediate emergency treatment with epinephrine.

• Oxygen, intravenous fluids, antihistamines, corticosteroids, pressor amines, and airway management, including intubation, should be administered as indicated.

For acute hypersensitivity/anaphylaxis reactions—

CIPROFLOXACIN

Summary of Differences

Indications: Also indicated to reduce the incidence or progression of inhalational anthrax following exposure to aerosolized *Bacillus anthracis.*

Pharmacology/pharmacokinetics: Distribution—Penetrates CSF
Distributed to skin, fat, muscle, bone, cartilage
Crosses placenta

Precautions: Drug interactions—Interacts with aminophylline, oxtriphylline, and theophylline; phenytoin; urinary alkalizers; warfarin

Side/adverse effects: Phlebitis (parenteral dosage form only)

Additional Dosing Information

Diet/Nutrition

The presence of food in the stomach may delay the rate of absorption of oral ciprofloxacin; however, the overall absorption is not affected. Therefore, ciprofloxacin may be taken with meals or on an empty stomach. Ciprofloxacin should NOT be taken with dairy products or calcium-fortified juices alone; however, ciprofloxacin may be taken with a meal that contains these products Ciprofloxacin should be taken with a full glass (240 mL) of water.

Crystalluria has been reported, especially in patients with alkaline urine (pH 7 or above). Therefore, alkalinization of the urine should be avoided. Although crystalluria has been reported only rarely in humans, fluid intake should be sufficient to maintain urine output of at least 1200 to 1500 mL per day in adults.

Bioequivalence information

The oral suspension and tablet dosage forms of ciprofloxacin are bioequivalent.

Ciprofloxacin immediate-release tablets are not interchangeable with ciprofloxacin extended-release tablets.

Equivalent oral dosage for conversion from intravenous dosage based on equivalent AUC dosing regimens:

• Intravenous, 200 mg every twelve hours—Oral, 250 mg every twelve hours

• Intravenous, 400 mg every twelve hours—Oral, 500 mg every twelve hours

• Intravenous, 400 mg every eight hours—Oral, 750 mg every twelve hours

Parenteral dosage forms only

Parenteral ciprofloxacin should be administered by intravenous infusion over a period of at least 60 minutes to minimize patient discomfort and reduce the risk of venous irritation.

Oral Dosage Forms

Note: Bracketed uses in the *Dosage Forms* section refer to categories of use and/or indications that are not included in U.S. product labeling.

The dosing and strengths of the dosage forms available are expressed in terms of ciprofloxacin base.

CIPROFLOXACIN FOR ORAL SUSPENSION

Usual adult dose

Anthrax, inhalational (treatment)[1]—
Oral, 500 mg (base) every 12 hours for 60 days.

Bone and joint infections—
Mild or moderate: Oral, 500 mg (base) every twelve hours for at least four to six weeks.
Severe or complicated: Oral, 750 mg (base) every twelve hours for at least four to six weeks.

Diarrhea, infectious—
Mild to severe: Oral, 500 mg (base) every twelve hours for five to seven days.

Gonorrhea, endocervical and urethral—
Oral, 250 mg (base) as a single dose.

Intra-abdominal infections—
Oral, 500 mg (base) every twelve hours for seven to fourteen days, in combination with oral metronidazole.

Lower respiratory tract infections—
Mild to moderate: Oral, 500 mg (base) every twelve hours for seven to fourteen days.
Severe or complicated: Oral, 750 mg (base) every twelve hours for seven to fourteen days.

[Meningococcal carriers]—
Oral, 750 mg (base) as a single dose.

Prostatitis, chronic—
Mild or moderate: Oral, 500 mg (base) every twelve hours for twenty-eight days.

Sinusitis, mild or moderate[1] or
Typhoid fever—
Oral, 500 mg (base) every twelve hours for ten days.

Skin and soft tissue infections—
Mild or moderate: Oral, 500 mg (base) every twelve hours for seven to fourteen days.
Severe or complicated: Oral, 750 mg (base) every twelve hours for seven to fourteen days.

Urinary tract infections—
Acute uncomplicated: Oral, 100 or 250 mg (base) every twelve hours for three days.
Mild or moderate: Oral, 250 mg (base) every twelve hours for seven to fourteen days.
Severe or complicated: Oral, 500 mg (base) every twelve hours for seven to fourteen days.

Note: Adults with impaired renal function may require a reduction in dose as follows:

Creatinine clearance (mL/min)/(mL/sec)	Dose (base)
> 50/0.83	See *Usual adult dose*
30–50/0.5–0.83	250–500 mg every 12 hours
5–29/0.08–0.48	250–500 mg every 18 hours
Hemodialysis or Peritoneal dialysis patients	250–500 mg every 24 hours after dialysis

In patients with severe infection and severe renal function impairment, a unit dose of 750 mg may be administered at the intervals noted above; however, these patients should be monitored carefully and serum concentrations of ciprofloxacin should be measured periodically.

Usual adult prescribing limits

1.5 grams (base) daily.

Usual pediatric dose

Children up to 18 years of age—Use is not recommended in infants, children, or adolescents since fluoroquinolones cause arthropathy in immature animals. However, ciprofloxacin has been given to pediatric patients, as indicated below, when alternative therapy could not be used. Based on pharmacokinetic studies, dosing for patients with cystic fibrosis should be higher and at more frequent intervals than for patients without cystic fibrosis. Dosing for cystic fibrosis patients also should be decreased as body weight increases.

Anthrax, inhalational (treatment)[1]—
Oral, 15 mg per kg of body weight per dose (base), not to exceed 500 mg per dose, every 12 hours for 60 days.

Pyelonephritis or[1]
Urinary tract infection[1]—
Oral, 10 to 20 mg per kg of body weight per dose, not to exceed 750 mg per dose, administered every 12 hours. Total duration of administration is 10 to 21 days.

[Cystic fibrosis, pulmonary exacerbations][1]—
For children 14 to 28 kg of body weight: Oral, 28 to 20 mg (base) per kg of body weight every twelve hours, up to 2 grams per day.
For children 28 to 42 kg of body weight: Oral, 20 to 15 mg (base) per kg of body weight every twelve hours, up to 2 grams per day.

[For other infections][1]—
Oral, 10 to 15 mg (base) per kg of body weight twice a day, up to 1.5 grams per day.

Note: Pediatric patients with impaired renal function were excluded from the clinical trial of complicated urinary tract infection and pyelonephritis. No information is available on the dosing adjustments necessary for pediatric patients with moderate to severe renal insufficiency (creatinine clearance of less than 50 mL per min per 1.73 square meters of body surface area.

Usual geriatric dose
See *Usual adult dose.*

Strength(s) usually available
U.S.—
250 mg (base) per 5 mL (5%) (Rx) [*Cipro* (sucrose)].
500 mg (base) per 5 mL (10%) (Rx) [*Cipro* (sucrose)].

Canada—
Not commercially available.

Packaging and storage
Prior to reconstitution, store below 25 °C (77 °F). Protect from freezing. After reconstitution, store below 30 °C (86 °F). Protect from freezing.

Preparation of dosage form
To prepare the oral suspension, the small bottle containing the microcapsules should be emptied into the large bottle containing the diluent. **Water should not be added to the suspension**. The large bottle should be closed and shaken vigorously for about 15 seconds.

Stability
The suspension is stable for 14 days when stored in a refrigerator or at room temperature (below 30 °C [86 °F]).

Auxiliary labeling
- Shake well before use.
- Take with a full glass of water.
- May cause dizziness or lightheadedness.
- Continue medicine for full time of treatment.
- Avoid too much sun or use of sunlamp.
- Take ciprofloxacin at least 2 hours before or 6 hours after antacids containing magnesium or aluminum, as well as sucralfate, metal cations such as iron, and multivitamin preparations with zinc, or didanosine (Videx®) chewable/buffered tablets or the pediatric powder for oral solution.

CIPROFLOXACIN HYDROCHLORIDE AND CIPROFLOXACIN BETAINE EXTENDED-RELEASE TABLETS

Usual adult dose
Pyelonephritis, uncomplicated—
Oral, 1000 mg (base) every twenty-four hours for seven to fourteen days.

Urinary tract infections, complicated—
Oral, 1000 mg (base) every twenty-four hours for seven to fourteen days.

Urinary tract infections, uncomplicated (acute cystitis)—
Oral, 500 mg (base) every twenty-four hours for three days.

Note: Adults with impaired renal function may require a reduction in dose as follows:
- In patients with uncomplicated urinary tract infections: no dosage adjustment is required
- In patients with complicated urinary tract infections and acute uncomplicated pyelonephritis:Creatinine clearance less than 30 mL per minute: reduce dose from 1000 mg to 500 mg dailyFor patients on hemodialysis or peritoneal dialysis: administer after the dialysis procedure is completed

Adults with impaired hepatic function: no dosage adjustment is required in patients with stable chronic cirrhosis; studies have not been done in patients with acute hepatic insufficiency

Usual pediatric dose
Children up to 18 years of age—Safety and effectiveness of ciprofloxacin extended-release tablets in pediatric patients have not been established.

Usual geriatric dose
See *Usual adult dose.*

Note: The extended-release tablets contain two types of ciprofloxacin drug substance, ciprofloxacin hydrochloride and ciprofloxacin betaine (base). Dose is given as ciprofloxacin equivalent.

Strength(s) usually available
U.S.—
500 mg (base) (Rx) [*Cipro XR* (crospovidone; hypromellose; magnesium stearate; polyethylene glycol; silica colloidal anhydrous; succinic acid; titanium dioxide)].
1000 mg (base) (Rx) [*Cipro XR* (crospovidone; hypromellose; magnesium stearate; polyethylene glycol; silica colloidal anhydrous; succinic acid; titanium dioxide)].

Canada—
500 mg (base) (Rx) [*Cipro XL*].
1000 mg (base) (Rx) [*Cipro XL*].

Packaging and storage
Stor at 25 °C (77 °F); excursions permitted between 15 and 30 °C (59 and 86 °F)

Auxiliary labeling
- Swallow whole. Do not crush or chew.
- Drink plenty of fluids while taking this medicine.
- May cause dizziness.
- Finish all of this medication unless otherwise directed.
- Avoid extended exposure to sunlight or tanning beds while taking this drug. Severe burns may result.
- Ask your pharmacist about important information about your prescription.

CIPROFLOXACIN HYDROCHLORIDE TABLETS

Usual adult dose
See *Ciprofloxacin for Oral Suspension.*

Usual adult prescribing limits
See *Ciprofloxacin for Oral Suspension.*

Usual pediatric dose
See *Ciprofloxacin for Oral Suspension.*

Usual geriatric dose
See *Ciprofloxacin for Oral Suspension.*

Strength(s) usually available
U.S.—
100 mg (base) (Rx) [*Cipro*].
250 mg (base) (Rx) [*Cipro*].
500 mg (base) (Rx) [*Cipro*].
750 mg (base) (Rx) [*Cipro*].

Canada—
100 mg (base) (Rx) [*Cipro*].
250 mg (base) (Rx) [*Cipro*].
500 mg (base) (Rx) [*Cipro*].
750 mg (base) (Rx) [*Cipro*].

Packaging and storage
Store below 30 °C (86 °F).

Auxiliary labeling
- Take with a full glass of water.
- May cause dizziness or lightheadedness.
- Continue medicine for full time of treatment.
- Avoid too much sun or use of sunlamp.
- Take ciprofloxacin at least 2 hours before or 6 hours after antacids containing magnesium or aluminum, as well as sucralfate, metal cations such as iron, and multivitamin preparations with zinc, or didanosine (Videx®) chewable/buffered tablets or the pediatric powder for oral solution.

Parenteral Dosage Forms

Note: Bracketed uses in the *Dosage Forms* section refer to categories of use and/or indications that are not included in U.S. product labeling.

CIPROFLOXACIN INJECTION USP

Usual adult dose
Anthrax, inhalational (treatment)[1]—
Intravenous, 400 mg every 12 hours. Total duration of administration is 60 days.

Bone and joint infections—
Mild or moderate: Intravenous infusion, 400 mg every twelve hours for at least 4 to 6 weeks.
Severe or complicated: Intravenous infusion, 400 mg every eight hours for at least 4 to 6 weeks.
Intra-abdominal infections—
Intravenous infusion, 400 mg every twelve hours, in combination with parenteral metronidazole.
Lower respiratory tract infections; or
Skin and soft tissue infections—
Mild or moderate: Intravenous infusion, 400 mg every twelve hours for seven to fourteen days.
Severe or complicated: Intravenous infusion, 400 mg every eight hours for seven to fourteen days.
Neutropenia, febrile, empiric therapy[1]—
Severe: Intravenous infusion, 400 mg every eight hours, in combination with piperacillin 50 mg per kg of body weight every four hours (up to 24 grams per day), for seven to fourteen days.
Pneumonia, nosocomial—
Mild to severe: Intravenous infusion, 400 mg every eight hours for ten to fourteen days.
Prostatitis, chronic—
Intravenous infusion, 400 mg every twelve hours for 28 days.
Sinusitis, mild to moderate[1]—
Intravenous infusion, 400 mg every twelve hours for 10 days.
[Septicemia]—
Intravenous infusion, 400 mg every twelve hours.
Urinary tract infections—
Mild or moderate: Intravenous infusion, 200 mg every twelve hours for seven to fourteen days.
Severe or complicated: Intravenous infusion, 400 mg every twelve hours for seven to fourteen days.

Note: Adults with impaired renal function may require a reduction in dose as follows:

Creatinine clearance (mL/min)/(mL/sec)	Dose (base)
≥ 30/0.5	See *Usual adult dose*
5–29/0.08–0.48	200–400 mg every 18 to 24 hours

Usual pediatric dose

Children up to 18 years of age—Use is not recommended in infants, children, or adolescents since fluoroquinolones cause arthropathy in immature animals. However, ciprofloxacin has been given to pediatric patients, as indicated below, when alternative therapy could not be used. Based on pharmacokinetic studies, dosing for patients with cystic fibrosis should be higher and at more frequent intervals than for patients without cystic fibrosis. Dosing for cystic fibrosis patients also should be decreased as body weight increases.
Anthrax, inhalational (treatment)[1]—
Intravenous, 10 mg per kg of body weight per dose, not to exceed 400 mg per dose, administered every 12 hours. Total duration of administration is 60 days.
Pyelonephritis or[1]
Urinary tract infection[1]—
Intravenous, 6 to 10 mg per kg of body weight per dose, not to exceed 400 mg per dose, administered every 8 hours. Total duration of administration is 10 to 21 days.
[Cystic fibrosis, pulmonary exacerbations][1]—
Intravenous infusion, 10 to 15 mg per kg every eight hours, up to 1.2 grams per day.
[For other infections][1]—
Neonates: Intravenous infusion, 3.5 to 20 mg per kg of body weight every twelve hours.
Infants and children: Intravenous infusion, 7.5 to 10 mg per kg of body weight every twelve hours, up to 800 mg per day.

Note: Pediatric patients with impaired renal function were excluded from the clinical trial of complicated urinary tract infection and pyelonephritis. No information is available on the dosing adjustments necessary for pediatric patients with moderate to severe renal insufficiency (creatinine clearance of less than 50 mL per min per 1.73 square meters of body surface area.

Usual geriatric dose

See *Usual adult dose.*

Strength(s) usually available

U.S.—
200 mg per 20 mL (Rx) [*Cipro I.V.* (in sterile water for injection; requires dilution prior to administration)].
200 mg per 100 mL (Rx) [*Cipro I.V.* (in 5% dextrose injection; premixed)].
400 mg per 40 mL (Rx) [*Cipro I.V.* (in sterile water for injection; requires dilution prior to administration)].
400 mg per 200 mL (Rx) [*Cipro I.V.* (in 5% dextrose injection; premixed)].
1200 mg per 120 mL (Rx) [*Cipro I.V.* (in sterile water for injection; requires dilution prior to administration)].
Canada—
200 mg per 20 mL (Rx) [*Cipro I.V.* (in sterile water for injection; requires dilution prior to administration)].
400 mg per 40 mL (Rx) [*Cipro I.V.* (in sterile water for injection; requires dilution prior to administration)].

Packaging and storage

Store in a cool place (between 5 and 30 °C [41 and 86 °F]) or at controlled room temperature (between 20 and 25 °C [68 and 77 °F]), unless otherwise specified by manufacturer. Protect from light and freezing.

Preparation of dosage form

To prepare a solution for intravenous infusion, the concentrate in sterile water for injection should be withdrawn aseptically from the vial and diluted to a final concentration of 1 to 2 mg per mL with a suitable intravenous solution (see manufacturer's package insert). *Solutions that come from the manufacturer in 5% dextrose injection should not be diluted prior to intravenous infusion.* The resulting solution should be infused over a period of at least 60 minutes by direct infusion or through a Y-type intravenous infusion set. It is recommended that administration of any other solutions be discontinued during infusion of ciprofloxacin.

Stability

When diluted with appropriate intravenous fluids (see manufacturer's package insert) to concentrations from 0.5 to 2 mg per mL, solutions retain their potency for up to 14 days when refrigerated or stored at room temperature.

Incompatibilities

Ciprofloxacin is incompatible with aminophylline, amoxicillin, cefepime, clindamycin, dexamethasone, floxacillin, furosemide, heparin, and phenytoin.
If ciprofloxacin is to be given concurrently with another medication, each medication should be administered separately according to the recommended dosage and route of administration for each medication.

[1]Not included in Canadian product labeling.

ENOXACIN

Summary of Differences

Precautions: Drug interactions—
Enoxacin has the greatest effect in decreasing the clearance of caffeine and theophylline, increasing the risk of toxicity for these medications.
Interacts also with bismuth and digoxin
Medical considerations—Contraindicated in patients with tendinitis

Additional Dosing Information

Diet/Nutrition

The effect of food on the absorption of enoxacin tablets has not been studied; it is recommended that enoxacin be taken at least 1 hour before or 2 hours after a meal; however, decreased gastric acidity has been shown to decrease the bioavailability of enoxacin.
Caffeine-containing products (e.g., coffee, tea, chocolate, certain carbonated beverages) should be avoided during treatment with enoxacin.

Oral Dosage Forms

ENOXACIN TABLETS

Usual adult dose

Gonorrhea—
Oral, 400 mg as a single dose.
Urinary tract infections, endocervical and urethral—
Complicated: Oral, 400 mg every twelve hours for fourteen days.
Uncomplicated: Oral, 200 mg every twelve hours for seven days.

Note: Adults with impaired renal function may require a reduction in dose as follows:

Creatinine clearance (mL/min)/(mL/sec)	Dose
> 30/0.5	See *Usual adult dose*
≤ 30/0.5	50% of the recommended dose every 12 hours

Usual pediatric dose
Children up to 18 years of age—Use is not recommended in infants, children, or adolescents since fluoroquinolones cause arthropathy in immature animals.

Usual geriatric dose
See *Usual adult dose.*

Strength(s) usually available
U.S.—
200 mg (Rx) [*Penetrex*].
400 mg (Rx) [*Penetrex*].
Canada—
Not commercially available.

Packaging and storage
Store below 40 °C (104 °F), preferably between 15 and 30 °C (59 and 86 °F), in a tight container.

Auxiliary labeling
- Take with a full glass of water.
- May cause dizziness, lightheadedness, or drowsiness.
- Continue medicine for full time of treatment.

GATIFLOXACIN

Summary of Differences
Pharmacology/pharmacokinetic: Longer half-life; may be dosed once a day; does not inhibit cytochrome P450 isoenzymes and is not an enzyme inducer.
Precautions: Drug interactions—does not significantly interact with cimetidine, digoxin, glyburide, midazolam, theophylline, and warfarin.
Side effects—does not show phototoxicity when compared with placebo and had a lower potential for producing delayed photosensitivity skin reactions than ciprofloxacin or lomefloxacin.

Additional Dosing Information
Bioequivalence information
Dosage adjustment is not necessary when switching treatment of gatifloxacin from injection to tablets.

Diet/Nutrition
Gatifloxacin may be taken with or without food.
Antacids with aluminum and magnesium, vitamins containing iron or zinc, and sucralfate should not be taken within 4 hours after taking gatifloxacin.

For parenteral dosage forms only
Gatifloxacin injection should be administered only by slow intravenous infusion over a period of 60 minutes

Oral Dosage Forms
GATIFLOXACIN FOR ORAL SUSPENSION
Usual adult dose
See *Gatifloxacin tablets.*

Note: Adults with renal function impairment, creatinine clearance < 40 mL/min including patients on hemodialysis and on chronic ambulatory peritoneal dialysis, may require a reduction in dose. See *Gatifloxacin tablets*

Usual pediatric dose
Children up to 18 years of age—Use is not recommended in infants, children, or adolescents since fluoroquinolones cause arthropathy in immature animals.

Usual geriatric dose
See *Gatifloxacin tablets.*

Strength(s) usually available
U.S.—
200 mg per 5 mL (when reconstituted according to manufacturer's instructions) (available in 1-,2-,3-, and 4-gram bottles) (Rx) [*Tequin* (stearic acid; xylitol; aspartame; spray dried artificial guarana flavor; flavor cream de vanilla powder [natural and artificial] with 5% silicon dioxide; microcrystalline cellulose with sodium carboxymethylcellulose; methylparaben; titanium dioxide; sucrose)].
Canada—
Not commercially available

Packaging and storage
Prior to constitution, store at 25 °C (77 °F); excursions permitted to between 15 and 30 °C (59 and 86 °F).

Preparation of dosage form
Prepare a suspension at time of dispensing as follows:
- Tap the bottle until all the powder flows freely.
- Add approximately 1/2 of the total amount of water for constitution according to the table below.
- Shake bottle vigorously for about one minute to suspend the powder.
- Add the remainder of the water and shake again.
- Each bottle will provide the volume of 40 mg per mL of oral suspension indicated in the table below

Bottle size	Amount* of water to be added	Gatifloxacin concentration after constitution
25 mL (1 g)	12 mL	40 mg/mL
50 mL (2 g)	23 mL	40 mg/mL
75 mL (3 g)	34 mL	40 mg/mL
100 mL (4 g)	46 mL	40 mg/mL

*The water should be added in two approximately equal portions.

Stability
After reconstitution, gatifloxacin oral suspension is stable for 14 days under refrigeration, 2° to 8° C (36° to 46° F).

Auxiliary labeling
- Shake well. Refrigerate
- May cause dizziness, drowsiness, or lightheadedness.
- Avoid too much sun exposure or use of sunlamp.
- Continue medicine for full time of treatment.

GATIFLOXACIN TABLETS
Usual adult dose
Bronchitis, bacterial exacerbations—
Oral, 400 mg every 24 hours for 7 to 10 days.
Gonorrhea, endocervical and rectal in women; and urethral in men—
Oral, 400 mg single dose.
Pneumonia, community-acquired—
Oral, 400 mg every 24 hours for 7 to 14 days.
Pyelonephritis—
Oral, 400 mg every 24 hours for 7 to 10 days.
Sinusitis, acute—
Oral, 400 mg every 24 hours for 10 days.
Urinary tract infections, bacterial, uncomplicated—
Oral, 400 mg single dose; or 200 mg every 24 hours for 3 days.
Urinary tract infections, bacterial, complicated—
Oral, 400 mg every 24 hours for 7 to 10 days.

Note: Adults with renal function impairment, creatinine clearance < 40 mL/min including patients on hemodialysis and on chronic ambulatory peritoneal dialysis, may require a reduction in dose as follows:

Creatinine clearance	Initial dose	Subsequent dose*
≥ 40 mL/min	400 mg	400 mg every day
< 40 mL/min	400 mg	200 mg every day
Hemodialysis	400 mg	200 mg every day
Continuous peritoneal dialysis	400 mg	200 mg every day

*Start of subsequent dose on Day 2 of dosing

Usual pediatric dose
Children up to 18 years of age—Use is not recommended in infants, children, or adolescents since fluoroquinolones cause arthropathy in immature animals.

Usual geriatric dose
See *Usual adult dose*

Strength(s) usually available
U.S.—
200 mg (Rx) [*Tequin* (methylcellulose; polysorbate 80)].
400 mg [*Tequin* (methylcellulose; polysorbate 80)].
Canada—
Not commercially available.

Packaging and storage
Store at 25 °C (77 °F); excursion permitted to between 15 and 30 °C (59 and 86 °F).

Auxiliary labeling
- May cause dizziness, drowsiness, or lightheadedness.
- Avoid too much sun exposure or use of sunlamp.
- Continue medicine for full time of treatment.

Parenteral Dosage Forms

GATIFLOXACIN INTRAVENOUS SOLUTION—PREMIX BAGS

Usual adult dose

Bronchitis, bacterial exacerbations—
Intravenous infusion, 400 mg every 24 hours for 7 to 10 days.

Gonorrhea, endocervical and rectal in women; and urethral in men—
Intravenous infusion, 400 mg single dose.

Pneumonia, community-acquired—
Intravenous infusion, 400 mg every 24 hours for 7 to 14 days.

Pyelonephritis—
Intravenous infusion, 400 mg every 24 hours for 7 to 10 days.

Sinusitis, acute—
Intravenous infusion, 400 mg every 24 hours for 10 days.

Urinary tract infections, bacterial, uncomplicated—
Intravenous infusion, 400 mg single dose; or 200 mg every 24 hours for 3 days.

Urinary tract infections, bacterial, complicated—
Intravenous infusion, 400 mg every 24 hours for 7 to 10 days.

Note: Adults with renal function impairment, creatinine clearance < 40 mL/min including patients on hemodialysis and on chronic ambulatory peritoneal dialysis, may require a reduction in dose as follows:

Creatinine clearance	Initial dose	Subsequent dose*
≥ 40 mL/min	400 mg	400 mg every day
< 40 mL/min	400 mg	200 mg every day
Hemodialysis	400 mg	200 mg every day
Continuous peritoneal dialysis	400 mg	200 mg every day

*Start of subsequent dose on Day 2 of dosing

Usual pediatric dose

Children up to 18 years of age—Use is not recommended in infants, children, or adolescents since fluoroquinolones cause arthropathy in immature animals.

Usual geriatric dose

See *Usual adult dose*

Strength(s) usually available

U.S.—
200 mg per 100 ml (Rx) [*Tequin* (in 5% dextrose)].
400 mg per 200 ml (Rx) [*Tequin* (in 5% dextrose)].

Canada—
Not commercially available.

Packaging and storage

Store at 25 °C (77 °F); excursion permitted to between 15 and 30 °C (59 and 86 °F). Do not freeze.

Stability

Gatifloxacin injection contains no preservative or bacteriostatic agent. Because of this, the premix bags are for single use only; any unused portion remaining in the bag should be discarded.

Incompatibilities

Because there are only limited data on the compatibility of other substances with gatifloxacin injection, additives or other medications should not be added to gatifloxacin injection or infused simultaneously through the same intravenous line.

This product should be inspected visually for any particulate matter before administration. Samples with visible particles should be discarded.

GATIFLOXACIN INTRAVENOUS SOLUTION—SINGLE-USE VIALS

Usual adult dose

Bronchitis, bacterial exacerbations—
Intravenous infusion, 400 mg every 24 hours for 7 to 10 days.

Gonorrhea, endocervical and rectal in women; and urethral in men—
Intravenous infusion, 400 mg single dose.

Pneumonia, community-acquired—
Intravenous infusion, 400 mg every 24 hours for 7 to 14 days.

Pyelonephritis—
Intravenous infusion, 400 mg every 24 hours for 7 to 10 days.

Sinusitis, acute—
Intravenous infusion, 400 mg every 24 hours for 10 days.

Urinary tract infections, bacterial, uncomplicated—
Intravenous infusion, 400 mg single dose; or 200 mg every 24 hours for 3 days.

Urinary tract infections, bacterial, complicated—
Intravenous infusion, 400 mg every 24 hours for 7 to 10 days.

Note: Adults with renal function impairment, creatinine clearance < 40 mL/min including patients on hemodialysis and on chronic ambulatory peritoneal dialysis, may require a reduction in dose as follows:

Creatinine clearance	Initial dose	Subsequent dose*
≥ 40 mL/min	400 mg	400 mg every day
< 40 mL/min	400 mg	200 mg every day
Hemodialysis	400 mg	200 mg every day
Continuous peritoneal dialysis	400 mg	200 mg every day

*Start of subsequent dose on Day 2 of dosing

Usual pediatric dose

Children up to 18 years of age—Use is not recommended in infants, children, or adolescents since fluoroquinolones cause arthropathy in immature animals.

Usual geriatric dose

See *Usual adult dose*

Strength(s) usually available

U.S.—
200 mg per 20 ml (requires dilution prior to administration) (Rx) [*Tequin*].
400 mg per 40 ml (requires dilution prior to administration) (Rx) [*Tequin*].

Packaging and storage

Store at 25 °C (77 °F); excursion permitted to between 15 and 30 °C (59 and 86 °F).

Preparation of dosage form

To prepare a 200–mg dose for intravenous injection, withdraw 20 mL of gatifloxacin from the vial and dilute with a compatible intravenous solution (see manufacturer's labeling instruction) to a final concentration of 2 mg/mL or a final volume of 100 mL. To prepare a 400–mg dose for intravenous injection, withdraw 40 mL of gatifloxacin from the vial and dilute with a compatible intravenous solution (see manufacturer's labeling instruction) to a final concentration of 2 mg/mL or a final volume of 200 mL.

Stability

When diluted in a compatible intravenous solution to a concentration of 2 mg/mL, gatifloxacin is stable for 14 days when stored between 20 and 26 °C (68 and 77 °F) or under refrigeration between 2 and 8 °C (36 and 46 °F). Diluted solution that are frozen and stored between −25 and −10 °C (−13 to 14 °F) are stable for 6 months. Frozen solution may be thawed at controlled room temperature. Thawed solution are stable for 14 days when stored between 20 and 25 °C (68 and 77 °F) or when stored under refrigeration between 2 and 8 °C (36 and 46 °F). Solutions should not be refrozen.

Gatifloxacin injection contains no preservative or bacteriostatic agent. Because of this, the vials are for single use only; any unused portion remaining in the vial should be discarded.

Incompatibilities

Because there are only limited data on the compatibility of other substances with gatifloxacin injection, additives or other medications should not be added to gatifloxacin injection or infused simultaneously through the same intravenous line.

This product should be inspected visually for any particulate matter before administration. Samples with visible particles should be discarded.

LEVOFLOXACIN

Summary of Differences

Indications: Also indicated to prevent the development of inhalational anthrax following exposure to aerosolized *Bacillus anthracis*.

Precautions: Medical considerations—Diabetes mellitus

Additional Dosing Information

Bioequivalence information

Oral and parenteral dosage forms of levofloxacin are bioequivalent on a mg-per-mg basis; therefore, oral and parenteral routes of administration are considered to be interchangeable. Levofloxacin tablet and oral solution formulations are bioequivalent.

Diet/Nutrition
Levofloxacin oral solution should be taken 1 hour before eating or 2 hours after eating.
Levofloxacin tablets may be taken with or without food.
Antacids, vitamins containing iron or zinc, or sucralfate should not be taken within 2 hours before or 2 hours after taking levofloxacin.

For parenteral dosage forms only
Levofloxacin should be administered only by slow intravenous infusion over a period of not less than 60 minutes and up to 90 minutes, depending on the dose to avoid hypotension that may result from rapid intravenous injection.

Oral Dosage Forms

LEVOFLOXACIN ORAL SOLUTION

Usual adult dose
Anthrax, inhalation (treatment)—
Oral, 500 mg every twenty-four hours for 60 days.

Note: Levofloxacin administration should begin as soon as possible after suspected or confirmed exposure to aerosolized *B. anthracis.* This indication is based on a surrogate endpoint. Levofloxacin plasma concentrations achieved in humans are reasonably likely to predict clinical benefit.

Safety of levofloxacin in adults for durations of therapy beyond 28 days has not been studied. Prolonged levofloxacin therapy in adults should only be used when risk/benefit has been considered.

Bronchitis, bacterial exacerbations, treatment—
Oral, 500 mg every twenty-four hours for seven days.
Pneumonia, community-acquired, treatment—
Oral, 500 mg every twenty-four hours for seven to fourteen days, or oral, 750 mg every twenty-four hours for five days. Efficacy of 750 mg regimen has been demonstrated to be effective for infections caused by *Streptococcus pneumoniae* (excluding MDRSP), *Haemophilus influenzae, Mycoplasma pneumoniae,* and *Chlamydia pneumoniae.*
Pneumonia, nosocomial—
Oral, 750 mg every twenty-four hours for seven to fourteen days.
Prostatitis—
Oral, 500 mg every twenty-four hours for twenty-eight days.
Pyelonephritis, treatment—
Oral, 250 mg every twenty-four hours for ten days.
Sinusitis, treatment—
Oral, 500 mg every twenty-four hours for ten to fourteen days.
Skin and soft tissue infections, complicated, treatment—
Oral, 750 mg every twenty-four hours for seven to fourteen days.
Skin and soft tissue infections, uncomplicated, treatment—
Oral, 500 mg every twenty-four hours for seven to ten days.
Urinary tract infections, bacterial, complicated, treatment—
Oral, 250 mg every twenty-four hours for ten days.
Urinary tract infections, bacterial, uncomplicated, treatment—
Oral, 250 mg every twenty-four hours for three days.

Note: For patients with impaired renal function with *acute bacterial exacerbation of bronchitis, community acquired pneumonia, sinusitis, uncomplicated skin and soft tissue infections, chronic bacterial prostatitis, or inhalational anthrax (post-exposure)*, dosage adjustment is as follows:
- Creatinine clearance 50 to 80 mL per minute: no dosage adjustment
- Creatinine clearance 20 to 49 mL per minute: Oral, 500 mg initially then oral, 250 mg every twenty-four hours
- Creatinine clearance 10 to 19 mL per minute: Oral, 500 mg initially then oral, 250 mg every **forty-eight** hours
- Hemodialysis: Oral, 500 mg initially then oral, 250 mg every **forty-eight** hours
- CAPD: Oral, 500 mg initially then oral, 250 mg every **forty-eight** hours

For patients with impaired renal function with *complicated skin and soft tissue infections, nosocomial pneumonia or community acquired pneumonia*, dosage adjustment is as follows:
- Creatinine clearance 50 to 80 mL per minute: no dosage adjustment
- Creatinine clearance 20 to 49 mL per minute: Oral, 750 mg initially then oral, 750 mg every **forty-eight** hours
- Creatinine clearance 10 to 19 mL per minute: Oral, 750 mg initially then oral, 500 mg every **forty-eight** hours
- Hemodialysis: Oral, 750 mg initially then oral, 500 mg every **forty-eight** hours
- CAPD: Oral, 750 mg initially then oral, 500 mg every **forty-eight** hours

For patients with impaired renal function with *complicated urinary tract infection or acute pyelonephritis*, dosage adjustment is as follows:
- Creatinine clearance greater than or equal to 20 mL per minute: no dosage adjustment
- Creatinine clearance 10 to 19 mL per minute: Oral, 250 mg initially then oral, 250 mg every **forty-eight** hours

For patients with impaired renal function with *uncomplicated urinary tract infection*, no dosage adjustment is required.

Usual pediatric dose
Safety and efficacy have not been established.

Strength(s) usually available
U.S.—
25 mg per mL (Rx) [*Levaquin* (artificial and natural flavors; ascorbic acid; benzyl alcohol; caramel color; glycerin; hydrochloric acid; propylene glycol; purified water; sodium hydroxide; sucralose; sucrose)].
Canada—
Not commercially available.

Packaging and storage
Store at 25 °C (77 °F); excursions permitted between 15 and 30 °C (59 and 86 °F)

Auxiliary labeling
- Take on an empty stomach - 1 hour before or 2 hours after eating.
- Do not take dairy products, iron, or antacids 2 hours before to 2 hours after this drug.
- Drink plenty of fluids while taking this medication.
- May cause dizziness or drowsiness.
- Avoid extended exposure to sunlight or tanning beds while taking this drug. Severe burns may result.
- Finish all of this medication unless otherwise directed.

LEVOFLOXACIN TABLETS

Usual adult dose
Anthrax, inhalation (treatment)—
Oral, 500 mg every twenty-four hours for 60 days.

Note: Levofloxacin administration should begin as soon as possible after suspected or confirmed exposure to aerosolized *B. anthracis.* This indication is based on a surrogate endpoint. Levofloxacin plasma concentrations achieved in humans are reasonably likely to predict clinical benefit.

Safety of levofloxacin in adults for durations of therapy beyond 28 days has not been studied. Prolonged levofloxacin therapy in adults should only be used when risk/benefit has been considered.

Bronchitis, bacterial exacerbations—
Oral, 500 mg every twenty-four hours for seven days.
Pneumonia, community-acquired—
Oral, 500 mg every twenty-four hours for seven to fourteen days or oral, 750 mg every twenty-four hours for five days. Efficacy of 750 mg regimen has been demonstrated to be effective for infections caused by *Streptococcus pneumoniae* (excluding MDRSP), *Haemophilus influenzae, Mycoplasma pneumoniae,* and *Chlamydia pneumoniae.*

Note: Canadian manufacturer recommends 10 to 14 days for severe infections.

Pneumonia, nosocomial, treatment—
Oral, 750 mg every twenty-four hours for seven to fourteen days.
Prostatitis, bacterial, chronic, treatment—
Oral, 500 mg every twenty-four hours for twenty-eight days.
Pyelonephritis or
Urinary tract infections, complicated—
Oral, 250 mg every twenty-four hours for ten days.
Sinusitis, acute maxillary—
Oral, 500 mg every twenty-four hours for ten to fourteen days.
Skin and soft tissue infections, complicated, treatment—
Oral, 750 mg every twenty-four hours for seven to fourteen days.

Note: Canadian manufacturer recommends 500 mg every twelve hours for seven to fourteen days.

Skin and soft tissue infections, uncomplicated—
Oral, 500 mg every twenty-four hours for seven to ten days.
Urinary tract infections, bacterial, uncomplicated, treatment—
Oral, 250 mg every twenty-four hours for three days.

Note: For patients with impaired renal function with *acute bacterial exacerbation of bronchitis, community acquired pneumonia, sinus-*

itis, uncomplicated skin and soft tissue infections, chronic bacterial prostatitis, or inhalational anthrax (post-exposure), dosage adjustment is as follows:
• Creatinine clearance 50 to 80 mL per minute: no dosage adjustment
• Creatinine clearance 20 to 49 mL per minute: Oral, 500 mg initially then oral, 250 mg every twenty-four hours
• Creatinine clearance 10 to 19 mL per minute: Oral, 500 mg initially then oral, 250 mg every **forty-eight** hours
• Hemodialysis: Oral, 500 mg initially then oral, 250 mg every **forty-eight** hours
• CAPD: Oral, 500 mg initially then oral, 250 mg every **forty-eight** hours

For patients with impaired renal function with *complicated skin and soft tissue infections, nosocomial pneumonia or community acquired pneumonia*, dosage adjustment is as follows:
• Creatinine clearance 50 to 80 mL per minute: no dosage adjustment
• Creatinine clearance 20 to 49 mL per minute: Oral, 750 mg initially then oral, 750 mg every **forty-eight** hours
• Creatinine clearance 10 to 19 mL per minute: Oral, 750 mg initially then oral, 500 mg every **forty-eight** hours
• Hemodialysis: Oral, 750 mg initially then oral, 500 mg every **forty-eight** hours
• CAPD: Oral, 750 mg initially then oral, 500 mg every **forty-eight** hours

For patients with impaired renal function with *complicated urinary tract infection or acute pyelonephritis*, dosage adjustment is as follows:
• Creatinine clearance greater than or equal to 20 mL per minute: no dosage adjustment
• Creatinine clearance 10 to 19 mL per minute: Oral, 250 mg initially then oral, 250 mg every **forty-eight** hours

For patients with impaired renal function with *uncomplicated urinary tract infection*, no dosage adjustment is required.

Usual pediatric dose

Children up to 18 years of age—Use is not recommended in infants, children, or adolescents since fluoroquinolones cause arthropathy in immature animals.

Strength(s) usually available

U.S.—
250 mg (Rx) [*Levaquin* (synthetic red iron oxide)].
500 mg (Rx) [*Levaquin* (microcrystalline cellulose; magnesium stearate; titanium dioxide; synthetic red iron oxide; synthetic yellow iron oxide)].
750 mg (Rx) [*Levaquin* (hydroxypropyl methylcellulose; crospovidone; magnesium stearate; polyethylene glycol; titanium dioxide; polysorbate 80)].

Canada—
250 mg (Rx) [*Levaquin*].
500 mg (Rx) [*Levaquin*].

Packaging and storage

Store below 40 °C (104 °F), preferably between 15 and 30 °C (59 and 86 °F) in a well-closed container.

Auxiliary labeling

- Take with a full glass of water.
- May cause dizziness, drowsiness, or lightheadedness.
- Avoid too much sun exposure or use of sunlamp.
- Continue medicine for full time of treatment.

Parenteral Dosage Forms

LEVOFLOXACIN FOR INJECTION

Usual adult dose

Anthrax, inhalation (treatment)—
Intravenous infusion, 500 mg, administered over a 60-minute period, every twenty-four hours for 60 days.

Note: Levofloxacin administration should begin as soon as possible after suspected or confirmed exposure to aerosolized *B. anthracis*. This indication is based on a surrogate endpoint. Levofloxacin plasma concentrations achieved in humans are reasonably likely to predict clinical benefit.

Safety of levofloxacin in adults for durations of therapy beyond 28 days has not been studied. Prolonged levofloxacin therapy in adults should only be used when risk/benefit has been considered.

Bronchitis, bacterial exacerbations—
Intravenous infusion, 500 mg every twenty-four hours for seven to fourteen days.

Pneumonia, community-acquired—
Intravenous infusion, 500 mg every twenty-four hours for seven to fourteen days or intravenous infusion, 750 mg administered over a 90-minute period, every twenty-four hours for five days. Efficacy of 750 mg regimen has been demonstrated to be effective for infections caused by *Streptococcus pneumoniae* (excluding MDRSP), *Haemophilus influenzae*, *Mycoplasma pneumoniae*, and *Chlamydia pneumoniae*.

Pneumonia, nosocomial—
Intravenous infusion, 750 mg every twenty-four hours for seven to fourteen days.

Prostatitis, bacterial, treatment—
Intravenous infusion, 500 mg every twenty-four hours for twenty-eight days.

Pyelonephritis or
Urinary tract infections, complicated—
Intravenous infusion, 250 mg every twenty-four hours for ten days.

Sinusitis, acute maxillary—
Intravenous infusion, 500 mg every twenty-four hours for ten to fourteen days.

Skin and soft tissue infections, complicated, treatment—
Intravenous infusion, 750 mg every twenty-four hours for seven to fourteen days.

Skin and soft tissue infections, uncomplicated, treatment—
Intravenous infusion, 500 mg every twenty-four hours for seven to ten days.

Urinary tract infections, bacterial, complicated, treatment—
Intravenous infusion, 250 mg every twenty-four hours for ten days.

Urinary tract infections, bacterial, uncomplicated, treatment—
Intravenous infusion, 250 mg every twenty-four hours for three days.

Note: For patients with impaired renal function with *acute bacterial exacerbation of bronchitis, community acquired pneumonia, sinusitis, uncomplicated skin and soft tissue infections, chronic bacterial prostatitis, or inhalational anthrax (post-exposure)*, dosage adjustment is as follows:
• Creatinine clearance 50 to 80 mL per minute: no dosage adjustment
• Creatinine clearance 20 to 49 mL per minute: Intravenous infusion, 500 mg initially then intravenous infusion, 250 mg every twenty-four hours
• Creatinine clearance 10 to 19 mL per minute: Intravenous infusion, 500 mg initially then intravenous infusion, 250 mg every **forty-eight** hours
• Hemodialysis: Intravenous infusion, 500 mg initially then intravenous infusion, 250 mg every **forty-eight** hours
• CAPD: Intravenous infusion, 500 mg initially then intravenous infusion, 250 mg every **forty-eight** hours

For patients with impaired renal function with *complicated skin and soft tissue infections, nosocomial pneumonia or community acquired pneumonia*, dosage adjustment is as follows:
• Creatinine clearance 50 to 80 mL per minute: no dosage adjustment
• Creatinine clearance 20 to 49 mL per minute: Intravenous infusion, 750 mg initially then intravenous infusion, 750 mg every **forty-eight** hours
• Creatinine clearance 10 to 19 mL per minute: Intravenous infusion, 750 mg initially then intravenous infusion, 500 mg every **forty-eight** hours
• Hemodialysis: Intravenous infusion, 750 mg initially then intravenous infusion, 500 mg every **forty-eight** hours
• CAPD: Intravenous infusion, 750 mg initially then intravenous infusion, 500 mg every **forty-eight** hours

For patients with impaired renal function with *complicated urinary tract infection or acute pyelonephritis*, dosage adjustment is as follows:
• Creatinine clearance greater than or equal to 20 mL per minute: no dosage adjustment
• Creatinine clearance 10 to 19 mL per minute: Intravenous infusion, 250 mg initially then intravenous infusion, 250 mg every **forty-eight** hours

For patients with impaired renal function with *uncomplicated urinary tract infection*, no dosage adjustment is required.

Usual pediatric dose

Use is not recommended in infants, children, or adolescents since fluoroquinolones cause arthropathy in immature animals.

Strength(s) usually available

U.S.—
500 mg per 20 mL (requires dilution prior to administration) (Rx) [*Levaquin*].

Canada—
500 mg per 20 mL (requires dilution prior to administration) (Rx) [*Levaquin*].

Packaging and storage
Store below 40 °C (104 °F), preferably between 15 and 30 °C (59 and 86 °F). Protect from light.

Preparation of dosage form
Levofloxacin concentrate must be further diluted with compatible intravenous fluids prior to intravenous administration. The concentration of the resulting diluted solution must be 5 mg/mL prior to administration.
To prepare a 250-mg dose for intravenous infusion, withdraw 10 mL of levofloxacin for injection from the vial and dilute with 40 mL of a compatible intravenous solution (see manufacturer's labeling instructions), for a total volume of 50 mL. To prepare a 500-mg dose, withdraw 20 mL of levofloxacin for injection from the vial and dilute with 80 mL of a compatible intravenous solution (see manufacturer's labeling instructions), for a total volume of 100 mL.
To prepare a 750-mg dose for intravenous infusion, withdraw 30 mL of levofloxacin concentrate for injection from the vial and dilute with 120 mL of a compatible intravenous solution, for a total volume of 150 mL.

Stability
When diluted to a concentration of 5 mg per mL, levofloxacin for injection is stable for 72 hours when stored at or below 25 °C (77 °F) and for 14 days when refrigerated (5 °C [41 °F]) in plastic intravenous containers. Diluted solutions that are frozen in glass bottles or plastic containers are stable for 6 months when stored at −20 °C (−4 °F). Frozen solutions should be thawed at room temperature or in a refrigerator. They should not be thawed in a microwave or by water-bath immersion. Thawed solutions should not be refrozen.
Levofloxacin for injection contains no preservative or bacteriostatic agent. Because of this, the vials are for single use only; any unused portion remaining in the vial should be discarded.

Incompatibilities
Because there is only limited data on the compatibility of other substances with levofloxacin for injection, additives or other medications should not be added to levofloxacin for injection in the single-use vials or infused simultaneously through the same intravenous line.
This product should be inspected visually for any particulate matter before administration. Samples with visible particles should be discarded.

LEVOFLOXACIN INJECTION

Usual adult dose
See *Levofloxacin for Injection.*

Usual pediatric dose
See *Levofloxacin for Injection.*

Strength(s) usually available
U.S.—
250 mg per 50 mL (in dextrose solution) (Rx) [*Levaquin* (5% Dextrose)].
500 mg per 100 mL (in dextrose solution) (Rx) [*Levaquin* (5% Dextrose)].
750 mg per 150 mL (Rx) [*Levaquin* (5% Dextrose)].
Canada—
250 mg per 50 mL (in dextrose solution) (Rx) [*Levaquin* (5% Dextrose)].
500 mg per 100 mL (in dextrose solution) (Rx) [*Levaquin* (5% Dextrose)].

Packaging and storage
Store at or below 25 °C (77 °F); however, brief exposure at up to 40 °C (104 °F) does not adversely affect the product. Protect from excessive heat, freezing, and light.

Stability
Levofloxacin injection in flexible containers is for single use only; any unused portion should be discarded.

Incompatibilities
Because there are only limited data on the compatibility of other substances with levofloxacin injection, additives or other medications should not be added to levofloxacin injection in flexible containers or infused simultaneously through the same intravenous line.
This product should be inspected visually for any particulate matter before administration. Samples with visible particles should be discarded.
Levofloxacin pre-mix injection flexible containers are for single use only; any unused portion should be discarded. Do not use levofloxacin flexible containers in series connections.

LOMEFLOXACIN

Summary of Differences

Pharmacology/pharmacokinetics: Longer half-life; may be dosed once a day.
Precautions: Drug interactions—Does not significantly interfere with the clearance of caffeine and theophylline.

Additional Dosing Information

Diet/Nutrition
When lomefloxacin was administered with food, the extent of absorption was only slightly decreased. Lomefloxacin may be taken with or without food.

Oral Dosage Forms

Note: The dosing and strength of the dosage form available are expressed in terms of lomefloxacin base.

LOMEFLOXACIN TABLETS

Usual adult dose
Bronchitis, bacterial exacerbations[1]—
Oral, 400 mg (base) once a day for ten days.
Urinary tract infections, prophylaxis[1]—
Transrectal biopsy patients: Oral, 400 mg (base) as a single dose one to six hours prior to the start of surgery.
Transurethral surgical patients: Oral, 400 mg (base) as a single dose two to six hours prior to the start of surgery.
Urinary tract infections, treatment[1]—
Complicated: Oral, 400 mg (base) once a day for fourteen days.
Uncomplicated, due to *Escherichia coli*: Oral, 400 mg (base) once a day for three days.
Uncomplicated, due to *Klebsiella pneumoniae, Proteus mirabilis*, or *Staphylococcus saprophyticus*: Oral, 400 mg (base) once a day for ten days.

Note: Adults with impaired renal function may require a reduction in dose as follows:

Creatinine clearance (mL/min)/(mL/sec)	Dose (base)
> 40/0.67	See *Usual adult dose*
≤ 40/0.67 or Hemodialysis	400 mg for first dose, then 200 mg once a day

Usual pediatric dose
Children up to 18 years of age—Use is not recommended in infants, children, and adolescents since fluoroquinolones cause arthropathy in immature animals.

Usual geriatric dose
See *Usual adult dose.*

Strength(s) usually available
U.S.—
400 mg (base) (Rx) [*Maxaquin* (scored; lactose)].
Canada—
Not commercially available.

Packaging and storage
Store below 40 °C (104 °F), preferably between 15 and 30 °C (59 and 86 °F), in a tight container.

Auxiliary labeling
- Take with a full glass of water.
- May cause dizziness, lightheadedness, or drowsiness.
- Continue medicine for full time of treatment.

[1]Not included in Canadian product labeling.

MOXIFLOXACIN

Summary of Differences

Pharmacology/pharmacokinetic: Longer half-life; may be dosed once a day.
Precautions: Drug interactions—does not significantly interact with digoxin, glyburide, probenecid, ranitidine, theophylline, and warfarin.
Side effects: Prolongs QT interval in some patients; does not show phototoxicity when compared with placebo.

Additional Dosing Information

Diet/Nutrition
Food does not significantly affect the absorption. May be taken with or without food.

Oral Dosage Forms

MOXIFLOXACIN TABLETS

Usual adult dose
Bronchitis, bacterial exacerbations—
Oral, 400 mg once a day for 5 days.
Pneumonia, community-acquired—
Oral, 400 mg once a day for 7 to 14 days.
Sinusitis, acute—
Oral, 400 mg once a day for 10 days.
Skin and soft tissue infections (treatment)—
Oral, 400 mg once a day for 7 days

Usual pediatric dose
Children up to 18 years of age—Use is not recommended in infants, children, and adolescents since moxifloxacin causes arthropathy in immature animals.

Usual geriatric dose
See *Usual adult dose.*

Strength(s) usually available
U.S.—
400 mg (base) (Rx) [*Avelox*].
Canada—
Not commercially available.

Packaging and storage
Store at 25 °C (77 °F); excursion permitted between 15 and 30 °C (59 and 86 °F). Avoid high humidity.

Auxiliary labeling
- Take moxifloxacin at least 4 hours before or 8 hours after antacids containing magnesium or aluminum, as well as sucralfate, metal cations such as iron, and multivitamin preparations with zinc, or didanosine (Videx®) chewable/buffered tablets or the pediatric powder for oral solution.
- Take with a full glass of water.
- May cause dizziness, lightheadedness, or drowsiness.
- Continue medicine for full time of treatment.
- Avoid too much sun or use of sunlamp.

Parenteral Dosage Forms

MOXIFLOXACIN INJECTION

Usual adult dose
Bronchitis, bacterial exacerbations—
Intravenous, 400 mg once a day for 5 days.
Pneumonia, community-acquired—
Intravenous, 400 mg once a day for 7 to 14 days.
Sinusitis, acute—
Intravenous, 400 mg once a day for 10 days.
Skin and soft tissue infections (treatment)—
Intravenous, 400 mg once a day for 7 days

Usual pediatric dose
Children up to 18 years of age—Use is not recommended in infants, children, and adolescents since moxifloxacin causes arthropathy in immature animals.

Usual geriatric dose
See *Usual adult dose.*

Strength(s) usually available
U.S.—
400 mg (base) per 250 mL (Rx) [*Avelox I.V.* (in 0.8% sodium chloride; water for injection; may contain hydrochloric acid (pH adjustment); may contain sodium hydroxide (pH adjustment))].
Canada—
Not commercially available.

Packaging and storage
Store at 25 °C (77 °F); excursions permitted between 15 and 30 °C (59 and 86 °F).

Stability
Since moxifloxacin premix flexible bags are for single-use only, any unused portion should be discarded.

Incompatibilities
Since only limited data are available on the compatibility of moxifloxacin intravenous injection with other intravenous substances, additives or other medications should not be added to moxifloxacin injection or infused simultaneously through the same intravenous line. See the manufacturer's package insert for a list of compatible infusion solutions.

Auxiliary labeling
- Do not refrigerate—Product precipitates upon refrigeration.
- For intravenous infusion only. Moxifloxacin and gatifloxacin injections are not intended for intramuscular, intrathecal, intraperitoneal, or subcutaneous administration.
- Moxifloxacin is available in ready-to-use flexible bags so no further dilution of this preparation is necessary.
- This product should be visually inspected for particulate matter prior to administration. Samples containing visible particulates should not be used.

NORFLOXACIN

Summary of Differences

Precautions: Drug interactions—Cyclosporine; warfarin

Additional Dosing Information

Diet/Nutrition
The presence of food in the stomach may slightly decrease or delay absorption of norfloxacin. Therefore, norfloxacin preferably should be taken with a full glass (240 mL) of water on an empty stomach (either 1 hour before or 2 hours after meals or milk ingestion).
In studies with volunteers, crystalluria has been reported, especially with high doses (1200 or 1600 mg) and alkaline urine (pH 7 or above). Although crystalluria has not been reported with usual adult doses (400 mg twice a day), fluid intake should be sufficient to maintain urine output of at least 1200 to 1500 mL per day in adults.

Oral Dosage Forms

Note: Bracketed uses in the *Dosage Forms* section refer to categories of use and/or indications that are not included in U.S. product labeling.

NORFLOXACIN TABLETS USP

Usual adult dose
[Diarrhea, infectious][1]—
Oral, 400 mg every eight to twelve hours for five days.
Gonorrhea, endocervical and urethral—
Oral, 800 mg as a single dose.
Prostatitis, acute or chronic[1]—
Oral, 400 mg every twelve hours for twenty-eight days.
Urinary tract infections—
Uncomplicated, due to *Escherichia coli*, *Klebsiella pneumoniae*, or *Proteus mirabilis*: Oral, 400 mg every twelve hours for three days.
Uncomplicated, due to other indicated organisms: Oral, 400 mg every twelve hours for seven to ten days.
Note: Adults with impaired renal function may require a reduction in dose as follows:

Creatinine clearance (mL/min)/(mL/sec)	Dose
> 30/0.5	See *Usual adult dose*
≤ 30/0.5	400 mg once a day

Usual adult prescribing limits
1.2 grams per day for [infectious diarrhea][1].
800 mg per day for all other indications.

Usual pediatric dose
Children up to 18 years of age—Use is not recommended in infants, children, or adolescents since fluoroquinolones cause arthropathy in immature animals.

Usual geriatric dose
See *Usual adult dose.*

Strength(s) usually available
U.S.—
400 mg (Rx) [*Noroxin*].
Canada—
400 mg (Rx) [*Noroxin*].

Packaging and storage
Store below 40 °C (104 °F), preferably between 15 and 30 °C (59 and 86 °F), in a tight container.

Auxiliary labeling
- Take with a full glass of water.
- Take on empty stomach.
- May cause dizziness, lightheadedness, or drowsiness.
- Continue medicine for full time of treatment.

[1]Not included in Canadian product labeling.

OFLOXACIN

Summary of Differences

Precautions: Pregnancy—Crosses the placenta.
Breast-feeding—Highly concentrated in breast milk.
Drug interactions—Ofloxacin has a minor effect on the metabolism of theophylline; probenecid prolongs elimination half-life and increases risk of toxicity.
Side/adverse effects: Phlebitis (for parenteral dosage form only).
General dosing information: Unlike intravenous ciprofloxacin, the dose of intravenous ofloxacin does not need to be changed from the oral dose.

Additional Dosing Information

Diet/Nutrition
Food has minor influence on the absorption of ofloxacin, causing only a slight decrease in the peak serum concentration and the area under the serum concentration-time curve (AUC). Therefore, ofloxacin may be taken with or without food.

For parenteral dosage forms only
Ofloxacin injection should be administered only by slow intravenous infusion over 60 minutes. Rapid or bolus injection may result in hypotension.

Oral Dosage Forms

OFLOXACIN TABLETS

Usual adult dose
Bronchitis, bacterial exacerbations or
Pneumonia, community-acquired or
Skin and soft tissue infections, uncomplicated—
Oral, 400 mg every twelve hours for ten days.
Chlamydial infections, endocervical or urethral, with or without concurrent gonorrhea—
Oral, 300 mg every twelve hours for seven days.
Gonorrhea, uncomplicated, endocervical and urethral—
Oral, 400 mg as a single dose.
Pelvic inflammatory disease, acute—
Oral, 400 mg every twelve hours for ten to fourteen days.
Prostatitis—
Oral, 300 mg every twelve hours for six weeks.
Urinary tract infections—
Complicated: Oral, 200 mg every twelve hours for ten days.
Cystitis, due to *Escherichia coli* or *Klebsiella pneumoniae*: Oral, 200 mg every twelve hours for three days.
Cystitis, due to other indicated organisms: Oral, 200 mg every twelve hours for seven days.

Note: Adults with impaired renal function may require a reduction in dose as follows:

Creatinine clearance (mL/min)/(mL/sec)	Dose (% of *Usual adult dose*)	Dosing interval (hr)
> 50/0.83	100	12
20–50/0.33–0.83	100	24
< 20/0.33	50	24

Usual adult prescribing limits
400 mg per day for patients with severe hepatic function impairment (e.g., cirrhosis with or without ascites).

Usual pediatric dose
Children up to 18 years of age—Use is not recommended in infants, children, or adolescents since fluoroquinolones cause arthropathy in immature animals.

Usual geriatric dose
See *Usual adult dose*.

Strength(s) usually available
U.S.—
200 mg (Rx) [*Floxin* (lactose)].
300 mg (Rx) [*Floxin* (lactose)].
400 mg (Rx) [*Floxin* (lactose)].
Canada—
200 mg (Rx) [*Floxin* (lactose)].
300 mg (Rx) [*Floxin* (lactose)].
400 mg (Rx) [*Floxin* (lactose)].

Packaging and storage
Store below 30 °C (86 °F). Store in a well-closed container.

Auxiliary labeling
- Take with a full glass of water.
- Continue medicine for full time of treatment.
- Do not take antacids, or zinc or iron preparations, within 2 hours of taking this medicine.

Parenteral Dosage Forms

OFLOXACIN IN DEXTROSE INJECTION

Usual adult dose
Bronchitis, bacterial exacerbations or
Pneumonia, community-acquired or
Skin and soft tissue infections, uncomplicated—
Intravenous infusion, 400 mg, administered over a period of sixty minutes, every twelve hours for ten days.
Chlamydial infections, endocervical or urethral, with or without concurrent gonorrhea—
Intravenous infusion, 300 mg, administered over a period of sixty minutes, every twelve hours for seven days.
Gonorrhea, uncomplicated—
Intravenous infusion, 400 mg, administered over a period of sixty minutes, as a single dose.
Pelvic inflammatory disease, acute—
Intravenous infusion, 400 mg, administered over a period of sixty minutes, every twelve hours for ten to fourteen days.
Prostatitis—
Intravenous infusion, 300 mg, administered over a period of sixty minutes, every twelve hours for six weeks. There are no safety data presently available to support the use of parenteral ofloxacin for more than ten days. After ten days, treatment should be switched to the oral dosage form or another appropriate therapy.
Urinary tract infections—
Complicated: Intravenous infusion, 200 mg, administered over a period of sixty minutes, every twelve hours for ten days.
Cystitis, due to *Escherichia coli* or *Klebsiella pneumoniae*: Intravenous infusion, 200 mg, administered over a period of sixty minutes, every twelve hours for three days.
Cystitis, due to other indicated organisms: Intravenous infusion, 200 mg, administered over a period of sixty minutes, every twelve hours for seven days.

Note: Adults with renal function impairment may require a reduction in dose as follows:

Creatinine clearance (mL/min)/(mL/sec)	Dose (% of *Usual adult dose*)	Dosing interval (hr)
> 50/0.83	100	12
20–50/0.33–0.83	100	24
< 20/0.33	50	24

Usual adult prescribing limits
400 mg per day for patients with severe hepatic function impairment (e.g., cirrhosis with or without ascites).

Usual pediatric dose
Children up to 18 years of age—Use is not recommended in infants, children, or adolescents since fluoroquinolones cause arthropathy in immature animals.

Usual geriatric dose
See *Usual adult dose*.

Strength(s) usually available
U.S.—
200 mg per 50 mL (Rx) [*Floxin I.V.* (in 5% dextrose injection)].
400 mg per 100 mL (Rx) [*Floxin I.V.* (in 5% dextrose injection)].
Canada—
Not commercially available.

Packaging and storage
Store below 30 °C (86 °F). Protect from freezing and light.

Preparation of dosage form

Premixed ofloxacin in dextrose injection in flexible containers requires no further dilution prior to administration (see manufacturer's labeling for instructions). Since these injections contain no preservatives or bacteriostatic agent, they should be used promptly after opening; unused portions should be discarded.

Do not use the flexible containers in series connections. This may result in air embolism due to residual air being drawn from the primary container before administration of the fluid from the secondary container is complete.

Stability

Frozen solutions should be thawed at room temperature or in a refrigerator. They should not be thawed in a microwave or by water-bath immersion. Thawed solutions should not be refrozen.

Ofloxacin in dextrose injection contains no preservatives or bacteriostatic agent. It should not be used if injection is discolored or contains a precipitate.

Incompatibilities

Because only limited data are available on the compatibility of ofloxacin in dextrose injection with other intravenous substances, additives or other medications, including cefepime, should not be added to the preparation or infused simultaneously through the same intravenous line.

OFLOXACIN INJECTION

Usual adult dose

See *Ofloxacin in Dextrose Injection*.

Usual adult prescribing limits

See *Ofloxacin in Dextrose Injection*.

Usual pediatric dose

See *Ofloxacin in Dextrose Injection*.

Usual geriatric dose

See *Ofloxacin in Dextrose Injection*.

Strength(s) usually available

U.S.—

400 mg per 10 mL (Rx) [*Floxin I.V.* (in sterile water for injection; requires dilution prior to administration)].

Canada—

Not commercially available.

Packaging and storage

Store below 30 °C (86 °F). Protect from freezing and light.

Preparation of dosage form

Ofloxacin in sterile water for injection requires dilution prior to administration. To prepare a solution at a concentration of 4 mg per mL for intravenous administration, add the volume of appropriate diluent (see manufacturer's package insert) as indicated below:

Dose	Volume of ofloxacin concentrate to withdraw from vial	Volume of diluent to add
200 mg	5 mL	45 mL
300 mg	7.5 mL	67.5 mL
400 mg	10 mL	90 mL

The diluted solution should be administered only by intravenous infusion over a period of at least 60 minutes. Since these injections contain no preservatives or bacteriostatic agent, they should be used promptly after opening; unused portions should be discarded.

Stability

When diluted to a concentration between 0.4 and 4 mg/mL, ofloxacin injection is stable for 72 hours when stored at or below 24 °C (75 °F) or for 14 days when refrigerated at 5 °C (41 °F) in glass bottles or plastic intravenous containers. Solutions that are diluted and frozen are stable for 6 months when stored at −20 °C (−4 °F). Once thawed, the solution is stable for up to 14 days when refrigerated (2 to 8 °C [36 to 46 °F]).

Frozen solutions should be thawed at room temperature or in a refrigerator. They should not be thawed in a microwave or by water-bath immersion. Thawed solutions should not be refrozen.

Ofloxacin injection contains no preservatives or bacteriostatic agent. It should not be used if injection is discolored or contains a precipitate.

Incompatibilities

Because only limited data are available on the compatibility of ofloxacin injection with other substances, additives or other medications, including cefepime, should not be added to the preparation or infused simultaneously through the same intravenous line.

SPARFLOXACIN

Summary of Differences

Precautions: Medical considerations/Contraindications—
QTc-interval prolongation was observed in healthy volunteers
Contraindicated in patients with history of photosensitivity
Not recommended for patients with ongoing proarrhythmic conditions

Drug interactions—Medications that prolong the QTc interval are contraindicated

Laboratory value alterations—May produce false-negative test result for *Mycobacterium tuberculosis*

Side/adverse effects: More frequent phototoxicity or QTc-interval prolongation; vaginitis (more frequent)

Additional Dosing Information

Diet/Nutrition

May be taken with meals or on an empty stomach.

May be taken with caffeine-containing products or milk or other dairy products.

Treatment of photosensitivity or phototoxicity

Sparfloxacin-induced photosensitivity or phototoxicity should be treated within 2 weeks of onset of symptoms to prevent lichenoid tissue reaction.

Oral Dosage Forms

SPARFLOXACIN TABLETS

Usual adult dose

Bronchitis, bacterial exacerbations or
Pneumonia, community-acquired—

Oral, 400 mg on the first day, then 200 mg every twenty-four hours for a total of ten days of therapy.

Note: The recommended dose for patients with renal function impairment (creatinine clearance less than 50 mL per minute) is 400 mg on the first day, then 200 mg every forty-eight hours for a total of nine days of therapy.

Usual adult prescribing limits

400 mg.

Usual pediatric dose

Children up to 18 years of age—Use is not recommended in infants, children, or adolescents since fluoroquinolones cause arthropathy in immature animals.

Strength(s) usually available

U.S.—

200 mg (Rx) [*Zagam*].

Canada—

Not commercially available.

Packaging and storage

Store below 40 °C (104 °F), preferably between 15 and 30 °C (59 and 86 °F).

Auxiliary labeling

- Take with a full glass of water.
- Do not take antacids or iron preparations within 4 hours of this medicine.
- May cause dizziness or lightheadedness.
- Avoid too much sun or use of sunlamp.
- Continue medicine for full time of treatment.

Revised: 04/11/2005

Table 1. Pharmacology/Pharmacokinetics

Drug	Bioavailability (%)	Half-life (hr) Normal renal function	Half-life (hr) Impaired renal function	Time to peak serum concentration (hr)	Peak serum concentration after dose mcg/mL	Peak serum concentration after dose Dose (mg)	Peak urine concentration after dose mcg/mL	Peak urine concentration after dose Dose (mg)
Ciprofloxacin								
Oral	70–80*	4†	6–8	1–2	1.2–1.4	250	> 200	250
					2.4–4.3	500		
					3.4–4.3	750		
					5.4	1000		
IV		5–6		End of infusion	2.1	200	> 200	200
					4.6	400	> 400	400
Enoxacin								
Oral	90	3–6	9–10	1–3	0.9	200		
					2	400		
Gatifloxacin								
Oral	96			1–2	2	200		
		7.1	11.2–30.7		3.8	400		
IV		12.3		End of infusion	2.4	200		
		13.9			4.6	400		
Levofloxacin								
Oral	99	4–8	6–28	1–2	5.7	500		
IV					6.4	500		
Lomefloxacin								
Oral	95–98		21–45	1.5	0.8	100	> 300	400
					1.4	200		
					3–5.2	400		
Moxifloxacin								
Oral	90	12		1–3	4.5	400		
IV		14.8		End of infusion	4.2–4.6	400		
Norfloxacin								
Oral	30–70*	3–4	6–9	1–2	1.4–1.6	400	98–200	400
					2.5	800		
Ofloxacin		4.7–7#	15–60**					
Oral	95–100			1–2	1.5–2.6	200		
					4.6–5	400		
IV				End of infusion	2.3–2.7	200		
					5.5–7.2	400		
Sparfloxacin								
Oral	92	16–30		3–6	1.3	400		
					1.1	200		

*Absorption delayed in presence of food, although overall absorption not substantially affected.
†Half-life of ciprofloxacin slightly prolonged in elderly patients (approximately 6 hours).
#Half-life of ofloxacin slightly prolonged in elderly patients (approximately 6 to 8.5 hours).
**Half-life of ofloxacin also prolonged in patients who have cirrhosis with ascites (approximately 7.3 to 19.5 hours).

Table 2. Pharmacology/Pharmacokinetics*

Drug	Protein binding (%)	Renal excretion (% unchanged/hrs)	Metabolism (%)	Biliary excretion (%)	Vol_D (liter/kg)	Removal by dialysis HD (%)	Removal by dialysis PD (%)
Ciprofloxacin	20–40		20		2	<10	< 10
Oral		40–50/24		20–35			
IV		50–70/24		15			
Enoxacin	40†	40–60/48	20	18	1.6	< 5	
Gatifloxacin	20	70/48	<1	5	1.5–2	14	11‡§
Levofloxacin	24–38	79–87/48			1.09–1.26	12	12
Lomefloxacin	10	60–80/48	5	10	1.8–2.5	< 3	< 3
Moxifloxacin	50	20	55	25	1.7–2.7		
Norfloxacin	10–15	26–40/24–48	20	28–30	3.2	< 10	
Ofloxacin	20–25	70–90/36	3	4–8	0.9–1.8	10–30	2–10
Sparfloxacin	45	50/24			3.9		

*Abbreviations: Vol_D = volume of distribution; HD = hemodialysis; PD = peritoneal dialysis; NS = not significant.
†Approximately 14% of enoxacin is bound to plasma proteins in patients with impaired renal function.
‡Recovered over 4 hours
§Recovered over 8 days

FLUOROURACIL Systemic

VA CLASSIFICATION (Primary/Secondary): AN300/OP109

Commonly used brand name(s): *Adrucil*.

Another commonly used name is 5-FU.

Note: For a listing of dosage forms and brand names by country availability, see *Dosage Forms* section(s).

Category

Antineoplastic.

Indications

Note: Bracketed information in the *Indications* section refers to uses that are not included in U.S. product labeling.

Accepted

Carcinoma, colorectal (treatment)
Carcinoma, breast (treatment)
Carcinoma, gastric (treatment) or
Carcinoma, pancreatic (treatment)—Fluorouracil is indicated for palliative treatment of carcinoma of the colon, rectum, breast, stomach, and pancreas in patients considered to be incurable by surgery or other means.

[Carcinoma, bladder (treatment)]
[Carcinoma, prostatic (treatment)]
[Carcinoma, ovarian, epithelial (treatment)]
[Carcinoma, cervical (treatment)][1]
[Carcinoma, endometrial (treatment)][1]
[Carcinoma, anal (treatment)]
[Carcinoma, esophageal (treatment)]
[Carcinoma, skin (treatment)]
[Hepatoblastoma (treatment)]
[Carcinoma, hepatocellular, primary (treatment)][1] or
[Carcinoma, head and neck (treatment)]—Fluorouracil is also indicated for treatment of bladder carcinoma, prostatic carcinoma, epithelial ovarian carcinoma, cervical carcinoma, endometrial carcinoma, anal carcinoma, esophageal carcinoma, metastatic tumors of skin carcinoma, and hepatoblastoma, and is used by intra-arterial injection for treatment of hepatic tumors and head and neck tumors.

[Carcinoma, adrenocortical (treatment)][1]
[Carcinoma, vulvar (treatment)][1]
[Carcinoma, penile (treatment)][1] or
[Carcinoid tumors (treatment)][1]—Fluorouracil, in combination therapy, is reasonable medical therapy at some point in the management of adrenocortical carcinoma (Evidence rating: IIID), vulvar carcinoma (Evidence rating: IIID), penile carcinoma (Evidence rating: IIID), and carcinoid tumors (gastrointestinal and neuroendocrine tumors) (Evidence rating: IA).

Note: Although fluorouracil has been used for treatment of malignant pleural effusions, the USP Division of Information Development Hematology-Oncology Advisory Panel believes there is insufficient evidence to support the effectiveness of fluorouracil in the treatment of malignant pleural effusions.

[Glaucoma, open-angle (treatment)][1]—Fluorouracil is used for the treatment of glaucoma during or following trabeculectomy surgery.

Acceptance not established

Use of fluorouracil for the treatment of islet cell carcinoma has not been established.

---

[1]Not included in Canadian product labeling.

Pharmacology/Pharmacokinetics

Physicochemical characteristics

Molecular weight—130.08.

Mechanism of action/Effect

Fluorouracil is an antimetabolite of the pyrimidine analog type. Fluorouracil is considered to be cell cycle–specific for the S phase of cell division. Activity results from its conversion to an active metabolite in the tissues, and includes inhibition of DNA and RNA synthesis.

Other actions/effects

Fluorouracil inhibits fibroblast proliferation and formation of scar tissue following trabeculectomy surgery for the treatment of glaucoma.

Distribution

Distributes into tumors, intestinal mucosa, bone marrow, liver, and other tissues; crosses the blood-brain barrier.

Biotransformation

Rapidly, via a complex metabolic pathway in the tissues to produce an active metabolite, floxuridine monophosphate. Catabolic degradation occurs in the liver.

Half-life

Intravenous—
Approximately 16 minutes.

Elimination

Primary route—Respiratory (approximately 90% as carbon dioxide).
Secondary route—Renal (approximately 7 to 20% unchanged; 90% of this in the first hour).

Precautions to Consider

Carcinogenicity

Secondary malignancies are potential delayed effects of many antineoplastic agents, although it is not clear whether the effect is related to their mutagenic or immunosuppressive action. The effect of dose and duration of therapy is also unknown, although risk seems to increase with long-term use.

Antimetabolites have been shown to be carcinogenic in animals and may be associated with an increased risk of development of secondary carcinomas in humans, although the risk appears to be less than with alkylating agents.

Long-term carcinogenicity studies in animals have not been done. However, studies in rats at oral doses of 0.01, 0.3, 1, or 3 mg per rat 5 days a week for 52 weeks, followed by a 6-month observation period, found no evidence of carcinogenicity. In addition, studies in male rats at intravenous doses of 33 mg per kg of body weight (mg/kg) once a week for 52 weeks, followed by observation for the rest of their lifetimes, found no evidence of carcinogenicity. Incidence of lung adenomas was unchanged in female mice given 1 mg of fluorouracil intravenously once a week for 16 weeks.

Mutagenicity

Very high levels of fluorouracil produce oncogenic changes in cultured C3H/10T1/2 mouse embryo cells. In addition, fluorouracil has been found to be mutagenic in several strains of *Salmonella typhimurium*, including TA 1535, TA 1537, and TA 1538, and in *Saccharomyces cerevisiae*, but not in *Salmonella typhimurium* strains TA 92, TA 98, and TA 100. A positive effect was also observed in the micronucleus test on bone marrow cells of the mouse, and very high concentrations of fluorouracil produced chromosomal breaks in hamster fibroblasts *in vitro* .

Pregnancy/Reproduction

Fertility—Gonadal suppression, resulting in amenorrhea or azoospermia, may occur in patients taking antineoplastic therapy, especially with the alkylating agents. In general, these effects appear to be related to the dose and duration of therapy and may be irreversible. Prediction of the degree of testicular or ovarian function impairment is complicated by the common use of combinations of several antineoplastics, which makes it difficult to assess the effects of individual agents.

In male rats given intraperitoneal doses of 125 or 250 mg/kg, fluorouracil induced chromosomal aberrations and changes in chromosomal organization of spermatogonia. In addition, inhibition of spermatogonial differentiation by fluorouracil resulted in transient infertility. However, fluorouracil did not produce any abnormalities at doses of up to 80 mg/kg per day in a strain of mouse that is sensitive to the induction of sperm head abnormalities after exposure to a range of chemical mutagens and carcinogens.

In female rats given intraperitoneal doses of 25 or 50 mg/kg per week for 3 weeks during the pre-ovulatory phase of oogenesis, fluorouracil significantly reduced the incidence of fertile matings, delayed the development of pre- and post-implantation embryos, increased the incidence of pre-implantation lethality, and induced chromosomal anomalies in these embryos. A limited study in rabbits with single doses of 25 mg/kg or five daily doses of 5 mg/kg found no effect on ovulation, no apparent effect on implantation, and only a limited effect in producing zygote destruction.

Pregnancy—Adequate and well-controlled studies in humans have not been done.

First trimester—

It is usually recommended that use of antineoplastics, especially combination chemotherapy, be avoided whenever possible, especially during the first trimester. Although information is limited because of the relatively few instances of antineoplastic administration during pregnancy, the mutagenic, teratogenic, and carcinogenic potential of these medications must be considered.

One case of multiple congenital anomalies has been reported with fluorouracil administration in the first trimester.

Other hazards to the fetus include adverse reactions seen in adults.

In general, use of a contraceptive is recommended during cytotoxic drug therapy.

Teratogenic effects—

Fluorouracil has been reported to be teratogenic in mice given single intraperitoneal doses of 10 to 40 mg/kg on days 10 and 12 of gestation, in rats given 12 to 37 mg/kg intraperitoneally between days 9 and 12 of gestation, and in hamsters given 3 to 9 mg intramuscularly between days 8 and 11 of gestation; these dosages, which are one to three times the maximum recommended human dose (MRHD), produced malformations including cleft palates, skeletal defects, and deformed appendages, paws, and tails. Teratogenicity did not occur in monkeys given divided doses of 40 mg/kg between days 20 and 24 of gestation.

Nonteratogenic effects—

Studies of effects of fluorouracil on perinatal and postnatal development in animals have not been done. However, in rats fluorouracil crosses the placenta and enters into fetal circulation, and use has resulted in increased resorptions and embryo deaths. Abortion occurred in all pregnant monkeys given doses of fluorouracil higher than 40 mg/kg.

FDA Pregnancy Category D.

Breast-feeding

It is not known whether fluorouracil is distributed into breast milk. Although very little information is available regarding distribution of antineoplastic agents into breast milk, breast-feeding is not recommended during chemotherapy because of the risks to the infant (adverse effects, mutagenicity, carcinogenicity).

Pediatrics

Appropriate studies on the relationship of age to the effects of fluorouracil have not been performed in the pediatric population. However, pediatrics-specific problems that would limit the usefulness of this medication in children are not expected.

Geriatrics

Although appropriate studies on the relationship of age to the effects of fluorouracil have not been performed in the geriatric population, geriatrics-specific problems are not expected to limit the usefulness of this medication in the elderly. However, elderly patients are more likely to have age-related renal function impairment, which may require reduction of dosage in patients receiving fluorouracil.

Dental

The bone marrow depressant effects of fluorouracil may result in an increased incidence of microbial infection, delayed healing, and gingival bleeding. Dental work, whenever possible, should be completed prior to initiation of therapy or deferred until blood counts have returned to normal. Patients should be instructed in proper oral hygiene during treatment, including caution in use of regular toothbrushes, dental floss, and toothpicks.

Fluorouracil also commonly causes ulcerative stomatitis, which may be associated with considerable discomfort.

Drug interactions and/or related problems

The following drug interactions and/or related problems have been selected on the basis of their potential clinical significance (possible mechanism in parentheses where appropriate)—not necessarily inclusive (» = major clinical significance):

Blood dyscrasia-causing medications (see *Appendix II*)
(leukopenic and/or thrombocytopenic effects of fluorouracil may be increased with concurrent or recent therapy if these medications cause the same effects; dosage adjustment of fluorouracil, if necessary, should be based on blood counts)

» Bone marrow depressants, other (see *Appendix II*) or
Radiation therapy
(additive bone marrow depression may occur; dosage reduction may be required when two or more bone marrow depressants, including radiation, are used concurrently or consecutively)

Leucovorin
(concurrent use may increase the therapeutic and toxic effects of fluorouracil; although the two medications may be used together for therapeutic advantage, dosage adjustment may be necessary)

Vaccines, killed virus
(because normal defense mechanisms may be suppressed by fluorouracil therapy, the patient's antibody response to the vaccine may be decreased. The interval between discontinuation of medications that cause immunosuppression and restoration of the patient's ability to respond to the vaccine depends on the intensity and type of immunosuppression-causing medication used, the underlying disease, and other factors; estimates vary from 3 months to 1 year)

» Vaccines, live virus
(because normal defense mechanisms may be suppressed by fluorouracil therapy, concurrent use with a live virus vaccine may potentiate the replication of the vaccine virus, may increase the side/adverse effects of the vaccine virus, and/or may decrease the patient's antibody response to the vaccine; immunization of these patients should be undertaken only with extreme caution after careful review of the patient's hematologic status and only with the knowledge and consent of the physician managing the fluorouracil therapy. The interval between discontinuation of medications that cause immunosuppression and restoration of the patient's ability to respond to the vaccine depends on the intensity and type of immunosuppression-causing medication used, the underlying disease, and other factors; estimates vary from 3 months to 1 year. Immunization with oral poliovirus vaccine should also be postponed in persons in close contact with the patient, especially family members)

Anticoagulants, coumarin-derivative, such as warfarin
(concurrent use may increase the anticoagulant effect; adjustment of anticoagulant dosage based on frequent prothrombin-time determinations is recommended)

Laboratory value alterations

The following have been selected on the basis of their potential clinical significance (possible effect in parentheses where appropriate)—not necessarily inclusive (» = major clinical significance).

With physiology/laboratory test values
Albumin, plasma
(may be decreased because of drug-induced protein malabsorption)

Medical considerations/Contraindications

The medical considerations/contraindications included have been selected on the basis of their potential clinical significance (reasons given in parentheses where appropriate)—not necessarily inclusive (» = major clinical significance).

This medication should be used with extreme caution when the following medical problems exist:

» Bone marrow depression
» Chickenpox, existing or recent (including recent exposure) or
» Herpes zoster
(risk of severe generalized disease)
» Hepatic function impairment
(reduced biotransformation; lower dosage is recommended)
» Infection
» Renal function impairment
(reduced elimination; lower dosage is recommended)
» Sensitivity to fluorouracil
» Tumor cell infiltration of bone marrow
» Extreme caution should be used also in patients who have had previous cytotoxic drug therapy with alkylating agents or high-dose pelvic radiation therapy; a lower dosage is recommended.

Patient monitoring

The following are especially important in patient monitoring (other tests may be warranted in some patients, depending on condition; » = major clinical significance):

Alanine aminotransferase (ALT [SGPT]) values and
Aspartate aminotransferase (AST [SGOT]) values and
Bilirubin concentrations, serum and
Lactate dehydrogenase (LDH) values
(recommended prior to initiation of therapy and at periodic intervals during therapy; frequency varies according to clinical state, agent, dose, and other agents being used concurrently)

» Examination of patient's mouth for ulceration
(recommended before administration of each dose)

» Hematocrit or hemoglobin and
» Leukocyte count, total and, if appropriate, differential and
» Platelet count
(determinations recommended prior to initiation of therapy and at periodic intervals during therapy; frequency varies according to clinical state, agent, dose, and other agents being used concurrently)

Side/Adverse Effects

Note: Many "side effects" of antineoplastic therapy are unavoidable and represent the medication's pharmacologic action. Some of these (for example, leukopenia and thrombocytopenia) are actually used as parameters to aid in individual dosage titration.

Adverse effects associated with prolonged use of an arterial catheter include arterial ischemia, thrombosis, bleeding at the catheter site, blocked catheters, leakage at the site, embolism, fibromyositis, infection at the catheter site, abscesses, and thrombophlebitis.

The following side/adverse effects have been selected on the basis of their potential clinical significance (possible signs and symptoms in parentheses where appropriate)—not necessarily inclusive:

Those indicating need for medical attention

Incidence more frequent

Diarrhea; esophagopharyngitis (heartburn); ***leukopenia or infection*** (fever or chills; cough or hoarseness; lower back or side pain; painful or difficult urination)—usually asymptomatic; ***ulcerative stomatitis*** (sores in mouth and on lips)

Note: *Esophagopharyngitis* may lead to sloughing and ulceration.

Leukopenia usually occurs by 9 to 14 days after each course of treatment; the nadir of leukocyte count occurs about 9 to 14 days after the first day of a course of therapy (uncommonly, as long as 20 days) and usually recovers by about 30 days. Severity of bone marrow depression varies and determines subsequent dosage of fluorouracil.

Incidence less frequent

Gastrointestinal ulceration (black, tarry stools; severe nausea and vomiting; stomach cramps); ***thrombocytopenia*** (unusual bleeding or bruising; black, tarry stools; blood in urine or stools; pinpoint red spots on skin)—usually asymptomatic

Incidence rare

Cerebellar syndrome, acute (trouble with balance); ***myocardial ischemia*** (chest pain; shortness of breath); ***palmar-plantar erythrodysesthesia syndrome*** (tingling of hands and feet, followed by pain, redness, and swelling); ***pneumopathy*** (cough; shortness of breath)

Note: *Myocardial ischemia* may occur several hours after a dose; it usually develops after the second or later doses.

The *palmar-plantar erythrodysesthesia syndrome* is also known as hand-foot syndrome. It begins with tingling of hands and feet and may progress over the next few days to pain when holding objects or walking. Symmetrical swelling and erythema of palms and soles, with tenderness of the distal phalanges, occurs, possibly accompanied by desquamation. Symptoms gradually resolve over 5 to 7 days following withdrawal of fluorouracil. The syndrome may also be treatable with oral pyridoxine.

Those indicating need for medical attention only if they continue or are bothersome

Incidence more frequent

Dermatitis (skin rash and itching, usually on extremities and less frequently on trunk); ***loss of appetite; nausea and vomiting; weakness***

Note: *Gastrointestinal distress* usually occurs on about the fourth day of therapy and subsides 2 or 3 days after the medication is stopped. *Weakness* usually occurs immediately and persists for 12 to 36 hours after administration.

Incidence less frequent

Dry skin and fissuring

Those not indicating need for medical attention

Incidence more frequent

Alopecia (loss of hair)

Those indicating the need for medical attention if they occur after medication is discontinued

Bone marrow depression (black, tarry stools; blood in urine or stools; cough or hoarseness; fever or chills; lower back or side pain; painful or difficult urination; pinpoint red spots on skin; unusual bleeding or bruising)

Patient Consultation

As an aid to patient consultation, refer to *Advice for the Patient, Fluorouracil (Systemic)*.

In providing consultation, consider emphasizing the following selected information (» = major clinical significance):

Before using this medication

» Conditions affecting use, especially:
- Sensitivity to fluorouracil
- Pregnancy—Use not recommended because of mutagenic, teratogenic, and carcinogenic potential; advisability of using contraception; telling physician immediately if pregnancy is suspected
- Breast-feeding—Not recommended because of risk of serious side effects
- Other medications, especially other bone marrow depressants or previous cytotoxic drug or radiation therapy
- Other medical problems, especially chickenpox, herpes zoster, hepatic function impairment, infection, or renal function impairment

Proper use of this medication

Caution with combination therapy; taking each medication at the right time

Frequency of nausea and vomiting; importance of continuing medication despite stomach upset

» Proper dosing

Precautions while using this medication

» Importance of close monitoring by the physician

» Avoiding immunizations unless approved by physician; other persons in patient's household should avoid immunizations with oral poliovirus vaccine; avoiding persons who have taken oral poliovirus vaccine or wearing a protective mask that covers nose and mouth

Caution if bone marrow depression occurs:

» Avoiding exposure to persons with infections, especially during periods of low blood counts; checking with physician immediately if fever or chills, cough or hoarseness, lower back or side pain, or painful or difficult urination occurs

» Checking with physician immediately if unusual bleeding or bruising; black, tarry stools; blood in urine or stools; or pinpoint red spots on skin occur

Caution in use of regular toothbrush, dental floss, or toothpick; physician, dentist, or nurse may suggest alternatives; checking with physician before having dental work done

Not touching eyes or inside of nose unless hands are washed immediately before

Using caution to avoid accidental cuts with use of sharp objects such as safety razor or fingernail or toenail cutters

Avoiding contact sports or other situations where bruising or injury could occur

Side/adverse effects

May cause adverse effects such as blood problems and cancer; importance of discussing possible effects with physician

Signs of potential side effects, especially diarrhea, esophagopharyngitis, leukopenia, infection, ulcerative stomatitis, gastrointestinal ulceration, thrombocytopenia, acute cerebellar syndrome, myocardial ischemia, palmar-plantar erythrodysesthesia, and pneumopathy

Physician or nurse can help in dealing with side effects

Possibility of hair loss; normal hair growth should return after treatment has ended

General Dosing Information

Patients receiving fluorouracil should be under supervision of a physician experienced in antimetabolite chemotherapy and should be hospitalized at least during the first course of treatment.

Dosage subsequent to the initial dose should be adjusted to meet the individual requirements of each patient, based on the patient's hematologic response to the previous dose. An additional course of fluorouracil should be given only after toxic effects from the first course have subsided.

Fluorouracil is recommended for parenteral use only. Fluorouracil should not be administered intrathecally because of neurotoxicity.

Administration of fluorouracil by slow intravenous infusion over 2 to 24 hours appears to reduce the toxicity, although rapid injections (over 1 to 2 minutes) may be more effective.

When fluorouracil is given intra-arterially, use of an appropriate infusion pump is recommended to ensure a uniform rate of infusion. In selected patients, a portable pump may be used.

Fluorouracil is an extremely toxic medication; therapy should be discontinued promptly at the first sign of:
- Diarrhea
- Esophagopharyngitis
- Gastrointestinal ulceration and bleeding
- Hemorrhage from any site
- Leukopenia, marked, or rapidly falling leukocyte (particularly granulocyte) count
- Stomatitis
- Thrombocytopenia
- Vomiting, intractable

Therapy may be reinitiated at a lower dose when side effects have subsided.

Special precautions are recommended in patients who develop thrombocytopenia as a result of administration of fluorouracil. These may include extreme care in performing invasive procedures; regular inspection of intravenous sites, skin (including perirectal area), and mucous membrane surfaces for signs of bleeding or bruising; limiting frequency of venipuncture and avoiding intramuscular injections; testing urine, emesis, stool, secretions for occult blood; care in use of regular toothbrushes, dental floss, toothpicks, safety razors, and fingernail and toenail cutters; avoiding constipation; and using caution to prevent falls and other injuries. Such patients should avoid alcohol and aspirin intake because of the risk of gastrointestinal bleeding. Platelet transfusions may be required.

Patients who develop leukopenia should be observed carefully for signs of infection. Antibiotic support may be required. In neutropenic patients who develop fever, broad-spectrum antibiotic coverage should be initiated empirically, pending bacterial cultures and appropriate diagnostic tests.

Safety considerations for handling this medication

There is limited but increasing evidence and concern that personnel involved in the preparation and administration of parenteral antineoplastics may be at some risk because of the potential mutagenicity, teratogenicity, and/or carcinogenicity of these agents, although the actual risk is unknown. USP advisory panels recommend cautious handling both in preparation and disposal of antineoplastic agents. Precautions that have been suggested include:

- Use of a biological containment cabinet during reconstitution and dilution of parenteral medications and wearing of disposable surgical gloves and masks.
- Use of proper technique to prevent contamination of the medication, work area, and operator during transfer between containers (including proper training of personnel in this technique).
- Cautious and proper disposal of needles, syringes, vials, ampuls, and unused medication.

A number of medical centers have developed detailed guidelines for handling of antineoplastic agents.

Combination chemotherapy

Fluorouracil may be used in combination with other agents in various regimens. As a result, incidence and/or severity of side effects may be altered and different dosages (usually reduced) may be used. For example, fluorouracil is part of the following chemotherapeutic combinations (some commonly used acronyms are in parentheses):

—cyclophosphamide, doxorubicin, and fluorouracil (CAF).
—cyclophosphamide, methotrexate, and fluorouracil (CMF).
—cyclophosphamide, methotrexate, fluorouracil, vincristine, and prednisone (CMFVP).
—fluorouracil, doxorubicin, and cyclophosphamide (FAC).
—fluorouracil, doxorubicin, and mitomycin (FAM).
—fluorouracil and leucovorin.

For specific dosages and schedules, consult the literature. For information regarding each agent, consult the individual monographs.

For treatment of side/adverse effects

The palmar-plantar erythrodysesthesia syndrome may be treated with oral pyridoxine in a dose of 100 to 150 mg per day.

Parenteral Dosage Forms

Note: Bracketed uses in the *Dosage Forms* section refer to categories of use and/or indications that are not included in U.S. product labeling.

FLUOROURACIL INJECTION USP

Usual adult and adolescent dose

Carcinoma, colorectal or
Carcinoma, breast or
Carcinoma, gastric or
Carcinoma, pancreatic or
[Carcinoma, bladder] or
[Carcinoma, prostatic] or
[Carcinoma, ovarian, epithelial]—

Initial—

Intravenous, 7 to 12 mg per kg of body weight per day for four days, then after three days if no toxicity has occurred, 7 to 10 mg per kg of body weight every three or four days, for a total course of two weeks or

Intravenous, 12 mg per kg of body weight per day for four days, then after one day if no toxicity has occurred, 6 mg per kg of body weight every other day for four or five doses, for a total course of twelve days.

Note: Poor-risk patients should receive a dose of 3 to 6 mg per kg of body weight per day for three days, then after one day if no toxicity has occurred, 3 mg per kg of body weight every other day for three doses.

Maintenance—

Intravenous, 7 to 12 mg per kg of body weight every seven to ten days or

Intravenous, 300 to 500 mg per square meter of body surface area per day for four or five days, repeated monthly.

Note: Although dosages are based on the patient's actual weight, use of estimated lean body mass (dry weight) is recommended in obese patients or those with weight gain due to edema, ascites, or other abnormal fluid retention.

Fluorouracil has also been administered in a regimen containing no loading dose, at an intravenous dose of 15 mg per kg of body weight or 500 to 600 mg per square meter of body surface area once a week.

[Carcinoma, cervical][1] or
[Carcinoma, endometrial][1] or
[Carcinoma, anal] or
[Carcinoma, esophageal] or
[Carcinoma, skin] or
[Hepatoblastoma] or
[Carcinoma, hepatocellular, primary][1] or
[Carcinoma, head and neck] or
[Carcinoma, adrenocortical][1] or
[Carcinoma, vulvar][1] or
[Carcinoma, penile][1] or
[Carcinoid tumors][1]—

Consult medical literature or manufacturer's literature for specific dosage.

[Glaucoma][1]—

Subconjunctivally, 5 mg (in 0.1 mL) postoperatively as needed following trabeculectomy surgery. Specific treatment regimens vary widely. For example, one regimen initiates dosing immediately in the post-operative period and continues dosing daily for 14 days, while another does not initiate dosing until 14 days after surgery and continues dosing intermittently for up to 37 days. Consult the medical literature for specific dosage regimens.

Note: A sponge soaked in fluorouracil 50 mg/mL is sometimes applied directly during trabeculectomy surgery.

Usual adult prescribing limits

For oncology use—800 mg daily (400 mg daily in poor-risk patients).

Usual pediatric dose

See *Usual adult and adolescent dose*.

Strength(s) usually available

U.S.—

50 mg per mL (10-mL vials) (Rx) [*Adrucil;* GENERIC].

Canada—

50 mg per mL (10- and 50-mL vials) (Rx) [*Adrucil;* GENERIC].

Packaging and storage

Store below 40 °C (104 °F), preferably between 15 and 30 °C (59 and 86 °F), unless otherwise specified by the manufacturer. Protect from light. Protect from freezing.

Preparation of dosage form

Fluorouracil Injection USP may be mixed with 5% dextrose injection or 0.9% sodium chloride injection for administration by intravenous infusion.

Note: The 50-mL vial is intended for intravenous admixture service use only. Entry into the vial should be made with a sterile dispensing device or transfer set that will accept a syringe hub; use of a syringe and needle is not recommended because of the risk of leakage and microbial and particulate contamination. Proper aseptic technique, under a laminar flow hood, should be used. Any unused portion should be discarded within 8 hours.

Stability

Although Fluorouracil Injection USP may discolor slightly during storage, potency and safety are not adversely affected. If a precipitate forms because of exposure to low temperatures, redissolve the medication by heating to 60 °C (140 °F) and shaking vigorously, then allow to cool to body temperature before using.

---

[1]Not included in Canadian product labeling.

Revised: 05/04/2001

FLUOROURACIL Topical

VA CLASSIFICATION (Primary): DE600

Commonly used brand name(s): *Carac; Efudex; Fluoroplex.*

Another commonly used name is 5-FU.

Note: For a listing of dosage forms and brand names by country availability, see *Dosage Forms* section(s).

Category

Antineoplastic, topical.

Indications

Note: Bracketed information in the *Indications* section refers to uses that are not included in U.S. product labeling.

Accepted

Actinic keratoses, multiple (treatment)
[Actinic cheilitis (treatment)][1]
[Leukoplakia, mucosal (treatment)][1]
[Radiodermatitis (treatment)][1]
[Bowen's disease (treatment)][1] or
[Erythroplasia of Queyrat (treatment)][1]—Topical fluorouracil is indicated for treatment of precancerous skin conditions including multiple actinic (solar) keratoses, actinic cheilitis, mucosal leukoplakia, radiodermatitis, Bowen's disease, and erythroplasia of Queyrat.

Carcinoma, skin (treatment)—Topical fluorouracil is indicated for treatment of superficial basal cell carcinomas (multiple lesions or difficult access sites), although conventional treatment is preferred whenever possible.

Note: The diagnosis should be established prior to treatment, since topical fluorouacil has not been proven effective in other types of basal cell carcinomas. Surgery is preferred with isolated, easily accessible basal cell carcinomas, since success with such lesions is almost 100%. The success rate with fluorouracil cream and solution is approximately 93%.

[1]Not included in Canadian product labeling.

Pharmacology/Pharmacokinetics

Physicochemical characteristics

Molecular weight—130.08.
pKa—8 and 13.

Mechanism of action/Effect

There is evidence that the metabolism of fluorouracil via the anabolic pathway blocks the methylation reaction of deoxyuridylic acid to thymidylic acid. In this manner fluorouracil interferes with the synthesis of DNA and, to a lesser extent, inhibits the formation of RNA. Since DNA and RNA are essential for cell division and growth, the effect of fluorouracil may be to create a thymine deficiency, which provokes unbalanced growth and death of the cell. The effects of DNA and RNA deprivation are most marked on cells that grow more rapidly and take up fluorouracil at a more rapid rate.

Absorption

Systemic absorption studies of topically applied fluorouracil have been performed on patients with actinic keratoses using tracer amounts of carbon-labeled fluorouracil added to a 5% preparation. All patients had been receiving nonlabeled fluorouracil until the peak of the inflammatory reaction occurred (2 to 3 weeks), ensuring that the time of maximum absorption was used for measurement. One gram of labeled preparation was applied to the entire face and neck and left in place for 12 hours. At the end of 3 days, urine samples were collected. The total recovery ranged between 0.48% and 0.94% with an average of 0.76%, indicating that approximately 5.98% of the topical dose was absorbed systemically. If applied twice daily, this would indicate systemic absorption of topical fluorouracil to be in the range of 5 to 6 mg per daily dose of 100 mg.

Distribution

In one clinical study, negligible amounts of labeled material were found in the plasma after 3 days of treatment with topically applied carbon-labeled fluorouracil.

Onset of action

2 to 3 days. A treatment period of 2 to 6 weeks is usually required to reach the erosion and necrosis stage, or up to 12 weeks in some patients with superficial basal cell carcinomas. Complete healing may not occur until 1 to 2 months after therapy is stopped.

Precautions to Consider

Carcinogenicity

Studies have not been done. However, morphological transformation of cells was produced by fluorouracil in three *in vitro* cell transformation assays. In one of these assays, a metabolite of fluorouracil produced morphological transformation, and injection of the transformed cells into immunosuppressed syngeneic mice produced malignant tumors.

Mutagenicity

Parenteral administration of fluorouracil in humans at cumulative doses of 240 mg to 1 gram has produced an increase in numerical and structural chromosome aberrations in peripheral blood lymphocytes. Fluorouracil is mutagenic in yeast cells, *Bacillus subtilis,* and *Drosophila* assays. It produced chromosome damage in an *in vitro* hamster fibroblast assay at concentrations of 1 and 2 mcg per liter and increased micronuclei formation in the bone marrow of mice at intraperitoneal doses within the human therapeutic dose range of 12 to 15 mg per kg of body weight (mg/kg) per day. Results of the dominant lethal mutation assay performed in mice were negative.

Pregnancy/Reproduction

Fertility—Parenteral fluorouracil impairs fertility in rats. In mice, single-dose intravenous and intraperitoneal injections of fluorouracil killed differentiated spermatogonia and spermatocytes at a dose of 500 mg/kg and produced abnormalities in spermatids at a dose of 50 mg/kg.

Pregnancy—Adequate and well-controlled studies with either the topical or the parenteral forms of fluorouracil have not been done in humans. However, topical fluorouracil may cause fetal harm when administered to a pregnant woman. One case of birth defect, cleft lip and palate, has been reported in the newborn of a patient using topical fluorouracil as recommended. One case of birth defect, ventricular septal defect, and some cases of miscarriage have been reported when topical fluorouracil was applied to mucous membrane areas. Multiple birth defects were reported in the fetus of a patient treated with intravenous fluorouracil.

Studies with topical fluorouracil have not been done in animals. Fluorouracil administered parenterally has been shown to be teratogenic in mice, rats, and hamsters when given at doses equivalent to the usual human intravenous dose. However, the amount of fluorouracil absorbed systemically after topical administration to actinic keratoses is minimal.

FDA Pregnancy Category X.

Breast-feeding

It is not known whether topical fluorouracil is distributed into breast milk. However, there is some systemic absorption of fluorouracil after topical administration. Therefore, because of the potential for serious adverse reactions in nursing infants, a decision should be made whether to discontinue nursing or to discontinue use of topical fluorouracil, taking into account the importance of topical fluorouracil treatment to the mother.

Pediatrics

Appropriate studies on the relationship of age to the effects of topical fluorouracil have not been performed in the pediatric population. Safety and efficacy have not been established.

Geriatrics

Appropriate studies on the relationship of age to the effects of topical fluorouracil have not been performed in the geriatric population. However, geriatrics-specific problems that would limit the usefulness of this medication in elderly patients are not expected.

Laboratory value alterations

The following have been selected on the basis of their potential clinical significance (possible effect in parentheses where appropriate)—not necessarily inclusive (» = major clinical significance).

With physiology/laboratory test values
Eosinophilia and
Leukocytosis and
Thrombocytopenia and
Toxic granulation
(may occur)

Medical considerations/Contraindications

The medical considerations/contraindications included have been selected on the basis of their potential clinical significance (reasons given in parentheses where appropriate)—not necessarily inclusive (» = major clinical significance).

Except under special circumstances, this medication should not be used when the following medical problem exists:

» Dihydropyrimidine dehydrogenase enzyme deficiency
(use is contraindicated in patients with dihydropyrimidine dehydrogenase [DPD] enzyme deficiency; may result in shunting of fluo-

rouracil to the anabolic pathway leading to cytotoxic activity and possible life-threatening toxicities such as diarrhea, neurotoxicity, neutropenia, and stomatitis)

» Hypersensitivity to fluorouracil or any of its components, such as parabens

Risk-benefit should be considered when the following medical problems exist:

Hemorrhagic ulcerated tissues
(significant systemic absorption and toxicity may occur)

Pre-existing dermatoses, especially chloasma and rosacea
(may be accentuated by the inflammatory response to fluorouracil)

Patient monitoring

The following may be especially important in patient monitoring (other tests may be warranted in some patients, depending on condition; » = major clinical significance):

Biopsy
(recommended to confirm diagnosis if actinic (solar) keratoses do not respond or if they recur after treatment, and to confirm cure of superficial basal cell carcinomas)

Side/Adverse Effects

The following side/adverse effects have been selected on the basis of their potential clinical significance (possible signs and symptoms in parentheses where appropriate)—not necessarily inclusive:

Those indicating need for medical attention

Incidence more frequent

Inflammatory response or allergic reaction (redness and swelling of normal skin)

Note: A delayed *hypersensitivity* reaction may occur. Patch testing for hypersensitivity may be inconclusive.

Those indicating need for medical attention only if they continue or are bothersome

Incidence more frequent

Burning feeling at site of application; contact dermatitis (skin rash); ***increased sensitivity of skin to sunlight; itching; oozing; soreness or tenderness of skin***

Incidence less frequent or rare

Darkening of skin; scaling; watery eyes

Patient Consultation

As an aid to patient consultation, refer to *Advice for the Patient, Fluorouracil (Topical)*.

In providing consultation, consider emphasizing the following selected information (» = major clinical significance):

Before using this medication

» Conditions affecting use, especially:
Hypersensitivity to fluorouracil or any of its components, such as parabens
Pregnancy—Use not recommended because of teratogenic potential; some systemic absorption occurs
Breast-feeding—Not recommended because of risk of serious side effects; some systemic systemic absorption occurs
Other medical problems, especially dihydropyrimidine dehydrogenase (DPD) enzyme deficiency

Proper use of this medication

» Compliance with therapy; applying enough medication to cover affected areas

Washing area to be treated with soap and water and drying thoroughly; using cotton-tipped applicator or fingertips to apply

» Washing hands immediately after application if fingertips are used

Possible unsightly and uncomfortable reaction during therapy and for several weeks after therapy is completed; possible temporary pink, smooth spot left during healing; checking with physician before discontinuing medication

» Proper dosing

Missed dose: Applying as soon as remembered; not applying if not remembered within a few hours; checking with physician if more than one dose is missed

» Proper storage

Precautions while using this medication

» Importance of close monitoring by physician

» Caution in applying medication; avoiding eyes, nose, and mouth

» Possible photosensitivity reactions during therapy and for 1 or 2 months after therapy is completed; avoiding sun; using protective clothing and sun block product; avoiding use of sunlamp, tanning bed, or tanning booth

Side/adverse effects

Signs of potential side effects, especially inflammatory response or allergic reaction

General Dosing Information

Patients using topical fluorouracil should be under supervision of a physician experienced in use of the medication.

Patients should be forewarned that the reaction in the treated areas may be unsightly during therapy and, usually, following cessation of therapy. Patients should be instructed to avoid exposure to ultraviolet rays during and immediately following treatment with topical fluorouracil because the intensity of the reaction may be increased. If topical fluorouracil is applied with the fingers, the hands should be washed immediately afterward. Topical fluorouracil should not be applied on the eyelids or directly into the eyes, nose, or mouth, because irritation may occur.

When topical fluorouracil is applied to a lesion, a response occurs in the following sequence: erythema, usually followed by vesiculation, desquamation, erosion, and epithelialization.

Fluorouracil cream or solution should be applied twice daily on actinic or solar keratoses in an amount sufficient to cover the lesions. Medication should be continued until the inflammatory response reaches the erosion stage, at which time use of topical fluorouracil should be terminated. The usual duration of therapy is from 2 to 4 weeks. Complete healing of the lesions may not be evident for 1 to 2 months following cessation of topical fluorouracil therapy.

In superficial basal cell carcinomas, only the 5% strength is recommended. Fluorouracil cream or solution should be applied twice daily in an amount sufficient to cover the lesions. Treatment should be continued for at least 3 to 6 weeks. Therapy may be required for as long as 10 to 12 weeks before the lesions are obliterated. As in any neoplastic condition, the patient should be followed for a reasonable period of time to determine if a cure has been obtained.

Occlusion of the skin with consequent hydration has been shown to increase percutaneous penetration of several topical preparations. Therefore, if any occlusive dressing is used in treatment of basal cell carcinoma, there may be an increase in the severity of inflammatory reactions in the adjacent normal skin. A porous gauze dressing may be applied for cosmetic reasons without an increase in reaction.

It is recommended that treatment with fluorouracil be discontinued if an excessive inflammatory response occurs on normal skin.

Do not apply fluorouracil to mucous membranes. Local inflammation and ulceration may occur. Cases of miscarriage and a ventricular septal defect birth defect have been reported when topical fluorouracil was applied to the mucous membrane areas during pregnancy.

Topical Dosage Forms

FLUOROURACIL CREAM

Usual adult dose

Actinic (solar keratoses)—
Topical, to the skin, as a 0.5% or 1% cream once or twice a day in a sufficient amount to cover the lesions. Usually the 0.5% strength is effective on the face and anterior scalp; 1% on the head, neck, and chest; 2 to 5% may be needed on the hands.

Superficial basal cell carcinomas—
Topical, to the skin, as a 5% cream twice a day in a sufficient amount to cover the lesions, for at least three to six weeks, and possibly up to twelve weeks.

Usual pediatric dose

Safety and efficacy have not been established.

Strength(s) usually available

U.S.—
0.5% (Rx) [*Carac* (carbomer 940; dimethicone; glycerin; methyl gluceth-20; methyl methacrylate/glycol dimethacrylate crosspolymer; methylparaben; octyl hydroxy stearate; polyethylene glycol 400; polysorbate 80; propylene glycol; propylparaben; purified water; sorbitan monooleate; stearic acid; trolamine)].
1% (Rx) [*Fluoroplex* (benzyl alcohol)].
5% (Rx) [*Efudex* (methylparaben; propylparaben)].

Canada—
1% (Rx) [*Fluoroplex* (benzyl alcohol)].
5% (Rx) [*Efudex*].

Packaging and storage

Store below 40 °C (104 °F), preferably between 15 and 30 °C (59 and 86 °F), unless otherwise specified by the manufacturer. Store in a tight container.

Auxiliary labeling
- For the skin.
- Continue medicine for full course of treatment.
- Avoid overexposure to sun.

FLUOROURACIL TOPICAL SOLUTION

Usual adult dose
Actinic (solar keratoses)—
Topical, to the skin, as a 1 or 2% solution once or twice a day in a sufficient amount to cover the lesions. Usually the 1% strength is effective on the head, neck, and chest; 2 to 5% may be needed on the hands.

Superficial basal cell carcinomas—
Topical, to the skin, as a 5% solution twice a day in a sufficient amount to cover the lesions, for at least three to six weeks, and possibly up to twelve weeks.

Usual pediatric dose
Safety and efficacy have not been established.

Strength(s) usually available
U.S.—
1% (Rx) [*Fluoroplex*].
2% (Rx) [*Efudex* (methylparaben; propylparaben)].
5% (Rx) [*Efudex* (methylparaben; propylparaben)].

Canada—
1% (Rx) [*Fluoroplex*].

Packaging and storage
Store between 15 and 30 °C (59 and 86 °F), unless otherwise specified by manufacturer. Store in a tight container. Protect from freezing.

Auxiliary labeling
- For the skin.
- Continue medicine for full course of treatment.
- Avoid overexposure to sun.

Revised: 08/03/2004

FLUOXETINE Systemic

VA CLASSIFICATION (Primary/Secondary): CN603/CN900

Commonly used brand name(s): *Prozac; Prozac Weekly; Sarafem.*

Note: For a listing of dosage forms and brand names by country availability, see *Dosage Forms* section(s).

Category
Antidepressant; antiobsessional agent; antibulimic agent.

Indications

Accepted
Depressive disorder, major (treatment)—Fluoxetine is indicated for the treatment of major depressive disorder. Treatment of acute depressive episodes typically requires 6 to 12 months of antidepressant therapy. Patients with recurrent or chronic depression may require long-term treatment. Fluoxetine has shown effective maintenance of antidepressant response for up to 50 weeks of treatment in a placebo-controlled trial.

Obsessive-compulsive disorder (treatment)—Fluoxetine is indicated for the treatment of obsessions and compulsions in patients with obsessive-compulsive disorder.

Bulimia nervosa (treatment)—Fluoxetine is indicated for the treatment of binge-eating and vomiting behaviors in patients with moderate to severe bulimia nervosa.

Premenstrual dysphoric disorder (treatment)[1]—Fluoxetine is used to relieve the symptoms of premenstrual dysphoric disorder (PMDD). PMDD was formerly known as late luteal phase dysphoric disorder (LLPDD) and is distinguishable from the cyclic changes in mood commonly known as premenstrual syndrome (PMS) by its greater severity of symptoms. (Evidence rating: B-1)

[Premature ejaculation (treatment)][1]—Fluoxetine is indicated for the treatment of premature ejaculation.

[1]Not included in Canadian product labeling.

Pharmacology/Pharmacokinetics

Physicochemical characteristics
Chemical Group—Cyclic, propylamine-derivative. Chemically unrelated to tricyclic or tetracyclic antidepressants. Fluoxetine is a 50:50 racemic mixture of R- and S-fluoxetine.

Molecular weight—
Fluoxetine: 309.33.
Fluoxetine hydrochloride: 345.79.

Solubility—14 mg per mL water.

Mechanism of action/Effect
The antidepressant, antiobsessional, and antibulimic effects of fluoxetine are thought to be related to its effects on serotonergic neurotransmission. Fluoxetine is a potent and selective inhibitor of serotonin (5-HT) uptake, but not of norepinephrine or dopamine uptake, in the central nervous system (CNS). In depressed patients who had received 40 to 60 mg per day of fluoxetine for 6 weeks, the cerebrospinal fluid concentrations of the metabolites of 5-HT (5-HIAA), dopamine (HVA), and norepinephrine (HMPG) were reduced by 46%, 14%, and 18%, respectively. Because uptake inactivates serotonin by removing it from the synaptic cleft, uptake inhibition by fluoxetine enhances serotonergic function. As a consequence, the 5-HT_1 receptors are desensitized or downregulated after long-term fluoxetine administration. Fluoxetine does not interact directly with postsynaptic serotonin receptors, muscarinic-cholinergic receptors, histaminergic receptors, or alpha-adrenergic receptors. Fluoxetine does not appear to cause downregulation of postsynaptic beta-adrenergic receptors or a decrease in beta-adrenergic–stimulated cyclic adenosine monophosphate (cAMP) generation as do older antidepressant medications.

Other actions/effects
Fluoxetine may exhibit an acute anorectic effect and could potentially cause weight loss proportional to the degree of initial obesity as measured by the body mass index (BMI).

Fluoxetine and norfluoxetine inhibit the isoenzyme cytochrome P450 2D6 (CYP2D6) potently and CYP3A to a lesser extent. Fluoxetine is a moderately potent inhibitor of CYP2C9 and CYP2C19.

Fluoxetine blocks the uptake of 5-HT into human platelets as well as into neurons.

Absorption
Well-absorbed with a small first-pass effect. Food does not affect the extent of absorption, although the rate may be slightly decreased.

Distribution
Fluoxetine has a large volume of distribution. In eight patients being treated with fluoxetine for major depression or obsessive-compulsive disorder, the mean ratio of brain concentration to plasma concentration of fluoxetine plus its metabolites was 2.6.

Protein binding
High (94.5%).

Biotransformation
Metabolized by demethylation in the liver to the active metabolite, norfluoxetine, and other unidentified metabolites. *In vivo* studies indicate that cytochrome P450 2D6 (CYP2D6) is involved in fluoxetine metabolism. An *in vitro* study indicates that CYP2C9 and, to a lesser extent, CYP3A may also be involved in fluoxetine metabolism.

The active metabolite of fluoxetine, norfluoxetine, exists as a racemic mixture. The selective serotonin reuptake inhibition activity of S-norfluoxetine is comparable to that of fluoxetine. R-norfluoxetine is significantly less potent than the parent compound.

Half-life
Elimination—
Fluoxetine: 1 to 3 days after a single dose, and 4 to 6 days with long-term administration.
Norfluoxetine: 4 to 16 days after single dose or long-term administration.

After long-term or high-dose use, it may take 1 to 2 months for the active moieties to be eliminated from the body. In four patients who had received 80 mg of fluoxetine per day for 52 $\pm$ 8 weeks, the elimination half-lives of fluoxetine and norfluoxetine were found to be 8 days and 19.3 days, respectively. This extended elimination time may have reflected the increased plasma concentrations achieved with high dosing, since fluoxetine displays nonlinear pharmacokinetics, as well as the extensive distribution of fluoxetine in the body.

Onset of action
Depression—Effects have been seen in 1 to 3 weeks; however, response may require 4 to 6 weeks to occur.

Obsessive-compulsive disorder—Full effectiveness may not occur for 5 or more weeks.

Bulimia nervosa—Significant improvement has been seen in 1 week; however, response may require 4 to 6 weeks to occur.

Time to peak concentration

6 to 8 hours after a single oral dose of 40 mg.

Time to steady-state concentration

Approximately 4 weeks for fluoxetine and norfluoxetine.

Peak serum concentration

Single dose (40 mg)—
- Fluoxetine: 15 to 55 nanograms per mL. Fluoxetine exhibits nonlinear pharmacokinetics; higher doses lead to disproportionately higher plasma concentrations.

Multiple dose (40 mg a day for 30 days)—
- Fluoxetine: 91 to 302 nanograms per mL. After multiple dosing, plasma fluoxetine concentrations are higher than predicted by single-dose kinetics.
- Norfluoxetine: 72 to 258 nanograms per mL. Norfluoxetine appears to have linear kinetics.

Elimination

Renal—
- 80% excreted in the urine (11.6% fluoxetine, 7.4% fluoxetine glucuronide, 6.8% norfluoxetine, 8.2% norfluoxetine glucuronide, > 20% hippuric acid, 46% other). Renal function impairment does not alter fluoxetine or norfluoxetine pharmacokinetics; however, effects on other metabolites are unknown.

Biliary—
- Approximately 15% in the feces.

In dialysis—
- Not dialyzable because of high protein binding and large volume of distribution.

Precautions to Consider

Carcinogenicity

Two-year studies in rats and mice given dietary fluoxetine in doses equivalent to 1.2 and 0.7 times, respectively, the maximum recommended human dose (MRHD) on a mg per square meter of body surface area (mg/m^2) basis showed no evidence of carcinogenicity.

Mutagenicity

Fluoxetine and norfluoxetine have shown no genotoxic effects in the bacterial mutation assay, DNA repair assay in cultured rat hepatocytes, mouse lymphoma assay, or *in vivo* sister chromatid exchange assay in Chinese hamster bone marrow cells.

Pregnancy/Reproduction

Fertility—No evidence of adverse effects on fertility was seen in rats given fluoxetine doses of 0.9 to 1.5 times the MRHD on a mg/m^2 basis.

Pregnancy—A study comparing birth outcomes between women who took fluoxetine only during the first and second trimesters of pregnancy and women who took fluoxetine during the third trimester of pregnancy found an increased risk of premature delivery and poor neonatal adaptation, including respiratory difficulties, cyanosis on feeding, and jitteriness, in the neonates who had been exposed during the third trimester. In addition, the number of neonates exhibiting more than three minor anomalies was greater among neonates who had been exposed to fluoxetine during the first trimester than among neonates with no *in utero* exposure to fluoxetine. However, a previous analysis of birth outcomes among women taking various antidepressant medications during pregnancy, including 96 women taking fluoxetine, either as monotherapy or in combination with other medications, found the rates of adverse pregnancy outcome to be within the normal limits. Also, an analysis of the manufacturer's registry of fluoxetine-exposed pregnancies, which comprised 123 pregnancies at the time of analysis, found the rates of adverse outcome to be within the normal limits, as did a prospective study comparing pregnancy outcomes of 128 women who took fluoxetine during the first trimester with pregnancy outcomes of 128 age-matched controls who took medications known to be nonteratogenic during the first trimester. A study of preschoolers and young children revealed no differences in global intelligence, language development, or behavioral development between a group of 55 preschoolers and young children with *in utero* fluoxetine exposure, either during the first trimester or throughout gestation, and a group of 84 preschoolers and young children with no fluoxetine exposure.

Petechiae and a cephalohematoma, in addition to jitteriness and hypertonia, were reported in a newborn whose mother was receiving 60 mg per day of fluoxetine to treat obsessive-compulsive disorder. However, at a 5-month follow-up, the infant was normal. Serum fluoxetine and norfluoxetine concentrations on the infant's second day of life were 129 and 227 nanograms per mL, respectively.

No evidence of teratogenicity was found in studies in rats and rabbits receiving fluoxetine doses that were 1.5 and 3.6 times, respectively, the MRHD on a mg/m^2 basis. However, an increase in stillbirths and pup deaths during the first postpartum week was seen in rats given 1.5 times the MRHD on a mg/m^2 basis during gestation or 0.9 times the MRHD on a mg/m^2 basis during gestation and lactation.

Non-teratogenic effects—When exposed to fluoxetine and other selective serotonin reuptake inhibitors (SSRIs) or selective norepinephrine reuptake inhibitors (SNRIs) late in the third trimester, neonates have developed complications requiring prolonged hospitalization, respiratory support, and tube feeding and these can arise immediately upon delivery. Features consistent with a direct toxic effect of SSRIs and SNRIs or a drug discontinuation syndrome including respiratory distress, cyanosis, apnea, seizures, temperature instability, feeding difficulty, vomiting, hypoglycemia, hypotonia, hypertonia, hyperreflexia, tremor, jitteriness, irritability, and constant crying have been reported. In some cases, it should be noted that the clinical picture is consistent with serotonin syndrome. When treating a pregnant woman with fluoxetine during the third trimester, the physician should carefully consider the potential risks and benefits of treatment. The physician may consider tapering fluoxetine in the third trimester.

FDA Pregnancy Category C.

Labor and delivery—The effect of fluoxetine on labor and delivery is not known.

Breast-feeding

Fluoxetine is distributed into breast milk. In a study of 10 mothers and 11 nursing infants ranging in age from 20 to 747 days, the concentration of fluoxetine in breast milk was found to be linearly correlated with maternal fluoxetine dose and, in most cases, to peak within 6 hours after the dose was taken. Infant exposure to fluoxetine plus norfluoxetine was estimated using mean fluoxetine and norfluoxetine milk concentrations and an assumed milk intake of one liter per day. The estimated infant exposure was 10.8% (range 6.3 to 13.9%) of the maternal fluoxetine dose in mg per kg of body weight (mg/kg). Mothers in this study reported no adverse effects in the infants. However, in one case report, vomiting, watery stools, crying, and sleep disorders were reported in the 6-week-old infant of a nursing mother taking 20 mg of fluoxetine a day; these symptoms remitted when breast-feeding was interrupted and recurred when the infant was rechallenged with breast milk. Total drug exposure will be affected by the maturity of the metabolic and excretory systems of the infant, with very young infants having lower drug clearance and higher exposure. Use of fluoxetine in nursing mothers is not recommended. However, the risks and benefits to both the mother and the infant must be considered in each case.

Pediatrics

Fluoxetine is only approved for use in treating MDD in the pediatric population.

Fluoxetine has been studied for a variety of indications in over 300 patients 7 to 18 years of age. Most of the studies were open trials; almost all of the studies had 40 or fewer subjects; and results were variable. However, one randomized, double-blind, placebo-controlled study in 96 children 7 to 17 years of age (48 receiving 20 mg per day of fluoxetine and 48 receiving placebo), who were diagnosed with major depressive disorder, found fluoxetine to be superior to placebo in relieving depressive symptoms. The difference between the two groups became statistically significant after 5 weeks of treatment. Response in children 7 through 12 years of age did not differ from response in adolescents 13 through 17 years of age, nor was there a difference in response between males and females. Although the available information is insufficient to establish the efficacy of fluoxetine in children, it does provide some evidence of effectiveness of fluoxetine in the treatment of depression and obsessive-compulsive disorder.

Antidepressants increase the risk of suicidal thinking and behavior (suicidality) in children and adolescents with major depressive disorder (MDD) and other psychiatric disorders. Anyone considering the use of fluoxetine or any other antidepressant in a child or adolescent must balance this risk with the clinical need.

Pooled analyses of short-term placebo controlled trials of nine antidepressant drugs in children and adolescents with MDD, obsessive compulsive disorder, or other psychiatric disorders have revealed a greater risk of adverse events representing suicidality during the first few months of treatment in those receiving antidepressants.

Children may be more sensitive than adults to the behavioral adverse effects of fluoxetine, including mania or hypomania, social disinhibition, irritability, restlessness, and insomnia.

Geriatrics

No geriatric-specific problems have been documented in studies done to date that included elderly patients.

Pharmacogenetics

Approximately 2 to 10% of the adult population has a reduced ability to metabolize substrates of cytochrome P450 2D6 (CYP2D6). In these patients, the rate of S-fluoxetine metabolism is decreased, leading to higher plasma concentrations of S-fluoxetine and lower plasma concentrations of S-norfluoxetine than are seen in normal metabolizers. However, the metabolism of R-fluoxetine appears to be unaffected. The sum concentration of the four active moieties is not significantly different between patients with reduced CYP2D6 activity and patients with normal CYP2D6 activity.

Drug interactions and/or related problems

The following drug interactions and/or related problems have been selected on the basis of their potential clinical significance (possible mechanism in parentheses where appropriate)—not necessarily inclusive (» = major clinical significance):

Note: Because fluoxetine is a potent inhibitor of cytochrome P450 2D6 (CYP2D6) there is a potential for interaction with medications that are metabolized by this enzyme, other than those listed below, such as flecainide, metoprolol, risperidone, and vinblastine. A reduction in the dosage of medications that are metabolized by CYP2D6 may be needed when they are used concurrently with fluoxetine or within 5 weeks of discontinuing fluoxetine.

Fluoxetine also inhibits CYP3A, CYP2C9, and CYP2C19. Possible interactions with medications that are metabolized by these isoenzymes, other than those listed below, such as nifedipine (CYP3A), diclofenac (CYP2C9), and omeprazole (CYP2C19), should be considered.

Combinations containing any of the following medications, depending on the amount present, may also interact with this medication.

Alcohol
(although fluoxetine has not been shown to alter alcohol metabolism and does not appear to potentiate cognitive or psychomotor effects of alcohol in healthy subjects, concomitant use is not recommended)

» Alprazolam or
Diazepam
(concurrent use with fluoxetine may prolong the half-lives of these medications; decreased psychomotor performance has been reported with concurrent use of alprazolam but not with concurrent use of diazepam)

» Antidepressants, tricyclic (TCAs)
(plasma concentrations of the TCAs and/or their active metabolites may be increased twofold to tenfold when they are used with or within 3 or more weeks after discontinuation of fluoxetine; although beneficial effects of the combination have been reported, there have been reports of serious adverse effects, including seizures and death; if these medications are to be administered concurrently or if TCA therapy is to be initiated shortly after the discontinuation of fluoxetine, the initial TCA dosage should be reduced and TCA plasma concentrations should be monitored)

» Aspirin or
» Nonsteroidal anti-inflammatory drugs [NSAIDs] or
» Other drugs that interfere with homostasis
(caution should be used; concomitant use potentiates risk of bleeding)

» Astemizole
(because of the possibility that fluoxetine may inhibit the metabolism of astemizole, leading to increased blood levels and risk of cardiac arrhythmias, including *torsades de pointes*, concurrent use is not recommended)

Carbamazepine
(although small drug interaction studies have yielded conflicting results regarding the effect of fluoxetine on the plasma concentrations of carbamazepine and its metabolite, carbamazepine-10,11-epoxide, there have been reports of increased anticonvulsant concentrations and toxicity after the initiation of fluoxetine treatment in patients stabilized on carbamazepine)

Cyproheptadine
(may reverse the therapeutic effects of fluoxetine)

Electroconvulsive therapy
(prolonged seizures have been reported in patients on concomitant fluoxetine therapy)

Clozapine or
Haloperidol or
Loxapine or
Molindone or
Phenothiazines or
Pimozide or
Thioxanthenes
(caution in concurrent use of other CNS-active medications with fluoxetine is recommended because of a potentially increased risk of side effects)

(elevated concentrations of clozapine, fluphenazine, and haloperidol have been reported in patients receiving concomitant fluoxetine)

(cases of bradycardia and mental status changes have been reported with concurrent pimozide and fluoxetine use)

» Highly protein-bound medications, especially:
Anticoagulants including
Warfarin or
Digitalis or digitoxin
(caution in concurrent use with fluoxetine is recommended because of possible displacement of either medication from protein-binding sites, leading to increased plasma concentrations of the free [unbound] medications and increased risk of adverse effects such as increased bleeding; careful coagulation monitoring for patients on anticoagulant therapy when fluoxetine is started or discontinued)

(increased international normalized ratio [INR] measurements and increased bleeding have been reported when warfarin and fluoxetine were used concurrently; the mechanism of this interaction is unknown; careful coagulation monitoring is recommended when treatment with fluoxetine is initiated or discontinued)

Lithium
(both increased and decreased lithium concentrations, as well as some cases of lithium toxicity, have been reported with concomitant fluoxetine use; close monitoring of lithium concentrations is recommended)

Maprotiline or
Trazodone
(plasma concentrations of these medications may be doubled when fluoxetine is used concurrently)

» Moclobemide
(because of the potentially fatal effects of concomitant use of fluoxetine and nonselective, irreversible monoamine oxidase [MAO] inhibitors, and the increased risk of development of the serotonin syndrome with concomitant use of fluoxetine and the selective, reversible, MAO type A inhibitor moclobemide, concurrent use is not recommended; a wash-out period of 7 days is advised between discontinuing moclobemide and initiating fluoxetine therapy, and a wash-out period of 5 weeks [approximately 5 half-lives of norfluoxetine] is advised between discontinuing fluoxetine and initiating moclobemide therapy)

» Monoamine oxidase (MAO) inhibitors, including furazolidone, procarbazine, and selegiline
(concurrent use of fluoxetine with MAO inhibitors may result in confusion, agitation, restlessness, gastrointestinal symptoms, hyperpyretic episodes, severe convulsions, hypertensive crises, the serotonin syndrome, or death. Concurrent use is **contraindicated**, and at least 14 days should elapse between discontinuation of an MAO inhibitor and initiation of fluoxetine. However, because of the long half-lives of fluoxetine and its active metabolite, at least 5 weeks [approximately 5 half-lives of norfluoxetine] should elapse between discontinuation of fluoxetine and initiation of therapy with an MAO inhibitor. Deaths following the initiation of an MAO inhibitor shortly after stopping fluoxetine administration have been reported)

» Phenytoin
(elevated plasma phenytoin concentrations resulting in symptoms of toxicity have been reported when fluoxetine was used concurrently with phenytoin; caution and close monitoring are suggested)

» Serotonergics or other medications or substances with serotonergic activity (see *Appendix II*)
(increased risk of developing the serotonin syndrome, a rare but potentially fatal hyperserotonergic state; symptoms typically occur shortly [hours to days] after the addition of a serotonergic agent to a regimen that includes serotonin-enhancing drugs or an increase in dosage of a serotonergic agent; symptoms include agitation, diaphoresis, diarrhea, fever, hyperreflexia, incoordination, mental status changes [confusion, hypomania], myoclonus, shivering, or tremor)

(use of tramadol with fluoxetine increases the risk of having seizures)

(there have been reports of agitation, restlessness, and gastrointestinal distress occurring with concurrent use of tryptophan and fluoxetine)

Sumatriptan
(rare reports of weakness, hyperreflexia, and incoordination following use of an SSRI and sumatriptan; appropriate observation of patient advised if concomitant use is clinically warranted)

» Thioridazine
(concomitant use **contraindicated** due to potential risk of serious ventricular arrhythmias and sudden death associated with elevated plasma levels of thioridazine; should not be administered with fluoxetine or within a minimum of 5 weeks after fluoxetine has been discontinued)

Medical considerations/Contraindications

The medical considerations/contraindications included have been selected on the basis of their potential clinical significance (reasons given in parentheses where appropriate)—not necessarily inclusive (» = major clinical significance).

Except under special circumstances, this medication should not be used when the following medical problem exists:

» Hypersensitivity to fluoxetine

Risk-benefit should be considered when the following medical problems exist:

» Bipolar disorder or risk of
(may increase likelihood of precipitation of a mixed/manic episode or mania/hypomania in these patients; prior to initiating fluoxetine treatment, patient should be adequately screened to determine if they are at risk for bipolar disorder; such screening should include a detailed psychiatric history, including a family history of suicide, bipolar disorder, and depression.)

Diabetes mellitus
(glycemic control may be altered due to improved peripheral and hepatic insulin action occurring with fluoxetine use; adjustment of insulin and/or oral hypoglycemic dosage with fluoxetine initiation or discontinuation)

Diseases affecting metabolism or hemodynamic responses
(caution is advisable in these patients)

» Hepatic function impairment
(metabolism of fluoxetine is delayed; lower doses or less frequent dosing is recommended in patients with liver disease)

Neurological impairment, including developmental delay or
Seizures, history of
(risk of seizures may be increased)

Parkinson's disease
(exacerbation has been reported)

Renal function impairment
(metabolites that are excreted renally may accumulate; however, routine dosage adjustments are not required)

Weight loss
(although weight loss occurring with fluoxetine use in bulimia trials averaged 0.45 kg [about 1 pound], significant weight loss may be an undesirable effect of fluoxetine use in some patients)

Patient monitoring

The following may be especially important in patient monitoring (other tests may be warranted in some patients, depending on condition; » = major clinical significance):

» Careful supervision of patients including those with:
» Abnormal behaviors (i.e., agitation, panic attacks, or hostility) or
» Clinical worsening of their depression
» Suicidal ideation and behavior (suicidality)
(recommended especially during early treatment phase prior to peak effectiveness of fluoxetine or at the time of increases or decreases in dose; prescribing the smallest amount of medication necessary for good patient management is recommended to prevent overdosing; consideration should be given to changing the therapeutic regimen, including possibly discontinuing the medicine, in patients whose depression is persistently worse or whose emergent suicidality or other symptoms are severe, abrupt in onset, or were not part of the patient's presenting symptoms)

Electrolytes, serum
(recommended in bulimic patients prior to initiation of fluoxetine treatment since electrolyte disturbances, which can occur due to vomiting, may lower the seizure threshold or may cause cardiac conduction abnormalities)

» Symptoms associated with discontinuation
(patients should be monitored for symptoms upon discontinuation; a gradual reduction in dose rather than abrupt cessation is recommended whenever possible; previously prescribed dose may be considered if intolerable symptoms occur following a decrease in the dose or upon discontinuation of treatment)

Weight
(recommended in bulimic patients periodically during treatment because of anorexia associated with fluoxetine use)

Side/Adverse Effects

The following side/adverse effects have been selected on the basis of their potential clinical significance (possible signs and symptoms in parentheses where appropriate)—not necessarily inclusive:

Those indicating need for medical attention

Incidence more frequent

Akathisia (inability to sit still; restlessness); ***sexual dysfunction, including abnormal ejaculation; anorgasmia; decreased libido; genital anesthesia (rare); or impotence*** (decreased sexual drive or ability); ***skin rash, hives, or itching***

Note: *Skin rash, hives, or itching* has been associated with systemic signs or symptoms, including arthralgia, carpal tunnel syndrome, edema, fever, leukocytosis, lymphadenopathy, mild transaminase elevations, proteinuria, and respiratory distress. Some patients have experienced syndromes resembling serum sickness. Rarely, systemic events involving the lung, kidney, or liver have developed in patients with skin rash. Deaths have occurred. However, most patients with fluoxetine-associated skin rash recovered with discontinuation of fluoxetine and/or with treatment with steroids or antihistamines. Fluoxetine should be discontinued if the patient develops skin rash or other allergic symptomatology for which no alternate etiology can be identified.

Incidence less frequent

Chills or fever; joint or muscle pain

Incidence rare

Abnormal bleeding (purple or red spots on skin); ***breast enlargement or pain; dyspnea*** (trouble in breathing); ***galactorrhea*** (unusual secretion of milk)—in females; ***hypoglycemia*** (anxiety; chills; cold sweats; confusion; cool pale skin; difficulty in concentration; drowsiness; excessive hunger; fast heartbeat; headache; nervousness; shakiness; unsteady walk; unusual tiredness or weakness); ***hyponatremia*** (confusion; drowsiness; dryness of mouth; increased thirst; lack of energy; seizures)—especially in geriatric or volume-depleted patients; ***mania or hypomania*** (talking, feeling, and acting with excitement and activity that cannot be controlled); ***movement disorders*** (unusual or incomplete body or facial movements); ***palpitation*** (fast or irregular heartbeat); ***seizures; serotonin syndrome*** (diarrhea; fever; increased sweating; mood or behavior changes; overactive reflexes; racing heartbeat; restlessness; shivering or shaking)

Note: *Dyspnea* may indicate a rare pulmonary event involving an inflammatory process and/or fibrosis.

Hyponatremia results from the syndrome of inappropriate antidiuretic hormone (SIADH). The majority of these occurrences have been in older patients and in patients taking diuretics or who were volume depleted..

Movement disorders are more likely to occur in patients with risk factors, such as pre-existing movement disorders or comedication with drugs associated with movement disorders. *Movement disorders* have also been reported since market introduction of fluoxetine.

The *serotonin syndrome* is most likely to occur shortly (hours to days) after a dosage increase or the addition of another serotonergic agent to the patient's regimen and may include cardiac arrhythmias, coma, disseminated intravascular coagulation, hypertension or hypotension, renal failure, respiratory failure, seizures, or severe hyperthermia. Although the serotonin syndrome has not been reported in patients receiving fluoxetine monotherapy, it has been reported in patients receiving monotherapy with other selective serotonin reuptake inhibitors and the possibility of occurrence with fluoxetine monotherapy exists.

Incidence not determined—Observed during clinical practice, estimates of frequency can not be determined

Anaphylactoid events (cough; difficulty swallowing; dizziness; fast heartbeat; hives; itching, puffiness or swelling of the eyelids or around the eyes, face, lips or tongue; shortness of breath; skin rash; tightness in chest; unusual tiredness or weakness; wheezing); ***angioedema*** (large, hive-like swelling on face, eyelids, lips, tongue, throat, hands, legs, feet, sex organs); ***aplastic anemia*** (chest pain; chills; cough; fever; headache; shortness of breath; sores, ulcers, or white spots on lips or in mouth; swollen or painful glands; tightness in chest; unusual bleeding or bruising; unusual tiredness or weakness; wheezing); ***atrial fibrillation*** (fast or irregular heartbeat; dizziness; fainting); ***bronchospasm*** (cough; difficulty breathing; noisy breathing; shortness of breath; tightness in chest; wheezing); ***cataract*** (blindness; blurred vision; decreased vision); ***cerebral vascular accident*** (sudden weakness in arms or legs; sudden, severe chest pain); ***cholestatic jaundice*** (abdominal or stomach pain; chills; clay-colored stools; dark urine; diarrhea; dizziness; fever; headache; itching; loss of appetite; nausea; rash; unpleasant breath odor; unusual tiredness or weakness; vomiting of blood; yellow eyes or skin); ***dyskinesia*** (twitching, twisting, uncontrolled repetitive movements of tongue, lips, face, arms, or legs); ***eosinophilic pneumonia*** (chest pain; dry cough; fever; general feeling of tiredness or weakness; rapid breathing; shortness of breath; skin rash; wheezing); ***epidermal necrolysis*** (redness, tenderness, itching, burning, or peeling of skin; red or irritated eyes; sore throat, fever, and chills); ***erythema nodosum*** (fever; pain in ankles or knees, painful, red lumps under the skin, mostly on the legs); ***heart arrest*** (stopping of heart; no blood pressure or pulse; unconsciousness); ***hepatic failure/necrosis*** (abdominal or stomach pain; black, tarry stools; chills; continuing vomiting; light-colored stools; dark urine; dizziness; fever; headache; itching; loss of appetite; nausea; rash; unpleasant breath odor; unusual tiredness or weakness; vomiting of blood; yellow eyes or skin); ***hyperprolactinemia*** (swelling of breasts or unusual milk production); ***hypoglycemia*** (anxiety; blurred vision; chills; cold sweats; coma; confusion; cool, pale skin; depression; dizziness; fast heartbeat; headache; increased hunger; nausea; nervousness; nightmares; seizures; shakiness; slurred speech; unusual tiredness or weakness); ***immune-related hemolytic anemia*** (back, leg, or stomach pains; bleeding gums; chills; dark urine; difficulty breathing; fatigue; fever; general body swelling; headache; loss of appetite; nausea or vomiting; nosebleeds; pale skin; sore throat; yellowing of the eyes or skin); ***kidney failure*** (agitation; coma; confusion; decreased urine output; depression; dizziness; headache; hostility; irritability; lethargy; muscle twitching; nausea; rapid weight gain; seizures; stupor; swelling of face, ankles, or hands; unusual tiredness or weakness); ***laryngospasm*** (shortness of breath; trouble in breathing; tightness in chest; or wheezing); ***neuroleptic malignant syndrome-like events*** (convulsions; difficulty in breathing; fast heartbeat; high fever; high or low blood pressure; increased sweating; loss of bladder control; severe muscle stiffness; unusually pale skin; tiredness); ***optic neuritis*** (blindness; blue-yellow color blindness; blurred vision; decreased vision; eye pain); ***pancreatitis*** (bloating; chills; constipation; darkened urine; fast heartbeat; fever; indigestion; loss of appetite; nausea; pains in stomach, side, or abdomen, possibly radiating to the back; vomiting; yellow eyes or skin); ***pancytopenia*** (high fever; chills; unexplained bleeding or bruising; bloody, black, or tarry stools; pale skin; unusual tiredness or weakness; cough; shortness of breath; sores, ulcers, or white spots on lips or in mouth; swollen glands); ***pulmonary embolism*** (anxiety; chest pain; cough; fainting; fast heartbeat; sudden shortness of breath or troubled breathing; dizziness or lightheadedness); ***pulmonary hypertension*** (shortness of breath); ***QT prolongation*** (dizziness or fainting; pounding heartbeat; fast or irregular heartbeat); ***Stevens-Johnson syndrome*** (blistering, peeling, loosening of skin; chills; cough; diarrhea; itching; joint or muscle pain; red, irritated eyes; red skin lesions, often with a purple center; sore throat; sores, ulcers, or white spots in mouth or on lips; unusual tiredness or weakness); ***sudden unexpected death; suicidal ideation*** (thoughts of killing oneself; changes in behavior); ***thrombocytopenia*** (black, tarry stools; bleeding gums; blood in urine or stools; pinpoint red spots on skin; unusual bleeding or bruising); ***thrombocytopenic purpura*** (unusual bleeding or bruising; bloody nose; heavier menstrual periods; pinpoint red spots on skin; black, tarry stools; blood in urine; black, tarry stools; unusual tiredness or weakness; fever skin rash); ***torsades de pointes-type arrhythmias*** (chest pain or discomfort; irregular or slow heart rate; fainting; shortness of breath); ***urticaria*** (hives or welts; itching; redness of skin; skin rash); ***ventricular tachycardia*** (fainting; fast, pounding, or irregular heartbeat or pulse; palpitations); ***violent behaviors*** (use of extreme physical or emotional force)

Those indicating need for medical attention only if they continue or are bothersome

Incidence more frequent

Anxiety or nervousness; anorexia (decreased appetite); ***asthenia*** (tiredness or weakness); ***diarrhea; drowsiness; headache; increased sweating; insomnia*** (trouble in sleeping); ***nausea; tremor*** (trembling or shaking)

Incidence less frequent or rare

Abnormal dreams; alopecia (hair loss); ***changes in vision; chest pain; dizziness or lightheadedness; frequent urination; gastrointestinal effects, including change in sense of taste; constipation; dryness of mouth; increased appetite; stomach cramps, gas, or pain; vomiting; weight gain; or weight loss; menstrual pain; photosensitivity*** (increased sensitivity of skin to sunlight); ***vasodilation*** (feeling of warmth or heat; flushing or redness of skin, especially on face and neck); ***yawning***

Incidence not determined—Observed during clinical practice, estimates of frequency can not be determined

Confusion (mood or mental changes); ***exfoliative dermatitis*** (cracks in the skin; loss of heat from the body; red, swollen skin; scaly skin); ***gynecomastia*** (swelling of the breasts or breast soreness in both females and males); ***hyperprolactinemia*** (swelling of breasts or unusual milk production); ***priapism*** (painful or prolonged erection of the penis)

Those indicating need for medical attention if they occur after medication is discontinued

Agitation; anxiety; confusion (mood or mental changes); ***dizziness; dysphoric mood*** (feeling of distress); ***emotional lability*** (crying; depersonalization; dysphoria; euphoria; mental depression; paranoia; quick to react or overreact emotionally; rapidly changing moods)
fatigue (unusual tiredness or weakness)
headache; hypomania (actions that are out of control; irritability; nervousness; talking, feeling, and acting with excitement)
insomnia (sleeplessness; trouble sleeping; unable to sleep)
irritability
lethargy (unusual drowsiness, dullness, tiredness, weakness or feeling of sluggishness)
malaise (general feeling of discomfort or illness)
nausea; paresthesias (such as electrical shock sensations) (burning, crawling, itching, numbness, prickling, "pins and needles", or tingling feelings)
sweating; vaginal bleeding
vertigo (feeling that body or surroundings are turning)

Note: *Dizziness* and *vertigo* have been reported to occur in short bursts of a few seconds each.

Discontinuation symptoms have been reported less frequently with fluoxetine than with other selective serotonin reuptake inhibitors, probably due to the long half-lives of fluoxetine and its active metabolite, norfluoxetine. The symptoms may begin up to 3½ weeks after discontinuation of fluoxetine and may require several weeks to resolve.

Overdose

For specific information on the agents used in the management of fluoxetine overdose, see:

- *Charcoal, Activated (Oral-Local)* monograph; and/or
- *Diazepam* in *Benzodiazepines (Systemic)* monograph.

For more information on the management of overdose or unintentional ingestion, **contact a Poison Control Center** (see *Poison Control Center Listing*).

Clinical effects of overdose

The following effects have been selected on the basis of their potential clinical significance (possible signs and symptoms in parentheses where appropriate)—not necessarily inclusive:

Note: Patients who take an overdose of fluoxetine only, with no other substances, may remain asymptomatic.

Agitation and restlessness; drowsiness; hypomania (talking, feeling, and acting with excitement and activity that cannot be controlled); ***nausea and vomiting; seizures; tachycardia*** (fast heartbeat); ***tremor*** (trembling or shaking)

Treatment of overdose

There is no specific antidote for fluoxetine overdose. Treatment is essentially symptomatic and supportive.

To decrease absorption—Administering activated charcoal with sorbitol.

Specific treatment—Administering an anticonvulsant such as diazepam, if necessary, for seizure control.

Monitoring—Monitoring cardiovascular function (ECG).

Supportive care—Maintaining respiratory function. Maintaining body temperature. Patients in whom intentional overdose is confirmed or suspected should be referred for psychiatric consultation.

Note: Dialysis, forced diuresis, hemoperfusion or exchange transfusions are unlikely to be of benefit due to the large volume of distribution and high degree of protein binding of fluoxetine.

If a tricyclic antidepressant has been coingested, the tricyclic toxicity may be prolonged due to inhibition of metabolism by fluoxetine.

Patient Consultation

As an aid to patient consultation, refer to *Advice for the Patient, Fluoxetine (Systemic)*.

In providing consultation, consider emphasizing the following selected information (» = major clinical significance):

Before using this medication

» Conditions affecting use, especially:
  Hypersensitivity to fluoxetine
  Pregnancy—Should be used during pregnancy only if potential benefit justifies potential risk to fetus
  Complications including prolonged hospitalization, respiratory support and tube feeding in neonates exposed to fluoxetine and other SSRIs late in the third trimester; physician should carefully consider potential risks and benefits when treating a pregnant woman in her third trimester
  Breast-feeding—Not recommended; vomiting, watery stools, crying, and sleep disturbance were reported in one infant; in several other infants, no problems were reported
  Use in children—Because of Food and Drug Administration [FDA] reports of the occurrence of suicidality in clinical trials for various antidepressant drugs in pediatric patients with major depressive disorder [MDD], fluoxetine must be used with caution in treating pediatric patients for MDD.
  Contraindicated medications—Monamine oxidase (MAO) inhibitors, Thioridazine
  Other medications, especially alprazolam; aspirin; astemizole; highly protein-bound medications such as anticoagulants (including warfarin), digitalis, or digitoxin; moclobemide; nonsteroidal anti-inflammatory drugs (NSAIDs); other drugs that interfere with homostasis; phenytoin; serotonergics or other medications or substances with serotonergic activity; or tricyclic antidepressants
  Other medical problems, especially bipolar disorder or risk of; or hepatic function impairment

Proper use of this medication

» Compliance with therapy; not taking more or less medicine than prescribed
  Taking with or without food, as directed by physician
  Taking with food if medicine causes stomach upset
» May require 4 weeks or longer of therapy to obtain antidepressant effects; may require 5 weeks or longer to obtain full antiobsessional effects; antibulimic effects may be seen after 1 week of therapy but may require 4 weeks or longer to occur
» Proper dosing
  Missed dose: Skipping the missed dose and continuing on regular schedule with next dose; not doubling doses
» Proper storage

Precautions while using this medication

  Regular visits to physician to check progress of therapy
  Checking with physician before discontinuing medication
» Importance of patient tapering off of the medication as directed by the physician
» Importance of patient or caregiver notifying physician immediately if any signs of abnormal behavior, worsening depression or suicidality occur
» Importance of patient notifying physician immediately if rash or other signs of an allergic reaction occur
» Not taking fluoxetine within 2 weeks of discontinuing an MAO inhibitor; not taking an MAO inhibitor for at least 5 weeks after discontinuing fluoxetine
  Avoiding use of alcoholic beverages
» Stopping fluoxetine and checking with physician as soon as possible if skin rash or hives occurs
  For diabetic patients: possible change in blood sugar levels; discussing with physician
» Possible drowsiness, impairment of judgment, thinking, or motor skills; caution when driving or doing jobs requiring alertness

Side/adverse effects

  Signs of potential side effects, especially akathisia; sexual dysfunction; skin rash, hives, or itching; chills or fever; joint or muscle pain; abnormal bleeding; breast enlargement or pain; dyspnea; galactorrhea, in females; hypoglycemia; hyponatremia; mania or hypomania; movement disorders; seizures; or serotonin syndrome
  Signs of potential side effects observed during clinical practice, especially anaphylactoid events, angioedema, aplastic anemia, atrial fibrillation, bronchospasm, cataract, cerebral vascular accident, cholestatic jaundice, dyskinesia, eosinophilic pneumonia, epidermal necrolysis, erythema nodosum, heart arrest, hepatic failure/necrosis, hyperprolactinemia, hypoglycemia, immune-related hemolytic anemia, kidney failure, neuroleptic malignant syndrome-like events, optic neuritis, pancreatitis, pancytopenia, pulmonary embolism, pulmonary hypertension, QT prolongation, Stevens-Johnson syndrome, sudden unexpected death, suicidal ideation, thrombocytopenia, thrombocytopenic purpura, torsades de pointes-type arrhythmias, urticaria, ventricular tachycardia, or violent behaviors
  Signs of discontinuation symptoms, especially agitation, anxiety, confusion, dizziness, dysphoric mood, emotional lability, fatigue, headache, hypomania, insomnia, irritability, lethargy, malaise, nausea, paresthesias (such as electrical shock sensations), sweating, vaginal bleeding, or vertigo

General Dosing Information

Because of the long elimination half-lives of fluoxetine and norfluoxetine, dosing changes are not reflected in plasma for several weeks. This must be taken into consideration when titrating to a final dose.

Potentially suicidal patients, particularly those who may use alcohol excessively, should not have access to large quantities of this medication since these patients may continue to exhibit suicidal tendencies until significant improvement occurs. Some clinicians recommend that the patient be supplied with the least amount of medication necessary for satisfactory patient management.

Patients should be periodically reassessed to determine the need for continued treatment.

There have been reports of adverse events occurring upon discontinuation of fluoxetine and other SSRIs and SNRIs, especially when discontinuation is abrupt. Patients should be monitored for discontinuation symptoms, regardless of the indication for which fluoxetine was prescribed. If intolerable symptoms occur following a decrease in dose or upon discontinuation of treatment, then resuming the previously prescribed dose may be considered. Subsequently the physician may continue decreasing the dose, but at a more gradual rate. Plasma fluoxetine and norfluoxetine concentration decrease gradually at the conclusion of therapy which may minimize the risk of discontinuation symptoms with this drug.

In a study comparing 20 mg per day and 60 mg per day of fluoxetine to placebo, there was no statistically significant added benefit for the 60 mg per day dose compared with the 20 mg per day dose.

Diet/Nutrition

Fluoxetine may be taken with food to lessen possible stomach upset.

Bioequivalence information

Fluoxetine hydrochloride oral capsules and oral solution are bioequivalent.

For treatment of adverse effects

Akathisia—Fluoxetine dosage reduction, addition of propranolol, or both may lessen or eliminate akathisia.

Discontinuation symptoms—Although tapering fluoxetine when discontinuing therapy generally is not required, patients who experience distressing symptoms upon discontinuation may benefit from reinstitution of fluoxetine followed by a gradual tapering of the dosage.

Serotonin syndrome—Serotonergic medications should be discontinued. Treatment is essentially symptomatic and supportive. The nonspecific serotonergic receptor antagonists cyproheptadine and methysergide have been reported to be of some use in shortening the duration of the syndrome.

Skin rash or hives—Fluoxetine should be discontinued on appearance of skin rash or hives. Treatment with antihistamines and/or steroids may be necessary.

Oral Dosage Forms

Note: Bracketed uses in the *Dosage Forms* section refer to categories of use and/or indications that are not included in U.S. product labeling.

The available dosage forms contain fluoxetine hydrochloride, but dosage and strength are expressed in terms of fluoxetine base.

FLUOXETINE HYDROCHLORIDE CAPSULES USP

Usual adult dose

Antidepressant or
Antiobsessional agent—
  Oral, initially 20 mg (base) a day as a single morning dose. The dose may be increased as needed and tolerated at intervals of four to eight weeks.
  Note: Some clinicians begin fluoxetine therapy with a single morning dose of 5 to 10 mg (base).
  The manufacturer states that, in the treatment of depression or obsessive-compulsive disorder, doses over 20 mg (base) a

day may be taken as a single morning dose or in two divided doses, in the morning and at noon.

For maintenance or continued or extended treatment of depression, a weekly dosing regimen with the 90 mg (base) capsule may be initiated 7 days following the last daily dose of 20 mg. Therapeutic equivalence of the 90-mg capsule given once a week with the 20-mg capsule given daily for delaying time to relapse of depression has not been established. Therefore, a daily dosing regimen should be reconsidered if the results from a weekly dosing regimen are unsatisfactory.

Antibulimic agent—

Oral, the target dose is 60 mg (base) a day as a single morning dose. Patients may need to be titrated up to this dose over several days.

Premenstrual dysphoric disorder[1]—

Initial treatment: Oral, 20 mg per day given continuously (i.e., every day of menstrual cycle) or intermittently (i.e., starting a daily dose 14 days prior to anticipated onset of menstruation through the first full day of menses and repeating with each new cycle).

Maintenance/continuation treatment: Oral, 20 mg per day continuously for periods up to 6 months and 20 mg per day intermittently for periods up to 3 months.

Dosing regimen should be determined based on individual patient characteristics.

[Premature ejaculation][1]—

Oral, initially 20 mg (base) a day as a single morning dose. The dose may be increased as needed and tolerated up to 60 mg a day.

Note: For all indications, patients with hepatic function impairment should receive a lower dosage or less frequent dosing. Also, for elderly patients and patients who have concurrent illness or who are taking multiple medications, a lower dosage or less frequent dosing should be considered. For patients with renal function impairment, dosage adjustments are not routinely required.

Usual adult prescribing limits

For a daily dosing regimen—80 mg (base) a day.

For a weekly dosing regimen—90 mg (base) one day per week

Usual pediatric dose

Safety and efficacy have not been established.

Usual geriatric dose

See *Usual adult dose*.

For post menstrual dysphoria disorder—This diagnosis is not applicable to postmenopausal women.

Note: Dosage for elderly patients is often initiated at 10 mg (base) a day and usually does not exceed 60 mg (base) a day.

Strength(s) usually available

U.S.—

10 mg (base) (Rx) [*Prozac* (FD&C Blue No. 1; gelatin; iron oxide; silicon; starch; titanium dioxide)].

20 mg (base) (Rx) [*Prozac* (FD&C Blue No. 1; gelatin; iron oxide; silicon; starch; titanium dioxide)].

40 mg (base) (Rx) [*Prozac* (FD&C Blue No. 1; FD&C Yellow No.6; gelatin; iron oxide; silicon; starch; titanium dioxide)].

90 mg (base) (Rx) [*Prozac Weekly* (FD&C Blue No. 2; FD&C Yellow No. 10; gelatin; hydroxypropyl methylcellulose; hydroxypropyl methylcellulose acetate succinate; sodium lauryl sulfate; sucrose; sugar spheres; talc; titanium dioxide; triethyl citrate)].

10 mg (base) (Rx) [*Sarafem* (dimethicone; FD& C Blue No. 1; FD &C Red No. 3; FD&C Yellow No. 6; gelatin; sodium lauryl sulfate; starch; titanium dioxide)].

20 mg (base) (Rx) [*Sarafem* (dimethicone; FD&C Blue No. 1; FD&C Red No. 3; FD&C Yellow No. 6; gelatin; sodium lauryl sulfate; starch; titanium dioxide)].

Canada—

10 mg (base) (Rx) [*Prozac* (benzyl alcohol; carboxymethylcellulose sodium; edetate calcium disodium; FD&C Blue No. 1; gelatin; iron oxide black; iron oxide yellow; methylparaben; silicone; sodium lauryl sulfate; sodium propionate; starch; titanium dioxide)].

20 mg (base) (Rx) [*Prozac* (benzyl alcohol; carboxymethylcellulose sodium; edetate calcium disodium; FD&C Blue No. 1; gelatin; iron oxide yellow; methylparaben; silicone; sodium lauryl sulfate; sodium propionate; starch; titanium dioxide)].

Packaging and storage

Store below 40 °C (104 °F), preferably between 15 and 30 °C (59 and 86 °F), unless otherwise specified by manufacturer. Store in a tight, light-resistant container.

Auxiliary labeling

- May cause drowsiness. Be careful when driving or operating machinery. Use caution until you become familiar with its effects
- Avoid alcoholic beverages.
- Tell your doctor about all medications you are taking; prescription and nonprescription

FLUOXETINE HYDROCHLORIDE ORAL SOLUTION

Usual adult dose

See *Fluoxetine Capsules USP*.

Usual adult prescribing limits

See *Fluoxetine Capsules USP*.

Usual pediatric dose

See *Fluoxetine Capsules USP*.

Usual geriatric dose

See *Fluoxetine Capsules USP*.

Strength(s) usually available

U.S.—

20 mg (base) per 5 mL (Rx) [*Prozac* (alcohol 0.23%; benzoic acid; flavoring agent; glycerin; purified water; sucrose)].

Canada—

20 mg (base) per 5 mL (Rx) [*Prozac* (benzoic acid; glycerin; mint flavor; purified water; sucrose)].

Packaging and storage

Store below 40 °C (104 °F), preferably between 15 and 30 °C (59 and 86 °F), in a tight, light-resistant container, unless otherwise specified by manufacturer. Protect from freezing.

Stability

Fluoxetine oral solution has been shown to be stable for up to 8 weeks at temperatures of 5 and 30 °C (41 and 86 °F) when diluted to strengths of 1 mg/mL or 2 mg/mL with deionized water, Simple Syrup British Pharmacopeia, Syrup NF, Aromatic Elixir NF, or grape-cranberry drink.

Auxiliary labeling

- May cause drowsiness. Be careful when driving or operating machinery. Use caution until you become familiar with its effects
- Avoid alcoholic beverages.
- Tell your doctor about all medications you are taking; prescription and nonprescription

Additional information

The oral solution is mint-flavored.

FLUOXETINE HYDROCHLORIDE ORAL TABLETS

Usual adult dose

See *Fluoxetine Capsules USP*.

Usual adult prescribing limits

See *Fluoxetine Capsules USP*.

Usual pediatric dose

See *Fluoxetine Capsules USP*.

Usual geriatric dose

See *Fluoxetine Capsules USP*.

Strength(s) usually available

U.S.—

10 mg (base) (Rx) [*Prozac* (microcrystalline cellulose; magnesium stearate; crospovidone; hydroxypropyl methylcellulose; titanium dioxide; polyethylene glycol; yellow iron oxide; FD&C Blue No. 1 aluminum lake; polysorbate 80)].

Packaging and storage

Store at controlled room temperature, preferably between 15 and 30 °C (59 and 86 °F).

Auxiliary labeling

- May cause drowsiness. Be careful when driving or operating machinery. Use caution until you become familiar with its effects
- Avoid alcoholic beverages.
- Tell your doctor about all medications you are taking; prescription and nonprescription

[1]Not included in Canadian product labeling.

Revised: 02/01/2005

FLUOXYMESTERONE—See *Androgens (Systemic)*

FLUPENTHIXOL—See *Thioxanthenes (Systemic)*

FLUPHENAZINE—See *Phenothiazines (Systemic)*

FLURANDRENOLIDE—See *Corticosteroids (Topical)*

FLURAZEPAM—See *Benzodiazepines (Systemic)*

FLURBIPROFEN—See *Anti-inflammatory Drugs, Nonsteroidal (Ophthalmic), Anti-inflammatory Drugs, Nonsteroidal (Systemic)*

FLUTAMIDE—See *Antiandrogens, Nonsteroidal (Systemic)*

FLUTICASONE—See *Corticosteroids (Nasal), Corticosteroids (Topical)*

FLUTICASONE Inhalation-Local

VA CLASSIFICATION (Primary/Secondary): RE110/RE190

Commonly used brand name(s): *Flovent; Flovent Diskus; Flovent Rotadisk.*

Note: For a listing of dosage forms and brand names by country availability, see *Dosage Forms* section(s).

Category

Anti-inflammatory (inhalation); antiasthmatic.

Indications

Note: Bracketed information in the *Indications* section refers to uses that are not included in the U.S. product labeling.

Accepted

Asthma, chronic (treatment)—Fluticasone is indicated for the maintenance treatment of asthma as prophylactic therapy in adult and pediatric patients 4 years of age and older. It is also indicated for patients requiring oral corticosteroid therapy for asthma. Many of the patients may be able to reduce or eliminate their requirement for oral corticosteroids over time.

[Pulmonary disease, chronic obstructive (treatment)[1]]—Fluticasone is indicated in the treatment of chronic obstructive pulmonary disease (COPD).

Unaccepted

Fluticasone is not indicated in the primary treatment of status asthmaticus or other acute asthma symptoms where intensive measures, such as rapid bronchodilation, are required.

[1]Not included in Canadian product labeling.

Pharmacology/Pharmacokinetics

Physicochemical characteristics

Source—Synthetic.

Molecular weight—Fluticasone propionate: 500.58.

Mechanism of action/Effect

Fluticasone acts as a human glucocorticoid receptor agonist with an affinity for the receptor that is 18 times greater than that of dexamethasone, almost twice that of beclomethasone-17-monopropionate, and over three times that of budesonide.

Studies have demonstrated that the clinical effectiveness of inhaled fluticasone is due to its direct local effect rather than an indirect effect through systemic absorption.

The anti-inflammatory actions of fluticasone may contribute to its efficacy in asthma; however, its precise mechanisms are unknown. Glucocorticoids have been shown to inhibit mast cells, eosinophils, basophils, lymphocytes, macrophages, and neutrophils. Glucocorticoids also inhibit production or secretion of cell mediators such as histamine, leukotrienes, cytokines, and eicosanoids.

Absorption

Inhalation aerosol—Systemic bioavailability averages approximately 30% of the dose delivered from the actuator of fluticasone propionate.

Powder for inhalation—Systemic bioavailability of fluticasone propionate averages about 13.5% of the nominal dose.

Oral—Studies using radiolabeled and nonradiolabeled drug have demonstrated that the systemic bioavailability is less than 1%, primarily due to incomplete absorption and presystemic metabolism in the intestine and liver.

Distribution

The average volume of distribution (Vol_D) is 4.2 liters per kilogram of body weight (L/kg).

Protein binding

Plasma proteins—Very high (91%). Fluticasone is weakly and reversibly bound to erythrocytes. It is not significantly bound to transcortin.

Biotransformation

The total clearance of fluticasone is high, with renal clearance accounting for less than 0.02%. In humans, one circulating metabolite, formed through the cytochrome P450 3A4 pathway, the 17-β carboxylic acid derivative, is detectable; *in vitro* studies using human lung cytosol show that this metabolite has significantly less affinity for the glucocorticoid receptor than does the parent drug.

Half-life

After intravenous administration—7.8 hours.

Onset of action

Improvement following inhalation can occur within 24 hours.

Peak plasma concentration

Inhalation aerosol—Ranges from 0.1 to 1 nanogram per mL following an 880-microgram (mcg) dose.

Powder for inhalation—Ranges from 0.1 to 1 nanogram per mL following a 1000-mcg dose.

Time to peak effect

Maximum benefit may not be achieved for 1 to 2 weeks or longer after starting treatment.

Duration of action

Asthma stability persists for several days after withdrawal of corticosteroids.

Elimination

Fecal, as parent drug and metabolites.

Renal, less than 5% as metabolites.

Precautions to Consider

Carcinogenicity/Tumorigenicity

Fluticasone showed no tumorigenic potential in a 78-week study in mice given oral doses of up to 1000 mcg per kg of body weight (mcg/kg) (approximately 2 and 10 times the maximum recommended daily [MRD] human inhalation dose) on a mcg per square meter of body surface area (mcg/m²) basis in adults and children, respectively, and in a 104-week study in rats given inhalation doses of up to 57 mcg/kg (approximately one fourth the MRD human inhalation dose) in adults and comparable to the MRD human dose in children, on a mcg/m² basis.

Mutagenicity

Fluticasone was not mutagenic at high oral or subcutaneous doses in *in vitro* tests in prokaryotic or eukaryotic cells or in human peripheral lymphocytes or in an *in vivo* mouse micronucleus test. No clastogenic effect was seen in cultured human *in vitro* or mouse assays. Fluticasone did not delay erythroblast division in bone marrow *in vitro*.

Pregnancy/Reproduction

Fertility—No evidence of impairment of fertility was seen in male and female rats given fluticasone subcutaneously in doses of up to 50 mcg/kg (approximately one fourth or one fifth the MRD human inhalation dose of the inhalation aerosol or powder for inhalation, respectively, on a mcg/m² basis). However, prostate weight was significantly reduced at a subcutaneous dose of 50 mcg/kg.

Pregnancy—Adequate and well-controlled studies in humans have not been done. Fluticasone should be used during pregnancy only if the potential benefit justifies the potential risk to the fetus.

Inhalation aerosol—Less than 0.008% of a dose crosses the placenta following oral administration of fluticasone to rats and rabbits in doses of 100 mcg/kg and 300 mcg/kg (approximately one half and three times the MRD human inhalation dose), respectively, on a mcg/m² basis. Studies in mice and rats given fluticasone subcutaneously in doses of 45 mcg/kg and 100 mcg/kg (approximately one tenth and one half the MRD human inhalation) on a mcg/m² basis, respectively, showed fetal toxicity characteristic of potent glucocorticoids, including embryonic growth retardation, omphalocele, cleft palate, and retarded cranial ossification. No teratogenicity was seen in rats at inhalation doses up to 68.7 mcg per kg (less than the maximum recommended daily inhalation dose in adults on a mcg per m^2 basis). In rabbits, fetal weight reduction and cleft palate were observed following subcutaneous doses of 4 mcg/kg (approximately one twenty-fifth of the MRD human inhalation dose) on a mcg/m^2 basis. However, following oral administration of fluticasone to rabbits in doses of 300 mcg/kg (approximately three times the MRD human inhalation dose) on a mcg/m^2 basis, no maternal effects or increased incidence of external, visceral, or skeletal fetal defects were shown.

Powder for inhalation—Studies in mice and rats at subcutaneous doses of 45 and 100 mcg/kg, respectively (approximately one tenth and one third, respectively, the MRD inhalation dose in adults on a mcg/m^2 basis) found fetal toxicity characteristic of potent corticosteroid compounds, including embryonic growth retardation, omphalocele, cleft palate, and retarded cranial ossification. Studies in rabbits at subcutaneous doses of 4 mcg/kg (approximately one thirtieth the MRD inhalation dose in adults on a mcg/m^2 basis) found fetal weight reduction and cleft palate. However, no teratogenic effects were reported at oral doses of up to 300 mcg/kg (approximately twice the MRD inhalation dose in adults on a mcg/m^2 basis); in addition, no fluticasone propionate was detected in the plasma in this study, consistent with the established low bioavailability following oral administration. Fluticasone propionate crosses the placenta following oral administration of 100 mcg/kg to rats or 300 mcg/kg to rabbits (approximately one third and two times, respectively, the MRD inhalation dose in adults on a mcg/m^2 basis).

Experience suggests that rodents are more susceptible to the teratogenic effects of pharmacologic doses of oral glucocorticoids than are humans. Additionally, because production of glucocorticoid increases naturally during pregnancy, most women will require a lower exogenous glucocorticoid dose and many may not need glucocorticoid treatment during pregnancy.

FDA Pregnancy Category C.

Breast-feeding

It is not known whether fluticasone is distributed into human breast milk. However, subcutaneous administration of radiolabeled fluticasone to lactating rats, in doses of approximately one twentieth the maximum human daily inhalation aerosol dose of 10 mcg/kg (approximately one twenty-fifth of the dose of the powder for inhalation) in adults on a mcg/m^2 basis, resulted in measurable radioactivity in milk. Because other corticosteroids are distributed into human breast milk, caution should be exercised when fluticasone propionate inhalation aerosol or powder is administered to nursing women.

Pediatrics

Clinical trials in 1300 children with asthma showed that fluticasone aerosol (200 micrograms per day [mcg/day]) and fluticasone powder for inhalation (100 and 200 mcg/day) are effective in the treatment of childhood asthma.

Safety and efficacy in children younger than 4 years of age have not been established.

Plasma concentrations of fluticasone after an inhaled dose of 100 mcg were higher in children 4 to 11 years of age (median 58.7 picograms per mL) than in adults (median 39.5 picograms per mL).

Orally inhaled corticosteroids, including fluticasone, are valuable and highly effective therapies in the management of asthma in pediatric patients. The Food and Drug Administration (FDA) and its advisory committees consider these products to be safe and effective in children when used according to their labeling guidelines. However, recent controlled clinical studies have shown that inhaled corticosteroids may cause a reduction in growth velocity in pediatric patients. In these studies (over a period of about 1 year), the mean reduction in growth velocity was approximately 1 centimeter (cm) per year (range 0.3 to 1.8 cm). This reduction appears to be related to the dose and the duration of exposure to the inhaled corticosteroid. This effect was observed in the absence of laboratory evidence of hypothalamic-pituitary-adrenal (HPA) axis suppression, which suggests that growth velocity is a more sensitive indicator of systemic corticosteroid exposure in pediatric patients than are some commonly used tests of HPA axis function. The long-term effects of this reduction in growth velocity, including the impact on the final adult height, are unknown. The potential for "catch up" growth following the discontinuation of treatment has not been adequately studied.

In another 52-week study, 325 prepubescent children (4 to 11 years of age; mean age of 8.5 years) were given 50 and 100 mcg twice daily doses of fluticasone propionate inhalation powder. Those given placebo compared with those given 50 mcg and 100 mcg showed mean velocity growth rates of 6.32 cm per year, 6.07 cm per year and 5.66 cm per year, respectively. In children who remained prepubertal, growth rates were 6.10 cm per year in the placebo group, 5.91 cm per year in the 50 mcg group and 5.67 cm per year in the 100 mcg group. The range of expected growth in children 8.5 years of age is: boys—3rd percentile=3.8 cm/year, 50th percentile=5.4 cm/year, and 97th percentile=7.0 cm/year; girls—3rd percentile=4.2 cm/year, 50th percentile=5.7 cm/year, and 97th percentile=7 cm/year. The clinical significance of these growth data is not certain.

The growth of pediatric patients receiving orally inhaled corticosteroids should be monitored routinely, for example, via stadiometry. The potential effects on growth velocity of prolonged treatment with inhaled corticosteroids should be weighed against the clinical benefits obtained and the availability of safe and effective noncorticosteroid treatment alternatives. To minimize the systemic effects of orally inhaled corticosteroids, the dose should be titrated to the lowest effective dose for the patient.

In addition, patients using fluticasone may be more susceptible to infection; therefore, exposure to chickenpox or measles should be avoided.

Geriatrics

Studies performed with the inhalation aerosol in 574 patients and with the powder for inhalation in 173 patients 65 years of age and older have not demonstrated geriatrics-specific problems that would limit the usefulness of fluticasone in the elderly.

Surgical

Surgical—Because of the possibility of systemic absorption of inhaled corticosteroids, postoperative patients treated with these drugs should be observed carefully for evidence of inadequate adrenal response.

Critical/Emergency care

Because of the possibility of systemic absorption of inhaled corticosteroids, patients treated with these drugs should be observed carefully during periods of stress for evidence of inadequate adrenal response.

Drug interactions and/or related problems

The following drug interactions and/or related problems have been selected on the basis of their potential clinical significance (possible mechanism in parentheses where appropriate)—not necessarily inclusive (» = major clinical significance):

Note: Combinations containing any of the following medications, depending on the amount present, may also interact with this medication.

Cytochrome P450 3A4 isoenzyme inhibitors, other
(may cause increased plasma concentrations of fluticasone or reductions in plasma cortisol area under the curve [AUC])

Ketoconazole
(concurrent use with fluticasone propionate powder for inhalation has been reported to lead to increased plasma fluticasone concentrations, decreased plasma cortisol AUC, and no effect on urinary excretion of cortisol; this effect may be related to inhibition, by ketoconazole, of the cytochrome P450 3A4 isoenzyme system, which is involved in metabolism of fluticasone)

» Ritonavir
(may cause significantly increased fluticasone concentration and reduced serum cortisol concentration; postmarketing use reports of concomitant use resulting in systemic corticosteroid effects including Cushing syndrome and adrenal suppression; coadministration not recommended unless potential benefit outweighs potential risk)

Laboratory value alterations

The following have been selected on the basis of their potential clinical significance (possible effect in parentheses where appropriate)—not necessarily inclusive (» = major clinical significance).

With physiology/laboratory test values
Hypothalamic-pituitary-adrenal (HPA) axis function as assessed by short cosyntropin test
(may occasionally be decreased with high doses)

Medical considerations/Contraindications

The medical considerations/contraindications included have been selected on the basis of their potential clinical significance (reasons given in parentheses where appropriate)—not necessarily inclusive (» = major clinical significance).

Except under special circumstances, this medication should not be used when the following medical problems exist:

» Allergy to lactose or milk for fluticasone powder for inhalation

» Herpes simplex, ocular or
» Infections, systemic, bacterial, fungal, parasitic, or viral, untreated
(possible increased risk of severe, uncontrollable infections)

Hypersensitivity to fluticasone or any of the ingredients of the preparation

» Tuberculosis, pulmonary, active or quiescent
(may be exacerbated or reactivated)

Patient monitoring

The following may be especially important in patient monitoring (other tests may be warranted in some patients, depending on condition; » = major clinical significance):

» Growth and development in children and adolescents
(careful monitoring of growth, for example via stadiometry, is recommended periodically during therapy with inhaled corticosteroids)

Side/Adverse Effects

Note: Some clinically important cases of growth suppression have been reported for orally inhaled corticosteroids. See also *Pediatrics* section.

Rarely, systemic corticosteroid effects such as hypercorticism and adrenal suppression may occur, especially with the use of higher doses.

The following side/adverse effects have been selected on the basis of their potential clinical significance (possible signs and symptoms in parentheses where appropriate)—not necessarily inclusive:

Those indicating need for medical attention

Incidence more common—>3%

Oropharyngeal candidiasis (white patches in mouth or throat)

Incidence less common—1–3%

Conjunctivitis (redness or discharge of eye, eyelid, or lining of the eyelid); ***dyspnea*** (shortness of breath); ***gastroenteritis/colitis*** (diarrhea; lower abdominal pain; vomiting); ***nausea; otitis media*** (ear ache; fever); ***pelvic inflammatory disease*** (lower abdominal pain); ***tonsillitis*** (trouble in swallowing; fever; sore throat); ***vaginal candidiasis*** (creamy white vaginal discharge); ***vaginitis/vulvovaginitis*** (increased vaginal discharge; itching; pain on passing urine); ***vomiting***

Incidence rare

Angioedema (large hives); ***bronchospasm, paradoxical or hypersensitivity-induced*** (shortness of breath; tightness in chest; troubled breathing; wheezing); ***cushingoid features*** (bone fractures; diabetes mellitus [increased hunger, thirst, or urination]; excessive facial hair in women; fullness or roundness of face, neck, and trunk; high blood pressure; impotence in males; lack of menstrual periods; muscle wasting; weakness; growth velocity retardation in children or adolescents); ***glaucoma; increased intraocular pressure; or cataracts*** (blindness; blurred vision; eye pain); ***hypersensitivity reaction, immediate or delayed,*** (swelling of face, lips, or eyelids); ***such as skin rash or urticaria*** (hives and rash); ***systemic eosinophilic conditions (e.g., Churg-Strauss syndrome)*** (cardiac complications; neuropathy [numbness and weakness of hands and feet]; vasculitic rash [skin rash]; worsening asthma [shortness of breath, troubled breathing, wheezing])

Incidence not determined—Observed during clinical practice; estimates of frequency can not be determined

Anaphylactic reaction (cough; difficulty swallowing; dizziness; fast heartbeat; hives; itching, puffiness or swelling of the eyelids or around the eyes, face, lips or tongue; shortness of breath; skin rash; tightness in chest; unusual tiredness or weakness; wheezing)—very rare, includes patients with severe milk protein allergy; ***asthma exacerbation*** (cough; difficulty breathing; noisy breathing; shortness of breath; tightness in chest; wheezing); ***chest tightness; facial and oropharyngeal edema*** (swelling of the face, mouth, or throat; tightness in throat; trouble breathing); ***growth velocity reduction in children/adolescents; immediate bronchospasm*** (cough; difficulty breathing; noisy breathing; shortness of breath; tightness in chest; wheezing)

Those indicating need for medical attention only if they continue or are bothersome

Incidence more frequent—> 3%

Bronchitis (cough; shortness of breath); ***dysphonia*** (hoarseness or other voice changes); ***fatigue*** (unusual tiredness); ***influenza*** (fever; general aches and pains; diarrhea; headache; loss of appetite; weakness); ***diarrhea; insomnia*** (trouble in sleeping); ***malaise*** (general feeling of illness); ***nasal problems, such as nasal congestion*** (stuffy nose); ***nasal discharge; rhinitis*** (runny or stuffy nose); ***pain in nasal sinuses; or sinusitis*** (headache); ***nasopharyngitis*** (sore nose or throat); ***upper respiratory infections*** (greenish-yellow mucus; stuffy nose)

Incidence less frequent

Abdominal pain or discomfort (stomach pain or burning); ***dermatitis*** (rash); ***dizziness; dysmenorrhea*** (faintness; nausea; vomiting; irregular or painful menstrual period); ***epistaxis*** (bloody mucus or unexplained nosebleeds); ***eye irritation; giddiness; irritation due to inhalant; joint pain; migraines; mouth irritation; muscle soreness, sprain, or strain; sneezing***

Incidence rare

Aggression; agitation; depression; ecchymoses, or contusions (bruising); ***pruritus*** (itching); ***restlessness; weight gain***

Incidence not determined—Observed during clinical practice; estimates of frequency can not be determined

Aphonia (loss of voice); ***hyperactivity*** (restlessness; trouble sitting still)—very rarely and primarily in children; ***hyperglycemia*** (abdominal pain; blurred vision; dry mouth; fatigue; flushed, dry skin; fruit-like breath odor; increased hunger; increased thirst; increased urination; nausea; sweating; troubled breathing unexplained weight loss; vomiting); ***irritability***—very rarely and primarily in children; ***osteoporosis*** (pain in back, ribs, arms, or legs; decrease in height); ***sore throat; wheezing*** (difficulty in breathing or troubled breathing)

Overdose

Clinical effects of overdose

The following effects have been selected on the basis of their potential clinical significance (possible signs and symptoms in parentheses where appropriate)—not necessarily inclusive:

Chronic

Hypercorticism (e.g. Cushing's syndrome) (bone fractures; diabetes mellitus [increased hunger, thirst, or urination]; excessive facial hair in women; fullness or roundness of face, neck, and trunk; high blood pressure; impotence in males; lack of menstrual periods; muscle wasting; weakness)

Treatment of overdose

The fluticasone dose should be reduced gradually, consistent with accepted procedures for reducing systemic corticosteroids and for management of the patient's asthma symptoms.

Patient Consultation

As an aid to patient consultation, refer to *Advice for the Patient, Fluticasone (Inhalation-Local)*.

In providing consultation, consider emphasizing the following selected information (» = major clinical significance):

Before using this medication

» Conditions affecting use, especially:
Hypersensitivity to fluticasone propionate or any ingredients of the preparation
Breast-feeding—Cautious use in nursing women because other corticosteroids pass into breast milk
Use in children—Chronic use may result in decreased growth velocity; monitoring of growth and development is important; exposure to chickenpox or measles should be avoided
Other medications, especially ritonavir
Other medical problems, especially active or quiescent pulmonary tuberculosis, allergy to lactose or milk when using the powder for inhalation, herpes simplex infection of the eye, or untreated systemic bacterial, fungal, parasitic, or viral infections

Proper use of this medication

» Not using to relieve acute asthma attacks; continuing use of fluticasone even if using other medications for asthma attack
» Importance of not using more than the amount prescribed
» Compliance with therapy by using every day in regularly spaced doses
Rinsing mouth with water after each dose; not swallowing rinse water
» Reading patient instructions carefully; checking frequently with health care professional for proper use of inhaler
» Proper dosing
Missed dose: Using as soon as possible; using any remaining doses for that day at regularly spaced intervals; not doubling doses
» Proper storage

For inhalation aerosol
Testing inhaler before using first time
Proper administration technique
Proper cleaning procedure for inhaler

For powder for inhalation
Proper loading technique for inhaler
Proper administration technique
Proper cleaning procedure for inhaler

Precautions while using this medication

» Checking with physician in the following circumstances:
Periods of unusual stress
A severe asthma attack occurs
Asthma symptoms do not improve or condition worsens
Exposure to chickenpox or measles occurs

Carrying medical identification stating that supplemental systemic corticosteroid therapy may be required in emergency situations, periods of unusual stress, or acute asthma attack

» Caution if any kind of surgery or emergency treatment is required; informing health care professional that inhalation corticosteroid is being used

Side/adverse effects

Signs of potential side effects, especially angioedema, bronchospasm (paradoxical or hypersensitivity-induced), cataracts, conjunctivitis, cushingoid features, dyspnea, gastroenteritis/colitis, glaucoma, hypersensitivity reactions (immediate or delayed), increased intraocular pressure, nausea, oropharyngeal candidiasis, otitis media, pelvic inflammatory disease, systemic eosinophilic conditions, tonsillitis, vaginal candidiasis, vaginitis/vulvovaginitis, vomiting

Signs of potential side effects observed during clinical practice, especially anaphylactic reaction, asthma exacerbation, chest tightness, facial and oropharyngeal edema, growth velocity reduction in children/adolescents, or immediate bronchospasm

General Dosing Information

Pharmacologic doses of fluticasone should be carefully titrated to the minimum effective dose to control asthma symptoms and prevent systemic effects. This is especially important for pediatric patients. See also *Pediatrics* section.

Caution is recommended when patients are transferred from systemic corticosteroids to inhaled fluticasone because deaths due to adrenal insufficiency have occurred in asthmatic patients during and after transfer from systemic corticosteroids to less systemically available inhaled corticosteroids. After withdrawal from systemic corticosteroids, several months are required for recovery of hypothalamic-pituitary-adrenal (HPA) function. Patients who have been maintained on the equivalent of 20 mg or more of prednisone per day may be most susceptible, particularly when their systemic corticosteroids have been almost completely withdrawn. During this period of HPA suppression, patients may exhibit signs and symptoms of adrenal insufficiency when exposed to trauma, surgery, infection (particularly gastroenteritis), or other conditions associated with severe electrolyte loss. In recommended doses, fluticasone by inhalation may control asthma symptoms during these episodes but supplies lower-than-normal physiological amounts of glucocorticoid systemically and does not provide the mineralocorticoid activity necessary for coping with these emergencies. During periods of stress or if a severe asthma attack occurs, patients who have been withdrawn from systemic corticosteroids should be instructed to immediately resume oral corticosteroids in large doses and to contact their physician for further instructions. These patients should also be instructed to carry a warning card indicating that they may need systemic corticosteroids during periods of stress or if a severe asthma attack occurs.

After at least 1 week of fluticasone inhalation therapy, the dose of oral corticosteroid should be tapered slowly. The daily prednisone dose should be reduced no faster than by 2.5 mg per day on a weekly basis. Reduction of the prednisone dose should be done only when lung function, asthma symptoms, and as-needed beta-adrenergic bronchodilator use are better than or comparable to that seen before starting the prednisone dose reduction. Careful monitoring of lung function forced expiratory volume (FEV) or a.m. peak expiratory flow rate (PEFR), beta-adrenergic agonist use, and asthma symptoms is recommended during withdrawal of oral corticosteroids. In addition, patients should be observed for signs and symptoms of adrenal insufficiency, such as fatigue, hypotension, lassitude, nausea, vomiting, or weakness.

Transfer of patients from systemic corticosteroid therapy to fluticasone propionate by inhalation may unmask conditions previously suppressed by the systemic corticosteroid therapy, such as rhinitis, conjunctivitis, eczema, and arthritis. During withdrawal from oral corticosteroids, some patients may experience symptoms of systemically active corticosteroid withdrawal, such as joint and/or muscular pain, lassitude, and depression, despite maintenance or even improvement of respiratory function.

If bronchospasm, with an immediate increase in wheezing, occurs after dosing, it should be treated immediately with a fast-acting inhaled bronchodilator. It is recommended that treatment with inhaled fluticasone be discontinued and alternative therapy instituted.

Patients who are on medications that suppress the immune system are more susceptible to infections; therefore, children or adults using fluticasone who have not had diseases such as chickenpox or measles should avoid exposure. If the patient is exposed to chickenpox, prophylaxis with varicella zoster immune globulin (VZIG) may be indicated. If the patient is exposed to measles, prophylaxis with intramuscular pooled immune globulin (IG) may be indicated. If chickenpox develops, treatment with antiviral agents may be considered.

After asthma stability has been achieved with the initial dose of fluticasone, titration to the lowest effective dose is desirable to reduce the possibility of side effects. For patients who do not respond adequately to the initial dose after 2 weeks, higher doses may provide better asthma control.

If symptoms of hypercorticism or adrenal suppression occur, the dosage of fluticasone should be reduced slowly.

For treatment of adverse effects

Recommended treatment consists of the following:

- Appropriate local or systemic antifungal therapy should be given to treat localized infections of *Candida albicans* while fluticasone therapy is continued. Interruption of fluticasone therapy rarely is required.

Inhalation Dosage Forms

FLUTICASONE PROPIONATE INHALATION AEROSOL

Usual adult and adolescent dose

Asthma, chronic (treatment)—

Previous asthma therapy consisting of bronchodilators alone: Oral inhalation, 88 to 440 mcg two times a day.

Previous asthma therapy including inhaled corticosteroids: Oral inhalation, 88 to 440 mcg two times a day. Initial doses above 88 mcg two times a day may be considered for patients with inadequate asthma control or those who have required inhaled corticosteroids in the higher dosing range for that medication.

Previous asthma therapy including systemic corticosteroids: Oral inhalation, 880 mcg two times a day. After at least one week of therapy, slow reduction of the oral corticosteroid dosage may be considered.

Canadian labeling recommends: Oral inhalation, 100 to 500 mcg two times a day. Patients should be given starting dose of inhaled fluticasone propionate which is appropriate for the severity of their disease, as follows:

Mild asthma: 100 to 250 mcg two times a day.

Moderate asthma: 250 to 500 mcg two times a day.

Severe asthma: 500 mcg two times a day. Very severe asthma such as in patients currently requiring oral corticosteroids may use doses up to 1000 mcg two times a day.

Pulmonary disease, chronic obstructive (treatment)—

Oral inhalation, 500 mcg two times a day.

Usual adult and adolescent prescribing limits

1660 mcg per day for patients previously taking oral corticosteroids.

880 mcg per day for patients previously using inhaled corticosteroids or bronchodilators alone.

Canadian labeling recommends doses up to 2000 mcg per day.

Usual pediatric dose

Asthma, chronic (treatment)—

Children younger than 12 years of age: Safety and efficacy have not been established.

Children 12 years of age and older: See *Usual adult and adolescent dose.*

Canadian labeling recommends:

For children 16 years of age and older: See *Usual adult and adolescent dose.*

For children 4 to 16 years of age: Oral inhalation, 50 to 100 mcg two times a day; the dose should then be adjusted until control is achieved or reduced to the lowest effective dose according to individual response.

For children up to 4 years of age: Safety and efficacy have not been established.

Usual geriatric dose

See *Usual adult and adolescent dose.*

Strength(s) usually available

U.S.—

Note: Each strength is available as a 7.9-gram and a 13-gram canister that provides 60 and 120 metered sprays, respectively.

44 mcg per metered spray (Rx) [*Flovent* (chlorofluorocarbons)].

110 mcg per metered spray (Rx) [*Flovent* (chlorofluorocarbons)].

220 mcg per metered spray (Rx) [*Flovent* (chlorofluorocarbons)].

Canada—

Note: Each strength is available in aluminum canisters that provide either 60 or 120 metered sprays.

25 micrograms per metered spray (Rx) [*Flovent* (chlorofluorocarbons)].

50 micrograms per metered spray (Rx) [*Flovent* (chlorofluorocarbons)].

125 micrograms per metered spray (Rx) [*Flovent* (chlorofluorocarbons)].

250 micrograms per metered spray (Rx) [*Flovent* (chlorofluorocarbons)].

Packaging and storage
Store between 2 and 30 °C (36 and 86 °F). Store canister with nozzle end down. Protect from freezing and direct sunlight.

Auxiliary labeling
• Shake well before using.

Note
Include patient instructions when dispensing.

Demonstrate administration technique.

Additional information
This product contains trichlorofluoromethane and dichlorodifluoromethane, substances that harm public health and the environment by destroying ozone in the upper atmosphere.

FLUTICASONE PROPIONATE POWDER FOR INHALATION

Usual adult and adolescent dose
Asthma, chronic (treatment)—

Previous asthma therapy consisting of bronchodilators alone: Oral inhalation, starting dose of 100 mcg two times a day; up to 500 mcg two times a day.

Previous asthma therapy including inhaled corticosteroids: Oral inhalation, starting dose of 100 to 250 mcg two times a day; up to 500 mcg two times a day. Initial doses above 100 mcg two times a day may be considered for patients with inadequate asthma control or those who have required inhaled corticosteroids in the higher dosing range.

Previous asthma therapy including systemic corticosteroids: Oral inhalation, starting dose of 500 to 1000 mcg two times a day; up to 1000 mcg two times a day. After at least one week of therapy, slow reduction of the oral corticosteroid dosage may be considered.

Canadian labeling recommends: Oral inhalation, 100 to 500 mcg two times a day. Patients should be given starting dose of inhaled fluticasone propionate which is appropriate for the severity of their disease, as follows:

Mild asthma: 100 to 250 mcg two times a day.

Moderate asthma: 250 to 500 mcg two times a day.

Severe asthma: 500 mcg two times a day. Very severe asthma such as in patients currently requiring oral corticosteroids may use doses up to 1000 mcg two times a day.

Usual adult and adolescent prescribing limits
2000 mcg per day for patients previously taking oral corticosteroids.

1000 mcg per day for patients previously using inhaled corticosteroids or bronchodilators alone.

Note: The 2000-mcg-per-day limit recommendation is based on clinical data from a study using fluticasone inhalation aerosol; no dosing-limit studies have been done with the powder for inhalation.

Usual pediatric dose
Asthma, chronic (treatment)—

Children older than 12 years of age: See *Usual adult and adolescent dose*.

Children 4 to 11 years of age:

Previous asthma therapy consisting of bronchodilators alone—Oral inhalation, starting dose of 50 mcg two times a day; up to 100 mcg two times a day.

Previous asthma therapy including inhaled corticosteroids—Oral inhalation, starting dose of 50 mcg two times a day; up to 100 mcg two times a day.

Children younger than 4 years of age: Safety and efficacy have not been established.

Canadian labeling recommends:

For children 16 years of age and older: See *Usual adult and adolescent dose*.

For children 4 to 16 years of age: Oral inhalation, 50 to 100 mcg two times a day; the dose should then be adjusted until control is achieved or reduced to the lowest effective dose according to individual response.

For children up to 4 years of age: Safety and efficacy have not been established.

Usual pediatric prescribing limits
Children 4 to 11 years of age—200 mcg per day.

Usual geriatric dose
See *Usual adult and adolescent dose*.

Strength(s) usually available
U.S.—

Note: This product is supplied with 15 disks and one inhaler device per carton. The disks are in a white plastic tube that is protected from moisture by a foil pouch. Each circular disk comes in a double-foil pack containing four blisters of the medication.

50 mcg per disk (delivering 44 mcg) (Rx) [*Flovent Rotadisk* (lactose)].

100 mcg per disk (delivering 88 mcg) (Rx) [*Flovent Rotadisk* (lactose)].

250 mcg per disk (delivering 220 mcg) (Rx) [*Flovent Rotadisk* (lactose)].

Canada—

Note: The product is supplied with a plastic inhaler device containing a foil strip with 60 blisters.

50 micrograms per blister (Rx) [*Flovent Diskus* (lactose)].

100 micrograms per blister (Rx) [*Flovent Diskus* (lactose)].

250 micrograms per blister (Rx) [*Flovent Diskus* (lactose)].

500 micrograms per blister (Rx) [*Flovent Diskus* (lactose)].

Packaging and storage
Store between 20 and 25 °C (68 and 77 °F). Protect from moisture.

Canadian product should be stored between 2 and 30 °C (36 and 86 °F) in a dry place. Protect from frost and direct sunlight.

Note
Include patient instructions when dispensing.

Demonstrate administration technique.

Revised: 11/15/2005
Developed: 10/16/1996

FLUTICASONE AND SALMETEROL Inhalation–Local

VA CLASSIFICATION (Primary/Secondary): RE 190/RE110/RE120

Commonly used brand name(s): *Advair 125; Advair 250; Advair Diskus*.

Note: For a listing of dosage forms and brand names by country availability, see *Dosage Forms* section(s).

Category
Antiasthmatic; anti–inflammatory (inhalation); bronchodilator.

Indications
Note: Bracketed information in the *Indications* section refers to uses that are not included in the U.S. product labeling.

Accepted
Asthma, chronic (treatment)—The combination of fluticasone and salmeterol is indicated for long term, twice-daily, maintenance treatment of asthma in patients 4 years of age and older.

Pulmonary disease, chronic obstructive (treatment)—The combination of fluticasone and salmeterol is indicated for the twice daily maintenance of treatment of airflow obstruction in patients with COPD associated with chronic bronchitis.

Note: The only approved dosage strength of the powder for inhalation for treatment of COPD associated with chronic bronchitis in the US is 250/50. In Canada the approved dosage strengths of the powder for inhalation for treatment of COPD, including emphysema and chronic bronchitis, is 250/50 or 500/50.

[Asthma, chronic (treatment)]—The combination of fluticasone and salmeterol aerosol for inhalation is indicated for treatment of reversible obstructive airway disease in patients 12 years of age and older.

[Pulmonary disease, chronic obstructive (treatment)]—The combination of fluticasone and salmeterol is indicated for treatment of chronic obstructive pulmonary disease.

Unaccepted
The combination of fluticasone and salmeterol is not indicated for use in the treatment of acute bronchospasm. It is contraindicated for use in the primary treatment of status asthmaticus or other acute episodes where intensive measures are required.

Fluticasone and salmeterol inhalation powder should not be the first medicine prescribed to treat a patient's asthma. It should be used only for patients who have not adequately responded to other asthma medications, such as inhaled corticosteroids. The National Heart, Lung, and Blood Institute (NHLBI) and World Health Organization (WHO) guidelines recommend inhaled corticosteroids as the first step in controller therapy, with long-beta$_2$-agonists (LABA) as an optional add-on therapy if low-to-medium dose inhaled corticosteroids do not adequately control the patient's asthma. Since this combination contains both a LABA and a corticosteroid, FDA, therefore, advises it only be started in asthma patients who have not responded adequately to low to medium dose inhaled corticosteroids without LABAs or in patients with asthma who are already taking both an inhaled corticosteroid and a LABA.

Pharmacology/Pharmacokinetics

Physicochemical characteristics

Molecular weight—
Fluticasone: 500.6.
Salmeterol: 603.8.

Mechanism of action/Effect

Fluticasone acts as a human glucocorticoid receptor agonist with an affinity for the receptor that is 18 times greater than that of dexamethasone, almost twice that of beclomethasone-17-monopropionate, and over three times that of budesonide. The anti-inflammatory actions of fluticasone may contribute to its efficacy in asthma; however, its precise mechanisms are unknown. Corticosteroids have been shown to inhibit mast cells, eosinophils, basophils, lymphocytes, macrophages, and neutrophils. Corticosteroids also inhibit production or secretion of cell mediators such as histamine, leukotrienes, cytokines, and eicosanoids

Salmeterol is a long acting beta-adrenergic agonist. It acts by stimulating $beta_2$-adrenergic receptors in the lungs to relax bronchial smooth muscle, thereby relieving bronchospasm. This action is believed to result from increased production of cyclic adenosine 3,5-monophosphate (cyclic 3,5-AMP; cAMP) and ensuing reduction in intracellular calcium concentration caused by activation of the enzyme adenylate cyclase that catalyzes the conversion of adenosine triphosphate (ATP) to cAMP. Increased cAMP concentrations, in addition to relaxing bronchial smooth muscle, inhibit release of mediators of immediate hypersensitivity from cells, especially from mast cells.

Absorption

Fluticasone—Oral bioavailability is less than 1%, due to incomplete absorption and presystemic metabolism in the intestine and liver. Systemic bioavailability via the DISKUS device averages 18%

Salmeterol—Systemic levels are low or undetectable after inhalation, due to small doses.

Distribution

Volume of distribution (Vol_D)—
Fluticasone: 4.2 L per kg (L/kg)

Protein binding

Fluticasone—Very high (91%)
Salmeterol—Very high (96%)

Biotransformation

Fluticasone—Total clearance is high; average 1093 mL per minute. The primary metabolite is the 17β-carboxylic acid derivative of fluticasone (via cytochrome P450 3A4).

Salmeterol—Metabolized by hydroxylation

Half-life

Elimination—
Fluticasone: 7.8 hours
Salmeterol: 5.5 hours

Time to peak concentration

Fluticasone—1 to 2 hours following administration.
Salmeterol—5 minutes following administration.

Peak plasma concentration

Fluticasone—Ranged from undetectable to 266 pg per mL after a 500 mcg twice daily dose. Mean concentration: 110 pg per mL

Salmeterol—Mean concentrations: 167 pg per mL over 20 minutes following a chronic dosing schedule.

Elimination

Fluticasone—
Renal: Less than 5 %
Fecal: Remainder of dose

Salmeterol—
Renal: 25 %
Fecal: 60 %

Precautions to Consider

Carcinogenicity/Tumorigenicity/Mutagenicity

Fluticasone—

There was no tumorigenic potential in a 78-week study in mice given oral doses of up to 1000 mcg/kg (approximately 4 times the maximum recommended daily [MRD] inhalation dose mcg per m²) and in a 104-week study in rats given inhalation doses of up to 57 mcg/kg (less than the maximum recommended daily [MRD] inhalation dose in adults mcg per m²). Fluticasone was not mutagenic in prokaryotic or eukaryotic cells *in vitro* . No clastogenic effect was seen in cultured human *in vitro* or mouse micronucleus test.

Salmeterol—

An 18-month study in mice showed that salmeterol, administered orally in doses of 1.4 mg/kg and above (20 times the maximum daily inhalation dose in adults based on comparison of area under the plasma concentration-time curves [AUCs]), caused a dose-related increase in the incidences of smooth muscle hyperplasia, cystic glandular hyperplasia, leiomyomas of the uterus, and ovarian cysts. The incidence of leiomyomas were not found to be statistically significant. No tumors were seen at 0.2 mg/ kg (3 times the maximum recommended daily inhalation dose based on the areas under the plasma concentration-time curves)

A 24-month study in rats given salmeterol orally and by inhalation in doses of 0.68 mg/kg and above (approximately 60 times the maximum recommended daily inhalation dose in adults on a mg per m² basis) showed dose-related increases in the incidences of mesovarian leiomyomas and ovarian cysts. No tumors were seen at 0.21 mg/kg (approximately 20 times the maximum recommended daily inhalation dose in adults on a mg per m² basis). Similar results have been reported in rodents with other beta-adrenergic bronchodilators and the relevance of these findings in humans use is unknown. Salmeterol was not mutagenic in *in vitro* tests in microbial or mammalian genes. No clastogenic effect was seen in *in vitro* human lymphocytes or in an *in vivo* rat micronucleus test.

Pregnancy/Reproduction

Fertility—

Fluticasone—

No evidence of impairment of fertility was was seen in studies done on male and female rats at subcutaneous doses up to 50 mcg/kg (less than the maximum recommended daily inhalation dose in adults on a mcg/ m² basis). Prostate weight was significantly reduced at a subcutaneous dose of 50 mcg/kg.

Salmeterol—

No effects on fertility were found in male and female rats treated with salmeterol at oral doses up to 2 mg/kg (approximately 180 times the maximum recommended daily inhalation dose in adults on a mg/ m² basis).

Pregnancy—

Fluticasone and Salmeterol combination—

No evidence of enhanced toxicity was seen in studies done using the combination of fluticasone and salmeterol as compared to the use of the drugs individually. In mice, the combination of 150 mcg/ kg subcutaneously of fluticasone (less than the maximum recommended daily inhalation dose in adults on a mg per m² basis) with 10 mg/kg orally of salmeterol (approximately 450 times the maximum recommended daily inhalation dose in adults on a mg per m² basis) was teratogenic. Cleft palate, fetal death, increased implantation loss and delayed ossification were seen. These observations are characteristic of glucocorticoids. No developmental toxicity was observed at combination doses up to 40 mcg/kg subcutaneously of fluticasone (less than the maximum recommended daily inhalation dose in adults on a mg per m² basis) and up to 1.4 mg/kg orally of salmeterol (approximately 65 times the maximum recommended daily inhalation dose in adults on a mg/ m² basis)

In rats, there was no teratogenicity observed at combination doses up to 30 mcg/kg subcutaneously of fluticasone (less than the maximum recommended daily inhalation dose in adults on a mg per m² basis) and up to 1 mg/ kg of salmeterol (approximately 90 times the MRD inhalation dose in adults on a mcg/ m² basis). Combining 100 mcg/kg subcutaneously of fluticasone (less than the maximum recommended daily inhalation dose in adults on a mg/ m² basis) with 10 mg/ kg orally of salmeterol (approximately 900 times the MRD inhalation dose in adults on a mcg/m² basis) produced maternal toxicity, decreased placental weight, decreased fetal weight, umbilical hernia, delayed ossification, and changes in the occipital bone.

There are no adequate and well controlled studies of the combination of fluticasone and salmeterol in pregnant women. It should be used during pregnancy only when the potential benefit justifies the potential risk to the fetus.

FDA Pregnancy Category C

Fluticasone—

Studies in mice and rats at subcutaneous doses of Fluticasone at 45 and 100 mcg/kg, respectively (less than or equivalent to the MRD inhalation dose in adults on a mcg/m² basis) found fetal toxicity characteristic of potent corticosteroid compounds, including embryonic growth retardation, omphalocele, cleft palate, and retarded cranial ossification. Studies in rabbits at subcutaneous doses of 4 mcg/kg (less than the MRD inhalation dose in adults on a mcg/m² basis) found fetal weight reduction and cleft palate. However, no teratogenic effects were reported at oral doses of up to 300 mcg/kg (approximately 5 times the MRD inhalation dose in adults on a mcg/m² basis); in addition, no fluticasone propionate was detected in the plasma in this study, consistent with the established low bioavailability following oral administration.

Fluticasone propionate crosses the placenta following a subcutaneous dose of 100 mcg /kg to mice (less than the MRD inhalation dose in adults on a mcg/m² basis); subcutaneous or oral administration of 100 mcg/kg to rats (approximately equivalent to the MRD in adults on a mcg/m² basis) or 300 mcg/kg to rabbits (approximately 5 times the MRD inhalation dose in adults on a mcg/m² basis).

Experience suggests that rodents are more susceptible to the teratogenic effects of pharmacologic doses of oral glucocorticoids than are humans. Additionally, because production of glucocorticoid increases naturally during pregnancy, most women will require a lower exogenous glucocorticoid dose and many may not need glucocorticoid treatment during pregnancy.

Pregnancy Category C

Salmeterol—

Rats given oral doses of 2 mg/kg of salmeterol (approximately 180 times the maximum recommended daily inhalation dose (MRD) in adults on a mg/m² basis) experienced no teratogenic effects. In pregnant Dutch rabbits given oral doses of 1 mg per kg and above (approximately 50 times the MRD based on the comparison of the AUCs) toxic effects were shown in the fetus. The developed effects were considered to be characteristic of beta-adrenergic stimulation (i.e., precocious eyelid openings, cleft palate, sternebral fusion, limb and paw flexures, and delayed ossification of the frontal cranial bones). No significant effects occurred at 20 times the recommended human clinical dose based on AUC comparisons. New Zealand white rabbits were less sensitive, and the exposure to oral doses of 10 mg/kg (approximately 1800 times the recommended human clinical dose based on mg/m² basis) produced only delayed ossification of frontal bones.

Salmeterol crossed the placenta following oral administration of 10 mg/kg to mice and rats (approximately 450 and 900 times, respectively, the recommended human clinical dose based on mg/m² basis)

Pregnancy Category C

Labor and delivery—There are no well controlled human studies that have investigated the effects of the combination of fluticasone and salmeterol on pre term labor or labor at term. Because of the potential for beta-agonist interference with uterine contractility, the use of the drug for management of asthma during labor should be restricted to those patients in whom the benefit clearly outweighs the risk.

Breast-feeding

It is not known whether the combination of fluticasone and salmeterol is distributed into breast milk. Caution should be used when administering to nursing women.

Fluticasone—It is not known whether fluticasone is distributed into breast milk, however other corticosteroids have been detected in human milk. After subcutaneous administration of tritiated fluticasone at a 10 mcg per kg dose (less than the maximum recommended daily inhalation dose in adults on a mg per m² basis) to lactating rats resulted in measurable radioactivity in milk.

Salmeterol—It is not known whether salmeterol is distributed into breast milk, however salmeterol xinafoate is distributed in rat's milk.

Pediatrics

The safety and efficacy of fluticasone and salmeterol have not been established in children with asthma under 4 years of age. Recent controlled clinical studies have shown that inhaled corticosteroids may cause a reduction in growth velocity in pediatric patients. This effect was observed in the absence of laboratory evidence of hypothalamic-pituitary-adrenal (HPA) axis suppression, which suggests that growth velocity is a more sensitive indicator of systemic corticosteroid exposure in pediatric patients than are some commonly used tests of HPA axis function.

The long-term effects of this reduction in growth velocity, including the impact on the final adult height, are unknown. The potential for "catch up" growth following the discontinuation of treatment has not been adequately studied. The growth of pediatric patients receiving orally inhaled corticosteroids should be monitored routinely. If the patient appears to have growth suppression, the possibility that they are particularly sensitive to the effects of corticosteroids should be considered. The potential effects on growth velocity of prolonged treatment with inhaled corticosteroids should be weighed against the clinical benefits obtained and the availability of safe and effective noncorticosteroid treatment alternatives. To minimize the systemic effects of orally inhaled corticosteroids, the dose should be titrated to the lowest effective dose for the patient.

Geriatrics

Appropriate studies performed to date have not demonstrated geriatrics-specific problems that would limit the usefulness of fluticasone and salmeterol in the elderly. However, elderly patients are more likely to have age related medical problems such as cardiovascular disease which may require adjustment of dosing and using caution in patients receiving fluticasone and salmeterol.

Drug interactions and/or related problems

The following drug interactions and/or related problems have been selected on the basis of their potential clinical significance (possible mechanism in parentheses where appropriate)—not necessarily inclusive (» = major clinical significance):

Note: Combinations containing any of the following medications, depending on the amount present, may also interact with this medication.

» Antidepressants, tricyclic or
» Monoamine oxidase (MAO) inhibitors
(extreme caution should be used within 2 weeks of discontinuation or if medications are currently being used; salmeterol action on the vascular system may be potentiated by these agents)

» Beta-adrenergic receptor blocking agents, systemic
(caution should be used as may produce severe bronchospasm in asthmatic patients; pulmonary effects of beta-agonists may be blocked by these drugs; cardioselective beta-adrenergic blockers may be a safer alternative)

» $Beta_2$-adrenergic agonist, long-acting such as
Salmeterol, additive
(do not use additional salmeterol or other inhaled long acting $beta_2$-agonist for prevention of exercise-induced bronchospasm)

Diuretics, potassium-depleting or
Diuretics, thiazide
(caution is advised in the coadministration; changes in ECG or hypokalemia can be acutely worsened by these agents)

Ketoconazole or
Cytochrome P450 inhibitors such as
» Ritonavir
(concurrent use of ritonavir and fluticasone and salmeterol combination; may increase fluticasone exposure, resulting in significantly reduced serum cortisol concentration)

Laboratory value alterations

The following have been selected on the basis of their potential clinical significance (possible effect in parentheses where appropriate)—not necessarily inclusive (» = major clinical significance).

With physiology/laboratory test values

Electrocardiogram
(flattening of the T wave, prolongation of the QT_c interval, and ST segment depression have been seen in patients after administration of beta-agonists.)

Glucose
(Blood glucose concentrations may be increased)

Potassium, serum
(beta agonist medications may produce significant hypokalemia in some patients, possibly via intracellular shunting; generally transient and does not require supplementation)

Medical considerations/Contraindications

The medical considerations/contraindications included have been selected on the basis of their potential clinical significance (reasons given in parentheses where appropriate)—not necessarily inclusive (» = major clinical significance).

Except under special circumstances, this medication should not be used when the following medical problem exists:

» Asthma, acutely deteriorating or significantly worsening
(therapy should not be initiated in patients with a history of corticosteroid dependence, frequent hospitalizations, intubation, mechanical ventilation or low pulmonary function as a result of asthma; results could be life threatening)

» Asthma attack, severe or
» Electrolyte loss, severe or
» Infection or
» Psychological stress or
» Surgery or
» Trauma
(the combination of fluticasone and salmeterol should not be used for transferring patients from systemic corticosteroid therapy during periods of stress or severe asthma attack; deaths due to adrenal insufficiency have occurred; supplementary systemic corticosteroids may be needed.)

» Tuberculosis, pulmonary, active or quiescent
(may be exacerbated or reactivated)

» Herpes simplex, ocular, or

» Infections, systemic, bacterial, fungal, parasitic, or viral, untreated (possible increased risk of severe, uncontrolled infections; worsening chickenpox, measles and Candida infections may occur, prophylactic vaccinations or antiviral treatments may be warranted; caution if taking other immunosuppressant therapies)

» Hypersensitivity to fluticasone or salmeterol or any of the ingredients used in their preparation

» Status asthmaticus (use of fluticasone and salmeterol is contraindicated for primary treatment)

Risk-benefit should be considered when the following medical problems exist:

» Cardiac arrhythmias or

» Coronary insufficiency or

» Hypertension (sympathomimetic amines may cause increased blood pressure and heart rate; caution is warranted)

» Diabetes mellitus, preexisting or

» Ketoacidosis (clinically significant changes in blood glucose and/or serum potassium have occurred)

Eosinophilic conditions (caution; use may worsen this condition)

Osteoporosis, patients with major risk factors for, such as:
Advanced age or
Chronic use of drugs that can reduce bone mass (e.g., anticonvulsants and corticosteroids)
Osteoporosis, family history, or
Poor nutrition or
Sendentary lifestyle or
Tobacco use (use of inhalation powder may pose additional risks)

Seizure disorder or
Thyrotoxicosis (sympathomimetic amines may cause worsening of condition; caution is warranted)

Patient monitoring

The following may be especially important in patient monitoring (other tests may be warranted in some patients, depending on condition; » = major clinical significance):

Bone mineral density (BMD) (patients with major risk factors for BMD may be at additional risk with use of fluticasone and salmeterol; if significant reductions in BMD are seen, use of medication to treat or prevent osteoporosis should be strongly considered.)

Eye examination (regular eye examinations, especially for cataracts or glaucoma, should be considered)

» Growth and development in children and adolescents (careful monitoring of growth, for example via stadiometry, is recommended periodically during therapy with inhaled corticosteroids)

Pulmonary function monitoring (objective measures of lung function are essential for diagnosis and for guiding therapeutic decision-making in the treatment of asthma; measurement of forced expiratory airflow, using a spirometer or a peak flowmeter, is recommended at periodic intervals)

Side/Adverse Effects

The following side/adverse effects have been selected on the basis of their potential clinical significance (possible signs and symptoms in parentheses where appropriate)—not necessarily inclusive:

Long-acting $beta_2$-adrenergic agonists, such as salmeterol, have been associated with an increased risk of serious asthma exacerbations and asthma-related death.

Those indicating need for medical attention

Angioedema (large, hive-like swelling on face, eyelids, lips, tongue, throat, hands, legs, feet, sex organs); ***bronchospasm, paradoxical*** (cough; difficulty breathing; noisy breathing; shortness of breath; tightness in chest; wheezing)—may be life threatening; needs immediate treatment; ***cataracts*** (blindness; blurred vision; decreased vision); ***eosinophilia*** (black, tarry stools; chest pain; chills; cough; fever; painful or difficult urination; shortness of breath; sore throat; sores, ulcers, or white spots on lips or in mouth; swollen glands; unusual bleeding or bruising; unusual tiredness or weakness); ***glaucoma*** (blindness; blurred vision; decreased vision; eye pain; headache; nausea or vomiting; tearing); ***hypersensitivity reactions*** (difficulty in breathing or swallowing; fast heartbeat; shortness of breath; skin itching, rash, or redness; swelling of face, throat, or tongue); ***increase in intraocular pressure*** (blurred vision; change in vision; loss of vision); ***neuropathy*** (burning, tingling, numbness or pain in the hands, arms, feet, or legs; sensation of pins and needles; stabbing pain); ***rash; urticaria*** (hives or welts; itching; redness of skin; skin rash); ***vasculitic rash***

Those indicating the need for medical attention only if they continue or are bothersome

Incidence more frequent

Choking; headaches; stridor or laryngeal spasm, irritation or swelling (high-pitched noise when breathing); ***pharyngitis*** (body aches or pain; congestion; cough; dryness or soreness of throat; fever; hoarseness; runny nose; tender, swollen glands in neck; trouble in swallowing; voice changes); ***upper respiratory tract infection*** (cough; fever; sneezing; sore throat); ***upper respiratory inflammation***

Incidence less frequent

Bronchitis (cough producing mucus; difficulty breathing; shortness of breath; tightness in chest; wheezing); ***blood in nasal mucosa*** (bloody nose); ***candidiasis*** (white patches in the mouth or throat or on the tongue); ***chest pain; cough; diarrhea; dysphonia*** (hoarseness; sore throat; voice changes); ***gastrointestinal discomfort and pain; keratitis or conjunctivitis*** (irritation or inflammation of eye); ***muscle pain; nausea; nervousness; palpitations*** (fast, irregular, pounding, or racing heartbeat or pulse); ***rapid heart rate; rhinitis*** (stuffy nose; runny nose; sneezing); ***rhinorrhea*** (runny nose); ***sinusitis*** (pain or tenderness around eyes and cheekbones; fever; stuffy or runny nose; headache; cough; shortness of breath); ***sleep disorders; tremors; viral gastrointestinal infection*** (abdominal or stomach pain; diarrhea; loss of appetite; nausea; weakness); ***viral respiratory infection*** (flu-like symptoms)

Overdose

For more information on the management of overdose or unintentional ingestion, **contact a poison control center** (see *Poison Control Center Listing*).

Clinical effects of overdose

The following effects have been selected on the basis of their potential clinical significance (possible signs and symptoms in parentheses where appropriate)—not necessarily inclusive:

Angina (chest pain or tightness; fast or irregular heartbeat; shortness of breath); ***arrhythmias*** (chest pain or tightness; fast or irregular heartbeat; shortness of breath); ***cardiac arrest; dizziness; dry mouth; fatigue; headaches; hypercorticism*** (darkening of skin; diarrhea; dizziness; fainting; loss of appetite; mental depression; nausea; skin rash; unusual tiredness or weakness; vomiting); ***hyperglycemia*** (blurred vision; dry mouth; fatigue; flushed, dry skin; fruit-like breath odor; increased hunger; increased thirst); ***hypertension*** (high blood pressure); ***hypokalemia*** (convulsions; decreased urine; dry mouth; irregular heartbeat; increased thirst; loss of appetite; mood changes; muscle pain or cramps; nausea or vomiting; numbness or tingling in hands, feet, or lips; shortness of breath; unusual tiredness or weakness); ***hypotension*** (blurred vision; confusion; dizziness, faintness, or light-headedness when getting up from a lying or sitting position; sudden sweating; unusual tiredness or weakness); ***insomnia*** (trouble in sleeping); ***malaise*** (general feeling of discomfort or illness; unusual tiredness or weakness); ***muscle cramps; nervousness; palpitation*** (fast, irregular, pounding, or racing heartbeat or pulse); ***seizures; tachycardia*** (fainting; fast, pounding, or irregular heartbeat or pulse; palpitations); ***tremors***

Treatment of overdose

To decrease absorption—

Discontinue fluticasone and salmeterol and begin appropriate symptomatic therapy. A cardioselective beta-receptor blocker may be considered, but it can produce bronchospasm.

There is insufficient evidence to support the benefit of dialysis for overdosage of salmeterol.

Monitoring—

Cardiac monitoring is recommended.

Supportive care—

Patients in whom intentional overdose is confirmed or suspected should be referred for psychiatric consultation.

Patient Consultation

As an aid to patient consultation, refer to *Advice for the Patient, Fluticasone and Salmeterol (Inhalation-Local).*

In providing consultation, consider emphasizing the following selected information (» = major clinical significance):

Before using this medication

» Conditions affecting use, especially:

Hypersensitivity to fluticasone, salmeterol, or any of the ingredients in the preparation.

Chronic use of fluticasone may result in decreased growth velocity; monitoring of growth and development is important; exposure to chickenpox or measles should be avoided

Elderly patients who have cardiovascular disease may have increased chances of side effects from this medicine.

Other medications, especially tricyclic antidepressants, beta-adrenergic blocking agents, beta$_2$-adrenergic agonist, monoamine oxidase inhibitors, or ritonavir

Other medical conditions, especially asthma, acutely deteriorating or significantly worsening, pulmonary, active, or quiescent tuberculosis, cardiac arrhythmias, coronary insufficiency, diabetes mellitus, electrolyte loss, hypertension, ketoacidosis, ocular herpes simplex, psychological stress, severe asthma attack, surgery, systemic, bacterial, fungal, parasitic, or viral infections, status asthmaticus, or trauma

Proper use of this medication

» Not using to relieve acute asthma attacks

» Having rapid-acting inhaled beta-adrenergic bronchodilator available for symptomatic relief of acute asthma attacks

» Not prescribing fluticasone/salmeterol as the first medication to treat a patient's asthma; only administering if patient has not responded to other asthma-controller medications, such as low-to-medium dose inhaled corticosteroids

» Using only for patients for an additional therapy in patients not adequately controlled on other asthma-controller medications or whose disease severity clearly warrants initiation of treatment with 2 maintenance therapies

» Advising patient to continue taking this medicine or other asthma medications that have been prescribed unless treatment has been discussed with their healthcare provider

» Proper administration technique: reading patient instructions carefully before using

» Compliance with therapy by using everyday in regular spaced doses

Gargling and rinsing mouth with water after each dose; not swallowing rinse water

» Proper dosing

Missed dose: Taking as soon as possible; using any remaining doses for day at regularly spaced intervals; not doubling doses

» Proper storage

Precautions while using this medication

» Importance of contacting your doctor if asthma symptoms do not improve, if there is an increased use of short-acting beta$_2$-agonist inhaler, or a decrease in peak flow patients.

» Importance of checking regular visits to physician to check for usefulness of therapy and to check for side effects from therapy.

» Advising patients that this medicine may increase the chances of a severe asthma episode occurring

Importance of checking with your doctor if you are exposed to chicken pox or measles.

Side/adverse effects

Signs of adverse effects, especially angioedema, paradoxical bronchospasm, cataracts, eosinophilia, glaucoma, hypersensitivity reactions, increase in intraocular pressure, neuropathy rash, urticaria, or vasculitic rash

General Dosing Information

Fluticasone and salmeterol combination should not be used in patients during rapidly deteriorating or potentially life-threatening episodes of asthma.

Patients should be advised to continue using this medicine or other asthma medicines that have been prescribed unless they have discussed with their health care provider whether or not to continue treatment.

Due to a possible increased risk of asthma-related death with the use of salmeterol, physicians should only prescribed fluticasone/salmeterol for asthma patients not adequately controlled on other asthma-controller medications (e.g., low- to medium-dose inhaled corticosteroids) or whose disease severity clearly warrants initiation of treatment with 2 maintenance therapies.

Improvement in asthma control following inhaled administration of fluticasone/salmeterol can occur within 30 minutes. However, maximum benefit may not be achieved for 1 week or longer after starting treatment. Individual patients will experience a variable time to onset and degree of symptom relief.

For patients not responding adequately to the starting dosage following 2 weeks of therapy, replacing the current strength of fluticasone/salmeterol with a higher strength may provide additional improvement in asthma control.

If a fluticasone/salmeterol dose regimen that was previously effective fails to provide adequate improvement in asthma control, the therapeutic regimen should be reevaluated and additional therapeutic options (e.g., replacing the current strength with a higher strength, adding additional inhaled corticosteroid, or initiating oral corticosteroids) should be considered.

Caution is recommended when patients are transferred from systemic corticosteroids to inhaled corticosteroids because deaths due to adrenal insufficiency have occurred in asthmatic patients during and after transfer from systemic corticosteroids to less systemically available inhaled corticosteroids. After withdrawal from systemic corticosteroids, several months are required for recovery of hypothalamic-pituitary-adrenal (HPA) function. Patients who have been maintained on the equivalent of 20 mg or more of prednisone per day may be most susceptible, particularly when their systemic corticosteroids have been almost completely withdrawn. During this period of HPA suppression, patients may exhibit signs and symptoms of adrenal insufficiency when exposed to trauma, surgery, infection (particularly gastroenteritis), or other conditions associated with severe electrolyte loss. Although inhaled corticosteroids may provide control of the asthma symptoms in recommended doses, they supply lower-than-normal physiological amounts of glucocorticoid systemically and does not provide the mineralocorticoid activity necessary for coping with these emergencies. During periods of stress or if a severe asthma attack occurs, patients who have been withdrawn from systemic corticosteroids should be instructed to immediately resume oral corticosteroids in large doses and to contact their physician for further instructions. These patients should also be instructed to carry a warning card indicating that they may need systemic corticosteroids during periods of stress or if a severe asthma attack occurs.

Transfer of patients from systemic corticosteroid therapy to fluticasone and salmeterol combination may unmask conditions previously suppressed by the systemic corticosteroid therapy, such as rhinitis, conjunctivitis, eczema, and arthritis.

If paradoxical bronchospasm occurs after dosing, it should be treated immediately with a short-acting inhaled bronchodilator. It is recommended that treatment with fluticasone and salmeterol combination be discontinued and alternative therapy instituted.

Patients who are on medications that suppress the immune system are more susceptible to infections; therefore, children or adults using fluticasone and salmeterol combination who have not had diseases such as chickenpox or measles should avoid exposure. If the patient is exposed to chickenpox, prophylaxis with varicella zoster immune globulin (VZIG) may be indicated. If the patient is exposed to measles, prophylaxis with intramuscular pooled immune globulin (IG) may be indicated. If chickenpox develops, treatment with antiviral agents may be considered.

Titration to the lowest effective dose is desirable to avoid unnecessary side effects.

A short-acting inhaled beta$_2$-agonist should be prescribed in addition to the fluticasone and salmeterol combination to relieve the acute asthma symptoms that the patient may experience. Fluticasone/salmeterol should not be used to treat acute symptoms.

Patients should be monitored for increased use of short-acting inhaled beta$_2$-agonist, which is an indication of deteriorating asthma.

Patients should be educated to recognize the signs of deteriorating asthma control and the need to seek medical attention promptly if the circumstances occur.

A long-acting inhaled beta$_2$-agonist should not be used in conjunction with the combination of fluticasone and salmeterol.

Salmeterol is not a replacement for inhaled corticosteroids, which should be continued at the same dose and not stopped or reduced, when initiating therapy with salmeterol.

Recommended dosage should not be exceeded.

The fluticasone and salmeterol inhaler should never be used with a spacer, and patients should rinse their mouth out after using inhaler.

The following techniques should be followed when using the DISKUS device: do not exhale into the device, do not take apart or wash the device, use the device in the horizontal position

Patients should not stop taking fluticasone or salmeterol without the guidance of a physician, since symptoms may recur, which may be life threatening.

Inhalation Dosage Forms

Note: Bracketed use in the Dosage Forms section refer to categories of use and/or indications that are not included in U.S. product labeling.

The available dosage forms of this combination contain fluticasone propionate and salmeterol xinafoate, but the dosing and strengths of salmeterol are expressed in terms of the salmeterol base.

FLUTICASONE PROPIONATE AND SALMETEROL INHALATION AEROSOL

Usual adult and adolescent dose

[Antiasthmatic, chronic]—

Oral inhalation, two inhalations (25 mcg salmeterol and 125 or 250 mcg fluticasone propionate) twice daily.

Usual pediatric dose

Antiasthmatic, chronic—

Children up to 12 years of age: Safety and efficacy have not been established.

Usual geriatric dose

See *Usual adult and adolescent dose*

Strength(s) usually available

U.S.—

Not commercially available

Canada—

125 mcg of fluticasone propionate and 25 mcg of salmeterol base (Rx) [*Advair 125* (HFA-134a [1,1,1,2-tetrafluoroethane) propellant)].

250 mcg of fluticasone propionate and 25 mcg of salmeterol base (Rx) [*Advair 250* (HFA-134a [1,1,1,2-tetrafluoroethane) propellant)].

Packaging and storage

Store between 15° and 25°C. Protect from frost and direct sunlight. Contents under pressure. Container may explode if heated. Do not place near any source of heat.

The therapeutic effect of this medication may decrease when the canister is cold.

Auxiliary labeling

- For inhalation only
- You should take this medicine exactly as prescribed. Do not skip or discontinue unless directed.

Note

Include patient instructions when dispensing.

Demonstrate administration technique.

FLUTICASONE PROPIONATE AND SALMETEROL INHALATION POWDER

Usual adult dose

Antiasthmatic, chronic—

For patients not currently on an inhaled corticosteroid and whose disease therapy warrants treatment with two maintenance therapies, including those patients on non-corticosteroid maintenance therapy, recommended starting dose is one inhalation (100 mcg fluticasone and 50 mcg salmeterol or 250 mcg fluticasone and 50 mcg salmeterol) twice daily (morning and evening, approximately 12 hours apart)

The recommended starting dosages for patients 12 years of age and older are based upon patients' current asthma therapy. For patients not adequately controlled on an inhaled corticosteroid, the following table provides the recommended starting dosage:

Current **Daily Dose** of Inhaled Corticosteroid		Recommended Strength and Dosing Schedule of Fluticasone/Salmeterol
Beclamethasone dipropionate HFA inhalation aerosol	≤160 mcg	100/50 twice daily
	320 mcg	250/50 twice daily
	640 mcg	500/50 twice daily
Budesonide inhalation aerosol	≤400 mcg	100/50 twice daily
	800 to 1200 mcg	250/50 twice daily
	1600 mcg	500/50 twice daily
Flunisolide inhalation aerosol	≤1000 mcg	100/50 twice daily
	1250 to 2000 mcg	250/50 twice daily
Flunisolide HFA inhalation aerosol	≤320 mcg	100/50 twice daily
	640 mcg	250/50 twice daily
Fluticasone propionate HFA inhalation aerosol	≤176 mcg	100/50 twice daily
	440 mcg	250/50 twice daily
	660 to 880 mcg	500/50 twice daily
Fluticasone propionate inhalation powder	≤200 mcg	100/50 twice daily
	500 mcg	250/50 twice daily
	1000 mcg	500/50 twice daily
Mometasone furoate inhalation powder	220 mcg	100/50 twice daily
	440 mcg	250/50 twice daily
	880 mcg	500/50 twice daily
Triamcinolone acetonide inhalation aerosol	≤1000 mcg	100/50 twice daily
	1100 to 1600 mcg	250/50 twice daily

Note: Fluticasone/salmeterol should not be used for transferring patients from systemic corticosteroid therapy.

Note: For patients on an inhaled corticosteroid: Dosing is variable, depending on the inhaled corticosteroid that the patient is receiving. See package insert for details. Dosing ranges from 100 mg of fluticasone and 50 mg of salmeterol twice daily to 500 mg of fluticasone and 50 mg of salmeterol twice daily.

Pulmonary disease, chronic obstructive (treatment)—

250 mcg fluticasone and 50 mcg salmeterol twice daily.

Note: In Canada the 500/50 is also indicated for treatment of COPD

Usual adult prescribing limits

Administration of more than twice a day, or a higher number of inhalations (more than 1 inhalation twice a day) of the prescribed strength is not recommended. Maximum dose should not exceed 500 mcg fluticasone and 50 mcg salmeterol twice daily.

Usual pediatric dose

Antiasthmatic chronic—

Children 12 years of age and older: See *Usual adult dose*.

Children 4 to 11 years of age: One inhalation of 100 mcg fluticasone and 50 mcg of salmeterol twice daily (morning and evening, approximately 12 hours apart).

Children up to 4 years of age: Safety and efficacy have not been established.

Usual geriatric dose

See *Usual adult dose*

Strength(s) usually available

U.S.—

100 mcg of fluticasone propionate and 50 mcg of salmeterol base (Rx) [*Advair Diskus* (lactose)].

250 mcg of fluticasone propionate and 50 mcg of salmeterol base (Rx) [*Advair Diskus* (lactose)].

500 mcg of fluticasone propionate and 50 mcg of salmeterol base. (Rx) [*Advair Diskus* (lactose)].

Canada—

100 mcg of fluticasone propionate and 50 mcg of salmeterol base (Rx) [*Advair Diskus* (lactose)].

250 mcg of fluticasone propionate and 50 mcg of salmeterol base (Rx) [*Advair Diskus* (lactose)].

500 mcg of fluticasone propionate and 50 mcg of salmeterol base (Rx) [*Advair Diskus* (lactose)].

Packaging and storage

Store at 20° to 25°C (68° to 77°F). Store in a dry place away from direct heat or sunlight.

Stability

Device should be discarded 1 month after removal from the moisture protective foil overwrap pouch, or after every blister has been used, whichever comes first.

Auxiliary labeling

- Keep out of reach of children

Note

Include patient instructions when dispensing.

Demonstrate administration technique.

Revised: 04/05/2006
Developed: 12/4/2000

FLUVASTATIN—See *HMG-CoA Reductase Inhibitors (Systemic)*

FLUVOXAMINE Systemic

VA CLASSIFICATION (Primary/Secondary): CN900/CN603

Commonly used brand name(s): *Luvox*.

Note: For a listing of dosage forms and brand names by country availability, see *Dosage Forms* section(s).

Category

Antiobsessional agent; antidepressant.

Indications

Note: Bracketed information in the *Indications* section refers to uses that are not included in U.S. product labeling.

Accepted

Obsessive-compulsive disorder (treatment)—Fluvoxamine is used to relieve symptoms of obsessive-compulsive disorder (OCD) in children[1] and adults. The effectiveness of using fluvoxamine for longer than 10 weeks has not been evaluated in placebo-controlled trials.

[Depressive disorder, major (treatment)]—Fluvoxamine is used to relieve symptoms of depressive illness. The effectiveness of using fluvoxamine for longer than 10 weeks has not been evaluated in placebo-controlled trials. However, treatment of acute depressive episodes typically requires 6 to 12 months of antidepressant therapy. Patients with recurrent or chronic depression may require long-term treatment.

---

[1]Not included in Canadian product labeling.

Pharmacology/Pharmacokinetics

Physicochemical characteristics

Chemical Group—2-aminoethyl oxime ethers of aralkylketones. Fluvoxamine is chemically unrelated to other selective serotonin reuptake inhibitors (SSRIs) or clomipramine.

Molecular weight—
Fluvoxamine base: 318.3.
Fluvoxamine maleate: 434.41.

Solubility—Fluvoxamine maleate is sparingly soluble in water and freely soluble in ethanol.

Mechanism of action/Effect

The mechanism of action of fluvoxamine as an antiobsessional agent and as an antidepressant is presumed to be linked to its specific serotonin (5-hydroxytryptamine [5-HT]) reuptake inhibition in brain neurons. Fluvoxamine potently and specifically inhibits presynaptic neuronal reuptake of 5-HT by blocking the membrane pump mechanism for neuronal 5-HT reuptake, thereby facilitating serotonergic transmission and decreasing 5-HT turnover. Noradrenergic and dopaminergic functioning is generally unaffected by fluvoxamine. *In vitro* studies have shown fluvoxamine to possess no significant affinity for histaminergic, alpha-adrenergic, beta-adrenergic, muscarinic, dopaminergic, 5-HT_1, or 5-HT_2 receptors.

Other actions/effects

Fluvoxamine inhibits serotonin (5-HT) uptake by platelets as well as by neurons.

Fluvoxamine is a potent inhibitor of cytochrome P450 1A2 (CYP1A2). *In vitro* studies have also shown fluvoxamine to inhibit CYP3A4 and CYP2C9, and to weakly inhibit CYP2D6.

Absorption

Fluvoxamine is well absorbed, but bioavailability is about 50%, probably due to first-pass metabolism. Absorption is nonlinear over a dosage range of 100 to 300 mg per day, and higher doses of fluvoxamine lead to higher plasma concentrations than predicted by lower dose kinetics. Food does not significantly affect oral bioavailability.

Distribution

The mean apparent volume of distribution for fluvoxamine is approximately 25 liters per kg of body weight (L/kg), reflecting the lipophilic nature of fluvoxamine and suggesting extensive tissue distribution. Fluvoxamine is distributed into breast milk.

Protein binding

High (approximately 77%), primarily to albumin.

Biotransformation

Fluvoxamine is extensively metabolized in the liver, primarily by oxidative demethylation and oxidative deamination. The specific cytochrome P450 isoenzymes involved in fluvoxamine metabolism have yet to be completely identified. However, a study comparing fluvoxamine kinetics in poor and extensive metabolizers of CYP2D6 substrates indicates that the CYP2D6 isoenzyme is involved in fluvoxamine metabolism. Nine metabolites have been identified, none of which shows significant pharmacologic activity.

Half-life

Elimination—
15 to 20 hours; may be slightly increased after multiple dosing.

Onset of action

Antiobsessional agent—3 to 10 weeks.
Antidepressant—2 to 3 weeks.

Time to peak concentration

About 3 to 8 hours with a single dose or at steady-state.

Time to steady-state concentration

Steady-state plasma concentrations of fluvoxamine are attained in about 10 days of multiple dosing.

Steady-state plasma concentrations

At steady state, fluvoxamine demonstrates nonlinear pharmacokinetics over a dosage range of 50 to 150 mg twice a day, and plasma concentrations after multiple dosing are greater than those predicted by single-dose kinetics. In 30 healthy volunteers, maximum steady-state plasma fluvoxamine maleate concentrations reached 88, 283, and 546 nanograms/mL (0.203, 0.651, and 1.26 micromoles/L) following dosing regimens of 100, 200, and 300 mg per day, respectively. A correlation between plasma fluvoxamine concentration and efficacy has not been demonstrated.

In one kinetics study, mean maximum plasma concentrations were 40% higher in elderly patients (66 to 73 years of age) than in younger subjects (19 to 35 years of age).

Elimination

Renal; 94% within 71 hours following a single oral dose of 5 mg of fluvoxamine maleate, about 3% as unchanged drug. A comparison of mean minimum plasma concentrations at 4 and 6 weeks of treatment in 13 patients with renal function impairment (creatinine clearance of 5 to 45 mL per minute) receiving 50 mg of fluvoxamine two times per day showed comparable values, indicating no accumulation of medication.

Precautions to Consider

Carcinogenicity/Mutagenicity

There was no evidence of carcinogenicity or mutagenicity in animal or *in vitro* studies with fluvoxamine.

Pregnancy/Reproduction

Fertility—Fertility studies in male and female rats that received up to two times the maximum recommended human dose (MRHD) of fluvoxamine on a mg per square meter of body surface area (mg/m^2) basis showed no effect on mating performance, duration of gestation, or pregnancy rate.

Pregnancy—Adequate and well-controlled studies have not been done in humans. Fluvoxamine should be used during pregnancy only if the potential benefit justifies the potential risk to the fetus.

In teratology studies conducted in rats and rabbits receiving daily oral fluvoxamine doses approximately two times the MRHD on a mg/m^2 basis, no fetal malformations were seen. In other reproductive studies in which pregnant rats were dosed through weaning, there was an increase in pup mortality at birth at doses greater than or equal to two times the MRHD on a mg/m^2 basis, and decreases in postnatal pup survival at all doses tested (0.1 through 4 times the MRHD on a mg/m^2 basis). While the results of a cross-fostering study implied that at least some of these results probably occurred secondarily to maternal toxicity, a direct drug effect on the fetuses or pups could not be ruled out.

FDA Pregnancy Category C.

Labor and delivery—The effect of fluvoxamine on labor and delivery in humans is unknown.

Breast-feeding

Fluvoxamine is distributed into breast milk, but does not appear to accumulate in breast milk. In one woman receiving fluvoxamine at a dosage of 100 mg two times a day, plasma and breast milk fluvoxamine base concentrations were 0.31 mg per L (mg/L; 0.97 micromole/L) and 0.09 mg/L (0.28 micromole/L), respectively, 4.75 hours after a 100-mg dose. The decision of whether to discontinue nursing or to discontinue the drug should take into account the potential for serious adverse effects from exposure to fluvoxamine in the nursing infant as well as the potential benefits of fluvoxamine maleate tablet therapy to the mother.

Pediatrics

Appropriate studies performed to date have not demonstrated pediatrics-specific problems that would limit the usefulness of fluvoxamine in children.

Because decreased appetite and weight loss are associated with fluvoxamine use, monitoring of weight and growth parameters is recommended in children receiving long-term treatment with fluvoxamine.

Antidepressants increase the risk of suicidal thinking and behavior (suicidality) in children and adolescents with major depressive disorder (MDD) and other psychiatric disorders. Anyone considering the use of fluvoxamine or any other antidepressant in a child or adolescent must balance this risk with the clinical need.

Pooled analyses of short-term placebo controlled trials of nine antidepressant drugs in children and adolescents with MDD, obsessive compulsive disorder, or other psychiatric disorders have revealed a greater risk of adverse events representing suicidality during the first few months of treatment in those receiving antidepressants.

Note: Although fluvoxamine data was reviewed with the other antidepressant drugs data, it should be noted that it is not approved as an antidepressant in the United States.

Geriatrics

No differences in safety or efficacy were seen between elderly and younger subjects in studies that included geriatric patients. However, fluvoxamine clearance is reduced by about 50% in elderly patients, and elderly patients may be less tolerant of adverse effects. A reduced initial fluvoxamine dosage and slower dosage titration may be appropriate in elderly patients.

Pharmacogenetics

About 2 to 10% of the adult population are poor metabolizers of CYP2D6 substrates. A study comparing fluvoxamine single-dose kinetics in poor and extensive metabolizers found the mean maximum plasma concentration, the area under the plasma concentration-time curve (AUC), and the elimination half-life of fluvoxamine to be 52%, 200%, and 62% higher, respectively, in the poor metabolizers. This indicates that fluvoxamine is metabolized, at least in part, by the CYP2D6 isoenzyme.

Drug interactions and/or related problems

The following drug interactions and/or related problems have been selected on the basis of their potential clinical significance (possible mechanism in parentheses where appropriate)—not necessarily inclusive (» = major clinical significance):

Note: Fluvoxamine is a potent inhibitor of cytochrome P450 1A2 (CYP1A2). *In vitro* studies have also shown fluvoxamine to inhibit CYP3A4 and CYP2C9, and to weakly inhibit CYP2D6. Interactions with medications other than those listed below that are metabolized by these enzymes, particularly medications having a narrow therapeutic window such as phenytoin, should be considered. If fluvoxamine is coadministered with a drug that is eliminated via oxidative metabolism and that has a narrow therapeutic window, plasma concentrations and/or pharmacodynamic effects of the latter drug should be monitored closely.

CYP2D6 appears to be involved in fluvoxamine metabolism. Therefore, interactions with medications that inhibit this isoenzyme, such as quinidine, should also be considered.

Combinations containing any of the following medications, depending on the amount present, may also interact with this medication.

Alcohol
(although studies indicate that there is no significant pharmacokinetic or pharmacodynamic interaction between fluvoxamine and alcohol, concomitant use is not recommended)

» Alosetron
(fluvoxamine has been shown to increase mean alosetron plasma concentrations approximately 6-fold and prolonged the half-life by approximately 3-fold; therefore, coadministration is **contraindicated**)

» Antidepressants, tricyclic (TCAs)
(coadministration of fluvoxamine with amitriptyline, clomipramine, or imipramine has resulted in significantly increased plasma concentrations of the TCAs; a reduced TCA dosage and monitoring of TCA plasma concentrations should be considered)

Antipsychotics of the butyrophenone type, including haloperidol
(concurrent administration has resulted in significantly increased serum concentrations of the antipsychotic or of two- to tenfold increases in fluvoxamine serum concentration)

» Astemizole or
» Cisapride or
» Terfenadine
(astemizole, cisapride, and terfenadine are metabolized via the cytochrome P450 3A4 [CYP3A4] isoenzyme; *in vitro* studies show that fluvoxamine is an inhibitor of this isoenzyme and, therefore, could block metabolism of these agents; other agents that block metabolism of astemizole, cisapride, or terfenadine via this isoenzyme have caused increased concentrations of these drugs, resulting in potentially fatal QT prolongation and *torsades de pointes*; coadministration of astemizole, cisapride, or terfenadine with fluvoxamine is **contraindicated**)

» Benzodiazepines that are metabolized by hepatic oxidation, such as
Alprazolam or
Bromazepam or
Diazepam or
Midazolam or
Triazolam
(fluvoxamine is likely to reduce the clearance of these benzodiazepines; concurrent use has been shown to reduce the clearance of alprazolam, bromazepam, diazepam, and the active metabolite of diazepam, *N*-desmethyldiazepam, by 50% or more, and to impair psychomotor performance and memory; when alprazolam is to be used with fluvoxamine, the initial alprazolam dosage should be reduced by at least 50%; it is recommended that diazepam not be used concurrently with fluvoxamine because of the probability of accumulation of diazepam and its active metabolite; benzodiazepines such as lorazepam, oxazepam, and temazepam, which are metabolized by glucuronidation, are unlikely to be affected by fluvoxamine)

» Beta-adrenergic blocking agents that are metabolized hepatically, such as
Metoprolol or
Propranolol
(coadministration of fluvoxamine with propranolol in healthy volunteers resulted in mean minimum propranolol plasma concentrations increasing fivefold; potentiation of propranolol-induced heart rate reduction and exercise diastolic pressure reduction were seen in this study; similarly, cases of bradycardia, hypotension, and orthostatic hypotension have been reported with the coadministration of fluvoxamine with metoprolol; if concurrent use is undertaken, reductions in initial beta-blocking agent dosage and cautious titration are recommended; the beta-adrenergic blocking agent atenolol undergoes minimal hepatic metabolism and effects on atenolol plasma concentrations have not been reported)

Caffeine or
» Theophylline
(clearance of caffeine and theophylline are decreased, probably due to inhibition of cytochrome P450 1A2 [CYP1A2] by fluvoxamine; symptoms of theophylline toxicity, including arrhythmias, headache, tiredness, tremor, or vomiting have been reported with concurrent use of theophylline and fluvoxamine; if theophylline is coadministered with fluvoxamine, the theophylline dosage should be reduced to one third of the usual daily maintenance dosage, and theophylline plasma concentrations should be monitored)

Carbamazepine
(elevated carbamazepine plasma concentrations and symptoms of toxicity have been reported following coadministration with fluvoxamine, although one small study found no change in plasma concentrations of carbamazepine or its active metabolite, carbamazepine-10,11-epoxide)

» Clozapine
(coadministration of clozapine with fluvoxamine has resulted in threefold and greater elevations of serum concentrations of clozapine and clinical symptoms of toxicity; patients receiving the combination should be closely monitored)

Diltiazem
(concurrent administration of diltiazem with fluvoxamine has resulted in bradycardia)

Methadone
(significantly increased methadone plasma concentration-to-dose ratios have been reported when fluvoxamine was added to the regimens of patients on methadone maintenance; symptoms of opioid intoxication were reported in one patient; one case of opioid withdrawal symptoms was reported when fluvoxamine was discontinued; fluvoxamine treatment should be initiated and discontinued with caution in patients receiving methadone)

» Monoamine oxidase (MAO) inhibitors, including furazolidone, procarbazine, and selegiline
(serious and sometimes fatal reactions have occurred in patients receiving another serotonin reuptake inhibitor with an MAO inhibitor; reactions have included hyperthermia, rigidity, myoclonus, autonomic instability with rapid fluctuation of vital signs, and mental status changes including extreme agitation progressing to delirium and coma; some cases presented with features resembling neuroleptic malignant syndrome [NMS]; concurrent use of an MAO inhibitor and fluvoxamine is **contraindicated**; at least 14 days should elapse between the discontinuation of one medication and the initiation of the other)

» Serotonergics or other medications or substances with serotonergic activity (see *Appendix II*)
(increased risk of developing the serotonin syndrome, a rare but potentially fatal hyperserotonergic state which may occur in patients receiving serotonergic medications such as fluvoxamine, usually in combination; symptoms typically occur shortly [hours to days] after the addition of a serotonergic agent to a regimen that includes other serotonin-enhancing drugs or after an increase in dosage of a serotonergic agent; symptoms include agitation, dia-

phoresis, diarrhea, fever, hyperreflexia, incoordination, mental status changes [confusion, hypomania], myoclonus, shivering, or tremor)

(concurrent use of lithium and fluvoxamine has resulted in seizures as well as a case resembling the serotonin syndrome, which included hyperreflexia, tremor, and decreased coordination; the combination of these agents should be administered with caution)

(severe vomiting has been reported with the combined use of tryptophan and fluvoxamine)

Smoking tobacco

(bioavailability of fluvoxamine is significantly decreased in smokers as compared with nonsmokers, possibly due to induction of metabolism of fluvoxamine)

» Tizanidine

(study of effects of fluvoxamine on tizanidine showed increased C_{max}, elimination half-life, and AUC; blood pressure and heart rate were decreased; drowsiness was significantly increased and performance on a psychomotor task was significantly impaired; concomitant use is **contraindicated**)

» Warfarin

(fluvoxamine administered concomitantly with warfarin for 2 weeks resulted in warfarin plasma concentration increases of up to 98% and prolonged prothrombin times; patients receiving both medications should have their prothrombin times monitored and anticoagulant doses adjusted accordingly)

Medical considerations/Contraindications

The medical considerations/contraindications included have been selected on the basis of their potential clinical significance (reasons given in parentheses where appropriate)—not necessarily inclusive (» = major clinical significance).

Risk-benefit should be considered when the following medical problems exist:

Drug abuse or dependence, or history of

(patients with a history of drug abuse should be observed closely for signs of misuse or abuse, as with any new central nervous system [CNS] agent)

» Hepatic function impairment

(fluvoxamine elimination half-life is increased; initial fluvoxamine dosage should be reduced, and titration should proceed slowly; an increased dosing interval may be considered)

Mania or hypomania, history of

(condition may be re-activated)

Neurological impairment, including developmental delay or

» Seizure disorders, history of

(risk of seizures may be increased; if seizures occur, fluvoxamine should be discontinued)

Sensitivity to fluvoxamine maleate

Patient monitoring

The following may be especially important in patient monitoring (other tests may be warranted in some patients, depending on condition; » = major clinical significance):

Careful supervision of depressed patients including those with:

Abnormal behaviors (i.e., agitation, panic attacks, hostility) or

Clinical worsening of their depression or

Suicidal ideation and behavior (suicidality)

(recommended especially during early treatment phase before peak effectiveness of fluvoxamine is achieved or at the time of increases or decreases in dose; prescribing the smallest number of tablets necessary for good patient management is recommended to decrease the risk of overdose; consideration should be given to changing the therapeutic regimen, including possibly discontinuing the medicine, in patients whose depression is persistently worse or whose emergent suicidality or other symptoms are severe, abrupt in onset, or were not part of the patient's presenting symptoms)

Monitoring of growth parameters and weight in children

(recommended during long-term treatment because of anorexia and weight loss associated with fluvoxamine use)

Side/Adverse Effects

The following side/adverse effects have been selected on the basis of their potential clinical significance (possible signs and symptoms in parentheses where appropriate)—not necessarily inclusive:

Those indicating need for medical attention

Incidence more frequent

Sexual dysfunction, including abnormal ejaculation; anorgasmia; decreased libido; delayed orgasm; or impotence (change in sexual performance or desire)

Incidence less frequent

Behavior, mood, or mental changes, including agitation; anxiety; apathy; confusion; disinhibition; hallucinations (rare); malaise; mania or hypomania; nervousness; panic attack (rare); or psychotic reaction; dyspnea (trouble in breathing); ***myoclonus*** (twitching); ***urinary retention*** (trouble in urinating)

Incidence rare

Abnormal bleeding (nose bleed; unusual bruising); ***blurred vision; extrapyramidal effects, including akinesia or hypokinesia*** (absence of or decrease in body movements); ***ataxia*** (clumsiness or unsteadiness); ***dyskinesia*** (unusual or incomplete body movements); ***or dystonia*** (unusual or sudden body or facial movements; inability to move eyes); ***hyperkinesia*** (increase in body movements); ***menstrual changes; seizures; serotonin syndrome*** (agitation; confusion; diarrhea; fever; overactive reflexes; poor coordination; restlessness; shivering; sweating; talking or acting with excitement you cannot control; trembling or shaking; twitching)—usually following an increase in dosage; ***skin rash; syndrome of inappropriate antidiuretic hormone (SIADH)*** (difficult urination; irritability; muscle twitching; weakness); ***toxic epidermal necrolysis*** (redness, tenderness, itching, burning or peeling of skin; red or irritated eyes; sore throat, fever, and chills); ***unusual lactation*** (unusual secretion of milk)—in females

Note: Cardiac arrhythmias, coma, disseminated intravascular coagulation, hyper- or hypotension, renal failure, respiratory failure, seizures, and severe hyperthermia have been reported effects of the *serotonin syndrome*.

Those indicating need for medical attention only if they continue or are bothersome

Incidence more frequent

Asthenia or fatigue (unusual tiredness or weakness); ***constipation; dizziness; drowsiness; headache; insomnia*** (trouble in sleeping); ***nausea; vomiting***

Incidence less frequent

Abdominal pain; anorexia (decreased appetite); ***diarrhea; dryness of mouth; dyspepsia*** (heartburn); ***increased sweating; palpitation*** (feeling of fast or irregular heartbeat); ***tachycardia*** (fast heartbeat); ***taste perversion*** (change in sense of taste); ***tremor*** (trembling or shaking); ***unusual weight gain or loss; urinary frequency; vertigo*** (feeling of constant movement of self or surroundings)

Incidence rare

Abnormal dreaming; flatulence (gas); ***polydypsia*** (increased thirst); ***yawning***

Those indicating the need for medical attention if they occur after medication is discontinued

Confusion; decreased energy; dizziness; headache; irritability; nausea; problems with memory; weakness

Note: Discontinuation symptoms usually start 24 to 72 hours after discontinuing fluvoxamine, and continue for 7 to 14 days.

Overdose

For specific information on the agents used in the management of fluvoxamine overdose, see *Charcoal, Activated (Oral-Local)* monograph.

For more information on the management of overdose or unintentional ingestion, **contact a Poison Control Center** (see *Poison Control Center Listing*).

Clinical effects of overdose

Note: Overdose with fluvoxamine alone has resulted in death. However, patients have recovered completely from overdoses of 9000 to 10,000 mg.

The clinical effects of fluvoxamine overdose may be similar to side effects seen at therapeutic doses, but may be more severe or several may occur together.

The following effects have been selected on the basis of their potential clinical significance (possible signs and symptoms in parentheses where appropriate)—not necessarily inclusive:

Acute

Most commonly observed effects

Diarrhea; dizziness; drowsiness; nausea; vomiting

Other notable signs and symptoms

Bradycardia (slow heartbeat); ***coma; dryness of mouth; electrocardiogram (ECG) abnormalities; hypotension;*** (low blood pressure) ***liver function abnormalities; mydriasis*** (large pupils); ***myoclonus*** (twitching); ***seizures; tachycardia*** (fast heartbeat); ***tremor*** (trembling or shaking); ***urinary retention*** (trouble in urinating)

Symptoms that may be secondary to vomiting or loss of consciousness

Aspiration pneumonitis; hypokalemia; respiratory difficulties

Treatment of overdose

There is no specific antidote for fluvoxamine. Treatment is essentially symptomatic and supportive.

To decrease absorption—The stomach should be emptied as soon as possible by emesis or gastric lavage. The administration of activated charcoal may be useful up to 24 hours post-ingestion, since absorption may be delayed in overdose.

Monitoring—Electrocardiogram (ECG) and vital signs monitoring is necessary. Because of prolonged absorption, monitoring should be continued for at least 48 hours.

Supportive care—Adequate airway, oxygenation, and ventilation must be maintained. Patients in whom intentional overdose is confirmed or suspected should be referred for psychiatric consultation.

Note: Dialysis and forced diuresis are not likely to be of benefit because of the large volume of distribution of fluvoxamine.

In managing overdose, the possibility of multiple drug involvement should be considered.

Patient Consultation

As an aid to patient consultation, refer to *Advice for the Patient, Fluvoxamine (Systemic)*.

In providing consultation, consider emphasizing the following selected information (» = major clinical significance):

Before using this medication

» Conditions affecting use, especially:
- Hypersensitivity to fluvoxamine maleate
- Pregnancy—Risk/benefit considerations
- Breast-feeding—Fluvoxamine is distributed into breast milk; risk and benefits should be considered
- Use in children—Growth and weight monitoring is recommended during long-term treatment.
- Because of Food and Drug Administration [FDA] reports of the occurrence of suicidality in clinical trials for various antidepressant drugs in pediatric patients with major depressive disorder [MDD], fluvoxamine must be used with caution in treating pediatric patients for MDD.
- Use in the elderly—Clearance is reduced; elderly may be more sensitive to adverse effects
- Contraindicated medications—Alosetron, astemizole, cisapride, monoamine oxidase (MAO) inhibitors, terfenadine, and tizanidine—
- Other medications, especially benzodiazepines that are metabolized by hepatic oxidation, beta-adrenergic blocking agents that are metabolized hepatically, clozapine, other serotonergics or medications or substances with serotonergic activity, theophylline, tricyclic antidepressants, or warfarin
- Other medical problems, especially hepatic function impairment or history of seizure disorders

Proper use of this medication

» Compliance with therapy; not taking more or less medicine than prescribed

Taking with or without food, on a full or empty stomach.

» May require several weeks of therapy to obtain therapeutic effects

» Proper dosing

Missed dose: If taking once a day, taking the missed dose as soon as possible if remembered the same day; continuing on regular schedule with next dose; not doubling doses

If taking two times a day, skipping the missed dose and continuing on regular schedule with next dose; not doubling doses

» Proper storage

Precautions while using this medication

» Regular visits to physician to check progress of therapy

» Not taking alosetron, astemizole, cisapride, terfenadine, or tizanidine while taking fluvoxamine

» Not taking fluvoxamine or an MAO inhibitor within 14 days of each other

Avoiding use of alcoholic beverages

» Notifying physician as soon as possible if skin rash, hives, or other sign of allergic reaction occurs

» Possible drowsiness, impairment of thinking, vision, or motor skills; caution when driving or doing jobs requiring alertness, clear vision, or good muscle control

Checking with physician before discontinuing medication; gradual dosage reduction may be required to avoid discontinuation symptoms

Side/adverse effects

Signs of potential side effects, especially sexual dysfunction; behavior, mood, or mental changes; dyspnea; myoclonus; urinary retention; abnormal bleeding; blurred vision; extrapyramidal effects; menstrual changes; seizures; serotonin syndrome; skin rash; syndrome of inappropriate antidiuretic hormone; toxic epidermal necrolysis; unusual lactation (in females)

General Dosing Information

Although the long-term efficacy of fluvoxamine has not been documented in clinical trials, obsessive-compulsive disorder and depression may be frequently recurring or chronic conditions and it is reasonable to consider continuing drug therapy in a responding patient. The patient should be maintained on the lowest effective dosage, and be reassessed periodically to determine the need for continued therapy.

If obsessive-compulsive symptoms do not improve within 10 to 12 weeks, treatment with fluvoxamine should be reconsidered.

Potentially suicidal patients, particularly those who use alcohol excessively, should not have access to large quantities of this medication. Some clinicians recommend that the patient be supplied with the least amount of medication necessary for satisfactory patient management.

Skin rash, hives, or any other sign of allergic reaction should be reported to the physician as soon as possible.

Discontinuation of fluvoxamine treatment should be achieved by a gradual reduction in dosage to reduce the occurrence of discontinuation symptoms. A reduction rate of 50 mg per day every 5 to 7 days has been proposed.

Diet/Nutrition

Fluvoxamine may be taken with or without food, on a full or empty stomach.

For treatment of adverse effects

Serotonin syndrome—Treatment is essentially symptomatic and supportive. The nonspecific serotonergic receptor antagonists cyproheptadine and methysergide have been reported to be of some use in shortening the duration of the serotonin syndrome.

Oral Dosage Forms

Note: Bracketed uses in the Dosage Forms section refer to categories of use and/or indications that are not included in U.S. product labeling.

FLUVOXAMINE MALEATE TABLETS

Usual adult dose

Antiobsessional agent or
[Antidepressant]—

Oral, initially 50 mg in a single dose at bedtime. The dosage may be increased as needed and tolerated in increments of 50 mg a day at intervals of four to seven days. If the daily dosage exceeds 100 mg, it should be taken in two divided doses. If the doses are not equal, the larger dose should be taken at bedtime.

Note: In patients with hepatic function impairment, initial fluvoxamine dosage should be reduced, and titration should proceed slowly; an increased dosing interval may be considered.

Some clinicians recommend an initial dosage of 25 mg once a day in all adult patients to reduce the incidence of adverse effects.

Usual adult prescribing limits

300 mg per day.

Usual pediatric dose

Antiobsessional agent[1]—

Children younger than 8 years of age: Safety and efficacy have not been established.

Children 8 to 17 years of age: Oral, initially 25 mg in a single dose at bedtime. The dosage may be increased as needed and tolerated in increments of 25 mg a day at intervals of four to seven days. If the daily dosage exceeds 50 mg, it should be administered in two divided doses. If the doses are not equal, the larger dose should be administered at bedtime.

Usual pediatric prescribing limits

Antiobsessional agent—

Children 8 to 17 years of age: 200 mg a day.

Usual geriatric dose

See *Usual adult dose*.

Note: In elderly patients, modifications of the initial dosage and subsequent titration may be appropriate. Some clinicians recommend an initial dosage of 25 mg once a day and a maximum dosage of 100 mg two times a day for elderly patients.

Strength(s) usually available

U.S.—

25 mg (Rx) [*Luvox* (carnauba wax; hydroxypropyl methylcellulose; mannitol; polyethylene glycol; polysorbate 80; pregelatinized po-

tato starch; silicon dioxide; sodium stearyl fumarate; corn starch; titanium dioxide)].

50 mg (Rx) [*Luvox* (scored; carnauba wax; hydroxypropyl methylcellulose; mannitol; polyethylene glycol; polysorbate 80; pregelatinized potato starch; silicon dioxide; sodium stearyl fumarate; corn starch; synthetic iron oxides; titanium dioxide)].

100 mg (Rx) [*Luvox* (scored; carnauba wax; hydroxypropyl methylcellulose; mannitol; polyethylene glycol; polysorbate 80; pregelatinized potato starch; silicon dioxide; sodium stearyl fumarate; corn starch; synthetic iron oxides; titanium dioxide)].

Canada—

50 mg (Rx) [*Luvox* (scored)].

100 mg (Rx) [*Luvox* (scored)].

Packaging and storage

Store at controlled room temperature, between 15 and 30 °C (59 and 86 °F), in a tight container, unless otherwise specified by manufacturer. Protect from humidity.

Auxiliary labeling

- Avoid alcoholic beverages.
- May cause drowsiness.

Note

Dispense in tight container.

[1]Not included in Canadian product labeling.

Selected Bibliography

Claassen V, Davies, JE, Hertting G, et al. Fluvoxamine, a specific 5-hydroxytryptamine uptake inhibitor. Br J Pharmacol 1977; 60: 505-16.

Wilde MI, Plosker GL, Benfield P. Fluvoxamine: an updated review of its pharmacology, and therapeutic use in depressive illness. Drugs 1993; 46(5): 895-924.

Revised: 06/08/2005
Developed: 04/16/1998

FOLIC ACID Systemic

VA CLASSIFICATION (Primary): VT120

Commonly used brand name(s): *Apo-Folic; Folvite; Novo-Folacid.*

Another commonly used name is Vitamin B_9.

Note: For a listing of dosage forms and brand names by country availability, see *Dosage Forms* section(s).

Category

Nutritional supplement (vitamin); diagnostic aid (folate deficiency)

Note: Folic acid (vitamin B_9) is a water-soluble vitamin.

Indications

Note: Bracketed information in the *Indications* section refers to uses that are not included in U.S. product labeling.

Accepted

Folic acid deficiency (prophylaxis and treatment)—Folic acid is indicated for prevention and treatment of folic acid deficiency states, including megaloblastic anemia and in anemias of nutritional origin, pregnancy, infancy, or childhood. Folic acid deficiency may occur as a result of inadequate nutrition or intestinal malabsorption but does not occur in healthy individuals receiving an adequate balanced diet. Simple nutritional deficiency of individual B vitamins is rare since dietary inadequacy usually results in multiple deficiencies. For prophylaxis of folic acid deficiency, dietary improvement, rather than supplementation, is advisable. For treatment of folic acid deficiency, supplementation is preferred.

Folic acid should not be given until the diagnosis of pernicious anemia has been ruled out, since it corrects the hematologic manifestations and masks pernicious anemia while allowing neurologic damage to progress.

Deficiency of folic acid may lead to megaloblastic and macrocytic anemias and glossitis.

Recommended intakes may be increased and/or supplementation may be necessary in the following persons or conditions (based on documented folic acid deficiency):

Alcoholism
Anemia, hemolytic
Fever, chronic
Gastrectomy
Hemodialysis, chronic
Infants—low-birthweight, breast-fed, or those receiving unfortified formulas such as evaporated milk or goat's milk
Intestinal diseases—celiac disease, tropical sprue, persistent diarrhea
Malabsorption syndromes associated with hepatic-biliary disease—hepatic function impairment, alcoholism with cirrhosis
Stress, prolonged

Some unusual diets (e.g., reducing diets that drastically restrict food selection) may not supply minimum daily requirements of folic acid. Supplementation is necessary in patients receiving total parenteral nutrition (TPN) or undergoing rapid weight loss or in those with malnutrition, because of inadequate dietary intake.

Recommended intakes for all vitamins and most minerals are increased during pregnancy. Many physicians recommend that pregnant women receive multivitamin and mineral supplements, especially those pregnant women who do not consume an adequate diet and those in high-risk categories (i.e., women carrying more than one fetus, heavy cigarette smokers, and alcohol and drug abusers). Taking excessive amounts of a multivitamin and mineral supplement may be harmful to the mother and/or fetus and should be avoided.

Some studies have found that folic acid supplementation alone or in combination with other vitamins given before conception and during early pregnancy may reduce the incidence of neural tube defects in infants.

Recommended intakes for all vitamins and most minerals are increased during breast-feeding.

Recommended intakes may be increased by the following medications: Analgesics (long-term use), anticonvulsants, epoetin, estrogens, sulfasalazine.

[Folate deficiency (diagnosis)][1]—Folic acid is being used in the diagnosis of folate deficiency.

Unaccepted

Folic acid has not been proven effective for prevention of mental disorders or in the treatment of normocytic, refractory, or aplastic anemias.

[1]Not included in Canadian product labeling.

Pharmacology/Pharmacokinetics

Physicochemical characteristics

Molecular weight—441.41.

Mechanism of action/Effect

Folic acid, after conversion to tetrahydrofolic acid, is necessary for normal erythropoiesis, synthesis of purine and thymidylates, metabolism of amino acids such as glycine and methionine, and the metabolism of histidine.

Absorption

Commercially available folic acid is almost completely absorbed from the gastrointestinal tract (mostly in the upper duodenum), even in the presence of malabsorption due to tropical sprue. However, absorption of food folates is impaired in malabsorption syndromes.

Protein binding

Extensive (to plasma proteins).

Storage

Hepatic (large proportion).

Biotransformation

Hepatic. Folic acid is converted (in the presence of ascorbic acid) in the liver and plasma to its metabolically active form (tetrahydrofolic acid) by dihydrofolate reductase.

Peak serum concentration:

30 to 60 minutes.

Elimination

Renal (almost entirely as metabolites). Excess beyond daily needs is excreted, largely unchanged, in urine.

In dialysis—Folic acid is removed by hemodialysis; therefore, dialysis patients should receive increased amounts (100 to 300% of USRDA [United States Recommended Daily Allowances]).

Precautions to Consider

Pregnancy/Reproduction

Pregnancy—Problems in humans have not been documented with intake of normal daily recommended amounts. Folic acid crosses the placenta. However, adequate and well-controlled studies in humans have not shown that folic acid causes adverse effects on the fetus.

Some studies have found that folic acid supplementation alone or in combination with other vitamins given before conception and during early pregnancy may reduce the incidence of neural tube defects in infants.

FDA Pregnancy Category A.

Breast-feeding
Folic acid is distributed into breast milk. However, problems in humans have not been documented with intake of normal daily recommended amounts.

Pediatrics
Problems in pediatrics have not been documented with intake of normal daily recommended amounts.

Folic acid injection that contains benzyl alcohol as a preservative should not be used in newborn and immature infants. The use of benzyl alcohol in neonates has been associated with a fatal toxic syndrome consisting of metabolic acidosis and CNS, respiratory, circulatory, and renal function impairment.

Geriatrics
Problems in geriatrics have not been documented with intake of normal daily recommended amounts.

Drug interactions and/or related problems
The following drug interactions and/or related problems have been selected on the basis of their potential clinical significance (possible mechanism in parentheses where appropriate)—not necessarily inclusive (» = major clinical significance):

Note: Combinations containing any of the following medications, depending on the amount present, may also interact with this medication.

Analgesics, long-term use or
Anticonvulsants, hydantoin or
Carbamazepine or
Estrogens or
Oral contraceptives or
Phenobarbital or
Primidone
(requirements for folic acid may be increased in patients receiving these medications)
(concurrent use with folic acid may decrease the effects of hydantoin anticonvulsants by antagonism of their central nervous system [CNS] effects; an increase in hydantoin dosage may be necessary for patients who receive folic acid supplementation)

Antacids, aluminum- or magnesium-containing
(prolonged use of aluminum- and/or magnesium-containing antacids may decrease folic acid absorption by lowering the pH of the small intestine; patients should be advised to take antacids at least 2 hours after folic acid)

Antibiotics
(may interfere with the microbiologic method of assay for serum and erythrocyte folic acid concentrations and cause falsely low results)

Cholestyramine
(concurrent use with folic acid may interfere with absorption of folic acid; folic acid supplementation taken at least 1 hour before or 4 to 6 hours after cholestyramine is recommended in patients receiving cholestyramine for prolonged periods)

Methotrexate or
Pyrimethamine or
Triamterene or
Trimethoprim
(act as folate antagonists by inhibiting dihydrofolate reductase; most significant with high doses and/or prolonged use; leucovorin calcium must be used instead of folic acid in patients receiving these medications)

Sulfonamides, including sulfasalazine
(inhibit absorption of folate; folic acid requirements may be increased in patients receiving sulfasalazine)

Zinc supplements
(some studies have found that folate may decrease the absorption of zinc, but not in the presence of excessive zinc; other studies have found no inhibition)

Laboratory value alterations
The following have been selected on the basis of their potential clinical significance (possible effect in parentheses where appropriate)—not necessarily inclusive (» = major clinical significance):

With physiology/laboratory test values
Vitamin B_{12} concentrations in blood
(may be reduced by large and continuous doses of folic acid)

Medical considerations/Contraindications
The medical considerations/contraindications included have been selected on the basis of their potential clinical significance (reasons given in parentheses where appropriate)—not necessarily inclusive (» = major clinical significance).

Risk-benefit should be considered when the following medical problems exist:

» Pernicious anemia
(folic acid will correct hematologic abnormalities but neurologic problems will progress irreversibly; doses of folic acid greater than 0.4 mg per day are not recommended until pernicious anemia has been ruled out, except during pregnancy and lactation)

Sensitivity to folic acid

Side/Adverse Effects
Note: No side effects other than an allergic reaction have been reported with folic acid administration, even at doses of up to 10 times the recommended dietary allowances (RDA) for 1 month.

The following side/adverse effects have been selected on the basis of their potential clinical significance (possible signs and symptoms in parentheses where appropriate)—not necessarily inclusive:

Those indicating need for medical attention
Incidence rare

Allergic reaction, specifically; bronchospasm (shortness of breath; troubled breathing; tightness of chest; wheezing); ***erythema*** (reddened skin); ***fever; general malaise*** (general weakness or discomfort); ***skin rash or itching***

Note: Side effects including abdominal bloating and gas, anorexia, confusion, depression, difficulty in concentrating, excitement, irritability, impaired judgment, nausea, trouble in sleeping, and unpleasant taste were reported in a study of patients taking 15 mg daily.

Patient Consultation
As an aid to patient consultation, refer to *Advice for the Patient, Folic Acid (Vitamin B_9) (Systemic).*

In providing consultation, consider emphasizing the following selected information (» = major clinical significance):

Description of use
Description should include function in the body, signs of deficiency, and unproven uses

Importance of diet
Importance of proper nutrition; supplement may be needed because of inadequate dietary intake

Food sources of folic acid; effects of processing

Not using vitamins as substitute for balanced diet

Recommended daily intake for folic acid

Before using this dietary supplement
» Conditions affecting use, especially:
Other medical problems, especially pernicious anemia

Proper use of this medication
» Proper dosing
Missed dose: No cause for concern because of length of time necessary for depletion; remembering to take as directed

» Proper storage

Side/adverse effects
Signs of potential side effects, especially allergic reaction, specifically bronchospasm, erythema, fever, general malaise, skin rash, or itching

General Dosing Information
Because of the infrequency of single B vitamin deficiencies, combinations are commonly administered. Many commercial combinations of B vitamins are available.

For parenteral dosage forms only
In most cases, parenteral administration is indicated only when oral administration is not acceptable (for example, in nausea, vomiting, preoperative and postoperative conditions) or possible (for example, in malabsorption syndromes or following gastric resection).

Diet/Nutrition
Recommended dietary intakes for folic acid are defined differently worldwide.

For U.S.—
The Recommended Dietary Allowances (RDAs) for vitamins and minerals are determined by the Food and Nutrition Board of the National Research Council and are intended to provide adequate nutrition in most healthy persons under usual environmental stresses. In addition, a different designation may be used by the

FDA for food and dietary supplement labeling purposes, as with Daily Value (DV). DVs replace the previous labeling terminology United States Recommended Daily Allowances (USRDAs).

For Canada—
Recommended Nutrient Intakes (RNIs) for vitamins, minerals, and protein are determined by Health and Welfare Canada and provide recommended amounts of a specific nutrient while minimizing the risk of chronic diseases.

Daily recommended intakes for folic acid are generally defined as follows:

Persons	U.S. (mcg)	Canada (mcg)
Infants and children		
Birth to 3 years of age	25–50	50–80
4 to 6 years of age	75	90
7 to 10 years of age	100	125–180
Adolescent and adult males	150–200	150–220
Adolescent and adult females	150–180	145–190
Pregnant females	400	445–475
Breast-feeding females	260–280	245–275

These are usually provided by adequate diets.

Best dietary sources of folic acid include vegetables, especially green vegetables; potatoes; cereal and cereal products; fruits; and organ meats (liver, kidney). Heat destroys folic acid (50 to 90%) in foods.

Oral Dosage Forms

Note: Bracketed uses in the *Dosage Forms* section refer to categories of use and/or indications that are not included in U.S. product labeling.

FOLIC ACID TABLETS USP

Usual adult and adolescent dose

Deficiency (prophylaxis)—
Oral, amount based on normal daily recommended intakes:

Persons	U.S. (mcg)	Canada (mcg)
Adolescent and adult males	150–400	150–220
Adolescent and adult females	150–400	145–190
Pregnant females	400 to 800	445–475
Breast-feeding females	260–800	245–275

Deficiency (treatment)—
Treatment dose is individualized by prescriber based on severity of deficiency.

[Diagnostic aid (folate deficiency)][1]—
Oral, 100 to 200 mcg (0.1 to 0.2 mg) a day for ten days plus low dietary folic acid and vitamin B_{12}.

Usual pediatric dose

Deficiency (prophylaxis)—
Oral, amount based on normal daily recommended intakes:

Persons	U.S. (mcg)	Canada (mcg)
Infants and children		
Birth to 3 years of age	25–	50–80
4 to 6 years of age	75–400	90
7 to 10 years of age	100–400	125–180

Deficiency (treatment)—
Treatment dose is individualized by prescriber based on severity of deficiency.

Strength(s) usually available

U.S.—
100 mcg (Rx) [GENERIC].
400 mcg (Rx) [GENERIC].
800 mcg (Rx) [GENERIC].
1 mg (Rx) [*Folvite*; GENERIC].

Canada—
5 mg (Rx) [*Apo-Folic* (scored); *Folvite* (scored); *Novo-Folacid*; GENERIC].

Note: Some strengths of these folic acid preparations may exceed the dosage range recommended by USP DI Advisory Panels based on the amount necessary to meet normal nutritional needs.

Packaging and storage

Store below 40 °C (104 °F), preferably between 15 and 30 °C (59 and 86 °F), unless otherwise specified by manufacturer. Store in a well-closed container.

Parenteral Dosage Forms

Note: Bracketed uses in the *Dosage Forms* section refer to categories of use and/or indications that are not included in U.S. product labeling.

FOLIC ACID INJECTION USP

Usual adult and adolescent dose

Deficiency (prophylaxis)—
Intravenous infusion, as part of total parenteral nutrition solutions, the specific amount determined by individual patient need.

Deficiency (treatment)—
Intramuscular, intravenous, or deep subcutaneous: 250 mcg (0.25 mg) to 1 mg a day until a hematologic response occurs.

[Diagnostic aid (folate deficiency)][1]—
Intramuscular, 100 to 200 mcg (0.1 to 0.2 mg) a day for ten days plus low dietary folic acid and vitamin B_{12}.

Usual pediatric dose

See *Usual adult and adolescent dose*.

Note: Folic acid injection that contains benzyl alcohol as a preservative should not be used in newborn and immature infants. The use of benzyl alcohol in neonates has been associated with a fatal toxic syndrome consisting of metabolic acidosis and CNS, respiratory, circulatory, and renal function impairment.

Strength(s) usually available

U.S.—
5 mg (base) per mL (Rx) [*Folvite* (benzyl alcohol 1.5%); GENERIC].
10 mg per mL (Rx) [GENERIC].

Canada—
5 mg (base) per mL (Rx) [*Folvite*].

Packaging and storage

Store below 40 °C (104 °F), preferably between 15 and 30 °C (59 and 86 °F), unless otherwise specified by manufacturer. Protect from light. Protect from freezing.

[1]Not included in Canadian product labeling.

Revised: 12/30/1999

FOLLITROPIN ALFA Systemic†

VA CLASSIFICATION (Primary): HS106

Commonly used brand name(s): *Gonal-F*.

Note: For a listing of dosage forms and brand names by country availability, see *Dosage Forms* section(s).

†Not commercially available in Canada.

Category

Gonadotropin; infertility therapy agent.

Indications

General Considerations

Special attention should be given to the underlying cause of female infertility in both female and male partners before follitropin alfa treatment is initiated.

Accepted

Infertility, female (treatment)—Follitropin alfa is indicated in the treatment of female infertility to stimulate ovarian follicular development in patients with ovulatory dysfunction not due to primary ovarian failure, such as anovulation or oligo-ovulation. Follitropin alfa replaces physiologic concentrations of follicle-stimulating hormone (FSH). It is used in conjunction with a properly timed injection of human chorionic gonadotropin (hCG) when the patient produces no ovulatory surge of endogenous luteinizing hormone (LH). In studies of patients using follitropin alfa for no more than three cycles for ovulation induction, the cumulative ovulation rate of 81% produced a cumulative pregnancy rate of 37%, which resulted in 63% single births, 14% multiple births, and 23% of pregnancies not reaching term.

Infertility, male (treatment)—Follitropin alfa is indicated for the induction of spermatogenesis in men with primary and secondary hypogonadotropic hypogonadism in whom the cause of infertility is not due to primary testicular failure.

Reproductive technologies, assisted—Follitropin alfa is indicated to stimulate the development of multiple oocytes in ovulatory patients enrolled in an assisted reproductive technology (ART) program, such as embryo transfer (ET) or *in vitro* fertilization (IVF). In some studies, patients were pretreated with a gonadotropin-releasing hormone agonist (GnRHa) to down-regulate the pituitary in order to reduce FSH and LH activity, giving control of hypothalamic-pituitary axis function and timing of exogenous gonadotropins (follitropin alfa and hCG) administration to the investigator or clinician. Follitropin alfa is used in conjunction with a properly timed injection of hCG when the patient produces no ovulatory surge of endogenous LH. In studies of patients undergoing ART, pregnancy outcome may be influenced by several factors, such as number of oocytes being inseminated, fertilization rate of oocytes, and number of embryos transferred *in utero* in a single treatment cycle. Many variables that will be different among patients and/or treatment protocols influence these results.

Pharmacology/Pharmacokinetics

Physicochemical characteristics

Source—Follitropin alfa is derived from genetically modified Chinese hamster ovary (CHO) cells cultured in bioreactors. It is then purified to a consistent follicle-stimulating hormone (FSH) isoform profile by means of immunochromatography.

Chemical Group—The primary and tertiary structures of follitropin alfa are identical to that of human FSH.

Molecular weight—10,205.88 for the alpha subunit of 92 amino acids; 12,485.34 for the beta subunit of 111 amino acids.

Other characteristics—

Follitropin alfa may contain up to 15% of oxidized follitropin alfa.

Mechanism of action/Effect

Infertility, female or reproductive technologies, assisted—Follitropin alfa replaces deficient or abnormal FSH serum concentrations in patients experiencing ovulatory function impairment. Specifically, follitropin alfa, a recombinant FSH, stimulates follicle recruitment and follicular growth and maturation. Follitropin alfa's ability to increase serum concentrations of inhibin, estradiol, and total ovarian follicular volume varies widely among individuals. The rise in the serum inhibin concentration is an early indicator of follicular development; its concentration declines quickly after follitropin alfa treatment is discontinued. Total growth of ovarian follicles lags behind increasing FSH serum concentrations, and ovarian follicular growth continues to increase for a time with declining FSH serum concentrations. Maximum ovarian follicular volume correlates better with inhibin or estradiol serum concentrations than it does with FSH serum concentrations. Anovulatory patients who need luteinizing hormone (LH) activity at mid-cycle receive an injection of human chorionic gonadotropin (hCG) to stimulate ovulation and to continue follicular maturation. Follitropin alfa is not useful for patients experiencing infertility due to primary ovarian failure.

Before consecutive administration of gonadotropins as single agents to increase recruitment of multiple follicles, some assisted reproductive technology protocols include pretreatment with a gonadotropin-releasing hormone agonist (GnRHa) to suppress the pituitary release of gonadotropins. Once the pituitary is suppressed, the patient's physiologic concentrations of gonadotropins are then replaced.

Absorption

Absorption of follitropin alfa is slower than its elimination, and the pharmacokinetics are considered to be dependent on the absorption rate.

Distribution

Human tissue or organ distribution of subcutaneous follitropin alfa administration has not been determined.

Biotransformation

Biotransformation has not been studied in humans.

Half-life

Distribution—Intravenous: 2 to 5 hours.

Elimination

Renal, 12.5% of total clearance.

Precautions to Consider

Cross-sensitivity and/or related problems

Patients hypersensitive to follicle-stimulating hormone (FSH) preparations may be hypersensitive to follitropin alfa also.

Carcinogenicity

Long-term studies have not been done in animals to evaluate the carcinogenic potential of follitropin alfa.

Mutagenicity

Follitropin alfa was not found to be mutagenic in a series of tests, including the bacterial and mammalian cell mutation tests, a chromosomal aberration test, and a micronucleus test.

Pregnancy/Reproduction

Use of follitropin alfa in treatment of infertility or as an adjunct with assisted reproduction technologies is associated with a high incidence of multiple gestations and multiple births. This may increase the risk of neonatal prematurity, as well as other complications associated with multiple gestations.

Fertility—Follitropin alfa is used before a natural or artificial luteinizing hormone (LH) surge to develop and recruit follicles in humans.

Impaired fertility has been reported in rats given 40 international units per kg (IU/kg) or more of body weight once a day for extended periods.

Pregnancy—Use of follitropin alfa during pregnancy is unnecessary and not recommended. Ovarian hyperstimulation syndrome (OHSS), which may be induced by follitropin alfa therapy, is more common, more severe, and protracted in patients who conceive.

FDA Pregnancy Category X.

Breast-feeding

It is not known whether follitropin alfa is distributed into breast milk.

Medical considerations/Contraindications

The medical considerations/contraindications included have been selected on the basis of their potential clinical significance (reasons given in parentheses where appropriate)—not necessarily inclusive (» = major clinical significance).

Risk-benefit should be considered when the following medical problems exist:

» Abnormal uterine or genital bleeding, undiagnosed
(may delay diagnosis of endocrinopathology, such as endometrial hyperplasia or hormone-dependent carcinoma; inducing fertility and pregnancy may not be advisable for such patients)

» Adrenal function impairment, uncontrolled or
» Thyroid function impairment, uncontrolled or
» Tumors, intracranial or sex hormone-dependent
(increasing estrogen concentrations may make these conditions worse)

Asthma
(may be exacerbated)

Hypersensitivity to FSH preparations

» Ovarian cyst or enlargement, undetermined cause
(increased risk of further enlargement)

» Primary ovarian failure or
Primary testicular failure
(follitropin alfa is ineffective in patients with primary ovarian or testicular failure)

Patient monitoring

The following may be especially important in patient monitoring (other tests may be warranted in some patients, depending on condition; » = major clinical significance):

Note: Patients should be examined for ovarian hyperstimulation syndrome (OHSS) every other day during treatment with follitropin alfa and for 14 days posttreatment.

For female patients

Daily basal body temperature and/or
Progesterone, serum
(measurement of serum progesterone concentrations can be made prior to follitropin alfa therapy to confirm anovulation. An increase in serum progesterone concentrations or a rise in basal body temperature can confirm ovulation)

» Estradiol, serum and/or
» Ultrasonography of ovaries and uterus
(ultrasonography and monitoring of serum estradiol concentrations can be used to monitor follicular development, predict timing for human chorionic gonadotropin [hCG] administration, detect ovarian enlargement, and aid in minimizing risk of OHSS and multiple gestation)
(ultrasonography of the ovaries can determine approximate time of ovulation by viewing fluid in the cul-de-sac, ovarian stigmata, collapsed follicle, or secretory endometrium. Ultrasonography is especially useful for evaluating the number of developing follicles, which is not predictable from serum estrogen concentration data)

Pregnancy test
(pregnancy can be confirmed by testing for serum hCG)

For male patients

Testosterone, serum
(in order to increase effectiveness, normal levels should be reached before and maintained during treatment)

For male partners

Sperm count and determinations of sperm motility and

Testosterone, serum (baseline measurement of sperm count and activity in male partners is recommended to evaluate success of follitropin alfa treatment in females. If semen analysis is abnormal, serum testosterone concentration in the male partner may be measured)

Side/Adverse Effects

Note: Serious pulmonary and vascular complications have been reported in patients who have received gonadotropins. Arterial thromboembolism has been reported both in association with and separate from ovarian hyperstimulation syndrome (OHSS) in patients who have received follitropin alfa. Complications resulting from thromboembolism have included venous thrombophlebitis, pulmonary embolism, pulmonary infarction, stroke, arterial occlusion necessitating limb amputation, and, in rare cases, death. Serious pulmonary complications that have occurred include atelectasis, acute respiratory distress syndrome, and, rarely, death.

The following side/adverse effects have been selected on the basis of their potential clinical significance (possible signs and symptoms in parentheses where appropriate)—not necessarily inclusive:

Those indicating need for medical attention

Incidence more frequent

For patients treated for female infertility or patients pretreated with a gonadotropin-releasing hormone agonist (GnRHa) undergoing artificial reproductive technologies (ART)

Abdominal or pelvic pain—9 to 10%; ***diarrhea***—8%; ***flatulence*** (passing of gas)—4 to 7%; ***influenza-like or cold symptoms, including sinusitis; pharnygitis; and upper respiratory tract infection*** (body aches or pain; coughing; fever; headache; loss of voice; runny nose; unusual tiredness or weakness)—4 to 12%; ***intermenstrual bleeding*** (uterine bleeding between menstrual periods)—4 to 9%; ***nausea***—5 to 14%; ***ovarian enlargement, mild and uncomplicated*** (abdominal bloating; abdominal pain)—20%, usually regresses after 2 to 3 weeks

For patients treated for female infertility

Acne—4%; ***breast pain or tenderness***—4%; ***emotional lability*** (mood swings)—5%; ***ovarian cysts*** (abdominal or pelvic pain; mild bloating)—15.3%; ***ovarian hyperstimulation syndrome (OHSS)*** (abdominal pain, severe; nausea; rapid weight gain; vomiting)—7%

Note: When comparing follitropin alfa to urofollitropin in one study of 454 patients treated for ovulation induction, 15% of patients using follitropin alfa and 29% of patients using urofollitropin developed *ovarian cysts*. Conversely, 7% of patients using follitropin alfa developed *ovarian hyperstimulation syndrome (OHSS)* while 4% of patients using urofollitropin developed OHSS; 0.8% of all patients were considered to have severe cases. Ovarian cysts and OHSS did not occur in two studies of 237 patients enrolled in an ART program who were pretreated with gonadotropin-releasing hormone agonists to down-regulate the pituitary before follitropin alfa or urofollitropin treatment was initiated.

Incidence less frequent

For patients treated for female infertility or patients pretreated with a GnRHa undergoing ART—1 to 3%

Dizziness; dysmenorrhea (painful menstrual periods); ***leukorrhea*** (white vaginal discharge); ***redness, pain, or swelling at injection site; somnolence*** (sleepiness); ***vaginal hemorrhage*** (heavy nonmenstrual vaginal bleeding)

For patients treated for female infertility—1 to 3%

Dyspepsia (stomach discomfort); ***hypotension*** (dizziness; lightheadedness; fainting); ***lesion on cervix; migraine; nervousness***

For patients pretreated with a GnRHa undergoing ART—1 to 2%

Anorexia (loss of appetite); ***chest pain or palpitations*** (fast, racing heartbeat); ***pruritus*** (itching of skin); ***unusual thirst***

Those indicating possible need for medical attention if they occur after medication is discontinued

OHSS (abdominal pain, severe; nausea; rapid weight gain; vomiting)—usually within seven to ten days after treatment discontinuation

Patient Consultation

As an aid to patient consultation, refer to *Advice for the Patient, Follitropin Alfa (Systemic)*.

In providing consultation, consider emphasizing the following selected information (» = major clinical significance):

Before using this medication

» Conditions affecting use, especially:

Hypersensitivity to follicle-stimulating hormone (FSH) preparations

Pregnancy—Use during pregnancy is not needed or recommended; increased risk of multiple gestations and their associated complications and protracted ovarian hyperstimulation syndrome (OHSS) in patients who conceive

Other medical problems, especially abnormal uterine or genital bleeding, undiagnosed; adrenal function impairment, uncontrolled; intracranial or sex hormone–dependent tumors; ovarian cyst or enlargement, undetermined cause; primary ovarian failure; or thyroid function impairment, uncontrolled

Proper use of this medication

» Carefully reading patient instructions provided

For those patients self-administering the medication

Proper preparation of medication; using proper technique to prevent contamination of the medication, work area, and patient during transfer between containers

Proper administration; using proper needle and syringe

Knowing proper dose to use and not using more than prescribed

Carefully selecting and rotating injection sites as directed by physician

Disposing of needles, syringes, ampuls, and unused medication properly

Alerting physician when last dose of follitropin alfa is given and knowing that another drug called human chorionic gonadotropin may be required as a single injection 24 hours after the last dose of follitropin alfa

» Proper dosing

Missed dose: Calling physician for advice; do not double doses

» Proper storage

Precautions while using this medication

» Understanding the duration of treatment and the importance of required frequent monitoring by physician during treatment and for at least 2 weeks after follitropin alfa treatment is stopped

» Importance of following physician's instructions for recording basal body temperature, if requested, and timing of intercourse

Understanding that dizziness can occur with use of follitropin alfa and may impair driving, using machines, or other dangerous tasks

Side/adverse effects

Signs of potential side effects, especially:

For patients treated for female infertility or patients pretreated with a GnRHa undergoing ART—Abdominal or pelvic pain; diarrhea; flatulence; influenza-like or cold symptoms, including sinusitis, pharnygitis, and upper respiratory tract infection; intermenstrual bleeding; nausea; ovarian enlargement, mild and uncomplicated; dizziness; dysmenorrhea; leukorrhea; redness, pain, or swelling at injection site; somnolence; or vaginal hemorrhage

For patients treated for female infertility—Acne; breast pain or tenderness; emotional lability; ovarian cysts; ovarian hyperstimulation syndrome; dyspepsia; hypotension; lesion on cervix; migraine; or nervousness

For patients pretreated with a GnRHa undergoing ART—Anorexia; chest pain or palpitations; pruritus; or unusual thirst

General Dosing Information

Patients receiving follitropin alfa should be under the supervision of a physician experienced in the treatment of gynecologic or endocrinologic disorders and willing to devote considerable time to case-management.

Dosage varies considerably and must be adjusted to meet the individual requirements of each patient on the basis of clinical response.

If the ovaries are abnormally enlarged on the last day of follitropin alfa treatment, human chorionic gonadotropin (hCG) should not be administered to minimize risk of ovarian hyperstimulation syndrome (OHSS). OHSS develops rapidly (between 24 and 72 hours) and is distinct from uncomplicated ovarian enlargement. Patients should be monitored for 2 weeks after treatment ends, since the risk of OHSS reaches its maximal potential at 7 to 10 days post-treatment.

Patients self-injecting follitropin alfa should be given the patient information sheet and instructed on how to prepare the medication and injection site, administer the medication, and safely discard used items. Injection sites should be rotated and medication administered to upper thigh or at waistline.

For patients treated for ovulation induction

Conception should be attempted daily beginning within 24 hours of administration of hCG until ovulation is thought to have occurred.

If ovulation does not occur after any cycle of therapy, the therapeutic regimen employed should be re-evaluated. After three to six cycles of nonovulatory menses, the appropriateness of continuing the use of follitropin alfa for ovulation induction should be reconsidered.

Bioequivalence information

According to physicochemical tests and assays, the primary and tertiary structures of follitropin alfa, follitropin beta, and human follicle-stimulating hormone (FSH) are indistinguishable from one another. These hormones are similar to human menopausal urine-derived follicle-stimulating hormone (urofollitropin) but without urinary protein for the nonpurified dosage form, and to menotropins without the urinary protein or luteinizing hormone (LH) components.

Safety considerations for handling this medication
Precautions include:
- Use of proper technique to prevent contamination of the medication, work area, and operator during transfer between containers, including proper training in this technique for those patients self-administering the medication
- Cautious and proper disposal of needles, syringes, vials, ampuls, and unused medication.

For treatment of adverse effects
Recommended treatment for OHSS consists of the following:
- Stopping treatment with follitropin alfa (or hCG).
- Hospitalizing patients with severe OHSS; less severe cases may spontaneously resolve at onset of menses.
- Managing electrolyte and fluid imbalances.

Parenteral Dosage Forms

FOLLITROPIN ALFA FOR INJECTION

Usual adult dose

Infertility, female—

Subcutaneous, 75 international units (IU) a day, usually for fourteen days, then the dose is increased by 37.5 IU at weekly intervals if clinically indicated after measurement of the serum estradiol concentration and follicular development. Total dose should not routinely exceed 300 IU a day. Total length of treatment should not exceed thirty-five days, unless serum estradiol indicates imminent follicular development. Treatment should be discontinued if the ovaries become abnormally enlarged or abdominal pain occurs; at this time the patient should be advised not to have sexual intercourse. To complete follicular development and to induce ovulation in the absence of a luteinizing hormone (LH) surge, human chorionic gonadotropin (hCG) is administered one day after the last dose of follitropin alfa treatment, unless the serum estradiol concentration exceeds 2000 picograms per mL.

Infertility, male—

Subcutaneous, 150 international units (IU) three times a week in conjunction with 1000 USP Units of human chorionic gonadotropin (hCG) (or the dose required to maintain serum testosterone levels within the normal range) three times a week, once normal testosterone levels are reached. The dosage may be increased to a maximum dose of 300 IU three times a week if azoospermia persists. The treatment with follitropin alfa may need to last for up to eighteen months to achieve adequate spermatogenesis.

Note: Follitropin alfa must be given in conjunction with hCG. Prior to concomitant therapy with follitropin alfa and hCG, pretreatment with hCG alone at the dose of 1000 to 2250 USP Units two to three times a week is required. The dose of hCG may be increased and the pretreatment should be continued for a period sufficient (may need three to six months) to achieve serum testosterone levels within the normal range.

Reproductive technologies, assisted—

Subcutaneous, 150 international units (IU) once a day, beginning cycle Day 2 or Day 3 until follicles are developed sufficiently. Dose adjustment can be considered after the first five days of treatment, and then adjusted every three to five days thereafter; dose should be adjusted by no more than 75 to 150 IU per day for each adjustment interval. For most patients, treatment should not exceed ten days. Doses greater than 450 IU a day are not recommended. For patients with suppressed endogenous gonadotropins, treatment may begin at 225 IU once a day. To complete follicular development in all patients not experiencing an LH surge, hCG is administered one day after the last dose of follitropin alfa treatment.

Usual adult prescribing limits
Males: 300 IU three times a week.

Strength(s) usually available
U.S.—

37.5 International Units (Rx) [*Gonal-F* (inactive dibasic sodium phosphate 1.11 mg; monobasic sodium phosphate monohydrate 0.45 mg; sucrose 30 mg)].

75 International Units (Rx) [*Gonal-F* (inactive dibasic sodium phosphate 1.11 mg; monobasic sodium phosphate monohydrate 0.45 mg; sucrose 30 mg)].

150 International Units (Rx) [*Gonal-F* (inactive dibasic sodium phosphate 1.11 mg; monobasic sodium phosphate monohydrate 0.45 mg; sucrose 30 mg)].

Packaging and storage
Store between 2 and 25 °C (36 and 77 °F). Protect from light.

Preparation of dosage form
Using standard aseptic technique, follitropin alfa is reconstituted by adding 0.5 to 1 mL of Sterile Water for Injection USP to each ampul. A total concentration of 225 IU per 0.5 mL should not be exceeded.

Stability
The solution should be used immediately after reconstitution and any unused material discarded. The solution should not be used if it is cloudy or discolored.

Auxiliary labeling
- Protect from light.

Note
Include patient package information when dispensing.

Revised: 12/28/2000
Developed: 01/26/1998

FOLLITROPIN BETA Systemic

VA CLASSIFICATION (Primary): HS106

Commonly used brand name(s): *Follistim*.

Note: For a listing of dosage forms and brand names by country availability, see *Dosage Forms* section(s).

Category

Gonadotropin; infertility therapy agent.

Indications

General Considerations
Special attention should be given to the underlying cause of female infertility in both female and male partners before follitropin beta treatment is initiated.

Accepted
Infertility, female (treatment)—Follitropin beta is indicated in the treatment of female infertility to stimulate ovarian follicular development in patients with ovulatory dysfunction not due to primary ovarian failure, such as anovulation or oligo-ovulation. Follitropin beta replaces physiologic concentrations of follicle-stimulating hormone (FSH). It is used in conjunction with a properly timed injection of human chorionic gonadotropin (hCG) when the patient produces no ovulatory surge of endogenous luteinizing hormone (LH). In studies of patients unresponsive to clomiphene using follitropin beta for no more than three cycles for ovulation induction, the cumulative ovulation rate of 85% produced a cumulative pregnancy rate of 23%, which resulted in 63% single births, 6% multiple births, and 31% of pregnancies not reaching term.

Reproductive technologies, assisted—Follitropin beta is indicated to stimulate the development of multiple oocytes in ovulatory patients enrolled in an assisted reproductive technology (ART) program, such as embryo transfer (ET) or *in vitro* fertilization (IVF). In some studies, patients were pretreated with a gonadotropin-releasing hormone agonist (GnRHa) to down-regulate the pituitary in order to reduce FSH and LH activity, giving control of hypothalamic-pituitary axis function and timing of exogenous gonadotropins (follitropin beta and hCG) administration to the investigator or clinician. Follitropin beta is used in conjunction with a properly timed injection of hCG when the patient produces no ovulatory surge of endogenous LH. In studies of patients undergoing ART, pregnancy outcome may be influenced by several factors, such as number of oocytes being inseminated, fertilization rate of oocytes, and number of embryos transferred *in utero* in a single treatment cycle. Many variables that will be different among patients and/or treatment protocols influence these results.

Pharmacology/Pharmacokinetics

Physicochemical characteristics
Source—Follitropin beta is derived from a product produced from genetically modified Chinese hamster ovary (CHO) cells. Afterwards, it is purified to a consistent follicle-stimulating hormone (FSH) isoform profile.

Chemical Group—The primary and tertiary structures of follitropin beta are identical to that of human FSH.

Molecular weight—10,205.88 for the alpha subunit of 92 amino acids; 12,485.34 for the beta subunit of 111 amino acids.

Other characteristics—

Follitropin beta may contain up to 20% oxidized follitropin beta.

Mechanism of action/Effect

Infertility, female, or reproductive technologies, assisted—Follitropin beta replaces deficient or abnormal FSH serum concentrations in patients experiencing ovulatory function impairment. Specifically, follitropin beta, a recombinant FSH, stimulates follicle recruitment and follicular growth and maturation. Follitropin beta's ability to increase serum concentrations of inhibin, estradiol, and total ovarian follicular volume varies widely among individuals. The rise in the serum inhibin concentration is an early indicator of follicular development; its concentration declines quickly after follitropin beta treatment is discontinued. Total growth of ovarian follicles lags behind increasing FSH serum concentrations, and ovarian follicular growth continues to increase for a time with declining FSH serum concentrations. Maximum ovarian follicular volume correlates better with inhibin or estradiol serum concentrations than it does with FSH serum concentrations. Anovulatory patients who need luteinizing hormone (LH) activity at mid-cycle receive an injection of human chorionic gonadotropin (hCG) to stimulate ovulation and to continue follicular maturation. Follitropin beta is not useful for patients experiencing infertility due to primary ovarian failure.

Before consecutive administration of gonadotropins as single agents to increase recruitment of multiple follicles, some assisted reproductive technology protocols include pretreatment with a gonadotropin-releasing hormone agonist (GnRHa) to suppress the pituitary release of gonadotropins. Once the pituitary is suppressed, the patient's physiologic concentrations of gonadotropins are replaced.

Absorption

The area under the plasma concentration-time curve (AUC) for the subcutaneous and intramuscular routes for administering follitropin beta are considered equivalent; however, the peak plasma concentration (C_{max}) differs.

Half-life

Elimination—

The mean half-lives for 7-day treatment for the following doses of follitropin beta given intramuscularly once a day are:

75 international units (IU)—26.9 hours ± 7.8 hours.

150 IU—30.1 hours ± 6.2 hours.

225 IU—28.9 hours ± 6.5 hours.

The mean half-life for a single dose of 300 IU of follitropin beta given intramuscularly is 43.9 ± 14.1 hours.

Peak serum concentration

A 7-day treatment of 75 IU, 150 IU, and 225 IU of follitropin beta given once a day to pituitary-suppressed females produced the following mean peak serum concentrations (C_{max}):

75 IU—Intramuscular, 4.7 ± 1.5 IU per liter (IU/L). Subcutaneous, 4.3 ± 0.6 IU/L.

150 IU—Intramuscular, 9.5 ± 2.6 IU/L. Subcutaneous—8.5 ± 0.6 IU/L.

225 IU—Intramuscular, 11.3 ± 1.8 IU/L. Subcutaneous—13.9 ± 1.8 IU/L.

A single dose of 300 IU of follitropin beta given intramuscularly to healthy, gonadotropin-deficient females produced a C_{max} of 4.3 ± 1.7 IU/L.

Precautions to Consider

Cross-sensitivity and/or related problems

Patients hypersensitive to follicle-stimulating hormone (FSH) preparations may be hypersensitive to follitropin beta also.

Carcinogenicity

Long-term studies have not been done in animals to evaluate the carcinogenic potential of follitropin beta.

Mutagenicity

Follitropin beta was not found to be mutagenic in the Ames test and an *in vitro* chromosomal aberration test using human lymphocytes.

Pregnancy/Reproduction

Use of follitropin beta in treatment of infertility or as an adjunct with assisted reproduction technologies is associated with a high incidence of multiple gestations and multiple births. This may increase the risk of neonatal prematurity, as well as other complications associated with multiple gestations.

Fertility—Follitropin beta is used before a natural or an artificial luteinizing hormone (LH) surge to develop and recruit follicles in humans.

Pregnancy—Follitropin beta is not needed or recommended for use during pregnancy. Ovarian hyperstimulation syndrome (OHSS), which may be induced by follitropin beta therapy, is more common, more severe, and protracted in patients who conceive.

FDA Pregnancy Category X.

Breast-feeding

It is not known whether follitropin beta is distributed into breast milk.

Pharmacogenetics

Although drug clearance was comparable between groups of European women and Japanese women, the Japanese women absorbed more of a single 300 IU dose of follitropin beta given intramuscularly based on their lower body weight.

Medical considerations/Contraindications

The medical considerations/contraindications included have been selected on the basis of their potential clinical significance (reasons given in parentheses where appropriate)—not necessarily inclusive (» = major clinical significance).

Risk-benefit should be considered when the following medical problems exist:

» Abnormal uterine or genital bleeding, undiagnosed
(may delay diagnosis of endocrinopathology, such as endometrial hyperplasia or hormone-dependent carcinoma; inducing fertility and pregnancy may not be advisable for such patients)

» Adrenal function impairment, uncontrolled or
» Thyroid function impairment, uncontrolled or
» Tumors, intracranial or sex hormone-dependent
(increasing estrogen concentrations may make these conditions worse)

Asthma
(may be exacerbated)

Hypersensitivity to FSH preparations

» Ovarian cyst or enlargement, undetermined cause
(increased risk of further enlargement)

» Primary ovarian failure
(follitropin beta is ineffective in patients with primary ovarian failure)

Patient monitoring

The following may be especially important in patient monitoring (other tests may be warranted in some patients, depending on condition; » = major clinical significance):

Note: Patients should be examined for ovarian hyperstimulation syndrome (OHSS) every other day during treatment with follitropin beta and for 14 days posttreatment.

For female patients

Daily basal body temperature and/or
Progesterone, serum
(measurement of serum progesterone concentrations can be made prior to follitropin beta therapy to confirm anovulation. An increase in serum progesterone concentrations or a rise in basal body temperature can confirm ovulation)

» Estradiol, serum and/or
Examination, cervical secretions or vaginal cytology and
» Ultrasonography of ovaries and/or uterus
(ultrasonography and monitoring of serum estradiol concentrations can be used to monitor follicular development, predict time of human chorionic gonadotropin [hCG] administration, detect ovarian enlargement, and aid in minimizing risk of OHSS and multiple gestation)
(ultrasonography of the ovaries and endometrial lining can help confirm if ovulation occurs by viewing fluid in the cul-de-sac, ovarian stigmata, collapsed follicle, or secretory endometrium. Ultrasonography is especially helpful for evaluating the number of follicles, which is not predictable from serum estrogen concentration data)
(when evaluating follicular development, estrogenic changes of vaginal cytology or changes in volume or appearance of cervical mucus may be assessed as an adjunct to direct measurement of serum estradiol concentrations or viewing of the ovaries or endometrial lining by ultrasonography)

Pregnancy test
(pregnancy can be confirmed by testing for serum hCG)

For male partners

Sperm count and determinations of sperm motility and
Testosterone, serum
(baseline measurement of sperm count and activity in male partners is recommended to evaluate success of follitropin beta treat-

ment in females. If semen analysis is abnormal, serum testosterone concentration in the male partner may be measured)

Side/Adverse Effects

Note: Serious pulmonary and vascular complications and arterial thromboembolism have been reported both in association with and separate from ovarian hyperstimulation syndrome in patients who have received gonadotropins. Complications resulting from thromboembolism have included venous thrombophlebitis, pulmonary embolism, pulmonary infarction, stroke, arterial occlusion necessitating limb amputation, and, in rare cases, death. Serious pulmonary complications that have occurred include atelectasis, acute respiratory distress syndrome, and, rarely, death.

The following side/adverse effects have been selected on the basis of their potential clinical significance (possible signs and symptoms in parentheses where appropriate)—not necessarily inclusive:

Those indicating need for medical attention

Incidence more frequent

For patients treated for female infertility or patients pretreated with a gonadotropin-releasing hormone agonist (GnRHa) undergoing assisted reproductive technology (ART)

Ovarian hyperstimulation syndrome (OHSS) (abdominal pain, severe; nausea; rapid weight gain; vomiting)—7.6% for treatment of female infertility and 5.2% for ART

Incidence less frequent

For patients treated for female infertility or patients pretreated with a GnRHa undergoing ART

Abdominal pain—2.5 to 2.9%

For patients treated for female infertility

Ovarian cyst—2.9%

For patients pretreated with a GnRHa undergoing ART

Redness, pain, or swelling at site of injection—1.7%

Those indicating need for medical attention only if they continue or are bothersome

Breast tenderness; dermatological symptoms, such as dry skin; hair loss; hives; and skin rash; dizziness; dyspnea (difficulty in breathing); ***influenza-like symptoms, such as body aches or pain; chills; fever; headache; nausea; unusual tiredness; tachycardia*** (fast, racing heart); ***tachypnea*** (quick, shallow breathing)

Note: The above side/adverse effects have not been reported in patients specifically receiving follitropin beta but have been reported for patients receiving gonadotropins and may potentially occur for follitropin beta.

Those indicating possible development of OHSS and/or the need for medical attention if they occur after medication is discontinued

OHSS (abdominal pain, severe; nausea; rapid weight gain; vomiting)—usually occurring within 7 to 10 days after treatment discontinuation

Patient Consultation

As an aid to patient consultation, refer to *Advice for the Patient, Follitropin Beta (Systemic)*.

In providing consultation, consider emphasizing the following selected information (» = major clinical significance):

Before using this medication

» Conditions affecting use, especially:

Hypersensitivity to follicle-stimulating hormone (FSH) preparations

Pregnancy—Use during pregnancy is not needed or recommended; increased risk of multiple gestations and their associated complications and protracted ovarian hyperstimulation syndrome (OHSS) in patients who conceive

Other medical problems, especially abnormal uterine or genital bleeding, undiagnosed; adrenal function impairment, uncontrolled; intracranial or sex hormone–dependent tumors; ovarian cyst or enlargement, undetermined cause; primary ovarian failure; or thyroid function impairment, uncontrolled

Proper use of this medication

Carefully reading patient instructions provided

For patients self-administering the medication

Proper preparation of medication; using proper technique to prevent contamination of the medication, work area, and patient during transfer between containers

Proper administration; using proper needle and syringe

Knowing proper dose to use and not using more than prescribed

Carefully selecting and rotating injection sites as directed by physician

Disposing of needles, syringes, vials, and unused medication properly

Alerting physician when last dose of follitropin beta is given and knowing that another drug called human chorionic gonadotropin may be required as a single injection 24 hours after the last dose of follitropin beta

» Proper dosing

Missed dose: Calling physician for advice; do not double doses

» Proper storage

Precautions while using this medication

» Understanding the duration of treatment and the importance of being monitored every other day by physician during treatment and for at least 2 weeks after treatment stops

» Importance of following physician's instructions for recording basal body temperature, if requested, and timing of intercourse

» If abdominal pain occurs, discontinuing treatment of follitropin beta, notifying physician, not having injection of hCG, and avoiding sexual intercourse

Understanding that dizziness can occur with use of follitropin beta and may impair driving, using machines, or other dangerous tasks

Side/adverse effects

Signs of potential side effects, especially:

For patients treated for female infertility or patients pretreated with a GnRHa undergoing ART—Ovarian hyperstimulation syndrome; abdominal pain

For patients treated for female infertility—Ovarian cyst

For patients pretreated with a GnRHa undergoing ART—Redness, pain, or swelling at site of injection

General Dosing Information

Patients receiving follitropin beta should be under the supervision of a physician experienced in the treatment of gynecologic or endocrine disorders. Patient and physician should be willing to devote considerable time to case-management.

Dosage varies considerably and must be adjusted to meet the individual requirements of each patient, on the basis of clinical response.

If the ovaries are abnormally enlarged on the last day of follitropin beta treatment, hCG should not be administered to minimize risk of ovarian hyperstimulation syndrome (OHSS). OHSS develops rapidly (between 24 and 72 hours) and is distinct from uncomplicated ovarian enlargement. Patients should be monitored every other day for 2 weeks after treatment ends, since the risk of OHSS reaches its maximal potential at 7 to 10 days posttreatment.

Patients self-injecting follitropin beta should be given the patient information sheet and instructed on how to prepare the medication and injection site, administer the medication, and safely discard used items. Injection sites should be rotated and medication administered subcutaneously to upper thigh or at waistline or administered intramuscularly to the upper outer quadrant of the buttocks.

For patients treated for ovulation induction

Conception should be attempted daily beginning within 24 hours of administration of hCG until ovulation is thought to have occurred.

If ovulation does not occur after any cycle of therapy, the therapeutic regimen employed should be re-evaluated. After three to six cycles of nonovulatory menses, the appropriateness of continuing the use of follitropin beta for ovulation induction should be reconsidered.

Bioequivalence information

According to physicochemical tests and assays, the primary and tertiary structures of follitropin alfa, follitropin beta, and human follicle-stimulating hormone (FSH) are indistinguishable from one another, but alfa and beta forms are based on different international reference standards. These hormones are similar to formulations of human menopausal urine-derived follicle-stimulating hormone (urofollitropin), but without urinary protein for the nonpurified dosage form. Also, follitropin beta's action is similar to that of menotropins, but follitropin beta does not contain the urinary protein or luteinizing hormone (LH) components.

Safety considerations for handling this medication

Precautions include:

• Use of proper technique to prevent contamination of the medication, work area, and operator during transfer between containers, including proper training in this technique for patients self-administering the medication.

• Cautious and proper disposal of needles, syringes, vials, ampuls, and unused medication.

For treatment of adverse effects

Ovarian enlargement, ovarian cyst formation, or ovarian hyperstimulation syndrome (OHSS)—

• Discontinuing therapy until ovarian size has returned to baseline. Human chorionic gonadotropin should also be withheld for that cycle.

• Prohibiting intercourse until ovarian size has returned to baseline to prevent cyst rupture.

• Reducing dosage of follitropin beta in next course of therapy.

• Most cases of ovarian enlargement, ovarian cyst formation, or OHSS will spontaneously resolve when menses begins. In selected cases, hospitalization of the patient and bed rest may be necessary.

• Limiting performance of pelvic examinations since they may result in rupture of ovarian cysts and hemoperitoneum.

• When treating OHSS, the general purpose of therapy is to prevent hemoconcentration and minimize risk of thromboembolism and renal injury.

—*Acute phase of OHSS*: The electrolyte imbalance should be corrected cautiously while an acceptable intravascular volume is maintained; in the acute phase, intravascular volume deficit cannot be completely corrected without increasing third space fluid volume.

• Specific treatment:

—Avoiding diuretic use since it reduces intravascular volume further.

—Administering intravenous fluids, electrolytes, and Albumin Human USP as needed to maintain adequate urine output and to avoid hemoconcentration.

—Administering analgesics as needed.

• Monitoring:

—Monitoring fluid intake and output, body weight, hematocrit, serum and urine electrolytes, urine specific gravity, blood urea nitrogen (BUN) and creatinine, total protein with albumin:globulin ratio, coagulation studies, and abdominal girth daily or as often as required.

—Monitoring serum potassium concentrations and electrocardiogram for development of hyperkalemia.

• Supportive care:

—Removing ascitic, pleural, or pericardial fluid *only* if it is imperative for relief of symptoms such as respiratory distress or cardiac tamponade; to do so may increase risk of injury to the ovary.

—In patients who require surgery to control bleeding from ovarian cyst rupture, employing surgical measures that also maximally conserve ovarian tissue.

—*Intermediate phase of OHSS*: Once patient is stabilized, minimize third spacing of fluids.

• Specific treatment:

—Avoiding diuretic use.

—Restricting or cautiously replacing potassium, sodium, and fluids as required, based on monitoring of serum electrolyte concentrations.

—*Resolution phase of OHSS*: In this phase, the third space fluid shifts to the intravascular compartment, resulting in decreased hematocrit value and increased urinary output.

• Monitoring: Peripheral and/or pulmonary edema may result if mobilized third space fluid volume exceeds renal output.

• Specific treatment: Administering diuretics when required to manage pulmonary edema.

Parenteral Dosage Forms

FOLLITROPIN BETA FOR INJECTION

Usual adult dose

Infertility, female—

Subcutaneous or intramuscular, 75 international units (IU) once a day, for up to fourteen days. Then the dose is increased by 37.5 IU at weekly intervals if clinically indicated after measurement of the serum estradiol concentration and follicular development. Total daily dose should not routinely exceed 300 IU. Treatment should be discontinued if the ovaries become abnormally enlarged or abdominal pain occurs, and the patient should be advised to avoid sexual intercourse.

To complete follicular development and to induce ovulation in the absence of a luteinizing hormone (LH) surge, human chorionic gonadotropin (hCG) is administered one day after the last dose of follitropin beta treatment. Human chorionic gonadotropin should not be injected if the ovaries are abnormally enlarged or the ovarian response is inappropriate, as shown by serum estradiol concentrations or ultrasonography.

Reproductive technologies, assisted—

Subcutaneous or intramuscular, 150 to 225 international units (IU) once a day, beginning cycle Day 2 or Day 3 for the first four days of treatment. Dose may then be adjusted according to an individual's ovarian response; daily maintenance doses of 75 to 300 IU for six to twelve days are usually sufficient. About 10% of patients who do not respond may need higher doses of 375 to 600 IU.

After a sufficient number of follicles are produced, hCG is administered one day after the last dose of follitropin beta treatment to complete follicular development in all patients not experiencing an LH surge, unless the ovaries are abnormally enlarged. Egg retrieval is attempted thirty-four to thirty-six hours later.

Strength(s) usually available

U.S.—

75 International Units (Rx) [*Follistim* (polysorbate 20; sucrose 25 mg; sodium citrate dihydrate 7.35 mg)].

Packaging and storage

Store between 2 and 25 °C (36 and 77 °F). Protect from light.

Preparation of dosage form

Using standard aseptic technique, follitropin beta is reconstituted by adding 1 mL of 0.45% Sodium Chloride Injection USP to a vial of follitropin beta to make 75 IU per mL. The vial should be swirled slowly, not shaken. For larger doses, the contents of the first vial can be used as the diluent for subsequent vials; up to four vials can be used to make a solution of 300 IU per mL. After reconstitution, the solution should be checked to determine that it is thoroughly mixed, clear, and free of particles before combining the contents of the next vial of follitropin beta.

Stability

The solution should be used immediately after reconstitution and any unused material discarded. The solution should not be used if it is cloudy or discolored.

Auxiliary labeling

• Protect from light.

Note

Include patient package information when dispensing.

Revised: 02/24/1998

FONDAPARINUX Systemic†

INN: Fondaparin Sodium

VA CLASSIFICATION (Primary): BL119

Commonly used brand name(s): *Arixtra*.

Note: For a listing of dosage forms and brand names by country availability, see *Dosage Forms* section(s).

†Not commercially available in Canada.

Category

Antithrombotic.

Indications

Accepted

Deep vein thrombosis (prophylaxis)—Fondaparinux is indicated for the prophylaxis of deep vein thrombosis, which may lead to pulmonary embolism in patients undergoing hip fracture surgery, hip replacement surgery, knee replacement surgery, or in patients undergoing abdominal surgery who are at risk for thromboembolic complications.

Deep vein thrombosis, acute (treatment)—Fondaparinux is indicated for the treatment of acute deep vein thrombosis when administered in conjunction with warfarin sodium.

Pulmonary embolism, acute (treatment)—Fondaparinux is indicated for the treatment of acute pulmonary embolism when administered in conjunction with warfarin sodium when initial therapy is administered in the hospital.

Pharmacology/Pharmacokinetics

Physicochemical characteristics

Molecular weight—1728.

pH—5.0 to 8.0

Mechanism of action/Effect

Antithrombotic—the antithrombotic activity of fondaparinux is the result of antithrombin III [ATIII]-mediated selective inhibition of Factor Xa. By selectively binding to ATIII, fondaparinux potentiates the innate neutralization of Factor Xa by ATIII. Neutralization of Factor Xa interrupts the blood coagulation cascade and thus inhibits thrombin formation and thrombus development.

Fondaparinux does not inactivate thrombin (activated Factor II) and has no known effect on the platelet function. At the recommended dose, fondaparinux does not affect fibrinolytic activity or bleeding time.

Absorption
Absolute bioavailability—100%

Distribution
Volume of distribution (Vol_D)—Steady state and non-steady state: 7 to 11 L; distributes mainly in the blood and only to a minor extent in extravascular fluid.

Protein binding
Very high (94%)—To antithrombin III [ATIII]

Fondaparinux does not bind significantly to other plasma proteins (including platelet Factor 4 or red blood cells).

Half-life
Elimination—17 to 21 hours

Time to peak concentration
Following subcutaneous administration of 2.5 mg to young male subjects—2 hours

Peak plasma concentration:
Following subcutaneous administration of 2.5 mg to young male subjects—0.34 mg per liter

Duration of action
Following discontinuation of fondaparinux, its anticoagulant effects may persist for 2 to 4 days in patients with normal renal function. In patients with impaired renal function, the anticoagulant effects may persist even longer.

Elimination
Renal—In patients with normal renal function following a single subcutaneous or intravenous dose of fondaparinux, up to 77% of the dose is eliminated in the urine as unchanged drug in 72 hours.

Note: Fondaparinux elimination is prolonged 25 to 55% in patients with mild to severe renal impairment, 25% in patients over the age of 75, and 30% in patients weighing less than 50 kg of body weight. See *Fondaparinux (Systemic)—Medical considerations/Contraindications*

Precautions to Consider

Carcinogenicity
Appropriate studies in animals have not been done to evaluate the carcinogenic potential of fondaparinux.

Mutagenicity
Fondaparinux was not genotoxic in the Ames test, the mouse lymphoma cell forward mutation test, the human lymphocyte chromosome aberration test, the rat hepatocyte unscheduled DNA synthesis test, or the rat micronucleus test.

Pregnancy/Reproduction
Fertility—Fondaparinux was found to have no effect on fertility and reproductive performance of male and female rats at subcutaneous doses up to 10 mg per kg of body weight per day (32 times the recommended human dose based on body surface area).

Pregnancy—Adequate and well-controlled studies in pregnant women have not been done. Because animal reproduction studies are not always predictive of human response, this drug should be used during pregnancy only if clearly needed.

Reproduction studies done in pregnant rats and pregnant rabbits up to 10 mg per kg of body weight per day (respectively 32 and 65 times the human dose based on body surface area) have revealed no evidence of impaired fertility or harm to the fetus due to fondaparinux.

FDA Pregnancy Category B

Breast-feeding
It is not known whether fondaparinux is distributed into human breast milk. Because many drugs are distributed into human milk, caution should be exercised when fondaparinux sodium is administered to a nursing mother.

Fondaparinux has been found to be distributed into the milk of lactating rats.

Pediatrics
No information is available on the relationship of age to the effects of fondaparinux in the pediatric population. Safety and efficacy have not been established.

Geriatrics
The risk of fondaparinux-associated major bleeding increased with age by 1.8% in patients less than 65 years old, 2.2% in patients 65 to 74 years of age and 2.7% in those 75 years of age or older. Additionally, serious adverse events increased with age for patients receiving fondaparinux. Careful attention to dosing directions and concomitant medications, especially antiplatelet medication, is recommended. Elderly patients are more likely to have age-related renal function impairment, which may require monitoring.

Drug interactions and/or related problems
The following drug interactions and/or related problems have been selected on the basis of their potential clinical significance (possible mechanism in parentheses where appropriate)—not necessarily inclusive (» = major clinical significance):

Note: In clinical studies, the concomitant use of fondaparinux with oral anticoagulants (warfarin), platelet inhibitors (acetylsalicylic acid), NSAIDs (piroxicam) and digoxin did not significantly affect the pharmacokinetics/pharmacodynamics of fondaparinux.

Medications that may enhance the risk of hemorrhage should be discontinued prior to initiation of fondaparinux therapy. If co-administration is essential, close monitoring may be necessary.

Laboratory value alterations
The following have been selected on the basis of their potential clinical significance (possible effect in parentheses where appropriate)—not necessarily inclusive (» = major clinical significance).

With physiology/laboratory test values

Alanine aminotransferase (ALT [SGPT]) and
Aspartate aminotransferase (AST [SGOT])
(serum levels may be increased during fondaparinux therapy to levels greater than three times the upper limit of normal and are fully reversible; the elevation is rarely associated with increases in bilirubin)

Note: Since aminotransferase determinations are important in the differential diagnosis of myocardial infarction, liver disease and pulmonary emboli, elevations that might be caused by fondaparinux should be interpreted with caution.

Medical considerations/Contraindications
The medical considerations/contraindications included have been selected on the basis of their potential clinical significance (reasons given in parentheses where appropriate)—not necessarily inclusive (» = major clinical significance).

Except under special circumstances, this medication should not be used when the following medical problem exists:

» Bleeding, active major or
» Endocarditis, bacterial or
» Thrombocytopenia associated with a positive *in vitro* test for anti-platelet antibody in the presence of fondaparinux
(fondaparinux is contraindicated in patients with active major bleeding, bacterial endocarditis or in patients with thrombocytopenia associated with a positive *in vitro* test for anti-platelet antibody in the presence of fondaparinux.)

» Body weight less than 50 kilograms
(risk of major bleeding episodes was doubled during clinical trials; prophylactic therapy **contraindicated** in patients weighing <50 kg undergoing hip fracture, hip replacement or knee replacement surgery, and abdominal surgery; should be used with caution in treatment of deep vein thrombosis and pulmonary embolism)

» Hypersensitivity to fondaparinux

» Renal impairment, severe
(risk of major bleeding episodes is increased; fondaparinux elimination is prolonged in patients with severe renal impairment (creatine clearance < 30 mL per min); in patients undergoing elective hip surgery or hip fracture surgery, the total clearance of fondaparinux is approximately 55% lower in patients with severe renal impairment.)

Risk-benefit should be considered when the following medical problems exist:

Any medical procedure or condition in which the risk of bleeding or hemorrhage is present, such as: (risk of epidural or spinal hematoma, which can result in long-term or permanent paralysis; this risk is increased with the use of indwelling epidural catheters or by the concomitant use of medications that affect hemostasis, such as nonsteroidal anti-inflammatory drugs, platelet inhibitors, or other anticoagulants; the risk also may be increased by traumatic or repeated epidural or spinal puncture.)

» Anesthesia, epidural or spinal

» Stroke, hemorrhagic,
» Surgery, brain, ophthalmological, or spinal, recent
» Ulcerative and angiodysplastic gastrointestinal disease, active
» Bleeding diathesis
» Bleeding disorders, congenital or acquired or
» Diabetic retinopathy, recent history ofor
» Gastrointestinal ulceration, recent or history ofor
» Hemorrhage, recent history ofor
» Hypertension, uncontrolled arterialor
» Platelet defects, or
» Thrombocytopenia, heparin-induced
(caution is recommended)
» Renal impairment, mild or moderate
(risk of major bleeding episodes is increased; fondaparinux elimination is prolonged in patients with mild or moderate renal impairment (respectively, creatinine clearance 50 to 80 mL per minutes and 30 to 50 mL per minute); in patients undergoing elective hip surgery or hip fracture surgery, the total clearance of fondaparinux is approximately 25% lower in patients with mild renal impairment and 40% lower in patients with moderate renal impairment; use with caution in patients with a history of heparin-induced thrombocytopenia.)

Patient monitoring

The following may be especially important in patient monitoring (other tests may be warranted in some patients, depending on condition; » = major clinical significance):

» Blood counts, complete, including
Platelet count
(recommended routinely during the course of treatment; any degree of thrombocytopenia should be closely monitored and fondaparinux should be discontinued if the platelet count falls below 100,000 per mm^3)

» Blood tests, occult
(recommended routinely during the course of treatment with fondaparinux injection)

» Neurologic status
(monitor for signs and symptoms of neurological impairment; if neurologic compromise is noted, urgent treatment is necessary.)

» Renal function, including serum creatinine concentration
(should be assessed routinely throughout treatment; fondaparinux should be discontinued immediately in patients who develop severe renal impairment or labile renal function.)

Note: Routine coagulation tests such as prothrombin time and activated partial thromboplastin time are relatively insensitive measures of fondaparinux activity and are unsuitable for patient monitoring.

Side/Adverse Effects

The following side/adverse effects have been selected on the basis of their potential clinical significance (possible signs and symptoms in parentheses where appropriate)—not necessarily inclusive:

Note: Spinal or epidural hematomas, which may result in long-term or permanent paralysis, can occur with the use of anticoagulants and neuroaxial (spinal/epidural) anesthesia or spinal puncture. The risk of these events may be higher with post-operative use of indwelling epidural catheters or concomitant use of other drugs affecting hemostasis such as NSAIDs.

Those indicating need for medical attention

Incidence more frequent

Anemia (pale skin; troubled breathing with exertion; unusual bleeding or bruising; unusual tiredness or weakness)

Incidence less frequent

Hematoma (collection of blood under skin; deep, dark purple bruises; itching, pain, redness, or swelling at place of injection); ***hemorrhage, post-operative*** (bleeding)—including intracranial, cerebral and retroperitoneal hemorrhage; ***hypokalemia*** (convulsions; decreased urine; dry mouth; irregular heartbeat; increased thirst; loss of appetite; mood changes; muscle pain or cramps; nausea or vomiting; numbness or tingling in hands, feet, or lips; shortness of breath; unusual tiredness or weakness); ***hypotension*** (blurred vision; confusion; dizziness, faintness, or lightheadedness when getting up from a lying or sitting position; sudden sweating; unusual tiredness or weakness); ***thrombocytopenia, moderate*** (black, tarry stools; bleeding gums; blood in urine or stools; pinpoint red spots on skin; unusual bleeding or bruising)—platelet count between 50,000 and 100,000 mm^3; ***urinary tract infection*** (bladder pain; bloody or cloudy urine; difficult, burning, or painful urination; frequent urge to urinate; lower back or side pain); ***wound infection, post-operative*** (red, tender, or oozing skin at incision)

Incidence rare

Thrombocytopenia, severe (black, tarry stools; bleeding gums; blood in urine or stools; pinpoint red spots on skin; unusual bleeding or bruising)—platelet count less than 50,000 mm^3

Those indicating need for medical attention only if they continue or are bothersome

Incidence more frequent

Constipation (difficulty having a bowel movement); ***edema*** (swelling); ***fever; insomnia*** (sleeplessness; trouble sleeping; inability to sleep); ***local irritation*** (injection site bleeding; pruritus; rash); ***nausea; rash; vomiting***

Incidence less frequent

Bullous eruption (skin blisters); ***confusion; diarrhea; dizziness; dyspepsia*** (acid or sour stomach; belching; heartburn; indigestion; stomach discomfort, upset or pain); ***headache; pain; pneumonia*** (chest pain; cough; fever or chills; sneezing; shortness of breath; sore throat; troubled breathing; tightness in chest; wheezing); ***purpura*** (pinpoint red or purple spots on skin); ***surgical site reaction*** (unusual changes to site of surgery); ***urinary retention*** (decrease in urine volume; decrease in frequency of urination; difficulty in passing urine; dribbling urine; painful urination); ***wound drainage, increased***

Overdose

Clinical effects of overdose

The following effects have been selected on the basis of their potential clinical significance (possible signs and symptoms in parentheses where appropriate)—not necessarily inclusive:

Hemorrhagic complications (abdominal pain or swelling; back pain; blood in eyes; blood in urine; black, sticky stools; bruising or purple areas on skin; coughing up blood; decreased alertness; dizziness; headache; joint pain or swelling; nosebleeds)

Treatment of overdose

There is no antidote for fondaparinux.

Fondaparinux therapy should be discontinued following an overdose associated with bleeding complications and appropriate treatment should be initiated.

To enhance elimination—
Data obtained during studies in patients undergoing chronic intermittent hemodialysis suggest that fondaparinux clearance can increase by 20% during hemodialysis

Supportive care—
Treatment should be symptomatic and supportive.
Patients in whom intentional overdose is confirmed or suspected should be referred for psychiatric consultation.

Patient Consultation

As an aid to patient consultation, refer to *Advice for the Patient, Fondaparinux (Systemic)*.

In providing consultation, consider emphasizing the following selected information (» = major clinical significance):

Before using this medication

» Conditions affecting use, especially:
Hypersensitivity to fondaparinux
Use in the elderly—The risk of fondaparinux-associated major bleeding increased with age; serious adverse events increased with age for patients receiving fondaparinux; careful attention to dosing directions and concomitant medications, especially antiplatelet medication, is recommended; elderly patients are more likely to have age-related renal function impairment, which may require monitoring.
Other medical problems, especially active major bleeding, bacterial endocarditis, body weight less than 50 kilograms, congenital or acquired bleeding disorders, bleeding diathesis, recent history of diabetic retinopathy, epidural or spinal anesthesia, gastrointestinal ulceration, recent history of hemorrhage, hemorrhagic stroke, renal impairment, platelet defects; recent surgery, thrombocytopenia, ulcerative and angiodysplastic gastrointestinal disease, or uncontrolled hypertension.

Proper use of this medication

» Not administering before 6 hours after surgery; associated with increased risk of major bleeding
» Proper injection technique
» Safe handling and disposal of syringe
» Proper dosing

Missed dose: Taking as soon as possible; not taking if almost time for next scheduled dose; not doubling doses

» Proper storage

Precautions while using this medication

» Need to inform all physicians and dentists that this medication is being used.

» Notifying physician immediately if signs and symptoms of bleeding occur

Side/adverse effects

Signs of potential side effects, especially anemia, hematoma, hemorrhage, hypokalemia, hypotension, thrombocytopenia, urinary tract infection, or wound infection (post-operative).

General Dosing Information

Fondaparinux cannot be used interchangeably (unit for unit) with heparin, low molecular weight heparins or heparinoids.

Administration of fondaparinux before 6 hours after surgery has been associated with an increased risk of major bleeding.

Fondaparinux is administered by subcutaneous injection into the fatty tissue once daily; injection sites should be rotated. Fondaparinux must not be injected intramuscularly.

Parenteral Dosage Forms

FONDAPARINUX SODIUM INJECTION

Usual adult dose

Deep vein thrombosis, prophylaxis—

Subcutaneous, 2.5 mg once a day

Treatment should be initiated after hemostasis has been established and the initial dose given 6 to 8 hours after surgery. Administration of fondaparinux less than 6 hours after surgery has been associated with an increased risk of major bleeding.

Deep vein thrombosis (treatment) or
Pulmonary embolism (treatment)—

Subcutaneous, 5 mg (body weight <50 kg), 7.5 mg (body weight 50 to 100 kg), or 10 mg (body weight >100 kg) once day with fondaparinux treatment continuing for at least 5 days and until a therapeutic oral anticoagulant effect is established (INR 2 to 3). Concomitant treatment with warfarin sodium should be initiated as soon as possible, usually within 72 hours.

Usual adult prescribing limits

Deep vein thrombosis, prophylaxis—

Following hip or knee replacement surgeries: The usual duration of treatment is 5 to 9 days; up to 11 days of treatment has been tolerated.

In patients undergoing hip fracture surgery: An extended prophylaxis course of up to 24 additional days is recommended and a total of 32 days (peri-operative and extended prophylaxis) has been tolerated.

Following abdominal surgery: The usual duration of treatment is 5 to 9 days; up to 10 days of treatment has been administered.

Deep vein thrombosis (treatment) or
Pulmonary embolism (treatment)—

The usual duration of treatment is 5 to 9 days; up to 26 days of treatment has been administered.

Usual pediatric dose

Safety and efficacy have not been established.

Usual geriatric dose

See *Usual adult dose.*

Note: Dose selection for elderly patients should be cautious because of the greater frequency of geriatric-specific problems.

Usual geriatric prescribing limits

See *Usual adult prescribing limits.*

Strength(s) usually available

U.S.—

2.5 mg of fondaparinux sodium in 0.5 mL (Rx) [*Arixtra* (sodium chloride; water)].

5 mg of fondaparinux sodium in 0.4 mL (Rx) [*Arixtra* (sodium chloride; water)].

7.5 mg of fondaparinux sodium in 0.6 mL (Rx) [*Arixtra* (sodium chloride; water)].

10 mg of fondaparinux sodium in 0.8 mL (Rx) [*Arixtra* (sodium chloride; water)].

Packaging and storage

Store at 25 °C (77 °F), USP Controlled Room Temperature, excursions permitted to 15 to 30 °C (59 to 86°F)

Preparation of dosage form

The pre-filled syringe should be visually inspected prior to administration for particulate matter and discoloration.

To avoid loss of drug when using the pre-filled syringe, do not expel the air bubble from the syringe before the injection.

Incompatibilities

Fondaparinux should not be mixed with other injections or infusions.

Auxiliary labeling

- Keep out of the reach of children
- For single dose only. Discard unused drug

Revised: 08/22/2005
Developed: 07/22/2002

FORMOTEROL—See *Bronchodilators, Adrenergic (Inhalation-Local)*

FORMOTEROL Inhalation-Local

VA CLASSIFICATION (Primary): RE 120

Commonly used brand name(s): *Foradil; Oxeze.*

Note: For a listing of dosage forms and brand names by country availability, see *Dosage Forms* section(s).

Category

Bronchodilator, adrenergic (inhalation).

Indications

Accepted

Asthma (adjunctive treatment)—Formoterol is indicated to treat asthma concomitantly with short-acting beta$_2$-agonists, inhaled or systemic corticosteroids and theophylline therapy.

Note: Canadian product information states formoterol is indicated in patients who are using optimal corticosteroid treatment and experiencing regular or frequent breakthrough symptoms requiring regular use of short-acting bronchodilators.

Asthma (treatment)—Formoterol is indicated for long-term maintenance treatment of asthma in adult and children 5 years of age and older with reversible obstructive airway disease, including patients with symptoms of nocturnal asthma,

Note: Canadian product information states formoterol is indicated in treatment of asthma in adults and children ages 6 and older.

Chronic obstructive pulmonary disease [COPD] (treatment)—Formoterol is indicated as long-term, twice-daily administration in the treatment of patients with chronic obstructive pulmonary disease including chronic bronchitis and emphysema.

Exercise-induced bronchospasm [EIB] (prevention)[1]—Formoterol is indicated for the acute prevention of exercise-induced bronchospasm when administered on an occasional, as needed basis.

Unaccepted

Not to be used in patients whose asthma can be managed by occasional use of short-acting inhaled β_2-agonists.

Formoterol inhalation powder should not be the first medicine prescribed to treat a patient's asthma. It should be used only for patients who have not adequately responded to other asthma medications, such as inhaled corticosteroids. The National Heart, Lung, and Blood Institute (NHLBI) and World Health Organization (WHO) guidelines recommend inhaled corticosteroids as the first step in controller therapy, with long-beta$_2$-agonists as an option if low-to-medium dose inhaled corticosteroids do not adequately control the patient's asthma.

[1]Not included in Canadian product labeling.

Pharmacology/Pharmacokinetics

Physicochemical characteristics

Molecular weight—840.9.

pKa—

Phenolic group: 7.9.

Amino group: 9.2.

Mechanism of action/Effect
Formoterol is a long-acting selective stimulator of the beta$_2$adrenergic receptors in bronchial smooth muscle. This stimulation causes relaxation of smooth muscle fibers and produces bronchodilation.

Bioavailability:
Pulmonary: 21-37%
Total systemic: 46%

Protein binding
Moderate (61 to 64%)
Serum albumin binding was 31 to 38% over a range of 5 to 500 ng per mL.

Biotransformation
Hepatic via cytochrome P450 isozymes (CYP2D6, CYP2C19, CYP2C9 and CYP2A6) and non-450 pathways (glucuronidation, O-demethylation and direct conjugation).

Half-life
Mean terminal: 10 hours.

Onset of action
1–3 minutes

Time to peak concentration
5 minutes following a single 120 mcg (10 times the recommended clinical dose) inhaled dose.

Peak serum concentration
92 picograms per mL following inhalation of a single 120 mcg dose.

Duration of action
12 hours

Elimination
Following inhalation—
- Primarily eliminated via metabolism
- In asthma patients following a 12 or 24 mcg dose: 10% and 15 to 18% excreted unchanged in the urine, respectively
- In COPD patients following a 12 or 24 mcg dose: 7% and 6 to 9% excreted unchanged in the urine, respectively

Following oral administration—
- In healthy patients following an 80 mcg dose: 59 to 62% excreted in the urine and 32 to 34% excreted in the feces. Renal clearance from the blood was 150 mL per min.

Precautions to Consider

Carcinogenicity
Carcinogenic potential of formoterol has been evaluated in drinking water and dietary studies in both rats and mice. The incidence of ovarian leiomyomas in rats was increased at doses of 15 mg per kg and above in the drinking water study and at 20 mg per kg in the dietary study. The incidence of benign ovarian theca-cell tumors in rats was increased at doses of 0.5 mg per kg and above in the dietary study. The incidence of adrenal subcapsular adenomas and carcinomas was increased in male mice at doses of 69 mg per kg and above in the drinking water study, but not at doses up to 50 mg per kg in the dietary study. The incidence of hepatocarcinomaswas increased in the dietary study at doses of 20 and 50 mg per kg in female mice and 50 mg per kg in male mice.Uterine leiomyomas and leiomyosarcomashave been found in mice following oral administration of formoterol. Similarly, mesovarian leiomyomas have been found in rats following inhalation of formoterol.These are expected findings in mice and rats administered beta-stimulating agents.

Mutagenicity
Formoterol was not shown to be mutagenic or clastogenic in any of the following: bacterial and mammalian cell mutagenicity tests, chromosome analyses tests in mammalian cells, unscheduled DNA synthesis repair tests in human fibroblasts or in rat hepatocytes, transformation assay in mammalian fibroblasts and micronucleus tests in mice and in rats.

Pregnancy/Reproduction
Fertility—Reproduction studies in rats revealed no impairment of fertility at oral doses up to 3 mg per kg (approximately 1000 times the maximum recommended daily inhalation dose in humans on a mg per m basis).

Pregnancy—There are no adequate and well-controlled studies in pregnant women.Safety and efficacy in pregnant women has not been established.

In animal studies formoterol has been shown to cause stillbirth and neonatal mortality at oral doses of 6 mg per kg (approximately 2000 times the maximum recommended daily inhalation dose in humans on a mg per m$_2$ basis) and above in rats receiving the drug during the late stage of pregnancy. When formoterol was given to rats throughout organogenesis, oral doses of 0.2 mg per kg and above delayed ossification of the fetus, and doses of 6 mg per kg and above decreased fetal weight.

Formoterol did not cause malformations in rats or rabbits following oral administration.

Note: Canadian product information states the following findings regarding the use of formoterol during pregnancy: Rat studies have found that placental weights increase and maternal weights decrease following inhaled doses of .004–1.2 mg per kg of formoterol. No teratogenic effects were seen at any dosing level.

Studies in rabbits have demonstrated an increase in both maternal and placental weight following oral formoterol doses of .2, 3.5 and 60 mg per kg. A higher percentage of liver cysts, extra ribs and reduced and/or asymmetric/bipartite sternbrae in the fetuses was noted following maternal doses of 60 mg per kg (7000–11000 times the recommended human exposure)

FDA Pregnancy Category C

Labor and delivery—There are no adequate and well controlled studies on the effects of formoterol when used during labor. However, β_2-agonists such as formoterol have the potential for interference with uterine contractility and should only be used when the potential benefit to the mother outweighs the potential risk to the fetus.

Breast-feeding
There are no adequate and well-controlled studies in nursing women.It is not known whether formoterol is distributed in human breast milk. However, it is distributed in rat milk after oral administration. Risk-benefit should be carefully considered before administering formoterol to nursing mothers.

Pediatrics
Appropriate studies on the relationship of age to the effect of formoterol have not been performed in children less than 5 years of age. Use in children less than 5 years of age is not recommended due to limited clinical data.

Note: Canadian product information states that use in children less than 6 years of age is not recommended

Geriatrics
Appropriate studies performed to date have not demonstrated geriatrics-specific problems that would limit the usefulness of formoterol in the elderly. However, greater sensitivity of some older individuals cannot be ruled out.

Drug interactions and/or related problems
The following drug interactions and/or related problems have been selected on the basis of their potential clinical significance (possible mechanism in parentheses where appropriate)—not necessarily inclusive (» = major clinical significance):

Note: Combinations containing any of the following medications, depending on the amount present, may also interact with this medication.

Adrenergic drugs, additional
(may potentiate the pharmacologically predictable sympathetic effects of formoterol)

Alcohol or
Levodopa or
Levothyroxine or
Oxytocin
(may impair cardiac tolerance towards beta$_2$-sympathomimetics)

» Antidepressants, tricyclic or
» Disopyramide or
» Phenothiazines or
» Procainamide or
» Quinidine
(concomitant treatment may prolong the QTc interval and increase the risk of ventricular arrhythmias)

» Beta-receptor blocking agents
(may partly or totally inhibit the effect of beta-stimulants; beta-blockers with less predominant beta$_2$blocking effects should be considered; patients should be monitored for deterioration in pulmonary function; dosage adjustment of either drug may be necessary)

Diuretics, non potassium-sparing or
Digitalis glycosides or
Methylxanthines or
Steroids
(may potentiate the hypokalemic effect of beta$_2$ agonists and lead to an increased disposition towards arrhythmias in patients. ECG

changes and/or hypokalemia that may result from the administration of non-potassium-sparing diuretics can be acutely worsened by beta-agonists)

Halogenated hydrocarbons
(may increase risk of arrhythmias in patients receiving halogenated hydrocarbon anesthesia)

» Monoamine oxidase inhibitors, including furazolidine and procarbazine
(concomitant treatment may prolong the QTc interval and increase the risk of ventricular arrhythmias; may increase chance of hypertensive reactions)

Laboratory value alterations

The following have been selected on the basis of their potential clinical significance (possible effect in parentheses where appropriate)—not necessarily inclusive (» = major clinical significance).

With physiology/laboratory test values

Blood pressure
(clinically significant changes in systolic and/or diastolic blood pressure have been seen infrequently in controlled clinical studies, but may necessitate the discontinuation of formoterol.)

Electrocardiogram
(prolonged QTc interval, flattening of the T wave and ST segment depression reported)

Glucose, blood
(concentrations may be increased, possibly due to glycogenolysis; clinically significant changes may be more pronounced following nebulization or with frequent use of higher doses or an overdose)

Potassium, serum
(concentrations may be decreased, possibly through intracellular shunting; the decrease is dose-related, is usually transient, and may not require supplementation; effects may be more pronounced following frequent use of higher doses or an overdose)

Pulse rate
(clinically significant increases in pulse rate may occur. Although reported as an uncommon occurrence, it may necessitate the discontinuation of formoterol.)

Medical considerations/Contraindications

The medical considerations/contraindications included have been selected on the basis of their potential clinical significance (reasons given in parentheses where appropriate)—not necessarily inclusive (» = major clinical significance).

Except under special circumstances, this medication should not be used when the following medical problems exist:

Acutely deteriorating asthma
(increased risk of adverse events, contraindicated)

» Hypersensitivity to formoterol or
» Inhaled lactose

» Tachyarrhythmias

Risk-benefit should be considered when the following medical problems exist:

» Cardiovascular disorders, especially:
» Cardiac arrhythmias,
» Coronary insufficiency and
» Hypertension
» Convulsive disorders
» Thyrotoxicosis
» Unusual responsiveness to sympathomimetic amines
(changes in systolic and/or diastolic blood pressure, pulse rate and electrocardiograms have been reported in controlled clinical studies)

» Cardiac decompensation, severe or
Hypertrophic obstructive cardiomyopathy or
Ischemic heart disease
(may require special care and supervision, with particular emphasis on dosage limits)

Hyperthyroidism, uncontrolled
(unusually responsive to sympathomimetic amines; signs and symptoms of excessive beta-adrenergic stimulation are more likely to occur)

Idiopathic hypertrophic subvalvular aortic stenosis
(may lead to an increase in the pressure gradient between the left ventricle and the aorta)

» Diabetes
(additional blood glucose monitoring is recommended)

Patient monitoring

The following may be especially important in patient monitoring (other tests may be warranted in some patients, depending on condition; » = major clinical significance):

Pulmonary function monitoring
(objective measures of lung function are essential for diagnosis and for guiding therapeutic decision-making in the treatment of asthma; measurement of forced expiratory air flow, using a spirometer or a peak expiratory flowmeter, is recommended at periodic intervals)

Side/Adverse Effects

Note: Adverse reactions to formoterol are similar in nature to other selective beta$_2$-adrenoreceptor agonists; for example, angina, hypertension or hypotension, tachycardia, arrhythmias, nervousness, headache, tremor, dry mouth, palpitation, muscle cramps, nausea, dizziness, fatigue, malaise, hypokalemia, hyperglycemia, metabolic acidosis and insomnia.

Long-acting beta$_2$-adrenergic agonists, such as formoterol, have been associated with an increased risk of serious asthma exacerbations and asthma-related death.

The following side/adverse effects have been selected on the basis of their potential clinical significance (possible signs and symptoms in parentheses where appropriate)—not necessarily inclusive:

Those indicating need for medical attention

Incidence more frequent

Infection, viral (chills; cough or hoarseness; fever; cold, flu-like symptoms); ***upper respiratory infection*** (cough; fever; sneezing or sore throat)

Incidence less frequent

Bronchitis (cough producing mucus; difficulty breathing; shortness of breath; tightness in chest; wheezing); ***chest infection; chest pain*** (chest pain or discomfort); ***dyspnea*** (shortness of breath; difficult or labored breathing; tightness in chest; wheezing); ***fever; pharyngitis*** (body aches or pain; congestion; cough; dryness or soreness of throat; fever; hoarseness; runny nose; tender, swollen glands in neck; trouble in swallowing; voice changes); ***sinusitis*** (pain or tenderness around eyes and cheekbones; fever; stuffy or runny nose; headache; cough; shortness of breath or troubled breathing; tightness of chest or wheezing); ***tonsillitis*** (congestion; fever; sore throat; swollen glands); ***trauma***

Incidence rare

Bronchospasm (cough;; difficulty breathing; noisy breathing; shortness of breath; tightness in chest; wheezing); ***hypokalemia*** (convulsions; decreased urine; dry mouth; irregular heartbeat; increased thirst; or loss of appetite); ***tachycardia*** (fainting; fast pounding, or irregular heartbeat or pulse; palpitations or pounding in the ears)

Those indicating need for medical attention only if they continue or are bothersome

Incidence more frequent

Headache

Incidence less frequent

Agitation; anxiety; back pain; cramps; dizziness; dry mouth; dysphonia (hoarseness; sore throat; voice changes); ***exanthema*** (skin rash); ***insomnia*** (sleeplessness; trouble sleeping; unable to sleep); ***pruritus*** (itching skin); ***rash; restlessness; sleep disturbances; sputum, increased*** (increased mucous in throat and lungs); ***tremor*** (trembling or shaking of hands or feet; shakiness in legs, arms, hands, feet); ***urticaria*** (hives or welts; itching; redness of skin; skin rash)

Overdose

For more information on the management of overdose or unintentional ingestion, **contact a poison control center** (see *Poison Control Center Listing*).

Clinical effects of overdose

Note: The expected signs and symptoms with overdosage of formoterol are those of excessive beta-adrenergic stimulation and/or any of the signs and symptoms listed under *side and adverse effects.*

The following effects have been selected on the basis of their potential clinical significance (possible signs and symptoms in parentheses where appropriate)—not necessarily inclusive:

Angina (arm, back or jaw pain; chest pain or discomfort; chest tightness or heaviness; fast or irregular heartbeat; shortness of breath; sweating; nausea); ***arrhythmias*** (dizziness; fainting; fast, slow, or irregular heartbeat); ***cardiac arrest*** (stopping of heart; no blood pressure or pulse; unconsciousness); ***dizziness; dry mouth; fatigue;***

headache; hyperglycemia (blurred vision; increased hunger or thirst; increased urination); ***hypertension*** (blurred vision; dizziness, severe or continuing; nervousness; headache; pounding in the ears; slow or fast heartbeat); ***hypokalemia*** (convulsions; decreased urine; dry mouth; irregular heartbeat; increased thirst; loss of appetite; mood changes; muscle pain or cramps; nausea or vomiting; numbness or tingling in hands, feet, or lips; shortness of breath; unusual tiredness or weakness); ***hypotension*** (dizziness or light-headedness); ***insomnia*** (trouble sleeping; unable to sleep); ***malaise*** (general feeling of discomfort or illness; unusual tiredness or weakness); ***metabolic acidosis*** (shortness of breath; troubled breathing); ***muscle cramps; muscle tremor; nausea; nervousness; palpitation; seizures*** (convulsions; muscle spasm or jerking of all extremities; sudden loss of consciousness); ***tachycardia*** (fainting; fast pounding, or irregular heartbeat or pulse; palpitations)

Treatment of overdose

There is no clinical experience on the management of overdose

Treatment should be symptomatic and supportive

The judicious use of a cardioselective beta-receptor blocker may be considered, bearing in mind that such medication can produce bronchospasm.

Cardiac monitoring is recommended.

There is insufficient evidence to determine if dialysis is beneficial for overdosage of formoterol.

Supportive care—

Patients in whom intentional overdose is confirmed or suspected should be referred for psychiatric consultation.

Patient Consultation

As an aid to patient consultation, refer to *Advice for the Patient, Formoterol (Inhalation-Local).*

In providing consultation, consider emphasizing the following selected information (» = major clinical significance):

Before using this medication

» Conditions affecting use, especially:

Hypersensitivity to formoterol or inhaled lactose

Carcinogenicity—Carcinogenic potential of formoterol has been evaluated in drinking water and dietary studies in both rats and mice. The incidence of ovarian leiomyomas in rats was increased at doses of 15 mg per kg and above in the drinking water study and at 20 mg per kg in the dietary study. The incidence of benign ovarian theca-cell tumors in rats was increased at doses of 0.5 mg per kg and above in the dietary study. The incidence of adrenal subcapsular adenomas and carcinomas was increased in male mice at doses of 69 mg per kg and above in the drinking water study, but not at doses up to 50 mg per kg in the dietary study. The incidence of hepatocarcinomas was increased in the dietary study at doses of 20 and 50 mg per kg in female mice and 50 mg per kg in male mice. Uterine leiomyomas have been found in mice following oral administration of formoterol. Similarly, mesovarian leiomyomas have been found in rats following inhalation of formoterol

Use in children—Not indicated for children less than 5 years of age

Note: Canadian product information states that formoterol is not indicated for children less than 6 years of age

Critical/Emergency care

Not using for treatment of acute symptoms

Other medications, especially antidepressants (tricyclic), beta-receptor blocking agents, disopyramide, furazolidine, monoamine oxidase inhibitors, phenothiazines, procainamide, procarbazine, quinidine, and terfenadine

Other medical problems, especially arrhythmias, cardiac decompensation (severe), cardiovascular disorders, coronary insufficiency, convulsive disorders, diabetes, hypertension (severe), tachyarrhythmias, thyrotoxicosis and unusual responsiveness to sympathomimetic amines.

Proper use of this medication

» Importance of not using to relieve an acute asthma attack

» Having a rapid-acting inhaled beta-adrenergic bronchodilator available for symptomatic relief of acute asthma attacks

» Not prescribing formoterol as the first medication to treat a patient's asthma; only administering if patient has not responded to other asthma-controller medications, such as low-to-medium dose inhaled corticosteroids

» Advising patient to continue taking formoterol or other asthma medications that have been prescribed unless treatment has been discussed with their healthcare provider

» Reading patient instructions carefully before using

» Importance of not using more medication than prescribed; not using more than two times a day or less than 12 hours apart

Knowing correct administration technique for using inhaler

» Proper dosing

Missed dose: Taking as soon as possible; not taking if almost time for next scheduled dose; not doubling doses; using rapid-acting inhaled bronchodilator if symptoms occur before next dose is due

Proper storage

Precautions while using this medication

» Regular visits to physician at least every 6 to 12 months to check progress

» Checking with physician immediately if difficulty in breathing persists after use of this medication or if condition becomes worse

» For patients also using anti-inflammatory medication, checking with physician before stopping or reducing anti-inflammatory therapy

» Advising patients that this medicine may increase the chances of a severe asthma episode occurring

Side/adverse effects

Signs of potential side effects, especially viral infection, upper respiratory infection, bronchitis, chest infection, chest pain, dyspnea, fever, pharyngitis, sinusitis, tonsillitis, bronchospasms, hypokalemia, tachycardia or trauma.

General Dosing Information

Corticosteroid therapy should not be stopped or reducedwhen formoterol therapy is initiated.

Patients should be advised to continue using formoterol or other asthma medicines that have been prescribed unless they have discussed with their health care provider whether or not to continue treatment.

Formoterol should not be used to treat acute symptoms or in patients with significantly worsening symptoms.

Need for increased use to treat symptoms indicates deterioration of asthma control and the need to reassess the patient's therapy. Fatalities have been reported in association with excessive use of inhaled sympathomimetic drugs in patients with asthma. The exact cause of death is unknown, but cardiac arrest following an unexpected development of a severe acute asthmatic crisis and subsequent hypoxia is suspected.

A satisfactory clinical response to formoterol does not eliminate the need for continued treatment with an anti-inflammatory agent.

When beginning treatment with formoterol, patients who have been taking inhaled, short-acting $beta_2$-agonists on a regular basis should be instructed to discontinue the regular use of these drugs and use them only for symptomatic relief of acute asthma symptoms.

With use in exercise induced bronchospasm, formoterol should be taken 15 minutes prior to exercise and not be re-dosed for 12 hours.

The inhaler should never be washed and the patient should always use the new inhaler that comes with each refill.

Formoterol should never be used with a spacer.

Patients should handle capsules with dry hands. In rare instances the gelatin capsule might break into small pieces, but should be caught by the screen built into the inhaler. Tiny pieces of gelatin might however reach the mouth or throat. The capsule is less likely to shatter when pierced once.

Patients should be instructed to never exhale into the device.

The inhaler should only be used for formoterol capsules and not be used with any other medication.

Inhalation Dosage Forms

FORMOTEROL FUMARATE DIHYDRATE POWDER FOR INHALATION

Usual Adult and Adolescent Dose

Asthma, chronic (treatment)—

Oral inhalation, 12 mcg every 12 hours

Note: Canadian product information states that some patients may need up to 24 mcg every 12 hours.

Chronic Obstructive Pulmonary Disease [COPD] (treatment)—

Oral inhalation, 12 mcg every 12 hours.

Note: Canadian product information states that 12 or 24 mcg should be taken every 12 hours.

Exercise-induced bronchospasm [EIB] (prevention)[1]—

12 mcg at least 15 minutes before exercise administered on an occasional as needed basis.

Note: Additional doses should not be used for 12 hours after administration; regular, twice-daily dosing has not been studied in preventing EIB; patients who are receiving formoterol twice daily for maintenance treatment of their asthma should not use additional doses for prevention of EIB and may require a short-acting bronchodilator.

Usual adult prescribing limits
Up to 24 mcg daily.

Note: Canadian product information states that up to 24 mcg twice daily can be prescribed.

Usual pediatric dose
Asthma, chronic treatment—
Children 5 years of age and older: See *Usual adult and adolescent dose*

Note: Canadian product information states that in children 6 years of age and older: See *Usual adult and adolescent dose*

Usual pediatric prescribing limits
Up to 24 mcg daily.

Note: Canadian product information states that up to 24 mcg twice daily can be prescribed.

Usual geriatric dose
See *Usual adult dose.*

Usual geriatric prescribing limits
See *Usual adult prescribing limits.*

Strength(s) usually available
U.S.—
12 mcg per capsule for inhalation (Rx) [*Foradil* (lactose)].
Canada—
6 mcg per metered dose (Rx) [*Oxeze* (lactose)].
12 mcg per metered dose (Rx) [*Oxeze* (lactose)].
12 mcg per capsule for inhalation (Rx) [*Foradil* (lactose)].

Packaging and storage
Prior to dispensing—store in a refrigerator, 2° to 8°C (36° to 46°F)
After dispensing to patient—store at 20° to 25°C (68° to 77°F)
Protect from heat and moisture.

Note: Capsules should always be stored in the blister and only removed from the blister immediately before use.

Note: Canadian product information states to store between 15 and 25 °C

---

[1]Not included in Canadian product labeling.

Revised: 12/02/2005
Developed: 03/05/2001

FOSAMPRENAVIR Systemic

VA CLASSIFICATION (Primary): AM830
Commonly used brand name(s): *LEXIVA; TELZIR.*

Note: For a listing of dosage forms and brand names by country availability, see *Dosage Forms* section(s).

Category
Antiviral (systemic).

Indications
Accepted
Human immunodeficiency virus (HIV) infection (treatment)—Fosamprenavir is indicated in combination with other antiretroviral agents for the treatment of HIV infections in adults.

Pharmacology/Pharmacokinetics
Physicochemical characteristics
Molecular weight—623.7 (fosamprenavir calcium).
Solubility—Approximately 0.31 mg per mL (mg/mL) in water at 25 °C.

Mechanism of action/Effect
Fosamprenavir is rapidly converted to amprenavir by cellular phosphatases in vivo. Amprenavir is an inhibitor of HIV-1 protease. Amprenavir binds to the active site of HIV-1 protease and thereby prevents the processing of viral Gag and Gag-Pol polyprotein precursors, resulting in the formation of immature non-infectious viral particles.

Absorption
The following are area under the curve (AUC) values of amprenavir based on the drug therapy regimen administered:
- Fosamprenavir 1400 mg twice per day—27.6 to 39.2 mcg hr per mL (median 33 mcg hr per mL)
- Fosamprenavir 1400 mg once per day plus ritonavir 200 mg once per day—59.7 to 80.8 mcg hr per mL (median 69.4 mcg hr per mL)
- Fosamprenavir 700 mg twice per day plus ritonavir 100 mg twice per day—69 to 90.6 mcg hr per mL (median 79.2 mcg hr per mL)

Fosamprenavir may be taken with or without food. Administering fosamprenavir in the fed state compared to the fasted state was associated with no significant changes in absorption.
Absolute oral bioavailability of amprenavir following fosamprenavir administration in humans has not been established.
Healthy patients AUC—12 ± 4.38 mcg hr per mL
Patients with moderate cirrhosis AUC—significantly greater at 25.76 ± 14.68 mcg hr per mL
Patients with severe cirrhosis AUC—significantly greater at 38.66 ± 16.08 mcg hr per mL

Protein binding
Very high (approximately 90%); primarily bound to alpha$_1$-acid glycoprotein; higher amounts of unbound amprenavir present as amprenavir serum concentrations increase.

Biotransformation
In the gut epithelium during absorption, fosamprenavir is rapidly and almost completely hydrolyzed to amprenavir and inorganic phosphate prior to reaching the systemic circulation. Amprenavir is metabolized in the liver by the cytochrome P450 3A4 enzyme with 2 major metabolites resulting from oxidation of the tetrahydrofuran and aniline moieties. Glucuronide conjugates of oxidized metabolites have been identified as minor metabolites in urine and feces.

Half-life
Plasma elimination half-life of amprenavir—approximately 7.7 hours

Time to peak concentration
T_{max} amprenavir—1.5 to 4 hours (median 2.5 hours) following administration of a single dose of fosamprenavir
The following are time to peak concentrations (T_{max}) of amprenavir based on the drug therapy regimen administered:
Fosamprenavir 1400 mg twice per day—0.8 to 4 hours (median 1.3 hours)
Fosamprenavir 1400 mg once per day plus ritonavir 200 mg once per day—0.8 to 5 hours (median 2.1 hours)
Fosamprenavir 700 mg twice per day plus ritonavir 100 mg twice per day—0.75 to 5 hours (median 1.5 hours)

Peak serum concentration
Peak plasma concentration (C_{max}):—
The following are C_{max} values of amprenavir based on the drug therapy regimen administered:
Fosamprenavir 1400 mg once per day plus ritonavir 200 mg once per day—6.32 to 8.28 mcg per mL (median 7.24 mcg per mL)
Fosamprenavir 1400 mg twice per day—4.06 to 5.72 mcg per mL (median 4.82 mcg per mL)
Fosamprenavir 700 mg twice per day plus ritonavir 100 mg twice per day—5.38 to 6.86 mcg per mL (median 6.08 mcg per mL)
Patients with severe cirrhosis C_{max}—significantly greater at 9.43 ± 2.61 mcg per mL
Minimum plasma concentration (C_{min}):—
The following are C_{min} values of amprenavir based on the drug therapy regimen administered:
Fosamprenavir 1400 mg twice per day—0.27 to 0.46 mcg per mL (median 0.35 mcg per mL)
Fosamprenavir 1400 mg once per day plus ritonavir 200 mg once per day—1.16 to 1.81 mcg per mL (median 1.45 mcg per mL)
Fosamprenavir 700 mg twice per day plus ritonavir 100 mg twice per day—1.77 to 2.54 mcg per mL (median 2.12 mcg per mL)

Elimination
Minimal excretion of unchanged amprenavir in urine and feces (less than 1% in urine and undetectable in feces)
Renal—14% of radiolabeled amprenavir as metabolites
Fecal—75% of radiolabeled amprenavir as metabolites; two metabolites accounted for greater than 90% of the radiocarbon in fecal samples
Renal impairment impact on amprenavir elimination has not been studied; however, renal impairment is not expected to significantly impact am-

prenavir elimination due to minimal renal excretion of unchanged amprenavir.

Precautions to Consider

Cross-sensitivity and/or related problems

Hypersensitivity to fosamprenavir or to any components of the product, to amprenavir, or to sulfonamides; because fosamprenavir contains a sulfonamide moiety and the potential for cross-sensitivity between fosamprenavir and sulfonamides is unknown, caution should be used

Carcinogenicity

Carcinogenicity studies of fosamprenavir in rats and mice are in progress; however, results are available from carcinogenicity studies with amprenavir. Carcinogenic potential of amprenavir was evaluated in mice and rats and showed an increase in the incidence of benign hepatocellular adenomas and an increase in the combined incidence of hepatocellular adenomas plus carcinoma in males of both species at the highest doses tested (2 and 4 times, respectively, the human exposure at the recommended dose of 1200 mg twice daily). Administration of amprenavir did not cause a statistically significant increase in the incidence of any other benign or malignant neoplasm in mice or rats.

Mutagenicity

Fosamprenavir was not mutagenic or genotoxic in a battery of *in vitro* and *in vivo* assays, including bacterial reverse mutation (Ames), mouse lymphoma, rat micronucleus and chromosome aberrations in human lymphocytes.

Pregnancy/Reproduction

Fertility—The effects of fosamprenavir on fertility and general reproductive performance were evaluated in male and female rats administered a dose 3 to 4 times higher than the maximum recommended human dose [MRHD]. Fosamprenavir did not impair mating or fertility of male or female rats and did not affect the development and maturation of sperm from treated rats.

Pregnancy—There are no adequate and well-controlled studies in pregnant women. Fosamprenavir should be used during pregnancy only if the potential benefit justifies the potential risk to the fetus.

An Antiretroviral Pregnancy Registry has been established to monitor maternal-fetal outcomes of pregnant women exposed to fosamprenavir. Physicians are encouraged by the manufacturer to register patients by calling (800) 258-4263.

Abortions were associated with amprenavir administration in rabbits. Increased skeletal abnormalities were found in the offspring of rabbits and rats; in rabbits the systemic exposure at the highest tested dose was approximately one twentieth of the exposure seen at the recommended human dose; in rats, the systemic exposure was one half of that associated with the recommended human dose. Reduced body weights (10% to 20%) occurred in the offspring of rats dosed in the prenatal and postnatal periods; systemic exposure was approximately twice the exposure in humans at the recommended human dose. Surviving pups born to female rats given fosamprenavir showed an increases time to successful mating, an increased length of gestation, a reduced number of uterine implantation sites per litter and reduced gestational body weights compared to control animals.

FDA Pregnancy Category C

Breast-feeding

It is not known whether amprenavir is distributed into breast milk. Amprenavir is distributed into milk in rats.

The Centers for Disease Control and Prevention recommend that HIV-infected mothers not breast-feed their infants to avoid risking postnatal transmission of HIV. Because of both the potential for HIV transmission and the potential for serious adverse reactions in nursing infants, mothers should be instructed not to breast-feed if they are receiving fosamprenavir.

Pediatrics

Safety and efficacy have not been established.

Geriatrics

No information is available on the relationship of age to the effects of amprenavir in geriatric patients. However, dose selection for an elderly patient should be cautious, reflecting the greater frequency of decreased hepatic, renal, or cardiac function, and of concomitant disease or other drug therapy.

Pharmacogenetics

Pharmacokinetics of fosamprenavir do not differ between males and females or between blacks and non-blacks.

Drug interactions and/or related problems

The following drug interactions and/or related problems have been selected on the basis of their potential clinical significance (possible mechanism in parentheses where appropriate)—not necessarily inclusive (» = major clinical significance):

Note: Combinations containing any of the following medications, depending on the amount present, may also interact with this medication.

» Amiodarone or
» Lidocaine (systemic) or
» Quinidine or
» Tricyclic antidepressants
(may cause serious or life-threatening adverse events; caution should be used and therapeutic concentration monitoring recommended when coadministered with fosamprenavir)

» Antacids
(may cause decrease in C_{max} and AUC of amprenavir)

» Atorvastatin
(may increase atorvastatin plasma concentration; use ≤20 mg per day of atorvastatin with careful monitoring; may consider other HMG-CoA reductase inhibitors such as fluvastatin, pravastatin, or rosuvastatin in combination with fosamprenavir)

Benzodiazepines, including
Alprazolam or
Clorazepate or
Diazepam or
Flurazepam
(decrease in benzodiazepine dose may be needed; increase in serum concentration of benzodiazepine with concomitant use; clinical significance is unknown)

» Bepridil
(use with caution; increased bepridil exposure may be associated with life-threatening reactions such as cardiac arrhythmias)

Calcium channel blockers, including
Amlodipine or
Diltiazem or
Felodipine or
Isradipine or
Nicardipine or
Nifedipine or
Nimodipine or
Nisoldipine or
Verapamil
(should use caution and clinical monitoring of patient is recommended; concomitant use may increase serum concentrations of calcium channel blocking agents)

» Carbamazepine or
» Phenobarbital or
» Phenytoin
(use with caution; fosamprenavir may be less effective due to decreased amprenavir plasma concentrations with concomitant use)

» Cisapride
(**contraindicated** due to potential for serious and/or life-threatening reactions such as cardiac arrhythmias)

Clarithromycin
(may increase amprenavir concentrations)

» Cyclosporine or
» Sirolimus (rapamycin) or
» Tacrolimus
(may increase serum concentration of immunosuppressant; therapeutic concentration monitoring is recommended for immunosuppressant agents when coadministered with fosamprenavir)

CYP3A4 substrates, inhibitors or inducers or
Medications metabolized by CYP3A4
(caution should be used)

» Delavirdine
(should not be coadministered with fosamprenavir; may lead to loss of virologic response and possible resistance to delavirdine)

Dexamethasone
(use with caution; fosamprenavir may be less effective due to decreased amprenavir plasma concentrations with concomitant use)

Efavirenz or
Nevirapine
(may decrease amprenavir concentration; safety and efficacy for appropriate combination doses have not been established; dosage adjustment of ritonavir recommended for once daily dosing with fosamprenavir/ritonavir combination and efavirenz [twice daily dosing: adjustment not required])

» Ergot derivatives, including

Dihydroergotamine or
Ergonovine or
Ergotamine or
Methylergonovine
(**contraindicated** due to potential for serious and/or life-threatening reactions such as acute ergot toxicity characterized by peripheral vasospasm and ischemia of the extremities and other tissues)

» Flecainide or
» Propafenone
(if fosamprenavir and ritonavir are coadministered, then flecainide or propafenone use is **contraindicated** due to potential for serious and/or life-threatening reactions such as cardiac arrhythmias secondary to increases in plasma concentrations of antiarrhythmics)

» Fluticasone
(concomitant use may increase fluticasone plasma concentrations; should be used with caution and alternatives to fluticasone should be considered, particularly for long-term use; coadministration of fosamprenavir/ritonavir and fluticasone not recommended unless potential benefit to patient outweighs risk of systemic corticosteroid side effects)

Histamine H_2-receptor antagonists or
Proton-pump inhibitors
(use with caution; fosamprenavir may be less effective due to decreased amprenavir plasma concentrations with concomitant use)

» HMG-CoA reductase inhibitors, including
Atorvastatin or
Lovastatin or
Simvastatin
(potential for serious reactions such as risk of myopathy including rhabdomyolysis)

Indinavir or
Nelfinavir
(may increase amprenavir concentration; safety and efficacy for appropriate combination doses have not been established)

» Itraconazole or
» Ketoconazole
(increased monitoring for adverse events; dose reduction of itraconazole or ketoconazole may be needed; high doses of itraconazole or ketoconazole not recommended with fosamprenavir/ritonavir combination)

Lopinavir/ritonavir
(may decrease amprenavir and lopinavir concentrations; increased rate of adverse events observed with coadministration; safety and efficacy of appropriate combination doses have not been established)

Methadone
(coadministration may decrease plasma levels of methadone; dosage increase of methadone may be needed)

» Midazolam or
» Triazolam
(**contraindicated** due to potential for serious and/or life-threatening reactions such as prolonged or increased sedation or respiratory depression)

» Oral contraceptives, including
Ethinyl estradiol/norethindrone
(may decrease amprenavir concentration; may increase ethinyl estradiol/norethindrone concentration and hormonal levels may be altered; alternative methods of non-hormonal contraception recommended)

» PDE5 inhibitors, including
Sildenafil or
Vardenafil
(may increase sildenafil and vardenafil plasma concentrations and increase risk for hypotension, visual changes, and priapism; use with caution at reduced dose of sildenafil or vardenafil with increased monitoring for adverse events; for fosamprenavir/ritonavir combination, use vardenafil at reduced dose with increased monitoring for adverse events)

» Pimozide
(**contraindicated** due to potential for serious and/or life-threatening reactions such as cardiac arrhythmias)

» Rifabutin
(may cause increase of rifabutin and rifabutin metabolite concentrations; required rifabutin dose reduction by at least half the recommended dose; complete blood count should be performed weekly and as clinically indicated to monitor for neutropenia in patients receiving fosamprenavir and rifabutin concomitantly; with fosamprenavir/ritonavir combination, a rifabutin dose reduction by at least 75% of the usual dose is recommended)

» Rifampin
(should not be coadministered with fosamprenavir; reduces amprenavir plasma concentrations by about 90%; may lead to loss of virologic response and possible resistance to fosamprenavir or to the class of protease inhibitors)

» Saquinavir
(may decrease amprenavir concentration; effect on saquinavir not established; safety and efficacy of appropriate combination doses have not been established)

» St. John's wort
(St. John's wort or any product containing it should not be coadministered with fosamprenavir; may lead to loss of virologic response and possible resistance to fosamprenavir or to the class of protease inhibitors)

» Trazodone
(concomitant use with or without ritonavir may increase plasma concentrations of trazodone; if trazodone is used with a CYP3A4 inhibitor such as fosamprenavir, combination should be used with caution and lower dose of trazodone should be considered)

» Warfarin
(may affect warfarin concentrations; recommended monitoring of international normalized ratio [INR])

Zidovudine
(amprenavir and zidovudine concentrations may be increased)

Note: For information on other potential drug interactions for ritonavir that may affect fosamprenavir/ritonavir coadministration, refer to *Ritonavir (Systemic)*.

Laboratory value alterations

The following have been selected on the basis of their potential clinical significance (possible effect in parentheses where appropriate)—not necessarily inclusive (» = major clinical significance).

With physiology/laboratory test values

Alanine aminotransferase (ALT [SGPT], serum and
Aspartate aminotransferase (AST [SGOT], serum
(values may be elevated)

Glucose, plasma or
Lipase, serum
Triglycerides, serum
(concentrations may be increased)

Neutrophil count
(may be decreased)

Medical considerations/Contraindications

The medical considerations/contraindications included have been selected on the basis of their potential clinical significance (reasons given in parentheses where appropriate)—not necessarily inclusive (» = major clinical significance).

Except under special circumstances, this medication should not be used when the following medical problem exists:

» Hypersensitivity to fosamprenavir, amprenavir, or any components of this product
(fosamprenavir use contraindicated)

Risk-benefit should be considered when the following medical problems exist:

Diabetes mellitus
(protease inhibitors may exacerbate pre-existing diabetes mellitus; may require dose adjustments of insulin or oral hypoglycemic agents in these patients)

Hemophilia
(spontaneous bleeding has been reported in patients with hemophilia types A and B treated with protease inhibitors; a causal relationship has not been established)

» Hepatic function impairment
(cautions should be exercised; fosamprenavir principally metabolized by the liver, dose reductions may be required)

Hepatitis B or
Hepatitis C
(may be at increased risk for developing transaminase elevations; patients should be monitored closely during fosamprenavir treatment)

Hypersensitivity to sulfonamides
(caution should be used; fosamprenavir contains a sulfonamide moiety; potential for cross-sensitivity between drugs in the sulfonamide class and fosamprenavir unknown)

Patient monitoring

The following may be especially important in patient monitoring (other tests may be warranted in some patients, depending on condition; » = major clinical significance):

Blood glucose determinations
(development of hyperglycemia or diabetes may be associated with the use of protease inhibitors)

Blood coagulation times
(monitoring of blood coagulation times may be appropriate, particularly in patients with hemophilia)

Cholesterol and triglyceride testing
(should be performed prior to initiating therapy and periodically during therapy)

Immune reconstitution syndrome
(reported in patients treated with fosamprenavir; during initial phase of combination antiretroviral treatment, patients whose immune system responds may develop inflammatory response to indolent or residual opportunistic infections [*Mycobacterium avium* infection, cytomegalovirus, *Pneumocystis jirovecii* pneumonia (PCP), or tuberculosis] which may necessitate further evaluation and treatment)

Liver function tests
(monitor before initiating fosamprenavir and periodically, or if clinical signs or symptoms of hyperlipidemia or elevated liver function tests occur during therapy)

Side/Adverse Effects

The following side/adverse effects have been selected on the basis of their potential clinical significance (possible signs and symptoms in parentheses where appropriate)—not necessarily inclusive:

Those indicating need for medical attention

Incidence more frequent

Hypertriglyceridemia (large amount of triglyceride in the blood)—in protease inhibitor-experienced adult patients; ***skin rash***—severe or life-threatening or if accompanied by systemic symptoms

Incidence less frequent

Depressive/mood disorders (depression mood or mental changes); ***hyperglycemia*** (abdominal pain; blurred vision; dry mouth; fatigue; flushed, dry skin; fruit-like breath odor; increased hunger; increased thirst; increased urination; nausea; sweating; troubled breathing; unexplained weight loss; vomiting)—in protease inhibitor-experienced adult patients

Incidence rare

Acute hemolytic anemia (back, leg, or stomach pains; bleeding gums; chills; dark urine; difficulty breathing; fatigue; fever; general body swelling; headache; loss of appetite; nausea or vomiting; nosebleeds; pale skin; sore throat; yellowing of the eyes or skin); ***Stevens-Johnson syndrome*** (blistering, peeling, loosening of skin; chills; cough; diarrhea; itching; joint or muscle pain; red irritated eyes; red skin lesions often with a purple center; sore throat; sores, ulcers, or white spots in mouth or on lips; unusual tiredness or weakness)

Those indicating need for medical attention only if they continue or are bothersome

Incidence more frequent

Nausea; rash, mild or moderate; pruritus (itching skin)

Incidence less frequent

Abdominal pain (stomach pain); ***diarrhea; fatigue*** (unusual tiredness or weakness); ***headache; oral paresthesia*** (burning or prickling sensation around the mouth); ***vomiting***

Frequency unknown

Breast enlargement; central obesity; cushingoid appearance (increased fat deposits on face, neck, and trunk); ***dorsocervical fat enlargement*** (buffalo hump); ***facial wasting; fat redistribution; peripheral wasting***

Note: These fat redistribution side effects have been observed in patients receiving antiretroviral therapy, including fosamprenavir. The mechanism and long-term consequences of these events are currently unknown. A causal relationship has not been established

Overdose

For more information on the management of overdose or unintentional ingestion, **contact a poison control center** (see *Poison Control Center Listing*).

Treatment of overdose

There is no known antidote for fosamprenavir. It is not known whether amprenavir can be removed by perioneal dialysis or hemodialysis.

Monitoring—
Monitor for evidence of toxicity

Supportive care—
Standard supportive treatment should be applied as necessary
Patients in whom intentional overdose is confirmed or suspected should be referred for psychiatric consultation.

Patient Consultation

As an aid to patient consultation, refer to *Advice for the Patient, Fosamprenavir (Systemic)*.

In providing consultation, consider emphasizing the following selected information (» = major clinical significance):

Before using this medication

» Conditions affecting use, especially:

Hypersensitivity to amprenavir, fosamprenavir or any components of this product, or to sulfonamides

Carcinogenic potential of amprenavir evaluated in mice and rats showed an increase in the incidence of benign hepatocellular adenomas and an increase in the combined incidence of hepatocellular adenomas plus carcinoma in males of both species at the highest doses tested.

Pregnancy—Should be used during pregnancy only if the potential benefit justifies the potential risk to the fetus

Breast-feeding—HIV-infected mothers should not breast-feed if they are receiving fosamprenavir

Use in children—Safety and efficacy have not been established in pediatric patients.

Use in the elderly—Dose selection should be cautious, reflecting the greater frequency of decreased hepatic, renal, or cardiac function, and of concomitant disease or other drug therapy.

Other medications, especially amiodarone, antacids, atorvastatin, bepridil, carbamazepine, cisapride, cyclosporine, delavirdine, ergot derivatives, flecainide, fluticasone, HMG-CoA reductase inhibitors, itraconazole, ketoconazole, lidocaine (systemic), midazolam, oral contraceptives, PDE5 inhibitors, phenobarbital, phenytoin, pimozide, propafenone, quinidine, rifabutin, rifampin, saquinavir, sirolimus (rapamycin), St. John's wort, tacrolimus, trazodone, triazolam, tricyclic antidepressants, vardenafil, or warfarin

Other medical problems, especially hepatic function impairment

Proper use of this medication

» Importance of taking fosamprenavir exactly as prescribed and not skipping or discontinuing unless directed

» Importance of compliance with therapy and being under the supervision of a doctor

» For oral suspension: Taking without food and on an empty stomach

» Not sharing medication with others

» Not taking any other medications (prescription or nonprescription) without first consulting your physician

» Importance of taking fosamprenavir in combination with other antiretroviral medications

» Proper dosing
Missed dose: Taking as soon as possible; not taking if almost time for next scheduled dose; not doubling doses

Proper storage

Precautions while using this medication

» Using alternate or additional contraceptive measures if oral contraceptives are taken during fosamprenavir therapy because the efficacy of oral contraceptives may be reduced with use of fosamprenavir

For patients with diabetes: checking with physician if changes in blood glucose concentrations occur

» Regular visits to physician to check progress and for blood tests and monitoring of blood glucose concentrations

» Being aware that fosamprenavir therapy does not reduce the risk of transmitting HIV to others through sexual contact or contamination through blood

Side/adverse effects

Signs of potential side effects, especially hypertriglyceridemia, skin rash (severe or life-threatening), depressive/mood disorders, hyperglycemia, acute hemolytic anemia, or Stevens-Johnson syndrome

General Dosing Information

Once-daily administration of fosamprenavir plus ritonavir is not recommended for protease inhibitor-experienced patients.

The protease inhibitor-experienced patient study was not large enough to reach a definitive conclusion that fosamprenavir/ritonavir and lopinavir/ritonavir are clinically equivalent.

During the initial phase of treatment, patients responding to antiretroviral therapy may develop an inflammatory response to indolent or residual opportunistic infections (such as MAC, CMV, PCP, and TB), which may necessitate further evaluation and treatment

Diet/Nutrition

Fosamprenavir tablets may be taken with or without food.

Fosamprenavir oral suspension should be taken without food on an empty stomach.

Oral Dosage Forms

FOSAMPRENAVIR CALCIUM ORAL SUSPENSION

Usual adult dose

See *Fosamprenavir Tablets*.

Usual pediatric dose

See *Fosamprenavir Tablets*.

Usual geriatric dose

See *Fosamprenavir Tablets*.

Strength(s) usually available

U.S.—

Not commercially available

Canada—

50 mg/mL (base) (Rx) [*TELZIR* (grape bubblegum and peppermint flavoring; hypromellose; sucralose; propylene glycol; methyl parahydroxybenzoate; propyl parahydroxybenzoate; polysorbate 80; calcium chloride dihydrate; artificial grape bubblegum flavor; natural peppermint flavor; purified water)].

Packaging and storage

Store between 2 and 30 °C (36 and 86 °F). Do not freeze.

The suspension should be discarded 28 days after first opening.

Auxiliary labeling

- Take on an empty stomach - 1 hour before or 2 to 3 hours after eating.
- Do not take this medication with food.
- You should take this medication exactly as prescribed. Do not skip or discontinue unless directed.
- Ask your doctor or pharmacist before using nonprescription drugs

FOSAMPRENAVIR CALCIUM TABLETS

Usual adult dose

Human immunodeficiency virus (HIV) infection (treatment)—

Fosamprenavir alone for therapy-naive patientsOral, 1400 mg twice daily

Fosamprenavir with ritonavir for therapy-naive patientsOral, 1400 mg fosamprenavir with 200 mg ritonavir once daily or divided into two daily doses

Fosamprenavir with ritonavir for protease inhibitor-experienced patientsOral, 700 mg fosamprenavir with 100 mg ritonavir twice daily

Once-daily dosing of fosamprenavir with ritonavir is **not** recommended in protease inhibitor-experienced patients.

Note: Dosage adjustment for ritonavir when fosamprenavir plus ritonavir are administered with efavirenz—additional 100 mg per day for a total of 300 mg ritonavir recommended for once daily dosing. No dosage adjustment of ritonavir is required for twice daily dosing of fosamprenavir with efavirenz and ritonavir

Higher-than-approved dose combinations of fosamprenavir plus ritonavir are not recommended for use.

When administering ritonavir as part of a combination therapy regimen, refer to *Ritonavir (Systemic)* for detailed dosing information.

Note: Dosing adjustment for patients with hepatic impairment:

- Mild or moderate impairment (Child-Pugh score ranging from 5 to 8)—Oral, 700 mg twice daily (without concurrent ritonavir) with caution
- Severe impairment (Child-Pugh score ranging from 9 to 12)—Should not be used because dose cannot be reduced below 700 mg

There is no data on the use of fosamprenavir in combination with ritonavir in patients with any degree of hepatic impairment.

Usual pediatric dose

Human immunodeficiency virus (HIV) infection (treatment)—

Safety and efficacy have not been established.

Usual geriatric dose

See *Usual adult dose*.

Strength(s) usually available

U.S.—

700 mg (base) (Rx) [*LEXIVA* (colloidal silicon dioxide; croscarmellose sodium; magnesium stearate; microcrystalline cellulose; povidone K30; hypromellose; iron oxide red; titanium dioxide; triacetin)].

Canada—

700 mg (base) (Rx) [*TELZIR* (colloidal silicon dioxide; croscarmellose sodium; magnesium stearate; microcrystalline cellulose; povidone K30; hypromellose; iron oxide red; titanium dioxide; triacetin)].

Packaging and storage

Store at controlled room temperature of 25 °C (77 °F), excursions permitted between 15 and 30 °C (59 and 86 °F) in a tightly closed container.

Auxiliary labeling

- This medication can be taken with or without food
- You should take this medication exactly as prescribed. Do not skip or discontinue unless directed.
- Ask your doctor or pharmacist before using nonprescription drugs

Revised: 10/28/2005
Developed: 04/02/2004

FOSINOPRIL—See *Angiotensin-converting Enzyme (ACE) Inhibitors (Systemic)*

FOSPHENYTOIN—See *Anticonvulsants, Hydantoin (Systemic)*

FROVATRIPTAN Systemic†

VA CLASSIFICATION (Primary): CN105

Commonly used brand name(s): *Frova*.

Note: For a listing of dosage forms and brand names by country availability, see *Dosage Forms* section(s).

†Not commercially available in Canada.

Category

Antimigraine agent.

Indications

General Considerations

Frovatriptan should only be prescribed for patients who have an established clear diagnosis of migraine.

Accepted

Headache, migraine (treatment)—Frovatriptan is indicated for the acute treatment of migraine attacks with or without aura in adults

Unaccepted

Frovatriptan is not indicated in the management of hemiplegic or basilar migraine.

Frovatriptan is not indicated for use in cluster headache, which is present in an older, predominately male population. Safety and efficacy of frovatriptan in this condition have not been established.

Frovatriptan is not intended for the prophylactic therapy of migraine.

Pharmacology/Pharmacokinetics

Physicochemical characteristics

Molecular weight—Frovatriptan succinate: 379.4.

Solubility—Frovatriptan succinate: soluble in water.

Mechanism of action/Effect

Frovatriptan is a 5-HT receptor agonist that binds with high affinity to 5-HT_{1B} and 5-HT_{1D} receptors. Frovatriptan has no significant effects on $GABA_A$ mediated channel activity and has no significant affinity for benzodiazepine binding sites.

Frovatriptan is believed to act on extracerebral, intracranial arteries and to inhibit excessive dilation of these vessels in migraine.

Absorption

The absolute bioavailability of an oral dose of frovatriptan is about 20% in males and 30% in females. The rate and extent of absorption are not affected by administration with food.

Distribution

Volume of distribution (Vol_D)—Steady state: 4.2 L per kg in males and 3.0 L per kg in females.

Protein binding

Low (approximately 15%) to serum proteins.

Biotransformation

In vitro cytochrome P450 1A2 is the principal enzyme involved in the metabolism of frovatriptan. The desmethyl metabolite has lower affinity for 5-$HT_{1B/1D}$ receptors as compared to the parent compound and the N-acetyl desmethyl metabolite has no significant affinity for 5-HT receptors. Other metabolites' receptor activity is unknown.

Half-life

Elimination—

Intravenous administration: Approximately 26 hours

Time to peak concentration

Oral—2 to 4 hours.

Administration with food delays time to peak concentration by one hour.

Time to peak effect

Relief of headache (i.e., moderate or severe pain being reduced to mild or no pain)—

Oral (single 2.5 mg dose): Within 2 hours in 37 to 46% of patients

Elimination

Renal; following a single oral 2.5 mg dose of radiolabeled frovatriptan, 32% of the dose was recovered in urine. Radiolabeled compounds excreted in the urine were unchanged frovatriptan, hydroxylated frovatriptan, N-acetyl desmethyl frovatriptan, hydroxylated N-acetyl desmethyl frovatriptan, desmethyl frovatriptan and several other minor metabolites.

Fecal; following a single oral 2.5 mg dose of radiolabeled frovatriptan, 62% of the dose was recovered in feces.

Precautions to Consider

Carcinogenicity/Tumorigenicity

The carcinogenic potential of frovatriptan was evaluated in an 84-week study in mice, a 104-week study in rats and a 26-week study in transgenic mice. There were no increases in tumor incidence in the 84-week mouse study at doses producing 140 times the exposure achieved at the maximum recommended daily human dose based on blood AUC comparisons. In the rat study, there was a statistically significant increase in the incidence of pituitary adenomas in males only at a dose that produced 250 times the exposure achieved at the maximum recommended daily human dose based on AUC comparisons. In the transgenic mouse study, there was an increased incidence of subcutaneous sarcomas in females dosed at 390 and 630 times the human exposure based on AUC comparisons. The incidence of sarcomas was not increased at lower doses that achieved exposures 180 and 60 times the human exposure. These sarcomas were physically associated with subcutaneously implanted animal identification transponders. There were no other increases in tumor incidence of any type in any dose group. These sarcomas are not considered to be relevant to humans.

Mutagenicity

Frovatriptan was clastogenic in human lymphocyte cultures, in the absence of metabolic activation. In the bacterial reverse mutation assay (Ames test), frovatriptan produced an equivocal response in the absence of metabolic activation. No mutagenic or clastogenic activities were seen in an *in vitro* mouse lymphoma assay, an *in vivo* mouse bone marrow micronucleus test, or an *ex vivo* assay for unscheduled DNA synthesis in rat liver.

Pregnancy/Reproduction

Fertility—Studies in male and female rats at doses of 100, 500, and 1000 mg per kg per day showed an increase at all dose levels in the number of females that mated on the first day of pairing compared to control animals. This occurred in conjunction with a prolongation of the estrous cycle. Females also had a decreased mean number of corpora lutea and a lower number of live fetuses per litter, which suggested a partial impairment of ovulation. There were no other fertility-related effects.

Pregnancy—Adequate and well-controlled studies have not been done in humans.

Studies in rats receiving oral doses of frovatriptan throughout the period of organogenesis at doses of 100, 500, and 1000 mg per kg per day revealed a dose related increased incidence of litters and total numbers of fetuses with dilated ureters, unilateral and bilateral pelvic cavitation, hydronephrosis and hydroureters. A no-effect dose for renal effects was not established. This signifies a syndrome of related effects on a specific organ in the developing embryo which is consistent with a slight delay in fetal maturation. This delay was also indicated by a treatment related increased incidence of incomplete ossification of the sternebrae, skull and nasal bones in all treated groups. Slightly lower fetal weights and an increased incidence of early embryonic deaths were observed in treated rats. When pregnant rabbits were dosed throughout organogenesis at doses up to 80 mg per kg per day, no effects on fetal development were observed.

FDA Pregnancy Category C

Breast-feeding

It is not known whether frovatriptan is distributed into human breast milk. However, frovatriptan is distributed into the milk of lactating rats with the maximum concentration being four times higher than that seen in blood.

Pediatrics

No information is available on the relationship of age to the effects of frovatriptan in the pediatric population. Safety and efficacy have not been established. Frovatriptan is not recommended for use in patients up to 18 years of age.

Geriatrics

Mean blood concentrations of frovatriptan in elderly subjects (age 65 to 77 years) were 1.5 to 2-times higher than those seen in younger adults. However, since there are no differences in half-life between the two populations, there are no recommended therapy adjustments.

Pharmacogenetics

Bioavailability was higher, and systemic exposure to frovatriptan was approximately two-fold greater, in females than males, regardless of age. However, since there are no differences in half-life between the two populations, there are no recommended therapy adjustments.

Drug interactions and/or related problems

The following drug interactions and/or related problems have been selected on the basis of their potential clinical significance (possible mechanism in parentheses where appropriate)—not necessarily inclusive (» = major clinical significance):

Note: Combinations containing any of the following medications, depending on the amount present, may also interact with this medication.

Ergotamine tartrate
(concurrent use with ergotamine tartrate has resulted in a 25% decrease in the area under the plasma concentration-time curve [AUC] and peak plasma concentration of frovatriptan.)

Oral contraceptives
(concurrent use with oral contraceptives has resulted in a 30% increase in the area under the plasma concentration-time curve [AUC] and peak plasma concentration of frovatriptan.)

Other 5-hydroxytryptamine agonists or
Ergotamine containing medications such as:
Dihydroergotamine or
Methysergide
(a delay of 24 hours between administration of dihydroergotamine, ergotamine, or methysergide or other 5-hydroxytryptamine agonists and frovatriptan is recommended because of the possibility of additive and/or prolonged vasoconstriction)

Propranolol
(concurrent use with propranolol increased the area under the plasma concentration-time curve [AUC] in males by 60% and in females by 29%. The peak plasma concentration was increased by 23% in males and 16% in females; however the half-life of frovatriptan in both populations, though slightly longer in females, was not affected by concomitant administration of propranolol.)

Selective serotonin reuptake inhibitors, such as:
Fluoxetine or
Fluvoxamine or
Paroxetine or
Sertraline
(concurrent use may result in weakness, hyperreflexia, and incoordination; careful observation of the patient is recommended)

Medical considerations/Contraindications

The medical considerations/contraindications included have been selected on the basis of their potential clinical significance (reasons given in parentheses where appropriate)—not necessarily inclusive (» = major clinical significance).

Except under special circumstances, this medication should not be used when the following medical problem exists:

» Cerebrovascular syndromes, especially:
» Strokes, any type
» Ischemic attacks, transient
(5-hydroxytryptamine [5-HT_1] agonists may cause cerebral hemorrhage, stroke, subarachnoid hemorrhage or other cerebrovascular events; caution is recommended when administering frovatriptan to patients at risk for cerebrovascular events)

» Coronary artery disease, predisposition to
(5-HT$_1$ agonists have caused serious coronary adverse effects; patients in whom coronary artery disease is a possibility on the basis of age or the presence of other risk factors, such as diabetes, hypercholesterolemia, hypertension, obesity, a strong family history of coronary artery disease, female gender with physiological or surgical menopause, male gender over 40 years or age, or tobacco smoking should be evaluated for the presence of cardiovascular disease before frovatriptan is prescribed; even after a satisfactory evaluation, the advisability of administering the patient's first dose under medical supervision should be considered)

» Hypersensitivity to frovatriptan

» Hypertension, uncontrolled
(may be exacerbated)

» Ischemic heart disease, especially:
» Angina pectoris or
» Ischemia, silent, documented or
» Myocardial infarction, history of, or
» Prinzmetal's variant angina or
» Vasospastic coronary artery disease or
» Other significant underlying cardiovascular disease
(frovatriptan may cause coronary vasospasms and an increased risk of myocardial ischemia and/or infarction.)

» Peripheral vascular disease, especially:
» Ischemic bowel disease or
» Raynaud's syndrome
(5-HT$_1$ agonists may cause vasospastic reactions other than coronary artery spasm; peripheral vascular ischemia and colonic ischemia with abdominal pain and bloody diarrhea have been reported with 5-HT$_1$ agonists)

Patient monitoring

The following may be especially important in patient monitoring (other tests may be warranted in some patients, depending on condition; » = major clinical significance):

Electrocardiogram (ECG)
(monitoring is recommended immediately following the first dose of frovatriptan for patients with cardiovascular risk factors and for long-term intermittent frovatriptan users)

Note: Patients who experience signs or symptoms suggestive of angina following dosing should be evaluated for the presence of coronary artery disease [CAD].

Note: Frovatriptan and/or its metabolites may bind to the melanin of the eye and could cause toxicity in these tissues after extended use. Although no specific recommendations for ophthalmologic monitoring are made, prescribers should be aware of the possibility of long-term ophthalmologic effects.

Side/Adverse Effects

Note: Serious cardiac events, including some that have been fatal, have occurred following use of 5-HT$_1$ agonists. These events are extremely rare and most have been reported in patients with risk factors predictive of coronary artery disease [CAD]. Events reported have included coronary artery vasospasm, transient myocardial ischemia, myocardial infarction, ventricular tachycardia and ventricular fibrillation.

The following side/adverse effects have been selected on the basis of their potential clinical significance (possible signs and symptoms in parentheses where appropriate)—not necessarily inclusive:

Those indicating need for medical attention

Incidence less frequent
Chest pain

Those indicating need for medical attention only if they continue or are bothersome

Incidence more frequent
Dizziness

Incidence less frequent
Dry mouth; dyspepsia (acid or sour stomach; belching; heartburn; indigestion; stomach discomfort, upset or pain); ***fatigue*** (unusual tiredness or weakness); ***flushing*** (feeling of warmth; redness of the face, neck, arms and occasionally, upper chest); ***headache; hot or cold sensation; nausea; paresthesia*** (tingling, burning, or prickly sensations); ***skeletal pain; somnolence*** (sleepiness or unusual drowsiness)

Overdose

For more information on the management of overdose or unintentional ingestion, **contact a poison control center** (see *Poison Control Center Listing*).

Clinical effects of overdose

Overdose has not been reported in humans. No adverse effects were reported in male and female patients with migraine who received single oral doses up to 40 mg or in healthy male subjects who received single oral doses up to 100 mg.

Treatment of overdose

There is no known specific antidote to frovatriptan.

It is not known whether hemodialysis or peritoneal dialysis affects the clearance of frovatriptan.

Monitoring—
The patient should be monitored closely for at least 48 hours, due to an elimination half-life of 26 hours.

Supportive care—
Treatment should be symptomatic and supportive
Patients in whom intentional overdose is confirmed or suspected should be referred for psychiatric consultation.

Patient Consultation

As an aid to patient consultation, refer to *Advice for the Patient, Frovatriptan (Systemic)*.

In providing consultation, consider emphasizing the following selected information (» = major clinical significance):

Before using this medication

» Conditions affecting use, especially:
Hypersensitivity to frovatriptan
Other medical problems, especially cerebrovascular syndromes (especially, strokes and transient ischemic attacks), coronary artery disease (predisposition to), hypertension (uncontrolled), ischemic heart disease (especially, silent, documented ischemia, myocardial infarction (history of), Prinzmetal's variant angina, vasospastic coronary artery disease), other significant underlying cardiovascular disease, and peripheral vascular disease (especially, ischemic bowel disease and Raynaud's syndrome).

Proper use of this medication

» Not administering if atypical headache symptoms are present; checking with physician instead
Administering after onset of headache pain
» Taking an additional dose, if needed, for return of migraine 2 hours or more after initial relief was obtained, but taking no more than three doses within a 24-hour period
Additional benefit may be obtained if the patient lies down in a quiet, dark room after administering medication
» Not using additional doses if a first dose does not provide substantial relief; additional frovatriptan is not likely to be effective in these circumstances; taking alternate medication as previously advised by physician, then checking with physician as soon as possible
» Compliance with prophylactic therapy, if prescribed
» Proper dosing
Proper storage

Precautions while using this medication

Checking with physician if usual dose fails to relieve three consecutive headaches, or frequency and/or severity of headaches increases
Avoiding alcohol, which aggravates headaches
» Caution if drowsiness or dizziness occurs

Side/adverse effects

Signs of potential side effects, especially chest pain

General Dosing Information

The dose may be repeated after 2 hours if the headache returns, but no more than three doses should be given within a 24-hour period. Efficacy of a second dose if the initial dose is ineffective has not been established.

Frovatriptan should be given with fluids.

Oral Dosage Forms

Note: Frovatriptan tablets contain frovatriptan succinate. However, dosage and strength are expressed in terms of frovatriptan base

FROVATRIPTAN SUCCINATE TABLETS

Usual adult dose

Antimigraine agent—
Oral, 2.5 mg (base) as a single dose. If necessary, an additional dose may be taken after two hours.

Note: There is no evidence that a second dose of frovatriptan is effective in patients who do not respond to a first dose of the drug for the same headache.

Usual adult prescribing limits
Not more than 7.5 mg within twenty-four hours

Note: The safety of treating an average of more than four migraine attacks in a 30-day period has not been established.

Usual pediatric dose
Use is not recommended in patients up to 18 years of age.

Usual geriatric dose
See *Usual adult dose*.

Usual geriatric prescribing limits
See *Usual adult prescribing limits*.

Strength(s) usually available
U.S.—
2.5 mg (base) (Rx) [*Frova* (lactose NF; microcrystalline cellulose NF; colloidal silicon dioxide NF; sodium starch glycolate NF; magnesium stearate NF; hydroxypropylmethylcellulose USP; polyethylene glycol 3000 USP; triacetin USP; titanium dioxide USP)].

Packaging and storage
Store at 25°C (77°F); excursions permitted between 15 to 30 °C (59 to 86 °F).
Protect from moisture and light.

Auxiliary labeling
- Take with fluid

Developed: 07/02/2002

FRUCTOSE, DEXTROSE, AND PHOSPHORIC ACID Oral-Local

VA CLASSIFICATION (Primary): GA609
Commonly used brand name(s): *Emetrol*.

NOTE: The *Fructose, Dextrose, and Phosphoric Acid (Oral-local)* monograph is maintained on the *USP DI* electronic data base. A copy of the most recent revision of the complete monograph can be accessed on the *USP DI* Updates Online website. See the front cover of book for details on accessing the site.

The information that follows is selectively abstracted from the complete monograph and is provided to facilitate drug use review and patient counseling.

Note: For a listing of dosage forms and brand names by country availability, see *Dosage Forms* section(s).

Category
Antiemetic.

Indications
Accepted
Fructose, dextrose, and phosphoric acid oral solution is used for the symptomatic relief of nausea and vomiting. However, to date, there is insufficient evidence to establish effectiveness (FDA Category III).

Patient Consultation
As an aid to patient consultation, refer to *Advice for the Patient, Fructose, Dextrose, and Phosphoric Acid (Oral)*.
In providing consultation, consider emphasizing the following selected information (» = major clinical significance):

Before using this medication
» Conditions affecting use, especially:
Intolerance to fructose, dextrose, or phosphoric acid
Risk of fluid and electrolyte loss due to vomiting
Risk of fluid and electrolyte loss due to vomiting
Other medical problems, especially diabetes mellitus, symptoms of appendicitis, or inflamed bowel

Proper use of this medication
Following physician's or manufacturer's instructions
Not diluting or taking fluids before or after dose
» Proper dosing
» Proper storage

Precautions while using this medication
» Checking with physician if symptoms do not improve or become worse
» Not taking if symptoms of appendicitis or inflamed bowel are present; checking with physician for proper diagnosis

Side/adverse effects
Signs of potential side effects, especially fructose intolerance

Oral Dosage Forms
FRUCTOSE, DEXTROSE, AND PHOSPHORIC ACID ORAL SOLUTION

Usual adult and adolescent dose
Antiemetic—Oral, 15 to 30 mL. Dose may be repeated every fifteen minutes until distress subsides, but should not be taken for more than one hour (five doses) without consulting a physician.

Note: For morning sickness, dose should be taken on arising and repeated every three hours as needed.

Usual pediatric dose
Antiemetic—
Children up to 3 years of age: Use is not recommended.
Children over 3 years of age: Oral, 5 to 10 mL. Dose may be repeated every fifteen minutes until distress subsides, but should not be taken for more than one hour (five doses) without consulting a physician.

Usual geriatric dose
See *Usual adult and adolescent dose*.

Strength(s) usually available
U.S.—
1.87 grams of fructose, 1.87 grams of dextrose, and 21.5 mg of phosphoric acid, per 5 mL (OTC) [*Emetrol*].
Canada—
1.87 grams of fructose, 1.87 grams of dextrose, and 21.5 mg of phosphoric acid, per 5 mL (OTC) [*Emetrol*].

Revised: 05/12/1993

FULVESTRANT Systemic†

VA CLASSIFICATION (Primary): AN500
Commonly used brand name(s): *Faslodex*.

Note: For a listing of dosage forms and brand names by country availability, see *Dosage Forms* section(s).

†Not commercially available in Canada.

Category
Antineoplastic.

Indications
Accepted
Carcinoma, breast (treatment)—Fulvestrant is indicated for the treatment of hormone receptor positive metastatic breast cancer in postmenopausal women with disease progression following antiestrogen therapy.

Pharmacology/Pharmacokinetics
Physicochemical characteristics
Chemical Group—Estrogen receptor antagonist
Molecular weight—606.77.

Mechanism of action/Effect
Fulvestrant is an estrogen receptor antagonist that binds to the estrogen receptor in a competitive manner with affinity comparable to estradiol. Fulvestrant down regulates the estrogen receptors (ER) protein in human breast cancer cells.
Clinical studies demonstrate down regulation of ER increases with increasing dose. This down regulation is associated with a dose-related decrease in the expression of the progesterone receptor, an estrogen-related protein. These effects on the ER pathway were also associated with a decrease in Ki67 labeling index, a marker of cell proliferation.

Vol_D
Steady state—3 to 5 liters per kilogram; distribution is extensive and rapid; largely extravascular.

Protein binding
Very high (99%); bound to plasma proteins; VLDL, LDL and HDL lipoprotein fractions appear to be the major binding components.

Biotransformation
Metabolism appears to involve combinations of a number of pathways, including oxidation, aromatic hydroxylation, conjugation with glucu-

ronic acid and/or sulfate at the 2, 3 and 17 positions of the steroid nucleus, and oxidation of the side chain sulfoxide. Studies using human liver preparations and recombinant human enzymes indicate that cytochrome P-450 3A4 (CYP3A4) is the only P-450 isoenzyme involved in the oxidation of fulvestrant; however, the relative contribution of P-450 and non-P-450 routes *in vivo* is unknown.

Half-life
Approximately 40 days

Steady-state concentration:
Following administration of 250 milligrams of fulvestrant intramuscularly every month—after 3 to 6 doses.

Peak plasma concentration:
Following an intramuscular injection—approximately 7 days; concentration is maintained for at least one month.

Elimination
Rapidly cleared by hepatobiliary route at a rate of about 10.5 milliliters plasma per minute per kilogram.
Fecal—approximately 90%
Renal—negligible (<1%)

Pharmacokinetic Profile
The following table represents the mean pharmacokinetic parameters after intramuscular administration of 250 milligrams of fulvestrant

Pharmacokinetic Parameters	C_{max} (ng/mL)	AUC (ng.d/mL)	CL (mL/min)
Single dose	8.5 ± 5.4	131 ± 62	690 ± 226
Multiple dose (Steady-state)	15.8 ± 2.4	328 ± 48	

Precautions to Consider

Tumorigenicity
Studies in rats have found an increased incidence of benign ovarian granulosa cell tumors and testicular Leydig cell tumors.

Mutagenicity
Fulvestrant was not mutagenic or clastogenic in multiple *in vitro* tests.

Pregnancy/Reproduction
Fertility—In female rats, fulvestrant administered at doses ≥ 0.01 mg per kg per day (approximately one-hundredth of the human recommended dose based on body surface area [BSA] for two weeks prior to and for one week following mating) caused a reversible reduction in fertility and embryonic survival. No adverse effects on female fertility and embryonic survival were evident in animals dosed at 0.001 mg per kg per day (approximately one-thousandth of the human dose based on BSA).

The effects of fulvestrant on the fertility of male animals has not been studied. In a 6-month toxicology study, male rats treated with doses larger than the human recommended equivalent resulted in loss of spermatozoa from the seminiferous tubules, seminiferous tubular atrophy, and degenerative changes in the epididymides.

Pregnancy—Fulvestrant is contraindicated in pregnant women. Women of childbearing potential should be advised not to become pregnant while receiving fulvestrant. Use of fulvestrant has not been studied in pregnant women. If the patient becomes pregnant while receiving fulvestrant, the patient should be apprised of the potential hazard to the fetus, or potential risk for loss of the pregnancy.

Fulvestrant crosses the placenta and has been shown to cause fetal harm in rats and rabbits. Risk benefit must be carefully considered when this medication is required in life-threatening situations or in serious diseases for which other medications cannot be used or are ineffective.

In studies in rats, intramuscular doses of fulvestrant caused an increased incidence of fetal abnormalities and death. Similarly, rabbits failed to maintain pregnancy and the fetuses showed an increased incidence of skeletal variations.

FDA Pregnancy Category D

Breast-feeding
It is not known whether fulvestrant is distributed into human breast milk. However, fulvestrant is distributed into the milk of lactating rats. Because of the potential for serious adverse reactions from fulvestrant in nursing infants, a decision should be made whether to discontinue nursing or discontinue the drug taking into consideration the importance of the drug to the mother.

Pediatrics
Fulvestrant is not indicated for use in children. Appropriate studies have not been performed on the relationship of age to the effects of fulvestrant in the pediatric population. Safety and efficacy have not been established.

Geriatrics
Appropriate studies on the relationship of age to the effects of fulvestrant have not been performed in the geriatric population. No geriatrics-specific problems have been identified. However, when tumor response was considered by age, objective response rates were greater in patients under 65 years of age (complete response 24%; partial response 22%) than in patients 65 years of age and older (complete response 16%; partial response 11%).

There was no difference in fulvestrant pharmacokinetic profile related to age (range 33 to 89 years) in patients with breast cancer.

Pharmacogenetics
No differences in fulvestrant pharmacokinetics were observed related to race, gender, or menopausal status.

Drug interactions and/or related problems
The following drug interactions and/or related problems have been selected on the basis of their potential clinical significance (possible mechanism in parentheses where appropriate)—not necessarily inclusive (» = major clinical significance):

Note: Combinations containing any of the following medications, depending on the amount present, may also interact with this medication.

» Anticoagulants
(may increase the risk of bleeding or bruising associated with the intramuscular administration of fulvestrant)

Medical considerations/Contraindications
The medical considerations/contraindications included have been selected on the basis of their potential clinical significance (reasons given in parentheses where appropriate)—not necessarily inclusive (» = major clinical significance).

Except under special circumstances, this medication should not be used when the following medical problem exists:
» Bleeding diathesis or
» Thrombocytopenia
(these conditions may increase the risk of bleeding or bruising associated with the intramuscular administration of fulvestrant)

» Hepatic impairment, moderate to severe
(safety and efficacy have not been evaluated in patients with moderate to severe hepatic impairment)

» Hypersensitivity to fulvestrant

Patient monitoring
The following may be especially important in patient monitoring (other tests may be warranted in some patients, depending on condition; » = major clinical significance):

» Pregnancy testing
(recommended before starting treatment with fulvestrant; women of childbearing potential should be asked about pregnancy status periodically during treatment with fulvestrant and advised not to become pregnant while receiving fulvestrant)

Side/Adverse Effects

The following side/adverse effects have been selected on the basis of their potential clinical significance (possible signs and symptoms in parentheses where appropriate)—not necessarily inclusive:

Those indicating need for medical attention
Incidence more frequent
Peripheral edema (bloating or swelling of face, arms, hands, lower legs, or feet; rapid weight gain; tingling of hands or feet; unusual weight gain or loss)

Those indicating need for medical attention only if they continue or are bothersome
Incidence more frequent
Abdominal pain; anorexia (loss of appetite; weight loss); ***asthenia*** (lack or loss of strength); ***back pain; bone pain; chest pain; constipation; cough, increased; depression*** (discouragement; feeling sad or empty; irritability; lack of appetite; loss of interest or pleasure; tiredness; trouble concentrating; trouble sleeping); ***diarrhea; dizziness; dyspnea*** (shortness of breath; difficult or labored breathing; tightness in chest; wheezing); ***fever; flu syndrome*** (chills; cough; diarrhea; fever; general feeling of discomfort or illness; headache; joint pain; loss of appetite; muscle aches and pains; nausea; runny nose; shivering; sore throat; sweating; trouble sleeping; unusual tiredness or weakness; vomiting); ***headache; injection site pain; insomnia*** (sleeplessness; trouble sleeping; unable to sleep); ***nausea; pain; paresthe-***

sia (burning, crawling, itching, numbness, prickling, "pins and needles", or tingling feelings); ***pelvic pain; pharyngitis*** (body aches or pain; congestion; cough; dryness or soreness of throat; fever; hoarseness; runny nose; tender, swollen glands in neck; trouble in swallowing; voice changes); ***skin rash; vasodilation*** (feeling of warmth or heat; flushing or redness of skin, especially on face and neck; headache; feeling faint, dizzy, or light-headedness; sweating); ***urinary tract infection*** (bladder pain; bloody or cloudy urine; difficult, burning, or painful urination; frequent urge to urinate; lower back or side pain); ***vomiting***

Incidence less frequent

Accidental injury; anemia (pale skin; troubled breathing with exertion; unusual bleeding or bruising; unusual tiredness or weakness); ***anxiety*** (fear; nervousness); ***arthritis*** (pain, swelling, or redness in joints; muscle pain or stiffness; difficulty in moving); ***sweating***

Incidence rare

Leukopenia (black, tarry stools; chest pain; chills; cough; fever; painful or difficult urination; shortness of breath; sore throat; sores, ulcers, or white spots on lips or in mouth; swollen glands; unusual bleeding or bruising; unusual tiredness or weakness); ***myalgia*** (joint pain; swollen joints; muscle aching or cramping; muscle pains or stiffness; difficulty in moving); ***thromboembolic phenomena*** (pain in chest, groin, or legs, especially the calves; difficulty breathing; severe, sudden headache; slurred speech; sudden, unexplained shortness of breath; sudden loss of coordination; sudden, severe weakness or numbness in arm or leg; vision changes); ***vaginal bleeding; vertigo*** (dizziness or lightheadedness; feeling of constant movement of self or surroundings; sensation of spinning)

Overdose

For more information on the management of overdose or unintentional ingestion, **contact a poison control center** (see *Poison Control Center Listing*).

Clinical effects of overdose

There is no clinical experience with overdosage in humans. No adverse effects were seen in healthy male and female volunteers who received intravenous fulvestrant, which resulted in peak plasma concentrations that were approximately 10 to 15 times those seen after intramuscular injection. Animal studies have shown no effects other than those related directly or indirectly to antiestrogen activity following intramuscular administration of fulvestrant at doses higher than recommended in humans.

Treatment of overdose

Supportive care—

Treatment should be symptomatic and supportive.

Patients in whom intentional overdose is confirmed or suspected should be referred for psychiatric consultation.

Patient Consultation

As an aid to patient consultation, refer to *Advice for the Patient, Fulvestrant (Systemic)*.

In providing consultation, consider emphasizing the following selected information (» = major clinical significance):

Before using this medication

» Conditions affecting use, especially:

Pregnancy—Do not take fulvestrant during pregnancy. Fulvestrant crosses the placenta and has been shown to cause fetal harm in animals. Tell your physician immediately if pregnancy is suspected. Do not become pregnant while receiving fulvestrant.

Breast-feeding—It is not known whether fulvestrant is distributed into human breast milk. Because of the potential for serious adverse reactions in nursing infants, a decision should be made whether or not to discontinue nursing, taking into consideration the importance of the drug to the mother.

Use in the elderly—When tumor response was considered by age, objective response rates were greater in patients under 65 years of age.

Other medications, especially anticoagulants

Other medical problems, especially bleeding diathesis, thrombocytopenia, or moderate to severe hepatic impairment

Proper use of this medication

Importance of proper intramuscular use

Importance of proper handling and disposal of needles and syringes

» Proper dosing: Administer one dose each month, on the same day each month (e.g., first day of month).

If dosing schedule is once a month: administer missed dose as soon as possible; do not double doses or administer more often than one dose every 30 days.

Proper storage: Store in refrigerator. Protect from light by storing in the original carton until time of use.

Precautions while using this medication

» Regular visits to physician to check progress during therapy

» For women of reproductive age—Importance of not becoming pregnant while receiving fulvestrant

Side/adverse effects

Signs of potential side effects, especially peripheral edema

General Dosing Information

For the two 2.5-mL syringe package only, both syringes must be administered to receive the 250 mg recommended monthly dose.

The injection should be administered slowly into the buttock.

Safety considerations for handling this medication

Using care in handling contaminated needles to avoid HIV (AIDS), HBV (Hepatitis) and other infectious diseases due to accidental needlesticks; not recapping or removing contaminated needles, unless there is no alternative or that such action is required by a specific medical procedure.

Using a one-handed technique and activating away from self and others for greatest safety.

Keeping hands behind the needle at all times during use and disposal and not autoclaving the needle.

Discarding syringe in an approved sharps collector in accordance with applicable regulations after single use.

Parenteral Dosage Forms

FULVESTRANT INJECTION

Usual adult dose

Carcinoma, breast—

Intramuscular, 250 mg once monthly as a single 5-mL injection or two concurrent 2.5-mL injections

Note: Safety and efficacy of fulvestrant have not been evaluated in patients with moderate to severe hepatic impairment. No dosage adjustment is recommended in patients with mild hepatic impairment.

Mild hepatic impairment is defined as:

- alanine aminotransferase [ALT] concentration greater than the upper limit of normal (ULN) but less than two times the ULN or
- any two of the following 3 parameters were between one and two times the ULN:

aspartate aminotransferase [AST]
alkaline phosphatase
total bilirubin

Usual pediatric dose

Carcinoma, breast—

Safety and efficacy have not been established.

Usual geriatric dose

See *Usual adult dose*.

Strength(s) usually available

U.S.—

250 mg of fulvestrant per 5-mL prefilled syringe (50 mg/mL) (Rx) [*Faslodex* (alcohol; benzyl alcohol; benzyl benzoate; castor oil)].

125 mg of fulvestrant per 2.5-mL prefilled syringe (50 mg/mL) (Rx) [*Faslodex* (contains two 5-mL prefilled syringes containing 2.5 mL; alcohol; benzyl alcohol; benzyl benzoate; castor oil)].

Canada—

Not commercially available

Packaging and storage

Store between 2 and 8°C (36 and 46°F). Protect from light by storing in the original carton until time of use.

Auxiliary labeling

- For intramuscular (I.M.) use only
- Refrigerate
- Protect from light

Additional information

See the manufacturer's package insert for instructions for intramuscular use, handling and disposal of fulvestrant injection.

Revised: 03/10/2004
Developed: 01/21/2003

FUROSEMIDE—See *Diuretics, Loop (Systemic)*

GABAPENTIN Systemic

VA CLASSIFICATION (Primary/Secondary): CN400/CN900

Commonly used brand name(s): *Neurontin; Novo-Gabapentin.*

Another commonly used name is GBP.

Note: For a listing of dosage forms and brand names by country availability, see *Dosage Forms* section(s).

Category

Anticonvulsant; Antineuralgic.

Indications

Note: Bracketed information in the *Indications* section refers to uses that are not included in U.S. product labeling.

Accepted

Epilepsy (treatment adjunct)—Gabapentin is indicated as an adjunct to other anticonvulsant medications (in the treatment of partial seizures with or without secondary generalization in adults and adolescents)[1] with epilepsy. Gabapentin is also indicated as adjunctive therapy for the treatment of partial seizures in pediatric patients 3 years of age and older with epilepsy.[1]

Postherpetic Neuralgia[1]—Gabapentin is indicated for the management of postherpetic neuralgia in adults.

[Pain, peripheral neuropathic, diabetic (treatment)][1]—Gabapentin is indicated for the treatment of diabetic peripheral neuropathic pain.

[1]Not included in Canadian product labeling.

Pharmacology/Pharmacokinetics

Physicochemical characteristics

Chemical Group—Cyclohexane-acetic acid derivative. Structural analog to gamma-aminobutyric acid (GABA).

Molecular weight—171.24.

pKa—3.68 and 10.7.

Solubility—Freely soluble in water and both basic and acidic aqueous solutions.

Partition coefficient—The log of the partition coefficient (n-octanol/0.05M phosphate buffer) at pH 7.4 is −1.25.

Mechanism of action/Effect

Anticonvulsant action—The mechanism of action is unknown. Gabapentin does not interact with GABA receptors, is not metabolized to a GABA agonist or to GABA, and does not inhibit GABA uptake or degradation. In rats, gabapentin interacts with a novel binding site on cortical neurons that may be associated with the L-system amino acid transporter of brain cell membranes.

Analgesic action—The mechanism of action is unknown. Gabapentin prevents pain-related behavior in response to a normally innocuous stimulus (allodynia) and exaggerated response to painful stimuli (hyperalgesia) in animal models. In models of neuropathic pain in rats or mice, gabapentin prevents pain-related responses. Pain-related responses after peripheral inflammation were also decreased by gabapentin. Immediate pain-related behaviors (rat tail flick test, formalin footpad acute phase, acetic acid abdominal constriction test, footpad heat irradiation test) were not altered by gabapentin.

Absorption

Rapid. Gabapentin is absorbed in part by the L-amino acid transport system, which is a carrier-mediated, saturable transport system; as the dose increases, bioavailability decreases. Bioavailability ranges from approximately 60% for a 900 mg dose per day to approximately 27% for a 4800 milligram dose per day.

Food has a slight effect on the rate and extent of absorption of gabapentin (14% increase in AUC).

Distribution

Volume of distribution (Vol_D) is approximately 50 to 60 L. Gabapentin penetrates the blood–brain barrier, yielding cerebrospinal fluid (CSF) concentrations approximately equal to 20% of corresponding steady-state plasma trough concentrations in patients with epilepsy. Brain tissue concentrations in one patient undergoing temporal lobectomy were approximately 80% of corresponding plasma concentrations.

Protein binding

Very low—less than 3% circulates bound to plasma protein.

Biotransformation

Gabapentin is not metabolized.

Half-life

Elimination—

Normal renal function: 5 to 7 hours.

Impaired renal function (creatinine clearance < 30 mL/minute): 52 hours.

In hemodialysis: In 11 anuric patients, a single 400-mg oral dose of gabapentin had an elimination half-life of 132 hours on days when patients did not receive dialysis, and 3.8 hours during dialysis.

Time to peak concentration

2 to 4 hours.

Therapeutic serum concentration

The therapeutic serum concentration range for gabapentin is not well defined. However, in one study it was noted that seizure frequency decreased significantly only in patients with gabapentin serum concentrations > 2 mg/L (11.7 micromoles/L). After receiving gabapentin 400 mg three times per day for one week, patients maintained on phenytoin had minimum gabapentin plasma concentrations of 2 to 4.8 mg/L (11.7 to 28 micromoles/L) and maximum gabapentin plasma concentrations of 3.6 to 8.6 mg/L (21 to 50.2 micromoles/L). Titration of dosage is based on clinical response.

Food increases C_{max} by 14%.

Note: Steady-state pharmacokinetics of gabapentin in patients with epilepsy were similar to those in healthy subjects.

Elimination

Renal—Entire absorbed dose, as unchanged drug. Gabapentin clearance is directly proportional to creatinine clearance. Higher oral clearance values were observed in children <5 years of age when normalized per body weight. In infants < 1 year of age, clearance was highly variable.

In dialysis—Gabapentin can be removed from plasma by hemodialysis.

Precautions to Consider

Carcinogenicity/Tumorigenicity

In two-year carcinogenicity studies, a statistically significant increase in the incidence of pancreatic acinar cell adenomas and carcinomas was found in male rats receiving doses of gabapentin that produced plasma concentrations 10 times higher than those seen in humans receiving 3600 mg per day. Tumors were noninvasive, did not metastasize, did not affect survival, and did not occur in female rats or in mice. The significance to humans is unknown.

Mutagenicity

No evidence of mutagenicity was found in appropriate *in vitro* and *in vivo* testing. Gabapentin was negative in the Ames test, and negative in the *in vitro* HGPRT forward mutation assay in Chinese hamster lung cells; it did not produce significant increases in chromosomal aberrations in the *in vitro* Chinese hamster lung cell assay; it was negative in the *in vivo* chromosomal aberration assay and in the *in vivo* micronucleus test in Chinese hamster bone marrow.

Pregnancy/Reproduction

Fertility—No adverse effect on fertility was seen in rats given up to 5 times an equivalent human dose of 3600 mg on a mg per square meter of body surface area (mg/m^2) basis.

Pregnancy—Gabapentin should be used during pregnancy only if the benefit justifies the potential risk to the fetus.

Adequate and well-controlled studies have not been done in humans.

Gabapentin has been shown to be fetotoxic in rodents. Pregnant mice given 1 to 4 times an equivalent human dose of 3600 mg on a mg/m^2 basis during organogenesis produced offspring with delayed ossification of several bones in the skull, vertebrae, and limbs. Rats given approximately 1 to 5 times an equivalent human dose of 3600 mg on a mg/m^2 basis produced offspring with an increased incidence of hydroureter and hydronephrosis. In rabbits given < 1/4 to 8 times an equivalent human dose of 3600 mg on a mg/m^2 basis, an increased incidence of postimplantation fetal loss occurred.

FDA Pregnancy Category C.

Breast-feeding

Gabapentin is distributed into human breast milk following oral administration. A nursed infant could be exposed to a maximum dose of approximately 1 milligram per kilogram per day. Gabapentin should be used in women who are nursing only if the benefits clearly outweigh the risks.

Pediatrics

Safety and effectiveness of gabapentin in the management of postherpetic neuralgia in pediatric patients have not been established.

In pediatric patients below the age of 3 years, effectiveness of gabapentin as adjunctive therapy in the treatment of partial seizures has not been established.

In Canada, systematic studies to establish safety and efficacy in children have not been performed.

In controlled trials performed in pediatric patients age 3 to 12, there were associated occurrences of central nervous system related adverse events. These neuropsychiatric events included emotional liability, hostility, thought disorders (including concentration problems and change in school performance) and hyperkinesia (primarily restlessness and hyperactivity).

Adolescents

Appropriate studies on the relationship of age to the effects of gabapentin have not been performed in the adolescent population. However, clinical trials that included a limited number of patients aged 12 to 18 years revealed no adolescence-specific problems.

Geriatrics

Plasma clearance of gabapentin is reduced in the elderly, probably due to age-related renal function decline. Dosage reduction based on creatinine clearance is recommended. Further dosage adjustments should be based on clinical response.

In controlled clinical trials in patients with postherpetic neuralgia, patients 75 years of age and older experienced a larger treatment effect. Types and incidence of adverse events were similar across age groups except for peripheral edema and ataxia, which tended to increase in incidence with age.

Pharmacogenetics

Adequate and well-controlled studies in humans have not been done. No important racial differences or significant gender differences have been observed.

Drug interactions and/or related problems

The following drug interactions and/or related problems have been selected on the basis of their potential clinical significance (possible mechanism in parentheses where appropriate)—not necessarily inclusive (» = major clinical significance):

Note: Gabapentin does not induce or inhibit the hepatic mixed oxidase enzymes responsible for drug metabolism. Also, it does not interfere with the metabolism of commonly coadministered antiepileptic agents.

Combinations containing any of the following medications, depending on the amount present, may also interact with this medication.

Alcohol or
Central nervous system (CNS) depression-producing medications, other (see *Appendix II*)
(increased CNS depression may occur)

» Antacids, especially aluminum- and magnesium-containing
(antacid taken with or within 2 hours after gabapentin reduces gabapentin's bioavailability by 20%; gabapentin should be taken at least 2 hours after antacid)

Hydrocodone
(concomitant administration decreased hydrocodone C_{max} and AUC values in a dose-dependent manner and increased gabapentin AUC values by 14%)

» Morphine
(concomitant use increased mean gabapentin AUC values by 44%; patients may experience increases in CNS depressive events; decreases in dosing of either agent may be necessary)

Naproxen
(may increase the amount of gabapentin absorbed by 12 to 15%.; no dosing recommendations are given)

Laboratory value alterations

The following have been selected on the basis of their potential clinical significance (possible effect in parentheses where appropriate)—not necessarily inclusive (» = major clinical significance).

With diagnostic test results

Dipstick tests for urinary protein (e.g., Ames N-Multistix SG, Chemstrip 3)
(gabapentin causes a false positive result; the sulfosalicylic acid precipitation procedure should be used to detect urinary protein in patients taking gabapentin)

With physiology/laboratory test values

Blood glucose in patients with diabetes mellitus or
White blood cell counts
(may be decreased or increased)

Liver function tests
(may be elevated)

Medical considerations/Contraindications

The medical considerations/contraindications included have been selected on the basis of their potential clinical significance (reasons given in parentheses where appropriate)—not necessarily inclusive (» = major clinical significance).

Risk-benefit should be considered when the following medical problems exist:

» Hypersensitivity to gabapentin or any ingredients in the formulation

» Renal function impairment
(elimination may be prolonged in patients not receiving hemodialysis, and shortened in patients during hemodialysis; dosage adjustment based on creatinine clearance is recommended)

Side/Adverse Effects

Antiepileptic drugs should not be abruptly discontinued because of the possibility of increasing seizure frequency.

Sudden and unexplained death occurred in 8 patients among a cohort of 2203 patients treated, which could represent seizure-related deaths.

The following side/adverse effects have been selected on the basis of their potential clinical significance (possible signs and symptoms in parentheses where appropriate)—not necessarily inclusive:

Note: Adverse effects from gabapentin therapy are generally mild to moderate in severity, and tend to diminish with continued use.

Those indicating need for medical attention

Incidence more frequent

Ataxia (clumsiness or unsteadiness)—may be dose-related; ***nystagmus*** (continuous, uncontrolled, back-and-forth and/or rolling eye movements)

In pediatric patients 3 to 12 years of age

Neuropsychiatric problems, including emotional lability (anxiety; behavior problems; crying; false sense of well-being; mental depression; reacting too quickly, too emotionally, or overreacting; rapidly changing moods); ***hostility*** (aggressive behavior; suspiciousness or distrust); ***hyperkinesia*** (hyperactivity or increase in body movements; restlessness); ***and thought disorders*** (concentration problems and change in school performance)

Incidence less frequent

Amnesia (loss of memory); ***depression, irritability, or other mood or mental changes; fracture*** (pain or swelling in arms or legs); ***leukopenia*** (black, tarry stools; chest pain; chills; cough; fever; painful or difficult urination; shortness of breath; sore throat; sores, ulcers, or white spots on lips or in mouth; swollen glands; unusual bleeding or bruising; unusual tiredness or weakness)

Incidence is not determined—Observed during clinical practice

Angioedema (large, hive-like swelling on face, eyelids, lips, tongue, throat, hands, legs, feet, sex organs); ***erythema multiforme*** (blistering, peeling, loosening of skin; chills; cough; diarrhea; fever; itching; joint or muscle pain; red irritated eyes; sore throat; sores, ulcers, or white spots in mouth or on lips; unusual tiredness or weakness); ***hyponatremia*** (coma; confusion; convulsions; decreased urine output; dizziness; fast or irregular heartbeat; headache; increased thirst; muscle pain); ***jaundice*** (chills; clay-colored stools; dark urine; dizziness; fever; headache; itching; loss of appetite; nausea; abdominal or stomach pain; rash; unpleasant breath odor; unusual tiredness or weakness; vomiting of blood; yellow eyes or skin); ***Stevens-Johnson syndrome*** (blistering, peeling, loosening of skin; chills; cough; diarrhea; itching; joint or muscle pain; red irritated eyes; red skin lesions, often with a purple center; sore throat; sores, ulcers, or white spots in mouth or on lips; unusual tiredness or weakness)

Those indicating need for medical attention only if they continue or are bothersome

Incidence more frequent

Abnormal thinking (confusion; delusions; dementia); ***asthenia*** (lack or loss of strength); ***diarrhea; dizziness; fatigue*** (unusual tiredness or weakness); ***fever; infection*** (fever or chills; cough or hoarseness; lower back or side pain; painful or difficult urination); ***myalgia*** (muscle ache or pain); ***peripheral edema*** (swelling of hands, feet, or lower legs); ***somnolence*** (drowsiness)—may be dose-related; ***tremor*** (trembling or shaking); ***viral infection*** (chills; cough or hoarseness; fever; cold or flu-like symptoms); ***vision abnormalities, including blurred vision and diplopia*** (double vision)

Incidence less frequent or rare

Abdominal pain; abnormal gait (change in walking and balance; clumsiness, or unsteadiness); ***abrasion*** (pain, redness, rash, swelling, or bleeding where the skin is rubbed off); ***amblyopia*** (blurred vision; change in vision; impaired vision); ***appetite increased or decreased; back pain; bronchitis*** (cough producing mucus; difficulty breathing; shortness of breath; tightness in chest; wheezing); ***conjunctivitis*** (redness, pain, swelling of eye, eyelid, or inner lining of eyelid; burning, dry or itching eyes; discharge; excessive tearing); ***cough; dental abnormalities; dryness of mouth or throat; dysarthria*** (slurred speech); ***flatulence*** (bloated full feeling; excess air or gas in stomach or intestines; passing gas); ***frequent urination; gastrointestinal effects, including constipation, diarrhea, dyspepsia,*** (indigestion); ***nausea, and vomiting; headache; hypesthesia*** (increased sensitivity to pain; increased sensitivity to touch; tingling in the hands and feet); ***hyperglycemia*** (abdominal pain; blurred vision; dry mouth; fatigue; flushed, dry skin; fruit-like breath odor; increased hunger; increased thirst; increased urination; nausea; sweating; troubled breathing; unexplained weight loss; vomiting); ***hypotension*** (low blood pressure); ***incoordination; impotence*** (decrease in sexual desire or ability); ***injury, accidental; insomnia*** (trouble in sleeping); ***nervousness; otitis media*** (earache; redness or swelling in ear); ***pharyngitis*** (body aches or pain; congestion; cough; dryness or soreness of throat; fever; hoarseness; runny nose; tender, swollen glands in neck; trouble in swallowing; voice changes); ***pruritus*** (itching skin); ***respiratory infection*** (cough; fever; sneezing; sore throat); ***rhinitis*** (runny nose); ***skin rash; tinnitus*** (noise in ears); ***trouble in thinking; twitching; vasodilatation*** (feeling of warmth or heat; flushing or redness of skin, especially on face and neck; headache; feeling faint, dizzy, or lightheadedness; sweating); ***weight gain***

Overdose

For more information on the management of overdose or unintentional ingestion, **contact a Poison Control Center** (see *Poison Control Center Listing*).

Clinical effects of overdose

Note: Some of the effects of gabapentin overdose may be similar to adverse effects seen at therapeutic doses; they may be more severe, or several adverse effects may occur together. Saturation of the carrier-mediated absorption pathway at higher gabapentin doses may limit drug absorption at the time of overdose and subsequently reduce the toxicity from overdose.

The following effects have been selected on the basis of their potential clinical significance (possible signs and symptoms in parentheses where appropriate)—not necessarily inclusive:

Diarrhea; diplopia (double vision); ***dysarthria*** (slurred speech); ***lethargy*** (sluggishness); ***somnolence*** (drowsiness)

Treatment of overdose

Note: There is no specific antidote for gabapentin overdose.

Specific treatment—Hemodialysis (may be indicated by clinical state or in patients with significant renal impairment)

Supportive care—Patients in whom intentional overdose is confirmed or suspected should be referred for psychiatric consultation.

Patient Consultation

As an aid to patient consultation, refer to *Advice for the Patient, Gabapentin (Systemic)*.

In providing consultation, consider emphasizing the following selected information (» = major clinical significance):

Before using this medication

» Conditions affecting use, especially:
- Hypersensitivity to gabapentin
- Pregnancy—Gabapentin should be used during pregnancy only if the benefit justifies the potential risk to the fetus.
- FDA Pregnancy Category C
- Breast-feeding—is distributed into human breast milk following oral administration
- Use in children—Safety and effectiveness of gabapentin in the management of postherpetic neuralgia in pediatric patients have not been established.
- In pediatric patients below the age of 3 years, effectiveness of gabapentin as adjunctive therapy in the treatment of partial seizures has not been established.
- In Canada, systematic studies to establish safety and efficacy in children have not been performed.
- Neuropsychiatric events, including emotional liability, hostility, thought disorders (including concentration problems and change in school performance) and hyperkinesia (primarily restlessness and hyperactivity), have been reported in pediatric patients.
- Use in the elderly—Elderly patients may excrete gabapentin more slowly; dosage reduction based on creatinine clearance and dosage adjustment based on clinical response are recommended
- Other medications, especially antacids and morphine.
- Other medical problems, especially renal function impairment

Proper use of this medication

» Compliance with therapy; not taking more or less medicine than prescribed; not missing any doses

Importance of not exceeding 12-hour interval between any 2 doses while on 3-times-a-day dosing schedule

» Importance of dissolving each dose as needed when a liquid dosage form is required; not dissolving any doses to save for later use

Gabapentin may be taken with or without food.

Missed dose: Taking as soon as possible; if less than 4 hours until next dose, do not take the missed dose and return to your regular dosing schedule. Do not allow more than 12 hours to go by between doses. If this happens, call your doctor right away.

» Proper storage

Precautions while using this medication

» Importance of regular visits to physician to check progress of therapy

» Discussing alcohol use or use of other CNS depressants with physician

» Possible blurred or double vision, dizziness, drowsiness, impairment of thinking or motor skills; caution when driving or doing jobs requiring alertness

Possible false positive results with dipstick tests for urinary protein; using the sulfosalicylic acid precipitation procedure to determine presence of urinary protein

» Not discontinuing gabapentin abruptly; consulting physician about gradually reducing dosage

Side/adverse effects

Ataxia; nystagmus; neuropsychiatric problems (including emotional lability, hostility, hyperkinesia, and thought disorders); amnesia, depression, irritability, or other mood or mental changes; fracture; leukopenia

(Signs of potential side effects observed during clinical practice, especially angioedema, erythema multiforme, hyponatremia, jaundice, and Steven Johnson Syndrome.)

General Dosing Information

Gabapentin dosage is titrated to clinical effect, not to plasma concentration.

Adverse effects are generally mild to moderate in severity, and tend to diminish with continued use of gabapentin.

Anticonvulsant medications should not be discontinued abruptly because of the possibility of increased seizure frequency. If gabapentin is to be discontinued, or if another anticonvulsant medication is to be added to the patient's therapy, the change should be made gradually, over a minimum period of one week, to avoid loss of seizure control.

Diet/Nutrition

Gabapentin may be taken with or without food.

Oral Dosage Forms

Note: Bracketed uses in the *Dosage Forms* section refer to categories of use and/or indications that are not included in U.S. product labeling.

GABAPENTIN CAPSULES

Usual adult and adolescent dose

Anticonvulsant—

Usual adult and adolescent dose: Oral, initially 300 mg three times a day. The dosage may be gradually increased based on clinical response. Dosages of 900 to 1800 mg per day are effective for most patients. However, dosages as high as 2400 to 3600 mg per day have been well tolerated.

Note: Dosage may be increased more slowly to avoid CNS adverse effects.

When taking gabapentin three times a day, the maximum time between doses should not exceed twelve hours.

For patients with renal function impairment: See *Usual geriatric dose*.

Postherpetic neuralgia[1]—

Usual adult dose: Oral, initial single dose of 300 milligram on day 1; 600 milligrams per day (divided, two times a day) on day 2; 900 milligrams per day (divided, three times a day) on day 3. Dose may be titrated up to a maximum daily dose of 1800 milligrams (divided, three times a day). Additional benefits were not demonstrated at doses greater than 1800 milligrams per day.

Note: For patients with renal function impairment: See *Usual geriatric dose*.

[Diabetic peripheral neuropathic pain][1]—

Usual adult dose: Oral, initially 900 mg per day titrated to a maximum of 3600 mg per day.

Note: Adults with renal function impairment may require a reduction in dose as follows:
—Creatinine clearance (CrCl) > 60: Up to 1800 mg a day.
—CrCl = 30-60 mL per minute: 300 mg two times a day.
—CrCl = 15-30 mL per minute: 300 mg per day.
—CrCl < 15 mL per minute: 300 mg every other day.

Usual adult and adolescent prescribing limits
3600 mg per day

Usual pediatric dose
Anticonvulsant—
Children 3 years to 12 years—The starting dose should range from 10 to 15 mg per kg of body weight per day, divided into three doses. The effective dose should be reached by upward titration over a period of approximately 3 days.
• Ages 5 years and older—The effective dose is 25 to 35 mg per kg of body weight per day given in divided doses (three times a day)
• Ages 3 years and 4 years—The effective dose is 40 mg per kg of body weight per day given in divided doses (three times a day)
Children 12 years of age and over: See *Usual adult and adolescent dose.*

Note: The maximum time interval between doses should not exceed 12 hours.
The use of gabapentin has not been studied in patients less that 12 years of age with compromised renal function.

Usual pediatric prescribing limit
Dosages of up to 50 mg per kg of body weight per day have been well tolerated in long-term clinical studies.

Usual geriatric dose
Anticonvulsant—
Oral, initial dosage recommendations, based on creatinine clearance, are as follows. Dosage adjustments may be based on clinical response.

Dosage in Renal Impairment—USA

Creatinine Clearance (mL per minute)	Total Daily Dose (mg per day)	Dosage Regimen (mg)				
≥ 60	900 to 3600	300 three times a day	400 three times a day	600 three times a day	800 three times a day	1200 three times a day
30 to 59	400 to 1400	200 two times a day	300 two times a day	400 two times a day	500 two times a day	700 two times a day
15 to 29	200 to 700	200 once a day	300 once a day	400 once a day	500 once a day	700 once a day
15	100 to 300	100 once a day	125 once a day	150 once a day	200 once a day	300 once a day
Post-Hemodialysis Supplemental Dose (mg)						
Hemodialysis	125	150	200	250	350	

Note: Maintenance dose is based on estimates of creatinine clearance as indicated in table above. Supplemental post-hemodialysis dose is administered after each 4 hours of hemodialysis.

Dosage in Renal Impairment—Canada

Creatinine Clearance (mL per minute)	Total Daily Dose (mg per day)	Dosage Regimen (mg)
> 60	1200	400 three times a day
30 to 60	600	300 two times a day
15 to 30	300	300 once a day
<15	150	300 once every other day

Note: For patients undergoing hemodialysis: Oral, 300 to 400 mg initially for patients who have never received gabapentin, then 200 to 300 mg following each four hours of hemodialysis.

Postherpetic neuralgia[1]—
See *Usual adult and adolescent dose*

Strength(s) usually available
U.S.—
100 mg (Rx) [*Neurontin* (lactose)].
300 mg (Rx) [*Neurontin* (lactose)].
400 mg (Rx) [*Neurontin* (lactose)].
Canada—
Note: Capsule shells may contain gelatin, titanium dioxide, silicon dioxide, sodium lauryl sulfate, yellow iron oxide, red iron oxide, and FD&C Blue No. 2.
100 mg (Rx) [*Neurontin* (lactose); GENERIC].
300 mg (Rx) [*Neurontin* (lactose); GENERIC].
400 mg (Rx) [*Neurontin* (lactose); GENERIC].

Packaging and storage
Store at 25 °C (77 °F), excursions permitted between 15 and 30 °C (59 and 86 °F), in a well-closed container, unless otherwise specified by manufacturer.

Preparation of dosage form
For patients who cannot take oral solids—Individual doses may be dissolved in juice or sprinkled over soft foods, such as applesauce, immediately before use. However, gabapentin solutions degrade over time and should be freshly prepared and taken immediately after preparation.

Auxiliary labeling
• May cause blurred vision.
• May cause dizziness.
• May cause drowsiness. Alcohol may intensify this effect.
• This medication can be taken with or without food

GABAPENTIN ORAL SOLUTION

Usual adult and adolescent dose
See *Gabapentin Capsules*

Usual adult and adolescent prescribing limits
See *Gabapentin Capsules*

Usual pediatric dose
See *Gabapentin Capsules*
Children 12 years of age and over: See *Usual adult and adolescent dose.*

Usual pediatric prescribing limits
See *Gabapentin Capsules*

Usual geriatric dose
See *Gabapentin Capsules*

Strength(s) usually available
U.S.—
50 mg per mL (Rx) [*Neurontin* (glycerin; xylitol; purified water; artificial cool strawberry anise flavor)].
Canada—
Not commercially available.

Packaging and storage
Store refrigerated, 2 to 8 °C (36 to 46 °F)

Auxiliary labeling
• May cause blurred vision.
• May cause dizziness.
• May cause drowsiness. Alcohol may intensify this effect.
• Refrigerate
• This medication can be taken with or without food

GABAPENTIN TABLETS

Usual adult and adolescent dose
See *Gabapentin Capsules*

Usual adult and adolescent prescribing limits
See *Gabapentin Capsules*

Usual pediatric dose
See *Gabapentin Capsules*
Children 12 years of age and over: See *Usual adult and adolescent dose.*

Usual pediatric prescribing limits
See *Gabapentin Capsules*

Usual geriatric dose
See *Gabapentin Capsules*

Strength(s) usually available
U.S.—
600 mg (Rx) [*Neurontin* (poloxamer 407; copolyvidonum; cornstarch; magnesium stearate; hydroxypropyl cellulose; talc; candellila wax; purified water; synthetic black iron oxide; pharmaceutical shellac; pharmaceutical glaze; propylene glycol; ammonium hydroxide; isopropyl alcohol; n-butyl alcohol)].
800 mg (Rx) [*Neurontin* (poloxamer 407; copolyvidonum; cornstarch; magnesium stearate; hydroxypropyl cellulose; talc; candellila wax;

purified water; synthetic yellow iron oxide; synthetic red iron oxide; hypromellose; propylene glycol; methanol; isopropyl alcohol; deionized water)].

Canada—

800 mg (Rx) [*Novo-Gabapentin*].

Packaging and storage

Store at 25 °C (77 °F); excursions permitted to 15 and 30 °C (59° and 86 °F)

Auxiliary labeling

- May cause blurred vision.
- May cause dizziness.
- May cause drowsiness. Alcohol may intensify this effect.
- This medication can be taken with or without food

[1]Not included in Canadian product labeling.

Selected Bibliography

Product Information: Neurontin®, gabapentin. Pfizer Inc., New York, NY, (PI revised 8/2003) reviewed 9/2003.

Product Information: Neurontin®, gabapentin. Pfizer Canada Inc., Kirkland, Quebec (PI revised 1/2001) reviewed 9/2003.

Revised: 10/03/2003

GADOBENATE Systemic†

VA CLASSIFICATION (Primary): DX900

Commonly used brand name(s): *MultiHance*.

Note: For a listing of dosage forms and brand names by country availability, see *Dosage Forms* section(s).

†Not commercially available in Canada.

Category

Diagnostic aid, paramagnetic (brain disorders; spine disorders).

Indications

Accepted

Brain imaging, magnetic resonance or

Spinal imaging, magnetic resonance—Gadobenate is indicated for intravenous use in magnetic resonance imaging (MRI) of the CNS in adults to visualize lesions with abnormal blood brain barrier or abnormal vascularity of the brain, spine, and associated tissues.

Pharmacology/Pharmacokinetics

Physicochemical characteristics

Molecular weight—Gadobenate: 1058.2.

pH—6.5 to 7.5.

Osmolality—1.97 osmol/kg at 37° C; 6.9 times that of plasma and is hypertonic under conditions of use.

Viscosity—5.3 mPas at 37° C.

Density—1.220 g/mL at 20° C.

Mechanism of action/Effect

Gadobenate dimeglumine is a paramagnetic agent. It develops a magnetic moment when placed in a magnetic field, resulting in a large local magnetic field which can enhance the relaxation rates of water protons in its vicinity leading to an increase of signal intensity (brightness) of tissue.

Magnetic resonance imaging (MRI) is based primarily on differences in proton density and proton relaxation dynamics. When placed in a magnetic field, gadobenate dimeglumine decreases the T1 and T2 relaxation time in target tissues. At the recommended dose, the effect is observed with greatest sensitivity in the T1-weighted sequences.

Distribution

Volume of distribution (Vol_D)—from 0.074 +/- 0.017 to 0.158 +/- 0.038 L/kg, central compartment; 0.170 +/- 0.016 to 0.282 +/- 0.079 L/kg, by area.

Protein binding

No appreciable binding to human serum proteins.

Biotransformation

There is no detectable biotransformation of gadobenate ion, and dissociation *in vivo* has been shown to be minimal.

Half-life

Distribution—0.084 +/- 0.012 to 0.0605 +/- 0.072 hours.

Elimination—1.17 +/- 0.26 to 2.02 +/- 0.60 hours.

Elimination—6.1+/- 3.0 to 9.5 +/- 3.1 hours for moderate and severe renal impairment.

Elimination—1.2+/- 0.29 hours for patients with end-stage renal disease on dialysis compared to 42.4 +/- 24.4 hours when off dialysis.

Elimination

Urine: 78% to 96%.

Feces: 0.6% to 4%.

Clearance, plasma: 0.093 +/- 0.010 to 0.133 +/- 0.270 L/hr/kg.

Clearance, renal: 0.082 +/- 0.007 to 0.104 +/- 0.039 L/hr/kg.

Precautions to Consider

Carcinogenicity

Long-term animal studies have not been performed to evaluate the carcinogenic potential of gadobenate.

Mutagenicity

Gadobenate dimeglumine has not been shown to be mutagenic or clastogenic in the *in vitro* bacteria reverse mutation assay, *in vitro* gene mutation assay in mammalian cells, *in vitro* chromosomal aberration assay, *in vitro* unscheduled DNA synthesis assay, and in the *in vivo* micronucleus assay in rats.

Pregnancy/Reproduction

Fertility—No effects on fertility or reproductive performance were revealed in male rats given IV doses of gadobenate at 2 mmol/kg/day for 13 weeks or in female rats for 32 days. Non reversible vacuolation in testes and abnormal spermatogenic cells were observed in male rats given IV doses of gadobenate at 3 mmol/kg/day for 28 days. The effects were not reported in dogs at doses up to 11 times the human dose on body surface area, for 28 days and monkey at doses 10 times the human dose on body surface area, for 14 days.

Pregnancy—Adequate and well controlled studies in humans have not been done. Gadobenate should be used during pregnancy only if potential benefit justifies the potential risk to the fetus.

Gadobenate has been shown to have teratogenic effects including microphthalmia, small eye and focal retinal fold in rabbits given IV doses at 2 mmol/kg/day during organogenesis (day 6 to 18). Intravenous doses at 3 mmol/kg/day have shown increases in intrauterine deaths in rabbits.

No evidence of teratogenic effects, systemic toxicity or adverse effects on birth, survival, growth, development and fertility of the F1 generation in rats was observed following doses up to 2 mmol/kg/day in peri- and post-natal gadobenate studies.

FDA Pregnancy Category C

Breast-feeding

It is not known to what extent that gadobenate dimeglumine is distributed into human milk. Breast-feeding should be discontinued prior to the administration of gadobenate and should not be restarted until at least 24 hours after the administration of gadobenate.

Studies in rats have shown that less than 0.5% of the administered dose is transferred from the mothers' milk to neonates.

Pediatrics

Safety and effectiveness in pediatric patients have not been established.

Geriatrics

Appropriate studies to date have not demonstrated geriatrics-specific problems that would limit the usefulness of gadobenate in the elderly. However, elderly patients are more likely to have age-related renal function impairment and may, therefore, require monitoring of renal function.

Pharmacogenetics

No effects on the pharmacokinetics of gadobenate due to sex have been found; however, clearance appeared to decrease slightly with increasing age.

Pharmacokinetic differences due to race have not been studied.

Drug interactions and/or related problems

The following drug interactions and/or related problems have been selected on the basis of their potential clinical significance (possible mechanism in parentheses where appropriate)—not necessarily inclusive (» = major clinical significance):

Note: Combinations containing any of the following medications, depending on the amount present, may also interact with this medication.

Alkaloids such as
  Vincristine or
Antracyclines such as
  Doxorubicin or
  Daunorubicin or

Cisplatin or
Etoposide or
Methotrexate or
Paclitaxel or
Tamoxifen or
Vinca
(may compete for the canalicular multispecific organic anion transporter [cMOAT also referred to as MRP2 or ABCC2] sites)

Laboratory value alterations

The following have been selected on the basis of their potential clinical significance (possible effect in parentheses where appropriate)—not necessarily inclusive (» = major clinical significance).

With physiology/laboratory test values
Alkaline phosphatase values, serum or
Alanine aminotransferase (ALT [SGPT]) values, serum or
Aspartate aminotransferase (AST [SGOT]) values, serum or
GGT or
Iron, serum or
LDH
(values may be increased)

Ferritin, serum
(transient increases were observed in some patients)

Zinc, urine
(transient increases were detected in patients with renal disease)

Diagnostic interference

The following drug interactions and/or related problems have been selected on the basis of their potential clinical significance (possible mechanism in parentheses where appropriate)—not necessarily inclusive (» = major clinical significance):

With Results of *this* test
Due to medical problems or conditions
Metabolic disorders such as
Dubin Johnson syndrome
(caution; cMOAT sites may be affected)

Medical considerations/Contraindications

The medical considerations/contraindications included have been selected on the basis of their potential clinical significance (reasons given in parentheses where appropriate)—not necessarily inclusive (» = major clinical significance).

Except under special circumstances, this medication should not be used when the following medical problem exists:

» Hypersensitivity or known allergic reaction to gadobenate, gadolinium or any product ingredient, including benzyl alcohol

Risk-benefit should be considered when the following medical problems exist:

» Anemia, hemolytic
(possible increased risk of hemolysis)

Hepatic metabolic disorders such as
Willebrands' disease or
Wilsons' disease
(transient asymptomatic elevations in bilirubin may occur)

Cardiac abnormalities or
Metabolic abnormalities or
Other abnormalities that predispose to cardiac arrhythmias
(caution should be exercised)

» Sickle cell disease
(in *in vitro* studies, deoxygenated sickle erythrocytes have been shown to align perpendicular to a magnetic field, which may result in vascular occlusion *in vivo*)

Patient monitoring

The following may be especially important in patient monitoring (other tests may be warranted in some patients, depending on condition; » = major clinical significance):

» Allergy, history of or
» Drug reactions or
» Hypersensitivity-like disorders
(patients should be closely observed during and for several hours after drug administration)

Side/Adverse Effects

The following side/adverse effects have been selected on the basis of their potential clinical significance (possible signs and symptoms in parentheses where appropriate)—not necessarily inclusive:

Those indicating need for medical attention

Incidence rare

Acute necrotizing pancreatitis (bloating; chills; constipation; darkened urine; fast heartbeat; fever; indigestion; loss of appetite; nausea; pains in stomach, side, or abdomen, possibly radiating to the back; vomiting; yellow eyes or skin); ***acute pulmonary edema*** (chest pain; difficult, fast, noisy breathing, sometimes with wheezing blue lips and fingernails; pale skin; increased sweating; coughing that sometimes produces a pink frothy sputum; shortness of breath; swelling in legs and ankles); ***anaphylactic reaction*** (cough; difficulty swallowing; dizziness; fast heartbeat; hives; itching; puffiness or swelling of the eyelids or around the eyes, face, lips or tongue; shortness of breath; skin rash; tightness in chest; unusual tiredness or weakness; wheezing); ***aphasia*** (problems with speech or speaking); ***bradycardia*** (chest pain or discomfort; lightheadedness; dizziness or fainting; shortness of breath; slow or irregular heartbeat; unusual tiredness); ***convulsions*** (seizures); ***dyspnea*** (shortness of breath; difficult or labored breathing; tightness in chest; wheezing); ***ECG abnormality; facial edema*** (swelling of the face); ***hematuria*** (blood in urine); ***hemolysis*** (abdominal pain; back pain; dark urine; decreased urination; fever; tiredness; yellow eyes or skin); ***hyperventilation*** (deep or fast breathing with dizziness, numbness to feet, hands and around mouth); ***hypesthesia*** (burning, crawling, itching, numbness, prickling, "pins and needles", or tingling feelings); ***hypocalcemia*** (abdominal cramps; confusion; convulsions; difficulty in breathing; irregular heartbeats; mood or mental changes; muscle cramps in hands, arms, feet, legs, or face; numbness and tingling around the mouth, fingertips, or feet; shortness of breath; tremor); ***hyponatremia*** (coma; confusion; convulsions; decreased urine output; dizziness; fast or irregular heartbeat headache increased thirst muscle pain or cramps nausea or vomiting shortness of breath swelling of face, ankles, or hands unusual tiredness or weakness); ***leukocytosis*** (chills; cough; eye pain; fever; general feeling of illness; headache; sore throat; unusual tiredness); ***leukopenia*** (black, tarry stools; chest pain; chills; cough; fever; painful or difficult urination; shortness of breath; sore throat; sores, ulcers, or white spots on lips or in mouth; swollen glands; unusual bleeding or bruising; unusual tiredness or weakness); ***lung edema*** (swelling of lung); ***myocardial ischemia*** (chest pain or discomfort; nausea; pain or discomfort in arms, jaw, back or neck; shortness of breath; sweating; vomiting); ***paralysis; paresthesia*** (burning, crawling, itching, numbness, prickling, "pins and needles", or tingling feelings); ***pulmonary embolus*** (anxiety; chest pain; cough; fainting; fast heartbeat; sudden shortness of breath or troubled breathing; dizziness or lightheadedness)

Those indicating need for medical attention only if they continue or are bothersome

Incidence less frequent

Headache; injection site reaction (bleeding, blistering, burning, coldness, discoloration of skin; feeling of pressure, hives, infection, inflammation, itching, lumps, numbness, pain, rash, redness, scarring, soreness, stinging, swelling, tenderness, tingling, ulceration, or warmth at site of injection); ***nausea; vasodilatation*** (feeling of warmth or heat; flushing or redness of skin, especially on face and neck; headache; feeling faint, dizzy, or light-headedness; sweating)

Rare

Abdominal pain (stomach pain); ***abnormal lab tests; abnormal vision*** (changes in vision); ***albuminuria*** (cloudy urine); ***arrhythmia*** (dizziness; fainting; fast, slow, or irregular heartbeat); ***asthenia*** (lack or loss of strength); ***atrial fibrillation*** (fast or irregular heartbeat; dizziness; fainting); ***back pain; basophilia; bilirubinemia*** (chills; clay-colored stools; dark urine; dizziness; fever; headache; itching; loss of appetite; nausea; abdominal or stomach pain; area rash; unpleasant breath odor; unusual tiredness or weakness; vomiting of blood; yellow eyes or skin); ***chest pain; chills; cold feeling; constipation*** (difficulty having a bowel movement (stool)); ***diarrhea; dizziness; dry mouth; dyspepsia*** (acid or sour stomach; belching; heartburn; indigestion; stomach discomfort upset or pain); ***ear pain; eye disorder; fecal incontinence*** (loss of bowel control); ***fever; glycosuria*** (sugar in the urine); ***hemiplegia*** (inability to move legs or arms; paralysis of one side of the body); ***hyperglycemia*** (abdominal pain; blurred vision; dry mouth; fatigue; flushed; dry skin; fruit-like breath odor; increased hunger; increased thirst; increased urination; nausea; sweating; troubled breathing; unexplained weight loss; vomiting); ***hyperkalemia*** (abdominal pain; confusion; irregular heartbeat; nausea or vomiting; nervousness; numbness or tingling in hands, feet, or lips; shortness of breath; difficult breathing; weakness or heaviness of legs); ***hyperlipidemia*** (large amount of fat in the blood); ***hypertension*** (blurred vision; dizziness; nervousness; headache; pounding in the ears; slow or fast heartbeat); ***hypotension*** (blurred vision; confusion; dizziness, faintness, or lightheadedness when getting up from a lying or sitting position suddenly; sweating; unusual tiredness or weakness); ***hypoglycemia*** (anxiety; blurred vision; chills; cold sweats; coma; confusion; cool pale skin; depression; dizziness; fast heartbeat; headache; increased hunger; nausea; nervousness; nightmares; seizures; shakiness; slurred speech; unusual tiredness or weakness); ***hypoproteinemia*** (abdominal pain; diarrhea; fat in the stool); ***hypertonia*** (excessive muscle tone; muscle tension or tightness; muscle stiffness); ***increased cough; increased pruritus in patients with cirrhosis*** (increased itching in patients with cirrhosis); ***increased salivation*** (increased watering of mouth); ***infection*** (fever or chills; cough or hoarseness; lower back or side pain; painful or difficult urination); ***injection site inflammation*** (redness or swelling of skin); ***injection site pain; laryngismus*** (spasm of throat); ***malaise*** (general feeling of discomfort or illness; unusual tiredness or weakness); ***myalgia*** (joint pain, swollen joints, muscle aching or cramping, muscle pains or stiffness, difficulty in moving); ***myositis*** (muscle pain; unusual tiredness or weakness); ***pain; palpitations*** (fast, irregular, pounding, or racing heartbeat or pulse); ***parosmia*** (transient, mild, pleasant aromatic odor); ***peripheral edema*** (swelling of hands, ankles, feet, or lower legs); ***pruritus*** (itching skin); ***rash; rhinitis*** (stuffy nose; runny nose; sneezing); ***stupor*** (decreased awareness or responsiveness; severe sleepiness); ***supraventricular extrasystoles*** (rapid or irregular heartbeat); ***sweating; syncope*** (fainting); ***tachycardia*** (fast, pounding, or irregular heartbeat or pulse); ***taste perversion*** (change in taste; bad unusual or unpleasant (after) taste); ***thirst; tinnitus*** (continuing ringing or buzzing or other unexplained noise in ears; hearing loss); ***tremor*** (trembling or shaking of hands or feet; shakiness in legs, arms, hands, feet); ***urinary frequency*** (increased need to urinate; passing urine more often); ***urinary incontinence*** (loss of bladder control); ***urinary tract infection*** (bladder pain; bloody or cloudy urine; difficult, burning, or painful urination; frequent urge to urinate; lower back or side pain); ***urinary urgency*** (frequent strong or increased urge to urinate); ***urticaria*** (hives or welts; itching; redness of skin; skin rash); ***ventricular extrasystoles*** (extra heart beat); ***vomiting***

Overdose

For more information on the management of overdose or unintentional ingestion, **contact a poison control center** (see *Poison Control Center Listing*).

Treatment of overdose

There is no known specific antidote to gadobenate. Treatment is generally symptomatic and supportive.

To enhance elimination—
  Gadobenate has been shown to be dialyzable.

Supportive care—
  Support of vital functions and prompt institution of symptomatic care.

Patient Consultation

As an aid to patient consultation, refer to *Advice for the Patient, Gadobenate (Systemic)*.

In providing consultation, consider emphasizing the following selected information (» = major clinical significance):

Description of use

Action in the body: Accumulates in brain and spinal lesions creating a local magnetic field; visualization of lesions possible with MR instruments

Before having this test

» Conditions affecting use, especially:
  Hypersensitivity to gadobenate or known allergic reactions to gadolinium or other ingredients, including benzyl alcohol.
  Pregnancy—Gadobenate should be used during pregnancy only if potential benefit justifies the potential risk to the fetus.
  Breast-feeding—Breast-feeding should be discontinued prior to the administration of gadobenate and should not be restarted until at least 24 hours after the administration of gadobenate.
  Use in children—Safety and effectiveness in pediatric patients have not been established.
  Other medical problems, especially allergy, history of; hemolytic anemia, drug reactions, hypersensitivity-like disorders, or sickle cell disease

Proper use of this medication

» Proper dosing
» Proper storage

Preparation for this test

» Special preparatory instructions may apply; patient should inquire in advance

Side/adverse effects

Signs of potential side effects, especially acute necrotizing pancreatitis, acute pulmonary edema, anaphylactic reaction, bradycardia, convulsions, dyspnea, hematuria, hemolysis, hypocalcemia, hyponatremia, lung edema, myocardial ischemia, paralysis, or pulmonary embolus

General Dosing Information

Diagnostic procedures that involve the use of contrast agents should be carried out under the direction of a physician with prerequisite training and a thorough knowledge of the procedure to be performed.

Using sterile technique, gadobenate should be drawn into a plastic disposable syringe and used immediately. If non-disposable equipment is used, scrupulous care should be taken to prevent residual contamination with traces of cleansing agents. Any residual product must be discarded according to regulations of disposal of such material.

For complete injection of gadobenate, ensure that the IV needle or cannula is correctly inserted into a vein and, the injection should be followed by a saline flush of at least 5 milliliters.

Caution should be exercised when contrast-enhanced interpretations are made in the absence of a companion unenhanced MRI; lesions seen on unenhanced images may not all be seen on contrast-enhanced images.

Use caution to avoid local extravasation during intravenous administration of gadobenate.

Treatment of Adverse Effects

Appropriate facilities should be available for coping with complications of the procedures, including emergency treatment of life threatening, or fatal, anaphylactic or cardiovascular reactions, or other idiosyncratic reactions, especially in patients with a history of hypersensitivity, or a history of asthma or other allergic respiratory disorders.

If extravasation occurs, patients should be monitored and treated as necessary if local reactions develop.

Parenteral Dosage Forms

Note: Bracketed information in the *Indications* section refers to uses that are not included in U.S. product labeling.

GADOBENATE DIMEGLUMINE INJECTION

Usual adult dose

Brain and spinal lesions imaging, magnetic resonance—
  Intravenous rapid bolus injection, 0.1 mmol (0.2 mL) per kg of body weight.

Usual pediatric dose

Safety and effectiveness in pediatric patients have not been established.

Usual geriatric dose

See *Usual adult dose*.

Strength(s) usually available

U.S.—
  529 mg of gadobenate dimeglumine per mL (Rx) [*MultiHance*].

Packaging and storage

Store at 25 °C (77 °F), excursions permitted to 15- 30°C (59-86°F). Do not freeze.

Preparation of dosage form

Gadobenate is a clear colorless solution. Visually inspect for particulate matter and discoloration prior to administration. If particulate matter or discoloration is present, do not use.

Incompatibilities

Concurrent medications or parenteral nutrition should not be physically mixed with gadobenate and should not be administered in the same intravenous line because of potential incompatibility.

Auxiliary labeling

• Do not freeze.

Developed: 01/12/2006

GALANTAMINE Systemic†

VA CLASSIFICATION (Primary): CN900

Commonly used brand name(s): *Razadyne; Razadyne ER*.

Note: For a listing of dosage forms and brand names by country availability, see *Dosage Forms* section(s).

†Not commercially available in Canada.

Category

Dementia symptoms treatment adjunct.

Indications

Accepted

Dementia, Alzheimer-type, mild to moderate (treatment)—Galantamine is indicated for the treatment of mild to moderate dementia of the Alzheimer's type.

Unaccepted

Individuals with *mild cognitive impairment* (MCI) demonstrate isolated memory impairment greater than expected for their age and education, but DO NOT meet current diagnostic criteria for Alzheimer's disease. Deaths occurred in two clinical trials in subjects with MCI.

Pharmacology/Pharmacokinetics

Physicochemical characteristics

Molecular weight—368.27.

Mechanism of action/Effect

The cause of cognitive impairment in Alzheimer's Disease is not fully understood, it has been shown that acetylcholine producing neurons degenerate. The cholinergic loss has been correlated with cognitive impairment and a density of amyloid plaques.

Galantamine is a tertiary alkaloid and it competes with and is a reversible inhibitor of acetylcholinesterase. The exact mechanism of galantamine is not known, but it is believed to enhance cholinergic function.

There is no evidence that galantamine alters the underlying dementing process, and its effect may lessen as the disease progresses due to fewer cholinergic neurons remaining functionally intact.

Absorption

Galantamine is rapidly and completely absorbed. The absolute oral bioavailability is about 90%. Galantamine shows linear pharmacokinetics with doses ranging from 8 to 32 mg per day.

Distribution

Mean volume of distribution (Vol_D) is 175 L.

Protein binding

Low (18%)

Biotransformation

Galantamine is metabolized by hepatic cytochrome P450 enzymes.

Half-life

Elimination—7 Hours

Time to peak concentration

Approximately 1 hour

Elimination

Renal. After intravenous or oral administration, about 20% of the dose was excreted as unchanged galantamine in the urine in 24 hours (renal clearance of about 65 mL/min), about 20–25% of the total plasma clearance of about 300 mL/min.

Precautions to Consider

Carcinogenicity

In a 24 month oral carcinogenicity study done in rats a slight increase in endometrial carcinomas were observed at doses of 10 mg/kg/day (4 times the Maximum Recommended Human Dose [MRHD]) on a mg/m^2 basis or 6 times on a exposure [AUC] basis and 30 mg/kg/day (12 times the MRHD on a mg/m^2 basis or 19 times on an AUC basis). No increases in neoplastic changes were seen in females at 2.5 mg/kg/day (equivalent to the MRHD on a mg/m^2 basis or 2 times on an AUC basis) or in males up to the highest dose tested of 30 mg/kg/day (12 times the MRHD on a mg/m^2 basis and AUC basis).

Galantamine was not carcinogenic in a 6 month oral carcinogenicity study in transgenic (P 53 deficient) mice up to 20 mg/kg/day, or in a 24 month oral carcinogenicity study in male and female mice up to 10 mg/kg/day (2 times the MRHD on a mg/m^2 basis and equivalent on a AUC basis).

Mutagenicity

Galantamine was not shown to be genotoxic in the *in vitro* Ames *S. typhimurium* or *E. coli* reverse mutation assay, *in vitro* mouse lymphoma assay, *in vivo* micronucleus test in mice, or *in vitro* chromosome aberration assay in Chinese hamster ovary cells.

Pregnancy/Reproduction

Fertility—No evidence of impaired fertility was seen in rats given up to 16 mg/kg/day (7 times the MRHD on a mg/m^2 basis) for 14 days prior to mating in females and for 60 days prior to mating in males.

Pregnancy—Studies have not been done in humans. Galantamine should be used during pregnancy only if the potential benefit justifies the potential risk to the fetus.

In a study where female rats were dosed from day 14 and male rats were dosed from day 60 prior to mating through the period of organogenesis, a slightly increased incidence of skeletal variations were observed at doses of 8 mg/kg/day (3 times the MRHD on a mg/m^2 basis) and 16 mg/kg/day. In a study where pregnant rats were dosed from the beginning of organogenesis through day 21 and post partum, pup weights were decreased at 8 and 16 mg/kg/day, but no adverse effects on other postnatal developmental parameters were seen. The doses causing the above effects in rats produced slight maternal toxicity. No major malformations were caused in rats given up to 16 mg/kg/day. No drug related teratogenic effects were observed in rabbits given up to 40 mg/kg/day (32 times the MRHD on a mg/m^2 basis) during the period of organogenesis.

FDA Pregnancy Category B

Breast-feeding

It is not known whether galantamine is distributed into breast milk. However, there is no indication for use in nursing women.

Pediatrics

No information is available on the relationship of age to the effects of galantamine. Safety and efficacy have not been established. Use in children is not recommended.

Geriatrics

Data from studies in patients with Alzheimer's disease indicate that the galantamine concentrations are 30 to 40% higher than in healthy young subjects.

Drug interactions and/or related problems

The following drug interactions and/or related problems have been selected on the basis of their potential clinical significance (possible mechanism in parentheses where appropriate)—not necessarily inclusive (» = major clinical significance):

Note: Combinations containing any of the following medications, depending on the amount present, may also interact with this medication.

Anesthesia
(galantamine is likely to exaggerate the neuromuscular blockade effects of succinylcholine-type and similar neuromuscular blocking agents during anesthesia.)

Anticholinergics
(concurrent use may decrease the effects of these medications)

Cimetidine or
Paroxetine
(may increase the bioavailability of galantamine)

Bethanechol or
Cholinergic agonists, other or
Cholinesterase inhibitors, other or
Neuromuscular blocking agents, similar or
Succinylcholine
(synergistic effect with concurrent use of cholinesterase inhibitors and succinylcholine, other cholinesterase inhibitors, similar neuromuscular blocking agents, or cholinergic agonists such as bethanechol)

Erythromycin or
Ketoconazole
(concurrent use may increase the area under the curve for galantamine)

Nonsteroidal anti-inflammatory drugs (NSAIDs)
(galantamine may increase gastric acid secretion, which may contribute to gastrointestinal irritation; patient should be monitored for occult gastrointestinal bleeding)

Medical considerations/Contraindications

The medical considerations/contraindications included have been selected on the basis of their potential clinical significance (reasons given in parentheses where appropriate)—not necessarily inclusive (» = major clinical significance).

Except under special circumstances, this medication should not be used when the following medical problem exists:

» Known hypersensitivity to galantamine or any excipients used in the formulation

Risk-benefit should be considered when the following medical problems exist:

» Asthma, active or history of or
» Obstructive pulmonary disease
(because of the cholinomimetic action of galantamine, caution should be used)

» Cardiovascular conditions such as
Bradycardia or
Heart block
(vagotonic effect on heart may exacerbate pre-existing conditions)

» Epilepsy or history of seizures
(galantamine may have some potential to cause generalized convulsions)

Hepatic impairment or
Renal impairment
(dose titration of extended-release capsules should proceed cautiously with moderate impairment; use of extended-release capsules not recommended for severe impairment)

» Mild cognitive impairment (MCI)
(individuals with this condition demonstrate isolated memory impairment greater than expected for their age and education, but do not meet current diagnostic criteria for Alzheimer's disease)

» Urinary tract obstruction
(may cause bladder outflow obstruction)

» Ulcers, active or history of
(increased gastric acid secretion may exacerbate or reactivate condition)

Note: Because of their pharmacological action, cholinesterase inhibitors may be expected to increase gastric acid secretion due to increased cholinergic activity. Therefore, patients should be monitored closely for symptoms of active or occult gastrointestinal bleeding, especially those at increased risk for developing ulcers (e.g. those with a history of ulcer or those receiving concurrent anti-inflammatory drugs [NSAIDs]).

Patient monitoring

The following may be especially important in patient monitoring (other tests may be warranted in some patients, depending on condition; » = major clinical significance):

» Gastrointestinal effects
(galantamine has been shown to produce nausea, vomiting, diarrhea, anorexia and weight loss.)

Side/Adverse Effects

The following side/adverse effects have been selected on the basis of their potential clinical significance (possible signs and symptoms in parentheses where appropriate)—not necessarily inclusive:

Those indicating need for medical attention

Less frequent

Bradycardia (chest pain or discomfort; lightheadedness, dizziness or fainting; shortness of breath; slow or irregular heartbeat; unusual tiredness)

Incidence not determined—Observed during clinical practice; estimates of frequency can not be determined

Aggression (attack, assault, force); ***dehydration*** (confusion; decreased urination; dizziness; dry mouth; fainting; increase in heart rate; lightheadedness; rapid breathing; sunken eyes; thirst; unusual tiredness or weakness; wrinkled skin)—including rare, severe cases leading to renal insufficiency and renal failure; ***hypokalemia*** (convulsions; decreased urine; dry mouth; irregular heartbeat; increased thirst; loss of appetite; mood changes; muscle pain or cramps; nausea or vomiting; numbness or tingling in hands, feet, or lips; shortness of breath; unusual tiredness or weakness); ***upper and lower GI bleed*** (bloody or black, tarry stools; vomiting of blood or material that looks like coffee grounds; severe stomach pain; constipation)

Those indicating need for medical attention only if they continue or are bothersome

Incidence more frequent

Anorexia (loss of appetite; weight loss); ***depression*** (discouragement; feeling sad or empty; irritability; lack of appetite; loss of interest or pleasure; tiredness; trouble concentrating; trouble sleeping); ***diarrhea; nausea; urinary tract infection*** (bladder pain; bloody or cloudy urine; difficult, burning, or painful urination; frequent urge to urinate; lower back or side pain); ***vomiting; weight decrease***

Incidence less frequent

Abdominal pain; anemia (pale skin; troubled breathing, exertional; unusual bleeding or bruising; unusual tiredness or weakness); ***bradycardia*** (slow or irregular heartbeat (less than 50 beats per minute); lightheadedness; dizziness or fainting; unusual tiredness); ***dizziness; dyspepsia*** (indigestion); ***fatigue*** (unusual tiredness or weakness); ***headache; hematuria*** (blood in urine; lower back pain; pain or burning while urinating); ***insomnia*** (sleeplessness; trouble sleeping; unable to sleep); ***rhinitis*** (stuffy nose); ***somnolence*** (sleepiness; unusual drowsiness); ***syncope*** (high or low blood pressure; dizziness; lightheadedness; feeling faint); ***tremor***

Overdose

For specific information on agents used in the management of galantamine toxicity or overdose, see *Atropine* in the *Anticholinergics/Antispasmodics (Systemic)* monograph.

For more information on the management of overdose or unintentional ingestion, **contact a poison control center** (see *Poison Control Center Listing*).

Clinical effects of overdose

The following effects have been selected on the basis of their potential clinical significance (possible signs and symptoms in parentheses where appropriate)—not necessarily inclusive:

Bradycardia (slow heart beat); ***convulsions and collapse*** (seizures); ***defecation; hypotension*** (low blood pressure; dizziness; fainting); ***gastrointestinal cramping; increased salivation*** (drooling; watering of the mouth); ***increased sweating; lacrimation*** (tearing of the eyes); ***muscle weakness or fasciculations; respiratory depression*** (slow or troubled breathing)—increasing muscular weakness may affect respiratory muscles, resulting in death; ***severe nausea and vomiting; urination***

Note: The clinical effects mentioned above are symptoms of cholinergic crisis.

Note: In one postmarketing report, a patient who had been taking 4 mg per day galantamine for one week inadvertently took 32 mg (8 tablets) on a single day. She developed bradycardia, QT prolongation, ventricular tachycardia and torsades de pointes accompanied by a brief loss of consciousness and required hospital treatment. Two other cases of accidental ingestion of 32 mg (nausea, vomiting and dry mouth; nausea, vomiting, and substernal chest pain) and of 40 mg (vomiting) all resulted in brief hospitalizations followed by full recovery. Another patient who was prescribed 16 mg per day of oral solution, inadvertently took 160 mg (40 mL) and experienced sweating, vomiting, bradycardia, and near-syncope one hour later, which required hospitalization with symptoms resolving within 24 hours.

Treatment of overdose

To enhance elimination—
It is not known whether galantamine and it's metabolites can be removed by dialysis.

Specific treatment—
Tertiary anticholinergics may be used as an antidote for galantamine overdosage. See the package insert or *Atropine* in the *Anticholinergics/Antispasmodics (Systemic)* monograph for specific dosing guidelines.

Monitoring—
Atypical responses in blood pressure and heart rate have been reported with other cholinomimetics when coadministered with quaternary anticholinergics.

Supportive care—
General supportive measures should be utilized.
Patients in whom intentional overdose is confirmed or suspected should be referred for psychiatric consultation.

Patient Consultation

As an aid to patient consultation, refer to *Advice for the Patient, Galantamine (Systemic)*.

In providing consultation, consider emphasizing the following selected information (» = major clinical significance):

Before using this medication

» Conditions affecting use, especially:
Hypersensitivity to galantamine or any excipients used in the formulation
Pregnancy—Risk-benefit considerations
Surgical—Galantamine is a cholinesterase inhibitor and may prolong or exaggerate succinylcholine-type muscle relaxation during anesthesia.
Other medical problems, especially asthma, cardiovascular conditions (such as bradycardia, hypotension), epilepsy or history of seizures, mild cognitive impairment (MCI), obstructive pulmonary disease, urinary tract obstruction, and peptic ulcer

Proper use of this medication

» Not taking more medication than the amount prescribed because of increased risk of adverse effects
Taking doses at regular intervals, preferably with meals
Taking doses at regular intervals for maximum efficacy
Importance of adequate fluid intake during treatment
Following instruction sheet for proper administration of oral solution
» Proper dosing

Missed dose: Taking as soon as possible if remembered within an hour or so; not taking if remembered later; not doubling doses

» Proper storage

Precautions while using this medication

» Importance of complying with monitoring schedule and keeping appointments with physician and/or laboratory

Informing physician when new symptoms arise or when previously noted symptoms increase in severity

» Caution if any kind of surgery or emergency treatment is required; informing physician or dentist in charge that galantamine is being taken

» Caution if dizziness, clumsiness, or unsteadiness occurs

» Suspected overdose: Getting emergency help at once

Side/adverse effects

Signs of potential side effects, especially abdominal pain, anemia, anorexia, bradycardia, diarrhea, dizziness, dyspepsia, fatigue, headache, hematuria, insomnia, nausea, rhinitis, somnolence, syncope, tremors, vomiting, and weight loss

Signs of potential side effects observed during clinical practice, especially aggression, dehydration, hypokalemia, or upper and lower GI bleed

General Dosing Information

For oral dosing forms:

Dose escalation should follow a minimum of four weeks at the prior dose.

Patients and/or caregivers should be advised to ensure adequate fluid intake during treatment.

If galantamine therapy has been interrupted for several days or longer, the patient should be restarted at the lowest dose and the dose escalated to their current dose.

Galantamine should be taken twice a day, preferably with the morning and evening meal.

The abrupt withdrawal of galantamine was not associated with an increased frequency of adverse events in comparison with those continuing to receive the same doses of the drug. The beneficial effects of galantamine are lost, however, when the drug is discontinued.

Diet/Nutrition

For tablets and oral solution: The recommended administration is twice per day, preferably with the morning and evening meals.

For extended-release capsules: The recommended administration is once per day in the morning, preferably with food.

Oral Dosage Forms

Note: The available dosage form contains galantamine hydrobromide, but dosage and strength are expressed in terms of galantamine base.

GALANTAMINE HYDROBROMIDE EXTENDED-RELEASE CAPSULES

Usual adult dose

Alzheimer's dementia—

Oral, starting dose is 8 mg once daily in the morning, preferably with food. After a minimum of 4 weeks, dose should be increased to initial maintenance dose of 16 mg once daily. A further increase to 24 mg once daily may be attempted after a minimum of 4 weeks at the 16 mg once daily dose. Dose increases should be based upon assessment of clinical benefit and tolerability of the previous dose.

Note: In patients with moderately impaired hepatic function (Child-Pugh score of 7 to 9), the dose should generally not exceed 16 mg per day. In patients with severe hepatic impairment (Child-Pugh score of 10 to 15), use of galantamine extended-release capsules is not recommended.

In patients with moderate renal impairment, the dose should generally not exceed 16 mg per day. In patients with severe renal impairment (creatinine clearance < 9 mL per minute), use of galantamine extended-release capsules is not recommended.

Usual pediatric dose

Safety and efficacy have not been established.

Usual geriatric dose

See *Usual adult dose*.

Strength(s) usually available

U.S.—

8 mg (base) (Rx) [*Razadyne ER* (gelatin; diethyl phthalate; ethylcellulose; hypromellose; polyethylene glycol; titanium dioxide; sugar spheres (sucrose and starch))].

16 mg (base) (Rx) [*Razadyne ER* (gelatin; diethyl phthalate; ethylcellulose; hypromellose; polyethylene glycol; titanium dioxide; sugar spheres (sucrose and starch); red ferric oxide)].

24 mg (base) (Rx) [*Razadyne ER* (gelatin; diethyl phthalate; ethylcellulose; hypromellose; polyethylene glycol; titanium dioxide; sugar spheres (sucrose and starch); red ferric oxide; yellow ferric oxide)].

Packaging and storage

Store at 25 °C (77 °F); excursions permitted to 15 to 30°C (59 to 86 °F).

Auxiliary labeling

• Keep out of reach of children.

GALANTAMINE HYDROBROMIDE ORAL SOLUTION

Usual adult dose

See *Galantamine Tablets*

Usual pediatric dose

Safety and efficacy have not been established.

Usual geriatric dose

See *Galantamine Tablets*

Strength(s) usually available

U.S.—

4 mg per mL (base) (Rx) [*Razadyne* (methyl parahydroxybenzoate; propyl parahydroxybenzoate; sodium saccharin; sodium hydroxide; purified water)].

Note: In April 2005, the manufacturer changed the product name from *Reminyl* to *Razadyne*.

Packaging and storage

Store at 25 °C (77 °F); excursions permitted to 15 to 30°C (59 to 86 °F). Do not freeze.

Auxiliary labeling

• Keep out of reach of children.

GALANTAMINE HYDROBROMIDE TABLETS

Usual adult dose

Alzheimer's dementia—

Oral, starting dose is 4 mg twice a day. After at least 4 weeks of treatment, if the dose is being tolerated well, the dose may be increased to 8 mg twice daily. Additional increases to 12 mg twice a day should be attempted after a minimum of 4 weeks at the previous dose.

Note: For patients with moderate renal or hepatic impairment (Child-Pugh score of 7 to 9), the dose should not exceed 16 mg/day (8 mg twice a day). In patients with severe hepatic impairment (Child-Pugh score of 10–15) or severe renal impairment (Cl_{cr} < 9 mL/min), use is not recommended.

Usual pediatric dose

Safety and efficacy have not been established.

Usual geriatric dose

See *Usual adult dose*.

Strength(s) usually available

U.S.—

Note: In April 2005, the manufacturer changed the product name from *Reminyl* to *Razadyne*.

4 mg (base) (Rx) [*Razadyne* (colloidal silicon dioxide; crospovidone; hydroxypropyl methylcellulose; lactose monohydrate; magnesium stearate; microcrystalline cellulose; propylene glycol; talc; titanium dioxide; yellow ferric oxide)].

8 mg (base) (Rx) [*Razadyne* (colloidal silicon dioxide; crospovidone; hydroxypropyl methylcellulose; lactose monohydrate; magnesium stearate; microcrystalline cellulose; propylene glycol; talc; titanium dioxide; red ferric oxide)].

12 mg (base) (Rx) [*Razadyne* (colloidal silicon dioxide; crospovidone; hydroxypropyl methylcellulose; lactose monohydrate; magnesium stearate; microcrystalline cellulose; propylene glycol; talc; titanium dioxide; red ferric oxide; FD&C yellow #6 aluminum lake)].

Packaging and storage

Store at 25 °C (77 °F), excursions permitted to 15 to 30°C (59–86 °F).

Auxiliary labeling

• Keep out of reach of children.

Revised: 05/10/2005
Developed: 05/17/2001

GALLAMINE — See *Neuromuscular Blocking Agents (Systemic)*

GALLIUM NITRATE Systemic†

VA CLASSIFICATION (Primary): HS309

Commonly used brand name(s): *Ganite*.

Note: For a listing of dosage forms and brand names by country availability, see *Dosage Forms* section(s).

†Not commercially available in Canada.

Category

Antihypercalcemic.

Indications

Accepted

Hypercalcemia, associated with neoplasms (treatment)—Gallium nitrate is indicated in the treatment of hypercalcemia of malignancy that is inadequately managed by oral hydration alone. It is used with saline hydration and may be used with diuretics.

Acceptance not established

Gallium nitrate has been used to treat moderate to severe symptoms of Paget's disease of bone (osteitis deformans), characterized by abnormal and accelerated bone metabolism in one or more bones. However, data are limited and further study is required to define the role of gallium nitrate in this condition.

Pharmacology/Pharmacokinetics

Physicochemical characteristics

Source—Gallium nitrate is a hydrated nitrate salt of the group IIIa element gallium.

Molecular weight—417.87.

Mechanism of action/Effect

In vivo studies indicate that gallium nitrate preferentially accumulates in metabolically active areas of high bone turnover, where it reversibly inhibits osteoclast-mediated bone resorption.

Hypercalcemia of malignancy—Bone resorption is increased in the presence of neoplastic tissue. Gallium nitrate inhibits abnormal bone resorption and reduces the flow of calcium from the resorbing bone into the blood, effectively decreasing total and ionized serum calcium. When kidney function is adequate for the fluid load, hydration with saline increases urine output and the use of diuretics increases the rate of calcium excretion.

Distribution

Vol_D—1.27 liters per kg of body weight (L/kg).

Biotransformation

None.

Half-life

Alpha—1 hour.

Beta—24 hours, but lengthens to 72 to 115 hours with prolonged intravenous infusion.

Duration of action

Studies have reported a median duration of 6 to 8 days (range, 0 to 15+ days).

Elimination

Renal.

Precautions to Consider

Carcinogenicity

Long-term carcinogenicity studies have not been performed in animals.

Mutagenicity

Gallium nitrate has not been found to be mutagenic in standard tests such as Ames and chromosomal aberration studies on human lymphocytes.

Pregnancy/Reproduction

Pregnancy—Studies have not been done in humans.

Studies have not been done in animals.

FDA Pregnancy Category C.

Breast-feeding

It is not known whether gallium nitrate is distributed into breast milk. It is recommended that mothers taking gallium nitrate not breast-feed because of potentially serious adverse effects in nursing infants.

Pediatrics

No information is available on the relationship of age to the effects of gallium nitrate in pediatric patients. Safety and efficacy have not been established.

Geriatrics

Although appropriate studies on the relationship of age to the effects of gallium nitrate have not been performed in the geriatric population, no geriatrics-specific problems have been documented to date. However, elderly patients are more likely to have age-related renal function impairment, which may require caution in patients receiving gallium nitrate.

Drug interactions and/or related problems

The following drug interactions and/or related problems have been selected on the basis of their potential clinical significance (possible mechanism in parentheses where appropriate)—not necessarily inclusive (» = major clinical significance):

» Nephrotoxic medications, other (See *Appendix II*)
(the possibility of additive toxicity should be considered if these medications are used concurrently with gallium nitrate)

Laboratory value alterations

The following have been selected on the basis of their potential clinical significance (possible effect in parentheses where appropriate)—not necessarily inclusive (» = major clinical significance).

With diagnostic test results

Gallium citrate Ga 67 scintigraphy for tumor or abscess localization
(gallium nitrate competes with gallium citrate Ga 67 for plasma protein binding sites, resulting in reduced tumor or abscess uptake and increased skeletal uptake, increased renal excretion, and reduced liver uptake of gallium citrate Ga 67)

Medical considerations/Contraindications

The medical considerations/contraindications included have been selected on the basis of their potential clinical significance (reasons given in parentheses where appropriate)—not necessarily inclusive (» = major clinical significance).

Except under special circumstances, this medication should not be used when the following medical problem exists:

» Renal function impairment when serum creatinine is greater than 2.5 mg per deciliter (mg/dL)
(condition may be exacerbated)

Risk-benefit should be considered when the following medical problem exists:

» Renal function impairment when serum creatinine is 2 to 2.5 mg/dL
(frequent monitoring of patient's renal status is recommended; gallium nitrate treatment should be discontinued if serum creatinine exceeds 2.5 mg/dL)

Patient monitoring

The following may be especially important in patient monitoring (other tests may be warranted in some patients, depending on condition; » = major clinical significance):

Albumin concentrations, serum and
Calcium concentrations, serum and
Phosphorus concentrations, serum
(serum calcium should be monitored daily, serum phosphorus two times a week, and serum albumin before and after each course of therapy; serum proteins, especially albumin, may influence the ratio of free and bound calcium; corrected serum calcium values should be calculated by using an established algorithm; albumin-corrected serum calcium determinations may be useful when the signs and symptoms of hypercalcemia are inconsistent with unadjusted calcium values)

» Renal function determinations, especially serum creatinine and blood urea nitrogen (BUN)
(recommended daily to every 2 to 3 days during therapy; treatment should be discontinued if serum creatinine is greater than 2.5 mg per dL)

Side/Adverse Effects

The following side/adverse effects have been selected on the basis of their potential clinical significance (possible signs and symptoms in parentheses where appropriate)—not necessarily inclusive:

Note: Decreased serum bicarbonate, possibly secondary to mild respiratory alkalosis, has been reported. It has been asymptomatic and has not required specific treatment.

Those indicating need for medical attention

Incidence more frequent

Hypophosphatemia (bone pain; loss of appetite; muscle weakness); ***nephrotoxicity*** (blood in urine; greatly increased or decreased frequency of urination or amount of urine; increased thirst; loss of appetite; nausea; vomiting)

Incidence less frequent

Hypocalcemia (abdominal cramps; confusion; muscle spasms)

Incidence rare

Anemia (unusual tiredness or weakness)—with doses of up to 1400 mg per square meter of body surface area

Those indicating need for medical attention only if they continue or are bothersome

Incidence more frequent

Diarrhea; metallic taste; nausea; vomiting

Patient Consultation

As an aid to patient consultation, refer to *Advice for the Patient, Gallium Nitrate (Systemic)*.

In providing consultation, consider emphasizing the following selected information (» = major clinical significance):

Before using this medication

» Conditions affecting use, especially:

Breast-feeding—Not known if distributed into breast milk; may cause potentially serious adverse effects in nursing infants

Other medications, especially nephrotoxic medications

Other medical problems, especially renal function impairment

Proper use of this medication

» Proper dosing

» Proper storage

Precautions while using this medication

Importance of close monitoring by physician

Side/adverse effects

Signs of potential adverse effects, especially hypophosphatemia, nephrotoxicity, hypocalcemia, and anemia

General Dosing Information

The daily dose is usually diluted in 1000 mL of 0.9% sodium chloride injection or 5% dextrose injection. The diluted dose should be administered over a period of twenty-four hours. The solution can also be delivered undiluted via a metered ambulatory infusion pump.

During acute therapy for hypercalcemia,patients should maintain a urinary output of at least 2000 mL per day to decrease the chance of nephrotoxicity.

Parenteral Dosage Forms

GALLIUM NITRATE INJECTION

Usual adult and adolescent dose

Hypercalcemia (treatment)—

Intravenous infusion, 100 to 200 mg per square meter of body surface area per day, administered over a period of twenty-four hours, for five days.

Note: If serum calcium concentrations decrease to normal in less than five days, treatment should be discontinued.

Some clinicians recommend that therapy be repeated, if needed, after a waiting period of two to four weeks.

Usual pediatric dose

Safety and efficacy have not been established.

Usual geriatric dose

Safety and efficacy have not been established.

Strength(s) usually available

U.S.—

25 mg per mL (Rx) [*Ganite*].

Canada—

Gallium nitrate is not commercially available in Canada; however, it is available by emergency drug release from the Health Protection Branch.

Packaging and storage

Store below 40 °C (104 °F), preferably between 15 and 30 °C (59 and 86 °F), unless otherwise specified by manufacturer.

Preparation of dosage form

The daily dose is usually diluted in 1000 mL of 0.9% sodium chloride injection or 5% dextrose injection.

Stability

Diluted solution may be stored at controlled room temperature for 48 hours and under refrigeration for 7 days without loss of potency.

Revised: 08/05/1997

GALSULFASE Systemic†

VA CLASSIFICATION (Primary): HS451

Commonly used brand name(s): *Naglazyme.*

Note: For a listing of dosage forms and brand names by country availability, see *Dosage Forms* section(s).

†Not commercially available in Canada.

Category

Enzyme replenisher.

Indications

Note: Bracketed information in the *Indications* section refers to uses that are not included in U.S. product labeling.

Accepted

Mucopolysaccharidosis VI (treatment)—Galsulfase is indicated for patients with Mucopolysaccharidosis VI. Galsulfase has been shown to improve walking and stair-climbing capacity.

Pharmacology/Pharmacokinetics

Physicochemical characteristics

Source—Galsulfase is a normal variant form of the polymorphic human enzyme, N-acetylgalactosamine 4-sulfatase that is produced by recombinant DNA technology in a Chinese hamster ovary cell line.

Molecular weight—Galsulfase: Approximately 56kD.

pH—Approximately 5.8

Specific activity—Approximately 70 U/mg protein content

Mechanism of action/Effect

Mucopolysaccharidosis VI is characterized by the deficiency of N-acetylgalactosamine 4-sulfatase, resulting in the accumulation of the glycosaminoglycans (GAG) substrate, dermatan sulfate throughout the body, leading to widespread cellular, tissue, and organ dysfunction. Galsulfase provides exogenous enzyme for uptake into lysosomes and increases the catabolism of GAG. This uptake into the lysosomes is most likely mediated by the mannose-6-phosphate-terminated oligosaccharide chains of galsulfase binding to specific mannose-6-phosphate receptors.

Absorption

AUC: Patients with MPS VI received 1 mg/kg of galsulfase as 4-hour infusions weekly for 24 weeks.

- Week 1: 2.3 range (1 to 3.5) h-mcg/mL
- Week 24: 4.3 range (0.3 to 14.2) h-mcg/mL

- Week 1: 9 (6 to 21) minutes
- Week 24: 26 (8 to 40) minutes

Peak plasma concentration

- Week 1: 0.8 range (0.4 to 1.3) mcg/mL
- Week 24: 1.5 range (0.2 to 5.5) mcg/mL

- Clearance—week 1: 7.2 mL/kg/min
- Clearance—week 24: 3.7 mL/kg/min

Precautions to Consider

Carcinogenicity/Mutagenicity

Studies done to determine the carcinogenic and mutagenic potential of galsulfase have not been conducted.

Pregnancy/Reproduction

Fertility—Reproductive studies done in rats given doses of galsulfase up to 3 mg/kg/day have revealed no evidence of impaired fertility.

Pregnancy—Adequate and well controlled studies in humans have not been done. Studies in animals have not shown that galsulfase causes adverse effects in the fetus. Because animal reproduction studies are not always predictive of human response, this drug should be used during pregnancy only if clearly needed.

A Clinical Surveillance Program has been established to better understand the variability and progression of MPS VI in the population as a whole and to monitor and evaluate treatments. The Clinical Surveillance Program will also monitor the effect of galsulfase on pregnant women and their offspring, and determine if galsulfase is distributed in breast milk. Patients should be encouraged to participate and advised that their participation may involve long term follow up. Information regarding the registry program may be found at www.MPSVI.com/CSP or by calling (866) 906–6100. Pregnant or nursing women are encouraged to participate in this program.

Studies done in rats given doses of galsulfase up to 3 mg/kg/day have revealed no harm to the fetus.

FDA Pregnancy Category B

Breast-feeding

It is not known whether galsulfase is distributed into breast milk. Because many drugs are distributed in human milk, caution should be exercised when galsulfase is administered to a nursing woman.

Pediatrics

Safety and efficacy in pediatric patients under 5 years of age have not been established.

Geriatrics

No information is available on the relationship of age to the effects of galsulfase in geriatric patients.

Drug interactions and/or related problems

The following drug interactions and/or related problems have been selected on the basis of their potential clinical significance (possible mechanism in parentheses where appropriate)—not necessarily inclusive (» = major clinical significance):

Note: No formal drug interaction studies have been conducted.

Medical considerations/Contraindications

The medical considerations/contraindications included have been selected on the basis of their potential clinical significance (reasons given in parentheses where appropriate)—not necessarily inclusive (» = major clinical significance).

Except under special circumstances, this medication should not be used when the following medical problem exists:

» Hypersensitivity to galsulfase or to any of its components

Risk-benefit should be considered when the following medical problems exist:

Febrile, acute or
Respiratory illness
(consider delaying galsulfase infusion)

Sleep apnea
(antihistamine pretreatment in patients with MPS VI may increase the risk of apneic episodes; evaluate airway patency prior to initiation of treatment)

Side/Adverse Effects

The following side/adverse effects have been selected on the basis of their potential clinical significance (possible signs and symptoms in parentheses where appropriate)—not necessarily inclusive:

Those indicating need for medical attention

Incidence less frequent

Chest pain; dyspnea (shortness of breath; difficult or labored breathing; tightness in chest wheezing); ***facial edema*** (swelling of the face); ***hypertension*** (blurred vision; dizziness; nervousness; headache pounding in the ears; slow or fast heartbeat); ***increased corneal opacification*** (blindness; blurred vision; decreased vision); ***umbilical hernia*** (hernia of the naval)

Incidence unknown

Infusion reactions, including (dizziness; fever or chills; facial swelling; headache; nausea or vomiting; shortness of breath skin rash; weakness); ***abdominal pain*** (stomach pain); ***angioneurotic edema*** (large, hive-like swelling on face, eyelids, lips, tongue, throat, hands, legs, feet, sex organs); ***apnea*** (bluish lips or skin, not breathing); ***bronchospasm*** (cough; difficulty breathing; noisy breathing; shortness of breath; tightness in chest; wheezing); ***hypotension*** (blurred vision confusion dizziness, faintness, or lightheadedness when getting up from a lying or sitting position suddenly sweating unusual tiredness or weakness); ***joint pain; nausea; respiratory distress*** (shortness of breath, troubled breathing, tightness in chest, or wheezing); ***retrosternal pain*** (pain behind the sternum); ***urticaria*** (hives or welts; itching; redness of skin; skin rash); ***vomiting***

Those indicating need for medical attention only if they continue or are bothersome

Incidence more frequent

Ear pain; gastroenteritis (abdominal or stomach pain diarrhea loss of appetite nausea weakness); ***immunogenicity*** (body produces substance that can bind to drug making it less effective or cause side effects); ***pain***

Incidence less frequent

Areflexia (loss of or increase in reflexes); ***conjunctivitis*** (redness, pain, swelling of eye, eyelid, or inner lining of eyelid; burning, dry or itching eyes; discharge; excessive tearing); ***malaise*** (general feeling of discomfort or illness; unusual tiredness or weakness); ***nasal congestion*** (stuffy nose); ***pharyngitis*** (body aches or pain; congestion; cough; dryness or soreness of throat; fever; hoarseness; runny nose; tender, swollen glands in neck; trouble in swallowing; voice changes); ***rigors*** (feeling unusually cold; shivering)

Observed during clinical trials

Arthralgia (pain in joints; muscle pain or stiffness; difficulty in moving); ***cough; fever; headache; otitis media*** (earache; redness or swelling in ear); ***upper respiratory infections*** (ear congestion; nasal congestion; chills; cough; fever; sneezing, or sore throat; body aches or pain; headache; loss of voice; runny nose; unusual tiredness or weakness; difficulty in breathing)

Overdose

For more information on the management of overdose or unintentional ingestion, **contact a poison control center** (see *Poison Control Center Listing*).

Treatment of overdose

There is no known specific antidote to galsulfase. Treatment is generally symptomatic and supportive.

Supportive care—
Patients in whom intentional overdose is confirmed or suspected should be referred for psychiatric consultation.

Patient Consultation

As an aid to patient consultation, refer to *Advice for the Patient, Galsulfase (Systemic)*.

In providing consultation, consider emphasizing the following selected information (» = major clinical significance):

Before using this medication

» Conditions affecting use, especially:
Hypersensitivity to galsulfase.
Pregnancy—Studies in humans have not been done. Studies in animals have not shown that galsulfase causes harm to the fetus. However, animal studies are not always predictive of human response. Galsulfase should be used in pregnancy only if clearly needed.
Breast-feeding—It is not known whether galsulfase is distributed into breast milk.
Use in children—Safety and efficacy in children under the age of 5 years have not been established.
Other medical problems, especially acute febrile, respiratory illness, or sleep apnea

Proper use of this medication

» Proper dosing
Missed dose: Talk to your doctor about rescheduling your next dose.
» Proper storage

Precautions while using this medication

» Importance of monitoring by the physician

Side/adverse effects

Signs of potential side effects, especially chest pain, dyspnea, facial edema, hypertension, increased corneal opacification, infusion reactions including abdominal pain, angioneurotic edema, apnea, bronchospasm, hypotension, joint pain, malaise, nausea, respiratory distress, retrosternal pain, urticaria, vomiting; or umbilical hernia

General Dosing Information

The concentrated galsulfase solution should be diluted in 0.9% Sodium Chloride Injection, USP using aseptic techniques in PVC containers, and administered with a PVC infusion set equipped with an in-line, low protein-binding 0.2 micrometer filter.

The initial infusion rate should be 6 mL/hr for the first hour. If tolerated, the rate of the infusion may be increased to 80 mL/hr for the remaining 3 hours.

Diluting galsulfase in a volume of 100 mL may be considered in patients 20 kg and under who are susceptible to fluid volume overload. The infusion rate should then be decreased so that the total volume infusion duration remains no less than 4 hours. If an infusion reaction occurs, the infusion time can be extended up to 20 hours.

The vial of galsulfase concentrate should not be used more than once.

Galsulfase contains no preservatives; therefore, any unused product or waste material should be discarded and disposed of in accordance with local requirements.

Treatment of adverse effects

Pretreatment with antipyretics and/or antihistamines is recommended 30 to 60 minutes prior to starting the galsulfase infusion.

If patient uses supplemental oxygen or continuous positive airway pressure (CPAP) during sleep, these treatments should be readily available during infusion. Extreme drowsiness/sleep may occur with antihistamine pretreatment.

If severe infusion reactions should occur, immediately discontinue galsulfase infusion and patients given appropriate care. Reconsider risk and benefits before re-administering galsulfase.

Parenteral Dosage Forms

GALSULFASE FOR INJECTION CONCENTRATE

Usual adult and adolescent dose

Enzyme replenisher—

Intravenous infusion, 1 mg/kg of body weight administered over a minimum of 4 hours, once weekly.

Usual pediatric dose

See *Usual adult and adolescent dose.* Safety and efficacy have not been established in children under 5 years of age.

Usual geriatric dose

Safety and efficacy have not been established.

Strength(s) usually available

U.S.—

5 mg of galsulfase per 5 mL vial (Rx) [*Naglazyme* (sodium chloride; sodium phosphate monobasic monohydrate; sodium phosphate dibasic heptahydrate; polysorbate 80)].

Packaging and storage

Store between 2 and 8°C (36 and 46 °F). Do not freeze.

Preparation of dosage form

On the day of use, the vial of galsulfase is to be diluted in 0.9% Sodium Chloride Injection USP to a final volume of 100 or 250 mL. Galsulfase should be prepared using PVC containers and administered with a PVC infusion set equipped with an in-line, low protein binding 0.2 micrometer filter.

- Determine the number of vials to be diluted. This is done based on the patient's weight and the recommended dose of 1 mg per kg of body weight. Round up to the nearest whole vial. Allow the vials to reach room temperature. Do not allow the vials to remain at room temperature longer than 24 hours prior to dilution. Do not heat or microwave vials.
- Before withdrawing the galsulfase concentrate from the vials, visually inspect each vial for particulate matter and discoloration. The solution should be clear to slightly opalescent and colorless to pale yellow. Do not use if there is particulate matter or if the solution is discolored.
- Remove and discard a volume of the 0.9% Sodium Chloride Injection from the 250 mL infusion bag equal to the volume of galsulfase concentrate to be added. If using a 100 mL infusion bag this is not necessary.
- Carefully withdraw the appropriate volume of galsulfase concentrate to be added. Use caution to avoid excessive agitation. Do not use a filter needle as this may cause agitation and denature the galsulfase rendering it inactive.
- Slowly and carefully add the galsulfase concentrate to the 0.9% Sodium Chloride Injection avoiding agitation.
- To insure proper distribution of galsulfase gently rotate the infusion bag. Do not shake.

Stability

Galsulfase does not contain a preservative. The product information for galsulfase states that the diluted solution should be used immediately. If immediate use is not possible, the diluted solution should be stored at 2 to 8 °C (36 to 46 °F). The diluted solution should not be stored longer than 48 hours from the time of preparation to completion of administration.

Incompatibilities

Galsulfase must not be mixed with other medicinal products in the same infusion line. The compatibility of galsulfase in solution with other products has not been evaluated.

The compatibility of diluted galsulfase with glass containers has not been determined.

Auxiliary labeling

- Do not freeze.
- Do not shake.
- Dilute medication before use.

Developed: 09/28/2005

GANCICLOVIR Systemic

VA CLASSIFICATION (Primary): AM890

Commonly used brand name(s): *Cytovene; Cytovene-IV.*

Another commonly used name is DHPG

Note: For a listing of dosage forms and brand names by country availability, see *Dosage Forms* section(s).

Category

Antiviral (systemic).

Indications

Note: Bracketed information in the *Indications* section refers to uses that are not included in U.S. product labeling.

Accepted

Cytomegalovirus retinitis (treatment)—Parenteral ganciclovir is indicated for induction and maintenance in the treatment of cytomegalovirus (CMV) retinitis in immunocompromised patients, including patients with acquired immunodeficiency syndrome (AIDS). Oral ganciclovir is indicated only for maintenance treatment of CMV retinitis in patients who have had a complete resolution of active retinitis after an induction course of parenteral ganciclovir; however, oral ganciclovir has been associated with a shorter time to CMV retinitis progression. [Intravitreal administration of ganciclovir has also been used in patients who have been unresponsive to intravenous ganciclovir, or in whom serious myelosuppression has precluded the continuation of intravenous therapy.]

Cytomegalovirus disease (prophylaxis)[1]—Parenteral ganciclovir is indicated for the prophylaxis of CMV disease in transplant patients who are at risk for the disease. Oral ganciclovir is indicated for the prophylaxis of CMV disease in solid organ transplant recipients and in patients with advanced human immunodeficiency virus (HIV) infection who are at risk for developing CMV disease.

[Cytomegalovirus disease (treatment)][1]—Parenteral ganciclovir is used in the treatment of severe CMV disease, including CMV pneumonia, CMV gastrointestinal disease, and disseminated CMV infections, in immunocompromised patients.

[Polyradiculopathy (treatment)][1]—Parenteral ganciclovir is used in the treatment of polyradiculopathy caused by CMV in patients with AIDS.

Resistance to ganciclovir has been reported. One paper described CMV disease refractory to ganciclovir therapy due to infections with a resistant virus, a susceptible virus that became resistant, and an infection first by a susceptible strain, and later by a genetically distinct, resistant one. The primary mechanism of resistance to ganciclovir is the decreased ability to form the active triphosphate moiety. Recurrence may be more frequent in patients treated with ganciclovir for prolonged periods (> 3 to 6 months).

Acceptance not established

Ganciclovir has been studied for the treatment of *symptomatic congenital CMV infection in neonates.* More data are needed to establish the place in therapy for ganciclovir for this indication.

[1]Not included in Canadian product labeling.

Pharmacology/Pharmacokinetics

Physicochemical characteristics

High pH (11).

Molecular weight—

Ganciclovir: 255.23.

Ganciclovir sodium: 277.22.

Mechanism of action/Effect

Ganciclovir is a prodrug that is structurally similar to acyclovir. Its antiviral activity results from its intracellular conversion to the triphosphate form. In cytomegalovirus (CMV)-infected cells, ganciclovir is thought to be rapidly phosphorylated to the monophosphate form by a CMV-encoded enzyme, then subsequently converted to the diphosphate and triphosphate forms by cellular kinases. Ganciclovir is phosphorylated much more rapidly in infected cells; however, uninfected cells can also produce low levels of ganciclovir-triphosphate. Ganciclovir-triphosphate competitively inhibits DNA polymerase by acting as a substrate and becoming incorporated into the DNA. This inhibits DNA synthesis by suppressing DNA chain elongation. The drug inhibits viral DNA polymerases more effectively than it does cellular polymerase. Chain elongation resumes when ganciclovir is removed.

Absorption
Ganciclovir is poorly absorbed after oral administration; bioavailability under fasting conditions is approximately 5%, and when administered with food, 6 to 9%.

Distribution
Ganciclovir is widely distributed to all tissues and crosses the placenta; however, there is no marked accumulation in any one type of tissue. Penetration into the cerebrospinal fluid averaged 38% in one study, and ranged from 7 to 67% in others. Ganciclovir also appears to have good intraocular penetration. In one patient, the subretinal fluid ganciclovir concentration was 7.2 micromoles per L with a corresponding plasma concentration of 8.2 micromoles per L 5.5 hours after a dose of 5 mg per kg of body weight (mg/kg), and 2.58 micromoles per L with a corresponding plasma concentration of 1.3 micromoles per L 8 hours after a subsequent dose of 5 mg/kg.

Vol_D (steady state)—Adults and neonates: Approximately 0.74 L per kg.

Protein binding
Low (1 to 2%).

Biotransformation
Little to no metabolism.

Half-life
Serum—

Intravenous:

Adults—Normal renal function: 2.5 to 3.6 hours (average, 2.9 hours).

Adults—Renal function impairment: 9 to 30 hours (creatinine clearance of 20 to 50 mL per minute [0.33 to 0.83 mL per second]).

Neonates—Approximately 2.4 hours.

Oral:

Normal renal function—3.1 to 5.5 hours.

Renal function impairment—15.7 to 18.2 hours (creatinine clearance of 10 to 50 mL per minute [0.17 to 0.83 mL per second]).

Vitreous fluid—

Approximately 13 hours.

Time to peak concentration
Intravenous—

End of infusion (approximately 1 hour).

Oral—

Fasting: Approximately 1.8 hours.

With food: Approximately 3 hours.

Peak concentrations
Intravenous—

Adults: 5 mg/kg over 1 hour—8.3 to 9 mcg/mL.

Neonates: 4 and 6 mg/kg over 1 hour—Approximately 5.5 and 7 mcg/mL, respectively.

Oral—

3 grams per day: 1 to 1.2 mcg/mL.

Intravitreal injection—

1000 mcg administered in five divided doses over 15 days: 16.2 mcg/mL; ganciclovir was not detected in plasma.

Elimination
Renal; almost 100% excreted unchanged in the urine by glomerular filtration and tubular secretion.

In dialysis—Plasma ganciclovir concentrations are reduced by approximately 50% after a single, 4-hour hemodialysis.

Precautions to Consider

Cross-sensitivity and/or related problems
Patients hypersensitive to acyclovir may also be hypersensitive to ganciclovir because of the chemical similarity of the two medications.

Carcinogenicity/Tumorigenicity
Ganciclovir is carcinogenic in animals and should be considered a potential carcinogen in humans. Ganciclovir was carcinogenic in the mouse at oral doses of 20 and 1000 mg per kg of body weight (mg/kg) per day (approximately 0.1 and 1.4 times, respectively, the mean drug exposure in humans following the recommended intravenous dose of 5 mg/kg, based on the area under the concentration-time curve [AUC]) comparisons. Mice given oral doses of 20 mg/kg per day showed a slightly increased incidence of tumors in the preputial and harderian glands in males, forestomach in males and females, and liver in females. Studies in mice given oral doses of 1000 mg/kg per day showed an increased incidence of tumors of the forestomach in males and females, preputial gland in males, and reproductive tissues and liver in females. All ganciclovir-induced tumors were of epithelial or vascular origin, except for histiocytic sarcoma of the liver. No carcinogenic effect occurred at a dose of 1 mg/kg per day.

Mutagenicity
Ganciclovir was mutagenic in mouse lymphoma cells at concentrations between 50 and 500 mcg/mL, and caused chromosomal damage *in vitro* in human lymphocytes at concentrations between 250 and 2000 mcg/mL. Parenteral ganciclovir was also clastogenic in the mouse micronucleus assay at doses of 150 and 500 mg/kg (2.8 to 10 times the human exposure based on area under the concentration-time curve [AUC] of a single intravenous dose of 5 mg/kg), but not at a dose of 50 mg/kg (exposure approximately comparable to the human dose based on AUC). Ganciclovir was not mutagenic in the Ames Salmonella assay at concentrations of 500 to 5000 mcg/mL.

Pregnancy/Reproduction
Fertility—Although data in humans have not been obtained, temporary or permanent suppression of fertility in women and spermatogenesis in men may occur.

In female mice, ganciclovir caused decreased mating behavior, decreased fertility, and increased death in utero at doses approximately 1.7 times the recommended human dose (based on the AUC of a single intravenous dose of 5 mg/kg). Ganciclovir was also found to cause decreased fertility in male mice, and hypospermatogenesis in mice and dogs following daily oral or intravenous administration of doses ranging from 0.2 to 10 mg/kg. Inhibition of spermatogenesis and subsequent infertility was reversible at lower doses and irreversible at higher doses in animals. Systemic drug exposure (as measured by AUC) at the lowest dose showing toxicity in each species ranged from 0.03 to 0.1 times the AUC of the recommended human intravenous dose.

Pregnancy—Adequate and well-controlled studies in humans have not been done. However, ganciclovir has been found to cross the placenta. Due to the high toxicity and mutagenic and teratogenic potential of ganciclovir, use during pregnancy should be avoided whenever possible. Women of childbearing age should use effective contraception. Men should use barrier contraception during, and for at least 90 days following, treatment with ganciclovir.

Ganciclovir was found to be carcinogenic in animals and teratogenic in rabbits, causing cleft palate, anophthalmia/microphthalmia, aplastic organs (kidneys and pancreas), hydrocephaly, bradygnathia, and fetal growth retardation. It also was found to be embryotoxic in mice, and to cause death in utero and maternal toxicity in both rabbits and mice. Fetal resorptions occurred in at least 85% of rabbits and mice administered 60 mg/kg per day and 108 mg/kg per day (2 times the human exposure based on AUC comparisons), respectively. Daily intravenous doses of 90 mg/kg administered to female mice prior to mating, during gestation, and during lactation caused hypoplasia of the testes and seminal vesicles in the month-old male offspring, as well as pathologic changes in the nonglandular region of the stomach. The drug exposure in mice as estimated by the AUC was approximately 1.7 times the human AUC.

FDA Pregnancy Category C.

Breast-feeding
It is not known whether ganciclovir is distributed into breast milk; however, it is likely that some drug will accumulate because of its pharmacokinetic properties. Because of the potential for serious adverse effects in nursing infants, breast-feeding should be stopped during ganciclovir therapy. Ganciclovir has caused irreversible toxicity in nursing animal pups.

Pediatrics
There is little information currently available on the use of ganciclovir in children, especially those up to the age of 12. At this time, the side effects seen in children appear to be similar to those seen in adults, especially granulocytopenia (17%) and thrombocytopenia (10%). However, the probability of long-term carcinogenicity and reproductive toxicity seen in animal studies should also be considered.

Geriatrics
No information is available on the relationship of age to the effects of ganciclovir in geriatric patients. However, elderly patients are more likely to have an age-related decrease in renal function, which may require an adjustment of dosage or dosing interval in patients receiving ganciclovir.

Dental
The neutropenic and thrombocytopenic effects of ganciclovir may result in an increased incidence of microbial infection, delayed healing, and gingival bleeding. Patients should be instructed in proper oral hygiene, including caution in use of regular toothbrushes, dental floss, and toothpicks.

Drug interactions and/or related problems
The following drug interactions and/or related problems have been selected on the basis of their potential clinical significance (possible

mechanism in parentheses where appropriate)—not necessarily inclusive (» = major clinical significance):

Note: Combinations containing any of the following medications, depending on the amount present, may also interact with this medication.

Blood dyscrasia-causing medications (see *Appendix II*) or
» Bone marrow depressants, other (see *Appendix II*) or
Radiation therapy
(concurrent use with ganciclovir may increase the bone marrow–depressant effects of these medications and radiation therapy)

Didanosine
(concurrent and sequential [2 hours apart] administration of didanosine with ganciclovir results in a significant increase in the steady-state area under the concentration-time curve [AUC] of didanosine [range, 72 to 111%]; when didanosine was administered 2 hours before oral ganciclovir, the steady-state AUC of ganciclovir was decreased by approximately 21%; there was no significant change in renal clearance of either medication)

Imipenem and cilastatin combination
(generalized seizures have been reported in patients receiving ganciclovir and imipenem and cilastatin combination concurrently)

» Nephrotoxic medications (see *Appendix II*)
(concurrent use with ganciclovir may increase serum creatinine; concurrent use with nephrotoxic medications, such as cyclosporine or amphotericin B, may increase the chance of renal function impairment; this may also decrease elimination of ganciclovir and increase the risk of toxicity)

Probenecid
(concurrent use with probenecid increases the AUC of ganciclovir by approximately 53% and decreases its renal clearance by approximately 22%; concurrent use of ganciclovir with probenecid, or other medications that inhibit renal tubular secretion, may reduce the renal clearance of ganciclovir and lead to toxicity)

» Zidovudine
(concurrent use of ganciclovir with zidovudine has been associated with severe hematologic toxicity in some patients, even when the zidovudine dose was reduced to 300 mg per day; concurrent use increases the AUC of zidovudine by approximately 14 to 19%; *in vitro* studies found concurrent use of these 2 drugs to be synergistically cytotoxic; concurrent administration should be used with caution)

Laboratory value alterations

The following have been selected on the basis of their potential clinical significance (possible effect in parentheses where appropriate)—not necessarily inclusive (» = major clinical significance).

With physiology/laboratory test values

Alanine aminotransferase (ALT [SGPT]), serum and
Alkaline phosphatase, serum and
Aspartate aminotransferase (AST [SGOT]), serum and
Bilirubin, serum
(values may be increased)

Blood urea nitrogen (BUN) or
Creatinine, serum
(values may be increased)

Medical considerations/Contraindications

The medical considerations/contraindications included have been selected on the basis of their potential clinical significance (reasons given in parentheses where appropriate)—not necessarily inclusive (» = major clinical significance).

Risk-benefit should be considered when the following medical problems exist:

» Absolute neutrophil count (ANC) < 500 cells/mm^3 or platelet count < 25,000 cells/mm^3

» Hypersensitivity to acyclovir or ganciclovir

» Renal function impairment
(because ganciclovir is excreted through the kidneys, the dose of ganciclovir should be reduced or the dosing interval increased in patients with renal function impairment)

Patient monitoring

The following may be especially important in patient monitoring (other tests may be warranted in some patients, depending on condition; » = major clinical significance):

» Complete blood counts (CBCs) and
» Platelet counts
(because ganciclovir may cause granulocytopenia and thrombocytopenia, neutrophil and platelet counts should be monitored prior to treatment, every 2 days during induction therapy, then at least weekly thereafter. Neutrophil and platelet counts should be performed daily in patients undergoing hemodialysis, patients with neutrophil counts less than 1000 cells/mm^3 at the beginning of treatment, and those in whom use of ganciclovir or other nucleoside analogs previously resulted in leukopenia. When severe neutropenia [absolute neutrophil count < 500 cells/mm^3] or severe thrombocytopenia [platelet count < 25,000 cells/mm^3] occurs, discontinuation of ganciclovir may be necessary; however, a small number of patients have been successfully treated with concurrent use of sargramostim [GM-CSF; granulocyte-macrophage colony stimulating factor] or filgrastin [G-CSF; granulocyte colony stimulating factor])

Liver function tests
(liver function tests, including serum ALT [SGPT] and AST [SGOT] values, and serum bilirubin concentration, should be monitored periodically since elevations, usually reversible, have occurred during ganciclovir therapy)

» Renal function determinations
(blood urea nitrogen and serum creatinine determinations should be monitored at least every 2 weeks since patients with renal function impairment will require an adjustment in dosage or dosage interval)

For treatment of cytomegalovirus [CMV] retinitis, in addition to the above

» Ophthalmologic examinations
(ophthalmologic examinations should be performed weekly during induction and every 4 weeks during maintenance since ganciclovir is not a cure for cytomegalovirus [CMV] retinitis, and progression of retinitis may occur during or following ganciclovir treatment; however, the frequency of examinations may vary, depending on the extent of disease, activity, and proximity to the macula and optic disc)

Side/Adverse Effects

The following side/adverse effects have been selected on the basis of their potential clinical significance (possible signs and symptoms in parentheses where appropriate)—not necessarily inclusive:

Those indicating need for medical attention

Incidence more frequent

For intravenous and oral administration

Granulocytopenia (sore throat and fever); ***thrombocytopenia*** (unusual bleeding or bruising)

Note: *Granulocytopenia* is usually reversible, with an overall incidence of approximately 40%; the incidence of dose-limiting toxicity is < 20%.

Thrombocytopenia is also usually reversible, with an overall incidence of approximately 20%; the incidence of dose-limiting toxicity is 5 to 10%.

Incidence less frequent

For intravenous and oral administration

Anemia (unusual tiredness and weakness); ***central nervous system (CNS) effects*** (mood or other mental changes; nervousness; tremor); ***hypersensitivity*** (fever; skin rash); ***phlebitis*** (pain at site of injection)

For intravitreal administration

Bacterial endophthalmitis; conjunctival scarring, mild; foreign body sensation; retinal detachment; scleral induration; or subconjunctival hemorrhage (decreased vision or any change in vision)

Those indicating need for medical attention only if they continue or are bothersome

Incidence less frequent

Gastrointestinal disturbances (abdominal pain; loss of appetite; nausea and vomiting)

Patient Consultation

As an aid to patient consultation, refer to *Advice for the Patient, Ganciclovir (Systemic).*

In providing consultation, consider emphasizing the following selected information (» = major clinical significance):

Before using this medication

» Conditions affecting use, especially:

Hypersensitivity to acyclovir or ganciclovir

Pregnancy—Use of ganciclovir during pregnancy should be avoided whenever possible. Ganciclovir crosses the placenta and has been found to be carcinogenic and teratogenic in animals. Use of effective contraception by men and women who are undergoing treatment and in men for 90 days following treatment is recommended.

Breast-feeding—Because of ganciclovir's potential for severe toxicity, breast-feeding should be stopped during therapy.

Use in children—There is little information currently available on the use of ganciclovir in children, especially those up to the age of 12; long-term carcinogenicity and reproductive toxicity due to ganciclovir use in children is unknown

Dental—The neutropenic and thrombocytopenic effects of ganciclovir may result in an increased incidence of microbial infection, delayed healing, and gingival bleeding

Other medications, especially other bone marrow depressants, nephrotoxic medications, or zidovudine

Other medical problems, especially renal function impairment, an absolute neutrophil count (ANC) < 500 cells/mm^3, or platelet count < 25,000 cells/mm^3

Proper use of this medication

» Taking ganciclovir capsules with food

» Importance of receiving medication for full course of therapy and on a regular schedule

» Proper dosing

Precautions while using this medication

To reduce the risk of bleeding during periods of low blood counts:

» Checking with physician immediately if getting an infection or fever or chills

» Checking with physician immediately if unusual bleeding or bruising; black, tarry stools; blood in urine or stools; or pinpoint red spots on skin occur

Using caution in use of regular toothbrushes, dental floss, and toothpicks; physician, dentist, or nurse may suggest alternative methods for cleaning teeth and gums; checking with physician before having dental work done

Using caution to avoid accidental cuts with use of sharp objects such as a safety razor or fingernail or toenail cutters

» Using contraception since ganciclovir has mutagenic and teratogenic potential; women should use effective contraception during treatment, and men should use barrier contraception during and for at least 90 days following treatment

» Regular visits to physician to check blood counts

» *For CMV retinitis*—Regular visits to ophthalmologist to examine eyes since progression of retinitis and visual loss may occur during ganciclovir therapy

Side/adverse effects

Signs of potential side effects, especially granulocytopenia, thrombocytopenia, anemia, CNS effects, hypersensitivity, and phlebitis when ganciclovir is administered intravenously or orally; and bacterial endophthalmitis, mild conjunctival scarring, foreign body sensation, retinal detachment, scleral induration, and subconjunctival hemorrhage when it is administered intravitreally

General Dosing Information

Ganciclovir is not a cure for cytomegalovirus infections. Maintenance therapy is almost always necessary in AIDS patients to prevent relapse, which is very common once the medication has been withdrawn.

Monitoring of serum ganciclovir concentrations has not been shown to be useful for ensuring efficacy or avoiding toxicity.

Ganciclovir sodium should be administered by intravenous infusion only. Intramuscular or subcutaneous injection will result in severe tissue irritation due to ganciclovir's high pH (11).

Intravenous infusions of ganciclovir should be administered at a constant rate *over at least a 1-hour period*, and patients must be adequately hydrated, to avoid increased toxicity. The recommended dosage, frequency, and infusion rate should not be exceeded.

Severe neutropenia or thrombocytopenia (absolute neutrophil count [ANC] < 500 cells/mm^3 or platelet count < 25,000 cells/mm^3) requires an interruption in therapy until there is evidence of bone marrow recovery (ANC ≥ 750 cells/mm^3); however, a small number of patients have been successfully treated with concurrent use of sargramostim (GM-CSF; granulocyte-macrophage colony stimulating factor).

Ganciclovir capsules should be taken with food for maximum absorption.

The dose of ganciclovir must be decreased in patients with renal function impairment.

Patients undergoing hemodialysis should not receive a dose in excess of 1.25 mg per kg of body weight (mg/kg) every 24 hours. On dialysis days, the dose of ganciclovir should be administered after hemodialysis has been performed since dialysis will reduce plasma ganciclovir concentrations by approximately 50%.

Ganciclovir capsules are indicated as an alternative to intravenous ganciclovir for maintenance therapy of CMV retinitis in immunocompromised patients, including those with AIDS. Oral ganciclovir should be used in patients in whom retinitis is stable and quiescent following appropriate induction therapy and for whom the risk of more rapid progression is balanced by the benefit associated with avoiding long-term daily intravenous infusions, usually requiring indwelling intravenous catheters.

Intravitreal administration of ganciclovir has been used in patients who have been unresponsive to intravenous ganciclovir, or in whom serious myelosuppression has precluded the continuation of intravenous therapy. Intravitreal doses of 200 micrograms have resulted in improvement or stabilization of retinitis and have been well tolerated. In one report describing a patient who received 28 intravitreal injections, plasma concentrations after intravitreal injections showed no significant systemic absorption. The elimination half-life of ganciclovir from the vitreous fluid was estimated to be 13.3 hours, and the intravitreal concentration remained above the ID_{50} of cytomegalovirus for approximately 62 hours after a single injection.

Safety considerations for handling this medication

Caution should be exercised in the handling and preparation of ganciclovir. Because ganciclovir shares some properties of anti-tumor agents (i.e., carcinogenicity and mutagenicity), it should be handled and disposed of according to guidelines issued for cytotoxic drugs. Ganciclovir solution is alkaline (pH 11). Avoid inhalation, ingestion, or direct contact of ganciclovir with the skin or mucous membranes. If contact does occur, wash area thoroughly with soap and water; rinse eyes thoroughly with plain water. Ganciclovir capsules should not be opened or crushed.

Oral Dosage Forms

GANCICLOVIR CAPSULES

Usual adult and adolescent dose

Cytomegalovirus retinitis—

Induction: Ganciclovir capsules should not be used for induction therapy. See *Ganciclovir Sodium for Injection.*

Maintenance: Oral, 1000 mg three times a day with food, or 500 mg six times a day every three hours with food, during waking hours.

Note: For maintenance, patients with impaired renal function may require a reduction in dose as follows:

Creatinine Clearance (mL/min)/(mL/sec)	Dose
≥ 70/1.17	See *Usual adult and adolescent dose*
50–69/0.83–1.15	1500 mg once a day, or 500 mg three times a day
25–49/0.42–0.82	1000 mg once a day, or 500 mg twice a day
10–24/0.17–0.40	500 mg once a day
< 10/0.17	500 mg three times a week, following hemodialysis

Cytomegalovirus disease (prophylaxis)[1]—

Oral, 1000 mg three times a day with food.

Note: Patients with impaired renal function may require a reduction in dose as follows:

Creatinine Clearance (mL/min)/(mL/sec)	Dose
≥ 70/1.17	See *Usual adult and adolescent dose*
50–69/0.83–1.15	1500 mg once a day, or 500 mg three times a day
25–49/0.42–0.82	1000 mg once a day, or 500 mg twice a day
10–24/0.17–0.40	500 mg once a day
< 10/0.17	500 mg three times a week, following hemodialysis

Usual pediatric dose

Dosage has not been established.

Strength(s) usually available

U.S.—

250 mg (Rx) [*Cytovene* (croscarmellose sodium; magnesium stearate; povidone; gelatin; titanium dioxide; yellow iron oxide)].

500 mg (Rx) [*Cytovene* (croscarmellose sodium; magnesium stearate; povidone; gelatin; titanium dioxide; yellow iron oxide)].

Canada—

250 mg (Rx) [*Cytovene* (croscarmellose sodium; gelatin; indigotine; iron oxide; magnesium stearate; povidone; titanium dioxide)].

500 mg (Rx) [*Cytovene* (croscarmellose sodium; gelatin; indigotine; iron oxide; magnesium stearate; povidone; titanium dioxide)].

Packaging and storage

Store below 40 °C (104 °F), preferably between 15 and 30 °C (59 and 86 °F), unless otherwise specified by manufacturer.

Auxiliary labeling
- Continue medicine for full time of treatment.

Note
Ganciclovir capsules should not be opened or crushed.

Because ganciclovir capsules are associated with a risk of more rapid rate of CMV retinitis progression they should be used as a maintenance treatment only in the patients for whom this risk is balanced by the benefit associated with avoiding daily intravenous infusions.

Parenteral Dosage Forms

GANCICLOVIR SODIUM FOR INJECTION

Usual adult and adolescent dose
Cytomegalovirus retinitis (treatment)—
Induction—
Intravenous infusion, 5 mg per kg of body weight, administered over at least one hour, every twelve hours for fourteen to twenty-one days.

Note: Doses of 7.5 to 15 mg per kg of body weight per day divided into two or three doses have been used, and treatment has been continued for longer than twenty-one days; if retinitis does not show significant improvement, the possibility of viral resistance should be considered.

Intravitreal injection, 200 mcg two times a week for three weeks.

Note: For induction, patients with impaired renal function may require a reduction in dose as follows:

Creatinine Clearance (mL/min)/(mL/sec)	Dose
≥ 70/1.17	See *Usual adult and adolescent dose*
50–69/0.83–1.15	2.5 mg per kg every twelve hours
25–49/0.42–0.82	2.5 mg per kg every twenty-four hours
10–24/0.17–0.40	1.25 mg per kg every twenty-four hours
< 10	1.25 mg per kg three times a week, following hemodialysis

Maintenance—
Intravenous infusion, 5 mg per kg of body weight a day, administered over at least one hour, once a day for seven days per week; or 6 mg per kg of body weight, administered over at least one hour, once a day for five days of the week.

Note: If CMV retinitis progresses during maintenance therapy, patients should be re-treated with the twice-a-day induction regimen.

Intravitreal injection, 200 mcg once a week.

Note: For maintenance, patients with impaired renal function may require a reduction in dose as follows:

Creatinine Clearance (mL/min)/(mL/sec)	Dose
≥ 70/1.17	See *Usual adult and adolescent dose*
50–69/0.83–1.15	2.5 mg per kg every twenty-four hours
25–49/0.42–0.82	1.25 mg per kg every twenty-four hours
10–24/0.17–0.40	0.625 mg per kg every twenty-four hours
< 10	0.625 mg per kg three times a week, following hemodialysis

Cytomegalovirus disease (prophylaxis)—
Intravenous infusion, 5 mg per kg of body weight, administered over at least one hour, every twelve hours for seven to fourteen days; then 5 mg per kg of body weight, administered over at least one hour, once a day for seven days of the week, or 6 mg per kg of body weight, administered over at least one hour, once a day for five days of the week.

Usual pediatric dose
Dosage has not been established. However, induction doses of 7.5 to 10 mg per kg of body weight divided into two or three doses, and maintenance doses of 2.5 to 5 mg per kg of body weight a day have been used in children.

Strength(s) usually available
U.S.—
500 mg (Rx) [*Cytovene-IV* (sodium 46 mg)].
Canada—
500 mg (Rx) [*Cytovene*].

Packaging and storage
Store below 40 °C (104 °F), preferably between 15 and 30 °C (59 and 86 °F), unless otherwise specified by manufacturer.

Preparation of dosage form
To prepare initial dilution for intravenous infusion, 10 mL of sterile water for injection (without parabens) should be added to each 500-mg vial to provide 50 mg per mL. To ensure complete dissolution, the vial should be shaken until solution is clear. The resulting solution should be further diluted, usually with 100 mL of 0.9% sodium chloride injection, 5% dextrose injection, Ringer's injection, or lactated Ringer's injection. Final concentrations of 10 mg per mL or less are recommended.

Note: Caution should be exercised in the handling and preparation of ganciclovir. Because ganciclovir shares some properties of antitumor agents (i.e., carcinogenicity and mutagenicity), it should be handled and disposed of according to guidelines issued for cytotoxic drugs. Ganciclovir solution is alkaline (pH 11). Avoid inhalation, ingestion, or direct contact of ganciclovir with the skin or mucous membranes. If contact does occur, wash area thoroughly with soap and water; rinse eyes thoroughly with plain water.

Stability
The manufacturer states that after reconstitution, solutions at concentrations of 50 mg per mL retain their potency for 12 hours at room temperature. Refrigeration is not recommended. After further dilution for intravenous infusion, it is recommended that solutions be used within 24 hours since nonbacteriostatic infusion solutions must be used; refrigerate the diluted solution; do not freeze.

However, studies have found that ganciclovir, when diluted to concentrations of 1, 5, and 10 mg per mL in 5% dextrose injection and 0.9% sodium chloride injection, was stable when assayed at 28 and 35 days. These solutions were refrigerated in polyvinyl chloride (PVC) bags and syringes. Ganciclovir was also stable when 5 and 10 mg per mL solutions were frozen in PVC bags for 28 days.

Incompatibilities
Parabens are incompatible with ganciclovir sodium and may cause precipitation.

[1]Not included in Canadian product labeling.

Selected Bibliography

Markham A, Faulds D. Ganciclovir. An update of its therapeutic use in cytomegalovirus infections. Drugs 1994; 48(3): 455-84.

Revised: 04/04/2001

GATIFLOXACIN Ophthalmic†

VA CLASSIFICATION (Primary): OP201

Note: For a listing of dosage forms and brand names by country availability, see *Dosage Forms* section(s).

†Not commercially available in Canada.

Category

Antibacterial (ophthalmic).

Indications

Accepted
Conjunctivitis, bacterial (treatment)—Gatifloxacin ophthalmic solution is indicated for the treatment of bacterial conjunctivitis caused by *Cornyebacterium propinquum, Haemophilus influenzae, Staphylococcus aureus, Staphylococcus epidermidis, Streptococcus mitis*, and *Streptococcus pneumoniae*.

Note: Efficacy for Cornyebacterium propinquum and Streptococcus mitis was studied in fewer than ten infections.

Pharmacology/Pharmacokinetics

Physicochemical characteristics
Chemical Group—8-methoxy-fluoroquinolone
Molecular weight—Gatifloxacin: 402.42.
pH—Approximately 6
Osmolality—260 to 330 mOsmol/kg

Mechanism of action/Effect
Gatifloxacin's antibacterial action results from inhibition of DNA gyrase and topoisomerase IV, which are essential enzymes involved in the

replication, transcription, repair and partitioning of the chromosomal DNA during bacterial cell division. This mechanism of action is different from that of aminoglycoside, macrolide, and tetracycline antibiotics. Therefore gatifloxacin may be active against pathogens that are resistant to these antibodies, and these antibiotics may be active against pathogens that are resistant to gatifloxacin.

There is no cross-resistance between gatifloxacin and aminoglycoside, macrolide, and tetracycline antibiotics, but cross-resistance has been observed between gatifloxacin and other fluoroquinolones.

Absorption

Serum gatifloxacin levels, were below the lower limit of quantification (5 ng per mL) at all time points after doses of 0.3% or 0.5% solution, given up to 2 drops 8 times daily.

Precautions to Consider

Cross-sensitivity and/or related problems

Patients sensitive to other quinolones may be sensitive to this medication also.

Carcinogenicity

In 18 month to 2 years studies, there was no increase in neoplasms among mice or rats given doses of gatifloxacin in the diet, 1000 to 3000 times higher than the maximum recommended ophthalmic dose.

Mutagenicity

Gatifloxacin was found to be mutagenic in the *in vitro* mammalian cell mutation and chromosome aberration assays, the *in vitro* unscheduled DNA synthesis in rat hepatocytes and, in 1 of 5 strains used in the bacterial reverse mutation assay. Gatifloxacin was not mutagenic in *in vivo* micronucleus tests in mice, cytogenetics tests in rats, and DNA repair test in rats.

Pregnancy/Reproduction

Fertility—There were no adverse effects on fertility or reproduction in rats given oral doses of gatifloxacin approximately 4500 times higher than the maximum recommended ophthalmic dose.

Pregnancy—No teratogenic effects were observed in rats or rabbits following oral doses approximately 1000-fold higher than the maximum recommended ophthalmic dose. However, in doses of approximately 3000-fold higher than the maximum recommended ophthalmic dose, defects such as skeletal/craniofacial malformations, delayed ossification, atrial enlargement and reduced fetal weights were observed in rats. In a perinatal/postnatal study, doses approximately 4500 times the maximum recommended ophthalmic dose increased late post-implantation loss and neonatal/perinatal mortalities were observed. Since there are no adequate and well controlled studies in humans, and animal studies are not always predictive of human response, gatifloxacin should only be administered during pregnancy if the potential benefit justifies the potential risk to the fetus.

FDA Pregnancy Category C

Breast-feeding

It is not known whether gatifloxacin is distributed into human milk. However, gatifloxacin is distributed into the breast milk of rats. Because many drugs are distributed in human milk, caution should be exercised when gatifloxacin is administered to a nursing woman.

Pediatrics

Safety and effectiveness in infants below the age of one year have not been established.

Geriatrics

Appropriate studies performed to date have not demonstrated geriatrics-specific problems that would limit the usefulness of gatifloxacin in the elderly.

Drug interactions and/or related problems

Drug interaction studies for gatifloxacin ophthalmic solution have not been done. However, it has been shown that systemic administration of some quinolones may elevate plasma concentrations of theophylline, interfere with metabolism of caffeine, and enhance the effects of the oral anticoagulant warfarin and its derivatives. It has also been associated with transient elevations in serum creatinine in patients concomitantly receiving systemic cyclosporine.

Medical considerations/Contraindications

The medical considerations/contraindications included have been selected on the basis of their potential clinical significance (reasons given in parentheses where appropriate)—not necessarily inclusive (» = major clinical significance).

Except under special circumstances, this medication should not be used when the following medical problem exists:

» Hypersensitivity to gatifloxacin or any of its components, or other fluoroquinolones

Side/Adverse Effects

Note: In some patients receiving systemic quinolones, including gatifloxacin, serious and occasionally fatal hypersensitivity reactions have occurred. Some reactions were accompanied by cardiovascular collapse, loss of consciousness, angioedema (including laryngeal, pharyngeal or facial), airway obstruction, dyspnea, urticaria, and itching. Serious acute hypersensitivity reactions may require immediate emergency treatment.

The following side/adverse effects have been selected on the basis of their potential clinical significance (possible signs and symptoms in parentheses where appropriate)—not necessarily inclusive:

Those indicating need for medical attention

Incidence more frequent

Conjunctival irritation; keratitis (eye redness, irritation, or pain)

Incidence less frequent

Chemosis (swelling of the membrane covering the white part of the eye); ***conjunctival hemorrhage*** (bloody eye; redness of eye); ***eye pain; reduced visual acuity*** (decrease in vision)

Those indicating need for medical attention only if they continue or are bothersome

Incidence more frequent

Increased lacrimation (watering of eyes); ***papillary conjunctivitis*** (redness, pain, swelling of eye, eyelid, or inner lining of eyelid; burning, dry or itching eyes; discharge; excessive tearing)

Incidence less frequent

Dry eye; eye discharge; eye irritation (red, sore eyes); ***eyelid edema*** (swelling of eyelids); ***headache; red eye; taste disturbance*** (change in taste; bad unusual or unpleasant (after)taste)

Overdose

For more information on the management of overdose or unintentional ingestion, **contact a poison control center** (see *Poison Control Center Listing*).

Treatment of overdose

There is no known specific antidote to gatifloxacin. Treatment is generally symptomatic and supportive.

Supportive care—

Patients in whom intentional overdose is confirmed or suspected should be referred for psychiatric consultation.

Patient Consultation

As an aid to patient consultation, refer to *Advice for the Patient, Gatifloxacin (Ophthalmic).*

In providing consultation, consider emphasizing the following selected information (» = major clinical significance):

Before using this medication

» Conditions affecting use, especially:
  Sensitivity to gatifloxacin or other quinolones
  Use in children—Safety and effectiveness in infants below the age of one year have not been established.

Proper use of this medication

» Avoiding contamination of the applicator tip with material from the eye, fingers or other surfaces

» Proper dosing
  Missed dose: Taking as soon as possible; not taking if almost time for next scheduled dose; not doubling doses

» Proper storage

Precautions while using this medication

The importance of not wearing contact lenses while signs or symptoms of bacterial conjunctivitis exist

(Discontinuing use of gatifloxacin and contacting physician if rash or allergic reaction occurs)

Side/adverse effects

Signs of potential side effects, especially, chemosis, conjunctival hemorrhage, conjunctival irritation, eye pain, keratitis, reduced visual acuity

General Dosing Information

Gatifloxacin ophthalmic solution is not for injection into the eye, nor should it be introduced directly into the anterior chamber of the eye.

If hypersensitivity develops, therapy with ophthalmic gatifloxacin should be discontinued.

Patients should be advised not be wear contacts if they have signs and symptoms of bacterial conjunctivitis.

As with other anti-infectives, prolonged use may result in overgrowth of non-susceptible organisms including fungi. Should superinfection occur, discontinue use and institute alternative therapy.

Avoid contaminating the applicator tip with material from the eye, fingers or other source.

For treatment of adverse effects
Recommended treatment includes
- Discontinue gatifloxacin treatments if an allergic reaction occurs.
- Patients with serious hypersensitivity reactions should be given emergency medical treatment including administration of oxygen and airway management.

Ophthalmic Dosage Forms

GATIFLOXACIN OPHTHALMIC SOLUTION

Usual adult and adolescent dose
Bacterial conjunctivitis—

Topical, Days 1 and 2—Instill one drop in the affected eye(s) every two hours while awake, up to eight times daily; Days 3 through 7—Instill one drop in the affected eye(s) up to four times daily while awake.

Usual pediatric dose
Bacterial conjunctivitis—

Infants up to 1 year of age: Safety and efficacy have not been established.

Children over 1 year of age: See *Usual adult and adolescent dose.*

Usual geriatric dose
See *Usual adult dose.*

Strength(s) usually available
U.S.—

0.3% (3 mg/mL) (Rx) [*Zymar* (benzalkonium chloride 0.005%; edetate disodium; purified water; sodium chloride; hydrochloric acid and/or; sodium hydroxide)].

Packaging and storage
Store between 15 and 25 °C (59 and 77 °F). Protect from freezing.

Auxiliary labeling
- For the eye.
- Not for injection.

Developed: 11/06/2003

GEFITINIB Systemic†

VA CLASSIFICATION (Primary): AN300

Commonly used brand name(s): *Iressa.*

Note: For a listing of dosage forms and brand names by country availability, see *Dosage Forms* section(s).

†Not commercially available in Canada.

Category
Antineoplastic.

Indications
Note: Bracketed information in the *Indications* section refers to uses that are not included in U.S. product labeling.

Accepted
Carcinoma, lung, non-small cell (treatment)—Gefitinib is indicated as continued monotherapy for the treatment of patients with locally advanced or metastatic non-small cell lung carcinoma after failure of both platinum-based and docetaxel chemotherapies who are or have benefited from gefitinib therapy.

The effectiveness of gefitinib is based on objective response rates, not clinical benefit or increased survival.

Unaccepted
In two large, controlled, randomized trials in first line treatment of non-small cell lung cancer there was no benefit in adding gefitinib to doublet, platinum based chemotherapy. Therefore gefitinib is not indicated for use in this setting.

Carcinoma, lung, non-small cell (initial treatment)—Other treatment options (including another epidermal growth factor receptor with positive survival data) should be used in patients with locally advanced or metastatic non-small cell lung cancer who have received one or two prior chemotherapy regimens and are refractory/intolerant to their most recent regimen.

Pharmacology/Pharmacokinetics

Physicochemical characteristics
Molecular weight—Gefitinib: 446.9.

pKa—Gefitinib has a pKa of 5.4 and 7.2 and therefore ionizes progressively in solution as the pH falls.

Solubility—Gefitinib is sparingly soluble at pH 1, but is practically insoluble above pH 7 the solubility drops sharply between pH 4 and pH 6. In non-aqueous solvents, gefitinib is freely soluble in glacial acetic acid and dimethylsulphoxide, soluble in pyridine, and sparingly soluble tetrahydrofuran, and slightly soluble in methanol, ethanol (99.5%), ethyl acetate, propan-2-ol, and acetonitrile.

Mechanism of action/Effect
The mechanism of the clinical antitumor action of gefitinib is not fully characterized. Gefitinib inhibits the intracellular phosphorylation of numerous tyrosine kinases associated with transmembrane cell surface receptors. This includes the tyrosine kinases associated with the epidermal growth factor receptor (EGFR-TK), which is expressed on the cell surface of many normal cells and cancer cells.

Absorption
Gefitinib is absorbed slowly after oral administration with mean bioavailability of 60%. Bioavailability is not significantly altered by food.

Distribution
Volume of distribution (Vol_D)—steady state: 1400 L following intravenous administration.

Protein binding
High (90%), primarily to serum albumin and alpha$_1$-acid glycoproteins.

Biotransformation
Gefitinib undergoes extensive hepatic metabolism, predominantly by CYP3A. Three sites of biotransformation have been identified: metabolism of the N-propoxymopholine group, demethylation of the methoxy-substituent on the quinazoline, and oxidative defluorination of the halogenated phenyl group.

Five metabolites were identified in human plasma. Only O-desmethyl gefitinib has exposure comparable to gefitinib. Although similar EGFR-TK activity to gefitinib it had only 1/14 of the potency of gefitinib in one of the cell based assays.

Half-life
Elimination—About 48 hours.

Time to peak concentration
Gefitinib is slowly absorbed, with peak plasma levels occurring 3 to 7 hours after administration.

Steady state plasma concentration are achieved within 10 days.

Elimination
Fecal excretion—86%

Renal elimination—Less than 4% of drug and metabolites

Clearance—Gefitinib is cleared primarily by the liver, with total plasma clearance of 595 mL/min following intravenous administration.

Precautions to Consider

Carcinogenicity
Carcinogenicity studies with gefitinib have not been done.

Mutagenicity
Genotoxicity studies of *in vitro* bacterial mutation, mouse lymphoma, and human lymphocyte assays and an *in vivo* rat micronucleus test did not cause genetic damage.

Pregnancy/Reproduction
Pregnancy—Gefitinib crosses the placenta and has been shown to cause adverse effects in the fetus of animals. Therefore, women of child-bearing potential must be advised to avoid becoming pregnant while using gefitinib.

Studies done in rats given oral doses of 5 mg per kg, about 1/5 the recommended human dose on a mg per m^2 basis resulted in a reduction in the number of offspring born alive. This effect was more severe at 20 mg per kg and was accompanied by high neonatal mortality soon after parturition. However a dose of 1 mg per kg caused no adverse effects.

FDA Pregnancy Category D

Breast-feeding
It is not known whether gefitinib is distributed into human breast milk. However, gefitinib and its metabolites are distributed into the milk of rats, at levels 11 to 19 times higher than in blood after oral doses of 5 mg per kg. Because many drugs are distributed into human milk and

because of the potential for serious adverse effects to the nursing infants, gefitinib is not recommended for use while breast feeding.

Pediatrics

Safety and effectiveness of gefitinib in pediatric patients have not been established.

In clinical trials gefitinib alone or with radiation in pediatric patients with primary Central Nervous System (CNS) tumors, cases of CNS hemorrhage and death have been reported.

Geriatrics

Appropriate studies performed to date have not demonstrated geriatrics-specific problems that would limit the usefulness of gefitinib in the elderly.

Pharmacogenetics

In population based data analyses, no relationships were identified between predicted steady state trough concentrations and patient age, body weight, gender, or ethnicity.

Drug interactions and/or related problems

The following drug interactions and/or related problems have been selected on the basis of their potential clinical significance (possible mechanism in parentheses where appropriate)—not necessarily inclusive (» = major clinical significance):

Note: Combinations containing any of the following medications, depending on the amount present, may also interact with this medication.

» CYP3A4 inducers, such as
  Phenytoin, or
  Rifampin
  (increase the metabolism of gefitinib and decrease its plasma concentration; a dose increase of gefitinib should be considered)

» CYP3A4 inhibitors, potent, such as
  Ketoconazole, or
  Itraconazole
  (caution; concomitant administration decreases gefitinib metabolism and increases its plasma concentrations)

» Histamine H_2-receptor antagonists, such as
  Cimetidine, or
  Ranitidine
  (may reduce plasma concentrations of gefitinib, and therefore may reduce efficacy)

» Metoprolol
  (increased by 30% when given in combination with gefitinib)

» Vinorelbine
  (concomitant use with gefitinib may exacerbate the neutropenic effect of vinorelbine)

» Warfarin
  (caution; international normalized ratio [INR] elevations and/or bleeding events have occurred when taken with gefitinib)

Medical considerations/Contraindications

The medical considerations/contraindications included have been selected on the basis of their potential clinical significance (reasons given in parentheses where appropriate)—not necessarily inclusive (» = major clinical significance).

Except under special circumstances, this medication should not be used when the following medical problem exists:

» Hypersensitivity to gefitinib or any of its components

Risk-benefit should be considered when the following medical problems exist:

» Hepatic function impairment
  (gefitinib exposure may be increased)

» Idiopathic pulmonary fibrosis
  (caution; an increased mortality compared to patients without concurrent idiopathic pulmonary fibrosis has been observed in patients whose conditions worsen while receiving gefitinib therapy)

» Renal function impairment, severe
  (gefitinib should be administered with caution, the effects on the pharmacokinetics of gefitinib is not known)

» Caution, in patients who have had previous chemotherapy or radiation therapy because of the possible increased risk of pulmonary toxicity.

Patient monitoring

The following may be especially important in patient monitoring (other tests may be warranted in some patients, depending on condition; » = major clinical significance):

» Liver function testing, such as
  Alkaline phosphatase, and
  Bilirubin, and
  Transaminases
  (periodic testing is advised as asymptomatic increases in liver transaminases may occur; discontinuation of gefitinib should be considered if changes are severe)

» Prothrombin time or INR
  (patients taking concomitant warfarin and gefitinib should be monitored for changes to INR or prothrombin time)

Side/Adverse Effects

Interstitial lung disease (ILD) has been observed in some patients at an incidence of about 1%. Approximately 1/3 of those cases have been fatal. The adverse events have been described as interstitial pneumonia, pneumonitis and alveolitis. ILD occurred more frequently in patients who have received prior radiation therapy or chemotherapy.

Non-clinical studies have indicated that gefitinib has the potential to inhibit the cardiac QT interval.

The following side/adverse effects have been selected on the basis of their potential clinical significance (possible signs and symptoms in parentheses where appropriate)—not necessarily inclusive:

Those indicating the need for medical attention

Incidence less frequent

Amblyopia (blurred vision, change in vision, impaired vision); ***conjunctivitis*** (redness, pain, swelling of eye, eyelid, or inner lining of eyelid; burning, dry or itching eyes; discharge; excessive tearing); ***dyspnea*** (shortness of breath; difficult or labored breathing; tightness in chest, wheezing); ***peripheral edema*** (bloating or swelling of face, arms, hands, lower legs, or feet; rapid weight gain; tingling of hands or feet, unusual weight gain or loss)

Incidence unknown

Aberrant eyelash growth; allergic reactions (fainting or loss of consciousness; fast or irregular breathing; swelling of eyes or eyelids; trouble in breathing, tightness in chest, and/or wheezing; skin rash; itching); ***angioedema*** (large, hive-like swelling on face, eyelids, lips, tongue, throat, hands, legs, feet, sex organs); ***corneal membrane sloughing*** (blurry vision; eye irritation or redness; severe stinging in the eye); ***corneal ulcer*** (eye irritation or redness); ***epidermal necrolysis*** (redness, tenderness, itching, burning, or peeling of skin; red or irritated eyes; sore throat; fever; and chills); ***erythema multiforme*** (blistering, peeling, loosening of skin; chills; cough; diarrhea; fever; itching; joint or muscle pain; red irritated eyes; sore throat; sores, ulcers, or white spots in mouth or on lips; unusual tiredness or weakness); ***eye pain; hemorrhage, including; epistaxis*** (bloody nose); ***hematuria*** (blood in urine); ***interstitial lung disease*** (cough; fever; shortness of breath); ***ocular hemorrhage*** (red or bloodshot eye; change in vision; seeing floating spots before the eyes); ***ocular ischemia*** (changes in vision; eye pain); ***pancreatitis*** (bloating; chills; constipation; darkened urine; fast heartbeat; fever; indigestion; loss of appetite; nausea; pains in stomach, side, or abdomen, possibly radiating to the back; vomiting; yellow eyes or skin); ***urticaria*** (hives or welts; itching; redness of skin; skin rash)

Those indicating need for medical attention only if they continue or are bothersome

Incidence more frequent

Acne (blemishes on the skin, pimples); ***anorexia*** (loss of appetite, weight loss); ***asthenia*** (lack or loss of strength); ***diarrhea; dry skin; nausea; pruritus*** (itching skin); ***rash; vomiting; weight loss***

Incidence less frequent

Mouth ulcer (irritation or soreness of mouth); ***vesiculobullous rash*** (blisters under the skin, large, hard skin blisters)

Overdose

For more information on the management of overdose or unintentional ingestion, **contact a poison control center** (see *Poison Control Center Listing*).

The acute toxicity of gefitinib up to 500 mg in clinical studies has been low.

Daily doses of up to 1000 mg was administered during clinical trials in a limited number of patients. Diarrhea and skin rash were observed at a higher frequency and severity.

Clinical effects of overdose

The following effects have been selected on the basis of their potential clinical significance (possible signs and symptoms in parentheses where appropriate)—not necessarily inclusive:

Diarrhea; skin rash

Treatment of overdose

There is no known specific antidote to gefitinib. Treatment is generally symptomatic and supportive.

Supportive care—
Managing diarrhea appropriately.
Patients in whom intentional overdose is confirmed or suspected should be referred for psychiatric consultation.

Patient Consultation

As an aid to patient consultation, refer to *Advice for the Patient, Gefitinib (Systemic)*.

In providing consultation, consider emphasizing the following selected information (» = major clinical significance):

Before using this medication

» Conditions affecting use, especially:
Hypersensitivity to gefitinib or any of its components
Pregnancy—Not recommended for use during pregnancy. Gefitinib crosses the placenta, and has been shown to cause adverse effects in the fetus of animals. Women of childbearing potential must be advised to avoid becoming pregnant while taking gefitinib.
Breast-feeding—Use is not recommended; although not known if distributed into human breast milk, potential for serious adverse effects in nursing infant exist; gefitinib and its metabolites are distributed into the milk of rats
Other medications, especially CYP3A4 inducers, such as phenytoin or rifampin; CYP3A4 inhibitors such as itraconazole or ketoconazole; histamine H_2-receptor antagonists such as cimetidine or ranitidine; metoprolol, vinorelbine, and warfarin
Other medical problems, especially hepatic function impairment, idiopathic pulmonary fibrosis, prior chemotherapy or radiation therapy, and severe renal impairment

Proper use of this medication

» Proper dosing
Missed dose: Taking as soon as possible; not taking if almost time for next scheduled dose; not doubling doses
» Proper storage

Precautions while using this medication

» Checking with physician if severe or persistent diarrhea, nausea, anorexia occur
» Checking with physician if onset or worsening of shortness of breath, cough or fever
» Checking with physician if eye irritations or any new symptoms occur

Side/adverse effects

Signs of potential side effects, especially allergic reactions, amblyopia, angioedema, conjunctivitis, dyspnea, epidermal necrolysis, erythema multiforme, hemorrhage, including epistaxis, and hematuria; ocular hemorrhage, pancreatitis, peripheral edema, and urticaria.

General Dosing Information

Gefitinib may be taken with or without food.

For patients that have difficulty swallowing solids, the gefitinib tablet can be dissolved without crushing the tablet in a half a glass of non-carbonated drinking water. After drinking, the glass should then be rinsed with another half a glass of water and then drink the contents. The liquid can also be administered through a naso-gastric tube.

Higher doses of gefitinib do not give a better response and cause increased toxicity.

Treatment of adverse effects

Patients with poorly tolerated diarrhea or skin adverse drug reactions may be successfully managed by providing a brief (up to 14 days) therapy interruption followed by reinstatement of the 250 mg daily dose.

In the event of acute onset or worsening of pulmonary symptoms, such as dyspnea, cough or fever, gefitinib therapy should be interrupted and a prompt investigation and treatment of the symptoms should be initiated. If interstitial lung disease is confirmed gefitinib should be discontinued and appropriate treatment given to the patient.

If development of new eye symptoms occur, including an aberrant eyelash, gefitinib therapy should be interrupted and symptoms managed appropriately. After the symptoms have resolved, a decision should be made regarding reinstatement of gefitinib therapy.

Oral Dosage Forms

GEFITINIB TABLETS

Usual adult dose

Carcinoma, lung, non-small cell (treatment)—
Oral, 250 mg daily

Note: For patients receiving a potent CYP3A4 inducer such as rifampicin or phenytoin, a dose increase to 500 mg daily should be considered in the absence of severe drug reaction.

Usual pediatric dose

Safety and efficacy in pediatric patients have not been established.

Usual geriatric dose

See *Usual adult dose.*

Strength(s) usually available

U.S.—
250 mg (Rx) [*Iressa* (croscarmellose; hypromellose; lactose monohydrate; magnesium stearate; microcrystalline cellulose; polyethylene glycol 300; povidone; red ferric oxide; sodium lauryl sulfate; titanium dioxide; yellow ferric oxide)].

Packaging and storage

Store at controlled room temperature 20 to 25 °C (68 to 77°F).

Auxiliary labeling

Cytotoxic agent. Please dispose of properly.

Revised: 07/14/2005
Developed: 12/03/2003

GEMCITABINE Systemic

VA CLASSIFICATION (Primary): AN300

Commonly used brand name(s): *Gemzar*.

Note: For a listing of dosage forms and brand names by country availability, see *Dosage Forms* section(s).

Category

Antineoplastic.

Indications

Note: Bracketed information in the *Indications* section refers to uses that are not included in U.S. product labeling.

Accepted

Carcinoma, breast (treatment)[1]—Gemcitabine in combination with paclitaxel is indicated for the first-line treatment of patients with metastatic breast cancer after failure of prior anthracycline-containing adjuvant chemotherapy, unless anthracyclines are clinically contraindicated.

Carcinoma, pancreatic (treatment)—Gemcitabine is indicated as first-line therapy for locally advanced (nonresectable Stage II or III) or metastatic (Stage IV) adenocarcinoma of the pancreas. It is also indicated as second-line therapy for patients who have previously been treated with fluorouracil. Treatment with gemcitabine is primarily palliative.

Carcinoma, lung, non-small cell—Gemcitabine is indicated in combination with cisplatin as first-line therapy for inoperable, locally advanced (Stage IIIA or IIIB) or metastatic (Stage IV) non-small cell lung carcinoma.

[Carcinoma, biliary tract (treatment)][1] or
[Carcinoma, gallbladder (treatment)][1]—Gemcitabine is indicated for the treatment of locally advanced, unresectable, or metastatic biliary tract (i.e., cholangiocarcinoma, biliary tree carcinoma, bile duct carcinoma) and gallbladder carcinomas.

[Carcinoma, bladder][1]—Gemcitabine is indicated for treatment of metastatic bladder (urothelial) carcinoma, based on response rates (both complete and partial responses) achieved in clinical trials.

[Carcinoma, ovarian, epithelial (treatment)][1]—Gemcitabine is indicated, alone or in combination with other chemotherapeutic agents, as reasonable medical therapy at some point in the management of patients with advanced or relapsed epithelial ovarian carcinoma (Evidence rating: IIID).

[Lymphomas, Hodgkin's (treatment)][1] or
[Lymphomas, non-Hodgkin's (treatment)][1]—Gemcitabine is indicated, alone or in combination with other agents, for the treatment of relapsed Hodgkin's and non-Hodgkin's lymphomas (T-cell and B-cell).

[Tumors, germ cell (treatment)][1]
[Tumors, germ cell, ovarian (treatment)][1]
[Tumors, germ cell, testicular (treatment)][1]—Gemcitabine is indicated for the treatment of relapsed/refractory, progressive, metastatic, or nonseminomatous gonadal (i.e., testicular, ovarian) and extragonadal germ cell tumors.

Acceptance not established

Use of gemcitabine for the treatment of primary breast carcinoma has not been established, due to insufficient efficacy data.

Use of gemcitabine for the treatment of mesotheliomas has not been established. Although case reports state objective and subjective benefit in few patients, most phase II trials of an adequate sample size do not demonstrate an established benefit of gemcitabine therapy.

Use of gemcitabine for the treatment of advanced, metastatic, unresectable, refractory/relapsed sarcomas has not been established, due to insufficient data regarding efficacy and few well-conducted studies.

Use of gemcitabine for the treatment of advanced, metastatic, unresectable, relapsed/refractory, renal cell carcinoma has not been established, due to insufficient date regarding response/efficacy as a single agent and lack of peer-reviewed evidence.

Use of gemcitabine for the treatment of carcinoma of unknown primary site (CUPS) has not been established, due to insufficient data supporting efficacy. The role of gemcitabine in combination regimens has not been defined. Single-agent use needs more support.

[1]Not included in Canadian product labeling.

Pharmacology/Pharmacokinetics

Physicochemical characteristics

Chemical Group—Gemcitabine is a nucleoside (deoxycytidine) analog.

Molecular weight—Gemcitabine hydrochloride: 299.66.

pH—2.7 to 3.3 (after reconstitution).

pKa—3.6.

Solubility—Practically insoluble in ethanol and polar organic solvents; soluble in water.

Mechanism of action/Effect

Gemcitabine is an antimetabolite of the pyrimidine analog type. Gemcitabine is cell cycle–specific for the S phase and for the G_1/S phase boundary of cell division. Activity occurs as a result of intracellular conversion to two active metabolites, gemcitabine diphosphate and gemcitabine triphosphate. Gemcitabine diphosphate inhibits the enzyme responsible for catalyzing synthesis of deoxynucleoside triphosphates required for DNA synthesis, and gemcitabine triphosphate competes with endogenous deoxynucleoside triphosphates for incorporation into DNA. The gemcitabine diphosphate–induced reduction in intracellular concentrations of deoxynucleoside triphosphates results in increased incorporation of gemcitabine triphosphate into DNA and, consequently, in inhibition of DNA synthesis. DNA polymerase epsilon is unable to remove the incorporated gemcitabine triphosphate and repair the DNA strands.

Other actions/effects

Gemcitabine is a potent radiation sensitizer. In *in vitro* studies, it produced significant radiosensitization even in lower-than-cytotoxic concentrations.

Distribution

The volume of distribution is significantly affected by the duration of the gemcitabine infusion and the gender of the patient.

- Short infusion (< 70 minutes)—50 liters per square meter of body surface area (L/m^2), indicating that gemcitabine is not distributed extensively into tissues.
- Long infusion (70 to 285 minutes)—370 L/m^2, indicating slow equilibration within the tissue compartment.

Protein binding

Very low (< 10%).

Biotransformation

Gemcitabine undergoes intracellular metabolism, via nucleoside kinases, to produce two active metabolites (gemcitabine diphosphate and gemcitabine triphosphate) and also undergoes deamination to an inactive uracil metabolite.

Half-life

Gemcitabine—Elimination:

- Short infusions (< 70 minutes)—
  - Females:
    - 29 years of age—49 minutes.
    - 45 years of age—57 minutes.
    - 65 years of age—73 minutes.
    - 79 years of age—94 minutes.
  - Males:
    - 29 years of age—42 minutes.
    - 45 years of age—48 minutes.
    - 65 years of age—61 minutes.
    - 79 years of age—79 minutes.
- Long infusions (70 to 285 minutes)—245 to 638 minutes, depending on age and gender.

Gemcitabine triphosphate metabolite—Terminal (from peripheral blood mononuclear cells): 1.7 to 19.4 hours.

Elimination

Renal—92 to 98% of a single dose of radiolabeled gemcitabine (1000 mg per square meter of body surface area, given over 30 minutes to five patients) was recovered within 1 week, primarily as the inactive uracil metabolite (approximately 89% of the excreted dose) and secondarily as unchanged gemcitabine (less than 10% of the excreted dose).

Clearance is affected by age and gender as follows:

- Females—
  - 29 years of age: 69.4 liters per hour per square meter of body surface area (L/hr/m^2).
  - 45 years of age: 57 L/hr/m^2.
  - 65 years of age: 41.5 L/hr/m^2.
  - 79 years of age: 30.7 L/hr/m^2.
- Males—
  - 29 years of age: 92.2 L/hr/m^2.
  - 45 years of age: 75.7 L/hr/m^2.
  - 65 years of age: 55.1 L/hr/m^2.
  - 79 years of age: 40.7 L/hr/m^2.

Precautions to Consider

Carcinogenicity

Secondary malignancies are potential delayed effects of many antineoplastic agents, although it is not clear whether the effect is related to their mutagenic or immunosuppressive action. The effect of dose and duration of therapy is also unknown, although risk seems to increase with long-term use. The risk of secondary malignancies developing after gemcitabine therapy is not known.

Long-term animal studies to evaluate the carcinogenic potential of gemcitabine have not been done.

Mutagenicity

Gemcitabine was mutagenic in *in vitro* (mouse lymphoma assay) and *in vivo* (mouse micronucleus assay) mammalian test systems. However, it was not mutagenic in the Ames test, *in vivo* sister chromatid exchange, or in *in vitro* (chromosomal aberration assays and unscheduled DNA synthesis) test systems.

Pregnancy/Reproduction

Fertility—Intraperitoneal administration to male mice of 0.5 mg per kg of body weight (mg/kg) per day (0.14% of the recommended human dose on a mg per square meter of body surface area [mg/m^2] basis) resulted in moderate to severe hypospermatogenesis, decreased fertility, and decreased implantations. The hypospermatogenesis was reversible. Gemcitabine did not impair fertility, but caused maternal toxicity in female mice given doses of 1.5 mg/kg per day (0.5% of the recommended human dose on a mg/m^2 basis).

Pregnancy—Studies in humans have not been done.

It is usually recommended that use of antineoplastics, especially combination chemotherapy, be avoided whenever possible, especially during the first trimester. Although information is limited because of the relatively few instances of antineoplastic administration during pregnancy, the mutagenic, teratogenic, and carcinogenic potential of these medications must be considered.

Other potential hazards to the fetus include adverse reactions seen in adults.

In general, use of a contraceptive is recommended during therapy with cytotoxic medications.

Gemcitabine caused fetal malformations (fusion of the pulmonary artery and absence of the gallbladder) in rabbits given 0.1 mg/kg per day (0.17% of the recommended human dose on a mg/m^2 basis). The medication was embryotoxic (causing decreased fetal viability, reduced live litter sizes, and delayed development), and teratogenic (causing cleft palate and incomplete ossification) in mice given 1.5 mg/kg per day (0.5% of the recommended human dose on a mg/m^2 basis). In mice, embryolethality or fetotoxicity occurred with intravenous doses as low as 0.25 mg/kg per day (0.08% of the recommended human dose on a mg/m^2 basis).

FDA Pregnancy Category D.

Breast-feeding

Although very little information is available regarding distribution of antineoplastic agents into breast milk, breast-feeding is not recommended while gemcitabine is being administered, because of the risks to the infant (adverse effects, mutagenicity, carcinogenicity). It is not known whether gemcitabine or its metabolites are distributed into breast milk.

Pediatrics

Appropriate studies on the relationship of age to the effects of gemcitabine have not been performed in the pediatric population. Safety and efficacy have not been established.

The maximum tolerated dose of gemcitabine in pediatric patients with refractory leukemia was shown to be 10 mg/m^2/min for 360 min three times a week during a Phase 1 trial.

A Phase 2 trial in pediatric patients with relapsed acute lymphoblastic leukemia and acute myelogenous leukemia observed adverse reactions similar to those seen in the adult population, including: bone marrow suppression, febrile neutropenia, elevation of serum transaminases, nausea, and rash.

Geriatrics

Appropriate studies performed to date have not demonstrated geriatrics-specific problems that would limit the usefulness of gemcitabine in the elderly. Although some pharmacokinetic parameters are altered in geriatric patients (increased elimination half-life and decreased clearance), no adjustment of the initial dose is recommended for patients older than 65 years of age. However, the risk of hematologic toxicity requiring reduction, delay, or omission of subsequent doses is higher in elderly patients than in younger adults. Specifically, Grade 3 or 4 thrombocytopenia is more likely to occur in elderly men and women and Grade 3 or 4 neutropenia is more likely to occur in elderly women. Nonhematologic toxicities did not occur more frequently in patients older than 65 years of age than in younger adults.

Dental

The bone marrow depressant effects of gemcitabine may result in an increased incidence of microbial infection, delayed healing, and gingival bleeding. Dental work, whenever possible, should be completed prior to initiation of therapy or deferred until blood counts have returned to normal. Patients should be instructed in proper oral hygiene during treatment, including caution in use of regular toothbrushes, dental floss, and toothpicks.

Gemcitabine causes stomatitis, usually mild, in a minority of patients (incidence 11% or lower in various clinical trials).

Drug interactions and/or related problems

The following drug interactions and/or related problems have been selected on the basis of their potential clinical significance (possible mechanism in parentheses where appropriate)—not necessarily inclusive (» = major clinical significance):

Blood dyscrasia-causing medications (see *Appendix II*)
(leukopenic and/or thrombocytopenic effects of gemcitabine may be increased with concurrent or recent therapy if these medications cause the same effects; dosage adjustment of gemcitabine, if necessary, should be based on blood counts)

» Bone marrow depressants, other (see *Appendix II*) or
» Radiation therapy
(additive bone marrow depression may occur; dosage reduction may be required when two or more bone marrow depressants, including radiation, are used concurrently or consecutively)
(gemcitabine is a potent radiosensitizer; depending on the site being irradiated, concurrent use of gemcitabine may cause severe, life-threatening esophagitis or pneumonitis; in one study, gemcitabine with radiation therapy caused severe stomatitis or pharyngeal damage requiring patients to be fed via feeding tube for as long as 10 to 12 months, even when gemcitabine was given in doses as low as 300 mg per square meter of body surface area [25% or less of the usual adult dose])

Cisplatin
(cisplatin may decrease the clearance of gemcitabine)

» Immunosuppressants, other, such as:
Azathioprine
Chlorambucil
Corticosteroids, glucocorticoid
Cyclophosphamide
Cyclosporine
Mercaptopurine
Muromonab CD-3
Tacrolimus
(concurrent use with gemcitabine may increase the risk of infection)

Paclitaxel
(no direct interaction of these medications has been observed; however, the potential for a pharmacokinetic interaction may exist)

Vaccines, killed virus
(because normal defense mechanisms may be suppressed by gemcitabine therapy, the patient's antibody response to the vaccine may be decreased. The interval between discontinuation of medications that cause immunosuppression and restoration of the patient's ability to respond to the vaccine depends on the intensity and type of immunosuppression-causing medication used, the underlying disease, and other factors; estimates vary from 3 months to 1 year)

» Vaccines, live virus
(because normal defense mechanisms may be suppressed by gemcitabine therapy, concurrent use with a live virus vaccine may potentiate the replication of the vaccine virus, may increase the side/adverse effects of the vaccine virus, and/or may decrease the patient's antibody response to the vaccine; immunization of these patients should be undertaken only with extreme caution, after careful review of the patient's hematologic status, and only with the knowledge and consent of the physician managing the gemcitabine therapy. The interval between discontinuation of medications that cause immunosuppression and restoration of the patient's ability to respond to the vaccine depends on the intensity and type of immunosuppression-causing medication used, the underlying disease, and other factors; estimates vary from 3 months to 1 year. In addition, immunization with oral poliovirus vaccine should be postponed in persons in close contact with the patient, especially family members)

Laboratory value alterations

The following have been selected on the basis of their potential clinical significance (possible effect in parentheses where appropriate)—not necessarily inclusive (» = major clinical significance).

With physiology/laboratory test values
Alanine aminotransferase (ALT [SGPT]) and
Alkaline phosphatase and
Aspartate aminotransferase (AST [SGOT]) and
Bilirubin concentrations, serum
(values may be increased; in clinical trials, Grade 3 or 4 increases in ALT, alkaline phosphatase, AST, and bilirubin occurred in 10%, 9%, 8%, and 3% of all patients and in 11%, 20%, 17%, and 8% of pancreatic cancer patients, respectively. However, continuation of gemcitabine therapy despite these elevations produced no evidence of increasing hepatotoxicity)

Blood urea nitrogen (BUN) and
Creatinine, serum
(concentrations may be increased)

» Hemoglobin/hematocrit and
» Leukocyte count and
» Platelet count
(may be decreased)

Medical considerations/Contraindications

The medical considerations/contraindications included have been selected on the basis of their potential clinical significance (reasons given in parentheses where appropriate)—not necessarily inclusive (» = major clinical significance).

Risk-benefit should be considered when the following medical problems exist:

» Bone marrow depression
(will be exacerbated; reduction, delay, or omission of a gemcitabine dose may be necessary)

» Chickenpox, existing or recent (including recent exposure) or
» Herpes zoster
(risk of severe generalized disease)

Hepatic function impairment, severe or
Renal function impairment
(caution is recommended; gemcitabine has not been studied in patients with these medical problems)
(caution and careful monitoring of patients with renal function impairment are also recommended because hemolytic-uremic syndrome has been reported in a few patients during or immediately following gemcitabine therapy)

» Hypersensitivity to gemcitabine

» Infection
(gemcitabine may decrease the patient's ability to fight an infection)

» Caution should be used also in patients who have had previous cytotoxic chemotherapy or radiation therapy

Patient monitoring

The following may be especially important in patient monitoring (other tests may be warranted in some patients, depending on condition; » = major clinical significance):

Alanine aminotransferase (ALT [SGPT]) and
Alkaline phosphatase and
Aspartate aminotransferase (AST [SGOT]) and
Bilirubin, serum and
Blood urea nitrogen (BUN) and
Creatinine concentrations, serum
(determinations recommended prior to initiation of gemcitabine therapy and at appropriate intervals during therapy)

» Hemoglobin concentration and
» Leukocyte count, total and, if appropriate, differential and
» Platelet count
(determinations recommended prior to each course of gemcitabine therapy; reduction, delay, or omission of a dose may be required, depending on cell counts)

Side/Adverse Effects

Note: Many "side effects" of antineoplastic therapy are unavoidable and represent the medication's pharmacologic action. Some of these (for example, leukopenia and thrombocytopenia) are actually used as parameters to aid in individual dosage titration.

The following side/adverse effects have been selected on the basis of their potential clinical significance (possible signs and symptoms in parentheses where appropriate)—not necessarily inclusive:

Those indicating need for medical attention

Incidence more frequent

Anemia (unusual tiredness or weakness); ***dyspnea*** (shortness of breath)—may be due to underlying disease; ***edema*** (swelling of fingers, feet, or lower legs); ***fever***—may occur in the absence of infection, usually in conjunction with other flu-like symptoms; ***hematuria*** (blood in urine); ***leukopenia or neutropenia***—usually asymptomatic; ***proteinuria*** (cloudy urine); ***skin rash, with or without itching; thrombocytopenia*** (unusual bleeding or bruising; black, tarry stools; blood in urine or stools; pinpoint red spots on skin)—usually asymptomatic; symptoms occur less frequently

Note: Bone marrow suppression (*anemia*, *leukopenia*, and *thrombocytopenia*) is the dose-limiting adverse effect.

Edema is usually peripheral, but rarely may become generalized.

Typically, gemcitabine-induced *skin rashes* are mild to moderate in severity and consist of macular or finely granular maculopapular eruptions on the trunk and extremities.

Incidence less frequent

Bronchospasm (shortness of breath, troubled breathing, tightness in chest, and/or wheezing); ***cardiovascular effects, including arrhythmia*** (fast or irregular heartbeat); ***cerebrovascular accident*** (headache, sudden and severe; slurred speech or inability to speak; weakness in arm and/or leg on one side of the body, sudden and severe); ***hypertension*** (high blood pressure); ***or myocardial infarction*** (pain in chest, arm, or back; pressure or squeezing in chest); ***febrile neutropenia or other infection*** (fever or chills; cough or hoarseness; lower back or side pain; painful or difficult urination); ***hemorrhage***

Note: In clinical trials, *cardiovascular effects* occurred mostly in patients with a prior history of cardiovascular disease, and *hemorrhage* occurred mostly in patients with pancreatic carcinoma.

Severe infections associated with *leukopenia* or *neutropenia* occurred in approximately 1% of patients in clinical studies.

Incidence rare

Anaphylactoid reaction (change in facial skin color; shortness of breath, troubled breathing, tightness in chest, and/or wheezing; skin rash, hives, and/or itching; swelling or puffiness of the face, especially the eyelids or area around the eyes); ***heart failure*** (coughing; noisy, rattling, or troubled breathing); ***hemolytic-uremic syndrome*** (black, tarry stools; blood in urine or stools; fever; increased or decreased urination; pinpoint red spots on skin; swelling of face, fingers, feet, or lower legs; unusual bleeding or bruising; unusual tiredness or weakness; yellow eyes or skin); ***lung toxicity, parenchymal, or pneumonitis*** (coughing; shortness of breath); ***pulmonary edema*** (coughing; noisy, rattling, or troubled breathing)

Note: In clinical trials, *hemolytic-uremic syndrome* occurred in 6 of 2429 patients. Four cases occurred during gemcitabine treatment and two shortly after treatment had ended. This complication may result in irreversible renal failure requiring dialysis.

Heart failure and *pulmonary edema* have been reported in patients being treated for lung carcinoma.

Those indicating need for medical attention only if they continue or are bothersome

Incidence more frequent

Constipation; diarrhea; flu-like syndrome (chills; cough; fever; general feeling of illness; headache; loss of appetite; muscle pain; runny nose; sweating; trouble in sleeping; weakness); ***nausea and vomiting***

Note: Weakness, while often occurring as part of a *flu-like syndrome*, may also occur as an isolated symptom.

Nausea and vomiting are usually mild to moderate in severity, but may be severe in up to 15% of patients.

Incidence less frequent

Irritation, pain, or redness at injection site—if extravasation occurs; ***paresthesia*** (numbness or tingling of hands or feet); ***somnolence*** (drowsiness, severe); ***stomatitis*** (sores, ulcers, or white spots on lips and in mouth)

Note: Gemcitabine is not a vesicant. Extravasation has not caused injection site necrosis.

Paresthesia is usually mild; however, severe paresthesia may occur rarely.

Those not indicating need for medical attention

Incidence more frequent

Alopecia (loss of hair)—usually minimal

Note: Complete hair loss, which was reversible after discontinuation of treatment, occurred in less than 0.5% of patients in clinical trials.

Overdose

For more information on the management of overdose, **contact a Poison Control Center** (see *Poison Control Center Listing*).

Clinical effects of overdose

The following effects have been selected on the basis of their potential clinical significance (possible signs and symptoms in parentheses where appropriate)—not necessarily inclusive:

Acute and chronic

Bone marrow suppression, including anemia (unusual tiredness or weakness); ***leukopenia or neutropenia, possibly with infection*** (chills; cough or hoarseness; lower back or side pain; painful or difficult urination); ***and thrombocytopenia*** (unusual bleeding or bruising; black, tarry stools; blood in urine or stools; pinpoint red spots on skin); ***paresthesia*** (numbness or tingling of hands or feet); ***skin rash, severe***

Treatment of overdose

There is no specific antidote to gemcitabine.

The patient's blood count should be monitored and supportive therapy given, as needed. Severe bone marrow depression may require transfusion of needed blood components. Patients who develop leukopenia should be observed carefully for signs of infection. Antibiotic support may be required. In neutropenic patients who develop fever, broad-spectrum antibiotic coverage should be initiated empirically, pending bacterial cultures and appropriate diagnostic tests.

Patient Consultation

As an aid to patient consultation, refer to *Advice for the Patient, Gemcitabine (Systemic)*.

In providing consultation, consider emphasizing the following selected information (» = major clinical significance):

Before using this medication

» Conditions affecting use, especially:
Hypersensitivity to gemcitabine
Pregnancy—Use not recommended because of mutagenic, teratogenic, embryotoxic, and fetotoxic potential; advisability of using contraception; telling physician immediately if pregnancy is suspected
Breast-feeding—Not recommended because of risk of serious adverse effects
Use in the elderly—Seriously low blood counts are more likely to occur in older patients
Other medications, especially other bone marrow depressants, other immunosuppressants, or other cytotoxic medication or radiation therapy
Other medical problems, especially chickenpox or recent exposure, herpes zoster, infection, or previous cytotoxic medication or radiation therapy

Proper use of this medication

Frequency of flu-like syndrome or nausea and vomiting; importance of continuing medication despite stomach upset or otherwise feeling ill

» Proper dosing

Precautions while using this medication

» Importance of close monitoring by the physician; periodic blood tests required to monitor blood counts

» Avoiding immunizations unless approved by physician; other persons in patient's household should avoid immunizations with oral poliovirus vaccine; avoiding persons who have taken oral poliovirus vaccine or wearing a protective mask that covers nose and mouth

» Checking with physician immediately if dyspnea develops or worsens during treatment

Caution if bone marrow depression occurs:

» Avoiding exposure to persons with bacterial infections, especially during periods of low blood counts; checking with physician immediately if fever or chills, cough or hoarseness, lower back or side pain, or painful or difficult urination occur

» Checking with physician immediately if unusual bleeding or bruising; black, tarry stools; blood in urine or stools; or pinpoint red spots on skin occur

Caution in use of regular toothbrush, dental floss, or toothpick; physician, dentist, or nurse may suggest alternatives; checking with physician before having dental work done

Not touching eyes or inside of nose unless hands are washed immediately before

Using caution to avoid accidental cuts with use of sharp objects such as safety razor or fingernail or toenail cutters

Avoiding contact sports or other situations where bruising or injury could occur

Side/adverse effects

May cause adverse effects such as blood problems; importance of discussing possible effects with physician

Signs of potential side effects, especially anemia; dyspnea; edema; fever; hematuria; proteinuria; skin rash; thrombocytopenia; bronchospasm; cardiovascular effects; febrile neutropenia or other infection; hemorrhage; anaphylactoid reaction; hemolytic-uremic syndrome; and lung toxicity or pneumonitis

Physician or nurse can help in dealing with side effects

Possibility that some adverse effects may occur after treatment has ended; notifying physician if symptoms of serious adverse effects noted

Possibility of hair loss; normal hair growth should return after treatment has ended

General Dosing Information

Patients receiving gemcitabine should be under the supervision of a physician experienced in cancer chemotherapy. Gemcitabine may be administered on an outpatient basis.

Gemcitabine is to be administered only by intravenous infusion.

Adverse effects associated with gemcitabine therapy may occur more frequently and be more severe if gemcitabine is administered more frequently than once weekly or infused over a time period longer than 60 minutes.

If gemcitabine-induced pneumonitis is confirmed or suspected, treatment should be discontinued permanently.

Special precautions are recommended in patients who develop thrombocytopenia as a result of administration of gemcitabine. These may include extreme care in performing invasive procedures; regular inspection of intravenous sites, skin (including perirectal area), and mucous membrane surfaces for signs of bleeding or bruising; limiting frequency of venipuncture and avoiding intramuscular injections; testing urine, emesis, stool, and secretions for occult blood; care in use of regular toothbrushes, dental floss, toothpicks, safety razors, and fingernail and toenail cutters; avoiding constipation; and using caution to prevent falls and other injuries. Such patients should avoid alcohol and aspirin intake because of the risk of gastrointestinal bleeding. Platelet transfusions may be required.

Patients who develop leukopenia should be observed carefully for signs of infection. Antibiotic support may be required. In neutropenic patients who develop fever, broad-spectrum antibiotic coverage should be initiated empirically, pending bacterial cultures and appropriate diagnostic tests.

Safety considerations for handling this medication

There is limited but increasing evidence and concern that personnel involved in preparation and administration of parenteral antineoplastics may be at some risk because of the potential mutagenicity, teratogenicity, and/or carcinogenicity of these agents, although the actual risk is unknown. USP advisory panels recommend cautious handling both in preparation and disposal of antineoplastic agents. Precautions that have been suggested include:

- Use of a biological containment cabinet during reconstitution and dilution of parenteral medications and wearing of disposable surgical gloves and masks.
- Use of proper technique to prevent contamination of the medication, work area, and operator during transfer between containers (including proper training of personnel in this technique).
- Cautious and proper disposal of needles, syringes, vials, ampuls, and unused medication.

A number of medical centers have developed detailed guidelines for handling of antineoplastic agents.

Direct contact of skin or mucosa with gemcitabine requires immediate washing with soap and water or thoroughly flushing with water, respectively.

Parenteral Dosage Forms

Note: Bracketed uses in the *Dosage Forms* section refer to categories of use and/or indications that are not included in U.S. product labeling.

GEMCITABINE FOR INJECTION

Usual adult dose

Carcinoma, breast—

Intravenous infusion (over thirty minutes), 1250 mg per square meter of body surface area on Days 1 and 8 of each 21-day cycle. Paclitaxel should be administered at 175 mg per square meter of body surface area on Day 1 as a 3-hour intravenous infusion before gemcitabine administration.

Dose Modification for Hematological Toxicity—Dosage adjustments are based on granulocyte and platelet counts taken on Day 8 of therapy. Gemcitabine dosage should be modified according to the following guidelines if marrow suppression is detected.

Day 8 Dosage Reduction Guidelines for Gemcitabine in Combination with Paclitaxel

Absolute granulocyte count (x 10^6 per L)		Platelet count (x 10^6 per L)	Percent of full dose
≥ 1200	and	> 75,000	100
1000 to 1199	or	50,000 to 75,000	75
700 to 999	and	≥ 50,000	50
< 700	or	< 50,000	Hold dose

Dose Modification for Severe (Grade 3 or 4) Non-Hematological Toxicity—Gemcitabine should be held or decreased by 50% depending on the judgment of the treating physician for severe (Grade 3 or 4) non-hematological toxicity, except alopecia and nausea/vomiting. For paclitaxel dosage adjustment, see manufacturer's prescribing information.

Carcinoma, pancreatic—

Intravenous infusion (over thirty minutes), 1000 mg per square meter of body surface area, once a week for up to seven weeks (depending on toxicity experienced by the patient), followed by a one-week rest. Each subsequent cycle of therapy consists of administering the medication once a week for three weeks followed by a one-week rest.

Carcinoma, lung, non-small cell—

Intravenous infusion (over thirty minutes), 1000 mg per square meter of body surface area per day on days one, eight, and fifteen of a regimen that is repeated every twenty-eight days or

Intravenous infusion (over thirty minutes), 1250 mg per square meter of body surface area per day on days one and eight of a regimen that is repeated every twenty-one days.

Note: Gemcitabine is given in combination with cisplatin 100 mg per square meter of body surface area, administered intravenously on day one of either the twenty-one- or twenty-eight-day regimen, after infusion of gemcitabine.

[Carcinoma, bladder][1]—

Intravenous infusion (over thirty minutes), 1000 to 1200 mg per square meter of body surface area, once a week for three weeks, followed by a one-week rest.

Note: In the treatment of [breast carcinoma][1] doses of 600 (with cisplatin) or 800 to 1250 mg per square meter of body surface area, by intravenous infusion, once a week for two or three weeks, followed by a one-week rest have been used. In the treatment of [epithelial ovarian carcinoma][1] doses of 800 to 1250 mg per square meter of body surface area, once a week, for two or three weeks, followed by a one- to two-week rest have been used.

Note: The development of neutropenia and thrombocytopenia may require an adjustment of gemcitabine dosage. If the absolute granulocyte and platelet counts measured prior to each dose are—500 to 999 × 10^6 cells per liter and 50,000 to 99,000 × 10^6 cells per liter, respectively: The dosage of gemcitabine should be decreased to 75% of the full dose. However, some oncologists recommend that, because treatment for pancreatic carcinoma and lung carcinoma is primarily palliative, gemcitabine should be withheld until cell counts recover, then resumed at the lower dose level.

Less than 500 × 10^6 cells per liter and 50,000 × 10^6 cells per liter, respectively: Gemcitabine should be withheld until cell counts recover.

If one complete cycle of therapy (seven weeks or three weeks) at the recommended initial dose is well tolerated (i.e., the granulocyte count nadir remains higher than 1500 × 10^6 cells per liter, the platelet count nadir exceeds 100,000 × 10^6 cells per liter, and nonhematologic toxicities are no more severe than Grade 1), the dose of gemcitabine for the next cycle may be increased by 25% (e.g., from 1000 to 1250 mg per square meter of body surface area). If the medication remains well tolerated during a complete cycle at this higher dose (i.e., toxicities remain within the specified parameters), the dose may be increased a second time (e.g., from 1250 to 1500 mg per square meter of body surface area).

[Carcinoma, biliary tract][1] or
[Carcinoma, gallbladder][1] or
[Tumors, germ cell][1] or
[Tumors, germ cell, ovarian][1] or
[Tumors, germ cell, testicular][1]—
Because several doses and regimens using gemcitabine are showing activity, no individual dose/regimen is listed here. Consult medical literature and/or experts in the field of oncology for information on dosage.

[Lymphomas, Hodgkin's][1] or
[Lymphomas, non-Hodgkin's][1]—
Patients have benefited from intravenous doses of 1000 to 1250 mg/m^2 (up to 1500 mg/m^2 in some patients), by 30-minute infusion, on days 1, 8, and 15 of a 28-day treatment cycle, for up to 9 treatment cycles.

Usual pediatric dose
Safety and efficacy have not been established.

Usual geriatric dose
See *Usual adult dose.*

Strength(s) usually available
U.S.—
200 mg (single-dose vial) (Rx) [*Gemzar* (mannitol 200 mg; sodium acetate 12.5 mg)].
1 gram (single-dose vial) (Rx) [*Gemzar* (mannitol 1 gram; sodium acetate 62.5 mg)].

Canada—
200 mg (single-dose vial) (Rx) [*Gemzar* (mannitol 200 mg; sodium acetate 12.5 mg)].
1 gram (single-dose vial) (Rx) [*Gemzar* (mannitol 1 gram; sodium acetate 62.5 mg)].

Packaging and storage
Store between 20 and 25 °C (68 and 77 °F), unless otherwise specified by manufacturer.

Preparation of dosage form
Gemcitabine for injection is reconstituted for intravenous use by adding 5 or 25 mL of 0.9% sodium chloride injection (without preservative) to the 200-mg or 1-gram vial, respectively, producing a clear, colorless to light straw-colored solution containing 38 mg of gemcitabine per mL. Incomplete dissolution may occur if gemcitabine is reconstituted to a concentration greater than 40 mg per mL. The resulting solution may be further diluted with 0.9% sodium chloride injection, if necessary, to a concentration as low as 0.1 mg per mL.

Stability
After reconstitution, gemcitabine injections are stable for 24 hours at controlled room temperature (20 to 25 °C [68 to 77 °F]).

Unused portions of gemcitabine injection should be discarded.

Reconstituted gemcitabine should not be refrigerated because of the possibility of crystal formation.

Auxiliary labeling
- Do not refrigerate.

[1]Not included in Canadian product labeling.

Selected Bibliography

Gebbia V, Giuliani F, Verderame F, et al. Treatment of inoperable and/or metastatic biliary tree carcinomas with single-agent gemcitabine or in combination with levofolinic acid and infusional fluorouracil: results of a multicenter phase II study. J Clin Oncol. 2001; 19(20): 4089-91.

Landonio G, Sartore-Bianchi A, Giannetta L, et al. Controversies in the management of brain metastases: the role of chemotherapy. Forum (Genova) 2001; 11(1): 59-74.

Revised: 09/14/2005
Developed: 08/21/1997

GEMFIBROZIL Systemic

VA CLASSIFICATION (Primary): CV359

Commonly used brand name(s): *Apo-Gemfibrozil; Gen-Fibro; Lopid; Novo-Gemfibrozil; Nu-Gemfibrozil.*

Note: For a listing of dosage forms and brand names by country availability, see *Dosage Forms* section(s).

Category
Antihyperlipidemic.

Indications

Accepted
Hyperlipidemia (treatment)—Gemfibrozil is indicated in the treatment of hyperlipidemia and to reduce the risk of coronary heart disease *only* in those patients with type IIb hyperlipidemia without history of or symptoms of existing coronary heart disease, who have not responded to diet, exercise, weight loss, or other pharmacologic therapy (bile acid sequestrants and niacin) alone *and* who have the triad of low high density lipoprotein (HDL) cholesterol levels, elevated low density lipoprotein (LDL) cholesterol levels, and elevated triglycerides.

Gemfibrozil is also recommended for use in patients with severe primary hyperlipidemia (types IV and V hyperlipidemia) and a significant risk of coronary artery disease, abdominal pain typical of pancreatitis, or pancreatitis, who have not responded to diet or other measures alone. Its use is limited in type III hyperlipidemia because of its limited effect on cholesterol concentrations. It is not useful in the treatment of type I hyperlipidemia.

Gemfibrozil is not indicated for treatment of patients with type IIa hyperlipidemia or patients with low HDL cholesterol as their only lipid abnormality because the potential benefits do not outweigh the risks.

Caution and close observation are recommended in patients with high triglyceride concentrations, since in some of these patients treatment with gemfibrozil is associated with significant increases in low density lipoprotein (LDL)-cholesterol concentrations.

For additional information on initial therapeutic guidelines related to the treatment of hyperlipidemia, see *Appendix III.*

Gemfibrozil is not recommended for community-wide prevention of ischemic heart disease.

Studies have suggested that control of elevated cholesterol and triglycerides may not lessen the danger of cardiovascular disease and mortality, although incidence of nonfatal myocardial infarctions may be decreased.

Pharmacology/Pharmacokinetics

Physicochemical characteristics
Molecular weight—250.34.

Mechanism of action/Effect
Gemfibrozil reduces plasma triglyceride (very low-density lipoprotein [VLDL]) concentrations and increases high-density lipoprotein (HDL) concentrations. Although gemfibrozil may slightly reduce total and low-density lipoprotein (LDL) cholesterol concentrations, use of gemfibrozil in patients with elevated triglycerides associated with type IV hyperlipidemia often results in significant increases in LDL; LDL concentrations are not significantly affected by gemfibrozil in patients with Type IIb hyperlipidemia (although HDL is significantly increased). The mechanism of this action is not completely understood but may involve inhibition of peripheral lipolysis; reduced hepatic extraction of free fatty acids, which reduces hepatic triglyceride production; inhibition of synthesis and increased clearance of VLDL carrier, apolipoprotein B, which also reduces VLDL production; and, according to animal studies, reduced incorporation of long-chain fatty acids into newly formed triglycerides, accelerated turnover and removal of cholesterol from the liver (stimulates incorporation of cholesterol precursors into liver sterols), and increased excretion of cholesterol in the feces.

Absorption
Well absorbed from gastrointestinal tract.

Biotransformation
Hepatic.

Half-life
Single dose—1.5 hours.
Multiple doses—1.3 hours.

Onset of action
Reduction of plasma VLDL concentrations—2 to 5 days.

Time to peak concentration
1 to 2 hours.

Time to peak effect
Reduction of plasma VLDL concentrations—4 weeks (major effect; further decreases occur over several months).

Elimination
Renal (70%; largely unchanged)/fecal (6%).

Precautions to Consider

Carcinogenicity/Tumorigenicity
During long term follow-up of patients in the Helsinki Heart Study, there was a trend toward an increased incidence of basal cell carcinomas and deaths attributed to cancer in the group of patients originally randomized to gemfibrozil. However, these data did not reach statistical significance.

Long-term studies in male rats have shown gemfibrozil to have a tumorigenic effect. Studies in rats given gemfibrozil for prolonged periods found an increased incidence of benign and malignant hepatic tumors in male and female rats, as well as benign testicular (Leydig cell) tumors in male rats, at doses of 1 and 10 times the human dose.

Pregnancy/Reproduction
Fertility—Studies in male rats given gemfibrozil at doses 0.6 to 2 times the human dose (based on surface area) for 10 weeks revealed a dose-related decrease in fertility.

Pregnancy—Studies in humans have not been done.

Studies in female rats given gemfibrozil at 0.6 to 2 times the human dose (based on surface area) before and throughout gestation resulted in a dose-related decrease in conception rate and an increase in skeletal variations, including anophthalmia. At the high dose level an increase in stillbirths and reduction in pup weight during lactation were observed. In addition, similar doses given to female rats from gestation day 15 through weaning resulted in decreased birth weights and pup growth suppression during lactation.

Gemfibrozil, given at doses 1 to 3 times the human dose (based on surface area) to female rabbits during organogenesis, caused decreased litter sizes and, at the high dose, an increased incidence of parietal bone variations.

FDA Pregnancy Category C.

Breast-feeding
It is not known whether gemfibrozil is excreted in breast milk. Problems in humans have not been documented; however, any decision regarding breast-feeding during therapy should take into account that gemfibrozil has a tumorigenic effect in rats.

Pediatrics
Appropriate studies on the relationship of age to the effects of gemfibrozil have not been performed in the pediatric population. However, use in children under 2 years of age is not recommended since cholesterol is required for normal development.

Geriatrics
No information is available on the relationship of age to the effects of gemfibrozil in geriatric patients. However, elderly patients are more likely to have age-related renal function impairment, which may require reduction of dosage in patients receiving gemfibrozil.

Drug interactions and/or related problems
The following drug interactions and/or related problems have been selected on the basis of their potential clinical significance (possible mechanism in parentheses where appropriate)—not necessarily inclusive (» = major clinical significance):

» Anticoagulants, coumarin- or indandione-derivative
(concurrent use with gemfibrozil may significantly increase the anticoagulant effect of these medications; adjustment of anticoagulant dosage based on frequent prothrombin-time determinations is recommended)

Chenodiol or
Ursodiol
(effect may be decreased when chenodiol or ursodiol is used concurrently with gemfibrozil, which tends to increase cholesterol saturation of bile)

» Lovastatin
(concurrent use with gemfibrozil may be associated with an increased risk of rhabdomyolysis, significant increases in creatine kinase [CK] concentrations, and myoglobinuria that leads to acute renal failure; may be seen as early as 3 weeks or as late as several months after initiation of combined therapy; monitoring of CK has not been shown to prevent severe myopathy or renal damage)

Laboratory value alterations
The following have been selected on the basis of their potential clinical significance (possible effect in parentheses where appropriate)—not necessarily inclusive (» = major clinical significance).

With physiology/laboratory test values
Alanine aminotransferase (ALT [SGPT]), serum and
Alkaline phosphatase, serum and
Aspartate aminotransferase (AST [SGOT]), serum and
Bilirubin, serum and
Creatine kinase (CK), plasma and
Lactate dehydrogenase (LDH), serum
(concentrations may be increased, indicating liver function abnormalities)

Hematocrit and
Hemoglobin concentrations and
Leukocyte counts
(may be mildly decreased, but usually stabilize with continued administration)

Potassium
(serum concentrations may be decreased)

Medical considerations/Contraindications
The medical considerations/contraindications included have been selected on the basis of their potential clinical significance (reasons given in parentheses where appropriate)—not necessarily inclusive (» = major clinical significance).

Except under special circumstances, this medication should not be used when the following medical problem exists:

» Primary biliary cirrhosis
(use of gemfibrozil may further raise the cholesterol)

Risk-benefit should be considered when the following medical problems exist:

Gallbladder disease or
Gallstones
(increased risk of biliary complications, including possible formation of gallstones)

» Hepatic function impairment
(reduced biotransformation; reduced dosage is recommended)

» Renal function impairment, severe
(reduced clearance leads to increased incidence of side effects; reduced dosage is recommended)
(gemfibrozil may worsen pre-existing renal insufficiency)

Sensitivity to gemfibrozil

Patient monitoring
The following may be especially important in patient monitoring (other tests may be warranted in some patients, depending on condition; » = major clinical significance):

Blood counts, complete and
Cholesterol, serum and
Liver function tests and
Triglycerides, serum
(determinations recommended prior to initiation of therapy and at periodic intervals during therapy)

Side/Adverse Effects
Note: Because of the chemical, pharmacologic, and clinical similarity of gemfibrozil to clofibrate, the possibility of similar long-term effects should be kept in mind. Studies with clofibrate have associated long-term use of the medication with an increased incidence of deaths from noncardiovascular causes and have also found a greatly increased incidence of cholelithiasis and cholecystitis requiring surgery in clofibrate users (see *Clofibrate [Systemic]).* In addition, studies have suggested that control of elevated cholesterol and triglycerides may not lessen the danger of cardiovascular disease and mortality, although incidence of nonfatal myocardial infarctions may be decreased.

Subcapsular bilateral cataracts and unilateral cataracts have been reported in 10% and 6.3%, respectively, of male rats given 10 times the human dose.

The following side/adverse effects have been selected on the basis of their potential clinical significance (possible signs and symptoms in parentheses where appropriate)—not necessarily inclusive:

Those indicating need for immediate medical attention
Incidence rare

Anemia or leukopenia (cough or hoarseness; fever or chills; lower back or side pain; painful or difficult urination); ***gallstones*** (severe stomach pain with nausea and vomiting); ***myositis*** (muscle pain, unusual tiredness or weakness)

Note: Gemfibrozil may increase cholesterol secretion into the bile.

Those indicating need for medical attention only if they continue or are bothersome

Incidence more frequent

Stomach pain, gas, or heartburn

Incidence less frequent

Diarrhea; nausea or vomiting; skin rash; unusual tiredness

Patient Consultation

As an aid to patient consultation, refer to *Advice for the Patient, Gemfibrozil (Systemic)*.

In providing consultation, consider emphasizing the following selected information (» = major clinical significance):

Before using this medication

Potential serious toxicity because of similarity to clofibrate

» Diet as preferred therapy

» Conditions affecting use, especially:

Sensitivity to gemfibrozil

Pregnancy—High doses in animals cause birth defects and an increase in fetal deaths

Breast-feeding—High doses associated with increased incidence of tumors in rats; consider when deciding whether to breast-feed

Use in children—Not recommended in children under 2 years of age since cholesterol is required for normal development

Other medications, especially lovastatin or oral anticoagulants

Other medical problems, especially primary biliary cirrhosis, hepatic function impairment, or severe renal function impairment

Proper use of this medication

» Importance of not taking more or less medication than the amount prescribed

Taking 30 minutes before morning and evening meal

» Compliance with prescribed diet

» Proper dosing

Missed dose: Taking as soon as possible; not taking if almost time for next dose; not doubling doses

» Proper storage

Precautions while using this medication

» Importance of close monitoring by physician

» Checking with physician before discontinuing medication; blood lipid concentrations may increase significantly

Side/adverse effects

Signs of potential side effects, especially gallstones, leukopenia, anemia, and myositis

General Dosing Information

If response is inadequate after 3 months of treatment, gemfibrozil therapy should be withdrawn.

When gemfibrozil is discontinued, an appropriate hypolipidemic diet and monitoring of serum lipids are recommended until the patient stabilizes, since a rise in serum triglyceride and cholesterol concentrations to the original base may occur.

If results of hepatic function tests rise significantly or show significant abnormalities, it is recommended that gemfibrozil therapy be withdrawn and not resumed; laboratory abnormalities are usually reversible.

If gallstones are found, gemfibrozil therapy should be withdrawn.

If patients receiving gemfibrozil experience muscle pain or weakness, evaluation for myositis (including serum CK determinations) is recommended. It is recommended that gemfibrozil be withdrawn if myositis is suspected or diagnosed.

Diet/Nutrition

Gemfibrozil should be taken 30 minutes before the morning and evening meals.

Oral Dosage Forms

GEMFIBROZIL CAPSULES USP

Usual adult dose

Antihyperlipidemic—

Oral, 1.2 grams a day in two divided doses thirty minutes before the morning and evening meals.

Usual pediatric dose

Dosage has not been established.

Strength(s) usually available

U.S.—

Not commercially available.

Canada—

300 mg (Rx) [*Lopid; Apo-Gemfibrozil; Gen-Fibro; Nu-Gemfibrozil;* GENERIC].

Packaging and storage

Store below 30 °C (86 °F), unless otherwise specified by manufacturer. Store in a tight container.

GEMFIBROZIL TABLETS

Usual adult dose

Antihyperlipidemic—

Oral, 1.2 grams a day in two divided doses thirty minutes before the morning and evening meals.

Usual pediatric dose

Dosage has not been established.

Strength(s) usually available

U.S.—

600 mg (Rx) [*Lopid* (scored; methylparaben; propylparaben); GENERIC].

Canada—

600 mg (Rx) [*Lopid; Apo-Gemfibrozil; Gen-Fibro; Novo-Gemfibrozil; Nu-Gemfibrozil;* GENERIC].

Packaging and storage

Store below 30 °C (86 °F), unless otherwise specified by manufacturer. Store in a tight container.

Selected Bibliography

National Cholesterol Education Program. Second Report of the Expert Panel on Detection, Evaluation, and Treatment of High Blood Cholesterol in Adults (Adult Treatment Panel II). Circulation 1994; 89(3): 1329-445.

Knodel LC, Talbert RL. Adverse effects of hypolipidaemic drugs. Med Toxicol 1987; 2: 10-32.

Frick MH, Elo O, Haapa K, et al. Helsinki Heart Study: Primary-prevention trial with gemfibrozil in middle-aged men with dyslipidemia. N Engl J Med 1987; 317: 1237-45.

Revised: 08/12/1998

GEMIFLOXACIN Systemic†

VA CLASSIFICATION (Primary): AM402

Commonly used brand name(s): *Factive*.

Note: For a listing of dosage forms and brand names by country availability, see *Dosage Forms* section(s).

†Not commercially available in Canada.

Category

Antibacterial (systemic).

Indications

Accepted

Chronic bronchitis, acute bacterial exacerbation of (treatment)—Gemifloxacin is indicated in the treatment of acute bacterial exacerbations of chronic bronchitis caused by *Haemophilus influenzae, Haemophilus parainfluenza, Moraxella catarrhalis*, or *Streptococcus pneumoniae*.

Pneumonia, community-acquired (treatment)—Gemifloxacin is indicated in the treatment of mild to moderate community-acquired pneumonia caused by *Chlamydia pneumoniae, H. influenzae, Klebsiella pneumoniae, M. catarrhalis, Mycoplasma pneumoniae*, and *S. pneumoniae* (including multidrug-resistant strains of *S. pneumoniae*).

Pharmacology/Pharmacokinetics

Physicochemical characteristics

Source—Synthetic.

Chemical Group—Fluoroquinolone; broad spectrum antibacterial agent

Molecular weight—485.49.

Mechanism of action/Effect

Note: Gemifloxacin inhibits DNA synthesis through inhibition of DNA gyrase and topoisomerase IV (TOPO IV) which are essential to bacterial growth. The main mechanism of resistance is due to mutations in DNA gyrase or TOPO IV.

Resistance to gemifloxacin develops slowly via multistep mutations and efflux in a manner similar to other fluoroquinolones.

Absorption
Rapidly absorbed from the gastrointestinal tract after oral administration; may be taken with or without food
AUC: 9.93 ± 3.07 μg/mL/hr
Bioavailability: 71%

Distribution
Widely distributed in the body after oral administration; concentrations of gemifloxacin in bronchoalveolar lavage fluid exceed those in plasma; penetrates well into lung tissue and fluids

Vol_D: 4.18 L/kg

Protein binding
60 to 70%; concentration independent

Biotransformation
Hepatic; Metabolites formed are minor (< 10 % of administered oral dose); N-acetyl gemifloxacin and E-isomer of gemifloxacin, carbamyl glucuronide of gemifloxacin are the principal metabolites.Gemifloxacin is not metabolized by CYP450 enzymes.

Half-life
Elimination—7 ± 2 hours (range 4—12 hours)

Time to Peak plasma concentration:
0.5 to 2 hours following oral administration

C_{max}: 1.61 ± 0.51 μg/mL

Time to steady state concentration:
3 days

Elimination
Fecal: 61 %
Renal: 36 % as unchanged drug and metabolites in urine.
Mean renal clearance: 11.6 ± 3.9 L/hr; indicates active secretion is involved in renal excretion
In dialysis—
Hemodialysis removes approximately 20 to 30% of an oral dose of gemifloxacin from plasma.

Precautions to Consider

Cross-sensitivity and/or related problems
Patients allergic to one fluoroquinolone or other chemically related quinolone derivatives (e.g., cinoxacin, nalidixic acid) may be allergic to other fluoroquinolones also.

Carcinogenicity
Long term studies in animals to determine the carcinogenic potential of gemifloxacin have not been conducted.

Mutagenicity
Gemifloxacin was not mutagenic in 4 bacterial strains (TA 98, TA 100, TA 1535, TA 1537) used in an Ames *Salmonella* reversion assay. It did not induce micronuclei in the bone marrow of mice following intraperitoneal doses of up to 40 mg/kg and it did not induce unscheduled DNA synthesis in hepatocytes from rats which received oral doses up to 1600 mg/kg. Gemifloxacin was clastogenic *in vitro* in the mouse lymphoma and human lymphocyte chromosome aberration assays. It was clastogenic *in vivo* in the rat micronucleus assay at oral and intravenous dose levels (≥ 800 mg/kg and ≥40 mg/kg, respectively) that produced bone marrow toxicity. Fluoroquinolone clastogenicity is apparently due to inhibition of mammalian topoisomerase activity which has threshold implications.

Pregnancy/Reproduction
Fertility—Gemifloxacin did not affect the fertility of male or female rats at AUC levels following oral administration (216 and 600 mg/kg/day) that were approximately 3–to 4–fold higher than the AUC levels at the clinically recommended dose.

Pregnancy—Adequate and well controlled studies in humans have not been done. Gemifloxacin should not be used in pregnant women unless the potential benefit outweighs the risk to the fetus.

Gemifloxacin treatment during organogenesis caused fetal growth retardation in mice (oral dosing at 450 mg/kg/day), rats (oral dosing at 600 mg/kg/day) and rabbits (IV dosing at 40 mg/kg/day) at AUC levels which were 2–, 4–, and 3–fold those in women given oral doses of 320 mg. In rats, this growth retardation appeared to be reversible in a pre- and post-natal development study (mice and rats were not studied for the reversibility of this effect). Treatment of pregnant rats at 8–fold clinical exposure (based on AUC comparisons) caused fetal brain and ocular malformations in the presence of maternal toxicity. The overall no-effect exposure level in pregnant animals was approximately 0.8– to 3–fold clinical exposure.

FDA Pregnancy Category C

Breast-feeding
It is not known if gemifloxacin is distributed into human breast milk. However, gemifloxacin is distributed into the breast milk of rats. Gemifloxacin should not be used in nursing mothers unless the potential benefit to the mother outweighs the risk.

Pediatrics
Appropriate studies on the relationship of age to the effects of gemifloxacin have not been done. Safety and efficacy have not been established in patients up to 18 years of age. Fluoroquinolones have been shown to cause arthropathy and osteochondrosis in immature animals of several species.

Geriatrics
Appropriate studies on the relationship of age to the effects of gemifloxacin have not demonstrated geriatrics-specific problems that would limit the usefulness of gemifloxacin in the elderly. The risk of tendon effects may be increased in patients receiving concomitant corticosteroids, especially the elderly.

Drug interactions and/or related problems
The following drug interactions and/or related problems have been selected on the basis of their potential clinical significance (possible mechanism in parentheses where appropriate)—not necessarily inclusive (» = major clinical significance):

Note: Unlike other fluoroquinolones, gemifloxacin does not alter the repeat dose pharmacokinetics of digoxin, theophylline or an ethinyl estradiol/levonorgestrol oral contraceptive in healthy subjects.

Concomitant administration of gemifloxacin and calcium carbonate, cimetidine, omeprazole or an estrogen/progesterone oral contraceptive produced minor changes in the pharmacokinetics of gemifloxacin, which were not considered clinically significant.

Combinations containing any of the following medications, depending on the amount present, may also interact with this medication.

» Antiarrhythmic agents, class Ia or class III such as
Amiodarone
Procainamide
Quinidine
Sotalol
(use should be avoided in patients receiving these antiarrhythmics; fluoroquinolones may prolong the QT interval in some patients)

» Antacids, aluminum- and/or magnesium-containing or
» Didanosine or
» Ferrous sulfate or
» Multivitamins containing zinc or other metal cations
(systemic availability is reduced when concomitantly administered; these drugs should not be taken within 3 hours before or 2 hours after taking gemifloxacin)

Antipsychotics or
» Cisapride or
» Erythromycin or
Tricyclic antidepressants
(use gemifloxacin with caution, the risk of QTc prolongation may be greater when gemifloxacin is used with these drugs.)

Corticosteroids
(concomitant use of corticosteroids and gemfloxacin may increase the risk for tendon effects in some patients, especially the elderly)

Probenecid
(concurrent use of gemifloxacin with probenecid reduced the mean renal clearance by approximately 50%, resulting in a mean increase of 45% in gemifloxacin area-under-the curve [AUC] and a prolongation of mean half-life by 1.6 hours; mean gemifloxacin C_{max} increased by 8%)

» Sucralfate
(oral bioavailability of gemifloxacin was significantly reduced when sucralfate was administered 3 hours before gemifloxacin; gemifloxacin should be taken at least 2 hours before sucralfate)

Warfarin
(gemifloxacin had no significant effect on warfarin therapy in healthy subjects; because some quinolones have been reported to enhance the anticoagulant effects of warfarin or its derivatives in patients, patients should be monitored)

Laboratory value alterations
The following have been selected on the basis of their potential clinical significance (possible effect in parentheses where appropriate)—not necessarily inclusive (» = major clinical significance).

With physiology/laboratory test values
Alanine aminotransferase (ALT [SGPT]) and
Alkaline phosphatase (AKT) and

Aspartate aminotransferase (AST [SGOT]) and
Gammaglutamyl transferase (GGT) and
(serum values may be increased; elevations resolved with cessation of therapy)

Calcium
(values may be increased or decreased)

Creatinine phosphokinase or
Blood urea nitrogen or
Serum creatinine or
Total bilirubin or
Potassium
(values may be increased)

Platelets or
Neutrophils or
Hematocrit or
Hemoglobin or
Red blood cells
(may be increased or decreased)

Sodium or
Albumin or
Total protein
(may be decreased)

Medical considerations/Contraindications

The medical considerations/contraindications included have been selected on the basis of their potential clinical significance (reasons given in parentheses where appropriate)—not necessarily inclusive (» = major clinical significance).

Except under special circumstances, this medication should not be used when the following medical problem exists:

» Electrolyte disorders, uncorrected, including:
» Hypokalemia or
» Hypomagnesemia
(use should be avoided in patients with these conditions)

» Hypersensitivity to gemifloxacin, fluoroquinolone antibiotic agents, or any of the product components

» QTc prolongation, history of
(use should be avoided in patients with a history of prolongation of the QTc interval)

Risk-benefit should be considered when the following medical problems exist:

Central nervous system (CNS) disorders, including epilepsy or predisposed to seizures
(fluoroquinolones can cause CNS effects, gemifloxacin should be used with caution and should be discontinued if symptoms occur)

Proarrhythmic conditions, such as
Bradycardia, clinically significant or
Myocardial ischemia, acute
(gemifloxacin should be used with caution in patients with these conditions)

Renal impairment or
Hepatic impairment
(gemifloxacin levels may be increased leading to increased risk of QTc prolongation)

Patient monitoring

The following may be especially important in patient monitoring (other tests may be warranted in some patients, depending on condition; » = major clinical significance):

» Diarrhea
(pseudomembranous colitis has been reported with nearly all antibiotic agents, and ranges in severity from mild to life-threatening; it is important to consider this diagnosis in patients who present with diarrhea subsequent to the administration of any antibacterial agent; once diagnosed therapeutic measures should be instituted)

» Hypersensitivity reactions
(serious and occasionally fatal hypersensitivity reactions and/or anaphylactic reactions have been reported; reactions may occur following the first dose; gemifloxacin should be discontinued immediately at the first sign of an immediate type 1 hypersensitivity skin rash or any other manifestation of a hypersensitivity reaction)

Liver function tests
(recommended in patients with baseline liver disease)

Prothrombin time or
Anticoagulation tests, other
(because some quinolones have been reported to enhance the anticoagulant effects of warfarin or its derivatives the prothrombin time or other suitable coagulation tests should be closely monitored if a quinolone antimicrobial is administered concomitantly with warfarin or its derivatives)

» Rash
(gemifloxacin treatment should be discontinued in patients developing a rash while on treatment; rashes usually appear 8 to 10 days after start of therapy; rashes are more common in patients <40 years of age, especially females and post-menopausal females taking hormone replacement therapy; incidence of rash correlated with longer treatment duration [>7 days])

Side/Adverse Effects

Serious and occasionally fatal hypersensitivity and/or anaphylactic reactions have been reported in patients receiving fluoroquinolone therapy. These reactions may occur following the first dose. Some reactions have been accompanied by cardiovascular collapse, hypotension/shock, seizure, loss of consciousness, tingling, angioedema (including tongue, laryngeal, throat, or facial edema/swelling), airway obstruction (including bronchospasm, shortness of breath and acute respiratory distress), dyspnea, urticaria, itching, and other serious skin reactions. Gemifloxacin should be discontinued immediately at the appearance of any sign of an immediate type 1 hypersensitivity skin rash or any other manifestation of a hypersensitivity reaction; the need for continued fluoroquinolone therapy should be evaluated.

There have been reports of ruptures of the tendons in the shoulder or hand, or of the Achilles tendon, requiring surgical repair or resulting in prolonged disability, in patients receiving quinolones. The risk of tendon effects may be increased in patients receiving concomitant corticosteroids, especially the elderly, based on post-marketing surveillance reports. Patients should discontinue gemifloxacin if they experience pain, inflammation, or rupture of a tendon. They should rest and refrain from exercise until the diagnosis of tendinitis or tendon rupture has been excluded. Tendon rupture can occur at any time during or after gemifloxacin therapy.

The most common form of rash associated with gemifloxacin was described as maculopapular and mild to moderate in severity; some were described as urticarial in appearance. Rash was more common in women younger than 40 years of age and usually appeared 8 to 10 days after starting therapy and usually resolved in 7 to 14 days. Some rashes reported were severe but there were not documented cases in the clinical trials of more serious skin reactions associated with morbidity and mortality.

Central nervous system (CNS) effects have been reported infrequently. As with other fluoroquinolones, gemifloxacin should be used with caution in patients with CNS diseases such as epilepsy or patients predisposed to convulsions. Although not seen in gemifloxacin clinical trials, convulsions, increased intracranial pressure, and toxic psychosis have been reported in patients receiving other fluoroquinolones. CNS stimulation may lead to tremors, restlessness, anxiety, lightheadedness, confusion, hallucinations, paranoia, depression, insomnia and rarely suicidal thoughts or acts. If these reactions occur the drug should be discontinued and appropriate measures instituted.

The following side/adverse effects have been selected on the basis of their potential clinical significance (possible signs and symptoms in parentheses where appropriate)—not necessarily inclusive:

Those indicating need for medical attention

Incidence less frequent

Rash

Incidence rare

Anemia (pale skin; troubled breathing with exertion; unusual bleeding or bruising; unusual tiredness or weakness); ***bilirubinemia*** (yellow eyes or skin); ***dyspnea*** (shortness of breath; difficult or labored breathing; tightness in chest; wheezing); ***eosinophilia*** (black, tarry stools; chest pain; chills; cough; fever; painful or difficult urination; shortness of breath; sore throat; sores, ulcers, or white spots on lips or in mouth; swollen glands; unusual bleeding or bruising; unusual tiredness or weakness); ***fungal infection; granulocytopenia*** (fever; chills; cough; sore throat; ulcers, sores, or white spots in mouth; shortness of breath; unusual tiredness or weakness); ***leukopenia*** (black, tarry stools chest pain; chills; cough; fever; painful or difficult urination; shortness of breath; sore throat; sores, ulcers, or white spots on lips or in mouth; swollen glands; unusual bleeding or bruising; unusual tiredness or weakness); ***peripheral neuropathy*** (burning, numbness, tingling, or painful sensations; weakness in arms, hands, legs, or feet; unsteadiness or awkwardness); ***pharyngitis*** (body aches or pain; congestion; cough; dryness or soreness of throat; fever; hoarseness; runny nose; tender, swollen glands in neck; trouble in swallowing; voice changes); ***pneumonia*** (chest pain; cough; fever or chills; sneezing; shortness of breath; sore throat; troubled breathing; tightness in chest; wheezing); ***pruritus*** (itching skin); ***thrombocytopenia*** (black, tarry stools; bleeding gums; blood in urine or stools; pinpoint red spots on skin; unusual bleeding or bruising); *urticaria* (hives or welts; itching; redness of skin; skin rash)

Those indicating need for medical attention only if they continue or are bothersome

Incidence less frequent

Diarrhea; headache; nausea

Incidence rare

Abdominal pain; abnormal urine; anorexia (loss of appetite; weight loss); ***arthralgia*** (pain in joints; muscle pain or stiffness; difficulty in moving); ***asthenia*** (lack or loss of strength); ***back pain; constipation*** (difficulty having a bowel movement (stool)); ***dermatitis*** (blistering, crusting, irritation, itching, or reddening of skin; cracked, dry, scaly skin; swelling); ***dizziness; dry mouth; dyspepsia*** (acid or sour stomach; belching; heartburn; indigestion; stomach discomfort upset or pain); ***eczema*** (skin rash encrusted, scaly and oozing); ***fatigue*** (unusual tiredness or weakness); ***flushing*** (feeling of warmth redness of the face, neck, arms and occasionally, upper chest); ***gastroenteritis*** (abdominal or stomach pain; diarrhea; loss of appetite; nausea; weakness); ***hot flashes*** (feeling of warmth; redness of the face, neck, arms and occasionally, upper chest; sudden sweating); ***hyperglycemia*** (abdominal pain; blurred vision; dry mouth; fatigue; flushed, dry skin; fruit-like breath odor; increased hunger; increased thirst; increased urination; nausea; sweating; troubled breathing; unexplained weight loss; vomiting); ***insomnia*** (sleeplessness); ***leg cramps; myalgia*** (joint pain; swollen joints; muscle aching or cramping; muscle pains or stiffness; difficulty in moving); ***nervousness; non-specified gastrointestinal disorder; pain; photosensitivity*** (increased sensitivity of skin to sunlight); ***somnolence*** (sleepiness or unusual drowsiness); ***taste perversion*** (change in taste; bad unusual or unpleasant (after)taste); ***tremor*** (trembling or shaking of hands or feet; shakiness in legs, arms, hands, feet); ***vertigo*** (dizziness or lightheadedness; feeling of constant movement of self or surroundings; sensation of spinning); ***visual abnormality; vomiting***

Overdose

In the event of an acute oral overdose, the stomach should be emptied by inducing vomiting or gastric lavage, the patient should be carefully observed, and appropriate hydration maintained. Hemodialysis removes approximately 20 to 30% of an oral dose of gemifloxacin from plasma.

Mortality occurred at oral gemifloxacin doses of 1600 mg/kg in rats and 320 mg/kg in mice. The minimum lethal overdose in these species were 160 and 80 mg/kg respectively. Toxic signs after administration of a single high oral dose (400 mg/kg) of gemifloxacin to rodents included ataxia, lethargy, piloerection, tremor, and clonic convulsions.

For more information on the management of overdose or unintentional ingestion, **contact a Poison Control Center** (see *Poison Control Center Listing*).

Treatment of overdose

Any signs or symptoms of overdosage should be treated symptomatically.

Supportive care—Patients in whom intentional overdose is confirmed or suspected should be referred for psychiatric consultation.

Patient Consultation

As an aid to patient consultation, refer to *Advice for the Patient, Gemifloxacin (Systemic)*.

In providing consultation, consider emphasizing the following selected information (» = major clinical significance):

Before using this medication

» Conditions affecting use, especially:

Hypersensitivity to gemifloxacin, fluoroquinolone antibiotic agents, or any of the product components

Pregnancy—Not recommended for use during pregnancy

Breast-feeding—Gemifloxacin should not be used in nursing mothers unless the potential benefit to the mother outweighs the risk

Use in children—Safety and effectiveness in children and adolescents less than 18 years of age have not been established.

Other medications, especially antiarrhythmic agents, class Ia or class III; antacids, aluminum- and/or magnesium-containing; antipsychotics; cisapride; didanosine; erythromycin; ferrous sulfate; multivitamins containing zinc or other metal cations; sucralfate; tricyclic antidepressants

Other medical problems, especially hypokalemia; hypomagnesemia; QTc prolongation

Proper use of this medication

» This medicine should only be used to treat bacterial infections. This medicine will not treat viral infections such as the common cold.

» Gemifloxacin may be taken with or without food

Compliance with full course of therapy

Importance of maintaining adequate fluid intake

» Proper dosing; not exceeding the recommended dose and duration

Missed dose: Taking as soon as possible; Do not take more than 1 dose of gemifloxacin in one day

» Proper storage

Precautions while using this medication

Checking with physician if no improvement within a few days

» Avoiding concurrent use of antacids, didanosine, ferrous sulfate, and multivitamins that contain zinc or other metals; taking these products at least 3 hours before or 2 hours after administration of gemifloxacin; gemifloxacin should be taken at least 2 hours before sucralfate

(Avoid concurrent use of Class IA and Class III antiarrhythmic agents, cisapride, erythromycin, antipsychotics, and tricyclic antidepressants.)

» Possible phototoxicity reactions; using broad spectrum sunblock if in bright sunlight

» Discontinuing gemifloxacin at the first sign of skin rash or other allergic reaction and instructing patient to contact physician

» Caution when driving or doing anything else requiring alertness because of possible dizziness, drowsiness, or light-headedness

» Discontinuing gemifloxacin and notifying physician if pain, inflammation, or rupture of a tendon is experienced; resting and refraining from exercise until the diagnosis of tendinitis or tendon rupture has been excluded

» Discontinuing gemifloxacin and contacting physician if patient is develops signs or symptoms of a hypersensitivity reaction or anaphylactic reaction

» Discontinuing gemifloxacin and contacting physician if patient develops seizures

» Telling physician about cardiac medical history; checking with physician if palpitations, fainting spells, chest pain (recent), or other cardiac symptoms develop.

» Contact your doctor if you develop severe diarrhea while taking this medicine or after you have finished taking all of the medicine.

Side/adverse effects

Signs of potential side effects, especially rash, anemia, bilirubinemia, dyspnea, eosinophilia, fungal infection, granulocytopenia, leukocytopenia, peripheral neuropathy, pharyngitis, pneumonia, pruritus, thrombocytopenia, urticaria

General Dosing Information

For oral dosing forms:

Gemifloxacin can be taken with or without food. It should be swallowed whole and taken with fluids.

To reduce the development of drug-resistant bacteria and maintain the effectiveness of gemifloxacin and other antibacterial drugs, gemifloxacin should be used only to treat infections that are proven or strongly suspected to be caused by susceptible bacteria. When culture and susceptibility information are available, they should be considered in selecting or modifying antibacterial therapy. In the absence of such data, local epidemiology and susceptibility patterns may contribute to the empiric selection of therapy.

Adequate hydration of patients receiving gemifloxacin should be maintained to prevent the formation of highly concentrated urine.

For information pertaining to microbiology refer to manufacturer's package insert.

For treatment of adverse effects

• Some patients may develop antibiotic-associated pseudomembranous colitis (AAPMC), caused by *Clostridium difficile* toxin, during or following administration of gemifloxacin. Mild cases may respond to discontinuation of the drug alone. Moderate to severe cases may require fluid, electrolyte, and protein replacement.

• In cases not responding to the above measures or in more severe cases, oral doses of an antibacterial medication effective against *Clostridium difficile* should be administered.

For antibiotic-associated pseudomembranous colitis (AAPMC)—

• Some patients may develop serious and occasionally fatal hypersensitivity and/or anaphylactic reactions while receiving fluoroquinolone therapy.

As with other drugs, serious acute hypersensitivity reactions may require treatment with epinephrine and other resuscitative measures, including oxygen, intravenous fluids, antihistamines, corticosteroids, pressor amines and airway management as clinically indicated.

For Hypersensitivity Reactions—

Oral Dosage Forms

GEMIFLOXACIN MESYLATE TABLETS

Usual adult dose

Chronic bronchitis, acute bacterial exacerbations of, treatment—
Oral, 320 mg every twenty-four hours for five days.

Pneumonia, community-acquired, treatment—
Oral, 320 mg every twenty-four hours for seven days.

Note: Dose adjustment in patients with creatinine clearance >40 mL/min is not required. Modification of the dosage is recommended for patients with creatinine clearance ≤ 40 mL/min.

Creatinine Clearance (mL/min)	Dose
> 40	See Usual Dosage
≤ 40	160 mg q24 hours

Patients requiring routine hemodialysis or continuous ambulatory peritoneal dialysis (CAPD) should receive 160 mg q 24 hours.

When only serum creatinine clearance is known, the following formula may be used to estimate creatinine clearance:
- Men: Creatinine Clearance (mL/min) = (Weight (kg) x (140 – age))/(72 x serum creatinine[mg/dL])
- Women: 0.85 x the value calculated for men

Note: No dosage adjustment is recommended in patients with mild (Child-Pugh Class A), moderate (Child-Pugh Class B), or severe (Child-Pugh Class C) hepatic impairment.

Usual adult prescribing limits

The recommended dose and duration should not be exceeded.

Usual pediatric dose

Safety and efficacy have not been established.

Usual geriatric dose

See *Usual adult dose.*

Usual geriatric prescribing limits

See *Usual adult prescribing limits.*

Strength(s) usually available

U.S.—
320 mg (base) (Rx) [*Factive* (crospovidone; hydroxypropyl methylcellulose; magnesium stearate; microcrystalline cellulose; polyethylene glycol; povidone; titanium dioxide)].

Packaging and storage

Store at 25 °C (77 °F), excursions permitted to 15-30 °C (59-86 °F). Protect from light.

Auxiliary labeling

- May be taken with or without food.
- Swallow tablet whole with liberal amount of liquid
- Take at the same time each day.
- Avoid excessive exposure to sunlight
- May cause dizziness or drowsiness

Revised: 11/15/2004
Developed: 12/18/2003

GEMTUZUMAB OZOGAMICIN Systemic†

VA CLASSIFICATION (Primary): AN900

Commonly used brand name(s): *Mylotarg.*

Note: For a listing of dosage forms and brand names by country availability, see *Dosage Forms* section(s).

†Not commercially available in Canada.

Category

Antineoplastic; Monoclonal antibody.

Indications

Accepted

Leukemia, acute myeloid (treatment)—Gemtuzumab ozogamicin is indicated for the treatment of patients with CD33 positive acute myeloid leukemia in first relapse who are 60 years of age or older and who are not considered candidates for other cytotoxic chemotherapy.

Pharmacology/Pharmacokinetics

Physicochemical characteristics

Source—Recombinant DNA-derived humanized monoclonal antibody conjugated with a cytotoxic antitumor antibiotic, calicheamicin, isolated from fermentation of a bacterium, *Micromonospora echinospora* sp. *calichensis.*

Molecular weight—151 to 153 kilodaltons.

Mechanism of action/Effect

Gemtuzumab ozogamicin is cytotoxic to the CD33 positive HL-60 human leukemia cell line. Gemtuzumab ozogamicin binds to the CD33 antigen expressed by hematopoietic cells which results in formation of a complex that is internalized. Once internalized, the calicheamicin derivative is released inside the lysosomes of the myeloid cell and binds to DNA which results in DNA double strand breaks and cell death. This results in significant inhibition of colony formation in cultures of adult leukemic bone marrow cells.

Half-life

Elimination—45 and 100 hours, total and unconjugated calicheamicin, respectively, after the first recommended 9 mg/m^2 dose given over 2 hours. After a second 9 mg/m^2 dose, the half-life of total calicheamicin increases to 60 hours while the half-life of unconjugated calicheamicin remains unchanged.

Precautions to Consider

Cross-sensitivity and/or related problems

Patients sensitive to anti-CD33 antibody or calicheamicin derivatives may also be sensitive to gemtuzumab ozogamicin.

Carcinogenicity/Mutagenicity

No long-term studies in animals have been performed to evaluate the carcinogenic potential of gemtuzumab ozogamicin. Gemtuzumab ozogamicin was clastogenic in the mouse *in vivo*micronucleus test. This positive result is consistent with the known ability of calicheamicin to cause double-stranded breaks in DNA.

Pregnancy/Reproduction

Fertility—Formal fertility studies have not been conducted in animals. When given weekly for 6 doses to rats, gemtuzumab ozogamicin caused atrophy of the seminiferous tubules, oligospermia, desquamated cells in the epididymis, and hyperplasia of the interstitial cells at the dose of 1.2 mg/kg/week (approximately 0.9 times the human dose on a mg/m^2 basis). These findings did not resolve following a 5-week recovery period.

Pregnancy—Gemtuzumab ozogamicin crosses the placenta and has been shown to cause adverse effects on the fetus. Risk-benefit must be carefully considered when this medication is required in life-threatening situations or in serious diseases for which other medications cannot be used or are ineffective. Gemtuzumab ozogamicin may cause fetal harm when administered to a pregnant woman. There are no adequate and well-controlled studies in pregnant women. If gemtuzumab ozogamicin is used in pregnancy or if the patient becomes pregnant while receiving it, the patient should be apprised of the potential hazard to the fetus. Women of childbearing potential should be advised to avoid becoming pregnant while receiving treatment with gemtuzumab ozogamicin. Daily treatment of pregnant rats with gemtuzumab ozogamicin during organogenesis caused dose-related decreases in fetal weight in association with dose-related decreases in fetal skeletal ossification beginning at 0.025 mg/kg/day. Doses of 0.060 mg/kg/day (approximately 0.04 times the recommended human single dose on a mg/m^2 basis) produced increased embryo-fetal mortality (increased numbers of resorptions and decreased numbers of live fetuses per litter). Gross external, visceral, and skeletal alterations at the 0.060 mg/kg/day dose level included digital malformations in one or both hind feet, absences of the aortic arch, wavy ribs, anomalies of the long bones in the forelimb(s), misshapen scapula, absence of vertebral centrum, and fused sternebrae. This dose was also associated with maternal toxicity (decreased weight gain, decreased food consumption).

FDA Pregnancy Category D.

Breast-feeding

It is not known if gemtuzumab ozogamicin is distributed into breast milk. Because many drugs, including immunoglobulins, are excreted in human milk, and because of the potential for serious adverse reactions in nursing infants from gemtuzumab ozogamicin, a decision should be made whether to discontinue nursing or to discontinue gemtuzumab ozogamicin, taking into account the importance of the drug to the mother.

Pediatrics
No information is available on the relationship of age to the effects of gemtuzumab ozogamicin in the pediatric population. Safety and efficacy have not been established.

Geriatrics
Elderly patients are more likely to have laboratory parameters associated with hepatic dysfunction. It is recommended that bilirubin, AST, and ALT levels be closely monitored.

Pharmacogenetics
There have been no clinically important differences in treatment-emergent adverse events between female and male patients.

Drug interactions and/or related problems
The following drug interactions and/or related problems have been selected on the basis of their potential clinical significance (possible mechanism in parentheses where appropriate)—not necessarily inclusive (» = major clinical significance):

Note: Combinations containing any of the following medications, depending on the amount present, may also interact with this medication.

Blood dyscrasia-causing medications (see *Appendix II*)
(anemic and/or thrombocytopenic effects of gemtuzumab ozogamicin may be increased with concurrent or recent therapy if these medications cause the same effects; dosage adjustment of gemtuzumab ozogamicin, if necessary, should be based on blood counts)

» Bone marrow depressants, other (see *Appendix II*) or
Radiation therapy
(additive bone marrow depression may occur; dosage reduction may be required when two or more bone marrow depressants, including radiation, are used concurrently or consecutively)

Vaccines, killed virus
(because normal defense mechanisms may be suppressed by gemtuzumab ozogamicin therapy, the patient's antibody response to the vaccine may be decreased. The interval between discontinuation of medications that cause immunosuppression and restoration of the patient's ability to respond to the vaccine depends on the intensity and type of immunosuppression-causing medication used, the underlying disease, and other factors; estimates vary from 3 months to 1 year)

» Vaccines, live virus
(because normal defense mechanisms may be suppressed by gemtuzumab ozogamicin therapy, concurrent use with a live virus vaccine may potentiate the replication of the vaccine virus, may increase the side/adverse effects of the vaccine virus, and/or may decrease the patient's antibody response to the vaccine; immunization of these patients should be undertaken only with extreme caution after careful review of the patient's hematologic status and only with the knowledge and consent of the physician managing the gemtuzumab ozogamicin therapy. The interval between discontinuation of medications that cause immunosuppression and restoration of the patient's ability to respond to the vaccine depends on the intensity and type of immunosuppression-causing medication used, the underlying disease, and other factors; estimates vary from 3 months to 1 year. In addition, immunization with oral poliovirus vaccine should be postponed in persons in close contact with the patient, especially family members)

Medical considerations/Contraindications
The medical considerations/contraindications included have been selected on the basis of their potential clinical significance (reasons given in parentheses where appropriate)—not necessarily inclusive (» = major clinical significance).

Except under special circumstances, this medication should not be used when the following medical problem exists:

» Previous allergic reaction to gemtuzumab ozogamicin or any of its components, including anti-CD33 antibody and calicheamicin derivatives

Risk-benefit should be considered when the following medical problems exist:

» Bone marrow depression, existing or
» Infection
(gemtuzumab ozogamicin will cause severe bone marrow depression in all patients when given at the recommended dose. Hematologic monitoring is required and systemic infections should be treated)

» Caution should be used also in patients who have had previous cytotoxic drug or radiation therapy

Caution should be used in patients that have had or are planning to have a hematopoietic stem-cell transplant
(increased risk of developing severe hepatic veno-occlusive disease)

» Chickenpox, existing or recent (including recent exposure) or
» Herpes zoster
(risk of severe generalized disease)

Hepatic function impairment
(gemtuzumab ozogamicin has not been studied in patients with bilirubin >2 mg/dL. Caution should be exercised when administering gemtuzumab ozogamicin in patients with hepatic impairment; increased risk of developing severe hepatic veno-occlusive disease)

High peripheral blast counts
(risk of pulmonary events and tumor lysis syndrome may be increased; consider leukoreduction or leukapheresis prior to starting gemtuzumab ozogamicin therapy)

Patient monitoring
The following may be especially important in patient monitoring (other tests may be warranted in some patients, depending on condition; » = major clinical significance):

» Electrolytes
(recommended during therapy with gemtuzumab ozogamicin due to possible occurrences of hypokalemia, hypomagnesia, and increased lactic dehydrogenase)

» Alanine aminotransferase (ALT [SGPT]) values and
» Aspartate aminotransferase (AST [SGOT]) values and
» Total bilirubin concentrations, serum
(recommended to monitor for abnormalities of liver function)

» Complete blood counts and
» Platelet counts
(recommended to monitor for myelosuppression, anemia, and thrombocytopenia)

» Vital signs
(recommended during infusion and for the four hours following infusion due to possible post-infusion symptom complex)

Side/Adverse Effects

The following side/adverse effects have been selected on the basis of their potential clinical significance (possible signs and symptoms in parentheses where appropriate)—not necessarily inclusive:

Those indicating need for medical attention
Incidence more frequent
Anemia (pale skin; troubled breathing, exertional; unusual bleeding or bruising; unusual tiredness or weakness); ***bleeding events, including epistaxis*** (unexplained nosebleeds); ***cerebral hemorrhage*** (blurred vision; headache sudden and severe; inability to speak; seizures; slurred speech; temporary blindness; weakness in arm and/or leg on one side of the body, sudden and severe); ***disseminated intravascular coagulation*** (blood in stools; blood in urine; bluish color of fingernails, lips, skin, palms, or nail beds; bruising; excessive sweating; persistent bleeding or oozing from puncture sites, mouth, or nose); ***intracranial hemorrhage*** (headache, sudden severe; weakness, sudden); ***hematuria*** (blood in urine; lower back pain; pain or burning while urinating); ***ecchymosis*** (bruising; large, flat, blue or purplish patches in the skin); ***hepatotoxicity, including hyperbilirubinemia and hepatic veno-occlusive disease*** (yellow eyes or skin; upper abdominal pain; rapid weight gain); ***abnormal levels in ALT and AST; and concurrent elevations in transaminases and bilirubin; hypokalemia*** (convulsions; decreased urine; dry mouth; irregular heartbeat; increased thirst; loss of appetite; mood changes; muscle pain or cramps; nausea or vomiting; numbness or tingling in hands, feet, or lips; shortness of breath; unusual tiredness or weakness); ***hypomagnesemia*** (muscle trembling or twitching); ***infections, including sepsis*** (chills; confusion; delirium; dizziness; light-headedness; fainting; fast heartbeat; fever; rapid, shallow breathing); ***pneumonia*** (chest pain; cough; fever or chills; sneezing; shortness of breath; sore throat; troubled breathing; tightness in chest; wheezing); ***and Herpes simplex*** (burning or stinging of skin; painful cold sores or blisters on lips, nose, eyes, or genitals); ***infusion-related reactions, including chills; fever; nausea or vomiting; dyspnea*** (troubled breathing); ***headache; hypotension*** (dizziness; fainting); ***hypertension*** (blurred vision; dizziness; severe or continuing dull nervousness; headache; pounding in the ears; slow or fast heartbeat); ***hypoxia; and hyperglycemia*** (blurred vision dry mouth; fatigue; flushed, dry skin; fruit-like breath odor; increased hunger; increased thirst; increased urination; loss of consciousness; nausea; stomachache; sweating; troubled breathing; vomiting); ***lactic dehydrogenase increased; mucositis or stomatitis*** (cracked lips; diarrhea; difficulty in swallowing; sores, ulcers, or white spots on lips, tongue, or inside mouth; swelling or in-

flammation of the mouth); ***myelosuppression*** (black, tarry stools; blood in urine or stools; cough or hoarseness; fever or chills; lower back or side pain; painful or difficult urination; pinpoint red spots on skin; unusual bleeding or bruising); ***neutropenic fever; peripheral edema*** (bloating or swelling of face, arms, hands, lower legs, or feet; rapid weight gain; tingling of hands or feet; unusual weight gain or loss); ***petechiae*** (small red or purple spots on skin); ***renal failure*** (lower back or side pain; decreased frequency or amount of urine; bloody urine; increased thirst; loss of appetite; nausea; vomiting, unusual tiredness, or weakness; swelling of face, fingers, lower legs; weight gain; troubled breathing; increased blood pressure)—secondary to tumor lysis syndrome; ***tachycardia*** (fainting; fast, pounding, or irregular heartbeat or pulse; palpitations); ***thrombocytopenia*** (black, tarry stools; chest pain; chills; cough; fever; painful or difficult urination; shortness of breath; sore throat; sores, ulcers, or white spots on lips or in mouth; swollen glands; unusual bleeding or bruising; unusual tiredness or weakness); ***tumor lysis syndrome*** (joint pain; lower back or side pain; stomach pain; swelling of feet or lower legs); ***vaginal hemorrhage*** (heavy nonmenstrual vaginal bleeding)

Note: Severe myelosuppression occurs in all patients when gemtuzumab ozogamicin is used at recommended doses.

Infusion-reaction symptoms generally occur after the end of the 2–hour intravenous infusion and resolve after 2 to 4 hours with supportive therapy including acetaminophen, diphenhydramine, and intravenous fluids. Fewer infusion-related events are observed after the second dose.

Those indicating need for medical attention only if they continue or are bothersome

Incidence more frequent

Abdomen enlarged (swelling of abdominal or stomach area; full or bloated feeling or pressure in the stomach); ***abdominal pain; anorexia*** (loss of appetite; weight loss); ***arthralgia*** (pain, swelling, or redness in joints; muscle pain or stiffness; difficulty in moving); ***asthenia*** (lack or loss of strength); ***back pain; constipation; cough increased; depression*** (mood or mental changes); ***diarrhea*** (increase in bowel movements; loose stools; soft stools); ***dizziness; dyspepsia*** (acid or sour stomach; belching; heartburn; indigestion; stomach discomfort upset); ***insomnia*** (sleeplessness; trouble sleeping; unable to sleep); ***local skin reactions*** (dry, red, hot, or irritated skin); ***nonspecific skin rash; pain; pharyngitis; pulmonary physical finding, including; rales; rhonchi; and changes in breath sounds; rhinitis*** (stuffy nose; runny nose; sneezing)

Incidence less frequent

Antibody formation

Those not indicating need for medical attention

Incidence less frequent

Immune response

Overdose

For more information on the management of overdose or unintentional ingestion, **contact a poison control center** (see *Poison Control Center Listing*).

Treatment of overdose

General supportive measures should be followed in case of overdose. Blood pressure and blood counts should be carefully monitored. Gemtuzumab ozogamicin is not dialyzable.

Patients in whom intentional overdose is known or suspected should be referred for psychiatric consultation.

Patient Consultation

As an aid to patient consultation, refer to *Advice for the Patient, Gemtuzumab ozogamicin (Systemic)*.

In providing consultation, consider emphasizing the following selected information (» = major clinical significance):

Before using this medication

» Conditions affecting use, especially:

Hypersensitivity to gemtuzumab ozogamicin or any of its components: anti-CD33 antibody, calicheamicin derivatives, or inactive ingredients

Pregnancy—Use is not recommended because of potential harm to fetus; advisability of using contraception and informing physician immediately if pregnancy is suspected.

Breast-feeding—Not recommended because of potential serious adverse effects.

Use in the elderly—Patients 60 years old and older may more consistently have laboratory parameters associated with hepatic dysfunction than patients less than 60 years old while receiving gemtuzumab ozogamicin.

Other medications, especially other bone marrow depressants or previous cytotoxic drug or radiation therapy

Other medical problems, especially bone marrow depression, infection, chickenpox, and herpes zoster

Proper use of this medication

» Proper dosing

» Proper storage

Precautions while using this medication

» Importance of close monitoring by physician

» Avoiding immunizations unless approved by physician; other persons in patient's household should avoid immunizations with oral poliovirus vaccine; avoiding other persons who have taken oral poliovirus vaccine or wearing a protective mask that covers nose and mouth

(Caution if bone marrow depression occurs)

» Avoiding exposure to persons with bacterial infections, especially during periods of low blood counts; checking with physician immediately if fever or chills, cough or hoarseness, lower back or side pain, or painful or difficult urination occur

» Checking with physician immediately if unusual bleeding or bruising; black, tarry stools; blood in urine or stools; or pinpoint red spots on skin occur

Caution in use of regular toothbrush, dental floss, or toothpick; physician, dentist, or nurse may suggest alternatives; checking with physician before having dental work done

Not touching eyes or inside of nose unless hands washed immediately before

Using caution to avoid accidental cuts with use of sharp objects such as safety razor or fingernail or toenail cutters

Avoiding contact sports or other situations where bruising or injury could occur

Side/adverse effects

Signs of potential side effects, especially anemia, bleeding events (including epistaxis), cerebral hemorrhage, disseminated intravascular coagulation, intracranial hemorrhage, hematuria, ecchymosis, hepatotoxicity (including hyperbilirubinemia, hepatic veno-occlusive disease, and abnormal levels in ALT and AST), hypokalemia, hypomagnesemia, infections (including sepsis, pneumonia, and Herpes simplex), infusion-related reactions (including chills, fever, nausea or vomiting, dyspnea, headache, hypotension, hypertension, hypoxia, and hyperglycemia), increased lactic dehydrogenase, mucositis or stomatitis, myelosuppression, neutropenic fever, peripheral edema, petechiae, renal failure, tachycardia, thrombocytopenia, tumor lysis syndrome, or vaginal hemorrhage

General Dosing Information

Gemtuzumab ozogamicin may be given peripherally or through a central line. A separate IV line equipped with a low protein-binding 1.2–micron terminal filter must be used for administration of the drug.

To reduce the incidence of post-infusion symptom complex, patients should receive diphenhydramine 50 mg orally and acetaminophen 650 to 1000 mg orally one hour prior to gemtuzumab ozogamicin administration; thereafter, two additional doses of acetaminophen 650 to 1000 mg orally every 4 hours as needed should be given.

Special precautions are recommended in patients who develop thrombocytopenia as a result of administration of gemtuzumab ozogamicin. These may include: extreme care in performing invasive procedures; regular inspection of intravenous sites, skin (including perirectal area), and mucous membrane surfaces for signs of bleeding or bruising; limiting frequency of venipuncture and avoiding intramuscular injections; testing urine, emesis, stool and secretions for occult blood; care in use of toothbrushes, dental floss, toothpicks, safety razors, and fingernail and toenail cutters; avoiding constipation; and using caution to prevent falls and other injuries. Such patients should avoid alcohol and any aspirin intake because of the risk of gastrointestinal bleeding. Platelet transfusions may be required.

Tumor lysis syndrome may be a consequence of leukemia treatment. Appropriate measures (e.g., hydration and allopurinol), must be taken to prevent hyperuricemia.

Safety considerations for handling this medication

Procedures for handling and disposal of anticancer drugs should be considered. There is limited but increasing evidence and concern that personnel involved in preparation and administration of parenteral antineoplastic agents may be at some risk because of the potential mutagenicity, teratogenicity, and/or carcinogenicity of these agents, although the actual risk is unknown. USP advisory panels recommend cautious handling both in preparation and disposal of antineoplastic agents. Precautions that have been suggested include

• Use of a biological containment cabinet during reconstitution and dilution of parenteral medications and wearing of disposable surgical gloves, goggles, gowns, and masks.

• Pregnant personnel should not come in contact with antineoplastic medication containers or mixing supplies.

• Use of proper technique to prevent contamination of the medication, work area, and operator during transfer between containers (including proper training of personnel in this technique).

• Cautious and proper disposal of needles, syringes, vials, ampules, and unused medication.

• Use of proper technique in handling spills, including the use of dilute sodium hypochlorite solution (1% active chlorine) and water, and proper disposal of waste.

Parenteral Dosage Forms

GEMTUZUMAB OZOGAMICIN FOR INJECTION

Note: Gemtuzumab ozogamicin should not be administered as an intravenous push or bolus. Gemtuzumab ozogamicin should be administered under the supervision of physicians experienced in the treatment of acute leukemia and in facilities equipped to monitor and treat leukemia patients.

Note: Physicians should consider leuko reduction with hydroxyurea or leukopheresis to reduce the white blood count to below 30,000 per microliter prior to administration

Usual adult dose

Leukemia, acute myeloid (treatment)—

Intravenous infusion, 9 mg per square meter (mg/m^2) administered over 2 hours. The recommended treatment course with gemtuzumab ozogamicin is a total of 2 doses with 14 days between the doses. Full recovery from hematologic toxicities is not a requirement for administration of the second dose.

Usual pediatric dose

Safety and efficacy have not been established.

Usual geriatric dose

See *Usual adult dose.*

Strength(s) usually available

U.S.—

5 mg of lyophilized powder per 20 mL single-vial package (Rx) [*Mylotarg* (dextran 40; sucrose; sodium chloride; monobasic and dibasic sodium phosphate)].

Packaging and storage

Store between 2 and 8 °C (36 and 46 °F). Protect from light.

Preparation of dosage form

All preparation of gemtuzumab ozogamicin should take place in a biologic safety hood with the fluorescent light off. Prior to reconstitution, allow drug vials to come to room temperature. Reconstitute the contents of the vial with 5 mL Sterile Water for Injection, USP, using sterile syringes. Gently swirl each vial. Each vial should be inspected for complete solution and for particulate matter. The final concentration of drug in the vial is 1 mg per mL. Withdraw the desired volume from each vial and inject into a 100 mL IV bag of 0.9% Sodium Chloride Injection. Place the 100–mL IV bag into an UV protection bag.

Stability

While in the vial, the reconstituted drug may be stored in the refrigerator and protected from light for up to 8 hours. The diluted drug solution in the IV bag should be used immediately.

Incompatibilities

No physical biochemical compatibility studies have been conducted to evaluate the coadministration of gemtuzumab ozogamicin with other agents. Gemtuzumab ozogamicin should not be infused concomitantly in the same intravenous line with other agents.

Auxiliary labeling

• Keep from heat and light.

Selected Bibliography

Revised: 08/22/2002
Developed: 08/28/2000

GENTAMICIN—See *Aminoglycosides (Systemic), Gentamicin (Ophthalmic), Gentamicin (Otic), Gentamicin (Topical)*

GENTAMICIN Ophthalmic

VA CLASSIFICATION (Primary): OP201

Commonly used brand name(s): *Alcomicin; Garamycin; Genoptic Liquifilm; Genoptic S.O.P.; Gentacidin; Gentafair; Gentak; Ocu-Mycin; Spectro-Genta.*

Another commonly used name is gentamycin.

Note: For a listing of dosage forms and brand names by country availability, see *Dosage Forms* section(s).

Category

Antibacterial (ophthalmic).

Indications

Accepted

Blepharitis, bacterial (treatment)
Blepharoconjunctivitis (treatment)
Conjunctivitis, bacterial (treatment)
Corneal ulcers (treatment)
Dacryocystitis (treatment)
[Episcleritis (treatment)]
Keratitis, bacterial (treatment)
Keratoconjunctivitis, bacterial (treatment) or
Meibomianitis (treatment)—Ophthalmic gentamicin is indicated in the treatment of blepharitis, blepharoconjunctivitis, conjunctivitis, dacryocystitis, keratitis, keratoconjunctivitis, and acute meibomianitis caused by coagulase-negative and coagulase-positive staphylococci, *Streptococcus pyogenes, S. pneumoniae, Pseudomonas aeruginosa,* indole-positive and indole-negative *Proteus* species, *Escherichia coli, Klebsiella pneumoniae, Hemophilus influenzae, H. aegyptius, Enterobacter aerogenes (Aerobacter aerogenes), Moraxella lacunata* (Morax-Axenfeld bacillus), *Serratia marcescens* and *Neisseria* species, including *N. gonorrhoeae.*

Note: Not all species or strains of a particular organism may be susceptible to gentamicin.

Pharmacology/Pharmacokinetics

Physicochemical characteristics

Chemical Group—Aminoglycosides.

pH—Gentamicin sulfate ophthalmic solution is buffered to pH of approximately 7.

Mechanism of action/Effect

Aminoglycoside; actively transported across the bacterial cell membrane, binds to a specific receptor protein on the 30 S subunit of bacterial ribosomes, and interferes with an initiation complex between mRNA (messenger RNA) and the 30 S subunit, inhibiting protein synthesis. DNA may be misread, thus producing nonfunctional proteins; polyribosomes are split apart and are unable to synthesize protein.

Note: Aminoglycosides are bactericidal, while most other antibiotics that interfere with protein synthesis are bacteriostatic.

Absorption

May be absorbed in minute quantities following topical application to the eye.

Precautions to Consider

Cross-sensitivity and/or related problems

Patients sensitive to one aminoglycoside may be sensitive to other aminoglycosides also.

Pregnancy/Reproduction

Problems in humans have not been documented.

Pregnancy Category C.

Postpartum—

Gentamicin given to pregnant rats in daily doses approximately 500 times the maximum recommended ophthalmic human dose resulted in offspring with decreased body and kidney weights.

Breast-feeding

Problems in humans have not been documented.

Pediatrics

Appropriate studies on the relationship of age to the effects of this medicine have not been performed in neonates. Safety and efficacy have not been established.

Geriatrics

Appropriate studies on the relationship of age to the effects of this medicine have not been performed in the geriatric population. However, no geriatrics-specific problems have been documented to date.

Medical considerations/Contraindications

The medical considerations/contraindications included have been selected on the basis of their potential clinical significance (reasons given in parentheses where appropriate)—not necessarily inclusive (» = major clinical significance).

Risk-benefit should be considered when the following medical problem exists:

Sensitivity to gentamicin

Side/Adverse Effects

The following side/adverse effects have been selected on the basis of their potential clinical significance (possible signs and symptoms in parentheses where appropriate)—not necessarily inclusive:

Those indicating need for medical attention

Incidence less frequent

Allergic reaction or Hypersensitivity (itching, redness, swelling, or other sign of irritation not present before therapy); ***Conjunctivitis*** (redness of eye, eyelid, or inner lining of eyelid)

Incidence rare

Corneal ulcers, bacterial or fungal (blurred vision, eye pain, sensitivity to light, and/or tearing); ***Hallucinations*** (seeing, hearing, or feeling things that are not there); ***Thrombocytopenia*** (black, tarry stools; blood in urine or stools; unusual bleeding or bruising)

Those indicating need for medical attention only if they continue or are bothersome

Incidence less frequent

Burning or stinging

Those not indicating need for medical attention

For ophthalmic ointment dosage form only

Blurred vision

Patient Consultation

As an aid to patient consultation, refer to *Advice for the Patient, Gentamicin (Ophthalmic)*.

In providing consultation, consider emphasizing the following selected information (» = major clinical significance):

Before using this medication

» Conditions affecting use, especially:

Sensitivity to gentamicin or to any related antibiotic, such as amikacin, kanamycin, neomycin, netilmicin, streptomycin, or tobramycin

Proper use of this medication

Proper administration technique

» Compliance with full course of therapy

» Proper dosing

Missed dose: Applying as soon as possible; not applying if almost time for next dose

» Proper storage

Precautions while using this medication

Check with physician if no improvement within a few days

Avoid wearing contact lenses during treatment

Side/adverse effects

Blurred vision may occur for a few minutes after application of ophthalmic ointments

Signs of potential side effects, especially allergic reaction or hypersensitivity, conjunctivitis, bacterial or fungal corneal ulcers, hallucinations, or thrombocytopenia

General Dosing Information

Gentamicin sulfate ophthalmic solution is not for subconjunctival injection or for direct injection into the anterior chamber of the eye.

Although some manufacturers recommend a dose of 2 drops of an ophthalmic solution at appropriate intervals, the conjunctival sac will usually hold only 1 drop.

At night the ophthalmic ointment may be used as an adjunct to the ophthalmic solution to provide prolonged contact with the medication.

In infections of the tear sacs (dacryocystitis), often occurring in children with nonpatent tear passages, hot compresses and gentle massage of the area over the tear duct may be useful adjuncts to treatment with the ophthalmic solution.

Ophthalmic Dosage Forms

GENTAMICIN SULFATE OPHTHALMIC OINTMENT USP

Usual adult and adolescent dose

Antibacterial (ophthalmic)—

Topical, to the conjunctiva, a thin strip (approximately 1 cm) of ointment to the affected eye every eight to twelve hours.

Usual pediatric dose

See *Usual adult and adolescent dose.*

Neonates—Safety and efficacy have not been established.

Strength(s) usually available

U.S.—

5 mg of gentamicin sulfate, equivalent to 3 mg of gentamicin base, per gram (Rx) [*Garamycin* (methylparaben; propylparaben); *Genoptic S.O.P.* (methylparaben; propylparaben); *Gentacidin; Gentafair* (may contain methylparaben; may contain propylparaben); *Gentak* (methylparaben; propylparaben); *Ocu-Mycin;* GENERIC (may contain methylparaben; may contain propylparaben)].

Canada—

5 mg of gentamicin sulfate, equivalent to 3 mg of gentamicin base, per gram (Rx) [*Garamycin* (methylparaben; propylparaben)].

Packaging and storage

Store below 30 °C (86 °F). Store in a collapsible ophthalmic ointment tube. Protect from freezing.

Auxiliary labeling

- For the eye.
- Continue medicine for full time of treatment.

GENTAMICIN SULFATE OPHTHALMIC SOLUTION USP

Usual adult and adolescent dose

Antibacterial (ophthalmic)—

Mild to moderate infections: Topical, to the conjunctiva, 1 to 2 drops into the affected eye every four hours.

Severe infections: Topical, to the conjunctiva, 1 to 2 drops into the affected eye as often as once every hour.

Usual pediatric dose

See *Usual adult and adolescent dose.*

Neonates—Safety and efficacy have not been established.

Strength(s) usually available

U.S.—

5 mg of gentamicin sulfate, equivalent to 3 mg of gentamicin base, per mL (Rx) [*Garamycin* (benzalkonium chloride); *Genoptic Liquifilm* (polyvinyl alcohol 1.4%; benzalkonium chloride); *Gentacidin* (benzalkonium chloride); *Gentafair* (may contain benzalkonium chloride); *Gentak* (benzalkonium chloride 0.01%); *Ocu-Mycin; Spectro-Genta;* GENERIC (may contain benzalkonium chloride)].

Canada—

5 mg of gentamicin sulfate, equivalent to 3 mg of gentamicin base, per mL (Rx) [*Alcomicin* (benzalkonium chloride 0.01%); *Garamycin* (benzalkonium chloride)].

Packaging and storage

Store below 30 °C (86 °F). Store in a tight container. Protect from freezing.

Auxiliary labeling

- For the eye.
- Continue medicine for full time of treatment.

Note

Dispense in original unopened container.

Revised: 07/18/2000

GLATIRAMER ACETATE Systemic

VA CLASSIFICATION (Primary): IM409; CN900

Commonly used brand name(s): *Copaxone.*

Another commonly used name is copolymer-1.

Note: For a listing of dosage forms and brand names by country availability, see *Dosage Forms* section(s).

Category

Multiple sclerosis (MS) therapy agent.

Indications

General Considerations

Because glatiramer acetate can modify immune response, consideration must be given to the possibility that it may interfere with useful immune function. Theoretically, for example, it could interfere with the recognition of foreign antigens in a manner that would undermine the body's defenses against infections and tumor surveillance. There is no evidence of this, although no systematic evaluation of this risk has been conducted.

Because glatiramer acetate is an antigenic material, its use possibly could induce unwanted host responses. There is no evidence that this occurs in humans, although no systematic evaluation of this risk has been conducted. Studies in rats and monkeys, however, have suggested that immune complexes are deposited in the renal glomeruli. Furthermore, in a controlled trial of 125 patients with relapsing-remitting multiple sclerosis who received 20 mg of glatiramer acetate subcutaneously every day for 2 years, serum IgG levels reached approximately three times the baseline values in 80% of patients within 3 to 6 months of initiation of treatment. These values decreased to about 50% greater than baseline during the remainder of treatment.

Although treatment with glatiramer acetate is intended to minimize the autoimmune response to myelin, the possibility remains that continued alteration of cellular immunity due to long-term treatment may result in untoward effects.

Accepted

Multiple sclerosis (treatment)—Glatiramer acetate is indicated for reduction of the frequency of relapses in patients with relapsing-remitting multiple sclerosis.

Pharmacology/Pharmacokinetics

Physicochemical characteristics

Chemical Group—Glatiramer acetate is composed of the acetate salts of synthetic polypeptides, containing four naturally occurring amino acids: L-glutamic acid, L-alanine, L-tyrosine, and L-lysine, with an average molar fraction of 0.141, 0.427, 0.095, and 0.338, respectively.

Molecular weight—The average molecular weight of glatiramer acetate is 4700 to 11,000 daltons.

Mechanism of action/Effect

The mechanism of action is unknown. However, glatiramer acetate is believed to modify immune processes that are thought to be responsible for the pathogenesis of multiple sclerosis (MS). Glatiramer acetate reduces the incidence and severity of experimentally induced allergic encephalomyelitis; this condition can be induced in several animal species through immunization against myelin-containing material derived from the central nervous system (CNS), and often is used as an experimental animal model of MS.

The ability of glatiramer acetate to modify immune functions raises concerns regarding its potential to alter naturally occurring immune responses. Results of a limited battery of tests designed to evaluate this risk were negative; however, the possibility cannot be absolutely excluded.

Pharmacokinetics

Pharmacokinetic studies have not been performed in humans. Partly on the basis of animal studies, a substantial fraction of subcutaneously injected glatiramer acetate is assumed to be hydrolyzed locally. Some fraction of the injected material is presumed to enter the lymphatic circulation, enabling it to reach regional lymph nodes, and some may enter the systemic circulation intact.

Precautions to Consider

Carcinogenicity

Studies to assess the carcinogenic potential of glatiramer acetate in mice and rats are in progress.

Mutagenicity

Glatiramer acetate was not mutagenic in four strains of *Salmonella typhimurium* and two strains of *Escherichia coli* (Ames test) or in the *in vitro* mouse lymphoma assay in L5178Y cells. Glatiramer acetate was found to be clastogenic in two separate *in vitro* chromosomal aberration assays in cultured human lymphocytes; it was not clastogenic in an *in vivo* mouse bone marrow micronucleus assay.

Pregnancy/Reproduction

Fertility—In a multigeneration reproduction and fertility study in rats, glatiramer acetate at subcutaneous doses of up to 36 mg per kg of body weight (mg/kg) (18 times the recommended human daily dose) had no adverse effects on reproductive parameters.

Pregnancy—Adequate and well-controlled studies in humans have not been done.

In reproduction studies in rats and rabbits receiving subcutaneous doses of glatiramer acetate up to 37.5 mg/kg during the period of organogenesis, no adverse effects on embryo/fetal development occurred. In a prenatal and postnatal study in which rats received subcutaneous glatiramer acetate doses of up to 36 mg/kg from day 15 of pregnancy through lactation, no significant effects on delivery or on offspring growth and development were observed.

FDA Pregnancy Category B.

Breast-feeding

It is not known whether glatiramer acetate is distributed into human milk.

Pediatrics

Safety and efficacy have not been established in patients younger than 18 years of age.

Geriatrics

Glatiramer acetate has not been studied specifically in elderly patients.

Drug interactions and/or related problems

Note: Interactions between glatiramer acetate and other medications have not been fully evaluated. Results from clinical trials do not suggest any significant interactions of glatiramer acetate with other therapies commonly used in multiple sclerosis patients, including concurrent use of corticosteroids for up to 28 days. Glatiramer acetate has not been evaluated formally in combination with interferon beta; however, ten patients who switched from therapy with interferon beta to glatiramer acetate have not reported any serious or unexpected adverse events thought to be related to treatment.

Medical considerations/Contraindications

The medical considerations/contraindications included have been selected on the basis of their potential clinical significance (reasons given in parentheses where appropriate)—not necessarily inclusive (» = major clinical significance).

Risk-benefit should be considered when the following medical problem exists:

Sensitivity to glatiramer acetate or mannitol

Side/Adverse Effects

Note: Approximately 10% of patients exposed to glatiramer acetate in premarketing studies experienced a constellation of symptoms immediately after injection. Symptoms included flushing, chest pain, palpitations, anxiety, dyspnea, constriction of the throat, and urticaria. These symptoms were invariably transient and self-limited and did not require specific treatment. In general, these symptoms appear several months after the initiation of therapy, although they may occur earlier in the course of treatment, and a patient may experience one or several episodes of these symptoms. It is not certain if this constellation of symptoms represents a specific syndrome. Whether these episodes are mediated by an immunologic or nonimmunologic mechanism, or whether several similar episodes seen in a particular patient have identical mechanisms is not known.

Approximately 26% of patients receiving glatiramer acetate in the premarketing multicenter controlled trial experienced at least one episode of transient chest pain, as compared with 10% of the patients receiving placebo. Some, but not all, of these episodes occurred in the context of the immediate postinjection reaction. Chest pain usually lasted only a few minutes, was often unassociated with other symptoms, and appeared to have no important sequelae. Electrocardiogram (ECG) monitoring was not performed during these episodes. Chest pain episodes usually began at least 1 month after initiation of treatment, and some patients experienced more than one episode. The pathogenesis of this symptom is unknown.

The following side/adverse effects have been selected on the basis of their potential clinical significance (possible signs and symptoms in parentheses where appropriate)—not necessarily inclusive:

Those indicating need for medical attention

Incidence more frequent

Anxiety; arthralgia (joint pain); ***chest pain; dyspnea*** (troubled breathing); ***facial edema*** (swelling or puffiness of face); ***hypertonia*** (excessive muscle tone); ***injection-site reactions; including hemorrhage*** (bleeding); ***induration*** (hard lump); ***inflammation; pain; pruritus*** (itching); ***redness; urticaria*** (hives or welts); ***lymphadenopathy*** (swollen lymph glands); ***neck pain; palpitations*** (irregular or pounding heartbeat); ***vaginal moniliasis*** (vaginal yeast infection); ***vasodilatation*** (flushing)

Incidence less frequent

Agitation; bronchitis (tightness in chest or wheezing); ***chills; confusion; ecchymosis*** (purple spots under the skin); ***edema*** (bloating or swelling); ***flu-like syndrome*** (chills; fever; muscle aches); ***infection; laryngismus*** (spasm of throat); ***migraine; pain; peripheral edema*** (swelling of fingers, arms, feet, or legs); ***skin nodules*** (small lumps under the skin); ***skin rash; syncope*** (fainting); ***urinary urgency*** (strong urge to urinate); ***urticaria*** (hives)

Incidence rare

Anorexia (loss of appetite); ***back pain; diarrhea; dysmenorrhea or other menstrual changes; ear pain; hematuria*** (blood in urine); ***hypertension*** (high blood pressure); ***hyperventilation*** (fast breathing); ***impotence*** (decreased sexual ability); ***nystagmus*** (continuous, uncontrolled back-and-forth and/or rolling eye movements); ***oral moniliasis*** (irritation of mouth and tongue [thrush]); ***speech problems; suspicious Papanicolaou test; tachycardia*** (fast or racing heartbeat); ***vertigo*** (sensation of motion, usually whirling, either of oneself or of one's surroundings); ***vision problems***

Those indicating need for medical attention only if they continue or are bothersome

Incidence more frequent

Asthenia (unusual tiredness or weakness); ***nausea; sweating, increased; tremor*** (trembling); ***vomiting***

Incidence less frequent

Rhinitis (runny nose); ***weight gain***

Overdose

For information on the management of overdose or unintentional ingestion, **contact a Poison Control Center** (see *Poison Control Center Listing*).

Patient Consultation

In providing consultation, consider emphasizing the following selected information (» = major clinical significance)

Before using this medication

» Conditions affecting use, especially:
Sensitivity to glatiramer acetate or mannitol

Proper use of this medication

» Receiving instructions in self-injection techniques to assure safe administration
» Carefully reading patient instructions contained in package
» Importance of using medication exactly as directed
» Not discontinuing medication without checking with physician
» Proper dosing
Missed dose: Using as soon as remembered; not using if not remembered until next day; not doubling doses
» Proper storage

Side/adverse effects

Signs of potential side effects, especially anxiety, arthralgia, chest pain, dyspnea, facial edema, hypertonia, injection-site reactions, lymphadenopathy, neck pain, palpitations, vaginal moniliasis, vasodilatation, agitation, bronchitis, chills, confusion, ecchymosis, edema, flu-like syndrome, infection, laryngismus, migraine, pain, peripheral edema, skin nodules, skin rash, syncope, urinary urgency, urticaria, anorexia, back pain, diarrhea, dysmenorrhea or other menstrual changes, ear pain, hematuria, hypertension, hyperventilation, impotence, nystagmus, oral moniliasis, speech problems, suspicious Papanicolaou test, tachycardia, vertigo, and vision problems

General Dosing Information

Patients should be instructed in self-injection techniques to assure safe administration.

Patients should be instructed not to change the dose or dosing schedule and not to discontinue the medication without consulting physician.

Parenteral Dosage Forms

GLATIRAMER ACETATE FOR INJECTION

Usual adult dose

Relapsing-remitting multiple sclerosis—
Subcutaneously, 20 mg a day.

Usual pediatric dose

Safety and efficacy in patients up to 18 years of age have not been established.

Strength(s) usually available

U.S.—
20 mg (Rx) [*Copaxone* (diluent—Sterile Water for Injection; Mannitol USP)].

Packaging and storage

Vials containing glatiramer acetate should be stored between 2 and 8 °C (36 and 46 °F) and protected from light. If refrigeration is not available, vials containing glatiramer acetate may be stored between 15 and 30 °C (59 and 86 °F) for up to one week. Vials containing diluent should be stored between 15 and 30 °C (59 and 86 °F).

Preparation of dosage form

The contents of the diluent vial are transferred into the lyophilized glatiramer acetate vial using aseptic technique. The vial is gently swirled and allowed to stand at room temperature until the solid material is completely dissolved; this occurs in about 5 minutes. If particulate matter remains, glatiramer acetate should not be used, and the vial should be discarded.

After reconstitution, the solution should be withdrawn into a sterile syringe fitted with a new 27-gauge needle and injected subcutaneously.

Stability

Glatiramer acetate contains no preservatives and should be used immediately after reconstitution or must be discarded.

Auxiliary labeling

- Store glatiramer acetate vials in refrigerator.

Additional information

The manufacturer has established a program entitled Shared Solutions™ to provide support to any patient with multiple sclerosis; the program is accessible with a toll-free telephone number.

Revised: 05/21/1998

GLICLAZIDE—See *Antidiabetic Agents, Sulfonylurea (Systemic)*

GLIMEPIRIDE—See *Antidiabetic Agents, Sulfonylurea (Systemic)*

GLIPIZIDE—See *Antidiabetic Agents, Sulfonylurea (Systemic)*

GLIPIZIDE AND METFORMIN Systemic

VA CLASSIFICATION (Primary): HS509

Commonly used brand name(s): *Metaglip*.

NOTE: The *Glipizide and Metformin (Systemic)* monograph is maintained on the *USP DI* electronic database. A copy of the most recent revision of the complete monograph can be accessed on the *USP DI* Updates Online website. See the front cover of book for details on accessing the site. The information that follows is selectively abstracted from the complete monograph and is provided to facilitate drug use review and patient counseling.

Note: For a listing of dosage forms and brand names by country availability, see *Dosage Forms* section(s).

Category

Antidiabetic agent.

Indications

Accepted

Diabetes, type 2 (treatment)—The combination of glipizide and metformin is indicated as an initial therapy as an adjunct to diet and exercise to improve glycemic control in patients with type 2 diabetes whose hyperglycemia cannot be controlled by diet and exercise alone. The combination of glipizide and metformin also is indicated as second-line therapy when diet, exercise, and initial treatment with a sulfonylurea or metformin do not result in adequate glycemic control in patients with type 2 diabetes.

Patient Consultation

As an aid to patient consultation, refer to *Advice for the Patient, Glipizide and Metformin (Systemic).*

In providing consultation, consider emphasizing the following selected information (» = major clinical significance):

Before using this medication

» Conditions affecting use, especially:
- Hypersensitivity to glipizide or metformin
- Pregnancy—Diet or diet/insulin is recommended to prevent maternal and fetal problems; importance of controlling and monitoring blood glucose during pregnancy; alerting physician if planning to become pregnant; stopping therapy one month before due date
- FDA Pregnancy Category C
- Breast-feeding—It is not known whether glipizide or metformin passes into human breast milk.
- Use in children—Safety and efficacy have not been established in children.
- Use in the elderly—Elderly patients should not be titrated to the maximum dose. Elderly patients may be more susceptible to hypoglycemia and it may be difficult to recognize signs and symptoms of hypoglycemia in these patients. Glipizide and metformin should not be used in patients 80 years of age or older unless measurement of creatinine clearance demonstrates that renal function is not reduced.
- Surgical—Treatment should be temporarily suspended for any surgical procedure (except minor procedures); should not be restarted until oral intake has been reestablished to pre-surgical levels and renal function is normal.
- Other medications, especially alcohol, beta-adrenergic blocking agents, cimetidine, fluconazole, furosemide, and miconazole
- Other medical problems, especially adrenal insufficiency, alcohol intoxication, cardiovascular collapse, congestive heart failure, debilitated physical condition, dehydration, diagnostic studies using iodinated contrast media, inadequate diet or malnutrition, kidney disease or dysfunction, liver disease or dysfunction, metabolic acidosis, myocardial infarction, pituitary insufficiency, and septicemia

Proper use of this medication

» Importance of adherence to recommended regimens for diet, exercise, and glucose monitoring

Taking medication with meals to reduce gastrointestinal symptoms

» Proper dosing

Missed dose: Taking as soon as possible; not taking if almost time for next scheduled dose; not doubling doses

Proper storage

Precautions while using this medication

» Regular visits to physician to check progress

» Recognizing symptoms of lactic acidosis, such as abdominal discomfort; decreased appetite; diarrhea; fast, shallow breathing; general feeling of discomfort; muscle pain or cramping; or unusual sleepiness, tiredness, or weakness

» Getting immediate emergency medical help if symptoms of lactic acidosis occur

» Carefully following special instructions of health care team:
- Discussing use of alcohol
- Not taking other medications unless discussed with physician
- Getting counseling for family members to help them assist the patient with diabetes; also, special counseling for pregnancy planning and contraception
- Making travel plans that include readiness for diabetic emergencies and eating meals at the usual times, even with changing time zones

» Preparing for and understanding what to do in case of diabetic emergency; carrying medical history and current medication list and wearing medical identification

» Recognizing symptoms of hypoglycemia: anxiety; behavior change similar to drunkenness; blurred vision; cold sweats; coma; confusion; cool, pale skin; difficulty in concentrating; drowsiness; excessive hunger; fast heartbeat; headache (continuing); nausea; nervousness; nightmares; restless sleep; seizures; shakiness; slurred speech; and unusual tiredness or weakness

» Recognizing what brings on symptoms of hypoglycemia, such as delaying or missing a meal or snack; drinking significant amounts of alcohol; exercising more than usual; having an illness, including vomiting or diarrhea; taking certain medications; or using other antidiabetic medication

» Knowing what to do if symptoms of hypoglycemia occur, such as eating glucose tablets or gel, corn syrup, honey, or sugar cubes; drinking fruit juice, nondiet soft drink, or sugar dissolved in water; or injecting glucagon if symptoms are severe

» Recognizing symptoms of hyperglycemia and ketoacidosis: blurred vision; drowsiness; dry mouth; flushed, dry skin; fruit-like breath odor; increased urination (frequency and volume); ketones in urine; loss of appetite; somnolence (sleepiness); stomachache, nausea, or vomiting; tiredness; troubled breathing (rapid and deep); unconsciousness; and unusual thirst

» Recognizing what brings on symptoms of hyperglycemia, such as exercising less than usual, having a fever or infection, not taking enough or skipping a dose of antidiabetic medication, or overeating or not following meal plan

» Knowing what to do if symptoms of hyperglycemia occur, such as checking blood glucose and contacting a member of the health care team

Side/adverse effects

Signs of potential side effects, especially hypoglycemia, infection, hypertension, megaloblastic anemia, and lactic acidosis

Oral Dosage Forms

GLIPIZIDE AND METFORMIN HYDROCHLORIDE TABLETS

Usual adult dose

Type 2 diabetes—

As initial therapy: Oral, 2.5 mg of glipizide and 250 mg of metformin once a day with a meal. Dosage may be increased in increments of one tablet per day every two weeks up to a maximum of 10 mg of glipizide and 2000 mg of metformin per day given in divided doses until glycemic control is attained.

As second-line therapy: Oral, 2.5 mg of glipizide and 500 mg of metformin or 5 mg of glipizide and 500 mg of metformin two times a day, with the morning and evening meals. Dosage may be increased in increments of no more than 5 mg of glipizide and 500 mg of metformin until the minimum dose necessary to achieve glycemic control. The starting dose should not exceed the daily doses of glipizide or metformin already being taken.

For patients whose FPG exceeds 280 to 320 mg/dL: As initial therapy: Oral, 2.5 mg of glipizide and 500 mg of metformin twice daily. The efficacy of patients whose FPG exceeds 320 mg/dL has not been established.

Note: When switching patients from a sulfonylurea plus metformin to the glipizide and metformin combination, the initial dose should not exceed the daily dose of glipizide (or equivalent dose of another sulfonylurea) and metformin that was being taken. The decision to switch to the nearest equivalent dose or to titrate should be based on clinical judgement.

Usual adult prescribing limits

20 mg glipizide and 2000 mg metformin daily

Usual pediatric dose

Safety and efficacy have not been established

Usual geriatric dose

See *Usual adult dose.* The initial and maintenance dose should be conservative in patients with advanced age due to the potential for decreased renal function.

Note: This medication should not be initiated in patients 80 years of age or older unless it can be demonstrated that renal function is not reduced. Maximum doses are not advised for use in elderly patients.

Strength(s) usually available

U.S.—

2.5 mg of glipizide and 250 mg of metformin hydrochloride (Rx) [*Metaglip* (microcrystalline cellulose; povidone; croscarmellose sodium; magnesium stearate)].

2.5 mg of glipizide and 500 mg of metformin hydrochloride (Rx) [*Metaglip* (microcrystalline cellulose; povidone; croscarmellose sodium; magnesium stearate)].

5 mg of glipizide and 500 mg of metformin hydrochloride (Rx) [*Metaglip* (microcrystalline cellulose; povidone; croscarmellose sodium; magnesium stearate)].

Auxiliary labeling

- Take with food
- Avoid alcohol while on this medication
- Keep out of reach of children

Developed: 07/18/2003

GLUCAGON Systemic

VA CLASSIFICATION (Primary/Secondary): HS508/AD900; DX900; GA801

Commonly used brand name(s): *Glucagon Diagnostic Kit; Glucagon Emergency Kit; Glucagon Emergency Kit for Low Blood Sugar.*

Note: For a listing of dosage forms and brand names by country availability, see *Dosage Forms* section(s).

Category

Antihypoglycemic; diagnostic aid adjunct (antispasmodic); antispasmodic; antidote (to beta-adrenergic blocking agents; to calcium channel blocking agents).

Indications

Note: Bracketed information in the *Indications* section refers to uses that are not included in U.S. product labeling.

Accepted

Hypoglycemia (treatment)—Glucagon is indicated in the correction of severe hypoglycemic conditions. Its efficacy is dependent upon the availability of glycogen in the liver. Glucagon may be used together with glucose without decreasing the effects of either, such as in patients in a very deep state of coma (e.g., Stage IV or Stage V of Himwich) in which intravenous glucose is given in addition to glucagon for a more immediate response.

Radiography, gastrointestinal, adjunct—Glucagon is indicated in barium radiographic examinations to produce hypotonicity and relaxation of the esophagus, stomach, duodenum, small bowel, and colon. Glucagon is administered to provide relaxation of smooth musculature, and to decrease peristalsis, thereby reducing patient discomfort, slowing emptying, and improving the examination quality.

[Abdominal imaging, digital angiographic, adjunct][1] or
[Abdominal imaging, computed tomographic (CT), adjunct][1] or
[Abdominal imaging, magnetic resonance, adjunct][1] or
[Pelvic imaging, magnetic resonance, adjunct][1]—Glucagon is indicated to inhibit bowel peristalsis in abdominal digital vascular imaging, abdominal and pelvic magnetic resonance imaging, and in abdominal CT scanning to prevent motion-related artifact.

[Bleeding, gastrointestinal (diagnosis adjunct)][1]—Glucagon may be beneficial as an adjuvant to Tc 99m–labeled red blood cells in the scintigraphic diagnosis of small bowel hemorrhage.

[Hysterosalpingography, adjunct][1]—Glucagon is used rarely by some clinicians to eliminate possible spasm of the fallopian tubes during hysterosalpingography in those patients whose fallopian tubes are not visualized during examination.

[Toxicity, beta-adrenergic blocking agent (treatment)][1]—Glucagon administered in large intravenous doses is indicated to treat the cardiotoxic effects, specifically bradycardia and hypotension, in overdoses of beta-adrenergic blocking agents. Glucagon may be used with isoproterenol or dobutamine. Supplemental potassium may be necessary for treated patients since glucagon tends to reduce serum potassium.

[Toxicity, calcium channel blocking agent (treatment)][1]—Glucagon is indicated in the treatment of myocardial depression caused by calcium channel blocking agents in those patients in whom conventional therapies have been ineffective.

[Esophageal obstruction, foreign body (treatment)][1]—Glucagon is indicated in the treatment of lower esophageal obstruction due to foreign bodies, including food boluses.

Unaccepted

Glucagon is of little or no help in the treatment of hypoglycemia in conditions in which hepatic glycogen stores are depleted, such as starvation, adrenal insufficiency, or chronic hypoglycemia.

Glucagon should not be used to treat birth asphyxia or hypoglycemia in premature infants or in infants who have had intrauterine growth retardation.

Glucagon has been used as an aid in the diagnosis of insulinoma and pheochromocytoma; however, USP advisory panels do not generally recommend glucagon for this use because of questions about safety.

[1]Not included in Canadian product labeling.

Pharmacology/Pharmacokinetics

Physicochemical characteristics

Source—
Animal origin: Beef or pork pancreas..
Recombinant DNA (rDNA) origin: Synthesized using rDNA process involving genetically altered *Escherichia coli*.

Chemical Group—Glucagon is a single-chain polypeptide containing 29 amino acid residues. It is chemically unrelated to insulin. One USP Unit of glucagon is equivalent to 1 International Unit of glucagon and to 1 mg of glucagon.

Molecular weight—3482.82.

pH—Reconstituted solution (animal origin): 2.5 to 3.

Mechanism of action/Effect

Promotes hepatic glycogenolysis and gluconeogenesis. Stimulates adenylate cyclase to produce increased cyclic adenosine monophosphate (cAMP), which is involved in a series of enzymatic activities. The resultant effects are increased concentrations of plasma glucose, a relaxant effect on smooth musculature, and a positive chronotropic and inotropic myocardial effect. Hepatic stores of glycogen are necessary for glucagon to elicit an antihypoglycemic effect.

Distribution

Vol_D—0.25 L per kg of body weight.

Biotransformation

Primarily hepatic and renal through enzymatic proteolysis.

Half-life

In plasma—
Animal origin: 3 to 6 minutes.
rDNA origin: 8 to 18 minutes.

Onset of action

Antihypoglycemic action—
Intravenous: 5 to 20 minutes.
Intramuscular: 15 to 26 minutes.
Subcutaneous: 30 to 45 minutes.
Smooth muscle relaxation—
Intravenous:
0.25 to 2 USP Units—45 seconds to 1 minute.
Intramuscular:
1 USP Unit—8 to 10 minutes.
2 USP Units—4 to 7 minutes.

Time to peak plasma concentration

Intramuscular—13 minutes.
Subcutaneous—20 minutes.

Peak plasma concentration

Intramuscular—6.9 nanograms per mL (nanograms/mL).
Subcutaneous—7.9 nanograms/mL.

Duration of action

Antihypoglycemic action—
90 minutes.
Smooth muscle relaxation—
Intravenous:
0.25 to 0.5 USP Units—9 to 17 minutes.
2 USP Units—22 to 25 minutes.
Intramuscular:
1 USP Unit—12 to 27 minutes.
2 USP Units—21 to 32 minutes.

Precautions to Consider

Cross-sensitivity and/or related problems

Patients who are allergic to beef or pork proteins may be allergic to animal origin glucagon.

Carcinogenicity

Studies to determine the carcinogenic potential of glucagon have not been done.

Mutagenicity

The increase in colony counts found with the Ames assay was attributed to difficulties in performing the assay with peptides and not to the mutagenic activity of glucagon.

Pregnancy/Reproduction

Fertility—Studies in rats administered glucagon at doses of up to 2 mg per kg of body weight (mg/kg) two times a day (up to 40 times the human dose based on body surface area) have not shown that glucagon causes impaired fertility.

Pregnancy—Adequate and well-controlled studies in humans have not been done.

Studies in rats administered glucagon at doses of up to 2 mg/kg two times a day (up to 40 times the human dose based on body surface area) have not shown that glucagon causes adverse effects in the fetus.

FDA Pregnancy Category B.

Breast-feeding

It is not known whether glucagon is distributed into breast milk. However, problems in humans have not been documented. Because glucagon is inactivated by gastric acid, problems are unlikely. Also, glucagon has a short half-life and generally is used only for a short time.

Pediatrics

Appropriate studies performed to date have not demonstrated pediatrics-specific problems that would limit the usefulness of glucagon in children.

Geriatrics

Appropriate studies on the relationship of age to the effects of glucagon have not been performed in the geriatric population. However, geriatrics-specific problems that would limit the usefulness of this medication in the elderly are not expected.

Drug interactions and/or related problems

The following drug interactions and/or related problems have been selected on the basis of their potential clinical significance (possible mechanism in parentheses where appropriate)—not necessarily inclusive (» = major clinical significance):

Anticoagulants, coumarin- or indandione-derivative
(concurrent use with glucagon may potentiate the anticoagulant effects; enhanced anticoagulant activity has been reported with unusually high doses of glucagon such as 25 mg or more per day for 2 or more days)

Beta-adrenergic blocking agents
(the transient increases in blood pressure and pulse rate caused by glucagon may be more pronounced with concurrent use)

Laboratory value alterations

The following have been selected on the basis of their potential clinical significance (possible effect in parentheses where appropriate)—not necessarily inclusive (» = major clinical significance):

With physiology/laboratory test values

Blood pressure and
Pulse rate
(transient increases may occur)

Potassium
(serum concentrations may be decreased with use of large doses)

Medical considerations/Contraindications

The medical considerations/contraindications included have been selected on the basis of their potential clinical significance (reasons given in parentheses where appropriate)—not necessarily inclusive (» = major clinical significance).

Risk-benefit should be considered when the following medical problems exist:

Allergy to beef or pork proteins, history of

» Insulinoma, or history of
(blood glucose concentrations may be decreased as a result of insulin released by the insulinoma in response to glucagon's antihypoglycemic effect)

» Pheochromocytoma
(increased risk of hypertension due to stimulation of the release of catecholamines)

Sensitivity to glucagon

For use as a diagnostic aid adjunct (in addition to those listed above)

» Diabetes mellitus
(increased risk of hyperglycemia)

Patient monitoring

The following may be especially important in patient monitoring (other tests may be warranted in some patients, depending on condition; » = major clinical significance):

For treatment of hypoglycemia

Blood glucose determinations
(recommended every 15 minutes until blood glucose concentrations return to normal, then hourly for an additional 3 to 4 hours)

For treatment of calcium channel blocking agent toxicity

Calcium, total and
Calcium, total ionized
(recommended to determine efficacy; failure of glucagon therapy may be associated with hypocalcemia and hypercalcemia)

Side/Adverse Effects

The following side/adverse effects have been selected on the basis of their potential clinical significance (possible signs and symptoms in parentheses where appropriate)—not necessarily inclusive:

Those indicating need for medical attention

Incidence less frequent

Allergic reaction (dizziness; lightheadedness; skin rash; trouble in breathing)

Those indicating need for medical attention only if they continue or are bothersome

Incidence less frequent or rare

Fast heartbeat; nausea; vomiting

Note: The incidence of *nausea* and *vomiting* is generally dependent upon dose (it is higher with the 2-mg dose than with lower doses) and, with intravenous use, the rate of injection; these effects may be diminished by slower intravenous administration.

Overdose

For specific information on the agents used in the management of glucagon overdose, see:

- *Phentolamine (Systemic)* monograph; and/or
- *Potassium Supplements (Systemic)* monograph.

For more information on the management of overdose or unintentional ingestion, **contact a Poison Control Center** (see *Poison Control Center Listing*).

Clinical effects of overdose

The following effects have been selected on the basis of their potential clinical significance (possible signs and symptoms in parentheses where appropriate)—not necessarily inclusive:

Continuing nausea; continuing vomiting; diarrhea; gastric hypotonicity; hypertension; hypokalemic syndrome (severe weakness of extremities and trunk; loss of appetite; nausea; vomiting; irregular heartbeat; muscle cramps or pain)

Treatment of overdose

Due to the short half-life of glucagon, treatment of glucagon overdose is primarily symptomatic and supportive. Also, because it is a polypeptide, glucagon would be destroyed rapidly in the gastrointestinal tract if it were unintentionally ingested.

Specific treatment—Treating hypokalemia with potassium supplementation and hypertension with phentolamine.

Monitoring—Monitoring of serum electrolytes, especially potassium; monitoring blood glucose concentrations and blood pressure.

Supportive care—Replacing fluids as necessary, due to excessive nausea and vomiting. Patients in whom intentional overdose is confirmed or suspected should be referred for psychiatric consultation.

Patient Consultation

As an aid to patient consultation, refer to *Advice for the Patient, Glucagon (Systemic)*.

In providing consultation, consider emphasizing the following selected information (» = major clinical significance):

Before using this medication

» Conditions affecting use, especially:
Sensitivity to glucagon
Other medical problems, especially diabetes mellitus (for diagnostic procedures only), insulinoma or history of, or pheochromocytoma

Proper use of this medication

» Using medication only as directed by physician; explaining proper use to family member or friend; reviewing use on a regular basis

» Reading directions in glucagon kit before medication is actually needed; knowing how to reconstitute and inject properly

» Not keeping after expiration date on vial; checking date regularly; replacing medication before it expires; discarding unused portion after mixing

» Proper dosing

Proper storage

Precautions while using this medication

» Recognizing what brings on symptoms of hypoglycemia, such as using too much insulin or oral antidiabetic medication; delaying or missing a meal or snack; illness, especially vomiting or diarrhea; and exercising more than usual

» Recognizing early symptoms of hypoglycemia: anxiety, behavior change similar to drunkenness, blurred vision, cold sweats, confusion, cool pale skin, difficulty in concentrating, drowsiness, excessive hunger, fast heartbeat, headache, nausea, nervousness, nightmares, restless sleep, shakiness, slurred speech, and unusual tiredness and weakness; unless corrected, will lead to unconsciousness, seizures, and possibly death

Being aware that symptoms of hypoglycemia vary among individuals; learning to recognize own symptoms; checking blood sugar if hypoglycemia is suspected

» Knowing what to do if symptoms of mild hypoglycemia occur: eating glucose tablets or gel, corn syrup, honey, or sugar cubes; drinking fruit juice, nondiet soft drink, or sugar dissolved in water; also eating a small snack, such as crackers and cheese, half a sandwich, or drinking a glass of milk when scheduled meal is longer than 1 hour away; not eating hard candy or mints because the sugar does not get into the blood stream quickly enough; not eating foods high in fat, such as chocolate, because fat slows gastric emptying; checking blood sugar after 10 to 20 minutes

» Going to the doctor or hospital immediately if symptoms do not improve after eating or drinking a source of sugar

» Administering glucagon and calling the patient's physician if seizures or unconsciousness occurs; preventing choking by not forcing the patient to eat or drink anything

Steps to be taken after glucagon is injected for hypoglycemia:

» After the injection, turning the patient onto the left side to prevent choking if vomiting occurs

» If the patient does not regain consciousness within 15 minutes, giving second dose; simultaneously, getting emergency help

When the patient is conscious enough to swallow, initially giving some form of sugar to take orally, then having patient eat crackers and cheese or half a sandwich or drink a glass of milk to prevent hypoglycemia from recurring before the next scheduled meal or snack

Monitoring blood glucose concentrations throughout episode, treatment, and hourly for 3 to 4 hours after the patient regains consciousness

» If nausea and vomiting prevent the patient from swallowing some form of sugar for an hour after injection, getting medical assistance

» Keeping physician informed of hypoglycemic episodes and use of glucagon

» Replacing supply of glucagon as soon as possible

At all times wearing medical identification and carrying identification card that lists medical condition and medications

Side/adverse effects

Signs of potential side effects, especially allergic reaction

General Dosing Information

Glucagon should not be used in concentrations greater than 1 USP Unit (1 mg) per mL.

For use as an antihypoglycemic

Prior to the administration of glucagon, a rapid blood glucose test should be performed to confirm that the patient has low blood sugar. A physician should be contacted at the time of glucagon administration. Blood glucose should also be monitored throughout the hypoglycemic episode, treatment period, and for 3 to 4 hours after the patient regains consciousness.

Patient response usually occurs within 15 minutes after administration of glucagon. An additional dose may be given if no response is evident within this time. Medical care will be needed if response is not obtained following a second glucagon injection; intravenous glucose will be required if the patient fails to respond to glucagon.

After the patient is sufficiently alert and oriented, oral supplemental sugar (glucose or sucrose) must be given to prevent secondary hypoglycemia. Patients with type 1 diabetes have less of an increase in blood glucose concentration than do patients with stable type 2 diabetes. Therefore, it is especially important that supplemental carbohydrates be given as soon as possible to patients with type 1 diabetes. Emergency room evaluation and/or hospital admission should be considered for all patients experiencing a hypoglycemic episode from oral antidiabetic agents (especially chlorpropamide), since hypoglycemia may recur after blood glucose concentrations are normalized.

If nausea and vomiting result from glucagon administration and the patient is unable to ingest some form of sugar for 1 hour, medical assistance should be obtained immediately. Severe hypoglycemia may rapidly recur in these circumstances.

Parenteral Dosage Forms

Note: Bracketed uses in the *Dosage Forms* section refer to categories of use and/or indications that are not included in U.S. product labeling.

One mg of glucagon is equivalent to 1 USP Unit of glucagon and to 1 International Unit (IU) of glucagon.

GLUCAGON FOR INJECTION (ANIMAL ORIGIN) USP

Usual adult and adolescent dose

Hypoglycemia—

Intramuscular, intravenous, or subcutaneous, 1 mg, repeated after fifteen minutes if necessary.

Radiography, gastrointestinal or
[Abdominal imaging, digital angiographic][1] or
[Abdominal imaging, computed tomographic or magnetic resonance][1] or
[Pelvic imaging, magnetic resonance][1] or
[Hysterosalpingography][1]—

Intravenous, 0.25 to 2 mg.

Note: For examination of the colon, the dose should be administered intramuscularly approximately ten minutes prior to the procedure.

Doses in the upper range and/or intramuscular administration may be preferred by some clinicians to achieve hypotonicity during the prolonged scan times associated with magnetic resonance imaging. The duration of action of glucagon is longer with intramuscular administration.

[Toxicity, beta-adrenergic blocking agent][1]—

Intravenous, initially, 50 to 150 mcg (0.05 to 0.15 mg) per kg of body weight over one minute, to be followed by a 1- to 5-mg-per-hour infusion.

[Toxicity, calcium channel blocking agent][1]—

Intravenous, initially 2 mg. Maintenance dosing is then titrated according to patient response.

[Esophageal obstruction due to foreign body][1]—

Intravenous, 0.5 to 2 mg, repeated after ten to twenty minutes if necessary.

Usual pediatric dose

Hypoglycemia—

For patients weighing up to 20 kg—

Intramuscular, intravenous, or subcutaneous: 0.5 mg or 20 to 30 mcg (0.02 to 0.03 mg) per kg of body weight, repeated after fifteen minutes if necessary.

For patients weighing 20 kg or over—

See *Usual adult and adolescent dose*.

Usual geriatric dose

See *Usual adult and adolescent dose*.

Strength(s) usually available

U.S.—

1 mg (1 USP Unit) (Rx) [*Glucagon Emergency Kit* (lactose 49 mg); GENERIC].

Canada—

1 mg (1 USP Unit) (Rx) [*Glucagon Emergency Kit* (lactose 49 mg); GENERIC].

Packaging and storage

Prior to reconstitution, store between 15 and 30 °C (59 and 86 °F), unless otherwise specified by manufacturer.

Preparation of dosage form

The entire contents of the diluent-filled syringe should be injected into the vial of glucagon. The vial then should be swirled gently until the glucagon is dissolved completely.

Stability

Glucagon should be used immediately after it is reconstituted. Any unused solution should be discarded.

Incompatibilities

Glucagon may precipitate from saline solution and solutions having a pH of 3 to 9.5.

Auxiliary labeling

• Discard unused portion.

Note

Make sure patient understands use of syringe supplied with kit.

Check patient's understanding of preparing and administering medication.

Make sure patient routinely checks expiration date of medication.

GLUCAGON FOR INJECTION (RECOMBINANT)

Usual adult and adolescent dose

See *Glucagon for Injection USP (Animal Origin)*.

Usual pediatric dose
See *Glucagon for Injection USP (Animal Origin)*.

Usual geriatric dose
See *Glucagon for Injection USP (Animal Origin)*.

Strength(s) usually available
U.S.—
1 mg (1 USP Unit) (Rx) [*Glucagon Diagnostic Kit* (lactose 49 mg); *Glucagon Emergency Kit for Low Blood Sugar* (lactose 49 mg)].

Canada—
Not commercially available.

Packaging and storage
Prior to reconstitution, store between 15 and 30 °C (59 and 86 °F), unless otherwise specified by manufacturer.

Preparation of dosage form
The entire contents of the diluent-filled syringe should be injected into the vial of glucagon. The vial then should be swirled gently until the glucagon is dissolved completely.

Stability
Glucagon should be used immediately after it is reconstituted. Any unused solution should be discarded.

Incompatibilities
Glucagon may precipitate from solutions having a pH of 3 to 9.5.

Auxiliary labeling
- Discard unused portion.

Note
Make sure patient understands use of syringe supplied with kit.

Check patient's understanding of preparing and administering medication.

Make sure patient routinely checks expiration date of medication.

[1]Not included in Canadian product labeling.

Revised: 01/29/1999

GLUTAMINE Systemic†

VA CLASSIFICATION (Primary/Secondary): GA900/TN503

Commonly used brand name(s): *NutreStore*.

Some other commonly used names are:
L-glutamine

Note: For a listing of dosage forms and brand names by country availability, see *Dosage Forms* section(s).

†Not commercially available in Canada.

Category
Nutritional supplement (amino acid).

Indications

Accepted
Bowel syndrome, short (treatment)—Glutamine is indicated, in conjunction with recombinant human growth hormone (rhGH) and a specialized oral diet (SOD), for the treatment of short bowel syndrome.

Pharmacology/Pharmacokinetics

Physicochemical characteristics
Molecular weight—L-glutamine: 146.15 d.

Mechanism of action/Effect
L-glutamine has important functions in regulation of gastrointestinal cell growth, function, and regeneration. Under normal conditions, glutamine concentration is maintained in the body by dietary intake and synthesis from endogenous glutamate. Glutamine concentration decreases and tissue glutamine metabolism increases during many catabolic disease states, and thus glutamine is often considered a "conditionally essential" amino acid.

Absorption
Highly variable depending on the length, segment, and presence/absence of ileal-cecal valve for the remnant bowel; 150 mcg/mL following a single dose of 0.1 gram per kilogram to six subjects.

Distribution
Volume of distribution (Vol_D)—Approximately 200 mL/kg, following an intravenous (IV) bolus dose

Biotransformation
Exogenous glutamine is expected to undergo similar metabolism to endogenous glutamine. Endogenous glutamine's metabolic activity includes the formation of glutamate, and synthesis of proteins, nucleotides, and amino sugars.

Half-life
Terminal—approximately 1 hour following an IV bolus dose.

Time to peak concentration
Approximately 30 minutes after administration.

Elimination
Metabolism is the major route. Eliminated by glomerular filtration and almost completely reabsorbed by renal tubules.

Precautions to Consider

Carcinogenicity/Mutagenicity
Long term studies in animals to determine the carcinogenic and mutagenic potential of L-glutamine have not been done.

Pregnancy/Reproduction
Fertility—Studies to evaluate the potential for impairment of fertility of L-glutamine have not been conducted.

Pregnancy—Studies have not been done in humans.

Studies have not been done in animals.

Glutamine should be given to a pregnant woman only if clearly needed.

FDA Pregnancy Category C

Labor and delivery—Unknown.

Breast-feeding
It is not known whether L-glutamine is distributed in human milk. Because many drugs are distributed in human milk, caution should be exercised when L-glutamine is administered to a nursing woman.

Pediatrics
Safety and effectiveness in pediatric patients have not been established.

Geriatrics
No information is available on the relationship of age to the effects of L-glutamine in geriatric patients. However, elderly patients are more likely to have greater frequency of decreased hepatic, renal or cardiac function as well as concomitant disease requiring individualized dose selection.

Drug interactions and/or related problems
The following drug interactions and/or related problems have been selected on the basis of their potential clinical significance (possible mechanism in parentheses where appropriate)—not necessarily inclusive (» = major clinical significance):

Note: Formal drug interaction studies have not been done.

Medical considerations/Contraindications
The medical considerations/contraindications included have been selected on the basis of their potential clinical significance (reasons given in parentheses where appropriate)—not necessarily inclusive (» = major clinical significance).

Risk-benefit should be considered when the following medical problems exist:

Hepatic function impairment
(increase in metabolized glutamine to glutamate and ammonia.)

Patient monitoring
The following may be especially important in patient monitoring (other tests may be warranted in some patients, depending on condition; » = major clinical significance):

» Hepatic function or
» Renal function
(routine monitoring recommended; glutamine is metabolized to glutamate and ammonia which may increase in patients with hepatic dysfunction.)

Side/Adverse Effects
The following side/adverse effects have been selected on the basis of their potential clinical significance (possible signs and symptoms in parentheses where appropriate)—not necessarily inclusive:

Those indicating need for medical attention
Incidence less frequent

Allergic reaction (cough; difficulty swallowing; dizziness; fast heartbeat; hives; itching; puffiness or swelling of the eyelids or around the eyes, face, lips or tongue; shortness of breath; skin rash; tightness in chest; unusual tiredness or weakness; wheezing); ***pancreatitis*** (bloating; chills; constipation; darkened urine; fast heartbeat; fever; indigestion; loss of appetite; nausea; pains in stomach, side, or abdomen, possibly radiating to the back; vomiting; yellow eyes or skin); ***pyelo-***

nephritis (chills; fever; frequent or painful urination; headache; stomach pain); ***renal calculus*** (blood in urine; difficult urination; pain in lower back; pain or burning while urinating; sudden decrease in amount of urine); ***sepsis*** (chills; confusion; dizziness; lightheadedness; fainting; fast heartbeat; fever; rapid, shallow breathing); ***vascular disorder*** (changes in skin color; cold hands and feet; pain, redness, or swelling in arm or leg)

Those indicating need for medical attention only if they continue or are bothersome

Incidence more frequent

Infection (fever or chills; cough or hoarseness; lower back or side pain; painful or difficult urination); ***tenesmus*** (frequent urge to defecate; straining while passing stool)

Incidence less frequent

Abdomen enlarged (swelling of abdominal or stomach area; full or bloated feeling; pressure in the stomach); ***arthralgia*** (pain in joints, muscle pain or stiffness difficulty in moving); ***abdominal pain*** (stomach pain); ***back pain; bacterial infection*** (fever or chills; cough or hoarseness; lower back or side pain; painful or difficult urination); ***breast pain, female; chest pain; Crohn's disease aggravated*** (diarrhea; fever; rectal bleeding; stomach pain; weight loss); ***constipation*** (difficulty having a bowel movement (stool)); ***dehydration*** (confusion; decreased urination; dizziness; dry mouth; fainting; increase in heart rate; lightheadedness; rapid breathing; sunken eyes; thirst; unusual tiredness or weakness; wrinkled skin); ***depression*** (discouragement; feeling sad or empty; irritability; lack of appetite; loss of interest or pleasure; tiredness; trouble concentrating; trouble sleeping); ***dizziness; dry mouth; ear or hearing symptoms; edema, facial*** (swelling of face); ***edema, peripheral*** (swelling of hands, ankles, feet, or lower legs); ***fatigue*** (unusual tiredness or weakness); ***flatulence*** (bloated full feeling; excess air or gas in stomach or intestines; passing gas); ***fever; flu-like disorder*** (chills; cough; diarrhea; fever; general feeling of discomfort or illness; headache; joint pain; loss of appetite; muscle aches and pains; nausea; runny nose; shivering; sore throat; sweating; trouble sleeping; unusual tiredness or weakness; vomiting); ***fungal vaginosis*** (change in the color, amount, or odor of vaginal discharge); ***gastric ulcer*** (loss of appetite; nausea; stomach bloating, burning, cramping, or pain; vomiting; weight loss); ***gastrointestinal fistula; headache; hemorrhoids*** (bleeding after defecation; uncomfortable swelling around anus); ***hepatic function, abnormal*** (abdominal or stomach pain; chills; light-colored stools; dark urine; diarrhea; dizziness; fever; headache; itching; loss of appetite; nausea; rash; unpleasant breath odor; unusual tiredness or weakness; vomiting of blood; yellow eyes or skin); ***hypoaesthesia*** (abnormal or decreased touch sensation); ***injection site pain; injection site reaction*** (bleeding, blistering, burning, coldness, discoloration of skin, feeling of pressure, hives, infection, inflammation, itching, lumps, numbness, pain, rash, redness, scarring, soreness, stinging, swelling, tenderness, tingling, ulceration, or warmth at site); ***insomnia*** (sleeplessness; trouble sleeping; unable to sleep); ***laryngitis*** (cough; dryness or soreness of throat; hoarseness; trouble in swallowing; voice changes); ***myalgia*** (joint pain; swollen joints; muscle aching or cramping; muscle pains or stiffness; difficulty in moving); ***nail disorder*** (discoloration of fingernails or toenails); ***nausea; pain; pharyngitis*** (body aches or pain; congestion; cough; dryness or soreness of throat; fever; hoarseness; runny nose; tender, swollen glands in neck; trouble in swallowing; voice changes); ***pruritis*** (itching skin); ***rash; rhinitis*** (stuffy nose; runny nose; sneezing); ***rigors*** (feeling unusually cold shivering); ***thirst; viral infection*** (chills; cough or hoarseness; fever; cold flu-like symptoms); ***vomiting***

Overdose

For more information on the management of overdose or unintentional ingestion, **contact a poison control center** (see *Poison Control Center Listing*).

Treatment of overdose

Supportive care—

Patients in whom intentional overdose is confirmed or suspected should be referred for psychiatric consultation.

Patient Consultation

As an aid to patient consultation, refer to *Advice for the Patient, Glutamine (Systemic)*.

In providing consultation, consider emphasizing the following selected information (» = major clinical significance):

Importance of diet

Importance of proper nutrition; may include specialized diet, enteral feedings, parenteral nutrition, fluid and micronutrient supplements.

Before using this medication

» Conditions affecting use, especially:

Pregnancy—Not recommended for use during pregnancy; glutamine should be given to a pregnant woman only if clearly needed

Breast-feeding—It is not known whether glutamine is distributed in human milk. Because many drugs are distributed in human milk, caution should be exercised when glutamine is administered to a nursing woman

Use in children—Safety and effectiveness in pediatric patients have not been established

Use in the elderly—Elderly patients may have greater frequency of decreased hepatic, renal or cardiac function as well as concomitant disease requiring individualized dose selection

Proper use of this medication

» Proper dosing

Missed dose: Taking as soon as possible; not taking if almost time for next scheduled dose; not doubling doses

» Proper storage

Precautions while using this medication

» Regular visits to physician to check progress

Side/adverse effects

Signs of potential side effects, especially allergic reaction, pancreatitis, pyelonephritis, renal calculus, sepsis, or vascular disorder

General Dosing Information

Glutamine should only be taken under the direction of a physician, registered dietician or nutritionist.

Glutamine administered with human growth hormone should be used in conjunction with optimal management including a specialized diet, enteral feedings, parenteral nutrition, fluid and micronutrient supplements.

A dose may be delayed for up to 2 hours in the event of a patient's transient intolerance to oral intake.

Diet/Nutrition

Optimal management of SBS may consist of a specialized oral diet (SOD) of high carbohydrate and low-fat, adjusted for an individual patient's requirements and preferences.

Oral Dosage Forms

Note: Bracketed information in the *Indications* section refers to uses that are not included in U.S. product labeling.

L-GLUTAMINE POWDER FOR ORAL SOLUTION

Usual adult dose

Bowel syndrome, short (treatment)—

Oral, 30 grams daily, (5 grams taken 6 times a day) taken with meals or snacks at 2 to 3 hour intervals while awake, for up to 16 weeks. Safety and efficacy have not been studied beyond 16 weeks of treatment.

Note: For optimal management of SBS, glutamine should be administered as a co-therapy with recombinant human growth hormone.

Usual pediatric dose

Safety and efficacy have not been established

Usual geriatric dose

See *Usual adult dose*.

Strength(s) usually available

U.S.—

5 g of L-glutamine powder (Rx) [*NutreStore*].

Packaging and storage

Store at 25 °C (77 °F), with excursions allowed to 15° to 30°C (59° to 86°C).

Preparation of dosage form

Each dose of L-glutamine should be reconstituted in 8-oz (250 mL) of water, prior to consumption. The volume of water may be varied according to the patient's preference.

Developed: 09/24/2004

GLYBURIDE—See *Antidiabetic Agents, Sulfonylurea (Systemic)*

GLYBURIDE AND METFORMIN

Systemic

VA CLASSIFICATION (Primary): HS509

Commonly used brand name(s): *Glucovance.*

NOTE: The *Glyburide and Metformin (Systemic)* monograph is maintained on the *USP DI* electronic database. A copy of the most recent revision of the complete monograph can be accessed on the *USP DI* Updates Online website. See the front cover of book for details on accessing the site. The information that follows is selectively abstracted from the complete monograph and is provided to facilitate drug use review and patient counseling.

Note: For a listing of dosage forms and brand names by country availability, see *Dosage Forms* section(s).

Category

Antidiabetic agent.

Indications

Accepted

Diabetes, type 2 (treatment)—The combination of glyburide and metformin is indicated as an adjunct to diet in the treatment of patients with type 2 diabetes (previously referred to as non-insulin-dependent diabetes mellitus [NIDDM]) whose blood glucose cannot be controlled by diet and exercise alone.The combination of glyburide and metformin also is indicated as second-line therapy when diet, exercise, and initial treatment with a sulfonylurea or metformin do not result in adequate glycemic control in patients with type 2 diabetes.

Patient Consultation

As an aid to patient consultation, refer to *Advice for the Patient, Glyburide and Metformin (Systemic)*

In providing consultation, consider emphasizing the following selected information (» = major clinical significance):

Before using this medication

» Conditions affecting use, especially:
- Hypersensitivity to glyburide or metformin
- Pregnancy—Diet or diet/insulin is recommended to prevent maternal and fetal problems; importance of controlling and monitoring blood glucose during pregnancy; alerting physician if planning to become pregnant
- Breast-feeding—It is not known whether glyburide or metformin passes into human breast milk.
- Other medications, especially alcohol, beta adrenergic blockers, cimetidine, or furosemide
- Other medical problems, especially acute or chronic metabolic acidosis, acute myocardial infarction, cardiovascular collapse, congestive heart failure, diabetic coma or ketoacidosis, diagnostic radiologic exams using intravascular iodinated contrast media, hepatic function impairment, major surgery, renal function impairment, septicemia, or severe dehydration

Proper use of this medication

» Importance of adherence to recommended regimens for diet, exercise, and glucose monitoring

Taking medication with meals to reduce gastrointestinal symptoms

» Proper dosing

Proper storage

Precautions while using this medication

» Regular visits to physician to check progress

» Recognizing symptoms of lactic acidosis, such as abdominal discomfort; decreased appetite; diarrhea; fast, shallow breathing; general feeling of discomfort; muscle pain or cramping; or unusual sleepiness, tiredness, or weakness

» Getting immediate emergency medical help if symptoms of lactic acidosis occur

» *Carefully following special instructions of health care team:*
- Discussing use of alcohol and tobacco
- Not taking other medications unless discussed with physician
- Getting counseling for family members to help the patient with diabetes; also, special counseling for pregnancy planning and contraception
- Making travel plans that include readiness for diabetic emergencies and eating meals at the usual times, even with changing time zones
- Preparing for and understanding what to do in case of diabetic emergency; carrying medical history and current medication list and wearing medical identification

» Recognizing symptoms of hypoglycemia: anxiety; behavior change similar to drunkenness; blurred vision; cold sweats; coma; confusion; cool, pale skin; difficulty in concentrating; drowsiness; excessive hunger; fast heartbeat; headache (continuing); nausea; nervousness; nightmares; restless sleep; seizures; shakiness; slurred speech; and unusual tiredness or weakness

» Recognizing what brings on symptoms of hypoglycemia, such as delaying or missing a meal or snack; drinking significant amounts of alcohol; exercising more than usual; having an illness, including vomiting or diarrhea; taking certain medications; or using other antidiabetic medication

» Knowing what to do if symptoms of hypoglycemia occur, such as eating glucose tablets or gel, corn syrup, honey, or sugar cubes; drinking fruit juice, nondiet soft drink, or sugar dissolved in water; or injecting glucagon if symptoms are severe

» Recognizing symptoms of hyperglycemia and ketoacidosis: blurred vision; drowsiness; dry mouth; flushed, dry skin; fruit-like breath odor; increased urination (frequency and volume); ketones in urine; loss of appetite; somnolence (sleepiness); stomachache, nausea, or vomiting; tiredness; troubled breathing (rapid and deep); unconsciousness; and unusual thirst

» Recognizing what brings on symptoms of hyperglycemia, such as exercising less than usual, having a fever or infection, not taking enough or skipping a dose of antidiabetic medication, or overeating or not following meal plan

» Knowing what to do if symptoms of hyperglycemia occur, such as checking blood glucose and contacting a member of the health care team

Side/adverse effects

Signs of potential side effects, especially hypoglycemia, upper respiratory infection, and lactic acidosis

Oral Dosage Forms

GLYBURIDE AND METFORMIN HYDROCHLORIDE TABLETS

Usual adult dose

Type 2 diabetes—

As initial therapy: Oral, 1.25 mg of glyburide and 250 mg of metformin one or two times a day with meals. Dosage may be increased in increments of 1.25 mg of glyburide and 250 mg of metformin per day every two weeks until the minimum dose necessary to achieve glycemic control is attained.

As second-line therapy: Oral, 2.5 mg of glyburide and 500 mg of metformin or 5 mg of glyburide and 500 mg of metformin two times a day, with the morning and evening meals. Dosage may be increased in increments of no more than 5 mg of glyburide and 500 mg of metformin until the minimum dose necessary to achieve glycemic control is attained.

Note: When switching patients from a sulfonylurea plus metformin to the glyburide and metformin combination, the initial dose should not exceed the daily dose of glyburide (or equivalent dose of another sulfonylurea) and metformin that was being taken.

Usual adult prescribing limits

20 mg glyburide and 2000 mg metformin daily.

Usual pediatric dose

Safety and efficacy have not been established.

Usual geriatric dose

See *Usual adult dose*.

Note: This medication should not be initiated in patients 80 years of age or older unless it can be demonstrated that renal function is not reduced. Maximum doses are not advised for use in elderly patients.

Strength(s) usually available

U.S.—

1.25 mg of glyburide and 250 mg of metformin hydrochloride (Rx) [*Glucovance* (microcrystalline cellulose; povidone; croscarmellose sodium; magnesium stearate)].

2.5 mg of glyburide and 500 mg of metformin hydrochloride (Rx) [*Glucovance* (microcrystalline cellulose; povidone; croscarmellose sodium; magnesium stearate)].

5 mg of glyburide and 500 mg of metformin hydrochloride (Rx) [*Glucovance* (microcrystalline cellulose; povidone; croscarmellose sodium; magnesium stearate)].

Auxiliary labeling
- Take with food.
- Keep out of reach of children.

Developed: 12/07/2000

GLYCERIN—See *Glycerin (Systemic), Laxatives (Local)*

GLYCOPYRROLATE—See *Anticholinergics/Antispasmodics (Systemic)*

GOLD SODIUM THIOMALATE—See *Gold Compounds (Systemic)*

GRANISETRON Systemic

VA CLASSIFICATION (Primary): GA605

Commonly used brand name(s): *Kytril*.

Note: For a listing of dosage forms and brand names by country availability, see *Dosage Forms* section(s).

Category

Antiemetic.

Indications

Note: Bracketed information in the *Indications* section refers to uses that are not included in U.S. product labeling.

General Considerations

Granisetron does not stimulate gastric or intestinal peristalsis. Therefore, it should not be used instead of nasogastric suction.

Accepted

Nausea and vomiting, cancer chemotherapy-induced (prophylaxis)—Granisetron is indicated for the prevention of nausea and vomiting associated with initial and repeat courses of moderately or severely emetogenic cancer chemotherapy, including high-dose cisplatin.

Studies have found intravenous granisetron to be as effective as high-dose metoclopramide plus dexamethasone, and superior to dexamethasone plus chlorpromazine or prochlorperazine in preventing nausea and vomiting induced by high-dose cisplatin, and by moderately emetogenic chemotherapy, respectively, during the acute phase lasting 24 hours after the start of chemotherapy. However, the dose of granisetron used in many of these studies was higher than the dose that is currently recommended. Unlike metoclopramide, granisetron has no dopamine receptor antagonist activity and thus does not induce extrapyramidal side effects.

Nausea and vomiting, cancer radiotherapy–induced (prophylaxis)—Granisetron is indicated for the prevention of nausea and vomiting associated with radiation, including total body irradiation and fractionated abdominal radiation.

Nausea and vomiting, cancer radiotherapy–induced (prophylaxis)[1]—Granisetron injection may be used to prevent the nausea and vomiting associated with total body or upper hemibody irradiation in patients undergoing bone marrow transplantation.

[1]Not included in Canadian product labeling.

Pharmacology/Pharmacokinetics

Physicochemical characteristics

Molecular weight—348.9.

pH—4.7 to 7.3

Mechanism of action/Effect

Antiemetic—Granisetron is a potent, selective antagonist of 5-hydroxytryptamine (serotonin) subtype 3 (5-HT_3) receptors. 5-HT_3 receptors are present peripherally on vagal nerve terminals and centrally in the area postrema of the brain. Cytotoxic drugs and radiation damage gastrointestinal mucosa, causing the release of serotonin from the enterochromaffin cells of the gastrointestinal tract. Stimulation of 5-HT_3 receptors causes transmission of sensory signals to the vomiting center via vagal afferent fibers to induce vomiting. By binding to 5-HT_3 receptors, granisetron blocks vomiting mediated by serotonin release.

Granisetron has little or no affinity for other serotonin receptors, including 5-HT_1, 5-HT_{1A}, 5-$HT_{1B/C}$, or 5-HT_2; for alpha$_1$-, alpha$_2$-, or beta-adrenoreceptors; for dopamine D_2 receptors; for histamine H_1 receptors; for benzodiazepine receptors; for picrotoxin receptors; or for opioid receptors. In most human studies, granisetron has had little effect on blood pressure, heart rate, or electrocardiogram (ECG). Other studies have found no effect on plasma prolactin or aldosterone concentrations.

Other actions/effects

Granisetron, administered in single or multiple oral doses to volunteers, reduced colonic transit time, perhaps by antagonizing the effects of serotonin on the cholinergic neurons of the colon. However, a single intravenous infusion (of 50 or 200 micrograms of granisetron per kg of body weight [mcg/kg]) administered to volunteers showed no effect on oro-cecal transit time.

Distribution

The volume of distribution in cancer patients following a 5-minute infusion of 40 mcg/kg was 2 to 3 L/kg. The volume of distribution in healthy volunteers following administration of a single 1-mg oral dose of granisetron was 3.94 L/kg. Granisetron distributes freely between plasma and erythrocytes.

Protein binding

Moderate (65%).

Biotransformation

Hepatic; undergoes *N*-demethylation and aromatic ring oxidation followed by conjugation. Animal studies suggest that some of the metabolites may have 5-HT_3 receptor antagonist activity.

Half-life

Intravenous—The elimination half-life in healthy volunteers following a single intravenous dose of 40 mcg/kg has been reported as 4 to 5 hours. The elimination half-life in cancer patients following a single intravenous dose of 40 mcg/kg has been reported as 9 to 12 hours. However, there is wide intrapatient and interpatient variability.

Oral—The elimination half-life in healthy volunteers following a single 1-mg dose has been reported as 6.23 hours.

Peak plasma concentration

Intravenous—Following a 5-minute infusion of 40 mcg of granisetron per kg of body weight, a mean peak plasma concentration of 63.8 nanograms per mL (nanograms/mL) was reported in adult cancer patients, and a mean value of 42.8 nanograms/mL was reported in healthy volunteers. Following a 3-minute infusion of 40 mcg of granisetron per kg of body weight to healthy volunteers, a mean peak plasma concentration of 64.3 nanograms/mL was reported in subjects 21 to 42 years of age, and a mean value of 57 nanograms/mL was reported in subjects 65 to 81 years of age.

Oral—Following an oral dose of 1 mg of granisetron twice a day for 7 days, a mean peak plasma concentration of 5.99 nanograms/mL (range, 0.63 to 30.9 nanograms/mL) was reported in adult cancer patients. Following a single oral dose of 1 mg, a mean value of 3.63 nanograms/mL (range, 0.27 to 9.14 nanograms/mL) was reported in healthy volunteers. When healthy volunteers received a single oral 10-mg dose of granisetron with food, the area under the plasma concentration-time curve (AUC) was decreased by 5% and the peak plasma concentration was increased by 30%.

Elimination

Predominantly hepatic. In healthy volunteers, approximately 8 to 15% of an intravenous dose, and 11% of an oral dose, of granisetron is recovered unchanged in the urine. The remainder of the dose is excreted as metabolites, 48 to 49% in the urine and 34 to 38% in the feces.

Precautions to Consider

Cross-sensitivity and/or related problems

Carcinogenicity/Tumorigenicity

In a 2-year study in rats, granisetron—given orally in doses corresponding to 20 and 101 times the recommended human oral dose (81 and 405 times the recommended human intravenous dose, respectively)—produced a statistically significant increase in the incidence of hepatocellular carcinomas and adenomas in males at 20 times the recommended oral dose and females at 101 times the recommended oral dose. In a 1-year study in rats, granisetron given orally in a dose corresponding to 405 times the recommended human oral dose (1622 times the recommended human intravenous dose) produced hepatocellular adenomas in males and females. A 2-year mouse carcinogenicity study of granisetron did not show a statistically significant increase in tumor incidence. However the study was not conclusive.

Mutagenicity

Granisetron was not mutagenic in the *in vitro* Ames test and mouse lymphoma cell forward mutation assay, the *in vivo* mouse micronucleus test, and *in vitro* and *ex vivo* rat hepatocyte unscheduled DNA synthesis (UDS) assays. However, granisetron produced a significant increase in UDS in HeLa cells *in vitro* and a significantly increased incidence of cells with polyploidy in an *in vitro* human lymphocyte chromosomal aberration test.

Pregnancy/Reproduction

Fertility—Granisetron was found to have no effect on the fertility and reproductive performance of male or female rats when given subcutaneously a dose corresponding to 97 times the recommended human intravenous dose (405 times the recommended human oral dose).

Pregnancy—Adequate and well-controlled studies have not been done in humans. Because animal reproduction studies are not always predictive of human response, this drug should be used during pregnancy only if clearly needed.

Studies in pregnant rats and rabbits given intravenous doses corresponding to 146 and 96 times the recommended human intravenous dose (507 and 255 times the recommended human oral dose), respectively, have not shown that granisetron causes adverse effects in the fetus.

FDA Pregnancy Category B.

Breast-feeding

It is not known whether granisetron is distributed into breast milk. Because many drugs are distributed into human milk, caution should be exercised when granisetron is administered to a nursing woman.

Pediatrics

Intravenous—Appropriate studies performed to date have not demonstrated pediatrics-specific problems that would limit the use of intravenous granisetron in children 2 years of age and older. Safety and efficacy in children up to 2 years of age have not been established.

Oral—Appropriate studies on the relationship of age to the effects of oral granisetron have not been performed in the pediatric population. Safety and efficacy have not been established.

Geriatrics

Studies performed in patients 65 years of age or older have not demonstrated geriatrics-specific problems that would limit the usefulness of granisetron in the elderly.

Drug interactions and/or related problems

The following drug interactions and/or related problems have been selected on the basis of their potential clinical significance (possible mechanism in parentheses where appropriate)—not necessarily inclusive (» = major clinical significance):

Note: Combinations containing any of the following medications, depending on the amount present, may also interact with this medication.

Enzyme inducers, hepatic, cytochrome P450 (see *Appendix II*) or
Enzyme inhibitors, hepatic, various (see *Appendix II*)
(because granisetron is metabolized by hepatic cytochrome P450 3A enzymes, inducers or inhibitors of this enzyme may alter granisetron's clearance and half-life)

Ketoconazole
(in *in vitro* human microsomal studies, ketoconazole inhibited ring oxidation of granisetron; clinical significance of this is unknown)

Phenobarbital
(hepatic enzyme induction with phenobarbital resulted in a 25% increase in total plasma clearance of intravenous granisetron; clinical significance of this change not known)

Laboratory value alterations

The following have been selected on the basis of their potential clinical significance (possible effect in parentheses where appropriate)—not necessarily inclusive (» = major clinical significance).

With physiology/laboratory test values
Alanine aminotransferase (ALT [SGPT]), serum and
Aspartate aminotransferase (AST [SGOT]), serum
(values may be increased)

Medical considerations/Contraindications

The medical considerations/contraindications included have been selected on the basis of their potential clinical significance (reasons given in parentheses where appropriate)—not necessarily inclusive (» = major clinical significance).

Except under special circumstances, this medication should not be used when the following medical problem exists:
» Hypersensitivity to granisetron or any of its components

Risk-benefit should be considered when the following medical problem exists:
Nausea and vomiting, chemotherapy-induced or
Post-abdominal surgery
(granisetron use in patients with these conditions may mask a progressive ileus and/or gastric distention)

Side/Adverse Effects

The following side/adverse effects have been selected on the basis of their potential clinical significance (possible signs and symptoms in parentheses where appropriate)—not necessarily inclusive:

Those indicating need for medical attention

Incidence less frequent

Fever; hypertension (blurred vision; dizziness; nervousness; headache; pounding in the ears; slow or fast heartbeat)

Incidence rare

Angina pectoris (arm, back or jaw pain; chest pain or discomfort; chest tightness or heaviness; fast or irregular heartbeat; shortness of breath; sweating; nausea); ***arrhythmias*** (irregular heartbeat); ***atrial fibrillation*** (fast or irregular heartbeat; dizziness; fainting); ***chest pain; fainting; hypersensitivity reaction*** (shortness of breath; skin rash, hives, and itching); ***hypotension*** (blurred vision; confusion; dizziness, faintness, or lightheadedness when getting up from a lying or sitting position suddenly; sweating; unusual tiredness or weakness)

Note: *Alopecia, anemia, anorexia, leukopenia,* and *thrombocytopenia* have also been reported. However, it is not clear whether these effects were caused by granisetron or by the chemotherapy.

Those indicating need for medical attention only if they continue or are bothersome

Incidence more frequent

Abdominal pain; asthenia (lack or loss of strength); ***constipation; diarrhea; headache; nausea and vomiting; unusual tiredness or weakness***

Incidence less frequent

Agitation; anxiety (fear; nervousness); ***dizziness; drowsiness; dyspepsia*** (heartburn; indigestion; sour stomach); ***insomnia*** (trouble in sleeping); ***somnolence*** (sleepiness or unusual drowsiness); ***unusual taste in mouth***

Patient Consultation

As an aid to patient consultation, refer to *Advice for the Patient, Granisetron (Systemic).*

In providing consultation, consider emphasizing the following selected information (» = major clinical significance):

Before receiving this medication

» Conditions affecting use, especially:
Hypersensitivity to granisetron or any of its components
Pregnancy—Should be used during pregnancy only if clearly needed

Proper use of this medication

Not using granisetron instead of nasogastric suction; granisetron does not stimulate gastric or intestinal peristalsis

» Proper dosing

Precautions while receiving this medication

Consulting physician if severe nausea and vomiting occur after administration of chemotherapy

Side/adverse effects

Signs of potential side effects, especially fever, hypertension, angina pectoris, arrhythmias, atrial fibrillation, chest pain, fainting, hypersensitivity reaction, and hypotension

Oral Dosage Forms

Note: The dosing and strength of the dosage form available are expressed in terms of granisetron base (not the hydrochloride salt).

GRANISETRON HYDROCHLORIDE ORAL SOLUTION

Usual adult and adolescent dose

Nausea and vomiting, cancer chemotherapy-induced, prophylaxis—
Oral, 2 mg (base) (10 mL) given up to one hour before chemotherapy. Alternatively, 1 mg (base) (5 mL) administered up to one hour prior to chemotherapy, then 1 mg (5 mL) administered twelve hours after the initial dose.

Nausea and vomiting, cancer radiotherapy–induced (prophylaxis)—
Oral, 2 mg (base) (10 mL) once daily. Two teaspoonfuls (each teaspoon equals 5 mL) are taken within 1 hour of radiation.

Note: Dosage adjustment is not required in the elderly, or in patients with hepatic or renal function impairment.

Usual pediatric dose

Safety and effectiveness have not been established in pediatric patients.

Usual geriatric dose

See *Usual adult and adolescent dose.*

Strength(s) usually available

U.S.—

2 mg per 10 mL (base) (Rx) [*Kytril* (orange color and flavor; citric acid anhydrous; FD&C Yellow No. 6; orange flavor; purified water; sodium benzoate; sorbitol)].

Packaging and storage

Store at 25 °C (77 °F); excursions permitted to 15 to 30 °C (59 to 86 °F), unless otherwise specified by manufacturer. Keep bottle closed tightly and stored in an upright position. Protect from light.

GRANISETRON HYDROCHLORIDE TABLETS

Usual adult and adolescent dose

Nausea and vomiting, cancer chemotherapy-induced, prophylaxis—

Oral, 2 mg (base) given up to one hour before chemotherapy. Alternatively, 1 mg (base) administered up to one hour prior to chemotherapy, then 1 mg administered twelve hours after the initial dose.

Nausea and vomiting, cancer radiotherapy–induced (prophylaxis)—

Oral, 2 mg (base) once daily. Two 1 mg tablets are taken within 1 hour of radiation.

Note: Dosage adjustment is not required in the elderly, or in patients with hepatic or renal function impairment.

Usual pediatric dose

Dosage has not been established.

Usual geriatric dose

See *Usual adult and adolescent dose.*

Strength(s) usually available

U.S.—

1 mg (base) (Rx) [*Kytril* (hydroxypropyl methylcellulose; lactose; magnesium stearate; microcrystalline cellulose; polyethylene glycol; polysorbate 80; sodium starch glycolate; titanium dioxide)].

Canada—

1 mg (base) (Rx) [*Kytril* (hydroxypropyl methylcellulose; lactose; magnesium stearate; microcrystalline cellulose; polyethylene glycol; polysorbate 80; sodium starch glycolate; titanium dioxide)].

Packaging and storage

Store between 15 and 30 °C (59 and 86 °F), unless otherwise specified by manufacturer. Protect from light.

Parenteral Dosage Forms

Note: Bracketed uses in the *Dosage Forms* section refer to categories of use and/or indications that are not included in U.S. product labeling.

The dosing and strength of the dosage form available are expressed in terms of granisetron base (not the hydrochloride salt).

GRANISETRON HYDROCHLORIDE INJECTION

Usual adult and adolescent dose

Nausea and vomiting, cancer chemotherapy-induced, prophylaxis; or [Nausea and vomiting, cancer radiotherapy–induced, prophylaxis][1]—

Intravenous, 10 mcg (base) per kg of body weight, administered within thirty minutes before initiation of emetogenic chemotherapy or radiotherapy. The dose may be administered undiluted over thirty seconds, or diluted with 5% dextrose injection or 0.9% sodium chloride injection and infused over five minutes. (See *Preparation of dosage form.*)

Note: Dosage adjustment is not required in the elderly, or in patients with hepatic or renal function impairment.

Usual pediatric dose

Children up to 2 years of age—Dosage has not been established.

Children 2 years of age and older—See *Usual adult and adolescent dose.*

Usual geriatric dose

See *Usual adult and adolescent dose.*

Strength(s) usually available

U.S.—

1 mg (base) per mL (Rx) [*Kytril* (sodium chloride 9 mg; citric acid 2 mg—in multi-dose vial; benzyl alcohol 10 mg—in multi-dose vial)].

Canada—

1 mg (base) per mL (Rx) [*Kytril* (sodium chloride 9 mg)].

Packaging and storage

Store between 2 and 30 °C (36 and 86 °F), unless otherwise specified by manufacturer. Do not freeze. Protect from light.

Preparation of dosage form

Granisetron may be diluted with 5% dextrose injection or 0.9% sodium chloride injection to a total volume of 20 to 50 mL.

Stability

Intravenous infusions of granisetron retain their potency for 24 hours at room temperature under normal lighting after dilution with 5% dextrose injection or 0.9% sodium chloride injection.

Incompatibilities

The chemical stability of granisetron with the following medications injected into Y-sites of administration sets has been verified:

Medication	*Concentration*
Cyclophosphamide	2 mg/mL
Cytarabine	2 mg/mL
Dacarbazine	1.7 mg/mL
Dexamethasone	0.24 mg/mL
Doxorubicin	0.2 mg/mL
Fluorouracil	2 mg/mL
Furosemide	0.4 mg/mL
Ifosfamide	4 mg/mL
Magnesium sulfate	4 grams/250 mL
Methotrexate	12.5 mg/mL
Potassium chloride	40 mEq/L

Additionally, granisetron admixed with dexamethasone and mannitol is stable for 24 hours. However, no data are available on the compatibility of granisetron injection with other substances; therefore, other medications should not be added to the preparation or infused simultaneously through the same intravenous line.

Caution

Granisetron dosage is expressed in terms of mcg; however, the vial concentration is identified in terms of mg per mL.

Granisetron hydrochloride injection that contains benzyl alcohol as a preservative must not be used in newborns and immature infants. The use of benzyl alcohol in neonates has been associated with a fatal toxic syndrome consisting of metabolic acidosis and central nervous system (CNS), respiratory, circulatory, and renal function impairment.

[1]Not included in Canadian product labeling.

Selected Bibliography

Plosker GL, Goa KL. Granisetron. A review of its pharmacological properties and therapeutic use as an antiemetic. Drugs 1991; 42: 805-24.

Joss RA, Dott CS, on behalf of the Granisetron Study Group. Clinical studies with granisetron, a new 5-HT_3 receptor antagonist for the treatment of cancer chemotherapy-induced emesis. Eur J Cancer 1993; 29A(1 Suppl): S22-S29.

Revised: 01/11/2006
Developed: 12/16/1994

GROWTH HORMONE Systemic

This monograph includes information on the following: 1) Somatrem; 2) Somatropin, Recombinant.

JAN: Somatropin—Human growth hormone

VA CLASSIFICATION (Primary): HS701

Commonly used brand name(s): *Genotropin[2]; Genotropin Miniquick[2]; Humatrope[2]; Norditropin[2]; Norditropin NordiFlex®[2]; Norditropin® cartridges[2]; Nutropin[2]; Nutropin AQ[2]; Protropin[1]; Saizen[2]; Serostim[2].*

Note: For a listing of dosage forms and brand names by country availability, see *Dosage Forms* section(s).

Category

Growth hormone.

Indications

Accepted

Growth failure:

Growth hormone deficiency–associated (treatment)

(Somatrem and recombinant somatropin are indicated in children for long-term treatment of growth failure caused by pituitary growth hormone (GH) deficiency (pituitary dwarfism), including GH deficiency caused by cranial irradiation. Failure to grow must be documented by a subnormal growth rate, and GH deficiency is usually identified by a lack of response to two standard pharmacologic stimuli that would normally provoke the release of somatropin or evidence of impaired spontaneous secretion or bioactivity of endogenous GH.)

(Recombinant somatropin (*Genotropin, Humatrope, Norditropin, Nutropin, Nutropin AQ, Saizen*) is also indicated in adults for treatment of growth failure caused by GH deficiency[1] when both of the following criteria are present and growth hormone deficiency is confirmed by an appropriate growth hormone stimulation test:

- GH deficiency of adult onset, alone or with multiple hormone deficiencies, such as hypopituitarism, as a result of hypothalamic or pituitary disease, radiation therapy, surgery, or trauma. Or GH deficiency of childhood onset that was not confirmed until adulthood; and
- Negative response to a standard growth hormone stimulation test, i.e., maximum peak of less than 5 nanograms per mL when measured by polyclonal antibody (RIA) or less than 2.5 nanograms per mL when measured by monoclonal antibody (IRMA).

Chronic renal insufficiency–associated (treatment)

(Recombinant somatropin (*Nutropin, Nutropin AQ*) is indicated in children for treatment of growth failure caused by chronic renal insufficiency. It has been shown to improve growth rate and correct the acquired height deficit seen in these patients. Somatropin may be used until the time of renal transplantation. However, there are insufficient data to establish benefit of therapy beyond 3 years.)

Prader-Willi syndrome (PWS)-associated (treatment)[1]

(Somatropin is indicated for long-term treatment of pediatric patients who have growth failure due to PWS and also have a diagnosis of growth hormone deficiency. The diagnosis of PWS should be confirmed by appropriate genetic testing.)

Turner's syndrome–associated (treatment)[1]

(Recombinant somatropin (*Humatrope, Nutropin, Nutropin AQ*) is indicated for long-term treatment of short stature associated with Turner's syndrome.)

Cachexia, acquired immunodeficiency syndrome (AIDS)-associated (treatment) or

Weight loss, AIDS-associated (treatment)—Recombinant somatropin (*Serostim*), in conjunction with the appropriate antiretroviral therapy, is indicated for treatment of AIDS-associated cachexia or weight loss.

Unaccepted

There are currently insufficient data to establish the efficacy and the long-term safety of the use of growth hormone in treating idiopathic short stature.

Growth hormone should not be used for growth promotion in pediatric patients with closed epiphyses.

Growth hormone is not indicated for the long-term treatment of pediatric patients who have growth failure due to genetically confirmed Prader-Willi syndrome unless they also have a diagnosis of growth hormone deficiency.

The use of human growth hormone in older males to change body composition (e.g., to decrease adiposity and to prevent decline in muscle mass) is not recommended.

Growth hormone is not indicated in patients with functioning renal allografts.

---

[1]Not included in Canadian product labeling.

Pharmacology/Pharmacokinetics

Physicochemical characteristics

Source—

Somatrem: Biosynthetic. A single polypeptide chain of 192 amino acids, one more (methionine) than naturally occurring human growth hormone, produced by a recombinant DNA process in *Escherichia coli.*

Somatropin, recombinant: Biosynthetic, produced by a recombinant DNA process in *E. coli;* same amino acid sequence as naturally occurring human growth hormone. A single polypeptide chain of 191 amino acids.

Molecular weight—

Somatrem: 22,256.39.

Somatropin: 22,125.19.

pH—

Genotropin (reconstituted solution): 6.7.

Humatrope (reconstituted solution): 7.5.

Norditropin (reconstituted solution): 7.3.

Nutropin (reconstituted solution): 7.4.

Nutropin AQ: 6.

Protropin (reconstituted solution): 7.8.

Saizen (reconstituted solution): 6.5 to 8.5.

Serostim (reconstituted solution): 7.4 to 8.5.

Mechanism of action/Effect

Human growth hormone is an anterior pituitary hormone. Most anabolic actions are thought to be mediated by insulin-like growth factor-I (IGF-I, which has also been known as somatomedin C), synthesized in the liver and other tissues in response to growth hormone stimulation. IGF-I concentrations are low in children with growth hormone deficiency but normalize in response to administration of exogenous growth hormone.

Growth hormone stimulates linear growth by affecting cartilaginous growth areas of long bones. It also stimulates growth by increasing the number and size of skeletal muscle cells, influencing the size of organs, and increasing red cell mass through erythropoietin stimulation.

Growth hormone influences metabolism of carbohydrates by decreasing insulin sensitivity and possibly by affecting glucose transport; of fats by causing mobilization of fatty acids; of minerals by causing the retention of phosphorus, sodium, and potassium through promotion of cellular growth; of proteins by increasing protein synthesis, which results in nitrogen retention; and of connective tissue by stimulating synthesis of chondroitin sulfate and collagen, and by increasing urinary excretion of hydroxyproline.

Other actions/effects

In adults, increases in lean body mass, total body water, and physical performance, and decreases in body fat and waist circumference, are seen with growth hormone therapy.

Absorption

Bioavailability—

Genotropin: Approximately 80% following subcutaneous administration of a 0.03-mg-per-kg of body weight dose in the thigh.

Humatrope: 63% and 75% following intramuscular and subcutaneous administration, respectively.

Nutropin, Nutropin AQ: 81 ± 20%.

Saizen: 70 to 80%.

Distribution

Localizes to highly perfused organs, especially the kidneys and liver.

Vol_D—

Genotropin: 1.3 ± 0.81 L per kg following administration to adults with growth hormone deficiency.

Humatrope: 0.07 L per kg following intravenous injection.

Nutropin, Nutropin AQ: At steady-state, 50 mL per kg of body weight in healthy adult males.

Saizen, Serostim: 12 ± 1.08 L following intravenous injection to healthy volunteers.

Biotransformation

Primarily renal, also hepatic. In renal cells, growth hormone is cleaved into its constituent amino acids, which are returned to the systemic circulation.

Half-life

Intravenous injection—Approximately 20 to 30 minutes (elimination).

Intramuscular or subcutaneous injection—Serum concentrations decline with a half-life of approximately 3 to 5 hours, reflecting continued release of the hormone from the injection site.

Duration of action

Approximately 12 to 48 hours.

Elimination

Biliary (approximately 0.1% of a dose as unchanged drug).

Precautions to Consider

Carcinogenicity/Mutagenicity

Carcinogenicity and mutagenicity testing have not been performed in animals or humans. Mutagenicity testing *in vitro* with recombinant somatropin did not reveal any mutagenic effects.

Anecdotal cases of acute and chronic leukemia have been reported in patients treated with human growth hormone, at an incidence slightly higher than that expected in the overall population. However, the exact relationship to human growth hormone therapy is unknown. Leukemia has also been reported in hypopituitary patients who have not been treated with growth hormone.

Pregnancy/Reproduction

Fertility—Studies in rats and rabbits administered doses of up to 31 and 62 times, respectively, the recommended human pediatric dose on a body surface area basis have not shown that somatropin causes impaired fertility.

Pregnancy—Studies have not been done in humans.

Studies in rats and rabbits administered doses of up to 31 and 62 times, respectively, the recommended human pediatric dose on a body surface area basis have not shown that somatropin causes adverse effects in the fetus.

Because animal reproduction studies are not always predictive of human response, somatropin should be used during pregnancy only if clearly needed.

FDA Pregnancy Category B (*Genotropin, Saizen, Serostim*).

FDA Pregnancy Category C (*Humatrope, Norditropin, Nutropin, Nutropin AQ, Protropin*).

Breast-feeding

It is not known whether growth hormone is distributed into breast milk.

Because many drugs are distributed in human milk, caution should be exercised when somatropin is administered to a nursing woman.

Pediatrics

Safety and efficacy in pediatric patients with acquired immunodeficiency syndrome (AIDS) have not been established.

Geriatrics

Appropriate studies on the relationship of age to the effects of growth hormone have not been performed in the geriatric population. However, geriatrics-specific problems that would limit the usefulness of this medication in the elderly are not expected. Elderly patients may be more sensitive to the action of *Saizen*, and may be more prone to develop adverse reactions.

Drug interactions and/or related problems

The following drug interactions and/or related problems have been selected on the basis of their potential clinical significance (possible mechanism in parentheses where appropriate)—not necessarily inclusive (» = major clinical significance):

Note: Combinations containing any of the following medications, depending on the amount present, may also interact with this medication.

Anabolic steroids or
Androgens or
Estrogens or
Thyroid hormones
(concurrent use of excessive doses of these hormones may accelerate epiphyseal closure, although hormone supplement therapy may be necessary in patients with deficiencies of these hormones to maintain the growth response to human growth hormone)

» Corticosteroids, glucocorticoid or
» Corticotropin (ACTH), especially with chronic therapeutic use
(inhibition of the growth response to human growth hormone may occur with chronic therapeutic use of corticotropin or with daily oral corticosteroid doses [per square meter of body surface area] in excess of:
Betamethasone: 300 to 450 mcg
Cortisone: 12.5 to 18.8 mg
Dexamethasone: 250 to 500 mcg
Hydrocortisone: 10 to 15 mg
Methylprednisolone: 2 to 3 mg
Prednisolone: 2.5 to 3.75 mg
Prednisone: 2.5 to 3.75 mg
Triamcinolone: 2 to 3 mg
Maximum parenteral corticosteroid doses are approximately one half maximum oral doses. In general, it is recommended that these doses not be exceeded during human growth hormone therapy and if larger doses are required, administration of human growth hormone should be postponed, except for brief administration of stress dosages during acute febrile illness or other acute stress; however, there is great interindividual variation. Also, concurrent use with corticotropin is not recommended; of the others, hydrocortisone or cortisone is usually preferred, except in extenuating circumstances)

Drugs metabolized by CYP3A4 enzymes
(formal drug interaction studies have not been conducted; growth hormone may be a CYP3A4 inducer; advisable to monitor clinical effectiveness of these drugs when administered concomitantly with growth hormone)

Laboratory value alterations

The following have been selected on the basis of their potential clinical significance (possible effect in parentheses where appropriate)—not necessarily inclusive (» = major clinical significance).

With physiology/laboratory test values
Alkaline phosphatase
(values may be increased)

Glucose tolerance
(may be reduced by high doses)

Inorganic phosphate
(serum concentrations may be increased to normal during treatment with growth hormone as a result of metabolic activity associated with bone growth as well as increased tubular reabsorption of phosphate by the kidneys)

Insulin-like growth factors (IGF-I)
(may increase after somatropin therapy)

Nonesterified fatty acids
(plasma concentrations may be increased as a result of lipid mobilization from body fat stores)

Parathyroid hormone
(concentrations may be increased)

Thyroid function
(serum thyroxine [T_4] concentration, radioactive iodine uptake [RAIU], and thyroxine-binding capacity may be slightly decreased; asymptomatic hypothyroidism usually occurs in less than 5%, but possibly up to 10 to 20%, of patients with hypopituitarism)

Medical considerations/Contraindications

The medical considerations/contraindications included have been selected on the basis of their potential clinical significance (reasons given in parentheses where appropriate)—not necessarily inclusive (» = major clinical significance).

Except under special circumstances, this medication should not be used when the following medical problems exist:

» Acute critical illness due to:
Complications following open heart or abdominal surgery or
Multiple accidental trauma or
Respiratory failure, acute
(growth hormone should not be initiated to treat patients with acute critical illness; safety of continuing growth hormone treatment in patients who concurrently develop the illnesses has not been established; therefore, potential benefit of treatment continuation with growth hormone in patients having acute critical illnesses should be weighed against the potential risk)

» Closed epiphyses in pediatric patients
(Somatropin should not be used for growth promotion in pediatric patients with closed epiphyses)

» Diabetic retinopathy, proliferative or preproliferative

» Hypersensitivity to somatropin, somatrem, benzyl alcohol or any component of the product

» Neoplasia, active
(any pre-existing neoplasia should be inactive and its treatment complete prior to instituting somatropin; if evidence of recurrent activity, somatropin should be discontinued)

» Prader-Willi syndrome with one or more risk factors including:
Obesity, severe, or
Respiratory impairment, severe, or
Respiratory infection, unidentified, or
Sleep apnea, history of, or
Upper airway obstruction, history of
(reports of fatalities after initiating therapy with growth hormone in pediatric patients with Prader-Willi syndrome; male patients with one or more of these factors may be at greater risk than females; patients with Prader-Willi syndrome should be evaluated for signs of upper airway obstruction and sleep apnea before initiation of growth hormone treatment if patients show signs of upper airway obstruction [including onset of or increased snoring] and/or new onset sleep apnea, treatment should be interrupted)

Risk-benefit should be considered when the following medical problems exist:

Diabetes mellitus or family history of diabetes mellitus
(may induce a state of insulin resistance; patients should be observed for evidence of glucose intolerance and caution should be used; adjustment of insulin dosage may be needed)

» Hypothyroidism, untreated
(interferes with growth response to human growth hormone; prior and/or concurrent thyroid hormone replacement therapy is recommended)

Malignancy, especially intracranial tumor, actively growing within the previous 12 months
(human growth hormone should not be used if there is evidence of progression or recurrent growth of an underlying tumor; antitu-

mor therapy and a reasonable period of observation should be complete before initiating growth hormone therapy)

Patient monitoring

The following may be especially important in patient monitoring (other tests may be warranted in some patients, depending on condition; » = major clinical significance):

Antibodies to growth hormone, serologic evaluation for
(in some cases, where growth rate falls during therapy and all other causes of growth inhibition have been ruled out, serologic evaluation for the presence of antibodies to growth hormone may be performed, with emphasis on binding capacity; antibodies to somatrem may be formed in the first 3 to 6 months of treatment but only rarely cause failure to respond to therapy; antibodies to recombinant somatropin have been detected in patients treated for 6 months or more; relative incidence of antibody formation is difficult to compare because different assays have been used; however, growth inhibition appears to be correlated more with high antibody binding capacity [exceeding 2 mg per L] than with growth hormone titer, and differences in antibody formation have demonstrated minimal clinical significance to date)

Bone age determinations
(recommended annually during therapy, especially in pubertal patients on concurrent androgen, estrogen, or thyroid replacement therapy since concurrent use may accelerate epiphyseal maturation)

Calcium concentrations, serum and
Parathyroid hormone concentrations, serum and
Phosphorus concentrations, serum and
Renal function determinations
(recommended periodically in patients with growth failure secondary to chronic renal insufficiency to detect progression of renal osteodystrophy)

Examinations to monitor intracranial lesion
(recommended at frequent intervals in patients with growth hormone deficiency secondary to an intracranial lesion)

Examinations to monitor progression of scoliosis
(although growth hormone has not been shown to increase the incidence of scoliosis, rapid growth can lead to progression of scoliosis; close monitoring is recommended)

Funduscopic examinations
(recommended upon initiation and periodically during the course of growth hormone therapy, to detect intracranial hypertension)

Glucose concentrations
(recommended periodically because growth hormone can cause insulin resistance)

Glucocorticoid therapy
(glucocorticoid replacement dose should be carefully monitored to avoid an inhibitory effect on grown in patients with coexisting ACTH deficiency)

Growth rate determinations from stadiometer measurements
(recommended every 3 to 6 months during therapy; if the growth rate does not exceed the pretreatment growth rate by at least 2 cm per year, the patient should be checked for noncompliance or the presence of antibodies or other medical problems such as hypothyroidism or malnutrition)

Hormonal replacement therapy
(standard hormonal replacement therapy should be monitored closely when somatropin therapy is initiated in patients with hypopituitarism and multiple hormone deficiencies)

Radiograph, hip
(recommended prior to growth hormone therapy in patients with chronic renal insufficiency because risk of slipped capital femoral epiphysis and avascular necrosis of the femoral head are increased in patients with advanced renal osteodystrophy)

» Signs of respiratory infection and/or
Weight control
(Prader-Willi syndrome patients should have effective weight control and be monitored for signs of respiratory infection, which should be diagnosed as early as possible and treated aggressively)

Thyroid function determinations
(recommended at regular intervals during therapy to detect hypothyroidism that develops during treatment; untreated hypothyroidism interferes with response to human growth hormone)

Side/Adverse Effects

Note: Prolonged use of excessive doses of human growth hormone in patients who are not growth hormone deficient may theoretically cause acromegalic features (face, hands, feet) and other problems associated with acromegaly, including organ enlargement, diabetes mellitus, atherosclerosis, hypertension, and nerve entrapment syndrome (carpal tunnel syndrome).

Development of antibodies to growth hormone may occur in a small number of patients. Interference with growth response has been seen only when antibody binding capacity exceeded 2 mg per L. For patients receiving somatrem who exhibit attenuation of growth response as a result of an increased production of antibodies, consideration should be given to transferring to somatropin. It has been suggested, although not proven, that methionine on the *N*-terminus of somatrem causes development of antibodies.

The following side/adverse effects have been selected on the basis of their potential clinical significance (possible signs and symptoms in parentheses where appropriate)—not necessarily inclusive:

Those indicating need for medical attention

Incidence more frequent

Hypertension (blurred vision; dizziness; nervousness; headache; pounding in the ears; slow or fast heartbeat); ***hypoaesthesia*** (abnormal or decreased touch sensation); ***otitis media or other ear disorders***—in patients with Turner's syndrome; ***paresthesias*** (burning, crawling, itching, numbness, prickling, "pins and needles", or tingling feelings)

Incidence less frequent

Chest pain

Incidence rare

Allergic reaction (skin rash or itching); ***intracranial hypertension*** (changes in vision; headache; nausea and vomiting; papilledema)—in children; ***lipodystrophy at site of injection*** (depression of the skin); ***pain and swelling at site of injection***; ***pancreatitis*** (abdominal pain or distension; nausea; vomiting); ***slipped capital femoral epiphysis*** (limp; pain in hip or knee)—in children

Note: Symptoms of *intracranial hypertension* usually occur within the first 8 weeks of therapy and resolve with a reduction in growth hormone dose or discontinuation of therapy.

The risk of *lipodystrophy* may be decreased by rotating injection sites.

Slipped capital femoral epiphyses may also occur in growth hormone–deficient children not treated with growth hormone.

Those indicating need for medical attention only if they continue or are bothersome

Incidence more frequent

Arthralgia (pain in joints; muscle pain or stiffness; difficulty in moving); ***back pain; bronchitis*** (cough producing mucus; difficulty breathing; shortness of breath; tightness in chest; wheezing); ***dizziness; hypothyroidism*** (constipation; depressed mood; dry skin and hair; feeling cold; hair loss; hoarseness or husky voice; muscle cramps and stiffness; slowed heartbeat; weight gain; unusual tiredness or weakness); ***influenza-like symptoms*** (chills; cough; diarrhea; fever; general feeling of discomfort or illness; headache; joint pain; loss of appetite; muscle aches and pains; nausea; runny nose; shivering; sore throat; sweating; trouble sleeping; unusual tiredness or weakness; vomiting); ***myalgia*** (joint pain; swollen joints; muscle aching or cramping; muscle pains or stiffness; difficulty in moving); ***rhinitis*** (stuffy nose; runny nose; sneezing); ***sweating, increased; upper respiratory tract infection*** (ear congestion; nasal congestion; chills; cough, fever, sneezing, or sore throat; body aches or pain; headache; loss of voice; runny nose; unusual tiredness or weakness; difficulty in breathing)

Incidence less frequent or rare

Carpal tunnel syndrome—mild and transient; ***dependent edema*** (swelling of legs and feet); ***depression*** (discouragement; feeling sad or empty; irritability; lack of appetite; loss of interest or pleasure; tiredness; trouble concentrating; trouble sleeping); ***generalized edema*** (swelling); ***gynecomastia*** (enlargement of breasts); ***headache; increased growth of nevi***; ***insomnia*** (sleeplessness; trouble sleeping; unable to sleep); ***joint pain; muscle pain***; ***nausea; peripheral edema*** (swelling of hands, feet, or lower legs); ***skeletal pain; unusual tiredness or weakness***

Overdose

For more information on the management of overdose or unintentional ingestion, **contact a Poison Control Center** (see *Poison Control Center Listing*).

Clinical effects of overdose

The following effects have been selected on the basis of their potential clinical significance (possible signs and symptoms in parentheses where appropriate)—not necessarily inclusive:

Acute

Hypoglycemia (anxiety; behavior change similar to drunkenness; blurred vision; cold sweats; confusion; cool, pale skin; difficulty in concentrating; drowsiness; excessive hunger; fast heartbeat; headache; nausea; nervousness; nightmares; restless sleep; shakiness; slurred speech; unusual tiredness or weakness)—initially; ***hyperglycemia*** (blurred vision; drowsiness; dry mouth; flushed, dry skin; fruit-like breath odor; increased frequency and volume of urination; ketones in urine; loss of appetite; nausea or vomiting; stomachache; tiredness; troubled breathing [rapid and deep]; unconsciousness; unusual thirst)—subsequently

Chronic

Acromegaly (amenorrhea; backache; changes in vision; excessive sweating; extreme weakness; headache; increase in hat, glove, or shoe size; joint pain; pain in extremities; polydipsia; polyuria)

Patient Consultation

As an aid to patient consultation, refer to *Advice for the Patient, Growth Hormone (Systemic)*.

In providing consultation, consider emphasizing the following selected information (» = major clinical significance):

Before using this medication

» Conditions affecting use, especially:

Hypersensitivity to any component of the growth hormone product prescribed (including benzyl alcohol in the bacteriostatic water for injection diluent)

Other medications, especially corticosteroids or corticotropin (ACTH)

Other medical problems, especially active neoplasia, acute critical illness, closed epiphyses in pediatric patients, diabetic retinopathy (proliferative or preproliferative), Prader-Willi syndrome, or untreated hypothyroidism

Proper use of this medication

» Proper preparation and administration of medication

» Carefully selecting and rotating injection sites

» Safe handling and disposal of needles and syringes; not reusing needles and syringes

» Proper dosing

» Proper storage

Precautions while using this medication

» Importance of regular visits to physician

Side/adverse effects

Signs of potential side effects, especially hypertension, hypoaesthesia, otitis media or other ear disorders (in patients with Turner's syndrome), paresthesias, chest pain, allergic reaction, intracranial hypertension (in children), lipodystrophy at site of injection, pain and swelling at site of injection, pancreatitis, and slipped capital femoral epiphysis (in children)

General Dosing Information

Patients receiving human growth hormone should be under the supervision of a physician trained in the use of and familiar with growth hormone therapy

The dosage and schedule of administration must be individualized for each patient.

For treatment of growth failure

The dosage of human growth hormone may be increased above the recommended dosage in older children with hypopituitarism, especially those who have open epiphyses.

Generally, after 2 or more years of treatment, growth rate will decrease if therapy is continued. Attenuation of growth may be spontaneous. However, if this occurs, the patient should be checked for poor compliance with therapy, other medical problems (such as malnutrition or hypothyroidism), or the presence of antibodies. An increased dose of human growth hormone may be effective. In some patients, low doses of androgens or estrogens may be given concomitantly to restore the response, as long as epiphyseal maturation of 11 years or greater is present.

Human growth hormone therapy should be continued as long as the patient is responsive, until the patient reaches a mature adult height, or until epiphyses close.

For treatment of acquired immunodeficiency syndrome (AIDS)-associated cachexia or wasting

In some *in vitro* studies, growth hormone at concentrations of 50 to 250 nanograms per mL has been shown to potentiate human immunodeficiency virus (HIV) replication. However, when antiretroviral agents didanosine, lamivudine, or zidovudine were added to the culture medium, no increase in virus production was seen. The antiretroviral activity of stavudine and zalcitabine also was not shown to be affected by growth hormone in *in vitro* studies. In clinical trials, no increase in virus production was seen in patients receiving growth hormone; however, all patients concomitantly received antiretroviral agents.

If weight loss continues after two weeks of growth hormone therapy, other causes such as opportunistic infection should be considered.

SOMATREM

Parenteral Dosage Forms

SOMATREM FOR INJECTION

Note: The specific activity of growth hormone is defined as International Units (IU) per mg of protein. In October 1994, a new standard was developed that changed the conversion amount from 2.6 IU per mg of growth hormone to 3 IU per mg of growth hormone. This change did not affect the milligram-per-kg dosing or the quantity (mg) of growth hormone per vial. The only change was the increase in the number of IUs per mg.

Usual pediatric dose

Growth hormone deficiency–associated growth failure—

Intramuscular or subcutaneous, up to 0.3 mg (0.9 IU) per kg of body weight a week with dosing and dosing regimen individualized according to the patient's needs. It is recommended that this dose be divided into the appropriate dose for daily injection (six or seven times per week). The subcutaneous route of administration is preferred to the intramuscular route.

Note: If the growth rate does not exceed the pretreatment growth rate by at least 2 cm per year, the patient should be checked for noncompliance or the presence of antibodies or other medical problems such as hypothyroidism or malnutrition. If increasing the dose is not effective, treatment should be discontinued and the patient re-evaluated.

Strength(s) usually available

U.S.—

5 mg (approximately 15 IU) per vial (Rx) [*Protropin* (mannitol 40 mg; sodium phosphate 1.7 mg; Bacteriostatic Water for Injection, USP [benzyl alcohol preserved])].

10 mg (approximately 30 IU) per vial (Rx) [*Protropin* (mannitol 40 mg; sodium phosphate 1.7 mg; Bacteriostatic Water for Injection, USP [benzyl alcohol preserved])].

Canada—

5 mg (approximately 15 IU) per vial (Rx) [*Protropin* (diluent—Bacteriostatic Water for Injection, USP)].

10 mg (approximately 30 IU) per vial (Rx) [*Protropin* (diluent—Bacteriostatic Water for Injection, USP)].

Packaging and storage

Prior to and following reconstitution, store between 2 and 8 °C (36 and 46 °F). Protect the lyophilized powder, diluent, and reconstituted solution from freezing.

Preparation of dosage form

Using standard aseptic technique, 1 to 5 mL of bacteriostatic water for injection (benzyl alcohol–preserved only) should be added to the 5-mg vial or 1 to 10 mL to the 10-mg vial and swirled gently to dissolve. The vial should not be shaken. Cloudy solution should not be used.

If somatrem is to be administered to a neonate or to a patient with a known sensitivity to any component of the diluent, Sterile Water for Injection, USP should be used for reconstitution. Benzyl alcohol used as a preservative has been associated with toxicity in neonates. Each vial should then be used only for one dose and any unused portion discarded.

Stability

When prepared with the diluent provided by the manufacturer, reconstituted solutions should be stored in the refrigerator and used within 14 days. If sterile water for injection is used for reconstitution, each vial should be used only for one dose and any unused portion discarded. If these procedures are not followed, sterility of the solution cannot be assured.

SOMATROPIN, RECOMBINANT

Parenteral Dosage Forms

SOMATROPIN, RECOMBINANT, INJECTION

Usual adult dose

Growth hormone deficiency–associated growth failure[1]—

Nutropin AQ or *Nutropin*—

Initial—

Subcutaneous, up to 0.006 mg (0.018 IU) per kg of body weight a day.

For *Saizen*: Subcutaneous, up to 0.005 mg per kg of body weight per day. Dosage and schedule of administration should be individualized for each patient.

Maintenance—

Patients up to 35 years of age: Subcutaneous, up to 0.025 mg (0.075 IU) per kg of body weight a day.

Patients 35 years of age or older: Subcutaneous, up to 0.0125 mg (0.0375 IU) per kg of body weight a day.

Note: The dose should be decreased if required by the occurrence of side effects or excessive insulin-like growth factor-I (IGF-I) levels.

In addition to adverse effects, determination of age- and gender-adjusted serum IGF-I levels and clinical response may be used to help guide dose titration. This approach will tend to result in doses that are larger for women compared with men, and smaller for AO growth hormone deficient patients compared with CO growth hormone deficient patients as well as older and obese patients.

Growth hormone deficiency–associated growth failure[1]—

Norditropin—

Subcutaneous, up to 0.004 mg per kg of body weight a day. The dose may be increased as tolerated to not more than 0.016 mg per kg of body weight a day after approximately 6 weeks.

Note: In addition to adverse effects, determination of age- and gender-adjusted serum IGF-I levels and clinical response may be used to help guide dose titration. This approach will tend to result in doses that are larger for women compared with men, and smaller for AO growth hormone deficient patients compared with CO growth hormone deficient patients as well as older and obese patients.

Usual adult prescribing limits

Saizen: May be increased to not more than 0.01 mg per kg of body weight per day after 4 weeks depending upon patient tolerance of treatment.

Usual pediatric dose

Growth hormone deficiency–associated growth failure—

Norditropin cartridge: Subcutaneous, 0.024 to 0.034 mg (0.072 to 0.102 IU) per kg of body weight a day, administered 6 to 7 times a week.

Nutropin AQ or *Nutropin:* Subcutaneous, up to 0.3 mg (0.9 IU) per kg of body weight a week divided into equal doses and administered daily.

In pubertal patients, a weekly dose of up to 0.7 mg per kg of body weight divided daily may be used.

Chronic renal insufficiency–associated growth failure—

Nutropin AQ or *Nutropin*—

Subcutaneous, up to 0.35 mg (1.05 IU) per kg of body weight a week divided into equal doses and administered daily.

Note: Recombinant somatropin therapy may be continued until the time of renal transplantation.

For patients requiring dialysis, it is recommended that somatropin be administered at the following times:

Hemodialysis—At night just before going to sleep or at least three to four hours after hemodialysis to prevent heparin-induced hematoma formation.

Chronic cycling peritoneal dialysis—In the morning after dialysis is completed.

Chronic ambulatory peritoneal dialysis—In the evening at the time of the overnight exchange.

Turner's syndrome–associated growth failure[1]—*Nutropin AQ*—

Subcutaneous, up to 0.375 mg (1.125 IU) per kg of body weight a week divided into the appropriate dose for daily injection (seven times per week) or, as an alternative, divided and injected three times a week (every other day).

Strength(s) usually available

U.S.—

Note: *Norditropin® cartridges* are intended for use only in the *NordiPen* delivery system.

Norditropin NordiFlex® are prefilled pens.

10 mg (approximately 30 IU) per 2 mL (Rx) [*Nutropin AQ* (sodium chloride 17.4 mg; phenol 5 mg; polysorbate 20 4 mg; sodium citrate 10 mM)].

5 mg (approximately 15 IU) per vial (Rx) [*Nutropin* (mannitol 45 mg; sodium phosphate 1.7 mg; glycine 1.7 mg; Bacteriostatic Water for Injection, USP (benzyl alcohol preserved))].

10 mg (approximately 30 IU) per vial (Rx) [*Nutropin* (mannitol 90 mg; sodium phosphate 3.4 mg; glycine 3.4 mg; Bacteriostatic Water for Injection, USP (benzyl alcohol preserved))].

5 mg per 1.5 mL (Rx) [*Norditropin® cartridges* (histidine [1 mg]; mannitol [60 mg]; phenol [4.5 mg]; poloxamer 188 [4.5 mg]); *Norditropin NordiFlex®* (histidine [1 mg]; mannitol [60 mg]; phenol [4.5 mg]; poloxamer 188 [4.5 mg])].

10 mg per 1.5 mL (Rx) [*Norditropin® cartridges* (histidine [1 mg]; mannitol [60 mg]; phenol [4.5 mg]; poloxamer 188 [4.5 mg]); *Norditropin NordiFlex®* (histidine [1 mg]; mannitol [60 mg]; phenol [4.5 mg]; poloxamer 188 [4.5 mg])].

15 mg per 1.5 mL (Rx) [*Norditropin® cartridges* (histidine [1 mg]; mannitol [60 mg]; phenol [4.5 mg]; poloxamer 188 [4.5 mg]); *Norditropin NordiFlex®* (histidine [1 mg]; mannitol [60 mg]; phenol [4.5 mg]; poloxamer 188 [4.5 mg])].

Canada—

5 mg (approximately 15 IU) per mL (Rx) [*Nutropin AQ*].

Packaging and storage

Nutropin AQ and Nutropin—Store between 2 and 8 °C (36 and 46 °F). Protect from freezing.

Norditropin cartridges and Norditropin NordiFlex prefilled pens: Prior to dispensing, store the delivery device at a temperature between 2 and 8 °C (36 and 46 °F). Protect from freezing and direct light.

Stability

Nutropin AQ: Stable for up to 28 days after initial use if stored in the refrigerator.

Nutropin: Stable for 14 days after reconstitution with Bacteriostatic Water for Injection, USP.

Norditropin cartridges: Once a cartridge has been inserted into the injector, it must be stored in the refrigerator and used within 4 weeks.

Norditropin NordiFlex: After initial injection, the prefilled pen must be stored in the refrigerator and used within 4 weeks; discard unused portion after 4 weeks

SOMATROPIN, RECOMBINANT, FOR INJECTION

Note: The specific activity of growth hormone is defined as International Units (IU) per mg of protein. In October 1994, a new standard was developed that changed the conversion amount from 2.6 IU per mg of growth hormone to 3 IU per mg of growth hormone. This change did not affect the milligram-per-kg dosing or the quantity (mg) of growth hormone per vial. The only change was the increase in the number of IUs per mg.

Usual adult dose

Growth hormone deficiency–associated growth failure[1]—

See *Somatropin, Recombinant, Injection.*

Acquired immunodeficiency syndrome (AIDS)-associated cachexia or AIDS-associated weight loss—

For patients weighing more than 55 kg: Subcutaneous, 6 mg a day at bedtime.

For patients weighing 45 to 55 kg: Subcutaneous, 5 mg a day at bedtime.

For patients weighing 35 to 44 kg: Subcutaneous, 4 mg a day at bedtime.

For patients weighing up to 35 kg: Subcutaneous, 0.1 mg per kg of body weight a day at bedtime.

Usual pediatric dose

Growth hormone deficiency–associated growth failure—

Genotropin, Norditropin: Subcutaneous, 0.16 to 0.24 (0.48 to 0.72 IU) per kg of body weight a week divided into the appropriate dose for daily injection (six or seven times per week).

Humatrope, Nutropin, Saizen: Intramuscular or subcutaneous, 0.18 to 0.3 mg (0.54 to 0.9 IU) per kg of body weight a week with dosing and dosing regimen individualized according to the patient's needs. This can be divided into the appropriate dose for daily injection (six or seven times per week) or, as an alternative, divided and injected three times a week (every other day). The subcutaneous route of administration is preferred to the intramuscular route.

Note: If the growth rate does not exceed the pretreatment growth rate by at least 2 cm per year, the patient should be checked for noncompliance or the presence of antibodies or other medical problems such as hypothyroidism or malnutrition. If increasing the dose is not effective, treatment should be discontinued and the patient re-evaluated.

Chronic renal insufficiency–associated growth failure—
See *Somatropin, Recombinant, Injection*.

Prader-Willi syndrome (PWS)-associated growth failure[1]—
Subcutaneous, 0.24 mg per kg of body weight per week divided into the appropriate dose for daily injection (six or seven times per week).

Turner's syndrome–associated growth failure[1]—
See *Somatropin, Recombinant, Injection*.

AIDS-associated cachexia or
AIDS-associated weight loss—
Safety and efficacy have not been established.

Strength(s) usually available

U.S.—
- 0.2 mg (approximately 0.6 IU) per two-chamber cartridge (Rx) [*Genotropin Miniquick*].
- 0.4 mg (approximately 1.2 IU) per two-chamber cartridge (Rx) [*Genotropin Miniquick*].
- 0.6 mg (approximately 1.8 IU) per two-chamber cartridge (Rx) [*Genotropin Miniquick*].
- 0.8 mg (approximately 2.4 IU) per two-chamber cartridge (Rx) [*Genotropin Miniquick*].
- 1 mg (approximately 3 IU) per two-chamber cartridge (Rx) [*Genotropin Miniquick*].
- 1.2 mg (approximately 3.6 IU) per two-chamber cartridge (Rx) [*Genotropin Miniquick*].
- 1.4 mg (approximately 4.2 IU) per two-chamber cartridge (Rx) [*Genotropin Miniquick*].
- 1.5 mg (approximately 4.5 IU) per two-chamber cartridge (Rx) [*Genotropin*].
- 1.6 mg (approximately 4.8 IU) per two-chamber cartridge (Rx) [*Genotropin Miniquick*].
- 1.8 mg (approximately 5.4 IU) per two-chamber cartridge (Rx) [*Genotropin Miniquick*].
- 2 mg (approximately 6 IU) per two-chamber cartridge (Rx) [*Genotropin Miniquick*].
- 4 mg (approximately 12 IU) per vial (Rx) [*Norditropin* (diluent—benzyl alcohol 1.5% per mL); *Serostim*].
- 5 mg (approximately 15 IU) per vial (Rx) [*Humatrope* (diluent—*m*-cresol 0.3%; glycerin 1.7%); *Nutropin* (diluent—benzyl alcohol 0.9% per mL); *Saizen* (34.2 mg sucrose; 1.16 mg O-phosphoric acid; sodium hydroxide to adjust pH; bacteriostatic water for injection containing benzyl alcohol 0.9%); *Serostim*].
- 5.8 mg (approximately 17.4 IU) per two-chamber cartridge (Rx) [*Genotropin*].
- 6 mg (approximately 18 IU) per vial (Rx) [*Serostim*].
- 8 mg (approximately 24 IU) per vial (Rx) [*Norditropin* (diluent—benzyl alcohol 1.5% per mL)].
- 8.8 mg (approximately 26.4 IU) per vial (Rx) [*Saizen* (60.2 mg sucrose; 2.05 mg O-phosphoric acid; sodium hydroxide to adjust pH; bacteriostatic water for injection containing benzyl alcohol 0.9%)].
- 10 mg (approximately 30 IU) per vial (Rx) [*Nutropin* (diluent—benzyl alcohol 0.9% per mL)].
- 13.8 mg (approximately 41.4 IU) per two-chamber cartridge (Rx) [*Genotropin*].

Canada—
- 3.33 mg (approximately 10 IU) per vial (Rx) [*Saizen* (diluent—benzyl alcohol)].
- 5 mg (approximately 15 IU) per vial (Rx) [*Humatrope* (diluent—*m*-cresol; glycerin); *Nutropin* (diluent—benzyl alcohol); *Serostim*].
- 6 mg (approximately 18 IU) per vial (Rx) [*Serostim*].
- 6.7 mg (approximately 20 IU) per cartridge (Rx) [*Humatrope*].
- 10 mg (approximately 30 IU) per vial (Rx) [*Nutropin* (diluent—benzyl alcohol)].
- 13.3 mg (approximately 40 IU) per cartridge (Rx) [*Humatrope*].
- 26.6 mg (approximately 80 IU) per cartridge (Rx) [*Humatrope*].

Packaging and storage

Prior to and following reconstitution, store *Genotropin, Humatrope, Norditropin, Nutropin,* and *Saizen* at a temperature between 2 and 8 °C (36 and 46 °F). Protect the lyophilized powder, diluent, and reconstituted solution from freezing and direct light.

Prior to dispensing, store the *Genotropin Miniquick* delivery device at a temperature between 2 and 8 °C (36 and 46 °F); it may be stored at or below 25 °C (77 °F) for up to 3 months after dispensing.

Prior to reconstitution, store *Serostim* at a temperature between 15 and 30 °C (59 and 86 °F). Following reconstitution, store *Serostim* at a temperature between 2 and 8 °C (36 and 46 °F). Protect the lyophilized powder, diluent, and reconstituted solution from freezing.

Preparation of dosage form

Genotropin is available as a two-chamber cartridge with the lyophilized powder in the front chamber and the diluent in the rear chamber. A reconstitution device to mix the powder and diluent is also provided. The manufacturers instructions for reconstitution should be followed.

Humatrope may be available as cartridges for use with pen injection devices. The manufacturer's instructions for reconstitution and administration should be followed.

For products that package the diluent and somatropin in separate vials, using standard aseptic technique the following amount of diluent should be added:

For *Humatrope*—1.5 to 5 mL of the diluent provided by the manufacturer should be added to the 5-mg vial.

For *Norditropin*—2 mL of the diluent provided by the manufacturer should be added to the 4-mg or 8-mg vial. The resulting somatropin concentration is 2 mg or 4 mg per mL when using the 4-mg or 8-mg vial, respectively.

For *Nutropin*—1 to 5 mL of the diluent provided by the manufacturer or bacteriostatic water for injection (benzyl alcohol–preserved only) should be added to the 5-mg vial, or 1 to 10 mL of the diluent provided by the manufacturer or bacteriostatic water for injection (benzyl alcohol–preserved only) should be added to the 10-mg vial.

For *Saizen*—5 mL of the diluent provided by the manufacturer should be added to the 3.33-mg vial, or 1 to 3 mL of the diluent provided by the manufacturer or bacteriostatic water for injection (benzyl alcohol–preserved only) should be added to the 5-mg vial or 2 to 3 mL of the diluent should be added to the 8.8-mg vial

Note: Benzyl alcohol as a preservative in Bacteriostatic Water for Injection, USP has been associated with toxicity in newborns. If sensitivity to the diluent occurs, *Saizen* may be reconstituted with Sterile Water for Injection, USP. When it is reconstituted in this manner, the reconstituted solution should be used immediately and any unused solution should be discarded.

For *Serostim*—1 mL of the diluent provided by the manufacturer should be added to the 4-mg, 5-mg, or 6-mg vial.

To mix the diluent with the somatropin, the diluent must be injected while aimed against the glass wall of the vial, then swirled gently to dissolve the contents of the vial. The vial should not be shaken. Cloudy solutions or those containing particulate matter should not be used.

If somatropin is to be administered to a neonate or to a patient with a known sensitivity to any component of the diluent, sterile water for injection should be used for reconstitution. Benzyl alcohol used as a preservative has been associated with toxicity in neonates. Each vial should then be used only for one dose and any unused portion discarded.

Stability

Genotropin—
1.5-mg cartridge and *Genotropin Miniquick*: Diluent contains no preservative. Stable for up to 24 hours if stored in the refrigerator following reconstitution. Both should be used only for one dose and any unused portion discarded.
5.8-mg and 13.8-mg cartridges: Diluent contains a preservative. Stable for up to 21 days if stored in the refrigerator following reconstitution.

Humatrope, Norditropin, Nutropin, Saizen—
Stable for up to 14 days if stored in the refrigerator following reconstitution with the diluent provided by the manufacturer. If sterile water for injection is used for reconstitution, each vial should be refrigerated and used within 24 hours.

Serostim—
Stable for up to 24 hours if stored in the refrigerator following reconstitution.

[1]Not included in Canadian product labeling.

Selected Bibliography

Frasier SD, Lippe BM. The rational use of growth hormone during childhood [review]. J Clin Endocrinol Metab 1990; 71(2): 269-73.

Product Information: Saizen®, somatropin (rDNA origin). Serono, Randolph, MA, (PI revised 07/2004) reviewed 11/2004.

Product Information: Norditropin®, somatropin (rDNA origin) injection. Novo Nordisk Pharmaceuticals Inc., Princeton, NJ. (PI revised 11/2004) reviewed 01/2005.

Revised: 01/24/2005

GUAIFENESIN Systemic

VA CLASSIFICATION (Primary): RE302

Commonly used brand name(s): *Anti-Tuss; Balminil Expectorant; Benylin-E; Breonesin; Calmylin Expectorant; Diabetic Tussin EX; Fenesin; Gee-Gee; Genatuss; Glycotuss; Glytuss; Guiatuss; Halotussin; Humibid L.A; Humibid Sprinkle; Hytuss; Hytuss-2X; Naldecon Senior EX; Organidin NR; Pneumomist; Resyl; Robitussin; Scot-tussin Expectorant; Sinumist-SR; Touro EX; Uni-tussin.*

Another commonly used name is glyceryl guaiacolate.

Note: For a listing of dosage forms and brand names by country availability, see *Dosage Forms* section(s).

Category

Expectorant.

Indications

Accepted

Cough (treatment)—Guaifenesin is indicated as an expectorant in the temporary symptomatic management of cough due to minor upper respiratory infections and related conditions, such as sinusitis, pharyngitis, and bronchitis, when these conditions are complicated by viscous mucus and congestion. However, because supporting data are very limited, there is some controversy about its effectiveness.

Pharmacology/Pharmacokinetics

Physicochemical characteristics

Molecular weight—198.22.

Mechanism of action/Effect

Guaifenesin is thought to act as an expectorant by increasing the volume and reducing the viscosity of secretions in the trachea and bronchi. Thus, it may increase the efficiency of the cough reflex and facilitate removal of the secretions; however, objective evidence for this is limited and conflicting.

Absorption

Readily absorbed from gastrointestinal tract.

Elimination

Renal, as inactive metabolites.

Precautions to Consider

Carcinogenicity/Tumorigenicity/Mutagenicity

Studies to determine the carcinogenicity, tumorigenicity, or mutagenicity of guaifenesin in animals have not been conducted.

Pregnancy/Reproduction

Pregnancy—Although adequate and well-controlled studies in pregnant women have not been done, the Collaborative Perinatal Project monitored 197 mother-child pairs exposed to guaifenesin during the first trimester. An increased occurrence of inguinal hernias was found in the neonates. However, congenital defects were not strongly associated with guaifenesin use during pregnancy in 2 large groups of mother-child pairs.

Studies have not been done in animals.

FDA Pregnancy Category C.

Breast-feeding

It is not known whether guaifenesin is distributed into breast milk. However, problems in humans have not been documented.

Pediatrics

Appropriate studies on the relationship of age to the effects of guaifenesin have not been performed in the pediatric population. However, no pediatrics-specific problems have been documented to date.

Caution is recommended in children up to 12 years of age with persistent or chronic cough, such as occurs with asthma, or if the cough is accompanied by excessive phlegm (mucus). The condition of these children may need a physician's evaluation before guaifenesin is administered.

Guaifenesin should not be given to children younger than 2 years of age unless recommended by a physician.

Geriatrics

Appropriate studies on the relationship of age to the effects of guaifenesin have not been performed in the geriatric population. However, no geriatrics-specific problems have been documented to date.

Laboratory value alterations

The following have been selected on the basis of their potential clinical significance (possible effect in parentheses where appropriate)—not necessarily inclusive (» = major clinical significance).

With diagnostic test results

5-hydroxyindoleacetic acid (5-HIAA), urine
(urinary determinations may be falsely increased when nitrosonaphthol reagent is used because of color interference by guaifenesin metabolites; guaifenesin should be discontinued 48 hours before collection of urine for this test)

Vanillylmandelic acid (VMA), urine
(guaifenesin or its metabolites may cause color interference with urinary determinations and may falsely elevate VMA test for catechols; guaifenesin should be discontinued 48 hours before collection of urine for this test)

Medical considerations/Contraindications

The medical considerations/contraindications included have been selected on the basis of their potential clinical significance (reasons given in parentheses where appropriate)—not necessarily inclusive (» = major clinical significance).

Risk-benefit should be considered when the following medical problem exists:

Sensitivity to guaifenesin

Side/Adverse Effects

The following side/adverse effects have been selected on the basis of their potential clinical significance (possible signs and symptoms in parentheses where appropriate)—not necessarily inclusive:

Those indicating need for medical attention only if they continue or are bothersome

Less frequent or rare

Diarrhea; dizziness; headache; nausea or vomiting; skin rash; stomach pain; urticaria (hives)

Patient Consultation

As an aid to patient consultation, refer to *Advice for the Patient, Guaifenesin (Systemic).*

In providing consultation, consider emphasizing the following selected information (» = major clinical significance):

Before using this medication

» Conditions affecting use, especially:
Sensitivity to guaifenesin
Pregnancy—Increased incidence of inguinal hernias in the babies of one group of women taking guaifenesin during pregnancy; however, this did not occur in other groups
Use in children—For self-medication, caution if cough is persistent or occurs with excessive phlegm; not administering to children younger than 2 years of age unless directed by a physician

Proper use of this medication

Proper administration
Importance of maintaining adequate fluid intake

» For extended-release dosage forms
Swallowing capsules whole or opening capsules and sprinkling contents on soft food, then swallowing without crushing or chewing
Not breaking (unless scored for breakage), crushing, or chewing tablets; swallowing tablet whole

» Proper dosing
Missed dose (if on a scheduled dosing regimen): Taking as soon as possible; not taking if almost time for next dose; not doubling doses

» Proper storage

Precautions while using this medication

Checking with physician if cough persists after medication has been used for 7 days or if fever, skin rash, continuing headache, or sore throat is present with cough

General Dosing Information

Before prescribing or recommending medication to suppress or modify cough, it is important that the underlying cause of the cough be assessed.

For self-medication, guaifenesin should not be taken for chronic cough unless directed by a physician.

Patient should be advised to maintain adequate hydration.

Oral Dosage Forms

GUAIFENESIN CAPSULES USP

Usual adult and adolescent dose

Expectorant—

Oral, 200 to 400 mg every four hours, not to exceed 2400 mg a day.

Usual pediatric dose

Expectorant—

Children 2 to 6 years of age: The liquid or extended-release capsule dosage forms may be preferable for children in this age group.

Children 6 to 12 years of age: Oral, 100 to 200 mg every four hours, not to exceed 1200 mg a day.

Usual geriatric dose

See *Usual adult and adolescent dose*.

Strength(s) usually available

U.S.—

200 mg (OTC) [*Breonesin; Hytuss-2X*].

Canada—

Not commercially available.

Packaging and storage

Store below 40 °C (104 °F), preferably between 15 and 30 °C (59 and 86 °F), unless otherwise specified by manufacturer. Store in a tight container.

GUAIFENESIN EXTENDED-RELEASE CAPSULES

Usual adult and adolescent dose

Expectorant—

Oral, 600 to 1200 mg every twelve hours, not to exceed 2400 mg a day.

Usual pediatric dose

Expectorant—

Children 2 to 6 years of age: Oral, 300 mg every twelve hours, not to exceed 600 mg a day.

Note: The liquid dosage forms may be preferable for children 2 to 6 years of age, who cannot always be relied upon to swallow the contents of the capsule without chewing.

Children 6 to 12 years of age: Oral, 600 mg every twelve hours, not to exceed 1200 mg a day.

Usual geriatric dose

See *Usual adult and adolescent dose*.

Strength(s) usually available

U.S.—

300 mg (Rx) [*Humibid Sprinkle*].

Canada—

Not commercially available.

Packaging and storage

Store between 15 and 30 °C (59 and 86 °F), unless otherwise specified by manufacturer. Store in a tight container.

Additional information

Extended-release capsules may be swallowed whole or opened and the contents sprinkled on soft food immediately prior to ingestion, then swallowed without crushing or chewing. Capsule contents should not be subdivided.

GUAIFENESIN ORAL SOLUTION

Usual adult and adolescent dose

See *Guaifenesin Capsules USP*.

Usual pediatric dose

Expectorant—

Children 6 months to 2 years of age—Dosage must be individualized by physician. A commonly used regimen is 25 to 50 mg every four hours, not to exceed 300 mg a day.

Children 2 to 6 years of age—Oral, 50 to 100 mg every four hours, not to exceed 600 mg a day.

Children 6 to 12 years to age—See *Guaifenesin Capsules USP*.

Usual geriatric dose

See *Usual adult and adolescent dose*.

Strength(s) usually available

U.S.—

100 mg per 5 mL (OTC) [*Diabetic Tussin EX* (alcohol free; sugar free); *Scot-tussin Expectorant* (alcohol 3.5%; sugar free)].

100 mg per 5 mL (Rx) [*Organidin NR* (sorbitol; alcohol free)].

200 mg per 5 mL (OTC) [*Naldecon Senior EX* (alcohol free; sugar free)].

Canada—

Not commercially available.

Packaging and storage

Store below 40 °C (104 °F), preferably between 15 and 30 °C (59 and 86 °F), unless otherwise specified by manufacturer. Store in a tight container. Protect from freezing.

GUAIFENESIN SYRUP USP

Usual adult and adolescent dose

See *Guaifenesin Capsules USP*.

Usual pediatric dose

See *Guaifenesin Oral Solution*.

Usual geriatric dose

See *Usual adult and adolescent dose*.

Strength(s) usually available

U.S.—

100 mg per 5 mL (OTC) [*Anti-Tuss* (alcohol 3.5%); *Genatuss* (alcohol 3.5%); *Guiatuss; Halotussin* (alcohol 3.5%); *Robitussin* (alcohol 3.5%); *Uni-tussin* (alcohol 3.5%); GENERIC].

Canada—

100 mg per 5 mL (OTC) [*Balminil Expectorant; Benylin-E* (alcohol 5%); *Calmylin Expectorant* (sorbitol; alcohol free); *Robitussin* (alcohol 3.5%)].

Packaging and storage

Store below 40 °C (104 °F), preferably between 15 and 30 °C (59 and 86 °F), unless otherwise specified by manufacturer. Store in a tight container. Protect from freezing.

GUAIFENESIN TABLETS USP

Usual adult and adolescent dose

See *Guaifenesin Capsules USP*.

Usual pediatric dose

See *Guaifenesin Capsules USP*.

Usual geriatric dose

See *Usual adult and adolescent dose*.

Strength(s) usually available

U.S.—

100 mg (OTC) [*Glycotuss; Hytuss* (scored; sugar free)].

200 mg (OTC) [*Gee-Gee; Glytuss*].

200 mg (Rx) [*Organidin NR* (scored)].

Canada—

100 mg (OTC) [*Resyl*].

Packaging and storage

Store below 40 °C (104 °F), preferably between 15 and 30 °C (59 and 86 °F), unless otherwise specified by manufacturer. Store in a tight container.

GUAIFENESIN EXTENDED-RELEASE TABLETS

Usual adult and adolescent dose

See *Guaifenesin Extended-release Capsules*.

Usual pediatric dose

See *Guaifenesin Extended-release Capsules*.

Strength(s) usually available

U.S.—

600 mg (Rx) [*Fenesin* (scored); *Humibid L.A* (scored); *Pneumomist* (scored); *Sinumist-SR* (scored); *Touro EX* (scored); GENERIC].

Canada—

Not commercially available.

Packaging and storage

Store between 15 and 30 °C (59 and 86 °F), unless otherwise specified by manufacturer. Store in a tight container.

Selected Bibliography

Irwin RS, Curley FJ, Bennett FM. Appropriate use of antitussives and protussives. Drugs 1993; 46(1): 80-91.

Revised: 06/27/2000

GUANFACINE Systemic†

VA CLASSIFICATION (Primary): CV409

Commonly used brand name(s): *Tenex*.

Note: For a listing of dosage forms and brand names by country availability, see *Dosage Forms* section(s).

†Not commercially available in Canada.

Category
Antihypertensive.

Indications

Accepted
Hypertension (treatment)—Guanfacine is indicated, usually in combination with a thiazide diuretic, in the treatment of hypertension.

Pharmacology/Pharmacokinetics

Physicochemical characteristics
Molecular weight—282.56.

Mechanism of action/Effect
Thought to be due to central alpha$_2$-adrenergic stimulation, which results in a decreased sympathetic outflow to the heart, kidneys, and peripheral vasculature; decreased systolic and diastolic blood pressure; and slightly decreased heart rate.

Other actions/effects
Growth hormone secretion stimulated by single doses (no effect with long-term use).

Absorption
Rapid and complete; bioavailability approximately 80%.

Protein binding
Moderate (70%; 50% to erythrocytes).

Biotransformation
Hepatic.

Half-life
Approximately 17 hours (range, 10–30 hours); 13 to 14 hours in younger patients.

Onset of action
Multiple doses—Within 1 week.

Time to peak plasma concentration
1 to 4 hours (average, 2.6 hours).

Time to peak effect
Single dose—8 to 12 hours.

Multiple doses—1 to 3 months.

Duration of action
Single dose—24 hours.

Elimination
Renal, approximately 40% unchanged.

In dialysis—Not significantly removed by dialysis (2.4%).

Precautions to Consider

Carcinogenicity
Studies in mice for 78 weeks at doses greater than 150 times the maximum recommended human dose and in rats for 102 weeks at doses greater than 100 times the maximum recommended human dose found no evidence of carcinogenicity.

Mutagenicity
Mutagenicity studies were negative.

Pregnancy/Reproduction
Fertility—Studies in male and female rats found no adverse effects on fertility.

Pregnancy—Adequate and well-controlled studies in humans have not been done.

Studies in rats and rabbits at doses 70 and 20 times the maximum recommended human dose, respectively, have not shown that guanfacine causes adverse effects in the fetus. Studies with doses of 100 and 200 times the maximum recommended human dose in rabbits and rats respectively, showed maternal toxicity and reduced fetal survival. Guanfacine crosses the placenta in rats.

FDA Pregnancy Category B.

Breast-feeding
It is not known whether guanfacine is distributed into human breast milk. However, problems have not been documented. Guanfacine is distributed into the milk of lactating rats.

Pediatrics
Appropriate studies on the relationship of age to the effects of guanfacine have not been performed in the pediatric population. Safety and efficacy have not been established.

Geriatrics
Appropriate studies on the relationship of age to the effects of guanfacine have not been performed in the geriatric population. However, the elderly may be more sensitive to the hypotensive and sedative effects.

Dental
Use of guanfacine may decrease or inhibit salivary flow, thus contributing to the development of caries, periodontal disease, oral candidiasis, and discomfort.

Drug interactions and/or related problems
The following drug interactions and/or related problems have been selected on the basis of their potential clinical significance (possible mechanism in parentheses where appropriate)—not necessarily inclusive (» = major clinical significance):

Note: Combinations containing any of the following medications, depending on the amount present, may also interact with this medication.

Alcohol or
Central nervous system (CNS) depression-producing medications (See *Appendix II*)
(concurrent use may enhance the CNS depressant effects of either these medications or guanfacine)

Anti-inflammatory drugs, nonsteroidal (NSAIDs), especially indomethacin
(may reduce antihypertensive effects of guanfacine; indomethacin, and possibly other NSAIDs, may antagonize the antihypertensive effect by inhibiting renal prostaglandin synthesis and/or by causing sodium and fluid retention; the patient should be carefully monitored to confirm that the desired effect is being obtained)

Hypotension-producing medications, other (See *Appendix II*)
(concurrent use may potentiate antihypertensive effects; although some antihypertensive and/or diuretic combinations are frequently used for therapeutic advantage, dosage adjustments may be necessary during concurrent use)

Sympathomimetics
(may reduce antihypertensive effects of guanfacine; the patient should be carefully monitored to confirm that the desired effect is being obtained)

Laboratory value alterations
The following have been selected on the basis of their potential clinical significance (possible effect in parentheses where appropriate)—not necessarily inclusive (» = major clinical significance).

With physiology/laboratory test values
Catecholamine concentrations, urinary, and
Vanillylmandelic acid (VMA), urinary, excretion
(values may be decreased but may increase on abrupt withdrawal)

Growth hormone, plasma
(concentrations may be increased transiently because of stimulation of growth hormone release, but are not elevated chronically with long-term use of guanfacine)

Medical considerations/Contraindications
The medical considerations/contraindications included have been selected on the basis of their potential clinical significance (reasons given in parentheses where appropriate)—not necessarily inclusive (» = major clinical significance).

Risk-benefit should be considered when the following medical problems exist:
Cerebrovascular disease or
Coronary insufficiency or
Myocardial infarction, recent
(may be aggravated by reduced blood pressure)

Hepatic function impairment, chronic
(increased sensitivity or prolonged guanfacine effect may occur, since guanfacine undergoes hepatic biotransformation)

Mental depression, history of
(may be aggravated by CNS effects of guanfacine)

Sensitivity to guanfacine

Patient monitoring
The following may be especially important in patient monitoring (other tests may be warranted in some patients, depending on condition; » = major clinical significance):

» Blood pressure measurements
(recommended at periodic intervals in patients being treated for hypertension; selected patients may be trained to perform blood

pressure measurements at home and report the results at regular physician visits)

Side/Adverse Effects

Note: Side/adverse effects are dose-related and incidence usually declines with continued administration.

The following side/adverse effects have been selected on the basis of their potential clinical significance (possible signs and symptoms in parentheses where appropriate)—not necessarily inclusive:

Those indicating need for medical attention

Incidence less frequent

Confusion; mental depression

Signs and symptoms of overdose

Difficulty in breathing; dizziness, extreme, or faintness; slow heartbeat; unusual tiredness or weakness, severe

Those indicating need for medical attention only if they continue or are bothersome

Incidence more frequent

Constipation; dizziness; drowsiness; dryness of mouth

Incidence less frequent

Conjunctivitis (dry, itching, or burning eyes); ***decreased sexual ability; headache; nausea or vomiting; trouble in sleeping; unusual tiredness or weakness***

Those indicating possible withdrawal and the need for medical attention if they occur after medication is discontinued

Sympathetic overactivity (anxiety or tenseness; chest pain; fast or irregular heartbeat; headache; increased salivation; nausea; nervousness; restlessness; shaking or trembling of hands and fingers; stomach cramps; sweating; trouble in sleeping; vomiting)

Note: *Sympathetic overactivity* is usually infrequent and mild and does not occur until 2 to 7 days after abrupt withdrawal of guanfacine. The risk appears to be increased in patients receiving divided doses totaling more than 4 mg per day. Rebound hypertension occurs less frequently.

Overdose

For more information on the management of overdose or unintentional ingestion, **contact a Poison Control Center** (see *Poison Control Center Listing*).

Treatment of overdose

Guanfacine overdose should be treated symptomatically, with careful cardiovascular monitoring. Treatment may include gastric lavage; isoproterenol infusion, as appropriate.

Patient Consultation

As an aid to patient consultation, refer to *Advice for the Patient, Guanfacine (Systemic)*.

In providing consultation, consider emphasizing the following selected information (» = major clinical significance):

Before using this medication

» Conditions affecting use, especially:
Sensitivity to guanfacine
Pregnancy—Use of extremely high doses in animals caused increased fetal deaths
Use in the elderly—Increased sensitivity to hypotensive effects

Proper use of this medication

Possible need for control of weight and diet, especially sodium intake

» Patient may not experience symptoms of hypertension; importance of taking medication even if feeling well

» Does not cure, but helps control hypertension; possible need for lifelong therapy; serious consequences of untreated hypertension

Taking at bedtime to reduce daytime drowsiness

» Proper dosing

Missed dose: Taking as soon as possible; checking with physician if two or more doses in a row are missed; possible reaction if stopped abruptly

» Proper storage

Precautions while using this medication

Making regular visits to physician to check progress

Checking with physician before discontinuing medication; gradual dosage reduction may be necessary to avoid rebound hypertension

Having enough medication on hand to get through weekends, holidays, and vacations; possibly carrying second prescription for emergency use

Caution if any kind of surgery (including dental surgery) or emergency treatment is required

» Not taking other medications, especially nonprescription sympathomimetics, unless discussed with physician

» Avoiding use of alcohol or other CNS depressants

» Caution when driving or doing things requiring alertness because of possible drowsiness

Possible dryness of mouth; using sugarless gum or candy, ice, or saliva substitute for relief; checking with dentist if dry mouth continues for more than 2 weeks

Side/adverse effects

Signs of potential side effects, especially confusion, mental depression, and withdrawal reaction

General Dosing Information

It is recommended that the daily dose be taken at bedtime to reduce daytime drowsiness.

Recent evidence suggests that withdrawal of antihypertensive therapy prior to surgery is not necessary, but that the anesthesiologist must be aware of such therapy. In addition, the possibility of withdrawal syndrome should be kept in mind if guanfacine is discontinued abruptly, although the syndrome does not generally occur until the patient has been without the drug for more than 2 days.

Guanfacine therapy should be discontinued if drug-related mental depression occurs.

Oral Dosage Forms

GUANFACINE HYDROCHLORIDE TABLETS

Note: The dosing and strengths of the dosage form available are expressed in terms of guanfacine base.

Usual adult dose

Antihypertensive—
Oral, 1 mg (base) once a day at bedtime, the dosage being increased after three to four weeks, if necessary, to 2 mg per day. If necessary, dosage may be further increased after an additional three to four weeks to 3 mg per day.

Note: If reduction in blood pressure is not maintained over 24 hours, divided daily dosing may be more effective, although the incidence of side/adverse effects may be increased.

Usual pediatric dose

Dosage has not been established.

Strength(s) usually available

U.S.—
1 mg (base) (Rx) [*Tenex* (lactose)].
2 mg (base) (Rx) [*Tenex* (lactose)].

Canada—
Not commercially available.

Packaging and storage

Store below 40 °C (104 °F), preferably between 15 and 30 °C (59 and 86 °F), in a tight container, unless otherwise specified by manufacturer. Protect from light.

Auxiliary labeling

- Avoid alcoholic beverages.
- Keep container tightly closed.

Note

Check refill frequency to determine compliance in hypertensive patients.

Selected Bibliography

Sorkin EM, Heel RC. Guanfacine: A review of its pharmacodynamic and pharmacokinetic properties, and therapeutic efficacy in the treatment of hypertension. Drugs 1986; 31: 301-36.

Cornish LA. Guanfacine hydrochloride: a centrally acting antihypertensive agent. Clin Pharm 1988 Mar; 7: 187-97.

The fifth report of the Joint National Committee on Detection, Evaluation, and Treatment of High Blood Pressure (JNC V). Arch Intern Med 1993; 153(2): 154-83.

Revised: 08/19/1998

HAEMOPHILUS B CONJUGATE VACCINE (HBOC—DIPHTHERIA CRM$_{197}$ PROTEIN CONJUGATE)—See *Haemophilus b Conjugate Vaccine (Systemic)*

HAEMOPHILUS B CONJUGATE VACCINE (PRP-D—DIPHTHERIA TOXOID CONJUGATE)—See *Haemophilus b Conjugate Vaccine (Systemic)*

HAEMOPHILUS B CONJUGATE VACCINE (PRP-OMP—MENINGOCOCCAL PROTEIN CONJUGATE)—See *Haemophilus b Conjugate Vaccine (Systemic)*

HAEMOPHILUS B CONJUGATE VACCINE (PRP-T—TETANUS PROTEIN CONJUGATE)—See *Haemophilus b Conjugate Vaccine (Systemic)*

HAEMOPHILUS B CONJUGATE VACCINE Systemic

This monograph includes information on the following: 1) Haemophilus b conjugate vaccine (HbOC—diptheria CRM$_{197}$ protein conjugate); 2) Haemophilus b conjugate vaccine (PRP-D—diphtheria toxoid conjugate); 3) Haemophilus b conjugate vaccine (PRP-OMP—meningococcal protein conjugate); 4) Haemophilus b conjugate vaccine (PRP-T—tetanus protein conjugate).

Note: It is recommended that, whenever possible, persons with indications for haemophilus b (Hib) vaccine be immunized with this newer, more immunogenic conjugate vaccine instead of with the polysaccharide vaccine. This is especially important for children 2 months to 24 months of age. See *Haemophilus b Polysaccharide Vaccine (Systemic)* for information on the polysaccharide vaccine.

This vaccine is not an immunizing agent against diphtheria, meningococcal disease, or tetanus.

VA CLASSIFICATION (Primary): IM100

Commonly used brand name(s): *Act-Hib*[4]; *Hibtiter*[1]; *Pedvaxhib*[3]; *Prohibit*[2].

Other commonly used names for HbOC are oligo-CRM and PRP-HbOC.

Note: For a listing of dosage forms and brand names by country availability, see *Dosage Forms* section(s).

Category

Immunizing agent (active).

Indications

Accepted

Haemophilus influenzae type b disease (prophylaxis)—Haemophilus b conjugate vaccine is indicated for routine immunization of all children 2 to 59 months of age against diseases caused by *Haemophilus influenzae* type b (Hib).

[Fractional-dose regimens of Hib conjugate vaccines may be used in developing countries where cost has limited their use][1].

Hib is a major cause of serious bacterial infection in early childhood. In developing countries, pneumonia and meningitis due to Hib are common in children under 12 months of age and the mortality from meningitis is high. Hib conjugate vaccines have brought Hib disease under control in industrialized countries. However, the cost of Hib conjugate vaccines has limited their use in developing countries. Fractional (one-half or one-third) doses of Hib conjugate vaccine have been shown to be highly effective. The use of fractional-dose regimens and the savings afforded by these regimens may represent the difference between vaccinating and not vaccinating infants against Hib in developing countries (See *Pharmacology/Pharmacokinetics*).

Note: *Act-Hib* (PRP-T), *Hibtiter* (HbOC), and *Pedvaxhib* (PRP-OMP) are licensed for use in infants and children 2 months of age and older. *Prohibit* (PRP-D) is licensed for use in children 15 months of age and older (U.S.) and in children 18 months of age and older (Canada).

There are no efficacy data available on the use of Hib vaccine for children 5 years of age and older and adults. Moreover, healthy adults and children 5 and older are not at risk for invasive Hib disease. However, studies suggest that patients in this age group who have chronic conditions associated with an increased risk of Hib disease, such as sickle cell disease, leukemia, splenectomy, or HIV infection, demonstrate good immune responses when immunized with Hib vaccine and may benefit from such immunization. Persons infected with human immunodeficiency virus (HIV) may receive this vaccine whether they are asymptomatic or symptomatic.

The following children should be included:

- Children attending day-care facilities.
- Children in residential institutions, such as orphanages.
- Children with chronic illnesses associated with increased risk of Hib disease. These illnesses include asplenia, sickle cell disease, antibody deficiency syndromes, immunosuppression, and Hodgkin's disease. Children scheduled to undergo immunosuppressive therapy, including that for Hodgkin's disease, should receive the conjugate vaccine at least 10 to 14 days prior to the therapy's initiation. The interval between discontinuation of therapy that causes immunosuppression and the restoration of the patient's ability to respond to an active immunizing agent depends on the intensity and type of immunosuppressive therapy used, the underlying disease, and other factors; estimates vary from 3 months to 1 year. Children with immunodeficiency syndromes secondary to deficient synthesis of immunoglobulins (e.g., agammaglobulinemia) probably will not benefit from immunization with the conjugate vaccine. Instead, passive immunity should be considered in these children.
- Infants and children under 24 months of age who have already had invasive Hib disease. Many infants and children under 24 months of age do not develop an adequate immune response to Hib disease and may contract the disease again if they are not immunized. The vaccine series can be initiated, or continued, at the time of discharge from the hospital. Children 24 months of age or older who contract Hib disease do not need to be immunized, since most children in this age group will develop protective levels of antibody from their illnesses.
- Children with asymptomatic or symptomatic human immunodeficiency virus (HIV) infection. Immunization is recommended even though immunization may be less effective than it would be for immunocompetent children.
- Children of certain racial groups, such as American Indian and Alaskan Eskimo. These racial groups appear to be at increased risk of Hib disease.
- Children of low socioeconomic status. Low socioeconomic status is often associated with crowded living conditions, which increase a child's risk of contact with Hib-infected persons.
- Children who have been previously immunized with the polysaccharide vaccine. Children previously immunized before 24 months of age should be reimmunized with the conjugate vaccine. Reimmunization should take place at least 2 months after the polysaccharide immunization. Children previously immunized at 24 months of age or older do not need to be reimmunized.

Even though they may be protected from invasive disease themselves, household, nursery, and day-care contacts, both adults and children, exposed to children with Hib disease may become asymptomatic carriers of Hib organisms and may infect unimmunized contacts. Therefore, the Immunization Practices Advisory Committee (ACIP) recommends that all contacts (whether immunized or unimmunized) of children with Hib disease receive rifampin chemoprophylaxis with the precautions that apply to the medication. Immunization of unimmunized contacts should not be used to prevent Hib disease in these contacts, because of the time required to generate an immunologic response. In addition, routinely immunizing health-care and day-care workers who may come into close contact with children with invasive Hib disease is not necessary, because healthy adults are not at risk for invasive Hib disease.

Unaccepted

This vaccine should not be used as an immunizing agent against diphtheria, tetanus, or meningococcal disease, even though there will be some increase in serum diphtheria or tetanus antitoxin levels or antibody levels to the outer membrane protein complex (OMPC) of *Neisseria meningitidis*, respectively, following immunization. No changes in the schedule for administration of diphtheria or tetanus toxoid or meningococcal vaccine are necessitated by the administration of this vaccine.

The conjugate vaccine protects against only *Haemophilus influenzae* type b (Hib). Protection against other strains of *H. influenzae*, such as non-encapsulated strains associated with recurrent upper respiratory disease (including otitis media and sinusitis) should not be anticipated following administration of this vaccine.

---

[1]Not included in Canadian product labeling.

Pharmacology/Pharmacokinetics

Physicochemical characteristics

Source—Purified capsular polysaccharide, a polymer of ribose, ribitol, and phosphate (PRP), from the bacterium *Haemophilus influenzae* type b (Hib). It has been conjugated in one of the following ways:
- For the diphtheria toxoid conjugate—The polysaccharide has been conjugated to the diphtheria toxoid via a 6-carbon linker molecule.
- For the diphtheria CRM_{197} protein conjugate—The oligosaccharide has been derived from the polysaccharide and has been bound directly to CRM_{197} (a nontoxic variant of diphtheria toxin) by reductive amination.
- For the meningococcal protein conjugate—The polysaccharide has been covalently bound to an outer membrane protein complex (OMPC) of the B11 strain of *Neisseria meningitidis* serogroup B.
- For the tetanus protein conjugate—The polysaccharide has been covalently bound to tetanus toxoid protein.

Mechanism of action/Effect

Haemophilus influenzae type b (Hib) bacteria are surrounded by polysaccharide capsules, which make these bacteria resistant to attack by white blood cells. However, human blood serum contains antibodies that render the bacteria vulnerable to attack. The vaccine, which is derived from the purified polysaccharide from Hib cells, stimulates production of anticapsular antibodies and provides active immunity to the *Haemophilus influenzae* type b bacteria.

Whereas the nonconjugated polysaccharide vaccine predominantly stimulates B-cells to produce antibodies (known as being T-cell independent), haemophilus b conjugate vaccine stimulates T-cells also. The additional stimulation of T-cells (known as being T-cell dependent) is particularly important in young children to ensure an adequate and persistent antibody response. Stimulation of T-cells also results in an anamnestic response to future doses of the conjugate or nonconjugate vaccine and to future natural exposure to *Haemophilus influenzae* type b, resulting in elevated antibody levels.

Protective effect

The exact protective level of anti-Haemophilus b polysaccharide antibody has not been established; however, 0.15 mcg per mL is considered by many experts to be protective, and 1 mcg per mL in post-immunization sera is considered indicative of long-term protection.

A study has shown that fractional (one-half or one-third) doses of Hib conjugate vaccines (PRP-T and PRP-CRM_{197}) can stimulate $\geq$ 0.15 mcg per mL antibody concentrations in 91–100% of immunized infants. This rate is similar to the 93% rate at which three full doses stimulated seroprotective concentrations. Therefore, the use of alternative regimens (i.e., fractional-dose regimens) and the savings afforded by fractional-dose regimens may represent the difference between vaccinating and not vaccinating infants against Hib in developing countries.

Antibody response to the vaccine is age related in children, with the immune response improving with increasing age.

Some differences in immunogenicity may exist among the different conjugates of haemophilus b conjugate vaccine; however, further studies are needed to confirm these differences and to evaluate their clinical relevance.

Haemophilus b conjugate vaccine is significantly more immunogenic than the nonconjugated polysaccharide vaccine.

Time to protective effect

Approximately 1 to 2 weeks for onset of a detectable antibody response to the vaccine.

Duration of protective effect

The duration of immunity of the conjugate vaccine is unknown.

Precautions to Consider

Cross-sensitivity and/or related problems

Patients sensitive to haemophilus b polysaccharide vaccine may be sensitive to the conjugate vaccine also.

Patients sensitive to diphtheria toxoid, meningococcal vaccine, or tetanus toxoid protein may be sensitive to the conjugate vaccines available in the U.S. and Canada. These vaccines contain either diphtheria toxoid, a nontoxic variant of diphtheria toxin, an outer membrane protein complex (OMPC) of *Neisseria meningitidis*, or tetanus toxoid protein.

Carcinogenicity/Mutagenicity

The conjugate vaccine has not been evaluated for its carcinogenic or mutagenic potential.

Pregnancy/Reproduction

Pregnancy—Studies have not been done in humans or animals.

FDA Pregnancy Category C.

Breast-feeding

Problems in humans have not been documented.

Pediatrics

Immunization is not recommended for children less than 2 months of age, since the safety and efficacy of the conjugate vaccine have not been established in this age group.

Geriatrics

Appropriate studies on the relationship of age to the effects of Hib vaccine have not been performed in the geriatric population. However, no geriatrics-specific problems have been documented to date.

Drug interactions and/or related problems

The following drug interactions and/or related problems have been selected on the basis of their potential clinical significance (possible mechanism in parentheses where appropriate)—not necessarily inclusive (» = major clinical significance):

Note: Combinations containing any of the following medications, depending on the amount present, may also interact with this medication.

Immunosuppressive agents or
Radiation therapy
(because normal defense mechanisms are suppressed by immunosuppressive agents or radiation treatment, the patient's antibody response to the conjugate vaccine may be decreased. If possible, children who are to undergo therapy with agents that cause immunosuppression, including treatment for Hodgkin's disease, should receive the vaccine at least 10 days, and preferably more than 14 days, before receiving the immunosuppressive agent; otherwise, it may be preferable to postpone the immunization until after the immunosuppressive therapy is completed. The interval between discontinuation of therapy that causes immunosuppression and the restoration of the patient's ability to respond to an active immunizing agent depends on the intensity and type of immunosuppressive therapy used, the underlying disease, and other factors; estimates vary from 3 months to 1 year. The precaution does not apply to corticosteroids used as replacement therapy, for short-term [less than 2 weeks] systemic therapy, or by other routes of administration that do not cause immunosuppression)

Laboratory value alterations

The following have been selected on the basis of their potential clinical significance (possible effect in parentheses where appropriate)—not necessarily inclusive (» = major clinical significance).

With diagnostic test results
Antigen detection tests
(there is a possibility that the conjugate vaccine may interfere with interpretation of antigen detection tests, such as latex agglutination and countercurrent immunoelectrophoresis, that are used for diagnosis of systemic Hib disease. PRP [a polymer of ribose, ribitol, and phosphate] derived from haemophilus b meningococcal protein conjugate vaccine may be detected in the urine of some persons for up to 7 days following immunization)

Medical considerations/Contraindications

The medical considerations/contraindications included have been selected on the basis of their potential clinical significance (reasons given in parentheses where appropriate)—not necessarily inclusive (» = major clinical significance).

Except under special circumstances, this medication should not be used when the following medical problems exist:

» Illness, acute or febrile
(administration of the conjugate vaccine should be postponed to avoid confusing the symptoms of the illness with the side effects of the vaccine; minor illnesses, such as mild upper respiratory infections, do not preclude administration of the vaccine)

Risk-benefit should be considered when the following medical problem exists:

Sensitivity to haemophilus b conjugate vaccine

Side/Adverse Effects

Note: Side effects generally are minor and last 48 hours or less; in addition, no serious systemic reactions have been observed.

In one person, thrombocytopenia was temporally noted; however, no causative relationship was established.

There are no significant differences in the frequency or types of side effects between haemophilus b polysaccharide vaccine and haemophilus b conjugate vaccine.

The following side/adverse effects have been selected on the basis of their potential clinical significance (possible signs and symptoms in parentheses where appropriate)—not necessarily inclusive:

Those indicating need for medical attention

Incidence rare

Anaphylactic reaction (difficulty in breathing or swallowing; hives; itching, especially of soles or palms; reddening of skin, especially around ears; swelling of eyes, face, or inside of nose; unusual tiredness or weakness, sudden and severe); ***convulsions***

Those indicating need for medical attention only if they continue or are bothersome

Incidence more frequent

Anorexia (loss of appetite); ***erythema at injection site*** (redness); ***fever up to 39°C (102.2°F)*** (usually resolves within 48 hours); ***irritability; lethargy*** (lack of interest; reduced physical activity); ***tenderness at injection site***

Incidence less frequent

Diarrhea; fever over 39°C (over 102.2°F) (usually resolves within 48 hours); ***induration*** (hard lump); ***swelling, or warm feeling at injection site; skin rash; urticaria*** (hives); ***vomiting***

Patient Consultation

As an aid to patient consultation, refer to *Advice for the Patient, Haemophilus B Conjugate Vaccine (Systemic)*.

In providing consultation, consider emphasizing the following selected information (» = major clinical significance):

Before receiving this vaccine

» Conditions affecting use, especially:

Sensitivity to haemophilus b conjugate vaccine, haemophilus b polysaccharide vaccine, diphtheria toxoid, meningococcal vaccine, or tetanus toxoid

Use in children—Not recommended for use in children up to 2 months of age

Other medical problems, especially fever or serious illness

Proper use of this medication

» Proper dosing

Side/adverse effects

Signs of potential side effects, especially anaphylactic reaction or convulsions

General Dosing Information

When sterilizing syringes before vaccination, care should be taken to avoid use of preservatives, antiseptics, detergents, and disinfectants, since the conjugate vaccine may be inactivated by these substances. Disposable syringes and needles are recommended.

The conjugate vaccine is for intramuscular administration only. It should not be administered intravenously.

This vaccine should not be used as an immunizing agent against diphtheria, meningococcal meningitis, or tetanus, even though there may be some slight increase in serum antitoxin or antibody levels following immunization. No changes in the schedule for administration of diphtheria or tetanus toxoid or meningococcal vaccine are necessitated by the administration of this vaccine.

Polysaccharide vaccines, including haemophilus b conjugate vaccine, may be administered concurrently with the vaccines listed below, using separate syringes for the parenterals, and the precautions that apply to each immunizing agent. If DTP, MMR, and IPV are administered concurrently with Hib conjugate vaccine, any 2 of the vaccines may be administered in the same deltoid, and any of these vaccines may be administered in the thigh. If any of the other vaccines listed below is to be administered concurrently with Hib conjugate vaccine, each parenteral vaccine should be administered at a separate body site.

- Polysaccharide vaccines, other, such as meningococcal polysaccharide vaccine or pneumococcal polyvalent vaccine.
- Influenza vaccine, whole or split virus.
- Diphtheria toxoid, tetanus toxoid, and/or pertussis vaccine.
- Live virus vaccines, such as measles, mumps, and/or rubella vaccines.
- Poliovirus vaccines (oral [OPV], inactivated [IPV], or enhanced-potency inactivated [enhanced-potency IPV]).
- Hepatitis B recombinant or plasma-derived vaccine.
- Immune globulin and disease-specific immune globulins.
- Inactivated vaccines, except cholera, typhoid (parenteral), and plague. It is recommended that cholera, typhoid (parenteral), and plague vaccines be administered on separate occasions because there are no data available on the concurrent administration of haemophilus b conjugate vaccine and these vaccines and because of these vaccines' propensity for causing side/adverse effects.

The first conjugate vaccine was licensed for use in the U.S. in December 1987. Persons immunized against Hib disease before that date can be presumed to have received the polysaccharide vaccine.

For treatment of adverse effects

Recommended treatment includes:

- For mild hypersensitivity reaction—Administering antihistamines, and, if necessary, glucocorticoids.
- For severe hypersensitivity or anaphylactic reaction—Administering epinephrine. Antihistamines or glucocorticoids may also be administered as required.

HAEMOPHILUS B CONJUGATE VACCINE (HbOC—DIPTHERIA CRM$_{197}$ PROTEIN CONJUGATE)

Parenteral Dosage Forms

HAEMOPHILUS B CONJUGATE VACCINE INJECTION (HbOC—diphtheria CRM$_{197}$ protein conjugate)

Usual adult and adolescent dose

Active immunizing agent—

Use is not recommended in these age groups, except for patients with certain chronic conditions associated with an increased risk of Hib disease.

Usual pediatric dose

Note: In countries where the cost of Hib conjugate vaccines has limited their use, fractional dose (one-half or one-third of the usual pediatric dose) regimens may be used as an alternative to the usual pediatric dose (See *Indications*).

Active immunizing agent—

Intramuscular, 0.5 mL, into the outer aspect of the upper arm (deltoid) or into the lateral mid thigh (vastus lateralis), according to the following dosage schedules:

In the U.S.—

Infants:

First dose—At 2 months of age.

Note: The vaccine series may be initiated as early as 6 weeks of age.

Second dose—At 4 months of age.

Third dose—At 6 months of age.

Booster—At 15 months of age.

Children up to 59 months of age who did not follow the above schedule:

Age 2 to 6 months of age at first dose—Three doses, two months apart, then a booster dose at 15 months of age or as soon as possible thereafter, but not less than two months after previous dose.

Age 7 to 11 months of age at first dose—Two doses, two months apart, then a booster dose at 15 months of age or as soon as possible thereafter, but not less than two months after previous dose.

Age 12 to 14 months of age at first dose—One dose, then a booster dose at 15 months of age or as soon as possible thereafter, but not less than two months after previous dose.

Age 15 to 59 months of age at first dose—One dose.

Note: An interval as short as 1 month between doses is acceptable, but is not optimal.

Any of the other conjugate vaccines may be used for the booster dose; however, there are no data demonstrating that a booster response will occur if one of these other vaccines is used. Ideally, the same conjugate vaccine should be used throughout the vaccination series, including the booster.

Children 5 years of age and older:

Use is not recommended, except for patients with certain chronic conditions associated with an increased risk of Hib disease.

In Canada—

Infants:

First dose—At 2 months of age.

Note: The vaccine series may be initiated as early as 6 weeks of age.

Second dose—At 4 months of age.

Third dose—At 6 months of age.

Booster—At 15 to 18 months of age.

Children up to 59 months of age who did not follow the above schedule:

Age 2 to 6 months of age at first dose—Three doses, two months apart, then a booster dose at 15 to 18 months of age or as soon as possible thereafter, but not less than two months after previous dose.

Age 7 to 11 months of age at first dose—Two doses, two months apart, then a booster dose at 15 to 18 months of age or as soon as possible thereafter, but not less than two months after previous dose.

Age 12 to 17 months of age at first dose—One dose, then a booster dose at 15 to 18 months of age or as soon as possible thereafter, but not less than two months after previous dose.

Age 18 to 59 months of age at first dose—One dose.

Note: An interval as short as 1 month between doses is acceptable, but is not optimal.

Any of the other conjugate vaccines may be used for the booster dose; however, there are no data demonstrating that a booster response will occur if one of these other vaccines is used. Ideally, the same conjugate vaccine should be used throughout the vaccination series, including the booster.

Children 5 years of age and older:

Use is not recommended.

Note: Children 5 years of age and older with certain chronic conditions associated with an increased risk of Hib disease may profit from Hib immunization.

Strength(s) usually available

U.S.—

10 mcg (0.01 mg) of purified haemophilus b saccharide and approximately 25 mcg (0.025 mg) of CRM_{197} protein, a nontoxic variant of diphtheria toxin, per 0.5 mL dose (Rx) [*Hibtiter* (in multidose vials—thimerosal 1:10,000)].

Canada—

10 mcg (0.01 mg) of purified haemophilus b saccharide and approximately 25 mcg (0.025 mg) of CRM_{197} protein, a nontoxic variant of diphtheria toxin, per 0.5 mL dose (Rx) [*Hibtiter*].

Packaging and storage

Store between 2 and 8 °C (35 and 46 °F), unless otherwise specified by manufacturer. Do not freeze.

HAEMOPHILUS B CONJUGATE VACCINE (PRP-D—DIPHTHERIA TOXOID CONJUGATE)

Parenteral Dosage Forms

HAEMOPHILUS B CONJUGATE VACCINE INJECTION (PRP-D—diphtheria toxoid conjugate)

Usual adult and adolescent dose

Active immunizing agent—

Use is not recommended in these age groups, except for patients with certain chronic conditions associated with an increased risk of Hib disease.

Usual pediatric dose

Note: In countries where the cost of Hib conjugate vaccines has limited their use, fractional dose (one-half or one-third of the usual pediatric dose) regimens may be used as an alternative to the usual pediatric dose (See *Indications*).

Active immunizing agent—

Intramuscular, 0.5 mL, into the outer aspect of the upper arm (deltoid) or into the lateral mid thigh (vastus lateralis), according to the following dosage schedules:

In the U.S.—

Infants and children up to 15 months of age: Use is not recommended.

Children 15 to 59 months of age who were not previously immunized: One dose.

Children 5 years of age and older: Use is not recommended, except for patients with certain chronic conditions associated with an increased risk of Hib disease.

In Canada—

Infants and children up to 18 months of age: Use is not recommended.

Children 18 to 60 months of age who were not previously immunized: One dose.

Children 5 years of age and older: Use is not recommended, except for patients with certain chronic conditions associated with an increased risk of Hib disease.

Strength(s) usually available

U.S.—

25 mcg (0.025 mg) of purified haemophilus b capsular polysaccharide and 18 mcg (0.018 mg) of diphtheria toxoid protein, per 0.5 mL dose (Rx) [*Prohibit* (thimerosal 1:10,000)].

Canada—

25 mcg (0.025 mg) of purified haemophilus b capsular polysaccharide and 18 mcg (0.018 mg) of diphtheria toxoid protein, per 0.5 mL dose (Rx) [*Prohibit* (thimerosal 1:10,000)].

Packaging and storage

Store between 2 and 8 °C (35 and 46 °F), unless otherwise specified by manufacturer. Do not freeze.

HAEMOPHILUS B CONJUGATE VACCINE (PRP-OMP—MENINGOCOCCAL PROTEIN CONJUGATE)

Parenteral Dosage Forms

HAEMOPHILUS B CONJUGATE VACCINE INJECTION (PRP-OMP—meningococcal protein conjugate)

Usual adult and adolescent dose

Active immunizing agent—

Use is not recommended in these age groups, except for patients with certain chronic conditions associated with an increased risk of Hib disease.

Usual pediatric dose

Note: In countries where the cost of Hib conjugate vaccines has limited their use, fractional dose (one-half or one-third of the usual pediatric dose) regimens may be used as an alternative to the usual pediatric dose (See *Indications*).

Active immunizing agent—

Intramuscular, 0.5 mL, into the outer aspect of the upper arm (deltoid) or into the lateral mid thigh (vastus lateralis), according to the following dosage schedules:

In the U.S.—

Infants:

First dose—At 2 months of age.

Note: the vaccine series may be initiated as early as 6 weeks of age.

Second dose—At 4 months of age.

Booster—At 12 months of age.

Children up to 59 months of age who did not follow the above schedule:

Age 2 to 6 months of age at first dose—Two doses, two months apart, then a booster dose at 12 months of age or as soon as possible thereafter, but not less than two months after previous dose.

Age 7 to 11 months of age at first dose—Two doses, two months apart, then a booster dose at 15 months of age or as soon as possible thereafter, but not less than two months after previous dose.

Age 12 to 14 months of age at first dose—One dose, then a booster dose at 15 months of age or as soon as possible thereafter, but not less than two months after previous dose.

Age 15 to 59 months of age at first dose—One dose.

Note: The U.S. manufacturer's labeling gives the age ranges and dosages as: 2 to 10 months of age at first dose—2 doses, 2 months apart, with a booster at 12 to 15 months; 11 to 14 months of age at first dose—2 doses, 2 months apart; 15 to 71 months of age at first dose—1 dose. These recommendations differ somewhat from those of the Immunization Practices Advisory Committee (ACIP) that are used above.

An interval as short as 1 month between doses is acceptable, but is not optimal.

Any of the other conjugate vaccines may be used for the 15-month booster dose; however, there are no data demonstrating that a booster response will occur if one of these other vaccines is used. Ideally, the same conjugate vaccine should be used throughout the vaccination series, including the booster.

Children 5 years of age and older:
Use is not recommended, except for patients with certain chronic conditions associated with an increased risk of Hib disease.

In Canada—
Infants:
First dose—At 2 months of age.
Note: The vaccine series may be initiated as early as 6 weeks of age.
Second dose—At 4 months of age.
Booster—At 12 months of age.
Children up to 59 months of age who did not follow the above schedule:
Age 2 to 6 months of age at first dose—Two doses, two months apart, then a booster dose at 12 months of age or as soon as possible thereafter, but not less than two months after previous dose.
Age 7 to 11 months of age at first dose—Two doses, two months apart, then a booster dose at 15 months of age or as soon as possible thereafter, but not less than two months after previous dose.
Age to 12 to 17 months of age at first dose—One dose, then a booster dose at 18 months of age or as soon as possible thereafter, but not less than two months after previous dose.
Age 18 to 59 months of age at first dose—One dose.
Note: An interval as short as 1 month between doses is acceptable, but is not optimal.
Any of the other conjugate vaccines may be used for the 15- or 18-month booster dose; however, there are no data demonstrating that a booster response will occur if one of these other vaccines is used. Ideally, the same conjugate vaccine should be used throughout the vaccination series, including the booster.
Children 5 years of age and older:
Use is not recommended.
Note: Children 5 years of age and older with certain chronic conditions associated with an increased risk of Hib disease may profit from Hib immunization.

Strength(s) usually available
U.S.—
15 mcg (0.015 mg) of purified haemophilus b capsular polysaccharide and 250 mcg (0.25 mg) of an outer membrane protein complex (OMPC) of the B11 strain of *Neisseria meningitidis* serogroup B, per 0.5 mL dose (Rx) [*Pedvaxhib* (in lyophilized product—lactose 2 mg; in diluent—aluminum 225 mcg as aluminum hydroxide; thimerosal 1:20,000)].

Canada—
15 mcg (0.015 mg) of purified haemophilus b capsular polysaccharide and 250 mcg (0.25 mg) of an outer membrane protein complex (OMPC) of the B11 strain of *Neisseria meningitidis* serogroup B, per 0.5 mL dose (Rx) [*Pedvaxhib* (in lyophilized product—lactose 2 mg; in diluent—aluminum 225 mcg as aluminum hydroxide; thimerosal 1:20,000)].

Packaging and storage
Store between 2 and 8 °C (35 and 45 °F), unless otherwise specified by manufacturer. Do not freeze reconstituted vaccine or aluminum hydroxide diluent.

Preparation of dosage form
Pedvaxhib should be reconstituted only with the aluminum hydroxide diluent that is supplied. The diluent should be agitated prior to its withdrawal. The vaccine should be agitated at the time of reconstitution, prior to withdrawal of the vaccine dose into the syringe, and prior to injection.

Stability
Pedvaxhib should be used as soon as possible after reconstitution. Reconstituted vaccine should be stored between 2 and 8 °C (35 and 46 °F) and discarded if not used within 24 hours.

Auxiliary labeling
- Shake gently before use.

HAEMOPHILUS B CONJUGATE VACCINE (PRP-T—TETANUS PROTEIN CONJUGATE)

Parenteral Dosage Forms

HAEMOPHILUS B CONJUGATE VACCINE INJECTION (PRP-T—tetanus protein conjugate)

Usual adult and adolescent dose
Active immunizing agent—
Use is not recommended in these age groups, except for patients with certain chronic conditions associated with an increased risk of Hib disease.

Usual pediatric dose
Note: In countries where the cost of Hib conjugate vaccines has limited their use, fractional dose (one-half or one-third of the usual pediatric dose) regimens may be used as an alternative to the usual pediatric dose (See *Indications*).

Active immunizing agent—
Intramuscular, 0.5 mL, into the outer aspect of the upper arm (deltoid) or into the lateral mid thigh (vastus lateralis), according to the following dosage schedules:
In the U.S.—
Infants:
First dose—At 2 months of age.
Note: The vaccine series may be initiated as early as 6 weeks of age.
Second dose—At 4 months of age.
Third dose—At 6 months of age.
Booster—At 15 months of age.
Children up to 59 months of age who did not follow the above schedule:
Age 2 to 6 months of age at first dose—Three doses, two months apart, then a booster dose at 15 months of age or as soon as possible thereafter, but not less than two months after previous dose.
Age 7 to 11 months of age at first dose—Two doses, two months apart, then a booster dose at 15 months of age or as soon as possible thereafter, but not less than two months after previous dose.
Age 12 to 14 months of age at first dose—One dose, then a booster dose at 15 months of age or as soon as possible thereafter, but not less than two months after previous dose.
Age 15 to 59 months of age at first dose—One dose.
Note: An interval as short as 1 month between doses is acceptable, but is not optimal.
Any of the other conjugate vaccines may be used for the booster dose; however, there are no data demonstrating that a booster response will occur if one of these other vaccines is used. Ideally, the same conjugate vaccine should be used throughout the vaccination series, including the booster.
Children 5 years of age and older:
Use is not recommended, except for patients with certain chronic conditions associated with an increased risk of Hib disease.

In Canada—
Infants:
First dose—At 2 months of age.
Note: The vaccine series may be initiated as early as 6 weeks of age.
Second dose—At 4 months of age.
Third dose—At 6 months of age.
Booster—At 18 months of age.
Children up to 59 months of age who did not follow the above schedule:
Age 3 to 6 months of age at first dose—Three doses, two months apart, then a booster dose at 18 months of age or as soon as possible thereafter, but not less than two months after previous dose.
Age 7 to 11 months of age at first dose—Two doses, two months apart, then a booster dose at 18 months of age or as soon as possible thereafter, but not less than two months after previous dose.
Age 12 to 14 months of age at first dose—One dose, then a booster dose at 18 months of age or as soon as possible

thereafter, but not less than two months after previous dose.

Age 15 to 59 months of age at first dose—One dose.

Note: An interval as short as 1 month between doses is acceptable, but is not optimal.

The booster dose may be given as early as 15 months of age or as soon as possible thereafter, but not less than two months after previous dose.

Any of the other conjugate vaccines may be used for the booster dose; however, there are no data demonstrating that a booster response will occur if one of these other vaccines is used. Ideally, the same conjugate vaccine should be used throughout the vaccination series, including the booster.

Children 5 years of age and older:

Use is not recommended, except for patients with certain chronic conditions associated with an increased risk of Hib disease.

Strength(s) usually available

U.S.—

10 mcg (0.01 mg) of purified haemophilus b capsular polysaccharide and 20 mcg (0.02 mg) of tetanus protein, per 0.5 mL dose (Rx) [*Act-Hib*].

Canada—

10 mcg (0.01 mg) of purified haemophilus b capsular polysaccharide and 20 mcg (0.02 mg) of tetanus protein, per 0.5 mL dose (Rx) [*Act-Hib*].

Packaging and storage

Store between 2 and 8 °C (35 and 46 °F), unless otherwise specified by manufacturer. Do not freeze the reconstituted vaccine.

Preparation of dosage form

Act-Hib should be reconstituted only with the 0.4% saline diluent that is supplied. The vaccine should be shaken gently until a clear, colorless solution results. (In Canada, *Act-Hib* may be reconstituted also with the Connaught-Canada brand of DTP vaccine).

Stability

Act-Hib should be discarded if it is not used immediately after reconstitution.

Selected Bibliography

Centers for Disease Control. ACIP update: prevention of Haemophilus influenzae type b disease. MMWR 1988 Jan 22; 37: 13-6.

Berkowitz CD, et al. Safety and immunogenicity of Haemophilus influenzae type b polysaccharide and polysaccharide diphtheria toxoid conjugate vaccines in children 15 to 24 months of age. J Pediatr 1987 Apr: 509-14.

Centers for Disease Control. Haemophilus b conjugate vaccines for prevention of Haemophilus influenzae type b disease among infants and children two months of age and older: recommendation of the Immunization Practices Advisory Committee (ACIP). MMWR 1991 Jan 11: 40 (RR-1).

Centers for Disease Control. Update on adult immunization: recommendations of the Immunization Practices Advisory Committee (ACIP). MMWR 1991 Nov 15: 40 (RR-12).

Weinberg GA, Granoff DM. Polysaccharide-protein conjugate vaccines for the prevention of Haemophilus influenzae type b disease. J Pediatr 1988 Oct; 113(4): 621-31.

Revised: 08/16/2000

HALAZEPAM—See *Benzodiazepines (Systemic)*

HALCINONIDE—See *Corticosteroids (Topical)*

HALOBETASOL—See *Corticosteroids (Topical)*

HALOPERIDOL Systemic

VA CLASSIFICATION (Primary/Secondary): CN709/CN900; GA609

Commonly used brand name(s): *Apo-Haloperidol; Haldol; Haldol Decanoate; Haldol LA; Novo-Peridol; PMS Haloperidol; Peridol.*

Note: For a listing of dosage forms and brand names by country availability, see *Dosage Forms* section(s).

Category

Antipsychotic; antidyskinetic (Gilles de la Tourette's syndrome; Huntington's chorea); antiemetic.

Indications

Note: Bracketed information in the *Indications* section refers to uses that are not included in U.S. product labeling.

Accepted

Psychotic disorders (treatment)—Haloperidol is indicated for the management of the manifestations of acute and chronic psychotic disorders including schizophrenia, manic states, and drug-induced psychoses, such as steroid psychosis. It may also be useful in the management of aggressive and agitated patients, including patients with organic mental syndrome or mental retardation. Haloperidol decanoate, a long-acting parenteral form, is intended for maintenance use in the management of patients requiring prolonged parenteral therapy, as in chronic schizophrenia.

Behavior problems, severe (treatment)—Haloperidol is effective in the treatment of children with severe behavior problems of apparently unprovoked, combative, explosive hyperexcitability. It is also effective in the *short-term* treatment of hyperactivity in children who show excessive motor activity with accompanying conduct disorders such as aggressiveness, impulsiveness, easy frustration, short attention span, and/or rapid mood fluctuations. In these two groups of children, haloperidol should be tried only in patients who fail to respond to psychotherapy or other non-neuroleptic medication.

Gilles de la Tourette's syndrome (treatment)—Haloperidol is used to control tics and vocalizations of Tourette's syndrome in children and adults.

[Autism, infantile (treatment)][1]—Haloperidol has been used to reduce abnormal behaviors, such as withdrawal, stereotypy, abnormal object relationships, fidgetiness, hyperactivity, negativism, angry affect, and labile affect, and may improve learning, in some patients with autism.

[Chorea, Huntington's (treatment)][1]—Because of its strong extrapyramidal effects, haloperidol is used to reduce disabling choreiform movements in Huntington's disease.

[Nausea and vomiting, cancer chemotherapy-induced (prophylaxis and treatment)][1]—Haloperidol is used as a second-line agent to control nausea and vomiting associated with antineoplastic therapy and surgery.

[1]Not included in Canadian product labeling.

Pharmacology/Pharmacokinetics

Note: Pharmacological effects of haloperidol are similar to the effects of piperazine-derivative phenothiazines, which include acetophenazine, fluphenazine, perphenazine, prochlorperazine, and trifluoperazine.

Physicochemical characteristics

Chemical Group—A butyrophenone derivative.

Molecular weight—

Haloperidol: 375.87.

Haloperidol decanoate: 530.12.

Other characteristics—

Haloperidol oral solution: pH 2.75–3.75.

Haloperidol injection: pH 3.0–3.8.

Mechanism of action/Effect

Although the complex mechanism of the therapeutic effect is not clearly established, haloperidol is known to produce a selective effect on the central nervous system (CNS) by competitive blockade of postsynaptic dopamine (D_2) receptors in the mesolimbic dopaminergic system and an increased turnover of brain dopamine to produce its tranquilizing effects. With subchronic therapy, depolarization blockade, or diminished firing rate of the dopamine neuron (decreased release) along with D_2 postsynaptic blockade results in the antipsychotic action.

The long-acting decanoate form acts as a pro-drug, slowly and steadily releasing haloperidol from the vehicle.

Other actions/effects

Blockade of dopamine receptors in the nigrostriatal dopamine pathway produces extrapyramidal motor reactions; blockade of dopamine receptors in the tuberoinfundibular system decreases growth hormone release and increases prolactin release by the pituitary. There is also some blockade of alpha-adrenergic receptors of the autonomic system.

Absorption
Oral—60%.

Distribution
The volume of distribution of haloperidol at steady state (Vd_{SS}) is 18 L per kg.

Protein binding
Very high (92%).

Biotransformation
Hepatic; extensive.

Half-life
Haloperidol, Elimination—
Oral: 24 hours (range, 12 to 37 hours).
Intramuscular: 21 hours (range, 17 to 25 hours).
Intravenous: 14 hours (range, 10 to 19 hours).
Haloperidol decanoate, Elimination—
Approximately 3 weeks (single or multiple doses).

Time to peak plasma concentration
Oral—3 to 6 hours.
Intramuscular—10 to 20 minutes.
Long-acting intramuscular—3 to 9 days, although variable. May occur on first day in some patients, notably the elderly.

Therapeutic plasma concentration
4 to 20 nanograms per mL (0.01 to 0.05 micromoles per L).

Elimination
Renal—
About 40% of a single oral dose is excreted in the urine within 5 days, 1% of which is unchanged drug. A mean clearance value of 12 mL per kg per minute has been reported.
Biliary—
15% of an oral dose is excreted in the feces by biliary elimination.

Precautions to Consider

Carcinogenicity/Tumorigenicity
Neuroleptic drugs (including haloperidol) elevate prolactin concentrations; the elevation persists during chronic administration. Tissue culture experiments indicate that approximately one third of human breast cancers are prolactin dependent *in vitro* , a factor of potential importance if the prescription of these drugs is contemplated in a patient with a previously detected breast cancer. Although disturbances such as galactorrhea, amenorrhea, gynecomastia, and impotence have been reported, the clinical significance of elevated serum prolactin concentrations is unknown for most patients. An increase in mammary neoplasms has been found in rodents after chronic administration of neuroleptic drugs. However, neither clinical studies nor epidemiologic studies conducted to date have shown an association between chronic administration of these drugs and mammary tumorigenesis; the available evidence is considered too limited to be conclusive at this time.

Mutagenicity
Haloperidol decanoate—No mutagenic potential was found in the Ames *Salmonella* microsomal activation assay.

Pregnancy/Reproduction
Fertility—Animal reproduction studies have shown decreased fertility with doses 2 to 20 times the usual maximum human dose of haloperidol.

Pregnancy—
For haloperidol—
Adequate studies in humans have not been done. However, there have been some reports of limb malformations with maternal use of haloperidol along with other drugs of suspected teratogenicity during the first trimester.
Some rodent studies have shown an increase in incidence of fetal resorption, delayed delivery, and neonatal death with doses 2 to 20 times the usual maximum human dose of haloperidol. Cleft palate has been observed in a study with mice given 15 times the human dose of haloperidol.
For haloperidol decanoate—
Adequate studies in humans have not been done.
Studies in rats given up to three times the usual maximum human dose showed an increase in incidence of fetal resorption, fetal mortality, and neonatal mortality.

FDA Pregnancy Category C.

Breast-feeding
Haloperidol is distributed into breast milk. Animal studies have shown that haloperidol is distributed into milk in quantities sufficient to cause sedation and motor function impairment in the nursing offspring. Breast-feeding during haloperidol therapy is not recommended.

Pediatrics
Haloperidol is not recommended for use in children up to 3 years of age. Children are highly susceptible to the extrapyramidal side effects, especially dystonias, of haloperidol.

Geriatrics
Geriatric patients tend to develop higher plasma concentrations of haloperidol because of changes in distribution due to decreases in lean body mass, total body water, and albumin, and often an increase in total body fat composition. These patients usually require lower initial dosage and a more gradual titration of dose.

Elderly patients appear to be more prone to orthostatic hypotension and exhibit an increased sensitivity to the anticholinergic and sedative effects of haloperidol. In addition, they are more prone to develop extrapyramidal side effects, such as tardive dyskinesia and parkinsonism. The symptoms of tardive dyskinesia are persistent, difficult to control, and, in some patients, appear to be irreversible. The symptoms may be masked during long-term treatment, but may appear if haloperidol is discontinued. There is no known effective treatment. Careful observation during haloperidol therapy for early signs of tardive dyskinesia and reduction of dosage or discontinuation of medication may prevent a more severe manifestation of the syndrome. It has been suggested that elderly patients receive half the usual adult dose. Patients with organic mental syndrome or acute confusional states should initially receive one-third to one-half the usual adult dose, with the dose being increased no more frequently than every 2 or 3 days, and preferably at intervals of 7 to 10 days. A periodic attempt should be made to discontinue medication as soon as the patient improves.

Dental
The peripheral anticholinergic effects of haloperidol may decrease or inhibit salivary flow, especially in middle-aged or elderly patients, thus contributing to the development of caries, periodontal disease, oral candidiasis, and discomfort.

Extrapyramidal reactions induced by haloperidol will result in increased motor activity of the head, face, and neck. Occlusal adjustments, bite registrations, and treatment for bruxism may be made less reliable.

The leukopenic and thrombocytopenic effects of haloperidol may result in an increased incidence of microbial infection, delayed healing, and gingival bleeding. If leukopenia or thrombocytopenia occurs, dental work should be deferred until blood counts have returned to normal. Patients should be instructed in proper oral hygiene, including caution in use of regular toothbrushes, dental floss, and toothpicks.

Drug interactions and/or related problems
The following drug interactions and/or related problems have been selected on the basis of their potential clinical significance (possible mechanism in parentheses where appropriate)—not necessarily inclusive (» = major clinical significance):

Note: Combinations containing any of the following medications, depending on the amount present, may also interact with this medication.

» Alcohol or
» CNS depression-producing medications, other (see *Appendix II*)
(concurrent use with haloperidol may result in increased CNS and respiratory depression and increased hypotensive effects)
(concurrent use with haloperidol may potentiate alcohol intoxication)

Amphetamines
(concurrent use may decrease stimulant effects of amphetamines due to alpha-adrenergic blockade by haloperidol; also, the antipsychotic effects of haloperidol may be reduced when amphetamines and haloperidol are used concurrently)

Anticholinergics or other medications with anticholinergic activity (see *Appendix II*) or
Antidyskinetic agents or
Antihistamines
(concurrent use with haloperidol may intensify anticholinergic side effects, especially those of confusion, hallucinations, nightmares, and increased intraocular pressure, because of secondary anticholinergic effects of haloperidol; also, patients should be advised to report occurrence of gastrointestinal problems since paralytic ileus may occur with concurrent therapy; in addition, antipsychotic effectiveness of haloperidol may be decreased because of reduced gastrointestinal absorption; dosage adjustments may be necessary)

Anticoagulants, coumarin- or indandione-derivative
(concurrent use with haloperidol may either increase or decrease anticoagulant activity; although the clinical significance has not been determined, caution is recommended)

Anticonvulsants, including barbiturates
(concurrent use with haloperidol may cause a change in the pattern and/or frequency of epileptiform seizures; dosage adjustments of anticonvulsants may be necessary; serum concentrations of haloperidol may be significantly reduced)

Antidepressants, tricyclic or
Maprotiline or
Monoamine oxidase (MAO) inhibitors, including furazolidone, procarbazine, or selegiline or
Trazodone
(concurrent use with haloperidol may prolong and intensify the sedative and anticholinergic effects of either these medications or haloperidol)

Bromocriptine
(concurrent use with haloperidol may increase serum prolactin concentrations and interfere with effects of bromocriptine; dosage adjustment of bromocriptine may be necessary)

Bupropion
(concurrent use of bupropion with haloperidol may lower the seizure threshold and increase the risk of major motor seizures)

Diazoxide
(concurrent use antagonizes the inhibition of insulin release by diazoxide)

Dopamine
(concurrent use may antagonize peripheral vasoconstriction produced by high doses of dopamine because of the alpha-adrenergic blocking action of haloperidol)

Ephedrine
(concurrent use may decrease the pressor response to ephedrine)

» Epinephrine
(concurrent use may block the alpha-adrenergic effects of epinephrine, possibly resulting in severe hypotension and tachycardia)

» Extrapyramidal reaction-causing medications, other (see *Appendix II*)
(concurrent use with haloperidol may increase the severity and frequency of extrapyramidal effects)

Fluoxetine
(caution in concurrent use of fluoxetine with haloperidol is recommended because of a potentially increased risk of CNS side effects, particularly extrapyramidal reactions)

Guanadrel or
Guanethidine
(concurrent use with haloperidol may decrease the hypotensive effects of these agents because of displacement from and inhibition of uptake into alpha-adrenergic neurons)

» Levodopa or
Pergolide
(concurrent use may decrease the therapeutic effects of these agents because of blockade of dopamine receptors by haloperidol)

» Lithium
(lithium is frequently used concurrently with haloperidol during the first week or two of treatment for acute manic episodes; lithium alone may be adequate thereafter, although some patients may continue to need both; however, concurrent use with haloperidol has been associated with irreversible neurological toxicity and brain damage, especially in patients with organic mental syndrome or other CNS impairment, although this interaction has been reported only with high doses; extrapyramidal symptoms may be increased by haloperidol's enhancement of dopamine blockade; patients should be monitored closely during concurrent use; dosage adjustments or discontinuation of treatment may be necessary)

(admixture of the liquid forms of lithium and haloperidol may result in precipitation of free haloperidol)

Metaraminol
(concurrent use with haloperidol usually decreases, but does not reverse or completely block, the pressor response to metaraminol, because of the alpha-adrenergic blocking action of haloperidol)

Methoxamine
(prior administration of haloperidol may decrease the pressor effect and duration of action of methoxamine because of the alpha-adrenergic blocking action of haloperidol)

Methyldopa
(concurrent use with haloperidol may cause unwanted mental effects such as disorientation and slowed or difficult thought processes)

Phenylephrine
(prior administration of haloperidol may decrease the pressor response to phenylephrine because of the alpha-adrenergic blocking action of haloperidol)

Laboratory value alterations

The following have been selected on the basis of their potential clinical significance (possible effect in parentheses where appropriate)—not necessarily inclusive (» = major clinical significance).

With diagnostic test results
ECG
(prolongation of the Q-T interval and changes compatible with configuration of *torsades de pointes* may occur)

Medical considerations/Contraindications

The medical considerations/contraindications included have been selected on the basis of their potential clinical significance (reasons given in parentheses where appropriate)—not necessarily inclusive (» = major clinical significance).

Except under special circumstances, this medication should not be used when the following medical problem exists:

» CNS depression, toxic, drug-induced, severe
(may be potentiated)

Risk-benefit should be considered when the following medical problems exist:

Alcoholism, active
(CNS depression may be potentiated; risk of heat stroke may be increased)

» Cardiovascular disease, severe, especially angina
(transient hypotension and anginal pain may be provoked)

» Epilepsy
(seizure threshold may be lowered)

Glaucoma or predisposition to
(may be potentiated because of secondary anticholinergic effects of haloperidol)

Hepatic function impairment
(metabolism may be altered)

Hyperthyroidism or thyrotoxicosis
(severe neurotoxicity such as rigidity and inability to walk or talk may result)

» Parkinson's disease
(may be potentiated)

Pulmonary insufficiency, such as asthma, emphysema, or acute pulmonary infections
(potentiation of breathing impairment may possibly lead to "silent pneumonias")

Renal function impairment
(excretion may be altered; more applicable to higher dosage since renal clearance of unchanged drug is relatively low)

» Sensitivity to haloperidol
(patients with known allergies or with a history of allergic reactions to other medications may also be sensitive to haloperidol)

» Urinary retention
(may be potentiated)

Patient monitoring

The following may be especially important in patient monitoring (other tests may be warranted in some patients, depending on condition; » = major clinical significance):

Blood cell counts and differential in patients with sore throat and fever or infections
(may be required during high-dose or prolonged therapy when symptoms of infection develop; if significant cellular depression occurs, medication should be discontinued and appropriate therapy initiated; rechallenge in recovered patients will usually cause a recurrence of agranulocytosis)

Careful observation for early signs of dehydration, such as lethargy and decreased sensation of thirst
(recommended at periodic intervals, especially in elderly or debilitated persons, for prevention of bronchopneumonia)

Careful observation for early symptoms of tardive dyskinesia
(recommended at periodic intervals, especially in the elderly and patients on high or extended maintenance dosage; since there is no known effective treatment if syndrome should develop, haloperidol should be discontinued, if clinically feasible, at earliest signs, usually fine, worm-like movements of the tongue, to stop further development)

Careful observation for early symptoms of tardive dystonia
(recommended at periodic intervals; since there is no known effective treatment if syndrome should develop, haloperidol should be discontinued, if clinically feasible, at the earliest signs)

Careful observation for signs of overdose or insufficient dosing with haloperidol decanoate
(recommended during initial dosing adjustments; since haloperidol decanoate slowly increases to steady state plasma concentration over 2 to 4 months, accumulation to excessive levels may occur; if psychotic symptoms reappear before next dose, therapy can be supplemented with short-acting forms of haloperidol)

Hepatic function determinations
(may be required at periodic intervals during high-dose or prolonged therapy or if jaundice or grippe-like symptoms occur, to detect liver function impairment)

Side/Adverse Effects

Note: A few cases of sudden and unexpected death have been reported in patients who were receiving haloperidol therapy. However, there is no definite evidence that haloperidol is a causative factor.

Children are highly susceptible to extrapyramidal effects.

Geriatric and debilitated patients are more prone to develop extrapyramidal side effects and orthostatic hypotension and usually require a lower initial dosage and a more gradual titration of dose.

The following side/adverse effects have been selected on the basis of their potential clinical significance (possible signs and symptoms in parentheses where appropriate)—not necessarily inclusive:

Those indicating need for medical attention

Incidence more frequent

Akathisia (restlessness or need to keep moving); ***dystonic extrapyramidal effects*** (muscle spasms of face, neck, and back; tic-like or twitching movements; twisting movements of body; inability to move eyes; weakness of arms and legs); ***parkinsonian extrapyramidal effects*** (difficulty in speaking or swallowing; loss of balance control; mask-like face; shuffling walk; stiffness of arms or legs; trembling and shaking of hands and fingers)

Note: *Akathisia* may appear within first 6 hours after dose; often indistinguishable from psychotic agitation; differentiation with benztropine may improve haloperidol-induced akathisia but not psychotic agitation.

Dystonic extrapyramidal effects appear most often in children and young adults and early in treatment; may subside within 24 to 48 hours after drug has been discontinued.

Parkinsonian extrapyramidal effects are more frequent in the elderly; symptoms may be seen in the first few days of treatment or after prolonged treatment, and can recur after even a single dose.

Incidence less frequent

Allergic reaction (red and raised, or acne-like skin rash); ***anticholinergic effects*** (difficult urination; hallucinations); ***CNS effect*** (hallucinations); ***decreased thirst, or unusual tiredness or weakness; orthostatic hypotension*** (dizziness, lightheadedness, or fainting); ***persistent tardive dyskinesia*** (lip smacking or puckering; puffing of cheeks; rapid or worm-like movements of tongue; uncontrolled chewing movements; uncontrolled movements of the arms and legs)

Note: *Decreased thirst* or *unusual tiredness or weakness* may precede dehydration, hemoconcentration, reduced pulmonary ventilation, and bronchopneumonia; occur most often in elderly or debilitated patients.

Tardive dyskinesia is more frequent in elderly patients, women, and patients with brain damage; initially dose related, but may increase with long-term treatment and total cumulative dose; may persist after discontinuation of haloperidol.

Incidence rare

Agranulocytosis (sore throat and fever; unusual bleeding or bruising); ***heat stroke*** (hot, dry skin; inability to sweat; muscle weakness; confusion); ***obstructive jaundice*** (yellow eyes or skin); ***neuroleptic malignant syndrome (NMS)*** (difficult or unusually fast breathing; fast heartbeat or irregular pulse; high fever; high or low [irregular] blood pressure; increased sweating; loss of bladder control; severe muscle stiffness; seizures; unusual tiredness or weakness; unusually pale skin); ***tardive dystonia*** (increased blinking or spasms of eyelid; unusual facial expressions or body positions; uncontrolled twisting movements of neck, trunk, arms, or legs)

Note: *Heat stroke,* caused by haloperidol-induced suppression of central and peripheral temperature regulation in the hypothalamus, may occur during environmental conditions of high heat and high humidity. The effectiveness of sweating as a cooling mechanism may be reduced by humid conditions and by the anticholinergic effects of haloperidol, used alone or in combination with other anticholinergic medications such as nonprescription cold medications or antihistamines. Adequate interior temperature control (air conditioning) must be maintained for institutionalized patients during hot weather because of the increased risk of heat stroke and NMS. Patients should be advised to avoid exertion, stay in cool areas, and avoid dehydration and other anticholinergic medications.

NMS may occur at any time during neuroleptic therapy, but is more commonly seen soon after start of therapy, or after patient has switched from one neuroleptic to another, during combined therapy with another psychotropic medication, or after a dosage increase. Along with the overt signs of skeletal muscle rigidity, hyperthermia, autonomic dysfunction, and altered consciousness, differential diagnosis may reveal leukocytosis (9500 to 26,000 cells per cubic millimeter), elevated liver function test values, and elevated creatine kinase (CK).

Those indicating need for medical attention only if they continue or are bothersome

Incidence more frequent

Blurred vision; changes in menstrual period; constipation; dryness of mouth; swelling or soreness in breasts in females; unusual secretion of milk; weight gain

Incidence less frequent

Decreased sexual ability; drowsiness; increased sensitivity of skin to sun; nausea or vomiting

Those indicating the need for medical attention if they occur after the medication is discontinued

Withdrawal emergent dyskinesia (trembling of fingers and hands; uncontrolled, repetitive movements of mouth, tongue, and jaw)—more frequent in elderly patients, women, and patients with brain damage

Overdose

For specific information on the agents used in the management of haloperidol overdose, see:

- *Albumin Human (Systemic)* monograph;
- *Benztropine* in *Antidyskinetics (Systemic)* monograph;
- *Charcoal, Activated (Oral-Local)* monograph;
- *Diphenhydramine* in *Antihistamines (Systemic)* monograph; and/or
- *Norepinephrine* in *Sympathomimetic Agents—Cardiovascular Use (Parenteral-Systemic)* monograph.

For more information on the management of overdose or unintentional ingestion, **contact a Poison Control Center** (see *Poison Control Center Listing*).

Clinical effects of overdose

In general, symptoms of overdose may be an exaggeration of adverse effects. Patient would appear comatose with respiratory depression and hypotension severe enough to produce a shock-like state.

The following effects have been selected on the basis of their potential clinical significance (possible signs and symptoms in parentheses where appropriate)—not necessarily inclusive:

Severe breathing difficulty; dizziness; severe drowsiness or comatose state; severe muscle trembling, jerking, stiffness, or uncontrolled movements; severe tiredness or weakness

Treatment of overdose

Treatment is essentially symptomatic and supportive.

To decrease absorption—
Inducing emesis or initiating gastric lavage, immediately followed by administration of activated charcoal.

Specific treatment—
Counteracting hypotension and circulatory collapse by use of intravenous fluids, plasma, or concentrated albumin, and vasopressor agents such as norepinephrine. Epinephrine should *not* be used since it may cause paradoxical hypotension.

Administering benztropine or diphenhydramine to manage severe extrapyramidal reactions.

Monitoring—
Monitoring ECG for signs of Q-T prolongation or *torsades de pointes.* Severe arrhythmias should be treated with appropriate antiarrhythmic measures.

Supportive care—
Establishing a patent airway.
Mechanically assisting respiration, if necessary.
Patients in whom intentional overdose is known or suspected should be referred for psychiatric consultation.

Note: Dialysis is not effective in removing excessive systemic haloperidol.

Patient Consultation

As an aid to patient consultation, refer to *Advice for the Patient, Haloperidol (Systemic).*

In providing consultation, consider emphasizing the following selected information (» = major clinical significance):

Before using this medication

» Conditions affecting use, especially:
  Sensitivity to haloperidol
  Pregnancy—Reports of limb malformations after maternal use of haloperidol with other drugs of suspected teratogenicity during first trimester; animal reproduction studies have shown a decrease in fertility, increased incidence of fetal resorption, delayed delivery, and neonatal death with very high doses
  Breast-feeding—Distributed into breast milk; animal studies have shown sedation, impaired motor function in nursing offspring; not recommended for use during breast-feeding
  Use in children—Children are more prone to extrapyramidal symptoms, especially dystonias
  Use in the elderly—Elderly patients are more likely to develop extrapyramidal, anticholinergic, hypotensive, and sedative effects; reduced dosage recommended
  Dental—Haloperidol-induced blood dyscrasias may result in infections, delayed healing, and bleeding; dry mouth may cause caries, candidiasis, periodontal disease, and discomfort; increased motor activity of face, head, and neck may interfere with some dental procedures
  Other medications, especially alcohol, other CNS depression-producing medications, epinephrine, other extrapyramidal reaction–producing medications, levodopa, or lithium
  Other medical problems, especially severe cardiovascular disease, severe CNS depression, Parkinson's disease, allergies, epilepsy, or urinary retention

Proper use of this medication

Taking with food or milk to reduce gastrointestinal irritation
Proper administration of oral liquid form:
  Using special dropper
  Mixing with water or a beverage such as orange juice, apple juice, tomato juice, or cola; not mixing with tea or coffee
» Importance of not taking more or less medication than the amount prescribed
» Compliance with therapy; may require several weeks of therapy to obtain desired effects
» Proper dosing
  Missed dose: Taking as soon as possible; taking any remaining doses for that day at regularly spaced intervals; not doubling doses
» Proper storage

Precautions while using this medication

Regular visits to physician to check progress of therapy
» Checking with physician before discontinuing medication; gradual dosage reduction may be needed
» Avoiding use of alcoholic beverages or other CNS depressants during therapy
» Possible drowsiness or dizziness; caution when driving, using machinery, or doing things requiring alertness
  Possible dizziness or lightheadedness: caution when getting up suddenly from a lying or sitting position
» Possible heat stroke: caution during exercise, hot baths, or hot weather
  Avoiding the use of over-the-counter medications for colds or allergies, to prevent increased anticholinergic effects and risk of heat stroke
» Caution if any kind of surgery, dental treatment, or emergency treatment is required; telling physician or dentist in charge about taking haloperidol because of possible drug interactions or blood dyscrasias
  Possible skin photosensitivity; avoiding unprotected exposure to sun; using protective clothing; using a sun block product that includes protection against both UVA-caused photosensitivity reactions and UVB-caused sunburn reactions; avoiding use of sunlamp, tanning bed, or tanning booth
  Possible dryness of mouth; using sugarless gum or candy, ice, or saliva substitute for relief; checking with physician or dentist if dry mouth continues for more than 2 weeks
  If taking liquid form, avoiding contact with skin (to prevent contact dermatitis)
  Observing precautions for up to 6 weeks with long-acting parenteral form

Side/adverse effects

» Stopping medication and notifying physician immediately if symptoms of neuroleptic malignant syndrome (NMS) appear
  Extrapyramidal effects are more likely to occur in children, the elderly, and debilitated patients
  Notifying physician as soon as possible if early symptoms of tardive dyskinesia appear
  Possibility of withdrawal symptoms
  Signs of potential side effects, especially akathisia, dystonias, parkinsonism, allergic reaction, anticholinergic effects, CNS effect, decreased thirst, unusual tiredness or weakness, orthostatic hypotension, tardive dyskinesia or dystonia, blood dyscrasias, heat stroke, obstructive jaundice, and neuroleptic malignant syndrome (NMS)

General Dosing Information

See also *Patient monitoring.*

Dosage must be individualized by titration from the lower dose range. After a favorable response is noted (usually within 3 weeks), the proper maintenance dosage should be determined by gradually decreasing to the lowest level of therapeutic dosage that will maintain an adequate clinical response.

The antiemetic effect of haloperidol may mask signs of drug toxicity or may obscure diagnosis of conditions in which the primary symptom is nausea.

When extended therapy is discontinued, a gradual reduction in haloperidol dosage over several weeks is recommended, since abrupt withdrawal may cause some patients on high or long-term dosage to experience withdrawal-emergent neurological symptoms.

Avoid skin contact with haloperidol oral solution; contact dermatitis has been reported.

For oral dosage forms only

Because undiluted haloperidol concentrated oral solution may irritate mucous membranes, the dose should be diluted with water or beverages having a pH less than 4 (such as orange juice, apple juice, tomato juice, or cola). The dilution should be prepared immediately prior to administration to prevent precipitation. If mixed with coffee, tea, or lithium citrate syrup, free haloperidol will precipitate.

For long-acting dosage form only

Patients being considered for haloperidol decanoate therapy should be first converted to oral haloperidol from any other neuroleptic they may have been taking to prevent unexpected adverse sensitivity to haloperidol.

Variations in patient response may require adjustments of dose and dosing intervals. Each patient must be carefully supervised to determine the optimal dosing interval and lowest effective dose, depending on patient's response, age, physical condition, symptoms, severity of illness, and drug history.

Effects of the extended-action injectable form may last up to 6 weeks in some patients. The side effects information and precautions apply during this period of time.

Diet/Nutrition

Haloperidol tablets may be taken with food or a full glass (240 mL) of water or milk if necessary to lessen gastrointestinal irritation.

To prevent mucosal irritation, haloperidol oral solution should be diluted in water or beverages such as orange juice, apple juice, tomato juice, or cola immediately prior to administration.

For treatment of adverse effects

Treatment is essentially symptomatic and supportive and includes the following

• *Discontinuing haloperidol immediately.* Neuroleptic malignant syndrome after injection of long-acting haloperidol decanoate may be difficult to treat because of this dosage form's long half-life.

• Hyperthermia—Administering antipyretics (aspirin or acetaminophen); using cooling blanket.

• Dehydration—Restoring fluids and electrolytes.

• Cardiovascular instability—Monitoring blood pressure and cardiac rhythm closely.

• Hypoxia—Administering oxygen; considering airway insertion and assisted ventilation.

• Muscle rigidity—Dantrolene sodium may be administered (100 to 300 mg per day in divided doses; 1.25 to 1.5 mg per kg of body weight, intravenously). Bromocriptine (5 to 7.5 mg every eight hours) has been used to reverse hyperpyrexia and muscle rigidity.

Neuroleptic malignant syndrome (NMS)—
Parkinsonism, severe—
Many authorities advise that the only appropriate treatment of extrapyramidal symptoms is reduction of the antipsychotic dosage, if possible. Oral antidyskinetic agents such as trihexyphenidyl, 2 mg three times per day, or benztropine, may be effective in treating more severe parkinsonism and acute motor restlessness but are used sparingly, and then usually for no longer than 3 months. Extrapyramidal symptoms may reappear if both haloperidol and the antidyskinetic agent are discontinued simultaneously. The antidyskinetic agent may have to be continued after haloperidol is discontinued because of different excretion rates. Milder effects may be treated by adjusting dosage.

Akathisia—
May be treated with antiparkinsonian medications, or with propranolol (30 to 120 mg per day), nadolol (40 mg per day), pindolol (5 to 60 mg per day), lorazepam (1 or 2 mg two or three times a day), or diazepam (2 mg two or three times a day).

Dystonia—
Acute dystonic postures or oculogyric crisis may be relieved by parenteral administration of benztropine (2 mg intramuscularly); or diphenhydramine (50 mg intramuscularly); or diazepam (5 to 7.5 mg intravenously), to be followed by oral antidyskinetic medication for one or two days to prevent recurrent dystonic episodes. Dosage adjustments of haloperidol may control these effects, and discontinuation of haloperidol may reverse severe symptoms in weeks to months.

Tardive dyskinesia or tardive dystonia—
No known effective treatment. Dosage of haloperidol should be lowered or medication discontinued, if clinically feasible, at earliest signs of tardive dyskinesia or tardive dystonia, to prevent possible irreversible effects.

Oral Dosage Forms

Note: Bracketed uses in the *Dosage Forms* section refer to categories of use and/or indications that are not included in U.S. product labeling.

HALOPERIDOL ORAL SOLUTION USP

Usual adult and adolescent dose

Antipsychotic; antidyskinetic—
Oral, 500 mcg (0.5 mg) to 5 mg two or three times a day initially, the dosage being gradually adjusted as needed and tolerated.

Usual adult prescribing limits

100 mg a day.

Usual pediatric dose

Psychotic disorders—
Children younger than 3 years of age: Safety and efficacy have not been established.
Children 3 to 12 years of age or 15 to 40 kg of body weight: Oral, initially 50 mcg (0.05 mg) per kg of body weight a day (in two or three divided doses), the daily dose being increased as needed and tolerated by 500-mcg (0.5 mg) increments at five- to seven-day intervals up to a total of 150 mcg (0.150 mg) per kg of body weight a day.

Nonpsychotic behavior disorders and Tourette's syndrome—
Children younger than 3 years of age: Safety and efficacy have not been established.
Children 3 to 12 years of age or 15 to 40 kg of body weight: Oral, initially 50 mcg (0.05 mg) per kg of body weight a day (in two or three divided doses), the daily dose being increased as needed and tolerated by 500-mcg (0.5 mg) increments at five- to seven-day intervals up to a total of 75 mcg (0.075 mg) per kg of body weight a day. Alternatively, some clinicians recommend that, in the treatment of Tourette's syndrome, the initial daily dose be administered at bedtime to avoid daytime sedation.

[Infantile autism][1]—
Children younger than 3 years of age: Safety and efficacy have not been established.
Children 3 to 12 years of age or 15 to 40 kg of body weight: Oral, 25 mcg (0.025 mg) per kg of body weight a day, up to 50 mcg (0.05 mg) per kg of body weight a day.

Note: There is little evidence that pediatric dosages exceeding 6 mg a day produce additional improvement in behavior or in tics.

Usual geriatric dose

Oral, 500 mcg (0.5 mg) to 2 mg two or three times a day, the dosage being increased gradually as needed and tolerated.

Note: The dose for debilitated patients is the same as the geriatric dose.

Strength(s) usually available

U.S.—
2 mg per mL (Rx) [*Haldol* (methylparaben); GENERIC].

Canada—
2 mg per mL (Rx) [*Apo-Haloperidol; Novo-Peridol; Peridol; PMS Haloperidol;* GENERIC].

Packaging and storage

Store below 40 °C (104 °F), preferably between 15 and 30 °C (59 and 86 °F), unless otherwise specified by manufacturer. Store in a tight, light-resistant container. Protect from freezing.

Incompatibilities

Insoluble precipitate of haloperidol is formed when mixed with coffee, tea or lithium citrate syrup.

Auxiliary labeling

- May cause drowsiness.
- Avoid alcoholic beverages.

Note

Avoid skin contact with liquid forms of this medication; contact dermatitis has been reported.

Each dose must be diluted in water or a beverage such as orange juice, apple juice, tomato juice, or cola, immediately prior to administration.

Provide patient with specially marked dosage dropper and explain use if necessary.

HALOPERIDOL TABLETS USP

Usual adult and adolescent dose

See *Haloperidol Oral Solution USP*.

Usual adult prescribing limits

See *Haloperidol Oral Solution USP*.

Usual pediatric dose

See *Haloperidol Oral Solution USP*.

Usual geriatric dose

See *Haloperidol Oral Solution USP*.

Strength(s) usually available

U.S.—
500 mcg (0.5 mg) (Rx) [*Haldol;* GENERIC].
1 mg (Rx) [*Haldol* (tartrazine); GENERIC].
2 mg (Rx) [*Haldol;* GENERIC].
5 mg (Rx) [*Haldol* (tartrazine); GENERIC].
10 mg (Rx) [*Haldol* (tartrazine); GENERIC].
20 mg (Rx) [*Haldol;* GENERIC].

Canada—
500 mcg (0.5 mg) (Rx) [*Apo-Haloperidol; Haldol; Novo-Peridol; Peridol* (scored); GENERIC].
1 mg (Rx) [*Apo-Haloperidol; Haldol* (tartrazine); *Novo-Peridol; Peridol* (scored); GENERIC].
2 mg (Rx) [*Apo-Haloperidol; Haldol* (metabisulfite); *Novo-Peridol; Peridol* (scored); GENERIC].
5 mg (Rx) [*Apo-Haloperidol; Haldol* (tartrazine); *Novo-Peridol; Peridol* (scored); GENERIC].
10 mg (Rx) [*Apo-Haloperidol; Haldol* (tartrazine); *Novo-Peridol; Peridol* (scored); GENERIC].
20 mg (Rx) [*Haldol* (metabisulfite); *Novo-Peridol;* GENERIC].

Packaging and storage

Store below 40 °C (104 °F), preferably between 15 and 30 °C (59 and 86 °F), unless otherwise specified by manufacturer. Store in a tight, light-resistant container.

Auxiliary labeling

- May cause drowsiness.
- Avoid alcoholic beverages.

Parenteral Dosage Forms

HALOPERIDOL INJECTION USP

Usual adult and adolescent dose

Acute psychosis—
Intramuscular, 2 to 5 mg initially, the dosage being repeated at one-hour intervals if necessary, or at four- to eight-hour intervals if symptoms are satisfactorily controlled.

Note: For the rapid control of acute psychosis or delirium, haloperidol has also been administered intravenously, in doses of 0.5 to 50 mg at a rate of 5 mg per minute, the dose being repeated as needed at 30-minute intervals. Alternatively, the dose of haloperidol can be diluted in 30 to 50 mL of compatible intravenous fluid and administered over 30 minutes.

Usual adult prescribing limits

Intramuscular: 100 mg daily.

Usual pediatric dose
Safety and efficacy have not been established.

Strength(s) usually available
U.S.—
5 mg per mL (Rx) [*Haldol* (methylparaben 1.8 mg; propylparaben 0.2 mg; lactic acid); GENERIC].
Canada—
5 mg per mL (Rx) [*Haldol* (methylparaben 1.8 mg; propylparaben 0.2 mg; lactic acid); GENERIC].

Packaging and storage
Store below 40 °C (104 °F), preferably between 15 and 30 °C (59 and 86 °F), unless otherwise specified by manufacturer. Protect from light. Protect from freezing.

Incompatibilities
Haloperidol injection may be precipitated by phenytoin or heparin.

HALOPERIDOL DECANOATE INJECTION

Note: The dosing of haloperidol decanoate injection is expressed in terms of haloperidol base (not the decanoate).

Usual adult and adolescent dose
Chronic psychosis—
Intramuscular, initially 10 to 15 times the previous daily oral dose of haloperidol, up to a maximum initial dose of 100 mg (base), at monthly intervals, the dosing interval and dose being adjusted as needed and tolerated.

Note: Administration is by deep intramuscular injection into gluteal region using Z-track technique. A 2-inch long, 21-gauge needle is recommended.
The maximum volume per injection site should not exceed 3 mL.

Usual adult prescribing limits
300 mg (base) per month.

Note: Monthly doses as high as 900 mg (base) have been reported.

Usual pediatric dose
Safety and efficacy have not been established.

Strength(s) usually available
U.S.—
50 mg (base) (70.52 mg of haloperidol decanoate) per mL (Rx) [*Haldol Decanoate* (benzyl alcohol 1.2%; sesame oil); GENERIC].
100 mg (base) (141.04 mg of haloperidol decanoate) per mL (Rx) [*Haldol Decanoate* (benzyl alcohol 1.2%; sesame oil); GENERIC].
Canada—
50 mg (base) (70.52 mg of haloperidol decanoate) per mL (Rx) [*Haldol LA* (benzyl alcohol 15 mg/mL)].
100 mg (base) (141.04 mg of haloperidol decanoate) per mL (Rx) [*Haldol LA* (benzyl alcohol 15 mg/mL)].

Packaging and storage
Store below 40 °C (104 °F), preferably between 15 and 30 °C (59 and 86 °F), unless otherwise specified by manufacturer. Protect from light. Protect from freezing. Do not refrigerate.

Note
Not to be administered intravenously.

[1]Not included in Canadian product labeling.

Revised: 08/24/1998

HALOTHANE—See *Anesthetics, Inhalation (Systemic)*

HEPARIN Systemic

VA CLASSIFICATION (Primary): BL110

Commonly used brand name(s): *Calcilean; Calciparine; HEP-LOCK U/P; Hepalean; Heparin Leo; Liquaemin.*

Note: For a listing of dosage forms and brand names by country availability, see *Dosage Forms* section(s).

Category
Anticoagulant.

Indications
Note: Bracketed information in the *Indications* section refers to uses that are not included in U.S. product labeling.

Note: Some of the indications for heparin therapy are identical to those for thrombolytic (alteplase [tissue-type plasminogen activator, recombinant], anistreplase [anisoylated plasminogen-streptokinase activator complex, APSAC], streptokinase, or urokinase) or coumarin- or indandione-derivative anticoagulant therapy. However, thrombolytic agents are used primarily to lyse obstructive thrombi and restore blood flow in a recently occluded blood vessel, whereas anticoagulants are used primarily to prevent thrombus formation and extension of existing thrombi. For treatment of acute deep venous thrombosis and acute pulmonary embolism, a thrombolytic agent may be the treatment of choice in selected patients. However, the selection of thrombolytic therapy or anticoagulant therapy as opposed to other forms of treatment, including vascular surgery, must be based on determination of the severity of thrombotic disease and assessment of patient condition and history.

Heparin is the anticoagulant of choice when an immediate effect is required. When long-term anticoagulant therapy is required, a coumarin or indandione derivative is usually administered as a follow-up to heparin therapy. However, in some patients (especially pregnant women) long-term anticoagulation with heparin may be desirable.

Accepted

Patency maintenance of indwelling venipuncture device—Heparin Lock Flush solution is indicated to maintain patency of an indwelling venipuncture device designed for intermittent injection or infusion therapy or blood sampling. Solution may be used following initial placement of the device in the vein, after each injection of a medication or after withdrawal of blood for laboratory.

Thrombosis, deep venous (prophylaxis and treatment) and
Thromboembolism, pulmonary (prophylaxis and treatment)—Heparin is indicated using a full-dose regimen in the treatment of patients with recent thrombosis or thrombophlebitis of the deep veins to prevent extension and embolization of the thrombus and to reduce the risk of pulmonary embolism or recurrent thrombus formation. In acute pulmonary embolism, full-dose heparin is indicated to decrease the risk of extension, recurrence, or death.

Heparin is also indicated using a low-dose regimen to prevent the development of venous thrombosis and pulmonary embolism following major abdominal or thoracic surgery in high-risk patients, such as patients with a history of thromboembolism and patients requiring prolonged immobilization following surgery, especially if they are 40 years of age or older. Low-dose heparin may be ineffective for this purpose in some patients, especially following hip surgery. Many clinicians question the validity of data showing the efficacy and safety of low-dose heparin prophylaxis.

[Low-dose heparin prophylaxis is also used to prevent thrombus formation in selected immobilized medical patients who are not at risk of hemorrhage.]

Heparin is also administered using an adjusted-dose regimen for prophylaxis against thromboembolic complications when low-dose heparin may not be effective, e.g., for general abdominal or thoracic surgery in very high-risk patients, high-risk orthopedic procedures such as elective hip surgery or knee reconstruction, and [the second half of the third trimester in pregnant women with a history of venous thrombosis or pulmonary embolism][1].

Adjusted-dose subcutaneous heparin is also recommended when long-term anticoagulation is required and use of a coumarin- or indandione-derivative anticoagulant is contraindicated or inadvisable (e.g., during pregnancy). In addition, after the dosage of heparin has been stabilized (i.e., the desired level of anticoagulation has been achieved and maintained for a 2-week period without additional dosage adjustment), further anticoagulant monitoring and dosage adjustment are not needed (except during pregnancy, when heparin requirements increase with the patient's blood volume as pregnancy progresses). Therefore, this regimen can be utilized for the long-term treatment of nonpregnant patients when anticoagulant therapy cannot be monitored on a regular basis.

Thromboembolism (prophylaxis)—Heparin is indicated prior to and during attempted cardioversion or surgery to prevent systemic thromboembolism that may occur in patients with chronic atrial fibrillation, especially those with rheumatic mitral stenosis, congestive heart failure, left atrial enlargement, or cardiomyopathy.

Heparin is indicated as adjunctive therapy in acute myocardial infarction to reduce the risk of thromboembolic complications, especially in high-risk patients such as those with shock, congestive heart failure, prolonged arrhythmias (especially atrial fibrillation), previous myocardial infarction, or history of venous thrombosis or pulmonary embolism. Also, heparin may be administered to help prevent reocclusion following thrombolytic therapy in patients with acute myocardial infarction.

[Heparin is also used to prevent catheter-induced thromboembolism during coronary angiography and percutaneous transluminal angioplasty.][1]

Blood clotting (prophylaxis)—Heparin is indicated to prevent blood clotting during extracorporeal circulation in cardiac surgery and dialysis procedures.

Heparin is indicated to prevent blood clotting during and following arterial surgery. It is administered systemically or by local intra-arterial injection.

Heparin is indicated to prevent blood clotting during blood transfusions and in blood sampling for laboratory purposes. However, heparinized blood should not be used for isoagglutinin, complement, or erythrocyte fragility tests, or for platelet counts. In addition, leukocyte counts should be performed within 2 hours after heparin is added to the blood sample.

Heparin is also available as a lock flush solution, which is not intended for anticoagulant therapy. This solution is used to maintain the patency of an indwelling intravascular device.

Coagulation, disseminated intravascular (treatment)—Although heparin is indicated as a temporary measure in the treatment of disseminated intravascular coagulation, especially if there is clinical evidence of intravascular thrombosis, its use in this condition is controversial. The underlying cause of the condition must be determined and treated.

Thromboembolism, arterial (treatment)—Heparin is indicated as adjunctive therapy for peripheral arterial embolism. It may prevent further thrombus formation when surgery must be delayed.

Thrombosis, cerebral (prophylaxis)—Heparin is indicated to decrease the risk of cerebral thrombosis and death in patients with progressive stroke (stroke-in-evolution).

[Thromboembolism, cerebral, recurrence (prophylaxis)][1]—Heparin is also used in the treatment of patients with recent cerebral embolism to decrease the risk of recurrence and death; however, this use is controversial. Although administration of an anticoagulant too soon after a cerebral embolism may increase the risk of cerebral hemorrhage, recent studies have indicated that the risk of early recurrence may be greater than the risk of anticoagulant therapy. It is recommended that heparin therapy be initiated only if the patient is not hypertensive and a computerized tomographic (CT) scan performed 24 hours or longer following the onset of the stroke shows no evidence of hemorrhagic transformation. If severe hypertension is present, or the embolic stroke is large, there is a risk of late hemorrhagic transformation and anticoagulant therapy should be delayed for several days. If hemorrhagic transformation is documented, anticoagulant therapy should be postponed for at least 8 to 10 days. Long-term anticoagulation is recommended.

Unaccepted

Prophylactic use of heparin (low-dose or full-dose) is not recommended for patients with bleeding disorders; patients having neurosurgery, ophthalmic surgery, or spinal anesthesia; or patients who are receiving a coumarin- or indandione-derivative anticoagulant or a platelet active agent.

[Heparin has also been used to reduce the risk of thrombosis and/or occlusion of the aortocoronary bypass following coronary bypass surgery; however, its efficacy has not been established and this use is controversial. Also, platelet aggregation inhibitors, especially aspirin, are more commonly used for this indication.]

Heparin Lock Flush solution is not to be used for anticoagulant therapy.

---

[1]Not included in Canadian product labeling.

Pharmacology/Pharmacokinetics

Physicochemical characteristics

Source—Derived from porcine intestines.

pH—Heparin Lock Flush solution: 5.0–7.5

Mechanism of action/Effect

Heparin acts indirectly at multiple sites in both the intrinsic and extrinsic blood clotting systems to potentiate the inhibitory action of antithrombin III (heparin cofactor) on several activated coagulation factors, including thrombin (factor IIa) and factors IXa, Xa, XIa, and XIIa, by forming a complex with and inducing a conformational change in the antithrombin III molecule. Inhibition of activated factor Xa interferes with thrombin generation and thereby inhibits the various actions of thrombin in coagulation. Heparin also accelerates the formation of an antithrombin III–thrombin complex, thereby inactivating thrombin and preventing the conversion of fibrinogen to fibrin; these actions prevent extension of existing thrombi. Larger doses of heparin are required to inactivate thrombin than are required to inhibit thrombin formation.

Heparin also prevents formation of a stable fibrin clot by inhibiting the activation of the fibrin stabilizing factor by thrombin. Heparin has no fibrinolytic activity.

Full-dose heparin prolongs partial thromboplastin time, thrombin time, whole blood clotting time, and activated clotting time (ACT).

Other actions/effects

Heparin reduces the concentration of triglycerides in plasma by releasing the enzyme lipoprotein lipase from tissues and stabilizing the enzyme. The resultant hydrolysis of triglycerides leads to increased blood concentrations of free fatty acids.

Protein binding

Very high; primarily to low-density lipoproteins; also bound to globulins and to fibrinogen.

Biotransformation

Hepatic; however, the primary route of removal from the circulation is uptake by the reticuloendothelial system.

Half-life

1 to 6 hours (average 1.5 hours); dose and route dependent and subject to inter- and intrapatient variation. May be increased above the average in patients with renal failure, hepatic function impairment, or obesity. May be decreased in patients with pulmonary embolism, infections, or malignancy.

Onset of action

Direct intravenous injection—Immediate.

Intravenous infusion—Immediate when infusion is preceded by the recommended intravenous loading dose. If no loading dose is given, the onset of action may depend upon the rate of infusion.

Subcutaneous—Generally within 20 to 60 minutes but subject to interpatient variability.

Elimination

Renal, usually as metabolites. However, after intravenous administration of high doses, up to 50% of a dose may be excreted unchanged.

In dialysis—Not removed via hemodialysis.

Precautions to Consider

Cross-sensitivity and/or related problems

Patients with a history of allergies, especially those who are allergic to swine, beef, or other animal proteins, may be allergic to this medication also (depending on heparin source).

Pregnancy/Reproduction

Pregnancy—Heparin does not cross the placenta and is the anticoagulant of choice for use during pregnancy because it does not affect blood clotting mechanisms in the fetus. Although heparin has not been reported to cause birth defects, use during pregnancy has been reported to increase the risk of stillbirth or prematurity. However, the underlying condition, rather than heparin itself, may have been responsible. Also, the reported incidence (13 to 22%) of these complications is lower than that reported with coumarin-derivative anticoagulants (31%). In addition, caution is recommended when heparin is used during the last trimester of pregnancy or during the postpartum period because of the increased risk of maternal bleeding.

Especially careful monitoring of the patient and attention to dosage are recommended during pregnancy. Heparin requirements increase, because of expansion of the patient's blood volume, as pregnancy progresses. Readjustment of heparin dosage may be needed following delivery.

FDA Pregnancy Category C.

Breast-feeding

Heparin is not distributed into breast milk. However, administration to lactating women has rarely been reported to cause rapid (within 2 to 4 weeks) development of severe osteoporosis and vertebral collapse.

Pediatrics

Appropriate studies performed to date have not demonstrated pediatrics-specific problems that would limit the usefulness of heparin in children. However, heparin injections that contain benzyl alcohol should not be administered to premature neonates because the preservative has been associated with a fatal "gasping syndrome" in these patients.

The 100 unit/mL concentration heparin lock flush solution should not be used in neonates or in infants who weigh less than 10 kg because of the risk of systemic anticoagulation. Caution is necessary when using the 10 unit/mL concentration in premature infants who weigh less than 1 kg who are receiving frequent flushes since a therapeutic heparin dose may be given to the infant in a 24–hour period.

Geriatrics

Patients 60 years of age or older, especially females, may be more susceptible to hemorrhaging during heparin therapy. Also, elderly patients are more likely to have age-related renal function impairment, which may increase the risk of bleeding in patients receiving anticoagulants.

Dental

Bleeding from gingival tissue may be a symptom of heparin overdose.

Heparin therapy increases the risk of localized hemorrhage during and following oral surgical procedures. Consultation with the prescribing physician may be advisable prior to oral surgery, to determine whether a temporary dosage reduction or withdrawal of heparin therapy is feasible. Also, local measures to minimize bleeding should be used at the time of surgery.

Drug interactions and/or related problems

The following drug interactions and/or related problems have been selected on the basis of their potential clinical significance (possible mechanism in parentheses where appropriate)—not necessarily inclusive (» = major clinical significance):

Note: Combinations containing any of the following medications, depending on the amount present, may also interact with this medication.

Interactions listed below may not apply to short-term use of heparin followed by protamine reversal, as in cardiovascular surgery.

In addition to the documented interactions listed below, the possibility should be considered that multiple effects leading to further impairment of blood clotting and/or increased risk of bleeding may occur if heparin is administered to a patient receiving any medication having a significant potential for causing hypoprothrombinemia, thrombocytopenia, or gastrointestinal ulceration or hemorrhage.

Acid citrate dextrose (ACD)–converted blood—blood collected in heparin and later converted to ACD blood
(heparin anticoagulant activity lasts for up to 22 days after conversion to ACD blood when refrigerated; use of ACD blood in heparin-treated patients may increase the risk of hemorrhage)

Adrenocorticoids, glucocorticoid or
Corticotropin, especially chronic therapeutic use or
Ethacrynic acid or
Salicylates, nonacetylated
(the potential occurrence of gastrointestinal ulceration or hemorrhage during therapy with these medications may cause increased risk of bleeding in patients receiving anticoagulant therapy)
(large [antirheumatic] doses of salicylates may cause hypoprothrombinemia, which may increase the risk of bleeding in patients receiving anticoagulant therapy)

Anticoagulants, coumarin- or indandione-derivative
(although these medications are commonly used concurrently with heparin, the fact that concurrent use may lead to a severe deficiency of vitamin K-dependent procoagulant factors, leading to increased risk of bleeding, must be considered)
(heparin may prolong the prothrombin time used for dosage adjustments of these agents)

Antihistamines or
Digitalis glycosides or
Nicotine or
Tetracyclines
(these medications may partially counteract the anticoagulant effect of heparin; heparin dosage adjustment may be required during and following concurrent use)

Anti-inflammatory drugs, nonsteroidal (NSAIDs) or
» Platelet aggregation inhibitors, other, (See *Appendix II*) especially:
» Aspirin
» Sulfinpyrazone
(inhibition of platelet function by these agents may lead to hemorrhage because it impairs a hemostatic mechanism on which heparin-treated patients depend to prevent bleeding)
(hypoprothrombinemia induced by large [antirheumatic] doses of aspirin, and the potential occurrence of gastrointestinal ulceration or hemorrhage during therapy with NSAIDs, aspirin, or sulfinpyrazone, may also cause increased risk of bleeding in patients receiving heparin therapy)

» Cefamandole or
» Cefoperazone or
» Cefotetan or
» Plicamycin or
» Valproic acid
(these medications may cause hypoprothrombinemia; in addition, plicamycin or valproic acid may inhibit platelet aggregation; concurrent use with heparin may increase the risk of hemorrhage and is not recommended)

Chloroquine or
Hydroxychloroquine
(these agents may cause thrombocytopenia, which may increase the risk of hemorrhage because heparin-treated patients depend on platelet aggregation to prevent bleeding)

» Methimazole or
» Propylthiouracil
(these medications may cause hypoprothrombinemia, which may enhance the anticoagulant effect of heparin and increase the risk of bleeding)

Nitroglycerin, intravenous
(the anticoagulant effect of heparin may be decreased in patients receiving nitroglycerin via intravenous infusion; adjustment of heparin dosage may be required to maintain the desired degree of anticoagulation during and following administration of a nitroglycerin infusion)

» Probenecid
(probenecid may increase and prolong the anticoagulant effect of heparin)

» Thrombolytic agents, such as:
» Alteplase (tissue-type plasminogen activator, recombinant)
» Anistreplase (anisoylated plasminogen-streptokinase activator complex; APSAC)
» Streptokinase
» Urokinase
(concurrent or sequential use with heparin increases the risk of bleeding complications; although heparin is sometimes given before, and is usually given to decrease the risk of reocclusion following, thrombolytic therapy, caution and especially careful monitoring of the patient are recommended)

Diagnostic interference

The following drug interactions and/or related problems have been selected on the basis of their potential clinical significance (possible mechanism in parentheses where appropriate)—not necessarily inclusive (» = major clinical significance):

With diagnostic test results

Blood pool imaging studies
(heparin may impair blood pool images by decreasing the radiolabeling of red blood cells with sodium pertechnetate Tc 99m)

^{125}I-fibrinogen uptake test
(some reports have indicated that heparin may cause false-negative test results in patients with actively forming or established venous thrombosis)

Platelet scintigraphy using indium In 111 oxyquinoline
(although studies of the effect of heparin on In 111–labeled platelet accumulation on venous thrombi have yielded contradictory results, the possibility should be considered that false negative test results may occur in heparin-treated patients)

Prothrombin-time test, one-stage
(may be prolonged; single intravenous injections or subcutaneous injection of full therapeutic doses of heparin may prolong the prothrombin time considerably because of the high concentrations of heparin in the blood, whereas usual prophylactic [low] doses of heparin given subcutaneously or full therapeutic doses given by continuous intravenous infusion usually do not increase the prothrombin time by more than a few seconds; to minimize problems, draw blood for the prothrombin time test just prior to, or at least 5 hours after, a single intravenous dose or 12 to 24 hours following subcutaneous injection of a full therapeutic dose)

Radionuclide imaging using technetium Tc 99m sulfur colloid
(heparin may reduce the quantity of technetium Tc 99m sulfur colloid reaching the site being studied by causing the radiotracer to accumulate in the lung, probably by increasing the number of free intravascular macrophages, which may migrate to, and phagocytize colloidal particles in, the pulmonary capillary bed)

Skeletal imaging, radionuclide
(subcutaneously administered heparin calcium may cause extraosseus accumulation of technetium Tc 99m medronate, technetium Tc 99m oxidronate, or technetium Tc 99m pyrophosphate, thereby interfering with the bone scan, if injected near the site to be studied; the interference involves precipitation of calcium, which may occur if the tissue concentration of calcium exceeds its solubility limits, and therefore does not occur with subcutaneously administered heparin sodium)

Thyroid function tests
(increases in serum thyroxine concentrations may occur, depending on the test method used; also, resin T_3 uptake may be increased)

With physiology/laboratory test values

Plasma free fatty acid concentration
(may be increased)

Plasma triglyceride concentration
(may be decreased)

Serum alanine aminotransferase (ALT [SGPT]) activity and
Serum aspartate aminotransferase (AST [SGOT]) activity
(may be increased during, and for a time following, heparin therapy; the usefulness of determinations of these enzymes in the differential diagnosis of myocardial infarction, pulmonary embolism, or liver disease may therefore be decreased)

Serum cholesterol concentration
(may be decreased with doses of 15,000 to 20,000 USP Units of heparin)

Medical considerations/Contraindications

The medical considerations/contraindications included have been selected on the basis of their potential clinical significance (reasons given in parentheses where appropriate)—not necessarily inclusive (» = major clinical significance).

Except under special circumstances, this medication should not be used when the following medical problems exist:

» Abortion, threatened or
» Aneurysm, cerebral or dissecting aorta, except in conjunction with corrective surgery or
» Cerebrovascular hemorrhage, confirmed or suspected
(increased risk of uncontrollable hemorrhage)

» Hemorrhage, active uncontrollable, except in disseminated intravascular coagulation

» Hypertension, severe uncontrolled
(increased risk of cerebral hemorrhage)

» Thrombocytopenia, severe, heparin-induced, within past several months
(risk of recurrence, which may cause resistance to heparin and new thromboembolic complications)

Risk-benefit should be considered when the following medical problems exist:

Allergic reaction to heparin, history of

Allergy or asthma, history of
(increased risk of allergic reactions because heparin is derived from animal tissue)

Any medical or dental procedure or condition in which the risk of bleeding or hemorrhage is present, such as:
» Anesthesia, regional or lumbar block
» Blood dyscrasias, hemorrhagic, especially thrombocytopenia or hemophilia; or other hemorrhagic tendency
» Childbirth, recent
Diabetes, severe
» Endocarditis, subacute bacterial
Gastrointestinal ulceration, history of
Intrauterine contraceptive device, use of
» Neurosurgery, recent or contemplated
» Ophthalmic surgery, recent or contemplated
» Pericarditis or pericardial effusion
Radiation therapy, recent
Renal function impairment, mild to moderate
» Renal function impairment, severe
» Spinal puncture, recent
» Surgery, major, or wounds resulting in large open surfaces
» Trauma, severe, especially to the central nervous system (CNS)
Tuberculosis, active
» Ulceration or other lesions of the gastrointestinal, respiratory, or urinary tract, active
» Vasculitis, severe

Hepatic function impairment, mild to moderate

» Hepatic function impairment, severe

Hypertension, mild to moderate
(increased risk of cerebral hemorrhage)

» Caution in use is also recommended for lactating women, who may develop severe osteoporosis after only 2 to 4 weeks of heparin therapy, and geriatric patients, who may be at increased risk of heparin-induced hemorrhage.

Patient monitoring

The following may be especially important in patient monitoring (other tests may be warranted in some patients, depending on condition; » = major clinical significance):

» Blood coagulation tests
(except in rare acute or emergency situations, should be performed prior to full-dose therapy to establish a baseline or control value; also, recommended prior to initiation of low-dose prophylaxis to identify pre-existing coagulation defects and aid in determining whether the patient is a suitable candidate for such treatment)

» Blood coagulation tests, heparin-specific, such as:
Activated clotting time (ACT) test or
Partial thromboplastin time (PTT) tests
(must be performed at periodic intervals during full-dose therapy as a guide to dosage, efficacy, and safety)
(PTT tests are used to establish dosage requirements during the initial phase of adjusted-dose therapy; they are also required at periodic intervals throughout adjusted-dose therapy, as a guide to dosage and efficacy, if the patient is pregnant)

Hematocrit determinations and
Stool tests for occult blood loss
(should be performed at regular intervals during full-dose therapy)

» Platelet counts
(recommended prior to initiation of therapy and at intervals of every 2 to 3 days during full-dose, adjusted-dose, or low-dose therapy to detect thrombocytopenia)

Side/Adverse Effects

Note: The occurrence of hemorrhage (especially in the gastrointestinal tract) during heparin therapy, especially if blood coagulation tests are within the therapeutic range, may indicate the presence of an underlying occult lesion such as a tumor or ulcer.

Two forms of reversible thrombocytopenia related to heparin therapy have been identified, either of which may occur in up to 30% of patients receiving the medication. A mild form may occur on the second to fourth day of heparin therapy and may improve despite continuing heparin usage. This condition is characterized by a moderate decrease in platelet count and by the absence of thrombotic or hemorrhagic complications; it may occur more frequently with bovine lung heparin than with porcine mucosal heparin. A severe form of thrombocytopenia, associated with the development of heparin-dependent antiplatelet antibodies resulting in greatly increased platelet aggregation, has also been reported. This condition usually occurs after the eighth day of therapy, although it has occurred within as little as 2 days in some patients, and is characterized by reduction of platelet count to as low as 5000 per cu. mm. and by increased resistance to heparin therapy. Continued use of heparin may lead to the "white clot syndrome", i.e., the formation of new thrombi composed primarily of fibrin platelet aggregates, which may cause thrombotic complications including organ infarction, skin necrosis, gangrene of the extremities, pulmonary embolism, and stroke. Rarely, hemorrhage may occur. This severe form of thrombocytopenia is independent of the source of heparin, dosage, or route of administration; however, patients who have recently received a prior course of heparin therapy may be at greater risk of developing this complication. Heparin should be discontinued immediately if severe thrombocytopenia occurs or is suspected. Severe thrombocytopenia may recur if heparin is administered to the patient within several months following the development of this complication.

Adrenal hemorrhage resulting in acute adrenal insufficiency has been reported to occur rarely during anticoagulant therapy. Diagnosis may be difficult because the initial symptoms (abdominal pain, apprehension, diarrhea, dizziness or fainting, headache, loss of appetite, nausea or vomiting, and weakness) are nonspecific and variable. If acute adrenal insufficiency is suspected, anticoagulant therapy must be discontinued and high-dose adrenocorticoid therapy (preferably with hydrocortisone, since other glucocorticoids do not provide sufficient sodium retention) instituted immediately. Delay of treatment while laboratory confirmation of the diagnosis is awaited may prove fatal to the patient. It has been proposed that abdominal computerized axial tomographic (CAT) scanning may be of use in diagnosing this condition more rapidly.

Heparin may suppress aldosterone synthesis. Rarely, with prolonged use, inhibition of renal function, hyperkalemia, and metabolic acidosis may result.

The following side/adverse effects have been selected on the basis of their potential clinical significance (possible signs and symptoms in parentheses where appropriate)—not necessarily inclusive:

Those indicating need for medical attention

Incidence less frequent or rare

Allergic reaction (fever with or without chills; runny nose; headache; nausea with or without vomiting; shortness of breath, troubled breathing, wheezing, or tightness in chest; skin rash, itching, or hives; tearing of eyes); ***anaphylactoid reaction, possibly including anaphylactic shock*** (changes in facial skin color; skin rash, hives, and/ or itching; fast or irregular breathing; puffiness or swelling of the eyelids or around the eyes; shortness of breath, troubled breathing, tightness in chest, and/or wheezing; sudden, severe decrease in blood pressure and collapse); ***chest pain; frequent or persistent erection; itching and burning feeling, especially on the plantar site of the feet; pain, coldness, and blue color of skin of arms or legs; peripheral neuropathy*** (numbness or tingling in hands or feet)

Note: Signs and symptoms suggestive of *ischemia* may occur in one or more limbs approximately 6 to 10 days following initiation of therapy. If heparin therapy is continued, progression of the reaction may lead to cyanosis, tachypnea, and headache. Protamine sulfate will not reverse these effects, which in the past have been attributed to an allergic vasospastic reaction. Whether these effects are actually identical to complications associated with heparin-induced thrombocytopenia has not been determined.

Signs and symptoms of hemorrhage indicating need for medical attention

Early signs of hemorrhage

Bleeding from gums when brushing teeth; heavy bleeding or oozing from cuts or wounds; unexplained bruising or purplish areas on skin; unexplained nosebleeds; unusually heavy or unexpected menstrual bleeding

Note: *Unexplained bleeding or bruising* may also indicate thrombocytopenia.

Signs and symptoms of internal bleeding—incidence 5 to 15%

Abdominal pain or swelling; back pain or backaches; blood in urine; bloody or black, tarry stools; constipation caused by hemorrhage-induced paralytic ileus or intestinal obstruction; coughing up blood; dizziness; headaches, severe or continuing; joint pain, stiffness, or swelling; vomiting of blood or material that looks like coffee grounds

Those occurring during long-term (6 months or longer) therapy and indicating need for medical attention

Osteoporosis (back or rib pain; decrease in height); ***unusual hair loss***

Those occurring at site of administration and indicating need for medical attention

Incidence less frequent or rare with deep subcutaneous injections

Hematoma (collection of blood under skin [blood blister]); ***histamine-like reaction; hives, localized; irritation, pain, redness, or ulceration; necrosis, cutaneous*** (peeling or sloughing of skin)—several cases of tissue necrosis, possibly associated with cutaneous hemorrhage, have also been reported following intravenous administration

Overdose

For specific information on the agents used in the management of heparin overdose, see the

Protamine (Systemic) monograph.

For more information on the management of overdose, **contact a Poison Control Center** (see *Poison Control Center Listing*).

Clinical effects of overdose

The following effects have been selected on the basis of their potential clinical significance (possible signs and symptoms in parentheses where appropriate)—not necessarily inclusive:

Early signs of excessive anticoagulation

Bleeding from gums when brushing teeth; heavy bleeding or oozing from cuts or wounds; unexplained bruising or purplish areas on skin; unexplained nosebleeds; unusually heavy or unexpected menstrual bleeding

Note: *Unexplained bleeding or bruising* may also indicate thrombocytopenia.

Signs and symptoms of internal bleeding

Abdominal pain or swelling; back pain or backaches; blood in urine; bloody or black, tarry stools; constipation caused by hemorrhage-induced paralytic ileus or intestinal obstruction; coughing up blood; dizziness; headaches, severe or continuing; joint pain, stiffness, or swelling; vomiting of blood or material that looks like coffee grounds

Treatment of overdose

For mild effects of heparin overdose, withdrawal of heparin therapy may be sufficient.

Specific treatment—

For more severe overdose, administration of the heparin antagonist protamine is required. One milligram of protamine sulfate will neutralize approximately 100 USP Units of heparin. However, heparin blood concentrations decrease rapidly following intravenous administration; 30 minutes after intravenous administration of heparin, half as much protamine sulfate may be sufficient to neutralize the remaining heparin. In most cases, it is recommended that protamine sulfate be administered intravenously, slowly (over a one-to three-minute period), and in doses not exceeding 50 mg in any ten-minute period. It is strongly recommended that blood coagulation tests be used to determine optimum protamine dosage, especially when neutralizing large doses of heparin given during cardiac or arterial surgery.

Because absorption of heparin may be prolonged following subcutaneous administration, it has been recommended that protamine (when used to neutralize heparin administered via that route) be administered as an initial loading dose of 25 to 50 mg that is followed by continuous intravenous infusion (over a period of 8 to 16 hours) of the remainder of the calculated dose. It is recommended that blood coagulation tests and/or direct titration of a sample of the patient's blood with protamine be used as a guide to protamine dosage.

When protamine is used to neutralize large doses of heparin, such as those used during cardiopulmonary bypass surgery, a rebound of heparin activity resulting in hemorrhage may occur despite initial complete neutralization of heparin. Prolonged monitoring of the patient is necessary; additional protamine should be administered as determined by coagulation test results. Also, it is recommended that no more than 100 mg of protamine sulfate be administered over a short period of time (2 hours) unless accurate titrations or other tests indicate that larger doses are required.

For severe hemorrhaging, transfusion of whole blood or plasma may also be required. This may dilute, but will not neutralize the effects of, heparin.

Patient Consultation

As an aid to patient consultation, refer to *Advice for the Patient, Heparin (Systemic)*.

In providing consultation, consider emphasizing the following selected information (» = major clinical significance):

Before using this medication

» Conditions affecting use, especially:

Allergies, especially to heparin or to swine, beef, or other animal proteins

Pregnancy—Although heparin does not cross the placenta and is not likely to adversely affect the fetus or neonate, there is a risk of maternal bleeding

Breast-feeding—Although heparin is not distributed into breast milk and poses no danger to the infant, severe osteoporosis and vertebral collapse may develop rapidly in lactating women

Use in the elderly—Increased risk of hemorrhage, especially in elderly females

Other medications, especially platelet aggregation inhibitors, hypoprothrombinemia-inducing medications, and probenecid

Other medical problems, especially hypertension; hemorrhagic blood dyscrasias; recent childbirth, spinal puncture, surgery, or other trauma; endocarditis; hepatic function impairment; renal function impairment; ulcers or other lesions of the gastrointestinal, respiratory, or urinary tract; and history of heparin-induced thrombocytopenia

Proper use of this medication

» Proper administration of injections at home (if applicable)

» Importance of strict compliance with dosage measurement and dosage schedule to achieve maximum effectiveness and to lessen chance of bleeding

» Regular visits to physician and regular blood coagulation tests to check progress during therapy

» Proper dosing

Missed dose: Using as soon as possible; not using if almost time for next dose; not doubling doses; keeping record of doses taken to avoid mistakes; keeping record of missed doses to give physician

» Proper storage—if dispensed to patient

Precautions while using this medication

» Not taking aspirin while using this medication; checking all medications for aspirin content; not taking ibuprofen or other platelet-active medications (unless prescribed by physician) while using heparin

» Need to inform all physicians and dentists that this medication is being used

Need to carry identification stating that medication is being used

Avoiding activities that may lead to injuries

Using care in brushing teeth and shaving

Side/adverse effects

Signs of potential side effects, especially allergic reactions, including anaphylaxis and anaphylactic shock; bleeding, including internal bleeding; chest pain; pain, coldness, or blue color of skin of arms or legs; peripheral neuropathy; skin necrosis; and local reactions at the injection site

Notifying physician immediately if signs and symptoms of bleeding are evident

General Dosing Information

Full-dose heparin is administered by deep subcutaneous (intrafat) injection, direct intravenous injection, or intravenous infusion. Heparin should not be administered by intramuscular injection because of the increased incidence of hematomas, irritation, and pain at the injection site. Low-dose heparin is generally administered by deep subcutaneous injection.

The deep subcutaneous (intrafat) injections should be made deep into fatty tissue such as above the iliac crest or into the abdominal fat layer, and the sites should be rotated to prevent formation of hematomas. Aspiration of blood should not be attempted, and the needle should not be moved while the solution is being injected. Other measures recommended to reduce the risk of tissue trauma during subcutaneous injections include use of a small needle, use of a concentrated heparin solution to minimize the injection volume, and injection of the solution into a 2 to 2.5 cm (l to 2 inch) area of fat which is grasped and held away from deeper tissues. The injection sites should not be massaged before or after the injections; however, application of pressure over the injection sites for up to two minutes following each injection has been recommended.

For intravenous administration, many clinicians prefer continuous intravenous infusion because several studies have indicated that a more constant degree of anticoagulation may be achieved with lower total daily dosages and that the incidence of bleeding complications may be decreased. However, other clinicians prefer intermittent intravenous administration. Use of an indwelling, rubber-capped needle (heparin-lock) has been recommended for intermittent intravenous therapy. Use of a constant infusion pump or mechanical syringe pump has been recommended for administration of the continuous intravenous infusion, to control the flow rate and infusion volume. **It is recommended that other medications not be added to infusion solutions containing heparin**, even if compatibility has been established, because changes in the infusion rate that may be needed to adjust heparin dosage will also affect the delivery rate of other medications present in the solution.

When heparin is administered using a full-dose regimen, the dosage must be individualized and adjusted according to the results of periodic coagulation tests. *Full-dose heparin therapy is contraindicated whenever suitable blood coagulation tests cannot be performed at the required intervals.* However, the effect of low-dose heparin usually does not require monitoring if the patient has normal pretreatment coagulation parameters. During the first day of treatment, a coagulation test is usually performed prior to each injection (if given via an intermittent dosage schedule). When the medication is given by continuous intravenous infusion, the test is usually performed 1½ to 2 hours after the infusion is started, then every 4 hours during the early stages of treatment. However, the frequency of testing must be adjusted to the needs of the individual patient. Coagulation tests should be performed at least once daily for the duration of therapy; however, increased monitoring may be necessary in patients who may be more sensitive to the effects of heparin, such as elderly patients or those with hypertension, renal function impairment, or hepatic function impairment.

When heparin is administered using an adjusted-dose regimen, dosage must be established according to the results of daily coagulation tests. When no dosage adjustments have been needed for two weeks, further monitoring at regular frequent intervals may be unnecessary for most patients. However, pregnant women should be monitored throughout therapy because their dosage requirements increase as pregnancy progresses.

The standard tests used for measuring heparin's general effect on clotting include the Lee-White whole blood clotting time, the whole blood activated partial thromboplastin time (WBAPTT), the activated partial thromboplastin time (APTT), and the activated clotting time (ACT). Other tests may be used in some cases. The Lee-White whole blood clotting time has been reported to be less reproducible than other tests and has largely been replaced by partial thromboplastin time tests. If the Lee-White whole blood clotting time is used to monitor therapy, the clotting time should be elevated to 2½ to 3 times the control value in minutes. The generally accepted value for the APTT is 1½ to 2½ times the control value in seconds. However, the specific reagent used must be considered when evaluating APTT test results because the various reagents used in the APTT test vary widely in their sensitivity to heparin. The generally accepted value for the ACT test is 2 to 3 times the control value in seconds. The ACT has been recommended as being particularly useful during extracorporeal circulation because it can be performed at the bedside; however, one study has indicated that the ACT may be ineffective for monitoring heparin dosage and protamine neutralization during cardiopulmonary bypass procedures in which hypothermia has been induced. Hypothermia may also interfere with the results of other coagulation tests. It is recommended that a single laboratory be employed for each patient, and that the laboratory understand the test will be used to monitor heparin therapy.

Because heparin is derived from animal tissue, it is recommended that patients with a history of allergies or asthma be given a test dose of 1000 USP Units before therapy is initiated.

Postsurgical patients and those with active thromboembolic disease (especially pulmonary embolism or myocardial infarction), infections with thrombosing tendency, malignancy, or a fever may be resistant to the effects of heparin and may require larger doses than other patients. Resistance to the effects of heparin also occurs in patients with familial antithrombin III deficiency. However, this type of resistance cannot always be overcome by increasing the dosage of heparin; a coumarin- or indandione-derivative anticoagulant is indicated for such patients. Also, local antithrombin III depletion resulting in loss of heparin effect may occur when heparin is administered intraperitoneally during peritoneal dialysis procedures.

If clinical evidence of thromboembolism occurs in a patient receiving low-dose heparin prophylaxis, full therapeutic doses of an anticoagulant should be administered. However, before full therapeutic doses of heparin are given, the possibility that the thrombosis may be due to the severe form of heparin-induced thrombocytopenia must be ruled out.

Heparin may be administered prior to or following thrombolytic therapy with alteplase (tissue-type plasminogen activator, recombinant), streptokinase, or urokinase. However, heparin should be discontinued and the patient's TT or APTT should be less than twice the control value prior to initiation of intravenous thrombolytic therapy. Also, following thrombolytic therapy, the patient's TT or APTT should return to less than twice the control value prior to administration of heparin.

When anticoagulant therapy is initiated with heparin and continued with a coumarin or indandione derivative, it is recommended that both agents be given concurrently until prothrombin time determinations indicate an adequate response to the coumarin or indandione derivative. The fact that early changes in prothrombin time may reflect initial depletion of factor VII rather than peak antithrombogenic activity must be kept in mind. Some clinicians recommend continuation of heparin therapy for several days after prothrombin time determinations have shown a reduction of activity to ensure that peak antithrombogenic activity has been reached.

Intramuscular injection of other medications is not recommended in patients receiving heparin because hematomas and bleeding into adjacent areas may occur.

A concentration of 400 to 600 USP Units of heparin per 100 mL of whole blood is usually used to prevent clotting during blood transfusion; a concentration of 70 to 150 USP Units of heparin per 10 to 20 mL of whole blood is usually used to prevent clotting in blood used for laboratory sampling. Consult manufacturers' prescribing information for specific directions. For use of heparin lock-flush solution in maintaining the patency of an indwelling venipuncture device, consult manufacturers' prescribing information. For use of heparin to prevent clotting during extracorporeal dialysis procedures, consult the equipment manufacturers' operating directions.

Parenteral Dosage Forms

Note: The following doses are given in USP Heparin Units. The strengths of heparin preparations available in the U.S. are labeled in USP Heparin Units per mL. The strengths of heparin preparations available in Canada may be labeled in USP Units or in International Units (IU) per mL. The strengths of heparin preparations available in many other countries, including the U.K., are labeled only in IU per mL. *USP Heparin Units are not identical to IU.* The relative potency between USP Units and IU may vary, depending upon the test method and specific reagents used to measure heparin activity. Also, a new International Standard for Heparin (used to calibrate potency in IU) was adopted in 1983. Therefore, equivalence in USP Units of dosages in clinical studies using heparin preparations labeled in IU may be difficult to determine. Consult current labeling for specific dosage recommendations for heparin preparations labeled in IU. At one time, 1 mg of heparin sodium was equivalent to 100 USP Units. However, this is no longer the case because of increased purification.

HEPARIN CALCIUM INJECTION USP

Usual adult dose

Full-dose (therapeutic) regimen—

Subcutaneous, deep (intrafat), 10,000 to 20,000 USP Units initially, then 8000 to 10,000 USP Units every eight hours or 15,000 to 20,000 USP Units every twelve hours, or as determined by coagulation test results. This dosage schedule is usually preceded by a loading dose of 5000 USP Units administered by intravenous injection.

Intravenous, 10,000 USP Units initially, then 5000 to 10,000 USP Units every four to six hours or 100 USP Units per kg of body weight every four hours, or as determined by coagulation test results. The dose may be administered undiluted or diluted with 50 to 100 mL of 0.9% sodium chloride injection.

Intravenous infusion, 20,000 to 40,000 USP Units in 1000 mL of 0.9% sodium chloride injection, administered over a twenty-four-hour period. This dosage schedule is usually preceded by a loading dose of 35 to 70 USP Units per kg of body weight or 5000 USP Units, administered by intravenous injection. The infusion is often administered at a rate of l000 USP Units per hour; however, dosage must be adjusted as determined by coagulation test results.

Note: Recommendations for specific indications include:

Heart and blood vessel surgery—Intravenous, initially not less than l50 USP Units per kg of body weight. Doses of 300 USP Units per kg of body weight are often used for procedures expected to last less than 60 minutes and doses of 400 USP units per kg of body weight are often used for procedures expected to last longer than 60 minutes. It is recommended that subsequent doses be based on coagulation test results.

Disseminated intravascular coagulation—Intravenous, 50 to 100 USP Units per kg of body weight every four hours, administered by continuous infusion or as a single injection. The medication should be discontinued if no improvement occurs within 4 to 8 hours.

Adjusted-dose regimen—

Subcutaneous, deep (intrafat), an established dose to be injected every twelve hours. The required dose is determined by adjusting heparin dosage until the midinterval (six hours after an injection) activated partial thromboplastin time (APTT) is maintained at one and one-half times the control value.

Low-dose (prophylactic) regimen—

Subcutaneous, deep (intrafat), 5000 USP Units two hours before surgery and every eight to twelve hours thereafter for seven days or until the patient is fully ambulatory, whichever is longer.

Usual pediatric dose

Intravenous, 50 USP Units per kg of body weight initially, then 50 to 100 USP Units per kg of body weight every four hours, or as determined by coagulation test results.

Intravenous infusion, 50 USP Units per kg of body weight as a loading dose initially, then 100 USP Units per kg of body weight added and absorbed every four hours or 20,000 USP Units per square meter of body surface every twenty-four hours, or as determined by coagulation test results.

Note: Recommendations for specific indications include:

Disseminated intravascular coagulation—Intravenous, 25 to 50 USP Units per kg of body weight every four hours, administered by continuous infusion or as a single injection. The medication should be discontinued if no improvement occurs within 4 to 8 hours.

Heart and blood vessel surgery—Intravenous, initially not less than l50 USP Units per kg of body weight. Doses of 300 USP Units per kg of body weight are often used for procedures expected to last less than 60 minutes. It is recommended that subsequent doses be based on coagulation test results.

Strength(s) usually available

U.S.—

Derived from porcine intestinal mucosa:

25,000 USP Units per mL (Rx) [*Calciparine* (in single unit-dose containers providing 5000 USP Units per 0.2 mL; 12,500 USP Units per 0.5 mL; and 20,000 USP Units per 0.8 mL)].

Canada—

Derived from porcine intestinal mucosa:

25,000 International Units (IU) per mL (Rx) [*Calcilean* (in single unit-dose containers providing 20,000 IU per 0.8 mL); *Calciparine* (in single unit-dose containers providing 5000 IU per 0.2 mL; 12,500 IU per 0.5 mL; and 20,000 IU per 0.8 mL)].

Packaging and storage

Store below 40 °C (104 °F), preferably between 15 and 30 °C (59 and 86 °F), unless otherwise specified by manufacturer. Protect from freezing.

Stability

Do not use if the solution is discolored or contains a precipitate. Some studies have indicated that loss of heparin activity may occur if heparin is diluted with 5% dextrose injection and the diluted solution is not used within 24 hours, or if diluted solutions of heparin in any diluent are stored in glass containers.

Incompatibilities

Heparin is strongly acidic and is incompatible with many solutions containing medications, although no loss of activity occurs when the agents are given via separate administration sites. Also, heparin may be incompatible with solutions containing a phosphate buffer, sodium carbonate, or sodium oxalate. It is recommended that heparin not be mixed, or administered through the same intravenous line, with other medications unless compatibility has first been established. In addition, heparin may be inactivated when used in conjunction with an artificial kidney because of an influx of calcium, magnesium, and acetate ions from the dialysate.

Note

When preparing the label, indicate that heparin calcium is of porcine mucosal origin.

HEPARIN LOCK FLUSH SOLUTION INJECTION

Usual adult dose

To prevent clot formation in a heparin lock set or central venous catheter—

Inject via the injection hub in a quantity sufficient to fill the entire device. The solution should be replaced every time the device is used. The solution will maintain coagulation within the device for up to 4 hours.

Strength(s) usually available

U.S.

10 USP units per mL [*HEP-LOCK U/P* (water; sodium chloride; monobasic sodium phosphate monohydrate; dibasic sodium phosphate anhydrous)].

100 USP units per mL [*HEP-LOCK U/P* (water; sodium chloride; monobasic sodium phosphate monohydrate; dibasic sodium phosphate anhydrous)].

Packaging and storage

Store at 20° to 25° C (68° to 77° F)

HEPARIN SODIUM INJECTION USP

Usual adult dose

Full-dose (therapeutic) regimen—

Subcutaneous, deep (intrafat), 10,000 to 20,000 USP Units initially, then 8000 to 10,000 USP Units every eight hours or 15,000 to 20,000 USP Units every twelve hours, or as determined by coagulation test results. This dosage schedule is usually preceded by a loading dose of 5000 USP Units administered by intravenous injection.

Intravenous, 10,000 USP Units initially, then 5000 to 10,000 USP Units every four to six hours or 100 USP Units per kg of body weight every four hours, or as determined by coagulation test results. The dose may be administered undiluted or diluted with 50 to 100 mL of 0.9% sodium chloride injection.

Intravenous infusion, 20,000 to 40,000 USP Units in 1000 mL of 0.9% sodium chloride injection, administered over a twenty-four-hour period. This dosage schedule is usually preceded by a loading dose of 35 to 70 USP Units per kg of body weight or 5000 USP Units, administered by intravenous injection. The infusion is often administered at a rate of l000 USP Units per hour; however, dosage must be adjusted as determined by coagulation test results.

Note: Recommendations for specific indications include:

Heart and blood vessel surgery—Intravenous, initially not less than l50 USP Units per kg of body weight. Doses of 300 USP Units per kg of body weight are often used for procedures expected to last less than 60 minutes and doses of 400 USP units per kg of body weight are often used for procedures expected to last longer than 60 minutes. It is recommended that subsequent doses be based on coagulation test results.

Disseminated intravascular coagulation—Intravenous, 50 to 100 USP Units per kg of body weight every four hours, administered by continuous infusion or as a single injection. The medication should be discontinued if no improvement occurs within 4 to 8 hours.

Adjusted-dose regimen—
Subcutaneous, deep (intrafat), an established dose to be injected every twelve hours. The required dose is determined by adjusting heparin dosage until the midinterval (six hours after an injection) activated partial thromboplastin time (APTT) is maintained at one and one-half times the control value.

Low-dose (prophylactic) regimen—
Subcutaneous, deep (intrafat), 5000 USP Units two hours before surgery and every eight to twelve hours thereafter for seven days or until the patient is fully ambulatory, whichever is longer.

Usual pediatric dose

Intravenous, 50 USP Units per kg of body weight initially, then 50 to 100 USP Units per kg of body weight every four hours, or as determined by coagulation test results.

Intravenous infusion, 50 USP Units per kg of body weight as a loading dose initially, then 100 USP Units per kg of body weight added and absorbed every four hours or 20,000 USP Units per square meter of body surface every twenty-four hours, or as determined by coagulation test results.

Note: Recommendations for specific indications include:

Disseminated intravascular coagulation—Intravenous, 25 to 50 USP Units per kg of body weight every four hours, administered by continuous infusion or as a single injection. The medication should be discontinued if no improvement occurs within 4 to 8 hours.

Heart and blood vessel surgery—Intravenous, initially not less than l50 USP Units per kg of body weight. Doses of 300 USP Units per kg of body weight are often used for procedures expected to last less than 60 minutes. It is recommended that subsequent doses be based on coagulation test results.

Strength(s) usually available

U.S.—

Note: Single unit-dose containers may also provide the quantities of heparin sodium listed above in volumes other than 1 mL.

Derived from beef lung: With preservative:
- 1000 USP Units per mL (Rx) [GENERIC].
- 5000 USP Units per mL (Rx) [GENERIC].
- 10,000 USP Units per mL (Rx) [GENERIC].
- 20,000 USP Units per mL (Rx) [GENERIC].

Derived from beef lung: Without preservative:
- 1000 USP Units per mL (Rx) [GENERIC].
- 5000 USP Units per mL (Rx) [GENERIC].

Derived from porcine intestinal mucosa: With preservative:
- 1000 USP Units per mL (Rx) [*Liquaemin* (benzyl alcohol); GENERIC].
- 2500 USP Units per mL (Rx) [GENERIC].
- 5000 USP Units per mL (Rx) [*Liquaemin* (benzyl alcohol); GENERIC].
- 7500 USP Units per mL (Rx) [GENERIC].
- 10,000 USP Units per mL (Rx) [*Liquaemin* (benzyl alcohol); GENERIC].
- 15,000 USP Units per mL (Rx) [GENERIC].
- 20,000 USP Units per mL (Rx) [*Liquaemin* (benzyl alcohol); GENERIC].
- 25,000 USP Units per mL (Rx) [GENERIC].
- 40,000 USP Units per mL (Rx) [*Liquaemin* (benzyl alcohol); GENERIC].

Derived from porcine intestinal mucosa: Without preservative:
- 1000 USP Units per mL (Rx) [*Liquaemin;* GENERIC].
- 5000 USP Units per mL (Rx) [*Liquaemin;* GENERIC].

Canada—

Derived from porcine intestinal mucosa: With preservative:
- 1000 International Units (IU) per mL (Rx) [*Heparin Leo* (chlorobutanol)].
- 1000 USP Units per mL (Rx) [*Hepalean* (benzyl alcohol); GENERIC].
- 10,000 IU per mL (Rx) [*Heparin Leo* (chlorobutanol)].
- 10,000 USP Units per mL (Rx) [*Hepalean* (benzyl alcohol); GENERIC].
- 25,000 IU per mL (Rx) [*Heparin Leo* (in 2-mL containers; chlorobutanol)].
- 25,000 USP Units per mL (Rx) [*Hepalean* (in single-dose containers providing 5000 USP Units in 0.2 mL and in 2-mL containers; benzyl alcohol)].

Derived from porcine intestinal mucosa: Without preservative:
- 1000 IU per mL (Rx) [*Heparin Leo*].
- 1000 USP Units per mL (Rx) [*Hepalean*].
- 10,000 IU per mL (Rx) [*Heparin Leo*].
- 25,000 IU per mL (Rx) [*Heparin Leo* (in single-dose containers providing 5000 IU in 0.2 mL)].

Packaging and storage

Store below 40 °C (104 °F), preferably between 15 and 30 °C (59 and 86 °F), unless otherwise specified by manufacturer. Protect from freezing.

Stability

Do not use if the solution is discolored or contains a precipitate. Some studies have indicated that loss of heparin activity may occur if heparin is diluted with 5% dextrose injection and the diluted solution is not used within 24 hours, or if diluted solutions of heparin in any diluent are stored in glass containers.

Incompatibilities

Heparin is strongly acidic and is incompatible with many solutions containing medications, although no loss of activity occurs when the agents are given via separate administration sites. Also, heparin may be incompatible with solutions containing a phosphate buffer, sodium carbonate, or sodium oxalate. It is recommended that heparin not be mixed, or administered through the same intravenous line, with other medications unless compatibility has first been established. In addition, heparin may be inactivated when used in conjunction with an artificial kidney because of an influx of calcium, magnesium, and acetate ions from the dialysate.

Note

When preparing the label, indicate the organ and species from which the heparin is derived.

Additional information

Heparin sodium injections that contain benzyl alcohol should not be administered to premature neonates because the preservative has been associated with a fatal "gasping syndrome" in these patients.

HEPARIN SODIUM IN DEXTROSE INJECTION

Usual adult dose

Intravenous infusion, 20,000 to 40,000 USP Units, administered over a twenty-four-hour period. This dosage schedule is usually preceded by a loading dose of 35 to 70 USP Units per kg of body weight or 5000 USP Units, administered by intravenous injection. The infusion is often administered at a rate of 1000 USP Units per hour; however, dosage must be adjusted as determined by coagulation test results.

Usual pediatric dose

Intravenous infusion, 50 USP Units per kg of body weight as a loading dose initially, then 100 USP Units per kg of body weight added and absorbed every four hours or 20,000 USP Units per square meter of body surface every twenty-four hours, or as determined by coagulation test results.

Strength(s) usually available

U.S.—

Derived from porcine intestinal mucosa:
- 20 USP Units per mL (10,000 USP Units per 500 mL), with 5% of dextrose (Rx) [GENERIC].
- 40 USP Units per mL (20,000 USP Units per 500 mL), with 5% of dextrose (Rx) [GENERIC].
- 50 USP Units per mL (12,500 USP Units per 250 mL and 25,000 USP Units per 500 mL), with 5% of dextrose (Rx) [GENERIC].
- 100 USP Units per mL (10,000 USP Units per 100 mL and 25,000 USP Units per 250 mL), with 5% of dextrose (Rx) [GENERIC].

Canada—

Derived from porcine intestinal mucosa:
- 40 USP Units per mL (20,000 USP Units per 500 mL), with 5% of dextrose (Rx) [GENERIC].

Packaging and storage

Store below 40 °C (104 °F), preferably between 15 and 30 °C (59 and 86 °F), unless otherwise specified by manufacturer. Protect from freezing.

Incompatibilities

Heparin is strongly acidic and is incompatible with many solutions containing medications, although no loss of activity occurs when the agents are given via separate administration sites. Also, heparin may be incompatible with solutions containing a phosphate buffer, sodium carbonate, or sodium oxalate. It is recommended that heparin not be mixed, or administered through the same intravenous line, with other medications unless compatibility has first been established.

HEPARIN SODIUM IN SODIUM CHLORIDE INJECTION

Usual adult dose

Intravenous infusion, 20,000 to 40,000 USP Units, administered over a twenty-four-hour period. This dosage schedule is usually preceded by a loading dose of 35 to 70 USP Units per kg of body weight or 5000 USP Units, administered by intravenous injection. The infusion is often administered at a rate of l000 USP Units per hour; however, dosage must be adjusted as determined by coagulation test results.

Usual pediatric dose

Intravenous infusion, 50 USP Units per kg of body weight as a loading dose initially, then 100 USP Units per kg of body weight added and absorbed every four hours or 20,000 USP Units per square meter of body surface every twenty-four hours, or as determined by coagulation test results.

Strength(s) usually available

U.S.—

Derived from porcine intestinal mucosa:

2 USP Units per mL (1000 USP Units per 500 mL and 2000 USP Units per 1000 mL), with 0.9% of sodium chloride (Rx) [GENERIC].

50 USP Units per mL (12,500 USP Units per 250 mL and 25,000 USP Units per 500 mL), with 0.45% of sodium chloride (Rx) [GENERIC].

100 USP Units per mL (25,000 USP Units per 250 mL), with 0.45% of sodium chloride (Rx) [GENERIC].

Canada—

Derived from porcine intestinal mucosa:

2 USP Units per mL (1000 USP Units per 500 mL and 2000 USP Units per 1000 mL), with 0.9% of sodium chloride (Rx) [GENERIC].

5 USP Units per mL (5000 USP Units per 1000 mL), with 0.9% of sodium chloride (Rx) [GENERIC].

Packaging and storage

Store below 40 °C (104 °F), preferably between 15 and 30 °C (59 and 86 °F), unless otherwise specified by manufacturer. Protect from freezing.

Incompatibilities

Heparin is strongly acidic and is incompatible with many solutions containing medications, although no loss of activity occurs when the agents are given via separate administration sites. Also, heparin may be incompatible with solutions containing a phosphate buffer, sodium carbonate, or sodium oxalate. It is recommended that heparin not be mixed, or administered through the same intravenous line, with other medications unless compatibility has first been established.

Revised: 02/01/2006

HEPATITIS A VACCINE INACTIVATED Systemic

VA CLASSIFICATION (Primary): IM100

Note: This monograph is specific for the inactivated whole virus vaccine derived from hepatitis A virus (HAV) and grown in human diploid cell (MRC-5) culture.

Commonly used brand name(s): *Havrix; Vaqta.*

Note: For a listing of dosage forms and brand names by country availability, see *Dosage Forms* section(s).

Category

Immunizing agent (active).

Indications

General Considerations

Hepatitis A virus (HAV), previously known as the infectious hepatitis virus, is acquired by ingesting uncooked or undercooked seafood from polluted water, swimming in polluted water, and by person-to-person spread. Food and water are the leading sources of HAV transmission because of the relative stability of the virus itself, poor sanitation in large areas of the world, and abundant HAV shedding in feces.

Travelers to HAV-endemic areas should avoid eating uncooked or undercooked food, especially fruits and vegetables contaminated by polluted water or human fecal fertilizer, and shellfish taken from polluted waters, and should peel fruits themselves. Travelers also should avoid drinking polluted water and the ice and drinks made from it, and should avoid swimming or bathing in polluted fresh or ocean water.

General improvement in hygiene, especially in water supplies and sewage disposal, in many industrialized and industrializing countries has resulted in a falling level of natural immunity to the disease. This in turn has led to a substantial rise in the proportion of persons with no protective antibodies, which places them at risk for HAV infection. It has been shown that seronegative travelers and military personnel visiting regions where HAV is endemic are at higher risk of hepatitis A. This higher risk has also been demonstrated in seronegative health care workers and day-care center staff.

In developing countries, HAV infection in children is frequent and typically mild, leading to the formation of antibodies and immunity. In such areas, there is at present little need for hepatitis A vaccine. However, in certain industrialized countries that have a higher level of sanitation, immunity is not acquired during childhood, and hepatitis A typically occurs in adults. Tourism is one of the largest businesses in many developing countries where hepatitis A is endemic, and susceptible travelers are at high risk of acquiring infection.

Many travel medicine experts estimate that the morbidity from HAV among international travelers is much higher than that from other vaccine-preventable infections. HAV infection accounts for 20 to 25% of clinically apparent acute hepatitis cases worldwide. In the U.S., 20 to 30% of all documented cases of acute viral hepatitis are due to HAV. Therefore, travelers to areas in which there is a recognized risk of exposure to HAV should take the necessary precautions. Risk is greatest for travelers to countries of Africa, Asia (except Japan), parts of the Caribbean, Central and South America, eastern Europe, the Mediterranean basin, the Middle East, and Mexico. For travelers to these areas of the world, risk of infection increases with duration of travel, and will be highest in those who live in or visit rural areas, travel through back country areas, or frequently eat or drink in settings of poor sanitation.

Accepted

Hepatitis A (prophylaxis)—*Havrix* brand hepatitis A vaccine inactivated is indicated for preexposure immunization against disease caused by hepatitis A virus (HAV) in persons 2 years of age or older. *Vaqta* brand hepatitis A vaccine inactivated is indicated for active immunization against disease caused by hepatitis A virus in persons 12 months of age and older. Primary immunization should be given at least 2 weeks prior to expected exposure to HAV.

Unless otherwise contraindicated, hepatitis A vaccine inactivated is indicated in persons 2 years or 12 months of age or older (*Havrix* or *Vaqta*, respectively) who are at increased risk of infection by HAV and for any person wishing to obtain immunity. Examples of groups identified as being at increased risk of infection include:

• International travelers. Persons from areas of low endemicity who travel to areas of intermediate or high endemicity are at risk for acquiring hepatitis A. These areas include, but are not limited to, Africa, Asia (except Japan), parts of the Caribbean, Central and South America, eastern Europe, the Mediterranean basin, the Middle East, and Mexico. Current advisories from the Centers for Disease Control and Prevention (CDC) should be consulted for information about specific locales. Immunization should be considered for persons traveling to areas where hepatitis A is highly endemic, for travel of long duration, and for those who travel repeatedly. Primary immunization with hepatitis A vaccine inactivated should be completed at least 2 weeks prior to expected exposure to HAV. Travelers to Australia, Canada, Japan, New Zealand, the U.S., and western Europe do not have a significantly increased risk of hepatitis A and, therefore, vaccination is not warranted.

• Military personnel identified as being at increased risk. Prevention of hepatitis A in military personnel is essential. This is especially important for military personnel from developed countries who are deployed in areas where hepatitis A is common, particularly during conflicts. Immunization should be considered for military personnel traveling to areas of higher endemicity for hepatitis A.

• People living in or relocating to areas of higher HAV endemicity.

• Populations that experience cyclic hepatitis A epidemics, such as Alaskan Eskimos and Native Americans. Hepatitis A is endemic in Native Americans; infection rates approach 100 cases per 100,000 people. In Alaskan Eskimos, large HAV epidemics occur every 10 to 12 years, resulting in thousands of cases of clinical illness and a few deaths. Studies have shown the effectiveness of the hepatitis A vaccine in Alaskan Eskimos. Consideration should be given to vaccination of these groups of people.

• Persons engaging in high-risk sexual activity, such as sexually active homosexual and bisexual males. Extensive hepatitis A outbreaks among homosexual men have been recognized in urban areas of the U.S., England, and Australia. Therefore, sexually active homosexual and bisexual men should be considered for vaccination with hepatitis A vaccine.

• Users of illicit injectable drugs. Within the past decade, hepatitis A outbreaks have been reported with increasing frequency among users of illicit injectable drugs, both in the U.S. and Europe. As these individuals may have underlying liver disease due to chronic infection with other hepatotropic viruses, they may be at higher risk for severe complications from hepatitis A. Consideration should be given to vaccination of these individuals.

• Residents of a community experiencing an outbreak of hepatitis A.

• Certain institutional workers, such as caretakers for the developmentally disabled.

• Employees of child day-care centers. Outbreaks have been recognized among children and employees in day-care centers, and in some instances these outbreaks may be the source of larger community epidemics. Outbreaks have been recognized predominantly in centers with children who are not toilet-trained, and where clinical disease occurs in staff, parents, and older siblings of day-care center children. The use of immune globulin (IG) has been well documented to control outbreaks of disease in these settings. Although use of hepatitis A vaccine has not yet been studied in the day-care center setting, the available data from efficacy studies suggest that the vaccine may be able to replace IG in control of day-care center outbreaks.

• Laboratory workers who handle live HAV.

• Handlers of primate animals that may be harboring HAV. Since viral hepatitis was recognized among primates caretakers, consideration should be given to vaccination of handlers of primate animals that may be harboring HAV.

• Patients with hemophilia. Outbreaks of HAV infection in patients with hemophilia receiving solvent detergent–treated factor concentrates have been reported primarily in Europe. However, in the U.S., three cases of HAV infection were reported in the mid-1990s in patients with hemophilia who received factor VIII concentrate from a single lot from one manufacturer. Available seroprevalence data in the U.S. from patients with hemophilia do not allow accurate determination of risk. Nevertheless, patients with hemophilia, especially those receiving solvent detergent–treated factor concentrates, may benefit from protection against HAV infection and should be considered for immunization. Preimmunization testing for anti-HAV antibody may be cost-effective because seroprevalence rates among persons with hemophilia may be higher.

• Food handlers. Food-borne outbreaks usually are associated with contamination of uncooked food during preparation by a food handler who is infected with HAV. The most effective means to prevent these outbreaks is by careful hygienic practices during food preparation. Little information is available concerning seroprevalence rates of HAV antibody in food handlers compared with that in the general population. Therefore, routine hepatitis A vaccination is not indicated in this population. However, economic, medicolegal, and public relations implications of a food-borne HAV outbreak from a commercial establishment may indicate that use of hepatitis A vaccine inactivated should be considered in some circumstances. Factors to consider in this decision include the nature of the food (e.g., materials for salads) as well as the demographic characteristics, the average duration of employment, and the number of food handlers.

• Persons with chronic liver disease, including those with alcoholic cirrhosis, chronic hepatitis B, chronic hepatitis C, autoimmune hepatitis, and primary biliary cirrhosis. Since clinical hepatitis A may be more severe in persons with chronic liver disease due to hepatitis viruses or other etiologies, vaccination of these persons should be considered. Although few data exist about the immunogenicity and protective efficacy of hepatitis A vaccine inactivated in persons with chronic liver disease, no reason exists to suspect that the hepatitis A vaccine inactivated would aggravate the chronic condition.

Unaccepted
Hepatitis A vaccine inactivated will not give protection from hepatitis caused by infectious agents other than HAV.

Pharmacology/Pharmacokinetics

Physicochemical characteristics
Source—Hepatitis A vaccine inactivated is a sterile suspension for intramuscular injection. The vaccine is a whole virus vaccine derived from hepatitis A virus (HAV), grown in human diploid cell (MRC-5) culture, and inactivated with formalin. The vaccine contains HAV antigen adsorbed onto aluminum provided as aluminum hydroxide.

Protective effect
Clinical studies in animals and humans have shown that hepatitis A vaccine inactivated is safe and highly immunogenic. Immunogenicity studies have shown that 70 to 90% of persons develop antibodies to HAV (anti-HAV) following a single dose, and nearly 100% of persons develop antibodies following two doses of vaccine. The presence of anti-HAV confers protection against hepatitis A infection. However, the lowest titer needed to confer protection has not been determined. Antibody levels obtained after a single dose of vaccine are often higher than those obtained after a single dose of IG, and substantial levels of anti-HAV neutralizing antibody are present in the majority of recipients of a complete immunization series. One immunogenicity study has suggested that simultaneous administration of large doses of immune globulin (IG) with the first vaccine dose may lower the active antibody response. However, the lowering of antibody titer levels does not appear great enough to have an impact on the protective effect of the vaccine.

Time to protective effect
After receiving the initial dose of hepatitis A vaccine, persons are considered protected in 4 weeks. For long-term protection, a second dose is needed 6 to 12 months later. For persons who will travel to high-risk areas in < 4 weeks after the initial vaccine dose, IG (0.02 mL per kg of body weight) should be administered simultaneously with the first dose of vaccine but at different injection sites.

Duration of protective effect
The duration of protection after vaccination is unknown. However, antibody decay studies suggest that measurable antibody will persist for many years. Continued observation of immunized persons will be required to determine the need for later booster doses of vaccine.

Precautions to Consider

Carcinogenicity/Mutagenicity
Hepatitis A vaccine inactivated has not been evaluated for its carcinogenic or mutagenic potential.

Pregnancy/Reproduction
Fertility—Hepatitis A vaccine inactivated has not been evaluated for its potential to impair fertility.

Pregnancy—Adequate and well-controlled studies have not been done in humans. However, hepatitis A vaccine inactivated, if indicated, should be given to pregnant women only if clearly needed. Although data on the safety of hepatitis A vaccine inactivated for the developing fetus are not available, no risk would be expected because the vaccine contains inactivated, purified viral proteins. In contrast, infection with the hepatitis A virus (HAV) in a pregnant woman can result in severe disease in the mother.

Studies have not been done in animals.

FDA Pregnancy Category C.

Breast-feeding
It is not known whether hepatitis A vaccine inactivated is distributed into breast milk. However, problems in humans have not been documented. Because many drugs are distributed into human breast milk, caution should be exercised when hepatitis A vaccine inactivated is administered to a woman who is breast-feeding.

Pediatrics
For *Havrix*—Children have the highest age-specific incidence of hepatitis A and are likely to play a role in its spread. Hepatitis A vaccine inactivated is well tolerated and highly immunogenic and effective in children 2 years of age and older. In a double-blind, controlled study in the U.S. involving 1037 children, aged 2 to 16 years, who were randomly assigned to receive either one intramuscular injection of inactivated hepatitis A vaccine or placebo, 25 cases of clinical hepatitis A occurred in the control group while none were noted in the vaccinated group, establishing a protective efficacy of 100%. A similar study performed in Thailand showed similar results. Safety and efficacy of hepatitis A vaccine inactivated in infants and children younger than 2 years of age have not been established, and use is not recommended.

For *Vaqta*—Safety and efficacy of hepatitis A vaccine inactivated in infants and children younger than 12 months of age have not been established.

Geriatrics
Appropriate studies performed to date have not demonstrated geriatrics-specific problems that would limit the usefulness of hepatitis A vaccine inactivated in the elderly. However, greater sensitivity of some older individuals cannot be ruled out.

Drug interactions and/or related problems
The following drug interactions and/or related problems have been selected on the basis of their potential clinical significance (possible mechanism in parentheses where appropriate)—not necessarily inclusive (» = major clinical significance):

Note: Combinations containing any of the following medications, depending on the amount present, may also interact with this medication.

Anticoagulant therapy
(should not be given unless the potential benefits clearly outweigh risk of administration; caution should be used with steps taken to avoid risk of hematoma following the injection)

Immunosuppressive agents or
Radiation therapy
(because normal defense mechanisms are suppressed, the patient's antibody response to hepatitis A vaccine inactivated may be decreased)

Laboratory value alterations

The following have been selected on the basis of their potential clinical significance (possible effect in parentheses where appropriate)—not necessarily inclusive (» = major clinical significance).

With physiology/laboratory test values
- Alanine aminotransferase (ALT [SGPT]) and
- Alkaline phosphatase and
- Aspartate aminotransferase (AST [SGOT])
  - (serum values may be increased)

Medical considerations/Contraindications

The medical considerations/contraindications included have been selected on the basis of their potential clinical significance (reasons given in parentheses where appropriate)—not necessarily inclusive (» = major clinical significance).

Except under special circumstances, this medication should not be used when the following medical problem exists:

» Hypersensitivity to any component of the hepatitis A vaccine
  (should not be administered to persons with a history of severe reaction to a prior dose of hepatitis A vaccine or to a vaccine component)

Risk-benefit should be considered when the following medical problem exists:

Acute infection or
Febrile illness
  (may be reason for delaying use of hepatitis A vaccine except when withholding entails greater risk)

Bleeding disorders such as
Hemophilia or
Thrombocytopenia
  (should be given with caution with steps taken to avoid risk of hematoma following the injection)

Immunocompromised patients
  (expected immune response may not be obtained)

Side/Adverse Effects

Note: Cases of convulsions, dizziness, encephalopathy, Guillain-Barré syndrome, multiple sclerosis, myelitis, neuropathy, and paresthesia have been reported following administration of hepatitis A vaccine inactivated. However, no causal relationship has been established.

Angioedema, dyspnea, erythema multiforme, hepatitis, hyperhidrosis, jaundice, lymphadenopathy, and syncope have been reported since market introduction of the vaccine, but the relationship to the vaccine is unclear.

The following side/adverse effects have been selected on the basis of their potential clinical significance (possible signs and symptoms in parentheses where appropriate)—not necessarily inclusive:

Those indicating need for medical attention

Incidence rare

Anaphylactic reaction (difficulty in breathing or swallowing; hives; itching, especially of soles or palms; reddening of skin, especially around ears; swelling of eyes, face, or inside of nose; unusual tiredness or weakness, sudden and severe)

Incidence not determined—Observed during clinical practice; estimates of frequency can not be determined

Cerebellar ataxia (shakiness and unsteady walk; unsteadiness, trembling, or other problems with muscle control or coordination); ***encephalitis*** (confusion; irritability; headache; seizures; stiff neck; vomiting); ***Guillain-Barre syndrome*** (sudden numbness and weakness in the arms and legs; inability to move arms and legs); ***thrombocytopenia*** (black, tarry stools; bleeding gums; blood in urine or stools; pinpoint red spots on skin; unusual bleeding or bruising)

Those indicating need for medical attention only if they continue or are bothersome

Incidence more frequent

Soreness at injection site—incidence 21 to 56%

Note: Local reactions are common but generally mild. Although rare, since market introduction of the vaccine, localized edema has also been reported following administration of the vaccine.

Incidence less frequent

Anorexia (lack of appetite); ***arm or back pain; asthenia/fatigue*** (lack or loss of strength); ***fever ≥ 37.7 °C (100 °F); headache; malaise*** (general feeling of discomfort or illness); ***menstruation disorder*** (change in pattern of monthly periods; change in amount of bleeding during periods; unusual stopping of menstrual bleeding; bleeding between periods); ***nasal congestion*** (stuffy nose); ***nausea; pain, soreness, bruising, tenderness or warmth at injection site***; ***pharyngitis*** (body aches or pain; congestion; cough; dryness or soreness of throat; fever; hoarseness; runny nose; tender, swollen glands in neck; trouble in swallowing; voice changes); ***stiffness; upper respiratory infection*** (cough; fever; sneezing; sore throat)

Incidence rare

Arthralgia, arthritis, or myalgia (aches or pain in joints or muscles); ***diarrhea or stomach cramps or pain; lymphadenopathy*** (swelling of glands in armpits or neck); ***pruritus*** (itching); ***urticaria*** (welts); ***vomiting***

Patient Consultation

As an aid to patient consultation, refer to *Advice for the Patient, Hepatitis A Vaccine Inactivated (Systemic)*.

In providing consultation, consider emphasizing the following selected information (» = major clinical significance):

Before using this medication

» Conditions affecting use, especially:
  Hypersensitivity to hepatitis A vaccine inactivated or any component of the vaccine
  Pregnancy—Should be given to a pregnant woman only if clearly needed
  Breast-feeding—Caution should be exercised when administering to a nursing woman
  Use in children—For *Havrix*—Use is not recommended in infants and children younger than 2 years of age
  For *Vaqta*—Use is not recommended in infants and children younger than 12 months of age
  Use in the elderly—No differences in safety and immunogenicity, but greater sensitivity of some older individuals can not be ruled out.

Proper use of this medication

» Proper dosing

Side/adverse effects

Signs of potential side effects, especially anaphylactic reaction
Signs of potential side effects observed during clinical practice, especially cerebellar ataxia, encephalitis, Guillain-Barre syndrome or thrombocytopenia

General Dosing Information

Appropriate precautions should be taken prior to vaccine injection to prevent allergic or other unwanted reactions. Precautions should include a review of the patient's history regarding possible sensitivity and the ready availability of epinephrine 1:1000 and other appropriate agents used for control of immediate allergic reactions.

Hepatitis A vaccine inactivated is administered by *intramuscular* injection. It should not be injected intravenously, intradermally, or subcutaneously.

The deltoid muscle (outer aspect of the upper arm) is the recommended site for the immunization of adults and older children. The vaccine should not be administered in the gluteal region since administration at this site may result in suboptimal response.

Vaccination of an immune person is not contraindicated and does not increase the risk of adverse effects. Prevaccination serologic testing may be indicated for adult travelers who probably have had prior hepatitis A virus (HAV) infection, if the cost of testing is less than the cost of vaccination and if testing will not interfere with completion of the vaccine series. Such persons may include those older than 40 years of age and those born in areas of the world having a high endemicity of HAV infection. Postvaccination testing for serologic response is not indicated.

The Advisory Committee on Immunization Practices (ACIP) offers the following recommendations for the use of inactivated hepatitis A vaccine among international travelers:

- All susceptible persons traveling to or working in countries with intermediate or high HAV endemicity (countries other than Australia, Canada, Japan, New Zealand, the U.S., and countries in Scandinavia and western Europe) should be vaccinated or receive immune globulin (IG) before departure. Hepatitis A vaccine at the age-appropriate dose is preferred for persons who plan to travel repeatedly to, or reside for long periods in, these high-risk areas. IG is recommended for travelers younger than 2 years of age.
- After receiving the initial dose of hepatitis A vaccine, persons are considered protected in 4 weeks. For long-term protection, a second dose is needed 6 to 12 months later. For persons who will travel to high-risk areas in less than 4 weeks after the initial vaccine dose, IG (0.02 mL per kg of body weight) should be administered simultaneously with the first dose of vaccine but at a different injection site.
- Persons who are allergic to a vaccine component or otherwise elect not to receive the vaccine should receive a single dose of IG (0.02 mL

per kg of body weight), which provides effective protection against hepatitis A for up to 3 months. IG should be administered at 0.06 mL per kg of body weight and must be repeated if travel is longer than 5 months.

Hepatitis A vaccine inactivated can be administered simultaneously with other vaccines and toxoids, including cholera, diphtheria, hepatitis B, Japanese encephalitis, rabies, tetanus, oral typhoid, and yellow fever, without affecting immunogenicity or increasing the frequency of adverse effects. However, during simultaneous administration, the vaccines should be given at separate injection sites. Hepatitis A and hepatitis B vaccines induce a similar immune response when given either separately or concomitantly.

When IG is given concurrently with the first dose of vaccine, the proportion of persons who develop protective levels of anti-HAV antibody is not affected, but antibody concentrations are lower. Because the final concentrations of anti-HAV antibody are substantially higher than those considered to be protective, this reduced immunogenicity is not expected to be clinically important.

Hepatitis A vaccine inactivated should replace IG for use in preexposure prophylaxis against HAV. On the other hand, hepatitis A vaccine inactivated has little to offer after a person has been exposed to HAV, because the need for protection is immediate and exposure is almost always limited to a brief period. Thus, when hepatitis A is recognized in a patient, close family member, or household contact, IG should be given for prophylaxis, optimally within two weeks after exposure.

Hepatitis A vaccine inactivated does not enhance disease progression in human immunodeficiency virus (HIV)-infected persons and can be administered safely to persons who are HIV-positive.

For treatment of adverse effects

Recommended treatment consists of the following:

- For mild hypersensitivity reaction—Administering antihistamines, and, if necessary, corticosteroids. In mild anaphylaxis, antihistamines or subcutaneous epinephrine may be all that is necessary if the condition is progressing slowly and is not life-threatening, regardless of the organ or system affected. Under these circumstances the risks associated with intravenous epinephrine administration outweigh the benefits.
- For severe hypersensitivity or anaphylactic reaction—Administering epinephrine. Antihistamines or corticosteroids may also be administered as required. Epinephrine is the treatment of choice for severe hypersensitivity or anaphylactic reaction. If the patient's condition is not stable, epinephrine should be infused. Norepinephrine may be preferable if there is no bronchospasm. For bronchospasm, epinephrine should be given with corticosteroids. Other bronchodilators, such as intravenous aminophylline or albuterol by nebulization, also should be considered.

Note: All cases of suspected or confirmed side/adverse effects following the administration of hepatitis A vaccine inactivated should be reported to the U.S. Department of Health and Human Services' Vaccine Adverse Events Reporting System (VAERS) at 1–800–822–7967.

Parenteral Dosage Forms

HEPATITIS A VACCINE INACTIVATED INJECTION

Usual adult dose

Hepatitis A (prophylaxis)—

Intramuscular, a single dose of 1440 enzyme linked immunosorbent assay (ELISA) Units (*Havrix*) or 50 Units (*Vaqta*).

Note: A booster dose is recommended six to eighteen months after the first dose of (*Vaqta*), or six to twelve months after the first dose of (*Havrix*).

Usual pediatric dose

Hepatitis A (prophylaxis)—

Children 2 to 18 years of age—Intramuscular, a single dose of 720 enzyme linked immunosorbent assay (ELISA) Units or two doses of 360 enzyme linked immunosorbent assay (ELISA) Units given one month apart (*Havrix*—U.S. and Canada).

Children 12 months to 18 years of age—Intramuscular, a single dose of 25 Units (*Vaqta*—U.S.).

For *Havrix*—Children younger than 2 years of age—Use is not recommended.

For *Vaqta*—Children younger than 12 months of age—Use is not recommended.

Note: A booster dose is recommended six to eighteen months after the first dose of (*Vaqta*—U.S.), or six to twelve months after the first dose of (*Havrix*—U.S. and Canada).

Strength(s) usually available

U.S.—

1440 enzyme linked immunosorbent assay (ELISA) units viral antigen, adsorbed on 0.5 mg of aluminum hydroxide in each 1-mL adult dose (Rx) [*Havrix* (formalin approximately 0.1 mg)].

360 enzyme linked immunosorbent assay (ELISA) units viral antigen, adsorbed on 0.25 mg of aluminum hydroxide in each 0.5-mL pediatric dose (Rx) [*Havrix* (formalin approximately 0.05 mg)].

720 enzyme linked immunosorbent assay (ELISA) units viral antigen, adsorbed on 0.25 mg of aluminum hydroxide in each 0.5-mL pediatric dose (Rx) [*Havrix* (formalin approximately 0.05 mg)].

50 units viral antigen, adsorbed on 0.45 mg of aluminum hydroxide in each 1-mL adult dose (Rx) [*Vaqta* (formaldehyde approximately 0.8 mcg)].

25 units viral antigen, adsorbed on 0.225 mg of aluminum hydroxide in each 0.5-mL pediatric dose (Rx) [*Vaqta* (formaldehyde approximately 0.4 mcg)].

Canada—

1440 enzyme linked immunosorbent assay (ELISA) units viral antigen, adsorbed on 0.5 mg of aluminum hydroxide in each 1-mL adult dose (Rx) [*Havrix* (formalin approximately 0.1 mg)].

360 enzyme linked immunosorbent assay (ELISA) units viral antigen, adsorbed on 0.25 mg of aluminum hydroxide in each 0.5-mL pediatric dose (Rx) [*Havrix* (formalin approximately 0.05 mg)].

50 units viral antigen, adsorbed on 0.45 mg of aluminum hydroxide in each 1-mL adult dose (Rx) [*Vaqta* (formaldehyde approximately 0.8 mcg)].

25 units viral antigen, adsorbed on 0.225 mg of aluminum hydroxide in each 0.5-mL pediatric dose (Rx) [*Vaqta* (formaldehyde approximately 0.4 mcg)].

Packaging and storage

Store between 2 and 8 °C (36 and 46 °F), unless otherwise specified by the manufacturer. Protect from freezing.

Preparation of dosage form

The vaccine should be used as supplied, and should not be diluted. The vial should be shaken well immediately before withdrawal of the dose. In addition, thorough agitation at the time of administration is necessary to maintain suspension of the vaccine. After agitation, the vaccine is a slightly opaque, white suspension. The vaccine should be discarded if the suspension does not appear homogenous.

Stability

Storage below the recommended temperature may reduce potency. Freezing destroys potency, and the vaccine should be discarded if freezing occurs.

Auxiliary labeling

- Do not freeze; discard if freezing occurs.
- Shake well.

Selected Bibliography

Centers for Disease Control. Recommendations of the Advisory Committee on Immunization Practices (ACIP): prevention of hepatitis A through active or passive immunization. MMWR Morb Mortal Wkly Rep 1996; 45(15): 1-30.

American Academy of Pediatrics. Hepatitis A. In: Peter G, editor. 1997 Red Book: report of the Committee on Infectious Diseases. 24th ed. Elk Grove Village, IL: American Academy of Pediatrics; 1997. p. 237-46.

Revised: 09/14/2005

HEPATITIS A VIRUS VACCINE INACTIVATED AND HEPATITIS B VIRUS VACCINE RECOMBINANT Systemic

VA CLASSIFICATION (Primary): IM100

Commonly used brand name(s): *Twinrix*.

Note: For a listing of dosage forms and brand names by country availability, see *Dosage Forms* section(s).

Category

Immunizing agent (active).

Indications

General Considerations

Hepatitis A—

Hepatitis A virus (HAV) is highly contagious and the predominant mode of transmission is person to person via the fecal-oral route. Infection is acquired by contaminated water or food, infected food handlers, after breakdown in usual sanitary conditions or after floods or natural disasters, by ingesting uncooked or undercooked shellfish (oysters, clams, mussels) from contaminated waters, during travel to areas of the world with poor hygienic conditions, among institutionalized children and adults, in day care centers, and by parenteral transmission, either by blood transfusions or by sharing needles with infected people.

Hepatitis B—

The hepatitis B virus (HBV) occurs throughout the world with highly variable prevalences. A human reservoir of persistently infected persons is present in nearly all communities of the world. In the United States, the primary means of transmission are parenteral drug abuse, unprotected sexual activity, occupationally acquired infection, or travelers returning from high prevalence countries.

After a person has been exposed to HBV, there is no definitive treatment for acute infection. Those who develop antibodies to HBsAg after active infection are protected against subsequent infection.

Accepted

Hepatitis A and Hepatitis B virus infection (prophylaxis)—Hepatitis A inactivated and hepatitis B recombinant combination vaccine is indicated for preexposure immunization against disease caused by hepatitis A virus (HAV) and infection by all known subtypes of hepatitis B virus in persons 18 years of age or older.

Unless otherwise contraindicated, hepatitis A and hepatitis B combination vaccine is indicated in persons 18 years of age or older who are at increased risk of infection due to behavior or occupational factors. Examples of groups identified as being at increased risk of infection include:

- International travelers; persons from areas of low endemicity who travel to areas of intermediate or high endemicity are at risk for acquiring hepatitis A. These areas include, but are not limited to, Africa, the Caribbean, Central America, eastern Europe, the Middle East, South America (temperate and tropical), south and southeast Asia (except Japan), southern Europe, and the former Soviet Union.
- Military personnel identified as being at increased risk for HBV, including military recruits.
- People living in, or relocating to, areas of higher HAV endemicity and who have risk factors for HBV.
- Persons engaging in high-risk sexual activity, such as sexually active homosexual and bisexual males.
- Users of illicit injectable drugs.
- Persons at risk through their work, such as laboratory workers who handle live hepatitis A and hepatitis B virus, police and other personnel who render first aid or medical assistance, and workers who come in contact with feces or sewage.
- Employees of child day-care centers and correctional facilities, residents of drug and alcohol treatment centers, and patients and staff in hemodialysis units.
- Patients who frequently receive blood products, including those people who have clotting-factor disorders, such as hemophiliacs and other recipients of therapeutic blood products.
- Persons with chronic liver disease, including those with alcoholic cirrhosis, chronic hepatitis C, autoimmune hepatitis, and primary biliary cirrhosis.
- Healthcare personnel who give first aid or emergency medical assistance.
- People who are at increased risk for HBV infection and who are close contacts of patients with acute or relapsing hepatitis A and individuals who are at increased risk for HAV infection and who are close contacts of those with hepatitis B infections either acute or chronic.

Unaccepted

Hepatitis A and hepatitis B vaccine will not give protection from hepatitis caused by agents such as hepatitis C virus, hepatitis E virus, or other pathogens that infect the liver.

Pharmacology/Pharmacokinetics

Physicochemical characteristics

Source—

Hepatitis A vaccine inactivated is a sterile suspension of inactivated hepatitis A virus (strain HM175) grown in MRC-5 cells and combined with purified surface antigen of the hepatitis B virus.

Hepatitis B recombinant vaccines are produced from *Saccharomyces cerevisiae* cells, which carry the gene for the hepatitis B surface antigen (HBsAg) in synthetic media that contain inorganic salts, amino acids, dextrose, and vitamins. Yeast-derived protein constitutes no more than 5% of the final product. Bulk preparations of each antigen are adsorbed separately onto aluminum salts and then pooled during formulation.

Protective effect—

Clinical studies were analyzed following administration of three doses of the hepatitis A and hepatitis B combination vaccine in healthy adults and it was shown to be safe and immunogenic. Immunogenicity studies have shown that 93.8%, 98.8%, and 99.9% of patients developed protective antibodies against HAV, and 30.8%, 78.2%, and 98.5% of patients developed protective antibodies against HBV after 1, 2, and 3 doses, respectively.

Time to protective effect

Protective antibodies against HAV were detected in 99.9% of patients, and protective antibodies against HBV were detected in 98.5% of patients one month after completion of the three dose series.

Duration of protective effect

The duration of protective effect by the combination vaccine is at least 4 years, as demonstrated by clinical studies.

Precautions to Consider

Pregnancy/Reproduction

Pregnancy—Studies have not been done in humans. It is unknown whether the combination of hepatitis A and hepatitis B vaccine can cause fetal harm or can affect reproductive capacity. It should be used in pregnant women only if the benefit outweighs the risk.

Studies have not been done in animals.

Note: Healthcare providers are encouraged to register pregnant women who received hepatitis A and hepatitis B vaccine in the SmithKline Beecham Pharmaceuticals vaccination registry by calling 1–800–366–8900 extension 5231.

FDA Pregnancy Category C.

Breast-feeding

It is not known whether the vaccine is distributed into human breast milk. However, many drugs are distributed into human breast milk, caution should be used when administering to nursing women.

Pediatrics

No information is available on the relationship of age to the effects of the combination hepatitis A and hepatitis B vaccine in the pediatric population. Safety and efficacy have not been established in patients under the age of 18 years.

Geriatrics

Appropriate studies on the relationship of age to the effects of the combination hepatitis A and hepatitis B vaccine in the geriatric population have not been performed. However, no specific geriatric problems have been documented to date.

Drug interactions and/or related problems

The following drug interactions and/or related problems have been selected on the basis of their potential clinical significance (possible mechanism in parentheses where appropriate)—not necessarily inclusive (» = major clinical significance):

» Anticoagulants
(caution is recommended because bleeding may occur following intramuscular administration of the hepatitis A inactivated and hepatitis B recombinant combination vaccine)

Immunosuppressive therapy
(because normal defense mechanisms are suppressed, the patient's antibody response to hepatitis A inactivated and hepatitis B recombinant combination vaccine may not be as expected)

Medical considerations/Contraindications

The medical considerations/contraindications included have been selected on the basis of their potential clinical significance (reasons given in parentheses where appropriate)—not necessarily inclusive (» = major clinical significance).

Except under special circumstances, this medication should not be used when the following medical problem exists:

» Hypersensitivity to any component of the vaccine
(there have been rare reports of anaphylaxis/anaphylactoid reactions following the use of hepatitis A vaccine inactivated; therefore, persons experiencing hypersensitivity reactions after a dose of hepatitis A vaccine inactivated or hepatitis B vaccine recombinant should not receive further doses of the combination hepatitis A and hepatitis B vaccine)

Risk-benefit should be considered when the following medical problems exist:

Allergy to yeast
(the manufacturing procedures used to make this vaccine result in a product that contains no more than 5% yeast protein)

» Bleeding disorders or
» Thrombocytopenia
(caution is recommended because bleeding may occur following intramuscular administration of the hepatitis A inactivated and hepatitis B recombinant combination vaccine)

Hepatitis A, current infection or
Hepatitis B, current infection
(hepatitis A inactivated and hepatitis B recombinant combination vaccine will not prevent infection in patients who have unrecognized hepatitis A or hepatitis B at the time of vaccination)

Illness, moderate or severe, with or without fever
(administration of the vaccine should be delayed, except when withholding the vaccine entails a greater risk to the patient than a possible superimposed reaction to the vaccine)

Immune deficiency conditions
(because normal defense mechanisms are suppressed, the patient's antibody response to hepatitis A inactivated and hepatitis B recombinant combination vaccine may not be as expected)

Side/Adverse Effects

Note: Results from two clinical studies indicated no relationship between Hepatitis B vaccine and the development of multiple sclerosis and that vaccination with hepatitis B does not appear to increase the short-term risk of multiple sclerosis relapse.

The following side/adverse effects have been selected on the basis of their potential clinical significance (possible signs and symptoms in parentheses where appropriate)—not necessarily inclusive:

Those indicating need for medical attention

Incidence rare

Anaphylactic reaction (difficulty in breathing or swallowing; hives; itching, especially of feet or hands; reddening of skin, especially around ears; swelling of eyes, face, or inside of nose; unusual tiredness or weakness, sudden and severe)—seen only with hepatitis A vaccine inactivated

Those indicating need for medical attention only if they continue or are bothersome

Incidence more frequent (> 10%)

Soreness at injection site

Incidence less frequent (1 to 10%)

Induration at injection site (hardening or thickening of skin at injection site); ***upper respiratory tract infection*** (cough; fever; sneezing; sore throat)

Incidence rare (less than 1%)

Abdominal pain; anorexia (loss of appetite; weight loss); ***arthralgia*** (pain, swelling, or redness in joints; difficulty in moving); ***back pain; dizziness; erythema*** (redness of skin; unusually warm skin); ***flushing*** (feeling of warmth; redness of the face, neck, arms and occasionally upper chest); ***injection site reactions, including ecchymoses*** (bruising; large, flat, blue or purplish patches in the skin); ***itching, redness, or swelling at injection site; influenza-like symptoms*** (nausea; vomiting); ***insomnia*** (sleeplessness; trouble sleeping); ***irritability and agitation; migraine*** (severe headache); ***myalgia*** (muscle pain); ***paresthesia*** (tingling, burning, or prickly sensations); ***petechiae*** (small, red or purple spots on skin); ***rash; respiratory tract illness*** (headache; sore throat; runny nose; fever); ***somnolence*** (sleepiness; unusual drowsiness); ***syncope*** (fainting or lightheadedness when getting up from a lying or sitting position; unusually fast heartbeat; palpitations); ***sweating; urticaria*** (hives or skin rash; itching); ***vertigo*** (feeling of constant movement of self or surroundings; sensation of spinning); ***weakness***

Patient Consultation

As an aid to patient consultation, refer to *Advice for the Patient, Hepatitis A Virus Vaccine Inactivated and Hepatitis B Virus Vaccine Recombinant (Systemic)*.

In providing consultation, consider emphasizing the following selected information (» = major clinical significance):

Before receiving this vaccine

» Conditions affecting use, especially:
Hypersensitivity to hepatitis A vaccine inactivated, hepatitis B vaccine recombinant, or any of their components
Other medications, especially anticoagulants
Other medical problems, especially bleeding disorders or thrombocytopenia

Proper use of this medication

» Proper dosing

Side/adverse effects

Signs of potential side effects, especially anaphylactic reaction

General Dosing Information

Before the injection of any vaccine, the health care professional should take all reasonable precautions to prevent allergic or other adverse reactions. The patient's history should be reviewed for possible vaccine sensitivity, previous vaccine related adverse reactions, and to determine that there is no contraindication to the vaccine being given.

Hepatitis A vaccine inactivated and hepatitis B vaccine recombinant is administered by *intramuscular* injection in the deltoid region. It should not be administered in the gluteal region because a suboptimal response may result. It also should not be injected intravenously, intradermally, or subcutaneously.

As with any vaccine, vaccination may not protect 100% of the recipients. As hepatitis D (caused by the delta virus) does not occur in the absence of the hepatitis B infection, it can be expected that prevention of hepatitis D infection will occur with vaccination with the combination hepatitis A and B vaccine.

Epinephrine injection and other appropriate agents used for the control of immediate allergic reactions must be immediately available should an acute anaphylactic reaction occur.

Patients should be informed of the importance of adhering to the immunization schedule. As with any vaccine it is important to question the patient concerning the occurrence of symptoms/signs after a previous dose of the same vaccine. If any suspected adverse events have occurred, the Vaccine Adverse Events Reporting System (VAERS) should be notified. The number for forms and information is 1–800–822–7967.

Parenteral Dosage Forms

HEPATITIS A VIRUS VACCINE INACTIVATED AND HEPATITIS B VIRUS VACCINE RECOMBINANT INJECTABLE SUSPENSION

Usual adult dose

Hepatitis A and Hepatitis B (prophylaxis)—
Intramuscular, into the deltoid muscle, 1 mL (720 enzyme linked immunosorbant assay [ELISA] units of inactivated hepatitis A virus and 20 mcg of hepatitis B surface antigen) for a total of three doses on a 0-, 1- and 6-month schedule.

Usual pediatric dose

Safety and efficacy have not been established.

Usual geriatric dose

See *Usual adult dose*.

Strength(s) usually available

U.S.—
Not less than 720 enzyme linked immunosorbent assay (ELISA) units of inactivated hepatitis A virus and 20 mcg of recombinant HBsAg protein per mL (Rx) [*Twinrix* (aluminum phosphate; aluminum hydroxide; amino acids; 2–phenoxyethanol 5 mg [as a preservative]; sodium chloride; phosphate buffer; polysorbate 20; water for injection; formalin [not more than 0.1 mg]; thimerosal [<1 mcg of mercury]; residual MRC-5 cellular proteins [not more than 2.5 mcg]; neomycin sulfate [not more than 20 nanograms per dose])].

Packaging and storage

Store refrigerated between 2 and 8 °C (36 and 46 °F). Protect from freezing.

Preparation of dosage form

The vaccine should be used as supplied, and should not be diluted. The full recommended dose of the vaccine should be used. The vial should be shaken well immediately before withdrawal of the dose. In addition, thorough agitation at the time of administration is necessary to maintain suspension of the vaccine. After agitation, the vaccine is a slightly opaque, white suspension. The vaccine should be discarded if the suspension does not appear homogenous. Any vaccine remaining in the vial should be discarded.

Auxiliary labeling

- Refrigerate. Do not freeze; discard if freezing occurs.
- Shake well.

Developed: 08/22/2001

HEPATITIS B IMMUNE GLOBULIN (Human) Systemic

VA CLASSIFICATION (Primary): IM402

Commonly used brand name(s): *Nabi-HB*.

Note: For a listing of dosage forms and brand names by country availability, see *Dosage Forms* section(s).

Category

Immunizing agent (passive).

Indications

Note: Bracketed information in the *Indications* section refers to uses that are not included in U.S. product labeling.

Accepted

Hepatitis B, following percutaneous or permucosal exposure (prophylaxis)—Hepatitis B immune globulin (human) is indicated for prophylaxis of hepatitis B infection following acute exposure to hepatitis B surface antigen (HBsAg)-positive blood, plasma, or serum.

Hepatitis B, following perinatal exposure (prophylaxis)—Hepatitis B immune globulin (human) is indicated for prophylaxis of hepatitis B infection in infants born to mothers positive for HBsAg with or without hepatitis B e antigen (HBeAg).

Hepatitis B, following sexual exposure (prophylaxis)—Hepatitis B immune globulin (human) is indicated for prophylaxis of hepatitis B infection in sexual partners of HBsAg-positive persons.

Hepatitis B, following household exposure (prophylaxis)—Hepatitis B immune globulin (human) is indicated for prophylaxis of hepatitis B infection in infants less than 12 months of age whose mother or primary caregiver is positive for HBsAg and in other household contacts with an identifiable blood exposure to the index patient.

[Hepatitis B virus infection, recurrence of in liver transplant recipients (prophylaxis)]—Long-term administration of hepatitis B immune globulin (human) is indicated to prevent the recurrence of hepatitis B virus infection in liver transplant recipients.

Pharmacology/Pharmacokinetics

Physicochemical characteristics

Source—The *Nabi-HB* manufacturing process includes a solvent/detergent treatment step (using tri-n-butyl phosphate and Triton X-100) that is effective in inactivating known enveloped viruses such as hepatitis B virus (HBV), hepatitis C virus (HCV), and human immunodeficiency virus (HIV). *Nabi-HB* is filtered using a Planova 35nm Virus Filter designed to increase product safety by reducing some known enveloped and non-enveloped viruses..

pH—6.25.

Protective action

Hepatitis B immune globulin (human) products provide passive immunization for individuals exposed to the hepatitis B virus as evidenced by a reduction in the attack rate of hepatitis B following use.

Protective effect

For an infant with perinatal exposure to a hepatitis B surface antigen (HBsAg)-positive and hepatitis B e antigen (HBeAg)-positive mother, a regimen combining one dose of hepatitis B immune globulin (human) with the hepatitis B vaccine series started soon after birth is 85–98% effective in preventing development of the HBV carrier state. A regimen involving either multiple doses of hepatitis B immune globulin (human) alone or the vaccine series alone has a 70–90% efficacy, while a single dose of hepatitis B immune globulin (human) alone has 50% efficacy.

Sexual partners of HBsAg-positive persons are at increased risk of acquiring HBV infection. A single dose of hepatitis B immune globulin (human) is 75% effective if administered within two weeks of the last sexual exposure to a person with acute hepatitis B.

Distribution

Volume of distribution (Vol_D)—15.3 ± 6.2L.

Half-life

24.8 ± 5.6 days.

Time to peak concentration

Maximum concentrations of hepatitis B immune globulin (human) were reached in 6.6 ± 3 days.

Precautions to Consider

Pregnancy/Reproduction

Pregnancy—Studies in humans have not been done.

Studies in animals have not been done.

FDA Pregnancy Category C.

Breast-feeding

It is not known whether hepatitis B immune globulin (human) is distributed in human breast milk.

Pediatrics

Appropriate studies performed to date have not demonstrated pediatrics-specific problems that would limit the usefulness of hepatitis B immune globulin (human) in children.

Geriatrics

No information is available on the relationship of age to the effects of hepatitis B immune globulin in geriatric patients.

Drug interactions and/or related problems

The following drug interactions and/or related problems have been selected on the basis of their potential clinical significance (possible mechanism in parentheses where appropriate)—not necessarily inclusive (» = major clinical significance):

Note: Combinations containing any of the following medications, depending on the amount present, may also interact with this medication.

» Vaccines, live virus
(vaccination with live virus vaccines [with the exception of the oral poliovirus and yellow fever vaccines] should be deferred until approximately three months after administration of hepatitis B immune globulin (human). It may be necessary to revaccinate persons who receive hepatitis immune globulin (human) shortly after live virus vaccination)

Medical considerations/Contraindications

The medical considerations/contraindications included have been selected on the basis of their potential clinical significance (reasons given in parentheses where appropriate)—not necessarily inclusive (» = major clinical significance).

Except under special circumstances, this medication should not be used when the following medical problem exists:

» Hypersensitivity to any human immune globulin, including hepatitis B immune globulin

Risk-benefit should be considered when the following medical problems exist:

» Coagulations disorders or
» Thrombocytopenia, severe
(intramuscular injections generally are contraindicated in patients with these conditions; therefore, hepatitis B immune globulin [human] should be used only if the expected benefits outweigh the potential risks)

» Immunoglobulin A (IgA) deficiency
(individuals who are deficient in IgA may have the potential to develop IgA antibodies and have an anaphylactoid reaction)

Patient monitoring

The following may be especially important in patient monitoring (other tests may be warranted in some patients, depending on condition; » = major clinical significance):

» Antibodies, hepatitis B surface antigen
(monthly monitoring is recommended for the first 3 months of therapy to prevent early reinfection in liver transplant recipients; thereafter, monitoring should continue on a periodic, but less frequent, schedule)

Side/Adverse Effects

The following side/adverse effects have been selected on the basis of their potential clinical significance (possible signs and symptoms in parentheses where appropriate)—not necessarily inclusive:

Note: Anaphylactic reactions have occurred rarely following administration of human immune globulins. However, there have been no reports of anaphylactic reactions following administration of hepatitis B immune globulin (human).

Products made from human plasma may carry a risk of transmitting infectious agents, e.g., viruses, and theoretically, the Creutzfeldt-Jakob disease agent.

Those indicating need for medical attention only if they continue or are bothersome

Incidence more frequent

Back pain; headache; malaise (general feeling of discomfort); ***myalgia*** (muscle aches or pain); ***nausea; pain at injection site***

Incidence less frequent or rare

Abdominal cramping; ache at injection site; arthralgia (joint pain); ***burning at injection site; chills; diarrhea; erythema at injection site*** (redness of skin; unusually warm skin); ***fatigue*** (unusual tiredness or weakness); ***heat at injection site; lightheadedness; retching*** (feeling as if you are going to vomit); ***skin rash***

Patient Consultation

As an aid to patient consultation, refer to *Advice for the Patient, Hepatitis B Immune Globulin (Human) (Systemic).*

In providing consultation, consider emphasizing the following selected information (» = major clinical significance):

Before using this medication

» Conditions affecting use, especially:
- Hypersensitivity to any human immune globulin, including hepatitis B immune globulin
- Other medications, especially vaccines produced from a live virus (except the oral poliovirus and yellow fever vaccines)
- Other medical problems, especially coagulation disorders, immunoglobulin A (IgA) deficiency, or severe thrombocytopenia

Proper use of this medication

Medication preferably injected into a muscle in the upper arm or outer thigh

» Proper dosing

General Dosing Information

Hepatitis B immune globulin is indicated for intramuscular use only. The preferred site of injection in infants and neonates is the anterolateral aspect of the upper thigh. The preferred sites of injection in other patients are the anterolateral aspect of the upper thigh and the deltoid muscle of the upper arm. If the buttock must be used, the injection should be made into the outer or upper quadrant and not into the central region. To minimize the possiblity of involving the sciatic nerve, the needle should be directed anteriorly rather than inferiorly or perpendicular to the skin.

Any infections thought by a physician possibly to have been transmitted by *Nabi-HB*™ should be reported by the physician or other health care provider to Nabi at 1-800-458-4244.

For prophylaxis following percutaneous or permucosal exposure to hepatitis B

Hepatitis B immune globulin should be administered as soon as possible following exposure. The degree of efficacy is not known if the product is given more than 7 days following exposure.

For prophylaxis following perinatal exposure to hepatitis B

The degree of efficacy is not known if hepatitis B immune globulin is given more than 48 hours following birth.

Parenteral Dosage Forms

Note: Bracketed uses in the *Dosage Forms* section refer to categories of use and/or indications that are not included in U.S. product labeling.

HEPATITIS B IMMUNE GLOBULIN USP

Note: Each vial of hepatits B immune globulin is labeled with the anti-hepatitis B surface antigen (anti-HBs) activity expressed in International Units (IU) per vial. This potency assignment is referenced to the World Health Organization (WHO) standard and exceeds the potency of anti-HBs activity in a U.S. reference hepatitis B immune globulin. The U.S. reference has been tested against the WHO standard and has been found to be equal to 208 IU per mL.

Usual adult dose

Percutaneous or permucosal exposure to hepatitis B—
- For unvaccinated patients—Intramuscular, 0.06 mL per kg of body weight followed by initiation of the hepatitis B virus vaccine recombinant vaccination series.
- For vaccinated patients—Intramuscular, if tests reveal < 10 mIU per mL of anti-HBs activity, 0.06 mL per kg of body weight in addition to a hepatitis B virus vaccine recombinant booster dose.

Sexual exposure to hepatitis B—

Intramuscular, 0.06 mL per kg of body weight followed by initiation of the hepatitis B virus vaccine recombinant vaccination series within 14 days of the last sexual contact or if sexual contact with the infected person will continue.

[Prevention of hepatitis B virus infection recurrence in liver transplant recipients]—

Because various dosing protocols are used by different liver transplant centers, the medical literature should be consulted for a specific dosage regimen.

Usual pediatric dose

Perinatal exposure to hepatitis B—
- For infants of HBsAg-positive mothers—Intramuscular, 0.5 mL within the first 12 hours after birth.
- For infants of mothers not screened for HBsAg—Intramuscular, 0.5 mL as soon as possible and within the first 7 days after birth if the mother is found to be HBsAg positive.

Household exposure to hepatitis B—

Infants less than 12 months of age: Intramuscular, 0.5 mL.

Note: Infants should receive standard hepatitis B virus vaccine recombinant vaccinations regardless of their mothers' infection status.

Strength(s) usually available

U.S.—

1 mL single dose vial (greater than 312 IU) (Rx) [*Nabi-HB* (glycine 0.15 M; polysorbate 80 0.01%; sodium chloride 0.075 M)].

5 mL single dose vial (greater than 1560 IU) [*Nabi-HB* (glycine 0.15 M; polysorbate 80 0.01%; sodium chloride 0.075 M)].

Packaging and storage

Store between 2 and 8°C (36 and 46°F), in a refrigerator. Do not freeze.

Stability

Administration of hepatitis B immune globulin should begin within 6 hours after entering the vial. Partially used vials should be discarded.

Incompatibilities

It is recommended that hepatitis B immune globulin be administered at a separate site and without mixing with intravenous fluids or other medications.

Revised: 06/02/2002
Developed: 09/10/2001

HEPATITIS B VACCINE RECOMBINANT Systemic

VA CLASSIFICATION (Primary): IM100

Note: This monograph is specific to the recombinant DNA hepatitis B vaccine derived from the surface antigen of hepatitis B virus (HBsAg) and produced in yeast (*Saccharomyces cerevisiae*) cells.

Commonly used brand name(s): *Engerix-B; Recombivax HB; Recombivax HB Dialysis Formulation.*

Another commonly used name is HB vaccine.

Note: For a listing of dosage forms and brand names by country availability, see *Dosage Forms* section(s).

Category

Immunizing agent (active).

Indications

General Considerations

Hepatitis B virus (HBV) (previously known as the serum hepatitis virus) infection is a major cause of acute and chronic hepatitis, cirrhosis, and primary hepatocellular carcinoma worldwide. It is estimated that more than 200 million persons are chronically infected with HBV worldwide, and up to 80% of new liver cancer cases each year are attributable to HBV infection.

Viral hepatitis is the second most reported disease in the U.S., with hepatitis B accounting for about 45% of cases. HBV infection is a significant cause of morbidity and mortality in the U.S., and there are approximately 200,000 to 300,000 new cases of hepatitis B infection each year. Among infected persons, approximately 4000 to 5000 die each year of HBV-induced chronic liver disease or hepatocellular carcinoma. It is estimated that more than 1 million Americans have chronic HBV infection. In the U.S., most persons infected with HBV acquire the infection during adolescence or young adulthood. HBV is transmitted primarily through sexual contact, intravenous drug use, regular household contact with a chronically infected person, or occupational exposure. However, for approximately one third of persons who have acute hepatitis B, the source of infection is unknown.

Because of lifestyle, occupation, or ethnicity, certain groups have a much higher risk of hepatitis B infection than the general population. These groups include health care workers, those undergoing dialysis, persons from areas in which HBV infection is endemic, homosexual men, heterosexual persons with multiple sex partners, intravenous drug users, household contacts of HBV carriers, children of carrier mothers, and clients and staff of programs for the developmentally disabled.

In pregnancy, HBV is thought to be transmitted primarily at the time of delivery. Vertical transmission is an effective route for neonatal infection, and 10 to 85% of infants born to hepatitis B surface antigen (HBsAg)–positive mothers will become infected, depending on the hepatitis B e antigen (HBeAg) status of the mother. Morbidity and mortality rates are significant higher among infected infants than in the general newborn population, with 90% having chronic infection, and 25% of this population ultimately dying of complications of liver disease. However, 90% of infections can be prevented if HBsAg–positive mothers are identified, and their offspring are treated promptly after delivery with hepatitis B immune globulin and hepatitis B vaccine.

The Centers for Disease Control and Prevention (CDC) and the American College of Obstetricians and Gynecologists recommend adding HBsAg to routine early prenatal tests and notifying the pediatrician as soon as possible as to the HBV status of the mother so the newborn can be given HBV vaccination and hepatitis B immune globulin as appropriate.

After a person has been exposed to HBV, appropriate immunoprophylactic treatment can effectively prevent infection. The mainstay of postexposure immunoprophylaxis is hepatitis B vaccine, but in some settings the addition of hepatitis B immune globulin will provide some increase in protection.

Coinfection with HBV and human immunodeficiency virus (HIV) is common in the U.S. The two viruses are transmitted through similar routes, including sexual contact, sharing of infected needles, and exposure to infected blood products. In one study, the prevalence of HBV markers in patients with acquired immune deficiency syndrome (AIDS) was reported to be as high as 89%. These patients are at high risk of developing a chronic carrier state, viremia, and chronic hepatitis. At present, no medication therapy can reliably treat patients with chronic HBV infection. Theoretically, early identification and vaccination of high-risk groups against HBV before they acquire HIV infection should produce the best response to the vaccine. However, this strategy has not been successful, and coinfection continues to be a significant cause of morbidity and mortality in these patients.

Accepted

Hepatitis B virus infection (prophylaxis)—Hepatitis B recombinant vaccine is indicated for immunization of persons of all ages against infection caused by all subtypes of hepatitis B virus. The dialysis formulation of hepatitis B recombinant vaccine is indicated for immunization of adult predialysis and dialysis patients.

Hepatitis B recombinant vaccine is also recommended in conjunction with hepatitis B immune globulin (HBIG) for postexposure prophylaxis.

Unless otherwise contraindicated, hepatitis B recombinant vaccine is recommended for all infants (whether at high or low risk), adolescents, and persons of all ages who live in areas of high prevalence of hepatitis B infection or who are, or will be, at increased risk of infection from hepatitis B virus. The Committee on Infectious Diseases of the American Academy of Pediatrics, the Advisory Committee on Immunization Practices of the Centers for Disease Control and Prevention, and the American Academy of Family Physicians recommend that all adolescents who have not previously received three doses of hepatitis B vaccine should initiate or complete the series at the 11- to 12-year-old visit to the physician.

Examples of groups identified as being at increased risk of infection include:

- Newborn infants, including those born to HBsAg-positive mothers whether or not the infants are HBeAg-positive. The routine hepatitis B vaccination series should begin at birth for all infants. Infants of HBsAg-positive mothers should receive the first dose of vaccine along with immunoprophylaxis with hepatitis B immune globulin.
- Health care personnel. HBV infection is a major infectious occupational hazard for healthcare and public safety workers. The risk of acquiring HBV infection from occupational exposure is dependent on the frequency of percutaneous and permucosal exposures to blood or blood products. Risk is often the highest during the professional training period of medical personnel. Therefore, immunization should be completed during training in the schools of medicine, dentistry, nursing, laboratory technology, and other allied health professions before workers have their first occupational contact with human blood.
- Employees in medical facilities, such as paramedical personnel and custodial staff, who may be exposed to the virus via blood, blood products, or other patient specimens.
- Patients and staff of institutions or residential settings for the developmentally disabled. Staff who work closely with patients, and the patients themselves, should be immunized. The risk in institutional environments is associated not only with blood exposure, but also with bites and contact with skin lesions and other infective secretions.
- Staff of nonresidential day-care programs for the developmentally disabled, such as schools and sheltered workshops. Staff who have clients who are HBV carriers are at a risk of HBV infection comparable to that of health care workers. Although the risk of HBV infection to other clients appears to be lower than the risk to staff, immunization of clients is recommended if a client who is an HBV carrier is aggressive or has special medical problems that increase the risk of others exposure to his or her blood or serous secretions.
- Sexually active homosexual and bisexual males, including those with human immunodeficiency virus (HIV) infection. Sexually active homosexual and bisexual males should be immunized regardless of their age or the duration of their homosexual practices. Males should be immunized as soon as possible after their homosexual activity begins or if they anticipate initiating homosexual activity.
- Sexually active heterosexual persons with multiple sexual partners. Heterosexual persons with multiple sexual partners are at increased risk of HBV infection; the risk increases with the number of sexual partners. Immunization is recommended for prostitutes, persons with a history of multiple sexual partners in the last 6 months, and persons who have recently or repeatedly acquired other sexually transmitted diseases.
- Hemodialysis patients. Although seroconversion rates and antibody to hepatitis B surface antigen (anti-HBs) titers are lower after vaccination in hemodialysis patients than in healthy persons, for the patients who do respond, hepatitis B recombinant vaccine will protect them from HBV infection and reduce the need for frequent serologic screening.
- Patients with renal disease. Some studies have shown higher seroconversion rates and antibody titers after vaccination for patients with uremia who were immunized before they required dialysis. Therefore, it is recommended that patients be immunized early in the course of renal disease.
- Users of illicit injection drugs. Injection drug abusers should be immunized as soon as possible after drug abuse begins.
- Patients with clotting disorders who receive clotting factor concentrates. These patients are at increased risk of HBV infection and should be immunized at the time that their specific clotting disorder is identified. Preimmunization testing for HBsAg may be cost-effective in patients who have already received multiple infusions of these blood products.
- Household and sexual contacts of HBV carriers. Household contacts of HBV carriers are at high risk, and their sexual contacts appear to be at the greatest risk, of HBV infection.
- Persons accepting orphans or adoptees from countries of high or intermediate HBV endemicity. The children should be tested for HBsAg. If the children are found to be positive, the adopting family members should be immunized.
- Populations with high endemicity of HBV infection, such as Alaskan Eskimos, Pacific Islanders, Haitian and Indochinese immigrants, and refugees from HBV-endemic areas.
- Inmates of long-term correctional facilities.
- International travelers. Immunization should be considered for travelers who plan to reside abroad for more than 6 months and will have close contact with the local population in areas with high levels of endemic HBV. Immunization also should be considered for short-term travelers who are likely to have sexual contact with, or contact with blood from, members of the local population in endemic areas.
- Military personnel identified as being at increased risk.
- Morticians and embalmers.
- Police and fire department personnel. Paramedical or other personnel who render first aid or medical assistance may be exposed to the hepatitis B virus.

Hepatitis D virus infection (prophylaxis)—Since hepatitis D infection (caused by the delta hepatitis virus) can occur only in the presence of hepatitis B infection, it can be expected that hepatitis D infection will be prevented by immunization with hepatitis B recombinant vaccine.

Unaccepted

Because this vaccine protects only against infection with subtypes of hepatitis B virus (and indirectly against infection with hepatitis D virus), immunization with hepatitis B recombinant vaccine is not an indication for, and will not provide protection against, hepatitis caused by other hepatitis viruses or by other viruses known to infect the liver.

Pharmacology/Pharmacokinetics

Physicochemical characteristics

Hepatitis B recombinant vaccines are produced from *Saccharomyces cerevisiae*, into which a plasmid containing the gene for the hepatitis B surface antigen (HBsAg) has been inserted. Purified HBsAg is obtained by lysis of the yeast cells and separation of the HBsAg from the yeast components. These vaccines contain more than 95% HBsAg protein. Yeast-derived protein constitutes no more than 5% of the final product. Hepatitis B recombinant vaccines are adsorbed with aluminum hydroxide (0.5 mg per mL). No substances of human origin are used in their manufacture.

Protective effect

Well-designed clinical trials have demonstrated the efficacy of hepatitis B recombinant vaccines. Immunization reduced the incidence of hepatitis B by 90 to 95% in cohorts of homosexual men and of health care workers frequently exposed to blood. Protection is evident within weeks after the first two doses of vaccine in adults and, in large prospective studies, is correlated with anti-HBs titers above 10 milli-International Units per milliliter (mIU/mL). Pre-exposure vaccination produces protective levels of antibody in 95 to 100% of infants after three doses, in 80 to 95% after two doses, and in 20 to 50% after one dose. For infants born to HBsAg-positive mothers, the average efficacy of postexposure prophylaxis with hepatitis B recombinant vaccine and hepatitis B immune globulin to prevent chronic infection is 95%; vaccination alone and the combined regimen have similar efficacy.

Studies have revealed that the percentage of infants who develop protective levels ($\geq$ 10 mIU/mL) of antibody to HBsAg (anti-HBs) and the final anti-HBs concentrations may be lower in premature infants given the hepatitis B recombinant vaccines beginning at birth than if the initial dose is delayed until they are older or weigh more than 2000 grams. In one study, the response rates for premature infants who received their first doses of hepatitis B recombinant vaccine at a weight of either 1000 to 1999 grams or 2000 grams or more were 79% and 91% respectively; the response rate was 100% for full-term infants. The second dose was given 1 month later, and the third dose was given approximately 5 months after the first dose.

In a study of premature Thai infants with gestational ages of 28 to 32 weeks, 11 of 14 (78%) developed protective levels of anti-HBs after receiving three 10-mcg doses of hepatitis B recombinant vaccine; doses were given at birth, 1 month of age, and 6 months of age. Eleven of 11 infants with gestational ages of 33 to 37 weeks developed protective levels. The overall response rate for premature infants was 22 of 25 (88%).

A third study in Italy revealed that 37 of 37 premature infants ($<$ 37 weeks' gestation) developed anti-HBs levels of 10 mIU/mL or greater after receiving 10-mcg doses of hepatitis B recombinant vaccine at birth, 1 month of age, and 3 months of age; or at birth, 1 month of age, and 6 months of age. Lower gestational age but not lower birth weight was associated with lower final antibody concentrations.

As is seen with other vaccines, serologic response of human immunodeficiency virus (HIV)-infected patients to both plasma-derived and recombinant HBV vaccines have been suboptimal. Protective antibody responses after three doses of hepatitis B recombinant vaccine were achieved in 28% of 32 HIV-infected patients, as compared with 88% of 75 HIV-negative individuals. An additional dose given 9 months after the last of three doses led to only one additional HIV-infected patient achieving protective level. The CD4+ cell count was significantly higher in responders than in nonresponders. In addition, nonresponders were significantly more likely to progress to HIV-related diseases within 24 months than were responders.

In one study, hepatitis B recombinant vaccine was administered to 16 HIV-positive and 68 HIV-negative patients. One month after the last vaccine of the series, low or no antibody response had occurred in 44% of the HIV-positive group as compared with only 9% in the HIV-negative group.

Duration of protective effect

Long-term protection (6 to 13 years) from hepatitis B virus (HBV) infection has been shown in approximately 3700 immunized persons from populations that continue to be exposed to HBV. Vaccine-induced antibody levels may decline with age. Loss of antibody has occurred in one third of adults and 15% of infants and children. Asymptomatic infections have been identified in approximately 3% of these individuals, and HBsAg-positive infections in less than 0.5%, but not all infections were chronic. Protection against HBV infection persists even when antibody titers subsequently decline; therefore, booster doses are not necessary.

In contrast, a lower proportion (50 to 60%) of vaccinated hemodialysis patients develops a protective antibody response. Booster doses are necessary to maintain protection against hepatitis B infection when antibody titers decline below protective levels. However, more than 50% of hemodialysis patients can be protected from hepatitis B infection by vaccination, and maintaining immunity among these patients will reduce the frequency and cost of serologic screening.

Precautions to Consider

Cross-sensitivity and/or related problems

Patients sensitive to the plasma-derived hepatitis B vaccine may be sensitive to the recombinant hepatitis B vaccine also.

Pregnancy/Reproduction

Pregnancy—Adequate and well-controlled studies have not been done in humans. However, risk from vaccination is largely theoretical; there is no convincing evidence of risk from vaccinating pregnant women. Hepatitis B recombinant vaccine is recommended for pregnant women at risk of hepatitis B infection. All pregnant women should be tested for the presence of hepatitis B virus surface antigen (HBsAg), and those infected with hepatitis B virus (HBV) should be monitored carefully to ensure that the infant receives hepatitis B immune globulin and begins the hepatitis B vaccine series shortly after birth.

Studies have not been done in animals.

FDA Pregnancy Category C.

Breast-feeding

It is not known whether the vaccine is distributed into breast milk. However, the vaccine does not affect the safety of breast-feeding for mothers or infants. Breast-feeding does not adversely affect immunization, and is not a contraindication for vaccination. Breast-fed infants should be vaccinated according to the routine, recommended schedule.

Pediatrics

Note: Because infants born to HBsAg-negative women are not at immediate risk of exposure to HBV, the first dose of vaccine can be deferred. Infants born to HBsAg-positive women, however, are at immediate risk of contracting HBV infection. Immunization, together with a dose of hepatitis B immune globulin, should be given at birth and these infants should be tested for anti-HBs antibody. Infants born to mothers who have not been screened should receive the first dose of hepatitis B vaccine at birth using the dose of vaccine recommended for infants born to HBsAg-positive mothers. Subsequent management of these infants is dependent on the results of the serologic screening of the mother.

Hepatitis B recombinant vaccine has been shown to be well tolerated and highly immunogenic in infants and children of all ages. Neonates also respond well, and maternally transferred antibodies do not interfere with the active immune response to the vaccine.

No published pediatrics-specific information is available for the dialysis formulation of hepatitis B recombinant vaccine. Safety and efficacy have not been established.

Although long-term carriage of HBV in children is usually asymptomatic, it may lead to chronic hepatitis, liver cirrhosis, and hepatocellular carcinoma in later life. Many studies have demonstrated the efficacy of hepatitis B vaccine in reducing long-term carriage in neonates at high risk. The World Health Organization (WHO) has endorsed the inclusion of hepatitis B vaccine in routine childhood immunization programs, especially in areas where hepatitis B is endemic. Studies suggest that universal hepatitis B vaccination of infants in the first year of life is effective in the improvement of the endemic status of the infection.

Premature infants born to HBsAg-positive mothers should receive immunoprophylaxis with hepatitis B recombinant vaccine and hepatitis B immune globulin, beginning at birth. For premature infants of HBsAg-negative mothers, the optimal timing of hepatitis B vaccination has not been determined. Some studies suggest that decreased seroconversion rates may occur in some premature infants with low birthweight (i.e., less than 2000 grams) following administration of hepatitis B recombinant vaccine at birth. Such low-birthweight premature infants born to HBsAg-negative mothers should receive the hepatitis B vaccine series at discharge from the nursery, if the infant weighs at least 2000 grams, or at 2 months of age along with diphtheria, tetanus, and pertussis vaccine; oral poliovirus vaccine; and haemophilus b conjugate vaccine.

Adolescents

Studies have shown that hepatitis B recombinant vaccine is highly immunogenic in adolescents and young adults when administered in varying three-dose schedules. Routine vaccination of adolescents 11 to 12 years of age who have not been vaccinated previously is an effective strategy for rapidly lowering the incidence of HBV infection and its transmission in the U.S. Studies performed in Canada, and Italy indicated that universal vaccination of this age group can be highly acceptable and efficient. An adolescent's visit to a physician at 11 to 12 years of age gives the provider an opportunity to initiate protection against HBV before the adolescent begins high-risk behaviors. Unvaccinated adolescents older than 12 years of age who are at increased risk for HBV infection also should be vaccinated.

Geriatrics

Studies have shown that the adult response to hepatitis B recombinant vaccine is inversely related to age: more than 90% response in young adults, 70% in persons 50 to 59 years of age, and 50 to 70% in persons 60 years of age and over. Other geriatrics-specific problems that would limit the usefulness of this medication in the elderly are not expected.

Drug interactions and/or related problems

The following drug interactions and/or related problems have been selected on the basis of their potential clinical significance (possible mechanism in parentheses where appropriate)—not necessarily inclusive (» = major clinical significance):

Note: Combinations containing any of the following medications, depending on the amount present, may also interact with this medication.

Immunosuppressive agents or
Radiation therapy
(because normal defense mechanisms are suppressed, the patient's antibody response to hepatitis B recombinant vaccine may be decreased. Larger vaccine doses [2 to 4 times the normal adult dose] or an increased number of doses [4 doses] may be required to induce protective levels of antibody in immunocompromised persons)

Laboratory value alterations

The following have been selected on the basis of their potential clinical significance (possible effect in parentheses where appropriate)—not necessarily inclusive (» = major clinical significance).

With physiology/laboratory test values
Erythrocyte sedimentation (SED) rate
(may be increased)

Medical considerations/Contraindications

The medical considerations/contraindications included have been selected on the basis of their potential clinical significance (reasons given in parentheses where appropriate)—not necessarily inclusive (» = major clinical significance).

Except under special circumstances, this medication should not be used when the following medical problem exists:

» Previous hypersensitivity reaction to hepatitis B recombinant vaccine (rare cases of anaphylaxis [1 per 600,000 vaccine doses administered] among vaccine recipients has been reported to the Vaccine Adverse Events Reporting System [VAERS]; although none of the persons who developed anaphylaxis died, this adverse event can be fatal; in addition, hepatitis B vaccine can, in rare instances, cause a life-threatening hypersensitivity reaction in some persons; therefore, subsequent vaccination with hepatitis B vaccine is contraindicated for persons who previously had anaphylactic responses to a dose of this vaccine)

Risk-benefit should be considered when the following medical problems exist:

Allergy to yeast
(hepatitis B recombinant vaccine is produced using yeast; a maximum of 1 or 5%, depending on the manufacturer, of yeast-derived protein may be present in the final vaccine; although there have not been any proven allergic reactions to the yeast, the possibility exists that they may occur)

Cardiopulmonary status, severely compromised
(a febrile or systemic reaction to the vaccine could pose a significant risk to persons with this condition)

Illness, moderate or severe, with or without fever
(administration of the vaccine should be delayed, except when withholding the vaccine entails a greater risk to the patient than a possible superimposed reaction to the vaccine)

Immune deficiency conditions
(antibody response to hepatitis B recombinant vaccine may be decreased; larger vaccine doses [2 to 4 times the normal adult dose] or an increased number of doses [4 doses] may be required to induce protective levels of antibody in immunocompromised persons)

Side/Adverse Effects

Note: In the U.S., an estimated 2.5 million adults received one or more doses of hepatitis B recombinant vaccine between 1986 and 1990, and available data concerning these vaccinees do not indicate an association between receipt of hepatitis B recombinant vaccine and Guillain-Barré syndrome (GBS). Moreover, large-scale hepatitis B immunization programs for infants in Alaska, New Zealand, and Taiwan have not established an association between vaccination and the occurrence of GBS. However, systematic surveillance for adverse reactions in these populations has been limited, and only a minimal number of children have received the recombinant vaccine. Any presumed risk for adverse events that could be causally associated with hepatitis B vaccination must be balanced against the expected risk for hepatitis B virus (HBV)-related liver disease. Currently, an estimated 2000 to 5000 persons in each U.S. birth cohort will die as a result of HBV–related liver disease because of the 5% lifetime risk for HBV infection.

Agitation, conjunctivitis, constipation, erythrocyte sedimentation rate increase, hepatic enzyme elevation, herpes zoster, hypesthesia, irritability, keratitis, migraine, myelitis, petechiae, radiculopathy, somnolence, Stevens-Johnson syndrome, syncope, tachycardia, thrombocytopenia, tinnitus, and visual disturbances also have been reported in temporal association with administration of hepatitis B recombinant vaccine, but their relationship to the vaccine is unclear.

The following side/adverse effects have been selected on the basis of their potential clinical significance (possible signs and symptoms in parentheses where appropriate)—not necessarily inclusive:

Those indicating need for medical attention

Incidence rare

Anaphylactic reaction (difficulty in breathing or swallowing; hives; itching, especially of feet or hands; reddening of skin, especially around ears; swelling of eyes, face, or inside of nose; unusual tiredness or weakness, sudden and severe); ***neuropathy*** (muscle weakness or numbness or tingling of limbs); ***optic neuritis*** (blurred vision or other vision changes); ***serum sickness-like reaction*** (aches or pain in joints, fever, or skin rash or welts)—may occur days or weeks following administration of the vaccine

Those indicating need for medical attention only if they continue or are bothersome

Incidence more frequent

Soreness at injection site—20 to 30%

Incidence less frequent (1 to 10% frequency)

Fatigue (unusual tiredness or weakness); ***fever of 37.7 °C (100 °F) or over; headache; induration*** (hard lump); ***erythema*** (redness); ***swelling; pain; pruritus*** (itching); ***ecchymosis*** (purple spot); ***tenderness; or warmth at injection site; vertigo*** (dizziness)

Incidence rare (less than 1% frequency)

Anorexia (lack of appetite); ***or decreased appetite; arthralgia, arthritis, or myalgia*** (aches or pain in joints or muscles); ***back pain; chills; diarrhea or abdominal cramps or pain*** (stomach cramps or pain); ***flushing*** (sudden redness of skin); ***hypotension*** (unusual tiredness or weakness); ***increased sweating; influenza-like symptoms or upper respiratory tract illness*** (headache, sore throat, runny nose, or fever); ***insomnia or sleep disturbance*** (trouble in sleeping); ***lymphadenopathy*** (swelling of glands in armpit or neck); ***malaise*** (general feeling of discomfort or illness); ***nausea or vomiting; nodule at injection site*** (lump at place of injection)—probably from the aluminum content of the vaccine and may persist for a few weeks; ***pruritus*** (itching); ***skin rash; or urticaria*** (welts); ***stiffness or pain in neck or shoulder***

Patient Consultation

As an aid to patient consultation, refer to *Advice for the Patient, Hepatitis B Vaccine Recombinant (Systemic).*

In providing consultation, consider emphasizing the following selected information (» = major clinical significance):

Before receiving this vaccine

» Conditions affecting use, especially:

Hypersensitivity to plasma-derived hepatitis B vaccine or recombinant hepatitis B vaccine or allergy to yeast

Use in the elderly—Compared with younger adults, persons over 50 years of age may be less likely to develop a protective antibody level following immunization with hepatitis B recombinant vaccine

Proper use of this medication

» Proper dosing

Side/adverse effects

Signs of potential side effects, especially anaphylactic reaction, neuropathy, optic neuritis, or serum sickness-like reaction

General Dosing Information

Although systemic reactions to hepatitis B recombinant vaccine are rare, anaphylaxis among vaccine recipients has been reported to the Vaccine Adverse Events Reporting System (VAERS). Therefore, appropriate precautions should be taken prior to hepatitis B recombinant vaccine injection to prevent allergic or any other unwanted reactions. Precautions should include review of the patient's history regarding possible sensitivity and the ready availability of 1:1000 epinephrine injection and other appropriate agents used for control of immediate allergic reactions.

Only persons who have not been infected with hepatitis B virus (HBV) previously need to be immunized with hepatitis B recombinant vaccine. Therefore, as a cost-effective measure, testing for prior HBV infection should be considered for adults in groups having a high prevalence of HBV infection (e.g., users of injection drugs, homosexual men, and household contacts of HBV carriers). If the group to be tested is also expected to have a high prevalence of carriers, it may be preferable to test for antibody to hepatitis B core antigen (anti-HBc), since this test identifies previously infected persons, both carriers and noncarriers. If the group to be tested is not expected to have a high rate of carriers, the test for antibody to hepatitis B surface antigen (anti-HBs) will be adequate, since this test identifies previously infected persons, except for carriers.

There is no harm but also no proven benefit in immunizing those already infected with HBV. Recent claims of a therapeutic response in carriers of hepatitis B surface antigen (HBsAg) have not been confirmed.

Although the dosages are different for the products of different manufacturers, the resulting immunogenicity of each is comparable. An immunization schedule started with one manufacturer's vaccine and dose may be completed with the other manufacturer's vaccine and dose. However, in the dialysis setting, the two vaccines should not be used interchangeably.

Because of the long incubation period of HBV, unrecognized infection may be present at the time of immunization; the vaccine may not prevent hepatitis B in already-infected patients.

Passively acquired antibody, whether acquired by administration of immune globulins or via the transplacental route, will not interfere with active immunization with hepatitis B recombinant vaccine. In addition, there is no interference with the induction of protective antibodies elicited by hepatitis B recombinant vaccine when hepatitis B immune globulin (HBIG) is administered at the same time at different body sites.

The Committee on Infectious Diseases of the American Academy of Pediatrics, the Advisory Committee on Immunization Practices of the Centers for Disease Control and Prevention, and the American Academy of Family Physicians offer the following recommendations for the use of hepatitis B recombinant vaccine among infants, children, and adolescents:

- Infants born to HBsAg-negative mothers should receive 2.5 mcg *Recombivax HB* or 10 mcg *Engerix-B*. A second dose should be administered 1 or more months after the first dose.
- Infants born to HBsAg-positive mothers should receive 0.5 mL HBIG within 12 hours of birth, and either 5 mcg *Recombivax HB* or 10 mcg *Engerix-B* at a separate injection site. A second dose should be administered at 1 to 2 months of age and a third dose at 6 months of age.
- Infants born to mothers whose HBsAg status is unknown should receive either 5 mcg *Recombivax HB* or 10 mcg *Engerix-B* within 12 hours of birth. A second dose should be administered at 1 month of age and a third dose at 6 months of age.
- Adolescents who have not previously received three doses of hepatitis B vaccine should initiate or complete the series at the 11- to 12-year-old visit to the physician. A second dose should be administered at least 1 month after the first dose, and a third dose should be administered at least 4 months after the first dose, and at least 2 months after the second dose.

If within 7 days after delivery, a mother of unknown HBsAg status is found to be HBsAg positive, the infant should receive HBIG immediately. In addition, immunization with the appropriate dosage of hepatitis B recombinant vaccine should be initiated or continued. If hepatitis B recombinant vaccine and HBIG are administered at the same time, they should be administered in the anterolateralaspects of opposite thighs. If a mother of unknown HBsAg status is found not to be HBsAg-positive, the infant should complete the immunization series with the appropriate dosage of hepatitis B recombinant vaccine.

For known or presumed exposure to the hepatitis B virus, HBIG should be administered according to its directions as soon as possible after exposure and within 24 hours if possible. (HBIG's value if given later than 7 days after exposure is unclear; in addition, the period after sexual exposure to HBV during which HBIG is effective is unknown, but extrapolation from other data suggests that this period does not exceed 14 days.) In addition, hepatitis B recombinant vaccine should be administered at a separate body site, using one of the following dosage schedules and the dosage that applies to it:

- If using *Recombivax HB*—At the same time as HBIG or within 7 days after exposure, then 1 month and 6 months after the first dose, for a total of three doses.
- If using *Engerix-B*—
  —At the same time as HBIG or within 7 days after exposure, then 1 month and 6 months after the first dose, for a total of three doses.
  —Alternatively, at the same time as HBIG or within 7 days after exposure, then 1 month, 2 months, and 12 months after the first dose, for a total of four doses.
- If the exposed person has begun, but not completed, immunization with hepatitis B recombinant vaccine, HBIG should be given as usual, and immunization with the vaccine should be completed as scheduled.

For travelers: Ideally, immunization with hepatitis B recombinant vaccine should begin at least 6 months before travel to allow completion of the full three-dose vaccine series (given at 0, 1, and 6 months). However, if there is less time available before travel than a full 6 months, the first three doses of an alternative four-dose schedule (given at 0, 1, 2, and 12 months) may provide earlier protection during travel if the doses can be administered before travel begins.

Although the alternative four-dose schedule (given at 0, 1, 2, and 12 months)(*Engerix-B*) provides a more rapid induction of immunity, there is no clear evidence that this schedule provides greater long-term protection than the standard three-dose schedule (given at 0, 1, and 6 months).

Vaccine doses administered at longer-than-recommended intervals (recommended intervals being 0, 1, and 6 months) provide equally satisfactory protection. However, optimal protection is not conferred until after the third dose. If the vaccine series is interrupted after the first dose, the second dose should be given as soon as possible, followed by the third dose 3 to 5 months later. Persons who receive the third dose later than 6 months after the initial dose should be given the third dose as soon as is practical. In healthy persons it is not considered necessary to perform postvaccination testing to ensure an adequate antibody response, in either of the above situations.

When sterilizing syringes and skin before vaccination, care should be taken to avoid contact of the vaccine with preservatives, antiseptics, detergents, and disinfectants, since the vaccine virus particles may be easily denatured by these substances.

The hepatitis B recombinant vaccine should be administered by intramuscular (IM) injection. The needle should be of sufficient length and bore to reach the muscle mass itself and to prevent vaccine from seeping into subcutaneous tissue. For adults, the suggested needle length is 1½ inches. For children, a 20- or 22-gauge needle 1 to 1¼ inches long is recommended. For small infants, a 25-gauge needle 5/8 inch long may be adequate. However, for persons at risk of hemorrhage following IM injections, the vaccine may be administered subcutaneously, although the subsequent antibody titer may be lower and there may be an increased risk of local reactions. The vaccine should not be administered intravenously or intradermally.

The deltoid muscle (outer aspect of the upper arm) is the recommended site for the immunization of adults and older children. For infants and young children, the anterolateral aspect of the thigh muscle is the recommended site. The vaccine should not be administered in the gluteal region (buttock), because the immunogenicity of the vaccine is substantially lowered.

The 40 mcg/mL strength (*Recombivax HB Dialysis Formulation*) is given in a three-dose regimen, with a total of three doses required. The 20 mcg/mL strength (*Engerix-B*) requires either one 2-mL injection or two separate 1-mL injections during a four-dose regimen for a total of either four or eight injections.

Larger vaccine doses (2 to 4 times the normal adult dose) or an increased number of doses (4 doses) may be necessary for immunocompromised persons (such as those on immunosuppressive medications or with human immunodeficiency virus [HIV] infection). However, although persons with HIV infection have an impaired response to hepatitis B recombinant vaccine, the immunogenicity of higher doses of the vaccine in these persons is unknown, and specific recommendations on dosage are not available.

Although postimmunization testing for serologic response and immunity is not routinely recommended, it is recommended for the following:

- Persons whose subsequent management depends on knowledge of their immune status, such as dialysis patients, medical staff, and infants born to HBsAg-positive mothers.
- Persons in whom a less-than-optimal response may be anticipated, such as those who were administered the vaccine in the buttock or subcutaneously, persons over 50 years of age, and persons with HIV infection or other immune deficiencies.
- Persons at occupational risk who may have HBV exposures necessitating postexposure prophylaxis.
- Postimmunization testing should be done 1 to 6 months after completion of the immunization series to provide definitive information on the response to the vaccine.

• Reimmunization of persons who did not originally respond to the primary series produces adequate antibody response in 15 to 25% after 1 additional dose and in 30 to 50% after 3 additional doses, when the original immunization was administered in the deltoid muscle. Data suggest that in more than 75% of persons who did not adequately respond to a primary vaccine series given in the buttock, reimmunization in the arm induces adequate antibody response.

In adult predialysis and dialysis patients, hepatitis B recombinant vaccine–induced protection is less complete and may persist only as long as antibody levels remain at or above 10 milliInternational Units (mIU) per mL. The need for additional doses of the vaccine should be assessed by annual antibody testing. It is recommended that additional doses of 40 mcg of hepatitis B recombinant vaccine be given when antibody levels decline to below 10 mIU per mL.

Hepatitis B recombinant vaccine, an inactivated product, can be administered concurrently with the following, using separate body sites (in infants, selecting separate sites in the same anterolateral aspect of the thigh muscle is preferable to administering hepatitis B recombinant vaccine in the buttock or deltoid muscle), separate syringes (for parenterals), and the precautions that apply to each immunizing agent:

• Polysaccharide vaccines, such as haemophilus b conjugate vaccine, haemophilus b polysaccharide vaccine, meningococcal polysaccharide vaccine, or pneumococcal polyvalent vaccine.
• Influenza virus vaccine, whole or split virus.
• Diphtheria toxoid, tetanus toxoid, and/or pertussis (whole cell or acellular) vaccine.
• Live virus vaccines, such as measles, mumps, and/or rubella vaccines.
• Poliovirus vaccines (oral [OPV], inactivated [IPV], or enhanced-potency inactivated [enhanced-potency IPV]).
• Immune globulin and disease-specific immune globulins.
• Inactivated vaccines, other, except cholera, typhoid (parenteral), and plague. It is recommended that cholera, typhoid (parenteral), and plague vaccines be administered on separate occasions because of these vaccines' propensity to cause side/adverse effects.

For treatment of adverse effects

Recommended treatment includes:

• For mild hypersensitivity reaction—Administering antihistamines, and, if necessary, corticosteroids. In mild anaphylaxis, antihistamines or subcutaneous epinephrine may be all that is necessary if the condition is progressing slowly and is not life-threatening, regardless of the organ or system affected. Under these circumstances the risks associated with intravenous epinephrine administration outweigh the benefits.
• For severe hypersensitivity or anaphylactic reaction—Administering epinephrine. Antihistamines or corticosteroids may also be administered as required. Epinephrine is the treatment of choice for severe hypersensitivity or anaphylactic reaction. If the patient's condition is not stable, epinephrine should be infused. Norepinephrine may be preferable if there is no bronchospasm. For bronchospasm, epinephrine should be given with corticosteroids. Other bronchodilators, such as intravenous aminophylline or albuterol by nebulization, also should be considered.

Parenteral Dosage Forms

STERILE HEPATITIS B VACCINE RECOMBINANT SUSPENSION

Usual adult and adolescent dose

Immunizing agent (active)—

Adolescents 11 to 19 years of age: Intramuscular, into the deltoid muscle, 5 mcg (*Recombivax HB*—U.S. and Canada), or 10 mcg (*Recombivax HB*—Canada), or 20 mcg (*Engerix-B*—U.S. and Canada), at initial visit, then one month and six months after the first dose, for a total of three doses.

Adults 19 years of age and older: Intramuscular, into the deltoid muscle, 10 mcg (*Recombivax HB*—U.S. and Canada) or 20 mcg (*Engerix-B*—U.S. and Canada), at initial visit, then one month and six months after the first dose, for a total of three doses.

Adult predialysis and dialysis patients—Intramuscular, into the deltoid muscle, 40 mcg (*Recombivax HB Dialysis Formulation*—U.S. and Canada), at initial visit, then one month and six months after the first dose, for a total of three doses;

or

40 mcg (*Engerix-B*—U.S. and Canada), at initial visit, then one month, two months, and six months after the first dose, for a total of four doses. The 20 mcg/mL strength (*Engerix-B*) requires either one 2-mL injection or two separate 1-mL injections during a four-dose regimen for a total of either four or eight injections.

Usual pediatric dose

Immunizing agent (active)—

Neonates born to hepatitis B surface antigen (HBsAg)-positive mothers: Intramuscular, into the anterolateral aspect of the thigh—5 mcg (*Recombivax HB*—U.S. and Canada), 10 mcg (*Engerix-B*—U.S. and Canada), within twelve hours after birth (preferably) or within seven days after birth, then one month and six months after the first dose, for a total of three doses;

10 mcg (*Engerix-B*—U.S. and Canada), within twelve hours after birth (preferably) or within seven days after birth, then one month, two months, and twelve months after the first dose, for a total of four doses.

Neonates born to mothers of unknown HBsAg status: Intramuscular, into the anterolateral aspect of the thigh: 5 mcg (*Recombivax HB*—U.S.), 10 mcg (*Engerix-B*—U.S. and Canada), within twelve hours after birth (preferably) or within seven days after birth, then:

Infants of mothers subsequently determined to be HBsAg-positive—

5 mcg (*Recombivax HB*—U.S.), 10 mcg (*Engerix-B*—U.S. and Canada), one month and six months after the first dose, for a total of three doses;

10 mcg (*Engerix-B*—U.S. and Canada), one month, two months, and twelve months after the first dose, for a total of four doses.

Infants of mothers subsequently determined to be HBsAg-negative—

2.5 mcg (*Recombivax HB*—U.S.), 10 mcg (*Engerix-B*—U.S. and Canada), one month and six months after the first dose, for a total of three doses.

Neonates born to HBsAg-negative mothers or

Infants and children up to 11 years of age: Intramuscular, into the anterolateral aspect of the thigh for neonates, infants, and young children and into the deltoid muscle for older children, 2.5 mcg (*Recombivax HB*—U.S. and Canada), 10 mcg (*Engerix-B*—U.S. and Canada), at initial visit, then one month and six months after the first dose, for a total of three doses.

Note: Physicians have a great deal of flexibility in scheduling the three-dose immunization series for full-term infants born to HBsAg-negative mothers. The recommended schedule is to give the first dose during the neonatal period or by two months of age, the second dose one to two months later, and the third dose at six to eighteen months of age. The vaccines, however, are highly immunogenic when given according to other schedules. Although the highest titers of anti-HBs are achieved when the last two doses of vaccine are spaced four months apart or longer, schedules with two-month intervals between doses have been shown to produce high rates of seroconversion. Some pediatricians have adopted other three-dose schedules in order to minimize the number of simultaneous injections. Schedules with intervals of up to ten months between the second and the third doses have been shown to be highly effective. Intervals longer than two months between the first two doses or more than one year between the second and the third dose have not been evaluated in controlled trials. The American Academy of Pediatrics currently recommends that children of all ages for whom a longer time than recommended has elapsed between doses of hepatitis B vaccine can complete the series without repeating a dose or starting the series over.

Strength(s) usually available

U.S.—

2.5 mcg (0.0025 mg) of hepatitis B surface antigen (HBsAg) protein per 0.5 mL (Rx) [*Recombivax HB* (0.25 mg aluminum as aluminum hydroxide; thimerosal 1:20,000)].

5 mcg (0.005 mg) of HBsAg protein per 0.5 mL (Rx) [*Recombivax HB* (0.25 mg aluminum as aluminum hydroxide; thimerosal 1:20,000)].

10 mcg (0.01 mg) of HBsAg protein per mL (Rx) [*Recombivax HB* (0.5 mg aluminum as aluminum hydroxide; thimerosal 1:20,000)].

10 mcg (0.01 mg) of HBsAg protein per 0.5 mL (Rx) [*Engerix-B* (0.25 mg aluminum as aluminum hydroxide; thimerosal 1:20,000)].

20 mcg (0.02 mg) of HBsAg protein per mL (Rx) [*Engerix-B* (0.5 mg aluminum as aluminum hydroxide; thimerosal 1:20,000)].

40 mcg (0.04 mg) of HBsAg protein per mL (Rx) [*Recombivax HB Dialysis Formulation* (0.5 mg aluminum as aluminum hydroxide; thimerosal 1:20,000)].

Canada—

5 mcg (0.005 mg) of HBsAg protein per 0.5 mL (Rx) [*Recombivax HB* (alum adjuvant; thimerosal 1:20,000)].

10 mcg (0.01 mg) of HBsAg protein per mL (Rx) [*Recombivax HB* (alum adjuvant; thimerosal 1:20,000)].

10 mcg (0.01 mg) of HBsAg protein per mL (Rx) [*Engerix-B* (0.25 mg aluminum as aluminum hydroxide; thimerosal 1:20,000)].

20 mcg (0.02 mg) of HBsAg protein per mL (Rx) [*Engerix-B* (0.5 mg aluminum as aluminum hydroxide; thimerosal 1:20,000)].

40 mcg (0.04 mg) of HBsAg protein per mL (Rx) [*Recombivax HB Dialysis Formulation* (thimerosal 1:20,000)].

Packaging and storage

Store between 2 and 8 °C (36 and 46 °F), unless otherwise specified by manufacturer. Protect from freezing.

Preparation of dosage form

The vaccine should be used as supplied, and should not be diluted. The vial should be shaken well immediately before withdrawal of the dose. In addition, thorough agitation at the time of administration is necessary to maintain suspension of the vaccine. After agitation, the vaccine is a slightly opaque, white suspension.

Stability

Storage above or below the recommended temperature may reduce potency. Freezing destroys potency, and the vaccine should be discarded if freezing occurs.

Auxiliary labeling

- Do not freeze; discard if freezing occurs.
- Shake well.

Revised: 06/20/1997

HISTAMINE H_2-RECEPTOR ANTAGONISTS Systemic

This monograph includes information on the following: 1) Cimetidine; 2) Famotidine; 3) Nizatidine; 4) Ranitidine.

VA CLASSIFICATION (Primary/Secondary):
Cimetidine—GA301/DE890
Famotidine—GA301
Nizatidine—GA301
Ranitidine—GA301

Commonly used brand name(s): *Acid Control*[2]; *Act*[2]; *Alti-Ranitidine*[4]; *Apo-Cimetidine*[1]; *Apo-Famotidine*[2]; *Apo-Nizatidine*[3]; *Apo-Ranitidine*[4]; *Axid*[3]; *Axid AR*[3]; *Dyspep HB*[2]; *Fluxid*[2]; *Gen-Cimetidine*[1]; *Gen-Famotidine*[2]; *Gen-Ranitidine*[4]; *Maalox H2 Acid Controller*[2]; *Mylanta AR Acid Reducer*[2]; *Novo-Cimetine*[1]; *Novo-Famotidine*[2]; *Novo-Ranitidine*[4]; *Nu-Cimet*[1]; *Nu-Famotidine*[2]; *Nu-Ranit*[4]; *PMS-Cimetidine*[1]; *Pepcid*[2]; *Pepcid AC*[2]; *Pepcid AC Acid Controller*[2]; *Pepcid I.V.*[2]; *Pepcid RPD*[2]; *Peptol*[1]; *Tagamet*[1]; *Tagamet HB*[1]; *Tagamet HB 200*[1]; *Ulcidine*[2]; *Ulcidine-HB*[2]; *Zantac*[4]; *Zantac 150*[4]; *Zantac 150 EFFERdose Tablets*[4]; *Zantac 25 EFFERdose Tablets*[4]; *Zantac 300*[4]; *Zantac 75*[4].

Note: For a listing of dosage forms and brand names by country availability, see *Dosage Forms* section(s).

Category

Histamine H_2-receptor antagonist—All drugs in this monograph are used as histamine H_2-receptor antagonists.

Antiulcer agent—All drugs in this monograph are used as antiulcer agents.

Gastric acid secretion inhibitor—All drugs in this monograph are used as gastric acid secretion inhibitors.

Urticaria therapy adjunct—Cimetidine.

Indications

Note: Bracketed information in the *Indications* section refers to uses that are not included in U.S. product labeling.

Accepted

Ulcer, duodenal (prophylaxis and treatment)—Histamine H_2-receptor antagonists are indicated in the short-term treatment of active duodenal ulcer. They are also indicated (at reduced dosage) in the prevention of duodenal ulcer recurrence in selected patients.

Ulcer, gastric (treatment)—Cimetidine, famotidine, nizatidine, and ranitidine are indicated in the short-term treatment of active benign gastric ulcer.

Ulcer, gastric (prophylaxis)—Cimetidine and ranitidine are indicated (at reduced dosage) in the prevention of gastric ulcer recurrence after the healing of acute ulcers.

Heartburn, acid indigestion, and sour stomach associated with hyperacidity (prophylaxis and treatment)—Nonprescription strengths of the histamine H_2-receptor antagonists cimetidine, famotidine, and ranitidine are indicated for relief of symptoms associated with hyperacidity, including heartburn, acid indigestion, and sour stomach. Nonprescription strengths of cimetidine, famotidine, nizatidine, and ranitidine are also indicated in prevention of hyperacidity symptoms brought on by the consumption of food or beverages.

Hypersecretory conditions, gastric (treatment)
Zollinger-Ellison syndrome (treatment)
Mastocytosis, systemic (treatment) or
Adenoma, multiple endocrine (treatment)—Cimetidine, famotidine, [nizatidine][1], and ranitidine are indicated in the treatment of pathological gastric hypersecretion associated with Zollinger-Ellison syndrome (alone or as part of multiple endocrine neoplasia Type-1), systemic mastocytosis, and multiple endocrine adenoma.

Gastroesophageal reflux disease [GERD] (treatment)—Cimetidine, famotidine, nizatidine[1], and ranitidine are indicated in the treatment of acute gastroesophageal reflux disease, which may or may not cause erosive or ulcerative esophagitis.

[Pancreatic insufficiency (treatment adjunct)][1]—Cimetidine is used to enhance pancreatic replacement by reducing peptic acid deactivation and to enhance the efficacy of orally administered pancreatic enzymes in patients with pancreatic insufficiency by reducing the secretion of hydrochloric acid. However, the efficacy of cimetidine in acute pancreatitis has not been established, and some studies have demonstrated that cimetidine may increase and prolong hyperamylasemia.

Bleeding, upper gastrointestinal (treatment)—Cimetidine, [famotidine][1], and [ranitidine] are used to treat upper gastrointestinal bleeding secondary to gastric ulcer, duodenal ulcer, or hemorrhagic gastritis.

Stress-related mucosal damage (prophylaxis and treatment)—[Parenteral ranitidine] is used to prevent and treat and parenteral cimetidine is indicated to prevent and used to treat upper gastrointestinal, stress-induced ulceration and bleeding, especially in intensive care patients. However, the efficacy of histamine H_2-receptor antagonists in treating hemorrhage in critically ill patients has not been established.

[Pneumonitis, aspiration (prophylaxis)]—Cimetidine, ranitidine, and famotidine also are used before anesthesia induction for the prophylaxis of aspiration pneumonitis.

Arthritis, rheumatoid (treatment adjunct)—[Cimetidine] and [ranitidine][1] are used for the relief of gastrointestinal symptoms associated with the use of nonsteroidal anti-inflammatory drugs in the treatment of rheumatoid arthritis.

[Urticaria, acute (treatment adjunct)][1]—Cimetidine is used in combination with an antihistamine to treat acute urticaria.

[1]Not included in Canadian product labeling.

Pharmacology/Pharmacokinetics

See *Table 1*, page 1584.

See *Table 2*, page 1585.

Physicochemical characteristics

Molecular weight—
Cimetidine: 252.34.
Famotidine: 337.43.
Nizatidine: 331.45.
Ranitidine: 350.87.

pKa—
Cimetidine: 7.09.
Cimetidine hydrochloride: 7.11.
Ranitidine: 8.2 and 2.7.

Mechanism of action/Effect

H_2-receptor antagonists inhibit basal and nocturnal gastric acid secretion by competitive inhibition of the action of histamine at the histamine H_2-receptors of the parietal cells. They also inhibit gastric acid secretion stimulated by food, betazole, pentagastrin, caffeine, insulin, and physiological vagal reflex.

Urticaria therapy adjunct—Cimetidine blocks H_2-receptors, which in part are responsible for the inflammatory response, in the cutaneous blood vessels of humans.

Other actions/effects

Cimetidine—Inhibits hepatic cytochrome P450 and P448 mixed function oxidase (microsomal enzyme) systems; antagonizes dihydrotestosterone (antiandrogenic action); produces transient and clinically insignificant increases in prolactin concentrations (with intravenous bolus administration only). May enhance gastromucosal defense and healing in acid-related disorders, particularly stress-induced ulceration and bleeding, by increasing production of gastric mucus, content of mucus glycoprotein, mucosal secretion of bicarbonate, gastric mucosal blood flow, endogenous mucosal prostaglandin synthesis, and rate of epithelial cell renewal.

Famotidine—Weak inhibitor of hepatic cytochrome P450 mixed function oxidase system.

Nizatidine—Weak inhibitor of hepatic cytochrome P450 mixed function oxidase system.

Ranitidine—Weak inhibitor of hepatic cytochrome P450 mixed function oxidase system; produces small, transient, and clinically insignificant increases in serum prolactin concentrations (reported with intravenous bolus administration of 100 mg or more).

Distribution

All H_2-receptor antagonists are distributed in breast milk and cerebrospinal fluid.

Onset of action

Famotidine—Oral: 1 hour.

Precautions to Consider

Cross-sensitivity and/or related problems

Patients sensitive to one of the histamine H_2-receptor antagonists may be sensitive to the other histamine H_2-receptor antagonists also.

Carcinogenicity/Mutagenicity/Tumorigenicity

It is not known whether the histamine H_2-receptor antagonists are carcinogenic or mutagenic in humans.

For cimetidine—Long-term toxicity studies in rats have shown a significantly higher incidence of benign Leydig cell tumors in cimetidine-treated groups than in controls at doses approximately 8 to 48 times the recommended human dose.

For famotidine—Studies in rats and mice with oral doses approximately 2500 times the recommended human dose showed no evidence of carcinogenicity. Results of the Ames test were negative. Studies in mice with a micronucleus test and a chromosomal aberration test showed no evidence of mutagenicity.

For nizatidine—Studies in rats and mice with oral doses many times the recommended human dose showed no evidence of carcinogenicity.

For ranitidine—Long-term studies in mice and rats with doses up to 2 grams per kg of body weight have not shown ranitidine to be carcinogenic.

Pregnancy/Reproduction

Fertility—For cimetidine: There has been no evidence of impaired mating performance or fertility in rats, rabbits, and mice at doses 40 times the human dose.

For famotidine: Studies in rats and rabbits with oral doses of up to 2000 and 500 mg per kg of body weight (mg/kg) per day, respectively, have not shown that famotidine impairs fertility.

For nizatidine: Studies in rats and rabbits with oral doses up to 300 and 55 times the human dose, respectively, have not shown that nizatidine impairs fertility.

For ranitidine: Studies in rats and rabbits at doses up to 160 times the human dose have not shown that ranitidine impairs fertility.

Pregnancy—

For cimetidine—

Adequate and well-controlled studies in humans have not been done.

Animal studies have shown that cimetidine crosses the placenta. Also, a study in rats exposed to cimetidine during intrauterine life and the immediate neonatal period showed a hypoandrogenization in adult life with decreased weights of androgen-dependent tissues and decreased concentrations of testosterone.

FDA Pregnancy Category B.

For famotidine—

Famotidine crosses the placenta. Adequate and well-controlled studies in humans have not been done.

Studies in rats and rabbits with oral doses of up to 2000 and 500 mg/kg per day, respectively, have not shown that famotidine has adverse effects on the fetus. Rabbits displaying a markedly decreased food intake at doses of 250 times the usual human dose experienced sporadic abortions.

FDA Pregnancy Category B.

For nizatidine—

Nizatidine crosses the placenta. Adequate and well-controlled studies in humans have not been done.

Rabbits treated with a dose equivalent to 300 times the human dose had abortions, a decreased number of live fetuses, and depressed fetal weights.

FDA Pregnancy Category B.

For ranitidine—

Ranitidine crosses the placenta. Adequate and well-controlled studies in humans have not been done.

Studies in rats and rabbits at doses up to 160 times the human dose have not shown that ranitidine causes adverse effects on the fetus.

FDA Pregnancy Category B.

Breast-feeding

Problems in humans have not been documented; however, cimetidine, famotidine, nizatidine, and ranitidine are distributed into breast milk and possibly could suppress gastric acidity, inhibit drug metabolism, and cause central nervous system (CNS) stimulation in the nursing infant. It has been found that very high acute and chronic milk/plasma ratios occur with the use of cimetidine; therefore, the Committee on Drugs of the American Academy of Pediatrics has recommended that cimetidine not be taken by mothers while they are breast-feeding. Although, at present, data for ranitidine are insufficient, it appears that high milk/plasma ratios may also occur with ingestion of ranitidine.

Pediatrics

For cimetidine—Studies performed to date have not demonstrated pediatrics-specific problems that would limit the usefulness of cimetidine in children for short-term (6 to 8 weeks) use. Cimetidine has been used for long-term treatment of chronic gastroesophageal reflux disease in children; however, cimetidine-induced cerebral toxicity and reported cimetidine effects on the hormonal system in adults may be of concern with long-term use in children.

For famotidine—Studies performed to date have not demonstrated pediatrics-specific problems that would limit the usefulness of famotidine in pediatric patients 6 to 16 years of age.

For nizatidine—Appropriate studies have not been performed in children up to 16 years of age.

For ranitidine—Studies performed to date have not demonstrated pediatrics-specific problems that would limit the usefulness of famotidine in pediatric patients one month and older. Safety and effectiveness in neonates less than one month of age have not been established.

Geriatrics

For cimetidine, famotidine, and ranitidine—Although appropriate studies on the relationship of age to the effects of these medicines have not been performed in the geriatric population, no geriatrics-specific problems have been documented to date. However, confusion is more likely to occur in elderly patients with impaired hepatic or renal function.

For nizatidine—Studies performed to date have not demonstrated geriatrics-specific problems that would limit the usefulness of nizatidine in the elderly.

Drug interactions and/or related problems

The following drug interactions and/or related problems have been selected on the basis of their potential clinical significance (possible mechanism in parentheses where appropriate)—not necessarily inclusive (» = major clinical significance):

Note: Only specific interactions between histamine H_2-receptor antagonists and other medications have been identified in this monograph. However, histamine H_2-receptor antagonists, by increasing gastric pH, have the potential to affect the bioavailability of those medications and dosage forms (e.g., enteric-coated) whose absorption is pH-dependent. Also, histamine H_2-receptor antagonists may prevent the degradation of acid-labile drugs.

In addition, because of cimetidine's documented ability to inhibit hepatic microsomal drug metabolism, elimination of other medications that require hepatic metabolism via the cytochrome (P450) system or that are highly extracted by the liver, may be decreased during concurrent use with cimetidine. This same possibility should be kept in mind for ranitidine, although ranitidine's ability to inhibit hepatic microsomal drug metabolism is significantly less than that for cimetidine. To date, there is no evidence that famotidine or nizatidine binds to cytochrome P450 to a significant extent, and interactions with medications metabolized by this system have not been reported; however, clinical experience with famotidine and nizatidine is very limited.

Combinations containing any of the following medications, depending on the amount present, may also interact with this medication.

For all histamine H_2-receptor antagonists

Antacids

(concurrent use with histamine H_2-receptor antagonists in the treatment of peptic ulcer may be indicated for the relief of pain; however, simultaneous administration of antacids of medium to high potency [80 mmol to 150 mmol HCl] is not recommended since absorption of histamine H_2-receptor antagonists may be decreased; patients should be advised not to take any antacids within one-half to one hour of taking histamine H_2-receptor antagonists)

Bone marrow depressants (see *Appendix II*)
(concurrent use with H_2-receptor antagonists may increase the risk of neutropenia or other blood dyscrasias)

» Itraconazole or
» Ketoconazole
(histamine H_2-receptor antagonists may increase gastrointestinal pH; concurrent administration with histamine H_2-receptor antagonists may result in a marked reduction in absorption of itraconazole or ketoconazole; patients should be advised to take histamine H_2-receptor antagonists at least 2 hours after itraconazole or ketoconazole)

Sucralfate
(although a decrease in absorption is only reported in the literature for cimetidine and ranitidine, concurrent use with sucralfate may decrease the absorption of any H_2-receptor antagonist; patients should be advised to take an H_2-receptor antagonist 2 hours before sucralfate)

For cimetidine

Alcohol
(some studies in humans have found increased blood alcohol levels when oral cimetidine was given in conjunction with alcohol; the clinical significance of this effect has not been documented)

» Anticoagulants, coumarin- or indandione-derivative or
» Antidepressants, tricyclic or
Benzodiazepines, especially chlordiazepoxide, diazepam, and midazolam or
Glipizide or
Glyburide or
» Metoprolol or
Metronidazole or
» Phenytoin or
» Propranolol or
» Xanthines, such as:
Aminophylline
Caffeine
Oxtriphylline
Theophylline
(inhibition of the cytochrome P450 enzyme system by cimetidine may cause a decrease in the hepatic metabolism of these medications, which may result in delayed elimination and increased blood concentrations, when these medications are used concurrently with cimetidine)
(monitoring of blood concentrations, or prothrombin time for anticoagulants, as a guide to dosage is recommended since dosage adjustment of these medications may be necessary during and after cimetidine therapy to prevent bleeding due to anticoagulant potentiation)
(concurrent use of phenytoin with cimetidine may increase the risk of ataxia due to increased blood concentrations of phenytoin)
(concurrent use of metoprolol or propranolol with cimetidine may require monitoring of blood pressure)

Calcium channel blocking agents
(concurrent use with cimetidine may result in accumulation of the calcium channel blocking agent as a result of inhibition of first-pass metabolism; caution and careful titration of the calcium channel blocking agent dose is recommended on initiation of therapy in patients receiving cimetidine)

Cyclosporine
(although this effect is rare, cimetidine has been reported to increase plasma concentrations of cyclosporine and may increase the risk of nephrotoxicity)

Lidocaine
(concurrent administration of lidocaine with cimetidine may result in reduced hepatic clearance of lidocaine, possibly resulting in delayed elimination and increased blood concentrations; lower doses of lidocaine may be required)

Paroxetine
(in one study, steady-state plasma concentrations of paroxetine were increased by approximately 50% during concurrent administration of cimetidine; although the clinical significance of this interaction has not been definitively established, initial dosage reductions are not thought to be necessary, but subsequent dose titration should be based on clinical effects)

Procainamide
(renal elimination of procainamide may be decreased due to competition between cimetidine and procainamide for active tubular secretion, resulting in increased blood concentration of procainamide)

Quinine
(concurrent use of quinine with cimetidine may reduce the clearance of quinine)

For ranitidine

Alcohol
(some studies in humans have found increased blood alcohol levels when oral ranitidine was given in conjunction with alcohol; the clinical significance of this effect has not been documented)

Glipizide or
Glyburide or
Metoprolol or
Midazolam or
Nifedipine or
Phenytoin or
Theophylline or
Warfarin
(ranitidine is a weak inhibitor of hepatic drug metabolism; isolated cases of drug interactions have been reported between ranitidine and glipizide, glyburide, metoprolol, midazolam, nifedipine, phenytoin, theophylline, and warfarin)
(monitoring of blood concentrations or prothrombin time for anticoagulants as a guide to dosage is recommended since dosage adjustment of these medications may be necessary during and after ranitidine therapy to prevent bleeding due to anticoagulant potentiation)
(concurrent use of phenytoin with ranitidine may increase the risk of ataxia due to increased blood concentrations of phenytoin)

Procainamide
(renal elimination of procainamide may be decreased due to competition between ranitidine and procainamide for active tubular secretion, resulting in increased blood concentration of procainamide)

Laboratory value alterations

The following have been selected on the basis of their potential clinical significance (possible effect in parentheses where appropriate)—not necessarily inclusive (» = major clinical significance).

With diagnostic test results

For all histamine H_2-receptor antagonists

» Gastric acid secretion test
(histamine H_2-receptor antagonists may antagonize the effect of pentagastrin and histamine in the evaluation of gastric acid secretory function; administration of histamine H_2-receptor antagonists is not recommended during the 24 hours preceding the test)

Skin tests using allergen extracts
(histamine H_2-receptor antagonists may inhibit the cutaneous histamine response, thus producing false-negative results; it is recommended that histamine H_2-receptor antagonists be discontinued before the diagnostic use of immediate skin tests)

For nizatidine only (in addition to those listed above for all histamine H_2-receptor antagonists)

Urine urobilinogen test
(a false-positive reaction may be produced during nizatidine therapy)

For ranitidine only (in addition to those listed above for all histamine H_2-receptor antagonists)

Urine protein test
(a false-positive reaction may be produced during ranitidine therapy; testing with sulphosalicylic acid is recommended)

With physiology/laboratory test values

For cimetidine

Creatinine and
Transaminase
(serum values may be increased)

Parathyroid hormone
(concentrations may be decreased, especially when abnormally elevated as in primary hyperparathyroidism)

Prolactin
(serum concentrations may be increased after intravenous bolus administration)

For famotidine

Transaminase
(serum values may be increased)

For nizatidine

Alanine aminotransferase (ALT [SGPT]) and
Alkaline phosphatase and
Aspartate aminotransferase (AST [SGOT])
(serum values may be increased)

For ranitidine

Creatinine and

Gamma-glutamyl transpeptidase and
Transaminase
(serum values may be increased)

Medical considerations/Contraindications

The medical considerations/contraindications included have been selected on the basis of their potential clinical significance (reasons given in parentheses where appropriate)—not necessarily inclusive (» = major clinical significance).

Except under special circumstances, this medication should not be used when the following medical problem exists:

» Hypersensitivity to any of the histamine H_2-receptor antagonists

Risk-benefit should be considered when the following medical problems exist:

» Acute porphyria, history of
(ranitidine should be avoided in these patients)

Cirrhosis, with history of portal systemic encephalopathy or
Hepatic function impairment or
» Renal function impairment
(decreased hepatic or renal clearance of histamine H_2-receptor antagonists may result in increased plasma concentrations thus increasing the risk of side effects, especially CNS effects; dosage reduction of histamine H_2-receptor antagonists or longer intervals between doses are recommended with renal function impairment and may be necessary with hepatic function impairment)

Immunocompromised patients
(decreased gastric acidity may increase the possibility of a hyperinfection of strongyloidiasis)

Phenylketonuria (PKU)
(the chewable tablet form and the oral disintegrating tablet form of Pepcid brand of famotidine, and the effervescent granule form and the effervescent tablet form of Zantac brand of ranitidine contain aspartame, which is metabolized to phenylalanine, and must be used with caution in patients with PKU)

Patient monitoring

The following may be especially important in patient monitoring (other tests may be warranted in some patients, depending on condition; » = major clinical significance):

Cyanocobalamin (vitamin B_{12}) concentration determinations
(monitoring may be needed in long-term treatment of patients likely to have impaired secretion of intrinsic factor, such as those with severe fundic gastritis, to prevent malabsorption of cyanocobalamin)

Side/Adverse Effects

Those indicating need for medical attention
Incidence rare

For all histamine H_2-receptor antagonists

Cardiac arrhythmias including bradycardia (slow heartbeat); ***tachycardia*** (fast, pounding, or irregular heartbeat); ***and atrioventricular block*** (dizziness; fainting; slow heartbeat; troubled breathing; unusual tiredness or weakness); ***dermatologic reactions, including erythema multiforme*** (blisters on palms of hands and soles of feet; fever; general feeling of discomfort or illness; joint pain; redness of skin); ***exfoliative dermatitis*** (chills; fever; redness and scaling of skin); ***pruritus*** (itching); ***Stevens-Johnson syndrome*** (bleeding or crusting sores on lips; chills; fever; muscle cramps; pain; skin rash or itching; sore throat; sores, ulcers, or white spots on lips, in mouth, or on genitals; weakness); ***toxic epidermal necrolysis*** (blisters; chills; fever; general feeling of discomfort or illness; muscle aches; peeling or sloughing of skin; red or irritated eyes; redness, tenderness, or burning of skin; sores or ulcers on lips or in mouth); ***fever; hematologic effects, including aplastic anemia*** (shortness of breath, troubled breathing, wheezing, or tightness in chest; sores, ulcers, or white spots on lips or in mouth; swollen or painful glands; unusual bleeding or bruising); ***leukopenia*** (chills; fever; sore throat); ***neutropenia*** (continuing sores or ulcers in mouth and throat; fever; sore throat); ***pancytopenia*** (fever; sore throat; sores or ulcers in mouth and throat; unusual bleeding or bruising); ***thrombocytopenia*** (unusual bleeding or bruising); ***and immune hemolytic anemia*** (back, leg, or stomach pain; fever; nausea, vomiting, or loss of appetite; unusual tiredness or weakness)—extremely rare; ***hepatic effects, including hepatitis*** (dark-colored urine; flu-like symptoms; light-colored stools); ***and jaundice*** (yellow eyes or skin); ***hypersensitivity reactions, including anaphylaxis*** (chills; coughing; difficulty in swallowing; fast heartbeat; fever; skin rash, hives, or itching; shortness of breath, troubled breathing, wheezing, or tightness in chest; swelling of face, lips, or eyelids); ***angioedema*** (swelling of face, mouth, lips, tongue, hands or feet; sudden difficult breathing); ***eosinophilia*** (fever; loss of appetite; muscle ache; unusual tiredness or weakness; weight loss); ***laryngeal edema*** (shortness of breath, troubled breathing, or unusually slow or irregular breathing); ***skin rash; urticaria*** (hives); ***vasculitis*** (inflammation of blood vessels); ***mood or mental changes, including anxiety; agitation; confusion; hallucinations*** (seeing, hearing, or feeling things that are not there); ***mental depression; nervousness; psychosis*** (severe mental illness); ***myalgia*** (muscle ache)

Note: *Blood dyscrasias* are more likely to occur in patients with serious concomitant illnesses or in those who also received antimetabolites, alkylating agents, or other medications and/or treatment known to produce neutropenia; appear to be reversible and tend to occur within the first 30 days of administration.

Cardiac effects reported for nizatidine are less than those of the other agents, and include short episodes of asymptomatic ventricular tachycardia in two patients.

Hepatic effects are usually reversible; rarely deaths have occurred; rare cases of hepatic failure have been reported, as have rare cases of cholestatic or mixed hepatocellular and cholestatic liver toxicity

Mental changes are especially likely to occur in severely ill elderly patients.

For cimetidine

Agranulocytosis (fever; sore throat; unusual tiredness or weakness); ***arthralgia*** (joint pain); ***pancreatitis*** (abdominal pain; fever; muscle ache; vomiting)

For famotidine

Agranulocytosis (fever; sore throat; unusual tiredness or weakness); ***arthralgia*** (joint pain); ***asthenia*** (unusual tiredness or weakness); ***bronchospasm*** (wheezing or troubled breathing, severe); ***fatigue*** (unusual tiredness or weakness); ***palpitations*** (fast, pounding, or irregular heartbeat)

For nizatidine

Amblyopia (changes in vision); ***anemia*** (unusual tiredness or weakness); ***asthenia*** (unusual tiredness or weakness); ***bronchospasm*** (wheezing or troubled breathing, severe); ***hyperuricemia*** (joint pain)—not associated with gout or nephrolithiasis; ***increased cough; infection, including pharnygitis and sinusitis; pain, including chest pain and back pain; serum sickness*** (fever; itching or hives; joint pain; skin rash)

For ranitidine

Agranulocytosis (fever; sore throat; unusual tiredness or weakness); ***arthralgia*** (joint pain); ***blurred vision; bronchospasm*** (wheezing or troubled breathing, severe); ***pancreatitis*** (abdominal pain; fever; muscle ache; vomiting); ***premature ventricular beats*** (fast or irregular heartbeat; sudden faintness or weakness)

Those indicating need for medical attention only if they continue or are bothersome
Incidence less frequent or rare

For all histamine H_2-receptor antagonists

Decreased libido (decrease in sexual desire); ***diarrhea; dizziness; gynecomastia*** (swelling of the breasts or breast soreness in both females and males); ***headache; impotence*** (decrease in sexual ability); ***somnolence*** (drowsiness)

Note: *Gynecomastia* occurs most commonly in patients with hypersecretory conditions who are treated with cimetidine for over a month. With the other agents, the incidence of gynecomastia is the same as that in the general population.

Decreased libido and *impotence* occur most commonly in patients with hypersecretory conditions who are treated with cimetidine, especially at high doses for longer than 12 months; at regular doses of cimetidine, as with the other histamine H2-receptor antagonists, incidence is the same as that in the general population.

For cimetidine

Alopecia (hair loss); ***interstitial nephritis*** (fever; increase or decrease in urination; skin rash or hives); ***polymyositis*** (fever; joint pain; muscle tenderness, weakness, or pain; skin rash; unusual tiredness or weakness; weight loss); ***urinary retention*** (difficulty in urinating)

For famotidine

Abdominal pain; alopecia (hair loss); ***anorexia*** (loss of appetite); ***constipation; dryness of mouth; dryness of skin; insomnia***

(trouble in sleeping); ***nausea; tinnitus*** (ringing or buzzing in ears); ***vomiting***

For nizatidine

Abdominal pain; constipation; dryness of mouth; increased sweating; insomnia (trouble in sleeping); ***nausea; rhinitis*** (runny nose); ***vomiting***

For ranitidine

Abdominal pain; alopecia (hair loss); ***constipation; insomnia*** (trouble in sleeping); ***nausea; vomiting***

Overdose

For specific information on the agents used in the management of overdose with histamine H_2-receptor antagonists, see:

- *Atropine* in *Anticholinergics/Antispasmodics (Systemic)* monograph;
- *Diazepam* in *Benzodiazepines (Systemic)* monograph; and/or
- *Lidocaine Hydrochloride (Systemic)*monograph.

For more information on the management of overdose or unintentional ingestion, **contact a Poison Control Center** (see *Poison Control Center Listing*).

Treatment of overdose

There is no specific antidote for overdose with histamine H_2-receptor antagonists; treatment is symptomatic and supportive with possible utilization of the following:

To decrease absorption—

Induction of emesis and/or use of gastric lavage.

Specific treatment—

For seizures—Treatment with intravenous diazepam.

For bradycardia—Treatment with atropine.

For ventricular arrhythmias—Treatment with lidocaine.

Monitoring—

Clinical monitoring should be instituted.

Supportive care—

Patients in whom intentional overdose is confirmed or suspected should be referred for psychiatric consultation.

Patient Consultation

As an aid to patient consultation, refer to *Advice for the Patient, Histamine H_2-receptor Antagonists (Systemic)*.

In providing consultation, consider emphasizing the following selected information (» = major clinical significance):

Before using this medication

» Conditions affecting use, especially:

Hypersensitivity to any of the H_2-receptor antagonists

Pregnancy—All cross placenta

Breast-feeding—Cimetidine, famotidine, nizatidine, and ranitidine are distributed into breast milk; nursing is not recommended during cimetidine therapy, because of high concentration in breast milk

Use in the elderly—Confusion more likely with cimetidine, famotidine, and ranitidine in elderly patients with impaired hepatic or renal function

Other medications, especially itraconazole, ketoconazole (with all histamine H_2-receptor antagonists); anticoagulants, metoprolol, phenytoin, xanthines (with cimetidine and possibly ranitidine only); propranolol or tricyclic antidepressants (with cimetidine only)

Other medical problems, especially acute porphyria, history of (for ranitidine), renal function impairment

Proper use of this medication

For patients taking nonprescription strengths: not taking maximum daily dose continuously for more than 2 weeks unless directed by physician; seeing physician promptly if having trouble swallowing or persistent abdominal pain

Dosing schedule for patients taking prescription strengths:

1 dose a day—Taking at bedtime

2 doses a day—Taking in the morning and at bedtime

Several doses a day—Taking with meals and at bedtime

For patients taking famotidine chewable tablets, chewing the tablet well before swallowing

For patients taking famotidine oral disintegrating tablets: leave tablets in unopened package until the time of use, then open pack with dry hands and place tablet on the tongue to dissolve and be swallowed with saliva.

For patients taking ranitidine effervescent granules or tablets: removing foil wrapping and dissolving dose in 6 to 8 ounces of water before drinking; *not chewing, swallowing whole, or dissolving on tongue*

For patients taking *Zantac EFFERdose* tablets: not taking if you have allergy to phenylalanine; these contain aspartame

For giving *Zantac EFFERdose* tablets to an infant: Proper use of medical dropper bottle or oral syringe

Taking antacids for relief of ulcer pain; not taking within one-half to one hour of histamine H_2-receptor antagonists

» Compliance with full course of therapy

» Proper dosing

Missed dose: Taking as soon as possible; not taking if almost time for next dose; not doubling doses

» Proper storage

Precautions while using this medication

Possible interference with gastric acid secretion tests or skin tests using allergens; need to inform physician of use of medication

Avoiding use of foods, drinks, or other medication that may cause gastrointestinal irritation

Discontinuing smoking or at least avoiding smoking after last dose of day

Avoiding alcoholic beverages

Checking with physician if condition does not improve or worsens

Side/adverse effects

Signs of possible side effects, especially cardiac arrhythmias, dermatologic reactions, fever, hematologic effects, hepatic effects, hypersensitivity reactions, mood or mental changes, myalgia, arthralgia, pancreatitis, asthenia, fatigue, palpitations, amblyopia, anemia, hyperuricemia, increased cough, infection, pain, serum sickness, blurred vision, premature ventricular beats

General Dosing Information

Use of histamine H_2-receptor antagonists in the treatment of duodenal ulcer rarely continues beyond 8 weeks, since no long-term, carefully monitored studies have been done with these medications. Also, most patients taking histamine H_2-receptor antagonists heal within 6 to 8 weeks.

Although the symptoms of duodenal ulcers may subside within 1 or 2 weeks after initiation of therapy, treatment should be continued for at least 4 to 6 weeks, unless healing has been documented by endoscopic examination or x-rays.

Histamine H_2-receptor antagonists may be used, in reduced doses, to prevent ulcer recurrence. However, until consequences of very long term use are fully determined, such use should be limited to patients likely to need surgical treatment, patients with concomitant illnesses in whom surgery would constitute a greater-than-usual risk, and patients with recurrent ulcers.

Initial titration of doses and subsequent dosage adjustment of histamine H_2-receptor antagonists is recommended in the long-term treatment of pathological hypersecretory conditions (e.g., Zollinger-Ellison syndrome, systemic mastocytosis, multiple endocrine adenomas). Doses of cimetidine should generally not exceed 2.4 grams per day; however, doses up to 12 grams per day have been used. Up to 160 mg of famotidine every 6 hours and up to 6 grams of ranitidine per day have been administered to some patients with severe Zollinger-Ellison syndrome.

The efficacy of histamine H_2-receptor antagonists in inhibiting nocturnal gastric acid secretion may be decreased by cigarette smoking. Patients with peptic ulcer disease should discontinue smoking, or at least avoid smoking after their last dose of the day.

Dosage of histamine H_2-receptor antagonists may need to be increased in burn patients to achieve adequate control of gastric pH, because of enhanced clearance of histamine H_2-receptor antagonists in these patients. Individualization of dosage should be based on monitoring of gastric pH and/or plasma concentrations of histamine H_2-receptor antagonists since their clearance varies in proportion to burn size.

No dosage adjustment of histamine H_2-receptor antagonists is necessary for hemodialysis and peritoneal dialysis patients, since only small amounts of the medications are removed.

For oral dosage forms only

In the treatment of peptic ulcer and other hypersecretory conditions, optimal therapeutic effect is obtained when histamine H_2-receptor antagonists are taken with meals and at bedtime. By administering histamine H_2-receptor antagonists with meals, maximum serum concentrations and antisecretory effects are achieved when the stomach is no longer protected by the buffering capacity of the food. However, more recent information indicates that ulcer healing rates may be greatest with a bedtime-only dosage regimen.

If required, antacids of standard neutralizing capacity (e.g., 13 mEq per 15 mL) may be administered concurrently with histamine H_2-receptor antagonists for the relief of pain. However, spacing of doses one-half to one hour apart is recommended, especially with antacids of greater neutralizing capacity, since absorption of histamine H_2-receptor antagonists may be decreased.

For parenteral dosage forms only

Parenteral administration may be indicated in hospitalized patients with pathological hypersecretory disorders or intractable ulcers, or in patients who are unable to take oral medication.

Rapid intravenous bolus administration of cimetidine, famotidine, or ranitidine is not recommended because it may increase the risk of cardiac arrhythmias and hypotension.

Diet/Nutrition

Patients with phenylketonuria (PKU) should be informed that the chewable tablet form of Pepcid AC brand of famotidine contains 1.4 mg of phenylalanine per 10-mg dose, the oral disintegrating tablet form of Pepcid RPD brand of famotidine contains 1.05 mg of phenylalanine per 20-mg dose, and the EFFERdose tablet forms of the Zantac brand of ranitidine contain 2.81 mg of phenylalanine per 25-mg dose and 16.84 mg of phenylalanine per 150-mg dose.

CIMETIDINE

Summary of Differences

Indications:

Also used in treatment of pancreatic insufficiency and as a treatment adjunct in acute urticaria.

Pharmacology/pharmacokinetics:

Other actions/effects—Inhibits hepatic cytochrome P450 and P448 mixed function oxidase (microsomal enzyme) systems; possesses antiandrogenic activity; increases prolactin concentration (with IV bolus injection); enhances gastromucosal defense and healing in stress-induced ulceration and bleeding.

Precautions:

Drug interactions and/or related problems—May interact with alcohol, anticoagulants, tricyclic antidepressants, benzodiazepines, glipizide, glyburide, metoprolol, metronidazole, phenytoin, propranolol, xanthines, calcium channel blocking agents, cyclosporine, lidocaine, procainamide, sucralfate, quinine.

Laboratory value alterations—May increase serum prolactin concentrations; may decrease parathyroid hormone concentrations.

Side/adverse effects:

Constipation has not been reported. Bronchospasms have not been reported as a side/adverse effect with cimetidine.

Oral Dosage Forms

Note: Bracketed uses in the *Dosage Forms* section refer to categories of use and/or indications that are not included in U.S. product labeling.

CIMETIDINE TABLETS USP

Usual adult and adolescent dose

Duodenal ulcer—

Treatment: Oral, 300 mg four times a day, with meals and at bedtime; 400 or 600 mg two times a day, in the morning and at bedtime; or 800 mg at bedtime.

Note: A 1600-mg dose of cimetidine at bedtime has been found to produce a more rapid healing in some ulcer patients who have an endoscopically demonstrated ulcer larger than 1 cm and are also heavy smokers.

Prophylaxis of recurrent duodenal ulcer: Oral, 300 mg two times a day, in the morning and at bedtime; or 400 mg at bedtime. Patients have been maintained on continued treatment with 400 mg at bedtime for periods of up to five years.

Gastric ulcer, benign, active—

Oral, 300 mg four times a day, with meals and at bedtime; or 600 mg two times a day, in the morning and at bedtime; or 800 mg at bedtime.

Heartburn, acid indigestion, and sour stomach—

Treatment: Oral, 200 mg with water as symptoms occur; dose may be repeated once in twenty-four hours

Prophylaxis: Oral, 100 to 200 mg with water up to one hour before consuming food or beverages expected to cause symptoms

Gastric hypersecretory conditions (e.g., Zollinger-Ellison syndrome, systemic mastocytosis, multiple endocrine adenomas)—

Oral, 300 mg four times a day, with meals and at bedtime, the dosage being adjusted as needed, and therapy continued for as long as clinically indicated.

Gastroesophageal reflux—

Oral, 800 to 1600 mg per day in divided doses for 12 weeks.

Upper gastrointestinal bleeding—

Oral, 300 mg every six hours; or 600 mg two times a day, in the morning and at bedtime.

Note: For patients with impaired renal function—Oral, 300 mg every twelve hours, the dosage being increased to 300 mg every eight hours or more frequently, if necessary. Further reduction in dosage may be required if hepatic function impairment is also present.

Usual adult prescribing limits

Up to 2.4 grams daily; however, doses up to 12 grams per day have been used in the treatment of pathological hypersecretory conditions.

Usual pediatric dose

Duodenal ulcer; or

Gastric ulcer—

Oral, 20 to 40 mg per kg of body weight a day in divided doses four times a day, with meals and at bedtime.

Gastroesophageal reflux—

Oral, 40 to 80 mg per kg of body weight a day in divided doses four times a day.

Note: In certain circumstances, doses may be titrated based on gastric pH.

Clinical experience with the use of cimetidine in children up to 16 years of age is limited; risk-benefit must be considered.

In children with impaired renal function, dosage should be reduced to 10 to 15 mg per kg of body weight a day, and the dosing interval increased to eight hours.

Usual geriatric dose

See *Usual adult and adolescent dose*.

Strength(s) usually available

U.S.—

100 mg (OTC) [*Tagamet HB;* GENERIC].
200 mg (OTC) [*Tagamet HB 200;* GENERIC].
200 mg (Rx) [*Tagamet* (film-coated); GENERIC].
300 mg (Rx) [*Tagamet* (film-coated); GENERIC].
400 mg (Rx) [*Tagamet* (film-coated); GENERIC].
800 mg (Rx) [*Tagamet* (film-coated); GENERIC].

Canada—

100 mg (OTC) [*Apo-Cimetidine* (film-coated)].
200 mg (Rx) [*Apo-Cimetidine* (film-coated); *Gen-Cimetidine* (film-coated); *Novo-Cimetine* (scored; film-coated); *Nu-Cimet* (film-coated); *PMS-Cimetidine* (film-coated); GENERIC].
300 mg (Rx) [*Apo-Cimetidine* (film-coated); *Gen-Cimetidine* (film-coated); *Novo-Cimetine* (scored; film-coated); *Nu-Cimet* (film-coated); *Peptol* (film-coated); *PMS-Cimetidine* (film-coated); *Tagamet* (film-coated); GENERIC].
400 mg (Rx) [*Apo-Cimetidine* (film-coated); *Gen-Cimetidine* (film-coated); *Novo-Cimetine* (scored; film-coated); *Nu-Cimet* (film-coated); *Peptol* (film-coated); *PMS-Cimetidine* (film-coated); *Tagamet* (film-coated); GENERIC].
600 mg (Rx) [*Apo-Cimetidine* (film-coated); *Gen-Cimetidine* (film-coated); *Novo-Cimetine* (scored; film-coated); *Nu-Cimet* (film-coated); *Peptol; PMS-Cimetidine* (film-coated); *Tagamet* (film-coated); GENERIC].
800 mg (Rx) [*Apo-Cimetidine* (film-coated); *Gen-Cimetidine* (film-coated); *Novo-Cimetine* (scored; film-coated); *Peptol; PMS-Cimetidine* (film-coated); GENERIC].

Packaging and storage

Store between 15 and 30 °C (59 and 86 °F), in a tight, light-resistant container.

Auxiliary labeling

- Continue medicine for full time of treatment.

Note

Tablets have a characteristic odor, which does not represent any risk to the patient.

CIMETIDINE HYDROCHLORIDE ORAL SOLUTION

Note: The dosing and strengths of the dosage forms available are expressed in terms of cimetidine base (not the hydrochloride salt).

Usual adult and adolescent dose

See *Cimetidine Tablets USP*.

Usual adult prescribing limits
See *Cimetidine Tablets USP*.

Usual pediatric dose
See *Cimetidine Tablets USP*.

Usual geriatric dose
See *Usual adult and adolescent dose*.

Strength(s) usually available
U.S.—
300 mg (base) per 5 mL (Rx) [*Tagamet* (light orange, mint-peach flavored; alcohol 2.8%); GENERIC].
Canada—
300 mg (base) per 5 mL (Rx) [*Tagamet* (light orange, bittersweet melon-pineapple flavored; alcohol 2.8%)].

Packaging and storage
Store between 15 and 30 °C (59 and 86 °F), in a tight, light-resistant container, unless otherwise specified by manufacturer. Protect from freezing.

Auxiliary labeling
• Continue medicine for full time of treatment.

Parenteral Dosage Forms

Note: Bracketed uses in the *Dosage Forms* section refer to categories of use and/or indications that are not included in U.S. product labeling.

CIMETIDINE HYDROCHLORIDE INJECTION

Note: The dosing and strengths of the dosage forms available are expressed in terms of cimetidine base (not the hydrochloride salt).

Usual adult and adolescent dose
Duodenal ulcer or
Gastric ulcer or
Gastric hypersecretory conditions (e.g., Zollinger-Ellison syndrome, systemic mastocytosis, multiple endocrine adenomas) or
Upper gastrointestinal bleeding—
Intramuscular, 300 mg (base) every six to eight hours.
Intravenous, 300 mg (base) every six to eight hours, diluted with a compatible intravenous solution and administered over a period of not less than five minutes.
Intravenous infusion, 300 mg (base) every six to eight hours, diluted in a compatible intravenous solution and administered over a fifteen- to twenty-minute period.
Note: If necessary, increases in dosage should be made by more frequent administration of a 300-mg dose.
Continuous intravenous infusion, 37.5 (base) mg per hour (900 mg per day), diluted in a compatible intravenous solution. The infusion rate should be adjusted to individual patient requirements.
Note: For patients requiring a rapid elevation of gastric pH, a loading dose of 150 mg may be administered by intravenous infusion before continuous infusion is begun.
Prophylaxis of stress-related mucosal bleeding—
Continuous intravenous infusion, 50 mg (base) per hour, diluted in a compatible intravenous solution for up to 7 days.
Note: Patients with a creatinine clearance less than 30 mL per minute should receive 25 mg per hour.
[Prophylaxis of aspiration pneumonitis]—
Intramuscular, 300 mg (base) one hour before induction of anesthesia, and 300 mg (base) given intramuscularly or intravenously every four hours until patient responds to verbal commands.
[Urticaria therapy adjunct]—
Intravenous, 300 mg over 15 to 20 minutes.
Note: For patients with impaired renal function—Intravenous, 300 mg (base) every twelve hours, the dosage being increased to 300 mg every eight hours or more frequently, if necessary. Further reduction in dosage may be required if hepatic function impairment is also present.

Usual adult prescribing limits
2.4 grams (base) daily.

Usual pediatric dose
Duodenal ulcer or
Gastric ulcer—
Intramuscular, 5 to 10 mg (base) per kg of body weight every six to eight hours.
Intravenous, 5 to 10 mg (base) per kg of body weight every six to eight hours, diluted to a suitable volume with a compatible intravenous solution and administered over a period of not less than two minutes.
Intravenous infusion, 5 to 10 mg (base) per kg of body weight every six to eight hours, diluted to a suitable volume with a compatible intravenous solution and administered over a fifteen- to twenty-minute period.
Note: In certain circumstances, doses may be titrated based on gastric pH.
Clinical experience with the use of cimetidine in children up to 16 years of age is limited; risk-benefit must be considered.
In children with impaired renal function, doses should be reduced and dosing interval increased.

Usual geriatric dose
See *Usual adult and adolescent dose*.

Strength(s) usually available
U.S.—
300 mg (base) per 2 mL (Rx) [*Tagamet;* GENERIC].
300 mg (base) per 50 mL (premixed) (Rx) [*Tagamet*].
Canada—
300 mg (base) per 2 mL (Rx) [*Novo-Cimetine; Tagamet*].
300 mg (base) per 50 mL (premixed) (Rx) [*Tagamet*].

Packaging and storage
Store between 15 and 30 °C (59 and 86 °F), unless otherwise specified by manufacturer. Protect from light. Protect from freezing.

Preparation of dosage form
Not for premixed dosage form
• For intravenous use, cimetidine hydrochloride injection must be diluted prior to use with a compatible intravenous solution, such as sodium chloride injection (0.9%).
• For intermittent intravenous infusion, cimetidine hydrochloride injection must be diluted prior to use in 50 mL of a compatible intravenous solution, such as dextrose injection (5%).

Stability
Diluted solutions of cimetidine hydrochloride injection are stable for 48 hours at room temperature.
Exposure to cold may lead to development of cloudiness. However, this is of no clinical significance, and solution clears on returning to room temperature.
Injection should not be used if discolored or if a precipitate is present.

FAMOTIDINE

Summary of Differences

Side/adverse effects: Loss of appetite, dryness of mouth or skin, ringing or buzzing in ears have been reported.
Bioequivalence: Famotidine tablets, oral suspension, and oral disintegrating tablets are bioequivalent.

Oral Dosage Forms

Note: Bracketed uses in the *Dosage Forms* section refer to categories of use and/or indications that are not included in U.S. product labeling.

FAMOTIDINE FOR ORAL SUSPENSION

Usual adult and adolescent dose
Duodenal ulcer—
Treatment: Oral, 40 mg once a day at bedtime or 20 mg two times a day.
Prophylaxis of recurrent duodenal ulcer: Oral, 20 mg at bedtime.
Gastric ulcer, benign, active—
Treatment: Oral, 40 mg once a day at bedtime.
Gastric hypersecretory conditions (e.g., Zollinger-Ellison syndrome, systemic mastocytosis, multiple endocrine adenomas)—
Oral, 20 mg every six hours, the dosage being adjusted as needed and therapy continued for as long as clinically indicated. Doses up to 160 mg every six hours have been administered to some patients with severe Zollinger-Ellison syndrome.
Gastroesophageal reflux—
Oral, 20 mg two times a day for up to six weeks.
Note: The recommended oral dose for esophagitis due to gastroesophageal reflux disease is 20 to 40 mg two times a day for up to twelve weeks.
[Prophylaxis of aspiration pneumonitis]—
Oral, 40 mg given either the night before or the morning of surgery.
Note: For patients with severely impaired renal function (creatinine clearance less than 10 mL per minute)—Oral, 20 mg at bedtime. Depending on patient's response, the dosing interval may have to be increased to thirty-six to forty-eight hours.

Usual pediatric dose
Duodenal ulcer or
Gastric ulcer—
Oral, initially 0.5 mg per kg of body weight a day, at bedtime or in two divided doses.
Gastroesophageal reflux disease—
For children weighing more than 10 kg: Oral, 1 to 2 mg per kg of body weight a day, in two divided doses.
For children weighing less than 10 kg: Oral, 1 to 2 mg per kg per day, in three divided doses.

Note: In certain circumstances, doses may be titrated based on gastric pH.

Usual pediatric prescribing limits
40 mg a day.

Usual geriatric dose
See *Usual adult and adolescent dose.*

Strength(s) usually available
U.S.—
40 mg per 5 mL (Rx) [*Pepcid* (cherry-banana-mint flavor; sucrose; sodium benzoate 0.1%; sodium methylparaben 0.1%; sodium propylparaben 0.02%)].
Canada—
Not commercially available.

Packaging and storage
Prior to constitution, store below 40 °C (104 °F), preferably between 15 and 30 °C (59 and 86 °F), unless otherwise specified by manufacturer.
After constitution, store below 30 °C (86 °F), unless otherwise specified by manufacturer. Protect from freezing.

Preparation of dosage form
At time of dispensing, slowly add 46 mL of purified water. Shake vigorously for 5 to 10 seconds immediately after adding the water and immediately before use.

Stability
Unused oral suspension of famotidine should be discarded after 30 days.

Auxiliary labeling
- Shake well.
- Continue medicine for full time of treatment.

FAMOTIDINE TABLETS USP

Usual adult and adolescent dose
Duodenal ulcer—
Treatment: Oral, 40 mg once a day at bedtime or 20 mg two times a day.
Prophylaxis of recurrent duodenal ulcer: Oral, 20 mg at bedtime.
Gastric ulcer, benign, active—
Treatment: Oral, 40 mg once a day at bedtime.
Heartburn, acid indigestion, and sour stomach—
Treatment: Oral, 10 mg at onset of symptoms; dose may be repeated once in twenty-four hours
Prophylaxis: Oral, 10 mg up to one hour before consuming food or beverages expected to cause symptoms
Gastric hypersecretory conditions (e.g., Zollinger-Ellison syndrome, systemic mastocytosis, multiple endocrine adenomas)—
Oral, 20 mg every six hours, the dosage being adjusted as needed and therapy continued for as long as clinically indicated. Doses up to 160 mg every six hours have been administered to some patients with severe Zollinger-Ellison syndrome.
Gastroesophageal reflux—
Oral, 20 mg two times a day for up to six weeks.
Note: The recommended oral dose for esophagitis due to gastroesophageal reflux disease is 20 to 40 mg two times a day for up to twelve weeks.
[Prophylaxis of aspiration pneumonitis]—
Oral, 40 mg given either the night before or the morning of surgery.

Note: For patients with severely impaired renal function (creatinine clearance less than 10 mL per minute)—Oral, 20 mg at bedtime. Depending on patient's response, the dosing interval may have to be increased to thirty-six to forty-eight hours

Usual pediatric dose
See *Famotidine for Oral Suspension.*

Usual geriatric dose
See *Usual adult and adolescent dose.*

Strength(s) usually available
U.S.—
10 mg (OTC) [*Mylanta AR Acid Reducer; Pepcid AC Acid Controller*].
20 mg (Rx) [*Pepcid*].
40 mg (Rx) [*Pepcid*].
Canada—
10 mg (OTC) [*Acid Control* (film-coated); *Act* (film-coated); *Apo-Famotidine; Dyspep HB* (film-coated); *Gen-Famotidine; Maalox H2 Acid Controller* (film-coated); *Pepcid AC* (film-coated); *Ulcidine-HB*].
20 mg (Rx) [*Apo-Famotidine* (film-coated); *Gen-Famotidine* (film-coated); *Novo-Famotidine* (film-coated); *Nu-Famotidine* (film-coated); *Pepcid* (film-coated); *Ulcidine* (film-coated); GENERIC].
40 mg (Rx) [*Apo-Famotidine* (film-coated); *Gen-Famotidine* (film-coated); *Novo-Famotidine* (film-coated); *Nu-Famotidine* (film-coated); *Pepcid* (film-coated); *Ulcidine* (film-coated); GENERIC].

Packaging and storage
Store below 40 °C (104 °F), preferably between 15 and 30 °C (59 and 86 °F), in a well-closed container, unless otherwise specified by manufacturer. Protect from light.

Auxiliary labeling
- Continue medicine for full time of treatment.

FAMOTIDINE TABLETS (CHEWABLE)

Usual adult and adolescent dose
See *Famotidine Tablets USP.*

Usual pediatric dose
See *Famotidine for Oral Suspension.*

Usual geriatric dose
See *Famotidine Tablets USP.*

Strength(s) usually available
U.S.—
10 mg (OTC) [*Pepcid AC* (phenylalanine 1.4 mg)].
Canada—
10 mg (OTC) [*Pepcid AC* (aspartame)].

Packaging and storage
Store between 15 and 30 °C (59 and 86 °F), in a well-closed container, unless otherwise specified by manufacturer.

Auxiliary labeling
- Chew tablets well before swallowing.

Caution
Pepcid AC brand of chewable tablets contain aspartame, which is metabolized to phenylalanine and must be used with caution in patients with phenylketonuria.

FAMOTIDINE ORAL DISINTEGRATING TABLETS

Note: Pepcid RPD and Fluxid brands of oral disintegrating tablets rapidly disintegrate on the tongue and do not require water to aid dissolution or swallowing.

Usual adult and adolescent dose
See *Famotidine Oral Tablets.*

Usual pediatric dose
See *Famotidine Oral Suspension.*

Usual geriatric dose
See *Famotidine Oral Tablets.*

Strength(s) usually available
U.S.—
20 mg (Rx) [*Fluxid* (citric acid; colloidal silicon dioxide; corn starch; crospovidone; hypromellose; magnesium stearate; mannitol; methacrylic acid copolymer; microcrystalline cellulose; natural and artificial cherry flavor; sodium bicarbonate; sucralose; sucrose)].
40 mg (Rx) [*Fluxid* (citric acid; colloidal silicon dioxide; corn starch; crospovidone; hypromellose; magnesium stearate; mannitol; methacrylic acid copolymer; microcrystalline cellulose; natural and artificial cherry flavor; sodium bicarbonate; sucralose; sucrose)].
20 mg (Rx) [*Pepcid RPD* (phenylalanine 1.05 mg; mint flavor)].
40 mg (Rx) [*Pepcid RPD* (phenylalanine 2.1 mg; mint flavor)].
Canada—
Not commercially available.

Packaging and storage
Store between 2 and 30 °C (36 and 86 °F), unless otherwise specified by manufacturer. Protect from light.

Auxiliary labeling
- Continue medicine for full time of treatment.

Caution
Pepcid RPD brand of oral disintegrating tablets contain aspartame, which is metabolized to phenylalanine and must be used with caution in patients with phenylketonuria.

Additional information

Proper handling/administration—With dry hands, peel back the foil backing of one blister. Gently remove the tablet and place it immediately on top of the tongue. It will dissolve in seconds, and should then be swallowed with saliva.

Parenteral Dosage Forms

Note: Bracketed uses in the *Dosage Forms* section refer to categories of use and/or indications that are not included in U.S. product labeling.

FAMOTIDINE INJECTION

Usual adult and adolescent dose

Duodenal ulcer or
Gastric ulcer, benign, active or
Gastric hypersecretory conditions (e.g., Zollinger-Ellison syndrome, systemic mastocytosis, multiple endocrine adenomas)—
Intravenous, 20 mg every twelve hours, diluted with a compatible intravenous solution and administered over a period of not less than two minutes.
Intravenous infusion, 20 mg every twelve hours, diluted with a compatible intravenous solution and administered over a fifteen- to thirty-minute period.
[Prophylaxis of aspiration pneumonitis]—
Intramuscular, 20 mg given either the night before or the morning of surgery.

Usual pediatric dose

Duodenal ulcer or
Gastric ulcer or
Gastroesophageal reflux disease—
For children ages one to 16 years: Intravenous, initially 0.25 mg per kg of body weight every twelve hours, injected over at least two minutes.
Intravenous infusion, initially 0.25 mg per kg of body weight every twelve hours, diluted to a suitable volume with a compatible intravenous solution and administered over a 15-minute period.
For children up to one year of age: Dosage has not been established.

Usual pediatric prescribing limits

40 mg a day.

Usual geriatric dose

See *Usual adult and adolescent dose*.

Strength(s) usually available

U.S.—
10 mg per mL (Rx) [*Pepcid I.V.*].
20 mg per 50 mL (premixed) [*Pepcid*].
Canada—
10 mg per mL (Rx) [*Pepcid I.V.* (benzyl alcohol 0.9%)].

Packaging and storage

Store between 2 and 8 °C (36 and 46 °F), unless otherwise specified by manufacturer. Protect from freezing.

Preparation of dosage form

For intravenous use, famotidine must be diluted prior to use with a compatible intravenous solution, such as sodium chloride injection (0.9%) to a total volume of either 5 or 10 mL.

For intravenous infusion, famotidine must be diluted prior to use in 100 mL of a compatible intravenous solution, such as dextrose injection (5%).

Caution—Famotidine products containing benzyl alcohol are not recommended for use in neonates (first 30 days of postnatal life). A fatal toxic syndrome consisting of metabolic acidosis, CNS depression, respiratory problems, renal failure, hypotension, and possibly seizures and intracranial hemorrhages has been associated with this use.

Stability

Diluted solutions of famotidine injection are stable for 48 hours at room temperature.

Injection should not be used if discolored or if a precipitate is present.

NIZATIDINE

Summary of Differences

Pharmacology/pharmacokinetics: Nizatidine is moderately protein bound, approximately 35%.

Precautions: Laboratory value alterations—Increases serum aspartate aminotransferase concentrations. May cause false-positive reaction with urine urobilinogen test.

Side/adverse effects: Agranulocytosis, joint or muscle pain, and loss of hair have not been reported with nizatidine. Increase in sweating has been reported.

Oral Dosage Forms

NIZATIDINE CAPSULES USP

Usual adult and adolescent dose

Duodenal ulcer—
Treatment: Oral, 300 mg once a day at bedtime or 150 mg two times a day.
Note: For patients with impaired renal function:
With creatinine clearance less than 20 mL per minute: Oral, 150 mg every other day.
With creatinine clearance from 20 to 50 mL per minute: Oral, 150 mg every day.

Duodenal ulcer, recurrent—
Prophylaxis: Oral, 150 mg once a day at bedtime.
Note: For patients with impaired renal function:
With creatinine clearance less than 20 mL per minute: Oral, 150 mg every three days.
With creatinine clearance from 20 to 50 mL per minute: Oral, 150 mg every other day.

Gastric ulcer, benign, active—
Treatment: Oral, 300 mg once a day at bedtime or 150 mg two times a day.

Gastroesophageal reflux[1]—
Oral, 150 mg two times a day.

Usual pediatric dose

Dosage has not been established.

Usual geriatric dose

See *Usual adult and adolescent dose.*

Strength(s) usually available

U.S.—
150 mg (Rx) [*Axid*].
300 mg (Rx) [*Axid*].
Canada—
150 mg (Rx) [*Apo-Nizatidine; Axid*].
300 mg (Rx) [*Apo-Nizatidine; Axid*].

Packaging and storage

Store between 15 and 30 °C (59 and 86 °F), in a well-closed container, unless otherwise specified by manufacturer.

Auxiliary labeling

- Continue medicine for full time of treatment.

NIZATIDINE TABLETS

Usual adult and adolescent dose

Heartburn, acid indigestion, and sour stomach—
Prophylaxis: Oral, 75 mg thirty to sixty minutes before consuming food or beverages expected to cause symptoms.

Usual pediatric dose

Dosage has not been established.

Usual geriatric dose

See *Usual adult and adolescent dose.*

Strength(s) usually available

U.S.—
75 mg (OTC) [*Axid AR*].
Canada—
Not commercially available.

Packaging and storage

Store between 20 and 25 °C (68 and 77 °F), in a well-closed container, unless otherwise specified by manufacturer. Protect from light.

[1]Not included in Canadian product labeling.

RANITIDINE

Summary of Differences

Pharmacology/pharmacokinetics:
Other actions/effects—
Weak inhibitor of P450 mixed function oxidase (microsomal enzyme) system; produces small, transient increase in prolactin concentration (with IV bolus injection).

Precautions:
Laboratory value alterations—May increase glutamyl transpeptidase. May cause false-positive reaction with urine protein test.

Drug interactions and/or related problems—May interact with alcohol, antacids, glipizide, glyburide, metoprolol, midazolam, nifedipine, phenytoin, theophylline, warfarin, procainamide, sucralfate.

Side/adverse effects:

Blurred vision has been reported.

Oral Dosage Forms

Note: The dosing and strengths of the dosage forms available are expressed in terms of ranitidine base (not the hydrochloride salt).

RANITIDINE HYDROCHLORIDE EFFERVESCENT GRANULES

Usual adult and adolescent dose

Duodenal ulcer—

Treatment: Oral, 150 mg two times a day or 300 mg at bedtime.

Prophylaxis of recurrent duodenal ulcer: Oral, 150 mg at bedtime.

Gastric ulcer, benign, active—

Treatment: Oral, 150 mg two times a day.

Prophylaxis of recurrent gastric ulcer: Oral, 150 mg at bedtime.

Gastric hypersecretory conditions (e.g., Zollinger-Ellison syndrome, systemic mastocytosis, multiple endocrine adenomas)—

Oral, 150 mg two times a day, the dosage being adjusted as needed and therapy continued as long as clinically indicated. Doses up to 6 grams per day have been used in severe cases.

Gastroesophageal reflux—

Oral, 150 mg two times a day.

Note: The recommended oral dose for the treatment of erosive esophagitis is 150 mg four times a day. For the prophylaxis of erosive esophagitis, the recommended oral dose is 150 mg two times a day.

Note: For patients with impaired renal function (creatinine clearance of less than 50 mL per minute)—Oral, 150 mg every twenty-four hours, the frequency of the dosage being increased to every twelve hours or more frequently, if necessary. Reductions in dosage may also be required if hepatic function impairment is present.

Usual pediatric dose

Duodenal ulcer or

Gastric ulcer—

Treatment: Oral, 2 to 4 mg per kg per day, divided into two doses, up to a maximum dose of 300 mg per day.Maintenance: Oral, 2 to 4 mg per kg once daily, up to a maximum dose of 150 mg per day.

Gastroesophageal reflux or

Erosive esophagitis treatment—

Treatment: Oral, 5 to 10 mg per kg per day, usually given as two divided doses.

Note: In certain circumstances, doses may be titrated based on gastric pH.

Usual geriatric dose

See *Usual adult and adolescent dose.*

Strength(s) usually available

U.S.—

Note: Not commercially available

Canada—

Not commercially available.

Packaging and storage

Store between 2 and 30 °C (36 and 86 °F), unless otherwise specified by manufacturer.

Preparation of dosage form

Dissolve each dose in 6 to 8 ounces (180 to 240 mL) of water before drinking.

Auxiliary labeling

- Continue medicine for full time of treatment.

Caution

Zantac EFFERdose Granules brand of effervescent granules contain aspartame, which is metabolized to phenylalanine and must be used with caution in patients with phenylketonuria. The aspartame in a 150-mg dose of Zantac EFFERdose Granules will be metabolized to 16.84 mg of phenylalanine.

Additional information

The total sodium content is 173.54 mg (7.55 mEq) per dose.

RANITIDINE HYDROCHLORIDE SYRUP USP

Usual adult and adolescent dose

Duodenal ulcer—

Treatment: Oral, 150 mg two times a day or 300 mg at bedtime.

Prophylaxis of recurrent duodenal ulcer: Oral, 150 mg at bedtime.

Gastric ulcer, benign, active—

Treatment: Oral, 150 mg two times a day.

Prophylaxis of recurrent gastric ulcer: Oral, 150 mg at bedtime.

Gastric hypersecretory conditions (e.g., Zollinger-Ellison syndrome, systemic mastocytosis, multiple endocrine adenomas)—

Oral, 150 mg two times a day, the dosage being adjusted as needed and therapy continued as long as clinically indicated. Doses up to 6 grams per day have been used in severe cases.

Gastroesophageal reflux—

Oral, 150 mg two times a day.

Note: The recommended oral dose for the treatment of erosive esophagitis is 150 mg four times a day. For the prophylaxis of erosive esophagitis, the recommended oral dose is 150 mg two times a day.

Note: For patients with impaired renal function (creatinine clearance of less than 50 mL per minute)—Oral, 150 mg every twenty-four hours, the frequency of the dosage being increased to every twelve hours or more frequently, if necessary. Reductions in dosage may also be required if hepatic function impairment is present.

Usual pediatric dose

Duodenal ulcer or

Gastric ulcer—

Treatment: Oral, 2 to 4 mg per kg per day, divided into two doses, up to a maximum dose of 300 mg per day.Maintenance: Oral, 2 to 4 mg per kg once daily, up to a maximum dose of 150 mg per day.

Gastroesophageal reflux or

Erosive esophagitis treatment—

Treatment: Oral, 5 to 10 mg per kg per day, usually given as two divided doses.

Note: In certain circumstances, doses may be titrated based on gastric pH.

Usual geriatric dose

See *Usual adult and adolescent dose.*

Strength(s) usually available

U.S.—

15 mg (base) per mL (Rx) [*Zantac* (alcohol 7.5%; butylparaben; dibasic sodium phosphate; hypromellose; peppermint flavor; monobasic potassium phosphate; propylparaben; purified water; saccharin sodium; sodium chloride; sorbitol)].

Canada—

75 mg (base) per 5 mL (Rx) [*Zantac* (peppermint flavored; alcohol 7.5%; butylparaben; flavor mint; propylparaben; sodium cyclamate; sorbitol)].

Packaging and storage

Store between 4 and 25 °C (39 and 77 °F), in a tight, light-resistant container, unless otherwise specified by manufacturer. Protect from freezing.

Auxiliary labeling

- Continue medicine for full time of treatment.

RANITIDINE HYDROCHLORIDE TABLETS USP

Usual adult and adolescent dose

Duodenal ulcer—

Treatment: Oral, 150 mg two times a day or 300 mg at bedtime.

Prophylaxis of recurrent duodenal ulcer: Oral, 150 mg at bedtime.

Gastric ulcer, benign, active—

Treatment: Oral, 150 mg two times a day.

Heartburn, acid indigestion, and sour stomach—

Treatment: Oral, 150 mg with a glass of water at onset of symptoms; dose may be repeated once in twenty-four hours.

Prophylaxis: Oral, 150 mg with a glass of water thirty to sixty minutes before consuming food or beverages expected to cause symptoms.

Gastric hypersecretory conditions (e.g., Zollinger-Ellison syndrome, systemic mastocytosis, multiple endocrine adenomas)—

Oral, 150 mg two times a day, the dosage being adjusted as needed and therapy continued as long as clinically indicated. Doses up to 6 grams per day have been used in severe cases.

Gastroesophageal reflux—

Oral, 150 mg two times a day.

Note: The recommended oral dose for erosive esophagitis is 150 mg four times a day.

Note: For patients with impaired renal function (creatinine clearance of less than 50 mL per minute)—Oral, 150 mg every twenty-four hours, the frequency of the dosage being increased to every twelve hours or more frequently, if necessary. Reductions in dosage may also be required if hepatic function impairment is present.

Usual adult prescribing limits

Heartburn, acid indigestion, and sour stomach (prophylaxis and treatment)—
Not more than 2 tablets (300 mg) in 24 hours

Usual pediatric dose

Duodenal ulcer or
Gastric ulcer—
Treatment: Oral, 2 to 4 mg per kg per day divided into two doses, up to a maximum dose of 300 mg per day.
Maintenance: Oral, 2 to 4 mg per kg per day, given once daily, up to a maximum dose of 150 mg per day.

Gastroesophageal reflux or
Erosive Esophagitis—
Treatment: Oral, 5 to 10 mg per kg per day, usually given as two divided doses.

Note: In certain circumstances, doses may be titrated based on gastric pH.

Heartburn, acid indigestion, and sour stomach (prophylaxis and treatment)—
Should not be given to children under 12 years of age unless directed by a doctor

Usual geriatric dose

See *Usual adult and adolescent dose*.

Strength(s) usually available

U.S.—
150 mg (base) (OTC) [*Zantac* (sugar-free; hypromellose; magnesium stearate; microcrystalline cellulose; synthetic red iron oxide; titanium dioxide; triacetin)].
150 mg (base) (Rx) [*Zantac 150* (film-coated; FD&C Yellow No. 6 Aluminum Lake; hypromellose; magnesium stearate; microcrystalline cellulose; titanium dioxide; triacetin; yellow iron oxide); GENERIC].
300 mg (base) (Rx) [*Zantac 300* (film-coated; croscarmellose sodium; D&C Yellow No. 10 Aluminum Lake; hypromellose; magnesium stearate; microcrystalline cellulose; titanium dioxide; triacetin); GENERIC].

Canada—
75 mg (base) (OTC) [*Zantac 75* (film-coated)].
150 mg (base) (Rx) [*Alti-Ranitidine* (film-coated); *Apo-Ranitidine* (film-coated); *Gen-Ranitidine* (film-coated); *Novo-Ranitidine* (film-coated); *Nu-Ranit* (film-coated); *Zantac* (film-coated)].
300 mg (base) (Rx) [*Alti-Ranitidine* (film-coated); *Apo-Ranitidine* (film-coated); *Gen-Ranitidine* (film-coated); *Novo-Ranitidine* (film-coated); *Nu-Ranit* (film-coated); *Zantac* (film-coated)].

Packaging and storage

Store between 15 and 30 °C (59 and 86 °F), unless otherwise specified by manufacturer. Store in a tight, light-resistant container.

Auxiliary labeling

- Continue medicine for full time of treatment.

RANITIDINE HYDROCHLORIDE EFFERVESCENT TABLETS

Usual adult and adolescent dose

Duodenal ulcer—
Treatment: Oral, 150 mg two times a day or 300 mg at bedtime.
Prophylaxis of recurrent duodenal ulcer: Oral, 150 mg at bedtime.

Gastric ulcer, benign, active—
Treatment: Oral, 150 mg two times a day.
Prophylaxis of recurrent gastric ulcer: Oral, 150 mg at bedtime.

Gastric hypersecretory conditions (e.g., Zollinger-Ellison syndrome, systemic mastocytosis, multiple endocrine adenomas)—
Oral, 150 mg two times a day, the dosage being adjusted as needed and therapy continued as long as clinically indicated. Doses up to 6 grams per day have been used in severe cases.

Gastroesophageal reflux—
Oral, 150 mg two times a day.

Note: The recommended oral dose for the treatment of erosive esophagitis is 150 mg four times a day. For the prophylaxis of erosive esophagitis, the recommended oral dose is 150 mg two times a day.

Note: For patients with impaired renal function (creatinine clearance of less than 50 mL per minute)—Oral, 150 mg every twenty-four hours, the frequency of the dosage being increased to every twelve hours or more frequently, if necessary. Reductions in dosage may also be required if hepatic function impairment is present.

Usual pediatric dose

Duodenal ulcer or
Gastric ulcer—
Treatment: Oral, 2 to 4 mg per kg per day, divided into two doses, up to a maximum dose of 300 mg per day.Maintenance: Oral, 2 to 4 mg per kg once daily, up to a maximum dose of 150 mg per day.

Gastroesophageal reflux or
Erosive esophagitis treatment—
Treatment: Oral, 5 to 10 mg per kg per day, usually given as two divided doses.

Note: In certain circumstances, doses may be titrated based on gastric pH.

Usual geriatric dose

See *Usual adult and adolescent dose*.

Strength(s) usually available

U.S.—
25 mg (base) (Rx) [*Zantac 25 EFFERdose Tablets* (aspartame; monosodium citrate anhydrous; povidone; sodium bicarbonate; sodium benzoate)].
150 mg (base) (Rx) [*Zantac 150 EFFERdose Tablets* (aspartame; monosodium citrate anhydrous; povidone; sodium bicarbonate)].

Canada—
Not commercially available.

Packaging and storage

Store between 2 and 30 °C (36 and 86 °F), unless otherwise specified by manufacturer.

Preparation of dosage form

Dissolve each dose in 6 to 8 ounces (180 to 240 mL) of water before drinking.

Auxiliary labeling

- Continue medicine for full time of treatment.
- Dissolve in water before use

Caution

Zantac EFFERdose Tablets brand of effervescent tablets contain aspartame, which is metabolized to phenylalanine and must be used with caution in patients with phenylketonuria. The aspartame in a 25-mg dose of Zantac EFFERdose Tablets will be metabolized to 2.81 mg of phenylalanine and the aspartame in a 150-mg dose of Zantac EFFERdose Tablets will be metabolized to 16.84 mg of phenylalanine.

Additional information

The total sodium content is 183.12 mg (7.96 mEq) per tablet.

Parenteral Dosage Forms

Note: Bracketed uses in the *Dosage Forms* section refer to categories of use and/or indications that are not included in U.S. product labeling.

The dosing and strengths of the dosage forms available are expressed in terms of ranitidine base (not the hydrochloride salt).

RANITIDINE HYDROCHLORIDE INJECTION USP

Usual adult and adolescent dose

Duodenal ulcer or
Gastric ulcer or
Gastric hypersecretory conditions (e.g., Zollinger-Ellison syndrome, systemic mastocytosis, multiple endocrine adenomas) and
[Prophylaxis of stress-related mucosal bleeding]—
Intramuscular, 50 mg every six to eight hours.
Intravenous, 50 mg every six to eight hours, diluted to a total volume of 20 mL with a compatible intravenous solution and administered over a period of not less than five minutes.
Intravenous infusion, 50 mg every six to eight hours, diluted in 100 mL of a compatible intravenous solution and administered over a fifteen- to twenty-minute period.
Continuous intravenous infusion, 6.25 mg per hour, diluted in a compatible intravenous solution.

Note: For gastric hypersecretory conditions, the infusion should be started at 1 mg per kg of body weight per hour and increased by 0.5 mg per kg of body weight per hour increments (if gastric acid output is greater than 10 mEq per hour or patient is symptomatic), up to 2.5 mg per kg of body weight per hour.

[Prophylaxis of aspiration pneumonitis]—
Intramuscular or slow intravenous injection, 50 mg administered forty-five to sixty minutes before induction of general anesthesia.

Note: For patients with impaired renal function (creatinine clearance of less than 50 mL per minute)—Intravenous, 50 mg every eighteen to twenty-four hours, the frequency of the dosage being increased to every twelve hours or more frequently, if necessary. Further reduction in dosage may be required if hepatic function impairment is also present.

Usual adult prescribing limits
400 mg a day.

Usual pediatric dose
Duodenal ulcer or
Gastric ulcer—
Intravenous infusion, 2 to 4 mg per kilogram of body weight a day, diluted to a suitable volume with a compatible intravenous solution and administered over a fifteen- to twenty-minute period
Gastroesophageal reflux—
Intravenous infusion, 2 to 8 mg per kg of body weight, diluted in a suitable volume with a compatible intravenous solution and administered over a fifteen- to twenty-minute period, three times a day.

Note: In certain circumstances, doses may be titrated based on gastric pH.

Usual geriatric dose
See *Usual adult and adolescent dose.*

Strength(s) usually available
U.S.—
50 mg (base) per 2 mL (Rx) [*Zantac* (phenol 0.5%)].
Canada—
50 mg (base) per 2 mL (Rx) [*Zantac*].

Packaging and storage
Store below 30 °C (86 °F), unless otherwise specified by manufacturer. Protect from light. Protect from freezing.

Preparation of dosage form
For 50 mg per 2 mL strength—
For intravenous use, ranitidine injection must be diluted prior to use to a total volume of 20 mL with a compatible intravenous solution, such as sodium chloride injection (0.9%).
For intermittent intravenous infusion, ranitidine injection must be diluted prior to use in 100 mL of a compatible intravenous solution, such as dextrose injection (5%).

Stability
Diluted solutions of ranitidine injection are stable for 48 hours at room temperature.
Injection should not be used if discolored or if a precipitate is present.
The bulk package of ranitidine should be discarded within twenty-four hours after it is opened.

RANITIDINE HYDROCHLORIDE IN SODIUM CHLORIDE INJECTION

Usual adult and adolescent dose
See *Ranitidine Injection USP*

Usual adult prescribing limits
See *Ranitidine Injection USP*

Usual pediatric dose
See *Ranitidine Injection USP*

Usual geriatric dose
See *Ranitidine Injection USP*

Strength(s) usually available
U.S.—
50 mg (base) per 50 mL (premixed), in 0.45% sodium chloride (Rx) [*Zantac*].
Canada—
50 mg (base) per 50 mL (premixed), in 0.45% sodium chloride (Rx) [*Zantac*].

Packaging and storage
Store between 2 °C and 25 °C (36 °F and 77 °F). Protect from light. Protect from freezing.

Note: Brief exposure to temperatures up to 40 °C (104 °F) has not adversely affected the premixed product.

Selected Bibliography

Feldman M, Burton M. Histamine$_2$-receptor antagonists standard therapy for acid-peptic diseases (first of two parts). N Engl J Med 1990; 323(24): 1672-80.

Feldman M, Burton M. Histamine$_2$-receptor antagonists standard therapy for acid-peptic diseases (second of two parts). N Engl J Med 1990; 323(25): 1749-55.

Revised: 01/21/2005

Table 1. Pharmacology/Pharmacokinetics

Drug	Absorption* (% oral bioavailability)	Protein binding	Biotransformation	Half-life (elimination): With normal renal function (hr)	Half-life (elimination): With reduced creatinine clearance (mL/min: hr)
Cimetidine	Rapid (60–70)	Low (15–20%)	Hepatic (30–40% of oral dose)	Oral: 2.0 Parenteral: 1.6–2.1†	20–50: 2.9 <20: 3.7 Anephric: 5
Famotidine	Rapid; incomplete (40–45)	Low (15–20%)	Hepatic (minimal first pass metabolism)	Oral/Parenteral: 2.5–3.5	<10: 20 or more
Nizatidine	Rapid (>90)	Moderate (35%)	Hepatic (minimal first pass metabolism)	Oral: 1–2	Anephric: 3.5–11
Ranitidine	Rapid (39–87)	Low (15%)	Hepatic	Oral: 2.5 Parenteral: 2–2.5	Oral—20–30: 8–9 Parenteral—25–35: 4.8

*Rate of absorption, but not extent, is delayed by food. Younger patients usually have better absorption of cimetidine than elderly patients. Absorption of famotidine and nizatidine is slightly increased by food, while the absorption of ranitidine is not significantly affected by the presence of food.

†In burn patients with thermal injury ranging from 6 to 80% of the body surface, and with normal renal function, elimination half-life of cimetidine has been found to be significantly reduced.

Table 2. Pharmacology/Pharmacokinetics

Drug	Mean serum concentration resulting in 50% inhibition* (ng/mL)	Time to peak concentration after oral dose (hr)	Time to peak effect (hr)	Duration of action (hr)	Elimination† (% excreted unchanged)
Cimetidine	500	0.75-1.5	Oral: 1–2	Nocturnal: 6–8 Basal: 4–5	Primarily renal (48% of oral dose; 75% of parenteral dose)‡
Famotidine	13	1–3	Oral: 1–3 Parenteral: 0.5	Nocturnal and basal: 10–12 (oral and IV)	Primarily renal (30–35% of oral dose; 65–70% of parenteral dose)
Nizatidine	295	0.5–3	Oral: 0.5–3	Nocturnal: Up to 12 Basal: Up to 8	Primarily renal (60% of oral dose)
Ranitidine	100	2–3	Oral: 1–3	Nocturnal: 13 Basal: 4	Primarily renal (30% of oral dose; 70% of parenteral dose)

*Refers to inhibition of pentagastrin-stimulated acid secretion.
†Trace amounts of H_2-receptor antagonists are removable by hemodialysis and peritoneal dialysis.
‡In burn patients with thermal injury ranging from 6 to 80% of the body surface, and with normal renal function, total clearance of cimetidine has been found to be significantly increased.

HISTRELIN Systemic†

VA CLASSIFICATION (Primary): AN500

Commonly used brand name(s): *Vantas*.

Note: For a listing of dosage forms and brand names by country availability, see *Dosage Forms* section(s).

†Not commercially available in Canada.

Category

Antineoplastic.

Indications

Accepted

Carcinoma, prostate—Histrelin is indicated in the palliative treatment of advanced prostate cancer.

Pharmacology/Pharmacokinetics

Physicochemical characteristics

Source—Synthetic.

Chemical Group—Nonapeptide; potent antagonistic activity against naturally occurring gonadotropin releasing-hormone (GnRH).

Molecular weight—Histrelin acetate: 1443.7.

Mechanism of action/Effect

Histrelin exerts its pharmacological action by an initial increase in circulating levels of luteinizing hormone (LH) and follicle stimulating hormone (FSH) leading to a transient increase in concentration of gonadal steroids. Continuous administration results in decreased levels of LH and FSH. In males, testosterone is reduced to castrate levels.

Absorption

The relative bioavailability for the histrelin implant in prostate cancer patients with normal renal and hepatic function compared to a subcutaneous bolus dose in healthy male volunteers is 92%.

Distribution

Volume of distribution (Vol_D): 58.4 +/− 7.86 L following a (500 mcg) subcutaneous bolus dose.

Biotransformation

A study using human hepatocytes identified a single metabolite resulting from C-terminal dealkylation. Peptide fragments from hydrolysis are also likely metabolites.

Half-life

Terminal—3.92 +/− 1.01 hr following a subcutaneous bolus dose in healthy volunteers.

Time to peak concentration

12 hours.

Peak serum concentration

1.10 +/− 0.375 ng/mL.

Time to peak effect

Medical castration occurs within 2 to 4 weeks after initiation of treatment.

Elimination

Clearance: 179 +/− 37.8 mL/min following a subcutaneous bolus dose in healthy volunteers; 174 +/− 56.5 mL/min following a 50 mg as histrelin acetate implant in 17 prostate cancer patients.

Special populations

Race: Data from Hispanics, Blacks and Caucasians demonstrated no differences among race on the pharmacokinetics of histrelin.

Renal Insufficiency: Serum concentrations of histrelin in renally impaired patients (CL_{cr}: 15-60 mL/min) was 50% higher than in patients with no renal impairment; however, the change in exposure is not clinically relevant.

Hepatic insufficiency: The pharmacokinetics of histrelin in hepatically impaired patients have not been determined.

Precautions to Consider

Carcinogenicity

Carcinogenicity studies were done in rats and mice. Rats given histrelin at doses of 5, 25, or 150 mcg/kg/day for two years revealed increased pituitary adenomas, pancreatic islet-cell adenomas in females, and non-dose-related testicular Leydig-cell tumors. In addition, increased stomach papillomas were seen in male rats given high doses. Mice given histrelin at doses of 20, 200, or 2000 mcg/kg/day for 18 months showed increases in mammary-gland adenocarcinomas in all treated females and increases in histiocytic sarcomas in females at the highest dose.

Mutagenicity

Saline extracts of implants with and without histrelin were negative in a battery of genotoxicity tests.

Mutagenicity studies with histrelin acetate have not been done.

Pregnancy/Reproduction

Fertility—Fertility studies done in rats and monkeys given subcutaneous daily doses of histrelin acetate up to 180 mcg/kg for 6 months demonstrated full reversibility of fertility suppression. The development and reproductive performance of offspring from histrelin treated parents has not been investigated.

Pregnancy—Histrelin is contraindicated in women. Risk-benefit must be carefully considered. Studies in animals have shown that histrelin causes major fetal abnormalities in animals.

Increased fetal mortality and decreased fetal body weight were observed in rats and rabbits. The effects of fetal mortality are expected consequences of altered hormonal levels. Spontaneous abortion may occur.

FDA Pregnancy Category X

Breast-feeding

Although very little information is available regarding the distribution of antineoplastic agents into breast milk, breast-feeding is not recommended during chemotherapy because of the potential risks to the infant.

Pediatrics
Histrelin is contraindicated in pediatric patients.

Geriatrics
Appropriate studies performed to date have not demonstrated geriatrics-specific problems that would limit the usefulness of histrelin in the elderly. Prostate cancer occurs primarily in an older patient population. Clinical studies with histrelin have been conducted primarily in patients ≥ 65 years of age.

Drug interactions and/or related problems
The following drug interactions and/or related problems have been selected on the basis of their potential clinical significance (possible mechanism in parentheses where appropriate)—not necessarily inclusive (» = major clinical significance):

Note: No pharmacokinetic-based drug-drug studies with histrelin have been done.

Laboratory value alterations
The following have been selected on the basis of their potential clinical significance (possible effect in parentheses where appropriate)—not necessarily inclusive (» = major clinical significance).

With diagnostic test results

Gonadal functions and
Pituitary gonadotropic
(may be suppressed during and after histrelin therapy)

Prostate-specific antigen (PSA), serum
(levels may decrease)

» Testosterone, serum
(transient increases may be seen during the first week of treatment)

Medical considerations/Contraindications
The medical considerations/contraindications included have been selected on the basis of their potential clinical significance (reasons given in parentheses where appropriate)—not necessarily inclusive (» = major clinical significance).

Except under special circumstances, this medication should not be used when the following medical problem exists:

» Hypersensitivity to GnRH, GnRH agonist analogs or to any components of histrelin

Risk-benefit should be considered when the following medical problems exist:

Hepatic insufficiency
(adequate studies have not been done)

Patient monitoring
The following may be especially important in patient monitoring (other tests may be warranted in some patients, depending on condition; » = major clinical significance):

Bone mineral density
(extended treatment may result in decreased bone mineral density; patients should be monitored)

Prostate-specific antigen (PSA), serum
(monitor for response to histrelin)

» Testosterone, serum and
(monitor for response to histrelin; results of testosterone determinations are dependent on type and precision of assay methodology; worsening of symptoms or onset of new symptoms may occur; cases of ureteral obstruction and spinal cord compression have been reported with LH-RH agonists; if spinal compression or renal impairment develop standard treatment should be instituted)

» Urinary tract obstruction or
» Vertebral lesions, metastatic
(observe closely during the first few weeks of therapy)

Side/Adverse Effects
The following side/adverse effects have been selected on the basis of their potential clinical significance (possible signs and symptoms in parentheses where appropriate)—not necessarily inclusive:

Those indicating need for medical attention
Incidence rare

Renal impairment (lower back/side pain; decreased frequency / amount of urine; bloody urine; increased thirst; loss of appetite; nausea; vomiting; unusual tiredness or weakness; swelling of face, fingers, lower legs; weight gain; troubled breathing; increased blood pressure)

Reported during clinical trials

Renal failure aggravated (back/side pain; decreased frequency / amount of urine bloody urine; increased thirst; loss of appetite; nausea; vomiting; unusual tiredness or weakness; swelling of face, fingers, lower legs; weight gain; troubled breathing; increased blood pressure)

Those indicating need for medical attention only if they continue or are bothersome
Incidence more frequent

Fatigue (unusual tiredness or weakness); ***hot flashes*** (feeling of warmth; redness of the face, neck, arms and occasionally, upper chest sudden; sweating); ***implant site reaction*** (infection, irritation, redness or swelling to skin, local); ***testicular atrophy*** (decrease in testicle size)

Incidence less frequent

Constipation (difficulty having a bowel movement (stool)); ***erectile dysfunction*** (loss in sexual ability, desire, drive, or performance; decreased interest in sexual intercourse; inability to have or keep an erection); ***erythema*** (flushing, redness of skin; unusually warm skin); ***gynecomastia*** (swelling of the breasts or breast soreness in both females and males); ***headache; insomnia*** (sleeplessness; trouble sleeping; unable to sleep); ***libido decreased*** (loss in sexual ability, desire, drive, or performance; decreased interest in sexual intercourse; inability to have or keep an erection); ***weight increased***

Incidence rare

Infection/inflammation (redness feeling of heat); ***swelling***

Reported during clinical trials

Abdominal discomfort (stomach soreness or discomfort); ***anemia*** (pale skin, troubled breathing with exertion, unusual bleeding or bruising, unusual tiredness or weakness); ***appetite increased; arthralgia*** (pain in joints; muscle pain or stiffness; difficulty in moving); ***back pain; bone pain; breast pain; breast tenderness; calculus renal*** (blood in urine; difficult urination; pain in lower back; pain or burning while urinating; sudden decrease in amount of urine); ***contusion*** (large, flat, blue or purplish patches in the skin); ***depression*** (discouragement; feeling sad or empty; irritability; lack of appetite; loss of interest or pleasure; tiredness; trouble concentrating; trouble sleeping); ***dizziness; dyspnea exertional*** (shortness of breath; difficult or labored breathing; tightness in chest; wheezing); ***dysuria*** (difficult or painful urination burning while urinating); ***feeling cold; food craving; fluid retention*** (decrease in amount of urine; noisy, rattling breathing; shortness of breath; swelling of fingers, hands, feet, or lower legs; troubled breathing at rest; weight gain); ***flushing*** (feeling of warmth redness of the face, neck, arms and occasionally, upper chest); ***genital pruritus (male)*** (itching or pain of the genital area); ***gynecomastia aggravated*** (swelling of the breasts or breast soreness in both females and males); ***hematoma*** (collection of blood under skin deep, dark purple bruise itching, pain, redness, or swelling); ***hematuria aggravated*** (blood in urine); ***hepatic disorder*** (dark urine; light-colored stools; loss of appetite; nausea and vomiting; unusual tiredness; yellow eyes or skin; fever with or without chills; stomach pain); ***hypercalcemia*** (abdominal pain; confusion; constipation; depression; dry mouth; headache; incoherent speech; increased urination; loss of appetite; metallic taste; muscle weakness; nausea; thirst; unusual tiredness; vomiting; weight loss); ***hypercholesterolemia*** (large amount of cholesterol in the blood); ***hypotrichosis*** (increased hair growth on forehead, back, arms, and legs); ***irritability; lethargy*** (unusual drowsiness; dullness; tiredness; weakness or feeling of sluggishness); ***malaise*** (general feeling of discomfort or illness; unusual tiredness or weakness); ***muscle twitching; myalgia*** (joint pain; swollen joints; muscle aching or cramping; muscle pains or stiffness; difficulty in moving); ***nausea; neck pain; night sweats; pain; pain in limb; palpitations*** (fast, irregular, pounding, or racing heartbeat or pulse); ***peripheral edema*** (bloating or swelling of face, arms, hands, lower legs, or feet; rapid weight gain; tingling of hands or feet; unusual weight gain or loss); ***pruritus*** (itching skin); ***sexual dysfunction*** (decreased sexual performance or desire abnormal ejaculation); ***stent occlusion; sweating increased; tremor*** (trembling or shaking of hands or feet; shakiness in legs, arms, hands, feet); ***urinary frequency*** (increased need to urinate; passing urine more often); ***urinary retention*** (decrease in urine volume; decrease in frequency of urination; difficulty in passing urine; [dribbling] painful urination); ***ventricular extrasystoles*** (extra heart beat); ***weakness; weight decreased***

Overdose
For more information on the management of overdose or unintentional ingestion, **contact a poison control center** (see *Poison Control Center Listing*).

Histrelin at doses up to 200 mcg/kg in rats and rabbits, or 2000 mcg/kg in mice (20 to 200 times the maximum recommended human dose of 10 mcg/kg day) produced no systemic toxicity.

Treatment of overdose

There is no known specific antidote to histrelin. Treatment is generally symptomatic and supportive.

Supportive care—

Patients in whom intentional overdose is confirmed or suspected should be referred for psychiatric consultation.

Patient Consultation

As an aid to patient consultation, refer to *Advice for the Patient, Histrelin (Systemic).*

In providing consultation, consider emphasizing the following selected information (» = major clinical significance):

Before using this medication

» Conditions affecting use, especially:

Hypersensitivity to GnRH, GnRH agonist analogs or to any component in histrelin.

Pregnancy—Histrelin is not indicated in women. Histrelin may cause fetal harm if administered to pregnant women.

Use in children—Histrelin is not indicated for use in children.

Proper use of this medication

» Proper dosing

» Proper storage

» Importance of reading the patient information leaflet.

» The importance of not removing the pressure bandage or wetting the inserted arm for 24 hours after insertion of the implant.

» The importance of refraining from heavy lifting and strenuous physical activity of the inserted arm for 7 days to allow the incision to fully close.

» The importance of not removing the surgical strips, rather allowing them to fall off on their own after several days.

Precautions while using this medication

» Regular visits to physician to check your progress and to ensure histrelin insert is in place and functioning in your body.

» Potential loss in bone mineral density with extended treatment.

Side/adverse effects

Signs of potential side effects, especially renal impairment

General Dosing Information

Histrelin implant is a surgical procedure. Adherence to recommended insertion and removal procedures is advised to minimize complications and implant expulsion.

Histrelin implant includes a kit containing all supplies necessary for insertion and removal of the implant.

Patients should be given and read the histrelin information leaflet.

Patients should be instructed to refrain from wetting the inserted arm for 24 hours, and avoid heavy lifting or strenuous exertion for 7 days after implant insertion.

Long periods of medical castration may have effects on bone density. Decreased bone density has been reported in men who have had orchiectomy or who have been treated with an LH-RH agonist analog.

Histrelin implant must be removed after 12 months. Another implant may be inserted to continue therapy.

It is important to properly dispose of the histrelin implant.

Histrelin implant is not radio-opaque and not visible through X-ray. If the implant is difficult to locate by palpation, ultrasound and CT scan may be used.

Parenteral Dosage Forms

HISTRELIN ACETATE IMPLANT

Usual adult dose

Carcinoma, prostatic—

Subcutaneous implant, one implant per 12 months.

Usual pediatric dose

Safety and efficacy have not been established.

Usual geriatric dose

See *Usual adult dose.*

Strength(s) usually available

U.S.—

50 mg (free base) per implant (Rx) [*Vantas* (benzoin methyl ether; Perkadox-16; stearic acid NF; trimethylolpropane trimethacrylate; Triton X-100; 2-hydroxyethyl methacrylate; 2-hydroxypropyl methacrylate)].

Packaging and storage

Store between 2 and 8 °C (36 and 46 °F) in the original container. Protect from light. Do not freeze.

Preparation of dosage form

See the manufacturer's package insert for instructions on inserting and removing the implant.

Auxiliary labeling

- Protect from light.
- Do not freeze.

Developed: 11/29/2005

HMG-COA REDUCTASE INHIBITORS Systemic

This monograph includes information on the following: 1) Atorvastatin; 2) Cerivastatin# †; 3) Fluvastatin; 4) Lovastatin; 5) Pravastatin; 6) Simvastatin.

VA CLASSIFICATION (Primary/Secondary): CV351/CV900

Commonly used brand name(s): *Altoprev*[4]; *Lescol*[3]; *Lipitor*[1]; *Mevacor*[4]; *Pravachol*[5]; *Zocor*[6]

Other commonly used names are: Epistatin [Simvastatin] Eptastatin [Pravastatin] Mevinolin [Lovastatin] Synvinolin [Cerivastatin#]

Note: For a listing of dosage forms and brand names by country availability, see *Dosage Forms* section(s).

*Not commercially available in U.S.

†Not commercially available in Canada.

#Products containing cerivastatin were withdrawn from the market by Bayer in August 2001

Category

HMG-CoA reductase inhibitor; antihyperlipidemic.

Indications

Note: Cerivastatin was removed from the market by Bayer in August 2001

Accepted

Hyperlipidemia (treatment)—3-Hydroxy-3-methylglutaryl coenzyme A (HMG-CoA) reductase inhibitors are indicated as adjuncts to diet in the treatment of primary hypercholesterolemia (heterozygous familial and nonfamilial) and mixed dyslipidemia (type IIa and IIb hyperlipoproteinemia) caused by elevated low-density lipoprotein cholesterol (LDL-C) concentrations in patients with a significant risk of coronary artery disease, who have not responded to diet or other measures alone. The HMG-CoA reductase inhibitors may also be useful for the reduction of elevated LDL-C concentrations in patients with combined hypercholesterolemia and hypertriglyceridemia,and for the reduction of total-C, LDL-C, apolipoprotein B (Apo B), and triglyceride (TG), and to increase HDL-C levels in patients with combined hypercholesterolemia and mixed dyslipidemia.

Atorvastatin[1] and simvastatin are indicated as adjunctive therapy with other lipid lowering treatments (*eg*, LDL apheresis) in homozygous familial hypercholesterolemia to reduce total cholesterol (total-C) and LDL-C.

Atorvastatin[1] and simvastatin[1] are indicated for the treatment of dysbetalipoproteinemia (type III hyperlipoproteinemia) in patients who did not respond adequately to diet.

Atorvastatin[1] and simvastatin[1] are indicated as adjunctive therapy to diet for the treatment of patients with elevated serum triglyceride levels (type IV hyperlipoproteinemia).

For additional information on initial therapeutic guidelines related to the treatment of hyperlipidemia, see *Appendix III.*

Coronary heart disease (prophylaxis)—Pravastatin and simvastatin are indicated to reduce the risk of total mortality by reducing the incidence of coronary death in patients without symptomatic cardiovascular disease. Lovastatin[1], pravastatin, and simvastatin are indicated to reduce the risk of myocardial infarction and the risk of undergoing myocardial revascularization procedures. Lovastatin[1] is also indicated to reduce the risk of unstable angina.

Fluvastatin and lovastatin are indicated to slow the progression of atherosclerosis in patients with coronary heart disease as part of a treatment strategy to lower total-C and LDL-C to target levels.

Stroke or transient ischemic attack (prophylaxis)[1]—Simvastatin is indicated to reduce the risk of stroke or transient ischemic attack in patients with coronary heart disease and hypercholesterolemia.

[1]Not included in Canadian product labeling.

Pharmacology/Pharmacokinetics

Physicochemical characteristics

Source—
Atorvastatin, cerivastatin, fluvastatin: Synthetic.
Lovastatin, pravastatin, simvastatin: Fungus-derived.

Molecular weight—
Atorvastatin calcium: 1209.42.
Cerivastatin sodium: 481.5.
Fluvastatin sodium: 433.45.
Lovastatin: 404.55.
Pravastatin sodium: 446.52.
Simvastatin: 418.57.

Mechanism of action/Effect

The active beta-hydroxy acid form of the 3-hydroxy-3-methylglutaryl coenzyme A (HMG-CoA) reductase inhibitors competitively inhibits the enzyme HMG-CoA reductase. Atorvastatin, cerivastatin, fluvastatin, and pravastatin are administered in the active (open acid) form, while lovastatin and simvastatin must be hydrolyzed to the beta-hydroxyacid in tissues.

Inhibition of HMG-CoA reductase prevents conversion of HMG-CoA to mevalonate, the rate-limiting step in cholesterol biosynthesis. The primary site of action of HMG-CoA reductase inhibitors is the liver. Inhibition of cholesterol synthesis in the liver leads to upregulation of LDL receptors and an increase in catabolism of LDL cholesterol. There may also be some reduction in LDL production as a result of inhibition of hepatic synthesis of very low-density lipoprotein (VLDL), the precursor of LDL. HMG-CoA reductase inhibitors reduce LDL cholesterol, VLDL cholesterol, and to a lesser extent, plasma triglyceride concentrations, and slightly increase high-density lipoprotein (HDL) concentrations.

Absorption

Atorvastatin—Rapidly absorbed; bioavailability of parent compound 14%. Grapefruit juice in large amounts has been shown to interfere with the metabolism of atorvastatin, causing increases in C_{max} and AUC

Cerivastatin—Bioavailability 60% (range 39 to 101%)

Fluvastatin—Rapidly and almost completely absorbed from the gastrointestinal tract (greater than 90%); bioavailability 19 to 29%.

Lovastatin—Reduced by approximately 30% when administered on an empty stomach rather than with food.

Pravastatin—Approximately 34%; bioavailability approximately 18%.

Simvastatin—Absorption in animal study averaged about 85%; bioavailability less than 5%

Protein binding

Atorvastatin—Very high (≥ 98%)
Cerivastatin—Very high (> 99%) (80% to albumin)
Fluvastatin—Very high (greater than 98%).
Lovastatin—Very high (greater than 95%).
Pravastatin—Moderate (50%).
Simvastatin—Very high (approximately 95%).

Biotransformation

Atorvastatin—Administered in active (open acid) form. Biotransformation by ortho- and parahydroxylation and beta-oxidation. Ortho- and parahydroxylated metabolites are pharmacologically active. Their *in vitro* inhibition of HMG-CoA reductase activity is equivalent to the parent compound.

Cerivastatin—Administered in active (open acid) form. Biotransformation by demethylation and hydroxylation. Certain metabolites (M1 and M23) are pharmacologically active with relative potency of 50% and 100% of the parent compound, respectively

Fluvastatin—Administered in active (open acid) form. Biotransformation by hydroxylation, N-dealkylation, and beta-oxidation; the major metabolic products present in plasma are pharmacologically inactive.

Lovastatin and simvastatin—By hydrolysis in tissues, to several metabolites, including a major active beta-hydroxy metabolite.

Pravastatin—Administered in active (open acid) form and converted to inactive metabolites and active metabolites with minimal activity.

Half-life

Atorvastatin—Elimination, approximately 14 hours
Cerivastatin—Elimination, 2 to 3 hours
Fluvastatin—Approximately 1.2 hours (range, 0.5 to 3.1 hours).
Lovastatin—3 hours.
Pravastatin—1.3 to 2.7 hours.
Pravastatin—Approximately 1 hour.
Simvastatin—1.3 to 2.4 hours.

Time to peak concentration

Atorvastatin—1 to 2 hours
Cerivastatin—Approximately 2.5 hours
Fluvastatin—0.5 to 0.7 hour.
Lovastatin
- Extended-release—14.2 hours
- Immediate-release—2 to 4 hours

Peak plasma concentration:

Lovastatin
- Extended-release (40 mg), steady state—5.5 ng per mL for lovastatin; 5.8 ng per mL for lovastatin acid
- Immediate-release (40 mg), steady state—7.8 ng per mL for lovastatin; 11.9 ng per mL for lovastatin acid

Duration of action

Lovastatin—After withdrawal of continuous therapy: 4 to 6 weeks.

Elimination

Atorvastatin—
Fecal (biliary): primary route of elimination
Renal: less than 2%

Cerivastatin—
Fecal (biliary): 70%
Renal: 24%

Fluvastatin—
Fecal (biliary): 90%.
Renal: 5%.

Lovastatin—
Fecal (biliary and unabsorbed): 83%.
Renal: 10%.

Pravastatin—
Fecal (biliary and unabsorbed): 70%.
Renal: 20%.

Simvastatin—
Fecal (biliary and unabsorbed): 60%.
Renal: 13%.

Precautions to Consider

Carcinogenicity

Atorvastatin—A 2-year carcinogenicity study in rats at doses of 10, 30, and 100 mg per kg of body weight (mg/kg) per day found 2 rare tumors (rhabdomyosarcoma and fibrosarcoma) in the high dose female rats (plasma drug concentration of approximately 16 times the mean human plasma drug concentration after an 80 mg oral dose). Administration of atorvastatin at 100, 200, or 400 mg/kg per day in mice (producing plasma values of 6 times the mean human drug exposure after an 80 mg dose) for 2 years resulted in a significant increase in liver adenomas in males and liver carcinomas in females.

Cerivastatin—A 2-year carcinogenicity study in rats at doses of 0.007, 0.034, or 0.158 mg/kg per day (plasma drug concentrations of the high dosage level equaled that of human exposure after a 0.4 mg daily oral dose) showed tumor incidences were comparable to those in controls. In mice given cerivastatin for 2 years at doses of 0.4, 1.8, 9.1, or 55 mg/kg per day (plasma drug concentrations in the range of human exposure at 0.4 mg/day) hepatocellular adenomas were significantly increased in males and females at doses ≥ 9.1 mg/kg, and hepatocellular carcinomas were significantly increased in males at ≥ 1.8 mg/kg.

Fluvastatin—A study in rats given fluvastatin in doses of 6, 9, and 18 to 24 mg per kg of body weight (mg/kg) per day (plasma drug concentrations of approximately 9, 13, and 26 to 35 times the mean human plasma drug concentration after a 40-mg dose) found a low incidence of forestomach squamous papillomas and one carcinoma of the forestomach at the 24 mg/kg dose. However, these results were thought to reflect prolonged hyperplasia induced by direct contact with fluvastatin sodium rather than a systemic drug effect. Similar results were found in mice studies. In addition, an increased incidence of thyroid follicular cell adenomas and carcinomas was found in male rats treated with the 18 to 24 mg/kg doses.

Lovastatin—Studies in male and female mice given lovastatin in doses of 500 mg/kg per day (a total plasma drug exposure [total HMG-CoA reductase inhibitory activity in extracted plasma] 3 to 4 times that of humans given the highest recommended dose) for 21 months found an increased incidence of hepatocellular carcinomas and adenomas. In female mice, an increase in pulmonary adenomas was observed at approximately 4 times the human drug exposure. The incidence of papillomas in nonglandular mucosa of the stomach was also increased beginning at exposures 1 to 2 times that of humans; however, the human stomach contains only glandular mucosa. In rats given lovastatin for 24 months at drug exposures between 2 and 7 times human exposure at 80 mg per day, a positive dose–response relationship for hepatocellular carcinogenicity was observed in males.

Pravastatin—A study in rats given pravastatin doses producing serum drug concentrations 6 to 10 times higher than those in humans receiving 40 mg showed an increased incidence of hepatocellular carcinomas in male rats at the highest dose. Administration of pravasta-

(producing plasma drug concentrations 0.5 to 5 times the human drug concentrations at 40 mg) in mice for 22 months resulted in an increased incidence of malignant lymphomas in females.

Simvastatin—A 72-week study in mice given simvastatin at doses producing serum concentrations 3, 15, and 33 times higher than the mean human plasma drug concentration after a 40-mg dose revealed increased incidences of liver adenomas, liver carcinomas, and lung adenomas in the middle- and high-dose groups. In addition, a higher incidence of Harderian gland (a gland of the eye in rodents) adenomas was observed in the high-dose group.

A 2-year study in rats exposed to simvastatin concentrations 45 times higher than those in humans given 40 mg revealed an increased incidence of thyroid follicular adenomas.

Mutagenicity

Atorvastatin—No evidence of mutagenicity or clastogenicity was found in the following *in vitro* tests with or without metabolic activation: the Ames test with *Salmonella typhimurium* and *Escherichia coli*, the HGPRT forward mutation assay in Chinese hamster lung cells, and the chromosomal aberration assay in Chinese hamster lung cells. *In vivo,* atorvastatin, was negative in the mouse micronucleus test.

Cerivastatin—No evidence of mutagenicity was found *in vitro* with or without metabolic activation in the following assays: microbial mutagen tests using mutant strains of *Salmonella typhimurium* or *Escherichia coli* , Chinese Hamster Ovary Forward Mutation Assay, Unscheduled DNA Synthesis in rat primary hepatocytes, chromosome aberrations in Chinese hamster ovary cells, and spindle inhibition in human lymphocytes. There was no evidence of genotoxicity *in vivo* in a mouse micronucleus test; however, there was equivocal evidence of mutagenicity in a mouse dominant lethal test.

Fluvastatin—No evidence of mutagenicity was observed in *in vitro* studies with or without rat-liver activation, including microbial mutagen tests, unscheduled DNA synthesis in rat primary hepatocytes, and chromosomal aberration tests. Additionally, there was no evidence of mutagenicity in *in vivo* rat or mouse micronucleus tests.

Lovastatin and *simvastatin*—A microbial mutagen test using mutant strains of *Salmonella typhimurium* with or without rat or mouse liver metabolic activation found no evidence of mutagenicity. There was also no evidence of damage to genetic material in *in vitro* alkaline elution assays using rat or mouse hepatocytes, a V-79 mammalian cell forward mutation study, an *in vitro* chromosome aberration study in CHO cells, or an *in vivo* chromosomal aberration assay in mouse bone marrow.

Pravastatin—No evidence of mutagenicity was observed in *in vitro* tests with or without liver metabolic activation, including microbial mutagen tests, a chromosomal aberration test, a gene conversion assay, a dominant lethal test in mice, and a micronucleus test in mice.

Pregnancy/Reproduction

Fertility—*Atorvastatin:* No changes in fertility in rats were observed at doses up to 175 mg/kg (15 times the human exposure). Aplasia and aspermia in the epididymis and lower epididymal weight were found at doses of 100 mg/kg per day (16 times the human exposure at the 80 mg dose). Lower testis weight was observed at doses of 30 and 100 mg/kg. Decreased sperm motility, decreased spermatid head concentration, and an increased number of abnormal sperms were observed in male rats given 100 mg/kg per day for 11 weeks prior to mating. No adverse effects on semen parameters, or reproductive organ histopathology were found in dogs given dose of 10, 40, or 120 mg/kg for 2 years.

Cerivastatin: No adverse effects on fertility or reproductive performance were observed in male and female rats at doses up to 0.1 mg/kg per day (peak plasma concentration [C_{max}] in the range of human exposure). At a dose of 0.3 mg/kg per day (C_{max} about 2 times human exposure), the length of gestation was marginally prolonged, stillbirths were increased, and the survival rate up to day 4 postpartum was decreased. In the fetuses (F1), a marginal reduction in fetal weight and delay in bone development was observed. In dogs given doses of 0.0008 mg/kg per day (C_{max} in the range of human exposure), atrophy, vacuolization of the germinal epithelium, spermatidic giant cells, and focal oligospermia were observed. At doses of 0.1 mg/kg per day (C_{max} about 20 times human exposure) ejaculate volume was small and libido was decreased in dogs. There was an increased number of morphologically altered spermatozoa, indicating disturbance of epididymal sperm maturation that was reversible when drug administration was discontinued.

Fluvastatin: No adverse effects on fertility or reproductive performance were observed in rats given fluvastatin sodium at doses of up to 6 mg/kg per day in females and 20 mg/kg per day in males.

Lovastatin: Testicular atrophy, decreased spermatogenesis, spermatocytic degeneration, and giant cell formation were seen in dogs given lovastatin starting at doses of 20 mg/kg per day. However, no adverse effects on fertility were observed in rats.

Pravastatin: No adverse effects on fertility or general reproductive performance were observed in rats given pravastatin at doses of up to 500 mg/kg per day.

Simvastatin: Decreased fertility was noted in rats given simvastatin for 34 weeks at 15 times the maximum human exposure level. However, this effect was not observed in another study in rats given simvastatin for 11 weeks at the same dosage level. Seminiferous tubule degeneration was observed in rats given simvastatin at a dose of 180 mg/kg per day (44 times the exposure level of humans given 40 mg per day). Testicular atrophy, decreased spermatogenesis, spermatocytic degeneration, and giant cell formation were observed in dogs given simvastatin at a dose of 10 mg/kg per day (7 times the human exposure level at a dose of 40 mg per day).

Pregnancy—HMG-CoA reductase inhibitors are not recommended for use during pregnancy or in women who plan to become pregnant in the near future.

Adequate and well-controlled studies in humans have not been done. However, because HMG-CoA reductase inhibitors interfere with biosynthesis of mevalonic acid, a cholesterol precursor that may have an essential function in DNA replication and, therefore, may be closely tied to fetal development (including synthesis of steroids and cell membranes), there is a possibility that fetal harm may be caused by administration of these medications during pregnancy. Vertebral anomalies, anal atresia, tracheo-esophageal fistula with esophageal atresia, and renal and radial dysplasias occurred in a neonate born to a mother who took lovastatin during the first trimester of pregnancy. However, a direct causal relationship has not been proven.

Use of birth control is recommended during use of these medications. If pregnancy occurs during HMG-CoA reductase inhibitor therapy, it is recommended that the HMG-CoA reductase inhibitor be discontinued for the duration of the pregnancy. Because of the long-term nature of antihyperlipidemic treatment, temporary suspension of therapy is not expected to be deleterious.

Atorvastatin—

No evidence of teratogenicity was found in rats at doses up to 300 mg/kg per day or rabbits at doses up to 100 mg/kg per day (30 and 20 times, respectively, the human exposure level based on surface area [mg/m^2]). Decreased rat pup survival at birth, neonate, weaning, and maturity in pups, and pup body weight were observed in the offspring of mothers dosed with 225 mg/kg per day(22 times the human exposure at 80 mg/day). Pup development was delayed at doses of 100 and 225 mg/kg per day.

FDA Pregnancy Category X.

Cerivastatin—

Studies in rats given cerivastatin at doses of 0.72 mg/kg (5 times the human exposure of a 0.4 mg oral dose) caused a significant increase in incomplete ossification of the lumbar center of the vertebrae. No anomalies or malformations were found in rabbits given 0.75 mg/kg (3 times the human exposure of a 0.4 mg oral dose). In pregnant rats given a single oral 2 mg/kg dose, cerivastatin crossed the placenta and was found in fetal liver, gastrointestinal tract, and kidneys.

FDA Pregnancy Category X.

Fluvastatin—

No evidence of teratogenicity was found in rats or rabbits given doses of up to 36 mg/kg and 10 mg/kg per day, respectively. Administration of fluvastatin at 12 and 24 mg/kg per day to female rats during the third trimester resulted in maternal mortality at or near term and postpartum. Fetal and neonatal deaths were also observed. These results were confirmed by a second study.

FDA Pregnancy Category X.

Lovastatin—

Studies in mice and rats at doses producing plasma concentrations 40 (mouse fetus) and 80 (rat fetus) times the human exposure found an increased incidence of skeletal malformations. No changes occurred in rats or mice at multiples of 8 and 4 times, respectively, or in rabbits at exposures up to 3 times the highest tolerated human exposure.

FDA Pregnancy Category X.

Pravastatin—

Studies in rats and rabbits given pravastatin at doses of 1000 mg/kg per day (240 times the human exposure based on surface area) and 50 mg/kg per day (20 times the human exposure based on surface area), respectively, did not reveal teratogenic effects.

FDA Pregnancy Category X.

Simvastatin—

No teratogenic effects were observed in rats or rabbits given simvastatin at doses of 25 mg/kg per day (6 times the human exposure based on surface area) and 10 mg/kg per day (4 times the human exposure based on surface area), respectively.

FDA Pregnancy Category X.

Breast-feeding

Use of HMG-CoA reductase inhibitors while breast-feeding is not recommended, because of the potential for serious adverse effects in nursing infants.

Atorvastatin—

It is not known if atorvastatin is distributed in the breast milk. Nursing rat pups had plasma and liver drug levels of 50% and 40%, respectively, of that in their mother's milk.

Cerivastatin—

Cerivastatin is distributed in the breast milk at a milk to plasma concentration ratio of 1.3 to 1.

Fluvastatin—

Fluvastatin is distributed into breast milk and is present in breast milk in a 2 to 1 ratio (milk to plasma).

Lovastatin—

It is not known whether lovastatin is distributed into human breast milk, but it is distributed into the milk of rats.

Pravastatin—

Trace amounts of pravastatin are distributed into human breast milk.

Simvastatin—

It is not known whether simvastatin is distributed into human breast milk.

Pediatrics

Appropriate studies on the relationship of age to the effects of HMG-CoA reductase inhibitors have not been performed in the pediatric population. Safety and efficacy have not been established.

Limited experience with use of atorvastatin, lovastatin, and simvastatin in children younger than 18 years of age seems to indicate that these medications are well tolerated and may be useful in severely hypercholesterolemic children who need medication therapy. However, the long-term safety of HMG-CoA reductase inhibitor use in children has not been studied. Use of these agents should be reserved for severe cases under the care of a lipid specialist. Caution is recommended in use of cholesterol-lowering agents in children younger than 10 years of age.

Atorvastatin—

Safety and effectiveness in patients 10 to 17 years of age with heterozygous familial hypercholesterolemia have been evaluated in a controlled clinical trial of 6 months duration in adolescent boys and postmenarchal girls. In this limited controlled study, there was no detectable effect on growth or sexual maturation in boys or on menstrual cycle length in girls. Adolescent females should be counseled on appropriate contraceptive methods while on atorvastatin therapy.

Geriatrics

Studies performed to date in a limited number of patients 65 years of age or older have not demonstrated geriatrics-specific problems that would limit the usefulness of HMG-CoA reductase inhibitors in the elderly.

Drug interactions and/or related problems

The following drug interactions and/or related problems have been selected on the basis of their potential clinical significance (possible mechanism in parentheses where appropriate)—not necessarily inclusive (» = major clinical significance):

Note: Combinations containing any of the following medications, depending on the amount present, may also interact with this medication.

Anticoagulants, coumarin- or indandione-derivative
(concurrent use with HMG-CoA reductase inhibitors may increase bleeding or prothrombin time; prothrombin time should be monitored in patients taking HMG-CoA reductase inhibitors with anticoagulants. However, atorvastatin, cerivastatin, fluvastatin, and pravastatin did not significantly affect prothrombin time when coadministered with warfarin; monitor prothrombin time (PT) before and during concurrent therapy with coumarin anticoagulants and simvastatin.)

Cholestyramine or
Colestipol
(concurrent use may decrease the bioavailability of HMG-CoA reductase inhibitors; therefore, when these agents are used with HMG-CoA reductase inhibitors for therapeutic advantage, it is recommended that the HMG-CoA reductase inhibitor be given 2 to 4 hours after cholestyramine or colestipol)

Azole antifungals or
» Cyclosporine or
» Gemfibrozil or
» Fibrates, other or
Immunosuppressants or
Macrolide antibiotics or
» Niacin
(concurrent use with HMG-CoA reductase inhibitors may be associated with an increased risk of rhabdomyolysis and acute renal failure; although cases have been reported only with lovastatin, the potential also exists with other HMG-CoA reductase inhibitors; combined therapy of HMG-CoA reductase inhibitors with gemfibrozil, other fibrates, niacin, or immunosuppressants should include careful monitoring for symptoms of myopathy or rhabdomyolysis)

(simvastatin dose should not exceed 10 mg/day when administered concurrently with niacin, fibrates, or cyclosporine)

(concurrent use with cerivastatin and gemfibrozil is contraindicated, due to rhabdomyolysis and associated renal failure)

For atorvastatin (in addition to those listed above):

Antacids
(concurrent use with atorvastatin may decrease plasma concentrations of atorvastatin approximately 35%)

» Oral contraceptives
(concurrent use with atorvastatin may increase AUC value for norethindrone and ethinyl estradiol by approximately 30% and 20% respectively)

For atorvastatin, fluvastatin, and simvastatin (in addition to those listed above)

» Digoxin
(concurrent use with atorvastatin, fluvastatin, or simvastatin may cause an elevation in serum digoxin concentrations)

For atorvastatin and simvastatin (in addition to those listed above)

» Grapefruit juice
(concurrent use with large amounts of grapefruit juice has been reported to significantly increase the serum concentrations and the area under the plasma concentration-time curve (AUC). In a study with 12 subjects, administration of grapefruit juice double-strength 200 mL three times a day resulted in a C_{max} decrease of about 24% of active atorvastatin compounds. An increase in AUC of active atorvastatin compounds was about 23%. The time to C_{max}(tmax) was increased from 1 hour to 4 hours. Grapefruit juice or other grapefruit products in large doses should not be taken before or after administration of atorvastatin)

(concurrent use with large amounts of grapefruit juice (> 1 quart per day) and simvastatin has been reported to significantly increase the plasma concentrations of simvastatin, increasing the risk of myopathy)

For fluvastatin:

Cimetidine or
Omeprazole or
Ranitidine
(concurrent use with fluvastatin results in a significant increase in the peak plasma concentration [C_{max}] of fluvastatin, [43%, 70%, and 50%, respectively] with an 18 to 23% decrease in plasma clearance)

Rifampin
(addition of fluvastatin in patients pretreated with rifampin results in significant reduction in C_{max} [59%] and area under the curve [AUC] [51%] for rifampin, and a large increase in plasma clearance of rifampin [95%])

For simvastatin (in addition to those listed above)

» HIV protease inhibitors or
» Nefazodone
(concurrent use with simvastatin may be associated with an increased risk of rhabdomyolysis and acute renal failure; concurrent use is not recommended)

» Verapamil
(concurrent use with simvastatin may be associated with an increased risk of myopathy; this effect is not seen with other calcium channel blockers)

Laboratory value alterations

The following have been selected on the basis of their potential clinical significance (possible effect in parentheses where appropriate)—not necessarily inclusive (» = major clinical significance).

With physiology/laboratory test values

Creatine kinase (CK) concentrations
(mild transient increases are common and may not be drug-related; drug-related marked increases, with myositis and possible renal failure, occur in about 0.5 to 1% of patients, although the incidence may be higher in organ transplant patients treated concurrently with immunosuppressants or gemfibrozil)

Transaminase, serum
(values may be increased, usually to less than 3 times the upper limit of normal; in slightly less than 1 to 2% of patients receiving HMG-CoA reductase inhibitors for at least 1 year, marked in-

creases to more than 3 times the upper limit of normal have occurred)

Medical considerations/Contraindications

The medical considerations/contraindications included have been selected on the basis of their potential clinical significance (reasons given in parentheses where appropriate)—not necessarily inclusive (» = major clinical significance).

Except under special circumstances, this medication should not be used when the following medical problem exists:

» Hepatic disease, active
(condition may be exacerbated)

Hypersensitivity to any HMG-CoA reductase inhibitor or any component of the medication

Risk-benefit should be considered when the following medical problems exist:

Alcoholism, active or in remission or
Hepatic disease, history of
(further increases in liver enzymes may occur)

» Organ transplant, with immunosuppressant therapy
(increased risk of rhabdomyolysis and renal failure)

» Serious conditions predisposing to the development of renal failure secondary to rhabdomyolysis, such as hypotension, severe acute infection, severe metabolic, endocrine, or electrolyte disorders, uncontrolled seizures, major surgery, or trauma
(increased risk of secondary renal failure if rhabdomyolysis occurs)

Patient monitoring

The following may be especially important in patient monitoring (other tests may be warranted in some patients, depending on condition; » = major clinical significance):

» Cholesterol, serum
(determinations recommended 4 weeks after initiation of therapy and at periodic intervals during therapy)

» Creatine kinase (CK), serum
(determinations recommended if patient develops muscle tenderness during therapy or during concurrent therapy with niacin or immunosuppressive medications; a level 10 times higher than the upper limit of normal (ULN) in a patient with unexplained muscle symptoms indicates myopathy)

» Liver function tests, including serum transaminase
(determinations recommended prior to initiation of therapy, every 6 weeks during the first 3 months of therapy, every 8 weeks during the remainder of the first year of therapy, and then at periodic intervals [approximately every 6 months])

Prothrombin time
(determinations recommended prior to initiation of therapy and frequently enough during early therapy to insure prothrombin time stability in patients patients taking coumarin anticoagulants concomitantly)

Side/Adverse Effects

Note: Recent data on patients receiving lovastatin do not reveal clinically significant differences between lovastatin and placebo in the incidence, type, or progression of lens opacities. To date, no increased incidence of lens opacities has been found with atorvastatin, cerivastatin, fluvastatin, pravastatin, or simvastatin.

Acute *pancreatitis* has been reported during clinical use with simvastatin and lovastatin. A causal relationship with the HMG-CoA reductase inhibitors has not been clearly established. However, onset of symptoms appears to occur within 3 months of initiation of therapy. Rapid regression of symptoms and laboratory anomalies has been observed upon discontinuation of the HMG-CoA reductase inhibitor. Patients should be advised to report immediately to physician acute onset of severe abdominal pain. Although reports of fluvastatin- or pravastatin-associated pancreatitis are lacking, patients taking these medications should also be properly advised, since the mechanism of the effect is poorly understood.

The following side/adverse effects have been selected on the basis of their potential clinical significance (possible signs and symptoms in parentheses where appropriate)—not necessarily inclusive:

Those indicating need for medical attention

Incidence less frequent or rare

Myalgia, myositis, or rhabdomyolysis (fever; muscle aches or cramps; unusual tiredness or weakness)

Note: *Rhabdomyolysis* may lead to renal failure. Incidence may be increased in patients treated with immunosuppressants, gemfibrozil, erythromycin, or niacin. Onset may occur weeks to months after initiation of treatment. Patients should be advised to report immediately to physician any unexplained muscle pain, tenderness, or weakness, especially if it is accompanied by malaise or fever.

Those indicating need for medical attention only if they continue or are bothersome

Incidence more frequent

Constipation, diarrhea, gas, heartburn, or stomach pain; dizziness; headache; nausea; skin rash

Incidence rare

Impotence (decreased sexual ability); ***insomnia*** (trouble in sleeping)

Patient Consultation

As an aid to patient consultation, refer to *Advice for the Patient, HMG-CoA Reductase Inhibitors (Systemic).*

In providing consultation, consider emphasizing the following selected information (» = major clinical significance):

Before using this medication

Diet as preferred therapy; importance of following prescribed diet

» Conditions affecting use, especially:

Sensitivity to any HMG-CoA reductase inhibitor

Pregnancy—Use not recommended in pregnancy or in women who plan to become pregnant in near future, because inhibited formation of cholesterol may impair fetal development; birth defects reported with lovastatin

Breast-feeding—Use not recommended, because of potentially serious adverse effects in nursing infants

Other medications, especially cyclosporine, gemfibrozil, other fibrates, niacin (with all HMG-CoA reductase inhibitors); digoxin (with atorvastatin, fluvastatin, and simvastatin); oral contraceptives (with atorvastatin only); HIV protease inhibitors, nefazodone (with simvastatin); verapamil (with simvastatin); or grapefruit juice in large amounts (with atorvastatin and simvastatin)

Other medical problems, especially, active hepatic disease; hypotension; major surgery; organ transplant with immunosuppressant therapy; severe infection; severe metabolic, endocrine, or electrolyte disorders; trauma; or uncontrolled seizures

Proper use of this medication

For all HMG-CoA reductase inhibitors

» Importance of not taking more or less medication than the amount prescribed

This medication does not cure the condition but instead helps control it.

» Compliance with prescribed diet

» Proper dosing

Missed dose: Taking as soon as possible; not taking if almost time for next dose; not doubling doses

» Proper storage

For atorvastatin and simvastatin

Importance of not taking atorvastatin or simvastatin with grapefruit juice in large amounts

For lovastatin

For extended-release tablets: Take at bedtime; tablets should be swallowed whole and not chewed, crushed, or cut.

(*For tablets:* Taking with meals, since medication is more effective with food)

Precautions while using this medication

» Importance of close monitoring by physician

» Notifying physician immediately if pregnancy is suspected; counseling women of child-bearing potential about appropriate contraceptive methods

» Checking with physician before discontinuing medications; blood lipid levels may increase significantly

» Caution if any kind of surgery (including dental surgery) or emergency treatment is required

Side/adverse effects

Signs of potential side effects, especially myalgia, myositis, or rhabdomyolysis

General Dosing Information

If serum transaminase concentrations increase to 3 times the upper limit of normal, HMG-CoA reductase inhibitor therapy should be withdrawn.

If creatine kinase (CK) concentrations are markedly increased or myositis occurs, HMG-CoA reductase inhibitor therapy should be withdrawn.

Diet/Nutrition

Nonpharmacologic management (dietary and weight control) of hypercholesterolemia is recommended as an adjunct to all pharmacologic therapy.

Concurrent administration of atorvastatin with 200 mL of grapefruit juice has been shown to decrease plasma concentration 24%

ATORVASTATIN

Summary of Differences

Indications:
Indicated for prevention of cardiovascular disease in adults.
Indicated for treatment of homozygous familial hypercholesterolemia.
Also indicated in Type III, Type IV hyperlipoproteinemia, and Types IIa and IIb.

Pharmacology/pharmacokinetics:
Biotransformation—Administered in active form and metabolized by ortho- and parahydroxylation and beta-oxidation to active metabolites.
Time to peak concentration—1 to 2 hours

Precautions:
Drug interaction and/or related problems—Interacts with antacids and oral contraceptives.

Additional Dosing Information

Can be taken at any time of the day, with or without food

Oral Dosage Forms

Note: The dosing and strengths of the dosage forms available are expressed in terms of atorvastatin base (not the calcium salt).

ATORVASTATIN CALCIUM TABLETS

Usual adult dose

Coronary heart disease (prophylaxis)—
Oral, 10 mg once per day.

Antihyperlipidemic—
Heterozygous familial and nonfamilial hypercholesterolemia and mixed dyslipidemia (Fredrickson type IIa and IIb):—
Initial—Oral, 10 or 20 mg (base) once a day. Oral, 40 mg (base) once a day in patients who require a large reduction in LDL-C (more than 45%). The dosage can be adjusted after assessing treatment response in 2 to 4 weeks.
Maintenance—Oral, 10 to 80 mg (base) once daily.

Homozygous familial hypercholesterolemia:—
Oral, 10 to 80 mg a day

Note: Atorvastatin should be used in these patients as an adjunct to other lipid-lowering treatments such as LDL apheresis, or if such treatments are unavailable.

Note: Dosage adjustments in patients with renal dysfunction is not necessary because renal disease does not affect the plasma concentrations nor LDL-C reduction of atorvastatin.

Adult prescribing limits

80 mg (base) per day.

Usual pediatric and adolescent dose

Antihyperlipidemic—
Heterozygous familial hypercholesterolemia in pediatric patients 10 to 17 years of age:—
Oral, 10 mg (base) once a day. The dosage can be adjusted after assessing treatment response in 2 to 4 weeks.
Maintenance—Oral, 10 to 20 mg (base) once daily.

Homozygous familial hypercholesterolemia:—
Dosage has not been established

Pediatric and adolescent prescribing limits

Heterozygous familial hypercholesterolemia in pediatric patients 10 to 17 years of age: 20 mg (base) per day.

Strength(s) usually available

U.S.—
10 mg (base) (Rx) [*Lipitor* (calcium carbonate; candelilla wax; croscarmellose sodium; hydroxypropyl cellulose; lactose monohydrate; magnesium stearate; microcrystalline cellulose; hypromellose; polyethylene glycol; talc; titanium dioxide; polysorbate 80; simethicone emulsion)].
20 mg (base) (Rx) [*Lipitor* (calcium carbonate; candelilla wax; croscarmellose sodium; hydroxypropyl cellulose; lactose monohydrate; magnesium stearate; microcrystalline cellulose; hypromellose; polyethylene glycol; talc; titanium dioxide; polysorbate 80; simethicone emulsion)].
40 mg (base) (Rx) [*Lipitor* (calcium carbonate; candelilla wax; croscarmellose sodium; hydroxypropyl cellulose; lactose monohydrate; magnesium stearate; microcrystalline cellulose; hypromellose; polyethylene glycol; talc; titanium dioxide; polysorbate 80; simethicone emulsion)].
80 mg (base) (Rx) [*Lipitor* (calcium carbonate; candelilla wax; croscarmellose sodium; hydroxypropyl cellulose; lactose monohydrate; magnesium stearate; microcrystalline cellulose; hypromellose; polyethylene glycol; talc; titanium dioxide; polysorbate 80; simethicone emulsion)].

Canada—
10 mg (base) (Rx) [*Lipitor* (calcium carbonate; candelilla wax; croscarmellose sodium; hydroxypropyl cellulose; lactose monohydrate; magnesium stearate; microcrystalline cellulose; hydroxypropylmethylcellulose; polyethylene glycol; talc; titanium dioxide; polysorbate 80; simethicone emulsion)].
20 mg (base) (Rx) [*Lipitor* (calcium carbonate; candelilla wax; croscarmellose sodium; hydroxypropyl cellulose; lactose monohydrate; magnesium stearate; microcrystalline cellulose; hydroxypropylmethylcellulose; polyethylene glycol; talc; titanium dioxide; polysorbate 80; simethicone emulsion)].
40 mg (base) (Rx) [*Lipitor* (calcium carbonate; candelilla wax; croscarmellose sodium; hydroxypropyl cellulose; lactose monohydrate; magnesium stearate; microcrystalline cellulose; hydroxypropylmethylcellulose; polyethylene glycol; talc; titanium dioxide; polysorbate 80; simethicone emulsion)].

Packaging and storage

Store at controlled room temperature 20 to 25 °C (68 to 77 °F)

CERIVASTATIN

Note: Products containing cerivastatin were withdrawn from the market by the manufacturer in August 2001.

Summary of Differences

Pharmacology/pharmacokinetics:
Biotransformation—Administered in active form and metabolized by demethylation and hydroxylation to active metabolites
Time to peak concentration—approximately 2.5 hours

Additional Dosing Information

Should be taken in the evening with or without food.

Oral Dosage Forms

CERIVASTATIN SODIUM TABLETS

Usual adult and adolescent dose

Antihyperlipidemic—
Heterozygous familial and nonfamilial and mixed dyslipidemia (Fredrickson type IIa and IIb): Initial—Oral, 0.4 mg once daily in the evening. The dosage can be adjusted at four-week intervals after assessing treatment response.
Maintenance—Oral, 0.4 mg to 0.8 mg once daily in the evening.

Note: For patients with significant renal impairment (creatinine clearance less than or equal to 60 mL/min/1.73m^2), the starting dose should be 0.2 or 0.3 mg once a day in the evening.

Usual adult prescribing limits

0.8 mg per day.

Usual pediatric dose

Safety and efficacy have not been established.

Strength(s) usually available

U.S.—
Not commercially available

Canada—
Not commercially available

Packaging and storage

Store below 25 °C (77 °F) protected from moisture. Store in a tight container.

FLUVASTATIN

Summary of Differences

Pharmacology/pharmacokinetics:
Biotransformation—By hydroxylation, N-dealkylation, and beta-oxidation to inactive metabolites.
Time to peak concentration—0.5 to 0.7 hour.

Additional Dosing Information

Can be taken with meals or on an empty stomach.

Oral Dosage Forms

Note: The dosing and strengths of the dosage forms available are expressed in terms of fluvastatin base (not the sodium salt).

FLUVASTATIN SODIUM CAPSULES

Usual adult and adolescent dose

Antihyperlipidemic—

Initial: Oral, 20 mg (base) once a day at bedtime, the dosage being adjusted at four-week intervals as needed and tolerated.

Maintenance: Oral, 20 to 40 mg (base) once a day in the evening.

Note: A 40-mg (base) daily dose may be split and taken two times a day.

Usual pediatric dose

Safety and efficacy have not been established.

Strength(s) usually available

U.S.—

20 mg (base) (Rx) [*Lescol* (gelatin; magnesium stearate; microcrystalline cellulose; pregelatinized starch; titanium dioxide)].

40 mg (base) (Rx) [*Lescol* (gelatin; magnesium stearate; microcrystalline cellulose; pregelatinized starch; titanium dioxide)].

Canada—

20 mg (base) (Rx) [*Lescol* (calcium carbonate; magnesium stearate; microcrystalline cellulose; pregelatinized starch; sodium bicarbonate; talc)].

40 mg (base) (Rx) [*Lescol* (calcium carbonate; magnesium stearate; microcrystalline cellulose; pregelatinized starch; sodium bicarbonate; talc)].

Packaging and storage

Store below 30 °C (86 °F) in a tight container. Protect from light.

LOVASTATIN

Summary of Differences

Pharmacology/pharmacokinetics:

Absorption—Reduced by one-third on empty stomach.

Biotransformation—By hydrolysis to active metabolites.

Time to peak concentration—2 to 4 hours.

Duration of action—After withdrawal of continuous therapy: 4 to 6 weeks.

Additional Dosing Information

Immediate release tablets should be taken with meals to maximize absorption.

Oral Dosage Forms

LOVASTATIN EXTENDED-RELEASE TABLETS

Usual adult and adolescent dose

Coronary heart disease (prophylaxis) or

Antihyperlipidemic—

Oral, 10 to 60 mg once a day in the evening at bedtime. A starting dose of 10 mg may be considered for patients requiring smaller reductions. The dosage adjustments should be made at intervals of four-weeks or more as needed and tolerated.

Note: For patients with complicated medical conditions (renal insufficiency, diabetes) the usual starting dose is 20 mg once a day given in the evening at bedtime. Higher doses should be used cautiously after considering the potential risks and benefits.

For patients on concomitant immunosuppressive therapy (cyclosporine), it is recommended that lovastatin therapy begin with 10 mg per day and not exceed 20 mg per day.

For patients on concomitant amiodarone or verapamil, the dose should not exceed 20 mg per day.

For patients with severe renal function impairment (creatinine clearance less than 30 mL per min), doses above 20 mg per day should be carefully considered and dosage titration should proceed cautiously.

Usual adult prescribing limits

60 mg per day.

Usual pediatric dose

Safety and efficacy have not been established.

Usual geriatric dose

Antihyperlipidemic—

Initially, oral 20 mg once a day given in the evening at bedtime. Higher doses should be used cautiously after considering the potential risks and benefits.

Strength(s) usually available

U.S.—

10 mg (Rx) [*Altoprev* (acetyltributyl citrate; butylated hydroxyanisole; candelilla wax; cellulose acetate; confectioner's sugar [contains corn starch]; FD&C yellow #6; glyceryl monostearate; hypromellose; hypromellose phthalate; lactose; methacrylic acid copolymer, type B; polyethylene glycols [PEG 400, PEG 8000]; polyethylene oxides; polysorbate 80; propylene glycol; silicon dioxide; sodium chloride; sodium lauryl sulfate; synthetic black iron oxide; red iron oxide; talc; titanium dioxide; triacetin)].

20 mg (Rx) [*Altoprev* (acetyltributyl citrate; butylated hydroxyanisole; candelilla wax; cellulose acetate; confectioner's sugar [contains corn starch]; FD&C yellow #6; glyceryl monostearate; hypromellose; hypromellose phthalate; lactose; methacrylic acid copolymer, type B; polyethylene glycols [PEG 400, PEG 8000]; polyethylene oxides; polysorbate 80; propylene glycol; silicon dioxide; sodium chloride; sodium lauryl sulfate; synthetic black iron oxide; red iron oxide; talc; titanium dioxide; triacetin)].

40 mg (Rx) [*Altoprev* (acetyltributyl citrate; butylated hydroxyanisole; candelilla wax; cellulose acetate; confectioner's sugar [contains corn starch]; FD&C yellow #6; glyceryl monostearate; hypromellose; hypromellose phthalate; lactose; methacrylic acid copolymer, type B; polyethylene glycols [PEG 400, PEG 8000]; polyethylene oxides; polysorbate 80; propylene glycol; silicon dioxide; sodium chloride; sodium lauryl sulfate; synthetic black iron oxide; red iron oxide; talc; titanium dioxide; triacetin)].

60 mg (Rx) [*Altoprev* (acetyltributyl citrate; butylated hydroxyanisole; candelilla wax; cellulose acetate; confectioner's sugar [contains corn starch]; FD&C yellow #6; glyceryl monostearate; hypromellose; hypromellose phthalate; lactose; methacrylic acid copolymer, type B; polyethylene glycols [PEG 400, PEG 8000]; polyethylene oxides; polysorbate 80; propylene glycol; silicon dioxide; sodium chloride; sodium lauryl sulfate; synthetic black iron oxide; red iron oxide; talc; titanium dioxide; triacetin)].

Canada—

Not commercially available.

Packaging and storage

Store at controlled room temperature 20 to 25 °C (68 to 77 °F). Avoid excessive heat and humidity.

Auxiliary labeling

- Take at bedtime.
- Swallow whole. Do not crush or chew.

LOVASTATIN TABLETS USP

Usual adult and adolescent dose

Coronary heart disease (prophylaxis)

Antihyperlipidemic—

Initial: Oral, 20 mg once a day with the evening meal, the dosage being adjusted at four-week intervals as needed and tolerated.

Maintenance: Oral, 20 to 80 mg per day, as a single dose or in divided doses, with meals.

Note: For patients on concomitant immunosuppressive therapy, it is recommended that lovastatin therapy begin with 10 mg per day and not exceed 20 mg per day.

For patients with severe renal function impairment (creatinine clearance less than 30 mL per min), doses above 20 mg per day should be carefully considered and dosage titration should proceed cautiously.

Usual adult prescribing limits

80 mg per day.

Usual pediatric dose

Safety and efficacy have not been established.

Strength(s) usually available

U.S.—

10 mg (Rx) [*Mevacor* (cellulose; lactose; magnesium stearate; starch; butylated hydroxyanisole (BHA) as preservative; red ferric oxide; yellow ferric oxide)].

20 mg (Rx) [*Mevacor* (cellulose; lactose; magnesium stearate; starch; butylated hydroxyanisole (BHA) as preservative; red ferric oxide; yellow ferric oxide; FD&C Blue 2)].

40 mg (Rx) [*Mevacor* (cellulose; lactose; magnesium stearate; starch; butylated hydroxyanisole (BHA) as preservative; red ferric oxide; yellow ferric oxide; FD&C Yellow 10; FD&C Blue 2)].

Canada—

20 mg (Rx) [*Mevacor* (butylated hydroxyanisole; indigotine on alumina; lactose; magnesium stearate; microcrystalline cellulose; pregelatinized starch)].

40 mg (Rx) [*Mevacor* (butylated hydroxyanisole; indigotine and quinoline yellow on alumina substratum; lactose; magnesium stearate; microcrystalline cellulose; pregelatinized starch)].

Packaging and storage

Store below 40 °C (104 °F), preferably between 15 and 30 °C (59 and 86 °F), in a tight, light-resistant container, unless otherwise specified by manufacturer.

Auxiliary labeling
• Take with meals.

PRAVASTATIN

Summary of Differences
Pharmacology/pharmacokinetics:
Biotransformation—Administered in active form.
Time to peak concentration—1 hour.

Additional Dosing Information
Can be taken with meals or on an empty stomach.

Oral Dosage Forms
PRAVASTATIN SODIUM TABLETS
Usual adult and adolescent dose
Antihyperlipidemic—
Initial—
Oral, 10 to 40 mg once a day at bedtime, the dosage being adjusted at four-week intervals as needed and tolerated.
Note: An initial dose of 10 mg once a day is recommended in patients with significant renal function impairment or hepatic function impairment, and for the elderly.
Maintenance—
10 to 40 mg once a day at bedtime.
Note: In the elderly, maintenance doses of 20 mg a day or less are usually effective.

Usual pediatric dose
Safety and efficacy have not been established.

Strength(s) usually available
U.S.—
10 mg (Rx) [*Pravachol* (croscarmellose sodium; lactose; magnesium oxide; magnesium stearate; microcrystalline cellulose; povidone; red ferric oxide)].
20 mg (Rx) [*Pravachol* (croscarmellose sodium; lactose; magnesium oxide; magnesium stearate; microcrystalline cellulose; povidone; yellow ferric oxide)].
40 mg (Rx) [*Pravachol* (croscarmellose sodium; lactose; magnesium oxide; magnesium stearate; microcrystalline cellulose; povidone; Green Lake Blend)].
Canada—
10 mg (Rx) [*Pravachol* (croscarmellose sodium; lactose; magnesium oxide; magnesium stearate; microcrystalline cellulose; povidone; red ferric oxide)].
20 mg (Rx) [*Pravachol* (croscarmellose sodium; lactose; magnesium oxide; magnesium stearate; microcrystalline cellulose; povidone; yellow ferric oxide)].
40 mg (Rx) [*Pravachol* (croscarmellose sodium; lactose; magnesium oxide; magnesium stearate; microcrystalline cellulose; povidone; FD&C yellow no. 10; FD&C blue no. 1)].

Packaging and storage
Store below 40 °C (104 °F), preferably between 15 and 30 °C (59 and 86 °F), in a well-closed container, unless otherwise specified by manufacturer.

SIMVASTATIN

Summary of Differences
Pharmacology/pharmacokinetics:
Biotransformation—By hydrolysis to active metabolites.
Time to peak concentration—1.3 to 2.4 hours.
Precautions:
Drug interactions and/or related problems—Elevation of serum digoxin.

Additional Dosing Information
Can be taken with meals or on an empty stomach.

Oral Dosage Forms
SIMVASTATIN TABLETS
Usual adult and adolescent dose
Antihyperlipidemic—
Initial: Oral, 20 mg once a day in the evening, the dosage being adjusted at four-week intervals. Oral, 40 mg once a day in the evening for patients requiring a large LDL-C reduction (more than 45%), dosage adjusted at four-week intervals.
Maintenance: 5 to 80 mg per day.
Note: For patients taking concurrent immunosuppressive medications, it is recommended that simvastatin therapy begin with 5 mg per day and not exceed 10 mg per day. For patients with severe renal insufficiency, begin therapy with 5 mg per day and closely monitor. For patients with homozygous familial hypercholesterolemia, the recommended dose (adjunct therapy to other lipid-lowering treatments or if other therapy not available) is 40 mg per day in the evening or 80 mg per day in 3 divided doses of 20 mg, 20 mg, and an evening dose of 40 mg.

Usual adult prescribing limits
80 mg per day.

Usual pediatric dose
Safety and efficacy have not been established.

Strength(s) usually available
U.S.—
5 mg (Rx) [*Zocor* (cellulose; hydroxypropyl cellulose; hydroxypropyl methylcellulose; iron oxides; lactose; magnesium stearate; talc; titanium dioxide; butylated hydroxyanisole as preservative)].
10 mg (Rx) [*Zocor* (cellulose; hydroxypropyl cellulose; hydroxypropyl methylcellulose; iron oxides; lactose; magnesium stearate; talc; titanium dioxide; butylated hydroxyanisole as preservative)].
20 mg (Rx) [*Zocor* (cellulose; hydroxypropyl cellulose; hydroxypropyl methylcellulose; iron oxides; lactose; magnesium stearate; talc; titanium dioxide; butylated hydroxyanisole as preservative)].
40 mg (Rx) [*Zocor* (cellulose; hydroxypropyl cellulose; hydroxypropyl methylcellulose; iron oxides; lactose; magnesium stearate; talc; titanium dioxide; butylated hydroxyanisole as preservative)].
80 mg (Rx) [*Zocor* (cellulose; hydroxypropyl cellulose; hydroxypropyl methylcellulose; iron oxides; lactose; magnesium stearate; talc; titanium dioxide; butylated hydroxyanisole as preservative)].
Canada—
5 mg (Rx) [*Zocor* (ascorbic acid; butylated hydroxyanisole; citric acid; hydroxypropyl cellulose; lactose; magnesium stearate; methylcellulose; microcrystalline cellulose; pregelatinized starch; red ferric oxide; talc; titanium dioxide; yellow ferric oxide)].
10 mg (Rx) [*Zocor* (ascorbic acid; butylated hydroxyanisole; citric acid; hydroxypropyl cellulose; lactose; magnesium stearate; methylcellulose; microcrystalline cellulose; pregelatinized starch; red ferric oxide; talc; titanium dioxide; yellow ferric oxide)].
20 mg (Rx) [*Zocor* (ascorbic acid; butylated hydroxyanisole; citric acid; hydroxypropyl cellulose; lactose; magnesium stearate; methylcellulose; microcrystalline cellulose; pregelatinized starch; red ferric oxide; talc; titanium dioxide; yellow ferric oxide)].
40 mg (Rx) [*Zocor* (ascorbic acid; butylated hydroxyanisole; citric acid; hydroxypropyl cellulose; lactose; magnesium stearate; methylcellulose; microcrystalline cellulose; pregelatinized starch; red ferric oxide; talc; titanium dioxide; yellow ferric oxide)].
80 mg [*Zocor* (ascorbic acid; butylated hydroxyanisole; citric acid; hydroxypropyl cellulose; lactose; magnesium stearate; methylcellulose; microcrystalline cellulose; pregelatinized starch; red ferric oxide; talc; titanium dioxide; yellow ferric oxide)].

Packaging and storage
Store below 40 °C (104 °F), preferably between 15 and 30 °C (59 and 86 °F), in a well-closed container, unless otherwise specified by manufacturer.

Selected Bibliography

Simvastatin
Todd P, Goa K. Simvastatin: a review of its pharmacological properties and therapeutic potential in hypercholesterolaemia. Drugs 1990; 40(4): 583-607.

Pravastatin
Jungnickel PW, Cantral KA, Maloley PA. Pravastatin: a new drug for the treatment of hypercholesterolemia. Clin Pharm 1992; 11: 677-89.

Fluvastatin
Levy RI, Troendle AJ, Fattu JM. A quarter century of drug treatment of dyslipoproteinemia, with a focus on the new HMG-CoA reductase inhibitor fluvastatin. Circulation 1993; 87(Suppl III): III45-III53.

General
Grundy SM. HMG-CoA reductase inhibitors for treatment of hypercholesterolemia. N Engl J Med 1988 Jul 7; 319: 24-33.

Indications

Note: Bracketed information in the *Indications* section refers to uses that are not included in U.S. product labeling.

Accepted

Absorption and dispersion of other injected drugs (adjuvant)—Hyaluronidase is indicated as an adjuvant to increase the absorption and dispersion of other injected drugs.

Hypodermoclysis (adjunct)—Hyaluronidase is indicated for hypodermoclysis.

Urography, subcutaneous (adjunct)—Hyaluronidase is indicated as an adjunct in subcutaneous urography for improving resorption of radiopaque agents.

Unaccepted

Hyaluronidase should not be injected into or around an infected or acutely inflamed area because of the danger of spreading a localized infection.

Hyaluronidase should not be used to reduce the swelling of bites and stings.

Hyaluronidase should not be applied directly to the cornea.

Hyaluronidase should not be used for intravenous injections because the enzyme is rapidly inactivated.

Pharmacology/Pharmacokinetics

Physicochemical characteristics

Source—
Purified bovine testicular hyaluronidase.
Purified ovine testicular hyaluronidase.

pH—
Purified bovine testicular hyaluronidase injection: approximately 6.8
Purified ovine testicular hyaluronidase for injection, reconstituted solution: approximately 6.8
Purified ovine testicular hyaluronidase injection: 6.4 to 7.2

Osmolality—
Purified bovine testicular hyaluronidase: 295 to 310 mOsm
Purified ovine testicular hyaluronidase for injection, reconstituted solution: 290 to 310 mOsm

Mechanism of action/Effect

Hyaluronidase is a spreading or diffusing substance. Hyaluronidase hydrolyzes hyaluronic acid. Hyaluronic acid is a polysaccharide found in the intercellular ground substance of connective tissue, and of certain specialized tissues, such as the umbilical cord and vitreous humor. Hyaluronic acid is also present in the capsules of type A and C hemolytic streptococci. Hyaluronidase splits the glucosaminidic bond between C_1 of the glucosamine moiety and the C_4 of glucuronic acid during hydrolysis of hyaluronic acid. The viscosity of the cellular cement is temporarily decreased by this hydrolysis and injected fluids, localized transudates or exudates diffuse more rapidly thus facilitating their absorption. Local interstitial pressure must be adequate to furnish the necessary mechanical impulse.

The blood of a number of mammalian species brings about the inactivation of hyaluronidase. Hyaluronidase is antigenic and repeated injections of relatively large amounts of this enzyme may result in the formation of neutralizing antibodies.

The reconstitution of the dermal barrier removed by intradermal injection of hyaluronidase to adult humans is incomplete at 24 hours and is inversely related to the dosage of enzyme administered for doses of 20, 2, 0.2, 0.02, and 0.002 Units per mL. The barrier is completely restored in all treated areas at 48 hours after hyaluronidase administration.

Other actions/effects

Based on human experimental study, hyaluronidase does not deter bone healing.

Duration of action

The reconstitution of the dermal barrier removed by intradermal injection of hyaluronidase to adult humans is incomplete at 24 hours and is inversely related to the dosage of enzyme administered for doses of 20, 2, 0.2, 0.02, and 0.002 Units per mL. The barrier is completely restored in all treated areas at 48 hours after hyaluronidase administration.

Precautions to Consider

Carcinogenicity

Long-term animal studies have not been performed to assess the carcinogenic potential of hyaluronidase. However, hyaluronidase is found in most tissues of the body.

Mutagenicity

Long-term animal studies have not been performed to assess the mutagenic potential of hyaluronidase. However, hyaluronidase is found in most tissues of the body.

Pregnancy/Reproduction

Fertility—Long-term animal studies have not been performed to assess whether hyaluronidase impaired fertility.

Male: Testicular degeneration has been reported following repeated injections of hyaluronidase producing organ specific antibodies.

Female: Hyaluronidase does not appear to adversely affect fertility in females. Human studies indicate that intravaginal hyaluronidase may have aided conception in sterility due to oligospermia.

Pregnancy—Adequate and well-controlled studies in humans or animals have not been done. Hyaluronidase should be used during pregnancy only if clearly needed.

FDA Pregnancy Category C

Labor and delivery—It is not known whether hyaluronidase has an effect on the fetus or the later growth development or functional maturation of the infant when hyaluronidase is used during labor. There are no reports of complications, increase in blood loss, or differences in cervical trauma when hyaluronidase was administered during labor.

Breast-feeding

It is not known whether hyaluronidase is distributed into breast milk. Because many drugs are distributed in human breast milk, caution should be exercised when hyaluronidase is administered to a nursing woman.

Pediatrics

Overhydration should be avoided in pediatric patients during hypodermoclysis by controlling the rate and total volume of the clysis.

Geriatrics

Appropriate studies performed to date have not demonstrated geriatrics-specific problems that would limit the usefulness of hyaluronidase in the elderly.

Drug interactions and/or related problems

The following drug interactions and/or related problems have been selected on the basis of their potential clinical significance (possible mechanism in parentheses where appropriate)—not necessarily inclusive (» = major clinical significance):

Note: When considering the administration of any other drug with hyaluronidase, consult appropriate references to determine the usual precautions for the use of the other drug.

Combinations containing any of the following medications, depending on the amount present, may also interact with this medication.

Anesthetic, local
(hastens the onset of analgesia and tends to reduce the swelling caused by local infiltration, but wider spread of local anesthetic solution increases its absorption which shortens its duration of action and tends to increase the incidence of systemic reaction)

ACTH or
Antihistamines or
Cortisone or
Estrogens or
Salicylates
(large doses of these drugs apparently render the tissues partly resistant to the action of hyaluronidase; larger amounts of hyaluronidase may be required for equivalent dispersing effect)

» Dopamine or
» Alpha agonists
(hyaluronidase should not be used to enhance the absorption and dispersion of dopamine and/or alpha agonist drugs)

Medical considerations/Contraindications

The medical considerations/contraindications included have been selected on the basis of their potential clinical significance (reasons given in parentheses where appropriate)—not necessarily inclusive (» = major clinical significance).

Except under special circumstances, this medication should not be used when the following medical problem exists:

» Hypersensitivity to hyaluronidase or any other ingredient in the formulation

Patient monitoring

The following may be especially important in patient monitoring (other tests may be warranted in some patients, depending on condition; » = major clinical significance):

» Fluid and electrolyte status
(For hypodermoclysis, observe effect closely with same precautions for restoring fluid and electrolyte balance as in intravenous injections)

Side/Adverse Effects

Hyaluronidase may enhance the adverse events associated with the co-administered drug product.

The following side/adverse effects have been selected on the basis of their potential clinical significance (possible signs and symptoms in parentheses where appropriate)—not necessarily inclusive:

Those indicating need for medical attention

Incidence rare

Allergic reactions including (cough; difficulty swallowing; dizziness; fast heartbeat; hives; itching; puffiness or swelling of the eyelids or around the eyes, face, lips or tongue; shortness of breath; skin rash; tightness in chest; unusual tiredness or weakness; wheezing); ***angioedema*** (large, hive-like swelling on face, eyelids, lips, tongue, throat, hands, legs, feet, or sex organs); ***urticaria*** (hives or welts; itching; redness of skin; skin rash)

Those indicating need for medical attention only if they continue or are bothersome

Incidence more frequent

Injection site reactions (bleeding, blistering, burning, coldness, discoloration of skin, feeling of pressure, hives, infection, inflammation, itching, lumps, numbness, pain, rash, redness, scarring, soreness, stinging, swelling, tenderness, tingling, ulceration, or warmth at injection site)

Incidence not determined

Edema (swelling)—with hypodermoclysis

Overdose

For more information on the management of overdose or unintentional ingestion, **contact a poison control center** (see *Poison Control Center Listing*).

Clinical effects of overdose

The following effects have been selected on the basis of their potential clinical significance (possible signs and symptoms in parentheses where appropriate)—not necessarily inclusive:

Chills; dizziness; edema, local (swelling); ***erythema*** (flushing; redness of skin; unusually warm skin); ***hypotension*** (blurred vision; confusion; dizziness, faintness, or lightheadedness when getting up from a lying or sitting position suddenly; sweating; unusual tiredness or weakness); ***nausea; tachycardia*** (fast, pounding, or irregular heartbeat or pulse); ***vomiting***

Treatment of overdose

Supportive care—

Hyaluronidase should be discontinued.

Treatment is supportive.

Patients in whom intentional overdose is confirmed or suspected should be referred for psychiatric consultation.

Patient Consultation

As an aid to patient consultation, refer to *Advice for the Patient, Hyaluronidase (Parenteral-Local)*.

In providing consultation, consider emphasizing the following selected information (» = major clinical significance):

Before using this medication

» Conditions affecting use, especially:

Pregnancy—Adequate and well-controlled studies in humans or animals have not been done. Hyaluronidase should be used during pregnancy only if clearly needed.

Breast-feeding—It is not known whether hyaluronidase is distributed into breast milk. Because many drugs are distributed in human breast milk, caution should be exercised when hyaluronidase is administered to a nursing woman.

Use in children—Overhydration should be avoided in pediatric patients during hypodermoclysis by controlling the rate and total volume of the clysis.

Use in the elderly—Appropriate studies performed to date have not demonstrated geriatrics-specific problems that would limit the usefulness of hyaluronidase in the elderly.

Other medications, especially dopamine or alpha agonists

Proper use of this medication

» Proper dosing

» Proper storage

Precautions while using this medication

» Tell your health care provider if you develop signs or symptoms of an allergic reaction.

Side/adverse effects

Signs of potential side effects, especially allergic reactions including angioedema or urticaria

General Dosing Information

For parenteral dosing forms:

Hyaluronidase should not be injected into or around an infected or acutely inflamed area because of the danger of spreading a localized infection.

Hyaluronidase should not be used to reduce the swelling of bites and stings.

Hyaluronidase should not be applied directly to the cornea.

Hyaluronidase should not be used for intravenous injections because the enzyme is rapidly inactivated.

Skin testing for hypersensitivity: A preliminary skin test for hypersensitivity to hyaluronidase can be performed. Administer 0.02 mL (3 Unites) of a 150 Unit per mL solution by intradermal injection. If a wheal with pseudopods appears within 5 minutes and persists for 20 to 30 minutes accompanied by localized itching, a positive reaction occurred and hyaluronidase should not be administered. The reaction is not considered positive if transient vasodilation at the site of the test is observed.

For hypodermoclysis, the dose, rate of injection, and type of solution must be adjusted carefully to the individual patient. Hypovolemia may occur when solutions devoid of inorganic electrolytes are given by hypodermoclysis.

For treatment of adverse effects

If sensitization occurs, discontinue hyaluronidase injection.

Parenteral Dosage Forms

Note: Bracketed information in the *Indications* section refers to uses that are not included in U.S. product labeling.

HYALURONIDASE (BOVINE DERIVED) INJECTION USP

Usual adult dose

Absorption and dispersion of injected drugs—

Subcutaneous, 50 to 300 Units added to the injection solution of another injected drug; most typically 150 Units is added

Hypodermoclysis—

Subcutaneous, 150 Units will facilitate absorption of 1000 mL or more of solution. Hyaluronidase injection can be injected into the clysis tubing close to the needle or alternatively can be injected under the skin prior to clysis.

For clysis, a needle is inserted with the tip lying free and movable between the skin and muscle using aseptic precautions. Clysis fluid should start in readily without lump or pain.

Urography, subcutaneous—

Subcutaneous, 75 Units of hyaluronidase is injected subcutaneously over each scapula, followed by injection of the contrast media at the same sites. The subcutaneous route of administration of urographic contrast media is indicated when intravenous administration cannot be successfully accomplished, particularly in infants and small children.

Usual pediatric dose

Absorption and dispersion of injected drugs—

See *Usual adult dose.*

Hypodermoclysis—

See *Usual adult dose.*

Hyaluronidase may be added to solutions of drugs for subcutaneous injection.

Urography, subcutaneous—

See *Usual adult dose.*

Usual pediatric prescribing limits

For hypodermoclysis: The daily dosage should not exceed 25 mL per kg of body weight in premature infants or during the neonatal period.

For hypodermoclysis: The rate of administration should not be greater than 2 mL per minute in premature infants or during the neonatal period. The rate and volume of administration should not exceed those employed for intravenous infusion for older pediatric patients.

Usual geriatric dose

Absorption and dispersion of injected drugs—

See *Usual adult dose.*

Hypodermoclysis—

See *Usual adult dose.*

Urography, subcutaneous—

See *Usual adult dose.*

Strength(s) usually available

U.S.—

150 Units of bovine hyaluronidase per mL (Rx) [*Amphadase* (2 mL glass vial with gray rubber stopper; sodium chloride; edetate disodium; calcium chloride; monobasic sodium phosphate buffer; thimerosal)].

Canada—
Not commercially available.

Packaging and storage
Store in refrigerator at 2 to 8 °C (36 to 46 °F); do not freeze

Incompatibilities
The benzodiazepines, furosemide, and phenytoin are incompatible with hyaluronidase.

Appropriate references should be consulted regarding chemical or physical incompatibilities before adding hyaluronidase to a solution containing another drug.

Auxiliary labeling
- Refrigerate - do not freeze

Caution
Parenteral drug products should be visually inspected for particulate matter and discoloration prior to administration, whenever solution and container permit.

Not recommended for IV use.

HYALURONIDASE (OVINE DERIVED) FOR INJECTION USP

Usual adult dose
Absorption and dispersion of injected drugs—
See *Hyaluronidase (Bovine Derived) Injection USP Usual adult dose.*

Hypodermoclysis—
See *Hyaluronidase (Bovine Derived) Injection USP Usual adult dose.*

Urography, subcutaneous—
See *Hyaluronidase (Bovine Derived) Injection USP Usual adult dose.*

Usual pediatric dose
Absorption and dispersion of injected drugs—
See *Hyaluronidase (Bovine Derived) Injection USP Usual adult dose.*

Hypodermoclysis—
See *Hyaluronidase (Bovine Derived) Injection USP Usual pediatric dose.*

Urography, subcutaneous—
See *Hyaluronidase (Bovine Derived) Injection USP Usual adult dose.*

Usual pediatric prescribing limits
See *Hyaluronidase (Bovine Derived) Injection USP Usual pediatric prescribing limits.*

Usual geriatric dose
Absorption and dispersion of injected drugs—
See *Hyaluronidase (Bovine Derived) Injection USP Usual adult dose.*

Hypodermoclysis—
See *Hyaluronidase (Bovine Derived) Injection USP Usual adult dose.*

Urography, subcutaneous—
See *Hyaluronidase (Bovine Derived) Injection USP Usual adult dose.*

Strength(s) usually available
U.S.—
6200 Units of lyophilized ovine hyaluronidase (Rx) [*Vitrase* (5 mL vial with rubber stopper; lactose; potassium phosphate dibasic; potassium phosphate monobasic)].

Canada—
Not commercially available.

Packaging and storage
Store unopened vial in refrigerator at 2 to 8 °C (35 to 46 °F).

Preparation of dosage form
See the manufacturer's package insert for detailed instructions. A 1 mL syringe and a 5-micron filter needle are supplied in the hyaluronidase (ovine derived) for injection kit.

The vial is reconstituted by adding 6.2 mL of sodium chloride injection, USP to the hyaluronidase vial to produce a solution with a concentration of 1000 Units per mL. Prior to administration, the reconstituted solution should be further diluted to the desired concentration, commonly 150 Units per mL. Following reconstitution, apply the 5-micron filter needle to the 1 mL syringe. Draw the desired amount of hyaluronidase into the syringe, and dilute according to the table below. Remove the filter needle and apply a needle appropriate for the intended injection. This solution should be used immediately after preparation.

Dilution of Reconstituted Hyaluronidase Solution

Desired Concentration	Amount of hyaluronidase reconstituted solution (1000 Units/mL)	Additional Sodium Chloride Injection
50 Units/mL	0.05 mL	0.95 mL
75 Units/mL	0.075 mL	0.925 mL
150 Units/mL	0.15 mL	0.85 mL
300 Units/mL	0.3 mL	0.7 mL

Stability
After reconstitution, store at controlled room temperature 20 to 25 °C (68 to 77 °F). Use within 6 hours.

The final diluted solution should be used immediately after preparation.

Incompatibilities
The benzodiazepines, furosemide, and phenytoin are incompatible with hyaluronidase.

Appropriate references should be consulted regarding chemical or physical incompatibilities before adding hyaluronidase to a solution containing another drug.

Caution
Parenteral drug products should be visually inspected for particulate matter and discoloration prior to administration, whenever solution and container permit.

Not recommended for IV use.

HYALURONIDASE (OVINE DERIVED) INJECTION USP

Usual adult dose
Absorption and dispersion of injected drugs—
See *Hyaluronidase (Bovine Derived) Injection USP Usual adult dose.*

Hypodermoclysis—
See *Hyaluronidase (Bovine Derived) Injection USP Usual adult dose.*

Urography, subcutaneous—
See *Hyaluronidase (Bovine Derived) Injection USP Usual adult dose.*

Usual pediatric dose
Absorption and dispersion of injected drugs—
See *Hyaluronidase (Bovine Derived) Injection USP Usual adult dose.*

Hypodermoclysis—
See *Hyaluronidase (Bovine Derived) Injection USP Usual pediatric dose.*

Urography, subcutaneous—
See *Hyaluronidase (Bovine Derived) Injection USP Usual adult dose.*

Usual pediatric prescribing limits
See *Hyaluronidase (Bovine Derived) Injection USP Usual pediatric prescribing limits.*

Usual geriatric dose
Absorption and dispersion of injected drugs—
See *Hyaluronidase (Bovine Derived) Injection USP Usual adult dose.*

Hypodermoclysis—
See *Hyaluronidase (Bovine Derived) Injection USP Usual adult dose.*

Urography, subcutaneous—
See *Hyaluronidase (Bovine Derived) Injection USP Usual adult dose.*

Strength(s) usually available
U.S.—
200 Units of ovine hyaluronidase per mL (Rx) [*Vitrase* (2 mL vial with rubber stopper; lactose NF; potassium phosphate dibasic USP; potassium phosphate monobasic NF; sodium chloride USP)].

Canada—
Not commercially available.

Packaging and storage
Store unopened vial in refrigerator between 2 and 8 °C (35 and 46 °F); do not freeze; protect from light

Incompatibilities
The benzodiazepines, furosemide, and phenytoin are incompatible with hyaluronidase.

Appropriate references should be consulted regarding chemical or physical incompatibilities before adding hyaluronidase to a solution containing another drug.

Auxiliary labeling
- Refrigerate - do not freeze

Caution
Parenteral drug products should be visually inspected for particulate matter and discoloration prior to administration, whenever solution and container permit.

Not recommended for IV use.

Developed: 02/28/2005

HYDRALAZINE Systemic

VA CLASSIFICATION (Primary/Secondary): CV402/CV900

Commonly used brand name(s): *Apo-Hydral; Apo-Hydralazine; Apresoline; Apresoline Injection; Novo-Hylazin.*

Note: For a listing of dosage forms and brand names by country availability, see *Dosage Forms* section(s).

Category

Antihypertensive; vasodilator, congestive heart failure.

Indications

Note: Bracketed information in the *Indications* section refers to uses that are not included in U.S. product labeling.

Accepted

Hypertension (treatment)—Hydralazine is indicated orally for the treatment of hypertension. Hydralazine is indicated intravenously when oral therapy cannot be given or when there is an urgent need to lower blood pressure, such as in hypertensive crisis or pre-eclampsia or eclampsia.

For additional information on initial therapeutic guidelines related to the treatment of hypertension, see *Appendix III*.

[Congestive heart failure (treatment)][1]—Hydralazine combined with isosorbide dinitrate (nonspecific vasodilator therapy) has been used as a supplement to the traditional congestive heart failure treatment of digitalis and diuretics. Although the hydralazine-isosorbide combination has demonstrated beneficial effects, its use remains controversial because of the results of the Veterans Administration Cooperative Vasodilator–Heart Failure Trials (V-HeFT I and II) that evaluated the effects of this combination in patients with mild to moderate congestive heart failure. In V-HeFT I, treatment of patients with hydralazine-isosorbide resulted in a favorable effect on left ventricular (LV) function (interpreted as a delay in the progression of LV dysfunction) and a 28% reduction in overall mortality when compared with treatment of patients receiving placebo. In V-HeFT II, treatment of patients with the angiotensin-converting enzyme (ACE) inhibitor enalapril resulted in a significantly lower average 2-year mortality rate (18%) than treatment of patients with hydralazine-isosorbide (25%), although treatment of patients with hydralazine-isosorbide resulted in a significant improvement in exercise performance and LV function when compared with those treated with enalapril. Since the conclusion of these trials, the statistical methods used in the V-HeFT I trial have been questioned, and the results, according to some scientists, are considered borderline significant. Although ACE inhibitors are considered the basis of treatment for heart failure, isosorbide dinitrate and hydralazine may be considered for the treatment of New York Heart Association (NYHA) class II and III heart failure when ACE inhibitors are not tolerated, as determined by the occurrence of symptomatic hypotension, azotemia, hyperkalemia, cough, rash, or angioneurotic edema.

[1]Not included in Canadian product labeling.

Pharmacology/Pharmacokinetics

Physicochemical characteristics

Molecular weight—Hydralazine hydrochloride: 196.64.
pKa—7.3.

Mechanism of action/Effect

Antihypertensive—Although the exact mechanism of antihypertensive action is not fully understood, hydralazine is thought to lower blood pressure by acting directly on arterial smooth muscle to cause vasodilation. By altering cellular calcium metabolism, hydralazine interferes with the movement of calcium, thereby affecting the contractile state of vascular smooth muscle. Vasodilation and a reduction in total peripheral vascular resistance occur, resulting in an increase in heart rate, stroke volume, and cardiac output.

Vasodilator, congestive heart failure—The beneficial effects of hydralazine in the treatment of congestive heart failure are thought to be due to a direct increase in cardiac output secondary to decreased systemic resistance and to the associated afterload reduction when hydralazine is used in combination with isosorbide dinitrate (additionally, isosorbide dinitrate decreases preload by decreasing resistance in venous capacitance vessels).

Other actions/effects

Hydralazine increases renin activity in plasma, possibly resulting from an increase in the secretion of renin by the renal juxtaglomerular cells in response to reflex sympathetic discharge. Increased renin activity leads to the production of angiotensin II, which stimulates the production of aldosterone, causing a reabsorption of sodium. Hydralazine also maintains or increases renal and cerebral blood flow.

Absorption

Hydralazine is rapidly and extensively absorbed (up to 90%) from the gastrointestinal tract and undergoes extensive first-pass metabolism by genetic polymorphic acetylation. Oral bioavailability of hydralazine is dependent upon acetylator phenotype. Bioavailability is approximately 31% in slow acetylators and 10% in fast acetylators.

Protein binding

High (87%).

Biotransformation

Hydralazine, when administered orally, undergoes extensive first-pass metabolism by genetic polymorphic acetylation, which is responsible for a threefold range of oral bioavailability. Intravenously administered hydralazine does not undergo first-pass metabolism and, therefore, is not affected by acetylator phenotype. After the drug reaches the systemic circulation, it is combined with endogenous aldehydes and ketones, including pyruvic acid, to form hydrazone metabolites. The active metabolites, hydralazine acetonide hydrazone and hydralazine pyruvate hydrazone, are equipotent with the parent, hydralazine.

Half-life

Apparent hydralazine (using nonselective assays)—
3 to 7 hours.
Hydralazine (using urine specific assay)—
Approximately 90 minutes.

Some references state a difference in half-life between slow and fast acetylators, but there is generally thought to be little difference.

The half-life of antihypertensive action is much longer than the plasma half-life, possibly because hydralazine persists within arteriolar walls.

Time to peak concentration

Oral tablets—1 to 2 hours.

Elimination

Renal—52 to 90%, primarily as metabolites.
Fecal—Approximately 10%.

Precautions to Consider

Cross-sensitivity and/or related problems

Patients sensitive to tartrazine (FD & C Yellow No. 5) may be sensitive to the tablets that contain this dye.

Carcinogenicity

A lifetime study in Swiss male and female albino mice given hydralazine continuously in their drinking water at a dose of about 250 mg per kg of body weight (mg/kg) per day (approximately 80 times the maximum recommended human dose) revealed an increase in the incidence of lung tumors (adenomas and adenocarcinomas).

Tumorigenicity

In a 2-year carcinogenicity study of rats, hydralazine given at dose levels of 15, 30, and 60 mg/kg per day (about 5 to 20 times the recommended human daily dose) produced a small, but statistically significant, increase in benign neoplastic nodules in male and female rats in the high-dose group and in female rats in the intermediate-dose group. Furthermore, benign interstitial cell tumors of the testes were significantly increased in male rats in the high-dose group.

Mutagenicity

Hydralazine was shown to be mutagenic in bacterial systems (gene mutation and DNA repair). Mutagenicity was also found in one of two rat and one rabbit hepatocyte *in vitro* DNA repair study. However, *in vivo* and *in vitro* studies using mouse lymphoma cells, germinal cells, and fibroblasts, Chinese hamster bone marrow cells, and human cell fibroblasts did not reveal any mutagenic potential of hydralazine.

Pregnancy/Reproduction

Pregnancy—Although hydralazine is one of the most commonly used drugs for acute blood pressure reduction in severe hypertension in pregnancy, few adequate and well-controlled studies of hydralazine in pregnant women have been done. Adverse effects that have occurred in pregnant women with hydralazine administration include anxiety, epigastric pain, flushing, headaches, hypotension, nausea, palpitations, reduction in placental perfusion, restlessness, tachycardia, tremors, and vomiting. Thrombocytopenia, leukopenia, petechial bleeding, and hematomas have been reported in newborns whose mothers took hydralazine orally, although these symptoms resolved spontaneously in 1 to 3 weeks. In patients with intrauterine growth retardation, intravenous use of hydralazine has caused fetal distress. The risk of fetal distress appears to be greater when vasodilation with hydralazine is undertaken without prior volume expansion. Hydralazine should be used during pregnancy only if the expected benefit justifies the potential risk to the fetus.

Studies in mice given hydralazine at 20 to 30 times the maximum daily human dose of 200 to 300 mg revealed teratogenic effects. Furthermore, studies in rabbits indicate teratogenic effects at doses 10 to 15 times the maximum daily human dose. Teratogenic effects observed were cleft palate and malformations of facial and cranial bones. However, hydralazine was not shown to be teratogenic in rats.

FDA Pregnancy Category C.

Breast-feeding

Hydralazine is distributed into breast milk.

Pediatrics

Appropriate studies on the relationship of age to the effects of hydralazine have not been performed in the pediatric population. However, the oral solution contains aspartame, which is metabolized to phenylalanine, and must be used with caution in children with phenylketonuria.

Geriatrics

Although extensive studies on the relationship of age to the effects of hydralazine have not been performed in the geriatric population, geriatrics-specific problems are not expected to limit the usefulness of hydralazine in the elderly. Renal clearance and apparent volume of distribution appear to be decreased and half-life appears to be increased in older hypertensive patients when compared with young healthy volunteers, although confirmation of these differences requires further investigation.

Pharmacogenetics

Acetylator phenotype is responsible for differences in oral bioavailability of hydralazine. Generally, all patients may be divided into two groups, slow and fast acetylators of hydralazine. Eskimo, Oriental, and American Indian populations have the lowest prevalence of slow acetylators, while Egyptian, Israeli, Scandinavian, other Caucasian, and black populations have the highest prevalence of slow acetylators.

In slow acetylators, the oral bioavailability of hydralazine is increased, which may explain why rapid acetylators generally require larger oral doses of hydralazine for the control of blood pressure. Slow acetylators, as a result of increased bioavailability, are exposed to higher plasma hydralazine concentrations than are rapid acetylators when a fixed, weight-adjusted oral dose is administered. This may explain why slow acetylators are more prone to develop adverse effects, such as hydralazine-induced systemic lupus erythematosus (SLE).

Drug interactions and/or related problems

The following drug interactions and/or related problems have been selected on the basis of their potential clinical significance (possible mechanism in parentheses where appropriate)—not necessarily inclusive (» = major clinical significance):

Note: Combinations containing any of the following medications, depending on the amount present, may also interact with this medication.

Anti-inflammatory drugs, nonsteroidal (NSAIDs), especially indomethacin
(may reduce antihypertensive effects of hydralazine; indomethacin, and possibly other NSAIDs, may antagonize the antihypertensive effect by inhibiting renal prostaglandin synthesis and/or by causing sodium and fluid retention)

» Diazoxide or
Hypotension-producing medications, other (see *Appendix II*)
(antihypertensive effects may be potentiated when these medications are used concurrently with hydralazine; concurrent use of diazoxide or other potent parenteral antihypertensive agents with hydralazine may result in a severe, additive hypotensive effect; although some antihypertensive and/or diuretic combinations are frequently used for therapeutic advantage, dosage adjustments may be necessary during concurrent use; patients should be continuously observed for excessive fall in blood pressure for several hours after concurrent administration of diazoxide or other potent parenteral antihypertensives)

Sympathomimetics, including
Epinephrine
(hydralazine may reduce pressor responses to epinephrine; contrarily, sympathomimetics may reduce the antihypertensive effects of hydralazine; the patient should be monitored carefully when sympathomimetics are used concurrently with hydralazine)

Laboratory value alterations

The following have been selected on the basis of their potential clinical significance (possible effect in parentheses where appropriate)—not necessarily inclusive (» = major clinical significance).

With physiology/laboratory test values
Direct antiglobulin (Coombs') tests
(may produce positive results)

Medical considerations/Contraindications

The medical considerations/contraindications included have been selected on the basis of their potential clinical significance (reasons given in parentheses where appropriate)—not necessarily inclusive (» = major clinical significance).

Except under special circumstances, this medication should not be used when the following medical problems exist:

» Coronary artery disease
(myocardial stimulation and increased myocardial oxygen demands may cause or aggravate ischemia and angina and reportedly may precipitate myocardial infarction)

» Hypersensitivity to hydralazine

» Mitral valvular disease, such as that associated with rheumatic heart disease
(hydralazine may increase pulmonary artery pressure in these patients)

Risk-benefit should be considered when the following medical problems exist:

Aortic aneurysm or
» Aortic dissection, acute
(reflexive increase in heart rate, cardiac output, and shear stress associated with hydralazine may exacerbate condition)

Cerebrovascular disease or accident
(hydralazine-induced decreases in blood pressure may increase cerebral ischemia)

Phenylketonuria
(the oral solution of hydralazine contains aspartame, which is metabolized to phenylalanine, and may be hazardous to patients with phenylketonuria)

Renal function impairment
(high plasma "apparent" hydralazine concentrations have occurred in patients with renal failure and, in one study, the two subjects with the lowest estimated creatinine clearances [39 and 45 mL per minute (mL/min)] had the longest half-lives and lowest clearances of hydralazine. Although evidence of increased hydralazine toxicity in renal failure has not been observed, caution should be used in dosing hydralazine in patients with severe renal function impairment)

Note: There is no substantial evidence that use of hydralazine in the treatment of hypertension in patients with systemic vasculitis or systemic lupus erythematosus (SLE) exacerbates the underlying disease process.

Patient monitoring

The following may be especially important in patient monitoring (other tests may be warranted in some patients, depending on condition; » = major clinical significance):

Antinuclear antibody (ANA) titer determinations and
Lupus erythematosus cell preparations
(may be indicated if arthralgia, fever, chest pain, continued malaise, or other unexplained symptoms develop that may be related to drug-induced SLE)

» Blood pressure measurements
(periodic monitoring is necessary for titration of dose according to the patient's response)

Complete blood counts (CBC)
(periodic monitoring may be necessary; blood dyscrasias, consisting of a reduction in hemoglobin and red cell count, leukopenia, agranulocytosis, and purpura, have been reported; hydralazine should be discontinued if these abnormalities occur)

Side/Adverse Effects

Note: Side/adverse effects are rare at lower dosages and are generally reversible.

Hepatotoxicity has been reported in a few patients.

The following side/adverse effects have been selected on the basis of their potential clinical significance (possible signs and symptoms in parentheses where appropriate)—not necessarily inclusive:

Those indicating need for medical attention

Incidence less frequent

Allergic reaction (skin rash or itching); ***angina pectoris*** (chest pain); ***cutaneous vasculitis*** (blisters on skin); ***lymphadenopathy*** (swelling of lymph glands); ***peripheral neuritis*** (numbness, tingling, pain, or weakness in hands or feet); ***sodium and water retention and edema*** (swelling of feet or lower legs); ***systemic lupus erythematosus (SLE)–like syndrome, including glomerulonephritis*** (blisters on skin; chest pain; general feeling of discomfort, illness, or weakness; muscle pain; joint pain; skin rash or itching; sore throat and fever)

Note: Long-term hydralazine therapy has been associated with a moderate incidence of a condition resembling *systemic lupus erythematosus* (SLE). Risk factors for development of hydralazine-induced SLE include high daily doses of hydralazine (greater than 200 mg per day), slow acetylator or HLA-DRw4 phenotype, and family history of autoimmune disease. Clinical symptoms may include adenopathy, arthralgias, arthritis, fever, malaise, myalgias, pericarditis with or without effusions, pleuritis with or without effusions, and, rarely, skin rash and glomerulonephritis. If SLE-like symptoms develop, hydralazine should be discontinued. Clinical symptoms usually resolve within days or weeks after discontinuation of hydralazine, although the resolution of laboratory value changes, such as a positive antinuclear antibody (ANA) titer, may take much longer. Approximately 30% of all patients receiving hydralazine develop a positive ANA within 1 year of continuous therapy. Development of a positive ANA titer is not strongly linked to development of clinical symptoms; therefore, screening asymptomatic patients using serial ANA titers is not recommended.

Attacks of *angina pectoris* and electrocardiographic changes showing myocardial ischemia have occurred as a result of hydralazine-induced myocardial stimulation.

Incidence rare

Blood dyscrasias, including agranulocytosis, leukopenia, and purpura (fever; general feeling of discomfort or illness; sore throat; weakness)

Those indicating need for medical attention only if they continue or are bothersome

Incidence more frequent

Anorexia (loss of appetite); ***diarrhea; headache; nausea or vomiting; palpitations*** (pounding heartbeat); ***tachycardia*** (fast heartbeat)

Note: In patients with severe heart failure, sympathetic tone is already high and there will be little or no change in heart rate.

Incidence less frequent

Constipation; dyspnea (shortness of breath); ***hypotension*** (dizziness or lightheadedness); ***lacrimation*** (watery eyes); ***nasal congestion*** (stuffy nose); ***redness or flushing of face***

Overdose

For specific information on the agents used in the management of hydralazine overdose, see:
- *Beta-adrenergic Blocking Agents (Systemic) monograph;* and/or
- *Charcoal, Activated (Oral-Local) monograph;* and/or
- *Sympathomimetic Agents—Cardiovascular Use (Parenteral-Systemic) monograph.*

For more information on the management of overdose or unintentional ingestion, **contact a Poison Control Center** (see *Poison Control Center Listing*).

Clinical effects of overdose

The following effects have been selected on the basis of their potential clinical significance (possible signs and symptoms in parentheses where appropriate)—not necessarily inclusive:

Headache; hypotension; myocardial ischemia and subsequent myocardial infarction (anxiety; cough; dizziness, lightheadedness, or fainting; nausea; prolonged abdominal, back, or chest pain that may radiate to the arms, shoulders, neck, chest, back, teeth, or jaw; shortness of breath, sudden; sweating, unusual; vomiting); ***flushing of skin; shock, severe; tachycardia*** (fast heartbeat)

Note: *Myocardial ischemia* with marked ST segment depression has been reported.

Treatment of overdose

To decrease absorption—

Evacuation of gastric contents. If conditions permit, activated charcoal may be administered.

Specific treatment—

For shock: Plasma expanders. If a vasopressor is required, care should be taken not to precipitate or aggravate cardiac arrhythmia.

For tachycardia: Beta-adrenergic blocking agents.

Monitoring—

Fluid and electrolyte status and renal function should be monitored.

Supportive care—

Support of cardiovascular system is most important. Patients in whom intentional overdose is confirmed or suspected should be referred for psychiatric consultation.

Patient Consultation

As an aid to patient consultation, refer to *Advice for the Patient, Hydralazine (Systemic).*

In providing consultation, consider emphasizing the following selected information (» = major clinical significance):

Before using this medication

» Conditions affecting use, especially:

Hypersensitivity to hydralazine

Pregnancy—Blood problems and fetal distress reported in infants of mothers who took hydralazine orally; high doses have caused birth defects in animals

Use in children—Aspartame-containing oral solution must be used with caution in children with phenylketonuria

Other medications, especially diazoxide

Other medical problems, especially acute aortic dissection, coronary artery disease, or mitral valvular disease, such as that associated with rheumatic heart disease

Proper use of this medication

Compliance with therapy; taking medication at the same times each day to maintain the therapeutic effect

» Proper dosing

Missed dose: Taking as soon as possible; not taking if almost time for next dose; not doubling doses

» Proper storage

For use as an antihypertensive

Possible need for control of weight and diet, especially sodium intake

» Patient may not experience symptoms of hypertension; importance of taking medication even if feeling well

» Does not cure, but helps control hypertension; possible need for lifelong therapy; checking with physician before discontinuing medication; serious consequences of untreated hypertension

For oral solution dosage form

May be mixed with fruit juice or applesauce just prior to administration

Precautions while using this medication

Making regular visits to physician to check progress

» Caution when driving or doing things requiring alertness because of possible headache or dizziness

Phenylketonuric patients:

The oral solution dosage form contains phenylalanine 1.4 mg per teaspoonful

For use as an antihypertensive:

» Not taking other medications, especially nonprescription sympathomimetics, unless discussed with physician

Side/adverse effects

Signs of potential side effects, especially allergic reaction, angina pectoris, cutaneous vasculitis, lymphadenopathy, peripheral neuritis, sodium and water retention, edema, SLE-like syndrome, and blood dyscrasias

General Dosing Information

In response to hydralazine-induced vasodilation, reflex tachycardia and fluid retention can occur when hydralazine is administered alone long-term. Concurrent administration of hydralazine with a diuretic and a beta-adrenergic blocking or other appropriate sympatholytic agent may prevent fluid retention and excessive sympathetic stimulation of the heart.

Incidence and severity of some of the side effects of hydralazine can be minimized if the dosage is increased slowly to its therapeutic level.

Recent evidence suggests that withdrawal of antihypertensive therapy prior to surgery is not necessary, but that the anesthesiologist must be made aware of such therapy.

Peripheral neuritis has been observed in some patients on hydralazine therapy. Evidence suggests that this may be due to an antipyridoxine effect. Discontinuation of hydralazine or continuation of hydralazine with supplemental vitamin B_6 (pyridoxine) 100 to 200 mg per day usually results in remission of the neuritis over a period of 4 to 6 weeks.

Due to differences in oral bioavailability between acetylator phenotypes, rapid acetylators may require a larger oral dose than slow acetylators require for the control of blood pressure.

To avoid a sudden increase in blood pressure, patients on hydralazine who have shown a significant decrease in blood pressure should have the medication withdrawn gradually at cessation of therapy.

For oral dosage forms

Food may enhance the bioavailability of hydralazine by reducing first-pass metabolism in the gastrointestinal wall. Consistent administration in relation to meals is recommended.

The oral solution of hydralazine may be mixed with fruit juice or applesauce just prior to administration.

For parenteral dosage forms

Most patients can be transferred to the oral dosage form of hydralazine within 24 to 48 hours after initiation of parenteral therapy.

Oral Dosage Forms

Note: Bracketed uses in the *Dosage Forms* section refer to categories of use and/or indications that are not included in U.S. product labeling.

HYDRALAZINE HYDROCHLORIDE ORAL SOLUTION

Usual adult dose

Hypertension—

Oral, initially 40 mg per day, divided into two or four doses, for the first two to four days, followed by 100 mg per day, divided into two or four doses, for the balance of the first week. For the second and subsequent weeks, 200 mg per day, divided into two or four doses. Maintenance dosage should be adjusted to the lowest effective dose.

Note: Hydralazine conventionally has been administered in four divided doses per day, the basis for this convention being the short plasma half-life of hydralazine. However, a study of the blood pressure-lowering effects of hydralazine in hypertensive patients found that there was no significant difference in efficacy when two-, three-, or four-dose regimens were used. A possible explanation for the lack of a difference may be that hydralazine is readily taken up by arterial blood vessels and released very slowly, prolonging the hypotensive effect.

[Congestive heart failure][1]—

Oral, initially, when administered concurrently with isosorbide dinitrate, 40 to 150 mg per day, divided into two, three, or four doses. If tolerated, the dose may be increased to up to 300 mg per day, divided into two, three, or four doses. Patients with low blood pressure, severe heart failure, or advanced age may be started at 30 mg per day in divided doses.

Usual adult prescribing limits

300 mg daily.

Usual pediatric dose

Hypertension—

Oral, 750 mcg (0.75 mg) per kg of body weight a day divided into two or four doses, the dosage being increased gradually over three or four weeks as needed, up to a maximum of 7.5 mg per kg of body weight or 200 mg a day.

Strength(s) usually available

U.S.—

Not commercially available. Compounding required for prescriptions.

Canada—

Not commercially available. Compounding required for prescriptions.

Packaging and storage

Package in a light-resistant glass or plastic 120-mL bottle, with a child-resistant cap. Store at refrigerator temperature, 2 to 8 °C (36 to 46 °F).

Preparation of dosage form

For a 0.1% oral solution (5 mg per 5 mL)— Hydralazine Hydrochloride USP	100	mg
For a 1% oral solution (50 mg per 5 mL)— Hydralazine Hydrochloride USP	1	gram
Remaining ingredients:		
Sorbitol solution USP (70%)	40	grams
Methylparaben NF	65	mg
Propylparaben NF	35	mg
Propylene Glycol USP	10	grams
Aspartame NF	50	mg
Purified Water, a sufficient quantity to make	100	mL

Dissolve the appropriate amount of hydralazine hydrochloride in 30 mL of purified water. Add aspartame and shake or stir until dissolved. Add sorbitol solution. In a separate container, dissolve the methylparaben and propylparaben in the propylene glycol and, while stirring, add this mixture to the solution containing the hydralazine hydrochloride. Add purified water to make 100 mL and mix.

Note: Contains 1.4 mg of phenylalanine per teaspoonful (5 mL).

Stability

Preparation is stable for 30 days after the day on which it was compounded.

Auxiliary labeling

- Store in refrigerator.
- Expiration date.
- Do not take other medicines without your doctor's advice.

HYDRALAZINE HYDROCHLORIDE TABLETS USP

Usual adult dose

Hypertension—

Oral, initially 40 mg per day, divided into two or four doses, for the first two to four days, followed by 100 mg per day, divided into two or four doses, for the balance of the first week. For the second and subsequent weeks, 200 mg per day, divided into two or four doses. Maintenance dosage should be adjusted to the lowest effective dose.

Note: Hydralazine conventionally has been administered in four divided doses per day, the basis for this convention being the short plasma half-life of hydralazine. However, a study of the blood pressure-lowering effects of hydralazine in hypertensive patients found that there was no significant difference in efficacy when two-, three-, or four-dose regimens were used. A possible explanation for the lack of a difference may be that hydralazine is readily taken up by arterial blood vessels and released very slowly, prolonging the hypotensive effect.

[Congestive heart failure][1]—

Oral, initially, when administered concurrently with isosorbide dinitrate, 40 to 150 mg per day, divided into two, three, or four doses. If tolerated, the dose may be increased to up to 300 mg per day, divided into two, three, or four doses. Patients with low blood pressure, severe heart failure, or advanced age may be started at 30 mg per day, divided into two or three doses.

Usual adult prescribing limits

300 mg daily.

Usual pediatric dose

Hypertension—

Oral, 750 mcg (0.75 mg) per kg of body weight a day divided into two or four doses, the dosage being increased gradually over three or four weeks as needed, up to a maximum of 7.5 mg per kg of body weight or 200 mg a day.

Strength(s) usually available

U.S.—

10 mg (Rx) [GENERIC].
25 mg (Rx) [GENERIC].
50 mg (Rx) [GENERIC].
100 mg (Rx) [GENERIC].

Canada—

10 mg (Rx) [*Apo-Hydral; Apresoline* (scored; tartrazine); *Novo-Hylazin;* GENERIC].
25 mg (Rx) [*Apo-Hydralazine; Apresoline* (lactose); *Novo-Hylazin;* GENERIC].
50 mg (Rx) [*Apo-Hydralazine; Apresoline* (lactose); *Novo-Hylazin;* GENERIC].

Note: The *Apresoline* brand name product is no longer commercially available in the U.S.

Packaging and storage

Store below 40 °C (104 °F), preferably between 15 and 30 °C (59 and 86 °F), unless otherwise specified by manufacturer. Store in a tight, light-resistant container.

Auxiliary labeling

- Do not take other medicines without your doctor's advice.

Parenteral Dosage Forms

HYDRALAZINE HYDROCHLORIDE INJECTION USP

Usual adult dose

Hypertension—

Intramuscular or intravenous, 5 to 40 mg, repeated as needed.

Pre-eclampsia or eclampsia: Intravenous, 5 mg every fifteen to twenty minutes. If a therapeutic response is not achieved after a total dose of 20 mg, another agent should be considered. Continuous intravenous infusion of hydralazine should be avoided because a rapid uncontrolled decline in blood pressure could increase the risk for development of fetal distress, necessitating cesarean delivery.

Usual pediatric dose

Hypertension—

Intramuscular or intravenous, 1.7 to 3.5 mg per kg of body weight a day, divided into four to six daily doses.

Strength(s) usually available

U.S.—

20 mg per mL (Rx) [GENERIC].

Canada—

20 mg per mL (Rx) [*Apresoline Injection*].

Note: The *Apresoline* brand name product is no longer commercially available in the U.S.

Packaging and storage

Store below 40 °C (104 °F), preferably between 15 and 30 °C (59 and 86 °F), unless otherwise specified by manufacturer. Protect from freezing.

Stability

Hydralazine hydrochloride injection should be used immediately after the ampul is opened.

Incompatibilities

Hydralazine hydrochloride injection may undergo color changes when added to infusion fluids. It is recommended that hydralazine hydrochloride injection not be added to infusion solutions.

[1]Not included in Canadian product labeling.

Selected Bibliography

Cohn JN, Archibald DG, Ziesche S, et al. Effect of vasodilator therapy on mortality in chronic congestive heart failure. Results of a Veterans Administration Cooperative Study. N Engl J Med 1986; 314: 1547-52.

Cohn JN, Johnson G, Ziesche S, et al. A comparison of enalapril with hydralazine-isosorbide dinitrate in the treatment of chronic congestive heart failure. N Engl J Med 1991; 325: 303-10.

Revised: 08/24/1998

HYDRALAZINE AND HYDROCHLOROTHIAZIDE Systemic

VA CLASSIFICATION (Primary): CV401

Commonly used brand name(s): *Apresazide*.

NOTE: The *Hydralazine and Hydrochlorothiazide (Systemic)* monograph is maintained on the *USP DI* electronic data base. A copy of the most recent revision of the complete monograph can be accessed on the *USP DI* Updates Online website. See the front cover of book for details on accessing the site.

For information on the specific components of this combination, see the *USP DI* monographs for *Diuretics, Thiazide (Systemic)* and *Hydralazine (Systemic)*.

The information that follows is selectively abstracted from the complete monograph and is provided to facilitate drug use review and patient counseling.

Note: For a listing of dosage forms and brand names by country availability, see *Dosage Forms* section(s).

Category

Antihypertensive.

Indications

Accepted

Hypertension (treatment)—Hydralazine and hydrochlorothiazide combination is indicated in the treatment of hypertension.

Fixed-dosage combinations are generally not recommended for initial therapy and are useful for subsequent therapy only when the proportion of the component agents corresponds to the dose of the individual agents, as determined by titration.

For additional information on initial therapeutic guidelines related to the treatment of hypertension, see *Appendix III*.

Patient Consultation

As an aid to patient consultation, refer to *Advice for the Patient, Hydralazine and Hydrochlorothiazide (Systemic)*.

In providing consultation, consider emphasizing the following selected information (» = major clinical significance):

Before using this medication

» Conditions affecting use, especially:

Sensitivity to hydralazine, hydrochlorothiazide, sulfonamide-type medications, bumetanide, furosemide, or carbonic anhydrase inhibitors

Pregnancy—Blood problems reported in infants of mothers who took hydralazine and birth defects found in animals; hydrochlorothiazide may cause jaundice, thrombocytopenia, hypokalemia in infant

Breast-feeding—Hydrochlorothiazide is distributed into breast milk

Use in the elderly—Increased sensitivity to hypotensive and electrolyte effects; increased risk of hydralazine-induced hypothermia

Other medications, especially diazoxide, digitalis glycosides, lithium

Other medical problems, especially coronary artery disease, rheumatic heart disease, anuria or severe renal function impairment, or infants with jaundice

Proper use of this medication

Diuretic effects of the medication and timing of doses to minimize inconvenience of diuresis

Possible need for control of weight and diet, especially sodium intake

» Patient may not experience symptoms of hypertension; importance of taking medication even if feeling well

» Does not cure, but helps control hypertension; possible need for lifelong therapy; checking with physician before discontinuing medication; serious consequences of untreated hypertension

Compliance with therapy; taking medication at the same times each day to maintain the therapeutic effect

» Proper dosing

Missed dose: Taking as soon as possible; not taking if almost time for next dose; not doubling doses

» Proper storage

Precautions while using this medication

Making regular visits to physician to check progress

» Not taking other medications, especially nonprescription sympathomimetics, unless discussed with physician

» Caution when driving or doing things requiring alertness because of possible headache or dizziness

» Caution when getting up suddenly from a lying or sitting position

» Caution in using alcohol, while standing for long periods or exercising, and during hot weather because of enhanced orthostatic hypotensive effects

» Possibility of hypokalemia; possible need for additional potassium in diet; not changing diet without first checking with physician

To prevent dehydration, checking with physician if severe nausea, vomiting, or diarrhea occurs and continues

Diabetics: May increase blood sugar levels

Possible photosensitivity; avoiding unprotected exposure to sun; using protective clothing and sun block product; avoiding use of sunlamp, tanning bed, or tanning booth

Side/adverse effects

Signs of potential side effects, especially electrolyte imbalance, agranulocytosis, allergic reaction, angina pectoris, cutaneous vasculitis, lymphadenopathy, peripheral neuritis, SLE-like syndrome, agranulocytosis, cholecystitis, pancreatitis, hepatic function impairment, hyperuricemia, gout, and thrombocytopenia

Oral Dosage Forms

HYDRALAZINE HYDROCHLORIDE AND HYDROCHLOROTHIAZIDE CAPSULES

Usual adult dose

Antihypertensive—

Oral, 1 capsule two times a day, as determined by individual titration with the component agents.

Note: Geriatric patients may be more sensitive to the effects of the usual adult dose.

Usual pediatric dose

Antihypertensive—

Oral, as determined by individual titration with the component agents.

Strength(s) usually available

U.S.—

25 mg of hydralazine hydrochloride and 25 mg of hydrochlorothiazide (Rx) [*Apresazide* (sodium bisulfite); GENERIC].

50 mg of hydralazine hydrochloride and 50 mg of hydrochlorothiazide (Rx) [*Apresazide* (sodium bisulfite); GENERIC].

Canada—

Not commercially available.

Auxiliary labeling

- Do not take other medicines without your doctor's advice.

Revised: 08/13/1998

HYDROCHLOROTHIAZIDE—See *Diuretics, Thiazide (Systemic)*

HYDROCODONE—See *Opioid (Narcotic) Analgesics (Systemic)*

HYDROCODONE AND IBUPROFEN Systemic

VA CLASSIFICATION (Primary): CN900

Note: Controlled substance classification

U.S.: Schedule III

Note: For a listing of dosage forms and brand names by country availability, see *Dosage Forms* section(s).

†Not commercially available in Canada.

Category

Analgesic.

Indications

Accepted

Pain (treatment)—Hydrocodone and ibuprofen combination is indicated for the short-term (< 10 days) management of acute pain.

Unaccepted

Hydrocodone and ibuprofen combination is not indicated for the treatment of osteoarthritis and rheumatoid arthritis.

Patient Consultation

As an aid to patient consultation, refer to *Advice for the Patient, Hydrocodone and Ibuprofen (Systemic)*.

In providing consultation, consider emphasizing the following selected information (» = major clinical significance):

Before using this medication

» Conditions affecting use, especially:

Sensitivity to hydrocodone or ibuprofen

Allergies to aspirin or any other nonsteroidal anti-inflammatory drugs (NSAIDs), or other opioid analgesics

Pregnancy—Regular use of opioids by pregnant women may cause physical dependence in the fetus and withdrawal symptoms in the neonate; use of NSAIDs are not recommended during the last trimester of pregnancy due to the potential adverse effects on renal blood flow

Breast-feeding—Use of hydrocodone and ibuprofen combination is not recommended for nursing mothers due to the potential adverse effects of ibuprofen on the neonate

Use in the elderly—Increased risk of toxicity, especially respiratory depression and gastrointestinal effects

Other medications, especially alcohol or other central nervous system (CNS) depressants; angiotensin-converting enzyme (ACE) inhibitors; anticoagulants, coumarin- or indandione-derivative; diuretics; lithium; methotrexate; monoamine oxidase (MAO) inhibitors; and tricyclic antidepressants

Other medical problems, especially allergic reaction; aspirin-induced nasal polyps associated with bronchospasm; coagulation disorders or platelet function disorders; peptic ulcer disease (active); renal disease (severe); renal function impairment; respiratory disease or impairment

Proper use of this medication

» Not taking more medication than prescribed

» Proper dosing

Missed dose: Taking as soon as possible; not taking if almost time for next dose; not doubling doses

» Proper storage

Precautions while using this medication

» Avoiding use of alcoholic beverages or other CNS depressants during therapy, unless prescribed or otherwise approved by physician

» Caution if dizziness, drowsiness, lightheadedness, false sense of well-being occurs, or vision problems occur

» Caution when getting up from a lying or sitting position

» Importance of immediately reporting to physician symptoms of edema, gastrointestinal bleeding or ulceration, cardiovascular events, unusual weight gain, or skin rash

Need to inform physician or dentist of use of medication if any kind of surgery (including dental) or emergency treatment is required

Possible dryness of mouth; using sugarless gum or candy, ice, or saliva substitute for relief; checking with dentist if dry mouth continues for more than 2 weeks

Side/adverse effects

Signs of potential side effects, especially allergic reaction; arrhythmia; bronchitis; dyspnea; fever; frequent urge to urinate; gastrointestinal effects, including esophagitis; gastritis; gastroenteritis; hypotension; melena; tachycardia; tinnitus; urinary incontinence; urinary retention

Oral Dosage Forms

HYDROCODONE AND IBUPROFEN TABLETS

Usual adult dose

Analgesic—

Oral, 1 tablet containing 7.5 mg of hydrocodone and 200 mg of ibuprofen every four to six hours as needed.

Usual adult prescribing limits

5 tablets containing 7.5 mg of hydrocodone and 200 mg of ibuprofen in twenty-four hours.

Usual pediatric dose

Safety and efficacy have not been established.

Usual geriatric dose

See *Usual adult dose*.

Note: Dosage adjustment may be required.

Strength(s) usually available

U.S.—

7.5 mg of hydrocodone and 200 mg of ibuprofen (Rx) [*Vicoprofen* (colloidal silicon dioxide; corn starch; croscarmellose sodium; hydroxypropyl methylcellulose; magnesium stearate; microcrystalline cellulose; polyethylene glycol; polysorbate 80; titanium dioxide)].

Auxiliary labeling

- May cause drowsiness.
- Avoid alcoholic beverages.
- May be habit-forming

Revised: 08/04/2005
Developed: 07/13/1998

HYDROCODONE-CONTAINING COMBINATIONS—See *Hydrocodone and Ibuprofen (Systemic)*

HYDROCORTISONE—See *Corticosteroids—Glucocorticoid Effects (Systemic), Corticosteroids (Ophthalmic), Corticosteroids (Rectal), Corticosteroids (Topical)*

HYDROFLUMETHIAZIDE—See *Diuretics, Thiazide (Systemic)*

HYDROMORPHONE—See *Opioid (Narcotic) Analgesics (Systemic)*

HYDROXOCOBALAMIN—See *Vitamin B_{12} (Systemic)*

HYDROXYCHLOROQUINE Systemic

VA CLASSIFICATION (Primary/Secondary): AP101/MS109; TN900

Commonly used brand name(s): *Plaquenil*.

Note: For a listing of dosage forms and brand names by country availability, see *Dosage Forms* section(s).

Category

Antiprotozoal; antirheumatic (disease-modifying); lupus erythematosus suppressant; antihypercalcemic; polymorphous light eruption suppressant; porphyria cutanea tarda suppressant.

Indications

Note: Bracketed information in the *Indications* section refers to uses that are not included in U.S. product labeling.

Accepted

Malaria (prophylaxis and treatment)—Hydroxychloroquine is indicated in the suppressive treatment and the treatment of acute attacks of malaria caused by *Plasmodium vivax*, *P. malariae*, *P. ovale*, and susceptible strains of *P. falciparum.* The radical cure of *P. vivax* and *P. ovale* malaria requires the concurrent or subsequent administration of primaquine.

Arthritis, rheumatoid (treatment)—Hydroxychloroquine is indicated in the treatment of acute and chronic rheumatoid arthritis. [It may be used in addition to nonsteroidal anti-inflammatory agents.]

Lupus erythematosus, discoid (treatment) or
Lupus erythematosus, systemic (treatment)—Hydroxychloroquine is indicated as a suppressant for chronic discoid and systemic lupus erythematosus.

[Arthritis, juvenile (treatment)][1]—Hydroxychloroquine is used in the treatment of juvenile arthritis.

[Hypercalcemia, sarcoid-associated (treatment)][1]—Hydroxychloroquine is used to reduce urinary calcium excretion and the levels of 1,25-dihydroxyvitamin D in the serum of sarcoid patients who are unable to take corticosteroids.

[Polymorphous light eruption (treatment)][1]—Hydroxychloroquine is used as a suppressant for polymorphous light eruption.

[Porphyria cutanea tarda (treatment)][1]—Hydroxychloroquine is used in the treatment of porphyria cutanea tarda.

[Urticaria, solar (treatment)][1] or
[Vasculitis, chronic cutaneous (treatment)][1]—Hydroxychloroquine is used in the treatment of solar urticaria and chronic cutaneous vasculitis unresponsive to other therapy.

Chloroquine-resistant strains of *P. falciparum*, originally seen only in Southeast Asia and South America, are now documented in all malarious areas except Central America west of the Canal Zone, the Middle East, and the Caribbean. Chloroquine is still the drug of choice for the treatment of susceptible strains of *P. falciparum* and the other 3 malarial species; however, chloroquine-resistant *P. vivax* has recently been reported.

Unaccepted

Hydroxychloroquine does not prevent relapses in patients with *P. vivax* or *P. ovale* malaria since it is not effective against exo-erythrocytic forms of the parasite. In these species, "hypnozoites", which remain dormant in the liver, are responsible for relapses.

[1]Not included in Canadian product labeling.

Pharmacology/Pharmacokinetics

Note: Because hydroxychloroquine concentrates in the cellular fraction of blood, hydroxychloroquine concentrations measured in the blood are higher than those measured in the plasma.

Physicochemical characteristics

Molecular weight—433.95.

Mechanism of action/Effect

Antiprotozoal—Malaria: Unknown, but may be based on ability of hydroxychloroquine to bind to and alter the properties of DNA. Also has been found to be taken up into the acidic food vacuoles of the parasite in the erythrocyte. This increases the pH of the acid vesicles, interfering with vesicle functions and possibly inhibiting phospholipid metabolism. In suppressive treatment, hydroxychloroquine inhibits the erythrocytic stage of development of plasmodia. In acute attacks of malaria, it interrupts erythrocytic schizogony of the parasite. Its ability to concentrate in parasitized erythrocytes may account for their selective toxicity against the erythrocytic stages of plasmodial infection.

Antirheumatic—Hydroxychloroquine is thought to act as a mild immunosuppressant, inhibiting the production of rheumatoid factor and acute phase reactants. It also accumulates in white blood cells, stabilizing lysosomal membranes and inhibiting the activity of many enzymes, including collagenase and the proteases that cause cartilage breakdown.

Absorption

Variable rate of absorption; absorption half-life of 3.6 hours (range, 1.9 to 5.5 hours). Bioavailability is approximately 74%.

Distribution

Widely distributed in body tissues such as the eyes, kidneys, liver, and lungs where retention is prolonged. Concentrations are 2 to 5 times higher in erythrocytes than in plasma. Very low concentrations in intestinal wall. Crosses the placenta, also.

Apparent Vol_D = 5,522 L (measured in blood); 44,257 L (measured in plasma).

Protein binding

Moderate (approximately 45%).

Biotransformation

Hepatic (partially), to active de-ethylated metabolites.

Half-life

Terminal elimination half-life—
In blood: Approximately 50 days.
In plasma: Approximately 32 days.

Time to peak concentration

Approximately 3.2 hours (range, 2 to 4.5 hours).

Peak concentrations

Steady state concentration in whole blood (achieved at 6 months)—
155 mg (base) daily: 948 nanograms per mL.
310 mg (base) daily: 1895 nanograms per mL.

Elimination

Renal; 23 to 25% of hydroxychloroquine excreted unchanged in the urine. Hydroxychloroquine is excreted very slowly; may persist in urine for months or years after medication is discontinued. Also excreted in bile.

Hemodialysis does not remove appreciable amounts of hydroxychloroquine from blood.

Precautions to Consider

Cross-sensitivity and/or related problems

Patients hypersensitive to chloroquine, a 4-aminoquinoline compound structurally similar to hydroxychloroquine, may also be hypersensitive to hydroxychloroquine.

Pregnancy/Reproduction

Pregnancy—Hydroxychloroquine crosses the placenta. Use is not recommended during pregnancy except in the suppression or treatment of malaria or hepatic amebiasis since malaria poses greater potential danger to the mother and fetus (i.e., abortion and death) than prophylactic administration of hydroxychloroquine. Hydroxychloroquine, given in weekly chemoprophylactic doses, has not been shown to cause adverse effects in the fetus. However, risk-benefit must be considered since 4-aminoquinolines, given in therapeutic doses, have been shown to cause central nervous system (CNS) damage, including ototoxicity (auditory and vestibular); congenital deafness; retinal hemorrhages; and abnormal retinal pigmentation. In addition, hydroxychloroquine has been shown to accumulate selectively in melanin structures of fetal eyes. It may be retained in ocular tissues for up to 5 months after elimination from the blood.

Breast-feeding

One case report found that a very small amount of hydroxychloroquine is distributed into breast milk; chloroquine is also distributed into breast milk. Although problems in humans have not been documented, risk-benefit must be considered since infants and children are especially sensitive to the effects of 4-aminoquinolines.

Pediatrics

Infants and children are especially sensitive to the effects of hydroxychloroquine and chloroquine. Fatalities have been reported following the ingestion of as little as 750 mg to 1 gram of chloroquine; hydroxychloroquine is assumed to be equally toxic. Long-term therapy with hydroxychloroquine is not generally recommended in children. However, it has been used in juvenile arthritis for as long as 6 months with little or no toxicity.

Geriatrics

No information is available on the relationship of age to the effects of hydroxychloroquine in geriatric patients.

Drug interactions and/or related problems

The following drug interactions and/or related problems have been selected on the basis of their potential clinical significance (possible mechanism in parentheses where appropriate)—not necessarily inclusive (» = major clinical significance):

Note: Combinations containing any of the following medications, depending on the amount present, may also interact with this medication.

Penicillamine
(concurrent use of penicillamine with hydroxychloroquine may increase penicillamine plasma concentrations, increasing the potential for serious hematologic and/or renal adverse reactions, as well as the possibility of severe skin reactions)

Medical considerations/Contraindications

The medical considerations/contraindications included have been selected on the basis of their potential clinical significance (reasons given in parentheses where appropriate)—not necessarily inclusive (» = major clinical significance).

Risk-benefit should be considered when the following medical problems exist:

» Blood disorders, severe
(hydroxychloroquine may cause blood dyscrasias, including agranulocytosis, aplastic anemia, neutropenia, or thrombocytopenia)

Gastrointestinal disorders, severe
(hydroxychloroquine may cause gastrointestinal irritation)

Glucose-6-phosphate dehydrogenase (G6PD) deficiency
(hydroxychloroquine may cause hemolytic anemia in G6PD-deficient patients, although this is unlikely when hydroxychloroquine is given in therapeutic doses)

» Hepatic function impairment
(because hydroxychloroquine is metabolized in the liver, hepatic function impairment may increase blood concentrations of hydroxychloroquine, increasing the risk of side effects)

Hypersensitivity to hydroxychloroquine or chloroquine

» Neurological disorders, severe
(hydroxychloroquine may cause neuromyopathy, ototoxicity, polyneuritis, or seizures)

Porphyria
(hydroxychloroquine may cause exacerbation of porphyria)

Psoriasis
(hydroxychloroquine may precipitate severe attacks of psoriasis)

» Renal function impairment
(because hydroxychloroquine is excreted very slowly in urine, renal function impairment may cause increased blood concentrations of hydroxychloroquine, increasing the risk of side effects)

» Retinal or visual field changes, presence of
(hydroxychloroquine may cause corneal opacities, keratopathy, or retinopathy)

Patient monitoring

The following may be especially important in patient monitoring (other tests may be warranted in some patients, depending on condition; » = major clinical significance):

» Ophthalmologic examinations, including visual acuity, expert slit lamp, funduscopic, visual field tests, central field screening with a red Amsler grid (Amsler's chart), and retinoscopy
(recommended before and at least every 6 months during prolonged daily therapy since irreversible retinal damage has been reported with long-term or high-dosage therapy; serious ocular injury has been thought to be correlated with a total cumulative dose of greater than 200 grams (base) of hydroxychloroquine; however, a daily dose of greater than 310 mg (base), or 5 mg (base) per kg daily, of hydroxychloroquine may be a more important determinant; any retinal or visual abnormality that is not fully explainable by difficulties of accommodation or corneal opacities should be monitored following discontinuation of therapy, since retinal changes and visual disturbances may progress even after cessation of therapy)

Side/Adverse Effects

Note: Side/adverse effects of hydroxychloroquine are usually dose-related. When hydroxychloroquine is used for the short-term treatment of malaria or other parasitic diseases, side/adverse effects are usually mild and reversible. However, following prolonged use and/or high-dose therapy, such as in the treatment of rheumatoid arthritis, lupus erythematosus, or polymorphous light eruption, side/adverse effects may be serious and sometimes irreversible.

Irreversible retinal damage may be more likely to occur when the daily dosage equals or exceeds the equivalent of 310 mg (base), or 5 mg (base) per kg daily, of hydroxychloroquine.

The following side/adverse effects have been selected on the basis of their potential clinical significance (possible signs and symptoms in parentheses where appropriate)—not necessarily inclusive:

Those indicating need for medical attention

Incidence less frequent

Ocular toxicity specifically corneal opacities (blurred vision or any other change in vision); ***keratopathy*** (blurred vision or any other change in vision); ***retinopathy*** (blurred vision or any other change in vision)

Note: The risk of *retinopathy* is reduced when the daily maintenance dose is less than 6.5 mg (5 mg base) per kg of body weight (mg/kg) and the cumulative dose is less than 200 grams, the duration of treatment is less than 10 years, and renal function is not impaired.

Incidence rare

Aplastic anemia (fatigue; weakness); ***blood dyscrasias, specifically agranulocytosis*** (sore throat and fever); ***emotional changes or psychosis*** (mood or other mental changes); ***neuromyopathy*** (increased muscle weakness); ***neutropenia*** (sore throat and fever); ***ototoxicity*** (any loss of hearing; ringing or buzzing in ears)—usually in patients with pre-existing auditory damage; ***seizures; thrombocytopenia*** (unusual bleeding or bruising)

Those indicating need for medical attention only if they continue or are bothersome

Incidence more frequent

Ciliary muscle dysfunction (difficulty in reading); ***gastrointestinal irritation*** (diarrhea; loss of appetite; nausea; stomach cramps or pain; vomiting); ***headache; itching*** (especially in black patients)—not an indication for discontinuation of therapy in black patients

Incidence less frequent

Bleaching of hair or increased hair loss; blue-black discoloration of skin, fingernails, or inside of mouth; dizziness or lightheadedness; nervousness or restlessness; skin rash or itching

Those indicating possible retinal changes, visual disturbances and the need for medical attention if they occur or progress after medication is discontinued

Blurred vision or any other change in vision

Overdose

For specific information on the agents used in the management of hydroxychloroquine overdose, see:

- *Charcoal, Activated (Oral-Local)* monograph;
- *Diazepam* in *Benzodiazepines (Systemic)* monograph; and/or
- *Sympathomimetic Agents—Cardiovascular Use (Parenteral-Systemic)* monograph.

For more information on the management of overdose or unintentional ingestion, **contact a Poison Control Center** (see *Poison Control Center Listing*).

Clinical effects of overdose

After ingestion of an overdose of hydroxychloroquine, toxic symptoms may occur within 30 minutes. These include drowsiness, visual disturbances, cardiovascular collapse, and seizures, followed by sudden respiratory and cardiac arrest.

Doses of chloroquine phosphate as small as 0.75 to 1 gram in children, and 2.25 to 3 grams in adults, may be fatal. It is assumed that hydroxychloroquine is equally toxic.

The following effects have been selected on the basis of their potential clinical significance (possible signs and symptoms in parenthesis where appropriate)—not necessarily inclusive:

Acute

Cardiovascular toxicities, specifically conduction disturbances or hypotension; neurotoxicity, specifically drowsiness; headache; hyperexcitability; seizures; or coma; respiratory and cardiac arrest; visual disturbances (blurred vision)

Treatment of overdose

Since there is no specific antidote, treatment of hydroxychloroquine overdose should be symptomatic and supportive with possible utilization of the following:

To decrease absorption—
Emptying stomach with gastric lavage.
Administering activated charcoal with a cathartic. The dose of activated charcoal should be 5 to 10 times the estimated dose of the drug ingested.

To enhance elimination—
Forcing diuresis and acidifying the urine, with ammonium chloride, for example, can help promote urinary excretion of 4-aminoquinolines. Adjusting the dose of the acidifying agent to maintain a urinary pH of 5.5 to 6.5. Monitoring of plasma potassium is recommended. Using with caution in patients with renal function impairment and/or metabolic acidosis.

Specific treatment—
For seizures: Treating repetitive seizures or status epilepticus with intravenous diazepam (in 2.5 to 5 mg increments).
For arrhythmias: Managing life-threatening ventricular arrhythmias or cardiac arrest appropriately, as per Advanced Cardiac Life Support guidelines.
For hypotension and circulatory shock: Administering fluids at a sufficient rate to maintain urine output. Administering intravenous pressors and/or inotropic drugs, such as norepinephrine, dopamine, isoproterenol, or dobutamine, if required. One study found that administration of a high-dose diazepam infusion improved hemodynamic function, and epinephrine decreased the myocardial depressant and vasodilatory effects of chloroquine overdose. This may also apply to a hydroxychloroquine overdose.

Monitoring—
Monitoring of plasma potassium is recommended.

Supportive care—
Securing and maintaining a patent airway, administering oxygen, and instituting assisted or controlled respiration as required. In severe overdoses, early mechanical ventilation has been suggested to prevent hypoxemia. Patients in whom intentional overdose is

known or suspected should be referred for psychiatric consultation.

Patient Consultation

As an aid to patient consultation, refer to *Advice for the Patient, Hydroxychloroquine (Systemic).*

In providing consultation, consider emphasizing the following selected information (» = major clinical significance):

Before using this medication

» Conditions affecting use, especially:
- Hypersensitivity to hydroxychloroquine or chloroquine
- Pregnancy—May cause toxicity to the fetus when given to mother in therapeutic doses; however, hydroxychloroquine has not been shown to cause adverse effects in the fetus when used as a prophylactic agent against malaria
- Use in children—Infants and children are especially sensitive to effects of hydroxychloroquine
- Other medical problems, especially impaired hepatic function, impaired renal function, presence of retinal or visual field changes, severe blood disorders, or severe neurologic disorders

Proper use of this medication

» Taking with meals or milk to minimize possible gastrointestinal irritation

» Keeping medication out of reach of children; fatalities reported with as few as 3 or 4 tablets (250-mg strength) of chloroquine phosphate; hydroxychloroquine is assumed to be equally toxic

» Importance of not taking more medication than the amount prescribed

» Compliance with full course of therapy

» Importance of not missing doses and taking medication on regular schedule

» Proper dosing

Missed dose: Taking as soon as possible; not taking if almost time for next dose; not doubling doses

» Proper storage

For prevention of malaria

Starting medication 1 to 2 weeks before entering malarious area to ascertain patient response and allow time to substitute another medication if reactions occur

» Continuing medication while staying in area and for 4 to 6 weeks after leaving area; checking with physician immediately if fever develops while traveling or within 2 months after departure from endemic area

For arthritis and lupus erythematosus

Importance of taking medication on regular schedule

May require up to 6 months for full benefit

For patients unable to swallow hydroxychloroquine tablets

Crushing tablets and putting each dose in capsules; contents of capsules may be mixed with jam, jelly, or jello

Precautions while using this medication

» Regular visits to physician for ophthalmologic examinations during or after long-term therapy

Checking with physician if no improvement within a few days (or a few weeks or months for arthritis)

» Caution if blurred vision, difficulty in reading, other change in vision, dizziness, or lightheadedness occurs

Mosquito-control measures to reduce the chance of getting malaria:
- Sleeping under mosquito netting
- Wearing long-sleeved shirts or blouses and long trousers to protect arms and legs between dusk and dawn
- Applying mosquito repellent to uncovered areas of skin between dusk and dawn

Side/adverse effects

Signs of potential side effects, especially ocular toxicity, blood dyscrasias, emotional or psychological changes, neuromyopathy, ototoxicity, and seizures

General Dosing Information

Long-term and/or high-dosage therapy may cause irreversible retinal damage and/or neurosensorial deafness.

Hydroxychloroquine should be discontinued if any of the following problems occur: any abnormality in visual acuity, visual fields, retinal macular changes, or any other visual symptoms; muscle weakness; or severe blood disorders.

Malaria-suppressive therapy should be started 1 to 2 weeks before the patient enters a malarious area and should be continued for 4 to 6 weeks after patient leaves the area. Starting the medication in advance will help to determine the patient's tolerance to the medication and allow time to substitute other antimalarials if the patient develops allergies to the medication or develops other adverse effects.

Hydroxychloroquine should be taken with meals or milk to minimize the possibility of gastrointestinal irritation.

Corticosteroids and/or nonsteroidal anti-inflammatory analgesics (including salicylates) may be given concurrently with hydroxychloroquine in the treatment of rheumatoid arthritis. These medications can usually be reduced gradually in dosage or discontinued after hydroxychloroquine has been given for several weeks.

When hydroxychloroquine is used in the treatment of rheumatoid arthritis, several months of therapy may be required for it to reach its maximum effectiveness. If improvement (such as reduced joint swelling and increased mobility) does not occur within 6 months, the medication should be discontinued.

Oral Dosage Forms

Note: Bracketed uses in the *Dosage Forms* section refer to categories of use and/or indications that are not included in U.S. product labeling.

HYDROXYCHLOROQUINE SULFATE TABLETS USP

Usual adult and adolescent dose

Malaria—

Suppressive: Oral, 400 mg (310 mg base) once every seven days.

Therapeutic: Oral, 800 mg (620 mg base) as a single dose; or 800 mg (620 mg base) initially, followed by 400 mg (310 mg base) in six to eight hours, and 400 mg (310 mg base) once a day on the second and third days.

Antirheumatic (disease-modifying)—

Oral, up to 6.5 mg (5 mg base) per kg of lean body weight daily, with meals or a glass of milk.

Note: In a small number of patients who experience side effects with the usual initial dose in the treatment of rheumatoid arthritis, a temporary reduction in the initial dose of hydroxychloroquine may be required. After five to ten days the dose may be gradually increased until the desired response is obtained.

If relapse occurs after withdrawal of hydroxychloroquine, therapy may be resumed or continued on an intermittent schedule if there are no ocular contraindications.

Lupus erythematosus suppressant—

Oral, up to 6.5 mg (5 mg base) per kg of lean body weight daily.

[Polymorphous light eruption suppressant][1]—

Oral, 200 mg (155 mg base) two or three times a day.

Usual pediatric dose

Malaria—

Suppressive: Oral, 6.4 mg (5 mg base) per kg of body weight, not to exceed the adult dose, once every seven days.

Therapeutic: Oral, 32 mg (25 mg base) per kg of body weight administered over a period of three days as follows: 12.9 mg (10 mg base) per kg of body weight, not to exceed a single dose of 800 mg (620 mg base); then 6.4 mg (5 mg base) per kg of body weight, not to exceed a single dose of 400 mg (310 mg base), six, twenty-four, and forty-eight hours after the first dose.

Note: Children are especially sensitive to the effects of the 4-aminoquinolines.

Long-term therapy with hydroxychloroquine is not recommended in children.

Strength(s) usually available

U.S.—

200 mg (equivalent to 155 mg base) (Rx) [*Plaquenil*].

Canada—

200 mg (equivalent to 155 mg base) (Rx) [*Plaquenil* (scored)].

Packaging and storage

Store below 40 °C (104 °F), preferably between 15 and 30 °C (59 and 86 °F), unless otherwise specified by manufacturer. Store in a well-closed container.

Preparation of dosage form

According to the manufacturer, the tablets may be crushed and each dose placed in a capsule. The contents of each compounded capsule may then be mixed with a teaspoonful of jam, jelly, or jello prior to administration. Preparation of hydroxychloroquine sulfate oral suspensions is not recommended.

Auxiliary labeling

- Continue medication for full time of treatment.
- Keep out of reach of children.

- Take with food or milk.
- May cause dizziness.

Note

Explain potential danger of accidental overdose in children.

Consider dispensing in unit-dose packaging in child-resistant containers ("double-barrier" packaging).

[1]Not included in Canadian product labeling.

Revised: 05/24/1999

HYDROXYPROGESTERONE—See *Progestins (Systemic)*

HYDROXYUREA Systemic

VA CLASSIFICATION (Primary/Secondary): AN300/BL400

Commonly used brand name(s): *Droxia; Hydrea.*

Note: For a listing of dosage forms and brand names by country availability, see *Dosage Forms* section(s).

Category

Antineoplastic; Antianemic.

Indications

Note: Bracketed information in the *Indications* section refers to uses that are not included in U.S. product labeling.

Accepted

Carcinoma, ovarian (treatment)[1] or

[Carcinoma, cervical (treatment)][1]—Hydroxyurea is indicated for treatment of recurrent, metastatic, or inoperable carcinoma of the ovary and for treatment of cervical carcinoma.

Carcinoma, head and neck (treatment adjunct)—Used with irradiation therapy for local control of primary squamous cell (epidermoid) carcinomas of the head and neck, excluding the lip.

Leukemia, chronic myelocytic (treatment)—Hydroxyurea is indicated for treatment of resistant chronic myelocytic leukemia.

Melanoma (treatment)—Hydroxyurea is indicated for the treatment of melanoma.

[Thrombocytosis, essential (treatment)][1] or

[Polycythemia vera (treatment)][1]—Hydroxyurea is indicated for treatment of essential thrombocytosis and polycythemia vera.

Sickle cell anemia, painful crises (prophylaxis)[1]—Hydroxyurea is indicated to reduce the frequency of painful crises and to reduce the need for blood transfusions in adult patients with sickle cell anemia with recurrent moderate to severe painful crises (generally at least 3 during the preceding 12 months).

[1]Not included in Canadian product labeling.

Pharmacology/Pharmacokinetics

Physicochemical characteristics

Molecular weight—76.05.

Mechanism of action/Effect

Hydroxyurea is classified as an antimetabolite. Hydroxyurea is thought to be cell cycle–specific for the S phase of cell division. The exact mechanism of antineoplastic activity is unknown but is thought to involve interference with synthesis of DNA, with no effect on synthesis of RNA or protein.

Pharmacologic effects of hydroxyurea that may contribute to its beneficial effects in sickle cell anemia include increasing hemoglobin F levels in red blood cells (RBCs), decreasing neutrophils, increasing the water content of RBCs, increasing deformability of sickled cells, and altering the adhesion of RBCs to the endothelium.

Absorption

Well absorbed from the gastrointestinal tract.

Distribution

Crosses the blood-brain barrier.

Volume of distribution (V_D)—Equal to total body water.

Concentrates in leukocytes (white blood cells) (WBCs) and erythrocytes (red blood cells) (RBCs).

Biotransformation

Hepatic.

Half-life

3 to 4 hours.

Time to peak concentration

1 to 4 hours.

Elimination

Renal—80% within 12 hours (50% unchanged). In adults with sickle cell anemia, the mean cumulative urinary excretion was 62% of the administered dose at 8 hours.

Hepatic—Saturable.

Respiratory—As carbon dioxide.

Precautions to Consider

Cross-sensitivity and/or related problems

Patients sensitive to tartrazine may be sensitive to the capsule dosage form available in Canada also, since the capsules may contain tartrazine.

Carcinogenicity

Secondary malignancies are potential delayed effects of many antineoplastic agents, although it is not clear whether the effect is related to their mutagenic or immunosuppressive action. The effect of dose and duration of therapy is also unknown, although risk seems to increase with long-term use. Although information is limited, available data seem to indicate that the carcinogenic risk is greatest with the alkylating agents.

Antimetabolites have been shown to be carcinogenic in animals and may be associated with an increased risk of development of secondary carcinomas in humans, although the risk appears to be less than with alkylating agents.

Tumorigenicity

An increased incidence of mammary tumors has been reported for female rats administered intraperitoneal hydroxyurea at 125 to 250 mg per kilogram (mg/kg) of body weight (about 0.6 to 1.2 times the maximum recommended human oral daily dose on a mg per square meter [mg/m^2] basis) three times a week for six months.

Hydroxyurea causes the transformation of rodent embryo cells to a tumorigenic phenotype.

Mutagenicity

Hydroxyurea is mutagenic *in vitro* to bacteria, fungi, protozoa, and mammalian cells.

Hydroxyurea is clastogenic *in vitro* (in hamster cells and human lymphoblasts) and *in vivo* (SCE assay in rodents, mouse micronucleus assay).

Pregnancy/Reproduction

Fertility—Gonadal suppression, resulting in amenorrhea or azoospermia, may occur in patients taking antineoplastic therapy, especially with the alkylating agents. In general, these effects appear to be related to dose and length of therapy and may be irreversible. Prediction of the degree of testicular or ovarian function impairment is complicated by the common use of combinations of several antineoplastics, which makes it difficult to assess the effects of individual agents. Hydroxyurea causes reversible germ cell toxicity.

Pregnancy—No adequate and well controlled studies have been done in pregnant women.

First trimester: It is usually recommended that use of antineoplastics, especially combination chemotherapy, be avoided whenever possible, especially during the first trimester. Although information is limited because of the relatively few instances of antineoplastic administration during pregnancy, the mutagenic, teratogenic, and carcinogenic potential of these medications must be considered.

Other hazards to the fetus include adverse reactions seen in adults.

In general, use of a contraceptive is recommended during cytotoxic drug therapy.

Hydroxyurea is teratogenic in animals. It is also embryotoxic, causing decreased fetal viability, decreased litter size, developmental delays, growth retardation, impaired learning ability, and malformations (partially ossified cranial bones, absence of eye sockets, hydrocephaly, bipartite sternebrae, missing lumbar vertebrae) at 180 mg/kg per day (about 0.8 times the maximum recommended human daily dose on a mg per square meter of body surface area basis) in rats and at 30 mg/kg per day (about 0.3 times the maximum recommended human daily dose on a mg per square meter of body surface area basis) in rabbits.

FDA Pregnancy Category D.

Breast-feeding
Hydroxyurea is excreted in human breast milk. Because of the potential for serious adverse effects, a decision should be made to discontinue nursing or discontinue the medication, taking into consideration the importance of the medication to the mother.

Pediatrics
Although appropriate studies on the relationship of age to the effects of hydroxyurea have not been performed in the pediatric population, children may be more sensitive to the effects of hydroxyurea.

Geriatrics
Although appropriate studies on the relationship of age to the effects of hydroxyurea have not been performed in the geriatric population, the elderly may be more sensitive to effects of hydroxyurea. In addition, because elderly patients are more likely to have decreased renal function, care should be taken in dose selection, and it may be useful to monitor renal function.

Dental
The bone marrow depressant effects of hydroxyurea may result in an increased incidence of microbial infection, delayed healing, and gingival bleeding. Dental work, whenever possible, should be completed prior to initiation of therapy or deferred until blood counts have returned to normal. Patients should be instructed in proper oral hygiene during treatment, including caution in use of regular toothbrushes, dental floss, and toothpicks.
Hydroxyurea may also cause stomatitis associated with considerable discomfort.

Drug interactions and/or related problems
The following drug interactions and/or related problems have been selected on the basis of their potential clinical significance (possible mechanism in parentheses where appropriate)—not necessarily inclusive (» = major clinical significance):

Allopurinol or
Colchicine or
» Probenecid or
» Sulfinpyrazone
(hydroxyurea may raise the concentration of blood uric acid; dosage adjustment of antigout agents may be necessary to control hyperuricemia and gout; allopurinol may be preferred to prevent or reverse hydroxyurea-induced hyperuricemia because of risk of uric acid nephropathy with uricosuric antigout agents)

Blood dyscrasia-causing medications (see *Appendix II*)
(leukopenic and/or thrombocytopenic effects of hydroxyurea may be increased with concurrent or recent therapy if these medications cause the same effects; dosage adjustment of hydroxyurea, if necessary, should be based on blood counts)

» Bone marrow depressants, other (see *Appendix II*) or
Radiation therapy
(additive bone marrow depression may occur; dosage reduction may be required when two or more bone marrow depressants, including radiation, are used concurrently or consecutively)

» Didanosine or
» Stavudine or
» Antiretroviral agents, other
(in HIV-infected patients, fatal and nonfatal pancreatitis, hepatotoxicity, hepatic failure, and peripheral neuropathy have been reported with concurrent treatment with other antiretroviral agents, especially didanosine with or without stavudine)

» Interferon therapy
(cutaneous vasculitic toxicities have occurred during therapy with hydroxyurea and were reported most often in patients with a history of, or currently receiving, interferon therapy)

Vaccines, killed virus
(because normal defense mechanisms may be suppressed by hydroxyurea therapy, the patient's antibody response to the vaccine may be decreased. The interval between discontinuation of medications that cause immunosuppression and restoration of the patient's ability to respond to the vaccine depends on the intensity and type of immunosuppression-causing medications used, the underlying disease, and other factors; estimates vary from 3 months to 1 year)

» Vaccines, live virus
(because normal defense mechanisms may be suppressed by hydroxyurea therapy, concurrent use with a live virus vaccine may potentiate the replication of the vaccine virus, may increase the side/adverse effects of the vaccine virus, and/or may decrease the patient's antibody response to the vaccine; immunization of these patients should be undertaken only with extreme caution after careful review of the patient's hematologic status and only with the knowledge and consent of the physician managing the hydroxyurea therapy. The interval between discontinuation of medications that cause immunosuppression and restoration of the patient's ability to respond to the vaccine depends on the intensity and type of immunosuppression-causing medications used, the underlying disease, and other factors; estimates vary from 3 months to 1 year. Patients with leukemia in remission should not receive live virus vaccine until at least 3 months after their last chemotherapy. Immunization with oral poliovirus vaccine should also be postponed in persons in close contact with the patient, especially family members)

Laboratory value alterations
The following have been selected on the basis of their potential clinical significance (possible effect in parentheses where appropriate)—not necessarily inclusive (» = major clinical significance).

With physiology/laboratory test values
Blood urea nitrogen (BUN) and
Creatinine, serum and
Uric acid, serum
(concentrations may occasionally be temporarily increased as a result of impairment of renal tubular function)

Medical considerations/Contraindications
The medical considerations/contraindications included have been selected on the basis of their potential clinical significance (reasons given in parentheses where appropriate)—not necessarily inclusive (» = major clinical significance).

Risk-benefit should be considered when the following medical problems exist:

» Anemia or
» Leukopenia or
» Neutropenia or
» Thrombocytopenia
(if severe, must be corrected with whole blood replacement before initiation of hydroxyurea therapy)

» Bone marrow depression

» Chickenpox, existing or recent (including recent exposure) or
» Herpes zoster
(risk of severe generalized disease)

Gout, history of or
Urate renal stones, history of
(risk of hyperuricemia)

» HIV infection, especially concurrent treatment with antiretroviral agents
(fatal and nonfatal pancreatitis, hepatotoxicity, hepatic failure, and peripheral neuropathy reported with concurrent treatment with other antiretroviral agents, especially didanosine with or without stavudine)

» History of receiving interferon therapy
(cutaneous vasculitic toxicities have occurred during therapy with hydroxyurea and were reported most often in patients with a history of, or currently, receiving interferon therapy)

» Infection

» Renal function impairment
(reduced elimination; lower dosage is recommended)

» Hypersensitivity to hydroxyurea

» Caution should be used in patients who have had previous cytotoxic drug therapy and radiation therapy.

Patient monitoring
The following may be especially important in patient monitoring (other tests may be warranted in some patients, depending on condition; » = major clinical significance):

Blood urea nitrogen (BUN) concentrations and
Creatinine concentrations, serum
(recommended prior to initiation of therapy and at periodic intervals during therapy; frequency varies according to clinical state, agent, dose, and other agents being used concurrently)

» Hematocrit or hemoglobin and
» Leukocyte count, total and, if appropriate, differential and
» Platelet count
(determinations recommended prior to initiation of therapy and at periodic intervals during therapy; frequency varies according to clinical state, agent, dose, and other agents being used concurrently)

Uric acid concentrations, serum
(recommended prior to initiation of therapy and at periodic intervals during therapy; frequency varies according to clinical state, agent, dose, and other agents being used concurrently)

Side/Adverse Effects

Note: Many "side effects" of antineoplastic therapy are unavoidable and represent the medication's pharmacologic action. Some of these (for example, leukopenia and thrombocytopenia) are actually used as parameters to aid in individual dosage titration.

Administration of hydroxyurea to patients with severe renal function impairment may produce visual and auditory hallucinations and pronounced hematologic toxicity.

Skin changes resembling atrophic lichen planus, including atrophy, brittle nails, darkening or redness of skin, and skin ulcers, have been reported rarely in patients receiving prolonged (over several years) daily treatment with hydroxyurea.

The following side/adverse effects have been selected on the basis of their potential clinical significance (possible signs and symptoms in parentheses where appropriate)—not necessarily inclusive:

Those indicating need for medical attention

Incidence more frequent

Anemia or erythrocytic or platelet abnormalities; leukopenia; neutropenia (cough or hoarseness; fever or chills; lower back or side pain; painful or difficult urination)—usually asymptomatic

Note: Self-limiting *megaloblastic erythropoiesis* occurs commonly early in the course of therapy; morphologic changes resemble pernicious anemia, but are not related to vitamin B_{12} or folic acid deficiency. Plasma iron clearance may be delayed and rate of iron utilization by erythrocytes reduced, but hydroxyurea does not appear to alter red blood cell survival time.

Onset of *leukopenia* occurs about 10 days after initiation of therapy.

Hematologic abnormalities usually recover 2 weeks after cessation of therapy.

Incidence less frequent

Melanonychia (blackening of fingernails and toenails); ***stomatitis*** (sores in mouth and on lips); ***thrombocytopenia*** (unusual bleeding or bruising; black, tarry stools; blood in urine or stools; pinpoint red spots on skin)—usually asymptomatic

Incidence rare

Hyperuricemia or uric acid nephropathy (joint pain; lower back or side pain; swelling of feet or lower legs); ***neurotoxicity or cerebral metastatic disease*** (confusion; convulsions; dizziness; hallucinations; headache); ***renal function impairment*** (difficulty in urination)

Note: *Hyperuricemia or uric acid nephropathy* occurs most commonly during initial treatment of patients with leukemia, as a result of rapid cell breakdown, which leads to elevated serum uric acid concentrations.

Incidence not determined—Observed during clinical practice; estimates of frequency can not be determined

Cutaneous vasculitic toxicities (blisters on skin); ***gangrene*** (cold, pale or a bluish color skin of the fingers or toes; itching skin; numbness or tingling of the fingers or toes; pain in the fingers or toes); ***vasculitic ulcerations*** (bleeding under skin; crater-like lesions; fever; weight loss; fatigue)

Those indicating need for medical attention only if they continue or are bothersome

Incidence more frequent—dose-related

Diarrhea; drowsiness—large doses; ***loss of appetite; nausea or vomiting***

Incidence less frequent

Constipation; exacerbation of postirradiation erythema (redness of skin at place of irradiation); ***skin rash and itching***

Those not indicating need for medical attention

Incidence less frequent

Loss of hair

Note: Normal *hair growth* usually returns after treatment has ended, although it may be slightly different in color or texture

Those indicating the need for medical attention if they occur after medication is discontinued

Bone marrow depression (black, tarry stools; blood in urine; cough or hoarseness; fever or chills; lower back or side pain; painful or difficult urination; pinpoint red spots on skin; unusual bleeding or bruising)

Overdose

For more information on the management of overdose or unintentional ingestion, **contact a Poison Control Center** (see *Poison Control Center Listing*).

Clinical effects of overdose

The following effects have been selected on the basis of their potential clinical significance (possible signs and symptoms in parentheses where appropriate)—not necessarily inclusive:

Edema of palms and soles (swelling of palms and soles of feet); ***scaling of hands and feet; severe generalized hyperpigmentation of the skin*** (darkening of skin color); ***soreness; stomatitis*** (sores in mouth and on lips); ***violet erythema*** (violet flushing of the skin)

Patient Consultation

As an aid to patient consultation, refer to *Advice for the Patient, Hydroxyurea (Systemic)*.

In providing consultation, consider emphasizing the following selected information (» = major clinical significance):

Before using this medication

» Conditions affecting use, especially:

Hypersensitivity to hydroxyurea

Pregnancy—Use not recommended because of mutagenic, teratogenic, and carcinogenic potential; advisability of using contraception; telling physician immediately if pregnancy is suspected

Breast-feeding—Hydroxyurea is excreted in human breast milk; not recommended because of risk of serious side effects

Use in children—Children may be more sensitive to effects

Use in the elderly—Elderly patients may be more sensitive to effects; cautious dose selection and renal function monitoring due to increased likelihood of renal impairment in elderly patients

Other medications, especially probenecid, sulfinpyrazone, other bone marrow depressants, didanosine, stavudine, other antiretroviral agents, interferon therapy, live virus vaccines, or previous cytotoxic drug or radiation therapy

Other medical problems, especially anemia, chickenpox, herpes zoster, infection (especially HIV treated with antiretroviral drugs), history of receiving interferon therapy, leukopenia, neutropenia, renal function impairment, or thrombocytopenia

Proper use of this medication

» Importance of not taking more or less medication than the amount prescribed

» Importance of handling this medicine with care and decreasing risk of exposure by wearing gloves and following safety instructions in the product information

For patients who cannot swallow capsules: Contents of capsules may be emptied into glass of water and taken immediately; some inert material may not dissolve and may float on surface

Caution in taking combination chemotherapy; taking each medication at the right time

Importance of ample fluid intake and subsequent increase in urine output to aid in excretion of uric acid

» Frequency of nausea, vomiting, and diarrhea; importance of continuing medication despite stomach upset

Checking with physician if vomiting occurs shortly after dose is taken

» Proper dosing

Missed dose: Not taking at all; not doubling doses

» Proper storage

Precautions while using this medication

» Importance of close monitoring by the physician

» Avoiding immunizations unless approved by physician; other persons in patient's household should avoid immunizations with oral poliovirus vaccine; avoiding other persons who have taken oral poliovirus vaccine or wearing a protective mask that covers nose and mouth

Caution if bone marrow depression occurs:

» Avoiding exposure to persons with infections, especially during period of low blood counts; checking with physician immediately if fever or chills, cough or hoarseness, lower back or side pain, or painful or difficult urination occurs

» Checking with physician immediately if unusual bleeding or bruising; black, tarry stools; blood in urine; or pinpoint red spots on skin occur

Caution in use of regular toothbrush, dental floss, or toothpick; physician, dentist, or nurse may suggest alternatives; checking with physician before having dental work done

Not touching eyes or inside of nose unless hands washed immediately before

Using caution to avoid accidental cuts with use of sharp objects such as safety razor or fingernail or toenail cutters
Avoiding contact sports or other situations where bruising or injury could occur

Side/adverse effects
Signs of potential side effects, especially anemia, erythrocytic or platelet abnormalities, leukopenia, neutropenia, melanonychia, stomatitis, thrombocytopenia, hyperuricemia or uric acid nephropathy, neurotoxicity, cerebral metastatic disease, or renal function impairment
Signs of potential side effects observed during clinical practice, especially cutaneous vasculitic toxicities, gangrene, or vasculitic ulcerations
Physician or nurse can help in dealing with side effects

General Dosing Information

Patients receiving hydroxyurea should be under supervision of a physician experienced in antimetabolite chemotherapy.

Dosage must be adjusted to meet the individual requirements of each patient, based on clinical response and appearance or severity of toxicity.

Dosage reduction may be necessary in children and in the elderly, who may be more sensitive to effects of the drug.

If the patient is unable to swallow capsules, the contents of the capsule may be emptied into a glass of water (some inert material may float on the surface) and taken immediately.

Development of uric acid nephropathy in patients with leukemia or lymphoma may be prevented by adequate oral hydration and, in some cases, administration of allopurinol. Alkalinization of urine may be necessary if serum uric acid concentrations are elevated.

If there is no clinical response after 6 weeks of therapy, the medication should be discontinued; if a response occurs, the medication may be continued indefinitely.

Combination therapy with radiation may be associated with more frequent and severe side effects of the radiation, including gastric distress and inflammation of mucous membranes at the irradiated site. Severe reactions may require temporary withdrawal of hydroxyurea therapy.

It is recommended that hydroxyurea therapy be temporarily withdrawn if marked leukopenia (particularly granulocytopenia) or thrombocytopenia occurs. Therapy may be resumed if, after 3 days, the counts rise significantly towards normal values; counts usually return to normal within 10 to 30 days after discontinuation of hydroxyurea. If anemia occurs, it may be corrected with whole blood replacement, without interruption of hydroxyurea therapy.

Special precautions are recommended in patients who develop thrombocytopenia as a result of administration of hydroxyurea. These may include extreme care in performing invasive procedures; regular inspection of intravenous sites, skin (including perirectal area), and mucous membrane surfaces for signs of bleeding or bruising; limiting frequency of venipuncture and avoiding intramuscular injections; testing urine, emesis, stool, and secretions for occult blood; care in use of regular toothbrushes, dental floss, toothpicks, safety razors, and fingernail and toenail cutters; avoiding constipation; and using caution to prevent falls and other injuries. Such patients should avoid alcohol and any aspirin intake because of the risk of gastrointestinal bleeding. Platelet transfusions may be required.

Patients who develop leukopenia should be observed carefully for signs of infection. Antibiotic support may be required. In neutropenic patients who develop fever, broad-spectrum antibiotic coverage should be initiated empirically, pending bacterial cultures and appropriate diagnostic tests.

When hydroxyurea is used in sickle cell anemia, the prophylactic administration of folic acid is recommended as hydroxyurea may mask the incidental development of folic acid deficiency.

Safety considerations for handling this medication

Hydroxyurea should be handled with care and exposure by people not taking this medicine should be avoided. To decrease the risk of exposure:

- Wear disposable gloves when handling hydroxyurea or bottles containing hydroxyurea.
- Wash hands before and after contact with the bottle or capsules.
- If powder from the capsule is spilled, it should be wiped up immediately with a damp disposable towel and discarded in a closed container, such as a plastic bag.
- Medicine should be kept away from children and pets.
- Doctor should be contacted for instructions on how to dispose of expired capsules.

To minimize the risk of dermal exposure, it is important that gloves be worn during all handling activities in clinical settings, pharmacies, storerooms, and home healthcare settings, including during unpacking and inspections, transport within a facility, and dose preparation and administration.

Oral Dosage Forms

HYDROXYUREA CAPSULES USP

Usual adult dose
Carcinoma, ovarian[1]—
Oral, 80 mg per kg of body weight in a single dose every third day, or 20 to 30 mg per kg of body weight per day in a single dose.
Carcinoma, head and neck, epidermoid—
Oral, 80 mg per kg of body weight in a single dose every third day, in combination with radiation therapy.
Note: Administration of hydroxyurea should begin at least seven days prior to initiation of radiation therapy, and should be continued under adequate observation during radiation therapy and indefinitely afterwards.

Leukemia, chronic myelocytic, resistant—
Oral, 20 to 30 mg per kg of body weight a day in a single dose or two divided daily doses.
Melanoma—
Oral, 80 mg per kg of body weight in a single dose every third day, or 20 to 30 mg per kg of body weight per day in a single dose.
Note: Although dosages are based on the patient's actual weight, use of estimated lean body mass (dry weight) is recommended in obese patients or those with abnormal fluid retention.
In general, use of intermittent dosage is associated with less risk of serious toxicity than continuous daily dosage.

Sickle cell anemia, painful crises—
Oral, 15 mg per kg of body weight per day as a single dose. If blood counts are within "acceptable" range, the dose may be increased by 5 mg/kg per day every 12 weeks until a maximum tolerated dose (the highest dose that does not produce "toxic" blood counts over 24 consecutive weeks), or 35 mg/kg per day, is reached.
Note: The dosage should be based on the patient's actual or ideal body weight, whichever is lower.
Blood counts in the "acceptable" range are defined as neutrophils $\geq$ 2500 cells/mm^3, platelets $\geq$ 95,000/mm^3, hemoglobin $>$ 5.3 g/dL, and reticulocytes $\geq$ 95,000/mm^3 if the hemoglobin concentration is $<$ 9 g/dL. Blood counts in the "toxic" range are defined as neutrophils $<$ 2000 cells/mm^3, platelets $<$ 80,000/mm^3, hemoglobin $<$ 4.5 g/dL, and reticulocytes $<$ 80,000/mm^3 if the hemoglobin concentration is $<$ 9 g/dL.

Usual pediatric dose
Dosage has not been established.

Strength(s) usually available
U.S.—
200 mg (Rx) [*Droxia*].
300 mg (Rx) [*Droxia*].
400 mg (Rx) [*Droxia*].
500 mg (Rx) [*Hydrea* (lactose); GENERIC].
Canada—
500 mg (Rx) [*Hydrea* (tartrazine 3 mg)].

Packaging and storage
Store below 40 °C (104 °F), preferably between 15 and 30 °C (59 and 86 °F), unless otherwise specified by manufacturer. Store in a tight container.

Auxiliary labeling
- Keep container tightly closed.

[1]Not included in Canadian product labeling.

Revised: 03/03/2006

HYDROXYZINE—See *Antihistamines (Systemic)*

HYOSCYAMINE—See *Anticholinergics/Antispasmodics (Systemic)*

IBANDRONATE Systemic†

VA CLASSIFICATION (Primary): HS301

Commonly used brand name(s): *Boniva.*

Note: For a listing of dosage forms and brand names by country availability, see *Dosage Forms* section(s).

†Not commercially available in Canada.

Category

Bone resorption inhibitor.

Indications

Accepted

Osteoporosis, postmenopausal (treatment adjunct)—Oral and injectable ibandronate are indicated for the treatment of osteoporosis in postmenopausal women. In postmenopausal women with osteoporosis, ibandronate increases bone mineral density and reduces the incidence of vertebral fractures.

Osteoporosis, postmenopausal (prophylaxis)—Oral ibandronate is indicated for the prevention of osteoporosis in postmenopausal women who are at risk of developing osteoporosis and for whom the desired clinical outcome is to maintain bone mass and to reduce the risk of future fracture.

Pharmacology/Pharmacokinetics

Physicochemical characteristics

Molecular weight—Ibandronate sodium monohydrate: 359.24.

Solubility—Ibandronate is freely soluble in water and practically insoluble in organic solvents.

Mechanism of action/Effect

The mechanism of action is based on the affinity of ibandronate for hydroxyapatite, which is part of the mineral matrix of bone. In postmenopausal women ibandronate inhibits osteoclast activity and reduces bone resorption and the elevated rate of bone turnover; thus, leading to a net gain in bone mass.

Absorption

Ibandronate is absorbed in the upper gastrointestinal tract. The mean bioavailability of ibandronate following a 2.5 mg oral dose is about 0.6% compared to intravenous dosing. Absorption is impaired by any kind of food or drink other than plain water, reducing bioavailability 90% if administered with a standard breakfast compared to fasting state. No significant reduction in bioavailability was observed when ibandronate was taken at least 60 minutes before a meal; however, both bioavailability and bone mineral density were reduced when taken less that 60 minutes before food or beverages.

Distribution

Ibandronate either rapidly binds to bone or is excreted into urine. The amount of the dose removed from the circulation via the bone is approximately 40% to 50% of the circulating dose.

Volume of distribution (Vol_D)—At least 90 L in humans

Protein binding

Very high (90.9–99.5%) serum; over a concentration range of 2 to 10 ng/mL

High (85.7%) serum; over a concentration range of 0.5 to 10 ng/mL

Biotransformation

In humans, there is no evidence that ibandronate is metabolized.

Half-life

Terminal—37 to 157 hours (upon oral administration of 150-mg tablet)

Time to peak plasma concentrations

Maximum plasma concentrations ranged from 0.5 to 2 hours in fasted healthy postmenopausal women.

Elimination

Renal—about 60 mL/min in healthy postmenopausal women, accounting for 50 to 60% of total clearance.

Total clearance—84 to 160 mL/min, relating to creatinine clearance.

Unabsorbed ibandronate is eliminated unchanged in the feces.

Precautions to Consider

Carcinogenicity/Tumorigenicity

In a 90–week carcinogenicity study when given oral doses 220 to 400 times the human exposure a dose related increased incidence of adrenal subcapsular adenoma/carcinoma was observed in female mice, which was statistically significant at 80 mg/kg/day. The relevance of these findings to humans is unknown.There were no significant drug related tumor findings in male and female rats in a 104–week carcinogenicity study when given oral doses 12 to 7 times the human exposure, or in a 78–week carcinogenicity study when given oral doses 475 to 70 times the human exposure.

Mutagenicity

Ibandronate was not genotoxic in the *in vivo* mouse micronucleus tests for chromosomal damage. There was also no evidence for mutagenic or clastogenic potential in the Ames test, the mammalian cell mutagenesis assay in Chinese hamster V79 cells, and the chromosomal aberration test in human peripheral lymphocytes each with and without metabolic activation.

Pregnancy/Reproduction

Fertility—Studies in female rats given oral doses of 16 mg/kg/day (45 times the recommended human exposure at the recommended daily oral dose of 2.5 mg and 13 times human exposure at the recommended once-monthly oral dose of 150 mg, based on AUC comparison) or at an intravenous dose of 1.2 mg per kg of body weight per day (117 times human exposure at the recommended intravenous dose of 3 mg every 3 months, based on cumulative AUC comparison) from 14 days prior to mating through gestation, decreased fertility, corpora lutea, and implantation sites.

In male rats treated for 28 days prior to mating, a decrease in sperm production and altered sperm morphology were observed at intravenous doses ≥0.3 mg per kg of body weight per day (≥40 times human exposure at the recommended intravenous dose of 3 mg every 3 months, based on cumulative AUC comparison).

Pregnancy—Ibandronate crosses the placenta. Adequate and well controlled studies in humans have not been done. Studies in animals have shown that ibandronate causes adverse effects in the fetus. Ibandronate should be used during pregnancy only if the potential benefit justifies the potential risk to the mother and fetus.

In animal studies when rats were given oral doses ≥3 times the recommended human exposure at the recommended daily oral dose of 2.5 mg or ≥1 times human exposure at the recommended once-monthly oral dose of 150 mg, based on AUC comparison beginning 14 days before mating through lactation, maternal deaths were observed at the time of delivery. Perinatal pup loss also occurred at oral doses 45 times the human exposure at the recommended daily oral dose of 2.5 mg and 13 times human exposure at the recommended once-monthly oral dose of 150 mg, based on AUC comparison and was likely related to maternal dystocia. A calcium supplementation of 32 mg/kg/day by subcutaneous injection did not completely prevent dystocia and periparturient mortality. A low incidence of postimplantation loss was observed in rats treated from 14 days before mating throughout lactation or during gestation, only at doses causing maternal dystocia and periparturient mortality. In another study rats given oral doses ≥5 mg/kg/day or intravenous doses of 0.05, 0.15, or 0.5 mg per kg of body weight per day from gestation day 17 through lactation day 21, maternal toxicity, including dystocia and mortality, fetal perinatal and postnatal mortality were observed. Periparturient mortality has also been observed with other bisphosphonates and appears to be related to inhibition of skeletal calcium mobilization resulting in hypocalcemia and dystocia.

Exposure of pregnant rats given oral doses ≥30 times the human exposure at the recommended daily oral dose of 2.5 mg, ≥9 times human exposure at the recommended once-monthly oral dose of 150 mg, and ≥47 times human exposure at the recommended intravenous dose of 3 mg every 3 months based on AUC comparison, during organogenesis resulted in increased fetal incidence of RPU (renal pelvis ureter) syndrome. Impaired pup neuromuscular development was observed after oral doses 45 times the human exposure at the recommended daily oral dose of 2.5 mg and 13 times human exposure at the recommended once-monthly oral dose of 150 mg, based on AUC comparison, given from 14 days before mating through lactation. Pups exhibited abnormal odontogeny that decreased food consumption and body weight gain at ≥18 times human exposure at the recommended intravenous dose of 3 mg every 3 months, based on cumulative AUC comparison.

Studies in pregnant rabbits given oral doses ≥8 times the recommended human dose of 2.5 mg/day and ≥4 times the recommended human dose of 150 mg per month, based on body surface area comparison, resulted in dose related maternal mortality. The deaths occurred prior to parturition and were associated with lung edema and hemorrhage. However no fetal anomalies were observed.

In rat studies with intravenous dosing during gestation, fetal weight and pup growth were reduced at doses ≥5 times human exposure at the recommended intravenous dose of 3 mg every 3 months, based on cumulative AUC comparison.

In rabbits given intravenous doses up to 0.2 mg per kg of body weight per day (19 times the recommended human intravenous dose of 3 mg every 3 months, based on cumulative body surface area comparison, mg/m^2) during the period of organogenesis, maternal mortality, reduced maternal body weight gain, decreased litter size due to increased resorption rate, and decreased fetal weight were observed.

FDA Pregnancy Category C

Breast-feeding

Ibandronate was distributed into the milk of rats after intravenous doses of 0.08 mg per kg of body weight. Ibandronate was present in breast milk at concentrations of 8.1 to 0.4 ng per mL from 2 to 24 hours after dose administration (average concentrations in milk of 1.5 times plasma concentrations. It is not known whether ibandronate is distributed into human breast milk. Because many drugs are distributed into human milk, caution should be exercised when ibandronate is administered to a nursing woman..

Pediatrics

Safety and effectiveness in pediatric patients have not been established.

Geriatrics

Appropriate studies performed to date have not demonstrated geriatrics-specific problems that would limit the usefulness of ibandronate in the elderly. However, some elderly patients may have a greater sensitivity than younger patients.

Pharmacogenetics

The pharmacokinetics of ibandronate are similar in both men and women.

Dental

Osteonecrosis of the jaw (ONJ) has been reported in patients treated with bisphosphonates. Most cases have been in cancer patients undergoing dental procedures, but some have occurred in patients with postmenopausal osteoporosis or other diagnoses. Known risk factors include a diagnosis of cancer, concomitant therapies (e.g., chemotherapy, radiotherapy, corticosteroids), and co-morbid disorders (e.g., anemia, coagulopathy, infection, pre-existing dental disease). For patients who develop ONJ while on bisphosphonate therapy, dental surgery may exacerbate the condition. For patients requiring dental procedures, there are no data available to suggest whether discontinuation of bisphosphonate treatment reduces the risk of ONJ. Clinical judgment of the treating physician should guide the management plan based on individual benefit/risk assessment.

Drug interactions and/or related problems

The following drug interactions and/or related problems have been selected on the basis of their potential clinical significance (possible mechanism in parentheses where appropriate)—not necessarily inclusive (» = major clinical significance):

Note: Combinations containing any of the following medications, depending on the amount present, may also interact with this medication.

Antacids or
Calcium supplements or
Products containing multivalent cations such as
Aluminum or
Iron or
Magnesium or
Vitamins
(may interfere with absorption of ibandronate and should, therefore, be taken at least 60 minutes after administration of ibandronate)

Aspirin or
NSAIDs
(caution should be exercised; additive gastrointestinal irritation may occur)

Laboratory value alterations

The following have been selected on the basis of their potential clinical significance (possible effect in parentheses where appropriate)—not necessarily inclusive (» = major clinical significance).

Alkaline phosphatase, total
(value may be decreased; expected with bisphosphonate treatment.)

Bone imaging agents
(bisphosphonates are known to interfere with the use of bone imaging agents)

Medical considerations/Contraindications

The medical considerations/contraindications included have been selected on the basis of their potential clinical significance (reasons given in parentheses where appropriate)—not necessarily inclusive (» = major clinical significance).

Except under special circumstances, this medication should not be used when the following medical problem exists:

» Hypersensitivity to ibandronate or any of its excipients

» Hypocalcemia, uncorrected or
Other disturbances of bone and mineral metabolism
(use is contraindicated; should be treated effectively before starting therapy with ibandronate, including adequate intake of calcium and vitamin D)

» Inability to stand or sit upright for at least 60 minutes

» Renal impairment, severe
(use is not recommended in patients with creatinine clearance less than 30 mL/min)

Risk-benefit should be considered when the following medical problems exist:

Gastrointestinal diseases such as
Dysphagia, or
Esophageal ulcer, or
Esophagitis, or
Gastric ulcer
(patients should be advised to comply to the dosing instructions to minimize the risk of these effects, and should be advised to discontinue use and seek medical attention if symptoms of esophageal irritation, pain on swallowing, retrosternal pain, or heartburn occur.)

Osteonecrosis of the jaw [ONJ] risk factors including:
Cancer diagnosis or
Concomitant therapies such as
Chemotherapy or
Corticosteroids or
Radiotherapy or
Co-morbid disorders such as
Anemia or
Coagulopathy or
Infection or
Pre-existing dental disease
(clinical judgment should guide management plan of each patient based on individual benefit/risk assessment; dental surgery may exacerbate condition; most cases have been in cancer patients undergoing dental procedures but some have occurred in patients with postomenopausal osteoporosis or other diagnosis)

Risk factors for developing osteoporosis and fractures including
Caucasian or Asian race or
Family history of osteoporosis or
High bone turnover or
Previous fracture or
Reduced BMD (at least 1.0 SD below the premenopausal mean) or
Smoking or
Thin body frame
(may be important when considering the use of ibandronate for *preventing* osteoporosis)

Side/Adverse Effects

Patients should be instructed to discontinue ibandronate and seek medical attention if signs or symptoms signaling a possible esophageal reaction (e.g., new or worsening dysphagia, pain on swallowing, retrosternal pain, or heartburn) occur.

Acute phase reaction (APR) symptoms have been reported with intravenous bisphosphonate use. In most cases, symptoms subsided within 24 to 48 hours with no specific treatment required.

The following side/adverse effects have been selected on the basis of their potential clinical significance (possible signs and symptoms in parentheses where appropriate)—not necessarily inclusive:

Those indicating need for medical attention

Incidence more frequent

Bronchitis (cough producing mucus; difficulty breathing; shortness of breath; tightness in chest; wheezing); ***hypertension*** (blurred vision; dizziness; nervousness; headache; pounding in the ears; slow or fast heartbeat); ***pneumonia*** (chest pain; cough; fever or chills; sneezing; shortness of breath; sore throat; troubled breathing; tightness in chest; wheezing); ***urinary tract infection*** (bladder pain; bloody or cloudy urine; difficult, burning, or painful urination; frequent urge to urinate; lower back or side pain)

Incidence less frequent

Allergic reaction (cough; difficulty swallowing; dizziness; fast heartbeat; hives; itching, puffiness or swelling of the eyelids or around the eyes, face, lips or tongue; shortness of breath; skin rash; tightness in chest; unusual tiredness or weakness; wheezing); ***cystitis*** (bloody or cloudy urine; difficult, burning, or painful urination; frequent urge to urinate); ***hypercholesterolemia*** (large amount of cholesterol in the blood); ***nerve root lesion*** (numbness; tingling; or weakness); ***pharyngitis*** (body aches or pain; congestion; cough; dryness or soreness of throat; fever; hoarseness; runny nose; tender, swollen glands in neck; trouble in swallowing; voice changes)

Incidence unknown

Osteonecrosis of the jaw (ONJ) (heavy jaw feeling; loosening of a tooth; pain, swelling, or numbness in the mouth or jaw)—mostly cases of cancer patients on bisphosphonate therapy and undergoing dental procedures; ***scleritis*** (eye redness; eye tenderness; decreased vision; increased tearing; sensitivity to light; severe eye pain); ***uveitis*** (eye pain; tearing; sensitivity of eye to light; redness of eye; blurred vision or other change in vision)

Incidence not determined—Observed during clinical practice; estimates of frequency can not be determined

Bone, joint, and/or muscle pain, severe and occasionally incapacitating

Note: In postmarketing experience, this side effect has been reported infrequently in patients taking bisphosphonates. Most of the patients were postmenopausal women. The time to onset of symptoms varied from one day to several months after starting the drug. Most patients had relief of symptoms after stopping. A subset had recurrence of symptoms when rechallenged with the same drug or another bisphosphonate.

Those indicating need for medical attention only if they continue or are bothersome

Incidence more frequent

Abdominal pain (stomach pain); ***back pain; diarrhea; dyspepsia*** (acid or sour stomach; belching; heartburn; indigestion; stomach discomfort upset or pain); ***headache; pain in extremity; upper respiratory infection*** (ear congestion; nasal congestion; chills; cough; fever; sneezing; sore throat; body aches or pain; headache; loss of voice; runny nose; unusual tiredness or weakness; difficulty in breathing)

Incidence less frequent

Arthralgia (pain in joints; muscle pain or stiffness; difficulty in moving); ***arthritis*** (pain, swelling, or redness in joints; muscle pain or stiffness; difficulty in moving); ***asthenia*** (lack or loss of strength); ***constipation*** (difficulty having a bowel movement [stool]); ***depression*** (discouragement; feeling sad or empty; irritability; lack of appetite; loss of interest or pleasure; tiredness; trouble concentrating; trouble sleeping); ***dizziness; gastritis*** (burning feeling in chest or stomach; tenderness in stomach area; stomach upset; indigestion); ***gastroenteritis*** (abdominal or stomach pain; diarrhea; loss of appetite; nausea; weakness); ***infection*** (fever or chills; cough or hoarseness; lower back or side pain; painful or difficult urination); ***influenza*** (chills; cough; diarrhea; fever; general feeling of discomfort or illness; headache; joint pain; loss of appetite; muscle aches and pains; nausea; runny nose; shivering; sore throat; sweating; trouble sleeping; unusual tiredness or weakness; vomiting); ***injection site reaction*** (bleeding, blistering, burning, coldness, discoloration of skin, feeling of pressure, hives; infection, inflammation, itching, lumps, numbness, pain, rash, redness, scarring, soreness, stinging, swelling, tenderness, tingling, ulceration, or warmth at site); ***joint disorder*** (difficulty in moving; muscle pain or stiffness; pain, swelling, or redness in joints); ***localized osteoarthritis*** (difficulty in moving; muscle pain or stiffness; pain, swelling, or redness in joints); ***myalgia*** (joint pain; swollen joints; muscle aching or cramping, muscle pains or stiffness, difficulty in moving); ***nasopharyngitis*** (stuffy or runny nose; muscle aches; unusual tiredness or weakness; fever; sore throat; headache); ***nausea; rash; tooth disorder; vertigo*** (dizziness or lightheadedness; feeling of constant movement of self or surroundings; sensation of spinning); ***vomiting***

Rare

Influenza-like illness (chills; cough; diarrhea; fever; general feeling of discomfort or illness; headache; joint pain; loss of appetite; muscle aches and pains; nausea; runny nose; shivering; sore throat; sweating; trouble sleeping; unusual tiredness or weakness; vomiting); ***insomnia*** (sleeplessness; trouble sleeping; unable to sleep)

Overdose

For more information on the management of overdose or unintentional ingestion, **contact a poison control center** (see *Poison Control Center Listing*).

Clinical effects of overdose

The following effects have been selected on the basis of their potential clinical significance (possible signs and symptoms in parentheses where appropriate)—not necessarily inclusive:

Dyspepsia (acid or sour stomach; belching; heartburn; indigestion; stomach discomfort upset or pain); ***esophagitis*** (difficulty in swallowing; pain or burning in throat; chest pain; heartburn; vomiting; sores, ulcers or white spots on lips or tongue or inside the mouth); ***gastritis*** (burning feeling in chest or stomach; tenderness in stomach area; stomach upset; indigestion); ***hypocalcemia*** (abdominal cramps; confusion; convulsions; difficulty in breathing; irregular heartbeats; mood or mental changes; muscle cramps in hands, arms, feet, legs, or face; numbness and tingling around the mouth, fingertips, or feet; shortness of breath; tremor); ***hypophosphatemia*** (bone pain; convulsions; loss of appetite; trouble breathing; unusual tiredness or weakness); ***ulcer; upset stomach***

Treatment of overdose

There is no known specific antidote to ibandronate. Treatment is generally symptomatic and supportive, possibly including:

To decrease absorption—

Milk or antacids should be given to bind ibandronate

To enhance elimination—

Dialysis would not be beneficial.

Specific treatment—

Due to the risk of esophageal irritation, vomiting should not be induced, and the patient should remain fully upright

Supportive care—

Patients in whom intentional overdose is confirmed or suspected should be referred for psychiatric consultation.

Patient Consultation

As an aid to patient consultation, refer to *Advice for the Patient, Ibandronate (Systemic)*.

In providing consultation, consider emphasizing the following selected information (» = major clinical significance):

Importance of diet

Importance of proper nutrition; supplement may be needed because of inadequate dietary intake.

Before using this medication

» Conditions affecting use, especially:

Hypersensitivity to ibandronate or any of its excipients

Pregnancy—Risk/benefit considerations

Breast-feeding—Caution should be exercised when ibandronate is administered to a nursing woman

Use in children—Safety and effectiveness not established

Dental—Osteonecrosis of the jaw (ONJ) reported in patients treated with bisphosphonates; dental surgery may exacerbate ONJ; physician should manage patient based on risk/benefit

Other medical problems, especially hypocalcemia uncorrected, inability to stand or sit upright for at least 60 minutes, or severe renal impairment

Proper use of this medication

» Taking with 6 to 8 ounces of plain water on empty stomach, at least 60 minutes before first food, beverage, or medication of the day

» Swallowing whole; not chewing or sucking on the tablet because of potential for oropharyngeal ulceration.

» Not lying down for at least 60 minutes after taking ibandronate

» Importance of receiving ibandronate injection intraveneously from a healthcare professional

Possible need for calcium and vitamin D supplementation

» Proper dosing

Missed dose: For the once daily 2.5-mg tablet—Not taking later in the day; continuing usual schedule the next morning.

For the once monthly 150-mg tablet—Taking if your next scheduled dose is more than 7 days away; waiting until your next scheduled dose if only 1 to 7 days away; not taking two 150-mg tablets within the same week

For the injection—Receiving missed dose as soon as it can be rescheduled; thereafter, scheduling every 3 months from the date of the last injection

Proper storage

Precautions while using this medication

» Contacting physician and discontinuing ibandronate immediately if signs or symptoms signaling a possible esophageal reaction occur including new or worsening dysphagia, pain on swallowing, retrosternal pain, or heartburn

Side/adverse effects

Signs of potential side effects, especially allergic reaction, bronchitis, cystitis, hypertension, hypercholesterolemia, nerve root lesion, osteonecrosis of the jaw (ONJ), pharyngitis, pneumonia, scleritis, urinary tract infection or uveitis

Signs of potential side effects observed during the clinical practice of bisphosphonates, especially severe and occasionally incapacitating bone, joint, and/or muscle pain

General Dosing Information

Hypocalcemia and other disturbances of bone and mineral metabolism should be treated effectively before ibandronate therapy is initiated.

For oral tablets

To facilitate delivery of ibandronate to the stomach and reduce esophageal irritation, patients should not lie down for at least 60 minutes after taking ibandronate and after first food of the day

Patients should not chew or suck the tablet because of a potential for oropharyngeal ulceration.

The ibandronate 150-mg tablet should be taken the same date each month.

The patient should be directed as follows if a monthly ibandronate dose is missed:

• If the patient's next scheduled ibandronate day is more than 7 days away, the patient should be instructed to take one ibandronate 150-mg in the morning following the date that it is remembered.

• The patient must not take two 150-mg tablets within the same week.

• If the patient's next scheduled ibandronate day is only 1 to 7 days away, the patient must wait until then to take their tablet.

• The patient should then return to taking one 150-mg tablet every month in the morning of their chosen day, according to their original schedule.

For injections

Ibandronate injection must only be administered intravenously by a healthcare professional. The safety and efficacy of ibandronate injection following non-intravenous routes of administration have not been established. Care should be taken not to administer ibandronate injection intra-arterially or paravenously as this could lead to tissue damage.

Diet/Nutrition

Ibandronate should be taken with 6 to 8 ounces of plain water. Some mineral waters have a higher concentration of calcium and therefore should not be used. Food and beverages will decrease the absorption of ibandronate. Waiting 60 minutes will improve the absorption of ibandronate.

Absorption of ibandronate is best when taken in the morning, at least 60 minutes before the first food, beverage, medication, or supplementation, including calcium, antacids, or vitamins of the day.

Some patients may be instructed to take calcium or vitamin D supplements if their dietary intake is inadequate. These supplements should be taken at least 60 minutes after taking ibandronate.

Oral Dosage Forms

IBANDRONATE SODIUM TABLETS

Usual adult dose

Postmenopausal osteoporosis (treatment)—

Oral, 2.5 mg once daily or one 150 mg tablet taken once monthly on the same date each month, administered at least sixty minutes before the first food, beverage (other than water), supplementation, (including calcium, antacids, or vitamins) or medication of the day. The dose should be taken with six to eight ounces of plain water.

Postmenopausal osteoporosis (prophylaxis)—

Oral, 2.5 mg once daily recommended; or alternatively, one 150 mg tablet taken once monthly on the same date each month may be considered; administered at least sixty minutes before the first food, beverage (other than water), supplementation, (including calcium, antacids, or vitamins) or medication of the day. The dose should be taken with six to eight ounces of plain water.

Note: No dose adjustment is necessary for patients with hepatic impairment or patients with mild or moderate renal impairment where creatinine clearance is equal to or greater than 30 mL/minute. Ibandronate is contraindicated in patients with severe renal impairment (creatinine clearance of less than 30 mL/minute).

Usual pediatric dose

Safety and efficacy have not been established.

Usual geriatric dose

See *Usual adult dose.*

Strength(s) usually available

U.S.—

2.5 mg (free acid) (Rx) [*Boniva* (film-coated; lactose monohydrate; povidone; microcrystalline cellulose; crospovidone; purified stearic acid; colloidal silicon dioxide; purified water)].

150 mg (free acid) (Rx) [*Boniva* (film-coated; lactose monohydrate; povidone; microcrystalline cellulose; crospovidone; purified stearic acid; colloidal silicon dioxide; purified water)].

Packaging and storage

Store at 25°C (77 °F); excursions permitted between 15° and 30°C (59° and 86°F).

Auxiliary labeling

• Take on empty stomach.
• Take with 6 to 8 oz of water at least 60 minutes prior to first food/beverage/drug of day. Do not lie down for 30 minutes.
• Swallow whole. Do not crush or chew.

Parenteral Dosage Forms

IBANDRONATE SODIUM INJECTION

Usual adult dose

Postmenopausal osteoporosis (treatment)—

Intravenous, 3 mg every 3 months administered over a period of 15 to 30 seconds.

Postmenopausal osteoporosis (prophylaxis)—

See *Ibandronate Sodium Tablets*. Injectable ibandronate is not indicated for the prophylaxis of postmenopausal osteoporosis.

Note: For patients with hepatic impairment, no dosage adjustment is necessary.

For patients with mild or moderate renal impairment (creatinine clearance ≥30 mL/minute), no dosage adjustment is necessary.

For patients with severe renal impairment (creatinine clearance <30 mL/minute), ibandronate injection should not be administered.

Usual adult prescribing limits

Ibandronate injection should not be administered more frequently than once every 3 months.

Usual pediatric dose

Safety and efficacy have not been established.

Usual geriatric dose

See *Usual adult dose.*

Strength(s) usually available

U.S.—

3 mg (free acid) per 3 mL (Rx) [*Boniva* (sodium chloride; glacial acetic acid; sodium acetate; water)].

Packaging and storage

Store at 25 °C (77 °F); excursions permitted between 15 and 30 °C (59 and 86 °F).

Incompatibilities

Ibandronate injection should not be mixed with calcium-containing solutions or other intravenously administered drugs.

Auxiliary labeling

• For single dose only. Discard unused drug.

Revised: 02/08/2006
Developed: 03/25/2004

IBRITUMOMAB TIUXETAN Systemic†

For information pertaining to the use of rituximab, a component of the ibritumomab tiuxetan therapeutic regimen, see *Rituximab (Systemic).*

VA CLASSIFICATION (Primary): AN900

Commonly used brand name(s): *Zevalin.*

Other commonly used names are:
IDEC-2B8 (ibritumomab tiuxetan)
IDEC-Y2B8 (yttrium-90-ibritumomab tiuxetan)
IDEC-In2B8 (indium-111-ibritumomab tiuxetan)
IDEC-129

Note: For a listing of dosage forms and brand names by country availability, see *Dosage Forms* section(s).

†Not commercially available in Canada.

Category

Monoclonal antibody; Antineoplastic (radioactive).

Indications

Accepted

Lymphomas, non-Hodgkin's (treatment)—Yttrium-90 Ibritumomab tiuxetan (co-administered with rituximab) is indicated for treatment of relapsed or refractory low-grade, follicular, or transformed B-cell non-Hodgkin's lymphoma, including rituximab refractory follicular non-Hodgkin's lymphoma.

Physical Properties

Nuclear Data

Radionuclide (half-life)	Mode of decay (product of decay)	Radiation mean energy (keV)	Mean number of disintegration
In 111 (67.3 hours)	Electron capture (Cadmium-111)	Gamma-2 (171.3)	0.902
		Gamma-3 (245.4)	0.94
Y 90 (64.1 hours)	Emission of beta particles (Zirconium-90)	Beta minus (750–935)	1

Pharmacology/Pharmacokinetics

Physicochemical characteristics

Source—

Ibritumomab tiuxetan therapeutic regimen kit for the preparation of Indium-111 (In-111) ibritumomab tiuxetan and Yttrium-90 (Y-90) ibritumomab tiuxetan.

Ibritumomab tiuxetan is an immunoconjugate resulting from a stable thiourea covalent bond between the monoclonal antibody ibritumomab and the linker-chelator tiuxetan.

The antibody moiety of ibritumomab, a murine IgG_1 kappa monoclonal antibody directed against the CD20 antigen, which is found on the surface of normal and malignant B lymphocytes. Ibritumomab is produced in Chinese hamster ovary cells and is composed of two kappa light chains of 213 amino acids each and two murine gamma 1 heavy chains of 445 amino acids each. More than 90% of B-cell non-Hodgkin's lymphomas (NHL) have CD20 antigen expressed on pre-B and mature B lymphocytes. The CD20 antige is not internalized upon antibody binding and is not shed from the cell surface.

The linker-chelator, tiuxetan, provides a high affinity, conformationally restricted chelation site for Indium-111 or Yttrium-90.

Molecular weight—148 kD.

Binding affinity—Ibritumomab has an approximate apparent affinity (K_D) for the CD20 antigen between 14 to 18 nM.

Radionuclide exposure—The exposure rate constant for 37 MBq (1 mCi) of In-111 is 8.3×10^{-4} C per kg body weight per hour (3.2 R per hr) at 1 cm.

Mechanism of action/Effect

Regions of ibritumomab bind to the CD20 antigen on B lymphocytes and induce apoptosis (programmed cell death) in CD20+ B-cell lines *in vitro* . Tiuxetan (chelator) tightly binds In-111 or Y-90. The chelator complex covalently links to the amino acids of exposed lysines and arginines contained within the antibody (ibritumomab). Beta emission from Y-90 induces cellular damage by the formation of free radicals in the target and neighboring cells.

Ibritumomab tiuxetan does not bind selectively to neoplastic cells; cross-reactivity was observed *in vitro* on lymphoid cells of the bone marrow, lymph node, thymus, red and white pulp of the spleen, lymphoid follicles of the tonsil, and lymphoid nodules of other organs such as large and small intestines. Nonlymphoid tissues or gonadal tissues were not observed to bind ibritumomab tiuxetan.

Other actions/effects

IgG and IgA median serum levels remained within the normal range throughout the period of B-cell depletion.

IgM median serum levels decreased (median 49 mg per dL, range 13 to 3990 mg per dL) after treatment and recovered to normal values by 6 months after treatment.

Distribution

Only 18% of known sites of disease were imaged when In-111 ibritumomab tiuxetan was administered without unlabeled ibritumomab.

Detection of sites of disease improved to 56% and 92% when In-111 ibritumomab tiuxetan was preceded by unlabeled ibritumomab 1 mg per kg of body weight or 2.5 mg per kg of body weight, respectively.

Half-life

The mean effective half-life of Y-90 activity in blood was 30 hours.

The mean area under the fraction of injected activity (FIA) versus time curve of Y-90 in blood was 39 hours.

Onset of action

The median number of B cells was zero (range, 0 to 1084 cells per cubic millimeter) at four weeks following administration of ibritumomab tiuxetan therapeutic regimen.

Time to peak concentration: In-111 ibritumomab tiuxetan—

Visual evaluation of whole-body planar anterior and posterior gamma images for biodistribution studies are acquired at 2 to 24 hours and 48 to 72 hours following administration of In-111 ibritumomab tiuxetan. A third image at 90 to 120 hours following administration of In-111 ibritumomab tiuxetan may be necessary to resolve ambiguities.

The radiopharmaceutical, In-111 ibritumomab tiuxetan, is expected to be easily detectable in the blood pool areas at the first time point, with less activity in the blood pool on later images. Low uptake is seen in lungs, kidneys, and urinary bladder. Moderately high to high uptake is seen in normal liver and spleen. Uptake localized to lymphoid aggregates in the bowel wall has been reported. Uptake by tumor in soft tissue may be visualized as areas of increased intensity and tumor-bearing areas in normal organs may be seen as areas of increased or decreased intensity.

Time to peak effect

The median number of B cells was zero (range, 0 to 1084 cells per cubic millimeter) at four weeks following administration of ibritumomab tiuxetan therapeutic regimen. By approximately 12 weeks following treatment, B cell recovery began in clinical studies.

Duration of action

The median level of B cells was within normal range (32 to 341 cells per cubic millimeter) by 9 months following administration of ibritumomab tiu... peutic regimen in clinical studies.

...etry

...nated radiation absorbed doses*

Organ	Y-90 ibritumomab tiuxetan (mGy/MBq) Median	Range	In-111 ibritumomab tiuxetan (mGy/MBq) Median	Range
Spleen†	9.4	1.8-14.4	0.9	0.2-1.2
Testes†	9.1	5.4-11.4	0.6	0.4-0.8
Liver†	4.8	2.3-8.1	0.7	0.3-1.1
Lower large intestinal wall†	4.8	3.1-8.2	0.4	0.2-0.6
Upper large intestinal wall†	3.6	2.0-6.7	0.3	0.2-0.6
Heart wall†	2.8	1.5-3.2	0.4	0.2-0.5
Lungs†	2.0	1.2-3.4	0.2	0.1-0.4
Small intestine†	1.4	0.8-2.1	0.2	0.1-0.3
Red marrow§	1.3	0.7-1.8	0.2	0.1-0.2
Urinary bladder wall‡	0.9	0.7-2.1	0.2	0.1-0.2
Bone surfaces§	0.9	0.5-1.2	0.2	0.1-0.2
Ovaries‡	0.4	0.3-0.5	0.2	0.2-0.2
Uterus‡	0.4	0.3-0.5	0.2	0.1-0.2
Adrenals‡	0.3	0.0-0.5	0.2	0.1-0.3
Brain‡	0.3	0.0-0.5	0.1	0.0-0.1
Breasts‡	0.3	0.0-0.5	0.1	0.0-0.1
Gallbladder wall‡	0.3	0.0-0.5	0.3	0.1-0.4
Muscle‡	0.3	0.0-0.5	0.1	0.0-0.1
Pancreas‡	0.3	0.0-0.5	0.2	0.1-0.3
Skin‡	0.3	0.0-0.5	0.1	0.0-0.1
Stomach‡	0.3	0.0-0.5	0.1	0.1-0.2
Thymus‡	0.3	0.0-0.5	0.1	0.1-0.2
Thyroid‡	0.3	0.0-0.5	0.1	0.0-0.1
Kidneys†	0.1	0.0-0.2	0.2	0.1-0.2
Total body‡	0.5	0.2-0.7	0.1	0.1-0.2

*Sequential whole body images and the MIRDOSE 3 software program were used to estimate the radiation-absorbed doses for In-111 ibritumomab tiuxetan and Y-90 ibritumomab tiuxetan. Absorbed dose estimates for the lower large intestine, upper large intestine, and small intestine have been modified (from standard MIRDOSE 3 output) to account for the assumption that activity is within the intestine wall rather than the intestine contents.

†Organ region of interest

§Sacrum region of interest

‡Whole body region of interest

Elimination
Renal—A median of 7.2% of the injected Y-90 activity was excreted in urine over 7 days.

Precautions to Consider

For information pertaining to the Precautions to Consider for rituximab, a component of the ibritumomab tiuxetan therapeutic regimen, see *Rituximab (Systemic)*.

Cross-sensitivity and/or related problems
Ibritumomab tiuxetan is contraindicated in patients with Type I hypersensitivity or anaphylactic reactions to murine proteins or to ibritumomab tiuxetan, rituximab, yttrium chloride or indium chloride.

Carcinogenicity/Mutagenicity
Long-term animal studies have not been performed to establish the carcinogenic or mutagenic potential for ibritumomab tiuxetan therapeutic regimen. Radiation is a potential carcinogen and mutagen.

Tumorigenicity
Of 349 patients treated, one developed a Grade 1 meningioma, three developed acute myelogenous leukemia, and two developed myelodysplastic syndrome following ibritumomab tiuxetan therapeutic regimen. The onset of the secondary malignancy was 8 to 34 months following ibritumomab tiuxetan therapeutic regimen and 4 to 14 years following the patients' diagnosis of non-Hodgkin's lymphoma.

Pregnancy/Reproduction
Fertility—Long-term animal studies have not been performed to determine the effects of ibritumomab tiuxetan therapeutic regimen on fertility in females or males. The ibritumoman tiuxetan therapeutic regimen results in a significant radiation dose to the testes; the radiation dose to the ovaries has not been established. There is potential risk that the ibritumomab tiuxetan therapeutic regimen could cause toxic effects on the female and male gonads. Effective contraception methods are recommended during treatment and for up to 12 months following ibritumomab tiuxetan therapeutic regimen.

Pregnancy—Ibritumomab tiuxetan crosses the placenta and has been shown to cause fetal harm. Risk benefit must be carefully considered when this medication is required in life-threatening situations or in serious diseases for which other medications cannot be used or are ineffective.

Y-90 ibritumomab tiuxetan can cause fetal harm when administered to a pregnant woman. Adequate and well-controlled studies in pregnant women are not available.

Women of childbearing potential should be advised to avoid becoming pregnant while receiving ibritumomab tiuxetan therapeutic regimen. Effective contraception methods are recommended during treatment and for up to 12 months following ibritumomab tiuxetan therapeutic regimen. The patient should be apprised of the potential hazard to the fetus if ibritumomab tiuxetan is used during pregnancy or if the patient becomes pregnant while receiving ibritumomab tiuxetan.

FDA Pregnancy Category D

Breast-feeding
It is not known if ibritumomab tiuxetan is distributed into breast milk. Breast-feeding is not recommended during ibritumomab tiuxetan therapeutic regimen because human IgG is distributed into human milk and the potential for ibritumomab tiuxetan exposure in the infant is unknown (adverse effects, mutagenicity, carcinogenicity). Formula feeding should be substituted for breast feeding.

Pediatrics
No information is available on the relationship of age to the effects of ibritumomab tiuxetan therapeutic regimen in the pediatric population. Safety and efficacy have not been established.

Geriatrics
Although appropriate studies on the relationship of age to the effects of ibritumomab tiuxetan therapeutic regimen have not been performed in the geriatric population, geriatrics-specific problems are not expected to limit the usefulness of ibritumomab tiuxetan in the elderly. However, some elderly patients may have greater sensitivity to the effects of ibritumomab tiuxetan therapeutic regimen.

No overall differences in safety or effectiveness were observed between older subjects (132 of 349 age 65 years and over; 41 of 349 age 75 years and over) and younger subjects in clinical studies of 349 patients treated with the ibritumomab tiuxetan therapeutic regimen.

For information pertaining to the Medication Advisory Screening of rituximab, a component of the ibritumomab tiuxetan therapeutic regimen, see *Rituximab (Systemic)*.

Drug interactions and/or related problems
The following drug interactions and/or related problems have been selected on the basis of their potential clinical significance (possible mechanism in parentheses where appropriate)—not necessarily inclusive (» = major clinical significance):

Combinations containing any of the following medications, depending on the amount present, may also interact with this medication.

Formal drug interaction studies have not been performed with ibritumomab tiuxetan.

» Anticoagulants
(Ibritumomab tiuxetan therapeutic regimen results in severe and prolonged cytopenias in most patients. The potential benefits of medications which interfere with coagulation should be weighed against the potential increased risks of bleeding and hemorrhage in these patients.)

» Bone marrow depressants (see *Appendix II*)
(Ibritumomab tiuxetan therapeutic regimen results in severe and prolonged cytopenias in most patients. Ibritumomab tiuxetan should not be administered to patients with impaired bone marrow reserves.)

» Platelet function, interferes with (see *Appendix II*)
(Ibritumomab tiuxetan therapeutic regimen results in severe and prolonged cytopenias in most patients. The potential benefits of medications which interfere with platelet function should be weighed against the potential increased risks of bleeding and hemorrhage in these patients.)

Vaccines
(The safety of immunization with live viral vaccines following the ibritumomab therapeutic regimen have not been studied.)
(The ability of patients who received the ibritumomab tiuxetan therapeutic regimen to generate a primary or anamnestic humoral response to any vaccine has not be studied.)
(The interval between discontinuation of medications that cause immunosuppression and restoration of the patient's ability to respond to the vaccine depends on the intensity and type of immunosuppression-causing medication used, the underlying disease, and other factors; estimates vary from 3 months to 1 year.)

Laboratory value alterations
The following have been selected on the basis of their potential clinical significance (possible effect in parentheses where appropriate)—not necessarily inclusive (» = major clinical significance).

With physiology/laboratory test values
» B-cell counts, or
» Neutrophil counts, or
» Platelet counts
(severe and prolonged decreases can be expected)

Blood pressure
(may be decreased, especially in patients with severe infusion reaction)

Hemoglobin concentrations, or
Hematocrit
(may be decreased)

Immunoglobulin concentrations
(IgM may be decreased)

Medical considerations/Contraindications
The medical considerations/contraindications included have been selected on the basis of their potential clinical significance (reasons given in parentheses where appropriate)—not necessarily inclusive (» = major clinical significance).

Except under special circumstances, this medication should not be used when the following medical problem exists:

» Biodistribution of In-111 ibritumomab tiuxetan, altered
Characterized by:
• The blood pool is not visualized on the first image indicating rapid clearance of the radiopharmaceutical by the reticuloendothelial system to the liver, spleen, and/or marrow
• Diffuse uptake in normal lung more intense than the cardiac blood pool on the first day image or more intense than the liver on the second or third day image
• Kidneys with greater intensity than the liver on the posterior view of the second or third day image
• Intense areas of uptake throughout the normal bowel comparable to uptake by the liver on the second or third day images

» Bone marrow reserve, impaired
Impaired bone marrow reserve is defined as any one of the following:
• Prior myeloablative therapy with stem cell support
• Prior external beam radiation to greater than 25% of active marrow
• Platelet count less than 100,000 cells per cubic millimeter

- Neutrophil count less than 1,500 cells per cubic millimeter
- Hypocellular bone marrow (≤15% cellularity or marked reduction in bone marrow precursors)
- Patients with a history of failed stem cell collection

» Hypersensitivity (type I) or previous anaphylactic reaction to ibritumomab tiuxetan

For information pertaining to the severe infusion reactions associated with rituximab, a component of the ibritumomab tiuxetan therapeutic regimen, see *Rituximab (Systemic)*

» Hypersensitivity (type I) or previous anaphylactic reaction to rituximab (Ibritumomab tiuxetan is not known to cross-react with rituximab, however a separate infusion of rituximab is administered as a component of the ibritumomab tiuxetan therapeutic regimen)

» Hypersensitivity (type I) or previous anaphylactic reaction to yttrium chloride

» Hypersensitivity (type I) or previous anaphylactic reaction to indium chloride

» Hypersensitivity (type I) or previous anaphylactic reaction to murine proteins

» Lymphoma marrow involvement ≥ 25%

Patient monitoring

The following may be especially important in patient monitoring (other tests may be warranted in some patients, depending on condition; » = major clinical significance):

» Complete blood counts and
» Platelet counts
(should be performed weekly following ibritumomab tiuxetan therapeutic regimen and continued until cell counts recover; in patients who develop severe cytopenia, monitor more frequently or as clinically indicated)
(careful monitoring for and management of cytopenias and their complications for up to 3 months after ibritumomab tiuxetan therapeutic regimen is recommended. Patients who develop leukopenia should be observed carefully for signs of infection. Antibiotic support may be required. In neutropenic patients who develop fever, broad-spectrum antibiotic coverage should be initiated empirically, pending bacterial cultures and appropriate diagnostic tests)

Side/Adverse Effects

Note: The ibritumomab tiuxetan therapeutic regimen includes an IV infusion of rituximab before the imaging and therapeutic dose of ibritumomab tiuxetan. Adverse events were followed for 12 weeks following the first rituximab infusion of the ibritumomab tiuxetan therapeutic regimen. All adverse events are included, regardless of relationship of the adverse event to the therapeutic intervention performed (rituximab, In-111 ibritumomab tiuxetan (radiolabeled), or Y-90 ibritumomab tiuxetan (radiolabeled). For information pertaining to the Side/Adverse Effects of rituximab, a component of the ibritumomab tiuxetan therapeutic regimen, see Rituximab (Systemic).

Note: **Creutzfeldt-Jakob disease (CJD)**—This product contains a derivative of human blood, albumin. It carries an extremely remote, theoretical risk for transmission of Creutzfeldt-Jakob disease (CJD).

Hypersensitivity reactions—Intravenous administration of proteins to patients may cause anaphylactic and other hypersensitivity reactions.

Human anti-mouse antibodies (HAMA) should be screened for in patients with prior exposure to murine proteins. Patients with evidence of HAMA may be at increased risk of allergic or serious hypersensitivity reactions during ibritumomab tiuxetan therapeutic regimen administration.

Infectious events—During the first 3 months after initiating ibritumomab tiuxetan therapeutic regimen, 29% of patients developed infections; 3% of patients developed serious infections (urinary tract infection, febrile neutropenia, sepsis, pneumonia, cellulitis, colitis, diarrhea, osteomyelitis, and upper respiratory tract infections) and 2% of patients developed life-threatening infections (sepsis, empyema, pneumonia, febrile neutropenia, fever, and biliary stent-associated cholangitis).

During follow-up from 3 months to 4 years after initiating ibritumomab tiuxetan therapeutic regimen, 6% of patients developed infections; 2% of patients developed serious infections (urinary tract infection, bacterial or viral pneumonia, febrile neutropenia, perihilar infiltrate, pericarditis, intravenous drug-associated viral hepatitis) and 1% of patients developed life-threatening infections (bacterial pneumonia, respiratory disease, sepsis).

Infusion reactions—Severe infusion reactions, including some fatalities, have been reported following rituximab infusion, an essential component of the ibritumomab tiuxetan therapeutic regimen. Fatalities occurred within 24 hours of rituximab infusion and 80% occurred in association with the first rituximab infusion with the time to onset of 30 to 120 minutes. The signs and symptoms associated with these fatal infusion reactions may include angioedema, bronchospasm, hypotension, or hypoxia. The most severe manifestations and sequelae may include acute respiratory distress syndrome, cardiogenic shock, myocardial infarction, pulmonary infiltrates, or ventricular fibrillation. Patients who develop severe infusion reactions should have rituximab, In-111 ibritumomab tiuxetan, and Y-90 ibritumomab tiuxetan infusions discontinued.

Immunogenicity—There were 8 of 211 (3.8%) patients who received the ibritumomab tiuxetan therapeutic regimen in clinical trials (followed for 90 days) with evidence of human anti-mouse antibody (HAMA) or human anti-chimeric antibody (HACA) at any time during the course of the study. Test results were considered positive for antibodies to ibritumomab or rituximab using kinetic enzyme immunoassays to ibritumomab or rituximab. The incidence of antibody positivity in an assay is highly dependent on the sensitivity and specificity of the assay and may be influenced by several factors including sample handling and concomitant medications. Comparisons of the incidence of HAMA/HACA to the ibritumomab tiuxetan therapeutic regimen with the incidence of antibodies to other products may be misleading.

Patients who are leukopenic may not demonstrate evidence of immunogenicity.

Viral disease transmission—This product contains a derivative of human blood, albumin. It carries an extremely remote risk for transmission of viral diseases.

Note: Many side effects of antineoplastic therapy are unavoidable and represent the medication's pharmacologic action.

The following side/adverse effects have been selected on the basis of their potential clinical significance (possible signs and symptoms in parentheses where appropriate)—not necessarily inclusive:

Those indicating need for medical attention

Incidence more frequent

Anemia (pale skin; troubled breathing with exertion; unusual bleeding or bruising; unusual tiredness or weakness); ***angioedema*** (large, hive-like swelling on face, eyelids, lips, tongue, throat, hands, legs, feet, sex organs); ***bronchospasm*** (cough; difficulty breathing; noisy breathing; shortness of breath; tightness in chest; wheezing); ***hemorrhage while thrombocytopenic*** (bleeding gums; coughing up blood; difficulty in breathing or swallowing; dizziness; headache; increased menstrual flow or vaginal bleeding; nosebleeds; paralysis; prolonged bleeding from cuts; red or dark brown urine; red or black, tarry stools; shortness of breath)—resulting in deaths; ***infection*** (fever or chills; cough or hoarseness; lower back or side pain; painful or difficult urination); ***neutropenia*** (chills; cough; fever; sore throat; sores, ulcers, or white spots on lips or in mouth; swollen glands); ***thrombocytopenia*** (black, tarry stools; bleeding gums; blood in urine or stools; pinpoint red spots on skin; unusual bleeding or bruising)

Note: The most frequently observed adverse event in clinical trials was hematologic events.

Hemoglobin— The median time to hemoglobin nadir was 68 days.

Neutropenia—In patients with normal baseline platelet counts (≥ 150,000 cells per cubic millimeter) treated with ibritumomab tiuxetan therapeutic regimen using 0.4 mCi per kilogram of body weight of Y-90 ibritumomab tiuxetan developed a median absolute neutrophil count nadir of 800 cells per cubic millimeter with a median duration of absolute neutrophil count less than 1,000 cells per cubic millimeter of 22 days.

In patients with mild thrombocytopenia at baseline (platelet count 100,000 to 149,000 cells per cubic millimeter) treated with modified ibritumomab tiuxetan therapeutic regimen using 0.3 mCi per kilogram of body weight of Y-90 ibritumomab tiuxetan developed a median absolute neutrophil count nadir of 600 cells per cubic millimeter with a median duration of absolute neutrophil count less than 1,000 cells per cubic millimeter of 29 days.

The median time to absolute neutrophil count nadir was 53 days.

Thrombocytopenia—In patients with normal baseline platelet counts (≥ 150,000 cells per cubic millimeter) treated with ibritumomab tiuxetan therapeutic regimen using 0.4 mCi per kilogram of body weight of Y-90 ibritumomab tiuxetan developed a median nadir of 41,000 cells per cubic millimeter with a median duration of platelets less than 50,000 cells per cubic millimeter of 24 days.

In patients with mild thrombocytopenia at baseline (platelet count 100,000 to 149,000 cells per cubic millimeter) treated with modified ibritumomab tiuxetan therapeutic regimen using 0.3 mCi per kilogram of body weight of Y-90 ibritumomab tiuxetan developed a median nadir of 24,000 cells per cubic millimeter with a median duration of platelets less than 50,000 cells per cubic millimeter of 35 days.

The median time to platelet count nadir was 62 days.

Treatment of hematologic toxicity—Erythropoietin was given to 8% of 211 patients of whom data were collected about growth factor use.

Filgrastim was given to 13% of 211 patients of whom data were collected about growth factor use.

Red blood cell transfusions were given to 22% of 211 patients of whom data were collected about transfusion use.

Incidence less frequent

Allergic reaction (cough; difficulty swallowing; dizziness; fast heartbeat; hives; itching; puffiness or swelling of the eyelids or around the eyes, face, lips or tongue; shortness of breath; skin rash; tightness in chest; unusual tiredness or weakness; wheezing); ***apnea*** (bluish lips or skin; not breathing); ***epistaxis*** (bloody nose that does not stop after pinching the nasal alae together and holding them continuously for 5 to 10 minutes); ***hemorrhage, gastrointestinal*** (black, tarry stools; bloody stools; vomiting of blood or material that looks like coffee grounds); ***infection, severe*** (chills; confusion; dizziness; lightheadedness; fainting; fast heartbeat; fever; rapid, shallow breathing); ***melena*** (bloody, black, or tarry stools); ***pain at site of tumor; pancytopenia*** (chest pain or discomfort; shortness of breath; unusual bleeding or bruising; bloody nose; unusual vaginal bleeding; pinpoint red spots on skin; bloody, black, or tarry stools; blood in urine; unusual tiredness or weakness; fever; skin rash; chills; cough; diarrhea; headache; pale skin; painful or difficult urination; sore throat; sores, ulcers, or white spots on lips or in mouth; swollen glands); ***petechia*** (small red or purple spots on skin)

Incidence rare

Encephalopathy (agitation; back pain; blurred vision; coma; confusion; dizziness; drowsiness; fever; hallucinations; headache; irritability; mood or mental changes; seizures; stiff neck; unusual tiredness or weakness; vomiting); ***hematemesis*** (vomiting of blood or material that looks like coffee grounds); ***hematoma, subdural*** (blurred vision; irregular heartbeat; nausea and vomiting; severe headache); ***hemorrhage, cerebral*** (blurred vision; headache, sudden and severe; inability to speak; seizures; slurred speech; temporary blindness; weakness in arm and/or leg on one side of the body, sudden and severe); ***hemorrhage, vaginal*** (heavy nonmenstrual vaginal bleeding); ***pulmonary edema*** (chest pain; difficult, fast, noisy breathing, sometimes with wheezing; blue lips and fingernails; pale skin; increased sweating; coughing that sometimes produces a pink frothy sputum; shortness of breath; swelling in legs and ankles); ***pulmonary embolus*** (anxiety; chest pain; cough; fainting; fast heartbeat; sudden shortness of breath or troubled breathing; dizziness or lightheadedness); ***tachycardia*** (fast, pounding, or irregular heartbeat or pulse); ***urticaria, severe*** (hives or welts; itching; redness of skin; skin rash)

Incidence unknown—Observed during clinical practice; estimates of frequency cannot be determined

Bullous dermatitis (skin blisters); ***erythema multiforme*** (blistering, peeling, loosening of skin; chills; cough; diarrhea; fever; itching; joint or muscle pain; red, irritated eyes; sore throat; sores, ulcers, or white spots in mouth or on lips; unusual tiredness or weakness); ***exfoliative dermatitis*** (cracks in the skin; loss of heat from the body; red, swollen skin, scaly skin); ***Stevens-Johnson syndrome*** (blistering, peeling, loosening of skin; chills; cough; diarrhea; itching; joint or muscle pain; red, irritated eyes; red skin lesions, often with a purple center; sore throat; sores, ulcers, or white spots in mouth or on lips; unusual tiredness or weakness); ***toxic epidermal necrolysis*** (blistering, peeling, loosening of skin; chills; cough; diarrhea; itching; joint or muscle pain; red, irritated eyes; red skin lesions, often with a purple center; sore throat; sores, ulcers, or white spots in mouth or on lips; unusual tiredness or weakness)

Those indicating need for medical attention only if they continue or are bothersome

Incidence more frequent

Abdominal enlargement (swelling of abdominal or stomach area; full or bloated feeling or pressure in the stomach); ***anorexia*** (loss of appetite, weight loss); ***anxiety*** (fear; nervousness); ***arthralgia*** (pain in joints; muscle pain or stiffness; difficulty in moving); ***asthenia*** (lack or loss of strength); ***chills***—seek medical attention if associated with signs or symptoms of infection; ***constipation*** (difficulty having a bowel movement (stool)); ***cough; dizziness; dyspnea*** (difficult or labored breathing; shortness of breath; tightness in chest; wheezing); ***ecchymoses*** (bruising; large, flat, blue or purplish patches in the skin); ***edema, peripheral*** (swelling of hands, ankles, feet, or lower legs); ***fever***—seek medical attention if associated with signs or symptoms of infection; ***flushing*** (feeling of warmth; redness of the face, neck, arms and occasionally, upper chest); ***gastrointestinal symptoms*** (abdominal pain or stomach pain; diarrhea or increased bowel movements; loose or liquid stools; nausea or feeling of upset stomach or feeling like you may vomit; vomiting); ***headache, mild*** (pain in one or more areas of the head.)—seek medical attention if severe; ***hypotension*** (blurred vision; confusion; dizziness; faintness or lightheadedness when getting up from a lying or sitting position; sudden sweating; unusual tiredness or weakness); ***insomnia*** (sleeplessness; trouble sleeping; unable to sleep); ***myalgia*** (joint pain; swollen joints; muscle aching or cramping; muscle pains or stiffness; difficulty in moving); ***pain; pain, back; pruritus*** (itching skin); ***rash; rhinitis*** (stuffy nose; runny nose; sneezing); ***throat irritation***

Incidence less frequent

Arthritis (pain, swelling, or redness in joints; muscle pain or stiffness; difficulty in moving); ***dyspepsia*** (acid or sour stomach; belching; heartburn; indigestion; stomach discomfort, upset or pain); ***urticaria, mild*** (hives or welts; itching; redness of skin; skin rash)

Those indicating need for medical attention only if they occur after 3 months of therapy

Incidence less frequent

Hemorrhage (bleeding gums; coughing up blood; difficulty in breathing or swallowing; dizziness; headache; increased menstrual flow or vaginal bleeding; nosebleeds; paralysis; prolonged bleeding from cuts; red or dark brown urine; red or black, tarry stools; shortness of breath); ***hemorrhage, cerebral*** (blurred vision; headache, sudden and severe; inability to speak; seizures; slurred speech; temporary blindness; weakness in arm and/or leg on one side of the body, sudden and severe); ***infection, severe*** (chills; confusion; dizziness; lightheadedness; fainting; fast heartbeat; fever; rapid, shallow breathing); ***leukemia, acute myelogenous*** (bone pain)—secondary malignancy occurred in 3 of 349 patients treated with ibritumomab tiuxetan; ***myelodysplastic syndrome***—secondary malignancy occurred in 2 of 349 patients treated with ibritumomab tiuxetan; ***neutropenia, febrile*** (black, tarry stools; chills; cough; fever; lower back or side pain; painful or difficult urination; pale skin; shortness of breath; sore throat; ulcers, sores, or white spots in mouth; unusual bleeding or bruising; unusual tiredness or weakness)

Overdose

For more information on the management of overdose or unintentional ingestion, **contact a nuclear medicine physician or radiation oncologist**.

Clinical effects of overdose

Severe hematological toxicities (without fatalities or second organ injury) were observed in clinical trials following doses as high as 0.52 mCi per kilogram of body weight (19.2 MBq per kilogram of body weight) of Y-90 ibritumomab tiuxetan.

In a limited number of patients, single doses of up to 50 mCi (1850 MBq) of Y-90 ibritumomab tiuxetan and multiple doses of 20 mCi (749 MBq) followed by 40 mCi (1480 MBq) of Y-90 ibritumomab tiuxetan were studied. Autologous stem cell support to manage hematological toxicity was required in some patients.

Treatment of overdose

Specific treatment—

There is no known specific antidote to ibritumomab tiuxetan. Treatment is generally symptomatic and supportive.

Monitoring—

Careful monitoring for and management of cytopenias and their complications for up to 3 months after administration of ibritumomab tiuxetan therapeutic regimens recommended.

Supportive care—

Management of cytopenias may include platelet transfusions, red blood cell transfusions, administration of growth factors such as erythropoietin, and/or autologous stem cell support.

Infections that develop due to neutropenia should be managed with appropriate antimicrobial therapy.

Patient Consultation

As an aid to patient consultation, refer to *Advice for the Patient, Ibritumomab Tiuxetan (Systemic)*.

In providing consultation, consider emphasizing the following selected information (» = major clinical significance):

Description of use

Action in the body: Localization at sites of tumor spread or growth, the Y-90 beta emission induces cellular damage by free radical formation in the target and neighboring cells.

Before using this medication

» Conditions affecting use, especially:

Not recommended for use in patients with Type I hypersensitivity or previous anaphylactic reactions to ibritumomab, indium, murine proteins, rituximab, or yttrium.

Carcinogenicity/Mutagenicity—Radiation is a potential carcinogen and mutagen. Ibritumomab tiuxetan results in a significant radiation dose to the testes.

Tumorigenicity—Of 349 patients treated, one developed a Grade 1 meningioma, three developed acute myelogenous leukemia, and two developed myelodysplastic syndrome following ibritumomab tiuxetan therapeutic regimen. The onset of the secondary malignancy was 8 to 34 months following ibritumomab tiuxetan therapeutic regimen and 4 to 14 years following the patients' diagnosis of non-Hodgkin's lymphoma.

Fertility—Y-90 ibritumomab tiuxetan results in significant radiation dose to the testes; the radiation dose to the ovaries has not been established. There is potential risk that the ibritumomab tiuxetan therapeutic regimen could cause toxic effects on the female and male gonads. Effective contraception methods are recommended during treatment and for up to 12 months following ibritumomab tiuxetan therapeutic regimen.

Pregnancy—Not recommended for use during pregnancy. Ibritumomab tiuxetan crosses the placenta and has been shown to cause fetal harm.

Breast-feeding—Not recommended during ibritumomab tiuxetan therapeutic regimen.

Use in children—Safety and efficacy have not been established.

Use in the elderly—No overall differences in safety or effectiveness were observed between older subjects (132 of 349 age 65 years and over; 41 of 349 age 75 years and over) and younger subjects in clinical studies of 349 patients treated with the ibritumomab tiuxetan therapeutic regimen.

Other medications, especially anticoagulants, bone marrow depressants, vaccines, platelet function altering medications, or previous cytotoxic drug therapy or radiation therapy.

Other medical problems, especially altered biodistribution of In-111 ibritumomab tiuxetan or impaired bone marrow reserve.

Precautions while using this medication

» Avoiding immunizations unless approved by physician; other persons in patient's household should avoid immunizations with oral poliovirus vaccine; avoiding other persons who have taken oral polio virus vaccine or wearing a protective mask that covers nose and mouth

» Caution if bone marrow depression occurs:

(Avoiding exposure to persons with bacterial infections, especially during periods of low blood counts; checking with physician immediately if fever or chills, cough or hoarseness, lower back or side pain, or painful or difficult urination occur)

(Checking with physician immediately if unusual bleeding or bruising; black, tarry stools; blood in urine or stools; or pinpoint red spots on skin occur)

(Caution in use of regular toothbrush, dental floss, or toothpick; physician, dentist, or nurse may suggest alternatives; checking with physician before having dental work done)

(Not touching eyes or inside of nose unless hands washed immediately before)

(Using caution to avoid accidental cuts with use of sharp objects such as safety razor or fingernail or toenail cutters)

(Avoid contact sports or other situations where bruising or injury could occur)

» Advising patient to seek out prompt medical attention if severe cutaneous or mucocutaneous reactions are experienced

In-111 ibritumomab tiuxetan and Y-90 ibritumomab tiuxetan are radiopharmaceuticals. Care should be taken to minimize radiation exposure to patients and to medical personnel, consistent with institutional good radiation safety practices and patient management procedures.

Side/adverse effects

Signs of potential side effects, especially anemia, angioedema, bronchospasm, hemorrhage, infection, neutropenia, thrombocytopenia, allergic reaction, apnea, epistaxis, gastrointestinal hemorrhage, severe infection, melena, pain at site of tumor, pancytopenia, petechia, encephalopathy, hematemesis, subdural hematoma, cerebral hemorrhage, pulmonary edema, pulmonary embolus, tachycardia, severe urticaria

Signs of potential side effects observed during clinical practice, especially bullous dermatitis, erythema multiforme, exfoliative dermatitis, Stevens-Johnson syndrome, or toxic epidermal necrolysis

General Dosing Information

For information pertaining to the General Dosing of rituximab, a component of the ibritumomab tiuxetan therapeutic regimen, see *Rituximab (Systemic)*.

Ibritumomab tiuxetan radiolabeled should be used only by physicians and other professionals qualified by training and experienced in the safe use and handling of radionuclides and who are authorized by the Nuclear Regulatory Commission (NRC) or the appropriate Agreement State agency, if required, or, outside the U.S., the appropriate authority.

Special precautions are recommended in patients who develop thrombocytopenia as a result of administration of ibritumomab tiuxetan therapeutic regimen. These may include: extreme care in performing invasive procedures; regular inspection of intravenous sites, skin (including perirectal area), and mucous membrane surfaces for signs of bleeding or bruising; limiting frequency of venipuncture and avoiding intramuscular injections; testing urine, emesis, stool and secretions for occult blood; care in use of toothbrushes, dental floss, toothpicks, safety razors, and fingernail and toenail cutters; avoiding constipation; and using caution to prevent falls and other injuries. Such patients should avoid alcohol and any aspirin intake because of the risk of gastrointestinal bleeding. Platelet transfusions may be required.

Patients who develop leukopenia should be observed carefully for signs of infection. Antibiotic support may be required. In neutropenic patients who develop fever, broad-spectrum antibiotic coverage should be initiated empirically, pending bacterial cultures and appropriate diagnostic tests.

Safety considerations for handling this medication

In-111 ibritumomab tiuxetan and Y-90 ibritumomab tiuxetan are radiopharmaceuticals. Care should be taken to minimize radiation exposure to patients and to medical personnel, consistent with institutional good radiation safety practices and patient management procedures, during and after radiolabeling of ibritumomab tiuxetan with In-111 or Y-90.

Guidelines for the receipt, storage, handling, dispensing, and disposal of radioactive materials are available from scientific, professional, state, federal, and international bodies. Handling of this radiopharmaceutical should be limited to those individuals who are appropriately qualified and authorized.

For treatment of adverse effects

Medications for the treatment of hypersensitivity reactions, including epinephrine, antihistamines, and corticosteroids, should be available for immediate use in the event of an allergic reaction during administration of ibritumomab tiuxetan therapeutic regimen.

Patients who develop severe infusion reactions should have rituximab, In-111 ibritumomab tiuxetan, and Y-90 ibritumomab tiuxetan infusions discontinued and appropriate medical treatment should be initiated.

Patients who experience a severe cutaneous or mucocutaneous reaction should not receive any further component of the ibritumomab tiuxetan therapeutic regimen and should receive prompt medical evaluation.

Due to the possibility of hypersensitivity reactions with the administration of rituximab as part of the ibritumomab tiuxetan regimen, premedication with acetaminophen and diphenhydramine should be administered with each dose of rituximab.

Parenteral Dosage Forms

Note: The dose of rituximab is lower when used as part of the ibritumomab tiuxetan therapeutic regimen, as compared to the dose of rituximab when used as a single agent.

IBRITUMOMAB TIUXETAN INJECTION

Usual adult dose

Lymphomas, non-Hodgkin's (treatment)—

Ibritumomab tiuxetan therapeutic regimen is administered in two steps:

- Step 1—Intravenous infusion, rituximab (not included in ibritumomab tiuxetan kit) 250 milligrams per square meter of body surface area preceding (within 4 hours) an intravenous push (over 10 minutes) dose of 5 mCi (1.6 milligrams total antibody dose) of In-111 ibritumomab tiuxetan.

• Wait seven to nine days following step 1. Assess biodistribution. If biodistribution is not acceptable, do not proceed.

• Step 2—Infusion, rituximab (not included in ibritumomab tiuxetan kit) 250 milligrams per square meter of body surface area preceding (within 4 hours) an intravenous push (over 10 minutes) dose of 0.4 mCi per kilogram of body weight of Y-90 ibritumomab tiuxetan.

Note: **Patients with mild thrombocytopenia**—The dose of Y-90 ibritumomab tiuxetan (in Step 2) should be reduced to 0.3 mCi per kilogram of body weight (11.1 MBq per kilogram of body weight) for patients with a baseline platelet count between 100,000 and 149,000 cells per cubic millimeter.

Do not treat patients with baseline platelet count less than 100,000 cells per cubic millimeter.

Rituximab dose—The dose of rituximab is lower when used as part of the ibritumomab tiuxetan therapeutic regimen, as compared to the dose of rituximab when used as a single agent.

Usual adult prescribing limits

Maximum allowable dose—The prescribed, measured, and administered dose of Y-90 ibritumomab tiuxetan should not exceed 32 mCi (1,184 MBq).

Usual pediatric dose

Lymphomas, non-Hodgkin's B-cell (treatment)—

The safety and efficacy have not been established.

Usual geriatric dose

See *Usual adult dose.*

Usual geriatric prescribing limits

See *Usual adult prescribing limits.*

Strength(s) usually available

U.S.—

3.2 mg of ibritumomab tiuxetan in 2 mL of 0.9% sodium chloride solution per vial (sterile, pyrogen-free; no preservatives) (Rx) [*Zevalin* (Kit contains 4 vials—1 vial of ibritumomab tiuxetan, 1 vial 50 mM sodium acetate (13.6 mg of sodium acetate trihydrate in 2 mL of Water for injection), 1 vial formulation buffer (750 mg of human albumin, 76 mg of sodium chloride, 21 mg of sodium phosphate dibasic heptahydrate, 4 mg of pentetic acid, 2 mg of potassium phosphate monobasic, and 2 mg of potassium chloride in 10 mL of water for injection adjusted to pH 7.1 with either sodium hydroxide or hydrochloric acid), and 1 empty reaction vial)].

Canada—

Not commercially available.

Packaging and storage

Before radiolabeling, store between 2 and 8ºC (36 and 46ºF), unless otherwise specified by manufacturer. Do not freeze.

Note: Product should be brought to room temperature before radiolabeling.

Indium-111 *(Zevalin)* should be stored between 2 and 8ºC (36 and 46ºF) until use and administered within 12 hours of radiolabeling.

Yttrium-90 *(Zevalin)* should be stored between 2 and 8ºC (36 and 46ºF) until use and administered within 8 hours of radiolabeling.

Preparation of dosage form

Read all directions thoroughly and assemble all materials before starting the radiolabeling procedure.

Significant differences exist in the preparation of the In-111 ibritumomab tiuxetan and the Y-90 ibritumomab tiuxetan dose.

See the manufacturer's package insert for instructions.

Preparation of the Indium-111 ***(Zevalin)*** dose

• The patient dose should be measured by a suitable radioactivity calibration system immediately prior to administration. The dose calibrator must be operated in accordance with the manufacturer's specifications and quality control for the measurement of In-111.

• Proper aseptic technique and precautions for handling radioactive materials should be employed. Waterproof gloves should be utilized in the preparation and during the determination of radiochemical purity of In-111 *(Zevalin)*. Appropriate shielding should be used during radiolabeling, and use of a syringe shield is recommended during administration to the patient.

• To prepare injection, a sterile, pyrogen-free indium In 111 chloride solution is used. The use of high purity In-111 chloride manufactured by Amersham Health, Inc. or Mallinckrodt, Inc. is required. Isotope solution must be buffered with sodium acetate before adding to the ibritumomab tiuxetan solution. See manufacturer's package insert for instructions.

• Determine radiochemical purity. See manufacturer's package insert for instructions.

• Indium-111 *(Zevalin)* should be stored between 2 and 8ºC (36 and 46ºF) until use and administered within 12 hours of radiolabeling.

• See *Usual adult dose* step 1 for dosage and administration of Indium-111 *(Zevalin)*.

• Discard needles, syringes, and vials in accordance with local, state, and federal regulations governing radioactive and biohazardous waste.

Preparation of the Yttrium-90 ***(Zevalin)*** dose

• The patient dose should be measured by a suitable radioactivity calibration system immediately prior to administration. The dose calibrator must be operated in accordance with the manufacturer's specifications and quality control for the measurement of Y-90.

• Proper aseptic technique and precautions for handling radioactive materials should be employed. Waterproof gloves should be utilized in the preparation and during the determination of radiochemical purity of Y-90 *(Zevalin)*. Appropriate shielding should be used during radiolabeling, and use of a syringe shield is recommended during administration to the patient.

• To prepare injection, a sterile, pyrogen-free yttrium Y 90 chloride solution is used. The use of high purity Y-90 chloride manufactured by MDS Nordion is required. Isotope solution must be buffered with sodium acetate before adding to the *(Zevalin)* solution. See manufacturer's package insert for instructions.

• Determine radiochemical purity. See manufacturer's package insert for instructions.

• Yttrium-90 *(Zevalin)* should be stored between 2 and 8ºC (36 and 46ºF) until use and administered within 8 hours of radiolabeling.

• See *Usual adult dose* step 2 for dosage and administration of Yttrium-90 *(Zevalin)*.

• Yttrium-90 *(Zevalin)* is suitable for administration on an outpatient basis. No special shielding is necessary, other than the use of vial and syringe shields for preparation and injection.

• Discard needles, syringes, and vials in accordance with local, state, and federal regulations governing radioactive and biohazardous waste.

Stability

Indium-111 *(Zevalin)* should be stored between 2 and 8ºC (36 and 46ºF) until use and administered within 12 hours of radiolabeling.

Yttrium-90 *(Zevalin)* should be stored between 2 and 8ºC (36 and 46ºF) until use and administered within 8 hours of radiolabeling.

Caution

Radioactive material.

Additional information

The ibritumomab tiuxetan vial contains a protein solution that may develop translucent particulates. These particulates will be removed by filtration prior to administration.

Revised: 07/29/2006
Developed: 11/18/2002

IBUPROFEN—See *Anti-inflammatory Drugs, Nonsteroidal (Systemic)*

IBUPROFEN AND OXYCODONE
Systemic†

VA CLASSIFICATION (Primary): CN101

U.S.: Schedule II

Commonly used brand name(s): *Combunox.*

Note: For a listing of dosage forms and brand names by country availability, see *Dosage Forms* section(s).

†Not commercially available in Canada.

Category

Analgesic.

Indications

Accepted

Pain, acute moderate to severe (treatment)—Oxycodone HCl and ibuprofen combination tablet is indicated for the short term (no more than 7 days) management of acute, moderate to severe pain.

Unaccepted

Ibuprofen/oxycodone is not a substitute for corticosteroids nor to treat corticosteroid insufficiency.

Pharmacology/Pharmacokinetics

Physicochemical characteristics

Molecular weight—
Ibuprofen—206.29.
Oxycodone HCl—351.83.

Mechanism of action/Effect

Ibuprofen—Ibuprofen is a nonsteroidal anti-inflammatory agent that possesses analgesic and antipyretic activities. Its mechanism of action is thought to be related to its inhibition of cyclooxygenase activity and prostaglandin synthesis. Ibuprofen is a peripherally acting analgesic and does not have any known effects on opiate receptors.

Oxycodone—Oxycodone is a semisynthetic opioid analgesic with multiple actions involving the central nervous system and smooth muscle. The mechanism of action of oxycodone is thought to be related to its binding to opiate receptors in the central nervous system. In addition to analgesia, oxycodone may produce sedation and respiratory depression.

Absorption

Ibuprofen—Rapid; bioavailability is not altered in the presence of food

Oxycodone—Rapid; bioavailability slightly increased (25%) in the presence of food

Protein binding

Ibuprofen—Very high (99%)

Oxycodone—Moderate (45%)

Biotransformation

Ibuprofen—Both the R- and S- isomers metabolized to two primary metabolites: (+)-2-4'-2-hydroxy-2-methyl-propyl) phenyl propionic acid and (+)-1-4'-2-carboxypropyl) phenyl propionic acid) which circulate in the plasma at low levels relative to the parent.

Oxycodone—Metabolized in the liver by means of N-demethylation, O-demethylation, 6-ketoreduction, and glucuronidation; major circulating metabolite is noroxycodone; oxymorphone is the end product of O-demethylation and is present in the plasma at low concentrations. Metabolism of oxycodone to oxymorphone occurs via CYP2D6.

Half-life

Ibuprofen—1.8 to 2.6 hours (elimination following single dose administration)

Oxycodone—3.1 to 3.7 hours (elimination following single dose administration)

Time to peak concentration

Ibuprofen—T_{max}: 1.6 to 3.1 hours

Oxycodone—T_{max}: 1.3 to 2.1 hours

Peak plasma concentration:

Ibuprofen—C_{max}: 18.5 to 34.3 mcg/mL. Repeated administration of ibuprofen/oxycodone every 6 hours does not result in any accumulation of ibuprofen

Oxycodone—C_{max}: 9.8 to 11.7 ng/mL. Repeated administration of ibuprofen/oxycodone every 6 hours results in approximately 50 to 65% increase in oxycodone C_{max}

Elimination

Ibuprofen—Urinary, less than 0.2% unchanged ibuprofen

Oxycodone—Urinary, approximately 4% unchanged oxycodone

Precautions to Consider

Cross-sensitivity and/or related problems

Patients known to be hypersensitive to other opioids may exhibit cross-sensitivity to oxycodone.

Carcinogenicity/Mutagenicity

Studies to evaluate the potential effects of ibuprofen/oxycodone on carcinogenicity and mutagenicity have not been conducted.

Pregnancy/Reproduction

Fertility—Studies to evaluate the potential effects of ibuprofen/oxycodone on impairment of fertility have not been conducted.

Pregnancy—Adequate and well-controlled studies in humans have not been done.

Animal studies were conducted in rat and rabbit models. Pregnant rats were treated with oral combination oxycodone/ibuprofen doses in mg per kg of body weight per day (0.25/20, 0.5/40, 1/80, 2/160) on days 7 to 16 of gestation. There was no developmental toxicity or teratogenicity evidence at any dose. However, maternal toxicity was noted at 0.5/40 doses and above. The highest dose of 2/160 tested in rats is equivalent to the maximum recommended human daily dose on a body surface area basis. This dose was associated with maternal toxicity (death, clinical signs, and decreased body weight).

Pregnant rabbits were given oral combination oxycodone/ibuprofen doses in mg per kg of body weight per day (0.38/30, 0.75/60, 1.5/120 or 3/240) on days 7 through 19 of gestation. Treatment was not teratogenic; however, maternal toxicity was noted at doses of 1.5/120 (reduced body weight and food consumption) and 3/240 (mortality). The no adverse effect level (NOAEL) for maternal toxicity, 0.75/60 mg/kg/day is 0.75-fold the proposed maximum daily human dose based upon body surface area. Developmental toxicity, as evidenced by delayed ossification and reduced fetal body weights, was noted at the highest dose, which is approximately 3 times the MRHD on a mg per m^2 basis and is likely due to maternal toxicity. The fetal NOAEL of 1.5/120 mg/kg/day dose is approximately 1.5 times the MRHD on a mg per m^2 basis.

Ibuprofen/oxycodone combination should be used during pregnancy only if the potential benefit justifies the potential risk to the fetus. *Due to the ibuprofen, the combination should not be used during the third trimester because it could cause problems in the unborn child (premature closure of the ductus arteriosus and pulmonary hypertension in the fetus/neonate).*

FDA Pregnancy Category C

Labor and delivery—Ibuprofen/oxycodone combination should not be used during the third trimester of pregnancy due to the potential for ibuprofen to inhibit prostaglandin synthetase which may prolong pregnancy and inhibit labor. Oxycodone is not recommended for use in women during and immediately prior to labor and delivery because oral opioids may cause respiratory depression in the newborn.

Breast-feeding

Ibuprofen is not distributed in breast milk in significant quantities. However, oxycodone is distributed in human milk and withdrawal symptoms and/or respiratory depression have been observed in neonates whose mothers were taking narcotic analgesics during pregnancy. Although adverse effects in the nursing infant have not been documented, withdrawal can occur in breast-feeding infants when maternal administration of an opioid analgesic is discontinued. Because of the potential for serious adverse reactions in nursing infants from the oxycodone present in ibuprofen/oxycodone combination, a decision should be made whether to discontinue nursing or to discontinue the drug, taking into account the importance of the drug to the mother.

Pediatrics

Safety and efficacy have not been established in pediatric patients under 14 years of age.

Adolescents

Safety and efficacy have been established in patients between the ages of 14 and 17 years of age. Appropriate studies performed to date have not demonstrated problems in ages 14 to 17 years of age that would limit the usefulness of ibuprofen/oxycodone in this age group.

Geriatrics

Appropriate studies performed to date have not demonstrated geriatrics-specifics problems that would limit the usefulness of ibuprofen/oxycodone in the elderly. However, greater sensitivity of some older individuals cannot be ruled out. Because the elderly may be more sensitive to the renal and gastrointestinal effects of NSAIDs as well as the possible increased risk of respiratory depression with opioids, extra caution should be used when treating the elderly with ibuprofen/oxycodone.

Drug interactions and/or related problems

The following drug interactions and/or related problems have been selected on the basis of their potential clinical significance (possible mechanism in parentheses where appropriate)—not necessarily inclusive (» = major clinical significance):

Note: Oxycodone is metabolized in part to oxymorphone via the cytochrome P_{450} isoenzyme CYP2D6. While this pathway may be blocked by a variety of drug (e.g., certain cardiovascular drugs and antidepressants), such blockade has not yet been shown to be of clinical significance with this agent. However, clinicians should be aware of this possible interaction.

Note: Combinations containing any of the following medications, depending on the amount present, may also interact with this medication.

Agonist/antagonist analgesics including
Buprenorphine or
Butorphanol or
Nalbuphine or
Pentazocine
(should be administered with caution to patients who are receiving oxycodone; agonist/antagonist analgesics may reduce the analgesic effect of oxycodone and/or may precipitate withdrawal symptoms in these patients)

» Alcohol or
» Central nervous system (CNS) depression-producing medications, other (see *Appendix II*)
(concurrent use with oxycodone may result in additive effects; interactive effects resulting in respiratory depression, hypotension, profound sedation, or coma may result if these drugs are taken in combination with the usual oxycodone dosage; dose of one or both agents should be reduced with concomitant use)

» Angiotensin-converting enzyme (ACE) inhibitors
(concurrent use with ibuprofen may reduce antihypertensive effects of the ACE inhibitor)

Anticholinergics
(concomitant use of anticholinergics and oxycodone preparations may produce paralytic ileus)

» Anticoagulants or
» Corticosteroids
(concomitant use with NSAIDs can inhibit platelet aggregation; patients should be carefully monitored)

Aspirin
(concomitant use not generally recommended because of potential for increased adverse effects)

» Diuretics
(ibuprofen has been shown to reduce natriuretic effects of diuretics in some patients, possibly by inhibiting renal prostaglandin synthesis; patient should be observed closely for signs of renal failure, as well as diuretic efficacy, during concomitant use)

» Lithium
(inhibition of renal prostaglandin activity by ibuprofen has been reported to result in an increase in the plasma concentration of lithium and a decrease in its renal clearance; increased monitoring for lithium toxicity is recommended during concomitant use)

» Methotrexate
(caution should be used when administered concomitantly; ibuprofen reported to competitively inhibit methotrexate accumulation in rabbit studies; this may indicate that ibuprofen could enhance methotrexate toxicity)

» Monoamine oxidase inhibitors (MAOIs)
(use of oxycodone not recommended concurrently or within 14 days of stopping MAOI treatment; have been reported to intensify effects of at least one opioid drug causing anxiety, confusion and significant respiratory depression or coma)

Neuromuscular blocking agents
(oxycodone may enhance neuromuscular blocking action or skeletal muscle relaxants and produce increased degree of respiratory depression)

» Warfarin
(warfarin and NSAIDs effects on GI bleeding are synergistic; greater risk of serious GI bleeding with concomitant use than with either drug alone)

Laboratory value alterations

The following have been selected on the basis of their potential clinical significance (possible effect in parentheses where appropriate)—not necessarily inclusive (» = major clinical significance).

With physiology/laboratory test values
Amylase, serum
(opioids like oxycodone may cause increases in levels)

Hemoglobin
(decrease may occur)

Liver function tests, including
SGOT (AST)
SGPT (ALT)
(values may be elevated, remain unchanged, or may be transient with continued therapy; however, if significant abnormalities occur, clinical signs and symptoms consistent with liver disease develop, or systemic manifestations such as eosinophilia or skin rash occur, ibuprofen/oxycodone combination should be discontinued)

Medical considerations/Contraindications

The medical considerations/contraindications included have been selected on the basis of their potential clinical significance (reasons given in parentheses where appropriate)—not necessarily inclusive (» = major clinical significance).

Except under special circumstances, this medication should not be used when the following medical problem exists:

» Allergic reaction, severe, such as anaphylaxis or angioedema, or asthma, induced by aspirin, other NSAIDs, history of, or other opioids, history of or
» Nasal polyps associated with bronchospasm, aspirin-induced
(high risk of severe allergic reactions because of cross-sensitivity; fatal reactions to NSAIDs have been reported in such patients; emergency help should be sought if anaphylactoid reaction occurs)

» Bronchial asthma, acute or severe or
» Hypercarbia or
» Respiratory depression, significant (in unmonitored settings or the absence of resuscitative equipment)

» Coronary artery bypass graft (CABG) surgery
(ibuprofen/oxycodone contraindicated for the treatment of peri-operative pain in this setting)

» Hypersensitivity to ibuprofen, oxycodone hydrochloride, or any component of the product

» Paralytic ileus, known or suspected

Risk-benefit should be considered when the following medical problems exist:

» Abdominal conditions, acute
(diagnosis or clinical course may be obscured by oxycodone administration)

Addison's disease or
Alcoholism, acute or
Central nervous system (CNS) depression or coma or
Convulsive disorders or
Delirium tremens or
Hepatic function impairment, severe or
Hypothyroidism or
Kyphoscoliosis associated with respiratory depression or
Prostatic hypertrophy or
Pulmonary function impairment or
Toxic psychosis or
Urethral stricture
(usual precautions should be observed with the possibility of respiratory depression, postural hypotension, and altered mental states kept in mind, especially in elderly or debilitated patients)

» Advanced renal disease
(ibuprofen/oxycodone treatment not recommended due to NSAID component; if therapy must be initiated; close monitoring of patient's kidney function is advisable)

Anemia
(may be exacerbated because anemia is sometimes seen in patients receiving ibuprofen; may be due to fluid retention, GI loss, or an incompletely described effect upon erythropoiesis)

Asthma, pre-existing
(should be used with caution)

Biliary tract disease including
Acute pancreatitis
(ibuprofen/oxycodone may cause spasm of sphincter of Oddi and should be used with caution in patients with these conditions)

» Cardiovascular disease or risk factors for
(greater risk of serious cardiovascular thrombotic events, myocardial infarction, and stroke, which can be fatal)

» Chronic obstructive pulmonary disease or
Cor pulmonale or
Decreased respiratory reserve or
Hypercapnia or
Hypoxia or
Respiratory depression, pre-existing
(should be used with extreme caution in these patients; even usual therapeutic doses may decrease respiratory drive to point of apnea; occurs most frequently in elderly or debilitated patients, usually following large initial doses in non-tolerant patients, or when opioids are given in conjunction with other agents that depress respiration)

» Circulatory shock
(should be administered with caution to these patients since vasodilatation produced by the drug may further reduce cardiac output and blood pressure)

Coagulation or platelet function disorders
(caution is recommended because prolonged bleeding effect may be exaggerated in these patients)

Complications of presumed noninfectious, noninflammatory painful conditions
(ibuprofen's antipyretic and anti-inflammatory activity may reduce fever and inflammation, thus diminishing their utility as diagnostic signs in detecting these conditions)

Conditions predisposing to and/or exacerbated by fluid retention, such as:
Compromised cardiac function or
Congestive heart disease or
Hypertension
(ibuprofen has been reported to cause fluid retention and edema; therefore, ibuprofen/oxycodone combination should be used with caution in patients with these conditions)

» Conditions predisposing to gastrointestinal (GI) effects, such as:
Alcoholism, active
Gastrointestinal bleeding, history of
Peptic ulcer disease, active or history of
Tobacco use, or recent history of
(NSAIDs should be used with extreme caution in patients with these and elderly or debilitated patients; shortest possible duration of NSAIDs use to minimize potential risk of GI events; alternate therapies should be considered for high risk patients; should remain alert for ulceration and bleeding even in the absence of previous GI tract symptoms and even short term therapy is not without risk)

Dehydration or
Heart failure or
Impaired renal function or
Liver dysfunction or
Renal disease, pre-existing or
(caution should be used; rehydration is advisable before initiating ibuprofen/oxycodone therapy in dehydrated patients; ibuprofen administration has resulted in renal toxicity including renal papillary necrosis and other renal pathologic changes; discontinuation of NSAID is usually followed by recovery to pretreatment state)

Drug abuse dependence, current or history of
(should be considered when prescribing due to increased risk of misuse, abuse or diversion of oxycodone [schedule II controlled substance])

» Head injury or
Increased intracranial pressure, pre-existing or
Intracranial lesions
(risk of respiratory depression and further elevation of cerebrospinal fluid pressure is increased; also, oxycodone produce adverse reactions that may obscure clinical course of head injury)

Lupus erythematosus or
Related connective tissue diseases
(aseptic meningitis with fever and coma has been observed rarely in patients on ibuprofen therapy; it is probably more likely to occur in patients with these conditions; if patient develops signs of meningitis while taking ibuprofen/oxycodone, possibility of its being related to ibuprofen should be considered)

Postoperative or
Pulmonary disease
(caution should be exercised because oxycodone suppresses the cough reflex)

Patient monitoring

The following may be especially important in patient monitoring (other tests may be warranted in some patients, depending on condition; » = major clinical significance):

Assessment of amount and frequency of medication use
(recommended at periodic intervals during to detect signs of dependence or abuse and help to limit abuse of opioids)

Blood pressure
(should be monitored closely during initiation of treatment and throughout course of therapy)

» Liver function tests or
» Renal function tests
(routine monitoring may be required during ibuprofen/oxycodone combination therapy in patients with severe hepatic or renal function impairment)

Side/Adverse Effects

The following side/adverse effects have been selected on the basis of their potential clinical significance (possible signs and symptoms in parentheses where appropriate)—not necessarily inclusive:

Those indicating need for medical attention

Incidence less frequent

Vasodilation (feeling of warmth or heat; flushing or redness of skin, especially on face and neck; headache; feeling faint, dizzy, or lightheadedness; sweating)

Incidence rare

Anemia (pale skin; troubled breathing with exertion; unusual bleeding or bruising; unusual tiredness or weakness); ***chest pain; hypertonia*** (excessive muscle tone, muscle tension or tightness; muscle stiffness); ***hypokalemia*** (convulsions; decreased urine; dry mouth; irregular heartbeat; increased thirst; loss of appetite; mood changes; muscle pain or cramps; nausea or vomiting; numbness or tingling in hands, feet, or lips; shortness of breath; unusual tiredness or weakness); ***hypotension*** (blurred vision; confusion; dizziness, faintness, or lightheadedness when getting up from a lying or sitting position suddenly; sweating; unusual tiredness or weakness); ***hypoxia*** (confusion; dizziness; fast heartbeat; shortness of breath; weakness); ***ileus*** (abdominal pain; severe constipation; severe vomiting); ***lung disorder*** (difficulty in breathing); ***syncope*** (fainting); ***tachycardia*** (fast, pounding, or irregular heartbeat or pulse); ***thrombophlebitis*** (changes in skin color; pain, tenderness, swelling of foot or leg); ***urinary frequency*** (increased need to urinate; passing urine more often); ***urinary retention*** (decrease in urine volume; decrease in frequency of urination; difficulty in passing urine [dribbling]; painful urination)

Incidence unknown

Exfoliative dermatitis (cracks in the skin; loss of heat from the body; red, swollen skin, scaly skin); ***fulminant hepatitis*** (abdominal or stomach pain; chills; clay-colored stools; dark urine; diarrhea; dizziness; fever; headache; itching; loss of appetite); ***hepatic failure*** (headache; stomach pain; continuing vomiting; dark-colored urine; general feeling of tiredness or weakness; light-colored stools; yellow eyes or skin); ***jaundice*** (chills; clay-colored stools; dark urine; dizziness; fever; headache; itching; loss of appetite; nausea; abdominal or stomach pain; area rash; unpleasant breath odor; unusual tiredness or weakness; vomiting of blood; yellow eyes or skin); ***liver necrosis*** (abdominal or stomach pain; black, tarry stools; chills; light-colored stools; dark urine; dizziness; fever; headache; itching; loss of appetite; nausea; rash; unpleasant breath odor; unusual tiredness or weakness; vomiting of blood; yellow eyes or skin); ***Stevens-Johnson Syndrome*** (blistering, peeling, loosening of skin; chills; cough; diarrhea; itching; joint or muscle pain; red irritated eyes; red skin lesions, often with a purple center; sore throat; sores, ulcers, or white spots in mouth or on lips; unusual tiredness or weakness); ***toxic epidermal necrolysis*** (blistering, peeling, loosening of skin; chills; cough; diarrhea; itching; joint or muscle pain; red irritated eyes; red skin lesions, often with a purple center; sore throat; sores, ulcers, or white spots in mouth or on lips; unusual tiredness or weakness)

Those indicating need for medical attention only if they continue or are bothersome

Incidence more frequent

Dizziness; headache; nausea; somnolence (sleepiness or unusual drowsiness); ***vomiting***

Incidence less frequent

Asthenia (lack or loss of strength); ***constipation*** (difficulty having a bowel movement (stool); ***diarrhea; dyspepsia*** (acid or sour stomach; belching; heartburn; indigestion; stomach discomfort, upset, or pain); ***fever; flatulence*** (bloated full feeling; excess air or gas in stomach or intestines; passing gas); ***sweat***

Rare

Abdominal pain (stomach pain); ***abnormal thinking*** (confusion; delusions; dementia); ***amblyopia*** (blurred vision; change in vision; impaired vision); ***anxiety*** (fear; nervousness); ***arthritis*** (pain, swelling, or redness in joints; muscle pain or stiffness; difficulty in moving); ***back pain; chills; constipation*** (difficulty having a bowel movement (stool)); ***dry mouth; ecchymosis*** (bruising, large, flat, blue or purplish patches in the skin); ***edema*** (swelling); ***enlarged abdomen; euphoria*** (false or unusual sense of well-being); ***hyperkinesia*** (increase in body movements); ***infection*** (fever or chills; cough or hoarseness; lower back or side pain; painful or difficult urination); ***insomnia*** (sleeplessness; trouble sleeping; unable to sleep); ***nervousness; pharyngitis*** (body aches or pain; congestion; cough; dryness or soreness of throat; fever; hoarseness; runny nose; tender, swollen glands in neck; trouble in swallowing; voice changes); ***rash; taste perversion***

Overdose

For specific information on the agents used in the management of ibuprofen and oxycodone combination overdose, see:

- *Charcoal, Activated (Oral-Local)* monograph; and/or
- *Naloxone (Systemic)* monograph.

For more information on the management of overdose or unintentional ingestion, **contact a Poison Control Center** (see *Poison Control Center Listing*).

Clinical effects of overdose

The following effects have been selected on the basis of their potential clinical significance (possible signs and symptoms in parentheses where appropriate)—not necessarily inclusive:

Acute and/or chronic

Ibuprofen

Abdominal pain (stomach pain); ***atrial fibrillation*** (fast or irregular heartbeat; dizziness; fainting); ***bradycardia*** (chest pain or discomfort; lightheadedness, dizziness, or fainting; shortness of breath; slow or irregular heartbeat; unusual tiredness); ***cardiovascular toxicity*** (blurred vision; chest pain; confusion; dizziness; fainting; lightheadedness; fast or irregular heartbeat; shortness of breath; sudden fainting; unusual tiredness or weakness); ***CNS depression*** (confusion; difficulty sleeping; disorientation; dizziness; drowsiness to profound coma; hallucination; headache; lethargy; lightheadedness; mood or other mental changes; trouble breathing; unusual tiredness or weakness); ***drowsiness*** (sleepiness); ***headache; hypotension*** (blurred vision; confusion; dizziness, faintness, or lightheadedness when getting up from a lying or sitting position suddenly; sweating; unusual tiredness or weakness); ***nausea; seizures*** (convulsions; muscle spasm or jerking of all extremities; sudden loss of consciousness; loss of bladder control); ***tachycardia*** (fast, pounding, or irregular heartbeat or pulse); ***tinnitus*** (continuing ringing or buzzing or other unexplained noise in ears; hearing loss); ***vomiting***

Note: Ibuprofen overdose toxicity is dependent on the amount of drug ingested and time elapsed since ingestion, although individual response may vary, necessitating individual evaluation of each case. Although uncommon, serious toxicity and death have been reported in the medical literature with ibuprofen overdosage.

Oxycodone

Bradycardia (chest pain or discomfort; lightheadedness, dizziness, or fainting; shortness of breath; slow or irregular heartbeat; unusual tiredness); ***cold and clammy skin; coma*** (change in consciousness, loss of consciousness); ***constricted pupils; death*** (no pulse; no blood pressure; no breathing); ***hypotension*** (blurred vision; confusion; dizziness, faintness, or lightheadedness when getting up from a lying or sitting position suddenly; sweating; unusual tiredness or weakness); ***respiratory depression*** (pale or blue lips, fingernails, or skin; difficult or troubled breathing; irregular, fast or slow, or shallow breathing; shortness of breath); ***skeletal muscle flaccidity; somnolence*** (sleepiness or unusual drowsiness); ***stupor*** (decreased awareness or responsiveness; severe sleepiness)

Treatment of overdose

To decrease absorption—Emptying the stomach via ipecac-induced emesis or gastric lavage. Emesis is most effective if initiated within 30 minutes of ingestion. Activated charcoal may also be used to reduce the absorption and reabsorption of ibuprofen. Induced emesis is NOT recommended in patients with impaired consciousness or overdoses greater than 400 mg per kg of body weight of the ibuprofen component in children because of the risk for convulsions and the potential for aspiration of gastric contents.

To enhance elimination—Administering urinary alkalizers may increase ibuprofen excretion.

Dialysis is not likely to be of value because of ibuprofen's high degree of protein binding.

Specific treatment—Cardiac arrest or arrhythmias may require cardiac massage or defibrillation.

Administering the opioid antagonist naloxone intravenously with simultaneous efforts at respiratory resuscitation. See the package insert or the *Naloxone (Systemic)* monograph for specific dosing guidelines for this product.

Monitoring—Continuing to monitor the patient and administering additional naloxone as needed to maintain adequate respiration. Management of hypotension, acidosis, and gastrointestinal bleeding may be necessary.

Supportive care—Establishing adequate respiratory exchange through provision of a patent airway and institution of assisted or controlled ventilation. Supportive measures (including oxygen and vasopressors) should be employed in the management of circulatory shock and pulmonary edema accompanying overdose, as indicated. Administering supportive measures as needed.

Patients in whom intentional overdose is confirmed or suspected should be referred for psychiatric consultation.

Patient Consultation

As an aid to patient consultation, refer to *Advice for the Patient, Ibuprofen and Oxycodone (Systemic)*.

In providing consultation, consider emphasizing the following selected information (» = major clinical significance):

Before using this medication

» Conditions affecting use, especially:

Hypersensitivity to ibuprofen, oxycodone, or any component of the product or to other opioids

Pregnancy—Risk benefit considerations; should not be used during third trimester due to potential for problems in the unborn child (premature closure of the ductus arteriosus and pulmonary hypertension in the fetus/neonate)

Breast-feeding—Risk benefit considerations

Use in children—Safety and efficacy in children younger than 14 years of age not established

Use in the elderly—Extra caution due to greater sensitivity possible with renal and gastrointestinal effects and possible increased risk of respiratory depression with opioids

Other medications, especially alcohol, ACE inhibitors, anticoagulants, CNS depression-producing medications, corticosteroids, diuretics, lithium, methotrexate, MAOIs, or warfarin

Other medical problems, especially acute abdominal conditions; acute or severe bronchial spasm; advanced renal disease; aspirin-induced nasal polyps associated with bronchospasm; cardiovascular disease (or risk factors for); chronic obstructive pulmonary disease; circulatory shock; conditions predisposing to gastrointestinal (GI) effects; coronary artery bypass graft (CABG) surgery; head injury; hypercarbia; known or suspected paralytic ileus; severe allergic reactions (such as anaphylaxis or angioedema, or asthmas, induced by aspirin, other NSAIDs or other opioids, history of); or significant respiratory depression

Proper use of this medication

» Taking only the amount prescribed no longer than ordered by the physician to avoid potential for abuse and unwanted effects

» Not sharing medicine with others

» Proper dosing

Missed dose: Taking as soon as possible; not taking if almost time for next scheduled dose; not doubling doses

» Proper storage

Precautions while using this medication

» Importance of regularly scheduled appointments with doctor to monitor blood pressure

» Avoiding use of alcoholic beverages or other CNS depressants during therapy, unless prescribed or otherwise approved by physician

» Contacting doctor if cardiovascular side effects (i.e., chest pain, shortness of breath, weakness, slurring of speech) occur

» Asking for medical advice if signs and symptoms of GI tract ulcerations and bleeding such as black tarry stools, vomiting of blood or material that looks like coffee grounds, severe or continuing stomach pain, discomfort or burning, trouble breathing, severe and continuing nausea, heartburn or indigestion occur

» Discontinuing drug and calling doctor immediately if any type of skin rash develops

» Importance of reporting any signs of liver toxicity

» Caution if dizziness, drowsiness, lightheadedness, false sense of well-being occurs, or vision problems occur

» Caution when getting up from a lying or sitting position

Importance of informing physician or dentist of use of medication if any kind of surgery (including dental) or emergency treatment is required

Possible dryness of mouth; using sugarless gum or candy, ice, or saliva substitute for relief; checking with dentist if dry mouth continues for more than 2 weeks

Side/adverse effects

Signs of potential side effects, especially vasodilation, anemia, chest pain, hypertonia, hypokalemia, hypotension, hypoxia, ileus, lung disorder, syncope, tachycardia, thrombophlebitis, urinary frequency, urinary retention, exfoliative dermatitis, fulminant hepatitis, hepatic failure, jaundice, liver necrosis, Stevens-Johnson Syndrome, or toxic epidermal necrolysis

General Dosing Information

Ibuprofen/oxycodone combination is for short-term use (no longer than 7 days).

Because oxycodone has the potential for being abused, record-keeping for prescribing information, including quantity, frequency, and renewal requests for ibuprofen/oxycodone combination is strongly advised.

Oral Dosage Forms

IBUPROFEN AND OXYCODONE TABLETS

Usual adult and adolescent dose

Pain, acute moderate to severe (treatment)—
Oral, recommended dose of one tablet (400 mg ibuprofen, 5 mg oxycodone).

Usual adult and adolescent prescribing limits

Should not exceed 4 tablets in a 24-hour period and should not exceed 7 days

Usual pediatric dose

Safety and efficacy have not been established in patients under 14 years of age.

Usual geriatric dose

See *Usual adult and adolescent dose.*

Usual geriatric prescribing limits

See *Usual adult and adolescent prescribing limits.*

Strength(s) usually available

U.S.—
400 ibuprofen/5 mg oxycodone hydrochloride (Rx) [*Combunox* (sodium starch glycolate; microcrystalline cellulose; colloidal silicon dioxide; stearic acid; calcium stearate; carboxymethylcellulose; povidone; titanium dioxide; polydextrose; hypromellose; triacetin; polyethylene glycol 8000)].

Packaging and storage

Store at 25 °C (77 °F); excursions permitted between 15 and 30 °C (59 and 86 °F).

Auxiliary labeling

- May cause drowsiness.
- Avoid alcoholic beverages.
- This medication may be habit forming.
- Caution: Federal law prohibits the transfer of this drug to any person other than the patient for whom it was prescribed.

Note

Controlled substance in the U.S.

Revised: 07/29/2006
Developed: 04/14/2005

IBUPROFEN-CONTAINING COMBINATIONS—See *Hydrocodone and Ibuprofen (Systemic)*

IFOSFAMIDE Systemic

VA CLASSIFICATION (Primary): AN100

Commonly used brand name(s): *IFEX.*

Note: For a listing of dosage forms and brand names by country availability, see *Dosage Forms* section(s).

Category

Antineoplastic.

Indications

Note: Bracketed information in the *Indications* section refers to uses that are not included in U.S. product labeling.

Accepted

Tumors, germ cell, testicular (treatment)[1]—Ifosfamide is indicated, in combination with other antineoplastic agents and a prophylactic agent against hemorrhagic cystitis (such as mesna), for treatment of germ cell testicular tumors.

[Carcinoma, head and neck (treatment)][1]—Ifosfamide is indicated as reasonable medical therapy for treatment of head and neck carcinoma. (Evidence rating: IIID)

[Sarcomas, soft-tissue (treatment)][1]
[Ewing's sarcoma (treatment)][1]
[Lymphomas, Hodgkin's (treatment)][1] or
[Lymphatics, non-Hodgkin's (treatment)][1]—Ifosfamide is used for treatment of soft-tissue sarcomas, Ewing's sarcoma, and Hodgkin's and non-Hodgkin's lymphomas.

[Carcinoma, breast (treatment)][1]
[Carcinoma, cervical (treatment)]
[Carcinoma, lung, small cell (treatment)][1]
[Carcinoma, lung, non-small cell (treatment)][1]
[Carcinoma, ovarian epithelial (treatment)][1]
[Leukemia, acute lymphocytic (treatment)][1]
[Neuroblastoma (treatment)][1] or
[Osteosarcoma (treatment)][1]—Ifosfamide is indicated for treatment of breast carcinoma, cervical carcinoma, small cell lung carcinoma, non-small cell lung carcinoma, ovarian epithelial carcinoma, acute lymphocytic leukemia, neuroblastoma, and osteosarcoma.

[Tumors, germ cell, ovarian (treatment)][1]—Ifosfamide, in combination therapy, is considered reasonable medical therapy at some point in the management of germ cell ovarian tumors (Evidence rating: IIID).

[Carcinoma, bladder (treatment)][1] or
[Carcinoma, endometrial (treatment)][1]—Ifosfamide, alone and in combination with other chemotherapeutic agents, is considered reasonable medical therapy at some point in the management of bladder carcinoma (Evidence rating: IIID) and endometrial carcinoma (Evidence rating: IIIA).

[Carcinoma, thymic (treatment)][1] or
[Thymoma (treatment)][1]—Ifosfamide is indicated for the treatment of relapsed or refractory thymoma and thymic carcinoma.

[Wilms' tumor (treatment)][1]—Ifosfamide is indicated, alone or in combination with other chemotherapeutic agents, as second-line therapy for the treatment of Wilms' tumor in patients who have not responded to or whose disease has progressed during previous treatment(Evidence rating: IIID).

[1]Not included in Canadian product labeling.

Pharmacology/Pharmacokinetics

Physicochemical characteristics

Molecular weight—261.09.

Mechanism of action/Effect

Ifosfamide is classified as an alkylating agent of the nitrogen mustard type. After metabolic activation, active metabolites of ifosfamide alkylate or bind with many intracellular molecular structures, including nucleic acids. The cytotoxic action is primarily due to cross-linking of strands of DNA and RNA, as well as inhibition of protein synthesis.

Distribution

Active metabolites cross the blood-brain barrier to only a limited extent.

Biotransformation

Hepatic (including initial activation and subsequent degradation). Metabolic pathways appear to be saturated at high doses.

Half-life

At single doses of 3.8 to 5 grams per square meter of body surface area—
Biphasic: Terminal—15 hours.

At doses of 1.6 to 2.4 grams per square meter of body surface area per day—Monophasic: 7 hours.

Elimination

Renal, 70 to 86%; 61% unchanged at single doses of 5 grams per square meter of body surface area. 12 to 18% unchanged at doses of 1.2 to 2.4 grams per square meter of body surface area.

Precautions to Consider

Carcinogenicity

Secondary malignancies are potential delayed effects of many antineoplastic agents, although it is not clear whether the effect is related to their mutagenic or immunosuppressive action. The effects of dose and duration of therapy are also unknown, although risk seems to increase with long-term use. Although information is limited, available data seem to indicate that the carcinogenic risk is greatest with the alkylating agents.

Studies in rats have found ifosfamide to be carcinogenic, with female rats showing a significant incidence of leiomyosarcomas and mammary fibroadenomas.

Mutagenicity

Ifosfamide has been shown to be mutagenic in bacterial studies *in vitro* and mammalian cells *in vivo*. *In vivo*, ifosfamide has induced mutagenic effects in mice and *Drosophila melanogaster* germ cells, and has induced a significant increase in dominant lethal mutations in male mice as well as recessive sex-linked lethal mutations in *Drosophila*.

Pregnancy/Reproduction

Fertility—Gonadal suppression, resulting in amenorrhea or azoospermia, may occur in patients taking antineoplastic therapy, especially with the alkylating agents. In general, these effects appear to be related to dose and length of therapy and may be irreversible. Prediction of the degree of testicular or ovarian function impairment is complicated by the common use of combinations of several antineoplastics, which makes it difficult to assess the effects of individual agents.

Pregnancy—First trimester: It is usually recommended that use of antineoplastics, especially combination chemotherapy, be avoided whenever possible, especially during the first trimester. Although information is limited because of the relatively few instances of antineoplastic administration during pregnancy, the mutagenic, teratogenic, and carcinogenic potential of these medications must be considered.

Other hazards to the fetus include adverse reactions seen in adults.

In general, use of a contraceptive is recommended during cytotoxic drug therapy.

Studies in animals have shown that ifosfamide is teratogenic in mice, rats, and rabbits given 0.05 to 0.075 times the human dose.

FDA Pregnancy Category D.

Breast-feeding

Ifosfamide is distributed into breast milk. Breast-feeding is not recommended during chemotherapy because of the risks to the infant (adverse effects, mutagenicity, carcinogenicity).

Pediatrics

Appropriate studies on the relationship of age to the effects of ifosfamide have not been performed in the pediatric population. However, no pediatrics-specific problems have been documented to date.

Geriatrics

No information is available on the relationship of age to the effects of ifosfamide in geriatric patients. However, elderly patients are more likely to have age-related renal function impairment, which may require caution.

Dental

The bone marrow depressant effects of ifosfamide may result in an increased incidence of microbial infection, delayed healing, and gingival bleeding. Dental work, whenever possible, should be completed prior to initiation of therapy or deferred until blood counts have returned to normal. Patients should be instructed in proper oral hygiene during treatment, including caution in use of regular toothbrushes, dental floss, and toothpicks.

Ifosfamide may also rarely cause stomatitis associated with considerable discomfort.

Drug interactions and/or related problems

The following drug interactions and/or related problems have been selected on the basis of their potential clinical significance (possible mechanism in parentheses where appropriate)—not necessarily inclusive (» = major clinical significance):

Note: Combinations containing any of the following medications, depending on the amount present, may also interact with this medication.

Blood dyscrasia-causing medications (see *Appendix II*)
(leukopenic and/or thrombocytopenic effects of ifosfamide may be increased with concurrent or recent therapy if these medications cause the same effects; dosage adjustment of ifosfamide, if necessary, should be based on blood counts)

» Bone marrow depressants, other (see *Appendix II*) or
» Radiation therapy
(additive bone marrow depression may occur; dosage reduction may be required when two or more bone marrow depressants, including radiation, are used concurrently or consecutively)

Hepatic enzyme inducers (see *Appendix II*)
(these agents may induce microsomal metabolism to increase formation of alkylating metabolites of ifosfamide; although it is unknown whether activity of ifosfamide is increased, neurotoxicity may be increased; caution is recommended)

Nephrotoxic medications
(prior or concurrent use with ifosfamide may increase ifosfamide's nephrotoxic effects)
(previous use of large cumulative doses of cisplatin may increase the risk of central nervous system (CNS) toxicity with ifosfamide)

Vaccines, killed virus
(because normal defense mechanisms may be suppressed by ifosfamide therapy, the patient's antibody response to the vaccine may be decreased. The interval between discontinuation of medications that cause immunosuppression and restoration of the patient's ability to respond to the vaccine depends on the intensity and type of immunosuppression-causing medication used, the underlying disease, and other factors; estimates vary from 3 months to 1 year)

» Vaccines, live virus
(because normal defense mechanisms may be suppressed by ifosfamide therapy, concurrent use with a live virus vaccine may potentiate the replication of the vaccine virus, may increase the side/adverse effects of the vaccine virus, and/or may decrease the patient's antibody response to the vaccine; immunization of these patients should be undertaken only with extreme caution after careful review of the patient's hematologic status and only with the knowledge and consent of the physician managing the ifosfamide therapy. The interval between discontinuation of medications that cause immunosuppression and restoration of the patient's ability to respond to the vaccine depends on the intensity and type of immunosuppression-causing medication used, the underlying disease, and other factors; estimates vary from 3 months to 1 year. Patients with leukemia in remission should not receive live virus vaccine until at least 3 months after their last chemotherapy. In addition, immunization with oral poliovirus vaccine should be postponed in persons in close contact with the patient, especially family members)

Laboratory value alterations

The following have been selected on the basis of their potential clinical significance (possible effect in parentheses where appropriate)—not necessarily inclusive (» = major clinical significance).

With physiology/laboratory test values

Alanine aminotransferase (ALT [SGPT]) and
Aspartate aminotransferase (AST [SGOT]) and
Lactate dehydrogenase (LDH)
(serum values may be increased as a sign of hepatotoxicity)

Bilirubin
(serum concentrations may be increased as a sign of hepatotoxicity)

Blood urea nitrogen (BUN) or
Creatinine, serum
(concentrations may be increased transiently as a sign of renal toxicity)

Creatinine clearance
(may be decreased transiently as a sign of renal toxicity)

Medical considerations/Contraindications

The medical considerations/contraindications included have been selected on the basis of their potential clinical significance (reasons given in parentheses where appropriate)—not necessarily inclusive (» = major clinical significance).

Risk-benefit should be considered when the following medical problems exist:

» Bone marrow depression
» Chickenpox, existing or recent (including recent exposure) or
» Herpes zoster
(risk of severe generalized disease)

» Hepatic function impairment
(effect of ifosfamide may be reduced or enhanced because of its dependence on hepatic microsomal enzyme activation and degradation)

» Infection

» Renal function impairment
(reduced elimination; incidence of CNS toxicity and renal toxicity may be increased; dosage reduction may be necessary)

Sensitivity to ifosfamide

Tumor cell infiltration of bone marrow
(bone marrow depression)

» Caution should be used also in patients who have had previous cytotoxic drug therapy or radiation therapy.

Patient monitoring

The following are especially important in patient monitoring (other tests may be warranted in some patients, depending on condition; » = major clinical significance):

Alanine aminotransferase (ALT [SGPT]) values, serum and
Alkaline phosphatase values, serum and
Aspartate aminotransferase (AST [SGOT]) values, serum and

Lactate dehydrogenase (LDH) values, serum
(recommended prior to initiation of therapy and at periodic intervals during therapy; frequency varies according to clinical state, agent, dose, and other agents being used concurrently)

Bilirubin, concentrations, serum and
Blood urea nitrogen (BUN) concentrations and
Creatinine concentrations, serum
(recommended prior to initiation of therapy and at periodic intervals during therapy; frequency varies according to clinical state, agent, dose, and other agents being used concurrently)

» Examination of urine for microscopic hematuria
(recommended prior to each dose)

» Hematocrit or hemoglobin and
» Leukocyte count, total and, if appropriate, differential and
» Platelet count
(determinations recommended prior to initiation of therapy and at periodic intervals during therapy; frequency varies according to clinical state, agent, dose, and other agents being used concurrently)

Phosphate concentrations, serum and
Potassium concentrations, serum
(recommended at periodic intervals during therapy)

Side/Adverse Effects

Note: Many "side effects" of antineoplastic therapy are unavoidable and represent the medication's pharmacologic action. Some of these (for example, leukopenia and thrombocytopenia) are actually used as parameters to aid in individual dosage titration.

The following side/adverse effects have been selected on the basis of their potential clinical significance (possible signs and symptoms in parentheses where appropriate)—not necessarily inclusive:

Those indicating need for medical attention

Incidence more frequent—dose-related

CNS effects or encephalopathy (agitation; confusion; hallucinations; unusual tiredness; less frequently, dizziness; rarely, seizures; coma); ***leukopenia; thrombocytopenia*** (rarely associated with unusual bleeding or bruising; black, tarry stools; blood in urine or stools; pinpoint red spots on skin); ***urotoxicity, including hemorrhagic cystitis; dysuria; urinary frequency*** (blood in urine; frequent urination; painful urination)

Note: *CNS effects and encephalopathy* do not appear to be dose-related. They may be associated with electroencephalogram (EEG) changes. Signs and symptoms usually resolve within 3 days after withdrawal of ifosfamide, but may persist longer. Fatalities have been reported.

Leukopenia is usually mild to moderate. Nadir of leukocyte count occurs within 7 to 14 days and counts usually recover by 21 days after a course.

With *thrombocytopenia*, nadir of platelet count occurs within 7 to 14 days and counts usually recover by 21 days after a course.

Urotoxicity may occur within a few hours or be delayed by several weeks; it is thought to be caused by a metabolite of ifosfamide (acrolein). Urotoxicity usually resolves a few days after withdrawal of ifosfamide, but may persist and may be fatal. Incidence is reduced by fractionation of dosage, adequate hydration, and administration of mesna.

Incidence less frequent

Hepatotoxicity; infection, resulting from leukopenia (fever or chills; cough or hoarseness; lower back or side pain; painful or difficult urination); ***nephrotoxicity; phlebitis*** (redness, swelling, or pain at site of injection)

Note: *Hepatotoxicity* is usually asymptomatic and detected on laboratory tests.

Nephrotoxicity is usually asymptomatic with signs of tubular damage detected on laboratory tests. Metabolic acidosis as a manifestation of *nephrotoxicity* has been reported to occur frequently in patients receiving high doses of ifosfamide. Renal tubular acidosis, Fanconi syndrome, and renal rickets have been reported.

Incidence rare

Cardiotoxicity; polyneuropathy; pulmonary toxicity (cough or shortness of breath); ***stomatitis*** (sores in mouth and on lips)

Those indicating need for medical attention only if they continue or are bothersome

Incidence more frequent

Nausea and vomiting

Note: *Nausea and vomiting* are usually controlled by antiemetics.

Those not indicating need for medical attention

Incidence more frequent

Loss of hair

Those indicating the need for medical attention if they occur after medication is discontinued

Hemorrhagic cystitis (blood in urine)

Patient Consultation

As an aid to patient consultation, refer to *Advice for the Patient, Ifosfamide (Systemic)*.

In providing consultation, consider emphasizing the following selected information (» = major clinical significance):

Before using this medication

» Conditions affecting use, especially:
Sensitivity to ifosfamide
Pregnancy—Use not recommended because of mutagenic, teratogenic, and carcinogenic potential; advisability of using contraception; telling physician immediately if pregnancy is suspected
Breast-feeding—Not recommended because of risk of serious side effects
Other medications, especially other bone marrow depressants, previous cytotoxic drug therapy or radiation therapy
Other medical problems, especially chickenpox, herpes zoster, hepatic function impairment, infection, renal function impairment

Proper use of this medication

Caution in taking combination therapy; taking each medication at the right time

Importance of ample fluid intake and subsequent increase in urine output, as well as frequent voiding (including at least once during night), to prevent hemorrhagic cystitis and aid in excretion of uric acid; following physician instructions for recommended fluid intake; some patients may require up to 3000 mL (3 quarts) per day

Probability of nausea and vomiting; importance of continuing medication despite stomach upset

» Proper dosing

Precautions while using this medication

» Importance of close monitoring by physician

» Avoiding immunizations unless approved by physician; other persons in patient's household should avoid immunizations with oral poliovirus vaccine; avoiding other persons who have taken oral poliovirus vaccine within the past several months or wearing a protective mask that covers nose and mouth

Caution if bone marrow depression occurs:

» Avoiding exposure to persons with infections, especially during periods of low blood counts; checking with physician immediately if fever or chills, cough or hoarseness, lower back or side pain, or painful or difficult urination occurs

» Checking with physician immediately if unusual bleeding or bruising; black, tarry stools; blood in urine or stools; or pinpoint red spots on skin occur

Caution in use of regular toothbrush, dental floss, or toothpick; physician, dentist, or nurse may suggest alternatives; checking with physician before having dental work done

Not touching eyes or inside of nose unless hands washed immediately before

Using caution to avoid accidental cuts with use of sharp objects such as safety razor or fingernail or toenail cutters

Avoiding contact sports or other situations where bruising or injury might occur

Side/adverse effects

May cause adverse effects such as blood problems; loss of hair; toxicity to lungs, heart, liver, or bladder; and cancer; importance of discussing possible effects with physician

Signs of potential side effects, especially CNS effects, leukopenia, thrombocytopenia, urotoxicity, hepatotoxicity, infection, nephrotoxicity, phlebitis, cardiotoxicity, polyneuropathy, pulmonary toxicity, and stomatitis

Physician or nurse can help in dealing with side effects

Possibility of hair loss; normal hair growth should return after treatment has ended

General Dosing Information

Patients receiving ifosfamide should be under supervision of a physician experienced in cancer chemotherapy.

A variety of dosage schedules and regimens of ifosfamide, alone or in combination with other antitumor agents, are used. The prescriber may consult the medical literature as well as the manufacturer's literature in choosing a specific dosage.

Dosage must be adjusted to meet the individual requirements of each patient, based on clinical response and appearance or severity of toxicity.

To reduce the risk of hemorrhagic cystitis, adequate hydration is recommended prior to ifosfamide treatment and for at least 72 hours following treatment to ensure ample urine output. Concurrent use of an agent to prevent hemorrhagic cystitis (such as mesna) is recommended. In addition, the patient should be encouraged to void frequently to prevent prolonged contact of irritating metabolites with bladder mucosa.

Development of mild bladder irritation (microscopic hematuria) may require adjustment of mesna dosage. Although concurrent use of mesna greatly reduces the risk, ifosfamide should be discontinued at the first sign of hemorrhagic cystitis. In severe cases, blood replacement may be necessary. Electrocautery diversion of urine flow, cryosurgery, and formaldehyde bladder instillations have been used. Resumption of therapy should be undertaken with caution since recurrence is common.

Each subsequent dose should be given only after microscopic hematuria, if present (defined as greater than 10 red blood cells per high power field), has resolved.

Ifosfamide therapy should be discontinued if severe CNS symptoms occur.

Special precautions are recommended in patients who develop thrombocytopenia as a result of administration of ifosfamide. These may include extreme care in performing invasive procedures; regular inspection of intravenous sites, skin (including perirectal area), and mucous membrane surfaces for signs of bleeding or bruising; limiting frequency of venipuncture and avoiding intramuscular injections; testing urine, emesis, stool, and secretions for occult blood; care in use of regular toothbrushes, dental floss, toothpicks, safety razors, and fingernail and toenail cutters; avoiding constipation; and using caution to prevent falls and other injuries. Such patients should avoid alcohol and any aspirin intake because of the risk of gastrointestinal bleeding. Platelet transfusions may be required.

Patients who develop leukopenia should be observed carefully for signs of infection. Antibiotic support may be required. In neutropenic patients who develop fever, broad-spectrum antibiotic coverage should be initiated empirically, pending bacterial cultures and appropriate diagnostic tests.

If marked leukopenia (particularly granulocytopenia) or thrombocytopenia occurs, ifosfamide therapy should be withdrawn until leukocyte and platelet counts return to satisfactory levels. Then therapy may be reinstituted, possibly at a lower dose.

Safety considerations for handling this medication

There is limited but increasing evidence and concern that personnel involved in preparation and administration of parenteral antineoplastics may be at some risk because of the potential mutagenicity, teratogenicity, and/or carcinogenicity of these agents, although the actual risk is unknown. USP advisory panels recommend cautious handling both in preparation and disposal of antineoplastic agents. Precautions that have been suggested include:

- Use of a biological containment cabinet during reconstitution and dilution of parenteral medications and wearing of disposable surgical gloves and masks.
- Use of proper technique to prevent contamination of the medication, work area, and operator during transfer between containers (including proper training of personnel in this technique).
- Cautious and proper disposal of needles, syringes, vials, ampuls, and unused medication.

A number of medical centers have developed detailed guidelines for handling of antineoplastic agents.

Combination chemotherapy

Ifosfamide may be used in combination with other agents in various regimens. As a result, incidence and/or severity of side effects may be altered and different dosages (usually reduced) may be used. For example, ifosfamide is part of the following chemotherapeutic combinations (some commonly used acronyms are in parentheses):

—etoposide, ifosfamide, and cisplatin (VIP).
—vinblastine, ifosfamide, and cisplatin (VeIP).

For specific dosages and schedules, consult the literature. For information regarding each agent, consult the individual monograph.

Parenteral Dosage Forms

Note: Bracketed uses in the *Dosage Forms* section refer to categories of use and/or indications that are not included in U.S. product labeling.

STERILE IFOSFAMIDE USP

Usual adult and adolescent dose

Germ cell testicular tumors[1]—

Intravenous infusion (over at least thirty minutes), 1.2 grams per square meter of body surface area per day for five consecutive days, the course being repeated every three weeks or after hematologic recovery.

Note: Mesna is also administered during ifosfamide therapy to reduce hemorrhagic cystitis.

[Carcinoma, breast][1] or
[Carcinoma, cervical] or
[Carcinoma, head and neck][1] or
[Carcinoma, lung, non-small cell][1] or
[Carcinoma, lung, small cell][1] or
[Carcinoma, ovarian epithelial][1] or
[Ewing's sarcoma][1] or
[Leukemia, acute lymphocytic][1] or
[Lymphomas, Hodgkin's][1] or
[Lymphomas, non-Hodgkin's][1] or
[Neuroblastoma][1] or
[Osteosarcoma][1] or
[Sarcomas, soft-tissue] or
[Tumors, germ cell, ovarian][1] or
[Carcinoma, bladder][1] or
[Carcinoma, endometrial][1] or
[Wilms' tumor][1]—

Consult medical literature or manufacturer's literature for information on appropriate dosage.

[Carcinoma, thymic][1] or
[Thymoma][1]—

Because several doses and regimens using ifosfamide are showing activity, no individual dose/regimen is listed here. Consult medical literature and/or experts in the field of oncology for information on dosage.

Usual pediatric dose

Dosage has not been established.

Strength(s) usually available

U.S.—

1 gram (Rx) [*IFEX* (plus 1 gram vial of mesna)].
3 grams (Rx) [*IFEX* (plus 1 gram vial of mesna)].

Canada—

1 gram (Rx) [*IFEX*].
2 grams (Rx) [*IFEX*].
3 grams (Rx) [*IFEX*].

Packaging and storage

Store below 40 °C (104 °F), preferably between 15 and 30 °C (59 and 86 °F), unless otherwise specified by manufacturer.

Preparation of dosage form

May be prepared for parenteral use by adding 20, 40, or 60 mL of sterile water for injection or bacteriostatic water for injection (benzyl alcohol– or paraben-preserved) to the 1-gram, 2-gram, or 3-gram vial, respectively, and shaking to dissolve, to provide a solution containing 50 mg of ifosfamide per mL. The resulting solution may be added to 5% dextrose injection, 0.9% sodium chloride injection, lactated Ringer's injection, or sterile water for injection for administration by intravenous infusion. Use of intermediate concentrations or mixtures of excipients (e.g., 2.5% dextrose injection, 0.45% sodium chloride injection, 5% dextrose and 0.9% sodium chloride injection) is also acceptable.

Caution: Use of diluents containing benzyl alcohol is not recommended for preparation of medications for use in neonates. A fatal toxic syndrome consisting of metabolic acidosis, CNS depression, respiratory problems, renal failure, hypotension, and possibly seizures and intracranial hemorrhages has been associated with this use.

Stability

Reconstituted or diluted solutions of ifosfamide are stable for up to 24 hours in a refrigerator (2 to 8 °C [36 to 46 °F]).

Note

Because ifosfamide for injection contains no preservative, caution in preparing and storing solutions is required to ensure sterility.

Ifosfamide and mesna may be mixed in the same infusion.

[1]Not included in Canadian product labeling.

Revised: 04/24/2002

ILOPROST Inhalation†

VA CLASSIFICATION (Primary): CV900

Commonly used brand name(s): *Ventavis*.

Note: For a listing of dosage forms and brand names by country availability, see *Dosage Forms* section(s).

†Not commercially available in Canada.

Category

Antihypertensive (pulmonary).

Indications

Accepted

Pulmonary arterial hypertension (treatment)—Iloprost is indicated for the treatment of pulmonary arterial hypertension (WHO Group I) in patients with NYHA class III or IV symptoms.

Pharmacology/Pharmacokinetics

Physicochemical characteristics

Source—Iloprost is a synthetic analogue of prostacyclin PGI_2. Iloprost consists of a mixture of the 4R and 4S diastereomers at a ratio of approximately 53:47.

Molecular weight—Iloprost: 360.49.

Solubility—Iloprost is an oily substance, soluble in methanol, ethanol, ethyl acetate, acetone and pH 7 buffer, sparingly soluble in buffer pH 9, and very slightly soluble in distilled water, buffer pH 3, and buffer pH 5.

Mechanism of action/Effect

Iloprost dilates systemic and pulmonary arterial vascular beds. It also affects platelet aggregation; however, the relevance of this to the treatment of pulmonary hypotension is unknown. The two diastereoisomers of iloprost, 4S and 4R isomer differ in potency in dilating blood vessels, 4S isomer is substantially more potent than the 4R isomer.

Absorption

The absolute bioavailability of inhaled iloprost has not been determined.

Distribution

Volume of distribution (Vol_D)—Steady-state: 0.7 to 0.8 L/kg in healthy subjects, following intravenous infusion.

Protein binding

Moderate 60% mainly to albumin; concentration-independent in the range of 30 to 3000 pg/mL.

Biotransformation

Iloprost is metabolized via beta-oxidation of the carboxyl side chain. The primary metabolite is tetranor-iloprost, which is found in urine in free and conjugated form. Tetranor-iloprost was found to be pharmacologically inactive in animal studies.

In vitro studies revealed that cytochrome P450-dependent metabolism plays only a minor in the biotransformation of iloprost.

Half-life

20 to 30 minutes following an intravenous administered dose of 1 to 3 ng/kg/min.

Peak serum concentration

Approximately 150 pg/mL following inhalation of 5 mcg dose in patients with pulmonary hypertension.

Elimination

Urine: 68%; 14 hours post-dose in healthy subjects.

Fecal: 12%; 14 hours post-dose in healthy subjects.

Clearance: approximately 20 mL/min/kg in normal subjects.

Precautions to Consider

Tumorigenicity

No evidence of tumorigenicity was revealed in Sprague-Dawley rats given oral doses of iloprost clathrate up to 125 mg/kg/day for 8 months, followed by 16 months at 100 mg/kg day or in mice given oral doses up to 125 mg/kg/day for up to 24 months.

Mutagenicity

No mutagenic potential was observed in bacterial and mammalian cells in the presence or absence of extrinsic metabolic activation. Iloprost was negative for chromosomal aberrations *in vitro* in human lymphocytes and was not clastogenic *in vivo* in NMRI/SPF mice.

Pregnancy/Reproduction

Fertility—No impairment in fertility was observed in male or female Han-Wistar rats given intravenous doses up to 1 mg/kg/day.

Pregnancy—Adequate and well controlled studies in pregnant women have not been done. Iloprost should be used during pregnancy only if the potential benefit justifies the potential risk to the fetus.

Studies done in pregnant rats given intravenous doses of iloprost at 0.01 mg/kg/day led to shortened digits of the thoracic extremity in fetuses and pups. However, in comparable studies in pregnant Sprague-Dawley rats given oral doses up to 50 mg/kg/day, and in pregnant rabbits given intravenous doses up to 0.5 mg/kg/day, and in pregnant monkeys given doses up to 0.04 mg/kg/day, no digital anomalies or other gross-structural abnormalities were observed in the fetus/pups. However, in gravid Sprague-Dawley rats significant increases in the number of non-viable fetuses was observed at a maternally toxic dose of iloprost at 250 mg/kg/day, and in Han Wistar rats was found to be embryolethal in 15 of 44 litters at an intravenous dose of 1 mg/kg/day.

FDA Pregnancy Category C

Breast-feeding

It is not known whether iloprost is distributed into human breast milk. Because many drugs are distributed in human milk and because of the potential for serious adverse reactions in nursing infants, a decision should be made taking into the account the importance of the drug to the mother.

Studies done in rats revealed higher mortality rates in the pups of lactating dams given intravenous doses of iloprost at doses of 1 mg/kg/day and maternally toxic oral doses of 250 mg/kg/day.

Pediatrics

Safety and efficacy in pediatric patients have not been established.

Geriatrics

No information is available on the relationship of age to the effects of iloprost in geriatric patients. However, elderly patients are more likely to have age related decreases in hepatic, renal, or cardiac function and concomitant disease or other drug therapy which may require caution in dosage selection usually starting at the low end of the dosing range.

Drug interactions and/or related problems

The following drug interactions and/or related problems have been selected on the basis of their potential clinical significance (possible mechanism in parentheses where appropriate)—not necessarily inclusive (» = major clinical significance):

Note: Combinations containing any of the following medications, depending on the amount present, may also interact with this medication.

Anticoagulants
(iloprost inhibits platelet function; increased risk of bleeding, particularly in patients maintained on anticoagulants.)

Antihypertensive drugs or
Vasodilators
(iloprost may increase the hypotensive effects)

Drugs that increase the risk of syncope
(syncope can occur particularly in association with physical exertion and may reflect a therapeutic gap or insufficient efficacy; the need to adjust the dose or a change in therapy should be considered)

Medical considerations/Contraindications

The medical considerations/contraindications included have been selected on the basis of their potential clinical significance (reasons given in parentheses where appropriate)—not necessarily inclusive (» = major clinical significance).

Except under special circumstances, this medication should not be used when the following medical problem exists:

» Hypersensitivity to iloprost or any of its ingredients

Risk-benefit should be considered when the following medical problems exist:

Asthma, severe
Chronic obstructive pulmonary disease
Pulmonary infections, acute
(caution; iloprost has not been evaluated in patients with these conditions)

Hepatic function impairment
(caution during iloprost therapy in patients with hepatic impairment; iloprost exposure increased with hepatic impairment)

» Hypotension
(iloprost should not be initiated in patients with systolic blood pressure less than 85 mm Hg)

Renal function impairment
(caution in treating patients with renal impairment; the effect of dialysis on iloprost exposure has not been evaluated)

Patient monitoring

The following may be especially important in patient monitoring (other tests may be warranted in some patients, depending on condition; » = major clinical significance):

» Vital signs
(monitor while initiating iloprost treatment)

Side/Adverse Effects

The following side/adverse effects have been selected on the basis of their potential clinical significance (possible signs and symptoms in parentheses where appropriate)—not necessarily inclusive:

Those indicating need for medical attention

Incidence unknown

Chest pain; congestive heart failure (chest pain; decreased urine output; dilated neck veins; extreme fatigue; irregular breathing; irregular heartbeat; shortness of breath; swelling of face, fingers, feet, or lower legs; tightness in chest; troubled breathing; weight gain; wheezing); ***dyspnea*** (shortness of breath; difficult or labored breathing; tightness in chest; wheezing); ***kidney failure; peripheral edema*** (bloating or swelling of face, arms, hands, lower legs, or feet; rapid weight gain; tingling of hands or feet; unusual weight gain or loss); ***supraventricular tachycardia*** (fainting; fast, pounding, or irregular heartbeat or pulse; palpitations)

Those indicating need for medical attention only if they continue or are bothersome

Incidence more frequent

Abnormal lab test; alkaline phosphate increased; back pain; cough increased; flu syndrome (chill; cough; diarrhea; fever; general feeling of discomfort or illness; headache; joint pain; loss of appetite; muscle aches and pains; nausea; runny nose; shivering; sore throat; sweating; trouble sleeping; unusual tiredness or weakness vomiting); ***flushing*** (feeling of warmth; redness of the face, neck, arms and occasionally, upper chest); ***GGT increased; headache; hemoptysis*** (coughing or spitting up blood); ***hypotension*** (blurred vision, confusion, dizziness, faintness, or lightheadedness when getting up from a lying or sitting position suddenly; sweating; unusual tiredness or weakness); ***insomnia*** (sleeplessness; trouble sleeping; unable to sleep); ***muscle cramps; nausea; palpitations*** (fast, irregular, pounding, or racing heartbeat or pulse); ***syncope*** (fainting); ***trismus*** (difficulty opening the mouth; lockjaw; muscle spasm, especially of neck and back); ***vomiting***

Incidence less frequent

Pneumonia (chest pain; cough; fever or chills; sneezing; shortness of breath; sore throat; troubled breathing; tightness in chest; wheezing); ***tongue pain***

Overdose

For more information on the management of overdose or unintentional ingestion, **contact a poison control center** (see *Poison Control Center Listing*).

Clinical effects of overdose

The following effects have been selected on the basis of their potential clinical significance (possible signs and symptoms in parentheses where appropriate)—not necessarily inclusive:

Diarrhea; flushing (feeling of warmth; redness of the face, neck, arms and occasionally, upper chest); ***headache; hypotension*** (blurred vision; confusion; dizziness, faintness, or lightheadedness when getting up from a lying or sitting position suddenly; sweating; unusual tiredness or weakness); ***nausea; vomiting***

Treatment of overdose

There is no known specific antidote to iloprost. Treatment is generally interruption of the inhalation session, monitoring and symptomatic measures.

Patients in whom intentional overdose is confirmed or suspected should be referred for psychiatric consultation.

Patient Consultation

As an aid to patient consultation, refer to *Advice for the Patient, Iloprost (Inhalation).*

In providing consultation, consider emphasizing the following selected information (» = major clinical significance):

Before using this medication

» Conditions affecting use, especially:
Hypersensitivity to iloprost or any of its ingredients

Pregnancy—Iloprost should be used during pregnancy only if the potential benefit justifies the potential risk to the fetus.

Breast-feeding—It is not known whether iloprost is distributed into human breast milk. Because many drugs are distributed in human milk and because of the potential for serious adverse reactions in nursing infants, a decision should be made taking into the account the importance of the drug to the mother.

Use in children—Safety and efficacy in pediatric patients have not been established.

Use in the elderly—Elderly patients may have age related decreases in hepatic, renal, or cardiac function and concomitant disease or other drug therapy, which may require caution in dosage selection usually starting at the low end of the dosing range.

Other medical problems, especially hypotension

Proper use of this medication

» The importance of proper administration techniques including dosing frequency, ampule dispensing, Prodose® AAD® System operation, and equipment cleaning.

» The importance of proper dosing intervals of not less than 2 hours apart

» The importance of a back-up Prodose® AAD® System, to avoid potential interruptions in drug delivery due to equipment malfunctions.

» Discarding any remaining solution in the medication chamber after each inhalation session

» Proper dosing
Missed dose: Taking as soon as possible; not doubling doses

» Proper storage

Precautions while using this medication

» Advising patients that they may have a drop in blood pressure and may become dizzy or faint

Side/adverse effects

Signs of potential side effects, especially chest pain, congestive heart failure, dyspnea, kidney failure, peripheral edema, or supraventricular tachycardia

General Dosing Information

The importance of advising patients to use iloprost only as prescribed with the Prodose® AAD® System, following the manufacturer's instructions.

The importance of proper administration techniques, including dosing frequency, ampule dispensing, Prodose® AAD® System operation, and equipment cleaning.

Advising patients that they may have a drop in blood pressure, and may become dizzy or faint; they should stand up slowly when getting up from a sitting or lying position. If fainting gets worse, a dosage reduction may be required.

Advising patients that iloprost should be inhaled at intervals of not less than 2 hours and the benefits of iloprost may not last 2 hours.

Patients should have easy access to a back-up Prodose® AAD® System to avoid potential interruptions in drug delivery due to equipment malfunctions.

The importance of discarding any remaining solution in the medication chamber after each inhalation session to prevent unpredictable dosing.

Considering alternative treatments such as intravenous epoprostenol in patients who deteriorate on iloprost treatment.

Treatment of adverse events

Pulmonary edema can occur when inhaled iloprost is administered to patients with pulmonary hypertension. Should signs of pulmonary edema occur, treatment should be stopped immediately as this may be a sign of pulmonary venous hypertension.

Inhalation Dosage Forms

Note: Bracketed information in the *Indications* section refers to uses that are not included in U.S. product labeling.

ILOPROST FOR INHALATION

Usual adult dose

Pulmonary arterial hypertension—
Inhalation, 2.5 mcg first dose; if well tolerated, dosing may be increased to 5 mcg and maintained at that dose, taken 6 to 9 times per day, but not more than every 2 hours during waking hours.

Note: Renal impairment: Dose adjustment is not required in patients not on dialysis. The effect of dialysis on iloprost is unknown.

Hepatic impairment: Caution should be exercised during iloprost therapy in patients with at least Child Pugh Class B hepatic impairment.

Usual adult prescribing limits
Up to 45 mcg (5 mcg 9 times per day).

Usual pediatric dose
Safety and efficacy in pediatric patients have not been established.

Usual geriatric dose
See *Usual adult dose.*

Usual geriatric prescribing limits
See *Usual adult prescribing limits.*

Strength(s) usually available
U.S.—

0.01 mg per mL (Rx) [*Ventavis* (ethanol; hydrochloric acid; sodium chloride; tromethamine; water for injection)].

Packaging and storage
Store between 20 and 25 °C (68 and 77 °F), excursions permitted to 15 and 30 °C (59 and 86 °F).

Preparation of dosage form
For each inhalation session, the entire contents of one ampule of iloprost should be transferred into the Prodose® AAD® System medication chamber immediately before use. See the manufacturer's package insert for instructions.

Incompatibilities
Direct mixing of iloprost with other medications in the Prodose® AAD® system has not been evaluated.

Auxiliary labeling
- May cause dizziness
- Do not take by mouth
- For inhalation only

Caution
Iloprost should not be allowed to come into contact with the skin or eyes; oral ingestion of iloprost should be avoided.

Developed: 06/09/2005

IMATINIB Systemic

VA CLASSIFICATION (Primary): AN300

Commonly used brand name(s): *Gleevec.*

Note: For a listing of dosage forms and brand names by country availability, see *Dosage Forms* section(s).

Category
Antineoplastic.

Indications
Note: Bracketed information in the *Indications* section refers to uses that are not included in U.S. product labeling.

Accepted
[Acute lymphoblastic leukemia, Philadelphia chromosome-positive, newly diagnosed, as part of combination chemotherapy]—Imatinib mesylate as part of combination therapy has demonstrated activity in the treatment of patients with Philadelphia chromosome-positive acute lymphoblastic leukemia. Complete responses exceed 90% with greater than 50% attaining minimal residual disease negativity. In light of subsequent stem cell transplantation, overall impact on survival remains to be determined. Various dosing and administration schedules result in different rates of hematologic and nonhematologic toxicities. Optimal dosing and timing of imatinib mesylate is not yet defined in this setting.

Leukemia, chronic myeloid (treatment)—Imatinib is indicated for the treatment of patients with chronic myeloid leukemia (CML) in blast crisis, accelerated phase, or in chronic phase after failure of interferon-alpha therapy.

Imatinib is indicated for the treatment of adult patients with newly diagnosed CML in chronic phase.

Imatinib is indicated for the treatment of pediatric patients with Ph+ chronic phase CML whose disease has recurred after stem cell transplant or who are resistant to interferon-alpha therapy.

Note: Effectiveness is based on overall hematologic and cytogenetic response rates. There are no controlled trials demonstrating a clinical benefit, such as improvement in disease-related symptoms or increased survival.

Tumors, gastrointestinal stromal (treatment)[1]—Imatinib is indicated for the treatment of Kit (CD117) positive unresectable and/or metastatic gastrointestinal stromal tumors (GISTs).

Acceptance not established
Use of imatinib for the *treatment of idiopathic hypereosinophilic syndrome* has not been established. USP Experts recognize that this is a rare disorder; however, they agree that more data are needed before this indication can be considered accepted.

[1]Not included in Canadian product labeling.

Pharmacology/Pharmacokinetics

Physicochemical characteristics
Molecular weight—589.7.

Solubility—Very soluble in water and soluble in aqueous buffers (pH ≤ 5.5), with variable solubility in non-aqueous solvents. Very slightly soluble to insoluble in neutral/alkaline aqueous buffers.

Mechanism of action/Effect
A protein-tyrosine kinase inhibitor, imatinib mesylate, inhibits the abnormally functioning Bcr-Abl tyrosine kinase which is produced by the Philadelphia chromosome abnormality found in chronic myeloid leukemia (CML). Imatinib inhibits cell proliferation and induces apoptosis (programmed cell death) in the Bcr-Abl cell lines and in the leukemic cells generated by CML. Imatinib also inhibits proliferation and induces apoptosis in gastrointestinal stromal tumor (GIST) cells, which express an activating c-kit mutation.

Other actions/effects
In vitro studies demonstrate that imatinib is not entirely selective, as it also inhibits c-Kit and the receptor tyrosine kinases for platelet-derived growth factor (PDGF) and stem cell factor (SCF) (including PDGF- and SCF-mediated cellular events).

Absorption
After oral administration, imatinib is well absorbed with a mean absolute bioavailability of 98%.

Protein binding
Very high (95%), mostly albumin and α_1-acid glycoprotein.

Biotransformation
Via hepatic metabolism and cytochrome P450 enzymes (especially CYP3A4), imatinib is converted to its main circulating active metabolite, a N-demethylated piperazine derivative. This derivative, as shown *in vitro* , has similar potency to imatinib and comprises about 15% of the AUC ("area under the curve") for imatinib.

Half-life
Elimination—Approximately 18 and 40 hours, for imatinib and its primary metabolite, respectively.

Time to peak concentration
2 to 4 hours.

Elimination
Fecal—68% within 7 days (20% of dose unchanged).

Renal—13% within 7 days (5% of dose unchanged).

Note: The pharmacokinetics of imatinib were similar in CML and GIST patients.

Precautions to Consider

Carcinogenicity and Tumorigenicity
The urogenital tract from a 2-year carcinogenicity study in rats receiving doses of 15, 30, and 60 mg per kg per day of imatinib mesylate showed renal adenomas/carcinomas, urinary bladder papillomas and papillomas/carcinomas of the preputial and clitoral gland. Evaluation of other organs in the rats is ongoing. The papilloma/carcinoma of the preputial/clitoral gland were noted at 30 and 60 mg per kg per day (approximately 0.5 to 4 times the human daily exposure at 400 mg per day). The kidney adenoma/carcinoma and the urinary bladder papilloma were noted at 60 mg per kg per day. No tumors in the urogenital tract were observed at 15 mg per kg per day.

Mutagenicity
Positive genotoxic effects were demonstrated in an *in vitro* mammalian cell assay (Chinese hamster ovary) for clastogenicity (chromosome aberrations) in the presence of metabolic activation. Two intermediates, present in the final product, are positive for mutagenesis in the Ames assay.One of these intermediates was also positive in the mouse lymphoma assay. Imatinib was not genotoxic when tested in an *in vitro* bacterial cell assay (Ames test), an *in vitro* mammalian cell assay (mouse lymphoma) and an *in vivo* rat micronucleus assay.

Pregnancy/Reproduction

Fertility—In both male and female rat fertility studies, negative effects were not seen when rats were given doses ≤ 20 mg per kg (mg/kg). After dosing male rats at 60 mg/kg (approximately equal to maximum clinical dose for humans or 800 mg/day, based on body surface area) for 70 days prior to mating, testicular and epididymal weights and percent motile sperm were decreased. After dosing female rats at 60 mg/kg, post-implantation fetal loss significantly increased and the number of live fetuses decreased.When female rats were dosed 14 days prior to mating and through to gestational Day 6, thee was no effect on mating or on number of pregnant females. Female rats dosed with 45 mg per kg of imatinib from gestational Day 6 until the end of lactation experienced red vaginal discharge on either Day 14 or 15.

Pregnancy—No adequate and well controlled studies have been done in pregnant women. Women of childbearing potential should be advised to avoid becoming pregnant. If imatinib is used during pregnancy or if the patient becomes pregnant while taking imatinib, the patient should be told of the potential hazard to the fetus.

Imatinib was teratogenic in rats when given during organogenesis at doses ≥ 100 mg/kg (approximately equal to the maximum clinical dose for humans or 800 mg/day, based on body surface area). These effects included: exencephaly or encephalocele, absent or reduced frontal bones, and absent parietal bones. At doses more than 100 mg/kg, total fetal loss occurred in all animals.

FDA Pregnancy Category D.

Breast-feeding

It not known whether imatinib or its metabolites are distributed into human breast milk. It is estimated that approximately 1.5% of a maternal dose of imatinib is distributed into breast milk. Although very little information is available regarding distribution of antineoplastic agents in human breast milk, breast-feeding is not recommended during chemotherapy because of the potential risks to the infant (adverse effects, mutagenicity, carcinogenicity). Imatinib is distributed into the milk of rats.

Pediatrics

Appropriate studies performed to date have not demonstrated pediatric-specific problems that would limit the usefulness of imatinib in children 3 years of age and older with Ph+ chronic phase CML with recurrence after stem cell transplantation or resistance to interferon-alpha therapy.Safety and efficacy have not been established for the treatment of other conditions in pediatric patients

Geriatrics

Appropriate CML clinical studies performed to date have not demonstrated geriatrics-specific problems that would limit the usefulness of imatinib in the elderly. A higher frequency of edema has occurred in patients > 65 years of age. In the GIST study, no obvious differences in the safety or efficacy were noted in patients >65 years; however, the small number of patients (29% >60 years and 10% >70 years) limits a formal analysis.

Dental

The bone marrow depressant effects of imatinib may result in an increased incidence of microbial infection, delayed healing, and gingival bleeding. Dental work, whenever possible, should be completed prior to initiation of therapy or deferred until blood counts have returned to normal. Patients should be instructed in proper oral hygiene during treatment, including caution in use of regular toothbrushes, dental floss, and toothpicks.

Drug interactions and/or related problems

The following drug interactions and/or related problems have been selected on the basis of their potential clinical significance (possible mechanism in parentheses where appropriate)—not necessarily inclusive (» = major clinical significance):

Note: Combinations containing any of the following medications, depending on the amount present, may also interact with this medication.

» Acetaminophen
(may increase systemic exposure to acetaminophen when administered concomitantly with imatinib)

Blood dyscrasia-causing medications (see *Appendix II*)
(neutropenic and/or thrombocytopenic effects of imatinib may be increased with concurrent or recent therapy if these medications cause the same effects; dosage adjustment of imatinib, if necessary, should be based on blood counts; cytopenias are dependent on the stage of disease and are more frequent in accelerated phase CML or blast crisis than in chronic phase CML)

» Bone marrow depressants, other (see *Appendix II*) or
Radiation therapy
(additive bone marrow depression may occur; dosage reduction may be required when two or more bone marrow depressants, including radiation, are used concurrently or consecutively)

» Enzyme Inducers, hepatic, cytochrome P450 (isoenzyme CYP3A4), including (see *Appendix II*):
Carbamazepine or
Dexamethasone or
Phenobarbital or
Phenytoin or
Rifampicin or
St. John's Wort
(CYP3A4 inducers may increase imatinib metabolism and therefore decrease imatinib plasma concentrations; alternative therapeutic agents with less enzyme induction potential should be considered)

» Enzyme Inhibitors, hepatic, cytochrome P450 (isoenzyme CYP3A4), including (see *Appendix II*):
Clarithromycin or
Erythromycin or
Grapefruit juice or
Itraconazole or
Ketoconazole
(CYP3A4 inhibitors may decrease imatinib metabolism and therefore increase imatinib plasma concentrations; caution is warranted; significant increase in imatinib plasma concentration with concurrent use of ketoconazole)

Enzyme Substrates, hepatic, cytochrome P450 (isoenzyme CYP2D6), including:
Beta-blockers
Cyclophosphamide or
Morphine or
Oxycodone or
Serotonin-H_3 antagonists
(imatinib may increase the plasma concentration of other CYP2D6 metabolized medications; imatinib inhibits the isoenzyme CYP2D6 *in vitro;* no specific studies have been performed; caution is recommended)

» Cyclosporine or
Dihydropyridine calcium channel blockers or
» Pimozide or
Simvastatin or
HMG-CoA reductase inhibitors, other, certain or
Triazolo-benzodiazepines
(imatinib may increase the plasma concentration of other CYP3A4 metabolized medications; use caution as some medications have a narrow therapeutic window)

Vaccines, killed virus
(because normal defense mechanisms may be suppressed by imatinib therapy, the patient's antibody response to the vaccine may be decreased. The interval between discontinuation of medications that cause immunosuppression and restoration of the patient's ability to respond to the vaccine depends on the intensity and type of immunosuppression-causing medications used, the underlying disease, and other factors; estimates vary from 3 months to 1 year)

» Vaccines, live virus
(because normal defense mechanisms may be suppressed by imatinib therapy, concurrent use with a live virus vaccine may potentiate the replication of the vaccine virus, may increase the side/adverse effects of the vaccine virus, and/or may decrease the patient's antibody response to the vaccine; immunization of these patients should be undertaken only with extreme caution after careful review of the patient's hematologic status and only with the knowledge and consent of the physician managing the imatinib therapy. The interval between discontinuation of medications that cause immunosuppression and restoration of the patient's ability to respond to the vaccine depends on the intensity and type of immunosuppression-causing medications used, the underlying disease, and other factors; estimates vary from 3 months to 1 year. Patients with leukemia in remission should not receive live virus vaccine until at least 3 months after their last chemotherapy. Immunization with oral poliovirus vaccine should also be postponed in persons in close contact with the patient, especially family members)

» Warfarin
(patients who require anticoagulation should receive low-molecular weight or standard heparin due to competitive metabolism with the CYP2C9 and CYP3A4 isoenzymes by imatinib)

Laboratory value alterations

The following have been selected on the basis of their potential clinical significance (possible effect in parentheses where appropriate)—not necessarily inclusive (» = major clinical significance).

With physiology/laboratory values

Alanine aminotransferase (ALT [SGPT]), serum and
Alkaline phosphatase, serum and
Aspartate aminotransferase (AST [SGOT]), serum and
Bilirubin, serum
Creatinine, serum
(values may be increased during therapy)

Albumin
(value may be decreased during therapy)

Medical considerations/Contraindications

The medical considerations/contraindications included have been selected on the basis of their potential clinical significance (reasons given in parentheses where appropriate)—not necessarily inclusive (» = major clinical significance).

Except under special circumstances, this medication should not be used when the following medical problem exists:

» Hypersensitivity to imatinib

Risk-benefit should be considered when the following medical problems exist:

» Anemia or
» Leukopenia or
» Neutropenia or
» Thrombocytopenia
(if severe, should be corrected before initiation of imatinib therapy; patients should be closely monitored)
» Bone marrow depression
» Caution should be used in patients who have had previous cytotoxic drug therapy and radiation therapy.
» Chickenpox, existing or recent (including recent exposure) or
» Herpes zoster
(risk of severe generalized disease)
» Hepatic impairment
(exposure to imatinib may be increased; patients should be closely monitored)
» Infection

Patient monitoring

The following are especially important in patient monitoring (other tests may be warranted in some patients, depending on condition; » = major clinical significance):

Alanine aminotransferase (ALT [SGPT]) and
Alkaline phosphatase, serum and
Aspartate aminotransferase (AST [SGOT]) and
Bilirubin, serum
(determinations recommended prior to initiation of therapy and then monthly or as clinically indicated; treatment with imatinib may cause Grade 3 severity liver function tests, especially seen in myeloid blast and accelerated phase clinical trials)

Blood urea nitrogen (BUN) concentrations and
Creatinine, serum
(recommended at periodic intervals during therapy; no long-term safety studies have been done on humans; some animal testing has demonstrated potential toxicity with long-term use)

» Hematocrit or hemoglobin and
» Leukocyte count, total and, if appropriate, differential and
» Platelet count
(complete blood counts recommended after start of therapy: weekly for 1 month, biweekly for the second month, then periodically as clinically indicated)

Weight
(monitor regularly for unexpected rapid weight gain; severe fluid retention and superficial edema reported in 1–8% of patients)

Side/Adverse Effects

Note: Many side effects of antineoplastic therapy are unavoidable and represent the medication's pharmacologic action. Some of these (for example, leukopenia, neutropenia, and thrombocytopenia) are actually used as parameters to aid in individual dosage titration.

The majority of patients treated with imatinib experienced adverse effects during treatment, most of which were mild to moderate in severity.

A mix of adverse effects represent local or general fluid retention including pleural effusion, ascites, pulmonary edema, and rapid weight gain (with or without superficial edema). Severe cases occurred in 2 to 8% of patients taking imatinib for CML. Severe superficial edema was reported in 2 to 5% of the patients with CML. In patients taking imatinib for GIST, severe superficial edema and severe fluid retention (pleural effusion, pulmonary edema and ascites) were reported in 1 to 6%. These adverse effects, which seem dose related, were more common in the blast crisis and accelerated phase studies (dose of 600 mg/day) and were more common in the elderly. Treatment of these effects were usually managed by treatment cessation and with diuretics and other supportive care measures. Some of these adverse effects can be serious or life threatening.

The overall safety profile of pediatric patients was similar to that of adults, except that musculoskeletal pain was less frequent and peripheral edema was not reported.

Adverse effects are reported without establishment of a cause and effect relationship to the treatment.

The following side/adverse effects have been selected on the basis of their potential clinical significance (possible signs and symptoms in parentheses where appropriate)—not necessarily inclusive:

Those indicating need for medical attention

Incidence more frequent (>25%)

Anemia (pale skin; troubled breathing, exertional; unusual bleeding or bruising; unusual tiredness or weakness); ***edema*** (decreased urination; rapid weight gain; bloating or swelling of face, hands, lower legs, and/or feet)—more common in the elderly; may involve local or general fluid retention, watch for pleural effusion or pulmonary edema; ***hemorrhage*** (bleeding problems); ***neutropenia*** (black, tarry stools; chest pain; chills; cough; fever; painful or difficult urination; shortness of breath; sore throat; sores, ulcers, or white spots on lips or in mouth; swollen glands; unusual bleeding or bruising; unusual tiredness or weakness)—episode duration usually lasts two to three weeks; ***thrombocytopenia*** (black, tarry stools; chest pain; chills; cough; fever; painful or difficult urination; shortness of breath; sore throat; sores, ulcers, or white spots on lips or in mouth; swollen glands; unusual bleeding or bruising; unusual tiredness or weakness)—episode duration usually lasts three to four weeks

Incidence less frequent (10–25%)

Dyspnea (shortness of breath; difficult or labored breathing); ***hypokalemia*** (convulsions; decreased urine; dry mouth; irregular heartbeat; increased thirst; loss of appetite; mood changes; muscle pain or cramps; nausea or vomiting; numbness or tingling in hands, feet, or lips; shortness of breath; unusual tiredness or weakness); ***influenza*** (chills; cough, nonproductive; fever, abrupt onset; general feeling of discomfort or illness; headache; muscle aches and pains; runny nose; shivering; sore throat; sweating; unusual tiredness or weakness); ***petechiae*** (small red or purple spots on skin); ***pneumonia*** (chest pain; cough; fever or chills; sneezing; shortness of breath; sore throat; troubled breathing; tightness in chest; wheezing); ***upper respiratory tract infection*** (ear congestion; nasal congestion; chills; cough; fever; sneezing; sore throat; body aches or pain; headache; loss of voice; runny nose; unusual tiredness or weakness; difficulty in breathing)

Incidence rare (<10%)

Cerebral hemorrhage (blurred vision; headache sudden and severe; inability to speak; seizures; slurred speech; temporary blindness; weakness in arm and/or leg on one side of the body, sudden and severe); ***gastrointestinal hemorrhage*** (black, tarry stools; bloody stools; vomiting of blood or material that looks like coffee grounds); ***tumor hemorrhage***—GIST only

Those indicating need for medical attention only if they continue or are bothersome

Incidence more frequent (>25%)

Abdominal pain (stomach pain); ***arthralgia*** (joint pain); ***diarrhea*** (increased bowel movements; loose stools); ***fatigue*** (unusual tiredness or weakness); ***headache; muscle cramps; musculoskeletal pain*** (muscle or bone pain); ***myalgia*** (muscle pain)—reported less frequent for CML; ***nausea and vomiting; skin rash; pyrexia*** (fever)—reported less frequent for GIST; ***weight gain***

Incidence less frequent (10–25%)

Anorexia (loss of appetite; weight loss); ***asthenia*** (lack or loss of strength); ***back pain; constipation*** (difficulty having a bowel movement (stool)); ***cough; dizziness; dyspepsia*** (acid indigestion; upset stomach); ***ecchymoses*** (bruising; large, flat, blue or purplish patches in the skin); ***epistaxis*** (bloody nose); ***flatulence*** (bloated full feeling; excess air or gas in stomach or intestines; passing gas); ***insomnia*** (sleeplessness; trouble sleeping; unable to sleep); ***lacrimation, increased*** (watering of eyes); ***nasopharyngitis*** (stuffy nose; sore throat); ***night sweats; pruritus*** (itching skin); ***rigors*** (feeling unusually cold; shivering); ***sore throat; taste disturbance*** (change in taste; bad unusual or unpleasant (after)taste); ***weakness***

Overdose

For more information on the management of overdose or unintentional ingestion, **contact a poison control center** (see *Poison Control Center Listing*).

Clinical effects of overdose

Experience with doses greater than 800 mg is limited.

Treatment of overdose

There is no known specific antidote to imatinib. Treatment is generally symptomatic and supportive.

Patients in whom intentional overdose is confirmed or suspected should be referred for psychiatric consultation.

Patient Consultation

As an aid to patient consultation, refer to *Advice for the Patient, Imatinib (Systemic)*.

In providing consultation, consider emphasizing the following selected information (» = major clinical significance):

Before using this medication

» Conditions affecting use, especially:
- Hypersensitivity to imatinib
- Studies in rats found renal adenomas/carcinomas, urinary bladder papillomas and papillomas/carcinomas of the preputial and clitoral gland. No tumors in the urogenital tract were observed at 15 mg per kg per day.
- Positive genotoxic effects were demonstrated in an *in vitro* mammalian cell assay (Chinese hamster ovary) for clastogenicity (chromosome aberrations). Imatinib was not genotoxic when tested in an *in vitro* bacterial cell assay (Ames test), an *in vitro* mammalian cell assay (mouse lymphoma) and an *in vivo* rat micronucleus assay.
- Pregnancy—Not recommended for use during pregnancy
- Breast-feeding—Not recommended because of risk of serious side effects
- Pediatric safety and efficacy only established in children over 3 years of age with Ph+ chronic phase CML whose disease has recurred after stem cell transplant or who are resistant to interferon-alpha
- Higher frequency of edema
- Other medications and foods, especially acetaminophen, bone marrow depressants, carbamazepine, clarithromycin, cyclosporine, dexamethasone, erythromycin, grapefruit juice, itraconazole, ketoconazole, phenobarbital, phenytoin, pimozide, rifampicin, St. John's Wort, vaccines (live virus), or warfarin
- Other medical problems, especially anemia, bone marrow depression, chicken pox, herpes zoster, infection, leukopenia, neutropenia, hepatic function impairment, or thrombocytopenia

Proper use of this medication

» Importance of not taking more or less medication than the amount prescribed

» Taking medication with food and water

Importance of not taking imatinib with grapefruit juice, grapefruit, or grapefruit-containing products.

» Proper dosing

Not taking at all; not doubling doses

Proper storage

Precautions while using this medication

» Importance of close monitoring by the physician

» Avoiding immunizations unless approved by physician; other persons in patient's household should avoid immunizations with oral poliovirus vaccine; avoiding other persons who have taken oral poliovirus vaccine or wearing a protective mask that covers nose and mouth

Caution if bone marrow depression occurs:

» Avoiding exposure to persons with infections, especially during period of low blood counts; checking with physician immediately if fever or chills, cough or hoarseness, lower back or side pain, or painful or difficult urination occurs

» Checking with physician immediately if unusual bleeding or bruising; black, tarry stools; blood in urine; or pinpoint red spots on skin occur

Caution in use of regular toothbrush, dental floss, or toothpick; physician, dentist, or nurse may suggest alternatives; checking with physician before having dental work done

Not touching eyes or inside of nose unless hands washed immediately before

Using caution to avoid accidental cuts with use of sharp objects such as safety razor or fingernail or toenail cutters

Avoiding contact sports or other situations where bruising or injury could occur

Side/adverse effects

Signs of potential side effects, especially anemia, edema, hemorrhage, neutropenia, thrombocytopenia, dyspnea, hypokalemia, petechiae, pneumonia, upper respiratory tract infection, cerebral hemorrhage, gastrointestinal hemorrhage, or tumor hemorrhage

General Dosing Information

Treatment with imatinib should be initiated by a physician experienced with CML or GIST treatment and should continue as long as the patient benefits.

Treatment with imatinib is often associated with cytopenias (neutropenia or thrombocytopenia). Complete blood counts should be done weekly for the first month, biweekly for the second month, and periodically as clinically indicated (e.g., every two to three months). Cytopenias are dependent on the disease stage and are more frequent in patients with accelerated phase CML of blast crisis than in patients with chronic phase CML. In the GIST trial, cytopenias were more frequent at a dose of 600 mg and in patients with Grade 3 disease.

Special precautions are recommended in patients who develop thrombocytopenia as a result of administration of imatinib. These may include: extreme care in performing invasive procedures; regular inspection of intravenous sites, skin (including perirectal area), and mucous membrane surfaces for signs of bleeding or bruising; limiting frequency of venipuncture and avoiding intramuscular injections; testing urine, emesis, stool and secretions for occult blood; care in use of toothbrushes, dental floss, toothpicks, safety razors, and fingernail and toenail cutters; avoiding constipation; and using caution to prevent falls and other injuries. Such patients should avoid alcohol and any aspirin intake because of the risk of gastrointestinal bleeding. Platelet transfusions may be required.

Patients who develop leukopenia should be observed carefully for signs of infection. Antibiotic support may be required. In neutropenic patients who develop fever, broad-spectrum antibiotic coverage should be initiated empirically, pending bacterial cultures and appropriate diagnostic tests.

Diet/Nutrition

Imatinib sometimes causes gastrointestinal irritation and should be taken with food and a large glass of water to minimize this problem.

Imatinib should not be taken with grapefruit juice due to the possible inhibition of the metabolism of imatinib by substances in grapefruit.

For treatment of adverse effects

Many toxicity-related problems, such as kidney and liver toxicity, or immunosuppression can usually be managed by dose reduction and/or treatment interruption. Toxicities may develop from long-term use (more than six months) of imatinib and no long-term safety data exists.

Oral Dosage Forms

Note: Bracketed uses in the *Dosage Forms* section refer to categories of use and/or indications that are not included in U.S. product labeling.

IMATINIB MESYLATE CAPSULES

Note: Dose and strength of imatinib mesylate are expressed in terms of the base.

Usual adult dose

Leukemia, chronic myeloid, accelerated phase or blast crisis—

Oral, 600 mg (base) once daily with a meal and a large glass of water. Treatment should continue as long as the patient continues to benefit.

Note: Dose increase to 800 mg daily (given as 400 mg twice daily) may be considered in the absence of severe adverse drug reaction and severe non-leukemia related neutropenia or thrombocytopenia in the following circumstances: disease progression (at any time); failure to achieve a satisfactory hematologic response after at least three months of treatment; loss of a previously achieved hematologic response.

Note: Treatment changes for severe hematologic reactions (after at least one month of treatment): if absolute neutrophil count (ANC) drops below 0.5 x 10^9 cells/L and/or platelets drop below 10 x 10^9 cells/L, see procedure list (below):
- Check if cytopenia is related to leukemia by marrow aspirate or biopsy procedure.
- If cytopenia is unrelated to leukemia, reduce imatinib dose to 400 mg/day.

• If cytopenia persists for 2 weeks, further reduce imatinib dose to 300 mg/day.
• If cytopenia persists for 4 weeks and is not related to leukemia, stop imatinib dosing until ANC increases to at least 1 x 10^9 cells/L and platelets increase to at least 20 x 10^9 cells/L. Then, resume treatment at 300 mg/day.

Note: If a severe non-hematologic adverse reaction occurs (severe hepatotoxicity or severe fluid retention), imatinib treatment should be stopped until the event subsides. Treatment can be restarted as appropriate depending on the initial severity of the event.

If bilirubin levels exceed more than 3 times the institutional upper limit of normal (IULN) or if liver transaminases exceed more than 5 times the IULN, stop imatinib treatment until bilirubin levels have dropped below 1.5 times the IULN or transaminase levels have dropped below 2.5 times the IULN. Then, imatinib treatment may continue at a reduced daily dose (i.e., from 600 to 400 mg).

Leukemia, chronic myeloid, chronic phase—
Oral, 400 mg (base) once daily with a meal and a large glass of water.

Note: Dose increase to 600 mg daily may be considered in the absence of severe adverse drug reaction and severe non-leukemia related neutropenia or thrombocytopenia in the following circumstances: disease progression (at any time); failure to achieve a satisfactory hematologic response after at least three months of treatment; loss of a previously achieved hematologic response.

Note: Treatment changes for severe hematologic reactions: if absolute neutrophil count (ANC) drops below 1 x 10^9 cells/L and/or platelets drop below 50 x 10^9 cells/L, see procedure list (below):

• Stop imatinib dosing until ANC increases to at least 1.5 x 10^9 cells/L and platelets increase to at least 75 x 10^9 cells/L.
• Resume imatinib treatment at dose of 400 mg/day.
• If cytopenia recurs with the ANC dropping below 1 x 10^9 cells/L and platelets dropping below 50 x 10^9 cells/L, then stop imatinib dosing until ANC increases to at least 1.5 x 10^9 cells/L and platelets increase to at least 75 x 10^9 cells/L. Then, resume treatment at 300 mg/day.

Note: If a severe non-hematologic adverse reaction occurs (severe hepatotoxicity or severe fluid retention), imatinib treatment should be stopped until the event subsides. Treatment can be restarted as appropriate depending on the initial severity of the event.

If bilirubin levels exceed more than 3 times the institutional upper limit of normal (IULN) or if liver transaminases exceed more than 5 times the IULN, stop imatinib treatment until bilirubin levels have dropped below 1.5 times the IULN or transaminase levels have dropped below 2.5 times the IULN. Then, imatinib treatment may continue at a reduced daily dose (i.e., from 400 to 300 mg).

Tumors, gastrointestinal stromal[1]—
Oral, 400 mg per day, increasing to 600 mg per day as needed.

[Acute lymphoblastic leukemia, Philadelphia chromosome-positive, newly diagnosed, as part of combination chemotherapy]—
Optimal dosing and timing of imatinib mesylate is not yet defined in this setting. Oral, 400 to 600 mg per day.

Usual pediatric dose
Safety and efficacy have not been established.

Usual geriatric dose
See *Usual adult dose*.

Strength(s) usually available
U.S.—
Not commercially available

Canada—
100 mg (base) (Rx) [*Gleevec* (colloidal anhydrous silica; colloidal silicon dioxide; crospovidone; gelatin; iron oxides; magnesium stearate; microcrystalline cellulose; titanium dioxide)].

Packaging and storage
Store at 25 °C (77 °F), excursions permitted between 15 and 30 °C (59 and 86 °F). Store in a tight container.

Auxiliary labeling
• Keep container tightly closed.

IMATINIB MESYLATE TABLETS
Note: Dose and strength of imatinib mesylate are expressed in terms of the base.

Usual adult dose
Leukemia, chronic myeloid, accelerated phase or blast crisis—
Oral, 600 mg (base) once daily with a meal and a large glass of water. Treatment should continue as long as the patient continues to benefit.

Note: Dose increase to 800 mg daily (given as 400 mg twice daily) may be considered in the absence of severe adverse drug reaction and severe non-leukemia related neutropenia or thrombocytopenia in the following circumstances: disease progression (at any time); failure to achieve a satisfactory hematologic response after at least three months of treatment; loss of a previously achieved hematologic response.

Note: Treatment changes for severe hematologic reactions (after at least one month of treatment): if absolute neutrophil count (ANC) drops below 0.5 x 10^9 cells/L and/or platelets drop below 10 x 10^9 cells/L, see procedure list (below):

• Check if cytopenia is related to leukemia by marrow aspirate or biopsy procedure.
• If cytopenia is unrelated to leukemia, reduce imatinib dose to 400 mg/day.
• If cytopenia persists for 2 weeks, further reduce imatinib dose to 300 mg/day.
• If cytopenia persists for 4 weeks and is not related to leukemia, stop imatinib dosing until ANC increases to at least 1 x 10^9 cells/L and platelets increase to at least 20 x 10^9 cells/L. Then, resume treatment at 300 mg/day.

Note: If a severe non-hematologic adverse reaction occurs (severe hepatotoxicity or severe fluid retention), imatinib treatment should be stopped until the event subsides. Treatment can be restarted as appropriate depending on the initial severity of the event.

If bilirubin levels exceed more than 3 times the institutional upper limit of normal (IULN) or if liver transaminases exceed more than 5 times the IULN, stop imatinib treatment until bilirubin levels have dropped below 1.5 times the IULN or transaminase levels have dropped below 2.5 times the IULN. Then, imatinib treatment may continue at a reduced daily dose (i.e., from 600 to 400 mg).

Leukemia, chronic myeloid, chronic phase—
Oral, 400 mg (base) once daily with a meal and a large glass of water.

Note: Dose increase to 600 mg daily may be considered in the absence of severe adverse drug reaction and severe non-leukemia related neutropenia or thrombocytopenia in the following circumstances: disease progression (at any time); failure to achieve a satisfactory hematologic response after at least three months of treatment; loss of a previously achieved hematologic response.

Note: Treatment changes for severe hematologic reactions: if absolute neutrophil count (ANC) drops below 1 x 10^9 cells/L and/or platelets drop below 50 x 10^9 cells/L, see procedure list (below):

• Stop imatinib dosing until ANC increases to at least 1.5 x 10^9 cells/L and platelets increase to at least 75 x 10^9 cells/L.
• Resume imatinib treatment at dose of 400 mg[1] or 600 mg.
• If cytopenia recurs with the ANC dropping below 1 x 10^9 cells/L and platelets dropping below 50 x 10^9 cells/L, then stop imatinib dosing until ANC increases to at least 1.5 x 10^9 cells/L and platelets increase to at least 75 x 10^9 cells/L. Then, resume treatment at 300 mg[2] if starting dose was 600 mg and 400 mg if starting dose was 600 mg.

Note: If a severe non-hematologic adverse reaction occurs (severe hepatotoxicity or severe fluid retention), imatinib treatment should be stopped until the event subsides. Treatment can be restarted as appropriate depending on the initial severity of the event.

If bilirubin levels exceed more than 3 times the institutional upper limit of normal (IULN) or if liver transaminases exceed more than 5 times the IULN, stop imatinib treatment until bilirubin levels have dropped below 1.5 times the IULN or transaminase levels have dropped below 2.5 times the IULN. Then, imatinib treatment may continue at a reduced daily dose (i.e., from 400 to 300 mg or 600 mg to 400 mg). In children, daily doses can be reduced under the same circumstances from 260 mg per m^2 per day to 200 mg per m^2 per day or from 340 mg per m^2 per day to 260 mg per m^2 per day.

Tumors, gastrointestinal stromal[1]—
Oral, 400 mg per day, increasing to 600 mg per day as needed.

[Acute lymphoblastic leukemia, Philadelphia chromosome-positive, newly diagnosed, as part of combination chemotherapy]—
Optimal dosing and timing of imatinib mesylate is not yet defined in this setting. Oral, 400 to 600 mg per day.

Note: If a severe non-hematologic adverse reaction occurs (severe hepatotoxicity or severe fluid retention), imatinib treatment should be stopped until the event subsides. Treatment can be restarted as appropriate depending on the initial severity of the event.

If bilirubin levels exceed more than 3 times the institutional upper limit of normal (IULN) or if liver transaminases exceed more than 5 times the IULN, stop imatinib treatment until bilirubin levels have dropped below 1.5 times the IULN or transaminase levels have dropped below 2.5 times the IULN. Then, imatinib treatment may continue at a reduced daily dose (i.e., from 400 to 300 mg or 600 mg to 400 mg). In children, daily doses can be reduced under the same circumstances from 260 mg per m² per day to 200 mg per m² per day or from 340 mg per m² per day to 260 mg per m² per day.

Usual pediatric dose

Leukemia, chronic myeloid, chronic phase—
Oral, 260 mg per m² per day for children with Ph+ chronic phase CML recurrent after stem cell transplant or who are resistant to interferon alpha therapy

Note: Daily doses may be increased under circumstances similar to those leading to an increase in adult chronic phase disease, from 260 mg per m² per day to 340 mg per m² per day as clinically indicated.

Usual geriatric dose

See *Usual adult dose.*

Strength(s) usually available

U.S.—
100 mg (base) (Rx) [*Gleevec* (colloidal silicon dioxide; crospovidone; hydroxypropyl methylcellulose; iron oxides; magnesium stearate; microcrystalline cellulose; polyethylene glycol; talc)].
400 mg (base) (Rx) [*Gleevec* (colloidal silicon dioxide; crospovidone; hydroxypropyl methylcellulose; iron oxides; magnesium stearate; microcrystalline cellulose; polyethylene glycol; talc)].

Canada—
100 mg (base) (Rx) [*Gleevec* (colloidal silicon dioxide; crospovidone; hydroxypropyl methylcellulose; iron oxides; magnesium stearate; microcrystalline cellulose; polyethylene glycol; talc)].
400 mg (base) (Rx) [*Gleevec* (colloidal silicon dioxide; crospovidone; hydroxypropyl methylcellulose; iron oxides; magnesium stearate; microcrystalline cellulose; polyethylene glycol; talc)].

Packaging and storage

Store at 25 °C (77 °F), excursions permitted between 15 and 30 °C (59 and 86 °F). Store in a tight container.

Auxiliary labeling

- Keep container tightly closed.

[1]Not included in Canadian product labeling.

Revised: 05/04/2006
Developed: 06/08/2001

IMIPENEM AND CILASTATIN Systemic

VA CLASSIFICATION (Primary): AM119

Commonly used brand name(s): *Primaxin; Primaxin IM; Primaxin IV.*

Note: For a listing of dosage forms and brand names by country availability, see *Dosage Forms* section(s).

Category

Antibacterial (systemic).

Indications

General Considerations

Imipenem is the first of a class of beta-lactam antibiotics called carbapenems. It has a very wide spectrum of activity *in vitro* , including most gram-positive and gram-negative aerobic and anaerobic bacteria. It is also stable in the presence of bacterial beta-lactamases. Imipenem is administered with an equal amount of cilastatin, a renal dehydropeptidase inhibitor that blocks the renal metabolism of imipenem and increases its urinary recovery. Cilastatin has no antibacterial activity or effect on beta-lactamases, and does not potentiate or antagonize the effects of imipenem.

Imipenem has excellent *in vitro* activity against aerobic gram-positive organisms, including most strains of staphylococci, streptococci, and some enterococci. Exceptions to this include *Enterococcus faecium*, which is usually resistant, and an increasing number of strains of methicillin-resistant *Staphylococcus aureus* and coagulase-negative staphylococci.

Imipenem also has excellent *in vitro* activity against most species of Enterbacteriaceae, including *Escherichia coli*, *Klebsiella* species, *Citrobacter* sp., *Morganella morganii*, and *Enterobacter* sp. It is slightly less potent *in vitro* against *Serratia marcescens*, *Proteus mirabilis*, indole-positive *Proteus* sp., and *Providencia stuartii.* Most strains of *Pseudomonas aeruginosa* are susceptible; however, increasing resistance has been seen in patients receiving imipenem who have advanced, refractory infections. Many strains of *Ps. cepacia* and virtually all strains of *Xanthamonas maltophilia* are resistant.

Most anaerobic species are inhibited by imipenem, including *Bacteroides* sp., *Fusobacterium* sp., and *Clostridium* sp. However, *C. difficile* is only moderately susceptible. Other susceptible organisms *in vitro* include *Campylobacter* sp., *Haemophilus influenzae*, *Neisseria gonorrhoeae*, including penicillinase-producing strains, *Yersinia enterocolitica*, *Nocardia asteroides*, and *Legionella* sp. *Chlamydia trachomatis* is resistant to imipenem.

Accepted

Bone and joint infections (treatment)—Intravenous imipenem and cilastatin combination is indicated in the treatment of bone and joint infections caused by susceptible organisms.

Endocarditis, bacterial (treatment)—Intravenous imipenem and cilastatin combination is indicated in the treatment of bacterial endocarditis caused by susceptible organisms.

Intra-abdominal infections (treatment)—Intravenous and intramuscular imipenem and cilastatin combination is indicated in the treatment of intra-abdominal infections caused by susceptible organisms.

Pelvic infections, female (treatment)—Intravenous and intramuscular imipenem and cilastatin combination is indicated in the treatment of female pelvic infections caused by susceptible organisms.

Pneumonia, bacterial (treatment)—Intravenous and intramuscular imipenem and cilastatin combination is indicated in the treatment of bacterial pneumonia caused by susceptible organisms.

Septicemia, bacterial (treatment)—Intravenous imipenem and cilastatin combination is indicated in the treatment of bacterial septicemia caused by susceptible organisms.

Skin and soft tissue infections (treatment)—Intravenous and intramuscular imipenem and cilastatin combination is indicated in the treatment of skin and soft tissue infections caused by susceptible organisms.

Urinary tract infections, bacterial (treatment)—Intravenous imipenem and cilastatin combination is indicated in the treatment of bacterial urinary tract infections caused by susceptible organisms.

[Melioidosis (treatment)][1]—Intravenous imipenem and cilastatin combination is indicated for the treatment of melioidosis.

Melioidosis is an infection with *Burkholdria pseudomallei*, previously known as *Pseudomonas pseudomallei.* It is endemic in areas of southeast Asia and the northern part of Australia. Melioidosis causes acute and chronic pulmonary disease, abscesses of the skin and internal organs, meningitis, brain abscess and cerebritis, and acute fulminant rapidly fatal sepsis. Infection with *B. pseudomallei* has a high mortality rate. It is more common among adults, individuals with diabetes, and individuals with chronic renal disease, but it can occur in normal hosts and children. Melioidosis can reactivate years after primary infection and result in chronic or acute life-threatening disease. Melioidosis should be considered as a potential diagnosis for any patient with exposure to areas of endemicity.

[Neutropenia, febrile (treatment)][1]—Intravenous imipenem and cilastatin combination is indicated for empiric treatment of febrile neutropenia.

In patients at high risk of severe infection, including patients with a history of recent bone marrow transplantation, with hypotension at presentation, with an underlying hematologic malignancy, or with severe or prolonged neutropenia, antimicrobial therapy alone may not be appropriate.

[1]Not included in Canadian product labeling.

Pharmacology/Pharmacokinetics

Physicochemical characteristics

Molecular weight—
- Imipenem: 317.36.
- Cilastatin sodium: 380.43.

pKa—
- Imipenem—
  - pKa_1—3.2
  - pKa_2—9.9
- Cilastatin sodium (with aqueous sodium hydroxide)—
  - pKa_1—2.0
  - pKa_2—4.4
  - pKa_3—9.2

Mechanism of action/Effect

Imipenem—Bactericidal; binds to penicillin-binding proteins (PBP) 1A, 1B, 2, 4, 5, and 6 of *E. coli* and to PBP 1A, 1B, 2, 4, and 5 of *Ps. aeruginosa*; this results in inhibition of bacterial cell wall synthesis; imipenem apparently has greatest affinity for PBP 1A, 1B, and 2, and the least affinity for PBP 3; imipenem's ability to bind to bacterial PBP 2 causes development of small spheres or ellipsoids without formation of filaments commonly seen with penicillins and cephalosporins, ultimately resulting in lysis and death; its lethal effect may also be related to binding to PBP 1A and 1B as well; imipenem is highly resistant to degradation by bacterial beta-lactamases and may demonstrate a "post-antibiotic" effect in some bacteria.

Cilastatin—A competitive, reversible, highly specific inhibitor of the renal dipeptidase, dehydropeptidase I (DHP I); cilastatin blocks tubular secretion of imipenem by competitive exclusion at its transport site, thereby preventing the renal metabolism of imipenem and resulting in significantly improved urinary recovery of imipenem; cilastatin may also prevent proximal renal tubular necrosis that occurs when imipenem is used alone; cilastatin does not inhibit bacterial beta-lactamases and has no intrinsic antibacterial activity.

Absorption

Bioavailability—
- Intramuscular:
  - Imipenem—95%.
  - Cilastatin—75%.

Distribution

Imipenem rapidly and widely distributed to most tissues and fluids; distributed to sputum, pleural fluid, peritoneal fluid, interstitial fluid, bile, aqueous humor, reproductive organs, and bone; highest concentrations found in pleural fluid, interstitial fluid, peritoneal fluid, and reproductive organs; low concentrations have been detected in the cerebrospinal fluid (CSF).

Vol_D—
- Neonates: 0.4 to 0.5 L/kg.
- Children (2 to 12 years old): Approximately 0.7 L/kg.
- Adults: 0.23 to 0.31 L/kg.

Protein binding

Imipenem—Low (20%).

Cilastatin—Moderate (40%).

Biotransformation

Imipenem—Renal; when given alone, imipenem is metabolized in the kidneys by hydrolysis of the beta-lactam ring caused by the renal dipeptidase, dehydropeptidase I (DHP I), resulting in low urinary concentrations; DHP I is an enzyme located on the brush border of the proximal renal tubular epithelium; DHP I acts only after imipenem has been cleared from the plasma by glomerular filtration or tubular secretion ("post-excretory" metabolism); metabolism occurs only in the tubular cell or glomerular filtrate; virtually all of the secreted fraction and approximately 75% of the filtered fraction are metabolized (a total of 60 to 95%).

Cilastatin—Metabolized to *N*-acetyl conjugate.

Half-life

Adults—
- Intravenous:
  - Normal renal function—
    - Imipenem: Approximately 1 hour.
    - Cilastatin: Approximately 1 hour.
  - Impaired renal function—
    - Imipenem: 2.9 to 4.0 hours.
    - Cilastatin: 13.3 to 17.1 hours.
- Intramuscular:
  - Normal renal function—
    - Imipenem: 2 to 3 hours.

Neonates—
- Intravenous:
  - Imipenem—1.7 to 2.4 hours.
  - Cilastatin—3.8 to 8.4 hours.

Children (2 to 12 years of age)—
- Intravenous: 1 to 1.2 hours.

Time to peak concentration

Intramuscular—
- Imipenem: Within 2 hours.
- Cilastatin: Within 1 hour.

Peak serum concentration

Imipenem—
- Intravenous: Approximately 14 to 24, 21 to 58, and 41 to 83 mcg per mL following a dose of 250 mg, 500 mg, and 1 gram, respectively, over 20 minutes.
- Intramuscular: Approximately 10 and 12 mcg per mL following a dose of 500 mg and 750 mg, respectively.

Cilastatin—
- Intravenous: Approximately 15 to 25, 31 to 49, and 56 to 80 mcg per mL following a dose of 250 mg, 500 mg, and 1 gram, respectively, over 20 minutes.
- Intramuscular: Approximately 24 and 33 mcg per mL following a dose of 500 mg and 750 mg, respectively.

Urine concentration

Imipenem—
- >10 mcg per mL up to 8 hours following a 500 mg intravenous dose.
- >10 mcg per mL for 12 hours following a 500 mg and 750 mg intramuscular dose.

Elimination

Imipenem alone—
- Renal; approximately 5 to 40% excreted in urine by both glomerular filtration and tubular secretion.

Cilastatin alone—
- Renal; approximately 70 to 78% excreted in urine within 10 hours, by both glomerular filtration and tubular secretion.
- Dialysis: Substantial amounts (approximately 40 to 82%) rapidly cleared from the blood by hemodialysis.

Imipenem with cilastatin—
- Renal; approximately 70 to 76% excreted in urine within 10 hours, by both glomerular filtration and active tubular secretion (approximately two-thirds of that amount by glomerular filtration and one-third by tubular secretion); no further urinary excretion detectable.
- Nonrenal; approximately 20 to 25% excreted by unknown nonrenal mechanism, possibly including up to 1 to 2% excreted via the bile in the feces.
- Dialysis: Substantial amounts (approximately 73 to 90%) rapidly cleared from the blood by hemodialysis. A 3-hour session of intermittent hemofiltration has removed approximately 75% of a given dose.

Precautions to Consider

Cross-sensitivity and/or related problems

Patients allergic to other beta-lactam antibacterials (e.g., penicillins, cephalosporins) may be allergic to imipenem also.

Although imipenem has been administered without incident to some patients with rash-type penicillin allergy, caution is recommended when imipenem is administered to patients with a history of penicillin anaphylaxis because of cross-reactivity.

Carcinogenicity/Mutagenicity

Gene toxicity studies such as the V79 mammalian cell mutation assay, Ames test, unscheduled DNA synthesis assay, and *in vivo* mouse cytogenicity test have shown no evidence of genetic damage with imipenem and cilastatin combination.

Pregnancy/Reproduction

Pregnancy—Studies in humans have not been done.

Studies in mice, rats, and rabbits given doses ranging from the usual human dose up to 33 times the usual human dose have not shown that imipenem, cilastatin, or the combination causes adverse effects on the fetus. Studies in pregnant cynomolgus monkeys given intravenous bolus doses of 40 mg per kg of body weight (mg/kg) per day or 160 mg/kg per day subcutaneously resulted in maternal toxicity, including emesis, inappetence, weight loss, diarrhea, abortion, and death. No significant toxicity was observed when non-pregnant cynomolgus monkeys were given subcutaneous doses of up to 180 mg/kg per day. When doses of 100 mg/kg per day were administered to pregnant cynomolgus monkeys at an intravenous infusion rate which mimics human clinical use, there was minimal maternal intolerance (occasional emesis), no maternal deaths, no teratogenicity, but an increase in embryonic loss relative to the control groups.

FDA Pregnancy Category C.

Breast-feeding
It is not known whether imipenem or cilastatin is distributed into breast milk. However, problems in humans have not been documented.

Pediatrics
The half-life of imipenem in neonates is longer (1.7 to 2.4 hours) than that in adults with normal renal function (approximately 1 hour). The half-life in older pediatric patients (2 to 12 years of age) is 1 to 1.2 hours.

The half-life of cilastatin in neonates is longer (3.8 to 8.4 hours) than that in adults with normal renal function (approximately 1 hour).

Appropriate studies have not been performed in children up to 12 years of age.

Geriatrics
No information is available on the relationship of age to the effects of imipenem and cilastatin combination in geriatric patients. However, elderly patients are more likely to have an age-related decrease in renal function, which may require a reduction of dosage in patients receiving imipenem and cilastatin.

Dental
Imipenem and cilastatin may cause glossitis (inflammation of the tongue), tongue papillar hypertrophy, and increased salivation.

Drug interactions and/or related problems
The following drug interactions and/or related problems have been selected on the basis of their potential clinical significance (possible mechanism in parentheses where appropriate)—not necessarily inclusive (» = major clinical significance):

Note: Combinations containing any of the following medications, depending on the amount present, may also interact with this medication.

Probenecid
(since concurrent use of probenecid results in only minimal increases in the serum concentrations and half-life of imipenem, concurrent use is not recommended where higher imipenem serum concentrations may be desirable)

Laboratory value alterations
The following have been selected on the basis of their potential clinical significance (possible effect in parentheses where appropriate)—not necessarily inclusive (» = major clinical significance).

With diagnostic test results

Positive direct antiglobulin (Coombs') tests
(may occur during therapy)

With physiology/laboratory test values

» Alanine aminotransferase (ALT [SGPT]), serum and
» Alkaline phosphatase, serum and
» Aspartate aminotransferase (AST [SGOT]), serum and
Lactate dehydrogenase (LDH), serum
(values may be transiently increased)

Bilirubin, serum and
Blood urea nitrogen (BUN) concentrations and
Creatinine, serum
(concentrations may be transiently increased)

Hematocrit (HCT) and
Hemoglobin (Hb) concentrations
(may be decreased)

Medical considerations/Contraindications
The medical considerations/contraindications included have been selected on the basis of their potential clinical significance (reasons given in parentheses where appropriate)—not necessarily inclusive (» = major clinical significance).

Risk-benefit should be considered when the following medical problems exist:

» Allergy to imipenem, cilastatin, or other beta-lactams (penicillin, cephalosporins)

» Central nervous system (CNS) disorders (e.g., brain lesions or history of seizures)
(seizures are more likely to occur in patients receiving higher doses of imipenem, or in patients with CNS lesions, a history of seizure disorders, or renal function impairment)

» Renal function impairment
(because imipenem and cilastatin are primarily excreted through the kidneys, this medicine must be administered in a reduced dosage to patients with impaired renal function)

Side/Adverse Effects
Note: The following side/adverse effects of imipenem and cilastatin combination are similar in nature and incidence to those of other beta-lactam antibacterials. However, the incidence of seizures is higher than that seen with other beta-lactam antibiotics; it is reported to be 1.5 to 2%. The risk of seizures increases in patients receiving more than 2 grams of imipenem per day, those with a pre-existing seizure disorder, and patients with decreased renal function.

The following side/adverse effects have been selected on the basis of their potential clinical significance (possible signs and symptoms in parentheses where appropriate)—not necessarily inclusive:

Those indicating need for medical attention
Incidence more frequent

Allergic reactions (fever; hives; itching; skin rash; wheezing); ***CNS toxicity*** (confusion; dizziness; seizures; tremors); ***thrombophlebitis*** (pain at site of injection)

Incidence less frequent

Infusion rate reaction (dizziness; nausea and vomiting; sweating; unusual tiredness or weakness)—occurs with too rapid an infusion rate

Incidence rare

Pseudomembranous colitis (abdominal or stomach cramps and pain, severe; diarrhea, watery and severe, which may also be bloody; fever)

Those indicating need for medical attention only if they continue or are bothersome
Incidence more frequent

Gastrointestinal disturbances (diarrhea; nausea and vomiting)

Those indicating the need for medical attention if they occur after medication is discontinued
Pseudomembranous colitis (severe abdominal or stomach cramps and pain; watery and severe diarrhea, which may also be bloody; fever)

Patient Consultation
As an aid to patient consultation, refer to *Advice for the Patient, Imipenem and Cilastatin (Systemic).*

In providing consultation, consider emphasizing the following selected information (» = major clinical significance):

Before using this medication
» Conditions affecting use, especially:
Allergy to imipenem or cilastatin; patients allergic to other beta-lactams may also be allergic to imipenem
Dental—Imipenem and cilastatin may cause glossitis, tongue papillar hypertrophy, and increased salivation
Other medical problems, especially CNS disorders or renal function impairment

Proper use of this medication
» Importance of receiving medication for full course of therapy and on regular schedule

» Proper dosing

Precautions while using this medication
» Continuing anticonvulsant therapy in patients with a history of seizures

» For severe diarrhea, checking with physician before taking any antidiarrheals; for mild diarrhea, taking kaolin- or attapulgite-containing, but not other, antidiarrheals; checking with physician or pharmacist if mild diarrhea continues or worsens

Side/adverse effects
Signs of potential side effects, especially allergic reactions, CNS toxicity, infusion rate reaction, pseudomembranous colitis, and thrombophlebitis

General Dosing Information
Intravenous doses of 250 or 500 mg of imipenem should be given over a 20- to 30-minute period in adults. Doses of 1 gram should be given over a 40- to 60-minute period. In pediatric patients, imipenem may be administered over a 20- to 30-minute period.

Intramuscular imipenem and cilastatin combination should be administered by deep IM injection into a large muscle mass, such as the gluteal muscles or lateral part of the thigh.

In patients receiving more than 2 grams of imipenem per day, there is an increased risk of seizures.

If a dose of this medication is missed, give it as soon as possible. However, if it is almost time for the next dose, skip the missed dose and go back to the regular dosing schedule. Do not double doses.

For treatment of adverse effects

Anticonvulsants should be continued in the treatment of patients receiving imipenem and cilastatin combination who have known seizure disorders. In patients who develop symptoms of CNS toxicity (e.g., focal tremors, myoclonus, or seizures) during treatment with imipenem, anticonvulsant therapy (e.g., phenytoin or benzodiazepines) should be initiated, and the dosage of imipenem should be reduced or the drug should be discontinued.

If an allergic reaction to imipenem and cilastatin combination occurs, the drug should be discontinued. Severe hypersensitivity reactions may require the administration of epinephrine or other emergency measures.

Some patients may develop nausea, vomiting, hypotension, dizziness, or sweating during administration of imipenem and cilastatin combination, especially after rapid infusion. If these symptoms develop, the rate of infusion should be slowed. If this is not effective, it may be necessary to discontinue the drug.

For antibiotic-associated pseudomembranous colitis (AAPMC)—

Some patients may develop AAPMC, caused by *Clostridium difficile* toxin, during or following administration of imipenem. Mild cases may respond to discontinuation of the drug alone. Moderate to severe cases may require fluid, electrolyte, and protein replacement.

In cases not responding to the above measures or in more severe cases, oral metronidazole, oral bacitracin, or oral vancomycin may be used. Oral vancomycin is effective in doses of 125 to 500 mg every 6 hours for 5 to 10 days. The dose of metronidazole is 250 to 500 mg every 8 hours for 5 to 10 days. Recurrences may be treated with a second course of these medications.

Cholestyramine and colestipol resins have been shown to bind *C. difficile* toxin *in vitro* . If cholestyramine or colestipol resin is administered in conjunction with oral vancomycin, the medications should be administered several hours apart since the resins have been shown to bind oral vancomycin also.

In addition, AAPMC may result in severe watery diarrhea which may occur during therapy or up to several weeks after therapy is discontinued. If diarrhea occurs, administration of antiperistaltic antidiarrheals is not recommended since they may delay the removal of toxins from the colon, thereby prolonging and/or worsening the diarrhea.

Parenteral Dosage Forms

IMIPENEM AND CILASTATIN FOR INJECTION USP

Usual adult and adolescent dose

Antibacterial—

Intravenous infusion, based on anhydrous imipenem content:

Mild infections—250 to 500 mg every six hours.

Moderate infections—500 mg every six to eight hours to 1 gram every eight hours.

Severe, life-threatening infections—500 mg every six hours to 1 gram every six to eight hours.

Note: Lower doses are used in the treatment of infections caused by gram-positive organisms, anaerobes, and highly susceptible gram-negative organisms. Infections caused by other gram-negative organisms require higher doses.

Uncomplicated urinary tract infections: 250 mg every six hours.

Complicated urinary tract infections: 500 mg every six hours.

Adults with impaired renal function may require a reduction in dose as given below. Doses are based on an average body weight of 70 kg. Patients weighing less than 70 kg should receive a proportional reduction in dosage.

Creatinine Clearance (mL/min/1.73 M ^{2})/(mL/sec)	Dose
>70/1.17	See *Usual adult and adolescent dose*
30–70/0.50–1.17	500 mg every 6 to 8 hours
20–30/0.33–0.50	500 mg every 8 to 12 hours
0–20/0–0.33	250 to 500 mg every 12 hours
Hemodialysis patients	Supplemental dose after hemodialysis, unless next dose scheduled within 4 hours

[Melioidosis][1]—

Intravenous, 50 mg per kg of body weight daily.

Adults with impaired renal function may require a reduction in dose as indicated above.

[Neutropenia, febrile][1]—

Intravenous, 500 mg every six hours to 1 gram every eight hours.

Adults with impaired renal function may require a reduction in dose as indicated above.

Usual adult prescribing limits

Up to a maximum of 50 mg (imipenem) per kg of body weight or 4 grams daily, whichever is lower.

Usual pediatric dose

Antibacterial or

[Melioidosis or][1]

[Neutropenia, febrile][1]—

Infants and children up to 12 years of age: Dosage has not been established.

Children 12 years of age and older: See *Usual adult and adolescent dose*.

Strength(s) usually available

U.S.—

250 mg (anhydrous imipenem) and 250 mg (cilastatin) (Rx) [*Primaxin IV*].

500 mg (anhydrous imipenem) and 500 mg (cilastatin) (Rx) [*Primaxin IV*].

Canada—

250 mg (anhydrous imipenem) and 250 mg (cilastatin) (Rx) [*Primaxin*].

500 mg (anhydrous imipenem) and 500 mg (cilastatin) (Rx) [*Primaxin*].

Packaging and storage

Prior to reconstitution, store below 30 °C (86 °F), unless otherwise specified by manufacturer.

Preparation of dosage form

To prepare initial dilution for intravenous infusion, add approximately 10 mL of diluent (see manufacturer's package insert) to each 250- or 500-mg vial (13-mL) and shake well. The resulting suspension should be transferred to not less than 100 mL of suitable intravenous fluids. Do not administer the initially prepared suspension intravenously. Add an additional 10 mL of diluent to each previously reconstituted vial and shake well. Transfer the remaining contents of the vial to the infusion container. Shake the resulting mixture well until clear. Do not administer a cloudy solution.

For reconstitution of piggyback infusion bottles (120-mL), add 100 mL of diluent (see manufacturer's package insert) to each 250- or 500-mg infusion bottle. Shake the resulting mixture well until clear. Do not administer a cloudy solution.

Stability

After reconstitution with sterile water for injection, solutions retain their potency for 8 hours at room temperature or for 48 hours if refrigerated at 4 °C (39 °F).

After reconstitution with 0.9% sodium chloride injection, solutions retain their potency for 10 hours at room temperature or for 48 hours if refrigerated at 4 °C (39 °F).

After reconstitution with other diluents, solutions retain their potency for 4 hours at room temperature or for 24 hours if refrigerated at 4 °C (39 °F).

Solutions of imipenem and cilastatin combination should not be frozen.

Solutions may vary from colorless to yellow in color; color changes within this range do not affect potency. Imipenem and cilastatin combination may become slightly discolored under strong ultraviolet (UV) light.

Incompatibilities

Extemporaneous admixtures of beta-lactam antibacterials and aminoglycosides may result in substantial mutual inactivation. If they are administered concurrently, they should be administered in separate sites. Do not mix them in the same intravenous bag or bottle.

IMIPENEM AND CILASTATIN FOR INJECTABLE SUSPENSION USP

Usual adult and adolescent dose

Antibacterial—

Intramuscular, mild to moderate infections:

Female pelvic infections and

Pneumonia and

Skin and soft tissue infections—500 to 750 mg every twelve hours.

Intra-abdominal infections—750 mg every twelve hours.

Note: Safety and efficacy have not been studied in patients with a creatinine clearance of less than 20 mL/min.

Usual adult prescribing limits

Up to 1500 mg daily.

Usual pediatric dose

Antibacterial—

Infants and children up to 12 years of age: Dosage has not been established.

Children 12 years of age and older: See *Usual adult and adolescent dose*.

Strength(s) usually available

U.S.—

500 mg (anhydrous imipenem) and 500 mg (cilastatin) (Rx) [*Primaxin IM*].

750 mg (anhydrous imipenem) and 750 mg (cilastatin) (Rx) [*Primaxin IM*].

Canada—

Not commercially available.

Packaging and storage

Prior to reconstitution, store below 30 °C (86 °F), unless otherwise specified by manufacturer.

Preparation of dosage form

To prepare initial dilution for intramuscular use, add 2 mL of 1% lidocaine injection (without epinephrine) to each 500-mg vial, or 3 mL of 1% lidocaine injection (without epinephrine) to each 750-mg vial.

Stability

After reconstitution with 1% lidocaine injection, the suspension should be used within one hour.

Suspensions are white to light tan in color; variations of color within this range do not affect the potency.

Incompatibilities

Intramuscular imipenem and cilastatin combination should not be mixed with or physically added to other antibiotics. However, it may be administered concomitantly, but at separate sites, with other antibiotics.

[1]Not included in Canadian product labeling.

Revised: 08/09/2000

IMIPRAMINE—See *Antidepressants, Tricyclic (Systemic)*

IMIQUIMOD Topical

VA CLASSIFICATION (Primary/Secondary): IM404/DE600

Commonly used brand name(s): *Aldara*.

Note: For a listing of dosage forms and brand names by country availability, see *Dosage Forms* section(s).

Category

Antineoplastic, topical; biological response modifier.

Indications

Accepted

Actinic keratoses (treatment)—Imiquimod is indicated for the topical treatment of clinically typical non-hyperkeratotic, non-hypertrophic actinic keratoses on the face or scalp in immunocompetent adults.

Carcinoma, skin (treatment)—Imiquimod is indicated for the topical treatment of biopsy-confirmed, primary superficial basal cell carcinoma (sBCC) in immunocompetent adults, with a maximum tumor diameter of 2 cm, located on the trunk (excluding anogenital skin), neck, or extremities (excluding hands and feet), only when surgical methods are medically less appropriate and patient follow-up can be reasonably assured.

Condyloma acuminatum (treatment)—Imiquimod is indicated for the treatment of external genital and perianal warts (condyloma acuminatum) in individuals 12 years of age and older. Imiquimod is not a cure and new warts may develop during treatment; effect of imiquimod on transmission of genital warts is not known.

Unaccepted

Imiquimod has not been evaluated for the treatment of urethral, intravaginal, cervical, rectal, or anal human papilloma viral disease and is not recommended for these uses.

The safety and effectiveness have not been established for treating other types of basal cell carcinomas, including nodular, morpheaform (fibrosing or sclerosing) types. The safety and effectiveness have not been established for treating superficial basal cell carcinoma (sBCC) lesions on the face, head, or anogenital area. The safety and effectiveness have not been established for treating patients with Basal Cell Nevus Syndrome or Xeroderma Pigmentosum.

Pharmacology/Pharmacokinetics

Physicochemical characteristics

Molecular weight—240.31.

Mechanism of action/Effect

The mechanism of action is not known. Imiquimod does not have direct antiviral activity. Studies of mice show that imiquimod may induce cytokines, including interferon-alpha, in mouse skin; clinical significance or relevance of this finding to humans is not known. Imiquimod potentially can exacerbate inflammatory conditions of the skin.

In one clinical trial that had a 4 to 6 ratio of females to males, 50% of patients, approximately 75% of females and 33% of males, experienced complete wart clearance after using imiquimod for 10 weeks (median, range 4 to 16 weeks). Of the remaining 50% of patients, 33% still had genital warts at 16 weeks and 17% withdrew from the clinical trial. Of those who had complete wart clearance at 10 weeks and could be followed for 12 additional weeks, 23% of patients remained wart-free.

Absorption

Percutaneous absorption is minimal for a median wart area of 69 square millimeters (mm^2) (range, 8 to 5525 mm^2).

Precautions to Consider

Carcinogenicity

In an oral (gavage) rat carcinogenicity study, imiquimod was administered to Wistar rats on a two time per week (up to 6 mg per kg of body weight per day) dosing schedule for 24 months. No treatment related tumors were noted up to the highest doses tested in this study.

In a dermal mouse carcinogenicity study, imiquimod cream (up to 5 mg per kg of body weight per application) we applied to the backs of mice three times per week for 24 months. A statistically significant increase in the incidence of liver adenomas and carcinomas was noted in high dose male mice compared to control male mice. An increased number of skin papillomas was observed in vehicle cream control group animals at the treated site only.

In a 52-week dermal photoco-carcinogenicity study, the median time to onset of skin tumor formation was decreased in hairless mice following chronic topical dosing (three times per week; 40 weeks of treatment followed by 12 weeks of observation) with concurrent exposure to UV radiation (5 days per week) with the imiquimod cream vehicle alone. No additional effect on tumor development beyond the vehicle effect was noted with the addition of the active ingredient, imiquimod, to the vehicle cream.

Mutagenicity

Imiquimod was not found to be mutagenic in a series of tests, including the Ames, mouse lymphoma, Chinese hamster ovary (CHO) chromosome aberration, human lymphocyte chromosome aberration, SHE cell transformation, rat and hamster bone marrow cytogenetics, and mouse dominant lethal test.

Pregnancy/Reproduction

Fertility—Daily oral administration of imiquimod to rats at 87 times the human MRHD, based on AUC comparisons, produced no impairment of fertility or reproduction.

Pregnancy—Adequate and well-controlled studies in humans have not been done. Problems in humans have not been documented. Imiquimod should be used during pregnancy only if the potential benefit justifies the potential risk to the fetus.

Researchers studied imiquimod's effect on reproduction in rats and rabbits. In the presence of maternal toxicity, fetal effects noted at 20 mg per kg of body weight per day (577 times MRHD based on AUC comparisons) given to pregnant female rats included increased resorptions, decreased fetal body weights, delays in skeletal ossification, bent limb bones, and two fetuses in one litter (2 of 1567 fetuses) demonstrated exencephaly, protruding tongues and low-set ears. Bent limb bones were noted when rats were administered 6 mg per kg per day (87 times MRHD based on AUC comparisons) of imiquimod. This fetal effect was also noted in the oral rat embryofetal development study conducted with imiquimod

FDA Pregnancy Category C.

Breast-feeding

It is not known whether topical imiquimod is distributed into breast milk. Problems in humans have not been documented.

Pediatrics

Safety and efficacy in patients with external genital/perianal warts less than 12 years of age have not been established. Safety and efficacy of imiquimod for actinic keratoses [AK] or superficial basal cell carcinoma (sBCC) in patients less than 18 years of age have not been established as AK and sBCC are not conditions generally seen within the pediatric population.

Geriatrics

Appropriate studies performed to date have demonstrated no geriatrics-specific problems that would limit the usefulness of imiquimod in the elderly. However, greater sensitivity of some older patients can not be ruled out.

Medical considerations/Contraindications

The medical considerations/contraindications included have been selected on the basis of their potential clinical significance (reasons given in parentheses where appropriate)—not necessarily inclusive (» = major clinical significance).

Except under special circumstances, this medication should not be used when the following medical problems exist:

» Sensitivity to imiquimod or any of its components including parabens

Risk-benefit should be considered when the following medical problem exists:

» Autoimmune conditions, pre-existing
(use with caution)

» Drug or surgical treatment affecting the skin, previous
(imiquimod treatment not recommended until the skin is completely healed from previous drug or surgical treatments)

Immunosuppression
(safety and efficacy of imiquimod in immunosuppressed patients not established)

Inflammatory skin conditions
(has the potential to exacerbate these conditions)

Sensitivity to sunlight
(exercise caution with imiquimod use; sunburn susceptibility can be heightened with use)

Sunburn
(patients should be advised to not use imiquimod until fully recovered from a sunburn)

Patient monitoring

The following may be especially important in patient monitoring (other tests may be warranted in some patients, depending on condition; » = major clinical significance):

Regular follow-up
(recommended for patients with superficial basal cell carcinoma treated with imiquimod)

Side/Adverse Effects

The following side/adverse effects have been selected on the basis of their potential clinical significance (possible signs and symptoms in parentheses where appropriate)—not necessarily inclusive:

Those indicating need for medical attention

Incidence more frequent

Application site reaction (burning, itching, redness, skin rash, swelling, or soreness at site)—can include bleeding, burning, induration, itching, pain stinging, or tenderness at target or remote site; ***erosion or excoriation of skin*** (self-induced skin lesion, such as a scratch)—30%, at site of application; ***fungal infection, including tinea cruris*** (itching in genital or other skin areas; scaling)—11% in females, 2% in males; ***scabbing***—4 to 13%, at site of application; ***sinusitis*** (pain or tenderness around eyes and cheekbones; fever; stuffy or runny nose; headache; cough; shortness of breath or troubled breathing; tightness of chest or wheezing); ***ulceration or vesicles on skin*** (blisters; open sores on skin)—3 to 5%, at site of application; ***upper respiratory tract infection*** (ear congestion; nasal congestion; chills; cough; fever; sneezing; sore throat; body aches or pain; headache; loss of voice; runny nose; unusual tiredness or weakness; difficulty in breathing)

Incidence less frequent

Atrial fibrillation (fast or irregular heartbeat; dizziness; fainting); ***chest pain***—treatment of sBCC; ***erythema, severe*** (redness of skin)—4%, at site of application; ***gout*** (ankle, knee, or great toe joint pain; joint stiffness or swelling; lower back or side pain)—treatment of sBCC; ***hernia*** (abdominal pain; lump in abdomen); ***hypercholesterolemia*** (high amount of cholesterol in the blood); ***hypertension*** (blurred vision; dizziness; nervousness; headache; pounding in the ears; slow or fast heartbeat)—treatment of sBCC; ***lymphadenopathy*** (swollen, painful, or tender lymph glands in neck, armpit, or groin)—treatment of sBCC; ***squamous carcinoma*** (persistent non-healing sore; reddish patch or irritated area; shiny bump; pink growth; white, yellow or waxy scar-like area); ***urinary tract infection*** (bladder pain; bloody or cloudy urine; difficult, burning, or painful urination; frequent urge to urinate; lower back or side pain); ***viral infection*** (chills; cough or hoarseness; fever; cold flu-like symptoms)

Incidence unknown—Observed during clinical practice, estimates of frequency can not be determined

Cardiac failure (chest pain or discomfort; dilated neck veins; extreme fatigue; irregular breathing; irregular heartbeat; shortness of breath; swelling of face, fingers, feet, or lower legs; weight gain; wheezing); ***cardiomyopathy*** (chest discomfort or pain; difficulty breathing; dizziness; faintness; fast, irregular or pounding heartbeat; shortness of breath; swelling of feet or lower legs; troubled breathing; unusual tiredness or weakness); ***cerebrovascular accident*** (blurred vision; headache; sudden and severe inability to speak; seizures; slurred speech; temporary blindness; weakness in arm and/or leg on one side of the body, sudden and severe); ***convulsions; ischemia*** (chest pain or discomfort; irregular heartbeat; nausea or vomiting; pain in the shoulders, arms, jaw or neck; sweating); ***myocardial infarction*** (chest pain or discomfort; pain in arms, jaw, back or neck; shortness of breath, nausea, sweating; vomiting); ***pulmonary edema*** (chest pain; difficult, fast, noisy breathing, sometimes with wheezing; blue lips and fingernails; pale skin; increased sweating; coughing that sometimes produces a pink frothy sputum; shortness of breath; swelling in legs and ankles); ***suicide***

Signs and symptoms of systemic effects

Influenza-like symptoms (diarrhea; fatigue; fever; headache; muscle pain)

Those indicating need for medical attention only if they continue or are bothersome

Incidence more frequent

Burning or stinging of skin, mild—26%, at remote site and at site of application; ***edema of skin*** (swelling of skin)—12 to 17%, at site of application; ***erythema, mild*** (redness of skin)—54 to 61%, at site of application; ***flaking of skin, mild***—18 to 25%, at site of application; ***headache***—treatment of sBCC; ***pain, soreness, or tenderness of skin, mild***—8%, at remote site and at site of application; ***pruritus, mild*** (itching of skin)—32%, at remote site and at site of application; ***rash***—at site of application

Incidence less frequent

Back pain—treatment of sBCC; ***fatigue*** (unusual tiredness or weakness)—treatment of sBCC; ***fever***—treatment of sBCC; ***hypopigmentation*** (lightening of normal skin color)—at site of application; ***nausea***—treatment of sBCC; ***rhinitis*** (stuffy nose; runny nose; sneezing)—treatment of sBCC

Incidence unknown—Observed during clinical practice, estimates of frequency can not be determined

Abnormal liver function (lab results that show problems with liver); ***agitation; angioedema*** (large, hive-like swelling on face, eyelids, lips, tongue, throat, hands, legs, feet, sex organs); ***arrhythmias*** (dizziness; fainting; fast, slow, or irregular heartbeat); ***capillary leak syndrome*** (cloudy urine; decrease or increase in amount of urine; fainting or lightheadedness; nausea; stomach pain; swelling of hands, ankles, feet, or lower legs); ***depression; dyspnea*** (shortness of breath; difficult or labored breathing; tightness in chest wheezing); ***exfoliative dermatitis*** (cracks in the skin; loss of heat from the body; red, swollen skin; scaly skin); ***insomnia*** (sleeplessness; trouble sleeping unable to sleep); ***multiple sclerosis aggravation; paresis*** (partial or slight paralysis); ***proteinuria*** (cloudy urine); ***syncope*** (fainting); ***thyroiditis*** (swelling of neck)

Patient Consultation

As an aid to patient consultation, refer to *Advice for the Patient, Imiquimod (Topical)*.

In providing consultation, consider emphasizing the following selected information (» = major clinical significance):

Before using this medication

» Conditions affecting use, especially:

Carcinogenicity—A significant increase in the incidence of liver adenomas and carcinomas was noted in high dose male mice compared to the control group in a dermal mouse carcinogenicity study.

Pregnancy—Potential risk benefit should be assessed for imiquimod use.

Use in children—Safety and efficacy have not been established in patients with external genital/perianal warts less than 12 years or patients with actinic keratoses or superficial basal cell carcinoma less than 18 years of age.

Other medical problems, especially previous drug or surgical treatments affecting the skin or sensitivity to imiquimod or any of its components

Proper use of this medication

» Not using occlusive dressing, such as bandages; if covering is needed, only using nonocclusive material, such as cotton gauze or cotton underclothes

Proper administration

» Importance of washing hands before and after administration to help avoid translocation of cream. Avoiding contact with eyes, lips, and nostrils

» Understanding amount to use and avoiding excessive administration

Allowing medication to remain on skin for 8 hours when treating actinic keratoses or superficial basal cell carcinoma and 6 to 10 hours when treating external genital warts; removing medication by thoroughly washing area with soap and water

Uncircumcised men treating warts under the foreskin should retract the foreskin and clean the area daily

Discarding any unused cream from the single-dose packet

» Proper dosing

Missed dose: Wait until the next evening to apply it, and then return to the normal dosing schedule

» Proper storage

Precautions while using this medication

» *For treatment of superficial basal cell carcinoma (sBCC):* Importance of keeping all appointments. Your doctor will need to check your progress at regular visits while you are using this medicine.

» Reporting severe local skin reactions and rare systemic reactions to physician

» Delaying next dose for several days when experiencing any discomfort or if severe reaction occurs as determined by physician

» Avoiding genital, oral, or anal sexual contact while the cream is on the skin; washing cream off before engaging in sexual activities. Also, oils in the cream may weaken latex contraceptive devices, such as cervical caps, condoms, and diaphragms

Imiquimod is not a cure for genital warts. New warts may develop during treatment with imiquimod.

Imiquimod will not keep you from spreading genital warts to other people.

» Avoiding use of other topical medications on the same treatment area, unless recommended by physician

» Not sharing medication with others

» Avoiding or minimizing exposure to sunlight and sunlamps during imiquimod use due to the concern for heightened sunburn susceptibility.

Importance of using protective clothing and sunscreen, especially patients who have considerable sun exposure or sensitivity to sunlight

Side/adverse effects

Application site reaction; erosion or excoriation of skin (at site of application); fungal infection, including tinea cruris; scabbing (at site of application); sinusitis; ulceration or vesicles (at site of application); upper respiratory tract infection; atrial fibrillation; chest pain; erythema, severe (at site of application); gout; hernia; hypercholesterolemia; hypertension; lymphadenopathy; squamous carcinoma; urinary tract infection; or viral infection

(Observed during clinical practice—Cardiac failure, cardiomyopathy, cerebrovascular accident, convulsions, ischemia, myocardial infarction, pulmonary edema or suicide)

(Signs or symptoms of systemic effects—Influenza-like symptoms, including myalgia)

General Dosing Information

Occlusive dressings, such as bandages, should be avoided. If covering is needed, patient should use nonocclusive material, such as cotton gauze or cotton underclothes.

It is important for patients to avoid transferring cream to uninvolved skin sites or to their partners during sexual contact and not to share medication with others. Patient should wash hands before and after administration to help avoid translocation of cream, especially to eyes, lips, and nostrils and should wash the treatment area thoroughly with mild soap and water before engaging in sexual activities. Also, oils in the cream can weaken latex contraceptive devices, such as cervical caps, condoms, and diaphragms, and reduce their efficacy. Patients should be made aware that new warts may develop during therapy, as imiquimod is not a cure. The effect of imiquimod on the transmission of genital/perianal warts is unknown.

Patient should understand correct amount of imiquimod to use and avoid excessive administration, discarding the unused portion in the single-dose packets. Patients should contact their physician promptly if they experience any sign or symptom at the application site that restricts or prohibits their daily activity or makes continued application of the cream difficult. A rest period of several days may be taken if required by the patient's discomfort or severity of the local skin reaction. Treatment with imiquimod can be resumed after the skin reaction has subsided.

Exposure to sunlight (including sunlamps) should be avoided or minimized during use of imiquimod cream because of concern for heightened sunburn susceptibility. Patients should be warned to use protective clothing including hats and to use sunscreen when using imiquimod. Patients who may have considerable sun exposure, e.g., due to their occupations, and those patients with inherent sensitivity to sunlight should exercise caution when using imiquimod.

Imiquimod treatment should continue for the full 16 weeks. However, the treatment period should not be extended beyond 16 weeks due to missed doses or rest periods.

Safety and efficacy have not been established for imiquimod in the treatment of actinic keratosis with repeated use of more than one treatment course in the same 25 cm^2 area. The safety of imiquimod applied to areas of skin greater than 25 cm^2 for the treatment of AK has not been established.

The diagnosis of superficial basal cell carcinoma should be confirmed prior to treatment.

For treatment of adverse effects

Recommended treatment consists of the following:

- Discontinuing medication or decreasing frequency of dosing as needed.
- Using nonocclusive dressing, such as gauze, or cotton underclothes to help manage skin reactions.

Topical Dosage Forms

IMIQUIMOD CREAM

Usual adult dose

Actinic keratosis—

Topical, to the defined treatment area on the face or scalp (but not both concurrently), two times per week prior to normal sleeping hours, leaving on the skin approximately 8 hours per application and removing with mild soap and water

Note: Treatment area should be one contiguous area of approximately 25 cm^2. Imiquimod should be applied to the entire treatment area (e.g., the forehead, scalp, or one cheek).

Basal cell carcinoma—

Topical, to the defined treatment area, five times per week prior to normal sleeping hours, leaving on the skin approximately 8 hours per application and removing with mild soap and water.

The treatment area should include 1 cm margin of skin around the tumor.

Target Tumor Diameter	Size of Cream Droplet to be Used (diameter)	Approximate Amount of Cream to be Used
0.5 to < 1 cm	4 mm	10 mg
≥ 1 to < 1.5 cm	5 mm	25 mg
≥ 1.5 to < 2 cm	7 mm	40 mg

Condyloma acuminatum—

Topical, to the wart, once every other day (three times a week) prior to normal sleeping hours as a thin film, rubbing in well, leaving on skin for six to ten hours, then removing medication by washing with mild soap and water. Treatment is continued until wart is gone or for up to sixteen weeks.

Note: Each single-use packet containing 250 mg of cream is sufficient to cover a wart area of up to 20 square centimeters; excessive application should be avoided.

Usual adult prescribing limits

For actinic keratoses or condyloma acuminatum, treatment period should not exceed 16 weeks

For superficial basal cell carcinoma, treatment period should not exceed 6 weeks.

Usual pediatric dose

Actinic keratoses (treatment)—

Safety and efficacy have not been established in patients less than 18 years of age.

Basal cell carcinoma (treatment)—

Safety and efficacy have not been established in patients less than 18 years of age.

Condyloma acuminatum (treatment)—
Safety and efficacy have not been established in patients less than 12 years of age.

Usual geriatric dose

See *Usual adult dose.*

Strength(s) usually available

U.S.—
5% (Rx) [*Aldara* (benzyl alcohol; cetyl alcohol; glycerin; isostearic acid; methylparaben; polysorbate 60; propylparaben; purified water; sorbitan monostearate; stearyl alcohol; white petrolatum; xanthan gum)].

Canada—
5% (Rx) [*Aldara* (benzyl alcohol; cetyl alcohol; glycerin; isostearic acid; methylparaben; polysorbate 60; propylparaben; purified water; sorbitan monostearate; stearyl alcohol; white petrolatum; xanthan gum)].

Packaging and storage

Store below 25 °C (77 °F), preferably between 15 and 30 °C (59 and 86 °F). Protect from freezing.

Auxiliary labeling

- For external use only.
- Avoid contact in or around eyes
- For single dose only. Discard unused drug.
- Avoid extended exposure to sunlight or tanning beds while taking this drug. Severe burns may result.
- Keep out of reach of children

Revised: 10/19/2005
Developed: 11/13/1997

IMMUNE GLOBULIN INTRAVENOUS (Human) Systemic

VA CLASSIFICATION (Primary/Secondary): IM402/AM900; BL900; CV900; XX000

Commonly used brand name(s): *Gamimune N 10%; Gamimune N 10% S/D; Gamimune N 5%; Gamimune N 5% S/D; Gammagard Liquid; Gammagard S/D; Gammagard S/D 0.5 g; Gammar-P IV; Iveegam; Panglobulin; Polygam S/D; Sandoglobulin; Venoglobulin-I; Venoglobulin-S.*

Other commonly used names are IGIV and IVIG.

Note: For a listing of dosage forms and brand names by country availability, see *Dosage Forms* section(s).

Category

Immunizing agent (passive); platelet count stimulator (systemic); anti-Kawasaki disease (systemic); antibacterial (systemic); antiviral (systemic); antipolyneuropathy agent.

Indications

Note: Bracketed information in the *Indications* section refers to uses that are not included in U.S. product labeling.

Accepted

Note: The Food and Drug Administration (FDA) has approved specific brands of immune globulin intravenous (IGIV) preparations for specific indications. However, although IGIV preparations vary slightly, they are generally thought to be therapeutically equivalent and usually are selected on the basis of cost and convenience. Most physicians use IGIV preparations interchangeably (see *Pharmacology/Pharmacokinetics*).

Immunodeficiency, primary (treatment)—IGIV is indicated for the treatment of patients with primary immunodeficiency syndromes associated with defects in humoral immunity, such as congenital agammaglobulinemia (X-linked agammaglobulinemia), hypogammaglobulinemia, common variable immunodeficiency, X-linked immunodeficiency with hyperimmunoglobulin M, severe combined immunodeficiency, and Wiskott-Aldrich syndrome, to replace or boost immunoglobulin G (IgG). The beneficial effect of IGIV in the prophylactic management of these patients has been well documented.

The use of IGIV in IgG subclass deficiencies remains controversial and at present is recommended only for those patients who also demonstrate a deficiency in the ability to form antibodies against a variety of polysaccharide and protein antigens.

Thrombocytopenic purpura, idiopathic (treatment)—IGIV is indicated for the treatment of idiopathic thrombocytopenic purpura (ITP) when a rapid rise in the platelet count is required, such as prior to surgery, to control excessive bleeding, or to defer or avoid splenectomy. Not all patients will respond, however, and, if the platelet increment does occur, it may be transient. This treatment should not be considered curative, although remissions have occurred.

Kawasaki disease (treatment adjunct)—IGIV in conjunction with aspirin is indicated for the treatment of Kawasaki disease. Treatment with IGIV within the first 10 days of illness significantly reduces the prevalence of coronary artery abnormalities. In addition, IGIV has been shown to decrease the prevalence of giant coronary artery aneurysms (i.e., those with an internal diameter of > 8 mm) that are associated with the highest morbidity and mortality rates in Kawasaki disease.

Leukemia, chronic lymphocytic (treatment adjunct)—IGIV is indicated for the prevention of recurrent bacterial infections in patients with hypogammaglobulinemia associated with B-cell chronic lymphocytic leukemia (CLL).

Transplantation, bone marrow (treatment adjunct)—IGIV is indicated to prevent the risk of acute graft-versus-host disease, associated interstitial pneumonia (infectious or idiopathic), and infections (e.g., cytomegalovirus infections, varicella-zoster virus infection, and recurrent bacterial infection) after bone marrow transplantation (BMT) in patients 20 years of age or older in the first 100 days after transplantation. It is not indicated in BMT patients younger than 20 years of age, nor is it recommended for autologous transplants, because the benefit in these cases is slight.

Human immunodeficiency virus (HIV) infection, pediatric (treatment)—IGIV is indicated for use in HIV-infected children to reduce the risk of serious bacterial infections; however, there is no evidence to suggest that IGIV confers incremental benefit to antiretroviral therapy and prophylactic antibiotics administered according to current standards of practice. In children with advanced HIV disease who are receiving zidovudine, IGIV decreases the risk of serious bacterial infections. However, this benefit is apparent only in children who are not receiving co-trimoxazole as prophylaxis and for children with a CD4 count of greater than 200 to 400.

[Dermatomyositis (treatment)][1]—IGIV is used as a second-line agent in the treatment of dermatomyositis. Corticosteroids are the first-line agents in the treatment of dermatomyositis.

Dermatomyositis is a clinically distinct myopathy characterized by rash and a complement-mediated microangiopathy that results in the destruction of muscle fibers. In some patients the condition becomes resistant and causes severe physical disabilities. High-dose IGIV is a safe and effective treatment for refractory dermatomyositis. However, because dermatomyositis responds to corticosteroids, IGIV therapy should be reserved for corticosteroid-resistant patients or patients in whom corticosteroids are contraindicated.

[Guillain-Barré syndrome (treatment)][1]—IGIV is used in the treatment of Guillain-Barré syndrome (GBS). IGIV is the treatment of choice for adult patients with GBS, provided that they are so severely affected that they at least require aid to walk, that the disorder is diagnosed during the first 2 weeks of the illness, and that there are no contraindications to IGIV.

[Hyperimmunoglobulinemia E syndrome (treatment)][1]—IGIV is used in the treatment of hyperimmunoglobulinemia E syndrome.

Hyperimmunoglobulinemia E syndrome is an inflammatory skin disease characterized by severe eczema, recurrent staphylococcal infections of the skin and sinopulmonary tract, cold subcutaneous abscesses, and high serum immunoglobulin E (IgE) levels. IGIV is effective in the treatment of severe eczema in patients with hyperimmunoglobulinemia E syndrome and atopic dermatitis. IGIV also decreases enhanced IgE production both *in vivo* and *in vitro* .

[Lambert-Eaton myasthenic syndrome (treatment)][1]—IGIV is used in the treatment of Lambert-Eaton myasthenic syndrome.

The Lambert-Eaton myasthenic syndrome is a rare autoantibody-mediated disorder of neuromuscular transmission in which a reduction in the calcium-dependent release of acetylcholine from motor nerve terminals causes fatigable muscle weakness. Calcium-channel antibodies may be implicated in the reduction of functional calcium channels that underlies the disorder, and antibodies to P/Q-type calcium channels can be detected in the serum of 85 to 95% of patients. About 60% of patients with Lambert-Eaton myasthenic syndrome also have small cell lung cancer. Specific tumor therapy often is followed by clinical improvement, probably because tumor calcium-channel determinants are provoking the autoantibody response.

[Multifocal motor neuropathy (treatment)][1]—IGIV is indicated as a second-line agent in the treatment of multifocal motor neuropathy (MMN).

MMN is immune-mediated and treatable. It produces weakness that is typically distal and asymmetric, involves the arms early in the course of disease, and progresses slowly. Electrophysiologic abnormalities often include evidence of demyelination, especially focal conduction block, selectively on motor axons. High titers of serum immunoglobulin M (IgM) binding to GM1 ganglioside, alone or in a membrane environment, occur in 80 to 90% of patients with MMN. Treatments of MMN that commonly produce increased strength include IGIV and cyclophosphamide. Patients with MMN who had poor responses to other treatment regimens may show significant improvement after treatment with IGIV.

[Multiple sclerosis, relapsing-remitting (treatment)][1]—IGIV is used as a second-line agent in the treatment of relapsing-remitting multiple sclerosis.

Multiple sclerosis is the most common demyelinating disorder of the central nervous system and is characterized by repeated episodes of neurological dysfunction with variable remission. Monthly IGIV treatment is an effective and well-tolerated treatment for patients with relapsing-remitting multiple sclerosis.

[Neonates, high-risk, preterm, low-birth-weight, infections in (prophylaxis and treatment adjunct)][1]—IGIV is used for the prophylaxis of, and as a treatment adjunct in, infections in some high-risk, preterm, low-birth-weight neonates. Studies published before 1990 suggested that prophylactic IGIV reduced nosocomial infections in low-birth-weight infants. However, these studies enrolled small numbers of patients; employed varied designs, preparations, and doses; and included diverse study populations. The National Institute of Child Health and Human Development (NICHHD) Neonatal Research Network therefore performed a prospective, multicenter, randomized trial to test the hypothesis that the intravenous administration of immune globulin to infants with birth weights between 501 and 1500 grams would reduce the incidence of nosocomial infections. In this trial, the repeated prophylactic administration of IGIV failed to reduce the incidence of nosocomial infections significantly in premature infants weighing 501 to 1500 grams at birth. Furthermore, there were no significant differences in morbidity, mortality, or the duration of hospitalization between infants given IGIV and infants given no infusion or an infusion and placebo.

[Parvovirus B19 infection, chronic (treatment)][1]—IGIV is used in the treatment of chronic parvovirus B19 infection and severe anemia associated with bone marrow suppression.

Parvovirus B19 can cause aplastic anemia in sickle cell anemia and in immunodeficiency patients. High-dose IGIV can cure parvovirus B19 infection with reversal of anemia.

[Polyneuropathies, chronic inflammatory demyelinating (treatment)][1]—IGIV should be considered first-line treatment for chronic inflammatory demyelinating polyneuropathies. IGIV is used either alone or following therapeutic plasma exchange to prolong its effect. IGIV is considered easier to use than repeated therapeutic plasma exchange and to have fewer complications than long-term glucocorticoid therapy.

Acceptance not established

The safety and efficacy of immune globulin for the treatment of *stiff-person syndrome* have not been established.

---

[1]Not included in Canadian product labeling.

Pharmacology/Pharmacokinetics

Note: Although immune globulin intravenous (IGIV) preparations vary slightly, they are generally thought to be therapeutically equivalent and are therefore usually selected on the basis of cost and convenience. There are minor immunoglobulin A (IgA) and immunoglobulin G (IgG) subclass differences. Antibody titers also may vary from lot to lot and among different IGIV preparations. IGIV preparations with low IgA content should be used to minimize reactions in patients with hypogammaglobulinemia and concurrent IgA deficiency or when anti-IgA antibodies are present in a recipient (see *Side/Adverse Effects*).

Physicochemical characteristics

Source—

IGIV preparations consist of concentrated immunoglobulins (Ig), principally IgG, with a subclass distribution that largely reflects that of IgG in normal human serum. Pooled serum is collected from large numbers of donors, ranging from 1000 to more than 50,000, depending on the manufacturer. All U.S. IGIV manufacturers use Cohn-Oncley ethanol fractionation (fraction II) as an initial step in the preparation of immunoglobulin.

Subsequent steps differ among preparations and include ion exchange chromatography, ultrafiltration, enzymatic digestion, manipulation of the pH and salt concentration, and organic solvent-detergent partitioning. These procedures remove protein and other contaminants, minimize the concentration of IgG aggregates, and deactivate viral contaminants such as hepatitis B virus (HBV), hepatitis C virus (HCV), and human immunodeficiency virus (HIV). Donor serum samples are screened for antibodies to HIV, HCV, hepatitis B surface antigen, and elevated levels of alanine aminotransferase (ALT [SGPT]).

As a consequence of the 1994 HCV outbreak, the Food and Drug Administration (FDA) requires additional testing to detect HCV RNA by polymerase chain reaction (PCR) in all immunoglobulin preparations, including IGIV. Although the presence of HCV RNA in IGIV preparations may not necessarily correlate with infectivity, these measures should help prevent future transmission of HCV by IGIV preparations.

Mechanism of action/Effect

The mechanisms by which IGIV exerts a therapeutic effect in many disease states are unknown, but they are probably various immunomodulatory actions operating alone or in combination. Blockade of the Fc receptor on macrophages on the reticuloendothelial system in patients with immune cytopenia (e.g., idiopathic thrombocytopenic purpura [ITP]), appears to account for the major immediate effects of IGIV. The more long-term effects of IGIV can be attributed to the immunomodulatory effects of IGIV on T cells and macrophages, particularly cytokine synthesis, and B-cell immune function and its regulatory action on the membrane-damaging components of the complement system. In contrast, the effects of IGIV in Kawasaki disease and perhaps other diseases may be caused by the presence of specific antibodies in the IGIV that are capable of neutralizing bacterial or even viral toxins that can have profound effects on the host's immune and inflammatory systems. Undoubtedly no single mechanism accounts for all of the immune modulating effects of IGIV in these inflammatory/autoimmune processes.

Distribution

After an intravenous infusion of IGIV 2 grams per kg of body weight, the patient's serum IgG level increases fivefold and then declines by 50% in 72 hours before returning, in 21 to 28 days, to the pretreatment level. The marked initial decrease reflects extravascular redistribution. The IgG in the infusion easily enters the cerebrospinal fluid (CSF). During the first 48 hours of the infusion, when the serum IgG level is high, the concentration of IgG in the CSF increases as much as twofold, but it returns to normal within a week.

Biotransformation

During their circulating life span, IgG antibodies repeatedly exit and enter the vascular compartment. Most antibodies never encounter their specific target antigen and are eventually removed from the circulation and degraded at an unknown site. The rate of IGIV degradation is determined by the Fc region and by the IGIV concentration, so that degradation is accelerated in hypergammaglobulinemia and reduced in hypogammaglobulinemia.

Half-life

The half-life of most IGIV preparations is 18 to 32 days, similar to that of native IgG. The half-life of IGIV in neonates is similar to that in adults. There is, however, considerable individual variability, which reflects several factors including the immunoglobulin level before infusion, the peak immunoglobulin level after infusion, the presence of infection or burns, the reliability in determining immunoglobulin levels, and other factors.

Precautions to Consider

Pregnancy/Reproduction

Pregnancy—Studies have not been done in humans. However, intact immune globulins cross the placenta from maternal circulation increasingly after 30 weeks of gestation. IGIV should be administered to pregnant women only if clearly needed. In cases of maternal idiopathic thrombocytopenic purpura (ITP) where immune globulin intravenous (IGIV) was administered to the mother prior to delivery, the platelet response and clinical effect were similar in the mother and neonate.

Studies have not been done in animals.

FDA Pregnancy Category C.

Breast-feeding

It is not known whether IGIV is distributed into breast milk. However, problems in humans have not been documented.

Pediatrics

Appropriate studies on the relationship of age to the effects of IGIV have not been performed in the pediatric population. However, administration of high doses of IGIV to children with ITP did not cause any pediatrics-specific problems.

Geriatrics

Appropriate studies on the relationship of age to the effects of IGIV have not been performed in the geriatric population. However, no geriatrics-specific problems have been documented to date.

Drug interactions and/or related problems

The following drug interactions and/or related problems have been selected on the basis of their potential clinical significance (possible mechanism in parentheses where appropriate)—not necessarily inclusive (» = major clinical significance):

» Live virus vaccines

(live virus vaccines given parenterally can have diminished immunogenicity when given shortly before or during a period of several months after receipt of IGIV; high doses of IGIV have been demonstrated to inhibit the response to measles vaccine for a prolonged period; the duration of inhibition varies directly with the dose of IGIV administered; inhibition of immune response to rubella, while of shorter duration, also has been demonstrated; the appropriate suggested interval between IGIV administration and measles vaccination is 8 to 11 months, depending on the dose of IGIV administered)

(if IGIV must be given within 14 days after the administration of measles or measles-containing vaccines, these vaccines should be administered again after the recommended interval unless serologic testing indicates immunity, i.e., adequate serum antibodies were produced)

(the effect of administration of IGIV on the antibody response to varicella vaccine is not known; because of potential inhibition of the response, however, varicella vaccine should not be administered for at least 5 months after receipt of an IGIV preparation; in addition, IGIV preparations, if possible, should not be administered for 3 weeks after vaccination; if IGIV is given in this interval, the vaccine either should be revaccinated 5 months later or tested for varicella immunity at that time and revaccinated if seronegative)

(administration of IGIV does not interfere with the antibody response to oral polio vaccine [OPV] given as a booster dose to young adults who already had received primary immunization or to yellow fever vaccination; these vaccines can be administered simultaneously with IGIV, such as to travelers whose departure is imminent)

(in contrast to live virus vaccines, administration of IGIV preparations has not been demonstrated to cause significant inhibition of the immune responses to inactivated vaccines and toxoids)

» Nephrotoxic drugs

(IGIV products reported to be associated with acute renal failure; patients taking nephrotoxic drugs should be administered IGIV products at the minimum concentration available and the minimum rate of infusion practicable)

Medical considerations/Contraindications

The medical considerations/contraindications included have been selected on the basis of their potential clinical significance (reasons given in parentheses where appropriate)—not necessarily inclusive (» = major clinical significance).

Except under special circumstances, this medication should not be used when the following medical problems exist:

» Anaphylactic reaction to IGIV

(contraindicated in the setting of detectable IgA levels following IgG infusion; alternative therapy should be considered under these conditions)

» Immunoglobulin A (IgA) deficiencies, selective, in patients who have known antibody to IgA

(the use of IGIV preparations should be avoided in patients with known IgA deficiency where the IgA deficiency is the only concern, in whom anaphylaxis is more common, and in the presence of renal failure, which may be exacerbated; however, if a decision is made to administer IGIV, preparations that contain only small amounts of IgA are recommended; the first infusion should be administered in the hospital under medical supervision)

Risk-benefit should be considered when the following medical problems exist:

» Acute renal failure or

» Predisposition to acute renal failure including patients with

Age greater than 65 or

Diabetes mellitus or

Paraproteinemia or

Renal insufficiency, pre-existing or

Sepsis or

Volume depletion

(IGIV products reported to be associated with renal dysfunction, acute renal failure, osmotic nephrosis, and death; preliminary evidence suggests that IGIV preparations containing sucrose may present a greater risk for this complication [see *General Dosing Information*]; IGIV products should be administered at minimum concentration available and minimum rate of infusion practicable in patients with these conditions)

» Cardiovascular disease, history of or

» Thrombotic events, history of

(possible association between IGIV and thrombotic events; exact cause is unknown; caution should be exercised in the prescribing and infusion of IGIV in patients with these conditions)

» Cardiac function impairment in seriously ill patients

(these patients may be at increased risk for vasomotor or cardiac complications, such as elevated blood pressure and cardiac failure)

Sensitivity to immune globulins

(patients allergic to other immune globulins, either intramuscular or intravenous, may be allergic to IGIV also)

Sensitivity to maltose or sucrose

(these ingredients may be present in some IGIV products)

Patient monitoring

The following may be especially important in patient monitoring (other tests may be warranted in some patients, depending on condition; » = major clinical significance):

Blood urea nitrogen (BUN) and

Creatinine, serum and

Urine output

(determination recommended prior to initiation of therapy, particularly in patients judged to have a potential increased risk for developing acute renal failure, and again at appropriate intervals)

Side/Adverse Effects

Note: Immune globulin intravenous (IGIV) is a pooled plasma product, collected from large numbers of donors. Although potential blood donors are screened for antibodies to hepatitis B virus (HBV), hepatitis C virus (HCV), and human immunodeficiency virus (HIV), and the product is tested for the presence of certain current virus infections, and certain viruses are removed or inactivated, the risk of viral transmission cannot be ruled out. Because IGIV is made from human blood, it may carry a risk of transmitting infectious agents such as viruses and theoretically, the Creutzfeldt-Jakob disease [CJD] agent. All infections thought by a physician possibly to have been transmitted by an IGIV product should be reported by the physician or other healthcare provider to the manufacturer of that IGIV product. The physician should discuss risks and benefits of the IGIV product with the patient.

The reported incidence of adverse effects associated with the administration of IGIV ranges from 1 to 15%, but usually is less than 5%. Most of these reactions are mild and self-limited. Severe reactions occur very infrequently and usually do not contraindicate further IGIV therapy.

Adverse effects tend to be associated with rapid infusion rates in patients with concurrent acute infections, in previously untreated patients, or when significant time between infusions has transpired (more than 6-week intervals). Immediate minor reactions can be avoided or diminished by reducing either the rate or the volume of infusion.

A few investigators have given high concentrations (9% and 12% solutions) infused rapidly over a period of 20 to 40 minutes. This rapid rate can be tolerated by some patients; however, this should not be performed except by experts equipped to manage adverse reactions.

Therapy with IGIV increases serum viscosity. In patients with high normal serum viscosity in conditions such as cryoglobulinemia, hypercholesterolemia, or hypergammaglobulinemia, viscosity increases even further. Serum viscosity greater than 2.5 centipoise (normal 1.2 to 1.8 centipoise) increases the risk for thromboembolic events, which probably accounts for rare cases of stroke or pulmonary embolism after IGIV therapy. Therapy with IGIV also can induce a hyperviscosity syndrome in children with HIV infection who have high pretreatment levels of serum immunoglobulins. Reversible cerebral vasospasm has occurred in a patient treated with IGIV.

In patients with a history of migraine headache, IGIV therapy may trigger a migraine attack, which sometimes can be prevented by propranolol prophylaxis. The incidence of aseptic meningitis is also high in these patients. Therapy with IGIV was associated with stroke in a young woman with a history of migraine.

Aseptic meningitis develops in as many as 10% of patients treated with IGIV and is unrelated to the commercial source of the IGIV product, the infusion rate, or the underlying disease. Prophylaxis with intravenous corticosteroids often is ineffective. The symptoms respond to strong analgesia and subside in 24 to 48 hours. Additional diagnostic testing rarely is necessary.

Acute renal tubular necrosis, usually reversible, occurs rarely following IGIV therapy in patients who have pre-existing kidney disease and volume depletion, especially elderly, diabetic, or poorly hydrated patients. This complication has been associated with a high concentration of sucrose in some IGIV preparations. Osmotic tubular nephrosis, caused by intravenous solutions containing a concentration of hypertonic sucrose similar to that in IGIV preparations, is also a rare reaction; diluting the IGIV preparation and slowing the rate of infusion minimize the risk for this event.

After IGIV therapy, the erythrocyte sedimentation rate increases sixfold or more, probably as a result of enhanced rouleaux formation and reduced surface area caused by the infused gammaglobulin. The increase can persist for 2 to 3 weeks and should not be considered a sign of developing vasculitis.

Since IGIV preparations were first introduced in 1981, the Food and Drug Administration (FDA) has received over 114 adverse effect reports of renal dysfunction and/or acute renal failure associated with the administration of these products. Although acute renal failure was successfully managed in the majority of cases, deaths were reported in 17 patients. Many of the patients who died had serious underlying conditions. Preliminary evidence suggests that IGIV preparations containing sucrose may present a greater risk for this complication (see *General Dosing Information*).

The following side/adverse effects have been selected on the basis of their potential clinical significance (possible signs and symptoms in parentheses where appropriate)—not necessarily inclusive:

Those indicating need for medical attention

Incidence more frequent

Dyspnea (troubled breathing); ***tachycardia*** (fast or pounding heartbeat)

Incidence less frequent

Burning sensation in head; cyanosis (bluish coloring of lips or nail beds); ***faintness or lightheadedness; fatigue*** (unusual tiredness or weakness); ***wheezing***

Incidence rare

Anaphylactic reaction (difficulty in breathing or swallowing; hives; itching, especially of feet or hands; reddening of skin, especially around ears; swelling of eyes, face, or inside of nose; unusual tiredness or weakness, sudden and severe)

Note: A severe *anaphylactic reaction* may occur in patients who have a serious deficiency of immunoglobulin A (IgA) associated with anti-IgE or anti-IgG antibodies against IgA, which react with the IgA in the IGIV preparation. The reaction is rare and occurs primarily in patients with common variable immunodeficiency. The use of IGIV preparations should be avoided in patients with known IgA deficiency, in whom anaphylaxis is more common, and in the presence of renal failure, which may be exacerbated. However, if a decision is made to administer IGIV, preparations that contain only small amounts of IgA are recommended for treating patients with low serum IgA levels.

Frequency unknown

Renal dysfunction (decrease in urine output or decrease in urine-concentrating ability, cloudy urine); ***thrombotic events*** (severe headaches of sudden onset, sudden loss of coordination, pains in chest, groin, or legs, especially calves of legs, sudden onset of shortness of breath for no apparent reason, sudden onset of slurred speech, sudden vision changes)

Incidence not determined—Observed during clinical practice; estimates of frequency can not be determined

Abdominal pain (stomach pain); ***acute respiratory distress syndrome (ARDS)*** (shortness of breath; tightness in chest; troubled breathing; wheezing); ***apnea*** (bluish lips or skin; not breathing); ***bronchospasm*** (cough; difficulty breathing; noisy breathing; shortness of breath; tightness in chest; wheezing); ***bullous dermatitis*** (skin blisters); ***cardiac arrest*** (stopping of heart; no blood pressure or pulse; unconsciousness); ***coma*** (change in consciousness; loss of consciousness); ***epidermolysis*** (blistering, peeling, loosening of skin); ***erythema multiforme*** (blistering, peeling, loosening of skin; chills; cough; diarrhea; fever; itching; joint or muscle pain; red irritated eyes; sore throat; sores, ulcers, or white spots in mouth or on lips; unusual tiredness or weakness); ***hemolysis*** (abdominal pain; back pain; dark urine; decreased urination; fever; tiredness; yellow eyes or skin.); ***hypoxemia*** (bluish lips or skin); ***leukopenia*** (black, tarry stools; chest pain; chills; cough; fever; painful or difficult urination; shortness of breath; sore throat; sores, ulcers, or white spots on lips or in mouth; swollen glands; unusual bleeding or bruising; unusual tiredness or weakness); ***loss of consciousness; pancytopenia*** (high fever; chills; unexplained bleeding or bruising; bloody, black, or tarry stools; pale skin; unusual tiredness or weakness; cough; shortness of breath; sores, ulcers, or white spots on lips or in mouth; swollen glands); ***pulmonary edema*** (chest pain; difficult, fast, noisy breathing, sometimes with wheezing; blue lips and fingernails; pale skin; increased sweating; coughing that sometimes produces a pink frothy sputum; shortness of breath; swelling in legs and ankles); ***rigors*** (feeling unusually cold; shivering); ***seizures*** (convulsions; muscle spasm or jerking of all extremities; sudden loss of consciousness; loss of bladder control); ***Stevens-Johnson syndrome*** (blistering, peeling, loosening of skin; chills; cough; diarrhea; itching; joint or muscle pain; red irritated eyes; red skin lesions, often with a purple center; sore throat; sores, ulcers, or white spots in mouth or on lips; unusual tiredness or weakness); ***transfusion-related acute lung injury (TRALI)*** (shortness of breath; tightness in chest; troubled breathing; wheezing); ***tremor*** (trembling or shaking of hands or feet; shakiness in legs, arms, hands, feet); ***vascular collapse*** ()

Those indicating need for medical attention only if they continue or are bothersome

Incidence more frequent

Arthralgia (joint pain); ***backache or pain; headache; malaise*** (general feeling of discomfort or illness); ***myalgia*** (muscle pain); ***nausea; vomiting***

Incidence less frequent

Chest or hip pain; leg cramps; redness, rash, or pain at injection site; urticaria (hives)

Frequency unknown

Chills; fatigue (unusual tiredness or weakness); ***fever; flushing*** (feeling of warmth, redness of the face, neck, arms and occasionally, upper chest); ***hypertension, mild*** (high blood pressure); ***hypotension, mild or moderate*** (blurred vision, confusion, dizziness, faintness, or lightheadedness when getting up from a lying or sitting position suddenly, sweating, unusual tiredness or weakness); ***lightheadedness***

Patient Consultation

As an aid to patient consultation, refer to *Advice for the Patient, Immune Globulin Intravenous (Human) (Systemic).*

In providing consultation, consider emphasizing the following selected information (» = major clinical significance):

Before using this medication

» Conditions affecting use, especially:

Sensitivity to intramuscular or intravenous immune globulins

Pregnancy—Should be given to a pregnant woman only if clearly needed

Other medications, especially live virus vaccines or nephrotoxic drugs

Other medical problems, especially acute renal failure, anaphylactic reaction to IGIV, cardiac function impairment in seriously ill patients, cardiovascular disease, predisposition to acute renal failure including patients with age greater than 65, diabetes mellitus, paraproteinemia, pre-existing renal insufficiency, sepsis, or volume depletion, renal dysfunction, selective IgA deficiencies, or thrombotic events

Proper use of this medication

Waiting at least 2 to 3 weeks after receiving live virus vaccines before receiving IGIV, depending on the vaccine received

Waiting at least 5 to 11 months after receiving IGIV before receiving live virus vaccines, depending on the vaccine to be received

Importance of consulting manufacturer's product information for specific dosing as it may vary

» Proper dosing

Side/adverse effects

Signs of potential side effects, especially dyspnea, tachycardia, burning sensation in head, cyanosis, faintness or lightheadedness, fatigue, wheezing, and anaphylactic reaction

Signs of potential side effects observed during clinical practice, especially abdominal pain, acute respiratory distress syndrome (ARDS), apnea, bronchospasm, bullous dermatitis, cardiac arrest, epidermolysis, erythema multiforme, hemolysis, hypoxemia, leukopenia, loss of consciousness, pancytopenia, pulmonary edema, rigors, seizures, Stevens-Johnson syndrome, transfusion related acute lung injury (TRALI) or vascular collapse

General Dosing Information

Immune globulin intravenous (human) should only be administered intravenously. Other routes of administration have not been evaluated.

Anaphylactic reactions may occur in patients with a history of prior systemic allergic reactions or seizures following administration of human immunoglobulin preparations. Very rarely, an anaphylactoid reaction may occur in patients with no prior history of severe allergic reaction to human immunoglobulin (Ig) preparations. Patients previously sensitized to certain antigens, most commonly immunoglobulin A (IgA), may be at risk for immediate anaphylactoid and hypersensitivity reactions. Therefore, appropriate precautions should be taken prior to immune globulin intravenous (IGIV) injection to prevent allergic or any other unwanted reactions. Precautions should include review of the patient's history regarding possible sensitivity and the ready availability of 1:1000 epinephrine injection and other appropriate agents used for control of immediate allergic reactions.

In an effort to reduce the risk of acute renal failure and based on data that currently are available, the Food and Drug Administration (FDA) recommends that the following precautions be taken when considering administration of IGIV preparations:

- Patients should be adequately hydrated prior to the initiation of the infusion of IGIV.
- For patients at increased risk of developing acute renal failure, physicians should carefully weigh the potential benefits of administering sucrose-containing IGIV preparations against the risks of causing renal damage. IGIV products containing sucrose as a stabilizer accounted for a disproportionate share of the total number of IGIV products in reports associating renal dysfunction and acute renal failure with IGIV use.
- The recommended dose should not be exceeded. Reduction in dose, concentration, and/or rate of administration in patients at risk of acute renal failure has been proposed in order to reduce the risk of acute renal failure. Because no prospective data are presently available to identify a maximal safe dose, concentration, or rate of infusion for IGIV preparations for patients at risk for acute renal failure, the FDA recommends that, for such patients, prescribers reconstitute/dilute the product in such a manner as to produce both the minimum concentration and rate of infusion practicable. A recommendation by the manufacturer is to reduce the infusion rate to less than 13.3 mg IG per kg of body weight per minute. For sucrose-containing IGIV preparations a maximum infusion rate of 3 mg per kg of body weight per minute should not be exceeded.
- Renal function, including urine output, blood urea nitrogen (BUN), and serum creatinine, should be assessed prior to infusion of IGIV, particularly in patients judged to have a potential increased risk for developing acute renal failure, and again at appropriate intervals. If renal function deteriorates, discontinuation of IGIV should be considered.

The dosing regimen for IGIV in patients with primary immunodeficiencies is not standardized, and treatment is tailored to the needs of the individual based on clinical response and trough immunoglobulin G (IgG) levels. Although trough IgG levels of greater than 500 mg/dL appear beneficial in the majority of patients, the minimum serum concentration necessary for protection has not been established. Monthly doses of at least 100 mg per kg of body weight (mg/kg) are recommended, and most patients receive 200 to 400 mg/kg every 3 to 4 weeks. Comparative studies of dose, dosing schedules, and product selection in patients with primary immunodeficiencies have not been conducted. At present there are no data to suggest that clinically significant differences exist among IGIV preparations commercially available in the U.S., and thus it is reasonable to assume that they are therapeutically interchangeable.

Idiopathic thrombocytopenic purpura (ITP) is a disorder in which antiplatelet autoantibodies cause the destruction of platelets, resulting in thrombocytopenia. In children, ITP tends to be acute and short-lived, with only supportive management required. However, in many adults the disorder is chronic and often requires medical therapy or splenectomy. Treatment with high-dose IGIV causes a transient rise in the platelet count in both children and adults with ITP.

Although there is evidence to suggest efficacy in ITP, many questions remain regarding the use of IGIV. Some patients do not respond to therapy, and the treatment is not curative. A study comparing high-dose oral methylprednisolone with IGIV found no difference in the response of the platelet counts among the groups and concluded that these two therapies are equally effective in childhood ITP. It was suggested that the choice of treatment in childhood ITP be based on consideration of cost as well as on therapy-related risks.

Kawasaki disease represents one of the few conditions for which efficacy of IGIV has been demonstrated in carefully designed, prospective, controlled trials. When administered in conjunction with aspirin within 10 days of the onset of disease, IGIV resulted in a 65 to 78% decrease in the incidence of coronary artery abnormalities compared with treatment with aspirin alone. The recommended dosage regimen is a single 2 gram/kg of body weight dose. Because all studies of IGIV in Kawasaki disease involved concurrent administration of aspirin, the treatment regimen should include oral aspirin as well.

In hypogammaglobulinemic patients with chronic lymphocytic leukemia (CLL), IGIV at the recommended dosage of 400 mg/kg of body weight every 3 to 4 weeks has been shown to reduce bacterial infections significantly. However, treatment is costly and does not alter overall mortality.

The benefit of IGIV in the prevention of bacterial infections in human immunodeficiency virus (HIV)-infected children has been demonstrated in several trials. IGIV can delay the time to development of bacterial infections and decrease the frequency of hospitalizations in infants and children with CD4+ T-lymphocyte counts 200/mm^3 or higher, but it does not affect survival. Accordingly, the Working Group on Antiretroviral Therapy of the National Pediatric HIV Resource Center has recommended IGIV every 4 weeks for children with HIV-infection, including:

- Those with hypogammaglobulinemia, i.e., serum IgG concentration less than 250 mg/dL.
- Those with recurrent serious bacterial infections, i.e., defined as two or more infections such as bacteremia, meningitis, or pneumonia in a 1-year period.
- Those who fail to form antibodies to common antigens, such as measles, pneumococcal, and/or *Haemophilus influenzae* type b vaccine.
- Those living in areas where measles is highly prevalent and who have not developed an antibody response after two doses of measles, mumps, and rubella virus vaccine live.

IGIV is recommended for intravenous administration only. The intramuscular route has not been evaluated for this medication and is not recommended.

For some patients, intravenous administration of IGIV is not feasible because of poor venous access, severe side effects, or rapid IgG catabolism. Clinical studies demonstrated that the slow subcutaneous infusion of IGIV is a suitable alternative in these patients. The IgG concentration area under the curve after subcutaneous IGIV is equivalent to that of intravenous administration; however, peak serum levels usually are not obtained for 4 days. This slow release into the blood stream is advantageous when there has been prior anaphylaxis, aseptic meningitis, or rapid IgG catabolism. Subcutaneous IGIV permits selective patients to continue immunoglobulin therapy in a safe and effective fashion.

The infusion of IGIV should be at approximately room temperature for administration.

Diluents are product-specific. Only the specific diluent indicated by each manufacturer should be used for its particular product.

For treatment of adverse effects

Recommended treatment includes

- For reducing the incidence of adverse reactions—Adverse reactions often can be alleviated by reducing either the rate or the volume of infusion. For patients with repeated severe reactions unresponsive to these measures, hydrocortisone, 1 to 2 mg per kg of body weight, can be given intravenously 30 minutes before infusion. Utilizing a different IGIV preparation or pretreatment with diphenhydramine, acetaminophen, or aspirin also may be helpful. For prolonged infusions in patients with a history of side effects, the premedication can be repeated after 2 hours of medication.
- For mild hypersensitivity reaction—Administering antihistamines and, if necessary, corticosteroids. In mild anaphylaxis, antihistamines or subcutaneous epinephrine may be all that is necessary if the condition is progressing slowly and is not life-threatening, regardless of the organ or system affected. Under these circumstances, the risks associated with intravenous epinephrine administration outweigh the benefits.
- For severe hypersensitivity or anaphylactic reaction—Administering epinephrine. Antihistamines and/or corticosteroids also may be administered as required. Epinephrine is the treatment of choice for severe hypersensitivity or anaphylactic reaction. If the patient's condition is not stable, epinephrine should be infused. Norepinephrine may be preferable if there is no bronchospasm. For bronchospasm, epinephrine should be given with corticosteroids. Other bronchodilators, such as intravenous aminophylline or albuterol by nebulization, also should be considered.

Parenteral Dosage Forms

Note: Bracketed uses in the *Dosage Forms* section refer to categories of use and/or indications that are not included in U.S. product labeling.

Note: Rapid infusion rates and high doses of IGIV might be potential risk factors for thrombotic events in patients who are already at risk for thrombotic events. It is strongly recommended that the infusion concentration should be no more than 5%, and the infusion rate should be initiated no faster than 0.5 milliliter per kilogram of body weight per hour and advanced slowly only if well tolerated to a maximum rate of 4 milliliter per kilogram body weight per hour. Safety of the patient should be taken into account in determining the rate of infusion and percent of the solution concentration.

Dosing varies for different IGIV products. See the manufacturer's insert for the specific product being administered to determine appropriate dosing.

IMMUNE GLOBULIN INTRAVENOUS (HUMAN) INJECTION

Usual adult and adolescent dose

Immunodeficiency, primary (treatment)—

Intravenous, from 200 to 600 mg (4 to 12 mL) per kg of body weight once a month depending on which brand name product is being administered. Consult the manufacturer's product information for specific dosing information. As there are significant differences in the half-life of IgG among patients with primary immunodeficiency, the frequency and amount of immunoglobulin therapy may vary from patient to patient. The proper amount can be determined by monitoring clinical response. However, the minimum level of IgG required for protection has not been determined.

Idiopathic thrombocytopenic purpura (ITP) (treatment)—

Intravenous, 400 mg per kg of body weight per day for two to five consecutive days. If the patient's response to this five-day treatment period is inadequate, an additional 400 mg per kg of body weight may be administered as a single maintenance dose, repeated intermittently as needed.

Kawasaki disease (treatment adjunct)—

Intravenous, a single dose of 2 grams per kg of body weight may be administered. Because all studies have involved concurrent administration of aspirin, the treatment regimen should include aspirin, 100 mg per kg of body weight each day, until fever defervesces, then 3 to 5 mg per kg of body weight as a single daily dose for six to eight weeks if coronary artery abnormalities are not detected.

Usual pediatric dose

See *Usual adult and adolescent dose*.

Strength(s) usually available

U.S.—

500 mg protein in 10 mL solution (Rx) [*Gamimune N 5%* (maltose 9 to 11%); *Gamimune N 5% S/D* (maltose 9 to 11%)].

10% [*Gammagard Liquid* (sucrose-free)].

1 gram protein in 10 mL solution (Rx) [*Gamimune N 10%* (maltose 9 to 11%); *Gamimune N 10% S/D* (maltose 9 to 11%)].

2.5 grams protein in 50 mL solution (Rx) [*Gamimune N 5%* (maltose 9 to 11%); *Gamimune N 5% S/D* (maltose 9 to 11%)].

5 grams protein in 50 mL solution (Rx) [*Gamimune N 10%* (maltose 9 to 11%); *Gamimune N 10% S/D* (maltose 9 to 11%)].

5 grams protein in 100 mL solution (Rx) [*Gamimune N 5%* (maltose 9 to 11%); *Gamimune N 5% S/D* (maltose 9 to 11%)].

10 grams protein in 100 mL solution (Rx) [*Gamimune N 10%* (maltose 9 to 11%); *Gamimune N 10% S/D* (maltose 9 to 11%)].

10 grams protein in 200 mL solution (Rx) [*Gamimune N 5% S/D* (maltose 9 to 11%)].

20 grams protein in 200 mL solution (Rx) [*Gamimune N 10%* (maltose 9 to 11%); *Gamimune N 10% S/D* (maltose 9 to 11%)].

12.5 grams protein in 250 mL solution (Rx) [*Gamimune N 5%* (maltose 9 to 11%); *Gamimune N 5% S/D* (maltose 9 to 11%)].

Canada—

500 mg protein in 10 mL solution (Rx) [*Gamimune N 5%* (maltose 9 to 11%); *Gamimune N 5% S/D* (maltose 9 to 11%)].

1 gram protein in 10 mL solution (Rx) [*Gamimune N 10%* (maltose 9 to 11%); *Gamimune N 10% S/D* (maltose 9 to 11%)].

2.5 grams protein in 50 mL solution (Rx) [*Gamimune N 5%* (maltose 9 to 11%); *Gamimune N 5% S/D* (maltose 9 to 11%)].

5 grams protein in 50 mL solution (Rx) [*Gamimune N 10%* (maltose 9 to 11%); *Gamimune N 10% S/D* (maltose 9 to 11%)].

5 grams protein in 100 mL solution (Rx) [*Gamimune N 5%* (maltose 9 to 11%); *Gamimune N 5% S/D* (maltose 9 to 11%)].

10 grams protein in 100 mL solution (Rx) [*Gamimune N 10%* (maltose 9 to 11%); *Gamimune N 10% S/D* (maltose 9 to 11%)].

10 grams protein in 200 mL solution (Rx) [*Gamimune N 5% S/D* (maltose 9 to 11%)].

20 grams protein in 200 mL solution (Rx) [*Gamimune N 10%* (maltose 9 to 11%); *Gamimune N 10% S/D* (maltose 9 to 11%)].

12.5 grams protein in 250 mL solution (Rx) [*Gamimune N 5%* (maltose 9 to 11%); *Gamimune N 5% S/D* (maltose 9 to 11%)].

Packaging and storage

Store at 2 to 8 °C (36 to 46 °F), unless otherwise specified by manufacturer. Protect from freezing.

Preparation of dosage form

The medication may be diluted only with 5% dextrose in water.

Stability

A solution that has been frozen should be discarded.

The contents of any vial that has been entered should be used promptly. The solution should not be used if it is not clear and colorless. Partially used vials should be discarded.

Incompatibilities

Incompatibilities have not been evaluated. It is recommended that IGIV be administered through a separate line, by itself, and without mixing with other intravenous fluids (with the exception of 5% dextrose in water for this particular product) or medications.

IMMUNE GLOBULIN INTRAVENOUS HUMAN FOR INJECTION

Usual adult and adolescent dose

Immunodeficiency, primary (treatment)—

Intravenous, initially, 200 to 400 mg per kg of body weight once a month.

Idiopathic thrombocytopenic purpura (ITP) (treatment)—

Intravenous, 400 mg per kg of body weight per day for two to five consecutive days. If the patient's response is inadequate, 400 mg per kg of body weight may be administered as a single maintenance dose once every several weeks. In some patients, it may be necessary to increase the maintenance dose up to 800 mg or 1 gram per kg of body weight.

Bacterial infections secondary to B-cell chronic lymphocytic leukemia (CLL) (treatment adjunct)[1]—

Intravenous, 400 mg per kg of body weight once every three to four weeks.

Kawasaki disease (treatment adjunct)—

Intravenous, a single dose of 2 grams per kg of body weight may be administered. Because all studies have involved concurrent administration of aspirin, the treatment regimen should include aspirin, 100 mg per kg of body weight each day, until fever defervesces, then 3 to 5 mg per kg of body weight as a single daily dose for six to eight weeks if coronary artery abnormalities are not detected.

[Dermatomyositis (treatment)][1]—

Intravenous, 1 gram per kg of body weight for two days per month for three months.

[Guillain-Barré syndrome (GBS) (treatment)][1]—

Intravenous, 400 mg per kg of body weight a day for five days.

[Hyperimmunoglobulinemia E syndrome (treatment)][1]—

Intravenous, 400 mg per kg of body weight a day for five days.

[Lambert-Eaton myasthenic syndrome (treatment)][1]—

Intravenous, 1 gram per kg of body weight a day for two consecutive days.

[Multifocal motor neuropathy (MMN) (treatment)][1]—

Intravenous, 400 mg per kg of body weight a day for five days.

[Multiple sclerosis, relapsing-remitting (treatment)][1]—

Intravenous, 200 mg per kg of body weight a month for two years.

[Parvovirus B19 infection, chronic (treatment)][1]—

Intravenous, 400 mg per kg of body weight per day for five days followed by twice a week for two weeks.

Usual pediatric dose

See *Usual adult and adolescent dose*.

Strength(s) usually available

U.S.—

0.5 gram with 10 mL sterile water for injection as diluent (Rx) [*Gammagard S/D 0.5 g* (sucrose-free; sodium chloride 0.15 M; glucose 20 mg per mL; polyethylene glycol 2 mg per mL; glycine 0.3 M; human albumin 3 mg per mL); *Venoglobulin-I* (D-mannitol 20 mg per mL; human albumin 10 mg per mL; sodium chloride 5 mg per mL; polyethylene glycol ≤ 6 mg per mL)].

1 gram with 20 mL sterile water for injection as diluent (Rx) [*Gammar-P IV* (human albumin 3%; sucrose 5%; sodium chloride 0.5%; citric acid; sodium carbonate)].

1 gram with 33 mL sodium chloride injection as diluent (Rx) [*Sandoglobulin*].

1 gram for reconstitution with sterile 0.9% sodium chloride, 5% dextrose, or sterile water (Rx) [*Panglobulin* (preservative-free; 1.67 g sucrose per gram of protein; less than 20 mg sodium chloride per gram of protein)].

2.5 grams with 50 mL sterile water for injection as diluent (Rx) [*Gammagard S/D* (sucrose-free; sodium chloride 0.15 M; glucose 20 mg per mL; polyethylene glycol 2 mg per mL; glycine 0.3 M; human albumin 3 mg per mL); *Gammar-P IV* (human albumin 3%; sucrose 5%; sodium chloride 0.5%; citric acid; sodium carbonate); *Iveegam* (glucose 50 mg per mL; sodium chloride 3 mg per mL; polyethylene glycol < 0.5 gram per dL); *Venoglobulin-S* (D-sorbitol 50 mg per mL; human albumin ≤ 1.3 mg per mL; polyethylene glycol ≤ 100 mcg per mL; polysorbate 80 ≤ 100 mcg per mL; tri- *n*-butyl phosphate ≤ 10 mcg per mL)].

2.5 grams with or without 50 mL sterile water for injection as diluent (Rx) [*Polygam S/D* (sodium chloride 0.15 M; glucose 20 mg per mL; polyethylene glycol 2 mg per mL; glycine 0.3 M; human albumin 3 mg per mL); *Venoglobulin-I* (D-mannitol 20 mg per mL; human albumin 10 mg per mL; sodium chloride 5 mg per mL; polyethylene glycol ≤ 6 mg per mL)].

3 grams with or without 100 mL sodium chloride injection as diluent (Rx) [*Sandoglobulin*].

3 grams for reconstitution with sterile 0.9% sodium chloride, 5% dextrose, or sterile water (Rx) [*Panglobulin* (preservative-free; 1.67 g sucrose per gram of protein; less than 20 mg sodium chloride per gram of protein)].

5 grams with 100 mL sterile water for injection as diluent (Rx) [*Gammagard S/D* (sucrose-free; sodium chloride 0.15 M; glucose 20 mg per mL; polyethylene glycol 2 mg per mL; glycine 0.3 M; human albumin 3 mg per mL); *Gammar-P IV* (human albumin 3%; sucrose 5%; sodium chloride 0.5%; citric acid; sodium carbonate); *Iveegam* (glucose 50 mg per mL; sodium chloride 3 mg per mL; polyethylene glycol < 0.5 gram per dL); *Polygam S/D* (sodium chloride 0.15 M; glucose 20 mg per mL; polyethylene glycol 2 mg per mL; glycine 0.3 M; human albumin 3 mg per mL); *Venoglobulin-S* (D-sorbitol 50 mg per mL; human albumin ≤ 1.3 mg per mL; polyethylene glycol ≤ 100 mcg per mL; polysorbate 80 ≤ 100 mcg per mL; tri-*n*-butyl phosphate ≤ 10 mcg per mL)].

5 grams with or without 100 mL sterile water for injection as diluent (Rx) [*Venoglobulin-I* (D-mannitol 20 mg per mL; human albumin 10 mg per mL; sodium chloride 5 mg per mL; polyethylene glycol ≤ 6 mg per mL)].

6 grams with or without 200 mL sodium chloride injection as diluent (Rx) [*Sandoglobulin*].

6 grams for reconstitution with sterile 0.9% sodium chloride, 5% dextrose, or sterile water (Rx) [*Panglobulin* (preservative-free; 1.67 g sucrose per gram of protein; less than 20 mg sodium chloride per gram of protein)].

10 grams with 200 mL sterile water for injection as diluent (Rx) [*Gammagard S/D* (sucrose-free; sodium chloride 0.15 M; glucose 20 mg per mL; polyethylene glycol 2 mg per mL; glycine 0.3 M; human albumin 3 mg per mL); *Gammar-P IV* (human albumin 3%; sucrose 5%; sodium chloride 0.5%; citric acid; sodium carbonate); *Polygam S/D* (sodium chloride 0.15 M; glucose 20 mg per mL; polyethylene glycol 2 mg per mL; glycine 0.3 M; human albumin 3 mg per mL); *Venoglobulin-I* (D-mannitol 20 mg per mL; human albumin 10 mg per mL; sodium chloride 5 mg per mL; polyethylene glycol ≤ 6 mg per mL); *Venoglobulin-S* (D-sorbitol 50 mg per mL; human albumin ≤ 1.3 mg per mL; polyethylene glycol ≤ 100 mcg per mL; polysorbate 80 ≤ 100 mcg per mL; tri-*n*-butyl phosphate ≤ 10 mcg per mL)].

12 grams with or without 200 mL sodium chloride injection as diluent (Rx) [*Sandoglobulin*].

12 grams for reconstitution with sterile 0.9% sodium chloride, 5% dextrose, or sterile water (Rx) [*Panglobulin* (preservative-free; 1.67 g sucrose per gram of protein; less than 20 mg sodium chloride per gram of protein)].

Canada—

5 grams with 100 mL sterile water for injection as diluent (Rx) [*Iveegam* (glucose 50 mg ± 5 mg per mL; sodium chloride 3 mg ± 1 mg per mL)].

Packaging and storage

Store at 2 to 8 °C (36 to 46 °F), not to exceed 25 °C (77 °F) unless otherwise specified by manufacturer.Protect from freezing.

Preparation of dosage form

The diluent and lyophilized product should be brought to room temperature prior to reconstitution. When the diluent is added, dissolution usually occurs within a few minutes, although in rare cases, or when the product and/or diluent are cold, dissolution may take up to 20 minutes. The reconstituted solution should not be shaken, since excessive shaking will cause foaming. Reconstituted solution should be at approximately room temperature at the time of administration.

Stability

Only the specific diluent that the product's manufacturer indicates for that particular product should be used. The solution should not be used if it is not clear and colorless to slightly straw-colored, or if there is particulate matter present. Administration should begin promptly after reconstitution, or within 2 to 3 hours, according to the individual manufacturer's instructions. Partially used vials should be discarded.

Incompatibilities

Incompatibilities have not been evaluated. It is recommended that IGIV be administered through a separate line, by itself, and without mixing with other intravenous fluids (with the exception of the product's specified diluent) or medications.

Auxiliary labeling

- Do not shake. Excessive shaking will cause foaming

Caution

Certain components used in the packaging of some IGIV products contain natural rubber latex.

[1]Not included in Canadian product labeling.

Selected Bibliography

Product information: Gammagard S/D, immune globulin intravenous (human). Baxter Healthcare, Glendale, CA (PI revised 01/2001) reviewed 11/2003.

Product information: Panglobulin, immune globulin intravenous (human). American Red Cross Blood Services, Washington DC, MD (PI revised 09/2000) reviewed 11/2003.

FDA Center for Biologics Evaluation and Research [CBER] Information Sheet: FDA Interim Statement Regarding Immune Globulin Intravenous [IGIV] (August 27, 2002). Available at: www.fda.gov/cber/infosheets/igiv082702.htm.

Revised: 09/22/2005

INAMRINONE Systemic†

Note: The name of the drug amrinone was changed to inamrinone in the U.S. market in July 2000.

Note: Products containing inamrinone were withdrawn from the Canadian market by Sanofi Canada in July 2000.

VA CLASSIFICATION (Primary): CV900

Commonly used brand name(s):.

Note: For a listing of dosage forms and brand names by country availability, see *Dosage Forms* section(s).

†Not commercially available in Canada.

Category

Cardiotonic.

Indications

Note: Products containing inamrinone were withdrawn from the Canadian market by Sanofi Canada in July 2000.

Accepted

Congestive heart failure (treatment)—Inamrinone is indicated for the short-term management of congestive heart failure in patients who have not responded adequately to digitalis, diuretics, and/or vasodilators.

Pharmacology/Pharmacokinetics

Physicochemical characteristics

Molecular weight—187.20.

Mechanism of action/Effect

Not precisely known; but seems to be peripheral vasodilation, reducing both preload and afterload,and possibly also direct stimulation of cardiac contractility (positive inotropic effect)as a result of phosphodiesterase inhibition.

Other actions/effects

Slightly increases atrioventricular (AV) conduction velocity.

Protein binding
Low to moderate (10 to 49%).

Biotransformation
Hepatic.

Half-life
Adults—
Healthy volunteers: Approximately 3.6 hours.
Congestive heart failure: Approximately 5.0 to 8.3 hours (mean 5.8 hours).
Neonates and infants—
Less than 4 weeks: 12.7 to 22.2 hours.
More than 4 weeks: 3.8 to 6.8 hours.

Time to peak effect
Within 10 minutes.

Duration of action
Dose-related—
750 mcg (0.75 mg) per kg of body weight (mcg/kg): 30 minutes.
3 mg per kg of body weight (mg/kg): 2 hours.

Elimination
Renal—About 63%, as unchanged drug (10 to 40%) and metabolites.
Fecal—About 18%.

Precautions to Consider

Cross-sensitivity and/or related problems
Patients sensitive to bisulfites may also be sensitive to inamrinone, which contains sodium metabisulfite.

Carcinogenicity
A 2-year study in rats found no evidence of carcinogenicity.

Mutagenicity
Positive results were obtained in the mouse micronucleus test (at 7.5 to 10 times the maximum human dose) and in the Chinese hamster ovary chromosome aberration assay, indicating clastogenic potential and suppression of the number of polychromatic erythrocytes. However, negative results were obtained in the Ames Salmonella assay, mouse lymphoma study, and cultured human lymphocyte metaphase analysis.

Pregnancy/Reproduction
Pregnancy—Adequate and well-controlled studies in humans have not been done.

Studies in New Zealand white rabbits at oral doses of 16 and 50 mg per kg of body weight (mg/kg) have shown that inamrinone causes fetal skeletal and gross external malformations. These effects did not occur in French Hy/Cr rabbits at oral doses of 32 mg/kg per day or in rats receiving intravenous doses approximately equivalent to the recommended daily human dose.

In mutagenicity studies, gestation levels in rats were slightly prolonged at doses of 50 and 100 mg/kg per day. At the higher dose, dystocia occurred in dams and the incidence of stillbirths, decreased litter size, and poor pup survival was increased.

FDA Pregnancy Category C.

Breast-feeding
It is not known whether inamrinone is excreted in breast milk. However, problems in humans have not been documented.

Pediatrics
Studies and case reports of inamrinone use for pulmonary hypertension, congestive heart failure, and postoperative low cardiac output in approximately 30 neonates and infants and 6 children up to 24 months of age have not demonstrated pediatrics-specific problems that would limit the usefulness of inamrinone in pediatric patients.

Geriatrics
Although appropriate studies on the relationship of age to the effects of inamrinone have not been performed in the geriatric population, no geriatrics-specific problems have been documented to date. However, elderly patients are more likely to have age-related renal function impairment, which may require adjustment of dosage in patients receiving inamrinone.

Drug interactions and/or related problems
The following drug interactions and/or related problems have been selected on the basis of their potential clinical significance (possible mechanism in parentheses where appropriate)—not necessarily inclusive (» = major clinical significance):

Note: No untoward clinical manifestations have been observed in patients in which inamrinone was used concurrently with the following drugs: digitalis glycosides; lidocaine, quinidine; metoprolol, propranolol; hydralazine, prazosin; isosorbide dinitrate, nitroglycerin; chlorthalidone, ethacrynic acid, furosemide, hydrochlorothiazide, spironolactone; captopril; heparin, warfarin; potassium supplements; insulin; diazepam.

Disopyamide
(a single case report of excessive hypotension has been reported when inamrinone was used concurrently with disopyramide)

Laboratory value alterations
The following have been selected on the basis of their potential clinical significance (possible effect in parentheses where appropriate)—not necessarily inclusive (» = major clinical significance).

With physiology/laboratory test values
Blood pressure and
Potassium concentrations, serum
(may be decreased)

Hepatic enzymes
(serum concentrations may be increased)

Medical considerations/Contraindications
The medical considerations/contraindications included have been selected on the basis of their potential clinical significance (reasons given in parentheses where appropriate)—not necessarily inclusive (» = major clinical significance).

Except under special circumstances, this medication should not be used when the following medical problems exist:

» Aortic or pulmonic valvular disease, severe
(surgical relief of obstruction required)

» Hypersensitivity to inamrinone or bisulfites

Risk-benefit should be considered when the following medical problems exist:

Hepatic function impairment
(elimination reduced; dosage adjustment may be necessary)

» Hypertrophic subaortic stenosis
(inamrinone may aggravate outflow tract obstruction)

Myocardial infarction, acute
(clinical trials have not been carried out in patients in the acute phase of postmyocardial infarction; inamrinone is not recommended in these cases.)

Renal function impairment
(elimination reduced; dosage adjustment may be necessary)

Patient monitoring
The following may be especially important in patient monitoring (other tests may be warranted in some patients, depending on condition; » = major clinical significance):

» Blood pressure and
» Heart rate
(determinations at periodic intervals in patients receiving inamrinone; inamrinone infusion should be slowed or stopped in patients who develop an excessive fall in blood pressure)

» Body weight
(determinations recommended at periodic intervals to confirm efficacy of inamrinone)

Cardiac index and
Central venous pressure and
Pulmonary capillary wedge pressure
(determinations recommended at periodic intervals to confirm efficacy of inamrinone)

Hepatic function determinations and
Renal function determinations and
Serum electrolyte, especially potassium, concentrations
(recommended at periodic intervals in patients receiving inamrinone; hypokalemia secondary to improved cardiac output and resultant diuresis may contribute to risk of arrhythmias)
(dosage adjustment may be necessary in patients with existing or developing renal or hepatic function impairment)

» Platelet counts
(recommended prior to initiation and at periodic intervals during inamrinone therapy. Dosage of inamrinone may need to be reduced if thrombocytopenia occurs; in some cases, platelet levels stabilize with continuation at the same dose; any decision regarding a change in dosage should be based on monitoring of platelet counts; in some patients, withdrawal of inamrinone may be necessary)

Side/Adverse Effects

The following side/adverse effects have been selected on the basis of their potential clinical significance (possible signs and symptoms in parentheses where appropriate)—not necessarily inclusive:

Note: There have been several apparent hypersensitivity reactions in patients treated with oral inamrinone for about two weeks. Signs and symptoms were variable, but included pericariditis, pleuritis and ascites (1 case), myositis with interstitial shadowing on chest x-ray and elevated sedimentation rate (1 case) and vasculitis with nodular pulmonary densities, hypoxemia and jaundice (1 case). None of the cases were rechallenged so that attribution to inamrinone is not certain. However, possible hypersensitivity reactions should be considered in any patient maintained for a prolonged period on inamrinone.

Those indicating need for medical attention

Incidence less frequent

Arrhythmias (irregular heartbeat); ***hypotension*** (dizziness)

Incidence rare

Anorexia (loss of appetite, weight loss); ***burning at site of injection; chest pain or discomfort; hepatotoxicity*** (yellow eyes or skin); ***thrombocytopenia*** (unusual bleeding or bruising; black, sticky stools; blood in urine or stools; pinpoint red spots on skin)

Note: *Thrombocytopenia* occurs in about 2.4% of patients but is rarely symptomatic; more common with high doses or prolonged treatment.

Those indicating need for medical attention only if they continue or are bothersome

Incidence less frequent or rare

Abdominal pain (stomach pain); ***fever; nausea or vomiting***

Overdose

For more information on the management of overdose or unintentional ingestion, **contact a Poison Control Center** (see *Poison Contol Center Listing*).

Treatment of overdose

Treatment of overdose consists of general measures for circulatory support.

Patient Consultation

Note: Products containing inamrinone were withdrawn from the Canadian market by Sanofi Canada in July 2000.

As an aid to patient consultation, refer to *Advice for the Patient, Inamrinone (Systemic)*.

In providing consultation, consider emphasizing the following selected information (» = major clinical significance):

Before using this medication

» Conditions affecting use, especially:
Hypersensitivity to inamrinone or bisulfites.
Other medical problems, especially aortic or pulmonic valvular disease, severe or hypertrophic subaortic stenosis.

Proper use of this medication

» Proper dosing
Proper storage

Side/adverse effects

Signs of potential side effects, especially arrhythmias, hypotension, anorexia, burning at site of injection, chest pain, hepatotoxicity, or thrombocytopenia

General Dosing Information

Pretreatment with digitalis is recommended in patients with atrial flutter/fibrillation since inamrinone may increase ventricular response rates because of its slight enhancement of atrioventricular (AV) conduction.

Patients who have received vigorous diuretic therapy may need cautiously liberalized fluid and electrolyte intake to ensure an adequate cardiac filling pressure for response to inamrinone.

Caution is recommended to avoid extravasation of inamrinone infusion.

Tachyphylaxis to the hemodynamic effects of inamrinone occurs commonly, usually within 72 hours of initiation of therapy.

Parenteral Dosage Forms

Note: The dosing and strengths of the dosage forms available are expressed in terms of inamrinone base (not the lactate salt).

INAMRINONE INJECTION USP

Usual adult dose

Initial—Intravenous, 750 mcg (0.75 mg) (base) per kg of body weight, undiluted, given slowly over 2 to 3 minutes; may be repeated after thirty minutes if necessary.

Maintenance—Intravenous infusion, 5 to 10 mcg (0.005 to 0.01 mg) (base) per kg of body weight per minute, the dosage being adjusted according to clinical response.

Usual adult prescribing limits

Up to 10 mg (base) per kg of body weight per day, although some patients have been given doses up to 18 mg per kg per day for short durations.

Usual pediatric dose

Neonates—
Initial: Intravenous, 3.0 to 4.5 mg per kg of body weight in divided doses.
Maintenance: Intravenous infusion, 3 mcg (0.003 mg) to 5 mcg (0.005 mg) per kg of body weight per minute.

Infants—
Initial: Intravenous, 3.0 to 4.5 mg per kg of body weight in divided doses.
Maintenance: Intravenous infusion, 10 mcg (0.01 mg) per kg of body weight per minute.

Strength(s) usually available

U.S.—
With sodium metabisulphite:
5 mg (base) per mL (Rx) [GENERIC].

Canada—
Not commercially available

Packaging and storage

Store below 40 °C (104 °F), preferably between 15 and 30 °C (59 and 86 °F), unless otherwise specified by manufacturer. Protect from light. Protect from freezing.

Preparation of dosage form

For administration by intravenous infusion, inamrinone may be diluted in 0.45% or 0.9% sodium chloride injection, to produce a solution containing 1 to 3 mg of inamrinone (base) per mL.

Stability

Diluted solutions should be used within 24 hours.

Incompatibilities

Inamrinone should not be diluted with solutions containing dextrose since a chemical interaction occurs, developing slowly over 24 hours. However, inamrinone may be injected into running dextrose infusions through a Y-connector or directly into the tubing where preferable.

Furosemide should not be administered in intravenous lines containing inamrinone, since an immediate precipitate is formed.

Selected Bibliography

Bottorff MB, Rutledge DR, Pieper JA. Evaluation of intravenous amrinone: the first of a new class of positive inotropic agents with vasodilator properties. Pharmacotherapy 1985; 5(5): 227-37.

A symposium: amrinone. November 11, 1984, Miami, Florida. Am J Cardiol 1985 Jul 22; 56: 1B-42B.

Revised: 05/06/2002

INDAPAMIDE Systemic

VA CLASSIFICATION (Primary/Secondary): CV701/CV409

Commonly used brand name(s): *Apo-Indapamide; Gen-Indapamide; Lozide; Lozol; Novo-Indapamide; Nu-Indapamide.*

Note: For a listing of dosage forms and brand names by country availability, see *Dosage Forms* section(s).

Category

Antihypertensive; diuretic.

Indications

Accepted

Hypertension (treatment)—Indapamide is indicated, alone or in combination with other agents, for treatment of hypertension. Indapamide is effective in treating hypertension in patients with renal function impairment, although its diuretic effect is reduced.

Edema (treatment)—Indapamide is indicated for treatment of salt and fluid retention associated with congestive heart failure.

Pharmacology/Pharmacokinetics

Physicochemical characteristics
Molecular weight—365.83.
pKa—8.8.

Mechanism of action/Effect
Antihypertensive—Not clearly understood, but may involve both renal and extrarenal effects. The diuretic effect (reduction of extracellular fluid and blood volume) probably contributes only minimally since indapamide decreases blood pressure at a dose well below the effective diuretic dose. The antihypertensive effect is thought to be the result of reduction in peripheral vascular resistance.

Diuretic—Indapamide inhibits reabsorption of water and electrolytes, primarily as a result of action on the cortical diluting segment of the distal tubule.

Protein binding
High (71 to 79%), to plasma proteins. Also bound to elastin in vascular smooth muscle.

Biotransformation
Hepatic (extensive).

Half-life
In whole blood—Approximately 14 hours.
Terminal half-life of excretion of total radioactivity (^{14}C-labeled indapamide)—26 hours.

Onset of action
Antihypertensive—Multiple dose: 1 to 2 weeks.

Time to peak concentration
Within 2 hours.

Peak serum concentration
Approximately 260 nanograms per mL after oral administration of 5 mg.

Time to peak effect
Antihypertensive—
Single dose: Approximately 24 hours.
Multiple doses: 8 to 12 weeks.

Duration of action
Antihypertensive—Multiple doses: Up to 8 weeks.

Elimination
Renal—60 to 70% (5 to 7% unchanged).
Fecal—20 to 23%.

Precautions to Consider

Cross-sensitivity and/or related problems
Patients sensitive to other sulfonamide-type medications may be sensitive to indapamide also.

Carcinogenicity/Tumorigenicity
Studies in rats and mice found no evidence of carcinogenicity or tumorigenicity.

Pregnancy/Reproduction
Fertility—Studies in animals have not shown that indapamide causes adverse effects on the fetus at up to 6250 times the therapeutic human dose.

Pregnancy—Adequate and well-controlled studies in humans have not been done. However, pregnant women should be advised to contact physician before taking this medication, since routine use of diuretics during normal pregnancy is inappropriate and exposes mother and fetus to unnecessary hazard.

Studies in animals have not shown that indapamide causes adverse effects on the fetus at up to 6250 times the therapeutic human dose.

FDA Pregnancy Category B.

Breast-feeding
It is not known whether indapamide is distributed in breast milk. However, problems in humans have not been documented.

Pediatrics
Appropriate studies on the relationship of age to the effects of indapamide have not been performed in the pediatric population. Safety and efficacy have not been established.

Geriatrics
Although appropriate studies on the relationship of age to the effects of indapamide have not been performed in the geriatric population, the elderly may be more sensitive to the hypotensive and electrolyte effects. In addition, elderly patients are more likely to have age-related renal function impairment, which may require caution in patients receiving indapamide.

Drug interactions and/or related problems
The following drug interactions and/or related problems have been selected on the basis of their potential clinical significance (possible mechanism in parentheses where appropriate)—not necessarily inclusive (» = major clinical significance):

Note: Combinations containing any of the following medications, depending on the amount present, may also interact with this medication.

Amiodarone
(concurrent use of indapamide with amiodarone may lead to an increased risk of arrhythmias associated with hypokalemia)

Anticoagulants, coumarin- or indandione-derivative
(effects may be decreased when these medications are used concurrently with indapamide, as a result of reduction of plasma volume leading to concentration of procoagulant factors in the blood; in addition, diuretic-induced improvement of hepatic congestion may lead to improved hepatic function resulting in increased procoagulant factor synthesis; dosage adjustments may be necessary)

» Digitalis glycosides
(concurrent use with indapamide may enhance the possibility of digitalis toxicity associated with hypokalemia)

Hypotension-producing medications, other (See *Appendix II*)
(antihypertensive and/or diuretic effects may be increased when these medications are used concurrently with indapamide; although some antihypertensive and/or diuretic combinations are used frequently for therapeutic advantage, dosage adjustment may be necessary during concurrent use)

» Lithium
(concurrent use with indapamide is not recommended, as it may provoke lithium toxicity because of reduced renal clearance; in addition, lithium has nephrotoxic effects)

Neuromuscular blocking agents, nondepolarizing
(indapamide may induce hypokalemia, which may enhance the blockade of nondepolarizing neuromuscular blocking agents; serum potassium determinations may be necessary prior to administration of nondepolarizing neuromuscular blocking agents; careful postoperative monitoring of the patient may be necessary following concurrent or sequential use, especially if there is a possibility of incomplete reversal of neuromuscular blockade)

Sympathomimetics
(antihypertensive effects of indapamide may be reduced when it is used concurrently with sympathomimetics; the patient should be carefully monitored to confirm that the desired effect is being obtained)
(indapamide may decrease arterial responsiveness to norepinephrine, but does not usually significantly interfere with its clinical effects)

Laboratory value alterations
The following have been selected on the basis of their potential clinical significance (possible effect in parentheses where appropriate)—not necessarily inclusive (» = major clinical significance).

With physiology/laboratory test values

Calcium and
Protein-bound iodine (PBI)
(serum concentrations may be slightly decreased)

Plasma renin activity (PRA)
(may be increased)

Potassium and
Sodium
(serum concentrations may be decreased but usually remain within normal limits)

Uric acid
(serum concentrations may be increased but usually remain within normal limits)

Medical considerations/Contraindications
The medical considerations/contraindications included have been selected on the basis of their potential clinical significance (reasons given in parentheses where appropriate)—not necessarily inclusive (» = major clinical significance).

Risk-benefit should be considered when the following medical problems exist:

» Anuria or severe renal function impairment
(diuretic effect reduced; may precipitate azotemia)

Diabetes mellitus
(possible impaired glucose tolerance)
Gout, history of or
Hyperuricemia
(serum uric acid concentrations may be elevated)
Hepatic function impairment
(risk of dehydration, which may precipitate hepatic coma and death)
Sensitivity to indapamide or other sulfonamide-type medications
Sympathectomy
(antihypertensive effects may be enhanced)

Patient monitoring

The following may be especially important in patient monitoring (other tests may be warranted in some patients, depending on condition; » = major clinical significance):

Blood glucose concentration and
Blood urea nitrogen (BUN) concentration and
Uric acid concentration, serum
(determinations recommended prior to initiation of therapy and at periodic intervals during therapy)
» Blood pressure measurements
(recommended at periodic intervals in patients being treated for hypertension; selected patients may be trained to perform blood pressure measurements at home and report the results at regular physician visits)
Electrolyte concentrations, serum
(determinations recommended at periodic intervals for patients on long-term therapy, especially if they are also taking cardiac glycosides or systemic steroids, or when severe cirrhosis is present)

Side/Adverse Effects

The following side/adverse effects have been selected on the basis of their potential clinical significance (possible signs and symptoms in parentheses where appropriate)—not necessarily inclusive:

Those indicating need for medical attention

Incidence rare

Allergic reaction (skin rash, itching, or hives); ***electrolyte imbalance, specifically hyponatremia, hypochloremic alkalosis, or hypokalemia*** (dryness of mouth; increased thirst; irregular heartbeat; mood or mental changes; muscle cramps or pain; nausea or vomiting; unusual tiredness or weakness; weak pulse)

Note: *Electrolyte imbalance* is dose-related (*hypokalemia* occurs fairly frequently) but is not usually symptomatic.

Those indicating need for medical attention only if they continue or are bothersome

Incidence less frequent or rare

Anorexia (loss of appetite); ***diarrhea; headache; orthostatic hypotension as a result of volume depletion*** (dizziness or lightheadedness, especially when getting up from a lying or sitting position); ***trouble in sleeping; stomach upset***

Overdose

For more information on the management of overdose or unintentional ingestion, **contact a Poison Control Center** (see *Poison Control Center Listing*).

Treatment of overdose

Indapamide overdose should be treated by immediate evacuation of the stomach followed by supportive, symptomatic treatment and monitoring of serum electrolyte concentrations and renal function.

Patient Consultation

As an aid to patient consultation, refer to *Advice for the Patient, Indapamide (Systemic)*.

In providing consultation, consider emphasizing the following selected information (» = major clinical significance):

Before using this medication

» Conditions affecting use, especially:
Sensitivity to indapamide or other sulfonamide-type medications
Pregnancy—Routine use not recommended
Use in the elderly—Increased sensitivity to hypotensive and electrolyte effects
Other medications, especially digitalis glycosides or lithium
Other medical problems, especially anuria or severe renal function impairment

Proper use of this medication

Diuretic effects of the medication and timing of doses to minimize inconvenience of diuresis
Compliance with therapy; taking medication at the same time each day to maintain the therapeutic effect
» Proper dosing
Missed dose: Taking as soon as possible; not taking if almost time for next dose; not doubling doses
» Proper storage

For use as an antihypertensive
Possible need for control of weight and diet, especially sodium intake
» Patients may not experience symptoms of hypertension; importance of taking medication even if feeling well
» Does not cure but helps control hypertension; possible need for lifelong therapy; checking with physician before discontinuing therapy; serious consequences of untreated hypertension

Precautions while using this medication

Making regular visits to physician to check progress
» Possibility of hypokalemia; possible need for additional potassium in diet; not changing diet without first checking with physician
To prevent dehydration, checking with physician if severe nausea, vomiting, or diarrhea occurs and continues

For use as an antihypertensive:
» Not taking other medications, especially nonprescription sympathomimetics, unless discussed with physician

Side/adverse effects

Signs of potential side effects, especially allergic reaction and electrolyte imbalance

General Dosing Information

The lowest effective dosage should be utilized to minimize potential electrolyte imbalance.

When used to promote diuresis, a single daily dose is preferably taken on arising in order to minimize the effect of increased frequency of urination on sleep. Intermittent dosage schedules (drug-free days) may reduce the possibility of electrolyte imbalance or hyperuricemia resulting from therapy.

Concurrent administration of potassium supplements or potassium-sparing diuretics may be indicated in patients considered to be at higher risk for developing hypokalemia. Caution in administering potassium supplements is recommended, however, since loss of potassium is not clinically significant in most patients, and supplementation leads to a risk of development of hyperkalemia.

Recent evidence suggests that withdrawal of antihypertensive therapy prior to surgery is not necessary, but that the anesthesiologist must be aware of such therapy.

Oral Dosage Forms

INDAPAMIDE TABLETS

Usual adult dose

Diuretic—
Oral, 2.5 mg once a day, adjusted according to response after one (for edema) to four (for hypertension) weeks up to 5 mg once a day.

Note: Geriatric patients may be more sensitive to the effects of the usual adult dose.

Usual pediatric dose

Safety and efficacy have not been established.

Strength(s) usually available

U.S.—
1.25mg [*Lozol;* GENERIC].
2.5 mg (Rx) [*Lozol* (lactose); GENERIC].

Canada—
1.25 mg [*Lozide*].
2.5 mg (Rx) [*Lozide; Apo-Indapamide; Gen-Indapamide; Novo-Indapamide; Nu-Indapamide;* GENERIC].

Packaging and storage

Store below 40 °C (104 °F), preferably between 15 and 30 °C (59 and 86 °F), in a well-closed container, unless otherwise specified by manufacturer. Protect from light.

Note

Check refill frequency to determine compliance in hypertensive patients.

Selected Bibliography

Thomas JR. A review of 10 years of experience with indapamide as an antihypertensive agent. Hypertension 1985; 7 (Suppl 2): II152-6.

The fifth report of the Joint National Committee on Detection, Evaluation, and Treatment of High Blood Pressure (JNC V). Arch Intern Med 1993; 153(2): 154-83.

Revised: 08/18/1998

INDINAVIR Systemic

VA CLASSIFICATION (Primary): AM830

Commonly used brand name(s): *Crixivan*.

Another commonly used name isIDV

Note: For a listing of dosage forms and brand names by country availability, see *Dosage Forms* section(s).

Category

Antiviral (systemic).

Indications

General Considerations

Human immunodeficiency virus (HIV) isolates with reduced susceptibility to indinavir have been recovered from some patients treated with this medication. Resistance correlated with the accumulation of mutations that resulted in the expression of amino acid substitutions at eleven residue positions in the viral protease.

Cross-resistance between indinavir and reverse transcriptase inhibitors is thought to be unlikely because they affect different enzyme targets. However, cross-resistance was observed between indinavir and ritonavir, another protease inhibitor. Varying degrees of resistance have been noted between indinavir and other protease inhibitors.

Accepted

Human immunodeficiency virus (HIV) infection (treatment) or Immunodeficiency syndrome, acquired (AIDS) (treatment)—Indinavir is indicated in combination with the nucleoside analogs or as monotherapy for the treatment of HIV infection or AIDS.

Pharmacology/Pharmacokinetics

Physicochemical characteristics

Molecular weight—Indinavir sulfate: 711.88.

Mechanism of action/Effect

Indinavir binds to the protease active site and inhibits the activity of human immunodeficiency virus (HIV) protease, an enzyme required for the proteolytic cleavage of viral polyprotein precursors into individual functional proteins found in infectious HIV. This inhibition prevents cleavage of viral polyproteins and results in the formation of immature noninfectious viral particles.

Absorption

Rapidly absorbed when taken on an empty stomach. Administration of indinavir with a meal high in calories, fat, and protein resulted in an 84% reduction in peak plasma concentration (C_{max}) and a 77% reduction in area under the plasma concentration-time curve (AUC). Administration with a lighter meal resulted in little or no change in C_{max} or AUC.

Protein binding

Moderate (60%).

Biotransformation

Hepatic; seven metabolites have been identified. One is a glucuronide conjugate and six are oxidative metabolites; cytochrome P450 3A4 (CYP3A4) has been found to be the major enzyme responsible for formation of the oxidative metabolites.

Half-life

Approximately 1.8 hours.

Time to peak concentration

Approximately 0.8 hour after administration in the fasted state.

Elimination

Fecal—Approximately 83% of an administered radioactive dose was recovered in the feces. Radioactivity due to the parent medication in the feces was approximately 19%.

Renal—Approximately 19% of an administered radioactive dose was recovered in the urine. Radioactivity due to the parent medication in the urine was approximately 9%.

In dialysis—It is not known whether indinavir is dialyzable by peritoneal or hemodialysis.

Precautions to Consider

Carcinogenicity

In animal studies performed in mice, no increased incidence of any tumor type was observed. In rats, the highest dose tested was 640 mg/kg/day; at this dose a statistically significant increased incidence of thyroid adenomas was seen only in male rats. At that dose, daily systemic exposure in rats was approximately 1.3 times higher than daily systemic exposure in humans.

Mutagenicity

There has been no evidence of mutagenicity or genotoxicity in *in vitro* microbial mutagenesis (Ames) tests, *in vitro* alkaline elution assays for DNA breakage, *in vitro* and *in vivo* chromosomal aberration studies, and *in vitro* mammalian cell mutagenesis assays.

Pregnancy/Reproduction

Fertility—There were no effects on mating, fertility, or embryo survival in female rats and no effects on mating performance seen in male rats at doses providing systemic exposure comparable to or slightly higher than that attained with the clinical dose. Also, there were no effects observed on fertility or fecundity of untreated females mated with treated males.

Pregnancy—*An Antiretroviral Pregnancy Registry has been established to monitor the outcomes of pregnant women exposed to indinavir. Physicians are encouraged by the manufacturer to register patients by calling (800) 258-4263.*

Adequate and well-controlled studies have not been done in humans. Hyperbilirubinemia has occurred during treatment with indinavir; it is unknown whether administration to the mother in the perinatal period will exacerbate physiologic hyperbilirubinemia in neonates.

No evidence of teratogenicity was found in developmental toxicity studies performed in rats (at doses up to 640 mg/kg/day), dogs (at doses up to 80 mg/kg/day), and rabbits (at doses up to 240 mg/kg/day) administered doses comparable to or slightly greater than those administered to humans. No treatment related external or visceral changes were observed in rats. In rats, there were treatment-related increases over controls in the incidence of supernumerary ribs at exposures at or below those in humans, and of cervical ribs at exposures comparable to or slightly greater than those in humans. There were no external, visceral, or skeletal changes observed in rabbits or dogs. In all three species, there were no treatment-related effects on embryonic/fetal survival or fetal weights.

In rabbits, at a maternal dose of 240 mg/kg/day, no drug was detected in fetal plasma 1 hour after dosing. Fetal plasma drug levels 2 hours after dosing were approximately 3% of maternal plasma drug levels. In dogs, at a maternal dose of 80 mg/kg/day, fetal plasma drug levels were approximately 50% of maternal plasma drug level both 1 and 2 hours after dosing. In rats at maternal doses of 40 and 640 mg/kg/day, fetal plasma drug levels were approximately 10 to 15% and 10 to 20% of maternal plasma drug levels 1 to 2 hours after dosing, respectively.

Indinavir was administered to Rhesus monkeys during the third trimester of pregnancy (at doses up to 160 mg/kg twice daily) and to neonatal Rhesus monkeys (at doses up to 160 mg/kg twice daily). When administered to neonates, indinavir caused an exacerbation of the transient hyperbilirubinemia seen in this species after birth; serum bilirubin values were approximately four fold above controls at 160 mg/kg twice daily. A similar exacerbation did not occur in neonates after *in utero* exposure to indinavir during the third trimester of pregnancy. In Rhesus monkeys, fetal plasma drug levels were approximately 1 to 2% of maternal plasma drug levels approximately 1 hour after maternal dosing at 40, 80, or 160 mg/kg twice daily.

FDA Pregnancy Category C.

Breast-feeding

It is not known whether indinavir is distributed into human breast milk; however, there exists the potential for adverse effects in nursing infants. Nursing mothers are advised to discontinue breast-feeding if they are receiving indinavir.

Indinavir is distributed into the milk of lactating rats.

Pediatrics

The optimal dosing regimen for the use of indinavir in pediatric patients has not been established. A dose of 500 mg/m² every eight hours has been studied in uncontrolled studies of 70 children, 3 to 18 years of age. The pharmacokinetic profiles of indinavir at this dose were not comparable to profiles previously observed in adults receiving the recommended dose. Although viral suppression was observed in some of the 32 children who were followed on this regimen through 24 weeks, a substantially higher rate of nephrolithiasis was reported when compared to adult historical data. Physicians considering the use of indinavir in pediatric patients without other protease inhibitor options should be aware of the limited data available in this population and the increased risk of nephrolithiasis.

Geriatrics
No information is available on the relationship of age to the effects of indinavir in geriatric patients.

Pharmacogenetics
The effects of gender were compared in 10 HIV seropositive women to HIV seropositive men, and differences in indinavir exposure, peak concentrations, and trough concentrations were seen. The percent change in the AUC and C_{max} was shown to be a 13% decrease for females compared to males. The C_{8h} has shown a 22% decrease for females relative to males. The clinical significance of these differences is ot known.

The effects of race seemed to be comparable in Caucasians and Blacks based on pharmacokinetic studies including 42 Caucasians (26 HIV positive) and 16 Blacks (4 HIV positive).

Drug interactions and/or related problems
The following drug interactions and/or related problems have been selected on the basis of their potential clinical significance (possible mechanism in parentheses where appropriate)—not necessarily inclusive (» = major clinical significance):

Note: Combinations containing any of the following medications, depending on the amount present, may also interact with this medication.

» P450 CYP3A4 substrates such as:
» Cisapride or
» Ergot derivatives or
» Midazolam or
» Pimozide or
» Triazolam
(Indinavir should not be administered concurrently with cisapride, ergot derivatives, midazolam, pimozide, and triazolam; because competition for CYP3A4 by indinavir could result in inhibition of the metabolism of these medications and elevated plasma concentrations, there is a potential for serious and/or life-threatening side effects;)

Calcium Channel Blockers
(calcium channel blockers are metabolized by CYP3A4 which is inhibited by indinavir; coadministration could result in increased plasma concentrations of calcium channel blockers and may increase or prolong therapeutic effect)

Cimetidine
(concurrent administration does not affect the area under the plasma concentration-time curve [AUC] of indinavir)

Clarithromycin
(concurrent use results in a 29% increase in the AUC of indinavir and a 53% increase in the AUC of clarithromycin; dosing modification is not required)

Contraceptives, estrogen-containing, oral
(concurrent use of indinavir with an estrogen-containing oral contraceptive [*Ortho-Novum 1/35®*] results in a 24% increase in the AUC of ethinyl estradiol and a 26% increase in the AUC of norethindrone; dosing modification is not required)

CYP3A4 inducers, less potent, such as:
carbamazepine or
dexamethasone or
phenobarbital or
phenytoin
(interactions have not been studied; should be used with caution because concurrent administration could result in decreased plasma concentrations of indinavir)

» Delavirdine
(a dose reduction should be considered when administering delavirdine with indinavir due to an increase in indinavir plasma concentrations)

» Didanosine
(if indinavir and didanosine are both part of a treatment regimen, they should be administered at least 1 hour apart on an empty stomach; a normal acidic pH may be necessary for the optimal absorption of indinavir, and didanosine requires a buffer to increase the pH so that acid does not rapidly degrade didanosine)

» Efavirenz
(indinavir plasma concentrations, AUC and C_{max} were decreased by approximately 31% and 16%, respectively, as a result of enzyme induction; a dose adjustment for indinavir is recommended when administering efavirenz concurrently)

Fluconazole
(concurrent use results in a 19% decrease in the AUC of indinavir and no change in the AUC of fluconazole; dosing modification is not required)

Grapefruit juice
(administration of a single 400-mg dose of indinavir with grapefruit juice results in a 26% decrease in the AUC of indinavir; dosing modification is not required)

» HMG-CoA inhibitors:
» Lovastatin or
» Simvastatin
(concomitant use is not recommended, metabolized by the CYP3A4 pathway; increased risk of myopathy including rhabdomyolysis)

Isoniazid
(concurrent administration results in a 13% increase in the AUC of isoniazid and no change in the AUC of indinavir; dosing modification is not required)

» Itraconazole
(itraconazole inhibits P-450 3A4 that increases plasma concentrations of indinavir; a dosage reduction of indinavir is recommended)

» Ketoconazole
(concurrent use results in a 68% increase in the AUC of indinavir; a dosage reduction of indinavir is recommended when coadministered with ketoconazole)

Lamivudine or
Zidovudine
(concurrent administration of zidovudine and indinavir results in a 13% increase in the AUC of indinavir and a 17% increase in the AUC of zidovudine; administration of indinavir with zidovudine and lamivudine results in no change in the AUC of indinavir, a 36% increase in AUC of zidovudine and a 6% decrease in AUC of lamivudine; dosing modification is not required)

Quinidine
(administration of a single 400-mg dose of indinavir with 200 mg of quinidine sulfate results in a 10% decrease in the AUC of indinavir; dosing modification is not required)

» Rifabutin
(concurrent use results in a 32% decrease in the AUC of indinavir and a 204% increase in the AUC of rifabutin; dosage reduction of rifabutin is recommended when indinavir is coadministered with rifabutin.)

» Rifampin
(because rifampin is a potent inducer of CYP3A4 concurrent use with indinavir is not recommended; coadministration resulted in 89% ± 9% decrease in indinavir AUC.)

» St. John's Wort (*Hypericum perforatum*)
(concurrent use decreases the AUC_{0-8h} of indinavir from 36 to 79% and decreases C_{8h} from 49 to 99% may lead to loss of virological response and possible indinavir or protease inhibitor resistance; concurrent use is not recommended)

» Sildenafil
(coadministration substantially increases sildenafil plasma concentrations; increased risk of sildenafil associated side effects including hypotension, visual changes, and priapism; any sildenafil associated symptoms should be reported promptly; indinavir average peak concentration C_{max} was increased 48% and AUC_{0-8h} was increased 11%)

Sulfamethoxazole and trimethoprim combination
(concurrent administration results in no change in the AUC of indinavir and sulfamethoxazole, and a 19% increase in the AUC of trimethoprim; dosing modification is not required)

Stavudine
(concurrent administration results in no change in the AUC of indinavir and a 25% increase in the AUC of stavudine; dosing modification is not required)

Laboratory value alterations
The following have been selected on the basis of their potential clinical significance (possible effect in parentheses where appropriate)—not necessarily inclusive (» = major clinical significance).

With physiology/laboratory test values
Alanine aminotransferase (ALT [SGPT]), serum and
Amylase, serum and
Aspartate aminotransferase (AST [SGOT]), serum
(values may be increased)

» Bilirubin, total serum
(asymptomatic hyperbilirubinemia [total bilirubin ≥ 2.5 mg per dL], reported primarily as elevated indirect bilirubin, has occurred in

approximately 10% of patients treated with indinavir; this was associated with elevations in ALT or AST in less than 1% of patients; it also occurred more frequently at doses > 2.4 grams per day)

Glucose, plasma
(concentrations may be increased)

Serum triglycerides or
Serum cholesterol
(laboratory abnormalities have occurred during post-marketing experience with indinavir.)

Medical considerations/Contraindications

The medical considerations/contraindications included have been selected on the basis of their potential clinical significance (reasons given in parentheses where appropriate)—not necessarily inclusive (» = major clinical significance).

Except under special circumstances, this medication should not be used when the following medical problem exists:

» Hypersensitivity to indinavir

Risk-benefit should be considered when the following medical problems exist:

Hemophilia
(spontaneous bleeding has been reported in patients with hemophilia types A and B who are being treated with protease inhibitors; a causal relationship has not been established)

» Hepatitis
(hepatitis cases resulting in hepatic failure and death has been reported in patients with confounding medical conditions and/or were receiving concomitant therapy; a causal relationship has not been established)

» Hepatic function impairment
(it is recommended that the dosage of indinavir be lowered in patients with mild to moderate hepatic function impairment due to cirrhosis)

Hyperbilirubinemia
(it is unknown if indinavir will exacerbate the physiologic hyperbilirubinemia seen in neonates; indirect hyperbilirubinemia has occurred frequently during indinavir treatment and has infrequently been associated with increases in serum transaminases)

Patient monitoring

The following may be especially important in patient monitoring (other tests may be warranted in some patients, depending on condition; » = major clinical significance):

» Blood glucose determinations
(recommended to closely monitor patient's plasma glucose concentrations; development of hyperglycemia or diabetes may be associated with the use of protease inhibitors)

Side/Adverse Effects

Note: Nephrolithiasis/Urolithiasis (kidney stones) was reported in approximately 12.4% of adult patients and 29% in pediatric patients treated with indinavir. It was not usually associated with renal function impairment and resolved with hydration and temporary interruption of therapy. Nephrolithiasis/Urolithiasis was more likely to occur with increasing exposure to indinavir Acute hemolytic anemia, including cases resulting in death, have been reported in patients being treated with indinavir. Once a diagnosis is apparent, appropriate measures for the treatment of hemolytic anemia should be instituted, including discontinuation of indinavir.

The redistribution or accumulation of body fat, including central obesity, dorsocervical fat enlargement (buffalo hump), peripheral wasting, breast enlargement, and "cushingoid appearance" have been reported in patients on protease inhibitor therapy. A causal relationship between these events and use of protease inhibitors has not been confirmed.

The following side/adverse effects have been selected on the basis of their potential clinical significance (possible signs and symptoms in parentheses where appropriate)—not necessarily inclusive:

Those indicating need for medical attention

Incidence more frequent

Kidney stones (blood in urine; sharp back pain just below ribs)

Incidence less frequent

Jaundice (chills; clay-colored stools; dark urine; dizziness; fever; headache; itching; loss of appetite; nausea; abdominal or stomach pain; area rash; unpleasant breath odor; unusual tiredness or weakness; vomiting of blood; yellow eyes or skin)

Incidence rare

Anemia (pale skin; troubled breathing with exertion; unusual bleeding or bruising; unusual tiredness or weakness); ***diabetes or hyperglycemia*** (dry or itchy skin; fatigue; hunger, increased; thirst, increased; unexplained weight loss; urination, increased); ***ketoacidosis*** (confusion; dehydration; mouth odor, fruity; nausea; vomiting; weight loss)

Incidence not determined—Observed during clinical practice; estimates of frequency cannot be determined

Acute hemolytic anemia (back, leg, or stomach pains; bleeding gums; chills; dark urine; difficulty breathing; fatigue; fever; general body swelling); ***angina pectoris*** (arm, back or jaw pain; chest pain or discomfort; chest tightness or heaviness; fast or irregular heartbeat; shortness of breath; sweating; nausea); ***anaphylactoid reactions*** (cough; difficulty swallowing; dizziness; fast heartbeat; hives; itching; puffiness or swelling of the eyelids or around the eyes, face, lips or tongue; shortness of breath; skin rash; tightness in chest; unusual tiredness or weakness; wheezing); ***cardiovascular disorder*** (fainting; fast or slow heartbeat; irregular pulse; troubled breathing [dyspnea] on exertion); ***cerebrovascular disorder; crystalluria*** (blood in urine; difficult urination; pain in lower back; pain or burning while urinating; sudden decrease in amount of urine); ***diabetes mellitus*** (blurred vision; dry mouth; fatigue; flushed, dry skin; fruit-like breath odor; increased hunger; increased thirst; increased urination; loss of consciousness; nausea; stomachache; sweating; troubled breathing; unexplained weight loss; vomiting)—new onset or exacerbation of pre-existing diabetes; ***dysuria*** (difficult or painful urination; burning while urinating); ***hepatitis*** (dark urine; general tiredness and weakness; light-colored stools; nausea and vomiting; upper right abdominal pain; yellow eyes and skin)—including reports of hepatic failure; ***hemophilia, increased spontaneous bleeding; liver function abnormalities; myocardial infarction*** (chest pain or discomfort; pain or discomfort in arms, jaw, back or neck; shortness of breath; nausea; sweating; vomiting); ***nephritis, intersitial*** (fever; joint pain; skin rash; swelling of body or feet and ankles; unusual weight gain); ***pancreatitis*** (bloating; chills; constipation; darkened urine; fast heartbeat; fever; indigestion; loss of appetite; nausea; pains in stomach, side, or abdomen, possibly radiating to the back vomiting; yellow eyes or skin); ***pyelonephritis*** (chills; fever; frequent or painful urination; headache; stomach pain)—with or without bacteremia; ***rash, including erythema multiforme and Stevens Johnson syndrome*** (blistering, peeling, loosening of skin; chills; cough; diarrhea; fever; itching; joint or muscle pain; red irritated eyes; sore throat; sores, ulcers, or white spots in mouth or on lips; unusual tiredness or weakness)

Those indicating need for medical attention only if they continue or are bothersome

Incidence more frequent

Asthenia (generalized weakness); ***gastrointestinal disturbances*** (abdominal or stomach pain; diarrhea; nausea; vomiting); ***headache; insomnia*** (difficulty in sleeping); ***taste perversion*** (change in sense of taste)

Incidence less frequent

Acid regurgitation; anorexia (loss of appetite; weight loss); ***appetite increase; cough; dizziness; dyspepsia*** (acid or sour stomach; belching; heartburn; indigestion; stomach discomfort or pain); ***fever; malaise*** (general feeling of discomfort or illness); ***pruritus*** (itching skin); ***rash; somnolence*** (sleepiness)

Incidence not determined—Observed during clinical practice; estimates of frequency cannot be determined

abdominal distension; alopecia (hair loss; thinning of hair); ***arthralgia*** (pain in joints; muscle pain or stiffness; difficulty in moving); ***depression; hyperpigmentation*** (darkening of skin); ***oral paresthesia; paronychia*** (redness or soreness around fingernails; loosening of the fingernails); ***redistribution/accumulation of body fat; urticaria*** (hives or welts; itching, redness of skin; skin rash); ***vasculitis*** (redness, soreness or itching skin; fever; sores, welting or blisters)

Overdose

There are no reports of indinavir overdose in humans. Single oral and intraperitoneal doses of indinavir up to 20 times the human dose in rats and 10 times the human dose in mice did not result in any deaths.

For more information on the management of overdose or unintentional ingestion, **contact a Poison Control Center** (see *Poison Control Center Listing*).

Patient Consultation

As an aid to patient consultation, refer to *Advice for the Patient, Indinavir (Systemic)*.

In providing consultation, consider emphasizing the following selected information (» = major clinical significance)

Before using this medication

» Conditions affecting use, especially:
Hypersensitivity to indinavir

Pregnancy—Hyperbilirubinemia has occurred during treatment with indinavir; it is unknown whether administration to the mother in the perinatal period will exacerbate physiologic hyperbilirubinemia in the neonate

Breast-feeding—Indinavir is distributed into the milk of lactating rats; it is not known if indinavir is distributed into human breast milk; therefore, breast-feeding should be discontinued

Other medications, especially, cisapride, didanosine, delavirdine, efavirenz, ergot derivatives, HMG-CoA inhibitors, itraconazole, ketoconazole, lovastatin midazolam, pimozide, rifabutin, rifampin, simvastatin, St. John's wort, sildenafil, or triazolam

Other medical problems, especially hepatic function impairment and hepatitis

Proper use of this medication

» Importance of taking indinavir with water 1 hour before or 2 hours after a meal; indinavir may also be taken with other liquids (skim milk, juice, coffee, or tea) or with a light meal (dry toast with jelly, juice, and coffee with skim milk and sugar, or corn flakes, skim milk and sugar)

» Importance of drinking at least 1.5 liters (approximately 48 ounces) of liquids over each 24-hour period

» Importance of not taking more medication than prescribed; importance of not discontinuing indinavir without checking with physician

» Compliance with full course of therapy

» Importance of not missing doses and of taking at evenly spaced times

Not sharing medication with others

» Proper dosing

Missed dose: Taking as soon as possible; not taking if almost time for next dose; not doubling doses

» Proper storage; indinavir capsules are sensitive to moisture; indinavir should be stored and dispense in the original container and the desiccant should remain in the bottle

Precautions while using this medication

» Because indinavir may interact with other medications, not taking any other medications (prescription or nonprescription) without first consulting your physician

» Regular visits to physician for blood tests and monitoring of blood glucose concentrations

Side/adverse effects

Signs of potential side effects, especially anemia, diabetes or hyperglycemia, jaundice, nephrolithiasis/urolithiasis, and ketoacidosis

General Dosing Information

The recommended dose of indinavir is 800 mg every eight hours, whether it is used alone or in combination with other antiretroviral agents.

To help prevent kidney stones, it is recommended that patients drink at least 1.5 liters (approximately 48 ounces) of liquids over each 24-hour period. Patients who experience kidney stones may require temporary interruption of therapy (e.g., 1 to 3 days) during the acute episode or discontinuation of therapy.

Patients with mild to moderate hepatic function impairment due to cirrhosis require a dosage reduction to 600 mg every eight hours.

Diet/Nutrition

Administration of a single 400-mg dose of indinavir with grapefruit juice results in a 26% decrease in the area under the plasma concentration-time curve (AUC) of indinavir; dosing modification is not required.

Oral Dosage Forms

Note: The dosing and strengths of the dosage form available are expressed in terms of indinavir base (not the sulfate salt).

INDINAVIR SULFATE CAPSULES

Usual adult dose

Antiviral—

Single Therapy—Oral, 800 mg (base) every eight hours.

Concomitant Therapy—Delavirdine: Oral, indinavir 600 mg every 8 hours with delavirdine 400 mg three times a day

Efavirenz: Oral, indinavir 1000 mg every 8 hours with efavirenz

Itraconazole: Oral, indinavir 600 mg every 8 hours with itraconazole 200 mg twice daily

Ketoconazole: Oral, indinavir 600 mg every 8 hours

Rifabutin: Oral, indinavir 1000 mg every 8 hours and rifabutin dose reduced to half of the standard dose

Usual pediatric dose

Safety and efficacy have not been established.

Strength(s) usually available

U.S.—

100 mg (base) (Rx) [*Crixivan* (lactose)].
200 mg (base) (Rx) [*Crixivan* (lactose)].
333 mg (base) (Rx) [*Crixivan* (lactose)].
400 mg (base) (Rx) [*Crixivan* (lactose)].

Canada—

200 mg (base) (Rx) [*Crixivan*].
400 mg (base) (Rx) [*Crixivan*].

Packaging and storage

Store at room temperature, preferably between 15 and 30 °C (59 and 86 °F). Store in a tight container. Protect from moisture.

Indinavir should be dispensed and stored in the original container. The desiccant should remain in the original bottle.

Auxiliary labeling

- Take on an empty stomach or with a light meal.
- Drink plenty of fluids
- Continue medicine for full time of treatment.
- Do not take other medications without physician's advice.

Revised: 02/12/2003

INDOMETHACIN—See *Anti-inflammatory Drugs, Nonsteroidal (Ophthalmic), Anti-inflammatory Drugs, Nonsteroidal (Systemic), Indomethacin—For Patent Ductus Arteriosus (Systemic)*

INDOMETHACIN—For Patent Ductus Arteriosus Systemic

INN: Indometacin

VA CLASSIFICATION (Primary/Secondary):

Oral—MS102/MS400; CN850; CN105; CV900
Parenteral—CV900

Note: For information pertaining to use of indomethacin for other indications, see *Anti-inflammatory Drugs, Nonsteroidal (Systemic)*.

Commonly used brand name(s): *Apo-Indomethacin; Indameth; Indocid; Indocid PDA; Indocin; Indocin I.V; Novomethacin.*

Another commonly used name is indometacin.

Note: For a listing of dosage forms and brand names by country availability, see *Dosage Forms* section(s).

Category

Ductus arteriosus, patent, closure adjunct.

Indications

Note: Bracketed information in the *Indications* section refers to uses that are not included in U.S. product labeling.

Accepted

Ductus arteriosus, patent (treatment)—Intravenous indomethacin sodium is indicated to induce pharmacologic closure of a hemodynamically significant patent ductus arteriosus (PDA) in premature infants weighing 500 to 1750 grams. Evidence of a hemodynamically significant PDA (such as respiratory distress, continuous murmur, hyperactive precordium, enlarged heart, congestion in the lungs, and associated constitutional symptoms) should be present prior to therapy. In the U.S., indomethacin is FDA-approved for administration only if these signs and symptoms persist after 48 hours of conservative treatment, such as fluid restriction, diuretics, and respiratory support. [However, some neonatologists recommend that indomethacin therapy be instituted as soon as possible after identification of the PDA, especially if echocardiography shows the presence of a significant left-to-right shunt and/or the infant is being mechanically ventilated.][1]

Some investigators have not found successful closure to be associated with birth weight or postnatal age. However, others have reported the medication's efficacy to be decreased in infants >2 weeks of age (possibly because metabolism and/or clearance of indomethacin increases with neonatal age) and in infants weighing < 1000 grams (possibly because of insufficient muscular development in the ductal wall). Reopening of the ductus may occur following initial closure; although reclosure may occur spontaneously or in response to additional indomethacin, some infants may require surgery to achieve permanent closure.

[Indomethacin has also been administered orally (via a nasogastric tube) or rectally, as a suspension prepared from capsule contents, for this purpose.][1] However, intravenous administration is preferred because it produces more predictable indomethacin serum concentrations, leading to a higher closure rate (> 80%), than oral or rectal administration. Also, intravenous administration produces fewer gastrointestinal adverse effects than oral indomethacin.

[Indomethacin is not specifically approved by U.S. or Canadian regulatory agencies for administration to premature neonates without substantial evidence of a hemodynamically significant PDA. However, preliminary evidence suggests that administration at the first sign of a murmur (but no other symptoms) may prevent development of a symptomatic PDA in infants weighing < 1000 grams. These infants may be at greater risk of developing a symptomatic PDA than those with a murmur (but no other symptoms) weighing > 1000 grams.][1]

[1]Not included in Canadian product labeling.

Pharmacology/Pharmacokinetics

Physicochemical characteristics

Chemical Group—1–(4–chlorobenzoyl)–5–methoxy–2–methyl–1H–indole–3–acetic acid, sodium salt, trihydrate.

Molecular weight—
Indomethacin: 357.79.
Indomethacin sodium (trihydrate): 433.82.

pKa—4.5.

Mechanism of action/Effect

Indomethacin inhibits the activity of the enzyme cyclooxygenase to decrease the formation of precursors of prostaglandins and thromboxanes from arachidonic acid. Inhibition of prostaglandin synthesis (and the consequent reduction of prostaglandin activity) permits constriction of the patent ductus arteriosus, which may be due to excessive production, and/or increased sensitivity of the premature ductus to the dilating effects, of prostaglandins of the E series.

Other actions/effects

Indomethacin reversibly inhibits platelet aggregation.

Absorption

When administered via nasogastric tube—Poor and incomplete, possibly because of indomethacin's insolubility and/or abnormalities in gastric function (gastric acid secretion, gastric motility, etc.) or pH in premature neonates with a patent ductus arteriosus.

Protein binding

Has not been determined in the premature neonate. Very high (99%), to albumin, in adults.

Biotransformation

Hepatic; the rate of metabolism increases with neonatal age.

Half-life

Greatly prolonged as compared with that reported in adults; varies inversely with postnatal age and weight. The prolonged half-life may reflect extensive and/or repeated enterohepatic circulation and re-entry into plasma.

Infants <7 days of age—3 to 60 hours; average 20 hours.
Infants >7 days of age—4 to 38 hours; average 12 hours.
Infants <1000 grams—9 to 60 hours; average 21 hours.
Infants >1000 grams—3 to 52 hours; average 15 hours.

Peak serum concentration

Subject to wide individual variation when administered by any route but especially following oral administration.

Elimination

Renal and biliary excretion of metabolites and of unchanged indomethacin. In adults, 10 to 20% of a dose is excreted in the urine as unchanged indomethacin; the quantity excreted unchanged in the premature neonate has not been determined.

In dialysis—Indomethacin is not dialyzable.

Precautions to Consider

Drug interactions and/or related problems

The following drug interactions and/or related problems have been selected on the basis of their potential clinical significance (possible mechanism in parentheses where appropriate)—not necessarily inclusive (» = major clinical significance):

Note: In addition to the interactions listed below, the possibility should be considered that additive or multiple effects leading to impaired blood clotting and/or increased risk of bleeding may occur if indomethacin is used concurrently with any medication having a significant potential for causing hypoprothrombinemia, thrombocytopenia, or gastrointestinal ulceration or hemorrhage.

» Aminoglycosides or
» Digitalis glycosides
(indomethacin may decrease renal clearance of aminoglycosides or digitalis glycosides, leading to increased plasma concentrations, elimination half-lives, and risk of aminoglycoside or digitalis toxicity; careful observation is required when indomethacin is given concomitantly with digitalis; frequent electrocardiograms (ECG) and serum digitalis levels may be necessary; dosage adjustment of aminoglycosides may also be required, based on evidence of toxicity and/or measurement of plasma concentration)

Nephrotoxic medications, other (See *Appendix II*)
(concurrent use with indomethacin may increase the risk and/or severity of adverse renal effects)

Laboratory value alterations

The following have been selected on the basis of their potential clinical significance (possible effect in parentheses where appropriate)—not necessarily inclusive (» = major clinical significance).

With diagnostic test results
Urinary 5-hydroxyindoleacetic acid (5-HIAA) determinations
(false 5-HIAA concentration values may be measured via the Goldenberg modification of Undenfriend's method because indomethacin metabolites are structurally similar to 5-HIAA)

With physiology/laboratory test values
Bleeding time
(may be prolonged because of suppressed platelet aggregation; effects in the premature neonate may persist for several days after the medication is discontinued)

Blood glucose concentration
(may be decreased or, less frequently, increased)

Blood urea nitrogen (BUN) concentration and
Creatinine concentration, serum and
Glucose concentration, urine and
Potassium concentration, serum and
Protein (including albumin) concentrations, urine
(may be increased because indomethacin decreases glomerular filtration rate)

Note: Indomethacin may decrease both sodium and water excretion; however, water retention may exceed that of sodium so that the net effect is a reduction of serum sodium concentration (dilutional hyponatremia).

Chloride concentration, urine and
Creatinine clearance and
Free water clearance and
Glomerular filtration rate and
Osmolality, urine and
Potassium concentration, urine and
Sodium concentration, urine and
Sodium concentration, serum and
Urine volume
(may be decreased)

Leukocyte count and
Platelet count
(may be decreased)

Liver function tests, especially transaminase (AST [SGOT]; ALT [SGPT]) activity
(values may be increased; if significant abnormalities occur, clinical signs and symptoms consistent with liver disease develop, or systemic manifestations such as eosinophilia or rash occur, indomethacin should be discontinued)

Plasma renin activity (PRA)
(may be decreased; also, indomethacin may block the increase in PRA usually produced by bumetanide, furosemide, or indapamide)

Medical considerations/Contraindications

The medical considerations/contraindications included have been selected on the basis of their potential clinical significance (reasons given in parentheses where appropriate)—not necessarily inclusive (» = major clinical significance).

Except under special circumstances, this medication should not be used when the following medical problems exist:

» Bleeding, active, especially intracranial or gastrointestinal or
» Coagulation defects
(increased risk of severe hemorrhage because indomethacin inhibits platelet aggregation and may cause gastrointestinal bleeding)

» Enterocolitis, necrotizing, proven or suspected
(may be exacerbated)

» Heart disease, congenital, such as:
Coarctation of the aorta, severe
Pulmonary atresia

Tetralogy of Fallot, severe or
» Lesions, severely obstructive, left-sided, other
(patency of the ductus arteriosus may be required to provide satisfactory pulmonary or systemic blood flow; indomethacin should not be administered until the safety of inducing closure has been determined)
» Infection, untreated, confirmed or suspected
(symptoms of progression may be masked; also, sepsis may predispose the patient to renal insufficiency and increase the risk of renal impairment or failure; in addition, an unexpectedly high rate of treatment failure has been reported following indomethacin administration to infants with sepsis)
Jaundice, severe
(although no evidence of bilirubin displacement has been seen in controlled trials, indomethacin may cause displacement of bilirubin, thus increasing the risk of kernicterus in patients with severe jaundice, and should be used with caution)
» Renal function impairment, severe,
(may be exacerbated)
» Thrombocytopenia
(increased risk of severe hemorrhage because indomethacin inhibits platelet aggregation and may cause gastrointestinal bleeding; although platelets may be administered if necessary, indomethacin should be used only when the risk of surgery outweighs the risk of administering blood products)

Risk-benefit should be considered when the following medical problems exist:
Conditions predisposing to renal insufficiency, such as:
Congestive heart failure
Extracellular volume depletion
Hepatic function impairment
(increased risk of renal function impairment, including acute renal failure)

Patient monitoring

The following may be especially important in patient monitoring (other tests may be warranted in some patients, depending on condition; » = major clinical significance):

Electrolyte concentrations, serum and
Renal function tests
(monitoring recommended during and following indomethacin administration; if renal function impairment occurs, [as shown by: concomitant elevations of blood urea nitrogen and creatinine, and reductions in glomerular filtration rate and creatinine clearance; anuria or marked oliguria, with urinary output < 0.6 mL/kg per hour] therapy should be suspended until adequate renal function has been restored)

Side/Adverse Effects

The following side/adverse effects have been selected on the basis of their potential clinical significance (possible signs and symptoms in parentheses where appropriate)—not necessarily inclusive:

Those indicating need for medical attention

Incidence more frequent
Gastrointestinal problems (abdominal distention; bleeding [incidence 3% to 9%]; gastric perforation [incidence < 3%]; transient ileus; vomiting); ***renal function impairment***—incidence >40%

Note: *Renal function impairment* is characterized by decreases in urine volume; free water clearance; urine osmolality; glomerular filtration rate; creatinine clearance; and excretion of sodium, potassium, and chloride. Corresponding increases in blood urea nitrogen (BUN), blood creatinine, and serum potassium occur. Water retention may be greater than sodium retention, leading to dilutional hyponatremia.
Gastrointestinal problems have been reported more frequently with oral (via a nasogastric tube) than with intravenous administration.

Incidence less frequent
Bleeding problems; hypoglycemia

Note: *Bleeding problems* reported (in addition to gastrointestinal bleeding) include pulmonary hemorrhage, disseminated intravascular coagulopathy, microscopic hematuria, and oozing at needle puncture sites.
Intracranial hemorrhage, necrotizing enterocolitis, and retrolental fibroplasia have also been reported; however, the incidence in indomethacin-treated infants is not greater than that reported in other premature infants, who are known to be at risk for these complications.

Incidence rare
Acidosis; alkalosis; apnea; bradycardia; exacerbation of preexisting pulmonary infection

General Dosing Information

Sterile indomethacin sodium is to be administered intravenously only, over a 5- to 10-second period. Extravasation must be avoided because the solution is irritating to tissues.

Restriction of fluid intake (recommended for treatment of premature neonates with a patent ductus arteriosus) should be continued during indomethacin treatment.

Administration of 1 mg per kg of body weight (mg/kg) of furosemide immediately following indomethacin has been reported to prevent or reduce indomethacin-induced adverse renal effects without interfering with ductus arteriosus closure. However, furosemide administration is not a generally accepted measure for achieving this purpose. If a significant decrease in renal function occurs following a dose of indomethacin as indicated by a serum creatinine concentration greater than 1.2 to 1.4 mg per dL (106-124 micromols/L) or other appropriate tests, additional doses should be withheld until urine volume increases to normal levels (i.e., > 1 mL per kg of body weight per hour) and/or laboratory studies indicate return of normal renal function.

The medication should be discontinued if any severe adverse reaction, especially hepatic function impairment or disease, occurs.

If significant constriction or closure of the ductus arteriosus does not occur following 2 courses (3 doses per course) of indomethacin therapy, surgery may be required.

Reopening of the ductus arteriosus may occur following initial closure. Although spontaneous reclosure has occurred in many patients, additional indomethacin or surgery may be required.

For treatment of adverse effects or overdose

Recommended treatment may include:
- Discontinuing or temporarily suspending administration.
- Monitoring the patient and treating observed symptoms. The possibility must be considered that gastrointestinal ulceration or hemorrhage may not occur until several days after administration.

Hemodialysis is not effective in removing indomethacin from the circulation.

Oral Dosage Forms

Note: Bracketed uses in the *Dosage Forms* section refer to categories of use and/or indications that are not included in U.S. product labeling.

INDOMETHACIN CAPSULES USP

Usual pediatric dose

[Patent ductus arteriosus closure adjunct][1]—
Infants up to 48 hours of age at time of first dose—
Oral, via nasogastric tube, 200 mcg (0.2 mg) of indomethacin per kg of body weight initially. If necessary, one or two additional doses of 100 mcg (0.1 mg) of indomethacin per kg of body weight may be given at twelve- to twenty-four-hour intervals.

Infants 2 to 7 days of age at time of first dose—
Oral, via nasogastric tube, 200 mcg (0.2 mg) of indomethacin per kg of body weight initially. If necessary, one or two additional doses of 200 mcg (0.2 mg) of indomethacin per kg of body weight may be given at twelve- to twenty-four-hour intervals.

Infants over 7 days of age at time of first dose—
Oral, via nasogastric tube, 200 mcg (0.2 mg) of indomethacin per kg of body weight initially. If necessary, one or two additional doses of 250 mcg (0.25 mg) of indomethacin per kg of body weight may be given at twelve- to twenty-four-hour intervals.

Note: Some investigators have used initial doses of 300 mcg (0.3 mg) per kg of body weight.
The recommended dose may also be administered rectally (as a suspension prepared from capsule contents); however, intravenous administration is preferred if available.

Strength(s) usually available

U.S.—
25 mg (Rx) [*Indameth; Indocin;* GENERIC].
50 mg (Rx) [*Indameth; Indocin;* GENERIC].

Canada—
25 mg (Rx) [*Apo-Indomethacin; Indocid; Novomethacin*].
50 mg (Rx) [*Apo-Indomethacin; Indocid; Novomethacin*].

Packaging and storage

Store below 40 °C (104 °F), preferably between 15 and 30 °C (59 and 86 °F). Store in a well-closed container.

Parenteral Dosage Forms

INDOMETHACIN FOR INJECTION

Usual pediatric dose

Patent ductus arteriosus closure adjunct—

Infants up to 48 hours of age at time of first dose—

Intravenous, 200 mcg (0.2 mg) of indomethacin per kg of body weight initially. If necessary, one or two additional doses of 100 mcg (0.1 mg) of indomethacin per kg of body weight may be given at twelve- to twenty-four-hour intervals.

Infants 2 to 7 days of age at time of first dose—

Intravenous, 200 mcg (0.2 mg) of indomethacin per kg of body weight initially. If necessary, one or two additional doses of 200 mcg (0.2 mg) of indomethacin per kg of body weight may be given at twelve- to twenty-four-hour intervals.

Infants over 7 days of age at time of first dose—

Intravenous, 200 mcg (0.2 mg) of indomethacin per kg of body weight initially. If necessary, one or two additional doses of 250 mcg (0.25 mg) of indomethacin per kg of body weight may be given at twelve- to twenty-four-hour intervals.

Note: Some investigators have used initial doses of 300 mcg (0.3 mg) of anhydrous indomethacin per kg of body weight.

Strength(s) usually available

U.S.—

1 mg (Rx) [*Indocin I.V.*].

Canada—

1 mg (Rx) [*Indocid PDA*].

Note: Each vial contains indomethacin sodium trihydrate, equivalent to 1 mg indomethacin, as a lyophilized powder or plug.

Packaging and storage

Store below 30 °C (86 °F), unless otherwise directed by manufacturer. Protect from light.

Preparation of dosage form

Add 1 or 2 mL of preservative-free 0.9% sodium chloride injection or preservative-free sterile water for injection to the contents of the vial. A solution prepared using 1 mL of diluent contains 100 mcg (0.1 mg) of anhydrous indomethacin per 0.1 mL; a solution prepared using 2 mL of diluent contains 50 mcg (0.05 mg) of anhydrous indomethacin per 0.1 mL.

Stability

Sterile indomethacin sodium contains no preservatives. Therefore, the medication should be reconstituted immediately prior to use and any unused solution should be discarded.

Incompatibilities

Sterile indomethacin sodium contains no buffering agents. Further dilution of the reconstituted solution with intravenous infusion solutions is not recommended because free indomethacin may be precipitated if the pH of the solution is < 6.

[1]Not included in Canadian product labeling.

Revised: 12/21/1999

INFANT FORMULAS, HYPOALLERGENIC—See *Infant Formulas (Systemic)*

INFANT FORMULAS, MILK-BASED—See *Infant Formulas (Systemic)*

INFANT FORMULAS, SOY-BASED—See *Infant Formulas (Systemic)*

INFLIXIMAB Systemic

VA CLASSIFICATION (Primary/Secondary): GA400/MS109

Commonly used brand name(s): *Remicade*.

Another commonly used name is cA2.

Note: For a listing of dosage forms and brand names by country availability, see *Dosage Forms* section(s).

Category

Inflammatory bowel disease therapy agent; antirheumatic agent.

Indications

General Considerations

Since tumor necrosis factor-alpha (TNF-alpha) mediates inflammation and modulates cellular immune response, infliximab (and other anti–TNF-alpha therapies) may affect normal immune responses. At this time, it is not known whether long-term use of tumor necrosis inhibitors such as infliximab increases the incidence of infection or malignancy.

Accepted

Ankylosing spondylitis (treatment)[1]—Infliximab is indicated for reducing signs and symptoms in patients with active ankylosing spondylitis.

Arthritis, psoriatic (treatment)[1]—Infliximab is indicated for reducing signs and symptoms of active arthritis in patients with psoriatic arthritis.

Colitis, ulcerative (treatment)[1]—Infliximab is indicated for reducing signs and symptoms, achieving clinical remission and mucosal healing, and eliminating corticosteroid use in patients with moderately to severely active ulcerative colitis who have had an inadequate response to conventional therapy.

Crohn's disease (treatment)—Infliximab is indicated for reducing signs and symptoms and inducing and maintaining clinical remission in adult and pediatric patients with moderately to severely active Crohn's disease who have had an inadequate response to conventional therapy. Also, infliximab is indicated for reducing the number of draining rectovaginal and enterocutaneous fistulas and maintaining fistula closure in adult patients with fistulizing Crohn's disease.

Rheumatoid arthritis (treatment)—Infliximab, in combination with methotrexate, is indicated to reduce the signs and symptoms, inhibiting the progression of structural damage, and improving physical function in patients with moderately to severely active rheumatoid arthritis

[Psoriasis (treatment)][1]—Infliximab is indicated for the treatment of psoriasis

[Reactive arthritis (treatment)][1]—Infliximab is indicated for the treatment of reactive arthritis

[Inflammatory bowel disease arthritis (treatment)][1]—Infliximab is indicated for the treatment of inflammatory bowel disease arthritis

[1]Not included in Canadian product labeling.

Pharmacology/Pharmacokinetics

Note: During premarketing clinical trials, no pharmacokinetic differences were observed in patient subgroups defined by gender, age, weight, or hepatic or renal function.

Physicochemical characteristics

Source—Infliximab is a chimeric human-murine immunoglobulin ($IgG1_{kappa}$) monoclonal antibody composed of human constant and murine variable regions.

Molecular weight—Approximately 149,100 daltons.

Mechanism of action/Effect

Infliximab is a chimeric human-murine immunoglobulin ($IgG1_{kappa}$) monoclonal antibody that binds specifically to tumor necrosis factor-alpha (TNF-alpha), a proinflammatory cytokine. Infliximab neutralizes the biological activity of TNF-alpha; by binding to the soluble and transmembrane forms of TNF-alpha, it inhibits the binding of TNF-alpha to its receptors. Biological activities attributed to TNF-alpha include induction of proinflammatory cytokines, such as interleukin-1 (IL-1) and interleukin-6 (IL-6); enhancement of leukocyte migration by increasing endothelial layer permeability and expression of adhesion molecules by endothelial cells and leukocytes; stimulation of neutrophil and eosinophil functions; and induction of acute phase and other liver proteins. Cells expressing transmembrane TNF-alpha bound by infliximab can be lysed *in vitro* by complement or effector cells. Antibodies to TNF-alpha reduce disease activity in a cotton-top tamarin colitis model. Infliximab inhibits the functional activity of TNF-alpha in a wide variety of *in vitro* bioassays utilizing human fibroblasts, endothelial cells, neutrophils, B and T lymphocytes, and epithelial cells.

Mucosa and stools from patients with Crohn's disease have been found to contain elevated concentrations of TNF-alpha, correlating with increased disease activity. Treatment with infliximab reduces both infiltration of inflammatory cells and TNF-alpha production in inflamed areas of the intestine, and also reduces the proportion of mononuclear cells from the lamina propria able to express TNF-alpha and interferon gamma. After treatment with infliximab, patients with Crohn's disease have decreased levels of serum IL-6 and C-reactive protein (CRP) when compared with baseline. However, peripheral blood lymphocytes from infliximab-treated patients show no decrease in proliferative responses to *in vitro* mitogenic stimulation when compared with cells from untreated patients.

Infliximab does not neutralize the biological activity of TNF-beta (lymphotoxin alpha), a related cytokine that utilizes the same receptors as TNF-alpha.

Other actions/effects

Since TNF-alpha mediates inflammation and modulates cellular immune response, infliximab (and other anti-TNF therapies) may affect normal immune responses. In addition, some patients treated with infliximab develop human antichimeric antibodies (HACA), which may predispose them to infusion reactions. Anti-TNF therapy also may result in the formation of autoimmune antibodies, such as antibodies against double-stranded deoxynucleic acid (dsDNA).

Distribution

A single intravenous infusion of 5 mg per kg of body weight (mg/kg) resulted in a median volume of distribution (Vol_D) of 3 L. Vol_D was independent of the administered dose.

Half-life

A single intravenous infusion of 5 mg/kg of infliximab resulted in a terminal half-life of 9.5 days.

Peak serum concentration

A single intravenous infusion of 5 mg/kg of infliximab resulted in a median maximum serum concentration (C_{max}) of 118 mcg/mL. The C_{max} and area under the concentration-time curve (AUC) showed a direct and linear relationship with the administered dose.

Precautions to Consider

Cross-sensitivity and/or related problems

Patients sensitive to any murine (mouse) proteins or other component of this product may be sensitive to infliximab also.

Carcinogenicity

More malignancies have been observed in patients receiving infliximab compared to control groups. Fourteen patients were diagnosed with malignancies among 2897 infliximab-treated patients versus 1 patient among 1262 control patients, with median duration of follow-up of 0.5 year for infliximab-treated patients and 0.4 year for control patients. Common malignancies included breast, colorectal, and melanoma. The rate of expected malignancies in the general population was lower than expected for the control patients.

More lymphomas have been observed in patients receiving infliximab compared to control groups. Four patients were diagnosed with lymphomas among 4292 infliximab-treated patients versus no patients among 1265 control patients, with median duration of follow-up of 1 year for infliximab-treated patients and 0.5 year for control patients. Patients with Crohn's disease or rheumatoid arthritis, particularly patients with highly active disease and/or chronic exposure to immunosuppressant therapies, may be at higher risk (up to several fold) than the general population for lymphomas.

Tumorigenicity

A toxicity study was conducted with mice given cV1q anti-mouse TNFα to evaluate tumorigenicity. cV1q is an analogous antibody that inhibits the function of TNFα in mice. Weekly doses of 2 and 8 times the human dose for Crohn's disease were given and results indicated that cV1q did not cause tumorigenicity in mice.

Mutagenicity

No clastogenic or mutagenic effects of infliximab were observed in the *in vivo* mouse micronucleus test or the Ames test (*Salmonella-Escherichia coli* assay), respectively. Chromosomal aberrations were not observed in an assay performed using human lymphocytes.

Pregnancy/Reproduction

Fertility—Fertility was not impaired in a fertility and general reproduction toxicity study with the analogous mouse antibody in a 6-month chronic toxicity study.

Pregnancy—Studies have not been done in humans.

Animal reproduction studies have not been conducted with infliximab since it does not cross-react with TNF-alpha in species other than humans and chimpanzees. In a developmental toxicity study conducted in mice using an analogous antibody that selectively inhibits the functional activity of mouse TNF-alpha, no evidence of maternal toxicity, embryotoxicity, or teratogenicity was found. It is not known whether infliximab can cause fetal harm when administered to a pregnant woman or can affect reproduction capacity. Infliximab should be given to a pregnant woman only if clearly needed.

FDA Pregnancy Category B.

Breast-feeding

It is not known whether infliximab is distributed into breast milk or absorbed by the nursing infant.A decision should be made whether to discontinue nursing or to discontinue infliximab, taking into account the importance of infliximab to the mother.

Pediatrics

Safety and efficacy of infliximab in patients with juvenile rheumatoid arthritis and in pediatric patients with ulcerative colitis have not been established.

Safety and efficacy of infliximab have been established for reducing signs and symptoms and inducing and maintaining clinical remission in pediatric patients 6 years of age and older with moderately to severely active Crohn's disease who have had an inadequate response to conventional therapy. Infliximab has not been studied in children less than 6 years of age with Crohn's disease. Safety and efficacy of infliximab use for greater than a year in pediatric Crohn's disease patients have not been established in clinical trials.

It is recommended that pediatric Crohn's disease patients be brought up to date with all vaccinations prior to initiating infliximab therapy. The interval between vaccination and initiation of infliximab therapy should be in accordance with current vaccination guidelines.

Adolescents

Although causality is unclear, postmarketing cases of rare hepatosplenic T-cell lymphomas, which can be fatal, have been reported in adolescent and young adult patients with Crohn's disease who are taking infliximab.

Geriatrics

No information is available on the relationship of age to the effects of infliximab in geriatric patients. However, the incidence of infections in the elderly population is higher in general; caution should be used in treating these patients, since the impact of infliximab treatment on the incidence of infections is not known.

Drug interactions and/or related problems

The following drug interactions and/or related problems have been selected on the basis of their potential clinical significance (possible mechanism in parentheses where appropriate)—not necessarily inclusive (» = major clinical significance):

Note: Specific studies on drug interactions with infliximab have not been conducted. The majority of patients in premarketing clinical trials received other concomitant medications commonly used in the treatment of Crohn's disease, including antibiotics, antivirals, corticosteroids, mercaptopurine, methotrexate, azathioprine, and aminosalicylates.

» Anakinra
(concomitant use not recommended; serious infection and other similar toxicities to those seen with concomitant etanercept and anakinra therapy may also result from the combination of anakinra and other TNFα-blocking agents)

» Immunosuppressive therapy
(concomitant use along with the Crohn's disease or rheumatoid arthritis for which the patient is being treated could predispose them to infections; patients may also be more prone to developing lymphomas when being treated with immunosuppressive therapy and impact of treatment with infliximab concomitantly on this is unknown)

Live vaccines
(recommended that live vaccines not be given concurrently with infliximab; no data available on response to vaccination or on secondary transmission of infection by live vaccines in patients receiving anti-TNF therapy)

Laboratory value alterations

The following have been selected on the basis of their potential clinical significance (possible effect in parentheses where appropriate)—not necessarily inclusive (» = major clinical significance).

Liver enzymes
(marked elevations [5 times the upper limit of normal] have occurred in post-marketing reports; if liver enzyme abnormalities are found, infliximab should be discontinued and the abnormality investigated)

Medical considerations/Contraindications

The medical considerations/contraindications included have been selected on the basis of their potential clinical significance (reasons given in parentheses where appropriate)—not necessarily inclusive (» = major clinical significance).

Except under special circumstances, this medicine should not be used when the following medical problem exists:

» Congestive heart failure, moderate or severe
(infliximab should not be initiated in patients with moderate or severe congestive heart failure; treatment should be discontinued in patients whose congestive heart failure is worsening, and treatment discontinuation should be considered in patients with stable

concomitant congestive heart failure, especially in those who have not had a significant response to infliximab therapy.)

» Hypersensitivity to any murine (mouse) proteins or other component of infliximab

» Infections, chronic or
» Infections, invasive or
» Infections, opportunistic or
» Infections, recurrent, history of
(infliximab should not be administered to patients with a clinically important, active infection; caution should be exercised when considering the use of infliximab in patients with a chronic infection or a history of recurrent infection)

Risk-benefit should be considered when the following medical problem exists:

» Central nervous system demyelinating disorders, pre-existing or recent onset including or
CNS manifestation of systemic vasculitis or
Multiple sclerosis
» Seizure disorders, pre-existing or recent onset
(caution should be exercised in considering infliximab use in these patients; discontinuation of infliximab should be considered in patients who develop significant CNS adverse reactions)

Hepatitis B, chronic carrier
(infliximab use has been associated with reactivation of hepatitis B in patients who are carriers of the virus; these patients should be appropriately evaluated and monitored prior to and during treatment with infliximab)

» Hematologic abnormalities, ongoing or history of including:
» Leukopenia or
» Neutropenia or
» Pancytopenia or
» Thrombocytopenia
(caution should be exercised; discontinuation of therapy should be considered if patients develop signs and symptoms suggestive of blood dyscrasias)

» Malignancy, history of
(caution should be exercised; in clinical trials of TNFα-blocking agents, more cases of lymphoma have been observed among patients receiving TNF blockers; potential role of TNF blockers in development of malignancies not known)

» Tuberculosis, latent
(treatment of latent tuberculosis infection should be initiated prior to therapy with infliximab)

Patient monitoring

The following may be especially important in patient monitoring (other tests may be warranted in some patients, depending on condition; » = major clinical significance):

» Cardiac status
(patients with stable concomitant congestive heart failure should have cardiac status closely monitored)

» Infection
(patients should be monitored for signs and symptoms of infection while on or after treatment with infliximab; new infections should be closely monitored; infliximab therapy should be discontinued if patient develops serious infection)

Signs/symptoms of liver dysfunction
(should be evaluated for evidence of liver injury; severe hepatic reactions have occurred between two weeks to more than a year after initiating infliximab treatment)

» Tuberculosis
(patients should be evaluated for latent tuberculosis infection with a tuberculin skin test; patients, including those who are tuberculin skin test negative, should be monitored for signs and symptoms of active tuberculosis)

Side/Adverse Effects

Note: Tuberculosis (frequently disseminated or extrapulmonary), invasive fungal infections, and other opportunistic infections have been observed in patients receiving infliximab. Some of these infections have been fatal. If a patient develops a serious infection, infliximab therapy should be discontinued. Anti-tuberculosis treatment of patients with a reactive tuberculin skin test reduces the risk of TB reactivation in patients receiving treatment with infliximab. However, active tuberculosis has developed in patients receiving infliximab who were tuberculin skin test negative prior to receiving infliximab.

Cases of histoplasmosis, listeriosis, pneumocytosis, and tuberculosis have been observed in patients receiving infliximab. For patients residing in regions where histoplasmosis is endemic, the benefits and risks of infliximab treatment should be carefully considered before initiation of infliximab therapy.

Human antichimeric antibody (HACA) development may occur secondary to infliximab therapy. The majority of the HACA-positive patients were at low titer (≤ 1:20). Patients who were HACA-positive were more likely to experience an infusion reaction to the administration of infliximab. However, the incidence of positive HACA responses was lower among Crohn's disease patients who were receiving immunosuppressant therapies (such as 6-mercaptopurine, azathioprine, or corticosteroids) than among patients not receiving such therapies. Also, the clinical significance of HACA formation has been questioned since HACA-positive patients who received repeated treatment with infliximab have demonstrated sustained clinical benefit and have tolerated such treatment well.

Anti-TNF therapy may result in the formation of autoimmune antibodies and, rarely, the development of a lupus-like syndrome. If a patient develops symptoms suggestive of a lupus-like syndrome and is positive for antibodies against double-stranded deoxynucleic acid (dsDNA), infliximab treatment should be discontinued. In premarketing clinical trials, discontinuation of infliximab therapy in these patients resulted in resolution of symptoms and disappearance of the anti-dsDNA.

Patients with chronic Crohn's disease and long-term exposure to immunosuppressant therapies are more likely to develop infections and lymphomas. However, the effect of infliximab treatment on the incidence of infections or lymphomas is not known.

Caution should be used in the re-treatment of patients with infliximab following an extended period without treatment. In one study, 25% of patients who received infliximab 2 to 4 years following previous infliximab therapy presented with delayed adverse events including myalgia; rash; fever; polyarthralgia (including temporomandibular arthralgia); pruritus; facial, hand, or lip edema; dysphagia; urticaria; sore throat; and headache. Adverse effects appeared to be related to development of an immune response to infliximab. It is not clear if the formulation of the previous dose that most of these patients received initially, which differs from the current product formulation, contributed in a causal manner to the adverse reactions.

In a phase 2 trial of 150 patients with moderate to severe (NYHA class III-IV) congestive heart failure (CHF), higher incidences of mortality and hospitalization for worsening heart failure were seen in patients treated with infliximab, especially those treated with the higher dose of 10 mg/kg. At present, there are insufficient data to determine optimal patient management. However, it is recommended that treatment with infliximab be discontinued in patients with worsening CHF and treatment should not be initiated in patients with congestive heart failure.

The following side/adverse effects have been selected on the basis of their potential clinical significance (possible signs and symptoms in parentheses where appropriate)—not necessarily inclusive:

Those indicating need for medical attention

Incidence more frequent

Abdominal pain; bronchitis (cough; shortness of breath; tightness in chest; troubled breathing; wheezing); ***fatigue*** (unusual tiredness or weakness); ***infusion-related reactions, including fever; chills; pruritus*** (itching); ***urticaria*** (hives); ***chest pain; dyspnea*** (troubled breathing); ***facial flushing; headache; hypotension*** (dizziness; fainting); ***myalgia*** (muscle pain); ***nausea; upper respiratory tract infection*** (cough; fever; nasal congestion; runny nose; sneezing; sore throat); ***vomiting***

Note: *Infusion-related reactions* are more likely to occur in patients who have developed human antichimeric antibodies (i.e., HACA-positive).

Incidence less frequent

Back pain; cardiopulmonary reactions, including chest pain; dyspnea (troubled breathing); ***hypertension*** (headache; high blood pressure); ***or hypotension*** (dizziness; fainting; low blood pressure); ***cough; diarrhea; fever; headache; moniliasis, including dermal candidiasis*** (skin rash; cracks in skin at the corners of mouth; soreness or redness around fingernails and toenails); ***thrush*** (soreness or irritation of mouth or tongue; white patches in mouth and/or on tongue); ***and vaginitis*** (vaginal burning or itching and discharge); ***pain; pharyngitis*** (sore throat); ***pruritus*** (itching); ***rhinitis*** (runny nose); ***sinusitis*** (pain or tenderness around eyes and cheekbones; fever; headache; nasal congestion); ***urinary tract infection*** (difficult or painful urination; frequent urge to urinate; bloody or cloudy urine)

Incidence rare

Abdominal hernia (bulge of tissue through the wall of the abdomen); ***abscess*** (swollen, red, tender area of infection containing pus); ***adult respiratory distress syndrome*** (shortness of breath; tightness in chest; troubled breathing; wheezing); ***cholecystitis*** (stomach pain, severe; nausea; vomiting); ***dysuria*** (difficult or painful urination); ***falls; infection; intestinal obstruction*** (abdominal pain, severe; constipation; nausea; vomiting); ***intestinal perforation*** (abdominal pain, severe; troubled breathing; vomiting); ***intestinal stenosis*** (abdominal pain; nausea; vomiting); ***kidney infarction*** (back or side pain; nausea; vomiting); ***lupus erythematosus syndrome*** (skin rash, hives, or itching; fever; sore throat; swollen or painful glands; bone or joint pain; unusual tiredness or weakness); ***lymphoma*** (swollen glands; weight loss; general feeling of illness; black, tarry stools; yellow skin and eyes); ***palpitations*** (irregular or pounding heartbeat); ***pneumonia*** (cough; shortness of breath; troubled breathing; tightness in chest; wheezing); ***proctalgia*** (pain in rectum); ***skin rash; splenic infarction*** (abdominal pain; pain spreading to left shoulder); ***splenomegaly*** (abdominal pain; feeling of fullness); ***syncope*** (fainting); ***tendon injury; thrombocytopenia*** (usually asymptomatic; rarely, unusual bleeding or bruising; black, tarry stools; blood in urine or stools; pinpoint red spots on skin); ***ureteral obstruction*** (back or side pain, severe; nausea; vomiting)

Incidence not determined—Observed during clinical practice; estimates of frequency cannot be determined

Acute liver failure (headache; stomach pain; continuing vomiting; dark-colored urine; general feeling of tiredness or weakness; light-colored stools; yellow eyes or skin); ***anaphylactic-like reactions*** (cough; difficulty swallowing; dizziness; fast heartbeat; hives; itching, puffiness, or swelling of the eyelids or around the eyes, face, lips or tongue; shortness of breath; skin rash; tightness in chest; unusual tiredness or weakness; wheezing); ***bronchospasm, severe*** (cough; difficulty breathing; noisy breathing; shortness of breath; tightness in chest; wheezing); ***cholestasis*** (abdominal or stomach pain; chills; clay-colored stools; dark urine; diarrhea; dizziness; fever; headache; itching; loss of appetite; nausea; rash; unpleasant breath odor; unusual tiredness or weakness; vomiting of blood; yellow eyes or skin); ***Guillain-Barre syndrome*** (sudden numbness and weakness in the arms and legs; inability to move arms and legs); ***hepatitis*** (dark urine; general tiredness and weakness; light-colored stools; nausea and vomiting; upper right abdominal pain; yellow eyes and skin); ***hepatosplenic T-cell lymphomas*** (fatigue; painless swelling in neck, armpits or groin; weight loss; loss of appetite); ***Hodgkin's disease*** (swollen glands weight loss general feeling of illness black, tarry stools yellow skin and eyes); ***idiopathic thrombocytopenic purpura*** (unusual bleeding or bruising; bloody nose; heavier menstrual periods; pinpoint red spots on skin; black, tarry stools; blood in urine; unusual tiredness or weakness; fever; skin rash); ***interstitial pneumonitis/fibrosis*** (cough; difficult breathing; fever; shortness of breath); ***jaundice*** (chills; clay-colored stools; dark urine; dizziness; fever; headache; itching; loss of appetite; nausea; abdominal or stomach pain; area rash; unpleasant breath odor; unusual tiredness or weakness; vomiting of blood; yellow eyes or skin); ***laryngeal/pharyngeal edema*** (coughing; difficulty in breathing; difficulty in swallowing; hoarseness; shortness of breath; slow or irregular breathing; tightness in chest; wheezing); ***leukopenia*** (black, tarry stools; chest pain; chills; cough; fever; painful or difficult urination; shortness of breath; sore throat; sores, ulcers, or white spots on lips or in mouth; swollen glands; unusual bleeding or bruising; unusual tiredness or weakness); ***lymphoma*** (swollen glands weight loss general feeling of illness black, tarry stools yellow skin and eyes); ***neuropathies*** (burning, tingling, numbness or pain in the hands, arms, feet, or legs; sensation of pins and needles; stabbing pain); ***neutropenia*** (black, tarry, stools; chills; cough; fever; lower back or side pain; painful or difficult urination; pale skin; shortness of breath; sore throat; ulcers, sores, or white spots in mouth; unusual bleeding or bruising; unusual tiredness or weakness); ***non-Hodgkins lymphoma*** (swollen glands weight loss general feeling of illness black, tarry stools yellow skin and eyes); ***pancytopenia*** (high fever; chills; unexplained bleeding or bruising; bloody, black, or tarry stools; pale skin; unusual tiredness or weakness; cough; shortness of breath; sores, ulcers, or white spots on lips or in mouth; swollen glands); ***pericardial effusion*** (chest pain or discomfort; shortness of breath); ***seizure*** (convulsions; muscle spasm or jerking of all extremities; sudden loss of consciousness; loss of bladder control); ***systemic and cutaneous vasculitis*** (severe abdominal pain; redness, soreness or itching skin; fever; sores, welting or blisters); ***thrombocytopenia*** (black, tarry stools; bleeding gums; blood in urine or stools; pinpoint red spots on skin; unusual bleeding or bruising); ***thrombocytopenic purpura*** (unusual bleeding or bruising; bloody nose; heavier menstrual periods; pinpoint red spots on skin; black, tarry stools; blood in urine; unusual tiredness or weakness; fever; skin rash); ***transverse myelitis*** (back pain, sudden and severe; muscle weakness, sudden and progressing)

Note: In post-marketing experience, infections with various pathogens including viral, bacterial, fungal, and protozoal have been observed. Infections have been noted in all organ systems and have been reported in patients receiving infliximab alone or in combination with immunosuppressive agents.

Note: Rare post-marketing reports of *hepatosplenic T-cell lymphomas* have been reported in adolescent and young adult patients being treated for with infliximab for Crohn's disease. In all cases, patients were taking azathioprine or 6-mercaptopurine concomitantly. This disease is very aggressive with a fatal outcome within 2 years of diagnosis in most patients. The causal relationship between *hepatosplenic T-cell lymphomas* and infliximab remains unclear.

Overdose

Single infliximab doses of up to 20 mg per kg of body weight (mg/kg) have been administered without any direct toxic effect.

For information on the management of overdose, **contact a Poison Control Center** (see *Poison Control Center Listing*).

Treatment of overdose

The patient should be monitored for any signs or symptoms of adverse reactions or effects, and appropriate symptomatic treatment instituted immediately.

Patients in whom intentional overdose is confirmed or suspected should be referred for psychiatric consultation.

Patient Consultation

As an aid to patient consultation, refer to *Advice for the Patient, Infliximab (Systemic)*.

In providing consultation, consider emphasizing the following selected information (» = major clinical significance):

Before using this medication

» Conditions affecting use, especially:
- Hypersensitivity to any murine (mouse) proteins or other component of infliximab
- Pregnancy—Risk-benefit must be considered
- Breast-feeding—Risk-benefit must be considered
- Use in children—Safety and efficacy established in pediatric patients 6 years of age and older with Crohn's disease; importance of pediatric Crohn's patients being brought up to date with all vaccinations prior to infliximab therapy with an interval between vaccination and infliximab treatment that is in accordance with current vaccination guidelines
- Safety and efficacy in patients with juvenile rheumatoid arthritis and in pediatric patients with ulcerative colitis not established
- Use in adolescents—Rare post-marketing reports of hepatosplenic T-cell lymphomas in adolescents and young adults, especially in those receiving azathioprine or 6-mercaptopurine concomitantly, although causality unclear
- Use in the elderly—Caution should be used, since the effect of infliximab treatment on the incidence of infections is not known
- Other medications, especially anakinra or immunosuppressive therapy
- Other medical problems, especially central nervous system demyelinating disorders (pre-existing or recent onset), chronic, invasive, or opportunistic infections or history of recurrent infections, congestive heart failure (moderate or severe), hematologic abnormalities (ongoing or history of), latent tuberculosis infection, malignancies (history of), or seizure disorders (pre-existing or recent onset)

Proper use of this medication

Importance of reading patient information sheet before starting infliximab therapy and before each scheduled administration of infliximab.

» Proper dosing

» Proper storage

Precautions while using this medication

Check with doctor or nurse if chest pain, fever, chills, facial flushing, itching, hives, or troubled breathing occurs within a few hours after receiving infliximab

Importance of evaluating for latent tuberculosis infection with a tuberculin skin test

Importance of evaluating cardiac status with concomitant congestive heart disease

Checking with doctor immediately if signs of liver problems (skin and eyes turning yellow, dark brown-colored urine, right sided abdominal pain, fever and severe tiredness) develop

Telling doctor if lymphoma or other cancers have occurred in the past or if cancer develops while taking infliximab

Side/adverse effects

Signs of potential side effects, especially abdominal pain, bronchitis, fatigue, infusion-related reactions (including fever, chills, pruritus, urticaria, chest pain, dyspnea, facial flushing, headache, and hypotension), myalgia, nausea, upper respiratory tract infection, vomiting, back pain, cardiopulmonary reactions (including chest pain, dyspnea, hypertension, and hypotension), cough, diarrhea, fever, headache, moniliasis (including dermal candidiasis, thrush, and vaginitis), pain, pharyngitis, pruritus, rhinitis, sinusitis, urinary tract infection, abdominal hernia, abscess, adult respiratory distress syndrome, cholecystitis, dysuria, falls, infection, intestinal obstruction, intestinal perforation, intestinal stenosis, kidney infarction, lupus erythematosus syndrome, lymphoma, palpitations, pneumonia, proctalgia, skin rash, splenic infarction, splenomegaly, syncope, tendon injury, thrombocytopenia, and ureteral obstruction

Signs of potential side effects observed during clinical practice, especially acute liver failure, anaphylactic-like reactions, cholestasis, Guillain-Barre syndrome, hepatitis, hepatosplenic T-cell lymphomas, idiopathic thrombocytopenic purpura, interstitial pneumonitis/fibrosis, jaundice, laryngeal/pharyngeal edema, leukopenia, neuropathies, neutropenia, pancytopenia, pericardial effusion, seizure, severe bronchospasm, systemic and cutaneous vasculitis, thrombocytopenia, thrombotic thrombocytopenic purpura, and transverse myelitis

General Dosing Information

Caution should be used in the re-treatment of patients with infliximab following an extended period without treatment. The risk of potentially serious delayed adverse events should be weighed against the potential benefit of re-treatment if more than 2 years have elapsed since previous infliximab therapy. See *Side/Adverse Effects*.

Safety and efficacy of longer term use (greater than 1 year) of infliximab have not been established in pediatric patients being treated for Crohn's disease.

For treatment of adverse effects

Recommended treatment of hypersensitivity reactions consists of the following:

- Stopping the infusion if severe reactions occur.
- Providing symptomatic and supportive treatment. Epinephrine, corticosteroids, antihistamines, and acetaminophen should be available for immediate use.

Parenteral Dosage Forms

INFLIXIMAB FOR INJECTION

Usual adult dose

Ankylosing spondylitis (treatment)[1]—

Intravenous, 5 mg per kg of body weight followed with additional similar doses at 2 and 6 weeks after the first infusion, then every 6 weeks thereafter.

Arthritis, psoriatic (treatment)[1]—

Intravenous, 5 mg per kg of body weight administered as a single intravenous infusion over at least two hours, followed with additional doses at two and six weeks after the first infusion then every 8 weeks thereafter. Infliximab can be used with or without methotrexate.

Colitis, ulcerative (treatment)[1]—

Intravenous, 5 mg per kg of body weight given as an induction regimen at 0, 2, and 6 weeks followed by a maintenance regimen of 5 mg per kg of body weight given every 8 weeks thereafter for the treatment of moderately to severely active ulcerative colitis.

For moderately to severely active Crohn's disease in patients having an inadequate response to conventional therapy—

Intravenous, 5 mg per kg of body weight (mg/kg), administered as a single intravenous infusion over at least two hours, followed with additional doses at two and six weeks after the first infusion. Maintenance regimen of 5 mg per kg of body weight should be given every 8 weeks thereafter. For patients responding and then losing their response, consideration may be given to 10 mg per kg of body weight. Patients not responding by week 14 are unlikely to respond with continued dosing and discontinuation of infliximab should be considered.

For fistulizing Crohn's disease—

Intravenous, 5 mg/kg administered as an intravenous infusion over at least two hours, followed with additional doses at two and six weeks after the first infusion. Maintenance regimen of 5 mg per kg of body weight should be given every 8 weeks thereafter. For patients responding and then losing their response, consideration may be given to 10 mg per kg of body weight. Patients not responding by week 14 are unlikely to respond with continued dosing and discontinuation of infliximab should be considered.

For rheumatoid arthritis—

Intravenous, 3 mg per kg of body weight (mg/kg), administered as a single intravenous infusion over at least two hours, followed with additional doses at two and six weeks after the first infusion then every 8 weeks thereafter. For patients who have an incomplete response, consideration may be given to adjusting dose up to 10 mg per kg of body weight or treating as often as every 4 weeks. Infliximab should be administered in combination with methotrexate.

[Psoriasis (treatment)][1]—

Intravenous, 5 mg per kg of body weight administered as a single intravenous infusion over at least two hours, followed with additional doses at two and six weeks after the first infusion then every 8 weeks thereafter.

[Reactive arthritis (treatment)][1]—

Intravenous, 5 mg per kg of body weight administered as a single intravenous infusion over at least two hours, followed with additional doses at two and six weeks after the first infusion then every 8 weeks thereafter.

[Inflammatory bowel disease arthritis (treatment)][1]—

Intravenous, 5 mg per kg of body weight administered as a single intravenous infusion over at least two hours, followed with additional doses at two and six weeks after the first infusion then every 8 weeks thereafter.

Usual pediatric dose

Safety and efficacy have not been established for ankylosing spondylitis, psoriatic arthritis, ulcerative colitis, or rheumatoid arthritis in pediatric patients.

For moderately to severely active Crohn's disease in patients having an inadequate response to conventional therapy—

6 years of age and older: Intravenous, induction regimen of 5 mg per kg of body weight given at 0, 2 and 6 weeks followed by a maintenance regimen of 5 mg per kg of body weight every 8 weeks.

Less than 6 years of age: Safety and efficacy have not been established.

Usual geriatric dose

See *Usual adult dose*.

Strength(s) usually available

U.S.—

100 mg (Rx) [*Remicade* (polysorbate 80; monobasic sodium phosphate, monohydrate; dibasic sodium phosphate, dihydrate; sucrose)].

Canada—

100 mg (Rx) [*Remicade*].

Packaging and storage

Store between 2 and 8 °C (36 and 46 °F). Do not freeze.

Preparation of dosage form

Calculate the dose and the number of infliximab vials needed; calculate the total volume of reconstituted infliximab solution required.

Reconstitute each infliximab vial with 10 mL of Sterile Water for Injection USP. Using a 21-gauge or smaller needle, direct the stream of diluent to the glass wall of the infliximab vial. To dissolve the lyophilized powder, gently swirl the solution by rotating the vial. Avoid prolonged or vigorous agitation, and do not shake. (Foaming of the solution is not unusual.) Allow the reconstituted solution to stand for 5 minutes. The solution should be colorless to light yellow and opalescent. Because infliximab is a protein, the solution may develop a few translucent particles; however, if opaque particles, discoloration, or other foreign particles are present, do not use the solution.

The total volume of the reconstituted infliximab dose must be diluted to 250 mL with 0.9% Sodium Chloride Injection USP. Withdraw a volume of sodium chloride equal to the volume of reconstituted infliximab and discard. Slowly add the total volume of reconstituted infliximab solution to the infusion bottle or bag and mix gently. The infusion concentration should fall in the range of 0.4 mg/mL to 4 mg/mL.

The infusion solution must be administered over a period of not less than 2 hours and must use an infusion set with an in-line, sterile, nonpyrogenic, low–protein-binding filter with a pore size ≤ 1.2 micrometers (microns).

Stability

Infliximab vials do not contain antibacterial preservatives and should be used immediately after reconstitution. Infliximab intravenous infusions should begin within 3 hours of preparation. Any unused portion of infliximab infusion should be discarded.

Incompatibilities

No physical biochemical compatibility studies have been conducted to evaluate the coadministration of infliximab with other agents. Infliximab should not be infused concomitantly in the same intravenous line with other agents.

Auxiliary labeling

- Refrigerate - do not freeze.
- For single-dose only. Discard unused drug.
- Do not shake. Rotate vial gently.
- Please read patient information leaflet enclosed.

[1]Not included in Canadian product labeling.

Revised: 05/31/2006
Developed: 05/05/1999

INFLUENZA VIRUS VACCINE Systemic

VA CLASSIFICATION (Primary): IM100

Note: This monograph refers to the current (2006-2007 season) inactivated whole-virus influenza vaccine prepared from intact, purified virus particles. Purified surface-antigen and subvirion preparations of the inactivated vaccine are available. Manufacturer's prescribing information should be consulted for additional information regarding specific manufacturing processes.

Based on the detected antigenic changes in the circulating strains of influenza viruses in the U.S. and worldwide, the Advisory Committee on Immunization Practices (ACIP) recommends that the 2006-2007 trivalent influenza virus vaccine (inactivated and live) contain A/New Caledonia/20/99 (H1N1)-like, A/Wisconsin/67/2005 (H3N2)-like, and B/Malaysia/2506/2004-like antigens. For the A/Wisconsin/67/2005 (H3N2)-like antigen, manufacturers may use the antigenically equivalent A/Hiroshima/52/2005 virus; for the B/Malaysia/2506/2004-like antigen, manufacturers may use the antigenically equivalent B/Ohio/1/2005 virus.

Influenza vaccine with reduced thimerosal content became available for the 2003-2004 influenza season; however, supplies were limited. The 2006-2007 formula, Fluarix®, contains a trace amount of thimerosal (≤1 mcg mercury per dose).

Commonly used brand name(s): *FluMist; FluShield; Fluarix; Fluviral; Fluviral S/F; Fluvirin; Fluzone.*

Another commonly used name is flu vaccine.

Note: For a listing of dosage forms and brand names by country availability, see *Dosage Forms* section(s).

Category

Immunizing agent (active).

Indications

General Considerations

Influenza A viruses are classified into subtypes on the basis of their two surface antigens: hemagglutinin (H) and neuraminidase (N). Three subtypes of hemagglutinin (H1, H2, and H3) and two types of neuraminidase (N1 and N2) are recognized among influenza A viruses that have caused widespread human disease. Immunity to these antigens, especially to the hemagglutinin, reduces the likelihood of infection and lessens the severity of disease if infection occurs.

Note: Unlike influenza A, the influenza B viruses are not segregated into sub-types

Infection with a virus of one subtype confers little or no protection against viruses of other subtypes. Furthermore, over time, antigenic variation (antigenic drift) within a subtype may be so marked that infection or vaccination with one strain may not induce immunity to distantly related strains of the same subtype.

Although influenza B viruses have shown more antigenic stability than influenza A viruses, antigenic variations do occur in influenza B viruses. For these reasons, major epidemics of respiratory disease caused by new variants of influenza continue to occur. The antigenic characteristics of circulating strains provide the basis for selecting the virus strains included in each year's vaccine.

Typical influenza illness is characterized by abrupt onset of fever, myalgia, headache, rhinitis, sore throat, and nonproductive cough. Unlike other common respiratory illnesses, influenza can cause severe malaise lasting for several days. Cough and malaise can persist for greater than 2 weeks in some persons infected with influenza. More severe illness can result if influenza develops into viral pneumonia or if secondary bacterial pneumonia occurs. During influenza epidemics, high attack rates of acute illness result in increased numbers of visits to physicians' offices, walk-in clinics, and emergency rooms, and increased hospitalizations for management of lower respiratory tract complications.

Elderly persons and persons with underlying chronic health problems are at increased risk for complications of influenza. If they become ill with influenza, such members of high-risk groups are more likely than the general population to require hospitalization. During major epidemics, hospitalization rates for persons at high risk may increase twofold to fivefold, depending on the age group. Previously healthy children and younger adults may also require hospitalization for influenza-related complications, but the relative increase in their hospitalization rates is less than for persons who belong to high-risk groups.

An increase in mortality further indicates the impact of influenza epidemics. Increased mortality results not only from influenza and pneumonia, but also from cardiopulmonary and other chronic diseases that can be exacerbated by influenza. More than 90% of the deaths attributed to pneumonia and influenza occur among persons ≥ 65 years of age.

Because the proportion of elderly persons in the U.S. population is increasing, and because age and its associated chronic diseases are risk factors for severe influenza illness, the number of deaths attributed to influenza can be expected to increase unless control measures are implemented more vigorously. In addition, the number of persons < 65 years of age at increased risk for influenza-related complications is increasing. Better survival rates for organ-transplant recipients, the success of neonatal intensive-care units, and better management of diseases such as cystic fibrosis and acquired immunodeficiency syndrome (AIDS) contribute to a growing population of younger persons at high risk.

More than 8 million children and adolescents in the U.S., including 2.2 million persons 10 to 18 years of age who have asthma, have at least one medical condition that places them at high risk for complications associated with influenza. Such children and adolescents should be vaccinated annually against influenza; currently, however, few actually receive the vaccine.

Adolescents who meet any of the following criteria should be vaccinated against influenza:

- Adolescents who have chronic disorders of the pulmonary system (including those who have asthma) or the cardiovascular system.
- Adolescents who reside in long-term facilities.
- Adolescents who have required regular medical follow-up or hospitalization during the preceding year because of chronic metabolic disease (including those who have diabetes mellitus), renal dysfunction, hemoglobinopathy, or immunosuppression (including those who have immunosuppression caused by medication).
- Adolescents who receive long-term aspirin therapy and, therefore, may be at risk for contracting Reye's syndrome after an influenza infection.
- In addition, adolescents who have close contact with persons who meet any of these conditions or with persons ≥ 65 years of age should be administered influenza virus vaccine annually, to reduce the likelihood of their acquiring influenza infection.

In the U.S., influenza virus vaccine campaigns are targeted at approximately 35 million persons ≥ 65 years of age, and 33–39 million persons < 65 years of age who are at high risk for influenza-associated complications. National health objectives for the year 2000 include vaccination of at least 60% of persons at risk for severe influenza-related illnesses. Influenza virus vaccination levels among persons ≥ 65 years of age improved substantially from 1989 (33%) to 1999 (66%), thereby exceeding the year 2000 target for this age class. Vaccine coverage reached 68% during the 1999-2000 influenza season. The national health objective for this age group has now been upgraded to achieve vaccination coverage of at least 90% of all persons ≥ 65 years of age by the year 2010. In 2001, vaccination levels among all persons at high risk < 65 years of age was 29% and 41% for persons 50 to 64 years of age with chronic medical conditions.

Successful vaccination programs have combined education for health care workers, publicity and education targeted at potential recipients, a plan for identifying persons at high risk (usually by medical record review), and efforts to remove administrative and financial barriers that prevent persons from receiving the vaccine. Persons for whom influenza virus vaccine is recommended can be identified and vaccinated in the following settings:

• Outpatient clinics and physicians' offices. Staff in physicians' offices, clinics, health maintenance organizations, and employee health clinics should be instructed to identify and label the medical records of patients who should receive vaccination. Vaccination should be offered during visits beginning in September and lasting throughout the influenza season. The offer of vaccination and its receipt or refusal should be documented in the medical records. Patients in high-risk groups who do not have regularly scheduled visits during the fall should be reminded by mail or telephone of the need for vaccination. If possible, arrangements should be made to provide vaccination with minimal waiting time and at the lowest possible cost.

• Facilities providing episodic or acute care. Health care providers in these settings (e.g., emergency rooms and walk-in clinics) should be familiar with influenza virus vaccine recommendations. They should offer vaccination to persons in high-risk groups or should provide written information giving the reason for this vaccination, the locations where it is available, and the health care personnel to contact. Written information should be available in language(s) appropriate for the population served by the facility.

• Nursing homes and other residential long-term care facilities. Vaccination should be routinely provided to all residents of long-term care facilities with the concurrence of the attending physicians rather than by obtaining individual vaccination orders for each patient. Consent for vaccination should be obtained from the resident or a family member at the time of admission to the facility, and all residents should be vaccinated at one time, immediately preceding the influenza season. Residents admitted during the winter months after completion of the vaccination program should be vaccinated when they are admitted.

• Acute care hospitals. All persons ≥ 50 years of age and younger persons (including children) with-high risk conditions who are hospitalized at any time from September through March should be offered and strongly encouraged to receive the influenza virus vaccine before they are discharged. Household members and others with whom they will have contact also should receive written information about the need for influenza virus vaccination, and where it is available.

• Outpatient facilities providing continuing care to patients at high risk. All patients should be offered vaccination before the beginning of the influenza season. Patients admitted to such programs (e.g., hemodialysis centers, hospital specialty care clinics, and outpatient rehabilitation programs) during the winter months after the earlier vaccination program has been conducted should be vaccinated at the time of admission. Household members and others with whom they will have contact also should receive written information about the need for influenza virus vaccination, and where it is available.

• Visiting nurses and others providing home care to persons at high risk. Nursing care plans should identify patients in high-risk groups, and vaccination should be provided in the home if necessary. Caregivers and other persons in the household (including children) should be referred for vaccination.

• Facilities providing services to persons ≥50 years of age. In these facilities (e.g., retirement communities, assisted living facilities, and recreation centers), all unvaccinated residents/attendees should be offered vaccination on site before the influenza season begins. Education/publicity programs should also be provided; these programs should emphasize the need for influenza virus vaccination and provide specific information on the vaccination programs, their schedules, and locations.

• Clinics and other settings providing health care for travelers. Indications for influenza virus vaccination should be reviewed before travel, and vaccination should be offered, if appropriate.

• Health care workers. Administrators of all health care facilities should arrange for influenza vaccination to be offered to all personnel before the influenza season begins. Personnel should be provided with appropriate educational materials, and should be strongly encouraged to receive the vaccine. Particular emphasis should be placed on vaccination of persons who care for members of high risk groups (e.g., staff of intensive care units [including neonatal intensive care units], staff of medical/surgical units, and employees of nursing homes and long-term care facilities). Using a mobile cart to carry the vaccine doses to hospital wards or other work sites and making the vaccine available during night and weekend work shifts can enhance compliance, as can a follow-up campaign early in the course of a community outbreak.

An alternative strategy for controlling influenza type A infection among high-risk patients is the use of the antiviral agents amantadine and rimantadine, especially for chronically ill, institutionalized, or severely debilitated persons who have been or may be exposed to influenza type A during an outbreak. Amantadine and rimantadine are equally effective in the prevention and treatment of influenza type A infections. The neuraminadase inhibitors oseltamivir and zanamivir have also proven effective in reducing the duration of uncomplicated influenza A and B illness when administered within 2 days of symptom onset; however, neither have been approved for influenza prophylaxis. None of the four antiviral agents have been effective in the prevention of serious influenza-related complications.

Accepted

Influenza (prophylaxis)—Influenza virus vaccine is indicated for immunization against the selected virus strains contained in the vaccine.

Influenza virus vaccine live for intranasal administration is indicated for use in healthy children and adolescents, 6 months to 17 years of age, and healthy adults, 18 to 49 years of age. Influenza virus vaccine inactivated (subviron) for intramuscular injection is indicated for any person ≥ 6 months of age who, because of age or underlying medical condition, is at increased risk of complications of influenza, including:

• Targeted high-risk children. Yearly immunization is recommended for children 6 months of age and older with one or more specific risk factors. Data are insufficient regarding the potential severity of influenza in several of these groups of children; however, based on available data and knowledge of the pathophysiology of these disorders, children with the following risk factors warrant immunization:

—Those with asthma and other chronic pulmonary diseases. Influenza vaccination can be given safely and effectively to children with asthma regardless of asthma symptoms or concurrent prednisone therapy. Vaccination of all patients with moderate to severe asthma who visit clinics or emergency departments would improve the overall vaccination rate significantly.

—Those with hemodynamically significant cardiac disease.

—Those undergoing immunosuppressive therapy.

—Those with sickle-cell anemia and other hemoglobinopathies.

• Other high-risk children. Children who are potentially at increased risk for complicated influenza illness and who may benefit from influenza immunization are those with one or more of the following conditions:

• Human immunodeficiency virus (HIV) infection.

• Diabetes mellitus.

• Chronic metabolic diseases.

• Recipients of long-term aspirin therapy, such as children with rheumatoid arthritis or Kawasaki disease, who may have an increased risk of developing Reye's syndrome.

• Influenza virus vaccination also may be considered for children who are marginally immunocompromised as a result of any underlying condition, since even uncomplicated influenza can have adverse effects on the course of an underlying illness.

• Adults at increased risk for influenza-related complications:

—Persons ≥50 years of age.

—Residents of nursing homes and other long-term care facilities that house persons of any age with chronic medical conditions.

—Those with chronic disorders of the pulmonary or cardiovascular systems.

—Those who have required regular medical follow-up or hospitalization during the preceding year because of chronic metabolic diseases (including diabetes mellitus), renal dysfunction, hemoglobinopathies, or immunosuppression (including immunosuppression caused by medications).

—Women who will be pregnant during the influenza season should be vaccinated. Vaccination can occur in any trimester.

• Persons who can transmit influenza to others who are at high risk. Persons who are clinically or subclinically infected with influenza and who care for or live with members of high-risk groups can transmit influenza virus to them. Some persons at high risk (e.g., the elderly, transplant recipients, and persons with AIDS) can have a low antibody response to influenza vaccine. Efforts to protect these members of high-risk groups against influenza may be improved by reducing the likelihood of influenza virus exposure from their caregivers. Immunization of adults who are in close contact with children at high risk may be an important means of protecting these children, especially for infants < 6 months of age for whom vaccination is not recommended. Immunization of pregnant women may be beneficial to the neonates, as well, since transplacentally acquired antibody appears to protect neonates from infection with influenza A virus. Therefore, the following groups should be immunized:

—Physicians, nurses, and other personnel in both hospital and outpatient settings, including medical emergency response workers.

—Employees of nursing homes and long-term care facilities who have contact with patients or residents.

—Employees of assisted living and other residences for persons at high risk.

—Providers of home care to persons at high risk (e.g., visiting nurses and volunteer workers).

—Household contacts of persons at high risk, including children, siblings, and primary caretakers of children at high risk. HIV-infected children who are members of households with adults at high risk also should be immunized.

• General population. Physicians should administer influenza virus vaccine to any person who wishes to reduce the likelihood of becoming ill with influenza. Persons who provide essential community services should be considered for vaccination, to minimize disruption of essential activities during influenza outbreaks. Vaccination should be considered for groups of individuals whose close contact with each other facilitates rapid transmission of the virus infection resulting in disruption of routine activities. Examples are students in colleges, schools, and other institutions of learning, particularly those who reside in dormitories or who are members of athletic teams, and those living in residential institutions.

• Healthy young children. Recent studies, which attempt to separate the effects of RSV and influenza, report otherwise healthy children aged 0 to 4 years may be at increased risk for influenza-related hospitalization compared with older healthy children or older children with high-risk conditions. Vaccination of all children aged 6 to 23 months is recommended.Healthy children aged less than 6 months, the pediatric group at greatest risk for influenza-related complications, are not vaccinated because the influenza vaccine is not FDA approved for use in this population. Risk of transmission of influenza can be reduced if household contacts and out-of-home care givers are vaccinated.

• Persons infected with HIV. Limited information exists regarding the frequency and severity of influenza illness among HIV-infected persons, but reports suggest that symptoms may be prolonged and the risk for complications increased for some HIV-infected persons. Influenza vaccine has produced protective antibody titers against influenza in vaccinated HIV-infected persons who have minimal AIDS-related symptoms and high CD4+ T-lymphocyte cell counts. In patients who have advanced HIV infection–related disease and low CD4+ T-lymphocyte cell counts, however, influenza virus vaccine may not induce protective antibody titers; furthermore, a second dose of vaccine does not improve the immune response for these persons. Recent studies have examined the effect of influenza virus vaccination on replication of HIV type 1 (HIV-1). Although some studies have demonstrated a transient (i.e., 2- to 4-week) increase in replication of HIV-1 in the plasma or peripheral blood mononuclear cells of HIV-1–infected persons after vaccine administration, other studies using similar laboratory techniques have not indicated any substantial increase in replication. Decline in CD4+ T-lymphocyte cell counts and progression of clinical HIV infection–related disease have not been demonstrated among HIV-infected persons who receive influenza virus vaccine. Since influenza can result in serious illness and complications, and because influenza virus vaccination may result in protective antibody titers, vaccination will benefit many HIV-infected patients, including HIV-infected pregnant women.

• International travelers. The risk of exposure to influenza during foreign travel varies, depending on the season and destination. In the tropics, influenza outbreaks can occur throughout the year; in the southern hemisphere, most outbreaks occur between April and September. Because of the short incubation period for influenza, exposure to the virus during travel can result in clinical illness that begins while traveling, which could be an inconvenience or a potential danger, especially for persons at increased risk for complications. Travelers with organized tourist groups at any time of year may also be at risk for exposure if the group includes persons from areas of the world where influenza viruses are circulating.Persons preparing to travel should review their influenza vaccination histories. If they were not vaccinated during the previous fall or winter, they should consider receiving influenza vaccination before travel.

Unaccepted

The nasal mist influenza virus vaccine is not indicated for immunization of patients less than 5 years of age, patients 50 years of age and older, or for the therapy of influenza, nor will it protect against infections and illness caused by infectious agents other than influenza A or B viruses.

Pharmacology/Pharmacokinetics

Physicochemical characteristics

Source—

Each year's influenza vaccine contains three virus strains (usually two type A strains and one type B strain) representing the influenza viruses that are likely to circulate in the U.S. in the upcoming winter. The vaccine is made from highly purified, egg-grown viruses that have been made noninfectious (inactivated). Whole-virus, subvirion, and purified-surface-antigen preparations are available..

In collaboration with the World Health Organization (WHO), its international network of collaborating laboratories, and state and local health departments, the Centers for Disease Control and Prevention (CDC) conducts surveillance to monitor influenza activity and detect antigenic changes in the circulating strains of influenza viruses.

Mechanism of action/Effect

Humoral defenses against influenza infection are mainly conferred by serum and local immune globulin G (IgG) and immune globulin A (IgA) antibodies to the surface glycoproteins, hemagglutinin (H) and neuraminidase (N). Anti-H antibodies inhibit the attachment of the influenza virus to target cell membrane receptors and thus neutralize viral infectivity. Depending on their concentration, these antibodies can either provide complete protection from the acquisition of infection or prevent the development of serious illness. Protection studies have indicated that an anti-H antibody titer of $\geq$ 40 is the protection threshold beyond which serious illness is unlikely to develop.

Protective effect

Most vaccinated children and young adults develop high titers of postvaccination hemagglutinin-inhibition (HI) antibody. These antibodies protect the individual against illness caused by strains similar to those in the vaccine. Elderly persons and persons with certain chronic diseases may develop lower postvaccination antibody titers than healthy young adults and thus may remain susceptible to influenza-related upper respiratory tract infection. However, even if such persons develop influenza illness despite vaccination, the vaccine can be effective in preventing lower respiratory tract involvement or other complications, thereby reducing the risks of hospitalization and death.

The effectiveness of influenza vaccine in preventing or attenuating illness varies, depending primarily on the age and immunocompetence of the vaccine recipient and the degree of similarity between the virus strains included in the vaccine and those that circulate during the influenza season. When there is a good match between the vaccine and circulating viruses, influenza virus vaccine has been shown to prevent illness in approximately 70% of healthy persons $<$ 65 years of age. In these circumstances, studies have also indicated that the effectiveness of influenza virus vaccine in preventing hospitalization for pneumonia and influenza among elderly persons living in settings other than nursing homes or similar long-term care facilities ranges from 30 to 70%.

Among elderly persons residing in nursing homes, influenza virus vaccine is very effective in preventing severe illness, secondary complications, and death. Studies in this population have indicated that the vaccine can be 50 to 60% effective in preventing hospitalization and pneumonia, and 80% effective in preventing death, even though the vaccine's efficacy in preventing influenza illness may only be in the range of 30 to 40% among the frail elderly. Achieving a high rate of vaccination among nursing home residents can reduce the spread of infection in a facility, thus preventing disease through herd immunity.

Time to protective effect

Peak antibody protection against influenza strains included in the vaccine develops 2 weeks after vaccination in adults.

Duration of protective effect

Since the antigenic properties of influenza virus surface antigens frequently change, the vaccine-induced protective immunity is short-lived. For this reason, health authorities recommend annual revaccination of persons at risk, using influenza virus vaccines containing the expected epidemic strains for the next season.

Precautions to Consider

Carcinogenicity/Mutagenicity

Influenza virus vaccine has not been evaluated for its carcinogenic or mutagenic potential.

Pregnancy/Reproduction

Fertility—Influenza virus vaccine has not been evaluated for its potential to impair fertility.

Pregnancy—Influenza-associated excess mortality among pregnant women has not been documented except during the pandemics of 1918–19 and 1957–58. However, because death-certificate data often do not indicate whether a woman was pregnant at the time of death, studies conducted during interpandemic periods may underestimate the impact of influenza in this population. Case reports and limited studies suggest that pregnancy may increase the risk of serious medical complications of influenza, as a result of increases in heart rate, increases in stroke volume and oxygen consumption, decreases in lung capacity, and changes in immunologic functions. A recent study of the impact of influenza during 17 interpandemic influenza seasons documented that the relative risk of hospitalization for selected cardiorespiratory conditions among pregnant women increased from 1.4 during weeks 14 to 20 of gestation to 4.7 during weeks 37 to 42, as compared with rates among women who were 1 to 6 months postpartum. Women in their third trimesters of pregnancy were hospitalized at a rate comparable to that of nonpregnant women with high-risk medical conditions for whom influenza virus vaccine has traditionally been recommended. Using data from this study, it was estimated that an average of 1 to 2 hospitalizations among pregnant women could be prevented for every 1000 pregnant women immunized.

On the basis of these and other data suggesting that influenza infection may cause increased morbidity in women who are pregnant during the influenza season, the Advisory Committee on Immunization Practices (ACIP) of the Centers for Disease Control and Prevention (CDC) recommends that women who will be pregnant during the influenza season should be vaccinated with inactivated virus vaccine. Studies of influenza immunization of more than 2000 pregnant women have demonstrated no adverse fetal effects associated with influenza virus vaccine.

No data or evidence exists of any harm caused by the level of mercury exposure that might occur from influenza vaccination of pregnant women despite thimerosal use in U.S. vaccines since the 1930s. The benefit of inactivated influenza vaccine with reduced or standard thimerosal content to pregnant women for prevention of influenza-related complications outweighs the potential risk, if any, for thimerosal.

Inactivated influenza vaccination of HIV-infected pregnant women can result in the production of protective antibody titers and will benefit HIV-infected pregnant women by preventing serious influenza-related illness.

Adequate and well controlled studies have not been done using the nasal mist influenza virus vaccine live, and should, therefore, not be administered to pregnant women.

Studies have not been done in animals.

FDA Pregnancy Category C

Breast-feeding

Inactivated influenza vaccine does not affect the safety of breast-feeding for mothers or infants. Breast-feeding does not adversely affect the immune response and is not a contraindication for vaccination with inactivated virus vaccine.

It is not known whether the nasal mist influenza vaccine live is distributed into human breast milk. Therefore, as some viruses are distributed into human breast milk and because of the possibility of shedding vaccine virus, caution should be exercised when administering the nasal mist influenza vaccine live to nursing mothers.

Pediatrics

In immunosuppressed children receiving chemotherapy, inactivated influenza immunization with a new vaccine antigen results in a sufficient immune response in only a minority of children. The optimal time to immunize with inactivated influenza virus vaccine in children with malignancies who still must undergo chemotherapy is 3 to 4 weeks after chemotherapy has been discontinued and the peripheral granulocyte and lymphocyte counts are greater than 1000 per cubic millimeter. Children who are no longer receiving chemotherapy generally have high rates of seroconversion.

The immune response and safety of inactivated influenza vaccine in children with hemodynamically unstable cardiac disease (another large group of children potentially at high risk for complications of influenza) are comparable to those in healthy children.

The effect of corticosteroid therapy on inactivated influenza vaccine immunogenicity is unknown. Since a high dose of corticosteroids (i.e., a dose equivalent to either 2 mg per kg of body weight or a total of 20 mg per day of prednisone) may impair antibody responses, particularly in unvaccinated or previously uninfected persons, vaccination may be deferred temporarily during high-dose corticosteroid therapy, provided deferral does not compromise the likelihood of immunization before the start of the influenza season. Corticosteroid therapy should not unnecessarily delay the administration of influenza vaccine, particularly in children with asthma who require intermittent or maintenance corticosteroid therapy.

Infants younger than 6 months of age with high-risk conditions, especially those with compromised cardiopulmonary function may have the same or greater risk from influenza complications as of older children. However, no information is available about the reactivity, immunogenicity, or the efficacy of the inactivated influenza vaccine in infants during the first 6 months of life. In addition, the effect of influenza antigens in an inactivated vaccine on the infant's future immune response to influenza is unknown. Therefore, alternative methods of protection for young infants should be considered, including vaccination of household contacts and out-of-home care givers.

Recent studies, which attempt to separate the effects of RSV and influenza, report otherwise healthy children aged 0 to 4 years may be at increased risk for influenza-related hospitalization compared with older healthy children or older children with high-risk conditions. Vaccination with inactivated virus vaccine of all children aged 6 to 23 months is encouraged when feasible.

Children and young adults with cystic fibrosis (CF) will benefit from annual inactivated influenza vaccination. In a 10-year observational study with a cohort design of 38 children and young adults with CF, serum hemagglutinin-inhibition (HI) antibody titers were determined at the time of vaccination, and 4 weeks later each year in the fall before the influenza epidemic. While the prevaccination and postvaccination geometric mean serum HI antibody titers varied from year to year, no upward or downward trend was evident over the 10-year period. In addition, the majority of vaccinees had a presumably protective postvaccination serum HI titer ≥ 1:40 each year for all three vaccine strains.

In children with little previous experience with inactivated influenza, two doses of vaccine, administered 1 month apart, are necessary to produce a satisfactory antibody response. Children previously primed with a related strain of influenza virus by infection or vaccination almost uniformly exhibit a brisk antibody response to one dose of the vaccine.

Only the subvirion or purified surface-antigen vaccines (inactivated), i.e., those termed "split-virus" vaccines, should be used for children younger than 12 years of age.

The safety of the nasal mist influenza vaccine live in infants and children under 5 years of age has not been established.

Geriatrics

Although inactivated influenza vaccine reportedly provides 65 to 85% protection against influenza illness in young, healthy adults, studies of its effectiveness in high-risk groups, such as the elderly, have yielded inconsistent results. In observational studies of high-risk patients, respiratory illness during influenza epidemics occurred often, despite vaccination. A review of studies of influenza vaccination in nursing homes disclosed that the median protective effect in 16 outbreaks of influenza A was 26%, and it was only 19% in seven studies of influenza B outbreaks. Among noninstitutionalized elderly persons, the number of medical care visits for upper respiratory illnesses during two influenza outbreaks was the same for those who had received influenza vaccine and those who had not.

Despite the apparent ineffectiveness of inactivated influenza vaccination in preventing respiratory infection, other nonrandomized studies have shown that it reduces serious complications and mortality due to influenza in the elderly or chronically ill. In nursing homes, for example, significant reductions in pneumonia and mortality among vaccinees were documented during influenza A outbreaks.

Among noninstitutionalized elderly persons, compelling evidence for the effectiveness of inactivated influenza vaccine comes from retrospective studies of more than 10,000 elderly members of a prepaid health plan during four influenza epidemics from 1968 to 1981. Hospitalizations and deaths from influenza and pneumonia among elderly vaccinees with chronic illnesses were reduced by more than 70% during two of these outbreaks. Healthy elderly persons who received the vaccine also had fewer hospitalizations and deaths than their unvaccinated counterparts, although the differences were not statistically significant. During a third epidemic in which there was pronounced antigenic drift, a statistically insignificant trend toward protection against hospitalization and death among vaccine recipients was observed. Antigenic shift to a subtype different from that in the vaccine occurred during the fourth epidemic studied, and no protection from vaccination was observed. More recently, several case-control studies during the influenza seasons from 1989 to 1992 showed that influenza vaccination was 31 to 45% effective in preventing hospitalizations for pneumonia.

The safety of the nasal mist influenza vaccine live in patients 65 years and older has not been established.

Drug interactions and/or related problems

The following drug interactions and/or related problems have been selected on the basis of their potential clinical significance (possible mechanism in parentheses where appropriate)—not necessarily inclusive (» = major clinical significance):

Note: Combinations containing any of the following medications, depending on the amount present, may also interact with this medication.

Aminophylline or
Carbamazepine or
Phenobarbital or
Phenytoin or

Theophylline preparations or
Warfarin sodium
(influenza virus vaccine is listed in some references among the therapeutic agents that may increase theophylline levels or the anticoagulant effects of warfarin. Such warnings are apparently based on a report that influenza vaccination depresses hepatic cytochrome P450 activity and on case reports of complications or altered pharmacologic characteristics in vaccinated patients taking these medications. More recent studies have failed to show a significant impact of influenza virus vaccine on the laboratory or clinical effects of warfarin or theophylline, and patients taking these medications can be vaccinated safely without special precautions or monitoring.)

Antiviral compounds
(concurrent use of nasal mist influenza vaccine live and antiviral compounds that are active against influenza A and/or influenza B viruses is not recommended due to potential interference; nasal mist influenza vaccine live may be administered 48 hours after the cessation of antiviral therapy and antiviral agents may not be administered until two weeks after administration of the nasal mist influenza vaccine live)

» Aspirin therapy or
» Aspirin-containing therapy
(concomitant use of nasal mist influenza vaccine live in children or adolescents [5 to 17 years of age] who are receiving aspirin therapy or aspirin-containing therapy is contraindicated because of the association of Reye syndrome with aspirin and wild-type influenza infection)

Immunosuppressive agents or
Radiation therapy
(since normal defense mechanisms are suppressed, the patient's antibody response to inactivated influenza virus vaccine may be decreased. The precaution does not apply to corticosteroids used as replacement therapy, for short-term [less than 2 weeks] systemic therapy, or by other routes of administration that do not cause immunosuppression.)

» Immunosuppressive therapies, such as:
Alkylating drugs or
Antimetabolite drugs or
Corticosteroids (systemic) or
Immunosuppressive therapy or
Radiation therapy
(nasal mist influenza vaccine live should not be administered to patients who may be immunosuppressed or have altered or compromised immune status)

» Other vaccines
(nasal mist influenza vaccine live should not be administered with other vaccines)

Laboratory value alterations

The following have been selected on the basis of their potential clinical significance (possible effect in parentheses where appropriate)—not necessarily inclusive (» = major clinical significance).

Influenza virus diagnostic test
(nasopharyngeal secretions or swabs collected from patients vaccinated with nasal mist influenza virus vaccine live may test positive for influenza virus for up to three weeks following vaccination)

Human immunodeficiency virus (HIV), serum and
Hepatitis C virus (HCV), serum
(it was reported during one influenza season, that patients who receive influenza virus vaccine may develop false-positive results of enzyme-linked immunosorbent assays for HIV and HCV. Such false-positive test results are uncommon, probably occurring in less than 2% of vaccine recipients; results usually revert to negative within several months. There is no evidence that recipients of influenza virus vaccine are at increased risk of acquiring HIV or HCV infection. However, physicians should be aware of this laboratory test interaction in evaluating the results of the screening tests.)

Medical considerations/Contraindications

The medical considerations/contraindications included have been selected on the basis of their potential clinical significance (reasons given in parentheses where appropriate)—not necessarily inclusive (» = major clinical significance).

Except under special circumstances, this medication should not be used when the following medical problems exist:

» Asthma or reactive airway disease or
» Cardiovascular disease, chronic or
» Pulmonary disease, chronic
(nasal mist influenza vaccine live should not be administered to patients with a history of asthma, reactive airway disease or other chronic disorders of the cardiovascular and pulmonary systems; studies in children under 5 years of age were shown to have an increased rate of asthma within 42 days of vaccination)

» Febrile illness, severe
(to avoid confusing the manifestations of illness with possible side/adverse effects of vaccine.)

» Immune deficiency diseases or conditions, such as
Agammaglobulinemia or
Human immunodeficiency virus infection or
Immunodeficiency, combined or
Leukemia or
Lymphoma or
Malignancy or
Thymic abnormalities
(nasal mist influenza vaccine live should not be administered to patients with known or suspected immune deficiency)

» Metabolic diseases, chronic including:
Diabetes mellitus or
Hemoglobinopathies or
Renal dysfunction
(nasal mist influenza vaccine should not be administered to patients who have required medical follow-up or hospitalization due to chronic metabolic diseases)

» Respiratory disease, acute
(influenza virus vaccine should not be administered until the acute symptoms of the patient's illness have abated, since the symptoms of the condition may be confused with the possible side effects of the vaccine)

Risk-benefit should be considered when the following medical problems exist:

» Guillain-Barré syndrome (GBS), history of
(patients with a prior history of GBS have shown a greater likelihood of developing a recurrence of GBS following administration of influenza virus vaccine; although not absolutely contraindicated for patients with a history of GBS, certain authorities have recommended against vaccination in patients who are known to have developed GBS within 6 weeks of receiving the influenza virus vaccine, and who are not known to be at high risk for severe influenza-related complications; most authorities otherwise believe that the benefits of influenza virus vaccine justify the risk in patients with a history of GBS who are at high risk for development of severe complications associated with influenza)

» Hypersensitivity to eggs or egg products
(immediate, presumably allergic, reactions [e.g., hives, angioedema, allergic asthma, and systemic anaphylaxis] occur rarely after influenza vaccination. These reactions probably result from hypersensitivity to some vaccine component; the majority of reactions are most likely related to residual egg protein in the vaccine.)
(although current influenza vaccines contain only a small quantity of egg protein, this protein can induce immediate hypersensitivity reactions among persons who have severe egg allergy. Persons who have developed hives, have had swelling of the lips or tongue, or have experienced acute respiratory distress or collapse after eating eggs should consult a physician for appropriate evaluation to determine if influenza virus vaccine should be administered.)
(persons with documented immunoglobulin E [IgE]-mediated hypersensitivity to eggs, including those who have had occupational asthma or other allergic responses due to exposure to egg protein, may also be at increased risk of reactions from influenza vaccine, and similar consultation with a physician should be considered. The protocol for influenza virus vaccination developed by Murphy and Strunk may be considered for patients who have egg allergies and other medical conditions that place them at increased risk for influenza-associated complications.)

Hypersensitivity to influenza virus vaccine or any of its components which may include:
Hypersensitivity to gentamicin, streptomycin, or other aminoglycoside antibiotics or
Hypersensitivity to monosodium glutamate or
Hypersensitivity to sodium bisulfite or
(hypersensitivity reactions to any vaccine component can occur)
Hypersensitivity to thimerosal
(Exposure to vaccines containing thimerosal can lead to induction of hypersensitivity, most patients do not develop reactions to thimerosal when administered as a component of vaccines, even when patch or intradermal tests for thimerosal indicate hypersen-

sitivity; when reported, hypersensitivity to thimerosal usually has consisted of local, delayed-type hypersensitivity reactions) (thimerosal-free inactivated and live influenza virus vaccine formulations are available for use in thimerosal sensitized individuals)

Neurologic disorders, active
(influenza vaccine should not be administered to a patient with an active neurologic disorder; the vaccine should be considered only after the disease process has been stabilized.)

Side/Adverse Effects

Note: Because inactivated influenza vaccine contains only noninfectious viruses, it cannot cause influenza. Respiratory disease after vaccination represents coincidental illness unrelated to influenza vaccination.

Nasal mist influenza virus vaccine live contains live attenuated influenza viruses that replicate in the nasopharynx of the recipient and are shed in respiratory secretions. Transmission of virus from a vaccinated individual to a non-vaccinated individual via close contact may occur.

Unlike the 1976 swine influenza vaccine, subsequent vaccines prepared from other virus strains have not been clearly associated with an increased frequency of Guillain-Barré syndrome (GBS). However, a precise estimate of risk is difficult to determine for a rare condition such as GBS, which has an annual background incidence of only one to two cases per 100,000 in the adult population. Among persons who received the swine influenza vaccine, the rate of GBS that exceeded the background rate was slightly less than one case per 100,000 vaccinations.

An investigation of GBS cases in 1990–91 indicated no overall increase in frequency of GBS among persons who were administered influenza vaccine; a slight increase in GBS cases among vaccinated persons may have occurred in the age group of 18 to 64 years, but not among persons ≥ 65 years of age. In contrast to the swine influenza vaccine, the epidemiologic features of the possible associations of the 1990–91 vaccine and GBS were not as convincing. The rate of GBS cases after vaccination that was passively reported to the Vaccine Adverse Event Reporting System (VAERS) during 1993–94 was estimated to be approximately twice the average rate reported during other seasons (i.e., 1990–91, 1991–92, 1992–93, and 1994–5). The data currently available are not sufficient to determine whether this represents an actual risk. However, even if GBS were a true side effect, the very low estimated risk for GBS is less than that of severe influenza prevented by vaccination.

Whereas the incidence of GBS in the general population is very low, persons with a history of GBS have a substantially greater likelihood of subsequently developing GBS than persons without such a history. Thus, the likelihood of coincidentally developing GBS after influenza vaccination is expected to be greater among persons with a history of GBS than among persons with no history of this syndrome. Whether influenza vaccination is causally associated with the risk for recurrence is not known. Although it would seem prudent to avoid a subsequent influenza vaccination in a person known to have developed GBS within 6 weeks of a previous influenza vaccination, for most persons with a history of GBS who are at high risk of severe complications from influenza, the established benefits of influenza virus vaccination justify their yearly immunization.

The following side/adverse effects have been selected on the basis of their potential clinical significance (possible signs and symptoms in parentheses where appropriate)—not necessarily inclusive:

Those indicating need for medical attention

Incidence rare

Anaphylactic reaction, most likely to residual egg protein in the influenza virus vaccine (difficulty in breathing or swallowing; hives; itching, especially of feet or hands; reddening of skin, especially around ears; swelling of eyes, face, or inside of nose; unusual tiredness or weakness, sudden and severe)

Those indicating need for medical attention only if they continue or are bothersome

Incidence more frequent

Headache (nasal mist); nasal congestion (nasal mist); runny nose (nasal mist); tenderness, redness, or induration at the site of injection, lasting 1 or 2 days (tenderness, redness, or hard lump at place of injection)—incidence approximately 30%

Incidence less frequent

Abdominal pain (nasal mist); cough; diarrhea (nasal mist); fever, malaise, myalgia, and headache starting 6 to 12 hours after administration and persisting 1 or 2 days (aches or pains in muscles; general feeling of discomfort or illness)—most often affecting children and adults who have had no previous exposure to the influenza virus antigens in the vaccine; ***otitis media (nasal mist)*** (earache; redness or swelling in ear); ***sinusitis (nasal mist)*** (pain or tenderness around eyes and cheekbones; fever; stuffy or runny nose; headache; cough; shortness of breath or troubled breathing; tightness of chest; wheezing)

Note: Recent placebo-controlled trials suggest that in elderly persons and healthy young adults, split-virus influenza vaccine is not associated with higher rates of systemic symptoms (e.g., *fever, malaise, myalgia, and headache*) when compared with placebo injections.

Patient Consultation

As an aid to patient consultation, refer to *Advice for the Patient, Influenza Virus Vaccine (Systemic)*.

In providing consultation, consider emphasizing the following selected information (» = major clinical significance):

Before receiving this vaccine

» Conditions affecting use, especially:

Hypersensitivity to influenza virus vaccine or any of its components including eggs, monosodium glutamate, sodium bisulfite, thimerosal, gentamicin sulfate, streptomycin sulfate, or other aminoglycosides

Pregnancy—Nasal mist influenza vaccine live should not be administered to pregnant women. Inactivated influenza virus vaccine is available to immunize high-risk individuals such as pregnant women.

Breast-feeding—Caution should be exercised when administering nasal mist influenza vaccine live to nursing women due to the possibility of shedding vaccine virus.

Use in children—Use is not recommended for infants up to 6 months of age; for children 6 months to 12 years of age, only the split-virus vaccines (split, subvirion, or purified-surface-antigen type) should be used; if two doses are needed, they should be spaced 4 weeks apart.

Nasal mist influenza vaccine live is not recommended in infants and children under 5 years of age.

Use in the elderly—Inactivated influenza virus vaccine may be less effective in elderly persons; however, vaccine may be still effective in preventing other complications of influenza in these persons.

Nasal mist influenza vaccine live is not recommended for use in patients 50 years and older.

Other medications, especially aspirin therapy or aspirin-containing therapy in children or adolescents (for nasal mist), immunosuppressive therapies (for nasal mist), or other vaccines (for nasal mist)

Other medical problems, especially acute respiratory disease, allergy to eggs, acute respiratory disease, asthma, chronic cardiovascular disease, chronic metabolic diseases, chronic pulmonary disease, Guillain-Barré syndrome, hypersensitivity to influenza vaccine or any of its components including eggs, immune deficiencies diseases, reactive airway diseases, or severe febrile illness

Proper use of this medication

» Proper dosing

Precautions while receiving this vaccine

Not prescribing amantadine or rimantadine for influenza A treatment or chemoprophylaxis due to data indicating widespread resistance

Side/adverse effects

Signs of potential side effects, especially anaphylactic reaction

General Dosing Information

Appropriate precautions should be taken prior to vaccine injection to prevent allergic or any other unwanted reactions. This should include a review of the patient's history regarding possible sensitivity, and the ready availability of epinephrine 1:1000 and other appropriate agents (e.g., antihistamines) used to control immediate allergic reactions.

Inactivated influenza virus vaccine should not be administered to persons known to have anaphylactic hypersensitivity to eggs or to other components of the influenza vaccine without first consulting a physician. Use of an antiviral agent (i.e., oseltamivir or zanamivir) instead of influenza virus vaccine is an option for prevention of influenza A in such persons. However, persons who have a history of anaphylactic hypersensitivity to vaccine components but who are also at high risk of complications of influenza can benefit from the vaccine after appropriate allergy evaluation and desensitization procedures.

ACIP recommends that neither amantadine nor rimantadine be used for the treatment or chemoprophylaxis of influenza A in the U.S. because of recent data indicating widespread resistance of influenza virus to these medications. Until susceptibility to these drugs has been reestablished among circulating influenza A viruses, oseltamivir or zanamivir may be prescribed.

Children with severe chronic asthma at risk for adverse reactions to influenza virus vaccine should be identified, and appropriate steps should be taken to assure their proper immunization. With the protocol of administering increasing doses of the influenza virus vaccine in small increments, individuals with hypersensitivity to egg proteins can be safely and effectively immunized. Therefore, the following desensitization protocol for influenza virus vaccination developed by Murphy and Strunk may be considered for patients who have egg allergies and other medical conditions that place them at increased risk of influenza-associated complications.

Desensitization of the patient should be carried out by serial injections of diluted and undiluted influenza virus vaccine as indicated below at intervals of 15 minutes for a total cumulative dose of 0.5 mL undiluted influenza virus vaccine.

Schedules for desensitization:
- 0.05 mL of 1:100 dilution intramuscularly.
- 0.05 mL of 1:10 dilution intramuscularly.
- 0.05 mL of undiluted vaccine intramuscularly.
- 0.1 mL of undiluted vaccine intramuscularly.
- 0.15 mL of undiluted vaccine intramuscularly.
- 0.2 mL of undiluted vaccine intramuscularly.

Because of their decreased potential for causing febrile reactions, only split-virus vaccines should be used for children younger than 13 years of age. They may be labeled as split, subvirion, or purified-surface-antigen type vaccine. Immunogenicity and side effects of split- and whole-virus vaccines are similar among adults when vaccines are administered at the recommended dosage.

Elderly patients may develop lower antibody titers after immunization than healthy young adults and, therefore, may remain susceptible to influenza infection of the upper respiratory tract. Nonetheless, influenza virus vaccine may still be effective in preventing lower respiratory tract involvement or other complications of influenza.

During recent decades, data on influenza virus vaccine immunogenicity and side effects have been obtained for intramuscularly administered vaccine. Because recent influenza vaccines have not been adequately evaluated when administered by other routes, the intramuscular route is recommended.Inactivated influenza virus vaccine should not be injected intravenously. Adults and older children should be vaccinated in the deltoid muscle and infants and young children in the anterolateral aspect of the thigh.

Remaining influenza virus vaccine from the previous influenza season should not be used to provide protection for the current influenza season.

Beginning each September, when vaccine for the upcoming influenza season becomes available, persons at high risk who are seen by health care providers for routine care or as a result of hospitalization should be offered influenza virus vaccine. Opportunities to vaccinate persons at high risk of complications of influenza should not be missed.

The optimal time for organized vaccination campaigns for persons in high-risk groups is usually the period from October through mid-November. This period has been extended to include the first 2 weeks in October. In the U.S., influenza activity generally peaks between late December and early March. High levels of influenza activity infrequently occur in the contiguous 48 states before December. Administering the vaccine too far in advance of the influenza season should be avoided in facilities such as nursing homes, because antibody levels might begin to decline within a few months of vaccination. Vaccination programs can be undertaken as soon as the current vaccine is available, if regional influenza activity is expected to begin earlier than December.

Healthcare providers, state and local public health agencies, and facilities planning organized campaigns should develop outreach and infrastructure to provide immunization to more individuals than during the previous flu season. They should also develop contingency plans for timing and prioritization of administering the vaccine in case of the supply being delayed and/or reduced during the flu season.

ACIP emphasizes the importance of continuing to offer the vaccine throughout the flu season even after flu activity has been recorded in a community. All community vaccinators and public health agencies are encouraged to schedule clinics that serve target groups and help in extending the routine vaccination season by offering at least on clinic in December.

Children younger than 9 years of age who have not been vaccinated previously should receive two doses of vaccine at least 1 month apart for intramuscular injection and at least 6 weeks apart for nasal mist, to maximize the likelihood of a satisfactory antibody response to all three vaccine antigens. The second dose should preferably be administered before December. Live or inactivated vaccine can be used for either dose in children 5 to 9 years of age. If intramuscular injection is given first, then the nasal mist should be given less than 4 weeks later.If the nasal mist is used first, the second vaccine should be given 6 to 10 weeks later. If a child aged 6 months to less than 9 years of age received influenza vaccine for the first time during a previous season but did not receive a second dose of vaccine within the same season, only one dose of vaccine should be administered this season.

Note: Studies among adults receiving a second dose of vaccine during the same influenza season have shown little or no improvement in antibody response

Individuals at high risk for complications of influenza who were not vaccinated with influenza vaccine during the preceding fall or winter should consider receiving influenza vaccine before travel if they plan to: travel to the tropics; travel with large organized tourist groups at any time of year; or travel to the Southern Hemisphere during April to September.

Vaccine should be offered to both children and adults prior to, and even after, influenza activity is documented in a community.

The target groups for influenza and pneumococcal vaccination overlap considerably. For persons at high risk who have not been previously vaccinated with pneumococcal vaccine, health care providers should strongly consider administering both pneumococcal and influenza virus vaccines concurrently. Both vaccines can be administered at the same time at different body sites without increasing potential side effects. However, influenza virus vaccine is administered each year, whereas the pneumococcal vaccine is not. Children at high risk of influenza-related complications can receive influenza virus vaccine at the same time they receive other routine vaccinations, including pertussis vaccine (as DTP or as DTaP). Because influenza virus vaccine can cause fever when administered to young children, DTaP (which is less frequently associated with fever and other adverse reactions) is preferable.

The inactivated influenza vaccine is preferred only for persons who have close contact with severely immunosuppressed persons (e.g., patients with hematopoietic stem cell transplants) during those periods in which the immunosuppressed person requires care in a protective environment. There is no preference for inactivated influenza vaccine use by contacts of persons with lesser degrees of immunosuppression or other high risk conditions.

For intranasal dosage forms

The nasal mist influenza vaccine should under no circumstances be administered parenterally.

The nasal mist influenza vaccine should be thawed prior to administration. Do not refreeze after thawing.

Approximately 0.25 mL (half of the dose from a single nasal mist sprayer) is administered into each nostril while the recipient is in an upright position.

The dose-divider clip should be removed from the sprayer to administer the second half of the dose (0.25 mL) into the other nostril.

The used sprayer should be disposed of properly according to the standard procedures for biohazardous waste products.

Patients who have received the nasal mist influenza vaccine should avoid close contact with immunocompromised individuals for at least 21 days after receiving the vaccine.

For treatment of adverse effects

Recommended treatment includes:

- For mild hypersensitivity reaction—Administering antihistamines and, if necessary, corticosteroids. In mild anaphylaxis, antihistamines or subcutaneous epinephrine may be all that is necessary if the condition is progressing slowly and is not life-threatening, regardless of the organ or system affected. Under these circumstances, the risks associated with intravenous epinephrine administration outweigh the benefits.
- For severe hypersensitivity or anaphylactic reaction—Administering epinephrine. Antihistamines and/or corticosteroids also may be administered as required. Epinephrine is the treatment of choice for severe hypersensitivity or anaphylactic reaction. If the patient's condition is not stable, epinephrine may be infused. Norepinephrine may be preferable if there is no bronchospasm. For bronchospasm, epinephrine should be given with corticosteroids. Other bronchodilators, such as intravenous aminophylline or albuterol by nebulization, also should be considered.

Nasal Dosage Forms

INFLUENZA VIRUS VACCINE LIVE NASAL NASAL SOLUTION

Usual adult and pediatric dose

Influenza prophylaxis—

Adults and children 9 to 49 years of age: Intranasal, 0.5 mL as a single dose once each influenza season.

Usual pediatric dose

Influenza prophylaxis—

Children 5 to 8 years of age: Intranasal, 1 or 2 doses (0.5 mL), depending on whether the child has been previously vaccinated with nasal mist. The recommended schedule for patients who have previously received one dose of nasal mist influenza vaccine is one dose. If two doses are needed, they should be spaced at least 6 weeks apart. The dose is given each year.

Strength(s) usually available

U.S.

Each 0.5 mL dose contains $10^{6.5\text{-}7.5}$TCID$_{50}$ (median tissue culture infectious dose) of live attenuated influenza virus reassortants of the strains recommended by the U.S. Public Health Service for the present year's vaccine (Rx) [*FluMist* (preservative free; egg; sucrose; potassium phosphate; monosodium glutamate; gentamicin sulfate (trace))].

Canada—

Not commercially available.

Packaging and storage

Store at or below **minus** 15 °C (5 °F).

Do not refreeze after thawing.

Storage in a frost-free freezer should be avoided because the temperature could cycle above **minus** 15 °C (5 °F).

Stability

Storage above a constant temperature of **minus** 15 °C (5 °F) can negatively impact the stability of the product.

May be thawed in a refrigerator and stored at 2 to 8 °C (36 to 46 °F) for no more than 24 hours prior to use. Do not refreeze after thawing.

Parenteral Dosage Forms

INFLUENZA VIRUS VACCINE (Injection—Split virus [purified-surface-antigen type]) USP

Usual adult and adolescent dose

Influenza prophylaxis—

Adults and children 12 years of age and older: Intramuscular, 0.5 mL as a single dose.

Usual pediatric dose

Influenza prophylaxis—

Infants up to 6 months of age: Use is not recommended.

Infants 6 to 35 months of age: Two doses of 0.25 mL each, 4 weeks apart.

Children 3 to 8 years of age: Intramuscular, 0.5 mL of the split-virus vaccine. Two doses of 0.5 mL each, 4 weeks apart, are recommended for maximum protection in persons under 9 years of age who have not been previously vaccinated.

Children 9 to 12 years of age: Intramuscular, 0.5 mL as a single dose of the split-virus vaccine.

Usual geriatric dose

See *Usual adult and adolescent dose.*

Strength(s) usually available

U.S.

Each 0.5-mL dose contains the proportions, and not less than the microgram amounts, of hemagglutinin antigens (mcg HA) representative of the specific components recommended for the present year's vaccine (Rx) [*Fluarix* (octoxynol-10 ≤0.085 mg; alpha-tocopheryl hydrogen succinate ≤0.1 mg; polysorbate 80 ≤0.415 mg; thimerosal trace amounts [≤1 mcg mercury per dose]; may contain hydrocortisone ≤0.0016 mcg; may contain gentamicin sulfate ≤0.15 mcg; may contain ovalbumin ≤1 mcg; may contain formaldhyde ≤50 mcg; may contain sodium deoxycholate ≤50 mcg)].

Each 0.5-mL dose contains the proportions, and not less than the microgram amounts, of hemagglutinin antigens (mcg HA) representative of the specific components recommended for the present year's vaccine (Rx) [*Fluvirin* (thimerosal 0.01%)].

Canada—

Not commercially available.

Packaging and storage

Store between 2 and 8 °C (36 and 46 °F), unless otherwise specified by manufacturer. Do not freeze. Store in original package and protect from light.

Stability

Potency is destroyed by freezing; vaccine that has been frozen should not be used.

Auxiliary labeling

- Shake well.
- Do not freeze.

INFLUENZA VIRUS VACCINE (Injection—Split virus [split or subvirion type]) USP

Usual adult and adolescent dose

Influenza prophylaxis—

Adults and children 12 years of age and older: Intramuscular, 0.5 mL as a single dose.

Usual pediatric dose

Influenza prophylaxis—

Infants up to 6 months of age: Use is not recommended.

Infants 6 to 35 months of age: Intramuscular, 0.25 mL of the split-virus vaccine. Dose should be repeated in four or more weeks if the patient has not been previously vaccinated.

Children 3 to 8 years of age: Intramuscular, 0.5 mL of the split-virus vaccine. Two doses of 0.5 mL each, 4 weeks apart, are recommended for maximum protection in children under 9 years of age who have not been previously vaccinated.

Children 9 to 12 years of age: Intramuscular, 0.5 mL as a single dose of the split-virus vaccine.

Usual geriatric dose

See *Usual adult and adolescent dose.*

Strength(s) usually available

U.S.—

Note: Both of the preservative-free formulations contain a trace amount of thimerosal (≤ 0.5 micrograms Hg per 0.25 mL dose and ≤ 1.0 micrograms Hg per 0.5 mL dose) from the manufacturing process.

The 0.25-mL prefilled syringe is used for pediatric dosing. An alternative immunization method for children when one dose of 0.25 mL is indicated and the 0.5 mL prefilled syringe is being used, is to push the plunger of the 0.5 mL prefilled syringe exactly to the edge of the mark so that half of the volume is discarded. The remaining volume should then be injected.

Each 0.25-mL dose contains the proportions, and not less than the microgram amounts, of hemagglutinin antigens (mcg HA) representative of the specific components recommended for the present year's vaccine (Rx) [*Fluzone* (contains NO preservative)].

Each 0.5-mL dose contains the proportions, and not less than the microgram amounts, of hemagglutinin antigens (mcg HA) representative of the specific components recommended for the present year's vaccine (Rx) [*Fluzone* (contains NO preservative)].

Each 0.5-mL dose contains the proportions, and not less than the microgram amounts, of hemagglutinin antigens (mcg HA) representative of the specific components recommended for the present year's vaccine (Rx) [*FluShield* (1:10,000 thimerosal; gentamicin sulfate); *Fluzone* (1:10,000 thimerosal); GENERIC (may contain gentamicin sulfate; 1:10,000 thimerosal)].

Canada—

Each 0.5-mL dose contains the proportions, and not less than the microgram amounts, of hemagglutinin antigens (mcg HA) representative of the specific components recommended for the present year's vaccine (Rx) [*Fluviral S/F* (thimerosal 0.01%); *Fluzone* (thimerosal)].

Note: Gentamicin sulfate, streptomycin sulfate, neomycin, polymyxin, and/or sodium bisulfite may be used in the production of influenza virus vaccine. By current assay procedures, concentrations of these products are not detectable in the final vaccine; however, even in trace amounts they may be able to cause hypersensitivity reactions in susceptible persons.

Packaging and storage

Store between 2 and 8 °C (36 and 46 °F), unless otherwise specified by the manufacturer. Do not freeze.

Preparation of dosage form

This product should be visually inspected for particulate matter and/or discoloration prior to administration. Samples containing visible particulates should not be used.

Stability

Potency is destroyed by freezing; vaccine that has been frozen should not be used.

Auxiliary labeling

- Shake well.
- Do not freeze.

INFLUENZA VIRUS VACCINE (Injection—Whole virus) USP

Usual adult and adolescent dose

Influenza prophylaxis—

Adults and children 13 years of age and older: Intramuscular, 0.5 mL as a single dose.

Usual pediatric dose

Influenza prophylaxis—

Use is not recommended in children up to 12 years of age.

Note: Only split-virus influenza vaccines (split, subvirion, or purified-surface-antigen type) should be used for children up to 12 years of age because of the vaccines' lower potential for causing febrile adverse reactions when compared to the whole-virus influenza vaccine. None of the influenza virus vaccines is recommended for infants up to 6 months of age.

Usual geriatric dose

See *Usual adult and adolescent dose*.

Strength(s) usually available

U.S.—

Not commercially available.

Canada—

Each 0.5-mL dose contains the proportions, and not less than the microgram amounts, of hemagglutinin antigens (mcg HA) representative of the specific components recommended for the present year's vaccine (Rx) [*Fluviral* (thimerosal 0.01%); *Fluzone* (thimerosal)].

Packaging and storage

Store between 2 and 8 °C (35 and 46 °F), unless otherwise specified by manufacturer. Do not freeze.

Stability

Potency is destroyed by freezing; vaccine that has been frozen should not be used.

Auxiliary labeling

- Shake well.
- Do not freeze.

Selected Bibliography

Centers for Disease Control and Prevention (CDC). Prevention and control of influenza: recommendations of the Advisory Committee on Immunization Practices (ACIP). MMWR Morb Mortal Wkly Rep 2003; 52(RR-8): 1-35.

Centers for Disease Control and Prevention (CDC). Questions & Answers: The nasal-spray flu vaccine (live attenuated influenza vaccine [LAIV]). December 11, 2003. Available at: http://www.cdc.gov/flu/about/qa/nasalspray.html

Centers for Disease Control and Prevention (CDC). Prevention and control of influenza: recommendations of the Advisory Committee on Immunization Practices (ACIP). MMWR Morb Mortal Wkly Rep 2004; 53(RR-6): 1-40.

Revised: 07/31/2006

INSULIN Systemic

This monograph includes information on the following: 1) Buffered Insulin Human; 2) Extended Insulin Zinc†; 3) Extended Insulin Human Zinc; 4) Insulin; 5) Insulin Human; 6) Insulin Zinc; 7) Insulin Human Zinc; 8) Isophane Insulin; 9) Isophane Insulin Human; 10) Isophane Insulin Human and Insulin Human; 11) Prompt Insulin Zinc†.

INN:

Extended Insulin Zinc Suspension—Insulin Zinc Suspension (Crystalline)

Insulin Zinc Suspension—Compound Insulin Zinc Suspension

Prompt Insulin Zinc Suspension—Insulin Zinc Suspension (Amorphous)

BAN:

Extended Insulin Zinc Suspension—Insulin Zinc Suspension (Crystalline)

Prompt Insulin Zinc Suspension—Insulin Zinc Suspension (Amorphous)

JAN:

Extended Insulin Zinc Suspension—Crystalline Insulin Zinc Injection (Aqueous Suspension)

Insulin Human Injection—Insulin Human (Biosynthesis) and Insulin Human (Synthesis)

Isophane Insulin Suspension—Isophane Insulin Injection (Aqueous Suspension)

Insulin Zinc Suspension—Insulin Zinc Injection (Aqueous Suspension) and Insulin Zinc Purified Porcine (Suspension)

Prompt Insulin Zinc Suspension—Amorphous Insulin Zinc Injection (Aqueous Suspension)

VA CLASSIFICATION (Primary/Secondary): HS501/GA900; DX900

Commonly used brand name(s): *Humulin 10/90*[10]; *Humulin 20/80*[10]; *Humulin 30/70*[10]; *Humulin 40/60*[10]; *Humulin 50/50*[10]; *Humulin 70/30*[10]; *Humulin 70/30 Pen*[10]; *Humulin L*[7]; *Humulin N*[9]; *Humulin N Pen*[9]; *Humulin R*[5]; *Humulin R, Regular U-500 (Concentrated)*[5]; *Humulin U*[3]; *Humulin-L*[7]; *Humulin-N*[9]; *Humulin-R*[5]; *Humulin-U*[3]; *Lente*[6]; *Lente Iletin*[6]; *Lente Iletin II*[6]; *NPH Iletin*[8]; *NPH Iletin II*[8]; *NPH Purified Insulin*[8]; *Novolin 70/30*[10]; *Novolin 70/30 PenFill*[10]; *Novolin 70/30 Prefilled*[10]; *Novolin L*[7]; *Novolin N*[9]; *Novolin N PenFill*[9]; *Novolin N Prefilled*[9]; *Novolin R*[5]; *Novolin R PenFill*[5]; *Novolin R Prefilled*[5]; *Novolin ge 10/90 Penfill*[10]; *Novolin ge 20/80 Penfill*[10]; *Novolin ge 30/70*[10]; *Novolin ge 30/70 Penfill*[10]; *Novolin ge 40/60 Penfill*[10]; *Novolin ge 50/50 Penfill*[10]; *Novolin ge Lente*[7]; *Novolin ge NPH*[9]; *Novolin ge NPH Penfill*[9]; *Novolin ge Toronto*[5]; *Novolin ge Toronto Penfill*[5]; *Novolin ge Ultralente*[3]; *Regular (Concentrated) Iletin II, U-500*[4]; *Regular Iletin II*[4]; *Regular Insulin*[4]; *Velosulin BR*[1]; *Velosulin Human*[1]

Other commonly used names are:

Lente insulin [Insulin Zinc]

NPH insulin [Isophane Insulin]

Regular insulin [Insulin]

Semilente insulin [Prompt Insulin Zinc]

Ultralente insulin [Extended Insulin Zinc]

Note: For a listing of dosage forms and brand names by country availability, see *Dosage Forms* section(s).

*Not commercially available in U.S.

†Not commercially available in Canada.

Category

Antidiabetic agent; diagnostic aid (pituitary growth hormone reserve).

Indications

Note: Bracketed information in the *Indications* section refers to uses that are not included in U.S. product labeling.

Accepted

Diabetes, type 1—Insulin is indicated in the treatment of type 1 diabetes (previously called Type I, ketosis-prone, brittle, or juvenile-onset diabetes), which occurs in individuals who produce little or no endogenous insulin. One of two regimens (conventional or intensive therapy) is commonly used to treat this condition. The intensive regimen provides more rigid control of blood glucose than the conventional regimen does, but requires more frequent monitoring and more frequent dosage adjustment, and, unless insulin is administered via an insulin pump, a larger number of injections.

Diabetes, type 2—Insulin is indicated in the treatment of certain patients with type 2 diabetes (previously known as Type II, adult-onset, maturity-onset, ketosis-resistant, or stable diabetes), which occurs in individuals who produce or secrete insufficient quantities of endogenous insulin or who have developed resistance to endogenous insulin. Insulin therapy in type 2 diabetes is reserved for patients whose disease is not controlled by other measures, such as diet, exercise, or oral antidiabetic agents, or for patients who cannot tolerate oral antidiabetic agents.

Diabetes mellitus, gestational (GDM)

Diabetes mellitus, malnutrition-related or

Diabetes mellitus, other, associated with certain conditions or syndromes, such as: Pancreatic disease (congenital absence of the pancreatic islets, transient diabetes of the newborn, functional immaturity of insulin secretion in the neonate, or cystic fibrosis); endocrine disease (endocrine overactivity due to Cushing's syndrome, hyperthyroidism, pheochromocytoma, somatostatinoma, or aldosteronoma; or endocrine underactivity due to hypoparathyroidism-hypocalcemia, type I isolated growth hormone deficiency, or multitropic pituitary deficiency); or genetic syndromes, including inborn errors of metabolism (glycogen-storage disease type I or insulin-resistant syndromes, such as muscular dystrophies, late onset proximal myopathy, and Huntington's chorea)—Insulin is indicated for the treatment of GDM and for the treatment of diabetes mellitus associated with certain conditions and syndromes uncontrolled by other treatment measures (diet, exercise, and oral antidiabetic agents). Insulin requirements eventually increase during pregnancy for all patients with diabetes. Need for additional exogenous insulin usually stops postpartum for GDM patients due to hormonal and metabolic changes; however, in some patients, GDM progresses to type 1 or type 2 diabetes within 5 to 10 years. Insulin also is used to treat diabetes induced by hormones, medications, or chemicals. Insulin has been added to total parenteral nutrition or glucose solutions in order to facilitate glucose utilization in patients with poor glucose tolerance.

Insulin also is used to treat acute complications associated with diabetes, such as ketoacidosis, significant acidosis, ketosis, hyperglycemic hyperosmolar nonketotic coma, or diabetic coma. Also, temporary insulin dosing for patients with diabetes who do not usually require insulin or an increased insulin dose for patients with type 1 diabetes or patients with type 2 diabetes who require insulin may be warranted when these patients are subjected to physical stress (e.g., pregnancy, fever, severe infection, severe burns, major surgery, or other severe trauma).

Combination use of insulin and oral antidiabetic agents in patients with type 1 diabetes is controversial because many studies have indicated that oral antidiabetic agents are not effective in the treatment of these patients. Some patients with type 2 diabetes who are resistant to sulfonylureas alone may benefit from the combination of low-dose insulin and oral sulfonylurea agents for diabetes; however, resultant weight gain and effects of hyperinsulinemia should be considered. In addition, the combination of metformin and sulfonylurea agents has been used successfully before discontinuation of oral agents and initiation of insulin therapy.

Concentrated insulin (500 USP Insulin Units per mL) is used only to treat insulin-resistant patients needing a high dose (over 200 USP units) of insulin.

[Nephropathy, diabetic (prophylaxis)][1]
[Neuropathy, diabetic (prophylaxis) or][1]
[Retinopathy, diabetic (prophylaxis)][1]—Insulin, used in an intensified regimen, is indicated to prevent the development or slow the progression of microvascular complications, including diabetic nephropathy, neuropathy, and retinopathy, in patients with type 1 and type 2 diabetes.

In two large, long-term clinical trials (the Diabetes Control and Complications Trial [DCCT] and the Stockholm Diabetes Intervention Study [SDIS]), patients with type 1 diabetes who followed an intensified regimen that included at least three insulin injections each day realized improved microvascular outcomes compared with patients who followed a conventional regimen that included only one or two insulin injections each day. In addition to the three daily insulin injections, intensive therapy involved self-monitoring of blood glucose concentrations at least four times a day with adjustments in insulin dosage made as necessary, monthly clinic visits, individualized diabetes education, and continuous tutoring. The goal of intensive therapy was to achieve and maintain blood glucose concentrations and glycosylated hemoglobin (HbA_{1c}) values as close to normal as possible. In the DCCT, in which patients were followed for an average of 6.5 years, this goal was met by 44% of patients who achieved HbA_{1c} values of 6.05% or less at least one time during the study; however, less than 5% of patients were able to maintain values within the normal range. In the SDIS, in which patients were followed for 7.5 years, patients in the intensive therapy group achieved a mean HbA_{1c} value of slightly more than 7%. This value was higher than normal, but it was statistically significant compared with the baseline values obtained in the same group (9.5 ± 1.3%) and with the outcome values obtained in patients who received conventional therapy (8.5 ± 0.7%; P = 0.001). As a result of the lowered blood glucose concentrations achieved with intensive insulin therapy, the risk of development of nephropathy, neuropathy, and retinopathy was reduced by 35 to 76% in patients with no existing disease, and the progression of disease was slowed by approximately 55% in patients with mild forms of disease.

Intensive insulin therapy also has been shown to significantly reduce the risk of development of microvascular complications in patients with type 2 diabetes. Several long-term, randomized, controlled clinical trials, including the 10-year UK Prospective Diabetes Study (UKPDS), have demonstrated that patients who received intensive insulin therapy consisting of at least three insulin injections each day were able to maintain HbA_{1c} values of approximately 7%. This value was significantly lower than the HbA_{1c} values achieved by patients who received conventional therapy consisting of one of two insulin injections each day and, in the UKPDS, represented an 11% reduction over baseline values. Consequently, the onset and the progression of diabetic nephropathy, neuropathy, and retinopathy were effectively delayed in type 2 patients who followed an intensified regimen compared with type 2 patients who followed a conventional regimen.

[Growth hormone deficiency (diagnosis)][1]—Regular insulin administered intravenously is used to assess the capacity of the pituitary gland to release growth hormone. Reliable results may require that more than one test be performed, using either regular insulin or arginine. This test also may be used to obtain information regarding release of corticotropin from the pituitary. A physician experienced in the use of the insulin tolerance test should be present because of the risk of hypoglycemia.

[Hyperglycemia during intravenous nutrition in low birth weight infants (treatment)][1]—Insulin is indicated for the treatment of hyperglycemia caused by intravenous nutrition in low birth weight infants.

---

[1]Not included in Canadian product labeling.

Pharmacology/Pharmacokinetics

Physicochemical characteristics

Source—
- Bovine: Obtained from the pancreas of oxen; differs from human insulin by two amino acids at positions 8 and 10 on the A-chain and from porcine insulin by one amino acid at position 30 on the B-chain..
- Human: Derived by enzymatic modification of the one different amino acid (threonine for alanine) in porcine insulin (semi-synthetic) or derived by microbial synthesis (recombinant DNA process involving genetically engineered *Escherichia coli* or baker's yeast); identical to naturally occurring human insulin; contains 21 amino acids in the A-chain and 30 amino acids in the B-chain..
- Porcine: Obtained from pork pancreas; differs from human insulin by one amino acid at position 30 on the B-chain..

Molecular weight—
- Insulin (beef): 5733.61.
- Insulin (pork): 5777.66.
- Insulin Human (semisynthetic, biosynthetic): 5807.69.

Mechanism of action/Effect

Insulin is a polypeptide hormone that controls the storage and metabolism of carbohydrates, proteins, and fats. This activity occurs primarily in the liver, in muscle, and in adipose tissues after binding of the insulin molecules to receptor sites on cellular plasma membranes. Although the mechanisms of insulin's molecular actions in the cellular area are still being explored, it is known that cell membrane transport characteristics, cellular growth, enzyme activation and inhibition, and alterations in protein and fat metabolism are all influenced by insulin. More specifically, insulin promotes uptake of carbohydrates, proteins, and fats in most tissues. Also, insulin influences carbohydrate, protein, and fat metabolism by stimulating protein and free fatty acid synthesis, and by inhibiting release of free fatty acid from adipose cells. Insulin increases active glucose transport through muscle and adipose cellular membranes, and promotes conversion of intracellular glucose and free fatty acid to the appropriate storage forms (glycogen and triglyceride, respectively). Although the liver does not require active glucose transport, insulin increases hepatic glucose conversion to glycogen and suppresses hepatic glucose output. Even though the actions of exogenous insulin are identical to those of endogenous insulin, the ability to negatively affect hepatic glucose output differs because a smaller quantity of exogenous insulin reaches the portal vein.

Antidiabetic agent—
- Administered insulin substitutes for the lack of endogenous insulin secretion and partially corrects the disordered metabolism and inappropriate hyperglycemia of diabetes mellitus, which are caused by either an absolute deficiency or a reduction in the biologic effectiveness of insulin, or possibly both. Maintenance of good blood glucose control by insulin, which is facilitated by increasing glucose uptake and use, may slow the progression of the serious long-term complications of diabetes.

Diagnostic aid, pituitary growth hormone reserve—
- Regular insulin administered intravenously stimulates growth hormone secretion by producing hypoglycemia, which is used to evaluate pituitary growth hormone reserve.

Other actions/effects

Insulin increases the intracellular shift of potassium and magnesium and decreases renal excretion of sodium. Insulin decreases the synthesis of high density lipoprotein (HDL) cholesterol and increases the synthesis of very low density lipoprotein (VLDL) cholesterol in the liver. Insulin increases lipoprotein uptake and utilization in the lactating mammary gland. Also, insulin stimulates activity of and tissue response to the sympathetic nervous system. The growth-promoting action of insulin may contribute to an increase in peripheral vascular resistance through vascular hypertrophy.

USP Insulin Type	Onset of action† (hrs)	Time to peak† (hrs)	Duration of action† (hrs)
Intravenous Insulin injection U-100 (regular insulin) pork, purified pork, biosynthetic human, semisynthetic human	⅙–½	¼–½	½–1
Subcutaneous Insulin injection U-100 (regular insulin) pork, purified pork, biosynthetic human, semisynthetic human	½–1	2–4	5–7
Insulin injection U-500 (regular insulin) purified pork, biosynthetic human			24‡
Isophane insulin suspension U-100 (NPH insulin) mixed*, pork, purified pork, biosynthetic human	3–4	6–12	18–28
Isophane insulin suspension (70%) and insulin injection (30%) U-100 biosynthetic human	½	4–8	24
Insulin zinc suspension U-100 (lente insulin) mixed*, pork, purified pork, biosynthetic human	1–3	8–12	18–28
Extended insulin zinc suspension U-100 (ultralente) biosynthetic human	4–6	18–24	36
Prompt insulin zinc suspension U-100 (semilente)	1–3	2–8	12–16

*Mixed = Mixture of beef and pork insulins.
†Mean values; individual responses vary widely.
‡U-500 strength is absorbed slowly, resulting in a long duration of action.

Absorption

The rate of subcutaneous and intramuscular insulin absorption is highly variable (up to 50% interindividual and intraindividual variability) and is dependent on many factors including insulin formulation, injection site, injection technique, and route of injection. The addition of protamine or zinc to insulin produces a crystallized insulin in suspension that has a longer absorption phase (and a longer duration of action) than dissolved insulin does and is dependent on enzymatic degradation of the suspension at the injection site for absorption. Absorption of regular insulin, when mixed with equal or greater quantities of zinc insulin, may be slowed if the mixture is not injected immediately after preparation. Mixing regular insulin with isophane insulin does not alter the rate of absorption of either. Studies have shown that the absorption rate of human insulins is no different from, or only slightly higher than, the rate for animal insulins. The speed of injection and temperature of insulin do not alter absorption; however, capillary surface area and exercise do affect the intramuscular blood flow and can alter absorption. Exercising the limb into which the insulin was injected within 30 to 40 minutes postinjection may increase insulin absorption (delay of exercise may be warranted). Although longer-acting insulins have less pronounced variability in absorption among injection sites, the absorption rate for 12 USP Units of regular insulin given subcutaneously declined per region as follows: abdominal (87 minutes), deltoid (141 minutes), gluteal (155 minutes), and femoral (164 minutes). Finally, insulin absorption is faster with intramuscular injection than with subcutaneous injection, and is slower with very high insulin concentrations or high dose volumes.

A subcutaneous depot of insulin forms slowly at the injection site when a continuous subcutaneous infusion insulin pump is used, resulting in less variation in insulin availability and a smaller depot than occurs with use of subcutaneous injections. When injection sites are rotated, continued absorption from the first depot usually prevents plasma concentrations from decreasing to subtherapeutic values while another depot is forming.

Distribution

Distributed into most cells.

Biotransformation

Insulin—Hepatic and renal.

Isophane or zinc insulins—Split into protamine or zinc and insulin by subcutaneous enzymes prior to absorption.

Half-life

Insulin—5 to 6 minutes; can be longer in some patients with diabetes. Insulin antibodies, if present, bind to circulating plasma insulin and prolong its biologic half-life.

Elimination

Renal, 30 to 80%; unchanged insulin is reabsorbed.

Precautions to Consider

Cross-sensitivity and/or related problems

Patients intolerant of beef or pork insulins may use the alternative single-source insulin under the direction of their physician. Intolerance of beef insulin is more common than intolerance of pork insulin. Intolerance is often reduced by the use of purified pork insulin, biosynthetic human insulin, or semisynthetic human insulin.

Patients hypersensitive to protamine sulfate also may be hypersensitive to protamine-containing insulins. Patients who have become sensitized to protamine through administration of a protamine-containing insulin are at risk for severe anaphylactoid reactions if protamine sulfate is subsequently administered for reversal of heparin effect.

Pregnancy/Reproduction

Pregnancy—Insulin does not cross the placenta. However, maternal glucose and maternal insulin antibodies do cross the placenta and can cause fetal hyperinsulinemia and related problems, such as large-for-gestational-age infants and macrosomnia, possibly resulting in a need for early induced or cesarean delivery. Furthermore, high blood glucose concentrations occurring during early pregnancy (5 to 8 weeks gestation) have been associated with a higher incidence of major congenital abnormalities and, later in pregnancy, increased perinatal morbidity and mortality.

Women with diabetes must be educated about the necessity of maintaining strict metabolic control before conception and throughout pregnancy, especially during early pregnancy, to significantly decrease the risk of maternal mortality, congenital anomalies, and perinatal morbidity and mortality. A study reported that initial glycosylated hemoglobin (hemoglobin A_{1c}, a measurement of blood glucose control for the preceding 3 months) concentrations of 10% or more, 8 to 9.9%, and below 8% produced infant malformation rates of 35%, 12.9%, and 4.8%, respectively; the malformation rate in infants born to mothers who do not have diabetes is approximately 2%. Use of insulin rather than oral antidiabetic agents for the treatment of type 2 diabetes and gestational diabetes mellitus (GDM) permits maintenance of blood glucose at concentrations as close to normal as possible. Insulin requirements in pregnant patients with diabetes often are decreased during the first trimester. Requirements usually are increased in the last two trimesters of pregnancy in response to the anti-insulin hormone activity associated with increased concentrations of human placental estrogen, progesterone, chorionic gonadotropin, and prolactin; peripheral insulin resistance due to increasing levels of fatty acids and triglycerides; and increased degradation of insulin by the placenta.

Postpartum—

Insulin requirements drop quickly after childbirth, and GDM patients usually no longer need insulin. Inadequately controlled maternal blood glucose late in pregnancy may cause increased insulin production in the fetus, resulting in neonatal hypoglycemia. Treatment may be necessary until euglycemic control is established by the neonate.

Breast-feeding

Insulin is not distributed into breast milk. Problems in humans have not been documented. The insulin requirement in lactating women is reduced because of hormonal changes; in patients with type 1 diabetes, insulin requirements during lactation may be up to 27% lower than the patient's pre-pregnancy requirements. Daily monitoring for several months is important until insulin needs stabilize or until insulin is no longer needed.

Pediatrics

Insulin therapy in pediatric patients is similar to that in other age groups. However, strict intensive insulin therapy is not generally used for this age group because noncompliance may be a problem and because this regimen may be less beneficial before puberty while risks of hypoglycemia may be higher due to greater insulin sensitivity.

Adolescents

Insulin therapy in adolescents is similar to that in other age groups. Appropriate use of intensive insulin therapy may be beneficial when used cautiously. Patients with diabetes have a transient increase in insulin requirement (by approximately 20 to 50%) at puberty during the growth spurt only. Adolescent females usually require more insulin than do adolescent males because of increased insulin resistance; this is thought to be due, in part, to an increased secretion of growth hormone, but not to an increased secretion of sex hormones. Increased growth hormone secretion also may require alteration of the timing of insulin doses to overcome the prominent *dawn phenomenon* of hyperglycemia in adolescents of both sexes who have diabetes.

Geriatrics

Insulin therapy in older patients is similar to that in other age groups. However, strict intensive insulin therapy is not generally used. Also, dehydration, which may mask early symptoms of hypoglycemia and permit development of more severe symptoms; vision problems, which may lead to inaccurate dosage measurement and/or glucose monitoring; shakiness, which may interfere with measurement and self-administration of a dose; and lack of compliance with prescribed diet commonly occur in the elderly and may interfere with control of diabetes. Instructions may be needed to help the patient monitor urine or blood glucose if visual problems are present or early symptoms of hypoglycemia are missing or delayed, a particular problem in this age group. Special devices are available to help administer the insulin dose when help with visual clarity or steadiness is needed.

Drug interactions and/or related problems

The following drug interactions and/or related problems have been selected on the basis of their potential clinical significance (possible mechanism in parentheses where appropriate)—not necessarily inclusive (» = major clinical significance):

Note: Combinations containing any of the following medications, depending on the amount present, may also interact with this medication.

If the need exists to administer any medications that may affect metabolic or glycemic control of diabetes mellitus, blood glucose concentrations should be monitored by the patient or health care professional. This is particularly important when any medication is added to or removed from an established drug regimen. Subsequent adjustments in diet or insulin dosage or both may be necessary; these adjustments may differ depending on the severity of the diabetes mellitus and other factors.

» Alcohol
(consumption of moderate or large amounts of alcohol enhances insulin's hypoglycemic effect, increasing the risk of prolonged, severe hypoglycemia, especially under fasting conditions or when liver glycogen stores are low; small amounts of alcohol consumed with meals do not usually present problems)

Anabolic steroids, especially stanozolol, oxandrolone, and methandrostenolone or
Androgens
(increased tissue sensitivity to insulin and increased tissue resistance to glucagon may occur, resulting in hypoglycemia, especially when insulin resistance is present; a decrease in insulin dose may be required)

Antidiabetic agents, sulfonylurea or
Carbonic anhydrase inhibitors, especially acetazolamide
(these medications chronically stimulate the pancreatic beta cell to release insulin and increase receptor and tissue sensitivity to insulin; although concurrent use of these medications with insulin may increase the hypoglycemic response, the effect may be unpredictable)

(sulfonylurea antidiabetic agents have been used concurrently with insulin in treating a select group of patients with type 2 diabetes whose condition is not well-controlled with either agent alone; however, the long-term benefit of this use has not been established; many studies have shown there is generally no additional benefit from using sulfonylurea antidiabetic agents for the treatment of patients with type 1 diabetes)

Anti-inflammatory drugs, nonsteroidal (NSAIDs) or
Salicylates, large doses
(these medications inhibit synthesis of prostaglandin E [which inhibits endogenous insulin secretion], thereby increasing basal insulin secretion, the response to a glucose load, and the hypoglycemic effect of concurrently administered insulin; dosage adjustment of the NSAID or salicylate and/or insulin may be necessary, especially during and following chronic concurrent use)

» Beta-adrenergic blocking agents, including ophthalmics, if significant systemic absorption occurs
(beta-adrenergic blocking agents may inhibit insulin secretion, modify carbohydrate metabolism, and increase peripheral insulin resistance, leading to hyperglycemia; however, they also may cause hypoglycemia and block the normal catecholamine-mediated response to hypoglycemia [glycogenolysis and mobilization of glucose], thereby prolonging the time it takes to achieve euglycemia and increasing the risk of a severe hypoglycemic reaction. Selective beta$_1$-adrenergic blocking agents [such as acebutolol, atenolol, betaxolol, bisoprolol, and metoprolol] exhibit the above actions to a lesser extent; however, any of these agents can blunt some of the symptoms of developing hypoglycemia, such as increased heart rate or blood pressure [increased sweating may not be altered], making detection of this complication more difficult)

Chloroquine or
Quinidine or
Quinine
(concurrent use with insulin may increase the risk of hypoglycemia and increased blood insulin concentrations because of decreased insulin degradation)

» Corticosteroids
(these agents antagonize insulin's effects by stimulating release of catecholamines, causing hyperglycemia; corticosteroid-induced diabetes can occur in up to 14% of the patients taking systemic corticosteroids for several weeks or with prolonged use of topical corticosteroids, but this condition rarely produces acidosis or ketonuria even with high glucose concentrations; reversal of effects may take several weeks or months; changes in insulin dose may be necessary for patients with diabetes during and following concurrent use)

Diuretics, loop or
Diuretics, thiazide
(concurrent use with insulin may increase the risk of hyperglycemia because the potassium-depleting effect of these diuretics may inhibit insulin secretion and decrease tissue sensitivity to insulin)

Guanethidine or
Monoamine oxidase (MAO) inhibitors, including furazolidone, procarbazine, and selegiline
(epinephrine release by these agents may cause hyperglycemia; however, chronic use results in hypoglycemia; the mechanism of the latter is unknown but may include stored catecholamine depletion and interference with the compensatory adrenergic response to a fall in blood glucose; a change in dose of insulin before, during, and after treatment with these agents may be necessary)

Hyperglycemia-causing agents, such as:
Calcium channel blocking agents
Clonidine
Danazol
Dextrothyroxine
Diazoxide, parenteral
Epinephrine
Estrogen
Estrogen-progestin–containing oral contraceptives
Glucagon
Growth hormone
Heparin
Histamine H$_2$-receptor antagonists
Marijuana
Morphine
Nicotine
Phenytoin
Sulfinpyrazone
Thyroid hormones
(these medications may change metabolic control of glucose concentrations and, unless the changes can be controlled with diet, may necessitate an increase in the amount or a change in the timing of the insulin dose)

Hypoglycemia-causing agents, such as:
Angiotensin-converting enzyme inhibitors
Bromocriptine
Clofibrate
Ketoconazole
Lithium
Mebendazole
Pyridoxine
Sulfonamides
Theophylline
(these medications may change metabolic control of glucose concentrations and, unless the changes can be controlled with diet, may necessitate a decrease in the amount or a change in the timing of the insulin dose)

Octreotide
(octreotide can cause changes in the counterregulatory hormones secretion [insulin, glucagon, and growth hormone] and slow gastric emptying and gastrointestinal contractility, resulting in delayed

meal absorption and mild transient hypoglycemia or hyperglycemia in individuals with or without diabetes; in patients with diabetes, insulin therapy may need to be reduced following the initiation of octreotide and monitored for adjustments during and after octreotide treatment)

» Pentamidine
(pentamidine has a toxic effect on pancreatic beta cells, resulting in a biphasic effect on glucose concentration, i.e., initial insulin release and hypoglycemia followed by hypoinsulinemia and hyperglycemia with continued use of pentamidine; initially, insulin dose should be reduced, then the dose should be increased with continued use of pentamidine)

Tetracycline
(a delayed onset of increased tissue sensitivity to insulin may occur in patients with diabetes; this reaction has not occurred in individuals with normal glucose tolerance)

Tobacco, smoking
(may antagonize insulin effects by stimulating release of catecholamines, causing hyperglycemia; also, smoking reduces subcutaneous insulin absorption; dosage reduction of insulin may be necessary when an insulin-dependent patient suddenly stops smoking)

Medical considerations/Contraindications

The medical considerations/contraindications included have been selected on the basis of their potential clinical significance (reasons given in parentheses where appropriate)—not necessarily inclusive (» = major clinical significance).

Risk-benefit should be considered when the following medical problems exist:

Note: The following medical problems may necessitate a change in insulin therapy and are not intended as contraindications.

Allergy or local skin sensitivity to insulins
» Diarrhea or
» Gastroparesis or
» Intestinal obstruction or
» Vomiting or
» Other conditions causing delayed food absorption or malabsorption
(vomiting or delayed stomach emptying may require a change in timing of the insulin dose to realign peak action to peak blood glucose concentrations)

Hepatic disease
(insulin requirements are complex, and an increase or decrease of dosage may be needed partly because of modifications in hepatic metabolism of insulin and alterations in hepatic and plasma glucose concentrations)

» Hyperglycemia-causing conditions, such as:
Female hormonal changes or
Fever, high or
Hyperadrenalism, not optimally controlled or
Infection, severe or
Psychological stress
(these conditions may increase blood glucose, increase or change the insulin requirement, and necessitate more frequent blood glucose monitoring)
(insulin requirements may be increased near or during a menstrual cycle and may return to normal after menstruation; also, a change to intravenous insulin administration may be needed during labor when close glucose control is needed)

Hyperthyroidism, not optimally controlled
(hyperthyroidism increases both the activity and the clearance of insulin, making glycemic control difficult until the patient is euthyroid)

» Hypoglycemia-causing conditions, such as:
Adrenal insufficiency, not optimally controlled or
Pituitary insufficiency, not optimally controlled
(these conditions, by reducing blood glucose concentrations, may decrease the insulin requirement and necessitate more frequent blood glucose monitoring)
(also, untreated or not optimally controlled adrenal or pituitary insufficiency may increase tissue sensitivity to insulin and reduce the patient's insulin requirement)

Renal disease
(insulin requirements are complex, and an increase or decrease of dosage may be needed due to modifications in renal clearance of insulin)

Surgery or
Trauma
(hypoglycemia or hyperglycemia may occur, depending on the surgery or trauma; a change to intravenous insulin administration may be needed when close glucose control is necessary)

Patient monitoring

The following may be especially important in patient monitoring (other tests may be warranted in some patients, depending on condition; » = major clinical significance):

» Blood glucose determinations
(the concentration of blood or plasma glucose reflects the current degree of metabolic control and should be routinely monitored by the patient at home and by the physician [every 3 months and more often when the patient is not stabilized] to confirm that blood glucose concentration is maintained within agreed upon targets by the selected diet and dosing regimen; this is particularly important during dosage adjustments. Self-monitoring of blood glucose by the patient may require testing at multiple times during the day for intensive insulin therapy or once to several times a week for conventional insulin therapy)
(caution in interpreting blood glucose concentrations is needed because normal whole blood glucose values are approximately 15% lower than plasma glucose values. Normal fasting whole blood glucose for adults of all ages is 65 to 95 mg/dL [3.6 to 5.3 mmol/L]. Normal fasting serum glucose is 70 to 105 mg/dL [3.9 to 5.8 mmol/L] for adults younger than 60 years of age and 80 to 115 mg/dL [4.4 to 6.4 mmol/L] for adults 60 years of age or older. For children, normal fasting serum glucose is less than 130 mg/dL [7.2 mmol/L] and fasting whole blood glucose is less than 115 mg/dL [5.6 mmol/L]. For pregnant women with diabetes, normal fasting serum glucose is less than 105 mg/dL [5.8 mmol/L] and fasting whole blood glucose is less than 120 mg/dL [6.7 mmol/L]. Goals of intensive insulin therapy are to maintain fasting blood glucose between 60 and 120 mg/dL [3.3 and 6.7 mmol/L] and postprandial blood glucose at less than 180 mg/dL [10 mmol/L], while goals of conventional insulin therapy are based on the absence of symptoms of hyperglycemia and hypoglycemia)
(capillary blood glucose measurement provides important information when done properly, but caution is warranted because of potential errors in technique and readings; it has been suggested that the values be relied upon only if the reported glucose concentration for patients in whom diabetes is stable is between 75 mg/dL and 325 mg/dL [4.12 mmol/L and 17.88 mmol/L, respectively])

Body weight determinations
(significant increase in body weight may require increase in insulin dosage)

Glucose, urine or
Ketones, urine
(if blood glucose concentrations exceed 200 mg/dL [11.1 mmol/L], it may be necessary to monitor urine for the presence of glucose and ketones; normalization of glucose in the urine generally lags quantitatively behind serum glucose concentrations; test methods are generally capable of detecting serum glucose concentrations greater than 180 mg/dL [10 mmol/L])

Glycosylated hemoglobin (hemoglobin A_{1c}) determinations
(hemoglobin A_{1c} values [normal whole blood hemoglobin A_{1c} is 4 to 6% of total hemoglobin; specific values are laboratory-dependent] reflect the metabolic control over the preceding 3 months, but assessment of this parameter does not eliminate the need for daily blood glucose monitoring. Hemoglobin A_{1c} is falsely elevated in patients whose diabetes is unstable when the intermediate precursor is elevated [e.g., in alcoholism] and falsely lowered in conditions of shortened red blood cell life-span [e.g., in anemia and acute or chronic blood loss] or in patients with hemoglobinopathies [e.g., sickle cell disease])

pH measurements, serum or
Potassium concentrations, serum
(determinations may be important if the patient is hypoglycemic and ketoacidotic)

Side/Adverse Effects

The following side/adverse effects have been selected on the basis of their potential clinical significance (possible signs and symptoms in parentheses where appropriate)—not necessarily inclusive:

Those indicating need for medical attention

Incidence more frequent

Hypoglycemia—mild, including nocturnal hypoglycemia (anxiety; behavior change similar to drunkenness; blurred vision; cold sweats;

confusion; cool, pale skin; difficulty in concentrating; drowsiness; excessive hunger; fast heartbeat; headache; nausea; nervousness; nightmares; restless sleep; shakiness; slurred speech; unusual tiredness or weakness); ***hypoglycemia—severe*** (coma; seizures); ***weight gain***

Note: The occurrence of a recent episode of *hypoglycemia* may result in less severe symptoms appearing during a second episode. In children and the elderly, symptoms of *hypoglycemia* are variable and harder to identify. Furthermore, *nocturnal hypoglycemia* may be asymptomatic in 33% or more of affected patients. Also, rebound hyperglycemia may appear from ½ to 24 hours after moderate to severe hypoglycemia *(Somogyi phenomenon)*.

Hypoglycemic episodes, including severe hypoglycemic coma, occur more frequently with intensive insulin therapy than with conventional therapy.

Weight gain of 120% above ideal weight (mean of 4.6 kg after 5 years of treatment) is experienced by 12.7 patients per 100 patient-years during intensive insulin therapy and by 9.3 patients per 100 patient-years during conventional insulin therapy.

Incidence rare

Edema (swelling of face, fingers, feet, or ankles); ***lipoatrophy at injection site*** (depression of the skin at the injection site); ***lipohypertrophy at injection site*** (thickening of the skin at the injection site)

Note: *Edema* due to sodium retention caused by insulin is reversible over several days to a week after euglycemic recovery from severe hyperglycemia or ketoacidosis.

The risk of *lipoatrophy* may be reduced by injecting insulin into the periphery of the atrophic site in order to restore subcutaneous adipose tissue. The risk of *lipohypertrophy* may be decreased by rotating injection sites.

Patient Consultation

As an aid to patient consultation, refer to *Advice for the Patient, Insulin (Systemic)*.

In providing consultation, consider emphasizing the following selected information (» = major clinical significance):

Before using this medication

» Conditions affecting use, especially:

Allergy or local skin sensitivity to insulins

Pregnancy—Importance of controlling and monitoring blood glucose to meet changing needs for insulin during and after pregnancy and to prevent maternal and fetal problems, including fetal macrosomnia, congenital anomalies, and hyperglycemia; alerting physician to plans before becoming pregnant when possible

Breast-feeding—Insulin is not distributed into breast milk; however, the maternal requirement for insulin is less during breast-feeding because of hormonal changes; checking blood glucose every day for several months to help determine variable insulin dosing needs

Use in children—Use in children is similar to use in other age groups. However, prepubertal children have increased risk of hypoglycemia because they have greater sensitivity to insulin than do pubertal children

Use in adolescents—Use in adolescents is similar to use in other age groups. However, insulin needs increase by 20 to 50% at puberty and decrease afterwards; girls may need higher insulin doses than boys

Use in the elderly—Dehydration may mask early symptoms of hypoglycemia and permit development of more severe symptoms. Vision problems and shakiness may make accurate dosing and glucose monitoring difficult; special training and equipment are available to help overcome these problems

Other medications, especially alcohol, beta-adrenergic blocking agents, corticosteroids, or pentamidine

Other medical problems, especially adrenal insufficiency, pituitary insufficiency, or other conditions causing hypoglycemia; diarrhea, gastroparesis, intestinal obstruction, vomiting, or other conditions causing delayed food absorption or malabsorption; female hormonal changes, high fever, hyperadrenalism, psychological distress, severe infection, or other conditions causing hyperglycemia

Proper use of this medication

» Understanding what is meant by source of insulin (beef and pork, pork, mixed insulins, and human) and only buying insulin derived from the source and of the type and strength that are prescribed; otherwise, consulting physician

» Selecting syringe of proper units of measure for insulin capacity; syringe should be made to measure insulin in units to facilitate accurate dose measurement; a 3/10 cc syringe measures up to 30 USP Units, a ½ cc syringe measures up to 50 USP Units, and a 1 cc syringe measures up to 100 USP Units

Carefully selecting and rotating injection sites, following physician's recommendations

» Proper preparation of medication

» Measuring one type of insulin per dose

» Measuring and mixing two types of insulin per dose

» Proper administration technique

» *Using various injection devices*

Carefully reading patient instruction sheet contained in insulin or device package

Understanding how to use insulin in insulin devices such as automatic injectors, continuous subcutaneous insulin infusion pumps, disposable and nondisposable syringes, insulin pen devices, and insulin spray injectors

Disposing of syringes by separating needle from syringe, capping or clipping needle, and disposing in puncture-resistant container

» Compliance with therapy, including not taking more or less medication than directed

» Importance of adherence to recommended regimens for diet, exercise, blood sugar testing, changes in dose, and sick-day management

» Proper dosing

» Proper storage

Precautions while using this medication

» Regular visits to physician to check progress, especially during the first few weeks of treatment

» *Carefully following special instructions of health care team:*

Discussing use of alcohol

Discussing plans to stop chronic smoking of tobacco

Not taking other medications unless discussed with physician

Getting counseling for family members to help them assist the patient with diabetes; also, special counseling for pregnancy planning and contraception

Discussing travel arrangements, including transporting insulin and carrying medical history and extra supplies of insulin and syringes

» Preparing for and knowing what to do in case of an emergency by carrying medical history and current medication list; wearing medical identification; and keeping extra needed medical supplies, quick acting sugar, and nonexpired glucagon kit nearby

» Recognizing symptoms of hypoglycemia: Anxiety; behavior change similar to drunkenness; blurred vision; cold sweats; confusion; cool, pale skin; difficulty in concentrating; drowsiness; excessive hunger; fast heartbeat; headache; nausea; nervousness; nightmares; restless sleep; shakiness; slurred speech; and unusual tiredness or weakness

» Recognizing what brings on symptoms of hypoglycemia, such as delaying or missing a meal or snack, exercising more than usual, drinking significant amounts of alcohol, taking certain medications, using too much insulin, or sickness, including vomiting or diarrhea

» Knowing what to do if symptoms of hypoglycemia occur, such as eating glucose tablets or gel, corn syrup, honey, or sugar cubes; or drinking fruit juice, nondiet soft drink, or sugar dissolved in water; also, eating small snack, such as cheese and crackers, milk, or half sandwich when scheduled meal is longer than 1 hour away; not eating foods high in fat, such as chocolate because fat slows gastric emptying; or using glucagon injection if the patient becomes unconscious

» Recognizing symptoms of hyperglycemia and ketoacidosis: Blurred vision; drowsiness; dry mouth; flushed, dry skin; fruit-like breath odor; increased urination (frequency and volume); ketones in urine; loss of appetite; stomachache, nausea, or vomiting; tiredness; troubled breathing (rapid and deep); unconsciousness; and unusual thirst

» Recognizing what brings on symptoms of hyperglycemia, such as diarrhea, fever, or infection; not taking enough or skipping a dose of insulin; exercising less than usual; or overeating or not following meal plan

» Knowing what to do if symptoms of hyperglycemia occur, such as checking blood glucose and increasing the insulin dose (short term for supplementary or anticipatory doses) according to the individualized dosing schedule developed; contacting physician for more permanent dose changes; changing only one type of insulin dose (usually the first dose); anticipating how one change in an insulin dose affects other doses of the day; delaying a meal if blood glucose concentration exceeds 200 mg/dL (11.1 mmol/L); checking with physician when blood glucose concentration is above 240 mg/dL (13.3 mmol/L); not exercising when blood glucose concentration is above 240 mg/dL (13.3 mmol/L); or being hospitalized if ketoacidosis or coma occurs

Side/adverse effects

Signs of potential side effects, especially mild hypoglycemia, including nocturnal hypoglycemia; severe hypoglycemia; weight gain; edema; lipoatrophy or lipohypertrophy at injection site

General Dosing Information

In the U.S., the potency of insulin is expressed in terms of USP Insulin Units or USP Insulin Human Units. Bovine or porcine insulin contains not less than 26 USP Insulin Units per mg of insulin on the dried basis. Human insulin contains not less than 27.5 USP Insulin Human Units per mg of insulin on the dried basis. International Units cannot be compared directly to USP Units because the reference standards and the methodologies for manufacturing are different.

It is generally not recommended that patients whose diabetes is well-controlled with animal insulins automatically be switched to human insulins. Human insulins may not offer any significant advantage over the highly purified pork insulins, with the exception of reduced antibody concentrations, which may be a consideration for some patients, especially children, young adults, patients who are pregnant or considering pregnancy, patients with allergies, or patients using insulin intermittently. Patients should be informed of the possible need for dosage adjustment during the first 1 to 2 weeks following a change in the source (bovine and porcine, porcine, or human) of their insulin products and advised not to make such a change without first consulting their physicians.

Transferring patients from oral hypoglycemic agents to insulin can be immediate, although blood glucose concentrations should be evaluated for several days following the change and the prolonged effects of chlorpropamide should be considered when determining the insulin dose.

The vial of insulin must not be shaken hard before being used. Frothing or bubble formation can cause an incorrect dose. Contents are mixed well by rolling the bottle slowly between the palms of the hands or by gently tipping the bottle over a few times. Insulin should not be used if it looks lumpy or grainy, or sticks to the bottle. Also, regular insulin should not be used if it becomes viscous or cloudy; only clear, colorless solutions should be used.

Dilution of insulin preparations generally should be avoided. However, some pediatric doses may be too small to measure accurately. If needed, diluting from U-100 to U-10 has been suggested to aid in accurate dosing for very small doses in pediatric patients. Such dilutions are stable for 2 months when stored at 4 °C (39 °F) or until the date of expiration of the insulin, whichever occurs first. Occasionally insulin must be diluted to avoid crystallization in the catheters when it is administered as a low-dose infusion via an insulin pump. In these rare cases, dilution should be performed aseptically in a laminar flow hood using diluents and mixing vials provided or recommended by the manufacturer. The differences in strength, dosage volume, and expiration date should be clearly labeled by the pharmacist and emphasized to the patient. If insulin needs to be diluted during an emergency and the diluents are not readily available, 0.9% sodium chloride injection without preservative may be used for dilution of small insulin doses. However, these solutions are not stable and should be used promptly. Stinging or burning at the site of injection also may occur due to the lower pH of these solutions.

Different types of insulin are sometimes mixed in the syringe in proportions ordered by the physician in order to achieve a more accurate matching of insulin availability to the patient's requirements in a single dose. If insulins are to be mixed, several factors should be considered:

- Each patient should always follow the same sequence of mixing the separate insulin preparations. As a general rule, regular insulin should be drawn first to avoid contamination and clouding of the vial of regular insulin by the other insulin. A mixture of regular insulin and another insulin will have a longer duration of action than does regular insulin alone.
- Insulin zinc, prompt insulin zinc, and extended insulin zinc may be mixed in any proportion without loss of the characteristics of the individual insulins. Such mixtures are stable for up to 18 months.
- Unbuffered regular insulin and isophane insulin may be mixed in any proportion in a syringe and stored upright if possible. The prefilled syringe can be used immediately, stored at room temperature and used within 14 days, or stored in a refrigerator for use within 3 weeks. Mixtures containing buffered regular insulin should be used immediately.
- Mixing unbuffered regular insulin and insulin zinc insulins (lente, semilente, and ultralente) is not recommended because the excess zinc in the insulin zinc insulin can form an extra zinc insulin complex with the regular insulin. This can lengthen the insulin's duration of action and give unpredictable clinical results. However, if these insulins are combined, it is recommended that the mixture be used immediately.
- Phosphate buffered regular insulin or isophane insulins should not be mixed with insulin zinc insulins. Zinc phosphate may precipitate from the mixture, which can shorten the expected duration of action and provide unpredictable clinical results.
- Phosphate buffered regular insulin should not be mixed with any other insulin when used in an external insulin infusion pump because of the potential problem of precipitation.

After receiving insulin at first diagnosis of type 1 diabetes, 20 to 30% of patients appear to normalize for a few weeks or months (called the honeymoon phase). Some clinicians continue insulin treatment in small doses of 0.2 to 0.5 USP Units per kg of body weight during this time.

Conventional and intensive insulin therapies are individualized insulin regimens that provide different levels of blood glucose control. Conventional therapy consists of one or two insulin injections a day and daily self-monitoring of urine or blood glucose, but not daily adjustments of insulin dose. Intensive insulin therapy provides tighter blood glucose control via administration of three or more injections a day or by use of an insulin pump. Also, adjustments of insulin dose according to the results of self-monitoring of blood glucose determinations are performed at least four times a day and before anticipated dietary intake and exercise. The dosage and the timing of administration of insulin can vary greatly and must therefore be determined for each individual patient by the attending physician. Matching the patient's specific insulin needs over a 24-hour period through the use of short-acting and longer-acting preparations may decrease long-term complications of diabetes mellitus.

If a pattern of metabolic noncontrol ensues (blood glucose concentrations changing for 3 days), the total daily insulin dose usually is adjusted by changing only one type of insulin and only one segment of the daily dose; the first preprandial dose is the one most commonly changed because it more prominently affects the other doses of the day.

Insulin requirements may change with diet or physical activity. Algorithms can be developed to aid a patient with supplemental or anticipatory insulin dosing needs based on the patient's sensitivity to insulin. Supplemental doses of regular insulin can be used to correct excessive preprandial blood glucose concentrations after the basic dose of insulin is established. Anticipatory insulin doses are based on anticipated dietary or physical activity changes. Because of the increased risk of secondary hyperglycemia due to exercise, patients should be cautioned against exercising if the blood glucose concentration exceeds 240 mg/dL (13.3 mmol/L) or when a condition exists that causes low glucagon stores.

Additional low doses of regular insulin (1 to 2 USP Units for each 30 to 40 mg/dL [1.7 to 2.2 mmol/L] incremental rise above the target blood glucose concentration) every 3 to 4 hours may be needed on sick days. Patients should be warned to inform the physician if the concentration remains above 240 mg/dL (13.3 mmol/L) after three supplementary insulin doses or if symptoms of ketoacidosis develop.

The patient should always use only one brand or type of syringe and should consult the physician before changing brands or syringe types. Among different brands or syringe types, the unmeasured volume between the needle point and the bottom calibration on the syringe barrel (called dead space) may differ enough to cause improper dosage.

The use of a disposable syringe and needle to administer more than one injection is controversial. Although USP medical advisory panels do not recommend this practice, it must be recognized that some patients reuse disposable syringes and needles because of economic constraints. Where this is occurring, it must be emphasized that the syringe and needle be used only for one particular patient, the needle should be wiped with alcohol, and the needle's cap replaced after each use. Also, the syringe and needle should be reused only for a limited number of injections. Disposable syringes and needles should not be reused on a continuing basis.

For intravenous infusion

Regular insulin (Insulin Injection USP and Insulin Human Injection USP) in the 100-USP-Unit concentration is the only insulin type suitable for intravenous administration.

Insulin can be adsorbed to the surfaces of glass and plastic intravenous infusion containers (including polyvinyl chloride [PVC], ethylene vinyl acetate, and polyethylene). Adsorption is unpredictable and the clinical significance is uncertain. Recommendations for minimizing adsorption include adding 0.35% serum albumin human or approximately 5 mL of the patient's blood or using a syringe pump with a short cannula. For admixtures of insulin greater than 100 USP Units per 500 mL of intravenous solution, decant 50 mL of intravenous solution containing insulin through the administration apparatus and store for 30 minutes before using for optimal results. Afterwards, insulin dosage should be adjusted to meet the patient's targeted blood glucose concentration. Regular insulin is compatible with dextrose injection, 0.9% sodium chloride injection, and combinations of these.

For continuous subcutaneous insulin infusion pump

Generally, buffered regular insulin is used in insulin pumps, although unbuffered regular insulin has been used. Phosphate buffered regular insulin is less likely to crystallize and block insulin pump catheters and is preferred over unbuffered regular insulin. Following insulin pump manufacturers" recommendations and suggested maintenance procedures is important to ensure optimal performance and to avoid problems, such as insulin adhesion or clogging. Consult individual manufacturer's package inserts.

When initiating a continuous subcutaneous insulin infusion with an insulin pump, a priming dose may be needed. Without an initial priming dose, the depot forms at a very slow rate. Pumps with a short pulse-rate interval have little superiority over pumps with a longer interval in relation to the depot formation. An additional priming dose is not necessary when the infusion site is changed. Absorption of insulin from the depot at the first site continues after discontinuation of the infusion, preventing insulin concentrations from decreasing to subtherapeutic values while another depot is forming at the new site.

For treatment of adverse effects and/or overdose

Recommended treatment may include:

- For mild to moderate hypoglycemia:
  —Treating with immediate ingestion of a source of sugar, such as glucose gel, glucose tablets, fruit juice, corn syrup, nondiet soft drink, honey, sugar cubes, or table sugar dissolved in water. A frequently used source of sugar is a glassful of orange juice containing 2 or 3 teaspoonfuls of table sugar.
  —Documenting blood glucose and rechecking in 15 minutes.
  —Counseling patient to seek medical assistance promptly.
- For severe hypoglycemia or acute overdose, including coma:
  —Need for patient to obtain emergency medical assistance immediately.
  —Immediately treating with 50 mL of 50% dextrose injection given intravenously to stabilize the patient. Then administering a continuous infusion of 5 to 10% dextrose injection to maintain slight hyperglycemia (approximately 100 mg/dL blood glucose concentration) for up to 12 days. An adult who does not have diabetes usually exhibits a higher maximal hypoglycemic effect from insulin than does an adult who has diabetes. It is important to note that oral glucose cannot be relied upon to maintain euglycemia because 60% of an oral glucose dose is stored as hepatic glycogen with only 15% left for brain utilization and 15% for insulin-dependent tissues.
  —Glucagon, 1 to 2 mg administered intramuscularly, is useful for fast onset of action to mobilize hepatic glucose stores but may be ineffective or variable in its effect if glycogen stores are depleted.
  —Monitoring vital signs, arterial blood gases, blood glucose, and serum electrolytes (especially calcium, potassium, and sodium) as required. Initially, blood glucose concentrations should be monitored as frequently as every 1 to 3 hours. Blood urea nitrogen and serum creatinine concentrations also should be obtained.
- Cerebral edema—Managed with mannitol and dexamethasone.
- Hypokalemia—Managed with potassium supplements.

Other supportive measures also should be employed as needed.

BUFFERED INSULIN HUMAN

Parenteral Dosage Forms

Note: Bracketed uses in the *Dosage Forms section* refer to categories of use and/or indications that are not included in U.S. product labeling.

BUFFERED INSULIN HUMAN INJECTION

Usual adult and adolescent dose

Type 1 diabetes—

Initial—

Subcutaneous or continuous subcutaneous insulin infusion, a total insulin dose, using one or more types of insulin, is 0.5 to 1.2 USP Insulin Human Units per kg of body weight a day in divided doses, taking body fat, blood glucose, and insulin sensitivity into consideration. A few patients will require less than 0.5 USP Insulin Human Unit per kg of body weight a day. Dose titration to a targeted blood glucose goal is achieved over several days; a change in total daily insulin dose does not usually exceed 10% of the existing total daily insulin dose.

When using a continuous subcutaneous insulin infusion pump, the basal insulin dose (usually forty to sixty percent of the total insulin daily dose) is divided into a dose that can be continuously infused subcutaneously over twenty-four hours. Also, a premeal injection (also, forty to sixty percent of total insulin dose) can be delivered preprogrammed or manually by the patient through the insulin pump.

When using subcutaneous injections, regular human insulin is usually injected in low doses, i.e., less than 10 USP Insulin Human Units a dose.

Both subcutaneous injections and premeal injections of regular human insulin using a continuous subcutaneous insulin infusion pump generally are given fifteen to thirty minutes before one or more meals and/or a bedtime snack.

Maintenance—

Subcutaneous or continuous subcutaneous insulin infusion, dosage must be determined by the physician, based on blood glucose concentrations.

Type 2 diabetes—

Initial—

Subcutaneous, a total insulin dose, using one or more types of insulin, may vary from 5 to 10 USP Insulin Human Units per day to 0.7 to 2.5 USP Insulin Human Units per kg of body weight a day in divided doses, taking body fat, blood glucose, and insulin sensitivity into consideration. Dose titration to a targeted blood glucose goal is achieved over several days with changes of no more than 2 to 6 USP Insulin Human Units a day in the existing total daily insulin dose; again, with consideration of body weight. Very insulin-resistant patients using large doses, 200 USP Insulin Human Units or greater, may need to use a concentrated regular insulin (U-500) instead.

Regular human insulin is usually given in low doses, i.e., often less than 10 USP Insulin Human Units a dose, fifteen or thirty minutes before one or more meals and/or a bedtime snack.

Maintenance—

Subcutaneous, dosage must be determined by the physician, based on blood glucose concentrations.

Gestational diabetes mellitus—

Subcutaneous, dosage must be determined by the physician, based on blood glucose concentrations and gestational duration.

Diabetes mellitus, other, associated with certain conditions or syndromes—

Subcutaneous, dosage must be determined by the physician, based on body weight and blood glucose concentrations.

Note: For treatment of diabetic ketoacidosis, an optional loading dose of 0.15 USP Insulin Human Unit per kg of body weight is given intravenously, followed by 0.1 USP Insulin Human Unit per kg of body weight per hour by continuous infusion. The rate of insulin infusion should be decreased when the plasma glucose concentration reaches 300 mg per dL. Infusion of 5% dextrose injection should be started separately from the insulin infusion when plasma glucose concentration reaches 250 mg per dL. Thirty minutes before discontinuing the insulin infusion, an appropriate dose of insulin should be injected subcutaneously; intermediate-acting insulin has been recommended. Alternatively, a loading dose of 0.5 USP Insulin Human Unit per kg of body weight is injected intramuscularly, followed by 0.1 USP Insulin Human Unit per kg of body weight injected intramuscularly every hour until the blood glucose concentration reaches 300 mg per dL. Then to maintain blood glucose concentration at 250 mg per dL, 0.1 USP Insulin Human Unit per kg of body weight is injected intramuscularly every two hours as needed. With either type of insulin administration, capillary blood glucose should be monitored at least hourly and the insulin dose adjusted accordingly.

Insulin requirements may change during illness or events causing psychological or physical stress. Dosage changes for patients receiving conventional therapy should be determined by the physician, based on each patient's needs and insulin sensitivity. Patients receiving intensive therapy may adjust individual doses to compensate for anticipated changes in diet or exercise but should consult a physician if the permitted adjustments are inadequate and/or glucose monitoring indicates the need for a permanent change in the daily dose.

Some patients experience a honeymoon phase after initial therapy and lose their requirement for insulin altogether or require much less for a limited period of time (several months to several years).

Adolescents during puberty may require an increase in their total daily insulin dose.

[Growth hormone deficiency, diagnosis of][1]—

Intravenous, 0.05 to 0.15 USP Insulin Human Unit per kg of body weight as a single rapid injection.

Usual pediatric dose

Antidiabetic agent—

Subcutaneous, dosage must be determined by the physician, based on body weight and blood glucose concentrations.

[Hyperglycemia during intravenous nutrition in low birth weight infants (treatment)][1]—

Initial—

Intravenous, 0.05 USP Insulin Human Unit per kg of body weight per hour.

Maintenance—

Intravenous, 0.05 to 0.08 USP Insulin Human Unit per kg of body weight per hour as needed up to a maximum of 0.16 USP Insulin Human Unit per kg of body weight per hour.

Strength(s) usually available

U.S.—

100 USP Insulin Human Units per mL (OTC) [*Velosulin BR* (semisynthetic; phosphate buffered)].

Canada—

Note: *Velosulin Human* is available only through the Special Access Program in Ottawa.

100 USP Insulin Human Units per mL [*Velosulin Human* (semisynthetic; phosphate buffered)].

Packaging and storage

Store between 2 and 8 °C (36 and 46 °F). Protect from freezing.

Stability

Do not use if cloudy, discolored, or unusually viscous.

Auxiliary labeling

- Refrigerate.
- Do not freeze.

Note

Patients should be advised not to mix phosphate buffered insulin with zinc-containing insulins.

Also, patients should be advised not to mix phosphate buffered insulin with any other insulin when using a continuous subcutaneous external insulin pump.

Buffered insulin human is the preferred regular insulin for use in continuous subcutaneous infusion insulin pumps, but also may be injected subcutaneously or intramuscularly with an insulin syringe, or used intravenously. When this insulin is used in a continuous subcutaneous infusion insulin pump, the catheter tubing and the insulin in the reservoir must be changed every 48 hours or the manufacturer's recommendations followed for specific external insulin pumps.

[1]Not included in Canadian product labeling.

EXTENDED INSULIN ZINC

Parenteral Dosage Forms

EXTENDED INSULIN ZINC SUSPENSION (ULTRALENTE INSULIN) USP

Usual adult and adolescent dose

Type 1 diabetes—

Initial: Subcutaneous, a total insulin dose is 0.5 to 0.8 USP Insulin Unit per kg of body weight sometimes as a single dose, depending on insulin type, or 0.5 to 1.2 USP Insulin Units per kg of body weight per day in divided doses. Body fat, blood glucose, and insulin sensitivity also should be considered. This total daily dose of insulin may be provided by one or more types of insulin. A few patients will require less than 0.5 USP Insulin Unit per kg of body weight per day. Dose titration to a targeted blood glucose goal is achieved over several days; a change in total daily insulin dose does not usually exceed 10% of the existing total daily insulin dose. Extended insulin zinc is given once or twice a day thirty to sixty minutes before a meal and/or a bedtime snack.

Maintenance: Subcutaneous, dosage must be determined by the physician, based on blood glucose concentrations.

Type 2 diabetes—

Initial: Subcutaneous, a total insulin dose may vary from 5 to 10 USP Insulin Units per day to 0.7 to 2.5 USP Insulin Units per kg of body weight per day, taking body fat, blood glucose, and insulin sensitivity into consideration. This total daily dose of insulin may be provided by one or more types of insulin and, depending on insulin type, may be given as a single dose or as divided doses. Dose titration to a targeted blood glucose goal is achieved over several days with changes from the existing total daily insulin dose of no more than 2 to 6 USP Insulin Units a day; again, body weight should be considered. Very insulin-resistant patients using large doses, 200 USP Insulin Units or greater, may need to use a concentrated regular insulin (U-500) instead. Extended insulin zinc is given once or twice a day thirty or sixty minutes before a meal and/or a bedtime snack.

Maintenance: Subcutaneous, dosage must be determined by the physician, based on blood glucose concentrations.

Gestational diabetes mellitus—

Subcutaneous, dosage must be determined by the physician, based on blood glucose concentrations and gestational duration.

Diabetes mellitus, other, associated with certain conditions or syndromes—

Subcutaneous, dosage must be determined by the physician, based on body weight and blood glucose concentrations.

Note: Insulin requirements may change during illness or events causing psychological or physical stress. Dosage changes for patients receiving conventional therapy should be determined by the physician, based on each patient's needs and insulin sensitivity. Patients receiving intensive therapy may adjust individual doses to compensate for anticipated changes in diet or exercise but should consult a physician if the permitted adjustments are inadequate and/or glucose monitoring indicates the need for a permanent change in the daily dose.

Some patients experience a honeymoon phase after initial therapy and lose their requirement for insulin altogether or require much less for a limited period of time (several months to several years).

Adolescents during puberty may require an increase in their total daily insulin dose.

Usual pediatric dose

Antidiabetic agent—

Subcutaneous, dosage must be determined by the physician, based on body weight and blood glucose concentrations.

Strength(s) usually available

U.S.—

Not commercially available.

Canada—

Not commercially available.

Packaging and storage

Store between 2 and 8 °C (36 and 46 °F). Protect from freezing.

Stability

Do not use if precipitate has become clumped or granular in appearance.

Auxiliary labeling

- Shake gently.
- Refrigerate.
- Do not freeze.

Note

Extended insulin zinc suspension is sometimes mixed with other insulin types as directed by the physician.

EXTENDED INSULIN HUMAN ZINC

Parenteral Dosage Forms

EXTENDED INSULIN HUMAN ZINC SUSPENSION USP

Usual adult and adolescent dose

Type 1 diabetes—

Initial: Subcutaneous, a total insulin dose is 0.5 to 0.8 USP Insulin Human Unit per kg of body weight as a single dose, depending on insulin type, or 0.5 to 1.2 USP Insulin Human Units per kg of body weight per day in divided doses. Body fat, blood glucose, and insulin sensitivity also should be considered. This total daily dose of insulin may be provided by one or more types of insulin. A few patients will require less than 0.5 USP Insulin Human Unit per kg of body weight per day. Dose titration to a targeted blood glucose goal is achieved over several days; a change in total daily insulin dose does not usually exceed 10% of the existing total daily insulin dose. Extended insulin human zinc is given once or twice a day thirty to sixty minutes before a meal and/or a bedtime snack.

Maintenance: Subcutaneous, dosage must be determined by the physician, based on blood glucose concentrations.

Type 2 diabetes—
Initial: Subcutaneous, a total insulin dose may vary from 5 to 10 USP Insulin Human Units per day to 0.7 to 2.5 USP Human Insulin Units per kg of body weight per day, taking body fat, blood glucose, and insulin sensitivity into consideration. This total daily dose of insulin may be provided by one or more types of insulin and, depending on insulin type, may be given as a single dose or as divided doses. Dose titration to a targeted blood glucose goal is achieved over several days with changes from the existing total daily insulin dose of no more than 2 to 6 USP Insulin Human Units a day; again, body weight should be considered. Very insulin-resistant patients using large doses, 200 USP Insulin Human Units or greater, may need to use a concentrated regular insulin (U-500) instead. Extended insulin human zinc is given once or twice a day thirty to sixty minutes before a meal and/or a bedtime snack.
Maintenance: Subcutaneous, dosage must be determined by the physician, based on blood glucose concentrations.

Gestational diabetes mellitus—
Subcutaneous, dosage must be determined by the physician, based on blood glucose concentrations and gestational duration.

Diabetes mellitus, other, associated with certain conditions or syndromes—
Subcutaneous, dosage must be determined by the physician, based on body weight and blood glucose concentrations.

Note: Insulin requirements may change during illness or events causing psychological or physical stress. Dosage changes for patients receiving conventional therapy should be determined by the physician, based on each patient's needs and insulin sensitivity. Patients receiving intensive therapy may adjust individual doses to compensate for anticipated changes in diet or exercise but should consult a physician if the permitted adjustments are inadequate and/or glucose monitoring indicates the need for a permanent change in the daily dose.

Some patients experience a honeymoon phase after initial therapy and lose their requirement for insulin altogether or require much less for a limited period of time (several months to several years).

Adolescents during puberty may require an increase in their total daily insulin dose.

Usual pediatric dose
Antidiabetic agent—
Subcutaneous, dosage must be determined by the physician, based on body weight and blood glucose concentrations.

Strength(s) usually available
U.S.—
100 USP Insulin Human Units per mL (OTC) [*Humulin U* (biosynthetic)].

Canada—
100 USP Insulin Human Units per mL (OTC) [*Humulin-U* (biosynthetic); *Novolin ge Ultralente* (biosynthetic)].

Packaging and storage
Store between 2 and 8 °C (36 and 46 °F). Protect from freezing.

Stability
Do not use if precipitate has become clumped or granular in appearance.

Auxiliary labeling
- Shake gently.
- Refrigerate.
- Do not freeze.

INSULIN

Parenteral Dosage Forms

Note: Bracketed uses in the *Dosage Forms section* refer to categories of use and/or indications that are not included in U.S. product labeling.

INSULIN INJECTION (REGULAR INSULIN, CRYSTALLINE ZINC INSULIN) USP

Usual adult and adolescent dose
Type 1 diabetes—
Initial—
Subcutaneous or continuous subcutaneous insulin infusion, a total insulin dose, using one or more types of insulin, is 0.5 to 1.2 USP Insulin Units per kg of body weight a day in divided doses, taking body fat, blood glucose, and insulin sensitivity into consideration. A few patients will require less than 0.5 USP Insulin Unit per kg of body weight a day. Dose titration to a targeted blood glucose goal is achieved over several days; a change in total daily insulin dose does not usually exceed 10% of the existing total daily insulin dose.

When using a continuous subcutaneous insulin infusion pump, the basal insulin dose (usually forty to sixty percent of the total insulin daily dose) is divided into a dose that can be continuously infused subcutaneously over twenty-four hours. Also, a premeal injection (also, forty to sixty percent of total insulin dose) can be delivered preprogrammed or manually by the patient through the insulin pump.

When using subcutaneous injections, regular insulin usually is injected in low doses, i.e., often less than 10 USP Insulin Units a dose.

Both subcutaneous injections and premeal injections using a continuous subcutaneous insulin infusion pump of regular insulin generally are given fifteen to thirty minutes before one or more meals and/or a bedtime snack.

Maintenance—
Subcutaneous or continuous subcutaneous insulin infusion, dosage must be determined by the physician, based on blood glucose concentrations.

Type 2 diabetes—
Initial—
Subcutaneous, a total insulin dose, using one or more types of insulin, may vary from 5 to 10 USP Insulin Units per day to 0.7 to 2.5 USP Insulin Units per kg of body weight a day in divided doses, taking body fat, blood glucose, and insulin sensitivity into consideration. Dose titration to a targeted blood glucose goal is achieved over several days with changes from the existing total daily insulin dose of no more than 2 to 6 USP Insulin Units a day; again, with consideration of body weight. Very insulin-resistant patients using large doses, 200 USP Insulin Units or greater, may need to use a concentrated regular insulin (U-500) instead. Regular insulin usually is given in low doses, i.e., often less than 10 USP Insulin Units a dose, fifteen to thirty minutes before one or more meals and/or a bedtime snack.

Maintenance—
Subcutaneous, dosage must be determined by the physician, based on blood glucose concentrations.

Gestational diabetes mellitus—
Subcutaneous, dosage must be determined by the physician, based on blood glucose concentrations and gestational duration.

Diabetes mellitus, other, associated with certain conditions or syndromes—
Subcutaneous, dosage must be determined by the physician, based on body weight and blood glucose concentrations.

Note: For treatment of diabetic ketoacidosis, an optional loading dose of 0.15 USP Insulin Unit per kg of body weight is given intravenously, followed by 0.1 USP Insulin Unit per kg of body weight per hour by continuous infusion. The rate of insulin infusion should be decreased when the plasma glucose concentration reaches 300 mg per dL. Infusion of 5% dextrose injection should be started separately from the insulin infusion when plasma glucose concentration reaches 250 mg per dL. Thirty minutes before discontinuing the insulin infusion, an appropriate dose of insulin should be injected subcutaneously; intermediate-acting insulin has been recommended. Alternatively, a loading dose of 0.5 USP Unit per kg of body weight is injected intramuscularly, followed by 0.1 USP Insulin Unit per kg of body weight injected intramuscularly every hour until the blood glucose concentration reaches 300 mg per dL. Then to maintain blood glucose concentration at 250 mg per dL, 0.1 USP Insulin Unit per kg of body weight is injected intramuscularly every two hours as needed. With either type of insulin administration, capillary blood glucose should be monitored at least hourly and the insulin dose adjusted accordingly.

Insulin requirements may change during illness or events causing psychological or physical stress. Dosage changes for patients receiving conventional therapy should be determined by the physician, based on each patient's needs and insulin sensitivity. Patients receiving intensive therapy may adjust individual doses to compensate for anticipated changes in diet or exercise but should consult a physician if the permitted adjustments are inadequate and/or glucose monitoring indicates the need for a permanent change in the daily dose.

Some patients experience a honeymoon phase after initial therapy and lose their requirement for insulin altogether or require much less for a limited period of time (several months to several years).

Adolescents during puberty may require an increase in their total daily insulin dose.

[Growth hormone deficiency, diagnosis of][1]—
Intravenous, 0.05 to 0.15 USP Insulin Unit per kg of body weight as a single rapid injection.

Usual pediatric dose

Antidiabetic agent—
Subcutaneous, dosage must be determined by the physician, based on body weight and blood glucose concentrations.

[Hyperglycemia during intravenous nutrition in low birth weight infants (treatment)][1]—
Initial—
Intravenous, 0.05 USP Insulin Unit per kg of body weight per hour.

Maintenance—
Intravenous,
0.05 to 0.08 USP Insulin Unit per kg of body weight per hour as needed up to a maximum of 0.16 USP Insulin Unit per kg of body weight per hour.

Strength(s) usually available

U.S.—
100 USP Insulin Units per mL (OTC) [*Regular Iletin II* (purified pork); *Regular Insulin* (pork); *Regular Insulin* (purified pork)].
500 USP Insulin Units per mL (Rx) [*Regular (Concentrated) Iletin II, U-500* (purified pork)].

Canada—
100 USP Insulin Units per mL (OTC) [*Regular Iletin II* (pork)].

Packaging and storage

Store between 2 and 8 °C (36 and 46 °F). Protect from sunlight and from freezing.

Stability

Do not use if cloudy, discolored, or unusually viscous.

Auxiliary labeling

- Refrigerate.
- Do not freeze.

Note

The 500-Unit strength is available only with a prescription and is used only for the treatment of patients with insulin-resistant diabetes.

Insulin Injection USP is sometimes mixed with other insulin types as directed by physician.

Patients should be advised not to mix regular insulin with any other insulin when using a continuous subcutaneous external insulin pump.

Regular insulin can be used in continuous subcutaneous infusion insulin pumps, but also may be injected subcutaneously or intramuscularly with an insulin syringe, or used intravenously. Phosphate buffered insulin is preferred over non–phosphate buffered insulin in insulin pumps. When this insulin is used in a continuous subcutaneous infusion insulin pump, the catheter tubing and the insulin in the reservoir must be changed every 48 hours or the manufacturer's recommendations followed for specific external insulin pumps.

[1]Not included in Canadian product labeling.

INSULIN HUMAN

Parenteral Dosage Forms

Note: Bracketed uses in the *Dosage Forms section* refer to categories of use and/or indications that are not included in U.S. product labeling.

INSULIN HUMAN INJECTION (REGULAR INSULIN HUMAN) USP

Usual adult and adolescent dose

Type 1 diabetes—
Initial—
Subcutaneous or continuous subcutaneous insulin infusion, a total insulin dose, using one or more types of insulin, is 0.5 to 1.2 USP Insulin Human Units per kg of body weight a day in divided doses, taking body fat, blood glucose, and insulin sensitivity into consideration. A few patients will require less than 0.5 USP Insulin Human Unit per kg of body weight a day. Dose titration to a targeted blood glucose goal is achieved over several days; a change in total daily insulin dose does not usually exceed 10% of the existing total daily insulin dose.

When using a continuous subcutaneous insulin infusion pump, the basal insulin dose (usually forty to sixty percent of the total insulin daily dose) is divided into a dose that can be continuously infused subcutaneously over twenty-four hours. Also, a premeal injection (also, forty to sixty percent of total insulin dose) can be delivered preprogrammed or manually by the patient through the insulin pump.

When using subcutaneous injections, regular human insulin usually is injected in low doses, i.e., often less than 10 USP Insulin Human Units a dose.

Both subcutaneous injections and premeal injections of regular human insulin using a continuous subcutaneous insulin infusion pump generally are given fifteen to thirty minutes before one or more meals and/or a bedtime snack.

Maintenance—
Subcutaneous or continuous subcutaneous insulin infusion, dosage must be determined by the physician, based on blood glucose concentrations.

Type 2 diabetes—
Initial—
Subcutaneous, a total insulin dose, using one or more types of insulin, may vary from 5 to 10 USP Insulin Human Units per day to 0.7 to 2.5 USP Insulin Human Units per kg of body weight a day in divided doses, taking body fat, blood glucose, and insulin sensitivity into consideration. Dose titration to a targeted blood glucose goal is achieved over several days with changes from the existing total daily insulin dose of no more than 2 to 6 USP Insulin Human Units a day; again, with consideration of body weight. Very insulin-resistant patients using large doses, 200 USP Insulin Human Units or greater, may need to use a concentrated regular insulin (U-500) instead. Regular human insulin usually is given in low doses, i.e., often less than 10 USP Insulin Human Units a dose, fifteen to thirty minutes before one or more meals and/or a bedtime snack.

Maintenance—
Subcutaneous, dosage must be determined by the physician, based on blood glucose concentrations.

Gestational diabetes mellitus—
Subcutaneous, dosage must be determined by the physician, based on blood glucose concentrations and gestational duration.

Diabetes mellitus, other, associated with certain conditions or syndromes—
Subcutaneous, dosage must be determined by the physician, based on body weight and blood glucose concentrations.

Note: For treatment of diabetic ketoacidosis, an optional loading dose of 0.15 USP Insulin Human Unit per kg of body weight is given intravenously, followed by 0.1 USP Insulin Human Unit per kg of body weight per hour by continuous infusion. The rate of insulin infusion should be decreased when the plasma glucose concentration reaches 300 mg per dL. Infusion of 5% dextrose injection should be started separately from the insulin infusion when plasma glucose concentration reaches 250 mg per dL. Thirty minutes before discontinuing the insulin infusion, an appropriate dose of insulin should be injected subcutaneously; intermediate-acting insulin has been recommended. Alternatively, a loading dose of 0.5 USP Insulin Human Unit per kg of body weight is injected intramuscularly, followed by 0.1 USP Insulin Human Unit per kg of body weight injected intramuscularly every hour until the blood glucose concentration reaches 300 mg per dL. Then, to maintain blood glucose concentration at 250 mg per dL, 0.1 USP Insulin Human Unit per kg of body weight is injected intramuscularly every two hours as needed. With either type of insulin administration, capillary blood glucose should be monitored at least hourly and the insulin dose adjusted accordingly.

Insulin requirements may change during illness or events causing psychological or physical stress. Dosage changes for patients receiving conventional therapy should be determined by the physician, based on each patient's needs and insulin sensitivity. Patients receiving intensive therapy may adjust individual doses to compensate for anticipated changes in diet or exercise but should consult a physician if the permitted adjustments are inadequate and/or glucose monitoring indicates the need for a permanent change in the daily dose.

Some patients experience a honeymoon phase after initial therapy and lose their requirement for insulin altogether or require much less for a limited period of time (several months to several years).

Adolescents during puberty may require an increase in their total daily insulin dose.

[Growth hormone deficiency, diagnosis of][1]—
Intravenous, 0.05 to 0.15 USP Insulin Human Unit per kg of body weight as a single rapid injection.

Usual pediatric dose

Antidiabetic agent—

Subcutaneous, dosage must be determined by the physician, based on body weight and blood glucose concentrations.

[Hyperglycemia during intravenous nutrition in low birth weight infants (treatment)][1]—

Initial—Intravenous, 0.05 USP Insulin Human Unit per kg of body weight per hour. Maintenance—Intravenous, 0.05 to 0.08 USP Insulin Human Unit per kg of body weight per hour as needed up to a maximum of 0.16 USP Insulin Human Unit per kg of body weight per hour.

Strength(s) usually available

U.S.—

100 USP Insulin Human Units per mL (OTC) [*Humulin R* (biosynthetic); *Novolin R* (biosynthetic); *Novolin R PenFill* (biosynthetic); *Novolin R Prefilled* (biosynthetic; prefilled single use syringe contains 150 USP Units in 1.5 mL)].

500 USP Insulin Human Units per mL (Rx) [*Humulin R, Regular U-500 (Concentrated)* (biosynthetic)].

Canada—

100 USP Insulin Human Units per mL (OTC) [*Humulin-R* (biosynthetic); *Novolin ge Toronto* (biosynthetic); *Novolin ge Toronto Penfill* (biosynthetic)].

Packaging and storage

Store between 2 and 8 °C (36 and 46 °F). Protect from sunlight and from freezing.

Stability

Do not use if cloudy, discolored, or unusually viscous.

Auxiliary labeling

- Refrigerate.
- Do not freeze.

Note

The 500-Unit strength is available only with a prescription and is used only for the treatment of patients with insulin-resistant diabetes.

Insulin Human Injection USP is sometimes mixed with other insulin types as directed by the physician.

Patients should be advised not to mix insulin human with any other insulin when using a continuous subcutaneous infusion insulin pump.

Insulin human may be used in continuous subcutaneous infusion insulin pumps, but also may be injected subcutaneously or intramuscularly with an insulin syringe, or used intravenously. Phosphate buffered insulin is preferred over non–phosphate buffered insulin in insulin pumps. When this insulin is used in a continuous subcutaneous infusion insulin pump, the catheter tubing and the insulin in the reservoir must be changed every 48 hours or the manufacturer's recommendations followed for specific external insulin pumps.

[1]Not included in Canadian product labeling.

INSULIN ZINC

Parenteral Dosage Forms

INSULIN ZINC SUSPENSION (LENTE INSULIN) USP

Usual adult and adolescent dose

Type 1 diabetes—

Initial: Subcutaneous, a total insulin dose is 0.5 to 0.8 USP Insulin Unit per kg of body weight as a single dose, depending on insulin type, or 0.5 to 1.2 USP Insulin Units per kg of body weight per day in divided doses. Body fat, blood glucose, and insulin sensitivity also should be considered. This total daily dose of insulin may be provided by one or more types of insulin. A few patients will require less than 0.5 USP Insulin Unit per kg of body weight per day. Dose titration to a targeted blood glucose goal is achieved over several days; a change in total daily insulin dose does not usually exceed 10% of the existing total daily insulin dose. Insulin zinc is given thirty minutes before a meal and/or a bedtime snack.

Maintenance: Subcutaneous, dosage must be determined by the physician, based on blood glucose concentrations.

Type 2 diabetes—

Initial: Subcutaneous, a total insulin dose may vary from 5 to 10 USP Insulin Units per day to 0.7 to 2.5 USP Insulin Units per kg of body weight per day, taking body fat, blood glucose, and insulin sensitivity into consideration. This total daily dose of insulin may be provided by one or more types of insulin and, depending on insulin type, may be given as a single dose or as divided doses. Dose titration to a targeted blood glucose goal is achieved over several days with changes from the existing total daily insulin dose of no more than 2 to 6 USP Insulin Units a day; again, body weight should be considered. Very insulin-resistant patients using large doses, 200 USP Insulin Units or greater, may need to use a concentrated regular insulin (U-500) instead. Insulin zinc is given thirty minutes before a meal and/or a bedtime snack.

Maintenance: Subcutaneous, dosage must be determined by the physician, based on blood glucose concentrations.

Gestational diabetes mellitus—

Subcutaneous, dosage must be determined by the physician, based on blood glucose concentrations and gestational duration.

Diabetes mellitus, other, associated with certain conditions or syndromes—

Subcutaneous, dosage must be determined by the physician, based on body weight and blood glucose concentrations.

Note: Insulin requirements may change during illness or events causing psychological or physical stress. Dosage changes for patients receiving conventional therapy should be determined by the physician, based on each patient's needs and insulin sensitivity. Patients receiving intensive therapy may adjust individual doses to compensate for anticipated changes in diet or exercise but should consult a physician if the permitted adjustments are inadequate and/or glucose monitoring indicates the need for a permanent change in the daily dose.

Some patients experience a honeymoon phase after initial therapy and lose their requirement for insulin altogether or require much less for a limited period of time (several months to several years).

Adolescents during puberty may require an increase in their total daily insulin dose.

Usual pediatric dose

Antidiabetic agent—

Subcutaneous, dosage must be determined by the physician, based on body weight and blood glucose concentrations.

Strength(s) usually available

U.S.—

100 USP Insulin Units per mL (OTC) [*Lente Iletin II* (purified pork); *Lente* (purified pork)].

Canada—

100 USP Insulin Units per mL (OTC) [*Lente Iletin* (beef and pork); *Lente Iletin II* (pork)].

Packaging and storage

Store between 2 and 8 °C (36 and 46 °F). Protect from freezing.

Stability

Do not use if precipitate has become clumped or granular in appearance.

Auxiliary labeling

- Shake gently.
- Refrigerate.
- Do not freeze.

Note

Insulin zinc suspension is sometimes mixed with other insulin types as directed by the physician.

INSULIN HUMAN ZINC

Parenteral Dosage Forms

INSULIN HUMAN ZINC SUSPENSION USP

Usual adult and adolescent dose

Type 1 diabetes—

Initial: Subcutaneous, a total insulin dose is 0.5 to 0.8 USP Insulin Human Units per kg of body weight as a single dose, depending on insulin type, or 0.5 to 1.2 USP Insulin Human Units per kg of body weight per day in divided doses. Body fat, blood glucose, and insulin sensitivity also should be considered. This total daily dose of insulin may be provided by one or more types of insulin. A few patients will require less than 0.5 USP Insulin Human Unit per kg of body weight per day. Dose titration to a targeted blood glucose goal is achieved over several days; a change in total daily insulin dose does not usually exceed 10% of the existing total daily insulin dose. Insulin human zinc is given thirty minutes before a meal and/or a bedtime snack.

Maintenance: Subcutaneous, dosage must be determined by the physician, based on blood glucose concentrations.

Type 2 diabetes—

Initial: Subcutaneous, a total insulin dose may vary from 5 to 10 USP Insulin Human Units per day to 0.7 to 2.5 USP Insulin Human Units per kg of body weight per day, taking body fat, blood glucose, and insulin sensitivity into consideration. This total daily dose of insulin may be provided by one or more types of insulin and, depending on insulin type, may be given as a single dose or as divided doses. Dose titration to a targeted blood glucose goal is achieved over several days with changes from the existing total daily insulin dose of no more than 2 to 6 USP Insulin Human Units a day; again, body weight should be considered. Very insulin-resistant patients using large doses, 200 USP Insulin Human Units or greater, may need to use a concentrated regular insulin (U-500) instead. Insulin human zinc is given thirty minutes before a meal and/or a bedtime snack.

Maintenance: Subcutaneous, dosage must be determined by the physician, based on blood glucose concentrations.

Gestational diabetes mellitus—

Subcutaneous, dosage must be determined by the physician, based on blood glucose concentrations and gestational duration.

Diabetes mellitus, other, associated with certain conditions or syndromes—

Subcutaneous, dosage must be determined by the physician, based on body weight and blood glucose concentrations.

Note: Insulin requirements may change during illness or events causing psychological or physical stress. Dosage changes for patients receiving conventional therapy should be determined by the physician, based on each patient's needs and insulin sensitivity. Patients receiving intensive therapy may adjust individual doses to compensate for anticipated changes in diet or exercise but should consult a physician if the permitted adjustments are inadequate and/or glucose monitoring indicates the need for a permanent change in the daily dose.

Some patients experience a honeymoon phase after initial therapy and lose their requirement for insulin altogether or require much less for a limited period of time (several months to several years).

Adolescents during puberty may require an increase in their total daily insulin dose.

Usual pediatric dose

Antidiabetic agent—

Subcutaneous, dosage must be determined by the physician, based on body weight and blood glucose concentrations.

Strength(s) usually available

U.S.—

100 USP Insulin Human Units per mL (OTC) [*Humulin L* (biosynthetic); *Novolin L* (biosynthetic)].

Canada—

100 USP Insulin Human Units per mL (OTC) [*Humulin-L* (biosynthetic); *Novolin ge Lente* (biosynthetic)].

Packaging and storage

Store between 2 and 8 °C (36 and 46 °F). Protect from sunlight and from freezing.

Stability

Do not use if precipitate has become clumped or granular in appearance.

Auxiliary labeling

- Shake gently.
- Refrigerate.
- Do not freeze.

ISOPHANE INSULIN

Parenteral Dosage Forms

ISOPHANE INSULIN SUSPENSION (NPH INSULIN) USP

Usual adult and adolescent dose

Type 1 diabetes—

Initial: Subcutaneous, a total insulin dose is 0.5 to 0.8 USP Insulin Unit per kg of body weight as a single dose, depending on insulin type, or 0.5 to 1.2 USP Insulin Units per kg of body weight per day in divided doses. Body fat, blood glucose, and insulin sensitivity also should be considered. This total daily dose of insulin may be provided by one or more types of insulin. A few patients will require less than 0.5 USP Insulin Unit per kg of body weight per day. Dose titration to a targeted blood glucose goal is achieved over several days; a change in total daily insulin dose does not usually exceed 10% of the existing total daily insulin dose. Isophane insulin is given thirty to sixty minutes before a meal and/or a bedtime snack.

Maintenance: Subcutaneous, dosage must be determined by the physician, based on blood glucose concentrations.

Type 2 diabetes—

Initial: Subcutaneous, a total insulin dose may vary from 5 to 10 USP Insulin Units per day to 0.7 to 2.5 USP Insulin Units per kg of body weight per day, taking body fat, blood glucose, and insulin sensitivity into consideration. This total daily dose of insulin may be provided by one or more types of insulin and, depending on insulin type, may be given as a single dose or as divided doses. Dose titration to a targeted blood glucose goal is achieved over several days with changes from the existing total daily insulin dose of no more than 2 to 6 USP Insulin Units a day; again, body weight should be considered. Very insulin-resistant patients using large doses, 200 USP Insulin Units or greater, may need to use a concentrated regular insulin (U-500) instead. Isophane insulin is given thirty to sixty minutes before a meal and/or a bedtime snack.

Maintenance: Subcutaneous, dosage must be determined by the physician, based on blood glucose concentrations.

Gestational diabetes mellitus—

Subcutaneous, dosage must be determined by the physician, based on blood glucose concentrations and gestational duration.

Diabetes mellitus, other, associated with certain conditions or syndromes—

Subcutaneous, dosage must be determined by the physician, based on body weight and blood glucose concentrations.

Note: Insulin requirements may change during illness or events causing psychological or physical stress. Dosage changes for patients receiving conventional therapy should be determined by the physician, based on each patient's needs and insulin sensitivity. Patients receiving intensive therapy may adjust individual doses to compensate for anticipated changes in diet or exercise but should consult a physician if the permitted adjustments are inadequate and/or glucose monitoring indicates the need for a permanent change in the daily dose.

Some patients experience a honeymoon phase after initial therapy and lose their requirement for insulin altogether or require much less for a limited period of time (several months to several years).

Adolescents during puberty may require an increase in their total daily insulin dose.

Usual pediatric dose

Antidiabetic agent—

Subcutaneous, dosage must be determined by the physician, based on body weight and blood glucose concentrations.

Strength(s) usually available

U.S.—

100 USP Insulin Units per mL (OTC) [*NPH Iletin II* (purified pork); *NPH Purified Insulin* (purified pork)].

Canada—

100 USP Insulin Units per mL (OTC) [*NPH Iletin* (beef and pork); *NPH Iletin II* (pork)].

Packaging and storage

Store between 2 and 8 °C (36 and 46 °F). Protect from freezing.

Stability

Do not use if precipitate has become clumped or granular in appearance or clings to sides of vial.

Auxiliary labeling

- Shake gently.
- Refrigerate.
- Do not freeze.

Note

Isophane insulin suspension is sometimes mixed with insulin injection as directed by the physician.

ISOPHANE INSULIN HUMAN

Parenteral Dosage Forms

ISOPHANE INSULIN HUMAN SUSPENSION USP

Usual adult and adolescent dose

Type 1 diabetes—

Initial: Subcutaneous, a total insulin dose is 0.5 to 0.8 USP Insulin Human Unit per kg of body weight as a single dose, depending on insulin type, or 0.5 to 1.2 USP Insulin Human Units per kg of body weight per day in divided doses. Body fat, blood glucose, and insulin sensitivity also should be considered. This total daily dose of insulin may be provided by one or more types of insulin. A few patients will require less than 0.5 USP Insulin Human Unit per kg of body weight per day. Dose titration to a targeted blood glucose goal is achieved over several days; a change in total daily insulin dose does not usually exceed 10% of the existing total daily insulin dose. Isophane insulin human is given thirty minutes before a meal and/or a bedtime snack.

Maintenance: Subcutaneous, dosage must be determined by the physician, based on blood glucose concentrations.

Type 2 diabetes—

Initial: Subcutaneous, a total insulin dose may vary from 5 to 10 USP Insulin Human Units per day to 0.7 to 2.5 USP Insulin Human Units per kg of body weight per day, taking body fat, blood glucose, and insulin sensitivity into consideration. This total daily dose of insulin may be provided by one or more types of insulin and, depending on insulin type, may be given as a single dose or as divided doses. Dose titration to a targeted blood glucose goal is achieved over several days with changes from the existing total daily insulin dose of no more than 2 to 6 USP Insulin Human Units a day; again, body weight should be considered. Very insulin-resistant patients using large doses, 200 USP Insulin Human Units or greater, may need to use a concentrated regular insulin (U-500) instead. Isophane insulin human is given thirty minutes before a meal and/or a bedtime snack.

Maintenance: Subcutaneous, dosage must be determined by the physician, based on blood glucose concentrations.

Gestational diabetes mellitus—

Subcutaneous, dosage must be determined by the physician, based on blood glucose concentrations and gestational duration.

Diabetes mellitus, other, associated with certain conditions or syndromes—

Subcutaneous, dosage must be determined by the physician, based on body weight and blood glucose concentrations.

Note: Insulin requirements may change during illness or events causing psychological or physical stress. Dosage changes for patients receiving conventional therapy should be determined by the physician, based on each patient's needs and insulin sensitivity. Patients receiving intensive therapy may adjust individual doses to compensate for anticipated changes in diet or exercise but should consult a physician if the permitted adjustments are inadequate and/or glucose monitoring indicates the need for a permanent change in the daily dose.

Some patients experience a honeymoon phase after initial therapy and lose their requirement for insulin altogether or require much less for a limited period of time (several months to several years).

Adolescents during puberty may require an increase in their total daily insulin dose.

Usual pediatric dose

Antidiabetic agent—

Subcutaneous, dosage must be determined by the physician, based on body weight and blood glucose concentrations.

Strength(s) usually available

U.S.—

100 USP Insulin Human Units per mL (OTC) [*Humulin N* (biosynthetic); *Humulin N Pen* (biosynthetic); *Novolin N* (biosynthetic); *Novolin N PenFill* (biosynthetic); *Novolin N Prefilled* (biosynthetic; prefilled single-use syringe contains 150 USP Insulin Human Units in 1.5 mL)].

Canada—

100 USP Insulin Human Units per mL (OTC) [*Humulin-N* (biosynthetic); *Novolin ge NPH* (biosynthetic); *Novolin ge NPH Penfill* (biosynthetic)].

Packaging and storage

Store between 2 and 8 °C (36 and 46 °F). Protect from sunlight and from freezing.

Stability

Do not use if precipitate has become clumped or granular in appearance or clings to sides of vial.

Auxiliary labeling

- Shake gently.
- Gently rotate prefilled syringe up and down before injection.
- Refrigerate.
- Do not freeze.

ISOPHANE INSULIN HUMAN AND INSULIN HUMAN

Parenteral Dosage Forms

ISOPHANE INSULIN HUMAN SUSPENSION AND INSULIN HUMAN INJECTION

Usual adult and adolescent dose

Type 1 diabetes—

Initial: Subcutaneous, a total insulin dose is 0.5 to 0.8 USP Insulin Human Unit per kg of body weight as a single dose, depending on insulin type, or 0.5 to 1.2 USP Insulin Human Units per kg of body weight per day in divided doses. Body fat, blood glucose, and insulin sensitivity also should be considered. This total daily dose of insulin may be provided by one or more types of insulin. A few patients will require less than 0.5 USP Insulin Human Unit per kg of body weight per day. Dose titration to a targeted blood glucose goal is achieved over several days; a change in total daily insulin dose does not usually exceed 10% of the existing total daily insulin dose. Isophane insulin human and insulin human is given fifteen to thirty minutes before a meal and/or a bedtime snack.

Maintenance: Subcutaneous, dosage must be determined by the physician, based on blood glucose concentrations.

Type 2 diabetes—

Initial: Subcutaneous, a total insulin dose may vary from 5 to 10 USP Insulin Human Units per day to 0.7 to 2.5 USP Insulin Human Units per kg of body weight per day, taking body fat, blood glucose, and insulin sensitivity into consideration. This total daily dose of insulin may be provided by one or more types of insulin and, depending on insulin type, may be given as a single dose or as divided doses. Dose titration to a targeted blood glucose goal is achieved over several days with changes from the existing total daily insulin dose of no more than 2 to 6 USP Insulin Human Units a day; again, body weight should be considered. Very insulin-resistant patients using large doses, 200 USP Insulin Human Units or greater, may need to use a concentrated regular insulin (U-500) instead. Isophane insulin human and insulin human is given fifteen to thirty minutes before a meal and/or a bedtime snack.

Maintenance: Subcutaneous, dosage must be determined by the physician, based on blood glucose concentrations.

Gestational diabetes mellitus—

Subcutaneous, dosage must be determined by the physician, based on blood glucose concentrations and gestational duration.

Diabetes mellitus, other, associated with certain conditions or syndromes—

Subcutaneous, dosage must be determined by the physician, based on body weight and blood glucose concentrations.

Note: Insulin requirements may change during illness or events causing psychological or physical stress. Dosage changes for patients receiving conventional therapy should be determined by the physician, based on each patient's needs and insulin sensitivity. Patients receiving intensive therapy may adjust individual doses to compensate for anticipated changes in diet or exercise but should consult a physician if the permitted adjustments are inadequate and/or glucose monitoring indicates the need for a permanent change in the daily dose.

Some patients experience a honeymoon phase after initial therapy and lose their requirement for insulin altogether or require much less for a limited period of time (several months to several years).

Adolescents during puberty may require an increase in their total daily insulin dose.

Usual pediatric dose

Antidiabetic agent—

Subcutaneous, dosage must be determined by the physician, based on body weight and blood glucose concentrations.

Strength(s) usually available

U.S.—

100 USP Insulin Human Units per mL (50% isophane insulin human suspension and 50% insulin human injection) (OTC) [*Humulin 50/50* (biosynthetic)].

100 USP Insulin Human Units per mL (70% isophane insulin human suspension and 30% insulin human injection) (OTC) [*Humulin 70/30* (biosynthetic); *Humulin 70/30 Pen* (biosynthetic); *Novolin 70/30* (biosynthetic); *Novolin 70/30 PenFill* (biosynthetic); *Novolin 70/30 Prefilled* (biosynthetic; prefilled single-use syringe contains 150 USP Insulin Human Units in 1.5 mL)].

Canada—

100 USP Insulin Human Units per mL (10% insulin human injection and 90% isophane insulin human suspension) (OTC) [*Humulin 10/90* (biosynthetic); *Novolin ge 10/90 Penfill* (biosynthetic)].

100 USP Insulin Human Units per mL (20% insulin human injection and 80% isophane insulin human suspension) (OTC) [*Humulin 20/80* (biosynthetic); *Novolin ge 20/80 Penfill* (biosynthetic)].

100 USP Insulin Human Units per mL (30% insulin human injection and 70% isophane insulin human suspension) (OTC) [*Humulin 30/70* (biosynthetic); *Novolin ge 30/70* (biosynthetic); *Novolin ge 30/70 Penfill* (biosynthetic)].

100 USP Insulin Human Units per mL (40% insulin human injection and 60% isophane insulin human suspension) (OTC) [*Humulin 40/60* (biosynthetic); *Novolin ge 40/60 Penfill* (biosynthetic)].

100 USP Insulin Human Units per mL (50% insulin human injection and 50% isophane insulin human suspension) (OTC) [*Humulin 50/50* (biosynthetic); *Novolin ge 50/50 Penfill* (biosynthetic)].

Packaging and storage
Store between 2 and 8 °C (36 and 46 °F), unless otherwise specified by manufacturer. Protect from freezing.

Stability
Do not use if precipitate has become clumped or granular in appearance.

Auxiliary labeling
- Shake gently.
- Gently rotate prefilled syringe up and down before injection.
- Refrigerate.
- Do not freeze.

PROMPT INSULIN ZINC

Parenteral Dosage Forms

PROMPT INSULIN ZINC SUSPENSION (SEMILENTE INSULIN) USP

Usual adult and adolescent dose
Type 1 diabetes—

Initial: Subcutaneous, a total insulin dose is 0.5 to 0.8 USP Insulin Unit per kg of body weight as a single dose, depending on insulin type, or 0.5 to 1.2 USP Insulin Units per kg of body weight per day in divided doses. Body fat, blood glucose, and insulin sensitivity also should be considered. This total daily dose of insulin may be provided by one or more types of insulin. A few patients will require less than 0.5 USP Insulin Unit per kg of body weight per day. Dose titration to a targeted blood glucose goal is achieved over several days; a change in total daily insulin dose does not usually exceed 10% of the existing total daily insulin dose. Prompt insulin zinc is given thirty to sixty minutes before a meal and/or a bedtime snack.

Maintenance: Subcutaneous, dosage must be determined by the physician, based on blood glucose concentrations.

Type 2 diabetes—

Initial: Subcutaneous, a total insulin dose may vary from 5 to 10 USP Insulin Units per day to 0.7 to 2.5 USP Insulin Units per kg of body weight per day, taking body fat, blood glucose, and insulin sensitivity into consideration. This total daily dose of insulin may be provided by one or more types of insulin and, depending on insulin type, may be given as a single dose or as divided doses. Dose titration to a targeted blood glucose goal is achieved over several days with changes from the existing total daily insulin dose of no more than 2 to 6 USP Insulin Units a day; again, body weight should be considered. Very insulin-resistant patients using large doses, 200 USP Insulin Units or greater, may need to use a concentrated regular insulin (U-500) instead. Prompt insulin zinc is given thirty to sixty minutes before a meal and/or a bedtime snack.

Maintenance: Subcutaneous, dosage must be determined by the physician, based on blood glucose concentrations.

Gestational diabetes mellitus—

Subcutaneous, dosage must be determined by the physician, based on blood glucose concentrations and gestational duration.

Diabetes mellitus, other, associated with certain conditions or syndromes—

Subcutaneous, dosage must be determined by the physician, based on body weight and blood glucose concentrations.

Note: Insulin requirements may change during illness or events causing psychological or physical stress. Dosage changes for patients receiving conventional therapy should be determined by the physician, based on each patient's needs and insulin sensitivity. Patients receiving intensive therapy may adjust individual doses to compensate for anticipated changes in diet or exercise but should consult a physician if the permitted adjustments are inadequate and/or glucose monitoring indicates the need for a permanent change in the daily dose.

Some patients experience a honeymoon phase after initial therapy and lose their requirement for insulin altogether or require much less for a limited period of time (several months to several years). Adolescents during puberty may require an increase in their total daily insulin dose.

Usual pediatric dose
Antidiabetic agent—

Subcutaneous, dosage must be determined by the physician, based on body weight and blood glucose concentrations.

Strength(s) usually available
U.S.—

Not commercially available.

Canada—

Not commercially available.

Packaging and storage
Store between 2 and 8 °C (36 and 46 °F). Protect from freezing.

Stability
Do not use if precipitate has become clumped or granular in appearance.

Auxiliary labeling
- Shake gently.
- Refrigerate.
- Do not freeze.

Note
Prompt Insulin Zinc Suspension USP is sometimes mixed with other insulin types as directed by the physician.

Selected Bibliography

Koda-Kimble MA. Diabetes mellitus. In: Young LY, Koda-Kimble MA, editors. Applied therapeutics: the clinical use of drugs. 5th ed. Vancouver, WA: Applied Therapeutics Inc; 1992. p. 72(1)-72(53).

The Diabetes Control and Complications Trial Research Group. The effect of intensive treatment of diabetes on the development and progression of long-term complications in insulin-dependent diabetes mellitus. N Engl J Med 1993; 329(14): 977-86.

Revised: 04/03/2002

INSULIN ASPART Systemic†

VA CLASSIFICATION (Primary): HS501

Commonly used brand name(s): *NovoLog*.

Note: For a listing of dosage forms and brand names by country availability, see *Dosage Forms* section(s).

†Not commercially available in Canada.

Category
Antidiabetic agent.

Indications

Accepted
Diabetes mellitus, type 1 (treatment adjunct)

Diabetes mellitus, type 2 (treatment adjunct)—Insulin aspart is indicated for the treatment of adult patients with diabetes mellitus for the control of hyperglycemia. Insulin aspart has a more rapid onset and shorter duration of action than regular human insulin and, therefore, especially in patients with type 1 diabetes, insulin aspart should be used in regimens together with an intermediate or long-acting insulin.

Pharmacology/Pharmacokinetics

Physicochemical characteristics
Source—Human insulin analogue with a single substitution of amino acid (proline) at position B28 by aspartic acid. Insulin aspart is produced by recombinant DNA technology using *Saccharomyces cerevisiae* or baker's yeast.

Molecular weight—5825.8.

pH—7.2 to 7.6.

Mechanism of action/Effect
Insulin aspart, like regular types of human insulin, regulates glucose metabolism by binding to insulin receptors on muscle and fat cells and increases the cellular uptake of glucose. At the same time, insulin aspart inhibits the liver's conversion of stored glycogen into glucose and thus helps to lower blood glucose levels.

Absorption
In comparison studies with regular human insulin, insulin aspart was more rapidly absorbed after subcutaneous injection and also demonstrated significantly less intra-individual variability in time to maximum serum insulin concentration.

Insulin aspart also reached peak serum concentrations (in 40 to 50 minutes) approximately twice as quickly as compared with regular human insulin (in 80 to 120 minutes).

Distribution
In a clinical trial in type 1 diabetic patients, insulin aspart was given subcutaneously at a dose of 0.15 units (U) per kilogram (kg) of body weight and reached a mean maximum concentration of 82.1 mU/L, as compared to 35.9 mU/L for regular human insulin given at the same dose.

Protein binding
Very low (between 0 and 9%).

Half-life
Elimination—
81 minutes (in normal male volunteers, subcutaneous).

Onset of action
In a 6-hour study in type 1 diabetic patients, the maximum glucose-lowering effect of insulin aspart, given subcutaneously, was demonstrated between 1 and 3 hours, and lasts from 3 to 5 hours.

Time to peak concentration
Peak concentration is generally reached in 40 to 50 minutes.

Peak serum concentration
When type 1 diabetic patients were given a subcutaneous dose of 0.15 U/kg, the peak serum concentration reached an average of 82.1 mU/L.

Time to peak effect
In a 6-hour study in type 1 diabetic patients, the maximum glucose-lowering effect of insulin aspart, given subcutaneously, was demonstrated between 1 and 3 hours.

Duration of action
In a 6-hour study in type 1 diabetic patients, the maximum glucose-lowering effect of insulin aspart lasts from 3 to 5 hours as compared to 5 to 8 hours for regular human insulin. The time course of action for insulin aspart and insulin will vary in time considerably in different individuals or within the same individual.

Precautions to Consider

Cross-sensitivity and/or related problems
Production of antibodies cross-reactive to human insulin and insulin aspart was observed in patients participating in large clinical trials. The levels of such antibodies were higher in patients treated with insulin aspart as compared to regular human insulin. The clinical relevance of this antibody formation is unknown.

Carcinogenicity
Standard 2-year studies to evaluate the carcinogenic potential of insulin aspart have not been done in animals.

Tumorigenicity
In one-year studies, Sprague-Dawley rats were dosed subcutaneously with insulin aspart at 10, 50, and 200 units per kg of body weight (U/kg) per day (approximately 2, 8, and 32 times the human subcutaneous dose of 1 U/kg per day, based on unit per body surface area, respectively). At a dose of 200 U/kg per day (an equivalent dose of 32 times the human subcutaneous daily dose), insulin aspart increased the incidence of mammary gland tumors in females as compared to untreated controls (results are not significantly different than if using regular human insulin). The relevance of these results to humans in unknown.

Mutagenicity
No evidence of mutagenicity was found in the following series of genotoxic tests: Ames test, mouse lymphoma cell forward gene mutation test, human peripheral blood lymphocyte chromosome aberration test, *in vivo* micronucleus test in mice, and in *ex vivo* UDS test in rat liver hepatocytes.

Pregnancy/Reproduction
Fertility—No evidence of impaired fertility was observed in animal studies using male and female rats, at subcutaneous doses up to 200 U/kg per day (approximately 32 times the human subcutaneous dose, based on unit per body surface area).

Pregnancy—Adequate and well-controlled studies in humans have not been done. Both diabetics and patients with a history of gestational diabetes should maintain proper metabolic glucose control before conception and throughout the pregnancy term to improve fetal outcome. Insulin requirements often are decreased during the first trimester and increased during the second and third trimesters.

Both insulin aspart and regular human insulin were shown to cause pre- and post- implantation losses and visceral and skeletal abnormalities, in rats and in rabbits at doses of 200 U/kg per day and 10 U/kg per day, respectively (approximately 32 times and 3 times the human subcutaneous dose of 1 U/kg per day, based on unit per body surface area, in rats and in rabbits, respectively). The effects are thought to be secondary to maternal hypoglycemia at high doses.

FDA Pregnancy Category C.

Breast-feeding
It is not known whether insulin aspart is distributed into human breast milk. However, human insulin is distributed into breast milk and thus patient should use caution when taking insulin aspart.

Pediatrics
Appropriate studies on the relationship of age to the effects of insulin aspart have not been performed in the pediatric population. Safety and efficacy have not been established.

Geriatrics
Studies performed in approximately 36 patients 65 years of age or older have not demonstrated geriatrics-specific problems that would limit the usefulness of insulin aspart in the elderly.

Drug interactions and/or related problems
The following drug interactions and/or related problems have been selected on the basis of their potential clinical significance (possible mechanism in parentheses where appropriate)—not necessarily inclusive (» = major clinical significance):

Note: Combinations containing any of the following medications, depending on the amount present, may also interact with this medication.

Alcohol
Beta-adrenergic blockers
Clonidine
Lithium salts
Pentamidine
(these medications may change metabolic control of glucose concentrations; insulin requirements may be decreased *or* increased)
(pentamidine may cause hypoglycemia, sometimes followed by hyperglycemia)

Hyperglycemia-causing medications, such as:
Contraceptives, estrogen- and progestogen-containing, oral
Corticosteroids
Danazol
Diuretics
Estrogens
Isoniazid
Niacin
Phenothiazinessuch as chlorpromazine
Somatropin
Sympathomimetic agentssuch as epinephrine, salbutamol, or terbutaline
Thyroid hormones
(these medications may cause loss of glycemic control; insulin requirements may be increased)

Hypoglycemia-causing medications, such as:
Angiotensin Converting Enzyme (ACE) inhibitors
Antidiabetic agents, oral
Disopyramide
Fibrates
Fluoxetine
Monoamine oxidase (MAO) inhibitors
Propoxyphene
Salicylates
Somatostatin analogsuch as octreotide
Sulfonamides
(these medications may change metabolic control of glucose concentrations; insulin requirements may be decreased)

» Sympatholytic agents, such as:
Beta-adrenergic blockers
Clonidine
Guanethidine
Reserpine
(may blunt some of the symptoms of developing hypoglycemia making detection of this complication more difficult)

Laboratory value alterations
The following have been selected on the basis of their potential clinical significance (possible effect in parentheses where appropriate)—not necessarily inclusive (» = major clinical significance).

With physiology/laboratory test values
Alkaline phosphatase, serum
(some patients in controlled clinical trials experienced small but persistent increases in alkaline phosphatase lab values; clinical significance is unknown)

Medical considerations/Contraindications

The medical considerations/contraindications included have been selected on the basis of their potential clinical significance (reasons given in parentheses where appropriate)—not necessarily inclusive (» = major clinical significance).

Except under special circumstances, this medication should not be used when the following medical problem exists:

» Hypersensitivity to insulin aspart or
» Hypoglycemia

Risk-benefit should be considered when the following medical problems exist:

Hepatic function impairment or
Renal function impairment
(studies have shown increased concentrations of circulating insulin in patients with hepatic or renal function impairment; careful glucose monitoring and adjustment, possible reduction, of insulin aspart dosage may be necessary)

Patient monitoring

The following may be especially important in patient monitoring (other tests may be warranted in some patients, depending on condition; » = major clinical significance):

» Glucose concentrations, blood
(monitoring essential as a guide to therapeutic efficacy)

» Glycosylated hemoglobin determinations
(periodic monitoring recommended to assess long-term glycemic control)

» Potassium concentrations, serum
(determinations may be important if the patient is hypoglycemic, is fasting, has autonomic neuropathy, or is using potassium-lowering agents or taking agents sensitive to serum potassium level)

Side/Adverse Effects

The following side/adverse effects have been selected on the basis of their potential clinical significance (possible signs and symptoms in parentheses where appropriate)—not necessarily inclusive:

Those indicating need for medical attention

Incidence more frequent

Hypoglycemia (anxiety; behavior change similar to drunkenness; blurred vision; cold sweats; coma; confusion; depression; difficulty in concentrating; dizziness or lightheadedness; drowsiness; excessive hunger; fast heartbeat; headache; irritability or abnormal behavior; nervousness; nightmares; restless sleep; seizures; shakiness; slurred speech; tingling in the hands, feet, lips, or tongue)

Incidence less frequent or rare

Allergy, local (itching, redness, or swelling at injection site); ***allergy, systemic*** (decrease in blood pressure; rapid pulse; shortness of breath; skin rash or itching over the entire body; sweating; wheezing); ***hypokalemia*** (convulsions; decreased urine; dry mouth; irregular heartbeat; increased thirst; loss of appetite; mood changes; muscle pain or cramps; nausea or vomiting; numbness or tingling in hands, feet, or lips; shortness of breath; unusual tiredness or weakness); ***injection site reaction*** (bleeding; blistering; burning; coldness; discoloration of skin; feeling of pressure; hives; infection; inflammation; itching; lumps; numbness; pain; rash; redness; scarring; soreness; stinging; swelling; tenderness; tingling; ulceration; warmth); ***lipodystrophy*** (depression of the skin; indentation of the skin); ***pruritus*** (itching skin); ***rash***

Note: *Local allergic reactions* are usually minor and resolve in a few days to a few weeks although sometimes require discontinuation of treatment. In some cases, the reactions may be related to irritants in a skin cleansing agent or poor injection technique rather than to the medication.

Overdose

For specific information on the agent used in the management of insulin aspart overdose, see the *Glucagon (Systemic)* monograph.

For more information on the management of overdose or unintentional ingestion, **contact a poison control center** (see *Poison Control Center Listing*).

Clinical effects of overdose

The following effects have been selected on the basis of their potential clinical significance (possible signs and symptoms in parentheses where appropriate)—not necessarily inclusive:

Hypoglycemia (anxiety; behavior change similar to drunkenness; blurred vision; cold sweats; coma; confusion; depression; difficulty in concentrating; dizziness or lightheadedness; drowsiness; excessive hunger; fast heartbeat; headache; irritability or abnormal behavior; nervousness; nightmares; restless sleep; seizures; shakiness; slurred speech; tingling in the hands, feet, lips, or tongue)

Treatment of overdose

Specific treatment—

Mild hypoglycemia without neurologic symptoms or loss of consciousness should be treated with immediate ingestion of glucose and adjustments to medication dosage, meal patterns, or exercise.

Severe hypoglycemia including coma, seizures, or other neurologic impairment requires immediate emergency medical assistance. The patient should immediately be given intramuscular or subcutaneous glucagon, or intravenous glucose, and observed because relapse may occur following apparent clinical recovery.

Patient Consultation

As an aid to patient consultation, refer to *Advice for the Patient, Insulin Aspart (Systemic)*.

In providing consultation, consider emphasizing the following selected information (» = major clinical significance):

Before using this medication

» Conditions affecting use, especially:
Hypersensitivity to insulin aspart
Pregnancy—Importance of maintaining proper metabolic glucose control before conception and throughout pregnancy to improve fetal outcome; insulin requirements may change during pregnancy
Breast-feeding—Caution when taking insulin aspart
Other medications, especially sympatholytics
Other medical problems, especially hypoglycemia

Proper use of this medication

» Carefully selecting and rotating injection sites within the same region, in abdominal wall, thigh, or upper arm.
» Taking insulin apart within 5-10 minutes before the meal when used as a mealtime insulin
» Adhering to recommended regimens for diet, exercise, and glucose monitoring
» Proper dosing
» Proper storage

Precautions while using this medication

» Regular visits to physician to check progress, especially during the first few weeks of treatment
» *Carefully following special instructions of health care team:*
Discussing use of alcohol and tobacco
Not taking other medications unless discussed with physician
Getting counseling for family members to help the patient with diabetes; also, special counseling for pregnancy planning and contraception
Making travel plans that include readiness for diabetic emergencies and eating meals at the usual times, even with changing time zones

» Preparing for and understanding what to do in case of diabetic emergency; carrying medical history and current medication list and wearing medical identification

» Recognizing symptoms of hypoglycemia: anxiety; behavior change similar to drunkenness; blurred vision; cold sweats; coma; confusion; cool, pale skin; difficulty in concentrating; drowsiness; excessive hunger; fast heartbeat; headache (continuing); nausea; nervousness; nightmares; restless sleep; seizures; shakiness; slurred speech; and unusual tiredness or weakness

» Recognizing what brings on symptoms of hypoglycemia, such as delaying or missing a meal or snack; drinking significant amounts of alcohol; exercising more than usual; having an illness, including vomiting or diarrhea; taking certain medications; or using other antidiabetic medication

» Knowing what to do if symptoms of hypoglycemia occur, such as ingesting a source of glucose (not sucrose) or, if severe, injecting glucagon

» Recognizing symptoms of hyperglycemia and ketoacidosis: blurred vision; drowsiness; dry mouth; flushed, dry skin; fruit-like breath odor; increased urination (frequency and volume); ketones in urine; loss of appetite; somnolence (sleepiness); stomachache, nausea, or vomiting; tiredness; troubled breathing (rapid and deep); unconsciousness; and unusual thirst

» Recognizing what brings on symptoms of hyperglycemia, such as exercising less than usual, having a fever or infection, not taking enough or skipping a dose of antidiabetic medication, or overeating or not following meal plan

» Knowing what to do if symptoms of hyperglycemia occur, such as checking blood glucose and contacting a member of the health care team

Side/adverse effects

Signs of potential side effects, especially hypoglycemia, local allergy, systemic allergy, hypokalemia, and lipodystrophy or local reaction at injection site

General Dosing Information

The glucose-lowering capability of one unit of insulin aspart is equal to that of one unit of regular human insulin.

Because of the short duration of action of insulin aspart, supplementation with a longer acting insulin should be normally used to maintain proper glycemic control, especially in patients with type 1 diabetes. In addition, insulin aspart's duration of action may vary in different individuals (or sometimes in same individual) and is dependent on injection site, blood supply, temperature, and physical activity.

Any changes in patients' insulin dose should be made only under medical supervision. Dosage may need to be altered for changes in insulin strength, manufacturer, type (e.g., regular, NPH, analog), species (animal, human), or method of manufacture (rDNA versus animal-source insulin).

Adjustment of insulin dosage also may be necessary following a change in meal plan or amount of exercise, or following an acute illness, emotional disturbance, or period of stress.

Different types of insulin are sometimes mixed in the same syringe to achieve a more accurate matching of insulin availability to the patient's requirements in a single dose. If insulin aspart is to be mixed, several factors should be considered:

- Although no significant change in total bioavailability or time to peak concentration occurred when mixing insulin aspart with NPH human insulin immediately before injection, a decrease in the peak concentration of insulin aspart was demonstrated in healthy male volunteers (n = 24) in clinical study.
- If insulin aspart is mixed with NPH human insulin, insulin aspart should be drawn into the syringe first and then the mixture should be given immediately after mixing.
- Mixtures of insulin aspart and other insulin preparations should not be administered intravenously.
- Insulin aspart should not be mixed with crystalline zinc insulin preparations as no compatibility data exists.
- The effect of mixing insulin aspart with insulins of animal source or other manufacturers have not been studied.

Parenteral Dosage Forms

INSULIN ASPART INJECTION

Usual adult dose

Antidiabetic agent—

Subcutaneous, dosage should be individualized and determined by the physician and based on the patient's needs.

Note: When used in a meal-related regimen, 50 – 70% of the insulin dose should be provided by insulin aspart with the remainder of the dose provided by an intermediate- or long-acting insulin. Insulin aspart should generally be given immediately before a meal (start of meal within 5 – 10 minutes after injection).

Usual adult prescribing limits

Dose limit determined by physician but usually between 0.5 – 1.0 units per kg of body weight per day.

Usual pediatric dose

Safety and efficacy have not been established.

Usual geriatric dose

See *Usual adult dose.*

Usual geriatric prescribing limits

See *Usual adult prescribing limits.*

Strength(s) usually available

U.S.—

Note: Insulin aspart is available in 10 mL vials and 3 mL *PenFill*® cartridges. The cartridges are for use with Novo Nordisk's *NovoPen*® *3 Insulin Delivery Devices* and *NovoFine*® disposable needles.

100 Units of insulin aspart per mL (Rx) [*NovoLog* (Disodium hydrogen phosphate dihydrate 1.25 mg; glycerin 16 mg; metacresol 1.72 mg; phenol 1.50 mg; sodium chloride 0.58 mg; zinc 19.6 mcg)].

Packaging and storage

Store between 2 and 8 °C (36 and 46 °F). Protect from freezing. If refrigeration is not possible, insulin aspart may be stored unrefrigerated, at temperatures below 30 °C (86 °F) and protected from light, for up to 28 days.

Auxiliary labeling

- Refrigerate.
- Do not freeze.

Caution

Do not use if insulin aspart has been frozen or if solution has become viscous or cloudy.

Additional information

Insulin aspart is an aqueous, clear, and colorless solution.

Developed: 01/18/2001

INSULIN DETEMIR Systemic†

VA CLASSIFICATION (Primary): HS501

Commonly used brand name(s): *Levemir.*

Note: For a listing of dosage forms and brand names by country availability, see *Dosage Forms* section(s).

†Not commercially available in Canada.

Category

Antidiabetic agent.

Indications

Accepted

Diabetes mellitus, type 1 (treatment adjunct)

Diabetes mellitus, type 2 (treatment adjunct)—Insulin detemir is indicated for once or twice-daily subcutaneous administration in the treatment of adult patients with diabetes mellitus who require basal (long acting) insulin for the control of hyperglycemia.

Pharmacology/Pharmacokinetics

Physicochemical characteristics

Source—Insulin detemir is produced by recombinant DNA technology using *Saccharomyces cerevisiae* followed by chemical modification. Insulin detemir differs from human insulin in that the amino acid threonine at position B30 has been omitted, and a C14 fatty acid chain has been attached to the amino acid B29.

Molecular weight—Insulin detemir: 5916.9.

pH—approximately 7.4.

Mechanism of action/Effect

Insulin detemir regulates glucose metabolism by binding to insulin receptors. Receptor-bound insulin lowers blood glucose by facilitating cellular uptake of glucose into skeletal muscle and fat and by inhibiting output of glucose from the liver.

Absorption

In comparison studies with NPH human insulin, insulin detemir indicated a slower absorption after subcutaneous injection over 24 hours in healthy subjects and patients with diabetes.

The absolute bioavailability of insulin detemir is approximately 60%.

Distribution

Volume of distribution (Vol_D)—0.1 L/kg.

Protein binding

Very high 98% to albumin.

Half-life

Terminal—5 to 7 hours depending on dose.

Onset of action

Doses of insulin detemir from 0.2 to 0.4 U/kg exerts more than 50% of its maximum effect from 3 to 4 hours up to 14 hours following administration.

Time to peak concentration

Maximum peak concentration is generally reached between 6 to 8 hours following administration.

Duration of action

In a 24-hour study, the mean duration of action lasts from 5.7 hours at the lowest dose to 23.2 hours at the highest dose.

Precautions to Consider

Carcinogenicity

Standard 2-year studies to evaluate the carcinogenic potential of insulin detemir have not been done in animals.

Mutagenicity

Insulin detemir was negative for genotoxic potential in the *in vitro* reverse mutation study in bacteria, human peripheral blood lymphocyte chromosome aberration test, and the *in vivo* mouse micronucleus test.

Pregnancy/Reproduction

Pregnancy—Adequate and well-controlled studies in humans have not been done. Studies in animals have shown that insulin detemir causes adverse effects in the fetus.

Studies done in female rats before mating, during mating and throughout pregnancy given doses of insulin detemir up to 300 nmol/kg/day (3 times the recommended human dose) produced litters with visceral anomalies. Studies done in rabbits during organogenesis given doses of insulin detemir up to 900 nmol/kg/day, revealed drug-dose related increases in the incidence of fetuses with gall bladder abnormalities such as small, bilobed, bifurcated and missing gallbladders. Both studies included concurrent human insulin control groups indicating similar effects of embryotoxicity and teratogenicity.

FDA Pregnancy Category C

Breast-feeding

It is not known whether insulin detemir is distributed into breast milk. For this reason, caution should be exercised when insulin detemir is administered to a nursing mother. Patients with diabetes who are lactating may require adjustments in insulin dose, meal plan, or both.

Pediatrics

Safety and efficacy have not been established.

Geriatrics

Appropriate studies performed have not demonstrated geriatrics-specific problems that would limit the usefulness of insulin detemir in the elderly. However, higher insulin AUC levels (up to 35%) were found in elderly subjects due to a reduced clearance.

Pharmacogenetics

No overall differences in pharmacokinetics were observed between gender or race.

Drug interactions and/or related problems

The following drug interactions and/or related problems have been selected on the basis of their potential clinical significance (possible mechanism in parentheses where appropriate)—not necessarily inclusive (» = major clinical significance):

Note: Combinations containing any of the following medications, depending on the amount present, may also interact with this medication.

Alcohol or
Beta-adrenergic blockers or
Clonidine or
Lithium salts or
Pentamidine
(these medications may either potentiate or weaken the blood glucose-lowering effect of insulin; pentamidine may cause hypoglycemia, sometimes followed by hyperglycemia)

Antidiabetic, oral
(treatment may need to be adjusted when used concomitantly with insulin detemir)

Hyperglycemia-causing agents, such as:
Corticosteroids or
Danazol or
Diuretics or
Estrogens or
Isoniazid or
Oral contraceptives or
Phenothiazine derivatives or
Progestogens or
Somatropin or
Sympathomimetic agents or
Thyroid hormones
(these medications may affect glucose metabolism and may require insulin dosage adjustment and particularly close monitoring)

Hypoglycemia-causing agents, such as:
Antidiabetic drugs or
Angiotensin-converting enzyme (ACE) inhibitors or
Disopyramide or
Fibrates or
Fluoxetine or
Monoamine oxidase (MAO) inhibitors or
Octreotide or
Propoxyphene or
Salicylates or
Sulfonamides
(these medications may increase blood-glucose lowering effect of insulin)

» Sympatholytics, such as:
Beta-adrenergic blocking agents or
Clonidine or
Guanethidine or
Reserpine
(signs of hypoglycemia may be reduced or absent)

Medical considerations/Contraindications

The medical considerations/contraindications included have been selected on the basis of their potential clinical significance (reasons given in parentheses where appropriate)—not necessarily inclusive (» = major clinical significance).

Except under special circumstances, this medication should not be used when the following medical problem exists:

» Hypersensitivity to insulin detemir or to any of its excipients or
» Hypoglycemia

Risk-benefit should be considered when the following medical problems exist:

Intercurrent conditions, such as:
Emotional disturbances or
Illness or
Other stresses
(insulin requirements may be altered)

Hepatic function impairment or
Renal function impairment
(careful glucose monitoring and dose adjustments of insulin detemir may be necessary)

Patient monitoring

The following may be especially important in patient monitoring (other tests may be warranted in some patients, depending on condition; » = major clinical significance):

» Glucose concentrations, blood
(glucose monitoring is recommended for all patients with diabetes)

» Glycosylated hemoglobin (hemoglobin A_{1c}) determinations
(periodic monitoring recommended to assess long-term glycemic control)

Side/Adverse Effects

The following side/adverse effects have been selected on the basis of their potential clinical significance (possible signs and symptoms in parentheses where appropriate)—not necessarily inclusive:

Those indicating need for medical attention

Incidence unknown

Allergic reaction, including (cough; difficulty swallowing; dizziness; fast heartbeat; hives; itching; puffiness or swelling of the eyelids or around the eyes, face, lips or tongue; shortness of breath; skin rash; tightness in chest; unusual tiredness or weakness; wheezing); ***pruritus*** (itching skin); ***anaphylactic reaction*** (cough; difficulty swallowing; dizziness; fast heartbeat; hives; itching; puffiness or swelling of the eyelids or around the eyes, face, lips or tongue; shortness of breath; skin rash; tightness in chest; unusual tiredness or weakness; wheezing); ***hypersensitivity*** (fast heartbeat; fever; hives; itching; irritation; hoarseness; joint pain; stiffness or swelling; rash; redness of skin; shortness of breath; swelling of eyelids, face, lips, hands, or feet; tightness in chest; troubled breathing or swallowing; wheezing); ***hypoglycemia*** (anxiety; blurred vision; chills; cold sweats; coma; confusion; cool pale skin; depression; dizziness; fast heartbeat; headache; increased hunger; nausea; nervousness; nightmares; seizures; shakiness; slurred speech; unusual tiredness or weakness); ***rash***

Those indicating need for medical attention only if they continue or are bothersome

Incidence unknown

Edema (swelling); ***injection site reaction*** (bleeding, blistering, burning, coldness, discoloration of skin; feeling of pressure, hives, infection, inflammation, itching, lumps, numbness, pain, rash, redness, scarring, soreness, stinging, swelling, tenderness, tingling, ulceration, or warmth at site); ***lipodystrophy*** (redistribution or accumulation of body fat); ***sodium retention*** (decrease in amount of urine; noisy, rattling breathing; shortness of breath; swelling of fingers, hands, feet, or lower legs; troubled breathing at rest; weight gain); ***weight gain***

Overdose

For more information on the management of overdose or unintentional ingestion, **contact a poison control center** (see *Poison Control Center Listing*).

Clinical effects of overdose

The following effects have been selected on the basis of their potential clinical significance (possible signs and symptoms in parentheses where appropriate)—not necessarily inclusive:

Hypoglycemia (anxiety; blurred vision; chills; cold sweats; coma; confusion; cool pale skin; depression; dizziness; fast heartbeat; headache; increased hunger; nausea; nervousness; nightmares; seizures; shakiness; slurred speech; unusual tiredness or weakness)

Treatment of overdose

Specific treatment—

Mild hypoglycemia without neurologic symptoms or loss of consciousness should be treated with immediate ingestion of glucose and adjustments to medication dosage, meal patterns, or exercise.

Severe hypoglycemia including coma, seizures, or other neurologic impairment requires immediate emergency medical assistance. The patient should immediately be given intramuscular or subcutaneous glucagon, or intravenous glucose, and observed because relapse may occur following apparent clinical recovery.

Supportive care—

Patients in whom intentional overdose is confirmed or suspected should be referred for psychiatric consultation.

Patient Consultation

As an aid to patient consultation, refer to *Advice for the Patient, Insulin detemir.*

In providing consultation, consider emphasizing the following selected information (» = major clinical significance):

Before using this medication

» Conditions affecting use, especially:

Hypersensitivity to insulin detemir or any of its excipients

Pregnancy—Importance of maintaining glycemic control to improve fetal outcome; insulin requirements may change during pregnancy.

Breast-feeding—Women who are breast-feeding may require adjustments in their dosages of insulin detemir, in their meal plans, or in both.

Other medications, especially sympatholytics, such as beta-adrenergic blocking agents, clonidine, guanethidine, reserpine; or other insulin preparations

Other medical problems, especially hypoglycemia

Proper use of this medication

» The importance of carefully reading patient instruction sheet contained in insulin detemir before beginning treatment and after each refill for any new information and understanding:

How to prepare the medication

How to inject the medication

How to dispose of syringes, needles, and injection devices

» The importance of continued patient education and advice on insulin therapies, injection technique, life-style management, regular glucose monitoring, periodic glycosylated hemoglobin testing, recognition and management of hypo- and hyperglycemia, adherence to meal planning, complication of insulin therapy, timing of dosage, and instruction for use of injection devices.

» The importance of patient-performed blood glucose measurements to achieve effective glycemic control.

» Carefully selecting and rotating injection sites, following health care professional's recommendations

» Not diluting or mixing insulin detemir with any other insulin or solution.

» Proper dosing

» Proper storage

Precautions while using this medication

» Regular visits to physician to check progress, especially during the first few weeks of treatment

» *Carefully following special instructions of health care team:*

Discussing use of alcohol and tobacco

Not taking other medications unless discussed with physician

Getting counseling for family members to help the patient with diabetes; also, special counseling for pregnancy planning and contraception

Making travel plans that include readiness for diabetic emergencies and eating meals at the usual times, even with changing time zones

» Preparing for and understanding what to do in case of diabetic emergency; carrying medical history and current medication list and wearing medical identification

» Recognizing symptoms of hypoglycemia: anxiety; behavior change similar to drunkenness; blurred vision; cold sweats; coma; confusion; cool, pale skin; difficulty in concentrating; drowsiness; excessive hunger; fast heartbeat; headache (continuing); nausea; nervousness; nightmares; restless sleep; seizures; shakiness; slurred speech; and unusual tiredness or weakness

» Recognizing what brings on symptoms of hypoglycemia, such as delaying or missing a meal or snack; drinking significant amounts of alcohol; exercising more than usual; having an illness, including vomiting or diarrhea; taking certain medications; or using other antidiabetic medication

» Knowing what to do if symptoms of hypoglycemia occur, such as ingesting a source of glucose (not sucrose) or, if severe, injecting glucagon

» Recognizing symptoms of hyperglycemia and ketoacidosis: blurred vision; drowsiness; dry mouth; flushed, dry skin; fruit-like breath odor; increased urination (frequency and volume); ketones in urine; loss of appetite; somnolence (sleepiness); stomachache, nausea, or vomiting; tiredness; troubled breathing (rapid and deep); unconsciousness; and unusual thirst

Side/adverse effects

Signs of potential side effects, especially allergic reaction including pruritus; anaphylactic reaction, hypersensitivity, hypoglycemia, or rash

General Dosing Information

Insulin detemir should not be given intravenously or intramuscular because the prolonged duration of effect is dependent on injection into subcutaneous tissue.

Insulin detemir should be administered by subcutaneous injection in the thigh, abdominal wall, or upper arm; however, injection sites within an injection area should be rotated with each injection. Like other insulin products, the rate of absorption may be affected by dose, injection site, blood flow, temperature, and level of physical activity.

Insulin detemir is not to be used in insulin infusion pumps.

Patients treated with insulin detemir once daily should receive the dose with the evening meal or at bedtime.

Patients who require twice-daily dosing can receive the dose with either the evening meal, at bedtime, or 12 hours after the morning dose.

Changes in patients' insulin dose should be made cautiously and only under medical supervision. Dosage may need to be altered for changes in insulin strength, timing of dosing, manufacturer, type (e.g., regular, NPH, analog), species (animal, human), or method of manufacture (rDNA versus animal-source insulin).

Inadequate dosing and or discontinuation of treatment may lead to hyperglycemia and, in patients with type 1 diabetes, diabetic ketoacidosis.

Hypoglycemia depends on the action profile of the insulins used and may change when the treatment regimen or timing of dosing is changed.

Adjustments of insulin dosage may be necessary following a change in meal plan or amount of exercise, or following an acute illness, emotional disturbance, or period of stress.

The needle should not be recapped and should be disposed of in a puncture-resistant container. Such containers should be sealed and disposed of properly after each injection.

Parenteral Dosage Forms

Note: Bracketed information in the *Indications* section refers to uses that are not included in U.S. product labeling.

INSULIN DETEMIR INJECTION

Usual adult dose

Antidiabetic agent—

Subcutaneous, once or twice daily; dosage should be individualized and determined by the physician and based on the patient's needs.

Note: For patients with type 1 or type 2 diabetes on basal-bolus treatment: Changing the basal insulin to insulin detemir can be done on a unit to unit basis, and then adjusted to achieve glycemic targets.

For patients receiving only basal insulin: Changing the basal insulin to insulin detemir can be done on a unit-to-unit basis.

For insulin-naive patients with type 2 diabetes who are inadequately controlled on oral antidiabetic drugs: A starting dose of

0.1 to 0.2 U/kg once-daily in the evening or 10 units once- or twice-daily, and then adjusted to achieve glycemic targets.

For patients with renal impairment: Dose may need to be adjusted.

For patients with hepatic impairment: Dose may need to be adjusted.

Usual pediatric dose
Safety and efficacy have not been established.

Usual geriatric dose
See *Usual adult dose.*

Strength(s) usually available
U.S.—

Note: Insulin detemir is available in 10 mL vials, 3 mL *PenFill*® cartridges, 3 mL *InnoLet*® and 3 mL *FlexPen*®. The cartridges are for use with Novo Nordisk's 3 mL *PenFill*® compatible insulin delivery devices and *NovoFine*® disposable needles.

100 Units of insulin detemir per mL (Rx) [*Levemir* (disodium phosphate dihydrate; hydrochloric acid; m-cresol; mannitol; phenol; sodium chloride; sodium hydroxide; water for injection; zinc)].

Packaging and storage
Store between 2 and 8 °C (36 and 46 °F). Protect from freezing.
• Vials—After initial use should be stored in a refrigerator. If refrigeration is not possible, insulin detemir may be stored at room temperature, below 30 °C (86 °F) and protected from direct heat and light, for up to 42 days.
• *PenFill*® cartridges, *FlexPen*®, or *InnoLet*®—After initial use, a cartridge or a prefilled syringe may be used for up to 42 days if kept at room temperature, below 30 °C (86 °F) and protected from direct heat and light. In-use cartridges and prefilled syringes must not be stored in the refrigerator and must not be stored with the needle in place.

Incompatibilities
Insulin detemir should not be diluted or mixed with any other insulin or solution.

Auxiliary labeling
- Refrigerate.
- Do not freeze.

Caution
Do not use if insulin detemir has been frozen or if solution has become viscous or cloudy.

Additional information
Insulin detemir is an aqueous, clear, and colorless solution.

Developed: 09/08/2005

INSULIN GLARGINE Systemic

VA CLASSIFICATION (Primary): HS501

Commonly used brand name(s): *Lantus*®.

Another commonly used name is:
Glargine
HOE 71GT
HOE 901

Note: For a listing of dosage forms and brand names by country availability, see *Dosage Forms* section(s).

Category
Antidiabetic agent.

Indications

Accepted
Diabetes mellitus (treatment)—Insulin glargine is indicated in the treatment of diabetes mellitus for the control of hyperglycemia in adult and pediatric patients with type 1 diabetes and in adult patients with type 2 diabetes who require insulin.

Pharmacology/Pharmacokinetics

Physicochemical characteristics
Source—Analog of human insulin created by replacing the amino acid at position 21 of the A-chain (asparagine) with glycine and by adding two arginines to the C-terminus of the B-chain. Synthesized by recombinant DNA process involving a genetically engineered *Escherichia coli.*
Molecular weight—6063.
pH—4.

Mechanism of action/Effect
Like other types of insulin, the primary action of insulin glargine is to regulate glucose metabolism. Also, insulin glargine lowers the blood glucose concentration by stimulating glucose uptake especially by muscle and fat. It also inhibits hepatic glucose production.

Other actions/effects
Insulin also inhibits lipolysis in adipocytes, inhibits proteolysis, and enhances protein synthesis.

Absorption
Insulin glargine was formulated to have a low aqueous solubility at neutral pH. The insulin glargine solution has a pH of 4, and at this pH, it is completely soluble. However, in the neutral pH of the subcutaneous tissue, microprecipitates are formed from which small amounts of insulin glargine are slowly released. This results in a relatively constant concentration over 24 hours. There is no pronounced peak with insulin glargine.
Like other insulins, the time course of action of insulin glargine may vary between individuals and within the same individual. In contrast to other insulin products, the duration of action of insulin glargine was similar after subcutaneous injection into abdominal, deltoid, or thigh areas.

Biotransformation
In a human metabolism study, insulin glargine was partially metabolized at the carboxyl terminus of the B chain to two active metabolites, M1 (21^A-Gly-insulin) and M2 (21^A-Gly-des-30^B-Thr-insulin). These metabolites have *in vitro* activity similar to that of insulin.

Duration of action
24 hours

Precautions to Consider

Carcinogenicity
Two-year carcinogenicity studies were performed in mice and rats. Doses up to 0.455 mg/kg were used which is for the rat approximately 10 times and for the mouse approximately 5 times the recommended human subcutaneous starting dose of 10 International Units (0.008 mg/kg/day) based on mg per square meter of body surface area (mg/m^2). For female mice, the findings were not conclusive because excessive mortality occurred in all dose groups. Histiocytomas developed at injection sites in male rats (statistically significant) and male mice (not statistically significant) in groups receiving the acid vehicle. Female animals, saline control, or insulin comparator groups using a different vehicle did not develop histiocytomas. The relevance of these findings to humans is unknown.

Mutagenicity
Insulin glargine was not mutagenic in tests for detection of gene mutations in bacteria and mammalian cells (Ames- and HGPRT-test) and in tests for detection of chromosomal aberrations (cytogenetics in vitro in V79 cells and in vivo in Chinese hamsters).

Pregnancy/Reproduction
Pregnancy—Studies have not been done in humans.
However, women with diabetes or a history of gestational diabetes must be educated about the necessity of maintaining good glycemic control before conception and during pregnancy to improve fetal outcome. Insulin requirements often are decreased during the first trimester and increased during the second and third trimesters.
Administration of insulin glargine to female rats before mating, during mating, and throughout pregnancy at doses up to 0.36 mg per kilogram of body weight (approximately 7 times the recommended human subcutaneous starting dose of 10 International Units [0.008 mg/kg] based on mg/m^2) per day did not generally have effects that differed from regular human insulin. In Himalayan rabbits, doses of 0.072 mg per kilogram of body weight (approximately 2 times the recommended human subcutaneous starting dose of 10 International Units [0.008 mg/kg] based on mg/m^2) per day were administered during organogenesis. While the effects did not generally differ from regular human insulin, five rabbit fetuses from two litters of the high-dose group exhibited dilation of the cerebral ventricles. Otherwise, early embryonic development appeared normal.

FDA Pregnancy Category C.

Breast-feeding
It is not known whether insulin glargine is distributed into breast milk. Women who are breast-feeding may require adjustments in their dosages of insulin glargine, in their meal plans, or in both.

Pediatrics
Studies performed in patients 6 to 11 years of age with type 1 diabetes have not demonstrated pediatrics-specific problems that would limit the use of insulin glargine in children.

Adolescents
Studies performed in patients 12 to 15 years of age with type 1 diabetes have not demonstrated adolescent-specific problems that would limit the use of insulin glargine in teenagers.

Geriatrics
Appropriate studies performed to date have not demonstrated geriatrics-specific problems that would limit the usefulness of insulin glargine in the elderly. Compared to the entire study population, patients 65 years and older had an expected higher incidence of cardiovascular events in the insulin glargine and NPH human insulin-treated groups. Because hypoglycemia may be more difficult to detect in the elderly, the initial dose, dose increments, and maintenance dose should be conservative to minimize the chance of hypoglycemic reactions.

Drug interactions and/or related problems
The following drug interactions and/or related problems have been selected on the basis of their potential clinical significance (possible mechanism in parentheses where appropriate)—not necessarily inclusive (» = major clinical significance):

Note: Combinations containing any of the following medications, depending on the amount present, may also interact with this medication.

Hyperglycemia-causing agents, such as:
Corticosteroids
Danazol
Diuretics
Estrogens
Isoniazid
Oral contraceptives
Phenothiazine derivatives
Somatropin
Sympathomimetic agents or
Thyroid hormones
(these medications may cause loss of glycemic control; insulin requirements may be increased)

Hypoglycemia-causing agents, such as:
Alcohol
Antidiabetic agents
Angiotensin-converting enzyme (ACE) inhibitors
Disopyramide
Fibrates
Fluoxetine
Monoamine oxidase (MAO) inhibitors
Octreotide
Propoxyphene
Salicylates or
Sulfonamides
(these medications may improve glucose control; insulin requirements may be decreased)

Pentamidine
(may cause hypoglycemia followed by hyperglycemia)

» Sympatholytics, such as:
Beta-adrenergic blocking agents
Clonidine
Guanethidine or
Reserpine
(sympatholytics may mask some of the symptoms of hypoglycemia, making it more difficult to detect hypoglycemia)

Medical considerations/Contraindications
The medical considerations/contraindications included have been selected on the basis of their potential clinical significance (reasons given in parentheses where appropriate)—not necessarily inclusive (» = major clinical significance).

Except under special circumstances, this medication should not be used when the following medical problem exists:
» Hypoglycemia

Risk-benefit should be considered when the following medical problems exist:
» Diabetic ketoacidosis
(short-acting insulin administered intravenously is the preferred treatment for this condition)

Hypersensitivity to insulin glargine
Intercurrent conditions, such as:
Emotional disturbances
Infection or
Stress
(may require adjustments in insulin or insulin glargine dosage)

Hepatic function impairmentor

Renal function impairment
(adjustment of insulin glargine dosage may be necessary)

Patient monitoring
The following may be especially important in patient monitoring (other tests may be warranted in some patients, depending on condition; » = major clinical significance):

» Glucose concentrations, blood
(monitoring essential as a guide to therapeutic efficacy)

» Glycosylated hemoglobin (hemoglobin A_{1c}) determinations
(periodic monitoring recommended to assess long-term glycemic control)

Side/Adverse Effects
The following side/adverse effects have been selected on the basis of their potential clinical significance (possible signs and symptoms in parentheses where appropriate)—not necessarily inclusive:

Those indicating need for medical attention
Incidence more frequent

Hypoglycemia (anxiety; behavior change similar to drunkenness; blurred vision; cold sweats; coma; confusion; cool, pale skin; difficulty in concentrating; dizziness or lightheadedness; drowsiness; excessive hunger; fast heartbeat; headache; nausea; nervousness; nightmares; restless sleep; seizures; shakiness; slurred speech; tingling in the hands, feet, lips, or tongue)

Note: Recovery from hypoglycemia may be delayed because insulin glargine has a long duration of effect.

Incidence less frequent or rare

Allergy, systemic (decrease in blood pressure; rapid pulse; shortness of breath; skin rash or itching over the entire body; sweating; wheezing)—may be life-threatening

Those indicating need for medical attention only if they continue or are bothersome
Incidence less frequent

Injection site pain

Note: This reaction is usually mild and did not result in discontinuation of therapy.

Incidence rare

Allergy, local (itching, redness, or swelling at injection site) ; ***edema*** (bloating or swelling of face, hands, lower legs, and/or feet; rapid weight gain); ***lipoatrophy*** (depression of the skin at injection site); ***lipohypertrophy*** (thickening of the skin at injection site)

Note: Within a few days to a few weeks, these minor symptoms usually resolve. Continuous rotation of the injection site will also minimize this reaction.

Overdose
For specific information on the agent used in the management of insulin glargine overdose, see the

Glucagon (Systemic) monograph.

For more information on the management of overdose, **contact a Poison Control Center** (see *Poison Control Center Listing*).

Clinical effects of overdose
The following effects have been selected on the basis of their potential clinical significance (possible signs and symptoms—in parentheses where appropriate)not necessarily inclusive:

Hypoglycemia (anxiety; behavior change similar to drunkenness; blurred vision; cold sweats; coma; confusion; depression; difficulty in concentrating; dizziness or lightheadedness; drowsiness; excessive hunger; fast heartbeat; headache; irritability or abnormal behavior; nervousness; nightmares; restless sleep; seizures; shakiness; slurred speech; tingling in the hands, feet, lips, or tongue)

Treatment of overdose
Specific treatment—

Mild hypoglycemia without neurologic symptoms or loss of consciousness should be treated with immediate ingestion of glucose and adjustments to medication dosage and/or meal plan.

Severe hypoglycemia including coma, seizures, or other neurologic impairment requires immediate emergency medical assistance. The patient should immediately be given intramuscular or subcutaneous glucagon, or intravenous glucose, and observed because relapse may occur following apparent clinical recovery. See the package insert or *Glucagon (Systemic)* for specific dosing guidelines for the use of glucagon.

Supportive care—

Patients in whom intentional overdose is confirmed or suspected should be referred for psychiatric consultation.

Patient Consultation

As an aid to patient consultation, refer to *Advice for the Patient, Insulin Glargine (Systemic).*

In providing consultation, consider emphasizing the following selected information (» = major clinical significance):

Before using this medication

» Conditions affecting use, especially:
- Hypersensitivity to insulin glargine
- Pregnancy—Importance of maintaining glycemic control to improve fetal outcome; insulin requirements may change during pregnancy.
- Breast-feeding—Women who are breast-feeding may require adjustments in their dosages of insulin glargine, in their meal plans, or in both
- Other medications, especially sympatholytics
- Other medical problems, especially diabetic ketoacidosis or hypoglycemia

Proper use of this medication

» Carefully reading patient instruction sheet contained in insulin glargine package and understanding:
- How to prepare the medication
- How to inject the medication
- How to dispose of syringes, needles, and injection devices

» Carefully selecting and rotating injection sites, following health care professional's recommendations

» Taking insulin glargine once daily at bedtime

» Adhering to recommended regimens for diet, exercise, and glucose monitoring

» Proper dosing

Proper storage

Precautions while using this medication

» Regular visits to physician to check progress, especially during the first few weeks of treatment

» *Carefully following special instructions of health care team:*
- Discussing use of alcohol
- Not taking other medications unless discussed with physician
- Getting counseling for family members to help the patient with diabetes; also, special counseling for pregnancy planning and contraception
- Discussing travel arrangements, including transporting insulin glargine, carrying medical history and extra supplies of insulin glargine and syringes or injection devices, and adjusting dosage if traveling across more than two time zones

» Preparing for and knowing what to do in case of an emergency by carrying medical history and current medication list, wearing medical identification, keeping extra needed medical supplies and quick-acting sugar, and having nonexpired glucagon kit and needles nearby

» Recognizing what brings on symptoms of hypoglycemia, such as using other antidiabetic medication; delaying or missing a meal or snack; exercising more than usual; drinking significant amounts of alcohol; or sickness.

» Recognizing symptoms of hypoglycemia: anxiety; behavior change similar to drunkenness; blurred vision; cold sweats; confusion; difficulty in concentrating; dizziness or lightheadedness; drowsiness; excessive hunger; fast heartbeat; headache; irritability or abnormal behavior; nervousness; nightmares; restless sleep; shakiness; slurred speech; and tingling in the hands, feet, lips, or tongue

» Knowing what to do if symptoms of hypoglycemia occur, such as eating glucose tablets or gel, corn syrup, honey, or sugar cubes; drinking fruit juice, nondiet soft drink, or sugar dissolved in water; or injecting glucagon if symptoms are severe

» Recognizing what brings on symptoms of hyperglycemia, such as not taking enough or skipping a dose of insulin glargine or insulin; overeating or not following meal plan; having emotional stress or infection; or exercising less than usual

» Recognizing symptoms of hyperglycemia and ketoacidosis: blurred vision; drowsiness; dry mouth; flushed, dry skin; fruit-like breath odor; increased urination (frequency and volume); ketones in urine; loss of appetite; stomachache, nausea, or vomiting; tiredness; troubled breathing (rapid and deep); unconsciousness; and unusual thirst

» Knowing what to do if symptoms of hyperglycemia occur, such as checking blood glucose and contacting a member of the health care team

Side/adverse effects

Signs of potential side effects, especially hypoglycemia and systemic allergy

General Dosing Information

Insulin glargine should not be given intravenously because the prolonged duration of effect is dependent on injection into subcutaneous tissue.

One international unit is equal to one unit; therefore, the dose is the same whether it is expressed in international units or units.

The potency of insulin glargine is approximately the same as human insulin.

The glucose-lowering profile of insulin glargine is relatively constant over 24 hours.

Insulin glargine is administered once daily at bedtime. When patients are transferred from an intermediate- or long- acting insulin to insulin glargine, the dosage of the short-acting insulin or fast-acting insulin analog may require adjustment. The dosage of insulin glargine was usually NOT changed when patients were transferred from once-daily NPH human insulin or ultralente human insulin. For patients who were previously treated with twice-daily NPH human insulin, the initial dosage of insulin glargine was reduced by 20% and was subsequently based on patient response.

Absorption patterns are similar after subcutaneous injection into the arm, abdomen, or leg indicating lack of injection-site dependency; however, injection sites within an injection area should be rotated with each injection. Like other insulin products, the rate of absorption may be affected by exercise and other variables.

Changes in insulin strength, type (e.g., analog, NPH, regular), source (human or pork), method of manufacture (naturally occurring, recombinant DNA process), or manufacturer should be made cautiously and only under medical supervision. A change in any of these parameters may require an adjustment of insulin dosage.

Parenteral Dosage Forms

INSULIN GLARGINE INJECTION

Usual adult dose and adolescent dose

Diabetes mellitus, type 1—

Subcutaneous, dosage must be determined by the physician based on the patient's metabolic needs, eating habits, and other lifestyle variables. Insulin glargine is administered once daily at bedtime.

Diabetes mellitus, type 2—

Subcutaneous, for insulin-naive patients, the average initial dose is 10 International Units once daily at bedtime

Usual pediatric dose

See *Usual adult and adolescent dose* for children 6 years of age or older. Safety and efficacy have not been established in children less than 6 years old.

Usual geriatric dose

See *Usual adult dose.*

Strength(s) usually available

U.S.—

Note: Insulin glargine is available in 5-mL and 10-mL vials and 3-mL cartridges. The cartridges should be used with the *OptiPen*™ One Insulin Delivery Device

100 International Units (3.6378 mg) of insulin glargine per mL (Rx) [*Lantus*® (zinc 30 mcg; m-cresol 2.7 mg; glycerol 85% 20 mg; water for injection)].

Packaging and storage

Store unopened vials and cartridges in the refrigerator between 2 and 8 ° C (36 and 46 ° F). Do not store in the freezer. However, after a cartridge has been placed in the *OptiPen One* delivery device, it should not be refrigerated.

If refrigeration is not possible, the 10-mL vial and cartridge in use can be kept unrefrigerated for up to 28 days away from direct heat and light, as long as the temperature does not exceed 30° C(86° F). Unrefrigerated 10-mL vials and cartridges must be used within 28 days or they must be discarded.

If refrigeration is not possible, the 5–mL vial in use can be kept unrefrigerated for up to 14 days away from direct heat and light, as long as the temperature does not exceed 30° C (86° F). Unrefrigerated 5–mL vials must be used within 14 days or they must be discarded. If the 5–mL vial is refrigerated, it may be used for up to 28 days.

Stability

Insulin glargine should not be diluted or mixed with any other insulin or solution.

Auxiliary labeling
- Do not freeze.
- Refrigerate.

Developed: 08/07/2000

INSULIN GLULISINE Systemic†

VA CLASSIFICATION (Primary): HS501

Commonly used brand name(s): *Apidra*.

Note: For a listing of dosage forms and brand names by country availability, see *Dosage Forms* section(s).

†Not commercially available in Canada.

Category
Antidiabetic agent.

Indications
Note: Bracketed information in the *Indications* section refers to uses that are not included in U.S. product labeling.

Accepted
Diabetes mellitus, type 1 (treatment adjunct)

Diabetes mellitus, type 2 (treatment adjunct)—Insulin glulisine is indicated for the treatment of adult patients with diabetes mellitus for the control of hyperglycemia. Insulin glulisine has a more rapid onset and shorter duration of action than regular human insulin and, therefore, should be used in regimens that include a longer-acting insulin or basal insulin analog.

Pharmacology/Pharmacokinetics

Physicochemical characteristics
Source—Human insulin analogue with a substitution of (asparagine) at position B3 by lysine, and the substitution of lysine at position B29 by glutamic acid. Insulin glulisine is produced by recombinant DNA technology using *Escherichia coli* (K12).

Molecular weight—Insulin glulisine: 5823.

pH—
approximately 7.3

Mechanism of action/Effect
Insulin glulisine, like regular types of human insulin, regulates glucose metabolism. Insulins lower blood glucose levels by stimulating peripheral glucose uptake by skeletal muscle and fat, and by inhibiting the liver's conversion of stored glycogen into glucose.

Absorption
In comparison studies with regular human insulin, insulin glulisine was more rapidly absorbed after subcutaneous injection.

The absolute bioavailability of insulin glulisine after subcutaneous administration is about 70%, regardless of injection area.

Distribution
Volume of distribution (Vol_D)—13 L

Elimination
42 minutes after subcutaneous administration.

Time to peak concentration
Peak concentration is generally reached in 55 minutes (range 34 to 91 minutes).

Peak serum concentration
When type 1 diabetic patients were given a subcutaneous dose of 0.15 IU/kg, the peak serum concentration reached an average of 82 mcIU/mL (range 42 to 134 mcIU/mL).

Time to peak effect
In a 6-hour study in type 1 diabetic patients, the maximum glucose-lowering effect of insulin glulisine, given subcutaneously, was demonstrated between 1 and 3 hours.

Precautions to Consider

Cross-sensitivity and/or related problems
Production of antibodies cross-reactive to human insulin and insulin glulisine was observed. The levels of such antibodies remained near baseline during the first 6 months and then decreased in the following 6 months. The clinical relevance of this antibody formation is unknown and showed no correlation to change in HbA1c, insulin doses or incidences of hypoglycemia.

Carcinogenicity
Standard 2-year studies to evaluate the carcinogenic potential of insulin glulisine have not been done in animals.

Tumorigenicity
In one-year studies, Sprague-Dawley rats were given subcutaneous doses of insulin glulisine at 2.5, 5, 20 or 50 IU/kg twice daily. There was a non-dose dependent higher incidence of mammary gland tumors in females as compared to untreated controls (results were similar to using regular human insulin). The relevance of these results to humans is unknown.

Mutagenicity
No evidence of mutagenicity was found in the following series of genotoxic tests: Ames test, in vitro mammalian chromosome aberration test in V79 Chinese hamster cells, and *in vivo* mammalian erythrocyte micronucleus test in rats

Pregnancy/Reproduction
Fertility—No evidence of impaired fertility was observed in animal studies using male and female rats, at subcutaneous doses up to 10 IU/kg per day (approximately 2 times the human subcutaneous dose, based on unit per body surface area).

Pregnancy—Adequate and well-controlled studies in humans have not been done. Both diabetics and patients with a history of gestational diabetes should maintain proper metabolic glucose control before conception and throughout the pregnancy term to improve fetal outcome. Insulin requirements often are decreased during the first trimester and increased during the second and third trimesters.

Both insulin glulisine and regular human insulin were shown to cause pre- and post- implantation losses and skeletal defects, in rabbits at doses of 1.5 IU/kg per day The effects are thought to be secondary to maternal hypoglycemia at high doses.

FDA Pregnancy Category C

Breast-feeding
It is not known whether insulin glulisine is distributed into human breast milk. However, human insulin is distributed into breast milk and patients should use caution when taking insulin glulisine.

Pediatrics
Safety and effectiveness have not been established.

Geriatrics
Appropriate studies performed have not demonstrated geriatrics-specific problems that would limit the usefulness of insulin glulisine in the elderly. However, greater sensitivity of some older individuals cannot be ruled out.

Pharmacogenetics
A study performed comparing Caucasians and Japanese given subcutaneous insulin glulisine, showed Japanese subjects had greater initial exposure (33%) for the ratio of AUC (0–1hr) to AUC (0–clamp end) than that in Caucasians (21%) though the total exposures were similar.

Drug interactions and/or related problems
The following drug interactions and/or related problems have been selected on the basis of their potential clinical significance (possible mechanism in parentheses where appropriate)—not necessarily inclusive (» = major clinical significance):

Note: Combinations containing any of the following medications, depending on the amount present, may also interact with this medication.

Alcohol or
Beta-adrenergic blockers or
Clonidine or
Lithium salts or
Pentamidine
(may change metabolic control of glucose concentrations; insulin requirements may be decreased *or* increased)

(pentamidine may cause hypoglycemia, sometimes followed by hyperglycemia)

Hyperglycemia-causing medications, such as:
Antipsychotic medicines, atypical such as olanzapine and clozapine or
Contraceptives, estrogen- and progestogen-containing, oral or
Corticosteroids or
Danazol or
Diazoxide or

Diuretics or
Estrogens or
Glucagon or
Isoniazid or
Phenothiazines derivatives or
Protease inhibitors or
Somatropin or
Sympathomimetic agents such as epinephrine, albuterol and terbutaline or
Thyroid hormones
(may cause loss of glycemic control; insulin requirements may be increased)

Hypoglycemia-causing medications, such as:
Angiotensin converting enzyme (ACE) inhibitors or
Antidiabetic agents, oral or
Disopyramide or
Fibrates or
Fluoxetine or
Monoamine oxidase (MAO) inhibitors or
Pentoxifylline or
Propoxyphene or
Salicylates or
Sulfonamides
(these medications may change metabolic control of glucose concentrations; insulin requirements may be decreased)

» Sympatholytic agents, such as:
Beta-adrenergic blockers or
Clonidine or
Guanethidine or
Reserpine
(may blunt some of the symptoms of developing hypoglycemia making detection of this complication more difficult)

Medical considerations/Contraindications

The medical considerations/contraindications included have been selected on the basis of their potential clinical significance (reasons given in parentheses where appropriate)—not necessarily inclusive (» = major clinical significance).

Except under special circumstances, this medication should not be used when the following medical problem exists:

» Hypersensitivity to insulin glulisine

» Hypoglycemia
(use is contraindicated)

Risk-benefit should be considered when the following medical problems exist:

Hepatic function impairment or
Renal function impairment
(studies have shown insulin glulisine requirements may be reduced)

Patient monitoring

The following may be especially important in patient monitoring (other tests may be warranted in some patients, depending on condition; » = major clinical significance):

» Glucose concentrations, blood
(monitoring recommended for all patients with diabetes)

Side/Adverse Effects

The following side/adverse effects have been selected on the basis of their potential clinical significance (possible signs and symptoms in parentheses where appropriate)—not necessarily inclusive:

Those indicating need for medical attention

Incidence more frequent

Hypoglycemia (anxiety; blurred vision; chills; cold sweats; coma; confusion; depression; dizziness; fast heartbeat; headache; increased hunger; nausea; nervousness; nightmares; seizures; shakiness; slurred speech; unusual tiredness or weakness)

Incidence less frequent

Allergy, local (itching, redness, or swelling at injection site); ***allergy, systemic*** (decrease in blood pressure; rapid pulse; shortness of breath; skin rash or itching over the entire body; sweating; wheezing); ***injection site reaction*** (bleeding, blistering, burning, coldness, discoloration of skin; feeling of pressure; hives; infection, inflammation, itching, lumps, numbness, pain, rash, redness, scarring, soreness, stinging, swelling, tenderness, tingling, ulceration, or warmth at site); ***lipodystrophy*** (redistribution or accumulation of body fat); ***pruritus*** (itching skin); ***rash***

Overdose

For specific information on the agent used in the management of insulin glulisine overdose, see the *Glucagon (Systemic)* monograph.

Clinical effects of overdose

The following effects have been selected on the basis of their potential clinical significance (possible signs and symptoms in parentheses where appropriate)—not necessarily inclusive:

Hypoglycemia (anxiety; blurred vision; chills; cold sweats; coma; confusion; cool pale skin; depression; dizziness; fast heartbeat; headache; increased hunger; nausea; nervousness; nightmares; seizures; shakiness; slurred speech; unusual tiredness or weakness)

Treatment of overdose

Specific treatment—

Mild hypoglycemia without neurologic symptoms or loss of consciousness should be treated with immediate ingestion of glucose and adjustments to medication dosage, meal patterns, or exercise.

Severe hypoglycemia including coma, seizures, or other neurologic impairment requires immediate emergency medical assistance. The patient should immediately be given intramuscular or subcutaneous glucagon, or intravenous glucose, and observed because relapse may occur following apparent clinical recovery.

Supportive care—

Patients in whom intentional overdose is confirmed or suspected should be referred for psychiatric consultation.

Patient Consultation

As an aid to patient consultation, refer to *Advice for the Patient, Insulin Glulisine (Systemic)*.

In providing consultation, consider emphasizing the following selected information (» = major clinical significance):

Before using this medication

» Conditions affecting use, especially:
Hypersensitivity to insulin glulisine
Pregnancy—Importance of maintaining proper metabolic glucose control before conception and throughout pregnancy to improve fetal outcome; insulin requirements may change during pregnancy
Breast-feeding—Caution when taking insulin glulisine
Other medications, especially sympatholytics
Other medical problems, especially hypoglycemia

Proper use of this medication

» Carefully selecting and rotating injection sites within the same region, in abdominal wall, thigh, or upper arm.

» Taking insulin glulisine within 15 minutes before the meal or within 20 minutes after starting a meal when used as a mealtime insulin

» Adhering to recommended regimens for diet, exercise, and glucose monitoring

» Proper dosing

Proper storage

Precautions while using this medication

» Regular visits to physician to check progress, especially during the first few weeks of treatment

» *Carefully following special instructions of health care team:*
Discussing use of alcohol and tobacco
Not taking other medications unless discussed with physician
Getting counseling for family members to help the patient with diabetes; also, special counseling for pregnancy planning and contraception
Making travel plans that include readiness for diabetic emergencies and eating meals at the usual times, even with changing time zones

» Preparing for and understanding what to do in case of diabetic emergency; carrying medical history and current medication list and wearing medical identification

» Recognizing symptoms of hypoglycemia: anxiety; behavior change similar to drunkenness; blurred vision; cold sweats; coma; confusion; cool, pale skin; difficulty in concentrating; drowsiness; excessive hunger; fast heartbeat; headache (continuing); nausea; nervousness; nightmares; restless sleep; seizures; shakiness; slurred speech; and unusual tiredness or weakness

» Recognizing what brings on symptoms of hypoglycemia, such as delaying or missing a meal or snack; drinking significant amounts of alcohol; exercising more than usual; having an illness, including vomiting or diarrhea; taking certain medications; or using other antidiabetic medication

» Knowing what to do if symptoms of hypoglycemia occur, such as ingesting a source of glucose (not sucrose) or, if severe, injecting glucagon

» Recognizing symptoms of hyperglycemia and ketoacidosis: blurred vision; drowsiness; dry mouth; flushed, dry skin; fruit-like breath odor; increased urination (frequency and volume); ketones in urine; loss of appetite; somnolence (sleepiness); stomachache, nausea, or vomiting; tiredness; troubled breathing (rapid and deep); unconsciousness; and unusual thirst

» Recognizing what brings on symptoms of hyperglycemia, such as exercising less than usual, having a fever or infection, not taking enough or skipping a dose of antidiabetic medication, or overeating or not following meal plan

» Knowing what to do if symptoms of hyperglycemia occur, such as checking blood glucose and contacting a member of the health care team

Side/adverse effects

Signs of potential side effects, especially hypoglycemia, local allergy, systemic allergy, local reaction at injection site, lipodystrophy, pruritus, or rash

General Dosing Information

The glucose-lowering capability of one unit of insulin glulisine is equal to that of one unit of regular human insulin.

Because of its rapid onset of action and shorter duration of action, insulin glulisine should be given within 15 minutes before, or immediately after a meal.

Because of the short duration of action of insulin glulisine, supplementation with a longer acting insulin or insulin infusion pump therapy should be used to maintain proper glucose control. In addition, insulin glulisine duration of action may vary in different individuals (or sometimes in same individual) and is dependent on injection site, blood supply, temperature, and physical activity.

Any changes in patients' insulin dose should be made cautiously and only under medical supervision. Dosage may need to be altered for changes in insulin strength, manufacturer, type (e.g., regular, NPH, analog), or species (animal, human). Concomitant oral antidiabetic treatment may need to be adjusted.

Adjustment of insulin dosage also may be necessary following a change in meal plan or amount of exercise, or following an acute illness, emotional disturbance, or period of stress.

When used in an external insulin pump for subcutaneous infusion insulin glulisine should not be diluted or mixed with any other insulin.

Based on *in vitro* studies which have shown loss of m-cresol, and insulin degradation, insulin glulisine should not be used beyond 48 hours at 98.6°F (37°C) in infusion sets and reservoirs.

Different types of insulin are sometimes mixed in the same syringe to achieve a more accurate matching of insulin availability to the patient's requirements in a single dose. If insulin glulisine is to be mixed, several factors should be considered:

- Insulin glulisine should not be mixed with insulin preparations other than NPH.
- Although no significant change in total bioavailability or time to peak concentration occurred when mixing insulin glulisine with NPH human insulin immediately before injection, a decrease in the peak concentration of insulin glulisine was demonstrated in healthy volunteers (n = 32) in clinical study.
- If insulin glulisine is mixed with NPH human insulin, insulin glulisine should be drawn into the syringe first and then the mixture should be given immediately after mixing.
- Mixtures should not be administered intravenously.

Parenteral Dosage Forms

INSULIN GLULISINE INJECTION

Usual adult dose

Antidiabetic agent—

Subcutaneous, dosage should be individualized and determined by the physician and based on the patient's needs.

Note: Insulin glulisine should normally be used in regimens that include a longer-acting insulin or basal insulin analog. Insulin glulisine should be given within 15 minutes before a meal or within 20 minutes after starting a meal.

Usual pediatric dose

Safety and efficacy have not been established.

Usual geriatric dose

See *Usual adult dose.*

Strength(s) usually available

U.S.—

100 IU of insulin glulisine per mL (Rx) [*Apidra* (hydrochloric acid; m-cresol; polysorbate 20; sodium chloride; sodium hydroxide; tromethamine; water)].

Packaging and storage

Store between 2 and 8 °C (36 and 46 °F). Protect from light. Protect from freezing. If refrigeration is not possible, insulin glulisine may be stored unrefrigerated, at temperatures below 25 °C (77 °F) and protected from direct heat and light, for up to 28 days.

Insulin exposed to temperatures higher than 98.6°F (37°C) should be discarded.

Incompatibilities

Insulin glulisine should not be mixed with other insulins or with a diluent when used in the pump.

Auxiliary labeling

- Refrigerate.
- Do not freeze.

Caution

Do not use if insulin glulisine has been frozen or if solution has become viscous or cloudy.

Additional information

Insulin glulisine is an aqueous, clear, and colorless solution.

Developed: 07/29/2004

INSULIN HUMAN—See *Insulin (Systemic)*

INSULIN HUMAN, BUFFERED—See *Insulin (Systemic)*

INSULIN LISPRO Systemic

VA CLASSIFICATION (Primary): HS501

Commonly used brand name(s): *Humalog*.

Note: For a listing of dosage forms and brand names by country availability, see *Dosage Forms* section(s).

Category

Antidiabetic agent.

Indications

Accepted

Diabetes mellitus (treatment adjunct)—Insulin lispro is indicated in the treatment of diabetes mellitus for the control of hyperglycemia. Insulin lispro has a more rapid onset and shorter duration of action than regular human insulin and, therefore, in patients with type 1 diabetes, insulin lispro should be used in a regimen that includes a longer acting insulin. In patients with type 2 diabetes, insulin lispro may be used without a longer acting insulin when it is used in combination with a sulfonylurea agent.[1]

Insulin lispro may be used in an external insulin pump. It should not be mixed with any other insulin or diluted when used in the pump.

[1]Not included in Canadian product labeling.

Pharmacology/Pharmacokinetics

Physicochemical characteristics

Source—Analog of human insulin created by reversing amino acids at positions 28 (proline) and 29 (lysine) on the B-chain. Synthesized by recombinant DNA process involving genetically engineered *Escherichia coli.*.

Molecular weight—5808.

pH—7 to 7.8.

Mechanism of action/Effect

Like other types of insulin, the primary activity of insulin lispro is to control the metabolism of glucose. Also, like other types of insulin, insulin lispro acts in muscle and other tissues (except the brain) to increase intracellular transport of glucose and amino acids, promote anabolism, and inhibit protein catabolism. In the liver, insulin lispro promotes conversion of glucose to glycogen or fat, and inhibits gluconeogenesis.

Absorption

The rate of absorption of insulin lispro demonstrates inter- and intraindividual variability and is dependent upon many factors, including the site of injection; temperature of, and blood flow to, the site; and exercise. Insulin lispro was absorbed at a consistently faster rate than regular human insulin in healthy male volunteers given 0.2 USP Insulin Human Units of regular human insulin or insulin lispro at abdominal, deltoid, or femoral sites. Following abdominal administration of insulin lispro, serum drug concentrations were higher and the duration of action slightly shorter than following deltoid or femoral administration.

Bioavailability ranges from 55 to 77% following doses of 0.1 to 0.2 USP Insulin Human Units per kg of body weight.

Distribution

The volume of distribution ranges from 0.26 to 0.36 L per kg.

Biotransformation

Studies have not been done in humans. However, studies in animals indicate that the metabolism of insulin lispro is identical to that of regular human insulin.

Half-life

Elimination—

Intravenous: 26 and 52 minutes following doses of 0.1 and 0.2 USP Insulin Human Units, respectively (identical to that of regular human insulin).

Subcutaneous: 1 hour (versus 1.5 hours for regular human insulin).

Onset of action

Studies in healthy volunteers and patients with diabetes have shown that insulin lispro has a more rapid onset of action than regular human insulin.

Time to peak serum concentration

30 to 90 minutes following subcutaneous doses ranging from 0.1 to 0.4 USP Insulin Human Units per kg of body weight to healthy volunteers. Similar results were seen in patients with type 1 diabetes.

Time to peak effect

Studies in healthy volunteers and patients with diabetes have shown that insulin lispro has an earlier time to peak effect than regular human insulin.

Duration of action

Studies in healthy volunteers and patients with diabetes have shown that insulin lispro has a shorter duration of action than regular human insulin.

Precautions to Consider

Cross-sensitivity and/or related problems

Production of antibodies cross-reactive to human insulin and insulin lispro was observed in patients participating in large clinical trials. During the 12-month trials, the largest increase in antibody concentration to human insulin and insulin lispro was seen in patients new to insulin therapy.

Carcinogenicity

Long-term studies to evaluate the carcinogenic potential of insulin lispro have not been done in animals.

Mutagenicity

No evidence of mutagenicity was found in a series of *in vitro* and *in vivo* studies, including bacterial mutation tests, unscheduled DNA synthesis, mouse lymphoma assay, chromosomal aberration tests, and a micronucleus test.

Pregnancy/Reproduction

Fertility—No evidence of impaired fertility was found in animal studies.

Pregnancy—Studies have not been done in humans. However, women with diabetes must be educated about the necessity of maintaining glycemic control before conception and during pregnancy to improve fetal outcome. Insulin requirements often are decreased during the first trimester and increased during the second and third trimesters.

Studies in pregnant rats and rabbits given doses 4 and 0.3 times, respectively, the average human dose of 40 units per day based on body surface area have not shown that insulin lispro causes adverse effects in the fetus.

FDA Pregnancy Category B.

Breast-feeding

It is not known whether insulin lispro is distributed into breast milk. Women who are breast-feeding may require adjustments in their dosages of insulin lispro, in their meal plans, or in both.

Pediatrics

Studies performed in patients 3 years of age or older have not demonstrated pediatrics-specific problems that would limit the usefulness of insulin lispro in children.

Geriatrics

Studies performed in 338 patients 65 years of age or older (the majority of whom had type 2 diabetes) have not demonstrated geriatrics-specific problems that would limit the usefulness of insulin lispro in the elderly.

Drug interactions and/or related problems

The following drug interactions and/or related problems have been selected on the basis of their potential clinical significance (possible mechanism in parentheses where appropriate)—not necessarily inclusive (» = major clinical significance):

Note: Combinations containing any of the following medications, depending on the amount present, may also interact with this medication.

Antidiabetic agents, oral
(concurrent use may necessitate a decrease in insulin lispro dosage)

Hyperglycemia-causing agents, such as:
Corticosteroids
Estrogens
Isoniazid
Niacin
Oral contraceptives
Phenothiazines
Thyroid hormones
(these medications may cause loss of glycemic control; insulin requirements may be increased)

Hypoglycemia-causing agents, such as:
Alcohol
Angiotensin-converting enzyme (ACE) inhibitors
Monoamine oxidase (MAO) inhibitors, including furazolidone, procarbazine, and selegiline
Octreotide
Salicylates
Sulfonamides
(these medications may change metabolic control of glucose concentrations; insulin requirements may be decreased)

» Sympatholytics, such as beta-adrenergic blocking agents
(sympatholytics may mask some of the symptoms of developing hypoglycemia, making detection of this condition more difficult)

Medical considerations/Contraindications

The medical considerations/contraindications included have been selected on the basis of their potential clinical significance (reasons given in parentheses where appropriate)—not necessarily inclusive (» = major clinical significance).

Except under special circumstances, this medication should not be used when the following medical problem exists:

» Hypoglycemia

Risk-benefit should be considered when the following medical problems exist:

» Diarrhea or
» Vomiting
(may precipitate hypoglycemia; adjustment of insulin and/or insulin lispro dosage may be required)

» Fever or
» Infection
(may precipitate hyperglycemia; adjustment of insulin and/or insulin lispro dosage may be required)

Hepatic function impairment or
Renal function impairment
(studies have shown increased concentrations of circulating insulin in patients with hepatic or renal function impairment; careful glucose monitoring and adjustment of insulin lispro dosage may be necessary)

Hypersensitivity to insulin lispro

» Hypoglycemia-causing conditions, such as:
 Adrenal insufficiency
 Pituitary insufficiency

Patient monitoring

The following may be especially important in patient monitoring (other tests may be warranted in some patients, depending on condition; » = major clinical significance):

» Glucose concentrations, blood and/or urine
 (monitoring essential as a guide to therapeutic efficacy)

» Glycosylated hemoglobin (hemoglobin A_{1c}) determinations
 (periodic monitoring recommended to assess long-term glycemic control)

Side/Adverse Effects

The following side/adverse effects have been selected on the basis of their potential clinical significance (possible signs and symptoms in parentheses where appropriate)—not necessarily inclusive:

Those indicating need for medical attention

Incidence more frequent

Hypoglycemia (anxiety; behavior change similar to drunkenness; blurred vision; cold sweats; coma; confusion; depression; difficulty in concentrating; dizziness or lightheadedness; drowsiness; excessive hunger; fast heartbeat; headache; irritability or abnormal behavior; nervousness; nightmares; restless sleep; seizures; shakiness; slurred speech; tingling in the hands, feet, lips, or tongue)

Note: In patients with type 1 diabetes, the risk of *nocturnal hypoglycemia* is less with insulin lispro than with regular human insulin.

Incidence less frequent or rare

Allergy, local (itching, redness, or swelling at injection site); ***allergy, systemic*** (decrease in blood pressure; rapid pulse; shortness of breath; skin rash or itching over the entire body; sweating; wheezing)—may be life-threatening; ***hypokalemia*** (dryness of mouth; increased thirst; irregular heartbeat; mood or mental changes; muscle cramps or pain; nausea or vomiting; unusual tiredness or weakness; weak pulse); ***lipoatrophy at injection site*** (depression of the skin at injection site); ***lipohypertrophy at injection site*** (thickening of the skin at injection site)

Note: *Local allergic reactions* are usually minor and resolve within a few days to a few weeks. In some cases, the reactions may be related to irritants in a skin cleansing agent or poor injection technique rather than to the medication.

Overdose

For specific information on the agent used in the management of insulin lispro overdose, see the *Glucagon (Systemic)* monograph.

For more information on the management of overdose, **contact a Poison Control Center** (see *Poison Control Center Listing*).

Clinical effects of overdose

The following effects have been selected on the basis of their potential clinical significance (possible signs and symptoms—in parentheses where appropriate)not necessarily inclusive:

Hypoglycemia (anxiety; behavior change similar to drunkenness; blurred vision; cold sweats; coma; confusion; depression; difficulty in concentrating; dizziness or lightheadedness; drowsiness; excessive hunger; fast heartbeat; headache; irritability or abnormal behavior; nervousness; nightmares; restless sleep; seizures; shakiness; slurred speech; tingling in the hands, feet, lips, or tongue)

Treatment of overdose

Specific treatment—

Mild hypoglycemia without neurologic symptoms or loss of consciousness should be treated with immediate ingestion of glucose and adjustments to medication dosage and/or meal plan.

Severe hypoglycemia including coma, seizures, or other neurologic impairment requires immediate emergency medical assistance. The patient should immediately be given intramuscular or subcutaneous glucagon, or intravenous glucose, and observed because relapse may occur following apparent clinical recovery.

Patient Consultation

As an aid to patient consultation, refer to *Advice for the Patient, Insulin Lispro (Systemic)*.

In providing consultation, consider emphasizing the following selected information (» = major clinical significance):

Before using this medication

» Conditions affecting use, especially:
 Hypersensitivity to insulin lispro
 Pregnancy—Importance of maintaining glycemic control to improve fetal outcome; insulin requirements may change during pregnancy
 Breast-feeding—Women who are breast-feeding may require adjustments in their dosages of insulin lispro, in their meal plans, or in both
 Other medications, especially sympatholytics
 Other medical problems, especially adrenal insufficiency; diarrhea; fever; hypoglycemia; infection; pituitary insufficiency; or vomiting

Proper use of this medication

» Carefully reading patient instruction sheet contained in insulin lispro package and understanding:
 How to prepare the medication
 How to inject the medication
 How to use disposable insulin delivery device.
 How to use external insulin pump. How and when to change the infusion set, cartridge adapter, and insulin in the external insulin pump reservoir. How and when to change the insulin lispro 3-mL cartridge.
 How to dispose of syringes, needles, and injection devices

» Carefully selecting and rotating injection sites, following health care professional's recommendations

» Taking insulin lispro within 15 minutes before the meal when used as a mealtime insulin

» Adhering to recommended regimens for diet, exercise, and glucose monitoring

» Proper dosing

» Proper storage

Precautions while using this medication

» Regular visits to physician to check progress, especially during the first few weeks of treatment

» *Carefully following special instructions of health care team:*
 Discussing use of alcohol
 Not taking other medications unless discussed with physician
 Getting counseling for family members to help the patient with diabetes; also, special counseling for pregnancy planning and contraception
 Discussing travel arrangements, including transporting insulin lispro, carrying medical history and extra supplies of insulin lispro and syringes or injection devices, and adjusting dosage if traveling across more than two time zones

» Preparing for and knowing what to do in case of an emergency by carrying medical history and current medication list, wearing medical identification, keeping extra needed medical supplies and quick-acting sugar, and having nonexpired glucagon kit and needles nearby

» Recognizing what brings on symptoms of hypoglycemia, such as using other antidiabetic medication; delaying or missing a meal or snack; exercising more than usual; drinking significant amounts of alcohol; or sickness, such as vomiting or diarrhea

» Recognizing symptoms of hypoglycemia: anxiety; behavior change similar to drunkenness; blurred vision; cold sweats; confusion; depression; difficulty in concentrating; dizziness or lightheadedness; drowsiness; excessive hunger; fast heartbeat; headache; irritability or abnormal behavior; nervousness; nightmares; restless sleep; shakiness; slurred speech; and tingling in the hands, feet, lips, or tongue

» Knowing what to do if symptoms of hypoglycemia occur, such as eating glucose tablets or gel, corn syrup, honey, or sugar cubes; drinking fruit juice, nondiet soft drink, or sugar dissolved in water; or injecting glucagon if symptoms are severe

» Recognizing what brings on symptoms of hyperglycemia, such as not taking enough or skipping a dose of insulin lispro or insulin; overeating or not following meal plan; having a fever or infection; or exercising less than usual

» Recognizing symptoms of hyperglycemia and ketoacidosis: blurred vision; drowsiness; dry mouth; flushed, dry skin; fruit-like breath odor; increased urination (frequency and volume); ketones in urine; loss of appetite; stomachache, nausea, or vomiting; tiredness; troubled breathing (rapid and deep); unconsciousness; and unusual thirst

» Knowing what to do if symptoms of hyperglycemia occur, such as checking blood glucose and contacting a member of the health care team

Side/adverse effects

Signs of potential side effects, especially hypoglycemia, local allergy, systemic allergy, hypokalemia, and lipoatrophy or lipohypertrophy at injection site

General Dosing Information

The glucose-lowering capability of one unit of insulin lispro is equal to that of one unit of regular human insulin. However, patients taking insulin lispro may require a change in dosage from that used with other insulins. If an adjustment is needed, it may occur with the first dose or over a period of several weeks.

Because of the short duration of action of insulin lispro, supplementation with a longer acting insulin may be required to maintain glycemic control, especially in patients with type 1 diabetes except when using an external pump. However, in patients with type 2 diabetes, insulin lispro may be used without a longer-acting insulin when used in combination therapy with sulfonylurea agents.

Insulin lispro 3 times a day before meals plus sulfonylureas improved glycosylated hemoglobin (HbA_{1C}) concentrations to a greater extent than did insulin lispro 3 times a day plus human isophane insulin (NPH insulin) at bedtime or NPH insulin at bedtime plus sulfonylureas.

Changes in insulin strength, type (e.g., analog, NPH, regular), source (beef and pork, human, pork), method of manufacture (naturally occurring, recombinant DNA process), or manufacturer should be made cautiously and only under medical supervision. A change in any of these parameters may require an adjustment of insulin dosage. Adjustment of insulin dosage also may be necessary following a change in meal plan or amount of exercise, or following an acute illness, emotional disturbance, or period of stress.

Different types of insulin are sometimes mixed in the same syringe to achieve a more accurate matching of insulin availability to the patient's requirements in a single dose. If insulin lispro is to be mixed, several factors should be considered:

• Physicochemical changes in the mixture may occur (immediately or over time), resulting in a physiological response to the mixture that differs from the response to the individual insulin preparations. No decrease in absorption rate or in total bioavailability was seen when insulin lispro was mixed with human isophane insulin (NPH insulin) or with human extended insulin zinc suspension (ultralente insulin).

• When insulin lispro is mixed with longer acting insulins, the mixture should be administered within 15 minutes before a meal.

• When it is mixed with a longer acting insulin, insulin lispro should be drawn into the syringe first to prevent clouding by the longer acting insulin. The mixture should be used immediately and should not be administered intravenously.

• The effects of mixing insulin lispro with insulins of animal source or other manufacturers have not been studied.

Insulin lispro should not be diluted or mixed with any other insulin when used in the pump.

External insulin pump

If unexplained hyperglycemia or ketosis occurs during external insulin pump use, prompt identification and correction of the cause is necessary. The patient may require interim therapy with subcutaneous insulin injections.

Parenteral Dosage Forms

INSULIN LISPRO INJECTION

Usual adult and adolescent dose

Antidiabetic agent—

Subcutaneous, dosage must be determined by the physician based on the patient's metabolic needs, eating habits, and other lifestyle variables.

Note: When used as a mealtime insulin, insulin lispro should be administered within fifteen minutes before the meal or immediately after the meal.

Usual pediatric dose

See *Usual adult and adolescent dose.*

Note: To improve accuracy of dosing in pediatric patients, a diluent may be used. See *Preparation of dosage form.*

When used as a mealtime insulin, insulin lispro should be administered within fifteen minutes before the meal or immediately after the meal.

Usual geriatric dose

See *Usual adult and adolescent dose.*

Strength(s) usually available

U.S.—

Note: Insulin lispro is available in 10-mL vials, 1.5-mL cartridges, 3-mL cartridges, and 3-mL disposable insulin delivery devices. The 1.5-mL cartridges may be used with any of the following insulin delivery devices: Becton Dickinson and Company's *B-D® Pen* or Novo NordiskA/S's *NovoPen®*, *NovolinPen®*, or *NovoPen® 1.5*. The 3-mL cartridges are for use in the Owen Mumford, Ltd.'s *Autopen® 3 mL*insulin delivery device. The 3-mL cartridge may be used in the Owen Mumfor, Ltd.'s Autopen® 3 mL insulin delivery device and Disetronic D-Tron® or D-Tron® plus pumps.

100 USP Insulin Human Units per mL (Rx) [*Humalog* (glycerin 16 mg; dibasic sodium phosphate 1.88 mg; *m*-cresol 3.15 mg; zinc oxide content adjusted to provide 0.0197 mg zinc ion; phenol trace; water for injection)].

Canada—

Note: Insulin lispro is available in 10-mL vials, 1.5- and 3-mL cartridges, and 3-mL disposable insulin delivery devices.

100 USP Insulin Human Units per mL (Rx) [*Humalog* (glycerin 16 mg; dibasic sodium phosphate 1.88 mg; *m*-cresol 3.15 mg; zinc ion 0.0197 mg)].

Packaging and storage

Store between 2 and 8 °C (36 and 46 °F). Protect from freezing. If refrigeration is not possible, insulin lispro may be stored unrefrigerated, at temperatures not exceeding 30 °C (86 °F) and protected from direct light, for up to 28 days. Following insertion into a pen, the cartridge and pen should not be refrigerated.

Preparation of dosage form

Insulin lispro (*Humalog®*) may be diluted with Sterile Diluent for *Humalog®*, *Humulin® N*, *Humulin® 50/50*, *Humulin® 70/30*, and *NPH Iletin®* to a concentration of 1:10 (equivalent to U-10) or 1:2 (equivalent to U-50). *Do not dilute insulin lispro when used in an external insulin pump.*

Visually inspect parenteral drug products prior to administration whenever the solution and the container permit. The contents should not be injected if the solution is cloudy, contains particulate matter, is thickened, or is discolored.

Stability

Diluted insulin lispro can be used up to 28 days when stored at 5 °C (41 °F) or for 14 days when stored at 30 °C (86 °F).

A 3-mL cartridge used in the D-Tron® or D-Tron® plus should be discarded after 7 days, even if it still contains insulin lispro. Insulin lispro in the external insulin pump reservoir should be discarded every 48 hours.

Do not use insulin lispro if it has been frozen.

Do not use insulin lispro after its expiration date.

Incompatibilities

Care should be taken when mixing all insulins. A change in the peak action may occur. The American Diabetes Association warns in its Position Statement on Insulin Administration: "On mixing, physiochemical changes in the mixture may occur (either immediately or over time). As a result, the physiological response to the insulin mixture may differ from that of the injection of the insulins separately."

Studies have not been done on the effects of mixing insulin lispro with inulins produced by other manufacturers or insulins of animal source.

Auxiliary labeling

• Refrigerate.
• Do not freeze.

Revised: 11/10/2004
Developed: 08/04/1998

INSULIN ZINC—See *Insulin (Systemic)*

INSULIN ZINC, EXTENDED—See *Insulin (Systemic)*

INSULIN ZINC, EXTENDED, HUMAN—See *Insulin (Systemic)*

INSULIN ZINC, HUMAN—See *Insulin (Systemic)*

INSULIN ZINC, PROMPT—See *Insulin (Systemic)*

INTERFERON ALFA-2A, RECOMBINANT—See *Interferons, Alpha (Systemic)*

INTERFERON ALFA-2B, RECOMBINANT—See *Interferons, Alpha (Systemic), Ribavirin and Interferon Alfa-2b, Recombinant (Systemic)*

INTERFERON ALFACON-1 Systemic

VA CLASSIFICATION (Primary): IM404

Commonly used brand name(s): *Infergen.*

Note: For a listing of dosage forms and brand names by country availability, see *Dosage Forms* section(s).

Category

Biological response modifier.

Indications

Accepted

Hepatitis, chronic, active (treatment)—Recombinant interferon alfacon-1 is indicated in the treatment of chronic hepatitis C virus (HCV) infection associated with anti-HCV serum antibodies and/or HCV RNA, in patients 18 years of age or older who have compensated hepatic disease. In some of these patients, recombinant interferon alfacon-1 reduces serum alanine aminotransferase (ALT [SGPT]) concentrations to normal, reduces serum HCV RNA concentrations to undetectable levels (< 100 copies per mL), and improves liver histology.

Note: Other causes of hepatitis, such as viral hepatitis B or autoimmune hepatitis, should be ruled out prior to therapy with recombinant interferon alfacon-1.

Pharmacology/Pharmacokinetics

Note: Pharmacokinetic data for interferon alfacon-1 are the results of studies in normal, healthy individuals. No pharmacokinetic studies have been conducted in patients with chronic hepatitis C infection.

Physicochemical characteristics

Source—

Synthetic. A protein chain of 166 amino acids produced by a recombinant DNA process involving genetically engineered *Escherichia coli.* The amino acid sequence was derived by comparison of the sequences of several natural interferon alpha subtypes and assigning the most frequently observed amino acid in each corresponding position. Four additional amino acid changes were made to facilitate molecular construction. Interferon alfacon-1 differs from interferon alfa-2 at 20/166 amino acids (88% homology), and is 30% identical to interferon beta, which is closer than any natural alpha interferon subtype.

Following oxidation of recombinant interferon alfacon-1 to its native state, the purification procedure includes sequential passage over a series of chromatography columns.

Chemical Group—Type-I interferon, related to naturally occurring alpha and beta interferons.

Molecular weight—19,434 daltons.

pH—7 ± 0.2.

Mechanism of action/Effect

In general, type-I interferons have antiviral, antiproliferative, and immunomodulatory activities, and regulate the expression of cell surface major histocompatibility antigens (HLA class I and class II) and cytokines. Activities of type-I interferons occur as a result of binding to a cell-surface receptor and stimulation of production of several gene products, including 2′5′ oligoadenylate synthetase (2′5′ OAS) and beta-2 microglobulin.

Time to peak concentration

2′5′ OAS—24 hours.

Beta-2 microglobulin—24 to 36 hours.

Plasma concentrations of interferon alfacon-1 itself after subcutaneous administration are undetectable by either ELISA or inhibition of viral cytopathic effect. However, analysis of the interferon-induced gene products (2′5′ OAS and beta-2 microglobulin) reveals a statistically significant, dose-related increase in the area under the plasma concentration-time curve (AUC) ($p < 0.001$ for all comparisons).

Precautions to Consider

Cross-sensitivity and/or related problems

Patients sensitive to other *Escherichia coli*–derived products or to other alpha interferons may also be sensitive to interferon alfacon-1.

Carcinogenicity

Studies in humans or animals have not been done.

Mutagenicity

Interferon alfacon-1 was not found to be mutagenic in several *in vitro* assays, including the Ames bacterial mutagenicity test, or in an *in vivo* cytogenetic assay in human lymphocytes in the presence or the absence of metabolic activation.

Pregnancy/Reproduction

Fertility—Studies in male and female golden Syrian hamsters at subcutaneous doses as high as 100 mcg per kg of body weight (mcg/kg) given for 70 and 14 days before mating, respectively, and then through mating and to day 7 of pregnancy found no effect on reproductive performance or development of the offspring.

Pregnancy—Interferon alfacon-1 should not be used during pregnancy. If a woman becomes pregnant or plans to become pregnant while taking interferon alfacon-1, she should be informed of the potential hazards to the fetus. Males and females treated with interferon alfacon-1 should be advised to use effective contraception. Adequate and well-controlled studies in humans have not been done.

Studies in golden Syrian hamsters at 135 times the human dose and in cynomologus and rhesus monkeys at 9 to 81 times the human dose (based on body surface area) found embryolethal or abortifacient effects.

FDA Pregnancy Category C.

Breast-feeding

It is not known whether interferon alfacon-1 is distributed into breast milk.

Pediatrics

Safety and efficacy have not been established in patients up to 18 years of age. Use in pediatric patients is not recommended.

Drug interactions and/or related problems

The following drug interactions and/or related problems have been selected on the basis of their potential clinical significance (possible mechanism in parentheses where appropriate)—not necessarily inclusive (» = major clinical significance):

Note: Combinations containing any of the following medications, depending on the amount present, may also interact with this medication.

Blood dyscrasia-causing medications (see *Appendix II*) or
Bone marrow depressants, other (see *Appendix II*)
(leukopenic and/or thrombocytopenic effects of interferon alfacon-1 may be increased)

Medications metabolized by the cytochrome P450 enzyme system
(patients should be monitored closely for changes in concentrations of these medications during concurrent use with interferon alfacon-1)

Laboratory value alterations

The following have been selected on the basis of their potential clinical significance (possible effect in parentheses where appropriate)—not necessarily inclusive (» = major clinical significance).

With physiology/laboratory test values

Hemoglobin and
Hematocrit
(concentrations may be decreased)

Leukocyte counts (including neutrophils) and
Platelet counts
(counts may be decreased)

Thyroid function tests
(thyroxine [T_4] concentrations may be decreased and thyroid-stimulating hormone [TSH] concentrations may be increased, indicating possible hypothyroidism; thyroid supplements may be necessary in some patients)

Triglycerides
(serum concentrations may be increased to as much as three times pretreatment values; reversible upon withdrawal)

Medical considerations/Contraindications

The medical considerations/contraindications included have been selected on the basis of their potential clinical significance (reasons given in parentheses where appropriate)—not necessarily inclusive (» = major clinical significance).

Except under special circumstances, this medication should not be used when the following medical problems exist:

» Autoimmune hepatitis or
» Psychiatric disorders, severe, or history of
(use is not recommended)

Risk-benefit should be considered when the following medical problems exist:

» Autoimmune disease, history of
(caution is recommended because exacerbation of autoimmune disease has been reported with type-1 interferon therapy; use is not recommended in patients with autoimmune hepatitis)

» Bone marrow depression
(interferon alfacon-1 may cause leukopenia, which may be severe, and/or thrombocytopenia)

» Cardiac disease
(alpha interferons may cause hypertension, supraventricular arrhythmias, chest pain, and myocardial infarction)

» Endocrine disorders, history of
(interferon alfacon-1 may cause hypothyroidism, sometimes requiring administration of thyroid supplements)

» Hepatic disease, decompensated
(studies on the use of interferon alfacon-1 have not been done; use of interferon alfacon-1 is not recommended in patients with decompensated hepatic disease; if symptoms [ascites, coagulopathy, decreased serum albumin, jaundice] occur, interferon alfacon-1 therapy should be discontinued)

Immunosuppression, such as:
Transplantation
(caution is recommended)

» Mental depression, history of
(interferon alfacon-1 may cause mental depression, which may be severe and include suicidal thoughts or attempts)

» Sensitivity to interferon alfacon-1

Patient monitoring

The following may be especially important in patient monitoring (other tests may be warranted in some patients, depending on condition; » = major clinical significance):

» Absolute neutrophil count (ANC) and
» Platelet counts
(counts should be monitored prior to initiation of therapy, 2 weeks after initiation of therapy, and at periodic intervals during the 24 weeks of therapy, at the discretion of the physician)

» Albumin and
» Bilirubin and
» Creatinine and
» Hemoglobin and
» Thyroid-stimulating hormone (TSH) and
» Thyroxine (T_4)
(serum concentrations should be monitored prior to initiation of therapy, 2 weeks after initiation of therapy, and at periodic intervals during the 24 weeks of therapy, at the discretion of the physician)

Blood pressure measurements
(recommended at periodic intervals)

Electrocardiogram (ECG)
(recommended prior to initiation of therapy and at periodic intervals during therapy in patients with cardiac disease or advanced malignancy)

Monitoring for signs and symptoms of anaphylaxis
(recommended during and for at least 2 hours after administration)

Neuropsychiatric monitoring
(recommended especially in patients receiving high doses of alpha interferons)

Triglycerides
(serum concentrations should be monitored at periodic intervals during therapy)

Side/Adverse Effects

Note: Development of positive binding antibodies has been reported; the titer of neutralizing antibodies has not been measured. The response rate (as measured by serum alanine aminotransferase [ALT (SGPT)]) in hepatitis C was similar in patients who developed binding antibodies to those who did not. The most frequently observed time to first antibody response was week 16 of interferon therapy.

The following side/adverse effects have been selected on the basis of their potential clinical significance (possible signs and symptoms in parentheses where appropriate)—not necessarily inclusive:

Those indicating need for medical attention

Incidence more frequent

Anxiety; hematologic effects (leukopenia; thrombocytopenia); ***injection erythema*** (redness at site of injection); ***neurotoxicity*** (confusion; mental depression; nervousness; trouble in sleeping; trouble in thinking or concentrating)

Note: Depression may include suicidal ideation or suicide attempt. All patients should be monitored for evidence of depression. It is recommended that interferon alfacon-1 therapy be discontinued if severe mental depression, suicidal ideation, or other severe psychiatric disorders occur.

Incidence less frequent

Cardiovascular effects (chest pain; irregular heartbeat); ***hypoesthesia or paresthesia*** (numbness or tingling of fingers, toes, or face)

Incidence rare

Abnormality or loss of vision; allergic reaction (skin rash, hives, or itching); ***hypothyroidism***—usually asymptomatic

Those indicating need for medical attention only if they continue or are bothersome

Incidence more frequent

Abdominal pain; anorexia (decreased appetite); ***coughing; diarrhea; dizziness; dyspepsia*** (heartburn; indigestion); ***flu-like syndrome*** (aching muscles; fever and chills; headache; general feeling of discomfort or illness; pain in back or joints; unusual tiredness or weakness); ***nausea or vomiting; pharyngitis*** (sore throat)

Note: Although fever may be part of the flu-like syndrome caused by interferon alfacon-1, if persistent fever occurs other possible causes should be ruled out.

Those not indicating need for medical attention

Incidence less frequent

Alopecia (hair loss)

Overdose

For more information on the management of overdose or unintentional ingestion, **contact a Poison Control Center** (see *Poison Control Center Listing*).

Clinical effects of overdose

One patient enrolled in a phase I advanced malignancy clinical trial received 150 mcg interferon alfacon-1 (10 times the prescribed dosage) for 3 days. The patient experienced a mild increase in anorexia, chills, fever, and myalgia; increases in alanine aminotransferase (ALT [SGPT]), aspartate aminotransferase (AST [SGOT]), and lactate dehydrogenase (LDH) were reported. These laboratory values returned to normal or to the patient's baseline values within 30 days.

Treatment of overdose

Supportive care—Patients in whom intentional overdose is confirmed or suspected should be referred for psychiatric consultation.

Patient Consultation

In providing consultation, consider emphasizing the following selected information (» = major clinical significance):

Before using this medication

» Conditions affecting use, especially:
Sensitivity to interferon alfacon-1, other alpha interferons, or *Escherichia coli* –derived products
Pregnancy—Use is not recommended; contraception is recommended for both males and females receiving interferon alfacon-1 therapy
Use in children—Use is not recommended
Other medical problems, especially a history of autoimmune disease, endocrine disorders, mental depression, or psychiatric disorders; autoimmune hepatitis; bone marrow depression; cardiac disease; or decompensated hepatic disease

Proper use of this medication

» Compliance with therapy
» Reading patient directions carefully with regard to:
—Preparation of the injection
—Use of disposable syringes
—Proper administration technique
—Stability of the injection
Injecting at the same time each day

» Proper dosing
Missed dose: Checking with physician if dose is missed by more than a few hours
» Proper storage

Precautions while using this medication
» Importance of close monitoring by the physician
» Not changing brands of interferon without consulting with physician because of differences in dosage
» Frequency of fever and flu-like symptoms
» Checking with physician immediately if signs of mental depression, especially suicidal thoughts, occur
» Checking with physician if blurred vision or loss of visual field occurs

Side/adverse effects
Signs of potential side effects, especially anxiety, hematologic effects, injection erythema, neurotoxicity, cardiovascular effects, hypoesthesia or paresthesia, abnormality or loss of vision, allergic reaction, or hypothyroidism
Possibility of some hair loss

General Dosing Information

Patients receiving interferon alfacon-1 should be under the supervision of a physician experienced in immunomodulatory therapy.

If severe adverse effects occur, temporary withdrawal of interferon alfacon-1 is recommended. Dose reduction may be necessary if the adverse effect is intolerable. If the adverse effect does not become tolerable, the medication should be discontinued.

Dosage reduction may be necessary if leukopenia, especially granulocytopenia, is severe. If the absolute neutrophil count (ANC) decreases to less than 500 $\times 10^6$ per liter, it is recommended that interferon alfacon-1 therapy be withheld.

It is recommended that interferon alfacon-1 therapy be withheld if platelet counts fall to less than 50 $\times 10^9$ per liter.

If symptoms of hepatic decompensation (ascites, coagulopathy, decreased serum albumin, jaundice) occur, interferon alfacon-1 therapy should be discontinued.

If a hypersensitivity reaction (e.g., anaphylaxis, angioedema, bronchodilation, urticaria) occurs, it is recommended that interferon alfacon-1 therapy be discontinued immediately and appropriate medical treatment begun.

If the patient complains of any loss of visual acuity or disturbances in visual field, an eye examination should be performed to detect possible retinal hemorrhage, cotton wool spots, or retinal artery or vein obstruction.

Parenteral Dosage Forms

INTERFERON ALFACON-1 RECOMBINANT INJECTION

Usual adult dose
Hepatitis C, chronic, active—
Subcutaneous, 9 mcg per dose three times per week, at intervals of at least forty-eight hours for twenty-four weeks.

Note: Patients who relapse or do not respond, and who tolerated the initial dose, may be treated with 15 mcg per dose three times per week for six months.

If a severe adverse effect occurs, interferon alfacon-1 should be withheld temporarily. If the adverse effect is intolerable, dose reduction to 7.5 mcg may be necessary. Further decreases in dose are possible, but may result in decreased efficacy. If the adverse effect does not become tolerable, the medication should be discontinued.

In patients subsequently treated at a dose of 15 mcg, dose reductions in 3-mcg increments have been found to be necessary in 33% of patients.

Usual pediatric dose
Safety and efficacy have not been established in patients younger than 18 years of age. Use is not recommended.

Strength(s) usually available
U.S.—
9 mcg per 0.3 mL (Rx) [*Infergen* (sodium chloride 5.9 mg per mL)].
15 mcg per 0.5 mL (Rx) [*Infergen* (sodium chloride 5.9 mg per mL)].

Packaging and storage
Store between 2 and 8 °C (36 and 46 °F). Protect from freezing.

Note: Interferon alfacon-1 injection may be allowed to reach room temperature just prior to administration.

Stability
Any unused portion of the contents of a vial should be discarded.

Note
Do not shake.

Interferon alfacon-1 and interferon alfa-2a, -2b, -n1, and -n3 are not interchangeable.

Revised: 03/20/1998

INTERFERON ALFA-N1 (LNS)—See *Interferons, Alpha (Systemic)*

INTERFERON ALFA-N3—See *Interferons, Alpha (Systemic)*

INTERFERON, BETA-1A Systemic

VA CLASSIFICATION (Primary): CN900; IM409

Commonly used brand name(s): *Avonex; Rebif.*

Note: For a listing of dosage forms and brand names by country availability, see *Dosage Forms* section(s).

Category

Multiple sclerosis (MS) therapy agent; Biological response modifier.

Indications

Note: Bracketed information in the *Indications* section refers to uses that are not included in U.S. product labeling.

Accepted
Multiple sclerosis, relapsing-remitting (treatment)—Interferon beta-1a is indicated for treatment of relapsing forms of multiple sclerosis (MS) to slow the accumulation of physical disability and decrease the frequency of clinical exacerbations. The safety and efficacy in patients with chronic progressive MS have not been evaluated.

[Condyloma acuminatum (treatment)]—Interferon beta-1a is indicated for treatment of condyloma acuminatum to promote shrinkage of lesions.

Pharmacology/Pharmacokinetics

Physicochemical characteristics
Source—Synthetic. Interferon beta-1a is a 166 amino acid glycoprotein produced by recombinant DNA techniques. It is produced by mammalian cells (Chinese hamster ovary cells) into which the human interferon beta gene has been introduced. The amino acid sequence is identical to that of human interferon beta.

Chemical Group—Interferons are a family of naturally occurring proteins and glycoproteins produced by eukaryotic cells in response to viral infection and other biological inducers. Interferon beta, one member of this family, is produced by various cell types including fibroblasts and macrophages. Natural interferon beta and interferon beta-1a are glycosylated, with each containing a single *N*-linked complex carbohydrate moiety. Glycosylation of other proteins is known to affect their stability, activity, biodistribution, and half-life in blood. However, the effects of glycosylation of interferon beta on these properties have not been fully defined.

Molecular weight—Approximately 22,500 daltons.

pH—7.3 (reconstituted injection).

Specific activity—

Avonex: 200 million international units (IU) of antiviral activity per mg. The unit measurement is derived using the World Health Organization (WHO) natural interferon beta standard, Second International Standard for Interferon, Human Fibroblast (Gb-23-902-531)

Rebif: 270 million IU of antiviral activity per mg. The unit measurement is derived using an in-house natural hIFN-β National Institutes of Health (NIH) standard that is obtained from human fibroblasts (BILS 11), which has been calibrated against the NIH natural hIFN-β standard (GB 23–902–531).

Mechanism of action/Effect
Interferons are cytokines that mediate antiviral, antiproliferative, and immunomodulatory activities in response to viral infection and other biological inducers. Three major classes have been identified: alpha, beta, and gamma. Interferons alpha and beta form the Type 1 class

of interferons, and interferon gamma is a Type 2 interferon; these interferons have overlapping yet distinct biologic activities.

Interferon beta-1a exerts its biological effects by binding to specific receptors on the surface of human cells. This binding initiates a complex cascade of intracellular events that leads to the expression of numerous interferon-induced gene products and markers including 2′,5′-oligoadenylate synthetase, beta$_2$-microglobulin, and neopterin. The specific interferon-induced proteins and mechanisms by which interferon beta-1a exerts its effects in MS have not been fully defined.

Biological response markers (e.g., neopterin and beta$_2$-microglobulin) are induced by interferon beta-1a following parenteral doses of 15 to 75 mcg in both healthy subjects and treated patients. Concentrations of these markers increase within 12 hours of dosing, and remain elevated for at least 4 days. Peak biological response marker concentrations typically are observed 48 hours after dosing. The relationship of serum interferon beta-1a concentrations or of the concentrations of these induced biological response markers to the mechanisms by which interferon beta-1a exerts its effects in MS is unknown.

Pharmacokinetics

Pharmacokinetic information on patients with multiple sclerosis (MS) has not been evaluated. Serum concentrations of interferon beta-1a, as measured by its antiviral activity, are only slightly above detectable limits following a 30 mcg intramuscular dose, but increase with higher doses. Pharmacokinetic and pharmacodynamic profiles in healthy subjects following doses of 30 to 75 mcg have been determined.

Half-life

Elimination—

10 hours, following a 60-mcg dose administered intramuscularly.

8.6 hours, following a 60-mcg dose administered subcutaneously.

Time to peak concentration

9.8 (range, 3 to 15) hours following a 60-mcg dose administered intramuscularly.

7.8 hours (range, 3 to 18 hours) following a 60-mcg dose administered subcutaneously.

Note: Serum concentrations of interferon beta-1a may be sustained after its intramuscular administration due to prolonged absorption from the injection site.

Peak serum concentration

45 international units (IU) per mL following a 60-mcg dose administered intramuscularly.

30 IU per mL following a 60-mcg dose administered subcutaneously.

Systemic exposure, as determined by peak serum concentrations and area under the serum concentration-time curve (AUC) values, is greater following intramuscular than following subcutaneous administration.

Precautions to Consider

Carcinogenicity

No carcinogenicity data are available for interferon beta-1a in animals or humans.

Mutagenicity

Interferon beta-1a was not mutagenic in the Ames bacterial test or in an *in vitro* cytogenetic assay in human lymphocytes in the presence and absence of metabolic activation; these assays are designed to detect agents that interact directly with and cause damage to cellular DNA. Interferon beta-1a is a glycosylated protein that does not directly bind to DNA.

Pregnancy/Reproduction

Fertility—No studies have been conducted in healthy women or women with MS. It is not known if interferon beta-1a can affect human reproductive capacity.

Menstrual irregularities were observed in monkeys receiving interferon beta at a dose 100 times the recommended weekly human dose, based upon a body surface area comparison; anovulation and decreased serum progesterone concentrations also occurred transiently in some animals. These effects were reversible upon discontinuation of interferon beta treatment. Monkeys receiving interferon beta at a dose two times the recommended weekly human dose exhibited no changes in cycle duration or ovulation. In the placebo-controlled premarketing clinical trial, 6% of patients receiving placebo and 5% of patients receiving interferon beta-1a reported menstrual disorders. It is not known if, or for how long, menstrual irregularities will persist in women following treatment.

Pregnancy—Adequate and well-controlled studies have not been done in humans.

If a woman becomes pregnant or plans to become pregnant, it is recommended that interferon beta-1a therapy be discontinued due to potential risks to the fetus. If a woman becomes pregnant while taking interferon beta-1a, the physician is encouraged to enroll her in a manufacturer's pregnancy registry by calling 1-800-456-2255.

Studies in pregnant monkeys receiving 100 times the recommended weekly human dose, based on a body surface comparison, revealed no teratogenic or other adverse effects on fetal development; however, abortifacient activity was evident following administration of three to five doses. No abortifacient activity was seen in monkeys receiving two times the recommended weekly human dose, based on a body surface comparison. Although no teratogenic effects were demonstrated in these studies, it is not known if such effects would occur in humans.

FDA Pregnancy Category C.

Breast-feeding

It is not known whether interferon beta-1a is distributed into human breast milk. However, because of the potential for serious adverse reactions in nursing infants, discontinuation of interferon beta-1a or discontinuation of breast-feeding is recommended.

Pediatrics

Appropriate studies on the relationship of age to the effects of interferon beta-1a have not been performed in children up to 18 years of age. Safety and efficacy have not been established.

Geriatrics

No information is available on the relationship of age to the effects of interferon beta-1a in geriatric patients. In general, dose selection for an elderly patient should be cautious, usually starting at the low end of the dose range, reflecting the greater frequency of decreased hepatic, renal or cardiac function, and of concomitant disease or other drug therapy.

Drug interactions and/or related problems

The following drug interactions and/or related problems have been selected on the basis of their potential clinical significance (possible mechanism in parentheses where appropriate)—not necessarily inclusive (» = major clinical significance):

Note: Studies designed to evaluate drug interactions with interferon beta-1a have not been conducted. However, treatment of exacerbations with corticosteroids or ACTH, and concomitant administration of antidepressants and/or oral contraceptives to some patients during the placebo-controlled premarketing clinical trial did not result in unexpected adverse effects.

Other interferons have been shown to reduce cytochrome P450 oxidase-mediated drug metabolism. Formal studies in humans have not been conducted, but hepatic microsomes isolated from interferon beta-1a–treated monkeys showed no influence on hepatic cytochrome P450 enzyme-mediated metabolic activity.

Combinations containing any of the following medications, depending on the amount present, may also interact with this medication.

» Alcohol or

» Hepatotoxic drugs (See *Appendix II*)

(potential risk of hepatic injury should be considered prior to concomitant use or when adding new agent to regimen that includes interferon beta-1a)

» Myelosuppressive agents

(as with all interferon products, the potential for additive myelosuppressant effects exists)

Laboratory value alterations

The following have been selected on the basis of their potential clinical significance (possible effect in parentheses where appropriate)—not necessarily inclusive (» = major clinical significance).

With physiology/laboratory test values

Aspartate aminotransferase (AST [SGOT]) values

(during the placebo-controlled premarketing clinical trial, 3% of patients receiving interferon beta-1a had values greater than or equal to three times the upper limits of normal, as compared with 1% of the patients receiving placebo)

Eosinophil counts

(during the placebo-controlled premarketing clinical trial, 5% of patients receiving interferon beta-1a had counts $\leq$ 10%, as compared with 4% of patients receiving placebo)

Hematocrit

(during the placebo-controlled premarketing clinical trial, 3% of patients receiving interferon beta-1a had hematocrits $\leq$ 37% (males) and $\leq$ 32% (females), as compared with 1% of patients receiving placebo)

Hepatic transaminases, especially SGPT serum

(may be elevated; dose reduction should be considered if SGPT rises above 4 times the upper limit; dose may be gradually re-escalated when enzyme levels have normalized; post-marketing reports of asymptomatic elevation of hepatic transaminases and in some patients has recurred upon rechallenge with interferon beta-1a)

Serum neutralizing activity
(during the placebo-controlled premarketing clinical trial, 24% of patients treated with interferon beta-1a were found to have serum neutralizing activity at one or more time points tested; 15% of these patients tested positive for serum neutralizing activity at a level at which no placebo patient tested positive)

Medical considerations/Contraindications

The medical considerations/contraindications included have been selected on the basis of their potential clinical significance (reasons given in parentheses where appropriate)—not necessarily inclusive (» = major clinical significance).

Except under special circumstances, this medication should not be used when the following medical problem exists:

» Hypersensitivity to natural or recombinant interferon, human albumin, or any other component of the formulation

Risk-benefit should be considered when the following medical problems exist:

Cardiac disease, such as:
Anginaor
Arrhythmiasor
Congestive heart failure
(symptoms of influenza-like syndrome resulting from interferon beta-1a therapy may be stressful to patients with severe cardiac conditions)

» Depression, mental, especially with suicidal ideation or
» Psychiatric disorders, pre-existing, including
Psychosis or
» Other mood disorders
(condition may be exacerbated; patients should be monitored carefully; cessation of treatment with interferon beta-1a should be considered if patient develops depression or other severe psychiatric symptoms; postmarketing reports of these conditions; some of these patients improved upon cessation of interferon beta-1a dosing)

» Alcohol abuse or
» Elevated serum SGPT (greater than 2.5 times ULN) or
» Liver disease, active, or
» Significant liver disease, history of
(should be initiated with caution in these patients; treatment should be stopped if jaundice or other clinical symptoms of liver dysfunction appear)

» Seizure disorder
(condition may be exacerbated, although causal relationship to medication is not proven)

Patient monitoring

The following may be especially important in patient monitoring (other tests may be warranted in some patients, depending on condition; » = major clinical significance):

Blood chemistry values, including liver function tests
(recommended at periodic intervals during treatment)

Depression, especially suicidal ideation

Hepatic injury
(severe hepatic injury, including cases of hepatic failure, have been reported rarely; patients should be monitored for signs of hepatic injury)

Platelet counts and
White blood cell counts, complete and differential
(recommended at periodic intervals [1, 3, and 6 months] during treatment)

Note: Patients with myelosuppression may require more intensive monitoring of complete blood cell counts, with differential and platelet counts.

Thyroid function tests
(recommended every 6 months in patients with a history of thyroid dysfunction or as clinically indicated.)

Side/Adverse Effects

The lyophilized vial of *Avonex* contains albumin, a derivative of human blood. Based on effective donor screening and product manufacturing processes, it carries an extremely remote risk for transmission of viral diseases. A theoretical risk for transmission of Creutzfeldt-Jakob disease (CJD) also is considered extremely remote. No cases of transmission of viral diseases or CJD have been identified for albumin.

The following side/adverse effects have been selected on the basis of their potential clinical significance (possible signs and symptoms in parentheses where appropriate)—not necessarily inclusive:

Those indicating need for medical attention

Incidence more frequent

Anemia (unusual bleeding or bruising; unusual tiredness or weakness); ***asthenia*** (unusual tiredness or weakness); ***diarrhea; infection*** (fever; chills); ***influenza-like syndrome including arthralgia*** (joint pain); ***chills; fever; headache; and myalgia*** (muscle aches); ***nausea; pain***

Incidence less frequent

Abdominal pain; ataxia (clumsiness or unsteadiness); ***chest pain; decreased hearing; dizziness; dyspnea*** (troubled breathing); ***hypersensitivity reaction*** (coughing; difficulty in swallowing; hives or itching; swelling of face, lips, or eyelids; wheezing or difficulty in breathing); ***injection-site reactions*** (redness; swelling; tenderness); ***leukopenia*** (black, tarry stools; chest pain; chills; cough; fever; painful or difficult urination; shortness of breath; sore throat; sores, ulcers, or white spots on lips or in mouth; swollen glands; unusual bleeding or bruising; unusual tiredness or weakness); ***mental depression, especially with suicidal ideation*** (mood changes, especially with thoughts of suicide); ***muscle spasms; nevi*** (skin lesions); ***ovarian cyst*** (pelvic discomfort, aching, or heaviness); ***seizures; speech problems; syncope*** (fainting); ***upper respiratory infection*** (runny or stuffy nose; sneezing; sore throat); ***urticaria*** (hives or itching); ***vaginitis*** (pain or discharge from the vagina); ***vasodilation*** (flushing)

Note: Most injection site reactions are mild to moderate. Rare cases of skin ulceration and/or necrosis at the injection site have been reported with long term treatment.

Incidence rare

Anorexia (loss of appetite); ***herpes simplex*** (painful cold sores or blisters on lips, nose, eyes, or genitals); ***herpes zoster*** (painful blisters on trunk of body)—also known as "shingles"; ***malaise*** (general feeling of discomfort or illness); ***otitis media*** (earache); ***sinusitis*** (headache; stuffy nose)

Incidence not determined—Observed during clinical practice; estimates of frequency can not be determined

Anaphylaxis (cough; difficulty swallowing; dizziness; fast heartbeat; hives; itching, puffiness or swelling of the eyelids or around the eyes, face, lips or tongue; shortness of breath; skin rash; tightness in chest; unusual tiredness or weakness; wheezing); ***autoimmune hepatitis*** (dark urine; general tiredness and weakness; light-colored stools; nausea and vomiting; upper right abdominal pain; yellow eyes and skin); ***cardiomyopathy*** (chest discomfort or pain; difficulty breathing; dizziness; faintness; fast irregular or pounding heartbeat; shortness of breath; swelling of feet or lower legs; troubled breathing; unusual tiredness or weakness); ***congestive heart failure*** (chest pain; decreased urine output; dilated neck veins; extreme fatigue; irregular breathing; irregular heartbeat; shortness of breath; swelling of face, fingers, feet, or lower legs; tightness in chest; troubled breathing; weight gain; wheezing); ***hepatic failure*** (headache; stomach pain; continuing vomiting; dark-colored urine; general feeling of tiredness or weakness; light-colored stools; yellow eyes or skin); ***hepatic injury*** (pruritus; dark urine; persistent anorexia; yellow eyes or skin; influenza (flu)-like symptoms; right upper quadrant tenderness); ***hyperthyroidism*** (nervousness; sensitivity to heat; sweating; trouble sleeping; weight loss); ***hypothyroidism*** (constipation; depressed mood; dry skin and hair; feeling cold; hair loss; hoarseness or husky voice; muscle cramps and stiffness; slowed heartbeat; weight gain; unusual tiredness or weakness); ***idiopathic thrombocytopenia*** (unusual bleeding or bruising; bloody nose; heavier menstrual periods; pinpoint red spots on skin; black, tarry stools; blood in urine; black, tarry stools; unusual tiredness or weakness; fever; skin rash); ***orolingual edema*** (swelling of the mouth or throat; tightness in throat; trouble breathing); ***pancytopenia*** (high fever; chills; unexplained bleeding or bruising; bloody, black, or tarry stools; pale skin; unusual tiredness or weakness; cough; shortness of breath; sores, ulcers, or white spots on lips or in mouth; swollen glands); ***psychiatric disorders*** (mental depression; confusion; mood or other mental changes); ***seizures*** (convulsions; muscle spasm or jerking of all extremities; sudden loss of consciousness; loss of bladder control); ***skin rash; thrombocytopenia*** (black, tarry stools; bleeding gums; blood in urine or stools; pinpoint red spots on skin; unusual bleeding or bruising); ***vesicular rash*** (redness, blistering, peeling, or loosening of the skin)

Those indicating need for medical attention only if they continue or are bothersome

Incidence more frequent

Dyspepsia (heartburn; acid indigestion; sour stomach)

Incidence less frequent
Alopecia (hair loss); *insomnia* (trouble in sleeping)

Overdose

For information on the management of interferon beta-1a overdose, **contact a Poison Control Center** (see *Poison Control Center Listing*).

Patient Consultation

As an aid to patient consultation, refer to *Advice for the Patient, Interferon Beta-1a (Systemic).*

In providing consultation, consider emphasizing the following selected information (» = major clinical significance):

Before using this medication

» Conditions affecting use, especially:
Hypersensitivity to natural or recombinant interferon beta or albumin human
Pregnancy—Potential abortifacient effects; if pregnancy occurs, recommended discontinuation of interferon beta-1a due to potential risks to fetus
Breast-feeding—Not recommended due to potential serious adverse effects in the nursing infant
Other medications, especially alcohol, hepatotoxic drugs, or myelosuppressive agents and agents that are largely dependent on the hepatic cytochrome P450 system for clearance, such as anticonvulsants and some classes of antidepressants
Other medical problems, especially active liver disease, alcohol abuse, elevated serum SGPT, history of significant liver disease, hypersensitivity to natural or recombinant interferon, human albumin or any other component of the formulation, mental depression with suicidal ideation, other mood disorders, pre-existing psychiatric disorders including psychosis, and seizure disorder

Proper use of this medication

» Proper administration:
Importance of aseptic technique
Importance of training patient or caregiver in administration of intramuscular and subcutaneous injections
Importance of proper disposal of syringes and needles
» Proper dosing
Missed dose: Using as soon as remembered; the next injection should be scheduled at least 48 hours later
» Proper storage

Precautions while using this medication

» Importance of contacting physician immediately if signs and symptoms of liver injury or failure occur

Avoiding the use of alcohol due to the potential for serious liver problems

Checking with physician if signs or symptoms of depression or other psychiatric disorders including psychosis develop.

Side/adverse effects

Signs of potential side effects, especially anemia; asthenia; diarrhea; infection; influenza-like syndrome, including arthralgia, chills, fever, headache, and myalgia; nausea; pain; abdominal pain; ataxia; chest pain; decreased hearing; dizziness; dyspnea; hypersensitivity reaction; injection site reactions; leukopenia, mental depression, especially with suicidal ideation; muscle spasms; nevi; ovarian cyst; seizures; speech problems; syncope; upper respiratory infection; urticaria; vaginitis; vasodilation; anorexia; herpes simplex; herpes zoster; malaise; otitis media; and sinusitis

Signs of potential side effects observed during clinical practice, especially anaphylaxis, autoimmune hepatitis, cardiomyopathy, congestive heart failure, hepatic injury, hyperthyroidism, hypothyroidism, idiopathic thrombocytopenia, orolingual edema, pancytopenia, psychiatric disorders, seizures, skin rash, thrombocytopenia, and vesicular rash

General Dosing Information

For treatment of condyloma acuminatum, interferon beta-1a is best suited for patients with fewer than 9 lesions and who have failed other treatment. In the case of patients with 9 or more lesions, if the first treatment is successful, the remaining lesions could be treated with a second course of therapy. Interferon beta-1a should also be considered for patients for whom the side effects of other treatments (e.g., scarring) are of concern.

Interferon beta-1a is intended for use under the guidance and supervision of a physician. If it is determined that interferon beta-1a can be used outside of the physician's office, the person who will be administering the injections should be instructed in proper aseptic technique for reconstitution and injection, and in proper disposal of syringes and needles. Patients should also be advised to rotate sites for subcutaneous injections.If the patient is to self-administer interferon beta-1a, the physical ability of that patient to self-inject intramuscularly should be assessed. The first injection should be performed under the supervision of a qualified health care professional.

Concurrent use of analgesics and/or antipyretics may help ameliorate flu-like symptoms on treatment days.

For condyloma, all injections should be administered by a qualified health care professional.

For treatment of adverse effects

Recommended treatment consists of the following:

- Systemic acetaminophen may lessen the impact of influenza-like symptoms.
- An anesthetic cream such as lidocaine-prilocaine may lessen the pain of intralesional injections for condyloma acuminata

Parenteral Dosage Forms

INTERFERON BETA-1a FOR INJECTION

Usual adult dose

Multiple sclerosis, relapsing-remitting—
Avonex: Intramuscular, 30 mcg once a week.
Rebif: Subcutaneous, 22 mcg 3 times per week or 44 mcg 3 times per week. Dose should be administered at the same time (preferably late afternoon or evening) on the same three days (e.g., Monday, Wednesday, and Friday) at least 48 hours apart each week. Patients should be started at 20% of the prescribed dose three times per week and increased over a four week period to the targeted dose according to the following table:

	Recommended titration (% of final dose)	Titration dose for Rebif® 22 mcg	Titration dose for Rebif® 44 mcg	Injection volume mL
Weeks 1 to 2	20%	4.4 mcg	8.8 mcg	0.1 mL
Weeks 3 to 4	50%	11 mcg	22 mcg	0.25 mL
Weeks 5+	100%	22 mcg	44 mcg	0.5 mL

Note: Patients with leukopenia or elevated liver function tests may necessitate dose reductions of 20 to 50% until toxicity is resolved.

Condyloma acuminatum—
Rebif: Intra- or peri-lesional, 3.67 mcg (1 million IU) per lesion 3 times per week for 3 weeks

Usual adult prescribing limits

Safety of doses higher than 44 mcg subcutaneously 3 times per week have not been adequately evaluated. Maximum amount of interferon alfa-1a that can be safely administered has not been determined.

Usual pediatric dose

Safety and efficacy in children up to 18 years of age have not been established.

Strength(s) usually available

U.S.—
30 mcg prefilled syringe (Rx) [*Avonex* (albumin-free formulation; 0.79 mg sodium acetate trihydrate; 0.25 mg glacial acetic acid; 15.8 mg arginine hydrochloride; 0.025 polysorbate 20; water for injection)].
Note: *The prefilled syringe cap contains dry natural rubber.*
33 mcg (6.6 million International Units [IU]) per single-use vial (Rx) [*Avonex* (diluent: Sterile Water for Injection USP; Albumin Human USP 16.5 mg; Sodium Chloride USP 6.4 mg; Dibasic Sodium Phosphate USP 6.3 mg; Monobasic Sodium Phosphate USP 1.3 mg)].
22 mcg (6 million International Units [IU]) prefilled syringe (Rx) [*Rebif* (preservative-free; 2 mg human albumin; 27.3 mg mannitol; 0.4 mg sodium acetate; water for injection)].
44 mcg (12 million International Units [IU]) prefilled syringe (Rx) [*Rebif* (preservative-free; 4 mg human albumin; 27.3 mg mannitol; 0.4 mg sodium acetate; water for injection)].

Canada—
33 mcg (6.6 million International Units [IU]) per single-use vial (Rx) [*Avonex* (diluent: Sterile Water for Injection USP; albumin human USP; dibasic sodium phosphate USP; monobasic sodium phosphate USP; sodium chloride USP)].
11 mcg (3 million IU) (Rx) [*Rebif* (diluent: sodium chloride 0.9% in water; albumin human; mannitol; sodium acetate; sodium hydroxide)].

44 mcg (12 million IU) (Rx) [*Rebif* (diluent: sodium chloride 0.9% in water; albumin human; mannitol; sodium acetate; sodium hydroxide)].

Packaging and storage

Store between 2 and 8 °C (36 and 46 °F). Protect from freezing.

If refrigeration is not available, the vials may be stored at 25 °C (77 °F) for up to 30 days.

Once removed from the refrigerator, the prefilled syringes should be allowed to warm to room temperature (about 30 minutes) and used within 12 hours. Do not use external heat sources such as hot water to warm interferon beta-1a in a prefilled syringe. Do not expose to high temperatures. Protect from light. Do not use beyond the expiration date stamped on the syringe.

Preparation of dosage form

Relapsing-remitting multiple sclerosis—

Avonex, for intramuscular administration: The vials of drug and diluent should be allowed to come to room temperature before reconstitution. Using aseptic technique, 1.1 mL of the supplied diluent is transferred into the lyophilized interferon beta-1a vial. The vial should be swirled gently until the solid material is completely dissolved. If particulate matter remains or the reconstituted product is discolored, the vial should be discarded before use. Following reconstitution with the accompanying diluent, the resulting solution will contain 30 mcg of interferon beta-1a per mL. After reconstitution, I mL of solution should be withdrawn into a sterile syringe to be injected intramuscularly.

Note: *Avonex* supplied in prefilled syringes is ready to use and should not be diluted.

Rebif, for subcutaneous administration: To the 11–mcg vial, add 0.5 mL of diluent (sodium chloride 0.9% in water), for a final concentration of 22 mcg (6 million IU) per mL. To the 44–mcg vial, add 0.5 mL of diluent for a final concentration of 88 mcg (24 million IU) per mL.

Condyloma acuminatum—

Rebif, for intra- and peri-lesional administration: To the 11–mcg vial, add 0.3 mL of diluent (sodium chloride 0.9% in water) for a final concentration of 37 mcg (10 million IU) per mL. To the 44–mcg vial, add 1.2 mL of diluent for a final concentration of 37 mcg (10 million IU) per mL.

Note: *Rebif* supplied in prefilled syringes is ready to use and should not be diluted.

Stability

Interferon beta-1a contains no preservatives; after reconstitution, if not used immediately, it should be refrigerated and used within 6 hours.

Interferon beta-1a should be inspected visually for particulate matter and discoloration prior to use.

Auxiliary labeling

- Avoid alcohol while on this medication
- Refrigerate- Do not freeze.
- For single dose only. Discard unused drug.

Revised: 04/12/2005
Developed: 12/19/1997

INTERFERON, BETA-1B Systemic

VA CLASSIFICATION (Primary): CN900; IM409

Commonly used brand name(s): *Betaseron.*

Note: For a listing of dosage forms and brand names by country availability, see *Dosage Forms* section(s).

Category

Multiple sclerosis (MS) therapy agent.

Indications

Accepted

Multiple sclerosis (treatment)—Interferon beta-1b is indicated for use in ambulatory patients with relapsing-remitting multiple sclerosis (MS) to reduce the frequency of clinical exacerbations. The safety and efficacy of interferon beta-1b in chronic-progressive MS have not been evaluated.

Pharmacology/Pharmacokinetics

Physicochemical characteristics

Source—Synthetic. Interferon beta-1b is a sterile lyophilized protein product produced by recombinant DNA techniques. It is manufactured by bacterial fermentation of a strain of *Escherichia coli* that bears a genetically engineered plasmid containing the gene for human interferon $beta_{ser17}$. The native gene was obtained from human fibroblasts and altered in a way that substitutes serine for the cysteine residue found at position 17. Interferon beta-1b is a highly purified protein with 165 amino acids; it does not include the carbohydrate side chains found in the natural material.

Chemical Group—Interferons are a family of naturally occurring proteins. Three major classes have been identified: alfa, beta, and gamma. Interferon alfa, interferon beta-1b, and interferon gamma have overlapping yet distinct biologic activities; the activities of interferon beta-1b are species-restricted.

Molecular weight—Approximately 18,500 daltons.

Mechanism of action/Effect

Interferon beta-1b has both antiviral and immunoregulatory properties. The mechanism by which it exerts its effects in multiple sclerosis (MS) are not clearly understood. It is known, however, that the biologic response-modifying properties of interferon beta-1b are mediated through its interactions with specific cell receptors found on the surface of human cells. Binding of interferon beta-1b to these receptors induces the expression of a number of interferon-induced gene products (e.g., 2',5'-oligoadenylate synthetase, protein kinase, and indoleamine 2, 3-dioxygenase) that are believed to be the mediators of this interferon's biological actions.

Pharmacokinetics

Pharmacokinetic information on patients with multiple sclerosis (MS) receiving the recommended dose of interferon beta-1b is not available because serum concentrations following subcutaneous administration of ≤ 0.25 mg are low or undetectable. Healthy volunteers who received single or multiple daily subcutaneous doses of 0.5 mg generally had serum interferon beta-1b concentrations of less than 100 international units per mL (IU/mL). Pharmacokinetic parameters in non-MS patients following single and multiple intravenous doses of interferon beta-1b were comparable, and dosing three times a week for two weeks did not result in accumulation of interferon beta-1b in these patients.

Absorption

Bioavailability was approximately 50%, based on a total dose of 0.5 mg given as two subcutaneous injections at different sites to healthy volunteers.

Distribution

Mean steady-state volume of distribution (Vol_D) values ranged from 0.25 to 2.88 L per kg in healthy volunteers and non-MS patients who received single intravenous doses of up to 2 mg of interferon beta-1b.

Half-life

Terminal elimination—

Mean, 8 minutes to 4.3 hours in non-MS patients who received single intravenous doses of up to 2 mg of interferon beta-1b.

Time to peak concentration

1 to 8 hours following subcutaneous administration of 0.5 mg to healthy volunteers.

Peak serum concentration

Mean, 40 IU/mL following subcutaneous administration of 0.5 mg to healthy volunteers. Increases in serum concentrations were dose-proportional in non-MS patients receiving single intravenous doses of up to 2 mg of interferon beta-1b.

Elimination

Mean serum clearance values ranged from 9.4 to 28.9 mL/minute x kg, and were independent of dose.

Precautions to Consider

Carcinogenicity

No carcinogenicity data in humans or animals are available. However, the effect of interferon beta-1b on the morphological transformation of the mammalian cell line BALBc-3T3 was studied to evaluate carcinogenic potential, and no significant increases in transformation frequency were noted.

Mutagenicity

Interferon beta-1b was not mutagenic when assayed for genotoxicity in the Ames bacterial test in the presence or absence of metabolic activation.

Pregnancy/Reproduction

Fertility—The effects of interferon beta-1b on normally cycling human females are not known. Studies on female rhesus monkeys showed no apparent adverse effects on the menstrual cycle or on associated hormonal profiles when interferon beta-1b was administered at doses of up to 32 times the recommended human dose (based on body surface area comparison) over three consecutive menstrual cycles.

Pregnancy—Adequate and well-controlled studies have not been done in humans. Spontaneous abortions were reported in four women who participated in the premarketing clinical trial.

Studies in female rhesus monkeys demonstrated a dose-related abortifacient activity when interferon beta-1b was administered at doses ranging from 2.8 to 40 times the recommended human dose based on body surface area comparison. It is not known if animal doses can be extrapolated to human doses. Interferon beta-1b administered to female rhesus monkeys on gestation days 20 to 70 did not cause teratogenic effects; it is not known if teratogenic effects would occur in humans.

FDA Pregnancy Category C.

Breast-feeding

It is not known if interferon beta-1b is distributed into human milk; however, because of the potential for serious adverse reactions in nursing infants, risk-benefit must be considered.

Pediatrics

Safety and efficacy in children up to 18 years of age have not been established.

Geriatrics

The premarketing clinical trial of interferon beta-1b enrolled patients ranging from 18 to 50 years of age. No information is available on the effects of interferon beta-1b in geriatric patients.

Drug interactions and/or related problems

Note: Studies designed to evaluate drug interactions with interferon beta-1b have not been conducted. However, ACTH or corticosteroids have been administered for periods of up to 28 days to treat relapses in patients receiving interferon beta-1b. The effect of alternate-day administration on drug metabolism in MS patients is unknown. Interferon beta-1b administered to three cancer patients over a dose range of 0.025 to 2.2 mg led to dose-dependent inhibition of antipyrine elimination.

Laboratory value alterations

The following have been selected on the basis of their potential clinical significance (possible effect in parentheses where appropriate)—not necessarily inclusive (» = major clinical significance).

With physiology/laboratory test values

Alanine aminotransferase, serum (ALT [SGPT])
(values more than five times baseline occurred in 19% of patients receiving interferon beta-1b, as compared with 6% of patients receiving placebo in the premarketing clinical trial)

Aspartate aminotransferase, serum (AST [SGOT])
(values more than five times baseline occurred in 4% of patients receiving interferon beta-1b, as compared with 0% of patients receiving placebo in the premarketing clinical trial)

Bilirubin, total
(concentrations greater than 2.5 times the baseline occurred in 6% of patients receiving interferon beta-1b, as compared with 2% of patients receiving placebo in the premarketing clinical trial)

Glucose, blood
(concentrations of less than 55 mg/dL occurred in 15% of patients receiving interferon beta-1b, as compared with 13% of patients receiving placebo in the premarketing clinical trial)

Lymphocyte count
(counts less than 1500/mm^3 occurred in 82% of patients receiving interferon beta-1b, as compared with 67% of patients receiving placebo in the premarketing clinical trial)

Neutrophil count, absolute
(counts less than 1500/mm^3 occurred in 18% of patients receiving interferon beta-1b, as compared with 6% of patients receiving placebo in the premarketing clinical trial)

Protein, urine
(values greater than 1+ occurred in 5% of patients receiving interferon beta-1b, as compared with 3% of patients receiving placebo in the premarketing clinical trial)

White blood cell count
(counts less than 3000/mm^3 occurred in 16% of patients receiving interferon beta-1b, as compared with 5% of patients receiving placebo in the premarketing clinical trial)

Medical considerations/Contraindications

The medical considerations/contraindications included have been selected on the basis of their potential clinical significance (reasons given in parentheses where appropriate)—not necessarily inclusive (» = major clinical significance).

Risk-benefit should be considered when the following medical problems exist:

» Depression, mental, especially with suicidal ideation
(condition may be exacerbated; patients should be closely monitored)

Sensitivity to natural or recombinant interferon beta, Albumin Human USP, or dextrose

Patient monitoring

The following may be especially important in patient monitoring (other tests may be warranted in some patients, depending on condition; » = major clinical significance):

» Blood chemistry values, including liver function tests and
» Hemoglobin and
» Platelet counts and
» White blood cell counts, complete and differential
(recommended prior to initiation of therapy and at periodic intervals thereafter)

Side/Adverse Effects

Note: In the premarketing clinical trial, one suicide and four attempted suicides were observed among 372 study patients during a 3-year period. All five of these cases were patients receiving interferon beta-1b; no attempted suicides occurred in study patients who were not receiving interferon beta-1b. Depression and suicide also have been reported in patients receiving interferon alfa, a related compound. Patients should be informed of these side effects and instructed to report symptoms of depression and suicidal ideation immediately to the prescribing physician. If depression occurs, the patient should be closely monitored, and discontinuation of interferon beta-1b should be considered.

Injection site necrosis (ISN) was reported in 5% of patients in premarketing clinical trials. Although typically occurring within the first 4 months of interferon beta-1b therapy, postmarketing surveillance reports ISN occurring over a year after initiation of therapy. ISN may occur at single or multiple injection sites; lesions are typically 3 cm or less in diameter, although larger areas have been reported. While necrosis has commonly extended only to subcutaneous fat, there are reports of necrosis extending to and including fascia overlying muscle. In some lesions, vasculitis has been reported. Debridement and, infrequently, skin grafting have been required for some lesions. Any infection of the necrotic site should be treated appropriately. Time to healing varies depending on the severity of the necrosis; in most cases, healing has been associated with scarring. In some patients, healing of necrotic skin lesions has occurred while interferon beta-1b therapy has continued. The decision to discontinue therapy following a single site of necrosis is dependent on the extent of necrosis. If patients continue using interferon beta-1b after ISN has occurred, injection into the affected area should be avoided until the site is fully healed. If multiple lesions have occurred, therapy should be discontinued until healing is complete. Patients should be instructed to contact the physician promptly if any break in the skin, which may be associated with blue-black discoloration, swelling, or drainage of fluid from the injection site, occurs.

Other injection site reactions, including redness, pain, swelling, and discoloration, occurred in 85% of patients at one or more times during the controlled MS trial. In general, these reactions were transient and did not require discontinuation of therapy, but the nature and severity of all reported reactions need to be carefully assessed.

The following side/adverse effects have been selected on the basis of their potential clinical significance (possible signs and symptoms in parentheses where appropriate)—not necessarily inclusive:

Those indicating need for medical attention

Incidence more frequent

Abdominal pain; headache or migraine; hypertension (high blood pressure); ***injection site reactions including hypersensitivity*** (hives; itching; swelling); ***inflammation*** (redness; feeling of heat); ***necrosis*** (break in the skin, especially associated with blue-black discoloration, swelling, or drainage of fluid); ***and pain; influenza-like syndrome; including chills; fever; increased sweating; malaise*** (general feeling of discomfort or illness); ***and myalgia*** (muscle pain); ***palpitations*** (irregular or pounding heartbeat); ***sinusitis*** (headache; stuffy nose)

Incidence less frequent

Abnormal vision (any change in vision); ***breast pain; cystitis*** (bloody or cloudy urine; difficult, burning, or painful urination; frequent urge to urinate); ***dyspnea*** (troubled breathing); ***lymphadenopathy*** (swollen lymph glands); ***pain; pelvic pain; peripheral vascular disorder*** (cold hands and feet); ***tachycardia*** (fast or racing heartbeat); ***weight gain, unusual***

Incidence rare

Amnesia (loss of memory); ***breast neoplasm*** (abnormal growth in breast); ***confusion; conjunctivitis*** (red, itching, or swollen eyes); ***cyst*** (abnormal growth filled with fluid or semisolid material); ***edema, generalized*** (bloating or swelling); ***fibrocystic breast*** (benign lumps in breast); ***goiter*** (dry, puffy skin; increased weight gain; swelling of front part of neck; changes in menstrual periods; decreased sexual ability in males; feeling cold); ***hemorrhage*** (bleeding problems); ***hyperkinesia*** (hyperactivity); ***hypertonia*** (increased muscle tone); ***mental depression with suicidal ideation*** (depression with thoughts of suicide); ***seizure; speech disorder*** (problems in speaking); ***urinary urgency*** (increased urge to urinate); ***weight loss, unusual***

Those indicating need for medical attention only if they continue or are bothersome

Incidence more frequent

Asthenia (unusual tiredness or weakness); ***constipation; diarrhea; dizziness; dysmenorrhea or other menstrual disorders*** (menstrual pain or other menstrual changes); ***laryngitis***

Incidence less frequent

Alopecia (hair loss); ***anxiety; nervousness; somnolence*** (drowsiness); ***vomiting***

Overdose

For information on the management of overdose of interferon beta-1b, **contact a Poison Control Center** (see *Poison Control Center Listing*).

Patient Consultation

In providing consultation, consider emphasizing the following selected information (» = major clinical significance)

Before using this medication

» Conditions affecting use, especially:
- Sensitivity to interferon beta-1b, Albumin Human USP, or dextrose
- Pregnancy—Not recommended
- Breast-feeding—Possible need to avoid during interferon beta-1b therapy because of risk of serious adverse effects on infant
- Other medical problems, especially mental depression with suicidal ideation

Proper use of this medication

» Proper administration:
- Importance of aseptic technique
- Choosing an appropriate injection site
- Importance of rotating injection sites

» Proper dosing

Missed dose: Using as soon as remembered; the next injection should be scheduled about 48 hours later

» Proper storage

Side/adverse effects

Signs of potential side effects, especially abdominal pain; headache or migraine; hypertension; injection site reactions including hypersensitivity, inflammation, necrosis, and pain; influenza-like syndrome including chills, fever, increased sweating, malaise, and myalgia; palpitations; sinusitis; abnormal vision; breast pain; cystitis; dyspnea; lymphadenopathy; pain; pelvic pain; peripheral vascular disorder; tachycardia; unusual weight gain; amnesia; breast neoplasm; confusion; conjunctivitis; cyst; edema, generalized; fibrocystic breast; goiter; hemorrhage; hyperkinesia; hypertonia; mental depression with suicidal ideation; seizure; speech disorder; urinary urgency; unusual weight loss

General Dosing Information

Activity of interferon beta-1b is approximately 32 million international units (IU) per mg. The unit measurement is derived by comparing the antiviral activity of the product to the World Health Organization (WHO) reference standard of recombinant human interferon beta. Prior to 1993, a different analytical standard was used to determine potency; it assigned 54 million IU to 0.3 mg interferon beta-1b, as compared with the currently assigned potency of 9.6 million IU per 0.3 mg interferon beta-1b.

Patient understanding and use of aseptic self-injection techniques and procedures should be reevaluated periodically, particularly if injection site necrosis (ISN) has occurred.

Patient understanding of the importance of rotating areas of injection to minimize the likelihood of severe injection site reactions should be reinforced.

Taking interferon beta-1b at bedtime may help lessen the impact of influenza-like symptoms.

Parenteral Dosage Forms

INTERFERON BETA-1b FOR INJECTION

Usual adult dose

Relapsing-remitting multiple sclerosis—
Subcutaneously, 0.25 mg every other day.

Usual pediatric dose

Safety and efficacy in patients up to 18 years of age have not been established.

Strength(s) usually available

U.S.—
0.3 mg (Rx) [*Betaseron* (diluent: sodium chloride 0.54%; Albumin Human USP 15 mg; Dextrose USP 15 mg)].

Packaging and storage

Store between 2 and 8 °C (36 and 46 °F). Do not freeze.

If refrigeration is not possible, the drug and diluent should be kept as cool as possible (below 30 °C [86 °F]), stored away from heat and light, and used within 7 days.

Preparation of dosage form

Using aseptic technique, 1.2 mL of the supplied diluent should be transferred into the lyophilized interferon beta-1b vial. The vial should be swirled gently until the solid material is completely dissolved. If particulate matter remains or the reconstituted product is discolored, it should be discarded before use. Following reconstitution with the accompanying diluent, the resulting solution will contain 0.25 mg interferon beta-1b per mL.

After reconstitution, withdraw 1 mL of solution into a sterile syringe fitted with a new 27-gauge needle to be injected subcutaneously.

Stability

Interferon beta-1b contains no preservatives; after reconstitution, if not immediately used, it should be refrigerated and used within 3 hours.

Auxiliary labeling

- Refrigerate.
- Do not freeze.

Developed: 06/16/1998

INTERFERON, GAMMA Systemic†

VA CLASSIFICATION (Primary): IM404

Commonly used brand name(s): *Actimmune*.

Note: For a listing of dosage forms and brand names by country availability, see *Dosage Forms* section(s).

†Not commercially available in Canada.

Category

Biological response modifier; immunomodulator.

Indications

Accepted

Chronic granulomatous disease (treatment)—Interferon gamma-1b, recombinant, is indicated for reducing the frequency and severity of serious infections associated with chronic granulomatous disease

(CGD). Interferon gamma-1b appears to be effective in all genetic types of CGD.

Osteopetrosis (treatment)—Interferon gamma-1b is indicated for delaying time to disease progression in patients with severe, malignant osteopetrosis

Acceptance not established

There are insufficient data to establish the safety and efficacy of interferon gamma-1b in the treatment of *idiopathic pulmonary fibrosis*. The biological activity of interferon gamma in inducing myofibroblast apotosis suggests potential benefit in the treatment of idiopathic pulmonary fibrosis. Additionally, results of a placebo controlled, double-blind, randomized study indicated that interferon gamma-1b had a positive effect on increasing total lung capacity, increasing partial pressure of arterial oxygen, and potentially decreasing supplemental oxygen requirements. However, due to the small study size (n=18, 9 treatment and 9 control), extrapolating data to the larger population of patients with idiopathic pulmonary fibrosis is difficult.

Use of interferon gamma for the treatment of *epithelial ovarian carcinoma* has not been established, due to insufficient data supporting safety and efficacy.

There are insufficient data to establish the safety and efficacy of interferon gamma-1b in the treatment of *cutaneous, mucocutaneous, and visceral leishmaniasis*.

Pharmacology/Pharmacokinetics

Note: Pharmacokinetic studies have been conducted in healthy male subjects only.

Physicochemical characteristics

Source—Synthetic. Structurally identical to naturally occurring human gamma interferon. A protein chain of 140 amino acids produced by a recombinant DNA process involving genetically engineered *Escherichia coli*. Purification procedure involves conventional column chromatography.

Chemical Group—Related to naturally occurring gamma interferon. Interferons are produced and secreted by cells in response to viral infections or various synthetic and biologic stimuli; gamma interferon is produced mainly by T-lymphocytes.

Mechanism of action/Effect

In general, interferons have antiviral, antiproliferative, and immunomodulatory activities.

Naturally occurring gamma interferon, which is secreted by antigen-stimulated T-lymphocytes (mainly CD4+ [helper] cells, plus CD8+ [suppressor] cells and natural killer [NK] cells), probably interacts with other lymphokines (cytokines) such as interleukin-2 in a complex immunoregulatory network. Gamma interferon induces activation of quiescent macrophages in blood monocytes to phagocytes, which have augmented antimicrobial and tumoricidal activity involving release of toxic oxygen metabolites. Macrophage activation is critical in the cellular immune response to intracellular and extracellular pathogens. Gamma interferon also enhances antibody-dependent cellular cytotoxicity and NK cell activity, histocompatibility class I and class II antigen expression, lymphocyte proliferation, and monocyte Fc receptor expression. Treatment with gamma interferon is associated with increased serum concentrations of beta-2 microglobulin and H_2O_2 secretion by peripheral blood monocytes, as well as a temporary increase in the T4/T8 cell ratio. Gamma interferon is also known as Type II interferon (based on interferon receptor types) and immune interferon.

In chronic granulomatous disease (CGD; an inherited disorder characterized by deficient phagocyte oxidative metabolism), gamma interferon enhances phagocytic function, resulting in an increase in superoxide anion production by granulocytes and monocytes; gamma interferon also enhances the oxygen-independent antimicrobial activity of monocytes from patients with classic X-linked CGD.

In severe, malignant osteopetrosis (an inherited disorder characterized by an osteoclast defect leading to bone overgrowth and deficient phagocyte oxidative metabolism), gamma interferon enhances superoxide production by phagocytes *in situ*. Gamma interferon also enhances osteoclast function *in vitro*.

Other actions/effects

May inhibit the hepatic microsomal cytochrome P450 system.

Absorption

Intramuscular or subcutaneous—Slow; apparent fraction of dose absorbed is more than 89%.

Biotransformation

Unknown.

Half-life

Intramuscular—Mean: 2.9 hours

Intravenous—Mean: 38 minutes

Subcutaneous—Mean: 5.9 hours

Time to peak plasma concentration

Intramuscular—4 hours.

Subcutaneous: 7 hours.

Peak plasma concentration

After dose of 100 mcg per square meter of body surface—

Intramuscular: 1.5 nanograms per mL.

Subcutaneous: 0.6 nanograms per mL.

Note: Not related to blood monocyte activation capacity.

Elimination

In vitro studies indicate that rabbit livers and kidneys are capable of clearing gamma interferon from perfusate; in nephrectomized mice and squirrel monkeys, clearance of gamma interferon from blood is reduced but elimination is not prevented.

Precautions to Consider

Cross-sensitivity and/or related problems

Patients sensitive to any *Escherichia coli* product may also be sensitive to gamma interferon.

Carcinogenicity

Studies have not been done in either animals or humans.

Mutagenicity

Results of Ames tests using five different tester strains of bacteria with and without metabolic activation showed no evidence of mutagenicity. No evidence of chromosomal damage was found in a micronucleus assay in bone marrow cells of mice following two intravenous doses of 20 mg per kg of body weight (mg/kg).

Pregnancy/Reproduction

Fertility—In female cynomolgus monkeys, irregular menstrual cycles or absence of cyclicity occurred during treatment with daily subcutaneous doses of 30 mcg per kg of body weight (mcg/kg) or 150 mcg/kg (approximately 20 and 100 times the human dose), but not with doses of 3 mcg/kg.

Pregnancy—Adequate and well-controlled studies in humans have not been done.

Studies in primates at doses approximately 100 times the human dose found an increased incidence of abortions. No evidence of teratogenicity was found with intravenous doses of 2 to 100 times the human dose. Studies using recombinant murine gamma interferon in pregnant mice found increased incidences of uterine bleeding and abortifacient activity and decreased neonatal viability at maternally toxic doses; however, the clinical significance of this effect is unknown.

FDA Pregnancy Category C.

Breast-feeding

It is not known whether gamma interferon is excreted in breast milk. However, because of the potential for serious adverse effects in nursing infants, avoidance of breast-feeding should be considered while gamma interferon is being administered.

Pediatrics

Safety and efficacy in children less than 1 year of age have not been established. In one study, flu-like symptoms were twice as frequent in children 10 years of age or older as in those less than 10 years of age; the lowest incidence was in children 5 years of age or younger.

Geriatrics

No information is available on the relationship of age to the effects of gamma interferon in geriatric patients.

Drug interactions and/or related problems

The following drug interactions and/or related problems have been selected on the basis of their potential clinical significance (possible mechanism in parentheses where appropriate)—not necessarily inclusive (» = major clinical significance):

Note: Combinations containing any of the following medications, depending on the amount present, may also interact with this medication.

Blood dyscrasia-causing medications (See *Appendix II*)
(leukopenic and/or thrombocytopenic effects of gamma interferon, although usually not significant except at high doses, may be increased with concurrent or recent therapy if these medications cause the same effects; dosage adjustment of gamma interferon, if necessary, should be based on blood counts)

Bone marrow depressants, other (See *Appendix II*) or
Radiation therapy
(additive bone marrow depression may rarely occur; dosage reduction may be required when two or more bone marrow depressants, including radiation, are used concurrently or consecutively)

Laboratory value alterations

The following have been selected on the basis of their potential clinical significance (possible effect in parentheses where appropriate)—not necessarily inclusive (» = major clinical significance).

With physiology/laboratory test values

Alanine aminotransferase (ALT [SGPT]) and
Alkaline phosphatase and
Aspartate aminotransferase (AST [SGOT]) and
Lactate dehydrogenase (LDH)
(serum values may be slightly increased; dose related; reversible on withdrawal of gamma interferon)

Blood pressure
(may be decreased)

Cortisol concentrations, plasma
(may be increased; peak concentrations occur 2 to 4 hours after administration of gamma interferon)

Leukocyte counts (including neutrophils)
(may be decreased; dose-related)

Platelet counts
(may rarely be decreased)

Triglyceride concentrations, serum
(may be increased; dose-related; resolve after treatment is withdrawn)

Medical considerations/Contraindications

The medical considerations/contraindications included have been selected on the basis of their potential clinical significance (reasons given in parentheses where appropriate)—not necessarily inclusive (» = major clinical significance).

Risk-benefit should be considered when the following medical problems exist:

Bone marrow depression
(may be exacerbated)

» Cardiac disease, including symptoms of ischemia, congestive heart failure, or arrhythmia
(may be exacerbated as a result of the stress of the fever and chills that occur in patients receiving gamma interferon; no direct cardiotoxic effect of gamma interferon has been demonstrated)

» CNS function, compromised or
» Seizure disorders
(risk of CNS side effects)

» Multiple sclerosis or
» Systemic lupus erythematosus
(there is some evidence that these may be exacerbated; however, there is also some evidence of a helpful effect of gamma interferon)

» Sensitivity to gamma interferon or *Escherichia coli*–derived products

Caution should be used also in patients who have had previous cytotoxic drug therapy or radiation therapy.

Patient monitoring

The following may be especially important in patient monitoring (other tests may be warranted in some patients, depending on condition; » = major clinical significance):

Alanine aminotransferase (ALT [SGPT]) values, serum and
Aspartate aminotransferase (AST [SGOT]) values, serum and
Bilirubin concentrations, serum and
Lactate dehydrogenase (LDH) values, serum
(recommended prior to initiation of therapy and at periodic intervals during therapy)

» Leukocyte count, total and, if appropriate, differential and
» Platelet count
(determinations recommended prior to initiation of therapy and at periodic intervals during therapy)

Side/Adverse Effects

Note: Most side/adverse effects, except the flu-like syndrome, are dose-related.
Development of neutralizing antibodies has not been reported with interferon gamma-1b, although it has been reported with interferon gamma-4a.
Neutropenia and elevation of hepatic enzymes may occur at doses of 100 mcg per square meter of body surface per day and may be dose-limiting at doses above 250 mcg per square meter of body surface per day; they resolve after treatment is withdrawn. Thrombocytopenia and proteinuria are also rare.

The following side/adverse effects have been selected on the basis of their potential clinical significance (possible signs and symptoms in parentheses where appropriate)—not necessarily inclusive:

Those indicating need for medical attention

Incidence more frequent

Leukopenia (usually asymptomatic; rarely, fever or chills; cough or hoarseness; lower back or side pain; painful or difficult urination)

Note: In *leukopenia*, neutrophil counts usually do not fall out of the normal range and usually recover within 2 to 5 days after a dose.

Incidence rare

Hypotension (not symptomatic); ***neurotoxicity*** (confusion, parkinsonian symptoms [loss of balance control, mask-like face, shuffling walk, stiffness of arms or legs, trembling and shaking of hands and fingers, trouble in speaking or swallowing], trouble in thinking or concentrating, trouble in walking); ***thrombocytopenia*** (usually asymptomatic; rarely, unusual bleeding or bruising; black, tarry stools; blood in urine or stools; pinpoint red spots on skin)

Note: *Neurotoxicity* is usually reversible after withdrawal.

Those indicating need for medical attention only if they continue or are bothersome

Incidence more frequent

Diarrhea; flu-like syndrome (aching muscles; fever and chills; general feeling of discomfort or illness; headache; less frequently, back pain; joint pain); ***nausea or vomiting; skin rash; unusual tiredness***

Note: The *flu-like syndrome* occurs in most patients; it may decrease in severity with continued treatment. Severity is dose-related.

Incidence less frequent

Dizziness; loss of appetite; weight loss

Note: *Dizziness* is a CNS effect.

Patient Consultation

As an aid to patient consultation, refer to *Advice for the Patient, Interferon, Gamma (Systemic)*.

In providing consultation, consider emphasizing the following selected information (» = major clinical significance):

Before using this medication

» Conditions affecting use, especially:
Sensitivity to gamma interferon
Pregnancy—Abortifacient effects found in monkeys and mice
Breast-feeding—Possible need to avoid during gamma interferon therapy because of risk of serious adverse effects
Other medical problems, especially cardiac disease, compromised CNS function, multiple sclerosis, seizure disorders, and systemic lupus erythematosus

Proper use of this medication

» Compliance with therapy
» Reading patient directions carefully with regard to:
Preparation of the injection
Use of disposable syringes
Proper administration technique
Stability of the injection
Importance of ample fluid intake to reduce risk of hypotension
Administration at bedtime to minimize flu-like symptoms
» Proper dosing
Missed dose: Skipping missed dose and going back to regular schedule; not doubling doses; checking with physician
» Proper storage

Precautions while using this medication

» Importance of close monitoring by physician
» Frequency of fever and flu-like symptoms; possible need for acetaminophen before and after a dose is given

Side/adverse effects

Signs of potential side effects, especially leukopenia, neurotoxicity, and thrombocytopenia

General Dosing Information

Patients receiving gamma interferon should be under supervision of a physician experienced in immunomodulatory therapy.

The patient may be premedicated with acetaminophen at the time of gamma interferon dosing and the acetaminophen may be continued as needed to treat fever and headache.

If severe adverse effects occur, dosage reduction by 50% or temporary withdrawal of gamma interferon is recommended.

It is recommended that patients be well hydrated, especially during initial treatment with gamma interferon, to reduce the risk of hypotension associated with fluid depletion. Hypotension may require supportive treatment, including fluid replacement to maintain intravascular volume.

Patients who develop leukopenia should be observed carefully for signs of infection. Antibiotic support may be required. In neutropenic patients who develop fever, broad-spectrum antibiotic coverage should be initiated empirically, pending bacterial cultures and appropriate diagnostic tests. In some cases, it may be difficult to distinguish fever due to infection from fever associated with the flu-like syndrome.

Special precautions are recommended in patients who develop thrombocytopenia as a result of administration of gamma interferon. These may include extreme care in performing invasive procedures; regular inspection of intravenous sites, skin (including perirectal area), and mucous membrane surfaces for signs of bleeding or bruising; limiting frequency of venipuncture and avoiding intramuscular injections; testing urine, emesis, stool, and secretions for occult blood; care in use of regular toothbrushes, dental floss, toothpicks, safety razors, and fingernail and toenail cutters; avoiding constipation; and using caution to prevent falls and other injuries. Such patients should avoid alcohol and any aspirin intake because of the risk of gastrointestinal bleeding. Platelet transfusions may be required.

Parenteral Dosage Forms

INTERFERON GAMMA-1b, RECOMBINANT, INJECTION

Usual pediatric dose

Chronic granulomatous disease or
Osteopetrosis—

Body surface area greater than 0.5 square meter: Subcutaneous, 50 mcg (1 million International Units [IU]) per square meter of body surface area three times a week.

Body surface area less than or equal to 0.5 square meter: Subcutaneous, 1.5 mcg per kg of body weight three times a week.

Note: The activity expressed in International Units (1 million IU/50 mcg) was previously expressed as units (1.5 million U/50 mcg).

Note: The optimum injection sites are the right and left deltoid and anterior thigh.

Either sterilized glass or plastic disposable syringes may be used for administration.

Safety and efficacy in children less than 1 year of age have not been established.

Strength(s) usually available

U.S.—

200 mcg per mL (100 mcg [2 million IU] per 0.5-mL vial) (Rx) [*Actimmune* (mannitol; sodium succinate; polysorbate 20)].

Canada—

Not commercially available.

Packaging and storage

Store between 2 and 8 °C (36 and 46 °F), unless otherwise specified by manufacturer. Protect from freezing.

Stability

Contains no preservative; any unused portion should be discarded. Vials left at room temperature for a total time exceeding 12 hours should be discarded.

Note

Do not shake.

When dispensing for self-administration by the patient, make sure that patient instructions are included and that the patient understands how to prepare and administer the injection, including proper use of disposable syringes.

Selected Bibliography

Ijzermans JNM, Marquet RL. Interferon-gamma: a review. Immunobiol 1989; 179: 456-73.

Murray HW. Interferon-gamma, the activated macrophage, and host defense against microbial challenge. Ann Intern Med 1988 Apr; 108: 595-608.

Revised: 09/09/2002

INTERFERONS, ALPHA Systemic

This monograph includes information on the following: 1) Interferon Alfa-2a, Recombinant; 2) Interferon Alfa-2b, Recombinant; 3) Interferon Alfa-n1(Ins)*; 4) Interferon Alfa-n3†.

VA CLASSIFICATION (Primary/Secondary): IM404/AN900

Commonly used brand name(s): *Alferon N*[4]; *Intron A*[2]; *Roferon-A*[1]; *Wellferon*[3].

Note: For a listing of dosage forms and brand names by country availability, see *Dosage Forms* section(s).

*Not commercially available in U.S.
†Not commercially available in Canada.

Category

Biological response modifier; antineoplastic.

Indications

Note: Bracketed information in the *Indications* section refers to uses that are not included in U.S. product labeling.

Accepted

Leukemia, hairy cell (treatment)—Recombinant interferon alfa-2a, recombinant interferon alfa-2b, and interferon alfa-n1 (Ins) are indicated for treatment of hairy cell leukemia in splenectomized or nonsplenectomized patients. [Interferon alfa-n3] is also indicated for treatment of hairy cell leukemia.

Condyloma acuminatum (treatment)—Recombinant interferon alfa-2b[1], interferon alfa-n1 (Ins), and interferon alfa-n3 are indicated by intralesional injection for treatment of refractory or recurrent external condyloma acuminatum (genital warts).

Hepatitis, chronic, active (treatment)—[Recombinant interferon alfa-2a][1], recombinant interferon alfa-2b, interferon alfa-n1 (Ins)[1], and [interferon alfa-n3] are indicated for treatment of non-A, non-B/C hepatitis in patients 18 years of age or older with compensated liver disease who have a history of blood or blood product exposure and/or are HCV (hepatitis C virus) antibody positive. Safety and efficacy have not been established for treatment of patients with decompensated liver disease or for immune suppressed transplant recipients. Use is not recommended in patients with autoimmune hepatitis or a history of autoimmune disease.

Available data indicate that serum transaminase activity and markers of viral activity are reduced during alpha interferon treatment, although abnormalities may recur when treatment is withdrawn. Long-term effects of alpha interferon on development of chronic hepatitis are not established.

Hepatitis B, chronic (treatment)—Recombinant interferon alfa-2b[1] is indicated for treatment of chronic hepatitis B in patients 18 years of age or older with compensated liver disease and hepatitis B virus (HBV) replication. Patients must test positive for hepatitis B serum antigen for at least 6 months and have HBV replication with elevated serum alanine aminotransferase.

Kaposi's sarcoma, AIDS-associated (treatment)—Recombinant interferon alfa-2a and recombinant interferon alfa-2b are indicated for treatment of AIDS-associated Kaposi's sarcoma in selected patients 18 years of age and older. Interferon alfa-n1 (Ins)[1] and [interferon alfa-n3] are also indicated for this indication.

Carcinoma, bladder (treatment)—Interferon alfa-n1 (Ins)[1] and [interferon alfa-n3] are indicated for the treatment of superficial bladder carcinoma (intravesically).

Note: Recombinant interferon alfa-2a and recombinant interferon alfa-2b have been studied, in combination therapy, for intravesical use in the treatment of *bladder carcinoma* (Evidence rating: IIID). Although some medical experts agree that these medications may be useful in the management of bladder carcinoma, others state there is not enough medical literature or clinical experience to consider the use of these alpha interferons for this indication outside of a clinical trial setting.

Carcinoma, renal (treatment) or
Leukemia, chronic myelocytic (treatment)—[Recombinant interferon alfa-2a], [recombinant interferon alfa-2b][1], interferon alfa-n1 (Ins)[1], and [interferon alfa-n3] are indicated for the treatment of renal carcinoma and chronic myelocytic leukemia.

Papillomatosis, laryngeal (treatment)—[Recombinant interferon alfa-2b][1], interferon alfa-n1 (Ins), and [interferon alfa-n3] are indicated for treatment of laryngeal papillomatosis, including juvenile laryngeal papilloma.

Lymphomas, non-Hodgkin's (treatment)
Malignant melanoma (treatment)
Multiple myeloma (treatment) or
Mycosis fungoides (treatment)—[Recombinant interferon alfa-2a][1], recombinant interferon alfa-2b[1], interferon alfa-n1 (lns)[1], and [interferon alfa-n3] are indicated for treatment of non-Hodgkin's lymphomas, especially follicular small cleaved cell lymphoma (nodular poorly differentiated types), malignant melanoma, multiple myeloma, and mycosis fungoides.

[Carcinoid tumors (treatment)][1]—Alpha interferons are indicated as reasonable medical therapy in the management of carcinoid tumors (Evidence rating: IID).

[Carcinoma, ovarian, epithelial (treatment)][1] or
[Carcinoma, skin (treatment)]—Alpha interferons are indicated for treatment of epithelial ovarian (intraperitoneal administration) and skin (recombinant interferon alfa-2b) carcinomas.

[Polycythemia vera (treatment)][1]—Recombinant interferon alfa-2a and recombinant interferon alfa-2b are indicated as reasonable medical therapy at some point in the management of polycythemia vera (Evidence rating: IIID). However, these medications are not recommended for first-line treatment.

[Thrombocytosis, essential (treatment)][1]—Alpha interferons are indicated for treatment of essential thrombocytosis.

Although efficacy of all alpha interferons for various indications appears to be similar, differences in relative efficacy for a particular indication may exist.

Acceptance not established

Recombinant interferon alfa-2b, in combination therapy, has been studied for use in the treatment of *cervical carcinoma* (Evidence rating: IIID). Some medical experts consider this agent to be reasonable medical therapy at some point in the management of advanced cervical carcinoma (although it is not recommended as first-line treatment). However, other experts state that there is not enough medical literature or clinical experience to consider the use of recombinant interferon alfa-2b for the treatment of cervical carcinoma outside of a clinical trial setting.

Recombinant interferon alfa-2a and recombinant interferon alfa-2b have been studied, in combination therapy, for use in the treatment of *esophageal carcinoma* (Evidence rating: IIID). However, medical experts agree that, at this point in time, there is not enough medical literature or clinical experience to consider the use of these medications for the treatment of esophageal carcinoma outside of a clinical trial setting.

Unaccepted

Recombinant interferon alfa-2a and recombinant interferon alfa-2b, in combination therapy, have been shown in several studies to be ineffective in the treatment of *colorectal carcinoma* (Evidence rating: IIC). Their use is not recommended.

[1]Not included in Canadian product labeling.

Pharmacology/Pharmacokinetics

Physicochemical characteristics

Source—

Interferon alfa-2a, recombinant: Synthetic. A protein chain of 165 amino acids produced by a recombinant DNA process involving genetically engineered *Escherichia coli.* Has a lysine group at position 23. Purification procedure includes affinity chromatography using a murine monoclonal antibody. Contains only a single alpha interferon subtype.

Interferon alfa-2b, recombinant: Synthetic. A protein chain of 165 amino acids produced by a recombinant DNA process involving genetically engineered *Escherichia coli.* Has an arginine group at position 23. Purification is done by proprietary methods. Contains only a single alpha interferon subtype.

Interferon alfa-n1 (lns): A highly purified blend of natural human alpha interferons, obtained from human lymphoblastoid cells following induction with Sendai virus. Is a mixture of natural alpha interferon subtypes, but in different proportions than in human leukocyte interferon.

Interferon alfa-n3: A highly purified mixture of up to 14 natural human alpha interferon subtypes. A protein chain of approximately 166 amino acids. Manufactured from pooled units of human leukocytes that have been induced by incomplete infection with an avian virus (Sendai virus) to produce interferon alfa-n3. The manufacturing process includes immunoaffinity chromatography with a murine monoclonal antibody, acidification (pH 2) for 5 days at 4 °C, and gel filtration chromatography.

Chemical Group—Interferon alfa-n1 and -n3: Naturally occurring alpha interferons.Interferon alfa-2a and -2b, recombinant: Related to naturally occurring alpha interferons.Interferons are produced and secreted by cells in response to viral infections or various synthetic and biologic inducers; alpha interferons are produced mainly by leukocytes.

Mechanism of action/Effect

In general, interferons have antiviral, antiproliferative, and immunomodulatory activities. Antiviral and antiproliferative actions are thought to be related to alterations in synthesis of RNA, DNA, and cellular proteins, including oncogenes. The exact mechanism of antineoplastic activity is unknown, but may be related to any of these three actions.

Antiviral—Inhibit virus replication in virus-infected cells.
Antiproliferative—Suppress cell proliferation.
Immunomodulatory—Enhance phagocytic activity of macrophages and augment specific cytotoxicity of lymphocytes for target cells.

Absorption

Intralesional—Plasma concentrations achieved are below detectable levels; however, systemic effects have been reported, indicating some systemic absorption.

Intramuscular and subcutaneous—Greater than 80%.

Biotransformation

Renal, complete. Alpha interferons are totally filtered through the glomeruli and undergo rapid proteolytic degradation during tubular reabsorption.

Half-life

Recombinant interferon alfa-2a—
Intramuscular: 6 to 8 hours.
Intravenous infusion: 3.7 to 8.5 (mean 5.1) hours.

Recombinant interferon alfa-2b—
Intramuscular or subcutaneous: 2 to 3 hours.

Interferon alfa-n1—
Intravenous infusion: About 8 hours.

Note: Accumulation may occur with daily intramuscular dosing.

Onset of action

Hepatitis, chronic, active—Normalization of serum alanine aminotransferase (ALT) concentrations may occur as early as 2 weeks after initiation of treatment, although 6 months of treatment is usually recommended.

Time to peak concentration

Recombinant interferon alfa-2a (single dose)—
Intramuscular: 3.8 hours.
Subcutaneous: 7.3 hours.

Recombinant interferon alfa-2b (single dose)—
Intramuscular or subcutaneous: 3 to 12 hours.

Time to peak effect

Condyloma acuminatum—4 to 8 weeks after initiation of treatment.

Elimination

With systemic use—Renal; metabolites almost completely reabsorbed in renal tubules, with only negligible amounts of unchanged alpha interferon reappearing in systemic circulation.

Precautions to Consider

Cross-sensitivity and/or related problems

Patients sensitive to any alpha interferon may also be sensitive to any other alpha interferon.

Patients sensitive to mouse immunoglobulin may also be sensitive to recombinant interferon alfa-2a.

Patients sensitive to mouse immunoglobulin, egg protein, or neomycin may also be sensitive to interferon alfa-n3.

Carcinogenicity

Studies have not been done in either animals or humans.

Mutagenicity

Results of Ames tests and *in vitro* treatment of human lymphocyte cultures with recombinant alpha interferon at noncytotoxic concentrations showed no evidence of mutagenicity. However, both genotoxicity and protection from chromosomal abnormalities produced by gamma rays have been reported in association with human leukocyte interferon *in vitro.*

Pregnancy/Reproduction

Fertility—In humans, alpha interferon has been shown to affect the menstrual cycle and decrease serum estradiol and progesterone concentrations in adult females.

In Macaca mulatta (rhesus) monkeys given high doses (e.g., in the case of interferon alfa-n3, 326 times the average intralesional dose [120 times the maximum recommended dose]) intramuscularly daily, recombinant alpha interferon has been shown to cause menstrual cycle changes; normal menstrual rhythm returned when alpha interferon was withdrawn.

For interferon alfa-2a, recombinant: Has been shown to cause reversible menstrual irregularities, including prolonged or shortened menstrual periods and erratic bleeding with anovulation, in Macaca mulatta (rhesus) monkeys given 5 million and 25 million Units per kg of body weight per day.

For interferon alfa-n3: No menstrual changes were reported in humans.

Pregnancy—Adequate and well-controlled studies in humans have not been done.

For interferon alfa-2a, recombinant—

Studies in Macaca mulatta (rhesus) monkeys at doses approximately 20 to 500 times the therapeutic human dose found a significant increase in abortifacient activity but no evidence of teratogenic activity.

FDA Pregnancy Category C.

For interferon alfa-2b, recombinant—

Studies in Macaca mulatta (rhesus) monkeys at doses of 90 and 180 times the intramuscular or subcutaneous dose of 2 million Units per square meter of body surface area found an abortifacient effect.

FDA Pregnancy Category C.

For interferon alfa-n1 (Ins)—

Studies have not been done in animals.

For interferon alfa-n3—

Studies have not been done in animals.

FDA Pregnancy Category C.

Breast-feeding

It is not known whether alpha interferon is distributed into breast milk; in mice, mouse interferons are distributed into milk. However, because of the potential for serious adverse effects in nursing infants, avoidance of breast-feeding should be considered while alpha interferon is being administered.

Pediatrics

Appropriate studies on the relationship of age to the effects of alpha interferons have not been performed in the pediatric population.

Adolescents

Alpha interferons have been shown to affect the menstrual cycle in animals and decrease serum estradiol and progesterone concentrations in human females. These effects should be kept in mind when considering alpha interferon treatment in adolescent females.

Geriatrics

Although appropriate studies on the relationship of age to the effects of alpha interferons have not been performed in the geriatric population, neurotoxicity and cardiotoxicity may be more likely to occur in the elderly, who may have underlying central nervous system (CNS) and cardiac function impairment. In addition, elderly patients are more likely to have age-related renal function impairment, which may require caution in patients receiving alpha interferons.

Dental

The bone marrow depressant effects of alpha interferons may result in an increased incidence of microbial infection, delayed healing, and gingival bleeding. If leukopenia or thrombocytopenia occurs, dental work should be deferred until blood counts have returned to normal and patients should be instructed in proper oral hygiene, including caution in use of regular toothbrushes, dental floss, and toothpicks.

Interferon alfa-2a and alfa-2b may cause stomatitis and discomfort. Use of interferon alfa-2a or alfa-2b may decrease or inhibit salivary flow, thus contributing to the development of caries, periodontal disease, oral candidiasis, and discomfort.

Drug interactions and/or related problems

The following drug interactions and/or related problems have been selected on the basis of their potential clinical significance (possible mechanism in parentheses where appropriate)—not necessarily inclusive (» = major clinical significance):

Note: Combinations containing any of the following medications, depending on the amount present, may also interact with this medication.

The following information applies to systemic use.

Alcohol or
CNS depression-producing medications (see *Appendix II*)
(concurrent use may enhance the CNS depressant effects of either these medications or alpha interferon)

Blood dyscrasia-causing medications (see *Appendix II*)
(leukopenic and/or thrombocytopenic effects of interferon may be increased with concurrent or recent therapy if these medications cause the same effects; dosage adjustment of alpha interferon, if necessary, should be based on blood counts)

Bone marrow depressants, other (see *Appendix II*) or
Radiation therapy
(additive bone marrow depression may occur; dosage reduction may be required when two or more bone marrow depressants, including radiation, are used concurrently or consecutively)

Laboratory value alterations

The following have been selected on the basis of their potential clinical significance (possible effect in parentheses where appropriate)—not necessarily inclusive (» = major clinical significance).

With physiology/laboratory test values

Note: The following information applies to systemic use.

Alanine aminotransferase (ALT [SGPT]) and
Alkaline phosphatase and
Aspartate aminotransferase (AST [SGOT]) and
Lactate dehydrogenase
(serum values may be increased; dose-related; reversible on withdrawal of alpha interferon)

Blood pressure
(mild and transient increase may occur; hypotension is more likely and may occur during administration or up to 2 days after administration)

Hemoglobin concentrations and
Hematocrit
(may be decreased)

Leukocyte counts (including neutrophils) and
Platelet counts
(may be decreased; dose-related)

Prothrombin time (PT) and
Partial thromboplastin time (PTT)
(may be increased by recombinant interferon alfa-2b; dose-related)

Medical considerations/Contraindications

The medical considerations/contraindications included have been selected on the basis of their potential clinical significance (reasons given in parentheses where appropriate)—not necessarily inclusive (» = major clinical significance).

Risk-benefit should be considered when the following medical problems exist:

» Autoimmune disease, history of
(caution is recommended because alpha interferon may increase the activity of the immune system and thereby worsen the condition; use for treatment of non-A, non-B/C hepatitis or hepatitis B is not recommended)

Bone marrow depression
(may be exacerbated)

» Cardiac disease, severe, including recent myocardial infarction or
» Diabetes mellitus prone to ketoacidosis or
» Ischemic disorders or
» Pulmonary disease
(may be exacerbated as a result of the stress of the fever and chills that occur in most patients receiving alpha interferon)
(the risk of cardiotoxicity of alpha interferon may be increased in patients with a history of cardiac disease; myocardial infarction has been reported rarely)

» Chickenpox, existing or recent, including recent exposure or
» Herpes zoster
(risk of severe generalized disease)

» CNS function, compromised or

» Psychiatric conditions, severe, or history of or
» Seizure disorders
(risk of severe CNS side effects)

Hepatic disease, severe
(alpha interferons may elevate serum hepatic enzyme concentrations)

Herpes labialis, history of
(may be reactivated)

» Infectious disorders
(alfa interferons may aggravate fatal or life-threatening infectious disorders)

Renal disease, severe
(may be exacerbated by fever and dehydration caused by alpha interferon)

» Sensitivity to alpha interferon

Caution should be used also in patients who have had previous cytotoxic drug therapy or radiation therapy.

For treatment of non-A, non-B/C hepatitis, or hepatitis B (in addition to the above)

» Thyroid function impairment
(recombinant interferon alfa-2b has been reported to cause thyroid function abnormalities; serum thyroid-stimulating hormone [TSH] concentrations must be within normal limits before initiation of treatment)

For recombinant interferon alfa-2b and interferon alfa-n3 only (in addition to the above)

Coagulation disorders
(caution is recommended; recombinant interferon alfa-2b may prolong PT and PTT)

Patient monitoring

The following may be especially important in patient monitoring (other tests may be warranted in some patients, depending on condition; » = major clinical significance):

Note: The following information applies to systemic use.

Alanine aminotransferase (ALT [SGPT]) values and
Aspartate aminotransferase (AST [SGOT]) values and
Bilirubin concentrations, serum and
Lactate dehydrogenase (LDH) values
(recommended prior to initiation of therapy and at periodic intervals during therapy)

Blood pressure measurements
(recommended at periodic intervals)

Electrocardiogram (ECG)
(recommended prior to initiation of therapy and at periodic intervals during therapy in patients with cardiac disease or advanced malignancy)

» Blood count, complete (CBC)
» Hematocrit or hemoglobin and
» Platelet count and
» Total and, if appropriate, differential leukocyte count
(determinations recommended prior to initiation of therapy and at periodic intervals during therapy)

(alfa interferon therapy should be discontinued in patients who develop severe decreases in neutrophil or platelet counts)

Liver biopsy
(recommended prior to discontinuing alpha interferon treatment when hepatic enzyme values return to normal)

Neuropsychiatric monitoring
(recommended especially in patients receiving high doses of alpha interferon)

Thyroid-stimulating hormone (TSH) concentrations, serum
(recommended prior to initiation of treatment for non-A, non-B/C hepatitis, or hepatitis B and if symptoms of thyroid function impairment occur during treatment)

Side/Adverse Effects

See *Table 1*, page 1421.

Patient Consultation

As an aid to patient consultation, refer to *Advice for the Patient, Interferons, Alpha (Systemic).*

In providing consultation, consider emphasizing the following selected information (» = major clinical significance):

Before using this medication

» Conditions affecting use, especially:
Sensitivity to alpha interferons
Pregnancy—Abortifacient effects found in rhesus monkeys
Breast-feeding—Possible need to avoid breast-feeding during alpha interferon therapy because of risk of serious adverse effects in the nursing infant
Use in adolescents—Possible effects on menstrual cycle
Use in the elderly—Risk of cardiotoxic and neurotoxic effects may be increased
Other medical problems, especially history of autoimmune disease, severe cardiac disease, chickenpox, compromised CNS function, diabetes mellitus, herpes zoster, history of psychiatric disease, infectious disorders pulmonary disease, seizure disorders, and thyroid function impairment

Proper use of this medication

» Compliance with therapy
» Reading patient directions carefully with regard to:
—Preparation of the injection
—Use of disposable syringes
—Proper administration technique
—Stability of the injection
Importance of ample fluid intake to reduce risk of hypotension
Administration at bedtime to minimize inconvenience of fatigue
» Proper dosing
Missed dose: Skipping missed dose and going back to regular schedule; not doubling doses; checking with physician
» Proper storage

Precautions while using this medication

» Importance of close monitoring by physician

» Not changing brands of interferon without consulting physician because of differences in dosage

» Caution in taking alcohol or other CNS depressants during therapy

» Caution when driving or doing anything else requiring alertness because of possible fatigue and dizziness

» Frequency of fever and flu-like symptoms; possible need for acetaminophen before and after a dose is given

Caution if bone marrow depression occurs:

» Avoiding exposure to persons with bacterial infections, especially during periods of low blood counts; checking with physician immediately if fever or chills, cough or hoarseness, lower back or side pain, or painful or difficult urination occur

» Checking with physician immediately if unusual bleeding or bruising; black, tarry stools; blood in urine or stools; or pinpoint red spots on skin occur

Caution in use of regular toothbrush, dental floss, or toothpick; physician, dentist, or nurse may suggest alternatives; checking with physician before having dental work done

Not touching eyes or inside of nose unless hands washed immediately before

Using caution to avoid accidental cuts with use of sharp objects such as safety razor or fingernail or toenail cutters

Avoiding contact sports or other situations where bruising or injury could occur

Side/adverse effects

Signs of potential side effects, especially arthritis, cardiotoxicity,erythematosus syndrome, hemolytic anemia, neurotoxicity, peripheral neuropathy, leukopenia, thrombocytopenia and vasculitis

Possibility of minor hair loss; normal hair growth should return after treatment has ended

General Dosing Information

Strengths and dosages of recombinant interferon alfa-2a and alfa-2b, interferon alfa-n1, and interferon alfa-n3 are expressed in terms of Units. Units are determined by comparison of the antiviral activity of the interferon with the activity of the international reference preparation of human leukocyte interferon established by the World Health Organization (WHO).

Patients receiving alpha interferon should be under supervision of a physician experienced in immunomodulatory and/or cancer chemotherapy.

It is recommended that the patient be premedicated with acetaminophen at the time of alpha interferon dosing and that the acetaminophen be continued as needed to treat fever and headache. Dosage reduction of alpha interferon may be necessary if headache persists.

Patients who develop leukopenia should be observed carefully for signs of infection. Antibiotic support may be required. In neutropenic patients who develop fever, broad-spectrum antibiotic coverage should be initiated empirically, pending bacterial cultures and appropriate diagnostic tests. In some cases, it may be difficult to distinguish fever due to infection from fever associated with the flu-like syndrome.

Special precautions are recommended in patients who develop thrombocytopenia as a result of administration of alpha interferons. These may include extreme care in performing invasive procedures; regular inspection of intravenous sites, skin (including perirectal area), and mucous membrane surfaces for signs of bleeding or bruising; limiting frequency of venipuncture and avoiding intramuscular injections; testing urine, emesis, stool, and secretions for occult blood; care in use of regular toothbrushes, dental floss, toothpicks, safety razors, and fingernail and toenail cutters; avoiding constipation; and using caution to prevent falls and other injuries. Such patients should avoid alcohol and any aspirin intake because of the risk of gastrointestinal bleeding. Platelet transfusions may be required.

For systemic use

The subcutaneous route of administration is recommended for patients with thrombocytopenia or at risk for bleeding.

If severe adverse effects occur, dosage reduction by 50% or temporary withdrawal of alpha interferon is recommended.

It is recommended that patients be well hydrated, especially during initial treatment with alpha interferon, to reduce the risk of hypotension associated with fluid depletion. Hypotension may require supportive treatment, including fluid replacement to maintain intravascular volume.

INTERFERON ALFA-2a, RECOMBINANT

Summary of Differences

Pharmacology/pharmacokinetics:

Source—Synthetic; produced by a recombinant DNA process. Purification procedure includes affinity chromatography using a murine monoclonal antibody. Single alpha interferon subtype.

Half-life—

Intramuscular: 6 to 8 hours.

Intravenous infusion: 3.7 to 8.5 hours.

Time to peak concentration (single dose)—

Intramuscular: 3.8 hours.

Subcutaneous: 7.3 hours.

Parenteral Dosage Forms

INTERFERON ALFA-2a, RECOMBINANT, INJECTION

Usual adult dose

Hairy cell leukemia—

Induction: Intramuscular or subcutaneous, 3 million Units per day for sixteen to twenty-four weeks.

Maintenance: Intramuscular or subcutaneous, 3 million Units three times per week.

Kaposi's sarcoma, AIDS-associated—

Induction—

Intramuscular or subcutaneous, 36 million Units (1 mL) per day for ten to twelve weeks, or

Intramuscular or subcutaneous, 3 million Units per day on Days 1 to 3, 9 million Units per day on Days 4 to 6, and 18 million Units per day on Days 7 to 9, followed by 36 million Units (1 mL) per day for the remainder of the ten- to twelve-weeks induction period.

Maintenance—

Intramuscular or subcutaneous, 36 million Units (1 mL) three times per week.

Note: A variety of dosage schedules of interferon have been used for the unlabeled indications. Since these regimens are still largely investigational, the prescriber should consult the medical literature in choosing a specific dosage.

Usual pediatric dose

Dosage has not been established.

Strength(s) usually available

U.S.—

Note: The 10-million-Units-per-mL and 36-million-Units-per-mL strengths are for use for treatment of AIDS-associated Kaposi's sarcoma. They should *not* be used for treatment of hairy cell leukemia.

3 million Units per mL (Rx) [*Roferon-A* (sodium chloride; albumin; phenol)].

6 million Units per mL (18 million Units per vial) (Rx) [*Roferon-A* (sodium chloride; albumin; phenol)].

10 million Units per mL (9 million Units per 0.9-mL vial) (Rx) [*Roferon-A* (sodium chloride; albumin; phenol)].

36 million Units per mL (Rx) [*Roferon-A* (sodium chloride; albumin; phenol)].

Canada—

3 million Units per mL (Rx) [*Roferon-A* (sodium chloride; albumin; phenol)].

6 million Units per mL (Rx) [*Roferon-A* (phenol)].

Packaging and storage

Store between 2 and 8 °C (36 and 46 °F), unless otherwise specified by manufacturer. Protect from freezing.

Note

Do not shake.

When dispensing for self-administration by the patient, make sure that patient instructions are included and that the patient understands how to prepare and administer the injection, including proper use of disposable syringes.

Interferon alfa-2a, -2b, -n1, and -n3 are not interchangeable.

INTERFERON ALFA-2a, RECOMBINANT, FOR INJECTION

Usual adult dose

Hairy cell leukemia—

Induction: Intramuscular or subcutaneous, 3 million Units per day for sixteen to twenty-four weeks.

Maintenance: Intramuscular or subcutaneous, 3 million Units three times per week.

Note: A variety of dosage schedules of interferon have been used for the unlabeled indications. Since these regimens are still largely investigational, the prescriber should consult the medical literature in choosing a specific dosage.

Usual pediatric dose

Dosage has not been established.

Strength(s) usually available

U.S.—

18 million Units (Rx) [*Roferon-A* (diluent contains sodium chloride, albumin, phenol)].

Canada—

18 million Units (Rx) [*Roferon-A* (diluent contains sodium chloride, albumin, phenol)].

Packaging and storage

Store between 2 and 8 °C (36 and 46 °F), unless otherwise specified by manufacturer. Protect from freezing.

Preparation of dosage form

Interferon alfa-2a, recombinant, for injection is prepared for parenteral use by adding 3 mL of diluent (containing sodium chloride, albumin, and phenol) provided by the manufacturer and swirling gently to dissolve, producing a solution containing 6 million Units per mL.

Stability

Reconstituted solution of interferon alfa-2a, recombinant, for injection should be used within 30 days and stored between 2 and 8 °C (36 and 46 °F).

Note

When dispensing for self-administration by the patient, make sure that patient instructions are included and that the patient understands how to prepare and administer the injection, including proper use of disposable syringes.

Interferon alfa-2a, -2b, -n1, and -n3 are not interchangeable.

INTERFERON ALFA-2b, RECOMBINANT

Summary of Differences

Pharmacology/pharmacokinetics:
Source—Synthetic; produced by a recombinant DNA process. Purification is done by proprietary methods. Single alpha interferon subtype.
Half-life—Intramuscular or subcutaneous: 2 to 3 hours.
Time to peak concentration—Intramuscular or subcutaneous: 3 to 12 hours.

Precautions:
Laboratory value alterations—
Nadir of leukocyte and platelet counts is at 3 to 5 days, with recovery within 3 to 5 days after withdrawal.
Prothrombin time (PT) and partial thromboplastin time (PTT) may be increased.
Medical considerations/contraindications—
Caution in coagulation disorders.

Parenteral Dosage Forms

INTERFERON ALFA-2b, RECOMBINANT, FOR INJECTION

Usual adult dose

Hairy cell leukemia—
Intramuscular or subcutaneous, 2 million Units per square meter of body surface area three times per week.

Condyloma acuminatum[1]—
Intralesional, 1 million Units (using only the 10-million-Units-per-mL strength) per wart (up to five warts) three times a week on alternate days for three weeks. If response is not satisfactory twelve to sixteen weeks after the initial treatment course, a second course may be given. Patients with six to ten warts may be given a second (sequential) course of treatment at the same dose to treat up to five additional warts per course; for patients with more than ten warts, additional courses may be given as needed with up to five additional warts per course.

Kaposi's sarcoma, AIDS-associated—
Intramuscular or subcutaneous, 30 million Units (using 50-million-Units-per-mL strength) per square meter of body surface area three times a week.

Hepatitis, chronic, active—
Non-A, non-B/C hepatitis: Intramuscular or subcutaneous, 3 million Units three times per week. Patients who relapse may be retreated with the same dose to which they had previously responded.

Hepatitis B, chronic[1]—
Intramuscular or subcutaneous, 30 to 35 million Units per week, either as 5 million Units per day or 10 million Units three times per week, for sixteen weeks.

Malignant melanoma[1]—
Induction: Intravenous infusion, 20 million Units per square meter of body surface area for five consecutive days per week for four weeks.
Maintenance: Subcutaneous, 10 million Units per square meter of body surface area three times per week for forty-eight weeks.

Note: A variety of dosage schedules of interferon have been used for the unlabeled indications. Since these regimens are still largely investigational, the prescriber should consult the medical literature in choosing a specific dosage.

Usual pediatric dose

Safety and efficacy have not been established.

Strength(s) usually available

U.S.—

Note: The 10-million-Unit size is the only one that should be used for treatment of condyloma acuminatum. Dilution of the other available sizes (3, 5, 18, 25, or 50 million Units) that would be required for intralesional use with the volume of diluent recommended for preparing an intralesional injection would produce a hypertonic solution.

The 50-million-Unit size is a special formulation for use for treatment of AIDS-associated Kaposi's sarcoma or malignant melanoma. It should *not* be used for treatment of hairy cell leukemia or condyloma acuminatum.

3 million Units (Rx) [*Intron A* (albumin)].
5 million Units (Rx) [*Intron A* (albumin)].
10 million Units (Rx) [*Intron A* (albumin)].
18 million Units (Rx) [*Intron A* (albumin)].
25 million Units (Rx) [*Intron A* (albumin)].
50 million Units (Rx) [*Intron A* (albumin)].

Canada—
3 million Units (Rx) [*Intron A* (albumin)].
5 million Units (Rx) [*Intron A* (albumin)].
10 million Units (Rx) [*Intron A* (albumin)].

Packaging and storage

Store between 2 and 8 °C (36 and 46 °F), unless otherwise specified by manufacturer.

Preparation of dosage form

Interferon alfa-2b, recombinant, for injection is prepared for parenteral use by adding the appropriate amount of diluent (in the U.S., bacteriostatic water for injection provided by the manufacturer; in Canada, either sterile water for injection or bacteriostatic water for injection) and agitating gently to dissolve, producing a clear, colorless to light yellow solution.

Size (Units)	Diluent (mL)	Final concentration (Units/mL)
U.S.—		
For treatment of hairy cell leukemia		
3 million	1	3 million
5 million	1	5 million
10 million	2	5 million
25 million	5	5 million
For treatment of condyloma acuminatum		
10 million	1	10 million
For treatment of AIDS-associated Kaposi's sarcoma		
50 million	1	50 million
For treatment of malignant melanoma (induction or maintenance phase)		
3 million	1	3 million
5 million	1	5 million
10 million	1	10 million
18 million	1	18 million
25 million	5	5 million
50 million	1	50 million
For treatment of chronic hepatitis B		
5 million	1	5 million
10 million	1	10 million
For treatment of chronic active non-A, non-B/C hepatitis		
3 million	1	3 million
Canada—		
3 million	1	3 million
5 million	1	5 million
10 million	1	10 million

Stability

Reconstituted solutions of interferon alfa-2b, recombinant, prepared with sterile water for injection are stable for 24 hours when stored between 2 and 8 °C (36 and 46 °F); solutions prepared with bacteriostatic water for injection are stable for 1 month when stored between 2 and 8 °C (36 and 46 °F).

Note

When dispensing for self-administration by the patient, make sure that patient instructions are included and that the patient understands how to prepare and administer the injection, including proper use of disposable syringes.

Interferon alfa-2a, -2b, -n1, and -n3 are not interchangeable.

[1]Not included in Canadian product labeling.

INTERFERON ALFA-n1 (LNS)

Summary of Differences

Pharmacology/pharmacokinetics:
Source—Obtained from pooled units of human lymphoblastoid cells following induction with Sendai virus. Mixture of natural alpha interferon subtypes, but in different proportions than in human leukocyte interferon.
Half-life—Intravenous infusion: About 8 hours.

Parenteral Dosage Forms

INTERFERON ALFA-n1 (LNS) INJECTION

Usual adult dose

Hairy cell leukemia—

Induction: Intramuscular or subcutaneous, 3 million Units per day for sixteen to twenty-four weeks.

Maintenance: Intramuscular or subcutaneous, 3 million Units three times per week.

Condyloma acuminatum—

Intramuscular or subcutaneous, 1 to 3 million Units per square meter of body surface area five times a week for two weeks, followed by three times a week for four weeks. The same dose is then continued every other day or three times a week for one month.

Note: As an adjunct to laser surgery or cryosurgery, the dose is 1 million Units per square meter of body surface area intramuscularly or subcutaneously per day for seven days prior to and seven days following surgical resection of the lesions.

Note: A variety of dosage schedules of interferon have been used for the unlabeled indications. Since these regimens are still largely investigational, the prescriber should consult the medical literature in choosing a specific dosage.

Usual pediatric dose

Hairy cell leukemia or
Condyloma acuminatum—

Dosage has not been established.

Juvenile laryngeal papillomatosis—

For children older than 1 year of age—

Body surface area less than 0.5 square meter—Intramuscular or subcutaneous, 1.5 million Units per day for twenty-eight days, followed by maintenance dosage three times a week for at least six months.

Body surface area 0.5–1 square meter—Intramuscular or subcutaneous, 3 million Units per day for twenty-eight days, followed by maintenance dosage three times a week for at least six months.

Body surface area greater than 1 square meter—Intramuscular or subcutaneous, 5 million Units per day for twenty-eight days, followed by maintenance dosage three times a week for at least six months.

Strength(s) usually available

U.S.—

Not commercially available.

Canada—

3 million Units (Rx) [*Wellferon*].
10 million Units (Rx) [*Wellferon*].

Packaging and storage

Store between 2 and 8 °C (36 and 46 °F), unless otherwise specified by manufacturer. Protect from light.

Note

Interferon alfa-2a, -2b, -n1, and -n3 are not interchangeable.

INTERFERON ALFA-n3

Summary of Differences

Pharmacology/pharmacokinetics:

Source—Obtained from pooled units of human leukocytes that have been induced to produce interferon alfa-n3. Contains up to 14 natural alpha interferon subtypes. Human leukocyte interferon.

Precautions:

Medical considerations/contraindications—Caution in coagulation disorders.

Parenteral Dosage Forms

INTERFERON ALFA-n3 INJECTION

Usual adult dose

Condyloma acuminatum—

Intralesional (at the base of the wart, preferably using a 30 gauge needle), 250,000 Units two times a week for up to eight weeks.

Note: For large warts, it may be injected at several points around the periphery of the wart, using a total dose of 250,000 Units.

Safety and efficacy of more than one 8-week course have not been established.

A variety of dosage schedules of interferon have been used for the unlabeled indications. Since these regimens are still largely investigational, the prescriber should consult the medical literature in choosing a specific dosage.

Usual adult prescribing limits

2.5 million Units per treatment session.

Usual pediatric dose

Dosage has not been established.

Strength(s) usually available

U.S.—

5 million Units per mL (Rx) [*Alferon N* (phenol 3.3 mg per mL; human albumin 1 mg per mL)].

Canada—

Not commercially available.

Packaging and storage

Store between 2 and 8 °C (36 and 46 °F), unless otherwise specified by manufacturer. Protect from freezing.

Note

Do not shake.

Interferon alfa-2a, -2b, -n1, and -n3 are not interchangeable.

Revised: 09/12/2001

Table 1. Side/Adverse Effects

Note: Most side/adverse effects, except the flu-like syndrome, are dose-related. They are usually mild to moderate at systemic doses less than 10 million Units per day; hematologic and hepatic toxicities tend to be more frequent with doses above 10 million Units, and cardiovascular and neurologic toxicities tend to be more frequent with doses above 30 million Units. However, patient sensitivity varies.

Reduced blood pressure occurs frequently with systemic use but is rarely symptomatic; hypotension may occur during administration or up to two days after therapy, and may require supportive therapy including fluid replacement to maintain intravascular volume; hypertension may occur but is usually mild and transient.

Development of neutralizing antibodies has been reported. Relationship of the presence of neutralizing antibodies to loss of antitumor effects is controversial; a possible correlation with titer of neutralizing antibodies has been suggested but not confirmed. Differences in frequency of antibody formation have been reported among alpha interferons but relative frequency has not been studied prospectively. Differences may be related to the differences in the sensitivity of tests used in antibody detection, as well as to disease state, dose, schedule, and route of administration.

The following side/adverse effects have been selected on the basis of their potential clinical significance (possible signs and symptoms in parentheses where appropriate)—not necessarily inclusive:*	Indication				
	Hairy cell leukemia	Other malignancies	Condyloma acuminatum	Kaposi's sarcoma	Hepatitis
Those indicating need for medical attention					
Anemia (usually asymptomatic)	N/A	M	L	M	M
Autoimmune disorders including: vasculitis, arthritis, hemolytic anemia, and erythematosus syndrome	R	R	R	R	R
Cardiotoxicity (chest pain, irregular heartbeat) Note: Arrhythmias are usually supraventricular.	R	R	U	R	R
Hepatotoxicity (usually asymptomatic)	L	L	L	M	L
Hyperthyroidism or hypothyroidism (usually asymptomatic)	U	U	U	U	R

Table 1. Side/Adverse Effects *(continued)*

Note: Most side/adverse effects, except the flu-like syndrome, are dose-related. They are usually mild to moderate at systemic doses less than 10 million Units per day; hematologic and hepatic toxicities tend to be more frequent with doses above 10 million Units, and cardiovascular and neurologic toxicities tend to be more frequent with doses above 30 million Units. However, patient sensitivity varies.

Reduced blood pressure occurs frequently with systemic use but is rarely symptomatic; hypotension may occur during administration or up to two days after therapy, and may require supportive therapy including fluid replacement to maintain intravascular volume; hypertension may occur but is usually mild and transient.

Development of neutralizing antibodies has been reported. Relationship of the presence of neutralizing antibodies to loss of antitumor effects is controversial; a possible correlation with titer of neutralizing antibodies has been suggested but not confirmed. Differences in frequency of antibody formation have been reported among alpha interferons but relative frequency has not been studied prospectively. Differences may be related to the differences in the sensitivity of tests used in antibody detection, as well as to disease state, dose, schedule, and route of administration.

The following side/adverse effects have been selected on the basis of their potential clinical significance (possible signs and symptoms in parentheses where appropriate)—not necessarily inclusive:*	Indication				
	Hairy cell leukemia	Other malignancies	Condyloma acuminatum	Kaposi's sarcoma	Hepatitis
Ischemic attacks, transient (headache, numbness or tingling in arms or legs, trouble speaking)	R	R	R	R	R
Leukopenia (usually asymptomatic; rarely, fever or chills, cough or hoarseness, lower back or side pain, painful or difficult urination)	N/A	M	M	M	M
Neurotoxicity (confusion, mental depression, nervousness, trouble in sleeping, trouble in thinking or concentrating) Note: Usually reversible after withdrawal; in some patients, especially the elderly or those treated with high doses, stupor, obtundation, and coma have occurred.	L	L	L	L	L
Peripheral neuropathy (numbness or tingling of fingers, toes, or face)	L	L	L	L	R
Thrombocytopenia (usually asymptomatic; rarely, unusual bleeding or bruising; black, tarry stools; blood in urine or stools; pinpoint red spots on skin)	N/A	M	L	M	M
Those indicating need for medical attention only if they continue or are bothersome					
Blurred vision	L	L	L	L	L
Change in taste or metallic taste	M	M	R	M	R
Cold sores or stomatitis (sores in mouth and on lips)	L	L	R	R	R
Diarrhea	M	M	L	M	M
Dizziness Note: Dizziness is a CNS effect.	M	M	L	M	L
Dry mouth	M	M	R	M	L
Dry skin or itching	L	L	L	L	L
Flu-like syndrome (aching muscles, fever and chills, headache, general feeling of discomfort or illness; less frequently, joint pain, back pain) Note: Occurs in most patients; most pronounced in first week of treatment and gradually reduced, as a result of tachyphylaxis, within 2 to 4 weeks with continued treatment.	M	M	M	M	M
Increased sweating	L	L	L	L	L
Leg cramps	L	L	L	U	R
Loss of appetite Note: Loss of appetite tends to become more prominent with continued treatment and may necessitate dosage reduction; usually resolves within 4 weeks after withdrawal of alpha interferon.	M	M	L	M	M
Nausea or vomiting Note: Nausea or vomiting usually resolves within 3 to 5 days after withdrawal of alpha interferon.	M	M	M	M	M
Skin rash	M	M	L	M	L
Unusual tiredness Note: Unusual tiredness tends to become more prominent with continued treatment and may necessitate dosage reduction; usually resolves several weeks after withdrawal of alpha interferon.	M	M	M	M	M
Weight loss	R	R	R	L	R
Those not indicating need for medical attention					
Loss of hair, partial Note: Hair growth returns promptly after withdrawal of alpha interferon.	L	L	U	M	M

*Differences in frequency of occurrence may reflect either lack of clinical-use data or actual pharmacologic distinctions among agents (although their pharmacologic similarity suggests that side effects occurring with one may occur with the others). M = more frequent; L = less frequent; R = rare; U = unknown; X = does not occur; N/A = not applicable.

IOBENGUANE I 123—See *Iobenguane, Radioiodinated (Systemic—Diagnostic)*

IOBENGUANE I 131—See *Iobenguane, Radioiodinated (Systemic—Diagnostic)*

IOCETAMIC ACID—See *Cholecystographic Agents, Oral (Systemic)*

IODINATED I 125 ALBUMIN—See *Radioiodinated Albumin (Systemic)*

IODINATED I 131 ALBUMIN—See *Radioiodinated Albumin (Systemic)*

IOPANOIC ACID—See *Cholecystographic Agents, Oral (Systemic)*

IPODATE—See *Cholecystographic Agents, Oral (Systemic)*

IPRATROPIUM Inhalation-Local

VA CLASSIFICATION (Primary): RE150

Commonly used brand name(s): *Apo-Ipravent; Atrovent; Atrovent HFA; Kendral-Ipratropium.*

Note: For a listing of dosage forms and brand names by country availability, see *Dosage Forms* section(s).

Category

Bronchodilator.

Indications

Note: Bracketed information in the *Indications* section refers to uses that are not included in U.S. product labeling.

Accepted

Bronchitis, chronic (treatment) or

Emphysema, pulmonary (treatment) or

Pulmonary disease, chronic obstructive, other (treatment)—Ipratropium is indicated for maintenance treatment of bronchospasm associated with chronic obstructive pulmonary disease, including chronic bronchitis and pulmonary emphysema. Regular use of ipratropium results in at least as great an increase in airflow as that with use of other bronchodilators and fewer adverse effects. If additional bronchodilation is needed in these patients, an adrenergic bronchodilator may be used as an adjunct to ipratropium.

[Ipratropium is indicated as an adjunct to adrenergic bronchodilators for treatment of acute exacerbations of chronic obstructive pulmonary disease.]

[Asthma (treatment adjunct)]—Ipratropium is used as an adjunct to anti-inflammatory therapy or bronchodilators to prevent[1] exacerbations of asthma in patients who respond poorly to therapy or as an alternative to other bronchodilators in patients who develop significant side effects with these medications.

Ipratropium is used as an adjunct to adrenergic bronchodilators for the treatment of acute exacerbations of asthma. It is not used alone because it has a relatively slower onset of action and time to peak effect as compared with adrenergic bronchodilators.

Unaccepted

Ipratropium inhalation aerosol is not indicated for the initial treatment of acute episodes of bronchospasm where rescue therapy is required for rapid response.

[1]Not included in Canadian product labeling.

Pharmacology/Pharmacokinetics

Physicochemical characteristics

Source—A synthetic quaternary ammonium compound, chemically related to atropine.

Molecular weight—430.38.

Other characteristics—

Fairly stable in neutral solutions and in acid solutions; rapidly hydrolyzed in alkaline solutions

Mechanism of action/Effect

The bronchodilation produced by ipratropium is primarily a local, site-specific effect rather than a systemic effect. Ipratropium appears to produce bronchodilation by competitive inhibition of cholinergic receptors on bronchial smooth muscle. This effect antagonizes the action of acetylcholine at its membrane-bound receptor site and thereby blocks the bronchoconstrictor action of vagal efferent impulses.

Absorption

Systemic absorption is minimal following inhalation. Blood concentration and renal and fecal excretion studies have shown that ipratropium is poorly absorbed into the systemic circulation from both the surface of the lung and the gastrointestinal tract. At a dose of 14 times the recommended therapeutic inhalation dose, the peak plasma concentration is 0.06 nanograms/mL. Plasma concentrations after inhalation of usual doses are about 1000 times lower than equipotent oral or intravenous doses (15 and 0.15 mg, respectively).

Distribution

Studies in rats have shown that ipratropium does not penetrate the blood-brain barrier.

Biotransformation

Hepatic, for the small amount of ipratropium systemically absorbed; metabolites have little or no anticholinergic activity.

Onset of action

Within 5 to 15 minutes.

Time to peak effect

About 90 minutes (range, 1 to 2 hours).

Duration of action

About 3 to 4 hours in the majority of patients, but up to 6 to 8 hours in some patients.

Elimination

Primarily fecal; up to 90% of inhaled dose is swallowed and eliminated as unchanged drug. Absorbed portion of dose is excreted primarily in the urine.

Precautions to Consider

Cross-sensitivity and/or related problems

Patients sensitive to belladona alkaloids may be sensitive to ipratropium also, since ipratropium is chemically related to atropine. Although rare, allergic reactions to ipratropium metered-dose inhaler have been reported; however, the causative component has not been identified. Therefore, patients allergic to soybean protein or other legumes, such as peanuts, may be allergic to soya lecithin contained in the metered-dose inhaler as a suspending agent.

Carcinogenicity/Tumorigenicity

Two-year carcinogenicity studies in mice and rats have shown that ipratropium, at oral doses up to 1250 times the maximum recommended human daily dose, has no carcinogenic potential. Also, studies in mice and rats have shown that ipratropium, at oral doses up to 6 mg per kg of body weight (mg/kg), does not have a carcinogenic or tumorigenic effect.

Mutagenicity

Various studies in mice and hamsters have shown that ipratropium is not mutagenic.

Pregnancy/Reproduction

Fertility—Although studies in male and female rats have shown that ipratropium, at oral doses up to approximately 10,000 times the maximum recommended human daily dose, does not affect fertility, ipratropium has been shown to increase resorption and decrease conception rates when the medication was administered at doses above 18,000 times the maximum recommended human daily dose.

Pregnancy—Although adequate and well-controlled studies in humans have not been done, no increased risk of congenital malformation has been reported. Because animal reproduction studies are not always predictive of human response, ipratropium should be used during pregnancy only if clearly needed.

Reproduction studies with ipratropium in mice, rats, and rabbits given oral doses of 10, 100, and 125 mg per kg of body weight (mg/kg), respectively, and in rats and rabbits given inhalation doses of 1.5 and 1.8 mg/kg (or approximately 38 and 45 times the recommended human daily dose), respectively, have shown no evidence of teratogenic effects.

FDA Pregnancy Category B.

Breast-feeding

It is not known whether ipratropium is distributed into breast milk. However, problems in humans have not been documented. Although lipid-insoluble quaternary bases, such as ipratropium, are distributed into breast milk, it is unlikely that inhaled ipratropium would reach significant concentrations in maternal serum, and the concentration in breast milk would probably be undetectable. Because many drugs are distributed in human milk, caution should be exercised when ipratropium is administered to a nursing woman.

Pediatrics

Appropriate studies performed to date have not demonstrated pediatrics-specific problems that would limit the usefulness of ipratropium in children. Safety and effectiveness in the pediatric population have not been established.

Geriatrics
Studies performed to date on patients over 65 years of age have not demonstrated geriatrics-specific problems that would limit the usefulness of ipratropium inhalation in the elderly.

Drug interactions and/or related problems
The following drug interactions and/or related problems have been selected on the basis of their potential clinical significance (possible mechanism in parentheses where appropriate)—not necessarily inclusive (» = major clinical significance):

Note: Combinations containing any of the following medications, depending on the amount present, may also interact with this medication.

Anticholinergics, other, or other medications with anticholinergic activity (see *Appendix II*)
(concurrent use of other anticholinergics, including ophthalmic preparations, or other medications with anticholinergic action with ipratropium may result in additive effects)

Tacrine
(because tacrine is thought to act by increasing effective acetylcholine concentrations, concurrent use may decrease the effects of either ipratropium or tacrine)

Medical considerations/Contraindications
The medical considerations/contraindications included have been selected on the basis of their potential clinical significance (reasons given in parentheses where appropriate)—not necessarily inclusive (» = major clinical significance).

Except under special circumstance, this medication should not be used when the following medical condition exists:
» Hypersensitivity to ipratropium bromide or any other component or the product or
» Hypersensitivity to atropine or its derivatives

Risk-benefit should be considered when the following medical problems exist:
Bladder-neck obstruction or
Glaucoma, narrow-angle or
Prostatic hypertrophy
(should be used with caution)
» Glaucoma, angle-closure
(an acute attack may be precipitated or condition may be exacerbated if ipratropium inhalation aerosol is sprayed directly into the eyes or if a poorly fitting face mask is used with nebulized ipratropium inhalation solution, alone or in combination with an adrenergic bronchodilator)

Allergy to soya lecithin, soybean protein, or other legumes such as peanuts for patients using the metered-dose inhaler

Urinary retention
(rarely, condition may be aggravated)

Side/Adverse Effects
Note: Usual therapeutic doses of ipratropium generally do not cause systemic side/adverse effects because of the low blood concentrations achieved with the inhalation; however, the potential for systemic side/adverse effects exists.

Although rare, cases of precipitation or worsening of narrow-angle glaucoma and acute eye pain have been reported following use of ipratropium aerosol, and inhalation solution alone or in combination with an adrenergic bronchodilator, when the spray came into contact with the eyes.

Immediate hypersensitivity reactions may occur after administration of ipratropium bromide, as demonstrated by rare cases of urticaria, angioedema, rash, bronchospasm, anaphylaxis, and oropharyngeal edema.

Ipratropium inhalation aerosol may cause pardoxical bronchospasm. If this occurs, treatment should be stopped and other treatments considered.

The following side/adverse effects have been selected on the basis of their potential clinical significance (possible signs and symptoms in parentheses where appropriate)—not necessarily inclusive:

Those indicating need for medical attention
Incidence less frequent
Chronic obstructive pulmonary disease (COPD) exacerbation (increased cough, purulent sputum, wheezing, difficulty breathing)

Incidence rare
Bronchospasm, increased (increased wheezing; tightness in chest; difficulty in breathing); ***dermatitis, hypersensitivity-induced; angioedema*** (swelling of face, lips, or eyelids); ***skin rash; urticaria*** (hives); ***eye pain, acute; paralytic ileus*** (continuing constipation; lower abdominal pain or distention)—especially in patients with cystic fibrosis

Note: *Increased bronchospasm* may be due to sensitivity to benzalkonium chloride and edetate disodium present in the multiple-dose container of inhalation solution.

Incidence not determined—Observed during clinical practice; estimates of frequency can not be determined
Atrial fibrillation (fast or irregular heartbeat; dizziness; fainting); ***supraventricular tachycardia*** (fainting; fast, pounding, or irregular heartbeat or pulse; palpitations)

Those indicating need for medical attention only if they continue or are bothersome
Incidence more frequent
Bronchitis (cough producing mucus; difficulty breathing; shortness of breath; tightness in chest; wheezing); ***cough; dryness of mouth; unpleasant taste; upper respiratory tract infection*** (ear congestion; nasal congestion; chills; cough, fever, sneezing, or sore throat; body aches or pain; headache; loss of voice; runny nose; unusual tiredness or weakness; difficulty in breathing)

Incidence less frequent
Back pain; dyspepsia (acid or sour stomach; belching; heartburn; indigestion; stomach discomfort, upset, or pain); ***influenza-like symptoms*** (chills; cough; diarrhea; fever; general feeling of discomfort or illness; headache; joint pain; loss of appetite; muscle aches and pains; nausea; runny nose; shivering; sore throat; sweating; trouble sleeping; unusual tiredness or weakness; vomiting); ***sinusitis*** (pain or tenderness around eyes and cheekbones; fever; stuffy or runny nose; headache; cough; shortness of breath or troubled breathing; tightness of chest or wheezing); ***urinary tract infection*** (bladder pain; bloody or cloudy urine; difficult, burning, or painful urination; frequent urge to urinate; lower back or side pain)

Incidence rare
Blurred vision or other changes in vision; burning eyes; dizziness; headache; nausea; nervousness; palpitations (pounding heartbeat); ***sweating; trembling; urinary retention*** (difficult urination)

Overdose
For more information on the management of overdose or unintentional ingestion, **contact a poison control center** (see *Poison Control Center Listing*).

Acute overdosage by inhalation is unlikely since ipratropium bromide is not well–absorbed systemically.

Treatment of overdose
Cholinesterase inhibitors may be used for serious anticholinergic toxicity.

Patients in whom intentional overdose is confirmed or suspected should be referred for psychiatric evaluation.

Patient Consultation
As an aid to patient consultation, refer to *Advice for the Patient, Ipratropium (Inhalation)*.

In providing consultation, consider emphasizing the following selected information (» = major clinical significance):

Before using this medication
» Conditions affecting use, especially:
Hypersensitivity to ipratropium or any component of the product or to atropine or its derivatives; also, allergy to soya lecithin, soybean protein, or peanuts for patients using metered-dose inhaler
Pregnancy—Should be used during pregnancy only if clearly needed
Breast-feeding—Caution should be exercised if administering to a nursing woman
Use in children—Safety and efficacy not established
Other medical problems, especially angle-closure glaucoma

Proper use of this medication
» Using inhalation solution only with other bronchodilators when treating acute asthma attacks; helps control symptoms of lung disease
» Importance of not using ipratropium inhalation aerosol for the initial treatment of acute episodes of bronchospasm where rescue therapy is required for rapid response; the inhalation aerosol indicated for maintenance treatment
» Importance of not using more medication than the amount prescribed
» Avoiding contact with the eyes; closing eyes if necessary when inhaling; if accidentally sprayed into the eyes or if nebulized solution escapes into the eyes, irritation or blurring of vision may occur; rinsing eyes with cool water if necessary

Reading patient instructions carefully before using
» If using regularly, importance of using every day at regularly spaced times
» Proper dosing
Missed dose: If used regularly, using as soon as possible; using any remaining doses for that day at regularly spaced intervals
» Proper storage

For inhalation aerosol dosage form
Checking periodically with health care professional for proper use of inhaler to prevent improper technique and incorrect dosage
Keeping record of number of sprays used, if possible; not floating canister in water to test fullness
Testing or priming inhaler before using first time or first time in a while
Discarding canister after labeled number of metered dose sprays has been used, even if canister does not appear completely empty
Proper administration technique without spacer device
Proper administration technique with spacer device
Proper cleaning procedure for inhaler

For inhalation solution dosage form
Using only in nebulizer as instructed by physician
Preparing solution for nebulizer
Proper administration technique: using in a power-operated nebulizer with an adequate flow rate and equipped with a face mask or mouthpiece

Precautions while using this medication

» Checking with physician immediately if symptoms do not improve within 30 minutes after using this medication or if condition becomes worse

» Avoiding spraying medication in eyes and consulting physician immediately if any symptoms of precipitation or worsening of narrow-angle glaucoma, mydriasis, eye pain or discomfort, temporary blurring of vision, visual halos or colored images in association with red eyes from conjunctival and corneal congestion occur

» Importance of contacting physician immediately if hypersensitivity reactions occur after administration of this medicine such as rare cases of urticaria, angioedema, rash, bronchospasms, anaphylaxis, and oropharyngeal edema

For patients using ipratropium inhalation solution:
» If also using cromolyn inhalation solution, not mixing cromolyn inhalation solution with ipratropium inhalation solution containing the preservative benzalkonium chloride for use in a nebulizer

For patients using ipratropium inhalation aerosol:
» Discontinuing treatment with ipratropium inhalation aerosol and considering other treatments if paradoxical bronchospasm occurs
» Not using other inhaled medications without first contacting the physician
Advising patients that although taste and inhalation sensations of HFA and CFC formulations may be slightly different, safety and efficacy are comparable

Side/adverse effects

Signs of potential side effects, especially increased bronchospasm, COPD exacerbation, hypersensitivity-induced dermatitis, acute eye pain, and paralytic ileus
Signs of potential side effects observed during clinical practice, especially atrial fibrillation and supraventricular tachycardia

General Dosing Information

For nebulization of ipratropium bromide inhalation solution, a gas flow (oxygen or compressed air) of 6 to 10 liters per minute should be used. Nebulizers with either a face mask or mouthpiece have been used, although a mouthpiece may be preferable to a face mask because it reduces the risk of solution entering the eyes.

Patients should be advised on the use of ipratropium inhalation aerosol in relation to other inhaled drugs.

Patients should be advised to contact their physician immediately if they do not respond to the usual dose of ipratropium because this may be a sign of seriously worsening airflow obstruction or the development of concurrent illness requiring reassessment of therapy.

The contents of metered dose inhalers should generally not be floated in water to assess the contents since this method may not reliably predict the amount of medication remaining in the canister. A record should be kept of the number of inhalations used.

Although the taste and inhalation sensations of the HFA and CFC propellant formulations of the inhalation aerosol may be slightly different, they are comparable in terms of safety and efficacy.

Inhalation Dosage Forms

Note: Bracketed uses in the *Dosage Forms* section refers to indications that are not included in U.S. product labeling.

IPRATROPIUM BROMIDE INHALATION AEROSOL

Usual adult and adolescent dose

Bronchitis (treatment)
Emphysema, pulmonary (treatment) or
Pulmonary disease, chronic obstructive, other (treatment)—
Oral inhalation, 2 to 4 inhalations (36 to 72 mcg) three or four times a day. Some patients may require up to 6 to 8 inhalations (108 to 144 mcg) three times a day. For severe exacerbations, 6 to 8 inhalations may be administered, using a spacer device, every three to four hours.

[Asthma (treatment adjunct)]—
Oral inhalation, 1 to 4 inhalations (18 to 72 mcg) four times a day as necessary.

Usual adult and adolescent prescribing limits

The U.S. manufacturer recommends a maximum of twelve inhalations in twenty–four hours.The Canadian manufacturer recommends a maximum of 8 inhalations in twenty–four hours.

Usual pediatric dose

[Asthma (treatment adjunct)][1]—
Children up to 12 years of age: Oral inhalation, 1 to 2 inhalations (18 to 36 mcg) every six to eight hours as necessary.

Strength(s) usually available

U.S.—
18 mcg per metered spray (Rx) [*Atrovent* (dichlorodifluoromethane; dichlorotetrafluoroethane; trichloromonofluoromethane; soya lecithin)].
17 mcg per metered spray (Rx) [*Atrovent HFA* (HFA-134a [1,1,1,2-tetrafluoroethane] as propellant; purified water; dehydrated alcohol; anhydrous citric acid)].
Note: *Atrovent HFA* inhalation aerosol does not contain chlorofluorocarbons (CFCs) as the propellant.

Canada—
20 mcg per metered spray (Rx) [*Atrovent* (dichlorodifluoromethane; dichlorotetrafluoroethane; trichloromonofluoromethane; soya lecithin)].

Note: In Canada, metered dose inhalers are labeled according to the amount of ipratropium delivered at the valve; in the U.S., metered dose inhalers are labeled according to the amount of ipratropium delivered at the mouthpiece or actuator. Therefore, 20 mcg of ipratropium delivered at the valve is equivalent to 18 mcg delivered at the mouthpiece.

Packaging and storage

Store at 25 °C (77 °F); excursions permitted between 15 and 30 °C (59 and 86 °F), unless otherwise specified by manufacturer.

Auxiliary labeling

- For oral inhalation only.
- Shake well before using.
- You should take this medication exactly as prescribed. Do not skip or discontinue unless directed to.
- Store away from heat and direct sunlight.

Caution

Contents under pressure. Do not puncture or incinerate. Do not use or store near heat or open flame. Exposure to temperatures above 120 °F may cause bursting. Never throw the inhaler into a fire or incinerator.

Note

Include patient instructions when dispensing.

Demonstrate inhalation technique to patient when dispensing.

Additional information

The actuator supplied with the product should not be used with any other product canisters and other product actuators should not be used with this product. The correct amount of medication in each actuation cannot be assured after 200 actuations, even though the canister is not completely empty. The canister should be discarded when 200 actuations have been used.

IPRATROPIUM BROMIDE INHALATION SOLUTION

Usual adult and adolescent dose

Bronchitis (treatment)
Emphysema, pulmonary (treatment) or
Pulmonary disease, chronic obstructive, other (treatment)—
Oral inhalation, 250 to 500 mcg (0.25 to 0.5 mg), diluted, if necessary; dose is administered via nebulization three or four times a day,

every six to eight hours. For severe exacerbations of COPD, 500 mcg may be administered every four to eight hours.

[Asthma (treatment adjunct)]—
Oral inhalation, 500 mcg (0.5 mg), diluted, if necessary; dose is administered via nebulization three or four times a day, every six to eight hours as necessary.

Usual adult and adolescent prescribing limits
2 mg per twenty-four hours.

Usual pediatric dose
[Asthma (treatment adjunct)][1]—
Children up to 5 years of age: Safety and efficacy have not been established.
Children 5 to 12 years of age: Oral inhalation, 125 to 250 mcg (0.125 to 0.25 mg), diluted, if necessary, to three to five mL with preservative-free sterile sodium chloride inhalation solution 0.9%; dose is administered via nebulization every four to six hours as necessary.

Strength(s) usually available
U.S.—
Single-dose vial:
0.02% (200 mcg per mL [2.5 mL]) (Rx) [*Atrovent;* GENERIC].

Canada—
Single-dose vial:
0.0125% (125 mcg per mL [2 mL]) (Rx) [*Atrovent*].
0.025% (250 mcg per mL [1 or 2 mL]) (Rx) [*Atrovent*].
Multiple-dose vial:
0.025% (250 mcg per mL) (Rx) [*Apo-Ipravent* (benzalkonium chloride; EDTA-disodium); *Atrovent* (benzalkonium chloride; EDTA-disodium); *Kendral-Ipratropium*].

Packaging and storage
Prior to opening container, store between 15 and 30 °C (59 and 86 °F), unless otherwise specified by manufacturer. Protect from freezing. Protect from light.

Preparation of dosage form
Ipratropium inhalation solution can be diluted with preservative-free sterile 0.9% sodium chloride.

Stability
Solutions of ipratropium containing the preservative benzalkonium chloride may be diluted with preservative-free sterile sodium chloride inhalation solution 0.9%. The solution should be used within twenty-four hours from time of dilution when stored at room temperature and within forty-eight hours when stored in the refrigerator.

Preservative-free albuterol inhalation solution can be mixed in the nebulizer with ipratropium inhalation solution, if used within one hour.

Preservative-free ipratropium inhalation solution is recommended when combining ipratropium with cromolyn inhalation solution. This combination is compatible for up to one hour. Mixing ipratropium inhalation solution containing the preservative benzalkonium chloride with cromolyn in a nebulizer results in cloudiness of the solution, which is due to complexation between cromolyn sodium and benzalkonium chloride. No precipitation or significant decrease in the concentration of cromolyn or ipratropium occurs.

Auxiliary labeling
- For oral inhalation only.

Note
Include patient instructions for preparation of solution when dispensing.

[1]Not included in Canadian product labeling.

Selected Bibliography

Gross NJ. Ipratropium bromide. N Engl J Med 1988; 319: 486-94.

Spector SL, Nicklas RA, editors. Practice parameters for the diagnosis and treatment of asthma. J Allergy Clin Immunol 1995; 96: 786-9.

American Thoracic Society. Standards for the diagnosis and care of patients with chronic obstructive pulmonary disease. Am J Respir Crit Care Med 1995; 152 Suppl: 77S-120S.

Revised: 08/08/2005

IPRATROPIUM Nasal

VA CLASSIFICATION (Primary): NT900

Commonly used brand name(s): *Atrovent.*

Note: For a listing of dosage forms and brand names by country availability, see *Dosage Forms* section(s).

Category
Anticholinergic (nasal).

Indications

Accepted
Rhinorrhea associated with allergic and nonallergic perennial rhinitis (treatment)—Ipratropium nasal solution 0.03% is indicated for the symptomatic relief of rhinorrhea associated with allergic and nonallergic perennial rhinitis. However, ipratropium nasal solution 0.03% does not relieve nasal congestion, sneezing, or postnasal drip associated with allergic or nonallergic perennial rhinitis.

Rhinorrhea associated with the common cold (treatment)—Ipratropium nasal solution 0.06% is indicated for the symptomatic relief of rhinorrhea associated with the common cold. However, ipratropium nasal solution 0.06% does not relieve nasal congestion or sneezing associated with the common cold.

Pharmacology/Pharmacokinetics

Physicochemical characteristics
Source—A synthetic quaternary ammonium compound, chemically related to atropine..

Molecular weight—Ipratropium Bromide: 430.38.

Mechanism of action/Effect
Ipratropium antagonizes the actions of acetylcholine at parasympathetic, postganglionic, effector-cell junctions by competing with acetylcholine for receptor sites. When administered intranasally, ipratropium has a localized parasympathetic blocking action, which reduces watery hypersecretion from mucosal glands in the nose.

Absorption
Systemic absorption from the nasal mucosa is rapid but minimal following nasal administration.

Biotransformation
Hepatic, for the small amount of nasal ipratropium systemically absorbed; metabolites appear to have no anticholinergic activity.

Half-life
Elimination—About 3.5 hours (range, 1.5 to 4 hours).

Onset of action
Within 5 minutes.

Time to peak effect
1 to 4 hours.

Duration of action
About 4 to 8 hours.

Elimination
Absorbed portion of dose is excreted primarily in the urine; also excreted in the bile.

Precautions to Consider

Cross-sensitivity and/or related problems
Patients sensitive to belladonna alkaloids may be sensitive to ipratropium also, since ipratropium is chemically related to atropine.

Carcinogenicity
In a 2-year study in rats and mice, ipratropium administered in oral doses of up to 6 mg per kg of body weight (mg/kg) per day (approximately 70 and 36 times the maximum recommended daily intranasal dose in adults, respectively, and approximately 45 and 25 times the maximum recommended daily intranasal dose in children, respectively, on a mg per square meter of body surface area basis [mg/m^2]) showed no carcinogenic activity.

Mutagenicity
Ipratropium was not found to be mutagenic in the Ames test, mouse dominant lethal test, mouse micronucleus test, and chromosome aberration of bone marrow in Chinese hamsters test.

Pregnancy/Reproduction
Fertility—Fertility was unaffected in male and female rats administered ipratropium in oral doses of up to 50 mg/kg (approximately 600 times the maximum recommended daily intranasal dose in adults on a mg/m^2 basis). However, at an oral dose of 500 mg/kg (approximately 16,000 times the maximum recommended daily intranasal dose in adults on a mg/m^2 basis), ipratropium produced a decrease in the conception rate.

Pregnancy—Adequate and well-controlled studies in humans have not been done.

No evidence of teratogenic effects was found in reproduction studies (using inhalation of medication) conducted in rats and rabbits administered ipratropium in doses of 1.5 mg/kg and 1.8 mg/kg, respectively (approximately 20 and 45 times, respectively, the maximum recommended daily intranasal dose in adults on a mg/m² basis). In addition, no evidence of teratogenic effects was found in reproduction studies (using oral medication) conducted in mice, rats, and rabbits administered ipratropium in doses of 10 mg/kg, 1000 mg/kg, and 125 mg/kg, respectively (approximately 60, 12,000, and 3000 times, respectively, the maximum recommended daily intranasal dose in adults on a mg/m² basis). However, in rats administered oral doses of ipratropium above 90 mg/kg (approximately 1100 times the maximum recommended daily intranasal dose in adults on a mg/m² basis), embryotoxicity was observed as increased resorption. This effect was not considered relevant to human use, because of the large doses at which it was observed and the differences in the routes of administration between rats (oral) and humans (intranasal).

FDA Pregnancy Category B.

Breast-feeding

It is not known whether nasal ipratropium is distributed into breast milk. Problems in humans have not been documented.

Pediatrics

Rhinorrhea associated with the common cold (0.06% ipratropium nasal solution): For children under 5 years of age (in Canada, under 12 years of age)—Safety and efficacy have not been established.

Rhinorrhea associated with allergic and nonallergic perennial rhinitis (0.03% ipratropium nasal solution): For children under 6 years of age (in Canada, under 12 years of age)—Safety and efficacy have not been established.

Geriatrics

No information is available on the relationship of age to the effects of ipratropium nasal spray in geriatric patients.

Dental

Higher doses and prolonged use of ipratropium nasal spray may decrease or inhibit salivary flow, thus contributing to the development of caries, periodontal disease, oral candidiasis, and discomfort.

Drug interactions and/or related problems

The following drug interactions and/or related problems have been selected on the basis of their potential clinical significance (possible mechanism in parentheses where appropriate)—not necessarily inclusive (» = major clinical significance):

Note: Combinations containing any of the following medications, depending on the amount present, may also interact with this medication.

Anticholinergics, other, or other medications with anticholinergic activity (see *Appendix II*)
(concurrent use of other anticholinergics, including ophthalmic and oral inhalation preparations, or other medications with anticholinergic action with ipratropium nasal spray may result in additive effects)

Medical considerations/Contraindications

The medical considerations/contraindications included have been selected on the basis of their potential clinical significance (reasons given in parentheses where appropriate)—not necessarily inclusive (» = major clinical significance).

Risk-benefit should be considered when the following medical problems exist:

Bladder neck obstruction or
Glaucoma, angle-closure, or predisposition to or
Prostatic hypertrophy
(condition may be exacerbated, especially in patients who are taking another anticholinergic medication)
(an acute attack of angle-closure glaucoma may be precipitated or condition may be exacerbated if ipratropium nasal spray is sprayed directly into the eyes)

Sensitivity to ipratropium or belladonna alkaloids

Side/Adverse Effects

Note: Usual therapeutic doses of ipratropium given intranasally generally do not cause systemic side/adverse effects, because of the low blood concentrations achieved with nasal administration; however, the potential for systemic side/adverse effects exists.

In addition, acute overdose of ipratropium nasal spray is unlikely, since the medication is not well absorbed systemically.

Although other ipratropium products have been reported to cause allergic-type reactions, such as skin rash; angioedema of the tongue, lips, and face; urticaria; laryngospasm, and anaphylactic reactions, there are no reports of allergic-type reactions in the controlled clinical trials of nasal ipratropium.

There have been isolated reports of ocular complications (e.g., mydriasis, increased intraocular pressure, angle-closure glaucoma, and eye pain) when ipratropium inhalation aerosol was sprayed into the eyes; however, the aerosol product is no longer available. See also *General Dosing Information*.

There was no evidence of nasal rebound (i.e., clinically significant increase in rhinorrhea, posterior nasal drip, sneezing, or nasal congestion severity compared to baseline) upon discontinuation of clinical trials for the 0.03% nasal ipratropium.

The following side/adverse effects have been selected on the basis of their potential clinical significance (possible signs and symptoms in parentheses where appropriate)—not necessarily inclusive:

Those indicating need for medical attention

For the 0.03% nasal solution

Incidence less frequent

Epistaxis (nosebleeds); ***nasal dryness; pharyngitis*** (sore throat)

Incidence rare

Blurred vision; bowel obstruction (pain or cramping in abdomen); ***conjunctivitis*** (redness of eyes); ***dizziness; eye irritation; precipitation or worsening of angle-closure glaucoma*** (eye pain); ***prostate disorders or urinary retention*** (painful or difficult urination)

For the 0.06% nasal solution administered for 4 days

Incidence less frequent

Epistaxis (nosebleeds); ***nasal dryness***

Incidence rare

Blurred vision; bradycardia (slow heartbeat); ***bowel obstruction*** (pain or cramping in abdomen); ***conjunctivitis*** (redness of eyes); ***dizziness; heart palpitations*** (irregular heartbeat); ***pharyngitis*** (sore throat); ***precipitation or worsening of angle-closure glaucoma*** (eye pain); ***prostate disorders or urinary retention*** (painful or difficult urination); ***tachycardia*** (fast heartbeat); ***tinnitus*** (ringing or buzzing in ears)

Those indicating need for medical attention only if they continue or are bothersome

For the 0.03% nasal solution

Incidence less frequent or rare

Dry mouth or throat; nasal congestion, increased; nasal itching, burning, or irritation; nausea; runny nose, increased

For the 0.06% nasal solution administered for 4 days

Incidence less frequent or rare

Dry mouth or throat; nasal congestion, increased

Overdose

Acute overdosage is unlikely, since ipratropium bromide is not well absorbed systemically after intranasal or oral administration.

Patient Consultation

As an aid to patient consultation, refer to *Advice for the Patient, Ipratropium (Nasal)*.

In providing consultation, consider emphasizing the following selected information (» = major clinical significance):

Before using this medication

» Conditions affecting use, especially:
Sensitivity to ipratropium or belladonna alkaloids

Proper use of this medication

» Compliance with therapy; importance of not using more medication than the amount prescribed

» Keeping the nasal spray away from eyes; if the nasal spray gets in eyes, immediately flushing eyes with cool tap water for several minutes; if nasal spray gets in eyes, increased sensitivity to light (which may last a few hours), blurring of vision, or eye pain may occur; if eye pain or blurred vision occurs, checking with doctor as soon as possible

Reading patient instructions carefully before using

Checking with health care professional for proper use of spray device to prevent incorrect dosage

Priming spray device before using first time or if it has not been used for a while

Proper administration technique

Proper cleaning procedure for spray device

» Proper dosing

Missed dose: Using as soon as possible; not using if almost time for next dose; however, if almost time for next dose, skipping missed dose and going back to regular dosing schedule; not doubling doses

» Proper storage

Precautions while using this medication

» Some improvement in runny nose usually seen during the first full day of treatment; however, if using the 0.03% nasal spray, checking with physician if symptoms do not improve within 1 or 2 weeks or if condition becomes worse

Possible dryness of mouth or throat; using sugarless candy or gum, ice, or saliva substitute for relief; checking with physician or dentist if dryness of mouth continues for more than 2 weeks

Side/adverse effects

For the 0.03% nasal solution

Signs of potential side effects, especially epistaxis, nasal dryness, pharyngitis, blurred vision, bowel obstruction, conjunctivitis, dizziness, eye irritation, precipitation or worsening of angle-closure glaucoma, and prostate disorders or urinary retention

For the 0.06% nasal solution administered for 4 days

Signs of potential side effects, especially epistaxis, nasal dryness, blurred vision, bradycardia, bowel obstruction, conjunctivitis, dizziness, heart palpitations, pharyngitis, precipitation or worsening of angle-closure glaucoma, prostate disorders or urinary retention, tachycardia, and tinnitus

General Dosing Information

The smallest dose required to control symptoms should be used as a maintenance dose after the desired clinical response is achieved.

Prior to administration of ipratropium nasal spray, the nasal passages should be carefully cleared. During administration, the patient should not breathe in, so the medication will be deposited only on nasal mucosa. Following each spray, the patient should sniff deeply and breathe out through the nose. After spraying in the nostril and removing the unit, the patient should tilt the head backwards for a few seconds to let the spray spread over the back of the nose.

For treatment of adverse effects

There have been isolated reports of ocular complications (e.g., mydriasis, increased intraocular pressure, angle-closure glaucoma, and eye pain) when ipratropium inhalation aerosol was sprayed into the eyes (the aerosol product is no longer available). Eye pain or discomfort, blurred vision, visual halos, or colored images in association with red eyes from conjunctival and corneal congestion may be signs of acute angle-closure glaucoma. Should any combination of these symptoms develop, it is recommended that treatment with miotic ophthalmic drops be initiated and advice be sought from an eye specialist immediately.

Intranasal Dosage Form

IPRATROPIUM BROMIDE NASAL SOLUTION

Usual adult and adolescent dose

Rhinorrhea associated with allergic and nonallergic perennial rhinitis (treatment)—

Intranasal, 2 sprays of the 0.03% solution (21 mcg [0.021 mg] per metered spray) into each nostril two or three times a day.

Rhinorrhea associated with the common cold (treatment)—

Intranasal, 2 sprays of the 0.06% solution (42 mcg [0.042 mg] per metered spray) into each nostril three or four times a day. Safety and effectiveness have not been established for use beyond 4 days.

Usual adult prescribing limits

For the 0.03% nasal solution—12 metered sprays (252 mcg [0.252 mg]) per twenty-four hours.

For the 0.06% nasal solution—16 metered sprays (672 mcg [0.672 mg]) per twenty-four hours.

Usual pediatric dose

Rhinorrhea associated with allergic and nonallergic perennial rhinitis (treatment)—

Children up to 6 years of age (in Canada, up to 12 years of age)—Safety and efficacy have not been established.

Children 6 years of age and older (in Canada, 12 years of age and older)—See *Usual adult and adolescent dose*.

Rhinorrhea associated with the common cold (treatment)—

Children up to 5 years of age (in Canada, up to 12 years of age)—Safety and efficacy have not been established.

Children 5 years of age and older (in Canada, 12 years of age and older)—See *Usual adult and adolescent dose*.

Strength(s) usually available

U.S.—

0.03% (21 mcg [0.021 mg] per metered spray) (Rx) [*Atrovent* (benzalkonium chloride; edetate disodium; hydrochloric acid; sodium chloride; sodium hydroxide; purified water)].

0.06% (42 mcg [0.042 mg] per metered spray) (Rx) [*Atrovent* (benzalkonium chloride; edetate disodium; hydrochloric acid; sodium chloride; sodium hydroxide; purified water)].

Canada—

0.03% (21 mcg (0.021 mg) per metered spray (Rx) [*Atrovent* (benzalkonium chloride; edetate disodium; hydrochloric acid; sodium chloride; sodium hydroxide; purified water)].

0.06% (42 mcg (0.042 mg) per metered spray (Rx) [*Atrovent* (benzalkonium chloride; edetate disodium; hydrochloric acid; sodium chloride; sodium hydroxide; purified water)].

Packaging and storage

Store between 15 and 30 °C (59 and 86 °F), unless otherwise specified by manufacturer. Protect from freezing.

Auxiliary labeling

- For the nose.
- Keep away from the eyes.

Note

Include patient instructions when dispensing.

Demonstrate nasal administration technique to patient.

Additional information

For the 0.03% product—Each container yields 345 sprays (28 days of therapy at the maximum recommended dose of 2 sprays per nostril three times a day).

For the 0.06% product—Each container yields 165 sprays (10 days of therapy at the maximum recommended dose of 2 sprays per nostril four times a day).

Selected Bibliography

Borts MR, Druce HM. The use of intranasal anticholinergic agents in the treatment of nonallergic perennial rhinitis. J Allergy Clin Immunol 1992; 90: 1065-70.

Meltzer EO. Intranasal anticholinergic therapy of rhinorrhea. J Allergy Clin Immunol 1992; 90: 1055-64.

Revised: 06/11/1999

IPRATROPIUM AND ALBUTEROL Inhalation-Local

INN: Albuterol—Salbutamol; BAN: Albuterol—Salbutamol

VA CLASSIFICATION (Primary): RE190

Commonly used brand name(s): *Combivent; DuoNeb*.

Note: For a listing of dosage forms and brand names by country availability, see *Dosage Forms* section(s).

Category

Bronchodilator.

Indications

Accepted

Pulmonary disease, chronic obstructive (treatment)—Ipratropium and albuterol combination is indicated for the treatment of chronic obstructive pulmonary disease (COPD) in patients who are using an aerosol bronchodilator and who continue to have symptoms of bronchospasm that require treatment with a second bronchodilator.

Pharmacology/Pharmacokinetics

Physicochemical characteristics

Source—Ipratropium: A synthetic quaternary ammonium compound, chemically related to atropine.

Molecular weight—

Albuterol sulfate: 576.7.

Ipratropium bromide: 430.4.

Mechanism of action/Effect

Ipratropium and albuterol combination reduces bronchospasm through both anticholinergic and sympathomimetic mechanisms. Simultaneous administration of both drugs produces a greater bronchodilator effect than when either drug is used alone at recommended dosages.

Albuterol—Albuterol is a sympathomimetic agent that has a relatively high degree of selectivity for beta$_2$-adrenergic receptors. Activation of these receptors on airway smooth muscle leads to the activation of the enzyme adenylyl cyclase and to an increase in the intracellular concentration of cyclic-3, 5-adenosine monophosphate (cAMP). Increased cAMP concentrations indirectly lower intracellular ionic calcium, which results in airway smooth muscle relaxation.

Ipratropium—Ipratropium is an anticholinergic agent that produces a local, site-specific effect rather than a systemic effect. It appears to produce bronchodilation by inhibition of cholinergic receptors on bronchial smooth muscle.

Absorption

Albuterol—Rapidly and completely absorbed, although whether primarily from pulmonary or from gastrointestinal site is unknown.

Ipratropium—Not readily absorbed into the systemic circulation either from the surface of the lung or from the gastrointestinal tract, as confirmed by blood concentration and renal excretion studies.

Onset of action

Ipratropium and albuterol combination—In clinical trials, the median time to onset of a 15% increase in forced expiratory volume in 1 second (FEV_1) was 15 minutes.

Time to peak effect

Ipratropium and albuterol combination—1 hour.

Duration of action

Ipratropium and albuterol combination—4 to 5 hours.

Precautions to Consider

Cross-sensitivity and/or related problems

Patients allergic to soybean protein or other legumes, such as peanuts, may be allergic to the soya lecithin contained in the metered-dose inhaler.

Ipratropium—Patients sensitive to atropine or its derivatives may be sensitive to ipratropium.

Carcinogenicity/Tumorigenicity

Albuterol—A 2-year study in rats showed that albuterol, administered orally in doses of 20, 100, and 500 times the maximum recommended human inhalation dose, on a mg per square meter of body surface area (mg/m^2) basis, causes a dose-related increase in the incidence of benign leiomyomas of the mesovarium. This effect was blocked by the administration of propranolol in another study. An 18-month study in mice and a 99-week study in hamsters showed no evidence of tumorigenicity.

Ipratropium—Two-year studies in mice and rats have shown that ipratropium, at oral doses of up to 360 and 180 times, respectively, the maximum recommended human inhalation dose, on a mg/m^2 basis, has no carcinogenic potential.

Mutagenicity

Albuterol—*In vitro* studies with albuterol showed no evidence of tumorigenicity.

Ipratropium—Results of various *in vitro* mutagenicity studies were negative.

Pregnancy/Reproduction

Fertility—Albuterol: Reproduction studies in rats given albuterol sulfate revealed no evidence of impaired fertility.

Ipratropium: Although studies in rats have shown that ipratropium, at oral doses of up to approximately 3000 times the maximum recommended human inhalation dose, on a mg/m^2 basis, does not affect fertility, ipratropium has been shown to increase fetal resorption and decrease conception rates when administered at doses above approximately 5400 times the maximum recommended human inhalation dose, on a mg/m^2 basis.

Pregnancy—

Albuterol: Adequate and well-controlled studies in humans have not been done.

Mice given albuterol subcutaneously at doses one-tenth of, comparable to, and 10 times the maximum recommended human daily inhalation dose on a mg/m^2 basis showed cleft palate formation in 0%, 4.5%, and 9.3% of fetuses, respectively. In rabbits given oral albuterol at doses approximately 1000 times the maximum recommended human daily inhalation dose on a mg/m^2 basis showed cranioschisis in 37% of fetuses.

Ipratropium: Adequate and well-controlled studies in humans have not been done.

Reproduction studies in mice, rats, and rabbits revealed no evidence of teratogenicity.

FDA Pregnancy Category C.

Labor—Albuterol: Beta-adrenergic agonists have been shown to decrease uterine contractions when administered systemically.

Breast-feeding

It is not known whether ipratropium or albuterol is distributed into breast milk. However, problems in humans have not been documented.

Pediatrics

No information is available on the relationship of age to the effects of the metered-dose inhalation dosage form of ipratropium and albuterol in pediatric patients. Safety and efficacy have not been established.

Geriatrics

Appropriate studies performed to date have not demonstrated geriatrics-specific problems that would limit the usefulness of ipratropium and albuterol combination in older adults.

Drug interactions and/or related problems

The following drug interactions and/or related problems have been selected on the basis of their potential clinical significance (possible mechanism in parentheses where appropriate)—not necessarily inclusive (» = major clinical significance):

Note: Combinations containing any of the following medications, depending on the amount present, may also interact with this medication.

Anticholinergics, other, or other medications with anticholinergic activity (see Appendix II)
(concurrent use of other medications with anticholinergic activity together with ipratropium may result in additive effects)

Beta-adrenergic blocking agents
(concurrent use with adrenergic bronchodilators may result in mutual inhibition of therapeutic effects)

Laboratory value alterations

The following have been selected on the basis of their potential clinical significance (possible effect in parentheses where appropriate)—not necessarily inclusive (» = major clinical significance).

With physiology/laboratory test values

Electrocardiogram
(flattened T waves, prolongation of the QT_c interval, and ST segment depression have been reported with beta-adrenergic bronchodilators)

Potassium, serum
(beta-adrenergic bronchodilators may decrease serum potassium concentrations, especially when the recommended dose is exceeded)

Medical considerations/Contraindications

The medical considerations/contraindications included have been selected on the basis of their potential clinical significance (reasons given in parentheses where appropriate)—not necessarily inclusive (» = major clinical significance).

Risk-benefit should be considered when the following medical problems exist:

» Sensitivity to ipratropium, atropine, or albuterol

» Allergy to soya lecithin, soybean protein, or other legumes such as peanuts

For ipratropium

» Glaucoma, angle-closure
(an acute attack may be precipitated or condition may be exacerbated if ipratropium-containing inhalation aerosol is sprayed directly into the eyes)

Urinary retention
(rarely, condition may be aggravated)

For albuterol

Cardiac arrhythmias or
» Coronary insufficiency or
Hypertension
(although uncommon after administration of ipratropium and albuterol combination at recommended doses, albuterol can produce a clinically significant cardiovascular effect in some patients, as measured by pulse rate or blood pressure)

Side/Adverse Effects

The following side/adverse effects have been selected on the basis of their potential clinical significance (possible signs and symptoms in parentheses where appropriate)—not necessarily inclusive:

Those indicating need for medical attention

Incidence rare

Angioedema (swelling of the face, lips, or eyelids); ***bronchospasm, paradoxical or hypersensitivity-induced*** (shortness of breath; wheezing); ***chest discomfort or pain; irregular heartbeat; oropharyngeal edema*** (swelling of the mouth or throat); ***skin rash; tachycardia*** (fast heartbeat); ***urticaria*** (hives)

Those indicating need for medical attention only if they continue or are bothersome

Incidence less frequent (2 to 6%)

Coughing; headache; nausea

Incidence rare
Change in sense of taste; dizziness; dryness of mouth; nervousness; tremor

Patient Consultation

As an aid to patient consultation, refer to *Advice for the Patient, Ipratropium and Albuterol (Inhalation-Local).*

In providing consultation, consider emphasizing the following selected information (» = major clinical significance):

Before using this medication

» Conditions affecting use, especially:
Sensitivity to ipratropium, atropine, or albuterol; allergy to soya lecithin, soybean protein, or other legumes such as peanuts
Other medical problems, especially angle-closure glaucoma or coronary insufficiency

Proper use of this medication

Proper administration technique: reading patient instructions carefully before using
Performing three priming sprays before using inhalation aerosol for the first time or if not used for more than 24 hours
To administer inhalation solution, use a jet nebulizer (with face mask or mouthpiece) connected to compressor with good air flow
» Avoiding contact with eyes
» Importance of not using more medication than the recommended dose
» Proper dosing
Missed dose: Using as soon as possible; using any remaining doses for that day at regularly spaced intervals
» Proper storage

Precautions while using this medication

» Checking with physician immediately if difficulty in breathing persists after using this medication or if condition becomes worse

Side/adverse effects

Signs of potential side effects, especially angioedema, paradoxical or hypersensitivity-induced bronchospasm, chest discomfort or pain, irregular heartbeat, oropharyngeal edema, skin rash, tachycardia, and urticaria

General Dosing Information

Three priming sprays should be performed before the metered-dose inhaler is used for the first time or when it has not been used in more than 24 hours.

Inhalation solution should be administered via a jet nebulizer connected to an air compressor with adequate air flow, equipped with a mouthpiece or suitable face mask. Like all other nebulized treatment, the amount delivered to the lungs will depend on patient factors, the jet nebulizer used and the compressor performance. A Pari-LC-Plus™ nebulizer (with face mask or mouthpiece) connected to a PRONEB™ compressor was used in one U.S. clinical study. The safety and efficacy using other nebulizers and compressors have not been established.

Do not exceed the recommended dosage for the inhalation solution. Fatalities have been associated with the excessive use of inhaled products containing sympathomimetic amines and home use of nebulizers.

Inhalation Dosage Forms

Note: The strength of the dosage forms available are expressed in terms of albuterol base.

IPRATROPIUM BROMIDE AND ALBUTEROL SULFATE INHALATION AEROSOL

Usual adult dose

Pulmonary disease, chronic obstructive—
Oral inhalation, 2 inhalations four times a day and as required; however, the total number of inhalations should not exceed 12 inhalations in twenty-four hours.

Usual adult prescribing limits

12 inhalations in twenty-four hours.

Usual pediatric dose

Safety and efficacy have not been established.

Usual geriatric dose

See *Usual adult dose.*

Strength(s) usually available

U.S.—
18 mcg ipratropium bromide and 90 mcg albuterol (base) per metered spray (Rx) [*Combivent* (chlorofluorocarbons (CFCs))].

Packaging and storage

Store between 15 and 30 °C (59 and 86 °F); avoid excessive humidity.

Auxiliary labeling

- Shake well before using.
- For oral inhalation only.

Note

Include patient instructions when dispensing.

IPRATROPIUM BROMIDE AND ALBUTEROL SULFATE INHALATION SOLUTION

Usual adult dose

Pulmonary disease, chronic obstructive—
Oral inhalation, one 3 mL vial administered four times a day via nebulization; 2 additional 3 mL doses allowed per day, as needed.

Usual pediatric dose

Safety and efficacy have not been established.

Usual geriatric dose

See *Usual adult dose.*

Strength(s) usually available

U.S.—
0.5 mg (0.017%) ipratropium bromide and 2.5 mg (0.083%) albuterol (base) per 3 mL vial (Rx) [*DuoNeb* (sodium chloride; hydrochloric acid; edetate disodium)].

Packaging and storage

Store between 2 and 25 °C (36 and 77 °F); protect from light.

Auxiliary labeling

- For oral inhalation only.

Note

Include patient instructions when dispensing.

Revised: 07/03/2001
Developed: 06/17/1997

IRBESARTAN Systemic

VA CLASSIFICATION (Primary/Secondary): CV805/CV409
Commonly used brand name(s): *Avapro.*

Note: For a listing of dosage forms and brand names by country availability, see *Dosage Forms* section(s).

Category

Antihypertensive.

Indications

Accepted

Hypertension (treatment)—Irbesartan is indicated for the treatment of hypertension. It may be used alone or in combination with other antihypertensive medications.
For additional information on initial therapeutic guidelines related to the treatment of hypertension, see *Appendix III.*

Pharmacology/Pharmacokinetics

Physicochemical characteristics

Molecular weight—428.5.

Mechanism of action/Effect

Irbesartan is a nonpeptide angiotensin II antagonist that selectively blocks the binding of angiotensin II to the AT_1 receptor. In the renin-angiotensin system, angiotensin I is converted by angiotensin-converting enzyme (ACE) to form angiotensin II. Angiotensin II stimulates the adrenal cortex to synthesize and secrete aldosterone, which decreases the excretion of sodium and increases the excretion of potassium. Angiotensin II also acts as a vasoconstrictor in vascular smooth muscle. Irbesartan, by blocking the binding of angiotensin II to the AT_1 receptor, promotes vasodilation and decreases the effects of aldosterone. The negative feedback regulation of angiotensin II on renin secretion also is inhibited, but the resulting rise in plasma renin concentrations and consequent rise in angiotensin II plasma concentrations do not counteract the blood pressure-lowering effect that occurs.

Absorption

Rapid and complete; average absolute bioavailability ranges from 60 to 80%. Food does not affect the bioavailability of irbesartan.

Distribution
Volume of distribution (Vol_D)—53 to 93 liters. Irbesartan crosses the blood-brain barrier and placenta in low concentrations.

Protein binding
High (90%), primarily to albumin and $alpha_1$-acid glycoprotein.

Biotransformation
Irbesartan is metabolized by glucuronide conjugation and oxidation. Following oral or intravenous administration of radiolabeled irbesartan, more than 80% of the circulating plasma radioactivity is attributed to unchanged irbesartan. The primary metabolite is the inactive irbesartan glucuronide conjugate and accounts for approximately 6% of circulating metabolites. The remaining oxidative metabolites are considered to be inactive. *In vitro* studies indicate that irbesartan is oxidized primarily by the cytochrome P450 2C9 isoenzyme.

Half-life
Elimination—
11 to 15 hours.

Time to peak concentration
1.5 to 2 hours.

Elimination
Renal—Approximately 20%.
Fecal (biliary)—Approximately 80%.
In dialysis—
Irbesartan is not removable by hemodialysis.

Precautions to Consider

Carcinogenicity
No evidence of carcinogenicity was found in a 2-year study in male rats given irbesartan in doses of up to 500 mg per kg of body weight (mg/kg) per day or in female rats given irbesartan in doses of up to 1000 mg/kg per day or in mice given irbesartan in doses of up to 1000 mg/kg per day. In male and female rats, a 500 mg/kg dose represents 3 and 11 times, respectively, the maximum recommended human daily dose (MRHDD) of 300 mg of irbesartan. In female rats, a 1000 mg/kg dose represents approximately 21 times the MRHDD of 300 mg of irbesartan. For male and female mice a 1000 mg/kg dose represents approximately 3 and 5 times, respectively, the MRHDD of 300 mg of irbesartan.

Mutagenicity
Irbesartan was not found to be mutagenic in the Ames microbial test, rat hepatocyte DNA repair test, or V79 mammalian-cell forward gene mutation assay. Irbesartan was found to be negative for the induction of chromosomal aberrations in the *in vitro* human lymphocyte assay and in the *in vivo* mouse micronucleus study.

Pregnancy/Reproduction
Fertility—Irbesartan had no adverse effects on fertility or mating behavior of male or female rats given oral doses of ≤ 650 mg/kg per day. The 650 mg/kg dose of irbesartan represents approximately five times the MRHDD of 300 mg.

Pregnancy—Fetal exposure to drugs that act directly on the renin-angiotensin system during the second and third trimesters can cause hypotension, reversible or irreversible renal failure, anuria, neonatal skull hypoplasia, and death in the fetus or neonate. Irbesartan should be discontinued as soon as possible when pregnancy is detected, unless no alternative therapy can be used. If medication is continued, serial ultrasound examinations should be performed to assess the intra-amniotic environment. Perinatal diagnostic tests, such as contraction-stress testing (CST), a nonstress test (NST), or biophysical profiling (BPP) also may be appropriate during the applicable week of pregnancy.

Maternal oligohydramnios, which may result from decreased fetal renal function, has been reported, and is associated with fetal limb contractures, craniofacial deformation, and hypoplastic lung development. If oligohydramnios is observed, irbesartan should be discontinued unless it is considered lifesaving for the mother. Oligohydramnios may not appear until after the fetus has sustained irreversible damage. Other adverse effects that have been reported are prematurity, intrauterine growth retardation, and patent ductus arteriosus, although it is not clear how these effects are related to drug exposure. When limited to the first trimester, exposure to this medication does not appear to be associated with these adverse effects.

Infants exposed *in utero* to angiotensin II receptor antagonists should be observed closely for hypotension, oliguria, and hyperkalemia. Oliguria should be treated with support of blood pressure and renal perfusion. Dialysis or exchange transfusion may be necessary to reverse hypotension and/or substitute for disordered renal function.

Studies in pregnant rats given oral daily doses of 50, 180, and 650 mg/kg of irbesartan from day 0 to day 20 of gestation revealed increased incidences of renal pelvic cavitation, hydroureter, and/or absence of renal papilla in fetuses at doses ≥ 50 mg/kg (approximately equivalent to the MRHDD of 300 mg, based on a body surface area). Subcutaneous edema was observed in fetuses of rats given daily doses of ≥ 180 mg/kg. This dose represents approximately four times the maximum recommended human dose (MRHD) on a body surface area basis. Because these anomalies were not observed in rats given daily oral irbesartan doses of 50, 150, and 450 mg/kg limited to gestation days 6 through 15, they appear to reflect late gestational effects of irbesartan. In pregnant rabbits, oral daily doses of irbesartan of 30 mg/kg were associated with maternal mortality and abortion. In the surviving female rabbits given this dose (equivalent to approximately 1.5 times the MRHD on a body surface area basis), a slight increase in early resorptions and a corresponding decrease in live fetuses occurred. Irbesartan was found to cross the placental barrier in rats and rabbits. Radioactivity was present in the fetuses of rats and rabbits during late gestation following oral doses of radiolabeled irbesartan.

FDA Pregnancy Category C (first trimester).

FDA Pregnancy Category D (second and third trimesters).

Breast-feeding
It is not known whether irbesartan is distributed into breast milk, but irbesartan and/or its metabolite(s) is distributed into the milk of lactating rats at a low concentration. Because of the potential for adverse effects in the nursing infant, irbesartan should not be administered to nursing mothers.

Pediatrics
No information is available on the relationship of age to the effects of irbesartan in pediatric patients younger than 6 years of age. Safety and efficacy have not been established in patients younger than 6 years of age. Infants exposed *in utero* to angiotensin II receptor antagonists should be observed closely for hypotension, oliguria, and hyperkalemia. Oliguria should be treated with support of blood pressure and renal perfusion. Dialysis or exchange transfusion may be necessary to reverse hypotension and/or substitute for disordered renal function. See *Pregnancy/Reproduction* section.

Geriatrics
In subjects 65 to 80 years of age, irbesartan elimination half-life is not significantly altered, but the area under the plasma concentration-time curve (AUC) and maximum plasma concentration (C_{max}) values may be greater by 20 to 50% than those in subjects 18 to 40 years of age. No dosage adjustment is necessary in the elderly. However, the elderly may experience greater sensitivity to the effects of irbesartan.

Pharmacogenetics
In female patients with hypertension, irbesartan plasma concentrations are increased by 11 to 44%; however, no gender-related dosage adjustment is necessary. In healthy black subjects, the AUC is 25% greater than in white patients. Black patients, usually a low-renin population, may experience a smaller reduction in blood pressure with irbesartan treatment than white patients.

Drug interactions and/or related problems
The following drug interactions and/or related problems have been selected on the basis of their potential clinical significance (possible mechanism in parentheses where appropriate)—not necessarily inclusive (» = major clinical significance):

Note: Combinations containing any of the following medications, depending on the amount present, may also interact with this medication.

» Diuretics
(concurrent use with irbesartan may have additive hypotensive effects)

Medications that inhibit the cytochrome P450 2C9 isoenzyme or
Medications that are metabolized by cytochrome P450 2C9 (the isoenzyme responsible for irbesartan metabolism), such as
Tolbutamide
(*in vitro* studies show that irbesartan metabolism may be affected by medications that are metabolized by or inhibit the cytochrome P450 2C9 isoenzyme, although no clinically relevant interactions have been observed)

Laboratory value alterations
The following have been selected on the basis of their potential clinical significance (possible effect in parentheses where appropriate)—not necessarily inclusive (» = major clinical significance).

With physiology/laboratory test values
Creatinine, serum and
Blood urea nitrogen (BUN)
(increases in serum creatinine or BUN concentrations have occurred in patients with unilateral or bilateral renal artery stenosis who were treated with angiotensin-converting enzyme (ACE) in-

hibitors, and a similar effect may occur with irbesartan treatment; minor increases in concentrations occurred in 0.7% of patients treated with irbesartan in clinical trials)

Liver function tests
(incidence not determined; have been reported rarely in patients during clinical practice—increases in liver function tests have been reported in patients treated with irbesartan)

Medical considerations/Contraindications

The medical considerations/contraindications included have been selected on the basis of their potential clinical significance (reasons given in parentheses where appropriate)—not necessarily inclusive (» = major clinical significance).

Except under special circumstances, this medication should not be used when the following medical problem exists:

» Hypersensitivity to irbesartan

Risk-benefit should be considered when the following medical problems exist:

» Congestive heart failure, severe
(therapy with angiotensin receptor antagonists in these patients, who may be especially susceptible to changes in the renin-angiotensin-aldosterone system, has been associated with oliguria, azotemia, acute renal failure, and/or death)

Dehydration (sodium or volume depletion, due to excessive perspiration, vomiting, diarrhea, prolonged diuretic therapy, dialysis, or dietary salt restriction)
(a reduction in salt or fluid volume may increase the risk of symptomatic hypotension)

Renal artery stenosis, unilateral or bilateral or
Renal function impairment
(increases in serum creatinine or BUN concentrations have occurred in patients with unilateral or bilateral renal artery stenosis who were treated with ACE inhibitors and a similar effect may occur with irbesartan treatment; therapy with angiotensin receptor-antagonists in patients susceptible to changes in the renin-angiotensin-aldosterone system, such as patients with severe congestive heart failure, has been associated with oliguria, progressive azotemia, acute renal failure, and/or death)

Patient monitoring

The following may be especially important in patient monitoring (other tests may be warranted in some patients, depending on condition; » = major clinical significance):

» Blood pressure measurements
(periodic monitoring is necessary for titration of dose according to the patient's response)

Potassium, serum
(check periodically to monitor for hyperkalemia)

Side/Adverse Effects

The following side/adverse effects have been selected on the basis of their potential clinical significance (possible signs and symptoms in parentheses where appropriate)—not necessarily inclusive:

Those indicating need for medical attention

Incidence rare

Hypotension (dizziness, light-headedness, or fainting)—usually seen in volume- or salt-depleted patients receiving high doses of a diuretic

Note: *Hypotension* occurred in 0.4% of patients receiving irbesartan in clinical trials.

Incidence not determined—Observed during clinical practice

Angioedema (swelling on face, lips, throat, or tongue); ***hyperkalemia*** (confusion, irregular heartbeat, numbness or tingling in hands, feet, or lips, difficult breathing, or weakness or heaviness of legs)—has been rarely reported; ***jaundice*** (clay-colored stools, dark urine, itching, loss of appetite, stomach pain, yellow eyes or skin)

Those indicating need for medical attention only if they continue or are bothersome

Incidence less frequent

Anxiety and/or nervousness; diarrhea; dizziness; dyspepsia (belching; heartburn; stomach discomfort); ***fatigue*** (unusual tiredness); ***headache; musculoskeletal pain*** (muscle or bone pain); ***upper respiratory infection*** (cold symptoms)

Incidence not determined—Observed during clinical practice

urticaria (hives or welts, itching, redness of skin, or skin rash)

Overdose

For more information on the management of overdose or unintentional ingestion, **contact a Poison Control Center** (see *Poison Control Center Listing*).

Clinical effects of overdose

The following effects have been selected on the basis of their potential clinical significance (possible signs and symptoms in parentheses where appropriate)—not necessarily inclusive:

Acute and/or chronic

Bradycardia (slow heartbeat); ***hypotension*** (dizziness, lightheadedness, or fainting); ***tachycardia*** (fast heartbeat)

Treatment of overdose

Treatment should be symptomatic and supportive.

Supportive care—Patients in whom intentional overdose is confirmed or suspected should be referred for psychiatric consultation.

Patient Consultation

As an aid to patient consultation, refer to *Advice for the Patient, Irbesartan (Systemic)*.

In providing consultation, consider emphasizing the following selected information (» = major clinical significance):

Before using this medication

» Conditions affecting use, especially:

Hypersensitivity to irbesartan

Pregnancy—Fetal and neonatal hypotension, skull hypoplasia, renal failure, and death have been reported in humans; irbesartan should be discontinued as soon as possible when pregnancy is detected

Breast-feeding—Irbesartan is distributed into milk of lactating rats; use is not recommended in nursing mothers

Use in children—Safety and efficacy not established in children younger than 6 years of age

Use in the elderly—Elderly patients may experience greater sensitivity to the effects of irbesartan

Other medications, especially diuretics

Other medical problems, especially severe congestive heart failure

Proper use of this medication

» Compliance with therapy; taking medication at the same time each day to maintain the therapeutic effect

» Proper dosing

Missed dose: Taking as soon as possible; not taking if almost time for next scheduled dose; not doubling doses

» Proper storage

Precautions while using this medication

Regular visits to physician to check progress

» Notifying physician immediately if pregnancy is suspected because of possibility of fetal or neonatal injury and/or death

Not taking other medications without consulting the physician

» Caution when driving or doing other things requiring alertness because of possible dizziness

Checking with physician if severe nausea, vomiting, or diarrhea occurs and continues because of risk of dehydration, which may result in hypotension

Caution when exercising or during exposure to hot weather because of risk of dehydration, which may result in hypotension

Side/adverse effects

Signs of potential side effects, especially hypotension
(Observed during clinical practice; estimates of frequency can not be determined—angioedema, hyperkalemia or jaundice)

General Dosing Information

Dosage must be adjusted, on the basis of clinical response to meet the individual requirements of each patient.

Diet/Nutrition

Irbesartan may be administered with or without food.

For treatment of adverse effects

Recommended treatment consists of the following:

- Treatment of symptomatic hypotension involves placing the patient in a supine position and, if needed, administering normal saline intravenously.

Oral Dosage Forms

IRBESARTAN TABLETS

Usual adult dose

Hypertension—

Oral, initially 150 mg once a day. If blood pressure reduction is not adequate, the dosage may be increased to up to 300 mg once a day.

If blood pressure is not controlled by irbesartan alone, a low dose of a diuretic, such as hydrochlorothiazide, may be added. Patients not adequately controlled by the maximum irbesartan dose of 300 mg once a day are unlikely to derive additional benefit from a higher dose or twice-daily dosing.

In patients who are volume- and/or salt-depleted, such as those treated vigorously with diuretics or on hemodialysis, a lower initial dose of 75 mg of irbesartan is recommended.

Usual adult prescribing limits

300 mg.

Usual pediatric dose

Safety and efficacy have not been established in children younger than 6 years of age.

Hypertension—

Children 6 to 12 years of age: Oral, Initial dose of 75 mg once a day. Patients requiring further reduction in blood pressure should be titrated to 150 mg once a day.

Usual adolescent dose—

Adolescents 13 to 16 years of age: Oral, Initial dose of 150 mg once daily. Patients requiring further reduction in blood pressure should be titrated to 300 mg once a day.

Note: Irbesartan should not be administered to pediatric patients with creatinine clearance less than 30 mL per minute per 1.73 m^2.

Usual pediatric prescribing limits

Children: 150 mg daily

Adolescents: 300 mg daily

Strength(s) usually available

U.S.—

75 mg (Rx) [*Avapro*].

150 mg (Rx) [*Avapro*].

300 mg (Rx) [*Avapro*].

Packaging and storage

Store between 15 and 30 °C (59 and 86 °F).

Auxiliary labeling

- Do not take other medicines without your doctor's advice.

Revised: 11/17/2004

Developed: 01/05/1998

IRINOTECAN Systemic

VA CLASSIFICATION (Primary): AN900

Commonly used brand name(s): *Camptosar.*

Another commonly used name is CPT-11.

Note: For a listing of dosage forms and brand names by country availability, see *Dosage Forms* section(s).

Category

Antineoplastic.

Indications

Note: Bracketed information in the *Indications* section refers to uses that are not included in U.S. product labeling.

Accepted

Carcinoma, colorectal (treatment)—Irinotecan is indicated for treatment of metastatic carcinoma of the colon or rectum that has progressed during or recurred following first-line chemotherapy with fluorouracil (5-FU). Irinotecan is also indicated in a first-line combination chemotherapy regimen that includes 5-fluorouracil and leucovorin for patients with metastatic carcinoma of the colon or rectum.

[Carcinoma, lung, non-small cell (treatment)][1]—Irinotecan is indicated, alone or in combination with other active agents (e.g., cisplatin), at some point in the treatment of locally advanced and/or metastatic stage IIIB or IV non-small cell lung carcinoma.

[Extensive-stage small-cell lung cancer, first-line treatment, in combination with cisplatin]—The combination of irinotecan and cisplatin provides an effective alternative, with a different adverse effect profile, as compared to the combination of etoposide and cisplatin as first-line treatment for extensive-stage small-cell lung cancer (SCLC). Two phase 3, randomized clinical trials have compared the two regimens. A Japan Clinical Oncology Group (JCOG) trial was halted early due to improved overall survival in the irinotecan plus cisplatin group. A second, confirmatory clinical trial conducted in the United States, Australia, and Canada used different dosages of the regimens and found no difference in overall survival. Similar toxicity profiles were observed in both trials, with significantly more myelosuppression in the etoposide plus cisplatin arms and significantly more diarrhea in the irinotecan plus cisplatin arms. SWOG trial S0124 addresses the same regimens and schedules of the JCOG trial in the United States and differences in polymorphisms of UGT1A1 (as predictors of response and toxicity).

Acceptance not established

Use of irinotecan for the treatment of pancreatic carcinoma has not been established, due to insufficient data supporting efficacy and/or safety. The role of irinotecan in combination therapy has not been defined.

[1]Not included in Canadian product labeling.

Pharmacology/Pharmacokinetics

Physicochemical characteristics

Source—Semisynthetic derivative of camptothecin, an alkaloid extracted from plants, e.g., *Camptotheca acuminata.*

Molecular weight—Irinotecan hydrochloride: 677.2.

pH—3.5

Solubility—Slightly soluble in water and in organic solvents.

Mechanism of action/Effect

Irinotecan and its active metabolite, SN-38, inhibit the action of topoisomerase I, an enzyme that produces reversible single-strand breaks in DNA during DNA replication. These single-strand breaks relieve torsional strain and allow DNA replication to proceed. Irinotecan and SN-38 bind to the topoisomerase I–DNA complex and prevent religation of the DNA strand, resulting in double-strand DNA breakage and cell death.

Note: Although SN-38 is approximately 2 to 2000 times more potent than the parent compound in various *in vitro* cytotoxicity assays, the precise contribution of the metabolite to the activity of irinotecan in humans is not known because its protein binding is significantly higher, and its area under the plasma concentration-time curve (AUC) is much lower, than those of irinotecan.

Distribution

The volume of distribution (Vol_D) of the terminal elimination phase for irinotecan is 110 liters per square meter of body surface area.

Protein binding

Irinotecan—Moderate (30 to 68%), primarily to albumin.

SN-38 metabolite—Very high (95%), primarily to albumin.

Biotransformation

Primarily hepatic, via carboxylase-mediated cleavage of the carbamate bond. Conversion to the active metabolite (SN-38) is rapid. SN-38 undergoes conjugation to form a glucuronide metabolite, which is 50 to 100 times less active than SN-38. The disposition of irinotecan in humans is not completely clear.

Irinotecan and SN-38 both undergo reversible, pH-dependent conversion between their two forms, an active lactone and an inactive hydroxyacid. Whereas only the lactone form is present at an acidic pH, the hydroxyacid form predominates at physiologic pH.

Half-life

Terminal—

Irinotecan: Mean, 6 to 12 hours (5.5 hours in patients younger than 65 years of age and 6 hours in older patients).

SN-38 metabolite: Mean, 10 to 20 hours

Time to peak concentration

SN-38 metabolite—Peak plasma concentrations occur within 1 hour after administration of a 90–minute infusion.

Peak plasma concentration

Following a dose of 125 mg per square meter of body surface area (mg/m^2)—

Irinotecan: 1660 ± 797 nanograms per mL.

SN-38 metabolite: 26.3 ± 11.9 nanograms per mL.

Note: AUC values for 24 hours following a 125-mg/m^2 dose of irinotecan, administered as a 90-minute infusion, are 10,200 ± 3270 nanograms per mL per hour for irinotecan and 229 ± 108 nanograms per mL per hour for the SN-38 metabolite. Values in patients with hepatic metastases are somewhat higher. Also, dose-normalized values are 11% higher in patients 65 years of age or older than in younger patients.

Elimination

Renal—11 to 20% of a dose as unchanged irinotecan; < 1% of a dose as SN-38; 1 to 3% of a dose as SN-38 glucuronide.

Combined biliary and renal—In two patients, 25% of a 100-mg/m² dose and 50% of a 300-mg/m² dose were excreted within 48 hours after intravenous administration.

Total systemic clearance of irinotecan—13.3 ± 6.01 liters per hour per square meter of body surface area after a 125-mg/m² dose.

Note: The effect of hepatic or renal function impairment on elimination of irinotecan and its metabolites has not been formally studied. However, because relatively small quantities of irinotecan are eliminated via renal excretion, it is unlikely that renal function impairment would have a major influence on the pharmacokinetics of irinotecan.

Precautions to Consider

Carcinogenicity

Secondary malignancies are potential delayed effects of many antineoplastic agents, although it is not clear whether the effect is related to their mutagenic or immunosuppressive action. The effect of dose and duration of therapy is also unknown, although the risk seems to increase with long-term use. There is some evidence linking therapy with topoisomerase I inhibitors, such as irinotecan, to the development of acute leukemias associated with specific chromosomal translocations.

Long-term carcinogenicity studies in animals have not been done with irinotecan. However, a significant dose-related trend for the development of uterine horn endometrial stromal polyps and endometrial stromal sarcomas was found in studies in rats given 2 mg per kg of body weight (mg/kg) or 25 mg/kg once weekly for 13 weeks, then allowed to recover for 91 weeks. The 25-mg/kg dose produced maximum plasma concentration (C_{max}) and area under the plasma concentration-time curve (AUC) values equivalent to seven times and 1.3 times, respectively, the values for irinotecan in humans receiving 125 mg per square meter of body surface area (mg/m²).

Mutagenicity

Irinotecan was clastogenic in *in vitro* (chromosome aberrations in Chinese hamster ovary cells) and *in vivo* (micronucleus test in mice) mammalian test systems. However, neither irinotecan nor its active metabolite, SN-38, was mutagenic in the Ames test.

Pregnancy/Reproduction

Fertility—Irinotecan produced no significant effect on reproductive performance or fertility in rats and rabbits given up to 6 mg/kg per day. However, atrophy of male reproductive organs occurred in rodents given multiple daily intravenous doses of 20 mg/kg (producing C_{max} values approximately five times, and AUC values approximately equal to, the values for irinotecan in humans receiving 125 mg/m²), and in dogs given multiple daily intravenous doses of 0.4 mg/kg (producing C_{max} and AUC values approximately 50% and 6.6%, respectively, of the values for irinotecan in humans receiving 125 mg/m²).

Pregnancy—Adequate and well-controlled studies in humans have not been done. Patients should be apprised of potential hazard to the fetus if irinotecan is used during pregnancy or if patients become pregnant while receiving it. Women of childbearing potential should be advised to avoid pregnancy while receiving irinotecan treatment.

It is usually recommended that use of antineoplastics, especially combination chemotherapy, be avoided whenever possible, especially during the first trimester. Although information is limited because of the relatively few instances of antineoplastic therapy during pregnancy, the mutagenic, teratogenic, and carcinogenic potential of these medications must be considered.

Other potential hazards to the fetus include adverse reactions seen in adults.

In general, use of a contraceptive is recommended during therapy with cytotoxic medications.

Studies in rats have demonstrated that irinotecan crosses the placenta. Irinotecan was embryotoxic, causing increased postimplantation losses and decreased numbers of live fetuses, in rats and rabbits given 6 mg/kg per day (a dose that produced C_{max} and AUC values in rats that are approximately two times and 0.2 times the respective values in humans receiving 125 mg/m². In rabbits, this dose is equivalent to approximately half of the recommended human dose on a mg/m² basis). Also, irinotecan was teratogenic, causing external, visceral, and skeletal abnormalities in rats given more than 1.2 mg/kg per day (producing C_{max} and AUC values equivalent to two thirds and one fortieth the respective values in humans receiving 125 mg/m²) and in rabbits administered 6 mg/kg per day (a dose equivalent to approximately half of the recommended human dose on a mg/m² basis).

FDA Pregnancy Category D.

Breast-feeding

Although very little information is available regarding distribution of antineoplastic agents into breast milk, breast-feeding is not recommended while irinotecan is being administered because of the risks to the infant (adverse effects, mutagenicity, carcinogenicity). It is not known whether irinotecan is distributed into human breast milk.

Animal studies have shown that irinotecan is rapidly distributed into the milk of lactating rats. Four hours after administration, the concentration in milk was 65 times higher than the simultaneous plasma concentration, indicating that the medication accumulates in breast milk. Also, administration of 6 mg/kg per day of irinotecan to rat dams from the period following organogenesis through weaning caused lower female body weight and decreased learning ability in the offspring.

Pediatrics

Appropriate studies on the relationship of age to the effects of irinotecan have not been performed in the pediatric population. Safety and efficacy have not been established. Two open-label, single arm studies were evaluated. The adverse event profile in the first study was comparable to that observed in adults. However, the single agent irinotecan phase of the second study was halted due to the high rate (28.6%) of progressive disease and early deaths (14%). The adverse event profile was different in this study from that observed in adults with the most significant grade 3 or 4 adverse events being dehydration and dehydration associated with severe hypokalemia or hyponatremia, and grade 3-4 infections.

Geriatrics

Patients greater than 65 years of age may be at greater risk of late diarrhea. Careful monitoring is recommended. The starting dose of irinotecan should be reduced in patients 70 years and older for the once-every-3-week-dosage schedule. No dosage adjustment is recommended for the weekly dosage schedule in older adults.

Dental

The bone marrow depressant effects of irinotecan may result in an increased incidence of microbial infection, delayed healing, and gingival bleeding. Dental work, whenever possible, should be completed prior to initiation of therapy or deferred until blood counts have returned to normal. Patients should be instructed in proper oral hygiene during treatment, including caution in use of regular toothbrushes, dental floss, and toothpicks.

Irinotecan may cause stomatitis, which is usually mild. In clinical trials using single-agent irinotecan, stomatitis occurred in 12%, and was severe (U.S. National Cancer Institute [NCI] grades 3 or 4) in 1%, of the patients.

Drug interactions and/or related problems

The following drug interactions and/or related problems have been selected on the basis of their potential clinical significance (possible mechanism in parentheses where appropriate)—not necessarily inclusive (» = major clinical significance):

Note: Combinations containing any of the following medications, depending on the amount present, may also interact with this medication.

Blood dyscrasia-causing medications (see *Appendix II*)
(the leukopenic and/or thrombocytopenic effects of irinotecan may be increased with concurrent or recent therapy if these medications cause the same effects; dosage adjustment of irinotecan, if necessary, should be based on blood cell counts)

» Bone marrow depressants, other (see *Appendix II*) or
» Radiation therapy, current or history of
(additive bone marrow depression may occur; dosage reduction may be required when two or more bone marrow depressants, including radiation, are used concurrently or consecutively. Studies have shown that the risk of severe irinotecan-induced myelosuppression is significantly higher in patients who have received previous radiation therapy of the pelvis or abdomen. Concurrent use of irinotecan with radiation therapy has not been adequately studied and is not recommended)

Dexamethasone
(prophylactic use of dexamethasone as an antiemetic prior to irinotecan administration may result in hyperglycemia, especially in patients with a history of diabetes or glucose intolerance, and may also increase the occurrence of lymphocytopenia)

» Diuretics
(careful monitoring during concurrent therapy with irinotecan is recommended because diuretics may increase the severity of de-

hydration associated with irinotecan-induced diarrhea or vomiting; withholding diuretic treatment during periods of active diarrhea or vomiting may be prudent)

» Immunosuppressants, other, such as:
  Azathioprine
  Chlorambucil
  Corticosteroids, glucocorticoid
  Cyclophosphamide
  Cyclosporine
  Mercaptopurine
  Muromonab-CD3
  Mycophenolate
  Tacrolimus
  (concurrent use with irinotecan may increase the risk of infection)

» Laxatives
  (concurrent use with irinotecan may increase the risk of severe diarrhea and should be avoided)

Prochlorperazine
  (administration on the same day as irinotecan increased the incidence of akathisia in clinical trials of the weekly dosage schedule)

Vaccines, killed virus
  (because normal defense mechanisms may be suppressed by irinotecan therapy, the patient's antibody response to the vaccine may be decreased. The interval between discontinuation of medications that cause immunosuppression and restoration of the patient's ability to respond to the vaccine depends on the intensity and type of immunosuppression-causing medication used, the underlying disease, and other factors; estimates vary from 3 months to 1 year)

» Vaccines, live virus
  (because normal defense mechanisms may be suppressed by irinotecan therapy, concurrent use with a live virus vaccine may potentiate the replication of the vaccine virus, may increase the side/adverse effects of the vaccine virus, and/or may decrease the patient's antibody response to the vaccine; immunization of these patients should be undertaken only with extreme caution after careful review of the patient's hematologic status and only with the knowledge and consent of the physician managing the irinotecan therapy. The interval between discontinuation of medications that cause immunosuppression and restoration of the patient's ability to respond to the vaccine depends on the intensity and type of immunosuppression-causing medication used, the underlying disease, and other factors; estimates vary from 3 months to 1 year. In addition, immunization with oral poliovirus vaccine should be postponed in persons in close contact with the patient, especially family members)

Laboratory value alterations

The following have been selected on the basis of their potential clinical significance (possible effect in parentheses where appropriate)—not necessarily inclusive (» = major clinical significance).

With physiology/laboratory test values

Alkaline phosphatase, serum and
Aspartate aminotransferase (AST [SGOT]), serum
  (values may be increased, especially in patients with hepatic metastases)

Bilirubin
  (elevations of baseline bilirubin has **not** been associated with an increased risk of late diarrhea in clinical studies using the weekly dosage schedule)

» Hemoglobin concentration and
» Leukocyte count and
  Platelet count
  (may be decreased; anemia, leukopenia, and neutropenia were common in clinical trials, but severe thrombocytopenia was uncommon)

Medical considerations/Contraindications

The medical considerations/contraindications included have been selected on the basis of their potential clinical significance (reasons given in parentheses where appropriate)—not necessarily inclusive (» = major clinical significance).

Except under special circumstances, this medication should not be used when the following medical problem exists:

Hypersensitivity to irinotecan or any component of the drug

Risk-benefit should be considered when the following medical problems exist:

» Bone marrow depression, pre-existing or treatment-related
  (will be increased; delay, omission, and/or reduction of subsequent doses of irinotecan may be needed, depending on cell counts; a new course of irinotecan therapy should not be initiated until the granulocyte count has recovered to 1500 cells per cubic millimeter [cells/mm^3] and the platelet count has recovered to 100,000 cells/mm^3)

» Chickenpox, existing or recent (including recent exposure) or
» Herpes zoster
  (risk of severe, generalized disease)

» Hepatic function impairment
  (the risk of severe [U.S. National Cancer Institute (NCI) grade 3 or 4] neutropenia during the first course of irinotecan therapy may be substantially increased in patients with modest increases in serum bilirubin [concentrations between 1 and 2 mg/dL], and there is some evidence that patients with abnormal glucuronidation of bilirubin [e.g., patients with Gilbert's syndrome] may also be at relatively higher risk of irinotecan-induced myelosuppression. Studies have not been done in patients with more severe hepatic function impairment [serum bilirubin concentrations > 2 mg/dL or transaminase values > 3 times the upper limit of normal (ULN) in the absence of hepatic metastases, or transaminase values > 5 times the ULN in the presence of hepatic metastases]. A reduction in the initial dose of irinotecan should be considered)

» Infection, pre-existing
  (recovery may be impaired)

» Pulmonary disease or impairment
  (a potentially life-threatening syndrome consisting of dyspnea, fever, and reticulonodular pattern on chest radiograph occurred in some patients with pre-existing lung tumors or nonmalignant pulmonary disease in early clinical trials [conducted in Japan]; although the extent to which irinotecan may have been responsible for this complication has not been established, caution is recommended)

» Caution should also be used in patients who have had previous cytotoxic drug therapy or radiation therapy. In addition, caution should be used in patients with poor performance status because of a higher risk of diarrhea and neutropenia.

Patient monitoring

The following are especially important in patient monitoring (other tests may be warranted in some patients, depending on condition; » = major clinical significance):

» Bilirubin
  (prior to each course of irinotecan therapy; dosing recommendations have not been established for patients with bilirubin > 2 mg per deciliter)

» Diarrhea
  (ask patient about the number of stools per day and time of the last dose of antidiarrheal medicine prior to each course of irinotecan therapy; delay, omission, or dose adjustment of subsequent therapy cycle may be needed if bowel function does not return to pretreatment frequency of stools per day without antidiarrhea medication for at least 24 hours)

» Hemoglobin concentration and
» Leukocyte count, total and differential and
» Platelet count
  (determinations recommended prior to each course of irinotecan therapy; delay, omission, and/or reduction of subsequent doses is recommended if significant hematologic toxicity is present [e.g., granulocyte count lower than 1500 cells/mm^3 and/or platelet count lower than 100,000 cells/mm^3])

Infusion site
  (should be monitored for signs of inflammation; care should be taken to avoid extravasation and if extravasation should occur, flushing site with sterile water and applications of ice are recommended)

» Neutropenic fever
  (assess patient prior to each course of irinotecan therapy; omit dose until resolved, then decrease 2 dose levels)

» Nonhematologic toxicities
  (assess patient for other nonhematologic toxicities [excluding alopecia, anorexia, asthenia] prior to each course of irinotecan therapy; delay, omission, and/or reduction of subsequent doses may be needed to allow for recovery from treatment-related toxicity)

Side/Adverse Effects

Note: In addition to the side/adverse effects listed below, a potentially life-threatening syndrome consisting of dyspnea, fever, and a reticulonodular pattern on chest radiograph occurred in some patients in early clinical trials. Because this pulmonary syndrome appeared in patients with lung tumors or other pulmonary disease, the extent to which irinotecan may have contributed to this complication has not been established.

The following side/adverse effects have been selected on the basis of their potential clinical significance (possible signs and symptoms in parentheses where appropriate)—not necessarily inclusive:

Those indicating need for medical attention

Incidence more frequent

Abdominal enlargement (swelling of abdominal or stomach area; full or bloated feeling or pressure in the stomach); ***anemia*** (unusual tiredness or weakness, severe)—usually asymptomatic; ***ascites*** (stomach pain and bloating); ***cardiac dysfunction, mechanical*** (dizziness; fainting; fast, slow, or irregular heartbeat); ***diarrhea, possibly preceded by abdominal cramping and/or sweating; dyspnea*** (shortness of breath or troubled breathing)—may be associated with pulmonary metastases or other pre-existing lung disease; ***dysrhythmias*** (dizziness; fainting; fast, slow, or irregular heartbeat); ***edema*** (swelling); ***fever; hypotension*** (blurred vision; confusion; dizziness; faintness, or lightheadedness when getting up from a lying or sitting position suddenly; sweating; unusual tiredness or weakness); ***infection*** (fever or chills; cough or hoarseness; lower back or side pain; painful or difficult urination); ***ischemia*** (chest pain or discomfort; irregular heartbeat; nausea or vomiting; pain in the shoulders, arms, jaw or neck, sweating); ***jaundice*** (chills; clay-colored stools; dark urine; dizziness; fever; headache; itching; loss of appetite; nausea; abdominal or stomach pain; area rash; unpleasant breath odor; unusual tiredness or weakness; vomiting of blood; yellow eyes or skin); ***leukopenia***—usually asymptomatic; ***neutropenia***—usually asymptomatic; ***thrombocytopenia*** (black, tarry stools; blood in urine or stools; pinpoint red spots on skin; unusual bleeding or bruising)—usually asymptomatic; ***neutropenic infection*** (black, tarry stools; chills; cough; fever; lower back or side pain; painful or difficult urination; pale skin; shortness of breath; sore throat; ulcers, sores, or white spots in mouth; unusual bleeding or bruising; unusual tiredness or weakness); ***stomatitis*** (sores, ulcers, or white spots on lips or in mouth); ***thromboembolic events, including; angina pectoris*** (arm, back or jaw pain; chest pain or discomfort; chest tightness or heaviness; fast or irregular heartbeat; shortness of breath; sweating; nausea); ***arterial thrombosis*** (severe headaches of sudden onset; sudden loss of coordination; pains in chest, groin, or legs, especially calves of legs; sudden onset of shortness of breath for no apparent reason; sudden onset of slurred speech; sudden vision changes); ***cerebral infarct*** (blurred vision; confusion; numbness or tingling in face, arms, legs; severe headache; trouble speaking or walking); ***cerebrovascular accident*** (blurred vision; headache, sudden and severe; inability to speak; seizures; slurred speech; temporary blindness; weakness in arm and/or leg on one side of the body, sudden and severe); ***deep thrombophlebitis*** (changes in skin color; pain; tenderness; swelling of foot or leg); ***embolus, lower extremity*** (pain in legs; redness or swelling of leg); ***heart arrest*** (stopping of heart; no blood pressure or pulse; unconsciousness); ***myocardial infarct*** (chest pain or discomfort; pain or discomfort in arms, jaw, back or neck; shortness of breath; nausea; sweating; vomiting); ***myocardial ischemia*** (chest pain or discomfort; nausea; pain or discomfort in arms, jaw, back or neck; shortness of breath; sweating; vomiting); ***peripheral vascular disorder*** (cold hands and feet); ***pulmonary embolus*** (anxiety; chest pain; cough; fainting; fast heartbeat; sudden shortness of breath or troubled breathing; dizziness or lightheadedness); ***sudden death*** (no pulse; no blood pressure; no breathing); ***thrombophlebitis*** (changes in skin color; pain; tenderness; swelling of foot or leg); ***thrombosis*** (severe headaches of sudden onset; sudden loss of coordination; pains in chest, groin, or legs, especially calves of legs; sudden onset of shortness of breath for no apparent reason; sudden onset of slurred speech; sudden vision changes); ***vascular disorder*** (changes in skin color; cold hands and feet; pain, redness, or swelling in arm or leg)

Note: Phase I trials with irinotecan identified*diarrhea* as one of the medication's dose-limiting toxicities. Diarrhea may occur early (during or within 24 hours after administration of irinotecan) or late (more than 24 hours after administration of irinotecan; the median time to onset in clinical trials was 11 days), and may be severe. The early form of diarrhea is cholinergic in nature; it may be preceded by other symptoms of a cholinergic syndrome, including abdominal cramping, rhinitis, increased salivation, miosis, lacrimation, flushing and diaphoresis, and is usually short-lasting. Prophylactic or therapeutic administration of 0.25 to 1 mg of intravenous or subcutaneous atropine treatment should be considered (unless clinically contraindicated) for these patients.In clinical trials, early diarrhea occurred in 43%, and was severe (U.S. National Cancer Institute [NCI] grade 3 or 4) in 6.7%, of the patients. The late form of diarrhea may be severe and prolonged enough to cause life-threatening dehydration and electrolyte disturbances. In clinical trials, late diarrhea occurred in 83%, and was severe (NCI grade 3 or 4) in 31%, of the patients.The median durations of late diarrhea of any grade and of NCI grade 3 or 4 were 3 days and 7 days, respectively. Ulceration of the colon, sometimes with bleeding, has also been reported during therapy.

Neutropenia is the other dose-limiting toxicity of irinotecan. Although neutropenia occurred in 96.4%, and was severe (NCI grade 3 or 4) in 31.4%, of the patients in clinical trials, the incidence of neutropenic fever (grade 4 neutropenia with grade 2 or higher fever) was relatively low (5.8%). Deaths due to myelosuppression-related sepsis have been reported.

In patients receiving combination therapy including, irinotecan/5-FU/LV or 5-FU/LV in clinical trials, higher rates of hospitalization, neutropenic fever, thromboembolism, first-cycle treatment discontinuation and early deaths were observed in patients with a baseline performance status of 2 than in patients with a baseline performance status of 0 or 1.

Reports of thromboembolic events have been observed in patients receiving irinotecan-containing regimens; however, the specific cause of these events have not been determined.

Incidence less frequent

Dehydration (decreased urination; dizziness or lightheadedness, severe; dryness of mouth; fainting; increased thirst; wrinkled skin)—associated with severe diarrhea and/or vomitingand may lead to renal impairment and/or acute renal failure; ***hemorrhage*** (bleeding gums; coughing up blood; difficulty in breathing or swallowing; dizziness; headache; increased menstrual flow or vaginal bleeding; nosebleeds; paralysis; prolonged bleeding from cuts; red or dark brown urine; red or black, tarry stools; shortness of breath); ***neutropenic fever*** (fever or chills; cough or hoarseness; lower back or side pain; painful or difficult urination; sore throat); ***pneumonia*** (chest pain; cough, fever or chills; sneezing; shortness of breath sore throat troubled breathing tightness in chest wheezing)

Incidence rare

Allergic reactions, including anaphylactoid reactions (fast, irregular or troubled breathing; puffiness or swelling of the eyelids or around the eyes; shortness of breath; skin rash, hives, and/or itching; tightness in chest and/or wheezing); ***renal impairment or acute renal failure*** (lower back/side pain; decreased frequency/amount of urine; bloody urine; increased thirst; loss of appetite; nausea; vomiting; unusual tiredness or weakness; swelling of face, fingers, lower legs; weight gain; troubled breathing; increased blood pressure)

Note: There have been reports of renal impairment and acute renal failure, generally in patients who became infected and/or volume depleted from severe gastrointestinal toxicities.

Incidence not determined—Observed during clinical practice; estimates of frequency can not be determined

Colitis (stomach cramps; tenderness; pain; watery or bloody diarrhea; fever)

Note: Cases of colitis may be complicated by bleeding, ileus, infection or ulceration.

Those indicating need for medical attention only if they continue or are bothersome

Incidence more frequent

Abdominal cramps or pain; anorexia (loss of appetite; weight loss); ***accidental injury; asthenia*** (weakness); ***back pain; chills; constipation; cough; dizziness; dyspepsia*** (acid or sour stomach; belching; heartburn; indigestion; stomach discomfort, upset, or pain); ***flatulence*** (bloated full feeling; excess air or gas in stomach or intestines; passing gas); ***hand and foot syndrome*** (blistering, peeling, redness, and/or swelling of palms of hands or bottoms of feet; numbness, pain, tingling, or unusual sensations in palms of hands or bottoms of feet); ***headache; hepatomegaly*** (right upper abdominal pain and fullness); ***insomnia*** (sleeplessness; trouble sleeping; unable to sleep); ***mucositis*** (cracked lips; diarrhea; difficulty in swallowing; sores, ulcers, or white spots on lips, tongue, or inside mouth); ***nausea and vomiting; pain; rhinitis*** (runny nose); ***skin rash; somnolence*** (sleepiness or unusual drowsiness); ***sweating; syncope*** (fainting); ***vertigo*** (dizziness or lightheadedness; feeling of constant movement of self or surroundings, sensation of spinning); ***weight loss***

Note: *Nausea and vomiting*may occur early (within 24 hours after administration of irinotecan) or late (more than 24 hours after administration of irinotecan), and may be severe.

Incidence less frequent

Confusion

Those not indicating need for medical attention

Incidence more frequent

Alopecia (loss of hair); ***vasodilation*** (flushing)

Overdose

For specific information on the agents used in the management of irinotecan overdose, see the *Colony Stimulating Factors (Systemic)* monograph.

For more information on the management of overdose, **contact a Poison Control Center** (see *Poison Control Center Listing*).

Clinical effects of overdose

The following effects have been selected on the basis of their potential clinical significance (possible signs and symptoms in parentheses where appropriate)—not necessarily inclusive:

Acute and chronic

Diarrhea; leukopenia or neutropenia, including neutropenic fever (fever or chills; cough or hoarseness; lower back or side pain; painful or difficult urination; sore throat)

Note: Single doses as high as 750 mg per square meter of body surface area (mg/m^2) have been given to some participants in clinical trials. The adverse effects were similar to but more severe than those that typically occur with usual doses of irinotecan.

Treatment of overdose

It is recommended that the patient be hospitalized for close monitoring of vital functions and treatment of observed effects. Severe bone marrow depression may require transfusion of required blood components. A colony-stimulating factor may also be used to treat leukopenia or neutropenia. Febrile neutropenia should be treated empirically with broad-spectrum antibiotics, pending bacterial cultures and appropriate diagnostic tests.

Supportive care to prevent and treat dehydration associated with severe diarrhea is also recommended.

Patient Consultation

As an aid to patient consultation, refer to *Advice for the Patient, Irinotecan (Systemic)*.

In providing consultation, consider emphasizing the following selected information (» = major clinical significance):

Before using this medication

» Conditions affecting use, especially:

Hypersensitivity to irinotecan

Pregnancy—Use not recommended because of embryotoxic, teratogenic, and carcinogenic potential; advisability of using contraception and avoiding pregnancy; notifying physician immediately if pregnancy is suspected; apprising patient of potential hazard to fetus if drug is used during pregnancy

FDA Pregnancy Category D

Breast-feeding—Not recommended because of risk of serious side effects

Use in children—Safety and efficacy have not been established. However, a single agent irinotecan phase of one study was halted due to high rate of progressive disease and early death.

Use in the elderly—Increased risk of severe late diarrhea; close monitoring is recommended; reduced starting dose is recommended in selected older adults for the once-every-3-week dosage schedule

Other medications, especially other bone marrow depressants, diuretics, other immunosuppressants, laxatives, live virus vaccines, and radiation therapy or history of

Other medical problems, especially chickenpox, current or recent (including recent exposure); herpes zoster; hepatic function impairment; infection; pleural effusions; and pulmonary disease or impairment

Proper use of this medication

» Frequency of nausea and vomiting; importance of continuing treatment despite stomach upset; physician or nurse can advise on methods of minimizing discomfort

» Proper dosing

Precautions while using this medication

» Importance of close monitoring by the physician; need for periodic blood tests to check for asymptomatic side effects

» Avoiding immunizations unless approved by physician; other persons in patient's household should avoid immunizations with live vaccines (e.g., oral poliovirus vaccine, nasal influenza virus vaccine); avoiding other persons who have taken live vaccines or wearing a protective mask that covers the nose and mouth

Importance of monitoring infusion site for inflammation and avoiding extravasation; flushing site with sterile water and applying ice if extravasation occurs

Caution if diarrhea occurs:

» Notifying physician of occurrence immediately; informing physician if diarrhea is occurring within 24 hours after an infusion or was preceded by abdominal cramping or diaphoresis

» For late diarrhea (starting more than 24 hours after a dose): Can be life threatening. Starting treatment with loperamide as soon as an increased frequency or decreased consistency of bowel movement is noted, using a dosage regimen prescribed by physician or taking 4 mg initially, then 2 mg every 2 hours (or, at night, 4 mg every 4 hours), and continuing until free of diarrhea for 12 hours; not following maximum daily dosage recommendation for loperamide on nonprescription package labeling, which is insufficient for treating this complication
(Notify physician if the diarrhea is not controlled within 24 hours.)

» Notifying physician if vomiting also occurs

» Ensuring adequate fluid replacement; ingesting the type and quantity of fluid recommended by physician

Avoiding alcohol- or caffeine-containing beverages or medications, which can exacerbate fluid loss, and avoiding bran, raw fruits or vegetables, and fatty, fried, or spicy foods, which can aggravate diarrhea

» Notifying physician if signs and symptoms of dehydration (e.g., decreased urination, dizziness or lightheadedness, dryness of the mouth, fainting, increased thirst, wrinkled skin) occur

Caution if bone marrow depression occurs:

» Avoiding exposure to persons with infections, especially during periods of low blood counts; checking with physician immediately if fever with or without chills, cough or hoarseness, lower back or side pain, or painful or difficult urination occurs

» Checking with physician immediately if unusual bleeding or bruising; black, tarry stools; blood in urine or stools; or pinpoint red spots on skin occur

Caution in use of regular toothbrush, dental floss, or toothpick; physician, dentist, or nurse may suggest alternatives; checking with physician before having dental work done

Not touching eyes or inside of nose unless hands washed immediately before

Using caution to avoid accidental cuts when using sharp objects, such as safety razor or fingernail or toenail cutters

Avoiding contact sports or other situations where bruising or injury could occur

Side/adverse effects

May cause asymptomatic adverse effects such as bone marrow depression; importance of discussing possible effects with physician

Signs of potential side effects, especially abdominal enlargement, anemia, ascites, cardiac dysfunction, diarrhea with or without abdominal cramping and sweating, dyspnea, dysrhythmias, edema, fever, hypotension, infection, ischemia, jaundice, leukopenia, neutropenia, thrombocytopenia, neutropenic infection, stomatitis, thromboembolic events, dehydration, hemorrhage, neutropenic fever, pneumonia, allergic reactions, including anaphylactoid reactions, renal impairment or acute renal failure

Signs of potential side effects observed during clinical practice, especially colitis

Possibility of hair loss and of vasodilation

General Dosing Information

It is recommended that irinotecan be administered to patients only under the supervision of a physician experienced in cancer chemotherapy. It is also recommended that equipment and medications necessary for treatment of complications be readily available.

Irinotecan is to be given only by intravenous infusion. Care must be taken to avoid extravasation, and the infusion site should be monitored for signs of inflammation.

To reduce nausea and vomiting associated with irinotecan administration, patients should be premedicated with antiemetic agents, starting at least 30 minutes before the irinotecan infusion. A commonly used prophylactic regimen consists of 10 mg of dexamethasone plus a 5-hydroxytryptamine (serotonin) subtype 3 (5-HT$_3$) receptor antagonist (e.g., ondansetron or granisetron). Another antiemetic, e.g., prochlorperazine, may also be made available to the patient for postinfusion treatment of nausea and vomiting, if necessary.

Prophylactic administration of loperamide, to decrease the occurrence or severity of late diarrhea, is not recommended.

If severe (U.S. National Cancer Institute [NCI] grade 3 or 4) diarrhea or other toxicity occurs, further treatment should be withheld until recovery occurs.A delay of 1 or 2 weeks is usually sufficient. Treatment may then be resumed at a lower dose.However, if recovery does not occur within 2 weeks, discontinuation of treatment should be considered.

Special precautions are recommended for patients who develop thrombocytopenia (platelet count lower than 50,000 cells per cubic millimeter) during treatment. These may include extreme care in performing invasive procedures; regular inspection of intravenous access sites, skin (including the perirectal area), and mucous membrane surfaces for signs of bleeding or bruising; testing urine, emesis, stool, and secretions for occult blood; care in use of regular toothbrushes, dental floss, toothpicks, safety razors, and fingernail and toenail cutters; avoiding constipation; and using caution to prevent falls and other injuries. Such patients should avoid alcohol and aspirin intake because of the risk of gastrointestinal bleeding.

Treatment with irinotecan may be continued as long as a response is achieved or the disease remains stable, provided that therapy is well tolerated.

Outside of well-designed clinical studies, irinotecan should not be used in combination with the "Mayo Clinic" regimen of 5–fluorouracil/leucovorin (administered for 4–5 consecutive days every 4 weeks) due to reports of increased toxicity and toxic deaths.

Safety considerations for handling this medication

There is limited but increasing evidence and concern that personnel involved in the preparation and administration of parenteral antineoplastics may be at some risk because of the potential mutagenicity, teratogenicity, and/or carcinogenicity of these agents, although the actual risk is unknown. USP advisory panels recommend cautious handling both in preparation and disposal of antineoplastic agents. Precautions that have been suggested include:

- Use of a biological containment cabinet during reconstitution and dilution of parenteral medications and wearing of disposable surgical gloves and masks.
- Use of proper technique to prevent contamination of the medication, work area, and operator during transfer between containers (including proper training of personnel in this technique).
- Cautious and proper disposal of needles, syringes, vials, ampuls, and unused medication.

A number of medical centers have developed detailed guidelines for handling antineoplastic agents.

If irinotecan comes into contact with the skin, the skin should be washed immediately and thoroughly with soap and water. If the medication comes into contact with a mucous membrane, the area should be immediately and thoroughly flushed with water.

For treatment of adverse effects

For treatment of adverse effectsEarly diarrhea (occurring during, or within 24 hours following, an irinotecan infusion, sometimes preceded by abdominal cramping and/or diaphoresis)—0.25 to 1 mg of intravenous atropine, unless contraindicated.

Late diarrhea (occurring more than 24 hours postinfusion)—4 mg of loperamide immediately upon onset of increased frequency or decreased consistency of bowel movements, followed by 2 mg every 2 hours (at night, 4 mg every 4 hours) until diarrhea has been absent for at least 12 hours. Also, experience in a limited number of patients suggests that an alternative regimen consisting of 4 mg of loperamide every three hours plus 25 mg of diphenhydramine every six hours, starting immediately upon onset of increased frequency or decreased consistency of bowel movements, may decrease the occurrence of severe diarrhea significantly. Severe diarrhea also requires careful patient monitoring and fluid and electrolyte replacement as needed.Late diarrhea can be life threatening since it may be prolonged and may lead to dehydration, electrolyte imbalance, or sepsis. If severe diarrhea occurs, administration of irinotecan should be interrupted and subsequent doses reduced.

Leukopenia/neutropenia—Patients who develop leukopenia should be observed carefully for signs and symptoms of infection. Antibiotic support may be required. In neutropenic patients who develop fever, broad-spectrum antibiotic coverage should be initiated empirically, pending bacterial cultures and appropriate diagnostic tests. Use of a colony-stimulating factor may be considered. However, routine use of a colony-stimulating factor to prevent neutropenia during irinotecan treatment is not necessary.

Thrombocytopenia—Platelet transfusions may be required.

Extravasation-induced inflammation—Flushing the site with sterile water, then applying ice.

Parenteral Dosage Forms

Note: Bracketed uses in the *Dosage Forms* section refer to categories of use and/or indications that are not included in U.S. product labeling.

IRINOTECAN HYDROCHLORIDE INJECTION

Usual adult dose

Carcinoma, colorectal—

Single-agent—

Intravenous infusion (over ninety minutes), 125 mg per square meter of body surface area once a week for four weeks, followed by a rest period of two weeks. An alternate regimen of 240 to 350 mg per square meter of body surface area (infused over ninety minutes) every three weeks may also be used.

Note: Detailed guidelines for dosing adjustments related to toxicities are included in the manufacturer's product labeling.

When the weekly dosing regimen is used, dosage may be increased to up to 150 mg per square meter of body surface area or reduced to as low as 50 mg per square meter of body surface area, in increments of 25 or 50 mg per square meter of body surface area, according to individual patient tolerance.

When the weekly dosage regimen (single-agent) is used, a lower initial dose of 100 mg per square meter of body surface area once a week should be considered for patients with any of the following conditions: age ≥ 65 years, prior pelvic/abdominal irradiation, performance status of 2, and modestly elevated total serum bilirubin concentrations (1 to 2 mg/dL) because of the increased likelihood of first-course grade 3 or 4 neutropenia (graded according to U.S. National Cancer Institute [NCI] criteria). Although an appropriate initial dose has not been established for patients with pretreatment total serum bilirubin concentrations higher than 2 mg/dL, a starting dose that is even lower than 100 mg per square meter of body surface area should be considered.

In general, dosage should be decreased by 25 mg per square meter of body surface area if an NCI grade 2 toxicity occurs, by 25 to 50 mg per square meter of body surface area if an NCI grade 3 toxicity occurs, and by 50 mg per square meter of body surface area if an NCI grade 4 toxicity occurs. After a grade 2 toxicity, if using the lower dose for the remainder of that course of therapy results in adequate recovery, the original dosage may be used for the next course of treatment. After a grade 3 or 4 toxicity, irinotecan should be withheld until recovery to at least the grade 2 level has taken place, after which the lower dose should be used (unless further reduction is needed) for the duration of therapy. For toxicities occurring with the every-three-week dosage regimen, subsequent doses may be delayed and/or decreased by increments of 50 mg per square meter of body surface area as necessary.

After the first treatment, subsequent weekly chemotherapy treatments should be delayed in patients with active diarrhea until return of pretreatment bowel function for at least 24 hours without need for antidiarrhea medication. If grade 2,3, or 4 late diarrhea occur, subsequent doses of irinotecan should be decreased within the cycle

Combination-therapy with 5-Fluorouracil and Leucovorin—

Intravenous infusion (over ninety minutes), 125 mg per square meter of body surface area on days 1, 8, 15, 22 with the next course beginning on day 43. An alternate regimen of 180 mg per square meter of body surface area (infused over ninety minutes) on days 1, 15, and 29 with the next course beginning on day 43.

Note: Detailed guidelines for dosing adjustments related to toxicities are included in the manufacturer's product labeling.

In general, the dosage should be decreased by one dose level for an NCI grade 2 toxicity. For an NCI grade 3 or 4 toxicity that occurs during therapy, a dose should be omitted, and the dose should be decreased by 2 dose levels when recovery to ≤ grade 2 occurs.

[Carcinoma, lung, non-small cell][1]—

Because several doses and regimens using irinotecan are showing activity, no individual dose/regimen is listed here. Consult the medical literature and/or experts in the field of oncology for information on dosage. Support with rhG-CSF and antidiarrheals as needed.

Usual adult prescribing limits

Per single weekly dose, 150 mg per square meter of body surface area.

For single weekly dose in combination with 5-fluorouracil and leucovorin, 125 mg per square meter of body surface area.

Usual pediatric dose

Safety and efficacy have not been established.

Usual geriatric dose
See *Usual adult dose*.

Strength(s) usually available
U.S.—

20 mg per mL (40 mg per 2-mLand 100 mg per 5-mLsingle-use vials) (Rx) [*Camptosar* (sorbitol 45 mg; lactic acid 0.9 mg; hydrochloric acid or sodium hydroxide as needed to adjust pH)].

Canada—

20 mg per mL (40 mg per 2-mLand 100 mg per 5-mLsingle-use vials) (Rx) [*Camptosar* (sorbitol 45 mg; lactic acid 0.9 mg; hydrochloric acid or sodium hydroxide as needed to adjust pH)].

Packaging and storage
Store between 15 and 30 °C (59 and 86 °F), protected from light and freezing.

Preparation of dosage form
Irinotecan is prepared for administration by intravenous infusion by diluting the 20-mg-per-mL injection in 5% dextrose injection (preferred) or 0.9% sodium chloride injection to obtain a concentration of 0.12 to 2.8 mg per mL.

Stability
When diluted in 5% dextrose injection, irinotecan is stable for 48 hours if refrigerated at 2 to 8 °C (36 to 46 °F) and protected from light, or for up to 24 hours at room temperature (approximately 25 °C [77 °F]) in ambient fluorescent lighting.However, because irinotecan hydrochloride injection contains no antimicrobial preservative, the medication should preferably be used within 6 hours after dilution if kept at room temperature and within 24 hours after dilution if kept under refrigeration.

When diluted in 0.9% sodium chloride injection, irinotecan is stable for 24 hours at room temperature in ambient fluorescent lighting, but, because irinotecan hydrochloride injection contains no antimicrobial preservative, the medication should preferably be used within 6 hours after dilution if stored at room temperature or within 24 hours if refrigerated. Dilutions in 0.9% sodium chloride injection should not be refrigerated because of the possibility of precipitate formation.

The 2-mL and 5-mL vials of irinotecan are intended for single use only; unused portions of the injection should be discarded.

Incompatibilities
It is recommended that other medications not be added to the irinotecan infusion.

Auxiliary labeling
- Must be diluted prior to administration.
- Caution: Chemotherapy. Handle and dispose of properly.

[1]Not included in Canadian product labeling.

Selected Bibliography
Product Information: Camptosar®, irinotecan hydrochloride injection. Pharmacia & Upjohn Company, Kalamazoo, MI, (PI revised 05/2002) PI reviewed 01/2003.

Product Information: Camptosar®, irinotecan hydrochloride injection. Pharmacia Canada Inc., Mississauga, Ontario (PI revised 05/2002) PI reviewed 01/2003.

Revised: 07/19/2006
Developed: 06/26/1998

IRON DEXTRAN—See *Iron Supplements (Systemic)*

IRON SORBITOL—See *Iron Supplements (Systemic)*

IRON-POLYSACCHARIDE—See *Iron Supplements (Systemic)*

ISOCARBOXAZID—See *Antidepressants, Monoamine Oxidase (MAO) Inhibitor (Systemic)*

ISOETHARINE—See *Bronchodilators, Adrenergic (Inhalation-Local)*

ISOFLURANE—See *Anesthetics, Inhalation (Systemic)*

ISOFLUROPHATE—See *Antiglaucoma Agents, Cholinergic, Long-acting (Ophthalmic)*

ISOMETHEPTENE, DICHLORALPHENAZONE, AND ACETAMINOPHEN Systemic†

INN: Acetaminophen—Paracetamol

VA CLASSIFICATION (Primary/Secondary): CN103/CN105

Commonly used brand name(s): *Amidrine; Duradrin; I.D.A; Iso-Acetazone; Isocom; Midchlor; Midrin; Migquin; Migrapap; Migratine; Migrazone; Migrend; Migrex; Mitride.*

Note: For a listing of dosage forms and brand names by country availability, see *Dosage Forms* section(s).

†Not commercially available in Canada.

Category
Vascular headache suppressant (migraine)

Note: Some headache specialists question the validity of the term "vascular headache" because a correlation between dilatation of cerebral blood vessels and symptoms of migraine has not been demonstrated conclusively.

Indications
Accepted
Headache, migraine (treatment) and

Headache, tension-type (treatment)—Isometheptene, dichloralphenazone, and acetaminophen combination is indicated to relieve occasional migraine headaches (with or without aura) and coexisting migraine and tension-type headaches ("mixed" headache syndrome). However, the U.S. FDA has classified this combination as being "possibly" effective in the treatment of migraine headaches. This classification requires the submission of adequate and well-controlled studies in order to provide substantial evidence of effectiveness.

Note: Some headache specialists question the value of this formulation in pure tension-type headaches. However, the distinction between vascular, tension-type, and "mixed" headaches is often difficult or uncertain, and the medication may relieve some headaches characterized as tension-type.

Because frequent use of headache-aborting medications by headache-prone individuals may lead to tolerance and dependence, this medication is not recommended for regular use by patients who experience frequent, especially daily, headaches.

To reduce analgesic use, underlying problems that may contribute to tension-type headaches, such as inflammation or structural abnormalities in the cervical or temporomandibular areas, should be identified and treated. In some patients, application of heat, muscle relaxants, and/or physical therapy may be helpful. Other medications having the potential to cause habituation (e.g., benzodiazepines used as muscle relaxants) should be used as infrequently as possible.

Chronic tension-type headaches and severe migraines that occur more frequently than twice a month may require additional prophylactic treatment to reduce the frequency, severity, and/or duration of the headaches. The prophylactic agents most commonly used for tension-type headaches are tricyclic antidepressants, especially amitriptyline, and/or beta-adrenergic blocking agents, especially propranolol. For migraines, beta-adrenergic blocking agents, calcium channel blocking agents, tricyclic antidepressants, monoamine oxidase inhibitors, methysergide, pizotyline (not commercially available in the U.S.), and sometimes cyproheptadine (especially in children) are used as prophylaxis. The combination of amitriptyline plus propranolol has been found superior to either agent used alone as prophylaxis against "mixed" headaches.

Identification and avoidance of precipitating factors is also important in the overall management of the patient with migraine headaches. Relaxation and/or biofeedback techniques may also be helpful in controlling some types of headache, and may reduce the need for medication.

Pharmacology/Pharmacokinetics

Physicochemical characteristics

Molecular weight—
Isometheptene mucate: 492.7.
Dichloralphenazone: 519.04.
Acetaminophen: 151.16.

Mechanism of action/Effect

Isometheptene—The mechanism of action has not been established. Isometheptene is an indirect-acting sympathomimetic agent with vasoconstricting activity. It has been proposed that constriction of cerebral blood vessels reduces the pulsation in cerebral arteries that may be responsible for the pain of migraine headaches. However, studies have not consistently shown a significant correlation between dilatation of cerebral blood vessels and pain or other symptoms of migraine headaches, or between a vasoconstrictive action and relief of migraine.

Dichloralphenazone—A complex of chloral hydrate and antipyrine (INN: phenazone). It is present in this formulation as a mild sedative and relaxant.

Acetaminophen—The mechanism of analgesic action has not been fully determined. Acetaminophen may act predominantly by inhibiting prostaglandin synthesis in the central nervous system (CNS) and, to a lesser extent, through a peripheral action by blocking pain-impulse generation. The peripheral action may also be due to inhibition of prostaglandin synthesis or to inhibition of the synthesis or actions of other substances that sensitize pain receptors to mechanical or chemical stimulation.

Absorption

Acetaminophen—Rapid and almost complete; may be decreased if taken following a high-carbohydrate meal.

Distribution

In breast milk—Acetaminophen: Peak concentrations of 10 to 15 mcg per mL (66.2 to 99.3 micromoles/L) have been measured 1 to 2 hours following maternal ingestion of a single 650-mg dose.

Biotransformation

Dichloralphenazone—Hydrolyzed to the active compounds chloral hydrate and antipyrine. Chloral hydrate is metabolized in the liver and erythrocytes to the active metabolite trichloroethanol, which may be further metabolized to inactive metabolites. It is also metabolized in the liver and kidneys to inactive metabolites.

Acetaminophen—Approximately 90 to 95% of a dose is metabolized in the liver, primarily by conjugation with glucuronic acid, sulfuric acid, and cysteine. An intermediate metabolite, which may accumulate in overdosage after the primary metabolic pathways become saturated, is hepatotoxic and possibly nephrotoxic.

Half-life

Acetaminophen—
1 to 4 hours; does not change with renal failure but may be prolonged in acute overdosage, in some forms of hepatic disease, and in the elderly; may be somewhat shortened in children.
In breast milk: 1.35 to 3.5 hours.

Time to peak concentration

Acetaminophen—0.5 to 2 hours.

Peak plasma concentration

Acetaminophen—5 to 20 mcg per mL (with doses up to 650 mg).

Time to peak effect

Acetaminophen—1 to 3 hours.

Duration of action

Acetaminophen—3 to 4 hours.

Elimination

Acetaminophen—Renal, as metabolites, primarily conjugates; 3% of a dose may be excreted unchanged.

In dialysis:
Hemodialysis: 120 mL per minute (for unmetabolized drug); metabolites are also cleared rapidly.
Hemoperfusion: 200 mL per minute.
Peritoneal dialysis: <10 mL per minute.

Precautions to Consider

Note: The quantity of dichloralphenazone in this combination formulation does not provide full therapeutic doses of its active components chloral hydrate and antipyrine (phenazone). However, the possibility should be considered that precautions applying to chloral hydrate (see *Chloral Hydrate [Systemic]*) and to antipyrine may apply to ingestion of an overdose or to overuse of this combination medication.

Cross-sensitivity and/or related problems

Patients sensitive to aspirin are usually not sensitive to acetaminophen; however, acetaminophen has caused mild bronchospastic reactions in some aspirin-sensitive asthmatics (less than 5% of those tested).

Pregnancy/Reproduction

Fertility—Chronic toxicity studies in animals have shown that high doses of acetaminophen cause testicular atrophy and inhibition of spermatogenesis; the relevance of this finding to use in humans is not known.

Pregnancy—Acetaminophen crosses the placenta. However, problems in humans have not been documented.

Breast-feeding

Problems in humans have not been documented. Although peak concentrations of 10 to 15 mcg per mL (66.2 to 99.3 micromoles/L) of acetaminophen have been measured in breast milk 1 to 2 hours following maternal ingestion of a single 650-mg dose, neither acetaminophen nor its metabolites were detected in the urine of the nursing infants. The half-life in breast milk is 1.35 to 3.5 hours.

Pediatrics

No published information is available on the relationship of age to the effects of this combination medication in pediatric patients.

Geriatrics

No published information is available on the relationship of age to the effects of this combination medication in geriatric patients. Geriatric patients are more likely to have peripheral vascular disease, and are therefore more likely to be adversely affected by peripheral vasoconstriction, than are younger adults. However, isometheptene may be safer for elderly patients than the ergot derivatives used to abort acute vascular headaches. Also, elderly patients are more likely to have age-related renal function impairment, which may require caution in patients receiving acetaminophen and isometheptene.

Drug interactions and/or related problems

The following drug interactions and/or related problems have been selected on the basis of their potential clinical significance (possible mechanism in parentheses where appropriate)—not necessarily inclusive (» = major clinical significance):

Note: Combinations containing any of the following medications, depending on the amount present, may also interact with this medication.

Alcohol or
CNS depressants
(concurrent use with dichloralphenazone may cause additive sedation)

Alcohol, especially chronic abuse of or
Hepatic enzyme inducers (See *Appendix II*) or
Hepatotoxic medications, other (See *Appendix II*)
(risk of hepatotoxicity with single toxic doses of acetaminophen may be increased in alcoholics or in patients regularly taking other hepatotoxic medications or hepatic enzyme-inducing agents)
(chronic use of barbiturates [except butalbital] or primidone has been reported to decrease the therapeutic effects of acetaminophen, probably because of increased metabolism resulting from induction of hepatic microsomal enzyme activity; the possibility should be considered that similar effects may occur with other hepatic enzyme inducers)

» Monoamine oxidase (MAO) inhibitors
(concurrent use with an indirect-acting sympathomimetic such as isometheptene may cause sudden and severe hypertension and hyperpyrexia, which can reach crisis levels)

Laboratory value alterations

The following have been selected on the basis of their potential clinical significance (possible effect in parentheses where appropriate)—not necessarily inclusive (» = major clinical significance).

With diagnostic test results
Glucose, blood, determinations
(acetaminophen may cause values to be falsely decreased when measured by the glucose oxidase/peroxidase method but probably not when measured by the hexokinase [glucose-6-phosphate dehydrogenase (G6PD)] method)

5-Hydroxyindoleacetic acid (5-HIAA), serum, determinations
(acetaminophen may cause false-positive results with qualitative screening tests using nitrosonaphthol reagent; the quantitative test is unaffected)

Pancreatic function test using bentiromide
(administration of acetaminophen prior to the bentiromide test will invalidate test results because acetaminophen is also metabolized to an arylamine and will thus increase the apparent quantity of para-aminobenzoic acid [PABA] recovered; it is recommended

that acetaminophen be discontinued at least 3 days prior to administration of bentiromide)

Uric acid, serum, determinations
(acetaminophen may cause falsely increased values when the phosphotungstate uric acid test method is used)

With physiology/laboratory test values
Bilirubin, serum and
Lactate dehydrogenase (LDH), serum and
Prothrombin time and
Transaminase, serum
(values may be increased indicating acetaminophen-induced hepatotoxicity, especially in alcoholics, patients taking other hepatic enzyme inducers, or patients with pre-existing hepatic disease, when single toxic doses [>8 to 10 grams] are taken)

Medical considerations/Contraindications

The medical considerations/contraindications included have been selected on the basis of their potential clinical significance (reasons given in parentheses where appropriate)—not necessarily inclusive (» = major clinical significance).

Risk-benefit should be considered when the following medical problems exist:

» Alcoholism, active or
» Hepatic function impairment or
» Viral hepatitis
(increased risk of acetaminophen-induced hepatotoxicity)

Any condition in which the vasoconstrictive or other sympathomimetic effects of isometheptene may be hazardous, such as:
Cardiovascular or cerebrovascular insufficiency, including recent myocardial infarction or stroke
» Glaucoma, not optimally controlled
» Hypertension, not optimally controlled
» Organic heart disease
Peripheral vascular disease
» Renal function impairment, severe

Sensitivity to acetaminophen, dichloralphenazone, or to isometheptene, history of

Side/Adverse Effects

Note: The quantity of dichloralphenazone in this combination formulation does not provide full therapeutic doses of its active metabolites chloral hydrate and antipyrine (phenazone). However, the possibility should be considered that ingestion of an overdose or overuse of this combination medication may induce side effects characteristic of chloral hydrate (see *Chloral Hydrate [Systemic]*) and/or antipyrine.

The following side/adverse effects have been selected on the basis of their potential clinical significance (possible signs and symptoms in parentheses where appropriate)—not necessarily inclusive:

Those indicating need for medical attention

Incidence less frequent
Anemia or methemoglobinemia (unusual tiredness or weakness)

Incidence rare
Agranulocytosis (unexplained sore throat and fever); ***anemia*** (unusual tiredness or weakness); ***dermatitis, allergic*** (skin rash, hives, or itching); ***hepatitis*** (yellow eyes or skin); ***thrombocytopenia*** (unusual bleeding or bruising; black, tarry stools; blood in urine or stools; pinpoint red spots on skin)—usually asymptomatic

Symptoms of tolerance and/or dependence—with overuse
Headaches—more frequent, severe, and difficult to treat than previously

Those indicating need for medical attention only if they continue or are bothersome

Incidence more frequent
Drowsiness

Incidence less frequent or rare—dose-related
Dizziness; fast or irregular heartbeat

Overdose

For specific information on the agents used in the management of isometheptene, dichloralphenazone, and acetaminophen overdose, see:
- *Acetylcysteine (Systemic)* monograph.

For more information on the management of overdose or unintentional ingestion, **contact a poison control center** (see *Poison Control Center Listing*).

Clinical effects of overdose

The following effects have been selected on the basis of their potential clinical significance (possible signs and symptoms in parentheses where appropriate)—not necessarily inclusive:

Acute
Gastrointestinal upset (diarrhea; loss of appetite; nausea or vomiting; stomach cramps or pain); ***increased sweating***

Note: Early signs and symptoms of acetaminophen overdose, i.e., *gastrointestinal upset* and *increased sweating* often do not occur. However, when they do occur, they usually appear within 6 to 14 hours after ingestion of an overdose and persist for about 24 hours.

Chronic
Hepatotoxicity (pain, tenderness, and/or swelling in upper abdominal area)

Note: The first indications of overdosage may be signs and symptoms of possible *liver damage* and abnormalities in liver function tests, which may not occur until 2 to 4 days after ingestion of the overdose. Maximal changes in liver function tests usually occur 3 to 5 days after ingestion of the overdose.

Overt *hepatic disease or failure* may occur 4 to 6 days after ingestion of the overdose. *Hepatic encephalopathy* (with mental changes, confusion, agitation, or stupor), *convulsions, respiratory depression, coma, cerebral edema, coagulation defects, gastrointestinal bleeding, disseminated intravascular coagulation, hypoglycemia, metabolic acidosis, cardiac arrhythmias, and cardiovascular collapse* may occur.

Renal tubular necrosis leading to *renal failure* (signs may include bloody or cloudy urine and sudden decrease in amount of urine) has also been reported in acetaminophen overdose, usually, but not exclusively, in conjunction with acetaminophen-induced *hepatotoxicity.*

Treatment of overdose

For acetaminophen—

To decrease absorption—Emptying the stomach via induction of emesis or gastric lavage.

Removing activated charcoal (if used) by gastric lavage may be advisable. Although activated charcoal is recommended in cases of mixed drug overdose, it may interfere with absorption of orally administered acetylcysteine (antidote used to protect against acetaminophen-induced hepatotoxicity) and decrease its efficacy.

To enhance elimination—Instituting hemodialysis or hemoperfusion to remove acetaminophen from the circulation may be beneficial if acetylcysteine administration cannot be instituted within 24 hours following ingestion of a massive acetaminophen overdose. However, the efficacy of such treatment in preventing acetaminophen-induced hepatotoxicity is not known.

Specific treatment—Use of acetylcysteine. *It is recommended that acetylcysteine administration be instituted as soon as possible after ingestion of an overdose has been reported,* without waiting for the results of plasma acetaminophen determinations or other laboratory tests. Acetylcysteine is most effective if treatment is started within 10 to 12 hours after ingestion of the overdose; however, it may be of some benefit if treatment is started within 24 hours. See the package insert or *Acetylcysteine (Systemic)* monograph for specific dosing guidelines for use of this product.

Monitoring—Determining plasma acetaminophen concentration at least 4 hours following ingestion of the overdose. Determinations performed prior to this time are not reliable for assessing potential hepatotoxicity. Initial plasma concentrations above 150 mcg per mL (mcg/mL [993 micromoles/L]) at 4 hours, 100 mcg/mL (662 micromoles/L) at 6 hours, 70 mcg/mL (463.4 micromoles/L) at 8 hours, 50 mcg/mL (331 micromoles/L) at 10 hours, 20 mcg/mL (132.4 micromoles/L) at 15 hours, 8 mcg/mL (53 micromoles/L) at 20 hours, or 3.5 mcg/mL (23.2 micromoles/L) at 24 hours post-ingestion indicate possible hepatotoxicity and the need for completing the full course of acetylcysteine treatment. If the initial determination indicates a plasma concentration below those listed at the times indicated, cessation of acetylcysteine therapy can be considered. However, some clinicians advise that more than one determination should be performed to ascertain peak absorption and half-life of acetaminophen prior to considering discontinuation of acetylcysteine.

Monitoring renal and cardiac function and administering appropriate therapy as required.

Performing liver function tests (serum aspartate aminotransferase [AST; SGOT], serum alanine aminotransferase [ALT; SGPT], prothrombin time, and bilirubin) at 24-hour intervals for at least 96 hours postingestion if the plasma acetaminophen concentration indicates potential hepatotoxicity. If no abnormalities are detected within 96 hours, further determinations are not needed.

Supportive care—May include maintaining fluid and electrolyte balance, correcting hypoglycemia, and administering vitamin K_1 (if prothrombin time ratio exceeds 1.5) and fresh frozen plasma or clotting factor concentrate (if prothrombin time ratio exceeds 3.0).

For dichloralphenazone—

To decrease absorption—May include gastric lavage (endotracheal tube with inflated cuff should be in place to prevent aspiration of vomitus).

To enhance elimination—Hemodialysis may be effective in promoting the clearance of the active metabolite trichloroethanol.

Specific treatment—May include providing artificial respiration with oxygen.

Monitoring—Continuous cardiac monitoring is important, especially in patients with predisposing cardiac disease.

Supportive care—May include maintaining normal body temperature, maintaining appropriate fluid and electrolyte therapy and urinary output, and supporting respiration and circulation. Patients in whom intentional overdose is known or suspected should be referred for psychiatric consultation.

For isometheptene—

To decrease absorption—Emptying the stomach by induction of emesis or gastric lavage.

Monitoring—May include monitoring the patient, especially for signs and symptoms of excessive sympathetic stimulation or vasoconstriction, and treating observed symptoms as necessary.

Patient Consultation

As an aid to patient consultation, refer to *Advice for the Patient, Isometheptene, Dichloralphenazone, and Acetaminophen (Systemic)*.

In providing consultation, consider emphasizing the following selected information (» = major clinical significance):

Before using this medication

» Conditions affecting use, especially:

Allergic reaction to acetaminophen or to this combination medication, history of

Pregnancy—Acetaminophen crosses the placenta

Breast-feeding—Acetaminophen is excreted in breast milk

Other medications, especially monoamine oxidase inhibitors

Other medical problems, especially alcoholism (active), glaucoma, hypertension, heart disease, hepatic disease or viral hepatitis, and severe renal function impairment

Proper use of this medication

» Importance of not taking more medication than the amount prescribed; risk of tolerance and dependence with too frequent use; also, acetaminophen may cause liver damage with long-term use or greater than recommended doses

» Most effective when taken as soon as headache appears or at first sign of migraine attack (prodromal stage)

» Lying down in a quiet, dark room after taking initial dose

» Compliance with prophylactic therapy, if prescribed

Proper dosing

» Proper storage

Precautions while using this medication

» Checking with physician if usual dose fails to relieve headaches, or if frequency and/or severity of headaches increases; possibility that tolerance to the medication has developed and/or withdrawal (rebound) or chronic, daily headaches are occurring

» Caution if other medications containing acetaminophen are used

» Caution when driving or doing jobs requiring alertness because of possible drowsiness or dizziness, especially if also taking a CNS depressant.

» Avoiding use of alcohol, which increases the risk of liver toxicity with high doses of acetaminophen, especially in alcoholics; also, alcohol may aggravate or induce headache

Side/adverse effects

Signs of potential side effects, especially allergic dermatitis, blood dyscrasias, hepatotoxicity, and methemoglobinemia

General Dosing Information

Therapy is most effective when initiated at the first symptoms of a headache (during the prodrome, for migraine with aura).

After the first dose has been administered, it is recommended that the patient lie down and relax in a quiet, darkened room, because this contributes to relief of headaches.

In headache-prone individuals, frequent use of headache relievers may cause tolerance, leading to an increased dosage requirement, and to physical dependence, leading to both medication abuse and chronic (daily or near-daily) headaches. Patients who experience frequent headaches may also be dependent on a variety of other medications, including opioid analgesics, barbiturate-containing analgesic combinations, simple analgesics such as acetaminophen or aspirin, ergotamine, and antianxiety agents or sedatives.

Chronic headaches resulting from overmedication may be difficult to relieve, especially if the patient continues to take headache suppressants and/or analgesics. It is recommended that all such medications be discontinued. In-patient treatment may be necessary during detoxification. Naproxen, alone or together with amitriptyline, may reduce the severity of the headaches. Repetitive intravenous administration of dihydroergotamine (in conjunction with metoclopramide [to control dihydroergotamine-induced nausea and vomiting]) is recommended by some headache specialists to relieve chronic, intractable headaches associated with dependency on headache-aborting medications. Appropriate treatment for symptoms of withdrawal from other substances frequently used or abused by chronic headache patients may also be needed. In addition, appropriate prophylactic treatment should be initiated or adjusted to reduce the frequency and/or severity of future headaches.

Oral Dosage Forms

ISOMETHEPTENE MUCATE, DICHLORALPHENAZONE, AND ACETAMINOPHEN CAPSULES USP

Usual adult dose

Tension-type headache—

Oral, 1 or 2 capsules every four hours as needed, up to 8 capsules a day.

Vascular headache suppressant (migraine)—

Oral, 2 capsules at the start of the attack (during the prodrome, for migraine with aura), followed by 1 capsule every hour as needed, up to 5 capsules in twelve hours.

Usual pediatric dose

Dosage has not been established.

Strength(s) usually available

U.S.—

65 mg of isometheptene mucate, 100 mg of dichloralphenazone, and 325 mg of acetaminophen (Rx) [*Amidrine; Duradrin* (FD&C yellow No. 10); *I.D.A.* (FD&C yellow No. 10); *Iso-Acetazone; Isocom; Midchlor* (FD&C yellow No. 10); *Midrin* (FD&C yellow No. 6); *Migrapap; Migquin; Migratine; Migrazone; Migrend; Migrex; Mitride*; GENERIC].

Canada—

Not commercially available.

Packaging and storage

Store below 40 °C (104 °F), preferably between 15 and 30 °C (59 and 86 °F). Store in a well-closed container.

Selected Bibliography

Kunkel RS. Diagnosis and treatment of muscle contraction (tension-type) headaches. Med Clin N Amer 1991; 75: 595-603.

Anthony M. The treatment of migraine and other headaches. Curr Opin Neurol Neurosurg 1991; 4: 245-52.

Diamond S. Migraine headache. Med Clin N Amer 1991; 75: 545-66.

Revised: 12/22/1999

ISONIAZID Systemic

VA CLASSIFICATION (Primary): AM500

Commonly used brand name(s): *Isotamine; Laniazid; Nydrazid; PMS Isoniazid*.

Another commonly used name is INH.

Note: For a listing of dosage forms and brand names by country availability, see *Dosage Forms* section(s).

Category

Antibacterial (antimycobacterial).

Indications

Note: Bracketed information in the *Indications* section refers to uses that are not included in U.S. product labeling.

General Considerations

Tuberculosis is a highly infectious life-threatening bacterial disease with 8 million new cases and 3 million deaths reported worldwide each year to the World Health Organization (WHO). The vast majority of these cases are in developing countries; however, tuberculosis also has emerged as an important public health problem in the U.S. in recent years after the decline in number of cases observed between 1950 and 1980.

The resurgence of tuberculosis in the U.S. has been complicated by an increase in the proportion of patients with strains resistant to antituberculosis medications. Outbreaks of multidrug-resistant tuberculosis have been documented in hospitals and prisons. Drug-resistant tuberculosis, particularly that caused by strains resistant to isoniazid and rifampin, is much harder to treat and often is fatal. Among acquired immunodeficiency syndrome (AIDS) patients infected with tuberculosis bacilli resistant to both rifampin and isoniazid, a case-fatality rate of 91% has been reported. Recent investigations of outbreaks of multidrug-resistant tuberculosis have found an extraordinarily high case-fatality rate, with the median time to mortality being reached between 4 and 16 weeks. In almost all instances, these outbreaks have involved patients with severe immunosuppression by infection with the human immunodeficiency virus (HIV).

Acquired drug resistance develops during treatment for drug-sensitive tuberculosis with regimens that are poorly conceived or poorly complied with, allowing the emergence of naturally occurring drug-resistant mutations. Resistant organisms from affected patients may subsequently infect other people who have not been infected with *M. tuberculosis* previously, resulting in primary drug resistance.

Resistance to antituberculosis agents can develop not only in the strain that caused the initial disease, but also as a result of reinfection with a new strain of *M. tuberculosis* that is drug-resistant. Reinfection with a new multidrug-resistant *M. tuberculosis* strain can occur during therapy for the original infection or after completion of therapy. Most recent data suggest that outcomes can be improved if patients promptly begin therapy with two or more drugs that have *in vitro* activity against the multidrug-resistant isolate.

HIV infection is the strongest risk factor yet identified for the development of active tuberculosis disease in persons infected with tuberculosis. In addition, persons with HIV infection are at an increased risk of tuberculosis resulting either from newly acquired disease or from reactivation of latent infections. Tuberculosis is a major clinical manifestation of immunodeficiency induced by HIV. In hospital-based retrospective studies, high rates of tuberculosis have been found among patients with AIDS. In communities where tuberculosis and HIV infection are common, the prevalence of HIV seropositivity among patients with tuberculosis is greatly increasing.

WHO has estimated that 5.6 million people worldwide and 80,000 people in the U.S. are infected with both HIV and tuberculosis. Persons dually infected with *M. tuberculosis* and HIV have a high risk of developing clinically active tuberculosis. One study of HIV-positive drug users with positive tuberculin skin test results found a rate of the development of active tuberculosis to be 8 cases per 100 person-years (8% yearly) as compared with the 10% lifetime risk (1 to 3% risk within the first year after skin test conversion) in the general population.

Persons who are known to be HIV-infected and who are contacts of patients with infectious tuberculosis should be carefully evaluated for evidence of tuberculosis. If there are no findings suggestive of current tuberculosis, preventive therapy with isoniazid should be given. Because HIV-infected contacts are not managed in the same way as those who are not HIV-infected, HIV testing is recommended if there are known or suspected risk factors for their acquiring of HIV infection.

According to investigators at the National Institute of Allergy and Infectious Diseases (NIAID), levels of HIV in the bloodstream increase 5- to 160-fold in HIV-infected persons who develop active tuberculosis. Clinical and epidemiologic observations have demonstrated that HIV-infected individuals have an estimated 113-times higher risk and AIDS patients have a 170-times higher risk compared with uninfected persons. Furthermore, the problem of drug resistance may worsen as the HIV epidemic spreads. Immunosuppressed patients with HIV infection who subsequently become infected with *M. tuberculosis* have an extraordinarily high risk of developing active tuberculosis within a short period of time.

In addition to the convincing evidence that HIV infection increases the risk and worsens the course of tuberculosis, there is increasing clinical evidence that coinfection with *M. tuberculosis* accelerates progression of disease caused by HIV infection. Understanding the interaction of these two pathogens is clinically important, given the high prevalence of patients coinfected with HIV and *M. tuberculosis* in both the U.S. and Africa; it is estimated that by the year 2000 about 500,000 deaths per year will occur in coinfected patients worldwide.

Persons with a positive tuberculin skin test and HIV infection, and persons with a positive tuberculin skin test and at risk of acquiring HIV infection with unknown HIV status should be considered for tuberculosis preventive therapy regardless of age. One study showed that isoniazid prophylaxis in HIV-infected, tuberculin-positive individuals not only decreased the incidence of tuberculosis disease, but also delayed the progression to AIDS and death.

Twelve months of preventive therapy is recommended for adults and children with HIV infection and other conditions associated with immunosuppression. Persons with HIV infection should receive at least 6 months of preventive therapy. The American Academy of Pediatrics recommends that children receive 9 months of therapy.

Tuberculosis control programs should ensure that drug susceptibility tests are performed on all initial isolates of *M. tuberculosis* and the results are reported promptly to the primary care provider and the local health department. Tuberculosis control programs should monitor local drug resistance rates to assess the effectiveness of local tuberculosis control efforts and to determine the appropriateness of the currently recommended initial tuberculosis treatment regimen for the area.

Relapse of rifampin-resistant tuberculosis has been reported in HIV-infected patients. Reinfection with new strains of *M. tuberculosis* has also been reported in these patients. Rifampin-resistant tuberculosis is a serious threat because responses to therapy are more difficult to achieve and require long courses of treatment. Therefore, careful follow-up of HIV-infected patients with treated tuberculosis is essential.

Multidrug-resistant tuberculosis also has been transmitted to persons without HIV infection in health care facilities. Together with the lack of effective agents for second-line treatment and methods of prophylaxis, the transmission of multidrug-resistant strains of *M. tuberculosis* may create a substantial reservoir of latently infected people and the potential for clinical multidrug-resistant tuberculosis for many years to come.

Several studies have documented a high prevalence of extrapulmonary disease in HIV-infected patients with clinical tuberculosis disease, particularly in conjunction with pulmonary manifestations. Cutaneous miliary tuberculosis, also known as *tuberculosis cutis miliaris disseminata*, was in the past, a rare entity in adults, with only 24 cases reported in nearly a century. However, since the first reported case of cutaneous miliary tuberculosis in 1990 in a patient with AIDS, five additional cases have been reported in HIV-infected patients. Its appearance can be quite nondescript; therefore, a high level of suspicion must be maintained, particularly for patients with a CD4+ cell count of < 200 per cubic millimeter, in order to diagnose the condition and initiate therapy appropriately.

Accepted

Tuberculosis, latent infection (treatment)—Isoniazid is indicated alone in the treatment of latent tuberculosis infection in the following persons:

- Household members and other close contacts of patients with recently diagnosed tuberculosis who have a positive tuberculin skin test (PPD) of ≥ 5 mm; [tuberculin-negative children and adolescents who have been close contacts of infectious persons within the past 3 months are also candidates for preventative therapy until a repeat PPD is done 12 weeks after contact with the infectious source][1];
- [Human immunodeficiency virus (HIV)-infected persons of any age with a positive PPD of ≥ 5 mm or a past history of a positive PPD; also, persons with risk factors for HIV infection whose HIV status is unknown but who are suspected of having HIV infection][1];
- Positive PPD reactors of ≥ 5 mm with chest radiograph findings consistent with nonprogressive tuberculosis in whom there are neither positive bacteriologic findings nor a history of adequate chemotherapy for tuberculosis;
- [Children with a positive PPD of ≥ 5 mm who have an immunosuppressive condition, including HIV infection or immunosuppression due to corticosteroids][1];
- Adults with positive PPD reactions of ≥ 10 mm who are receiving immunosuppressives or prolonged therapy with corticosteroids, who have certain hematologic and reticuloendothelial diseases such as leukemia or Hodgkin's disease, who have diabetes mellitus or silicosis, or who have undergone gastrectomy;
- Children up to 4 years of age with a positive PPD of ≥ 10 mm who are at increased risk of dissemination because of their young age[1];
- [Children with a positive PPD of ≥ 10 mm who are at increased risk of dissemination because of medical risk factors other than immunosuppression due to corticosteroid therapy or HIV infection, such as

Hodgkin's disease, lymphoma, diabetes mellitus, chronic renal failure, and malnutrition][1];
• [Positive PPD reactors with a PPD ≥ 10 mm among intravenous drug abusers (IVDA) known to be HIV-negative, alcoholics, or homeless persons of any age, and children frequently exposed to these persons][1];
• [Positive PPD reactions of ≥ 10 mm in foreign-born persons up to 35 years of age, or children whose parents are from high-prevalence areas, such as Asia, Africa, or Latin America][1];
• [Positive PPD reactions of ≥ 10 mm in residents of long-term care facilities, prisons, nursing homes, and mental institutions, and children frequently exposed to these persons][1];
• [Positive PPD reactions of ≥ 10 mm in medically underserved low-income populations, up to 35 years of age, including high-risk racial or ethnic minority populations, especially blacks, Hispanics, and Native Americans][1]; or
• Recent converters, as indicated by a PPD increase of ≥ 10 mm within 2 years for those up to 35 years of age, and a PPD increase of ≥ 15 mm for those 35 years of age and older; [also, children 4 years of age and older with a PPD of ≥ 15 mm without any risk factors][1].

Tuberculosis (treatment)—Isoniazid is indicated, in combination with other antituberculars, in the treatment of all forms of tuberculosis, including tuberculous meningitis.

Resistance to isoniazid is a rapidly increasing problem. The primary cause of drug-resistance to antitubercular medications is inadequate therapy due to patient noncompliance. To try to avoid this continuing trend, administration of four-drug directly observed therapy (DOT) is currently recommended. (See *General Dosing Information.*)

Not all species or strains of a particular organism may be susceptible to isoniazid.

Unaccepted
Isoniazid is not recommended for use in the treatment of atypical mycobacterial infections, such as *Mycobacterium avium* complex (MAC), because isoniazid has weak activity against MAC compared to other antimycobacterial agents.

---

[1]Not included in Canadian product labeling.

Pharmacology/Pharmacokinetics

Note: Preliminary data suggest that patients coinfected with human immunodeficiency virus (HIV) and mycobacteria (*Mycobacterium tuberculosis* or *M. avium*) have altered pharmacokinetic profiles for antimycobacterial agents. In particular, malabsorption of these agents appears to occur frequently, and could seriously affect the efficacy of treatment.

Physicochemical characteristics
Molecular weight—137.14.

Mechanism of action/Effect
Isoniazid (INH) is a synthetic, bactericidal antitubercular agent that is active against many mycobacteria, primarily those that are actively dividing. Its exact mechanism of action is not known, but it may relate to inhibition of mycolic acid synthesis and disruption of the cell wall in susceptible organisms.

Absorption
Readily absorbed following oral administration; however, may undergo significant first pass metabolism. Absorption and bioavailability are reduced when isoniazid is administered with food.

Distribution
Widely distributed to all fluids and tissues, including cerebrospinal fluid (CSF), pleural and ascitic fluids, skin, sputum, saliva, lungs, muscle, and caseous tissue. INH crosses the placenta and is distributed into breast milk.

Vol_D—0.57 to 0.76 L per kg.

Protein binding
Very low (0 to 10%).

Biotransformation
Hepatic; isoniazid is acetylated by *N*-acetyl transferase to *N*-acetylisoniazid; it is then biotransformed to isonicotinic acid and monoacetylhydrazine. Monoacetylhydrazine is associated with hepatotoxicity via formation of a reactive intermediate metabolite when *N*-hydroxylated by the cytochrome P450 mixed oxidase system. The rate of acetylation is genetically determined; slow acetylators are characterized by a relative lack of hepatic *N*-acetyltransferase.

Half-life
Adults (including elderly patients)—
Fast acetylators: 0.5 to 1.6 hours.
Slow acetylators: 2 to 5 hours.
Acute and chronic liver disease: May be prolonged (6.7 hours vs 3.2 hours in controls).

Children (age 1.5 to 15 years)—
2.3 to 4.9 hours.

Neonates—
7.8 and 19.8 hours in two newborns who received isoniazid transplacentally. The long half-life may be due to the limited acetylation capacity of neonates.

Time to peak concentration
1 to 2 hours.

Peak serum concentration
3 to 7 mcg per mL after a single 300-mg oral dose.

Elimination
Renal; approximately 75–95% excreted by the kidneys within 24 hours, primarily as the inactive metabolites, *N*-acetylisoniazid and isonicotinic acid; of this amount, 93% of the isoniazid excreted in the urine may occur as the acetylated form in fast acetylators and 63% in slow acetylators, with the remainder, in both cases, occurring as the free or conjugated form.

Small amounts are excreted in feces.

In dialysis—
Significant amounts of isoniazid are removed from the blood by hemodialysis. A single 5-hour hemodialysis period has removed up to 73% of the isoniazid in the blood.
Peritoneal dialysis is of limited benefit.

Precautions to Consider

Cross-sensitivity and/or related problems
Patients hypersensitive to ethionamide, pyrazinamide, niacin (nicotinic acid), or other chemically related medications may be hypersensitive to this medication also.

Carcinogenicity/Tumorigenicity
Isoniazid has been shown to cause pulmonary tumors in a number of strains of mice. However, isoniazid has not been shown to be carcinogenic or tumorigenic in humans.

Pregnancy/Reproduction
Note: Tuberculosis in pregnancy should be managed in concert with an expert in the management of tuberculosis. Women who have only pulmonary tuberculosis are not likely to infect the fetus until after delivery, and congenital tuberculosis is extremely rare. *In utero* infections with tubercle bacilli, however, can occur after maternal bacillemia occurs at different stages in the course of tuberculosis. Miliary tuberculosis can seed the placenta and thereby gain access to the fetal circulation. In women with tuberculous endometritis, transmission of infection to the fetus can result from fetal aspiration of bacilli at the time of delivery. A third mode of transmission is through ingestion of infected amniotic fluid *in utero*.

If active disease is diagnosed during pregnancy, a 9-month regimen of isoniazid and rifampin, supplemented by an initial course of ethambutol if drug resistance is suspected, is recommended. Pyrazinamide usually is not given because of inadequate data regarding teratogenesis. Hence, a 9-month course of therapy is necessary for drug-susceptible disease. When isoniazid resistance is a possibility, isoniazid, ethambutol, and rifampin are recommended initially. One of these medications can be discontinued after 1 or 2 months, depending on results of susceptibility tests. If rifampin or isoniazid is discontinued, treatment is continued for a total of 18 months; if ethambutol is discontinued, treatment is continued for a total of 9 months. Prompt initiation of chemotherapy is mandatory to protect both the mother and fetus. If isoniazid or rifampin resistance is documented, an expert in the management of tuberculosis should be consulted.

Asymptomatic pregnant women with positive tuberculin skin tests and normal chest radiographs should receive preventive therapy with isoniazid for 9 months if they are HIV seropositive or have recently been in contact with an infectious person. For these individuals, preventive therapy should begin after the first trimester. In other circumstances in which none of these risk factors is present, although no harmful effects of isoniazid to the fetus have been observed, preventive therapy can be delayed until after delivery.

For all pregnant women receiving isoniazid, pyridoxine should be prescribed. Isoniazid, ethambutol, and rifampin appear to be relatively safe for the fetus. The benefit of ethambutol and rifampin for therapy of active disease in the mother outweighs the risk to the infant. Streptomycin and pyrazinamide should not be used unless they are essential to the control of the disease.

Pregnancy—Isoniazid crosses the placenta, resulting in fetal serum concentrations that may exceed maternal serum concentrations. However, problems in humans have not been documented.

Studies in rats and rabbits have shown that isoniazid may be embryocidal. However, isoniazid has not been shown to be teratogenic in mice, rats, or rabbits.

FDA Pregnancy Category C.

Breast-feeding

Isoniazid is distributed into breast milk. An estimated 0.75 to 2.3% of the daily adult dose could be ingested by the nursing infant. Problems in nursing newborns have not been documented and breast-feeding should not be discouraged. However, because isoniazid concentrations are so low in breast milk, breast-feeding cannot be relied upon for adequate tuberculosis prophylaxis or therapy for nursing infants.

Pediatrics

Note: If an infant is suspected of having congenital tuberculosis, a Mantoux tuberculin skin test, chest radiograph, lumbar puncture, and appropriate cultures should be performed promptly. Regardless of the skin test results, treatment of the infant should be initiated promptly with isoniazid, rifampin, pyrazinamide, and streptomycin or kanamycin. In addition, the mother should be evaluated for the presence of pulmonary or extrapulmonary (including uterine) tuberculosis. If the physical examination or chest radiograph support the diagnosis of tuberculosis, the patient should be treated with the same regimen as that used for tuberculous meningitis. The drug susceptibilities of the organism recovered from the mother and/or infant should be determined.

Possible isoniazid resistance should always be considered, particularly in children from population groups in which drug resistance is high, especially in foreign-born children from countries with a high prevalence of drug-resistant tuberculosis. For contacts who are likely to have been infected by an index case with isoniazid-resistant but rifampin-susceptible organisms, and in whom the consequences of the infection are likely to be severe (e.g., children up to 4 years of age), rifampin (10 mg per kg of body weight, maximum 600 mg, given daily in a single dose) should be given in addition to isoniazid (10 mg per kg, maximum 300 mg, given daily in a single dose) until susceptibility test results for the isolate from the index case are available. If the index case is known or proven to be excreting organisms resistant to isoniazid, then isoniazid should be discontinued and rifampin given for a total of 9 months. Isoniazid alone should be given if no proof of exposure to isoniazid-resistant organisms is found. Optimal therapy for children with tuberculosis infection caused by organisms resistant to isoniazid and rifampin is unknown. In deciding on therapy in this situation, consultation with an expert is advised.

Adjuvant treatment with corticosteroids in treating tuberculosis is controversial. Corticosteroids have been used for therapy in children with tuberculous meningitis to reduce vasculitis, inflammation, and, as a result, intracranial pressure. Data indicate that dexamethasone may lower mortality rates and lessen long-term neurologic impairment. The administration of corticosteroids should be considered in all children with tuberculous meningitis, and also may be considered in children with pleural and pericardial effusions (to hasten reabsorption of fluid), severe miliary disease (to mitigate alveolocapillary block), and endobronchial disease (to relieve obstruction and atelectasis). Corticosteroids should be given only when accompanied by appropriate antituberculosis therapy. Consultation with an expert in the treatment of tuberculosis should be obtained when corticosteroid therapy is considered.

Studies performed in children have not demonstrated pediatrics-specific problems that would limit the usefulness of isoniazid in children. However, newborn infants may have a limited acetylation capacity, prolonging the elimination half-life of isoniazid.

Children do not require routine hepatic function determinations unless they have pre-existing hepatic disease.

Pyridoxine supplementation is not usually required in children if dietary intake is adequate.

Geriatrics

Appropriate studies on the relationship of age to the effects of isoniazid have not been performed in the geriatric population. However, patients over 50 years of age are more likely to develop hepatitis while receiving isoniazid than are patients in younger age groups.

Pharmacogenetics

Patients can be divided into two groups: slow and rapid acetylators of isoniazid. Approximately 50% of blacks and Caucasians are slow acetylators; the majority of Eskimos and Asians are rapid acetylators. The rate of acetylation does not significantly alter the effectiveness of isoniazid. However, slow acetylation may lead to higher blood levels of isoniazid and thus, an increase in toxic reactions. Slow acetylators are characterized by a relative lack of hepatic *N*-acetyltransferase. Patients who are slow acetylators may be more prone to develop adverse effects, especially peripheral neuritis, and may require lower-than-usual doses. Rapid acetylators generally do not require higher doses, nor is isoniazid less effective in these patients.

Drug interactions and/or related problems

The following drug interactions and/or related problems have been selected on the basis of their potential clinical significance (possible mechanism in parentheses where appropriate)—not necessarily inclusive (» = major clinical significance):

Note: Combinations containing any of the following medications, depending on the amount present, may also interact with this medication.

Acetaminophen
(concurrent use of acetaminophen with isoniazid may increase the potential for hepatotoxicity and, possibly, nephrotoxicity; isoniazid is thought to induce cytochrome P450, resulting in a greater proportion of acetaminophen being converted to toxic metabolite)

» Alcohol
(concurrent daily use of alcohol may result in increased incidence of isoniazid-induced hepatotoxicity and increased metabolism of isoniazid; dosage adjustments of isoniazid may be necessary; patients should be monitored closely for signs of hepatotoxicity and should be advised to restrict intake of alcoholic beverages)

» Alfentanil
(chronic preoperative or perioperative use of isoniazid, a hepatic enzyme inhibitor, may decrease the plasma clearance and prolong the duration of action of alfentanil)

Antacids, especially aluminum-containing
(antacids may delay and decrease absorption and serum concentrations of orally administered isoniazid; concurrent use should be avoided, or patients should be advised to take oral isoniazid at least 1 hour before aluminum-containing antacids)

Anticoagulants, coumarin- or indandione-derivative
(concurrent use with isoniazid may result in increased anticoagulant effect because of the inhibition of enzymatic metabolism of anticoagulants)

Benzodiazepines
(isoniazid may decrease the hepatic metabolism of benzodiazepines, such as diazepam, chlordiazepoxide, flurazepam, and prazepam, that are metabolized by phase I reactions [*N*-demethylation and hydroxylation]; it may also impair the oxidation of triazolam, increasing plasma benzodiazepine concentrations; isoniazid may decrease first-pass metabolism and elimination of midazolam in the liver, probably by competitive inhibition at the cytochrome P450 binding sites, increasing steady-state plasma concentrations of midazolam)

» Carbamazepine
(concurrent use with isoniazid increases serum carbamazepine levels and toxicity, probably through inhibition of carbamazepine metabolism; also, carbamazepine may induce microsomal metabolism of isoniazid, increasing formation of an INH-reactive intermediate metabolite, which may lead to hepatotoxicity)

Cheese, such as Swiss or Cheshire, or
Fish, such as tuna, skipjack, or Sardinella
(concurrent ingestion with isoniazid may result in redness or itching of the skin, hot feeling, rapid or pounding heartbeat, sweating, chills or clammy feeling, headache, or lightheadedness; this is thought to be due to the inhibition of plasma monoamine oxidase and diamine oxidase by isoniazid, interfering with the metabolism of histamine and tyramine found in fish and cheese)

Corticosteroids, glucocorticoid
(concurrent use of prednisolone, and probably other related corticosteroids, with isoniazid may increase hepatic metabolism and/or excretion of isoniazid, leading to decreased plasma concentrations and effectiveness of isoniazid, especially in patients who are rapid acetylators; isoniazid dosage adjustments may be required)

Cycloserine
(concurrent use may result in increased incidence of central nervous system [CNS] effects such as dizziness or drowsiness; dosage adjustments may be necessary and patients should be monitored closely for signs of CNS toxicity)

» Disulfiram
(concurrent use in alcoholics may result in increased incidence of CNS effects such as dizziness, incoordination, irritability, or insom-

nia; reduced dosage or discontinuation of disulfiram may be necessary)

Enflurane
(isoniazid may increase formation of the potentially nephrotoxic inorganic fluoride metabolite when used concurrently with enflurane)

» Hepatotoxic medications, other (see *Appendix II*)
(concurrent use of other hepatotoxic medications with isoniazid may increase the potential for hepatotoxicity and should be avoided)

» Ketoconazole
(concurrent use of ketoconazole with isoniazid has been reported to decrease serum concentrations of ketoconazole; isoniazid should be used with caution when given concurrently with ketoconazole)

Neurotoxic medications, other (see *Appendix II*)
(concurrent use of other neurotoxic medications with isoniazid may produce additive neurotoxicity)

» Phenytoin
(concurrent use with isoniazid inhibits the metabolism of phenytoin, resulting in increased phenytoin serum concentrations and toxicity; phenytoin dosage adjustments may be necessary during and after isoniazid therapy, especially in slow acetylators of isoniazid)

Pyridoxine
(isoniazid may cause peripheral neuritis by acting as a pyridoxine antagonist or increasing renal excretion of pyridoxine; requirements for pyridoxine may be increased in patients receiving isoniazid concurrently)

» Rifampin
(concurrent use of rifampin with isoniazid may increase the risk of hepatotoxicity, especially in patients with pre-existing hepatic impairment and/or in fast acetylators of isoniazid; patients receiving rifampin and isoniazid concurrently should be monitored closely for signs of hepatotoxicity during the first 3 months of therapy)

Theophylline
(concurrent use may reduce the metabolism of theophylline, increasing theophylline plasma concentrations)

Laboratory value alterations

The following have been selected on the basis of their potential clinical significance (possible effect in parentheses where appropriate)—not necessarily inclusive (» = major clinical significance).

With diagnostic test results

Glucose, urine
(isoniazid may cause hyperglycemia with a secondary glycosuria, giving a positive response to copper sulfate tests; glucose enzymatic tests are not affected)

With physiology/laboratory test values

Alanine aminotransferase (ALT [SGPT]) and
Aspartate aminotransferase (AST [SGOT]) and
(values may be transiently and asymptomatically increased in approximately 10 to 20% of patients tested)

Bilirubin, serum
(concentrations may be transiently and asymptomatically increased in approximately 10 to 20% of patients tested)

Medical considerations/Contraindications

The medical considerations/contraindications included have been selected on the basis of their potential clinical significance (reasons given in parentheses where appropriate)—not necessarily inclusive (» = major clinical significance).

Risk-benefit should be considered when the following medical problems exist:

» Alcoholism, active or in remission, or
» Hepatic function impairment
(increased risk of hepatitis with daily consumption of alcohol or hepatic function impairment)

» Hypersensitivity to isoniazid, ethionamide, pyrazinamide, niacin (nicotinic acid), or other chemically related medications

Renal failure, severe
(there may be an increased risk of toxicity in patients who have severe renal failure [creatinine clearance < 10 mL/min])

Seizure disorders
(isoniazid may be neurotoxic and cause seizures)

Patient monitoring

The following may be especially important in patient monitoring (other tests may be warranted in some patients, depending on condition; » = major clinical significance):

Hepatic function determinations
(AST [SGOT], ALT [SGPT], and serum bilirubin determinations may be required prior to and monthly or more frequently during treatment; however, elevated serum enzyme values may not be predictive of clinical hepatitis and values may return to normal despite continued treatment; therefore, routine measurement of hepatic function is generally not recommended unless there is preexisting hepatic disease; patients should be instructed to report promptly any prodromal symptoms of hepatitis; if signs and symptoms of hepatotoxicity occur, isoniazid should be promptly discontinued; if isoniazid therapy must be reinstituted, very small and gradually increasing doses should be used, and then only after signs and symptoms of hepatotoxicity have cleared; isoniazid should be withdrawn immediately if any further evidence of hepatotoxicity occurs)

» Ophthalmologic examinations
(if symptoms of optic neuritis occur in either adults or children during treatment, ophthalmologic examinations may be required immediately and periodically thereafter; ophthalmologic examinations are not recommended in asymptomatic patients)

Side/Adverse Effects

Note: Isoniazid has been reported to cause severe, and sometimes fatal, age-related hepatitis. If signs and symptoms of hepatotoxicity occur, isoniazid should be discontinued promptly. The incidence of clinical hepatitis in young, healthy adults is 0.3%, but can increase to 2.6% for those who drink alcohol daily, have chronic liver disease, or are elderly.

Patients with advanced HIV disease have been reported to have an increased incidence of adverse reactions to antitubercular medications. This was not found in HIV-seropositive patients being treated for tuberculosis.

Pyridoxine deficiency is sometimes observed in adults receiving high doses of isoniazid and probably results from isoniazid's competition with pyridoxal phosphate for the enzyme apotryptophanase.

Peripheral neuritis usually is preventable by administering 10 to 25 mg of pyridoxine per day. It is recommended for patients at risk of neuritis, including those over 65 years of age, pregnant women, patients with diabetes mellitus, chronic renal failure, alcoholism, malnutrition, and those taking anticonvulsant medications.

The following side/adverse effects have been selected on the basis of their potential clinical significance (possible signs and symptoms in parentheses where appropriate)—not necessarily inclusive:

Those indicating need for medical attention

Incidence more frequent

Hepatitis (dark urine, yellow eyes or skin); ***hepatitis prodromal symptoms*** (loss of appetite, nausea or vomiting, unusual tiredness or weakness); ***peripheral neuritis*** (clumsiness or unsteadiness; numbness, tingling, burning, or pain in hands and feet)

Incidence rare

Blood dyscrasias (fever and sore throat, unusual bleeding and bruising, unusual tiredness or weakness); ***hypersensitivity*** (fever, joint pain, skin rash); ***neurotoxicity*** (seizures, mental depression, mood or other mental changes); ***optic neuritis*** (blurred vision or loss of vision, with or without eye pain)

Those indicating need for medical attention only if they continue or are bothersome

Incidence more frequent

Gastrointestinal disturbances (diarrhea, nausea and vomiting, stomach pain)

Incidence not reported

Local irritation at the site of intramuscular injections

Overdose

For specific information on the agents used in the management of isoniazid overdose, see

- *Pyridoxine (Systemic)* monograph;
- *Diazepam* in *Benzodiazepines (Systemic)* monograph; and/or
- *Thiopental* in *Barbiturates (Systemic)* monograph.

For more information on the management of overdose or unintentional ingestion, **contact a Poison Control Center** (see *Poison Control Center Listing*).

The information below applies to the clinical effects and treatment of isoniazid overdose.

Clinical effects of overdose

The following effects have been selected on the basis of their potential clinical significance (possible signs and symptoms in parentheses where appropriate)—not necessarily inclusive:

Acute and chronic effects

Gastrointestinal disturbances (severe nausea and vomiting); ***neurotoxicity*** (dizziness; slurred speech; lethargy; disorientation; hyperreflexia; seizures; coma)

Note: Patients may be asymptomatic for 30 minutes to 2 hours after an acute overdose. Early symptoms include *nausea and vomiting, dizziness, slurred speech, lethargy, disorientation,* and *hyperreflexia. Seizures* usually occur within 1 to 3 hours after ingestion, and are often repetitive and refractory to treatment with usual anticonvulsants. Lactic acid accumulation produces an anion-gap metabolic acidosis within a few hours, which is often severe and refractory to treatment with sodium bicarbonate. Hyperglycemia, glycosuria, and ketonuria have also been reported.

Treatment of overdose

To decrease absorption—

Because seizures may occur soon after ingestion, induction of emesis with ipecac is not recommended. Gastric lavage may be performed within 2 to 3 hours of ingestion, and activated charcoal and a cathartic may be administered if the patient's seizures are controlled and the airway protected.

Specific treatment—

Administering intravenous pyridoxine in a gram-for-gram dose, equivalent to the amount of isoniazid ingested; dose should be administered as a 5 or 10% solution in water for injection over 30 to 60 minutes. If the amount of isoniazid ingested is unknown, administering 5-gram doses of pyridoxine every 5 to 30 minutes until seizures stop or consciousness is regained.

Controlling seizures with diazepam, which acts synergistically with pyridoxine. Phenytoin should be used with caution, if at all, since isoniazid inhibits phenytoin metabolism. Thiopental has been effective in treating refractory seizures.

Carefully administering sodium bicarbonate if pyridoxine and diazepam do not control seizure activity. Use caution against overcorrection and watch for hypokalemia or hyperkalemia.

Supportive care—

Supportive measures such as establishing intravenous lines, hydration, correction of electrolyte imbalance, oxygenation, and support of ventilatory function are essential for maintaining the vital functions of the patient. Patients in whom intentional overdose is confirmed or suspected should be referred for psychiatric consultation.

Patient Consultation

As an aid to patient consultation, refer to *Advice for the Patient, Isoniazid (Systemic)*.

In providing consultation, consider emphasizing the following selected information (» = major clinical significance):

Before using this medication

» Conditions affecting use, especially:

Hypersensitivity to isoniazid, ethionamide, pyrazinamide, niacin (nicotinic acid), or other chemically related medications

Pregnancy—Isoniazid crosses the placenta; fetal serum concentrations may exceed maternal serum concentrations

Breast-feeding—Isoniazid is distributed into breast milk

Use in children—Children may be less susceptible to pyridoxine deficiency and hepatotoxicity than adults, unless they have pre-existing hepatic disease; newborn infants may have prolonged elimination

Use in the elderly—Patients over the age of 50 have the highest incidence of hepatitis

Other medicines, especially daily alcohol use, alfentanil, carbamazepine, disulfiram, other hepatotoxic medications, ketoconazole, phenytoin, or rifampin

Other medical problems, especially alcoholism, active or in remission, or hepatic function impairment

Proper use of this medication

Taking this medication with food or antacids, but not within 1 hour of aluminum-containing antacids, if gastrointestinal irritation occurs (oral only)

Proper administration technique for oral liquids

» Compliance with full course of therapy, which may take 6 months to 2 years

» Taking pyridoxine concurrently to prevent or minimize symptoms of peripheral neuritis; not usually required in children if dietary intake is adequate

» Proper dosing

Missed dose: Taking as soon as possible; not taking if almost time for next dose; not doubling doses

» Proper storage

Precautions while using this medication

» Regular visits to physician to check progress, as well as ophthalmologic examinations if signs of optic neuritis occur in either adults or children

Checking with physician if no improvement within 2 to 3 weeks

Checking with physician if vascular reactions occur following concurrent ingestion of cheese or fish with isoniazid

» Avoiding alcoholic beverages while taking this medication

» Need to report to physician promptly prodromal signs of hepatitis or peripheral neuritis

» Diabetics: False-positive reactions with copper sulfate urine glucose tests may occur

Side/adverse effects

Hepatitis may be more likely to occur in patients over 50 years of age

Signs of potential side effects, especially hepatitis, peripheral neuritis, blood dyscrasias, hypersensitivity, neurotoxicity, and optic neuritis

General Dosing Information

All patients may be divided into two groups: slow and fast acetylators of isoniazid. Patients who are slow acetylators may be more prone to development of adverse effects, especially peripheral neuritis, and may require lower-than-usual doses. Fast acetylators do not generally require higher doses, nor is isoniazid less effective in these patients. Eskimo, Oriental, and American Indian populations have the lowest prevalence of slow acetylators, while Egyptian, Israeli, Scandinavian, other Caucasian, and black populations have the highest prevalence of slow acetylators.

The duration of treatment with an antituberculosis regimen is at least 6 months, and may be continued for 2 years. Uncomplicated pulmonary tuberculosis is often successfully treated within 6 to 12 months. Several different treatment regimens are currently recommended.

The duration of antituberculosis therapy is based on the patient's clinical and radiographic responses, smear and culture results, and susceptibility studies of *Mycobacterium tuberculosis* isolates from the patient or the suspect source case. With directly observed therapy (DOT), clinical evaluation is an integral component of each visit for administration of medication. Careful monitoring of the clinical and bacteriologic responses to therapy on a monthly basis in sputum-positive patients is important.

If therapy is interrupted, the treatment schedule should be extended to a later completion date. Although guidelines cannot be provided for every situation, the following factors need to be considered in establishing a new date for completion:

- The length of interruption;
- The time during therapy (early or late) in which interruption occurred; and
- The patient's clinical, radiographic, and bacteriologic status before, during, and after interruption. Consultation with an expert is advised.

Therapy should be administered based on the following guidelines, published by the American Thoracic Society (ATS) and by the Centers for Disease Control and Prevention (CDC), and endorsed by the American Academy of Pediatrics (AAP).

- A 6-month regimen consisting of isoniazid, rifampin, and pyrazinamide given for 2 months followed by isoniazid and rifampin for 4 months is the preferred treatment for patients infected with fully susceptible organisms who adhere to the treatment course.
- Ethambutol (or streptomycin in children too young to be monitored for visual acuity) should be included in the initial regimen until the results of drug susceptibility studies are available, and unless there is little possibility of drug resistance (i.e., there is less than 4% primary resistance to isoniazid in the community, and the patient has had no previous treatment with antituberculosis medications, is not from a country with a high prevalence of drug resistance, and has no known exposure to a drug-resistant case).
- Alternatively, a 9-month regimen of isoniazid and rifampin is acceptable for persons who cannot or should not take pyrazinamide. Ethambutol (or streptomycin in children too young to be monitored for visual acuity) should also be included until the results of drug susceptibility studies are available, unless there is little possibility of drug resistance. If isoniazid resistance is demonstrated, rifampin and ethambutol should be continued for a minimum of 12 months.

- Consideration should be given to treating all patients with DOT. DOT programs have been demonstrated to increase adherence in patients receiving antituberculosis chemotherapy in both rural and urban settings.
- Multidrug-resistant tuberculosis (i.e., resistance to at least isoniazid and rifampin) presents difficult treatment problems. Treatment must be individualized and based on susceptibility studies. In such cases, consultation with an expert in tuberculosis is recommended.
- Children should be managed in essentially the same ways as adults, but doses of the medications must be adjusted appropriately and specific important differences between the management of adults and children addressed. However, optimal therapy of tuberculosis in children with HIV infection has not been established. The Committee on Infectious Diseases of the AAP recommends that therapy always should include at least three drugs initially, and should be continued for a minimum period of 9 months. Isoniazid, rifampin, and pyrazinamide with or without ethambutol or an aminoglycoside should be given for at least the first 2 months. A fourth drug may be needed for disseminated disease and whenever drug-resistant disease is suspected.
- Extrapulmonary tuberculosis should be managed according to the principles and with the drug regimens outlined for pulmonary tuberculosis, except in children who have miliary tuberculosis, bone/joint tuberculosis, or tuberculous meningitis. These children should receive a minimum of 12 months of therapy.
- A 4-month regimen of isoniazid and rifampin is acceptable therapy for adults who have active tuberculosis and who are sputum smear– and culture–negative, if there is little possibility of drug resistance.

ATS, CDC, and AAP recommend preventive treatment of tuberculosis infection in the following patients:

- Preventive therapy with isoniazid given for 6 to 12 months is effective in decreasing the risk of future tuberculosis disease in adults and children with tuberculosis infection demonstrated by a positive tuberculin skin test reaction.
- Persons with a positive skin test and any of the following risk factors should be considered for preventive therapy regardless of age:
  —Persons with HIV infection.
  —Persons at risk for HIV infection with unknown HIV status.
  —Close contacts of sputum-positive persons with newly diagnosed infectious tuberculosis.
  —Newly infected persons (recent skin test convertors).
  —Persons with medical conditions reported to increase the risk of tuberculosis (i.e., diabetes mellitus, corticosteroid therapy and other immunosuppressive therapy, intravenous drug users, hematologic and reticuloendothelial malignancies, end-stage renal disease, and clinical conditions associated with rapid weight loss or chronic malnutrition).

  In some circumstances, persons with negative skin tests should be considered for preventive therapy. These include children who are close contacts of infectious tuberculosis cases and anergic HIV-infected adults at increased risk of tuberculosis, tuberculin-positive adults with abnormal chest radiographs showing fibrotic lesions probably representing old healed tuberculosis, adults with silicosis, and persons who are known to be HIV-infected and who are contacts of patients with infectious tuberculosis.
- In the absence of any of the above risk factors, persons up to 35 years of age with a positive skin test who are in the following high-incidence groups should be also considered for preventive therapy:
  —Foreign-born persons from high-prevalence countries.
  —Medically underserved low-income persons from high-prevalence populations (especially blacks, Hispanics, and Native Americans).
  —Residents of facilities for long-term care (e.g., correctional institutions, nursing homes, and mental institutions).
- Twelve months of preventive therapy is recommended for adults and children with HIV infection and other conditions associated with immunosuppression. Persons without HIV infection should receive preventive therapy for at least 6 months.
- In persons younger than 35 years of age, routine monitoring for adverse effects of isoniazid should consist of a monthly symptom review. For persons 35 years of age and older, hepatic enzymes should be measured prior to starting isoniazid and monitored monthly throughout treatment, in addition to monthly symptom reviews.
- Persons who are presumed to be infected with isoniazid-resistant organisms should be treated with rifampin rather than with isoniazid.
- As with the treatment of active tuberculosis, the key to success of preventive treatment is patient adherence to the prescribed regimen. Although not evaluated in clinical studies, directly observed, twice-weekly preventive therapy may be appropriate for adults and children at risk, who cannot or will not reliably self-administer therapy.

The currently recommended regimen for treating tuberculosis is effective in treating HIV-infected patients with tuberculosis, and consists of isoniazid and rifampin for a minimum period of 6 months, plus pyrazinamide and either ethambutol or streptomycin for the first 2 months.

Because of the common association of tuberculosis with HIV infection, an increasing number of patients probably will be considered candidates for combined therapy with rifampin and protease inhibitors. Prompt initiation of appropriate pharmacologic therapy for patients with HIV infection who acquire tuberculosis is critical because tuberculosis may become rapidly fatal. The management of these patients is complex, requires an individualized approach, and should be undertaken only by or in consultation with an expert. In addition, all HIV-infected patients at risk for tuberculosis infection should be carefully evaluated and administered isoniazid preventive treatment if indicated, regardless of whether they are receiving protease inhibitor therapy.

For HIV-infected patients diagnosed with drug-susceptible tuberculosis and for whom protease inhibitor therapy is being considered but has not been initiated, the suggested management strategy is to complete tuberculosis treatment with a regimen containing rifampin before starting therapy with a protease inhibitor. The duration of the antituberculosis regimen is at least 6 months, and therapy should be administered according to the guidelines developed by ATS and CDC, including the recommendation to carefully assess clinical and bacteriologic response in patients coinfected with HIV and to prolong treatment if response is slow or suboptimal.

Most infants ≤ 12 months of age with tuberculosis are asymptomatic at the time of diagnosis, and the gastric aspirate cultures in these patients have a high yield for *M. tuberculosis*. When an infant is suspected of having tuberculosis, a thorough household investigation should be undertaken. A 6-month regimen of isoniazid and rifampin supplemented during the first 2 months by pyrazinamide has been found to be well-tolerated and effective in infants with pulmonary tuberculosis. Furthermore, twice-weekly DOT appears to be as effective as daily therapy, and is an essential alternative in patients for whom social issues prevent reliable daily therapy.

Physicians caring for children should be familiar with the clinical forms of the disease in infants to enable them to make an early diagnosis. Any child, especially one in a high-risk group or area, who has unexplained pneumonia, cervical adenitis, bone or joint infections, or aseptic meningitis should have a Mantoux tuberculin skin test performed, and a detailed epidemiologic history for tuberculosis should be obtained.

Management of a newborn infant whose mother, or other household contact, is suspected of having tuberculosis is based on individual considerations. If possible, separation of the mother, or contact, and infant should be minimized. The Committee on Infectious Diseases of the AAP offers the following recommendations in the management of the newborn infant whose mother, or any other household contact, has tuberculosis:

- *Mother, or any other household contact, with a positive tuberculin skin test reaction but no evidence of current disease:* Investigation of other members of the household or extended family to whom the infant may later be exposed is indicated. If no evidence of current disease is found in the mother or in members of the extended family, the infant should be tested with a Mantoux tuberculin skin test at 3 to 4 months of age. When the family members cannot be promptly tested, consideration should be given to administering isoniazid (10 mg per kg of body weight a day) to the infant until skin testing and other evaluation of the family members have excluded contact with a case of active tuberculosis. The infant does not need to be hospitalized during this time if adequate follow-up can be arranged, but adherence to medication administration should be closely monitored. The mother also should be considered for isoniazid therapy.
- *Mother with untreated (newly diagnosed) disease or disease that has been treated for 2 or more weeks and who is judged to be noncontagious at delivery:* Careful investigation of household members and extended family is mandatory. A chest radiograph and Mantoux tuberculin skin test should be performed on the infant at 3 to 4 months and at 6 months of age. Separation of the mother and infant is not necessary if adherence to treatment for the mother and infant is assured. The mother can breast-feed. The infant should receive isoniazid even if the tuberculin skin test and chest radiograph do not suggest clinical tuberculosis, since cell-mediated immunity of a degree sufficient to mount a significant reaction to tuberculin skin testing may develop as late as 6 months of age in an infant infected at birth. Isoniazid can be discontinued if the Mantoux skin test is negative at 3 to 4 months of age, the mother is adherent to treatment and has a satisfactory clinical response, and no other family members have infectious tuberculosis. The infant should be examined carefully at monthly intervals. If nonadherence is documented, the mother has an acid-fast bacillus (AFB)–positive sputum or smear, and supervision is impos-

sible, the infant should be separated from the ill family member and Bacillus Calmette-Guérin (BCG) vaccine may be considered for the infant. However, the response to the vaccine in infants may be delayed and inadequate for prevention of tuberculosis.

• *Mother has current disease and is suspected of having been contagious at the time of delivery:* The mother and infant should be separated until the infant is receiving therapy or the mother is confirmed to be noncontagious. Otherwise, management is the same as when the disease is judged to be noncontagious to the infant at delivery.

• *Mother has hematogenously spread tuberculosis (e.g., meningitis, miliary disease, or bone involvement):* The infant should be evaluated for congenital tuberculosis. If clinical and radiographic findings do not support the diagnosis of congenital tuberculosis, the infant should be separated from the mother until she is judged to be noncontagious. The infant should be given isoniazid until 3 or 4 months of age, at which time the Mantoux skin test should be repeated. If the skin test is positive, isoniazid should be continued for a total of 12 months. If the skin test is negative and the chest radiograph is normal, isoniazid may be discontinued, depending on the status of the mother and whether there are other cases of infectious tuberculosis in the family. The infant should continue to be examined carefully at monthly intervals.

Health care or correctional institutions experiencing outbreaks of tuberculosis that are resistant to isoniazid and rifampin, or that are resuming therapy for a patient with a prior history of antitubercular therapy, may need to begin five- or six-drug regimens as initial therapy. These regimens should include the four-drug regimen and at least three medications to which the suspected multidrug-resistant strain may be susceptible.

Patients with impaired renal function do not generally require a reduction in dose if the plasma creatinine concentration is less than 6 mg per 100 mL. If renal impairment is more severe or if patients are slow acetylators, a reduction in dose and/or serum determinations may be required. Slow acetylators may require dosage adjustments to ensure isoniazid serum concentrations of less than 1 mcg per mL measured 24 hours after the preceding dose. In anuric patients, one-half the usual maintenance dose is recommended.

For oral dosage forms only

Isoniazid may be taken with meals if gastrointestinal irritation occurs. Antacids may also be taken. However, isoniazid should be taken at least 1 hour before aluminum-containing antacids.

Oral absorption may be decreased if isoniazid is taken with food or antacids.

Oral Dosage Forms

ISONIAZID SYRUP USP

Usual adult and adolescent dose

Tuberculosis—

Treatment, latent infection: Oral, 300 mg once a day.

Treatment: In combination with other antituberculosis medications—

Oral, 300 mg of isoniazid once a day for the entire treatment period; or 15 mg per kg of body weight, up to 900 mg, two or three times a week, as specified by the treatment regimen.

Usual adult prescribing limits

300 mg daily.

Usual pediatric dose

Tuberculosis—

Treatment, latent infection: Oral, 10 mg per kg of body weight, up to 300 mg, once a day.

Treatment: In combination with other antituberculosis medications—

Oral, 10 to 20 mg of isoniazid per kg of body weight, up to 300 mg, once a day; or 20 to 40 mg per kg of body weight, up to 900 mg, two or three times a week, as specified by the treatment regimen.

Strength(s) usually available

U.S.—

50 mg per 5 mL (Rx) [*Laniazid;* GENERIC].

Canada—

50 mg per 5 mL (Rx) [*Isotamine; PMS Isoniazid*].

Packaging and storage

Store below 40 °C (104 °F), preferably between 15 and 30 °C (59 and 86 °F), unless otherwise specified by the manufacturer. Store in a tight, light-resistant container. Protect from freezing.

Auxiliary labeling

- Continue medicine for full time of treatment.
- Avoid alcoholic beverages.

Note

When dispensing, include a calibrated liquid-measuring device.

ISONIAZID TABLETS USP

Usual adult and adolescent dose

See *Isoniazid Syrup USP*.

Usual adult prescribing limits

See *Isoniazid Syrup USP*.

Usual pediatric dose

See *Isoniazid Syrup USP*.

Strength(s) usually available

U.S.—

50 mg (Rx) [*Laniazid;* GENERIC].

100 mg (Rx) [*Laniazid;* GENERIC].

300 mg (Rx) [*Laniazid;* GENERIC].

Canada—

50 mg (Rx) [*PMS Isoniazid*].

100 mg (Rx) [*PMS Isoniazid*].

300 mg (Rx) [*PMS Isoniazid*].

Packaging and storage

Store below 40 °C (104 °F), preferably between 15 and 30 °C (59 and 86 °F), unless otherwise specified by the manufacturer. Store in a well-closed, light-resistant container.

Auxiliary labeling

- Continue medicine for full time of treatment.
- Avoid alcoholic beverages.

Parenteral Dosage Forms

ISONIAZID INJECTION USP

Usual adult and adolescent dose

Tuberculosis—

Treatment, latent infection: Intramuscular, 300 mg once a day.

Treatment: In combination with other antituberculosis medications—

Intramuscular, 5 mg of isoniazid per kg of body weight, up to 300 mg, once a day for the entire treatment period; or 15 mg per kg of body weight, up to 900 mg, two or three times a week, as specified by the treatment regimen.

Usual adult prescribing limits

300 mg daily.

Usual pediatric dose

Tuberculosis—

Treatment, latent infection: Intramuscular, 10 mg per kg of body weight, up to 300 mg, once a day.

Treatment: In combination with other antituberculosis medications—

Intramuscular, 10 to 20 mg of isoniazid per kg of body weight, up to 300 mg, once a day; or 20 to 40 mg per kg of body weight, up to 900 mg, two or three times a week, as specified by the treatment regimen.

Strength(s) usually available

U.S.—

100 mg per mL (Rx) [*Nydrazid*].

Canada—

Not commercially available.

Packaging and storage

Store below 40 °C (104 °F), preferably between 15 and 30 °C (59 and 86 °F), unless otherwise specified by the manufacturer. Protect from light. Protect from freezing.

Note: Crystallization may occur at low temperatures. Upon warming to room temperature, the crystals will redissolve.

Selected Bibliography

The American Thoracic Society (ATS). Ad Hoc Committee on the Scientific Assembly on Microbology, Tuberculosis, and Pulmonary Infections. Treatment of tuberculosis and tuberculosis infection in adults and children. Clin Infect Dis 1995; 21: 9-27.

Revised: 06/30/2000

ISOPHANE INSULIN—See *Insulin (Systemic)*

ISOPHANE INSULIN, HUMAN—See *Insulin (Systemic)*

ISOPHANE INSULIN, HUMAN, AND INSULIN HUMAN (SYSTEMIC)—See *Insulin (Systemic)*

ISOPROTERENOL—See *Bronchodilators, Adrenergic (Inhalation-Local), Bronchodilators, Adrenergic (Systemic), Sympathomimetic Agents—Cardiovascular Use (Parenteral-Systemic)*

ISOSORBIDE DINITRATE—See *Nitrates (Systemic)*

ISOSORBIDE MONONITRATE—See *Nitrates (Systemic)*

ISOTRETINOIN Systemic

VA CLASSIFICATION (Primary/Secondary): DE751/DE890

Commonly used brand name(s): *Accutane; Accutane Roche.*

Another commonly used name is 13-*cis*-retinoic acid.

Note: For a listing of dosage forms and brand names by country availability, see *Dosage Forms* section(s).

Category

Antiacne agent (systemic); antirosacea agent (systemic); keratinization stabilizer (systemic).

Indications

Note: Bracketed information in the *Indications* section refers to uses that are not included in U.S. product labeling.

General Considerations

Note: **FOR INFORMATION REGARDING PROBLEMS THAT HAVE OCCURRED DURING PREGNANCY SEE THE *PREGNANCY/REPRODUCTION* SECTION OF *PRECAUTIONS TO CONSIDER.***

Because of the teratogenicity of isotretinoin and to minimize fetal exposure, isotretinoin is approved for marketing only under a special restricted distribution program approved by the Food and Drug Administration. This program is called iPLEDGE℠. Isotretinoin must only be prescribed by prescribers who are registered and activated with the iPLEDGE program. Isotretinoin must only be dispensed by a pharmacy registered and activated with iPLEDGE, and must only be dispensed to patients who are registered *and* meet all requirements of iPLEDGE.

Accepted

Severe recalcitrant nodular acne (treatment)—Isotretinoin is indicated in the treatment of severe, recalcitrant nodular acne, where severe is defined as numerous lesions of at least 5 millimeters in diameter that may be suppurative or hemorrhagic. [Isotretinoin is also indicated for severe, inflammatory acne and acne conglobata. Taking into consideration its potential adverse effects, isotretinoin may be considered in patients with moderately severe acne who are prone to scarring or dyspigmentation.] Because of its potential adverse effects, isotretinoin should be reserved for patients who are unresponsive to or intolerant of conventional therapy, including systemic antibiotics.

[Folliculitis, gram-negative (treatment)][1] or
[Rosacea, severe (treatment)][1]—Isotretinoin is used in the treatment of gram-negative folliculitis and severe rosacea.

[Hidradenitis suppurativa (treatment)][1]—Isotretinoin is used in the treatment of hidradenitis suppurativa and is more effective for less established conditions and for those mild in severity (less scarring). Complete suppression or prolonged remission is uncommon. Using isotretinoin as adjunctive therapy to intralesional steroids, systemic antibiotics, or local surgery has proved beneficial for some patients with hidradentitis suppurativa.

[Keratinization disorders][1]
[Ichthyosis, lamellar][1]
[Keratosis follicularis][1]
[Palmoplantar keratoderma][1]
[Pityriasis rubra pilaris][1]—Isotretinoin has been used for treatment of severe keratinization disorders, such as lamellar ichthyosis, keratosis follicularis (Darier's disease), palmoplantar keratoderma (keratosis palmaris et plantaris), and pityriasis rubra pilaris (PRP). Longer periods of isotretinoin therapy are usually required for keratinization disorders than for acne vulgaris, thus increasing the risk of side effects, including skeletal changes.

Unaccepted

Isotretinoin should not be used in the treatment of mild to moderate acne vulgaris that may be successfully controlled with topical acne medications and products or systemic antibiotics.

[1]Not included in Canadian product labeling.

Pharmacology/Pharmacokinetics

Physicochemical characteristics

Chemical Group—Vitamin A derivative (retinoid).
Molecular weight—300.44.
Chemical name—
Retinoic acid, 13-*cis*-.

Mechanism of action/Effect

The exact mechanism of action for isotretinoin is not known. Although isotretinoin is produced naturally in the body and is a retinoid, it does not bind directly to any of the two classes of nuclear retinoic acid receptors (RARs or RXRs) or their subclasses of receptors (alpha, beta, and gamma receptors). It does isomerize rapidly to all- *trans*-retinoic acid (tretinoin) and may metabolize to other compounds that act as a ligand for a retinoid receptor to alter gene expression and cause transcription or transrepression changes in protein synthesis. Other pathways outside of the retinoid receptor pathway may be responsible for the sebosuppressive action of isotretinoin.

Antiacne agent (systemic) and antirosacea agent (systemic)—The exact mechanism of action is not known. However, isotretinoin reduces sebaceous gland size and inhibits sebaceous gland activity, thereby decreasing sebum secretion. This action is probably responsible for the rapid initial clinical improvement in nodular acne. Isotretinoin also has been shown to decrease the number of *Propionibacterium acnes* organisms within the follicle. However, since isotretinoin has no effect on *P. acnes in vitro* , this action is probably a secondary effect due to decreased sebum secretion and the resulting decrease in nutrients and not a direct effect of isotretinoin. In addition, isotretinoin has been shown to have anti-keratinizing and anti-inflammatory actions. The exact role of these actions in clinical improvement of nodular acne is not known, especially with respect to prolonged remissions.

Hidradenitis suppurativa—If given early enough in the treatment of hidrandenitis suppurativa, isotretinoin may prevent a potentially affected apocrine gland from being occluded by ductal hypercornification.

Keratinization stabilizer (systemic)—Isotretinoin is thought to interfere with the terminal differentiation of keratinocytes.

Absorption

Rapidly absorbed from the gastrointestinal tract; amount absorbed increases when isotretinoin is taken with food. Data suggest that isotretinoin and 4-oxo-isotretinoin may be reabsorbed from the bile.

Distribution

Radiolabeled doses administered to rats showed high concentrations of radioactivity in many tissues after 15 minutes, maximizing at 1 hour and declining to nondetectable concentrations in most tissues after 24 hours. Low radioactive concentrations in rats were still detectable in the liver, ureter, ovary, and adrenal and lacrimal glands after 7 days.

Protein binding

Very high (99.9%), almost exclusively to albumin.

Biotransformation

Metabolized in liver and possibly in the gut wall. The major identified metabolite in blood and urine is 4-oxo-isotretinoin; other identified metabolites are tretinoin and 4-oxo-tretinoin.

Half-life

Isotretinoin—
10 to 20 hours, terminal half-life.
90 hours, biologic half-life, following a radiolabeled 80-mg dose.
4-oxo-isotretinoin (major metabolite)—25 hours (range 17 to 50 hours), elimination half-life.

Time to peak plasma concentration

Isotretinoin—Approximately 3 hours, following an 80-mg dose.

4-oxo-isotretinoin—6 to 20 hours, following an 80-mg dose of isotretinoin.

Peak plasma concentration

Isotretinoin—98 to 535 nanograms per mL (mean, 256 nanograms per mL) in acne patients, following an 80-mg dose. Steady-state blood concentration for isotretinoin is 160 ± 19 nanograms per mL, following doses of 40 mg twice a day.

4-oxo-isotretinoin—87 to 399 nanograms per mL, following an 80-mg dose of isotretinoin. Steady-state blood concentration for 4-oxo-isotretinoin concentration exceeded that of isotretinoin after about 6 hours, following doses of 40 mg of isotretinoin twice a day.

Elimination

Biliary or feces—83%.
Renal—65%.

Precautions to Consider

Cross-sensitivity and/or related problems

Patients sensitive to acitretin, etretinate, tretinoin, or vitamin A derivatives may be sensitive to this medication also, since isotretinoin is related to both retinoic acid and retinol (vitamin A). Also, paraben-sensitive patients may be sensitive to isotretinoin capsules, since the gelatin capsule contains the preservatives methylparaben and propylparaben.

Carcinogenicity/Tumorigenicity

Studies in the Fischer 344 rat given isotretinoin doses of 8 or 32 mg per kg of body weight (mg/kg) per day for more than 18 months show an increased incidence of pheochromocytoma and, at the higher dose, adrenal medullary hyperplasia. However, pheochromocytoma is known to occur with a relatively high frequency in the particular species of rat tested. At doses of 8 and 32 mg/kg per day, rats show a decreased incidence of hepatic adenomas, hepatic angiomas, and leukemia.

Mutagenicity

Isotretinoin was not found to be mutagenic in a series of tests or assays, including the Ames test (for one of two laboratories), Chinese hamster cell assay, mouse micronucleus test, *S. cerevisiae* D7 assay, *in vitro* clastogenesis assay with human-derived lymphocytes, and unscheduled DNA synthesis assay. In one laboratory, isotretinoin produced a weakly positive response for the Ames test when the test was conducted with metabolic activation.

Pregnancy/Reproduction

Fertility—Reproduction studies in male and female rats receiving isotretinoin in doses of 2, 8, or 32 mg/kg a day show no evidence of adverse effects on gonadal function, fertility, or conception rate. However, reproduction studies in male dogs receiving isotretinoin in doses of 20 or 60 mg/kg a day for approximately 30 weeks show incomplete testicular atrophy and microscopic evidence of depression of spermatogenesis. Studies in human males receiving isotretinoin for the treatment of nodular acne show no clinically significant changes in the number, motility, or morphology of spermatozoa in the ejaculate or in the production of ejaculate volume.

Pregnancy—**Isotretinoin is teratogenic in humans and is contraindicated during pregnancy. Because of the teratogenicity of isotretinoin and to minimize fetal exposure, isotretinoin is approved for marketing only under a special restricted distribution program approved by the Food and Drug Administration. This program is called iPLEDGE℠.** Isotretinoin must only be prescribed by prescribers who are registered and activated with the iPLEDGE program. Isotretinoin must only be dispensed by a pharmacy registered and activated with iPLEDGE, and must only be dispensed to patients who are registered *and* meet all requirements of iPLEDGE. Female patients of childbearing potential must access the iPLEDGE program via the internet (www.ipledgeprogram.com) or telephone (1-866-495-0654), before starting isotretinoin, on a monthly basis during therapy, and 1 month after the last dose to answer questions on the program requirements and to enter the patient's two chosen forms of contraception. Unless abstinence is the chosen method or if the patient has undergone a hysterectomy or is postmenopausal, it is required by the iPLEDGE program that the patient signifies that she uses two forms of effective contraception with at least one being a primary form to prevent pregnancy, starting 1 month before initiation of treatment, during treatment, and for 1 month after discontinuation of treatment

Isotretinoin is distributed in the semen of male patients taking isotretinoin. The amount delivered to a female partner is about 1 million times lower than an oral 40-mg dose of isotretinoin. The no-effect limit for isotretinoin-induced embryopathy is not known.

Although not every fetus exposed to isotretinoin has been affected, **the risk is high that an infant will have a deformity or abnormality if the pregnancy occurred while the mother was taking isotretinoin, even for a short period of time**. Whenever an unexpected pregnancy occurs during the time of teratogenic risk, the risk-benefit ratio of continuing the pregnancy must be considered. The risks include: 15% incidence of major malformations, 5% incidence of perinatal mortality, 16% incidence of premature birth, and 40% incidence of spontaneous abortion.

Major human fetal deformities or abnormalities associated with the use of isotretinoin include:

- Central nervous system (CNS) abnormalities, including hydrocephalus, microcephaly, and cranial nerve deficit;
- Eye abnormalities, including microphthalmia;
- Heart defects;
- Parathyroid deficiency;
- Skeletal or connective tissue abnormalities, including absence of terminal phalanges, alterations of the skull and cervical vertebra, and malformations of hip, ankle, and forearm; facial dysmorphia; cleft or high palate; low-set ears, micropinna, and small or absent external auditory canals; meningomyelocele; multiple synostoses; and syndactyly; and
- Thymus gland abnormality.

Cases of intelligence quotient scores lower than 85 have been reported with or without other CNS abnormalities.

One study of pregnant rats, who were given isotretinoin in doses of 5, 15, and 50 mg/kg a day on gestation days 7 through 15, produced no teratogenicity; in another study, isotretinoin was teratogenic in doses of 150 mg/kg a day. When rats were administered isotretinoin in doses of 5, 15, or 32 mg/kg a day on the 14th day of gestation through the 21st day of lactation, pup mortality increased, secondary to reduced maternal food intake.

In one study of pregnant New Zealand white rabbits given isotretinoin in doses of 1, 3, and 10 mg/kg of isotretinoin per day on the 7th through 18th days of gestation, no teratogenic or embryotoxic effects were seen at 1 and 3 mg/kg a day, but the 10 mg/kg dose caused nine of thirteen rabbits to abort and produced teratogenic effects in the remaining litters.

FDA Pregnancy Category X.

Breast-feeding

It is not known whether isotretinoin is distributed into breast milk. Isotretinoin should not be administered to women who are breast-feeding because of isotretinoin's potential to cause adverse effects in nursing infants.

Pediatrics

The long-term use of isotretinoin in children less than 12 years of age has not been studied. Although appropriate studies on the relationship of age to the effects of isotretinoin have not been performed in the pediatric population, many preteens have a high rate of clinical relapse for acne vulgaris. Prepubertal children may be more sensitive to some effects of isotretinoin. Adverse reactions reported in pediatric patients were similar to those described in adults except for the increased incidence of back pain and arthralgia (sometimes severe) and myalgia in pediatric patients.

Adolescents

Appropriate studies demonstrated that isotretinoin administered at a dose of 1 mg per kg of body weight per day given in two divided doses, was equally effective in treating severe recalcitrant nodular acne in both pediatric patients 13 to 17 years of age and adult patients. The use of isotretinoin in pediatric patients 12 to 17 years of age should be given careful consideration, especially for those patients where a known metabolic or structural bone disease exists. In an open-label extension study of ten patients 13 to 18 years of age who started a second course of isotretinoin 4 months after the first course, two patients showed a decrease in mean lumbar spine bone mineral density up to 3.25%.Adolescents may have a high rate of clinical relapse for acne vulgaris.

Geriatrics

Although appropriate studies on the relationship of age to the effects of isotretinoin have not been performed in the geriatric population, geriatrics-specific problems are not expected to limit the usefulness of isotretinoin in the elderly. However, elderly patients may experience an increase in some risks associated with isotretinoin therapy.

Dental

Isotretinoin can increase or decrease saliva production. Continuing dryness of the mouth may increase the risk of dental disease, including tooth decay, gum disease, and fungal infection. Having regular dental checkups and using artificial saliva or dissolving sugarless candy or ice in the mouth may help to reduce the incidence of dental problems. Patient should check with a physician or dentist if dry mouth continues for more than 2 weeks.

Drug interactions and/or related problems

The following drug interactions and/or related problems have been selected on the basis of their potential clinical significance (possible mechanism in parentheses where appropriate)—not necessarily inclusive (» = major clinical significance):

Note: Combinations containing any of the following medications, depending on the amount present, may also interact with this medication.

Anticonvulsants or
Corticosteroids, systemic or
Phenytoin
(caution should be exercised; studies have not been done to determine if there is an interactive effect on bone loss when these are used concomitantly with isotretinoin; these drug therapies may also cause osteoporosis/osteomalacia and/or affect vitamin D metabolism)

» Hormonal contraceptives
(did not induce clinically relevant changes in the pharmacokinetics of ethinyl estradiol and norethindrone and in the serum levels of progesterone, FSH, and LH in study of 31 premenopausal women given isotretinoin and oral norethindrone/ethinyl estradiol; *however, a drug interaction that decreases effectiveness of hormonal contraceptives has not been entirely ruled out;* although hormonal contraceptives are highly effective, there have been reports of pregnancy in women who have used oral contraceptives as well as topical/injectable/implantable/insertable hormonal birth control products, more frequently in women who use only a single method of contraception)

» Oral contraceptives, progestin-only
(contraceptive effect of progestins may be diminished with concurrent use of isotretinoin; women of childbearing potential must select and commit to use two forms of effective contraception simultaneously, unless absolute abstinence is the chosen method or the patient has undergone a hysterectomy)

Photosensitizing medications, other, such as sulfonamides, tetracyclines, or thiazide diuretics
(although isotretinoin is not phototoxic or photoallergenic, it may increase the patient's sensitivity to sunlight or ultraviolet light for several months as the horny layer of skin thins; concurrent use of isotretinoin and these medications may increase susceptibility to sunburn)

Retinoids, other, systemic, such as:
» Acitretin
» Tretinoin, oral
Vitamin A and its derivatives, including vitamin supplements containing vitamin A or
Retinoids, topical, such as adapalene, tazarotene, and tretinoin
(concurrent use of retinoids or doses of vitamin A larger than the minimum recommended daily allowance [RDA] increase the risk of clinical symptoms resembling those of excessive vitamin A intake or toxicity, also called hypervitaminosis A)

» Tetracyclines, oral, including minocycline
(concomitant treatment with isotretinoin should be avoided because isotretinoin has been associated with pseudotumor cerebri [benign intracranial hypertension] when administered with tetracyclines)

Laboratory value alterations

The following have been selected on the basis of their potential clinical significance (possible effect in parentheses where appropriate)—not necessarily inclusive (» = major clinical significance).

With physiology/laboratory test values
Alanine aminotransferase (ALT [SGPT]), serum and
Alkaline phosphatase (ALP), serum and
Aspartate aminotransferase (AST [SGOT]), serum and
Gamma-glutamyltransferase (GGT), serum and
Lactate dehydrogenase (LDH), serum
(increases in concentrations have occurred in about 10 to 20% of patients; some of these concentrations returned to normal levels with dosage reduction or continued administration of isotretinoin; if normalization does not readily occur or if hepatitis is suspected, isotretinoin should be discontinued)

Blood, urine and
Creatine phosphokinase (CPK) concentration, serum and
Glucose concentration, fasting, plasma or serum and
Uric acid concentration, urine and
Urinalysis, protein and
White cells in the urine
(increases have occurred; transient elevations of CPK concentrations have occurred in 12% of patients, including those engaging in vigorous physical activity)

High-density lipoprotein (HDL) concentration
(decreases in serum HDL concentrations have occurred in about 16% of patients; this effect is reversible upon discontinuation of medication)

Platelet counts, whole blood and
Sedimentation rate, erythrocyte (ESR), whole blood
(elevated sedimentation rates have been reported in about 40% of patients; increases in platelet counts have occurred in about 10 to 20% of patients)

Red blood cell indices, whole blood and
White blood cell count, whole blood including
Neutropenia, severe and
Agranulocytosis
(decreases have occurred in about 10 to 20% of patients)

Triglyceride, plasma and
Cholesterol, total, serum
(elevated plasma triglyceride concentrations occur in about 25% of patients and are dose-related. triglyceride concentrations greater than 500 mg/dL were experienced by 32 of 298 patients treated for all diagnoses and by 5 of 135 patients treated for nodular acne; elevation of serum triglycerides to concentrations in excess of 800 mg/dL occasionally has been associated with acute pancreatitis; isotretinoin use should be discontinued if hypertriglyceridemia cannot be controlled at an acceptable level or if symptoms of pancreatitis occur; a minimal increase in serum total cholesterol concentration has occurred in about 7% of patients; these effects are reversible upon discontinuation of medication)

Medical considerations/Contraindications

The medical considerations/contraindications included have been selected on the basis of their potential clinical significance (reasons given in parentheses where appropriate)—not necessarily inclusive (» = major clinical significance).

Except under special circumstances, this medication should not be used when the following medical problem exists:

» Hepatic insufficiency
» Hypersensitivity to isotretinoin, retinoids, parabens, or any other component of this medication
» Hypervitaminosis A
» Lipids, blood, excessive elevations of
» Renal insufficiency
(isotretinoin should not be given to these patients)

Risk-benefit should be considered when the following medical problems exist:

Age-related osteoporosis, genetic predisposition for or
Anorexia nervosa or
Childhood osteoporosis conditions, history of or
Osteomalacia or
Other disorders of bone metabolism
(caution should be used; effect of isotretinoin on bone loss is not established)

Conditions predisposing to hypertriglyceridemia, such as
High alcohol intake, or history of
Hypertriglyceridemia, family history of
Obesity
(isotretinoin may increase plasma triglyceride concentrations and, to a lesser extent, total cholesterol and may decrease high density lipoprotein [HDL] cholesterol concentrations, possibly increasing the risk of cardiovascular disease for patients with these conditions who take isotretinoin over a long period of time)

Diabetes mellitus, or family history of
(possible alteration in blood glucose concentrations; insulin requirements do not appear to be affected when isotretinoin is used

for treatment of acne for several months. Isotretinoin may increase plasma triglyceride concentrations and decrease HDL cholesterol concentrations, possibly increasing the risk of cardiovascular disease for patients with diabetes mellitus who take isotretinoin over a long period of time)

» Psychiatric disorders, history of
(depression, psychotic symptoms, and rarely, suicide attempts, suicide, and aggressive and/or violent behaviors have been reported in patients treated with isotretinoin; caution is advised when prescribing isotretinoin to patients with history of depression; isotretinoin should be discontinued immediately if symptoms of depression develop or worsen during treatment with isotretinoin and the patient should be referred for appropriate psychiatric evaluation and treatment)

Patient monitoring

The following may be especially important in patient monitoring (other tests may be warranted in some patients, depending on condition; » = major clinical significance):

Blood count, complete (CBC), whole blood
(baseline determinations are recommended prior to therapy and may be repeated as needed after 4 to 6 weeks of therapy)

Glucose, fasting, plasma or serum and/or
Glucose, 2-hour postprandial, plasma or serum
(recommended during therapy in patients known or suspected to have diabetes mellitus because some patients have experienced problems in controlling their blood glucose)

Evaluation of musculoskeletal system in pediatric patients
(patients 12 to 17 years of age may need to be evaluated if symptoms of back pain, arthralgia, myalgia, decrease in bone mineral density, calcification of tendons and ligaments, skeletal hyperostosis, and/or premature epiphyseal closure occur during treatment with isotretinoin)

Lipid profile, serum
(recommended under fasting conditions prior to therapy, then repeated at 1- or 2-week intervals until the lipid response to isotretinoin is established, which usually occurs within 4 weeks. After 1 month, the test is repeated only if there are significant increases in blood lipid concentrations, or if the patient has associated risk factors. Following consumption of alcohol, 36 hours should elapse before determining blood lipid concentrations)

Liver profile, serum
(recommended prior to therapy and at 1- or 2-week intervals until the hepatic function response is established, or as determined by the physician. Testing is repeated only if there are liver function abnormalities at 1 month. Since transient abnormalities of liver function have been reported, special monitoring is warranted for patients with a history of liver disease and for those patients undergoing vigorous physical exercise)

Occult blood, stool
(periodic monitoring recommended to detect inflammatory bowel disease)

Pregnancy testing
(recommended within 1 week of treatment initiation, on a monthly basis thereafter during treatment, and 1 month after treatment discontinuation; testing serves to remind the patient of the importance of avoiding pregnancy. If pregnancy occurs, patient should be counseled on whether to continue the pregnancy)

(physicians, pharmacists, and patients must all be registered with the pregnancy risk management program iPLEDGE™)

Vision
(carefully monitor patients for visual problems; if visual difficulties occur, isotretinoin should be discontinued and the patient should have an ophthalmological examination)

Side/Adverse Effects

Note: Most side/adverse reactions in nodular acne patients have been reversible upon discontinuation of therapy.

Studies in animals have shown that prolonged isotretinoin therapy increased the incidence of focal calcification; fibrosis and inflammation of the myocardium; calcification of coronary, pulmonary, and mesenteric arteries; and metastatic calcification of the gastric mucosa. Also, long bone fractures have been reported in rats given isotretinoin at a dosage of 32 mg per kg of body weight (mg/kg) per day for 15 weeks.

Patients may be at increased risk when participating in sports with repetitive impact where the risks of spondylolisthesis with and without pars fractures and hip growth plate injuries in early and late adolescence are known. There are spontaneous reports of fractures and/or delayed healing in patients while on treatment with isotretinoin or following cessation of isotretinoin treatment while involved in these activities. While causality to isotretinoin has not been established, an effect cannot be ruled out.

The following side/adverse effects have been selected on the basis of their potential clinical significance (possible signs and symptoms in parentheses where appropriate)—not necessarily inclusive:

Those indicating need for medical attention

Incidence more frequent

Arthralgia (bone or joint pain; difficulty in moving); ***burning, redness, itching, or other signs of inflammation of eyes***—incidence about 40% and 22% in pediatric patients; ***cheilitis*** (scaling, redness, burning, pain, or other signs of inflammation of lips)—incidence 90%; ***epistaxis*** (nosebleeds)—incidence of up to 80% in treatment of acne; ***skin infection***—incidence about 5%; ***skin rash***—incidence about 10%

Incidence rare

Bleeding or inflammation of gums; cataracts or corneal opacities (blurred vision or other changes in vision); ***decreased night vision*** (decreased vision after sunset and before sunrise)—may occur suddenly, may continue after treatment discontinuation; ***hepatitis*** (yellow eyes or skin); ***inflammatory bowel disease or regional ileitis*** (rectal bleeding; severe abdominal or stomach pain; severe diarrhea); ***mental depression; psychosis; or suicidal ideation*** (attempts at suicide or thoughts of suicide; changes in behavior); ***optic neuritis*** (pain or tenderness of eyes); ***pseudotumor cerebri*** (blurred vision or other changes in vision; headache, severe or continuing; nausea; vomiting); ***skeletal hyperostosis*** (back pain; bone or joint pain; difficulty in moving; stiff, painful muscles)—generally with long-term treatment

Note: If symptoms of *inflammatory bowel disease, visual disturbances,* or signs or symptoms of *pseudotumor cerebri* occur, isotretinoin should be discontinued. Inflammatory bowel disease or *regional ileitis* may not appear until months to a year or more after isotretinoin has been discontinued. Patients with signs or symptoms of pseudotumor cerebri should be referred to a neurologist for further diagnosis and care.

Although isotretinoin has caused *corneal opacities* and diffuse interstitial *skeletal hyperostosis* in patients treated for acne, these conditions occur more frequently when higher doses of isotretinoin are used in patients who are treated for keratinization disorders. A more extensive skeletal hyperostosis occurs in adults who use a mean dose of 2.24 mg of isotretinoin per kg of body weight a day. Premature closure of the epiphyses in children has occurred.

Mental depression, psychosis, suicidal ideation, suicide attempts, suicide, and *aggressive and/or violent behaviors* may occur rarely with isotretinoin treatment. Discontinuation of isotretinoin therapy may be insufficient; further evaluation may be necessary. A mechanism of action has not been established for these events.

Incidence not determined—Observed during clinical trials and clinical practice, frequency can not be determined

Acne fulminans (fever; general feeling of discomfort or illness; joint pain; loss of appetite; sudden onset of severe acne on chest and trunk; unusual tiredness or weakness; weight loss); ***aggression*** (attack, assault, or use of force); ***agranulocytosis*** (cough or hoarseness; fever with or without chills; general feeling of tiredness or weakness; lower back or side pain; painful or difficult urination; sore throat; sores, ulcers, or white spots on lips or in mouth; unusual bleeding or bruising); ***bronchospasms*** (cough; difficulty breathing; noisy breathing; shortness of breath; tightness in chest; wheezing)—with or without a history of asthma; ***chest pain, transient; colitis*** (stomach cramps, tenderness, or pain; watery or bloody diarrhea; fever); ***conjunctivitis*** (redness, pain, swelling of eye, eyelid, or inner lining of eyelid; burning, dry or itching eyes; discharge; excessive tearing); ***epiphyseal closure, premature*** (lack or slowing of normal growth in children); ***esophagitis or esophageal ulceration*** (difficulty in swallowing; pain or burning in throat; chest pain; heartburn; vomiting; sores, ulcers, or white spots on lips or tongue or inside the mouth); ***fractures and/or delayed healing***—in adolescents; ***glomerulonephritis*** (cloudy or bloody urine; high blood pressure; swelling of face, feet or lower legs);

hearing impairment (loss of hearing; change in hearing); ***herpes simplex, disseminated*** (burning or stinging of skin; painful cold sores or blisters on lips, nose, eyes, or genitals); ***hypersensitivity reaction, systemic*** (fast heartbeat; fever; hives; itching, irritation; hoarseness; joint pain, stiffness, or swelling; rash; redness of skin; shortness of breath; swelling of eyelids, face, lips, hands, or feet; tightness in chest; troubled breathing or swallowing; wheezing); ***lymphadenopathy*** (swollen, painful, or tender lymph glands in neck, armpit, or groin); ***neutropenia*** (black, tarry stools; chills; cough; fever; lower back or side pain; painful or difficult urination; pale skin; shortness of breath; sore throat; ulcers, sores, or white spots in mouth; unusual bleeding or bruising; unusual tiredness or weakness); ***osteopenia*** (bone pain, tenderness, or aching; loss of appetite; muscle weakness; unusual weight loss); ***osteoporosis*** (pain in back, ribs, arms, or legs; decrease in height); ***palpitation*** (fast, irregular, pounding, or racing heartbeat or pulse); ***pancreatitis*** (bloating; chills; constipation; darkened urine; fast heartbeat; fever; indigestion; loss of appetite; nausea; pains in stomach, side, or abdomen, possibly radiating to the back; vomiting; yellow eyes or skin); ***paronychia*** (loosening of the fingernails; redness or soreness around fingernails); ***photophobia*** (blurred vision; change in color vision; difficulty seeing at night; increased sensitivity of eyes to sunlight); ***pyogenic granuloma*** (sore in mouth or on gums; bleeding from sore in mouth); ***respiratory infection*** (cough; fever; sneezing; sore throat); ***rhabdomyolysis*** (dark-colored urine; fever; muscle cramps or spasms; muscle pain or stiffness; unusual tiredness or weakness); ***seizures*** (convulsions; muscle spasm or jerking of all extremities; sudden loss of consciousness; loss of bladder control); ***stroke*** (confusion; difficulty in speaking; slow speech; inability to speak; inability to move arms, legs, or facial muscles; double vision; headache); ***suicide*** (killing oneself); ***suicide attempts*** (attempts at killing oneself); ***syncope*** (fainting); ***tachycardia*** (fast, pounding, or irregular heartbeat or pulse); ***thrombocytopenia*** (black, tarry stools; bleeding gums; blood in urine or stools; pinpoint red spots on skin; unusual bleeding or bruising); ***thrombotic disease, vascular*** (severe headaches of sudden onset; sudden loss of coordination; pains in chest, groin, or legs, especially calves of legs; sudden onset of shortness of breath, for no apparent reason; sudden onset of slurred speech; sudden vision changes); ***urticaria*** (hives or welts, itching, redness of skin; skin rash); ***vasculitis*** (redness, soreness or itching skin; fever; sores, welting or blisters); ***violent behavior*** (use of extreme physical or emotional force); ***Wegener's granulomatosis*** (bloody or cloudy urine; cough or bloody cough; ear pain; loss or change in hearing; nose bleeds; pain or tenderness around eyes and cheekbones; stuffy or runny nose; swelling of face, feet, or lower legs; trouble breathing; unusual weight gain); ***xanthomas, eruptive*** (irregular yellow patch or lump on skin)

Those indicating need for medical attention only if they continue or are bothersome

Incidence more frequent

Back pain—29% in pediatric patients; ***delayed or exaggerated healing response*** (crusting of skin); ***difficulty in wearing contact lenses***—may continue after treatment discontinuation; ***dryness of eyes***—may continue after treatment discontinuation; ***dryness of mouth or nose***—incidence 80% in treatment of acne; ***dryness or itching of skin***—incidence 80% in treatment of acne; ***headache, mild***—incidence about 5%; ***increased sensitivity of skin to sunlight***—incidence about 5%; ***peeling of skin on palms of hands or soles of feet***—incidence about 5%; ***stomach upset***—incidence about 5%; ***thinning of hair***—incidence less than 10%, may continue after treatment discontinuation; ***unusual tiredness***—incidence about 5%

Incidence not determined—Observed during clinical trials and clinical practice, frequency can not be determined

Abnormal menses; alopecia (hair loss, thinning of hair)—persists in some cases; ***anemia*** (pale skin, troubled breathing with exertion, unusual bleeding or bruising, unusual tiredness or weakness); ***arthritis*** (pain, swelling, or redness in joints, muscle pain or stiffness, difficulty in moving); ***bone abnormalities; bruising; color vision disorder; dizziness; drowsiness; eczema*** (skin rash encrusted, scaly and oozing); ***edema*** (swelling); ***facial erythema*** (flushing, redness of face, unusually warm skin); ***fatigue; flushing; hair abnormalities; hirsutism*** (increased hair growth, especially on the face); ***hyperpigmentation*** (darkening of skin); ***hypertriglyceridemia*** (large amount of triglyceride in the blood); ***hypopigmentation*** (lightening of normal skin color, lightening of treated areas of dark skin); ***insomnia*** (sleeplessness, trouble sleeping, unable to sleep); ***lethargy*** (unusual drowsiness, dullness, tiredness, weakness or feeling of sluggishness); ***malaise*** (general feeling of discomfort or illness, unusual tiredness or weakness); ***nail dystrophy*** (changes in fingernails or toenails); ***nausea; nervousness; paresthesias*** (burning, crawling, itching, numbness, prickling, "pins and needles", or tingling feelings); ***pruritus*** (itching skin); ***seborrhea*** (dandruff, oily skin); ***skin fragility; sunburn susceptibility increased*** (rash, severe sunburn); ***sweating; tendonitis*** (joint pain or stiffness); ***tinnitus*** (continuing ringing or buzzing or other unexplained noise in ears, hearing loss); ***voice alteration; weakness; weight loss***

Note: Patients who experience tinnitus or hearing impairment should discontinue isotretinoin therapy and be referred for specialized care for further evaluation.

Overdose

For more information on the management of overdose or unintentional ingestion, **contact a Poison Control Center** (see *Poison Control Center Listing*).

Clinical effects of overdose

The following effects have been selected on the basis of their potential clinical significance (possible signs and symptoms in parentheses where appropriate)—not necessarily inclusive:

Acute and/or chronic

Abdominal pain; ataxia (shakiness and unsteady walk; unsteadiness; trembling, or other problems with muscle control or coordination); ***cheilosis*** (scaling of lips and fissures in the corners of the mouth); ***dizziness; drowsiness; facial flushing*** (redness to face; face is warm or hot to touch); ***intracranial pressure, elevated*** (headache, severe; nausea; vomiting); ***irritability; itchy skin***

Treatment of overdose

To decrease absorption—Evacuation of stomach should be considered within 2 hours of ingestion of acute overdose. Medication should be discontinued in patients with symptoms of overdose who were given therapeutic doses.

Monitoring—

- Monitor for increased intracranial pressure.
- Female patients of childbearing potential should have a pregnancy test at time of overdose and 1 month later; if positive, teratogenic risk and continuance of pregnancy should be discussed.
- Blood samples should be collected and isotretinoin and metabolite concentrations determined.
- Patients with isotretinoin overdose should not donate blood for at least 30 days.

Supportive care—Female patients of childbearing potential need to use two effective contraceptive methods for 1 month after overdose or until isotretinoin and its metabolites are no longer measurable in the blood.For 30 days following the overdose, male patients should use a condom or avoid reproductive sexual activity with a female who is or might become pregnant. Patients in whom intentional overdose is confirmed or suspected should be referred for psychiatric consultation.

Patient Consultation

As an aid to patient consultation, refer to *Advice for the Patient, Isotretinoin (Systemic)*.

In providing consultation, consider emphasizing the following selected information (» = major clinical significance):

Before using this medication

» Conditions affecting use, especially:

Hypersensitivity to isotretinoin, acitretin, etretinate, tretinoin, or vitamin A derivatives

Pregnancy—Not taking isotretinoin during pregnancy because it causes birth defects in humans. In addition, not taking if there is a chance that pregnancy may occur during treatment or within 1 month following treatment. Not taking isotretinoin unless an effective form of contraception is used for at least 1 month before beginning treatment. Contraception must be continued during treatment and for 1 month after isotretinoin is stopped

Requirement of physician, pharmacist, and women who could become pregnant to be registered with the pregnancy risk management program, iPLEDGE™

Isotretinoin is distributed in the semen of male patients taking isotretinoin. Amount of exposure to a female partner is about 1 million times lower than a 40-mg dose of isotretinoin.

FDA Pregnancy Category X.

Breast-feeding—It is not known whether this drug is distributed into human breast milk. Because of the potential for adverse effects, nursing mothers should not receive isotretinoin.

Use in children—Preadolescents may be more sensitive to the effects of isotretinoin and preadolescents and adolescents may experience high rates of relapse for acne vulgaris. Increased incidences of back pain, arthralgia and myalgia have occurred in pediatric patients.

Use in adolescents—Careful consideration should be given to isotretinoin use in adolescent patients 12 to 17 years of age, especially for patients with a known metabolic or structural bone disease.

Use in the elderly—Elderly patients may experience an increase in some risks associated with isotretinoin therapy.

Other medications, especially hormonal contraceptives, progestin-only oral contraceptives (birth control pill); retinoids, such as acitretin, tretinoin (oral); or tetracyclines (oral)

Other medical problems, especially hepatic insufficiency, hypervitaminosis A, excessive elevations of blood lipid values, renal insufficiency, or history of psychiatric disorder

Proper use of this medication

» Reading accompanying patient information before using this medication

» For women of reproductive potential—Special precautions, including registering with iPLEDGE via internet (www.ipledge.com) or phone (1-866-495-0654), are needed before beginning treatment to ensure that the patient is not pregnant, such as using an effective form of birth control for 1 month before initiating treatment, obtaining a negative pregnancy test after a normal menstrual period pattern has been established and within 1 week before initiating treatment, then starting medication on Day 2 or 3 of normal menses. Women of reproductive age or potential are required to use two forms of contraception during treatment, beginning at least 1 month before initiation of treatment with isotretinoin and continuing for 1 month after medication is discontinued

» Importance of patients receiving written warnings about rates of possible contraception failure (included in patient education kits) with oral contraceptives, as well as topical/injectable/implantable/insertable hormonal birth control products

» Taking isotretinoin dose with food and a full glass of liquid, like water. Taking with food is important for getting the right amount of medicine out of your stomach. Taking with a full glass of liquid will reduce chest or stomach discomfort that may occur from isotretinoin.

» Importance of not taking more medication than the amount prescribed

» Importance of not sharing medication with anyone else because of the risk of birth defects and other serious side effects.

» Importance of checking with your doctor before taking any medications including vitamins, herbal products, or over-the-counter (OTC) medicines. Some of these medicines or nutritional supplements (e.g., St. John's wort) may make your birth control pills not work.

» Proper dosing

Missed dose: Taking as soon as possible; not taking if almost time for next dose; not doubling doses

» Proper storage

Precautions while using this medication

» Regular visits to physician to check progress during therapy

» Stopping medication immediately and checking with physician if pregnancy is suspected, since isotretinoin causes birth defects in humans

» Checking with physician if skin condition does not improve within 1 to 2 months, full improvement may take 5 to 6 months; expecting that skin irritation may occur or skin condition may worsen within the first several weeks of treatment but will lessen in severity with continued use

» Not donating blood to a blood bank during treatment or for 30 days after isotretinoin therapy has been completed to prevent possibility of a pregnant patient receiving the blood

» Understanding that vision impairment can occur, including sudden night vision impairment, photophobia, blurred vision, or dryness of eyes. Vision problems can make driving a car or operating machinery dangerous.

Checking with physician anytime vision problems occur; wearing contact lenses may be uncomfortable

» Understanding that mood or behavior problems can occur, including having thoughts about hurting themselves; check with you doctor right away if unusual mood or behavior problems occur.

» Understanding that bone or muscle problems can occur, including joint pain, muscle pain or stiffness, or difficulty moving. Check with your doctor if these problems are bothersome.

Understanding that dental problems can occur resulting from dryness of mouth and may increase dental disease, including tooth decay, gum disease, and fungus infections; regular dental appointments are needed and use of sugarless candy or saliva substitute or melting ice in mouth may be necessary to lessen dental problems

» Minimizing exposure of skin to wind, cold temperatures, and sunlight, including limiting exposure on cloudy days, to avoid sunburn, dryness, or irritation, especially during the first months of treatment. Also, not using artificial sunlight or sunlamp, unless directed otherwise by physician

Using sunscreen preparations (minimum sun protection factor [SPF] of 15) and wearing protective clothing over exposed areas and UV-blocking sunglasses when sunlight exposure cannot be avoided; avoiding direct sunlight between 10 a.m. and 3 p.m.; checking with physician at any time skin becomes too dry or irritated; choosing proper skin products to reduce skin dryness or irritation

» Not using vitamin A or vitamin A-containing supplements in doses that exceed the minimum recommended daily allowances (RDA)

» Importance of not removing hair by wax epilation while taking isotretinoin and for 6 months after stopping isotretinoin. Isotretinoin can increase your chance of scarring from wax epilation.

» Importance of not having any cosmetic procedures to smooth your skin (e.g., dermabrasion, laser) while taking isotretinoin and for 6 months after stopping isotretinoin. Isotretinoin can increase your chance of scarring from these cosmetic procedures.

Patients with diabetes mellitus: Understanding that use of isotretinoin may alter blood glucose concentrations; insulin requirements do not appear to be affected when using isotretinoin for treatment of acne for several months

Side/adverse effects

Signs of potential side effects (some observed during clinical practice), especially arthralgia; burning, redness, itching, or other signs of inflammation of eye; cheilitis; epistaxis; skin infection; skin rash; bleeding or inflammation of gums; cataracts; corneal opacities; decreased night vision; hepatitis; inflammatory bowel disease; regional ileitis; mental depression, psychosis, or suicidal ideation; optic neuritis; pseudotumor cerebri; skeletal hyperostosis; acne fulminans; aggression; agranulocytosis; bronchospasms; transient chest pain; colitis; conjunctivitis; premature epiphyseal closure; esophagitis or esophageal ulceration; fractures and/or delayed healing; glomerulonephritis; hearing impairment; disseminated herpes simplex; hypersensitivity reaction; lymphadenopathy; neutropenia; osteopenia; osteoporosis; palpitation; pancreatitis; paronychia; photophobia; pyogenic granuloma; respiratory infection; rhabdomyolysis; seizures; stroke; suicide; suicide attempts; syncope; tachycardia; thrombocytopenia; vascular thrombotic disease; urticaria; vasculitis; violent behaviors; Wegener's granulomatosis; or eruptive xanthomas

General Dosing Information

Generally, the initial dose of isotretinoin should be individualized according to the patient's weight and the severity and location of the disease.

Diet/Nutrition

Isotretinoin should be given with food. Failure to take isotretinoin with food will significantly decrease absorption. If a dose increase is necessary, patients should first be questioned about their compliance with food instructions.

Patients should swallow the capsule with a full glass of liquid to decrease the risk of esophageal irritation.

For use as an anti-acne agent

Isotretinoin must only be dispensed

- in no more than a 30-day supply
- with an isotretinoin medication guide
- after authorization from the iPLEDGE program
- prior to the "do not dispense to patient after" date provide by the iPLEDGE program (within 7 days of the office visit)
- with a new prescription for refills and another authorization form the iPLEDGE program (No automatic refills are allowed.)

In addition, an isotretinoin medication guide must be given to the patient each time isotretinoin is dispensed, as required by law, for risk management for the patient. Isotretinoin must not be prescribed, dispensed or otherwise obtained through the internet or any other means outside of the iPLEDGE program. Only FDA-approved isotretinoin products must be distributed, prescribed, dispensed, and used. Patients must fill isotretinoin prescriptions only at US licensed pharmacies.

Micro-dosed progesterone preparations that do not contain an estrogen may be an inadequate method of contraception during isotretinoin therapy. Although other hormonal contraceptives are highly effective, there have been reports of pregnancy from women who have used combined oral contraceptives, as well as topical/injectable/implantable/insertable hormonal birth control products. These reports are more frequent for women who use only a single method of contraception. Patients must receive written warnings about the rates of possible contraception failure (included in patient education kits). It is not known if hormonal contraceptives differ in their effectiveness when used with isotretinoin. It is critically important the women of childbearing potential use two forms of effective contraception simultaneously.

Some medications may decrease effectiveness of birth control products. St. John's Wort, an over-the-counter herbal supplement for depression, should not be used concomitantly with hormonal contraceptives based on reports of breakthrough bleeding and pregnancies. Prescribers should consult the package insert of medication administered concomitantly with hormonal contraceptives and/or see *Estrogens and Progestins Oral Contraceptives (Systemic)* for specific drug interactions with hormonal contraceptives.

Isotretinoin doses of 0.5 and 1 mg per kilogram of body weight (mg/kg) a day provide initial clearing of nodular acne, but the need to re-treat the patient is less with the larger dose, providing that it can be tolerated by the patient. For best, long-lasting results and to lessen the chance of re-treatment, most physicians aim to achieve a cumulative isotretinoin dose of 100 to 150 mg/kg.

During the initial period of isotretinoin therapy, transient exacerbation of acne may occur. Severe flares sometimes occur. This usually can be prevented by starting with a lower initial dose for a short time, such as 0.5 mg/kg per day or less for 2 weeks.

Following 4 or more weeks of therapy, dosage adjustment should be based on response of the disease to isotretinoin and the occurrence of side effects.

Improvement in nodular acne may occur after 1 to 2 months, but marked improvement may require 4 to 5 months of therapy. Also, improvement may continue after discontinuation of isotretinoin use.

In most patients, a single course of therapy may result in complete and prolonged remission of severe nodular acne. However, if a second course of therapy is necessary, it should not be initiated for at least 8 weeks (possibly 16 to 20 weeks, depending on individual response) after completion of the first course. Improvement in the condition may continue following discontinuation of isotretinoin use. The optimal interval before retreatment has not been defined for patients who have not completed skeletal growth.

Long-term use of isotretinoin, even in low doses, has not been studied, and is not recommended. It is important that isotretinoin be given at the recommended doses for no longer than the recommended duration. The effect of long-term use of isotretinoin on bone loss is unknown.

Oral Dosage Forms

Note: Bracketed uses in the *Dosage Forms* section refer to categories of use and/or indications that are not included in U.S. product labeling.

ISOTRETINOIN CAPSULES

Usual adult and adolescent dose

Severe recalcitrant nodular acne—

Oral, 0.5 to 1 mg per kg of body weight per day given in two divided doses with food for 15 to 20 weeks. Once daily dosing is not recommended. The safety of once daily dosing with isotretinoin has not been established. For adult patients whose disease is very severe with scarring or is primarily manifested on the trunk may require dosage adjustments up to 2 mg per kg of body weight per day, as tolerated.

Note: In Canada, the duration of treatment with isotretinoin is 12 to 16 weeks. The daily dosage may be dosed either as a single dose or in two divided doses during the day, whichever is more convenient.

[Folliculitis, gram-negative][1] or
[Rosacea, severe][1]—

Oral, 0.5 to 1 mg per kg of body weight per day in two divided doses.

[Hidradenitis suppurativa (treatment)][1]—

Oral, 1 mg per kg of body weight per day for four months. A lower dose of 0.5 to 1 mg per kg may be effective if isotretinoin is used as adjunctive therapy.

[Keratinization disorders][1]—

Oral, up to 4 mg per kg of body weight per day, the dosage depending on the specific disease and its severity, for up to four months. Lowest dose to achieve clinical effect should be used.

Strength(s) usually available

U.S.—

10 mg (Rx) [*Accutane* (beeswax; butylated hydroxyanisole; edetate disodium; hydrogenated soybean oil flakes; hydrogenated vegetable oil; methylparaben; propylparaben; red iron oxide; soybean oil; titanium dioxide)].

20 mg (Rx) [*Accutane* (beeswax; butylated hydroxyanisole; edetate disodium; FD&C Red No. 3; FD&C Blue No. 1; hydrogenated soybean oil flakes; hydrogenated vegetable oil; methylparaben; propylparaben; soybean oil; titanium dioxide)].

40 mg (Rx) [*Accutane* (beeswax; butylated hydroxyanisole; D&C Yellow No. 10; edetate disodium; FD&C Yellow No. 6; hydrogenated soybean oil flakes; hydrogenated vegetable oil; methylparaben; propylparaben; soybean oil; titanium dioxide)].

Canada—

10 mg (Rx) [*Accutane Roche* (beeswax; canthaxanthin; gelatin; glycerin; hydrogenated hydrolyzed starch; mannitol; soybean and hydrogenated soybean oil; sorbitol; titanium dioxide)].

40 mg (Rx) [*Accutane Roche* (beeswax; gelatin; glycerin; methylparaben; propylparaben; quinoline yellow WS; soybean and hydrogenated soybean oil; sunset yellow FCF; titanium dioxide)].

Packaging and storage

Store between 15 and 30 °C (59 and 86 °F), in a tight, light-resistant container, unless otherwise specified by manufacturer.

Auxiliary labeling

- Do not take this medication if you become pregnant.
- Take with food.
- Take with a full glass of water.
- Avoid prolonged or excessive exposure to sunlight.
- May cause dizziness or blurred vision.
- This medication may impair your ability to drive or operate machinery. Use care until you become familiar with its effects.
- Ask your doctor or pharmacist before using nonprescription drugs.
- Vitamin A supplements should not be taken with this medication.
- Dry mouth may occur when taking this medication.
- A written prescription from the physician is necessary prior to refilling this prescription.

Note

Inform female patients of childbearing potential of their requirement to register with the iPLEDGE pregnancy risk management program.

Include patient directions when dispensing.

Counsel female patients about using two forms of birth control 1 month before starting treatment, during treatment, and for 1 month after discontinuing treatment.

Counsel male and female patients:
- Not to donate blood for transfusion during treatment and for at least 1 month after discontinuing treatment.
- Be aware that sudden night vision inadequacies can occur, which can be hazardous when operating a vehicle.

[1]Not included in Canadian product labeling.

Selected Bibliography

Med Watch 2002 Safety Alert- Dear Doctor Letter: Accutane®, isotretinoin (10/2002). Available at: http://www.fda.gov/medwatch/Safety/2002.

Product information: Accutane®, isotretinoin. Roche Laboratories, Nutley, NJ, (PI revised 08/2003) reviewed 12/2003.

Product Information: Accutane™ Roche®, isotretinoin. Hoffmann-La Roche Limited, Mississauga, Ontario, Canada (PI revised 05/15/2003) reviewed 01/2004.

Revised: 04/05/2006

ISRADIPINE—See *Calcium Channel Blocking Agents (Systemic)*

ITRACONAZOLE—See *Antifungals, Azole (Systemic)*

KANAMYCIN—See *Aminoglycosides (Systemic), Kanamycin (Oral-Local)*

KETAZOLAM—See *Benzodiazepines (Systemic)*

KETOCONAZOLE—See *Antifungals, Azole (Systemic)*

KETOCONAZOLE Topical

VA CLASSIFICATION (Primary): DE102

Commonly used brand name(s): *Nizoral A-D Shampoo; Nizoral Cream; Nizoral Shampoo.*

Note: For a listing of dosage forms and brand names by country availability, see *Dosage Forms* section(s).

Category

Antifungal (topical).

Indications

Note: Bracketed information in the *Indications* section refers to uses that are not included in U.S. product labeling.

Accepted

Tinea corporis (treatment) or
Tinea cruris (treatment)—Ketoconazole cream is indicated as a primary agent in the topical treatment of tinea corporis (ringworm of the body) and tinea cruris (ringworm of the groin; jock itch) caused by *Trichophyton rubrum, Trichophyton mentagrophytes*, and *Epidermophyton floccosum (Acrothesium floccosum).*

Tinea pedis (treatment)—Ketoconazole cream is indicated as a primary agent in the topical treatment of tinea pedis (athlete's foot).

Pityriasis versicolor (treatment)—Ketoconazole cream and ketoconazole 2% shampoo are indicated as primary agents in the topical treatment of pityriasis versicolor (tinea versicolor; "sun fungus") caused by *Malassezia furfur (Pityrosporon orbiculare).*

Candidiasis, cutaneous (treatment)—Ketoconazole cream is indicated as a primary agent in the topical treatment of cutaneous candidiasis caused by *Candida* species.

Dermatitis, seborrheic (treatment) or
Dermatitis, seborrheic (prophylaxis)—Ketoconazole cream and [ketoconazole 2% shampoo] are indicated in the treatment of seborrheic dermatitis. [Ketoconazole 2% shampoo] is indicated in the prophylaxis of seborrheic dermatitis.

Dandruff (treatment) or
Dandruff (prophylaxis)—Ketoconazole shampoo 1% and [ketoconazole shampoo 2%] are indicated in the treatment and prophylaxis of the flaking, scaling, and itching associated with dandruff.

[Paronychia (treatment)][1]
[Tinea barbae (treatment)][1] or
[Tinea capitis (treatment)][1]—Ketoconazole cream is used as a primary agent in the topical treatment of paronychia. Ketoconazole cream is used as a secondary agent in the topical treatment of tinea barbae and tinea capitis.

Not all species or strains of a particular organism may be susceptible to ketoconazole.

[1]Not included in Canadian product labeling.

Pharmacology/Pharmacokinetics

Physicochemical characteristics

Chemical Group—Imidazoles.
Molecular weight—531.44.

Mechanism of action/Effect

Fungistatic; may be fungicidal and sporocidal, depending on concentration; inhibits biosynthesis of ergosterol or other sterols, damaging the fungal cell membrane and altering its permeability; as a result, loss of essential intracellular elements may occur; also inhibits biosynthesis of triglycerides and phospholipids by fungi; in addition, inhibits oxidative and peroxidative enzyme activity, resulting in intracellular buildup of toxic concentrations of hydrogen peroxide, which may contribute to deterioration of subcellular organelles and cellular necrosis. In the treatment of *Candida albicans*, inhibits transformation of blastospores into invasive mycelial form.

Absorption

Shampoo—Ketoconazole 2% shampoo was not detected in the plasma of 39 patients who shampooed 4 to 10 times a week for 6 months or in 33 patients who shampooed 2 or 3 times a week for 3 to 26 months (mean: 16 months).

Cream—After a single topical application of ketoconazole cream to the chest, back, and arms of normal volunteers, systemic absorption of ketoconazole was not detected during the following 72-hour period, using a minimum detection level of 5 nanograms per mL in blood.

Precautions to Consider

Cross-sensitivity and/or related problems

Persons sensitive to miconazole or other imidazoles may be sensitive to ketoconazole also.

Carcinogenicity

A long-term feeding study in Swiss albino mice and Wistar rats has shown no evidence of carcinogenicity.

Mutagenicity

The dominant lethal mutation test in male and female mice, given single oral doses of ketoconazole as high as 80 mg per kg of body weight (mg/kg), has shown no mutations at any stage of germ cell development. The Ames *Salmonella* microsomal activator assay has also shown negative results.

Pregnancy/Reproduction

Pregnancy—Ketoconazole crosses the placenta. Adequate and well-controlled studies in humans have not been done.

Studies in rats, given oral doses of 80 mg/kg per day (10 times the maximum recommended human dose [MRHD]), have shown ketoconazole to be teratogenic, causing syndactyly and oligodactyly. However, these effects may be related to maternal toxicity, which was seen at this dose level.

FDA Pregnancy Category C.

Breast-feeding

It is not known whether ketoconazole cream, applied topically on a regular basis, is absorbed systemically in sufficient amounts to be distributed into breast milk in detectable quantities. However, no systemic absorption was detected following a single application of ketoconazole cream to the chest, back, and arms of healthy volunteers. In addition, ketoconazole shampoo was not detected in plasma after chronic shampooing. Therefore, topical ketoconazole is unlikely to be distributed into breast milk in significant amounts or to cause adverse effects in the nursing infant.

Pediatrics

No information is available on the relationship of age to the effects of this medicine in pediatric patients. Safety and efficacy have not been established.

Geriatrics

No information is available on the relationship of age to the effects of this medicine in geriatric patients.

Medical considerations/Contraindications

The medical considerations/contraindications included have been selected on the basis of their potential clinical significance (reasons given in parentheses where appropriate)—not necessarily inclusive (» = major clinical significance).

Risk-benefit should be considered when the following medical problems exist:

Sensitivity to topical ketoconazole
Sensitivity to sulfites present in ketoconazole cream

Side/Adverse Effects

The following side/adverse effects have been selected on the basis of their potential clinical significance (possible signs and symptoms in parentheses where appropriate)—not necessarily inclusive:

Those indicating need for medical attention

For the cream or shampoo—Incidence less frequent
Itching, stinging, or irritation not present before therapy

For the cream—Incidence rare
Contact dermatitis (skin rash)

Those indicating need for medical attention only if they continue or are bothersome

For the shampoo—Incidence less frequent
Dry skin; dryness or oiliness of the hair and scalp

For the shampoo—Incidence rare
Increase in normal hair loss

Overdose

For more information on the management of overdose or unintentional ingestion, **contact a Poison Control Center** (see *Poison Control Center Listing*).

Treatment of overdose

There has been no experience of overdose with ketoconazole cream. Ingestion of ketoconazole shampoo may result in nausea and vomiting due to the detergent.

To avoid aspiration—Gastric lavage or induced emesis should not be performed.

It has been reported that ketoconazole cannot be removed by hemodialysis.

Specific treatment—Use general supportive measures and appropriate routine overdose management.

Supportive care—Patients in whom intentional overdose is confirmed or suspected should be referred for psychiatric consultation.

Patient Consultation

As an aid to patient consultation, refer to *Advice for the Patient, Ketoconazole (Topical)*.

In providing consultation, consider emphasizing the following selected information (» = major clinical significance):

Before using this medication

» Conditions affecting use, especially:
Sensitivity to sulfites in ketoconazole cream or to topical ketoconazole
Pregnancy—Ketoconazole crosses the placenta; studies in animals found ketoconazole to be teratogenic

Proper use of this medication

» Avoiding contact with the eyes

For the cream form
Applying sufficient medication to cover affected and surrounding areas, and rubbing in gently
» Compliance with full course of therapy; fungal infections may require prolonged therapy

For the 1% shampoo form
Wetting hair and scalp with water
Applying adequate shampoo for lather and gently massaging in
Rinsing and repeating application
Rinsing thoroughly and drying hair

For the 2% shampoo form
Wetting hair and scalp with water
Applying shampoo to skin of affected area and wide margin surrounding area
Lathering and leaving in place for 5 minutes
Rinsing thoroughly and drying hair

» Proper dosing
Missed dose: Applying as soon as possible; not applying if almost time for next dose
» Proper storage

Precautions while using this medication

Checking with physician if skin condition becomes worse or if it does not improve within: 2 weeks for cutaneous candidiasis, pityriasis versicolor, tinea corporis, or tinea crucis; 4 weeks for seborrheic dermatitis; or 4 to 6 weeks for tinea pedis

For the cream form:
» Using hygienic measures to cure infection and prevent reinfection

For tinea pedis
Carefully drying feet, especially between toes, after bathing
Not wearing socks made from wool or synthetic materials; wearing clean, cotton socks and changing them daily or more often if feet perspire excessively
Wearing sandals or well-ventilated shoes
Using a bland, absorbent powder or an antifungal powder between toes, on feet, and in socks and shoes liberally once or twice daily; using the powder between administration times for the cream

For tinea cruris
Not wearing underwear that is tight-fitting or made from synthetic materials; wearing loose-fitting cotton underwear instead
Using a bland, absorbent powder or an antifungal powder on the skin between administration times for the cream

Side/adverse effects

Signs of potential side effects, especially itching, stinging, or irritation not present before therapy (for cream and shampoo); contact dermatitis (for cream)

General Dosing Information

Prolonged use of topical ketoconazole may rarely lead to skin sensitization, resulting in hypersensitivity reactions with subsequent topical or systemic use of the medication.

Tinea versicolor may cause hyper or hypopigmented patches on the body. Treatment of the infection may not result in normalization of the pigment for several months.

For cream dosage form

To reduce the possibility of recurrence of infection, tinea corporis and tinea cruris should be treated for at least 2 to 4 weeks. Candida and pityriasis versicolor should be treated for at least 2 to 3 weeks. Seborrheic dermatitis should be treated for at least 4 weeks or until clinical clearing occurs. Tinea pedis should be treated for approximately 4 to 6 weeks.

Topical Dosage Forms

Note: Bracketed uses in the *Dosage Forms* section refer to categories of use and/or indications that are not included in U.S. product labeling.

KETOCONAZOLE CREAM

Usual adult and adolescent dose

Tinea corporis or
Tinea cruris or
Tinea pedis or
Pityriasis versicolor—
Topical, to the affected skin and surrounding areas, once a day.
Candidiasis, cutaneous—
Topical, to the affected skin and surrounding areas, once a day. More resistant cases may require twice a day treatment.
Seborrheic dermatitis—
Topical, to the affected skin and surrounding areas, two times a day.
[Paronychia][1] or
[Tinea barbae][1] or
[Tinea capitis][1]—
Topical, to the affected skin and surrounding areas, two or three times a day.

Usual pediatric dose

Safety and efficacy have not been established.

Strength(s) usually available

U.S.—
2% (Rx) [*Nizoral Cream* (cetyl alcohol; isopropyl myristate; polysorbate 60; polysorbate 80; propylene glycol; purified water; sodium sulfite anhydrous; sorbitan monostearate; stearyl alcohol)].

Canada—
2% (Rx) [*Nizoral Cream*].

Packaging and storage

Store below 25 °C (77 °F), in a well-closed container, unless otherwise specified by manufacturer. Protect from freezing.

Auxiliary labeling

- For external use only.
- Continue medicine for full time of treatment.

KETOCONAZOLE SHAMPOO

Usual adult and adolescent dose

Dandruff—
1% shampoo—Topical, as a shampoo, every three or four days for up to 8 weeks, if needed, or as directed by physician. Prophylaxis: use only as needed to control dandruff.
[Dermatitis, seborrheic]—
2% shampoo—Topical, as a shampoo, twice a week for 2 to 4 weeks. Leave in place for 3 to 5 minutes before rinsing. Prophylaxis: once a week every 1 or 2 weeks.
Pityriasis versicolor—
2% shampoo—Topical, as a shampoo, to the affected skin and surrounding area(s), as a single application. Leave in place for 5 minutes before rinsing.

Usual pediatric dose
Safety and efficacy have not been established.

Strength(s) usually available
U.S.—
1% (OTC) [*Nizoral A-D Shampoo* (sodium lauryl ether sulfate; cocamide MEA; sodium cocoyl sarcosinate; glycol distearate; acrylic acid polymer; fragrance; sodium chloride; tetrasodium EDTA; butylated hydroxytoluene; quarternium-15; polyquarternium-7; sodium hydroxide; hydrochloric acid; FDC Blue No. 1)].
2% (Rx) [*Nizoral Shampoo* (coconut fatty acid diethanolemide; disodium monolauryl ether sulfosuccinate; FDC Red No. 40; hydrochloric acid; imidurea; laurimonium hydrolyzed animal collagen; macrogol 120 methyl glucose dioleate; perfume bouquet; sodium chloride; sodium hydroxide; sodium lauryl ether sulfate; purified water)].

Canada—
2% (Rx) [*Nizoral Shampoo*].

Packaging and storage
1% shampoo—Store between 2 and 30 °C (35 and 86 °F), unless otherwise specified by manufacturer. Protect from light. Protect from freezing.
2% shampoo—Store below 25 °C (77 °F), unless otherwise specified by manufacturer. Protect from light. Protect from freezing.

Auxiliary labeling
- For external use only.
- Keep away from eyes.

[1]Not included in Canadian product labeling.

Revised: 06/14/1999

KETOPROFEN—See *Anti-inflammatory Drugs, Nonsteroidal (Systemic)*

KETOROLAC Ophthalmic

VA CLASSIFICATION (Primary/Secondary): OP302/OP900

Commonly used brand name(s): *Acular*.

Note: For a listing of dosage forms and brand names by country availability, see *Dosage Forms* section(s).

Category
Anti-inflammatory, nonsteroidal (ophthalmic); antipruritic (ophthalmic).

Indications
Note: Bracketed information in the *Indications* section refers to uses that are not included in U.S. product labeling.

Accepted
Conjunctivitis, allergic (treatment)[1]—Ketorolac ophthalmic is indicated for the treatment of ocular itching caused by seasonal allergic conjunctivitis.

Inflammation, ocular (treatment)—Ketorolac is indicated for the treatment of postoperative inflammation in patients who have undergone cataract extraction.

[Inflammation, ocular (prophylaxis)]—Ketorolac ophthalmic is indicated for the prophylaxis of postoperative ocular inflammation in patients undergoing cataract extraction with or without implantation of an intraocular lens.

[1]Not included in Canadian product labeling.

Pharmacology/Pharmacokinetics

Physicochemical characteristics
Molecular weight—Ketorolac tromethamine: 376.41.
Osmolality—290 mOsmol per kg.
pKa—3.5.
pH—7.4.

Mechanism of action/Effect
Ketorolac is a nonsteroidal anti-inflammatory drug (NSAID) that is chemically related to indomethacin and tolmetin. Ocular administration of ketorolac reduces prostaglandin E_2 levels in aqueous humor, secondary to inhibition of prostaglandin biosynthesis.

Other actions/effects
Ketorolac ophthalmic has no significant effect on intraocular pressure.

Absorption
Negligible.

Distribution
Plasma—In a study where 26 subjects were administered 1 drop of 0.5% ketorolac ophthalmic solution in 1 eye 3 times a day for 21 days, 5 of 26 subjects had detectable (greater than 10 nanograms per mL) plasma levels of 11 to 22 nanograms per mL of ketorolac when they were tested 15 minutes after the first dose on day 10. When the subjects were tested on day 24, none had detectable plasma levels. In comparison, 10 mg of systemic ketorolac administered every 6 hours results in a steady state plasma level of approximately 960 nanograms per mL.

Aqueous humor—Eight of 9 patients administered 2 drops of 0.5% ketorolac ophthalmic solution in each eye 12 hours and 1 hour prior to cataract extraction had detectable (greater than or equal to 40 nanograms per mL) levels of 40 to 170 nanograms per mL (mean concentration 95 nanograms per mL) of ketorolac in the aqueous humor.

Precautions to Consider

Cross-sensitivity and/or related problems
Patients sensitive to aspirin; phenylacetic acid derivatives, such as diclofenac; or other systemic or ophthalmic nonsteroidal anti-inflammatory drugs (NSAIDs) may be sensitive to ketorolac also.

Tumorigenicity
No evidence of tumorigenicity was found in an 18-month study in mice given oral doses of ketorolac equivalent to the parenteral maximum recommended human dose (MRHD) and a 24-month study in rats given oral doses of ketorolac equivalent to 2.5 times the parenteral MRHD.

Mutagenicity
Ketorolac was not mutagenic in the Ames test, the unscheduled DNA synthesis and repair test, and in forward mutation assays. In addition, ketorolac did not cause chromosome breakage in the *in vivo* mouse micronucleus assay. However, at 1590 mcg per mL and higher concentrations of ketorolac, there was an increased incidence of chromosomal aberrations in Chinese hamster ovarian cells.

Pregnancy/Reproduction
Fertility—Male and female rats given ketorolac at oral doses of 9 mg per kg of body weight (mg/kg) and 16 mg/kg, respectively, did not show impairment of fertility.

Pregnancy—Adequate and well-controlled studies in humans have not been done.

Studies in rabbits and rats given ketorolac at oral doses of 3.6 mg/kg a day and 10 mg/kg a day, respectively, during organogenesis did not show evidence of teratogenicity. However, rats given oral doses of 1.5 mg/kg after gestation day 17 had a higher pup mortality rate.

FDA Pregnancy Category C.

Labor—Rats given oral doses of 1.5 mg/kg of ketorolac after gestation day 17 developed dystocia.

Breast-feeding
Problems in humans have not been documented.

Pediatrics
Appropriate studies on the relationship of age to the effects of ophthalmic ketorolac have not been performed in the pediatric population. Safety and efficacy have not been established.

Geriatrics
Appropriate studies on the relationship of age to the effects of ophthalmic ketorolac have not been performed in the geriatric population. However, no geriatrics-specific problems have been documented to date.

Drug interactions and/or related problems
The following drug interactions and/or related problems have been selected on the basis of their potential clinical significance (possible mechanism in parentheses where appropriate)—not necessarily inclusive (» = major clinical significance):

Note: Combinations containing any of the following medications, depending on the amount present, may also interact with this medication.

Any medication that may interfere with blood clotting or prolong bleeding time, such as:
Anticoagulants, coumarin- or indandione-derivative, or
Heparin or
Platelet aggregation inhibitors
(ophthalmic NSAIDs, such as ketorolac, may also increase the tendency to bleed; concurrent use may increase the risk of postoperative ocular bleeding)

Medical considerations/Contraindications

The medical considerations/contraindications included have been selected on the basis of their potential clinical significance (reasons given in parentheses where appropriate)—not necessarily inclusive (» = major clinical significance).

Risk-benefit should be considered when the following medical problems exist:

Hemophilia or other bleeding problems or coagulation defects or
Prolonged bleeding time
(increased risk of bleeding following ocular surgery)
Sensitivity to ophthalmic ketorolac

Side/Adverse Effects

The following side/adverse effects have been selected on the basis of their potential clinical significance (possible signs and symptoms in parentheses where appropriate)—not necessarily inclusive:

Those indicating need for medical attention

Incidence less frequent or rare
Hypersensitivity (itching, rash, redness, swelling, or other sign of irritation not present before therapy); ***keratitis, superficial*** (redness of the clear part of the eye); ***ocular irritation*** (itching, redness, tearing, or other sign of eye irritation not present before use of this medicine or becoming worse during use)

Those indicating need for medical attention only if they continue or are bothersome

Incidence more frequent
Stinging or burning upon instillation of medication

Patient Consultation

As an aid to patient consultation, refer to *Advice for the Patient, Ketorolac (Ophthalmic)*.

In providing consultation, consider emphasizing the following selected information (» = major clinical significance):

Before using this medication

» Conditions affecting use, especially:
Sensitivity to ophthalmic or systemic ketorolac; aspirin; phenylacetic acid derivatives, such as diclofenac; or other systemic or ophthalmic nonsteroidal anti-inflammatory drugs (NSAIDs)

Proper use of this medication

Proper administration; using a second drop if necessary; not touching applicator tip to any surface; keeping container tightly closed
» Proper dosing
Missed dose: Using as soon as possible; not using if almost time for next dose; using next dose at regularly scheduled time; not doubling doses
» Proper storage

Precautions while using this medication

Checking with doctor if symptoms do not improve or if they become worse
Expecting stinging or burning of eye upon administration of medication

Side/adverse effects

Signs of potential side effects, especially hypersensitivity; keratitis, superficial; or ocular irritation

General Dosing Information

The manufacturer recommends that patients not wear soft contact lenses during treatment with ketorolac ophthalmic solution. However, medical experts do not believe this precaution is necessary unless the patient has corneal epithelial problems and the medication is to be used more often than once every 1 to 2 hours. No significant problems have been documented with ophthalmic solutions that contain 0.03% or less of benzalkonium chloride as a preservative and are used as eye drops in patients with no significant corneal surface problems.

Ketorolac ophthalmic may be administered in conjunction with other ophthalmic medications, such as antibiotics, beta-adrenergic blocking agents, carbonic anhydrase inhibitors, cycloplegics, and mydriatics.

Ophthalmic Dosage Forms

Note: Bracketed uses in the *Dosage Forms* section refer to categories of use and/or indications that are not included in U.S. product labeling.

KETOROLAC TROMETHAMINE OPHTHALMIC SOLUTION

Usual adult and adolescent dose

Conjunctivitis, allergic (treatment)[1]—
Topical, to the conjunctiva, 1 drop in each eye four times a day.
Inflammation, ocular (treatment)—
In the U.S.: Topical, to the conjunctiva, 1 drop in the affected eye(s) four times a day beginning twenty-four hours after cataract surgery and continuing for two weeks.
[Inflammation, ocular (prophylaxis and treatment)]—
In Canada: Topical, to the conjunctiva, 1 drop in each eye every six to eight hours beginning twenty-four hours before surgery and continuing for three to four weeks.

Usual pediatric dose

Safety and efficacy have not been established.

Strength(s) usually available

U.S.—
0.5% (Rx) [*Acular* (benzalkonium chloride 0.01%)].
Canada—
0.5% (Rx) [*Acular* (benzalkonium chloride)].

Packaging and storage

Store between 15 and 30 °C (59 and 86 °F), unless otherwise specified by manufacturer. Protect from light.

Auxiliary labeling

- For the eye.

[1]Not included in Canadian product labeling.

Selected Bibliography

Ketorolac for seasonal allergic conjunctivitis. Med Lett Drugs Ther 1993 Sep 17; 35(905): 88-9.

Tinkelman DG, Rupp G, Kaufman H, et al. Double-masked, paired-comparison clinical study of ketorolac tromethamine 0.5% ophthalmic solution compared with placebo eyedrops in the treatment of seasonal allergic conjunctivitis. Surv Ophthalmol 1993 Jul-Aug; 38 Suppl: 133-40.

Ballas Z, Blumenthal M, Tinkelman DG, et al. Clinical evaluation of ketorolac tromethamine 0.5% ophthalmic solution for the treatment of seasonal allergic conjunctivitis. Surv Ophthalmol 1993 Jul-Aug; 38 Suppl: 141-8.

Revised: 11/20/1998
Developed: 08/11/1994

KETOROLAC Systemic

VA CLASSIFICATION (Primary): CN103
Commonly used brand name(s): *Toradol*.

Note: For a listing of dosage forms and brand names by country availability, see *Dosage Forms* section(s).

Category

Analgesic.

Indications

Note: Ketorolac, like other nonsteroidal anti-inflammatory drugs (NSAIDs), has antipyretic and anti-inflammatory, as well as analgesic actions. However, indications for specific NSAIDs may vary because of lack of specific testing and/or clinical-use data as well as the toxicity of the individual agent.

Accepted

Pain (treatment)—Ketorolac is indicated for the short-term management of moderately severe acute pain that would otherwise require treatment with an opioid analgesic. It is most commonly used to relieve postoperative pain. The oral dosage form is indicated only for continuation of therapy following initial parenteral administration. Because the risk of gastrointestinal bleeding and other severe adverse effects increases with the duration of treatment, **ketorolac should not be**

administered by any route or combination of routes for longer than 5 days.

Before ketorolac is used perioperatively, its platelet aggregation-inhibiting activity, which increases the risk of bleeding, must be considered. Postoperative hematomas and other signs of wound bleeding have been reported in ketorolac-treated patients. Therefore, **ketorolac should not be given prior to major surgery to prevent postoperative pain; nor should it be administered intraoperatively when control of bleeding is critical**. Also, ketorolac lacks the sedative and anti-anxiety activity usually desired in a preoperative medication.

[Pain, postoperative, in pediatric patients (treatment)][1]—Intravenous ketorolac is indicated for short term use in the treatment of postoperative pain in pediatric patients.

Unaccepted

Although ketorolac may be used for short-term (up to 5 days) treatment of moderately severe acute arthritic pain in patients who are not receiving chronic treatment with other NSAIDs, it is not recommended for the long-term treatment of chronic rheumatic disease.

Ketorolac is not recommended for treatment of mild pain or for long-term treatment of chronic pain.

---

[1]Not included in Canadian product labeling.

Pharmacology/Pharmacokinetics

Physicochemical characteristics

Molecular weight—376.41.

pKa—3.5.

Mechanism of action/Effect

Ketorolac is a nonsteroidal anti-inflammatory drug (NSAID) chemically related to indomethacin and tolmetin. Currently available NSAIDs inhibit the activity of the enzyme cyclo-oxygenase, leading to decreased formation of precursors of prostaglandins and thromboxanes from arachidonic acid. The resultant reduction in prostaglandin synthesis and activity may be at least partially responsible for many of the adverse, as well as the therapeutic, effects of these medications. Analgesia is probably produced via a peripheral action in which blockade of pain impulse generation results from decreased prostaglandin activity. However, inhibition of the synthesis or actions of other substances that sensitize pain receptors to mechanical or chemical stimulation may also contribute to the analgesic effect.

Other actions/effects

Ketorolac has anti-inflammatory and antipyretic actions that, together with its analgesic effects, may mask the onset and/or progression of an infection.

Ketorolac inhibits platelet aggregation. This effect is reversible (unlike aspirin-induced platelet inhibition, which persists for the life of the exposed platelets). Recovery of platelet function usually occurs within 24 to 48 hours following discontinuation of ketorolac.

Like other NSAIDs, ketorolac may cause gastrointestinal ulceration and bleeding. These effects probably result from ketorolac-induced reduction of the synthesis and activity of prostaglandins that exert a protective effect on the gastrointestinal mucosa; they may occur after parenteral as well as after oral administration. However, when administered orally, this acidic medication probably also exerts a direct irritant or erosive effect on the mucosa.

Like other NSAIDs, ketorolac may cause renal toxicity (i.e., sodium and fluid retention, decreased renal perfusion, and decreased renal function), probably by inhibiting the synthesis and activity of renal prostaglandins, which are directly involved in the maintenance of renal hemodynamics and sodium and fluid balance. Renal prostaglandins are especially important in maintaining renal function in the presence of generalized vasoconstriction or volume depletion.

Absorption

Intramuscular—Rapid and complete.

Oral—Rapid (more rapid than after intramuscular administration in some individuals) and complete. The rate, but not the extent, of absorption is decreased when the medication is taken with a high-fat meal. Absorption is not altered by concurrent administration with an antacid.

Distribution

The volume of distribution (Vol_D) of racemic ketorolac in patients with normal renal function is 0.15 to 0.33 L per kg of body weight. In patients with renal function impairment, the Vol_D of the active S-enantiomer of ketorolac is twice as large as in individuals with normal renal function, and the Vol_D of the inactive R-enantiomer is approximately 20% larger.

In breast milk—Maximum concentrations of 7.3 nanograms per mL (0.019 micromoles/L) 2 hours after the first dose and 7.9 nanograms per mL (0.021 micromoles/L) 2 hours after the fifth dose were measured in the breast milk of women receiving 10 mg of ketorolac, orally, 4 times a day. However, in 40% of the subjects tested, the concentration in breast milk did not reach the lowest detection limit of 5 nanograms per mL (0.013 micromoles/L).

Protein binding

Very high (> 99%).

Biotransformation

Primarily hepatic. Less than 50% of a dose is metabolized. The major metabolites are a glucuronide conjugate, which may also be formed in the kidney, and *p*-hydroxy ketorolac. Neither metabolite has significant analgesic activity.

Half-life

Terminal—

Individuals with normal renal function—

About 5.3 hours in healthy young adults (ranges, 3.5 to 9.2 hours after 30 mg intramuscularly, 4 to 7.9 hours after 30 mg intravenously, and 2.4 to 9.0 hours after 10 mg orally). Mean values are higher in healthy geriatric subjects, but remain within the same ranges reported for younger adults. Hepatic function impairment does not significantly prolong the half-life.

Patients with renal function impairment—

About 10.3 to 10.8 hours in patients with a serum creatinine of 1.9 to 5 mg per 100 mL (168 to 442 micromoles/L) (ranges, 5.9 to 19.2 hours after 30 mg intramuscularly and 3.4 to 18.9 hours after 10 mg orally). Values are even higher in patients receiving renal dialysis (13.6 [range, 8 to 39.1] hours after 30 mg intramuscularly).

Note: The above values apply to racemic ketorolac. In patients with normal renal function, terminal half-life values for the active S-enantiomer and the inactive R-enantiomer are approximately 2.5 hours and 5 hours, respectively.

Onset of action

Dose-dependent; generally within 30 minutes to 1 hour.

Time to peak plasma concentration

Intramuscular—

Single dose of up to 60 mg: 30 to 60 minutes.

Intravenous—

Single 15-mg dose: 1.1 ± 0.7 minutes.

Single 30-mg dose: 2.9 ± 1.8 minutes.

Oral—

Single 10-mg dose: 44 ± 34 minutes.

Time to steady-state plasma concentration

Intramuscular or oral—About 24 hours, when the medication is administered at 6-hour intervals.

Steady-state plasma concentration

With administration 4 times a day at 6-hour intervals—

Intramuscular—

15 mg: Average, 0.94 ± 0.29 mcg/mL (2.5 ± 0.77 micromoles/L).

30 mg: Average, 1.88 ± 0.59 mcg/mL (5 ± 1.57 micromoles/L).

Intravenous—

15 mg: Average, 1.09 ± 0.3 mcg/mL (2.89 ± 0.8 micromoles/L).

30 mg: Average, 2.17 ±0.59 mcg/mL (5.77 ± 1.57 micromoles/L).

Oral—

10 mg: Average, 0.59 ± 0.2 mcg/mL (1.57 ± 0.53 micromoles/L).

Note: Determination of minimum (trough) concentrations for each of the above routes of administration has shown that ketorolac concentrations do not decrease to subtherapeutic levels between doses.

Peak plasma concentration

Following administration of a single dose

Route*	Dose (mg)	Concentration	
		mcg/mL	micromoles/L
IM	15	1.14±0.32	3.03±0.85
	30	2.42±0.68	6.44±1.81
	60	4.5±1.27	11.97±3.38
IV	15	2.47±0.51	6.57±1.36
	30	4.65±0.96	12.37±2.55
PO	10	0.87±0.22	2.31±0.58

*IM = intramuscular; IV = intravenous; PO = oral.

Time to peak effect

Intramuscular or intravenous—1 to 2 hours.

Oral—2 to 3 hours.

Duration of action

Intramuscular or intravenous—4 to 6 hours.

Elimination

91% renal; approximately 6% biliary/fecal. The active S-enantiomer is cleared approximately twice as rapidly as the inactive R-enantiomer.

Average total clearance rates following administration of a single dose—
Healthy young adults:
Intramuscular, 30 mg—0.023 (range, 0.01 to 0.046) liters per hour per kg of body weight (L/hr/kg).
Intravenous, 30 mg—0.03 (range, 0.017 to 0.051) L/hr/kg.
Oral, 10 mg—0.025 (range, 0.013 to 0.05) L/hr/kg.
Elderly adults:
Intramuscular, 30 mg—0.019 (range, 0.013 to 0.034) L/hr/kg.
Oral, 10 mg—0.024 (range, 0.018 to 0.034) L/hr/kg.
Patients with hepatic function impairment:
Intramuscular, 30 mg—0.029 (range, 0.13 to 0.066) L/hr/kg.
Oral, 10 mg—0.033 (range, 0.019 to 0.051) L/hr/kg.
Patients with renal function impairment:
Serum creatinine 1.9 to 5 mg/100 mL (168 to 442 micromoles/L)—
Intramuscular, 30 mg: 0.015 (range, 0.005 to 0.043) L/hr/kg.
Oral, 10 mg: 0.016 (range, 0.007 to 0.052) L/hr/kg.
Renal dialysis patients—
Intramuscular, 30 mg: 0.016 (range, 0.003 to 0.036) L/hr/kg.
In dialysis—
Hemodialysis does not remove significant quantities of ketorolac from the body.

Precautions to Consider

Cross-sensitivity and/or related problems

Patients sensitive to aspirin or other nonsteroidal anti-inflammatory drugs (NSAIDs) may be sensitive to ketorolac also. Severe asthmatic and anaphylactoid reactions have occurred in such patients.

Tumorigenicity

No evidence of tumorigenicity was found in an 18-month study in mice receiving up to 2 mg per kg of body weight (mg/kg) per day or a 24-month study in rats receiving up to 5 mg/kg per day orally. These doses are considered, on the basis of area under the concentration-time curve (AUC) comparisons, to be equivalent to 0.9 and 0.5 times, respectively, the human exposure resulting from intramuscular or intravenous administration of 30 mg 4 times a day.

Mutagenicity

No evidence of mutagenicity was found in the Ames test, unscheduled DNA synthesis and repair, and forward mutation assays. Also, ketorolac did not cause chromosome breakage in the *in vivo* mouse micronucleus assay. However, in a concentration of 1590 mcg per mL (mcg/mL)(approximately 1000 times average human plasma concentrations), ketorolac increased the occurrence of chromosomal aberrations in Chinese hamster ovarian cells.

Pregnancy/Reproduction

Fertility—No impairment of fertility was observed in male rats given 9 mg/kg per day or female rats given 16 mg/kg per day, orally (53.1 and 50 mg per square meter of body surface area [mg/m^2] per day). These doses are equivalent to 0.9 and 1.6 times, respectively, the human exposure resulting from intramuscular or intravenous administration of 30 mg 4 times a day, based on AUC comparisons.

Pregnancy—

First trimester—

Adequate and well-controlled studies have not been done in pregnant women.

No teratogenicity occurred in offspring of rabbits receiving oral doses of up to 3.6 mg/kg per day (42.35 mg/m^2 per day; equivalent to 0.37 times the human exposure resulting from intramuscular or intravenous administration of 30 mg 4 times a day, based on AUC comparisons) or rats receiving orally up to 10 mg/kg per day (59 mg/m^2 per day; equivalent to the human exposure, based on AUC comparisons).

Second and third trimesters—

Although studies in pregnant women have not been done with ketorolac, chronic use of any NSAID during the second half of pregnancy is not recommended because of possible adverse effects in the fetus, such as premature closure of the ductus arteriosus, which may lead to persistent pulmonary hypertension in the newborn. Such effects have been documented in animal studies with other NSAIDs.

Chronic administration of 1.5 mg/kg per day (8.8 mg/m^2 per day) of ketorolac to rats after Day 17 of gestation caused dystocia and higher pup mortality. This dose is equivalent to 0.14 times the human exposure resulting from intramuscular or intravenous administration of 30 mg 4 times a day, based on AUC comparisons. Higher doses (9 mg/kg or more per day, administered to rats from Day 15 of gestation) significantly increased the length of gestation, in addition to increasing the incidence of maternal deaths associated with dystocia and decreasing birth weights and survival rates in the offspring.

FDA Pregnancy Category C.

Labor and delivery—When administered during labor, ketorolac crosses the placenta and inhibits platelet aggregation in the neonate. Ketorolac may cause adverse effects on uterine contractility and on the fetal ductus arteriosus, resulting in an increased risk of uterine bleeding and fetal circulatory disturbances, respectively. **Therefore, ketorolac should not be used during labor and delivery**.

Breast-feeding

Because of potential adverse effects in the nursing infant, use of ketorolac by nursing mothers is not recommended. Ketorolac is distributed into breast milk in small quantities. Maximum concentrations of 7.3 nanograms per mL (nanograms/mL) (0.019 micromoles/L) 2 hours after the first dose and 7.9 nanograms/mL (0.021 micromoles/L) 2 hours after the fifth dose were measured in the breast milk of women receiving 10 mg of ketorolac, orally, 4 times a day, although the concentration in breast milk failed to reach the lowest detection limit of 5 nanograms/mL (0.013 micromoles/L) in 40% of the subjects tested. Milk-to-plasma concentration ratios of 0.037 and 0.025 have been calculated after administration of a single dose and at steady-state, respectively.

Pediatrics

No information is available on the relationship of age to the effects of ketorolac in pediatric patients. Safety and efficacy in patients younger than 16 years of age have not been established.

Geriatrics

Studies have shown that clearance of ketorolac is reduced in healthy individuals 65 years of age or older, leading to significant prolongation of the elimination half-life. Also, geriatric patients are more likely to have age-related renal function impairment, which may further reduce ketorolac clearance and increase the risk of NSAID-induced renal or hepatic toxicity. The risk of gastrointestinal ulceration, bleeding, and perforation is higher in elderly patients receiving ketorolac than in younger adults. Also, ketorolac-induced gastrointestinal ulceration and/or bleeding is more likely to cause serious consequences, including fatalities, in geriatric patients. It is recommended that ketorolac be used with caution, in the lower of the recommended dosage regimens, and with careful monitoring of the patient.

Drug interactions and/or related problems

The following drug interactions and/or related problems have been selected on the basis of their potential clinical significance (possible mechanism in parentheses where appropriate)—not necessarily inclusive (» = major clinical significance):

Note: Combinations containing any of the following medications, depending on the amount present, may also interact with this medication.

All of the interactions listed below have not been documented with ketorolac. However, they have been reported with other NSAIDs and should be considered potential precautions to the use of ketorolac also.

In addition to the interactions listed below, the possibility should be considered that additive or multiple effects leading to impaired blood clotting and/or increased risk of bleeding may occur if any NSAID is used concurrently with any medication having a significant potential for causing hypoprothrombinemia, thrombocytopenia, or gastrointestinal ulceration or hemorrhage.

Acetaminophen
(prolonged concurrent use of acetaminophen with an NSAID may increase the risk of adverse renal effects; it is recommended that patients be under close medical supervision while receiving such combined therapy)

Alcohol or
Corticosteroids, glucocorticoid or
Corticotropin (chronic therapeutic use) or
Potassium supplements
(concurrent use with an NSAID may increase the risk of gastrointestinal side effects, including ulceration or hemorrhage)

» Anticoagulants, coumarin- or indanedione-derivative or
» Heparin or
» Thrombolytic agents, such as:
Alteplase
Anistreplase
Streptokinase
Urokinase
(ketorolac has not been shown to alter the pharmacokinetic or pharmacodynamic properties of warfarin or heparin; however, inhibition of platelet aggregation by ketorolac, and the potential occurrence of ketorolac-induced gastrointestinal ulceration or bleeding, may be hazardous to patients receiving anticoagulant or thrombolytic therapy; caution and careful monitoring of the patient are recommended, as there is evidence that administration of ke-

torolac to patients receiving an anticoagulant, possibly including low [prophylactic] doses of heparin [2500 to 5000 Units every 12 hours], increases the risk of bleeding and intramuscular hematoma formation)

Antihypertensives or
Diuretics
(increased monitoring of the response to any antihypertensive agent may be advisable when ketorolac is used concurrently because several other NSAIDs have been shown to reduce or reverse the effects of many antihypertensives, possibly by inhibiting renal prostaglandin synthesis and/or by causing sodium and fluid retention)
(NSAIDs may decrease the diuretic and natriuretic, as well as the antihypertensive, effects of diuretics, probably by inhibiting renal prostaglandin synthesis; ketorolac inhibited the diuretic effect of furosemide, decreasing sodium and urine output by about 20%, in a study in normovolemic healthy subjects)
(concurrent use of an NSAID and a diuretic may also increase the risk of renal failure secondary to a decrease in renal blood flow caused by inhibition of renal prostaglandin synthesis)
(concurrent use of ketorolac with an angiotensin-converting enzyme [ACE] inhibitor may also increase the risk of renal function impairment, especially in hypovolemic patients)

» Aspirin or other salicylates or
» Other NSAIDs
(concurrent use of aspirin or other NSAIDs with ketorolac is not recommended because of the potential for additive toxicity)
(concurrent use of ketorolac with antirheumatic doses of salicylates other than aspirin should be undertaken with caution and in reduced doses because therapeutic plasma concentrations of salicylate [30 mg per 100 mL (2.17 mmol per L)] decrease the protein binding of ketorolac sufficiently to potentially double the plasma concentration of free [unbound] ketorolac)

» Cefamandole or
» Cefoperazone or
» Cefotetan or
» Plicamycin or
» Valproic acid
(these medications may cause hypoprothrombinemia; in addition, plicamycin or valproic acid may inhibit platelet aggregation; concurrent use with an NSAID may increase the risk of bleeding because of additive interferences with blood clotting and/or the potential occurrence of gastrointestinal ulceration or hemorrhage during NSAID therapy)

Gold compounds
(although other NSAIDs are commonly used concurrently with gold compounds in the treatment of arthritis, the possibility should be considered that concurrent use of a gold compound with any NSAID, including ketorolac, may increase the risk of adverse renal effects)

» Lithium
(although the effect of ketorolac on lithium plasma concentration has not been studied, increases in lithium concentration have been reported during concomitant administration of ketorolac; increased monitoring of lithium plasma concentrations is recommended during and following concurrent use so that lithium dosage can be adjusted if necessary)

» Methotrexate
(the effect of ketorolac on methotrexate concentrations and/or toxicity has not been studied; however, administration of moderate- or high-dose methotrexate infusions to patients receiving other NSAIDs has resulted in severe, sometimes fatal, methotrexate toxicity, possibly because NSAIDs may reduce renal function, thereby decreasing methotrexate excretion; it is recommended that ketorolac not be administered for 24 hours prior to, and for at least 12 hours [or until the methotrexate plasma concentration has decreased to a nontoxic level] following, a high-dose methotrexate infusion)
(severe, sometimes fatal, methotrexate toxicity has also been reported with the relatively low to moderate doses of methotrexate used in the treatment of rheumatoid arthritis or psoriasis when an NSAID was given concurrently; it is recommended that concurrent use of ketorolac with low to moderate doses of methotrexate also be undertaken with caution, with methotrexate dosage being adjusted as determined by monitoring plasma methotrexate concentration and/or adequacy of the patient's renal function)

Nephrotoxic medications, other (see *Appendix II*)
(concurrent use with an NSAID may increase the risk and/or severity of adverse renal effects)

Platelet aggregation inhibitors, other (see *Appendix II*)
(concurrent use of any of these medications with an NSAID, including ketorolac, may increase the risk of bleeding because of additive inhibition of platelet aggregation as well as the potential occurrence of gastrointestinal ulceration or hemorrhage during NSAID therapy)

» Probenecid
(concurrent use with ketorolac is not recommended because probenecid decreases elimination of ketorolac, resulting in significantly increased ketorolac plasma concentrations [the area under the concentration-time curve (AUC) being increased about threefold, from 5.4 to 17.8 mcg per hour per mL] and half-life [which is more than doubled, to about 15 hours])

Laboratory value alterations

The following have been selected on the basis of their potential clinical significance (possible effect in parentheses where appropriate)—not necessarily inclusive (» = major clinical significance).

With physiology/laboratory test values

Bleeding time
(may be prolonged because ketorolac inhibits platelet aggregation; effects may persist for 24 to 48 hours after discontinuation of therapy)

Blood urea nitrogen (BUN) or
Creatinine, serum or
Potassium, serum
(may be increased)

Liver function tests, especially serum transaminase activity
(although borderline elevations in test values may occur in up to 15% of patients receiving ketorolac, significant elevations [3 times the upper limit] of serum transaminases have occurred in fewer than 1%; ketorolac therapy should be discontinued if significant abnormalities occur)

Medical considerations/Contraindications

The medical considerations/contraindications included have been selected on the basis of their potential clinical significance (reasons given in parentheses where appropriate)—not necessarily inclusive (» = major clinical significance).

Except under special circumstances, this medication should not be used when the following medical problems exist:

» Cerebrovascular bleeding, suspected or confirmed or
» Hemophilia or other bleeding problems including coagulation or platelet function disorders
(increased risk of bleeding because ketorolac inhibits platelet aggregation and may also cause gastrointestinal ulceration or hemorrhage)

» Gastrointestinal bleeding, active, recent, or history of or
» Gastrointestinal perforation, recent or
» Peptic ulceration, ulcerative colitis, or other ulcerative gastrointestinal disease, active or history of
(increased risk of gastrointestinal ulceration, perforation, and/or hemorrhage)

» Nasal polyps associated with bronchospasm, aspirin-induced, or angioedema, anaphylaxis, or other severe allergic reaction induced by aspirin, ketorolac, or other NSAIDs, history of
(high risk of severe allergic reactions because of cross-sensitivity)

» Renal function impairment, severe
(increased risk of renal failure)

Risk-benefit should be considered when the following medical problems exist:

» Allergic reaction, mild, such as allergic rhinitis, urticaria, or skin rash, induced by aspirin, ketorolac, or other NSAIDs, history of
(possibility of cross-sensitivity)

Asthma
(may be exacerbated)

Cholestasis or
Hepatitis, active
(although other forms of hepatic function impairment apparently do not alter the clearance of ketorolac, studies to assess the possible effect of cholestasis or active hepatitis on the pharmacokinetics of the medication have not been done)

Conditions predisposing to gastrointestinal toxicity, such as:
Alcoholism, active or
» Inflammatory bowel disease
Tobacco use, or recent history of
(caution and close supervision are recommended for patients in whom there is a significant risk of gastrointestinal toxicity; misoprostol or sucralfate should be considered as prophylaxis for those at high risk)

Conditions predisposing to and/or exacerbated by fluid retention, such as:
Compromised cardiac function or
Congestive heart disease or
Edema, pre-existing or
Hypertension
(ketorolac may cause fluid retention and edema)

Congestive heart failure or
Diabetes mellitus or
Edema, pre-existing or
Hepatic function impairment or
» Hypovolemia or
Sepsis
(increased risk of renal failure; caution and monitoring of urine output, serum urea, and serum creatinine are advised; hypovolemia should be corrected before ketorolac therapy is initiated)
(hepatotoxicity, as indicated by significant abnormalities in liver function tests, is more likely to occur in patients with pre-existing hepatic function impairment)

» Renal function impairment, mild to moderate
(ketorolac and its metabolites are excreted primarily via the kidney, which may also be a site of ketorolac metabolism; a substantial reduction in ketorolac clearance, leading to significant prolongation of its half-life, has been demonstrated in patients with renal function impairment; a reduction in dosage is recommended for patients with moderate elevations of serum creatinine)
(caution and careful monitoring of the patient are also recommended because of possible patient predisposition toward development of NSAID-induced adverse renal effects, including acute renal failure)

Systemic lupus erythematosus (SLE)
(increased risk of renal function impairment)

Side/Adverse Effects

In July 2005, the Food and Drug Administration (FDA) asked all manufacturers of NSAIDs, including ketorolac, to revise the labeling for their products to include a boxed warning, highlighting the potential for increased risk of cardiovascular (CV) events including stroke and the well described, serious potential life-threatening gastrointestinal (GI) bleeding associated with their use.

Note: The risk of adverse effects increases with the duration of treatment as well as with the total daily dose of ketorolac. In a long-term study in patients with chronic pain, oral administration of 10 mg 4 times a day of ketorolac caused more gastrointestinal toxicity than 650 mg 4 times a day of aspirin; the frequency of occurrence of gastrointestinal ulceration or bleeding was 0.69% after 3 months and 1.59% after 6 months in patients receiving ketorolac and 0% after 3 months and 0.73% after 6 months in patients receiving aspirin. An unusually large number of cases of upper gastrointestinal bleeding (20% of which were fatal) has been reported with ketorolac, mostly in elderly patients.

Studies have shown that there is also a substantial risk of gastrointestinal bleeding during short-term parenteral administration of ketorolac (a maximum of 20 doses, administered over 5 days), especially in patients older than 65 years of age and/or patients with a history of gastrointestinal perforation, ulcer, or bleeding (PUB). The following percentages of patients experienced clinically significant gastrointestinal bleeding in these studies:

Patient		Total dose/day (mg)			
Age(yr)	PUB History	≤60	>60–90	>90–120	>120
<65	No	0.4%	0.4%	0.9%	4.6%
	Yes	2.1%	4.6%	7.8%	15.4%
≥65	No	1.2%	2.8%	2.2%	7.7%
	Yes	4.7%	3.7%	2.8%	25%

The following side/adverse effects have been selected on the basis of their potential clinical significance (possible signs and symptoms in parentheses where appropriate)—not necessarily inclusive:

Those indicating need for medical attention

Incidence more frequent (4%)

Edema (swelling of face, fingers, lower legs, ankles, and/or feet; unusual weight gain)

Incidence less frequent (1 to 3%)

Hypertension (high blood pressure); ***purpura*** (small, red spots on skin; bruising); ***skin rash***—rarely including maculopapular rash, or itching; ***stomatitis*** (sores, ulcers, or white spots on lips or in mouth)

Incidence rare (< 1%)

Anaphylaxis or anaphylactoid reaction (changes in facial skin color; skin rash, hives, and/or itching; fast or irregular breathing; puffiness or swelling of the eyelids or around the eyes; shortness of breath, troubled breathing, tightness in chest, and/or wheezing); ***anemia*** (unusual tiredness or weakness); ***aseptic meningitis*** (fever; severe headache; drowsiness; confusion; stiff neck and/or back; general feeling of illness; nausea); ***asthma, bronchospasm, or dyspnea*** (shortness of breath, troubled breathing, tightness in chest, and/or wheezing); ***bleeding from wound, postoperatively; bloody stools; blurred vision or other vision change; cholestatic jaundice*** (dark urine; fever; itching; light-colored stools; pain, tenderness, and/or swelling in upper abdominal area; skin rash; swollen glands; yellow eyes or skin); ***convulsions; edema of tongue; eosinophilia; exfoliative dermatitis*** (fever with or without chills; red, thickened, or scaly skin; swollen and/or painful glands; unusual bruising); ***fainting; fever; flank pain, with or without hematuria and/or azotemia*** (pain in lower back and/or side; bloody or cloudy urine); ***gastrointestinal, usually peptic, ulceration, possibly with perforation and/or bleeding*** (abdominal pain, cramping, or burning, severe; bloody or black, tarry stools; vomiting of blood or material that looks like coffee grounds; nausea, heartburn, and/or indigestion, severe and continuing); ***hallucinations; hearing loss; hemolytic uremic syndrome; hepatitis*** (loss of appetite; nausea; vomiting; yellow eyes or skin; swelling in upper abdominal area); ***hives; hyperactivity*** (restlessness, severe); ***hypotension*** (low blood pressure); ***increase in frequency of urination; increased urine volume; laryngeal edema*** (shortness of breath or troubled breathing); ***leukopenia*** (rarely, fever or chills; cough or hoarseness; lower back or side pain; painful or difficult urination)—usually asymptomatic; ***mental depression; nephritis*** (bloody or cloudy urine; increased blood pressure; sudden decrease in amount of urine; swelling of face, fingers, feet, and/or lower legs; rapid weight gain); ***nosebleeds; oliguria*** (decrease in amount of urine); ***pancreatitis, acute*** (abdominal pain; fever with or without chills; swelling and/or tenderness in upper abdominal or stomach area); ***psychosis*** (mood changes; unusual behavior); ***pulmonary edema*** (difficult, fast, noisy breathing, sometimes with wheezing; blue lips and fingernails; pale skin; increased sweating); ***rectal bleeding; renal failure, acute*** (increased blood pressure; shortness of breath, troubled breathing, tightness in chest, and/or wheezing; sudden decrease in amount of urine; swelling of face, fingers, feet, and/or lower legs; continuing thirst; unusual tiredness or weakness; weight gain); ***rhinitis*** (runny nose); ***Stevens-Johnson syndrome*** (bleeding or crusting sores on lips; chest pain; fever with or without chills; muscle cramps or pain; skin rash; sores, ulcers, or white spots in mouth; sore throat); ***thrombocytopenia*** (rarely, unusual bleeding or bruising; black, tarry stools; blood in urine or stools; pinpoint red spots on skin)—usually asymptomatic; ***tinnitus*** (ringing or buzzing in ears); ***toxic epidermal necrolysis [Lyell's syndrome]*** (redness, tenderness, itching, burning, or peeling of skin; sore throat; fever with or without chills)

Note: *Hemolytic uremic syndrome* is characterized by hemolytic *anemia, renal failure, thrombocytopenia,* and *purpura.* These adverse effects may also occur independently of hemolytic uremic syndrome and are listed separately above.

Those indicating need for medical attention only if they continue or are bothersome

Incidence more frequent (> 3%)

Abdominal pain—[13%]; ***bruising at injection site; diarrhea***—[7%]; ***dizziness***—[7%]; ***drowsiness***—[6%]; ***headache***—[17%]; ***indigestion***—[12%]; ***nausea***—[12%]

Incidence less frequent (1 to 3%)

Bloated feeling or gas; burning or pain at injection site; constipation; feeling of fullness in gastrointestinal tract; increased sweating; vomiting

Overdose

For specific information on the agents used in the management of ketorolac overdose, see:
- *Antacids (Oral-Local)* monograph;
- *Charcoal, Activated (Oral-Local)* monograph;
- *Histamine H_2-receptor Antagonists (Systemic)* monograph;
- *Misoprostol (Systemic)* monograph;
- *Omeprazole (Systemic)* monograph; and/or
- *Sucralfate (Oral-Local)* monograph.

For more information on the management of overdose or unintentional ingestion, **contact a Poison Control Center** (see *Poison Control Center Listing*).

Factors that are associated with an increased risk of ketorolac toxicity (in addition to total daily dosage and duration of treatment) include hypovolemia; renal insufficiency; a patient history of gastrointestinal perforation, ulceration, or bleeding; and patient age of 65 years or older.

Clinical effects of overdose

The following effects have been selected on the basis of their potential clinical significance (possible signs and symptoms in parentheses where appropriate)—not necessarily inclusive:

Abdominal pain; gastrointestinal ulceration and bleeding; metabolic acidosis

Treatment of overdose

To decrease absorption—

Administering activated charcoal (if the medication was ingested orally). The initial dose of charcoal may be followed by a cathartic, such as magnesium citrate, if the charcoal is not pre-mixed with sorbitol. Gastric lavage may also be performed.

Induction of emesis may also be helpful.

To enhance elimination—Hemodialysis does not remove significant quantities of ketorolac from the body.

Specific treatment—

For treatment of abdominal pain: Administering an antacid. See the product label or *Antacids (Oral-Local)* for specific dosing guidelines.

For treatment of gastrointestinal ulceration or bleeding: Discontinuing ketorolac therapy immediately. Depending on the site and severity of the ulcer, administering antacids, histamine H_2-receptor antagonists (cimetidine, famotidine, nizatidine, ranitidine), misoprostol, omeprazole, and/or sucralfate. See the package inserts or *Antacids (Oral-Local), Histamine H_2-receptor Antagonists (Systemic), Misoprostol (Systemic), Omeprazole (Systemic),* or *Sucralfate (Oral-Local)* for specific dosing guidelines for these products.

Supportive care—Supportive measures, such as establishing intravenous lines, hydration, administration of plasma volume expanders, and support of ventilatory function, should be instituted as needed. Patients in whom intentional overdose is confirmed or suspected should be referred for psychiatric consultation.

Patient Consultation

As an aid to patient consultation, refer to *Advice for the Patient, Ketorolac (Systemic).*

In providing consultation, consider emphasizing the following selected information (» = major clinical significance):

Before using this medication

» Conditions affecting use, especially:

Sensitivity to ketorolac, aspirin, or any other nonsteroidal anti-inflammatory drug (NSAID)

Pregnancy—Crosses the placenta; use during second half of pregnancy may cause adverse effects on fetal or neonatal blood flow

Breast-feeding—Not recommended because of potential adverse effects in the infant; ketorolac is distributed into breast milk

Use in the elderly—Higher risk of gastrointestinal and/or renal toxicity, possibly because of reduced clearance in addition to increased sensitivity

Other medications, especially anticoagulants, aspirin or other salicylates, other NSAIDs, those cephalosporins that may adversely affect blood clotting, lithium, methotrexate, plicamycin, probenecid, and valproic acid

Other medical problems, especially bleeding (active, history of, or predisposition to), peptic ulcer or other ulcerative or inflammatory gastrointestinal tract disease (active or history of), and renal function impairment

Proper use of this medication

Proper administration:

For oral dosage form

Taking with food (a meal or snack) to reduce gastrointestinal irritation, or with an antacid

Taking with a full glass of water, then remaining in an upright position for at least 15 to 30 minutes, to reduce risk of esophageal irritation

For injection

Proper injection technique (if self-medicating at home)

» Not using more medication than prescribed or using for longer than 5 days

Not saving unused medication for the future, and not sharing it with others

» Proper dosing

Missed dose (scheduled dosing): Using as soon as possible; not using if almost time for next dose; not doubling doses

» Proper storage

Precautions while using this medication

» Not using acetaminophen concurrently for more than a few days, and not using aspirin, other salicylates, or other NSAIDs concurrently, unless combination therapy prescribed and monitored by physician or dentist

» Importance of immediately reporting to physician symptoms of edema, gastrointestinal bleeding or ulceration, cardiovascular events, unusual weight gain, or skin rash

» Caution if dizziness or drowsiness occurs; not driving, using machines, or doing anything else that requires alertness

Side/adverse effects

Signs of potential side effects, especially edema; hypertension; purpura; skin rash or itching; stomatitis; anaphylaxis or anaphylactoid reaction; aseptic meningitis; asthma, bronchospasm, or dyspnea; anemia; aseptic meningitis; bloody stools; blurred vision or other vision change; cholestatic jaundice; convulsions; edema of tongue; exfoliative dermatitis; fainting; fever; flank pain; gastrointestinal ulceration or bleeding; hallucinations; hearing loss; hemolytic uremic syndrome; hepatitis; hives; hyperactivity; hypotension; increase in frequency or volume of urination; laryngeal edema; leukopenia; mental depression; nephritis; nosebleeds; oliguria; pancreatitis, acute; psychosis; pulmonary edema; rectal bleeding; renal failure; rhinitis; Stevens-Johnson syndrome; thrombocytopenia; tinnitus; or toxic epidermal necrolysis

General Dosing Information

Ketorolac may be administered on a scheduled or on an as-needed basis, depending on the type and severity of pain.

Ketorolac may be administered intramuscularly, intravenously, or orally. An intravenous dose should be given over at least 15 seconds. An intramuscular injection should be given slowly, deep into the muscle. Ketorolac injection contains alcohol and should not be administered intrathecally or epidurally.

Because of the risk of anaphylaxis or other severe allergic reactions, equipment and medications to treat these complications should be available for immediate use when the first dose of ketorolac is administered.

Hypovolemia increases the risk of adverse renal effects and should be corrected before ketorolac therapy is instituted.

Ketorolac therapy should be initiated with parenteral administration, after which additional doses may be given parenterally or orally. However, **the duration of treatment by any route or combination of routes is not to exceed 5 days.** The patient should be transferred to another analgesic as quickly as possible.

Concurrent use of ketorolac with an opioid analgesic provides additive analgesia and may permit lower doses of both medications to be utilized. Breakthrough pain that occurs during ketorolac treatment may be treated with an opioid analgesic (unless contraindicated); **increasing the dose or the frequency of administration of ketorolac is not recommended.**

For treatment of adverse effects

For abdominal pain—Administering an antacid. See the product label or *Antacids (Oral-Local)* for specific dosing guidelines for these products.

For gastrointestinal ulceration or bleeding—Discontinuing ketorolac therapy immediately. Depending on the site and severity of the ulcer, administering antacids, histamine H_2-receptor antagonists (cimetidine, famotidine, nizatidine, ranitidine), misoprostol, omeprazole, and/or sucralfate. See the package inserts or *Antacids (Oral-Local), Histamine H_2-receptor Antagonists (Systemic), Misoprostol (Systemic), Omeprazole (Systemic),* or *Sucralfate (Oral-Local)* monographs for specific dosing guidelines for these products.

For severe hypersensitivity reactions (e.g., anaphylaxis or anaphylactoid reaction or laryngeal edema)—Depending on the nature and severity of the symptoms, administering epinephrine and corticosteroids, and, in some cases, antihistamines. See the package inserts or *Antihistamines (Systemic), Corticosteroids—Glucocorticoid Effects (Systemic),* or *Sympathomimetic Agents—Cardiovascular Use (Parenteral-Systemic)* monographs for specific dosing guidelines for individual agents.

For renal failure—Dialysis may be needed. However, dialysis is not likely to assist in removing ketorolac from the body after an overdose; decreased clearance and prolongation of half-life have been reported in patients receiving dialysis.

Oral Dosage Forms

KETOROLAC TROMETHAMINE TABLETS USP

Usual adult dose

Analgesic:—

Oral, as a continuation of initial parenteral therapy

Patients 16 to 64 years of age who weigh at least 50 kg and have normal renal function—

20 mg initially, followed by 10 mg up to four times a day at four- to six-hour intervals as needed.

Patients weighing less than 50 kg; and/or

Patients with renal function impairment—

10 mg up to four times a day, at four- to six-hour intervals as needed.

Note: The recommended doses and frequency of administration should not be increased if pain relief is inadequate or breakthrough pain occurs between doses. Supplemental doses of opioid analgesic may be used, if not contraindicated, to provide additional analgesia.

Usual adult prescribing limits

Oral, 40 mg per day. The duration of treatment (parenteral followed by oral administration) is not to exceed five days.

Usual pediatric dose

Patients up to 16 years of age—Safety and efficacy have not been established.

Usual geriatric dose

Analgesic—

Oral, as a continuation of initial parenteral therapy: 10 mg up to four times a day at four- to six-hour intervals as needed.

Note: The recommended doses and frequency of administration should not be increased if pain relief is inadequate or breakthrough pain occurs between doses. Supplemental doses of opioid analgesic may be used, if not contraindicated, to provide additional analgesia.

Usual geriatric prescribing limits

Oral, 40 mg per day. The duration of treatment (parenteral followed by oral administration) is not to exceed five days.

Strength(s) usually available

U.S.—

10 mg (Rx) [*Toradol* (lactose)].

Canada—

10 mg (Rx) [*Toradol* (lactose)].

Packaging and storage

Store between 15 and 30 °C (59 and 86 °F), unless otherwise specified by manufacturer. Protect from light and excessive humidity.

Parenteral Dosage Forms

Note: Bracketed uses in the *Dosage Forms* section refer to categories of use and/or indications that are not included in U.S. product labeling.

KETOROLAC TROMETHAMINE INJECTION USP

Usual adult dose

Analgesic: Patients 16 to 64 years of age who weigh at least 50 kg and have normal renal function—

Intramuscular, a single dose of 60 mg followed, if necessary, by oral ketorolac (see *Ketorolac Tromethamine Tablets USP*) or by other analgesic therapy, or

Intramuscular, 30 mg every six hours, up to a maximum of twenty doses given over five days, or

Intravenous, 30 mg as a single dose or as multiple doses administered every six hours, up to a maximum of twenty doses given over five days.

Patients weighing less than 50 kg; and/or

Patients with renal function impairment—

Intramuscular, a single dose of 30 mg followed, if necessary, by oral ketorolac (see *Ketorolac Tromethamine Tablets USP*) or by other analgesic therapy, or

Intramuscular, 15 mg every six hours, up to a maximum of twenty doses given over five days, or

Intravenous, 15 mg as a single dose or as multiple doses administered every six hours, up to a maximum of twenty doses given over five days.

Note: The recommended doses and frequency of administration should not be increased if pain relief is inadequate or breakthrough pain occurs between doses. Supplemental doses of opioid analgesic may be used, if not contraindicated, to provide additional analgesia.

Usual adult prescribing limits

Patients 16 to 64 years of age who weigh at least 50 kg and have normal renal function—

Intramuscular or intravenous, 120 mg per day. The duration of therapy is not to exceed five days.

Patients weighing less than 50 kg; and/or

Patients with renal function impairment—

Intramuscular or intravenous, 60 mg per day. The duration of therapy is not to exceed five days.

Usual pediatric dose

Patients up to 16 years of age—Safety and efficacy have not been established.

[Post operative pain management, short term use][1]—

Intravenous, 1 mg per kg of body weight alone or as an adjunct.

Usual geriatric dose

Analgesic—

Intramuscular, a single dose of 30 mg, followed, if necessary, by oral ketorolac (see *Ketorolac Tromethamine Tablets USP*) or by other analgesic therapy, or

Intramuscular, 15 mg every six hours, up to a maximum of twenty doses administered over five days, or

Intravenous, 15 mg as a single dose or as multiple doses administered every six hours, up to a maximum of twenty doses administered over five days.

Note: The recommended doses and frequency of administration should not be increased if pain relief is inadequate or breakthrough pain occurs between doses. Supplemental doses of opioid analgesic may be used, if not contraindicated, to provide additional analgesia.

Usual geriatric prescribing limits

Intramuscular or intravenous, 60 mg per day. The duration of therapy is not to exceed five days.

Strength(s) usually available

U.S.—

1.5% (15 mg per mL) (Rx) [*Toradol* (alcohol 10%)].

3% (30 mg per mL; 60 mg per 2 mL) (Rx) [*Toradol* (alcohol 10%)].

Canada—

1% (10 mg per mL) (Rx) [*Toradol* (alcohol 10%)].

1.5% (15 mg per mL) (Rx) [*Toradol* (alcohol 10%)].

3% (30 mg per mL; 60 mg per 2 mL) (Rx) [*Toradol* (alcohol 10%)].

Note: The product containing 60 mg in 2 mL is not recommended for intravenous administration.

Packaging and storage

Store between 15 and 30 °C (59 and 86 °F), unless otherwise specified by manufacturer. Protect from light.

Incompatibilities

Ketorolac and morphine should not be mixed in the same syringe.

[1]Not included in Canadian product labeling.

Selected Bibliography

O'Hara DA, Fragen RJ, Kinzer M, et al. Ketorolac tromethamine as compared with morphine sulfate for treatment of postoperative pain. Clin Pharmacol Ther 1987 May; 41: 556-61.

Revised: 08/04/2005

KETOTIFEN Ophthalmic

VA CLASSIFICATION (Primary): OP801

Commonly used brand name(s): *Zaditor*.

Note: For a listing of dosage forms and brand names by country availability, see *Dosage Forms* section(s).

Category

Antihistaminic (H_1-receptor), ophthalmic; mast cell stabilizer, ophthalmic; antiallergic, ophthalmic.

Indications

Accepted

Conjunctivitis, allergic (prophylaxis)—Ophthalmic ketotifen is indicated for the temporary prevention of itching of the eye due to allergic conjunctivitis.

Pharmacology/Pharmacokinetics

Physicochemical characteristics

Molecular weight—Ketotifen fumarate: 425.5.
pH—4.4 to 5.8

Mechanism of action/Effect

Ketotifen is a relatively selective, non-competitive histamine H_1-receptor antagonist and mast cell stabilizer. Ketotifen inhibits the release of mediators from cells involved in hypersensitivity reactions. Ketotifen also decreases chemotaxis and activation of eosinophils.

Onset of action

Within minutes of application.

Precautions to Consider

Mutagenicity

No mutagenicity was demonstrated in the following *in vitro* and *in vivo* models: Ames test, chromosomal aberration test with V79 Chinese hamster cells, micronucleus assay in mouse, and mouse dominant lethal test.

Pregnancy/Reproduction

Fertility—In male rats at oral doses ≥ 10 mg/kg per day (6667 times the maximum recommended human ocular dose [MRHOD] of 0.0015 mg/kg per day) for 70 days prior to mating, ketotifen caused mortality and decreased fertility. In female rats at oral doses of 50 mg/kg per day (33,333 times the MRHOD) for 15 days prior to mating, ketotifen did not impair fertility.

Pregnancy—Adequate and well-controlled studies in humans have not been done.

Ketotifen caused an increased incidence of retarded ossification of the sternebrae in the offspring of pregnant rabbits that have been given doses of 45 mg/kg per day (30,000 times the MRHOD) during organogenesis. However, no effects were observed in rabbits given doses up to 15 mg/kg per day (10,000 times the MRHOD) or rats treated with up to 100 mg/kg per day (66,667 times the MRHOD).

Ketotifen caused no biologically relevant embryofetal toxicity in pregnant rats given doses up to 100 mg/kg per day (66,667 times the MRHOD) and rabbits given doses up to 45 mg/kg per day (30,000 times the MRHOD) during organogenesis.

FDA Pregnancy Category C.

Postpartum—

In the offspring of the rats that received ketotifen orally from day 15 of pregnancy to day 21 postpartum at a dose of 15 mg/kg per day (33,333 times the MRHOD), the incidence of postnatal mortality was slightly increased, and body weight gain during the first 4 days postpartum was slightly decreased.

Breast-feeding

It is not known whether ophthalmic ketotifen is absorbed in sufficient quantities to be distributed into human breast milk. However, it has been found in the milk of nursing rats following oral administration.

Pediatrics

Appropriate studies on the relationship of age to the effects of ketotifen have not been performed in the pediatric population in children younger than 3 years of age. Safety and efficacy in children younger than 3 years of age have not been established.

Geriatrics

No information is available on the relationship of age to the effects of ophthalmic ketotifen in geriatric patients.

Medical considerations/Contraindications

The medical considerations/contraindications included have been selected on the basis of their potential clinical significance (reasons given in parentheses where appropriate)—not necessarily inclusive (» = major clinical significance).

Except under special circumstances, this medication should not be used when the following medical problem exist:

» Hypersensitivity to ketotifen or to any component of the ophthalmic solution, including benzalkonium chloride which is used as the preservative

Risk-benefit should be considered when the following medical problems exist:

» Eye irritation, contact lens-related
(ketotifen should not be used to treat contact lens related irritation)

Side/Adverse Effects

Note: In clinical trials, the side effects were generally mild and occurrences of the effects was similar to that of the underlying ocular disease being studied

The following side/adverse effects have been selected on the basis of their potential clinical significance (possible signs and symptoms in parentheses where appropriate)—not necessarily inclusive:

Those indicating need for medical attention

Incidence more frequent
Conjunctival injection (eye redness and swelling)—10 to 25%

Incidence less frequent—Less than 5%
Allergic reactions (eye redness; hives; itching; rash); ***conjunctivitis*** (eye redness and swelling); ***eye discharge; eye pain; increased itching of eyes; keratitis*** (eye redness, swelling and discomfort); ***rash***

Those indicating need for medical attention only if they continue or are bothersome

Incidence more frequent—10 to 25%
Headaches; rhinitis (stuffy or runny nose)

Incidence less frequent—Less than 5%
Burning or stinging; dry eyes; eyelid disorder; flu syndrome (fever, tiredness, achiness, and sore throat); ***lacrimation disorder*** (tearing); ***mydriasis*** (increase in size of pupils); ***pharyngitis*** (sore throat); ***photophobia*** (eye sensitivity to light)

Overdose

For more information on the management of overdose or unintentional ingestion, **contact a Poison Control Center** (see *Poison Control Center Listing*).

Clinical effects of overdose

No serious signs or symptoms occurred in clinical studies with ingestion of up to 20 mg of ketotifen fumarate. A 5 mL ketotifen bottle is equivalent to 1.725 mg of ketotifen fumarate.

Patient Consultation

As an aid to patient consultation, refer to *Advice for the Patient, Ketotifen (Ophthalmic)*.

In providing consultation, consider emphasizing the following selected information (» = major clinical significance):

Before using this medication

» Conditions affecting use, especially:
Hypersensitivity to ketotifen or components of the ophthalmic solution; ketotifen ophthalmic solution contains benzalkonium chloride, a preservative, which may be absorbed by soft contact lenses

Proper use of this medication

» Not wearing contact lenses if the eyes are red; not using ketotifen ophthalmic solution for contact lens–related irritation; removing contact lenses prior to administration; waiting at least 10 minutes after administration before reinserting lenses;

» Proper administration of eye drops

» Proper dosing
Missed dose: Applying as soon as possible; not applying if almost time for next dose; using next dose at regularly scheduled time; not doubling doses.

» Proper storage

Precautions while using this medication

» Checking with physician if symptoms do not improve or if condition worsens

Side/adverse effects

Signs of potential side effects, especially conjunctival injection, allergic reactions, conjunctivitis, eye discharge, eye pain, increased itching of eyes, keratitis, and rash

General Dosing Information

For topical ophthalmic use only. Not for injection or oral use.

Ketotifen contains benzalkonium chloride, which may be absorbed by soft contact lenses. Contact lenses should be removed prior to administration of ketotifen. Lenses may be reinserted 10 minutes after administration.

Ophthalmic Dosage Forms

Note: The dosing and strength of the dosage form available are expressed in terms of ketotifen base.

KETOTIFEN FUMARATE OPHTHALMIC SOLUTION

Usual adult and adolescent Dose

Allergic conjunctivitis (prophylaxis)—

Topical to the conjunctiva, 1 drop in each affected eye every 8 to 12 hours.

Usual pediatric dose

Allergic conjunctivitis (prophylaxis)—

Children younger than 3 years of age: Safety and efficacy have not been established.

Children 3 years of age and older: See *Usual adult and adolescent dose.*

Strength(s) usually available

U.S.—

Note: Each mL contains 0.345 mg ketotifen fumarate, which is equivalent to 0.25 mg ketotifen base.

0.025% (0.25 mg ketotifen [base] per mL) (Rx) [*Zaditor* (benzalkonium chloride 0.01%; glycerol; sodium hydroxide/hydrochloric acid; purified water)].

Packaging and storage

Store between 4 and 25 °C (39 and 77 °F).

Auxiliary labeling

- For the eye.

Revised: 10/28/1999
Developed: 10/13/1999

KETOTIFEN Systemic*

VA CLASSIFICATION (Primary): RE190

Commonly used brand name(s): *Apo-Ketotifen; Novo-Ketotifen; Zaditen.*

Note: For a listing of dosage forms and brand names by country availability, see *Dosage Forms* section(s).

*Not commercially available in U.S.

Category

Asthma prophylactic, systemic; Antiallergic, systemic.

Indications

Accepted

Asthma, atopic (prophylaxis)—Oral ketotifen is indicated as an add-on medication in the chronic treatment of mild atopic asthmatic children. Ketotifen is a prophylactic agent to be used on a continuous basis and is not effective in the acute prevention or treatment of acute asthma attacks.

Pharmacology/Pharmacokinetics

Physicochemical characteristics

Molecular weight—Ketotifen fumarate: 425.5.

pKa—Ka I = 8.43 ± 0.11.

Solubility—In the form of hydrogen fumarate it is readily soluble in water. Ketotifen is stable in slightly acidic solution.

Partition coefficient—

Chloroform/hydrochloric acid 0.1 N 1.2:1
n-Octanol/hydrochloric acid 0.1 N 0.7:1
Chloroform/phosphate buffer pH 6.8, 0.05 M >100:1
n-Octanol/phosphate buffer pH 6.8, 0.05 M >100:1

Mechanism of action/Effect

Ketotifen is a non-bronchodilator antiasthmatic drug which inhibits the effects of certain endogenous substances known to be inflammatory mediators, and thereby exerts antiallergic activity. Ketotifen possesses a powerful and sustained non-competitive histamine (H_1) blocking property. Ketotifen's antihistamine (H_1) effect seems to be distinct from its antiallergic properties. Properties of ketotifen which may contribute to its antiallergic activity and its ability to affect the underlying pathology of asthma include: *In Vivo* results: Inhibition of the development of airway hyperreactivity associated with activation of platelets by PAF (Platelet Activating Factor) or caused by neural activation following the use of sympathomimetic drugs or the exposure to allergen; inhibition of PAF-induced accumulation of eosinophils and platelets in the airways; suppression of the priming of eosinophils by human recombinant cytokines and thereby suppression of the influx of eosinophils into inflammatory loci; antagonism of bronchoconstriction due to leukotrienes. *In Vitro* results: Inhibition of the release of allergic mediators such as histamine, leukotrienes C_4 and D_4 (SRS-A) and PAF.

Absorption

Following oral administration absorption is at least 60%, and possibly even greater. The rate of absorption is rapid with an absorption half-life of 1 hour. Bioavailability is about 50% due to a large first pass effect.

Bioavailability is not affected by the intake of food.

Protein binding

High (75%)

The percentage of protein binding is concentration-independent.

Biotransformation

Ketotifen undergoes a large first pass effect in the liver (approximately 50%).

The main metabolite found in both plasma and urine is the inactive ketotifen-N-glucuronide. Nor-ketotifen, the N-demethylated metabolite, and the 10−hydroxyl derivative are the only other metabolites detectable in human urine. Both the 10−hydroxyl derivative and N-glucuronide conjugate may reform the intact product by *in vivo* reversibility.

The pattern of metabolism in children over the age of 3 years is the same as in adults, but the clearance is higher in children.

Half-life

Distribution—3 to 5 hours.

Elimination—21 hours.

Onset of action

Clinical improvements have been observed in some cases within the first week of treatment and generally reach statistical significance after ten weeks.

Time to peak concentration

2 to 4 hours.

Time to steady-state concentration

Less than 4 days.

Elimination

Within 48 hours, urinary excretion amounts to 1% as unchanged drug and 60% to 70% as metabolites.

Clearance is higher in children.

Precautions to Consider

Pregnancy/Reproduction

Fertility—In female rats treated orally with ketotifen fumarate at doses of 2, 10, and 50 mg/kg for two weeks, subsequent mating with untreated males showed no adverse effects on the fertility of the females at any dose level. In male rats treated orally for 70 days with 2, 10, and 50 mg/kg of ketotifen fumarate, no adverse effects were observed on fertility up to the dose of 10 mg/kg. In the 50 mg/kg group, a decreased copulation and fertility index was seen.

Pregnancy—Adequate and well-controlled studies in humans have not been done.

Following oral or intravenous administration in rats, ketotifen passes the maternal/fetal barrier; however, only low levels were found in the fetal tissues.

No teratogenic or embryolethal effects were seen when ketotifen was given to female rats in doses of 10, 30, 56, and 100 mg/kg/day between the sixth and fifteenth day of pregnancy. Maternal weight gain and total body weight were decreased at the 56 and 100 mg/kg/day dose levels. The 100 mg/kg dose was lethal to some of the adult animals. In rabbits, no teratogenic or embryolethal effects were seen following ketotifen treatment by gavage at daily doses of 5, 15, and 45 mg/kg between the sixth and eighteenth day of pregnancy.

In male rats treated orally for seventy days with 2, 10, and 50 mg/kg of ketotifen, no adverse effects were observed on the development of the offspring up to the dose of 10 mg/kg. In the 50 mg/kg group, an increased pre and postnatal mortality of the offspring was seen. However, high mortality occurred in males in the 10 and 50 mg/kg groups.

In female rats treated orally with ketotifen at doses of 2, 10, and 50 mg/kg for two weeks, subsequent mating with untreated males showed no adverse effects on the development of their offspring at any dose level. Impairment of weight gain and increased mortality was seen in mothers treated with 10 and 50 mg/kg.

In female rats treated orally with 2, 10, and 50 mg/kg of ketotifen from day fifteen postcoitum to day twenty-one postpartum, no adverse effects on the pre and postnatal development of the offspring were found in the two lower dose groups. However, the 50 mg/kg dose produced mortality in 10% of the mothers as well as an increase loss of pups, resulting in slightly decreased litter size and reduced weight gain during the first four days.

Postpartum—

In female rats treated orally with 2, 10, and 50 mg/kg of ketotifen from day fifteen postcoitum to day twenty-one postpartum, no adverse effects on the pre and postnatal development of the offspring were found in the two lower dose groups. However, the 50 mg/kg dose produced mortality in 10% of the mothers as well as an increase loss of pups, resulting in slightly decreased litter size and reduced weight gain during the first four days.

Breast-feeding

Ketotifen is distributed into the milk of rats and may be distributed into human breast milk. Women who take this medication should not breast-feed.

Pediatrics

Appropriate studies performed to date have not demonstrated pediatrics-specific problems that would limit the usefulness of ketotifen in children.

Geriatrics

No information is available on the relationship of age to the effects of ketotifen in geriatric patients.

Drug interactions and/or related problems

The following drug interactions and/or related problems have been selected on the basis of their potential clinical significance (possible mechanism in parentheses where appropriate)—not necessarily inclusive (» = major clinical significance):

Note: Combinations containing any of the following medications, depending on the amount present, may also interact with this medication.

» Antidiabetic agents, oral
(concomitant use with ketotifen may result in reversible thrombocytopenia; platelet counts are recommended during concurrent use)

» Alcohol or
» Antihistamines or
» Hypnotics or
» Sedatives
(concurrent use with ketotifen may potentiate the CNS depressant effects of these medications)

Laboratory value alterations

The following have been selected on the basis of their potential clinical significance (possible effect in parentheses where appropriate)—not necessarily inclusive (» = major clinical significance).

With physiology/laboratory test values
Liver enzymes
(elevated values were seen during clinical trials; however, no causal relationship could be established)

Medical considerations/Contraindications

The medical considerations/contraindications included have been selected on the basis of their potential clinical significance (reasons given in parentheses where appropriate)—not necessarily inclusive (» = major clinical significance).

Except under special circumstances, this medication should not be used when the following medical problem exists:

» Hypersensitivity to ketotifen or to any other component of the formulations, including benzoate compounds which are only present in the syrup.

Risk-benefit should be considered when the following medical problems exist:

» Diabetes mellitus
(carbohydrate content of the syrup (5 mL = 4 grams carbohydrate) should be taken into consideration; use ketotifen with caution if taking an oral antidiabetic agent)

» Epilepsy
(ketotifen may lower the seizure threshold)

Patient monitoring

The following may be especially important in patient monitoring (other tests may be warranted in some patients, depending on condition; » = major clinical significance):

» Platelet count
(recommended in patients taking oral antidiabetic agents concomitantly)

Side/Adverse Effects

Note: In one clinical trial, there was a relatively low incidence of adverse reactions reported. Adverse reactions were similar in both the ketotifen and placebo treated groups of patients.

The following side/adverse effects have been selected on the basis of their potential clinical significance (possible signs and symptoms in parentheses where appropriate)—not necessarily inclusive:

Those indicating need for medical attention

Incidence less frequent

Flu (chills; cough; diarrhea; fever; general feeling of discomfort or illness; headache; joint pain; loss of appetite; muscle aches and pains; nausea; runny nose; shivering; sore throat; sweating; trouble sleeping; unusual tiredness or weakness; vomiting); ***respiratory infection*** (cough; fever; sore throat)

Incidence rare

Cystitis (bloody or cloudy urine; difficult, burning, or painful urination; frequent urge to urinate); ***erythema multiforme*** (blistering, itching, peeling, or redness of skin; joint pain; muscle pain; unusual tiredness or weakness); ***hepatitis*** (abdominal or stomach pain; chills; clay-colored stools; dark urine; diarrhea; dizziness; fever; headache; itching; loss of appetite; nausea; rash; unpleasant breath odor; unusual tiredness or weakness; vomiting of blood; yellow eyes or skin); ***seizures*** (convulsions; muscle spasm or jerking of all extremities; sudden loss of consciousness)

Those indicating need for medical attention only if they continue or are bothersome

Incidence more frequent

Weight gain

Incidence less frequent or rare

Abdominal pain (stomach or abdomen pain); ***central nervous system (CNS) stimulation*** (excitation; irritability; insomnia; nervousness)—particularly in children; ***dizziness; dryness of mouth; epistaxis*** (bloody nose; unexplained nosebleeds); ***increased appetite; sedation*** (drowsiness); ***skin rash; sleep disturbance*** (trouble sleeping); ***swelling of eyelids***

Note: *Dizziness*, *dryness of mouth*, and *sedation* may occur at the beginning of ketotifen treatment but usually disappear with continued use.

Overdose

For specific information on the agents used in the management of ketotifen toxicity or overdose, see:
- *Barbiturates (Systemic)* monograph; and/or
- *Benzodiazepines (Systemic)* monograph; and/or
- *Charcoal, Activated (Oral-Local)* monograph; and/or
- *Physostigmine (Systemic)* monograph.

For more information on the management of overdose or unintentional ingestion, **contact a poison control center** (see *Poison Control Center Listing*).

Clinical effects of overdose

The following effects have been selected on the basis of their potential clinical significance (possible signs and symptoms in parentheses where appropriate)—not necessarily inclusive:

Acute

Coma (loss of consciousness)—reversible; ***confusion*** (disorientation); ***convulsions*** (seizures)—especially in children; ***hyperexcitability***—in children; ***hypotension*** (blurred vision; confusion; dizziness; faintness, or lightheadedness when getting up from a lying or sitting position; sweating; unusual tiredness or weakness); ***sedation*** (drowsiness)—mild to severe; ***tachycardia*** (fainting; fast, pounding, or irregular heartbeat or pulse; palpitations)

Treatment of overdose

Treatment is generally symptomatic and supportive, possibly including:

To decrease absorption—
If ingestion is very recent, emptying of the stomach may be considered. Administration of activated charcoal may be benefi-

cial. See the package insert or *Charcoal, Activated (Oral-Local)* for specific dosing guidelines for use of this product.

Specific treatment—

If necessary, specific or symptomatic treatment and monitoring of the cardiovascular system and physostigmine for anticholinergic effects are recommended. See the package insert or *Physostigmine (Systemic)* for specific dosing guidelines for use of this product.

If excitation or convulsions are present, short-acting barbiturates or benzodiazepine may be given. See the specific package inserts or *Barbiturates (Systemic)* or *Benzodiazepines (Systemic)* for specific dosing guidelines for use of these products.

Monitoring—

Monitor the cardiovascular system.

Supportive care—

Patients in whom intentional overdose is confirmed or suspected should be referred for psychiatric consultation.

Patient Consultation

As an aid to patient consultation, refer to *Advice for the Patient, Ketotifen (Systemic).*

In providing consultation, consider emphasizing the following selected information (» = major clinical significance):

Before using this medication

» Conditions affecting use, especially:

Hypersensitivity to ketotifen or to any other component of the formulations, including benzoate compounds which are only present in the syrup.

Breast-feeding—May be distributed into human breast milk; women taking ketotifen should not breast-feed

Other medications, especially antidiabetic agents (oral), alcohol, antihistamines, hypnotics, or sedatives

Other medical problems, especially diabetes mellitus or epilepsy

Proper use of this medication

» Helps prevent, but does not relieve, acute asthma attacks

» Ketotifen must be used continuously to be effective

Continuing current asthma medications unless otherwise directed by physician

» Ketotifen may be taken with or without food

» Proper dosing

Missed dose: Taking as soon as possible; not taking if almost time for next scheduled dose; not doubling doses

Proper storage

Precautions while using this medication

» Regular visits to physician to check progress during therapy

» Since drowsiness and, rarely, slight dizziness may occur in the early stages of therapy caution is advised; not driving, using machines, or doing anything else that requires alertness while taking ketotifen

» Occasionally, symptoms of central nervous system (CNS) stimulation, such as excitation, irritability, insomnia, and nervousness have been observed, particularly in children

» For patients with diabetes: Recognizing that ketotifen syrup contains 4 grams of carbohydrate in every 5 mL; glucose concentrations may be affected

Side/adverse effects

Signs of potential side effects, especially flu, respiratory infection, cystitis, erythema multiforme, hepatitis, and seizures

General Dosing Information

Ketotifen must be taken continuously to be effective. Clinical effectiveness is generally reached after 10 weeks of treatment. For patients not adequately responding within a few weeks, treatment should be maintained for a minimum of 2 to 3 months. Continuous use may reduce the frequency, severity, and duration of asthmatic symptoms or attacks, and lead to a reduction in daily requirements of concomitant antiasthmatic medication. If it is necessary to withdraw ketotifen, this should be done progressively over a period of 2 to 4 weeks.

To minimize initial sedation, a slow increase in dosage is recommended during the first week of treatment commencing with one half the daily recommended dosage given in two divided doses or in a single dose given in the evening, followed within 5 days, by an increase to the full therapeutic dose.

Existing asthma therapy should be maintained. A progressive reduction in dosage of other asthma drugs, where clinically indicated, should be attempted only after 6 to 12 weeks of ketotifen therapy. Reduction in the dosage of corticosteroids and/or ACTH should be completed in a gradual manner according to accepted and recommended methods. Patients should be monitored carefully during the dosage reduction period. If symptoms recur during the period of dosage reduction, the daily dose of the drug(s) should be raised immediately.

Diet/Nutrition

Ketotifen may be taken with or without food.

Oral Dosage Forms

KETOTIFEN FUMARATE SYRUP

Usual adult and adolescent dose

Asthma, atopic (prophylaxis)—

Oral, 5 mL (1 mg) twice daily, in the morning and evening.

Usual pediatric dose

Asthma, atopic (prophylaxis)—

Infants and children 6 months to 3 years of age: Oral, 0.25 mL (50 mcg or 0.05 mg) per kg of body weight twice daily, in the morning and evening.

Children older than 3 years of age: See *Usual adult and adolescent dose.*

Strength(s) usually available

U.S.—

Not commercially available.

Canada—

1 mg per 5 mL (Rx) [*Apo-Ketotifen* (artificial strawberry flavor; citric acid; glycerin; purified water; methylparaben; propylparaben; sodium citrate; sorbitol; sucrose); *Novo-Ketotifen* (alcohol; citric acid; strawberry flavor; methyl p-hydroxybenzoate; propyl-p-hydroxybenzoate; sodium phosphate; sorbitol solution; sucrose; water); *Zaditen* (alcohol; citric acid; propyl-p-hydroxybenzoate; sodium phosphate; methyl p-hydroxybenzoate; sorbitol solution; sucrose; strawberry flavor; water)].

Packaging and storage

Store at temperatures not exceeding 25 °C (77 °F).

Auxiliary labeling

- Avoid alcoholic beverages.
- May cause drowsiness.
- For oral use.

Caution

Patients who are sensitive to benzoate compounds should not use benzoate-containing brands of ketotifen syrup.

KETOTIFEN FUMARATE TABLETS

Usual adult and adolescent dose

Asthma, atopic (prophylaxis)—

Oral, 1 mg twice daily in the morning and evening.

Usual pediatric dose

Asthma, atopic (prophylaxis)—

Children older than 3 years of age—

See *Usual adult and adolescent dose*

Infants and children from 6 months to 3 years of age—

See *Ketotifen Fumarate Syrup.*

Strength(s) usually available

U.S.—

Not commercially available.

Canada—

1 mg (Rx) [*Novo-Ketotifen* (cornstarch; lactose; magnesium stearate; water); *Zaditen* (scored; calcium hydrogen phosphate, magnesium stearate, maize starch)].

Packaging and storage

Store at temperatures not exceeding 25 °C (77 °F), in a dry place.

Auxiliary labeling

- Avoid alcoholic beverages.
- May cause drowsiness.
- Swallow tablet whole.

Developed: 08/02/2000

LABETALOL—See *Beta-adrenergic Blocking Agents (Systemic)*

LACTULOSE—See *Laxatives (Local)*

LAMIVUDINE Systemic

VA CLASSIFICATION (Primary): AM840

Commonly used brand name(s): *3TC; Epivir; Epivir-HBV; Heptovir.*

Another commonly used name is 3TC

Note: For a listing of dosage forms and brand names by country availability, see *Dosage Forms* section(s).

Category

Antiviral (systemic).

Indications

Note: Bracketed information in the *Indications* section refers to uses that are not included in U.S. product labeling.

General Considerations

Lamivudine is the negative enantiomer of 2'-deoxy-3'-thiacytidine. Both the positive and negative enantiomers have *in vitro* activity against human immunodeficiency virus (HIV), but the negative enantiomer has greater activity and less toxicity. *In vitro* inhibition of DNA polymerase gamma, which is thought to be associated with peripheral neuropathy, is minimal.

Lamivudine has *in vitro* activity against HIV-1 and HIV-2, including zidovudine-resistant isolates, as well as hepatitis B virus. Lamivudine is indicated in combination with other antiretroviral agents for the treatment of HIV infection. Lamivudine and zidovudine have been found to act synergistically *in vitro* . This is thought to produce better efficacy than either medication alone. Resistance to lamivudine is associated with a mutation at codon 184 in HIV-1 reverse transcriptase; this can suppress the expression of pre-existing resistance to zidovudine in a number of different HIV isolates. Strains of HIV-1 resistant to both lamivudine and zidovudine have been isolated. Reduced sensitivity of hepatitis B virus (HBV) to lamivudine is related to mutations resulting in a methionine to valine or isoleucine substitution in the YMDD motif of the catalytic domain of HBV polymerase (position 552) and a leucine to methionine substitution at position 528.

Accepted

Hepatitis B, chronic (treatment)—Lamivudine is indicated in the treatment of chronic hepatitis B associated with evidence of hepatitis B viral replication and active liver inflammation. This use is based on 1–year histologic and serologic responses in patients with compensated chronic hepatitis B.

Human immunodeficiency virus (HIV) infection (treatment) or Immunodeficiency syndrome, acquired (AIDS) (treatment)—Lamivudine is indicated, in combination with zidovudineor other antiretroviral agents, in the treatment of HIV infection or AIDS when therapy is warranted based on clinical and/or immunological evidence of disease progression.

[Human immunodeficiency virus (HIV) infection, occupational exposure (prophylaxis)][1]—Lamivudine may be used prophylactically in health care workers at risk of acquiring HIV infection after occupational exposure to the virus. It is being used in combination with zidovudine and, in some cases, a protease inhibitor.

[1]Not included in Canadian product labeling.

Pharmacology/Pharmacokinetics

Physicochemical characteristics

Molecular weight—229.26.

Mechanism of action/Effect

Lamivudine, a synthetic nucleoside analogue, is phosphorylated intracellularly to its active 5'-triphosphate metabolite, lamivudine triphosphate (L-TP). The nucleoside analogue is incorporated into viral DNA by HIV reverse transcriptase and HBV polymerase, resulting in DNA chain termination. L-TP is a weak inhibitor of mammalian alpha-, beta-, and gamma-DNA polymerases.

Absorption

Rapidly absorbed; bioavailability in adults and adolescents is 80 to 88% and in children is approximately 66 to 68%. Food delays the peak serum concentration and the time to peak serum concentration; however, there is no significant difference in bioavailability. Therefore, lamivudine may be administered with or without food.

Distribution

Lamivudine is widely distributed. Lamivudine crosses the blood-brain barrier and is distributed into the cerebrospinal fluid (CSF) to a limited extent. In children, CSF concentrations ranged from 10 to 17% of the corresponding, non–steady-state serum concentration. Lamivudine crosses the placenta in rats, rabbits, and humans.

Apparent Vol_D= Approximately 1.3 liters per kg.

Protein binding

Low (36%).

Biotransformation

Trans-sulfoxide is the only known metabolite of lamivudine; serum concentrations of this metabolite have not been determined.

Half-life

Intracellular lamivudine triphosphate—
- 11 to 15 hours.

Lamivudine (serum)—
- Adults: 2.6 ± 0.5 hours.
- Children (4 months to 14 years of age): 1.7 to 2 hours.

Renal function impairment—
- Creatinine clearance, 10 to 40 mL per min (mL/min) (0.17 to 0.67 mL per sec [mL/sec])—Approximately 13.6 hours.
- Creatinine clearance, less than 10 mL/min (0.17 mL/sec)—Approximately 19.4 hours.

Time to peak concentration

Approximately 0.5 to 2 hours after a single 100–milligram dose.
- With food—
  - Approximately 3.2 hours.
- Fasting—
  - Approximately 1 hour.

Peak serum concentration

Adults and adolescents—
- 2 mg per kg of body weight (mg/kg): 1.5 micrograms per mL (mcg/mL) (6.5 micromoles per liter).

Children—
- 8 mg/kg: 1.1 mcg/mL (4.8 micromoles per liter).

Elimination

Renal; the majority of lamivudine is eliminated unchanged in the urine (68 to 71%); approximately 5.2% of the trans-sulfoxide metabolite is excreted in the urine within 12 hours. The renal clearance of lamivudine is greater than the glomerular filtration rate, implying active secretion into the renal tubules.

In dialysis—
- Hemodialysis increases lamivudine clearance by a mean of 24 mL/min, however, the length of dialysis treatment (i.e., 4 hours) may not be long enough to alter mean lamivudine exposure. Thus, dose modification beyond correction for creatinine clearance is not required after routine hemodialysis or peritoneal dialysis.
- It is not known whether lamivudine is removed by continuous (24 hour) hemodialysis.

Precautions to Consider

Carcinogenicity

Studies in mice and rats given lamivudine doses 10 times and 58 times the human therapeutic HIV dose, respectively, have shown no evidence of carcinogenic potential. Studies in mice and rats given 34 times and 200 times the human therapeutic hepatitis B dose, respectively, have shown no evidence of carcinogenic potential.

Mutagenicity

Lamivudine was not active in a microbial mutagenicity screen or in an *in vitro* cell transformation assay. It showed weak *in vitro* mutagenic activity in a cytogenic assay using cultured human lymphocytes and in the mouse lymphoma assay. However, lamivudine showed no evidence of *in vivo* genotoxic activity in rats at oral doses of up to 2000 mg per kg of body weight (mg/kg), which is approximately 65 times the recommended human dose based on body surface area.

Pregnancy/Reproduction

Fertility—Rats given doses of lamivudine up to 130 times the usual adult dose based on body surface area revealed no evidence of impaired fertility No evidence of impaired fertility or adverse effects on offspring were noted in rats given doses up to 4000 mg per kg daily (plasma levels 80 to 120 times those in humans).

Pregnancy—Adequate and well-controlled studies have not been done in humans. However, lamivudine has been found to cross the placenta in humans.

Lamivudine crosses the placenta in rats and rabbits. Studies have been done in rats and rabbits administered doses up to approximately 130 and 60 times the usual adult dose, respectively. Some evidence of embryo lethality in rabbits, but not in rats, at doses similar to the usual adult dose or higher has been seen.

Lamivudine should be used during pregnancy only if the potential benefits outweigh the risks.

FDA Pregnancy Category C.

Note: Physicians are encouraged to register patients in the Lamivudine Pregnancy Registry, a registry set up to monitor maternal-fetal outcomes of exposure to lamivudine during pregnancy, by calling 800–258–4263.

Breast-feeding

Lamivudine is distributed into human breast milk.

The Centers for Disease Control and Prevention and the manufacturer recommend that patients not breast-feed while taking lamivudine to avoid risking postnatal transmission of HIV infection and because of the potential for serious adverse reactions in nursing infants.

Pediatrics

In one study, pancreatitis was reported in 14 of 97 (14%) and paresthesias and peripheral neuropathies were seen in 13 of 97 (13%) of pediatric patients receiving lamivudine monotherapy. However, the patients who developed these complications had advanced HIV disease and a prior history of pancreatitis, most commonly associated with the use of didanosine. The combination of lamivudine and zidovudine should be used with caution in children with advanced HIV disease and/or a history of pancreatitis. In addition, an increase in serum transaminases (greater than 10 times the upper limits of normal) was observed in 3 of 89 (3%) of pediatric patients receiving lamivudine monotherapy.

The safety and pharmacokinetic properties of lamivudine in combination with antiretroviral agents other than zidovudine have not been established in pediatric patients. The safety and efficacy of twice-daily lamivudine in combination with other antiretroviral agents have been established in pediatric patients 3 months of age and older. Pharmacokinetic properties of lamivudine monotherapy were assessed in 57 children (ages 4.8 months to 16 years). The absolute bioavailability was 66 to 68%, which is less than the 86% seen in adults and adolescents. The mechanism for this diminished bioavailability in infants and children is unknown. The area under the serum concentration-time curve (AUC) was comparable for pediatric patients receiving a dose of 8 mg/kg per day and adults receiving a dose of 4 mg/kg per day.

Geriatrics

Although appropriate studies on the relationship of age to the effects of lamivudine have not been performed in the geriatric population, no geriatrics-specific problems have been documented to date. However, dose selection for an elderly patient should be cautious, reflecting the greater frequency of decreased hepatic, renal, or cardiac function, and of concomitant disease or other drug therapy. Because lamivudine is excreted by the kidney and elderly patients may be more likely to have decreased renal function, renal function should be monitored and dosage adjustments made accordingly

Lamivudine pharmacokinetics have not been studied in patients over 65 years of age.

Drug interactions and/or related problems

The following drug interactions and/or related problems have been selected on the basis of their potential clinical significance (possible mechanism in parentheses where appropriate)—not necessarily inclusive (» = major clinical significance):

Note: Lamivudine tablets and oral solution for treatment of human immunodeficiency virus (HIV) contain a higher dose than lamivudine tablets and oral solution for treatment of hepatitis B; the two formulations of lamivudine (higher- and lower-dose tablets/oral solution) should not be used concurrently. Combinations containing any of the following medications, depending on the amount present, may also interact with this medication.

Drugs associated with pancreatitis, such as alcohol, didanosine, intravenous pentamidine or sulfonamides
(pancreatitis was seen in 14% (14 of 97) of pediatric patients receiving lamivudine monotherapy; this population had advanced HIV disease and a history of pancreatitis; although no interactions have been documented to date, concurrent use of lamivudine with medications associated with the development of pancreatitis should be avoided or, if concurrent use is necessary, used with caution)

Drugs associated with peripheral neuropathy, such as dapsone, didanosine, isoniazid or stavudine
(paresthesias and peripheral neuropathy were seen in 13% (13 of 97) of pediatric patients with advanced HIV disease receiving lamivudine monotherapy; although no interactions have been documented to date, other medications associated with the development of neuropathy should be avoided or, if concurrent use is necessary, used with caution)

Indinavir
(concurrent administration of lamivudine 150 mg twice a day, indinavir 800 mg every eight hours, and zidovudine 200 mg every eight hours resulted in a 6% decrease in the AUC of lamivudine, no change in AUC of indinavir, and a 36% increase in the AUC of zidovudine; no adjustment in dose is necessary)

» Lamivudine and zidovudine
(lamivudine and zidovudine fixed dose combination tablet should not be administered concomitantly with lamivudine tablets or lamivudine oral solution.)

Sulfamethoxazole and trimethoprim combination
(concurrent sulfamethoxazole (800 mg)/trimethoprim (160 mg) once daily increased lamivudine AUC by 44% and decreased both oral and renal clearance by approximately 30%; pharmacokinetics of SMX/TMP were not altered; no dose adjustment is necessary unless the patient has renal impairment; it is unknown if higher doses of SMX/TMP have a greater effect on lamivudine pharmacokinetics)

» Zalcitabine
(Lamivudine and zalcitabine may inhibit the phosphorylation of one another and concurrent administration is not recommended)

Zidovudine
(in one small study, concurrent administration of lamivudine resulted in a 39% increase in the peak plasma concentration of zidovudine; although statistically significant, this increase is not thought to be significant to patient safety; no significant changes were observed in the AUC or total clearance of lamivudine or zidovudine)

Laboratory value alterations

The following have been selected on the basis of their potential clinical significance (possible effect in parentheses where appropriate)—not necessarily inclusive (» = major clinical significance).

With physiology/laboratory test values

Alanine aminotransferase (ALT [SGPT]) and
Aspartate aminotransferase (AST [SGOT]) and
Bilirubin
(values may be increased)

Amylase, serum
(values may be increased)

Creatine phosphokinase (CPK)
(may be elevated with lamivudine administration for chronic hepatitis B)

Hemoglobin concentration and
Neutrophil count
(values may be decreased)

Medical considerations/Contraindications

The medical considerations/contraindications included have been selected on the basis of their potential clinical significance (reasons given in parentheses where appropriate)—not necessarily inclusive (» = major clinical significance).

Except under special circumstances, this medication should not be used when the following medical problem exists:

» Hypersensitivity to lamivudine or any components of this product
(lamivudine use contraindicated in patients with previously demonstrated clinically significant hypersensitivity)

Risk-benefit should be considered when the following medical problems exist:

» Antiretroviral nucleoside exposure, history of or
» Pancreatitis, history of or
» Other significant risk factors for development of pancreatitis
(pancreatitis occurred in 14% (14 of 97) of pediatric patients receiving lamivudine monotherapy; these patients had advanced HIV disease and a history of pancreatitis; lamivudine should be used with extreme caution; treatment should be discontinued immediately if clinical signs, symptoms, or laboratory abnormalities suggestive of pancreatitis occur)

Co-infection with
» Human immunodeficiency virus [HIV]
» Hepatitis B virus [HBV]
(safety and efficacy of lamivudine has not been established in patients infected with both of these viruses; lamivudine-resistant hepatitis B variants have developed in patients infected with both HIV and HBV receiving lamivudine-containing antiretroviral regimens; post-treatment exacerbation of hepatitis has also been reported)

Concomitant infection with safety and efficacy of lamivudine has not been established in patients infected with both hepatitis B and either of these viruses

» Hepatitis C or

» Hepatitis delta

» Diabetes mellitus

(lamivudine oral solution contains 200 mg of sucrose per milliliter)

» Hepatic disease or

» Risk factors for hepatic disease or

» Obesity or

» Prolonged nucleoside exposure

(lactic acidosis and severe hepatomegaly with steatosis have been reported in patients with the use of nucleoside analogues alone or in combination; fatal cases have been reported; obesity and prolonged nucleoside exposure may be risk factors; majority of cases have been in women; treatment should be suspended in patients with evidence of lactic acidosis or pronounced hepatotoxicity which may include hepatomegaly and steatosis even in the absence of marked transaminase elevations)

(patients previously treated with zidovudine plus didanosine or zalcitabine may have developed resistance to lamivudine)

» Hepatic disease, decompensated or

» Organ transplant recipients

(safety and efficacy of lamivudine have not been established in patients with these conditions)

Peripheral neuropathy, or history of

(peripheral neuropathy occurred in approximately 13% (13 of 97) of pediatric patients receiving lamivudine monotherapy; these patients had advanced HIV disease; it has also been reported rarely in adults; lamivudine should be used with caution in patients who have peripheral neuropathy or a history of peripheral neuropathy)

» Renal function impairment

(decreased renal function has been found to result in an increase in the peak plasma concentration and elimination half-life of lamivudine; dosage modification is recommended in patients with a creatinine clearance of < 50 mL/min [0.83 mL/sec])

Patient monitoring

The following may be especially important in patient monitoring (other tests may be warranted in some patients, depending on condition; » = major clinical significance):

Alanine aminotransferase (ALT [SGPT]) and

Aspartate aminotransferase (AST [SGOT])

(an increase in serum transaminases [greater than 10 times the upper limits of normal] was observed in 3 of 89 (3%) of pediatric patients receiving lamivudine monotherapy)

(exacerbation of hepatitis has occurred following discontinuation of lamivudine; post-treatment clinical and laboratory follow-up should be maintained for at least 4 months)

» Amylase, serum, and

» Lipase, serum, and

» Triglycerides, serum

(lamivudine administration has been associated with pancreatitis in approximately 14% of pediatric patients; patients should be monitored for laboratory changes consistent with pancreatitis, such as elevated amylase, lipase, and triglyceride concentrations)

» Blood urea nitrogen (BUN) and

» Creatinine, serum

(blood urea nitrogen and serum creatinine concentrations should be monitored in patients with renal function impairment; an adjustment in dosage or dosage interval may be required)

» Hepatic function

(severe acute exacerbations of hepatitis B have been reported in patients who are co-infected with hepatitis B virus [HBV] and HIV and have discontinued anti-hepatitis B therapy [including lamivudine]; should be monitored closely with both clinical and laboratory follow-up for at least several months in patients who discontinue lamivudine; initiation of anti-hepatitis B therapy may be warranted)

Side/Adverse Effects

Note: Lactic acidosis and severe hepatomegaly with steatosis, including fatal cases, have been reported with the use of nucleoside analogs, including lamivudine, alone or in combination. A majority of these cases have been in women. Obesity and prolonged nucleoside exposure may be risk factors.

Lamivudine is given in combination with other antiretroviral agents. Some side effects, such as pancreatitis, peripheral neuropathy and hematologic abnormalities may be seen with other antiretroviral agents, such as zidovudine, and/or severe human immunodeficiency virus (HIV) disease; therefore, differentiation between the side effects of lamivudine and other medications or the complications of HIV disease may be difficult.

In one study, 14 of 97 pediatric patients (14%) being treated with lamivudine monotherapy developed pancreatitis; in a second pediatric study, 7 of 47 patients (15%) receiving lamivudine in combination therapy with other antiretroviral agents developed pancreatitis. Pancreatitis was most commonly seen in patients who had advanced HIV disease, as well as a prior history of pancreatitis, most commonly associated with the use of didanosine. The combination of lamivudine and zidovudine therapy should be used with caution in pediatric patients with a history of pancreatitis or other risk factors for pancreatitis. Pancreatitis was seen in only 3 of 656 adult patients (< 0.5%) who received lamivudine. Lamivudine should be discontinued immediately if any signs or symptoms of pancreatitis occur. In addition, an increase in serum transaminases (greater than 10 times the upper limits of normal) was observed in 3 of 89 (3%) of pediatric patients receiving lamivudine monotherapy.

Paresthesias and peripheral neuropathy were reported in 13% of pediatric patients and have been reported rarely in adults.

The following side/adverse effects have been selected on the basis of their potential clinical significance (possible signs and symptoms in parentheses where appropriate)—not necessarily inclusive:

Those indicating need for medical attention

Incidence more frequent

Pancreatitis (nausea; vomiting; severe abdominal or stomach pain)—more frequent in children; ***paresthesias and peripheral neuropathy*** (tingling, burning, numbness, or pain in the hands, arms, feet, or legs; sensation of pins and needles, stabbing pain; unsteadiness, awkwardness)—more frequent in children; ***skin rash; splenomegaly*** (abdominal pain; feeling of fullness)—more frequent in children

Incidence rare

Anemia (unusual tiredness or weakness); ***severe hepatomegaly with steatosis*** (abdominal discomfort; feeling of fullness)—more frequent in children (11%); ***lactic acidosis*** (abdominal discomfort; decreased appetite; diarrhea; fast, shallow breathing; general feeling of discomfort; muscle pain or cramping; nausea; shortness of breath; sleepiness; unusual tiredness or weakness); ***neutropenia*** (fever, chills, or sore throat)

Incidence not determined—Observed during clinical practice, estimates of frequency can not be determined

Anaphylaxis (cough, difficulty swallowing, dizziness, fast heartbeat, hives, itching, puffiness or swelling of the eyelids or around the eyes, face, lips or tongue, shortness of breath, skin rash, tightness in chest, unusual tiredness or weakness, wheezing); ***hepatitis B, post-treatment exacerbation*** (dark urine, general tiredness and weakness, light-colored stools, nausea and vomiting, upper right abdominal pain, yellow eyes and skin); ***rhabdomyolysis*** (dark-colored urine, fever, muscle cramps or spasms, muscle pain or stiffness, unusual tiredness or weakness); ***urticaria*** (hives or welts, itching, redness of skin, skin rash)

Those indicating need for medical attention only if they continue or are bothersome

Incidence more frequent

Abdominal pain or cramps (stomach pain or cramps); ***anorexia and/or decreased appetite*** (loss of appetite, weight loss); ***arthralgia*** (pain in joints, muscle pain or stiffness, difficulty in moving); ***cough; depressive disorders*** (recurring symptoms of discouragement, feeling sad or empty, irritability, lack of appetite, loss of interest or pleasure, tiredness, trouble concentrating, trouble sleeping); ***diarrhea; dizziness; ear discharge, erythema, pain or swelling*** (redness of skin; unusually warm skin)—more frequent in children; ***ear, nose, and throat infections; fatigue*** (unusual tiredness or weakness); ***headache; insomnia and other sleep disorders*** (trouble sleeping); ***lymphadenopathy*** (swollen, painful, or tender lymph glands in neck, armpit, or groin)—more frequent in children; ***malaise*** (general feeling of discomfort or illness, unusual tiredness or weakness); ***musculoskeletal pain*** (muscle or bone pain); ***myalgia*** (joint pain, swollen joints, muscle aching or cramping, muscle pains or stiffness, difficulty in moving); ***nasal discharge or congestion***—more frequent in children; ***nausea and/or vomiting; sore throat; stomatitis*** (canker sores; sores, ulcers, or white spots on lips or tongue or inside the mouth)—more frequent in children; ***wheezing***—more frequent in children

Incidence less frequent

Dyspepsia (acid or sour stomach, belching, heartburn, indigestion, stomach discomfort, upset, or pain)

Incidence not determined—Observed during clinical practice, estimates of frequency can not be determined

Abnormal breathing; alopecia (hair loss, thinning of hair); ***body fat redistribution/accumulation; hyperglycemia*** (abdominal pain, blurred vision, dry mouth, fatigue, flushed, dry skin, fruit-like breath odor, increased hunger, increased thirst, increased urination, nausea, sweating, troubled breathing, unexplained); ***pruritus*** (itching skin); ***weakness***

Overdose

For more information on the management of overdose or unintentional ingestion, **contact a poison control center** (see *Poison Control Center Listing*).

Clinical effects of overdose

There is one reported case in which an adult ingested 6 grams of lamivudine; no clinical signs and symptoms were noted and hematologic tests remained normal

Two cases of pediatric overdose were reported in study ACTG300. One case was a single dose of 7 mg/kg of lamivudine; the second case involved administration of 5 mg/kg of lamivudine twice daily for 30 days. There were no clinical signs or symptoms noted in either case.

Treatment of overdose

There is no known antidote for lamivudine.Standard supportive treatment should be applied and the patient should be monitored.

Because a negligible amount of lamivudine was removed via (4-hour) hemodialysis, continuous ambulatory peritoneal dialysis, and automated peritoneal dialysis, it is not known if continuous hemodialysis would provide clinical benefit in a lamivudine overdose event.

Patients in whom intentional overdose is known or suspected should be referred for psychiatric consultation.

Patient Consultation

As an aid to patient consultation, refer to *Advice for the Patient, Lamivudine (Systemic)*.

In providing consultation, consider emphasizing the following selected information (» = major clinical significance):

Before using this medication

» Conditions affecting use, especially:

Pregnancy—Lamivudine crosses the placenta. Lamivudine has caused embryo lethality in rabbits at doses similar to the usual adult dose or higher; physicians are encouraged to register pregnant patients. Lamivudine should be used during pregnancy only if the potential benefits outweigh the risks.

Breast-feeding—Lamivudine is distributed in human breast milk. It is recommended that patients not breast-feed while taking lamivudine.

Use in children—Lamivudine monotherapy has resulted in the development of pancreatitis in 14% (14 of 97) of children with advanced HIV disease and a prior history of pancreatitis, and paresthesias and peripheral neuropathies in 13% (13 of 97) of pediatric patients with advanced HIV disease; in addition, an increase in serum transaminases (greater than 10 times the upper limits of normal) was observed in 3 of 89 (3%) of pediatric patients receiving lamivudine monotherapy; the absolute bioavailability is 66 to 68% in children, less than the 86% seen in adults and adolescents

Use in the elderly—Dose selection should be cautious reflecting the greater frequency of age-related medical problems, especially decreased renal function.

Other medications, especially lamivudine with zidovudine tablets, or zalcitabine

Other medical problems, especially antiretroviral nucleoside exposure (or history of), diabetes mellitus, hepatic disease or risk factors for hepatic disease, hepatitis B, hepatitis C, hepatitis delta, history of pancreatitis, human immunodeficiency virus [HIV], hypersensitivity to lamivudine or any components of this product, obesity, organ transplant recipients, prolonged nucleoside exposure, renal function impairment, or significant risk factors for development of pancreatitis

Proper use of this medication

» Importance of not taking more medication than prescribed; importance of not discontinuing lamivudine or zidovudine without checking with physician

» Compliance with full course of therapy

» Importance of not missing doses and of taking at evenly spaced times

Proper administration technique for oral liquids

Not sharing medication with others

» Proper dosing

Missed dose: Taking as soon as possible; not taking if almost time for next dose; not doubling doses

» Proper storage

Precautions while using this medication

» Regular visits to physician for blood tests

» Importance of not taking other medications especially lamivudine with zidovudine or zalcitabine concurrently without checking with physician

» Informing patients co-infected with HIV and HBV that deterioration of liver disease has occurred in come cases when treatment with lamivudine was discontinued; advising patients to discuss any changes in regimen with their physician

Side/adverse effects

Signs of potential side effects, especially hepatomegaly with steatosis, lactic acidosis, pancreatitis, paresthesias, peripheral neuropathy, splenomegaly, anemia, neutropenia, or skin rash

Signs of potential side effects observed during clinical practice, especially anaphylaxis, post-treatment exacerbation of hepatitis B, rhabdomyolysis, or urticaria

General Dosing Information

Lamivudine may be taken on a full or empty stomach.

HIV counseling and testing should be offered to patients with hepatitis B before they initiate lamivudine therapy.

Lamivudine tablets and lamivudine oral solution for HIV patients *(Epivir)* contain a higher dose of the same active ingredient that is found in lamivudine tablets and oral solution for hepatitis B patients *(Epivir-HBV)* The formulation and dosage of lamivudine in *Epivir-HBV* is not appropriate for patients who are infected with both HIV and HBV.

Patients with HIV should receive only dosing forms appropriate for treatment with HIV.

If lamivudine *Epivir-HBV* is prescribed for a patient with unrecognized or untreated HIV infection, rapid emergence of HIV resistance is likely to result because of the subtherapeutic dose and the inappropriateness of monotherapy HIV treatment.

If a decision is made to administer lamivudine to patients dually infected with HIV and HBV, an appropriate combination regimen should be used.

Before beginning treatment of hepatitis B infection, patients should be assessed by a physician experienced in the management of chronic hepatitis B.

Oral Dosage Forms

Note: Bracketed uses in the *Dosage Forms* section refer to categories of use and/or indications that are not included in U.S. product labeling.

LAMIVUDINE ORAL SOLUTION

Usual adult and adolescent dose

Hepatitis B, chronic (treatment)—

Oral, 100 mg of lamivudine once a day. The optimum duration of treatment is unknown and the safety and efficacy of treatment beyond one year is unknown.

Hepatitis B, chronic (treatment): Recommended doses of lamivudine in accordance with renal function based on creatinine clearance:

- ≥50 mL per minute: Oral, 100 mg once daily
- 30 to 49 mL per minute: Oral, 100 first dose, then 50 mg once daily
- 15 to 29 mL per minute: Oral, 100 mg first dose, then 25 mg once daily
- 5 to 14 mL per minute: Oral, 35 mg first dose, then 15 mg once daily
- Less than 5 mL per minute: Oral, 35 mg first dose, then 10 mg once daily

Human immunodeficiency virus (HIV) infection (treatment) or Immunodeficiency syndrome, acquired (AIDS) (treatment)—

Adults and adolescents weighing 50 kg (110 pounds) or more: Oral, 150 mg of lamivudine twice a dayor 300 mg once a day in combination with other antiretroviral agents.

Adults weighing less than 50 kg (110 pounds): Oral, 2 mg per kg of body weight of lamivudine twice a day in combination with other antiretroviral agents.

HIV infection (treatment): Recommended doses of lamivudine in accordance with renal function based on creatinine clearance:

- ≥50 mL per minute: Oral, 150 mg twice daily or 300 mg once daily
- 30 to 49 mL per minute: Oral, 150 mg once daily
- 15 to 29 mL per minute: Oral, 150 mg first dose, then 100 mg once daily
- 5 to 14 mL per minute: Oral, 150 mg first dose, then 50 mg once daily
- Less than 5 mL per minute: Oral, 50 mg first dose, then 25 mg once daily

Note: No additional dosing of lamivudine is required after routine (4-hour) hemodialysis or peritoneal dialysis.

[Human immunodeficiency virus (HIV) infection, occupational exposure (prophylaxis)][1]—

Oral, 150 mg of lamivudine twice a day, in combination with zidovudine 200 mg three times a day, for four weeks. In certain cases, a protease inhibitor may also be added to the regimen.

Note: Lamivudine doses should be adjusted in accordance with renal function

Note: Patients that require treatment for both hepatitis B and either HIV or AIDS should follow the HIV/AIDS dosing regimen.

Usual pediatric dose

Hepatitis B, chronic (treatment)[1]—

Children over 17 years of age: See *Adult and adolescent dose.*

Children 2 to 17 years of age: Oral, 3 mg per kg of body weight once daily. The optimum duration of treatment is unknown and the safety and efficacy of treatment beyond one year is unknown.

Children under 2 years of age: Safety and efficacy have not been established.

Human immunodeficiency virus (HIV) infection (treatment) or Immunodeficiency syndrome, acquired (AIDS) (treatment)—

Children 16 years of age and older: See *Adult and adolescent dose.*

Children 3 months to 16 years of age: Oral, 4 mg per kg of body weight twice daily, up to a (maximum of 150 mg, twice a day) in combination with other antiretroviral agents.

Children up to 3 months of age: Safety and efficacy have not been established.

Note: In pediatric patients with renal impairment, a reduction in the dose and/or an increase in the dosing interval should be considered, though data are insufficient to recommend a specific dose adjustment.

Note: Patients that require treatment for both hepatitis B and either HIV or AIDS should follow the HIV/AIDS dosing regimen.

Usual pediatric prescribing limits

Hepatitis B, chronic (treatment)—Up to a maximum daily dose of 100 mg

Strength(s) usually available

U.S.—

10 mg per mL (Rx) [*Epivir* (artificial strawberry and banana flavors; citric acid, anhydrous; methylparaben; propylene glycol; propylparaben; sodium citrate dihydrate; 200 mg sucrose)].

5 mg per mL (Rx) [*Epivir-HBV* (artificial strawberry and banana flavors; citric acid, anhydrous; methylparaben; propylene glycol; propylparaben; sodium citrate dihydrate; sucrose)][1].

Canada—

10 mg per mL (Rx) [*3TC* (ethanol 6% v/v; methylparaben; propylparaben; sucrose)].

5 mg per mL (Rx) [*Heptovir* (methylparaben; propylparaben; propylene glycol; sodium citrate; sucrose)].

Packaging and storage

Store at 25 °C (77 °F) in a tight container.

Auxiliary labeling

- Continue medicine for full time of treatment.
- Oral solution contains sucrose.

Note

When dispensing, include a calibrated liquid-measuring device.

LAMIVUDINE TABLETS

Usual adult and adolescent dose

See *Lamivudine Oral Solution.*

Usual pediatric dose

See *Lamivudine Oral Solution.*

Strength(s) usually available

U.S.—

150 mg (Rx) [*Epivir* (hypromellose; magnesium stearate; microcrystalline cellulose; polyethylene glycol; polysorbate 80; sodium starch glycolate; titanium dioxide)].

100 mg (Rx) [*Epivir-HBV* (hypromellose; macrogol 400; magnesium stearate; microcrystalline cellulose; polysorbate 80; red iron oxide; sodium starch glycolate; titanium dioxide; yellow iron oxide)].

300 mg (Rx) [*Epivir* (black iron oxide; hypromellose; magnesium stearate; microcrystalline cellulose; polyethylene glycol; polysorbate 80; sodium starch glycolate; titanium dioxide)].

Canada—

150 mg (Rx) [*3TC*].

100 mg (Rx) [*Heptovir*].

Packaging and storage

Store at 25 °C (77 °F) with excursions permitted to 15 °C to 30 °C (59 to 86 °F) in a tight container.

Auxiliary labeling

- Continue medicine for full time of treatment.

[1]Not included in Canadian product labeling.

Revised: 02/04/2005
Developed: 08/08/1996

LAMIVUDINE AND ZIDOVUDINE Systemic

VA CLASSIFICATION (Primary): AM840

Commonly used brand name(s): *Combivir.*

NOTE: The *Lamivudine and Zidovudine (Systemic)* monograph is maintained on the *USP DI* electronic data base. A copy of the most recent revision of the complete monograph can be accessed on the *USP DI* Updates Online website. See the front cover of book for details on accessing the site.

For information on the specific components of this combination, see the *USP DI* monographs for *Lamivudine (Systemic),* and *Zidovudine (Systemic).*

The information that follows is selectively abstracted from the complete monograph and is provided to facilitate drug use review and patient counseling.

Note: For a listing of dosage forms and brand names by country availability, see *Dosage Forms* section(s).

Category

Antiviral (systemic).

Indications

General Considerations

Lamivudine and zidovudine are nucleoside inhibitors of reverse transcriptase in human immunodeficiency virus (HIV). Monotherapy with lamivudine or combination therapy with lamivudine and zidovudine has resulted in HIV isolates that were phenotypically and genotypically resistant to lamivudine within 12 weeks. In some patients harboring zidovudine-resistant virus at baseline, phenotypic sensitivity to zidovudine was restored by 12 weeks of therapy with lamivudine and zidovudine. Combination therapy with lamivudine and zidovudine delayed the emergence of mutations conferring resistance to zidovudine.

HIV strains resistant to both lamivudine and zidovudine have been isolated from patients after prolonged therapy with lamivudine and zidovudine. Dual resistance requires the presence of multiple mutations, the most essential of which appears to be at codon 333. The incidence of dual resistance and the duration of combination therapy required before dual resistance develops are unknown.

Cross-resistance among certain reverse transcriptase inhibitors has been recognized. However, cross-resistance between lamivudine and zidovudine has not been reported. In some patients treated with lamivudine alone or in combination with zidovudine, HIV isolates have emerged with a mutation at codon 184, which confers resistance to lamivudine. In the presence of this mutation, cross-resistance to didanosine and zalcitabine has been seen in some patients; the clinical significance of this is unknown. In some patients treated with zidovudine plus didanosine or zalcitabine, HIV isolates that are resistant to multiple drugs, including lamivudine, have emerged. Multiple drug resistance has been observed in 2 of 39 patients receiving zidovudine and didanosine combination therapy for 2 years.

Accepted

Human immunodeficiency virus (HIV) infection (treatment)—Lamivudine and zidovudine combination is indicated in the treatment of HIV infection.

Patient Consultation

As an aid to patient consultation, refer to *Advice for the Patient, Lamivudine and Zidovudine (Systemic).*

In providing consultation, consider emphasizing the following selected information (» = major clinical significance):

Before using this medication

» Conditions affecting use, especially:

Hypersensitivity to lamivudine or zidovudine or any component of the product

Pregnancy—Zidovudine crosses the placenta

Breast-feeding—Zidovudine is distributed into breast milk; it is recommended that HIV-infected mothers do not breast-feed their infants to avoid potential postnatal transmission of HIV

Use in children—Lamivudine and zidovudine combination is not recommended for use in children younger than 12 years of age

Use in adolescents—Lamivudine and zidovudine combination is not recommended for use in patients who weigh less than 50 kg

Other medications, especially abacavir/lamivudine/zidovudine combination, alpha interferons, doxorubicin, ganciclovir, lamivudine, other bone marrow depressants, ribavirin, stavudine, or zidovudine

Other medical problems, especially bone marrow depression, co-infection with HIV and HBV, hepatic disease, hepatic function impairment, hepatitis B virus infection, obesity, prolonged nucleoside exposure, renal function impairment, or risk factors for hepatic disease

Proper use of this medication

» Importance of not taking more medication than prescribed; importance of not discontinuing medication without checking with physician

» Importance of not missing doses and of taking at evenly spaced times

Not sharing medication with others

» Proper dosing

Missed dose: Taking as soon as possible; not taking if almost time for next dose; not doubling doses

» Proper storage

Precautions while using this medication

» Regular visits to physician for blood tests

» Importance of not taking other medications concurrently without checking with physician

» Informing patients co-infected with HIV and HBV that deterioration of liver disease has occurred in some cases when treatment with lamivudine and zidovudine was discontinued; advising patients to discuss any changes in regimen with their physician

Side/adverse effects

Signs of potential side effects, especially anemia, neutropenia, hepatotoxicity, myopathy or myositis, neuropathy, and pancreatitis

Signs of potential side effects observed during clinical practice, especially anaphylaxis, cardiomyopathy, erythema multiforme, hepatic steatosis, hepatitis B post-treatment exacerbation, lactic acidosis, paresthesias, peripheral neuropathy, rhabdomyolysis, seizures, splenomegaly, Stevens-Johnson syndrome, stomatitis, urticaria, or vasculitis

Oral Dosage Forms

LAMIVUDINE AND ZIDOVUDINE TABLETS

Usual adult and adolescent dose

Human immunodeficiency virus (HIV) infection—

Adults and adolescents 50 kg of body weight and over: Oral, 150 mg of lamivudine and 300 mg of zidovudine two times a day.

Adults and adolescents up to 50 kg of body weight: Use is not recommended.

Usual pediatric dose

Use is not recommended.

Usual geriatric dose

Dose selection for elderly patients should be cautious due to the greater frequency of geriatric-specific problems.

Strength(s) usually available

U.S.—

150 mg of lamivudine and 300 mg of zidovudine (Rx) [*Combivir*].

Revised: 10/27/2004
Developed: 11/14/1997

LAMOTRIGINE Systemic

VA CLASSIFICATION (Primary/Secondary): CN400/CN900

Commonly used brand name(s): *Lamictal*.

Another commonly used name is LTG .

Note: For a listing of dosage forms and brand names by country availability, see *Dosage Forms* section(s).

Category

Anticonvulsant; antimanic.

Indications

Note: Bracketed information in the *Indications* section refers to uses that are not included in U.S. product labeling.

Accepted

Bipolar disorder (treatment)—Lamotrigine is indicated for the maintenance treatment of Bipolar I disorder to delay the time to occurrence of mood episodes (depression, mania, hypomania, mixed episodes) in patients treated for acute mood episodes with standard therapy.

Epilepsy, partial seizures (treatment adjunct)—Lamotrigine is indicated as an adjunct to other anticonvulsant medications in the treatment of partial seizures in adults and pediatric patients 2 years of age and older with epilepsy.

Epilepsy, Lennox-Gastaut syndrome (treatment adjunct)—Lamotrigine is indicated as an adjunct to other anticonvulsant medications in the treatment of generalized seizures of Lennox-Gastaut syndrome in adult and pediatric patients 2 years of age and older.

Epilepsy, partial seizures (treatment)—Lamotrigine is indicated as monotherapy for treatment of partial seizures (in adults 16 years of age and older following withdrawal of a concomitantly used enzyme-inducing anticonvulsant medication)[1].

[Epilepsy (treatment)]—Lamotrigine is indicated as monotherapy for treatment of epilepsy following withdrawal of concomitantly used anticonvulsant medications.

Unaccepted

The effectiveness of lamotrigine in the acute treatment of mood episodes has not been established.

[1]Not included in Canadian product labeling.

Pharmacology/Pharmacokinetics

Physicochemical characteristics

Chemical Group—Phenyltriazine. Structurally unrelated to existing anticonvulsant medications.

Molecular weight—256.09.

pKa—5.7.

Mechanism of action/Effect

The exact mechanism of action is unknown. *In vitro* studies suggest that lamotrigine blocks voltage-sensitive sodium channels, thereby stabilizing neuronal membranes and inhibiting the presynaptic release of neurotransmitters, principally glutamate. Lamotrigine also may directly inhibit high-frequency sustained repetitive firing of sodium-dependent action potentials.

Other actions/effects

Lamotrigine is a weak dihydrofolate reductase inhibitor *in vitro* and in animal studies. No effect on folate concentrations has been noted in clinical studies. However, complete inhibition of erythropoiesis occurred in one patient with heterozygous beta-thalassemia, possibly due to inhibition of dihydrofolate reductase by lamotrigine.

Animal studies have shown that lamotrigine binds to melanin-containing tissues, such as eye tissues and pigmented skin. The long-term effects of this binding are not known, but no effects have been seen in humans.

The 2-*N*-methyl metabolite of lamotrigine causes cardiac conduction disturbances in dogs in a dose-dependent manner. This metabolite is present in trace amounts in the urine of people taking lamotrigine, but the clinical significance of its presence is unknown.

Absorption

Rapid. Bioavailability of lamotrigine is approximately 98% and is unaffected by food. Lamotrigine tablets and chewable/dispersible tablets are bioequivalent.

Distribution

Mean apparent volume of distribution (Vol_D) of lamotrigine following oral administration ranged from 0.9 to 1.3 liters per kg (L/kg). In a 10-year-old patient undergoing topectomy 4 hours post-dose, lamotrigine concentration in brain tissue was greater than unbound lamotrigine concentration in plasma. Lamotrigine is distributed into breast milk.

Protein binding

Moderate (55%).

Biotransformation

Hepatic glucuronic acid conjugation. Following multiple administration of 150 mg of lamotrigine twice a day to healthy volunteers taking no other medications, lamotrigine was found to induce its own metabolism, resulting in a 25% decrease in half-life and a 37% increase in apparent plasma clearance at steady-state, as compared to values obtained following a single lamotrigine dose in the same volunteers. Other evidence suggests that self-induction may not occur when lamotrigine is given as adjunctive therapy in patients receiving enzyme-inducing anticonvulsants. (Enzyme-inducing anticonvulsants include carbamazepine, phenobarbital, phenytoin, and primidone.)

The 2-*N*-methyl metabolite of lamotrigine is present in trace amounts in the urine of people taking lamotrigine, but the clinical significance of its presence is unknown.

Half-life

Elimination—

With no other medication: 25 ± 10 hours.

With enzyme-inducing anticonvulsants only: 14 ± 6 hours.

With valproic acid only: Approximately 59 hours.

With enzyme-inducing anticonvulsants and valproic acid: Approximately 28 hours.

In one study in patients who received a single 100-mg dose of lamotrigine, mean plasma elimination half-lives were 42.9 hours in 12 patients with chronic renal failure (mean creatinine clearance of 13 mL per minute); in six patients undergoing hemodialysis, mean elimination half-lives were 13 hours during hemodialysis and 57.4 hours between hemodialysis, as compared to 26.2 hours in healthy volunteers.

Time to peak concentration

1.4 to 4.8 hours. A second peak may be seen 4 to 6 hours after oral or intravenous administration; this peak may reflect enterohepatic recirculation.

Therapeutic plasma concentration

The therapeutic concentration range for lamotrigine has not been determined, and dosage titration should be based on clinical response rather than plasma concentrations.

Over a range of 50 to 400 mg given as a single dose, peak plasma concentrations increased linearly from 0.58 to 4.63 mg/L in healthy subjects. In two small studies of patients with epilepsy, plasma concentrations increased linearly with doses of 50 to 350 mg given two times a day.

Elimination

Renal—Approximately 94% (about 10% unchanged, 86% as glucuronide conjugates, less than 5% as other metabolites, and trace amounts as the 2-*N*-methyl metabolite).

Fecal—Approximately 2%.

In dialysis—In six patients, an average of approximately 20% (range, 5.6 to 35.1%) of lamotrigine in the body was removed in 4 hours of hemodialysis.

Precautions to Consider

Carcinogenicity

In animal studies, no evidence of carcinogenicity was seen following oral administration of lamotrigine for up to 2 years at maximum tolerated doses (30 mg per kilogram of body weight [mg/kg] per day in mice and 10 to 15 mg/kg per day in rats).

Mutagenicity

No evidence of mutagenicity was found in two gene mutation assays (the Ames test and the *in vitro* mammalian mouse lymphoma assay). Lamotrigine did not increase the incidence of structural or numerical chromosomal abnormalities in two cytogenic assays (the *in vitro* human lymphocyte assay and the *in vivo* rat bone marrow assay).

Pregnancy/Reproduction

Fertility—No adverse effect on fertility was seen in rats given up to 2.4 times the highest usual human maintenance dose of 8.33 mg/kg per day.

Pregnancy—Lamotrigine should be used during pregnancy only if the potential benefit justifies the potential risk to the fetus.

Folic acid supplementation should be considered for all women of childbearing potential who are taking lamotrigine.

Studies have not been done in humans.

Studies in rats and rabbits indicate that lamotrigine crosses the placenta, yielding placental and fetal concentrations comparable to concentrations in maternal plasma. No teratogenic effects were seen in studies in mice, rats, and rabbits employing up to 1.2 times an equivalent human dose of 500 mg of lamotrigine per day on a milligram per square meter of body surface area (mg/m^2) basis. However, maternal toxicity and secondary fetal toxicity resulting in reduced fetal weight and/or delayed ossification were seen in mice and rats. In rat dams that were administered an intravenous lamotrigine dose 0.6 times an equivalent human dose of 500 mg per day on a mg/m^2 basis, the incidence of intrauterine death without signs of teratogenicity was increased. Pregnant rats, receiving oral doses up to 0.3 times the equivalent human dose of 500 mg per day on a mg/m^2 basis during gestation days 15 to 20, showed evidence of maternal toxicity and consequent fetal death; food consumption and weight gain were reduced, the gestation period was slightly prolonged, and stillborn pups were found. Postnatal deaths also occurred, but some appeared to be drug-related and not secondary to the maternal toxicity. In addition, lamotrigine decreased fetal folate concentrations in rats, an effect known to be associated with teratogenicity in humans and animals.

FDA Pregnancy Category C.

Note: To facilitate monitoring of fetal outcomes of pregnant women exposed to lamotrigine, physicians are encouraged to register patients in the Antiepileptic Drug Pregnancy Registry before fetal outcome is known.

Labor and delivery—The effect of lamotrigine on labor and delivery is not known.

Breast-feeding

Lamotrigine is distributed into breast milk. However, the effects on the nursing infant are unknown. Because the effects on the infant exposed to lamotrigine by this route are unknown, breast-feeding while taking lamotrigine is not recommended.

Pediatrics

Lamotrigine is indicated as adjunctive therapy for partial seizures in patients above 2 years of age and for the generalized seizures of Lennox-Gastaut syndrome.

Safety and effectiveness for other uses in patients with epilepsy below the age of 16 years have not been established.

Safety and effectiveness in patients below the age of 18 years with bipolar disorder has not been established.

Life-threatening cutaneous reactions, including Stevens-Johnson syndrome and toxic epidermal necrolysis, have been reported in approximately 0.8% of pediatric patients receiving lamotrigine, as compared with 0.3% of adults. Deaths have occurred. (See *Side/Adverse Effects section.*).

Geriatrics

Appropriate studies on the relationship of age to the effects of lamotrigine have not been performed in the geriatric population. However, one single-dose pharmacokinetic study comparing 12 healthy volunteers 65 to 76 years of age and 12 healthy volunteers 26 to 38 years of age found that lamotrigine clearance was 37% lower, area under the concentration-time curve (AUC) was 55% higher, peak plasma concentration was 27% higher, and elimination half-life was 6 hours longer in the older group. In addition, elderly patients are more likely to have age-related renal function impairment, which may require dosage adjustment. It is recommended that elderly patients receive dosages at the low end of the normal range.

Pharmacogenetics

The apparent oral clearance of lamotrigine was 25% lower in nonwhite than in white subjects.

Drug interactions and/or related problems

The following drug interactions and/or related problems have been selected on the basis of their potential clinical significance (possible mechanism in parentheses where appropriate)—not necessarily inclusive (» = major clinical significance):

Note: The effects of lamotrigine on specific families of mixed-function oxidase isozymes have not been systematically evaluated. Possible interactions between lamotrigine and hepatic enzyme inducers or inhibitors not listed below should be considered.

Combinations containing any of the following medications, depending on the amount present, may also interact with this medication.

Acetaminophen
(half-life and area under the concentration-time curve of lamotrigine may be reduced slightly by chronic, high-dose acetaminophen use)

Alcohol or central nervous system (CNS) depression-producing medications, other (see *Appendix II*)
(lamotrigine may enhance the CNS depressant effects of these medications or alcohol)

» Carbamazepine or
» Phenobarbital or
» Phenytoin or
» Primidone
(clearance of lamotrigine is increased, possibly decreasing steady-state plasma concentrations by 40% or more; clearance may be expected to decrease when concomitant enzyme-inducing therapy is discontinued; initial lamotrigine dosage and rate of lamotrigine dosage escalation should be based on concomitant anticonvulsant therapy; monitoring of plasma concentrations of lamotrigine and other anticonvulsant medications should be considered, especially during dosage adjustments)

(an increased incidence of CNS adverse effects, including ataxia, blurred vision, diplopia, dizziness, or increased excitation, may occur with concomitant carbamazepine use; reduction of dosage of either lamotrigine or carbamazepine may reduce these effects)

Folate antagonists, other (see *Appendix II*)
(lamotrigine inhibits dihydrofolate reductase, and should be used with caution with other folate antagonists)

» Oral contraceptives or
» Other hormonal contraceptives or replacement
(dosage adjustments may be necessary for women receiving lamotrigine; possibility of decreased contraceptive efficacy in some patients can not be excluded and patients should promptly report changes in their menstrual pattern such as break-through bleeding)

Oxcarbazepine

(limited clinical data suggest higher incidence of headache, dizziness, nausea, and somnolence with concomitant use compared with oxcarbazepine or lamotrigine alone)

Rifampin

(rifampin significantly increased apparent clearance of lamotrigine by approximately 2-fold [AUC decreased by approximately 40%])

» Valproic acid

(half-life and plasma concentrations of lamotrigine are increased, probably due to competition for hepatic glucuronidation; lamotrigine plasma concentrations may be increased slightly more than twofold; half-life and plasma concentrations may be expected to decrease when valproic acid is discontinued; initial lamotrigine dosage, and rate of lamotrigine dosage escalation, should be based on concomitant anticonvulsant therapy; monitoring of plasma concentrations of lamotrigine and valproic acid should be considered, especially during dosage adjustments)

(disabling tremor and an increased incidence of rash, including severe rash, have occurred with concomitant valproic acid use)

(there is some evidence that the combination of lamotrigine and valproic acid may improve seizure control in patients who are refractory to either agent used alone, but controlled studies have not been done)

Medical considerations/Contraindications

The medical considerations/contraindications included have been selected on the basis of their potential clinical significance (reasons given in parentheses where appropriate)—not necessarily inclusive (» = major clinical significance).

Except under special circumstances, this medication should not be used when the following medical problem exists:

» Hypersensitivity to lamotrigine or its ingredients

Risk-benefit should be considered when the following medical problems exist:

Cardiac conduction abnormalities

(in one clinical trial, minor electrocardiogram [ECG] changes were seen in some patients with normal cardiac function who were taking lamotrigine; there is no experience with lamotrigine treatment in patients with cardiac conduction disturbances)

Hepatic function impairment

(lamotrigine metabolism may be decreased)

» Renal function impairment

(large interindividual differences in lamotrigine plasma concentrations were seen in uremic patients; elimination half-life is prolonged in patients with significant renal function impairment; patients with renal function impairment may require reduced maintenance doses)

» Thalassemia

(erythropoiesis may be decreased significantly)

Patient monitoring

The following may be especially important in patient monitoring (other tests may be warranted in some patients, depending on condition; » = major clinical significance):

» Careful supervision of depressed patients including those with:

Clinical worsening of their depression or

Suicidal ideation and behavior (suicidality)

(recommended especially at the beginning of course of treatment or at the time of dose changes; prescribing the smallest quantity of tablets necessary for good patient management is recommended to decrease the risk of overdose; consideration should be given to changing the therapeutic regimen, including possibly discontinuing the medicine, in patients whose depression is persistently worse or whose emergent suicidality or other symptoms are severe, abrupt in onset, or were not part of the patient's presenting symptoms)

Long-term ophthalmologic effects

(because lamotrigine binds to melanin, it could accumulate in melanin-rich tissues over time; availability of tests to detect potentially adverse consequences, if any, is unknown; although no specific recommendations for periodic ophthalmological monitoring, prescribers should be aware of possibility of long-term ophthalmic effects)

» Reassessment of the long-term need of the drug for bipolar disorder

(patients should be periodically reassessed to determine the need for maintenance treatment; there is no body of evidence available to answer the question of how long the patient should remain on lamotrigine therapy)

Side/Adverse Effects

Note: Serious cutaneous reactions requiring hospitalization, including Stevens-Johnson syndrome, angioedema, and rash associated with fever, lymphadenopathy, facial swelling, and/or hematologic and hepatologic abnormalities, have been reported in association with lamotrigine therapy. The incidence of these rashes is approximately 0.3% in adults and 0.8% in children up to 16 years of age. Since the rate of serious rash is greater in pediatric patients than it is in adult patients, the current U.S. product labeling for lamotrigine emphasizes the indication is for use in pediatric patients from 2 to 16 years of age only for the treatment of seizures associated with Lennox-Gastaut syndrome or in patients with partial seizures. In postmarketing experience worldwide, rare cases of toxic epidermal necrolysis and/or skin rash–related deaths also have been reported. Nearly all cases of life-threatening cutaneous reactions have occurred within 2 to 8 weeks of initiation of lamotrigine therapy. However, isolated cases also have been reported after prolonged therapy (e.g., 6 months). Therefore, the potential risk cannot be predicted by the duration of lamotrigine therapy. Similarly, the potential risk of serious or life-threatening cutaneous reactions cannot be predicted, since benign skin rashes also occur with lamotrigine therapy. (Approximately 10% of all patients exposed to lamotrigine in clinical trials developed a rash.) It has been suggested, although not yet proven, that the risk of skin rash may be increased by the coadministration of lamotrigine with valproic acid, by exceeding the recommended initial dose of lamotrigine, or by exceeding the recommended dose escalation for lamotrigine. Unless the rash clearly is not drug-related, lamotrigine should be discontinued at the first sign of rash. Discontinuation of lamotrigine therapy may not prevent a skin rash from becoming life-threatening or permanently disabling or disfiguring.

Disseminated intravascular coagulation and multi-organ failure have occurred very rarely in patients taking lamotrigine. Most cases have been in association with other serious medical events, such as status epilepticus and overwhelming sepsis, and it is uncertain whether these effects were related to lamotrigine use.

Prior to initiation of lamotrigine therapy, patients should be instructed that a skin rash or other symptoms of hypersensitivity (e.g., fever, lymphadenopathy) should be reported to the physician immediately, as they may signal the onset of a serious medical event.

An increased incidence of CNS adverse effects, including ataxia, blurred vision, diplopia, dizziness, or increased excitation, may occur with concomitant carbamazepine use; reduction of dosage of either lamotrigine or carbamazepine may reduce these effects.

Lamotrigine may be less sedating than other anticonvulsant medications.

The following side/adverse effects have been selected on the basis of their potential clinical significance (possible signs and symptoms in parentheses where appropriate)—not necessarily inclusive:

Those indicating need for medical attention

Incidence more frequent

Ataxia (clumsiness or unsteadiness); ***coordination abnormalities*** (poor coordination); ***skin rash; vision abnormalities, including blurred vision; and diplopia*** (double vision)

Note: It is recommended that any patient who acutely develops any combination of unexplained rash, fever, flu-like symptoms, or worsening of seizure control should discontinue lamotrigine and should be closely monitored; monitoring should include determinations of hepatic and renal function, and clotting parameters.

Ataxia, skin rash, blurred vision, and *diplopia* are dose-related.

Incidence less frequent

CNS toxicity, specifically anxiety; confusion; depression; irritability; other mood or mental changes; increased seizures; or nystagmus (continuous, uncontrolled back and forth and/or rolling eye movements); ***chest pain; infection***

Incidence rare

Amnesia (memory loss); ***angioedema*** (trouble in breathing; swelling of face, mouth, hands, or feet); ***blood dyscrasias, including anemia; eosinophilia; leukopenia; or thrombocytopenia*** (fever and sore throat; unusual bleeding or bruising; unusual tiredness or weakness); ***erythema multiforme, Stevens-Johnson syndrome, or toxic epidermal necrolysis*** (blistering, peeling, or loosening of skin; muscle cramps, pain, or weakness; red or irritated eyes; skin rash or itching; sore throat, fever, and chills; sores, ulcers, or white spots in mouth or on lips); ***fever; hypersensitivity syndrome*** (dark-colored urine; fever; flu-like symptoms; skin rash; facial swelling; swollen lymph nodes;

unusual tiredness or weakness; yellow eyes or skin); ***petechia*** (small red or purple spots on skin)

Incidence not determined—Observed during clinical practice; estimates of frequency can not be determined

Agranulocytosis (cough or hoarseness; fever with or without chills; general feeling of tiredness or weakness; lower back or side pain; painful or difficult urination, sore throat, sores, ulcers, or white spots on lips or in mouth, unusual bleeding or bruising); ***aplastic anemia*** (chest pain; chills; cough; fever; headache; shortness of breath; sores, ulcers, or white spots on lips or in mouth; swollen or painful glands; tightness in chest; unusual bleeding or bruising; unusual tiredness or weakness; wheezing); ***apnea*** (bluish lips or skin; not breathing); ***disseminated intravascular coagulation*** (blood in stools; blood in urine; bruising; confusion; coughing or vomiting blood; persistent bleeding or oozing from puncture sites, mouth, or nose, rash; shortness of breath); ***esophagitis*** (difficulty in swallowing; pain or burning in throat; chest pain; heartburn; vomiting; sores, ulcers, or white spots on lips or tongue or inside the mouth); ***exacerbation of Parkinsonian symptoms*** (difficulty swallowing; loss of balance control; mask-like face; shuffling walk; slowed movements; slurred speech; stiffness of arms and legs; tic-like [jerky] movements of head, face, mouth, and neck; trembling and shaking of fingers and hands)—in patients with preexisting Parkinson's disease; ***hemolytic anemia*** (back, leg, or stomach pains; bleeding gums; chills; dark urine; difficulty breathing; fatigue; fever; general body swelling; headache; loss of appetite; nausea or vomiting; nosebleeds; pale skin; sore throat; yellowing of the eyes or skin); ***lupus-like reaction*** (fever or chills; general feeling of discomfort or illness or weakness); ***multi-organ failure*** (chills; confusion; dizziness; lightheadedness; fainting; fast heartbeat; fever; rapid, shallow breathing); ***neutropenia*** (black, tarry, stools; chills; cough; fever; lower back or side pain; painful or difficult urination; pale skin; shortness of breath; sore throat; ulcers, sores, or white spots in mouth; unusual bleeding or bruising; unusual tiredness or weakness); ***pancreatitis*** (bloating; chills; constipation; darkened urine; fast heartbeat; fever; indigestion; loss of appetite; nausea; pains in stomach, side, or abdomen, possibly radiating to the back; vomiting; yellow eyes or skin); ***pancytopenia*** (high fever; chills; unexplained bleeding or bruising; bloody, black, or tarry stools; pale skin; unusual tiredness or weakness; cough; shortness of breath; sores, ulcers, or white spots on lips or in mouth; swollen glands); ***progressive immunosuppression*** (fever or chills; cough or hoarseness; lower back or side pain; painful or difficult urination); ***red cell aplasia*** (fever and sore throat; pale skin; unusual bleeding or bruising; unusual tiredness or weakness); ***rhabdomyolysis*** (dark-colored urine; fever; muscle cramps or spasms; muscle pain or stiffness; unusual tiredness or weakness)—in patients experiencing hypersensitivity reactions; ***tics*** (jerking of muscles all over the body); ***vasculitis*** (redness, soreness or itching skin; fever; sores, welting or blisters)

Those indicating need for medical attention only if they continue or are bothersome

Incidence more frequent

CNS effects, specifically dizziness; drowsiness; or headache; gastrointestinal effects, specifically nausea; or vomiting

Note: A higher incidence of *dizziness* is seen in females than in males. *Dizziness*, *nausea*, and *vomiting* are dose related.

Incidence less frequent or rare

Asthenia (loss of strength); ***constipation; diarrhea; dryness of mouth; dysarthria*** (slurred speech); ***dysmenorrhea*** (menstrual pain); ***dyspepsia*** (indigestion); ***insomnia*** (trouble in sleeping); ***pain; rhinitis*** (runny nose); ***tremor*** (trembling or shaking); ***weight loss, unusual***

Overdose

For specific information on the agents used in the management of lamotrigine overdose, see:

- *Charcoal, Activated (Oral-Local)* monograph.

For more information on the management of overdose or unintentional ingestion, **contact a Poison Control Center** (see *Poison Control Center Listing*).

Clinical effects of overdose

The following effects have been selected on the basis of their potential clinical significance (possible signs and symptoms—in parentheses where appropriate) not necessarily inclusive:

Acute effects

CNS toxicity, specifically severe ataxia (clumsiness or unsteadiness); ***coma; severe dizziness; severe drowsiness; severe dysarthria*** (slurred speech); ***or severe nystagmus*** (continuous, uncontrolled back and forth and/or rolling eye movements); ***severe dryness of mouth; electrocardiogram (ECG) changes, specifically prolonged QRS interval; severe headache; increased heart rate***

Note: Experience with lamotrigine overdose is very limited. Overdoses with lamotrigine have ranged from 1350 to over 4000 milligrams. Some of these clinical effects have occurred in only one patient, and general applicability to lamotrigine overdose is unknown.

Treatment of overdose

To decrease absorption—

Emesis may be induced or gastric lavage may be performed, if indicated, with precautions taken to protect the airway, keeping in mind the rapid absorption of lamotrigine. Activated charcoal also may be administered. These procedures may need to be repeated several times. The use of a cathartic to accelerate elimination of charcoal and medication from the lower gastrointestinal tract should be considered.

To enhance elimination—

Hemodialysis is of questionable efficacy. The extraction± ratio of lamotrigine in six patients with renal failure was 17 10% in 4 hours of hemodialysis.

Specific treatment—

There is no known antidote to lamotrigine overdose.

Monitoring—

Patient should be observed closely, with frequent monitoring of vital signs. Close electrocardiogram (ECG) monitoring may be advisable in patients showing QRS interval prolongation.

Supportive care—

General supportive care is the basis of lamotrigine overdose treatment. Patients in whom intentional overdose is confirmed or suspected should be referred for psychiatric consultation.

Patient Consultation

As an aid to patient consultation, refer to *Advice for the Patient, Lamotrigine (Systemic)*.

In providing consultation, consider emphasizing the following selected information (» = major clinical significance):

Before using this medication

» Conditions affecting use, especially:

Hypersensitivity to lamotrigine or its ingredients

Pregnancy—Crosses the placenta in animal studies; increases stillbirths and postnatal deaths among offspring of rats receiving less than maximum human dose; risk-benefit should be considered

Breast-feeding—Distributed into breast milk; effect on nursing infant is unknown; breast-feeding not recommended

Use in children—Serious cutaneous reactions are more likely to occur in children up to 16 years of age than in adults; safety and efficacy established in children 2 years of age and older as adjunct treatment for partial seizures and seizures associated with the Lennox-Gastaut syndrome only

Other medications, especially carbamazepine, phenobarbital, phenytoin, primidone, oral contraceptives, or valproic acid

Other medical problems, especially renal function impairment or thalassemia

Proper use of this medication

» Compliance with therapy; not taking more or less medicine than prescribed; not missing any doses

Taking with or without food or on a full or empty stomach, as directed by physician

Swallowing or chewing the chewable/dispersible tablets; alternatively, tablets may be dispersed in a small amount of water or diluted fruit juice, then swirled and consumed; partial quantities of dispersed tablets should not be administered

» Proper dosing

Missed dose: Taking as soon as possible; if almost time for next dose, skipping missed dose and returning to regular dosing schedule; not doubling doses

» Proper storage

Precautions while using this medication

» Regular visits to physician to check progress of therapy

» Importance of period assessments of maintenance use for bipolar disorder

» Notifying physician if patient is planning to stop or start using oral contraceptives or other female hormonal preparations

Importance of contacting physician if changes in menstrual pattern such a break-through bleeding occur while taking lamotrigine with oral contraceptives or other female hormonal preparations

» Discussing alcohol use and use of other CNS depressants with physician

» Possible blurred or double vision, dizziness, drowsiness, impairment of motor skills; caution when driving or doing jobs requiring alertness, coordination, or clear vision

» Immediately notifying physician if skin rash, fever, flu-like symptoms, swollen lymph glands, or increase in seizures occurs

» Seeking immediate medical attention if symptoms of worsening suicidality or emergence of suicidal ideation/behavior occur, especially if these symptoms are severe, abrupt in onset, or not part of patient's presenting symptoms

» Not discontinuing lamotrigine without consulting physician

Side/adverse effects

Signs of potential side effects, especially ataxia; coordination abnormalities; skin rash; vision abnormalities; anxiety, confusion, depression, irritability, other mood or mental changes, increased seizures, nystagmus; chest pain; infection; amnesia; angioedema; blood dyscrasias; erythema multiforme, Stevens-Johnson syndrome, or toxic epidermal necrolysis; fever; hypersensitivity syndrome; or petechia

Signs of potential side effects observed during clinical practice, especially agranulocytosis, aplastic anemia, apnea, disseminated intravascular coagulation, esophagitis, exacerbation of Parkinsonian symptoms, hemolytic anemia, lupus-like reaction, multi-organ failure, neutropenia, pancreatitis, pancytopenia, progressive immunosuppression, red cell aplasia, rhabdomyolysis, or vasculitis

General Dosing Information

Lamotrigine should be initiated at a low dose, and dosage escalation should proceed slowly, to minimize the occurrence of skin rash. The incidence of skin rash is highly dependent upon the initial rate of lamotrigine dosage escalation.

Prior to initiation of lamotrigine therapy, patients should be instructed that a skin rash or other symptoms of hypersensitivity (e.g., fever, flu-like symptoms, lymphadenopathy) should be reported to the physician immediately, as they may signal the onset of a serious medical event. Also, the physician should be notified immediately if an acute worsening of seizure control occurs.

Anticonvulsant medications ordinarily should not be discontinued abruptly because of the possibility of increased seizures. Lamotrigine dosage may be tapered over at least 2 weeks with the dose decreased by 50% each week, unless safety considerations require a more rapid withdrawal. Discontinuing carbamazepine, phenytoin, phenobarbital, or primidone should prolong the half-life of lamotrigine; discontinuing valproate should shorten the half-life of lamotrigine.

Diet/Nutrition

Folic acid supplementation should be considered for all women of childbearing potential who are taking lamotrigine.

Bioequivalence information

Lamotrigine tablets and lamotrigine chewable/dispersible tablets are bioequivalent.

Oral Dosage Forms

Note: Bracketed information in the *Dosage Forms* section refers to categories of use and/or indications that are not included in U.S. product labeling.

Lamotrigine therapy should be initiated at a low dose, and dosage escalation should proceed slowly, to minimize the risk of skin rash.

Enzyme-inducing anticonvulsants include carbamazepine, phenobarbital, phenytoin, and primidone.

LAMOTRIGINE TABLETS

Usual adult dose

Anticonvulsant, adjunctive treatment of Lennox-Gastaut syndrome

Anticonvulsant, adjunctive treatment of partial seizures—

With enzyme-inducing anticonvulsants only: Oral, 50 mg once a day for two weeks, then 100 mg a day, divided into two doses, for two weeks. To reach the usual maintenance dose of 300 to 500 mg a day (in two divided doses), subsequent daily doses should be increased by 100 mg a day every one to two weeks.

With enzyme-inducing anticonvulsants and valproic acid: Oral, 25 mg once every other day for two weeks, then 25 mg once a day for two weeks. To reach the usual maintenance dose of 100 to 400 mg a day (in one dose or two divided doses), subsequent daily doses should be increased by 25 to 50 mg a day every one to two weeks.

With valproic acid only: Lamotrigine dosing in patients receiving only concurrent valproic acid has not been established. However, lamotrigine dosing identical to that used in patients receiving lamotrigine with valproic acid and enzyme-inducing anticonvulsants has been used in some patients. Lamotrigine plasma concentrations in patients receiving only concurrent valproic acid may be up to two times those seen in patients who are also receiving enzyme-inducing anticonvulsants. Maintenance doses of adjunctive lamotrigine as high as 200 mg a day have been used in patients receiving only concurrent valproic acid.

Note: Since the effect of anticonvulsants (other than enzyme-inducing agents and valproic acid) on the metabolism of lamotrigine cannot be predicted, no specific dosing guidelines exist for concurrent use with these medications. Initial doses and dose escalations should be conservative; maintenance dosing would be expected to fall between the maintenance dose of lamotrigine when given with enzyme-inducing anticonvulsants and the maintenance dose of lamotrigine when given with enzyme-inducing anticonvulsants plus valproic acid.

Anticonvulsant, monotherapy of partial seizures following conversion from a single enzyme-inducing anticonvulsant medication[1]—

Lamotrigine should be added to the single enzyme-inducing anticonvulsant medication at a dose of 50 mg a day for the first two weeks, followed by 100 mg a day for the next two weeks. To reach the usual maintenance dose of 500 mg a day (in two divided doses), subsequent daily doses should be increased by 100 mg a day every one to two weeks. Once the maintenance dose of lamotrigine has been achieved, the enzyme-inducing anticonvulsant medication may be withdrawn over a four-week period by tapering the dose by 20% each week.

Anticonvulsant, monotherapy of partial seizures following conversion from adjunctive therapy with valproate

Bipolar disorder (treatment)—

Oral, target dose of 200 mg per day (100 mg per day in patients taking valproate and 400 mg per day in patients not taking valproate and taking either carbamazepine, phenytoin, phenobarbital, primidone, or rifampin). Treatment with lamotrigine is introduced, based on concurrent medications, according to the regimen outlined in the following table:

	For patients not taking carbamazepine, phenytoin, phenobarbital, primidone, or rifampin and not taking valproate	For patients taking valproate	For patients taking carbamazepine, phenytoin, phenobarbital, primidone, or rifampin and not taking valproate
Weeks 1 and 2	25 mg daily	25 mg every other day	50 mg daily
Weeks 3 and 4	50 mg daily	25 mg daily	100 mg daily, in divided doses
Week 5	100 mg daily	50 mg daily	200 mg daily, in divided doses
Week 6	200 mg daily	100 mg daily	300 mg daily, in divided doses
Week 7	200 mg daily	100 mg daily	up to 400 mg daily, in divided doses

Note: Carbamazepine, phenytoin, phenobarbital, primidone, and rifampin have been shown to increase the apparent clearance of lamotrigine.

Valproate has been shown to decrease the apparent clearance of lamotrigine.

If other psychotropic medications are withdrawn following stabilization, the dose of lamotrigine should be adjusted according to the following table:

	Discontinuation of psychotropic drugs (excluding carbamazepine, phenytoin, phenobarbital, primidone, rifampin, or valproate	After discontinuation of valproate	After discontinuation of carbamazepine, phenytoin, phenobarbital, primidone, or rifampin
		Current lamotrigine dose (mg/day) 100	Current lamotrigine dose (mg/day) 400
Week 1	Maintain current lamotrigine dose	150	400
Week 2	Maintain current lamotrigine dose	200	300
Week 3 onward	Maintain current lamotrigine dose	200	200

Anticonvulsant, monotherapy for treatment of epilepsy following withdrawal of concomitant anticonvulsant medications—

If the patient is transitioning from polytherapy, concomitant anticonvulsants may be decreased gradually by reducing the dose approximately twenty percent each week over a five-week period. Dosage may be tapered more slowly if clinically indicated.

Note: For patients with hepatic impairment—Initial escalation and maintenance doses should generally be reduced by approximately 50% and 75% in patients with moderate and severe hepatic impairment, respectively. Escalation and maintenance doses should be adjusted according to clinical response.

For patients with renal impairment—Initial doses of lamotrigine should be based on patients' AED regimen; reduced maintenance doses may be effective for patients with significant renal function impairment.

For women taking or starting oral contraceptives—

- For women not taking carbamazepine, phenytoin, phenobarbital, primidone, or rifampin, the maintenance dose of lamotrigine may need to be increased by as much as 2-fold over the recommended target maintenance dose, according to clinical response.
- For women taking lamotrigine in addition to carbamazepine, phenytoin, phenobarbital, primidone, or rifampin, no adjustment should be necessary.

For women stopping oral contraceptives—

- For women not taking carbamazepine, phenytoin, phenobarbital, primidone, or rifampin, the maintenance dose of lamotrigine may need to be decreased by as much as 50% of the maintenance dose with concurrent oral contraceptives, according to clinical response.
- For women taking lamotrigine in addition to carbamazepine, phenytoin, phenobarbital, primidone, or rifampin, no adjustment should be necessary.

For women taking other hormonal contraceptive preparations or hormone replacement therapy—The effect of these on the pharmacokinetics of lamotrigine has not been evaluated, the effect may be similar to oral contraceptives. Therefore, similar adjustments to the dosage of lamotrigine may be needed, based on clinical response.

Usual adult prescribing limits

With enzyme-inducing anticonvulsants only—700 mg a day in two divided doses.

With enzyme-inducing anticonvulsants and valproic acid—400 mg a day in two divided doses.

For treatment of bipolar disorder—doses above 200 mg per day not recommended

Usual pediatric dose

Note: Pediatric patients who weigh less than 6.7 kg (14.7 pounds) should not take lamotrigine because therapy cannot be initiated with the currently available tablet strengths.

Anticonvulsant, adjunctive treatment of Lennox-Gastaut syndrome

Anticonvulsant, adjunctive treatment of partial seizures—

Children 2 to 12 years of age—

With enzyme-inducing anticonvulsants only:

Initial—

Weeks one and two—Oral, 0.6 mg per kg of body weight per day in two divided doses, rounded down to the nearest whole tablet.

Weeks three and four—Oral, 1.2 mg per kg of body weight per day in two divided doses, rounded down to the nearest whole tablet.

Maintenance—

Oral, 5 to 15 mg per kg of body weight per day, with a maximum of 400 mg per day in two divided doses. To achieve the usual maintenance dose, subsequent daily doses should be increased every one to two weeks by 1.2 mg per kg of body weight, rounded down to the nearest whole tablet.

With enzyme-inducing anticonvulsants and valproic acid:

Initial—

Weeks one and two—Oral, 0.15 mg per kg of body weight per day, rounded down to the nearest whole tablet, and administered in one dose or two divided doses. If the initial calculated daily dose of lamotrigine is 2.5 to 5 mg, then 5 mg should be taken every other day for the first two weeks.

Weeks three and four—Oral, 0.3 mg per kg of body weight per day, rounded down to the nearest whole tablet, and administered in one dose or two divided doses.

Maintenance—

Oral, 1 to 5 mg per kg of body weight per day, with a maximum of 200 mg per day in one dose or two divided doses. To achieve the usual maintenance dose, subsequent daily doses should be increased every one to two weeks by 0.3 mg per kg of body weight, rounded down to the nearest whole tablet.

Note: It is likely that children weighing less than 30 kg may need the maintenance dose increased by as much as 50% based on clinical response.

Children older than 12 years of age—

With enzyme-inducing anticonvulsants only:

Initial—

Weeks one and two—Oral, 50 mg once a day.

Weeks three and four—100 mg a day in two divided doses.

Maintenance—

300 to 500 mg a day in two divided doses; maintenance dose may be achieved by increasing the dose by 100 mg a day every one to two weeks.

With enzyme-inducing anticonvulsants and valproic acid:

Initial—

Weeks one and two—Oral, 25 mg once every other day.

Weeks three and four—25 mg once a day.

Maintenance—

100 to 400 mg a day in one dose or two divided doses; maintenance dose may be achieved by increasing the dose every one to two weeks by 25 to 50 mg a day.

Note: The usual maintenance dose in children older than 12 years of age taking lamotrigine as an adjunct to valproic acid alone is 100 to 200 mg a day.

Usual pediatric prescribing limits

Children 2 to 12 years of age—

With enzyme-inducing anticonvulsants only: 400 mg a day (in two divided doses).

With enzyme-inducing anticonvulsants and valproic acid: 200 mg a day (in one dose or two divided doses).

Children 12 years of age and older—

See *Usual adult prescribing limits*.

Strength(s) usually available

U.S.—

25 mg (Rx) [*Lamictal* (scored; lactose)].

100 mg (Rx) [*Lamictal* (scored; lactose)].

150 mg (Rx) [*Lamictal* (scored; lactose)].

200 mg (Rx) [*Lamictal* (scored; lactose)].

Canada—

25 mg (Rx) [*Lamictal* (scored; lactose)].

100 mg (Rx) [*Lamictal* (scored; lactose)].

150 mg (Rx) [*Lamictal* (scored; lactose)].

Packaging and storage

Store between 15 and 25 °C (59 and 77 °F), in a well-closed container. Protect from light.

Auxiliary labeling

- May cause blurred vision.
- May cause dizziness.
- May cause drowsiness. Alcohol may intensify this effect.

LAMOTRIGINE TABLETS (CHEWABLE/DISPERSIBLE)

Note: Only wholly intact chewable/dispersible tablets of lamotrigine should be administered. If the calculated dose cannot be achieved using whole tablets, the dose should be rounded down to the nearest whole tablet.

Chewable/dispersible tablets may be swallowed whole, chewed, or dispersed in water or diluted fruit juice. If tablets are chewed, they should be followed with a small amount of water or diluted fruit juice to aid in swallowing.

Usual adult dose

See *Lamotrigine Tablets*.

Usual adult prescribing limits

See *Lamotrigine Tablets*.

Usual pediatric dose

See *Lamotrigine Tablets*.

Usual pediatric prescribing limits

See *Lamotrigine Tablets*.

Strength(s) usually available

U.S.—

2 mg (Rx) [*Lamictal* (blackcurrant flavor; saccharin sodium)].

5 mg (Rx) [*Lamictal* (blackcurrant flavor; saccharin sodium)].

25 mg (Rx) [*Lamictal* (blackcurrant flavor; saccharin sodium)].

Canada—

Not commercially available.

Packaging and storage
Store between 20 and 25 °C (68 and 77 °F). Protect from moisture.

Preparation of dosage form
If the tablets are not to be swallowed or chewed—The chewable/dispersible tablets should be placed in a small amount of liquid (enough to cover the medication, or about 1 teaspoonful). After the tablets are completely dispersed (approximately 1 minute), the solution should be swirled and the entire quantity consumed immediately. Partial quantities of the dispersed tablets should not be administered.

Auxiliary labeling
- May cause blurred vision.
- May cause dizziness.
- May cause drowsiness. Alcohol may intensify this effect.

---

[1]Not included in Canadian product labeling.

Selected Bibliography
Gilman JT. Lamotrigine: an antiepileptic agent for the treatment of partial seizures. Ann Pharmacother 1995 Feb; 29: 144-51.

Burstein AH. Lamotrigine. Pharmacotherapy 1995; 15(2): 129-43.

Fitton A, Goa KL. Lamotrigine: an update of its pharmacology and therapeutic use in epilepsy. Drugs 1995; 50(4): 691-713.

Revised: 09/23/2005
Developed: 05/23/1996

LANSOPRAZOLE Systemic

VA CLASSIFICATION (Primary): GA304

Commonly used brand name(s): *Prevacid; Prevacid I.V.*.

Note: For a listing of dosage forms and brand names by country availability, see *Dosage Forms* section(s).

Category
Gastric acid pump inhibitor; antiulcer agent.

Indications

Accepted
Gastroesophageal reflux disease [GERD] (prophylaxis and treatment)—Lansoprazole is indicated for the short-term treatment of heartburn and other symptoms associated with gastroesophageal reflux disease (GERD). Lansoprazole is indicated for the short-term (up to 8 weeks) treatment for symptom relief and healing of all grades of erosive esophagitis (associated with GERD). Lansoprazole may be indicated for an additional 8 weeks of treatment in patients in whom healing has not occurred. If erosive esophagitis recurs, an additional course of lansoprazole treatment may be considered. Lansoprazole also is indicated to maintain healing of erosive esophagitis.

Lansoprazole for injection is indicated as an alternative for the short-term treatment (up to 7 days) of all grades of erosive esophagitis when patients are unable to take the oral formulation. Once the patient is able to take medications orally, therapy can be switched to an oral formulation of lansoprazole for a total of 6 to 8 weeks.

Ulcer, gastric (treatment)—Lansoprazole is indicated for short-term (up to 8 weeks) treatment in patients with active benign gastric ulcer.

Ulcer, duodenal (prophylaxis and treatment)—Lansoprazole is indicated for short-term (up to 4 weeks) treatment for symptom relief and healing in patients with active duodenal ulcer. Lansoprazole also is indicated to maintain healing of duodenal ulcers.

Ulcer, duodenal, *Helicobacter pylori*–associated (treatment)—Lansoprazole is indicated in combination with amoxicillin plus clarithromycin for the treatment of duodenal ulcer associated with *H. pylori* infection. Lansoprazole also is indicated in combination with amoxicillin in patients who are either allergic or intolerant to clarithromycin or in whom resistance to clarithromycin is known or suspected. Eradication of *H. pylori* has been shown to reduce the risk of ulcer recurrence.

Hypersecretory conditions, gastric (treatment)—Lansoprazole is indicated for the long-term treatment of pathological hypersecretory conditions, including Zollinger-Ellison syndrome.

Acceptance not established
The safety and efficacy has not been demonstrated for the use of lansoprazole for injection as an initial treatment of erosive esophagitis.

Pharmacology/Pharmacokinetics
Note: A wide range of intersubject variability has been observed in the pharmacokinetic parameters of lansoprazole.

Physicochemical characteristics
Note: Lansoprazole is chemically and pharmacologically related to omeprazole.

Chemical Group—Substituted benzimidazole.

Molecular weight—369.37.

pKa—8.5.

pH—IV after first reconstitution with sterile water for injection: approximately 11

Mechanism of action/Effect
Lansoprazole is a selective and irreversible proton pump inhibitor. In the acidic environment of the gastric parietal cell, lansoprazole is converted to active sulphenamide derivatives that bind to the sulfhydryl group of (H^+, K^+)-adenosine triphosphatase [(H^+, K^+)-ATPase], also known as the proton pump. (H^+, K^+)-ATPase catalyzes the final step in the gastric acid secretion pathway. Lansoprazole's inhibition of (H^+, K^+)-ATPase results in inhibition of both centrally and peripherally mediated gastric acid secretion. The inhibitory effect is dose-related. Lansoprazole inhibits both basal and stimulated gastric acid secretion regardless of the stimulus.

Following oral administration, lansoprazole significantly decreases basal acid output and significantly increases the mean gastric pH and percent of time the gastric pH remains above 3 and 4. It also significantly reduces meal-stimulated gastric acid output and secretion volume, as well as pentagastrin-stimulated acid output. In addition, lansoprazole inhibits the normal increases in secretion volume, acidity, and acid output induced by insulin.

Lansoprazole does not have anticholinergic or histamine H_2-receptor antagonist properties.

Other actions/effects
Due to the normal physiologic effects caused by the inhibition of gastric acid secretion, blood flow in the antrum, pylorus, and duodenal bulb is decreased by about 17%; however, mucosal blood flow in the fundus of the stomach is not significantly affected by lansoprazole. Gastric emptying of digestible solids following intake of lansoprazole is significantly slowed. Lansoprazole increases serum pepsinogen levels and decreases pepsin activity under basal conditions and in response to meal stimulation or insulin injection. As with other agents that elevate intragastric pH, lansoprazole may cause an increase in the number of nitrate-reducing bacteria and an elevation in the nitrate concentration of gastric secretions in patients with gastric ulcer; however, significantly elevated nitrosamine levels have not been reported to date, suggesting no risk of carcinogenesis by this mechanism.

Lansoprazole and its active metabolites have demonstrated antimicrobial activity *in vitro* against *Helicobacter pylori*, a gram-negative bacilli strongly associated with peptic ulcers. Lansoprazole may influence the mucosal immune response to *H. pylori*. Mucosal *H. pylori*–specific IgA response is significantly enhanced after short-term treatment with lansoprazole, strongly suggesting that the secretory immune system is actively involved in host defense against *H. pylori*, and that the efficacy of such a system at the gastric mucosal level is crucial for complete eradication of *H. pylori*. Although lansoprazole alone has a relatively low clearance effect on *H. pylori*, it may enhance the ability of other agents to eradicate the organism; lansoprazole's activity as an antisecretory agent may be the more important factor explaining its effectiveness.

Lansoprazole has the ability to inhibit the hepatic cytochrome P450 enzyme system.

Absorption
Since lansoprazole is acid-labile, it is administered as a capsule containing enteric-coated granules to prevent gastric decomposition and to increase bioavailability. Once lansoprazole has left the stomach, absorption is rapid and relatively complete, with absolute bioavailability over 80%. Bioavailability may be decreased if lansoprazole is administered within 30 minutes of food intake as compared to that of a fasting state. Absorption may be delayed in patients with hepatic cirrhosis.

AUC 30 mg IV: 3192 ±1745 ng h/mL

Distribution
Distributed in tissue, particularly gastric parietal cells. Apparent oral volume of distribution following administration of 30 mg of lansoprazole is about 0.5 liters per kilogram (L/kg).

Protein binding
Very high (around 97%); protein binding remains constant over the concentration range of 0.05 to 5 mcg per mL. In patients with renal function impairment, protein binding may be decreased by 1 to 1.5%.

Biotransformation
Lansoprazole is extensively metabolized in the liver to two main excretory metabolites that are inactive. In the acidic environment of the gastric parietal cell, lansoprazole is converted to two active compounds that inhibit acid secretion by (H+, K+)-ATPase within the parietal cell canaliculus, but that are not present in the systemic circulation.

Half-life
Elimination—
- Normal renal function: Approximately 1.5 hours.
- Renal function impairment: Shortened elimination half-life.
- Elderly patients: 1.9 to 2.9 hours.
- Hepatic function impairment: 3.2 to 7.2 hours.

Onset of action
An increase in gastric pH is seen within 2 to 3 hours following a single 15-mg dose, 1 to 2 hours following a single 30-mg dose or a 15-mg multiple-dose regimen, and 1 hour following a 30-mg multiple-dose regimen.

Time to peak concentration
Approximately 1 to 2 hours. Time to peak concentration (t_{max}) is shorter when lansoprazole is administered in the morning as opposed to the evening.

Peak serum concentration
Mean peak serum concentrations (C_{max}) ranged from 0.75 to 1.15 milligrams per Liter (mg/L) following administration of a single oral 30-mg dose of lansoprazole to volunteers. Although there is no correlation with serum concentrations of lansoprazole per se, inhibition of gastric secretion appears to be dose-proportional. Serum concentrations after morning dosing may be increased by twofold or more as compared to evening dosing regimens. Both C_{max} and the area under the plasma concentration-time curve (AUC) decrease by about 50% when lansoprazole is administered within 30 minutes of food intake as opposed to fasting conditions. The concentration of lansoprazole and its active metabolites within the gastric parietal cell is the main determining factor of antisecretory efficacy.

Mean peak serum concentration (C_{max}): 1705 ± 292 ng/mL following a single 30 mg dose by IV infusion over 30 minutes

Duration of action
More than 24 hours. Following discontinuation of lansoprazole, gastric acid levels do not increase to half the basal output until 39 hours have elapsed. No rebound gastric acidity has been observed following discontinuation of lansoprazole. In patients with Zollinger-Ellison syndrome, the duration of action of lansoprazole is prolonged.

Elimination
Renal—Approximately 14 to 25% of a dose of lansoprazole is excreted in the urine, as conjugated and unconjugated hydroxylated metabolites. Less than 1% of unchanged lansoprazole is detectable in the urine.

Biliary/fecal—Approximately two-thirds of a dose of lansoprazole is detected as metabolites in the feces.

In dialysis—Lansoprazole and its metabolites are not significantly dialyzed; no appreciable fraction is removed by hemodialysis.

Note: Elimination is prolonged in healthy elderly subjects, in adult and elderly patients with mild renal impairment, and in patients with severe liver disease.

Precautions to Consider

Carcinogenicity
In 2-year studies in rats receiving up to 40 times the recommended human dose, lansoprazole produced dose-related gastric enterochromaffin-like (ECL) cell hyperplasia and ECL cell carcinoids in both male and female rats. Lansoprazole also increased the incidence of intestinal metaplasia of the gastric epithelium, and produced dose-related increases in the incidence of testicular interstitial adenomas. In a 1-year toxicity study in rats receiving 13 times the recommended human dose, testicular interstitial cell adenoma also occurred in 1 of 30 rats. In a 2-year study in mice receiving up to 80 times the recommended human dose, lansoprazole produced an increased incidence of liver tumors (hepatocellular adenomas and carcinomas), a dose-related increase in the incidence of gastric ECL cell hyperplasia, and adenomas of the rete testis in males.

Mutagenicity
Lansoprazole was not genotoxic in the Ames test, the *ex vivo* rat hepatocyte unscheduled DNA synthesis (UDS) test, the *in vivo* mouse micronucleus test, or the rat bone marrow cell chromosomal aberration test. It was positive in *in vitro* human lymphocyte chromosomal aberration assays.

Pregnancy/Reproduction
Fertility—Reproduction studies in rats and rabbits have shown no evidence of impaired fertility.

Pregnancy—Adequate and well-controlled studies in humans have not been done.

Reproductive studies in rats and rabbits at doses 40 times the recommended human dose have not shown that lansoprazole causes adverse effects in the fetus.

FDA Pregnancy Category B.

Breast-feeding
It is not known whether lansoprazole is distributed into breast milk. However, lansoprazole or its metabolites are distributed into the milk of rats. Because lansoprazole has been shown to cause tumorigenic effects in animals, a decision should be made as to whether nursing should be discontinued or the medication withdrawn, taking into account the importance of lansoprazole to the mother.

Pediatrics
Oral: The safety and effectiveness of lansoprazole have been established in pediatric patients 1 to 17 years of age for short-term treatment of symptomatic GERD and erosive esophagitis. Safety and effectiveness have not been established in patients less than one year of age.

Intravenous: The safety and effectiveness of lansoprazole for injection have not been established for pediatric patients.

Geriatrics
Studies in elderly patients indicate that the clearance of lansoprazole is decreased in the elderly, resulting in a 50 to 100% increase in the elimination half-life. Because the mean half-life in the elderly remains between 1.9 and 2.9 hours, repeated once-daily dosing does not result in accumulation of lansoprazole. However, subsequent doses higher than 30 mg a day should not be administered unless additional gastric acid suppression is necessary.

Drug interactions and/or related problems
The following drug interactions and/or related problems have been selected on the basis of their potential clinical significance (possible mechanism in parentheses where appropriate)—not necessarily inclusive (» = major clinical significance):

Note: Only specific interactions between lansoprazole and other medications have been identified in this monograph. However, lansoprazole, by increasing gastric pH, has the potential to affect the bioavailability of any medication whose absorption is pH-dependent. Also, lansoprazole may prevent the degradation of acid-labile drugs.

Possible interactions of lansoprazole with medications known to be metabolized by the hepatic cytochrome P450 enzyme system should be considered. To date, however, lansoprazole appears to interact minimally with other agents, and no clinically relevant interactions have been reported with antipyrine:arithromycin; diazepam; ibuprofen, indomethacin, or other nonsteroidal anti-inflammatory drugs (NSAIDs); oral contraceptives; phenytoin; prednisone or prednisolone; or propranolol.

Combinations containing any of the following medications, depending on the amount present, may also interact with this medication.

Ampicillin esters or
Digoxin or
Iron salts or
Ketoconazole
(lansoprazole causes prolonged inhibition of gastric acid secretion, and thereby may interfere with the absorption of these medications and others for which bioavailability is determined by gastric pH)

Cyanocobalamin
(lansoprazole appears to produce a dose-dependent decrease in the absorption of cyanocobalamin; this may be due to lansoprazole-induced hypochlorhydria or achlorhydria)

» Sucralfate
(lansoprazole absorption is delayed and bioavailability is decreased; lansoprazole should be taken at least 30 minutes prior to sucralfate)

Theophylline
(minor increases in the clearance of theophylline may occur, but the interaction is unlikely to be clinically significant; however, some patients may require adjustment of theophylline dosage when initiating or stopping lansoprazole therapy to maintain clinically effective concentrations of theophylline)

» Warfarin
(use with caution, concomitant use may increase International Normalized Ratio [INR]; monitor INR and prothrombin time)

Laboratory value alterations
The following have been selected on the basis of their potential clinical significance (possible effect in parentheses where appropriate)—not necessarily inclusive (» = major clinical significance).

Note: Although abnormalities in test values reported to date have generally not been of substantial clinical significance, the following have been selected on the basis of their *potential* clinical significance.

With physiology/laboratory test values

Alanine aminotransferase (ALT [SGPT]) and
Alkaline phosphatase and
Aspartate aminotransferase (AST [SGOT]) and
Bilirubin and
Gamma-glutamyltransferase (GGT) and
Globulins and
Lactate dehydrogenase (LDH)
(serum values may be increased)

Albumin/globulin (AG) ratio
(may be abnormal)

Cholesterol and
Electrolytes
(serum concentrations may be increased or decreased)

Creatinine, serum and
Glucocorticoids and
Triglycerides, serum and
Uric acid
(concentrations may be increased)

Gastrin, serum
(concentrations may be increased; median fasting gastrin concentrations may increase 50 to 100% from baseline but remain in the normal range following treatment with lansoprazole at doses of 15 to 60 mg; observations in over 2100 patients showed that elevations reached a plateau after 2 months of therapy and returned to baseline after treatment was discontinued)

Hematocrit and
Hemoglobin
(levels may be increased)

Platelet count and
Red blood cell (RBC) count and
White blood cell (WBC) count
(may be increased or decreased, and abnormalities may be present)

Medical considerations/Contraindications

The medical considerations/contraindications included have been selected on the basis of their potential clinical significance (reasons given in parentheses where appropriate)—not necessarily inclusive (» = major clinical significance).

Except under special circumstances, this medication should not be used when the following medical problem exists:

Hypersensitivity to lansoprazole

Risk-benefit should be considered when the following medical problems exist:

Hepatic function impairment
(dosage reduction may be required in patients with severe hepatic disease because of the prolonged plasma half-life of lansoprazole)

Phenylketonuria
(products that contain aspartame, which is metabolized to phenylalanine, may be hazardous to patients with phenylketonuria, especially young children; caution is recommended)

Side/Adverse Effects

The following side/adverse effects have been selected on the basis of their potential clinical significance (possible signs and symptoms in parentheses where appropriate)—not necessarily inclusive:

Those indicating need for medical attention

Incidence more frequent

Diarrhea; skin rash or itching

Incidence less frequent

Abdominal or stomach pain; arthralgia (joint pain); ***increased or decreased appetite; nausea; vomiting***

Incidence rare

Anxiety; constipation; influenza-like syndrome (flu-like symptoms); ***increased cough; mental depression; myalgia*** (muscle pain); ***thrombocytopenia*** (unusual bleeding or bruising); ***ulcerative colitis*** (diarrhea, abdominal pain, rectal bleeding); ***upper respiratory tract inflammation or infection*** (cold symptoms)

Incidence not determined—Observed during clinical practice, estimates of frequency can not be determined

Agranulocytosis (cough or hoarseness; fever with or without chills; general feeling of tiredness or weakness; lower back or side pain; painful or difficult urination; sore throat; sores, ulcers, or white spots on lips or in mouth; unusual bleeding or bruising); ***anaphylactoid-like reaction*** (cough; difficulty swallowing; dizziness; fast heartbeat; hives; itching; puffiness or swelling of the eyelids or around the eyes, face, lips or tongue; shortness of breath; skin rash; tightness in chest; unusual tiredness or weakness; wheezing); ***aplastic anemia*** (chest pain; chills; cough; fever; headache; shortness of breath; sores, ulcers, or white spots on lips or in mouth; swollen or painful glands; tightness in chest; unusual bleeding or bruising; unusual tiredness or weakness; wheezing); ***erythema multiforme*** (blistering, peeling, loosening of skin; chills; cough; diarrhea; fever; itching; joint or muscle pain; red irritated eyes; sore throat; sores, ulcers, or white spots in mouth or on lips; unusual tiredness or weakness); ***hemolytic anemia*** (back, leg, or stomach pains; bleeding gums; chills; dark urine; difficulty breathing; fatigue; fever; general body swelling; headache; loss of appetite; nausea or vomiting; nosebleeds; pale skin; sore throat; yellowing of the eyes or skin); ***hepatotoxicity*** (abdominal pain or tenderness; clay colored stools; dark urine; decreased appetite; fever; headache; itching; loss of appetite; nausea and vomiting; skin rash; swelling of feet or lower legs; unusual tiredness or weakness; yellow eyes or skin); ***leukopenia*** (black, tarry stools; chest pain; chills; cough fever; painful or difficult urination; shortness of breath; sore throat; sores, ulcers, or white spots on lips or in mouth; swollen glands; unusual bleeding or bruising; unusual tiredness or weakness); ***neutropenia*** (black, tarry, stools; chills; cough; fever; lower back or side pain; painful or difficult urination; pale skin; shortness of breath; sore throat; ulcers, sores, or white spots in mouth; unusual bleeding or bruising; unusual tiredness or weakness); ***pancreatitis*** (bloating; chills; constipation; darkened urine; fast heartbeat; fever; indigestion; loss of appetite; nausea; pains in stomach, side, or abdomen, possibly radiating to the back; vomiting; yellow eyes or skin); ***pancytopenia*** (high fever; chills; unexplained bleeding or bruising; bloody, black, or tarry stools; pale skin; unusual tiredness or weakness; cough; shortness of breath; sores, ulcers, or white spots on lips or in mouth; swollen glands); ***Stevens-Johnson syndrome*** (blistering, peeling, loosening of skin; chills; cough; diarrhea; itching; joint or muscle pain; red irritated eyes; red skin lesions, often with a purple center; sore throat; sores, ulcers, or white spots in mouth or on lips; unusual tiredness or weakness); ***thrombotic thrombocytopenic purpura*** (change in mental status; dark or bloody urine; difficulty speaking; fever; pale color of skin; pinpoint red spots on skin; seizures; weakness; yellow eyes or skin); ***toxic epidermal necrolysis*** (blistering, peeling, loosening of skin; chills; cough; diarrhea; itching; joint or muscle pain; red irritated eyes; red skin lesions, often with a purple center; sore throat; sores, ulcers, or white spots in mouth or on lips; unusual tiredness or weakness)

Those indicating need for medical attention only if they continue or are bothersome

Incidence more frequent

Dizziness; headache

Incidence less frequent

constipation (difficulty having a bowel movement (stool))—intravenous; ***injection site pain***—intravenous; ***injection site reaction*** (bleeding, blistering, burning, coldness, discoloration of skin, feeling of pressure, hives, infection, inflammation, itching, lumps, numbness, pain, rash, redness, scarring, soreness, stinging, swelling, tenderness, tingling, ulceration, or warmth at site)—intravenous; ***nausea, mild***

Incidence rare frequent

diarrhea, mild—intravenous; ***dyspepsia*** (acid or sour stomach; belching; heartburn; indigestion; stomach discomfort, upset or pain)—intravenous; ***paresthesia*** (burning, crawling, itching, numbness, prickling, “pins and needles”, or tingling feelings)—intravenous; ***rash***—intravenous; ***taste perversion*** (change in taste; bad, unusual or unpleasant (after) taste)—intravenous; ***vasodilatation*** (feeling of warmth or heat; flushing or redness of skin, especially on face and neck; headache; feeling faint, dizzy, or light-headedness; sweating)—intravenous; ***vomiting, mild***—intravenous

Incidence not determined—Observed during clinical practice, estimates of frequency can not be determined

Speech disorder (difficulty in speaking); ***urinary retention*** (decrease in urine volume; decrease in frequency of urination; difficulty in passing urine [dribbling]; painful urination)

Overdose

For information on the management of overdose or unintentional ingestion, **contact a poison control center** (see *Poison Control Center Listing*).

Clinical effects of overdose

Experience with lansoprazole overdose is limited. In one case in which a patient consumed 600 mg of lansoprazole, no adverse reaction was noted.

Treatment of overdose

There is no specific antidote for lansoprazole. Treatment is essentially symptomatic and supportive.

To decrease absorption—Any unabsorbed material should be removed from the gastrointestinal tract.

Monitoring—The patient should be carefully monitored.

To enhance elimination—Hemodialysis does not remove an appreciable fraction of the total quantity of lansoprazole or its metabolites.

Patients in whom intentional overdose is confirmed or suspected should be referred for psychiatric consultation.

Patient Consultation

As an aid to patient consultation, refer to *Advice for the Patient, Lansoprazole (Systemic).*

In providing consultation, consider emphasizing the following selected information (» = major clinical significance):

Before using this medication

» Conditions affecting use, especially:

Hypersensitivity to lansoprazole

Lansoprazole was carcinogenic in rats (doses 4 to 40 times the recommended human dose; testicular interstitial cell adenoma) and mice (doses 40 to 80 times the recommended human dose; hepatocellular adenoma plus carcinoma).

Pregnancy—Lansoprazole should only be used during pregnancy if clearly needed

Breast-feeding—Because of the potential for serious adverse effects, a decision should be made whether to discontinue nursing or to discontinue the drug, taking into account the importance of the drug to the mother.

Use in children—Oral: The safety and effectiveness of lansoprazole have been established in pediatric patients 1 to 17 years of age for short-term treatment of symptomatic GERD and erosive esophagitis. Safety and effectiveness have not been established in patients less than one year of age.

Intravenous: The safety and effectiveness of intravenous lansoprazole have not been established in pediatric patients.

Other medications, especially sucralfate or warfarin

Proper use of this medication

» Importance of taking the oral form before a meal, preferably in the morning

» Swallowing capsule whole without crushing, breaking, or chewing; however, if patient cannot swallow whole, capsule may be opened and intact granules sprinkled on one tablespoon of applesauce or dispersed in juice and swallowed immediately; granules should not be chewed or crushed

» Compliance with therapy

» Proper dosing

Missed dose: Taking as soon as possible; not taking if almost time for next dose; not doubling doses

» Proper storage

Precautions while using this medication

» Regular visits to physician to check progress

Side/adverse effects

Signs of potential side effects, especially diarrhea, skin rash or itching, abdominal or stomach pain, arthralgia, increased or decreased appetite, nausea, vomiting, anxiety, constipation, influenza-like syndrome, increased cough, mental depression, myalgia, thrombocytopenia, ulcerative colitis, upper respiratory tract inflammation or infection

Signs of potential side effects observed during clinical practice, especially agranulocytosis, anaphylactoid-like reaction, aplastic anemia, erythema multiforme, hemolytic anemia, hepatotoxicity, leukopenia, neutropenia, pancreatitis, pancytopenia, Stevens-Johnson syndrome, thrombocytopenia, thrombotic thrombocytopenic purpura, or toxic epidermal necrolysis

General Dosing Information

Since lansoprazole is acid-labile, it is administered as a capsule containing enteric-coated granules to prevent gastric decomposition and to increase bioavailability. Capsules should be swallowed whole, and not chewed or crushed. However, if the patient has difficulty swallowing capsules, the capsule may be opened and the intact granules may be sprinkled on one tablespoon of applesauce or dispersed in juice and swallowed immediately; granules should not be chewed or crushed. For patients who have a nasogastric tube in place, lansoprazole capsules may be opened and the intact granules mixed in 40 milliliters (mL) of apple juice and administered through the tube into the stomach. After administration, the tube should be flushed with additional apple juice to clear the tube.

Symptomatic response to therapy does not preclude the presence of gastric malignancy.

In patients with hypersecretory conditions such as Zollinger-Ellison syndrome, dosing should be adjusted according to individual needs and should continue for as long as clinically indicated. In general, treatment goals are to maintain basal acid output below 10 mEq per hour (<10 mmol/hr). Doses up to 90 mg two times a day have been administered, in some cases for as long as four years.

Lansoprazole may be taken with antacids.

For intravenous lansoprazole, an in-line filter is provided to remove precipitate that may form when the reconstituted drug product is mixed with IV solutions; filtration does not alter the amount of lansoprazole that is available for administration

Diet/Nutrition

Lansoprazole capsules should be taken before breakfast if dosing is once a day, and before meals if dosing is two or three times a day.

Oral Dosage Forms

LANSOPRAZOLE DELAYED-RELEASE CAPSULES

Usual adult dose

Gastroesophageal reflux disease—

Oral, 15 mg once a day for the relief of heartburn and regurgitation. For the treatment of erosive esophagitis, 30 mg once a day for eight weeks is recommended. An additional eight-week course may be helpful for patients who do not heal in the first eight weeks. For recurrence of erosive esophagitis, a third eight-week course of treatment may be considered. In patients requiring maintenance therapy, a dose of 15 mg once a day is recommended.

Ulcer, gastric—

Oral, 15 to 30 mg once a day, preferably in the morning before breakfast, for up to eight weeks.

Ulcer, duodenal—

Oral, 15 to 30 mg once a day, preferably in the morning before a meal, for up to four weeks. In patients requiring maintenance therapy, doses of 15 mg once a day have been used.

Ulcer, duodenal, associated with *H. pylori* infection—

Oral, triple therapy regimens of lansoprazole 30 mg, plus amoxicillin 1 gram, plus clarithromycin 500 mg, in which all three medications are taken before meals twice a day for ten to fourteen days. For dual therapy regimens, lansoprazole 30 mg plus amoxicillin 1 gram, with both medications taken before meals three times a day for fourteen days.

Note: For the eradication of *H. pylori*, amoxicillin and clarithromycin should not be administered to patients with renal impairment since the appropriate dosage in this patient population has not yet been established.

Hypersecretory conditions, gastric, including Zollinger-Ellison syndrome—

Oral, initially 60 mg once a day, preferably in the morning before a meal, the dosage being increased as needed, and therapy continued for as long as clinically indicated. Some patients have received doses as high as 90 mg two times a day for as long as four years. Daily dosages greater than 120 mg should be administered in divided doses.

Note: Dosage reduction should be considered in patients with severe hepatic function impairment; the dose generally should not exceed 30 mg a day in these patients.

Usual adult prescribing limits

For duodenal and gastric ulcers—

30 mg a day.

For hypersecretory conditions—

180 mg a day.

Usual pediatric dose

Safety and efficacy in children less than 1 year of age have not been established.

Gastroesophageal reflux disease—

For those between 1 and 11 years of age weighing less than 30 kg: Oral, 15 mg once daily for up to 12 weeks for the relief of heartburn, regurgitation or erosive esophagitis. For those between 11 and 17 years of age weighing more than 30 kg: Oral, 30 mg once daily for up to 12 weeks for the relief of heartburn, regurgitation or erosive esophagitis. For those between 12 and 17 years of age: Oral, 15 mg for up to 8 weeks for the relief of heartburn and regurgitation; 30 mg for up to 8 weeks for the relief of erosive esophagitis.

Usual geriatric dose

See *Usual adult dose.*

Usual geriatric prescribing limits

30 mg a day.

Strength(s) usually available
U.S.—
15 mg (Rx) [*Prevacid*].
30 mg (Rx) [*Prevacid*].
Canada—
15 mg (Rx) [*Prevacid*].
30 mg (Rx) [*Prevacid*].

Packaging and storage
Store below 40 °C (104 °F), preferably between 15 and 30 °C (59 and 86 °F), unless otherwise specified by manufacturer. Store in a tight container.

Preparation of dosage form
For patients who cannot take oral solids
The capsule may be opened and the intact granules may be sprinkled on one tablespoon of applesauce and swallowed immediately. Alternatively, the intact granules may be dispersed in juice and swallowed immediately. Lansoprazole granules have been shown to remain intact *in vitro* in apple, cranberry, grape, orange, pineapple, prune, tomato, or V-8 vegetable juice for up to thirty minutes. For administration via a nasogastric tube: the capsule may be opened and the intact granules mixed in 40 milliliters (mL) of apple juice and administered through the tube. After administration, the tube should be flushed with additional apple juice to clear the tube.

Auxiliary labeling
• Take before meals.

LANSOPRAZOLE DELAYED-RELEASE ORAL SUSPENSION

Usual adult dose
Gastroesophageal reflux disease—
Oral, 15 mg once a day for the relief of heartburn and regurgitation. For the treatment of erosive esophagitis, 30 mg once a day for eight weeks is recommended. An additional eight-week course may be helpful for patients who do not heal in the first eight weeks. For recurrence of erosive esophagitis, a third eight-week course of treatment may be considered. In patients requiring maintenance therapy, a dose of 15 mg once a day is recommended.
Ulcer, gastric—
Oral, 15 to 30 mg once a day, preferably in the morning before breakfast, for up to eight weeks.
Ulcer, duodenal—
Oral, 15 to 30 mg once a day, preferably in the morning before a meal, for up to four weeks. In patients requiring maintenance therapy, doses of 15 mg once a day have been used.
Ulcer, duodenal, associated with *H. pylori* infection—
Oral, triple therapy regimens of lansoprazole 30 mg, plus amoxicillin 1 gram, plus clarithromycin 500 mg, in which all three medications are taken before meals twice a day for ten to fourteen days. For dual therapy regimens, lansoprazole 30 mg plus amoxicillin 1 gram, with both medications taken before meals three times a day for fourteen days.
Note: For the eradication of *H. pylori*, amoxicillin and clarithromycin should not be administered to patients with renal impairment since the appropriate dosage in this patient population has not yet been established.
Hypersecretory conditions, gastric, including Zollinger-Ellison syndrome—
Oral, initially 60 mg once a day, preferably in the morning before a meal, the dosage being increased as needed, and therapy continued for as long as clinically indicated. Some patients have received doses as high as 90 mg two times a day for as long as four years. Daily dosages greater than 120 mg should be administered in divided doses.
Note: Dosage reduction should be considered in patients with severe hepatic function impairment; the dose generally should not exceed 30 mg a day in these patients.

Usual adult prescribing limits
For duodenal and gastric ulcers—
30 mg a day.
For hypersecretory conditions—
180 mg a day.

Usual pediatric dose
Safety and efficacy in children less than 1 year of age have not been established.
Gastroesophageal reflux disease—
For those between 1 and 11 years of age weighing less than 30 kg: Oral, 15 mg once daily for up to 12 weeks for the relief of heartburn, regurgitation or erosive esophagitis. For those between 11 and 17 years of age weighing more than 30 kg: Oral, 30 mg once daily for up to 12 weeks for the relief of heartburn, regurgitation or erosive esophagitis. For those between 12 and 17 years of age: Oral, 15 mg for up to 8 weeks for the relief of heartburn and regurgitation; 30 mg for up to 8 weeks for the relief of erosive esophagitis.

Usual geriatric dose
See *Usual adult dose*.

Usual geriatric prescribing limits
30 mg a day.

Strength(s) usually available
U.S.—
15 mg (Rx) [*Prevacid*].
30 mg (Rx) [*Prevacid*].
Canada—
15 mg (Rx) [*Prevacid*].
30 mg (Rx) [*Prevacid*].

Packaging and storage
Store below 40 °C (104 °F), preferably between 15 and 30 °C (59 and 86 °F), unless otherwise specified by manufacturer. Store in a tight container.

Preparation of dosage form
Empty the packet contents into a container containing 2 tablespoons of water. Stir well and drink immediately. If any material remains after drinking, add more water and drink immediately. **This product should not be administered through enteral administration tubes**

Auxiliary labeling
• Take before meals.

LANSOPRAZOLE DELAYED-RELEASE ORALLY DISINTEGRATING TABLETS

Usual adult dose
Gastroesophageal reflux disease—
Oral, 15 mg once a day for the relief of heartburn and regurgitation. For the treatment of erosive esophagitis, 30 mg once a day for eight weeks is recommended. An additional eight-week course may be helpful for patients who do not heal in the first eight weeks. For recurrence of erosive esophagitis, a third eight-week course of treatment may be considered. In patients requiring maintenance therapy, a dose of 15 mg once a day is recommended.
Ulcer, gastric—
Oral, 15 to 30 mg once a day, preferably in the morning before breakfast, for up to eight weeks.
Ulcer, duodenal—
Oral, 15 to 30 mg once a day, preferably in the morning before a meal, for up to four weeks. In patients requiring maintenance therapy, doses of 15 mg once a day have been used.
Ulcer, duodenal, associated with *H. pylori* infection—
Oral, triple therapy regimens of lansoprazole 30 mg, plus amoxicillin 1 gram, plus clarithromycin 500 mg, in which all three medications are taken before meals twice a day for ten to fourteen days. For dual therapy regimens, lansoprazole 30 mg plus amoxicillin 1 gram, with both medications taken before meals three times a day for fourteen days.
Note: For the eradication of *H. pylori*, amoxicillin and clarithromycin should not be administered to patients with renal impairment since the appropriate dosage in this patient population has not yet been established.
Hypersecretory conditions, gastric, including Zollinger-Ellison syndrome—
Oral, initially 60 mg once a day, preferably in the morning before a meal, the dosage being increased as needed, and therapy continued for as long as clinically indicated. Some patients have received doses as high as 90 mg two times a day for as long as four years. Daily dosages greater than 120 mg should be administered in divided doses.
Note: Dosage reduction should be considered in patients with severe hepatic function impairment; the dose generally should not exceed 30 mg a day in these patients.

Usual adult prescribing limits
For duodenal and gastric ulcers—
30 mg a day.
For hypersecretory conditions—
180 mg a day.

Usual pediatric dose
Safety and efficacy in children less than 1 year of age have not been established.
Gastroesophageal reflux disease—
For those between 1 and 11 years of age weighing less than 30 kg: Oral, 15 mg once daily for up to 12 weeks for the relief of heartburn, regurgitation or erosive esophagitis. For those between 11 and 17

years of age weighing more than 30 kg: Oral, 30 mg once daily for up to 12 weeks for the relief of heartburn, regurgitation or erosive esophagitis. For those between 12 and 17 years of age: Oral, 15 mg for up to 8 weeks for the relief of heartburn and regurgitation; 30 mg for up to 8 weeks for the relief of erosive esophagitis.

Usual geriatric dose
See *Usual adult dose.*

Usual geriatric prescribing limits
30 mg a day.

Strength(s) usually available
U.S.—
15 mg (Rx) [*Prevacid*].
30 mg (Rx) [*Prevacid*].
Canada—
Not commercially available

Packaging and storage
Store below 40 °C (104 °F), preferably between 15 and 30 °C (59 and 86 °F), unless otherwise specified by manufacturer. Store in a tight container.

Preparation of dosage form
Do not chew. Place on tongue and allow to disintegrate, with or without water, until particles can be swallowed.
For use with an Oral Syringe:
- Place a 15 mg tablet in oral syringe and draw up approximately 4 mL of water, or place a 30 mg tablet in oral syringe and draw up approximately 10 mL of water
- Shake gently
- After tablet has dispersed, administer within 15 minutes
- Refill the syringe with approximately 2 mL (5 mL for the 30 mg tablet) of water, shake gently and administer any remaining contents

For use with a Nasogastric Tube:
- Place a 15 mg tablet in ≥ 8 French syringe and draw up approximately 4 mL of water, or place a 30 mg tablet in oral syringe and draw up approximately 10 mL of water
- Shake gently
- After tablet has dispersed, inject through the nasogastric tube into the stomach within 15 minutes
- Refill the syringe with approximately 5 mL of water, shake gently and administer any remaining contents

Auxiliary labeling
- Take before meals.

Note
Prevacid Solutab brand of oral disintegrating tablets contain aspartame, which is metabolized to phenylalanine and must be used with caution in patients with phenylketonuria

Parenteral Dosage Forms

LANSOPRAZOLE FOR INJECTION

Usual adult dose
Erosive esophagitis (treatment)—
Intravenous, 30 mg of lansoprazole per day by intravenous infusion over 30 minutes for up to 7 days when patients are unable to take oral therapy. When the patient is able to take medications orally, oral lansoprazole therapy may be given for a total of 6 to 8 weeks.

Note: For patients with severe liver disease: dosage adjustment should be considered

For patients with renal impairment: no dosage adjustment is necessary

Usual adult prescribing limits
For erosive esophagitis—
30 mg a day

Usual pediatric dose
Safety and efficacy in children have not been established.

Usual geriatric dose
See *Usual adult dose.*

Usual geriatric prescribing limits
30 mg a day

Strength(s) usually available
U.S.—
30 mg (Rx) [*Prevacid I.V.* (60 mg mannitol; 10 mg meglumine; 3.45 mg sodium hydroxide)].
Canada—
Not commercially available

Packaging and storage
Store at 25 °C (77 °F); excursions permitted between 15 and 30 °C (59 and 86 °F), unless otherwise specified by manufacturer. Protect from light.

Preparation of dosage form
Reconstitution in vial and preparation of admixture:
Reconstitute vial with 5 mL of sterile water for injection, USP. The resulting solution contains lansoprazole 6 mg per mL.
Mix gently until the powder is dissolved.
Dilute the reconstituted solution in either 50 mL of 5% dextrose injection, USP, Lactated Ringer's injection, USP, or 0.9% sodium chloride injection, USP
Dispense with in-line filter provided. Filter should be primed prior to administration.
Reconstitution with Baxter's MINI-BAG Plus container:
Reconstitute directly into 50 mL of 5% dextrose injection, USP or 0.9% sodium chloride injection, USP using Baxter's MINI-BAG Plus container.
Dispense with in-line filter provided. Filter should be primed prior to administration.

Stability
Reconstituted solution can be stored for 1 hour at 25 °C (77 °F) prior to further dilution.
Admixture should be stored at 25 °C (77 °F) for: In 5% dextrose injection, USP: 12 hours
In Lactated Ringer's injection, USP: 24 hours
In 0.9% Sodium Chloride injection, USP: 24 hours
Baxter's MINI-BAG admixture should be stored at 25 °C (77 °F) for: In 5% dextrose injection, USP: 8 hours
In 0.9% Sodium Chloride injection, USP: 24 hours

Revised: 08/25/2005

LANTHANUM Oral-Local†

VA CLASSIFICATION (Primary): AD900
Commonly used brand name(s): *Fosrenol.*
Note: For a listing of dosage forms and brand names by country availability, see *Dosage Forms* section(s).

†Not commercially available in Canada.

Category
Antihyperphosphatemic.

Indications

Accepted
Hyperphosphatemia (treatment)—Lanthanum is indicated to reduce serum phosphate in patients with end-stage renal disease.

Pharmacology/Pharmacokinetics

Physicochemical characteristics
Source—Lanthanum is a naturally occurring rare earth element.
Molecular weight—Lanthanum (anhydrous): 457.8.
Solubility—Practically insoluble in water.

Mechanism of action/Effect
When lanthanum is taken with meals, it binds with phosphates released from food during digestion, which results in decreased serum phosphate and calcium phosphate concentrations.

Absorption
Very low (bioavailability <0.002%) following single or multiple oral dose to healthy subjects. Food effects on lanthanum have not been evaluated, however the timing of food intake (during and 30 minutes after) has a negligible effect on the systemic level of lanthanum.

Protein binding
Very high (> 99%) to human plasma proteins including albumin α1-acid glycoprotein and transferrin.

Biotransformation
Lanthanum is not metabolized and is not a substrate of CYP450.

Half-life
Elimination—53 hours in plasma.
Elimination—estimates from bone, range from 2 to 3.6 years.

Time to peak concentration
Steady state bone concentrations were not reached during the period studied.

Peak plasma concentration
Oral: 1 ng/mL

Steady state plasma concentration
Oral: approximately 0.6 ng/mL

Elimination
Fecal

Renal: less than 2% of total plasma clearance in healthy volunteers; not measured in the dialysate of treated ESRD patients.

Precautions to Consider

Carcinogenicity
Studies done in rats given oral doses of lanthanum carbonate (2.5 times the maximum recommended daily human dose [MRHD]) for up to 104 weeks, revealed no evidence of carcinogenic potential. However, mice given oral doses of lanthanum (1.3 times the MRHD) for up to 99 weeks had an increased incidence of glandular stomach adenomas in male mice.

Mutagenicity
Lanthanum carbonate was not found to be mutagenic in the Ames test (bacterial mutation assay), and an *in vitro* HGPRT gene mutation and chromosomal aberration assays in Chinese hamster ovary cells. Lanthanum was also negative in an oral mouse micronucleus assay at doses 1.7 times the MRHD and in a micronucleus and unscheduled DNA synthesis assays in rats given IV lanthanum chloride (> 2000 times the peak human plasma concentration.)

Pregnancy/Reproduction
Fertility—Lanthanum carbonate did not affect mating or impair fertility in male or female rats.

Pregnancy—Adequate and well-controlled studies in humans have not been done. The effect of lanthanum carbonate on absorption of vitamins and other nutrients has not been studied in pregnant women. Lanthanum is not recommended for use in pregnancy.

Studies in pregnant rabbits given oral doses of lanthanum (5 time the MRHD) produced a reduction in maternal body weight gain and food consumption, increased post-implantation loss, reduced fetal weights, and delayed fetal ossification. Rats given lanthanum carbonate (3.4 times the MRHD) from implantation through lactation showed reduction in body weight gain and delayed eye opening and sexual development in offspring. However, oral administration in pregnant rats given doses (3.4 times the MRHD) resulted in no evidence of harm to the fetus.

FDA Pregnancy Category C

Labor and delivery—The effects of lanthanum on labor and delivery in humans is unknown. No effects due to lanthanum carbonate were seen in animal studies.

Breast-feeding
It is not known if lanthanum carbonate is distributed into human breast milk. Because many drugs are distributed into breast milk, caution should be exercised when lanthanum is administered to a nursing woman.

Pediatrics
In long-term animal studies, lanthanum was deposited into developing bone including growth plate; however, no growth abnormalities were identified. The consequences of this deposition in pediatric patients in unknown. Therefore, the use of lanthanum in pediatric patients is not recommended.

Geriatrics
Appropriate studies performed to date have not demonstrated geriatrics-specific problems that would limit the usefulness of lanthanum in the elderly.

Drug interactions and/or related problems
The following drug interactions and/or related problems have been selected on the basis of their potential clinical significance (possible mechanism in parentheses where appropriate)—not necessarily inclusive (» = major clinical significance):

Compounds known to interact with antacids
(not recommended to be taken within two hours of dosing with lanthanum)

Medical considerations/Contraindications
The medical considerations/contraindications included have been selected on the basis of their potential clinical significance (reasons given in parentheses where appropriate)—not necessarily inclusive (» = major clinical significance).

Risk-benefit should be considered when the following medical problems exist:

» Bowel obstruction or
» Crohn's disease or
» Peptic ulcer, acute or
» Ulcerative colitis
(caution should be exercised if lanthanum is administered to patients with these conditions)

Side/Adverse Effects
The following side/adverse effects have been selected on the basis of their potential clinical significance (possible signs and symptoms in parentheses where appropriate)—not necessarily inclusive:

Those indicating need for medical attention
Incidence more frequent

Dialysis graft occlusion (dialysis graft blockage)

Those indicating need for medical attention only if they continue or are bothersome
Incidence more frequent

Abdominal pain (stomach pain); ***constipation*** (difficulty having a bowel movement (stool)); ***diarrhea; nausea; rhinitis*** (stuffy nose; runny nose; sneezing); ***vomiting***

Overdose
For more information on the management of overdose or unintentional ingestion, **contact a poison control center** (see *Poison Control Center Listing*).

Treatment of overdose
Supportive care—

There is no known specific antidote to lanthanum. Treatment is generally symptomatic and supportive.

Daily doses up to 4718 mg per day were well tolerated when administered with food in clinical trials.

Patients in whom intentional overdose is confirmed or suspected should be referred for psychiatric consultation.

Patient Consultation
As an aid to patient consultation, refer to *Advice for the Patient, Lanthanum (Oral-Local)*.

In providing consultation, consider emphasizing the following selected information (» = major clinical significance):

Before using this medication
» Conditions affecting use, especially:

Pregnancy—It is not known if lanthanum affects the absorption of vitamins in pregnancy. Lanthanum is not recommended for use in pregnancy.

Breast-feeding—It is not known if lanthanum is distributed into human breast milk. Because many drugs are distributed into breast milk, caution should be exercised when lanthanum is administered to a nursing woman.

Use in children—Safety and efficacy in pediatric patients have not been established.

Other medical problems, especially bowel obstruction, Crohn's disease, peptic ulcer, or ulcerative colitis.

Proper use of this medication
» Taking with meals
» Compliance with therapy
» Chewing tablet before swallowing; not swallowing whole
» Following prescribed diet
» Proper dosing
Taking as soon as possible; not taking if almost time for next scheduled dose; not doubling doses
Proper storage

Precautions while using this medication
» Regular visits to physician to check progress

Side/adverse effects
Signs of potential side effects, especially dialysis graft occlusion.

General Dosing Information
Treatment of hyperphosphatemia usually includes all of the following: reduction of dietary intake of phosphate, removal of phosphate by dialysis and inhibition of intestinal phosphate absorption with phosphate binders.

Diet/Nutrition
The importance of each tablet being taken with or immediately following a meal, and that the tablet be chewed completely before swallowing.

Oral Dosage Forms

LANTHANUM CARBONATE CHEWABLE TABLET

Usual adult dose
Hyperphosphatemia—

Initial: Oral, 750 to 1500 mg divided and taken with meals, depending on the patient's serum phosphates levels

Note: The dose should be titrated every 2 to 3 weeks until an acceptable serum phosphate level is reached. Serum phosphate levels should be monitored as needed during dose titration and on a regular basis thereafter. The average patient required a total daily dose between 1500 and 3000 mg to reduce plasma phosphate levels to less than 6 mg/dL. Doses were generally titered in increments of 750 mg/day.

Usual adult prescribing limits
Up to 3750 mg daily.

Usual pediatric dose
Safety and efficacy have not been established

Usual geriatric dose
See *Usual adult dose.*

Usual geriatric prescribing limits
See *Usual adult prescribing limits.*

Strength(s) usually available
U.S.—
250 mg (base) (Rx) [*Fosrenol* (dextrates [hydrated] NF; colloidal silicon dioxide NF; magnesium stearate NF; talc USP)].
500 mg (base) (Rx) [*Fosrenol* (dextrates [hydrated] NF; colloidal silicon dioxide NF; magnesium stearate NF; talc USP)].

Packaging and storage
Store at 25 °C (77 °F), excursions permitted to 15 and 30 °C (59 and 86 °F). Protect from moisture.

Auxiliary labeling
- Take with food.
- Chew tablets before swallowing.

Developed: 12/14/2004

LARONIDASE Systemic†

VA CLASSIFICATION (Primary): HS451

Commonly used brand name(s): *Aldurazyme.*

Note: For a listing of dosage forms and brand names by country availability, see *Dosage Forms* section(s).

†Not commercially available in Canada.

Category

Enzyme replenisher.

Indications

Accepted

Mucopolysaccharidosis I (treatment)—Laronidase is indicated as an enzyme replacement treatment for patients with Hurler and Hurler-Schele forms of Mucopolysaccharidosis I (MPS I) and for patients with Schele form who have moderate to severe symptoms. The risk benefit for treating mildly affected patients with Schele form has not been established.

Laronidase has been shown to improve pulmonary function and walking capacity. Laronidase has not been evaluated for effects on the central nervous system manifestations of the disorder.

Pharmacology/Pharmacokinetics

Physicochemical characteristics

Source—Laronidase is a polymorphic variant of the human enzyme, α-L-iduronidase that is produced by recombinant DNA technology in a Chinese hamster ovary cell line.

Molecular weight—Laronidase: approximately 83 kD.

pH—approximately 5.5

Mechanism of action/Effect

Mucopolysaccharidosis I (MPS I) is the deficiency of α-L-iduronidase, a lysosomal hydrolase which catalyses the hydrolysis of terminal α-L-iduronic acid residues of dermatan sulfate and heparan sulfate. Reduced or absent α-L-iduronidase activity results in the accumulation of GAG substrates and, dermatan, and heparan sulfates leading to widespread cellular, tissue, and organ dysfunction. Laronidase provides exogenous enzyme for uptake into lysosomes and increases the catabolism of GAG. This uptake into the lysosomes is most likely mediated by the mannose-6–phosphate-terminated oligosaccharide chains of laronidase binding to specific mannose-6–phosphate receptors.

Absorption

The mean area under the plasma concentration time curve (AUC) ranged from 4.5 to 6.9 mcg hour/mL.

Distribution

Volume of distribution (Vol_D)—0.24 to 0.6 L/kg.

Blood brain barrier: the ability of laronidase to cross the blood brain barrier has not been evaluated.

Half-life

Elimination—1.5 to 3.6 hours

Peak plasma concentration:

1.2 to 1.7 mcg/mL

Precautions to Consider

Carcinogenicity/Mutagenicity

Studies to determine the carcinogenic and mutagenic potential of laronidase have not been done.

Pregnancy/Reproduction

Fertility—Studies done in rats have not demonstrated impairment of fertility.

Pregnancy—Adequate and well controlled studies in humans have not been done. Studies in animals have not shown that laronidase causes adverse effects in the fetus. Because animal studies are not always predictive of human response laronidase should be used during pregnancy only if clearly needed.

Breast-feeding

A registry has been established to better understand the variability and progression of MPS I and to monitor and evaluate treatments. Patients should be encouraged to participate and advised that their participation may involve long term follow up. Information regarding the registry program may be found at www.MPSIregistry.com or by calling (800) 745–4447. Nursing women are encouraged to participate in this program.

It is not known whether laronidase is distributed into breast milk. Because many drugs are distributed into human milk, caution should be exercised when laronidase is administered to a nursing woman.

Pediatrics

Appropriate studies performed to date have not demonstrated pediatrics-specific problems that would limit the usefulness of laronidase in children 5 years of age and older. It is not known if children under 5 respond differently from older children.

Geriatrics

No information is available on the relationship of age to the effects of laronidase in geriatric patients.

Medical considerations/Contraindications

The medical considerations/contraindications included have been selected on the basis of their potential clinical significance (reasons given in parentheses where appropriate)—not necessarily inclusive (» = major clinical significance).

Risk-benefit should be considered when the following medical problems exist:

» Hypersensitivity to laronidase or any of its components, or
» Anaphylactic reaction, previous
(if the decision is made to administer laronidase, extreme care should be exercised with appropriate resuscitation measures readily available)

Side/Adverse Effects

The following side/adverse effects have been selected on the basis of their potential clinical significance (possible signs and symptoms in parentheses where appropriate)—not necessarily inclusive:

Those indicating need for medical attention

Incidence more frequent

Abscess (accumulation of pus; swollen, red, tender area of infection; fever); ***bilirubinemia*** (chills; clay-colored stools; dark urine; dizziness; fever; headache; itching; loss of appetite; nausea; abdominal or stomach pain; area rash; unpleasant breath odor; unusual tiredness or weakness; vomiting of blood; yellow eyes or skin); ***chest pain; hypotension*** (blurred vision; confusion; dizziness, faintness, or lightheadedness when getting up from a lying or sitting position suddenly; sweating; unusual tiredness or weakness); ***infusion reaction common*** (fever; headache; skin rash); ***thrombocytopenia*** (black, tarry stools; bleeding gums; blood in urine or stools; pinpoint red spots on skin; unusual bleeding or bruising)

Incidence less frequent

Infusion reaction, less common including; angioedema (large, hive-like swelling on face, eyelids, lips, tongue, throat, hands, legs, feet, sex organs); ***bronchospasm*** (cough; difficulty breathing; noisy breathing; shortness of breath; tightness in chest; wheezing); ***cough; dyspnea*** (shortness of breath; difficult or labored breathing; tightness in chest wheezing); ***pruritus*** (itching skin); ***urticaria*** (hives or welts; itching; redness of skin; skin rash)

Those indicating need for medical attention only if they continue or are bothersome
Incidence more frequent
Corneal opacity (blindness; blurred vision; decreased vision); ***dependent edema*** (swelling of legs and feet); ***facial edema*** (swelling or puffiness of face); ***hyperreflexia*** (overactive reflexes); ***immunogenicity*** (body produces substance that can bind to drug making it less effective or cause side effects); ***injection site reaction*** (bleeding, blistering, burning, coldness, discoloration of skin; feeling of pressure; hives, infection, inflammation, itching, lumps, numbness, pain, rash, redness, scarring, soreness, stinging, swelling, tenderness, tingling, ulceration, or warmth at site); ***paresthesias*** (burning, crawling, itching, numbness, prickling, "pins and needles", or tingling feelings); ***rash; upper respiratory tract infection*** (ear congestion; nasal congestion; chills; cough; fever; sneezing; sore throat; body aches or pain; headache; loss of voice; runny nose; unusual tiredness or weakness; difficulty in breathing); ***vein disorder*** (varicose or spider veins)

Overdose

For more information on the management of overdose or unintentional ingestion, **contact a poison control center** (see *Poison Control Center Listing*).

Treatment of overdose

There is no known specific antidote to laronidase. Treatment is generally symptomatic and supportive.

Supportive care—
Patients in whom intentional overdose is confirmed or suspected should be referred for psychiatric consultation.

Patient Consultation

As an aid to patient consultation, refer to *Advice for the Patient, Laronidase (Systemic)*.

In providing consultation, consider emphasizing the following selected information (» = major clinical significance):

Before using this medication

» Conditions affecting use, especially:
Hypersensitivity to laronidase.
Pregnancy—Studies in humans have not been done. Studies in animals have not shown that laronidase causes harm to the fetus. However, animal studies are not always predictive of human response. Laronidase should be used in pregnancy only if clearly needed.
Breast-feeding—It is not known whether laronidase is distributed into breast milk.
Use in children—Safety and efficacy in children under the age of 5 have not been established.

Proper use of this medication

» Proper dosing
Missed dose: Talk to your doctor about rescheduling your next dose.
» Proper storage

Precautions while receiving this medication

Importance of monitoring by the physician

Side/adverse effects

Signs of potential side effects, especially abscess, bilirubinemia, chest pain, hypotension, infusion reaction, or thrombocytopenia.

General Dosing Information

Pretreatment with antipyretics and/or antihistamines is recommended 60 minutes prior to starting the laronidase infusion.

The initial infusion rate of 10 mcg/kg/hr may be incrementally increased every 15 minutes over the first hour, as tolerated, until the maximum infusion rate of 200 mcg/kg/hr is reached. The maximum rate is then maintained for the remainder of the infusion.

Laronidase contains no preservatives; therefore, any unused product or waste material should be discarded and disposed of in accordance with local requirements.

Parenteral Dosage Forms

LARONIDASE INJECTION CONCENTRATE

Usual adult and adolescent dose

Enzyme replenisher—
Intravenous infusion, 0.58 mg/kg of body weight administered over 3 to 4 hours, once weekly.

Usual pediatric dose

See *Usual adult and adolescent dose.* Safety and efficacy have not been established in children under 5 years of age.

Usual geriatric dose

Safety and efficacy have not been established.

Strength(s) usually available

U.S.—
2.9 mg of laronidase per 5 mL vial (Rx) [*Aldurazyme* (sodium chloride; sodium phosphate monobasic monohydrate; sodium phosphate dibasic heptahydrate; polysorbate 80)].

Packaging and storage

Store between 2 and 8°C (36 and 46 °F). Do not freeze.

Preparation of dosage form

On the day of use, the vial of laronidase is to be diluted with 0.1% Albumin (Human) in 0.9% Sodium Chloride Injection USP to a final volume of 100 or 250 mL. Laronidase should be prepared using PVC containers and administered with a PVC infusion set equipped with an in-line, low protein binding 0.2 micrometer filter.
• Determine the number of vials to be diluted. This is done based on the patient's weight and the recommended dose of 0.58 mg per kg of body weight. Round up to the nearest whole vial. Allow the vials to reach room temperature. Do not heat or microwave.
• Before withdrawing the laronidase concentrate from the vials, visually inspect each vial for particulate and discoloration. The solution should be clear to slightly opalescent and colorless to pale yellow. Do not use if there is particulate matter or if the solution is discolored.
• Determine the volume of the infusion to be used. The final volume should be 100 mL (if weight is less than or equal to 20 kg) or 250 mL (if weight is greater than 20 kg).
• Prepare the infusion bag of 0.1% Albumin (Human) in 0.9% Sodium Chloride Injection, USP. Remove and discard a volume of 0.9% Sodium Chloride Injection equal to the volume of Albumin (Human) to be added to the infusion bag. Add the appropriate volume of Albumin (Human) to the bag and rotate gently to mix.
• Remove and discard a volume of the 0.1% Albumin in 0.9% Sodium Chloride Injection from the infusion bag equal to the volume of laronidase concentrate to be added.
• Carefully withdraw the appropriate volume of laronidase concentrate to be added. Use caution to avoid excessive agitation. Do not use a filter needle as this may cause agitation and denature the laronidase rendering it inactive.
• Slowly and carefully add the laronidase concentrate to the 0.1% Albumin in 0.9% Sodium Chloride Injection avoiding agitation.
• To insure proper distribution of laronidase gently rotate the infusion bag. Do not shake.

Stability

Laronidase does not contain a preservative. The product information for laronidase states that the diluted solution should be used immediately. If immediate use is not possible, the diluted solution should be stored at 2 to 8 °C (36 to 46 °F). The in use storage should not be longer than 36 hours from the time of preparation to completion of administration.

Incompatibilities

Laronidase must not be mixed with other medicinal products in the same infusion line. The compatibility of laronidase in solution with other products has not been evaluated.

Auxiliary labeling

- Do not freeze.
- Do not shake.
- Dilute medication before use.

Developed: 04/09/2004

LATANOPROST Ophthalmic

VA CLASSIFICATION (Primary): OP116

Commonly used brand name(s): *Xalatan.*

Note: For a listing of dosage forms and brand names by country availability, see *Dosage Forms* section(s).

Category

Antiglaucoma agent (ophthalmic); antihypertensive, ocular.

Indications

Accepted

Glaucoma, open-angle (treatment) or
Hypertension, ocular (treatment)—Latanoprost is indicated in the treatment of open-angle glaucoma or ocular hypertension in patients who are intolerant of other intraocular pressure (IOP)–lowering medications or insufficiently responsive (i.e., failed to achieve target IOP after multiple measurements over time) to another IOP-lowering medication. Latanoprost may be used alone or in combination with other antiglaucoma agents.

Acceptance not established

There is limited experience with latanoprost in the treatment of angle-closure, inflammatory, or neovascular glaucoma.

Pharmacology/Pharmacokinetics

Physicochemical characteristics

Chemical Group—Latanoprost is a prostaglandin $F_{2\text{-alpha}}$ analog.
Molecular weight—432.58.
pH—Approximately 6.7.

Mechanism of action/Effect

Latanoprost is a prostaglandin $F_{2\text{-alpha}}$ analog. It is believed to reduce intraocular pressure by increasing the outflow of aqueous humor. Studies suggest that the main mechanism of action is increased uveoscleral outflow.

Absorption

Latanoprost is an isopropyl ester prodrug. It is absorbed into the cornea, where it is hydrolyzed by esterases to latanoprost acid, which is biologically active.

Distribution

Vol_D—0.16 ± 0.02 L per kg (L/kg). Latanoprost acid has been measured in aqueous humor during the first 4 hours and in plasma only during the first hour, following ophthalmic administration.

Biotransformation

Latanoprost is an isopropyl ester prodrug. It is hydrolyzed by esterases in the cornea to latanoprost acid, which is biologically active. The portion of the latanoprost acid that reaches the systemic circulation is metabolized primarily by the liver to 1,2-dinor and 1,2,3,4-tetranor metabolites by fatty acid beta-oxidation.

Half-life

The elimination of latanoprost acid from plasma is rapid (half-life 17 minutes) after either ophthalmic or intravenous administration.

Onset of action

Approximately 3 to 4 hours after administration.

Time to peak concentration

Peak concentration in the aqueous humor is reached approximately 2 hours after ophthalmic administration.

Time to peak effect

8 to 12 hours after administration.

Elimination

Metabolites are eliminated mainly via the kidneys. Approximately 88 or 98% of the administered dose can be recovered in the urine after ophthalmic or intravenous dosing, respectively.

Precautions to Consider

Carcinogenicity

Latanoprost was not carcinogenic in mice and rats that were administered oral doses of up to 170 mcg per kg of body weight (mcg/kg) a day (approximately 2800 times the recommended maximum human dose) for up to 20 and 24 months, respectively.

Mutagenicity

Latanoprost was not mutagenic in bacteria, mouse lymphoma, or mouse micronucleus tests. *In vitro* and *in vivo* studies of unscheduled DNA synthesis in rats were negative. However, *in vitro* tests using human lymphocytes showed chromosome aberrations.

Pregnancy/Reproduction

Fertility—In animal studies, latanoprost was not found to have any effect on male or female fertility.

Pregnancy—Adequate and well-controlled studies in humans have not been done. Risk-benefit should be carefully considered when latanoprost is used during pregnancy.

In rabbits, 4 of 16 dams had no viable fetuses after receiving a dose approximately 80 times the maximum recommended human dose. The highest nonembryocidal dose in rabbits was approximately 15 times the maximum recommended human dose.

FDA Pregnancy Category C.

Breast-feeding

It is not known whether latanoprost or its metabolites are distributed into breast milk. Caution should be exercised when latanoprost is administered to nursing women.

Pediatrics

Appropriate studies on the relationship of age to the effects of latanoprost have not been performed in the pediatric population. Safety and efficacy have not been established.

Geriatrics

No information is available on the relationship of age to the effects of latanoprost in geriatric patients.

Drug interactions and/or related problems

The following drug interactions and/or related problems have been selected on the basis of their potential clinical significance (possible mechanism in parentheses where appropriate)—not necessarily inclusive (» = major clinical significance):

Note: Combinations containing any of the following medications, depending on the amount present, may also interact with this medication.

» Thimerosal-containing ophthalmic medications
(precipitation occurs when latanoprost is applied concurrently with thimerosal-containing ophthalmic medications; an interval of at least 5 minutes should elapse between applications of these medications)

Medical considerations/Contraindications

The medical considerations/contraindications included have been selected on the basis of their potential clinical significance (reasons given in parentheses where appropriate)—not necessarily inclusive (» = major clinical significance).

Except under special circumstances, this medication should not be used when the following medical problems exist:

» Hypersensitivity to latanoprost
» Hypersensitivity to benzalkonium chloride

Risk-benefit should be considered when the following medical problems exist:

» Aphakia or
» Macular edema, including cystoid macular edema, risk factors for or
» Pseudophakia
(macular edema, including cystoid macular edema, has been reported during treatment with latanoprost, mainly in patients with aphakia, in patients with pseudophakia who have a torn posterior lens capsule, or in patients with known risk factors for macular edema; latanoprost should be used with caution in these patients)

Hepatic function impairment or
Renal function impairment
(studies have not been done in patients with hepatic or renal function impairment; therefore, caution should be used when administering latanoprost in these patients)

Iritis or
Uveitis
(latanoprost should be used with caution in patients with active intraocular inflammation [iritis/uveitis])

Patient monitoring

The following may be especially important in patient monitoring (other tests may be warranted in some patients, depending on condition; » = major clinical significance):

Ophthalmic examinations
(patients should be examined regularly and, depending on the clinical situation, treatment may be stopped if increased brown pigmentation of iris occurs)

Side/Adverse Effects

Note: Changes in pigmented tissues may occur with use of latanoprost. Latanoprost may gradually change eye color by increasing the number of melanosomes (pigment granules) in the melanocytes, thereby increasing the amount of brown pigment in the iris. The mechanism of this increased pigmentation is probably not associated with proliferation of the melanocytes, but rather with stimulation of melanin production within the melanocytes of the iris stroma. The long-term effects on the melanocytes, the consequences of potential injury to the melanocytes, and the possibility of deposition of pigment granules to other areas of the eye are not known. The change in iris color occurs slowly and may not be noticeable for several months to years. Patients with mixed-color irides, such as blue-brown, gray-brown, green-brown, or yellow-brown, appear to be predisposed to the iris pigmentation changes. In addition, latanoprost has been reported to cause increased pigmentation of the periorbital tissue (eyelid). Also, latanoprost may gradually change eyelashes. The changes to the lashes include increased length, thickness, pigmentation, and the number of lashes. Patients should be advised of all the effects listed above and informed that if only one eye is treated with the medication, only one eye will be affected (heterochromia between the eyes). The changes in pigmentation and eyelash growth may be permanent.

Macular edema, including cystoid macular edema, has been reported during treatment with latanoprost, mainly in patients with aphakia, in patients with pseudophakia who have a torn posterior lens capsule, or in patients with known risk factors for macular edema. It is recommended that latanoprost be used with caution in these patients.

The following side/adverse effects have been selected on the basis of their potential clinical significance (possible signs and symptoms in parentheses where appropriate)—not necessarily inclusive:

Those indicating need for medical attention

Incidence more frequent

Blurred vision; increased length, thickness, pigmentation, and number of eyelashes (longer, thicker, and darker eyelashes); ***increased pigmentation of iris*** (increase in brown color in colored part of eye); ***increased pigmentation of periorbital tissue*** (darkening of eyelid skin color); ***punctate epithelial keratopathy*** (blurred vision, eye irritation, or tearing)

Incidence less frequent

Allergic skin reaction (skin rash); ***angina pectoris or other chest pain; eye pain; eyelid crusting, redness, swelling, discomfort, or pain; pain in muscles, joints, or back; upper respiratory tract infection, cold, or flu*** (cold or flu symptoms)

Incidence rare

Asthma; exacerbation of asthma (cough; difficulty breathing; noisy breathing; shortness of breath; tightness in chest; wheezing); ***conjunctivitis*** (redness of eye or inside of eyelid); ***corneal edema and erosions*** (swelling of the eye); ***diplopia*** (double vision); ***discharge from the eye; dyspnea*** (shortness of breath; difficult or labored breathing; tightness in chest; wheezing); ***intraocular inflammation, such as iritis or uveitis*** (eye pain, tearing, sensitivity of eye to light, redness of eye, or blurred vision or other change in vision); ***macular edema, including cystoid macular edema*** (blurred vision or other change in vision); ***toxic epidermal necrolysis*** (fever; pain in muscles; skin rash; sore throat)

Those indicating need for medical attention only if they continue or are bothersome

Incidence more frequent

Burning of eye; conjunctival hyperemia (redness of eye or inside of eyelid); ***foreign body sensation*** (feeling of something in eye); ***itching of eye; stinging of eye***

Incidence less frequent

Dryness of eye; photophobia (increased sensitivity of eyes to light); ***tearing***

Overdose

For more information on the management of overdose or unintentional ingestion, **contact a Poison Control Center** (see *Poison Control Center Listing*).

Clinical effects of overdose

Other than ocular irritation or conjunctival or episcleral hyperemia, the ocular effects of high doses of latanoprost are not known.

Following intravenous doses of 3 mcg per kg of body weight (mcg/kg) in healthy volunteers (which produced mean plasma concentrations that were 200 times the mean plasma concentrations produced by the usual clinical dose), no adverse reactions were observed. However, intravenous doses of 5.5 to 10 mcg/kg caused abdominal pain, dizziness, fatigue, hot flushes, nausea, and sweating.

Treatment of overdose

Treatment of overdose should be symptomatic.

Patient Consultation

As an aid to patient consultation, refer to *Advice for the Patient, Latanoprost (Ophthalmic)*.

In providing consultation, consider emphasizing the following selected information (» = major clinical significance):

Before using this medication

» Conditions affecting use, especially:

Hypersensitivity to latanoprost, benzalkonium chloride, or any other ingredient in the product

Mutagenicity—*In vitro* tests using human lymphocytes showed chromosome aberrations

Breast-feeding—Caution should be exercised when latanoprost is administered to nursing women, since it is not known whether latanoprost or its metabolites are distributed into breast milk

Other medications, especially thimerosal-containing ophthalmic medications

Other medical problems, especially aphakia; macular edema, including cystoid macular edema, risk factors for; and pseudophakia

Proper use of this medication

» Using medication only as directed; not using more of it or using it more often than directed; to do so may increase absorption and the chance of side effects

If physician ordered two different eye drops to be used together, waiting at least 5 minutes between applications of medications to prevent second medication from "washing out" the first one

» Importance of regular visits to physician to check eye pressure during therapy

Removing contact lenses prior to administration of latanoprost; reinserting lenses, if desired, at least 15 minutes after administration

» Proper administration technique; preventing contamination; not touching applicator tip to any surface; keeping container tightly closed

» Proper dosing

Missed dose: Applying as soon as possible; not applying if not remembered until next day; applying regularly scheduled dose

» Proper storage

Precautions while using this medication

» Possibility of iris of eye becoming more brown in color; change in color of iris is usually noticeable within several months to years while using medication; in addition, possibility of the darkening of eyelid skin color; also, possibility of increased length, thickness, pigmentation, and the number of lashes; iris, eyelid, and lash pigmentation and other lash changes may be permanent even if medication is stopped; the color and lash changes will occur only to the eye being treated; if only one eye is treated, there is a possibility of having differently colored eyes and differently appearing eyelashes

Possibility of medication causing eyes to become more sensitive to light than they are normally; wearing sunglasses and avoiding too much exposure to bright light may help lessen discomfort

Side/adverse effects

Signs of potential side effects, especially blurred vision; increased length, thickness, pigmentation, and number of eyelashes; increased pigmentation of iris; increased pigmentation of periorbital tissue; punctate epithelial keratopathy; allergic skin reaction; angina pectoris or other chest pain; eye pain; eyelid crusting, redness, swelling, discomfort, or pain; pain in muscles, joints, or back; upper respiratory tract infection, cold, or flu; asthma or exacerbation of asthma; conjunctivitis; corneal edema and erosions; diplopia; discharge from the eye; dyspnea; intraocular inflammation, such as iritis or uveitis; macular edema, including cystoid macular edema; toxic epidermal necrolysis

General Dosing Information

Latanoprost may be used alone or in combination with other antiglaucoma agents. If more than one ophthalmic medication is used, the medications should be administered at least 5 minutes apart.

Latanoprost contains benzalkonium chloride, which may be absorbed by contact lenses. Contact lenses should be removed prior to administration of latanoprost. Lenses may be reinserted 15 minutes after administration.

Once-daily dosing of latanoprost should not be exceeded. More frequent administration may decrease the intraocular pressure-lowering effect of the medication.

Ophthalmic Dosage Forms

LATANOPROST OPHTHALMIC SOLUTION

Usual adult and adolescent dose

Antiglaucoma agent (ophthalmic)

Antihypertensive, ocular—

Topical, to the conjunctiva, 1 drop in the affected eye(s) once a day in the evening.

Usual adult prescribing limits
No more than one dose per day.

Usual pediatric dose
Safety and efficacy have not been established.

Strength(s) usually available
U.S.—

Note: One drop contains approximately 1.5 mcg of latanoprost.

0.005% (50 mcg per mL) (Rx) [*Xalatan* (benzalkonium chloride 0.02%; sodium chloride; sodium dihydrogen phosphate monohydrate; disodium hydrogen phosphate anhydrous; water for injection)].

Packaging and storage
Store the unopened bottle between 2 and 8 °C (36 and 46 °F), unless otherwise specified by manufacturer. Protect from light.

Stability
Once the container has been opened, the medication may be stored at room temperature (up to 25 °C [77 °F]) for up to 6 weeks before discarding.

Incompatibilities
A precipitation occurs when latanoprost is applied concurrently with thimerosal-containing ophthalmic medications; an interval of at least 5 minutes should elapse between applications of these medications.

Auxiliary labeling
- For the eye.
- Keep container tightly closed.

Revised: 04/18/2000
Developed: 06/12/1997

LEFLUNOMIDE Systemic

VA CLASSIFICATION (Primary): MS109
Commonly used brand name(s): *Arava*.

Note: For a listing of dosage forms and brand names by country availability, see *Dosage Forms* section(s).

Category
Antirheumatic (disease-modifying).

Indications
General Considerations
For women of childbearing potential and men wishing to father a child, see the

Pregnancy/Reproduction section of

Precautions to Consider for restrictions on the use of leflunomide.

Accepted
Arthritis, rheumatoid, adult (treatment)—Leflunomide is indicated in adults for the treatment of active rheumatoid arthritis (RA) to reduce signs and symptoms, to inhibit structural damage as evidenced by x-ray erosion and joint space narrowing, and to improve physical function.

Pharmacology/Pharmacokinetics
Note: The active metabolite, A77 1726 (M1), of leflunomide is responsible for all of its pharmacological activity *in vivo.* Therefore, results of the pharmacokinetic studies were based on the activity of M1.

Physicochemical characteristics
Molecular weight—270.2.

Mechanism of action/Effect
Leflunomide, an immunomodulatory agent, inhibits dihydrooratate dehydrogenase. Anti-inflammatory effects have been demonstrated in *in vivo* and *in vitro* experimental models. In addition, leflunomide has antiproliferative activity.

Absorption
M1 metabolite is 80% bioavailable. Administration of leflunomide with a high-fat meal has no effect on the plasma concentration of M1.

Protein binding
M1—Very high (> 99%). In patients with chronic renal failure, the free fraction of M1 is increased twofold. However, the free fraction of M1 in rheumatoid arthritis patients is only slightly higher than in healthy volunteers.

Biotransformation
Leflunomide is metabolized to M1 and other minor active metabolites. An active metabolite, 4-trifluoromethylaniline, is present in plasma at low concentrations. Although the specific site of leflunomide metabolism is unknown, it has been suggested that the gastrointestinal wall and liver play a role in the metabolism.

Half-life
M1—2 weeks.

Time to peak concentration
M1—approximately 6 to 12 hours.

Elimination
Renal, approximately 43% of a radiolabeled leflunomide dose is excreted in the urine, primarily as leflunomide glucuronides and an oxalic acid derivative of M1. Fecal, approximately 48% of a radiolabeled leflunomide dose is eliminated in the feces, primarily as M1.

In dialysis—Studies have found that M1 is not removable by hemodialysis.

Precautions to Consider
Carcinogenicity
No carcinogenic effects of leflunomide were observed in a 2-year bioassay study in rats receiving oral doses of leflunomide of up to 6 mg per kg of body weight (mg/kg) per day (reflects an area under the plasma concentration-time curve [AUC] exposure of 1/40 of the maximum human M1 exposure).

Risk of malignancy, especially lymphoproliferative disorders, is increased with use of some immunosuppression. Leflunomide has potential for immunosuppression. No apparent increase in incidence of malignancies and lymphoproliferative disorders was reported in clinical trials; however, longer term- studies would be needed to determine increased risk potential of malignancy with leflunomide.

Mutagenicity
Leflunomide demonstrated no mutagenic activity in the Ames test, unscheduled DNA synthesis assay, or in the HGPRT gene mutation assay. However, a minor metabolite of leflunomide, 4-trifluoromethylaniline (TFMA), was demonstrated to be mutagenic in the Ames test and HGPRT gene mutation assay. There was no evidence of clastogenic activity with leflunomide or TFMA in the *in vivo* mouse micronucleus assay or in the cytogenic test in Chinese hamster bone marrow cells. However, there was evidence of clastogenic activity with TFMA in the *in vitro* assay for chromosome aberration in the Chinese hamster cells.

Pregnancy/Reproduction
Fertility—Fertility studies in adult males have not been done to evaluate the increased risk of male-mediated fetal toxicity. However, it is recommended that men intending to father a child minimize risks by discontinuing use of leflunomide and starting treatment with cholestyramine 8 grams three times a day for 11 days according to the manufacturers recommended drug elimination procedure for leflunomide.

No impairment of fertility was demonstrated in reproduction studies in male and female rats receiving doses of leflunomide of up to 4 mg/kg (reflects an AUC exposure of 1/30 of the maximum human M1 exposure).

Pregnancy—**Use of leflunomide is contraindicated during pregnancy** because of its potential to cause fetal harm.

Patients of childbearing potential may use leflunomide only if reliable contraception is being used and pregnancy has been excluded prior to starting leflunomide treatment. Pregnancy should be avoided during treatment with leflunomide and prior to the completion of the drug elimination procedure after receiving leflunomide. The drug elimination procedure should be used immediately if the patient becomes pregnant while taking leflunomide. If leflunomide is used by a pregnant woman, or if a woman becomes pregnant during treatment, she should be advised that this medication may harm the fetus. A pregnancy register has been established to monitor fetal outcomes of pregnant women exposed to leflunomide. Health care providers are encouraged to register such patients by calling 1-877-311-8972.

A study in rats during the organogenesis period showed that leflunomide doses of up to 15 mg/kg per day (reflects AUC exposure of 1/10 of the maximum human exposure) were teratogenic, resulting in anomalies such as anophthalmia or microphthalmia and internal hydrocephalus. In addition, leflunomide caused a decrease in maternal body weight and an increase in embryolethality with a decrease in the body weight of surviving fetuses.

A study in rabbits during the organogenesis period showed that leflunomide doses of up to 10 mg/kg per day (reflects an AUC exposure equivalent to the maximum human exposure) resulted in fused, dysplastic sternebrae. However, there were no teratogenic effects observed in rats or rabbits receiving leflunomide doses of 1 mg/kg.

In female rats receiving leflunomide at doses of 1.25 mg beginning 14 days before mating and continuing until the end of lactation, a 90% decrease in the postnatal survival of the offspring was observed.

FDA Pregnancy Category X.

Breast-feeding

It is not known whether leflunomide is distributed into the breast milk of humans and problems have not been documented. However, use is not recommended for nursing mothers.

Pediatrics

No information is available on whether the risk of leflunomide-induced adverse effects is increased in children up to 18 years of age. However, because of this medication's potential toxicity, use is not recommended in pediatric patients.

Safety and efficacy have not been fully evaluated in pediatric patients. In one safety study of pediatric patients ages 3 to 17 years, the most common adverse events reported were abdominal pain, diarrhea, nausea, vomiting, oral ulcers, upper respiratory tract infections, alopecia, rash, headache, and dizziness. Less common adverse events included anemia, hypertension and weight loss.

Geriatrics

Appropriate studies performed to date have not demonstrated geriatrics-specific problems that would limit the usefulness of leflunomide in the elderly. However, greater sensitivity of some older individuals cannot be ruled out. No dosage adjustment is needed in patients over 65 years of age.

Drug interactions and/or related problems

The following drug interactions and/or related problems have been selected on the basis of their potential clinical significance (possible mechanism in parentheses where appropriate)—not necessarily inclusive (» = major clinical significance):

Note: Combinations containing any of the following medications, depending on the amount present, may also interact with this medication.

Antimalarials or
Azathioprine or
D penicillamine or
Gold, intramuscular or oral
(concomitant use of leflunomide with these drugs has not been adequately studied)

Charcoal, activated or
Cholestyramine
(concurrent use of these medications will significantly decrease the plasma concentration of M1 by inhibiting gastrointestinal absorption)

» Hepatotoxic medications (see *Appendix II*), such as:
Methotrexate
(concurrent use with these medications may increase the risk of side effects and medication-induced hepatic toxicity; in a small study evaluating the concurrent use of leflunomide (100 mg per day followed by 10 to 20 mg per day) and methotrexate (10 to 25 mg per week with folate), an increased risk of hepatotoxicity was reported; dosage adjustment may be needed)

Rifampin
(concurrent use with rifampin may increase the plasma concentration of leflunomide; caution is recommended)

» Vaccines, live virus
(leflunomide may cause immunosuppression; use is not recommended)

Laboratory value alterations

The following have been selected on the basis of their potential clinical significance (possible effect in parentheses where appropriate)—not necessarily inclusive (» = major clinical significance).

With physiology/laboratory test values
Alanine aminotransferase (ALT [SGPT]), serum or
Alkaline phosphatase, serum or
Aspartate aminotransferase (AST [SGOT]), serum
(values may be increased)

Bilirubin, serum
(concentrations may be increased)

Medical considerations/Contraindications

The medical considerations/contraindications included have been selected on the basis of their potential clinical significance (reasons given in parentheses where appropriate)—not necessarily inclusive (» = major clinical significance).

Except under special circumstances, this medication should not be used when the following medical problems exist:

» Bone marrow dysplasia
» Immunodeficiency, severe
» Infections, severe or uncontrolled
(leflunomide may cause immunosuppression; use is not recommended)

» Hepatic disease
» Hepatic function impairment, severe
» Hepatitis B or C, positive serology
(may increase the risk of hepatotoxicity; rare cases of severe liver injury, including cases with fatal outcome; use is not recommended)

» Hypersensitivity to leflunomide or any other components of the product

Risk-benefit should be considered when the following medical problems exist:

» Hematologic abnormality, history of
(rare reports of pancytopenia, agranulocytosis and thrombocytopenia occurring in some patients with this condition)

» Renal function impairment
(studies in patients with chronic renal impairment have reported a twofold increase in the plasma concentration of leflunomide; caution is recommended)

Patient monitoring

The following may be especially important in patient monitoring (other tests may be warranted in some patients, depending on condition; » = major clinical significance):

» Hematocrit and
» Hemoglobin and
» Platelet and
» White blood cell counts
(should be monitored at baseline and monthly for six months following initiation of therapy and every 6 to 8 weeks thereafter; if concomitant use with methotrexate and/or other potential immunosuppressive agents, chronic monitoring should be monthly)

» Hepatic function tests
(values should be monitored at baseline and then monthly thereafter; monitoring may be continued according to individual patient's response after levels are stable)

» Interstitial lung disease
(post-marketing cases reported and associated with fatal outcomes; may occur acutely at any time during therapy; patient should be monitored for new onset or worsening pulmonary symptoms, such as cough and dyspnea, with or without associated fever; discontinuation of therapy and further investigation may be necessary)

Side/Adverse Effects

The following side/adverse effects have been selected on the basis of their potential clinical significance (possible signs and symptoms in parentheses where appropriate)—not necessarily inclusive:

Those indicating need for medical attention

Incidence more frequent

Bronchitis (congestion in chest; cough; difficult or painful breathing); ***hepatotoxicity*** (loss of appetite; nausea and/or vomiting; yellow eyes or skin); ***hypertension*** (dizziness; headache, severe or continuing); ***respiratory infection*** (cough; fever; sneezing; sore throat); ***urinary tract infection*** (bloody or cloudy urine; difficult, burning, or painful urination; frequent urge to urinate)

Incidence less frequent

Anemia (unusual tiredness or weakness); ***chest pain; dyspnea*** (shortness of breath); ***gastritis*** (burning feeling in chest or stomach; indigestion; tenderness in stomach area); ***gastroenteritis*** (severe abdominal pain; diarrhea; loss of appetite; nausea; weakness); ***palpitations*** (pounding heartbeat); ***paresthesias*** (burning, prickling, or tingling sensations in fingers and/or toes); ***synovitis*** (joint or muscle pain or stiffness); ***tachycardia*** (fast heartbeat); ***tenosynovitis*** (joint or muscle pain or stiffness)

Incidence not determined—Observed during clinical practice; estimates of frequency can not be determined

Acute hepatic necrosis (abdominal or stomach pain; black, tarry stools; chills; light-colored stools; dark urine; dizziness; fever; headache; itching; loss of appetite; nausea; rash; unpleasant breath odor; unusual tiredness or weakness; vomiting of blood; yellow eyes or skin); ***agranulocytosis*** (cough or hoarseness; fever with or without chills; general feeling of tiredness or weakness; lower back or side pain; painful or difficult urination; sore throat; sores, ulcers, or white spots on lips or in mouth; unusual bleeding or bruising); ***angioedema*** (large, hive-like swelling on face, eyelids, lips, tongue, throat, hands, legs, feet, sex organs); ***erythema multiforme*** (blistering, peeling, loosening of skin; chills; cough; diarrhea; fever; itching; joint or muscle pain; red irritated eyes; sore throat; sores, ulcers, or white spots in mouth or on lips; unusual tiredness or weakness); ***hepatic failure*** (headache; stomach pain; continuing vomiting; dark-colored urine; general feeling of tiredness or weakness; light-colored stools; yellow eyes or skin); ***hepatitis*** (dark urine; general tiredness and weakness; light-colored stools; nausea and vomiting; upper right abdominal pain; yellow eyes and skin); ***interstitial lung disease/pneumonitis*** (cough; difficult breathing; fever; shortness of breath); ***jaundice/cholestasis*** (chills; clay-colored stools; dark urine; dizziness; fever; headache; itching; loss of appetite; nausea; abdominal or stomach pain; area rash; unpleasant breath odor; unusual tiredness or weakness; vomiting of blood; yellow eyes or skin); ***leukopenia*** (black, tarry stools; chest pain; chills; cough; fever; painful or difficult urination; shortness of breath; sore throat; sores, ulcers, or white spots on lips or in mouth; swollen glands; unusual bleeding or bruising; unusual tiredness or weakness); ***neutropenia*** (black, tarry, stools; chills; cough; fever; lower back or side pain; painful or difficult urination; pale skin; shortness of breath; sore throat; ulcers, sores, or white spots in mouth; unusual bleeding or bruising unusual tiredness or weakness); ***opportunistic infections*** (fever or chills; cough or hoarseness; lower back or side pain; painful or difficult urination); ***pancreatitis*** (bloating; chills; constipation; darkened urine; fast heartbeat; fever; indigestion; loss of appetite; nausea; pains in stomach, side, or abdomen, possibly radiating to the back; vomiting; yellow eyes or skin); ***pancytopenia*** (high fever; chills; unexplained bleeding or bruising; bloody, black, or tarry stools; pale skin; unusual tiredness or weakness; cough; shortness of breath; sores, ulcers, or white spots on lips or in mouth; swollen glands); ***peripheral neuropathy*** (burning, numbness, tingling, or painful sensations; weakness in arms, hands, legs, or feet; unsteadiness or awkwardness); ***pulmonary fibrosis*** (fever; cough; shortness of breath); ***sepsis*** (chills; confusion; dizziness; lightheadedness; fainting; fast heartbeat; fever; rapid, shallow breathing); ***Stevens-Johnson syndrome/toxic epidermal necrolysis*** (blistering, peeling, loosening of skin; chills; cough; diarrhea; itching; joint or muscle pain; red irritated eyes; red skin lesions, often with a purple center; sore throat; sores, ulcers, or white spots in mouth or on lips; unusual tiredness or weakness); ***thrombocytopenia*** (black, tarry stools; bleeding gums; blood in urine or stools; pinpoint red spots on skin; unusual bleeding or bruising)

Those indicating need for medical attention only if they continue or are bothersome

Incidence more frequent

Abdominal pain (stomach pain); ***alopecia*** (hair loss); ***back pain; diarrhea; dizziness; dyspepsia*** (heartburn); ***headache; nausea and/or vomiting; skin rash; weight loss, unexplained***

Incidence less frequent

Acne; anorexia (decreased appetite); ***anxiety; conjunctivitis*** (red or irritated eyes); ***constipation; dry mouth; fever; flatulence*** (gas); ***malaise*** (unusual tiredness or weakness); ***mouth ulcer*** (irritation or soreness of mouth); ***pharyngitis*** (pain or burning in throat); ***pruritus*** (itching of the skin); ***rhinitis*** (runny nose); ***sinusitis*** (headache; runny nose)

Overdose

For specific information on the agents used in the management of leflunomide overdose, see:

- *Charcoal, Activated (Oral-Local)* monograph; or
- *Cholestyramine (Oral-Local)* monograph.

For more information on the management of overdose or unintentional ingestion, **contact a Poison Control Center** (see *Poison Control Center Listing*).

Treatment of overdose

To enhance elimination—

Administration of activated charcoal orally or via nasal gastric tube 50 grams every 6 hours for 24 hours post-ingestion.

Administration of cholestyramine 8 grams three times a day for 24 hours post-ingestion

Supportive care—General supportive measures should be instituted. Patients in whom intentional overdose is confirmed or suspected should be referred for psychiatric consultation.

Patient Consultation

As an aid to patient consultation, refer to *Advice for the Patient, Leflunomide (Systemic)*.

In providing consultation, consider emphasizing the following selected information (» = major clinical significance):

Before using this medication

» Conditions affecting use, especially:

Hypersensitivity to leflunomide or any other components of the product

Pregnancy—Use of leflunomide is contraindicated during pregnancy because of its potential harm to the fetus; advisability of using contraception; telling physician immediately if pregnancy is suspected

Breast-feeding—Use of leflunomide is not recommended for nursing mothers

Use in children—Use of leflunomide is not recommended in children

Use in the elderly—Greater sensitivity of some older adults can not be ruled out

Other medications, especially hepatotoxic medications or live vaccines

Other medical problems, especially bone marrow dysplasia, immunodeficiency, infection (severe or uncontrolled), hepatic disease, hepatic function impairment (severe), hepatitis B or C, history of hematologic abnormality, or renal function impairment

Proper use of this medication

» Importance of not taking more medication than the amount prescribed

» Proper dosing

Missed dose: Taking as soon as possible; skipping missed dose if almost time for next dose; not doubling doses

» Proper storage

Precautions while using this medication

» Regular visits to physician to check progress during therapy

» Stopping medication immediately and checking with physician if pregnancy is suspected, since leflunomide may cause birth defects in humans

» Men taking leflunomide should use condoms during sexual intercourse, since leflunomide may cause birth defects in the children of men taking this medication at the time of conception; men intending to father a child should discontinue leflunomide and contact their physician immediately

» Checking with doctor immediately if symptoms of interstitial lung disease (i.e., cough and dyspnea, with or without associated fever) occur

» Avoiding alcoholic beverages, which may increase the risk of hepatotoxicity

» Avoiding immunizations unless approved by physician

Side/adverse effects

Signs of potential side effects, especially bronchitis, hepatotoxicity, hypertension, respiratory infection, urinary tract infection, anemia, chest pain, dyspnea, gastritis, gastroenteritis, palpitations, paresthesias, synovitis, tachycardia, or tenosynovitis

Signs of potential side effects observed during clinical practice, especially acute hepatic necrosis, agranulocytosis, angioedema, erythema multiforme, hepatic failure, hepatitis, interstitial lung disease/pneumonitis, jaundice/cholestasis, leukopenia, neutropenia, opportunistic infections, pancreatitis, pancytopenia, peripheral neuropathy, pulmonary fibrosis, sepsis, Stevens-Johnson syndrome/toxic epidermal necrolysis, or thrombocytopenia

General Dosing Information

As a result of the long half-life of leflunomide, caution should be used in administering live vaccines after stopping leflunomide treatment.

After completing leflunomide treatment, the following elimination procedure is recommended by the manufacturer to obtain nondetectable plasma levels of leflunomide (0.02 mg/L):

- Administer cholestyramine 8 grams three times a day for 11 days. The 11 days do not have to be consecutive. However, to lower the plasma level rapidly, cholestyramine should be administered for 11 days consecutively.
- Use two different tests at least 14 days apart to confirm that plasma levels are less than 0.02 mg/L. If plasma levels are higher than 0.02 mg/L, additional cholestyramine treatment should be considered.

Note: If the elimination procedure is not used, it may take up to 2 years before plasma levels of M1 are less than 0.02 mg/L due to individual variation in drug clearance.

If a patient develops increased liver enzyme levels, the following guidelines are recommended for dosage adjustment or discontinuation based on the severity and persistence of the elevations:
• For elevations of alanine transferase (ALT [SGPT]) greater than two times the upper normal limit, the dose of leflunomide should be reduced to 10 mg a day.
• For elevations of ALT between two and three times the upper normal limit that persist despite the dose reduction, a liver biopsy is recommended if it is desirable to continue treatment with leflunomide.
• For elevations that are greater than three times the upper normal limit that continue with a dosage reduction and the administration of cholestyramine, leflunomide should be discontinued; then cholestyramine should be readministered with close monitoring and additional doses of cholestyramine as needed.

Oral Dosage Forms

LEFLUNOMIDE TABLETS

Usual adult dose

Arthritis, rheumatoid—

Oral, initially 100 mg once a day for three days, followed by a maintenance dose of 20 mg a day.

Note: Maintenance dose may be decreased to 10 mg a day according to patient response.

Usual adult prescribing limits

20 mg in twenty-four hours.

Usual pediatric dose

Safety and efficacy have not been established in children up to 18 years of age.

Usual geriatric dose

See *Usual adult dose.*

Strength(s) usually available

U.S.—

10 mg (Rx) [*Arava* (colloidal silicon dioxide; crospovidone; hydroxypropyl methylcellulose; lactose monohydrate; magnesium stearate; polyethylene glycol; povidone; starch; talc; titanium dioxide)].

20 mg (Rx) [*Arava* (colloidal silicon dioxide; crospovidone; hydroxypropyl methylcellulose; lactose monohydrate; magnesium stearate; polyethylene glycol; povidone; starch; talc; titanium dioxide; yellow ferric oxide)].

100 mg (Rx) [*Arava* (colloidal silicon dioxide; crospovidone; hydroxypropyl methylcellulose; lactose monohydrate; magnesium stearate; polyethylene glycol; povidone; starch; talc; titanium dioxide)].

Packaging and storage

Store at 25 °C (77 °F), excursions permitted between 15 and 30 °C (59 and 86 °F). Protect from light.

Revised: 12/21/2004
Developed: 12/01/1998

LENALIDOMIDE Systemic†

VA CLASSIFICATION (Primary): IM409

Commonly used brand name(s): *Revlimid.*

Note: For a listing of dosage forms and brand names by country availability, see *Dosage Forms* section(s).

†Not commercially available in Canada.

Category

Antianemic; antiangiogenesis agent; immunomodulator.

Indications

Accepted

Transfusional dependent anemia (treatment)—Lenalidomide is indicated for the treatment of patients with transfusion-dependent anemia due to Low- or Intermediate -1-risk myelodysplastic syndromes associated with a deletion 5q cytogenetic abnormality with or without additional cytogenetic abnormalities.

Pharmacology/Pharmacokinetics

Physicochemical characteristics

Molecular weight—Lenalidomide: 259.3.

Solubility—Lenalidomide is soluble in organic solvent/water mixtures, and buffered aqueous solvents and more soluble in organic solvents and low pH solutions. Solubility is significantly lower in less acidic buffers (0.4 to 0.5 mg/mL).

Mechanism of action/Effect

Lenalidomide inhibits the secretion of pro-inflammatory cytokines and increases the secretion of anti-inflammatory cytokines from peripheral blood mononuclear cells. In studies, lenalidomide inhibited growth of Namalwa cells (a human B cell lymphoma cell line with a deletion of one chromosome 5) but was less effective in inhibiting growth of KG-1 cells (human myeloblastic cell line, with a deletion of one chromosome 5) and other cell lines without chromosome 5 deletions. Lenalidomide inhibits cyclooxygenase-2 (COX-2) but not COX-1 expression *in vitro.*

Absorption

Rapidly absorbed following oral administration. Food has no effects on absorption, but reduces C_{max} by 36%.

Exposure (AUC) in multiple myeloma patients is 57% higher than in healthy male volunteers.

Multiple myeloma patients with mild renal impairment had a 56% greater AUC then those with normal renal function.

Protein binding

Low: approximately 30% to plasma protein.

Biotransformation

The metabolic profile of lenalidomide in humans has not been studied.

Half-life

Elimination—approximately 3 hours.

Time to peak plasma concentration

In healthy volunteers—between 0.625 and 1.5 hours post dose. AUC values increase proportionally with dose following single and multiple doses.

In multiple myeloma patients—between 0.5 and 4.0 hours post dose, both on Days 1 and 28.

Elimination

Urinary: approximately two-thirds unchanged drug. The process exceeds the glomerular filtration rate; and, therefore is partially or entirely active.

Precautions to Consider

Carcinogenicity

Carcinogenicity studies with lenalidomide have not been conducted.

Mutagenicity

Lenalidomide demonstrated no mutagenic effects in the Ames test, chromosome aberrations in cultured human peripheral blood lymphocytes, or mutation at the thymidine kinase (tk) locus of mouse lymphoma L5178Y cells. Lenalidomide did not increase morphological transformation on Syrian Hamster Embryo assay or induce micronuclei in the polychromatic erythrocytes of the bone marrow of male rats.

Pregnancy/Reproduction

Fertility—Fertility and early embryonic development studies done in rats given doses of lenalidomide up to 500 mg/kg, produced no parental toxicity and no adverse effects on fertility.

Pregnancy—*Any suspected fetal exposure to lenalidomide should be reported to the FDA via the Medwatch program at 1-800-FDA-1088 and also to Celgene Corporation at 1-888-4CELGEN (1-888-423-5436).*

Lenalidomide is contraindicated during pregnancy. Adequate and well-controlled studies in humans have shown that a similar drug, thalidomide causes serious and life threatening adverse effects in the fetus.

Lenalidomide is contraindicated in females who are or may become pregnant and who are not using the two required types of birth control or who are not continually abstaining from intercourse. If pregnancy does occur during treatment, lenalidomide should be discontinued immediately and the patient should be referred to an obstetrician/gynecologist experienced in reproductive toxicity for further evaluation and counseling.

Studies done in rabbits given lenalidomide at doses of 50 mg/kg (approximately 120 times the human dose of 10 mg based on body surface area) revealed embryocidal effects.

Studies done in rats given lenalidomide at doses of 500 mg/kg (about 600 times the human dose of 10 mg based on body surface area) showed no teratogenic effects. At doses of 100, 300 or 500 mg/kg/day, lenalidomide showed minimal maternal toxicity. Pre- and post-natal development studies done in female rats given 500 mg/kg revealed few adverse effects on the offspring, male offspring showed delayed sexual maturation and female offspring had slightly lower body weight gains during gestation when bred to male offspring.

FDA Pregnancy Category X

Breast-feeding

It is not known whether lenalidomide is distributed into human milk. Because many drugs are distributed in human milk and because of the potential for adverse effects in nursing infants, a decision should be made whether to discontinue nursing or to discontinue lenalidomide, taking into account the importance of the drug to the mother.

Pediatrics

Safety and effectiveness in pediatric patients below the age of 18 years have not been established.

Geriatrics

Appropriate studies performed to date have not demonstrated geriatrics-specific problems that would limit the usefulness of lenalidomide in the elderly. However, elderly patients are more likely to have age-related renal function impairment, which may require care in dosing selection and monitoring of renal function.

Pharmacogenetics

The pharmacokinetic effects of lenalidomide due to race and gender have not been studied.

Laboratory value alterations

The following have been selected on the basis of their potential clinical significance (possible effect in parentheses where appropriate)—not necessarily inclusive (» = major clinical significance).

With physiology/laboratory test values

Alanine aminotransferase (ALT [SGPT]), serum
(values may be increased.)

Medical considerations/Contraindications

The medical considerations/contraindications included have been selected on the basis of their potential clinical significance (reasons given in parentheses where appropriate)—not necessarily inclusive (» = major clinical significance).

Except under special circumstances, this medication should not be used when the following medical problem exists:

» Hypersensitivity to lenalidomide or to any of its components

Risk-benefit should be considered when the following medical problems exist:

Hepatic function impairment
(studies have not been done)

Multiple myeloma
(significant increased risk of deep venous thrombosis and pulmonary embolism)

Renal function impairment
(careful selection in dosing; may have increased risk of adverse reactions)

Patient monitoring

The following may be especially important in patient monitoring (other tests may be warranted in some patients, depending on condition; » = major clinical significance):

» Complete blood counts, including
Hematocrit and
Platelet count and
White blood cell counts with differential
(monitor weekly for the first 8 weeks and at least monthly thereafter for cytopenias; associations with significant neutropenia and thrombocytopenia.)

Pregnancy testing
(weekly during the first 4 weeks of therapy and every 4 weeks thereafter in women with regular menstrual cycles; every 2 weeks in women with irregular menstrual cycles)

Renal function
(monitor renal function in patients with renal function impairment)

Side/Adverse Effects

The following side/adverse effects have been selected on the basis of their potential clinical significance (possible signs and symptoms in parentheses where appropriate)—not necessarily inclusive:

Those indicating need for medical attention

Incidence more frequent

Dyspnea (shortness of breath; difficult or labored breathing; tightness in chest; wheezing); ***febrile neutropenia*** (black, tarry stools; chills; cough; fever; lower back or side pain; painful or difficult urination; pale skin; shortness of breath; sore throat; ulcers, sores, or white spots in mouth; unusual bleeding or bruising; unusual tiredness or weakness); ***hypokalemia*** (convulsions; decreased urine; dry mouth; irregular heartbeat; increased thirst; loss of appetite; mood changes; muscle pain or cramps; nausea or vomiting; numbness or tingling in hands, feet, or lips; shortness of breath; unusual tiredness or weakness); ***leukopenia*** (black, tarry stools; chest pain; chills; cough; fever; painful or difficult urination; shortness of breath; sore throat; sores, ulcers, or white spots on lips or in mouth; swollen glands; unusual bleeding or bruising; unusual tiredness or weakness); ***neutropenia*** (black, tarry, stools; chills; cough; fever; lower back or side pain; painful or difficult urination; pale skin; shortness of breath; sore throat; ulcers, sores, or white spots in mouth; unusual bleeding or bruising; unusual tiredness or weakness); ***thrombocytopenia*** (black, tarry stools; bleeding gums; blood in urine or stools; pinpoint red spots on skin; unusual bleeding or bruising)

Incidence unknown

Deep venous thrombosis (pain, redness, or swelling in arm or leg); ***pulmonary embolism*** (anxiety; chest pain; cough; fainting; fast heartbeat; sudden shortness of breath or troubled breathing; dizziness or lightheadedness)

Those indicating need for medical attention only if they continue or are bothersome

Incidence more frequent

Abdominal pain (stomach pain); ***anemia*** (pale skin; troubled breathing with exertion; unusual bleeding or bruising; unusual tiredness or weakness); ***anorexia*** (loss of appetite; weight loss); ***arthralgia*** (pain in joints; muscle pain or stiffness; difficulty in moving); ***asthenia*** (lack or loss of strength); ***back pain; bronchitis*** (cough producing mucus; difficulty breathing; shortness of breath; tightness in chest; wheezing); ***cellulitis*** (itching, pain, redness, swelling, tenderness, warmth on skin); ***chest pain; constipation*** (difficulty having a bowel movement (stool)); ***contusion*** (hemorrhage beneath unbroken skin); ***cough; depression*** (discouragement; feeling sad or empty; irritability; lack of appetite; loss of interest or pleasure; tiredness; trouble concentrating; trouble sleeping); ***diarrhea; dizziness; dry mouth; dry skin; dysgeusia*** (loss of taste; change in taste); ***dyspnoea exertional*** (difficult or labored breathing; shortness of breath); ***dysuria*** (difficult or painful urination; burning while urinating); ***ecchymosis*** (bruising; large, flat, blue or purplish patches in the skin); ***edema*** (swelling); ***edema peripheral*** (swelling of hands, ankles, feet, or lower legs); ***epistaxis*** (bloody nose); ***erythema*** (flushing, redness of skin; unusually warm skin); ***fatigue*** (unusual tiredness or weakness); ***headache; hypertension*** (blurred vision; dizziness; nervousness; headache; pounding in the ears; slow or fast heartbeat); ***hypoasthesia*** (abnormal or decreased touch sensation); ***hypomagnesaemia*** (drowsiness; loss of appetite; mood or mental changes; muscle spasms; [tetany] or twitching; seizures; nausea or vomiting; trembling; unusual tiredness or weakness); ***hypothyrodism, acquired*** (constipation; depressed mood; dry skin and hair; feeling cold; hair loss; hoarseness or husky voice; muscle cramps and stiffness; slowed heartbeat; weight gain; unusual tiredness or weakness); ***insomnia*** (sleeplessness; trouble sleeping; unable to sleep); ***loose stools; myalgia*** (joint pain; swollen joints; muscle aching or cramping; muscle pains or stiffness; difficulty in moving); ***nasopharyngitis*** (stuffy or runny nose; muscle aches; unusual tiredness or weakness; fever; sore throat; headache); ***nausea; night sweats; pain; pain in limb*** (pain in arms or legs); ***palpitations*** (fast, irregular, pounding, or racing heartbeat or pulse); ***peripheral neuropathy*** (burning, numbness, tingling, or painful sensations; weakness in arms, hands, legs, or feet; unsteadiness or awkwardness); ***pharyngitis*** (body aches or pain; congestion; cough; dryness or soreness of throat; fever; hoarseness; runny nose; tender, swollen glands in neck; trouble in swallowing; voice changes); ***pruritus*** (itching skin); ***pyrexia*** (fever); ***rash; rhinitis*** (stuffy nose; runny nose; sneezing); ***rigors*** (feeling unusually cold; shivering); ***sinusitis*** (pain or tenderness around eyes and cheekbones; fever; stuffy or runny nose; headache; cough; shortness of breath or troubled breathing; tightness of chest or wheezing); ***sweating increased; upper abdominal pain; upper respiratory tract infection*** (ear congestion; nasal congestion; chills, cough, fever, sneezing, or sore throat; body aches or pain; headache; loss of voice; runny nose; unusual tiredness or weakness; difficulty in breathing); ***vomiting***

Overdose

For more information on the management of overdose or unintentional ingestion, **contact a poison control center** (see *Poison Control Center Listing*).

Treatment of overdose

There is no known specific antidote to lenalidomide. Treatment is generally symptomatic and supportive.

Supportive care—

Patients in whom intentional overdose is confirmed or suspected should be referred for psychiatric consultation.

Patient Consultation

As an aid to patient consultation, refer to *Advice for the Patient, Lenalidomide (Systemic)*.

In providing consultation, consider emphasizing the following selected information (» = major clinical significance):

Before using this medication

» Conditions affecting use, especially:

Hypersensitivity to lenalidomide or to any of its components

Pregnancy—Not recommended for use during pregnancy

Breast-feeding—It is not known whether lenalidomide is distributed into human milk. Because many drugs are distributed in human milk and because of the potential for adverse effects in nursing infants, a decision should be made whether to discontinue nursing or to discontinue lenalidomide, taking into account the importance of the drug to the mother.

Use in children—Safety and effectiveness in pediatric patients below the age of 18 years have not been established.

Use in the elderly—Elderly patients may be more likely to have age-related renal function impairment, which may require care in dosing selection and monitoring of renal function.

Other medical problems, especially hepatic function impairment, multiple myeloma, or renal function impairment.

Proper use of this medication

» The importance of becoming educated and counseled on the requirements of the RevAssist program, and familiar with the RevAssist educational materials, Patient Medication Guide, and directing any questions to a physician or pharmacist prior to starting lenalidomide therapy.

» Taking the necessary precautions to avoid pregnancy during lenalidomide treatment by using one highly effective form of birth control plus an additional effective form of birth control at the same time.

» The importance of swallowing the capsule whole; do not break, chew, or open the capsule.

» Participating in a telephone survey and patient registry while taking lenalidomide.

» The importance of not donating blood while taking lenalidomide.

» The importance of not sharing this medication with anyone, even someone with similar symptoms.

» For male patients: not donating semen or sperm while taking lenalidomide.

» Proper dosing

Missed dose: Taking as soon as possible; not taking if almost time for next scheduled dose; not doubling doses

» Proper storage

Precautions while using this medication

» Regular visits to the physician every 4 weeks for pregnancy testing for women with regular menstrual cycles and every 2 weeks for women with irregular cycles.

» Calling your doctor or 1-888-688-2528 for emergency contraception information if you, for any reason, think you are pregnant or, for males, you think that your sexual partner may be pregnant.

» Seeking medical attention if you develop any shortness of breath, chest pain, or arm or leg swelling.

Side/adverse effects

Signs of potential side effects, especially deep venous thrombosis, dyspnea, febrile neutropenia, hypokalemia, leukopenia, neutropenia, pulmonary embolism, or thrombocytopenia.

General Dosing Information

Lenalidomide is prescribed only by licensed prescribers who are registered in the RevAssist program and understand the potential risk of teratogenicity if this drug is used during pregnancy.

Women of childbearing potential may be referred to a qualified provider of contraceptive methods.

Pregnancy test results must be verified by the prescriber and the pharmacist prior to dispensing lenalidomide.

Lenalidomide must only be dispensed to females of child bearing potential who are registered and meet all the conditions of the RevAssist program including:

• Understanding the risks associated with lenalidomide, and being able to reliably carry out the instructions.

• Being capable of complying with the contraceptive measures, pregnancy testing, patient registration, and patient survey as described in the RevAssist program.

• Have received both oral and written warnings of the risk of taking lenalidomide during pregnancy and exposing the fetus to the drug.

• Have received both oral and written warnings of the risk of possible contraception failure and needing to use two reliable forms of contraception, unless continuous abstinence is the chosen method.

• Have acknowledged in writing an understanding of the warnings and need for two reliable methods of contraception for 4 weeks prior to therapy, during therapy, during dose interruptions and for 4 weeks following discontinuation of therapy.

• Have had 2 negative pregnancy tests (sensitivity of at least 50 mIU/mL). The first test within 10-14 days, and the second test within 24 hours prior to receiving lenalidomide therapy.

• Having a parent or legal guardian read the educational materials and agree to try to ensure compliance in patients between 12 and 18 years of age.

Lenalidomide must only be dispensed to sexually active males who meet all the following conditions including:

• Understanding the risks associated with lenalidomide, and being able to reliably carry out the instructions.

• Being capable of complying with the contraceptive measures appropriate for men, patient registration, and patient survey as described in the RevAssist program.

• Have received both oral and written warnings of the risk of taking lenalidomide and exposing a fetus to the drug.

• Have received both oral and written warnings of the risk of possible contraception failure and that it is unknown whether lenalidomide is present in semen. And has been instructed to always use a condom during sexual contact with females of childbearing potential, even after a successful vasectomy.

• Have acknowledged in writing an understanding of the warnings and need to use a latex condom during any sexual contact with women of childbearing potential. Females of child bearing potential are considered to be sexually mature if they have not undergone a hysterectomy or who have not been postmenopausal for at least 24 consecutive months.

• Having a parent or legal guardian read the educational materials and agree to try to ensure compliance in patients between 12 and 18 years of age.

Pregnancy testing for women of childbearing potential should be weekly during the first 4 weeks of therapy and every 4 weeks thereafter in women with regular menstrual cycles. For women with irregular menstrual cycles, pregnancy testing should occur every 2 weeks.

If hormonal or IUD contraception is medically contraindicated, two other effective or highly effective methods may be used (e.g., latex condom, diaphragm, cervical cap or tubal ligation, or partner's vasectomy).

Treatment must be discontinued and pregnancy testing and counseling should be performed if a patient misses her period or if there is any abnormality in her pregnancy test or in her menstrual bleeding.

Patients may require the use of blood product support and/or growth factors.

Treatment of adverse effects

For venous thromboembolic events—Taking prophylactic measures should be done carefully taking into consideration a patient's underlying risk factors; it is not known whether prophylactic anticoagulation or antiplatelet therapy given concurrent with lenalidomide may lessen the potential.

Parenteral Dosage Forms

LENALIDOMIDE CAPSULES

Usual adult dose

Transfusional dependent anemia—

Oral, 10 mg with water daily. Dosing is continued or modified based upon clinical and laboratory findings.

Note: For patients who experience thrombocytopenia within 4 weeks of treatment at 10 mg daily—

Platelet counts:

• When platelet baseline counts ≥100,000/mcL fall to <50,000/mcL, interrupt treatment and resume at 5 mg daily when platelet counts are ≥50,000/mcL.

• When platelet baseline counts <100,000/mcL fall to 50% of the baseline value, interrupt treatment.

—When platelet baseline counts are ≥60,000/mcL and return to ≥50,000/mcL, resume at 5 mg daily.

—When platelet baseline counts are <60,000/mcL and return to ≥30,000/mcL, resume at 5 mg daily.

For patients who experience thrombocytopenia after 4 weeks of starting treatment at 10 mg daily—

• When platelet counts are < 30,000/mcL or <50,000/mcL and platelet transfusion, interrupt treatment; when counts return to ≥30,000/mcL (without hemostatic failure), resume at 5 mg daily.

For patients who experience thrombocytopenia at 5 mg daily—

- When platelet counts are < 30,000/mcL or <50,000/mcL and platelet transfusion, interrupt treatment; when counts return to ≥30,000/mcL (without hemostatic failure), resume at 5 mg every other day.

For patients who develop neutropenia within 4 weeks of starting treatment at 10 mg daily—

Neutrophil counts (ANC):

- When baseline ANC ≥1,000/mcL fall to <750/mcL interrupt treatment and resume treatment at 5 mg daily when ANC returns to ≥1,000/mcL.
- When baseline ANC <1,000/mcL fall to <500/mcL interrupt treatment and resume treatment at 5 mg daily when ANC returns to ≥500/mcL.

For patients who develop neutropenia after 4 weeks of starting treatment at 10 mg daily—

- When ANC counts are <500/mcL for ≥7 days or <500/mcL associated with fever (≥38.5°C), interrupt treatment and resume treatment at 5 mg daily when ANC returns to ≥500/mcL.

For patients who develop neutropenia at 5 mg daily—

- When ANC counts are <500/mcL for ≥7 days or <500/mcL associated with fever (≥38.5°C), interrupt treatment and resume treatment at 5 mg every other day when ANC returns to ≥500/mcL.

Usual pediatric dose
Safety and effectiveness in pediatric patients below the age of 18 years have not been established.

Usual geriatric dose
See *Usual adult dose*.

Strength(s) usually available
U.S.—

5 mg (Rx) [*Revlimid* (black ink; croscarmellose sodium; gelatin; lactose anhydrous; magnesium stearate; microcrystalline cellulose; titanium dioxide)].

10 mg (Rx) [*Revlimid* (black ink; croscarmellose sodium; FD&C blue #2; gelatin; lactose anhydrous; magnesium stearate; microcrystalline cellulose; titanium dioxide; yellow iron oxide)].

Packaging and storage
Store at 25 °C (77 °F); excursions permitted to 15 to 30°C (59 to 86°F).

Auxiliary labeling
- Swallow whole. Do not crush or chew.

Developed: 02/17/2006

LEPIRUDIN Systemic

VA CLASSIFICATION (Primary): BL113

Commonly used brand name(s): *Refludan*.

Another commonly used name is hirudin, recombinant.

Note: For a listing of dosage forms and brand names by country availability, see *Dosage Forms* section(s).

Category
Anticoagulant.

Indications

Accepted
Thrombocytopenia, heparin-induced (treatment)—Lepirudin is indicated for anticoagulation in patients with heparin-induced thrombocytopenia and associated thromboembolic disease in order to prevent further thromboembolic complications.

Pharmacology/Pharmacokinetics
Note: Pharmacokinetic behavior follows a two-compartment model.

Physicochemical characteristics
Source—Synthetic. Recombinant form of hirudin (a naturally occurring family of highly homologous isopolypeptides produced by the leech *Hirudo medicinalis*) that is produced by a recombinant DNA process involving yeast cells. A polypeptide composed of 65 amino acids, which differs from naturally occurring hirudin by substitution of leucine for isoleucine at the N-terminal end of the molecule and by absence of a sulfate group on the tyrosine at position 63.

Molecular weight—6979.5 daltons.

pH—Approximately 7.

Solubility—Freely soluble in water for injection or 0.9% sodium chloride injection.

Mechanism of action/Effect
A highly specific inhibitor of the thrombogenic activity of thrombin; one molecule of lepirudin binds to one molecule of thrombin. Produces dose-dependent increases in activated partial thromboplastin time (aPTT). Its action is independent of antithrombin III and it is not inhibited by platelet factor 4.

The pharmacodynamic response is directly related to lepirudin concentrations. No saturable effect has been observed at intravenous doses up to 500 mcg (0.5 mg) per kg of body weight.

Distribution
Essentially confined to extracellular fluids.

Biotransformation
Although conclusive data are not available, biotransformation is thought to involve release of amino acids via catabolic hydrolysis of the parent drug.

Half-life
Distribution—

10 minutes.

Elimination—

Young healthy volunteers: About 1.3 hours.

Renal function impairment, severe (creatinine clearance less than 15 mL per minute): Up to 2 days.

Hemodialysis: Up to 2 days.

Note: Elimination follows a first-order kinetics process.

Elimination
Renal, about 48% (35% unchanged).

In dialysis—

May be removable by hemofiltration or hemodialysis.

Note: Systemic clearance of lepirudin is proportional to the glomerular filtration rate (GFR) or creatinine clearance. Systemic clearance is about 25% lower in women than in men and about 20% lower in the elderly than in younger patients.

Precautions to Consider

Cross-sensitivity and/or related problems
Patients sensitive to other hirudins may also be sensitive to lepirudin.

Carcinogenicity
Long-term studies in animals have not been done.

Mutagenicity
Lepirudin was not found to be genotoxic in the Ames test, the Chinese hamster cell (V79/HGPRT) forward mutation test, the A549 human cell line unscheduled DNA synthesis (UDS) test, the Chinese hamster V79 cell chromosome aberration test, or the mouse micronucleus test.

Pregnancy/Reproduction
Fertility—Studies in male and female rats given intravenous doses up to 30 mg per kg of body weight (mg/kg) per day (180 mg per square meter of body surface area [mg/m^2] per day or 1.2 times the recommended maximum human total daily dose based on body surface area of 1.45 m^2 for a 50-kg subject) found no effect on fertility or reproductive performance.

Pregnancy—Adequate and well-controlled studies in humans have not been done.

Lepirudin has been found to cross the placenta after intravenous administration to pregnant rats. It is not known whether lepirudin crosses the placenta in humans. Because animal reproduction studies are not always predictive of human response, this drug should be used during pregnancy only if clearly needed.

Studies in rats and rabbits at intravenous doses up to 30 mg/kg per day (180 and 360 mg/m^2 per day or 1.2 and 2.4 times, respectively, the maximum recommended human total daily dose based on body surface area) found no evidence of fetal toxicity. However, an increase in maternal mortality due to undetermined causes was found in pregnant rats given 30 mg/kg per day during organogenesis and perinatal-postnatal periods.

FDA Pregnancy Category B.

Breast-feeding
It is not known whether lepirudin is distributed into human breast milk. However, risk-benefit should be considered because of the potential for serious adverse reactions in nursing infants from lepirudin.

Pediatrics
Safety and efficacy in pediatric patients have not been established. However, two children (11 and 12 years of age) were treated with lepirudin at doses ranging from 0.15 to 0.22 mg/kg per hour for 8 days, and 0.1 to 0.7 mg/kg per hour for 58 days, respectively, without serious adverse events.

Geriatrics
Appropriate studies performed to date have not demonstrated geriatrics-specific problems that would limit the usefulness of lepirudin in the elderly. However, elderly patients are more likely to have age-related renal function impairment, which may require adjustment of dosage in patients receiving lepirudin.

Systemic clearance in elderly patients is about 20% lower than in younger patients.

Drug interactions and/or related problems
The following drug interactions and/or related problems have been selected on the basis of their potential clinical significance (possible mechanism in parentheses where appropriate)—not necessarily inclusive (» = major clinical significance):

Note: Combinations containing any of the following medications, depending on the amount present, may also interact with this medication.

» Anticoagulants, coumarin-derivative or
» Platelet aggregation inhibitors
(concurrent use may increase the risk of bleeding; gradual reduction in dose/rate of lepirudin is recommended prior to switching to an oral anticoagulant)

» Thrombolytics, such as:
Alteplase, recombinant
Anistreplase
Reteplase
Streptokinase
Urokinase
(concurrent use may considerably increase the effect of lepirudin on activated partial thromboplastin time [aPTT] prolongation and increase the risk of bleeding complications such as intracranial bleeding)

Laboratory value alterations
The following have been selected on the basis of their potential clinical significance (possible effect in parentheses where appropriate)—not necessarily inclusive (» = major clinical significance).

With physiology/laboratory test values
Activated partial thromboplastin time (aPTT)
(lepirudin dose–related increases occur)
Thrombin time (TT)
(increased even at low doses of lepirudin)

Medical considerations/Contraindications
The medical considerations/contraindications included have been selected on the basis of their potential clinical significance (reasons given in parentheses where appropriate)—not necessarily inclusive (» = major clinical significance).

Except under special circumstances, this medication should not be used when the following medical problems exists:

» Hypersensitivity to hirudins or to any of the components of lepirudin (rDNA) for injection
(lepirudin use contraindicated in patients with known hypersensitivity)

Risk-benefit should be considered when the following medical problems exist:

» Conditions associated with a possible increased risk of bleeding, including
Anomaly of vessels or organs
Bacterial endocarditis
Bleeding, recent major (e.g., intracranial, gastrointestinal, intraocular, or pulmonary bleeding)
Cerebrovascular accident, stroke, intracerebral surgery, or other neuraxial procedures, recent
Hemorrhagic diathesis
Hypertension, severe uncontrolled
Peptic ulcer, recent active
Puncture of large vessels or organ biopsy, recent
Renal function impairment, severe
Surgery, recent major
(careful assessment of risk-benefit is recommended before initiation of treatment with lepirudin, because of the risk of life-threatening intracranial bleeding)

» Hepatic function impairment, severe, including cirrhosis
(may increase the anticoagulant effect of lepirudin as a result of reduced generation of vitamin K-dependent coagulation factors)

» Renal function impairment, known or suspected (creatinine clearance less than 60 mL per minute or serum creatinine greater than 1.5 mg per deciliter)
(dosage reduction of both the bolus intravenous injection and the intravenous infusion rate is recommended to prevent possible overdosage that may occur even with the standard dosing regimen)

Patient monitoring
The following may be especially important in patient monitoring (other tests may be warranted in some patients, depending on condition; » = major clinical significance):

» Activated partial thromboplastin time (aPTT)
(recommended prior to initiation of therapy, 4 hours after the start of the lepirudin infusion, and at least once a day during treatment; it is recommended that frequency of monitoring be increased in patients with renal function impairment, severe hepatic injury, or an increased risk of bleeding; the goal is to maintain the aPTT ratio [the patient's aPTT at a given time over an aPTT reference value, usually the median of the laboratory normal range for aPTT] between 1.5 and 2.5; it is recommended that lepirudin treatment not be initiated in patients with an aPTT ratio over 2.5 to avoid initial overdosing)

Note: At plasma lepirudin concentrations of 1500 nanograms per mL, the following aPTT ratios have been observed: nearly 3 for healthy volunteers, 2.3 for patients with heparin-induced thrombocytopenia, and 2.1 for patients with deep venous thrombosis.

Thrombin time (TT) is not suitable for routine monitoring of lepirudin therapy because TT has been found to exceed 200 seconds even at low plasma concentrations of lepirudin.

» Blood pressure and
» Hemoglobin tests
(an unexpected decrease in blood pressure or hemoglobin levels should lead to consideration of a hemorrhagic event)

Side/Adverse Effects
Note: Formation of *antihirudin antibodies* has been observed in about 40% of heparin-induced thrombocytopenia patients treated with lepirudin, which may increase the anticoagulant effect of lepirudin as a result of delayed renal elimination of active lepirudin-antihirudin complexes. Strict monitoring of aPTT is recommended during prolonged therapy. However, neither neutralization of lepirudin's effects nor allergic reactions associated with positive antibody test results have been observed.

Intracranial bleeding has been reported in patients with acute myocardial infarction who were treated with both lepirudin and thrombolytic therapy (rt-PA or streptokinase). There have been post marketing reports of intracranial bleeding in patients who received lepirudin without concomitant thrombolytic therapy.

The following side/adverse effects have been selected on the basis of their potential clinical significance (possible signs and symptoms in parentheses where appropriate)—not necessarily inclusive:

Those indicating need for medical attention
Incidence more frequent

Abnormal liver function (dark urine, light-colored stools, loss of appetite, nausea and vomiting, unusual tiredness, yellow eyes or skin, fever with or without chills, stomach pain); ***anemia or isolated drop in hemoglobin*** (pale skin, troubled breathing with exertion, unusual bleeding or bruising, unusual tiredness or weakness); ***bleeding complications; including bleeding from puncture sites and wounds; and hematoma*** (collection of blood under the skin); ***Hemorrhagic event*** (bleeding gums, coughing up blood, difficulty in breathing or swallowing, dizziness, headache, increased menstrual flow or vaginal bleeding, nosebleeds, paralysis, prolonged bleeding from cuts, red or dark brown urine, red or black, tarry stools shortness of breath)—the symptoms listed, an unexpected fall in hemoglobin, a fall in blood pressure, or any unexplained symptom should lead to consideration of a hemorrhagic event

Incidence less frequent

Allergic reaction (skin rash or itching); ***bleeding complications; hematuria*** (blood in urine); ***coughing up blood; nosebleed; and vaginal bleeding; heart failure*** (swelling of feet or lower legs); ***infection, unspecified*** (fever or chills, cough or hoarseness, lower back or side pain, painful or difficult urination); ***multiorgan failure; pneumonia*** (fever or chills; cough; shortness of breath)

Rare

Abnormal kidney function (decrease in urine output or decrease in urine-concentrating ability, cloudy urine); ***gastrointestinal and rectal bleeding*** (black, tarry stools; blood in stools; vomiting of blood or material that looks like coffee grounds); ***sepsis*** (chills, confusion, dizziness, lightheadedness, fainting, fast heartbeat, fever, rapid, shallow breathing)

Incidence not determined—Observed during clinical practice, estimates of frequency can not be determined

Anaphylactic reactions (cough, difficulty swallowing, dizziness, fast heartbeat, hives, itching, puffiness or swelling of the eyelids or around the eyes, face, lips or tongue, shortness of breath, skin rash, tightness in chest, unusual tiredness or weakness, wheezing); ***intracranial bleeding*** (confusion, headache, sudden severe weakness, nausea and vomiting)—in the absence of concomitant thrombolytic therapy

Overdose

For more information on the management of overdose or unintentional ingestion, **contact a poison control center** (see *Poison Control Center Listing*).

Clinical effects of overdose

The following effects have been selected on the basis of their potential clinical significance (possible signs and symptoms in parentheses where appropriate)—not necessarily inclusive:

Acute

Bleeding complications (bleeding gums, coughing up blood, difficulty in breathing or swallowing, dizziness, headache, increased menstrual flow or vaginal bleeding, nosebleeds, paralysis, prolonged bleeding from cuts, red or dark brown urine, red or black, tarry stools, shortness of breath)

Treatment of overdose

There is no specific antidote to lepirudin. If life threatening bleeding occurs and excessive plasma levels of lepirudin are suspected the following steps should be taken:

Discontinue lepirudin immediately.

Determine aPTT and other coagulation factor levels as appropriate.

Determine hemoglobin and prepare for blood transfusion if necessary.

Treat patient for shock as necessary and appropriate.

There is some evidence that hemofiltration or hemodialysis (using high-flux dialysis membranes with a cutoff point of 50,000 daltons, e.g., AN/69) may be effective.

General Dosing Information

In general, the dosage or infusion rate is adjusted according to the activated partial thromboplastin time (aPTT) ratio, which is the patient's aPTT at a given time over an aPTT reference value (usually the median of the laboratory normal range for aPTT). The target range for the aPTT ratio during treatment is 1.5 to 2.5, above which the risk of bleeding increases without an incremental increase in clinical efficacy.

It is recommended that lepirudin treatment not be initiated in patients with an aPTT ratio of over 2.5, to avoid initial overdosing.

Unless there is a clinical need to react immediately, it is recommended that any aPTT ratio that is out of the target range be confirmed at least once before altering the dose of lepirudin.

If the aPTT ratio is confirmed to be above 2.5, it is recommended that the lepirudin infusion be discontinued for 2 hours and the rate decreased by 50% when it is reinstituted (without repeating the initial bolus injection), followed by another determination of aPTT ratio 4 hours later.

If the aPTT ratio is confirmed to be below 1.5, it is recommended that the infusion rate be increased in increments of 20%, with determination of the aPTT ratio 4 hours after each increase.

When switching to oral anticoagulation, it is recommended that the dose of lepirudin be gradually reduced to produce an aPTT ratio just above 1.5 before initiation of oral anticoagulant therapy. Coumarin derivatives should be initiated only when platelet counts are normalizing. The intended maintenance dose should be started with no loading dose. To avoid prothrombotic effects when initiating coumarin, parenteral anticoagulation should continue for 4 to 5 days. Lepirudin may be discontinued as soon as the international normalized ratio (INR) stabilizes within the desired target range.

Lepirudin is almost exclusively excreted in the kidneys; therefore, the patient's renal function should be considered prior to administration. The initial intravenous injection and the continuous infusion rate must be reduced in case of known or suspected renal function impairment. Dosage adjustments should be based on creatinine clearance values, whenever available, as obtained from a reliable method (24-hour urine sampling). If creatinine clearance is not available, dosage adjustments should be based on serum creatinine values. See *Parenteral Dosage Forms* for dosage adjustments in renal function impairment.

There is limited information on the combined use of lepirudin and thrombolytic agents. An adjusted dosage regimen of lepirudin was used in nine patients with heparin-induced thrombocytopenia who presented with thromboembolic complications at baseline and were started on both lepirudin and thrombolytic therapy. See *Parenteral Dosage Forms* for specific dosing information on concomitant use of lepirudin and thrombolytic agents.

Parenteral Dosage Forms

LEPIRUDIN FOR INJECTION

Usual adult dose

Thrombocytopenia, heparin-induced (treatment)—

Initial: Intravenous (slowly, for example over fifteen to twenty seconds), 400 mcg (0.4 mg) per kg of body weight (up to 44 mg), followed by—

Intravenous infusion, at a rate of 150 mcg (0.15 mg) per kg of body weight per hour (up to 16.5 mg per hour, initially) for two to ten days or longer.

Creatinine clearance (mL/min)	Serum creatinine (mg/dL)	% of standard initial infusion rate	Infusion rate (mg/kg/hour)
45 - 60	1.6 - 2	50%	0.075
30 - 44	2.1 - 3	30%	0.045
15 - 29	3.1 - 6	15%	0.0225
< 15	> 6	avoid or stop infusion	

Dosage adjustments for patients with renal function impairment—

Recommended dose of initial intravenous injection for renal function impairment: 0.2 mg per kg of body weight. followed by—

Dosage adjustments for concomitant use with thrombolytic therapy—

Initial: intravenous, 0.2 mg per kg of body weight followed by—

Intravenous infusion, at rate of 0.1 mg per kg of body weight per hour

Note: Basing the initial dosage on the patient's body weight is valid for patients weighing up to 110 kg. However, for patients weighing more than 110 kg, the initial dosage should not be increased above 44 mg or the maximum infusion rate above 16.5 mg per hour.

Dosage is adjusted according to activated partial thromboplastin time (aPTT) ratio determinations.

Usual adult prescribing limits

In general, it is recommended that the infusion rate not exceed 0.21 mg per kg of body weight per hour without checking for coagulation abnormalities that might prevent an appropriate aPTT response.

Usual pediatric dose

Safety and efficacy have not been established.

Note: Two children (11 and 12 years of age) were treated with lepirudin at doses ranging from 150 to 220 mcg (0.15 to 0.22 mg) per kg of body weight per hour for eight days and 100 to 700 mcg (0.1 to 0.7 mg) per kg of body weight per hour for fifty-eight days, respectively, without serious adverse events.

Strength(s) usually available

U.S.—

50 mg (Rx) [*Refludan* (mannitol 40 mg; sodium hydroxide)].

Canada—

50 mg (Rx) [*Refludan* (mannitol 40 mg; sodium hydroxide)].

Packaging and storage

Store unopened vials between 2 and 25 °C (36 and 77 °F).

Preparation of dosage form

For rapid, complete reconstitution, inject 1 mL of diluent into the vial and shake gently.

Lepirudin for injection is reconstituted by adding 1 mL of water for injection or 0.9% sodium chloride injection to the 50-mg vial and shaking gently, producing a clear, colorless solution within a few seconds to less than 3 minutes and should be warmed to room temperature before using.

For further dilution, 0.9% sodium chloride injection or 5% dextrose injection are suitable.

Parenteral drug products should be inspected visually for particulate matter and discoloration before use. Do not use solutions that are cloudy or contain particles.

For administration by intravenous injection (bolus) (concentration of 5 mg/mL), the reconstituted solution is further diluted by transferring the solution to a sterile, single-use syringe (of at least 10 mL capacity) and adding sufficient water for injection, 0.9% sodium chloride injection, or

5% dextrose injection to produce a total volume of 10 mL of a solution containing 5 mg of lepirudin per mL.

For administration by continuous intravenous infusion (concentrations of 0.2 or 0.4 mg/ml), the contents of two vials of reconstituted solution (total of 100 mg of lepirudin) are transferred into an infusion bag containing 500 mL or 250 mL of 0.9% sodium chloride injection or 5% dextrose injection, producing a solution containing 0.2 or 0.4 mg of lepirudin per mL, respectively.

Stability

It is recommended that any unused portion of a vial be discarded and that the reconstituted solution be used immediately. For administration by intravenous infusion, the reconstituted solution is stable for up to 24 hours at room temperature.

Incompatibilities

Mixing with other drugs is not recommended.

Revised: 12/17/2003
Developed: 08/07/1998

LETROZOLE Systemic

VA CLASSIFICATION (Primary): AN500

Commonly used brand name(s): *Femara*.

Note: For a listing of dosage forms and brand names by country availability, see *Dosage Forms* section(s).

Category

Antineoplastic.

Indications

Accepted

Malignant tumor of breast (extended adjuvant, postmenopausal, following 5 years of tamoxifen therapy)—Letrozole is indicated for the extended adjuvant treatment of early breast cancer in postmenopausal women who have received 5 years of adjuvant tamoxifen therapy. The effectiveness of letrozole in extended adjuvant treatment of early breast cancer is based on an analysis of disease-free survival in patients treated for a median of 24 months. Further data will be required to determine long-term outcome.

Malignant tumor of breast (locally advanced or metastatic, postmenopausal, hormone receptor-positive or unknown, first-line)—Letrozole is indicated for first-line treatment of postmenopausal women with hormone receptor positive or hormone receptor unknown locally advanced or metastatic breast cancer.

Malignant tumor of breast (advanced, postmenopausal, following antiestrogen therapy)—Letrozole is indicated for treatment of advanced breast cancer in postmenopausal women with disease progression following antiestrogen therapy.

Malignant tumor of breast (adjuvant, postmenopausal, hormone receptor-positive)—Letrozole is indicated for the adjuvant treatment of postmenopausal women with hormone receptor-positive early breast cancer.

Pharmacology/Pharmacokinetics

Physicochemical characteristics

Molecular weight—285.31.

Solubility—Freely soluble in dichloromethane, slightly soluble in ethanol, and practically insoluble in water.

Mechanism of action/Effect

Letrozole is a nonsteroidal competitive inhibitor of aromatase and thus, in postmenopausal women, inhibits conversion of adrenal androgens (primarily androstenedione and testosterone) to estrogens (estrone and estradiol) in peripheral tissues and cancer tissue. As a result, letrozole interferes with estrogen-induced stimulation or maintenance of growth of hormonally responsive (estrogen and/or progesterone receptor positive or receptor unknown) breast cancers.

Other actions/effects

In human liver microsomes, letrozole strongly inhibits the cytochrome P450 (CYP) isoenzyme 2A6 (CYP 2A6) and moderately inhibits the CYP isoenzyme 2C19 (CYP 2C19).

Letrozole has not been shown to affect synthesis of adrenal corticosteroids, aldosterone, or thyroid hormones.

Absorption

Rapidly and completely absorbed. Absorption is not affected by food.

Distribution

The volume of distribution (Vol_D) is approximately 1.9 liters per kg of body weight.

Biotransformation

Hepatic, by the CYP isoenzymes 3A4 and 2A6 (CYP 3A4 and CYP 2A6), to an inactive carbinol metabolite and its ketone analog.

Half-life

Terminal—
Approximately 2 days.

Time to steady-state concentration

Plasma—2 to 6 weeks.

Note: Steady-state plasma concentrations are 1.5 to 2 times higher than would be predicted on the basis of single-dose measurements, indicating some nonlinearity in letrozole's pharmacokinetics with daily administration. However, steady-state concentrations are maintained for extended periods, without further accumulation of letrozole.

Elimination

Renal, approximately 90% of a dose (approximately 75% as the glucuronide conjugate of the inactive metabolite, 9% as two unidentified metabolites, and 6% unchanged).

Precautions to Consider

Carcinogenicity

A study in mice given doses of 0.6 to 60 mg per kg of body weight (mg/kg) per day by oral gavage (approximately 1 and 100 times, respectively, the maximum recommended daily human dose [MRHD] on a mg per square meter of body surface area [mg/m^2] basis) for up to 2 years found a dose-related increase in the incidence of benign ovarian stromal tumors. When the high-dose group was excluded because of low survival rates, a significant trend in the incidences of hepatocellular adenoma and carcinoma was shown in females. A study in rats given oral doses of 0.1 to 10 mg/kg per day (approximately 0.4 and 40 times the MRHD on a mg/m^2 basis, respectively) for up to 2 years found an increase in the incidence of benign ovarian stromal tumors with 10 mg/kg per day. Ovarian hyperplasia was also seen in female rats given 0.1 mg/kg or more per day.

Mutagenicity

Letrozole demonstrated no mutagenic effects in *in vitro* tests (Ames and *E. coli* bacterial tests), but was found to be a potential clastogen in *in vitro* assays (CHO K1 and CCL 61 Chinese hamster ovary cells). It was not clastogenic *in vivo* (micronucleus test in rats).

Pregnancy/Reproduction

Fertility—Fertility studies in animals have not been done. However, in male and female mice, rats, and dogs receiving repeated dosing with 0.6, 0.1, and 0.03 mg/kg, respectively (approximately 1, 0.4, and 0.4 times the MRHD on a mg/m^2 basis, respectively), letrozole caused sexual inactivity in females and atrophy of the reproductive tract in males and females.

Pregnancy—Studies in humans have not been done. Letrozole is indicated for use in postmenopausal women only. However, if a pregnant woman is exposed to the medication, she should be apprised of the possibility of fetal harm and/or loss of the pregnancy.

Studies in rats given doses of 0.003 mg/kg (approximately 1/100 of the MHRD on a mg/m^2 basis) or more during the period of organogenesis found embryotoxicity and fetotoxicity, including intrauterine mortality, increased resorption, increased postimplantation loss, decreased numbers of live fetuses, and fetal anomalies including absence and shortening of renal papilla, dilation of ureter, edema, and incomplete ossification of frontal skull and metatarsals. Also, letrozole was teratogenic in rats, causing fetal domed head and cervical/centrum vertebral fusion at a dose of 0.03 mg/kg (approximately 1/10 of the MRHD on a mg/m^2 basis). Studies in rabbits found fetotoxicity at doses of 0.02 mg/kg (approximately 1/10,000 of the MRHD on a mg/m^2 basis) and embryotoxicity at doses of 0.002 mg/kg or greater (about 1/100,000 of the MRHD on a mg/m^2 basis). Fetal anomalies included incomplete ossification of the skull, sternebrae, and fore- and hindlegs.

FDA Pregnancy Category D.

Breast-feeding

It is not known whether letrozole is distributed into human breast milk. Because many drugs are distributed in human milk, caution should be exercised when letrozole is administered to a nursing woman.

Pediatrics

No information is available on the relationship of age to the effects of letrozole in pediatric patients. Safety and efficacy have not been established.

Geriatrics

Clinical trials with letrozole included geriatric patients; the median age in the first-line randomized trial was 65 years, and 1/3 of the patients were 70 years of age or older. Time to tumor progression and tumor response rate were better in patients 70 years of age or older.The mean age in two second-line randomized trials was 64 years, and 30% of the patients were 70 years of age or older. There were no differences in response between patients 70 years of age or older and younger patients. Also, no age-related effects on the pharmacokinetics of letrozole were found in studies that included patients ranging in age from 35 years to more than 80 years.

Drug interactions and/or related problems

The following drug interactions and/or related problems have been selected on the basis of their potential clinical significance (possible mechanism in parentheses where appropriate)—not necessarily inclusive (» = major clinical significance):

Tamoxifen
(concomitant administration may reduce plasma concentrations of letrozole)

Laboratory value alterations

The following have been selected on the basis of their potential clinical significance (possible effect in parentheses where appropriate)—not necessarily inclusive (» = major clinical significance).

With physiology/laboratory test values

Calcium, serum
(concentrations may be increased in some patients)

Cholesterol, serum
(concentrations may be increased in some patients)

Alanine aminotransferase (ALT [SGPT]) and
Aspartate aminotransferase (AST [SGOT]) and
Bilirubin and
Gamma glutamyl transferase
(increases in serum values have been seen, but are most often associated with hepatic metastases)

Medical considerations/Contraindications

The medical considerations/contraindications included have been selected on the basis of their potential clinical significance (reasons given in parentheses where appropriate)—not necessarily inclusive (» = major clinical significance).

Except under special circumstances, this medication should not be used when the following medical problems exist:

Hypersensitivity to letrozole or any of its excipients

Risk-benefit should be considered when the following medical problems exist:

» Cirrhosis or
Hepatic function impairment or
» Hepatic function impairment, severe
(although modest increases in letrozole blood concentrations have been observed in individuals with hepatic function impairment due to cirrhosis, no dosage adjustment is recommended in mild to moderate hepatic function impairment; in patients with cirrhosis and severe hepatic dysfunction the dose should be reduced due to these patients experiencing approximately twice the exposure to a 2.5-dose of letrozole as healthy patients with normal liver function)

Renal function impairment
(no dosage adjustment is necessary when creatinine clearance is 10 mL per minute or more)

Patient monitoring

The following may be especially important in patient monitoring (other tests may be warranted in some patients, depending on condition; » = major clinical significance):

Alanine aminotransferase (ALT [SGPT])and
Aspartate aminotransferase (AST [SGOT])and
Bilirubinand
Gamma glutamyl transferase
(increases in serum values could be evidence of hepatic metastases)

Side/Adverse Effects

Note: Most side effects are mild to moderate. Letrozole was generally well tolerated across all studies as first-line and second-line treatment for breast cancer.

The following side/adverse effects have been selected on the basis of their potential clinical significance (possible signs and symptoms in parentheses where appropriate)—not necessarily inclusive:

Those indicating need for medical attention

Incidence more frequent (≥ 10%)

Dyspnea (shortness of breath)

Incidence less frequent (< 10%)

Bone fracture—less than 5% of patients; ***breast pain; chest pain; edema, peripheral*** (swelling of feet or lower legs); ***hypertension***—usually asymptomatic; ***mental depression***—less than 5% of patients; ***pleural effusion*** (chest pain; shortness of breath)—less than 5% of patients; ***viral infection*** (chills; cough or hoarseness; fever; cold; flu-like symptoms)

Incidence rare (≤ 2%)

Cerebrovascular events (confusion; severe or sudden headache; sudden loss of coordination; sudden slurring of speech); ***myocardial infarction*** (heart attack); ***myocardial ischemia*** (chest pain; fainting; fast heartbeat; increased sweating; nausea, continuing or severe nervousness; shortness of breath; weakness); ***pulmonary embolism*** (chest pain; cough; fainting; fast heartbeat; sudden shortness of breath or troubled breathing; dizziness or lightheadedness); ***thromboembolism*** (pain in chest, groin, or legs, especially the calves; severe, sudden headache; slurred speech; sudden, unexplained shortness of breath; sudden loss of coordination; sudden, severe weakness or numbness in arm or leg; vision changes)—specific symptoms dependent on site of thromboembolism, can result in stroke; ***vaginal bleeding***

Those indicating need for medical attention only if they continue or are bothersome

Incidence more frequent (> 10%)

Arthralgia (joint pain); ***back pain; bone pain; hot flashes*** (sudden sweating and feeling of warmth); ***myalgia*** (muscle pain); ***nausea***

Incidence less frequent (< 10%)

Anorexia (loss of appetite; weight loss); ***anxiety; asthenia*** (weakness); ***constipation; cough; diarrhea; dizziness; headache; hypercalcemia*** (abdominal pain; confusion; constipation; depression; dry mouth; headache; incoherent speech; increased urination; loss of appetite; metallic taste; muscle weakness; nausea; thirst; unusual tiredness; vomiting; weight loss); ***hypercholesterolemia (high cholesterol); increased sweating; insomnia*** (trouble sleeping); ***skin rash or itching; sleepiness; stomach pain or upset; unusual tiredness; vertigo*** (spinning or whirling sensation, altering sense of balance); ***vomiting; weight gain***

Incidence not determined—Observed during clinical practice; estimates of frequency can not be determined

Blurred vision; hepatic enzyme increased (asymptomatic)

Those not indicating need for medical attention

Incidence less frequent (< 5%)

Alopecia (loss of hair)

Overdose

For more information on the management of overdose or unintentional ingestion, **contact a Poison Control Center** (see *Poison Control Center Listing*).

Clinical effects of overdose

Isolated cases of letrozole overdose have been reported, in which the single highest dose taken was 62.5 mg or 25 tablets. No serious adverse events were reported. Due to the limited data available, no definitive treatment recommendations can be made.

Treatment of overdose

No specific treatment is recommended, although emesis could be induced if the patient is alert. Supportive care with frequent monitoring of vital signs is recommended.

Patients in whom overdose is confirmed or suspected should be referred for psychiatric evaluation.

Patient Consultation

As an aid to patient consultation, refer to *Advice for the Patient, Letrozole (Systemic)*.

In providing consultation, consider emphasizing the following selected information (» = major clinical significance):

Before using this medication

» Conditions affecting use, especially:
Hypersensitivity to letrozole or any of its excipients
Pregnancy—Intended for postmenopausal women only; accidental exposure during pregnancy may result in fetotoxicity and/or loss of the pregnancy
Other medical problems, especially cirrhosis or severe hepatic impairment

Proper use of this medication
» Compliance with prescribed regimen
» Proper dosing
Missed dose: Taking as soon as possible; not taking if almost time for next dose; not doubling doses
» Proper storage

Precautions while using this medication
Importance of close monitoring by physician
Caution if dizziness or drowsiness occurs; not driving or using machines while taking letrozole

Side/adverse effects
Stopping treatment and getting emergency help immediately if symptoms of myocardial infarction or thromboembolism occur, especially chest pain, dyspnea, hypertension, myocardial ischemia, peripheral edema, pleural effusion, and pulmonary embolism
Signs of other potential side effects, especially bone fracture, breast pain, mental depression, vaginal bleeding, and viral infection
Possibility of hair loss

General Dosing Information

Letrozole has no effect on cortisol or aldosterone secretion; therefore, glucocorticoid or mineralocorticoid replacement therapy is not required.

Patients should continue to take letrozole until tumor progression is evident.

Oral Dosage Forms

LETROZOLE TABLETS

Usual adult dose
Carcinoma, breast—
Oral, 2.5 mg once a day.
Note: • Renal impairment—If creatinine clearance is ≥ 10 mL/min: no dosage adjustment is required
• Hepatic impairment—If mild to moderate: no dosage adjustment is necessary
• Hepatic impairment—If cirrhosis or severe hepatic impairment: reduce dose by 50%, 2.5 mg every other day

Usual geriatric dose
Carcinoma, breast—
See *Usual adult dose*.

Strength(s) usually available
U.S.—
2.5 mg (Rx) [*Femara* (lactose monohydrate)].
Canada—
2.5 mg (Rx) [*Femara* (lactose)].

Packaging and storage
Store between 15 and 30 °C (59 and 86 °F), preferably at 25 °C (77 °F).

Revised: 01/03/2006
Developed: 09/30/1997

LEUCOVORIN Systemic

VA CLASSIFICATION (Primary/Secondary): VT120/AD900; BL400; AN400

Commonly used brand name(s): *Wellcovorin*.

Other commonly used names are citrovorum factor and folinic acid.

Note: For a listing of dosage forms and brand names by country availability, see *Dosage Forms* section(s).

Category

Antidote (to folic acid antagonists); antianemic; antineoplastic adjunct.

Indications

Accepted

Methotrexate toxicity (prophylaxis and treatment)
Pyrimethamine toxicity (prophylaxis and treatment) or
Trimethoprim toxicity (prophylaxis and treatment)—Leucovorin is indicated as an antidote to the toxic effects of folic acid antagonists such as methotrexate, pyrimethamine, or trimethoprim. Leucovorin also is indicated as a rescue after high-dose methotrexate therapy in osteosarcoma and as a part of chemotherapeutic treatment programs in the management of several forms of cancer.

Anemia, megaloblastic (treatment)—Leucovorin is indicated to treat megaloblastic anemias associated with sprue, nutritional deficiency, pregnancy, and infancy when oral folic acid therapy is not feasible.

Leucovorin is not recommended for use in the treatment of pernicious anemia or other megaloblastic anemias secondary to lack of vitamin B_{12}, since it may produce a hematologic remission while neurologic manifestations continue to progress.

Carcinoma, colorectal (treatment adjunct)—Leucovorin is indicated for use in combination with fluorouracil to prolong survival in the palliative treatment of patients with advanced colorectal cancer.

[Carcinoma, head and neck (treatment adjunct)][1]—Leucovorin is indicated for use in combination with agents such as fluorouracil or high-dose methotrexate, as second-line treatment of squamous cell head and neck carcinoma.

[Ewing's sarcoma (treatment adjunct) or][1]
[Lymphomas, non-Hodgkin's (treatment adjunct)][1]—Leucovorin is indicated for use in combination with high-dose methotrexate as second-line treatment of Ewing's sarcoma and non-Hodgkin's lymphomas.

[Tumors, trophoblastic (treatment adjunct)][1]—Leucovorin is indicated for use in combination with high-dose methotrexate as first-line treatment of gestational trophoblastic neoplasms.

Unaccepted

Leucovorin has not shown benefit over other regimens in the treatment of breast carcinomas.

Leucovorin has not shown benefit in the treatment of gastric carcinomas.

[1]Not included in Canadian product labeling.

Pharmacology/Pharmacokinetics

Physicochemical characteristics
Molecular weight—511.51.

Mechanism of action/Effect
Antidote (to folic acid antagonists)—Leucovorin is a reduced form of folic acid, which is readily converted to other reduced folic acid derivatives (e.g., tetrahydrofolate). Because it does not require reduction by dihydrofolate reductase as does folic acid, leucovorin is not affected by blockage of this enzyme by folic acid antagonists (dihydrofolate reductase inhibitors). This allows purine and thymidine synthesis, and thus DNA, RNA, and protein synthesis, to occur. Leucovorin may limit methotrexate action on normal cells by competing with methotrexate for the same transport processes into the cell. Leucovorin given at the appropriate time rescues bone marrow and gastrointestinal cells from methotrexate but has no apparent effect on pre-existing methotrexate nephrotoxicity.

Absorption
Rapidly absorbed after oral administration; saturation of absorption is reached at doses greater than 25 mg. Bioavailability is approximately 97% for a 25-mg dose, 75% for a 50-mg dose, and 37% for a 100-mg dose.

Distribution
Crosses blood-brain barrier in moderate amounts; largely concentrated in liver.

Biotransformation
Hepatic and intestinal mucosal, mainly to 5-methyltetrahydrofolate (active). After oral administration, leucovorin is substantially (greater than 90%) and rapidly (within 30 minutes) metabolized. Metabolism is less extensive (about 66% after intravenous and 72% after intramuscular administration) and slower with parenteral administration.

Half-life
Terminal half-life for total reduced folates—6.2 hours.

Onset of action
Oral—20 to 30 minutes.
Intramuscular—10 to 20 minutes.
Intravenous—Less than 5 minutes.

Time to peak serum reduced folate concentration
Oral—1.72 ± 0.8 hours.
Intramuscular—0.71 ± 0.09 hour.

Peak serum reduced folate concentration
After 15 mg dose—
Oral: 268 ± 18 nanograms per mL (approximately 1 micromolar [1 × 10^{-6} Molar]).
Intramuscular: 241 ± 17 nanograms per mL (approximately 1 micromolar [1 × 10^{-6} Molar]).

Duration of action
All routes—3 to 6 hours.

Elimination
Renal—80 to 90%.
Fecal—5 to 8%.

Precautions to Consider

Pregnancy/Reproduction
Pregnancy—Studies have not been done in either animals or humans.

FDA Pregnancy Category C.

Recommended for treatment of megaloblastic anemia caused by pregnancy.

Breast-feeding
It is not known whether leucovorin is distributed into breast milk. However, problems in humans have not been documented.

Pediatrics
Leucovorin may increase the frequency of seizures in susceptible pediatric patients by counteracting the anticonvulsant effects of barbiturates, hydantoin anticonvulsants, and primidone.

Geriatrics
No information is available on the relationship of age to the effects of leucovorin in geriatric patients. However, elderly patients are more likely to have age-related renal function impairment, which may require adjustment of dosage in patients receiving leucovorin as a rescue from the effects of high-dose methotrexate.

Drug interactions and/or related problems
The following drug interactions and/or related problems have been selected on the basis of their potential clinical significance (possible mechanism in parentheses where appropriate)—not necessarily inclusive (» = major clinical significance):

Note: Combinations containing any of the following medications, depending on the amount present, may also interact with this medication.

Anticonvulsants, barbiturate or
Anticonvulsants, hydantoin or
Primidone
(large doses of leucovorin may counteract the anticonvulsant effects of these medications)

Fluorouracil
(concurrent use of leucovorin may increase the therapeutic and toxic effects of fluorouracil; although the two medications may be used together for therapeutic advantage, caution is necessary)

Sulfamethoxazole and trimethoprim
(concurrent use of leucovorin may be associated with increased morbidity rates and treatment failure when used for the treatment of pneumonia due to *Pneumocystis carinii* in patients with human immunodeficiency virus (HIV) infection)

Medical considerations/Contraindications
The medical considerations/contraindications included have been selected on the basis of their potential clinical significance (reasons given in parentheses where appropriate)—not necessarily inclusive (» = major clinical significance).

Except under special circumstances, this medication should not be used when the following medical problems exist:

For treatment of anemia (as the sole agent)
» Pernicious anemia or
» Vitamin B_{12} deficiency
(may produce a partial hematologic response while neurologic manifestations continue to progress)

This medication should be used with caution when the following medical problems exist:
Sensitivity to leucovorin

Patient monitoring
The following may be especially important in patient monitoring (other tests may be warranted in some patients, depending on condition; » = major clinical significance):

For patients receiving high-dose methotrexate
» Creatinine clearance determinations
(recommended prior to initiation of high-dose methotrexate with leucovorin rescue therapy or if serum creatinine concentrations increase by 50% or more)

» Creatinine concentrations, serum
(recommended prior to and every 24 hours after each methotrexate dose, until plasma or serum methotrexate concentrations are less than 5×10^{-8} Molar, to detect developing renal function impairment and predict methotrexate toxicity. An increase of greater than 50% over the pretreatment concentration at 24 hours is associated with severe renal toxicity)

» Methotrexate concentrations, plasma or serum
(recommended by some clinicians every 12 to 24 hours after high-dose methotrexate administration to determine dose and duration of leucovorin treatment needed to maintain rescue. May aid in identifying patients with delayed methotrexate clearance; toxicity appears to be related at least as much to the length of time that methotrexate concentrations are elevated as to the peak concentrations achieved. In general, monitoring should continue until concentrations are less than 5×10^{-8} Molar)

» pH determinations, urine
(recommended prior to each dose of high-dose methotrexate therapy and about every 6 hours throughout leucovorin rescue, until plasma or serum methotrexate concentrations are less than 5×10^{-8} Molar, to ensure that pH remains greater than 7 so as to minimize the risk of methotrexate nephropathy from precipitation of methotrexate or metabolites in urine)

Side/Adverse Effects
The following side/adverse effects have been selected on the basis of their potential clinical significance (possible signs and symptoms in parentheses where appropriate)—not necessarily inclusive:

Those indicating need for medical attention
Incidence rare
Allergic reaction (skin rash, hives, or itching; wheezing); ***seizures***—reported with use in cancer chemotherapy

Patient Consultation
As an aid to patient consultation, refer to *Advice for the Patient, Leucovorin (Systemic).*

In providing consultation, consider emphasizing the following selected information (» = major clinical significance):

Before using this medication
» Conditions affecting use, especially:
Sensitivity to leucovorin
Use in children—May increase frequency of seizures in susceptible pediatric patients
Other medical problems, especially pernicious anemia or vitamin B_{12} deficiency (for treatment of anemia as the sole agent)

Proper use of this medication
» Importance of taking as directed and not missing doses; taking at evenly spaced times
» Checking with physician before discontinuing medication or if vomiting occurs shortly after dose is taken
» Proper dosing
Missed dose: Checking with physician right away; possible need for additional leucovorin; importance of not increasing dose unless directed by physician
» Proper storage

Side/adverse effects
Signs of potential side effects, especially allergic reaction and seizures

General Dosing Information
A 15-mg dose produces a serum reduced folate concentration of approximately 1 micromolar (1×10^{-6} Molar).

For use as an antidote to folic acid antagonists
Patients receiving leucovorin as a "rescue" from the toxic effects of methotrexate should be under supervision of a physician experienced in high-dose methotrexate therapy.

Leucovorin should be administered orally or parenterally. Leucovorin should not be administered intrathecally for the treatment of accidental overdoses of intrathecally administered folic acid antagonists. *Leucovorin may be harmful or fatal if administered intrathecally.*

Parenteral administration of leucovorin is recommended if it appears that absorption may be impaired as a result of nausea and vomiting.

High-dose methotrexate administration should not be initiated unless leucovorin is physically present and ready to be administered, since rescue is critical.

A variety of dosage schedules of leucovorin in combination with high-dose methotrexate have been used. Since this regimen is still largely investigational, the prescriber should consult the medical literature in choosing a specific dosage. Alkalinization of urine (with bicarbonate and/or acetazolamide) and intravenous hydration (1000 mL per square meter of body surface area over six hours prior to beginning the methotrexate infusion and 3000 mL per square meter of body surface area per day during the methotrexate infusion and for two days after the infusion is completed) are also important to prevent renal toxicity caused by methotrexate and/or its metabolites.

Administration of leucovorin should be consecutive to rather than simultaneous with methotrexate administration so as not to interfere with methotrexate's antineoplastic effects. However, leucovorin has been administered simultaneously with pyrimethamine and trimethoprim in oral or intramuscular doses ranging from 400 mcg (0.4 mg) to 5 mg to prevent megaloblastic anemia due to high doses of these medications.

In general, it is recommended that the first dose of leucovorin be administered within the first 24 to 42 hours of starting a high-dose methotrexate infusion (within 1 hour of an overdose), in a dosage to produce blood concentrations equal to or greater than methotrexate blood concentrations (leucovorin in a dose of 15 mg produces peak plasma concentrations of approximately 1 micromolar [1×10^{-6} Molar]). Duration of leucovorin administration varies with the dosage of methotrexate and plasma concentrations achieved (including rate of elimination); in general, leucovorin administration is continued until methotrexate concentrations fall to less than 5×10^{-8} Molar.

A larger dose and/or longer duration of leucovorin treatment may be required in patients with aciduria, ascites, dehydration, gastrointestinal obstruction, renal function impairment, or pleural or peritoneal effusions because excretion of methotrexate is slowed and the length of time for plasma methotrexate concentrations to decrease to nontoxic levels ($<5 \times 10^{-8}$ Molar) is increased. It is recommended that duration of leucovorin administration in these patients be based on determination of plasma methotrexate concentrations.

For use as an adjunct to fluorouracil for colorectal carcinoma

Patients receiving leucovorin in combination with fluorouracil should be under supervision of a physician experienced in cancer chemotherapy.

Oral Dosage Forms

Note: The dosing and strengths of the dosage forms available are expressed in terms of leucovorin base (not the calcium salt).

LEUCOVORIN CALCIUM TABLETS USP

Usual adult and adolescent dose

Antidote (to folic acid antagonists)—
To methotrexate—
Oral, 10 mg (base) per square meter of body surface area every six hours until methotrexate blood concentrations fall to less than 5×10^{-8} *M*.
To pyrimethamine or trimethoprim—
Prevention—Oral, 400 mcg (0.4 mg) to 5 mg (base) with each dose of the folic acid antagonist.
Treatment—Oral, 5 to 15 mg (base) per day.
Megaloblastic anemia, secondary to folate deficiency—
Oral, up to 1 mg (base) per day.

Note: Doses higher than 25 mg should be given parenterally because oral absorption is saturable at doses above 25 mg.

Usual pediatric dose

See *Usual adult and adolescent dose.*

Strength(s) usually available

U.S.—
5 mg (base) (Rx) [*Wellcovorin* (scored); GENERIC (scored)].
15 mg (base) (Rx) [GENERIC (scored)].
25 mg (base) (Rx) [*Wellcovorin* (scored)].
Canada—
5 mg (base) (Rx) [GENERIC (scored)].
15 mg (base) (Rx) [GENERIC (scored)].

Packaging and storage

Store below 40 °C (104 °F), preferably between 15 and 30 °C (59 and 86 °F), in a well-closed container. Protect from light.

Parenteral Dosage Forms

Note: The dosing and strengths of the dosage forms available are expressed in terms of leucovorin base (not the calcium salt).

LEUCOVORIN CALCIUM INJECTION USP

Usual adult and adolescent dose

Antidote (to folic acid antagonists)—
To methotrexate (inadvertent overdose)—
Intramuscular or intravenous, 10 mg (base) per square meter of body surface area every six hours until methotrexate blood concentrations fall to less than 5×10^{-8} Molar.

Note: If, at 24 hours following methotrexate administration, the serum creatinine is increased by 50% or greater over baseline or serum methotrexate is greater than 5×10^{-6} Molar, the dose of leucovorin should be 100 mg (base) per square meter of body surface area every three hours intravenously until methotrexate concentrations are reduced to appropriate levels.

To pyrimethamine or trimethoprim—
Prevention—Intramuscular, 400 mcg (0.4 mg) to 5 mg (base) with each dose of the folic acid antagonist.
Treatment—Intramuscular, 5 to 15 mg (base) per day.
Megaloblastic anemia, secondary to folate deficiency—
Intramuscular, up to 1 mg (base) per day.

Note: Because of its calcium content, leucovorin calcium injection should be administered by intravenous injection slowly, at a rate that does not exceed 160 mg of leucovorin per minute.

Usual pediatric dose

See *Usual adult and adolescent dose.*

Strength(s) usually available

U.S.—
Not commercially available.
Canada—
10 mg (base) per mL (Rx) [GENERIC (without preservative)].

Packaging and storage

Store in the refrigerator between 2 and 8 °C (36 and 46 °F). Protect from light.

Stability

Intravenous solutions containing leucovorin calcium in lactated Ringer's injection, Ringer's injection, or 0.9% sodium chloride injection are stable for up to 24 hours at room temperature. When diluted in 5% dextrose in water injection or 10% dextrose injection, intravenous solutions containing leucovorin calcium are stable for 12 hours at room temperature. When diluted in 10% dextrose in 0.9% sodium chloride injection, solutions are stable for 6 hours at room temperature.

Incompatibilities

Leucovorin calcium injection is incompatible with fluorouracil; precipitation will occur if these agents are combined in the same infusion solution.

LEUCOVORIN CALCIUM FOR INJECTION

Usual adult and adolescent dose

Antidote (to folic acid antagonists)—
To methotrexate (inadvertent overdose)—
Intramuscular or intravenous, 10 mg (base) per square meter of body surface area every six hours until methotrexate blood concentrations fall to less than 5×10^{-8} Molar.

Note: If, at 24 hours following methotrexate administration, the serum creatinine is increased 50% over baseline or serum methotrexate is greater than 5×10^{-6} Molar, the dose of leucovorin should be 100 mg (base) per square meter of body surface area every three hours intravenously until methotrexate concentrations are reduced to appropriate levels. *Only solutions prepared with sterile water for injection (i.e., without benzyl alcohol) should be used for doses greater than 10 mg per square meter of body surface area.*

To pyrimethamine or trimethoprim—
Prevention—Intramuscular, 400 mcg (0.4 mg) to 5 mg (base) with each dose of the folic acid antagonist.
Treatment—Intramuscular, 5 to 15 mg (base) per day.
Megaloblastic anemia, secondary to folate deficiency—
Intramuscular, up to 1 mg (base) per day.
Carcinoma, colorectal (treatment adjunct)—
Intravenous, 200 mg per square meter of body surface area over a minimum of three minutes, followed by fluorouracil 370 mg per square meter of body surface area intravenously, or
Intravenous, 20 mg per square meter of body surface area, followed by fluorouracil 425 mg per square meter of body surface area intravenously.
Either regimen is given daily for five days, and the course may be repeated at four-week intervals for two courses and then at four- to five-week intervals, as determined by toxicity to the previous course.

Note: Only solutions prepared with sterile water for injection (i.e., without benzyl alcohol) should be used, since the dose is greater than 10 mg per square meter of body surface area.
Because of its calcium content, leucovorin calcium for injection should be administered by intravenous injection slowly, at a rate that does not exceed 160 mg of leucovorin per minute.

Usual pediatric dose

Antidote (to folic acid antagonists) or

Megaloblastic anemia—See *Usual adult and adolescent dose.*

Carcinoma, colorectal (treatment adjunct)—Dosage has not been established.

Strength(s) usually available

U.S.—

50 mg (base) (Rx) [GENERIC (without preservative)].

100 mg (base) (Rx) [*Wellcovorin* (without preservative); GENERIC (without preservative)].

350 mg (base) (Rx) [GENERIC (without preservative)].

Canada—

50 mg (base) (Rx) [GENERIC (without preservative)].

100 mg (base) (Rx) [GENERIC (without preservative)].

350 mg (base) (Rx) [GENERIC (without preservative)].

Packaging and storage

Prior to reconstitution, store below 40 °C (104 °F), preferably between 20 and 25 °C (68 and 77 °F), unless otherwise specified by manufacturer. Protect from light.

Preparation of dosage form

Leucovorin calcium for injection is prepared for parenteral use by adding 5 or 10 mL of bacteriostatic water for injection (preserved with benzyl alcohol) to the vial containing 50 or 100 mg (base), respectively, producing a solution containing 10 mg per mL. If doses greater than 10 mg per square meter of body surface area are to be used, sterile water for injection should be used for reconstitution and the resulting solution used immediately.

Caution: Use of diluents containing benzyl alcohol is not recommended for preparation of medications for use in neonates. A fatal toxic syndrome consisting of metabolic acidosis, CNS depression, respiratory problems, renal failure, hypotension, and possibly seizures and intracranial hemorrhages has been associated with this use.

Stability

Reconstituted solutions prepared with bacteriostatic water for injection (preserved with benzyl alcohol) should be used within 7 days. Intravenous solutions containing leucovorin calcium in 10% dextrose injection, 10% dextrose in 0.9% sodium chloride injection, lactated Ringer's injection, or Ringer's injection have been found to maintain at least 90% of labeled potency when used within twenty-four hours.

Incompatibilities

Leucovorin calcium for injection is incompatible with fluorouracil; precipitation will occur if these agents are combined in the same infusion solution.

Revised: 08/14/2000

LEUPROLIDE Systemic

INN: Leuprorelin; BAN: Leuprorelin

VA CLASSIFICATION (Primary/Secondary): HS900/AN500

Commonly used brand name(s): *Eligard; Lupron; Lupron Depot; Lupron Depot-3 Month 11.25 mg; Lupron Depot-3 Month 22.5 mg; Lupron Depot-4 Month 30 mg; Lupron Depot-Ped; Lupron-3 Month SR Depot 22.5 mg; Viadur.*

Note: For a listing of dosage forms and brand names by country availability, see *Dosage Forms* section(s).

Category

Gonadotropin-releasing hormone analog; antiendometriotic agent; antineoplastic; gonadotropin inhibitor.

Indications

Bracketed information in the *Indications* section refers to uses that are not included in U.S. product labeling.

Accepted

Anemia due to uterine leiomyomas (treatment)[1]—Leuprolide, in conjunction with iron supplement therapy, is indicated for the preoperative hematologic improvement of patients with anemia caused by uterine leiomyomas (fibroids). Because some patients respond to iron supplementation alone, a 1-month trial period with iron should be considered prior to initiation of leuprolide therapy. Leuprolide may then be added if the response to iron supplementation is inadequate.

Carcinoma, prostatic (treatment)—Leuprolide is indicated for the palliative treatment of advanced prostatic cancer, especially as an alternative to orchiectomy or estrogen administration.

Endometriosis (treatment)—Leuprolide is indicated for management of endometriosis, including pain relief and reduction of endometriotic lesions.

Puberty, precocious, central (treatment)—Leuprolide is indicated for the treatment of central precocious puberty (CPP, idiopathic or neurogenic) in children with the onset of secondary sexual characteristics before the age of 8 years in females and 9 years in males. Prior to initiation of leuprolide therapy, clinical diagnosis should be confirmed by a prepubertal response to a gonadorelin stimulation test and by bone age that is advanced 1 year beyond the chronological age. Diagnosis of CPP should be confirmed before initiation of treatment with leuprolide by measuring serum sex steroids, height and weight, and basal gonadotropin levels, and by testing stimulation response to gonadorelin, assessing diagnostic imaging of the brain (including pituitary and hypothalamus), and performing pelvic ultrasound examinations.

Before beginning treatment for CPP with leuprolide, it is especially important to confirm that the patient is willing to comply with dosing requirements and the frequent monitoring required by the physician during the first 6 to 8 weeks of treatment to assure that suppression of gonadal-pituitary function is rapid.

[Carcinoma, breast (treatment)][1]—Leuprolide is indicated in the palliative treatment of advanced breast carcinoma in premenopausal and perimenopausal women.

[1]Not included in Canadian product labeling.

Pharmacology/Pharmacokinetics

Note: Pharmacokinetic studies of leuprolide use in children have not been done.

Physicochemical characteristics

Source—Synthetic gonadotropin-releasing hormone (GnRH) analog.

Molecular weight—Leuprolide acetate: 1269.48.

Mechanism of action/Effect

Like naturally occurring luteinizing hormone-releasing hormone (LHRH), initial or intermittent administration of leuprolide stimulates release of luteinizing hormone (LH) and follicle-stimulating hormone (FSH) from the anterior pituitary.

Prostatic carcinoma—LH and FSH release from the anterior pituitary transiently increases testosterone and dihydrotestosterone concentrations in males. However, continuous administration of leuprolide in the treatment of prostatic carcinoma suppresses secretion of gonadotropin-releasing hormone, with a resultant fall in testosterone concentrations and a pharmacologic castration.

Anemia due to uterine leiomyomas; endometriosis; or breast carcinoma—Initial stimulation of gonadotropins from the anterior pituitary is followed by prolonged suppression. Gonadotropin release from the anterior pituitary transiently increases estrone and estradiol concentrations in premenopausal females. However, continuous administration of leuprolide produces a decrease in estradiol, estrone, and progesterone concentrations to postmenopausal levels. As a consequence of suppression of ovarian function, both normal and ectopic endometrial tissues become inactive and atrophic. As a result, amenorrhea occurs.

Central precocious puberty—After an initial stimulation of gonadotropins and increase in the rate of pubertal development, testosterone and estradiol concentrations in males and females, respectively, decrease to prepubertal levels with continuous administration of therapeutic doses of leuprolide in children. Stimulated and basal gonadotropin concentrations also are reduced to prepubertal levels. As a result, menses stop, reproductive organ development decreases, and bone age velocity approaches normal, improving the child's chance of attaining the predicted adult height. Upon discontinuation of leuprolide, gonadotropins return to pubertal levels and normal maturation resumes.

Other actions/effects

Leuprolide also has some androgenic effects in females.

Absorption

Bioavailability after intramuscular injection of the depot formulation is estimated to be about 90%.

The leuprolide acetate implant delivers 120 micrograms of leuprolide acetate per day over 12 months.

Distribution

The mean steady-state volume of distribution following a single intravenous dose in healthy male volunteers was 27 L.

Protein binding
Moderate (46%).

Biotransformation
Metabolized to smaller inactive peptides, Metabolite I (a pentapeptide), Metabolites II and III (tripeptides), and Metabolite IV (a dipeptide).

Half-life
Approximately 3 hours following a 1-mg intravenous dose in healthy male volunteers.

Onset of action
Transient increases in testosterone and estradiol concentrations occur within the first week of therapy; a decline to castrate and postmenopausal levels, respectively, occurs within 2 to 4 weeks.

Time to peak concentration
3.75-mg depot—4 hours.
7.5-mg depot—4 hours.
22.5-mg depot—4 hours.

Peak plasma concentration
3.75-mg depot—4.6 to 10.2 nanograms per mL (nanograms/mL).
7.5-mg depot—20 nanograms/mL.
22.5-mg depot—48.9 nanograms/mL.

Steady-state serum concentration
After insertion of a leuprolide acetate implant, the mean serum leuprolide concentrations were 16.9 ng/mL at 4 hours and 2.4 ng/mL at 24 hours. Thereafter, leuprolide was released at a constant rate. Mean serum leuprolide concentrations were maintained at 0.9 ng/mL for 12 months.

Time to peak effect
Amenorrhea—Usually occurs after 1 to 2 months of therapy.
Prostatic carcinoma—Usually occurs after 2 to 4 weeks of therapy

Duration of action
Pituitary-gonadal system—Normal function is usually restored within 4 to 12 weeks after therapy is withdrawn.
Amenorrhea—Cyclic bleeding usually returns within 60 to 90 days after therapy is withdrawn.

Elimination
Less than 5% of a 3.75-mg dose was recovered in the urine as parent drug and Metabolite I.

Precautions to Consider

Cross-sensitivity and/or related problems
Patients sensitive to gonadorelin (GnRH), to components of any product, or to gonadotropin-releasing hormone analogs (GnRHa), such as buserelin, goserelin, histrelin, and nafarelin, may be sensitive to leuprolide also.

Carcinogenicity
Adults treated with doses of leuprolide as high as 10 mg a day for up to 3 years and 20 mg a day for up to 2 years have not shown clinical abnormalities of the pituitary.

Studies in rats and mice for 2 years at daily subcutaneous doses of 0.6 to 4 mg per kg of body weight (mg/kg) and up to 60 mg/kg, respectively, found an increased incidence of benign pituitary hyperplasia and benign pituitary adenomas at 24 months in the rats. Also, there was a significant, but not dose-related, increase of pancreatic islet-cell adenomas in female rats and, at the lower dose, interstitial cell adenomas in the testes of male rats.

Mutagenicity
Mutagenicity studies in bacterial and mammalian systems found no evidence of mutagenic effects.

Pregnancy/Reproduction
Fertility—In adult males: Suppression of testosterone secretion results in impairment of fertility. However, studies in adults administered leuprolide and similar analogs have shown reversal of fertility suppression when the medications were discontinued after continuous administration for periods of up to 24 weeks.

In adult females: Leuprolide usually induces anovulation and amenorrhea. This effect is reversible and the average time to return of menses is about 60 to 90 days following withdrawal of therapy. A nonhormonal contraceptive method should be used during leuprolide therapy.

Male and female children: Long-term posttreatment follow-up studies of fertility in children treated for central precocious puberty (CPP) have not been done.

Animal studies of adult and prepubertal rats and monkeys given leuprolide or other GnRH analogs showed functional reproductive recovery. Immature male and female rats given leuprolide in one study were normal when compared with controls, even though the histologic investigation showed that tubular degeneration in the testes occurred after a recovery period. The offspring of both sexes appeared normal.

Pregnancy—Leuprolide is not recommended for use during pregnancy; spontaneous abortion may occur.

Studies in rabbits at doses of 0.00024, 0.0024, and 0.024 mg/kg (1/600 to 1/6 the human adult dose; 1/1200 to 1/12 the human pediatric dose) on day 6 of pregnancy found a dose-related increase in major fetal abnormalities; these effects did not occur at similar doses in rats. The two higher doses in rabbits and the highest dose in rats were associated with increased fetal mortality and decreased fetal weights.

FDA Pregnancy Category X.

Breast-feeding
It is not known whether leuprolide passes into breast milk. However, because of potential adverse effects in the infant, breast-feeding is usually not recommended during treatment with leuprolide.

Pediatrics
For prostatic cancer: Safety and effectiveness of subcutaneous leuprolide has not been established and should not be used in pediatric patients.

Studies performed to date have not demonstrated pediatrics-specific problems that would limit the usefulness of leuprolide in children.

Geriatrics
Appropriate studies on the relationship of age to the effects of leuprolide have not been performed in the geriatric population. However, this medication is frequently used in elderly patients, especially for treatment of prostatic carcinoma, and geriatrics-specific problems that would limit the usefulness of this medication in the elderly are not expected.

Laboratory value alterations
The following have been selected on the basis of their potential clinical significance (possible effect in parentheses where appropriate)—not necessarily inclusive (» = major clinical significance).

With diagnostic test results
» Gonadal function testing and
» Pituitary gonadotropic function testing
(therapeutic doses of leuprolide suppress the pituitary-gonadal feedback regulatory system; baseline function usually is restored within 3 months after discontinuation of treatment)

With physiology/laboratory test values
Acid phosphatase
(transient increases in values may occur early in treatment of prostatic carcinoma, but usually decrease to or near baseline by the fourth week)

Alanine aminotransferase (ALT [SGPT]) and
Alkaline phosphatase and
Aspartate aminotransferase (AST [SGOT]) and
Lactate dehydrogenase (LDH)
(values may be increased)

Estradiol
(serum concentrations usually are increased during the first weeks of therapy in adult females but then decrease to postmenopausal levels)

Low-density lipoprotein (LDL) cholesterol and
Total cholesterol and
Triglycerides
(concentrations may be increased)

Platelet counts and
White blood cell counts
(may decrease; platelet count decrease may be transient, returning to normal during treatment)

Testosterone
(serum concentrations are usually increased during the first week of therapy for prostatic carcinoma but then decrease; castrate levels are reached within 2 to 4 weeks)

Medical considerations/Contraindications
The medical considerations/contraindications included have been selected on the basis of their potential clinical significance (reasons given in parentheses where appropriate)—not necessarily inclusive (» = major clinical significance).

Except under special circumstances, this medication should not be used when the following medical problem exists:
» Hypersensitivity to gonadorelin (synthetic gonadotropin-releasing hormone [GnRH]); gonadotropin-releasing hormone analogs (GnRHa), such as buserelin, goserelin, histrelin, leuprolide, and nafarelin; or benzyl alcohol

Risk-benefit should be considered when the following medical problems exist:

For treatment of endometriosis or of anemia due to uterine leiomyomas

Conditions causing decrease in bone density or

Osteoporosis, or history of, or family history of

(hypoestrogenism-induced loss of bone mineral density may occur in females treated with leuprolide and may be irreversible; major risk factors include chronic alcohol and/or tobacco abuse, family history of severe osteoporosis, and chronic use of medications, such as anticonvulsants or corticosteroids, that decrease bone mineral density; leuprolide should be used with caution in these patients)

» Uterine bleeding, undiagnosed abnormal

(use of leuprolide may delay diagnosis)

For treatment of prostatic carcinoma

» Urinary tract obstruction or history of

(existing urinary tract obstruction should be treated before beginning treatment with leuprolide; for patients with a history of urinary tract obstruction, there is an increased incidence of disease flare during initial leuprolide treatment because of the initial increase in serum testosterone concentrations; close monitoring is recommended during the first month of treatment; catheterization may be necessary on occurrence)

» Vertebral metastases

(worsening of symptoms during first few weeks of leuprolide therapy, with risk of neurologic problems, including paralysis)

Patient monitoring

The following may be especially important in patient monitoring (other tests may be warranted in some patients, depending on condition; » = major clinical significance):

Bone density assessment

(recommended as needed to monitor patient's response during long-term use of leuprolide, including treatment of endometriosis for longer than 6 months)

For treatment of central precocious puberty

Bone linear growth velocity and bone age velocity determinations and

Imaging studies

(recommended prior to treatment initiation and periodically during treatment, beginning 3 to 6 months after treatment initiation; diagnostic imaging studies should include radiography of the left hand and wrist [or non-dominate hand and wrist] for bone age determination, pelvic ultrasonography, and magnetic resonance imaging of the brain)

Dehydroepiandrosterone concentrations, serum and/or

Estradiol concentrations, serum and/or

Follicle-stimulating hormone concentrations, serum and/or

Human chorionic gonadotropin concentrations, serum and/or

Hydroxyprogesterone concentrations, serum and/or

Luteinizing hormone concentrations, serum and/or

Prolactin concentrations, serum and/or

Testosterone concentrations, serum

(recommended prior to treatment initiation to establish prepubertal gonadotropin response. If gonadal-pituitary function suppression is not apparent within 6 to 8 weeks after therapy with leuprolide is initiated and lack of patient compliance is ruled out, leuprolide should be discontinued and the diagnosis of gonadotropin-independent sexual precocity should be reconsidered. Other possible causes of sexual precocity include adrenal hyperplasia, testoxicosis, and hypothalamic or testicular tumors)

Gonadotropin-releasing hormone stimulation test

(recommended prior to treatment initiation to establish prepubertal gonadotropin response)

Pregnancy test

(recommended if treatment is not started during menstruation and in patients with irregular menstrual cycles)

For treatment of endometriosis

Pregnancy test

(recommended for females of reproductive potential if treatment is not started during menstruation, if irregular menstrual cycles exist, or if a scheduled dose is delayed)

For treatment of prostatic carcinoma

Acid phosphatase concentrations, plasma prostatic or serum and/or

Prostate-specific antigen (PSA) concentrations, serum and/or

Testosterone concentrations, serum

(recommended at periodic intervals to monitor response)

Bone scans

(recommended as needed to monitor response in patients at risk for vertebral metastases)

Imaging studies

(intravenous pyelogram, computerized tomography [CT] scan, and/or ultrasonography may be used to diagnose or assess patients at risk for obstructive uropathy; these are especially useful during the first week of therapy)

Side/Adverse Effects

Note: Many of the side/adverse effects of leuprolide are related to hypoestrogenism in females and hypotestosteronism in males. The reversibility of clinical hypogonadism produced by leuprolide has not been established for long-term use.

There is a risk of increased loss of vertebral trabecular bone density during treatment for endometriosis or for anemia due to uterine leiomyomas; this loss may be irreversible. However, the loss usually is small when the treatment period is limited to 3 months (for fibroids) or 6 months (for endometriosis), except in patients with existing risk factors (e.g., history of osteoporosis). Compared to pretreatment bone density values, bone density values measured by dual energy x-ray absorptiometry (DEXA) decreased by 3.9% for patients treated for endometriosis at 6 months; a 12-month measurement, 6 months after leuprolide discontinuation, showed the decrease as 2% in these patients. Decreased bone density also has been reported in men who have had orchiectomy or who have been treated with a gonadotropin–releasing hormone analog.

Note: During post-marketing surveillance, rare cases of pituitary apoplexy have been reported after the administration of gonadotropin-releasing hormone agonists, In a majority of these cases occurring within 2 weeks of the first dose, and some within the first hour. In these cases, pituitary apoplexy has presented as sudden headache, vomiting, visual changes, ophthalmoplegia, altered mental status, and sometimes cardiovascular collapse. **Immediate medical attention has been required.**

The following side/adverse effects have been selected on the basis of their potential clinical significance (possible signs and symptoms in parentheses where appropriate)—not necessarily inclusive:

Those indicating need for medical attention

Incidence less frequent—> 5%

In adult females and males

Cardiac arrhythmias or palpitations (fast or irregular heartbeat)—up to 19% in males

Incidence rare—< 5%

In adult females and males

Anaphylaxis (fast or irregular breathing; puffiness or swelling of the eyelids or around the eyes; shortness of breath, troubled breathing, tightness in chest, and/or wheezing; skin rash, hives, and/or itching; sudden, severe decrease in blood pressure and collapse); ***bone, muscle, or joint pain, continuing; paresthesias*** (numbness or tingling of hands or feet); ***syncope*** (fainting)

In adult females only

Androgenic effects (deepening of voice; increased hair growth); ***personality or behavioral changes*** (anxiety; mental depression; mood changes; nervousness)

In adult males only

Angina or myocardial infarction (pains in chest); ***pulmonary embolism*** (sudden shortness of breath); ***thrombophlebitis*** (pains in groin or legs, especially calves of legs)

In pediatric females and males ***Body pain; injection site reactions*** (burning, itching, redness, or swelling at place of injection); ***skin rash***

In pediatric females—expected within first few weeks

Uterine bleeding, continuing (vaginal bleeding); ***vaginal discharge, continuing*** (white vaginal discharge)

Incidence unknown—observed during clinical practice, estimates of frequency can not be determined

Pituitary apoplexy (altered mental status; cardiovascular collapse; double vision; headache, sudden; visual changes; vomiting)

Those indicating need for medical attention only if they continue or are bothersome

Incidence more frequent—> 50%

In adult females and males

Hot flashes (sudden sweating and feelings of warmth)

In adult females only

Amenorrhea (stopping of menstrual periods); ***or spotting*** (light, irregular vaginal bleeding)

Incidence less frequent—5 to 13%

In adult females and males

Blurred vision; decreased libido (decreased interest in sexual intercourse); ***dizziness; edema*** (swelling of feet or lower legs); ***headache***; ***injection site reaction*** (bleeding, bruising, burning, itching, pain, redness, or swelling at place of injection); ***nausea or vomiting***; ***swelling or increased tenderness of breasts; trouble in sleeping***; ***weight gain***

In adult females only

Endometriotic disease flare, transient (pelvic pain); ***vaginitis*** (burning, dryness, or itching of vagina)

Note: *An endometriotic disease flare*, with a transient increase in symptoms (pelvic pain, dysmenorrhea, dyspareunia, pelvic tenderness, induration), may occur shortly after initiation of therapy for endometriosis as a result of the temporary increase in serum estradiol.

In adult males only ***Constipation; decreased size of testicles; prostatic carcinoma disease flare, transient*** (bone pain); ***impotence*** (inability to have or keep an erection)

Note: A *prostatic carcinoma disease flare*, with a transient, sometimes severe, increase in bone or tumor pain, may occur shortly after initiation of therapy for prostatic carcinoma, usually associated with the increase in serum testosterone, but usually subsides with continued leuprolide treatment. Analgesics may be required during this time. Other signs and symptoms of prostatic carcinoma, including difficult urination and spinal compression, may also worsen transiently. In addition, worsening of neurologic signs and symptoms in patients with vertebral metastases may result in temporary weakness and paresthesias of the lower extremities; paralysis, with or without fatal complications, is possible.

Patient Consultation

As an aid to patient consultation, refer to *Advice for the Patient, Leuprolide (Systemic)*.

In providing consultation, consider emphasizing the following selected information (» = major clinical significance):

Before using this medication

» Conditions affecting use, especially:

Hypersensitivity to gonadorelin (GnRH), leuprolide or other GnRH analogs (GnRHa), or to other ingredients in the product's formulation, such as benzyl alcohol

Pregnancy/reproductionFor females and males: May impair fertility by suppressing sperm production in males and causing anovulation in most females, usually reversible after discontinuation

For females: Not recommended for use during pregnancy; may cause spontaneous abortion, causes birth defects in animals

Breast-feeding—Not recommended for use in nursing mothers

Use in children—Safety and effectiveness of subcutaneous leuprolide has not been established and should not be used in pediatric patients.

Other medical problems, especially undiagnosed abnormal vaginal bleeding (for endometriosis or uterine leiomyomas), urinary tract obstruction (for prostatic carcinoma), or vertebral metastases (for prostatic carcinoma)

Proper use of this medication

» Carefully reading patient instruction sheet contained in package

Using disposable syringes provided in kit

» Importance of not using more or less medication than the amount prescribed

» Importance of continuing medication despite side effects

» Proper dosing

Missed dose:

For daily dosing—Using as soon as remembered; not using if not remembered until next day; not doubling doses

For monthly or every 3 to 12 months dosing—Receiving as soon as remembered; returning to normal dosing schedule

» Proper storage

Precautions while using this medication

» Importance of close monitoring by the physician

For treatment of endometriosis or of anemia due to uterine leiomyomas:

Possibility of amenorrhea or irregular menstrual periods; checking with physician if regular menstruation does not occur within 60 to 90 days after discontinuation of medication

Notifying physician if regular menstruation persists during treatment; however, missing one or more successive doses of leuprolide may result in breakthrough menstrual bleeding

Advisability of using nonhormonal forms of contraception during therapy; not using oral contraceptives

» Stopping medication and checking with physician if pregnancy is suspected

Side/adverse effects

Signs of potential side effects, especially cardiac arrhythmias or palpitations (adults); anaphylaxis (adults); bone, muscle, or joint pain (adults); paresthesias (adults); syncope (adults); androgenic effects in females (adults); personality or behavioral changes in females (adults); angina or myocardial infarction in males (adults); pulmonary embolism in males (adults); thrombophlebitis in males (adults); body pain (children); injection site reactions (children); skin rash (children); uterine bleeding in females, continuing (children); and vaginal discharge, continuing (children), pituitary apoplexy (observed during clinical practice)

General Dosing Information

It is recommended that the intramuscular depot injection be administered by the physician. Parents or guardians may be instructed in how to give the subcutaneous injections at home to their child. Injection sites should be rotated periodically.

Leuprolide has approximately 15 to 50 times the activity of naturally occurring luteinizing hormone-releasing hormone (LHRH), and 80 to 100 times that of gonadotropin–releasing hormone (gonadorelin).

For treatment of anemia due to uterine leiomyomas

Therapy should continue uninterrupted for 3 months. Re-treatment is not recommended. However, if re-treatment is contemplated, bone density should be assessed prior to beginning treatment to verify that values are in the normal range.

For treatment of central precocious puberty

Dose must be individualized for each patient and titrated upward until patient's pituitary-gonadal axis is suppressed, according to clinical and/or laboratory parameters. Usually the dose that adequately suppresses the pituitary-gonadal axis is appropriate for the entire therapy; however, there are insufficient data to guide dosage adjustments as a child's weight changes, a special concern for children who started therapy at a very early age at a low dose. Careful monitoring for suppression of the pituitary-gonadal axis is required, especially 1 or 2 months after treatment initiation or following changes in dose.

If the patient responds and tolerates leuprolide therapy, treatment should continue until resumption of puberty is desired. Discontinuation of leuprolide therapy should be considered before the age of 11 years in females and 12 years in males. Normal function of pituitary-gonadal axis is restored within 4 to 12 weeks after treatment discontinuation.

For treatment of endometriosis

It is recommended that therapy begin with the first day of the menstrual cycle after pregnancy has been ruled out.

Development of amenorrhea is usually evidence of a clinical response, although spotting or bleeding from the atrophic endometrium can still occur.

Therapy should continue uninterrupted for 6 months. Re-treatment is not recommended. However, if re-treatment is contemplated, bone density should be assessed prior to beginning treatment to verify that values are in the normal range.

For treatment of prostatic carcinoma

Patients receiving leuprolide should be under supervision of a physician experienced in cancer chemotherapy.

Isolated short-term worsening of neurologic symptoms may contribute to paralysis with or without fatal complications in patients with vertebral metastases. For patients at risk, therapy may be initiated with daily leuprolide injection for the first 2 weeks to observe patient reaction, since worsening of symptoms occasionally requires discontinuation of therapy and possible surgical intervention.

For treatment of adverse effects

Recommended treatment:

- Bone pain—Mild oral analgesics with rest or, if severe, parenteral narcotics. Bone pain usually subsides after 2 weeks.
- Urinary obstruction, worsening of, in treatment of prostatic carcinoma—Catheterization. Urinary obstruction usually disappears after the first week of leuprolide therapy.

Parenteral Dosage Forms

LEUPROLIDE ACETATE IMPLANT

Usual adult dose

Carcinoma, prostatic—

Subcutaneous implant, one implant per 12 months

Note: The leuprolide acetate implant delivers approximately 120 micrograms of leuprolide acetate per day over 12 months.

Usual pediatric dose
Safety and efficacy have not been established.

Strength(s) usually available
U.S.—

65 mg (free base) per implant (Rx) [*Viadur* (dimethyl sulfoxide 104 mg; sodium chloride; sodium carboxymethyl cellulose; povidone; magnesium stearate; polyethylene glycol; sterile water for injection)].

Packaging and storage
Store at 25 ° C (77 ° F), excursions permitted to 15 to 30 ° C (59 to 86 ° F).

LEUPROLIDE ACETATE INJECTION

Usual adult dose
Carcinoma, prostatic—
Subcutaneous, 1 mg per day.

Usual pediatric dose
Puberty, precocious, central—
Subcutaneous, initially 50 mcg per kg of body weight per day as a single injection, increased as needed by increments of 10 mcg per kg of body weight per day to a maintenance dose. Younger children require larger doses on a mcg per kg of body weight basis; dose should be increased as weight increases throughout treatment.

Strength(s) usually available
U.S.—

Note: Packaging is labeled as *Lupron 14 Day Patient Administration Kit* (2.8 mL multiple dose vial and 1/2 cc 28-gauge 1/2-inch syringes) or *Lupron 28 Day Patient Administration Kit* (double the supplies of *Lupron 14 Day Patient Administration Kit*). Insulin syringes may be used also if volume is appropriately adjusted.

5 mg per mL (Rx) [*Lupron* (sodium chloride 6.3 mg; benzyl alcohol 9 mg; water for injection)].

Canada—

Note: Packaging includes multiple dose vial of 2.8 mL.

5 mg per mL(Rx) [*Lupron* (benzyl alcohol)].

Packaging and storage
In U.S.: Store below 25 °C (77 °F), unless otherwise specified by manufacturer. In Canada: Store between 2 and 8 °C (36 and 46 °F) before dispensing and between 15 and 30 °C (59 and 86 °F) after dispensing, unless otherwise specified by manufacturer. Protect from freezing. Protect from light.

Stability
Do not use if cloudy or discolored.

Auxiliary labeling
- Do not freeze.

LEUPROLIDE ACETATE FOR INJECTION

Note: Due to different release characteristics, a fractional dose of the 3-month or 4-month depot formulations is not equivalent to the same dose of the 1-month depot formulation and should not be given in its place.

Usual adult dose
Anemia due to uterine leiomyomas[1]
Intramuscular, 3.75 mg once a month for a maximum duration of three months or one 11.25-mg injection.

Carcinoma, prostatic—
Intramuscular, 7.5 mg once a month, 22.5 mg once every three months (eighty-four days), or 30 mg every four months.

Carcinoma, prostatic—
Subcutaneous, 7.5 mg once a month 22.5 mg once every three months, or 30 mg every four months.

Endometriosis—
Intramuscular, 3.75 mg once a month or 11.25 mg every three months for a maximum duration of six months.

Usual pediatric dose
Puberty, precocious, central—
Initial—
Intramuscular, 0.3 mg per kg of body weight every four weeks, using a minimum total dose of 7.5 mg every four weeks.
For children weighing ≤ 25 kg—Intramuscular, 7.5 mg every four weeks.
For children weighing 25 to 37.5 kg—Intramuscular, 11.25 mg every four weeks.
For children weighing > 37.5 kg—Intramuscular, 15 mg every four weeks.

Maintenance—
The dose may be increased as needed by increments of 3.75 mg every four weeks, up to a maximum total dose of 15 mg every four weeks.

Strength(s) usually available
U.S.—

Note: Packaged as single-use vial kits for *Lupron Depot 7.5 mg* and single-use vial kits and prefilled dual-chamber syringe kits for *Lupron Depot 3.75 mg* and for all pediatric formulations. Kits include alcohol swabs and syringes. All packaging includes the diluent. Inactive ingredients may differ among products and their diluents.

1-month release formulation:
3.75 mg vial [*Lupron Depot*].
7.5 mg vial (Rx) [*Lupron Depot; Lupron Depot-Ped; Eligard*].
11.25 mg vial (Rx) [*Lupron Depot-Ped*].
15 mg vial (Rx) [*Lupron Depot-Ped*].
3-month release formulation:
11.25 mg vial [*Lupron Depot-3 Month 11.25 mg*].
22.5 mg vial (Rx) [*Lupron Depot-3 Month 22.5 mg; Eligard*].
4-month release formulation:
30 mg vial (Rx) [*Lupron Depot-4 Month 30 mg; Eligard*].

Canada—

Note: Packaging of single-use vial kits includes alcohol swabs and syringes. All packaging includes the diluent. Inactive ingredients may differ among products and their diluents.

1-month release formulation:
3.75 mg vial [*Lupron Depot*].
7.5 mg vial (Rx) [*Lupron Depot; Eligard*].
11.25 mg vial (Rx) [*Lupron Depot*].
15 mg vial (Rx) [*Lupron Depot*].
3-month release formulation:
22.5 mg vial (Rx) [*Lupron-3 Month SR Depot 22.5 mg; Eligard*].

Packaging and storage
Store between 15 and 30 °C (59 and 86 °F), unless otherwise specified by manufacturer. Protect from freezing.
For Eligard® product store at 2–8°C (36–46°F).

Preparation of dosage form
Vial and ampule—Leuprolide acetate for injection is reconstituted with an appropriate volume of diluent provided by the manufacturer; the suspension should be shaken thoroughly to disperse particles evenly.
Prefilled dual-chamber syringe—For reconstitution, the manufacturer's instructions should be followed to release the diluent into the chamber of lyophilized microspheres. The suspension is then shaken gently to disperse the particles evenly.For Eligard® product the suspension is mixed by pushing the contents back and forth between two syringes.

Stability
Since leuprolide for injection and the diluent contain no preservatives, the reconstituted suspension should be used immediately after preparation and any unused portion should be discarded.

Auxiliary labeling
- Do not freeze.
- Shake well (after reconstitution).

[1]Not included in Canadian product labeling.

Revised: 11/29/2005

LEVALBUTEROL Inhalation-Local

VA CLASSIFICATION (Primary): RE120

Commonly used brand name(s): *Xopenex; Xopenex HFA.*

Note: For a listing of dosage forms and brand names by country availability, see *Dosage Forms* section(s).

Category
Bronchodilator, adrenergic (inhalation-local).

Indications

Accepted
Bronchospasm (treatment) or
Bronchospasm (prevention)—Levalbuterol is indicated for the treatment or prevention of bronchospasm due to reversible obstructive airway disease. Levalbuterol inhalation aerosol is indicated for use in adults, adolescents, and children 4 years of age and older.

Pharmacology/Pharmacokinetics

Physicochemical characteristics

Description—

Levalbuterol is an off-white, crystalline solid and is the (R)-enantiomer of the drug substance racemic albuterol.

Melting Point—Levalbuterol hydrochloride: 187 °C.

Molecular weight—

Levalbuterol hydrochloride: 275.8.

Levalbuterol tartrate: 628.71.

pH—Levalbuterol hydrochloride: 4. (3.3 to 4.5).

Solubility—

Levalbuterol hydrochloride: 180 mg/ml in water.

Levalbuterol tartrate: freely soluble in water; very slightly soluble in ethanol.

Mechanism of action/Effect

Levalbuterol binds to beta$_2$-adrenergic receptors on airway smooth muscle. This leads to the activation of adenylate cyclase and to an increase in the intracellular concentration of cyclic-3', 5'-adenosine monophosphate (cyclic AMP). This increase in cyclic AMP leads to the activation of protein kinase A, which inhibits the phosphorylation of myosin and lowers intracellular ionic calcium concentrations, resulting in relaxation of the smooth muscles of all airways. Levalbuterol relaxes the smooth muscle of the respiratory tree from the trachea to the terminal bronchioles. The increased cyclic AMP concentrations also inhibit the release of mediators from mast cells in the airway.

Other actions/effects

It should be noted that beta$_2$-adrenergic receptors comprise between 10% and 50% of cardiac beta-adrenergic receptors and therefore, in some patients, levalbuterol may have significant cardiovascular effects, such as changes in pulse rate, blood pressure, symptoms, and/or electrocardiographic (ECG) changes.

Absorption

Levalbuterol tartrate (following 90 mcg dose)—AUC_{0-6}=0.695 ng hr/mL in adults and adolescents (≥12 years); AUC_{0-6}=0.0.579 ng hr/mL in children (4 to 11 years)

Half-life

Levalbuterol hydrochloride—3.3 hours (single 1.25-mg inhalation dose); 4.0 hours (cumulative 5 mg inhalation dose given as 1.25 mg every 30 minutes for 4 doses).

Onset of action

Levalbuterol hydrochloride—The mean time to onset of a 15% increase in forced expiratory volume (FEV_1) over baseline was 10 to 17 minutes for 1.25-mg and 0.63-mg inhalation doses, respectively.

Time to peak concentration

Levalbuterol hydrochloride—0.2 hours following both a single 1.25-mg inhalation dose and a cumulative 5-mg inhalation dose (1.25 mg every 30 minutes for 4 doses).

Levalbuterol tartrate (following 90 mcg dose)—t_{max}=0.54 hours in adults and adolescents (≥12 years); t_{max}=0.76 hours in children (4 to 11 years)

Peak serum concentration

Levalbuterol hydrochloride—1.1 nanograms per milliliter (ng/ml) following a 1.25-mg single inhalation dose; 4.5 ng/ml following a cumulative 5-mg dose (1.25 mg every 30 minutes for 4 doses).

Levalbuterol tartrate (following 90 mcg dose)—0.199 ng/mL in adults and adolescents (≥12 years); 0.163 ng/mL in children (4 to 11 years)

Time to peak effect

Levalbuterol hydrochloride—The mean time to peak effect for inhalation doses of 0.63 mg and 1.25 mg was approximately 1.5 hours after 4 weeks of treatment.

Duration of action

Levalbuterol hydrochloride—The mean duration of effect (measured by a >15% increase in FEV_1 from baseline) was 5 and 6 hours after 0.63-mg and 1.25-mg inhalation doses, respectively, after 4 weeks of treatment. In some patients, the duration of effect was as long as 8 hours.

Elimination

Albuterol enantiomers—Renal, 80 to 100% of either the parent compound or the primary metabolite; Fecal; less than 20% of the drug

Racemic albuterol (intravenous administration)—Renal, 25 to 46% of the (R)-albuterol fraction of the dose was excreted as unchanged

HFA-134a propellant

HFA-134a propellant in the levalbuterol tartrate inhalation aerosol was found to be rapidly absorbed and rapidly eliminated, with an elimination half-life of 5 to 7 minutes. T_{max} and mean residence time are both extremely short, leading to a transient appearance of HFA-134a in the blood with no evidence of accumulation.

Precautions to Consider

Cross-sensitivity and/or related problems

Patients sensitive to racemic albuterol may be sensitive to levalbuterol. Immediate hypersensitivity reactions, including anaphylaxis, angioedema, bronchospasm, oropharyngeal edema, skin rash, and urticaria, may occur after administration of racemic albuterol.

Carcinogenicity

No carcinogenicity studies have been done with levalbuterol.

Tumorigenicity

No tumorigenic studies have been done with levalbuterol; however, there are data available on the tumorigenic effects of racemic albuterol. In a 2 year study in Sprague-Dawley rats, racemic albuterol sulfate caused a significant dose-related increase in the incidence of benign leiomyomas of the mesovarium at and above doses of 2 milligram per kilogram of body weight (mg/kg) (approximately 2 times the maximum recommended daily [MRD] human adult inhalation dose of levalbuterol-HCl, and 30 times the MRD adult and 15 times the MRD for children, respectively, of levalbuterol tartrate inhalation aerosol on a mg/m^2 basis). This effect has been blocked by the beta-adrenergic blocker, propranolol, in another study.

Additional studies of racemic albuterol in CD-1 mice and golden hamsters have shown no tumorigenicity at doses equivalent to 270 and 35 times, respectively, the MRD human adult inhalation dose of levalbuterol HCl, and 3800 times and 500 times the MRD adult dose and 1800 times and 240 times the MRD for children, respectively, of levalbuterol tartrate inhalation aerosol on a mg/m^2 basis.

Mutagenicity

Levalbuterol-HCl was not mutagenic in the Ames test or the CHO/HPRT Mammalian Forward Gene Mutation Assay. Levalbuterol HCl was not clastogenic in the *in vivo* micronucleus test in mouse bone marrow. Racemic albuterol sulfate was negative in an *in vitro* chromosomal aberration assay in CHO cell cultures..

Pregnancy/Reproduction

Fertility—No impairment of fertility studies have been done with levalbuterol-HCl; however, data are available from fertility studies with racemic albuterol. No evidence of impaired fertility was found in rats using oral doses of racemic albuterol up to 50 mg/kg (approximately 55 times the MRD human adult inhalation dose of levalbuterol HCl and approximately 750 times the MRD inhalation dose of levalbuterol tartrate for adults, on a mg/m^2 basis).

Pregnancy—Levalbuterol crosses the placenta. Well-controlled studies in humans have not been done. Because animal reproduction studies are not always predictive of human response, levalbuterol should be used during pregnancy only if the potential benefit justifies the potential risk to the fetus.

Note: During marketing experience of racemic albuterol, various congenital anomalies, including cleft palate and limb defects, have been rarely reported in the offspring of patients being treated with racemic albuterol. Some of the mothers were taking multiple medications during their pregnancies. No consistent pattern of defects can be discerned and a relationship between racemic albuterol use and congenital anomalies has not been established.

Studies in New Zealand white rabbits receiving doses up to 25 mg/kg (approximately 110 times and 750 times the MRD human adult inhalation dose of levalbuterol-HCl and levalbuterol tartrate, respectively, on a mg/m^2 basis), showed no teratogenicity. Racemic albuterol has been shown to cause cleft palate formation in 4.5 to 9.3% of mice and rabbits receiving subcutaneous doses slightly less than and equivalent to the MRD human adult inhalation dose of levalbuterol-HCl and approximately 2 to 20 times the MRD human adult inhalation dose of levalbuterol tartrate, on a mg/m^2 basis. Cleft palate did not result when a subcutaneous dose of 0.025 mg/kg (less than the MRD human adult inhalation dose) of levalbuterol-HCl and levalbuterol tartrate, on a mg/m^2 basis, was administered. Cranioschisis occurred in 37% of Stride Dutch rabbits receiving racemic albuterol at a dose of 50 mg/kg (equivalent to 110 times and 1500 times the MRD human adult inhalation dose of levalbuterol-HCl and levalbuterol tartrate, respectively, on a mg/m^2 basis). A study of pregnant rats receiving radiolabeled racemic albuterol demonstrated that drug-related material is transferred from the maternal circulation to the fetus.

FDA Pregnancy Category C.

Labor—Beta-adrenergic agonists, such as levalbuterol, have the potential to interfere with uterine contractility. Therefore, its use for the treatment of bronchospasm during labor should be restricted to those patients in whom the benefits clearly outweigh the risks. Levalbuterol-HCl and levalbuterol tartrate have not been approved for the management of tocolysis (preterm labor). Serious adverse reactions, including pulmonary edema, have been reported during or following treatment of premature labor with beta$_2$-agonists, including racemic albuterol.

Breast-feeding

It is not known whether levalbuterol is distributed into human breast milk. Because of the potential for tumorigenicity for racemic albuterol observed in animal studies, caution should be exercised when administering levalbuterol to a nursing woman.

Pediatrics

For levalbuterol hydrochloride inhalation solution: Appropriate studies on the relationship of age to the effects of levalbuterol have not been performed in children up to 12 years of age. Safety and efficacy have not been established.

For levalbuterol tartrate inhalation aerosol: Safety and efficacy in pediatric patients below the age of 4 years have not been established.

Geriatrics

Studies performed to date have not demonstrated geriatric-specific problems that would limit the usefulness of levalbuterol in the elderly, but these data are insufficient to determine its safety and efficacy in patients 65 years of age and older as compared to patients younger than 65 years of age.

For levalbuterol hydrochloride inhalation solution: In general, patients 65 years of age and older should be started at an inhalation dose of 0.63 mg levalbuterol solution and increased as tolerated, in conjunction with frequent clinical and laboratory monitoring.

For levalbuterol tartrate inhalation aerosol: In general, dose selection for an elderly patient should be cautious, usually starting at the lower end of the dosing range, reflecting the greater frequency of decreased hepatic, renal, or cardiac function, and of concomitant diseases or other drug therapy.

Note: Albuterol is known to be substantially excreted by the kidney, and the risk of toxic reactions may be greater in patients with impaired renal function. Because elderly patients are more likely to have decreased renal function, care should be taken in dose selection, and it may be useful to monitor renal function.

Drug interactions and/or related problems

The following drug interactions and/or related problems have been selected on the basis of their potential clinical significance (possible mechanism in parentheses where appropriate)—not necessarily inclusive (» = major clinical significance):

» Beta-adrenergic blocking agents, systemic
(concurrent use, especially propranolol, with adrenergic bronchodilators may result in mutual inhibition of therapeutic effects; beta-adrenergic blockage may antagonize the bronchodilating effect of levalbuterol; cardioselective beta-blockers could be considered, but caution is recommended with these agents as well)

» Digoxin
(concurrent use with levalbuterol may reduce serum digoxin levels, as in the case with racemic albuterol. Serum digoxin levels should be carefully evaluated in patients receiving digoxin and levalbuterol)

» Diuretics, non–potassium-sparing
(concurrent use of levalbuterol with non–potassium-sparing diuretics may worsen hypokalemia)

» Monoamine oxidase (MAO) inhibitors or
» Tricyclic antidepressants
(concurrent use, or within 2 weeks of discontinuation of MAO inhibitors or tricyclic antidepressants, with levalbuterol may potentiate the action of levalbuterol on the vascular system)

» Methylxanthines
(cardiac arrhythmia and sudden death have been reported in animals from concurrent use with levalbuterol)

» Short-acting sympathomimetic aerosol bronchodilators or Epinephrine
(concurrent use may potentiate cardiac effects)

Laboratory value alterations

The following have been selected on the basis of their potential clinical significance (possible effect in parentheses where appropriate)—not necessarily inclusive (» = major clinical significance).

With physiology/laboratory test values
Electrocardiogram (ECG)
(flattened T waves, ST segment depression, and prolongation of the QT$_c$ interval are reported rarely with adrenergic bronchodilators)
Potassium, serum
(concentration may decrease, resulting in hypokalemia)

Medical considerations/Contraindications

The medical considerations/contraindications included have been selected on the basis of their potential clinical significance (reasons given in parentheses where appropriate)—not necessarily inclusive (» = major clinical significance).

Except under special circumstances, this medication should not be used when the following medical problems exist:

» Cardiovascular disorders, such as coronary insufficiency or cardiac arrhythmias or
» Convulsive disorders
(concurrent use may worsen these conditions)

» Hypersensitivity to levalbuterol, racemic albuterol, or any other component of the product

» Hypertension
(clinically significant changes in systolic and diastolic blood pressure have been reported after the use of any beta-adrenergic bronchodilators)

» Sensitivity to adrenergic bronchodilators or other sympathomimetic amines

Risk-benefit should be considered when the following medical problems exist:

Diabetes mellitus
(use of levalbuterol may worsen blood glucose control and diabetic ketoacidosis)

Hyperthyroidism

Side/Adverse Effects

The following side/adverse effects have been selected on the basis of their potential clinical significance (possible signs and symptoms in parentheses where appropriate)—not necessarily inclusive:

Those indicating need for medical attention

Incidence more frequent
Tachycardia (fast heartbeat)

Incidence less frequent or rare
Allergic reaction, bronchospasm, or exacerbation of asthma (chest tightness; hives; shortness of breath; troubled breathing; wheezing); ***cardiovascular effects, specifically abnormal ECG changes, hypertension, hypotension, or syncope*** (high or low blood pressure; dizziness; light-headedness; feeling "faint"); ***chest pain; lung disorder*** (difficulty breathing)

Incidence not determined—Observed during clinical practice; estimates of frequency can not be determined
Anaphylaxis (cough; difficulty swallowing; dizziness; fast heartbeat; hives; itching, puffiness or swelling of the eyelids or around the eyes, face, lips or tongue; shortness of breath; skin rash; tightness in chest; unusual tiredness or weakness; wheezing); ***angioedema*** (large, hive-like swelling on face, eyelids, lips, tongue, throat, hands, legs, feet, sex organs); ***arrhythmias*** (dizziness; fainting; fast, slow, or irregular heartbeat); ***atrial fibrillation*** (fast or irregular heartbeat; dizziness; fainting); ***dyspnea*** (shortness of breath; difficult or labored breathing; tightness in chest; wheezing); ***extrasystoles*** (extra heartbeats); ***supraventricular tachycardia*** (fainting; fast, pounding, or irregular heartbeat or pulse; palpitations); ***urticaria*** (hives or welts; itching; redness of skin; skin rash)

Those indicating need for medical attention only if they continue or are bothersome

Incidence more frequent
Accidental injury—in children 4 to 11 years of age; ***anxiety; dizziness; dyspepsia*** (stomach pain or burning); ***hypertonia*** (muscle tightness); ***increased cough; influenza-like symptoms*** (fever; general aches and pains; headache; loss of appetite; weakness); ***leg cramps; migraines or other headaches; nervousness; pharyngitis*** (body aches or pain; congestion; cough; dryness or soreness of throat; fever; hoarseness; runny nose; tender, swollen glands in neck; trouble in swallowing; voice changes); ***rhinitis*** (runny nose); ***sinusitis*** (runny or stuffy nose); ***tremor; viral infection*** (chills; cough or hoarseness; fever); ***vomiting***

Incidence less frequent or rare
Acne (blemishes on the skin; pimples); ***bronchitis*** (cough producing mucus; difficulty breathing; shortness of breath; tightness in chest; wheezing)—in children 4 to 11 years of age; ***conjunctivitis*** (redness, pain, swelling of eye, eyelid, or inner lining of eyelid; burning, dry or itching eyes; discharge; excessive tearing); ***constipation*** (difficulty having a bowel movement [stool]); ***cyst*** (abnormal growth filled with fluid or semisolid material); ***dry mouth or throat; dysmenorrhea*** (pain, cramps, heavy bleeding); ***ear pain; epistaxis*** (bloody nose); ***eye itch; gastroenteritis*** (abdominal or stomach pain; diarrhea; loss of appetite; nausea; weakness); ***gastrointestinal effects*** (diarrhea;

vomiting); ***hematuria*** (blood in urine); ***herpes simplex*** (burning or stinging of skin; painful cold sores or blisters on lips, nose, eyes, or genitals); ***hypesthesia of the hand*** (numbness or decreased sensitivity); ***insomnia*** (sleeplessness); ***lymphadenopathy*** (fever; night sweats; weight loss); ***myalgia*** (muscle pain); ***nausea; pain; paresthesia*** (tingling sensation in extremities); ***rash; vaginal moniliasis*** (vaginal yeast infection)

Overdose

Although uncommon, fatalities have been reported in association with excessive use of inhaled sympathomimetics.

For more information on the management of overdose or unintentional ingestion, **contact a Poison Control Center** (see *Poison Control Center Listing*).

Clinical effects of overdose

The following effects have been selected on the basis of their potential clinical significance (possible signs and symptoms in parentheses where appropriate)—not necessarily inclusive:

Acute and/or chronic

The expected symptoms are those of excessive beta-adrenergic receptor stimulation; specifically:

Angina or cardiac arrest (chest pain); ***arrhythmia or palpitations*** (irregular heartbeat); ***dizziness; dry mouth; fatigue; headache; hypertension; hypokalemia*** (low potassium levels in the blood; irregular heartbeat); ***hypotension*** (impaired consciousness; light-headedness; sweating); ***insomnia*** (sleeplessness); ***malaise*** (general feeling of discomfort or illness); ***nausea; nervousness; seizures; sudden death; tachycardia*** (fast heartbeat); ***tremor***

Treatment of overdose

To enhance elimination—There is insufficient evidence to determine if dialysis is beneficial.

Supportive care—Treatment consists of discontinuation of levalbuterol together with symptomatic therapy. The use of a cardioselective beta-adrenergic receptor blocker may be considered, bearing in mind that this may induce bronchospasm.

Patient Consultation

As an aid to patient consultation, refer to *Advice for the Patient, Levalbuterol (Inhalation-Local)*.

In providing consultation, consider emphasizing the following selected information (» = major clinical significance):

Before using this medication

» Conditions affecting use, especially:

Hypersensitivity to levalbuterol or any component of the product, to racemic albuterol, or to adrenergic bronchodilators or other sympathomimetic amines

Pregnancy—Risk-benefit considerations; may have the potential to affect uterine contractility when used in labor

Not approved for preterm labor due to serious adverse reactions, including pulmonary edema

Breast-feeding—Caution should be exercised

Use in children—Levalbuterol hydrochloride: Safety and efficacy not established below 12 years of age

Levalbuterol tartrate: Safety and efficacy not established below 4 years of age

Levalbuterol hydrochloride: Starting dose of 0.63 mg and increased as tolerated with monitoring

Use in the elderly—Levalbuterol tartrate: Dose selection should be cautious

Other medications, especially beta-adrenergic blocking–agents (systemic), digoxin, diuretics (nonpotassium-sparing), methylxanthines, MAO inhibitors, short-acting sympathomimetic aerosol bronchodilators, and tricyclic antidepressants

Other medical problems, especially cardiovascular disorders (coronary insufficiency and cardiac arrhythmia), convulsive disorders (seizures), and hypertension

Proper use of this medication

» Reading patient instructions carefully before using

» Importance of not using more medication than the amount prescribed, because of the potential for enhanced absorption and increased severity of side effects

For inhalation aerosol dosage form

Checking periodically with health care professional for proper use of inhaler to prevent incorrect dosage

Keeping record of number of sprays used, if possible; not floating canister in water to test fullness

Testing or priming inhaler before using first time or if not used for a while

Discarding canister after labeled number of metered dose sprays has been used, even if canister does not appear completely empty

Proper administration technique

Proper administration technique with spacer device

Proper cleaning procedure for inhaler

Proper administration technique for use in nebulizer, administered over a period of 5 to 15 minutes

Not using solution if discolored or cloudy

Not mixing with another inhalation solution unless directed by physician

» Proper dosing

Missed dose: Using as soon as possible; skipping missed dose if almost time for next dose; not doubling doses

» Proper storage

Precautions while using this medication

Regular visits to physician to check progress during therapy

» Checking with physician immediately if difficulty in breathing persists after use of this medication, if condition worsens, or if using more often than prescribed

» Checking with physician before adding or stopping other inhaled drugs or asthma medications

Side/adverse effects

Signs of potential side effects, especially allergic reaction, bronchospasm, or exacerbation of asthma, cardiovascular effects, specifically abnormal ECG changes, hypertension, hypotension, or syncope, chest pain, lung disorder, and tachycardia

Signs of potential side effects observed during clinical practice, especially anaphylaxis, angioedema, arrhythmias, atrial fibrillation, dyspnea, extrasystoles, supraventricular, tachycardia, and urticaria

Inhaled Dosage Forms

LEVALBUTEROL HYDROCHLORIDE INHALATION SOLUTION

Usual adult and adolescent dose

Bronchodilator—

Inhaled, by nebulization, 0.63 mg to 1.25 mg administered three times a day, every six to eight hours.

Usual adult and adolescent prescribing limits

Up to 1.25 mg three times a day. If a previous effective dose fails to provide the expected relief, medical advice should be sought immediately, as this may be a sign of worsening asthma.

Usual pediatric dose

Bronchodilator—

Children up to 12 years of age: Safety and efficacy have not been established.

Children 12 years of age and older: See *Usual adult and adolescent dose*.

Usual geriatric dose

Bronchodilator—

Inhaled, by nebulization, 0.63 mg three times daily, every six to eight hours, may increase as tolerated.

Usual geriatric prescribing limits

Dose increases in this population should only be made in conjunction with frequent clinical and laboratory monitoring. See *Usual adult and adolescent prescribing limits*.

Strength(s) usually available

U.S.—

0.63 mg (base) (Rx) [*Xopenex* (sodium chloride)].

1.25 mg (base) (Rx) [*Xopenex* (sodium chloride)].

Packaging and storage

Store, in the protective foil pouch, below 40 °C (104 °F), preferably between 15 and 25 °C (59 and 77 °F), unless otherwise specified by manufacturer.

Protect from light and excessive heat.

Unopened vials should be kept in the pouch. Once the foil pouch is opened, the vials should be used within 2 weeks. Vials should be discarded if the solution is not colorless.

Preparation of dosage form

Levalbuterol inhalation solution is administered by nebulization. Nebulizer systems with established safety and efficacy when used with levalbuterol inhalation solution include the PARI LC Jet™ and the PARI LC Plus™ nebulizers and the PARI Master® and DURA-Neb® 2000 compressors. No diluent is necessary.

Incompatibilities
The drug compatibility (physical and chemical), efficacy, and safety of levalbuterol inhalation solution when mixed with other drugs in a nebulizer have not been established.

Auxiliary labeling
- For inhalation only; do not inject or use orally.
- Protect from light and excessive heat.

LEVALBUTEROL TARTRATE INHALATION AEROSOL

Usual adult and adolescent dose
Bronchodilator (prophylaxis or treatment)—

Inhaled, 90 mcg (2 inhalations) repeated every 4 to 6 hours. In some patients, 45 mcg (1 inhalation) repeated every 4 hours may be sufficient.

Usual pediatric dose
Bronchodilator—

Children up to 4 years of age: Safety and efficacy have not been established.

Children 4 years of age and older: See *Usual adult and adolescent dose.*

Usual geriatric dose
See *Usual adult and adolescent dose.*

Strength(s) usually available
U.S.—

45 mcg (base) per metered dose actuation (spray) (Rx) [*Xopenex HFA* (propellant HFA-134a [1,1,1,2-tetrafluoroethane]; dehydrated alcohol; oleic acid)].

Note: *Xopenex HFA* inhalation aerosol does not contain chlorofluorocarbons (CFCs) as the propellant.

Packaging and storage
Store between 20 and 25 °C (68 and 77 °F). Protect from freezing temperatures and direct sunlight. Store with the actuator down.

Auxiliary labeling
- For inhalation only
- Keep out of reach of children
- Store this medication in a dry area, away from light
- Do not freeze
- Shake well
- Avoid contact in or around eyes

Caution
Contents under pressure. Do not puncture or incinerate. Exposure to temperatures above 120 °F may cause bursting.

Additional information
The actuator supplied with the product should not be used with any other product canisters and other product actuators should not be used with this product. The correct amount of medication in each actuation cannot be assured after 200 actuations, even though the canister is not completely empty. The canister should be discarded when 200 actuations have been used.

Selected Bibliography
Xopenex HFA®, levalbuterol tartrate. Sepracor, Marlborough, MA, (PI revised 03/2005) reviewed 03/2005.

Revised: 03/25/2005

LEVETIRACETAM Systemic

VA CLASSIFICATION (Primary): CN400

Commonly used brand name(s): *Keppra.*

Note: For a listing of dosage forms and brand names by country availability, see *Dosage Forms* section(s).

Category
Anticonvulsant.

Indications

Accepted
Epilepsy, partial seizures (treatment adjunct)—Levetiracetam is indicated as adjunctive therapy in the treatment of partial onset seizures in adults and children 4 years of age and older with epilepsy.

Pharmacology/Pharmacokinetics

Physicochemical characteristics
Molecular weight—170.21.

Solubility—Very soluble in water (104 grams/100 mL); freely soluble in chloroform (65.3 grams/100 mL); freely soluble in methanol (53.6 grams/100 mL); soluble in ethanol (16.5 grams/100 mL); sparingly soluble in acetonitrile (5.7 grams/100 mL); and practically insoluble in n-hexane.

Mechanism of action/Effect
The exact mechanism of action is unknown but does not involve inhibitory and excitatory neurotransmission. Stereoselective binding of levetiracetam was confined to synaptic plasma membranes in the central nervous system with no binding occurring in peripheral tissue. Levetiracetam inhibits burst firing without affecting normal neuronal excitability, which suggests that it may selectively prevent hypersynchronization of epileptiform burst firing and propagation of seizure activity.

Absorption
Rapid and almost complete. Oral bioavailability of levetiracetam is 100%, and is not affected by food. Tablets and oral solution are bioequivalent in rate and extent of absorption

Distribution
Volume of distribution (Vol_D) is 0.7 L/kg

Protein binding
Very low (< 10%)

Biotransformation
Levetiracetam is not extensively metabolized. The major metabolic pathway is the enzymatic hydrolysis of the acetamide group. Cytochrome P450 isoenzyme system is not involved in the metabolism of levetiracetam. Levetiracetam and its major metabolite are neither inhibitors of or substrates for cytochrome P450 isoforms, epoxide hydrolase, or UDP-glucuronidation enzymes.

Half-life
Elimination—7 hours

Time to peak concentration
Oral—About 1 hour in fasted subjects. Food may delay the time to peak plasma concentration by 1.5 hours, and decrease the peak concentration by 20%.

Time to steady state concentration:
In patients with normal renal function, steady state is achieved after 2 days of multiple twice daily dosing.

Note: The pharmacokinetics of levetiracetam are linear over the dose range of 500 to 5000 mg.

Elimination
Renal excretion (glomerular filtration with subsequent partial tubular reabsorption) as unchanged drug represents 66% of the administered dose.

The inactive metabolite, ucb L057, is excreted by glomerular filtration and active tubular secretion.

With impaired renal function—

Levetiracetam clearance was reduced by 40% in patients with mild renal function impairment (creatinine clearance of 50-80 mL per minute per 1.73 square meters of body surface area [CLcr]), by 50% in patients with moderate renal function impairment (CLcr of 30-50 mL per minute), by 60% in patients with severe renal function impairment (CLcr less than 30 mL per minute), and by 70% in anuric (end stage renal disease) patients, as compared with the clearance in subjects with normal renal function (CLcr greater than 80 mL per minute). Dosage reductions based on creatinine clearance are necessary in patients with impaired renal function.

In patients on hemodialysis, approximately 50% of the pool of levetiracetam in the body is removed during a standard 4-hour procedure.

Precautions to Consider

Carcinogenicity
There was no evidence of carcinogenicity in a study in rats receiving 50, 300 and 1800 mg of levetiracetam per kg of body weight (mg/kg) per day for 104 weeks. The 1800 mg/kg per day dose corresponds to 6 times the maximum recommended daily human dose (MRHD) of 3000 mg on a mg per square meter of body surface area (mg/m²) basis and it also provided systemic exposure (area under the time-concentration curve[AUC]) approximately 6 times that achieved in humans receiving the MRHD.

Mutagenicity
Mutagenicity was not demonstrated in the Ames test or in the Chinese hamster ovary/HGPRT locus assay. It was not clastogenic in an *in*

vitro analysis of metaphase chromosomes obtained from Chinese hamster ovary cells or in an *in vivo* mouse micronucleus assay. The hydrolysis product and major human metabolite of levetiracetam (L057) was not mutagenic in the Ames test or the *in vitro* mouse lymphoma assay.

Pregnancy/Reproduction

Fertility—No adverse effects on male or female fertility or reproductive performance were observed in rats at doses up to 1800 mg/kg per day (approximately 6 times the maximum recommended human dose on a mg/m^2 or exposure basis).

Pregnancy—Adequate and well-controlled studies in humans have not been done. Studies in animals have shown that levetiracetam causes developmental toxicity at doses similar to or greater than human therapeutic doses. Doses ≥ 350 mg/kg per day (approximately equivalent to the maximum recommended human dose (MRHD) of 3000 mg on a mg/m^2 basis) was associated with increased incidences of minor fetal skeletal abnormalities and retarded offspring growth when administered to female rats throughout pregnancy and lactation. Doses of 1800 mg/kg per day (6 times the MRHD on a mg/m^2 basis) was associated with increased pup mortality and offspring behavioral alterations. The developmental no effect dose was 70 mg/kg per day (0.2 times the MRHD on a mg/m^2 basis).

Treatment of pregnant rabbits during the period of organogenesis resulted in increased embryofetal mortality and increased incidences of minor fetal skeletal abnormalities at doses ≥ 600 mg/kg per day (approximately 4 times MRHD on a mg/m^2 basis) and in decreased fetal weights and increased incidences of fetal malformations at a dose of 1800 mg/kg per day (12 times the MRHD on a mg/m^2 basis). The developmental no effect dose was 200 mg/kg per day (1.3 times MRHD on a mg/m^2 basis). Maternal toxicity was also observed at 1800 mg/kg per day.

Pregnant rats fed levetiracetam doses of 3600 mg/kg per day (12 times the MRHD) during the period of organogenesis produced offspring with decreased fetal weights and an increased incidence of fetal skeletal variations.

No adverse developmental or maternal effects in rats treated during the last third of gestation and throughout lactation at doses up to 1800 mg/kg per day (6 times the MRHD on a mg/m^2 basis).

FDA Pregnancy Category C

Note: To facilitate monitoring of fetal outcomes of pregnant women exposed to levetiracetam, physicians are encouraged to register patients in the Antiepileptic Drug Pregnancy Registry ((888) 233–2334) or the Keppra® Pregnancy registry ((888) 537–7734)before fetal outcome is known.

Labor and delivery—The effect of levetiracetam on labor and delivery is not known.

Breast-feeding

It is not known whether levetiracetam is distributed into breast milk. However, problems in humans have not been documented.

Pediatrics

Appropriate studies on the relationship of age to the effects of levetiracetam have not been performed in the pediatric population in children up to 4 years. Safety and efficacy have not been established.

One pharmacokinetic study in 24 patients 6 to 12 years of age showed that the apparent clearance of levetiracetam was approximately 40 % higher than that in adults following oral administration of a single 20 mg/kg dose.

Geriatrics

Appropriate studies performed to date have not demonstrated geriatric–specific problems that would limit the usefulness of levetiracetam in the elderly. However, elderly patients are more likely to have age–related renal function impairment which may require adjustment of dosage or dosing interval in patients receiving levetiracetam.

Pharmacogenetics

Due to the lack of important racial differences in creatinine clearance and the renal excretion of levetiracetam, pharmacokinetic differences due to race are not expected. Cross study comparisons between a small number of whites and Asians showed comparable pharmacokinetics.

Clearances adjusted for body weight, but not maximum concentration and area under the curve, were comparable between men and women.

Drug interactions and/or related problems

The following drug interactions and/or related problems have been selected on the basis of their potential clinical significance (possible mechanism in parentheses where appropriate)—not necessarily inclusive (» = major clinical significance):

Note: Studies to assess potential pharmacokinetic interactions with levetiracetam have shown no clinically relevant interactions with digoxin, oral contraceptives, or warfarin to date. Similarly, potential interactions with existing antiepileptic agents, including phenytoin, carbamazepine, valproic acid, phenobarbital, lamotrigine, gabapentin, and primidone, have not been demonstrated.

Probenecid
(no interaction between probenecid and levetiracetam was observed; however, probenecid decreased the renal clearance of ucb L057 [inactive metabolite of levetiracetam] by 60%.)

Laboratory value alterations

The following have been selected on the basis of their potential clinical significance (possible effect in parentheses where appropriate)—not necessarily inclusive (» = major clinical significance).

With physiology/laboratory test values
Hemoglobin
Hematocrit
Neutrophil count
Red blood cell count
White blood cell count
(minor decrease in values.)

Medical considerations/Contraindications

The medical considerations/contraindications included have been selected on the basis of their potential clinical significance (reasons given in parentheses where appropriate)—not necessarily inclusive (» = major clinical significance).

Except under special circumstances, this medication should not be used when the following medical problem exists:

» Hypersensitivity to levetiracetam

Risk-benefit should be considered when the following medical problems exist:

» Renal function impairment
(reduction in total body clearance of levetiracetam; dosage reduction is recommended.)

Side/Adverse Effects

The following side/adverse effects have been selected on the basis of their potential clinical significance (possible signs and symptoms in parentheses where appropriate)—not necessarily inclusive:

Note: Adverse events were usually mild to moderate in intensity.

Those indicating need for medical attention

Incidence less frequent

Ataxia (clumsiness or unsteadiness; problems with muscle control or coordination); ***diplopia*** (double vision); ***infection*** (fever or chills; cough or hoarseness; lower back or side pain; painful or difficult urination); ***mood or mental changes, including agitation; amnesia; anxiety; apathy; depersonalization; depression; emotional lability; hostility; and nervousness; sinusitis*** (pain or tenderness around eyes and cheekbones; fever; stuffy or runny nose; headache; cough; shortness of breath or troubled breathing; tightness of chest or wheezing)

Note: Four patients attempted suicide during the premarketing clinical trials, 1 successfully; these attempts occurred at 4 weeks to 6 months of therapy with levetiracetam. Psychotic symptoms and hallucinations also have been reported in a small number of patients, but resolved following discontinuation of levetiracetam.

One-half of all other behavioral symptoms occurred within the first 4 weeks of therapy.

In premarketing clinical trials, *ataxia* occurred most frequently within the first four weeks of treatment.

Incidence not determined—Observed during clinical practice; estimates of frequency cannot be determined

Leukopenia (black, tarry stools; chest pain; chills; cough; fever; painful or difficult urination; shortness of breath; sore throat; sores, ulcers, or white spots on lips or in mouth; swollen glands; unusual bleeding or bruising; unusual tiredness or weakness); ***neutropenia*** (black, tarry stools; chest pain; chills; cough; fever; painful or difficult urination; shortness of breath; sore throat; sores, ulcers, or white spots on lips or in mouth; swollen glands; unusual bleeding or bruising; unusual tiredness or weakness); ***pancreatitis*** (bloating; chills; constipation; darkened urine; fast heartbeat; fever; indigestion; loss of appetite; nausea; pains in stomach, side, or abdomen, possibly radiating to the back; vomiting; yellow eyes or skin); ***pancytopenia*** (high fever; chills; unexplained bleeding or bruising; bloody; black, or tarry stools; pale skin; unusual tiredness or weakness; cough; shortness of breath; sores, ulcers, or white spots on lips or in mouth; swollen glands); ***thrombocytopenia*** (black, tarry stools; bleeding gums; blood in urine or stools; pinpoint red spots on skin; unusual bleeding or bruising)

Those indicating need for medical attention only if they continue or are bothersome

Incidence more frequent

Asthenia (loss of strength or energy; muscle pain or weakness; unusual weak feeling)—predominantly occur during the first four weeks of treatment; ***dizziness***—predominantly occur during the first four weeks of treatment; ***headache; pain; pharyngitis*** (cough; dryness or soreness of throat; fever; hoarseness; runny nose; tender, swollen glands in neck; trouble in swallowing; voice changes); ***somnolence*** (sleepiness or unusual drowsiness)—predominantly occur during the first four weeks of treatment

Incidence less frequent

Anorexia (loss of appetite; weight loss); ***cough increased; paresthesia*** (burning, crawling, itching, numbness, prickling, pins and needles, or tingling feelings); ***rhinitis*** (sneezing; stuffy nose; runny nose); ***vertigo*** (dizziness or light-headedness; feeling of constant movement of self or surroundings; sensation of spinning)

Incidence not determined—Observed during clinical practice; estimates of frequency can not be determined

Alopecia (hair loss; thinning of hair)

Overdose

For more information on the management of overdose or unintentional ingestion, **contact a poison control center** (see *Poison Control Center Listing*).

Clinical effects of overdose

The following effects have been selected on the basis of their potential clinical significance (possible signs and symptoms in parentheses where appropriate)—not necessarily inclusive:

Experience with levetiracetam overdose is very limited. The highest known ingested dose was 6000 mg, and drowsiness was the only symptom reported in the few known cases of overdose.

Incidence not determined—Observed during clinical practice; estimates of frequency can not be determined

aggression; agitation; coma; depressed level of consciousness; respiratory depression (pale or blue lips, fingernails, or skin; difficult or troubled breathing; irregular, fast or slow, or shallow breathing; shortness of breath); ***somnolence*** (sleepiness or unusual drowsiness)

Treatment of overdose

Note: There is no specific antidote for levetiracetam overdose.

To decrease absorption—

Emesis or gastric lavage should be attempted if indicated.

To enhance elimination—

Standard hemodialysis should be considered, particularly, in select patients based on clinical state or renal impairment. Approximately 50% is removed in 4 hours.

Monitoring—

Monitor vital signs and clinical status.

Supportive care—

General supportive care.

Patients in whom intentional overdose is confirmed or suspected should be referred for psychiatric consultation.

Patient Consultation

As an aid to patient consultation, refer to *Advice for the Patient, Levetiracetam (Systemic)*.

In providing consultation, consider emphasizing the following selected information (» = major clinical significance):

Before using this medication

» Conditions affecting use, especially:

Hypersensitivity to levetiracetam.

Other medical problems, especially renal function impairment.

Proper use of this medication

» Compliance with therapy; not taking more or less medicine than prescribed; not missing any doses.

Missed dose: Contact your doctor if you miss a dose

» Proper storage

Precautions while using this medication

» Importance of regular visits to physician to check progress of therapy.

» Possible dizziness and somnolence; caution when driving or doing jobs requiring alertness.

» Not discontinuing levetiracetam abruptly; consulting a physician about gradually reducing dosage.

Side/adverse effects

Signs of potential side effects, especially ataxia, diplopia, infection, mood or mental changes including agitation, amnesia, anxiety, apathy, depersonalization,depression, emotional lability, hostility, and nervousness, and sinusitis.

General Dosing Information

May be taken with or without food.

If discontinuation of levetiracetam is necessary, dosage should be reduced gradually to minimize the potential of increased seizure frequency.

Only whole tablets should be administered.

Oral Dosage Forms

LEVETIRACETAM TABLETS

Usual adult dose

Anticonvulsant, adjunctive treatment of partial seizures—

Oral, initially 500 mg twice daily as an adjunct. Increase dose, as necessary, every 2 weeks in 1000 mg a day increments.

Note: Dosage adjustment required for patients with impaired renal function.

Creatinine Clearance (mL/min)	Dosage (mg)	Frequency
> 80	500 to 1500	Every 12 hours
50 to 80	500 to 1000	Every 12 hours
30 to 50	250 to 750	Every 12 hours
< 30	250 to 500	Every 12 hours

End-stage renal disease patients using dialysis–500 to 1000 mg every 24 hours with a supplemental dose of 250 to 500 mg following dialysis.

Usual adult prescribing limits

Up to 3000 mg a day.

Usual pediatric dose

Pediatric patients 16 years of age and older: See *Usual adult dose*

Pediatric patients 4 to 16 years of age: Oral, initially 20 mg per kg in 2 divided doses. The dose should be increased by 20 mg per kg every 2 weeks until the recommended daily dose of 60 mg per kg is reached.

Safety and efficacy have not been established in children less than 4 years of age.

Usual geriatric dose

See *Usual adult dose.*

Usual geriatric prescribing limits

See *Usual adult prescribing limits.*

Strength(s) usually available

U.S.—

250 mg (Rx) [*Keppra* (colloidal silicon dioxide; corn starch; hydroxypropyl methylcellulose; magnesium stearate; polyethylene glycol 4000; povidone; talc; titanium dioxide; FD&C Blue No. 2)].

500 mg (Rx) [*Keppra* (colloidal silicon dioxide; corn starch; hydroxypropyl methylcellulose; magnesium stearate; polyethylene glycol 4000; povidone; talc; titanium dioxide; yellow iron oxide; yellow iron oxide)].

750 mg (Rx) [*Keppra* (colloidal silicon dioxide; corn starch; hydroxypropyl methylcellulose; magnesium stearate; polyethylene glycol 4000; povidone; talc; titanium dioxide; FD&C Blue No. 2; FD&C Yellow No. 6; red iron oxide)].

Packaging and storage

Store at 25 °C (77 °F); excursions permitted between 15 and 30 °C (59 and 86 °F).

Auxiliary labeling

- May cause drowsiness.
- May cause dizziness.
- Be careful while driving or operating machinery. Use caution until you become familiar with the effects of this medicine.
- Swallow whole. Do not crush or chew

LEVETIRACETAM Oral Solution

Usual adult dose

Anticonvulsant, adjunctive treatment of partial seizures—

Oral, initially 500 mg twice daily as an adjunct. Increase dose, as necessary, every 2 weeks in 1000 mg a day increments.

Note: Dosage adjustment required for patients with impaired renal function.

Creatinine Clearance (mL/min)	Dosage (mg)	Frequency
> 80	500 to 1500	Every 12 hours
50 to 80	500 to 1000	Every 12 hours
30 to 50	250 to 750	Every 12 hours
< 30	250 to 500	Every 12 hours

End-stage renal disease patients using dialysis–500 to 1000 mg every 24 hours with a supplemental dose of 250 to 500 mg following dialysis.

Usual adult prescribing limits
Up to 3000 mg a day.

Usual pediatric dose
Pediatric patients 16 years of age and older: See *Usual adult dose*

Pediatric patients 4 to 16 years of age: Oral, initially 20 mg per kg in 2 divided doses. The dose should be increased by 20 mg per kg every 2 weeks until the recommended daily dose of 60 mg per kg is reached.

Safety and efficacy have not been established in children less than 4 years of age.

Note: Patients with body weight ≤ 20 kg should be dosed with oral solution.

Usual geriatric dose
See *Usual adult dose.*

Usual geriatric prescribing limits
See *Usual adult prescribing limits.*

Strength(s) usually available
U.S.—

100 mg (Rx) [*Keppra* (ammonium; glycyrrhizinate; citric acid monohydrate; glycerin; maltilol solution; methylparaben; potassium acesulfame; propylparaben; purified water; sodium citrate dihydrate; natural flavor, and; artificial flavor)].

Packaging and storage
Store at 25 °C (77 °F); excursions permitted between 15 and 30 °C (59 and 86 °F).

Auxiliary labeling
- May cause drowsiness.
- May cause dizziness.
- Be careful while driving or operating machinery. Use caution until you become familiar with the effects of this medicine.
- Swallow whole. Do not crush or chew

Revised: 02/01/2006
Developed: 04/14/2000

LEVOBETAXOLOL—See *Beta-adrenergic Blocking Agents (Ophthalmic)*

LEVOBUNOLOL—See *Beta-adrenergic Blocking Agents (Ophthalmic)*

LEVOBUPIVACAINE—See *Anesthetics (Parenteral-Local)*

LEVOCABASTINE Ophthalmic

VA CLASSIFICATION (Primary): OP801

Commonly used brand name(s): *Livostin.*

Note: For a listing of dosage forms and brand names by country availability, see *Dosage Forms* section(s).

Category
Antihistaminic (H_1-receptor) (ophthalmic); antiallergic (ophthalmic).

Indications

Accepted
Conjunctivitis, seasonal allergic (treatment)—Levocabastine is indicated in the treatment of seasonal allergic conjunctivitis.

Pharmacology/Pharmacokinetics

Physicochemical characteristics
Chemical Group—Levocabastine is a cyclohexylpiperidine derivative that has no structural relationship to other antihistamines.

Molecular weight—456.99.

pH—Ophthalmic suspension: 6 to 8.

Mechanism of action/Effect
Levocabastine is a potent, selective histamine H_1-receptor antagonist. It works by competing with histamine for H_1-receptor sites on effector cells. It thereby prevents, but does not reverse, responses mediated by histamine alone. Levocabastine does not block histamine release but, rather, prevents histamine binding and activity.

Absorption
Low; following ophthalmic administration of 0.05% levocabastine, mean plasma concentrations reached 1 to 2 nanograms per mL.

Biotransformation
Oral administration—10 to 20% is metabolized to the acylglucuronide of levocabastine.

Onset of action
Ophthalmic administration—Within 10 to 15 minutes.

Duration of action
Ophthalmic administration—At least 2 to 4 hours.

Elimination
Oral administration—
Renal, 70% (unchanged), 10 to 20% (as acylglucuronide).
Fecal, 10 to 20%.

Precautions to Consider

Carcinogenicity
Levocabastine was not carcinogenic when administered daily for up to 24 months in the diet of female mice, male mice, female rats, and male rats, in doses of up to 3.2 mg per kg of body weight (mg/kg), 49 mg/kg, 34 mg/kg, and 24 mg/kg, respectively, per day. However, female mice administered oral doses of 12.9 mg/kg per day of levocabastine (5000 times the maximum human ophthalmic dose) showed an increased incidence of pituitary gland adenoma and mammary gland adenocarcinoma. The increased incidence of these tumors was possibly related to the associated increase in prolactin levels.

Mutagenicity
Levocabastine was not mutagenic when tested in the Ames *Salmonella* reversion test, *Escherichia coli* test, *Drosophila melanogaster* test, mouse dominant lethal assay test, or rat micronucleus test.

Pregnancy/Reproduction
Fertility—Rats given oral doses of 20 mg/kg per day of levocabastine showed no evidence of impaired fertility.

Pregnancy—Adequate and well-controlled studies have not been done in humans.

Oral doses of levocabastine equivalent to 16,500 times the maximum human ophthalmic dose were shown to be teratogenic (causing polydactyly) in rats. Oral doses of levocabastine equivalent to 66,000 times the maximum human ophthalmic dose were shown to be teratogenic (causing polydactyly, hydrocephaly, and brachygnathia), embryotoxic, and maternotoxic in rats.

FDA Pregnancy Category C.

Breast-feeding
Levocabastine is distributed into breast milk. A study of a breast-feeding woman receiving the usual dose of ophthalmic levocabastine showed that the infant received a daily dose of 0.5 mcg of levocabastine.

Pediatrics
Appropriate studies on the relationship of age to the effects of levocabastine have not been performed in the pediatric population. Safety and efficacy have not been established for children up to 12 years of age.

Geriatrics
No information is available on the relationship of age to the effects of levocabastine in geriatric patients.

Medical considerations/Contraindications
The medical considerations/contraindications included have been selected on the basis of their potential clinical significance (reasons given in parentheses where appropriate)—not necessarily inclusive (» = major clinical significance).

Risk-benefit should be considered when the following medical problem exists:
Sensitivity to levocabastine

Side/Adverse Effects

Note: Ophthalmic levocabastine does not produce CNS depressive effects or clinically significant systemic antihistaminic effects in patients.

The following side/adverse effects have been selected on the basis of their potential clinical significance (possible signs and symptoms in parentheses where appropriate)—not necessarily inclusive:

Those indicating need for medical attention

Incidence less frequent

Headache

Incidence rare

Cough; dyspnea (troubled breathing); ***eyelid edema*** (swelling of eyelids); ***eye pain; fatigue*** (unusual tiredness or weakness); ***nausea; pharyngitis*** (sore throat); ***redness, tearing, discharge, or other eye irritation not present before therapy or becoming worse during therapy; skin rash; visual disturbances*** (change in vision or trouble in seeing)

Those indicating need for medical attention only if they continue or are bothersome

Incidence more frequent

Burning or stinging, transient, upon administration of medication

Incidence less frequent

Dry eyes; dry mouth; somnolence (feeling sleepy)

Patient Consultation

As an aid to patient consultation, refer to *Advice for the Patient, Levocabastine (Ophthalmic)*.

In providing consultation, consider emphasizing the following selected information (» = major clinical significance):

Before using this medication

» Conditions affecting use, especially:

Sensitivity to levocabastine

Carcinogenicity—Levocabastine is carcinogenic in female mice, but not in male mice or male or female rats.

Pregnancy—Levocabastine is teratogenic in rats.

Breast-feeding—Ophthalmic levocabastine is distributed into breast milk.

Use in children—Safety and efficacy have not been established for children up to 12 years of age

Proper use of this medication

Proper administration technique; not touching applicator tip to any surface; keeping container tightly closed

» Compliance with therapy; symptomatic response usually occurs within a few days

» Proper dosing

Missed dose: Using as soon as possible

» Proper storage

Precautions while using this medication

» Checking with physician if symptoms do not improve within 3 days or if condition becomes worse

After application, occasional stinging or burning may occur

Side/adverse effects

Signs of potential side effects, especially headache; cough; dyspnea; eye pain; eyelid edema; fatigue; nausea; pharyngitis; redness, tearing, discharge, or other eye irritation not present before therapy or becoming worse during therapy; skin rash; or visual disturbances.

General Dosing Information

The manufacturer recommends that patients not wear soft contact lenses during treatment with levocabastine ophthalmic suspension. However, medical experts do not believe this precaution is necessary unless the patient has corneal epithelial problems and the medication is to be used more often than once every 1 to 2 hours. No significant problems have been documented with the use of ophthalmic solutions containing 0.03% or less of benzalkonium chloride as a preservative in patients with no significant corneal surface problems.

If there is no improvement in the condition after 3 days of therapy, the medication should be withdrawn, since further therapy will not be useful.

Clinical studies to support the continuous treatment with levocabastine for longer than 16 weeks have not been done.

Ophthalmic Dosage Forms

LEVOCABASTINE HYDROCHLORIDE OPHTHALMIC SUSPENSION

Usual adult and adolescent dose

Antiallergic (ophthalmic) or

Antihistaminic (H_1-receptor) (ophthalmic)—

Topical, to the conjunctiva, 1 drop four times a day.

Note: In Canada, the initial dose is 1 drop two times a day, the dose being increased to 1 drop three or four times a day if needed.

Usual pediatric dose

Antiallergic (ophthalmic) or

Antihistaminic (H_1-receptor) (ophthalmic)—

Children up to 12 years of age: Safety and efficacy have not been established.

Children 12 years of age and older: See *Usual adult and adolescent dose*.

Strength(s) usually available

U.S.—

0.05% (Rx) [*Livostin* (benzalkonium chloride 0.15 mg)].

Canada—

0.05% (Rx) [*Livostin* (benzalkonium chloride 0.15 mg)].

Packaging and storage

Store between 15 and 30 °C (59 and 86 °F), unless otherwise specified by manufacturer. Protect from freezing.

Stability

The medication should be discarded 1 month after the applicator bottle is first opened.

The medication should be discarded if it has become discolored.

Auxiliary labeling

- For the eye.
- Shake well.

Selected Bibliography

Janssens M. Efficacy of levocabastine in conjunctival provocation studies. Doc Ophthalmol 1992; 82(4): 341-51.

Estelle F, Simons R, Simons KJ. Pharmacokinetic optimization of histamine H_1-receptor antagonist therapy. Clin Pharmacokinet 1991 Nov; 21(5): 372-93.

Dechant KL, Goa KL. Levocabastine: a review of its pharmacological properties and therapeutic potential as a topical antihistamine in allergic rhinitis and conjunctivitis. Drugs 1991 Feb; 41(2): 202-24.

Revised: 09/28/1998
Developed: 08/11/1994

LEVOCARNITINE Systemic

VA CLASSIFICATION (Primary): TN900

Commonly used brand name(s): *Carnitor*.

Another commonly used name is L-Carnitine.

Note: For a listing of dosage forms and brand names by country availability, see *Dosage Forms* section(s).

Category

Carnitine deficiency therapy agent.

Indications

Note: Bracketed information in the *Indications* section refers to uses that are not included in U.S. product labeling.

Accepted

Carnitine deficiency (treatment)—Levocarnitine is indicated for treatment of primary systemic carnitine deficiency, a genetic impairment of normal biosynthesis or utilization of levocarnitine from dietary sources, or for the treatment of secondary carnitine deficiency resulting from an inborn error of metabolism.

Deficiency of levocarnitine may lead to elevated triglyceride and free fatty acid concentrations, reduced ketogenesis, and lipid infiltration of liver and muscle. Severe, chronic deficiency may lead to hypoglycemia, life-threatening acidosis, progressive myasthenia, hypotonia, lethargy, hepatomegaly, hepatic encephalopathy, hepatic coma, cardiomegaly, congestive heart failure, cardiac arrest, muscle weakness and failure to thrive, neurologic disturbances, and impaired infant growth and development.

Carnitine deficiency, in end-stage renal disease (ESRD) patients on hemodialysis (prevention and treatment)[1]—Parenteral levocarnitine is indicated for the prevention and treatment of carnitine deficiency in patients with end-stage renal disease supported on hemodialysis.

[Carnitine deficiency, secondary to valproic acid toxicity (prophylaxis and treatment)][1]—Levocarnitine oral solution is used for the prevention and treatment of carnitine deficiency secondary to valproic acid toxicity.

Unaccepted

Levocarnitine has not been proven effective for treatment of abnormal plasma lipoprotein patterns or cardiac conditions unrelated to systemic carnitine deficiency. It has also not been proven effective for improvement of athletic performance.

[1]Not included in Canadian product labeling.

Pharmacology/Pharmacokinetics

Physicochemical characteristics

Molecular weight—161.20.

pH—

Oral solution—5.

Intravenous solution—6–6.5; adjusted with hydrochloric acid

Mechanism of action/Effect

Levocarnitine is necessary for normal mammalian fat utilization and energy metabolism. It facilitates entry of long-chain fatty acids into cellular mitochondria, where they are used during oxidation and energy production. It also exports acyl groups from subcellular organelles and from cells to urine before they accumulate to toxic concentrations.

Only the L isomer of carnitine (sometimes called vitamin B_T) affects lipid metabolism. The "vitamin B_T" form actually contains D,L-carnitine, which competitively inhibits levocarnitine and can cause deficiency.

Absorption

Bioavailability—

Oral—15% (tablets or solution).

Distribution

Vol_D—

29 L (0.39 liters per kg).

Protein binding

Not bound to plasma protein or albumin.

Biotransformation

Major metabolites include trimethylamine N-oxide and [^{3}H]-γ-butyrobetaine.

Half-life

Distribution—0.585 hours.

Elimination—17.4 hours

Time to peak concentration

Oral—

Solution: 3.3 hours.

Tablet: 3.3 hours.

Peak serum concentration

Oral—

80 nanomoles per mL.

Parenteral (following hemodialysis)—

1140–1190 micromoles per L (20 mg per kg dose, three times weekly, after dialysis session).

Elimination

Total body clearance—4 L/hour.

Fecal—<1%.

Renal—8.6% to 9.4% (after oral dosing); 75.6% (after single IV dose).

Plasma carnitine concentrations may be increased in patients with renal failure.

In dialysis—Removable by hemodialysis; deficiency may occur.

Precautions to Consider

Carcinogenicity

Studies have not been done in either animals or humans.

Mutagenicity

Studies in *Salmonella typhimurium*, *Saccharomyces cerevisiae*, and *Schizosaccharomyces pombe* found no evidence of mutagenicity.

Pregnancy/Reproduction

Pregnancy—Adequate and well-controlled studies have not been done in humans.

Studies in rats and rabbits at levocarnitine doses up to 3.8 times the usual adult dose (based on body surface area (mg/m^2)) have not demonstrated impaired fertility or fetal harm.

FDA Pregnancy Category B.

Breast-feeding

It is not known whether levocarnitine is distributed into breast milk. Problems in humans have not been documented. Carnitine occurs naturally in human milk.

Studies in dairy cows indicate that levocarnitine is distributed into dairy milk.

Pediatrics

Appropriate studies on the relationship of age to the effects of levocarnitine have not been performed in the pediatric population. However, pediatrics-specific problems that would limit the usefulness of this medicine in children are not expected.

Geriatrics

Appropriate studies on the relationship of age to the effects of levocarnitine have not been performed in the geriatric population. However, geriatrics-specific problems that would limit the usefulness of this medication in the elderly are not expected.

Drug interactions and/or related problems

The following drug interactions and/or related problems have been selected on the basis of their potential clinical significance (possible mechanism in parentheses where appropriate)—not necessarily inclusive (» = major clinical significance):

Valproic acid

(requirements for carnitine may be increased in patients receiving valproic acid)

Medical considerations/Contraindications

The medical considerations/contraindications included have been selected on the basis of their potential clinical significance (reasons given in parentheses where appropriate)—not necessarily inclusive (» = major clinical significance).

Risk-benefit should be considered when the following medical problems exist:

» Seizures

(Seizures may occur in patients with or without pre-existing seizure activity; increased seizure frequency and/or severity has been reported in patients with pre-existing seizure activity)

» End stage renal disease

(Administration of high doses of the oral formulations of levocarnitine for long periods of time is not recommended in patients with severely compromised renal function or in end stage renal disease patients on dialysis due to the fact that major metabolites formed following oral administration (trimethylamine [TMA] and trimethylamine-N-oxide [TMAO]) will accumulate since they cannot be efficiently removed by the kidneys. This does not occur to the same extent following intravenous administration. Only the intravenous form of levocarnitine is indicated for use in end stage renal disease patients on hemodialysis.)

Patient monitoring

The following may be especially important in patient monitoring (other tests may be warranted in some patients, depending on condition; » = major clinical significance):

Carnitine concentrations (free carnitine levels should be 35 to 60 micromoles per L) and

Free fatty acid concentrations and

Triglyceride concentrations

(plasma determinations recommended at periodic intervals to assess efficacy of levocarnitine; weekly to monthly monitoring during parenteral therapy is recommended)

Periodic blood chemistries

Vital signs

Overall clinical condition

Side/Adverse Effects

The following side/adverse effects have been selected on the basis of their potential clinical significance (possible signs and symptoms in parenthesis where appropriate)—not necessarily inclusive:

Those indicating need for medical attention

Incidence more frequent

Hypertension—in dialysis patients with end-stage renal disease (ESRD)

Incidence less frequent

Fever—in dialysis patients with ESRD; ***tachycardia*** (fast heartbeat)—in dialysis patients with ESRD

Incidence rare

Seizures—may occur in patients with or without seizure history; increased seizure frequency and/or severity has been reported in patients with pre-existing seizure activity

Those indicating need for medical attention only if they continue or are bothersome

Incidence more frequent

Abdominal or stomach cramps; diarrhea; headache—in dialysis patients with ESRD; ***nausea or vomiting***

Incidence less frequent

Body odor; gastritis (abdominal discomfort; loss of appetite)

Note: Gastrointestinal symptoms and levocarnitine-induced body odor are dose-related.

Incidence less frequent—In dialysis patients with ESRD

Amblyopia (blurred vision; change in vision; impaired vision); ***anorexia*** (loss of appetite; weight loss); ***asthenia*** (loss of strength or energy; muscle pain or weakness); ***depression; dizziness; hypercalcemia*** (abdominal pain; confusion; constipation; depression; dry mouth; headache; incoherent speech; increased urination; loss of appetite; metallic taste; muscle weakness; nausea; thirst; unusual tiredness; vomiting; weight loss); ***paresthesias*** (burning, crawling, itching, numbness, prickling, "pins and needles," or tingling feelings); ***peripheral edema*** (bloating or swelling of face, arms, hands, lower legs, or feet; rapid weight gain; tingling of hands or feet; unusual weight gain or loss)

Overdose

For more information on the management of overdose or unintentional ingestion, **contact a Poison Control Center** (see *Poison Control Center Listing*).

Clinical effects of overdose

There are no reports of toxicity from overdose of l-carnitine. Adverse effects Include nausea, vomiting, abdominal cramps, diarrhea, and drug-induced body odor.

Treatment of overdose

To enhance elimination

Removing levocarnitine from plasma via hemodialysis.

Supportive care—

Treatment is symptomatic and supportive.

Patient Consultation

As an aid to patient consultation, refer to *Advice for the Patient, Levocarnitine (Systemic)*.

In providing consultation, consider emphasizing the following selected information (» = major clinical significance):

Description of use

Description should include caution against confusion with the D,L-carnitine form

Before using this medication

» Conditions affecting use, especially:

Other medical problems, especially history of end stage renal disease (ESRD) and seizure activity

Proper use of this medication

Taking during or immediately following meals and consuming slowly to reduce gastrointestinal upset

Taking at evenly spaced times throughout day (every 3 or 4 hours).

» Proper dosing

Missed dose: Not taking at all and not doubling doses

» Proper storage

Precautions while using this medication

» Not changing brands or dosage forms of levocarnitine without checking with physician

Side/adverse effects

Signs of potential side effects, especially hypertension, fever, tachycardia, and seizures

General Dosing Information

Even spacing of doses throughout the day (every 3 or 4 hours) will help increase tolerance of levocarnitine. Gastrointestinal side effects are dose-related.

Diet/Nutrition

Levocarnitine oral solution may be given alone. However, to reduce gastrointestinal side effects caused by overly rapid ingestion, it is recommended that the solution be dissolved in drinks or other liquid foods and that no more than 10 mL (1 gram) be taken at each dose.

Levocarnitine tablets should be taken with meals to minimize gastrointestinal upset.

Bioequivalence information

There are few data showing the therapeutic equivalence of those levocarnitine products approved for drug use and those products sold as food supplements. However, Carnitor-brand tablets and oral solution are bioequivalent.

The effects of supplemental levocarnitine on either the signs and symptoms of carnitine deficiency or clinical outcomes have not been studied in the population of end stage renal disease hemodialysis patients being maintained on parenteral levocarnitine.

Oral Dosage Forms

LEVOCARNITINE ORAL SOLUTION USP

Usual adult and adolescent dose

Carnitine deficiency—

Oral/enteral, initially 1 gram once a day with food, the dosage being increased slowly as needed and tolerated. For a 50-kg patient, the usual dose is 1 gram one to three times a day with meals.

Usual pediatric dose

Carnitine deficiency—

Oral/enteral, initially 50 mg per kg of body weight a day with food, the dosage being increased slowly as needed and tolerated. The usual dose is 50 to 100 mg per kg of body weight a day with meals (maximum 3 grams a day).

Strength(s) usually available

U.S.—

100 mg per mL (Rx) [*Carnitor*].

Canada—

100 mg per mL (Rx) [*Carnitor*].

Packaging and storage

Store at controlled room temperature between 20 and 25° C (68 and 77° F).

Auxiliary labeling

- Take with meals.

Note

Not for parenteral use.

LEVOCARNITINE TABLETS USP

Note: Certain levocarnitine tablets are labeled and sold as food supplements only. These products have not been approved as drugs by the Food and Drug Administration for use in the treatment of carnitine deficiency. When used on prescription, one levocarnitine product should not be substituted for another unless otherwise directed by the patient's physician. There are no data showing the therapeutic equivalence of those products approved for drug use and those products sold as food supplements.

Usual adult and adolescent dose

Carnitine deficiency—

Oral, 990 milligrams two or three times a day with meals.

Usual pediatric dose

Carnitine deficiency—

Oral, initially 50 mg per kg of body weight a day with food, the dosage being increased slowly as needed and tolerated. The usual dose is 50 to 100 mg per kg of body weight a day with meals (maximum 3 grams a day).

Strength(s) usually available

U.S.—

330 mg (Rx) [*Carnitor*].

Canada—

330 mg (Rx) [*Carnitor*].

Packaging and storage

Store at controlled room temperature between 20 and 25 °C (68 and 77 °F).

Auxiliary labeling

- Take with meals.

Parenteral Dosage Forms

LEVOCARNITINE INJECTION

Usual adult dose

Carnitine deficiency—

Intravenous, 50 mg per kg (mg/kg) of body weight a day given by infusion or as a slow (2- to 3-minute) injection.

For severe metabolic crisis—

Intravenous, loading dose of 50 mg/kg of body weight, followed by a total of 50 mg/kg every 3 or 4 hours for one day, then 50 mg/kg a day. The highest dose administered has been 300 mg/kg.

Carnitine deficiency in patients with end-stage renal disease on hemodialysis (prevention and treatment)[1]—

Intravenous, initially: 10 to 20 mg per kg (mg/kg) of dry body weight a day given as a slow (2- to 3-minute) bolus injection into the venous return line after each dialysis session. Treatment should be given to those with pre-dialysis (trough) plasma levocarnitine levels below normal range (40 to 50 micromoles per L).

Intravenous, maintenance: Downward dose titrations are guided by trough plasma levocarnitine concentrations, with the earliest dose adjustment made after 3 to 4 weeks of therapy.

Pediatric dose—

See *Usual adult dose.*

Strength(s) usually available

U.S.—

200 mg per mL (Rx) [*Carnitor*].

Canada—

200 mg per mL (Rx) [*Carnitor*].

Packaging and storage

Store ampules at controlled room temperature between 20 and 25 °C (68 and 77 °F). Keep ampules in original container and protect from light. Ampules contain no preservative; discard any unused, opened ampules.

Stability

Solutions ranging in concentration between 0.5 and 8 mg per mL (250 to 4200 mg per 500 mL) prepared in Sodium Chloride 0.9% or Lactated Ringers are stable and compatible stored in polyvinyl chloride (PVC) containers at room temperature (25° C) for up to 24 hours.

[1]Not included in Canadian product labeling.

Revised: 08/01/2001
Developed: 09/02/1999

LEVOFLOXACIN—See *Fluoroquinolones (Systemic)*

LEVOFLOXACIN Ophthalmic

VA CLASSIFICATION (Primary): OP201

Commonly used brand name(s): *Quixin.*

Note: For a listing of dosage forms and brand names by country availability, see *Dosage Forms* section(s).

Category

Antibacterial (ophthalmic).

Indications

Accepted

Conjunctivitis, bacterial (treatment)—Levofloxacin ophthalmic solution is indicated in the treatment of conjunctivitis caused by susceptible strains of bacteria, including *Acinetobacter lwoffii, Corynebacterium* species, *Haemophilus influenzae, Serratia marcescens, Staphylococcus aureus* (methicillin-susceptible strains only), *Staphylococcus epidermidis* (methicillin-susceptible strains only), *Streptococcus pneumoniae, Streptococcus* (groups C/F), *Streptococcus* (group G), and *viridans group Streptococci.*

Pharmacology/Pharmacokinetics

Physicochemical characteristics

Chemical Group—

Fluoroquinolone

Levofloxacin is the pure (-)-(S)–enantiomer of ofloxacin.

Molecular weight—370.38.

pH—6.5

Mechanism of action/Effect

Levofloxacin's bactericidal action results from interference with the enzymes topoisomerase IV and DNA gyrase, which are needed for the synthesis of bacterial DNA.

Absorption

Fifteen subjects were treated with varying doses of levofloxacin over a 15 day testing period. The plasma concentration of levofloxacin ranged from 0.86 ng/ml on day 1 to 2.05 ng/ml on day 15. The highest level, 2.25 ng/ml, was recorded on day 4.

Precautions to Consider

Cross-sensitivity and/or related problems

Patients sensitive to other quinolones, such as cinoxacin, ciprofloxacin, nalidixic acid, norfloxacin, or ofloxacin, may be sensitive to this medication also.

Carcinogenicity

Rats and mice administered dietary levofloxacin for up to 2 years did not show carcinogenic effects. The highest dose, 100 mg per kg per day, was 875 times higher than the highest recommended human ophthalmic dose.

Mutagenicity

Levofloxacin was found to be mutagenic in the in vitro chromosomal aberration (CHL cell line) and *in vitro* sister chromatid exchange (CHL/IU cell line) assays. It was negative in the Ames bacterial mutation assay (*S. typhimurium* and *E. coli*), the CHO/HGPRT forward mutation assay, the mouse micronucleus test, the mouse dominant lethal test, the rat unscheduled DNA synthesis assay, and the *in vivo* mouse sister chromatid exchange assay.

Pregnancy/Reproduction

Fertility—Studies performed in rats administered levofloxacin in oral doses as high as 360 mg per kg per day, (3,150 times higher than the highest recommended human ophthalmic dose), revealed no evidence of impaired fertility.

Pregnancy—Adequate and well-controlled studies in humans have not been done. No teratogenic effects were found when rabbits were given 50 mg per kg per day of levofloxacin orally or 25 mg per kg per day intravenously, (400 and 200 times the highest recommended ophthalmic dose, respectively). Decreased fetal body weight and increased fetal mortality occurred in rats given oral levofloxacin at doses of 810 mg per kg per day, (7,000 times the highest recommended human ophthalmic dose).

FDA Pregnancy Category C.

Breast-feeding

It is not known whether ophthalmic levofloxacin is distributed into breast milk. However, based upon data from ofloxacin, it can be presumed that levofloxacin is excreted in human milk.

Pediatrics

The safety of levofloxacin in infants less than one year of age has not been determined. Although oral administration of quinolones have been shown to cause arthropathy in immature animals, there is no evidence that ophthalmic administration of levofloxacin has any negative effect on weight bearing joints.

Geriatrics

Appropriate studies performed to date have not demonstrated geriatrics-specific problems that would limit the usefulness of levofloxacin in the elderly.

Medical considerations/Contraindications

The medical considerations/contraindications included have been selected on the basis of their potential clinical significance (reasons given in parentheses where appropriate)—not necessarily inclusive (» = major clinical significance).

Except under special circumstances, this medication should not be used when the following medical problem exists:

Hypersensitivity to levofloxacin or other quinolones

Side/Adverse Effects

The following side/adverse effects have been selected on the basis of their potential clinical significance (possible signs and symptoms in parentheses where appropriate)—not necessarily inclusive:

Those indicating need for medical attention only if they continue or are bothersome

Incidence less frequent or rare

Allergic reactions (itching, pain, redness, or swelling of eye or eyelid; watering of eyes); ***fever; foreign body sensation*** (feeling of having something in the eye); ***headache; ocular problems, such as decreased vision; lid edema*** (swelling of eyelid); ***burning, dryness, itching, or pain; photophobia,*** (increased sensitivity of eyes to light); ***pharyngitis*** (body aches or pain; congestion; dryness or soreness of throat; fever; hoarseness; runny nose; tender, swollen glands in neck; trouble in swallowing; voice changes)

Overdose

For more information on the management of overdose or unintentional ingestion, **contact a poison control center** (see *Poison Control Center Listing*).

Treatment of overdose
Specific treatment—
There is no known specific antidote to levofloxacin. Treatment is generally symptomatic and supportive.
Patients in whom intentional overdose is confirmed or suspected should be referred for psychiatric consultation.

Patient Consultation

As an aid to patient consultation, refer to *Advice for the Patient, Levofloxacin (Ophthalmic).*

In providing consultation, consider emphasizing the following selected information (» = major clinical significance):

Before using this medication
» Conditions affecting use, especially:
Sensitivity to levofloxacin or other quinolones
Breast-feeding—Based on data from ofloxacin, it can be presumed that levofloxacin is distributed in human milk. However, levofloxacin has not been measured in human milk.
Use in children—Safety and efficacy have not been established in children below the age of one year.

Proper use of this medication
Proper administration technique
» Compliance with full course of therapy
» Proper dosing
Missed dose: Using as soon as possible; not using if almost time for next scheduled dose; not doubling doses
» Proper storage

Precautions while using this medication
Checking with physician if no improvement within a few days, or if infection gets worse
Possible photophobic reactions; wearing sunglasses and avoiding prolonged exposure to bright light

General Dosing Information

Levofloxacin ophthalmic solution is not for injection into the eye, nor should it be introduced directly into the anterior chamber of the eye.

If hypersensitivity develops, therapy with ophthalmic levofloxacin should be discontinued.

Patients should be advised not be wear contacts if they have signs and symptoms of bacterial conjunctivitis.

As with other antiinfectives, prolonged use may result in overgrowth of non-susceptible organisms. Should superinfection occur, discontinue use and consider alternative therapy.

For treatment of adverse effects
Recommended treatment includes
• Discontinue levofloxacin treatments if an allergic reaction occurs.
• Serious hypersensitivity reactions should receive emergency medical treatment including administration of oxygen and airway management.

Ophthalmic Dosage Forms

Note: The dosing and strengths of the dosage forms available are expressed in terms of levofloxacin base.

LEVOFLOXACIN OPHTHALMIC SOLUTION

Usual adult and adolescent dose
Bacterial conjunctivitis—
Topical, to the conjunctiva, Day 1 and 2: one to two drops in the affected eye(s) every 2 hours while awake, up to 8 times per day.
Days 3–7: one to two drops in the affected eye(s) every 4 hours while awake, up to 4 times per day.

Usual pediatric dose
Bacterial conjunctivitis—
Infants up to 1 year of age: Safety and efficacy have not been established.
Children over 1 year of age: See *Usual adult and adolescent dose.*

Strength(s) usually available
U.S.—
5.12 mg (5 mg base) per mL (Rx) [*Quixin* (benzalkonium chloride 0.005%; sodium chloride; hydrochloric acid and/or; sodium hydroxide)].

Packaging and storage
Store between 15 –25 °C (59 and 77 °F) in a tight container.

Auxiliary labeling
• For the eye.
• Continue medicine for full time of treatment.

Developed: 10/20/2000

LEVOFLOXACIN Systemic

VA CLASSIFICATION (Primary): AM402

Commonly used brand name(s): *Levaquin.*

Note: For a listing of dosage forms and brand names by country availability, see *Dosage Forms* section(s).

Category

Antibacterial (systemic).

Indications

Accepted

Anthrax, inhalation (treatment)—Levofloxacin is indicated to prevent the development of inhalational anthrax following exposure to *Bacillus anthracis.*

Levofloxacin has not been tested in human for the post-exposure prevention of inhalation anthrax. However, plasma concentrations achieved in humans are reasonably likely to predict efficacy.

Bronchitis, bacterial exacerbations (treatment)—Levofloxacin is indicated in the treatment of bacterial exacerbations of bronchitis caused by *Haemophilus influenzae, Haemophilus parainfluenzae, Moraxella catarrhalis, Staphylococcus aureus,* or *Streptococcus pneumoniae.*

Pneumonia, community-acquired (treatment)—Levofloxacin is indicated in the treatment of community-acquired pneumonia caused by *Chlamydia pneumoniae, H. influenzae, H. parainfluenzae, Klebsiella pneumoniae, Legionella pneumophila, M. catarrhalis, Mycoplasma pneumoniae, S. aureus,* or *S. pneumoniae* (including Multi-drug resistant strains [MDRSP]).

Note: MDRSP (Multi-Drug Resistant *Streptococcus pneumoniae*) isolates are strains resistant to two or more of the following antibiotics:
- penicillin (MIC greater than or equal to 2 mcg per mL)
- second generation cephalosporins
- macrolides
- tetracyclines
- trimethoprim and sulfamethoxazole

Pneumonia, nosocomial (treatment)—Levofloxacin is indicated in the treatment of nosocomial pneumonia due to *Escherichia coli, Haemophilus influenza, Klebsiella pneumoniae, Pseudomonas aeruginosa, Serratia marcescens, Staphylococcus aureus* or *Streptococcus pneumoniae.*

Prostatitis, bacterial (treatment)—Levofloxacin is indicated in the treatment of chronic bacterial prostatitis due to *Escherichia coli, Enterococcus faecalis,* or *Staphylococcus epidermidis.*

Pyelonephritis (treatment)—Levofloxacin is indicated in the treatment of pyelonephritis caused by *Escherichia coli.*

Sinusitis (treatment)—Levofloxacin is indicated in the treatment of sinusitis caused by *H. influenzae, M. catarrhalis,* or *S. pneumoniae.*

Skin and soft tissue infections, uncomplicated (treatment)—Levofloxacin is indicated in the treatment of uncomplicated skin and soft tissue infections caused by *S. aureus* or *Streptococcus pyogenes.*

Skin and soft tissue infections, complicated (treatment)—Levofloxacin is indicated in the treatment of complicated skin and soft tissue infections caused by *Enterococcus faecalis, Proteus mirabilis, S. aureus,* or *S. pyogenes.* [*Enterobacter cloacae, E. coli, K. pneumoniae* or- *Pseudomonas aeruginosa*]

Urinary tract infections, bacterial, complicated (treatment)—Levofloxacin is indicated in the treatment of complicated bacterial urinary tract infections caused by *E. cloacae, E. faecalis, E. coli, K. pneumoniae, P. mirabilis,* or *P. aeruginosa.*

Urinary tract infections, bacterial, uncomplicated (treatment)—Levofloxacin is indicated in the treatment of uncomplicated bacterial urinary tract infections caused by *E. coli, K. pneumoniae* or *Staphylococcus saprophyticus*

Pharmacology/Pharmacokinetics

Physicochemical characteristics
Chemical Group—Fluoroquinolone; levofloxacin is the L-isomer of the racemic medication, ofloxacin.
Molecular weight—370.38.

Mechanism of action/Effect
Levofloxacin acts by inhibiting DNA gyrase (bacterial topoisomerase II), an enzyme required for DNA replication, transcription, repair, and recombination.

Absorption
Rapidly and almost completely absorbed after oral administration. Bioavailability is approximately 99%.

Levofloxacin tablets may be taken with or without food. However, levofloxacin oral solution should be taken 1 hour before eating or 2 hours after eating.

Levofloxacin tablet and oral solution are bioequivalent.

AUC, 500 mg tablet q24h: 40.8 to 54.2 mcg hr per mL

Distribution
Widely distributed. Levofloxacin penetrates well into blister fluid and lung tissues.

Vol_D—74 to 112 L after single and multiple 500-mg or 750-mg doses.

Protein binding
Moderate (24 to 38%); mainly bound to serum albumin

Biotransformation
Levofloxacin is stereochemically stable and does not invert metabolically to its enantiomer, D-ofloxacin. It undergoes limited metabolism to desmethyl and N-oxide metabolites with little relevant pharmacological activity.

Half-life
Elimination—6 to 8 hours.

Time to peak concentration
Oral—Approximately 1 to 2 hours. Oral administration with food prolongs the time to peak concentration by approximately 1 hour; however, levofloxacin tablets may be taken without regard to food consumption.

Peak serum concentration
Oral—Approximately 5.7 mcg per mL after multiple doses of 500 mg. Oral administration with food decreases the peak concentration by approximately 14% following tablet and approximately 25% following oral solution.

Intravenous—Approximately 6.4 mcg per mL. The serum concentration profile of the intravenous infusion is similar and comparable to the extent of exposure (area under the plasma concentration-time curve [AUC]) seen with the tablets when equal doses are administered. Therefore, oral and intravenous routes of administration are considered to be interchangeable.

The mean plasma concentrations of levofloxacin associated with a statistically significant improvement in survival over placebo in the rhesus monkey model of inhalation anthrax are reached or exceeded in adult patients receiving oral and intravenous regimens.

Levofloxacin plasma concentrations achieved in humans serve as a surrogate endpoint reasonably likely to predict clinical benefit and provide the basis for inhalation anthrax treatment. The mean steady-state peak plasma concentration in human adults is as follows:

Oral, 500 mg once daily—4.3 to 5.9 mcg per mL

Intravenously, 500 mg once daily—5.2 to 7.2 mcg per mL

Total corresponding exposure for oral and intravenous was 41.1 to 54.7 mcg per mL and 42.9 to 53.7 mcg per mL, respectively.

Elimination
Renal—Approximately 87% of an orally administered dose is excreted unchanged in the urine within 48 hours; less than 5% of the orally administered dose is excreted as metabolites; renal clearance in excess of the glomerular filtration rate suggests that tubular secretion also occurs.

Fecal—Approximately 4% of an orally administered dose is excreted fecally within 72 hours.

In dialysis—

Levofloxacin is not efficiently removed by hemodialysis or peritoneal dialysis.

Precautions to Consider

Cross-sensitivity and/or related problems
Patients allergic to one fluoroquinolone or other chemically related quinolone derivatives (e.g., cinoxacin, nalidixic acid) may be allergic to other fluoroquinolones also.

Carcinogenicity/Tumorigenicity
In a long-term study in rats, levofloxacin did not show carcinogenic or tumorigenic potential after daily dietary administration for 2 years. The highest dose (100 mg per kg of body weight per day) was 1.4 times the recommended human dose based on body surface area or body weight. Levofloxacin was not photo-carcinogenic in a test for UV-induced skin tumors in hairless albino (Skh-1) mice at any levofloxacin dose level.

Mutagenicity
Levofloxacin was not mutagenic in the Ames test (*Salmonella typhimurium* and *Escherichia coli*), CHO/HGPRT forward mutation assay, mouse micronucleus test, mouse dominant lethal assay, rat unscheduled DNA synthesis assay, and the mouse sister chromatid exchange assay. It was positive in the *in vitro* chromosomal aberration (CHL cell line) and sister chromatid exchange (CHL/IU cell line) assays.

Pregnancy/Reproduction
Fertility—Levofloxacin had no effect on the fertility or reproductive performance of male and female rats at oral doses of up to 360 mg per kg of body weight (mg/kg) per day, corresponding to 4.2 times the maximum recommended human dose (MRHD) based on body surface area or at intravenous doses of up to 100 mg/kg per day, corresponding to 1.2 times the MRHD based on body surface area.

Pregnancy—Adequate and well-controlled studies in humans have not been done. Since levofloxacin has been shown to cause arthropathy in immature animals, use is recommended in pregnancy only if the potential benefit to the mother outweighs the potential risk to the fetus.

Levofloxacin was not teratogenic in rats at oral doses up to 810 mg per kg of body weight per day (9.4 times the maximum recommended human dose based on body surface area) or at intravenous doses up to 160 mg per kg of body weight per day (1.9 times the maximum recommended human dose based on body surface area). Decreased fetal body weight and increased fetal mortality occurred at oral doses of 810 mg per kg of body weight per day. Levofloxacin was not teratogenic in rabbits at oral doses up to 50 mg per kg of body weight per day (1.1 times the maximum recommended human dose based on body surface area) or at intravenous doses up to 25 mg per kg of body weight per day (0.5 times the maximum recommended human dose based on body surface area).

FDA Pregnancy Category C.

Breast-feeding
It is not known whether levofloxacin is distributed into breast milk; however, based on data for ofloxacin, it is expected that levofloxacin is distributed into human milk. Because of the potential for serious adverse effects in nursing infants, a decision should be made to either stop breast-feeding or discontinue taking levofloxacin.

Pediatrics
Safety and efficacy have not been established in patients up to 18 years of age. Fluoroquinolones have been shown to cause arthropathy and osteochondrosis in immature animals of several species.

For the indication of inhalation anthrax, the administration of levofloxacin to pediatric patients should be based on risk/benefit considerations for individual patients. Safety of levofloxacin in pediatric patients has not been established. There are no data from adequate and well-controlled clinical studies or postmarketing experience regarding the safety of levofloxacin in pediatric patients.

Geriatrics
Appropriate studies performed to date have not demonstrated geriatrics-specific problems that would limit the usefulness of levofloxacin in the elderly. However, greater sensitivity of some older individuals cannot be ruled out, especially drug-associated effects on the QT interval, increased risk of toxic reactions due to age-related renal function impairment, and an increased risk for tendinitis and tendon rupture.

Drug interactions and/or related problems
The following drug interactions and/or related problems have been selected on the basis of their potential clinical significance (possible mechanism in parentheses where appropriate)—not necessarily inclusive (» = major clinical significance):

Note: Unlike other fluoroquinolones, levofloxacin does not alter the pharmacokinetics of cyclosporine, digoxin, or theophylline, or warfarin.

Combinations containing any of the following medications, depending on the amount present, may also interact with this medication.

» Antacids, aluminum-, calcium-, and/or magnesium-containing or
» Didanosine or
» Ferrous sulfate or
» Sucralfate or
» Zinc

(antacids, didanosine, ferrous sulfate, sucralfate, and zinc may reduce absorption of levofloxacin by chelation, resulting in lower serum and urine concentrations; therefore, concurrent use is not recommended; it is recommended that levofloxacin be taken at least 2 hours before or 2 hours after taking any of these agents)

» Antiarrhythmic agents, class Ia or class III

(concurrent administration may increase the risk of cardiac arrhythmias through prolongation of the QT interval on the electrocardiogram)

» Antidiabetic agents
(concurrent administration has resulted in hyperglycemia or hypoglycemia, usually in diabetic patients who are taking oral hypoglycemic agents or insulin; careful monitoring of blood glucose is recommended)

» Anti-inflammatory drugs, nonsteroidal
(concurrent use may increase the risk of central nervous system [CNS] stimulation and seizures)

Cimetidine or
Probenecid
(concurrent use of levofloxacin with cimetidine or probenecid increases the area under the plasma concentration-time curve [AUC] by 27 to 38% and 30%, respectively, and decreases the clearance by 21 to 35%; although these differences are statistically significant, the changes are not considered high enough to warrant a change in dose)

Corticosteroids
(concomitant use with quinolones, including levofloxain, may increase risk of rupturing shoulder, hand, Achilles tendons or other tendons that may require surgical repair or result in prolonged disability, especially in the elderly)

» Warfarin
(post-marketing experience in patients suggests that levofloxacin enhances effects of warfarin; prothrombin time elevations in setting of concomitant use have been associated with episodes of bleeding; close monitoring of prothrombin time, INR, or other anticoagulation tests, and evidence of bleeding in patients administered levofloxacin concomitantly with warfarin)

Laboratory value alterations

The following have been selected on the basis of their potential clinical significance (possible effect in parentheses where appropriate)—not necessarily inclusive (» = major clinical significance).

With physiology/laboratory test values
» Glucose, blood
(concentrations may be increased or decreased)

Lymphocytes
(counts may be decreased)

Prothrombin time
(increased International Normalized Ratio (INR))

Medical considerations/Contraindications

The medical considerations/contraindications included have been selected on the basis of their potential clinical significance (reasons given in parentheses where appropriate)—not necessarily inclusive (» = major clinical significance).

Except under special circumstances, this medication should not be used when the following medical problem exists:

» Previous allergic reaction to levofloxacin or any other components of this product, or fluoroquinolones or other chemically related quinolone derivatives

Risk-benefit should be considered when the following medical problems exist:

» Bradycardia, significant
(levofloxacin may cause cardiac arrhythmias and prolongation of the QT interval in the presence of significant bradycardia)

CNS disorders, including cerebral arteriosclerosis or epilepsy
(levofloxacin may cause CNS stimulation or toxicity, increasing the risk of seizures in patients with these conditions)

» Diabetes mellitus
(levofloxacin has been reported to cause hyperglycemia and hypoglycemia, usually in diabetic patients who are taking oral hypoglycemic agents or insulin; diabetic patients should be carefully monitored)

» Hypokalemia
(levofloxacin may cause cardiac arrhythmias and prolongation of the QT interval in the presence of hypokalemia)

» Renal function impairment
(levofloxacin is renally excreted; it is recommended that patients with a creatinine clearance of less than 50 mL per minute receive a reduced dosage of levofloxacin)

Patient monitoring

The following may be especially important in patient monitoring (other tests may be warranted in some patients, depending on condition; » = major clinical significance):

» Diarrhea
(pseudomembranous colitis has been reported with nearly all antibiotic agents, and ranges in severity from mild to life-threatening; it is important to consider this diagnosis in patients who present with diarrhea subsequent to the administration of any antibacterial agent; once diagnosed therapeutic measures should be instituted)

» Hypersensitivity reactions
(serious and occasionally fatal hypersensitivity reactions and/or anaphylactic reactions have been reported; reactions may occur following the first dose; levofloxacin should be discontinued immediately at the first sign of an immediate type 1 hypersensitivity skin rash or any other manifestation of a hypersensitivity reaction)

Prothrombin time or
Anticoagulation tests, other
(because some quinolones have been reported to enhance the anticoagulant effects of warfarin or its derivatives the prothrombin time or other suitable coagulation tests should be closely monitored if a quinolone antimicrobial is administered concomitantly with warfarin or its derivatives)

Side/Adverse Effects

Note: There have been reports of ruptures of the Achilles tendon and of tendons in the shoulder and hand that required surgical repair or resulted in prolonged disability in patients taking levofloxacin or other fluoroquinolones. Patients should discontinue levofloxacin if they experience pain, inflammation, or rupture of a tendon. They should rest and refrain from exercise until the diagnosis of tendinitis or tendon rupture has been excluded. Tendon rupture can occur at any time during or after levofloxacin therapy.

The following side/adverse effects have been selected on the basis of their potential clinical significance (possible signs and symptoms in parentheses where appropriate)—not necessarily inclusive:

Those indicating need for medical attention

Incidence rare

Central nervous system (CNS) stimulation (agitation; confusion; hallucinations; psychosis, acute; tremors); ***hypersensitivity reactions*** (skin rash, itching, or redness); ***phototoxicity*** (blisters; itching; rash; redness; sensation of skin burning; swelling); ***pseudomembranous colitis*** (abdominal or stomach cramps and pain, severe; abdominal tenderness; diarrhea, watery and severe, which may also be bloody; fever); ***tendonitis or tendon rupture*** (pain, inflammation, or swelling in calves, shoulders, or hands)

Incidence not determined—Observed during clinical practice; estimates of frequency cannot be determined

Abnormal electroencephalogram (abnormal brain waves); ***allergic pneumonitis*** (difficult breathing); ***anaphylactic shock*** (sharp drop in blood pressure; hives); ***anaphylactoid reaction*** (cough; difficulty swallowing; dizziness; fast heartbeat; hives; itching; puffiness or swelling of the eyelids or around the eyes, face, lips or tongue; shortness of breath; skin rash; tightness in chest; unusual tiredness or weakness; wheezing); ***dysphonia*** (hoarseness; sore throat; voice changes); ***encephalopathy*** (blurred vision; coma; confusion; dizziness); ***eosinophilia*** (black, tarry stools; sore throat; swollen glands; unusual bleeding or bruising); ***erythema multiforme*** (blistering, peeling, loosening of skin; itching; joint or muscle pain); ***hemolytic anemia*** (bleeding gums; dark urine; fatigue; general body swelling); ***increased international normalized ratio/prothrombin time*** (increased bleeding time); ***multi-system organ failure*** (failure of the heart, lungs, kidneys and/or liver); ***peripheral neuropathy*** (burning, numbness, tingling, or painful sensations; weakness in arms, hands, legs, or feet; unsteadiness or awkwardness); ***rhabdomyolysis*** (dark-colored urine; fever; muscle cramps or spasms; muscle pain or stiffness; unusual tiredness or weakness); ***Stevens-Johnson Syndrome*** (blistering, peeling, loosening of skin; diarrhea itching; red skin); ***torsades de pointes*** (fast heartbeat; prolonged QT interval)

Those indicating need for medical attention if they continue or are bothersome

Incidence less frequent

CNS effects (dizziness; drowsiness; headache; lightheadedness; nervousness; trouble in sleeping); ***gastrointestinal effects*** (abdominal or stomach pain or discomfort; constipation; diarrhea; nausea; vomiting); ***taste perversion*** (change in sense of taste); ***vaginal candidiasis*** (vaginal itching and discharge)

Incidence not determined—Observed during clinical practice; estimates of frequency cannot be determined

Vasodilation (feeling of warmth or heat; flushing or redness of skin, especially on face and neck; headache; feeling faint, dizzy, or lightheadedness; sweating)

Those indicating possible pseudomembranous colitis and the need for medical attention if they occur after medication is discontinued

Abdominal or stomach cramps and pain, severe; abdominal tenderness; diarrhea, watery and severe, which may also be bloody; fever

Overdose

In the event of an acute levofloxacin overdose, the stomach should be emptied, the patient observed, and hydration maintained. Levofloxacin is not efficiently removed by hemodialysis or peritoneal dialysis.

Levofloxacin exhibits a low potential for acute toxicity. Mice, rats, dogs, and monkeys exhibited the following signs after receiving a single high dose of levofloxacin: ataxia, decreased locomotor activity, dyspnea, prostration, ptosis, seizures, and tremors. Doses greater than 1500 mg per kg of body weight (mg/kg) orally and 250 mg/kg intravenously produced significant morbidity in rodents.

For more information on the management of overdose or unintentional ingestion, **contact a Poison Control Center** (see *Poison Control Center Listing*).

Treatment of overdose

Supportive care—Patients in whom intentional overdose is confirmed or suspected should be referred for psychiatric consultation.

Patient Consultation

As an aid to patient consultation, refer to *Advice for the Patient, Levofloxacin (Systemic).*

In providing consultation, consider emphasizing the following selected information (» = major clinical significance):

Before using this medication

» Conditions affecting use, especially:

Previous drug allergy to levofloxacin or any other components of this product, or fluoroquinolones or other chemically related quinolone derivatives

Pregnancy—Levofloxacin is recommended for use during pregnancy only if the potential benefit to the mother outweighs the potential risk to the fetus, because levofloxacin has been shown to cause arthropathy in immature animals

Breast-feeding—It is not known whether levofloxacin is distributed into breast milk; however, caution should be exercised in making the decision whether to breast-feed, since levofloxacin has been shown to cause arthropathy in immature animals

Use in children—Safety and efficacy have not been established in children up to 18 years of age; for inhalation anthrax indication, risk/benefit should be considered in the individual patient; levofloxacin has been shown to cause arthropathy in immature animals

Use in the elderly—May have greater sensitivity due to levofloxacin effect on QT interval, increased risk of toxicity due to age-related renal function impairment, and increased risk of tendinitis and tendon rupture

Other medications, especially antidiabetic agents; aluminum-, calcium-, and/or magnesium-containing antacids; antiarrhythmic agents; didanosine; ferrous sulfate; nonsteroidal anti-inflammatory drugs; sucralfate; warfarin; or zinc

Other medical problems, especially bradycardia, diabetes mellitus, hypokalemia or renal function impairment

Proper use of this medication

» Levofloxacin *tablets* may be taken with or without food

Levofloxacin *oral solution* should be taken 1 hour before eating or 2 hours after eating.

Importance of maintaining adequate fluid intake

» Importance of beginning levofloxacin as soon as possible following suspected or confirmed exposure to anthrax

» Importance of not missing doses and taking at evenly spaced times

» Proper dosing

Missed dose: Taking as soon as possible; not taking if almost time for next dose; not doubling doses

» Proper storage

Precautions while using this medication

Checking with physician if no improvement within a few days

» Avoiding concurrent use of antacids, didanosine, ferrous sulfate, sucralfate, or zinc and levofloxacin; taking these products at least 2 hours before or 2 hours after administration of levofloxacin

(Avoid concurrent use of Class IA and Class III *antiarrhythmic agents.*)

» Possible phototoxicity reactions

» Discontinuing levofloxacin at the first sign of skin rash or other allergic reaction

» Caution when driving or doing anything else requiring alertness because of possible dizziness, drowsiness, or lightheadedness

» Discontinuing levofloxacin and notifying physician if pain, inflammation, or rupture of a tendon is experienced; resting and refraining from exercise until the diagnosis of tendinitis or tendon rupture has been excluded

» Discontinuing levofloxacin and contacting physician if patient is a diabetic being treated with insulin or an oral hypoglycemic agent and a hypoglycemic episode occurs

» Discontinuing levofloxacin and contacting physician if patient is hypokalemic and develops a fast, slow or irregular heartbeat

» Discontinuing levofloxacin and contacting physician if patient is bradycardic and develops a fast, slow or irregular heartbeat

Side/adverse effects

Signs of potential side effects, especially central nervous system stimulation, hypersensitivity reactions, phototoxicity, pseudomembranous colitis, tendinitis or tendon rupture, or torsades de pointes

Signs of potential side effects observed during post-marketing experience, especially abnormal electroencephalogram, allergic pneumonitis, anaphylactic shock, anaphylactoid reaction, dysphonia, encephalopathy, eosinophilia, erythema multiforme, hemolytic anemia, increased international normalized ration/prothrombin time, multi-system organ failure, peripheral neuropathy, rhabdomyolysis, Stevens-Johnson syndrome, or torsades de pointes

General Dosing Information

For parenteral dosage forms only

Because rapid intravenous injection may result in hypotension, levofloxacin should be administered only by slow intravenous infusion over a period of not less than 60 minutes and up to 90 minutes, depending on the dose.

Appropriate culture and susceptibility tests should be performed before treatment to isolate and identify the organism that is causing the infection and to determine their susceptibility to levofloxacin. Culture and susceptibility performed periodically during therapy will give information about the continued susceptibility of the pathogens and also about the possible emergence of bacterial resistance.

Levofloxacin concentrate for injection must be diluted prior to parenteral administration.

Diet/Nutrition

Levofloxacin oral solution should be taken 1 hour before eating a meal or 2 hours after eating a meal.

Levofloxacin tablets may be taken with or without food.

Bioequivalence information

The profile of serum levofloxacin concentration observed after intravenous administration is comparable to the extent of exposure (area under the plasma concentration-time curve) observed for oral administration of tablets when equal doses are administered (mg/mg). Therefore, the oral and intravenous routes of administration are considered to be interchangeable.

Levofloxacin tablet and oral solution are bioequivalent.

For treatment of adverse effects

• Some patients may develop antibiotic-associated pseudomembranous colitis (AAPMC), caused by *Clostridium difficile* toxin, during or after administration of levofloxacin. Mild cases may respond to discontinuation of the drug alone. Moderate to severe cases may require fluid, electrolyte, and protein replacement.

• In cases not responding to the above measures or in more severe cases, oral doses of an antibacterial medication effective against *C. difficile* should be administered.

• In addition, AAPMC may result in severe watery diarrhea, which may occur during therapy or up to several weeks after therapy is discontinued. If diarrhea occurs, administration of antiperistaltic antidiarrheals (e.g., diphenoxylate and atropine combination, loperamide, opiates) is not recommended since they may delay the removal of toxins from the colon, thereby prolonging and/or worsening the condition.

For antibiotic-associated pseudomembranous colitis (AAPMC)—

Oral Dosage Forms

LEVOFLOXACIN ORAL SOLUTION

Usual adult dose

Anthrax, inhalation (treatment)—

Oral, 500 mg every twenty-four hours for 60 days.

Note: Levofloxacin administration should begin as soon as possible after suspected or confirmed exposure to aerosolized *B. anthracis.* This indication is based on a surrogate endpoint. Levofloxacin plasma concentrations achieved in humans are reasonably likely to predict clinical benefit.

Safety of levofloxacin in adults for durations of therapy beyond 28 days has not been studied. Prolonged levofloxacin therapy in adults should only be used when risk/benefit has been considered.

Bronchitis, bacterial exacerbations, treatment—
Oral, 500 mg every twenty-four hours for seven days.

Pneumonia, community-acquired, treatment—
Oral, 500 mg every twenty-four hours for seven to fourteen days, or oral, 750 mg every twenty-four hours for five days. Efficacy of 750 mg regimen has been demonstrated to be effective for infections caused by *Streptococcus pneumoniae* (excluding MDRSP), *Haemophilus influenzae, Mycoplasma pneumoniae*, and *Chlamydia pneumoniae.*

Pneumonia, nosocomial—
Oral, 750 mg every twenty-four hours for seven to fourteen days.

Prostatitis—
Oral, 500 mg every twenty-four hours for twenty-eight days.

Pyelonephritis, treatment—
Oral, 250 mg every twenty-four hours for ten days.

Sinusitis, treatment—
Oral, either 750 mg every twenty-four hours for 5 days OR 500 mg every twenty-four hours for ten to fourteen days.

Skin and soft tissue infections, complicated, treatment—
Oral, 750 mg every twenty-four hours for seven to fourteen days.

Skin and soft tissue infections, uncomplicated, treatment—
Oral, 500 mg every twenty-four hours for seven to ten days.

Urinary tract infections, bacterial, complicated, treatment—
Oral, 250 mg every twenty-four hours for ten days.

Urinary tract infections, bacterial, uncomplicated, treatment—
Oral, 250 mg every twenty-four hours for three days.

Note: For patients with impaired renal function with *acute bacterial exacerbation of bronchitis, community acquired pneumonia, sinusitis, uncomplicated skin and soft tissue infections, chronic bacterial prostatitis, or inhalational anthrax (post-exposure)*, dosage adjustment is as follows:
- Creatinine clearance 50 to 80 mL per minute: no dosage adjustment
- Creatinine clearance 20 to 49 mL per minute: Oral, 500 mg initially then oral, 250 mg every twenty-four hours
- Creatinine clearance 10 to 19 mL per minute: Oral, 500 mg initially then oral, 250 mg every **forty-eight** hours
- Hemodialysis: Oral, 500 mg initially then oral, 250 mg every **forty-eight** hours
- CAPD: Oral, 500 mg initially then oral, 250 mg every **forty-eight** hours

For patients with impaired renal function with *complicated skin and soft tissue infections, nosocomial pneumonia or community acquired pneumonia*, dosage adjustment is as follows:
- Creatinine clearance 50 to 80 mL per minute: no dosage adjustment
- Creatinine clearance 20 to 49 mL per minute: Oral, 750 mg initially then oral, 750 mg every **forty-eight** hours
- Creatinine clearance 10 to 19 mL per minute: Oral, 750 mg initially then oral, 500 mg every **forty-eight** hours
- Hemodialysis: Oral, 750 mg initially then oral, 500 mg every **forty-eight** hours
- CAPD: Oral, 750 mg initially then oral, 500 mg every **forty-eight** hours

For patients with impaired renal function with *complicated urinary tract infection or acute pyelonephritis*, dosage adjustment is as follows:
- Creatinine clearance greater than or equal to 20 mL per minute: no dosage adjustment
- Creatinine clearance 10 to 19 mL per minute: Oral, 250 mg initially then oral, 250 mg every **forty-eight** hours

For patients with impaired renal function with *uncomplicated urinary tract infection*, no dosage adjustment is required.

Usual pediatric dose
Safety and efficacy have not been established.

Strength(s) usually available
U.S.—
25 mg per mL (Rx) [*Levaquin* (artificial and natural flavors; ascorbic acid; benzyl alcohol; caramel color; glycerin; hydrochloric acid; propylene glycol; purified water; sodium hydroxide; sucralose; sucrose)].

Canada—
Not commercially available.

Packaging and storage
Store at 25 °C (77 °F); excursions permitted between 15 and 30 °C (59 and 86 °F)

Auxiliary labeling
- Take on an empty stomach - 1 hour before or 2 hours after eating.
- Do not take dairy products, iron, or antacids 2 hours before to 2 hours after this drug.
- Drink plenty of fluids while taking this medication.
- May cause dizziness or drowsiness.
- Avoid extended exposure to sunlight or tanning beds while taking this drug. Severe burns may result.
- Finish all of this medication unless otherwise directed.

LEVOFLOXACIN TABLETS

Usual adult dose
Anthrax, inhalation (treatment)—
Oral, 500 mg every twenty-four hours for 60 days.

Note: Levofloxacin administration should begin as soon as possible after suspected or confirmed exposure to aerosolized *B. anthracis*. This indication is based on a surrogate endpoint. Levofloxacin plasma concentrations achieved in humans are reasonably likely to predict clinical benefit.

Safety of levofloxacin in adults for durations of therapy beyond 28 days has not been studied. Prolonged levofloxacin therapy in adults should only be used when risk/benefit has been considered.

Bronchitis, bacterial exacerbations, treatment—
Oral, 500 mg every twenty-four hours for seven days.

Pneumonia, community-acquired, treatment—
Oral, 500 mg every twenty-four hours for seven to fourteen days, or oral, 750 mg every twenty-four hours for five days. Efficacy of 750 mg regimen has been demonstrated to be effective for infections caused by *Streptococcus pneumoniae* (excluding MDRSP), *Haemophilus influenzae, Mycoplasma pneumoniae*, and *Chlamydia pneumoniae.*

Note: Canadian manufacturer recommends 10 to 14 days for severe infections.

Pneumonia, nosocomial, treatment—
Oral, 750 mg every twenty-four hours for seven to fourteen days.

Prostatitis, bacterial, chronic, treatment—
Oral, 500 mg every twenty-four hours for twenty-eight days.

Pyelonephritis, treatment—
Oral, 250 mg every twenty-four hours for ten days.

Sinusitis, treatment—
Oral, either 750 mg every twenty-four hours for 5 days OR 500 mg every twenty-four hours for ten to fourteen days.

Skin and soft tissue infections, complicated, treatment—
Oral, 750 mg every twenty-four hours for seven to fourteen days.

Note: Canadian manufacturer recommends 500 mg every twelve hours for seven to fourteen days.

Skin and soft tissue infections, uncomplicated, treatment—
Oral, 500 mg every twenty-four hours for seven to ten days.

Urinary tract infections, bacterial, complicated, treatment—
Oral, 250 mg every twenty-four hours for ten days.

Urinary tract infections, bacterial, uncomplicated, treatment—
Oral, 250 mg every twenty-four hours for three days.

Note: For patients with impaired renal function with *acute bacterial exacerbation of bronchitis, community acquired pneumonia, sinusitis, uncomplicated skin and soft tissue infections, chronic bacterial prostatitis, or inhalational anthrax (post-exposure)*, dosage adjustment is as follows:
- Creatinine clearance 50 to 80 mL per minute: no dosage adjustment
- Creatinine clearance 20 to 49 mL per minute: Oral, 500 mg initially then oral, 250 mg every twenty-four hours
- Creatinine clearance 10 to 19 mL per minute: Oral, 500 mg initially then oral, 250 mg every **forty-eight** hours
- Hemodialysis: Oral, 500 mg initially then oral, 250 mg every **forty-eight** hours
- CAPD: Oral, 500 mg initially then oral, 250 mg every **forty-eight** hours

For patients with impaired renal function with *complicated skin and soft tissue infections, nosocomial pneumonia or community acquired pneumonia*, dosage adjustment is as follows:
- Creatinine clearance 50 to 80 mL per minute: no dosage adjustment
- Creatinine clearance 20 to 49 mL per minute: Oral, 750 mg initially then oral, 750 mg every **forty-eight** hours

- Creatinine clearance 10 to 19 mL per minute: Oral, 750 mg initially then oral, 500 mg every **forty-eight** hours
- Hemodialysis: Oral, 750 mg initially then oral, 500 mg every **forty-eight** hours
- CAPD: Oral, 750 mg initially then oral, 500 mg every **forty-eight** hours

For patients with impaired renal function with *complicated urinary tract infection or acute pyelonephritis*, dosage adjustment is as follows:

- Creatinine clearance greater than or equal to 20 mL per minute: no dosage adjustment
- Creatinine clearance 10 to 19 mL per minute: Oral, 250 mg initially then oral, 250 mg every **forty-eight** hours

For patients with impaired renal function with *uncomplicated urinary tract infection*, no dosage adjustment is required.

Usual pediatric dose

Safety and efficacy have not been established.

Strength(s) usually available

U.S.—

250 mg (Rx) [*Levaquin* (hypromellose; crospovidone; microcrystalline cellulose; magnesium stearate; polyethylene glycol; titanium dioxide; polysorbate 80; synthetic red iron oxide)].

500 mg (Rx) [*Levaquin* (hypromellose; crospovidone; microcrystalline cellulose; magnesium stearate; polyethylene glycol; titanium dioxide; polysorbate 80; synthetic red iron oxide; synthetic yellow iron oxide)].

750 mg (Rx) [*Levaquin* (hypromellose; crospovidone; microcrystalline cellulose; magnesium stearate; polyethylene glycol; titanium dioxide; polysorbate 80)].

Canada—

250 mg (Rx) [*Levaquin* (hydroxypropyl methylcellulose; crospovidone; microcrystalline cellulose; magnesium stearate; polyethylene glycol; titanium dioxide; polysorbate 80; synthetic red iron oxide)].

500 mg (Rx) [*Levaquin* (hydroxypropyl methylcellulose; crospovidone; microcrystalline cellulose; magnesium stearate; polyethylene glycol; titanium dioxide; polysorbate 80; synthetic red iron oxide; synthetic yellow iron oxide)].

Packaging and storage

Store below 40 °C (104 °F), preferably between 15 and 30 °C (59 and 86 °F), unless otherwise specified by manufacturer.

Auxiliary labeling

- Continue medicine for the full time of treatment.
- Avoid too much sun exposure or use of sunlamp.
- Take with full glass of water.
- May cause dizziness, drowsiness, or lightheadedness.

Parenteral Dosage Forms

LEVOFLOXACIN FOR INJECTION

Usual adult dose

Anthrax, inhalation (treatment)—

Intravenous infusion, 500 mg, administered over a 60-minute period, every twenty-four hours for 60 days.

Note: Levofloxacin administration should begin as soon as possible after suspected or confirmed exposure to aerosolized *B. anthracis*. This indication is based on a surrogate endpoint. Levofloxacin plasma concentrations achieved in humans are reasonably likely to predict clinical benefit.

Safety of levofloxacin in adults for durations of therapy beyond 28 days has not been studied. Prolonged levofloxacin therapy in adults should only be used when risk/benefit has been considered.

Bronchitis, bacterial exacerbations, treatment—

Intravenous infusion, 500 mg, administered over a 60-minute period, every twenty-four hours for seven days.

Pneumonia, community-acquired, treatment—

Intravenous infusion, 500 mg, administered over a 60-minute period, every twenty-four hours for seven to fourteen days.or intravenous infusion, 750 mg administered over a 90-minute period, every twenty-four hours for five days. Efficacy of 750 mg regimen has been demonstrated to be effective for infections caused by *Streptococcus pneumoniae* (excluding MDRSP), *Haemophilus influenzae*, *Mycoplasma pneumoniae*, and *Chlamydia pneumoniae*.

Note: Canadian manufacturer recommends 10 to 14 days for severe infections.

Pneumonia, nosocomial—

Intravenous infusion, 750 mg administered over a 90-minute period, every twenty-four hours for seven to fourteen days.

Prostatitis—

Intravenous infusion, 500 mg administered over a 60-minute period, every twenty-four hours for twenty-eight days.

Pyelonephritis, treatment—

Intravenous infusion, 250 mg, administered over a 60-minute period, every twenty-four hours for ten days.

Sinusitis, treatment—

Intravenous infusion, 500 mg, administered over a 60-minute period, every twenty-four hours for ten to fourteen days.

Skin and soft tissue infections, complicated, treatment—

Intravenous infusion, 750 mg administered over a 90 minute period, every twenty-four hours for seven to fourteen days.

Note: Canadian manufacturer recommends 500 mg every twelve hours for seven to fourteen days.

Skin and soft tissue infections, uncomplicated, treatment—

Intravenous infusion, 500 mg administered over a 60-minute period, every twenty-four hours for seven to ten days.

Urinary tract infections, bacterial, complicated, treatment—

Intravenous infusion, 250 mg, administered over a 60-minute period, every twenty-four hours for ten days.

Urinary tract infections, bacterial, uncomplicated, treatment—

Intravenous infusion, 250 mg every twenty-four hours for three days.

Note: For patients with impaired renal function with *acute bacterial exacerbation of bronchitis, community acquired pneumonia, sinusitis, uncomplicated skin and soft tissue infections, chronic bacterial prostatitis, or inhalational anthrax (post-exposure)*, dosage adjustment is as follows:

- Creatinine clearance 50 to 80 mL per minute: no dosage adjustment
- Creatinine clearance 20 to 49 mL per minute: Intravenous infusion, 500 mg initially then intravenous infusion, 250 mg every twenty-four hours
- Creatinine clearance 10 to 19 mL per minute: Intravenous infusion, 500 mg initially then intravenous infusion, 250 mg every **forty-eight** hours
- Hemodialysis: Intravenous infusion, 500 mg initially then intravenous infusion, 250 mg every **forty-eight** hours
- CAPD: Intravenous infusion, 500 mg initially then intravenous infusion, 250 mg every **forty-eight** hours

For patients with impaired renal function with *complicated skin and soft tissue infections, nosocomial pneumonia or community acquired pneumonia*, dosage adjustment is as follows:

- Creatinine clearance 50 to 80 mL per minute: no dosage adjustment
- Creatinine clearance 20 to 49 mL per minute: Intravenous infusion, 750 mg initially then intravenous infusion, 750 mg every **forty-eight** hours
- Creatinine clearance 10 to 19 mL per minute: Intravenous infusion, 750 mg initially then intravenous infusion, 500 mg every **forty-eight** hours
- Hemodialysis: Intravenous infusion, 750 mg initially then intravenous infusion, 500 mg every **forty-eight** hours
- CAPD: Intravenous infusion, 750 mg initially then intravenous infusion, 500 mg every **forty-eight** hours

For patients with impaired renal function with *complicated urinary tract infection or acute pyelonephritis*, dosage adjustment is as follows:

- Creatinine clearance greater than or equal to 20 mL per minute: no dosage adjustment
- Creatinine clearance 10 to 19 mL per minute: Intravenous infusion, 250 mg initially then intravenous infusion, 250 mg every **forty-eight** hours

For patients with impaired renal function with *uncomplicated urinary tract infection*, no dosage adjustment is required.

Usual pediatric dose

Safety and efficacy have not been established.

Strength(s) usually available

U.S.—

500 mg per 20 mL (Rx) [*Levaquin*].

750 mg per 30 mL (Rx) [*Levaquin*].

Canada—

500 mg per 20 mL (Rx) [*Levaquin*].

Packaging and storage

Store below 40 °C (104 °F), preferably between 15 and 30 °C (59 and 86 °F), unless otherwise specified by the manufacturer. Protect from light.

Preparation of dosage form
Levofloxacin for injection must be further diluted with compatible intravenous fluids prior to intravenous administration. The concentration of the resulting diluted solution must be 5 mg/mL prior to administration.

To prepare a 250-mg dose for intravenous infusion, withdraw 10 mL of levofloxacin concentrate for injection from the vial and dilute with 40 mL of a compatible intravenous solution, for a total volume of 50 mL. To prepare a 500-mg dose, withdraw 20 mL of levofloxacin concentrate for injection from the vial and dilute with 80 mL of a compatible intravenous solution, for a total volume of 100 mL.

To prepare a 750-mg dose for intravenous infusion, withdraw 30 mL of levofloxacin concentrate for injection from the vial and dilute with 120 mL of a compatible intravenous solution, for a total volume of 150 mL.

Stability
When diluted to a concentration of 5 mg per mL, levofloxacin concentrate for injection is stable for 72 hours when stored at or below 25 °C (77 °F) and for 14 days when refrigerated (5 °C [41 °F]) in plastic intravenous containers. Diluted solutions that are frozen in glass bottles or plastic containers are stable for 6 months when stored at -20 °C (-4 °F). Frozen solutions should be thawed at room temperature or in a refrigerator. They should not be thawed in a microwave or by water bath immersion. Do not refreeze after initial thawing.

Incompatibilities
Because there is only limited data on the compatibility of other substances with levofloxacin concentrate for injection, additives or other medications should not be added to levofloxacin concentrate for injection in the single-use vials or infused simultaneously through the same intravenous line.

Note
This product should be inspected visually for any particulate matter before administration. Samples with visible particles should be discarded.

Levofloxacin concentrate for injection contains no preservative or bacteriostatic agent. Because of this, the vials are for single use only; any unused portion remaining in the vial should be discarded.

LEVOFLOXACIN INJECTION

Usual adult dose
See *Levofloxacin For Injection.*

Usual pediatric dose
See *Levofloxacin For Injection.*

Strength(s) usually available
U.S.—
250 mg per 50 mL (Rx) [*Levaquin*].
500 mg per 100 mL (Rx) [*Levaquin* (5% Dextrose)].
750 mg per 150 mL (Rx) [*Levaquin* (5% Dextrose)].

Canada—
250 mg per 50 mL (Rx) [*Levaquin* (5% Dextrose)].
500 mg per 100 mL (Rx) [*Levaquin* (5% Dextrose)].

Packaging and storage
Store at or below 25 °C (77 °F); however, brief exposure up to 40 °C (104 °F) does not adversely affect the product. Protect from excessive heat, freezing, and light.

Incompatibilities
Because there are only limited data on the compatibility of other substances with levofloxacin injection, additives or other medications should not be added to levofloxacin injection in the single-use vials or infused simultaneously through the same intravenous line.

Note
This product should be inspected visually for any particulate matter before administration. Samples with visible particles should be discarded.

Levofloxacin pre-mix injection flexible containers are for single use only; any unused portion should be discarded.

Do not use levofloxacin flexible containers in series connections

Revised: 04/19/2006
Developed: 07/31/1997

LEVONORGESTROL—See *Progestins (Systemic)*

LEVORPHANOL—See *Opioid (Narcotic) Analgesics (Systemic)*

LEVOTHYROXINE—See *Thyroid Hormones (Systemic)*

LIDOCAINE—See *Anesthetics (Mucosal-Local), Anesthetics (Parenteral-Local), Anesthetics (Topical), Lidocaine (Systemic)*

LIDOCAINE Systemic

VA CLASSIFICATION (Primary): CV300

Commonly used brand name(s): *Xylocaine; Xylocard.*

Note: For a listing of dosage forms and brand names by country availability, see *Dosage Forms* section(s).

Category
Antiarrhythmic.

Indications

Accepted
Arrhythmias, ventricular (treatment)—Lidocaine (systemic) is indicated and is the drug of choice in the acute management of ventricular arrhythmias, such as those resulting from acute myocardial infarction, digitalis toxicity, cardiac surgery, or cardiac catheterization.

Pharmacology/Pharmacokinetics

Physicochemical characteristics
pKa—7.86.

Mechanism of action/Effect
Antiarrhythmic—Lidocaine decreases the depolarization, automaticity, and excitability in the ventricles during the diastolic phase by a direct action on the tissues, especially the Purkinje network, without involvement of the autonomic system. Neither contractility, systolic arterial blood pressure, atrioventricular (AV) conduction velocity, nor absolute refractory period is altered by usual therapeutic doses. In the Vaughan Williams classification of antiarrhythmics, lidocaine is a class IB agent.

Distribution
Rapid. Volume of distribution (Vol_D)—About 1 liter per kg of body weight (L/kg); reduced in heart failure patients.

Protein binding
Moderate to high (60 to 80%; dependent on drug concentration).

Biotransformation
90% hepatic; active metabolites, monoethylglycinexylidide and glycinexylidide, may contribute to therapeutic and toxic effects, especially after infusions lasting 24 hours or more.

Half-life
1 to 2 hours (average about 100 minutes); dose-dependent (tends to be biphasic with the distribution phase of 7 to 9 minutes causing the short duration of action following an intravenous loading dose); increased to 3 hours or longer during prolonged intravenous infusions (longer than 24 hours).

Onset of action
Intravenous—Immediate (45 to 90 seconds).

Time to steady-state plasma concentration
Continuous intravenous infusion—3 to 4 hours (8 to 10 hours in patients with acute myocardial infarction).

Therapeutic plasma concentration
1.5 to 5 mcg/mL (concentrations exceeding 5 mcg/mL are considered to be in the toxic range).

Duration of action
Intravenous—10 to 20 minutes.

Elimination
Renal, 10% unchanged.
In dialysis—Very little removable by dialysis.

Precautions to Consider

Cross-sensitivity and/or related problems
Patients sensitive to other amide-type anesthetics or flecainide or tocainide may be sensitive to lidocaine also. Cross-sensitivity with procainamide or quinidine has not been reported.

Carcinogenicity/Mutagenicity
Long-term animal studies evaluating the carcinogenic or mutagenic potential of lidocaine have not been done.

Pregnancy/Reproduction
Pregnancy—Lidocaine crosses the placenta. Adequate and well-controlled studies in humans have not been done.

Studies in rats given doses up to 6.6 times the maximum human dose have not shown that lidocaine causes adverse effects in the fetus. However, lidocaine has been shown to constrict uterine arteries in sheep and in experimentally isolated uterine artery segments. Furthermore, studies in sheep have shown that lidocaine causes significant increases in fetal blood pressure and increases or decreases in fetal heart rate related to the rate of lidocaine infusion.

FDA Pregnancy Category B.

Breast-feeding
It is not known whether lidocaine is distributed into human breast milk. However, problems in humans have not been documented.

Pediatrics
Appropriate studies on the relationship of age to the effects of lidocaine have not been performed in the pediatric population. However, no pediatrics-specific problems have been documented to date.

Geriatrics
Elderly patients are more prone to the adverse effects of lidocaine. In patients over 65 years of age, dose and rate of infusion should be reduced by one half and adjusted slowly as needed and tolerated. In addition, elderly patients are more likely to have age-related renal function impairment, which may require dosage adjustment.

Drug interactions and/or related problems
The following drug interactions and/or related problems have been selected on the basis of their potential clinical significance (possible mechanism in parentheses where appropriate)—not necessarily inclusive (» = major clinical significance):

Note: Combinations containing any of the following medications, depending on the amount present, may also interact with this medication.

Antiarrhythmics, other
(although some antiarrhythmic agents may be used in combination for therapeutic advantage, combined use may sometimes potentiate risk of adverse cardiac effects)

» Anticonvulsants, hydantoin
(concurrent use with lidocaine may have additive cardiac depressant effects; hydantoin anticonvulsants may also promote increased hepatic metabolism of lidocaine, reducing its intravenous concentration)

Beta-adrenergic blocking agents, systemic and ophthalmic (if systemic absorption occurs)
(concurrent use may slow hepatic metabolism and increase the risk of toxicity of lidocaine because of reduced hepatic blood flow)

Cimetidine
(concurrent administration with lidocaine may result in reduced hepatic clearance of lidocaine, possibly resulting in delayed elimination and increased blood concentrations; monitoring of blood concentrations and clinical parameters as a guide to dosage is recommended)

Neuromuscular blocking agents
(effects may be potentiated when used concurrently with large doses [such as those over 5 mg per kg] of intravenous lidocaine)

Laboratory value alterations
The following have been selected on the basis of their potential clinical significance (possible effect in parentheses where appropriate)—not necessarily inclusive (» = major clinical significance).

With diagnostic test results

Bentiromide
(concurrent administration of lidocaine during a bentiromide test period will invalidate test results since lidocaine is also metabolized to arylamines and will thus increase the percent of PABA recovered; discontinuation of lidocaine at least 3 days prior to the administration of bentiromide is recommended)

Medical considerations/Contraindications
The medical considerations/contraindications included have been selected on the basis of their potential clinical significance (reasons given in parentheses where appropriate)—not necessarily inclusive (» = major clinical significance).

Except under special circumstances, this medication should not be used when the following medical problems exist:

» Adams-Stokes syndrome or
» Heart block, severe, including atrioventricular, intraventricular, or sinoatrial blocks
(heart block may be worsened)

Risk-benefit should be considered when the following medical problems exist:

» Congestive heart failure or
Hepatic function impairment or
» Reduced hepatic blood flow or
Renal function impairment
(accumulation may occur; dose and rate of infusion should be reduced by one half)

» Heart block, incomplete or
» Hypovolemia and shock or
» Sinus bradycardia or
» Wolff-Parkinson-White syndrome
(may be aggravated)

Sensitivity to lidocaine

Patient monitoring
The following may be especially important in patient monitoring (other tests may be warranted in some patients, depending on condition; » = major clinical significance):

Blood pressure determinations and
» Electrocardiograph (ECG) determinations
(recommended throughout therapy to help adjust dosage and detect toxicity; intravenous infusion of lidocaine should be promptly discontinued if ECG determinations show a prolonged PR interval and QRS complex or if arrhythmias occur or become worse)

Electrolyte concentrations, serum
(periodic to allow imbalance corrections during prolonged infusions)

Lidocaine concentrations, serum
(useful to avoid toxicity during prolonged or high-dose infusions or in patients receiving drugs that alter lidocaine clearance)

Side/Adverse Effects

Note: Adverse effects are dose- and age-related; incidence is increased in patients over 65 years of age.

Adverse cardiovascular effects at therapeutic doses are rare, except in patients with existing compromised ventricular function. Cardiac conduction disturbances are extremely rare. High plasma lidocaine concentrations may lead to hypotension, arrhythmias, heart block, and respiratory and cardiac arrest.

The following side/adverse effects have been selected on the basis of their potential clinical significance (possible signs and symptoms in parentheses where appropriate)—not necessarily inclusive:

Those indicating need for medical attention
Incidence rare

Allergic reaction (difficulty in breathing; itching; skin rash; swelling of skin)

Those indicating need for medical attention only if they continue or are bothersome
Incidence less frequent or rare

Pain at site of injection—with prolonged intravenous use

Incidence dose-related

With serum lidocaine concentrations of 1.5 to 6 mcg/mL

Anxiety or nervousness; dizziness; drowsiness; feelings of coldness, heat, or numbness

Overdose
For more information on the management of overdose or unintentional ingestion, **contact a Poison Control Center** (see *Poison Control Center Listing*).

Clinical effects of overdose
The following effects have been selected on the basis of their potential clinical significance (possible signs and symptoms in parentheses where appropriate)—not necessarily inclusive:

With serum lidocaine concentrations of 6 to 8 mcg/mL

Blurred or double vision; nausea or vomiting; ringing in ears; tremors or twitching

With serum lidocaine concentrations of > 8 mcg/mL

Difficulty in breathing; dizziness, severe, or fainting; seizures; slow heartbeat

Treatment of overdose
For severe reactions—
Stopping administration of lidocaine; monitoring patient closely.
Maintenance of airway and administration of oxygen.

Specific treatment—

For circulatory depression—Administration of a vasopressor (such as ephedrine or metaraminol) and intravenous fluids if necessary.

For seizures—If no satisfactory response to respiratory support is obtained, diazepam in 2.5-mg increments, or an ultra-short-acting barbiturate (such as thiopental or thiamylal) in 50- to 100-mg increments, is often beneficial. Caution must be maintained because of possible additive circulatory depression. If patient is under anesthesia, a short-acting muscle relaxant (such as succinylcholine) administered intravenously is sometimes helpful. When such relaxants are used, ability to provide artificial respiration is mandatory.

General Dosing Information

See also *Patient monitoring.*

Dosage should be adjusted to meet the individual requirements of each patient, on the basis of clinical response.

The use of lidocaine necessitates concurrent ECG monitoring and the availability of oxygen, resuscitation equipment, and emergency medications for the management of possible adverse reactions involving the cardiovascular system and/or central nervous system (CNS) as well as possible allergic reactions.

For intravenous administration

For intravenous regional anesthesia, a preservative-free, epinephrine-free lidocaine 0.5% injection should be administered.

The preferred diluent for lidocaine infusion is 5% dextrose injection.

Lidocaine must *not* be added to blood transfusions.

To achieve optimal control of lidocaine dosage and rate of administration, it is recommended that lidocaine be administered intravenously by means of an infusion pump, a microdrip regulator, or a similar device that allows precise adjustment of the flow rate.

A loading dose of lidocaine is commonly administered for the initial intravenous dose to partially compensate for its rapid perfusion and distribution, which tend to delay attainment of a therapeutic serum concentration. If the initial loading dose does not provide the desired effect within 5 minutes, a second loading dose reduced to one half to one third of the first dose may be given.

Dosage reduction may be required with prolonged intravenous infusions (longer than 24 hours) because of the risk of accumulation.

Parenteral Dosage Forms

LIDOCAINE HYDROCHLORIDE INJECTION (FOR CONTINUOUS INTRAVENOUS INFUSION) USP

Usual adult dose

Antiarrhythmic—

Continuous intravenous infusion (usually following a loading dose), 1 to 4 mg per minute (20 to 50 mcg per kg of body weight per minute).

Note: Infusion rates should be decreased in older patients and patients with congestive heart failure or hepatic dysfunction to avoid lidocaine toxicity.

Usual adult prescribing limits

300 mg (about 4.5 mg per kg of body weight) in any one-hour period.

Usual pediatric dose

Antiarrhythmic—

Continuous intravenous infusion (usually following a loading dose), 30 mcg (range, 20 to 50 mcg) (0.03 mg; range, 0.02 to 0.05 mg) per kg of body weight per minute. Rate of infusion should not exceed usual adult rate of 4 mg per minute.

Strength(s) usually available

U.S.—

4% w/v (40 mg per mL [1 gram per 25 mL or 2 grams per 50 mL]) (Rx) [*Xylocaine* (preservative-free); GENERIC (may contain methylparaben)].

10% w/v (100 mg per mL [1 gram per 10 mL]) (Rx) [GENERIC (may contain methylparaben)].

20% w/v (200 mg per mL [1 gram per 5 mL or 2 grams per 10 mL]) (Rx) [*Xylocaine* (preservative-free); GENERIC (may contain methylparaben)].

Canada—

2% (20 mg per mL [1 gram per 50 mL]) (Rx) [*Xylocard*].

20% (200 mg per mL [1 gram per 5 mL]) (Rx) [*Xylocard*].

Packaging and storage

Store below 40 °C (104 °F), preferably between 15 and 30 °C (59 and 86 °F). Protect from freezing.

Preparation of dosage form

To prepare solution for intravenous infusion, add 1 gram of lidocaine hydrochloride (25 mL of 4% or 5 mL of 20% Lidocaine Hydrochloride Injection USP) to 1 liter of 5% dextrose injection; the resultant concentration will be 1 mg per mL. Check manufacturer's package insert for additional dilution information.

Stability

After dilution in the appropriate intravenous solution for infusion, lidocaine hydrochloride is stable for at least 24 hours.

Auxiliary labeling

Following dilution, a label stating the concentration of the lidocaine hydrochloride contents with time and date of dilution should be placed on the infusion solution container.

LIDOCAINE HYDROCHLORIDE INJECTION (FOR DIRECT INTRAVENOUS INJECTION) USP

Usual adult dose

Antiarrhythmic—

Direct intravenous injection, 1 mg per kg of body weight (usually 50 to 100 mg) as a loading dose at a rate of about 25 to 50 mg per minute, the dose being repeated after five minutes if necessary; usually followed by continuous intravenous infusion of lidocaine to maintain antiarrhythmic effects.

Note: Geriatric patients may be more sensitive to the effects of the usual adult dose.

Usual adult prescribing limits

300 mg (about 4.5 mg per kg of body weight) in any one-hour period.

Usual pediatric dose

Antiarrhythmic—

Direct intravenous injection, 1 mg per kg of body weight as a loading dose at a rate of about 25 to 50 mg per minute, the dose being repeated after five minutes if necessary but not exceeding a total dose of 3 mg per kg; usually followed by continuous intravenous infusion of lidocaine to maintain antiarrhythmic effects.

Strength(s) usually available

U.S.—

1% w/v (10 mg per mL [50 mg per 5 mL or 100 mg per 10 mL]) (Rx) [*Xylocaine* (preservative-free); GENERIC (may contain methylparaben)].

2% w/v (20 mg per mL [100 mg per 5 mL]) (Rx) [*Xylocaine* (preservative-free); GENERIC (may contain methylparaben)].

Canada—

2% w/v (20 mg per mL [100 mg per 5 mL]) (Rx) [*Xylocard;* GENERIC].

Packaging and storage

Store below 40 °C (104 °F), preferably between 15 and 30 °C (59 and 86 °F). Protect from freezing.

Stability

When dilution is required, it should be done immediately prior to direct intravenous administration.

STERILE LIDOCAINE HYDROCHLORIDE USP

Usual adult dose

Antiarrhythmic—

Continuous intravenous infusion (usually following a loading dose), 1 to 4 mg per minute (20 to 50 mcg per kg of body weight per minute).

Note: Infusion rates should be decreased in older patients and patients with congestive heart failure or hepatic dysfunction to avoid lidocaine toxicity.

Usual adult prescribing limits

300 mg (about 4.5 mg per kg of body weight) in any one-hour period.

Usual pediatric dose

Antiarrhythmic—

Continuous intravenous infusion (usually following a loading dose), 30 mcg (0.03 mg) (range, 20 to 50 mcg) per kg of body weight per minute. Rate of infusion should not exceed usual adult rate of 4 mg per minute.

Strength(s) usually available

U.S.—

1 gram (Rx) [GENERIC].

2 grams (Rx) [GENERIC].

Canada—

Not commercially available.

Packaging and storage

Store below 40 °C (104 °F), preferably between 15 and 30 °C (59 and 86 °F).

Preparation of dosage form

Sterile Lidocaine Hydrochloride USP is prepared for continuous intravenous infusion by adding 1 or 2 grams to 1000 mL of 5% dextrose injection, producing a solution containing 1 or 2 mg of lidocaine hydrochloride per mL, respectively. Check manufacturer's package insert for additional dilution information.

Stability

After dilution in the appropriate intravenous solution for infusion, lidocaine hydrochloride is stable for at least 24 hours.

Auxiliary labeling

Following dilution, a label stating the concentration of the lidocaine hydrochloride contents with time and date of dilution should be placed on the infusion solution container.

LIDOCAINE HYDROCHLORIDE AND DEXTROSE INJECTION (FOR CONTINUOUS INTRAVENOUS INFUSION) USP

Usual adult dose

Antiarrhythmic—

Continuous intravenous infusion (usually following a loading dose), 1 to 4 mg per minute (20 to 50 mcg per kg of body weight per minute).

Note: Infusion rates should be decreased in older patients and patients with congestive heart failure or hepatic dysfunction to avoid lidocaine toxicity.

Usual adult prescribing limits

300 mg (about 4.5 mg per kg of body weight) in any one-hour period.

Usual pediatric dose

Antiarrhythmic—

Continuous intravenous infusion (usually following a loading dose), 30 mcg (range, 20 to 50 mcg) (0.03 mg; range, 0.02 to 0.05 mg) of lidocaine hydrochloride per kg of body weight per minute. Rate of infusion should not exceed usual adult rate of 4 mg per minute.

Strength(s) usually available

U.S.—

Lidocaine Hydrochloride:

0.1% w/v (1 mg per mL [250 mg per 250 mL, 500 mg per 500 mL, or 1 gram per 1000 mL]) (Rx) [GENERIC].

0.2% w/v (2 mg per mL [500 mg per 250 mL, 1 gram per 500 mL or 2 grams per 1000 mL]) (Rx) [GENERIC].

0.4% w/v (4 mg per mL [1 gram per 250 mL, 2 grams per 500 mL, or 4 grams per 1000 mL]) (Rx) [GENERIC].

0.8% w/v (8 mg per mL [2 grams per 250 mL, 4 grams per 500 mL, 8 grams per 1000 mL]) (Rx) [GENERIC].

Canada—

Lidocaine Hydrochloride:

0.1% w/v (1 mg per mL [250 mg per 250 mL, 500 mg per 500 mL, or 1 gram per 1000 mL]) (Rx) [GENERIC].

0.2% w/v (2 mg per mL [500 mg per 250 mL, 1 gram per 500 mL, or 2 grams per 1000 mL]) (Rx) [GENERIC].

0.4% w/v (4 mg per mL [1 gram per 250 mL, 2 grams per 500 mL, or 4 grams per 1000 mL]) (Rx) [GENERIC].

0.8% w/v (8 mg per mL [2 grams per 250 mL or 4 grams per 500 mL]) (Rx) [GENERIC].

Packaging and storage

Store below 40 °C (104 °F), preferably between 15 and 30 °C (59 and 86 °F). Protect from freezing.

Selected Bibliography

Anderson JL. Current understanding of lidocaine as an antiarrhythmic agent: a review. Clin Ther 1984; 1986(2): 125-44.

Revised: 12/15/2003

LIDOCAINE Topical

INN: none; BAN: Lignocaine

VA CLASSIFICATION (Primary): DE700

Commonly used brand name(s): *Lidoderm*.

Note: For a listing of dosage forms and brand names by country availability, see *Dosage Forms* section(s).

Category

Anesthetic (local).

Indications

General Considerations

In clinical studies, lidocaine topical systems were found to be superior to vehicle topical systems (placebo) in relieving the pain of postherpetic neuralgia.

Accepted

Postherpetic neuralgia (treatment)—Lidocaine topical systems are indicated for application to normal, intact skin, for relief of pain associated with postherpetic neuralgia.

Pharmacology/Pharmacokinetics

Physicochemical characteristics

Chemical Group—Lidocaine is an amide–type local anesthetic

Molecular weight—234.34.

pKa—7.9.

Partition coefficient—

Octanol–to–aqueous buffer solution (pH 7.4) partition coefficient—43

Mechanism of action/Effect

Lidocaine blocks both initiation and conduction of nerve impulses by decreasing ionic flux through the neuronal membrane. The penetration of lidocaine through intact skin will produce an analgesic effect but is not sufficient to produce complete sensory block.

Other actions/effects

This medication may produce erythema, edema, or an abnormal sensation at the application site. When lidocaine topical systems are used appropriately, systemic effects are unlikely due to the small amount of lidocaine absorbed.

Absorption

Systemic absorption of lidocaine from the topical system is dependent on the thickness of the skin, the duration of application, and the surface area over which it is applied. When used according to the recommended instructions, approximately 3% of the applied dose is absorbed.

Distribution

Lidocaine crosses the blood-brain barrier and the placenta, presumably by passive diffusion.

The volume of distribution (Vol_D) following intravenous administration is 0.7 to 2.7 liters per kilogram of body weight (L/kg).

Protein binding

High (70%), primarily to alpha–1–acid glycoprotein, at plasma concentrations produced by application of this topical product. At much higher plasma concentrations (1 to 4 micrograms per milliliter [mcg/mL]), binding is dependent on the concentration.

Biotransformation

Hepatic; rapid. Two metabolites (monoethylglycinexylidide and glycinexylidide) have pharmacologic activity similar to, but less potent than, lidocaine; another metabolite (2,6-xylidine) has unknown activity and may be more toxic than lidocaine, but blood levels of this metabolite are negligible following application of the lidocaine topical system. Whether metabolism occurs in the skin after topical application has not been determined.

Half-life

Elimination–81 to 149 minutes (mean 107 ± 22 minutes; determined after intravenous administration).

Time to peak concentration

Application to normal, intact skin–Time to peak plasma concentration is dependent on the thickness of the skin, the duration of application, and the surface area over which it is applied. In general, when 3 topical systems are applied to intact skin on a patient's back, covering an area of 420 square centimeters, and worn for 12 hours, the peak blood concentration of lidocaine occurs 11 hours after application.

Peak serum concentration

Application to normal, intact skin–Peak plasma concentration is dependent on the thickness of the skin, the duration of application, and the surface area over which it is applied. In general, when 3 topical systems are applied to intact skin on a patient's back, covering an area of 420 square centimeters, and worn for 12 hours, the mean peak blood concentration of lidocaine is about 0.13 mcg/mL. Concentrations higher than 0.25 mcg/mL have been reported.

Elimination

Lidocaine and its metabolites are renally excreted; < 10% is excreted as unchanged lidocaine. Systemic clearance is 0.33 to 0.90 L/min (mean 0.64 ± 0.18 L/min).

Precautions to Consider

Cross-sensitivity and/or related problems
Patients sensitive to other amide-type local anesthetics may be sensitive to lidocaine.

Carcinogenicity
The minor metabolite, 2,6-xylidine, has been shown to be carcinogenic in rats; however, the blood concentration of this metabolite is negligible following application of the lidocaine topical system.

Mutagenicity
Lidocaine hydrochloride was not shown to be mutagenic in the Salmonella/mammalian microsome test nor clastogenic in chromosome aberration assay with human lymphocytes and mouse micronucleus test.

Pregnancy/Reproduction
Fertility—Effects are unknown; studies have not been done.

Pregnancy—Lidocaine crosses the placenta. Adequate and well-controlled studies have not been done in humans. Studies in rats given subcutaneous injections of lidocaine at doses up to 30 milligrams per kilogram of body weight (mg/kg) have not shown evidence of harm to the fetus.

FDA Pregnancy Category B.

Labor and delivery—Studies of lidocaine topical systems have not been done in labor and delivery; however, lidocaine is not contraindicated in labor and delivery.

Breast-feeding
Lidocaine topical systems have not been studied in nursing mothers; however, lidocaine is distributed into breast milk and the milk:plasma ratio of lidocaine is 0.4.

Pediatrics
Appropriate studies on the relationship of age to the effects of the lidocaine topical system have not been performed in the pediatric population. Safety and efficacy have not been established.

Geriatrics
No information is available on the relationship of age to the effects of lidocaine topical systems in geriatric patients.

Drug interactions and/or related problems
The following drug interactions and/or related problems have been selected on the basis of their potential clinical significance (possible mechanism in parentheses where appropriate)—not necessarily inclusive (» = major clinical significance):

Note: Combinations containing any of the following medications, depending on the amount present, may also interact with this medication.

Anesthetics, local
(when used concomitantly with lidocaine topical systems, the amount absorbed from all formulations must be considered)

Antiarrhythmics
(class I antiarrhythmics such as tocainide and mexiletine should be used with caution in patients using lidocaine topical systems, since the toxic effects are additive and potentially synergistic)

Medical considerations/Contraindications
The medical considerations/contraindications included have been selected on the basis of their potential clinical significance (reasons given in parentheses where appropriate)—not necessarily inclusive (» = major clinical significance).

Except under special circumstances, this medication should not be used when the following medical problem exists:

» Sensitivity to lidocaine or other amide-type local anesthetics

Risk-benefit should be considered when the following medical problems exist :

» Burned, broken or inflamed skin
(absorption may be increased, resulting in higher blood levels of lidocaine)

» Hepatic function impairment, severe
(capacity for metabolizing lidocaine is reduced, which can result in higher blood levels of lidocaine and increase the risk of systemic effects)

Side/Adverse Effects
The following side/adverse effects have been selected on the basis of their potential clinical significance (possible signs and symptoms in parentheses where appropriate)—not necessarily inclusive:

Those indicating need for medical attention
Incidence rare

Acidosis; allergic and anaphylactoid reactions including; angioedema (swelling of face, mouth, hands, or feet); ***bronchospasm*** (cough; shortness of breath; wheezing); ***shock*** (fast heartbeat; rapid, shallow breathing; sweating or clammy skin; weakness); ***urticaria*** (hives; itching and redness of skin; swelling)—rarely, like other local anesthetics; ***bradycardia; cardiac arrest; CNS depression*** (drowsiness; loss of consciousness; slowed breathing); ***CNS stimulation*** (anxiety; apprehension; blurry or double vision; confusion; convulsions (seizures); dizziness or drowsiness; euphoria; light–headedness; nausea and vomiting; nervousness; ringing ears; sensations of cold, heat, or numbness; twitching or shaking); ***heart block; hypotension; hypoxia***

Note: Systemic effects are unlikely when recommended guidelines for use of this medication are followed, but central nervous system (CNS) toxicity and/or cardiovascular depression may occur if sufficiently high plasma concentrations of lidocaine are produced.

Incidence not determined—Observed during clinical practice, estimates of frequency can not be determined

Hypersensitivity reactions (difficulty in breathing and/or swallowing; fever; hives; nausea; reddening of the skin, especially around ears; swelling of eyes, face, or inside of nose; unusual tiredness or weakness)

Those indicating need for medical attention only if they continue or are bothersome
Incidence more frequent

Localized skin reactions (abnormal feeling at application site; itching; rash)—generally mild and transient, resolving spontaneously within a few minutes to hours

Incidence not determined—Observed during clinical practice, estimates of frequency can not be determined

Asthenia (lack or loss of strength); ***blurred vision; confusion; disorientation; dizziness; flushing; headache; hyperesthesia*** (increased sensitivity to pain, increased sensitivity to touch, tingling in the hands and feet); ***hypoesthesia*** (burning, crawling, itching, numbness, prickling, "pins and needles", or tingling feelings); ***lightheadedness; nausea; nervousness; metallic taste; paresthesia*** (burning, crawling, itching, numbness, prickling, "pins and needles", or tingling feelings); ***skin irritation; somnolence*** (sleepiness or unusual drowsiness); ***taste alteration; tinnitus*** (continuing ringing or buzzing or other unexplained noise in ears; hearing loss); ***tremor; visual disturbances; vomiting***

Overdose
For more information on the management of overdose or unintentional ingestion, **contact a poison control center** (see *Poison Control Center Listing*).

Clinical effects of overdose
Note: Excessive dosing by applying topical systems to larger areas or for longer than the recommended wearing time could result in increased absorption of lidocaine and high blood concentrations, leading to serious adverse effects.

The following effects have been selected on the basis of their potential clinical significance (possible signs and symptoms in parentheses where appropriate)—not necessarily inclusive:

Bradycardia; central nervous system (CNS) depression (drowsiness; loss of consciousness; slowed breathing); ***CNS stimulation*** (anxiety; blurry or double vision; confusion; convulsions (seizures); dizziness or drowsiness; nausea and vomiting; nervousness; ringing ears; twitching or shaking); ***hypotension***

Treatment of overdose
To decrease absorption—Remove any remaining medication from the skin surface.

To enhance elimination—Dialysis is of negligible value in the treatment of acute overdoses.

Specific treatment—Treatment is symptomatic.

Monitoring—Lidocaine blood concentration should be obtained; toxicity may occur at blood levels above 5 mcg/mL.

Supportive care—Secure and maintain a patent airway, administer 100% oxygen, and institute assisted or controlled respiration as needed. In some patients, endotracheal intubation may be required. Patients in whom intentional overdose is confirmed or suspected should be referred for psychiatric evaluation.

Patient Consultation
As an aid to patient consultation, refer to *Advice for the Patient, Lidocaine (Topical)*.

In providing consultation, consider emphasizing the following selected information (» = major clinical significance):

Before using this medication

» Conditions affecting use, especially:
Allergy to amide–type local anesthetics
Pregnancy—Crosses the placenta
Breast-feeding—Distributed into breast milk
Other medical problems, especially burned, broken, or inflamed skin, or hepatic disease

Proper use of this medication

» Do not apply to burned, broken, or inflamed skin
» Avoid contact with eyes; if inadvertent contact does occur, immediately wash out the eye with water or saline and protect the eye until sensation returns
» Proper dosing—Use only as directed; avoid applying more than the recommended number of topical systems or using the topical systems for longer than the recommended wearing time
» Proper storage—Store topical systems out of the reach of children and pets

Precautions while using this medication

» If irritation or a burning sensation occurs during application, remove the topical system(s) and do not reapply until the irritation subsides
» Wash hands after handling topical systems; avoid eye contact
» Used topical systems should be disposed of in such a way as to prevent access to them by children or pets

Side/adverse effects

Possibility of allergic reactions (anaphylactoid reactions, angioedema, bronchospasm, urticaria) and systemic effects (cardiovascular and/or CNS toxicity); obtaining medical assistance immediately if signs and/or symptoms occur

General Dosing Information

Contact with eyes should be avoided, because the medication may cause severe eye irritation. If contact with an eye occurs, immediately wash out the eye with water or saline and protect the eye until sensation returns.

The medication should not be applied to broken or inflamed skin.

If irritation or a burning sensation occurs during application, remove the topical system(s) and do not reapply until the irritation subsides.

Applying more than the recommended number of topical systems, longer application times, smaller patients, or impaired elimination could result in increased absorption of lidocaine and high blood concentrations, leading to serious adverse effects.

Avoid accidental exposure in children. Chewing or ingesting new or used topical systems could result in serious adverse effects. Store and dispose of topical systems out of the reach of children and pets.

Safety considerations for handling this medication

Wash hands after handling topical systems.

Avoid contact with eyes.

Store and dispose of topical systems out of the reach of children and pets.

For treatment of adverse effects

Remove any remaining medication from the skin surface.

For eye contact—Immediately wash out the eye with water or saline and protect the eye until sensation returns.

Topical Dosage Forms

LIDOCAINE TOPICAL SYSTEM

Usual adult dose

Postherpetic neuralgia—
Remove release liner and apply to intact skin, covering the most painful area(s). Topical systems may be cut into smaller sizes with scissors prior to removal of the release liner.
Smaller areas of treatment are recommended in debilitated patients and patients with hepatic function impairment.

Usual adult prescribing limits

Postherpetic neuralgia—
Up to 3 topical systems may be applied at one time and for up to twelve hours within a twenty–four hour period.

Usual pediatric dose

Safety and efficacy have not been established.

Usual geriatric dose

Postherpetic neuralgia—
See *Usual adult dose*

Strength(s) usually available

U.S.—
5% (each adhesive topical system [10 cm×14 cm] contains 700 mg lidocaine [50 mg per gram adhesive] in an aqueous base) (Rx) [*Lidoderm* (D–sorbitol; polyvinyl alcohol; urea)].

Packaging and storage

Store at 25° C (77° F); excursions permitted to 15 to 30° C (59 to 86° F). Keep envelope sealed at all times when not in use.

Auxiliary labeling

- For topical use only.
- Keep away from eyes.

Additional information

Each topical system is comprised of an adhesive material containing 5% lidocaine, which is applied to a non–woven polyester felt backing and covered with a polyethylene terephthalate (PET) film release liner.

Revised: 09/14/2005

LIDOCAINE AND PRILOCAINE Topical

INN: none; BAN: Lidocaine—Lignocaine

VA CLASSIFICATION (Primary): DE700

Commonly used brand name(s): *EMLA*.

Another commonly used name for lidocaine is lignocaine.

Note: For a listing of dosage forms and brand names by country availability, see *Dosage Forms* section(s).

Category

Anesthetic, local.

Indications

Note: Bracketed information in the *Indications* section refers to uses that are not included in U.S. product labeling.

Accepted

Anesthesia, local—Indicated for application to normal, intact skin, to provide topical anesthesia prior to procedures such as insertion of an intravascular cannula, venipuncture or other needle insertion; skin graft harvesting; the cleansing and debridement of leg ulcers; minor dermal procedures, such as laser treatment of port-wine stains and removal of mollusca, warts, or tattoos; lumbar puncture; and diathermy.

This topical anesthetic is also applied to the genital mucosa of men or [women], to provide anesthesia for infiltration of additional anesthetic prior to the surgical removal of localized lesions (e.g., removal of condolymata via carbon dioxide laser or thermocautery), or [to provide anesthesia for surgical removal of localized lesions] . It is used for this purpose only in adults; application to the mucosa of children is *not* recommended.

Unaccepted

Application of this medication to mucous membranes other than the genital mucosa of adults, especially application to the gums or other oral mucosa, is not recommended.

Application of this medication to the ear is not recommended because ototoxicity occurred in animal studies in which lidocaine and prilocaine topical cream was applied to the tympanic membrane or to the middle ear. Application of this medication to any area from which migration to or beyond the tympanic membrane is possible is not recommended.

Application of this medication to or near the eye is not recommended because corneal irritation can result.

Pharmacology/Pharmacokinetics

Note: Information reported below on various pharmacokinetic parameters and on the onset of action, time to peak effect, and duration of action after application to the skin was obtained in studies in Caucasians. Preliminary evidence from a study in a limited number of subjects indicates that the rate and extent of absorption are decreased, the onset of action and time to peak effect are increased, and the overall efficacy of the medication is reduced, after application to black skin.

Physicochemical characteristics

Chemical Group—Both lidocaine and prilocaine are amide-type local anesthetics.

Molecular weight—
Lidocaine: 234.34.
Prilocaine: 220.32.

Octanol-to-aqueous buffer solution (pH 7.4) partition ratio—
Lidocaine: 43.
Prilocaine: 25.

Mechanism of action/Effect

Local anesthetics block both the initiation and conduction of nerve impulses by decreasing the neuronal membrane's permeability to sodium ions. This reversibly stabilizes the membrane and inhibits depolarization, resulting in the failure of a propagated action potential and subsequent conduction blockade.

The base (nonionized) form of a local anesthetic is able to diffuse across neuronal membranes to produce local anesthesia much more readily than a salt (ionized) form of the agent. However, penetration through intact skin of effective concentrations of the highly lipophilic base form of an anesthetic is generally not achieved after application of topical formulations that contain single anesthetics. This lidocaine and prilocaine–containing formulation is an oil-in-water emulsion in which the oil phase is a eutectic mixture formed by combining equal parts by weight of lidocaine and prilocaine bases. Because the eutectic mixture is a liquid, the anesthetics need not be dissolved in oil before being incorporated into the water phase of the formulation; this increases the concentration of active substance in droplets of the emulsion and permits larger quantities of anesthetic to penetrate to the nerve endings in deeper skin layers.

The depth at which anesthesia is present after application to intact, healthy skin, as determined by needle insertion, increases with the length of time that the medication remains on the skin, about 3 mm after a 60-minute application, 4 mm after a 90-minute application, and 5 mm after a 120-minute application. However, when the medication remains on the skin for less than 120 minutes, the depth at which anesthesia is present may continue to increase for an additional 30 to 60 minutes after the anesthetic is removed, depending on the location at which the medication is applied.

Other actions/effects

This medication may produce vascular responses, i.e., vasoconstriction (manifested by blanching of the skin) and/or vasodilatation (manifested by erythema). In a study in which the medication was applied to normal skin, maximal blanching occurred after a 90-minute application, and erythema occurred only after a much longer application time (more than 3 hours). In another study in a limited number of patients, a product twice as strong as the formulation now commercially available in the U.S. and Canada produced vascular responses much more rapidly in skin affected by atopic dermatitis or eczema than in normal skin. In patients with atopic dermatitis or eczema, blanching and erythema occurred after application times of only 5 to 15 minutes and 30 to 60 minutes, respectively, whereas in individuals with normal skin, blanching and erythema occurred after application times of 30 to 60 minutes and 2 to 4 hours, respectively.

Absorption

Application to the skin—The rate and extent of systemic absorption are dependent on the thickness of the skin and the size of the area to which the medication is applied as well as the duration of application. In general, mean absorption rates in children and adults are 45 ± 16 mcg per square centimeter of skin area (mcg/cm²) per hour and 77 ± 36 mcg/cm² per hour for lidocaine and prilocaine, respectively. Absorption may be increased when the formulation is applied to broken or inflamed skin or to areas 2000 cm² or larger in size. Also, absorption is more rapid when the cream is applied to the skin of patients with atopic dermatitis and generalized eczema or other patients with damaged or thin skin.

Application to genital mucosa—The rate and extent of absorption are significantly greater than after application to normal, intact skin.

Distribution

Both lidocaine and prilocaine cross the blood-brain barrier and the placenta.

Note: The mean volumes of distribution at steady state, determined after intravenous administration, are 1.5 ± 0.3 liters per kg of body weight (L/kg) for lidocaine and 2.6 ± 1.3 L/kg for prilocaine.

Protein binding

Lidocaine—High (70%), primarily to alpha-1-acid glycoprotein, at plasma concentrations produced by application of this topical formulation. At much higher concentrations (> 1 mcg per mL [mcg/mL] [4.3 micromoles/L]), binding is dependent on the concentration.

Prilocaine—Moderate (40%).

Biotransformation

Lidocaine—Hepatic; rapid. One metabolite is active, but a less potent local anesthetic than the parent compound; another metabolite has no local anesthetic activity, but may be more toxic than lidocaine itself. Whether metabolism occurs in the skin after topical application has not been determined.

Prilocaine—Hepatic, by amidases; metabolism in renal tissues has also been demonstrated *in vitro*. One or more of the metabolic products is toxic (causing methemoglobinemia). Whether metabolism occurs in the skin after topical application has not been determined.

Half-life

Elimination (mean values)—
Lidocaine: 110 ± 24 minutes (determined after intravenous administration of lidocaine hydrochloride); may be increased in patients with cardiac or hepatic function impairment.
Prilocaine: 70 ± 48 minutes; may be increased in patients with hepatic or renal function impairment.

Onset of action

Application to the skin—Dependent on the epidermal and dermal thickness at the location to which the medication is applied; about 1 hour after application to intact skin, but much more rapid (less than 15 minutes) after application to skin areas affected by atopic dermatitis or eczema.

Time to peak serum concentration

Application to normal, intact skin—Dependent on the area to which the medication is applied and subject to interpatient variability; about 4 hours (range, 2 to 6 hours) when 60 grams is applied to a 400-cm² area of the thigh and allowed to remain, under an occlusive dressing, for 3 hours and 1.5 to 3 hours when 10 grams is applied to a 100-cm² area of the face and allowed to remain for 2 hours.

Peak serum concentration

Application to intact skin—
Lidocaine: The highest concentration measured after application of about 150 grams of the lidocaine and prilocaine formulation to up to 1300 cm² of intact skin for up to 3 hours is 1.1 mcg/mL (4.73 micromoles/L).
Prilocaine: The highest concentration measured after application of about 150 grams of the lidocaine and prilocaine formulation to up to 1300 cm² of intact skin for up to 3 hours is 0.2 mcg/mL (0.87 micromoles/L).
Note: The total quantity of prilocaine absorbed over a given time is greater than that of lidocaine, even though equal quantities of each are present in the formulation. However, prilocaine's larger volume of distribution and more rapid clearance result in lower plasma concentrations.

Time to peak effect

Application to intact skin—About 2 to 3 hours. In general, 1 hour of application under occlusion produces sufficient anesthesia for procedures such as intravascular catheter placement or venipuncture; 2 hours of application under occlusion produces sufficient anesthesia for procedures such as split skin graft harvesting. However, one study showed that 2 hours of application under occlusion may be required to provide sufficient anesthesia for venipuncture in children with black skin.

Application to genital mucosa—Sufficient anesthesia for removal of localized lesions occurs about 5 to 7 minutes after application; efficacy begins to decrease as soon as 10 to 15 minutes after application.

Duration of action

Application to intact skin—Effective anesthesia following a 1- or 2-hour application generally persists for an additional 1 or 2 hours after the medication is removed. However, the duration of anesthesia is dependent on the blood flow in the underlying tissue; efficacy may decline more rapidly in highly perfused areas, such as the face. One study demonstrated that a relatively short duration follows a rapid onset and a more prolonged duration follows a delayed onset.

Elimination

Lidocaine—More than 98% of the quantity absorbed is eliminated in the urine; less than 3% as unchanged lidocaine and the remainder as metabolites. Mean systemic clearance is 13 ± 3 mL per minute per kg of body weight (mL/min/kg).

Prilocaine—Renal; less than 3% as unchanged prilocaine. Mean systemic clearance is 38 ± 15 mL/min/kg.

Precautions to Consider

Note: In the animal studies reported in the *Carcinogenicity*, *Mutagenicity*, and *Pregnancy/Reproduction* sections below, the doses administered to, or blood concentrations achieved in, the animals are compared to the equivalent in humans of a Single Dermal Administration (SDA), defined as a single application of 60 grams of the local anesthetic formulation over 400 square centimeters (cm ^{2}) of the skin area of a 50-kg person for 3 hours.

Cross-sensitivity and/or related problems

Patients sensitive to other amide-type local anesthetics may rarely be sensitive to lidocaine and/or prilocaine also.

Carcinogenicity

Lidocaine—

A 2-year study showed the metabolite 2,6-xylidine to be carcinogenic, causing carcinomas, adenomas, and rhabdomyosarcomas in the nasal cavities of both male and female rats; subcutaneous fibromas and/or fibrosarcomas in both male and female rats; and neoplastic nodules of the liver in female rats when given in daily oral doses of 150 mg per kg of body weight (mg/kg) per day (900 mg per square meter of body surface area [mg/m^2] [60 times the SDA] per day). Statistically significant increases in nasal carcinomas and/or adenomas in male and female rats did not occur with oral doses of 50 mg/kg per day (300 mg/m^2 [30 times the SDA] per day), and no nasal tumors occurred with oral doses of 15 mg/kg per day (90 mg/m^2 [6 times the SDA] per day).

Prilocaine—

The metabolite ortho-toluidine, given chronically to mice in oral doses of 150 to 2400 mg/kg per day (900 to 14,400 mg/m^2 [60 to 90 times the SDA] per day) or to rats in oral doses of 150 to 800 mg/kg per day (900 to 4800 mg/m^2 [60 to 320 times the SDA] per day), was carcinogenic in both species at all dosage levels tested. Tumors included hepatocarcinomas and adenomas in female mice; hemangiosarcomas and hemangiomas in male and female mice; sarcomas of multiple organs and transitional-cell carcinomas and papillomas of the urinary bladder in both sexes of rats; subcutaneous fibromas, fibrosarcomas, and mesotheliomas in male rats; and mammary gland fibroadenomas and adenomas in female rats.

Mutagenicity

Lidocaine—

No evidence of mutagenicity was shown with lidocaine hydrochloride in the Ames *Salmonella* /mammalian microsome test or analysis of structural chromosome aberrations in human lymphocytes *in vitro* , or in the mouse micronucleus test *in vivo*. The metabolite 2,6-xylidine was weakly mutagenic in the Ames test only under metabolic activation conditions. The metabolite was also mutagenic at the thymidine kinase locus, with or without activation, and induced chromosome aberrations and sister chromatid exchanges at concentrations at which the substance precipitated out of solution (1.2 mg/mL). No evidence of genotoxicity was found in the *in vivo* assays measuring unscheduled DNA synthesis in rat hepatocytes, chromosome damage in polychromatic erythrocytes, or preferential killing of DNA repair-deficient bacteria in liver, lung, kidney, testes, and blood extracts from mice. However, covalent binding studies of DNA from liver and ethmoid turbinates in rats indicate that the metabolite may be genotoxic under certain conditions *in vivo.*

Prilocaine—

The metabolite ortho-toluidine produced positive results in *Escherichia coli* DNA repair and phage-induction assays in a concentration of 0.5 mcg/mL. Urine concentrates from rats given the metabolite (300 mg/kg orally [300 times the SDA]) were mutagenic for *Salmonella typhimurium* with metabolic activation. Several other tests on the metabolite, including reverse mutations in five different *Salmonella typhimurium* strains with or without activation and with single strand breaks in DNA of V79 Chinese hamster cells, were negative.

Pregnancy/Reproduction

Fertility—

Prilocaine—

Studies in rats given 300 mg/kg intramuscularly as the hydrochloride salt (188 times the SDA) have not shown evidence of impaired fertility.

Pregnancy—

Lidocaine and prilocaine mixture—

Adequate and well-controlled studies have not been done in humans.

Studies in rats given subcutaneous injections of an aqueous mixture of the hydrochloride salts of lidocaine and prilocaine (40 mg/kg of each [equivalent to 29 times the SDA for lidocaine and 25 times the SDA for prilocaine] per day) have not shown evidence of teratogenicity, embryotoxicity, or fetotoxicity. Also, studies in rats with the individual anesthetics (30 mg/kg subcutaneously [22 times the SDA] of lidocaine hydrochloride or 300 mg/kg intramuscularly [188 times the SDA] of prilocaine hydrochloride) have not shown evidence of harm to the fetus.

FDA Pregnancy Category B.

Breast-feeding

Lidocaine is, and prilocaine probably is, distributed into breast milk in small quantities. The risk of adverse effects in nursing infants is considered to be minimal.

Pediatrics

Neonates (up to 1 month of age)—

Use in neonates is not recommended because of the risk of methemoglobinemia.

Infants and children—

Application to the mucosa of pediatric patients is not recommended.

Methemoglobin concentrations are increased in infants and children after application of this medication. Although the concentrations generally do not reach clinically significant levels, overt methemoglobinemia developed after use of the anesthetic mixture in a 3-month-old infant who was also receiving other medication known to cause methemoglobinemia. It is recommended that the anesthetic formulation not be used for infants up to 12 months of age who are receiving such medications. Also, a study in children 1 to 6 years of age found that methemoglobin concentrations remain elevated for 24 hours after a 2-hour application of 5 grams of the medication. The possibility of cumulative effects on methemoglobin concentrations should be considered if the medication is needed on a daily basis.

Studies have shown that, because of fearfulness in children younger than 7 years of age, this medication provides less overall benefit (as determined by reaction to needle insertion) to these patients than it does to older children and adults. Use of this product does not eliminate the need for emotional and psychological support for young children who are undergoing medical or surgical procedures.

Geriatrics

No information is available on the relationship of age to the effects of this lidocaine and prilocaine topical formulation in geriatric patients. However, experience with other local anesthetic formulations has shown that geriatric patients are more likely than younger adults to develop local anesthetic–induced systemic toxicity after the medications are administered by injection or applied to mucous membranes.

Drug interactions and/or related problems

The following drug interactions and/or related problems have been selected on the basis of their potential clinical significance (possible mechanism in parentheses where appropriate)—not necessarily inclusive (» = major clinical significance):

Note: Combinations containing any of the following medications, depending on the amount present, may also interact with this medication.

Anesthetics, general
(symptoms of local anesthetic–induced CNS toxicity, which may occur if excessive quantities of the medication are absorbed, may be masked if the local anesthetic is used in conjunction with a general anesthetic)

Anesthetics, local, other or
Structurally related medications, such as mexiletine or tocainide
(the risk of systemic toxicity may be increased, especially if large quantities of the lidocaine and prilocaine topical formulation are used concurrently with any of these medications)

Methemoglobinemia-inducing medications, other, especially:
- Acetaminophen, chronic use of
- Chloroquine
- Dapsone
- Nitrates or nitrites, including nitrofurantoin, nitroglycerin, and nitroprusside
- Para-aminosalicylic acid
- Phenacetin—not commercially available in the U.S. or Canada
- Phenobarbital
- Phenytoin
- Primaquine
- » Sulfonamides, including mafenide

(concurrent use with the lidocaine and prilocaine topical formulation may increase the risk of overt methemoglobinemia, especially in infants; concurrent use in infants younger than 12 months of age is not recommended)

Laboratory value alterations

The following have been selected on the basis of their potential clinical significance (possible effect in parentheses where appropriate)—not necessarily inclusive (» = major clinical significance).

With diagnostic test results
Skin tests, intradermal or epicutaneous
(application of the lidocaine- and prilocaine-containing topical anesthetic prior to skin testing may reduce flare induced by injection of histamine [often used as a positive control for these tests]; false-negative interpretation of weakly positive tests may result)

Medical considerations/Contraindications

The medical considerations/contraindications included have been selected on the basis of their potential clinical significance (reasons given in parentheses where appropriate)—not necessarily inclusive (» = major clinical significance).

Risk-benefit should be considered when the following medical problems exist:

Note: Caution is recommended in geriatric, acutely ill, or debilitated patients, who may be predisposed to local anesthetic–induced systemic toxicity.

» Any situation in which absorption may be increased, such as:
Application to open wounds, burns, or broken or inflamed skin or
Atopic dermatitis or
Eczema
(the rate and extent of anesthetic absorption may be increased, leading to a higher risk of systemic toxicity; application to open wounds is not recommended)
(in burn patients, the presence of a pre-existing hemoglobin abnormality [carboxyhemoglobin] may also increase the risk of systemic toxicity)
(a study in a limited number of patients has shown that, after the medication is applied to skin affected by atopic dermatitis or eczema, the onset of action is more rapid than after application to healthy skin; a shorter application time may be appropriate for patients with these conditions, but additional clinical experience is needed before guidelines for use in these patients can be established)

Connective tissue disease, Ehlers Danlos Type III
(a study in a limited number of patients has shown that the topical lidocaine and prilocaine formulation does not provide adequate anesthesia in individuals with this condition)

» Glucose-6-phosphate dehydrogenase (G6PD) deficiency or other predisposition to methemoglobinemia or
» Methemoglobinemia, congenital or idiopathic
(medication may induce, or exacerbate pre-existing, methemoglobinemia)

Hepatic function impairment, severe
(capacity for metabolizing the anesthetics is reduced, which increases the risk of systemic effects)

» Sensitivity to lidocaine, prilocaine, or other amide-type local anesthetics, history of
(increased risk of allergic reaction)

Side/Adverse Effects

Note: Like other local anesthetics, lidocaine and prilocaine (individually) have rarely caused allergic and anaphylactoid reactions, including angioedema, bronchospasm, urticaria, and shock.

Systemic effects are unlikely when recommended guidelines for use of this medication are followed, but central nervous system (CNS) toxicity and/or cardiovascular depression may occur if sufficiently high plasma concentrations of the anesthetics are produced. Early signs of cardiovascular depression include bradycardia and hypotension. If treatment is not initiated promptly, decreases in cardiac output, total peripheral resistance, and mean arterial pressure may occur and may progress to hypoxia, acidosis, heart block, and cardiac arrest.

CNS toxicity induced by local anesthetics consists of CNS stimulation and/or CNS depression. CNS stimulation (signs and symptoms may include apprehension, nervousness, or euphoria; confusion; dizziness, light-headedness, or drowsiness; blurred or double vision; nausea and vomiting; ringing or buzzing in the ears; sensations of heat, cold, or numbness; and twitching, tremors, or convulsions) often occurs first, followed by CNS depression, characterized by drowsiness, unconsciousness, and respiratory depression and arrest. However, CNS excitation may be transient or absent, so that drowsiness may be the first sign of CNS toxicity in some patients, especially children.

The following side/adverse effects have been selected on the basis of their potential clinical significance (possible signs and symptoms in parentheses where appropriate)—not necessarily inclusive:

Those indicating need for medical attention

Incidence rare

Methemoglobinemia (blue or blue-purple color of lips, fingernails, or skin; fatigue; weakness; breathing problems; rapid heartbeat; headache; dizziness; collapse; altered mental status; dark urine)

Note: If *methemoglobinemia* is relatively mild, cyanosis may be the only sign. The other signs and symptoms occur when *methemoglobinemia* is severe and/or the patient cannot tolerate the reduced oxygen-carrying capacity of the blood.

Those indicating need for medical attention only if they continue or are bothersome

Incidence more frequent

Localized skin reactions (burning feeling, swelling, itching, or skin rash at place of application); ***vasoconstriction*** (very white skin at place of application); ***vasodilatation*** (red skin at place of application)

Note: *Localized skin reactions* generally resolve spontaneously within 1 or 2 hours. The adhesive in the occlusive dressing may also cause localized *sensitivity reactions* manifested by skin rash, itching, and/or redness.
Vasoconstriction-induced blanching generally occurs first and may be followed, depending on the application time, by *vasodilatation-induced erythema.*

Overdose

For specific information on the agents used in the management of lidocaine and prilocaine overdose, see:

- *Ascorbic Acid (Systemic)* monograph;
- *Benzodiazepines (Systemic)* monograph;
- *Methylene Blue (Systemic)* monograph; and/or
- *Sympathomimetic Agents—Cardiovascular Use (Parenteral-Systemic)* monograph.

For more information on the management of overdose or unintentional ingestion, **contact a Poison Control Center** (see *Poison Control Center Listing*).

Clinical effects of overdose

The following effects have been selected on the basis of their potential clinical significance (possible signs and symptoms in parentheses where appropriate)—not necessarily inclusive:

Acute and chronic

Circulatory depression; convulsions; methemoglobinemia

Treatment of overdose

To decrease absorption—
For systemic reactions caused by excessive absorption: Removing any remaining medication from the skin surface.

Specific treatment—
For circulatory depression: Administering a vasopressor and intravenous fluids.
For seizures: Administering an anticonvulsant. Benzodiazepines are most commonly used. Because intravenously administered benzodiazepines may cause respiratory and circulatory depression, especially when administered rapidly, medications and equipment needed for support of respiration and for resuscitation must be immediately available.
For methemoglobinemia: Administering methylene blue and/or ascorbic acid.

Supportive care—
Securing and maintaining a patent airway, administering 100% oxygen, and instituting assisted or controlled respiration as needed. In some patients, endotracheal intubation may be required.

Patient Consultation

As an aid to patient consultation, refer to *Advice for the Patient, Lidocaine and Prilocaine (Topical).*

In providing consultation, consider emphasizing the following selected information (» = major clinical significance):

Before using this medication

» Conditions affecting use, especially:
Sensitivity to lidocaine, prilocaine, or other amide-type local anesthetics
Use in children—Increased risk of adverse effect (methemoglobinemia) in infants younger than 1 year of age; use of medication does not eliminate need for comforting frightened children
Use in the elderly—Possibility of increased risk of systemic effects, based on experience with local anesthetics administered by other routes

Other medications, especially sulfonamides
Other medical problems, especially conditions that may increase absorption and methemoglobinemia or predisposition to (e.g., glucose-6-phosphate dehydrogenase deficiency)

Proper use of this medication

» Using only for appropriate indications, as directed by physician or nurse
» Not applying to open wounds, burns, or broken or inflamed skin, unless otherwise directed by physician or nurse
» Avoiding contact with eyes; if inadvertent contact does occur, not touching eyes and contacting physician immediately
» Avoiding contact with lips or mouth
» Following instructions provided by physician or nurse and/or patient information provided by manufacturer
» Contacting health care provider if any questions about method, site, or time of application
» Proper application technique for cream:
 Applying a thick layer of medication to specified area or areas; not spreading the medication
 Unless applying to genital area, covering the medication with an occlusive dressing; sealing tightly, making sure a thick layer remains under the dressing; not disturbing the dressing; not covering the medication with an occlusive dressing if the medication is applied to the genital area
 If directed to do so, removing the dressing after 1 or 2 hours, wiping off the medication, then cleaning the area with antiseptic solution; if not directed to do so, keeping medication and dressing in place until removed by physician or nurse
» Proper application technique for disc:
 Applying anesthetic disc to specified area, and leaving in place for 1 hour; making sure the disc stays in place and attached to skin during this time
» Proper dosing
» Proper storage

Precautions while using this medication

» Monitoring small children after administration, to make sure they do not disturb the dressing and/or ingest any medication
» Caution that injury may occur undetected while numbness persists in the affected area; using care to prevent injury (e.g., not scratching, rubbing, or exposing the affected area to extreme hot or cold temperatures) until sensation has returned

Side/adverse effects

Possibility of allergic reactions (anaphylactoid reactions, angioedema, bronchospasm, urticaria) and systemic effects (cardiovascular and/or CNS toxicity); obtaining medical assistance immediately if signs and/or symptoms occur
(Signs and symptoms of other potential adverse effects, especially methemoglobinemia)

General Dosing Information

Contact with the eyes should be avoided, because the medication may cause severe corneal irritation. Also, the anesthetic effect results in loss of protective reflexes, which may allow damage to the eye. If contact with an eye occurs, the eye should be washed with water or 0.9% sodium chloride solution and protected against injury until sensation returns.

The medication should not be applied to open wounds.

Although application of the medication to small sites (approximately 20 to 25 square centimeters [2 inches square]) may take place at home, before the patient travels to a medical appointment, it is recommended that the medication be applied to larger sites only under the supervision of medical personnel (e.g., in the office, clinic, or hospital).

The optimal application time may depend on the thickness and structure of the surface to which the medication is applied as well as the procedure being performed.

Prior to the procedure, the dressing should be removed, the medication wiped off, and the entire skin area cleaned with an antiseptic solution.

Application of this medication to the ear is not recommended because ototoxicity was noted in animal studies in which lidocaine and prilocaine topical cream was applied to the tympanic membrane or to the middle ear. Application of this medication to any area from which migration beyond the tympanic membrane is possible is not recommended.

This medication may not provide sufficient anesthesia when used as the sole anesthetic agent for cryotherapy for the removal of genital warts on men. In this case, application of lidocaine and prilocaine topical cream should be followed by infiltration of lidocaine to provide sufficient anesthesia for this procedure.

Topical Dosage Forms

Note: Bracketed uses in the *Dosage Forms* section refer to categories of use and/or indications that are not included in U.S. product labeling.

LIDOCAINE AND PRILOCAINE CREAM

Usual adult dose

Anesthesia, topical—
 Dermal procedures—
 Topical, to intact skin, a thick layer to be applied and covered with an occlusive dressing.
 For minor procedures involving a small area (e.g., intravascular cannulation, venipuncture)—2.5 grams, applied over twenty to twenty-five square centimeters of skin surface area and allowed to remain in contact with the skin surface for at least one hour. A second site may be prepared, to be used if a technical problem with cannulation or needle insertion should arise at the first site.
 For major dermal procedures involving larger areas (e.g., split thickness skin graft harvesting)—2 grams per ten square centimeters of skin surface area. The medication should be allowed to remain in contact with the skin surface for at least two hours.
 For laser treatment (removal of warts, tattoos, etc.)—1 to 2 grams per ten square centimeters of skin surface area.

 Note: A study performed in children has shown that application of smaller quantities of medication in a thin layer over a given surface area is not as effective as the recommended thick layer.

 Longer application times may be needed after application to black skin.

 Genital mucosal procedures (e.g., removal of condylomata or other localized lesions)—
 Topical, to the mucosa, 2.5 grams. Covering the medication with an occlusive dressing is not necessary. The medication should be allowed to remain in contact with the mucosa for 5 to 10 minutes, after which the procedure should be started immediately or infiltration with additional local anesthetic should be performed immediately.

Usual adult prescribing limits

Dermal procedures—
 The maximum recommended duration of exposure is four to five hours. Leaving the medication on the skin for longer than five hours is not likely to provide additional benefit, and may actually result in decreased anesthetic efficacy as well as an increased risk of systemic toxicity.

Usual pediatric dose

Anesthesia, topical—
 Neonates up to 1 month of age—
 Use is not recommended.

 Infants and children—
 Dermal procedures: See *Usual adult dose.*

Usual pediatric prescribing limits

Dermal procedures—
 The maximum recommended area of application in pediatric patients of various weights is—
 Up to 10 kg—100 square centimeters.
 10 to 20 kg—600 square centimeters.
 More than 20 kg—2000 square centimeters.

Usual geriatric dose

See *Usual adult dose.*

Strength(s) usually available

U.S.—
 5% (2.5% [25 mg per gram] of each anesthetic) (Rx) [*EMLA*].
Canada—
 5% (2.5% [25 mg per gram] of each anesthetic) (OTC) [*EMLA*].

Packaging and storage

Store between 15 and 30 °C (59 and 86 °F), unless otherwise specified by manufacturer. Protect from freezing.

Auxiliary labeling

- For topical use only.
- Keep away from eyes.
- Keep away from mouth.

LIDOCAINE AND PRILOCAINE TOPICAL DISC

Usual adult dose

Anesthesia, topical—

Dermal procedures—

Topical, to intact skin, one anesthetic disc should be applied and allowed to remain in contact with the skin surface for at least one hour.

A second site may be prepared, to be used if a technical problem with cannulation or needle insertion should arise at the first site.

Usual pediatric dose

Anesthesia, topical—

Neonates up to 1 month of age—

Use is not recommended.

Infants and children—

Dermal procedures: See *Usual adult dose*.

Usual pediatric prescribing limits

A maximum of two discs may be applied.

Usual geriatric dose

See *Usual adult dose*.

Strength(s) usually available

U.S.—

1 gram of the anesthetic emulsion (Rx) [*EMLA*].

Canada—

1 gram of anesthetic emulsion (OTC) [*EMLA*].

Packaging and storage

Store between 15 and 30 °C (59 and 86 °F), unless otherwise specified by manufacturer. Protect from freezing.

Auxiliary labeling

- For topical use only.
- Keep away from eyes.
- Keep away from mouth.

Selected Bibliography

Halperin DL, Koren G, Attias D, et al. Topical skin anesthesia for venous, subcutaneous drug reservoir and lumbar punctures in children. Pediatrics 1989; 84: 281-4.

Steward DJ, editor. Management of childhood pain: new approaches to procedure-related pain. J Pediatr 1993; 122(5 Pt 2): S1-S46.

Revised: 08/05/1998

LINEZOLID Systemic

VA CLASSIFICATION (Primary): AM900

Commonly used brand name(s): *Zyvox; Zyvox™*.

Another commonly used name is:

U-100766

PNU-10076

Note: For a listing of dosage forms and brand names by country availability, see *Dosage Forms* section(s).

Category

Antibacterial (systemic).

Indications

General Considerations

To reduce the development of drug-resistant bacteria and maintain the effectiveness of linezolid formulations and other antibacterial drugs, linezolid should be used only to treat or prevent infections that are proven or strongly suspected to be caused by bacteria.

Time-kill studies demonstrated that linezolid is bacteriostatic against enterococci and staphylococci and bactericidal against the majority of strains of streptococci.

Linezolid is a synthetic antibacterial agent. Linezolid belongs to a new antibiotic class called the oxazolidinones.

The mode of action of linezolid is different from that of other classes of antibacterials.

During clinical trials, resistance to linezolid developed in 6 patients with an infection caused by *Enterococcus faecium*. During compassionate use of linezolid, resistance developed in 8 patients infected with *Enterococcus faecium* and one patient infected with *Enterococcus faecalis*. Resistance may have developed due to use of a lower than recommended dose of linezolid, a retained prosthetic device, or an undrained abscess.

Accepted

Pneumonia, community-acquired (treatment)—Intravenous and oral linezolid is indicated in the treatment of community acquired pneumonia caused by penicillin-susceptible strains of *Streptococcus pneumoniae* or methicillin-susceptible strains of *Staphylococcus aureus*.

Pneumonia, nosocomial (treatment)—Intravenous and oral linezolid is indicated in the treatment of nosocomial pneumonia caused by methicillin-susceptible and methicillin-resistant *Staphylococcus aureus* or penicillin-susceptible strains of *Streptococcus pneumoniae*.

Skin and soft tissue infections, complicated (treatment)—Intravenous and oral linezolid is indicated in the treatment of complicated skin and soft tissue infections, including diabetic foot infections, without concomitant osteomyelitis, caused by *Staphylococcus aureus* (methicillin-susceptible and methicillin-resistant), *Streptococcus pyogenes*, or *Streptococcus agalactiae*. Patients with decubitus ulcers were not included in the clinical trials.

Skin and soft tissue infections, uncomplicated (treatment)—Oral linezolid is indicated in the treatment of uncomplicated skin and soft tissue infections caused by methicillin-susceptible strains of *Staphylococcus aureus* or *Streptococcus pyogenes*.

Vancomycin-resistant *Enterococcus faecium* infections—Intravenous and oral linezolid is indicated in the treatment of vancomycin-resistant *Enterococcus faecium* infections.

Pharmacology/Pharmacokinetics

Physicochemical characteristics

Source—Linezolid is a synthetic antibacterial agent.

Chemical Group—Oxazolidinone

Molecular weight—337.35.

Mechanism of action/Effect

The mechanism of action for linezolid is different than that of other antibacterial agents; therefore, cross-resistance between linezolid and other classes of antibiotics is unlikely. Linezolid acts via inhibition of protein synthesis. It binds to a site on the bacterial 23S ribosomal RNA of the 50S subunit and prevents the formation of a functional 70S initiation complex. This step is essential for the bacterial translation process.

Absorption

Well absorbed after oral administration; absolute bioavailability approximately 100%; food has no effect.

The following are AUC values of linezolid doses in adults

- 400 mg tablet (single dose)—55.1 mcg h/mL
- 400 mg tablet every 12 hours—73.4 mcg h/mL
- 600 mg tablet (single dose)—91.4 mcg h/mL
- 600 mg tablet every 12 hours—138 mcg h/mL
- 600 mg oral suspension (single dose)—80.8 mcg h/mL
- 600 mg intravenous injection (single dose)—80.2 mcg h/mL
- 600 mg intravenous injection every 12 hours—89.7 mcg h/mL

AUC is lower for pediatric patients compared with adults and a wider variability of linezolid AUC across all pediatric age groups as compared with adults. Most pre-term neonates less than 7 days of age (gestational age less than 34 weeks) have larger AUC values than many full-term neonates and older infants.

Distribution

Distributed to well-perfused tissues; volume of distribution slightly lower in women than men.

Vol_D (steady state)—40 to 50 L.

Protein binding

Low, approximately 31%

Biotransformation

Linezolid is primarily metabolized via oxidation of the morpholine ring. Two inactive metabolites are formed: the aminoethoxyacetic acid metabolite and the hydroxyethyl glycine metabolite.The hydroxyethyl glycine metabolite is formed via a non-enzymatic chemical oxidation mechanism *in vitro* .

In vitro studies have not shown that linezolid is metabolized by human cytochrome P450 enzymes Linezolid does not inhibit the cytochrome P450 enzymes.

Elimination–

The following are elimination half life values of linezolid doses in adults

- 400 mg tablet (single dose)—5.2 hours
- 400 mg tablet every 12 hours—4.69 hours
- 600 mg tablet (single dose)—4.26 hours
- 600 mg tablet every 12 hours—5.4 hours
- 600 mg oral suspension (single dose)—4.6 hours

- 600 mg intravenous injection (single dose)—4.4 hours
- 600 mg intravenous injection every 12 hours—4.8 hours

Pediatrics ranging in age from greater than 7 days of age to 11 years of age have a shorter half-life compared with adults.

Time to peak concentration

The following are T_{max} values of linezolid doses in adults

- 400 mg tablet (single dose)—1.52 hours
- 400 mg tablet every 12 hours—1.12 hours
- 600 mg tablet (single dose)—1.28 hours
- 600 mg tablet every 12 hours—1.03 hours
- 600 mg oral suspension (single dose)—0.97 hours
- 600 mg intravenous injection (single dose)—0.50 hours
- 600 mg intravenous injection every 12 hours—0.51 hours

Fat food, when given with linezolid, decreases T_{max} by 1.5 to 2.2 hours.

Peak serum concentration

The following are C_{max} values of linezolid doses in adults

- 400 mg tablet (single dose)—8.1 mcg/mL
- 400 mg tablet every 12 hours—11 mcg/mL
- 600 mg tablet (single dose)—12.7 mcg/mL
- 600 mg tablet every 12 hours—21.2 mcg/mL
- 600 mg oral suspension (single dose)—11 mcg/mL
- 600 mg intravenous injection (single dose)—12.9 mcg/mL
- 600 mg intravenous injection every 12 hours—15.1 mcg/mL

C_{max} is decreased by about 17% when high fat food is given with linezolid.

Elimination

Nonrenal clearance is responsible for about 65% of the total clearance of linezolid under steady-state conditions. At steady-state, about 30%, 40%, and 10% of the dose appear in the urine as linezolid, metabolite B, and metabolite A, respectively. The renal clearance of linezolid is low which suggests net tubular reabsorption.

Almost no parent drug appears in the feces; however, about 6% and 3% of metabolite B and metabolite A appear in the feces.

With increasing doses, a small degree of nonlinearity in clearance was observed with increasing doses of linezolid; however, the difference in clearance was small and did not affect the elimination half-life.

The following are systemic clearance values of linezolid doses in adults

- 400 mg tablet (single dose)—146 mL/min
- 400 mg tablet every 12 hours—110 mL/min
- 600 mg tablet (single dose)—127 mL/min
- 600 mg tablet every 12 hours—80 mL/min
- 600 mg oral suspension (single dose)—141 mL/min
- 600 mg intravenous injection (single dose)—138 mL/min
- 600 mg intravenous injection every 12 hours—123 mL/min

Clearance of linezolid varies as a function of age. With the exclusion of pre-term neonates less than one week of age, clearance is most rapid in the youngest age groups ranging from greater than 7 days of age to 11 years of age. As age of pediatric patients increase, the clearance of linezolid gradually decreases, and by adolescence mean clearance values approach those observed for the adult population. There is wider variability in linezolid clearance across all pediatric age groups as compared with adults.

Precautions to Consider

Carcinogenicity/Tumorigenicity/Mutagenicity

Although lifetime studies in animals have not been conducted to evaluate the carcinogenic potential of linezolid, no mutagenic or clastogenic potential was found in a battery of tests, including the Ames and AS52 assays, an *in vitro* unscheduled DNA synthesis (UDS) assay, an *in vitro* chromosome aberration assay in human lymphocytes, and an *in vivo* mouse micronucleus assay.

Pregnancy/Reproduction

Fertility—Linezolid did not affect the fertility or reproductive performance of adult female rats. It reversibly decreased fertility and reproductive performance in adult male rats when given at doses ≥ 50 mg/kg/day, with exposures approximately equal to or greater than the expected human exposure level (exposure comparisons are based on AUCs). Epithelial cell hypertrophy in the epididymis may have contributed to the decreased fertility by affecting sperm maturation. Similar epididymal changes were not seen in dogs. Although the concentrations of sperm in the testes were in the normal range, the concentrations in the cauda epididymis were decreased, and sperm from the vas deferens had decreased motility.

Mildly decreased fertility occurred in juvenile male rats treated with linezolid through most of their period of sexual development (50 mg/kg/day from days 7 to 36 of age, and 100 mg/kg/day from days 37 to 55 of age, with exposures ranging from 0.4–fold to 1.2–fold that expected in humans based on AUCs).No histopathological evidence of adverse effects was observed in the male reproductive tract.

Pregnancy—Adequate and well-controlled studies in humans have not been done. Linezolid should be used during pregnancy only if the potential benefit justifies the potential risk to the fetus.

Linezolid was not teratogenic in mice or rats at exposure levels 4–fold (in mice) or equivalent to (in rats) the expected human exposure level, based on AUCs.

In mice, embryo and fetal toxicities were seen only at doses that caused maternal toxicity (clinical signs and reduced body weight gain). A dose of 450 mg/kg/day (6.5–fold the estimated human exposure level based on AUCs) correlated with increased postimplantational embryo death, including total litter loss, decreased fetal body weights, and an increased incidence of costal cartilage fusion.

In rats, mild fetal toxicity was observed at 15 and 50 mg/kg/day (exposure levels 0.22–fold to approximately equivalent to the estimated human exposure, respectively, based on AUCs). The effects consisted of decreased fetal body weights and reduced ossification of sternebrae, a finding often seen in association with decreased body weights. Slight maternal toxicity, in the form of reduced body weight gain, was seen at 50 mg/kg/day.

When female rats were treated with 50 mg/kg/day (approximately equivalent to the estimated human exposure based on AUCs) of linezolid during pregnancy and lactation, survival of pups was decreased on postnatal days 1 to 4. Pups permitted to mature to reproductive age, when mated, showed an increase in preimplantation loss, with a corresponding decrease in fertility.

FDA Pregnancy Category C.

Breast-feeding

It is not known whether linezolid is distributed into human breast milk. Because many drugs are distributed in human milk, caution should be exercised when linezolid is administered to a nursing women.

Linezolid and its metabolites are excreted in the milk of lactating rats. Concentrations of linezolid were similar in milk and maternal plasma of rats.

Pediatrics

Safety and effectiveness of linezolid have been established for pediatric patients ranging in age from birth through 11 years for the treatment of nosocomial pneumonia, complicated skin and skin structure infections, community acquired pneumonia, and vancomycin-resistant *Enterococcus faecium* infections and ages 5 through 17 years for the treatment of uncomplicated skin and skin structure infections.

Geriatrics

Appropriate studies performed to date have not demonstrated geriatrics-specific problems that would limit the usefulness of linezolid in the elderly.

Pharmacogenetics

The volume of distribution and mean oral clearance are lower in females than males; however, the mean apparent elimination-rate constant and half-life are not significantly different between genders. Drug exposure in females is not expected to increase beyond levels known to be well tolerated.

Drug interactions and/or related problems

The following drug interactions and/or related problems have been selected on the basis of their potential clinical significance (possible mechanism in parentheses where appropriate)—not necessarily inclusive (» = major clinical significance):

Note: Combinations containing any of the following medications, depending on the amount present, may also interact with this medication.

» Bone marrow depressants, other (see *Appendix II*)
(leukopenic and/or thrombocytopenic effects of these medications may be increased; weekly monitoring of the complete blood count is recommended during concurrent therapy)

» Adrenergic agents such as
Dopamine or
Epinephrine
(initial dose should be reduced and titrated to achieve the desired response)

» Pseudoephedrine
(systolic blood pressure increased by 32 mm Hg after administration of linezolid with pseudoephedrine)

» Serotonergics (see *Appendix II*) including
Selective serotonin reuptake inhibitors (SSRIs)
(concurrent use may result in development of signs and symptoms of serotonin syndrome such as cognitive dysfunction or hyperpyrexia; caution is recommended; discontinuation of either one or both agents should be considered if signs and symptoms develop)

» Tyramine-containing foods and beverages, such as aged cheese (0 to 15 mg of tyramine per ounce); fermented, pickled, or air-dried

meats (0 to 15 mg of tyramine per ounce); red wine (0 to 6 mg of tyramine per 8 ounces); sauerkraut (8 mg of tyramine per 8 ounces); soy sauce (5 mg of tyramine per 1 teaspoon); and tap beer (4 mg of tyramine per 12 ounces)
(concurrent use of linezolid with 100 mg or more of tyramine per meal may cause a significant pressor response)

Laboratory value alterations

The following have been selected on the basis of their potential clinical significance (possible effect in parentheses where appropriate)—not necessarily inclusive (» = major clinical significance).

With physiology/laboratory test values
Hemoglobin and
Neutrophils and
Platelet count and
White blood count
(values may be decreased during therapy)
(in comparator-controlled phase 3 trials, 2.4% [range 0.3 to 10%] of patients taking linezolid developed substantially low platelet counts [defined as less than 75% of the lower limit of normal and/or baseline] compared with 1.5% [range 0.4 to 7%] of patients taking a comparator medication)

Alanine aminotransferase (ALT [SGPT]) and
Alkaline phosphatase and
Amylase and
Aspartate aminotransferase (AST [SGOT] and
Bilirubin, total and
Blood urea nitrogen and
Creatinine and
Lactate dehydrogenase (LDH) and
Lipase
(values may be transiently increased during therapy)

Medical considerations/Contraindications

The medical considerations/contraindications included have been selected on the basis of their potential clinical significance (reasons given in parentheses where appropriate)—not necessarily inclusive (» = major clinical significance).

Except under special circumstances, this medication should not be used when the following medical problem exists:

» Hypersensitivity to linezolid or any component of the product

Risk-benefit should be considered when the following medical problems exist:

» Bone marrow depression
(including anemia, leukopenia, pancytopenia, and thrombocytopenia has been reported; discontinuation should be considered in cases of worsening myelosuppression)

» Diarrhea
(important to consider diagnosis of pseudomembranous colitis, which may range in severity from mild to life-threatening, before administration of any antibacterial agent in patients who present with diarrhea)

» Phenylketonuria
(each 5 mL of the oral suspension contains 20 mg of phenylalanine)

Patient monitoring

The following may be especially important in patient monitoring (other tests may be warranted in some patients, depending on condition; » = major clinical significance):

» Complete blood count
(weekly monitoring is recommended, especially in patients who receive linezolid for more than 2 weeks, patients who have preexisting bone marrow depression, patients who concurrently receive medications that produce bone marrow depression, or patients who have a chronic infection and received previous or receive concurrent antibiotic therapy)

» Culture and sensitivity test

Side/Adverse Effects

Lactic acidosis has been reported with the use of linezolid. In reported cases, patients experienced repeated episodes of nausea and vomiting. Patients who develop recurrent nausea or vomiting, unexplained acidosis, or a low bicarbonate level while receiving linezolid should receive immediate medical evaluation.

If symptoms of visual impairment appear, such as changes in visual acuity, changes in color vision, blurred vision, or visual field defect, prompt ophthalmic evaluation is recommended. If peripheral or optic neuropathy occurs, the continued use of linezolid in these patients should be weighed against the potential risks.

Note: Peripheral and optic neuropathy have primarily been reported in patient treated with linezolid for longer than the maximum recommended duration of 28 days. In cases of optic neuropathy that progressed to loss of vision, patients were treated for extended periods beyond the maximum recommended duration.

The following side/adverse effects have been selected on the basis of their potential clinical significance (possible signs and symptoms in parentheses where appropriate)—not necessarily inclusive:

Those indicating need for medical attention

Incidence more frequent
Diarrhea

Incidence less frequent or rare
Anemia (unusual tiredness or weakness); ***leukopenia*** (chills; cough; fever; hoarseness; lower back or side pain; painful or difficult urination); ***oral moniliasis*** (sore mouth or tongue; white patches in mouth, tongue, or throat); ***pancytopenia*** (exertional dyspnea; headache; unusual tiredness or weakness); ***pseudomembranous colitis*** (abdominal cramps or pain, severe; diarrhea, severe and watery, may also be bloody; fever); ***thrombocytopenia*** (black, tarry stools; blood in urine or stools; pinpoint red spots on skin; unusual bleeding or bruising); ***vaginal moniliasis*** (discharge from the vagina; itching of the vagina)

Note: Mild cases of *pseudomembranous colitis* usually respond to discontinuation of the medication alone. Moderate to severe cases usually necessitate treatment with fluids and electrolytes, protein supplementation, and an antibacterial agent with activity against *Clostridium difficile*.
Linezolid-associated *thrombocytopenia* appears to be dependent on duration of therapy (generally greater than 2 weeks of treatment). For most patients, the platelet count returned to normal or baseline during the follow-up period. No clinical adverse events were identified in clinical trials. In the compassionate use program, bleeding events were identified in patients with thrombocytopenia; however, the role of linezolid in these events cannot be determined.

Incidence not determined—Observed during clinical practice; estimates of frequency can not be determined
Lactic acidosis (abdominal discomfort; decreased appetite; diarrhea; fast, shallow breathing; general feeling of discomfort; muscle pain or cramping; nausea; shortness of breath; sleepiness; unusual tiredness or weakness); ***optic neuropathy*** (blindness; blurred vision; decreased vision; eye pain); ***peripheral neuropathy*** (burning, numbness, tingling, or painful sensations; weakness in arms, hands, legs, or feet; unsteadiness or awkwardness)

Note: *Serotonin syndrome*(e.g., cognitive dysfunction, hyperpyrexia, hyperreflexia, incoordination) has been reported in patients receiving concomitant serotonergic agents, including antidepressants such as selective serotonin reuptake inhibitors (SSRIs).

Those indicating need for medical attention only if they continue or are bothersome

Incidence more frequent
Nausea

Incidence less frequent or rare
Dizziness; dysgeusia (bad taste in the mouth; change in sense of taste; loss of taste); ***headache; tongue discoloration; vomiting***

Overdose

For more information on the management of overdose or unintentional ingestion, **contact a poison control center** (see *Poison Control Center Listing*).

Treatment of overdose

There is no known specific antidote to linezolid. Treatment is generally supportive. In a phase 1 clinical trial, approximately 30% of a linezolid dose was removed during a 3–hour hemodialysis session. Hemodialysis was initiated 3 hours after the dose of linezolid. Hemodialysis may facilitate removal of linezolid.No information is available for removal of linezolid with peritoneal dialysis or hemoperfusion.

Patient Consultation

As an aid to patient consultation, refer to *Advice for the Patient, Linezolid (Systemic)*.

In providing consultation, consider emphasizing the following selected information (» = major clinical significance):

Before using this medication

» Conditions affecting use, especially:
Hypersensitivity to linezolid or any component of the product
Pregnancy—Risk-benefit considerations

Breast-feeding—Caution should be exercised when administering linezolid to a nursing woman

Use in children—Safety and efficacy established in children from birth through 11 years of age for all indications except treatment of uncomplicated skin and skin structure infections which is indicated for children ages 5 to 17 years

Other medications, especially adrenergic agents, other bone marrow depressants, pseudoephedrine, serotonergics including selective serotonin reuptake inhibitors (SSRIs), or tyramine-containing foods or beverages

Other medical problems, especially bone marrow depression, diarrhea, or phenylketonuria

Proper use of this medication

» Importance of receiving medication for full course of therapy and on regular schedule

» Prescribing linezolid only in the presence of a proven or strongly suspected bacterial infection or prophylactic indication to avoid increased risk of development of drug-resistant bacteria

» Proper administration technique for oral liquid

» Proper dosing

Missed dose: Taking as soon as possible; not taking if almost time for next scheduled dose; not doubling doses

Proper storage

Precautions while using this medication

» If your symptoms do not improve within a few days or if they become worse, check with your doctor

» Importance of contacting physician immediately for medical evaluation if recurrent nausea or vomiting, unexplained acidosis, or a low bicarbonate level occur; these could be signs of lactic acidosis.

Contacting eye doctor promptly for evaluation if symptoms of visual impairment such as changes in color vision, blurred vision, or visual field defect occur; these could be symptoms of peripheral or optic neuropathy

» For oral suspension—Importance of contacting physician or pharmacist if you have phenylketonuria; the oral suspension formulation contains phenylalanine

Caution if bone marrow depression occurs:

» Avoiding exposure to persons with bacterial infections, especially during periods of low blood counts; checking with physician immediately if fever or chills, cough or hoarseness, lower back of side pain, or painful or difficult urination occur

» Checking with physician immediately if unusual bleeding or bruising; black, tarry stools; blood in urine or stools; or pinpoint red spots on skin occur

Not touching eyes or inside of nose unless hands washed immediately before

Using caution to avoid accidental cuts with use of sharp objects such as safety razor or fingernail or toenail cutters

Avoiding contact sports or other situations where bruising or injury could occur

» Avoiding large amounts of tyramine-containing foods and beverages

Side/adverse effects

Signs of potential side effects, especially diarrhea, anemia, leukopenia, oral moniliasis, pancytopenia, pseudomembranous colitis, thrombocytopenia, and vaginal moniliasis

Signs of potential side effects observed during clinical practice, especially lactic acidosis, optic neuropathy, or peripheral neuropathy

(Post-marketing reports of serotonin syndrome in patients receiving concomitant serotonergic agents including SSRIs)

General Dosing Information

For oral dosing forms:

The use of antibiotics may promote the overgrowth of nonsusceptible organisms. Should superinfection occur during therapy, appropriate measures should be taken.

Linezolid has not been studied in patients with uncontrolled hypertension, pheochromocytoma, carcinoid syndrome, or untreated hyperthyroidism.

Safety and efficacy of linezolid formulations given for longer than 28 days have not been evaluated in controlled clinical trials.

Diet/Nutrition

Linezolid tablets and suspension may be taken with or without food.

Bioequivalence information

Dosage adjustment is not necessary when switching patients from intravenous to oral linezolid because the oral bioavailability is approximately 100%.

Treatment of pseudomembranous colitis

Mild cases—Usually respond to drug discontinuation alone

Moderate to severe cases—Consideration should be given to management with fluids and electrolytes, protein supplementation, and treatment with an antibacterial agent clinically effective against *Clostridium difficile.*

For parenteral dosing forms:

Linezolid injection should be administered as an intravenous infusion over 30 to 120 minutes.

Linezolid intravenous infusion bag should not be used in a series connection.

Additives should not be made to the linezolid infusion bag.

If linezolid injection is given concomitantly with another drug, each drug should be administered separately according to the administration guidelines for each drug.

If the same intravenous line is used for administration of several drugs, the line should be flushed before and after administration of linezolid injection.

Oral Dosage Forms

LINEZOLID TABLETS

Usual adult and adolescent dose

Pneumonia, community-acquired (treatment)—
Oral, 600 mg every 12 hours for 10 to 14 days.

Pneumonia, nosocomial (treatment)—
Oral, 600 mg every 12 hours for 10 to 14 days.

Skin and soft tissue infections, complicated (treatment)—
Oral, 600 mg every 12 hours for 10 to 14 days.

Skin and soft tissue infections, uncomplicated (treatment)—
Adults: Oral, 400 mg every 12 hours for 10 to 14 days.
Adolescents: Oral, 600 mg every 12 hours for 10 to 14 days.

Vancomycin-resistant Enterococcus faecium infections—
Oral, 600 mg every 12 hours for 14 to 28 days.

Usual adult and adolescent prescribing limits

Up to 1200 mg daily. Safety and efficacy not established for longer than 28 days.

Usual pediatric dose

Pneumonia, community-acquired (treatment)—
Oral, 10 mg per kg of body weight every 8 hours for 10 to 14 days.

Pneumonia, nosocomial (treatment)—
Oral, 10 mg per kg of body weight every 8 hours for 10 to 14 days.

Skin and soft tissue infections, complicated (treatment)—
Oral, 10 mg per kg of body weight every 8 hours for 10 to 14 days.

Skin and soft tissue infections, uncomplicated (treatment)—
Children less than 5 years of age: Oral, 10 mg per kg of body weight every 8 hours for 10 to 14 days.
Children 5 to 11 years of age: Oral, 10 mg per kg of body weight every 12 hours for 10 to 14 days.

Vancomycin-resistant *Enterococcus faecium* infections—
Oral, 10 mg per kg of body weight every 8 hours for 14 to 28 days.

Note: Neonates less than 7 days of age (gestational age less than 34 weeks) should be initiated with a dosing regimen of 10 mg per kg of body weight every 12 hours. Consideration may be given to the use of 10 mg per kg of body weight every 8 hours in neonates with a sub-optimal clinical response. All neonatal patients should receive 10 mg per kg of body weight every 8 hours by 7 days of life.

Usual geriatric dose

See *Usual adult and adolescent dose.*

Usual geriatric prescribing limits

See *Usual adult and adolescent prescribing limits.*

Note: Dosage adjustment is not necessary for patients with renal insufficiency. Since the metabolites may accumulate in patients with renal insufficiency, the potential risks should be weighed carefully in this patient population.

Dosage adjustment is not necessary for patients with mild-to-moderate hepatic insufficiency; however, data are not available for patients with severe hepatic insufficiency.

Note: The sodium content is 0.1 mEq per tablet regardless of strength.

Strength(s) usually available

U.S.—

400 mg (Rx) [*Zyvox* (corn starch; microcrystalline cellulose; hydroxypropyl methylcellulose; sodium starch glycolate; polyethylene glycol; titanium dioxide; carnauba wax)].

600 mg (Rx) [*Zyvox* (corn starch; microcrystalline cellulose; hydroxypropyl methylcellulose; sodium starch glycolate; polyethylene glycol; titanium dioxide; carnauba wax)].

Packaging and storage
Store at 25 °C (77 °F); excursions permitted to 15 to 30 °C (59 and 86 °F). Store in a tight, light-resistant container.

Auxiliary labeling
- Continue medication for full course of treatment.

LINEZOLID FOR ORAL SUSPENSION

Usual adult and adolescent dose
See *Linezolid Tablets.*

Usual adult and adolescent prescribing limits
See *Linezolid Tablets*

Usual pediatric dose
See *Linezolid Tablets*

Usual geriatric dose
See *Linezolid Tablets.*

Usual geriatric prescribing limits
See *Linezolid Tablets.*

Note: The sodium content is 0.4 mEq per 5 mL.

Strength(s) usually available
U.S.—

100 mg of linezolid per 5 mL (when reconstituted according to manufacturer's instructions) (Rx) [*Zyvox* (sucrose; citric acid; sodium citrate; microcrystalline cellulose; carboxymethylcellulose sodium; aspartame; xanthan gum; mannitol; sodium benzoate; colloidal silicon dioxide; sodium chloride; flavors)].

Packaging and storage
Store at 25 °C (77 °F); excursions permitted to 15 to 30 °C (59 and 86 °F). Store in a tight, light-resistant container.

Preparation of dosage form
To prepare the oral suspension, add 123 mL of distilled water in two portions. After adding the first half, shake vigorously. Then add the second portion and shake vigorously to obtain a uniform suspension.

Stability
Suspension retains its potency for 21 days from date of reconstitution when stored at room temperature.

Auxiliary labeling
- Continue medication for full course of treatment.
- Do not shake.
- Beyond-use date.

Parenteral Dosage Forms

LINEZOLID INJECTION

Usual adult and adolescent dose
Pneumonia, community-acquired (treatment)—
Intravenous, 600 mg every 12 hours for 10 to 14 days.

Pneumonia, nosocomial (treatment)—
Intravenous, 600 mg every 12 hours for 10 to 14 days.

Skin and soft tissue infections, complicated (treatment)—
Intravenous, 600 mg every 12 hours for 10 to 14 days.

Vancomycin-resistant Enterococcus faecium infections—
Intravenous, 600 mg every 12 hours for 14 to 28 days.

Usual adult and adolescent prescribing limits
Up to 1200 mg daily. Safety and efficacy not established for longer than 28 days.

Usual pediatric dose
Pneumonia, community-acquired (treatment)—
Intravenous, 10 mg per kg of body weight every 8 hours for 10 to 14 days.

Pneumonia, nosocomial (treatment)—
Intravenous, 10 mg per kg of body weight every 8 hours for 10 to 14 days.

Skin and soft tissue infections, complicated (treatment)—
Intravenous, 10 mg per kg of body weight every 8 hours for 10 to 14 days.

Vancomycin-resistant *Enterococcus faecium* infections—
Intravenous, 10 mg per kg of body weight every 8 hours for 14 to 28 days.

Note: Neonates less than 7 days of age (gestational age less than 34 weeks) should be initiated with a dosing regimen of 10 mg per kg of body weight every 12 hours. Consideration may be given to the use of 10 mg per kg of body weight every 8 hours in neonates with a sub-optimal clinical response. All neonatal patients should receive 10 mg per kg of body weight every 8 hours by 7 days of life.

Usual geriatric dose
See *Usual adult and adolescent dose.*

Usual geriatric prescribing limits
See *Usual adult and adolescent prescribing limits.*

Note: Dosage adjustment is not necessary for patients with renal insufficiency. Since the metabolites may accumulate in patients with renal insufficiency, the potential risks should be weighed carefully in this patient population.

Dosage adjustment is not necessary for patients with mild-to-moderate hepatic insufficiency; however, data are not available for patients with severe hepatic insufficiency.

Note: The sodium content is 5 mEq, 3.3 mEq, and 1.7 mEq for the 300-mL bag, 200-mL bag, and the 100-mL bag, respectively.

Strength(s) usually available
U.S.—

200 mg of linezolid per 100 mL (Rx) [*Zyvox*™ (sodium citrate; citric acid; dextrose)].

400 mg of linezolid per 200 mL (Rx) [*Zyvox*™ (sodium citrate; citric acid; dextrose)].

600 mg of linezolid per 300 mL (Rx) [*Zyvox*™ (sodium citrate; citric acid; dextrose)].

Packaging and storage
Store at 25 °C (77 °F); excursions permitted to 15 to 30 °C (59 and 86 °F). Protect from freezing. Store infusion bags in the overwrap until ready to use.

Stability
Parenteral drug products should be inspected visually for particulate matter prior to administration.

Incompatibilities
When administered via simulated Y-site injection, linezolid was incompatible with amphotericin B, ceftriaxone sodium, chlorpromazine HCl, diazepam, erythromycin lactobionate, pentamidine isothionate, phenytoin sodium, and trimethoprim-sulfamethoxazole. Additionally, chemical incompatibility resulted when linezolid injection was combined with ceftriaxone sodium.If other drugs are administered via the same intravenous line, the line should be flushed before and after administering linezolid with an infusion solution compatible with linezolid injection and with any other drugs administered via this common line. Intravenous solutions *compatible* with linezolid injection include: 5% Dextrose injection, 0.9% Sodium Chloride injection, and Lactated Ringer's injection.

Additional information
Linezolid injection may exhibit a yellow color that can intensify over time without adversely affecting potency.

Check for minute leaks by firmly squeezing the bag. If leaks are detected, discard the solution, as sterility may be impaired.

Revised: 08/04/2005
Developed: 08/17/2000

LIOTHYRONINE—See *Thyroid Hormones (Systemic)*

LIOTRIX—See *Thyroid Hormones (Systemic)*

LISINOPRIL—See *Angiotensin-converting Enzyme (ACE) Inhibitors (Systemic)*

LITHIUM Systemic

VA CLASSIFICATION (Primary/Secondary): CN750/CN900; BL400

Commonly used brand name(s): *Carbolith; Cibalith-S; Duralith; Eskalith; Eskalith CR; Lithane; Lithizine; Lithobid; Lithonate; Lithotabs.*

Note: For a listing of dosage forms and brand names by country availability, see *Dosage Forms* section(s).

Category
Antimanic; antidepressant therapy adjunct; granulopoietic; vascular headache prophylactic.

Indications

Note: Bracketed information in the *Indications* section refers to uses that are not included in U.S. product labeling.

Accepted

Bipolar disorder (treatment)—Lithium is indicated as the primary agent in the treatment of acute manic and hypomanic episodes in bipolar disorder, and for maintenance therapy to help diminish the intensity and frequency of subsequent manic episodes in patients with a history of mania.

Lithium is used in some patients as the agent of choice in the prevention of bipolar depression. Clinicians have observed a diminished intensity and frequency of severe depressive episodes.

[Depression, mental (treatment)][1]—Lithium is used alone for maintenance therapy in unipolar depression, and for acute and maintenance therapy in schizoaffective disorder. It is also used to augment the antidepressant effect of tricyclic or monoamine oxidase (MAO) inhibitor antidepressants in the treatment of major unipolar depression in patients not responsive to antidepressants alone.

[Headache, vascular (prophylaxis)][1]—Lithium is used to reduce the frequency of the occurrence of episodic and chronic cluster headaches.

[Neutropenia (treatment)][1]—Lithium is used to reduce the incidence of infection in patients with chemotherapy-induced neutropenia and in patients with chronic or acquired neutropenia.

---

[1]Not included in Canadian product labeling.

Pharmacology/Pharmacokinetics

Physicochemical characteristics

Molecular weight—
- Lithium carbonate: 73.89.
- Lithium citrate: 282.00.

Other characteristics—
- A monovalent cation easily assayed in biological fluids; salts share some chemical characteristics with salts of sodium and potassium

Mechanism of action/Effect

Antimanic—Has not been established. The mood-stabilizing effect has been postulated to relate to a reduction of catecholamine neurotransmitter concentration, possibly mediated by lithium ion (Li^+) effect on Na^+K^+ adenosine triphosphatase (Na^+K^+ATPase) to produce improved transneuronal membrane transport of sodium ion. An alternate postulate is that lithium may decrease cyclic adenosine monophosphate (cyclic AMP) concentrations, which would result in decreased sensitivity of hormonal-sensitive adenylcyclase receptors. Another hypothesis is the "second messenger" theory of lithium's interference with lipid inositol metabolism. This theory postulates that a group of improperly regulated neurons may be the underlying cause of manic symptoms. A phospholipase C-type enzyme hydrolyzes the plasma membrane–located lipid, phosphatidylinositol biphosphate, to diacyglycerol and inositol triphosphate, postsynaptic second messengers that contribute to chronic cell stimulation by altering electrical activity in the neuron. Inositol formed during this process is recycled by the inositol phospholipid–synthesizing enzymes in the CNS. There is evidence that cells in the CNS do not have access to plasma sources of inositol but, instead, depend on the synthesis of inositol for the transduction of neuronal signals. Lithium, in therapeutic concentrations, blocks the activity of the enzyme, inositol-1-phosphatase, resulting in a depletion of neuronal inositol and ultimately a decrease in the levels of phosphatidylinositol biphosphate. The lipid will no longer be able to stimulate the formation of adequate quantities of the second messengers or alter electrical activity. Subsequent cells in the CNS become relatively insensitive to the agonist stimulation, and clinical improvement results.

Granulopoietic—The exact mechanism of action has not been established; however, studies have shown that lithium stimulates granulopoiesis, enhances marrow proliferation, elevates neutrophil production, and increases the granulocyte pool.

Vascular headache prophylactic—Specific mechanism has not been established. It has been postulated that the action of lithium in cluster headaches may be directly related to changes in platelet serotonin and histamine concentrations.

Antidepressant—Has not been established. However, the mechanism may involve enhancement of serotonergic activity and downregulation of beta-receptors.

Absorption

Rapid; complete within 6 to 8 hours. Absorption rate of slow-release capsules is slower and the total amount of lithium absorbed is lower than with other dosage forms.

Protein binding

Not bound to plasma proteins.

Biotransformation

None.

Half-life (average)

Elimination—
- Adults: 24 hours.
- Adolescents: 18 hours.
- Elderly patients: Up to 36 hours.

Note: When therapy is initiated, the serum concentration decreases rapidly during the initial 5 or 6 hours, followed by a more gradual decline over the next 24 hours.

Time to peak serum concentration

Syrup—0.5 hours.
Capsules or tablets—1 to 3 hours.
Extended-release tablets—4 hours.
Slow-release capsules—3 hours.
Steady-state serum concentrations—4 days.

Therapeutic serum concentration

Bipolar disorder—
- Acute: 0.8 to 1.2 mEq per liter, occasionally up to 1.5 mEq per liter.
- Maintenance: 0.5 to 1.0 mEq per liter. Occasionally may require same concentration range as acute illness.

Onset of therapeutic action

Clinical improvement—1 to 3 weeks.

Elimination

Renal—
- 95% unchanged; rapid initially, slower with extended therapy; 80% may be actively reabsorbed in the proximal tubule; rate of excretion decreases with age.

Fecal—
- <1%.

Sweat—
- 4 to 5%.

Precautions to Consider

Pregnancy/Reproduction

Pregnancy—First trimester: Use of lithium is not recommended during pregnancy, especially in the first trimester, because of possible teratogenicity. Lithium crosses the placenta and is present in almost equal concentrations in the fetal and maternal serum. Data from lithium birth registers suggest an increased incidence of neonatal goiter and congenital cardiovascular malformations, especially Ebstein's anomaly.

FDA Pregnancy Category D.

Delivery—Lithium toxicity may be manifested as hypotonia, lethargy, and cyanosis in newborn infants of mothers taking lithium at term. Risk-benefit must be considered.

Breast-feeding

Lithium is excreted in breast milk at a concentration about one-half that in maternal serum. Signs and symptoms of lithium toxicity such as hypotonia, hypothermia, cyanosis, and electrocardiogram (ECG) changes have been reported in some infants. With rare exceptions, infants should not be breast-fed while the mother is receiving lithium therapy.

Pediatrics

Appropriate studies on the relationship of age to the effects of lithium have not been performed in the pediatric population. However, lithium may decrease bone formation or density in children by altering parathyroid hormone concentrations. Also, lithium is deposited in bone, replacing calcium in hydroxyapatite, an effect more pronounced in immature bone.

Geriatrics

Geriatric patients and patients with organic mental disease usually require lower lithium dosage, lower serum concentration, and more frequent monitoring than younger adults because renal clearance rate and distribution volume are reduced. Lithium is more toxic to the central nervous system (CNS) in the elderly, even when serum lithium concentrations are within the therapeutic range for younger adults. Also, the elderly possibly may be more prone to develop lithium-induced goiter and clinical hypothyroidism. Excessive thirst and larger volume of urine as early side effects of lithium therapy may be more frequent in the elderly.

Drug interactions and/or related problems

The following drug interactions and/or related problems have been selected on the basis of their potential clinical significance (possible

mechanism in parentheses where appropriate)—not necessarily inclusive (» = major clinical significance):

Note: Combinations containing any of the following medications, depending on the amount present, may also interact with this medication.

Amphetamines
(concurrent use with lithium may antagonize the CNS stimulating effects of amphetamines)

Angiotensin-converting enzyme (ACE) inhibitors
(reversible increases in serum lithium concentrations and toxicity have been reported during concurrent use with ACE inhibitors; frequent monitoring of serum lithium concentrations is recommended during concurrent use)

Antidepressants, tricyclic
(since tricyclics may cause a swing into mania and a rapid recycling between mania and depression, lithium plasma concentrations at or greater than 0.8 mEq per liter may be needed to prevent the tricyclic switch process)

» Acetazolamide
(may lower lithium concentrations by increasing urinary lithium excretion)

» Anti-inflammatory drugs, nonsteroidal (NSAIDs)
(concurrent use may increase the toxic effects of lithium by decreasing its renal excretion, thereby increasing the steady-state plasma lithium concentration by 39 to 50%; patient should be observed for symptoms of lithium toxicity, and increased monitoring of lithium plasma concentrations is recommended during concurrent use)

Atracurium or
Pancuronium or
Succinylcholine
(neuromuscular blocking effects may be potentiated or prolonged when these medications are used concurrently with chronic lithium therapy)

Calcium channel blocking agents
(concurrent use with lithium may increase the risk of neurotoxicity in the form of ataxia, tremors, nausea, vomiting, diarrhea, and/or tinnitus; caution is recommended)

» Calcium iodide or
» Iodinated glycerol or
» Potassium iodide
(concurrent use with lithium may potentiate the hypothyroid and goitrogenic effects of either these medications or lithium)

Carbamazepine or
Desmopressin or
Lypressin or
Posterior pituitary or
Vasopressin
(lithium may decrease the antidiuretic effect of these medications when used concurrently)
(lithium may prevent or decrease carbamazepine-induced leukopenia with a possible increase in therapeutic effect when carbamazepine is used to treat psychotic disorders or bipolar conditions)

» Chlorpromazine and possibly other phenothiazines
(concurrent use with lithium may reduce gastrointestinal absorption of the phenothiazine, thereby decreasing its serum concentrations by as much as 40%; phenothiazines, especially chlorpromazine, increase intracellular lithium concentration; concurrent use may increase rate of renal excretion of lithium; extrapyramidal symptoms, delirium, and cerebellar function impairment may be increased, especially in elderly patients; also, nausea and vomiting, early indications of lithium toxicity, may be masked by the antiemetic effect of some phenothiazines; admixture of lithium citrate syrup with any liquid forms of phenothiazines may form a precipitate of the free phenothiazine)

» Diuretics
(concurrent use with lithium may provoke severe lithium toxicity by delaying renal excretion of lithium and consequently increasing serum and red blood cell lithium concentrations; close monitoring of lithium plasma concentrations is essential since sodium and lithium reabsorption in the proximal tubule is increased, due to the body sodium deficit; a reduction in lithium dosage may be necessary)

Fludrocortisone
(in one published case report, lithium antagonized the mineralocorticoid effects of fludrocortisone; increased fludrocortisone dose and dietary sodium supplementation were required during concurrent use)

» Haloperidol
(lithium is frequently used concurrently with haloperidol during the first 1 or 2 weeks of treatment for acute manic episodes, but lithium alone may be adequate thereafter. However, concurrent use with lithium has been reported, in a few cases, to be associated with irreversible neurological toxicity and brain damage, especially in patients with organic mental syndrome or other CNS impairment, although this interaction is controversial; extrapyramidal symptoms may be increased by enhancement of dopamine blockade by haloperidol; patients should be monitored closely during concurrent use; dosage adjustments may be necessary)
(admixture of the liquid forms of lithium and haloperidol may precipitate free haloperidol)

Methyldopa
(concurrent use may increase the risk of lithium toxicity even though serum lithium concentrations remain within the recommended therapeutic range)

Metronidazole
(concurrent use may promote renal retention of lithium, leading to lithium toxicity; reducing the dose or discontinuing the use of lithium may be necessary during metronidazole therapy; if not feasible to discontinue, frequent monitoring of serum creatinine, electrolyte and lithium concentrations, and urine osmolality to detect possible nephrogenic diabetes insipidus are recommended)

» Molindone
(concurrent use with lithium may produce neurotoxic symptoms such as confusion, delirium, seizures, somnambulism, or abnormal electroencephalogram [EEG] changes)

Norepinephrine
(concurrent use with lithium may decrease the pressor response to norepinephrine; a higher dose of norepinephrine may be required to achieve the desired effect)

Selective serotonin reuptake inhibitors, such as:
Fluoxetine or
Fluvoxamine or
Paroxetine or
Sertraline
(concurrent use with lithium has been reported to result in symptoms such as agitation, confusion, diarrhea, dizziness, and tremor; lithium concentrations may be altered, leading to toxicity; close monitoring of lithium concentrations is recommended)

Sodium-containing medications or foods, especially sodium bicarbonate or sodium chloride
(high sodium intake enhances lithium excretion, possibly resulting in decreased efficacy)

Urea
(may increase the renal excretion of lithium, thereby decreasing its effects)

Xanthines such as:
Aminophylline
Caffeine
Dyphylline
Oxtriphylline
Theophylline
(concurrent use of these medications with lithium increases urinary excretion of lithium, thereby possibly reducing its therapeutic effect)

Laboratory value alterations

The following have been selected on the basis of their potential clinical significance (possible effect in parentheses where appropriate)—not necessarily inclusive (» = major clinical significance).

With physiology/laboratory test values

Glucose, blood
(may be increased during treatment with lithium; concentrations return to normal when lithium administration is discontinued)

Parathyroid hormone, immunoreactive and
Calcium
(serum concentrations may rise above normal after long-term therapy)

Medical considerations/Contraindications

The medical considerations/contraindications included have been selected on the basis of their potential clinical significance (reasons given in parentheses where appropriate)—not necessarily inclusive (» = major clinical significance).

Except under special circumstances, this medication should not be used when the following medical problem exists:

» Leukemia, history of
(leukemia may be reactivated by lithium)

Risk-benefit should be considered when the following medical problems exist:

» Cardiovascular disease
(may be exacerbated; possible interference with lithium excretion)

» CNS disorders, such as epilepsy and parkinsonism
(may be exacerbated; lithium-induced neurotoxicity may be masked)

» Dehydration, severe
(risk of toxicity is increased; the loss of large volumes of body fluid as in prolonged vomiting, diarrhea, or profuse perspiration due to fever, exercise, saunas, or hot baths may result in increased serum lithium concentration; such loss of body fluid may necessitate dosage adjustment of lithium and/or the supplemental intake of sodium and fluids until hydration status and electrolytes are stable)

Diabetes mellitus
(serum insulin concentration may be increased)

Goiter or
Hypothyroidism
(latent hypothyroidism may be induced in predisposed or elderly patients)

Hyperparathyroidism
(calcium metabolism may be altered after long-term use)

» Infections, severe
(fever with prolonged sweating, diarrhea, or vomiting may necessitate a decrease in lithium dosage to prevent lithium toxicity)

Organic mental disease or
Schizophrenia
(patients may be hypersensitive to lithium and exhibit increased confusion, seizures, or electroencephalogram [EEG] changes at normal serum lithium concentrations)

Psoriasis
(may be aggravated by lithium; dosage adjustments of lithium and/or other medications may be necessary)

» Renal insufficiency or
» Urinary retention
(lithium excretion may be delayed, leading to toxicity)

Sensitivity to lithium

Caution should be used also in severely debilitated patients or in patients on a sodium-restricted diet because these conditions may increase the risk of toxicity by delaying renal excretion of lithium.

Patient monitoring

The following may be especially important in patient monitoring (other tests may be warranted in some patients, depending on condition; » = major clinical significance):

Calcium concentrations, serum and
Phosphate concentrations, serum
(determinations recommended in children under 12 years of age prior to initiation of therapy and periodically during treatment since lithium increases parathyroid hormone concentrations and risk of hypercalcemia and hypophosphatemia)

» Electrocardiogram (ECG)
(recommended at least once prior to therapy in all patients, and especially in patients over 40 years of age and those with a history suggestive of cardiovascular disease; should be repeated if symptoms such as palpitations, irregular pulse, weight gain with edema, or diminished consciousness occur; also, lithium may cause the benign effect of flattening of T-waves and prominent U-waves)

Electrolyte concentrations, serum
(determinations recommended prior to therapy to detect preexisting hyponatremia, which will decrease lithium excretion)

Height and
Weight evaluation
(baseline weight measurement prior to therapy and every 3 months are recommended; weight gain, possibly due to a high intake of calorie-containing liquids as a result of lithium-induced polydipsia or to fluid retention to balance the increase in cations, may lead to a patient's noncompliance with lithium therapy; in children, height and weight charts should be maintained, and lithium therapy re-evaluated or discontinued if there is any decrease in growth rate)

» Lithium concentrations, serum
(determinations recommended once or twice weekly during treatment of acute manic episode until serum concentrations and patient's clinical condition have stabilized; recommended at least every 2 to 3 months during remission when patient is stabilized; blood samples should be drawn in the morning immediately prior to the next dose, 10 to 14 hours following the previous dose, when there is maximal stability in serum concentration. Some side effects may occur at serum lithium concentrations below 1.5 mEq per liter, and mild to moderate toxic reactions are likely to occur at concentrations from 1.5 to 2.5 mEq per liter. Serum lithium concentrations should not be permitted to exceed 1.5 mEq per liter during the acute treatment phase; concentrations above 2.0 mEq per liter in chronic consumption of lithium can produce complex and serious clinical problems. Severe toxicity can occur at 2.5 mEq per liter. Close monitoring is recommended if lithium is used during the last trimester of pregnancy, used concurrently with any other medication, and used in the elderly when renal clearance rate and distribution volume are reduced)

Pregnancy test, beta-HCG
(recommended prior to initiation of therapy in all women of childbearing potential)

» Renal function determinations
(close assessment recommended prior to initiation of lithium therapy and periodically thereafter, even in asymptomatic patients with stable serum lithium concentrations; blood urea nitrogen [BUN]; serum creatinine; and urinalysis should be performed prior to initiating therapy to determine hydration status, renal flow, and presence of pre-existing renal concentrating defect)

Thyroid function determinations
(serum thyroxine and thyroxine-stimulating hormone [TSH] should be evaluated at baseline before lithium therapy is initiated and at 6-month intervals during therapy; patient should be monitored for symptoms of hypothyroidism; maintenance of adequate thyroid function is important in children to maintain a satisfactory growth rate)

» White blood cell count, total and differential
(recommended prior to therapy and repeated if signs of unusual tiredness or weakness develop because of possible rare leukemia that may develop during lithium therapy; however, the association of lithium with leukemia is controversial; benign leukocytosis may be reversible on discontinuation of therapy)

Side/Adverse Effects

Note: The occurrence and severity of lithium–associated side/adverse effects are generally related directly to the serum lithium concentrations as well as to individual patient sensitivity to lithium. Lithium–related effects tend to occur with increasing frequency and severity at higher concentrations.

The following side/adverse effects have been selected on the basis of their potential clinical significance (possible signs and symptoms in parentheses where appropriate)—not necessarily inclusive:

Those indicating need for medical attention

Incidence less frequent

Cardiovascular problems (fainting; fast or slow heartbeat; irregular pulse; troubled breathing [dyspnea] on exertion); ***extrapyramidal symptoms*** (muscle dysfunction or rigidity); ***leukocytosis*** (unusual tiredness or weakness); ***genitourinary effects*** (glucose or protein in the urine); ***nephrogenic diabetes insipidus*** (frequent urination; increased thirst)—may persist after discontinuation of lithium; ***neurologic effects*** (blackout spells; confusion, poor memory or stupor; dizziness; slurred speech); ***weight gain***

Note: *Sinus node function impairment, sinoatrial block,* or *ventricular irritability* may occur at therapeutic serum lithium concentrations; possibly reversible when lithium is discontinued.

Leukocytosis is usually reversible upon discontinuation of lithium, but a rare leukemia may develop during lithium therapy.

Incidence rare

Blue color and pain in fingers and toes; coldness of arms and legs; pseudotumor cerebri (dizziness; eye pain; headache; nausea or vomiting; noises in ears; vision problems)

Note: If undetected, *pseudotumor cerebri* may result in enlargement of blind spot, constriction of visual fields, and eventual blindness, due to optic atrophy.

Symptoms of hypothyroidism

Dry, rough skin; hair loss; hoarseness; mania (unusual excitement); ***mental depression; sensitivity to cold; swelling of feet or lower legs; swelling of neck***

Those indicating need for medical attention only if they continue or are bothersome

Incidence more frequent

Diarrhea; increased thirst; nausea, mild; stress incontinence or urinary urgency (increased frequency of urination; loss of bladder control); ***trembling of hands, slight***

Note: *Stress incontinence* or *urinary urgency* is dose-related; more common in women; usually begins 2 to 7 years after start of treatment with lithium.

Incidence less frequent

Acne or skin rash; bloated feeling or pressure in the stomach; muscle twitching, slight

Overdose

For specific information on the agents used in the management of lithium overdose, see:

- *Acetazolamide* in *Carbonic Anhydrase Inhibitors (Systemic)* monograph; and/or
- *Mannitol (Systemic)* monograph.

For more information on the management of overdose or unintentional ingestion, **contact a poison control center** (see *Poison Control Center Listing*).

Clinical effects of overdose

The following effects have been selected on the basis of their potential clinical significance (possible signs and symptoms in parentheses where appropriate)—not necessarily inclusive:

Early symptoms of toxicity

Diarrhea; drowsiness; lack of coordination; loss of appetite; muscle weakness; nausea or vomiting; slurred speech; trembling

Late symptoms of toxicity

Ataxia (clumsiness or unsteadiness); ***blurred vision; confusion; convulsions; dizziness; increase in amount of urine; tinnitus*** (ringing in the ears); ***trembling, severe***

Treatment of overdose

No specific antidote is available. Early toxic symptoms can usually be treated by reducing or stopping administration of lithium and resuming treatment at a lower dosage after 24 to 48 hours.

Treatment of more severe toxicity or acute overdose may include the following:

To decrease absorption—

Inducing vomiting or using small volume (100 mL) gastric lavage (in acute overdose).

To enhance elimination—

Utilizing intermittent hemodialysis if plasma lithium does not drop more than 10% every 3 hours or half-life is greater than 36 hours. Since plasma lithium determinations immediately after dialysis do not take into account the rebound increase that occurs as lithium redistributes from tissue to blood, determinations must be obtained 6 hours later.

Possibly increasing lithium excretion with single dose of intravenous acetazolamide or using mannitol as an osmotic diuretic.

Monitoring—

Measuring plasma lithium concentrations every 3 hours until lithium is less than 1.0 mEq per liter.

Monitoring patient closely.

Supportive care—

Maintaining electrolyte balance and body fluids.

Regulating kidney function.

Maintaining adequate respiration.

Preventing infection.

Patients in whom intentional overdose is known or suspected should be referred for psychiatric consultation.

Patient Consultation

As an aid to patient consultation, refer to *Advice for the Patient, Lithium (Systemic)*

In providing consultation, consider emphasizing the following selected information (» = major clinical significance):

Before using this medication

» Conditions affecting use, especially:

Sensitivity to lithium

Pregnancy—Lithium crosses placenta; contraindicated in first trimester because of possible neonatal goiter and cardiovascular malformations; at delivery, hypotonia, lethargy, and cyanosis in newborns of mothers taking lithium at term

Breast-feeding—Excreted in breast milk; may cause hypotonia, hypothermia, cyanosis, and ECG changes in some babies

Use in children—May decrease bone formation or density

Use in the elderly—Elderly more prone to develop CNS toxicity, hypothyroidism and goiter; lower doses and more frequent monitoring required

Other medications, especially acetazolamide, iodine-containing preparations, nonsteroidal anti-inflammatory drugs, chlorpromazine (and possibly other phenothiazines), diuretics, haloperidol, or molindone

Other medical problems, especially history of leukemia, cardiovascular disease, epilepsy, parkinsonism, severe dehydration, renal insufficiency, urinary retention, or severe infections with prolonged sweating, vomiting, or diarrhea

Proper use of this medication

Taking after a meal or snack to prevent laxative action and to decrease the severity of stomach upset, tremors, or weakness by slowing absorption rate

» Importance of adequate fluid (2.5 to 3 liters each day) and sodium intake

» Importance of not taking more medication than the amount prescribed

» Compliance with therapy; improvement in condition may require 1 to 3 weeks; importance of maintaining adequate blood levels even though symptoms improved

» Proper dosing

Missed dose: Taking as soon as possible, unless within 4 hours (6 hours for extended-release tablets or slow-release capsules) of next scheduled dose; not doubling doses

» Proper storage

For extended-release or slow-release dosage form

Swallowing tablet or capsule whole

Not breaking, crushing, or chewing

For syrup dosage form

Diluting dose with fruit juice or other flavored beverage before taking

Precautions while using this medication

» Regular visits to physician to check progress during therapy; importance of serum lithium monitoring

Caution in drinking large amounts of coffee, tea, or colas because of diuretic effect

» Possible drowsiness or dizziness; caution if driving or doing jobs requiring alertness

» Caution during exercise, saunas, and hot weather

» Caution during illnesses that cause high fevers with profuse sweating, vomiting, or diarrhea

» Caution on self-imposed dieting

» Importance of patient and family knowing early symptoms of overdose or toxicity

For slow-release dosage form:

» Not using interchangeably with any other dosage form

Side/adverse effects

» Early symptoms of lithium overdose or toxicity:

(Diarrhea)
(Drowsiness)
(Lack of coordination)
(Loss of appetite)
(Muscle weakness)
(Nausea or vomiting)
(Slurred speech)
(Trembling)

Side effects are more likely to occur in the elderly

Signs of potential side effects, especially cardiovascular problems, extrapyramidal symptoms, genitourinary problems, leukocytosis, nephrogenic diabetes insipidus, neurologic effects, weight gain, blue color and pain in fingers and toes, coldness of arms and legs, pseudotumor cerebri, symptoms of hypothyroidism

General Dosing Information

Warning—Lithium toxicity can occur with doses at or near therapeutic serum concentrations. Facilities for prompt and accurate serum lithium determinations must be available during therapy. Accurate patient evaluation requires both clinical and laboratory analysis.

During the acute manic phase, the patient may have a greater ability to tolerate lithium. This tolerance decreases as the manic symptoms subside and often necessitates a corresponding dosage adjustment.

During the acute manic phase, lithium administration of 300 (8 mEq) to 600 mg three times a day should usually produce effective serum concentrations ranging from 0.8 to 1.2 mEq per liter, with weekly adjustments based on plasma lithium concentrations. An increase of 8 mEq a day will increase plasma concentrations by 0.3±0.1 mEq per liter. The maintenance dose of 300 mg three or four times a day usually produces effective serum concentrations ranging from 0.5 to 1.0 mEq per liter.

If a satisfactory therapeutic response to lithium at the highest tolerated serum concentrations within the therapeutic range is not achieved within 3 weeks, lithium therapy should be discontinued.

Slow-release lithium carbonate capsules and tablets are not bioequivalent to other lithium dosage forms and should not be used interchangeably with them.

Diet/Nutrition

Since lithium decreases sodium reabsorption by the renal tubules, a normal diet with an average consumption of salt and adequate fluid intake, 2.5 to 3 liters of fluid per day, is essential to prevent sodium depletion leading to lithium toxicity.

This medication may be taken with food, juice, or milk, if necessary, to lessen laxative action, stomach irritation, tremors, or weakness, by slowing absorption of lithium. The syrup must be diluted in juice or other flavored beverage before administration.

For treatment of adverse effects

Early side effects—If slight hand tremor, mild nausea or diarrhea, unusual drowsiness, or acne do not subside with continued treatment, a reduction in lithium dosage may be necessary. If hand tremor is especially bothersome, shifting a majority of the dose to bedtime, decreasing caffeine intake, or adding a beta-blocker such as propranolol may be helpful.

Suppression of thyroid activity—May necessitate thyroid hormone replacement therapy.

Urinary incontinence—Lowering dose of lithium whenever possible, adding an anticholinergic agent or an antidepressant with anticholinergic properties, or switching to another medication for treatment of bipolar disorder.

Polyuria—Lowering dose of lithium alone, whenever possible. If the lower plasma lithium concentration is inadequate to maintain a response, adding a thiazide diuretic and reducing the lithium dose by 50%, then readjusting it to reproduce the original plasma lithium concentration, may be effective. Alternatively, extended-release or slow-release lithium products can improve the patient's renal concentrating ability.

Weight gain—May be safely and effectively treated by limiting calorie intake with emphasis on adequate fluid and sodium intake.

Oral Dosage Forms

LITHIUM CARBONATE CAPSULES USP

Usual adult and adolescent dose

Antimanic—

Acute mania: Oral, initially 300 to 600 mg (8 to 16 mEq) three times a day, the dosage being adjusted as needed and tolerated at weekly intervals.

Maintenance: Oral, 300 mg three or four times a day, the dosage being adjusted as needed and tolerated.

Note: Geriatric or debilitated patients usually require a lower dosage.

Usual adult prescribing limits

Up to 2.4 grams a day.

Usual pediatric dose

Antimanic—

Children up to 12 years of age: Oral, initially 15 to 20 mg (0.4 to 0.5 mEq) per kg of body weight a day in two or three divided doses, the dosage being adjusted at weekly intervals, based on plasma lithium concentrations.

Children 12 to 18 years of age: See *Usual adult and adolescent dose*.

Strength(s) usually available

U.S.—

150 mg (Rx) [GENERIC].
300 mg (Rx) [*Eskalith; Lithonate;* GENERIC].
600 mg (Rx) [GENERIC].

Canada—

150 mg (Rx) [*Carbolith*].
300 mg (Rx) [*Carbolith; Lithane*].

Packaging and storage

Store below 40 °C (104 °F), preferably between 15 and 30 °C (59 and 86 °F), unless otherwise specified by manufacturer. Store in a well-closed container.

Auxiliary labeling

- May cause drowsiness.
- Take after a meal or snack.

LITHIUM CARBONATE SLOW-RELEASE CAPSULES

Usual adult and adolescent dose

Antimanic—

Acute mania: Oral, initially 600 to 900 mg a day on the first day, the dosage being increased, thereafter, to 1200 to 1800 mg a day in three divided doses, as needed and tolerated.

Maintenance: Oral, 900 to 1200 mg a day in three divided doses, the dosage being adjusted as needed and tolerated.

Usual adult prescribing limits

Up to 2.4 grams a day.

Usual pediatric dose

Antimanic—

Children up to 12 years of age: Dosage has not been established.

Children 12 to 18 years of age: See *Usual adult and adolescent dose*.

Usual geriatric dose

Antimanic—

Oral, 600 to 1200 mg a day in three divided doses.

Strength(s) usually available

U.S.—

Not commercially available.

Canada—

150 mg (Rx) [*Lithizine*].
300 mg (Rx) [*Lithizine*].

Note: Not bioequivalent to other lithium dosage forms and should not be used interchangeably with them.

Packaging and storage

Store below 40 °C (104 °F), preferably between 15 and 30 °C (59 and 86 °F), unless otherwise specified by manufacturer. Store in a well-closed container.

Auxiliary labeling

- Swallow whole.
- May cause drowsiness.

LITHIUM CARBONATE TABLETS USP

Usual adult and adolescent dose

See *Lithium Carbonate Capsules USP*.

Usual adult prescribing limits

See *Lithium Carbonate Capsules USP*.

Usual pediatric dose

See *Lithium Carbonate Capsules USP*.

Strength(s) usually available

U.S.—

300 mg (Rx) [*Lithotabs;* GENERIC].

Canada—

300 mg (Rx) [*Lithane*].

Packaging and storage

Store below 40 °C (104 °F), preferably between 15 and 30 °C (59 and 86 °F), unless otherwise specified by manufacturer. Store in a well-closed container.

Auxiliary labeling

- May cause drowsiness.
- Take after a meal or snack.

LITHIUM CARBONATE EXTENDED-RELEASE TABLETS

Usual adult and adolescent dose

Antimanic—

Acute mania: Oral, 450 to 900 mg two times a day or 300 to 600 mg three times a day, the dosage being adjusted as needed and tolerated.

Maintenance: Oral, 450 mg two times a day or 300 mg three times a day, the dosage being adjusted as needed and tolerated.

Note: Geriatric or debilitated patients usually require a lower dosage.

Usual adult prescribing limits

Up to 2.4 grams a day.

Usual pediatric dose

Antimanic—

Children up to 12 years of age: Dosage has not been established.

Children 12 to 18 years of age: See *Usual adult and adolescent dose*.

Strength(s) usually available

U.S.—

300 mg (Rx) [*Lithobid*].
450 mg (Rx) [*Eskalith CR* (scored)].

Canada—

300 mg (Rx) [*Duralith* (scored)].

Packaging and storage

Store below 40 °C (104 °F), preferably between 15 and 30 °C (59 and 86 °F), in a well-closed container, unless otherwise specified by manufacturer.

Auxiliary labeling

- Swallow whole.
- May cause drowsiness.
- Take after a meal or snack.

LITHIUM CITRATE SYRUP USP

Usual adult and adolescent dose

Antimanic—

Acute mania: Oral, the equivalent of 300 to 600 mg (8 to 16 mEq) of lithium carbonate three times a day, the dosage being adjusted as needed and tolerated.

Maintenance: Oral, the equivalent of 300 mg of lithium carbonate three or four times a day, the dosage being adjusted as needed and tolerated.

Note: Geriatric or debilitated patients usually require a lower dosage.

Usual adult prescribing limits

Up to the equivalent of 2.4 grams of lithium carbonate a day.

Usual pediatric dose

Antimanic—

Children up to 12 years of age: Oral, initially the equivalent of 15 to 20 mg (0.4 to 0.5 mEq) of lithium carbonate per kg of body weight a day in two or three divided doses, the dosage being adjusted at weekly intervals, based on plasma lithium concentrations.

Children 12 to 18 years of age: See *Usual adult and adolescent dose.*

Strength(s) usually available

U.S.—

8 mEq of lithium ion (equivalent to approximately 300 mg of lithium carbonate) per 5 mL (Rx) [*Cibalith-S;* GENERIC].

Canada—

Not commercially available.

Packaging and storage

Store between 15 and 30 °C (59 and 86 °F), unless otherwise specified by manufacturer. Store in a tight container. Protect from freezing.

Incompatibilities

Lithium citrate syrup should not be mixed with or administered at the same time as other medication, solid or liquid, that contains a basic form, such as chlorpromazine concentrate, haloperidol, thioridazine, or trifluoperazine, and tricyclic antidepressants.

Auxiliary labeling

- May cause drowsiness.
- Take after a meal or snack.
- Dilute with juice or other beverage before taking.

Revised: 02/02/2000

LOMEFLOXACIN—See *Fluoroquinolones (Systemic)*

LOMUSTINE Systemic

VA CLASSIFICATION (Primary): AN100

Commonly used brand name(s): *CeeNU.*

Another commonly used name is CCNU.

Note: For a listing of dosage forms and brand names by country availability, see *Dosage Forms* section(s).

Category

Antineoplastic.

Indications

Note: Bracketed information in the *Indications* section refers to uses that are not included in U.S. product labeling.

Accepted

Tumors, brain, primary (treatment)

[Carcinoma, colorectal (treatment)][1]

[Carcinoma, lung, non-small cell (treatment)] or

[Carcinoma, breast (treatment)]—Lomustine is indicated for treatment of both primary and metastatic brain tumors, in patients who have already received appropriate surgical or radiotherapeutic procedures. It is also indicated for treatment of colorectal carcinoma, non-small-cell lung carcinoma, and advanced breast carcinoma after conventional therapy has failed.

Lymphomas, Hodgkin's (treatment)—Lomustine is indicated for treatment of Hodgkin's disease, as secondary therapy in combination with other drugs in patients who relapse while being treated with primary therapy or in patients who fail to respond to primary therapy.

[Multiple myeloma (treatment)][1]—Lomustine is also indicated for treatment of multiple myeloma.

[Melanoma, malignant (treatment)]—Lomustine is indicated for treatment of malignant melanoma, alone or in combination with other drugs.

---

[1]Not included in Canadian product labeling.

Pharmacology/Pharmacokinetics

Physicochemical characteristics

Molecular weight—233.70.

Mechanism of action/Effect

Lomustine is an alkylating agent of the nitrosourea type. Lomustine (and/or its metabolites) interferes with the function of DNA and RNA. It is cell cycle-phase nonspecific. Lomustine also acts to inhibit DNA synthesis by inhibiting key enzymatic processes.

Absorption

Well and rapidly absorbed from the gastrointestinal tract.

Distribution

Crosses the blood-brain barrier.

Protein binding

Moderate (50%; metabolites).

Biotransformation

Hepatic; rapid and complete (active metabolites).

Half-life

Biologic—Approximately 94 minutes.

Chemical—Approximately 15 minutes.

Metabolites—Prolonged; 16 to 48 hours.

Elimination

Renal (totally as metabolites); some enterohepatic circulation is believed to occur.

Fecal (less than 5%).

Respiratory (10%).

Precautions to Consider

Carcinogenicity/Mutagenicity

Secondary malignancies are potential delayed effects of many antineoplastic agents, although it is not clear whether the effect is related to their mutagenic or immunosuppressive action. The effect of dose and duration of therapy is also unknown, although risk seems to increase with long-term use. Although information is limited, available data seem to indicate that the carcinogenic risk is greatest with the alkylating agents.

Long-term use of nitrosoureas in humans has been reported to be possibly associated with development of secondary malignancies (acute leukemia) and bone marrow dysplasias.

Lomustine is carcinogenic in rats and mice at the approximate clinical dose and, like other alkylating agents, is probably carcinogenic in humans.

Pregnancy/Reproduction

Fertility—Gonadal suppression, resulting in amenorrhea or azoospermia, may occur in patients taking antineoplastic therapy, especially with the alkylating agents. In general, these effects appear to be related to dose and length of therapy and may be irreversible. Prediction of the degree of testicular or ovarian function impairment is complicated by the common use of combinations of several antineoplastics, which makes it difficult to assess the effects of individual agents.

Lomustine suppresses gonadal function in male rats (at higher than the human dose) and in humans.

Pregnancy—Adequate and well-controlled studies in humans have not been done.

First trimester: It is usually recommended that use of antineoplastics, especially combination chemotherapy, be avoided whenever possible, especially during the first trimester. Although information is limited because of the relatively few instances of antineoplastic administration during pregnancy, the mutagenic, teratogenic, and carcinogenic potential of these medications must be considered.

Other hazards to the fetus include adverse reactions seen in adults.

In general, use of a contraceptive is recommended during cytotoxic drug therapy.

Lomustine is embryotoxic in rats and rabbits and teratogenic in rats at doses approximately equivalent to the human dose.

FDA Pregnancy Category D.

Breast-feeding

Lomustine is distributed into breast milk. Breast-feeding is not recommended during chemotherapy because of the risks to the infant (adverse effects, mutagenicity, carcinogenicity).

Pediatrics
Appropriate studies on the relationship of age to the effects of lomustine have not been performed in the pediatric population. However, pediatrics-specific problems that would limit the usefulness of this medication in children are not expected.

Geriatrics
No information is available on the relationship of age to the effects of lomustine in geriatric patients. However, elderly patients are more likely to have age-related renal function impairment, which may require caution in patients receiving lomustine.

Dental
The bone marrow depressant effects of lomustine may result in an increased incidence of microbial infection, delayed healing, and gingival bleeding. Dental work, whenever possible, should be completed prior to initiation of therapy or deferred until blood counts have returned to normal. Patients should be instructed in proper oral hygiene during treatment, including caution in use of regular toothbrushes, dental floss, and toothpicks.

Lomustine may also cause stomatitis that is associated with considerable discomfort.

Drug interactions and/or related problems
The following drug interactions and/or related problems have been selected on the basis of their potential clinical significance (possible mechanism in parentheses where appropriate)—not necessarily inclusive (» = major clinical significance):

Blood dyscrasia-causing medications (see *Appendix II*)
(leukopenic and/or thrombocytopenic effects of lomustine may be increased with concurrent or recent therapy if these medications cause the same effects; dosage adjustment of lomustine, if necessary, should be based on blood counts)

» Bone marrow depressants, other (see *Appendix II*) or
Radiation therapy
(additive bone marrow depression may occur; dosage reduction may be required when two or more bone marrow depressants, including radiation, are used concurrently or consecutively)

Vaccines, killed virus
(because normal defense mechanisms may be suppressed by lomustine therapy, the patient's antibody response to the vaccine may be decreased. The interval between discontinuation of medications that cause immunosuppression and restoration of the patient's ability to respond to the vaccine depends on the intensity and type of immunosuppression-causing medication used, the underlying disease, and other factors; estimates vary from 3 months to 1 year)

» Vaccines, live virus
(because normal defense mechanisms may be suppressed by lomustine therapy, concurrent use with a live virus vaccine may potentiate the replication of the vaccine virus, may increase the side/adverse effects of the vaccine virus, and/or may decrease the patient's antibody response to the vaccine; immunization of these patients should be undertaken only with extreme caution after careful review of the patient's hematologic status and only with the knowledge and consent of the physician managing the lomustine therapy. The interval between discontinuation of medications that cause immunosuppression and restoration of the patient's ability to respond to the vaccine depends on the intensity and type of immunosuppression-causing medication used, the underlying disease, and other factors; estimates vary from 3 months to 1 year. Immunization with oral poliovirus vaccine should also be postponed in persons in close contact with the patient, especially family members)

Laboratory value alterations
The following have been selected on the basis of their potential clinical significance (possible effect in parentheses where appropriate)—not necessarily inclusive (» = major clinical significance).

With physiology/laboratory test values
Hepatic function tests
(may be elevated transiently and reversibly)

Medical considerations/Contraindications
The medical considerations/contraindications included have been selected on the basis of their potential clinical significance (reasons given in parentheses where appropriate)—not necessarily inclusive (» = major clinical significance).

Risk-benefit should be considered when the following medical problems exist:

» Bone marrow depression
» Chickenpox, existing or recent (including recent exposure) or
» Herpes zoster
(risk of severe generalized disease)
» Infection
» Pulmonary function impairment, especially with a baseline below 70% of the forced vital capacity (FVC) or carbon monoxide diffusion capacity (DL_{CO})
(increased risk of pulmonary toxicity)
» Renal function impairment
» Sensitivity to lomustine
» Caution should be used also in patients who have had previous cytotoxic drug therapy and radiation therapy.

Patient monitoring
The following may be especially important in patient monitoring (other tests may be warranted in some patients, depending on condition; » = major clinical significance):

Alanine aminotransferase (ALT [SGPT]) values, serum and
Aspartate aminotransferase (AST [SGOT]) values, serum and
Bilirubin values, serum and
Lactate dehydrogenase (LDH) values, serum
(recommended prior to initiation of therapy and at periodic intervals during therapy; frequency varies according to clinical state, agent, dose, and other agents being used concurrently)

» Blood urea nitrogen (BUN) concentrations and
» Creatinine concentrations, serum
(recommended prior to initiation of therapy and at periodic intervals during therapy; frequency varies according to clinical state, agent, dose, and other agents being used concurrently)

» Hematocrit or hemoglobin and
» Leukocyte count, total and, if appropriate, differential and
» Platelet count
(determinations recommended prior to initiation of therapy and at periodic intervals during and after therapy; frequency varies according to clinical state, agent, dose, and other agents being used concurrently)

Pulmonary function tests
(recommended prior to initiation of therapy and at periodic intervals during therapy)

Side/Adverse Effects
Note: Many "side effects" of antineoplastic therapy are unavoidable and represent the medication's pharmacologic action. Some of these (for example, leukopenia and thrombocytopenia) are actually used as parameters to aid in individual dosage titration.

The following side/adverse effects have been selected on the basis of their potential clinical significance (possible signs and symptoms in parentheses where appropriate)—not necessarily inclusive:

Those indicating need for medical attention
Incidence more frequent

Immunosuppression or leukopenia or infection (fever or chills; cough or hoarseness; lower back or side pain; painful or difficult urination)—usually asymptomatic; ***thrombocytopenia*** (unusual bleeding or bruising; black, tarry stools; blood in urine or stools; pinpoint red spots on skin)—usually asymptomatic

Note: Maximum *thrombocytopenia* occurs about 4 weeks after a dose and persists for 1 to 2 weeks. Maximum *leukopenia* occurs about 4 to 6 weeks after a dose and persists for 1 to 2 weeks. Recovery usually occurs within 6 to 7 weeks after administration. Severity of bone marrow depression varies and determines subsequent dosage of lomustine.

Incidence less frequent

Anemia (unusual tiredness or weakness); ***neurotoxicity*** (awkwardness; confusion; slurred speech; unusual tiredness)—not definitely attributed to medication; ***renal toxicity and failure*** (decrease in urination; swelling of feet or lower legs)—especially with long-term therapy; ***stomatitis*** (sores in mouth and on lips)

Incidence rare

Hepatotoxicity—usually asymptomatic; ***pulmonary infiltrates and/or fibrosis*** (cough; shortness of breath)

Note: *Pulmonary toxicity* has occurred after cumulative doses ranging from 600 to 1240 mg or therapy of 6 months or more.

Those indicating need for medical attention only if they continue or are bothersome
Incidence more frequent

Loss of appetite; nausea and vomiting

Note: *Loss of appetite* may persist for 2 to 3 days after a dose.

Nausea and vomiting occur 3 to 6 hours after a dose and usually persist less than 24 hours.

Incidence less frequent

Darkening of skin; diarrhea; skin rash and itching

Those not indicating need for medical attention

Incidence less frequent

Loss of hair

Those indicating the need for medical attention if they occur after medication is discontinued

Bone marrow depression (black, tarry stools; blood in urine or stools; cough or hoarseness; fever or chills; lower back or side pain; painful or difficult urination; pinpoint red spots on skin; unusual bleeding or bruising)

Note: Cumulative myelosuppression may occur with repeated doses.

Patient Consultation

As an aid to patient consultation, refer to *Advice for the Patient, Lomustine (Systemic)*.

In providing consultation, consider emphasizing the following selected information (» = major clinical significance):

Before using this medication

» Conditions affecting use, especially:
  - Sensitivity to lomustine
  - Pregnancy—Use not recommended because of mutagenic, teratogenic, and carcinogenic potential; advisability of using contraception; telling physician immediately if pregnancy is suspected
  - Breast-feeding—Not recommended because of risk of serious side effects
  - Other medications, especially other bone marrow depressants or previous cytotoxic drug or radiation therapy
  - Other medical problems, especially chickenpox, herpes zoster, infection, pulmonary function impairment, or renal function impairment

Proper use of this medication

» Importance of not taking more or less medication than the amount prescribed

Explanation of different kinds of capsules included in one container

Caution in taking combination therapy; taking each medication at the right time

Frequency of nausea and vomiting, which usually lasts less than 24 hours; taking on an empty stomach to reduce nausea

Checking with physician if vomiting occurs shortly after dose is taken

» Proper dosing

Precautions while using this medication

» Importance of close monitoring by the physician

» Avoiding immunizations unless approved by physician; other persons in patient's household should avoid immunizations with oral poliovirus vaccine; avoiding other persons who have taken oral poliovirus vaccine or wearing a protective mask that covers nose and mouth

Caution if bone marrow depression occurs:

» Avoiding exposure to persons with infections, especially during periods of low blood counts; checking with physician immediately if fever or chills, cough or hoarseness, lower back or side pain, or painful or difficult urination occurs

» Checking with physician immediately if unusual bleeding or bruising; black, tarry stools; blood in urine or stools; or pinpoint red spots on skin occur

Caution in use of regular toothbrush, dental floss, or toothpick; physician, dentist, or nurse may suggest alternatives; checking with physician before having dental work done

Not touching eyes or inside of nose unless hands washed immediately before

Using caution to avoid accidental cuts with use of sharp objects such as safety razor or fingernail or toenail cutters

Avoiding contact sports or other situations where bruising or injury could occur

Side/adverse effects

May cause adverse effects such as blood problems, loss of hair, and cancer; importance of discussing possible effects with physician

Signs of potential side effects, especially immunosuppression, leukopenia, infection, thrombocytopenia, anemia, neurotoxicity, renal toxicity, stomatitis, hepatotoxicity, and pulmonary infiltrates and/or fibrosis

Physician or nurse can help in dealing with side effects

General Dosing Information

Patients receiving lomustine should be under supervision of a physician experienced in cancer chemotherapy.

A variety of dosage schedules and regimens of lomustine, alone or in combination with other antitumor agents, are used. The prescriber may consult the medical literature as well as the manufacturer's literature in choosing a specific dosage.

Treatment with lomustine is continued as long as the medication is effective. If no response occurs after 1 or 2 courses, a response is unlikely.

Some cross-resistance has been reported between lomustine and carmustine.

Frequency and duration of nausea and vomiting may be reduced in some patients by administration of antiemetics prior to dosing and by administration of lomustine to fasting patients.

Dosage subsequent to the initial dose should be adjusted to meet the individual requirements of each patient based on the hematological response of the patient to the previous dose. An additional course of lomustine should be given only after circulating blood elements have returned to acceptable levels (leukocytes above 4000 per cubic millimeter and platelets above 100,000 per cubic millimeter).

Because of the delayed and cumulative bone marrow suppression caused by lomustine, the medication should be given no more frequently than every 6 weeks.

Special precautions are recommended in patients who develop thrombocytopenia as a result of administration of lomustine. These may include extreme care in performing invasive procedures; regular inspection of intravenous sites, skin (including perirectal area), and mucous membrane surfaces for signs of bleeding or bruising; limiting frequency of venipuncture and avoiding intramuscular injections; testing urine, emesis, stool, and secretions for occult blood; care in use of regular toothbrushes, dental floss, toothpicks, safety razors, and fingernail and toenail cutters; avoiding constipation; and using caution to prevent falls and other injuries. Such patients should avoid alcohol and any aspirin intake because of the risk of gastrointestinal bleeding. Platelet transfusions may be required.

Patients who develop leukopenia should be observed carefully for signs of infection. Antibiotic support may be required. In neutropenic patients who develop fever, broad-spectrum antibiotic coverage should be initiated empirically, pending bacterial cultures and appropriate diagnostic tests.

Combination chemotherapy

Lomustine may be used in combination with other agents in various regimens. As a result, incidence and/or severity of side effects may be altered and different dosages (usually reduced) may be used. For example, lomustine is part of the following chemotherapeutic combinations (some commonly used acronyms are in parentheses):

—lomustine, doxorubicin, and vinblastine (CAVE).

—cyclophosphamide, methotrexate, and lomustine (CMC).

For specific dosages and schedules, consult the literature. For information regarding each agent, consult the individual monographs.

Oral Dosage Forms

Note: Bracketed uses in the *Dosage Forms* section refer to categories of use and/or indications that are not included in U.S. product labeling.

LOMUSTINE CAPSULES

Usual adult and adolescent dose

Tumors, brain, primary or
[Carcinoma, colorectal][1] or
[Carcinoma, lung, non-small cell] or
[Carcinoma, breast] or
Lymphomas, Hodgkin's or
[Multiple myeloma][1] or
[Melanoma, malignant]—

Initial: As a single agent—Oral, 100 to 130 mg per square meter of body surface area as a single dose, repeated every six weeks. A lower dose is used when lomustine is combined with other agents.

Note: In patients with suppressed bone marrow function, dosage is reduced to 100 mg per square meter of body surface area as a single dose, repeated every six weeks.

A suggested dosage adjustment schedule for subsequent doses is:

Nadir after Prior Dose (cells per cubic millimeter)		% of Prior Dose To Be Given
Leukocytes	Platelets	
>4000	>100,000	100
3000–3999	75,000–99,999	100
2000–2999	25,000–74,999	70
<2000	<25,000	50

Usual pediatric dose
See *Usual adult and adolescent dose.*

Strength(s) usually available
U.S.—

Note: Available only in a dose pack that contains a total of 300 mg (2 capsules of each strength) and provides enough medication for titration of a single dose. The total prescribed dose, to within 10 mg, can be obtained using the appropriate combination of capsules.

10 mg (Rx) [*CeeNU* (mannitol)].
40 mg (Rx) [*CeeNU* (mannitol)].
100 mg (Rx) [*CeeNU* (mannitol)].

Canada—

Note: Available also in a dose pack that contains a total of 300 mg (2 capsules of each strength) and will provide enough medication for titration of a single dose. The total prescribed dose, to within 10 mg, can be obtained using the appropriate combination of capsules.

10 mg (Rx) [*CeeNU* (mannitol)].
40 mg (Rx) [*CeeNU* (mannitol)].
100 mg (Rx) [*CeeNU* (mannitol)].

Packaging and storage
Store below 40 °C (104 °F), preferably between 15 and 30 °C (59 and 86 °F), in a well-closed container, unless otherwise specified by manufacturer.

Auxiliary labeling
• There may be two or more different types of capsules in this container. This is not an error. It is important that you take all of the capsules so that you receive the right dose of the medicine.
• Take on an empty stomach.

Note
A patient information label should be attached, explaining the difference in appearance of the capsules and advising the patient that all of the capsules together constitute one dose.

No more than one dose should be dispensed at a time and refills supplied only after direct verbal or written order by the physician.

[1]Not included in Canadian product labeling.

Revised: 09/30/1997

LOPERAMIDE Oral-Local

VA CLASSIFICATION (Primary): GA208

Commonly used brand name(s): *Apo-Loperamide; Diarr-Eze; Imodium; Imodium A-D; Imodium A-D Caplets; Kaopectate II; Loperacap; Maalox Anti-Diarrheal; Nu-Loperamide; PMS-Loperamide; Pepto Diarrhea Control; Rho-Loperamide.*

Note: For a listing of dosage forms and brand names by country availability, see *Dosage Forms* section(s).

Category

Antidiarrheal.

Indications

Note: Bracketed information in the *Indications* section refers to uses that not included in U.S. product labeling.

Note: The efficacy of any antidiarrheal medication for treatment of most cases of nonspecific diarrhea is questionable. *Preferred treatment consists of fluid and electrolyte replacement, nutritional therapy, and, if possible, elimination of the underlying cause of the diarrhea.*

Accepted
Diarrhea (treatment)—Loperamide is indicated in adults for the control and symptomatic relief of acute nonspecific diarrhea and of chronic diarrhea associated with inflammatory bowel disease. Loperamide is also indicated to reduce the volume of discharge from ileostomies, colostomies, and other intestinal resections.

[Loperamide may be used in children to treat diarrhea caused by rapid transit when the anatomy of the bowel has been altered by disease or by surgical procedures.][1]

Traveler's diarrhea (treatment)—Loperamide is indicated for symptomatic relief of secretory diarrhea produced by bacteria, viruses, and parasites.

Unaccepted
Loperamide is not recommended for use in children up to 6 years of age unless directed by a physician. Loperamide is also not recommended for routine use or as the first line of therapy for treatment of diarrhea resulting from infection or food allergy in otherwise healthy, older children.

Loperamide should not be used if diarrhea is accompanied by fever or if there is blood or mucus in the stool.

[1]Not included in Canadian product labeling.

Pharmacology/Pharmacokinetics

Physicochemical characteristics
Molecular weight—513.51.
pKa—8.6.

Mechanism of action/Effect
Loperamide acts on receptors along the small intestine to decrease circular and longitudinal muscle activity. Loperamide exerts its antidiarrheal action by slowing intestinal transit and increasing contact time, and perhaps also by directly inhibiting fluid and electrolyte secretion and/or stimulating salt and water absorption.

Other actions/effects
High doses may inhibit gastric acid secretion.

Absorption
Not well absorbed from gastrointestinal tract.

Protein binding
Very high (97%).

Biotransformation
Hepatic.

Half-life
9.1 to 14.4 (average 10.8) hours.

Time to peak concentration
Capsules—5 hours.
Oral solution—2.5 hours.

Duration of action
Up to 24 hours.

Elimination
Fecal/renal.

Precautions to Consider

Carcinogenicity
Carcinogenic potential was not documented in a study using rats administered doses up to 133 times the maximum human dose.

Pregnancy/Reproduction
Fertility—Reproduction studies in rats and rabbits have shown that loperamide administered in doses up to 30 times the human therapeutic dose does not interfere with fertility.

Pregnancy—Adequate and well-controlled studies have not been done in humans.

Reproduction studies in rats and rabbits have shown that loperamide administered in doses up to 30 times the human therapeutic dose did not cause harm to the offspring, or produce teratogenic effects. Higher doses, however, impaired maternal and neonate survival.

FDA Pregnancy Category B.

Breast-feeding
It is not known whether loperamide is distributed into breast milk. However, in a pre- and post-natal study, loperamide administered to female nursing rats at a dose of 40 mg per kg of body weight caused a decrease in pup survival.

Pediatrics
Loperamide is not recommended for use in children up to 6 years of age unless directed by a physician, or for routine use or as initial therapy in children older than 6 years of age.

Oral rehydration therapy is the preferred treatment for children with diarrhea because loperamide may mask dehydration and depletion of electrolytes. Dehydration may further increase the variability in the response to loperamide.

Children, especially those under 3 years of age, are more susceptible to the opiate-like effects (CNS effects) of loperamide.

Geriatrics

In geriatric patients with diarrhea, caution is recommended because loperamide may mask dehydration and depletion of electrolytes. Dehydration may further increase the variability in the response to loperamide.

Drug interactions and/or related problems

The following drug interactions and/or related problems have been selected on the basis of their potential clinical significance (possible mechanism in parentheses where appropriate)—not necessarily inclusive (» = major clinical significance):

» Opioid (narcotic) analgesics
(concurrent use of loperamide with an opioid analgesic may increase the risk of severe constipation)

Medical considerations/Contraindications

The medical considerations/contraindications included have been selected on the basis of their potential clinical significance (reasons given in parentheses where appropriate)—not necessarily inclusive (» = major clinical significance).

Except under special circumstances, this medication should not be used when the following medical problems exist:

» Colitis, severe
(patient may develop toxic megacolon)

» Diarrhea associated with *Clostridium difficile* resulting from treatment with broad-spectrum antibiotics
(loperamide may prolong transit time, causing a delay in the removal of toxins from the colon, thereby prolonging and/or worsening the diarrhea)

» Dysentery, acute, characterized by bloody stools and elevated temperature
(sole treatment with loperamide may be inadequate; antibiotic therapy may be required)

» Previous allergic reaction to loperamide

Risk-benefit should be considered when the following medical problems exist:

» Dehydration
(rehydration therapy is essential if signs or symptoms of dehydration, such as dryness of mouth, excessive thirst, wrinkled skin, decreased urination, and dizziness or lightheadedness, are present; fluid loss may have serious consequences, such as circulatory collapse and renal failure, especially in young children)

Diarrhea caused by infectious organisms
(bacterial diarrhea may, on rare occasions, worsen due to the increased contact time between the mucosa and the penetrating microorganism; however, there is no evidence of this occurring in actual practice)

Hepatic function impairment
(loperamide undergoes extensive first pass metabolism in the liver; therefore, patients with hepatic function impairment may have an increased risk of developing CNS toxicity)

Side/Adverse Effects

Note: Adverse effects may be difficult to distinguish from the diarrheal syndrome itself and are usually self-limited.

The following side/adverse effects have been selected on the basis of their potential clinical significance (possible signs and symptoms in parentheses where appropriate)—not necessarily inclusive:

Those indicating need for medical attention

Incidence rare

Allergic reaction (skin rash); ***toxic megacolon*** (bloating; constipation; loss of appetite; severe stomach pain with nausea and vomiting)

Those indicating need for medical attention only if they continue or are bothersome

Incidence rare

Dizziness or drowsiness; dryness of mouth

Overdose

For specific information on the agents used in the management of loperamide, see:

- *Charcoal, Activated (Oral-Local)* monograph; and/or
- *Naloxone (Systemic)* monograph.

For more information on the management of overdose or unintentional ingestion, **contact a Poison Control Center** (see *Poison Control Center Listing*).

Clinical effects of overdose

Although human data are inconclusive, animal pharmacological and toxicological data indicate that overdosage may result in CNS depression, constipation, and gastrointestinal irritation.

Treatment of overdose

Note: Treatment of loperamide overdose is similar to treatment for narcotic overdosage and involves the following:

To decrease absorption—Administration of activated charcoal promptly after ingestion. If vomiting has occurred spontaneously after ingestion of loperamide overdose, a slurry of 100 grams of activated charcoal should be administered as soon as fluids can be retained. Gastric lavage if vomiting has not occurred.

Specific treatment—Use of narcotic antagonists (e.g., naloxone), if necessary.

Monitoring—Prolonged and careful monitoring.

Supportive care—Support of respiration. Patients in whom intentional overdose is confirmed or suspected should be referred for psychiatric consultation.

Patient Consultation

As an aid to patient consultation, refer to *Advice for the Patient, Loperamide (Oral)*.

In providing consultation, consider emphasizing the following selected information (» = major clinical significance):

Before using this medication

» Conditions affecting use, especially:
Allergy to loperamide
Use in children—Not recommended for use in children unless directed by a physician; may mask symptoms of dehydration; variability in response to loperamide; increased susceptibility to CNS effects
Use in the elderly—May mask symptoms of dehydration; variability in response to loperamide
Other medical problems, especially acute dysentery, dehydration, diarrhea caused by antibiotics, or severe colitis

Proper use of this medication

» Not using if diarrhea is accompanied by fever or blood or mucus in the stool; contacting physician

» Importance of not taking more medication than the amount prescribed

Proper administration technique for oral solution

» Importance of maintaining adequate hydration and proper diet

» Proper dosing

Missed dose: Not taking missed dose; not doubling doses

» Proper storage

Precautions while using this medication

Regular visits to physician to check progress during prolonged therapy

» Consulting physician if diarrhea is not controlled within 48 hours and/or fever develops

Side/adverse effects

Signs of potential side effects, especially allergic reaction or toxic megacolon

General Dosing Information

Reduction of intestinal motility in patients with traveler's diarrhea may result in prolonged fever by slowing expulsion of infectious organisms that penetrate intestinal mucosa (for example, *Shigella, Salmonella*, and certain strains of *Escherichia coli*).

Inhibition of peristalsis may produce fluid retention in the bowel, which may aggravate and mask dehydration and depletion of electrolytes, especially in young children, and may also increase variability in the response to the medication. If dehydration or electrolyte imbalance occurs, loperamide therapy should be withheld until appropriate corrective therapy has begun.

In patients with acute ulcerative colitis, treatment with loperamide should be discontinued promptly in the event of abdominal distention or other symptoms that may indicate impending toxic megacolon.

Neither tolerance to the antidiarrheal effects nor physical dependence on loperamide has been reported in humans, although a morphine-like dependence has occurred in monkeys receiving high doses.

In acute diarrhea, treatment with loperamide should be discontinued after 48 hours if improvement does not occur. In chronic diarrhea, if no improvement has occurred after at least 10 days of treatment with the maximum dose, loperamide is unlikely to be effective, although further administration may be the only alternative when diet and specific treatment are inadequate.

Oral Dosage Forms

LOPERAMIDE HYDROCHLORIDE CAPSULES USP

Usual adult and adolescent dose

Acute diarrhea or
Traveler's diarrhea—
Oral, 4 mg after first loose bowel movement, followed by 2 mg after each subsequent loose bowel movement.

Chronic diarrhea—
Initial: Oral, 4 mg, followed by 2 mg after each subsequent loose bowel movement until diarrhea is controlled.
Maintenance: Oral, 4 to 8 mg a day in divided daily doses as needed.

Usual adult prescribing limits

16 mg per day.

Note: Maximum daily dosage for self-medication with loperamide using the over-the-counter product is 8 mg.

Usual pediatric dose

Note: Although loperamide is not recommended for routine use in children, the following pediatric doses have been used to treat diarrhea caused by specific motility disorders.

Acute diarrhea or
Traveler's diarrhea—
Children up to 6 years of age—
Use is not recommended unless directed by a physician.

Children 6 to 12 years of age—
Initial:
Oral, 80 to 240 mcg (0.08 to 0.24 mg) per kg of body weight a day in two or three divided doses; or, for
Children 6 to 8 years of age: Oral, 2 mg two times a day.
Children 8 to 12 years of age: Oral, 2 mg three times a day.
Maintenance:
Oral, 1 mg per 10 kg of body weight administered only after a loose stool.

Children older than 12 years of age—
See *Usual adult and adolescent dose.*

Chronic diarrhea—
Dosage has not been established.

Note: In general, oral rehydration therapy and dietary treatment of diarrhea in children are preferred whenever possible.

Strength(s) usually available

U.S.—
2 mg (Rx) [*Imodium* (lactose); GENERIC].
Canada—
2 mg (OTC) [*Imodium* (lactose); *Loperacap*].

Packaging and storage

Store below 40 °C (104 °F), preferably between 15 and 30 °C (59 and 86 °F), in a well-closed, light-resistant container, unless otherwise specified by manufacturer.

LOPERAMIDE HYDROCHLORIDE ORAL SOLUTION

Usual adult and adolescent dose

See *Loperamide Hydrochloride Capsules USP*.

Usual adult prescribing limits

8 mg per day for no more than two days.

Usual pediatric dose

Note: Although loperamide is not recommended for routine use in children, the following pediatric doses have been used to treat diarrhea caused by specific motility disorders.

Acute diarrhea or
Traveler's diarrhea—
Children up to 2 years of age—
Use is not recommended unless directed by a physician.

Children 2 to 11 years of age—
Initial:
Oral, 80 to 240 mcg (0.08 to 0.24 mg) per kg of body weight a day in two or three divided doses; or, for
Children 2 to 5 years of age: Oral, only under the direction of a physician, 1 mg after first loose bowel movement, followed by 1 mg after each subsequent loose bowel movement, not to exceed a total daily dose of 3 mg.
Children 6 to 8 years of age: Oral, 2 mg after first loose bowel movement, followed by 1 mg after each subsequent loose bowel movement, not to exceed a total daily dose of 4 mg.
Children 9 to 11 years of age: Oral, 2 mg after first loose bowel movement, followed by 1 mg after each subsequent loose bowel movement, not to exceed a total daily dose of 6 mg.
Maintenance:
Oral, 1 mg per 10 kg of body weight administered only after a loose stool.

Children 12 years of age and older—
See *Usual adult and adolescent dose.*

Note: In general, oral rehydration therapy and dietary treatment of diarrhea in children are preferred whenever possible.

Strength(s) usually available

U.S.—
1 mg per 5 mL (OTC) [*Imodium A-D* (alcohol 5.25%); *Maalox Anti-Diarrheal; Pepto Diarrhea Control* (alcohol 5.25%); GENERIC].
Canada—
1 mg per 5 mL (OTC) [*Diarr-Eze; Imodium* (alcohol 4.07%); *PMS-Loperamide*].

Packaging and storage

Store below 40 °C (104 °F), preferably between 15 and 30 °C (59 and 86 °F), unless otherwise specified by manufacturer. Protect from freezing.

LOPERAMIDE HYDROCHLORIDE TABLETS USP

Usual adult and adolescent dose

See *Loperamide Hydrochloride Capsules USP*.

Usual adult prescribing limits

8 mg per day for no more than two days.

Usual pediatric dose

Note: Although loperamide is not recommended for routine use in children, the following pediatric doses have been used to treat diarrhea caused by specific motility disorders.

Acute diarrhea or
Traveler's diarrhea—
Children up to 6 years of age—
Use is not recommended unless directed by a physician.

Children 6 to 11 years of age—
Initial:
Oral, 80 to 240 mcg (0.08 to 0.24 mg) per kg of body weight a day in two or three divided doses; or, for
Children 6 to 8 years of age: Oral, 2 mg after first loose bowel movement, followed by 1 mg after each subsequent loose bowel movement, not to exceed a total daily dose of 4 mg.
Children 9 to 11 years of age: Oral, 2 mg after first loose bowel movement, followed by 1 mg after each subsequent loose bowel movement, not to exceed a total daily dose of 6 mg.
Maintenance:
Oral, 1 mg per 10 kg of body weight administered only after a loose stool.

Children 12 years of age and older—
See *Usual adult and adolescent dose.*

Note: In general, oral rehydration therapy and dietary treatment of diarrhea in children are preferred whenever possible.

Strength(s) usually available

U.S.—
2 mg (OTC) [*Imodium A-D Caplets* (lactose); *Kaopectate II* (lactose); *Maalox Anti-Diarrheal; Pepto Diarrhea Control* (lactose); GENERIC].
Canada—
2 mg (OTC) [*Apo-Loperamide; Diarr-Eze; Imodium; Nu-Loperamide; PMS-Loperamide* (scored); *Rho-Loperamide*; GENERIC].

Packaging and storage

Store below 40 °C (104 °F), preferably between 15 and 30 °C (59 and 86 °F), in a well-closed, light-resistant container.

Selected Bibliography

Ericsson CD, DuPont HL. Travelers' diarrhea: approaches to prevention and treatment. Clin Infect Dis 1993; 16: 616-26.
Ericsson CD, Johnson PC. Safety and efficacy of loperamide. Am J Med 1990; 88(6A Suppl): 10S-14S.
Brownlee HJ. Family practitioner's guide to patient self-treatment of acute diarrhea. Am J Med 1990; 88(6A Suppl): 27S-29S.

Revised: 09/29/2000

LOPINAVIR AND RITONAVIR
Systemic

VA CLASSIFICATION (Primary): AM830

Commonly used brand name(s): *Kaletra.*

Note: For a listing of dosage forms and brand names by country availability, see *Dosage Forms* section(s).

Category

Antiviral (systemic).

Indications

General Considerations

Cross-resistance among protease inhibitors has been observed; however, the potential for protease inhibitor cross-resistance in HIV-1 isolates from patients treated with lopinavir and ritonavir has not yet been determined.

Accepted

Human immunodeficiency virus (HIV) infection (treatment)—The combination of lopinavir and ritonavir is indicated in combination with other antiretroviral agents for the treatment of HIV-infection. This indication is based no analyses of plasma HIV RNA levels and CD_4 cell counts in controlled studies of lopinavir and ritonavir of 48 weeks duration and in smaller uncontrolled dose-ranging studies of lopinavir and ritonavir of 144–204 weeks duration.

Pharmacology/Pharmacokinetics

Physicochemical characteristics

Molecular weight—
Lopinavir: 628.8.
Ritonavir: 720.95.

Solubility—Lopinavir: Freely soluble in methanol and ethanol, soluble in isopropanol, and practically insoluble in water.

Mechanism of action/Effect

Lopinavir: Lopinavir inhibits the human immunodeficiency virus (HIV) protease and prevents cleavage of the Gag-Pol polyprotein, thus reducing the probability of viral particles reaching a mature, infectious state. The antiviral activity of the combination product is due to the lopinavir component.

Ritonavir: Ritonavir acts to increase plasma levels of lopinavir by inhibiting the CYP3A-mediated metabolism of lopinavir.

Absorption

Capsules and oral solution: Twice daily dosing—The absorption of the combination of lopinavir and ritonavir is favorably affected by the presence of food. Administration with a high fat meal increases the area under the curve (AUC) of lopinavir by 97% and the maximum concentration (C_{max}) by 43% for the capsules and by 130% and 56%, respectively, for the oral solution relative to administration during a fasting state.

Capsules and oral solution: Once daily dosing—Lopinavir AUC over a 24 hour dosing interval averaged 154.1±61.4 mcg*h/mL

Tablets: No clinically significant changes in C_{max} and AUC were observed following lopinavir/ritonavir tablet administration under fed conditions compared to fasted conditions. Relative to fasting, administration of tablets with a moderate fat meal (500 to 682 Kcal, 23 to 25% calories from fat) increased lopinavir AUC and C_{max} by 26.9% and 17.6%, respectively. Relative to fasting, administration of tablets with a high fat meal (872 Kcal, 56% from fat) increased lopinavir AUC by 18.9% but not C_{max}. Therefore, lopinavir/ritonavir tablets may be taken with or without food.

Protein binding

Lopinavir: Very high (98–99%); predominantly to alpha-1-acid glycoprotein and albumin.

Biotransformation

The combination of lopinavir and ritonavir has been shown to inhibit CYP2D6 *in vitro* , but to a lesser extent than CYP3A. It does not inhibit CYP2C9, CYP2C19, CYP2E1, CYP2B6, or CYP1A2 at clinically relevant concentrations.

Lopinavir: Extensively metabolized by CYP3A to at least 13 oxidative metabolites.

Ritonavir: Has been shown to induce its own metabolism; furthermore, it is a potent CYP3A inhibitor, resulting in increased plasma levels of lopinavir.

Half-life

Lopinavir: 5–6 hours.

Time to peak concentration

Lopinavir: 4 hours following multiple doses of 400 mg of lopinavir and 100 mg of ritonavir for 3 to 4 weeks in HIV-positive patients; 6 hours following multiple doses of 800 mg lopinavir and 200 mg ritonavir once daily for four weeks with food.

Peak plasma concentration:

Lopinavir: 9.6± 4.4 micrograms per mL following multiple doses of 400 mg of lopinavir and 100 mg of ritonavir for 3 to 4 weeks in HIV-positive patients.Following multiple doses of 800 mg lopinavir and 200 mg ritonavir once daily for four weeks with food, 11.8±3.7 mcg per mL

Doseforms—Plasma concentrations of lopinavir and ritonavir after administration of two 200/50 mg lopinavir/ritonavir tablets are comparable to three 133.3/33.3 mg capsules under fed conditions with less pharmacokinetic variability.

Elimination

Following a single dose of 400 mg of lopinavir and 100 mg of ritonavir—
Fecal: 82.6 ± 2.5 % accounted for after 8 days.
Renal: 10.4 ± 2.3% accounted for after 8 days.

Precautions to Consider

Carcinogenicity

Lopinavir and Ritonavir: Studies in mice and rats have shown an increase in the incidence of benign hepatocellular adenomas and an increase in the combined incidence of hepatocellular adenomas plus carcinoma in both males and females in mice and females in rats at doses that produced approximately 1.6–2.2 times (mice) and 0.5 times (rats) the human exposure at the recommended dose of 400 mg lopinavir and 100 mg ritonavir twice daily.

Ritonavir: Incidences of both adenomas and combined adenomas and carcinomas in the liver increased with increasing doses (50, 100, or 200 mg per kg of body weight [mg/kg] per day) of ritonavir in male mice. The highest dose was approximately 4 times greater than the maximum recommended human dose. No carcinogenic effects were seen in female mice given doses as high as 9 times the recommended human dose or in rats given 7, 15, or 30 mg/kg per day.

Mutagenicity

Neither lopinavir nor ritonavir was found to be mutagenic or clastogenic in the Ames bacterial reverse mutation assay using *S. typhimurium* and *E. coli*, the mouse lymphoma assay, and the mouse micronucleus test and chromosomal aberration assays in human lymphocytes.

Pregnancy/Reproduction

Fertility—Neither male nor female rats experienced any effects on fertility following lopinavir/ritonavir doses of 10/5, 30/15, or 100/50 mg/kg per day (the exposures at high doses were approximately 0.7-fold for lopinavir and 1.8-fold for ritonavir of the exposures in humans at the recommended therapeutic dose).

Pregnancy—Studies in humans have not been done. Because animal reproduction studies are not always predictive of human response, this drug should be used during pregnancy only if clearly needed.

Early reabsorption, decreased fetal viability, decreased fetal body weight, and increased incidence of skeletal variations and skeletal ossification delays were seen in rats given a maternally toxic dosage of lopinavir and ritonavir (the exposures in rats were approximately 0.7-fold for lopinavir and 1.8-fold for ritonavir of the exposures in humans at the recommended therapeutic dose). Developmental toxicity manifested as a decrease in survival of rat pups between birth and postnatal day 21 was seen in rats at doses of 40/20 mg/kg per day. In contrast, no embryonic or fetal developmental toxicities were seen in rabbits given maternally toxic doses of 80/40 mg/kg per day (approximately 0.6 and 1 time the recommended human dose of lopinavir and ritonavir, respectively).

To monitor maternal-fetal outcomes of pregnant women exposed to lopinavir and ritonavir combination an Antiretroviral Pregnancy Registry has been established. Physicians are encouraged to register patients by calling 1–800–258–4263.

FDA Pregnancy Category C

Breast-feeding

It is not known whether lopinavir and ritonavir is distributed in human milk. However, lopinavir has been shown to be distributed in rat milk. Because of both the potential for HIV transmission and the potential for serious adverse effects in nursing infants, mothers should be instructed not to breast-feed if they are taking the combination of lopinavir and ritonavir.

The Centers for Disease Control and Prevention recommend that HIV-infected mothers refrain from breast-feeding their infants to avoid risking postnatal transmission of HIV.

Pediatrics

No information is available on the relationship of age to the effects of the lopinavir and ritonavir twice-daily dosing regimen in pediatric patients up to 6 months of age or the lopinavir and ritonavir once-daily dosing regimen in pediatric patients of any age. Safety and efficacy have not been established.

Appropriate studies performed to date have not demonstrated pediatrics-specific problems that would limit the usefulness of the lopinavir and ritonavir twice-daily dosing regimen in children 6 months to 12 years of age.

Geriatrics

No information is available on the relationship of age to the effects of lopinavir and ritonavir in geriatric patients. Dose selection should be done with caution as elderly people are more likely to have age related problems such as decreased hepatic, renal, or cardiac function, and of concomitant disease or other drug therapy.

Drug interactions and/or related problems

The following drug interactions and/or related problems have been selected on the basis of their potential clinical significance (possible mechanism in parentheses where appropriate)—not necessarily inclusive (» = major clinical significance):

Note: Combinations containing any of the following medications, depending on the amount present, may also interact with this medication.

Abacavir or
Zidovudine
(lopinavir and ritonavir may induce glucuronidation, thus reducing the plasma concentration of abacavir or zidovudine; clinical significance is unknown)

» Amiodarone or
» Bepridil or
» Lidocaine (systemic) or
» Quinidine
(concentrations of antiarrhythmics may be increased, caution is warranted; therapeutic monitoring of antiarrhythmic concentration may be necessary)

» Amprenavir
(concomitant use may result in increased concentrations of amprenavir and decreased concentrations of lopinavir; increased dose of lopinavir and ritonavir and decreased dose of amprenavir may be necessary when coadministered)
(amprenavir should not be administered concomitantly with the lopinavir and ritonavir once-daily dosing regimen)

» Astemizole or
» Cisapride or
» Flecainide or
» Pimozide or
» Propafenone or
» Terfenadine
(may cause serious and/or life threatening cardiac arrhythmias; concomitant use is contraindicated)

Atovaquone
(atovaquone concentration may be decreased; increase in atovaquone dose may be required; clinical significance is unknown)

» Atorvastatin or
» Lovastatin or
» Simvastatin
(concentration of lipid lowering agents is increased; dose of atorvastatin should be lowered to the lowest possible level when used in combination with lopinavir and ritonavir; consider using pravastatin or fluvastatin)
(concomitant use of lovastatin or simvastatin with lopinavir and ritonavir may result in serious reactions such as myopathy, including rhabdomyolysis; concomitant use is not recommended)

» Carbamazepine or
» Dexamethasone or
» Phenobarbital or
» Phenytoin
(concentration of lopinavir may be decreased with concurrent use, resulting in decreased effectiveness of lopinavir; caution is warranted)
(the lopinavir and ritonavir once-daily dosing regimen should not be administered concomitantly with carbamazepine, phenobarbital, or phenytoin)

» Clarithromycin
(concentration of clarithromycin may be increased with concomitant administration; for patients with renal impairment, the dosage should be adjusted)

» Cyclosporine or
» Sirolimus or
» Tacrolimus
(concentrations of the immunosuppressants cyclosporine, sirolimus, and tacrolimus may be increased if administered concomitantly with lopinavir and ritonavir; therapeutic monitoring of immunosuppressant levels is recommended)

Delavirdine
(lopinavir concentrations may be increased; appropriate doses of lopinavir and ritonavir when used concomitantly with delavirdine have not been established)

Didanosine
(didanosine administration requires an empty stomach; administer didanosine one hour before or two hours after the combination of lopinavir and ritonavir capsules or oral solution; lopinavir/ritonavir tablets can be taken at the same time as didanosine without food)

» Dihydroergotamine or
» Ergonovine or
» Ergotamine or
» Methylergonovine
(potential for serious and life-threatening acute ergot toxicity, characterized by peripheral vasospasm and ischemia of the extremities or other tissues, exists; concomitant use is contraindicated)

Disulfiram or
Metronidazole
(lopinavir and ritonavir oral solution contains alcohol, which can produce a disulfiram-like reaction when administered concurrently with disulfiram or metronidazole)

» Efavirenz or
» Nevirapine
(lopinavir concentration may be decreased due to induction of CYP3A by efavirenz and nevirapine; increased dosage of lopinavir and ritonavir may be required)
(increasing dose to 3 lopinavir/ritonavir tablets coadministered twice daily with efavirenz significantly increased lopinavir plasma concentrations approximately 35% and ritonavir concentrations approximately 56% to 92% compared to 2 lopinavir/ritonavir tablets twice daily without efavirenz)
(neither efavirenz nor nevirapine should be administered concomitantly with the lopinavir and ritonavir once-daily dosing regimen)

» Ethinyl estradiol
(ethinyl estradiol concentrations may be decreased; alternative or additional contraceptive measures should be used when estrogen-based oral contraceptives or with the contraceptive patch are administered with lopinavir and ritonavir)

» Felodipine or
» Nicardipine or
» Nifedipine or
(dihydropyridine calcium channel blocker concentrations may be increased; caution is warranted; clinical monitoring of patients is recommended)

» Fluticasone, inhaled or nasal
(coadministration not recommended unless potential benefit outweighs risk; concomitant use with ritonavir increases fluticasone propionate plasma concentrations resulting in significantly reduced serum cortisol concentrations; Cushing's syndrome and adrenal suppression have been reported)

Fosamprenavir or
» Indinavir or
» Saquinavir
(concomitant use may result in decreased peak plasma concentrations of indinavir and increased trough concentrations of indinavir, and saquinavir; decreased dose of indinavir or saquinavir is recommended)
(the lopinavir and ritonavir once-daily dosing regimen has not been studied in combination with indinavir or saquinavir)

» Itraconazole or
» Ketoconazole or
Voriconazole
(azole antifungal concentrations may be increased; high doses of ketoconazole or itraconazole(>200 mg/day) are not recommended when taken with lopinavir and ritonavir)
(concurrent use of voriconazole with lopinavir and ritonavir has not been studied)

Methadone
(methadone concentration may be decreased; dose of methadone may need to be increased when taken with lopinavir and ritonavir)

» Midazolam or
» Triazolam
(prolonged or increased sedation or respiratory depression may occur; concomitant use is contraindicated)
» Nelfinavir
(concomitant use may increase nelfinavir concentration; dose of lopinavir/ritonavir may need to be increased and nelfinavir dose may need to be decreased)
(nelfinavir should not be administered concomitantly with the lopinavir and ritonavir once-daily dosing regimen)
» Rifabutin
(increased concentrations of rifabutin and rifabutin metabolite may occur; rifabutin dosage reduction is recommended)
» Rifampin
(may lead to loss of virologic response and possible resistance to lopinavir and ritonavir or to the class of protease inhibitors or other co-administered antiretroviral agents)
Ritonavir
(safety and efficacy of additional doses of ritonavir have not been established)
» Sildenafil
» Tadalafil or
» Vardenafil
(concomitant use is likely to produce a large increase in the plasma concentration of PDE5 inhibitors, which may result in adverse effects such as hypotension, prolonged erection, syncope, and visual changes)
» St. John's wort (hypericum perforatum)
(concomitant use is likely to produce decreased concentrations of lopinavir and ritonavir resulting in suboptimal lopinavir concentrations, loss of virologic response, and possible resistance to lopinavir and ritonavir; concomitant use is not recommended)
Tenofovir
(lopinavir and ritonavir may increase concentrations of tenofovir)
» Trazodone
(concomitant use with ritonavir increases plasma concentrations of trazodone; nausea, dizziness, hypotension, and syncope have been observed following coadministration; ritonavir and trazodone should be used with caution and a lower dose of trazodone should be considered)
» Warfarin
(warfarin concentrations may be affected; International Normalized Ratio (INR) monitoring is recommended)

Laboratory value alterations

The following have been selected on the basis of their potential clinical significance (possible effect in parentheses where appropriate)—not necessarily inclusive (» = major clinical significance).

With physiology/laboratory test values
Alanine aminotransferase (ALT [SGPT]) and
Aspartate aminotransferase (AST [SGOT]) and
Gamma glutamyl transferase (GGT)
(values may be increased)
» Amylase or
» Cholesterol, total or
» Triglycerides
(large increases have been reported)
Bilirubin
(increased concentrations have been observed)
Glucose
(levels may be increased)
Neutrophils
(counts may be decreased)
Phosphorus, inorganic
(concentrations may be decreased)
Platelets
(decreased counts have been observed in pediatric patients)
Sodium
(decreased or increased concentrations have been observed in pediatric patients)
Uric acid
(levels may be increased)

Medical considerations/Contraindications

The medical considerations/contraindications included have been selected on the basis of their potential clinical significance (reasons given in parentheses where appropriate)—not necessarily inclusive (» = major clinical significance).

Except under special circumstances, this medication should not be used when the following medical problem exists:
» Hypersensitivity to either lopinavir or ritonavir or any components of the product

Risk-benefit should be considered when the following medical problems exist:
» Diabetes mellitus
(may exacerbate existing diabetes or increase blood sugar levels; adjustments in the dosage of insulin or oral antidiabetic agent may be necessary)
Hemophilia A or
Hemophilia B
(although a causal relationship has not been established, increased bleeding, including spontaneous skin hematomas and hemarthrosis, has been reported in patients receiving protease inhibitors; additional factor VIII may be given and treatment with protease inhibitors may be continued or reintroduced)
» Hepatic function impairment or
» Hepatitis B or
» Hepatitis C
(lopinavir is principally metabolized in the liver; caution is warranted due to the potential for increased lopinavir concentrations; patients with current transaminase elevations may be at risk for further elevation or hepatic decompensation)
» Pancreatitis, history of
(risk of recurrence may be increasedespecially in patients with advanced HIV disease or patients with a history of pancreatitis; antiretroviral therapy should be suspended as clinically appropriate)

Patient monitoring

The following may be especially important in patient monitoring (other tests may be warranted in some patients, depending on condition; » = major clinical significance):
» Alanine aminotransferase (ALT [SGPT]), serum and
» Aspartate aminotransferase (AST [SGOT]), serum
(Patients with hepatic impairment or toxicity should have increased ALT and AST monitoring, especially in the first several months of treatment.)
Amylase or
Lipase, serum
(patients with advanced HIV disease or a history of pancreatitis may be at increased risk for pancreatitis; periodic monitoring of amylase or serum lipase values may useful; patients with clinical symptoms of nausea, vomiting, or abdominal pain should be evaluated for pancreatitis, including abnormalities in laboratory values such as amylase or serum lipase)
» Cholesterol, total and
» Triglycerides
(testing is recommended prior to initiation of lopinavir and ritonavir and periodically during the course of therapy)

Side/Adverse Effects

The redistribution or accumulation of body fat, including central obesity, dorsocervical fat enlargement (buffalo hump), peripheral wasting, breast enlargement, and "cushingoid appearance" have been reported in patients on protease inhibitor therapy. A causal relationship between these events and use of protease inhibitors has not been confirmed.

Pancreatitis has been observed in patients receiving lopinavir/ritonavir therapy, including those who developed marked triglyceride elevations. In some cases, fatalities have been observed. Pancreatitis should be considered if clinical symptoms including, nausea, vomiting, abdominal or abnormalities in serum lipase or amylase values.

The incidence of diarrhea was greater for once daily dosing when compared with twice daily dosing (57% vs. 35%).

The following side/adverse effects have been selected on the basis of their potential clinical significance (possible signs and symptoms in parentheses where appropriate)—not necessarily inclusive:

Those indicating need for medical attention

Incidence less frequent
Diabetes mellitus or hyperglycemia (blurred vision; dry mouth; fatigue; flushed, dry skin; fruit-like breath odor; increased hunger; increased thirst; increased urination; loss of consciousness; nausea; stomachache; sweating; troubled breathing; unexplained weight loss; vomiting); ***pancreatitis*** (bloating; chills; constipation; darkened urine; fast heartbeat; fever; indigestion; loss of appetite; pains in stomach, side, or abdomen, possibly radiating to the back; yellow eyes or skin)

Note: If *pancreatitis* should occur, therapy with lopinavir and ritonavir and other antiretroviral agents should be suspended.

Incidence not determined—Observed during clinical practice; estimates of frequency cannot be determined

Bradyarrhythmias (chest pain or discomfort; lightheadedness, dizziness or fainting; shortness of breath; slow or irregular heartbeat; unusual tiredness); *erythema multiforme* (blistering, peeling, loosening of skin; chills; cough; diarrhea; fever; itching; joint or muscle pain; red irritated eyes; sore throat; sores, ulcers, or white spots in mouth or on lips; unusual tiredness or weakness); *Stevens Johnson syndrome* (blistering, peeling, loosening of skin; chills; cough; diarrhea; fever; itching; joint or muscle pain; red irritated eyes; sore throat; sores, ulcers, or white spots in mouth or on lips; unusual tiredness or weakness)

Those indicating need for medical attention only if they continue or are bothersome

Incidence more frequent

Diarrhea; nausea

Incidence less frequent

Abdominal pain; abnormal stools; asthenia (lack or loss of strength); *dyspepsia* (acid or sour stomach; belching; heartburn; indigestion; stomach discomfort, upset or pain); *headache; insomnia* (trouble in sleeping); *pain; skin rash; vomiting*

Those not indicating need for medical attention

Incidence not determined—Observed during clinical practice; estimates of frequency cannot be determined

Redistribution of body fat

Overdose

For more information on the management of overdose or unintentional ingestion, **contact a poison control center** (see *Poison Control Center Listing*).

Lopinavir and ritonavir oral solution contains 42.4% alcohol (v/v). Accidental ingestion by a child could result in significant alcohol–related toxicity and could approach the potential lethal dose of alcohol.

Treatment of overdose

Treatment is essentially symptomatic and supportive.

To decrease absorption—

Induction of emesis or use of gastric lavage to empty the stomach. Activated charcoal also may be administered.

To enhance elimination—

Dialysis is not likely to be effective because lopinavir is highly protein-bound.

Monitoring—

Vital signs and clinical status of the patient.

Supportive care—

Patients in whom intentional overdose is confirmed or suspected should be referred for psychiatric consultation.

Patient Consultation

As an aid to patient consultation, refer to *Advice for the Patient, Lopinavir and Ritonavir (Systemic).*

In providing consultation, consider emphasizing the following selected information (» = major clinical significance):

Before using this medication

» Conditions affecting use, especially:

Hypersensitivity to either lopinavir or ritonavir or any component of the product

Pregnancy—Should be used during pregnancy only if clearly needed

Breast-feeding—The Centers for Disease Control and Prevention recommend that HIV-infected mothers refrain from breast-feeding their infants to avoid risking postnatal transmission of HIV.

Use in children—Safety and effectiveness of the twice-daily dosing regimen have not been established in children below the age of 6 months.

Safety and effectiveness of the once-daily dosing regimen have not been established in the pediatric population.

Use in the elderly—Dose selection should be done with caution as elderly people are more likely to have age related problems such as decreased hepatic, renal, or cardiac function, and of concomitant disease or other drug therapy.

Other medications, especially amiodarone, amprenavir, atorvastatin, astemizole, bepridil, carbamazepine, cisapride, clarithromycin, cyclosporine, dexamethasone, dihydroergotamine, efavirenz, ergonovine, ergotamine, ethinyl estradiol, felodipine, flecainide, fluticasone (inhaled or nasal), indinavir, itraconazole, ketoconazole, lidocaine, lovastatin, methylergonovine, midazolam, nelfinavir, nevirapine, nicardipine, nifedipine, phenobarbital, phenytoin, pimozide, propafenone, quinidine, rifabutin, rifampin, saquinavir, sildenafil, simvastatin, sirolimus, St. John's wort, tacrolimus, terfenadine, trazodone, triazolam, voriconazole, or warfarin.

Other medical problems, especially diabetes mellitus, hepatic function impairment, hepatitis B, hepatitis C, or history of pancreatitis

Proper use of this medication

Reading patient package insert carefully

» Find out about medicines that should **NOT** be taken with lopinavir and ritonavir.

» For oral solution dosage form, using calibrated dosing syringe to measure dose.

» For tablet dosage form, swallowing whole and not crushing or chewing

» For capsule and oral solution dosage forms, importance of taking medication with food

» Importance of not taking more medication than prescribed; importance of not discontinuing lopinavir and ritonavir without checking with physician

» Proper dosing

Missed dose: Taking as soon as possible; not taking if almost time for next scheduled dose; not doubling doses

» Proper storage

Precautions while using this medication

» Regular visits to physician

When taking oral solution, limiting alcohol intake because dosage form contains 42% alcohol

» Importance of using an additional or alternative contraceptive if taking estrogen-containing oral contraceptives or using estrogen containing contraceptive patch.

» Importance of reporting any side effects, especially dizziness, fainting, changes in vision, if you are also taking sildenafil, tadalafil, or vardenafil.

Side/adverse effects

Signs of potential side effects, especially diabetes mellitus, hyperglycemia, or pancreatitis

(Signs of potential side effects observed during clinical practice, especially bradyarrhythmias, erythema multiforme, or Stevens Johnson Syndrome)

General Dosing Information

Once daily administration is not recommended in therapy-experienced patients.

Diet/Nutrition

For optimal absorption, lopinavir and ritonavir capsules and oral solution should be taken with food.

Lopinavir and ritonavir tablets may be taken with or without food.

Oral Dosage Forms

LOPINAVIR AND RITONAVIR CAPSULES

Usual adult and adolescent dose

Antiviral—

Oral, 400 mg of lopinavir and 100 mg of ritonavir (3 capsules) two times a day with food. The dose may be increased to 533 mg of lopinavir and 133 mg of ritonavir (4 capsules) two times a day with food when used in combination with amprenavir, efavirenz, nelfinavir, or nevirapine. Nelfinavir dose should be decreased to 1000 mg twice per day when coadministered. The dose of rifabutin should be reduced by at least 75% of the usual daily dose (i.e., 150 mg three times per week) when taken in combination with lopinavir and ritonavir. The dose of sildenafil should be reduced to 25 mg every 48 hours when taken in combination with lopinavir and ritonavir. Clarithromycin doses should be reduced by 50% in patients with creatinine clearance (CL_{CR}) 30 to 60 mL/min and 75% in patients with CL_{CR}<30 mL/min when taken in combination with lopinavir and ritonavir.

Oral, 800 mg of lopinavir and 200 mg of ritonavir (6 capsules) once-daily with food in therapy-naive patients only. The once-daily regimen should not be administered in combination with efavirenz, nevirapine, amprenavir, or nelfinavir. The dose of rifabutin should be reduced by at least 75% of the usual daily dose (i.e., 150 mg three times per week) when taken in combination with lopinavir and ritonavir. The dose of sildenafil should be reduced to 25 mg every 48 hours when taken in combination with lopinavir and ritonavir. Clarithromycin doses should be reduced by 50% in patients with creatinine clearance (CL_{CR}) 30 to 60 mL/min and 75% in patients with CL_{CR}<30 mL/min when taken in combination with lopinavir and ritonavir.

Note: The renal clearance of lopinavir is negligible. A decrease in total body clearance is not expected in patients with renal insufficiency.

Caution should be exercised when administering lopinavir and ritonavir to subjects with hepatic impairment. Lopinavir and ritonavir has not been studied in patients with severe hepatic hepatic impairment.

Usual pediatric dose

This dosage form is usually not used in children. See *Lopinavir and Ritonavir Oral Solution*.

The once-daily dosing regimen has not been evaluated in pediatric patients

Usual geriatric dose

See *Usual adult and adolescent dose.*

Strength(s) usually available

U.S.—

133.3 mg of lopinavir and 33.3 mg of ritonavir per capsule (Rx) [*Kaletra* (FD&C Yellow No. 6; gelatin; glycerin; oleic acid; polyoxyl 35 castor oil; propylene glycol; sorbitol special; titanium dioxide; water)].

Canada—

Note: May contain fractionated coconut-oil and lecithin blend.

133.3 mg of lopinavir and 33.3 mg of ritonavir per capsule (Rx) [*Kaletra* (FD&C Yellow No. 6; gelatin; glycerin; oleic acid; polyoxyl 35 castor oil; propylene glycol; sorbitol special; titanium dioxide; water)].

Packaging and storage

Store between 2 and 8 °C (36 and 46 °F). Protect from excessive heat.

Stability

If stored at room temperature (less than 25 °C or 77 °F), capsules should be used within 2 months.

If refrigerated, capsules will remain stable until the expiration date printed on the label.

Auxiliary labeling

- May be stored in refrigerator. If stored at room temperature discard unused drug in 2 months.
- Find out about medicines that should **NOT** be taken with this medicine.

LOPINAVIR AND RITONAVIR ORAL SOLUTION

Usual adult and adolescent dose

Antiviral—

Oral, 400 mg of lopinavir and 100 mg of ritonavir (5 mL) two times a day with food. The dose may be increased to 533 mg of lopinavir and 133 mg of ritonavir (6.5 mL) two times a day with food when used in combination with amprenavir, efavirenz, nelfinavir or nevirapine.

Oral, 800 mg of lopinavir and 200 mg of ritonavir (10 mL) once-daily with food in therapy-naive patients only. The once-daily regimen should not be administered in combination with efavirenz, nevirapine, amprenavir, or nelfinavir.

Usual pediatric dose

Note: Dosing is based on the lopinavir component of the lopinavir and ritonavir oral solution.

The manufacturer recommends that the prescriber calculate the appropriate milligram dose for each individual child less than 12 years old and determine the corresponding volume of oral solution or number of capsules. However, the dosing below provides guidelines for oral solution based on body weight. When possible the dose should be administered using a calibrated dosing syringe.

Antiviral—

Children weighing 7 to <15 kg: Oral, 12 mg/kg twice daily, with food

- 7 to 10 kg: 1.25 mL
- >10 kg to <15 kg: 1.75 mL

Children weighing 15 to 40 kg: Oral, 10 mg/kg twice daily, with food

- 15 to 20 kg: 2.25 mL
- >20 to 25 kg: 2.75 mL
- >25 to 30 kg: 3.5 mL
- >30 to 35 kg: 4 mL
- >35 to 40 kg: 4.75 mL

Children weighing more than 40 kg: See *Usual adult and adolescent dose.*

Children weighing 7 to <15 kg: Oral, 13 mg/kg twice daily, with food

- 7 to 10 kg: 1.5 mL
- >10 kg to <15 kg: 2 mL

Children weighing 15 to 45 kg: Oral, 11 mg/kg twice daily, with food

- 15 to 20 kg: 2.5 mL
- >20 to 25 kg: 3.25 mL
- >25 to 30 kg: 4 mL
- >30 to 35 kg: 4.5 mL
- >35 to 40 kg: 5 mL (or 3 capsules)
- >40 to 45 kg: 5.75 mL

Children weighing more than 45 kg: See *Usual adult and adolescent dose.*

For children 6 months to 12 years of age:—

Without amprenavir or efavirenz or nevirapine—:

Concomitant therapy with amprenavir, efavirenz or nevirapine—:

For children up to 6 months of age—

Safety and efficacy have not been established.

The once-daily dosing regimen has not been evaluated in pediatric patients

Note: In Canada, dosing in children 6 months to 12 years of age (without efavirenz or nevirapine concomitant therapy)—Oral, 230 milligrams of lopinavir and 57.5 milligrams of ritonavir per square meter of body surface area twice daily with food; up to a maximum dose of 400 milligrams of lopinavir and 100 milligrams of ritonavir twice daily.

In Canada, dosing in children 6 months to 12 years of age (with efavirenz or nevirapine concomitant therapy)—Oral, 300 milligrams of lopinavir and 75 milligrams of ritonavir per square meter of body surface area twice daily with food; up to a maximum dose of 533 milligrams of lopinavir and 133 milligrams of ritonavir twice daily.

Usual pediatric prescribing limits

In children greater than 40 kg (without concomitant efavirenz or nevirapine)—up to a maximum dose of 400 mg of lopinavir and 100 mg of ritonavir (5 mL or 3 capsules) twice daily.

In children greater than 45 kg (with concomitant efavirenz or nevirapine)—up to a maximum dose of 533 mg of lopinavir and 133 mg of ritonavir (6.5 mL or 4 capsules) twice daily.

Usual geriatric dose

See *Usual adult and adolescent dose.*

Strength(s) usually available

U.S.—

80 mg of lopinavir per mL and 20 mg of ritonavir per mL (Rx) [*Kaletra* (Acesulfame potassium; alcohol (42.4% v/v); artificial cotton candy flavor; citric acid; glycerin; high fructose corn syrup; Magnasweet-110 flavor; menthol; natural and artificial vanilla flavor; peppermint oil; polyoxyl 40 hydrogenated castor oil; povidone; propylene glycol; saccharin sodium; sodium chloride; sodium citrate; water)].

Canada—

80 mg of lopinavir per mL and 20 mg of ritonavir per mL (Rx) [*Kaletra* (Acesulfame potassium; alcohol (42.4% v/v); artificial cotton candy flavor; citric acid; glycerin; high fructose corn syrup; Magnasweet-110 flavor; menthol; natural and artificial vanilla flavor; peppermint oil; polyoxyl 40 hydrogenated castor oil; povidone; propylene glycol; saccharin sodium; sodium chloride; sodium citrate; water)].

Packaging and storage

Store between 2 and 8 °C (36 and 46 °F). Avoid excessive heat

Stability

If stored at room temperature (less than 25 °C or 77 °F), solution should be used within 2 months.

If refrigerated, solution will remain stable until the expiration date printed on the label.

Auxiliary labeling

- May be stored in refrigerator. If stored at room temperature discard unused drug in 2 months.
- Find out about medicines that should **NOT** be taken with this medicine.

LOPINAVIR AND RITONAVIR TABLETS

Usual adult and adolescent dose

Antiviral—

Oral, 400 mg of lopinavir and 100 mg of ritonavir (2 tablets) two times a day with or without food. Or, for therapy-naive patients only: Oral, 800 mg of lopinavir and 200 mg of ritonavir (4 tablets) once-daily with food.

Concomitant therapy: Antiretroviral-naive patients—Oral, 400 mg of lopinavir and 100 mg of ritonavir (2 tablets) can be used twice daily in combination with efavirenz, nevirapine, fosamprenavir or nelfinavir with no dose adjustment.

Treatment-experienced patients—A dose increase of lopinavir and ritonavir to 600 mg/150 mg (3 tablets) twice-daily may be considered when used in combination with efavirenz, nevirapine, fosamprenavir without ritonavir, or nelfinavir where decreased susceptibility to lopinavir is clinically suspected (by treatment history or laboratory evidence).

Lopinavir/ritonavir tablets should not be administered as a once-daily regimen in combination with efavirenz, nevirapine, amprenavir, or nelfinavir.

Usual pediatric dose

This dosage form is usually not used in children. See *Lopinavir and Ritonavir Oral Solution*.

The once-daily dosing regimen has not been evaluated in pediatric patients

Usual geriatric dose

See *Usual adult and adolescent dose*.

Strength(s) usually available

U.S.—

200 mg of lopinavir and 50 mg of ritonavir per tablet (Rx) [*Kaletra* (film-coated; copovidone; sorbitan monolaurate; colloidal silicon dioxide; sodium stearyl fumarate; hypromellose; titanium dioxide; polyethylene glycol 400; hydroxypropyl cellulose; talc; polyethylene 3350; yellow ferric oxide E172; polysorbate 80)].

Canada—

Not commercially available

Packaging and storage

Store between 20 and 25 °C (68 and 77 °F); excursions permitted to 15 and 30 °C (59 and 86 °F). Dispense in original container. Exposure to high humidity outside original container for longer than 2 weeks is not recommended.

Auxiliary labeling

- Does not require refrigeration
- This medication can be taken with or without food.
- Swallow whole. Do not crush or chew.
- Find out about medicines that should **NOT** be taken with this medicine.

Revised: 11/10/2005
Developed: 01/18/2001

LORACARBEF Systemic†

VA CLASSIFICATION (Primary): AM119

Commonly used brand name(s): *Lorabid*.

Note: For a listing of dosage forms and brand names by country availability, see *Dosage Forms* section(s).

†Not commercially available in Canada.

Category

Antibacterial (systemic).

Indications

General Considerations

Loracarbef is the first of a new class of beta-lactam antibiotics called carbacephems. Carbacephems are related structurally to cephalosporins. Loracarbef is chemically identical to cefaclor except that the sulfur atom in the dihydrothiazine ring has been replaced by a methylene group. Carbacephems have greater chemical stability than cephalosporins.

Loracarbef has *in vitro* activity against most pathogens responsible for upper respiratory tract infections. It is active *in vitro* against *Streptococcus pneumoniae*, as well as beta-lactamase positive and negative *Haemophilus influenzae* and *Moraxella catarrhalis*. Loracarbef may not be active against bacteria such as penicillin-resistant *S. pneumoniae* and nonbeta-lactamase-producing ampicillin-resistant *H. influenzae*. Loracarbef has good activity *in vitro* against *S. pyogenes* (group A streptococci), and groups B, C, and G streptococci. *Enterococcus* species (group D streptococci) are resistant. Most strains of *Staphylococcus aureus* are susceptible to loracarbef; however, beta-lactamase-producing strains may be less susceptible and methicillin-resistant staphylococci are resistant.

Some gram-negative bacteria have *in vitro* susceptibility to loracarbef, including *Escherichia coli*, *Salmonella* species, *Klebsiella pneumoniae*, *Proteus mirabilis*, and *Citrobacter diversus*. However, strains of *E. coli* and *K. pneumoniae* with high production of beta-lactamase may be resistant. *Citrobacter freundii*, *Proteus vulgaris*, *Klebsiella oxytoca*, *Serratia marcescens*, *Morganella morganii*, *Enterobacter* species, *Providencia* species, and *Pseudomonas* species are all resistant to loracarbef.

Accepted

Bronchitis, bacterial exacerbation of (treatment)—Loracarbef is indicated in the treatment of bacterial exacerbations of bronchitis caused by susceptible organisms.

Otitis media (treatment)—Loracarbef is indicated in the treatment of otitis media caused by susceptible organisms.

Pharyngitis, streptococcal (treatment)—Loracarbef is indicated in the treatment of streptococcal pharyngitis caused by susceptible organisms.

Pneumonia (treatment)—Loracarbef is indicated in the treatment of pneumonia caused by susceptible organisms.

Sinusitis (treatment)—Loracarbef is indicated in the treatment of sinusitis caused by susceptible organisms.

Skin and soft tissue infections (treatment)—Loracarbef is indicated in the treatment of skin and soft tissue infections caused by susceptible organisms.

Urinary tract infections, bacterial (treatment)—Loracarbef is indicated in the treatment of bacterial urinary tract infections caused by susceptible organisms.

Pharmacology/Pharmacokinetics

Physicochemical characteristics

Chemical Group—Carbacephems are chemically similar to cephalosporins

Molecular weight—367.8.

Mechanism of action/Effect

Bactericidal; binds to essential target proteins of the bacterial cell wall, leading to inhibition of cell wall synthesis and cellular lysis.

Absorption

Well absorbed (90%) from the gastrointestinal tract. When administered with food, the peak plasma concentration (C_{max}) decreases by 50 to 60%, and the time to peak plasma concentration (T_{max}) increases by 30 to 60 minutes; however, the total absorption remains unchanged.

Distribution

Concentrations in middle ear fluid, skin-blister fluid, and tonsillar tissue are approximately 40 to 50% of the simultaneous plasma concentration. Concentration in urine is still in the therapeutic range for most organisms 6 to 12 hours after administration. Cerebrospinal fluid (CSF) levels are not available.

Protein binding

Approximately 25%.

Biotransformation

There is no evidence of metabolism in humans.

Half-life

Single dose—
- Normal renal function:
  - Approximately 1 hour.
- Creatinine clearance:
  - 10 to 50 mL/min (0.17 to 0.83 mL/sec)—Approximately 5.6 hours.
  - <10 mL/min (0.17 mL/sec)—Approximately 32 hours.

Time to peak concentration

Capsules—Approximately 1.2 hours.
Suspension—0.5 to 0.8 hour.

Peak serum concentration

Single dose—
- Capsule:
  - 200 mg—Approximately 8 mcg/mL.
  - 400 mg—Approximately 14 mcg/mL.
- Suspension:
  - 400 mg—Approximately 17 mcg/mL.
  - 7.5 mg/kg—Approximately 13 mcg/mL.
  - 15 mg/kg—Approximately 19 mcg/mL.

Elimination

Renal; virtually all of loracarbef (87 to 97%) is excreted unchanged in the urine.

In dialysis—Hemodialysis reduces the half-life of loracarbef to approximately 4 hours.

Precautions to Consider

Cross-sensitivity and/or related problems

Patients allergic to cephalosporins or penicillins may be allergic to loracarbef. Loracarbef should be administered with caution to penicillin-allergic patients since the cross-reactivity among beta-lactam antibiotics is approximately 10%.

Carcinogenicity

Lifetime carcinogenic studies in animals have not been performed.

Mutagenicity

No mutagenic potential was found in bacterial mutation tests or in *in vitro* and *in vivo* mammalian systems.

Pregnancy/Reproduction

Fertility—Fertility and reproductive performance were not affected in rats given doses of loracarbef up to 33 times the maximum human exposure in mg per kg of body weight (mg/kg).

Pregnancy—Adequate and well-controlled studies in humans have not been done.

Studies in mice, rats, and rabbits given doses up to 33 times the maximum human exposure of loracarbef in mg/kg have revealed no evidence of harm to the fetus.

FDA Pregnancy Category B.

Breast-feeding

It is not known whether loracarbef is distributed into breast milk.

Pediatrics

Appropriate studies on the relationship of age to the effects of loracarbef have not been performed in children up to 6 months of age. The pharmacokinetics and clinical response to loracarbef in children 6 months to 17 years of age are very similar to those in adults.

Geriatrics

Appropriate studies performed to date have not demonstrated geriatrics-specific problems that would limit the usefulness of loracarbef in the elderly. However, elderly patients are more likely to have age-related renal function impairment, which may require a dosage adjustment in patients receiving loracarbef.

Drug interactions and/or related problems

The following drug interactions and/or related problems have been selected on the basis of their potential clinical significance (possible mechanism in parentheses where appropriate)—not necessarily inclusive (» = major clinical significance):

Note: Combinations containing any of the following medications, depending on the amount present, may also interact with this medication.

» Probenecid
(probenecid decreases the renal tubular secretion of loracarbef, increasing the area-under-the-curve [AUC] by approximately 80% and the half-life from 1 hour to 1.5 hours)

Laboratory value alterations

The following have been selected on the basis of their potential clinical significance (possible effect in parentheses where appropriate)—not necessarily inclusive (» = major clinical significance).

With physiology/laboratory test values
Alanine aminotransferase (ALT [SGPT]), serum or
Alkaline phosphatase, serum or
Aspartate aminotransferase (AST [SGOT]), serum
(values may be increased transiently)

Blood urea nitrogen (BUN) or
Creatinine, serum
(concentrations may be increased transiently)

Leukocyte count and
Platelet count
(may be decreased; transient leukopenia, thrombocytopenia, eosinophilia have been seen on rare occasion)

Medical considerations/Contraindications

The medical considerations/contraindications included have been selected on the basis of their potential clinical significance (reasons given in parentheses where appropriate)—not necessarily inclusive (» = major clinical significance).

Except under special circumstances, this medication should not be used when the following medical problem exists:

» Previous allergic reaction (anaphylaxis) to penicillins or cephalosporins

Risk-benefit should be considered when the following medical problem exists:

» Renal function impairment
(loracarbef is excreted renally; patients with renal function impairment may require a reduced dosage)

Side/Adverse Effects

The following side/adverse effects have been selected on the basis of their potential clinical significance (possible signs and symptoms in parentheses where appropriate)—not necessarily inclusive:

Those indicating need for medical attention

Incidence less frequent
Hypersensitivity (itching; skin rash)

Those indicating need for medical attention only if they continue or are bothersome

Incidence more frequent
Gastrointestinal disturbances (abdominal pain; anorexia; diarrhea; nausea and vomiting)

Incidence rare
Central nervous system disturbances (dizziness; headache; drowsiness; insomnia; nervousness); ***vaginitis*** (vaginal itching and discharge)

Patient Consultation

As an aid to patient consultation, refer to *Advice for the Patient, Loracarbef (Systemic).*

In providing consultation, consider emphasizing the following selected information (» = major clinical significance):

Before using this medication

» Conditions affecting use, especially:
Allergy to penicillins or cephalosporins
Other medications, especially probenecid
Other medical problems, especially renal function impairment

Proper use of this medication

Taking at least 1 hour before or 2 hours after meals
» Compliance with full course of therapy, especially in streptococcal infections
» Importance of not missing doses and taking at evenly spaced times
» Proper dosing
Missed dose: Taking as soon as possible; not taking if almost time for next dose; not doubling doses
» Proper storage

Precautions while using this medication

Checking with physician if no improvement within a few days
» May cause diarrhea—
For severe diarrhea, checking with physician before taking any antidiarrheals
For mild diarrhea, kaolin- or attapulgite-containing, but not other, antidiarrheals may be tried
Checking with physician or pharmacist if mild diarrhea continues or worsens

Side/adverse effects

Signs of potential side effects, especially hypersensitivity reactions

General Dosing Information

Therapy should be continued for at least 10 days in group A beta-hemolytic streptococcal infections to prevent acute rheumatic fever or glomerulonephritis.

Because loracarbef has a high degree of chemical stability, refrigeration of the reconstituted oral suspension is not required.

Adults and children with renal function impairment require a reduction in dose as follows:

Creatinine Clearance (mL/min)/(mL/sec)	Dose
≥50/0.83	See *Usual adult and adolescent dose*
10–49/0.17–0.82	One-half the *Usual adult and adolescent dose* or administer the *Usual adult and adolescent dose* at twice the regular dosing interval
<10/0.17	*Usual adult and adolescent dose* given every 3 to 5 days
Hemodialysis patients	Administer after hemodialysis

Diet/Nutrition

Loracarbef should be taken on an empty stomach (1 hour before or 2 hours after meals).

Oral Dosage Forms

LORACARBEF CAPSULES

Usual adult and adolescent dose

Bronchitis, bacterial exacerbations—
Oral, 200 to 400 mg every twelve hours for seven days.

Pharyngitis, streptococcal—
Oral, 200 mg every twelve hours for ten days.

Pneumonia, caused by *S. pneumoniae* or *H. influenzae*—
Oral, 400 mg every twelve hours for fourteen days.

Sinusitis—
Oral, 400 mg every twelve hours for ten days.

Skin and soft tissue infections—
Oral, 200 mg every twelve hours for seven days.
Urinary tract infections—
Uncomplicated cystitis—Oral, 200 mg every twenty-four hours for seven days.
Uncomplicated pyelonephritis—Oral, 400 mg every twelve hours for fourteen days.

Usual pediatric dose
Otitis media—
Oral, 15 mg per kg of body weight every twelve hours for ten days.
Pharyngitis, streptococcal: Oral, 7.5 mg per kg of body weight every twelve hours for ten days.
Skin and soft tissue infections—
Oral, 7.5 mg per kg of body weight every twelve hours for seven days.

Strength(s) usually available
U.S.—
200 mg (Rx) [*Lorabid*].
400 mg (Rx) [*Lorabid*].
Canada—
Not commercially available.

Packaging and storage
Store below 40 °C (104 °F), preferably between 15 and 30 °C (59 and 86 °F), unless otherwise specified by manufacturer. Store in a tight container.

Auxiliary labeling
- Continue medicine for full time of treatment.
- Take on an empty stomach.

LORACARBEF FOR ORAL SUSPENSION

Usual adult and adolescent dose
See *Loracarbef Capsules*.

Usual pediatric dose
See *Loracarbef Capsules*.

Strength(s) usually available
U.S.—
100 mg per 5 mL (when reconstituted according to the manufacturer's instructions) (Rx) [*Lorabid*].
200 mg per 5 mL (when reconstituted according to the manufacturer's instructions) (Rx) [*Lorabid*].
Canada—
Not commercially available.

Packaging and storage
Store below 40 °C (104 °F), preferably between 15 and 30 °C (59 and 86 °F), unless otherwise specified by manufacturer. Store in a tight container. Discard reconstituted suspension after 14 days.

Auxiliary labeling
- Continue medicine for full time of treatment.
- Shake well.
- Take on an empty stomach.

Revised: 06/20/1995

LORATADINE—See *Antihistamines (Systemic)*

LORAZEPAM—See *Benzodiazepines (Systemic)*

LOSARTAN Systemic

VA CLASSIFICATION (Primary/Secondary): CV805/CV409

Commonly used brand name(s): *Cozaar*.

Other commonly used names are DuP 753 and MK594.

Note: For a listing of dosage forms and brand names by country availability, see *Dosage Forms* section(s).

Category

Antihypertensive; angiotensin II receptor antagonist.

Indications

Accepted

Hypertension (treatment)—Losartan is indicated for the treatment of hypertension. It may be used alone or in combination with other antihypertensive agents, including diuretics.

For additional information on initial therapeutic guidelines related to the treatment of hypertension, see *Appendix III*.

Hypertension with left ventricular hypertrophy (treatment)—Losartan is indicated to reduce the risk of stroke in patients with hypertension and left ventricular hypertrophy, but there is evidence that this benefit dose not apply to Black patients.

Nephropathy, diabetic (treatment)—Losartan is indicated for the treatment of diabetic nephropathy with an elevated serum creatinine and proteinuria (urinary albumin to creatinine ratio ≥300 mg/g) in patients with type 2 diabetes and a history of hypertension. In this population, losartan reduces the rate of progression of nephropathy as measured by the occurrence of doubling of serum creatinine or end stage renal disease (need for dialysis or renal transplantation).

Pharmacology/Pharmacokinetics

Physicochemical characteristics

Molecular weight—Losartan potassium: 461.01.

Mechanism of action/Effect

Losartan is a nonpeptide angiotensin II receptor antagonist with high affinity and selectivity for the AT_1 receptor. Losartan blocks the vasoconstrictor and aldosterone-secreting effects of angiotensin II by inhibiting the binding of angiotensin II to the AT_1 receptor. AT_1 receptor blockade results in an increase in plasma renin activity (PRA) followed by increases in plasma angiotensin II concentration. The potential clinical consequences of these increases are not clear. Angiotensin II agonist effects have not been demonstrated.

Other actions/effects

In vitro platelet aggregometry shows that losartan appears to be a weak antagonist to human platelet thromboxane A_2/prostaglandin H_2 (TP) receptors. The clinical relevance of this effect is presently unclear. Losartan also appears to have a uricosuric effect. However, the clinical significance of this effect has not been delineated.

Absorption

Well-absorbed following oral administration. Bioavailability is approximately 33%.

Protein binding

Losartan—Very high (98.7%).
Carboxylic acid metabolite—Very high (99.8%).

Biotransformation

Losartan undergoes substantial first-pass metabolism by the cytochrome P450 system. Biotransformation results in a major active carboxylic acid metabolite that is 10 to 40 times more potent than the parent compound and is responsible for most of the pharmacologic activity. In addition, there are 5 minor metabolites that are much less active than the parent compound.

Half-life

Elimination—
Losartan: Approximately 2 hours.
Carboxylic acid metabolite: Approximately 6 to 9 hours.

Time to peak concentration

Losartan—Approximately 1 hour.
Carboxylic acid metabolite—Approximately 2 to 4 hours.

Time to peak effect

Approximately 6 hours.

Duration of action

Single dose—24 hours or more.

Elimination

Renal—Approximately 35% (4% of dose as parent and 6% of dose as active metabolite).
Fecal (biliary)—Approximately 60%.
In dialysis—Losartan and its carboxylic acid metabolite are not removable by hemodialysis.

Precautions to Consider

Carcinogenicity

Losartan was not carcinogenic in rats and mice given maximally tolerated doses of 270 mg per kg of body weight (mg/kg) per day and 200 mg/kg per day, respectively, for 105 and 92 weeks, respectively. However, female rats had a slightly higher incidence of pancreatic acinar adenoma. The maximally tolerated doses of losartan provided systemic exposures of up to 160 times (rats) and 30 times (mice) the exposure of a 50 kg human given 100 mg per day.

Mutagenicity

Losartan was not mutagenic in a number of *in vitro* and *in vivo* assays.

Pregnancy/Reproduction

Fertility—Studies in male rats given oral doses of up to 150 mg/kg per day did not reveal adverse effects on fertility or reproductive performance. However, toxic doses of 300 and 200 mg/kg per day given to females resulted in significant decreases in the number of corpora lutea, implants, and live fetuses. The relationship of these findings to losartan is uncertain.

Pregnancy—Medications affecting the renin-angiotensin system, such as losartan, can cause fetal and neonatal morbidity and mortality when administered to pregnant women. Losartan should be discontinued as soon as possible when pregnancy is detected.

Fetal exposure to medications affecting the renin-angiotensin system during the second and third trimesters of pregnancy have been associated with hypotension, neonatal skull hypoplasia, anuria, renal failure, and even death in the newborn. Maternal oligohydramnios has also been reported, probably reflecting decreasing fetal renal function. Oligohydramnios in this setting has been associated with fetal limb contractures, craniofacial deformation, and hypoplastic lung development. Prematurity, intrauterine growth retardation, and patent ductus arteriosus also have been reported. However, it is not clear that these occurrences were related to drug exposure.

It is recommended that infants exposed *in utero* to losartan be closely observed for hypotension, oliguria, and hyperkalemia. Oliguria should be treated with support of blood pressure and renal perfusion. If oligohydramnios is observed, losartan should be discontinued unless it is considered lifesaving for the mother. Oligohydramnios, however, may not appear until after the fetus has sustained irreversible damage.

Losartan exposure during late gestation at doses approximately 3 times the maximum recommended human dose on a mg per square meter of body surface area basis produced adverse effects in rat fetuses and neonates, including decreased body weight, delayed physical and behavioral development, mortality, and renal toxicity.

FDA Pregnancy Category C (first trimester) and D (second and third trimesters).

Breast-feeding

It is not known whether losartan is distributed into breast milk. However, significant concentrations of losartan and its active metabolite are present in the milk of rats. Because of the potential for adverse effects on the nursing infant, a decision should be made whether to discontinue nursing or discontinue the drug, taking into account the importance of the drug to the mother.

Pediatrics

No information is available on the relationship of age to the effects of losartan in pediatric patients. Safety and efficacy have not been established in children younger than 6 years of age.

Geriatrics

Use of losartan in a limited number of patients 65 years of age and over has not demonstrated geriatrics-specific problems that would limit the usefulness of losartan in the elderly, but greater sensitivity of some older individuals cannot be ruled out.

Pharmacogenetics

In the Losartan Intervention For Endpoint reduction in hypertension (LIFE) study, Black patients with hypertension and left ventricular hypertrophy had a lower risk of stroke on atenolol than on losartan. Given the difficulty in interpreting subset differences in large trials, it cannot be known whether the observed difference is the result of chance. However, the LIFE study does not provide evidence that the benefits of losartan on reducing the risk of cardiovascular events in hypertensive patients with left ventricular hypertrophy apply to Black patients.

Drug interactions and/or related problems

The following drug interactions and/or related problems have been selected on the basis of their potential clinical significance (possible mechanism in parentheses where appropriate)—not necessarily inclusive (» = major clinical significance):

Note: Combinations containing any of the following medications, depending on the amount present, may also interact with this medication.

Anti-inflammatory drugs, nonsteroidal (NSAIDs), especially indomethacin
(NSAIDs may antagonize the antihypertensive effect of losartan by inhibiting renal prostaglandin synthesis and/or causing sodium and fluid retention; the patient should be carefully monitored to confirm that the desired effect is being obtained)

Blood from blood bank (may contain up to 30 mEq [mmol] of potassium per L of plasma or up to 65 mEq [mmol] per L of whole blood when stored for more than 10 days) or
Cyclosporine or
Diuretics, potassium-sparing or
Low-salt milk (may contain up to 60 mEq [mmol] of potassium per liter) or
Potassium-containing medications or
Potassium supplements or substances containing high concentrations of potassium or
Salt substitutes (most contain substantial amounts of potassium)
(concurrent administration with losartan may result in hyperkalemia since reduction of aldosterone production induced by losartan may lead to elevation of serum potassium; determination of serum potassium concentrations is recommended if concurrent use of these agents is necessary)

» Diuretics
(symptomatic hypotension may occur after initiation of losartan therapy in patients taking a diuretic; caution and a lower starting dose are recommended)

Fluconazole
(concomitant use decreased active metabolite concentration and increased losartan concentration)

Hypotension-producing medications, other (See *Appendix II*)
(concurrent use with losartan may produce additive hypotensive effects)

Sympathomimetics
(concurrent use of these agents may reduce the antihypertensive effects of losartan; the patient should be carefully monitored to confirm that the desired effect is being obtained)

Laboratory value alterations

The following have been selected on the basis of their potential clinical significance (possible effect in parentheses where appropriate)—not necessarily inclusive (» = major clinical significance).

With physiology/laboratory test values

Alanine aminotransferase (ALT) and
Aspartate aminotransferase (AST)
(transient increases have been reported rarely; these increases were infrequently greater than 2 or 3 times the upper limit of normal)

Bilirubin, serum
(concentrations may be increased)

Hemoglobin and
Hematocrit
(small increases occur frequently, but are rarely of clinical significance)

Potassium, serum
(concentrations may be slightly increased as a result of reduced aldosterone concentrations)

Uric acid, serum
(concentrations may be decreased, reflecting losartan's uricosuric effect)

Uric acid, urine
(concentrations may be increased; losartan appears to significantly increase uric acid excretion; this effect appears to be related to the parent compound, losartan, and not the carboxylic acid metabolite)

Medical considerations/Contraindications

The medical considerations/contraindications included have been selected on the basis of their potential clinical significance (reasons given in parentheses where appropriate)—not necessarily inclusive (» = major clinical significance).

Except under special circumstances, this medication should not be used when the following medical problem exists:

» Hypersensitivity to losartan or any component of the product

Risk-benefit should be considered when the following medical problems exist:

» Hepatic function impairment
(increased plasma concentrations may occur; total plasma clearance of losartan may be 50% lower and oral bioavailability about 2 times higher than in individuals with normal hepatic function; lower dosages are recommended)

» Renal artery stenosis, bilateral or in a solitary kidney
(increased risk of renal function impairment)

Renal function impairment, moderate to severe
(losartan area under the curve [AUC] may be increased by approximately 50%; however, dosage adjustments are not necessary unless patient is volume-depleted)

(in patients whose renal function is dependent on the renin-angiotensin-aldosterone system, especially those with congestive heart failure, there may be a risk of losartan-induced renal failure)

» Caution is recommended in patients who are sodium- or volume-depleted. Symptomatic hypotension may occur following initiation of losartan therapy. Sodium- or volume-depletion should be corrected or a lower starting dose is recommended in these patients.

Patient monitoring

The following may be especially important in patient monitoring (other tests may be warranted in some patients, depending on condition; » = major clinical significance):

» Blood pressure measurements
(recommended at periodic intervals; selected patients may be taught to monitor their blood pressure at home and report the results at regular physician visits)

Potassium, serum
(check periodically to monitor for hyperkalemia)

Renal function determinations
(recommended at periodic intervals, especially in patients who are sodium- and volume-depleted as a result of diuretic therapy or who have severe congestive heart failure)

Side/Adverse Effects

Note: A case of angioedema has been reported in a patient being treated with losartan.

The following side/adverse effects have been selected on the basis of their potential clinical significance (possible signs and symptoms in parentheses where appropriate)—not necessarily inclusive:

Those indicating need for medical attention

Incidence less frequent

Dizziness; upper respiratory infection (cough, fever, or sore throat)

Incidence unknown—Observed during clinical practice, estimates of frequency can not be determined

Angioedema (large, hive-like swelling on face, eyelids, lips, tongue, throat, hands, legs, feet, sex organs); ***hepatitis*** (dark urine; general tiredness and weakness; light-colored stools; nausea and vomiting; upper right abdominal pain; yellow eyes and skin); ***hyperkalemia*** (dizziness; fast heartbeat; high blood pressure; irritability; muscle twitching; restlessness; seizures; swelling of feet or lower legs; weakness); ***hyponatremia*** (coma; confusion; convulsions; decreased urine output; dizziness; fast or irregular heartbeat; headache; increased thirst muscle pain or cramps nausea or vomiting shortness of breath swelling of face, ankles, or hands unusual tiredness or weakness); ***rhabdomyolysis*** (dark-colored urine; fever; muscle cramps or spasms; muscle pain or stiffness; unusual tiredness or weakness); ***thrombocytopenia*** (black, tarry stools; bleeding gums; blood in urine or stools; pinpoint red spots on skin; unusual bleeding or bruising); ***vasculitis including; Henoch-Schonlein purpura*** (blood in urine; bloody or black, tarry stools; fever; large, flat, blue or purplish patches in the skin; painful knees and ankles; raised red swellings on the skin, the buttocks, legs or ankles; stomach pain)

Those indicating need for medical attention only if they continue or are bothersome

Incidence more frequent

Headache

Incidence less frequent

Back pain; diarrhea; fatigue; nasal congestion

Incidence rare

Cough, dry; insomnia (trouble in sleeping); ***leg pain; muscle cramps or pain; sinus problems***

Overdose

For more information on the management of overdose or unintentional ingestion, **contact a Poison Control Center** (see *Poison Control Center Listing*).

Clinical effects of overdose

The following effects have been selected on the basis of their potential clinical significance (possible signs and symptoms in parentheses where appropriate)—not necessarily inclusive:

Bradycardia due to vagal stimulation; hypotension; tachycardia

Treatment of overdose

Symptomatic and supportive.

Patient Consultation

As an aid to patient consultation, refer to *Advice for the Patient, Losartan (Systemic)*.

In providing consultation, consider emphasizing the following selected information (» = major clinical significance):

Before using this medication

» Conditions affecting use, especially:
Hypersensitivity to losartan
Pregnancy—Can cause fetal and neonatal morbidity and mortality; not recommended for use during pregnancy
Use in children—Safety and efficacy not established in children younger than 6 years of age
Other medications, especially diuretics
Other medical problems, especially hepatic and renal function impairment, renal artery stenosis, or sodium or volume depletion

Proper use of this medication

Compliance with therapy; taking medication at the same time(s) each day to maintain the therapeutic effect

Possible need for control of weight and diet, especially sodium intake; risks associated with sodium depletion; not taking salt substitutes or using low-salt milk unless approved by physician

» Patient may not experience symptoms of hypertension; importance of taking medication even if feeling well

» Does not cure, but helps control hypertension; possible need for lifelong therapy; checking with physician before discontinuing medication; serious consequences of untreated hypertension

Recommending oral suspension that can be prepared by the pharmacist if patient is unable to swallow tablets

May be taken with or without food

» Proper dosing
Missed dose: Taking as soon as possible; not taking if almost time for next dose; not doubling doses

» Proper storage

Precautions while using this medication

» Notifying physician immediately if pregnancy is suspected

Making regular visits to physician to check progress

» Not taking other medications, especially nonprescription sympathomimetics, unless discussed with physician

Caution when driving or doing other things requiring alertness, because of possible dizziness, especially after initial dose of losartan in patients taking diuretics

To prevent dehydration and hypotension, checking with physician if severe nausea, vomiting, or diarrhea occurs and continues

Caution when exercising or during hot weather because of the risk of dehydration and hypotension due to reduced fluid volume

» Caution in using alcohol because of the risk of dehydration and hypotension due to reduced fluid volume

Side/adverse effects

Signs of potential side effects, especially dizziness or upper respiratory infection

Signs of potential side effects observed during clinical practice, especially angioedema, hepatitis, hyperkalemia, hyponatremia, rhabdomyolysis, thrombocytopenia, or vasculitis (including Henoch-Schonlein purpura)

General Dosing Information

Dosage must be adjusted to meet the individual requirements of each patient, on the basis of clinical response.

An oral suspension can be prepared by the pharmacist using losartan tablets. See the instructions in the *General Route of Administration* section of this monograph.

Although there does not appear to be a rebound effect after abrupt withdrawal of losartan, gradual dosage reduction is recommended to minimize any risk of a rebound effect.

Recent evidence suggests that withdrawal of antihypertensive therapy prior to surgery may be undesirable. However, the anesthesiologist must be aware of such therapy.

Diet/Nutrition

Losartan may be taken with or without food.

Oral Dosage Forms

LOSARTAN POTASSIUM TABLETS

Usual adult dose

Antihypertensive—
Initial—
Oral, 50 mg once a day.
Note: In patients with possible volume depletion and patients with a history of hepatic function impairment an initial dose of 25 mg once a day is recommended.

Maintenance—
Oral, 25 to 100 mg a day. Dose may be given once a day or divided into two doses.

Note: If adequate blood pressure control is not achieved by losartan alone, a low dose of a diuretic may be added for an additive effect.

Hypertension with left ventricular hypertrophy (treatment)—
Oral, usual starting dose 50 mg once daily. Hydrochlorothiazide 12.5 mg once daily should be added and/or losartan dose should be increased to 100 mg once daily followed by an increase in hydrochlorthiazide to 25 mg once daily based on blood pressure response.

Hypertrophy, diabetic (treatment)—
Oral, usual starting dose 50 mg once daily. Dose should be increased to 100 mg once daily based on blood pressure response.

Note: Losartan may be administered with insulin and other commonly used hypoglycemic agents (e.g., sulfonylureas, glitazones and glucosidase inhibitors.

Usual pediatric dose

Antihypertensive—
Children younger than 6 years of age—Safety and efficacy have not been established.
Children 6 years of age and older—Oral, initial dose of 0.7 mg per kg of body weight per day up to 50 mg per day.

Note: Losartan should not be administered to pediatric patients with creatinine clearance less than 30 mL per minute per 1.73 m^2.

Usual pediatric prescribing limits

1.4 mg per kg of body weight per day up to 100 mg per day

Strength(s) usually available

U.S.—
25 mg (Rx) [*Cozaar* (potassium 2.12 mg [0.054 mEq]; microcrystalline cellulose; lactose hydrous; pregelatinized starch; magnesium stearate; hydroxypropyl cellulose; hypromellose; titanium dioxide; D&C yellow No. 10 aluminum lake; FD&C blue No. 2 aluminum lake)].
50 mg (Rx) [*Cozaar* (potassium 4.24 mg [0.108 mEq]; microcrystalline cellulose; lactose hydrous; pregelatinized starch; magnesium stearate; hydroxypropyl cellulose; hypromellose; titanium dioxide; D&C yellow No. 10 aluminum lake; FD&C blue No. 2 aluminum lake)].
100 mg (Rx) [*Cozaar* (potassium 8.48 mg [0.216 mEq]; microcrystalline cellulose; lactose hydrous; pregelatinized starch; magnesium stearate; hydroxypropyl cellulose; hypromellose; titanium dioxide; D&C yellow No. 10 aluminum lake; FD&C blue No. 2 aluminum lake)].

Canada—
25 mg (Rx) [*Cozaar*].
50 mg (Rx) [*Cozaar*].
100 mg (Rx) [*Cozaar*].

Packaging and storage

Store at 25 °C (77 °F), preferably between 15 and 30 °C (59 and 86 °F), in a tightly closed container. Protect from light.

Preparation of dosage form

To prepare a suspension (200 mL of a 2.5 mg/mL suspension)—
• Add 10 ml of purified water to an 8 ounce (240 mL) amber polyethylene terephthalate (PET) bottle containing ten 50-mg losartan tablets
• Immediately shake for at least 2 minutes
• Let the concentrate stand for 1 hour and then shake for 1 minute to disperse the tablet contents
• Separately prepare a 50/50 volumetric mixture of Ora-Plus™ and Ora-Sweet SF™.
• Add 190 mL of the 50/50 Ora-Plus™/Ora-Sweet SF™ mixture to the tablet and water slurry in the PET bottle and shake for 1 minute to disperse the ingredients.
• The suspension should be refrigerated at 2 to 8 °C (36 to 46 °F) and can be stored for up to 4 weeks.
• Shake the suspension prior to each use and return promptly to the refrigerator

Auxiliary labeling

• Do not take other medicines without your doctor's advice.

Selected Bibliography

Goldberg AI, Dunlay MC, Sweet CS. Safety and tolerability of losartan potassium, an angiotensin II receptor antagonist, compared with hydrochlorothiazide, atenolol, felodipine ER, and angiotensin-converting enzyme inhibitors for the treatment of systemic hypertension. Am J Cardiol 1995; 75: 793-5.

Revised: 08/03/2005

LOSARTAN AND HYDROCHLOROTHIAZIDE Systemic

VA CLASSIFICATION (Primary): CV408

Commonly used brand name(s): *Hyzaar*.

NOTE: The *Lasartan and Hydrochlorothiazide (Systemic)* monograph is maintained on the *USP DI* electronic data base. A copy of the most recent revision of the complete monograph can be accessed on the *USP DI* Updates Online website. See the front cover of book for details on accessing the site.

For information on the specific components of this combination, see the *USP DI* monographs for *Losartan (Systemic)*, and *Diuretics, Thiazide (Systemic)*.

The information that follows is selectively abstracted from the complete monograph and is provided to facilitate drug use review and patient counseling.

Note: For a listing of dosage forms and brand names by country availability, see *Dosage Forms* section(s).

Category

Antihypertensive.

Indications

Accepted

Hypertension (treatment)—Losartan and hydrochlorothiazide combination is indicated for the treatment of hypertension.

Fixed-dosage combinations are generally not recommended for initial therapy and are useful for subsequent therapy only when the proportion of the component agents corresponds to the dose of the individual agents, as determined by titration. The fixed combination is indicated for initial therapy when the hypertension is severe enough that the value of achieving prompt blood pressure control exceeds the risk of initiating combination therapy in these patients.

For additional information on initial therapeutic guidelines related to the treatment of hypertension, see *Appendix III*.

Hypertensive patients with left ventricular hypertrophy (treatment)[1]—Losartan and hydrochlorothiazide is indicated to reduce the risk of stroke in patients with hypertension and left ventricular hypertrophy.

[1]Not included in Canadian product labeling.

Patient Consultation

As an aid to patient consultation, refer to *Advice for the Patient, Losartan and Hydrochlorothiazide (Systemic)*.

In providing consultation, consider emphasizing the following selected information (» = major clinical significance):

Before using this medication

» Conditions affecting use, especially:
Hypersensitivity to losartan, thiazide diuretics, or sulfonamide-type medications
Pregnancy—Not recommended for use during pregnancy; can cause fetal and neonatal morbidity and mortality
Breast-feeding—Hydrochlorothiazide is distributed into breast milk
Other medications, especially lithium, potassium-sparing diuretics, potassium supplements, or salt substitutes containing potassium
Other medical problems, especially anuria, hepatic function impairment, renal artery stenosis, or renal function impairment

Proper use of this medication

Compliance with therapy; taking medication at the same time each day to maintain the therapeutic effect
Possible need for control of weight and diet, especially sodium intake; risks associated with sodium depletion; not taking salt substitutes or using low-salt milk unless approved by physician
» Patient may not experience symptoms of hypertension; importance of taking medication even if feeling well
» Does not cure, but helps control, hypertension; possible need for lifelong therapy; checking with physician before discontinuing medication; serious consequences of untreated hypertension
May be taken with or without food
» Proper dosing
Missed dose: Taking as soon as possible; not taking if almost time for next dose; not doubling doses
» Proper storage

Precautions while using this medication

» Notifying physician immediately if pregnancy is suspected

Making regular visits to physician to check progress

» Not taking other medications, especially nonprescription sympathomimetics, unless discussed with physician

Caution when driving or doing other things requiring alertness, because of possible dizziness, especially after first dose of losartan and hydrochlorothiazide combination

To prevent dehydration and hypotension, checking with physician if severe nausea, vomiting, or diarrhea occurs and continues

Caution when exercising or during hot weather because of the risk of dehydration and hypotension due to reduced fluid volume

» Caution in using alcohol because of the risk of dehydration and hypotension due to reduced fluid volume

Diabetics: May increase blood sugar levels

Side/adverse effects

Signs of potential side effects, especially dizziness, electrolyte imbalance, upper respiratory tract infection, agranulocytosis, cholecystitis, pancreatitis, edema, palpitations, skin rash, or thrombocytopenia

Signs of potential side effects observed during clinical practice, especially angioedema, hepatitis, hyperkalemia, hyponatremia, rhabdomyolysis, or vasculitis (including Henoch-Schonlein purpura

Oral Dosage Forms

LOSARTAN POTASSIUM AND HYDROCHLOROTHIAZIDE TABLETS

Usual adult dose

Antihypertensive—

Oral, 1 or 2 tablets (50-12.5 mg tablet) once a day, or 1 tablet (100-25 mg tablet or 100–12.5 mg tablet) once a day as determined by individual titration with the component agents. A twice-a-day regimen at the same total daily dose may be considered if the antihypertensive effect measured at trough using once-a-day dosing is inadequate.

Severe hypertension (treatment)—

Oral, 1 tablet (50-12.5 mg tablet) once daily. For patients who do not respond adequately to 1 tablet after 2 to 4 weeks of therapy, the dosage may be increased to 1 (100-25 mg) tablet once daily.

Hypertension with left ventricular hypertrophy (treatment)—

Oral, 1 tablet (50-12.5 mg tablet) once daily. For patients who do not respond adequately to 1 tablet after 2 to 4 weeks of therapy, the dosage may be increased to 1 (100–12.5 or 100-25 mg) tablet once daily.

Note: For patients with renal impairment, the usual regimens of therapy with losartan/hydrochlorothiazide may be followed as long as the patient's creatinine clearance is greater than 30 mL per minute. In patients with more severe renal impairment, loop diuretics are preferred to thiazides, so losartan/hydrochlorothiazide is not recommended.

For patients with hepatic impairment, losartan/hydrochlorothiazide is not recommended for titration because the appropriate 25 mg starting dose of losartan cannot be given.

Usual adult prescribing limits

Losartan: Can be administered once or twice daily at total daily doses up to 100 mg.

Hydrochlorothiazide: Can be administered once daily at total daily doses up to 50 mg.

The maximum combination dose is 1 tablet containing 100 mg losartan and 25 mg hydrochlorothiazide once daily.

Usual pediatric dose

Safety and efficacy have not been established.

Strength(s) usually available

U.S.—

50 mg of losartan potassium and 12.5 mg of hydrochlorothiazide (Rx) [*Hyzaar* (D&C yellow No. 10 aluminum lake; hydroxypropyl cellulose; hypromellose; lactose hydrous; magnesium stearate; microcrystalline cellulose; pregelatinized starch; titanium dioxide)].

100 mg of losartan potassium and 12.5 mg of hydrochlorothiazide (Rx) [*Hyzaar* (D&C yellow No. 10 aluminum lake; hydroxypropyl cellulose; hypromellose; lactose hydrous; magnesium stearate; microcrystalline cellulose; pregelatinized starch; titanium dioxide; carnauba wax)].

100 mg of losartan potassium and 25 mg of hydrochlorothiazide (Rx) [*Hyzaar* (D&C yellow No. 10 aluminum lake; hydroxypropyl cellulose; hypromellose; lactose hydrous; magnesium stearate; microcrystalline cellulose; pregelatinized starch; titanium dioxide)].

Auxiliary labeling

• Do not take other medicines without your doctor's advice.

Revised: 11/29/2005

LOTEPREDNOL Ophthalmic

VA CLASSIFICATION (Primary): OP301

Commonly used brand name(s): *Alrex; Lotemax.*

Note: For a listing of dosage forms and brand names by country availability, see *Dosage Forms* section(s).

Category

Corticosteroid (ophthalmic); anti-inflammatory (steroidal), ophthalmic.

Indications

Accepted

Conjunctivitis, seasonal allergic (treatment)—Ophthalmic loteprednol 0.2% is indicated for temporary relief of the signs and symptoms of seasonal allergic conjunctivitis.

Inflammation, postoperative (treatment)—Ophthalmic loteprednol 0.5% is indicated for the treatment of postoperative inflammation following ocular surgery.

Ocular conditions, inflammatory (treatment)—Ophthalmic loteprednol 0.5% is indicated for treatment of steroid-responsive inflammatory ocular conditions of the palpebral and bulbar conjunctiva, cornea, and anterior segment of the globe, including allergic conjunctivitis, acne rosacea, superficial punctate keratitis, herpes zoster keratitis, iritis, cyclitis, and selected infective conjunctivitides when the benefits in terms of diminished edema and inflammation outweigh the risk of corticosteroid use.

Pharmacology/Pharmacokinetics

Physicochemical characteristics

Source—Synthetic. Structurally similar to other corticosteroids, except for the absence of the number 20 position ketone group.

Molecular weight—466.96.

pH—Ophthalmic suspension: 5.3 to 5.6.

Tonicity—250 to 310 milliosmoles per kg of body weight (mOsmol/kg).

Mechanism of action/Effect

Corticosteroids suppress the inflammatory response to a variety of inciting agents and probably delay or slow healing. They inhibit edema, fibrin deposition, capillary dilation, leukocyte migration, capillary proliferation, fibroblast proliferation, deposition of collagen, and scar formation, all of which are associated with inflammation. While the exact mechanism of action of ocular corticosteroids is not known, they are thought to act by induction of phospholipase A_2 inhibitory proteins, collectively called lipocortins, which are postulated to control the biosynthesis of potent mediators of inflammation, such as prostaglandins and leukotrienes by inhibiting the release of their common precursor, arachidonic acid.

Other actions/effects

Corticosteroids may increase intraocular pressure.

Absorption

A bioavailability study with administration of one drop of 0.5% loteprednol in each eye eight times a day for 2 days or four times a day for 42 days found that plasma concentrations of loteprednol etabonate and its primary inactive metabolite were below the limit of quantitation at all sampling times, which suggests limited (less than 1 nanogram per mL) systemic absorption.

Biotransformation

Extensive, to inactive carboxylic acid metabolites.

Precautions to Consider

Cross-sensitivity and/or related problems

Patients sensitive to other corticosteroids may be sensitive to loteprednol.

Carcinogenicity

Long-term animal studies have not been done.

Mutagenicity

Loteprednol was not found to be mutagenic *in vitro* in the Ames test, the mouse lymphoma tk assay, or in a chromosome aberration test in human lymphocytes, or *in vivo* in the single dose mouse micronucleus assay.

Pregnancy/Reproduction

Fertility—Studies in male and female rats administered loteprednol etabonate (route of administration not specified) prior to and during mating in doses of up to 50 and 25 mg per kg of body weight (mg/kg) per day, respectively (1500 and 750 times, respectively, the maximum daily dose of the 0.2% ophthalmic suspension or 600 and 300 times, respectively, the maximum daily dose of the 0.5% ophthalmic suspension), found no impairment of fertility.

Pregnancy—Studies in rabbits administered loteprednol etabonate in oral doses of 3 mg/kg per day (85 and 35 times the maximum daily clinical dose of the 0.2% and 0.5% ophthalmic suspension, respectively) during the period of organogenesis found loteprednol to be embryotoxic (delayed ossification) and teratogenic (increased incidence of meningocele, abnormal left common carotid artery, and limb flexures). The no-observed-effect level (NOEL) for these effects was 0.5 mg/kg per day (15 and 6 times the maximum daily clinical dose of the 0.2% and 0.5% ophthalmic suspension, respectively). Oral administration of loteprednol etabonate to rats during the period of organogenesis also produced teratogenicity (absent innominate artery at doses of ≥ 5 mg/kg per day and cleft palate and umbilical hernia at doses of ≥ 50 mg/kg per day) and embryotoxicity (increased post-implantation losses at 100 mg/kg per day and decreased fetal body weight and skeletal ossification at doses of ≥ 50 mg/kg per day). Treatment of rats with loteprednol etabonate (route of administration not specified) at doses of 0.5 mg/kg per day (15 and 6 times the maximum clinical dose of the 0.2% and 0.5% ophthalmic suspension, respectively) during organogenesis did not result in any reproductive toxicity. Maternal toxicity (significantly reduced body weight gain during treatment) occurred in rats at doses of ≥ 5 mg/kg per day (route of administration not specified) during the period of organogenesis. Oral administration of 50 mg/kg per day (a maternally toxic dose) to rats from the start of the fetal period through the end of lactation produced decreased growth and survival and retarded development in the offspring during lactation; the NOEL for these effects was 5 mg/kg per day. No effect on the duration of parturition or gestation was observed in rats with oral doses of up to 50 mg/kg per day during the fetal period.

FDA Pregnancy Category C.

Breast-feeding

It is not known whether ophthalmic corticosteroids could result in sufficient systemic absorption to produce detectable quantities in human breast milk. Caution should be exercised when ophthalmic corticosteroids are administered to women who breast-feed.

Pediatrics

Safety and efficacy have not been established.

Geriatrics

No information is available on the relationship of age to the effects of loteprednol in geriatric patients.

Medical considerations/Contraindications

The medical considerations/contraindications included have been selected on the basis of their potential clinical significance (reasons given in parentheses where appropriate)—not necessarily inclusive (» = major clinical significance).

Except under special circumstances, this medication should not be used when the following medical problems exist:

» Fungal diseases, ocular, or
» Herpes simplex keratitis, epithelial (dendritic keratitis) or
» Infections of the eye, other, including acute, purulent infections or
» Mycobacterial infection, ocular or
» Viral diseases, such as vaccinia, varicella, and other viral diseases of the cornea and conjunctiva
(corticosteroids decrease resistance to bacterial, fungal, and viral infections; application may mask or exacerbate existing infections and encourage the development of new or secondary infections)

Risk-benefit should be considered when the following medical problems exist:

Cataract surgery
(use of corticosteroids after cataract surgery may delay healing and increase the incidence of bleb formation)

» Diseases causing thinning of the cornea or sclera
(use may result in perforation)

Glaucoma
(prolonged use of corticosteroids may result in glaucoma, with damage to the optic nerve and defects in visual acuity and visual fields; corticosteroids should be used with caution in the presence of glaucoma)

Sensitivity to loteprednol or other corticosteroids

Patient monitoring

The following may be especially important in patient monitoring (other tests may be warranted in some patients, depending on condition; » = major clinical significance):

Intraocular pressure determinations
(recommended if loteprednol is administered for 10 days or longer)

Ophthalmologic examinations, including slit-lamp biomicroscopy and, if appropriate, fluorescein staining
(recommended before continuing therapy beyond 14 days)

Side/Adverse Effects

Note: Prolonged use of corticosteroids may result in glaucoma, damage to the optic nerve, defects in visual acuity and visual fields, and posterior subcapsular cataract formation.

Prolonged use of corticosteroids may also result in secondary ocular infections, including herpes simplex, due to suppression of host response, and perforation of the globe where there is thinning of the cornea or sclera.

Fungal infections of the cornea are prone to develop during long-term corticosteroid treatment. Fungal invasion should be considered in any persistent corneal ulceration where a corticosteroid is, or was, in use. Fungal cultures are recommended when appropriate.

Some side/adverse effects reported with ophthalmic loteprednol may resemble the disease being treated.

The following side/adverse effects have been selected on the basis of their potential clinical significance (possible signs and symptoms in parentheses where appropriate)—not necessarily inclusive:

Those indicating need for medical attention

Incidence more frequent—5 to 15%

Blurred vision or other change in vision; chemosis (swelling of the membrane covering the white part of the eye); ***injection*** (redness or swelling of the eye)

Incidence less frequent—< 5%

Conjunctivitis or keratoconjunctivitis (redness of eye, eyelid, or inner lining of eyelid); ***corneal abnormalities; eyelid erythema*** (redness of eyelid); ***eye discomfort, irritation, or pain; increased intraocular pressure; ocular discharge*** (discharge from the eye); ***papillae*** (tiny bumps on the inner lining of eyelid); ***uveitis*** (eye pain, tearing, sensitivity of eye to light, redness of eye, or blurred vision or other change in vision)

Those indicating need for medical attention only if they continue or are bothersome

Incidence more frequent—5 to 15%

Burning when medicine is applied; dry eye; epiphora (watery eye); ***foreign body sensation*** (feeling of something in the eye); ***headache; itching; pharyngitis*** (sore throat); ***photophobia*** (increased sensitivity of eyes to light); ***rhinitis*** (runny nose)

Patient Consultation

As an aid to patient consultation, refer to *Advice for the Patient, Loteprednol (Ophthalmic)*.

In providing consultation, consider emphasizing the following selected information (» = major clinical significance):

Before using this medication

» Conditions affecting use, especially:
Sensitivity to loteprednol or other corticosteroids
Pregnancy—Teratogenic and embryotoxic in animals
Other medical problems, especially diseases causing thinning of the cornea or sclera; fungal diseases, ocular; herpes simplex keratitis, epithelial (dendritic keratitis); infections of the eye, other, including acute, purulent infections or mycobacterial infection, ocular; or viral diseases, such as vaccinia, varicella, and other viral diseases of the cornea and conjunctiva

Proper use of this medication

Shaking suspension well before instilling
» If using the 0.5% strength, not wearing soft contact lenses while using medication
» If using the 0.2% strength, not wearing soft contact lenses if eyes are red; if eyes are not red, removing soft contact lenses before administration and waiting 10 minutes afterward before reinserting lenses
» Proper administration technique; preventing contamination; not touching applicator tip to any surface

» Proper dosing
Missed dose: Using as soon as remembered; not using if almost time for next dose; not doubling doses
» Proper storage

Precautions while using this medication
Need for ophthalmologic examinations during long-term therapy
» Checking with physician if symptoms do not improve or if condition becomes worse

Side/adverse effects
Signs of potential side effects, especially blurred vision or other change in vision; chemosis; injection; conjunctivitis or keratoconjunctivitis; corneal abnormalities; eyelid erythema; eye discomfort, irritation, or pain; increased intraocular pressure; ocular discharge; papillae; or uveitis

General Dosing Information

If signs and symptoms fail to improve after 2 days of therapy, the patient should be re-evaluated.

For the 0.2% ophthalmic solution—Patients should not wear contact lenses if their eyes are red. Patients whose eyes are not red should remove soft contact lenses while administering loteprednol and wait at least 10 minutes afterward before reinserting the lenses.

For the 0.5% ophthalmic solution—Patients should not wear soft contact lenses while being treated with loteprednol.

Ophthalmic Dosage Forms

LOTEPREDNOL OPHTHALMIC SUSPENSION

Usual adult dose
Seasonal allergic conjunctivitis—
Topical, to the conjunctiva, 1 drop of the 0.2% ophthalmic suspension in the affected eye(s) four times a day.
Ocular disorders, inflammatory—
Topical, to the conjunctiva, 1 or 2 drops of the 0.5% ophthalmic suspension in the affected eye(s) four times a day.
Note: During the first week of treatment, the dose may be increased, if necessary, up to 1 drop every hour. Therapy should not be discontinued prematurely.
Postoperative inflammation—
Topical, to the conjunctiva, 1 or 2 drops of the 0.5% ophthalmic suspension in the affected eye(s) four times a day beginning twenty-four hours after surgery and continuing throughout the first two weeks of the postoperative period.

Usual pediatric dose
Seasonal allergic conjunctivitis or
Ocular disorders, inflammatory or
Postoperative inflammation—
Safety and efficacy have not been established.

Strength(s) usually available
U.S.—
0.2% (Rx) [*Alrex* (benzalkonium chloride 0.01%; edetate disodium; glycerin; povidone; tyloxapol; hydrochloric acid and/or sodium hydroxide)].
0.5% (Rx) [*Lotemax* (benzalkonium chloride 0.01%; edetate disodium; glycerin; povidone; tyloxapol; hydrochloric acid and/or sodium hydroxide)].

Packaging and storage
Store container upright between 15 and 25 °C (59 and 77 °F). Keep from freezing.

Auxiliary labeling
• For the eye.
• Shake well.

Developed: 08/14/1998

LOTEPREDNOL AND TOBRAMYCIN Ophthalmic†

VA CLASSIFICATION (Primary): OP350

Commonly used brand name(s): *Zylet.*

Note: For a listing of dosage forms and brand names by country availability, see *Dosage Forms* section(s).

†Not commercially available in Canada.

Category

Anti-inflammatory (steroidal), ophthalmic; corticosteroid (ophthalmic); antibacterial (ophthalmic).

Indications

General Considerations
Tobramycin is active against staphylococci, including *Staphylococcus aureus* and *Staphylococcus epidermidis* (coagulase-positive and coagulase-negative), including penicillin-resistant strains. It is also active against streptococci, including some of the Group A beta-hemolytic species, some nonhemolytic species, and some *Streptococcus pneumoniae*. In addition, it is active against *Pseudomonas aeruginosa, Escherichia coli, Klebsiella pneumoniae, Enterobacter aerogenes, Proteus mirabilis, Morganella morganii*, most *Proteus vulgaris* strains, *Haemophilus influenzae*, and *Haemophilus aegyptius, Moraxella lacunata, Acinetobacter calcoaceticus*, and some *Neisseria* species.

Accepted
Inflammation, ocular (treatment) and
Ocular infections, superficial (treatment)—Loteprednol and tobramycin are indicated for steroid-responsive inflammatory ocular conditions for which a corticosteroid is indicated and where superficial bacterial ocular infection or a risk of bacterial ocular infection exists.

Ocular steroids are indicated in inflammatory conditions of the palpebral and bulbar conjunctiva, cornea and anterior segment of the globe such as allergic conjunctivitis, acne rosacea, superficial punctate keratitis, herpes zoster, iritis, cyclitis, and where the inherent risk of steroid use in certain infective conjunctivitides is accepted to obtain a diminution in edema and inflammation. They are also indicated in chronic anterior uveitis and corneal injury from chemical, radiation or thermal burns, or penetration of foreign bodies.

Pharmacology/Pharmacokinetics

Physicochemical characteristics
Molecular weight—
Loteprednol etabonate: 466.96.
Tobramycin: 467.52.
Solubility—Loteprednol etabonate is highly lipid soluble.
Tonicity—
260 to 320 milliosmoles per kg (mOsmol/kg).

Mechanism of action/Effect
Loteprednol—
There is no accepted explanation for the mechanism of action of ocular corticosteroids. However, corticosteroids are thought to act by induction of phospholipase A_2 inhibitory proteins, called lipocortins. It is postulated that these proteins control the biosynthesis of potent mediators of inflammation such as prostaglandins and leukotrienes by inhibiting the release of their common precursor arachidonic acid. Arachidonic acid is released from membrane phospholipids by phospholipase A_2.
Tobramycin—
The antibiotic combination of this combination provides action against susceptible organisms.

Absorption
Less than 1 ng/mL systemic absorption occurs with 0.5% loteprednol in normal volunteers.

Biotransformation
Loteprednol—
Based on *in vivo* and *in vitro* studies, loteprednol etabonate undergoes extensive metabolism to inactive carboxylic acid metabolites.

Precautions to Consider

Cross-sensitivity and/or related problems
Cross-sensitivity to other aminoglycoside antibiotics.

Carcinogenicity
Long term studies to evaluate the carcinogenic potential of loteprednol etabonate and tobramycin have not been conducted.

Mutagenicity
Loteprednol etabonate was not genotoxic *in vitro* in the Ames test, the mouse lymphoma TK assay, a chromosome aberration test in human lymphocytes, or in an *in vivo* mouse micronucleus assay.

Pregnancy/Reproduction
Fertility—
Loteprednol etabonate—
Studies done in male and female rats given oral doses of loteprednol etabonate at 50 mg/kg/day and 25 mg/kg/day prior to

and during mating showed no evidence of impaired fertility in either gender.

Tobramycin—

No impairment of fertility was observed in rats given subcutaneous doses of tobramycin at 100 mg/kg/day.

Pregnancy—Adequate and well controlled studies in humans have not been done. Loteprednol and tobramycin should be used during pregnancy only if the potential benefit justifies the potential risk to the fetus.

Loteprednol etabonate—

Studies done in rats and rabbits given oral doses of loteprednol etabonate during organogenesis at 5 and 3 mg/kg/day was found to be teratogenic. Oral doses at 50 mg/kg/day in rats during late pregnancy and throughout the weaning period revealed a decrease in growth and survival of pups without dystocia. No adverse effects in the pups were observed at 5 mg/kg/day.

Tobramycin—

Studies done in rats and rabbits given parenteral doses of tobramycin up to 100 mg/kg/day showed no harm to fetuses.

FDA Pregnancy Category C

Breast-feeding

It is not known whether topical ophthalmic administration of corticosteroids could result in sufficient systemic absorption to produce detectable quantities in human milk. Systemic steroids are distributed into human milk and could suppress growth, interfere with endogenous corticosteroid production, or cause other untoward effects. Caution should be exercised when loteprednol and tobramycin combination is administered to a nursing woman.

Pediatrics

Safety and effectiveness in pediatric patients have not been established.

Geriatrics

Appropriate studies to date have not demonstrated geriatrics-specific problems that would limit the usefulness of loteprednol and tobramycin in the elderly.

Drug interactions and/or related problems

The following drug interactions and/or related problems have been selected on the basis of their potential clinical significance (possible mechanism in parentheses where appropriate)—not necessarily inclusive (» = major clinical significance):

Aminoglycoside antibiotics
(monitor total serum concentration with concomitant administration of tobramycin and systemic aminoglycoside antibiotics)

Medical considerations/Contraindications

The medical considerations/contraindications included have been selected on the basis of their potential clinical significance (reasons given in parentheses where appropriate)—not necessarily inclusive (» = major clinical significance).

Except under special circumstances, this medication should not be used when the following medical problem exists:

» Fungal diseases, ocular, or
» Herpes simplex keratitis, epithelial (dendritic keratitis) or
» Mycobacterial infection, ocular or
» Viral diseases, such as vaccinia, varicella, and other viral diseases of the cornea and conjunctiva
» Hypersensitivity to loteprednol or tobramycin or to any of its ingredients and to other corticosteroids

Risk-benefit should be considered when the following medical problems exist:

Cataract surgery
(use of corticosteroids after cataract surgery may delay healing and increase the incidence of bleb formation)

» Diseases causing thinning of the cornea or sclera
(use may result in perforation)

» Glaucoma
(administer with caution; prolonged use of corticosteroids may result in glaucoma with damage to the optic nerve, defects in visual acuity and fields of vision, and in posterior subcapsular cataract formation.)

» Purulent conditions of the eye, acute
(steroids may mask or enhance existing infection)

Patient monitoring

The following may be especially important in patient monitoring (other tests may be warranted in some patients, depending on condition; » = major clinical significance):

Intraocular pressure determinations
(monitor if administered for 10 days or longer)

Serum concentration, total
(monitor total serum concentration with concomitant administration of tobramycin and systemic aminoglycoside antibiotics)

Side/Adverse Effects

The following side/adverse effects have been selected on the basis of their potential clinical significance (possible signs and symptoms in parentheses where appropriate)—not necessarily inclusive:

Those indicating need for medical attention

Incidence more frequent

Increased intraocular pressure; punctate keratitis, superficial (painful irritation of the clear front part of the eye)

Incidence less frequent—≤ 4%

Conjunctival erythema (redness of lid); ***corneal deposits*** (irritation and swelling of the eye; decreased vision or any change in vision); ***eyelid disorder*** (eyelid burning, redness, itching, pain, or tenderness); ***hypersensitivity*** (fast heartbeat; fever; hives; itching; irritation; hoarseness; joint pain; stiffness or swelling; rash; redness of skin; shortness of breath; swelling of eyelids, face, lips, hands, or feet; tightness in chest; troubled breathing or swallowing; wheezing); ***lid itching and swelling; ocular discharge*** (discharge from the eye); ***ocular discomfort*** (pain in eye); ***ocular toxicity*** (blurred vision or blue-green halos seen around objects dry eyes sensitivity of eyes to light); ***vision disorders*** (blurred vision or other changes in vision)

Incidence unknown

Bacterial ocular infection (blurred vision or other change in vision; eye pain; redness of eye; sensitivity of eye to light; tearing)

Those indicating need for medical attention only if they continue or are bothersome

Incidence more frequent

Burning; headache; itching; lacrimation disorder (dry eyes); ***photophobia*** (increased sensitivity of eyes to light); ***stinging***

Patient Consultation

As an aid to patient consultation, refer to *Advice for the Patient, Loteprednol and Tobramycin (Ophthalmic).*

In providing consultation, consider emphasizing the following selected information (» = major clinical significance):

Before using this medication

» Conditions affecting use, especially:

Hypersensitivity to loteprednol or tobramycin or to any its ingredients or to other corticosteroids

Pregnancy—Adequate and well controlled studies in humans have not been done. Loteprednol and tobramycin should be used during pregnancy only if the potential benefit justifies the potential risk to the fetus.

Breast-feeding—It is not known whether topical ophthalmic administration of corticosteroids could result in sufficient systemic absorption to produce detectable quantities in human milk. Caution should be exercised when loteprednol and tobramycin combination is administered to a nursing woman.

Use in children—Safety and effectiveness in pediatric patients have not been established.

Other medical problems, especially acute purulent conditions of the eye, cataract surgery, diseases causing thinning of the cornea or sclera, glaucoma, herpes simplex keratitis, ocular fungal diseases, ocular mycobacterial infection, or viral diseases, such as vaccinia, varicella, and other viral diseases of the cornea and conjunctiva

Proper use of this medication

» Not touching the dropper tip to any surface as this may contaminate the suspension
» Importance of not wearing soft contact lenses while using loteprednol and tobramycin ophthalmic solution
» Decreasing use gradually as clinical signs improve
» The importance of not discontinuing therapy prematurely
The importance of using only if the imprinted neckband is intact
» Proper dosing
Missed dose: Using as soon as possible; not using if almost time for next scheduled dose; not doubling doses
» Proper storage

Precautions while using this medication

» Importance of regular visits to physician to check progress
» Checking with doctor if symptoms do not improve or if condition becomes worse

Side/adverse effects

Signs of potential side effects, especially bacterial ocular infection, conjunctival erythema, corneal deposits, eyelid disorder, hypersensitivity, ocular discharge, increased intraocular pressure, lid itching and swelling, ocular discomfort, ocular toxicity, superficial punctate keratitis, vision disorders

General Dosing Information

Patients should be advised not to touch the dropper tip to any surface as this may contaminate the suspension.

Patients should be advised not to wear soft contact lenses while using loteprednol and tobramycin ophthalmic solution.

The initial prescription and renewal beyond 14 days should be made only after examination with the aid of magnification and fluorescein staining.

If signs and symptoms fail to improve after 2 days of therapy, the patient should be re-evaluated.

Use should decrease gradually as clinical signs improve.

It is important to not discontinuing therapy prematurely.

Not prescribing more than 20 mL initially or refilling without further evaluation.

Treatment of adverse effects

The development of secondary infections has occurred after use of combinations containing steroids and antimicrobials and following suppression of host responses. If super infection occurs, appropriate therapy should be initiated.

Ophthalmic Dosage Forms

LOTEPREDNOL ETABONATE AND TOBRAMYCIN OPHTHALMIC SUSPENSION

Usual adult dose

Ocular disorders (treatment)—

Topical, to the conjunctival sac, 1 or 2 drops every four to six hours. During the initial 24 to 48 hours the dosing may be increased to every one to two hours.

Usual pediatric dose

Safety and effectiveness in pediatric patients have not been established.

Usual geriatric dose

See *Usual adult dose*.

Strength(s) usually available

U.S.—

0.5% loteprednol etabonate and 0.3% tobramycin (Rx) [*Zylet* (benzalkonium chloride; edetate disodium; glycerin; povidone; purified water; sodium hydroxide; sulfuric acid; tyloxapol)].

Packaging and storage

Store between 15 and 25 °C (59 and 77 °F). Protect from freezing.

Auxiliary labeling

- Shake well
- For the eye
- Keep out of reach of children

Developed: 06/09/2005

LOVASTATIN—See *HMG-CoA Reductase Inhibitors (Systemic)*

LOXAPINE Systemic

VA CLASSIFICATION (Primary/Secondary): CN709/CN900

Commonly used brand name(s): *Loxapac; Loxitane; Loxitane C; Loxitane IM.*

Note: For a listing of dosage forms and brand names by country availability, see *Dosage Forms* section(s).

Category

Antipsychotic; antianxiety agent–antidepressant.

Indications

Note: Bracketed information in the *Indications* section refers to uses that are not included in U.S. product labeling.

Accepted

Psychotic disorders (treatment)—Loxapine is indicated for the management of symptoms and characteristics of psychotic conditions.

[Anxiety associated with mental depression (treatment)][1]—Loxapine has been used to treat anxiety neurosis with depression.

[1]Not included in Canadian product labeling.

Pharmacology/Pharmacokinetics

Note: The pharmacological effects of loxapine are similar to those of phenothiazines.

Physicochemical characteristics

Chemical Group—A tricyclic dibenzoxazepine derivative.

Molecular weight—

Loxapine: 327.81.

Loxapine succinate: 445.90.

pKa—6.6.

Mechanism of action/Effect

Although the exact mechanism of action has not been completely established, loxapine is thought to improve psychotic conditions by blocking dopamine at postsynaptic receptor sites in the brain.

Other actions/effects

Antiemetic—Inhibits the medullary chemoreceptor trigger zone.

Sedative—May cause indirect reduction of stimuli to the brain reticular activating system.

Biotransformation

Hepatic. Major active metabolites are 8-hydroxyloxapine, 7-hydroxyloxapine, and 8-hydroxyamoxapine.

Half-life

Oral—

3 to 4 hours.

Intramuscular—

12 hours.

Onset of action

30 minutes.

Time to peak effect

1½ to 3 hours.

Duration of action

Up to 12 hours.

Elimination

Biliary, as unconjugated metabolites. Renal, as conjugated metabolites.

Precautions to Consider

Cross-sensitivity and/or related problems

Patients sensitive to amoxapine (a dibenzoxazepine derivative) may be sensitive to loxapine also.

Carcinogenicity/Tumorigenicity

Most neuroleptic medications have been found to cause increased serum prolactin concentrations. Although the clinical significance of this increase is not known for most patients, *in vitro* studies have shown approximately ⅓ of human breast cancers to be prolactin dependent. Additionally, an increase in mammary neoplasms has been found in rodents after chronic administration of neuroleptics. However, a definite association between the chronic administration of these medications and mammary tumorigenesis is considered inconclusive because of limited evidence available.

Pregnancy/Reproduction

Pregnancy—Problems in humans have not been documented.

Fetotoxic effects, such as increased fetal resorptions and decreased fetal weight, were seen in rats and mice given doses within the range of the human therapeutic dose.

FDA Pregnancy Category C.

Breast-feeding

It is not known whether loxapine is excreted in breast milk. However, loxapine and its metabolites have been found in the milk of lactating dogs.

Pediatrics

Appropriate studies on the relationship of age to the effects of loxapine have not been performed in the pediatric population. Safety and efficacy have not been established.

Geriatrics

Geriatric patients tend to develop higher plasma concentrations of loxapine because of changes in distribution due to decreases in lean body mass, total body water, and albumin, and often an increase in total body fat composition. These patients usually require lower initial dosage and a more gradual titration of dose.

Elderly patients also appear to be more prone to orthostatic hypotension and exhibit an increased sensitivity to the anticholinergic and sedative effects of loxapine. In addition, they are more prone to develop extrapyramidal side effects, such as tardive dyskinesia and parkinsonism. The signs of tardive dyskinesia are persistent, difficult to control, and, in some patients, appear to be irreversible. There is no known effective treatment. The symptoms may be masked during long treatment but may appear if loxapine is discontinued. Careful observation during treatment for early signs of tardive dyskinesia and reduction of dosage or discontinuation of medication may prevent a more severe manifestation of the syndrome.

Dental

The peripheral anticholinergic effects of loxapine may decrease or inhibit salivary flow, especially in middle-aged or elderly patients, thus contributing to the development of caries, periodontal disease, oral candidiasis, and discomfort.

Extrapyramidal reactions induced by loxapine will result in increased motor activity of the head, face, and neck. Occlusal adjustments, bite registrations, and treatment for bruxism may be made less reliable.

The leukopenic and thrombocytopenic effects of loxapine may result in an increased incidence of microbial infection, delayed healing, and gingival bleeding. Although the occurrence is rare with loxapine, if leukopenia or thrombocytopenia occurs, dental work should be deferred until blood counts have returned to normal. Patients should be instructed in proper oral hygiene, including caution in use of regular toothbrushes, dental floss, and toothpicks.

Drug interactions and/or related problems

The following drug interactions and/or related problems have been selected on the basis of their potential clinical significance (possible mechanism in parentheses where appropriate)—not necessarily inclusive (» = major clinical significance):

Note: Combinations containing any of the following medications, depending on the amount present, may also interact with this medication.

Although not all of the following interactions have been documented specifically for loxapine, a potential exists for their occurrence because of loxapine's close pharmacological similarity to phenothiazine medications.

» Alcohol or
» Central nervous system (CNS) depression-producing medications, other, especially anesthetics, barbiturates, and opioid (narcotic) analgesics (See *Appendix II*)
(concurrent use may potentiate and prolong the CNS depressant effects of either these medications or loxapine; dosage adjustments to approximately ½ to ¼ of the usual dose may be necessary)

Amphetamines
(concurrent use may decrease the effects of amphetamines since loxapine produces alpha-adrenergic blockade)

Antacids or
Antidiarrheals, adsorbent
(concurrent use may inhibit the absorption of orally administered loxapine)

Anticholinergics or other medications with anticholinergic activity (See *Appendix II*) or
Antidyskinetic agents
(concurrent use with loxapine may intensify anticholinergic effects of both medications; patients should be advised to report gastrointestinal problems since paralytic ileus may occur; antidyskinetic agents should not be used for prophylaxis of pseudoparkinsonism during therapy with loxapine)

Anticonvulsants
(loxapine may lower the seizure threshold; dosage adjustment of anticonvulsant medications may be necessary; potentiation of anticonvulsant effects does not occur)

Antidepressants, tricyclic or
Monoamine oxidase (MAO) inhibitors, including furazolidone, procarbazine, and more than 10 mg of selegiline a day
(concurrent use may prolong and intensify the sedative and anticholinergic effects of either these medications or loxapine; serum concentrations of the antidepressant may be increased when it is administered concomitantly with loxapine; dosage reduction of antidepressant may be necessary)

Bromocriptine
(concurrent use with loxapine may antagonize effects of bromocriptine on serum prolactin activity; dosage adjustment of bromocriptine may be necessary)

Carbamazepine
(in addition to enhancement of CNS depressant effects and lowering of seizure threshold, the concurrent use of carbamazepine with loxapine, and possibly other neuroleptics, may decrease plasma concentrations of the neuroleptic; patient should be observed for clinical signs of ineffectiveness of loxapine and dosage adjusted accordingly)

Dopamine
(when dopamine is used concurrently with loxapine, alpha-adrenergic blocking action of loxapine may antagonize peripheral vasoconstriction produced by high doses of dopamine)

Ephedrine
(when used concurrently with loxapine, alpha-adrenergic blocking action of loxapine may decrease the pressor response to ephedrine)

Epinephrine
(alpha-adrenergic effects of epinephrine may be blocked when epinephrine is used concurrently with loxapine, possibly resulting in severe hypotension and tachycardia)

» Extrapyramidal reaction-causing medications, other (See *Appendix II*)
(concurrent use with loxapine may increase the severity and frequency of extrapyramidal effects)

» Guanadrel or
» Guanethidine
(concurrent use with loxapine may decrease the hypotensive effects of these agents because of their displacement from and inhibition of uptake by adrenergic neurons)

Levodopa
(concurrent use may inhibit the antiparkinsonian effects of levodopa by blocking dopamine receptors in the brain)

Metaraminol
(concurrent use usually decreases, but does not reverse or completely block, the pressor effect of metaraminol)

Methoxamine
(prior administration of alpha-adrenergic blocking agents such as loxapine may block the pressor effect and decrease the duration of action of methoxamine)

Ototoxic medications, especially ototoxic antibiotics
(concurrent use with loxapine may mask the symptoms of ototoxicity such as tinnitus, dizziness, or vertigo)

Phenylephrine or
Norepinephrine
(prior administration of loxapine may decrease the pressor response to phenylephrine or norepinephrine because of the alpha-adrenergic blocking action of loxapine, but severe hypotension associated with overdosage of loxapine would be expected to respond to either agent)

Medical considerations/Contraindications

The medical considerations/contraindications included have been selected on the basis of their potential clinical significance (reasons given in parentheses where appropriate)—not necessarily inclusive (» = major clinical significance).

Except under special circumstances, this medication should not be used when the following medical problems exist:

» CNS depression, drug-induced, severe or
» Comatose states
(may be exacerbated)

Risk-benefit should be considered when the following medical problems exist:

» Alcoholism, active
(CNS depression may be potentiated)

Cardiovascular disease
(increased risk of arrhythmias and hypotension)

Glaucoma, or predisposition to or
Parkinson's disease or
Urinary retention
(may be exacerbated)

» Hepatic function impairment
(metabolism may be altered)

Prostatic hypertrophy, symptomatic
(risk of urinary retention)

Seizure disorders
(seizure threshold may be lowered)

Sensitivity to amoxapine or loxapine

Patient monitoring

The following may be especially important in patient monitoring (other tests may be warranted in some patients, depending on condition; » = major clinical significance):

Blood cell counts
(may be required at periodic intervals during high-dose or prolonged therapy)

Careful observation for early symptoms of tardive dyskinesia
(recommended at periodic intervals, especially in the elderly and patients on high or extended maintenance dosage; loxapine should be discontinued if early symptoms of tardive dyskinesia appear, since there is no known effective treatment)

Hepatic function determinations and
Urine tests for bilirubin and bile
(may be required if jaundice or grippe-like symptoms occur)

Ophthalmologic examination
(may be advisable at periodic intervals during high-dose or prolonged therapy since deposition of particulate matter in the lens and cornea has occurred with some other antipsychotic medications)

Side/Adverse Effects

The following side/adverse effects have been selected on the basis of their potential clinical significance (possible signs and symptoms in parentheses where appropriate)—not necessarily inclusive:

Those indicating need for medical attention

Incidence more frequent

Akathisia (restlessness or need to keep moving); ***extrapyramidal effects, parkinsonian*** (difficulty in speaking or swallowing; loss of balance control; mask-like face; shuffling walk; slowed movements; stiffness of arms and legs; trembling and shaking of fingers and hands); ***tardive dyskinesia, persistent*** (lip smacking or puckering; puffing of cheeks; rapid or worm-like movements of tongue; uncontrolled movements of the arms and legs; uncontrolled chewing movements)

Note: *Parkinsonian extrapyramidal effects* are more common during first few days of treatment or following dosage increases.

Tardive dyskinesia is initially dose related, but may increase with long-term treatment and total cumulative dose; may persist after discontinuation of loxapine.

Incidence less frequent

Allergic reaction (skin rash); ***anticholinergic effect*** (difficult urination); ***constipation, severe***—may lead to paralytic ileus; ***extrapyramidal effects, dystonic*** (difficulty in swallowing; inability to move eyes; muscle spasms, especially of the neck and back; twisting movements of body)—may be severe

Incidence rare

Agranulocytosis (sore throat and fever; unusual bleeding or bruising); ***jaundice, obstructive*** (yellow eyes or skin); ***neuroleptic malignant syndrome [NMS]*** (convulsions; difficult or unusually fast breathing; fast heartbeat or irregular pulse; high fever; high or low [irregular] blood pressure; increased sweating; loss of bladder control; severe muscle stiffness or rigidity; unusual tiredness or weakness; unusually pale skin); ***tardive dystonia*** (increased blinking or spasms of eyelid; unusual facial expressions or body positions; uncontrolled twisting movements of neck, trunk, arms, or legs)

Note: *NMS* may occur at any time during neuroleptic therapy, but is more commonly seen soon after start of therapy, or after patient has switched from one neuroleptic to another, during combined therapy with another psychotropic medication, or after a dosage increase. Along with the overt signs of skeletal muscle rigidity, hyperthermia, autonomic dysfunction, and altered consciousness, differential diagnosis may reveal leukocytosis (9500 to 26,000 cells per cubic millimeter), elevated liver function tests, and elevated creatine phosphokinase (CPK).

Those indicating need for medical attention only if they continue or are bothersome

Incidence more frequent

Blurred vision; confusion; drowsiness; dryness of mouth; hypotension, orthostatic (dizziness, lightheadedness, or fainting)

Incidence less frequent

Constipation, mild; decreased sexual ability; enlargement of breasts, in males and females; headache; increased sensitivity of skin to sun; missing menstrual periods; nausea or vomiting; trouble in sleeping; unusual secretion of milk; weight gain

Those indicating the need for medical attention if they occur after the medication is discontinued

Dizziness; dyskinesia, withdrawal emergent (uncontrolled, repetitive movements of mouth, tongue, and jaw); ***nausea and vomiting; stomach upset or pain; trembling of fingers and hands***

Overdose

For specific information on the agents used in the management of loxapine overdose, see:

- *Norepinephrine* and *Phenylephrine* in *Sympathomimetic Agents—Cardiovascular Use (Parenteral-Systemic)* monograph.

For more information on the management of overdose or unintentional ingestion, **contact a Poison Control Center** (see *Poison Control Center Listing*).

Clinical effects of overdose

The following effects have been selected on the basis of their potential clinical significance (possible signs and symptoms in parentheses where appropriate)—not necessarily inclusive:

Dizziness; drowsiness, severe, or comatose state; muscle trembling, jerking, stiffness, or uncontrolled movements, severe; troubled breathing, severe; unusual tiredness or weakness, severe

Treatment of overdose

No specific antidote for loxapine is available. Treatment is symptomatic and supportive.

Specific treatment—
In event of severe hypotension, epinephrine should not be used, since it may further lower blood pressure in presence of partial adrenergic blockade. Norepinephrine or phenylephrine may be effective.

Supportive care—
Oxygen, intravenous fluids, anticonvulsant therapy, and anticholinergic agents may be indicated.

Patients in whom intentional overdose is known or suspected should be referred for psychiatric consultation.

Note: Because of the antiemetic effect of loxapine, centrally acting emetics, such as syrup of ipecac, may have little effect.

Patient Consultation

As an aid to patient consultation, refer to *Advice for the Patient, Loxapine (Systemic)*.

In providing consultation, consider emphasizing the following selected information (» = major clinical significance):

Before using this medication

» Conditions affecting use, especially:
Sensitivity to loxapine or amoxapine
Pregnancy—Studies in rats showed an increased number of fetal resorptions and decreased fetal weight.
Use in the elderly—Elderly patients are more likely to develop extrapyramidal, anticholinergic, hypotensive, and sedative effects; reduced dosage recommended.
Dental—Loxapine-induced blood dyscrasias may result in infections, delayed healing, and bleeding; dry mouth may cause caries and candidiasis; increased motor activity of face, head, and neck may interfere with some dental procedures.
Other medications, especially alcohol, other CNS depression-producing medications, other extrapyramidal reaction–producing medications, guanadrel, or guanethidine
Other medical problems, especially severe CNS depression, active alcoholism, or hepatic function impairment

Proper use of this medication

Taking with food, milk, or water to reduce stomach irritation
Measuring oral solution only with dropper provided by manufacturer
Mixing oral solution with orange or grapefruit juice just before each dose
» Compliance with therapy; not taking more or less medicine, nor taking more often, than directed
» Proper dosing
Missed dose: Taking as soon as possible; not taking if within 1 hour of next dose; returning to regular dosing schedule; not doubling doses
» Proper storage

Precautions while using this medication

Regular visits to physician to check progress of therapy
» Checking with physician before discontinuing medication; gradual dosage reduction may be needed
» Avoiding use of alcoholic beverages or other CNS depressants during therapy

Avoiding use of antacids or antidiarrheal medication within 2 hours of taking loxapine

» Possible drowsiness; caution when driving, using machines, or doing other things requiring alertness while taking loxapine

Possible dizziness or lightheadedness; caution when getting up suddenly from a lying or sitting position

Possible skin photosensitivity; avoiding unprotected exposure to sun; using protective clothing; using a sun block product that includes protection against both UVA-caused photosensitivity reactions and UVB-caused sunburn reactions; avoiding use of sunlamp, tanning bed, or tanning booth

Possible dryness of the mouth: using sugarless gum or candy, ice, or saliva substitute for relief; checking with physician or dentist if dry mouth continues for more than 2 weeks

» Caution if any kind of surgery, dental treatment, or emergency treatment is required

Side/adverse effects

Side effects are more likely to occur in the elderly

Signs of potential side effects, especially tardive dyskinesia, akathisia, dystonias, parkinsonian effects, anticholinergic effects, allergic skin reactions, agranulocytosis, obstructive jaundice, neuroleptic malignant syndrome (NMS), constipation (severe)

» Stopping medication and notifying physician immediately if symptoms of NMS appear, especially muscle rigidity, fever, difficult or fast breathing, seizures, fast heartbeat, increased sweating, loss of bladder control, unusually pale skin, unusual tiredness or weakness

» Notifying physician immediately if early symptoms of tardive dyskinesia appear, such as fine worm-like movements of the tongue or other uncontrolled movements of the mouth, tongue, jaw, or arms and legs; dosage adjustment or discontinuation may be needed to prevent irreversibility

Possibility of withdrawal symptoms

General Dosing Information

Dosage must be individualized by titration from the lower dose range over the first 7 to 10 days of therapy until effective control of psychotic symptoms is obtained. After such control is established, the dosage is gradually decreased to the lowest level that will maintain an adequate clinical response.

Loxapine has an antiemetic effect that may mask signs of overdose of other medication or may obscure diagnosis of conditions whose main symptoms include nausea. However, since the antiemetic effect of loxapine is central, nausea is not affected when it results from vestibular stimulation or local gastrointestinal irritation.

Upon cessation of extended maintenance therapy, a gradual reduction in loxapine dosage is recommended since abrupt withdrawal may cause some patients to experience transient dyskinetic signs, nausea, vomiting, gastritis, trembling, and dizziness.

For oral dosage forms only

The oral solution should be measured only with the dropper provided by the manufacturer and diluted with orange or grapefruit juice just before each dose.

For parenteral dosage form only

Because hypotension is a possible side effect of loxapine, intramuscular administration is used for bedfast patients or for appropriate acute ambulatory patients who can be closely monitored. Patients should remain lying down for at least ½ hour after the injection to avoid possible acute orthostatic hypotensive effects.

Diet/Nutrition

This medication may be taken with food or a full glass (240 mL) of water or milk if necessary to lessen stomach irritation.

For treatment of adverse effects

Treatment is essentially symptomatic and supportive and includes the following

- *Discontinuing loxapine immediately.*
- Hyperthermia—Administering antipyretics (aspirin or acetaminophen); using cooling blanket.
- Dehydration—Restoring fluids and electrolytes.
- Cardiovascular instability—Monitoring blood pressure and cardiac rhythm closely.
- Hypoxia—Administering oxygen; consider airway insertion and assisted ventilation.
- Muscle rigidity—Dantrolene sodium may be administered (100 to 300 mg a day in divided doses; 1.25 to 1.5 mg per kg of body weight intravenously). Bromocriptine (5 to 7.5 mg every eight hours) has been used to reverse hyperpyrexia and muscle rigidity.

Neuroleptic malignant syndrome—

Parkinsonism—

Many authorities advise that the only appropriate treatment of extrapyramidal symptoms is reduction of the antipsychotic dosage, if possible. Oral antidyskinetic agents such as trihexyphenidyl, 2 mg three times a day, or benztropine, may be effective in treating more severe parkinsonism and acute motor restlessness but should be used sparingly, only when side effects appear, and then usually for no longer than 3 months. Milder effects may be treated by adjusting dosage. In the elderly patient, the use of amantadine, 100 to 200 mg at bedtime, minimizes severe anticholinergic effects that may occur with other antidyskinetics.

Akathisia—

May respond to antiparkinsonian drugs or propranolol (30 to 80 mg a day); nadolol (40 mg a day); pindolol (5 to 60 mg a day), lorazepam (1 or 2 mg two or three times a day), or diazepam (2 mg two or three times a day), but often requires dosage reduction of loxapine.

Dystonia—

Acute dystonic postures or oculogyric crisis may be relieved by parenteral administration of benztropine (2 mg intramuscularly); diphenhydramine (50 mg intramuscularly); or diazepam (5 to 7.5 mg intravenously), to be followed by oral antidyskinetic medication for one or two days to prevent recurrent dystonic episodes. Dosage adjustments of loxapine may control these effects, and discontinuation of loxapine may reverse severe symptoms.

Tardive dyskinesia or tardive dystonia—

No known effective treatment. Dosage of loxapine should be lowered or medication discontinued, if clinically feasible, at earliest signs of tardive dyskinesia or tardive dystonia, to prevent irreversible effects.

Oral Dosage Forms

Note: The dosing and strengths of the dosage forms available are expressed in terms of loxapine base.

LOXAPINE HYDROCHLORIDE ORAL SOLUTION

Usual adult dose

Antipsychotic—

Initial: Oral, 10 mg (base) two times a day, the dosage being increased gradually during the first seven to ten days as needed for symptomatic control and as tolerated.

Maintenance: Oral, 15 to 25 mg (base) two to four times a day.

Note: This dosage form is intended primarily for institutional use.

Dose to be measured only with calibrated dropper provided by manufacturer.

Severely disturbed patients—Initial: Oral, 10 to 25 mg (base) two times a day.

Usual adult prescribing limits

Up to 250 mg (base) a day.

Usual pediatric dose

Children up to 16 years of age—Safety and efficacy have not been established.

Usual geriatric dose

Initial, oral, 3 to 5 mg (base) two times a day.

Strength(s) usually available

U.S.—

25 mg (base) per mL (Rx) [*Loxitane C* (propylene glycol)].

Canada—

25 mg (base) per mL (Rx) [*Loxapac*].

Packaging and storage

Store below 40 °C (104 °F), preferably between 15 and 30 °C (59 and 86 °F), in a well-closed container, unless otherwise specified by manufacturer. Protect from freezing.

Auxiliary labeling

- Take by mouth.
- May cause drowsiness.
- Avoid alcoholic beverages.
- Must be diluted before use.

Note

When dispensing, include the manufacturer-provided graduated dropper for dose measuring.

Explain administration technique and the necessary dilution in orange or grapefruit juice.

LOXAPINE SUCCINATE CAPSULES

Usual adult dose

See *Loxapine Hydrochloride Oral Solution.*

Usual pediatric dose
See *Loxapine Hydrochloride Oral Solution.*

Strength(s) usually available
U.S.—
5 mg (base) (Rx) [*Loxitane;* GENERIC].
10 mg (base) (Rx) [*Loxitane;* GENERIC].
25 mg (base) (Rx) [*Loxitane;* GENERIC].
50 mg (base) (Rx) [*Loxitane;* GENERIC].
Canada—
Not commercially available.

Packaging and storage
Store below 40 °C (104 °F), preferably between 15 and 30 °C (59 and 86 °F), in a well-closed container, unless otherwise specified by manufacturer.

Auxiliary labeling
- May cause drowsiness.
- Avoid alcoholic beverages.

LOXAPINE SUCCINATE TABLETS

Usual adult dose
See *Loxapine Hydrochloride Oral Solution.*

Usual pediatric dose
See *Loxapine Hydrochloride Oral Solution.*

Strength(s) usually available
U.S.—
Not commercially available.
Canada—
5 mg (base) (Rx) [*Loxapac*].
10 mg (base) (Rx) [*Loxapac*].
25 mg (base) (Rx) [*Loxapac*].
50 mg (base) (Rx) [*Loxapac*].

Packaging and storage
Store below 40 °C (104 °F), preferably between 15 and 30 °C (59 and 86 °F), in a well-closed container, unless otherwise specified by manufacturer.

Auxiliary labeling
- May cause drowsiness.
- Avoid alcoholic beverages.

Parenteral Dosage Forms

Note: The dosing and strengths of the dosage forms available are expressed in terms of loxapine base.

LOXAPINE HYDROCHLORIDE INJECTION

Usual adult dose
Intramuscular, 12.5 to 50 mg (base) every four to six hours as needed and tolerated.

Note: For intramuscular administration only. Not for intravenous use.

Usual adult prescribing limits
Up to 250 mg (base) a day.

Usual pediatric dose
Children up to 16 years of age—Safety and efficacy have not been established.

Strength(s) usually available
U.S.—
50 mg (base) per mL (Rx) [*Loxitane IM* (polysorbate 80 [5% w/v]; propylene glycol [70% v/v])].
Canada—
50 mg (base) per mL (Rx) [*Loxapac*].

Packaging and storage
Store below 40 °C (104 °F), preferably between 15 and 30 °C (59 and 86 °F), unless otherwise specified by manufacturer. Protect from light. Protect from freezing.

Stability
A darkening of the solution to a light amber will not alter potency or effectiveness. Do not use if markedly discolored or if a precipitate is present.

Note
Advise patient to remain lying down for ½ hour following administration to avoid severe orthostatic hypotension.

Revised: 01/29/1993

LUTROPIN ALFA Systemic†

VA CLASSIFICATION (Primary): HS106

Commonly used brand name(s): *Luveris.*

Note: For a listing of dosage forms and brand names by country availability, see *Dosage Forms* section(s).

†Not commercially available in Canada.

Category

Gonadotropin; infertility therapy adjunct.

Indications

General Considerations
Special attention should be given to selection of patients:
- Patients should have baseline serum hormone levels of LH < 1.2 IU/L and FSH < 5 IU/L.
- Before treatment is given, a thorough gynecologic and endocrinologic evaluation must be performed. This should include an assessment of pelvic anatomy and exclusion of pregnancy.
- Patient should have a negative progestin challenge test.
- A thorough diagnostic evaluation should be performed in patients who demonstrate abnormal uterine bleeding or other signs of endometrial abnormalities before starting lutropin alfa and follitropin alfa therapy.
- Evaluation of the partner's fertility potential should be included in the initial evaluation.

Accepted
Infertility, female (treatment)—Lutropin alfa, concomitantly administered with Gonal-f® (follitropin alfa) is indicated for stimulation of follicular development in infertile hypogonadotropic hypogonadal women with profound LH deficiency (LH < 1.2 IU/L). A definite effect on pregnancy in this population has not been demonstrated.

Unaccepted
The safety and effectiveness of concomitant administration of lutropin alfa with any other recombinant human FSH or urinary human FSH are unknown.

Pharmacology/Pharmacokinetics

Physicochemical characteristics
Source—Lutropin alfa is composed of recombinant human luteinizing hormone (r-hLH), derived from genetically modified Chinese Hamster Ovary (CHO) cells. The lutropin alfa is secreted by the CHO cell into the culture medium and then purified using a series of chromatographic steps.
Chemical Group—Its structure and glycosylation pattern are very similar to that of pituitary-derived human luteinizing hormone (hLH).
pH—7.5 to 8.5 after reconstitution

Mechanism of action/Effect
Lutropin alfa possess physicochemical, immunological, and biochemical activities comparable to those of human pituitary LH. During the follicular phase LH stimulates theca cells in the ovaries to secrete androgens, which are the substrates used to produce estradiol. Estradiol supports Follicle-Stimulating Hormone (FSH)-induced follicular development. Lutropin alfa is administered concomitantly with follitropin alfa for stimulation of a potentially competent follicle and indirect preparation of the reproductive tract for implantation and pregnancy.

Absorption
The absolute mean bioavailability following a single subcutaneous injection to healthy female volunteers is 56 ± 23%; there are no statistical differences between intramuscular and subcutaneous routes of administration for bioavailability.
AUC, subcutaneous: 44 ± h IU per L.

Distribution
Rapid.

Volume of distribution (Vol_D)—Steady state: approximately 10 L.

Biotransformation
The primary effect resulting from the administration of lutropin alfa is an increase in estradiol secretion by the follicles, the growth of which is stimulated by FSH.

Half-life
Terminal—Intravenous: 11 hours
Terminal—Subcutaneous: 18 hours

Time to peak serum concentration

Subcutaneous: 4 to 16 hours; there were no statistical differences between the intramuscular and subcutaneous routes of administration for t_{max}.

Peak serum concentration

Subcutaneous: 1.1 ± 0.3 IU/L; there were no statistical differences between the intramuscular and subcutaneous routes of administration for C_{max}.

Elimination

Renal: less than 5% unchanged; total body clearance approximately 2 to 3 liters per hour

Precautions to Consider

Carcinogenicity

Long-term studies have not been done in animals to evaluate the carcinogenic potential of lutropin alfa.

There have been infrequent reports of ovarian neoplasms, both benign and malignant, in women who have undergone multiple drug regimens for ovulation induction. However, a causal relationship has not been established.

Mutagenicity

Lutropin alfa was not found to be mutagenic in a series of tests, including bacterial and mammalian cell mutation tests, chromosomal aberration assay in human lymphocytes and *in vivo* mouse micronucleus tests.

Pregnancy/Reproduction

Fertility—Fertility studies in animals have shown impaired fertility in animals exposed to high doses of lutropin alfa, and increased pre- and post-implantation losses were observed in female rats and rabbits given lutropin alfa at doses of 10 IU/kg/day and higher.

Pregnancy—Lutropin alfa is contraindicated in pregnant women and may cause serious adverse effects in the fetus.

Studies in rats given doses 10 IU/kg/day and higher during the late pregnancy showed affects in postnatal survival and growth of newborns.

There is no evidence that use of any gonadotropin drug product for treatment of infertility is associated with and increased risk of congenital malformations.

FDA Pregnancy Category X

Breast-feeding

It is not known whether lutropin alfa is distributed into human breast milk. Because many drugs are distributed into human breast milk, caution should be exercised if lutropin is administered to a nursing woman.

Pediatrics

Lutropin alfa is not indicated in pediatric patients.

Geriatrics

Lutropin alfa is not indicated in geriatric patients.

Laboratory value alterations

The following have been selected on the basis of their potential clinical significance (possible effect in parentheses where appropriate)—not necessarily inclusive (» = major clinical significance).

With diagnostic test results

Liver function tests, transient

(abnormalities that are suggestive of hepatic dysfunction may also be associated with OHSS.)

Medical considerations/Contraindications

The medical considerations/contraindications included have been selected on the basis of their potential clinical significance (reasons given in parentheses where appropriate)—not necessarily inclusive (» = major clinical significance).

Except under special circumstances, this medication should not be used when the following medical problem exists:

» Abnormal uterine or genital bleeding, undiagnosed
(patients in later reproductive life have a greater predisposition to endometrial carcinoma as well as a higher incidence of anovulatory disorders; before starting lutropin alfa and follitropin alfa therapy a thorough diagnostic evaluation should always be performed in patients who demonstrate abnormal uterine bleeding or other signs of endometrial abnormalities.)

» Adrenal function impairment, uncontrolled or
» Thyroid function impairment, uncontrolled or
» Tumors, intracranial or sex hormone-dependent
(increasing estrogen concentrations may make these conditions worse)

» Hypersensitivity to hLH preparations or one of their excipients

» Ovarian cyst or enlargement, undetermined cause
(use is contraindicated.)

» Primary ovarian failure
(lutropin alfa is contraindicated in patients with primary ovarian failure)

Risk-benefit should be considered when the following medical problems exist:

» Thrombophlebitis, active
(potential for the occurrence of arterial thromboembolism exists)

Patient monitoring

The following may be especially important in patient monitoring (other tests may be warranted in some patients, depending on condition; » = major clinical significance):

» Estradiol, serum and/or
» Ultrasonography of ovaries and uterus
(ultrasonography and monitoring of serum estradiol concentrations can be used to monitor follicular development, predict timing of the ovulatory trigger, as well as detect ovarian enlargement, and aid in minimizing risk of OHSS and multiple gestation)
(ultrasonography of the ovaries can determine approximate time of ovulation by viewing fluid in the cul-de-sac, ovarian stigmata, collapsed follicle, or secretory endometrium; ultrasonography is especially useful for evaluating the number of developing follicles, which is not predictable from serum estrogen concentration data)

» Ovarian response
(careful monitoring can minimize the risk of overstimulation; if the ovaries are abnormally enlarged on the last day of therapy, hCG should not be administered in this course of therapy to reduce the risk of ovarian hyperstimulation syndrome (OHSS).)

Pregnancy test
(pregnancy can be confirmed by testing for serum hCG)

Side/Adverse Effects

The following side/adverse effects have been selected on the basis of their potential clinical significance (possible signs and symptoms in parentheses where appropriate)—not necessarily inclusive:

Those indicating need for medical attention

Incidence more frequent

Injection site reaction (bleeding, blistering, burning, coldness, discoloration of skin, feeling of pressure, hives, infection, inflammation, itching, lumps, numbness, pain, rash, redness, scarring, soreness, stinging, swelling, tenderness, tingling, ulceration, or warmth at injection site); ***ovarian cyst*** (bloating; stomach or pelvic discomfort, aching, or heaviness); ***ovarian hyperstimulation*** (abdominal pain; bloating; diarrhea; severe nausea; rapid weight gain; vomiting)

Adverse events reported subsequent to pregnancy; incidence unknown

Congenital abnormalities; ectopic pregnancy; postpartum fever; premature labor; spontaneous abortion

Adverse events reported during menotropin therapy; incidence unknown

Adnexal torsion—as a complication of ovarian enlargement; ***hemoperitoneum*** (blood in the peritoneal cavity); ***mild to moderate ovarian enlargement; pulmonary complications*** (shortness of breath or troubled breathing); ***vascular complications*** (changes in skin color; cold hands and feet; pain, redness, or swelling in arm or leg)

Those indicating need for medical attention only if they continue or are bothersome

Incidence more frequent

Abdominal pain (stomach pain); ***breast pain, female; fatigue*** (unusual tiredness or weakness); ***flatulence*** (bloated full feeling; excess air or gas in stomach or intestines; passing gas); ***headache; nausea; pain***

Incidence less frequent

Constipation (difficulty having a bowel movement (stool)); ***diarrhea; dysmenorrhoea*** (pain; cramps; heavy bleeding); ***ovarian disorder; upper respiratory tract infection*** (ear congestion; nasal congestion; chills; cough; fever; sneezing, or sore throat; body aches or pain; headache; loss of voice; runny nose; unusual tiredness or weakness; difficulty in breathing)

Overdose

For more information on the management of overdose or unintentional ingestion, **contact a poison control center** (see *Poison Control Center Listing*).

Clinical effects of overdose

The following effects have been selected on the basis of their potential clinical significance (possible signs and symptoms in parentheses where appropriate)—not necessarily inclusive:

Multiple gestation; ovarian hyperstimulation (abdominal pain; bloating; diarrhea; severe nausea; rapid weight gain; vomiting)

Treatment of overdose

There is no known specific antidote to lutropin alfa. Treatment is generally symptomatic and supportive.

Supportive care—

Patients in whom intentional overdose is confirmed or suspected should be referred for psychiatric consultation.

Patient Consultation

As an aid to patient consultation, refer to *Advice for the Patient, Lutropin alfa (Systemic)*.

In providing consultation, consider emphasizing the following selected information (» = major clinical significance):

Before using this medication

» Conditions affecting use, especially:

Hypersensitivity to hLH preparations or one of their excipients

Pregnancy—Use during pregnancy contraindicated; increased risk of multiple gestations and their associated complications and protracted ovarian hyperstimulation syndrome (OHSS) in patients who conceive

Breast-feeding—It is not known whether lutropin alfa is distributed into human breast milk. Because many drugs are distributed into human breast milk, caution should be exercised if lutropin is administered to a nursing woman.

Use in children—Not indicated in pediatric patients

Use in the elderly—Not indicated in geriatric patients

Other medical problems, especially abnormal uterine or genital bleeding, undiagnosed; adrenal function impairment, uncontrolled; intracranial or sex hormone–dependent tumors; ovarian cyst or enlargement, undetermined cause; or primary ovarian failure

Proper use of this medication

» Carefully reading patient instructions provided

For those patients self-administering the medication

Proper preparation of medication; using proper technique to prevent contamination of the medication, work area, and patient during transfer between containers

Proper administration; using proper needle and syringe

Knowing proper dose to use and not using more than prescribed

Carefully selecting and rotating injection sites as directed by physician

Disposing of needles, syringes, vials, and unused medication properly

Alerting physician when last doses of lutropin alfa and follitropin alfa are given and knowing that another drug called human chorionic gonadotropin may be required as a single injection 24 hours after the last dose of lutropin alfa and follitropin alfa.

» Proper dosing

Missed dose: Calling physician for advice; not doubling doses

» Proper storage

Precautions while using this medication

» Understanding the duration of treatment and the importance of required frequent monitoring by physician during treatment and for at least 2 weeks after lutropin alfa and follitropin alfa treatment is stopped

» Importance of following physician's instructions for recording basal body temperature, if requested, and timing of intercourse

Side/adverse effects

Signs of potential side effects, especially injection site reaction, ovarian cyst, or ovarian hyperstimulation

Signs of potential side effects reported subsequent to pregnancy, especially congenital abnormalities, ectopic pregnancy, postpartum fever, premature labor, or spontaneous abortion

Signs of potential side effects reported during menotropin therapy especially adnexal torsion as a complication of ovarian enlargement, hemoperitoneum, ovarian enlargement mild to moderate, pulmonary complications, or vascular complications

General Dosing Information

Prior to therapy with lutropin alfa, patients should be informed of the duration of treatment and monitoring required, the risks of OHSS, multiple births and other possible adverse reactions.

Patients receiving lutropin alfa should be under the supervision of a physician thoroughly familiar with infertility problems and their management and willing to devote considerable time to case-management.

Doses administered in subsequent cycles should be individualized for each patient based on response in the preceding cycles.

To complete follicular development and effect ovulation in the absence of an endogenous LH surge, human chorionic gonadotropin (hCG) should be given on the day after the last dose of lutropin alfa and follitropin alfa treatment.

If the ovaries are abnormally enlarged on the last day of lutropin alfa treatment, human chorionic gonadotropin (hCG) should not be administered to minimize risk of ovarian hyperstimulation syndrome (OHSS). OHSS develops rapidly (between 24 and 72 hours) and is distinct from uncomplicated ovarian enlargement. Patients should be monitored for 2 weeks after treatment ends, since the risk of OHSS reaches its maximal potential at 7 to 10 days post-treatment.

Patients self-injecting lutropin alfa should be given the patient information sheet and instructed on how to prepare the medication and injection site, administer the medication, and safely discard used items. Injection sites should be rotated.

Conception should be attempted daily beginning within 24 hours of administration of hCG until ovulation is thought to have occurred.

For treatment of adverse effects

Recommended treatment for OHSS consists of the following:

- Stopping treatment with lutropin alfa (or hCG).
- Hospitalizing patients with severe OHSS; less severe cases may spontaneously resolve at onset of menses.
- Managing electrolyte and fluid imbalances.

Parenteral Dosage Forms

LUTROPIN ALFA FOR INJECTION

Usual adult dose

Infertility, female—

Subcutaneous, 75 international units (IU) a day concomitantly administered with 75 to 150 IU of follitropin alfa as two separate injections until adequate follicular development is indicated by ovary ultrasonography and serum estradiol. Treatment duration should not normally exceed 14 days unless signs of imminent follicular development are present.

Usual pediatric dose

Safety and effectiveness in pediatric patients have not been established.

Usual geriatric dose

Safety and effectiveness in geriatric patients have not been established.

Strength(s) usually available

U.S.—

75 International Units (Rx) [*Luveris* (dibasic sodium phosphate dihydrate; L-methionine; monobasic sodium phosphate monohydrate; phosphoric acid; polysorbate; sodium hydroxide; sterile water for injection; sucrose)].

Canada—

Not commercially available.

Packaging and storage

Store refrigerated or at room temperature 2 to 25 °C (36 to 77 °F), in the original package. Protect from light.

Preparation of dosage form

Using standard aseptic technique, lutropin alfa is reconstituted by adding 1 mL of Sterile Water for Injection, USP to each vial. Mix gently, do not shake.The reconstituted solution should be visually inspected for particulate matter and discoloration prior to administration.

Stability

The solution should be used immediately after reconstitution and any unused material discarded. The solution should not be used if it is cloudy or discolored.

Auxiliary labeling

- Protect from light.
- Do not shake. Rotate vial gently.

Note

Include patient package information when dispensing.

Developed: 11/17/2004

MAGALDRATE—See *Antacids (Oral-Local)*

MAGNESIUM CHLORIDE—See *Magnesium Supplements (Systemic)*

MAGNESIUM CITRATE—See *Laxatives (Local), Magnesium Supplements (Systemic)*

MAGNESIUM GLUCEPTATE—See *Magnesium Supplements (Systemic)*

MAGNESIUM GLUCONATE—See *Magnesium Supplements (Systemic)*

MAGNESIUM HYDROXIDE—See *Antacids (Oral-Local), Laxatives (Local), Magnesium Supplements (Systemic)*

MAGNESIUM LACTATE—See *Magnesium Supplements (Systemic)*

MAGNESIUM OXIDE—See *Antacids (Oral-Local), Laxatives (Local), Magnesium Supplements (Systemic)*

MAGNESIUM PIDOLATE—See *Magnesium Supplements (Systemic)*

MAGNESIUM SALICYLATE—See *Salicylates (Systemic)*

MAGNESIUM SULFATE—See *Laxatives (Local), Magnesium Sulfate (Systemic), Magnesium Supplements (Systemic)*

MAGNESIUM SULFATE Systemic

VA CLASSIFICATION (Primary/Secondary): TN406/CN400; GU900; CV300

Note: For a listing of dosage forms and brand names by country availability, see *Dosage Forms* section(s).

Category

Anticonvulsant; electrolyte replenisher; tocolytic; antiarrhythmic.

Indications

Note: Bracketed information in the *Indications* section refers to uses that are not included in U.S. product labeling.

Accepted

Seizures, in toxemia of pregnancy (prophylaxis and treatment)—Intravenous magnesium sulfate is indicated for the prevention and immediate control of life-threatening seizures in the treatment of severe toxemias (pre-eclampsia and eclampsia) of pregnancy.

Hypomagnesemia (prophylaxis and treatment)—Magnesium sulfate is indicated for replacement therapy in magnesium deficiency, especially in acute hypomagnesemia accompanied by signs of tetany similar to those of hypocalcemia.

In patients receiving total parenteral nutrition, magnesium sulfate is added to the nutrient admixture to prevent or treat magnesium deficiency.

[Premature labor (treatment)][1]—Magnesium sulfate may be used as a tocolytic agent in the management of premature labor.

[Tachycardia, ventricular, polymorphous (treatment)][1]—Magnesium sulfate is used in the treatment of torsades de pointes. It is not effective in congenital QT interval prolongation syndromes.

Acceptance not established

There is insufficient data to establish safety and efficiacy of magnesium sulfate for the treatment of *acute asthma exacerbations.*

Early studies seemed to show that intravenous magnesium sulfate administered in the setting of *acute myocardial infarction* reduced the mortality rate. Pooled data from eight randomized controlled trials showed that intravenous magnesium administered within 24 to 48 hours after onset of symptoms decreased ventricular tachycardia and fibrillation by 49% and the incidence of cardiac arrest by 58% in patients who had not been treated with thrombolytic agents. Intravenous magnesium also reduced the early mortality rate in patients with suspected myocardial infarction in the second Leicester Intravenous Magnesium Intervention Trial (LIMIT-2). Magnesium's efficacy appeared to be independent of that of thrombolytic or antiplatelet therapy. In this study, little effect was seen on arrhythmic events, but the incidence of left ventricular failure was reduced in the treatment group.

However, recent data from the large randomized controlled trial, the Fourth International Study of Infarct Survival (ISIS-4), seem to challenge these earlier studies. ISIS-4 showed that intravenous magnesium was ineffective in significantly reducing mortality, independent of thrombolytic or antiplatelet therapy, in patients with suspected acute myocardial infarction. There was no significant evidence that magnesium had any effect on 5-week mortality, and follow-up at one year did not indicate any beneficial effect. In direct contrast to the results of some earlier studies, administration of intravenous magnesium was associated with small but significant increases in heart failure, cardiogenic shock, and in deaths attributed to cardiogenic shock.

Differences in study design, particularly between ISIS-4 and LIMIT-2, may explain the conflicting results. Intravenous magnesium was administered later in the course of myocardial infarction in ISIS-4, as compared to LIMIT-2. The ISIS-4 study was not designed to detect a highly time-dependent effect of magnesium on reperfusion injury. Therefore, because of conflicting evidence from these studies, it remains controversial whether the **routine** use of intravenous magnesium sulfate in the setting of acute myocardial infarction is beneficial.

[1]Not included in Canadian product labeling.

Pharmacology/Pharmacokinetics

Physicochemical characteristics

Molecular weight—246.48.

Other characteristics—

Magnesium sulfate, as the hydrated salt, contains approximately 10% of the labeled weight as magnesium and 49% as anhydrous magnesium sulfate. Doses are calculated based on the hydrate weight unless otherwise stated. One gram of magnesium sulfate heptahydrate ($MgSO_4 \cdot 7H_2O$) is equivalent to 8.12 mEq of magnesium.

Mechanism of action/Effect

Anticonvulsant—

Exact mechanism is not clearly understood. Magnesium may decrease the amount of acetylcholine released at the myoneuronal junction, resulting in depression of neuromuscular transmission. Magnesium also may have a direct depressant effect on smooth muscle and may cause central nervous system (CNS) depression.

Antiarrhythmic—

The exact mechanism of magnesium's antiarrhythmic effect is not clear. Magnesium may decrease myocardial cell excitability by contributing to the re-establishment of ionic equilibrium and stabilizing cell membranes. Magnesium also appears to modulate the sodium current, the slow inward calcium current, and at least one potassium current.

Myocardial infarction—

Possible mechanisms include antiarrhythmic action or direct cardioprotection. Magnesium's cardioprotective action may involve coronary vasodilation, reduction in peripheral vascular resistance, platelet aggregation inhibition, and an effect on the calcium current.

Tocolytic—

The exact mechanism is not known. It is speculated that magnesium may decrease myometrial contractility by altering calcium uptake, binding, and distribution in smooth muscle cells. Magnesium has been shown to increase uterine blood flow secondary to vasodilation of uterine vessels.

Onset of action

Anticonvulsant—

Intramuscular—About 1 hour.

Intravenous—Nearly immediate.

Therapeutic serum concentrations
Anticonvulsant—4 to 7 mEq per L (2 to 3.5 mmol per L).

Duration of action
Anticonvulsant—
Intramuscular—3 to 4 hours.
Intravenous—About 30 minutes.

Elimination
Renal, at a rate proportional to the plasma concentration and glomerular filtration rate.

Precautions to Consider

Pregnancy/Reproduction
Pregnancy—Parenteral magnesium sulfate has been administered to pregnant women in the treatment of pre-eclampsia and eclampsia (toxemia) of pregnancy and as a tocolytic agent. It readily crosses the placenta and rapidly attains fetal serum concentrations that approximate those in the mother. Magnesium's effects in the neonate may be similar to those in the mother and may include hypotonia, drowsiness, and respiratory depression. Bony abnormalities and congenital rickets have been reported in neonates born to mothers treated with parenteral magnesium sulfate for prolonged periods of time (4 to 13 weeks' duration).

FDA Pregnancy Category A.

Breast-feeding
Magnesium sulfate is distributed into breast milk. Milk concentrations are approximately twice those in maternal serum.

Pediatrics
Appropriate studies on the relationship of age to the effects of magnesium sulfate have not been performed in the pediatric population. However, no pediatrics-specific problems have been documented to date.

Geriatrics
Appropriate studies on the relationship of age to the effects of magnesium sulfate have not been performed in the geriatric population. However, elderly patients are more likely to have age-related renal function impairment, which may require dosage reduction in patients receiving magnesium sulfate.

Drug interactions and/or related problems
The following drug interactions and/or related problems have been selected on the basis of their potential clinical significance (possible mechanism in parentheses where appropriate)—not necessarily inclusive (» = major clinical significance):

Note: Combinations containing any of the following medications, depending on the amount present, may also interact with this medication.

Calcium (intravenous salts)
(concurrent use may neutralize effects of parenteral magnesium sulfate; calcium gluconate and calcium gluceptate are used to antagonize the toxic effects of hypermagnesemia; also, calcium sulfate may precipitate when a calcium salt is admixed with magnesium sulfate in the same intravenous solution; however, calcium salts and magnesium sulfate may be administered concurrently through separate intravenous lines if required in post-parathyroidectomy "hungry bones" syndrome or tetany associated with hypocalcemia and hypomagnesemia)

CNS depression-producing medications, other (see *Appendix II*)
(CNS depressant effects may be potentiated when these medications are used concurrently with parenteral magnesium sulfate)

Digitalis glycosides
(parenteral magnesium sulfate must be administered with extreme caution in digitalized patients, especially if intravenous calcium salts are also employed; cardiac conduction changes and heart block may occur)

Neuromuscular blocking agents
(concurrent use with parenteral magnesium sulfate may result in severe and unpredictable potentiation of neuromuscular blockade)

Nifedipine
(concurrent use of parenteral magnesium sulfate with nifedipine may produce an exaggerated hypotensive response)

Laboratory value alterations
The following have been selected on the basis of their potential clinical significance (possible effect in parentheses where appropriate)—not necessarily inclusive (» = major clinical significance).

With diagnostic test results
Reticuloendothelial cell imaging
(parenteral magnesium sulfate may impair reticuloendothelial cell imaging with technetium Tc 99m sulfur colloid by causing clumping of colloidal particles with subsequent entrapment in the vasculature of the lungs rather than in the liver, spleen, and bone marrow)

Medical considerations/Contraindications
The medical considerations/contraindications included have been selected on the basis of their potential clinical significance (reasons given in parentheses where appropriate)—not necessarily inclusive (» = major clinical significance).

Except under special circumstances, this medication should not be used when the following medical problems exist:

» Heart block
(magnesium may exacerbate this condition)

» Renal failure (creatinine clearance < 20 mL per minute)
(clearance of magnesium decreased; risk of magnesium toxicity)

Risk-benefit should be considered when the following medical problems exist:

Myasthenia gravis
(magnesium sulfate may precipitate an acute myasthenic crisis by decreasing the sensitivity of the motor endplate to acetylcholine)

» Renal function impairment, severe
(risk of developing hypermagnesemia and magnesium toxicity; patients with severely impaired renal function should receive no more than 20 grams of magnesium sulfate [162 mEq of magnesium] within a 48-hour period; caution is recommended against administering intravenous magnesium too rapidly in patients with oliguria or severe renal failure; close monitoring of serum magnesium concentration is recommended)

Respiratory disease
(increased risk of respiratory depression)

Patient monitoring
The following may be especially important in patient monitoring (other tests may be warranted in some patients, depending on condition; » = major clinical significance):

Blood pressure monitoring
(recommended at periodic intervals)

Cardiac function monitoring (ECG) and
Magnesium concentrations, serum
(recommended at periodic intervals during therapy as indicated by the clinical situation; normal average serum magnesium concentrations are 1.6 to 2.6 mEq per L [0.8 to 1.2 mmol per L])

Deep tendon reflexes, especially patellar reflex or knee jerk determinations
(used as an indication of CNS depression prior to administration of repeated doses; suppression of reflex may be related to impending respiratory arrest. The patellar reflex should be tested before each dose and, if the reflex is absent, no additional doses should be given until a positive response is obtained. The disappearance of the reflex is a useful sign for detecting excessive magnesium serum concentrations)

Renal function determinations, especially urine output
(recommended at periodic intervals; urine output should be at least 100 mL per 4 hours)

Respiration rate determination
(rate should be at least 16 breaths per minute prior to each parenteral dose of magnesium sulfate, since respiratory depression is the most critical side effect of this medication, rapidly proceeding to fatal respiratory paralysis)

Side/Adverse Effects
The following side/adverse effects have been selected on the basis of their potential clinical significance (possible signs and symptoms in parentheses where appropriate)—not necessarily inclusive:

Note: Although the side/adverse effects are stratified according to serum magnesium concentrations and early signs and symptoms of hypermagnesemia, these effects may occur early or late in the course of hypermagnesemia and may not always correlate with serum magnesium concentrations.

Those indicating need for prompt medical attention
Signs of hypermagnesemia—in order of increasing serum magnesium concentrations:

Effect	Serum magnesium concentration (mEq per L)
Deep tendon reflexes present, but possibly hypoactive	4 to 7
Prolonged PQ interval; widened QRS interval on ECG	5 to 10
Loss of deep tendon reflexes	8 to 10
Respiratory paralysis	10 to 13
Altered cardiac conduction	15
Cardiac arrest	25

Early signs and symptoms of hypermagnesemia
Bradycardia; diplopia; flushing; headache; hypotension; nausea; shortness of breath; slurred speech; vomiting; weakness

Overdose

For more information on the management of overdose or unintentional ingestion, **contact a Poison Control Center** (see *Poison Control Center Listing*).

Clinical effects of overdose

For clinical effects of overdose, see signs of hypermagnesemia in *Side/ Adverse Effects* section.

Treatment of overdose

Blood pressure and respiratory support; artificial respiration is often required.

Slow injection of intravenous calcium gluconate, 5 to 10 mEq of calcium or 10 to 20 mL of a 10% solution (diluted if desirable with 0.9% sodium chloride injection) to reverse heart block or respiratory depression.

Subcutaneous administration of physostigmine (0.5 to l mg) may be helpful; however, routine use is not recommended because of its toxicity.

Dialysis may be required to remove magnesium sulfate if renal function is reduced.

General Dosing Information

Magnesium sulfate injection 50% must be diluted to a concentration of 20% or less prior to intravenous infusion.

The rate of intravenous injection should generally not exceed 150 mg per minute, except in severe eclampsia with seizures.

Parenteral Dosage Forms

Note: Bracketed uses in the *Dosage Forms* section refer to categories of use and/or indications that are not included in U.S. product labeling.

MAGNESIUM SULFATE INJECTION USP

Usual adult and adolescent dose

Seizures, in toxemia of pregnancy—

Intravenous, 4 to 5 grams (32 to 40 mEq [16 to 20 mmol] of magnesium) in 250 mL of 5% dextrose injection USP or 0.9% sodium chloride infused over thirty minutes. Simultaneously, intramuscular doses of up to 10 grams (5 grams or 10 mL of undiluted 50% solution in each buttock) are given. Alternatively, the initial intravenous dose of 4 grams may be given by diluting the 50% solution to a 10 or 20% concentration; the diluted fluid (40 mL of a 10% solution or 20 mL of a 20% solution) may then be injected intravenously over a period of three to four minutes. Subsequently, 4 to 5 grams are injected intramuscularly into alternate buttocks every four hours as needed. Alternatively, after the initial intravenous dose, some clinicians administer 1 or 2 grams per hour as an intravenous infusion.

Hypomagnesemia—

Severe deficiency—

Intramuscular, 250 mg (2 mEq [1 mmol] of magnesium) per kg of body weight administered within a four-hour period.

Intravenous infusion, 5 grams (40 mEq [20 mmol] of magnesium) in 1 L of 5% dextrose injection or 0.9% sodium chloride injection, administered slowly over a three-hour period.

Mild deficiency—

Intramuscular, 1 gram (8 mEq [4 mmol] of magnesium) as a 50% solution, administered every six hours for four doses (a total of 32.5 mEq of magnesium) per twenty-four hours.

Total parenteral nutrition (TPN)—

Intravenous infusion, 1 to 3 grams (8 to 24 mEq [4 to 12 mmol] of magnesium) a day.

Note: Up to 6 grams a day may be necessary in selected patients, such as in patients with short bowel syndrome.

[Ventricular tachycardia, polymorphous][1]—

Intravenous, 2 grams (16 mEq [8 mmol] of magnesium) given over one to two minutes; the dose may be repeated if the arrhythmia is not controlled after five to fifteen minutes. Additionally, an intravenous infusion of 3 to 20 mg per minute may be needed.

[Premature labor][1]—

Initial: Intravenous, 4 to 6 grams (32 to 48 mEq [16 to 24 mmol] of magnesium) infused over twenty to thirty minutes.

Maintenance: Intravenous infusion, 1 to 3 grams (8 to 24 mEq [4 to 12 mmol] of magnesium) per hour until contractions abate.

Note: Extreme care must be used in the parenteral administration of magnesium sulfate in order to avoid toxic serum concentrations.

Geriatric patients often require lower dosages because of reduced renal function.

An intravenous preparation of a calcium salt (e.g., 10% calcium gluconate or gluceptate) should be readily available when magnesium sulfate is administered.

Usual adult prescribing limits

40 grams (320 mEq [160 mmol] of magnesium) a day.

Usual pediatric dose

Total parenteral nutrition (TPN)—

Intravenous infusion, 0.25 to 1.25 grams (2 to 10 mEq [1 to 5 mmol] of magnesium) a day.

Strength(s) usually available

U.S.—

10% w/v (1 gram [8 mEq of magnesium] per 10 mL) (Rx) [GENERIC].
12.5% w/v (1.25 grams [10 mEq of magnesium] per 10 mL) (Rx) [GENERIC].
50% w/v (5 grams [40 mEq of magnesium] per 10 mL) (Rx) [GENERIC].

Canada—

20% w/v (2 grams [16 mEq of magnesium] per 10 mL) (Rx) [GENERIC].
50% w/v (5 grams [40 mEq of magnesium] per 10 mL) (Rx) [GENERIC].

Packaging and storage

Store between 15 and 30 °C (59 and 86 °F). Protect from freezing.

Incompatibilities

Formation of a precipitate may result when magnesium sulfate is mixed with solutions containing:

Alcohol (in high concentrations)
Alkali carbonates and bicarbonates
Alkali hydroxides
Arsenates
Barium
Calcium
Clindamycin phosphate
Heavy metals
Hydrocortisone sodium succinate
Phosphates
Polymyxin B sulfate
Procaine hydrochloride
Salicylates
Strontium
Tartrates

The potential for incompatibility will often be influenced by changes in the concentration of reactants and the pH of the solutions.

Separation of intravenous fat emulsions may occur with concentrations of magnesium greater than 20 mEq per mL in total parenteral nutrition admixtures.

It has been reported that magnesium may reduce the antibiotic activity of streptomycin, tetracycline, and tobramycin when given together.

[1]Not included in Canadian product labeling.

Revised: 11/26/2002

MALT SOUP EXTRACT—See *Laxatives (Local)*

MANGANESE CHLORIDE—See *Manganese Supplements (Systemic)*

MANGANESE SULFATE—See *Manganese Supplements (Systemic)*

MAZINDOL—See *Appetite Suppressants (Systemic)*

MEASLES VIRUS VACCINE LIVE Systemic

VA CLASSIFICATION (Primary): IM100

Note: This monograph is specific for the measles virus vaccine live derived from Enders' attenuated Edmonston strain and grown in cell cultures of chick embryos.

Commonly used brand name(s): *Attenuvax*.

Note: For a listing of dosage forms and brand names by country availability, see *Dosage Forms* section(s).

Category

Immunizing agent (active).

Indications

General Considerations

Persons can generally be considered immune to measles only if they have documentation of adequate immunization with measles vaccine on or after their first birthdays, if they have laboratory evidence of measles immunity, or if they have a physician's diagnosis of measles infection.

Most individuals born before 1957 can generally be considered immune to measles because of probable previous infection. However, birth before 1957 provides only presumptive evidence of immunity, and measles can still occur in some persons born before 1957.

Although serologic tests may be conducted to determine the susceptibility of persons of unknown immunity, studies have indicated, no evidence of increased risk of adverse reactions to vaccination with measles virus vaccine live in persons already immune to measles.

Monovalent measles vaccine should be used to immunize infants 6 to 12 months of age during measles epidemics, although the combined measles-mumps-rubella or measles-rubella vaccines can be used if the monovalent measles vaccine is not available.

Measles, mumps, and rubella virus vaccine should be used for vaccinating individuals who are likely to be susceptible to more than one of these viruses, unless otherwise contraindicated.

Vaccines containing the measles antigen should be administered to persons 12 to 15 months of age or older under routine conditions.

Accepted

Measles (prophylaxis)—Measles virus vaccine live is indicated for immunization against measles (rubeola; morbilli; coughing, hard, red, or ten-day measles). The main objective of measles immunization is to prevent transmission of measles virus and to prevent severe complications, such as pneumonia, ear infections, sinusitis, encephalitis, subacute sclerosing panencephalitis, and death, which may develop from a measles infection. The risk of serious complications and death from a natural measles infection is greater for adults and infants than for children and adolescents.

Unless otherwise contraindicated, all susceptible persons should be immunized against measles, including:

- Children 12 to 15 months of age. All children 12 to 15 months of age should receive measles virus vaccine live, preferably as measles, mumps, and rubella virus vaccine live, as part of the routine childhood immunization schedule. The slightly lower response to the first dose of measles virus vaccine live when administered at 12 months of age compared with administration at 15 months of age has limited clinical importance because a second dose of the measles, mumps, and rubella virus vaccine live is recommended routinely for all children, enhancing the likelihood of seroconversion among children who do not respond to the first dose. Both the American Academy of Pediatrics (AAP) and the Advisory Committee on Immunization Practices (ACIP) recommend administration of measles virus vaccine live, preferably as the measles, mumps, and rubella virus vaccine live, at 12 to 15 months of age and a second dose prior to elementary school entery. Infants up to 12 months of age may retain maternal measles-neutralizing antibodies that may interfere with the immune response to measles virus vaccine live. Therefore, children vaccinated when younger than 12 months of age should be revaccinated with two additional doses of measles-containing vaccine.
- Adolescents who didn't receive a second dose of measles-containing vaccine. Because the recommendation for a second dose of measles, mumps, and rubella virus vaccine was made in 1989, many children born before 1985 (and some children born after 1985, depending on local policy) may not have received the second vaccine dose. Therefore, a second dose of measles-containing vaccine (preferably as measles, mumps, and rubella virus vaccine) is recommended for all adolescents who have not received two doses of the measles, mumps, and rubella virus vaccine at ≥ 12 months of age.
- International travelers. Persons without evidence of measles immunity who travel abroad should be vaccinated against measles because measles is endemic and even epidemic in many countries throughout the world. From 1985 to 1991, 993 reported cases of measles in the U.S. were attributable to exposure in foreign countries, and additional cases occurred in contacts of these imported cases. Therefore, vaccination against measles is especially important for international travelers. These persons should receive either a single antigen vaccine or a combined antigen vaccine as appropriate prior to international travel. However, the measles, mumps, and rubella virus vaccine live is preferred for persons likely to be susceptible to more than one of these viruses; and if a single-antigen measles vaccine is not readily available, travelers should receive the measles, mumps, and rubella virus vaccine live regardless of their immune status to mumps and rubella. Infants 6 to 12 months of age should receive a dose of monovalent measles vaccine before departure. If a single-antigen measles vaccine is not readily available, these infants should receive the measles, mumps, and rubella virus vaccine live. They should be revaccinated at 12 to 15 months of age with the measles, mumps, and rubella virus vaccine live, at least 1 month after the initial measles vaccination, so that children 16 months of age or older should have received two doses of measles-containing vaccine to assure immunity.

Pharmacology/Pharmacokinetics

Mechanism of action/Effect

Vaccination with measles virus vaccine live induces measles hemagglutination inhibiting (HI) antibodies, which provide active immunity against measles infection.

Protective effect

A single injection of the vaccine has been shown to induce measles HI antibodies in 97% or more of susceptible persons. In one recent study in which children randomly received the measles, mumps, and rubella virus vaccine live at either 12 or 15 months of age, the measles antibody response to the vaccine was 93% among children vaccinated at 12 months of age and 98% among those vaccinated at 15 months of age. Among children of mothers born after 1961, who probably had received measles vaccine and were less likely to have had measles infection than women born in previous years, the seroconversion rate was 96% among children vaccinated at 12 months of age and 98% among those vaccinated at 15 months of age.

Duration of protective effect

Vaccine-induced antibody levels have been shown to persist for at least 13 years without substantial decline. However, continued surveillance will be necessary to determine further duration of antibody persistence.

Precautions to Consider

Note: In the past, persons who had a history of anaphylactic reactions following egg ingestion were considered to be at increased risk for serious reactions after receipt of measles-containing vaccines, which are produced in chick embryo fibroblasts. Protocols for skin testing were developed for persons receiving the vaccine who had had anaphylactic reactions after egg ingestion. However, the predictive value of such skin testing and the need for special protocols when vaccinating egg-allergic persons with measles-containing vaccines is uncertain. The results of recent studies suggest that anaphylactic reactions to measles-containing vaccines are not associated with hypersensitivity to egg antigens, but with some other component of the vaccines. The risk for serious allergic reaction to these vaccines in egg-allergic patients is extremely low, and skin testing is not necessarily predictive of vaccine hypersensitivity.

Cross-sensitivity and/or related problems

Patients allergic to systemic or topical neomycin may be allergic to the measles virus vaccine live because each 0.5-mL dose contains approximately 25 mcg of neomycin, which is used in the production of the vaccine to prevent bacterial overgrowth in the viral culture. A history of hypersensitivity reactions, such as delayed-type allergic reaction (contact dermatitis), to neomycin generally does not preclude immunization. However, anaphylaxis from topically or systemically administered neomycin precludes immunization.

Patients allergic to gelatin also may be allergic to measles virus vaccine live, since gelatin is used as a stabilizer in the production of measles, mumps, and rubella virus vaccine and its component vaccines. The literature contains a single case report of a person with an anaphylactic sensitivity to gelatin who had an anaphylactic reaction after receipt of the measles, mumps, and rubella virus vaccine licensed in the U.S. Similar cases have occurred in Japan. Therefore, such persons should be vaccinated with measles, mumps, and rubella virus vaccine and its component vaccines with extreme caution.

Pregnancy/Reproduction

Pregnancy—Live measles vaccine, when given as a component of measles and rubella virus vaccine live or measles, mumps, and rubella virus vaccine live should not be given to women known to be pregnant or who are considering becoming pregnant within the next 3 months. Women who are given monovalent measles vaccine should not become pregnant for at least 30 days after vaccination. This precaution is based on the theoretical risk of fetal infection, although no evidence substantiates this theoretical risk. In considering the importance of protecting adolescents and young adults against measles, asking women if they are pregnant, excluding those who are, and explaining the theoretical risks to others before vaccination should be sufficient precautions.

Studies have not been done in animals.

FDA Pregnancy Category C.

Breast-feeding

It is not known whether this vaccine is distributed into breast milk. However, problems in humans have not been documented.

Pediatrics

Infants up to 15 months of age may fail to respond to measles virus vaccine live due to the presence of residual circulating measles antibody of maternal origin. This effect usually starts to wane after the child reaches 6 months of age. However, children born to younger mothers might respond well to measles vaccine administered at 12 months of age. In one study, children randomly received measles vaccine at either 12 or 15 months of age. The antibody response to measles virus vaccine live was 93 to 95% when the vaccine was administered at 12 months of age, and 98% when it was administered at 15 months of age. Among children of mothers born after 1961, who probably had received a measles vaccine and who therefore were less likely to have had measles infection than women born in previous years, the seroconversion rate was 96% among those children vaccinated at 12 months of age and 98% among those vaccinated at 15 months of age. Based on these findings, the Committee on Infectious Diseases of the American Academy of Pediatrics (AAP) and the Advisory Committee on Immunization Practices (ACIP) of the Centers for Disease Control and Prevention recommend administration of the first dose of measles-containing vaccine at 12 to 15 months of age. Both AAP and ACIP recommend that all children receive a second dose of measles-containing vaccine. The second dose of measles-containing vaccine (preferably as measles, mumps, and rubella virus vaccine live) is routinely recommended at 4 to 6 years of age, but may be administered at any visit, provided at least 1 month has elapsed since receipt of the first dose. The preadolescent health visit at 11 to 12 years of age can serve as a catch up opportunity to verify vaccination status and administer the vaccine to those children who have not yet received two doses of a measles-containing vaccine. Children who received the monovalent measles vaccine rather than the measles, mumps, and rubella virus vaccine live on or after their first birthdays also should receive a primary dose of mumps and rubella vaccines, and doses of measles, mumps, and rubella virus vaccine live or other measles-containing vaccines should be separated by at least 1 month.

If exposure to measles infection has occurred within 72 hours or is imminent, children between 6 and 15 months of age can be vaccinated, provided that those vaccinated before their first birthdays are revaccinated at 15 months of age. There is some evidence to suggest, however, that infants immunized at less than 12 months of age may not develop sustained antibody levels when reimmunized later. The advantage of early protection must be weighed against the chance for failure to respond adequately on reimmunization.

Children with end-stage renal disease receiving maintenance hemodialysis have a degree of immunosuppression that reduces their response to vaccination. Therefore, it may be necessary to monitor postvaccination antibody levels in children with end-stage renal disease, and to revaccinate those children who have failed to demonstrate seroconversion.

It is also very important to vaccinate human immunodeficiency virus (HIV)-infected children against measles.

Adolescents

The sustained decline of measles in the U.S. has been associated with a shift in occurrence from children to infants and young adults. From 1990 to 1994, 47% of reported cases occurred in persons aged 10 years or older, compared with only 10% from 1960 to 1964. During the 1980s, outbreaks of measles occurred among school-age children in schools with measles vaccination levels of ≥ 98%. Primary vaccine failure was considered the principal contributing factor in these outbreaks. As a result, beginning in 1989, a two-dose measles-vaccination schedule for students in primary schools, secondary schools, and colleges and universities was recommended. This two-dose vaccination schedule provides protection to ≥ 98% of persons vaccinated.

Drug interactions and/or related problems

The following drug interactions and/or related problems have been selected on the basis of their potential clinical significance (possible mechanism in parentheses where appropriate)—not necessarily inclusive (» = major clinical significance):

Note: Combinations containing any of the following medications, depending on the amount present, may also interact with this medication.

Blood products or
Immune globulins
(concurrent administration with measles virus vaccine live may interfere with the patient's immune response to the virus because of the possibility of antibodies to measles virus in these products. Measles virus vaccine live should be administered at least 14 days before, or 3 to 11 months after, administration of blood products or immune globulins, depending on the product and dose received)

» Immunosuppressive agents or
» Radiation therapy
(because normal defense mechanisms are suppressed, concurrent use with measles virus vaccine live may potentiate the replication of the vaccine virus, may increase the side/adverse effects of the vaccine, and/or may decrease the patient's antibody response to measles vaccine. The interaction may be severe enough to cause death. The interval between discontinuing medications that cause immunosuppression and regaining the ability to respond to measles virus vaccine live depends on the intensity and type of immunosuppressive medication used, the underlying disease, and other factors; estimates vary from 3 months to 1 year. Patients with leukemia in remission should not receive measles virus vaccine live until at least 3 months after their last chemotherapy. The precaution does not apply to corticosteroids used as replacement therapy, for short-term [less than 2 weeks] systemic therapy, or by other routes of administration that do not cause immunosuppression)

Live virus vaccines, other
(data are lacking on impairment of antibody responses to rubella, measles, mumps, or oral poliovirus vaccine (OPV) when these vaccines are administered on different days within 1 month of each other; however, OPV and measles, mumps, and rubella virus vaccine live [or its individual component vaccines] can be administered at any time before, with, or after each other, if indicated)

Laboratory value alterations

The following have been selected on the basis of their potential clinical significance (possible effect in parentheses where appropriate)—not necessarily inclusive (» = major clinical significance).

With diagnostic test results

» Tuberculin skin test
(short-term suppression lasting several weeks may occur, starting 4 to 7 days after vaccination, and may result in false-negative tests; if required, tuberculin skin tests should be done before, simultaneously with, or at least 4 to 6 weeks after administration of measles vaccine)

Skin tests, other
(decreased responsiveness to skin test antigens may occur because of vaccine-induced transient suppression of delayed-type hypersensitivity; the period of time for which responsiveness is decreased depends upon the particular skin test used)

Medical considerations/Contraindications

The medical considerations/contraindications included have been selected on the basis of their potential clinical significance (reasons given in parentheses where appropriate)—not necessarily inclusive (» = major clinical significance).

Except under special circumstances, this medication should not be used when the following medical problems exist:

» Febrile illness
(the decision to administer or delay vaccination because of a current or recent febrile illness depends largely on the cause of the illness and the severity of symptoms; minor illnesses, such as upper respiratory infection, do not preclude administration of vaccine; for persons whose compliance with medical care cannot be assured, every opportunity should be taken to provide appropriate vaccinations)
(children with moderate or severe febrile illnesses can be vaccinated as soon as they have recovered from the acute phase of the illness; this wait avoids superimposing adverse effects of vaccination on the underlying illness or mistakenly attributing a manifestation of the underlying illness to the vaccine; performing routine physical examinations or measuring temperatures are not prerequisites for vaccinating infants and children who appear to be in good health; Asking the parent or guardian if the child is ill, postponing vaccination for children with moderate or severe febrile illnesses, and vaccinating those without contraindications are appropriate procedures in childhood immunization programs)

» Immune deficiency conditions, congenital or hereditary, family history of, or
» Immune deficiency conditions, primary or acquired
(replication of vaccine viruses can be enhanced in persons with immune-deficiency diseases and in persons with immunosuppression, as occurs with leukemia, lymphoma, generalized malignancy, or therapy with alkylating agents, antimetabolites, radiation, or large doses of corticosteroids; evidence based on case reports has linked measles vaccine and measles infection to subsequent death in some severely immunocompromised children; of the more than 200 million doses of measles vaccine administered in the U.S., fewer than five such deaths have been reported; patients who have such conditions or are undergoing such therapies [excluding most HIV-infected patients] should not be given measles virus vaccine live)

(patients with leukemia in remission who have not received chemotherapy for at least 3 months may receive live virus vaccines; the exact amount of systemically absorbed corticosteroids and the duration of administration needed to suppress the immune system of an otherwise healthy child are not well defined; most experts agree that corticosteroid therapy usually does not contraindicate administration of live virus vaccine when such therapy is short-term [i.e., less than 2 weeks], low to moderate dose, long-term alternate-day treatment with short-acting preparations, maintenance physiologic doses [replacement therapy], or administered topically [skin or eyes], by aerosol, or by intraarticular, bursal, or tendon injection; although of recent theoretical concern, no evidence of increased severe reactions to live vaccines has been reported among persons receiving corticosteroid therapy by aerosol, and such therapy is not in itself a reason to delay vaccination)

(the immunosuppressive effects of corticosteroid treatment vary, but many clinicians consider a dose equivalent to either 2 mg per kg (mg/kg) of body weight or a total of 20 mg per day of prednisone as sufficiently immunosuppressive to raise concern about the safety of vaccination with live virus vaccines; corticosteroids used in greater than physiologic doses also can reduce the immune response to vaccines; physicians should wait at least 3 months after discontinuation of therapy before administering a live-virus vaccine to patients who have received high systemically absorbed doses of corticosteroids for ≥ 2 weeks)

(measles-containing vaccine is recommended for HIV-infected persons without evidence of measles immunity who are not severely immunocompromised; because of a reported case of pneumonitis in a measles vaccinee who had an advanced case of acquired immunodeficiency syndrome (AIDS), and because of other evidence indicating a diminished antibody response to measles vaccination among severely immunocompromised persons, it is important to withhold measles-containing vaccines from HIV-infected persons with evidence of severe immunosuppression)

Risk-benefit should be considered when the following medical problems exist:

Hypersensitivity to neomycin

(patients allergic to systemic or topical neomycin may be allergic to the measles virus vaccine live because each 0.5-mL dose contains approximately 25 mcg of neomycin, which is used in the production of the vaccine to prevent bacterial overgrowth in the viral culture. A history of hypersensitivity reactions, such as delayed-type allergic reaction (contact dermatitis), to neomycin generally does not preclude immunization. However, a history of anaphylaxis due to topically or systemically administered neomycin precludes immunization)

Allergy to gelatin

(patients allergic to gelatin also may be allergic to measles virus vaccine live, since gelatin is used as a stabilizer in the production of the vaccine)

Thrombocytopenia or vaccine-associated thrombocytopenia

(persons who experienced thrombocytopenia with the first dose of vaccine may develop thrombocytopenia with additional doses. These persons should have serological testing performed in order to determine the need for additional doses of vaccine. The risk-benefit ratio should be evaluated before vaccination is considered in such cases)

Conditions requiring avoidance of fever, such as cerebral injury or history of febrile seizures

(because of possible vaccine-induced fever)

Sensitivity to measles virus vaccine live

Patient monitoring

The following may be especially important in patient monitoring (other tests may be warranted in some patients, depending on condition; » = major clinical significance):

Seroconversion test

(may be performed at 4 or more weeks following vaccination in patients in whom immunity is considered crucial [e.g., persons traveling outside the U.S. or women in high-risk areas who intend to become pregnant], since vaccination with measles virus vaccine live may not result in seroconversion in all susceptible patients)

Side/Adverse Effects

Note: More than 240 million doses of measles vaccine were distributed in the U.S. from 1963 through 1993. The vaccine has an excellent record of safety. From 5 to 15% of vaccinees develop a temperature of 103 °F (39.4 °C) or higher beginning 5 to 12 days after vaccination and usually lasting several days. Most persons with fever are otherwise asymptomatic.

Transient rashes have been reported in approximately 5% of vaccinees. Central nervous system (CNS) conditions, including encephalitis and encephalopathy, have been reported with a frequency of less than one per million doses administered. The incidence of encephalitis or encephalopathy after measles vaccination of healthy children is lower than the observed incidence of encephalitis of unknown etiology. This finding suggests that the reported severe neurologic disorders that have been temporally associated with measles vaccination were not caused by the vaccine. These adverse events should be anticipated only in susceptible vaccinees and do not appear to be age-related. After revaccination, most reactions should be expected to occur only among the small proportion of persons who failed to respond on the first dose.

Measles vaccine significantly reduces the likelihood of developing subacute sclerosing panencephalitis (SSPE), as evidenced by the near elimination of SSPE cases after widespread measles vaccination began. SSPE has been reported rarely in children who do not have a history of natural measles infection but who have received measles vaccine. The available evidence suggests that at least some of these children may have had an unidentified measles infection before vaccination and that the SSPE probably resulted from the natural measles infection. The administration of live measles vaccine does not increase the risk for SSPE, regardless of whether the vaccinee has had measles infection or has previously received live measles vaccine.

The following side/adverse effects have been selected on the basis of their potential clinical significance (possible signs and symptoms in parentheses where appropriate)—not necessarily inclusive:

Those indicating need for medical attention

Incidence more frequent—5 to 15%

Fever over 39.4 °C (103 °F)

Incidence rare

Anaphylactic reaction (difficulty in breathing or swallowing; hives; itching, especially of soles or palms; reddening of skin, especially around ears; swelling of eyes, face, or inside of nose; unusual tiredness or weakness, sudden and severe); ***encephalitis or meningoencephalitis*** (confusion, severe or continuing headache, irritability, stiff neck, or vomiting); ***ocular palsies*** (double vision); ***thrombocytopenic purpura*** (bruising or purple spots on skin); ***Lymphadenopathy*** (swelling of glands in neck); ***swelling, blistering, or pain at injection site, severe and extensive***

Those indicating need for medical attention only if they continue or are bothersome

Incidence more frequent

Burning or stinging at injection site—due to acid pH of vaccine; ***fever of 37.7 °C (100 °F) or less***

Incidence less frequent

Allergic reaction, delayed-type, cell-mediated (itching, swelling, redness, tenderness, or hard lump at injection site); ***fever between 37.7 and 39.4 °C (100 and 103 °F); skin rash***

Patient Consultation

As an aid to patient consultation, refer to *Advice for the Patient, Measles Virus Vaccine Live (Systemic).*

In providing consultation, consider emphasizing the following selected information (» = major clinical significance):

Before receiving this vaccine

» Conditions affecting use, especially:

Sensitivity to measles vaccine or allergy to gelatin or neomycin

Pregnancy—Use of measles vaccine during pregnancy or pregnancy within 3 months of immunization is not recommended

Use in children—Use is not recommended for infants up to 12 months of age, unless risk of measles infection is high

Other medications, especially immunosuppressive agents or radiation therapy

Other medical problems, especially febrile illness, primary or acquired immune deficiency conditions, or family history of congenital or hereditary immune deficiency conditions

Proper use of this medication

Waiting at least 14 days after receiving vaccine before receiving blood products or immune globulin

Waiting at least 3 to 11 months after administration of blood products or immune globulins before receiving vaccine, depending on the product and dose received

» Proper dosing

Precautions after receiving this vaccine

» Not becoming pregnant for 3 months without first checking with physician, because of theoretical risk of birth defects

Checking with physician before receiving tuberculin skin test within 4 to 6 weeks of this vaccine, since the results of the test may be affected by the measles vaccine

Side/adverse effects

Fever and skin rash may occur from 5 to 12 days after vaccination and usually last several days.

Signs of potential side effects, especially fever over 39.4 °C (103 °F), anaphylactic reaction, encephalitis, meningoencephalitis, ocular palsies, or thrombocytopenic purpura

General Dosing Information

The American Academy of Pediatrics (AAP) and the Advisory Committee on Immunization Practices (ACIP) recommend that all children 12 to 15 months of age receive two doses of measles-containing vaccine, preferably as measles, mumps, and rubella virus vaccine live. Children who received monovalent measles vaccine rather than the measles, mumps, and rubella virus vaccine live on or after their first birthdays also should receive a primary dose of mumps and rubella vaccines; and doses of measles, mumps, and rubella virus vaccine live or other measles-containing vaccines should be separated by at least 1 month.

The dosage of measles vaccine is the same for both children and adults.

When sterilizing syringes and skin before vaccination, care should be taken to avoid preservatives, antiseptics, detergents, and disinfectants, since the vaccine virus is easily inactivated by these substances.

To prevent inactivation of the vaccine, it is recommended that only the diluent provided by the manufacturer be used for vaccine reconstitution.

A 25-gauge, 5/8th-inch needle is recommended for administration of the vaccine.

Measles vaccine is administered subcutaneously. It should not be injected intravenously.

Previous recommendations, based on data from persons who received low doses of immune globulin (IG) preparations, stated that measles, mumps, and rubella virus vaccine live and its individual component vaccines could be administered as early as 6 weeks to 3 months after administration of IG. However, recent evidence suggests that high doses of IG can inhibit the immune response to measles vaccine for more than 3 months. The duration of interference of IG preparations with the immune response to the measles virus vaccine live is dose-related. Therefore, measles virus vaccine live should be administered at least 14 days before, or 3 to 11 months after administration of IG.

Measles virus vaccine live generally should not be administered simultaneously with IG preparations. However, if administration of an IG preparation becomes necessary because of imminent exposure to disease, measles, mumps, and rubella virus vaccine live or its component vaccines can be administered simultaneously with the IG preparation, although vaccine-induced immunity might be compromised. The vaccine should be administered at a site remote from that chosen for the IG inoculation. Unless serologic testing indicates that specific antibodies have been produced, vaccination should be repeated after the recommended interval.

If administration of an IG preparation becomes necessary after measles, mumps, and rubella virus vaccine live or its individual component vaccines have been administered, interference may occur. Usually, vaccine virus replication and stimulation of immunity will occur 1 to 2 weeks after vaccination. Therefore, if the interval between administration of any of these vaccines and subsequent administration of an IG preparation is less than 14 days, vaccination should be repeated after the recommended interval, unless serologic testing indicates that antibodies have been produced.

Although measles, mumps, and rubella vaccines are commercially available as a combination vaccine (measles, mumps, and rubella virus vaccine live) and, as such, are administered as a single injection, the commercially available individual vaccines should not be mixed in the same syringe or administered at the same body site.

ACIP continues to recommend measles, mumps, and rubella virus vaccine live for HIV-infected persons without evidence of measles immunity. Severely immunocompromised and other symptomatic HIV-infected patients who are exposed to measles should receive IG, regardless of prior vaccination status. In addition, health-care providers should weigh the risks and benefits of measles vaccination or IG prophylaxis for severely immunocompromised HIV-infected patients who are at risk for measles exposure because of outbreaks or international travel.

Because the immunologic response to both live and killed antigen vaccines may decrease as HIV disease progresses, vaccination early in the course of HIV infection may be more likely to induce an immune response. Therefore, HIV-infected infants without severe immunosuppression should routinely receive measles, mumps, and rubella virus vaccine live as soon as possible upon reaching their first birthday. Evaluation and testing of asymptomatic persons to detect HIV infection are not necessary before deciding to administer measles, mumps, and rubella virus vaccine live or other measles-containing vaccine.

Because of a reported case of pneumonitis in a measles vaccinee who had an advanced case of acquired immunodeficiency syndrome (AIDS), and because of other evidence indicating a diminished antibody response to measles vaccination among severely immunocompromised persons, ACIP is re-evaluating the recommendations for vaccination of severely immunocompromised HIV-infected persons.

In the interim, it may be prudent to withhold measles-containing vaccines from HIV-infected persons with evidence of severe immunosuppression, defined by one of the following criteria:

- CD4+ T-lymphocyte count < 750 for children < 12 months of age, < 500 for children 1 to 5 years of age, or < 200 for persons ≥ 6 years of age; or
- CD4+ T-lymphocytes constituting < 15 % of total lymphocytes for children < 13 years of age, or < 14 % for persons ≥ 13 years of age.

If immediate protection against measles is required for persons with contraindications to measles vaccination, passive immunization with IG, 0.25 mL per kg (mL/kg) [0.11 mL per pound] of body weight (maximum dose 15 mL), should be given as soon as possible after known exposure. Exposed symptomatic HIV-infected and other immunocompromised persons should receive IG regardless of their previous vaccination status; however, IG in usual doses may not be effective in such patients. For immunocompromised persons, the recommended dose is 0.5 mL/kg of body weight if IG is administered intramuscularly (maximum dose 15 mL). This corresponds to a dose of protein approximately 82.5 mg per kg (mg/kg) (maximum dose 2475 mg). Intramuscular IG may not be needed if a patient with HIV infection is receiving 100 to 400 mg/kg intravenous IG (IGIV) at regular intervals and the last dose was given within 3 weeks of exposure to measles. Because the amounts of protein administered are similar, high-dose IGIV may be as effective as IG given intramuscularly. However, no data are available concerning the effectiveness of IGIV in preventing measles.

In general, simultaneous administration of the most widely used live and inactivated vaccines does not impair antibody responses or increase rates of adverse effects. Vaccines recommended for administration at 12 to 15 months of age can be administered at either one or two visits. There are equivalent antibody responses and no clinically significant increases in the frequency of adverse events when diphtheria toxoid, tetanus toxoid, and pertussis vaccine (DTP), measles, mumps, and rubella virus vaccine live, oral poliovirus vaccine (OPV) or inactivated poliovirus vaccine (IPV) and *H. influenzae* type b conjugate vaccine (HbCV) are administered either simultaneously at different sites or at separate times. If a child might not be brought back for future vaccinations, all vaccines (including DTP [or DTaP], measles, mumps, and rubella virus vaccine live, OPV [or IPV], varicella, HbCV, and hepatitis B vaccines may be administered simultaneously, as appropriate to the child's age and previous vaccination status.

For treatment of adverse effects

Recommended treatment includes

- For mild hypersensitivity reaction—Administering antihistamines and, if necessary, corticosteroids.
- For severe hypersensitivity or anaphylactic reaction—Administering epinephrine. Antihistamines or corticosteroids may also be administered as required.

Parenteral Dosage Forms

MEASLES VIRUS VACCINE LIVE (FOR INJECTION) USP

Usual adult and adolescent dose

Immunizing agent (active)—

Subcutaneous, 0.5 mL, preferably into the outer aspect of the upper arm:

First dose—At initial visit.

Second dose—At least one month after the first dose.

Usual pediatric dose

Immunizing agent (active)—

Infants up to 12 months of age—Use is not recommended.

Infants and children 12 months of age and older—See *Usual adult and adolescent dose.*

Note: The Committee on Infectious Diseases of the American Academy of Pediatrics (AAP) and the Advisory Committee on Immunization Practices (ACIP) recommend that all children receive a second dose of measles-containing vaccine. The second dose of measles-containing vaccine (preferably as measles, mumps, and rubella virus vaccine live) is routinely recommended at 4 to 6 years of age, but may be administered at any visit, provided at least one month has elapsed since receipt of the first dose. The preadolescent health visit at 11 to 12 years of age can serve as a catch up opportunity to verify vaccination status and administer the vaccine to those children who have not yet received two doses of a measles containing vaccine.

Strength(s) usually available

U.S.—

Not less than the equivalent of 1000 median tissue culture infective dose [$TCID_{50}$] of the U.S. Reference Measles Virus in each 0.5 mL dose (Rx) [*Attenuvax* (neomycin approximately 25 mcg)].

Canada—

Not less than the equivalent of 1000 median tissue culture infective dose [$TCID_{50}$] of a reference measles virus in each 0.5 mL dose (Rx) [GENERIC (may contain neomycin)].

Packaging and storage

Store the lyophilized form of the vaccine, the diluent, and the reconstituted form of the vaccine between 2 and 8 °C (36 and 46 °F), unless otherwise specified by the manufacturer.

Alternatively, the diluent for the single-dose vials may be stored between 15 and 30 °C (59 and 86 °F).

Protect both the lyophilized form and the reconstituted form of the vaccine from light.

Preparation of dosage form

To reconstitute, only the diluent provided by the manufacturer should be used, since it is free of preservatives and other substances that might inactivate the vaccine.

The entire volume of diluent (approximately 0.5 mL) should be withdrawn into the syringe. All the diluent in the syringe is injected into the vial of lyophilized vaccine and agitated to mix thoroughly. The entire contents should be withdrawn into the syringe and the total volume of restored vaccine injected subcutaneously.

Stability

Both the lyophilized and the reconstituted vaccine should be protected from light, which may inactivate the virus.

Use the reconstituted vaccine as soon as possible. Discard unused reconstituted vaccine after 8 hours.

The reconstituted vaccine is clear yellow. It should not be used if it is discolored.

Incompatibilities

Preservatives or other substances may inactivate the vaccine; therefore, only the diluent supplied by the manufacturer should be used for reconstitution.

Also, a sterile syringe free of preservatives, antiseptics, and detergents should be used for each injection and/or reconstitution of the vaccine because these substances may inactivate the live virus vaccine.

Auxiliary labeling

- Protect from light.
- Store in refrigerator.
- Discard reconstituted vaccine if not used within 8 hours.

Note

The date and time of reconstitution should be indicated on the vial if the reconstituted vaccine is not used at once.

Revised: 07/23/1997

MEASLES, MUMPS, AND RUBELLA VIRUS VACCINE LIVE Systemic

VA CLASSIFICATION (Primary): IM100

Note: This monograph is specific for the sterile lyophilized preparation of a more attenuated line of measles virus, derived from Enders' attenuated Edmonston strain and grown in cell cultures of chick embryo, the Jeryl Lynn (B level) strain of mumps virus grown in cell cultures of chick embryo, and the Wistar RA 27/3 strain of live attenuated rubella virus grown in human diploid cell (WI-38) culture.

Commonly used brand name(s): *M-M-R II*.

Note: For a listing of dosage forms and brand names by country availability, see *Dosage Forms* section(s).

Category

Immunizing agent (active).

Indications

General Considerations

Measles is an acute disease characterized by fever, cough, coryza, conjunctivitis, an erythematous maculopapular rash, and a pathognomonic enanthema (Koplik's spots). Complications such as otitis media, bronchopneumonia, laryngotracheobronchitis (croup), and diarrhea occur more commonly in young children than in older patients. Acute encephalitis, which frequently results in permanent brain damage, occurs in approximately 1 of every 1000 cases. Death, predominantly due to respiratory and neurologic complications, occurs in 1 to 2 of every 1000 cases reported in the U.S.

Subacute sclerosing panencephalitis (SSPE), a rare degenerative central nervous system (CNS) disease characterized by behavioral and intellectual deterioration and convulsions, is a result of a persistent measles virus infection that develops years after the original infection. Widespread use of measles vaccine has essentially eliminated SSPE from the U.S.

Measles illness during pregnancy is responsible for increased rates of premature labor, spontaneous abortion, and low birth weight in affected infants. Birth defects, with no definable pattern of malformation, have been reported in infants born to women infected with measles during pregnancy, but measles infection has not been confirmed as the cause of the malformations.

Measles can be severe and prolonged in immunocompromised persons, particularly those who have certain leukemias, lymphomas, or human immunodeficiency virus (HIV) infection. In these persons, measles may occur without the typical rash, and they may shed measles virus for several weeks after the acute illness.

Mumps is a systemic disease characterized by bilateral or, less commonly, unilateral parotitis. Parotitis may be preceded by fever, headache, malaise, myalgia, and anorexia. Only 30 to 40% of mumps infections produce typical acute parotitis; 15 to 20% of infections are asymptomatic, and up to 50% of infections are associated with nonspecific or primarily respiratory symptoms. Inapparent infection may be more common in adults than in children; parotitis occurs more commonly in children 2 to 9 years of age. Serious complications of mumps infection can occur without evidence of parotitis.

Most serious complications of mumps are more common in adults than in children. Although orchitis may occur in 38% of postpubertal men in whom mumps develops, sterility is thought to occur only rarely.

Aseptic meningitis affects 4 to 6% of persons with clinical cases of mumps and typically is mild. However, mumps meningoencephalitis can cause permanent sequelae, including paralysis, seizures, cranial nerve palsies, aqueductal stenosis, and hydrocephalus. In the prevaccine era, mumps was a major cause of sensorineural deafness in children. Deafness may be sudden in onset, bilateral, and permanent.

Among women in whom mumps develops during the first trimester of pregnancy, an increased risk for fetal death has been observed. However, mumps infection during pregnancy is not associated with congenital malformations.

Postnatal rubella usually is a mild disease characterized by an erythematous, maculopapular, discrete rash, generalized lymphadenopathy (most commonly suboccipital, postauricular, and cervical), and slight fever. Transient polyarthralgia and polyarthritis occasionally occur in children and are common in adolescents and adults, especially females. Encephalitis and thrombocytopenia are rare complications.

The most important consequences of rubella are the miscarriages, stillbirths, fetal anomalies, and therapeutic abortions that result when rubella infection occurs during early pregnancy, especially during the first trimester. An estimated 20,000 cases of congenital rubella syndrome (CRS) occurred during the 1964–1965 epidemic, the last U.S. rubella epidemic before rubella vaccine became available. Fetal infection without clinical signs of CRS can occur during any stage of pregnancy.

The anomalies most commonly associated with CRS are auditory (e.g., sensorineural deafness), ophthalmic (e.g., cataracts, microphthalmia, glaucoma, chorioretinitis), cardiac (e.g., patent ductus arteriosus, peripheral pulmonary artery astenosis, atrial or ventricular septal defects), and neurologic (e.g., microcephaly, meningoencephalitis, mental retardation). In addition, infants with CRS frequently exhibit both intrauterine and postnatal growth retardation. Other conditions sometimes observed in patients who have CRS include radiolucent bone defects, hepatosplenomegaly, thrombocytopenia, and purpuric skin lesions.

Accepted

Measles, mumps, and rubella (prophylaxis)—Measles, mumps, and rubella virus vaccine is indicated for simultaneous immunization against measles (rubeola; morbilli; coughing, hard, red, or 10-day measles), mumps, and rubella (German measles) in persons 12 to 15 months of age or older. The main objective of measles, mumps, and rubella immunization is to prevent severe complications and death, which may arise from measles, mumps, and/or rubella infections (see *General Considerations*).

Unless otherwise contraindicated, all susceptible persons 12 to 15 months of age or older should be immunized against measles, mumps, and rubella, including:

• Preschool-aged children. Children should receive the first dose of measles, mumps, and rubella virus vaccine live at 12 to 15 months of age (i.e., on or after their first birthday). In areas where risk for measles is high, initial vaccination with measles, mumps, and rubella virus vaccine live is recommended for all children as soon as possible upon reaching the first birthday (i.e., at age 12 months). An area where measles risk is high is defined as:

—A country with a large inner-city population.

—A country where a recent measles outbreak has occurred among unvaccinated preschool-aged children.

—A country in which more than five cases of measles have occurred among preschool-aged children during each of the last 5 years.

• School-aged children and adolescents. The second dose of measles, mumps, and rubella virus vaccine live is recommended for children 4 to 6 years of age (i.e., before a child enters kindergarten or first grade).

• Adults. Persons born in 1957 or later who are 18 years of age or older and who do not have a medical contraindication should receive at least one dose of measles, mumps, and rubella virus vaccine live unless they have documentation of vaccination with at least one dose of measles, mumps, and rubella-containing vaccine or other acceptable evidence of immunity to these three diseases. Persons born before 1957 can generally be considered immune to measles and mumps. In addition, persons born before 1957, except women who could become pregnant, generally can be considered immune to rubella.

• Women of childbearing potential. Measles, mumps, and rubella virus vaccine live should be offered to all women of childbearing age (i.e., adolescent girls and premenopausal adult women) who do not have acceptable evidence of rubella immunity whenever they make contact with the health care system. Opportunities to vaccinate susceptible women include occasions when their children undergo routine examinations or vaccinations. The continuing occurrence of rubella among women of childbearing age indicates the need to continue vaccination of susceptible adolescent and adult women of childbearing age, and the absence of evidence of vaccine teratogenicity indicates that the practice is safe.

• Postpartum women who do not plan to breast-feed, preferably before discharge from the hospital. Although problems in humans have not been documented, postpartum women who plan to breast-feed should consult their physicians to consider risk-benefit before receiving immunization with measles, mumps, and rubella virus vaccine live.

• Persons traveling outside the U.S. These persons should receive measles, mumps, and rubella virus vaccine live prior to international travel.

• Persons infected with HIV. Measles, mumps, and rubella virus vaccine live is recommended for all asymptomatic HIV-infected persons who do not have evidence of severe immunosuppression and for whom measles vaccination would otherwise be indicated. Measles, mumps, and rubella virus vaccine live also should be considered for all symptomatic HIV-infected persons who do not have evidence of severe immunosuppression. Testing asymptomatic persons for HIV infection is not necessary before administering measles, mumps, and rubella virus vaccine live or other measles-containing vaccine.

Some persons vaccinated according to earlier recommendations for use of individual measles, mumps, and/or rubella vaccines or measles, mumps, and rubella virus vaccine live should be revaccinated to ensure that they are adequately protected. Unless one of its component vaccines is contraindicated, measles, mumps, and rubella virus vaccine live should be used for revaccination in the following situations:

• Previous vaccination with live measles, rubella, and mumps vaccines. Persons vaccinated with live measles, rubella, and mumps vaccines before their first birthday who were not revaccinated on or after their first birthday should be considered unvaccinated. Unless they have other acceptable evidence of immunity to measles, rubella, and mumps, these persons should be revaccinated with measles, mumps, and rubella virus vaccine live.

• Previous vaccination with inactivated measles vaccine or measles vaccine of unknown type. Inactivated (killed) measles vaccine was available in the U.S. only from 1963 to 1967 but was available through the early 1970s in some other countries. It was frequently administered as a series of two or three injections. Because persons who received inactivated vaccine are at risk for developing severe atypical measles syndrome when exposed to the natural virus, they should receive two doses of measles, mumps, and rubella virus vaccine live or other live measles vaccine, separated by at least 28 days. Persons who received inactivated vaccine followed within 3 months by live virus vaccine should also be revaccinated with two more doses of measles, mumps, and rubella virus vaccine live or other live measles vaccine. Revaccination is particularly important when the risk for exposure to natural measles virus is increased (i.e., during international travel). Persons vaccinated during 1963 through 1967 with vaccine of unknown type may have received inactivated vaccine and also should be revaccinated. Persons who received a vaccine of unknown type after 1967 need not be revaccinated unless the original vaccination occurred before their first birthday or was accompanied by immune globulin (Ig) or measles immune globulin (MIg). However, such persons should receive a second dose before entering college, beginning work within a health care facility, or undertaking international travel.

• Previous vaccination with inactivated mumps vaccine or mumps vaccine of unknown origin. A killed mumps virus vaccine was licensed for use in the U.S. from 1950 through 1978. Although this vaccine induced antibody, the immunity was transient. The number of doses of killed mumps vaccine administered between licensure of live attenuated mumps vaccine in 1967 until the killed vaccine was withdrawn in 1978 is unknown but appears to have been limited. Revaccination with measles, mumps, and rubella virus vaccine live should be considered for certain persons vaccinated before 1979 with either killed mumps vaccine or mumps vaccine of unknown type who are at high risk for mumps infection (e.g., persons who work in health care facilities during a mumps outbreak). No evidence exists that persons who have had mumps disease or who have previously received mumps vaccine (killed or live) are at increased risk for local or systemic reactions upon receiving measles, mumps, and rubella virus vaccine live or live mumps vaccine.

Pharmacology/Pharmacokinetics

Physicochemical characteristics

Source—Measles, mumps, and rubella virus vaccine live contains a sterile lyophilized preparation of a more attenuated line of measles virus, derived from Enders' attenuated Edmonston strain and grown in cell cultures of chick embryo, the Jeryl Lynn (B level) strain of mumps virus grown in cell cultures of chick embryo, and the Wistar RA 27/3 strain of live attenuated rubella virus grown in human diploid cell (WI-38) culture. The vaccine viruses are the same as those used in the manufacture of measles virus vaccine live, mumps virus vaccine live, and rubella virus vaccine live. The three viruses are mixed before being lyophilized.

Mechanism of action/Effect

Following subcutaneous injection, measles, mumps, and rubella virus vaccine live produces a modified, noncommunicable measles, mumps, and rubella infection and provides active immunity to measles, mumps, and rubella.

Protective effect

Clinical studies of 279 triple seronegative children 11 months to 7 years of age demonstrated that measles, mumps, and rubella virus vaccine live is highly immunogenic and generally well tolerated. In these studies, a single injection of measles, mumps, and rubella virus vaccine live induced measles hemagglutinin-inhibition (HI) antibodies in 95%, mumps neutralizing antibodies in 96%, and rubella HI antibodies in 99% of susceptible individuals. The presence of these antibodies has been correlated with clinical protection and their absence considered indicative of susceptibility to these diseases.

Studies have shown that measles, mumps, and rubella virus vaccine live is as effective in producing immunity as each of the separate vaccines, and that the immunity induced by immunization with measles, mumps, and rubella virus vaccine is long-lasting and may even be lifelong.

The RA 27/3 rubella strain in measles, mumps, and rubella virus vaccine live elicits higher immediate postvaccination HI, complement-fixing, and neutralizing antibody levels than do other strains of rubella vaccine and has been shown to induce a broader profile of circulating antibodies, including anti-theta and anti-iota precipitating antibodies. The RA 27/3 rubella strain immunologically simulates natural infection more closely than other rubella vaccine viruses. The increased levels and broader profile of antibodies produced by RA 27/3 strain rubella virus vaccine appear to correlate with greater resistance to subclinical reinfection with the wild virus, and provide a greater probability of lasting immunity.

Duration of protective effect

The immunity conferred by measles, mumps, and rubella virus vaccine appears to be long-lasting. Vaccine-induced antibody levels following administration of measles, mumps, and rubella virus vaccine live have been shown to persist for up to 11 years without substantial decline. Protective antibodies have been observed 21 years after measles vaccination and 18 years after rubella vaccination. Administration of a second dose of vaccine some years after the first dose may ensure that protective antibody titers are maintained. Continued surveillance will be necessary to determine further duration of antibody persistence. Continuous serosurveillance is important to monitor the immunity status in the population and especially to ensure that the immunity is sufficient during childbearing years.

Precautions to Consider

Pregnancy/Reproduction

Pregnancy—Although adequate studies have not been done in humans, use in pregnant women is not recommended. Considerable complications, including increased rates of spontaneous abortion, premature births, low-birth-weight neonates, and, possibly, congenital defects, have been observed with natural measles infection during pregnancy, and the possibility exists that the measles vaccine may cause similar effects.

Although mumps vaccine virus has not been isolated from electively aborted fetuses of women who were vaccinated during pregnancy, the vaccine virus may infect the placenta. In addition, natural mumps infection can infect the placenta and fetus, but there is no evidence that natural mumps infection during pregnancy causes congenital malformations. Therefore, there is no reason to suspect or evidence to indicate that mumps vaccine would cause congenital malformations.

Rubella vaccine virus crosses the placenta and has been recovered from the products of conception of some aborted fetuses of women who received the vaccine just prior to or during pregnancy; however, from 1971 through 1988, the Centers for Disease Control (CDC) monitored 210 pregnant women who had received the RA 27/3 strain of rubella virus vaccine 3 months before or after conception and carried their pregnancies to term. Although some neonates had serological evidence of rubella virus infection, none had malformations associated with congenital rubella syndrome. Therefore, vaccination of a pregnant woman should not in itself indicate the need for abortion, although the final decision rests with the woman and her physician. The risk of congenital rubella syndrome associated with maternal infection with the wild virus during the first trimester of pregnancy is at least 20%. Although the risk of teratogenicity is not known, and appears to be minimal, there is still a theoretical risk of fetal abnormality caused by the vaccine virus.

It is recommended that pregnancy be avoided for 3 months following vaccination.

Studies have not been done in animals.

FDA Pregnancy Category C.

Breast-feeding

It is not known whether measles or mumps vaccine is distributed into breast milk. Although rubella vaccine may be distributed into breast milk and infants may subsequently show serological evidence of rubella infection or mild clinical illness typical of acquired rubella, studies have not shown that these effects cause serious clinical problems.

Pediatrics

Infants younger than 15 months of age may fail to respond to the measles component of the vaccine due to the presence of residual circulating measles antibody of maternal origin. This effect usually starts to wane after the child reaches 6 months of age. However, children born to younger mothers might respond well to measles vaccine administered at 12 months of age. In one study, children randomly received measles vaccine at either 12 or 15 months of age. The measles antibody response to measles, mumps, and rubella virus vaccine was 93 to 95% when the vaccine was administered at 12 months of age, and 98% when it was administered at 15 months of age. Among children of mothers born after 1961, who probably had received a measles vaccine and were less likely to have had measles infection than women born in previous years, the seroconversion rate was 96% among children vaccinated at 12 months of age and 98% among those vaccinated at 15 months of age. Based on these findings, the Committee on Infectious Diseases of the American Academy of Pediatrics (AAP) and the Advisory Committee on Immunization Practices (ACIP) recommend administration of the first dose of measles, mumps, and rubella virus vaccine live at 12 to 15 months of age. Both AAP and ACIP recommend that all children receive a second dose of measles-containing vaccine. The second dose of measles, mumps, and rubella virus vaccine live is routinely recommended at 4 to 6 years of age or at 11 to 12 years of age, but may be administered at any visit, provided at least 1 month has elapsed since receipt of the first dose. Children who were vaccinated when younger than 12 months of age should be revaccinated at 15 months of age. Children who received monovalent measles vaccine rather than measles, mumps, and rubella virus vaccine on or after their first birthdays also should receive a primary dose of mumps and rubella vaccines, and doses of measles, mumps, and rubella virus vaccine or other measles-containing vaccines should be separated by at least 1 month.

If exposure to measles infection has occurred within 72 hours or is imminent, children between 6 and 15 months of age can be vaccinated, provided that those vaccinated before their first birthdays are revaccinated at 15 months of age. There is some evidence to suggest, however, that infants immunized before 12 months of age may not develop sustained antibody levels when later reimmunized. The advantage of early protection must be weighed against the chance for failure to respond adequately on reimmunization.

It is also very important to vaccinate HIV-infected children against measles.

Children with end-stage renal disease receiving maintenance hemodialysis have a degree of immunosuppression that reduces their response to vaccination. One small trial showed that 80% of these vaccinated children developed antibodies to measles and rubella, while only 50% developed mumps antibodies. Moreover, only 30% developed antibodies to all three viruses. Therefore, it may be necessary to monitor postvaccination antibody levels in children with end-stage renal disease, and to revaccinate those children who have failed to demonstrate seroconversion.

AAP recommends the routine use of measles vaccine (including measles, mumps, and rubella virus vaccine live) in patients with nonanaphylactic allergy to eggs and in patients with allergies to chicken and chickenfeathers. One recent study showed that measles, mumps, and rubella virus vaccine live can be administered safely in a single dose to children with allergy to eggs, even those with severe hypersensitivity.

Drug interactions and/or related problems

The following drug interactions and/or related problems have been selected on the basis of their potential clinical significance (possible mechanism in parentheses where appropriate)—not necessarily inclusive (» = major clinical significance):

Note: Combinations containing any of the following medications, depending on the amount present, may also interact with this medication.

Blood products or
Immune globulins
(concurrent administration with measles, mumps, and rubella virus vaccine live may interfere with the patient's immune response to the vaccine because of the possibility of antibodies to measles, mumps, and rubella viruses in these products; measles, mumps, and rubella virus vaccine live should be administered at least 14 days before, or more than 5 to 6 months after, administration of blood products or immune globulins)

» Immunosuppressive agents or
» Radiation therapy
(because normal host defense mechanisms are suppressed, concurrent use with measles, mumps, and rubella virus vaccine live may potentiate the replication of the vaccine virus, increase the side/adverse effects of the vaccine virus, and/or decrease the patient's antibody response to measles, mumps, and rubella virus vaccine live. The reaction may be severe enough to cause death. The interval between discontinuing medications that cause immunosuppression and regaining the ability to respond to measles, mumps, and rubella virus vaccine live depends on the intensity and type of immunosuppressive medication being used, the underlying disease, and other factors; estimates vary from 3 months to 1 year. Patients with leukemia that is in remission should not receive measles, mumps, and rubella virus vaccine live until at least 3 months after their last dose of chemotherapy. This precaution does not apply to corticosteroids used as replacement therapy, for short-term [less than 2 weeks] systemic therapy, or for other routes of administration that do not cause immunosuppression)

Laboratory value alterations

The following have been selected on the basis of their potential clinical significance (possible effect in parentheses where appropriate)—not necessarily inclusive (» = major clinical significance).

With diagnostic test results
» Tuberculin skin test
(short-term suppression lasting several weeks may occur and may result in false-negative tests; if required, tuberculin skin tests should be done before, simultaneously with, or at least 8 weeks after administration of measles, mumps, and rubella virus vaccine)

Skin tests, other
(decreased responsiveness to skin test antigens may occur because of vaccine-induced transient suppression of delayed-type hypersensitivity; the period of time for which responsiveness is decreased depends upon the particular skin test used)

With physiology/laboratory test values
Platelets, blood
(counts may be decreased)

Medical considerations/Contraindications

The medical considerations/contraindications included have been selected on the basis of their potential clinical significance (reasons given in parentheses where appropriate)—not necessarily inclusive (» = major clinical significance).

Except under special circumstances, this medication should not be used when the following medical problems exist:

» Febrile illness, severe
(manifestations of illness may be confused with possible side/adverse effects of vaccine; however, minor illnesses, such as upper respiratory infection, do not preclude administration of vaccine)

» Immune deficiency conditions, congenital or hereditary, family history of or

» Immune deficiency conditions, primary or acquired
(because of reduced or suppressed defense mechanisms, the use of live virus vaccines, including measles, mumps, and rubella virus vaccine live, may potentiate the replication of the vaccine virus, and/or may decrease the patient's antibody response to measles, mumps, and rubella)
(persons with leukemia that is in remission may receive live virus vaccines if at least 3 months have passed since the last chemotherapy treatment)
(persons infected with human immunodeficiency virus [HIV] may receive measles, mumps, and rubella virus vaccine live if they are not severely lymphopenic)
(when there is a family history of congenital or hereditary immune deficiency conditions, the patient should not be vaccinated until immune competence is demonstrated)

Risk-benefit should be considered when the following medical problems exist:

Allergy to eggs
(patients allergic to eggs also may be allergic to measles, mumps, and rubella virus vaccine live, since measles and mumps virus vaccines are produced in chick embryo cell cultures. A history of hypersensitivity reactions other than anaphylaxis generally does not preclude immunization. In addition, no allergy to measles, mumps, and rubella virus vaccine live has been found in patients allergic to chicken feathers or chicken)

Allergy to gelatin
(patients allergic to gelatin also may be allergic to measles, mumps, and rubella virus vaccine live, since gelatin is used as a stabilizer in the production of the vaccine)

Allergy to neomycin
(patients allergic to neomycin also may be allergic to measles, mumps, and rubella virus vaccine live, since neomycin is used in the production of the vaccine)

Sensitivity to measles, mumps, and rubella virus vaccine

Thrombocytopenia or history of vaccine-associated thrombocytopenia
(persons who experienced thrombocytopenia with the first dose of vaccine may develop thrombocytopenia with additional doses. These persons should have serological testing performed in order to determine the need for additional doses of vaccine. The risk-benefit ratio should be evaluated before considering vaccination in such cases)

Patient monitoring

The following may be especially important in patient monitoring (other tests may be warranted in some patients, depending on condition; » = major clinical significance):

Seroconversion test
(may be performed 6 to 8 weeks following vaccination in patients for whom immunity is considered crucial [e.g., persons traveling outside the U.S. or women in high-risk areas who intend to become pregnant], since vaccination with measles, mumps, and rubella virus vaccine live may not result in seroconversion in all susceptible patients)

Side/Adverse Effects

Note: The side/adverse effects associated with the use of measles, mumps, and rubella virus vaccine live are the same as those expected to follow administration of the monovalent vaccines given separately. However, it is very important to differentiate between vaccine-induced side/adverse effects and natural infection.

Encephalitis with resultant residual permanent CNS impairment (encephalopathy) develops in approximately 1 per 1000 persons infected with measles virus. Whether attenuated live viral measles vaccine can also produce such a syndrome has been a concern since the earliest days of measles vaccine use.

Although cases of encephalopathy have been reported after administration of measles-containing vaccine, lack of a unique clinical syndrome or specific laboratory test hampered causality assessment. However, four independent passive surveillance systems in the U.S. have reported cases of encephalopathy in which a similar timing of reported events following vaccine administration was apparent. In all four case series, onset of encephalopathies followed a nonrandom distribution with onset approximately 10 days after vaccination, a timing consistent with onset of encephalopathy after infection with wild measles virus. Although this pattern may be in part attributable to consistent biases of these passive surveillance systems, it is also consistent with a causal relationship between measles vaccine and encephalopathies. During the period in which these four systems have collected data, 166 cases of encephalopathy occurring 6 to 15 days after vaccination have been identified and an estimated 313 million cases of measles-containing vaccines have been distributed (i.e., approximately 1 case per 2 million doses distributed). Thus, encephalopathy occurs less frequently after administration of measles vaccine than after measles infection.

Cases of Guillain-Barré syndrome (GBS) occurring after administration of measles, mumps, and rubella virus vaccine live or its component vaccines have been reported, but the Institute of Medicine (IOM) judged the evidence insufficient to accept or reject a causal relationship. Some studies provide evidence against this potential association. After mass vaccination campaigns that involved approximately 8 million doses of measles and rubella virus vaccine in the United Kingdom and more than 70 million doses of measles virus vaccine in Latin America, evaluations of GBS incidence demonstrated no increases over background rates.

Measles vaccination substantially reduces the occurrence of subacute sclerosing panencephalitis (SSPE), as evidenced by the near-elimination of SSPE cases after widespread measles vaccination. SSPE has been reported rarely among children who had no history of natural measles infection, but who had received measles vaccine. Evidence indicates that at least some of these children had unrecognized measles infection before they were vaccinated and that the SSPE was directly related to natural measles infection. The administration of live measles vaccine does not increase the risk for SSPE, even among persons who have previously had measles disease or received live measles vaccine.

Persons who are immune to measles, mumps, and/or rubella virus because of past vaccination or infection usually do not experience side/adverse effects from the vaccine. However, some recipients of inactivated measles vaccine who were later revaccinated with live measles vaccine had adverse reactions to the live vaccine; the percentage who reported adverse reactions ranged from 4 to 55%. In most cases, these reactions were mild (e.g., local swelling and erythema, low-grade fever lasting 1 to 2 days), but rarely more severe reactions (e.g., prolonged high fevers, extensive local reactions) were reported. However, natural measles infection is more likely to cause serious illness among recipients of inactivated measles vaccine than is live measles virus vaccine.

Excretion of small amounts of the live attenuated rubella virus from the nose or throat has occurred in the majority of susceptible individuals 7 to 28 days after vaccination. There is, however, no confirmed evidence to indicate that the vaccine virus is transmitted to susceptible persons who are in contact with the vaccinated individuals.

The following side/adverse effects have been selected on the basis of their potential clinical significance (possible signs and symptoms in parentheses where appropriate)—not necessarily inclusive:

Those indicating need for medical attention

Incidence more frequent
Fever higher than 39.4 °C (103 °F)

Incidence less frequent
Optic neuritis (pain or tenderness of eyes)—may occur from 1 to 4 weeks after immunization, lasting less than 1 week

Incidence rare
Anaphylactic reaction (difficulty in breathing or swallowing; hives; itching, especially of soles or palms; reddening of skin, especially around ears; swelling of eyes, face, or inside of nose; unusual tired-

ness or weakness, sudden and severe); ***encephalitis or meningoencephalitis*** (confusion; headache, severe or continuing; irritability; stiff neck; or vomiting); ***ocular palsies*** (double vision); ***orchitis in postpubescent and adult men*** (pain, tenderness, or swelling in testicles and scrotum); ***peripheral neuropathy, polyneuritis, or polyneuropathy*** (pain, numbness, or tingling of hands, arms, legs, or feet)—may occur from 1 to 4 weeks after immunization, lasting less than 1 week; ***seizures*** (convulsions); ***thrombocytopenic purpura*** (bruising or purple spots on skin)

Note: Hypersensitivity reactions, usually consisting of urticaria or a wheal and flare at injection site, occur rarely after administration of measles, mumps, and rubella virus vaccine live or any of its component vaccines. Immediate *anaphylactic reaction* to these vaccines is very rare. The reported rate of possible anaphylaxis after vaccination with measles-containing vaccine is less than 1 case per 1 million doses distributed. Allergic reactions including rash, pruritus, and purpura have been temporally associated with vaccination but are uncommon, usually mild, and of brief duration.

Surveillance of adverse reactions in the U.S. and other countries indicates that measles, mumps, and rubella virus vaccine live can, in rare instances, cause clinically apparent *thrombocytopenia* within 2 months after vaccination. In prospective studies, the reported frequency of clinically apparent thrombocytopenia after immunization with measles, mumps, and rubella virus vaccine live ranged from 1 case per 30,000 vaccinated children in Finland and Great Britain to 1 case per 40,000 in Sweden, with temporal clustering of cases occurring 2 to 3 weeks after vaccination. Based on passive surveillance, the reported frequency of thrombocytopenia was approximately 1 case per 100,000 vaccine doses distributed in Canada and France, and approximately 1 case per 1 million doses distributed in the U.S. The clinical course of these cases usually was transient and benign, although hemorrhage occurred rarely. The risk of thrombocytopenia during rubella or measles infection is much greater than the risk after vaccination. Based on case reports, the risk of measles, mumps, and rubella virus vaccine live–associated thrombocytopenia may be increased for persons who have previously had immune thrombocytopenic purpura, particularly for those who had thrombocytopenic purpura after an earlier dose of measles, mumps, and rubella virus vaccine live.

Those indicating need for medical attention only if they continue or are bothersome

Incidence more frequent

Fever between 37.7 and 39.4 °C (100 and 103 °F); lymphadenopathy or parotitis (swelling of glands in neck)—may occur from 1 to 4 weeks after immunization, lasting less than 1 week; ***reaction to acid pH of vaccine*** (burning or stinging at injection site); ***skin rash***

Incidence less frequent

Allergic reaction, delayed-type, cell-mediated (itching, swelling, redness, tenderness, or hard lump at injection site); ***arthralgia or arthritis*** (aches or pain in joints)—may occur from 1 to 10 weeks after immunization, lasting less than 1 week; ***malaise*** (vague feeling of bodily discomfort)—may occur from 1 to 4 weeks after immunization, lasting less than 1 week; ***mild headache, sore throat, or runny nose***—may occur from 1 to 4 weeks after immunization, lasting less than 1 week; ***nausea***

Note: One study showed that the RA 27/3 strain of rubella vaccine administered to susceptible adult women is not associated with clinically important acute or chronic joint disease. Therefore, rubella vaccination should continue to be used to protect susceptible adult women from rubella in order to advance the goal of eliminating the congenital rubella syndrome. The incidence of *arthralgia or arthritis* is increased greatly in women of childbearing age. Generally the older the woman, the greater the incidence, severity, and duration of arthralgia or arthritis. However, even in older women, the symptoms generally are well tolerated and rarely interfere with normal activities. No persistent joint disorders have been reported.

Patient Consultation

As an aid to patient consultation, refer to *Advice for the Patient, Measles, Mumps, and Rubella Virus Vaccine Live (Systemic).*

In providing consultation, consider emphasizing the following selected information (» = major clinical significance):

Before receiving this vaccine

» Conditions affecting use, especially:

Sensitivity to measles, mumps, and rubella virus vaccine live, or allergy to eggs, gelatin, or neomycin

Pregnancy—Use of measles, mumps, and rubella virus vaccine during pregnancy or pregnancy within 3 months of immunization is not recommended

Breast-feeding—Consulting physician if breast-feeding is considered

Use in children—Use is not recommended for infants younger than 12 months of age

Other medications, especially immunosuppressive agents or radiation therapy

Other medical problems, especially severe febrile illness, family history of congenital or hereditary immune deficiency conditions, or primary or acquired immune deficiency conditions

Proper use of this medication

» Proper dosing

Precautions after receiving this vaccine

» Not becoming pregnant for 3 months because of possible problems during pregnancy

Checking with physician before receiving:
- Tuberculin skin test within 8 weeks of this vaccine, since the results of the test may be affected by the vaccine
- Any other live-virus vaccines within 1 month of this vaccine
- Blood transfusions or other blood products within 2 weeks of this vaccine
- Gamma globulin or other globulins within 2 weeks of this vaccine

Side/adverse effects

Signs of potential side effects, especially fever higher than 39.4 °C (103 °F), optic neuritis, anaphylactic reaction, encephalitis or meningoencephalitis, ocular palsies, orchitis in postpubescent and adult males, peripheral neuropathy, polyneuritis, or polyneuropathy, seizures, and thrombocytopenic purpura

General Dosing Information

The dosage of measles, mumps, and rubella virus vaccine live is the same for both children and adults.

Measles, mumps, and rubella virus vaccine live is administered subcutaneously. It should not be injected intravenously.

When sterilizing syringes and skin before vaccination, care should be taken to avoid preservatives, antiseptics, detergents, and disinfectants, because the vaccine virus is easily inactivated by these substances.

To prevent inactivation of the vaccine, it is recommended that only the diluent provided by the manufacturer be used.

A 25-gauge, 5/8th-inch needle is recommended for administration of the vaccine.

Although measles, mumps, and rubella vaccines are available as a combination vaccine (measles, mumps, and rubella virus vaccine live) and, as such, are administered as a single injection, the commercially available individual vaccines should not be mixed in the same syringe or administered at the same body site.

Simultaneous administration of measles, mumps, and rubella virus vaccine live, diphtheria and tetanus toxoids and pertussis vaccine (DTP), and oral poliovirus vaccine (OPV) has resulted in rates of seroconversion and of side effects similar to those observed when the vaccines are administered at separate times. Since simultaneous administration of common vaccines is not known to affect the efficacy or safety of any of the routinely recommended childhood vaccines, if return of a vaccine recipient for further immunization is doubtful, simultaneous administration of all vaccines (DTP, OPV or poliovirus vaccine inactivated enhanced-potency [eIPV], measles, mumps, and rubella virus vaccine live, varicella virus vaccine live, hepatitis B vaccine, and *Haemophilus influenzae* type b vaccine [Hib]) appropriate for the age and previous vaccination status of the recipient is recommended.

For treatment of adverse effects

Recommended treatment consists of the following:
- For mild hypersensitivity reaction—Administering antihistamines, and, if necessary, corticosteroids.
- For severe hypersensitivity or anaphylactic reaction—Administering epinephrine. Antihistamines or corticosteroids also may be administered as required.

Parenteral Dosage Forms

MEASLES, MUMPS, AND RUBELLA VIRUS VACCINE LIVE (FOR INJECTION) USP

Usual adult and adolescent dose

Immunizing agent (active)—

Subcutaneous, 0.5 mL, preferably into the outer aspect of the upper arm.

Usual pediatric dose

Immunizing agent (active)—

Infants up to 12 months of age: Use is not recommended.

Infants and children 12 months of age and older: See *Usual adult and adolescent dose.*

Note: The Committee on Infectious Diseases of the American Academy of Pediatrics (AAP) and the Advisory Committee on Immunization Practices (ACIP) recommend that all children receive a second dose of measles-containing vaccine. The second dose of measles, mumps, and rubella virus vaccine live is routinely recommended at 4 to 6 years of age or at 11 to 12 years of age, but may be administered at any visit, provided at least 1 month has elapsed since receipt of the first dose.

Strength(s) usually available

U.S.—

Not less than the equivalent of 1000 $TCID_{50}$ of the U.S. Reference Measles Virus, not less than the equivalent of 20,000 $TCID_{50}$ of the U.S. Reference Mumps Virus, and not less than the equivalent of 1000 $TCID_{50}$ of the U.S. Reference Rubella Virus in each 0.5-mL dose (Rx) [*M-M-R II* (neomycin approximately 25 mcg)].

Canada—

Not less than the equivalent of 1000 $TCID_{50}$ of the U.S. Reference Measles Virus, not less than the equivalent of 20,000 $TCID_{50}$ of the U.S. Reference Mumps Virus, and not less than the equivalent of 1000 $TCID_{50}$ of the U.S. Reference Rubella Virus in each 0.5-mL dose (Rx) [*M-M-R II* (neomycin approximately 25 mcg)].

Packaging and storage

Store the lyophilized form of the vaccine, the diluent, and the reconstituted form of the vaccine between 2 and 8 °C (36 and 46 °F).

Alternatively, the diluent for the single-dose vials may be stored between 15 and 30 °C (59 and 86 °F).

Protect both the lyophilized form and the reconstituted form of the vaccine from light.

Preparation of dosage form

To reconstitute, use only the diluent provided by the manufacturer, since it is free of preservatives and other substances that might inactivate the vaccine.

Single-dose vial—The entire volume of diluent (approximately 0.5 mL) should be withdrawn into the syringe. All the diluent in the syringe should be injected into the vial of lyophilized vaccine and agitated to mix thoroughly. The entire contents of the vial should be withdrawn into the syringe and the total volume of restored vaccine injected subcutaneously.

10-dose vial (in U.S., available only to government agencies/institutions)—The entire contents (7 mL) of the diluent vial should be withdrawn into the syringe to be used for reconstitution. All of the diluent in the syringe should be injected into the 10-dose vial of lyophilized vaccine and agitated to mix thoroughly. The 10-dose container can be used with either syringes or a jet injector. Since the vaccine and diluent do not contain preservatives, special care should be taken to prevent contamination of the multiple-dose vial of vaccine. In addition, the vial should be stored properly until the reconstituted vaccine is used. Unused vaccine should be discarded after 8 hours.

Stability

Both the lyophilized and the reconstituted vaccine should be stored between 2 and 8 °C (36 and 46 °F) and protected from light. Improper storage and protection may inactivate the vaccine.

The reconstituted vaccine should be used as soon as possible. Unused reconstituted vaccine should be discarded after 8 hours.

The reconstituted vaccine is clear yellow. It should not be used if it is discolored.

Incompatibilities

Preservatives or other substances may inactivate the vaccine; therefore, only the diluent supplied by the manufacturer should be used for reconstitution.

A sterile syringe free of preservatives, antiseptics, disinfectants, and detergents should be used for each injection and/or reconstitution of the vaccine. These substances may inactivate the live virus vaccine.

Auxiliary labeling

- Protect from light.
- Store in refrigerator.
- Discard reconstituted vaccine if not used within 8 hours.

Note: The date and the time of reconstitution should be indicated on the vial if the reconstituted vaccine is not used at once.

Revised: 04/15/1999

MEBENDAZOLE Systemic

VA CLASSIFICATION (Primary): AP200

Commonly used brand name(s): *Vermox.*

Note: For a listing of dosage forms and brand names by country availability, see *Dosage Forms* section(s).

Category

Anthelmintic (systemic).

Indications

Note: Bracketed information in the *Indications* section refers to uses that are not included in U.S. product labeling.

Accepted

Ascariasis (treatment)—Mebendazole is indicated as a primary agent for ascariasis caused by *Ascaris lumbricoides* (common roundworm).

Enterobiasis (treatment)—Mebendazole is indicated as a primary agent for enterobiasis caused by *Enterobius vermicularis* (pinworm).

Hookworm infection (treatment)—Mebendazole is indicated as a primary agent for hookworm disease caused by *Ancylostoma duodenale* (common hookworm; Old World hookworm) and *Necator americanus* (American hookworm; New World hookworm).

Intestinal roundworm, multiple (treatment)—Mebendazole is indicated in the treatment of multiple intestinal roundworm infections.

Trichuriasis (treatment)—Mebendazole is indicated as a primary agent for trichuriasis caused by *Trichuris trichiura* (whipworm).

[Capillariasis (treatment)][1]—Mebendazole is used in the treatment of capillariasis caused by *Capillaria philippinensis.*

[Gnathostomiasis (treatment)][1]—Mebendazole is used in the treatment of gnathostomiasis caused by *Gnathostoma spinigerum.*

[Hydatid disease, alveolar (treatment)][1]—Mebendazole is used in the treatment of alveolar hydatid disease caused by *Echinococcus multilocularis (E. alveolaris).*

[Hydatid disease, unilocular (treatment)][1]—Mebendazole is used in the treatment of unilocular hydatid disease caused by *E. granulosus.* Mebendazole is used as a secondary agent in patients in whom surgery is contraindicated or has failed, in after-spill during surgery, or in recurrences. Very high doses may be effective.

[Trichinosis (treatment)][1]—Mebendazole is used as a secondary agent in the treatment of trichinosis (trichinellosis) caused by *Trichinella spiralis* (pork worm). Systemic corticosteroids are used concurrently, especially in patients with severe symptoms, to minimize inflammatory reactions to *Trichinella* larvae.

Not all species or strains of a particular helminth may be susceptible to mebendazole. In addition, efficacy varies with respect to pre-existing diarrhea, gastrointestinal transit time, and degree of infection.

[1]Not included in Canadian product labeling.

Pharmacology/Pharmacokinetics

Physicochemical characteristics

Molecular weight—295.30.

Mechanism of action/Effect

Vermicidal; may also be ovicidal for ova of most helminths; mebendazole causes degeneration of parasite's cytoplasmic microtubules and thereby selectively and irreversibly blocks glucose uptake in susceptible adult intestine-dwelling helminths and their tissue-dwelling larvae; inhibition of glucose uptake apparently results in depletion of the parasite's glycogen stores; this, in turn, results in reduced formation of adenosine triphosphate (ATP) required for survival and reproduction of the helminth; corresponding energy levels are gradually reduced until death of the parasite ensues; mebendazole does not appear to affect serum glucose concentrations in humans, however.

Absorption

Poorly absorbed (approximately 5 to 10%) from gastrointestinal tract; absorption may be increased when taken with food, especially fatty food.

Distribution

Distributed to serum, cyst fluid, liver, omental fat, and pelvic, pulmonary, and hepatic cysts; highest concentrations found in liver; relatively high concentrations also found in muscle-encysted *Trichinella spiralis* larvae; also crosses the placenta.

Protein binding

High to very high (90–95%).

Biotransformation
Primarily hepatic; metabolized to inactive amino, hydroxy, and hydroxy-amino metabolites; primary metabolite is 2-amino-5-benzoylbenzimidazole.

Half-life
Normal hepatic function—2.5 to 5.5 hours (range: 2.5 to 9 hours).
Impaired hepatic function (cholestasis)—Approximately 35 hours.

Time to peak serum concentration
2 to 5 hours (range—0.5 to 7 hours).

Peak serum concentration
Following a dose of 100 mg twice a day for 3 days—
Mebendazole: Not more than 0.03 mcg per mL.
2-Amino metabolite: Not more than 0.09 mcg per mL.

Serum concentrations up to 0.5 mcg per mL have been reported in chronic, high-dose therapy.

Elimination
Fecal—Approximately 95% excreted unchanged or as the primary metabolite (2-amino derivative) in feces.
Renal—Approximately 2 to 5% excreted unchanged or as the primary metabolite in urine.

Precautions to Consider

Carcinogenicity
Carcinogenicity studies in mice and rats given doses as high as 40 mg per kg of body weight (mg/kg) daily for over two years have not shown mebendazole to be carcinogenic.

Mutagenicity
Dominant lethal mutation studies in mice given single doses as high as 640 mg/kg have not shown that mebendazole is mutagenic. The spermatocyte test, the F_1 translocation test, and the Ames test produced negative results.

Pregnancy/Reproduction
Fertility—Studies in mice given doses of up to 40 mg/kg for 60 days prior to gestation in males and 14 days in females have not shown that mebendazole causes adverse effects on the fetus or offspring. However, mebendazole has been shown to cause slight maternal toxicity at this dose.

Pregnancy—Mebendazole crosses the placenta. A post-marketing survey in pregnant women who inadvertently took mebendazole during the first trimester has not shown an incidence of spontaneous abortion or malformation greater than that of the general population. In a total of 170 deliveries at term, mebendazole has not been shown to be teratogenic in humans.

Studies in rats given single oral doses as low as 10 mg/kg have shown that mebendazole is teratogenic and embryotoxic.

FDA Pregnancy Category C.

Breast-feeding
It is not known whether mebendazole is distributed into breast milk. However, problems in humans have not been documented.

Pediatrics
Appropriate studies on the relationship of age to the effects of mebendazole have not been performed in children up to 2 years of age. However, no pediatrics-specific problems have been documented to date in children over the age of 2.

Geriatrics
No information is available on the relationship of age to the effects of mebendazole in geriatric patients.

Drug interactions and/or related problems
The following drug interactions and/or related problems have been selected on the basis of their potential clinical significance (possible mechanism in parentheses where appropriate)—not necessarily inclusive (» = major clinical significance):

Note: Combinations containing any of the following medications, depending on the amount present, may also interact with this medication.

Carbamazepine
(in patients receiving high doses of mebendazole for treatment of tissue-dwelling organisms such as *Echinococcus multilocularis* or *E. granulosus* [hydatid disease], carbamazepine has been shown to lower mebendazole plasma concentrations by induction of hepatic microsomal enzymes and to impair the therapeutic response; if carbamazepine is being used for seizures, replacement with valproic acid is recommended; treatment of intestinal helminths such as whipworms or hookworms does not appear to be affected by the rate of hepatic metabolism of mebendazole)

Laboratory value alterations
The following have been selected on the basis of their potential clinical significance (possible effect in parentheses where appropriate)—not necessarily inclusive (» = major clinical significance).

With physiology/laboratory test values
» Alanine aminotransferase (ALT [SGPT]), serum, and
» Alkaline phosphatase, serum, and
» Aspartate aminotransferase (AST [SGOT]), serum, and
Blood urea nitrogen (BUN)
(values may be transiently increased)

Hemoglobin, serum
(concentration may be decreased)

Medical considerations/Contraindications
The medical considerations/contraindications included have been selected on the basis of their potential clinical significance (reasons given in parentheses where appropriate)—not necessarily inclusive (» = major clinical significance).

Risk-benefit should be considered when the following medical problems exist:

Crohn's ileitis or
Ulcerative colitis
(may increase absorption and toxicity of mebendazole, especially in high-dose therapy)

» Hepatic function impairment
(mebendazole is metabolized primarily in liver; prolonged half-life and drug accumulation may occur, with an increased incidence of side effects; dosage may need to be decreased)

Hypersensitivity to mebendazole

Patient monitoring
The following may be especially important in patient monitoring (other tests may be warranted in some patients, depending on condition; » = major clinical significance):

For pinworms
» Perianal examinations
(cellophane tape swabs of the perianal area to detect the presence of eggs may be required prior to and starting 1 week following treatment with mebendazole, especially in patients with persisting symptoms; swabs should be taken every morning prior to defecation and bathing for at least 3 days to determine efficacy or proof of cure; perianal examinations may also be required to detect the presence of adult worms in the perianal area; no patient should be considered cured unless perianal swabs have been negative for 7 consecutive days)

For roundworms, whipworms, and capillariasis
» Stool examinations
(may be required prior to and approximately 1 to 3 weeks following treatment with mebendazole to determine efficacy or proof of cure; because of colonic mixing, eggs may persist in the stool for up to 1 week following cure)

For patients on high-dose therapy
» Complete blood counts (CBCs)
(may be required prior to and periodically during the first month of treatment with mebendazole since high-dose mebendazole may cause granulocytopenia, neutropenia, and/or leukopenia; CBC's performed two or three times a week from day 10 through day 25, and weekly thereafter, are recommended)

Side/Adverse Effects
The following side/adverse effects have been selected on the basis of their potential clinical significance (possible signs and symptoms in parentheses where appropriate)—not necessarily inclusive:

Those indicating need for medical attention
Incidence rare
Hypersensitivity (fever; skin rash or itching); ***neutropenia*** (sore throat and fever; unusual tiredness and weakness)—with high doses, reversible

Those indicating need for medical attention only if they continue or are bothersome
Incidence less frequent
Gastrointestinal disturbances (abdominal pain or upset; diarrhea; nausea or vomiting)

Incidence rare
Alopecia (hair loss)—with high doses; ***dizziness; headache***

Overdose

For more information on the management of overdose or unintentional ingestion, **contact a Poison Control Center** (see *Poison Control Center Listing*).

In accidental overdose, gastrointestinal symptoms may occur and may last up to a few hours.

Treatment of overdose

Supportive care—

Supportive therapy necessary to maintain the vital functions of the patient may be administered.

Patient Consultation

As an aid to patient consultation, refer to *Advice for the Patient, Mebendazole (Systemic)*.

In providing consultation, consider emphasizing the following selected information (» = major clinical significance):

Before using this medication

» Conditions affecting use, especially:
Hypersensitivity to mebendazole
Pregnancy—Mebendazole crosses the placenta
Other medical problems, especially hepatic function impairment

Proper use of this medication

Reading patient instructions before taking medication

No special preparations or other measures (e.g., dietary restrictions or fasting, concurrent medications, purging, or cleansing enemas) required before, during, or immediately after therapy

Chewing tablets, swallowing whole, or crushing tablets and mixing with food

» Compliance with full course of therapy; second course may be required in some infections

» Proper dosing
Missed dose: Taking as soon as possible; not taking if almost time for next dose; not doubling doses

» Proper storage

For pinworms
Treating all household members concurrently; treating again in 2 to 3 weeks

For patients on high-dose therapy
» Taking with meals, especially fatty ones, to increase absorption; checking with physician if on low-fat diet

Precautions while using this medication

Regular visits to physician to check progress, especially in high-dose therapy

Checking with physician if no improvement within a few days

For hookworms or whipworms:
Importance of taking iron supplements daily during treatment and for up to 6 months following treatment if patient is anemic at the time of therapy

For pinworms:
Washing (not shaking) all bedding and nightclothes after treatment to prevent reinfection
Other measures may be recommended by some physicians

Side/adverse effects

Signs of potential side effects, especially hypersensitivity and neutropenia

General Dosing Information

No special preparations (e.g., dietary restrictions or fasting, concurrent medications, purging, or cleansing enemas) are required before, during, or immediately after treatment with mebendazole.

Mebendazole tablets may be chewed, swallowed whole, or crushed and mixed with food.

Patients who are heavily infected with helminths may require more prolonged treatment.

For high-dose therapy

In the treatment of tissue-dwelling helminth infections, the administration of much higher doses of mebendazole may be necessary because of poor absorption.

Mebendazole should preferably be taken with meals, especially fatty ones. This increases the bioavailability, absorption, and serum concentrations of mebendazole.

For hookworms and whipworms

In the treatment of hookworms and whipworms, especially in patients who are heavily infected or who have inadequate dietary intake of iron, concurrent iron therapy may be required if anemia is present. Iron therapy may need to be continued for up to 6 months to replenish iron stores.

For pinworms

Because of the high probability of transfer of pinworms, it is usually recommended that all members of the household be treated concurrently.

Retreatment is recommended 2 to 3 weeks following initial treatment.

Oral Dosage Forms

Note: Bracketed uses in the *Dosage Forms* section refer to categories of use and/or indications that are not included in U.S. product labeling.

MEBENDAZOLE TABLETS (CHEWABLE) USP

Usual adult and adolescent dose

Ascariasis; or
Trichuriasis; or
Hookworm—
Oral, 100 mg two times a day, morning and evening, for three days. May be repeated in two to three weeks if required.

Enterobiasis—
Oral, 100 mg as a single dose. Repeat in two to three weeks.

Intestinal roundworm, multiple—
Oral, 100 mg two times a day, morning and evening, for three days.

[Capillariasis][1]—
Oral, 200 mg two times a day for twenty days.

[Gnathostomiasis][1]—
Oral, 200 mg every three hours for six days.

[Hydatid disease][1]—
Oral, 13.3 to 16.7 mg per kg of body weight three times a day for up to three to six months.

[Trichinosis][1]—
Oral, 200 to 400 mg three times a day for three days, then 400 to 500 mg three times a day for ten days.

Usual adult prescribing limits

[Hydatid disease][1]—Doses up to 200 mg per kg of body weight daily have been used.

Usual pediatric dose

Children up to 2 years of age—Dosage has not been established.

Children 2 years of age and over—Ascariasis, [capillariasis][1], enterobiasis, intestinal roundworm infections, trichuriasis, and uncinariasis: See *Usual adult and adolescent dose*.

Note: In the treatment of infections caused by tissue-dwelling organisms in which high doses are required, dosage should be based on the patient's body weight.

Strength(s) usually available

U.S.—
100 mg (Rx) [*Vermox;* GENERIC].

Canada—
100 mg (Rx) [*Vermox* (scored)].

Packaging and storage

Store below 40 °C (104 °F), preferably between 15 and 30 °C (59 and 86 °F), unless otherwise specified by manufacturer. Store in a well-closed container.

Auxiliary labeling

- May be chewed, crushed, or swallowed whole.
- Take with meals (high-dose therapy).
- Continue medication for full time of treatment.

[1]Not included in Canadian product labeling.

Revised: 08/01/1995

MECASERMIN Systemic†

VA CLASSIFICATION (Primary): HS900

Commonly used brand name(s): *Increlex*.

Note: For a listing of dosage forms and brand names by country availability, see *Dosage Forms* section(s).

†Not commercially available in Canada.

Category

Insulin-like growth factor-1 replenisher.

Indications

Accepted

Growth failure (treatment)—Mecasermin (rDNA origin) injection is indicated for the long-term treatment of growth failure in children with severe primary IGF-1 deficiency (Primary IGFD) or with growth hormone (GH) gene deletion who have developed neutralizing antibodies to GH. Severe Primary IGFD is defined by:

- height standard deviation score ≤−3 and
- basal IGF-1 standard deviation score ≤−3 and
- normal or elevated growth hormone (GH)

Severe primary IGFD includes patients with mutations in the GH receptor (GHR), post-GHR signaling pathway, and IGF-1 gene defects; they are not GH deficient; and therefore, they cannot be expected to respond adequately to exogenous GH treatment.

Unaccepted

Mecasermin is not intended for use in subjects with secondary forms of IGF-1 deficiency, such as GH deficiency, malnutrition, hypothyroidism, or chronic treatment with pharmacologic doses of anti-inflammatory steroids.

Pharmacology/Pharmacokinetics

Physicochemical characteristics

Molecular weight—rhIGF-1: 7649 daltons.
pH—Approximately 5.4

Mechanism of action/Effect

Mecasermin (rDNA origin) injection contains human insulin-like growth factor-1 (rhIGF-1) by recombinant DNA technology. Mecasermin provides IGF-1, which is the principal mediator of statural growth, in children with severe IGF-1 deficiency. During normal growth, growth hormone (GH) binds to its receptor in the liver, and the other tissues which stimulates the synthesis and secretion of IGF-1. In target tissues, the type 1 IGF-1 receptor, which is homologous to the insulin receptor, is activated by IGF-1, leading to intracellular signaling which stimulated multiple processes leading to statural growth. The metabolic actions of IGF-1 are in part directed at stimulating the uptake of glucose, fatty acids, and amino acids so that metabolism supports growing tissues.

Other actions/effects

IGF-1 suppresses hepatic glucose production and stimulates peripheral glucose use giving it hypoglycemic potential. IGF-1 has inhibitory effects on insulin secretion.

Absorption

Bioavailability of rhIGF-1 after subcutaneous injection in healthy subjects reported to be close to 100%; absolute bioavailability of mecasermin given subcutaneously to subjects with primary insulin-like growth factor-1 deficiency (Primary IGFD) has not been determined

$AUC_{(0-8)}$—2932 hr*ng per mL

Distribution

Volume of distribution (Vol_D)—0.184 to 0.33 L per kg at a mecasermin dose of 0.045 mg per kg of body weight; estimated to increase as mecasermin dose increases

Protein binding

In blood, IGF-1 is bound to six IGF binding proteins with greater than 80% bound as a complex with IGFBP-3 and an acid-labile subunit. IGFBP-3 is greatly reduced in subjects with severe Primary IGFD, resulting in increased clearance of IGF-1 in these subjects relative to healthy subjects.

Biotransformation

Both the liver and kidney have been shown to metabolize IGF-1.

Half-life

Elimination—Estimated 5.8 hours following a single subcutaneous dose of 0.12 mg per kg of body weight in pediatric patients with severe Primary IGFD

Time to peak concentration

2 hours

Peak plasma concentration:

234 ng per mL

Precautions to Consider

Carcinogenicity

Mecasermin was administered subcutaneously to Sprague Dawley rats at doses of 0.25, 1, 4, and 10 mg per kg of body weight per day for up to 2 years. An increased incidence of adrenal medullary hyperplasia and pheochromocytoma was observed in male rats at doses of 1 mg per kg of body weight per day and greater (≥1 time the clinical exposure with MRHD based on AUC) and female rats at all dose levels (≥3 times the clinical exposure with MRHD). An increased incidence of keratoacanthoma in the skin was observed in male (4 mg and 10 mg/kg/day) and female rats (10 mg/kg/day). An increased incidence of mammary gland carcinoma in both male and female rats was observed in those treated with 10 mg/kg/day. Based on excess mortality secondary to IGF-1 induced hypoglycemia, these skin and mammary tumor findings were only observed at doses that exceeded the maximum tolerated dose.

Mutagenicity

Mecasermin was not clastogenic in the *in vitro* chromosome aberration assay and the *in vivo* mouse micronucleus assay.

Pregnancy/Reproduction

Fertility—Mecasermin was administered intravenously to rats at doses up to 4 mg per day (4 times the clinical exposure with the MRHD based on AUC) with no effects on fertility observed in males or females.

Pregnancy—Adequate and well-controlled studies in human fetuses have not been done. Therefore, there is insufficient medical information to determine whether there are significant risks to a fetus.

Studies have been done in Sprague Dawley rats administered doses up to 16 mg per kg of body weight per day (mg/kg/day; 20 times the MRHD based on body surface area comparison) and in New Zealand white rabbits administered dose up to 2 mg/kg/day (2 times the MRHD). No embryo-fetal developmental abnormalities were observed in rats. In rabbits, the NOAEL for maternal toxicity was 2 mg/kg/day and the NOAEL for fetal toxicity was 0.5 mg/kg/day (2 times the MRHD). There was no teratogenicity at doses up to 2 mg/kg/day.

FDA Pregnancy Category C

Breast-feeding

It is not known whether mecasermin is distributed into human milk. Because many drugs are distributed in human milk, caution should be exercised when mescasermin is administered to a nursing woman.

Pediatrics

Mecasermin has not been studied in children less than 2 years of age.

Note: This product contains benzyl alcohol as a preservative. Benzyl alcohol as a preservative has been associated with neurologic toxicity in neonates.

Geriatrics

Safety and effectiveness of mecasermin in patients aged 65 and over have not been evaluated.

Laboratory value alterations

The following have been selected on the basis of their potential clinical significance (possible effect in parentheses where appropriate)—not necessarily inclusive (» = major clinical significance).

With physiology/laboratory test values

Alanine aminotransferase (ALT [SGPT]) and
(occasional elevations noted)

Aspartate aminotransferase (AST [SGOT]) and
Lactate dehydrogenase, serum
(mild elevations found before and during treatment; none led to treatment discontinuation)

Cholesterol and
Triglycerides
(elevations to above the upper limit of normal observed before and during treatment)

Medical considerations/Contraindications

The medical considerations/contraindications included have been selected on the basis of their potential clinical significance (reasons given in parentheses where appropriate)—not necessarily inclusive (» = major clinical significance).

Except under special circumstances, this medication should not be used when the following medical problem exists:

» Closed epiphyses
(mecasermin should not be used for growth promotion in these patients)

» Hypersensitivity to mecasermin (IGF-1) or any of the inactive ingredients

» Neoplasia, active or suspected
(mecasermin is **contraindicated** and therapy should be discontinued if evidence of neoplasia develops)

Risk-benefit should be considered when the following medical problems exist:

» Hypothyroidism or
» Nutritional deficiencies
(should be corrected before initiating mecasermin treatment)

Patient monitoring

The following may be especially important in patient monitoring (other tests may be warranted in some patients, depending on condition; » = major clinical significance):

Funduscopic examination
(recommended initially and periodically during course of therapy for intracranial hypertension [IH])

Lymphoid tissue (tonsillar) hypertrophy complications
(complications, such as snoring, sleep apnea, and chronic middle-ear effusions; patients should have periodic examinations to rule out these complications and receive appropriate treatment if necessary)

Progression of scoliosis or
Slipped capital femoral epiphysis
(can occur in patients who experience rapid growth and should be monitored during treatment)

Soft tissues of the face
(should be monitored for thickening during mecasermin treatment)

Side/Adverse Effects

Renal and splenic lengths measured by ultrasound increased rapidly during the first years of mecasermin therapy. This lengthening subsequently slowed down; however, renal and/or splenic length in some patients reached or surpassed the 95th percentile.

As with any exogenous protein administration, local or systemic allergic reactions may occur.

The following side/adverse effects have been selected on the basis of their potential clinical significance (possible signs and symptoms in parentheses where appropriate)—not necessarily inclusive:

Those indicating need for medical attention

Incidence more frequent

Cardiac murmur (chest pain; rapid heartbeat; breathlessness; fatigue; bluish skin color or fingertips); ***convulsions*** (seizures); ***hypoacusis*** (loss of hearing); ***hypoglycemia*** (anxiety; blurred vision; chills; cold sweats; coma; confusion; cool pale skin; depression; dizziness; fast heartbeat; headache; increased hunger; nausea; nervousness; nightmares; seizures; shakiness; slurred speech; unusual tiredness or weakness); ***lipohypertrophy*** (thickening of the skin); ***thymus hypertrophy***

Incidence not known

Intercranial hypertension (IH) (headache; nausea and vomiting; blurred vision; change in ability to see colors, especially blue or yellow); ***slipped capital femoral epiphysis*** (limp; pain in hip or knee)

Those indicating need for medical attention only if they continue or are bothersome

Incidence more frequent

Abnormal tympanometry (); ***arthralgia*** (pain in joints; muscle pain or stiffness; difficulty in moving); ***bruising*** (large, flat, blue or purplish patches in the skin); ***dizziness; ear pain; fluid in middle ear*** (); ***headache; otitis media*** (earache; redness or swelling in ear); ***pain in extremity*** (pain in arms or legs); ***snoring; tonsillar hypertrophy*** (); ***vomiting***

Overdose

For more information on the management of overdose or unintentional ingestion, **contact a poison control center** (see *Poison Control Center Listing*).

Clinical effects of overdose

The following effects have been selected on the basis of their potential clinical significance (possible signs and symptoms in parentheses where appropriate)—not necessarily inclusive:

Acute

Hypoglycemia (anxiety; blurred vision; chills; cold sweats; coma; confusion; cool pale skin; depression; dizziness; fast heartbeat; headache; increased hunger; nausea; nervousness; nightmares; seizures; shakiness; slurred speech; unusual tiredness or weakness)

Chronic

Acromegaly (stop in menstruation; backache; changes in vision; excessive sweating; extreme weakness; frequent urination; headache; increase in hands and feet size; increased thirst; increased volume of pale, diluted urine; joint pain; pain in extremities)

Treatment of overdose

Specific treatment—

Directing treatment of acute overdose at reversing hypoglycemia by giving oral glucose or food

If overdose results in loss of consciousness, giving intravenous glucose or parenteral glucagon to reverse the hypoglycemic effects

Supportive care—

Patients in whom intentional overdose is confirmed or suspected should be referred for psychiatric consultation.

Patient Consultation

As an aid to patient consultation, refer to *Advice for the Patient, Mecasermin (Systemic).*

In providing consultation, consider emphasizing the following selected information (» = major clinical significance):

Before using this medication

» Conditions affecting use, especially:
Hypersensitivity to mecasermin (IGF-1), benzyl alcohol or any of the other inactive ingredients
Pregnancy—Insufficient information to determine risk
Breast-feeding—Caution should be used
Use in children—Not studied in children under 2 years of age; product contain benzyl alcohol which has been associated with neurologic toxicity in neonates
Other medical problems, especially active or suspected neoplasia, closed epiphyses, nutritional deficiencies, or thyroid deficiencies

Proper use of this medication

» Only giving injection subcutaneously (under the skin) and never intravenously (in a vein) or intramuscularly (in a muscle)
» Proper preparation and administration of medication
» Carefully selecting and rotating injection sites
» Safe handling and disposal of needles and syringes; not reusing needles and syringes
» Importance of giving shortly before or after (20 minutes either way) a meal or snack
» *Importance of not administering dose when the meal or snack is omitted.*
» Not increasing dose to make up for one or more missed dose(s)
» Proper dosing
Missed dose: Calling the doctor for instructions; not doubling doses
» Proper storage

Precautions while using this medication

» Regular visits to doctor for periodic examinations
» Recognizing signs and symptoms of hypoglycemia including: anxiety; blurred vision; chills; cold sweats; coma; confusion; cool pale skin; depression; dizziness; fast heartbeat; headache; increased hunger; nausea; nervousness; nightmares; seizures; shakiness; slurred speech; unusual tiredness or weakness.
» Importance of having a source of sugar on hand such as orange juice, candy, glucose gel, or milk for symptoms of hypoglycemia
Avoiding high risk activities such as driving within 2 to 3 hours after mecasermin injection, especially at the beginning of mecasermin treatment

Side/adverse effects

Signs of potential side effects, especially cardiac murmur, convulsions, hypoacusis, hypoglycemia, lipohypertrophy, thymus hypertrophy, intercranial hypertension (IH), or slipped capital femoral epiphysis

General Dosing Information

Treatment with mecasermin should be directed by physicians who are experienced in the diagnosis and management of patients with growth disorders.

The intravenous administration of mecasermin is contraindicated.

Mecasermin is not a substitute for growth hormone (GH) treatment.

Mecasermin should be administered using sterile disposable syringes and needles. Syringes should be of small enough volume that the prescribed dose can be withdrawn from the vial with reasonable accuracy.

Injection sites should be rotated to a different site with each injection.

Subsequent doses of mecasermin should never be increased to make up for one or more omitted dose(s).

Diet/Nutrition

Mecasermin should be administered shortly (20 minutes) before or after a meal or snack, because mecasermin has insulin-like hypoglycemic effects. Special attention should be paid to small children because their oral intake may not be consistent.

If a patient is unable to eat shortly before or after a dose for any reason, that dose of mecasermin should be withheld.

For treatment of adverse effects

If an allergic reaction occurs, treatment should be interrupted and prompt medical attention should be sought.

Hypoglycemia should be treated by giving oral glucose or food.

If treating severe hypoglycemia with loss of consciousness, intravenous glucose or parenteral glucagon should be given.

Parenteral Dosage Forms

MECASERMIN (rDNA origin) INJECTION

Usual adult dose

Mecasermin has not been studied in adults.

Usual pediatric dose

Growth failure (treatment)—

Subcutaneously, initially, 0.04 to 0.08 mg (40 to 80 micrograms) per kg of body weight twice daily within 20 minutes before or after a snack or meal. If well tolerated for one week, dose may be increased by 0.04 mg per kg twice daily.

Note: If hypoglycemia occurs with recommended doses, despite adequate food intake, the dose should be reduced.

Usual pediatric prescribing limits

Up to 0.12 mg per kg given twice daily. Doses greater than 0.12 mg per kg given twice daily have not been evaluated in children with Primary IGFD and, due to potential hypoglycemic effects, should not be used.

Usual geriatric dose

Safety and effectiveness of mecasermin in adults aged 65 and over have not been evaluated.

Strength(s) usually available

U.S.—

10 mg of mecasermin (rDNA origin) per 1-mL vial sterile solution (Rx) [*Increlex* (multiple-dose; 9 mg/mL benzyl alcohol; 5.84 mg/mL sodium chloride; polysorbate 20; 0.05M acetate)].

Packaging and storage

Store refrigerated between 2 and 8 °C (35 and 46 °F). Avoid freezing the vials. Protect from direct light.

Stability

Vials of mecasermin are stable for 30 days after initial vial entry when stored between 2 and 8 °C (35 and 46 °F).

Auxiliary labeling

- Refrigerate—Do not freeze.
- Protect from light.
- Expiration date

Caution

Patients should avoid any high-risk activities (e.g., driving, etc.) within 2 to 3 hours after dosing, especially during initial mecasermin treatment, until a well-tolerated dose has been established.

Additional information

Vial contents should be clear without particulate matter. If solution is cloudy or contains particulate matter, it must not be injected.

Mescasermin should not be used after its expiration date (stated on the label). Remaining unused material should be discarded.

Developed: 03/24/2006

MECHLORETHAMINE Systemic

INN: Chlormethine

VA CLASSIFICATION (Primary): AN100

Commonly used brand name(s): *Mustargen.*

Other commonly used names are chlormethine and nitrogen mustard.

Note: For a listing of dosage forms and brand names by country availability, see *Dosage Forms* section(s).

Category

Antineoplastic.

Indications

Accepted

Lymphomas, Hodgkin's (treatment) or

Lymphomas, non-Hodgkin's (treatment)—Mechlorethamine is indicated for the palliative treatment of Hodgkin's disease (stages III and IV) and for treatment of some non-Hodgkin's lymphomas, including lymphosarcoma.

Malignant effusions, pericardial (treatment)

Malignant effusions, peritoneal (treatment) or

Malignant effusions, pleural (treatment)—Mechlorethamine is indicated by intracavitary administration for palliative treatment of metastatic carcinoma resulting in effusion.

Mycosis fungoides (treatment)—Mechlorethamine is indicated for treatment of mycosis fungoides.

[Lymphomas, cutaneous T-cell (treatment)][1]—Mechlorethamine is indicated for second-line topical treatment of cutaneous T-cell lymphomas.

Mechlorethamine has been used for bronchogenic carcinoma, chronic lymphocytic leukemia, chronic myelocytic leukemia, and polycythemia vera; however, it *has been replaced* by safer and more effective agents.

[1]Not included in Canadian product labeling.

Pharmacology/Pharmacokinetics

Physicochemical characteristics

Molecular weight—192.52.

pKa—6.1.

Mechanism of action/Effect

Mechlorethamine is a bifunctional alkylating agent and is cell cycle-phase nonspecific. Activity occurs as a result of formation of an unstable ethylenimmonium ion, which alkylates or binds with many intracellular molecular structures, including nucleic acids. Its cytotoxic action is primarily due to cross-linking of strands of DNA and RNA, as well as inhibition of protein synthesis. With intracavitary use, mechlorethamine causes sclerosis and an inflammatory reaction on serous membranes, leading to adherence of serosal surfaces.

Other actions/effects

Has weak immunosuppressive activity.

Absorption

Mechlorethamine is incompletely absorbed following intracavitary administration, probably because of rapid deactivation by body fluids.

Biotransformation

Rapidly deactivated in body fluids and tissues.

Onset of action

Effects occur within a few seconds or minutes.

Elimination

Apparently renal (less than 0.01% unchanged).

Precautions to Consider

Carcinogenicity/Mutagenicity

Secondary malignancies are potential delayed effects of many antineoplastic agents, although it is not clear whether the effect is related to their mutagenic or immunosuppressive action. The effect of dose and duration of therapy is also unknown, although risk seems to increase with long-term use. Although information is limited, available data seem to indicate that the carcinogenic risk is greatest with the alkylating agents.

Mechlorethamine has been associated with an increased risk of development of secondary carcinomas in animals and humans.

Pregnancy/Reproduction

Fertility—Gonadal suppression, resulting in amenorrhea or azoospermia, may occur in patients taking antineoplastic therapy, especially with the alkylating agents. In general, these effects appear to be related to dose and length of therapy and may be irreversible. Prediction of the degree of testicular or ovarian function impairment is complicated by the common use of combinations of several antineoplastics, which makes it difficult to assess the effects of individual agents.

Mechlorethamine causes testicular atrophy and interferes with spermatogenesis.

Pregnancy—Although several successful pregnancies have been reported, there is evidence that mechlorethamine is teratogenic, especially when administered early in pregnancy.

First trimester: It is usually recommended that use of antineoplastics, especially combination chemotherapy, be avoided whenever possible, especially during the first trimester. Although information is limited because of the relatively few instances of antineoplastic administration during pregnancy, the mutagenic, teratogenic, and carcinogenic potential of these medications must be considered.

Other hazards to the fetus include adverse reactions seen in adults.

In general, use of a contraceptive is recommended during cytotoxic drug therapy.

FDA Pregnancy Category D.

Breast-feeding

Although very little information is available regarding distribution of antineoplastic agents into breast milk, breast-feeding is not recommended while mechlorethamine is being administered because of the risks to the infant (adverse effects, mutagenicity, carcinogenicity). It is not known whether mechlorethamine is distributed into breast milk.

Pediatrics

Appropriate studies on the relationship of age to the effects of mechlorethamine have not been performed in the pediatric population. However, pediatrics-specific problems that would limit the usefulness of this medication in children are not expected.

Geriatrics

No information is available on the relationship of age to the effects of mechlorethamine in geriatric patients.

Dental

The bone marrow depressant effects of mechlorethamine may result in an increased incidence of microbial infection, delayed healing, and gingival bleeding. Dental work, whenever possible, should be completed prior to initiation of therapy or deferred until blood counts have returned to normal. Patients should be instructed in proper oral hygiene during treatment, including caution in use of regular toothbrushes, dental floss, and toothpicks.

Mechlorethamine may also rarely cause stomatitis associated with considerable discomfort.

Drug interactions and/or related problems

The following drug interactions and/or related problems have been selected on the basis of their potential clinical significance (possible mechanism in parentheses where appropriate)—not necessarily inclusive (» = major clinical significance):

Note: Combinations containing any of the following medications, depending on the amount present, may also interact with this medication.

Allopurinol or
Colchicine or
» Probenecid or
» Sulfinpyrazone
(mechlorethamine may raise the concentration of blood uric acid; dosage adjustment of antigout agents may be necessary to control hyperuricemia and gout; allopurinol may be preferred to prevent or reverse mechlorethamine-induced hyperuricemia because of risk of uric acid nephropathy with uricosuric antigout agents)

Blood dyscrasia-causing medications (see *Appendix II*)
(leukopenic and/or thrombocytopenic effects of mechlorethamine may be increased with concurrent or recent therapy if these medications cause the same effects; dosage adjustment of mechlorethamine, if necessary, should be based on blood counts)

» Bone marrow depressants, other (see *Appendix II*) or
Radiation therapy
(additive bone marrow depression may occur; dosage reduction may be required when two or more bone marrow depressants, including radiation, are used concurrently or consecutively)

Vaccines, killed virus
(because normal defense mechanisms may be suppressed by mechlorethamine therapy, the patient's antibody response to the vaccine may be decreased. The interval between discontinuation of medications that cause immunosuppression and restoration of the patient's ability to respond to the vaccine depends on the intensity and type of immunosuppression-causing medication used, the underlying disease, and other factors; estimates vary from 3 months to 1 year)

» Vaccines, live virus
(because normal defense mechanisms may be suppressed by mechlorethamine therapy, concurrent use with a live virus vaccine may potentiate the replication of the vaccine virus, may increase the side/adverse effects of the vaccine virus, and/or may decrease the patient's antibody response to the vaccine; immunization of these patients should be undertaken only with extreme caution after careful review of the patient's hematologic status and only with the knowledge and consent of the physician managing the mechlorethamine therapy. The interval between discontinuation of medications that cause immunosuppression and restoration of the patient's ability to respond to the vaccine depends on the intensity and type of immunosuppression-causing medication used, the underlying disease, and other factors; estimates vary from 3 months to 1 year. Immunization with oral poliovirus vaccine should also be postponed in persons in close contact with the patient, especially family members)

Laboratory value alterations

The following have been selected on the basis of their potential clinical significance (possible effect in parentheses where appropriate)—not necessarily inclusive (» = major clinical significance).

With physiology/laboratory test values
Isocitric acid dehydrogenase (ICD)
(values may be increased, indicating hepatotoxicity)

Cholinesterase
(plasma values may be decreased)

Uric acid
(concentrations in blood and urine may be increased)

Medical considerations/Contraindications

The medical considerations/contraindications included have been selected on the basis of their potential clinical significance (reasons given in parentheses where appropriate)—not necessarily inclusive (» = major clinical significance).

Risk-benefit should be considered when the following medical problems exist:

» Bone marrow depression

» Chickenpox, existing or recent (including recent exposure) or
» Herpes zoster
(risk of severe generalized disease)

Gout, history of or
Urate renal stones, history of
(risk of hyperuricemia)

» Infection

Sensitivity to mechlorethamine

» Tumor cell infiltration of bone marrow

» Caution should be used also in patients who have had previous cytotoxic drug therapy or radiation therapy.

Patient monitoring

The following are especially important in patient monitoring (other tests may be warranted in some patients, depending on condition; » = major clinical significance):

Alanine aminotransferase (ALT [SGPT]) values, serum and
Aspartate aminotransferase (AST [SGOT]) values, serum and
Lactate dehydrogenase (LDH) values, serum
(determinations recommended prior to initiation of therapy and at periodic intervals during therapy; frequency varies according to clinical state, agent, dose, and other agents being used concurrently)

» Audiometric testing
(may be recommended at periodic intervals in patients receiving high doses)

» Hematocrit or hemoglobin and
» Leukocyte count, total and, if appropriate, differential and
» Platelet count
(determinations recommended prior to initiation of therapy and at periodic intervals during therapy; frequency varies according to clinical state, agent, dose, and other agents being used concurrently)

Bilirubin concentrations, serum and
Uric acid concentrations, serum
(determinations recommended prior to initiation of therapy and at periodic intervals during therapy; frequency varies according to clinical state, agent, dose, and other agents being used concurrently)

X-ray examination
(recommended after intracavitary administration to detect reaccumulation of fluid)

Side/Adverse Effects

Note: Many "side effects" of antineoplastic therapy are unavoidable and represent the medication's pharmacologic action. Some of these (for example, leukopenia and thrombocytopenia) are actually used as parameters to aid in individual dosage titration.

Systemic effects are unpredictable following intracavitary administration.

Pain after intracavitary administration and nausea, vomiting, and diarrhea after intraperitoneal injection occur frequently and may persist for 2 or 3 days.

The following side/adverse effects have been selected on the basis of their potential clinical significance (possible cause in parentheses where appropriate)—not necessarily inclusive:

Those indicating need for medical attention

Incidence more frequent

Gonadal suppression (missing menstrual periods); ***idiosyncratic reaction or precipitation of herpes zoster*** (painful rash); ***leukopenia, immunosuppression, or infection*** (fever or chills, cough or hoarseness, lower back or side pain, painful or difficult urination)—usually asymptomatic; ***thrombocytopenia*** (unusual bleeding or bruising; black, tarry stools; blood in urine or stools; pinpoint red spots on skin)—usually asymptomatic

Note: *Lymphocytopenia* usually occurs within 24 hours after the first dose. Significant granulocytopenia usually occurs within 6 to 8 days and lasts 10 days to 3 weeks.

Incidence more frequent with high doses or regional perfusion

Ototoxicity (dizziness; ringing in the ears; loss of hearing)

Incidence less frequent

Hyperuricemia or uric acid nephropathy (joint pain; lower back or side pain; swelling of feet or lower legs); ***thrombosis, thrombophlebitis, or extravasation*** (pain or redness at the site of injection)

Note: *Hyperuricemia or uric acid nephropathy* occurs most commonly during initial treatment of patients with leukemia or lymphoma, as a result of rapid cell breakdown that leads to elevated serum uric acid concentrations.

Pain or redness at the site of injection may persist for 4 to 6 weeks.

Incidence rare

Allergic reaction (shortness of breath, itching, wheezing); ***hepatotoxicity*** (yellow eyes or skin); ***peptic ulcer*** (black, tarry stools); ***peripheral neuropathy*** (numbness, tingling, or burning of fingers, toes, or face)

Note: An *allergic reaction* may also occur in patients previously treated with topical mechlorethamine.

Those indicating need for medical attention only if they continue or are bothersome

Incidence more frequent

Nausea and vomiting

Note: *Nausea and vomiting* occur in 90% of patients, usually within 1 to 3 hours of a dose; vomiting usually subsides within 8 hours, while nausea may persist for 24 hours.

Incidence less frequent

Diarrhea; loss of appetite; metallic taste; neurotoxicity (confusion; drowsiness; headache)—especially with high doses; ***weakness***

Those not indicating need for medical attention

Incidence less frequent

Loss of hair

Those indicating the need for medical attention if they occur after medication is discontinued

Bone marrow depression (black, tarry stools; blood in urine or stools; cough or hoarseness; fever or chills; lower back or side pain; painful or difficult urination; pinpoint red spots on skin; unusual bleeding or bruising)

Patient Consultation

As an aid to patient consultation, refer to *Advice for the Patient, Mechlorethamine (Systemic).*

In providing consultation, consider emphasizing the following selected information (» = major clinical significance):

Before using this medication

» Conditions affecting use, especially:

Sensitivity to mechlorethamine

Pregnancy—Use not recommended because of mutagenic, teratogenic, and carcinogenic potential; advisability of using contraception; telling physician immediately if pregnancy is suspected

Breast-feeding—Not recommended because of risk of serious side effects

Other medications, especially other bone marrow depressants, probenecid, sulfinpyrazone, or other cytotoxic drug or radiation therapy

Other medical problems, especially chickenpox, herpes zoster, or infection

Proper use of this medication

Caution in taking combination therapy; taking each medication at the right time

Importance of ample fluid intake and subsequent increase in urine output to aid in excretion of uric acid

Frequency of nausea, vomiting, and loss of appetite; importance of continuing medication despite stomach upset

» Proper dosing

Precautions while using this medication

» Importance of close monitoring by the physician

» Avoiding immunizations unless approved by physician; other persons in patient's household should avoid immunizations with oral poliovirus vaccine; avoiding persons who have taken oral poliovirus vaccine or wearing a protective mask that covers nose and mouth

Caution if bone marrow depression occurs:

» Avoiding exposure to persons with infections, especially during periods of low blood counts; checking with physician immediately if fever or chills, cough or hoarseness, lower back or side pain, or painful or difficult urination occurs

» Checking with physician immediately if unusual bleeding or bruising; black, tarry stools; blood in urine or stools; or pinpoint red spots on skin occur

Caution in use of regular toothbrush, dental floss, or toothpick; physician, dentist, or nurse may suggest alternatives; checking with physician before having dental work done

Not touching eyes or inside of nose unless hands are washed immediately before

Using caution to avoid accidental cuts with use of sharp objects such as safety razor or fingernail or toenail cutters

Avoiding contact sports or other situations where bruising or injury could occur

» Possibility of local tissue injury and scarring if infiltration of intravenous solution occurs; telling doctor or nurse right away about redness, pain, or swelling at injection site

Side/adverse effects

Importance of discussing possible effects, including cancer, with physician

Signs of potential side effects, especially gonadal suppression, idiosyncratic reaction, precipitation of herpes zoster, leukopenia, immunosuppression, infection, thrombocytopenia, ototoxicity, hyperuricemia, uric acid nephropathy, thrombosis, thrombophlebitis, extravasation, allergic reaction, hepatotoxicity, peptic ulcer, and peripheral neuropathy

Physician or nurse can help in dealing with side effects

Possibility of hair loss; normal hair growth should return after treatment has ended

General Dosing Information

For intravenous and intracavitary use

Patients receiving mechlorethamine should be under supervision of a physician experienced in cancer chemotherapy or immunosuppressive therapy.

A variety of dosage schedules, regimens, and routes of administration of mechlorethamine, alone or in combination with other antitumor agents, are used. The prescriber may consult the medical literature as well as the manufacturer's literature in choosing a specific dosage.

Dosage must be adjusted to meet the individual requirements of each patient, based on clinical response and appearance or severity of toxicity.

Although dosages are based on the patient's actual weight, use of estimated lean body mass (dry weight) is recommended in obese patients or those with weight gain due to edema, ascites, or other abnormal fluid retention.

Because mechlorethamine may contribute to the development of amyloidosis, it is recommended that the medication be used only if foci of acute and chronic suppurative inflammation are absent.

Severity of nausea and vomiting may be reduced in some patients by administration of antiemetics, in addition to sedatives such as barbiturates or chlorpromazine, prior to dosing.

Administration of mechlorethamine at night is recommended if sedation for side effects is required.

Development of uric acid nephropathy in patients with leukemia or lymphoma may be prevented by adequate oral hydration and, in some cases, administration of allopurinol. Alkalinization of urine may be necessary if serum uric acid concentrations are elevated.

It is recommended that mechlorethamine therapy be withdrawn if leukocyte (particularly granulocyte) or platelet levels fall markedly. Therapy may be resumed at a lower dosage when leukocyte and platelet counts return to satisfactory levels.

Special precautions are recommended in patients who develop thrombocytopenia as a result of administration of mechlorethamine. These may include extreme care in performing invasive procedures; regular inspection of intravenous sites, skin (including perirectal area), and mucous membrane surfaces for signs of bleeding or bruising; limiting frequency of venipuncture and avoiding intramuscular injections; testing urine, emesis, stool, and secretions for occult blood; care in use of regular toothbrushes, dental floss, toothpicks, safety razors, and fingernail and toenail cutters; avoiding constipation; and using caution to prevent falls and other injuries. Such patients should avoid alcohol and aspirin intake because of the risk of gastrointestinal bleeding. Platelet transfusions may be required.

Patients who develop leukopenia should be observed carefully for signs of infection. Antibiotic support may be required. In neutropenic patients who develop fever, broad-spectrum antibiotic coverage should be initiated empirically, pending bacterial cultures and appropriate diagnostic tests.

For intravenous use only

Mechlorethamine may be administered by intravenous push, although injection into the tubing of a running intravenous infusion is preferred to reduce the risk of local toxicity. Administration by intravenous infusion is not recommended because of deactivation of the medication by the solution. The injection should be completed within a few minutes.

Avoid high concentration and prolonged contact with the medication, especially in cases of elevated pressure in the antebrachial vein.

If extravasation occurs, the reaction may be minimized by prompt infiltration of the area with sterile isotonic sodium thiosulfate (0.125 Molar) or 1% lidocaine and application of an ice compress for 6 to 12 hours.

For intracavitary use only

Administration of mechlorethamine by the intracavitary route is not recommended in patients receiving other systemic bone marrow depressants concurrently.

Prior removal of excess fluid (paracentesis) improves contact of the medication with the peritoneal and pleural linings.

Prior administration of analgesics usually is required to offset pain of treatment.

For intrapleural or intrapericardial injection, a thoracentesis needle is used. For intraperitoneal injection, mechlorethamine is given through a rubber catheter inserted into the trocar used for paracentesis or through an 18-gauge needle inserted at another site. Slow injection with frequent aspiration is recommended to prevent or detect extravasation and to ensure adequate dissemination of the medication.

Changing the position of the patient (prone, supine, right side, left side, knee-chest) every 5 to 10 minutes for an hour ensures uniform distribution of the medication in the serous cavity.

Remaining fluid is removed by paracentesis 24 to 36 hours later.

Intrapleural administration may produce increased pleural fluid as a result of pleural irritation by mechlorethamine.

Safety considerations for handling this medication

There is limited but increasing evidence and concern that personnel involved in preparation and administration of parenteral antineoplastics may be at some risk because of the potential mutagenicity, teratogenicity, and/or carcinogenicity of these agents, although the actual risk is unknown. USP advisory panels recommend cautious handling both in preparation and disposal of antineoplastic agents. Precautions that have been suggested include:

- Use of a biological containment cabinet during reconstitution and dilution of parenteral medications and wearing of disposable surgical gloves and masks.
- Use of proper technique to prevent contamination of the medication, work area, and operator during transfer between containers (including proper training of personnel in this technique).
- Cautious and proper disposal of needles, syringes, vials, ampuls, and unused medication.

A number of medical centers have developed detailed guidelines for handling of antineoplastic agents.

Combination chemotherapy

Mechlorethamine may be used in combination with other agents in various regimens. As a result, incidence and/or severity of side effects may be altered and different dosages (usually reduced) may be used. For example, mechlorethamine is part of the following chemotherapeutic combination (a commonly used acronym is in parentheses):
—mechlorethamine, vincristine, procarbazine, and prednisone (MOPP).

For specific dosages and schedules, consult the literature. For information regarding each agent, consult the individual monographs.

Parenteral Dosage Forms

MECHLORETHAMINE HYDROCHLORIDE FOR INJECTION USP

Usual adult and adolescent dose

Lymphomas, Hodgkin's or
Lymphomas, non-Hodgkin's or
Mycosis fungoides—
Intravenous, total dose of 400 mcg (0.4 mg) per kg of body weight as a single dose or divided into two or four successive daily doses.

Malignant effusions, pericardial or
Malignant effusions, peritoneal or
Malignant effusions, pleural—
Intracavitary, 400 mcg (0.4 mg) per kg of body weight, or 200 mcg (0.2 mg) per kg of body weight by the intrapericardial route.

Note: Total dosage in patients who have received prior cytotoxic drug therapy or radiation therapy should not exceed 200 to 300 mcg (0.2 to 0.3 mg) per kg of body weight.

Usual adult prescribing limits

Total intravenous dose exceeding 400 mcg (0.4 mg) per kg of body weight may result in severe bone marrow depression, bleeding, sepsis, and death, although 800 mcg (0.8 mg) of mechlorethamine per kg of body weight, as a single agent, is tolerated in some patients.

Usual pediatric dose

See *Usual adult and adolescent dose*.

Strength(s) usually available

U.S.—
10 mg (Rx) [*Mustargen*].

Canada—
10 mg (Rx) [*Mustargen*].

Packaging and storage

Store below 40 °C (104 °F), preferably between 15 and 30 °C (59 and 86 °F), unless otherwise specified by manufacturer. Protect from light and humidity.

Preparation of dosage form

Mechlorethamine Hydrochloride for Injection USP is reconstituted for intravenous use by adding 10 mL of sterile water for injection or 0.9% sodium chloride injection to the vial and, with the needle still in the rubber stopper, shaking to dissolve, producing a clear, colorless solution containing 1 mg of mechlorethamine hydrochloride per mL.

Mechlorethamine Hydrochloride for Injection USP is reconstituted for intracavitary use by adding 10 mL of sterile water for injection or 0.9% sodium chloride injection to the vial (50 to 100 mL of 0.9% sodium chloride injection has also been used) and shaking to dissolve.

Stability

Solution should be freshly reconstituted immediately (less than 15 minutes) prior to each dose. Any unused portion should be discarded.

Note

Do not use if solution is discolored or if droplets of water appear in the vial.

Avoid inhalation of powder or vapors. If accidental contact with skin or mucous membranes occurs, immediately and thoroughly irrigate the affected part with a large volume of water for at least 15 minutes, followed by 2% sodium thiosulfate solution; if eye contact occurs, irrigation is performed with 0.9% sodium chloride solution or a balanced salt ophthalmic irrigating solution.

Any equipment used for administration of mechlorethamine (rubber gloves, tubing, glassware, etc.) should be neutralized immediately after use by soaking in an aqueous solution containing equal volumes of 5% sodium thiosulfate and 5% sodium bicarbonate for 45 minutes, washing away excess reagents and reaction products with water. Unused solution is neutralized by adding an equal volume of the sodium thiosulfate–bicarbonate solution and allowing the mixture to stand for 45 minutes. Vials that have contained mechlorethamine should be treated in the same way before disposal.

Revised: 08/14/2000

MECLIZINE Systemic

INN: Meclozine

BAN: Meclozine

VA CLASSIFICATION (Primary/Secondary): GA609/CN550

Commonly used brand name(s): *Antivert; Antivert/25; Antivert/50; Bonamine; Bonine; Dramamine II; Meclicot; Medivert.*

Note: For a listing of dosage forms and brand names by country availability, see *Dosage Forms* section(s).

Category

Antiemetic; antivertigo agent.

Indications

Note: Bracketed information in the *Indications* section refers to uses that are not included in U.S. product labeling.

Accepted

Motion sickness (prophylaxis and treatment)—Meclizine is indicated for the prophylaxis and treatment of nausea, vomiting, and dizziness associated with motion sickness.

Vertigo (prophylaxis and treatment)—The U.S. Food and Drug Administration (FDA) has classified meclizine as possibly effective in the management of vertigo associated with diseases affecting the vestibular system, such as labyrinthitis and Meniere's disease. This classification requires the submission of adequate and well-controlled studies to provide substantial evidence of effectiveness.

[Nausea and vomiting, radiotherapy-induced (prophylaxis and treatment)]—Meclizine is indicated for the prophylaxis and treatment of nausea, vomiting, and dizziness associated with radiotherapy.

Pharmacology/Pharmacokinetics

Physicochemical characteristics

Molecular weight—481.90.

Mechanism of action/Effect

Antiemetic; antivertigo agent—The mechanism by which meclizine exerts its antiemetic, anti-motion sickness, and antivertigo effects is not precisely known but may be related to its central anticholinergic actions. It diminishes vestibular stimulation and depresses labyrinthine function. An action on the medullary chemoreceptive trigger zone may also be involved in the antiemetic effect.

Other actions/effects

Meclizine also has antihistaminic, anticholinergic, and central nervous system (CNS) depressant effects.

Half-life

6 hours.

Onset of action

1 hour.

Duration of action

8 to 24 hours.

Precautions to Consider

Pregnancy/Reproduction

Pregnancy—Epidemiological studies in pregnant women have not shown that meclizine causes an increase in the risk of fetal abnormalities.

Studies in rats have shown that meclizine causes cleft palate when given in doses corresponding to 25 to 50 times the recommended human dose.

FDA Pregnancy Category B.

Breast-feeding

Meclizine may be distributed into breast milk. However, problems in humans have not been documented.

Because of its anticholinergic actions, meclizine may inhibit lactation.

Pediatrics

No information is available on the relationship of age to the effects of meclizine in pediatric patients. However, it is known that pediatric patients exhibit increased sensitivity to anticholinergic agents, which are related pharmacologically to meclizine.

Geriatrics

No information is available on the relationship of age to the effects of meclizine in geriatric patients. However, it is known that geriatric patients exhibit increased sensitivity to anticholinergic agents, which are related pharmacologically to meclizine. Therefore, constipation, dryness of mouth, and urinary retention (especially in males) are more likely to occur in the elderly.

Dental

Prolonged use of meclizine may decrease or inhibit salivary flow, thus contributing to the development of caries, periodontal disease, oral candidiasis, and discomfort.

Drug interactions and/or related problems

The following drug interactions and/or related problems have been selected on the basis of their potential clinical significance (possible mechanism in parentheses where appropriate)—not necessarily inclusive (» = major clinical significance):

Note: Combinations containing any of the following medications, depending on the amount present, may also interact with this medication.

» Alcohol or
» CNS depression-producing medications, other (see *Appendix II*)
(concurrent use may potentiate the CNS depressant effects of either these medications or meclizine)

Anticholinergics or other medications with anticholinergic activity (see *Appendix II*)
(concurrent use with meclizine may potentiate anticholinergic effects)

Apomorphine
(prior administration of meclizine may decrease the emetic response to apomorphine)

Laboratory value alterations

The following have been selected on the basis of their potential clinical significance (possible effect in parentheses where appropriate)—not necessarily inclusive (» = major clinical significance).

With diagnostic test results
Skin tests using allergen extracts
(may inhibit the cutaneous histamine response, thus producing false-negative results; it is recommended that meclizine be discontinued at least 72 hours before testing begins)

Medical considerations/Contraindications

The medical considerations/contraindications included have been selected on the basis of their potential clinical significance (reasons given in parentheses where appropriate)—not necessarily inclusive (» = major clinical significance).

Risk-benefit should be considered when the following medical problems exist:

Bladder neck obstruction or
Prostatic hyperplasia, symptomatic
(anticholinergic effects of meclizine may precipitate urinary retention)

Gastroduodenal obstruction
(decrease in motility and tone may occur, aggravating obstruction and gastric retention)

Glaucoma, angle-closure, predisposition to
(increased intraocular pressure may precipitate an acute attack of angle-closure glaucoma)

Pulmonary disease, chronic obstructive
(reduction in bronchial secretion may cause inspissation and formation of bronchial plugs)

Sensitivity to meclizine

Side/Adverse Effects

The following side/adverse effects have been selected on the basis of their potential clinical significance (possible signs and symptoms in parentheses where appropriate)—not necessarily inclusive:

Those indicating need for medical attention only if they continue or are bothersome

Incidence more frequent
Drowsiness

Incidence less frequent or rare
Blurred vision; dryness of mouth, nose, and throat

Overdose

For specific information on the agents used in the management of meclizine overdose, see:

- *Charcoal, Activated (Oral-Local)* monograph;
- *Diazepam* in *Benzodiazepines (Systemic)* monograph;
- *Ipecac (Oral-Local)* monograph;
- *Norepinephrine* and/or *Phenylephrine* in *Sympathomimetic Agents—Cardiovascular Use (Parenteral-Systemic)* monograph;
- *Physostigmine (Systemic)*monograph.

For more information on the management of overdose or unintentional ingestion, **contact a Poison Control Center** (see *Poison Control Center Listing*).

Clinical effects of overdose

The following effects have been selected on the basis of their potential clinical significance (possible signs and symptoms in parentheses where appropriate)—not necessarily inclusive:

CNS depression, including drowsiness and coma; hypotension—especially in the elderly; ***anticholinergic effects, including blurred vision, constipation, or dryness of mouth, nose, or throat***—especially in children; ***CNS stimulation, including hallucinations, insomnia (trouble in sleeping), and seizures***—especially in children

Treatment of overdose

There is no specific antidote for meclizine overdose. Treatment is primarily symptomatic and supportive.

To decrease absorption—If ingestion is recent (i.e., within 1 hour), induce emesis with syrup of ipecac or perform gastric lavage. Activated charcoal may be used.

Specific treatment—Hypotension may be corrected with vasopressors such as norepinephrine or phenylephrine; epinephrine should not be used because it may lower blood pressure further. Physostigmine may be used to counteract the anticholinergic effects. Intravenous diazepam may be used to treat seizures that do not respond to physostigmine.

Supportive care—The patient should be kept calm to minimize excitement. Patients in whom intentional overdose is confirmed or suspected should be referred for psychiatric consultation.

Patient Consultation

As an aid to patient consultation, refer to *Advice for the Patient, Meclizine/Buclizine/Cyclizine (Systemic)*.

In providing consultation, consider emphasizing the following selected information (» = major clinical significance):

Before using this medication

» Conditions affecting use, especially:
- Sensitivity to meclizine
- Pregnancy—No increase in fetal abnormalities in human studies; animal studies have shown meclizine to cause cleft palate at doses above recommended human dose
- Breast-feeding—May be distributed into breast milk; may inhibit lactation due to anticholinergic effects
- Use in children—Possible increased susceptibility to anticholinergic side effects
- Use in the elderly—Possible increased susceptibility to anticholinergic side effects
- Other medications, especially alcohol and other CNS depressants

Proper use of this medication

Not taking more medication than the amount recommended

» Proper dosing

Missed dose (if on a regular dosing regimen): Taking as soon as possible; not taking if almost time for next dose; not doubling doses

» Proper storage

Precautions while using this medication

Possible interference with skin tests using allergens; need to inform physician of use of this medication

» Avoiding use of alcohol or other CNS depressants

» Caution if drowsiness occurs

Possible dryness of mouth; using sugarless candy or gum, ice, or saliva substitute for relief; checking with physician or dentist if dry mouth continues for more than 2 weeks

General Dosing Information

For prophylaxis of motion sickness, this medication should be taken at least 1 hour before exposure to conditions that may precipitate motion sickness.

Oral Dosage Forms

Note: Bracketed uses in the *Dosage Forms* section refer to categories of use and/or indications that are not included in U.S. product labeling.

MECLIZINE HYDROCHLORIDE CAPSULES

Usual adult and adolescent dose

Motion sickness (prophylaxis and treatment)—Oral, 25 to 50 mg one hour before travel. Dose may be repeated every twenty-four hours as needed.

Vertigo (prophylaxis and treatment)—Oral, 25 to 100 mg a day as needed, in divided doses.

[Nausea and vomiting, radiotherapy-induced (prophylaxis and treatment)]—Oral, 50 mg two to twelve hours prior to radiotherapy.

Usual pediatric dose

Antiemetic or
Antivertigo agent—
- Children up to 12 years of age: Use is not recommended unless directed by a physician.
- Children 12 years of age or older: See *Usual adult and adolescent dose.*

Usual geriatric dose

See *Usual adult and adolescent dose.*

Note: Geriatric patients may be more sensitive to the effects of the usual adult dose.

Strength(s) usually available

U.S.—
Not commercially available.

Canada—
Not commercially available.

Packaging and storage

Store below 40 °C (104 °F), preferably between 15 and 30 °C (59 and 86 °F), in a well-closed container, unless otherwise specified by manufacturer.

Auxiliary labeling

- May cause drowsiness.
- Avoid alcoholic beverages.

MECLIZINE HYDROCHLORIDE TABLETS USP

Usual adult and adolescent dose

See *Meclizine Hydrochloride Capsules.*

Usual pediatric dose

See *Meclizine Hydrochloride Capsules.*

Usual geriatric dose

See *Meclizine Hydrochloride Capsules.*

Strength(s) usually available

U.S.—
- 12.5 mg (Rx) [*Antivert; Meclicot;* GENERIC].
- 25 mg [*Antivert/25; Dramamine II; Meclicot;* GENERIC].
- 30 mg (Rx) [*Medivert*].
- 50 mg (Rx) [*Antivert/50* (scored); GENERIC].

Canada—
Not commercially available.

Packaging and storage

Store below 40 °C (104 °F), preferably between 15 and 30 °C (59 and 86 °F), unless otherwise specified by manufacturer. Store in a well-closed container.

Auxiliary labeling

- May cause drowsiness.
- Avoid alcoholic beverages.

MECLIZINE HYDROCHLORIDE TABLETS (CHEWABLE) USP

Usual adult and adolescent dose

See *Meclizine Hydrochloride Capsules.*

Usual pediatric dose

See *Meclizine Hydrochloride Capsules.*

Usual geriatric dose

See *Meclizine Hydrochloride Capsules.*

Strength(s) usually available

U.S.—
- 25 mg [*Bonine;* GENERIC].

Canada—
- 25 mg (Rx) [*Bonamine* (scored; fruit-flavored)].

Packaging and storage

Store between 15 and 30 °C (59 and 86 °F), unless otherwise specified by manufacturer. Store in a well-closed container.

Auxiliary labeling

- May cause drowsiness.
- Avoid alcoholic beverages.
- May be chewed, swallowed whole, or allowed to dissolve in the mouth.

Revised: 02/24/1999

MECLOCYCLINE—See *Tetracyclines (Topical)*

MECLOFENAMATE—See *Anti-inflammatory Drugs, Nonsteroidal (Systemic)*

MEDROGESTONE—See *Progestins (Systemic)*

MEDROXYPROGESTERONE—See *Progestins (Systemic)*

MEDROXYPROGESTERONE AND ESTRADIOL Systemic

VA CLASSIFICATION (Primary): HS104

Commonly used brand name(s): *Lunelle*.

Note: For a listing of dosage forms and brand names by country availability, see *Dosage Forms* section(s).

Category

Contraceptive, systemic.

Indications

Accepted

Pregnancy, prevention of—The combination of estradiol and medroxyprogesterone in a monthly contraceptive injection is indicated for the prevention of pregnancy.

Pharmacology/Pharmacokinetics

Physicochemical characteristics

Molecular weight—
Medroxyprogesterone acetate: 386.53.
Estradiol cypionate: 396.57.

Mechanism of action/Effect

The combination of medroxyprogesterone and estradiol inhibits the secretion of gonadotropins, which prevents follicular maturation and ovulation.

Other possible mechanisms include thickening and reduction in volume of cervical mucus, which decreases sperm penetration and also endometrial thinning which leads to a reduction in the likelihood of implantation.

Absorption

Medroxyprogesterone and estradiol absorption is prolonged after an intramuscular injection

Protein binding

Medroxyprogesterone acetate—High (86%); Binds primarily to serum albumin, and no binding occurs with sex-hormone-binding globulin (SHBG)

Estradiol—High (97%); Binds primarily to sex-hormone-binding globulin (SHBG) and albumin. Also binds to α-1-glycoproteins and transcortin.

Biotransformation

Medroxyprogesterone acetate—Metabolism primarily involves ring A or side-chain reductions, loss of the acetyl group, hydroxylation in the 2-, 6-, and 21- positions or a combination of the positions; result is numerous derivatives.

Estradiol cypionate—Undergoes ester hydrolysis and releases the parent, active compound 17β-estradiol (E_2). E_2 is primarily metabolized into estrone and estriol, which are metabolized into their sulfate and glucuronide forms.

Half-life

Medroxyprogesterone acetate—Elimination: 15 days

17β-estradiol (E_2)—Elimination: 7-8 days

Time to peak concentration

Medroxyprogesterone acetate—1 to 10 days post injection

17β-estradiol (E_2)—1 to 7 days post injection

Peak serum concentration

Medroxyprogesterone acetate—1.25 ng/mL (mean C_{max})

17β-estradiol (E_2)—0.25 ng/mL (mean C_{max})

Precautions to Consider

Carcinogenicity

No long term studies have been done with the combination of medroxyprogesterone and estradiol to evaluate the risk of carcinoma of the female reproductive organs.

Numerous epidemiological studies have been done on the incidence of breast, endometrial, ovarian, and cervical cancer in women using oral contraceptives. In spite of the many studies that have been done on the relationship between oral contraceptive use and breast and cervical cancers, a cause and effect relationship has not been established.

Tumorigenicity

Benign hepatic adenomas are associated with oral contraceptive use, although the incidence of these is rare in the United States. The risk increases after 4 or more years of use. These benign hepatic adenomas may rupture and may cause death through intra-abdominal hemorrhage.

Mutagenicity

Clinical studies do not suggest an increased risk of mutagenicity or teratogenicity, including any development of fetal cardiac anormalies and limb reduction defects, when oral contraceptives are inadvertently taken during early pregnancy.

Pregnancy/Reproduction

Fertility—Return of ovulation and fertility was observed 63 to 112 days post treatment in 11 out of the 14 women participating in a study who received three monthly injections.

Another study showed that 52% of the women ovulated during the first post-treatment month, and 72% during the second post-treatment month.

Pregnancy—The use of the combination of medroxyprogesterone and estradiol is contraindicated during pregnancy.

No long term studies have been done with the combination of medroxyprogesterone and estradiol, but studies have been done with combination oral contraceptives. These studies have shown that combination oral contraceptives do not appear to increase the risk of birth defects when they are used before pregnancy. Studies have also shown that oral contraceptives, when taken inadvertently during early pregnancy, do not seem to have a teratogenic effect.

Unexpected pregnancies in women who receive medroxyprogesterone and estradiol are uncommon, and have not shown congenital malformations or other adverse events.

Any patient who has missed two consecutive menstrual periods or if the injection interval was not followed the patient should not be administered another injection until it has been determined that there is no possibility of pregnancy.

FDA Pregnancy Category X.

Breast-feeding

It is not known whether medroxyprogesterone and estradiol combination is distributed into the breast milk. However, nursing mothers who have been administered estrogen have shown to have a decreased quantity and quality of breast milk. Small amounts of combined hormonal contraceptive steroids have been detected in the breast milk of nursing mothers and a few adverse effects on their children have been reported, such as jaundice and breast enlargement.

Long term follow up of children whose mothers used a combined hormonal contraceptive while breast feeding have shown no deleterious effects.

It is recommended that nursing mothers should not start taking combined hormonal contraceptives until six weeks post partum.

Pediatrics

No information is available on the relationship of age to the effects of the combination of medroxyprogesterone and estradiol in the pediatric population. Safety and efficacy have not been established.

Adolescents

Although appropriate studies on the relationship of age to the effects of medroxyprogesterone and estradiol combination have not been performed in the adolescent population, safety and efficacy are expected to be the same for postpubertal adolescents under 16 years of age and users older than 16 years. Use of medroxyprogesterone and estradiol is not indicated prior to menarche.

Geriatrics

No information is available on the relationship of age to the effects of the combination of medroxyprogesterone and estradiol in geriatric patients. Safety and efficacy have not been established.

Drug interactions and/or related problems

The following drug interactions and/or related problems have been selected on the basis of their potential clinical significance (possible mechanism in parentheses where appropriate)—not necessarily inclusive (» = major clinical significance):

Note: Combinations containing any of the following medications, depending on the amount present, may also interact with this medication.

Acetaminophen or
Ascorbic acid
(concurrent use may increase plasma concentrations of some synthetic estrogens, possibly by the inhibition of conjugation.)

» Aminoglutethamide
(may decrease the serum concentration of medroxyprogesterone thus decreasing contraceptive efficacy)

» Carbamazepine or
» Phenobarbital or
» Phenytoin
(concurrent use has been shown to increase the metabolism of some synthetic estrogens and progestins, which could result in decreased contraceptive efficacy)

Phenylbutazone
(concurrent use may result in a reduction in contraceptive effectiveness and an increased incidence of menstrual irregularities)

» Rifampin
(concurrent use may cause increased metabolism of some synthetic estrogens and progestins, possibly resulting in decreased contraceptive efficacy and menstrual irregularities)

St. John's Wort (hypericum perforatum)
(concurrent use may induce hepatic enzymes (cytochrome P450) and p-glycoprotein transporter and may reduce effectiveness and may cause breakthrough bleeding)

Note: Combined hormonal contraceptives containing some synthetic estrogens may inhibit the metabolism of other compounds. Increased plasma concentrations of cyclosporine, prednisolone, and theophylline has been reported with concomitant use.

Combined hormonal contraceptives may also induce the conjugation of other compounds. Decreased plasma concentrations of acetaminophen and increased clearance of clofibric acid, morphine, salicylic acid, and temazepam have been noted when these drugs were administered concomitantly.

Laboratory value alterations

The following have been selected on the basis of their potential clinical significance (possible effect in parentheses where appropriate)—not necessarily inclusive (» = major clinical significance).

With diagnostic test results

Endocrine and liver function tests and blood components

Antithrombin 3
(decreased)

Norepinephrine-induced platelet aggregability
(increased)

Clotting factors VII, VIII, IX, and X or
Prothrombin
(increased)

Sex hormone-binding globulin (SHBG), serum or
Thyroid–binding globulin (TBG) or
Triglycerides
(SHBG and TBG are increased by combined hormonal contraceptives. The serum concentrations of total sex steroids and corticoids also increase, but free or biologically active levels remain unchanged. The total thyroid hormone also increases, but free thyroid concentration is unchanged)
(triglycerides may be increased by combined hormonal contraceptives)

Thyroid function tests

Thyroxine (T_4) determinations
(the amount of T_4 that is protein bound, which is measured by column or by radioimmunoassay, elevates because of increased thyroid binding globulin [TBG]; serum free T_4 concentrations are unchanged)

Triiodothyronine (T_3) determinations
(T_3 resin uptake is decreased because of increased TBG)

With physiology/laboratory test values

Folic acid, serum or
Glucose, plasma or serum
(glucose tolerance may be decreased by combined hormonal contraceptives. Serum folate levels may be depressed, which may be clinically significant if a woman becomes pregnant shortly after discontinuing combined hormonal contraceptive therapy)

The following tests may be affected by progestins

Cortisol or
Estradiol or
Pregnanediol or
Progesterone or
Testosterone
(plasma and urinary steroid levels are decreased)

Gonadotropins
(levels may be decreased)

Sex hormone-binding globulin
(concentrations are decreased)

Note: Pathologists should be advised of combined hormonal contraceptive therapy when relevant tissue samples are submitted.

Medical considerations/Contraindications

The medical considerations/contraindications included have been selected on the basis of their potential clinical significance (reasons given in parentheses where appropriate)—not necessarily inclusive (» = major clinical significance).

Except under special circumstances, this medication should not be used when the following medical problems exist:

» Carcinoma, breast, known or suspected or
» Carcinoma, endometrium or
» Neoplasia, estrogen–dependent, known or suspected
(use of estrogen–containing contraceptives may worsen condition and should be discontinued)

» Cerebrovascular disease, active or history of or
» Coronary artery disease, active or history of
(oral contraceptives have been shown to increase the risk of cerebrovascular events, and overall the greatest risk is in women who are over 35 years old, hypertensive and smoke)
(an increased risk of myocardial infarction has been associated with the use of oral contraceptives, which is primarily in smokers or women with other underlying risk factors for coronary artery disease such as hypertension, hypercholesterolemia, morbid obesity, and diabetes. A substantially increased incidence of myocardial infarction and mortality rates associated with circulatory disease has been shown in women over 35 years of age or older with smoking)

» Hepatic disease, cholestatic, active, or history of, or
» Hepatic tumors, benign or malignant, or history of
(condition may be worsen and use of estrogen–containing contraceptives should be discontinued)

» Thrombophlebitis, thrombosis, or thromboembolic disorders, active or history of
(increased risk in women using oral contraceptives is well established; if any occur or are suspected then the combination of medroxyprogesterone and estradiol should not be readministered)

» Uterine bleeding, abnormal or undiagnosed
(persistent or severe bleeding should be investigated to rule out the possibility of organic pathology; in the event of amenorrhea pregnancy should be ruled out)

Risk-benefit should be considered when the following medical problems exist:

Diabetes with vascular involvement

Emotional disorders
(patients who become significantly depressed while taking combined hormonal contraceptives should stop the medication and change to another method of contraception to determine if the condition is drug related; women who have a history of depression should be carefully observed; if depression recurs then discontinuation should be considered)

Gallbladder disease, or history of, especially gallstones
(combined hormonal contraceptives may worsen existing disease, and may accelerate the development of this disease in previously asymptomatic women; women with a history of combined hormonal contraceptive-related cholestasis are more likely to have the condition reoccur with subsequent combined hormonal contraceptive use)

Headaches
(focal neurological symptoms or migraine headaches that are recurrent, persistent or severe require evaluation of cause before further injections are given)

Hypersensitivity to any of the ingredients contained in the medroxyprogesterone and estradiol combination injection

» Hypertension
(increase in blood pressure has been observed, and is more likely in older patients with continued use)

Liver dysfunction
(steroid hormones may be poorly metabolized in patients with impaired liver function, resulting in a worsening of the condition; therefore, combined hormonal contraceptives should be discontinued)

Lipid Disorders
(patients being treated for hyperlipidemias should be followed closely as some progestins will elevate LDL levels and may make hyperlipidemias more difficult to control)

Patient monitoring

The following may be especially important in patient monitoring (other tests may be warranted in some patients, depending on condition; » = major clinical significance):

Hepatic function determinations and

» Physical examination
(the physical examination should include special reference to blood pressure, breasts, abdomen and pelvic organs, including cervical cytology, and relevant laboratory tests)

(women with a family history of breast cancer or who have breast nodules should be monitored carefully)

(special attention to rule out malignancy should be given to patients complaining of persistent or recurrent abnormal uterine bleeding)

Lipid profile, serum and
Lipoprotein profile, serum
(needed for patients who are being treated for hyperlipidemias)

Side/Adverse Effects

The following side/adverse effects have been selected on the basis of their potential clinical significance (possible signs and symptoms in parentheses where appropriate)—not necessarily inclusive:

Note: Increased risk of arterial thromboembolism, cerebral hemorrhage or thrombosis, gallbladder disease, hepatic adenomas or benign liver tumors, hypertension, myocardial infarction, pulmonary embolism, and thrombophlebitis has been associated with the use of combined hormonal contraceptives.

Those indicating need for medical attention

Incidence more frequent

Anaphylactic reactions (cough; difficulty swallowing; dizziness; fast heartbeat; hives; itching; puffiness or swelling of the eyelids or around the eyes, face, lips or tongue; shortness of breath; skin rash; tightness in chest; unusual tiredness or weakness; wheezing); ***cholestatic jaundice*** (loss of appetite; nausea; rash; unpleasant breath odor; unusual tiredness or weakness; vomiting of blood; yellow eyes or skin); ***corneal curvature changes***—i.e. steepening; ***edema*** (decreased urination; rapid weight gain; bloating or swelling of face, hands, lower legs, and/or feet)

Those indicating need for medical attention only if they continue or are bothersome

Incidence more frequent

Abdominal pain; acne; alopecia (hair loss; thinning of hair); ***amenorrhea*** (stopping of menstrual bleeding over several months); ***asthenia*** (lack or loss of strength); ***breast tenderness/pain; decreased libido; depression; decrease in lactation when given immediately postpartum; dizziness; dysmenorrhea; emotional lability*** (crying; depersonalization; dysphoria; euphoria; mental depression; paranoia; quick to react or overreact emotionally; rapidly changing moods); ***enlarged abdomen; headache; melasma*** (brown, blotchy spots on exposed skin); ***menorrhagia*** (increased amount of menstrual bleeding occurring at regular monthly periods); ***metrorrhagia*** (normal menstrual bleeding occurring earlier, possibly lasting longer than expected); ***nausea; nervousness; rash, allergic; reduced carbohydrate tolerance; vaginal moniliasis*** (vaginal yeast infection); ***vulvovaginal disorder; weight change***

Overdose

For more information on the management of overdose or unintentional ingestion, **contact a poison control center** (see *Poison Control Center Listing*).

Clinical effects of overdose

The following effects have been selected on the basis of their potential clinical significance (possible signs and symptoms in parentheses where appropriate)—not necessarily inclusive:

Nausea; menstrual irregularities; vaginal bleeding; vomiting

Treatment of overdose

There is no known specific antidote to medroxyprogesterone and estradiol combination. Treatment is generally symptomatic and supportive.

Supportive care—

Patients in whom intentional overdose is confirmed or suspected should be referred for psychiatric consultation.

Patient Consultation

As an aid to patient consultation, refer to *Advice for the Patient, Medroxyprogesterone and Estradiol (Systemic)*.

In providing consultation, consider emphasizing the following selected information (» = major clinical significance):

Before using this medication

» Conditions affecting use, especially:

Hypersensitivity to estrogens or progestins

Pregnancy—Not indicated for use during pregnancy

Breast-feeding—Combined hormonal contraceptives are distributed into breast milk. Not recommended to start taking combined hormonal contraceptives until six weeks postpartum

Use in adolescents—Careful counseling may be required to increase compliance

Other medications, especially aminoglutethamide, carbamazepine, phenobarbital, phenytoin, or rifampin

Other medical problems, especially carcinoma of the reproductive organs or breasts, cerebrovascular disease, coronary artery disease, genital bleeding that is abnormal or undiagnosed, hypertension, and thrombophlebitis, thrombosis, or thromboembolic disorders

Proper use of this medication

» Proper dosing

Missed dose: If dose exceeds 33 days then pregnancy must be ruled out before another injection is given

Precautions while using this medication

» Regular visits to physician every 12 months to check progress and have a physical exam

No protection of transmission of human immunodeficiency virus (HIV) or acquired immunodeficiency syndrome (AIDS) and other sexually transmitted diseases (STDs)

Side/adverse effects

Signs of potential side effects, especially anaphylactic reactions, cholestatic jaundice, corneal curvature changes and edema

General Dosing Information

The first injection should be given within the first 5 days of the onset of a normal menstrual period or within 5 days of a complete first trimester abortion.

The first injection for postpartum administration should be given no earlier than 4 weeks if patient is not breast-feeding, and no earlier than 6 weeks if patient is breast-feeding.

The second injection should be monthly (every 28 to 30 days) not to exceed 33 days. If the patient has exceeded the prescribed schedule then pregnancy should be considered, and should be ruled out before another injection is given.

Do not shorten the injection interval, as this could lead to a change in the patient's menstrual pattern.

Do not use bleeding episodes to guide the injection schedule.

When switching from other methods of contraception the injection should be given in manner that continuous contraceptive coverage is insured, based on the mechanism of action of both methods.

Patients should be counseled that this contraceptive does not provide protection against HIV Infection (AIDS) and other sexually transmitted diseases.

Parenteral Dosage Forms

MEDROXYPROGESTERONE AND ESTRADIOL FOR INJECTION

Usual adult dose

Contraceptive—

Intramuscular, 0.5 mL, into the deltoid, gluteus maximus, or anterior thigh, once a month (every 28 to 30 days).

Usual pediatric dose

Safety and efficacy have not been established.

Usual geriatric dose

Safety and efficacy have not been established.

Strength(s) usually available

U.S.—

25 mg medroxyprogesterone acetate and 5 mg estradiol cypionate (Rx) [*Lunelle* (monthly contraceptive injection; methylparaben (0.9 mg); polyethylene glycol (14.28 mg); polysorbate 80 (0.95 mg); propylparaben (0.1 mg); sodium chloride (4.28 mg))].

Packaging and storage

Store at 25 °C (77 °F), excursions permitted to 15 °C- 30 °C (59–86 °F).

Preparation of dosage form

Should be shaken vigorously before administration.

Auxiliary labeling

- Shake well.

Developed: 01/24/2001

MEDRYSONE—See *Corticosteroids (Ophthalmic)*

MEFENAMIC ACID—See *Anti-inflammatory Drugs, Nonsteroidal (Systemic)*

MEFLOQUINE Systemic

VA CLASSIFICATION (Primary): AP101

Commonly used brand name(s): *Lariam*.

Note: For a listing of dosage forms and brand names by country availability, see *Dosage Forms* section(s).

Category

Antimalarial.

Indications

General Considerations

Malaria transmission occurs in large areas of Central and South America, Hispaniola, sub-Saharan Africa, the Indian subcontinent, Southeast Asia, the Middle East, and Oceania. The estimated risk of a traveler acquiring malaria varies markedly from area to area. Country-specific information on malaria risk can be obtained from the Centers for Disease Control and Prevention (CDC) or from the CDC's web site at http://www.cdc.gov/travel/yellowbk.

Travelers to malarious areas should be advised to use an appropriate drug regimen and personal protection measures to prevent malaria. Because of the nocturnal feeding habits of *Anopheles* mosquitoes, malaria transmission occurs primarily between dusk and dawn. Therefore, travelers should take protective measures to reduce contact with mosquitoes especially during these hours (see *Patient Consultation*). However, travelers should be informed that regardless of methods employed, malaria still may be contracted.

Asplenic travelers are at increased risk of severe malaria and should take extra precautions to avoid contracting the disease. These precautions should involve careful use of antimosquito measures, strict compliance with appropriate chemoprophylaxis, and avoidance of unnecessary visits to malarious areas.

Drug resistance to chloroquine has been confirmed or is probable in all countries with *Plasmodium falciparum* malaria except the Dominican Republic, Haiti, countries in Central America west of the Panama Canal Zone, Egypt, and most countries in the Middle East. In addition, resistance to both chloroquine and sulfadoxine and pyrimethamine is widespread in Thailand, Myanmar, Cambodia, and the Amazon basin area of South America, and resistance also has been reported sporadically in sub-Saharan Africa. Resistance to mefloquine has been confirmed in those areas of Thailand (Thai-Cambodian border) with malaria transmission.

The appropriate chemoprophylactic regimen is determined by the traveler's risk of acquiring malaria in the area to be visited and by the risk of exposure to chloroquine-resistant *P. falciparum*. Indications for prophylaxis for children are identical to those for adults. Chemoprophylaxis should begin 1 to 2 weeks before arrival in the endemic area, allowing time for development of adequate blood concentration of the chemoprophylactic agent and evaluation of any adverse reactions (see *General Dosing Information*).

Accepted

Malaria (prophylaxis)—Mefloquine is indicated for the prophylaxis of *P. falciparum* and *Plasmodium vivax* malaria infections, including prophylaxis of chloroquine-resistant strains of *P. falciparum* and *P. vivax*.

Malaria (treatment)—Mefloquine is indicated for the treatment of mild to moderate acute malaria caused by mefloquine-susceptible strains of *P. falciparum* (both chloroquine-susceptible and resistant strains) or by both chloroquine-susceptible and resistant strains of *P. vivax*.

Pharmacology/Pharmacokinetics

Physicochemical characteristics

Chemical Group—Mefloquine is a 4-quinolinemethanol derivative. It is a 2-aryl substituted chemical structural analog of quinine.

Molecular weight—Mefloquine hydrochloride: 414.78.

Mechanism of action/Effect

Mefloquine is an antimalarial agent that acts as a blood schizonticide. However, the exact mechanism of action is unknown.

Absorption

Well absorbed from the gastrointestinal tract.

Distribution

Distributed into blood, urine, cerebrospinal fluid (CSF), and tissues; concentrated in erythrocytes; also distributed into breast milk in low concentrations (approximately 3 to 4% of the ingested dose).

Apparent Vol_D—9 to 29 L/kg (median 20 L/kg).

Protein binding

Very high (98%).

Biotransformation

Hepatic (partial); metabolized primarily to the carboxylic acid metabolite.

Half-life

Absorption—0.36 to 2 hours.

Elimination—15 to 33 days.

Time to peak concentration

2 to 12 hours.

Peak plasma concentration

Approximately 1 mcg/mL after a single dose of 1 gram.

Elimination

Biliary/fecal; eliminated very slowly, primarily through bile into the feces. Subtherapeutic concentrations may persist in the blood for up to several months or more.

Renal; approximately 5% of the oral dose is excreted unchanged in the urine.

Precautions to Consider

Cross-sensitivity and/or related problems

Patients hypersensitive to quinidine, quinine, or related medications may be hypersensitive to this medication also.

Carcinogenicity

Two-year feeding studies in rats and mice, fed doses of up to 30 mg per kg of body weight (mg/kg) daily, have not shown that mefloquine is carcinogenic.

Mutagenicity

Mefloquine has not been shown to be mutagenic in the Ames test, host-mediated assays in mice, fluctuation tests, and mouse micronucleus assays, with or without prior metabolic activation. In addition, mefloquine has not been shown to be mutagenic in modified Ames tests utilizing *Salmonella typhimurium* strains, with or without microsomal activation.

Pregnancy/Reproduction

Fertility—Studies in adult human males, at doses of 250 mg once a week for 22 weeks, have not shown that mefloquine causes any adverse effects on spermatozoa.

However, studies in rats given doses of 5, 20, and 50 mg/kg daily have shown that mefloquine causes adverse effects on fertility in males at doses of 50 mg/kg daily and in females at doses of 20 and 50 mg/kg daily. In addition, degenerative lesions in the epididymides of male rats have been reported at doses of 20 and 50 mg/kg daily for 13 weeks.

Note: Pregnant women should avoid traveling to areas where chloroquine-resistant *Plasmodium falciparum* malaria is endemic. If travel to the malarious area and mefloquine chemoprophylaxis are considered necessary, women of childbearing potential should be warned to take reliable contraceptive precautions while taking mefloquine and for 3 months after the last dose.

Pregnancy—Adequate and well-controlled studies in humans have not been done. However, a review of data from clinical trials and reports of inadvertent use of mefloquine during pregnancy suggests that its use is not associated with adverse fetal or pregnancy outcomes such as birth defects, stillbirths, or spontaneous abortions.

Malaria in pregnant women results in a higher mortality rate and greater morbidity than in other adults. The risks of malaria in pregnancy may far outweigh any harmful effects of chemoprophylaxis. Therefore, mefloquine may be considered for prophylactic use in women who are pregnant or likely to become pregnant when exposure to chloroquine-resistant *P. falciparum* is unavoidable.

Mefloquine has been demonstrated to be teratogenic and embryotoxic in rats and rabbits.

FDA Pregnancy Category C.

Breast-feeding

Mefloquine is distributed into breast milk in low concentrations (approximately 3 to 4%) following administration of a 250-mg dose. According to the Canadian manufacturer, the amount of mefloquine distributed into breast milk is of no prophylactic value to the infant. Because of the potential for serious adverse reactions in nursing infants from mefloquine, a decision should be made whether to discontinue the drug, taking into account the importance of the drug to the mother.

Pediatrics

Although the safety and efficacy of mefloquine have not been well studied, it has been effective in preventing and treating malaria caused by *P. falciparum* in children. Two studies of mefloquine in children living in endemic areas for *P. falciparum* were conducted. All children in these studies had at least a low level of parasitemia and 18 to 40% had significant parasitemia with or without mild malaria symptoms. When given 20 to 30 mg of mefloquine per kg of body weight as a single dose, all children with fever became afebrile, and 92% of those with significant parasitemia had a satisfactory response to treatment. While incomplete follow-up was obtained in these studies, nausea and vomiting occurred in approximately 10 and 20%, respectively, and dizziness was seen in approximately 40% of children.

Children of any age can contract malaria. Consequently, the indications for prophylaxis are identical to those described for adults. Safety and efficacy of mefloquine for the treatment of malaria in pediatric patients below the age of 6 months have not been established. Limited data suggest that mefloquine also is well tolerated by infants and children who weigh less than 15 kg. Therefore, mefloquine may be considered for use when travel to areas with chloroquine-resistant *P. falciparum* is unavoidable.

Children who cannot take mefloquine or doxycycline can be given chloroquine for prophylaxis in chloroquine-sensitive areas. The combination of chloroquine and proguanil for sub-Saharan Africa has lower efficacy. Children should avoid travel to areas with chloroquine-resistant *P. falciparum* malaria unless they can take a highly effective antimalarial agent, such as mefloquine, doxycycline, or primaquine. Primaquine is safe and highly effective in children provided that their glucose-6-phosphate dehydrogenase (G6PD) level is normal.

Geriatrics

Although appropriate studies on the relationship of age to the effects of mefloquine have not been performed in the geriatric population, no geriatrics-specific problems have been documented to date. However, since electrocardiographic abnormalities have been observed in individuals treated with mefloquine and underlying cardiac disease is more prevalent in elderly than in younger patients, the benefits of mefloquine therapy should be weighed against the possibility of adverse cardiac effects in elderly patients.

Drug interactions and/or related problems

The following drug interactions and/or related problems have been selected on the basis of their potential clinical significance (possible mechanism in parentheses where appropriate)—not necessarily inclusive (» = major clinical significance):

Note: Combinations containing any of the following medications, depending on the amount present, may also interact with this medication.

» Anticonvulsants such as
Carbamazepine or
Phenobarbital or
Phenytoin or
Valproic acid
(concomitant use may reduce seizure control by lowering plasma levels of the anticonvulsant; therefore, patient blood level of antiseizure medications should be monitored and dosage adjusted appropriately)

» Chloroquine
(concurrent use of chloroquine with mefloquine may increase the risk of seizures)

» Halofantrine
(data on the use of halofantrine after administration of mefloquine suggest a significant, potentially fatal, prolongation of the QTc interval of the ECG; therefore, halofantrine should not be given simultaneously with or after mefloquine)

» Quinidine or
» Quinine
(concurrent use of these agents with mefloquine may result in sinus bradycardia, prolonged QT intervals, or cardiac arrest; the risk of seizures may also be increased with quinine; if concurrent use is necessary, close monitoring of patient response is recommended; in addition, mefloquine should be administered at least 12 hours after the last dose of quinidine or quinine)

» Typhoid vaccine, oral, live
(attenuation of immunization with mefloquine cannot be excluded with concurrent use; vaccinations with attenuated live bacteria should be completed at least 3 days before the first dose of mefloquine)

Laboratory value alterations

The following have been selected on the basis of their potential clinical significance (possible effect in parentheses where appropriate)—not necessarily inclusive (» = major clinical significance).

With physiology/laboratory test values
Alanine aminotransferase (ALT [SGPT]), serum, and
Aspartate aminotransferase (AST [SGOT]), serum and
Leukocytes
(values may be transiently increased in patients taking mefloquine)
Thrombocytes
(may be transiently reduced)

Medical considerations/Contraindications

The medical considerations/contraindications included have been selected on the basis of their potential clinical significance (reasons given in parentheses where appropriate)—not necessarily inclusive (» = major clinical significance).

Except under special circumstances, this medication should not be used when the following medical problem exists: :

» Hypersensitivity to mefloquine or related compounds such as quinine and quinidine
(mefloquine use contraindicated)

» Psychiatric conditions such as
Active depression or recent history of depression or
Generalized anxiety disorder or
Psychosis or
Schizophrenia or
Other major psychiatric disorders or
» Convulsions, history of
(mefloquine use contraindicated in patients with any of these conditions)

Risk-benefit should be considered when the following medical problems exist:

Compromised cardiovascular system
(effects of mefloquine have not been evaluated; benefits of mefloquine therapy should be weighed against the possibility of adverse effects in patients with cardiac disease)

» Depression, previous history of
(should be used with caution)

» Epilepsy or
» Seizure disorder, history of
(mefloquine may increase the risk of seizures)

Liver function impairment
(elimination of mefloquine may be prolonged leading to higher plasma levels)

Patient monitoring

The following may be especially important in patient monitoring (other tests may be warranted in some patients, depending on condition; » = major clinical significance):

Liver function tests
(should be performed during prolonged prophylaxis)

Ophthalmic examinations, periodic
(long-term use in rat studies resulted in dose-related ocular lesions)

Psychiatric symptoms such as
Anxiety, acute or
Confusion or
Depression or
Restlessness
(if these occur, mefloquine should be discontinued and substituted with an alternative drug)

Side/Adverse Effects

Note: Mefloquine is well tolerated and rarely has been associated with serious adverse effects when used for prophylaxis. Serious adverse effects are more frequent with the higher doses of mefloquine used in the treatment of malaria. However, serious side effects of mefloquine may be difficult to distinguish from the symptoms of acute malaria infection.

Although mefloquine is well tolerated when used for prophylaxis, monitoring the occurrence of severe adverse reactions is important because such reactions are possible. During prophylactic use, if psychiatric symptoms such as acute anxiety, depression, restlessness, or confusion occur, these may be related to a more serious adverse event. In these cases, the drug must be discontinued and an alternative medication should be substituted. Patients who experience serious adverse reactions following a prophylactic dose of mefloquine should consult their physician, and the reactions should be reported to the Centers for Disease Control and Prevention (CDC) Malaria Section (telephone number: 1-770-488-7760).

Postmarketing observation indicates that more severe neuropsychiatric disorders have been reported occasionally such as sensory and motor neuropathies (including paresthesia, tremor, and ataxia), convulsions, agitation or restlessness, anxiety, depression, mood changes, panic attacks, forgetfulness, confusion, hallucinations, aggression, psychotic or paranoid reactions and encephalopathy. Rare cases of suicidal ideation and suicide have been reported though no relationship to drug administration has been confirmed.

Adverse reactions may occur or persist up to several weeks after the last dose of mefloquine due to its long half-life.

The following side/adverse effects have been selected on the basis of their potential clinical significance (possible signs and symptoms in parentheses where appropriate)—not necessarily inclusive:

Those indicating need for medical attention

Incidence rare

Arrhythmia (irregular heartbeat); ***bradycardia*** (chest pain or discomfort, lightheadedness, dizziness or fainting, shortness of breath, slow or irregular heartbeat, unusual tiredness); ***central nervous system (CNS) disturbances or neuropsychiatric toxicity*** (anxiety; confusion; depression; hallucinations; psychotic manifestations, such as mood or mental changes, mental depression, and/or restlessness); ***encephalopathy*** (confusion; headache, severe or continuing; irritability; stiff neck; vomiting); ***erythema multiforme and/or Stevens-Johnson syndrome*** (aching joints and muscles; blistering, loosening, peeling, or redness of skin; chills, fever, and/or sore throat; red or irritated eye; sores, ulcers, and/or white spots in mouth or on lips; unusual tiredness or weakness)

Incidence not determined—Observed during clinical practice, estimates of frequency can not be determined

Atrioventricular [AV] block (chest pain, dizziness, fainting, pounding, slow heartbeat, troubled breathing, unusual tiredness or weakness); ***chest pain; dyspnea*** (shortness of breath, difficult or labored breathing, tightness in chest, wheezing); ***extrasystoles*** (extra heartbeats); ***hearing impairment; hypertension*** (dizziness, severe or continued headache); ***hypotension*** (unusual tiredness or weakness, severe); ***palpitation*** (fast, irregular, pounding, or racing heartbeat or pulse); ***seizures*** (convulsions, muscle spasm or jerking of all extremities, sudden loss of consciousness, loss of bladder control); ***syncope*** (fainting); ***tachycardia*** (fast, pounding, or irregular heartbeat or pulse); ***visual disturbance*** (blurred or loss of vision; disturbed color perception; night blindness; double vision; tunnel vision; halos around lights; overbright appearance of lights)

Those indicating need for medical attention only if they continue or are bothersome

Incidence more frequent

Abdominal pain (stomach pain); ***arthralgia and/or myalgia*** (aches and pain in joints and/or muscles); ***chills; diarrhea; dizziness; emotional problems; fever; headache; loss of balance; nausea; tinnitus*** (continuing ringing or buzzing or other unexplained noise in ears, hearing loss); ***vomiting***

Incidence less frequent

Abnormal dreams; anorexia (loss of appetite); ***asthenia*** (unusual tiredness or weakness); ***insomnia*** (trouble in sleeping)

Incidence rare

Alopecia (loss of hair)

Incidence not determined—Observed during clinical practice, estimates of frequency can not be determined

Dyspepsia (acid or sour stomach, belching, heartburn, indigestion, stomach discomfort, upset, or pain); ***edema*** (swelling); ***erythema*** (flushing, redness of skin, unusually warm skin); ***exanthema*** (skin rash with a general disease); ***fatigue*** (unusual tiredness or weakness); ***malaise*** (general feeling of discomfort or illness, unusual tiredness or weakness); ***muscle cramps or weakness; pruritis*** (itching skin); ***rash; sweating; urticaria*** (hives or welts, itching, redness of skin, skin rash)

Overdose

For more information on the management of overdose or unintentional ingestion, **contact a Poison Control Center** (see *Poison Control Center Listing*).

Treatment of overdose

Since there is no known specific antidote, the following procedure is recommended in case of overdose:

To decrease absorption—

Vomiting should be induced or gastric lavage should be performed, as appropriate, to empty the stomach.

Specific treatment—

Cardiac function and neurologic and psychiatric status should be monitored for at least 24 hours. Vomiting and/or diarrhea should be treated with standard fluid therapy. Symptomatic treatment should also be given.

Supportive care—

Supportive measures such as maintaining an open airway, respiration, and circulation may be necessary. Patients in whom intentional overdose is confirmed or suspected should be referred for psychiatric consultation.

Patient Consultation

As an aid to patient consultation, refer to *Advice for the Patient, Mefloquine (Systemic)*.

In providing consultation, consider emphasizing the following selected information (» = major clinical significance):

Before using this medication

» Conditions affecting use, especially:

Allergies to mefloquine, quinidine, quinine, or related medications

Pregnancy—Pregnant women should postpone travel to malarious areas; however, if travel to high-risk areas is unavoidable, mefloquine should be given to pregnant women because the risk to both the mother and the fetus of complications due to malaria exceeds the risk of the harmful effects of mefloquine

Breast-feeding—Distributed into breast milk in low concentrations; however, the amount of mefloquine distributed into breast milk will not protect the infant from acquiring malaria. Due to the potential for serious adverse reactions in nursing infants from mefloquine, a decision should be made whether to discontinue the drug, taking into account the importance of the drug to the mother.

Use in children—Children should avoid travel to areas with chloroquine-resistant *Plasmodium falciparum* malaria, unless they can take a highly effective antimalarial agent, such as mefloquine Safety and efficacy of mefloquine for the treatment of malaria have not been established in pediatric patients less than 6 months of age.

Other medications, especially anticonvulsants such as carbamazepine, phenobarbital, phenytoin and valproic acid, chloroquine, halofantrine, quinidine, quinine, or typhoid vaccine

Other medical problems, especially convulsions, epilepsy, hypersensitivity to mefloquine or related compounds such as quinine and quinidine, psychiatric conditions such as active depression or history of depression, generalized anxiety disorder, psychosis, schizophrenia, or seizure disorder

Proper use of this medication

Taking with full glass (240 mL) of water and with food

Crushing tablet and suspending in water, milk, or other beverage if patient is unable to swallow it whole

» Proper storage

For prevention of malaria symptoms

The importance of reading the medication guide before starting mefloquine for prevention of malaria

Starting medication 1 week before entering malarious area to ascertain response and allow time to substitute another medication if reactions occur

» Continuing medication while staying in area and for 4 weeks after leaving area

» Checking with physician immediately if fever or "flu-like" symptoms develop while traveling in, or within several months after departure from, endemic area

» Importance of not missing doses and taking medication on a regular schedule

» Proper dosing

Missed dose: Taking as soon as possible; not taking if almost time for next dose; not doubling doses; intermittent dosing may result in less adequate protection

For treatment of malaria

» Compliance with therapy

Importance of readministering medication according to physician's instructions to pediatric patients who have vomited after the first administration

Precautions while using this medication

» Caution if visual disturbances, dizziness, light-headedness, or hallucinations occur

Mosquito-control measures to help prevent malaria:

- Remaining in air-conditioned or well-screened rooms to reduce human-mosquito contact
- Sleeping under mosquito netting, preferably impregnated with pyrethrum-containing insecticide
- Wearing long-sleeved shirts or blouses and long trousers to protect arms and legs when mosquitoes are out
- Applying mosquito repellents containing *N,N*-diethyl-*m*-toluamide (DEET) to uncovered areas of skin when mosquitoes are out

• Using a pyrethrum-containing flying insect spray to kill mosquitoes

» Taking mefloquine at least 12 hours after the last dose of quinidine or quinine

For treatment of malaria:

Checking with physician if no improvement within a few days

Side/adverse effects

Signs of potential side effects, especially abnormal dreams, asthenia, arrhythmias, CNS disturbances or neuropsychiatric toxicity, encephalopathy, erythema multiforme and/or Stevens-Johnson syndrome, and seizures

Signs of potential side effects observed during clinical practice, especially atrioventricular [AV] block, chest pain, dyspnea, extrasystoles, hearing impairment, hypertension, hypotension, neuropsychiatric disorders (especially anxiety, depression, restlessness, or confusion), palpitation, syncope, tachycardia, and visual disturbance

General Dosing Information

Antimalarial chemoprophylaxis should be recommended depending on the estimated risk of infection. Weekly mefloquine is recommended for most travelers to areas with chloroquine-resistant *Plasmodium falciparum.* However, chloroquine should be used in areas with chloroquine-sensitive *P. falciparum.*

Mefloquine prophylaxis should begin before arrival in malarious areas. Any potential side effects should be evaluated and treated by the traveler's physician before departure. Malaria prophylaxis should continue during travel in the malarious areas and for 4 weeks after leaving these areas.

The effects of mefloquine on travelers receiving comedication, particularly diabetics or patients using anticoagulants, should be checked before departure.

When standard weekly dosing is used, side effects usually occur between the third and seventh dose. Some studies suggest that side effects can be predicted within 1 week of initiating therapy by using a loading dose of 250 mg daily for 3 days, followed by weekly dosing.

Mefloquine should not be taken on an empty stomach and should be administered with at least 8 oz. (240 mL) of water.

Mefloquine tablets may be crushed and suspended in a small amount of water, milk, or other beverage for administration to small children and other persons unable to swallow them whole.

Patients with acute *P. vivax* malaria, treated with mefloquine, are at high risk of relapse because mefloquine does not eliminate exoerythrocytic (hepatic phase) parasites. To avoid relapse, after initial treatment of the acute infection with mefloquine, patients should subsequently be treated with an 8-aminoquinolone (e.g., primaquine). There are insufficient clinical data to document the effect of mefloquine in malaria caused by *Plasmodium ovale* or *Plasmodium malariae.*

If a full malaria treatment course with mefloquine does not lead to improvement within 48 to 72 hours, alternative treatment should be prescribed. Similarly, if previous prophylaxis with mefloquine has failed, mefloquine should not be used for curative treatment.

In pediatric patients, the administration of mefloquine has been associated with early vomiting which can be a possible cause of treatment failure. If a significant loss of mefloquine is observed after administration due to vomiting, it should be dosed again as follows:

• Less than 30 minutes—additional full dose of mefloquine should be given

• 30 to 60 minutes—additional half dose of mefloquine should be given

If vomiting recurs and improvement is not observed within a reasonable period of time, the patient should be monitored closely and alternative malaria treatment considered.

Mefloquine should not be used for self-treatment because of the frequency of serious side effects (e.g., hallucinations, convulsions) that have been associated with the high doses of mefloquine used for the treatment of malaria.

For travel to areas of risk where chloroquine-resistant *P. falciparum* exists, mefloquine alone should be used. Mefloquine can be used for long-term prophylaxis. In some countries a fixed combination of mefloquine and sulfadoxine and pyrimethamine is marketed under the name *Fansimef. Fansimef* should not be confused with mefloquine and is not recommended for prophylaxis of malaria, because of the potential for severe adverse reactions associated with prophylactic use of sulfadoxine and pyrimethamine.

Persons who travel to areas where drug-resistant *P. falciparum* is endemic and for whom mefloquine is not recommended should use an alternative regimen, as follows:

• Doxycycline alone taken daily is an alternative regimen for travelers who cannot tolerate mefloquine or for whom mefloquine is not recommended. Doxycycline is as effective as mefloquine for travel to most malarious areas. It is also the only available effective prophylactic agent for travelers to malaria-endemic areas of Thailand bordering Myanmar and Cambodia.

• Chloroquine alone taken weekly is recommended only for those travelers to areas with drug-resistant *P. falciparum* who cannot use mefloquine or doxycycline. Chloroquine with daily proguanil may be more effective than chloroquine alone. However, the combination of chloroquine and proguanil for sub-Saharan Africa has lower efficacy. Therefore, travelers should avoid areas with chloroquine-resistant *P. falciparum* malaria unless they can take a highly effective antimalarial agent, such as mefloquine, doxycycline, or primaquine.

Primaquine in an adult dose of 30 mg per day (2 tablets daily) has been shown to provide excellent protection against *P. falciparum* and *P. vivax* malaria in Indonesia, Kenya, and Colombia. If primaquine is considered for treatment, glucose-6-phosphate dehydrogenase (G6PD) level should be determined prior to primaquine administration.

Oral Dosage Forms

MEFLOQUINE HYDROCHLORIDE TABLETS

Note: The dosing below is based on the product available in the U.S., in which a 250-mg tablet is equivalent to 228 mg of mefloquine base. The product available in Canada and other countries is 250 mg of mefloquine base, equivalent to 274 mg of mefloquine hydrochloride. To avoid confusion, the dosing below is expressed in the salt form (i.e., mefloquine hydrochloride).

Usual adult and adolescent dose

Malaria (prophylaxis)—

Oral, 250 mg once a week, starting one week before arrival in endemic area, then weekly on the same day of each week and preferably after the main meal during travel in malarious areas and for four weeks after leaving those areas.

Malaria (treatment)—

Oral, 1250 mg as a single dose, or 16.5 mg per kg of body weight as a single dose. Alternatively, 750 mg followed by 500 mg 8 hours later may be considered.

Usual pediatric dose

Malaria (prophylaxis)—

Infants and children 5 to 9 kg of body weight: Oral, 5 mg per kg of body weight (approximately 1/8 tablet), once a week, starting one week before travel, then weekly during travel in malarious areas and for four weeks after leaving endemic areas.

Note: Approximate tablet fraction based on a dosage of 5 mg per kg of body weight. Exact doses for children weighing less than 10 kg may best be prepared and dispensed by the pharmacist. Experience with mefloquine is limited in infants less than 3 months old or weighing less than 5 kg.

Children 10 to 19 kg of body weight—Oral, 62.5 mg (¼ tablet) once a week, starting one week before arrival in endemic area, then weekly in malarious areas and for four weeks after leaving endemic areas.

Children 20 to 30 kg of body weight—Oral, 125 mg (½ tablet) once a week, starting one to two weeks before travel, then weekly during travel in malarious areas and for four weeks after leaving endemic areas.

Children 31 to 45 kg of body weight—Oral, 187.5 mg (¾ tablet) once a week, starting one to two weeks before travel, then weekly during travel in malarious areas and for four weeks after leaving endemic areas.

Children over 45 kg of body weight—See *Usual adult and adolescent dose.*

Malaria (treatment)—

Oral, 20 to 25 mg per kg of body weight divided into two doses taken 6 to 8 hours apart. Taking as two doses may reduce the occurrence or severity of adverse effects.

The safety and efficacy of mefloquine to treat malaria in patients below the age of 6 months have not been established. Experience with mefloquine is limited in infants less than 3 months of age or weighing less than 5 kg.

Strength(s) usually available

U.S.—

250 mg (228 mg base) (Rx) [*Lariam* (scored; ammonium-calcium alginate; corn starch; crospovidone; lactose; magnesium stearate; microcrystalline cellulose; poloxamer #331; talc)].

Canada—

274 mg (250 mg base) (Rx) [*Lariam* (cross-scored [both sides])].

Packaging and storage

Store between 15 and 30 °C (59 and 86 °F), unless otherwise specified by manufacturer.

Auxiliary labeling

- Take with food and full glass of water.
- May cause dizziness or vision problems.
- Continue medication for full time of treatment.

Revised: 12/02/2003

MEGESTROL—See *Progestins (Systemic)*

MELOXICAM—See *Anti-inflammatory Drugs, Nonsteroidal (Systemic)*

MELOXICAM Systemic

VA CLASSIFICATION (Primary): MS102

Commonly used brand name(s): *Mobic; Mobicox.*

Note: For a listing of dosage forms and brand names by country availability, see *Dosage Forms* section(s).

Category

Antirheumatic (nonsteroidal anti-inflammatory).

Indications

Accepted

Arthritis, juvenile rheumatoid (treatment)—Meloxicam is indicated for relief of the signs and symptoms of pauciarticular or polyarticular course Juvenile Rheumatoid Arthritis in patients 2 years of age and older.

Arthritis, rheumatoid (treatment)—Meloxicam is indicated for relief of the signs and symptoms of rheumatoid arthritis.

Osteoarthritis (treatment)—Meloxicam is indicated for the relief of the signs and symptoms of osteoarthritis.

Pharmacology/Pharmacokinetics

Physicochemical characteristics

Chemical Group—An oxicam derivative

Molecular weight—351.4.

pKa—1.1 and 4.2.

Solubility—Insoluble in water, in strong acids and bases, slightly soluble in methanol.

Partition coefficient—0.1 in *n*-octanol/buffer pH 7.4

Mechanism of action/Effect

Meloxicam is a nonsteroidal anti-inflammatory drug that exhibits anti-inflammatory, analgesic, and antipyretic activities in animal models. The of action of meloxicam may be related to prostaglandin synthetase (cyclooxygenase) inhibition.

Absorption

Absolute bioavailability of a single oral dose is 89%. Neither the rate nor the extent of absorption is affected by multiple dose administration. Administration with food does not affect the extent of absorption.

Distribution

Vol_D—10 L

Penetration into red blood cells is less than 10%.

Concentrations in synovial fluid after a single oral dose range from 40% to 50% of those in plasma. The free fraction in synovial fluid is 2.5 times higher than in plasma, due to the lower albumin content in synovial fluid.

Protein binding

Very high (99.4%)

Biotransformation

Almost completely metabolized to 4 pharmacologically inactive metabolites. Metabolized largely by cytochrome P450 2C9.

Half-life

Elimination—15 to 20 hours

Time to peak concentration

5 to 6 hours

Peak serum concentration

1.05 micrograms/mL in healthy male adults at steady state, with a 7.5–mg dose

Elimination

Only traces of unchanged parent compound are excreted in the urine (0.2%) and feces (1.6%). Excretion is predominantly in the form of metabolites and occurs to an equal extent in the urine and feces.

Precautions to Consider

Cross-sensitivity and/or related problems

Patients who have experienced asthma, urticaria, or allergic-type reactions after taking aspirin or other nonsteroidal anti-inflammatory drugs (NSAIDs) should not be given meloxicam; severe, anaphylactic-like reactions to NSAIDs have been reported in such patients.

Carcinogenicity

No carcinogenic effect of meloxicam was observed in rats given oral doses up to 0.8 mg/kg/day (approximately 0.4–fold the human dose of 15 mg/day for a 50 kg adult based on body surface area conversion) for 104 weeks or in mice given oral doses up to 8.0 mg/kg/day (approximately 2.2–fold the human dose) for 99 weeks.

Mutagenicity

Meloxicam was not mutagenic in an Ames assay. No clastogenic effect was observed in the chromosome aberration assay with human lymphocytes or in the *in vivo* micronucleus test in mouse bone marrow.

Pregnancy/Reproduction

Fertility—Meloxicam did not impair male and female fertility in rats at oral doses up to 9 and 5 mg/kg/day, respectively (4.9–fold and 2.5–fold the human dose of 15 mg/day for a 50 kg adult based on body surface area conversion).

Pregnancy—Adequate and well-controlled studies in humans have not been done. Meloxicam may cause premature closure of the ductus arteriosus. Therefore, use of meloxicam is not recommended during pregnancy, especially late pregnancy.

Meloxicam crosses the placenta.

Meloxicam caused an increased incidence of septal defect of the heart at an oral dose 64.5–fold the human dose (15 mg/day for a 50 kg adult based on body surface area conversion) and embryolethality at oral doses greater than 5.4 times the human dose in rabbits treated throughout organogenesis. Meloxicam was not teratogenic in rats at a dose equivalent to 2.2 times the human dose when given throughout organogenesis. An increased incidence of stillbirths occurred in rats given doses ≥ 1 mg/kg/day throughout organogenesis. When female rats were given meloxicam at half the human dose 2 weeks before mating and during early embryonic development, there was increased incidence of embryolethality. The birth index, the number of live births, and neonatal survival were reduced in rats given oral doses ≥0.125 mg/kg/day (0.07–fold the human dose) during the late gestation and lactation periods.

FDA Pregnancy Category C

Labor and delivery—Studies in rats with meloxicam showed an increased incidence of stillbirths, increased length of delivery time, and delayed parturition at doses 0.5–fold the human dose of 15 mg/day for a 50 kg adult based on body surface area conversion, and decreased pup survival at an oral dose of 2.1–fold the human dose given throughout organogenesis. Similar results were observed in rats at 0.07–fold the human dose given during late gestation and the lactation period.

Breast-feeding

Studies of distribution of meloxicam into human breast milk have not been done. However, meloxicam has been found in the milk of lactating rats at concentrations higher than those in plasma. Because many drugs are distributed in human milk and because of the potential for serious adverse reactions in nursing infants from meloxicam, a decision should be made whether to discontinue nursing or to discontinue the drug, taking into account the importance of the drug to the mother.

Pediatrics

For treatment of osteoarthritis and rheumatoid arthritis—No information is available on the relationship of age to the effects of meloxicam in children up to 18 years of age. Safety and efficacy have not been established.

For treatment of juvenile rheumatoid arthritis—Safety and effectiveness in pediatric patients from 2 to 17 years of age have been evaluated.

Geriatrics

As with any NSAID, caution should be exercised in treating the elderly (65 years and older). Elderly patients are at greater risk for serious gastrointestinal events.

Plasma concentrations of meloxicam and steady state pharmacokinetics in elderly men (≥65 years of age) were similar to those in young males. Elderly females (≥65 years of age) had a 47% higher AUC and 32% higher C_{max} when compared to younger females (≤55 years of age). Despite the difference in total concentrations, the adverse event profiles were comparable in elderly men and elderly women.

Drug interactions and/or related problems

The following drug interactions and/or related problems have been selected on the basis of their potential clinical significance (possible mechanism in parentheses where appropriate)—not necessarily inclusive (» = major clinical significance):

Note: Combinations containing any of the following medications, depending on the amount present, may also interact with this medication.

Angiotensin-converting enzyme (ACE) inhibitors
(meloxicam may diminish antihypertensive effect of the ACE inhibitor; the clinical significance of this interaction should be considered; also, the risk of renal failure is increased in patients taking meloxicam with ACE inhibitors)

» Aspirin
(concurrent administration of low-dose aspirin and meloxicam may result in an increased rate of gastrointestinal ulceration or other complications)

Furosemide
(other nonsteroidal anti-inflammatory drugs can reduce the natriuretic effect of furosemide; meloxicam does not affect the pharmacodynamics and pharmacokinetics of furosemide; nevertheless, during concomitant therapy, patients should be observed closely for signs of declining renal function, as well as to assure diuretic efficacy)

» Lithium
(meloxicam can elevate plasma lithium level and reduce renal lithium clearance; patients on lithium treatment should be closely monitored when meloxicam is introduced or withdrawn)

Methotrexate
(caution should be used with concomitant use; NSAIDs could enhance toxicity of methotrexate)

Warfarin or other anticoagulants
(may increase risk of bleeding complications when a new medication is introduced; close monitoring is recommended)

Laboratory value alterations

The following have been selected on the basis of their potential clinical significance (possible effect in parentheses where appropriate)—not necessarily inclusive (» = major clinical significance).

With physiology/laboratory test values

Alanine aminotransferase (ALT [SGPT]), serum and
Aspartate amino transferase (AST [SGOT]), serum
(values may increase during therapy; liver function test abnormalities may return to normal despite continued use; however, if significant abnormalities occur, clinical signs and symptoms consistent with liver disease develop, or systemic manifestations such as eosinophilia or rash occur, use of meloxicam should be discontinued)

Medical considerations/Contraindications

The medical considerations/contraindications included have been selected on the basis of their potential clinical significance (reasons given in parentheses where appropriate)—not necessarily inclusive (» = major clinical significance).

Except under special circumstances, this medication should not be used when the following medical problem exists:

» Coronary artery bypass graft (CABG) surgery
(meloxicam is contraindicated for the treatment of peri-operative pain in the setting of CABG surgery)

» Hypersensitivity to meloxicam

» Nasal polyps associated with bronchospasm, aspirin-induced
(high risk of severe allergic reaction)

» Previous allergic/anaphylactic reaction to aspirin or other NSAIDs

Risk-benefit should be considered when the following medical problems exist:

Alcoholism, active

» Gastrointestinal bleeding, active, or pre-existing

» Peptic ulcer disease, active

Tobacco use
(may increase risk of gastrointestinal bleeding; meloxicam should be used with caution in these patients)

Asthma
(if asthma is of the aspirin-sensitive type, may cause severe bronchospasm)

» Cardiovascular (CV) disease or

» Risk factors for CV disease
(may be at greater risk of serious CV thrombotic events; lowest effective dose of meloxicam for shortest duration should be used with physicians and patients remaining alert for development of signs and symptoms of such events)

Extracellular volume depletion
(patients should be rehydrated before beginning therapy with meloxicam)

Conditions predisposing to and/or exacerbated by fluid retention, such as:

Compromised cardiac function
Congestive heart disease
Edema, pre-existing
Hypertension
(meloxicam may cause fluid retention or edema; also, risk of renal failure is increased in patients with congestive heart disease)

Hepatic function impairment
(may increase the risk of renal toxicity)

Renal function impairment
(may increase risk of renal toxicity; caution should be used in patients with pre-existing renal function impairment)

» Renal function impairment, severe
(long-term studies have not been done in patients with severe renal function impairment; use of meloxicam is not recommended in these patients; however, if meloxicam is used in patients with severe renal impairment, close monitoring is recommended)

Patient monitoring

The following may be especially important in patient monitoring (other tests may be warranted in some patients, depending on condition; » = major clinical significance):

Hematocrit and
Hemoglobin
(monitoring is recommended in patients who have developed signs and symptoms of anemia or blood loss during prolonged therapy with meloxicam)

Alanine aminotransferase ALT [SGPT], serum and
Aspartate aminotransferase AST [SGOT], serum
(in the presence of signs or symptoms of liver dysfunction during therapy, evaluate for more severe hepatic reaction; if elevations persist, discontinuation of therapy may be necessary)

Side/Adverse Effects

In July 2005, the Food and Drug Administration (FDA) asked all manufacturers of NSAIDs, including meloxicam, to revise the labeling for their products to include a boxed warning, highlighting the potential for increased risk of cardiovascular (CV) events including stroke and the well described, serious potential life-threatening gastrointestinal (GI) bleeding associated with their use.

The following side/adverse effects have been selected on the basis of their potential clinical significance (possible signs and symptoms in parentheses where appropriate)—not necessarily inclusive:

Those indicating need for medical attention

Less frequent

Albuminuria (cloudy urine); ***allergic reaction*** (cough; difficulty swallowing; dizziness; fast heartbeat; hives; itching, puffiness or swelling of the eyelids or around the eyes, face, lips or tongue; shortness of breath; skin rash; tightness in chest; unusual tiredness or weakness; wheezing); ***angina pectoris*** (arm, back or jaw pain; chest pain or discomfort; chest tightness or heaviness; fast or irregular heartbeat; shortness of breath; sweating; nausea); ***angioedema*** (large, hive-like swelling on face, eyelids, lips, tongue, throat, hands, legs, feet, sex organs); ***arrhythmia*** (dizziness; fainting; fast, slow, or irregular heartbeat); ***asthma*** (cough; difficulty breathing; noisy breathing; shortness of breath; tightness in chest; wheezing); ***bilirubinemia*** (yellow eyes or skin); ***bronchospasm*** (cough; difficulty breathing; noisy breathing; shortness of breath; tightness in chest; wheezing); ***bullous eruption*** (skin blisters); ***cardiac failure*** (chest pain or discomfort; dilated neck veins; extreme fatigue; irregular breathing; irregular heartbeat; shortness of breath; swelling of face, fingers, feet, or lower legs; weight gain; wheezing); ***colitis*** (stomach cramps, tenderness, pain; watery or bloody diarrhea; fever); ***convulsions*** (seizures); ***duodenal ulcer*** (burning upper abdominal pain; loss of appetite; nausea; vomiting); ***dyspnea*** (shortness of breath; difficult or labored breathing; tightness in chest; wheezing); ***face edema*** (swelling or puffiness of face); ***gastric ulcer*** (loss of appetite; nausea; stomach bloating, burning, cramping, or pain; vomiting; weight loss); ***hematemesis*** (vomiting of blood or material that looks like coffee grounds); ***hematuria*** (blood in urine); ***hemorrhagic duodenal or gastric ulcer*** (black, tarry stools; bloody stools; vomiting of blood or material that looks like coffee grounds); ***hepatitis*** (dark urine; general tiredness and weakness; light-colored stools; nausea and vomiting; upper right abdominal pain; yellow eyes and skin); ***hypertension*** (blurred vision; dizziness; nervousness; headache; pounding in the ears; slow or fast heartbeat); ***hypotension*** (blurred vision; confusion; dizziness, faintness, or lightheadedness when getting up from a lying or sitting position suddenly; sweating; unusual tiredness or weakness); ***intestinal perforation*** (severe abdominal pain; cramping; burning; bloody, black, or tarry stools; trouble breathing; vomiting of material that looks like coffee grounds; severe and continuing nausea, heartburn and/or indigestion); ***leukopenia*** (black, tarry stools; chest pain; chills; cough; fever; painful or difficult urination; shortness of breath; sore throat; sores, ulcers, or white spots on lips or in mouth; swollen glands; unusual bleeding or bruising; unusual tiredness or weakness); ***melena*** (bloody, black, or tarry stools); ***myocardial infarction*** (chest pain or discomfort; pain or discomfort in arms, jaw, back or neck; shortness of breath; nausea; sweating; vomiting); ***palpitation*** (fast, irregular, pounding, or racing heartbeat or pulse); ***pancreatitis*** (bloating; chills; constipation; darkened urine; fast heartbeat; fever; indigestion; loss of appetite; nausea; pains in stomach, side, or abdomen, possibly radiating to the back; vomiting; yellow eyes or skin); ***perforated duodenal or gastric ulcer*** (severe abdominal pain; cramping; burning; bloody, black, or tarry stools, trouble breathing; vomiting of material that looks like coffee grounds; severe and continuing nausea; heartburn and/or indigestion); ***photosensitivity reaction*** (increased sensitivity of skin to sunlight; itching; redness or other discoloration of skin; severe sunburn; skin rash); ***pruritus*** (itching skin); ***purpura*** (pinpoint red or purple spots on skin); ***renal failure*** (lower back/side pain; decreased frequency/amount of urine; bloody urine; increased thirst; loss of appetite; nausea; vomiting; unusual tiredness or weakness; swelling of face, fingers, lower legs; weight gain; troubled breathing; increased blood pressure); ***stomatitis ulcerative*** (canker sores; sores, ulcers, or white spots on lips or tongue or inside the mouth); ***syncope*** (fainting); ***tachycardia*** (fast, pounding, or irregular heartbeat or pulse); ***thrombocytopenia*** (black, tarry stools; bleeding gums; blood in urine or stools; pinpoint red spots on skin; unusual bleeding or bruising); ***tremor*** (trembling or shaking of hands or feet; shakiness in legs, arms, hands, feet); ***urticaria*** (hives or welts; itching; redness of skin; skin rash); ***vasculitis*** (redness, soreness or itching skin; fever; sores, welting or blisters)

Incidence rare

Agranulocytosis (cough or hoarseness; fever with or without chills; general feeling of tiredness or weakness; lower back or side pain; painful or difficult urination; sore throat; sores, ulcers, or white spots on lips or in mouth; unusual bleeding or bruising); ***anaphylactoid reaction*** (difficulty swallowing; puffiness or swelling of the eyelids or around the eyes, face, lips or tongue; shortness of breath; tightness in chest; wheezing); ***anemia*** (unusual tiredness or weakness); ***erythema multiforme*** (blistering, peeling, loosening of skin; chills; cough; diarrhea; fever; itching; joint or muscle pain; red irritated eyes; sore throat; sores, ulcers, or white spots in mouth or on lips; unusual tiredness or weakness); ***exfoliative dermatitis*** (cracks in the skin; loss of heat from the body; red, swollen skin, scaly skin); ***gastrointestinal bleeding or hemorrhage*** (bloody or black, tarry stools; vomiting of blood or material that looks like coffee grounds; severe stomach pain); ***interstitial nephritis*** (bloody or cloudy urine; fever; skin rash; swelling of feet or lower legs; greatly decreased frequency of urination or amount of urine,); ***jaundice*** (chills; clay-colored stools; dark urine; dizziness; fever; headache; itching; loss of appetite; nausea; abdominal or stomach pain; area rash; unpleasant breath odor; unusual tiredness or weakness; vomiting of blood; yellow eyes or skin); ***liver failure*** (headache; stomach pain; continuing vomiting; dark-colored urine; general feeling of tiredness or weakness; light-colored stools; yellow eyes or skin); ***shock*** (cold clammy skin; confusion; dizziness; lightheadedness; fast, weak pulse; sweating; wheezing); ***Stevens-Johnson syndrome*** (blistering, peeling, loosening of skin; chills; cough; diarrhea; itching; joint or muscle pain; red irritated eyes; red skin lesions, often with a purple center; sore throat; sores, ulcers, or white spots in mouth or on lips; unusual tiredness or weakness); ***toxic epidermal necrolysis*** (blistering, peeling, loosening of skin; chills; cough; diarrhea; itching; joint or muscle pain; red irritated eyes; red skin lesions, often with a purple center; sore throat; sores, ulcers, or white spots in mouth or on lips; unusual tiredness or weakness)

Incidence unknown—Observed during clinical practice; estimates of frequency can not be determined

Cardiovascular thrombotic events (severe headaches of sudden onset; sudden loss of coordination; pains in chest, groin, or legs, especially calves of legs; sudden onset of shortness of breath for no apparent reason; sudden onset of slurred speech; sudden vision changes); ***gastrointestinal ulceration*** (abdominal or stomach pain, cramping, or burning; black, tarry stools; constipation; diarrhea; vomiting of blood or material that looks like coffee grounds; nausea; heartburn; indigestion); ***stroke*** (confusion; difficulty in speaking; slow speech; inability to speak; inability to move arms, legs, or facial muscles; double vision; headache)

Those indicating need for medical attention only if they continue or are bothersome

Incidence more frequent

Diarrhea; dyspepsia (heartburn; indigestion)—less frequent with shorter duration of use; ***flatulence*** (gas)

Incidence less frequent or rare

Abdominal pain; abnormal dreaming; abnormal vision (changes in vision); ***alopecia*** (hair loss; thinning of hair); ***anxiety; appetite increased; confusion; conjunctivitis*** (redness, pain, swelling of eye, eyelid, or inner lining of eyelid; burning, dry or itching eyes; discharge; excessive tearing); ***constipation; dehydration*** (confusion; decreased urination; dizziness; dry mouth; fainting; increase in heart rate; lightheadedness; rapid breathing; sunken eyes; thirst; unusual tiredness or weakness; wrinkled skin); ***depression*** (discouragement; feeling sad or empty; irritability; lack of appetite; loss of interest or pleasure; tiredness; trouble concentrating; trouble sleeping); ***dry mouth; eructation*** (belching; bloated full feeling; excess air or gas in stomach); ***esophagitis*** (difficulty in swallowing; pain or burning in throat; chest pain; heartburn; vomiting; sores, ulcers, or white spots on lips or tongue or inside the mouth); ***fatigue*** (unusual tiredness or weakness); ***fever; gastritis*** (burning feeling in chest or stomach; tenderness in stomach area; stomach upset; indigestion); ***gastroesophageal reflux*** (heartburn, vomiting); ***hot flushes; malaise*** (general feeling of discomfort or illness; unusual tiredness or weakness); ***nausea and/or vomiting; nervousness; paresthesia*** (burning, crawling, itching, numbness, prickling, "pins and needles", or tingling feelings); ***somnolence*** (sleepiness); ***sweating increased; taste perversion*** (change in taste; bad unusual or unpleasant [after]taste); ***tinnitus*** (continuing ringing or buzzing or other unexplained noise in ears; hearing loss); ***vertigo*** (dizziness or lightheadedness; feeling of constant movement of self or surroundings; sensation of spinning); ***weight decrease or increase***

Overdose

For specific information on the agents used in the management of meloxicam toxicity or overdose, see:

- *Charcoal, activated (Oral-local)* monograph; and/or
- *Cholestyramine (Oral-local)* monograph.

For more information on the management of overdose or unintentional ingestion, **contact a poison control center** (see *Poison Control Center Listing*).

Clinical effects of overdose

The following effects have been selected on the basis of their potential clinical significance (possible signs and symptoms in parentheses where appropriate)—not necessarily inclusive:

Note: The following symptoms describe overdose of nonsteroidal anti-inflammatory drugs (NSAIDs) in general.

Anaphylactoid reaction (difficulty swallowing; dizziness; fast heartbeat; puffiness or swelling of the eyelids or around the eyes, face, lips or tongue; shortness of breath; skin rash; tightness in chest; unusual tiredness or weakness; wheezing); ***cardiac arrest*** (chest pain); ***convulsions; drowsiness; lethargy*** (extreme tiredness or weakness); ***epigastric pain*** (pain in chest, upper stomach, or throat; heartburn); ***gastrointestinal bleeding*** (bloody or black, tarry stools; vomiting of blood or material that looks like coffee grounds; severe stomach pain); ***hepatic dysfunction*** (dark urine; unusual tiredness; yellow eyes or skin; fever with or without chills; stomach pain); ***hypertension*** (blurred vision; dizziness, severe or continuing; pounding in the ears; slow or fast heartbeat); ***nausea or vomiting; renal failure, acute*** (confusion; decreased urine output; dizziness; headache; rapid weight gain; stupor; swelling of face, ankles, or hands; unusual tiredness or weakness); ***respiratory depression*** (blue lips, fingernails, or skin; difficult or troubled breathing; irregular, fast or slow, or shallow breathing)

Treatment of overdose

Forced diuresis, alkalinization of urine, hemodialysis, or hemoperfusion may NOT be useful due to high protein binding.

Patients should be managed with symptomatic and supportive care, possibly including
- Activated charcoal—recommended for patients who present 1 to 2 hours after overdose
- Cholestyramine
- Gastric lavage—if performed within one hour of overdose

To decrease absorption—

Patients in whom intentional overdose is confirmed or suspected should be referred for psychiatric consultation.

Patient Consultation

As an aid to patient consultation, refer to *Advice for the Patient, Meloxicam (Systemic)*.

In providing consultation, consider emphasizing the following selected information (» = major clinical significance):

Before using this medication

» Conditions affecting use, especially:

Allergies to aspirin or to any of the nonsteroidal anti-inflammatory drugs (NSAIDs)

Pregnancy—Crosses the placenta. Not recommended for use during pregnancy, especially late pregnancy because of possible premature closure of the ductus arteriosus

Breast-feeding—Not recommended because of risk of serious side effects

Use in the elderly—Greater risk for serious gastrointestinal events in the elderly

Other medications, especially aspirin and lithium

Other medical problems, especially coronary artery bypass graft (CABG) surgery; allergic reaction induced by aspirin, other nonsteroidal anti-inflammatory drugs (NSAIDs); aspirin-induced nasal polyps associated with bronchospasm; gastrointestinal bleeding (active or pre-existing); peptic ulcer disease (active); cardiovascular disease; risk factors for cardiovascular disease; renal function impairment (severe)

Proper use of this medication

» Not taking more medication than prescribed

» Proper dosing

Missed dose: Taking as soon as possible; not taking if almost time for next scheduled dose; not doubling doses

» Proper storage

Precautions while using this medication

» Regular visits to physician during prolonged therapy

» Possibility that use of alcohol may increase the risk of ulceration

» Not taking two or more nonsteroidal anti-inflammatory drugs (NSAIDs), including ketorolac, concurrently, and not taking acetaminophen or aspirin or other salicylates for more than a few days while receiving NSAID therapy, unless concurrent use is prescribed by, and patient remains under the care of, a physician or dentist

» Importance of immediately reporting to physician symptoms of edema, gastrointestinal bleeding or ulceration, cardiovascular events, unusual weight gain, or skin rash

» Notifying physician immediately if symptoms of hepatotoxicity occur, such as fever, fatigue, itching of the skin, lethargy, nausea, or stomach pain

» Possibility of anaphylaxis

Side/adverse effects

» *Obtaining emergency treatment if symptoms of any of the following occur*

» Anaphylactoid reaction

» *Stopping medication and checking with physician immediately if symptoms of the following occur*

» Bleeding or hemorrhage

Signs of potential side effects, especially agranulocytosis, albuminuria, allergic reaction, anemia, angina pectoris, angioedema, arrhythmia, asthma, bilirubinemia, bronchospasm, bullous eruption, cardiac failure, cardiovascular thrombotic events, colitis, convulsions, duodenal ulcer, dyspnea, erythema multiforme, exfoliative dermatitis, face edema, gastric ulcer, gastrointestinal bleeding or hemorrhage, gastrointestinal ulceration, hematemesis, hematuria, hemorrhagic duodenal ulcer, hemorrhagic gastric ulcer, hepatitis, hypertension, hypotension, interstitial nephritis, intestinal perforation, jaundice, leukopenia, liver failure, melena, myocardial infarction, palpitation, pancreatitis, perforated duodenal ulcer, perforated gastric ulcer, photosensitivity reaction, pruritus, purpura, renal failure, shock, Stevens-Johnson syndrome, stomatitis ulcerative, stroke, syncope, tachycardia, thrombocytopenia, toxic epidermal necrolysis, tremor, urticaria, or vasculitis

General Dosing Information

Meloxicam should not be substituted for corticosteroid treatment or to treat corticosteroid insufficiency.

The pharmacological activity of meloxicam in reducing inflammation and possibly fever may diminish the utility of these diagnostic signs in detecting complications.

Meloxicam should not be substituted for aspirin for cardiovascular prophylaxis.

Diet/Nutrition

May be taken without regard to timing of meals and antacids

Bioequivalence information

Mobic brand meloxicam oral suspension 7.5 mg per 5 mL or 15 mg per 10 mL may be substituted for *Mobic* tablets 7.5 mg or 15 mg, respectively.

Oral Dosage Forms

MELOXICAM ORAL SUSPENSION

Usual adult dose

Osteoarthritis or rheumatoid arthritis—

See *Meloxicam Tablets*.

Usual adult prescribing limits

See *Meloxicam Tablets*.

Usual pediatric dose

For treatment of osteoarthritis and rheumatoid arthritis—See *Meloxicam Tablets*.

Juvenile rheumatoid arthritis—

Oral, recommended dose of 0.125 mg per kg of body weight once daily. Juvenile rheumatoid arthritis dosing using the oral suspension should be individualized based on the weight of the child as follows:

Weight	0.125 mg/kg of body weight	
	Dose (1.5 mg/mL)	Delivered Dose
12 kg (26 lb)	1 mL	1.5 mg
24 kg (54 lb)	2 mL	3 mg
36 kg (80 lb)	3 mL	4.5 mg
48 kg (106 lb)	4 mL	6 mg
≥60 kg (132 lb)	5 mL	7.5 mg

Note: To improve dosing accuracy in smaller weight children, the use of the meloxicam oral suspension is recommended.

Usual pediatric prescribing limits

Up to 7.5 mg once daily.

Usual geriatric dose

See *Usual adult dose*.

Strength(s) usually available

U.S.—

7.5 mg per 5 mL (Rx) [*Mobic* (colloidal silicon dioxide; hydroxyethylcellulose; sorbitol; glycerol; xylitol; monobasic sodium phosphate (dihydrate); saccharin sodium; sodium benzoate; citric acid (monohydrate); raspberry flavor; purified water)].

Canada—

Not commercially available

Packaging and storage

Store at 25 °C (77 °F); excursions permitted between 15 and 30 °C (59 and 86 °F). Keep container tightly closed.

Auxiliary labeling

- Keep out of reach of children.
- Shake gently

MELOXICAM TABLETS

Usual adult dose

Osteoarthritis or rheumatoid arthritis—

Oral, 7.5 mg once a day. Some patients may receive additional benefit by increasing the dose to 15 mg once daily.

Usual adult prescribing limits

Up to 15 mg once a day

Usual pediatric dose

For treatment of osteoarthritis and rheumatoid arthritis—Safety and efficacy have not been established

Juvenile rheumatoid arthritis—

See *Meloxicam Oral Suspension*.

Usual pediatric prescribing limits

Up to 7.5 mg once daily.

Usual geriatric dose
See *Usual adult dose.*

Strength(s) usually available
U.S.—

7.5 mg (Rx) [*Mobic* (colloidal silicon dioxide, crospovidone, lactose monohydrate, magnesium stearate, microcrystalline cellulose, povidone, sodium citrate dihydrate)].

15 mg (Rx) [*Mobic* (colloidal silicon dioxide; crospovidone; lactose monohydrate; magnesium stearate; microcrystalline cellulose; povidone; sodium citrate dihydrate)].

Canada—

7.5 mg (Rx) [*Mobicox* (anhydrous colloidal silica; crospolyvidone; lactose; magnesium stearate; microcrystalline cellulose; polyvidone; sodium citrate)].

15 mg (Rx) [*Mobicox* (anhydrous colloidal silica; crospolyvidone; lactose; magnesium stearate; microcrystalline cellulose; polyvidone; sodium citrate)].

Packaging and storage
Store between 15 and 30 °C (59 and 86 °F), in a tight container. Keep in a dry place.

Auxiliary labeling
- Keep out of reach of children
- Swallow tablet whole.

Revised: 09/13/2005
Developed: 06/08/2000

MELPHALAN Systemic

VA CLASSIFICATION (Primary): AN100

Commonly used brand name(s): *Alkeran.*

Other commonly used names are L-PAM and phenylalanine mustard.

Note: For a listing of dosage forms and brand names by country availability, see *Dosage Forms* section(s).

Category
Antineoplastic.

Indications
Note: Bracketed information in the *Indications* section refers to uses that are not included in U.S. product labeling.

Accepted
Carcinoma, ovarian, epithelial (treatment) or
[Carcinoma, breast (treatment)][1]—Melphalan is indicated for the palliative treatment of nonresectable epithelial carcinoma of the ovary. It is also indicated for treatment of breast carcinoma.

[Melanoma, malignant (treatment)]—Melphalan is indicated for regional limb perfusion as an adjuvant to surgery to treat metastatic melanoma of the extremity.

Multiple myeloma (treatment) or
[Waldenström's macroglobulinemia (treatment)][1]—Melphalan is indicated for the palliative treatment of multiple myeloma and Waldenström's macroglobulinemia.

[Lymphomas, Hodgkin's (treatment)][1]—Melphalan is indicated as a component of conventional-dose salvage combination therapy for relapsed, resistant Hodgkin's lymphomas.

[Leukemia, chronic myelocytic (treatment)][1]—Melphalan, as part of a high-dose chemotherapy regimen prior to bone marrow transplantation, is considered reasonable medical therapy at some point in the management of chronic myelocytic leukemia (Evidence rating: IIID).

[Carcinoma, endometrial (treatment)][1]—Melphalan, in combination with other agents, is considered reasonable medical therapy at some point in the management of endometrial carcinoma (Evidence rating: IIA).

[1]Not included in Canadian product labeling.

Pharmacology/Pharmacokinetics
Physicochemical characteristics
Molecular weight—305.21.

Mechanism of action/Effect
Melphalan is an alkylating agent of the nitrogen mustard type. Melphalan is a bifunctional alkylating agent and is cell cycle-phase nonspecific. Activity occurs as a result of formation of an unstable ethylenimmonium ion, which alkylates or binds with many intracellular molecular structures including nucleic acids. Its cytotoxic action is primarily due to cross-linking of strands of DNA and RNA, as well as inhibition of protein synthesis.

Absorption
Variably and incompletely absorbed from the gastrointestinal tract. Absorption is decreased in the presence of food.

Distribution
Apparent volume of distribution (Vol_D)—steady-state: 0.5 liter per kg of body weight (L/kg).

Protein binding
Moderate to high (60 to 90%), primarily to albumin and alpha$_1$-acid glycoprotein; 30% is irreversibly bound to plasma proteins.

Biotransformation
Deactivated in plasma by hydrolysis.

Half-life
Distribution—Approximately 10 minutes.

Terminal—Approximately 90 minutes; the average terminal half-life of melphalan in the perfusion circuit during regional hyperthermic perfusion is 26 to 53 minutes.

Elimination
Primarily nonrenal.

In dialysis—Not removable by hemodialysis or hemoperfusion.

Precautions to Consider
Cross-sensitivity and/or related problems
Patients sensitive to chlorambucil may also be sensitive (in form of skin rash) to melphalan.

Carcinogenicity/Mutagenicity
Secondary malignancies are potential delayed effects of many antineoplastic agents, although it is not clear whether the effect is related to their mutagenic or immunosuppressive action. The risk may increase with increasing dose and duration of therapy. In one study, the 10-year risk of developing secondary acute leukemia or myeloproliferative syndrome was less than 2% for cumulative doses under 600 mg, but 19.5% for cumulative doses of 730 to 9652 mg of melphalan. This does not mean that there is a cumulative dose below which there is no risk of the induction of secondary malignancy. The potential benefits from melphalan therapy must be weighed on an individual basis against the possible risk of the induction of a second malignancy. Melphalan has been associated with an increased risk of development of secondary malignancies, including acute nonlymphocytic leukemia and myeloproliferative syndrome, in humans.

Melphalan produces chromosomal aberrations in human cells both *in vitro* and *in vivo.*

Pregnancy/Reproduction
Fertility—Gonadal suppression, resulting in amenorrhea or azoospermia, may occur in patients taking melphalan. These effects may be related to the dose and length of therapy and may be irreversible. Prediction of the degree of testicular or ovarian function impairment is complicated by the common use of combinations of several antineoplastics, which makes it difficult to assess the effects of individual agents.

Pregnancy—Adequate and well-controlled studies in humans have not been done. However, melphalan is believed to be potentially harmful to the fetus.

In a study in rats, oral administration of melphalan at a dose of 6 to 18 mg per square meter of body surface area per day (mg/m^2/day) resulted in abnormalities in the development of the brain, eyes, mandible, and tail.

FDA Pregnancy Category D.

In general, use of a contraceptive is recommended during cytotoxic drug therapy.

Breast-feeding
It is not known whether melphalan is distributed into breast milk. Breast-feeding is not recommended while melphalan is being administered, because of the risks to the infant (adverse effects, mutagenicity, carcinogenicity). A decision should be made whether to discontinue nursing or discontinue the drug, taking into consideration the importance of the drug to the mother.

Pediatrics
Appropriate studies on the relationship of age to the effects of melphalan have not been performed in the pediatric population. Safety and efficacy in pediatric patients have not been established.

Geriatrics
No information is available on the relationship of age to the effects of melphalan in geriatric patients. However, geriatric patients are more

likely to have age-related renal function impairment, which may require adjustment of dosage.

Dental

The bone marrow depressant effects of melphalan may result in an increased incidence of microbial infection, delayed healing, and gingival bleeding. Dental work, whenever possible, should be completed prior to initiation of therapy or deferred until blood counts have returned to normal. Patients should be instructed in proper oral hygiene during treatment, including caution in use of regular toothbrushes, dental floss, and toothpicks.

Melphalan may cause stomatitis, especially when high doses are used.

Drug interactions and/or related problems

The following drug interactions and/or related problems have been selected on the basis of their potential clinical significance (possible mechanism in parentheses where appropriate)—not necessarily inclusive (» = major clinical significance):

Note: Combinations containing any of the following medications, depending on the amount present, may also interact with this medication.

Blood dyscrasia-causing medications (see *Appendix II*)
(leukopenic and/or thrombocytopenic effects of melphalan may be increased with concurrent or recent therapy if these medications cause the same effects; dosage adjustment of melphalan, if necessary, should be based on white blood cell and platelet counts)

» Bone marrow depressants, other (see *Appendix II*) or
Radiation therapy
(additive bone marrow depression may occur; dosage reduction may be required when two or more bone marrow depressants, including radiation, are used concurrently or consecutively)

Carmustine
(intravenous melphalan may be synergistic with carmustine in causing lung toxicity)

Cimetidine
(reduced serum concentration of melphalan may result, perhaps due to decreased absorption)

Cyclosporine
(increased risk of nephrotoxicity)

Interferons, alpha
(increased elimination of melphalan may occur, perhaps due to fever induced by alpha interferons)

Nalidixic acid
(increased incidence of hemorrhagic necrotic enterocolitis in pediatric patients)

Vaccines, killed virus
(because normal defense mechanisms may be suppressed by melphalan therapy, the patient's antibody response to the vaccine may be decreased. The interval between discontinuation of medications that cause immunosuppression and restoration of the patient's ability to respond to the vaccine depends on the intensity and type of immunosuppression-causing medication used, the underlying disease, and other factors; estimates vary from 3 months to 1 year)

» Vaccines, live virus
(because normal defense mechanisms may be suppressed by melphalan therapy, concurrent use with a live virus vaccine may potentiate the replication of the vaccine virus, may increase the side/adverse effects of the vaccine virus, and/or may decrease the patient's antibody response to the vaccine; immunization of these patients should be undertaken only with extreme caution after careful review of the patient's hematologic status and only with the knowledge and consent of the physician managing the melphalan therapy. The interval between discontinuation of medications that cause immunosuppression and restoration of the patient's ability to respond to the vaccine depends on the intensity and type of immunosuppression-causing medication used, the underlying disease, and other factors; estimates vary from 3 months to 1 year. Patients with leukemia in remission should not receive live virus vaccine until at least 3 months after their last chemotherapy. Oral poliovirus vaccine should not be administered to persons in close contact with the patient, especially family members)

Laboratory value alterations

The following have been selected on the basis of their potential clinical significance (possible effect in parentheses where appropriate)—not necessarily inclusive (» = major clinical significance).

With physiology/laboratory test values

Uric acid concentrations in blood and urine
(may be increased)

Urinary 5-hydroxyindoleacetic acid (5-HIAA) concentrations
(may be increased, possibly as a result of tumor cell destruction with accompanying release of metabolites)

Medical considerations/Contraindications

The medical considerations/contraindications included have been selected on the basis of their potential clinical significance (reasons given in parentheses where appropriate)—not necessarily inclusive (» = major clinical significance).

Except under special circumstances, this medication should not be used when the following medical problem exists:

» Hypersensitivity to melphalan

Risk-benefit should be considered when the following medical problems exist:

» Bone marrow depression

» Chickenpox, existing or recent (including recent exposure) or

» Herpes zoster
(risk of severe generalized disease)

Gout, history of, or
Urate renal stones, history of
(risk of hyperuricemia)

» Infection

» Renal function impairment
(effect on toxicity difficult to predict; possible increased risk of bone marrow depression)

» Caution should be used also in patients who have had previous cytotoxic drug therapy or radiation therapy within 3 to 4 weeks.

Patient monitoring

The following are especially important in patient monitoring (other tests may be warranted in some patients, depending on condition; » = major clinical significance):

» Blood counts, complete (CBC) with differential, including
Hematocrit
Hemoglobin
Platelet count
White blood cell count
(recommended prior to initiation of therapy and at periodic intervals during therapy; frequency varies according to the patient's condition, the dose of melphalan administered, and other drugs being administered concurrently)

Blood urea nitrogen (BUN) concentrations and
Serum creatinine concentrations
(recommended prior to initiation of therapy and at periodic intervals during therapy)

Serum uric acid concentrations
(recommended prior to initiation of therapy and at periodic intervals during therapy)

Side/Adverse Effects

The following side/adverse effects have been selected on the basis of their potential clinical significance (possible cause in parentheses where appropriate)—not necessarily inclusive:

Those indicating need for medical attention

Incidence more frequent—dose-related

Neutropenia, with or without infection (fever or chills; cough or hoarseness; lower back or side pain; painful or difficult urination)—usually asymptomatic; uncommon after limb perfusion; ***thrombocytopenia*** (unusual bleeding or bruising; black, tarry stools; blood in urine or stools; pinpoint red spots on skin)—usually asymptomatic

Note: *Myelosuppression* usually occurs within 2 to 3 weeks of initiation of therapy, although *neutropenia* may occur within 5 days in a few patients. The nadir of leukocyte and platelet counts usually occurs within 3 to 5 weeks, and leukocyte and platelet counts usually return to normal within 4 to 8 weeks.

Incidence less frequent or rare

Hypersensitivity reactions, including anaphylaxis (fast or irregular heartbeat; shortness of breath; sudden skin rash or itching; troubled breathing); ***hyperuricemia or uric acid nephropathy*** (joint pain; lower back or side pain; swelling of feet or lower legs); ***mucositis*** (diarrhea; difficulty in swallowing)—dose-related; ***pulmonary fibrosis*** (shortness of breath); ***skin or soft tissue injury*** (redness and/or soreness in arm or leg)—with isolated limb perfusion; ***stomatitis*** (sores in mouth and on lips); ***vasculitis, severe, recurrent*** (redness and/or soreness at the infusion site)

Note: *Hypersensitivity reactions* have occurred in approximately 2% of patients receiving multiple courses of intravenous melphalan.

Hyperuricemia or uric acid nephropathy occurs most commonly during initial treatment of patients with leukemia or lymphoma, as a result of rapid cell breakdown which leads to elevated serum uric acid concentrations.

Those indicating need for medical attention only if they continue or are bothersome

Incidence less frequent

Nausea and vomiting—dose-related

Those indicating the need for medical attention if they occur after medication is discontinued

Bone marrow depression (black, tarry stools; blood in urine or stools; cough or hoarseness; fever or chills; lower back or side pain; painful or difficult urination; pinpoint red spots on skin; unusual bleeding or bruising)

Note: Cumulative *myelosuppression* may occur with repeated dosing.

Overdose

For specific information on the agents used in the management of melphalan overdose, see the *Colony Stimulating Factors (Systemic)* monograph.

For more information on the management of overdose or unintentional ingestion, **contact a Poison Control Center** (see *Poison Control Center Listing*).

Clinical effects of overdose

The following effects have been selected on the basis of their potential clinical significance (possible signs and symptoms in parentheses where appropriate)—not necessarily inclusive:

Acute and chronic

Anemia (unusual bleeding or bruising; unusual tiredness or weakness); ***colitis*** (abdominal cramping and pain); ***mucositis, severe*** (difficulty in swallowing; diarrhea); ***nausea and vomiting; neutropenia, possibly with infection*** (chills; cough or hoarseness; lower back or side pain; painful or difficult urination); ***stomatitis*** (painful sores in the mouth); ***thrombocytopenia*** (unusual bleeding or bruising; black, tarry stools; blood in urine or stools; pinpoint red spots on skin)

Treatment of overdose

Supportive care

There is no specific antidote to melphalan; care of patients with melphalan overdose should be supportive. One pediatric patient who was inadvertently administered a dose of 254 mg per square meter of body surface area (mg/m^2) of melphalan survived with standard supportive care. Melphalan can not be removed from the plasma by hemodialysis or hemoperfusion.

The patient's blood count parameters should be monitored closely for 3 to 6 weeks following the overdose, and supportive therapy should be given as needed. Severe bone marrow depression may require transfusion of needed blood components. Patients who develop leukopenia should be observed carefully for signs of infection. Antibiotic support may be required. Treatment with colony stimulating factors may shorten the duration of pancytopenia. Nutritional support with parenteral nutrition may be used in cases of overdose if mucositis prevents the oral intake of nutrition.

Patient Consultation

As an aid to patient consultation, refer to *Advice for the Patient, Melphalan (Systemic)*.

Consider advising the patient on the following (» = major clinical significance):

Before using this medication

» Conditions affecting use, especially:
- Hypersensitivity to melphalan
- Carcinogenicity—Increased risk of secondary malignancies
- Pregnancy—Advisability of using contraception; telling physician immediately if pregnancy is suspected
- Breast-feeding—Not recommended because of the potential risk to the infant
- Other medications, especially other bone marrow depressants and live virus vaccines, or previous cytotoxic drug therapy or radiation therapy within 3 to 4 weeks
- Other medical problems, epecially bone marrow depression, chickenpox or recent exposure, herpes zoster, infection, or renal function impairment

Proper use of this medication

» Importance of not taking more or less medication than the amount prescribed

Caution in taking combination chemotherapy; taking each medication at the right time

Importance of ample fluid intake and subsequent increase in urine output to aid in excretion of uric acid

» Frequency of nausea and vomiting; importance of continuing medication despite stomach upset

Checking with physician if vomiting occurs shortly after dose is taken

» Proper dosing

Missed dose: Not taking at all; not doubling doses

» Proper storage

Precautions while using this medication

» Importance of close monitoring by the physician

» Avoiding immunizations unless approved by physician;" other persons in patients household should avoid immunizations with oral poliovirus vaccine; avoiding other persons who have taken oral poliovirus vaccine or wearing a protective mask that covers nose and mouth

Caution if bone marrow depression occurs:

» Avoiding exposure to persons with infections, especially during periods of low blood counts; checking with physician immediately if fever, chills, cough, hoarseness, lower back or side pain, or painful or difficult urination occurs

» Checking with physician immediately if unusual bleeding or bruising; black, tarry stools; blood in urine or stools; or pinpoint red spots on skin occur

Caution in use of regular toothbrush, dental floss, or toothpick; checking with physician before having dental work done

Not touching eyes or inside of nose unless hands washed immediately before

Using caution to avoid accidental cuts with use of sharp objects such as safety razor or fingernail or toenail cutters

Avoiding contact sports or other situations where bruising or injury could occur

Side/adverse effects

May cause adverse effects such as blood problems and cancer; importance of discussing possible effects with physician

Signs of potential side effects, especially neutropenia, with or without infection; thrombocytopenia; hypersensitivity reactions, including anaphylaxis; hyperuricemia or uric acid nephropathy; mucositis; pulmonary fibrosis; skin or soft tissue injury; stomatitis; severe, recurrent vasculitis

General Dosing Information

Patients receiving melphalan should be under the supervision of a physician experienced in cancer chemotherapy.

Although systemic complications are less common with isolated limb perfusion of melphalan compared with orally or intravenously administered melphalan, severe local reactions, rarely requiring amputation, are possible. Isolated limb perfusion should be used only by physicians well trained in the technique.

A variety of dosage schedules and regimens of melphalan, alone or in combination with other antitumor agents, are used. The prescriber may consult the medical literature as well as the manufacturer's literature in choosing a specific dosage.

Dosage must be adjusted to meet the individual requirements of each patient, based on clinical response and degree of bone marrow depression. This is especially important because of unreliable absorption of orally administered melphalan.

Although melphalan is eliminated primarily by nonrenal mechanisms, increased bone marrow toxicity has been observed in patients with renal function impairment who receive melphalan. The manufacturer recommends consideration of dosage reduction in patients with renal function impairment receiving melphalan intravenously, and careful observation of patients with renal function impairment receiving melphalan orally.

Development of uric acid nephropathy in patients with leukemia or lymphoma may be prevented by adequate oral hydration and, in some cases, administration of allopurinol. Alkalinization of urine may be necessary if serum uric acid concentrations are elevated.

It is recommended that melphalan therapy be discontinued if marked leukopenia (particularly granulocytopenia) or thrombocytopenia occurs. Therapy may be resumed at a lower dosage when the clinical and laboratory examinations are satisfactory.

Special precautions are recommended in patients who develop thrombocytopenia as a result of administration of melphalan. These may include extreme care in performing invasive procedures; regular inspection of intravenous sites, skin (including perirectal area), and mucous membrane surfaces for signs of bleeding or bruising; limiting frequency of venipuncture and avoiding intramuscular injections; testing urine, emesis, stool, and secretions for occult blood; care in use of regular toothbrushes, dental floss, toothpicks, safety razors, and fingernail and toenail cutters; avoiding constipation; and using caution to prevent falls and other injuries. Such patients should avoid alcohol and any aspirin intake because of the risk of gastrointestinal bleeding. Platelet transfusions may be required.

Patients who develop leukopenia should be observed carefully for signs of infection. Antibiotic support may be required.

Development of a hypersensitivity reaction requires immediate discontinuation of infusion and initiating symptomatic treatment. It is recommended that melphalan (oral and intravenous formulations) not be readministered if a hypersensitivity reaction occurs.

Safety considerations for handling this medication

There is evidence that personnel involved in preparation and administration of parenteral antineoplastics may be at some risk because of the potential mutagenicity, teratogenicity, and/or carcinogenicity of these agents, although the actual risk is unknown. USP advisory panels recommend cautious handling both in preparation and disposal of antineoplastic agents. Precautions that have been suggested include:

- Use of a biological containment cabinet during reconstitution and dilution of parenteral medications and wearing of disposable surgical gloves and masks.
- Use of proper technique to prevent contamination of the medication, work area, and operator during transfer between containers (including proper training of personnel in this technique).
- Cautious and proper disposal of needles, syringes, vials, ampuls, and unused medication.

Detailed guidelines for the handling of cytotoxic and hazardous antineoplastic agents have been developed by various groups, including the American Society of Health-System Pharmacists (ASHP) and the Office of Occupational Medicine, Occupational Safety and Health Administration (OSHA).

Direct contact of skin or mucosa with melphalan requires immediate washing with soap and water or thoroughly flushing with water, respectively.

Combination chemotherapy

Melphalan may be used in combination with other agents in various regimens. As a result, incidence and/or severity of side effects may be altered and different dosages may be used. For specific dosages and schedules, consult the literature. For information regarding each agent, consult the individual monographs.

For treatment of adverse effects

Recommended treatment consists of the following:

- Controlling hypersensitivity reactions with antihistamines and/or corticosteroids.

Oral Dosage Forms

MELPHALAN TABLETS USP

Usual adult dose

Multiple myeloma—

Oral, 150 mcg (0.15 mg) per kg of body weight a day for seven days, followed by a rest period of at least three weeks, during which time the leukocyte count will fall. When white cell and platelet counts are rising, a maintenance dose of 50 mcg (0.05 mg) per kg of body weight a day may be instituted, or

Oral, 100 to 150 mcg (0.1 to 0.15 mg) per kg of body weight a day for two to three weeks, or 250 mcg (0.25 mg) per kg of body weight a day for four days, followed by a rest period of two to four weeks. When leukocyte counts rise above 3000 to 4000 per cubic millimeter and platelet counts above 100,000 per cubic millimeter, a maintenance dose of 2 to 4 mg a day may be instituted, or

Oral, 7 mg per square meter of body surface area or 250 mcg (0.25 mg) per kg of body weight a day for five days every five to six weeks, adjusted to produce mild leukopenia and thrombocytopenia.

Ovarian carcinoma, epithelial—

Oral, 200 mcg (0.2 mg) per kg of body weight a day for five days, repeated every four to five weeks if blood counts return to normal.

[Carcinoma, endometrial (treatment)][1]—

Consult medical literature and manufacturer's literature for specific dosage.

Usual pediatric dose

Children up to 12 years of age—Safety and efficacy have not been established.

Usual geriatric dose

See *Usual adult dose*

Strength(s) usually available

U.S.—

2 mg (Rx) [*Alkeran* (scored; lactose; sucrose)].

Canada—

2 mg (Rx) [*Alkeran* (scored)].

Packaging and storage

Store below 40 °C (104 °F), preferably between 15 and 30 °C (59 and 86 °F), unless otherwise specified by manufacturer. Store in a well-closed, light-resistant container.

Note

Dispense in a glass container.

Parenteral Dosage Forms

Note: Bracketed uses in the Dosage Forms section refer to categories of use and/or indications that are not included in U.S. product labeling.

MELPHALAN HYDROCHLORIDE FOR INJECTION

Usual adult dose

Multiple myeloma—

Intravenous infusion, 16 mg per square meter of body surface area (mg/m^2) administered over 15 to 20 minutes at two-week intervals for four doses; then at four-week intervals after recovery from toxicity. Dosage adjustments may be made, based on white blood cell and platelet counts at the nadir.

[Malignant melanoma]—

Upper extremity—

Arterial infusion, by hyperthermic isolated limb perfusion technique, 1 mg per kg of body weight, not to exceed 80 mg, in three equally divided doses at five-minute intervals.

Lower extremity—

Arterial infusion, by hyperthermic isolated limb perfusion technique, 1.5 mg per kg of body weight, not to exceed 120 mg, in three equally divided doses at five-minute intervals.

Note: The following perfusion guidelines are recommended by the manufacturer:

- Temperature of the perfusate should not exceed 42.5 °C (108.5 °F)
- Temperature of the limb should not exceed 42 °C (107.6 °F)
- Flow-rate—250 to 600 mL per minute (mL/min)
- Perfusate—650 to 750 mL of heparinized whole blood or an equal mixture of lactated Ringer's solution and washed packed red blood cells
- Perfusion duration—Not to exceed one hour

[Leukemia, chronic myelocytic (treatment)][1]—

Consult medical literature and manufacturer's literature for specific dosage.

Usual pediatric dose

Safety and efficacy have not been established.

Usual geriatric dose

See *Usual adult dose*

Strength(s) usually available

U.S.—

50 mg (Rx) [*Alkeran* (lyophilized powder; povidone 20 mg)].

Canada—

50 mg (Rx) [*Alkeran* (lyophilized powder; povidone 20 mg)].

Packaging and storage

Store between 15 and 30 °C (59 and 86 °F). Protect from light.

Preparation of dosage form

For intravenous infusion—

Reconstitute the vial of melphalan with 10 mL of the diluent supplied by the manufacturer, for a concentration of 5 mg per mL (mg/mL).

Immediately dilute the dose to be administered in 0.9% sodium chloride injection, USP, to a final concentration no greater than 0.45 mg/mL.

For isolated limb perfusion—

Reconstitute the vial of melphalan with 10 mL of the diluent supplied by the manufacturer, for a concentration of 5 mg per mL (mg/mL).

Stability

Melphalan reconstituted as directed to a concentration of 5 mg/mL is stable for up to two hours at 30 °C (86 °F). The reconstituted solution should not be refrigerated because refrigeration will cause a precipitate to form.

Melphalan infusions prepared to a final concentration of 0.1 to 0.45 mg/mL in 0.9% sodium chloride injection are stable for up to 50 minutes when stored at 30 °C (86 °F), and up to four hours at 20 °C (68 °F).

Unused portions of melphalan should be discarded.

Incompatibilities

Melphalan 0.1 mg per mL (mg/mL) in 0.9% sodium chloride injection is incompatible for Y-site administration with amphotericin B, chlorpromazine hydrochloride, daunorubicin hydrochloride, idarubicin hydrochloride, lorazepam, methylprednisolone sodium succinate, and prochlorperazine edisylate.

Auxiliary labeling

- Do not refrigerate.
- Protect from light.

[1]Not included in Canadian product labeling.

Revised: 03/10/2004

MEMANTINE Systemic

VA CLASSIFICATION (Primary): CN900

Commonly used brand name(s): *Ebixa*; *Namenda*.

Note: For a listing of dosage forms and brand names by country availability, see *Dosage Forms* section(s).

Category

Dementia symptoms treatment adjunct.

Indications

Accepted

Dementia, Alzheimer's type, moderate to severe (treatment)—Memantine is indicated for treatment of moderate to severe dementia of the Alzheimer's type.

Pharmacology/Pharmacokinetics

Physicochemical characteristics

Molecular weight—245.76.

Solubility—Soluble in water.

Mechanism of action/Effect

Persistent activation of central nervous system N-methyl-D-aspartate (NMDA) receptors by the excitatory amino acid glutamate has been hypothesized to contribute to the symptomatology of Alzheimer's disease. Memantine is postulated to exert its therapeutic effect through its action as a low to moderate affinity uncompetitive (open-channel) NMDA receptor antagonist which binds preferentially to the NMDA receptor-operated cation channels. There is no evidence that memantine prevents or slows neurodegeneration in patients with Alzheimer's disease.

Memantine showed low to negligible affinity for GABA, benzodiazepine, dopamine, adrenergic, histamine and glycine receptors and for voltage-dependent Ca^{2+}, Na^+ or K^+ channels. Memantine also showed antagonistic effects at the $5HT_3$ receptor with a potency similar to that for the NMDA receptor and blocked nicotinic acetylcholine receptors with one-sixth to one-tenth the potency. *In vitro* studies have shown that memantine does not affect the reversible inhibition of acetylcholinesterase by donepezil, galantamine, or tacrine.

Absorption

Oral administration—highly absorbed; food has no effect

Distribution

Vol_D—9 to 11 L per kg

Protein binding

45%; plasma

Half-life

Terminal elimination—60 to 80 hours

Time to peak concentration

3 to 7 hours

Elimination

Urine, unchanged 57 to 87%

Remainder is converted primarily to three polar metabolites: the N-gludantan conjugate, 6-hydroxy memantine, and 1-nitroso-deaminated memantine. These metabolites possess minimal NMDA receptor antagonist activity. The hepatic microsomal CYP450 enzyme system does not play a significant role in the metabolism of memantine.

Renal clearance involves active tubular secretion moderated by pH dependent tubular reabsorption.

Special Populations

Gender: Following multiple dose administration of memantine 20 mg twice a day females had about 45% higher exposure than males, but there was no difference in exposure when body weight was taken into account.

Precautions to Consider

Carcinogenicity

There was no evidence of carcinogenicity on 113–week oral study in mice at doses up to 40 mg per kg per day (10 times the maximum recommended human dose [MRHD] on a mg per m² basis). There was also no evidence of carcinogenicity in rats orally dosed at up to 40 mg per kg per day for 71 weeks followed by 20 mg per kg per day (20 times and 10 times the MRHD on a mg per m² basis, respectively) through 128 weeks.

Mutagenicity

Memantine produced no evidence of genotoxic potential when evaluated in the *in vitro S. typhimurium* and *E. coli* reverse mutation assays, the *in vitro* chromosomal aberration test in human lymphocytes, the *in vivo* cytogenesis assay for chromosome damage in rats, and the *in vivo* mouse micronucleus assay. The results were equivocal in an *in vitro* gene mutation assay using Chinese hamster V79 cells.

Pregnancy/Reproduction

Fertility—No impairment of fertility or reproductive performance was seen in rats administered up to 18 mg per kg per day (9 times the human MRHD on a mg per m² basis) orally from 14 days prior to mating through gestation and lactation in females, or for up to 60 days prior to mating in males.

Pregnancy—There are no adequate and well-controlled studies of memantine in pregnant women. Memantine should be used during pregnancy only if the potential benefit justifies the potential risk to the fetus.

Memantine given orally to pregnant rats and pregnant rabbits during the period of organogenesis was not teratogenic up to the highest doses tested (18 mg per kg per day in rats and 30 mg per kg per day in rabbits, which are 9 and 30 times, respectively, the maximum recommend human dose [MRHD] on a mg per m² basis).

Slight maternal toxicity, decreased pup weights, and an increased incidence of non-ossified cervical vertebrae were seen at an oral dose of 18 mg per kg per day in a study in which rats were given oral memantine beginning pre-mating and continuing through the postpartum period. Slight maternal toxicity and decreased pup weights were also seen at this dose in a study in which rats were treated from day 15 of gestation through the postpartum period. The no-effect dose for these effects was 6 mg per kg, which is 3 times the MRHD on a mg per m² basis.

FDA Pregnancy Category B

Breast-feeding

It is not known whether memantine is distributed into human breast milk. Because many drugs are distributed into breast milk, caution should be used when administering memantine to a nursing mother.

Pediatrics

Appropriate studies on the relationship of age to the effects of memantine have not been performed in the pediatric population. Safety and efficacy have not been established.

Geriatrics

Appropriate studies on the relationship of age to the effects of memantine have not been performed in the geriatric population. However, no geriatrics specific problems have been reported to date.

Pharmacogenetics

Gender—Following multiple dose administration of memantine 20 mg twice a day females had about 45% higher exposure than males, but there was no difference in exposure when body weight was taken into account.

Drug interactions and/or related problems

The following drug interactions and/or related problems have been selected on the basis of their potential clinical significance (possible mechanism in parentheses where appropriate)—not necessarily inclusive (» = major clinical significance):

Note: Combinations containing any of the following medications, depending on the amount present, may also interact with this medication.

Hydrochlorothiazide
(memantine decreased the AUC and C_{max} of HCTZ by 20%)

NMDA antagonists, such as
Amantadine or
Dextromethorphan or

Ketamine
(combined use of memantine and other NMDA antagonists has not been evaluated and should be approached with caution)

Triamterene or
Cimetidine or
Nicotine or
Ranitidine or
Quinidine
(coadministration of drugs which undergo renal cationic tubular secretion could potentially result in altered plasma levels of both agents; however, coadministration of memantine and triamterene did not affect the bioavailability of either agent)

Carbonic anhydrase inhibitors or
Sodium bicarbonate
(drugs that alkalinize the urine would be expected to reduce the renal elimination of memantine; the clearance of memantine was reduced by about 80% under alkaline urine conditions at pH 8; alterations of urine pH towards the alkaline state may lead to an accumulation of the drug with a possible increase in adverse effects)

Medical considerations/Contraindications

The medical considerations/contraindications included have been selected on the basis of their potential clinical significance (reasons given in parentheses where appropriate)—not necessarily inclusive (» = major clinical significance).

Except under special circumstances, this medication should not be used when the following medical problem exists:

» Hypersensitivity to memantine or any excipients used in the formulation

Risk-benefit should be considered when the following medical problems exist:

Renal tubular acidosis or
Urinary tract infections, severe
(memantine should be used with caution as these conditions can alter urine pH towards an alkaline condition; alkaline conditions can lead to an accumulation of the drug with a possible increase in adverse effects)

» Neurological conditions
(memantine has not been systematically evaluated in patients with a seizure disorder; in clinical trials seizures occurred on 0.2% of patients treated with memantine and 0.5% of patients treated with placebo)

Genitourinary conditions
(conditions that increase the urine pH may decrease the urinary elimination of memantine resulting in increased plasma levels of memantine)

Renal impairment, mild to moderate
(may increase absorption and terminal half-life; dosage adjustment not necessary)

» Renal impairment, severe
(dosage adjustment is recommended)

Side/Adverse Effects

The following side/adverse effects have been selected on the basis of their potential clinical significance (possible signs and symptoms in parentheses where appropriate)—not necessarily inclusive:

Memantine has been commercially available outside the United States since 1982, and has been evaluated in clinical trials in patients with neuropathic pain, Parkinson's disease, organic brain syndrome, and spasticity. The following adverse events of possible importance for which there is inadequate data to determine the causal relationship have been reported to be temporally associated with memantine treatment in more than one patient: acne, bone fracture, carpal tunnel syndrome, hyperlipidemia, impotence, otitis media, and thrombocytopenia.

Those indicating need for medical attention

Incidence less frequent

Hypertension (blurred vision; dizziness; nervousness; headache; pounding in the ears; slow or fast heartbeat); ***peripheral edema*** (bloating or swelling of face, arms, hands, lower legs, or feet; rapid weight gain; tingling of hands or feet; unusual weight gain or loss)

Incidence not determined—Observed during clinical practice; estimates of frequency can not be determined

Acute pancreatitis (bloating; chills; constipation; darkened urine; fast heartbeat; fever; indigestion; loss of appetite; nausea; pains in stomach, side, or abdomen, possibly radiating to the back; vomiting; yellow eyes or skin); ***acute renal failure*** (agitation; coma; confusion; decreased urine output; depression; dizziness; headache; hostility; irritability; lethargy; muscle twitching; nausea; rapid weight gain; seizures; stupor; swelling of face, ankles, or hands; unusual tiredness or weakness); ***aspiration pneumonia*** (infection from breathing foreign substance into the lungs); ***atrioventricular block*** (chest pain; dizziness; fainting, pounding, slow heartbeat; troubled breathing; unusual tiredness or weakness); ***bone fracture*** (pain or swelling in arms or legs without any injury); ***cerebral infarction*** (blurred vision; confusion, numbness or tingling in face, arms, legs; severe headache; trouble speaking or walking); ***claudication*** (pain, tension, and weakness upon walking that subsides during periods of rest); ***dyskinesia*** (twitching, twisting, uncontrolled repetitive movements of tongue, lips, face, arms, or legs); ***grand mal convulsions*** (total body jerking; loss of bladder control; loss of consciousness); ***hepatic failure*** (headache; stomach pain; continuing vomiting; dark-colored urine; general feeling of tiredness or weakness; light-colored stools; yellow eyes or skin); ***ileus*** (abdominal pain; severe constipation; severe vomiting); ***intracranial hemorrhage*** (confusion; headache; sudden severe weakness; nausea and vomiting); ***neuroleptic malignant syndrome*** (convulsions; difficulty in breathing; fast heartbeat; high fever; high or low blood pressure; increased sweating; loss of bladder control; severe muscle stiffness; unusually pale skin; tiredness); ***prolonged QT interval*** (irregular heartbeat; recurrent fainting); ***Stevens-Johnson syndrome*** (blistering, peeling, loosening of skin; chills; cough; diarrhea; itching; joint or muscle pain; red irritated eyes; red skin lesions, often with a purple center; sore throat; sores, ulcers, or white spots in mouth or on lips; unusual tiredness or weakness); ***sudden death*** (no pulse; no blood pressure; no breathing); ***supraventricular tachycardia*** (fainting; fast, pounding, or irregular heartbeat or pulse; palpitations); ***tachycardia*** (fast, pounding, or irregular heartbeat or pulse); ***tardive dyskinesia*** (lip smacking or puckering; puffing of cheeks; rapid or worm-like movements of tongue; uncontrolled chewing movements; uncontrolled movements of arms and legs); ***thrombocytopenia*** (black, tarry stools; bleeding gums; blood in urine or stools; pinpoint red spots on skin; unusual bleeding or bruising)

Those indicating need for medical attention only if they continue or are bothersome

Incidence more frequent

Confusion; dizziness; headache

Incidence less frequent

Abnormal gait (change in walking and balance; clumsiness or unsteadiness); ***agitation*** (anxiety; nervousness; restlessness; irritability; dry mouth; shortness of breath; hyperventilation; trouble sleeping; irregular heartbeats; shaking); ***anorexia*** (loss of appetite; weight loss); ***anxiety*** (fear; nervousness); ***arthralgia*** (pain in joints; muscle pain or stiffness; difficulty in moving); ***back pain; bronchitis*** (cough producing mucus; difficulty breathing; shortness of breath; tightness in chest; wheezing); ***constipation*** (difficulty having a bowel movement (stool)); ***coughing; depression*** (discouragement; feeling sad or empty; irritability; lack of appetite; loss of interest or pleasure; tiredness; trouble concentrating; trouble sleeping); ***diarrhea; dyspnea*** (shortness of breath; difficult or labored breathing; tightness in chest; wheezing); ***fatigue*** (unusual tiredness or weakness); ***hallucination*** (seeing, hearing, or feeling things that are not there); ***influenza like syndrome*** (chills; cough; diarrhea; fever; general feeling of discomfort or illness; headache; joint pain; loss of appetite; muscle aches and pains); ***insomnia; nausea; pain; somnolence*** (sleepiness or unusual drowsiness); ***upper respiratory tract infection*** (cough; sore throat); ***urinary incontinence*** (loss of bladder control); ***urinary tract infection*** (bladder pain; bloody or cloudy urine; difficult, burning, or painful urination; frequent urge to urinate; lower back or side pain); ***vomiting***

Incidence not determined—Observed during clinical practice; estimates of frequency can not be determined

Carpal tunnel syndrome (burning, numbness, pain, or tingling in all fingers except smallest finger); ***chest pain; colitis*** (stomach cramps; tenderness; pain; watery or bloody diarrhea; fever); ***dysphagia*** (difficulty swallowing); ***gastritis*** (burning feeling in chest or stomach; tenderness in stomach area; stomach upset; indigestion); ***gastroesophageal reflux*** (heartburn; vomiting); ***hyperlipidemia*** (large amount of fat in the blood); ***hypoglycemia*** (anxiety; blurred vision; chills; cold sweats; coma; confusion; cool pale skin; depression; dizziness; fast heartbeat; headache; increased hunger; nausea; nervousness; nightmares; seizures; shakiness; slurred speech; unusual tiredness or weakness); ***impotence*** (loss in sexual ability, desire, drive, or performance; decreased interest in sexual intercourse; inability to have or keep an erection); ***malaise*** (general feeling of discomfort or illness; unusual tiredness or weakness); ***restlessness***

Overdose

For more information on the management of overdose or unintentional ingestion, **contact a poison control center** (see *Poison Control Center Listing*).

In a documented case of overdosage with up to 400 mg memantine the patient experienced restlessness, psychosis, visual hallucinations, somnolence, stupor, and loss of consciousness. The patient recovered without permanent sequelae.

Treatment of overdose

To enhance elimination—

Elimination of memantine can be enhanced by acidification of urine.

Supportive care—

As in any cases of overdose, general supportive measures should be utilized, and treatment should be symptomatic.

Patients in whom intentional overdose is confirmed or suspected should be referred for psychiatric consultation.

Patient Consultation

As an aid to patient consultation, refer to *Advice for the Patient, Memantine (Systemic).*

In providing consultation, consider emphasizing the following selected information (» = major clinical significance):

Before using this medication

» Conditions affecting use, especially:

Hypersensitivity to memantine or any of its components

Other medical problems, especially neurological conditions and severe renal impairment

Proper use of this medication

Proper administration of oral solution: Using dosing syringe to administer prescribed amount

» Proper dosing; care givers should understand proper administration and dose escalation

Missed dose: Taking as soon as possible; not taking if almost time for next scheduled dose; not doubling doses

» Proper storage

Side/adverse effects

Signs of potential side effects, especially hypertension, peripheral edema

Signs of potential side effects observed during clinical practice, especially acute pancreatitis, acute renal failure, aspiration pneumonia, atrioventricular block, bone fracture, cerebral infarction, claudication, dyskinesia, grand mal convulsions, hepatic failure, ileus, intracranial hemorrhage, neuroleptic malignant syndrome, prolonged QT interval, Stevens-Johnson syndrome, sudden death, supraventricular tachycardia, tachycardia, tardive dyskinesia, or thrombocytopenia

General Dosing Information

For oral dosing forms:

Memantine is a low to moderate affinity uncompetitive NMDA antagonist that did not produce any evidence of drug-seeking behavior or withdrawal symptoms upon discontinuation in 2,504 patients who participated in clinical trials at therapeutic doses. Post marketing data, outside the U.S., retrospectively collected, has provided no evidence of drug abuse or dependence.

Diet/Nutrition

May be taken with or without food.

Oral Dosage Forms

MEMANTINE HYDROCHLORIDE ORAL SOLUTION

Usual adult dose

See *Memantine Tablets.*

Strength(s) usually available

U.S.—

2 mg per mL (Rx) [*Namenda* (alcohol-free and sugar-free; sorbitol solution (70%); methyl paraben; propylparaben; propylene glycol; glycerin; natural peppermint flavor #104; citric acid; sodium citrate; purified water)].

Packaging and storage

Store at 25 °C (77 °F); excursions permitted to 15 to 30 °C (59 to 86 °F).

Preparation of dosage form

The following are instructions for administering the oral solution dosage form:

• Remove oral dosing syringe along with the cap and plastic tube from the bag and attach to tube to the cap.

• Open the child-resistant cap on the bottle by pushing down on the cap while turning the cap counter-clockwise (to the left) and remove the cap and seal from the bottle.

• Insert the plastic tube fully into the bottle and screw the cap tightly onto the bottle by turning the cap clockwise (to the right).

• Keeping the bottle upright on the table, remove the lid to uncover the opening on the top of the cap. With the plunger fully depressed, insert the tip of the syringe firmly into the opening of the cap.

• While holding the syringe, gently pull the plunger of the syringe up to draw medicine into the syringe.

• Remove the syringe from the cap opening. Invert the syringe (point tip upwards) and slowly press the plunger to a level that pushed out any large air bubbles that may be present. Keep the plunger in this position.

• Re-insert the tip of the syringe into the cap opening. While holding the syringe, continue to gently pull out the plunger until the bottom of the black ring of the plunger reaches the appropriate mark on the syringe that corresponds to the dose prescribed.

• Remove the syringe from the bottle and swallow the oral solution directly from the syringe. **Do not mix with any other liquid.**

• After use, reseal the bottle by snapping the attached lid closed.

• Rinse the empty syringe by inserting the open end of the syringe into a glass of water, pulling the plunger out to draw in water, and pushing the plunger in to remove the water. Repeat several times. Allow the syringe to air dry.

MEMANTINE HYDROCHLORIDE TABLETS

Usual adult dose

Alzheimer's dementia—

Oral, Starting dose is 5 mg daily; Target dose is 20 mg per day. May be taken with or without food.

Dose should be increased in 5 mg increments to 10 mg per day (5 mg twice a day), 15 mg per day (5 mg and 10 mg as separate doses), and 20 mg per day (10 mg twice a day). The minimum recommended interval between dose increases is one week.

Note: In patients with mild to moderate renal impairment, no dosage adjustment is needed.

A target dose of 5 mg twice per day is recommended in patients with severe renal impairment (creatinine clearance of 5 to 29 mL per minute based on the Cockroft-Gault equation):

• For males: CL_{cr}= [140− age (years) x Weight (kg)/[72 x serum creatinine (mg per dL)]

• For females: CL_{cr}= 0.85 x [140− age (years) x Weight (kg)/[72 x serum creatinine (mg per dL)]

Strength(s) usually available

U.S.—

5 mg (Rx) [*Namenda* (microcrystalline cellulose; lactose monohydrate; colloidal silicon dioxide; talc; magnesium stearate)].

10 mg (Rx) [*Namenda* (microcrystalline cellulose; lactose monohydrate; colloidal silicon dioxide; talc; magnesium stearate)].

Canada—

10 mg (Rx) [*Ebixa*].

Packaging and storage

Store at 25 °C (77 °F), excursions permitted to 15 to 30°C (59 to 86°F).

Auxiliary labeling

• Keep out of reach of children

Note

Caregivers should be instructed in the recommended administration (twice per day for doses above 5 mg) and dose escalation (minimum interval of one week between dose increases).

Revised: 09/23/2005

Developed: 03/02/2004

MENADIOL—See *Vitamin K (Systemic)*

MENINGOCOCCAL POLYSACCHARIDE VACCINE Systemic

VA CLASSIFICATION (Primary): IM100

Note: This monograph refers to the vaccine containing the polysaccharides from *Neisseria meningitidis* serogroups A, C, Y, and W-135.

Commonly used brand name(s): *Menomune.*

Note: For a listing of dosage forms and brand names by country availability, see *Dosage Forms* section(s).

Category
Immunizing agent (active).

Indications
General Considerations
Meningococcal disease is an infection caused by *Neisseria meningitidis*. Meningococcal disease manifests most commonly as meningitis and/or meningococcemia that can progress rapidly to purpura fulminans, shock, and death. *N. meningitidis* is transmitted from person to person via respiratory secretions; carriage usually is asymptomatic.

N. meningitidis causes both endemic and epidemic disease, principally meningitis and meningococcemia. As a result of the control of *Haemophilus influenzae* type b infections, *N. meningitidis* has taken their place as the leading cause of bacterial meningitis in children and young adults in the U.S., with an estimated 2600 cases each year. The case-fatality rate is 13% for meningitic disease (defined as the isolation of *N. meningitidis* from cerebrospinal fluid) and 11.5% for persons who have *N. meningitidis* isolated from blood, despite therapy with antimicrobial agents (e.g., penicillin) to which U.S. strains remain clinically sensitive.

The incidence of meningococcal disease peaks in late winter to early spring. Attack rates are highest among children 3 to 12 months of age and then steadily decline among older age groups. Based on multistate surveillance conducted between 1989 and 1991, serogroup B organisms accounted for 46% of all cases and serogroup C for 45%; serogroups W-135 and Y and strains that could not be serotyped accounted for most of the remaining cases. Recent data indicate that the proportion of cases caused by serogroup Y strains is increasing. Serogroup A, which rarely causes disease in the U.S., is the most common cause of epidemics in Africa and Asia. In the U.S., localized community outbreaks of serogroup C disease and a statewide serogroup B epidemic have been reported.

Persons who have certain medical conditions are at increased risk for developing meningococcal infection. Meningococcal disease is particularly common among persons who have component deficiencies in the terminal common complement pathway; many of these persons experience multiple episodes of infection. Asplenic persons also may be at increased risk for acquiring meningococcal disease with particularly severe infections. Persons who have other diseases associated with immunosuppression (e.g., those caused by human immunodeficiency virus [HIV] and *Streptococcus pneumoniae*) may be at higher risk for acquiring meningococcal disease and for disease caused by some other encapsulated bacteria. Evidence suggests that HIV-infected persons are not at substantially increased risk for epidemic serogroup A meningococcal disease; however, such patients may be at increased risk for sporadic meningococcal disease or disease caused by other meningococcal serogroups. Previously, military recruits had high rates of meningococcal disease, particularly serogroup C disease; however, since the initiation of routine vaccination of recruits with the bivalent A and C meningococcal vaccine in 1971, the high rates of meningococcal disease caused by those serogroups have decreased substantially and cases occur infrequently. Military recruits now routinely receive the quadrivalent A, C, Y, W-135 meningococcal vaccine.

The decision to implement mass vaccination to prevent meningococcal disease depends on whether the occurrence of more than one case of the disease represents an outbreak or an unusual clustering of endemic meningococcal disease. Because the number of cases in outbreaks usually is small, this determination is not easily made without evaluation and analysis of the pattern of disease occurrence. Mass vaccination campaigns are expensive, require a massive public health effort, and can create unwarranted concern among the public. However, mass vaccination can prevent unnecessary morbidity and mortality. Epidemiologists in state and local health departments should determine whether mass vaccination should be implemented to prevent meningococcal disease.

Accepted
Meningitis, meningococcal (prophylaxis)—Meningococcal polysaccharide vaccine is indicated for immunization against meningococcal disease caused by *Neisseria meningitidis*, Group A, Group C, Group Y, or Group W-135.

Routine vaccination of civilians with the quadrivalent meningococcal polysaccharide vaccine is not recommended because of its relative ineffectiveness in children younger than 2 years of age, among whom risk for endemic disease is highest, and its relatively short duration of protection. However, meningococcal polysaccharide vaccine is useful for controlling serogroup C meningococcal outbreaks.

In general, use of meningococcal polysaccharide vaccine should be restricted to persons 2 years of age and older; however, children as young as 3 months of age may be vaccinated to elicit short-term protection against serogroup A meningococcal disease.

Routine vaccination with meningococcal polysaccharide vaccine is recommended for certain high-risk groups, including:

- Military recruits. Before the advent of routine administration of meningococcal vaccine to military personnel in 1971, military recruits were at high risk, especially for the serogroup C disease.
- Persons with anatomic or functional asplenia. Asplenic persons seem to be at increased risk of developing meningococcal disease and experience particularly severe infections. Persons who have had their spleens removed because of trauma or nonlymphoid tumors have acceptable antibody responses to the vaccine.

In addition, immunization should be considered for:

- Household or institutional contacts of persons with meningococcal disease as an adjunct to antibiotic chemoprophylaxis. However, antimicrobial chemoprophylaxis of close contacts of patients who have sporadic cases of meningococcal disease is the primary means for prevention of meningococcal disease in the U.S.
- Research, industrial, and clinical laboratory personnel who routinely are exposed to *N. meningitidis* in solutions that may be aerosolized.
- Travelers to countries having epidemic meningococcal disease, particularly travelers who will have prolonged contact with the local populace. Vaccination with meningococcal polysaccharide vaccine may benefit travelers to and those residing in countries in which *N. meningitidis* is hyperendemic or epidemic. Epidemics of meningococcal disease are recurrent in that part of sub-Saharan Africa known as the "meningitis belt," which extends from Senegal in the west to Ethiopia in the east. Epidemics in the meningitis belt usually occur during the dry season (i.e., from December to June); thus, vaccination is recommended for travelers visiting this region during that time. Epidemics occasionally are identified in other parts of the world and have occurred in Saudi Arabia, Kenya, Tanzania, Burundi, and Mongolia. Information concerning the geographic areas for which vaccination is recommended can be obtained from international health clinics for travelers, state health departments, and the Centers for Disease Control and Prevention (CDC).

Revaccination may be indicated for persons in the above high-risk categories, particularly children at high-risk who were first immunized before they were 4 years of age; such children should be considered for revaccination after 2 or 3 years if they remain at high risk. Although the need for revaccination of older children and adults has not been determined, antibody levels decline rapidly over 2 to 3 years, and if indications still exist for immunization, revaccination may be considered within 3 to 5 years.

Unaccepted
Because this vaccine protects against only *Neisseria meningitidis* serogroups A, C, Y, and W-135, protection against other serogroups, such as serogroup B, is not an indication for immunization with this vaccine.

Pharmacology/Pharmacokinetics
Physicochemical characteristics
Source—Meningococcal polysaccharide vaccine consists of 50 mcg each of the respective (A, C, Y, and W-135) purified bacterial capsular polysaccharides.

Mechanism of action/Effect
Meningococcal bacteria are surrounded by polysaccharide capsules, which make the bacteria resistant to attack by white blood cells. However, human blood serum contains antibodies that render the bacteria vulnerable to attack. The vaccine, which is composed of the purified capsular polysaccharides from bacterial cells, stimulates production of these antibodies and provides active immunity to the four serogroups of *N. meningitidis* bacteria represented in the vaccine.

The vaccine will not stimulate protection against infections caused by organisms other than those in Groups A, C, Y, and W-135.

Protective effect
The immunogenicity and clinical efficacy of the serogroups A and C meningococcal vaccines have been well established. The serogroup A polysaccharide induces antibody in some children as young as 3 months of age, although a response comparable with that among adults is not achieved until 4 or 5 years of age. The serogroup C component is poorly immunogenic in recipients who are younger than 18 to 24 months of age. The serogroups A and C vaccines have demonstrated estimated clinical efficacies of 85 to 100% in children 5 years of age and older and adults and are useful in controlling epidemics. Serogroups Y and W-135 polysaccharides are safe and immunogenic in adults and in children 2 years of age and older. Although clinical protection has not been documented, vaccination with Y and W-135

polysaccharides induces bactericidal antibody. The antibody responses to each of the four polysaccharides in the quadrivalent vaccine are serogroup-specific and independent.

Time to protective effect
Protective levels of antibody usually are achieved within 7 to 10 days after vaccination. Cases of serogroup C meningococcal disease occurring in vaccinated persons within 10 days after vaccination should not be considered vaccine failures.

Duration of protective effect
The duration of protective effect provided by meningococcal polysaccharide vaccines is limited. In one study vaccine efficacy declined from 87 to 54% 1 and 3 years, respectively, after vaccination. This decline was particularly marked in children younger than 4 years of age, in whom vaccine efficacy was not significantly different from nil 3 years after vaccination. These clinical observations are supported by the results of serologic surveys. In another study, it was shown that in children meningococcal antibody levels decline to background levels 2 years after immunization with meningococcal polysaccharide vaccines.

Precautions to Consider

Pregnancy/Reproduction
Pregnancy—Studies of vaccination during pregnancy have not documented adverse effects among either pregnant women or neonates. In addition, these studies have documented high antibody levels in maternal and umbilical cord blood following vaccination during pregnancy. Antibody levels in the infants decreased during the first few months after birth; subsequent response to meningococcal vaccination was not affected. These observations have been confirmed in more recent studies of other polysaccharide vaccines administered during pregnancy. Based on data from studies involving use of meningococcal vaccines and other polysaccharide vaccines administered during pregnancy, altering meningococcal vaccination recommendations during pregnancy is unnecessary.

Studies have not been done in animals.

FDA Pregnancy Category C.

Breast-feeding
Problems in humans have not been documented.

Pediatrics
Meningococcal polysaccharide vaccine is less immunogenic in children younger than 2 years of age for prevention of sporadic disease. Therefore, use of meningococcal polysaccharide vaccine should be restricted to persons 2 years of age and older; however, children as young as 3 months of age may be vaccinated to elicit short-term protection against serogroup A meningococcal disease. Two doses of meningococcal polysaccharide vaccine administered 3 months apart should be considered for children 3 to 18 months of age.

Geriatrics
Appropriate studies on the relationship of age to the effects of this vaccine have not been performed in the geriatric population. However, no geriatrics-specific problems have been documented to date.

Drug interactions and/or related problems
The following drug interactions and/or related problems have been selected on the basis of their potential clinical significance (possible mechanism in parentheses where appropriate)—not necessarily inclusive (» = major clinical significance):

Note: Combinations containing any of the following medications, depending on the amount present, may also interact with this medication.

Immunosuppressive agents or
Radiation therapy
(because normal defense mechanisms are suppressed, the patient's antibody response to the meningococcal polysaccharide vaccine may be decreased. The precaution does not apply to corticosteroids used as replacement therapy, for short-term [less than 2 weeks] systemic therapy, or by other routes of administration that do not cause immunosuppression)

Medical considerations/Contraindications
The medical considerations/contraindications included have been selected on the basis of their potential clinical significance (reasons given in parentheses where appropriate)—not necessarily inclusive (» = major clinical significance).

Risk-benefit should be considered when the following medical problems exist:

Febrile illness, severe
(to avoid confusing manifestations of illness with possible side/adverse effects of vaccine; minor illnesses, such as upper respiratory infection, do not preclude administration of vaccine)

Sensitivity to meningococcal polysaccharide vaccine

Sensitivity to thimerosal

Side/Adverse Effects
The following side/adverse effects have been selected on the basis of their potential clinical significance (possible signs and symptoms in parentheses where appropriate)—not necessarily inclusive:

Those indicating need for medical attention
Incidence rare

Anaphylactic reaction (difficulty in breathing or swallowing; hives; itching, especially of soles or palms; reddening of skin, especially around ears; swelling of eyes, face, or inside of nose; unusual tiredness or weakness, sudden and severe)

Those indicating need for medical attention only if they continue or are bothersome
Incidence more frequent

Erythema at injection site (redness)—lasting 1 or 2 days; ***tenderness, soreness, or pain at injection site***

Incidence less frequent

Chills; fatigue (tiredness or weakness); ***fever over 37.8 °C (100 °F); headache; induration at injection site*** (hard lump); ***malaise*** (general feeling of discomfort or illness)

Patient Consultation
As an aid to patient consultation, refer to Advice for the Patient, *Meningococcal Polysaccharide Vaccine (Systemic).*

In providing consultation, consider emphasizing the following selected information (» = major clinical significance):

Before receiving this vaccine
» Conditions affecting use, especially:
Sensitivity to meningococcal vaccine or thimerosal; the vaccine contains thimerosal

Proper use of this medication
» Proper dosing

Side/adverse effects
Signs of potential side effects, especially anaphylactic reaction

General Dosing Information
Systemic reactions to meningococcal polysaccharide vaccine are rare. However, appropriate precautions should be taken prior to meningococcal polysaccharide vaccine injection to prevent allergic or any other unwanted reactions. Precautions should include review of the patient's history regarding possible sensitivity and the ready availability of 1:1000 epinephrine injection and other appropriate agents used for control of immediate allergic reactions.

Meningococcal polysaccharide vaccine is administered subcutaneously as a single 0.5-mL dose for both children and adults. It should not be administered intramuscularly, intradermally, or intravenously.

Meningococcal polysaccharide vaccine may be administered concurrently with other vaccines, using separate body sites, separate syringes, and the precautions that apply to each immunizing agent.

Revaccination may be indicated for persons at high risk of infection, particularly children at high risk who were first immunized before they were 4 years of age; such children should be considered for revaccination after 2 or 3 years if they remain at high risk.

In the U.S. and Canada, the vaccine is available in a 10-dose vial for use with either a needle and syringe or a jet injector and in a 50-dose vial for use only with a jet injector. During use it is possible that the nozzle of the jet injector apparatus may become contaminated with blood or serum. In one instance, such contamination has been reported to be associated with transmission of hepatitis B disease. Therefore, if blood or serum contamination occurs, the nozzle should be disassembled, cleansed, and sterilized before continued use to prevent the possibility of transmission of hepatitis or other infectious agents from one person to another. Any partially used reconstituted vaccine that has been administered with a jet injector apparatus should **not** be reused and should be discarded.

For treatment of adverse effects
Recommended treatment includes
- For mild hypersensitivity reaction—Administering antihistamines, and, if necessary, corticosteroids.

• For severe hypersensitivity or anaphylactic reaction—Administering epinephrine. Antihistamines or corticosteroids may also be administered as required.

Parenteral Dosage Forms

MENINGOCOCCAL POLYSACCHARIDE VACCINE FOR INJECTION

Usual adult and adolescent dose

Immunizing agent (active)—
Subcutaneous, 0.5 mL.

Usual pediatric dose

Immunizing agent (active)—
See *Usual adult and adolescent dose*.

Strength(s) usually available

U.S.—
50 mcg of polysaccharide from each of the four serogroups of meningococci represented in the vaccine in each 0.5 mL dose (Rx) [*Menomune* (thimerosal 1:10,000; lactose 2.5 to 5 mg)].

Canada—
50 mcg of polysaccharide from each of the four serogroups of meningococci represented in the vaccine in each 0.5 mL dose (Rx) [*Menomune* (thimerosal 1:10,000; lactose 2.5 to 5 mg)].

Packaging and storage

Store both the freeze-dried and the reconstituted vaccine between 2 and 8 °C (36 and 46 °F), unless otherwise specified by manufacturer. Protect from freezing.

Preparation of dosage form

• Reconstitute the vaccine using only the diluent supplied by the manufacturer.
• Draw up the appropriate amount of diluent into a suitably sized syringe and inject the diluent into the vial containing the vaccine.
• Shake the vial until the vaccine is dissolved.

Stability

Solution should not be used if there is extraneous particulate matter and/or discoloration prior to administration.

The date of reconstitution should be recorded on the label of the vaccine vial.

Single-dose vials of vaccine should be used within 24 hours of reconstitution.

Multidose vials of vaccine that have been reconstituted for administration by syringe should be discarded after 5 days.

Multidose vials of vaccine that have been reconstituted for administration by jet injector should be administered promptly. Partially used vials of vaccine should be discarded immediately.

Revised: 02/02/1999

MENINGOCOCCAL VACCINE, DIPHTHERIA CONJUGATE Systemic†

VA CLASSIFICATION (Primary): IM100

Commonly used brand name(s): *Menactra*.

Some other commonly used names are:
Meningococcal (Groups A, C, Y and W-135) Polysaccharide Diphtheria Toxoid Conjugate Vaccine
MCV4

Note: This monograph refers to the vaccine containing the polysaccharides from *Neisseria meningitidis* serogroups A, C, Y, and W-135.

Note: For a listing of dosage forms and brand names by country availability, see *Dosage Forms* section(s).

†Not commercially available in Canada.

Category

Immunizing agent (active).

Indications

General Considerations

The meningococcus bacterium, *N meningitidis*, causes both endemic and epidemic disease, principally meningitis and meningococcemia. At least 13 meningococcal serogroups have been identified based on antigenic differences in their capsular polysaccharides. Five serogroups (A, B, C, Y and W-135) are responsible for nearly all cases of meningococcal disease worldwide. Early clinical manifestations of meningococcal disease are often difficult to distinguish from other, more common but less serious illnesses. Onset and progression of disease can be rapid; in most cases (60%), infected individuals are symptomatic for less than 24 hours before seeking medical care. Even with administration of appropriate antimicrobials and other adjunctive therapies, the case fatality rate has remained at approximately 10%. In cases of fluminant septicemia, the case fatality rate may reach 40%. Approximately 11 to 19% of meningococcal disease survivors have sequelae such as hearing loss and neurologic disability, or loss of skin, digits or limbs as a result of ischemia.

In the United States, overall rates of meningococcal disease during the period of 1967 to 2002 have remained stable, with yearly case counts varying from 1323 to 3525, reflecting a cyclical pattern with peaks occurring every 10 to 15 years. The age-specific incidence of meningococcal disease continues to be highest among infants younger than one year old, among whom serogroup B predominates. The rate of meningococcal disease also peaks during adolescence and early adulthood.

From 1989 to 2002, the proportion of all meningococcal cases due to serogroup Y increased from 2% to 29%, while serogroups B and C decreased from 46% and 45% of cases, to 24% and 34%, respectively. The remaining cases were caused by serogroup W-135 and other strains. In 2002, serogroups C and Y accounted for 42% and 24% of meningococcal cases, respectively, in adolescents and adults 18 to 49 years of age.

Globally, serogroup A is the most common cause of epidemics in Africa and Asia, but a rare cause of disease in the US. Outbreaks of serogroup W-135 have been reported among pilgrims returning from the Hajj to Saudi Arabia in 2000 and 2001.

Accepted

Meningitis, meningococcal (prophylaxis)—Meningococcal polysaccharide diphtheria toxoid conjugate vaccine is indicated for active immunization of adolescents and adults 11-55 years of age for the prevention of invasive meningococcal disease caused by *N meningitidis* serogroups A, C, Y and W-135.

Unaccepted

Meningococcal polysaccharide diphtheria toxoid conjugate vaccine is not indicated for the prevention of meningitis caused by other microorganisms or for the prevention of invasive meningococcal disease caused by *N meningitidis* serogroup B.

Meningococcal polysaccharide diphtheria toxoid conjugate vaccine is not indicated for treatment of meningococcal infections.

Meningococcal polysaccharide diphtheria toxoid conjugate vaccine is not indicated for immunization against diphtheria.

Pharmacology/Pharmacokinetics

Physicochemical characteristics

Source—Each dose of the vaccine if formulated to contain 4 micrograms each of meningococcal A, C, Y, and W-135 polysaccharides conjugated to approximately 48 micrograms of diphtheria toxoid protein carrier.

Mechanism of action/Effect

The presence of bactericidal anti-capsular meningococcal antibodies has been associated with protection from invasive meningococcal disease. Meningococcal polysaccharide diphtheria toxoid conjugate vaccine induces the production of bactericidal antibodies specific to the capsular polysaccharides of serogroups A, C, Y and W-135.

Protective effect

Results from a clinical trial conducted in 881 adolescents aged 11 to 18 years of age with undetectable titers (i.e., less than 8 at day 0) showed seroconversion rates (defined as ≥4-fold rise in Day 28 serum bactericidal assay [SBA] titers) for Serogroups A, C, Y, and W-135 of 100%, 99%, 98%, and 99%, respectively. In a clinical trial conducted in 2554 adults aged 18 to 55 years of age, seroconversion rates for Serogroups A, C, Y, and W-135 were 100%, 99%, 91%, and 97%, respectively.

As with any vaccine, meningococcal diphtheria conjugate vaccine may not protect 100% of individuals.

Duration of protective effect

The need for, or timing of, a booster dose of meningococcal diphtheria conjugate vaccine has not yet been determined.

Precautions to Consider

Cross-sensitivity and/or related problems

Known hypersensitivity to diphtheria toxoid

Carcinogenicity/Mutagenicity

Meningococcal diphtheria conjugate vaccine has not been evaluated in animals for its carcinogenic or mutagenic potentials.

Pregnancy/Reproduction

Fertility—Meningococcal diphtheria conjugate vaccine has not been evaluated in animals for impairment of fertility.

Pregnancy—Studies have not been done in humans. Because animal studies are not always predictive of human response, meningococcal vaccine diphtheria conjugate should be used during pregnancy only if clearly needed. Health care providers are encouraged to register pregnant women who receive this vaccine in the manufacturer's vaccination pregnancy registry by calling 1-800-822-2463.

Animal reproduction studies were performed in mice using 900 times the human dose adjusted by body weight of meningococcal diphtheria conjugate vaccine with no effects on fertility, maternal health, embryo/fetal survival, or postnatal development. Skeletal examinations showed one fetus (1 of 234) in the vaccine group with a cleft palate. None were observed in the concurrent control group of 174. There are no data suggesting that this isolated finding is vaccine related, and no other skeletal and organ malformations were observed in this study.

FDA Pregnancy Category C

Breast-feeding

It is not known whether meningococcal vaccine is distributed into human breast milk. Because many drugs are distributed in human milk, caution should be exercised when this vaccine is administered to a nursing woman.

Pediatrics

The Advisory Committee on Immunization Practices (ACIP) recommends vaccination of young adolescents (defined as persons aged 11 to 12 years) with meningococcal vaccine (MCV4) at the preadolescent health-care visit.

Safety and efficacy in children below 11 years of age have not been established.

Adolescents

For those adolescents who have not previously received MCV4, ACIP recommends vaccination before high school entry (at approximately age 15 years) as an effective strategy to reduce meningococcal disease incidence among adolescents and young adults.

Geriatrics

Safety and efficacy in adults older than 55 years of age have not been established.

Drug interactions and/or related problems

The following drug interactions and/or related problems have been selected on the basis of their potential clinical significance (possible mechanism in parentheses where appropriate)—not necessarily inclusive (» = major clinical significance):

Note: Combinations containing any of the following medications, depending on the amount present, may also interact with this medication.

» Anticoagulant therapy
(should not be given concomitantly because of risk of hemorrhage unless potential benefit clearly outweighs risk of administration; if decision is made to administer to patient, it should be given with caution and steps taken to avoid risk of bleeding or hematoma formation following injection)

Immunosuppressive therapies including
Alkylating agents or
Antimetabolites or
Corticosteroids (used in greater than physiologic doses) or
Cytoxic drugs or
Irradiation
(may reduce immune response to vaccines)

Medical considerations/Contraindications

The medical considerations/contraindications included have been selected on the basis of their potential clinical significance (reasons given in parentheses where appropriate)—not necessarily inclusive (» = major clinical significance).

Except under special circumstances, this medication should not be used when the following medical problem exists:

» Guillain-Barre syndrome (GBS), history of
(should not receive meningococcal vaccine, diphtheria conjugate)

» Hypersensitivity to meningococcal vaccine diphtheria conjugate or any component of the product including diphtheria toxoid or

» Hypersensitivity to dry natural rubber latex or

» Life-threatening reaction after previous administration of a vaccine containing similar components

Risk-benefit should be considered when the following medical problems exist:

» Hemophilia or

» Thrombocytopenia
(should not be given because of risk of hemorrhage unless potential benefit clearly outweighs risk of administration; if decision is made to administer to patient, it should be given with caution and steps taken to avoid risk of bleeding or hematoma formation following injection)

Illness, recent or acute
(the ACIP has published guidelines for vaccination of these persons [refer to www.cdc.gov])

Immunosuppression
(immune response to meningococcal diphtheria conjugate vaccine administered to immunosuppressed persons has not been studied)

Side/Adverse Effects

The US Department of Health and Human Services has established the Vaccine Adverse Event Reporting System (VAERS) to accept all reports of suspected adverse events after the administration of any vaccine. Reporting of all adverse events occurring after vaccine administration is encouraged from vaccine recipients, parents/guardians and the health care provider. Adverse events following immunization should be reported to VAERS. Reporting forms and information about reporting requirements or completion of the form can be obtained from VAERS through a toll-free number 1-800-822-7967. Reporting forms may also be obtained at the FDA web site at www.vaers.org. Health-care providers should also report these events to the manufacturer by calling 1-800-822-2463.

In September 2005, the Food and Drug Administration (FDA) and Centers for Disease Control and Prevention (CDC) alerted consumers and health care providers to five reports of Guillain-Barre syndrome (GBS) following meningococcal conjugate vaccine administration. It is unknown whether or not these cases are causal. The five reports occurred in patients 17 or 18 years of age and all are reported to be recovering or to have recovered. Because of the serious nature of these reports, any individuals with knowledge of cases of GBS following meningococcal conjugate vaccine administration are asked to report them to VAERS.

The following side/adverse effects have been selected on the basis of their potential clinical significance (possible signs and symptoms in parentheses where appropriate)—not necessarily inclusive:

Those indicating need for medical attention

Incidence rare

Anaphylactic reaction (cough; difficulty swallowing; dizziness; fast heartbeat; hives; itching; puffiness or swelling of the eyelids or around the eyes, face, lips or tongue; shortness of breath; skin rash; tightness in chest; unusual tiredness or weakness; wheezing)

Incidence not determined—Observed during clinical practice; estimates of frequency can not be determined

Guillain-Barre syndrome (sudden numbness and weakness in the arms and legs; inability to move arms and legs); ***transverse myelitis*** (back pain, sudden and severe; muscle weakness, sudden and progressing)

Those indicating need for medical attention only if they continue or are bothersome

Incidence more frequent

Anorexia (loss of appetite; weight loss); ***arthralgia*** (pain in joints; muscle pain or stiffness; difficulty in moving); ***chills; diarrhea; fatigue*** (unusual tiredness or weakness); ***fever; headache; induration at injection site*** (hard lump at injection site); ***malaise*** (general feeling of discomfort or illness; unusual tiredness or weakness); ***pain, redness, or swelling at injection site***

Incidence less frequent

Rash; vomiting

Patient Consultation

As an aid to patient consultation, refer to *Advice for the Patient, Meningococcal Vaccine, Diphtheria Conjugate (Systemic).*

In providing consultation, consider emphasizing the following selected information (» = major clinical significance):

Before using this medication

» Conditions affecting use, especially:

Hypersensitivity to this vaccine or any of its components including diphtheria toxoid or to dry natural rubber latex, or to any other vaccines containing similar components

Pregnancy—Should be used during pregnancy only if clearly needed

Breast-feeding—Caution should be exercised when administering this vaccine to a nursing woman

Use in children—ACIP recommends vaccination of young adolescents (defined as persons aged 11 to 12 years)

Safety and efficacy not established in children younger than 11 years of age

Use in adolescents—If an adolescent has not received the vaccine previously, ACIP recommends before high school entry (at approximately age 15 years)

Use in the elderly—Safety and efficacy not established in adults older than 55 years of age

Other medications, especially anticoagulant therapy

Other medical problems, especially hemophilia history of Guillain-Barre syndrome, or thrombocytopenia

Proper use of this medication

» Proper dosing

Proper storage

Precautions while using this medication

» Importance of contacting physician immediately if signs of anaphylactic reaction occur

» Contacting physician immediately if sudden and increasing weakness in arms and legs occur

Encouraging patients and explaining how to report all adverse events to the Vaccine Adverse Event Reporting System (VAERS)

Side/adverse effects

Signs of potential side effects, especially anaphylactic reaction

Signs of potential side effects observed during clinical practice, especially Guillain-Barre syndrome and transverse myelitis

General Dosing Information

Before administration, all appropriate precautions should be taken to prevent adverse reactions. This includes a review of the patient's previous immunization history, the presence of any contraindications to immunization, the current health status, and history concerning possible sensitivity to the vaccine, similar vaccine, or to latex.

Concomitant use of meningococcal diphtheria conjugate vaccine with tetanus and diphtheria vaccine did not result in reduced tetanus, diphtheria, or meningococcal antibody responses compared with meningococcal diphtheria conjugated vaccine administered 28 days after tetanus and diphtheria. However, for meningococcal serogroups C, Y, and W-135, the proportion of participants with a 4-fold or greater rise in SBA-BR titer was higher when meningococcal diphtheria conjugate vaccine was given concomitantly with tetanus and diphtheria toxoids adsorbed for adult use (Td) than when the vaccine was given one month following Td. The clinical relevance of this finding has not been fully evaluated.

Concomitant use of meningococcal diphtheria conjugate vaccine with typhoid Vi polysaccharide vaccine did not result in reduced antibody responses to any of the vaccine antigens.

The safety and immunogenicity of concomitant administration of meningococcal diphtheria conjugate vaccine with vaccines other than typhoid Vi polysaccharide or tetanus and diphtheria vaccines have not been determined.

With concomitant administration, the vaccines should be given at separate injections sites with different syringes and NOT mixed in the same syringe.

This vaccine should not be administered intravenously, subcutaneously, or intradermally.

Before injection, the skin at the injection side should be cleaned and prepared with a suitable germicide.

The need for, or timing of, a booster dose of meningococcal diphtheria conjugate vaccine has not yet been determined.

Safety considerations for handling this medication

Special care should be taken to avoid subcutaneous injection of this vaccine since safety and efficacy have not been established using this route of administration.

Use of a separate, sterile syringe and needle or a sterile disposable unit for each patient to prevent transmission of blood borne infectious agents from person to person

Cautious and proper disposal of needles and syringes according to biohazardous waste guidelines

For treatment of adverse effects

As a precautionary measure in case of anaphylactic or serious allergic reactions, epinephrine injection (1:1000) and other appropriate agents and equipment must be immediately available.

Parenteral Dosage Forms

MENINGOCOCCAL VACCINE, DIPHTHERIA CONJUGATE INJECTION

Usual adult and adolescent dose

Meningitis, meningococcal (prophylaxis)—

Intramuscular injection, 0.5 mL preferably in the deltoid region. After insertion of the needle, aspirate to ensure that the needle has not entered a blood vessel

Usual pediatric dose

For young adolescents aged 11 to 12 years, see *adult and adolescent dose*.

Safety and efficacy in children less than 11 years of age have not been established.

Usual geriatric dose

Safety and efficacy in adults older than 55 years of age have not been established.

Strength(s) usually available

U.S.—

0.5 mL meningococcal (4 mcg each of groups A, C, Y and W-135) polysaccharide diphtheria toxoid conjugate vaccine (Rx) [*Menactra* (preservative-free; sodium phosphate buffered isotonic sodium chloride solution)].

Packaging and storage

Store between 2 and 8 °C (35 and 46 °F). Do not freeze. Protect from light.

Stability

Parenteral drug products should be inspected visually for container integrity, particulate matter and discoloration prior to administration whenever solution and container permit.

Do not use after expiration date.

Auxiliary labeling

- Refrigerate - Do not freeze.
- Protect from light.

Caution

The stopper of the vial contains dry natural rubber latex, which may cause allergic reactions in latex-sensitive individuals.

Product that has been exposed to freezing should not be used.

Additional information

Meningococcal diphtheria conjugate vaccine must not be mixed with any vaccine in the same syringe. Therefore, separate injections sites and different syringes should be used in case of concomitant administration.

Revised: 11/10/2005
Developed: 03/11/2005

MENTHYL ANTHRANILATE—See *Sunscreen Agents (Topical)*

MEPENZOLATE—See *Anticholinergics/Antispasmodics (Systemic)*

MEPERIDINE—See *Opioid (Narcotic) Analgesics (Systemic)*

MEPHENTERMINE—See *Sympathomimetic Agents—Cardiovascular Use (Parenteral-Systemic)*

MEPHENYTOIN—See *Anticonvulsants, Hydantoin (Systemic)*

MEPHOBARBITAL—See *Barbiturates (Systemic)*

MEPIVACAINE—See *Anesthetics (Parenteral-Local)*

MEQUINOL AND TRETINOIN
Topical†

VA CLASSIFICATION (Primary): DE900

Commonly used brand name(s): *Solagé*.

Some other commonly used names are:
Other commonly used names for mequinol are: hydroquinone methyl ether and 4–hydroxyanisole. Other commonly used names for tretinoin are: retinoic acid, all-*trans*-retinoic acid, and vitamin A acid.

Note: For a listing of dosage forms and brand names by country availability, see *Dosage Forms* section(s).

†Not commercially available in Canada.

Category

Hypopigmenting agent (topical).

Indications

Accepted

Solar lentigines (treatment)—Mequinol and tretinoin topical solution is indicated as an adjunct to a comprehensive skin care and sun avoidance program for the treatment of solar lentigines.

Acceptance not established

The safety and efficacy of mequinol and tretinoin topical solution for the prevention or treatment of melasma or postinflammatory hyperpigmentation have not been established.

Pharmacology/Pharmacokinetics

Physicochemical characteristics

Molecular weight—
Mequinol: 124.14.
Tretinoin: 300.44.

Chemical names—
Mequinol: 4–hydroxyanisole or hydroquinone monomethyl ether
Tretinoin: retinoic acid or all-*trans*-retinoic acid

Mechanism of action/Effect

Solar lentigines are localized, pigmented, macular lesions of the skin on areas of the body chronically exposed to sunlight.

Mequinol is a depigmenting agent; it is more potent and possibly more effective than hydroquinone (e.g., Melanex®) and is claimed to have a low propensity for leucoderma. The mechanism of depigmenting effects of mequinol remain unclear; speculations include oxidation by tyrosinase to cytotoxic products in melanocytes, a direct/selective toxic effect on melanocytes, or inhibition of melanin formation.

Tretinoin is a retinoid which acts via retinoic acid receptors (RARs), and also demonstrates a depigmenting effect. The mechanism of tretinoin in actinic lentigines is unclear; inhibition of tyrosinase activity has been suggested.

Other actions/effects

Both mequinol and tretinoin have been used singly as depigmenting agents. Topical tretinoin alone (e.g., Retin-A®) has been used extensively for photoaging.Melanocyte-toxic actions of mequinol have led to preclinical investigation and systemic clinical use in malignant melanoma.

Absorption

The percutaneous absorption of tretinoin from topical mequinol/tretinoin was approximately 4% in one study involving healthy subjects.

Biotransformation

Mequinol—Extensively metabolized.

Half-life

Elimination—The elimination half-life of tretinoin ranges from 0.5 to 2 hours after oral doses. Mequinol exhibited an elimination half-life of 30 to 90 minutes following intravenous infusion of 5 or 10 g/m² over 3 to 5 hours in melanoma patients; similar values were reported after intraarterial infusion.

Onset of action

Within 24 weeks.

Time to peak concentration

Following topical application (0.8 mL) to a 400-cm² area of the back (healthy subjects), peak plasma levels of mequinol occurred in 2 hours.

Peak plasma concentration:

Mequinol: mean 9.92 (range, 4.22 to 23.62) nanograms per mL (ng/mL).

Tretinoin—Concentrations did not increase above normal endogenous levels in one study in healthy subjects.

Duration of action

Up to 6 months.

Note: Following discontinuation of treatment, some degree of repigmentation of treated lesions was observed over time.

Elimination

Mequinol—Metabolites are renally eliminated.

Precautions to Consider

Cross-sensitivity and/or related problems

Patients sensitive to acitretin, etrinate, isotretinoin, or other vitamin A derivatives may be sensitive to mequinol and tretinoin, since tretinoin is a vitamin A derivative.

Carcinogenicity/Tumorigenicity

A study in CD-1 mice receiving topical mequinol and tretinoin at daily doses of 80 and 0.4 mg per kg of body weight (mg/kg) (240 and 1.2 mg per square meter of body surface area [mg/m²]), respectively, approximately 5 times the maximum possible human exposure, revealed that the combination was not carcinogenic. In a photocarcinogenicity study using hairless albino mice, median time to onset of tumors decreased. The number of tumors increased in all dose groups, ranging from 24 to 240 mg/m² mequinol and 0.12 to 1.2 mg/m² tretinoin, following chronic topical dosing with intercurrent exposure to ultraviolet radiation for up to 40 weeks.

Mutagenicity

Mequinol was non-mutagenic in the Ames/Salmonella assay. Mequinol and tretinoin topical solution was non-genotoxic in an *in vivo* dermal micronucleus assay in rats, but exposure to bone marrow was not demonstrated.

Pregnancy/Reproduction

Fertility—No impairment in fertility was seen in a dermal reproduction study in which rats received a dose of 80 and 0.4 mg/kg (480 and 2.4 mg/m²) of mequinol and tretinoin, respectively, applied to 5% of their total body surface area. This dose is approximately 11 times the corresponding maximum possible human exposure, assuming 100% bioavailability following topical application.

Pregnancy—Adequate and well-controlled studies in humans have not been done. Mequinol and tretinoin topical solution may cause fetal harm if administered to a pregnant woman. Mequinol and tretinoin topical solution is not recommended during pregnancy.

Studies in animals have shown that mequinol and tretinoin topical solution causes fetal harm. Other studies have shown no teratogenic effect.

FDA Pregnancy Category X

Breast-feeding

It not known whether the mequinol and tretinoin topical solution is distributed into breast milk. Because many drugs are distributed in breast milk, caution should be exercised when administered to nursing women.

Pediatrics

The safety and effectiveness of mequinol and tretinoin topical solution have not been established in pediatric patients. Use in children is not recommended.

Geriatrics

Studies performed to date have not demonstrated geriatrics-specific problems that would limit the usefulness of mequinol and tretinoin topical solution in the elderly.

Non-whites

The local cutaneous safety and efficacy of mequinol and tretinoin topical solution in non-whites have not been adequately established.

Drug interactions and/or related problems

The following drug interactions and/or related problems have been selected on the basis of their potential clinical significance (possible

mechanism in parentheses where appropriate)—not necessarily inclusive (» = major clinical significance):

Note: Combinations containing any of the following medications, depending on the amount present, may also interact with this medication.

» Photosensitizing medications, such as:
Fluoroquinolones
Phenothiazines
Sulfonamides
Tetracyclines
Thiazide diuretics
(concurrent use is not recommended because of the possibility of augmented phototoxicity)

Alcohol containing products, topical, or those with strong drying effects, such as:
Astringents
Spices or lime, topical
Medicated soaps or shampoos
Permanent wave solutions
Electrolysis, hair depilatories or waxes
(caution is recommended because of the possibility of increased irritation)

Medical considerations/Contraindications

The medical considerations/contraindications included have been selected on the basis of their potential clinical significance (reasons given in parentheses where appropriate)—not necessarily inclusive (» = major clinical significance).

Risk-benefit should be considered when the following medical problems exist:

» Eczema
(tretinoin may cause severe irritation)

Personal history, or family history of vitiligo
(may experience hypopigmentation on untreated areas)

Sensitivity to mequinol or tretinoin

» Sunburn, or
Frequent exposure to sunlight or sunlamps
(discontinue use until fully recovered from sunburn; because of heightened burning susceptibility, exposure of sunlight to treated areas should be avoided or minimized)

Side/Adverse Effects

Note: Mequinol and tretinoin topical solution is a dermal irritant. The effect of continued irritation of the skin when this medication is used for more than 52 weeks is not known.

The following side/adverse effects have been selected on the basis of their potential clinical significance (possible signs and symptoms in parentheses where appropriate)—not necessarily inclusive:

Those indicating need for medical attention

Incidence more frequent

Burning, tingling, or stinging sensation of skin, severe; erythema, severe (severe redness of skin); ***pruritus, severe*** (severe itching of skin); ***desquamation, severe*** (severe peeling of skin)

Incidence less frequent

Allergic reaction, contact; vesicular bulla (large blisters on the skin)

Those indicating need for medical attention only if they continue or are bothersome

Incidence more frequent

Burning sensation, stinging, or tingling of skin, mild; erythema, mild (redness of skin; unusually warm skin, mild); ***desquamation, mild*** (chapping and slight peeling of skin); ***pruritus*** (itching of skin); ***skin irritation; halo hypopigmentation*** (lightening of skin around treated area); ***hypopigmentation*** (lightening of skin on treated area)

Incidence less frequent

Crusting of skin; dry skin; hypopigmentation, persistent (lightening of skin on treated area)—beyond 120 days; ***skin rash***

Patient Consultation

As an aid to patient consultation, refer to *Advice for the Patient, Mequinol and Tretinoin (Topical).*

In providing consultation, consider emphasizing the following selected information (» = major clinical significance):

Before using this medication

» Conditions affecting use, especially:
Sensitivity to mequinol or to etretinate, isotretinoin, tretinoin, or vitamin A derivatives
Pregnancy—Not recommended during pregnancy
Other medications, especially photosensitizing agents
Other medical problems, especially eczema and sunburn

Proper use of this medication

» Importance of not using more medication or more frequently than prescribed

» Not applying medication to windburned or sunburned skin or on open wounds

» Avoiding contact with the eyes, mouth, nose, and mucous membranes

Reading patient directions carefully before use

Proper administration technique

Using the applicator tip on the solar lentigines, avoiding surrounding skin

Not showering or bathing for at least 6 hours after application.

Waiting 30 minutes after application before using cosmetics

» Proper dosing

Missed dose: Applying next dose at regularly scheduled time; not doubling doses

» Proper storage

Precautions while using this medication

May cause transient stinging, burning, or irritation; checking with physician if irritation becomes severe or if spots become darker

» Either checking with health care professional before using or avoiding use of irritating hair products (permanents or hair removal products), sun-sensitizing skin products (could contain limes or spices), alcohol-containing skin products, or drying or abrasive skin products (some cosmetics or soaps or skin cleansers)

» Minimizing exposure of treated areas to sunlight, wind, and cold temperatures to avoid sunburn, dryness, or irritation. Also, avoiding use of artificial sunlight or sunlamp

Using sunscreen preparations (minimum sun protection factor [SPF] of 15) or wearing protective clothing over treated areas when sunlight exposure cannot be avoided

» Checking with doctor at any time skin becomes too dry or irritated; choosing proper skin product to reduce skin dryness or irritation

Side/adverse effects

Signs of potential side effects, especially burning, tingling, or stinging sensation of skin (severe); erythema (severe); pruritus (severe); desquamation (severe); contact allergic reaction; and vesicular bulla

General Dosing Information

Mequinol and tretinoin topical solution should not be applied to mucous membranes; contact near the eyes, lips, or nose should be avoided.

If local irritation occurs, patients should use less medication, decrease the frequency of applications, discontinue use temporarily, or discontinue use permanently.

Patients should be counseled on the importance of protecting the skin from the sun, wind, cold temperatures, and excessive dryness by using sunscreens of at least SPF 15, moisturizers, and protective clothing. Artificial sunlight, such as sunlamps, should be avoided.

Any topical products, or cosmetic agents should not be applied simultaneously but should be delayed at least 30 minutes after the application of mequinol and tretinoin.

Treated areas of skin should not be washed for at least 6 hours after applying mequinol and tretinoin.

The efficacy of using mequinol and tretinoin topical solution for greater than 24 weeks has not been established. Application of larger amounts of medication than recommended will not lead to more rapid or better results but may cause increased redness, peeling, discomfort, or hypopigmentation of the skin.

Upon discontinuation of mequinol and tretinoin, gradual repigmentation will likely occur.

Results of controlled studies described by the manufacturer (n=421) indicate the superiority of topical tretinoin 0.01%/mequinol 2% over placebo (vehicle) in solar (actinic) lentigines, with moderate or marked improvement of facial lesions occurring in 57% and 15% of patients, respectively, after 24 weeks of treatment; slight improvement was seen in an additional 28% and 36% of patients in these groups. Similar intragroup efficacy rates were seen for forearm/back-of-hand lesions at 24 weeks (moderate/marked improvement in 54% and 14% and slight improvement in 26% and 33% of patients assigned to tretinoin/mequinol and placebo, respectively). Complete clearing of facial and forearm/back-of-hand lesions was evident in 3% and 1% of patients, respectively, treated with the combination product. However, following a 24-week posttreatment follow-up period, varying degrees of repigmentation were observed. Concurrent use of topical sunscreens was not allowed in these studies.

Topical Dosage Forms

MEQUINOL AND TRETINOIN TOPICAL SOLUTION

Usual adult and adolescent dose

Solar lentigines—

Topical, to the skin of affected areas, twice daily, morning and evening at least 8 hours apart

Usual pediatric dose

Use is not recommended.

Strength(s) usually available

U.S.—

Mequinol 2%, tretinoin 0.01% (Rx) [*Solagé* (ethyl alcohol 77.8% v/v)].

Canada—

Not commercially available.

Packaging and storage

Store between 15 and 30 °C (59 and 86 °F). Keep away from heat and open flame. Protect from light.

Auxiliary labeling

- For external use only.
- Avoid prolonged or excessive exposure to direct and/or artificial sunlight while using this medication.

Note

Include patient instructions when dispensing.

Developed: 04/26/2000

MERCAPTOPURINE Systemic

VA CLASSIFICATION (Primary/Secondary): AN300/IM403; MS103; GA900

Commonly used brand name(s): *Purinethol*.

Another commonly used name is 6-MP.

Note: For a listing of dosage forms and brand names by country availability, see *Dosage Forms* section(s).

Category

Antineoplastic; immunosuppressant.

Indications

Note: Bracketed information in the *Indications* section refers to uses that are not included in U.S. product labeling.

Accepted

Leukemia, acute lymphocytic (treatment) or

Leukemia, acute nonlymphocytic (treatment)—Mercaptopurine is indicated for remission induction and maintenance therapy of acute lymphocytic and acute nonlymphocytic leukemia.

[Leukemia, chronic myelocytic (treatment)]—Mercaptopurine is indicated for treatment of chronic myelocytic leukemia.

[Lymphomas, non-Hodgkin's (treatment)][1]—Mercaptopurine is indicated for treatment of some pediatric non-Hodgkin's lymphomas.

[Bowel disease, inflammatory (treatment)][1]—Mercaptopurine is also used in the treatment of regional enteritis (Crohn's disease) and ulcerative colitis.

[Arthritis, psoriatic (treatment)][1]—Mercaptopurine is used in the treatment of selected cases of severe psoriatic arthritis.

Extreme caution is recommended in use of mercaptopurine for non-neoplastic conditions because of potential carcinogenicity with long-term use of this agent.

[1]Not included in Canadian product labeling.

Pharmacology/Pharmacokinetics

Physicochemical characteristics

Molecular weight—170.19.

pKa—7.6.

Mechanism of action/Effect

Mercaptopurine is an antimetabolite of the purine analog type. Mercaptopurine is cell cycle–specific for the S phase of cell division. Activity occurs as the result of activation in the tissues and may include inhibition of DNA synthesis with a lesser effect on RNA synthesis.

Absorption

Variably and incompletely (up to 50%) absorbed from the gastrointestinal tract.

Distribution

Crosses the blood-brain barrier, but in insufficient amounts to treat meningeal leukemia.

Protein binding

Low (20%).

Biotransformation

Hepatic (activation and catabolism); degradation primarily by xanthine oxidase.

Half-life

Triphasic—45 minutes, 2.5 hours, and 10 hours.

Elimination

Renal (7 to 39% unchanged).

In dialysis—Removable by dialysis.

Precautions to Consider

Carcinogenicity/Mutagenicity

Secondary malignancies are potential delayed effects of many antineoplastic agents, although it is not clear whether the effect is related to their mutagenic or immunosuppressive action. The effect of dose and duration of therapy is also unknown, although risk seems to increase with long-term use. Although information is limited, available data seem to indicate that the carcinogenic risk is greatest with the alkylating agents.

Antimetabolites have been shown to be carcinogenic in animals and may be associated with an increased risk of development of secondary carcinomas in humans, although the risk appears to be less than with alkylating agents.

Mercaptopurine causes chromosome abnormalities in animals and humans and dominant-lethal mutations in male mice.

Pregnancy/Reproduction

Fertility—Gonadal suppression, resulting in amenorrhea or azoospermia, may occur in patients taking antineoplastic therapy, especially with the alkylating agents. In general, these effects appear to be related to dose and length of therapy and may be irreversible. Prediction of the degree of testicular or ovarian function impairment is complicated by the common use of combinations of several antineoplastics, which makes it difficult to assess the effects of individual agents.

Pregnancy—Mercaptopurine is not recommended during pregnancy.

First trimester: It is usually recommended that use of antineoplastics, especially combination chemotherapy, be avoided whenever possible, especially during the first trimester. Although information is limited because of the relatively few instances of antineoplastic administration during pregnancy, the mutagenic, teratogenic, and carcinogenic potential of these medications must be considered.

Other hazards to the fetus include adverse reactions seen in adults.

In general, use of a contraceptive is recommended during cytotoxic drug therapy.

Mercaptopurine is embryopathic in rats and has been associated with an increased risk of abortion or premature births in humans; the risk of teratogenicity in surviving offspring has not been studied.

FDA Pregnancy Category D.

Breast-feeding

Although very little information is available regarding distribution of antineoplastic agents into breast milk, breast-feeding is not recommended while mercaptopurine is being administered because of the risks to the infant (adverse effects, mutagenicity, carcinogenicity). It is not known whether mercaptopurine is distributed into breast milk.

Pediatrics

Appropriate studies on the relationship of age to the effects of mercaptopurine have not been performed in the pediatric population. However, pediatrics-specific problems that would limit the usefulness of this medication in children are not expected.

Geriatrics

No information is available on the relationship of age to the effects of mercaptopurine in geriatric patients. However, elderly patients are more likely to have age-related renal function impairment, which may require dosage reduction in patients receiving mercaptopurine.

Dental

The bone marrow depressant effects of mercaptopurine may result in an increased incidence of microbial infection, delayed healing, and gingival bleeding. Dental work, whenever possible, should be completed prior to initiation of therapy or deferred until blood counts have returned to normal. Patients should be instructed in proper oral hygiene during

treatment, including caution in use of regular toothbrushes, dental floss, and toothpicks.

Mercaptopurine may also cause stomatitis that is associated with considerable discomfort.

Drug interactions and/or related problems

The following drug interactions and/or related problems have been selected on the basis of their potential clinical significance (possible mechanism in parentheses where appropriate)—not necessarily inclusive (» = major clinical significance):

Note: Combinations containing any of the following medications, depending on the amount present, may also interact with this medication.

» Allopurinol or
Colchicine or
» Probenecid or
» Sulfinpyrazone
(concurrent use with allopurinol may result in greatly increased mercaptopurine activity and toxicity because of inhibition of metabolism; careful monitoring is recommended. It is recommended that mercaptopurine dosage be reduced to one-third to one-fourth of the usual dosage in patients receiving 300 to 600 mg of allopurinol a day concurrently to reduce or prevent hyperuricemia or to slow the metabolism of mercaptopurine. In addition, mercaptopurine may raise the concentration of blood uric acid; dosage adjustment of antigout agents may be necessary to control hyperuricemia and gout; concurrent use of uricosuric antigout agents should be avoided because of the risk of uric acid nephropathy)

Anticoagulants, coumarin- or indandione-derivative
(mercaptopurine may increase anticoagulant activity and/or increase the risk of hemorrhage as a result of decreased hepatic synthesis of procoagulant factors and interference with platelet formation or may reduce anticoagulant activity by means of increased prothrombin synthesis or activation)

Blood dyscrasia-causing medications (see *Appendix II*)
(leukopenic and/or thrombocytopenic effects of mercaptopurine may be increased with concurrent or recent therapy if these medications cause the same effects; dosage adjustment of mercaptopurine, if necessary, should be based on blood counts)

» Bone marrow depressants, other (see *Appendix II*) or
Radiation therapy
(additive bone marrow depression may occur; dosage reduction may be required when two or more bone marrow depressants, including radiation, are used concurrently or consecutively)

» Hepatotoxic medications, other (see *Appendix II*)
(concurrent use may increase the risk of hepatotoxicity and should be avoided)

» Immunosuppressants, other, such as:
Azathioprine
Chlorambucil
Corticosteroids, glucocorticoid
Corticotropin (ACTH)
Cyclophosphamide
Cyclosporine
Muromonab-CD3
(concurrent use with mercaptopurine may increase the risk of infection and development of neoplasms)

Vaccines, killed virus
(because normal defense mechanisms may be suppressed by mercaptopurine therapy, the patient's antibody response to the vaccine may be decreased. The interval between discontinuation of medications that cause immunosuppression and restoration of the patient's ability to respond to the vaccine depends on the intensity and type of immunosuppression-causing medication used, the underlying disease, and other factors; estimates vary from 3 months to 1 year)

» Vaccines, live virus
(because normal defense mechanisms may be suppressed by mercaptopurine therapy, concurrent use with a live virus vaccine may potentiate the replication of the vaccine virus, may increase the side/adverse effects of the vaccine virus, and/or may decrease the patient's antibody response to the vaccine; immunization of these patients should be undertaken only with extreme caution after careful review of the patient's hematologic status and only with the knowledge and consent of the physician managing the mercaptopurine therapy. The interval between discontinuation of medications that cause immunosuppression and restoration of the patient's ability to respond to the vaccine depends on the intensity and type of immunosuppression-causing medication used, the underlying disease, and other factors; estimates vary from 3 months to 1 year. Patients with leukemia in remission should not receive live virus vaccine until at least 3 months after their last chemotherapy. Immunization with oral poliovirus vaccine should also be postponed in persons in close contact with the patient, especially family members)

Laboratory value alterations

The following have been selected on the basis of their potential clinical significance (possible effect in parentheses where appropriate)—not necessarily inclusive (» = major clinical significance).

With diagnostic test results
Glucose and
Uric acid
(serum concentrations may be falsely increased when the sequential multiple analyzer [SMA] is used)

With physiology/laboratory test values
Uric acid
(concentrations in blood and urine may be increased)

Medical considerations/Contraindications

The medical considerations/contraindications included have been selected on the basis of their potential clinical significance (reasons given in parentheses where appropriate)—not necessarily inclusive (» = major clinical significance).

Risk-benefit should be considered when the following medical problems exist:

» Bone marrow depression

» Chickenpox, existing or recent (including recent exposure) or
» Herpes zoster
(risk of severe generalized disease)

Gout, history of, or
Urate renal stones, history of
(risk of hyperuricemia)

» Hepatic function impairment
(lower dosage recommended)

» Infection

» Renal function impairment
(lower dosage recommended)

Sensitivity to mercaptopurine

» Caution should be used also in patients who have had previous cytotoxic drug therapy and radiation therapy.

Patient monitoring

The following are especially important in patient monitoring (other tests may be warranted in some patients, depending on condition; » = major clinical significance):

» Alanine aminotransferase (ALT [SGPT]) values, serum and
» Aspartate aminotransferase (AST [SGOT]) values, serum and
» Bilirubin concentrations, serum and
» Lactate dehydrogenase (LDH) values, serum
(recommended prior to initiation of therapy and at periodic intervals during therapy; frequency varies according to clinical state, agent, dose, and other agents being used concurrently)

Blood urea nitrogen (BUN) concentrations and
Creatinine concentrations, serum
(recommended prior to initiation of therapy and at periodic intervals during therapy; frequency varies according to clinical state, agent, dose, and other agents being used concurrently)

» Hematocrit or hemoglobin and
» Leukocyte count, total and, if appropriate, differential and
» Platelet count
(determinations recommended prior to initiation of therapy and at periodic intervals during therapy; frequency varies according to clinical state, agent, dose, and other agents being used concurrently)

Uric acid concentrations, serum
(recommended prior to initiation of therapy and at periodic intervals during therapy; frequency varies according to clinical state, agent, dose, and other agents being used concurrently)

Note: In patients with acute leukemia and high total leukocyte counts, a rapid fall in leukocyte count may occur with mercaptopurine therapy. Daily blood counts are recommended in these patients.

Side/Adverse Effects

Note: Many "side effects" of antineoplastic therapy are unavoidable and represent the medication's pharmacologic action. Some of these (for example, leukopenia and thrombocytopenia) are actually used as parameters to aid in individual dosage titration.

The following side/adverse effects have been selected on the basis of their potential clinical significance (possible signs and symptoms in parentheses where appropriate)—not necessarily inclusive:

Those indicating need for medical attention

Incidence more frequent

Anemia (unusual tiredness or weakness); ***hepatotoxicity or biliary stasis*** (yellow eyes or skin); ***immunosuppression, leukopenia, or infection*** (fever or chills; cough or hoarseness; lower back or side pain; painful or difficult urination)—usually asymptomatic; ***thrombocytopenia*** (unusual bleeding or bruising; black, tarry stools; blood in urine or stools; pinpoint red spots on skin)—usually asymptomatic

Note: *Anemia* occurs with high doses.

Leukopenia and *thrombocytopenia* (usually mild) may begin 5 to 6 days after initiation of therapy and persist about 7 days after withdrawal.

Incidence less frequent

Hyperuricemia or uric acid nephropathy (joint pain; lower back or side pain; swelling of feet or lower legs); ***loss of appetite or nausea and vomiting***

Note: *Hyperuricemia and uric acid nephropathy* occur most commonly during initial treatment of patients with leukemia or lymphoma, as a result of rapid cell breakdown which leads to elevated serum uric acid concentrations.

Crystals of mercaptopurine have been found in urine of children receiving high dosage (1000 mg per square meter of body surface daily).

Loss of appetite or nausea and vomiting may be symptoms of overdosage.

Incidence rare

Gastrointestinal ulceration (black, tarry stools; stomach pain); ***stomatitis*** (sores in mouth and on lips)

Note: *Stomatitis* is common with large doses.

Those indicating need for medical attention only if they continue or are bothersome

Incidence less frequent

Darkening of skin; diarrhea; headache; skin rash and itching; weakness

Those indicating need for medical attention if they occur after medication is discontinued

Bone marrow depression (black, tarry stools; blood in urine or stools; cough or hoarseness; fever or chills; lower back or side pain; painful or difficult urination; pinpoint red spots on skin; unusual bleeding or bruising); ***hepatotoxicity*** (yellow eyes or skin)

Patient Consultation

As an aid to patient consultation, refer to *Advice for the Patient, Mercaptopurine (Systemic)*.

In providing consultation, consider emphasizing the following selected information (» = major clinical significance):

Before using this medication

» Conditions affecting use, especially:
- Sensitivity to mercaptopurine
- Pregnancy—Use not recommended because of mutagenic, teratogenic, and carcinogenic potential; advisability of using contraception; telling physician immediately if pregnancy is suspected
- Breast-feeding—Not recommended because of risk of serious side effects
- Other medications, especially allopurinol, other bone marrow depressants, other hepatotoxic medications, other immunosuppressants, probenecid, sulfinpyrazone, or previous cytotoxic drug or radiation therapy
- Other medical problems, especially chickenpox, herpes zoster, hepatic function impairment, infection, or renal function impairment

Proper use of this medication

» Importance of not taking more or less medication than the amount prescribed

Caution in taking combination therapy; taking each medication at the right time

Importance of ample fluid intake and subsequent increase in urine output to aid in excretion of uric acid

Checking with physician if vomiting occurs shortly after dose is taken

» Proper dosing

Missed dose: Not taking at all; not doubling doses

» Proper storage

Precautions while using this medication

» Importance of close monitoring by the physician

» Possibility of increased toxicity if alcohol is ingested

» Avoiding immunizations unless approved by physician; other persons in patient's household should avoid immunizations with oral poliovirus vaccine; avoiding persons who have taken oral poliovirus vaccine or wearing a protective mask that covers nose and mouth

Caution if bone marrow depression occurs:

» Avoiding exposure to persons with infections, especially during periods of low blood counts; checking with physician immediately if fever or chills, cough or hoarseness, lower back or side pain, or painful or difficult urination occurs

» Checking with physician immediately if unusual bleeding or bruising; black, tarry stools; blood in urine or stools; or pinpoint red spots on skin occur

Caution in use of regular toothbrush, dental floss, or toothpick; physician, dentist, or nurse may suggest alternatives; checking with physician before having dental work done

Not touching eyes or inside of nose unless hands washed immediately before

Using caution to avoid accidental cuts with use of sharp objects such as safety razor or fingernail or toenail cutters

Avoiding contact sports or other situations where bruising or injury could occur

Caution if any laboratory tests required; possible interference with serum glucose and uric acid values measured by sequential multiple analyzer (SMA)

Side/adverse effects

Importance of discussing possible effects, including cancer, with physician

Signs of potential side effects, especially anemia, hepatotoxicity, biliary stasis, immunosuppression, leukopenia, infection, thrombocytopenia, hyperuricemia, uric acid nephropathy, loss of appetite, nausea and vomiting, gastrointestinal ulceration, and stomatitis

Physician or nurse can help in dealing with side effects

General Dosing Information

Patients receiving mercaptopurine should be under supervision of a physician experienced in immunosuppressive and antimetabolite chemotherapy.

A variety of dosage schedules and regimens of mercaptopurine, alone or in combination with other antitumor agents, are used. The prescriber may consult the medical literature as well as the manufacturer's literature in choosing a specific dosage.

Dosage must be adjusted to meet the individual requirements of each patient, based on clinical response and appearance or severity of toxicity.

Development of uric acid nephropathy in patients with leukemia or lymphoma may be prevented by adequate oral hydration. Alkalinization of urine may be necessary if serum uric acid concentrations are elevated. Allopurinol should be administered with caution and only if uric acid concentrations are unacceptably high.

It is recommended that mercaptopurine dosage be reduced to one-third to one-fourth of the usual dosage in patients receiving 300 to 600 mg of allopurinol a day concurrently to reduce or prevent hyperuricemia or to slow the metabolism of mercaptopurine.

Because the actions of mercaptopurine may be delayed, it is recommended that mercaptopurine therapy be discontinued promptly at the first sign of marked leukopenia (particularly granulocytopenia) or thrombocytopenia, hemorrhage or bleeding tendencies, or jaundice. Therapy may be resumed at one-half the previous dosage when the leukocyte count remains constant for 2 or 3 days, or rises.

In acute leukemia, mercaptopurine may be administered despite the presence of thrombocytopenia and bleeding; stoppage of bleeding and increase in platelet count have occurred during treatment in some cases and platelet transfusions may be useful in others.

Special precautions are recommended in patients who develop thrombocytopenia as a result of administration of mercaptopurine. These may include extreme care in performing invasive procedures; regular inspection of intravenous sites, skin (including perirectal area), and mucous membrane surfaces for signs of bleeding or bruising; limiting frequency of venipuncture and avoiding intramuscular injections; testing urine, emesis, stool, and secretions for occult blood; care in use of regular toothbrushes, dental floss, toothpicks, safety razors, and fingernail and toenail cutters; avoiding constipation; and using caution to prevent falls and other injuries. Such patients should avoid alcohol and aspirin intake because of the risk of gastrointestinal bleeding. Platelet transfusions may be required.

Patients who develop leukopenia should be observed carefully for signs of infection. Antibiotic support may be required. In neutropenic patients who develop fever, broad-spectrum antibiotic coverage should be initiated empirically, pending bacterial cultures and appropriate diagnostic tests.

Combination chemotherapy

Mercaptopurine may be used in combination with other agents in various regimens. As a result, incidence and/or severity of side effects may be altered and different dosages (usually reduced) may be used.

Oral Dosage Forms

Note: Bracketed uses in the *Dosage Forms* section refer to categories of use and/or indications that are not included in U.S. product labeling.

MERCAPTOPURINE TABLETS USP

Usual adult dose

Leukemia, acute lymphocytic or
Leukemia, acute nonlymphocytic—

Initial: Oral, 2.5 mg per kg of body weight or 80 to 100 mg per square meter of body surface area (to the nearest 25 mg) a day in single or divided doses. If there is no clinical improvement and no leukocyte depression after four weeks at this dosage, an increase in dosage to 5 mg per kg of body weight a day may be attempted.

Maintenance: Oral, 1.5 to 2.5 mg per kg of body weight or 50 to 100 mg per square meter of body surface area a day.

[Inflammatory bowel disease][1]—

Oral, 1.5 mg per kg of body weight per day, the dosage being adjusted as necessary. If there is no clinical improvement and no leukocyte depression after two to three months at this dosage, a gradual increase in dosage to 2.5 mg per kg of body weight per day may be attempted.

Usual pediatric dose

Leukemia, acute lymphocytic or
Leukemia, acute nonlymphocytic—

Oral, 2.5 mg per kg of body weight or 75 mg per square meter of body surface area (to the nearest 25 mg) a day in single or divided doses.

Strength(s) usually available

U.S.—

50 mg (Rx) [*Purinethol* (scored; lactose)].

Canada—

50 mg (Rx) [*Purinethol* (scored)].

Packaging and storage

Store below 40 °C (104 °F), preferably between 15 and 30 °C (59 and 86 °F), unless otherwise specified by manufacturer. Store in a well-closed container.

[1]Not included in Canadian product labeling.

Revised: 05/22/2002

MEROPENEM Systemic

VA CLASSIFICATION (Primary): AM119

Commonly used brand name(s): *Merrem I.V.*

Note: For a listing of dosage forms and brand names by country availability, see *Dosage Forms* section(s).

Category

Antibacterial (systemic).

Indications

General Considerations

Meropenem is a carbapenem antibiotic. It has significant stability to hydrolysis by penicillinases and cephalosporinases produced by gram-positive and gram-negative organisms, with the exception of metallo–beta-lactamases.

Cross-resistance is sometimes seen with strains resistant to other carbapenems.

Meropenem has been shown to act synergistically with aminoglycosides *in vitro* against some isolates of *Pseudomonas aeruginosa*.

Accepted

Intra-abdominal infections (treatment)—Meropenem is indicated as a single agent in the treatment of intra-abdominal infections, including complicated appendicitis and peritonitis caused by susceptible organisms, in adults and children 3 months of age and older.

Meningitis, bacterial (treatment)—Meropenem is indicated as a single agent in the treatment of bacterial meningitis caused by susceptible organisms, in children 3 months of age and older. Meropenem has been found to be effective in eliminating concurrent bacteremia associated with bacterial meningitis.

Skin and skin structure infections, complicated (treatment)—Meropenem for injection is indicated as single agent therapy for the treatment of complicated skin and skin structure infections due to *Staphylococcus aureus* (beta-lactamase and non-beta-lactamase producing, methicillin-susceptible isolates only), *Streptococcus pyogenes*, *Streptococcus agalactiae*, viridans group streptococci, *Enterococcus faecalis* (excluding vancomycin-resistant isolates), *Pseudomonas aeruginosa*, *Escherichia coli*, *Proteus mirabilis*, *Bacteroides fragilis* and *Peptostreptococcus* species.

[Neutropenia, febrile (treatment)][1]—Meropenem is indicated for empiric treatment of febrile neutropenia.

In patients at high risk of severe infection, including patients with a history of recent bone marrow transplantation, with hypotension at presentation, with an underlying hematologic malignancy, or with severe or prolonged neutropenia, antimicrobial therapy alone may not be appropriate.

Unaccepted

Meropenem should not be used to treat methicillin-resistant staphylococci.

[1]Not included in Canadian product labeling.

Pharmacology/Pharmacokinetics

Physicochemical characteristics

Chemical Group—Carbapenem antibiotic.

Molecular weight—437.52.

pH—Between 7.3 and 8.3 after reconstitution.

Mechanism of action/Effect

Bactericidal; meropenem inhibits cell wall synthesis by penetrating the cell wall of most gram-positive and gram-negative bacteria to reach penicillin-binding–protein (PBP) targets. Its strongest affinity is toward PBPs 2, 3, and 4 of *Escherichia coli* and *Pseudomonas aeruginosa*, and PBPs 1, 2, and 4 of *Staphylococcus aureus*. Bactericidal concentrations are typically one to two times the bacteriostatic concentrations; the exception is *Listeria monocytogenes*, against which lethal activity has not been observed.

Distribution

Well distributed into most body fluids and tissues, including the cerebrospinal fluid (CSF); CSF concentrations match or exceed those concentrations required to inhibit most susceptible bacteria.

Protein binding

Low (approximately 2%).

Biotransformation

Meropenem is primarily excreted unchanged; however, there is one metabolite which is microbiologically inactive.

Half-life

Approximately 1 hour in adults and children 2 years of age and older with normal renal function.

Approximately 1.5 hours in children 3 months to 2 years of age.

Time to peak concentration

Approximately 1 hour after the start of the infusion.

Peak serum concentration

500 mg at the end of a 30-minute infusion—Approximately 23 mcg per mL (mcg/mL).

1 gram at the end of a 30-minute infusion—Approximately 49 mcg/mL.

500 mg at the end of a 5-minute injection—Approximately 45 mcg/mL.

1 gram at the end of a 5-minute injection—Approximately 112 mcg/mL.

Elimination

Renal—Approximately 70% of an administered dose is recovered in the urine as unchanged meropenem over 12 hours.

In dialysis—Meropenem and its metabolite are hemodialyzable; however, there is inadequate information on the use of meropenem in patients receiving hemodialysis and no information on the usefulness of hemodialysis to treat an overdose. There is also no information with regard to the effectiveness of peritoneal dialysis in the removal of meropenem.

Precautions to Consider

Cross-sensitivity and/or related problems
Patients allergic to other beta-lactam antibacterials (e.g., penicillins, cephalosporins, imipenem) may be allergic to meropenem also.

Carcinogenicity
Carcinogenicity studies have not been performed.

Mutagenicity
No evidence of mutagenic potential was found when the bacterial reverse mutation test, the Chinese hamster ovary HGPRT assay, cultured human lymphocytes cytogenic assay, and the mouse micronuclear test were performed with meropenem.

Pregnancy/Reproduction
Fertility—No impairment of fertility was seen when meropenem was studied in rats at doses of up to 1000 mg per kg of body weight (mg/kg) per day, and in cynomolgus monkeys at doses of up to 360 mg/kg per day. These doses are comparable to 1.8 and 3.7 times, respectively, the human exposure at the usual dose of 1 gram every 8 hours, based on area under the plasma concentration-time curve (AUC).

Pregnancy—Adequate and well-controlled studies in humans have not been done. Because animal reproduction studies are not always predictive of human response, this drug should be used during pregnancy only if clearly needed.

Studies have been performed in rats at doses of up to 1000 mg/kg per day, and cynomolgus monkeys at doses of up to 360 mg/kg per day. These doses are comparable to 1.8 and 3.7 times, respectively, the human exposure at the usual dose of 1 gram every 8 hours, based on AUC. These studies showed no harm to the fetus due to meropenem, although there were slight changes in fetal body weight at doses of 250 mg/kg per day (0.4 times the human exposure at the usual dose of 1 gram every 8 hours, based on AUC) and higher in rats.

FDA Pregnancy Category B.

Breast-feeding
It is not known whether meropenem is distributed into breast milk. Because many drugs are distributed into human milk, caution should be exercised when meropenem is administered to a nursing woman.

Pediatrics
Safety and efficacy have not been established in children less than 3 months of age. However, use of meropenem in children 3 months of age and older with bacterial meningitis is supported by evidence from adequate and well-controlled studies. Use of meropenem in children 3 months of age and older with intra-abdominal infections is supported by evidence from adequate and well-controlled studies in adults, with additional data from pediatric pharmacokinetics studies and controlled clinical trials in pediatric patients. Use of meropenem in pediatric patients with complicated skin and skin structure infections is supported by evidence from an adequate and well-controlled study with adults and additional data from pediatric pharmacokinetics studies.

Geriatrics
No information is available on the relationship of age to the effects of meropenem in geriatric patients. However, elderly patients are more likely to have an age-related decrease in renal function, which may require a reduction of dosage in patients receiving meropenem.

Drug interactions and/or related problems
The following drug interactions and/or related problems have been selected on the basis of their potential clinical significance (possible mechanism in parentheses where appropriate)—not necessarily inclusive (» = major clinical significance):

Note: Combinations containing the following medication, depending on the amount present, may also interact with this medication.

» Probenecid
(probenecid competes with meropenem for active tubular secretion, inhibiting the renal excretion of meropenem; this results in a 38% increase in the elimination half-life and a 56% increase in the extent of systemic exposure to meropenem; concurrent administration is not recommended)

Valproic acid
(there is evidence that meropenem may reduce serum levels of valproic acid to subtherapeutic levels [therapeutic range considered to be 50 to 100 mcg per mL total valproate])

Laboratory value alterations
The following have been selected on the basis of their potential clinical significance (possible effect in parentheses where appropriate)—not necessarily inclusive (» = major clinical significance).

With diagnostic test results
Partial thromboplastin time and
Prothrombin time
(may be shortened or prolonged)
Positive direct or indirect antiglobulin (Coombs') tests

With physiology/laboratory test values
Alanine aminotransferase (ALT [SGPT]) and
Alkaline phosphatase and
Aspartate aminotransferase (AST [SGOT]) and
Bilirubin and
Lactate dehydrogenase (LDH)
(serum values may be increased)

Blood urea nitrogen (BUN) and
Creatinine, serum
(concentrations may be transiently increased)

Hematocrit and
Hemoglobin concentrations and
White blood count
(may be decreased)
Platelet count
(may be increased or decreased)

Medical considerations/Contraindications
The medical considerations/contraindications included have been selected on the basis of their potential clinical significance (reasons given in parentheses where appropriate)—not necessarily inclusive (» = major clinical significance).

Except under special circumstances, this medication should not be used when the following medical problem exists:

» Hypersensitivity to meropenem or any component of the product or other beta-lactam antibacterials (e.g., penicillins, cephalosporins, imipenem)

Risk-benefit should be considered when the following medical problems exist:

» Central nervous system (CNS) disorders (e.g., brain lesions or history of seizures) or
» Meningitis, bacterial
(seizures are more likely to occur in patients with CNS lesions, a history of seizure disorders, bacterial meningitis, and/or renal function impairment)

» Renal function impairment
(because meropenem is primarily excreted through the kidneys, it must be administered in a reduced dosage to patients with impaired renal function; dosage adjustment is also recommended in elderly patients; also, thrombocytopenia has been observed in patients with renal function impairment, but no clinical bleeding has been reported)

Patient monitoring
The following may be especially important in patient monitoring (other tests may be warranted in some patients, depending on condition; » = major clinical significance):

Alanine aminotransferase (ALT [SGPT]), serum and
Alkaline phosphatase, serum and
Aspartate aminotransferase (AST [SGOT]), serum and
Bilirubin, serum and
Lactate dehydrogenase (LDH), serum
(periodic monitoring is advisable during prolonged therapy)

Blood urea nitrogen (BUN) concentrations and
Creatinine, serum
(periodic monitoring is advisable during prolonged therapy)

Hematocrit and
Hemoglobin concentrations and
Platelet count
White blood count
(periodic monitoring is advisable during prolonged therapy)

Side/Adverse Effects

Note: The incidence of seizures was reported to be 0.5% in patients treated for infections outside the CNS during clinical trials. All patients who experienced seizures had pre-existing contributing factors, including a prior history of seizures or CNS abnormality and concurrent administration of medications with seizure potential. Adherence to the recommended dose is strongly recommended, especially in patients with known factors that predispose them to seizure activity.

Thrombocytopenia has been seen in patients with renal dysfunction; however, no clinical bleeding has been reported.

The following side/adverse effects have been selected on the basis of their potential clinical significance (possible signs and symptoms in parentheses where appropriate)—not necessarily inclusive:

Those indicating need for medical attention

Incidence more frequent

Inflammation at site of injection (redness and swelling at site of injection)

Incidence less frequent

Apnea (bluish lips or skin; not breathing); ***pruritus*** (itching skin); ***sepsis*** (chills; confusion; dizziness; lightheadedness; fainting; fast heartbeat; fever; rapid, shallow breathing); ***shock*** (cold clammy skin; confusion, dizziness, lightheadedness; fast, weak pulse; sweating; wheezing); ***skin rash and itching; thrombophlebitis*** (pain at site of injection)

Incidence rare

Bleeding events (black, bloody stools; black, bloody vomit; nosebleed); ***gastrointestinal hemorrhage*** (black, tarry stools; bloody stools; vomiting of blood or material that looks like coffee grounds); ***hemoperitoneum*** (abdominal pain or swelling; dizziness; fast heartbeat; unusual tiredness or weakness); ***melena*** (bloody, black, or tarry stools); ***pseudomembranous colitis*** (abdominal or stomach cramps and pain, severe; diarrhea, watery and severe, which may also be bloody; fever); ***seizures*** (convulsions)

Incidence not determined—Observed during clinical practice; estimates of frequency can not be determined

Agranulocytosis (cough or hoarseness; fever with or without chills; general feeling of tiredness or weakness; lower back or side pain; painful or difficult urination; sore throat; sores, ulcers, or white spots on lips or in mouth; unusual bleeding or bruising); ***angioedema*** (large, hive-like swelling on face, eyelids, lips, tongue, throat, hands, legs, feet, sex organs); ***erythema multiforme*** (blistering, peeling, loosening of skin; chills; cough; diarrhea; fever; itching; joint or muscle pain; red irritated eyes; sore throat; sores, ulcers, or white spots in mouth or on lips; unusual tiredness or weakness); ***leukopenia*** (black, tarry stools; chest pain; chills; cough; fever; painful or difficult urination; shortness of breath; sore throat; sores, ulcers, or white spots on lips or in mouth; swollen glands; unusual bleeding or bruising; unusual tiredness or weakness); ***neutropenia*** (black, tarry, stools; chills; cough; fever; lower back or side pain; painful or difficult urination; pale skin; shortness of breath; sore throat; ulcers, sores, or white spots in mouth; unusual bleeding or bruising; unusual tiredness or weakness); ***Stevens-Johnson syndrome*** (blistering, peeling, loosening of skin; chills; cough; diarrhea; itching; joint or muscle pain; red irritated eyes; red skin lesions, often with a purple center; sore throat; sores, ulcers, or white spots in mouth or on lips; unusual tiredness or weakness); ***toxic epidermal necrolysis*** (blistering, peeling, loosening of skin; chills; cough; diarrhea; itching; joint or muscle pain; red irritated eyes; red skin lesions, often with a purple center; sore throat; sores, ulcers, or white spots in mouth or on lips; unusual tiredness or weakness)

Those indicating need for medical attention only if they continue or are bothersome

Incidence more frequent

Anemia (pale skin; troubled breathing with exertion; unusual bleeding or bruising; unusual tiredness or weakness); ***gastrointestinal disturbances*** (constipation; diarrhea; nausea and vomiting); ***pain***

Incidence less frequent

Accidental injury; constipation (difficulty having a bowel movement (stool)); ***diarrhea; gastrointestinal disorder*** (diarrhea; loss of appetite; nausea or vomiting; stomach pain, fullness, or discomfort; indigestion; passing of gas); ***headache; hypoglycemia*** (anxiety; blurred vision; chills; cold sweats; coma; confusion; cool pale skin; depression; dizziness; fast heartbeat; headache; increased hunger; nausea; nervousness; nightmares; seizures; shakiness; slurred speech; unusual tiredness or weakness); ***nausea/vomiting; peripheral vascular disorder*** (cold hands and feet); ***pharyngitis*** (body aches or pain; congestion; cough; dryness or soreness of throat; fever; hoarseness; runny nose; tender, swollen glands in neck; trouble in swallowing; voice changes); ***pneumonia*** (chest pain; cough; fever or chills; sneezing; shortness of breath; sore throat; troubled breathing; tightness in chest; wheezing); ***rash***

Rare

Epistaxis (bloody nose)

Those indicating the need for medical attention if they occur after medication is discontinued

Pseudomembranous colitis (abdominal or stomach cramps and pain, severe; diarrhea, watery and severe, which may also be bloody; fever)

Overdose

No cases of overdose have been reported in humans to date. The largest dose of meropenem administered in clinical trials has been 2 grams every 8 hours and no increased safety risks have been seen.

Large doses (2200 to 4000 mg per kg of body weight) of meropenem were administered to rats and mice; toxicities included ataxia, dyspnea, convulsions, and mortalities.

For more information on the management of overdose or unintentional ingestion, **contact a Poison Control Center** (see *Poison Control Center Listing*).

Treatment of overdose

There is no specific information available for the treatment of meropenem overdose. In the event of an overdose, the medication should be discontinued and supportive care administered until meropenem can be eliminated through the kidneys. Meropenem and its metabolite are dialyzable; however, there is no information available on the use of hemodialysis in the event of an overdose.

Supportive care—Patients in whom intentional overdose is confirmed or suspected should be referred for psychiatric consultation.

Patient Consultation

As an aid to patient consultation, refer to *Advice for the Patient, Meropenem (Systemic)*.

In providing consultation, consider emphasizing the following selected information (» = major clinical significance)

Before using this medication

» Conditions affecting use, especially:
- Hypersensitivity to meropenem or any component of the product or other beta-lactam antibiotics
- Other medications, especially probenecid
- Other medical problems, especially bacterial meningitis, central nervous system disorders, or renal function impairment

Proper use of this medication

» Importance of receiving medication for full course of therapy and on regular schedule

» Proper dosing

Precautions while using this medication

» Continuing anticonvulsant therapy in patients with a history of seizures

» For severe diarrhea, checking with physician before taking any antidiarrheals; for mild diarrhea, taking kaolin- or attapulgite-containing, but not other, antidiarrheals; checking with physician or pharmacist if mild diarrhea continues or worsens

Side/adverse effects

Signs of potential side effects, especially inflammation at site of injection, apnea, pruritus, sepsis, shock, skin rash and itching, thrombophlebitis, bleeding events, gastrointestinal hemorrhage, hemoperitoneum, melena, pseudomembranous colitis, and seizures

Signs of potential side effects observed during clinical practice, especially, agranulocytosis, angioedema, erythema multiform, leukopenia, neutropenia, Stevens-Johnson syndrome, and toxic epidermal necrolysis

General Dosing Information

For treatment of adverse effects

Anticonvulsants should be continued in the treatment of patients receiving meropenem who have known seizure disorders. In patients who develop symptoms of CNS toxicity (e.g., focal tremors, myoclonus, or seizures) during treatment with meropenem, anticonvulsant therapy (e.g., phenytoin or benzodiazepines) should be initiated, and the dosage of meropenem should be reduced or the drug should be discontinued.

For serious anaphylactic reactions, emergency treatment should include epinephrine, oxygen, intravenous corticosteroids, and airway management.

For antibiotic-associated pseudomembranous colitis (AAPMC)—

Some patients may develop AAPMC, caused by *Clostridium difficile* toxin, during or following administration of meropenem. Mild cases may respond to discontinuation of the drug alone. Moderate to severe cases may require fluid, electrolyte, and protein replacement. In cases not responding to the above measures or in more severe cases, treatment with an antibacterial medication effective against AAPMC may be necessary.

Parenteral Dosage Forms

MEROPENEM FOR INJECTION

Usual adult and adolescent dose

Antibacterial—

Intravenous, 1 gram, administered by intravenous infusion over fifteen to thirty minutes or by rapid intravenous injection over three to five minutes, every eight hours.

Skin and skin structure infections, complicated (treatment)—

Intravenous, 500 mg, administered by intravenous infusion over fifteen to thirty minutes or by rapid intravenous injection over three to five minutes, every 8 hours. Adults with impaired renal function may require a reduction in dose as given above.

Note: No dosage adjustment is necessary in patients with impaired hepatic function.

Adults with impaired renal function may require a reduction in dose as given below:

Creatinine Clearance (mL/min)/(mL/sec)	Dose
≥ 51/0.85	See *Usual adult and adolescent dose*
26–50/0.43–0.83	1 gram every 12 hours
10–25/0.17–0.42	500 mg every 12 hours
< 10/0.17	500 mg every 24 hours

No dosage adjustment is necessary in patients with impaired hepatic function.

[Neutropenia, febrile][1]—

Intravenous, 1 gram, administered by intravenous infusion over twenty to thirty minutes, every eight hours. Adults with impaired renal function may require a reduction in dose as given above.

Usual pediatric dose

Intra-abdominal infections—

Children 3 months of age and older and weighing up to 50 kg of body weight: Intravenous, 20 mg per kg of body weight, administered by intravenous infusion over fifteen to thirty minutes or by rapid intravenous injection over three to five minutes, every eight hours.

Children weighing 50 kg of body weight and over: Intravenous, 1 gram, administered by intravenous infusion over fifteen to thirty minutes or by rapid intravenous injection over three to five minutes, every eight hours.

Infants up to 3 months of age: Safety and efficacy have not been established.

Meningitis—

Children 3 months of age and older and weighing up to 50 kg of body weight: Intravenous, 40 mg per kg of body weight, administered by intravenous infusion over fifteen to thirty minutes or by rapid intravenous injection over three to five minutes, every eight hours.

Children weighing 50 kg of body weight and over: Intravenous, 2 grams, administered by intravenous infusion over fifteen to thirty minutes or by rapid intravenous injection over three to five minutes, every eight hours.

Infants up to 3 months of age: Safety and efficacy have not been established.

Skin and skin structure infections, complicated (treatment)—

Children 3 months of age and older and weighing up to 50 kg of body weight: Intravenous, 10 mg per kg of body weight, administered by intravenous infusion over fifteen to thirty minutes or by rapid intravenous injection over three to five minutes, every eight hours.

Children weighing 50 kg of body weight and over: Intravenous, 500 mg, administered by intravenous infusion over fifteen to thirty minutes or by rapid intravenous injection over three to five minutes, every eight hours.

Infants up to 3 months of age: Safety and efficacy have not been established.

[Neutropenia, febrile][1]—

Children 3 months of age and older and weighing up to 50 kg of body weight: Intravenous, 20 mg per kg of body weight, administered by intravenous infusion over twenty to thirty minutes, every eight hours.

Children weighing 50 kg of body weight and over: Intravenous, 1 gram, administered by intravenous infusion over twenty to thirty minutes, every eight hours.

Infants up to 3 months of age: Safety and efficacy have not been established.

Usual pediatric prescribing limits

For complicated skin and skin structure infections: 500 mg every 8 hours
For intra-abdominal infections: 1 gram every 8 hours
For meningitis: 2 grams every eight hours.

Strength(s) usually available

U.S.—

500 mg per 20 mL (Rx) [*Merrem I.V.* (sodium 45.1 mg)].
1 gram per 30 mL (Rx) [*Merrem I.V.* (sodium 90.2 mg)].

Packaging and storage

Store at controlled temperature between 20 and 25 °C (68 and 77 °F).

Preparation of dosage form

For rapid intravenous injection—Add 10 mL of sterile water for injection to the 500-mg-in-20-mL vial and 20 mL of sterile water for injection to the 1-gram-in-30-mL vial, for a final concentration of approximately 50 mg per mL. Shake to dissolve and let stand until clear.

For intravenous infusion—The infusion bottles (500 mg in 100 mL and 1 gram in 100 mL) may be reconstituted with 0.45% sodium chloride injection, 0.9% sodium chloride injection, or 5% dextrose injection. Alternatively, a 500-mg or 1-gram injection vial may be reconstituted, the resultant solution added to an intravenous container and further diluted with an appropriate infusion fluid.

Stability

For rapid intravenous injection—Reconstituted meropenem with sterile water for injection maintains its potency at controlled room temperature between 15 and 25 °C (59 and 77 °F) for up to 2 hours or for up to 12 hours under refrigeration at 4 °C (39 °F).

For intravenous infusion—Reconstituted meropenem with 0.9% sodium chloride injection maintains its potency at controlled room temperature between 15 and 25 °C (59 and 77 °F) for up to 2 hours or for up to 18 hours under refrigeration at 4 °C (39 °F). Reconstituted meropenem with 5% dextrose injection maintains its potency at controlled room temperature between 15 and 25 °C (59 and 77 °F) for up to 1 hour or for up to 8 hours under refrigeration at 4 °C (39 °F).

Incompatibilities

Compatibility of meropenem with other medications has not been established. Meropenem should not be mixed with or physically added to solutions containing other medications.

Note

Reconstituted meropenem should be visually inspected for particulate matter and discoloration prior to administration.

Additional information

Warning: Do not use flexible container in series connections.

[1]Not included in Canadian product labeling.

Revised: 01/13/2006
Developed: 02/27/1997

MESALAMINE Oral-Local

INN: Mesalazine
BAN: Mesalazine
VA CLASSIFICATION (Primary): GA400

Commonly used brand name(s): *Asacol; Mesasal; Pentasa; Salofalk.*

Other commonly used names are 5-aminosalicylic acid and 5-ASA.

Note: For a listing of dosage forms and brand names by country availability, see *Dosage Forms* section(s).

Category

Bowel disease (inflammatory) suppressant.

Indications

Note: Bracketed information in the *Indications* section refers to uses that are not included in U.S. product labeling.

Accepted

Bowel disease, inflammatory (prophylaxis and treatment)—Mesalamine is indicated to treat and to maintain remission of mild to moderate ulcerative colitis or [Crohn's disease].

Pharmacology/Pharmacokinetics

Physicochemical characteristics

Molecular weight—153.14.

Mechanism of action/Effect

Bowel disease (inflammatory) suppressant—

Uncertain. Mucosal production of arachidonic acid metabolites, both through the cyclooxygenase and lipoxygenase pathways, is increased in patients with inflammatory bowel disease. Mesalamine appears to diminish inflammation by inhibiting cyclooxygenase and lipoxygenase, thereby decreasing the production of prostaglandins, and leukotrienes and hydroxyeicosatetraenoic acids (HETEs), respectively.

It is also believed that mesalamine acts as a scavenger of oxygen-derived free radicals, which are produced in greater numbers in patients with inflammatory bowel disease.

Absorption
20 to 30% absorbed following oral administration. The site of mesalamine release and absorption within the gastrointestinal tract varies among the different formulations.

Asacol—Coated with an acrylic-based resin, Eudragit S, which dissolves at pH 7 or greater, releasing mesalamine into the distal ileum and the colon.

Mesasal and *Salofalk*—Coated with an acrylic-based resin, Eudragit L, which dissolves at pH 6 or greater, releasing mesalamine into the distal ileum and the colon.

Pentasa—Microgranules of mesalamine individually coated with ethylcellulose, which allows continuous release of mesalamine into the small (jejunum and ileum) and large (colon) bowel, independent of luminal pH.

Biotransformation
Absorbed mesalamine is rapidly acetylated to *N*-acetyl-5-aminosalicylic acid (Ac-5-ASA) in the intestinal mucosal wall and the liver.

Half-life
Elimination—
- Asacol:
  - Mesalamine—3 hours.
  - Ac-5-ASA—10 hours.
- Pentasa:
  - Because of the continuous release and absorption of mesalamine throughout the gastrointestinal tract, the true elimination half-life cannot be determined following oral administration.
- Salofalk:
  - Ac-5-ASA—
    - 5 to 10 hours.

Time to peak concentration
Asacol—4 to 12 hours.
Mesasal—6.5 to 7 hours.
Pentasa—3 hours.

Peak serum concentration
Mesasal—
- Mesalamine: 1.2 mcg per mL following a single 500-mg oral dose.
- Ac-5-ASA: 1.9 mcg per mL following a single 500-mg oral dose.

Pentasa—
- Mesalamine: 1 mcg per mL following a single 1-gram oral dose.
- Ac-5-ASA: 1.8 mcg per mL following a single 1-gram oral dose.

Elimination
Fecal—
- *Asacol:* Approximately 80% of an administered dose is recovered in the feces.
- *Pentasa:* Approximately 13% of an administered dose is recovered in the feces.
- *Salofalk:* Partially recovered unchanged in the feces.

Renal—
- Excreted in the urine as the Ac-5-ASA metabolite.

Precautions to Consider

Cross-sensitivity and/or related problems
Patients sensitive to olsalazine, sulfasalazine, or salicylates may be sensitive to mesalamine also.

Carcinogenicity
Long-term studies in animals have not been performed to evaluate the carcinogenic potential of mesalamine.

Mutagenicity
No evidence of mutagenicity was observed in an *in vitro* Ames test or in an *in vivo* mouse micronucleus test.

Pregnancy/Reproduction
Fertility—Oligospermia and infertility in men, which have been reported in association with sulfasalazine, have not been seen with mesalamine.

Mesalamine was found to have no effect on the fertility and reproductive performance of male and female rats when given orally at a dose corresponding to 7 times the maximum human dose.

Pregnancy—Mesalamine crosses the placenta. Adequate and well-controlled studies have not been done in humans.

Studies in pregnant rats and rabbits given doses of 1000 and 800 mg per kg of body weight (mg/kg) per day, respectively, have not shown that mesalamine causes adverse effects in the fetus.

FDA Pregnancy Category B.

Breast-feeding
Mesalamine and its metabolite, *N*-acetyl-5-aminosalicylic acid, are distributed into breast milk. However, problems in humans have not been documented.

Pediatrics
Appropriate studies on the relationship of age to the effects of mesalamine have not been performed in the pediatric population. Safety and efficacy have not been established.

Geriatrics
No information is available on the relationship of age to the effects of mesalamine in geriatric patients. However, elderly patients are more likely to have age-related renal function impairment, which may require caution in patients receiving mesalamine.

Drug interactions and/or related problems
The following drug interactions and/or related problems have been selected on the basis of their potential clinical significance (possible mechanism in parentheses where appropriate)—not necessarily inclusive (» = major clinical significance):

Note: Combinations containing any of the following medications, depending on the amount present, may also interact with this medication.

Lactulose
(acidification of the colonic lumen by lactulose may impair release of mesalamine from delayed- or extended-release formulations)

Omeprazole
(omeprazole may increase gastrointestinal pH; concurrent use may result in an increase in the absorption of mesalamine)

Laboratory value alterations
The following have been selected on the basis of their potential clinical significance (possible effect in parentheses where appropriate)—not necessarily inclusive (» = major clinical significance).

With physiology/laboratory test values

Alanine aminotransferase (ALT [SGPT]) and
Alkaline phosphatase and
Aspartate aminotransferase (AST [SGOT])
(values may be increased, but return to normal with either continuation or discontinuation of therapy)

Bilirubin, serum
(concentration may be increased, but returns to normal with either continuation or discontinuation of therapy)

Medical considerations/Contraindications
The medical considerations/contraindications included have been selected on the basis of their potential clinical significance (reasons given in parentheses where appropriate)—not necessarily inclusive (» = major clinical significance).

Risk-benefit should be considered when the following medical problems exist:

Renal function impairment
(increased risk of interstitial nephritis and nephrotic syndrome)

Sensitivity to mesalamine, olsalazine, sulfasalazine, or salicylates

Stenosis, pyloric
(prolonged gastric retention may delay release of mesalamine)

Patient monitoring
The following may be especially important in patient monitoring (other tests may be warranted in some patients, depending on condition; » = major clinical significance):

Blood urea nitrogen (BUN) and
Creatinine, serum and
Urinalysis
(determinations recommended prior to, and periodically during, therapy)

Side/Adverse Effects
The following side/adverse effects have been selected on the basis of their potential clinical significance (possible signs and symptoms in parentheses where appropriate)—not necessarily inclusive:

Those indicating need for medical attention
Incidence less frequent

Acute intolerance syndrome (abdominal or stomach cramps or pain, severe; bloody diarrhea; fever; headache, severe; skin rash and itching)

Note: Prompt withdrawal of mesalamine is recommended at the first signs of *acute intolerance syndrome.*

Incidence rare

Hepatitis (yellow eyes or skin); ***pancreatitis*** (back or stomach pain, severe; fast heartbeat; fever; nausea or vomiting; swelling of the stomach); ***pericarditis*** (anxiety; blue or pale skin; chest pain, possibly moving to the left arm, neck, or shoulder; chills; shortness of breath; unusual tiredness or weakness)

Those indicating need for medical attention only if they continue or are bothersome

Incidence more frequent

Abdominal or stomach cramps or pain, mild; diarrhea, mild; dizziness; headache, mild; nausea or vomiting; rhinitis (runny or stuffy nose or sneezing); ***unusual tiredness or weakness***

Incidence less frequent or rare

Acne; alopecia (loss of hair); ***anorexia*** (loss of appetite); ***back or joint pain; dyspepsia*** (indigestion); ***gas or flatulence***

Overdose

For specific information on the agents used in the management of mesalamine overdose, see:

- *Charcoal, Activated (Oral-Local)* monograph;
- *Ipecac (Oral-Local)* monograph; and/or
- *Salicylates (Systemic)* monograph.

For more information on the management of overdose or unintentional ingestion, **contact a Poison Control Center** (see *Poison Control Center Listing*).

Clinical effects of overdose

The following effects have been selected on the basis of their potential clinical significance (possible signs and symptoms in parentheses where appropriate)—not necessarily inclusive:

Acute effects

Confusion; diarrhea, severe or continuing; dizziness or lightheadedness; drowsiness, severe; fast or deep breathing; headache, severe or continuing; hearing loss or ringing or buzzing in ears, continuing; nausea or vomiting, continuing

Treatment of overdose

There has been no clinical experience with mesalamine overdosage. However, because mesalamine is an aminosalicylate, the symptoms of overdose may mimic the symptoms of salicylate overdose; therefore, measures used to treat salicylate overdose may be applied to mesalamine overdose.

To decrease absorption—The stomach may be emptied by induction of emesis with ipecac syrup (with care being taken to guard against aspiration) or by gastric lavage. Activated charcoal may also be administered.

Supportive care—Fluid and electrolyte imbalance should be corrected by the administration of appropriate intravenous therapy. Vital functions should be monitored and supported. Patients in whom intentional overdose is confirmed or suspected should be referred for psychiatric consultation.

Patient Consultation

As an aid to patient consultation, refer to *Advice for the Patient, Mesalamine (Oral).*

In providing consultation, consider emphasizing the following selected information (» = major clinical significance):

Before using this medication

» Conditions affecting use, especially:
  Sensitivity to mesalamine, olsalazine, sulfasalazine, or salicylates
  Pregnancy—Crosses the placenta
  Breast-feeding—Distributed into breast milk

Proper use of this medication

Swallowing capsules or tablets whole without breaking, crushing, or chewing

Taking medicine before meals and at bedtime with a full glass (8 ounces) of water

» Compliance with full course of therapy

» Not switching brands without consulting physician

» Proper dosing

Missed dose: Taking as soon as possible; not taking if almost time for next dose; not doubling doses

» Proper storage

Precautions while using this medication

Regular visits to physician to check progress

Patient may notice small beads or empty tablet in stool left over after medication is absorbed

Side/adverse effects

Signs of potential side effects, especially acute intolerance syndrome, hepatitis, pancreatitis, and pericarditis

General Dosing Information

Mesalamine should be taken before meals and at bedtime with a full glass (8 ounces) of water.

Oral Dosage Forms

Note: Bracketed uses in the *Dosage Forms* section refer to categories of use and/or indications that are not included in U.S. product labeling.

MESALAMINE EXTENDED-RELEASE CAPSULES

Usual adult dose

Ulcerative colitis; or
[Crohn's disease] —
  1 gram four times a day for up to eight weeks.

Usual pediatric dose

Safety and efficacy have not been established.

Usual geriatric dose

See *Usual adult dose.*

Strength(s) usually available

U.S.—
  250 mg (Rx) [*Pentasa* (acetylated monoglyceride; castor oil; colloidal silicon dioxide; ethylcellulose; hydroxypropyl methylcellulose; starch; stearic acid; sugar; talc; white wax)].

Canada—
  250 mg (Rx) [*Pentasa*].

Packaging and storage

Store at controlled room temperature between 15 and 30 °C (59 and 86 °F).

Auxiliary labeling

- Take with a full glass (8 ounces) of water.

MESALAMINE DELAYED-RELEASE TABLETS

Note: There are differences in the rate and site of absorption among the various brands of mesalamine delayed-release tablets; therefore, these preparations are not bioequivalent, and one brand should not be substituted for another unless otherwise directed by the patient's physician.

Usual adult dose

Ulcerative colitis; or
[Crohn's disease]—
  Asacol: 800 mg three times a day for six weeks.
  Mesasal: 1.5 to 3 grams daily in divided doses.
  Salofalk: 1 gram three or four times a day.

Maintenance of remission of ulcerative colitis—
  Asacol: 1.6 grams daily in divided doses.

Usual pediatric dose

Safety and efficacy have not been established.

Usual geriatric dose

See *Usual adult dose.*

Strength(s) usually available

U.S.—
  400 mg (Rx) [*Asacol* (Eudragit S)].

Canada—
  250 mg (Rx) [*Salofalk* (Eudragit L)].
  400 mg (Rx) [*Asacol* (Eudragit S)].
  500 mg (Rx) [*Mesasal* (Eudragit L); *Salofalk* (Eudragit L)].

Packaging and storage

Store at controlled room temperature between 15 and 30 °C (59 and 86 °F).

Auxiliary labeling

- Take with a full glass (8 ounces) of water.

MESALAMINE EXTENDED-RELEASE TABLETS

Usual adult dose

See *Mesalamine Extended-release Capsules.*

Usual pediatric dose

Safety and efficacy have not been established.

Usual geriatric dose

See *Mesalamine Extended-release Capsules.*

Strength(s) usually available

U.S.—
  Not commercially available.

Canada—
250 mg (Rx) [*Pentasa*].
500 mg (Rx) [*Pentasa*].

Packaging and storage

Store at controlled room temperature between 15 and 30 °C (59 and 86 °F).

Auxiliary labeling

- Take with a full glass (8 ounces) of water.

Selected Bibliography

Thomson ABR. Review article: new developments in the use of 5-aminosalicylic acid in patients with inflammatory bowel disease. Aliment Pharmacol Ther 1991; 5: 449-70.

Revised: 08/14/1998
Developed: 03/17/1995

MESALAMINE Rectal-Local

INN: Mesalazine
BAN: Mesalazine
VA CLASSIFICATION (Primary): RS100
Commonly used brand name(s): *Canasa; Rowasa; Salofalk*.
Other commonly used names are 5-aminosalicylic acid and 5-ASA.
Note: For a listing of dosage forms and brand names by country availability, see *Dosage Forms* section(s).

Category

Bowel disease (inflammatory) suppressant.

Indications

Note: Bracketed information in the *Indications* section refers to uses that are not included in U.S. product labeling.

Accepted

Bowel disease, inflammatory (treatment)—Mesalamine rectal suspension is indicated for the treatment of mild to moderate distal ulcerative colitis, proctosigmoiditis, and proctitis.

Mesalamine suppositories are indicated for the treatment of active ulcerative proctitis.

[Bowel disease, inflammatory (prophylaxis)]—Mesalamine rectal suspension is indicated to help maintain remission of distal ulcerative colitis.

Pharmacology/Pharmacokinetics

Physicochemical characteristics

Molecular weight—153.14.
pKa—5.8.

Mechanism of action/Effect

Bowel disease (inflammatory) suppressant—
Uncertain. Mucosal production of arachidonic acid metabolites, both through the cyclooxygenase and lipoxygenase pathways, is increased in patients with inflammatory bowel disease. Mesalamine appears to diminish inflammation by inhibiting cyclooxygenase and lipoxygenase, thereby decreasing the production of prostaglandins, and leukotrienes and hydroxyeicosatetraenoic acids (HETEs), respectively.

It is also believed that mesalamine acts as a scavenger of oxygen-derived free radicals, which are produced in greater numbers in patients with inflammatory bowel disease.

Absorption

Ten to 35% absorbed from the colon; extent of absorption is determined by the length of time the drug is retained in the colon.

Distribution

The distribution of absorbed mesalamine is not known.

Biotransformation

Absorbed mesalamine is acetylated to *N*-acetyl-5-ASA(Ac-5-ASA); however, it is not known whether acetylation takes place at colonic or systemic sites. Ac-5-ASA is further acetylated (deactivated) in at least 2 sites, the colonic epithelium and the liver.

Half-life

Elimination—
Mesalamine: 0.5 to 1.5 hours.
Ac-5-ASA: 5 to 10 hours.

Elimination

Unabsorbed—Fecal.
Absorbed—Renal; 10 to 30% of administered dose is excreted in the urine within 24 hours as the Ac-5-ASA metabolite.

Precautions to Consider

Cross-sensitivity and/or related problems

Patients sensitive to olsalazine, sulfasalazine, or salicylates may be sensitive to mesalamine also.

Carcinogenicity/Tumorigenicity

In a 2-year study in rats given mesalamine orally in doses up to 320 mg per kg of body weight (mg/kg) per day, no increase in the incidence of neoplastic lesions was found.

Mutagenicity

No evidence of mutagenicity was observed in an Ames mutagen test using *Salmonella typhimurium*. In addition, there was neither evidence of reverse mutations in an assay using an *Escherichia coli* strain, nor evidence of adverse chromosomal effects in an *in vivo* mouse micronucleus assay in doses of 600 mg/kg or in an *in vivo* sister chromatid exchange test in doses up to 610 mg/kg.

Pregnancy/Reproduction

Fertility—The oligospermia and infertility in men associated with sulfasalazine has very rarely been reported among patients treated with mesalamine.

Mesalamine was found to have no effect on the fertility of rats when given orally in doses up to 320 mg/kg per day.

Pregnancy—Adequate and well-controlled studies in humans have not been done.

Studies in rats and rabbits at oral doses 5 to 8 times the maximum recommended human dose, respectively, have not shown that mesalamine causes adverse effects in the embryo or the fetus. Because animal reproduction studies are not always predictive of human response, this drug should be used in pregnancy only if clearly needed.

FDA Pregnancy Category B.

Breast-feeding

It is not known whether rectally administered mesalamine or its metabolites are distributed into breast milk. Orally administered mesalamine and its metabolite, *N*-acetyl-5-aminosalicylic acid, are distributed into breast milk. Because may drugs are distributed into human milk, caution should be exercised when mesalamine suppositories are administered to a nursing woman.

Pediatrics

Appropriate studies on the relationship of age to the effects of mesalamine have not been performed in the pediatric population. Safety and efficacy have not been established.

Geriatrics

No information is available on the relationship of age to the effects of mesalamine in geriatric patients. However, elderly patients are more likely to have age-related renal function impairment, which may require caution and renal function monitoring in patients receiving mesalamine.

Laboratory value alterations

The following have been selected on the basis of their potential clinical significance (possible effect in parentheses where appropriate)—not necessarily inclusive (» = major clinical significance).

Liver enzymes
(levels may be elevated)

Medical considerations/Contraindications

The medical considerations/contraindications included have been selected on the basis of their potential clinical significance (reasons given in parentheses where appropriate)—not necessarily inclusive (» = major clinical significance).

Except under special circumstances, this medication should not be used when the following medical problem exists:

» Hypersensitivity to mesalamine (5-aminosalicylic acid), olsalazine, sulfasalazine, or to the suppository vehicle [saturated vegetable fatty acid esters (Hard Fat, NF)] or to salicylates (including aspirin)

Risk-benefit should be considered when the following medical problems exist:

» Hypersensitivity to sulfasalazine
(caution should be exercised; these patients should be instructed to discontinue therapy promptly if signs of acute intolerance syndrome symptoms (e.g., cramping, acute abdominal pain, bloody diarrhea, fever, headache and rash) occur; if rechallenge is clearly needed to confirm hypersensitivity, close supervision is required and consideration given to a reduced dose)

Renal function impairment
(although absorption of mesalamine is limited, the possibility of increased risk of renal damage should be considered)

Patient monitoring

The following may be especially important in patient monitoring (other tests may be warranted in some patients, depending on condition; » = major clinical significance):

Blood urea nitrogen (BUN) and
Creatinine, serum and
Urinalysis
(determinations may be required in patients with renal function impairment and in patients concurrently using oral medications, such as sulfasalazine, that liberate mesalamine)

Side/Adverse Effects

The following side/adverse effects have been selected on the basis of their potential clinical significance (possible signs and symptoms in parentheses where appropriate)—not necessarily inclusive:

Those indicating need for medical attention

Incidence less frequent or rare

Acute intolerance syndrome (abdominal or stomach cramps or pain, severe; bloody diarrhea; fever; headache, severe; skin rash); ***colitis*** (stomach cramps, tenderness, pain; watery or bloody diarrhea; fever); ***hepatitis*** (yellow eyes or skin); ***inflammatory bowel disease (including melena and hematochezia)*** (bright red blood in the stool; bloody, black, or tarry stools; severe abdominal or stomach pain; severe diarrhea); ***pancreatitis*** (back or stomach pain, severe; fast heartbeat; fever; nausea or vomiting; swelling of the stomach); ***pericarditis*** (anxiety; blue or pale skin; chest pain, possibly moving to the left arm, neck, or shoulder; chills; shortness of breath; unusual tiredness or weakness)

Note: Prompt withdrawal of mesalamine is recommended at the first signs of the *acute intolerance syndrome,* particularly in patients with a known allergy to sulfasalazine.

In some cases of pericarditis, discontinuation of mesalamine may be warranted. However, rechallenge with mesalamine can be performed under careful clinical observation should continued mesalamine use be necessary.

There have been two reports in the literature of serious adverse events: one patient developed leukopenia and thrombocytopenia after seven months of treatment with one 500-mg suppository; and one patient with rash and fever similar to a sulfasalazine reaction.

Incidence not determined—Observed during clinical practice; estimates of frequency can not be determined

Fibrosing alveolitis (cough; shortness of breath; troubled breathing); ***nephrotoxicity*** (blood in urine; change in frequency of urination or amount of urine; difficulty in breathing; drowsiness; increased thirst; loss of appetite; nausea or vomiting; swelling of feet or lower legs; weakness); ***neutropenia*** (black, tarry, stools; chills; cough; fever; lower back or side pain; painful or difficult urination; pale skin; shortness of breath; sore throat; ulcers, sores, or white spots in mouth; unusual bleeding or bruising; unusual tiredness or weakness); ***pancytopenia*** (high fever; chills; unexplained bleeding or bruising; bloody, black, or tarry stools; pale skin; unusual tiredness or weakness; cough; shortness of breath; sores, ulcers, or white spots on lips or in mouth; swollen glands)

Note: Cases of pancreatitis and fibrosing alveolitis have been reported as manifestations of inflammatory bowel disease as well.

Those indicating need for medical attention only if they continue or are bothersome

Incidence more frequent

Abdominal or stomach cramps or pain, mild; gas or flatulence; headache, mild; ; nausea

Incidence less frequent or rare

Acne; alopecia (loss of hair); ***diarrhea; dizziness; leg or joint pain; rectal irritation or pain***

Patient Consultation

As an aid to patient consultation, refer to *Advice for the Patient, Mesalamine (Rectal).*

In providing consultation, consider emphasizing the following selected information (» = major clinical significance):

Before using this medication

» Conditions affecting use, especially:
Hypersensitivity to mesalamine, olsalazine, sulfasalazine or to the suppository vehicle, or to salicylates (including aspirin)
Fertility—Very rare cases of oligospermia and infertility in men reported with mesalamine use
Pregnancy—Should be used in pregnancy only if clearly needed
Breast-feeding—Caution should be exercised when administering to nursing woman
Use in the elderly—Elderly patients may be more likely to have renal function impairment that may require caution and monitoring of renal function

Proper use of this medication

Carefully reading and following patient directions for enema or suppository dosage forms
Emptying bowel immediately prior to enema or suppository, for best results
» Compliance with full course of therapy
» Proper dosing
Missed dose: Mesalamine enema—Using as soon as possible if remembered same night; using next dose at regularly scheduled time; not doubling doses
Mesalamine suppository—Using as soon as possible unless almost time for next dose; not doubling doses
» Proper storage

Precautions while using this medication

Regular visits to physician to check progress
Importance of contacting physician immediately if signs/symptoms of acute intolerance syndrome (e.g., cramping, acute abdominal pain, bloody diarrhea, fever, headache and rash) develop
Checking with physician if signs of rectal irritation occur
May stain clothing, fabrics, painted surfaces, marble, granite, vinyl, or other surfaces with which it comes into contact
Baseline liver function tests recommended before starting medication

Side/adverse effects

Signs of potential side effects, especially acute intolerance syndrome, anal irritation or pain, colitis, hepatitis, inflammatory bowel disease (melena and hematochezia), pancreatitis, and pericarditis
Signs of potential side effects observed during clinical practice, especially fibrosing alveolitis, nephrotoxicity, neutropenia, and pancytopenia

General Dosing Information

The mesalamine enema should be used at bedtime with the objective of retaining the rectal suspension for at least 8 hours. The 500-mg mesalamine suppository should be used two to three times a day and the 1000-mg suppository should be used once daily at bedtime with the objective of retaining it for 1 to 3 hours or longer, if possible, to achieve maximum benefit.

For best results, bowel should be emptied immediately prior to the rectal administration of mesalamine.

Response to therapy with mesalamine may occur within 3 to 21 days; however, the usual course of therapy is from 3 to 6 weeks depending on symptoms and sigmoidoscopic examinations.

After remission, some patients may be maintained on mesalamine enema on a less than nightly schedule; however, the possibility of relapse increases as the frequency of mesalamine enema administration is decreased.

Studies to date have not determined if mesalamine suppositories modify the relapse rate after remission; however, it is recommended that abrupt discontinuation be avoided.

Mesalamine rectal suppositories will cause staining of direct contact surfaces, including but not limited to fabrics, flooring, painted surfaces, marble, granite, vinyl, and enamel.

Rectal Dosage Forms

Note: Bracketed uses in the *Dosage Forms* section refer to categories of use and/or indications that are not included in U.S. product labeling.

MESALAMINE RECTAL SUPPOSITORIES

Usual adult and adolescent dose

Bowel disease, inflammatory (treatment)—
Rectal, 500 mg two times a day with possible increase to 3 times daily if inadequate response at two weeks for three to six weeks.
Rectal, 1000 mg once daily at bedtime

Usual pediatric dose
Safety and efficacy have not been established.

Usual geriatric dose
See *Usual adult and adolescent dose.*

Strength(s) usually available
U.S.—
500 mg (Rx) [*Canasa* (hard fat); *Rowasa* (hard fat)].
1000 mg (Rx) [*Canasa* (hard fat)].
Canada—
250 mg (Rx) [*Salofalk* (hard fat)].
500 mg (Rx) [*Salofalk* (hard fat)].

Packaging and storage
Store between 19 and 26 °C (66 and 79 °F). Do not refrigerate. Protect from light, heat, and humidity.

Auxiliary labeling
- Rectal use only
- May stain clothing

MESALAMINE RECTAL SUSPENSION

Usual adult and adolescent dose
Bowel disease, inflammatory (treatment)—
Rectal, 4 grams as a retention enema each night for three to six weeks.
[Bowel disease, inflammatory (prophylaxis)]—
Rectal, 2 grams as a retention enema each night. Alternatively, 4 grams every other, or every third night.

Usual pediatric dose
Safety and efficacy have not been established.

Usual geriatric dose
See *Usual adult and adolescent dose.*

Strength(s) usually available
U.S.—
4 grams per 60-mL unit (Rx) [*Rowasa* (potassium metabisulfite; carbomer 943P; edetate disodium; potassium acetate; water; xanthan gum; sodium benzoate)].
Canada—
2 grams per 60-mL unit (Rx) [*Salofalk* (potassium metabisulfite; sodium benzoate)].
4 grams per 60-mL unit (Rx) [*Salofalk* (potassium metabisulfite; sodium benzoate)].

Packaging and storage
Store between 15 and 30 °C (59 and 86 °F), unless otherwise specified by manufacturer.

Stability
Mesalamine rectal suspension may darken with time. Slight darkening will not affect potency; however, enemas with a dark brown color should be discarded.

Auxiliary labeling
- For rectal use.
- Shake well.
- Will stain clothing.

Selected Bibliography

Biddle WL, Greenberger NJ, Swan JT, et al. 5-Aminosalicylic acid enemas: effective agent in maintaining remission in left-sided ulcerative colitis. Gastroenterology 1988; 94: 1075-9.

Guarino J, Chatzinoff M, Berk T, et al. 5-Aminosalicylic acid enemas in refractory distal ulcerative colitis: long-term results. Am J Gastroenterol 1987; 82: 732-7.

Revised: 04/20/2006

MESNA Systemic

VA CLASSIFICATION (Primary): AD900

Commonly used brand name(s): *MESNEX; Uromitexan.*

Note: For a listing of dosage forms and brand names by country availability, see *Dosage Forms* section(s).

Category
Hemorrhagic cystitis prophylactic.

Indications
Note: Bracketed information in the *Indications* section refers to uses that are not included in U.S. product labeling.

Accepted
Hemorrhagic cystitis, oxazaphosphorine-induced (prophylaxis)—Mesna is indicated to reduce the incidence of ifosfamide-induced or [cyclophosphamide-induced] hemorrhagic cystitis. Mesna is not effective in preventing hematuria due to other pathologic conditions such as thrombocytopenia, and does not affect other toxicities of oxazaphosphorines.

Pharmacology/Pharmacokinetics

Physicochemical characteristics
Molecular weight—164.18.
Other characteristics—Mesna injection: pH is 6.5 to 8.5.

Mechanism of action/Effect
Mesna disulfide, which is physically inert, is reduced in the kidney (in the renal tubular epithelium) to mesna, which binds to and detoxifies urotoxic metabolites of oxazophosphorines (for ifosfamide, 4-hydroxyifosfamide and acrolein).

Distribution
Apparent volume of distribution (Vol_D)—0.652 liter per kg.

Biotransformation
Rapid, by oxidation to one metabolite, mesna disulfide (dimesna).

Half-life
Mesna—0.36 hour.
Dimesna—1.17 hours.

Elimination
Renal, rapid, by glomerular filtration; 32% as mesna and 33% as dimesna.

Precautions to Consider

Carcinogenicity
Studies have not been done.

Mutagenicity
Mesna was not found to be mutagenic in the Ames *Salmonella typhimurium* test, mouse micronucleus assay, and frequency of sister chromatid exchange and chromosomal aberrations in PHA-stimulated lymphocytes in *in vitro* assays.

Pregnancy/Reproduction
Pregnancy—Studies in humans have not been done.
Studies in rats and rabbits at oral doses up to 1000 mg per kg of body weight (mg/kg) have not shown that mesna causes adverse effects on the fetus.

FDA Pregnancy Category B.

Breast-feeding
It is not known whether mesna is distributed into breast milk. However, problems in humans have not been documented.

Pediatrics
Appropriate studies on the relationship of age to the effects of mesna have not been performed in the pediatric population. However, no pediatrics-specific problems have been documented to date.

Geriatrics
No information is available on the relationship of age to the effects of mesna in geriatric patients.

Laboratory value alterations
The following have been selected on the basis of their potential clinical significance (possible effect in parentheses where appropriate)—not necessarily inclusive (» = major clinical significance).

With physiology/laboratory test values
Ketones, urinary
(false-positive results may be produced; in this test, a red-violet color develops, which returns to violet with the addition of glacial acetic acid)

Medical considerations/Contraindications
The medical considerations/contraindications included have been selected on the basis of their potential clinical significance (reasons given in parentheses where appropriate)—not necessarily inclusive (» = major clinical significance).

Risk-benefit should be considered when the following medical problems exist:
» Sensitivity to mesna
» Sensitivity to other thiol compounds

Patient monitoring

The following may be especially important in patient monitoring (other tests may be warranted in some patients, depending on condition; » = major clinical significance):

Examination of urine for microscopic hematuria (recommended prior to administration of each dose of ifosfamide or cyclophosphamide and mesna)

Side/Adverse Effects

Note: Since mesna is used in combination with ifosfamide and other chemotherapeutic agents with documented toxicities, it is difficult to distinguish the adverse reactions that may be due to mesna from those caused by the concomitantly administered cytostatic agents.

The following side/adverse effects have been selected on the basis of their potential clinical significance (possible signs and symptoms in parentheses where appropriate)—not necessarily inclusive:

Those indicating need for medical attention

Incidence rare

Allergic reaction (skin rash or itching)

Those indicating need for medical attention only if they continue or are bothersome

Incidence less frequent

Diarrhea; nausea or vomiting; unpleasant taste

Patient Consultation

As an aid to patient consultation, refer to *Advice for the Patient, Mesna (Systemic).*

In providing consultation, consider emphasizing the following selected information (» = major clinical significance):

Before using this medication

» Conditions affecting use, especially:
Sensitivity to mesna or other thiol compounds

Proper use of this medication

» Proper dosing

Side/adverse effects

Signs of potential side effects, especially allergic reaction

General Dosing Information

Patients receiving mesna should be under supervision of a physician experienced in cancer chemotherapy.

Mesna injection has been developed as an agent to prevent ifosfamide-induced hemorrhagic cystitis. It will not prevent or alleviate any of the other adverse reactions or toxicities associated with ifosfamide therapy.

Mesna does not prevent hemorrhagic cystitis in all patients. Up to 6% of patients treated with mesna have developed hematuria. If hematuria develops when mesna is given with ifosfamide according to the recommended dosage schedule, depending on the severity of the hematuria, dosage reductions or discontinuation of ifosfamide therapy may be initiated.

Parenteral Dosage Forms

MESNA INJECTION

Usual adult and adolescent dose

Prophylaxis of ifosfamide-induced hemorrhagic cystitis—
Intravenous injection, rapid, in a dosage equal to 20% of the ifosfamide dosage (w/w) at the time of ifosfamide administration and four and eight hours after each dose of ifosfamide (i.e., the total daily dose of mesna is equal to 60% of the total daily dose of ifosfamide) each day that ifosfamide is administered. For example, patients receiving a daily ifosfamide dose of 1.2 grams per square meter of body surface area should receive 240 mg of mesna per square meter of body surface area at zero, four, and eight hours after administration of each dose of ifosfamide.

Note: If the dose of ifosfamide is adjusted, the dose of mesna should be adjusted accordingly.

Usual pediatric dose

Dosage has not been established.

Strength(s) usually available

U.S.—
100 mg per mL (Rx) [*MESNEX*].

Canada—
100 mg per mL (Rx) [*Uromitexan*].

Packaging and storage

Store below 40 °C (104 °F), preferably between 15 and 30 °C (59 and 86 °F), unless otherwise specified by the manufacturer.

Preparation of dosage form

Mesna injection is prepared for intravenous administration by adding it to a sufficient quantity of 5% dextrose injection, 5% dextrose and sodium chloride injection, 0.9% sodium chloride injection, or lactated Ringer's injection to produce a solution containing 20 mg of mesna per mL.

Stability

Diluted solutions of mesna are chemically and physically stable for 24 hours at 25 °C (77 °F). However, it is recommended that diluted solutions be refrigerated and used within 6 hours. Because exposure to oxygen causes mesna to be oxidized to dimesna, any unused portion of an ampul should be discarded.

Incompatibilities

Mesna injection is incompatible with cisplatin injection.

Revised: 09/30/1997

MESORIDAZINE—See *Phenothiazines (Systemic)*

METAPROTERENOL—See *Bronchodilators, Adrenergic (Inhalation-Local), Bronchodilators, Adrenergic (Systemic)*

METARAMINOL—See *Sympathomimetic Agents—Cardiovascular Use (Parenteral-Systemic)*

METAXALONE—See *Skeletal Muscle Relaxants (Systemic)*

METFORMIN Systemic

VA CLASSIFICATION (Primary): HS503

Commonly used brand name(s): *Apo-Metformin; Gen-Metformin; Glucophage; Glucophage XR; Glumetza; Glycon; Novo-Metformin; Nu-Metformin.*

Note: For a listing of dosage forms and brand names by country availability, see *Dosage Forms* section(s).

Category

Antihyperglycemic agent.

Indications

Accepted

Type 2 diabetes (treatment)—Metformin is indicated in patients with type 2 diabetes to control hyperglycemia that cannot be controlled by diet management, exercise, or weight reduction, or when insulin therapy is not required or feasible. It is used as monotherapy or as an adjunct to sulfonylureas or insulin[1] when either alone does not achieve adequate glycemic control. It can be tried if primary or secondary failure of sulfonylureas occurs. However, caution and clinical judgment should be used when combining metformin with maximum doses of sulfonylureas for treating nonobese patients with type 2 diabetes who clearly are not responding to the sulfonylureas; insulin may be the preferred treatment in such cases.

[Polycystic ovary syndrome (treatment)][1]—Metformin is indicated for the treatment of polycystic ovary syndrome.

[1]Not included in Canadian product labeling.

Pharmacology/Pharmacokinetics

Physicochemical characteristics

Chemical Group—Biguanide.
Molecular weight—165.63.
pKa—2.8 and 11.5 at 32 °C (90 °F).

Mechanism of action/Effect

Metformin potentiates the effect of insulin by mechanisms not fully understood. Metformin does not stimulate pancreatic beta cells to increase secretion of insulin; insulin secretion must be present for metformin to work properly. It is postulated that metformin decreases hepatic glucose production and improves insulin sensitivity by increasing peripheral glucose uptake and utilization.

Specifically, it is thought that metformin may increase the number and/or affinity of insulin receptors on cell surface membranes, especially at peripheral receptor sites, and help to correct down regulation of the insulin receptor. This effect increases the sensitivity to insulin at receptor and postreceptor binding sites and increases glucose uptake peripherally. Insulin concentrations remain unchanged or are slightly reduced as glucose metabolism improves. At therapeutic doses, metformin does not cause hypoglycemia in diabetic or nondiabetic individuals. In addition, metformin's metabolic effects increase hepatic glycogen stores in diabetic patients (but not in nondiabetic patients), reduce fatty acid oxidation and acetyl coenzyme A formation, and may decrease intestinal glucose absorption. Glucose uptake and free fatty acid oxidation are effects considered to be caused by non–insulin-mediated mechanisms. Some studies have shown lipid-lowering effects in both diabetic and nondiabetic patients, while others have shown no clear evidence that metformin decreases lipid concentrations in all diabetic patients. These effects could manifest as weight reduction with nominal disturbance of the metabolic rate.

Other actions/effects

Metformin interferes with the absorption of vitamin B_{12} by competitive inhibition of calcium-dependent binding of the intrinsic factor–vitamin B_{12} complex to its receptor; anemia in predisposed individuals is possible.

Absorption

Absorbed over 6 hours; bioavailability is 50 to 60% under fasting conditions. Food delays absorption (lowers peak concentration by 40%) and decreases the extent of absorption (lowers area under the concentration-time curve [AUC] by 25%).

Distribution

Apparent volume of distribution is 654 ± 358 L. Main sites of concentration without accumulation are the intestinal mucosa and the salivary glands; also, the erythrocyte mass may be a compartment of distribution.

Protein binding

Negligible.

Biotransformation

Metformin is not metabolized.

Half-life

Plasma elimination—6.2 hours, mean, based on an initial elimination of 1.7 to 3 hours and terminal elimination of 9 to 17 hours.

Time to peak concentration

2.25 ± 0.44 hours.

Peak serum concentration

At steady-state—Approximately 1 to 2 mcg per mL (6.04 to 12.08 mmol per L).

Elimination

Renal—Up to 90% of a dose, eliminated unchanged. The renal clearance is 450 to 513 mL per minute (mL/minute).

Fecal—Up to 30% of a dose.

In dialysis—Hemodialysis with clearance of 170 mL/minute prevents accumulation of metformin.

Precautions to Consider

Carcinogenicity

A study in rats and in mice for 104 weeks and 91 weeks, respectively, at three times the recommended human daily dose showed no evidence of carcinogenicity.

Tumorigenicity

A study in male rats showed no evidence of tumorigenicity; however, female rats given three times the recommended human daily dose on a mg per kg of body weight (mg/kg) basis, or 900 mg a day, had an increased incidence of benign stromal uterine polyps.

Mutagenicity

Metformin was not found to be mutagenic in the Ames test, gene mutation test (mouse lymphoma cells), chromosome aberration test (human lymphocytes), or *in vivo* micronuclei formation test (mouse bone marrow).

Pregnancy/Reproduction

Fertility—Problems in humans have not been documented.

No evidence of impairment of fertility was found in male or female rats given twice the recommended human daily dose of metformin.

Pregnancy—Adequate and well-controlled studies in humans have not been done. Control of blood glucose during pregnancy with diet alone or a combination of diet and insulin is recommended, while use of all oral antidiabetic agents is discouraged. Use of insulin rather than metformin for the treatment of type 2 diabetes and gestational diabetes mellitus (GDM) permits maintenance of blood glucose at concentrations as close to normal as possible. High blood glucose concentrations have been associated with a higher incidence of major congenital abnormalities early in pregnancy (5 to 8 weeks gestation) and high perinatal morbidity and mortality later in pregnancy. A study reported infant malformation rates of 35, 12.9, and 4.8% when initial hemoglobin A_{1c} (an indicator of blood glucose control for the preceding 3 months) was 10% or more, 8 to 9.9%, and below 8%, respectively. The malformation rate in infants born to mothers who do not have diabetes is approximately 2%.

Teratological studies in albino rats found no abnormalities.

FDA Pregnancy Category B.

Breast-feeding

Problems in humans have not been documented. Metformin is distributed into breast milk.

Pediatrics

Appropriate studies performed to date have not demonstrated pediatrics specific problems in children that would limit the usefulness of metformin tablets in children older than 10 years of age.

No information is available on the relationship of age to the effects of metformin *extended release* tablets in pediatric patients. Safety and efficacy have not been established for metformin *extended release* tablets in pediatric patients less than 17–years-old.

Adolescents

No information is available on the relationship of age to the effects of metformin *extended release* tablets in adolescent patients. Safety and efficacy have not been established.

Appropriate studies performed to date have not demonstrated adolescent specific problems that would limit the usefulness of metformin tablets in children and adolescents up to 16 years of age.

Geriatrics

Appropriate studies performed to date have not demonstrated geriatrics-specific problems that would limit the usefulness of metformin in the elderly. However, because of possible gastrointestinal intolerance, it is recommended that treatment be initiated with low doses that are adjusted gradually, according to renal clearance. Maximum doses should not be used. Elderly patients are more likely to have age-related renal function impairment or peripheral vascular disease, which may require adjustment of dosage or dosage interval, or discontinuation of treatment when appropriate.

Drug interactions and/or related problems

The following drug interactions and/or related problems have been selected on the basis of their potential clinical significance (possible mechanism in parentheses where appropriate)—not necessarily inclusive (» = major clinical significance):

Note: Combinations containing any of the following medications, depending on the amount present, may also interact with this medication.

Administration of any medication that may affect metabolic or glycemic control of diabetes mellitus requires careful monitoring of blood glucose concentrations by the patient or health care professional. This is particularly important when any medication is added to or removed from an established treatment regimen. Subsequent adjustments in diet or in dose of antidiabetic agent or both may be necessary; these adjustments may differ depending on the severity of the diabetes.

» Alcohol, acute or chronic ingestion of
(excessive intake may elevate blood lactate concentrations or increase the risk of developing hypoglycemia, especially when alcohol is ingested without meals)

» Cimetidine or

» Other cationic medications excreted by renal tubular transport, such as:
- Amiloride
- Calcium channel blocking agents, especially nifedipine
- Digoxin
- Morphine
- Procainamide
- Quinidine
- Quinine
- Ranitidine
- Triamterene
- Trimethoprim

Vancomycin
(cimetidine inhibits the renal tubular secretion of metformin, decreases renal clearance of metformin by 27% over 24 hours, and can significantly increase plasma concentrations of metformin by 60% for up to 6 hours when cimetidine and metformin are taken together; clinical significance is not known, but dosage reduction of metformin potentially may be needed)
(nifedipine increased absorption of metformin in a single-dose study, resulting in a 9% increase in area under the concentration-time curve [AUC] and a 20% increase in peak plasma concentration with no change in half-life and urinary excretion; clinical significance is not known; it is not known whether similar effects are produced by other calcium channel blocking agents)
(other cationic medications excreted by renal tubular transport have the potential to increase metformin's plasma concentration or interfere with renal clearance; careful monitoring of blood glucose would be especially appropriate when these medications are given concurrently with metformin)

» Furosemide
(in one study, furosemide increased metformin's AUC by 15% in normal healthy volunteers; renal clearance was not affected; clinical significance is not known, but dosage reduction of metformin potentially may be needed)

Hyperglycemia-causing medications, such as:
Contraceptives, estrogen-containing, oral
Corticosteroids
Diuretics, thiazide
Estrogens
Isoniazid
Niacin
Phenothiazines, especially chlorpromazine
Phenytoin
Sympathomimetic agents
Thyroid hormones
(these medications may contribute to hyperglycemia; an increased dose of metformin or a change to another antidiabetic agent may be needed)

Hypoglycemia-causing medications, such as:
Clofibrate
Monoamine oxidase (MAO) inhibitors
Probenecid
Propranolol
Rifabutin
Rifampin
Salicylates
Sulfonamides, long-acting
Sulfonylureas
(these medications may cause hypoglycemia and decrease the dosage of metformin needed; although studies with many of these agents in combination with metformin have not been done, it is expected that those medications that are highly protein-bound will cause fewer problems when used with metformin than when used with some of the sulfonylurea antidiabetic agents)

Laboratory value alterations

The following have been selected on the basis of their potential clinical significance (possible effect in parentheses where appropriate)—not necessarily inclusive (» = major clinical significance).

With diagnostic test results
Ketones, urine
(may produce false-positive tests)

With physiology/laboratory test values
Cholesterol, total, serum or
Lipoproteins, low-density (LDL), serum or
Triglycerides, serum
(the effects of metformin on these lipid subfractions in patients with type 2 diabetes are inconsistent and may depend on weight control; further studies are needed to fully characterize these effects. Generally, concentrations of cholesterol, low-density lipoproteins, or triglycerides may be lowered or unchanged in metformin users. This is thought to be independent of metformin's glucose-lowering effect; it may involve suppression of free fatty acid oxidation and lipid oxidation or reduction in the triglyceride content of the LDL and very low-density lipoprotein [VLDL] fractions by metformin)

Lactate, fasting, serum
(may increase to the upper range of normal, 2 mEq/L [2 mmol/L], or show no change with therapeutic doses; although the source is unknown, any small increase is thought to be due to glucose metabolism in the splanchnic beds, not in skeletal muscle)

Lipoproteins, high-density (HDL), serum
(may be slightly increased or unchanged)

Medical considerations/Contraindications

The medical considerations/contraindications included have been selected on the basis of their potential clinical significance (reasons given in parentheses where appropriate)—not necessarily inclusive (» = major clinical significance).

Except under special circumstances, this medication should not be used when the following medical problems exist:

» Any condition needing close blood glucose control, such as:
Burns, severe
Dehydration
Diabetic coma
Diabetic ketoacidosis
Hyperosmolar nonketotic coma
Infection, severe
Surgery, major
Trauma, severe
(risks of side effects related to uncontrolled blood glucose or lactic acidosis may be increased, and metformin should be discontinued; insulin controls blood glucose best in patients with these conditions; also, metformin should be discontinued 2 days prior to surgery)

» Conditions associated with hypoxemia, such as:
Cardiorespiratory insufficiency
Cardiovascular collapse
Congestive heart failure
Myocardial infarction, acute or

» Hepatic disease, severe, acute, or chronic or

» Lactic acidosis, active or history of or

» Renal function impairment or renal disease
(lactic acidosis is associated with these conditions and the risk is further increased when metformin is given concurrently)
(risk of lactic acidosis increases with the degree of renal dysfunction, impairment of renal clearance, and age of patient; patients who have demonstrated fasting serum lactate values above the upper limit of normal should not receive metformin)

» Diagnostic or medical examinations using intravascular iodinated contrast media such as:
Angiography
Cholangiography, intravenous
Computed tomography (CT) scan
Pyelography
Urography
(because of the increased risk of lactic acidosis, metformin should be discontinued at the time of or prior to medical or diagnostic examinations requiring use of contrast media that can cause functional oliguria; metformin therapy should be withheld for 48 hours after the procedure and should not be reinstated until after renal function returns to normal)

» Hypersensitivity to metformin

Risk-benefit should be considered when the following medical problems exist:

» Diarrhea or
» Gastroparesis or
» Intestinal obstruction or
» Vomiting or
» Other conditions causing delayed food absorption
(conditions that decrease or delay stomach emptying may require a modification of metformin dose or a change to insulin)

» Hyperglycemia-causing conditions, such as:
Female hormonal changes
Fever, high
Hypercortisolism, not optimally treated
Psychological stress
(these conditions, by increasing blood glucose, may increase the need for more frequent glucose monitoring and increase the need for a temporary or permanent dose increase of metformin or a change to insulin if blood glucose is uncontrolled)

» Hyperthyroidism, not optimally controlled
(hyperthyroidism aggravates diabetes mellitus by increasing plasma glucose concentrations and glucose absorption and impairing glucose tolerance; thyroid hormone has dose-dependent biphasic effects on glycogenolysis and gluconeogenesis, which can make glycemic control difficult until the patient is euthyroid; patients with hyperthyroidism may require an increased dose of metformin until euthyroidism is achieved)

» Hypoglycemia-causing conditions, such as:
Adrenal insufficiency, not optimally controlled
Debilitated physical condition
Malnutrition

Pituitary insufficiency, not optimally controlled
(these conditions, which inherently predispose patients to the risk of developing hypoglycemia, increase the patient's risk of developing severe hypoglycemia during metformin treatment; reduction of metformin dose or more frequent blood glucose monitoring may be required)

» Hypothyroidism, not optimally controlled
(this condition is associated with reduced glucose absorption and altered glucose and lipoprotein metabolism; lower-than-normal doses of metformin may be needed when hypothyroid conditions exist, although an increase in metformin dose may be required when initiating thyroid treatment; glucose control may be difficult until the patient is euthyroid)

Patient monitoring

The following may be especially important in patient monitoring (other tests may be warranted in some patients, depending on condition; » = major clinical significance):

Folic acid concentrations, serum and
Vitamin B_{12} concentrations, serum
(recommended every 1 or 2 years during long-term metformin therapy because metformin may interfere with their absorption)

» Glucose concentration, blood or serum
(blood or serum glucose reflects the current degree of metabolic control and should be routinely self-monitored by the patient at home and by the physician [every 3 months, or more often when patient is not stabilized] to confirm that blood glucose concentration is maintained within agreed-upon targets by the selected diet and dosing regimen; this is particularly important during dosage adjustments. Self-monitoring of blood glucose by the patient may require testing several times a day or once to several times a week)
(caution in interpreting blood glucose concentrations is needed because normal whole blood glucose values are approximately 15% lower than serum glucose values; glucose values are also laboratory- and method-specific. Normal fasting whole blood glucose for adults of all ages is 65 to 95 mg/dL [3.6 to 5.3 mmol/L]. Normal fasting serum glucose is 70 to 105 mg/dL [3.9 to 5.8 mmol/L] for adults younger than 60 years of age and 80 to 115 mg/dL [4.4 to 6.4 mmol/L] for adults 60 years of age or older. For pregnant women with diabetes, a normal fasting serum glucose is less than 105 mg/dL [5.8 mmol/L] and a fasting whole blood glucose is less than 120 mg/dL [6.7 mmol/L])
(capillary blood glucose measurement provides important information when done properly, but caution is warranted because of potential errors in technique and readings; it has been suggested that the values be relied upon only if the reported glucose concentration for patients whose diabetes is stable is between 75 mg/dL and 325 mg/dL [4.16 mmol/L and 17.88 mmol/L, respectively])

Glucose concentrations, urine and
Ketone concentrations, urine
(if blood glucose concentrations exceed 200 mg/dL [11.1 mmol/L], monitoring of urine for the presence of glucose and ketones may be necessary; normalization of glucose in the urine generally lags quantitatively behind serum glucose concentrations; test methods are generally capable of detecting glucose concentrations in the urine greater than 180 mg/dL [10 mmol/L])

» Glycosylated hemoglobin (hemoglobin A_{1c}) determinations
(monitoring should be done every 3 months or as often as necessary; assessment of this parameter does not eliminate the need for daily blood glucose monitoring. Hemoglobin A_{1c} values reflect the blood glucose control over the preceding 3 months. Normal whole blood hemoglobin A_{1c} is approximately 4 to 6% of total hemoglobin; specific values are laboratory-dependent. Hemoglobin A_{1c} is falsely elevated in patients whose diabetes is unstable when the intermediate precursor is elevated [e.g., in alcoholism] and falsely lowered in conditions of shortened red blood cell life span [e.g., in anemia and acute or chronic blood loss] or in patients with hemoglobinopathies [e.g., sickle cell disease])

Hematocrit and
Hemoglobin concentrations and
Red blood cell indices
(recommended upon initiation of metformin therapy and annually thereafter)

Physical examinations
(regular examinations as often as necessary to reassess appropriateness of continuation of metformin therapy)

» Renal function assessment
(recommended annually or more often for patients in whom the risk of developing lactic acidosis is increased)

Side/Adverse Effects

The following side/adverse effects have been selected on the basis of their potential clinical significance (possible signs and symptoms in parentheses where appropriate)—not necessarily inclusive:

Those indicating need for medical attention

Incidence rare

Anemia, megaloblastic (tiredness; weakness); ***hypoglycemia*** (anxiety; behavior change similar to drunkenness; blurred vision; cold sweats; confusion; cool, pale skin; difficulty in concentrating; drowsiness; excessive hunger; fast heartbeat; headache; nausea; nervousness; nightmares; restless sleep; shakiness; slurred speech; unusual tiredness or weakness); ***lactic acidosis*** (diarrhea; fast, shallow breathing; muscle pain or cramping; unusual sleepiness; unusual tiredness or weakness)

Note: *Hypoglycemia* does not usually occur with use of metformin unless predisposing conditions or factors are present, such as unusual fasting, concurrent use of other antidiabetic agents, or toxic doses of metformin. Metformin, in combination with sulfonylureas, has been reported to lower basal glucose concentrations typically by at least 20% more than do sulfonylureas used alone.
Lactic acidosis is a potentially fatal complication. The cases reported have occurred primarily in patients in whom a contraindication existed; otherwise, the risk is minimal with use of metformin. Patients usually presented not with symptoms of lactic acidosis, but rather with acute symptoms of other problems that resulted in metformin accumulation because of renal function impairment or failure in conditions such as myocardial infarction or renal or hepatic disease.

Those indicating need for medical attention only if they continue or are bothersome

Incidence more frequent

Anorexia (loss of appetite); ***diarrhea; dyspepsia*** (stomachache); ***flatulence*** (passing of gas); ***headache; metallic taste; nausea; vomiting; weight loss***

Note: *Diarrhea, dyspepsia,* and *nausea* occur less frequently when small doses are used initially and, along with *headache* and *metallic taste,* are transient. If *diarrhea* occurs after several months of metformin therapy, lactic acidosis should be considered.

Overdose

For more information on the management of overdose or unintentional ingestion, **contact a Poison Control Center** (see *Poison Control Center Listing*).

Clinical effects of overdose

The following effects have been selected on the basis of their potential clinical significance (possible signs and symptoms in parentheses where appropriate)—not necessarily inclusive:

Hypoglycemia; lactic acidosis

Patient Consultation

As an aid to patient consultation, refer to *Advice for the Patient, Metformin (Systemic).*

In providing consultation, consider emphasizing the following selected information (» = major clinical significance):

Before using this medication

» Conditions affecting use, especially:
Hypersensitivity to metformin
Pregnancy—Use of any oral antidiabetic medication is discouraged during pregnancy; diet or diet/insulin is recommended to prevent maternal and fetal problems; importance of controlling and monitoring blood glucose during pregnancy; alerting physician if planning to become pregnant
Breast-feeding—Metformin is distributed into breast milk
Use in the elderly—Age-related renal function impairment or peripheral vascular disease may require discontinuation of metformin treatment or special precautions in the elderly
Other medications, especially alcohol, amiloride, calcium channel blocking agents, cimetidine, digoxin, furosemide, morphine, procainamide, quinidine, quinine, ranitidine, triamterene, trimethoprim, vancomycin, or any other cationic medication excreted by renal transport
Other medical problems, especially hepatic disease (severe, acute, or chronic); hyperthyroidism or hypothyroidism (not optimally controlled); lactic acidosis (active or history of); renal function impairment or renal disease; conditions associated

with hypoxemia; conditions causing delayed food absorption (e.g., diarrhea, gastroparesis, intestinal obstruction, or vomiting); conditions causing hyperglycemia or hypoglycemia; or conditions needing close blood glucose control

Proper use of this medication

» Compliance with therapy, including not taking more or less medication than directed

» Alternative dosing or therapy changes for modifications in blood glucose testing, diet, exercise, fluid replacement, and sick-day management

For extended-release tablets: swallowing whole, not chewing or crushing

» Proper dosing

Missed dose: Taking as soon as possible; not taking if almost time for next dose; not doubling doses

» Proper storage

Precautions while using this medication

» Regular visits to physician to check progress

» Carefully following special instructions of health care team:

Discussing use of alcohol

Not taking other medications unless discussed with physician

Getting counseling for family members to help them assist the patient with diabetes; also, special counseling for pregnancy planning and contraception

Travel considerations

» Preparing for and understanding what to do in case of an emergency; having or wearing medical identification and keeping a glucagon kit and quick-acting source of sugar close by

» Informing physician of metformin therapy when medical examinations that require administration of contrast media are scheduled or when surgery is scheduled; metformin should be discontinued before surgery or appropriate medical tests and may be reinstated 48 hours postprocedure if renal function is normal

» Recognizing symptoms of lactic acidosis, such as diarrhea, fast and shallow breathing, severe muscle pain or cramping, unusual sleepiness, and unusual tiredness and weakness

» Knowing what to do if symptoms of lactic acidosis occur, such as checking blood glucose and getting immediate emergency medical help; checking with physician if vomiting occurs

» Recognizing symptoms of hypoglycemia, such as anxiety; behavior change similar to drunkenness; blurred vision; cold sweats; confusion; cool, pale skin; difficulty in concentrating; drowsiness; excessive hunger; fast heartbeat; headache; nausea; nervousness; nightmares; restless sleep; shakiness; slurred speech; and unusual tiredness and weakness

» Recognizing what brings on symptoms of hypoglycemia, such as delaying or missing a meal or snack, exercising more than usual, drinking significant amounts of alcohol, taking certain medications, using too much antidiabetic medication (insulin or a sulfonylurea), or illness, especially with vomiting or diarrhea

» Knowing what to do if symptoms of hypoglycemia occur, such as using glucagon in emergency situations including when unconsciousness occurs; eating glucose tablets or gel, sugar cubes, corn syrup, or honey; or drinking fruit juice, nondiet soft drink, or sugar dissolved in water; not eating foods high in fat, such as chocolate, since fat slows gastric emptying; also, eating a small snack, such as crackers or half sandwich, when scheduled meal is longer than 1 hour away

» Recognizing symptoms of hyperglycemia and ketoacidosis, such as blurred vision; drowsiness; dry mouth; flushed, dry skin; fruit-like breath odor; increased frequency and volume of urination; ketones in urine; loss of appetite; nausea or vomiting; stomachache; tiredness; troubled breathing (rapid and deep); unconsciousness; and unusual thirst

» Recognizing what brings on symptoms of hyperglycemia, such as fever or infection; not taking enough or missing a dose of antidiabetic medication; exercising less than usual; taking certain medications; or overeating or not following meal plan

» Knowing what to do if symptoms of hyperglycemia occur, such as checking blood glucose and contacting a member of the health care team

Side/adverse effects

Signs and symptoms of potential side effects, especially megaloblastic anemia, hypoglycemia, and lactic acidosis

General Dosing Information

Individual determination of the minimum dose of metformin that lowers blood glucose adequately is recommended. Short-term treatment during periods of transient loss of glucose control may be sufficient for some patients. Some clinicians recommend that metformin be discontinued annually or semi-annually to assess its continued contribution to the control of blood glucose concentrations, especially if there are progressive signs of secondary failure. Metformin should be discontinued if it is not significantly contributing to disease management.

Metformin should be withdrawn or the dose reduced temporarily if vomiting occurs. Treatment may be resumed cautiously after the possibility of lactic acidosis has been excluded.

When transferring a patient from a sulfonylurea to metformin, no transition period is necessary, except when chlorpropamide has been used for treatment. Chlorpropamide's prolonged action requires more frequent monitoring for hypoglycemia during the first 2 weeks following the transition.

When adding a sulfonylurea to maximum doses of metformin or metformin to maximum doses of a sulfonylurea, even if primary or secondary failure of a sulfonylurea has occurred, the new medication should be added gradually and titrated to the lowest effective dose. Both agents should be discontinued and insulin should be initiated if the patient does not respond to maximum doses within 3 months (or less, depending on clinician's decision).

When switching patients from metformin tablets to metformin extended-release tablets, the results of a clinical trial suggests that patients may safely change to once daily administration at their same total daily dose, up to 2000 mg once daily. Following a change the patient's glycemic control should be closely monitored and dosage adjustments made accordingly.

Diet/Nutrition

Metformin should be taken with food to reduce gastrointestinal symptoms.

For treatment of adverse effects and/or overdose

Recommended treatment consists of the following:

For treatment of lactic acidosis

- Hemodialysis with sodium bicarbonate has been used but is controversial because published information concerning outcome is lacking and few cases of metformin-induced lactic acidosis have been reported; peritoneal dialysis also has been used, but hemodialysis is thought to be the preferred method when dialysis is needed, such as in patients with shock syndrome. Because of metformin's rapid renal elimination, dialysis is probably not necessary when renal function can be restored. Dialysis solutions containing lactate as the buffering agent should not be used in cases of metformin-induced lactic acidosis.

For mild to moderate hypoglycemia

- Treating with immediate ingestion of a source of glucose, such as glucose gel, glucose tablets, fruit juice, corn syrup, nondiet soft drinks, honey, sugar cubes, or table sugar dissolved in water. A frequently used source of glucose is a glassful of orange juice containing 2 or 3 teaspoonfuls of table sugar.
- Documenting blood glucose and rechecking in 15 minutes.
- Counseling patient to seek medical assistance promptly.
- Possible adjustment of metformin dosage.
- Possible adjustment of meal pattern.

For severe hypoglycemia or acute overdose, including coma

Note: Dextrose administration is the basis for treatment of hypoglycemia; however, an exposure to sudden hyperglycemia caused by a rapid injection of hypertonic dextrose injection may further stimulate the sulfonylurea-primed pancreas when sulfonylureas are used with metformin to release more insulin, worsening the hypoglycemia.

- Counseling patient to obtain emergency medical assistance immediately.
- Immediately treating with 50 mL of 50% dextrose injection given intravenously to stabilize the patient. Then, administering a continuous infusion of 5 to 10% dextrose injection to maintain slight hyperglycemia (approximately 100 mg/dL [5.55 mmol/L] blood glucose concentration) for up to 12 days. Intravenous dextrose therapy should not be terminated suddenly. Oral dextrose cannot be relied upon to maintain euglycemia because 60% of an oral dextrose dose is stored as hepatic glycogen with only 15% left for brain utilization and 15% for insulin-dependent tissues.
- Glucagon, 1 to 2 mg administered intramuscularly, is useful for fast onset of action to mobilize hepatic glucose stores but may be ineffective or variable in its effect if glycogen stores are depleted. Therefore, glucagon should be administered after dextrose administration.
- Diazoxide (200 mg orally every 4 hours or 300 mg intravenously over a 30-minute period every 4 hours) can be used for patients who

do not respond to dextrose therapy or for patients in a coma as an aid to dextrose infusion to reduce hypoglycemia; the patient must be monitored for sodium concentration and hypotension.

- Emesis can be induced with ipecac syrup if the metformin overdose is recent (within the past 30 minutes) and if the patient is alert, has an intact gag reflex, and is not obtunded or convulsing. Otherwise, gastric lavage is required after endotracheal tube placement.
- Gastric decontamination by administration of repeated doses of oral activated charcoal with the appropriate cathartic may be attempted, although the usefulness of this regimen has not been established.
- Monitoring vital signs, arterial blood gases, blood glucose, and serum electrolytes (especially calcium, potassium, and sodium) as required. Initially, blood glucose concentrations should be monitored as frequently as every 1 to 3 hours. Blood urea nitrogen and serum creatinine concentrations should also be obtained.
- Cerebral edema—Managing with mannitol and dexamethasone.
- Hypokalemia—Managing with potassium supplements.
- Hospitalization for 6 to 91 hours (mean, 24 hours), because the hypoglycemia may be recurrent and prolonged.
- Other supportive measures should also be employed as needed.

Oral Dosage Forms

METFORMIN HYDROCHLORIDE TABLETS

Usual adult dose

Antihyperglycemic agent—

As monotherapy—

Initial—Oral, 500 mg two times a day, taken with morning and evening meals. The daily dose may be increased by 500 mg at weekly intervals as needed. An alternative dose is 850 mg a day, taken with the morning meal. The daily dose may be increased by 850 mg at fourteen-day intervals.

Maintenance—Oral, 500 or 850 mg two to three times a day, taken with meals.

In combination with a sulfonylurea—

The dosage of each agent must be adjusted until the desired degree of glycemic control is achieved.

In combination with insulin[1]—

Oral, initially 500 mg a day. The dosage may be increased by 500 mg at weekly intervals as needed.

Note: The current insulin dose should be continued upon initiation of metformin therapy. However, the insulin dose should be decreased by 10 to 25% when the fasting plasma glucose concentration decreases to less than 120 mg per dL (6.7 mmol per L).

Usual adult prescribing limits

2550 mg a day.

Usual pediatric dose

Antihyperglycemic agent—

Children up to 10 years of age—Safety and efficacy have not been established.

Children 10 years of age and over—Initial: Oral, 500 mg two times a day, given with meals. Dose increases should be made in increments of 500 mg weekly up to a maximum of 2000 mg per day, given in divided doses.

[Polycystic ovary syndrome][1]—

Initial: Oral, 500 mg two times a day, given with meals. Maintenance: Oral, 500 mg three times a day or 850 mg two times a day.

Usual pediatric prescribing limits

2000 mg a day

Usual geriatric dose

See *Usual adult dose*. For some sensitive individuals, lower initial doses may be needed. Maximum doses are not advised for use in the elderly.

Strength(s) usually available

U.S.—

500 mg (Rx) [*Glucophage* (scored; povidone; magnesium stearate)].
850 mg (Rx) [*Glucophage* (scored; povidone; magnesium stearate)].
1000 mg (Rx) [*Glucophage* (scored; povidone; magnesium stearate)].

Canada—

500 mg (Rx) [*Apo-Metformin* (scored); *Gen-Metformin; Glucophage* (scored); *Glycon; Novo-Metformin* (scored); *Nu-Metformin* (scored)].
850 mg (Rx) [*Apo-Metformin; Glucophage; Novo-Metformin; Nu-Metformin*].

Packaging and storage

Store between 15 and 30 °C (59 and 86 °F) in a light-resistant container, unless otherwise specified by manufacturer.

Auxiliary labeling

- Take with food.
- Do not drink alcohol.

METFORMIN HYDROCHLORIDE EXTENDED-RELEASE TABLETS

Usual adult dose

Antihyperglycemic agent—

As monotherapy—

Dual hydrophilic polymer matrix system ER tablet (e.g. Glucophage® ER): Initial—Oral, 500 mg once daily, taken with the evening meal. The daily dose may be increased by 500 mg at weekly intervals as needed, up to a maximum of 2000 mg once daily with the evening meal.

If glycemic control is not achieved with once daily dosing of 2000 mg, a trial of 1000 mg twice daily should be considered.

If still higher doses of metformin are required for control, they should be administered as the regular-release dosage form, as described above. See *Usual adult dose*.

Maintenance—Oral, 500 to 2000 mg once daily, or 500 to 1000 mg two times daily, taken with meals.

Polymer-based system ER tablet (e.g. Glumetza™): Initial—Oral, 1000 mg once daily, taken with the evening meal. The daily dose may be increased by 500 mg at weekly intervals as needed, up to a maximum of 2000 mg once daily with the evening meal.

If glycemic control is not achieved with once daily dosing of 2000 mg, a trial of 1000 mg twice daily should be considered.

In combination with a sulfonylurea—

The dosage of each agent must be adjusted until the desired control is achieved.

In combination with insulin—

Oral, initially 500 mg a day. The dosage may be increased by 500 mg at weekly intervals as needed.

Note: The current insulin dose should be continued upon initiation of metformin therapy. However, the insulin dose should be decreased by 10 to 25% when the fasting plasma glucose concentration decreases to less than 120 mg per dL (6.7 mmol per L).

Usual adult prescribing limits

2000 mg a day.

Usual pediatric dose

Antihyperglycemic agent—

Children up to 17 years of age—Safety and efficacy have not been established.

Children 17 years of age and over—See *Usual adult dose*.

Usual geriatric dose

See *Usual adult dose*. For some sensitive individuals, lower initial doses may be needed. Maximum doses are not advised for use in the elderly.

Strength(s) usually available

U.S.—

500 mg (Rx) [*Glucophage XR* (hydroxypropyl methylcellulose; magnesium stearate; microcrystalline cellulose; sodium carboxymethyl cellulose)].
500 mg (Rx) [*Glumetza* (coloring; hypromellose; magnesium stearate; microcrystalline cellulose; polyethylene oxide)].
750 mg (Rx) [*Glucophage XR* (sodium carboxymethyl cellulose; hydroxypropyl methylcellulose; magnesium stearate)].
1000 mg (Rx) [*Glumetza* (crospovidone; dibutyl sebacate; ethylcellulose; glyceryl behenate; polyvinyl alcohol; polyvinylpyrrolidone; silicon dioxide)].

Packaging and storage

Store at 20 to 25 °C (68 to 77 °F) in a light-resistant container.

Auxiliary labeling

- Take with food.
- Do not drink alcohol.
- Swallow whole. Do not crush or chew.

[1]Not included in Canadian product labeling.

Selected Bibliography

Watkins PJ. Guidelines for good practice in the diagnosis and treatment of non-insulin–dependent diabetes mellitus. Report of a joint working party of the British Diabetic Association, the Research Unit of the Royal College of Physicians, and the Royal College of General Practitioners. J R Coll Physicians Lond 1993 Jul; 27(3): 259-66.

Aguilar C, Reza A, Garcia JE, et al. Biguanide related lactic acidosis: incidence and risk factors. Arch Med Res 1992 Spring; 23(1): 19-24.

Revised: 07/13/2005

METFORMIN AND PIOGLITAZONE Systemic†

VA CLASSIFICATION (Primary): HS509

Commonly used brand name(s): *Actoplus Met.*

Note: For a listing of dosage forms and brand names by country availability, see *Dosage Forms* section(s).

†Not commercially available in Canada.

Category

Antidiabetic agent.

Indications

Accepted

Diabetes, type 2 (treatment)—Metformin/pioglitazone combination is indicated as an adjunct to diet and exercise to improve glycemic control in patients with type 2 diabetes who are already treated with a combination of metformin and pioglitazone or whose diabetes is not adequately controlled with metformin alone, or for those patients who have initially responded to pioglitazone alone and require additional glycemic control.

Unaccepted

Metformin/pioglitazone is not indicated in patients with New York Heart Association (NYHA) Class III or IV cardiac status.

Metformin/pioglitazone should not be used in patients with type 1 diabetes or for the treatment of diabetic ketoacidosis.

Pharmacology/Pharmacokinetics

Physicochemical characteristics

Molecular weight—

Metformin hydrochloride—165.62.

Pioglitazone hydrochloride—392.9.

pKa—Metformin—12.4.

Solubility—

Metformin—Freely soluble in water; practically insoluble in acetone, ether, and chloroform.

Pioglitazone—Soluble in N,N-dimethylformamide; slightly soluble in anhydrous ethanol; very slightly soluble in acetone and acetonitrile; practically insoluble in water; insoluble in ether.

pH—Metformin hydrochloride 1% aqueous solution—6.68

Mechanism of action/Effect

Metformin and pioglitazone, antihyperglycemic agents acting with different mechanisms of action, improve glycemic control in patients with type 2 diabetes.

Metformin improves glucose tolerance in patients with type 2 diabetes by lowering basal and postprandial plasma glucose levels. Metformin decreases hepatic glucose production, decreases intestinal glucose absorption, and improves insulin sensitivity by increasing peripheral glucose uptake and utilization.

Pioglitazone is effective only in the presence of insulin. Its primary action is to decrease insulin resistance at peripheral sites and in the liver, resulting in increased insulin-dependent glucose disposal and decreased hepatic glucose output. These effects are accomplished through selective binding at the peroxisome proliferator–activated receptor-gamma (PPAR-gamma), which are found in adipose tissue, skeletal muscle, and the liver. Activation of these receptors modulates transcription of several insulin-responsive genes that control glucose and lipid metabolism.

Absorption

Metformin/pioglitazone—Administration of one tablet containing 15 mg of pioglitazone and 850 mg of metformin with food resulted in no overall change in pioglitazone exposure and no change in metformin AUC.

Metformin—Under fasting conditions, the bioavailability of a 500-mg metformin hydrochloride tablet is approximately 50 to 60%. Due to a lack of dose proportionality, increased doses of metformin may not result in greater bioavailability. In contrast, after administration of a single 850-mg dose of metformin with food, the absorption of metformin showed a 40% lower peak concentration, a 25% lower area under the plasma concentration-time curve (AUC), and a 35-minute longer time to peak plasma concentration. The clinical relevance of these changes is unknown.

Pioglitazone—Following oral administration in the fasting state, pioglitazone is first measurable in serum within 30 minutes, with peak concentrations observed within 2 hours. Food slightly delays the time to achieve peak serum concentrations to 3 to 4 hours but does not alter the extent of absorption.

Distribution

Metformin: Apparent volume of distribution (Vol_D)—654 L (296 to 1012 L) following a single oral dose of 850 mg

Pioglitazone—Mean apparent volume of distribution (Vol_D)—0.63 L per kg of body weight (0.22 to 1.04 L per kg of body weight) following single-dose administration

Protein binding

Metformin—Negligible

Pioglitazone—Very high (> 99%); in human serum, primarily to serum albumin. Metabolites are more than 98% bound to serum albumin.

Biotransformation

Metformin—Not metabolized.

Pioglitazone—Extensively metabolized in the liver to several active metabolites (Metabolite III - keto derivative, Metabolite IV - hydroxy derivative, and Metabolite II - hydroxy derivative). The metabolites also partly convert to glucuronide or sulfate conjugates. Cytochrome (CYP) P450 isoforms involved in the hepatic metabolism of pioglitazone are CYP2C8 and CYP3A4. The extrahepatic isoform, CYP1A1, is also involved in the metabolism of pioglitazone.

Half-life

Metformin—6.2 hours (plasma); 17.6 hours (blood). The longer elimination half-life in blood suggests that metformin may distribute into red blood cells.

Pioglitazone—3 to 7 hours (mean serum half-life); 16 to 24 hours (total pioglitazone)

Time to peak concentration

Metformin—35 minute prolongation of time to peak plasma concentration if taken with food; steady-state concentration is reached in 24 to 48 hours.

Pioglitazone—2 hours; may be increased to 3 to 4 hours if taken with food.

Steady-state plasma concentration

Metformin—Generally less than 1 microgram per mL.

Elimination

Metformin—

Renal—Up to 90% of a dose as unchanged drug

Biliary—None

Pioglitazone—

Biliary/fecal—It is assumed that most of a dose is excreted into bile as active drug or metabolites and is eliminated in the feces.

Renal—15% to 30%, primarily as metabolites and their conjugates; renal elimination of pioglitazone is negligible.

Apparent clearance—5 to 7 liters per hour

Precautions to Consider

Note: No animal studies have been done that combine both metformin and pioglitazone. Animal data is based only on individual products.

Carcinogenicity

Metformin—

Long-term studies were done using rats and mice, given doses up to 900 and 1500 mg/kg (approximately four times the recommended human daily dose based on body surface area) per day, respectively. No carcinogenicity was found in male rats and mice or in female mice. However, in female rats, the 900 mg/kg per day dose had an increased incidence of benign stromal uterine polyps.

Pioglitazone—

During a 2-year carcinogenicity study conducted in male and female rats, no drug-induced tumors were observed except for benign and/or malignant transitional cell neoplasms of the urinary bladder. These were observed only in male rats at doses of 4 mg per kg of body weight (mg/kg) per day and above (approximately equal to the maximum recommended human oral dose based on mg per square meter of body surface area [mg/m²]). Oral doses up to 63 mg/kg (approximately 14 times the maximum recommended human oral dose of 45 mg based on mg/m²) were used in this study. Drug-induced tumors were not observed in any organ in male and female mice given oral doses up to 100 mg/kg per day (approximately 11 times the maximum recommended human oral dose based on mg/m²).

Urinary tract tumors have been reported in rodents taking experimental drugs with dual PPAR alpha/gamma activity; however, pioglitazone is a selective agonist for PPAR gamma.

During clinical trials, no new cases of bladder tumors were detected in more than 1800 patients treated with pioglitazone. Abnormal urinary cytology was observed in 0.72% and 0.88% of patients treated with pioglitazone and placebo, respectively.

Mutagenicity

Metformin—

In vitro mutagenic tests, specifically the Ames test (*S. typhimurium*), gene mutation test (mouse lymphoma cells), and the chromosomal aberrations test (human lymphocytes), revealed no evidence of mutagenicity. The *in vivo* mouse micronucleus test was also negative for any mutagenic findings.

Pioglitazone—

No evidence of mutagenicity was found in the Ames bacterial assay, a mammalian cell forward gene mutation assay, an *in vitro* cytogenetics assay, an unscheduled DNA synthesis assay, and an *in vivo* micronucleus assay.

Pregnancy/Reproduction

Fertility—

Metformin—

The fertility of male or female rats was unaffected at doses up to 600 mg per kg of body weight per day, approximately 3 times the maximum recommended human daily dose based on body surface area.

Pioglitazone—

Pioglitazone therapy may cause resumption of ovulation in premenopausal anovulatory patients with insulin resistance. As a result, these patients may be at an increased risk for pregnancy while taking pioglitazone. Therefore, adequate contraception in premenopausal women is recommended.

No evidence of impaired fertility was found in male and female rats given pioglitazone in oral doses of 40 mg/kg per day (approximately 9 times the maximum recommended human oral dose based on mg/m^2) throughout mating and gestation.

Pregnancy—There are no adequate and well-controlled studies in pregnant women with metformin/pioglitazone or its individual components. Because current information strongly suggests that abnormal blood glucose levels during pregnancy are associated with a higher incidence of congenital anomalies, as well as increased neonatal morbidity and mortality, it is recommended that insulin be used during pregnancy to maintain blood glucose levels as close to normal as possible. Metformin/pioglitazone should not be used during pregnancy unless the potential benefit justifies the potential risk to the fetus.

FDA Pregnancy Category C

Metformin—

Metformin was not teratogenic in rats or rabbits at doses up to 600 mg per kg of body weight per day. For rabbits, this dosage is comparable to 6 times the maximum human daily dose of 2000 mg and in rats, the dosage compares to 2 times the maximum human daily dose.

Pioglitazone—

Teratogenicity was not observed in rats treated with oral pioglitazone at doses of up to 80 mg/kg/day or in rabbits treated with up to 160 mg/kg/day during organogenesis (approximately 17 and 40 times the maximum recommended human oral dose based on mg/m^2, respectively). In rats treated with oral pioglitazone at doses of 40 mg/kg/day and above (approximately 10 times the maximum recommended human oral dose based on mg/m^2), delayed parturition and embryotoxicity were observed. Delayed postnatal development, attributed to decreased body weight was observed in rats treated with oral pioglitazone at doses of 10 mg/kg and above (approximately 2 times the maximum recommended human oral dose based on mg/m^2) during late gestation and lactation. No functional or behavioral toxicity was observed in offspring of rats. In rabbits, embryotoxicity was observed at a dose of 160 mg/kg (approximately 40 times the maximum recommended human oral dose).

Breast-feeding

No studies have been conducted with metformin/pioglitazone. It is not known whether metformin, pioglitazone, or both are distributed into human milk. Because many drugs are distributed into human milk, metformin/pioglitazone should not be administered to a breast-feeding woman. If metformin/pioglitazone is discontinued and diet alone is inadequate for controlling blood glucose, insulin therapy should be considered.

In studies performed with the individual components, both pioglitazone and metformin are distributed into the milk of lactating rats.

Pediatrics

Safety and efficacy of metformin/pioglitazone in pediatric patients have not been established.

Geriatrics

Appropriate studies performed to date have not demonstrated geriatrics-specific problems that would limit the usefulness of metformin and pioglitazone in the elderly. However, aging is associated with reduced renal function and metformin/pioglitazone should be used with caution as age increases. Care should be taken in dose selection and should be based on careful and regular monitoring of renal function. This medication should not be initiated in patients 80 years of age or older unless it can be demonstrated that renal function is not reduced. Generally, elderly patients should not be titrated to the maximum dose of this medication.

Drug interactions and/or related problems

The following drug interactions and/or related problems have been selected on the basis of their potential clinical significance (possible mechanism in parentheses where appropriate)—not necessarily inclusive (» = major clinical significance):

Note: Combinations containing any of the following medications, depending on the amount present, may also interact with this medication.

» Alcohol
(known to potentiate the effect of metformin on lactate metabolism; patients should be warned against acute or chronic excessive intake of alcohol while receiving metformin/pioglitazone)

» Beta-adrenergic blocking agents
(may make it difficult to recognize hypoglycemia)

» Cimetidine or
Other cationic medications excreted by renal tubular transport, such as:
Amiloride or
Digoxin or
Morphine or
Procainamide or
Quinidine or
Quinine or
Ranitidine or
Triamterene or
Trimethoprim or
Vancomycin
(cimetidine competes with metformin and, therefore, inhibits the renal tubular secretion of metformin, resulting in a 60% increase in C_{max} and a 40% increase in AUC)
(other cationic drugs excreted by renal tubular transport theoretically have the potential to increase metformin plasma concentration or interfere with renal clearance; careful patient monitoring and dose adjustment recommended with concomitant use)

» Furosemide
(furosemide increased metformin C_{max} by 22% and AUC by 15%; no information is available regarding chronic coadministration)

Hyperglycemia-causing medications, such as:
Calcium channel blocking agents or
Corticosteroids or
Diuretics, other or
Diuretics, thiazide or
Estrogens or
Isoniazid or
Nicotinic acid or
Oral contraceptives or
Phenothiazines or
Phenytoin or
Sympathomimetic agents or
Thyroid hormones
(concomitant use may lead to loss of glycemic control; patient should be closely observed)

» Insulin or
» Oral hypoglycemic agents
(concomitant use with pioglitazone may be at risk for hypoglycemia; reduction in dose of one of these agents may be necessary)

Nifedipine
(nifedipine increased metformin C_{max} by 20% and AUC by 9% and increased amount excreted in the urine)

Laboratory value alterations

The following have been selected on the basis of their potential clinical significance (possible effect in parentheses where appropriate)—not necessarily inclusive (» = major clinical significance).

With physiology/laboratory test values

Creatine phosphokinase levels
(may be elevated)

Hematocrit and
Hemoglobin
(may be decreased)

Hepatic enzymes
(postmarketing reports of elevated levels to 3 or more times the upper limit of normal)

Vitamin B_{12} levels
(rare decrease to subnormal levels possibly due to interference with B_{12} absorption from the B_{12}-intrinsic factor complex; very rarely associated with anemia and appears to be rapidly reversible with either discontinuation of metformin or supplementation of vitamin B_{12})

Medical considerations/Contraindications

The medical considerations/contraindications included have been selected on the basis of their potential clinical significance (reasons given in parentheses where appropriate)—not necessarily inclusive (» = major clinical significance).

Except under special circumstances, this medication should not be used when the following medical problem exists:

» Conditions associated with hypoxemia, such as:
Cardiovascular collapse or
Congestive heart failure, acute, or
Myocardial infarction, acute, or

» Dehydration, severe or

» Septicemia
(associated with lactic acidosis and may also cause prerenal azotemia)

» Diabetic ketoacidosis, with or without coma, or

» Metabolic acidosis, acute or chronic

» Diagnostic radiologic studies using intravascular iodinated contrast media, such as:
Angiography or
Cholangiography, intravenous or
Computed tomography (CT) scan or
Urography, intravenous or

» Surgery, major
(increased risk of lactic acidosis due to acute renal function change; metformin/pioglitazone should be discontinued at time of or prior to medical or diagnostic examinations requiring use of contrast media that can cause functional oliguria; therapy should be withheld for 48 hours after procedure and should not be restarted until after renal function returns to normal)

» Hypersensitivity to metformin, pioglitazone or any other component of the product

» Renal disease or dysfunction (creatinine clearance ≥ 1.4 mg/dL in females or ≥ 1.5 mg/dL in males)

Risk-benefit should be considered when the following medical problems exist:

Adrenal insufficiency
Debilitation
Malnourishment
Older age
Pituitary insufficiency
(more susceptible to hypoglycemic effects; hypoglycemia may be difficult to recognize in elderly)

Edema
(postmarketing of worsening edema with metformin/pioglitazone; should be used with caution in these patients)

» Hepatic impairment
(do not administer if patient has active liver disease or ALT>2.5 times upper limit of normal)

Patient monitoring

The following may be especially important in patient monitoring (other tests may be warranted in some patients, depending on condition; » = major clinical significance):

» ALT, serum
(prior to initiation of therapy in all patients and periodically thereafter)

Anion gap and
Electrolyte concentrations and
Lactic acid, blood and
Lactate/pyruvate ratio and
Metformin concentration, plasma and
pH, blood
(may be useful in confirming diagnosis of lactic acidosis, which is characterized by an increased anion gap, electrolyte disturbances, blood lactic acid concentration greater than 5 millimoles/L, an increased lactic acid/pyruvate ratio, plasma metformin concentration greater than 5 mcg/mL, and a decreased blood pH)

» Fasting plasma and

» Glucose concentration in blood, serum, or urine
(fasting plasma glucose concentrations should be routinely monitored)

» Hemoglobin (HbA1c measurements)
(monitoring is recommended every 3 months to assess the efficacy of therapy)

Hematocrit and
Hemoglobin concentrations and
Red blood cell indices
(initial and periodic monitoring of hematologic factors should be done, at least once annually)

» Ketone bodies, urine
(if ketone bodies reach a high level, patient could develop ketoacidotic shock)

» Renal function assessment
(recommended prior to initiation of therapy and thereafter annually or more often in patients in whom the risk of developing lactic acidosis is increased)

Vitamin B_{12} concentrations
(although megaloblastic anemia is a rare finding, check for possible vitamin B_{12} deficiency recommended every 2 to 3 years)

Side/Adverse Effects

The following side/adverse effects have been selected on the basis of their potential clinical significance (possible signs and symptoms in parentheses where appropriate)—not necessarily inclusive:

Those indicating need for medical attention

Incidence more frequent

Urinary tract infection (bladder pain; bloody or cloudy urine; difficult, burning, or painful urination; frequent urge to urinate; lower back or side pain)

Incidence less frequent

Anemia (pale skin; troubled breathing with exertion; unusual bleeding or bruising; unusual tiredness or weakness)

Incidence rare

Hypoglycemia (anxiety; blurred vision; chills; cold sweats; coma; confusion; cool pale skin; depression; dizziness; fast heartbeat; headache; increased hunger; nausea; nervousness; nightmares; seizures; shakiness; slurred speech; unusual tiredness or weakness); ***lactic acidosis*** (abdominal discomfort; decreased appetite; diarrhea; fast, shallow breathing; general feeling of discomfort; muscle pain or cramping; nausea; shortness of breath; sleepiness; unusual tiredness or weakness)

Those indicating need for medical attention only if they continue or are bothersome

Incidence more frequent

Diarrhea; dizziness; nausea; upper respiratory tract infection (ear congestion; nasal congestion; chills cough, fever, sneezing, or sore throat; body aches or pain; headache; loss of voice; runny nose; unusual tiredness or weakness; difficulty in breathing)

Incidence less frequent

Edema lower limb (swelling of legs and feet); ***headache; sinusitis*** (pain or tenderness around eyes and cheekbones; fever; stuffy or runny nose; headache; cough; shortness of breath or troubled breathing; tightness of chest or wheezing); ***weight increased***

Overdose

For more information on the management of overdose or unintentional ingestion, **contact a poison control center** (see *Poison Control Center Listing*).

Clinical effects of overdose

Metformin—Overdose of metformin has occurred, including ingestion of amounts greater than 50 grams.

Pioglitazone—During clinical trials, one patient took pioglitazone at a dose of 120 mg a day for 4 days followed by 180 mg for 7 days. The patient did not have any clinical symptoms during this period.

The following effects have been selected on the basis of their potential clinical significance (possible signs and symptoms in parentheses where appropriate)—not necessarily inclusive:

Hypoglycemia (anxiety; blurred vision; chills; cold sweats; coma; confusion; cool pale skin; depression; dizziness; fast heartbeat; headache; increased hunger; nausea; nervousness; nightmares; seizures; shakiness; slurred speech; unusual tiredness or weakness)—for metformin; ***lactic acidosis*** (abdominal discomfort; decreased appetite; diarrhea; fast, shallow breathing; general feeling of discomfort; muscle pain or cramping; nausea; shortness of breath; sleepiness; unusual tiredness or weakness)—for metformin

Treatment of overdose

To enhance elimination—Metformin is dialyzable with a clearance of up to 170 mL per minute under good hemodynamic conditions. Therefore, hemodialysis may be useful for removal of accumulated metformin.

Supportive care—Patients in whom intentional overdose is confirmed or suspected should be referred for psychiatric consultation.

Patient Consultation

As an aid to patient consultation, refer to *Advice for the Patient, Metformin and Pioglitazone (Systemic)*.

In providing consultation, consider emphasizing the following selected information (» = major clinical significance):

Before using this medication

» Conditions affecting use, especially:

Hypersensitivity to metformin, pioglitazone or any other component of the product

Pregnancy—Risk/benefit considerations; recommending adequate contraception in premenopausal anovulatory women due to increased risk of pregnancy; importance of maintaining blood glucose levels using insulin during pregnancy

Breast-feeding—Should not be administered to a nursing woman

Use in children—Safety and efficacy not established in pediatric patients

Use in the elderly—Basing dose selection on careful and regular monitoring of renal function; not titrating elderly patients to the maximum dose of metformin and pioglitazone

Other medications, especially [example in alphabetical order: corticosteroids, cyclosporine, hepatic enzyme inducers, hepatotoxic medications (especially troleandomycin), ritonavir, theophylline, tobacco smoking, or troglitazone]

Other medical problems, especially conditions associated with hypoxemia, diabetic ketoacidosis (with or without coma), diagnostic radiologic studies using intravascular iodinated contrast media, hepatic impairment, major surgery, metabolic acidosis (acute or chronic), renal disease or dysfunction, severe dehydration, or septicemia,

Proper use of this medication

» Importance of adherence to recommended regimens for diet, exercise, and glucose monitoring

» Proper dosing

Missed dose: Taking as soon as possible; not taking if almost time for next scheduled dose; not doubling doses

» Proper storage

Precautions while using this medication

» Regular visits to physician to check progress

» Recognizing symptoms of lactic acidosis, such as abdominal discomfort; decreased appetite; diarrhea; fast, shallow breathing; general feeling of discomfort; muscle pain or cramping; or unusual sleepiness, tiredness, or weakness

» Getting immediate emergency medical help if symptoms of lactic acidosis occur

» *Carefully following special instructions of health care team:*

Discussing use of alcohol and tobacco and importance of avoiding alcohol use

Not taking other medications unless discussed with physician

Getting counseling for family members to help the patient with diabetes; also, special counseling for pregnancy planning and contraception

Making travel plans that include readiness for diabetic emergencies and eating meals at the usual times, even with changing time zones

» Preparing for and understanding what to do in case of diabetic emergency; carrying medical history and current medication list and wearing medical identification

» Recognizing symptoms of hypoglycemia: anxiety; behavior change similar to drunkenness; blurred vision; cold sweats; coma; confusion; cool, pale skin; difficulty in concentrating; drowsiness; excessive hunger; fast heartbeat; headache (continuing); nausea; nervousness; nightmares; restless sleep; seizures; shakiness; slurred speech; and unusual tiredness or weakness

» Recognizing what brings on symptoms of hypoglycemia, such as delaying or missing a meal or snack; drinking significant amounts of alcohol; exercising more than usual; having an illness, including vomiting or diarrhea; taking certain medications; or using other antidiabetic medication

» Knowing what to do if symptoms of hypoglycemia occur, such as eating glucose tablets or gel, corn syrup, honey, or sugar cubes; drinking fruit juice, nondiet soft drink, or sugar dissolved in water; or injecting glucagon if symptoms are severe

» Recognizing symptoms of hyperglycemia and ketoacidosis: blurred vision; drowsiness; dry mouth; flushed, dry skin; fruit-like breath odor; increased urination (frequency and volume); ketones in urine; loss of appetite; somnolence (sleepiness); stomachache, nausea, or vomiting; tiredness; troubled breathing (rapid and deep); unconsciousness; and unusual thirst

» Recognizing what brings on symptoms of hyperglycemia, such as exercising less than usual, having a fever or infection, not taking enough or skipping a dose of antidiabetic medication, or overeating or not following meal plan

» Knowing what to do if symptoms of hyperglycemia occur, such as checking blood glucose and contacting a member of the health care team

Side/adverse effects

Signs of potential side effects, especially urinary tract infection, anemia, hypoglycemia, or lactic acidosis

General Dosing Information

The use of antihyperglycemic therapy in the management of type 2 diabetes should be individualized on the basis of effectiveness and tolerability within the recommended daily doses. Selecting the starting dose should be based on the patient's current regimen of pioglitazone and/or metformin.

Safety and efficacy of metformin/pioglitazone in patients previously treated with other oral hypoglycemic agents and switched to metformin/pioglitazone have not been established. Any change in therapy of type 2 diabetes should be initiated with care and appropriate monitoring as changes in glycemic control can occur.

Sufficient time should be given to assess adequacy of therapeutic response. Ideally, the response to therapy should be evaluated using A1C which is a better indicator of long-term glycemic control than FPG alone. It is recommended that patients be treated with metformin/pioglitazone for a period of time adequate to evaluate change in A1C (8 to 12 weeks) unless glycemic control as measured by FPG deteriorates.

Diet/Nutrition

Metformin/pioglitazone should be given in divided daily doses with meals to reduce the side effects associated with metformin. gastrointestinal

For treatment of adverse effects

For lactic acidosis—This condition should be treated as a medical emergency in a hospital setting. Metformin/pioglitazone must be discontinued immediately and general supportive measures should be promptly instituted. Because metformin is dialyzable, prompt hemodialysis is recommended to correct the acidosis and remove the accumulated metformin. Such management often results in prompt reversal of symptoms and recovery.

Oral Dosage Forms

METFORMIN HYDROCHLORIDE AND PIOGLITAZONE HYDROCHLORIDE TABLETS

Usual adult dose

Type 2 diabetes—

For patients inadequately controlled on metformin monotherapy—Oral, based on the usual starting dose of pioglitazone (15 to 30 mg daily), metformin/pioglitazone may be initiated at either the 15 mg/500 mg or 15 mg/850 mg tablet strength once or twice daily, and gradually titrated after assessing adequacy of therapeutic response.

For patients who initially responded to pioglitazone monotherapy and require additional glycemic control—Oral, based on the usual starting dose of metformin (500 mg twice daily or 850 mg daily), metformin/pioglitazone may be initiated at either the 15 mg/500 mg twice daily or 15 mg/850 mg tablet strength once daily, and gradually titrated after assessing adequacy of therapeutic response.

For patients switching from combination therapy of pioglitazone plus metformin as separate tablets—Oral, metformin/pioglitazone may be initiated with either the 15 mg/500 mg or 15 mg/850 mg tablet strengths based on the dose of pioglitazone and metformin already being taken.

Usual adult prescribing limits
Maximum recommended daily dose of 2550 mg metformin and 45 mg pioglitazone

Usual pediatric dose
Safety and efficacy have not been established in pediatric patients.

Usual geriatric dose
See *Usual adult dose.*

Note: The initial and maintenance dosing should be conservative in patients with advanced age, due to the potential for decreased renal function in this population. This medication should not be initiated in patients 80 years of age or older unless it can be demonstrated that renal function is not reduced. Maximum doses are not advised for use in elderly patients.

Strength(s) usually available
U.S.—

15 mg pioglitazone hydrochloride (as the base) and 500 mg metformin hydrochloride (Rx) [*Actoplus Met* (film-coated; povidone; microcrystalline cellulose; croscarmellose sodium; magnesium stearate; hypromellose 2910; polyethylene glycol 8000; titanium dioxide; talc)].

15 mg pioglitazone hydrochloride (as the base) and 850 mg metformin hydrochloride (Rx) [*Actoplus Met* (film-coated; povidone; microcrystalline cellulose; croscarmellose sodium; magnesium stearate; hypromellose 2910; polyethylene glycol 8000; titanium dioxide; talc)].

Packaging and storage
Store at 25 °C (77 °F), excursions permitted to 15 to 30 °C (59 to 86 °F). Keep container tightly closed, and protect from moisture and humidity.

Auxiliary labeling
- Avoid alcoholic beverages.
- Take with food.
- Keep out of reach of children.

Developed: 04/12/2006

METHADONE—See *Opioid (Narcotic) Analgesics (Systemic)*

METHAMPHETAMINE—See *Amphetamines (Systemic)*

METHANTHELINE—See *Anticholinergics/Antispasmodics (Systemic)*

METHARBITAL—See *Barbiturates (Systemic)*

METHAZOLAMIDE—See *Carbonic Anhydrase Inhibitors (Systemic)*

METHDILAZINE—See *Antihistamines, Phenothiazine-derivative (Systemic)*

METHICILLIN—See *Penicillins (Systemic)*

METHIMAZOLE—See *Antithyroid Agents (Systemic)*

METHOCARBAMOL—See *Skeletal Muscle Relaxants (Systemic)*

METHOHEXITAL—See *Anesthetics, Barbiturate (Systemic)*

METHOTREXATE—For Cancer
Systemic

VA CLASSIFICATION (Primary): AN300

Commonly used brand name(s):

Another commonly used name is amethopterin.

Note: For a listing of dosage forms and brand names by country availability, see *Dosage Forms* section(s).

Category
Antineoplastic.

Indications
Note: Bracketed information in the *Indications* section refers to uses that are not included in U.S. product labeling.

Accepted
Carcinoma, breast (treatment)
Carcinoma, head and neck (treatment)
Carcinoma, lung, non-small cell (treatment)[1]
Carcinoma, lung, small cell (treatment)[1] or
Tumors, trophoblastic, gestational (treatment)—Methotrexate is indicated for treatment of breast carcinoma, head and neck cancers (epidermoid), non-small cell lung carcinoma (especially squamous cell types), small cell lung carcinoma, and gestational trophoblastic tumors (gestational choriocarcinoma, chorioadenoma destruens, hydatidiform mole).

[Carcinoma, cervical (treatment)][1]
[Carcinoma, ovarian, epithelial (treatment)][1]
[Carcinoma, bladder (treatment)]
[Carcinoma, colorectal (treatment)][1]
[Carcinoma, esophageal (treatment)][1]
[Carcinoma, gastric (treatment)]
[Carcinoma, pancreatic (treatment)][1] or
[Carcinoma, penile (treatment)][1]—Methotrexate is indicated for treatment of cervical carcinoma, ovarian carcinoma, bladder carcinoma, colorectal carcinoma, esophageal carcinoma, gastric carcinoma, pancreatic carcinoma, and penile carcinoma.

Leukemia, acute lymphocytic (treatment) or
Leukemia, meningeal (prophylaxis and treatment)—Methotrexate is indicated for treatment of acute lymphocytic leukemia and prophylaxis and treatment of meningeal leukemia.

[Leukemia, acute nonlymphocytic (treatment)][1]—Methotrexate is indicated for treatment of acute nonlymphocytic leukemia.

Lymphomas, non-Hodgkin's (treatment)—Methotrexate is indicated for treatment of non-Hodgkin's lymphomas, including advanced cases of lymphosarcoma (particularly in children) and Burkitt's lymphoma.

[Lymphomas, Hodgkin's (treatment)][1]—Methotrexate is indicated for treatment of Hodgkin's disease.

Mycosis fungoides (treatment)—Methotrexate is indicated for treatment of advanced cases of mycosis fungoides.

Osteosarcoma (treatment)—Methotrexate is indicated in high doses along with leucovorin rescue, in combination with other agents, for treatment of nonmetastatic osteosarcoma in patients who have undergone primary surgical treatment.

[Sarcomas, soft tissue (treatment)][1]—Methotrexate is indicated for treatment of soft tissue sarcomas.

[Carcinomatous meningitis (treatment)][1]—Methotrexate is indicated for treatment of carcinomatous menigitis (intrathecal and intraventricular administration) (Evidence rating: IIID).

[Tumors, brain (treatment)][1]—Methotrexate is indicated for treatment of central nervous system (CNS) lymphomas.

Note: Although methotrexate has been used for treatment of multiple myeloma, the USP Division of Information Development Hematology-Oncology Advisory Panel believes there is insufficient evidence to support the effectiveness of methotrexate in the treatment of multiple myeloma.

Unaccepted
Methotrexate has not shown benefit in the treatment of primary gliomas.

[1]Not included in Canadian product labeling.

Pharmacology/Pharmacokinetics

Physicochemical characteristics
Molecular weight—454.44.

Mechanism of action/Effect
Methotrexate is an antimetabolite of the folic acid analog type. Methotrexate is cell cycle–specific for the S phase of cell division. Activity is due to inhibition of DNA synthesis, repair, and cellular replication; inhibition occurs as a result of relatively irreversible binding of methotrexate with dihydrofolate reductase, which prevents reduction of dihydrofolate to the active tetrahydrofolate. Growth of rapidly proliferating cells (malignant cells, bone marrow, fetal cells, buccal and intestinal mucosa, cells of the urinary bladder, spermatogonia) is affected more severely than growth of most normal tissues and skin.

Other actions/effects
Also has mild immunosuppressant activity.

Absorption
Widely variable and dose-dependent. At doses of 30 mg per square meter of body surface area (mg/m^2), the mean bioavailability of methotrexate is approximately 60%. At doses greater than 80 mg/m^2, absorption is significantly decreased, possibly due to a saturation effect. Food may delay absorption and decrease the peak concentration.

Distribution
Methotrexate crosses the blood-brain barrier (from blood to central nervous system [CNS]) in only limited amounts when administered orally or parenterally (dose-related); however, high concentrations can be found in cerebrospinal fluid following its intrathecal administration.

Following intravenous administration—Initial Vol_D is approximately 0.18 L per kg (L/kg).

Steady state Vol_D is approximately 0.4 to 0.8 L/kg.

Protein binding
Moderate (approximately 50%), primarily to albumin.

Biotransformation
Hepatic; intracellular, to active polyglutamated forms, small amounts of which are retained in tissues for extended periods of time.

Half-life
Terminal—
- Low doses: 3 to 10 hours.
- High doses: 8 to 15 hours.

Note: There is wide interindividual variation in clearance rates. Small amounts of methotrexate and its metabolites are protein-bound and may remain in tissues (kidneys, liver) for weeks to months; the presence of fluid loads, such as ascites or pleural effusion, and renal function impairment will also delay clearance.

Time to peak serum concentration
Oral—Approximately 40 minutes to 4 hours, following a dose of 15 mg/m^2.

Intramuscular—30 to 60 minutes.

Elimination
Single dose—
- Renal (unchanged), 80 to 90% in the first 24 hours; some accumulation of polyglutamates in tissues occurs with repeated doses.
- Biliary, 10% or less.

Precautions to Consider

Carcinogenicity/Mutagenicity
Secondary malignancies are potential delayed effects of many antineoplastic agents, although it is not clear whether the effect is related to their mutagenic or immunosuppressive action. The effect of dose and duration of therapy is also unknown, although risk seems to increase with long-term use.

Antimetabolites have been shown to be carcinogenic in animals, and may be associated with an increased risk of development of secondary carcinomas in humans, although the risk appears to be less than with alkylating agents.

Carcinogenicity studies with methotrexate in animals have been inconclusive. However, there is evidence that methotrexate causes chromosomal damage to animal somatic cells and human bone marrow cells.

Pregnancy/Reproduction
Fertility—Gonadal suppression, resulting in amenorrhea or azoospermia, may occur in patients taking antineoplastic therapy, especially with the alkylating agents. In general, these effects appear to be related to dose and length of therapy and may be irreversible. Prediction of the degree of testicular or ovarian function impairment is complicated by the common use of combinations of several antineoplastics, which makes it difficult to assess the effects of individual agents. Methotrexate appears to have only a slight effect on gonadal function; however, reversible impairment of fertility, defective oogenesis and spermatogenesis, and menstrual function impairment have been reported.

Pregnancy—Methotrexate crosses the placenta and has been shown to cause adverse effects in the fetus. Methotrexate is a potent abortifacient.

First trimester: It is usually recommended that use of antineoplastics, especially combination chemotherapy, be avoided whenever possible, especially during the first trimester. Although information is limited because of the relatively few instances of antineoplastic administration during pregnancy, the mutagenic, teratogenic, and carcinogenic potential of these medications must be considered.

Other hazards to the fetus include adverse reactions seen in adults.

In general, use of a contraceptive is recommended during cytotoxic drug therapy.

FDA Pregnancy Category X.

Breast-feeding
Methotrexate is distributed into breast milk; breast-feeding is not recommended while methotrexate is being administered because of the risks to the infant (adverse effects, mutagenicity, carcinogenicity).

Pediatrics
Caution should be used in neonates and infants because of reduced renal and hepatic function.

Geriatrics
Although appropriate studies with methotrexate have not been performed in the geriatric population, caution should be used in the elderly because of possible reduced renal and hepatic functions and reduced folate stores. Dosage adjustment, especially on the basis of renal function status, may be necessary.

Dental
The bone marrow depressant effects of methotrexate may result in an increased incidence of microbial infection, delayed healing, and gingival bleeding. Dental work, whenever possible, should be completed prior to initiation of therapy or deferred until blood counts have returned to normal. Patients should be instructed in proper oral hygiene during treatment, including caution in use of regular toothbrushes, dental floss, and toothpicks.

Methotrexate also commonly causes ulcerative stomatitis associated with considerable discomfort.

Drug interactions and/or related problems
The following drug interactions and/or related problems have been selected on the basis of their potential clinical significance (possible mechanism in parentheses where appropriate)—not necessarily inclusive (» = major clinical significance):

Note: Combinations containing any of the following medications, depending on the amount present, may also interact with this medication.

» Acyclovir, parenteral
(concurrent administration of intrathecal methotrexate with acyclovir may result in neurological abnormalities; use with caution)

» Alcohol or
» Hepatotoxic medications, other (see *Appendix II*)
(concurrent use may increase the risk of hepatotoxicity)

Allopurinol or
Colchicine or
» Probenecid or
» Sulfinpyrazone
(methotrexate may raise the concentration of blood uric acid; dosage adjustment of antigout agents may be necessary to control hyperuricemia and gout; allopurinol may be preferred to prevent or reverse methotrexate-induced hyperuricemia because of risk of uric acid nephropathy with uricosuric antigout agents)

Anticoagulants, coumarin- or indandione-derivative
(methotrexate may increase anticoagulant activity and/or increase the risk of hemorrhage as a result of decreased hepatic synthesis of procoagulant factors and interference with platelet formation)

» Anti-inflammatory drugs, nonsteroidal (NSAIDs)
(concurrent use of phenylbutazone with methotrexate may increase the risk of agranulocytosis or bone marrow depression and is not recommended; also, phenylbutazone may displace methotrexate from its protein-binding sites and decrease its renal clearance, leading to increased methotrexate plasma concentration and risk of toxicity, especially during high-dose methotrexate infusion therapy. If concurrent use with phenylbutazone cannot be avoided, especially careful monitoring of the patient for plasma methotrexate concentrations or signs of methotrexate toxicity and/or adequacy of renal function is recommended; also, phenylbuta-

zone therapy should be discontinued for 7 to 12 days prior to, and for at least 12 hours [depending on plasma methotrexate concentrations] following, administration of a high-dose methotrexate infusion)

(administration of high-dose methotrexate infusions to patients receiving diflunisal or ketoprofen has resulted in severe and [with ketoprofen] sometimes fatal methotrexate toxicity; a few fatalities have also occurred in patients receiving intermediate-dose methotrexate infusions concurrently with indomethacin, possibly because of decreased methotrexate excretion leading to increased and prolonged methotrexate plasma concentration; however, severe methotrexate toxicity did not occur when ketoprofen was administered 12 hours following completion of the methotrexate infusion. It is recommended that NSAID therapy be discontinued for 24 to 48 hours [for diflunisal] or 12 to 24 hours [for ketoprofen] prior to, and for at least 12 hours [depending on plasma methotrexate concentrations] following, a high-dose methotrexate infusion and that indomethacin be discontinued for 24 to 48 hours prior to, and for at least 12 hours [depending on plasma methotrexate concentrations] following, administration of an intermediate- or high-dose methotrexate infusion)

(although not well documented, the possibility exists that other NSAIDs may also decrease methotrexate excretion and increase its plasma concentration to potentially toxic levels; it is recommended that NSAID therapy be discontinued for 12 to 24 hours [for NSAIDs with a short elimination half-life] to up to 10 days [for piroxicam] prior to, and for at least 12 hours [depending on plasma methotrexate concentrations] following, administration of a high-dose methotrexate infusion)

(severe, sometimes fatal, methotrexate toxicity has also been reported with low to moderate doses in patients receiving diclofenac, indomethacin, naproxen, or phenylbutazone; it is recommended that use of NSAIDs with low to moderate doses of methotrexate be undertaken with caution, with methotrexate dosage being adjusted by monitoring plasma methotrexate concentrations and/or adequacy of renal function)

» Asparaginase
(concurrent use may block the effects of methotrexate by inhibiting cell replication; this inhibition of methotrexate's action appears to correlate with suppression of asparagine concentrations. Some studies indicate that administration of asparaginase 9 to 10 days before or within 24 hours after methotrexate does not produce this inhibition of antineoplastic effect and may reduce the gastrointestinal and hematological effects of methotrexate)

Blood dyscrasia-causing medications (see *Appendix II*)
(leukopenic and/or thrombocytopenic effects of methotrexate may be increased with concurrent or recent therapy if these medications cause the same effects; dosage adjustment of methotrexate, if necessary, should be based on blood counts)

» Bone marrow depressants, other (see *Appendix II*) or
Radiation therapy
(additive bone marrow depression may occur; dosage reduction may be required when two or more bone marrow depressants, including radiation, are used concurrently or consecutively)

(leukoencephalopathy has been reported following intravenous methotrexate administration to patients who have received craniospinal irradiation)

Cytarabine
(administration of cytarabine 48 hours before or 10 minutes after initiation of methotrexate therapy may result in a synergistic cytotoxic effect; however, evidence is inconclusive and dosage adjustment based on routine hematologic monitoring is recommended)

Folic acid
(may interfere with the antifolate effects of methotrexate)

Neomycin, oral
(may decrease absorption of oral methotrexate)

Penicillins
(concurrent use with methotrexate has resulted in decreased clearance of methotrexate and in methotrexate toxicity; this is thought to be due to competition for renal tubular secretion; patients should be closely monitored; leucovorin doses may need to be increased and administered for longer periods of time)

Phenytoin
(concurrent use may result in increased methotrexate toxicity; this is thought to be due to displacement of methotrexate from serum albumin by phenytoin)

» Probenecid
(concurrent use may inhibit renal excretion of methotrexate and result in toxic plasma concentrations; if used concurrently with probenecid, methotrexate dosage should be decreased, the patient observed for signs of toxicity, and/or plasma methotrexate concentrations monitored)

Pyrimethamine or
Triamterene or
Trimethoprim
(concurrent use may rarely increase the toxic effects of methotrexate because of similar folic acid antagonist actions)

» Salicylates and other weak organic acids
(concurrent use may inhibit renal tubular secretion of methotrexate and result in toxic plasma concentrations; salicylates may also increase plasma concentrations by displacing methotrexate from binding sites; if methotrexate is used concurrently with these medications, the patient should be observed for signs of toxicity and/or methotrexate plasma concentration monitored. In addition, it is recommended that salicylate therapy be discontinued for 24 to 48 hours prior to, and for at least 12 hours [depending on plasma methotrexate concentrations] following, administration of a high-dose methotrexate infusion)

Sulfonamides
(in addition to increased risk of hepatotoxicity that may occur when sulfonamides are used concurrently with other hepatotoxic medications, medications that cause displacement from plasma protein binding may theoretically produce toxic plasma concentrations of methotrexate when used concurrently, although clinical significance has not been established)

Theophylline
(methotrexate may decrease theophylline clearance. Monitoring of serum theophylline concentrations is recommended when it is used concurrently with methotrexate)

Vaccines, killed virus
(because normal defense mechanisms may be suppressed by methotrexate therapy, the patient's antibody response to the vaccine may be decreased. The interval between discontinuation of medications that cause immunosuppression and restoration of the patient's ability to respond to the vaccine depends on the intensity and type of immunosuppression-causing medication used, the underlying disease, and other factors; estimates vary from 3 months to 1 year)

» Vaccines, live virus
(because normal defense mechanisms may be suppressed by methotrexate therapy, concurrent use with a live virus vaccine may potentiate the replication of the vaccine virus, may increase the side/adverse effects of the vaccine virus, and/or may decrease the patient's antibody response to the vaccine; immunization of these patients should be undertaken only with extreme caution after careful review of the patient's hematologic status and only with the knowledge and consent of the physician managing the methotrexate therapy. The interval between discontinuation of medications that cause immunosuppression and restoration of the patient's ability to respond to the vaccine depends on the intensity and type of immunosuppression-causing medication used, the underlying disease, and other factors; estimates vary from 3 months to 1 year. Patients with leukemia in remission should not receive live virus vaccine until at least 3 months after their last chemotherapy. Immunization with oral poliovirus vaccine should also be postponed in persons in close contact with the patient, especially family members)

Laboratory value alterations

The following have been selected on the basis of their potential clinical significance (possible effect in parentheses where appropriate)—not necessarily inclusive (» = major clinical significance).

With diagnostic test results
Assay for folate
(methotrexate may inhibit the organism used in the assay and interfere with detection of folic acid deficiency)

With physiology/laboratory test values
Isocitric acid dehydrogenase (ICD)
(values may be increased, indicating hepatotoxicity)

Serum aspartate aminotransferase (AST [SGOT])
(values may be increased transiently during high-dose therapy)

Uric acid concentrations in blood and urine
(may be increased)

Medical considerations/Contraindications

The medical considerations/contraindications included have been selected on the basis of their potential clinical significance (reasons

given in parentheses where appropriate)—not necessarily inclusive (» = major clinical significance).

Except under special circumstances, this medication should not be used when the following medical problem exists:

» Immunodeficiency

Risk-benefit should be considered when the following medical problems exist:

Aciduria (urine pH less than 7) or
» Ascites or
Dehydration or
Gastrointestinal obstruction or
» Pleural or peritoneal effusions or
» Renal function impairment
(risk of methotrexate toxicity is increased because elimination of methotrexate may be impaired and accumulation may occur; even small doses may lead to severe myelosuppression and mucositis; larger doses and/or increased duration of leucovorin treatment, if used, may be necessary, along with careful monitoring of methotrexate concentrations)
(a lower dosage of methotrexate and careful monitoring of plasma or serum methotrexate concentrations are recommended for patients with impaired renal function)
» Bone marrow depression
» Chickenpox, existing or recent (including recent exposure) or
» Herpes zoster
(risk of severe generalized disease)
Gout, history of or
Urate renal stones, history of
(risk of hyperuricemia)
» Hepatic function impairment
» Infection
» Mucositis, oral
Nausea and vomiting
(inadequate hydration secondary to severe nausea and vomiting may result in increased methotrexate toxicity)
» Peptic ulcer
Sensitivity to methotrexate
» Ulcerative colitis
» Caution should be used also in patients who have had previous cytotoxic drug therapy and radiation therapy, and in cases of general debility.

Patient monitoring

The following are especially important in patient monitoring (other tests may be warranted in some patients, depending on condition; » = major clinical significance):

» Blood urea nitrogen (BUN) concentrations and
Creatinine clearance and/or
» Serum creatinine concentrations
(recommended prior to initiation of therapy and at periodic intervals during therapy; frequency varies according to clinical state, agent, dose, and other agents being used concurrently)
Bone marrow aspiration studies and
Liver biopsy
(may be useful during high-dose or long-term therapy or if hematologic or hepatic function test results are abnormal; also recommended in patients who have received a cumulative dose of 1500 mg)
Examination of patient's mouth for ulceration
(recommended before administration of each dose)
» Hematocrit or hemoglobin and
» Platelet count and
» Total and, if appropriate, differential leukocyte count
(determinations recommended prior to initiation of therapy and at periodic intervals during therapy; frequency varies according to clinical state, agent, dose, and other agents being used concurrently)
» Serum alanine aminotransferase (ALT [SGPT]) and
» Serum aspartate aminotransferase (AST [SGOT]) and
» Serum lactate dehydrogenase (LDH)
(determinations recommended prior to initiation of therapy and at periodic intervals during therapy; frequency varies according to clinical state, agent, dose, and other agents being used concurrently)
» Serum bilirubin concentrations and
Serum uric acid concentrations
(recommended prior to initiation of therapy and at periodic intervals during therapy; frequency varies according to clinical state, agent, dose, and other agents being used concurrently)

For patients receiving high-dose methotrexate

» Creatinine clearance determinations
(recommended prior to initiation of high-dose methotrexate with leucovorin rescue therapy or if serum creatinine concentrations increase by 50% or more)
» Plasma or serum methotrexate concentrations
(recommended by some clinicians every 12 to 24 hours after high-dose methotrexate administration to determine dose and duration of leucovorin treatment needed to maintain rescue. May aid in identifying patients with delayed methotrexate clearance; toxicity appears to be related at least as much to the length of time that methotrexate concentrations are elevated as to the peak concentrations achieved. In general, monitoring should continue until concentrations are less than 5×10^{-8} Molar [M])
» Serum creatinine concentrations
(recommended prior to and every 24 hours after each methotrexate dose, until plasma or serum methotrexate concentrations are less than 5×10^{-8} M, to detect developing renal function impairment and predict methotrexate toxicity. An increase of greater than 50% over the pretreatment concentration at 24 hours is associated with severe renal toxicity)
» Urine pH determinations
(recommended prior to each dose of high-dose methotrexate therapy and about every 6 hours throughout leucovorin rescue, until plasma or serum methotrexate concentrations are less than 5×10^{-8} M, to ensure that pH remains greater than 7, so as to minimize the risk of methotrexate nephropathy due to precipitation of methotrexate or its metabolites in the urine)

Side/Adverse Effects

Note: Many "side effects" of antineoplastic therapy are unavoidable and represent the medication's pharmacologic action. Some of these (for example, leukopenia and thrombocytopenia) are actually used as parameters to aid in individual dosage titration.
Incidence and severity of side effects, particularly hepatotoxicity, appear to be related to dosage frequency and duration of methotrexate therapy. Toxicity tends to occur less frequently and be less severe with a total dose administered as intermittent weekly dosage than with prolonged daily dosage.

The following side/adverse effects have been selected on the basis of their potential clinical significance (possible signs and symptoms in parentheses where appropriate)—not necessarily inclusive:

Those indicating need for medical attention

Incidence more frequent

Gastrointestinal ulceration and bleeding, enteritis, or intestinal perforation, which may be fatal (black, tarry stools; bloody vomit; diarrhea; stomach pain); ***leukopenia, bacterial infection, or septicemia*** (fever or chills; cough or hoarseness; lower back or side pain; painful or difficult urination)—usually asymptomatic; ***thrombocytopenia*** (unusual bleeding or bruising; black, tarry stools; blood in urine or stools; pinpoint red spots on skin)—usually asymptomatic; ***stomatitis, ulcerative*** (sores in mouth and on lips)

Note: With development of *leukopenia* and *thrombocytopenia*, the nadir of the leukocyte and platelet counts occurs after 7 to 10 days, with recovery 7 days later.

Incidence more frequent (with high-dose therapy)

Renal failure, azotemia, hyperuricemia, or severe nephropathy (blood in urine; joint pain; swelling of feet or lower legs); ***severe acute methotrexate toxicity, cutaneous vasculitis, or reactivation of sunburn or increased erythematous response to ultraviolet therapy*** (reddening of skin)

Note: *Hyperuricemia* and *uric acid nephropathy* occur most commonly during initial treatment of patients with leukemia or lymphoma, as a result of rapid cell breakdown which leads to elevated serum uric acid concentrations. With high-dose methotrexate therapy, symptoms resembling uric acid nephropathy may also be due to renal tubular damage resulting from precipitation of methotrexate or metabolites in the urine.

Incidence less frequent, more frequent with prolonged, daily therapy

Hepatotoxicity, including liver atrophy, necrosis, cirrhosis, fatty changes, periportal fibrosis (dark urine; yellow eyes or skin); ***pneumonitis, potentially fatal, or pulmonary fibrosis*** (cough; shortness of breath)

Incidence less frequent, more frequent with intrathecal or prolonged high-dose administration

Central nervous system (CNS) effects, increased cerebrospinal fluid pressure, leukoencephalopathy, demyelination, or chemical arachnoiditis (back pain; blurred vision; confusion; convulsions; dizziness; drowsiness; fever; headache; unusual tiredness or weakness)

Those indicating need for medical attention only if they continue or are bothersome

Incidence more frequent

Loss of appetite; nausea or vomiting

Incidence less frequent

Acne; boils; pale skin; skin rash or itching

Those not indicating need for medical attention

Incidence less frequent

Alopecia (loss of hair)

Those indicating need for medical attention if they occur after medication is discontinued

CNS toxicity (encephalopathy, especially after intrathecal administration, or CNS leukemia) (back pain; blurred vision; confusion; convulsions; dizziness; drowsiness; fever; headache; unusual tiredness or weakness)

Overdose

For specific information on the agents used in the management of methotrexate overdose, see *Leucovorin (Systemic)*.

For more information on the management of overdose or unintentional ingestion, **contact a Poison Control Center** (see *Poison Control Center Listing*).

Treatment of overdose

Leucovorin should be administered as soon as possible following accidental methotrexate overdosage. The efficacy of leucovorin in reducing methotrexate toxicity decreases as the time between methotrexate administration and the initiation of leucovorin therapy increases.

Specific treatment—Preventing precipitation of methotrexate and metabolites in renal tubules by systemic hydration and urinary alkalization.

High dose leucovorin therapy, alkaline diuresis, rapid cerebrospinal fluid drainage, and ventriculolumbar perfusion may be necessary for treating intrathecal overdosage.

Monitoring—Monitoring of serum methotrexate concentration is necessary to determine the required dose and duration of treatment with leucovorin.

Supportive care—Intensive systemic supportive care is necessary following intrathecal overdose.

Patients in whom intentional overdose is confirmed or suspected should be referred for psychiatric consultation.

Note: Dialysis is of limited value in the treatment of overdose.

Patient Consultation

As an aid to patient consultation, refer to *Advice for the Patient, Methotrexate—For Cancer (Systemic)*.

In providing consultation, consider emphasizing the following selected information (» = major clinical significance):

Before using this medication

» Conditions affecting use, especially:
- Sensitivity to methotrexate
- Pregnancy—Use not recommended because of mutagenic, teratogenic, and carcinogenic potential; advisability of using contraception; telling physician immediately if pregnancy is suspected
- Breast-feeding—Not recommended because of risk of serious side effects
- Use in children—Newborns and other infants may be more sensitive to effects
- Use in the elderly—Side/adverse effects may be more frequent
- Other medications, especially acyclovir, alcohol or other hepatotoxic medications, asparaginase, live virus vaccines, nonsteroidal anti-inflammatory drugs (NSAIDs), other bone marrow depressants, previous cytotoxic drug therapy or radiation therapy, probenecid, sulfinpyrazone, or salicylates
- Other medical problems, especially chickenpox, herpes zoster, hepatic function impairment, renal function impairment, infection, oral mucositis, peptic ulcer, or ulcerative colitis

Proper use of this medication

» Importance of not taking more or less medication than the amount prescribed

Caution in taking combination therapy; taking each medication at the right time

Importance of ample fluid intake and subsequent increase in urine output to prevent nephrotoxicity and aid in excretion of uric acid

» Frequency of nausea and vomiting; importance of continuing medication despite stomach upset

Checking with physician if vomiting occurs shortly after dose is taken

» Proper dosing

Missed dose: Not taking at all; not doubling doses

» Proper storage

Precautions while using this medication

» Importance of close monitoring by physician

» Avoiding alcoholic beverages, which may increase hepatotoxicity

Possible photosensitivity reactions; avoiding too much unprotected exposure to sun or overuse of sunlamp

» Avoiding salicylate-containing products and NSAIDs, which may increase toxicity

» Avoiding immunizations unless approved by physician; other persons in patient's household should avoid immunizations with oral poliovirus vaccine; avoiding other persons who have taken oral poliovirus vaccine or wearing a protective mask that covers nose and mouth

Caution if bone marrow depression occurs:

» Avoiding exposure to persons with infections, especially during periods of low blood counts; checking with physician immediately if fever or chills, cough or hoarseness, lower back or side pain, or painful or difficult urination occurs

» Checking with physician immediately if unusual bleeding or bruising; black, tarry stools; blood in urine or stools; or pinpoint red spots on skin occur

Caution in use of regular toothbrush, dental floss, or toothpick; physician, dentist, or nurse may suggest alternatives; checking with physician before having dental work done

Not touching eyes or inside of nose unless hands are washed immediately before

Using caution to avoid accidental cuts with use of sharp objects such as safety razor or fingernail or toenail cutters

Avoiding contact sports or other situations where bruising or injury could occur

Side/adverse effects

May cause adverse effects such as blood problems; stomach, kidney, or liver problems; or cancer; importance of discussing possible effects with physician

Signs of potential side effects, especially gastrointestinal ulceration and bleeding, enteritis, intestinal perforation, leukopenia, bacterial infection, septicemia, thrombocytopenia, ulcerative stomatitis, renal failure, azotemia, hyperuricemia, severe nephropathy, severe acute methotrexate toxicity, cutaneous vasculitis, reactivation of sunburn or reaction to ultraviolet light, hepatotoxicity, pneumonitis, pulmonary fibrosis, and CNS effects

Physician or nurse can help in dealing with side effects

Possibility of hair loss; normal hair growth should resume after treatment has ended

General Dosing Information

Patients receiving methotrexate should be under supervision of a physician experienced in antineoplastic chemotherapy.

A variety of dosage schedules and regimens of methotrexate, alone or in combination with other antitumor agents, are used. The prescriber may consult the medical literature as well as the manufacturer's literature in choosing a specific dosage.

Dosage must be adjusted to meet the individual requirements of each patient, based on clinical response and appearance or severity of toxicity.

In general, use of intermittent courses of methotrexate is associated with less risk of serious toxicity than prolonged, daily dosage.

A significant amount of methotrexate passes into systemic circulation after intrathecal administration and may produce toxic levels in patients also receiving systemic methotrexate therapy; an adjustment in systemic dosage may be necessary.

Development of uric acid nephropathy in patients with leukemia or lymphoma may be prevented by adequate oral hydration and, in some cases, administration of allopurinol. Alkalinization of urine may be necessary if serum uric acid concentrations are elevated.

If severe bone marrow depression occurs, withdrawal of methotrexate may be necessary. However, in some patients with acute leukemia, methotrexate may be administered despite the presence of thrombocytopenia and bleeding; stoppage of bleeding and increase in platelet count have occurred during treatment in some cases and platelet transfusions may be useful in others.

Special precautions are recommended in patients who develop thrombocytopenia as a result of administration of methotrexate. These may include extreme care in performing invasive procedures; regular inspection of intravenous sites, skin (including perirectal area), and mucous membrane surfaces for signs of bleeding or bruising; limiting frequency of venipuncture and avoiding intramuscular injections; testing urine, emesis, stool, and secretions for occult blood; care in use of regular toothbrushes, dental floss, toothpicks, safety razors, and fingernail and toenail cutters; avoiding constipation; and using caution to prevent falls and other injuries. Such patients should avoid alcohol and any aspirin intake because of the risk of gastrointestinal bleeding. Platelet transfusions may be required.

Patients who develop leukopenia should be observed carefully for signs of infection. Antibiotic support may be required. In neutropenic patients who develop fever, broad-spectrum antibiotic coverage should be initiated empirically, pending bacterial cultures and appropriate diagnostic tests.

It is recommended that methotrexate therapy be interrupted if diarrhea or ulcerative stomatitis occurs, because of the risk of hemorrhagic enteritis and fatal intestinal perforation.

It is recommended that methotrexate therapy be interrupted if pulmonary symptoms (especially a dry, unproductive cough) occur, because of the risk of potentially irreversible pulmonary toxicity.

For use in high-dose methotrexate therapy

Because of its ability to bypass the effects of methotrexate, leucovorin calcium (folinic acid, citrovorum factor) is administered as a "rescue" from the hematologic and gastrointestinal effects of high-dosage methotrexate.

High-dose methotrexate administration should not be initiated unless leucovorin is physically present and ready to be administered, since rescue is critical.

Methotrexate administration should not be initiated unless creatinine clearance is greater than 60 mL per minute and serum creatinine concentrations are normal. If renal function impairment develops during therapy, methotrexate should be withdrawn until creatinine clearance improves to acceptable levels.

Methotrexate administration also should not be initiated if:
—White blood cell count is less than 1500 per microliter
—Neutrophil count is less than 200 per microliter
—Platelet count is less than 75,000 per microliter
—Bilirubin is greater than 1.2 mg per dL
—Alanine aminotransferase (ALT [SGPT]) values are greater than 450 units

Methotrexate administration also should be delayed until healing of stomatitis is evident and until after complete drainage of persistent pleural effusions.

A variety of dosage schedules of leucovorin in combination with high-dose methotrexate have been used. The prescriber should consult the medical literature in choosing a specific dosage. Alkalinization of urine (with bicarbonate and/or acetazolamide) and intravenous hydration (1000 mL per square meter of body surface area over 6 hours prior to beginning the methotrexate infusion and 3000 mL per square meter of body surface area per day during the methotrexate infusion and for 2 days after the infusion is completed) are also important to prevent renal toxicity caused by methotrexate and/or its metabolites.

Administration of leucovorin should be consecutive to rather than simultaneous with methotrexate administration so as not to interfere with methotrexate's antineoplastic effects.

In general, it is recommended that the first dose of leucovorin be administered 24 hours after a high-dose methotrexate infusion is started (within 1 hour of an overdose), in a dosage to produce blood concentrations equal to or greater than methotrexate blood concentrations (leucovorin in a dose of 15 to 25 mg per square meter of body surface area produces peak plasma concentrations of approximately 1 micromolar or 1×10^{-6} M). Duration of leucovorin administration varies with the dosage of methotrexate and plasma concentrations achieved (including rate of elimination); in general, leucovorin administration is continued until methotrexate concentrations fall to less than 5×10^{-8} M.

A larger dose and/or longer duration of leucovorin treatment may be required in patients with aciduria, ascites, dehydration, gastrointestinal obstruction, renal function impairment, or pleural or peritoneal effusions because excretion of methotrexate is slowed and the length of time for plasma methotrexate concentrations to decrease to nontoxic levels ($< 5 \times 10^{-8}$ M) is increased. It is recommended that duration of leucovorin administration in these patients be based on determination of plasma methotrexate concentrations.

For parenteral use

Methotrexate may be administered intramuscularly, intravenously (rapid or continuous infusion), intrathecally, intra-arterially, or intraventricularly.

Caution is recommended in making sure that the appropriate diluent for the intended route of administration is used when preparing methotrexate for administration.

Safety considerations for handling this medication

There is limited but increasing evidence and concern that personnel involved in preparation and administration of parenteral antineoplastics may be at some risk because of the potential mutagenicity, teratogenicity, and/or carcinogenicity of these agents, although the actual risk is unknown. USP advisory panels recommend cautious handling both in preparation and disposal of antineoplastic agents. Precautions that have been suggested include:
• Use of a biological containment cabinet during reconstitution and dilution of parenteral medications and wearing of disposable surgical gloves and masks.
• Use of proper technique to prevent contamination of the medication, work area, and operator during transfer between containers (including proper training of personnel in this technique).
• Cautious and proper disposal of needles, syringes, vials, ampuls, and unused medication.

A number of medical centers have developed detailed guidelines for handling of antineoplastic agents.

Combination chemotherapy

Methotrexate may be used in combination with other agents in various regimens. As a result, incidence and/or severity of side effects may be altered and different dosages (usually reduced) may be used. For example, methotrexate is part of the following chemotherapeutic combinations (some commonly used acronyms are in parentheses):
—cyclophosphamide, doxorubicin, methotrexate, and procarbazine (CAMP).
—cyclophosphamide, methotrexate, and fluorouracil (CMF).
—cyclophosphamide, methotrexate, fluorouracil, vincristine, and prednisone (CMFVP).

For specific dosages and schedules, consult the literature. For information regarding each agent, consult the individual monographs.

Oral Dosage Forms

Note: Bracketed uses in the *Dosage Forms* section refer to categories of use and/or indications that are not included in U.S. product labeling.

METHOTREXATE TABLETS USP

Usual adult dose

Choriocarcinoma or
Chorioadenoma destruens or
Hydatidiform mole—
Oral, 15 to 30 mg per day for five days, the course being repeated three to five times, with one to two weeks between courses. Usually, one or two courses are given after normalization of urinary human chorionic gonadotropin (HCG) concentrations.

Acute lymphocytic leukemia—
Induction: Oral, 3.3 mg per square meter of body surface area per day in combination with prednisone or other agents.
Maintenance: Oral, 30 mg per square meter of body surface area per week in two divided doses.

Burkitt's lymphoma—
Stages I–II: Oral, 10 to 25 mg per day for four to eight days, the course being repeated several times, with seven to ten days between courses.
Stage III: Oral, as for Stage I–II, in combination with other agents.

Lymphosarcoma (Stage III)—
Oral, 625 mcg (0.625 mg) to 2.5 mg per kg of body weight per day.

Mycosis fungoides—
Oral, 2.5 to 10 mg a day for weeks or months.

Carcinoma, breast or
Carcinoma, head and neck or
Carcinoma, lung, non-small cell[1] or
Carcinoma, lung, small cell[1] or
[Carcinoma, cervical][1] or
[Carcinoma, ovarian, epithelial][1] or
[Carcinoma, bladder] or
[Carcinoma, colorectal][1] or
[Carcinoma, esophageal][1] or
[Carcinoma, gastric] or
[Carcinoma, pancreatic][1] or
[Carcinoma, penile][1] or
[Leukemia, acute nonlymphocytic][1] or
[Lymphomas, Hodgkin's][1] or
[Sarcomas, soft tissue][1]—
Consult medical literature or manufacturer's literature for specific dosage.

Usual pediatric dose

Antineoplastic—
Oral, 20 to 40 mg per square meter of body surface area, once a week.

Strength(s) usually available

U.S.—

2.5 mg (Rx) [GENERIC (lactose; magnesium stearate; pregelatinized starch)].

Canada—

2.5 mg (Rx) [GENERIC].

Packaging and storage

Store below 40 °C (104 °F), preferably between 15 and 30 °C (59 and 86 °F), unless otherwise specified by manufacturer. Store in a well-closed container. Protect from light.

Auxiliary labeling

- Avoid alcoholic beverages.
- Do not take other medicines without advice from your doctor.
- Avoid overexposure to sun.

Parenteral Dosage Forms

Note: Bracketed uses in the *Dosage Forms* section refer to categories of use and/or indications that are not included in U.S. product labeling.

The dosing and strengths of dosage forms available are expressed in terms of methotrexate base.

METHOTREXATE SODIUM INJECTION USP

Usual adult dose

Choriocarcinoma or
Chorioadenoma destruens or
Hydatidiform mole—

Intramuscular, 15 to 30 mg (base) per day for five days, the course being repeated three to five times with one to two weeks between courses. Usually, one or two courses are given after normalization of urinary human chorionic gonadotropin (HCG) concentrations.

Acute lymphocytic leukemia—

Induction—

Intravenous or intramuscular, 3.3 mg (base) per square meter of body surface area per day in combination with prednisone or other agents.

Maintenance—

Intramuscular, 30 mg (base) per square meter of body surface area per week in two divided doses; or

Intravenous, 2.5 mg (base) per kg of body weight every fourteen days.

Osteosarcoma—

Intravenous infusion (over four hours), 12 grams (base) per square meter of body surface area, followed by leucovorin rescue (usually 15 mg orally every six hours for ten doses starting at twenty-four hours after the methotrexate infusion is started), on weeks 4, 5, 6, 7, 11, 12, 15, 16, 29, 30, 44, and 45 after surgery on a combination chemotherapy schedule that also includes doxorubicin, cisplatin, bleomycin, cyclophosphamide, and dactinomycin. The dose may be increased, if necessary, to 15 grams (base) per square meter of body surface area to achieve a peak serum methotrexate concentration of 1×10^{-3} M per liter.

Note: *High-dose methotrexate administration should not be initiated unless leucovorin is physically present and ready to be administered, since rescue is critical.*

If the patient is vomiting or cannot take oral medication, leucovorin may be administered intravenously or intramuscularly at the same dose as the oral dose.

Mycosis fungoides—

Intramuscular, 50 mg (base) once a week or 25 mg (base) two times a week.

Carcinoma, breast or
Carcinoma, head and neck or
Carcinoma, lung, non-small cell[1] or
Carcinoma, lung, small cell[1] or
[Carcinoma, cervical][1] or
[Carcinoma, ovarian, epithelial][1] or
[Carcinoma, bladder] or
[Carcinoma, colorectal][1] or
[Carcinoma, esophageal][1] or
[Carcinoma, gastric] or
[Carcinoma, pancreatic][1] or
[Carcinoma, penile][1] or
[Leukemia, acute nonlymphocytic][1] or
[Lymphomas, Hodgkin's][1] or
[Sarcomas, soft tissue][1]—

Consult medical literature or manufacturer's literature for specific dosage.

Usual pediatric dose

Antineoplastic—

Intramuscular, 20 to 40 mg (base) per square meter of body surface area, once a week.

Strength(s) usually available

U.S.—

25 mg (base) per mL (Rx) [GENERIC (with and without preservative)].

Canada—

2.5 mg (base) per mL (Rx) [GENERIC (with and without preservative)].
10 mg (base) per mL (Rx) [GENERIC (without preservative)].
25 mg (base) per mL (Rx) [GENERIC (with and without preservative)].

Packaging and storage

Store below 40 °C (104 °F), preferably between 15 and 30 °C (59 and 86 °F), unless otherwise specified by the manufacturer. Protect from light.

Preparation of dosage form

Methotrexate Sodium Injection USP may be further diluted with an appropriate preservative-free medium such as 0.9% sodium chloride injection or 5% dextrose injection.

Stability

If stored for 24 hours at a temperature of 21 to 25 °C (70 to 77 °F), a diluted solution of methotrexate sodium injection maintains 90% of its labeled potency. However, preservative-free solutions should be diluted immediately prior to use and any unused portion discarded.

METHOTREXATE SODIUM FOR INJECTION USP

Usual adult dose

Meningeal leukemia—

Induction: Intrathecal, 12 mg (base) every two to five days until the cell count of the cerebrospinal fluid (CSF) returns to normal.

Prophylaxis: Intrathecal, 12 mg (base) at an interval determined by consultation of the medical literature.

Choriocarcinoma or
Chorioadenoma destruens or
Hydatidiform mole—

Intramuscular, 15 to 30 mg (base) per day for five days, the course being repeated three to five times, with one to two weeks between courses. Usually, one or two courses are given after normalization of urinary human chorionic gonadotropin (HCG) concentrations.

Acute lymphocytic leukemia—

Induction—

Intravenous or intramuscular, 3.3 mg (base) per square meter of body surface area per day in combination with prednisone or other agents.

Maintenance—

Intramuscular, 30 mg (base) per square meter of body surface area per week in two divided doses; or

Intravenous, 2.5 mg (base) per kg of body weight every fourteen days.

Osteosarcoma—

Intravenous infusion (over four hours), 12 grams (base) per square meter of body surface area, followed by leucovorin rescue (usually 15 mg orally every six hours for ten doses starting at twenty-four hours after the methotrexate infusion is started), on weeks 4, 5, 6, 7, 11, 12, 15, 16, 29, 30, 44, and 45 after surgery on a combination chemotherapy schedule that also includes doxorubicin, cisplatin, bleomycin, cyclophosphamide, and dactinomycin. The dose may be increased, if necessary, to 15 grams (base) per square meter of body surface area to achieve a peak serum methotrexate concentration of 1×10^{-3} M per liter.

Note: *High-dose methotrexate administration should not be initiated unless leucovorin is physically present and ready to be administered, since rescue is critical.*

If the patient is vomiting or cannot take oral medication, leucovorin may be administered intravenously or intramuscularly in the same dose as the oral dose.

Mycosis fungoides—

Intramuscular, 50 mg (base) once a week or 25 mg (base) two times a week.

[Carcinomatous meningitis][1]—

Intrathecal or intraventricular; consult medical literature or manufacturer's literature for specific dosage.

Carcinoma, breast or
Carcinoma, head and neck or
Carcinoma, lung, non-small cell[1] or
Carcinoma, lung, small cell[1] or
[Carcinoma, cervical][1] or
[Carcinoma, ovarian, epithelial][1] or
[Carcinoma, bladder] or

[Carcinoma, colorectal][1] or
[Carcinoma, esophageal][1] or
[Carcinoma, gastric] or
[Carcinoma, pancreatic][1] or
[Carcinoma, penile][1] or
[Leukemia, acute nonlymphocytic][1] or
[Lymphomas, Hodgkin's][1] or
[Sarcomas, soft tissue][1]—
Consult medical literature or manufacturer's literature for specific dosage.

Usual pediatric dose

Meningeal leukemia—
For children up to 1 year of age: Intrathecal, 6 mg (base) every two to five days until the cell count of the CSF returns to normal.
For children 1 year of age: Intrathecal, 8 mg (base) every two to five days until the cell count of the CSF returns to normal.
For children 2 years of age: Intrathecal, 10 mg (base) every two to five days until the cell count of the CSF returns to normal.
For children 3 years of age and over: Intrathecal, 12 mg (base) every two to five days until the cell count of the CSF returns to normal.

Antineoplastic, other—
Intramuscular, 20 to 40 mg (base) per square meter of body surface area, once a week.

Strength(s) usually available

U.S.—
20 mg (base) (Rx) [GENERIC (without preservative)].
1 gram (base) (Rx) [GENERIC (without preservative)].

Canada—
20 mg (base) (Rx) [GENERIC (without preservative)].

Packaging and storage

Store below 40 °C (104 °F), preferably between 15 and 30 °C (59 and 86 °F), unless otherwise specified by manufacturer. Protect from light.

Preparation of dosage form

For intrathecal use, methotrexate sodium for injection (containing no preservative) is recommended. It must be reconstituted immediately prior to use with an appropriate volume of a sterile, preservative-free medium such as 0.9% sodium chloride injection to yield a solution containing 1 mg (base) per mL.

For intravenous or intramuscular use, the 20-mg vial of methotrexate sodium for injection is diluted with an appropriate volume of a sterile, preservative-free medium, such as 5% dextrose injection or 0.9% sodium chloride injection, to yield a solution containing not more than 25 mg (base) per mL. The 1-gram vial should be diluted with 19.4 mL of 5% dextrose injection or 0.9% sodium chloride injection to yield a solution containing 50 mg (base) per mL. For high dose intravenous use, methotrexate sodium for injection should only be diluted in 5% dextrose injection.

Stability

Solutions without preservative should be freshly reconstituted immediately prior to each dose; any unused portion should be discarded.

[1]Not included in Canadian product labeling.

Revised: 08/01/2000

METHOTRIMEPRAZINE—See *Phenothiazines (Systemic)*

METHOXAMINE—See *Sympathomimetic Agents—Cardiovascular Use (Parenteral-Systemic)*

METHOXSALEN Systemic

VA CLASSIFICATION (Primary/Secondary): DE801/DE890; AN900

Note: **Methoxsalen soft gelatin capsules should not be used interchangeably with the hard gelatin capsules, since the soft gelatin capsule dosage form exhibits significantly greater bioavailability and earlier photosensitization onset time than does the hard gelatin capsule dosage form.**

Commonly used brand name(s): *8-MOP; Oxsoralen; Oxsoralen-Ultra; Ultra MOP.*

Note: For a listing of dosage forms and brand names by country availability, see *Dosage Forms* section(s).

Category

Repigmenting agent (systemic); antipsoriatic (systemic); antineoplastic; hair growth stimulant, alopecia areata (systemic)

Note: Methoxsalen is used in conjunction with ultraviolet light A (UVA). This mode of treatment is known as PUVA (psoralen plus ultraviolet light A).

Methoxsalen soft gelatin capsules should not be used interchangeably with the hard gelatin capsules, since the soft gelatin capsule dosage form exhibits significantly greater bioavailability and earlier photosensitization onset time than does the hard gelatin capsule dosage form.

Indications

Note: Bracketed information in the *Indications* section refers to uses that are not included in U.S. product labeling.

Accepted

Mycosis fungoides (treatment)[1]—Photopheresis, using methoxsalen hard gelatin capsules [or soft gelatin capsules] with ultraviolet radiation of white blood cells, is indicated for use with the UVAR System in the palliative treatment of the skin manifestations of mycosis fungoides (also known as cutaneous T-cell lymphoma) in persons who have not been responsive to other forms of treatment. [PUVA is also used in the treatment of mycosis fungoides.][1]

Psoriasis (treatment)—PUVA, using methoxsalen hard gelatin capsules or soft gelatin capsules, is indicated in the treatment of severe, refractory, disabling psoriasis that has not responded to other therapy.

Vitiligo (treatment)—PUVA, using methoxsalen hard gelatin capsules [or soft gelatin capsules], is indicated for repigmentation in the treatment of vitiligo. PUVA is not effective in producing pigmentation in leukoderma of infectious origin or in albinism. Patients with albinism or patients who are intolerant to sunlight still may benefit from methoxsalen's ability to increase their tolerance to sunlight.

[Alopecia areata (treatment)][1]
[Dermatitis, atopic (treatment)]
[Dermatoses, inflammatory (treatment)][1]
[Eczema (treatment)][1]
[Lichen planus (treatment)][1] or
[Skin intolerance to sunlight]—PUVA is also used in the treatment of alopecia areata, atopic dermatitis, inflammatory dermatoses, eczema, and lichen planus. Methoxsalen, with natural light or with UVA light, also is used to increase skin tolerance to sunlight.

Unaccepted

The unsupervised use of methoxsalen to promote tanning is dangerous and should be discouraged.

[1]Not included in Canadian product labeling.

Pharmacology/Pharmacokinetics

Physicochemical characteristics

Molecular weight—216.19.

Mechanism of action/Effect

Methoxsalen is a psoralen derivative with photosensitizing activity. Exact mechanism of erythemogenic, melanogenic, and cytotoxic response in the epidermis is unknown, but may involve increased tyrosinase activity in melanin-producing cells, as well as inhibition of DNA synthesis, cell division, and epidermal turnover. Successful pigmentation requires the presence of functioning melanocytes.

Absorption

Methoxsalen is variably (approximately 95%) absorbed from the gastrointestinal tract. It has been postulated that poor response in some patients may be due to poor absorption.

Protein binding

High.

Biotransformation

Activated by long-wavelength UVA in the range of 320 to 400 nanometers (nm). Further metabolism: hepatic.

Half-life

Hard gelatin capsule—1.1 hours.
Soft gelatin capsule—Approximately 2 hours.

Onset of action

Vitiligo—Up to 6 months or longer.
Psoriasis—30 treatments (10 weeks or longer).
For intolerance of skin to sunlight—1 hour.
Tanning—Within a few days.

Time to peak photosensitivity

Hard gelatin capsule—3.9 to 4.25 hours.

Soft gelatin capsule—1.5 to 2.1 hours.

Mean minimal erythema dose (MED)

Substantially fewer Joules per square cm are required with the soft gelatin capsule dosage form than with the hard gelatin capsule dosage form.

Peak serum concentration

Hard gelatin capsule—1.5 to 6 hours (mean of 3 hours), when administered with 8 ounces of milk.

Soft gelatin capsule—0.5 to 4 hours (mean of 1.8 hours), when administered with 8 ounces of milk.

Duration of action

Increased sensitivity of skin to sunlight—Approximately 8 hours.

Elimination

Renal—As metabolites (80 to 90% in 8 hours; 95% in 24 hours).
Fecal—4 to 10%.

Precautions to Consider

Carcinogenicity

Psoralens have been found to augment UVA-induced carcinogenicity in laboratory animals. In addition, studies in humans treated with systemic methoxsalen plus UVA have shown an increase in the risk of squamous cell carcinoma. The possibility of increased risk may exist also for topical methoxsalen and systemic trioxsalen. This risk appears to be greatest in patients with predisposing risk factors, such as fair skin or a hypersensitivity to sunlight; a history of skin cancer, exposure to ionizing radiation, or excessive exposure to sunlight; or a history of treatment with tar and UVB (prolonged), arsenicals, or topical nitrogen mustard.

Pregnancy/Reproduction

Pregnancy—Studies have not been done in humans.
Studies have not been done in animals.

FDA Pregnancy Category C.

Breast-feeding

It is not known whether methoxsalen is distributed into breast milk. However, problems in humans have not been documented.

Pediatrics

Children up to 12 years of age—Appropriate studies on the relationship of age to the effects of methoxsalen have not been performed; however, some side effects are more likely to occur in children up to 12 years of age, since these children may be more sensitive to the effects of methoxsalen.

Children 12 years of age and over—Appropriate studies on the relationship of age to the effects of methoxsalen have not been performed in this age group. However, no problems specific to this age group have been documented to date.

Geriatrics

Although appropriate studies on the relationship of age to the effects of methoxsalen have not been performed in the geriatric population, no geriatrics-specific problems have been documented to date.

Drug interactions and/or related problems

The following drug interactions and/or related problems have been selected on the basis of their potential clinical significance (possible mechanism in parentheses where appropriate)—not necessarily inclusive (» = major clinical significance):

Note: Combinations containing any of the following medications, depending on the amount present, may also interact with this medication.

Furocoumarin-containing foods, such as limes, figs, parsley, parsnips, mustard, carrots, and celery
(although there have been no reports of serious reactions, caution and avoidance of these foods are recommended because of the risk of additive phototoxicity)

Photosensitizing medications, other
(concurrent use of methoxsalen with these medications, systemic or topical, may cause additive photosensitizing effects; concurrent use with coal tar or coal tar derivatives or with trioxsalen is not recommended)
(concurrent use of systemic methoxsalen with phenothiazines may potentiate intraocular photochemical damage to the choroid, retina, and lens)

» Caution should be used also in evaluating for treatment and subsequently treating patients with a history of having taken arsenicals or having received x-rays, cytotoxic therapy, or coal tar and ultraviolet light B (UVB) therapy because of the increased risk of skin cancer

Laboratory value alterations

The following have been selected on the basis of their potential clinical significance (possible effect in parentheses where appropriate)—not necessarily inclusive (» = major clinical significance).

With physiology/laboratory test values
Hepatic function tests
(abnormal hepatic function tests have been reported, but the relationship to the medication is not clear)

Medical considerations/Contraindications

The medical considerations/contraindications included have been selected on the basis of their potential clinical significance (reasons given in parentheses where appropriate)—not necessarily inclusive (» = major clinical significance).

Risk-benefit should be considered when the following medical problems exist:

» Albinism or
» Hydroa or
» Leukoderma of infectious origin or
» Lupus erythematosus, acute or
Polymorphic light eruptions or
» Porphyria or
» Xeroderma pigmentosum
(these conditions are associated with photosensitization)

» Aphakia
(increased risk of retinal damage due to lack of lenses)

Cardiovascular disease, severe
(because of the potential heat stress or the prolonged standing associated with each UVA treatment, patients with this problem should be carefully monitored and, if possible, not treated in a vertical UVA chamber)

» Cataracts

Gastrointestinal diseases

Hepatic function impairment
(metabolism may be impaired)

Infection, chronic

Sensitivity to methoxsalen

» Skin cancer, history of

Sunlight allergy, or family history of
(PUVA may cause photoallergic contact dermatitis or precipitate sunlight allergy)

» Caution should be used also in evaluating for treatment and subsequently treating patients with a history of having taken arsenicals or having received x-rays, cytotoxic therapy, or coal tar and ultraviolet light B (UVB) therapy because of the increased risk of skin cancer

Patient monitoring

The following may be especially important in patient monitoring (other tests may be warranted in some patients, depending on condition; » = major clinical significance):

Antinuclear antibodies test and
Complete blood count and
Hepatic function tests and
Renal function tests
(recommended prior to initiation of therapy)

Monitoring for melanoma and other skin carcinomas
(recommended in patients receiving methoxsalen for prolonged periods, since long-term safety has not been established)

Ophthalmic examination
(recommended prior to initiation of therapy and yearly thereafter during therapy)

Side/Adverse Effects

Note: Cataracts have been reported with psoralen use; however, risk is very low in patients who wear UVA-absorbing, wraparound sunglasses when exposed to sunlight or ultraviolet light during the 24 hours after taking methoxsalen.

There is an increased risk of skin cancer with psoralen use. This risk appears to be greatest in patients with predisposing risk factors, such as fair skin or a hypersensitivity to sunlight; a history of skin cancer, exposure to ionizing radiation, or excessive exposure to sunlight; or a history of treatment with tar and UVB (prolonged), arsenicals, or topical nitrogen mustard.

Premature aging of the skin may occur as a result of prolonged PUVA therapy. This effect is permanent and is similar to the results of excessive exposure to sunlight.

Toxic hepatitis has been reported in patients treated with methoxsalen, but the relationship to the medication is not clear.

The following side/adverse effects have been selected on the basis of their potential clinical significance (possible signs and symptoms in parentheses where appropriate)—not necessarily inclusive:

Those indicating need for medical attention

Symptoms of overdose or overexposure to ultraviolet light

Blistering and peeling of skin; reddened, sore skin; swelling, especially in feet or lower legs

Those indicating need for medical attention only if they continue or are bothersome

Incidence more frequent

Itching of skin; nausea

Incidence less frequent

Dizziness; headache; mental depression; nervousness; trouble in sleeping

Overdose

For more information on the management of overdose or unintentional ingestion, **contact a Poison Control Center** (see *Poison Control Center Listing*).

Clinical effects of overdose

The following effects have been selected on the basis of their potential clinical significance (possible signs and symptoms in parentheses where appropriate)—not necessarily inclusive:

Blistering and peeling of skin; reddened, sore skin; swelling, especially in feet or lower legs

Treatment of overdose

To decrease absorption—

Inducing emesis, if it can be accomplished within the first 2 to 3 hours after ingestion, since maximum blood levels are reached by that time.

Specific treatment—

For overdosage of methoxsalen: Keeping patient in a darkened room for at least 24 hours following methoxsalen ingestion to prevent the possibility of sun exposure and subsequent burn injury.

For overexposure to sunlight or ultraviolet light: Keeping patient in a darkened room for at least 24 hours following ingestion of methoxsalen to prevent the possibility of further sun exposure and subsequent burn injury while assessment of the extent of damage is made.

Monitoring—

Observing patient for erythema greater than Grade 2 (Grade 2 being marked erythema with no edema) occurring within 24 hours, which may signal the beginning of a potentially serious burn, since peak erythemal reaction to PUVA usually occurs approximately 48 hours following methoxsalen ingestion.

Supportive Care—

Treating patient symptomatically for burns, depending on their extent and severity.

Patient Consultation

As an aid to patient consultation, refer to *Advice for the Patient, Methoxsalen (Systemic)*.

In providing consultation, consider emphasizing the following selected information (» = major clinical significance):

Before using this medication

» Conditions affecting use, especially:

Sensitivity to methoxsalen

Diet—Avoiding eating furocoumarin-containing foods (limes, figs, parsley, parsnips, mustard, carrots, celery)

Other medical problems, especially acute lupus erythematosus; albinism; aphakia; cataracts; hydroa; leukoderma of infectious origin; porphyria; xeroderma pigmentosum; history of skin cancer; history of having taken arsenicals; history of having received x-rays, cytotoxic therapy, or coal tar and ultraviolet light B (UVB) therapy

Not using for suntanning purposes

Proper use of this medication

Usually comes with patient instructions; reading carefully before using medication

» May take 6 to 8 weeks to work; importance of not increasing the dosage of medication or exposure to ultraviolet light because of the risk of serious burns

The hard capsule dosage form may be taken with food or milk (the soft capsule dosage form may be taken with low-fat food or low-fat milk) to reduce gastrointestinal irritation

» Proper dosing

Late or missed dose: Notifying physician for rescheduling of light treatment

» Proper storage

Precautions while using this medication

Importance of regular visits to physician to have progress checked, including eye examinations

» Protecting skin from sunlight, even through window glass or on cloudy days, for at least 24 hours before and 8 hours following treatment; protecting lips with sun block lipstick that has a skin protection factor (SPF) of at least 15

Possibility of continued skin sensitivity to sunlight because of medication; using extra precautions for at least 48 hours following each treatment; not sunbathing anytime during course of treatment

» Wearing special sunglasses during daylight hours (even in indirect light, such as through window glass or on cloudy days) for 24 hours following each dose of medication

» Possibility of dry skin or itching; checking with physician before treating

» Possible long-term effects (cataracts, premature skin aging, carcinogenesis)

Side/adverse effects

Slight reddening of skin 24 to 48 hours after treatment is normal response to therapy

There is an increased risk of developing skin cancer. The body should be examined regularly and the physician shown skin sores that do not heal, new skin growths, and skin growths that have changed in appearance or feel

Premature aging of the skin may occur as a result of prolonged PUVA therapy. This effect is permanent and is similar to the results of excessive exposure to sunlight

Signs of potential side effects, especially blistering and peeling of skin; reddened, sore skin; swelling, especially in feet or lower legs

Note: Some side effects are more likely to occur in children.

General Dosing Information

Patients receiving methoxsalen should be under the supervision of a physician experienced in PUVA therapy.

Although dosage of methoxsalen is generally based on body weight, usually no change in dose is necessary if the patient's weight changes. However, if the physician believes the weight change to be significant enough to warrant an alteration, adjustment of UVA exposure time should be made instead of adjustment of methoxsalen dosage.

Exposure to sunlight or ultraviolet light should be carefully controlled and adjusted on an individual basis according to skin type and tolerance. Exposure time to sunlight should be reduced at high altitudes or at midday.

Skin should be protected from sunlight, even through window glass or on a cloudy day, for at least 24 hours before and 8 hours following oral PUVA treatment by protective clothing, such as long-sleeved shirts, full-length slacks, wide-brimmed hat, and gloves and by using a sun block product that has a skin protection factor of at least 15 on body areas that cannot be covered by clothing. In addition, lips should be protected with a sun block lipstick that has a skin protection factor of at least 15. Also, since the skin continues to be sensitive to sunlight for some time after treatment, the patient should avoid overexposure to sunlight for 48 hours following administration of methoxsalen. In addition, the patient should not sunbathe anytime during the course of treatment.

If a scheduled treatment is missed, the dose of UVA at the next treatment should not be increased; if more than one treatment is missed, the subsequent dose of UVA should be reduced in proportion to the number of treatments missed to reduce the risk of painful erythema.

Repigmentation occurs most rapidly on fleshy areas (face, abdomen, buttocks) and more slowly on the extremities and bony areas (hands and feet).

Tolerance to the effects of methoxsalen may occur when pigmentation precedes erythema by a long period of time. Hyperpigmentation reduces subsequent responsiveness.

Use of psoralen derivatives to promote suntanning has resulted in serious reactions, including acute generalized dermatitis, blistering, and edema; residual edema of the legs and cutaneous damage have been reported.

For skin intolerance to sunlight
Treatment should be limited to 14 days, since methoxsalen's effect to stimulate any new pigment production will have been accomplished by that time.

For treatment of psoriasis
Some clinicians recommend an increased dose in the treatment of psoriasis if there is no response after 15 treatments at the recommended dose. A lower-than-recommended dose eventually may produce the same effect, but it usually occurs more slowly.

Lack of response in psoriasis may be associated with a general phototoxic reaction; this may be confirmed by temporary withdrawal for 2 weeks, with subsequent improvement in the condition. If improvement does not occur, treatment with methoxsalen is considered to be a failure.

Patients with pre-existing erythrodermic psoriasis require special care because the erythema may obscure a possible treatment-related phototoxic erythema. These patients should be treated similar to patients with sun-sensitive skin types.

Diet/Nutrition
Methoxsalen hard gelatin capsules may be taken with food or milk (the soft gelatin capsules may be taken with low-fat food or low-fat milk) to reduce gastrointestinal irritation, or the dose may be split in two and the two halves taken one-half hour apart.

Bioequivalence information
Methoxsalen soft gelatin capsules should not be used interchangeably with the hard gelatin capsules, since the soft gelatin capsule dosage form exhibits significantly greater bioavailability and earlier photosensitization onset time than does the hard gelatin capsule dosage form.

For treatment of adverse effects
Recommended treatment consists of the following:

- Burning or blistering of skin—Temporary withdrawal of therapy is recommended.
- Hepatic function impairment—Reduction in dosage or withdrawal of methoxsalen therapy.

Oral Dosage Forms
Note: Bracketed uses in the *Dosage Forms* section refer to categories of use and/or indications that are not included in U.S. product labeling.

METHOXSALEN CAPSULES (XXI) (HARD GELATIN) USP

Usual adult and adolescent dose
[Dermatitis, atopic] or
Psoriasis or
Mycosis fungoides[1]—

Oral, 600 mcg (0.6 mg) per kg of body weight, two hours before measured periods of high-intensity UVA exposure, two or three times a week or as determined by the patient's schedule for UVA exposures (at least forty-eight hours apart). Dose may be increased by 10 mg after the fifteenth treatment, according to directions in the manufacturer's labeling. Exposure time should be based on skin type and response to therapy, according to the manufacturer's directions for the specific light source being used. Frequency of exposure may be gradually reduced for maintenance treatment; UVA exposure may be adjusted according to response.

Note: A commonly used dosage schedule according to weight is:

Weight (kg)	Dose (mg)
< 30	10
30–50	20
51–65	30
66–80	40
81–90	50
91–115	60
> 115	70

Vitiligo—

Oral, 20 mg a day, two to four hours before measured periods of UVA exposure, two or three times a week (at least forty-eight hours apart).

Sunlight—Initial exposure time should not exceed fifteen minutes for light skin colors, twenty minutes for medium skin colors, or twenty-five minutes for dark skin colors; may subsequently be increased five minutes each treatment, based on erythema and tenderness.

Artificial light—Initial exposure time should not exceed one-half of that producing erythema after sunlight exposure, or should be based on the minimal phototoxic dose (MPD) and manufacturer's directions for the specific light source being used. The MPD can be determined by irradiating several areas of skin 2 cm in diameter; a range of light exposure times is used and the time that produces erythema at seventy-two hours after exposure is the MPD.

[Skin intolerance to sunlight]—

Orally, 20 mg a day one hour before measured exposure to sunlight or to ultraviolet A light, for up to fourteen days.

Sunlight—Initial exposure time should not exceed fifteen minutes for light skin colors, twenty minutes for medium skin colors, or twenty-five minutes for dark skin colors; subsequently may be increased by five minutes for each treatment, depending on degree of erythema and tenderness.

Note: A commonly used dosage schedule according to weight is:

Weight (kg)	Dose (mg)
< 30	10
30–50	20
51–65	30
66–80	40
81–90	50

Usual pediatric dose
Children up to 12 years of age—Dosage has not been established.
Children 12 years of age and over—See *Usual adult and adolescent dose*.

Strength(s) usually available
U.S.—
10 mg (Rx) [*8-MOP* (tartrazine)].
Canada—
10 mg (Rx) [*Oxsoralen*].

Packaging and storage
Store below 40 °C (104 °F), preferably between 15 and 30 °C (59 and 86 °F) unless otherwise specified by manufacturer. Store in a tight, light-resistant container.

Auxiliary labeling
- Take with food or milk.

Note
Methoxsalen soft gelatin capsules should not be used interchangeably with the hard gelatin capsules.

METHOXSALEN CAPSULES (XXII) (SOFT GELATIN) USP

Usual adult and adolescent dose
[Dermatitis, atopic] or
Psoriasis—

Oral, 400 mcg (0.4 mg) per kg of body weight, one and one-half to two hours before measured periods of high-intensity UVA exposure, two or three times a week or as determined by the patient's schedule for UVA exposures (at least forty-eight hours apart). Exposure time should be based on skin type and response to therapy, according to the manufacturer's directions for the specific light source being used. Frequency of exposure may be gradually reduced for maintenance treatment; UVA exposure may be adjusted according to response.

Note: **The soft capsule dosage form exhibits significantly greater bioavailability and earlier photosensitization onset time than the hard capsule dosage form.** When this dosage form is used, the patient's minimum phototoxic dose (MPD) and phototoxic peak time after drug administration should be determined prior to initiation of photochemotherapy. The manufacturer's directions should be consulted for full information concerning dosage and administration.

[Skin intolerance to sunlight]—

Orally, 20 mg a day one hour before measured exposure to sunlight or to ultraviolet A light, for up to fourteen days.

Sunlight—Initial exposure time should not exceed fifteen minutes for light skin colors, twenty minutes for medium skin colors, or twenty-five minutes for dark skin colors; subsequently may be increased by five minutes for each treatment, depending on degree of erythema and tenderness.

Note: A commonly used dosage schedule according to weight is:

Weight (kg)	Dose (mg)
< 30	10
30–50	20
51–65	30
66–80	40
81–90	50

[Vitiligo]—[1]
Oral, 20 mg a day, one hour before measured periods of ultraviolet light exposure or black fluorescent light, two or three times a week (at least forty-eight hours apart).

Sunlight—Initial exposure time should not exceed fifteen minutes for light skin colors, twenty minutes for medium skin colors, or twenty-five minutes for dark skin colors; subsequently may be increased five minutes each treatment, based on degree of erythema and tenderness.

Artificial light—Initial exposure time should not exceed one half of that producing erythema after sunlight exposure, or should be based on the minimal phototoxic dose (MPD) and manufacturer's directions for the specific light source being used. The MPD can be determined by irradiating several areas of skin 2 cm in diameter; a range of light exposure times is used and the time that produces erythema at seventy-two hours after exposure is the MPD.

Usual pediatric dose
Children up to 12 years of age—Dosage has not been established.
Children 12 years of age and over—See *Usual adult and adolescent dose.*

Strength(s) usually available
U.S.—
10 mg (Rx) [*Oxsoralen-Ultra*].
Canada—
10 mg (Rx) [*Ultra MOP; Oxsoralen-Ultra*].

Packaging and storage
Store below 40 °C (104 °F), preferably between 15 and 30 °C (59 and 86 °F), in a tight container, unless otherwise specified by manufacturer. Protect from light.

Auxiliary labeling
• Take with low-fat food or milk.

Note
Methoxsalen soft gelatin capsules should not be used interchangeably with the hard gelatin capsules.

[1]Not included in Canadian product labeling.

Revised: 07/08/1998

METHOXYFLURANE—See *Anesthetics, Inhalation (Systemic)*

METHSCOPOLAMINE—See *Anticholinergics/Antispasmodics (Systemic)*

METHSUXIMIDE—See *Anticonvulsants, Succinimide (Systemic)*

METHYCLOTHIAZIDE—See *Diuretics, Thiazide (Systemic)*

METHYLCELLULOSE—See *Laxatives (Local)*

METHYLERGONOVINE Systemic†

INN: Methylergometrine

VA CLASSIFICATION (Primary): GU600

Commonly used brand name(s): *Methergine.*

Another commonly used name is methylergometrine.

Note: For a listing of dosage forms and brand names by country availability, see *Dosage Forms* section(s).

†Not commercially available in Canada.

Category
Uterine stimulant.

Indications
Note: Bracketed information in the *Indications* section refers to uses that are not included in U.S. product labeling.

Accepted
Hemorrhage, postpartum (prophylaxis and treatment)
Hemorrhage, postabortal (prophylaxis and treatment)—Methylergonovine is indicated in the prevention or treatment of postpartum or postabortal uterine bleeding due to uterine atony or subinvolution. Its use is not recommended prior to delivery of the placenta since placental entrapment may occur.
[Abortion, incomplete (treatment)]—In cases of incomplete abortion, methylergonovine may be used to hasten expulsion of uterine contents.

Unaccepted
Methylergonovine is not as effective in treatment of migraine as other ergot alkaloids and use is not recommended.

Methylergonovine is not indicated for induction or augmentation of labor, to induce abortion, or in cases of threatened spontaneous abortion because of its propensity to produce nonphysiologic, tetanic contractions and its long duration of action.

Pharmacology/Pharmacokinetics

Physicochemical characteristics
Chemical Group—Amine ergot alkaloid.
Molecular weight—455.51.

Mechanism of action/Effect
Uterine stimulant—
Methylergonovine directly stimulates the uterine muscle to increase force and frequency of contractions. When usual doses of methylergonovine are used, these contractions precede periods of relaxation; when larger doses are used, basal uterine tone is elevated and these relaxation periods will be decreased. Contraction of the uterine wall around bleeding vessels at the placental site produces hemostasis. The sensitivity of the uterus to the oxytocic effect is much greater toward the end of pregnancy. The oxytocic actions of methylergonovine are greater than its vascular effects.

Vasoconstriction—
Methylergonovine, like other ergot alkaloids, produces arterial vasoconstriction by stimulation of alpha-adrenergic and serotonin receptors and inhibition of endothelial-derived relaxation factor release. It is a less potent vasoconstrictor than ergotamine.

Other actions/effects
Methylergonovine has minor actions on the central nervous system (CNS). In the CNS, methylergonovine is a partial agonist and partial antagonist at some serotonin and dopamine receptors. Methylergonovine also possesses weak dopaminergic antagonist actions in certain blood vessels and partial agonist actions at serotonin receptors in umbilical and placental blood vessels. It does not possess significant alpha-adrenergic blocking activity.

Absorption
Absorption is rapid after oral (60%) and intramuscular (78%) administration.

Distribution
Rapidly, primarily to plasma and extracellular fluid following intravenous administration; distribution to tissues also occurs rapidly.

In a study in women who had received 125 mcg of methylergonovine orally 3 times a day for 5 days, concentrations in breast milk ranged from less than 0.5 (limit of detection) to 1.3 nanograms per mL at 1 hour after a 250 mcg oral dose and from 0 to 1.2 nanograms per mL at 8 hours.

Biotransformation
Likely hepatic, with extensive first-pass metabolism.

Half-life
Intravenous—
2 to 3 minutes or less (alpha phase).
20 to 30 minutes or longer (beta phase).

Onset of action
Contraction of uterus, postpartum—
Oral: 5 to 10 minutes.
Intramuscular: 2 to 5 minutes.
Intravenous: Immediate.

Time to peak concentration
In a study in postpartum patients, peak plasma concentrations occurred at 3 hours after a 250 mcg oral dose. In a study in healthy fasting males, peak plasma concentrations occurred at 30 minutes.

Peak serum concentration

In a study in postpartum patients, peak plasma concentrations were 3 nanograms per mL after a 250 mcg oral dose. In a study in healthy fasting males, similar concentrations were achieved. Women given 125 mcg by mouth 3 times a day for 5 days had plasma concentrations within the range of 0.6 to 4.4 nanograms per mL at 1 hour after a 250 mcg oral dose and from 0 to 0.6 nanograms per mL at 8 hours.

Duration of action

Contraction of uterus, postpartum—
- Oral: Approximately 3 hours.
- Intramuscular: Approximately 3 hours.
- Intravenous: 45 minutes (although rhythmic contractions may persist for up to 3 hours).

Elimination

Primarily renal excretion of metabolites; some fecal. Renal elimination of unchanged drug is responsible for less than 5% of total elimination. Methylergonovine does not appear to accumulate after multiple doses.

Precautions to Consider

Cross-sensitivity and/or related problems

Patients sensitive to other ergot derivatives may be sensitive to this medication also, although there is some degree of variation among ergot alkaloids in their ability to elicit oxytocic, CNS, or vasoconstrictive effects.

Pregnancy/Reproduction

Pregnancy—Methylergonovine is contraindicated during pregnancy. Tetanic contractions may result in decreased uterine blood flow and fetal distress.

Labor and delivery—High doses of methylergonovine administered prior to delivery may cause uterine tetany and fetal distress. Methylergonovine should *not* be administered prior to delivery of the placenta. Administration prior to delivery of the placenta may cause captivation of the placenta or missed diagnosis of twin gestation, due to excessive uterine contraction.

Breast-feeding

Problems in humans have not been documented. Ergot alkaloids are excreted in breast milk. However, very little passes into breast milk in humans. In a study in women who had received 125 mcg of methylergonovine orally 3 times a day for 5 days, concentrations in breast milk ranged from less than 0.5 (limit of detection) to 1.3 nanograms per mL at 1 hour after a 250 mcg oral dose and from 0 to 1.2 nanograms per mL at 8 hours.

Inhibition of lactation has not been reported for methylergonovine. However, studies have shown that methylergonovine may interfere with the secretion of prolactin (to a lesser degree than bromocriptine) in the immediate postpartum period. This could result in delayed or diminished lactation with prolonged use.

Ergot alkaloids have the potential to cause chronic ergot poisoning in the infant only if used in the mother in higher-than-recommended doses or if used for a longer period of time than is generally recommended.

Pediatrics

In newborns, elimination of methylergonovine may be prolonged. Neonates inadvertently administered ergonovine in overdose amounts have developed respiratory depression, myoclonic movements, purpuric symptoms, mild jaundice, and severe peripheral vasoconstriction.

Geriatrics

No information is available on the effects of methylergonovine in geriatric patients.

Drug interactions and/or related problems

The following drug interactions and/or related problems have been selected on the basis of their potential clinical significance (possible mechanism in parentheses where appropriate)—not necessarily inclusive (» = major clinical significance):

Note: Combinations containing any of the following medications, depending on the amount present, may also interact with this medication.

Anesthetics, general, especially halothane
(peripheral vasoconstriction may be potentiated by the concurrent use of general anesthetics with methylergonovine)
(concurrent use of halothane in concentrations greater than 1% may interfere with the oxytocic actions of methylergonovine, resulting in severe uterine hemorrhage)

Bromocriptine or
Ergot alkaloids, other
(the incidence of rare cases of hypertension, strokes, seizures, and myocardial infarction associated with the postpartum use of bromocriptine or other ergot alkaloids may be increased with the use of ergot alkaloids)

Nicotine or
Smoking, tobacco
(nicotine absorption from heavy smoking may result in enhanced vasoconstriction)

Nitroglycerin or
Antianginal agents, other
(ergot alkaloids may induce coronary vasospasm, lowering the efficacy of nitroglycerin or other antianginal agents; increased doses of nitroglycerin or antianginal agents and/or use of intracoronary nitroglycerin may be necessary)

Vasoconstrictors, other, including those present in local anesthetics or
Vasopressors
(concurrent use may result in enhanced vasoconstriction; dosage adjustments may be necessary)
(the pressor effect of sympathomimetic pressor amines may be potentiated, resulting in potentially severe hypertension, headache, and rupture of cerebral blood vessels; gangrene developed in a patient receiving both dopamine and ergonovine infusions)

Laboratory value alterations

The following have been selected on the basis of their potential clinical significance (possible effect in parentheses where appropriate)—not necessarily inclusive (» = major clinical significance).

With physiology/laboratory test values

Blood pressure or
Central venous pressure
(may be elevated due to peripheral vasoconstriction primarily of postcapillary vessels; less likely with methylergonovine than ergonovine; has sometimes been associated with preeclampsia, history of hypertension, intravenous administration of methylergonovine, or concurrent use of local anesthetics containing vasoconstrictors; hypotension has also been reported)

Heart rate
(may be decreased due primarily to an increase in vagal tone, and possibly to decreased central sympathetic activity and direct depression of the myocardium)

Prolactin
(serum concentrations may be decreased)

Medical considerations/Contraindications

The medical considerations/contraindications included have been selected on the basis of their potential clinical significance (reasons given in parentheses where appropriate)—not necessarily inclusive (» = major clinical significance).

Except under special circumstances, this medication should not be used when the following medical problems exist:

» Angina pectoris, unstable or
» Myocardial infarction, recent
(vasospasm caused by methylergonovine may precipitate angina or myocardial infarction)

» Cardiovascular disease or
» Coronary artery disease
(patients may be more susceptible to angina or myocardial infarction caused by methylergonovine-induced vasospasm)

» Cerebrovascular accident, history of or
» Transient ischemic attack, history of
(patients may be susceptible to recurrence due to increases in blood pressure)

» Eclampsia or
» Preeclampsia
(may be exacerbated; patients may be more likely to develop methylergonovine-induced hypertension; headaches, severe cardiac arrhythmias, seizures, and cerebrovascular accidents have occurred)

» Hypertension, severe, or history of
(may be exacerbated)

» Occlusive peripheral vascular disease or
» Raynaud's phenomenon, severe
(may be exacerbated; a patient with Raynaud's phenomenon developed impalpable arterial pulses with use of ergonovine)

Risk-benefit should be considered when the following medical problems exist:

Allergy or sensitivity to methylergonovine or other ergot alkaloids

» Hepatic function impairment
(impaired metabolism of methylergonovine may result in ergot overdose)

Hypocalcemia
(oxytocic response to methylergonovine may be reduced; cautious use of intravenous calcium gluconate may restore oxytocic response to methylergonovine)

» Mitral valve stenosis or
» Venoatrial shunts
(vasospasm caused by methylergonovine may precipitate angina or myocardial infarction)

» Renal function impairment

» Sepsis
(possible increased sensitivity to effects of methylergonovine)

Patient monitoring

The following may be especially important in patient monitoring (other tests may be warranted in some patients, depending on condition; » = major clinical significance):

Blood pressure determinations and
Pulse rate determinations and
Uterine response
(recommended at frequent intervals after parenteral therapy to monitor for adverse reactions; especially important with intravenous administration or before repeating doses)

Side/Adverse Effects

Note: Because the duration of therapy with methylergonovine is generally short, many of the side effects seen with other ergot alkaloids do not occur.

The following side/adverse effects have been selected on the basis of their potential clinical significance (possible signs and symptoms in parentheses where appropriate)—not necessarily inclusive:

Those indicating need for medical attention

Incidence less frequent

Bradycardia (slow heartbeat); ***coronary vasospasm*** (chest pain)

Incidence rare

Allergic reaction, including shock; cardiac arrest or ventricular arrhythmias, including fibrillation and tachycardia (irregular heartbeat); ***dyspnea*** (unexplained shortness of breath); ***hypertension, sudden and severe*** (sudden, severe headache; blurred vision; seizures); ***myocardial infarction*** (crushing chest pain; unexplained shortness of breath)—has occurred with the use of ergot preparations in the postpartum period; ***peripheral vasospasm*** (itching of skin; pain in arms, legs, or lower back; pale or cold hands or feet; weakness in legs)—dose-related

Those indicating need for medical attention only if they continue or are bothersome

Incidence more frequent

Nausea—especially after intravenous use; ***uterine cramping; vomiting***—especially after intravenous use

Note: *Uterine cramping* will occur to some degree in all patients and is indicative of efficacy. However, dosage reduction may be required in occasional patients with severe or intolerable uterine cramps.

Incidence less frequent

Abdominal or stomach pain; diarrhea; dizziness; sweating; tinnitus (ringing in the ears)

Overdose

For specific information on the agents used in the management of methylergonovine overdose, see:

- *Charcoal, Activated (Oral-Local)* monograph;
- *Chlorpromazine* in *Phenothiazines (Systemic)* monograph;
- *Diazepam* in *Benzodiazepines (Systemic)* monograph;
- *Hydralazine (Systemic)* monograph;
- *Laxatives (Local)* monograph;
- *Nitroglycerin* in *Nitrates (Systemic)* monograph;
- *Nitroprusside (Systemic)* monograph;
- *Phentolamine (Systemic)* monograph;
- *Phenytoin* in *Anticonvulsants, Hydantoin (Systemic)* monograph; and/or
- *Tolazoline (Parenteral-Systemic)* monograph.

For more information on the management of overdose or unintentional ingestion, **contact a Poison Control Center** (see *Poison Control Center Listing*).

Clinical effects of overdose

The following effects have been selected on the basis of their potential clinical significance (possible signs and symptoms in parentheses where appropriate)—not necessarily inclusive:

Acute

Angina (chest pain); ***bradycardia*** (slow heartbeat); ***confusion; drowsiness; fast, weak pulse; miosis*** (small pupils); ***peripheral vasoconstriction, severe*** (coolness, paleness, or numbness of arms or legs; muscle pain; weak or absent arterial pulse in arms or legs; tingling, itching, and coolness of skin); ***respiratory depression*** (decreased breathing rate or trouble in breathing; bluish color of skin or inside of nose or mouth); ***seizures; tachycardia*** (fast heartbeat); ***unconsciousness; unusual thirst; uterine tetany*** (severe cramping of the uterus)

Chronic

Formication (false feeling of insects crawling on the skin); ***gangrene*** (dry, shriveled appearance of skin on hands, lower legs, or feet); ***hemiplegia*** (paralysis of one side of the body); ***thrombophlebitis*** (pain and redness in an arm or leg)

Note: Chronic overdose symptoms are unlikely with proper use since treatment is of short duration.

Treatment of overdose

Immediate discontinuation of methylergonovine. Since there is no specific antidote for the management of methylergonovine overdose, treatment is primarily supportive and symptomatic and may include the following:

To decrease absorption—
Gastrointestinal decontamination for oral overdose, preferably with multiple doses of activated charcoal and an appropriate cathartic. Gastric lavage may also be considered.

Specific treatment—
Use of nitroglycerin for treatment of myocardial ischemia. Intracoronary nitroglycerin may be necessary.
Use of diazepam or phenytoin for treatment of seizures.
Use of sodium nitroprusside, tolazoline, or phentolamine for treatment of peripheral ischemia.
Use of sodium nitroprusside, chlorpromazine 15 mg, or hydralazine for treatment of severe hypertension.

Monitoring—
Frequent monitoring of vital signs, arterial blood gases, and electrolytes. Electrocardiogram monitoring to assess cardiac function and perfusion. Monitoring of serum methylergonovine levels is not predictive of the outcome of overdose.

Supportive care—
May include maintaining an open airway and breathing, maintaining proper fluid and electrolyte balance, correcting hypertension, and controlling seizures. Patients in whom intentional overdose is known or suspected should be referred for psychiatric consultation.

Patient Consultation

As an aid to patient consultation, refer to *Advice for the Patient, Ergonovine/Methylergonovine (Systemic)*.

In providing consultation, consider emphasizing the following selected information (» = major clinical significance):

Before using this medication

» Conditions affecting use, especially:
Allergies or sensitivity to methylergonovine or other ergot alkaloids
Pregnancy—Should not be used prior to delivery or delivery of the placenta
Breast-feeding—Ergot alkaloids are excreted in breast milk
Other medical problems, especially cardiac or vascular disease, hepatic function impairment, severe hypertension or history of hypertension, renal function impairment, and sepsis

Proper use of this medication

» Importance of not using more medication or using for longer than prescribed; risk of ergotism and gangrene with prolonged use

» Proper dosing
Missed dose: Not taking missed dose; not doubling doses

» Proper storage

Precautions while using this medication

Notifying physician if infection develops, since infection may cause increased sensitivity to medication

Side/adverse effects

Signs of potential side effects, especially allergic reaction, coronary vasospasm or other cardiovascular complications, dyspnea, severe hypertension, or peripheral vasospasm

General Dosing Information

Antiemetic medications such as prochlorperazine may be administered prior to use of methylergonovine.

For parenteral dosage forms only

Because the risk of severe adverse effects is increased with intravenous use of methylergonovine, such use is recommended only for emergencies such as excessive uterine bleeding.

If intravenous use is warranted, administration must be done slowly, over a period of at least 1 minute; some clinicians recommend dilution of the solution with normal saline before administration.

In some patients who do not respond to methylergonovine because of hypocalcemia, cautious intravenous administration of calcium gluconate (provided the patient is not receiving digitalis) may restore the oxytocic action.

Oral Dosage Forms

METHYLERGONOVINE MALEATE TABLETS USP

Usual adult and adolescent dose

Uterine stimulant—

Oral, 200 to 400 mcg (0.2 to 0.4 mg) two to four times a day (every six to twelve hours) until the danger of uterine atony and hemorrhage has passed.

Note: Generally, a treatment course of 48 hours is sufficient. However, in some patients, treatment for up to 7 days may be necessary, especially when used for treatment of incomplete abortion. Oral administration usually follows an initial parenteral dose.

Strength(s) usually available

U.S.—

200 mcg (0.2 mg) (Rx) [*Methergine*].

Canada—

Not commercially available.

Packaging and storage

Store below 40 °C (104 °F), preferably between 15 and 30 °C (59 and 86 °F), unless otherwise specified by manufacturer. Store in a tight container. Protect from light.

Parenteral Dosage Forms

METHYLERGONOVINE MALEATE INJECTION USP

Usual adult and adolescent dose

Uterine stimulant—

Intramuscular or intravenous, 200 mcg (0.2 mg), repeated in two to four hours if necessary, up to five doses.

Strength(s) usually available

U.S.—

200 mcg (0.2 mg) per mL (Rx) [*Methergine*].

Canada—

Not commercially available.

Packaging and storage

Store below 40 °C (104 °F), preferably between 15 and 30 °C (59 and 86 °F), unless otherwise specified by manufacturer. Protect from light. Protect from freezing.

Stability

Discolored solutions or solutions containing visible particles should not be used.

Revised: 06/07/1993

METHYLPHENIDATE Systemic

VA CLASSIFICATION (Primary): CN802

Note: Controlled substance classification

U.S.: Schedule II

Canada: C

Commonly used brand name(s): *Concerta; Daytrana; Metadate® CD; PMS-Methylphenidate; Riphenidate; Ritalin; Ritalin LA®; Ritalin SR; Ritalin-SR.*

Note: For a listing of dosage forms and brand names by country availability, see *Dosage Forms* section(s).

Category

Central nervous system stimulant.

Indications

Note: Bracketed information in the *Indications* section refers to uses that are not included in U.S. product labeling.

Accepted

Attention-deficit hyperactivity disorder (treatment)—Methylphenidate is used as the primary agent in a total treatment program that includes other remedial measures (psychological, educational, and social) to stabilize children age 6 to 12 years [and adults][1] with attention-deficit hyperactivity disorder (ADHD). This complex behavioral syndrome has been known in the past as hyperkinetic child syndrome, minimal brain damage, minimal cerebral dysfunction, or minor cerebral dysfunction.

Narcolepsy (treatment)—Methylphenidate is indicated in the management of the symptoms of narcolepsy.

[Depressive disorder secondary to medical illness (treatment)][1]—Methylphenidate may be useful in selected patients whose medical condition complicates treatment with conventional antidepressants.

Unaccepted

Methylphenidate is *not* recommended for the treatment of depressive disorders amenable to treatment with conventional antidepressants, for the prevention or treatment of normal fatigue states, or for children who exhibit symptoms secondary to environmental factors and/or psychiatric disorders, including psychosis.

---

[1]Not included in Canadian product labeling.

Pharmacology/Pharmacokinetics

Physicochemical characteristics

Molecular weight—269.77.

Solubility—Freely soluble in water and methanol, soluble in alcohol, slightly soluble in chloroform and acetone.

Mechanism of action/Effect

Central nervous system (CNS) stimulant—Although the primary mechanism is largely unknown, the effects of methylphenidate appear to be mediated by blockage of the reuptake mechanism of dopaminergic neurons. In children with attention-deficit hyperactivity disorder, methylphenidate decreases motor restlessness and enhances the ability to pay attention. In narcolepsy, methylphenidate appears to act at the cerebral cortex and subcortical structures, including the thalamus, to produce CNS stimulation, resulting in increased motor activity, increased mental alertness, diminished sense of fatigue, brighter spirits, and mild euphoria.

Absorption

Rapidly and extensively absorbed. Bioavailability is limited and is widely variable between patients due to extensive first-pass metabolism. Food may increase absorption rate but does not affect the extent of absorption. The absolute oral bioavailability of methylphenidate in children is 30% (range 10 to 52%)

Distribution

The volume of distribution (Vol_D) in children is about 20 L per kg of body weight (range, 11 to 33 L/kg).

Protein binding

Low (about 15%).

Biotransformation

Methylphenidate is metabolized primarily by de-esterification to ritalinic acid (α-phenyl-2-piperidine acetic acid, PPAA), which has little to no pharmacologic activity.

Half-life

Plasma half-life—

Ritalin and Ritalin-SR brands of methylphenidate:

Children: 2.4 hours (mean)

Adults: 2.1 hours (mean)

Concerta brand of methylphenidate: approximately 3.5 hours

Ritalin LA brand of methylphenidate:

Children: 2.5 hours (mean)

Adults: 3.5 hours (mean)

Metadate® CD brand of methylphenidate: approximately 6.8 hours

Daytrana™ brand of methylphenidate:

Children 6 to 12 years of age: 3 to 4 hours (d-methylphenidate); 1.4 to 2.9 hours (l-methylphenidate)

Time to peak serum concentration

Prompt-release tablets—

About 2 hours in children and adults (range in children, 0.3 to 4.4 hours).

Extended-release tablets—
Ritalin LA brand of methylphenidate extended-release tablets: 1.8 hours (first peak)
Ritalin-SR brand of methylphenidate extended-release tablets: 4.7 hours (range, 1.3 to 8.2 hours) in children
Concerta brand of methylphenidate extended-release tablets: 6 to 8 hours
Metadate® CD brand of methylphenidate: first peak concentration reached in 1.5 hours and a second peak reached in 4.5 hours.
Note: In 25 to 30% of patients only one observed peak concentration of methylphenidate with Metadate® CD. The first peak concentration was delayed by approximately one hour after ingestion of a high-fat meal.

Peak plasma concentration:
Ritalin and Ritalin-SR brands of methylphenidate—
Following administration of 0.3 mg of methylphenidate per kg of body weight (mg/kg):
Children—10.8 nanograms per mL
Adults—7.8 nanograms per mL
Note: Peak plasma concentrations showed marked variability between subjects.
Ritalin LA brand of methylphenidate—
Following administration of 40 mg of Ritalin LA: an early maximum concentration of 10.2 nanograms per mL due to the immediate release component and a later maximum concentration of 15.3 nanograms per mL representative of the extended release component.
Concerta brand of methylphenidate—
Following administration of 18 mg of methylphenidate: 3.7 nanograms per mL
Metadate® CD brand of methylphenidate—
Following administration of 20 mg of Metadate® CD: an early maximum concentration of 8.6 nanograms per ml due to the immediate release component, and a later maximum concentration of 10.9 nanograms per mL representative of the extended release component.
Note: the peak plasma concentration was increased by 30% when Metadate® CD 40 mg was administered following a high-fat meal.
Daytrana™ brand of methylphenidate—
Following 6 weeks of therapy with 9 hour wear times when applied to alternating hips, the mean peak d-methylphenidate (d-MPH) plasma concentration was 39 ng per mL (range, 0 to 114 ng per mL)
Varied inversely based on age ranging from 25 ng per mL (range, 2 to 80 ng per mL) in 12 year olds, to 53 ng per mL (range 18 to 83 ng per mL) in 6 year olds.
Daytrana™ mean peak d-MPH concentrations were approximately 1.9-fold higher than the highest concentrations after a once-daily oral methylphenidate formulation over a period of 7.5 to 10.5 hours when T_{max} typically occurs. The Daytrana™ peak concentrations on chronic dosing were also higher than C_{maxs} seen with Daytrana™ after single dosing, or 4 days of multiple dosing. With single Daytrana™ doses, peak concentrations were comparable to C_{maxs} from single doses of the once daily oral MPH formulation.
Note: Dose-proportionality was demonstrated in peak plasma concentrations and area under the concentration-time curve (AUC) values for all brands of methylphenidate.

Elimination
Renal—
For Ritalin brands of methylphenidate: 78 to 97% within 48 to 96 hours after an oral dose, < 1% as unchanged methylphenidate
For Concerta brand of methylphenidate: About 90% recovered in urine, approximately 80% as the PPAA metabolite.
Time to peak urinary excretion in children was 1.9 hours (range, 0.3 to 4.4 hours) for Ritalin brand of prompt-release methylphenidate tablets, and 4.7 hours (range, 1.3 to 8.2 hours) for Ritalin-SR brand of methylphenidate extended-release tablets.
An average of 67% of a dose of Ritalin-SR brand of methylphenidate extended-release tablets was excreted in children, as compared to 86% in adults.
Fecal—
1 to 3% within 48 to 96 hours after an oral dose.

Precautions to Consider

Carcinogenicity/Tumorigenicity
In a lifetime carcinogenicity study in a mouse strain that is sensitive to the development of hepatic tumors (B6C3F1 mice), methylphenidate caused an increase in hepatocellular adenomas (benign tumors) at a dose of approximately 60 mg per kg of body weight (mg/kg) a day, or approximately 2.5 times a human dose of 60 mg a day on a mg per square meter of body surface area (mg/m^2) basis. In the same study, male mice showed an increase in hepatoblastomas (rare malignant tumors). There was no increase in total malignant hepatic tumors. A similar study in F344 rats showed no increase in tumors. The significance of these findings to humans is unknown.

Mutagenicity
No mutagenic potential was found in the Ames reverse mutation assay or in the *in vitro* mouse lymphoma cell forward mutation assay. A weak clastogenic response was found in an *in vitro* assay in cultured Chinese Hamster Ovary cells. *In vivo* assays of genotoxic potential of methylphenidate have not been performed. The significance of these findings to humans is unknown.

Pregnancy/Reproduction
Fertility—Studies in male and female mice given up to 160 mg pre kg per day (80 times the human dose based on body surface area) found no effect on fertility
Pregnancy—There are no adequate and well controlled studies in pregnant women. Methylphenidate should be used during pregnancy only if the potential benefit justifies the risk to the fetus..
Studies in rabbits have shown that methylphenidate can cause teratogenic effects.
FDA Pregnancy Category C

Breast-feeding
It is not known whether methylphenidate is distributed into breast milk. Because many drugs are distributed into human milk, caution should be exercised if methylphenidate is administered to a nursing woman.

Pediatrics
The safety and efficacy of methylphenidate in children less than 6 years of age have not been established. Long-term effects of methylphenidate in children are not well established. Children are more prone than adults to develop anorexia, insomnia, stomach pain, tachycardia, and weight loss. Monitoring of growth (both height and weight gain) has been recommended during long-term therapy since chronic administration of methylphenidate may be associated with growth inhibition, although data are inadequate to determine this conclusively. Some clinicians may recommend medication-free periods during methylphenidate treatment to evaluate the need for continued therapy.

Geriatrics
No information is available on the relationship of age to the effects of methylphenidate in geriatric patients.

Drug interactions and/or related problems
The following drug interactions and/or related problems have been selected on the basis of their potential clinical significance (possible mechanism in parentheses where appropriate)—not necessarily inclusive (» = major clinical significance):
Note: Combinations containing any of the following medications, depending on the amount present, may also interact with this medication.
Anticholinergics or other medications with anticholinergic activity (see *Appendix II*)
(concurrent use may intensify anticholinergic effects because of secondary anticholinergic effects of methylphenidate)
Anticonvulsants, especially phenytoin, phenobarbital, and primidone or
Anticoagulants, coumarin- or indanedione-derivative or
Phenylbutazone
(serum concentrations of these medications may be increased because of inhibition of metabolism by methylphenidate, possibly resulting in toxicity; dosage adjustments may be necessary)
Antidepressants, tricyclic, especially desipramine and imipramine or
Selective serotonin reuptake inhibitors
(serum concentrations of these medications may be increased because of inhibition of metabolism by methylphenidate, possibly resulting in toxicity; also, concurrent use may antagonize the effects of methylphenidate)
Antihypertensives or
Diuretics used as antihypertensives
(hypotensive effects may be reduced when these medications are used concurrently with methylphenidate; the patient should be carefully monitored to confirm that the desired effect is being obtained)
» Clonidine or
Centrally acting alpha-2 agonists
(serious adverse events have been reported in concomitant use with clonidine)

» CNS stimulation-producing medications, other (see *Appendix II*)
(concurrent use with methylphenidate may result in additive CNS stimulation to excessive levels, causing nervousness, irritability, insomnia, or possibly seizures or cardiac arrhythmias; close observation is recommended)

Guanethidine
(methylphenidate may decrease the hypotensive effects of guanethidine)

» Monoamine oxidase (MAO) inhibitors, including furazolidone, procarbazine, and selegiline
(concurrent use may potentiate the effects of methylphenidate, possibly resulting in a hypertensive crisis; methylphenidate should not be administered during or within 14 days following the administration of MAO inhibitors)

» Pimozide
(methylphenidate may provoke tics; before therapy with pimozide is initiated, methylphenidate should be withdrawn to determine the cause of observed tics; pimozide is not indicated for the treatment of tics caused by other medications)

Vasopressors
(pressor effects may be potentiated when vasopressors are used concurrently with methylphenidate)

Laboratory value alterations

The following have been selected on the basis of their potential clinical significance (possible effect in parentheses where appropriate)—not necessarily inclusive (» = major clinical significance).

Blood pressure
(may be increased or decreased)

Medical considerations/Contraindications

The medical considerations/contraindications included have been selected on the basis of their potential clinical significance (reasons given in parentheses where appropriate)—not necessarily inclusive (» = major clinical significance).

Except under special circumstances, this medication should not be used when the following medical problems exist:

» Anxiety, tension, or agitation, severe or
» Depressive disorder amenable to treatment with conventional antidepressants or
» Glaucoma or
» Motor tics other than Tourette's disorder
(may be exacerbated)

Hypersensitivity to methylphenidate

Risk-benefit should be considered when the following medical problems exist:

» Cardiac abnormalities, structural
(stimulant products should generally not be used; sudden death reported in association with CNS stimulant treatment at usual doses in children with this condition)

Emotional instability, including history of drug dependence or alcoholism
(increased potential for addiction or abuse; careful supervision is recommended during withdrawal from abusive use since severe depression may occur)

Epilepsy or other seizure disorders
(seizure threshold may be lowered)

Gastrointestinal obstructions, pathologic or iatrogenic
(increased chance of obstructions due to nondeformable controlled-release tablet design)

» Gilles de la Tourette's syndrome, family history or diagnosis of
(motor and vocal tics may be exacerbated; however, some patients, under close supervision, may benefit from cautious trials)

Heart failure or
» Hypertension or
Hyperthyroidism or
Myocardial infarction
(may be exacerbated)

Psychosis
(symptoms of behavior disturbance and thought disorder may be exacerbated in children with psychoses)

Patient monitoring

The following may be especially important in patient monitoring (other tests may be warranted in some patients, depending on condition; » = major clinical significance):

Assessment of amount and frequency of medication use
(recommended at periodic intervals to detect signs of dependence or abuse during long-term therapy)

Blood pressure determinations
(recommended at periodic intervals during therapy, especially for patients with hypertension)

Complete blood cell, differential, and platelet counts
(recommended at periodic intervals for patients on prolonged therapy)

Monitoring of growth, both height and weight gain, in children
(recommended during long-term therapy, since data are inadequate to determine whether chronic administration of methylphenidate may be associated with growth inhibition)

Reassessment of need for therapy for behavioral syndrome in children
(interruption of therapy at periodic intervals is recommended to determine if a recurrence of behavioral symptoms is sufficient to continue therapy; tapering of dose may be necessary to prevent withdrawal symptoms)

» Re-evaluation of the long-term usefulness of the transdermal patch
(periods off medication are recommended to assess the patient's functioning without therapy; effectiveness for long term use [i.e., more than 7 weeks] has not been systematically evaluated in controlled trials)

Side/Adverse Effects

Contact sensitization can occur with methylphenidate transdermal system use. Sensitization should be suspected if erythema is accompanied by evidence of a more intense local reaction (edema, papules, vesicles) that does not significantly improve within 48 hours or spreads beyond the patch site. Patients sensitized by use of methylphenidate transdermal patches may develop systemic sensitization or other systemic reactions if methylphenidate-containing products are taken by other routes. Systemic sensitization manifestations may include a flare up of previous dermatitis or of prior positive patch test sites, or generalized skin eruptions in previously unaffected skin. Other systemic reactions may include headache, fever, malaise, arthralgia, diarrhea, or vomiting.

The following side/adverse effects have been selected on the basis of their potential clinical significance (possible signs and symptoms in parentheses where appropriate)—not necessarily inclusive:

Those indicating need for medical attention

Incidence more frequent

Hypertension (increased blood pressure); ***tachycardia*** (fast heartbeat)—especially with doses greater than 0.5 mg per kg of body weight (mg/kg)

Incidence less frequent

Angina (chest pain); ***arthralgia*** (joint pain); ***dyskinesia*** (uncontrolled movements of the body); ***fever; skin rash or hives; thrombocytopenia*** (rarely, unusual bleeding or bruising; black tarry stools; blood in urine or stools; pinpoint red spots on skin)—usually asymptomatic

Note: *Arthralgia, fever, skin rash or hives,* and *thrombocytopenia* may be indicative of a hypersensitivity reaction to methylphenidate. Rarely, exfoliative dermatitis and erythema multiforme have occurred.

Incidence rare

Allergic contact dermatitis (blistering, burning, crusting, dryness, flaking of skin; itching, scaling, severe redness, soreness, swelling of skin)—with transdermal patch; ***blurred vision or other changes in vision; contact sensitization*** (blistering, burning, itching, peeling, skin rash, redness, swelling, or other signs of irritation)—with transdermal patch; ***convulsions; muscle cramps; Tourette's syndrome*** (uncontrolled vocal outbursts and/or tics [uncontrolled repeated body movements])

Incidence not determined

Abnormal liver function; anemia (pale skin; troubled breathing with exertion; unusual bleeding or bruising; unusual tiredness or weakness); ***cerebral arteritis and/or occlusion*** (confusion; severe or sudden headache; sudden loss of coordination; sudden slurring of speech); ***erythema multiforme*** (blistering, peeling, loosening of skin; chills; cough; diarrhea; fever; itching; joint or muscle pain; red irritated eyes; sore throat; sores, ulcers, or white spots in mouth or on lips unusual tiredness or weakness); ***exfoliative dermatitis*** (cracks in the skin; loss of heat from the body; red, swollen skin; scaly skin); ***leukopenia*** (black, tarry stools; chest pain; chills; cough; fever; painful or difficult urination; shortness of breath; sore throat; sores, ulcers, or white spots on lips or in mouth; swollen glands; unusual bleeding or bruising; unusual tiredness or weakness); ***palpitations*** (fast, irregular, pounding, or racing heartbeat or pulse); ***urticaria*** (hives or welts; itching; redness of skin; skin rash)

With prolonged use or at high doses

Psychosis, toxic (changes in mood; confusion; delusions; depersonalization; hallucinations); ***weight loss***—possibly more frequent in children

Those indicating need for medical attention only if they continue or are bothersome

Incidence more frequent

Anorexia (loss of appetite)—usually transient; possibly more frequent in children; ***CNS stimulation*** (nervousness; trouble in sleeping)—possibly more frequent in children; ***edema*** (swelling at site of application)—with transdermal patch; ***erythema*** (flushing, redness of skin; unusually warm skin)—with transdermal patch; ***nasal congestion*** (stuffy nose); ***papules*** (small, rounded bumps rising from the skin)—with transdermal patch; ***vesicles*** (blisters under the skin)—with transdermal patch

Incidence less frequent

Anger; anxiety (fear; nervousness); ***dizziness; drowsiness; headache; hypomania*** (actions that are out of control; irritability; nervousness; talking, feeling, and acting with excitement); ***insomnia*** (sleeplessness; trouble sleeping; unable to sleep); ***nasopharyngitis*** (stuffy or runny nose; muscle aches; unusual tiredness or weakness; fever; sore throat; headache); ***nausea; scalp hair loss; stomach pain***—possibly more frequent in children; ***vomiting***

Those indicating possible withdrawal and the need for medical attention if they occur after medication is discontinued

Mental depression, severe; unusual behavior; unusual tiredness or weakness

Overdose

For specific information on the agents used in the management of methylphenidate overdose, see:

- *Barbiturates (Systemic)* monograph.

For more information on the management of overdose or unintentional ingestion, **contact a Poison Control Center** (see *Poison Control Center Listing*).

Clinical effects of overdose

The following effects have been selected on the basis of their potential clinical significance (possible signs and symptoms in parentheses where appropriate)—not necessarily inclusive:

Agitation; cardiac arrhythmias (fast or irregular heartbeat); ***confusion; delirium*** (extreme confusion); ***dryness of mouth or mucous membranes; euphoria*** (false sense of well-being); ***fever; flushing; hallucinations*** (seeing, hearing, or feeling things that are not there); ***headache, severe; hyperpyrexia*** (fever); ***hyperreflexia*** (overactive reflexes); ***increased blood pressure; increased sweating; muscle twitching; mydriasis*** (large pupils); ***palpitation*** (fast, pounding, or irregular heartbeat); ***seizures***—may be followed by coma; ***tachycardia*** (fast, pounding, or irregular heartbeat or pulse); ***tremors*** (trembling or shaking); ***vomiting***

Treatment of overdose

Since there is no specific antidote for overdose with methylphenidate, treatment is symptomatic and supportive.

To decrease absorption—

Emptying stomach by gastric lavage.

Specific treatment—

For severe intoxication, administering a short-acting barbiturate before gastric lavage using carefully titrated dosage.

Using external cooling procedures for hyperpyrexia.

For transdermal system—Removing all patches immediately and cleansing the area(s) to remove any remaining adhesive. The continuing absorption of methylphenidate from the skin, even after patch removal, should be considered when treating patients with overdose.

Supportive care—

Maintaining quiet, protective surroundings to minimize external stimulation and to protect patient against self-injury.

Maintaining adequate circulatory and respiratory function.

Patients in whom intentional overdose is confirmed or suspected should be referred for psychiatric consultation.

Note: Usefulness of peritoneal dialysis or extracorporeal hemodialysis in the treatment of methylphenidate overdose has not been established.

Patient Consultation

As an aid to patient consultation, refer to *Advice for the Patient, Methylphenidate (Systemic)*.

In providing consultation, consider emphasizing the following selected information (» = major clinical significance):

Before using this medication

» Conditions affecting use, especially:

Hypersensitivity to methylphenidate or any components of the product

Use in children—Children more likely to develop stomach pain, trouble in sleeping, fast heartbeat, loss of appetite, and weight loss; safety and efficacy not established in children less than 6 years of age

Other medications, especially clonidine, other CNS stimulation-producing medications, MAO inhibitors, or pimozide

Other medical problems, especially severe anxiety, tension, or agitation; depressive disorder amenable to conventional treatment; glaucoma; heart failure, hypertension; hyperthyroidism; motor tics; myocardial infarction; structural cardiac abnormalities; or Tourette's syndrome

Proper use of this medication

» Importance of not using more medication than the amount prescribed, because of possible habit-forming potential

» For transdermal system:

- Importance of reading patient leaflet information
- Encouraging patient to use the administration chart to monitor application and removal time of patch
- Importance of proper application and disposal of the patch
- Applying patch to hip area and avoiding waistline where clothing may cause patch to rub off
- Importance of wearing patch for no more than 9 hours per day

Taking with or after a meal or snack, except *Concerta* brand of methylphenidate extended-release tablets which do not have to be taken with food.

Informing patient that methylphenidate transdermal patch can be worn without regard to food

Taking the last dose of the day of the prompt-release tablets before 6 p.m. to minimize insomnia

Not increasing dose if medication seems less effective after a few weeks; checking with physician

Proper administration for extended-release dosage form: Swallowing whole; not breaking, crushing, or chewing

Appearance of intact tablet shells and insoluble core components in stool to be expected when taking Concerta brand of methylphenidate extended-release tablets

» Proper dosing

Missed dose: Taking as soon as possible; taking any remaining doses for that day at regularly spaced intervals; not doubling doses

» Proper storage

Precautions while using this medication

Regular visits to physician to check progress and to monitor for adverse effects during therapy

Possible dizziness, drowsiness, or changes in vision; not driving, riding a bicycle, operating machinery, or doing anything else that could be dangerous until effects of medication are known.

» Checking with physician if symptoms of allergic contact dermatitis occur

» Checking with physician before discontinuing medication after long-term and/or high-dose therapy; gradual dosage reduction may be necessary to avoid withdrawal symptoms

» Suspected psychological or physical dependence; checking with physician

Side/adverse effects

Possibility of withdrawal effects

Signs of potential side effects, especially hypertension, tachycardia, abnormal liver function, anemia, cerebral arteritis and/or occlusion, leukopenia, palpitations, exfoliative dermatitis, erythema multiforme, angina, arthralgia, dyskinesia, fever, skin rash or hives, thrombocytopenia, allergic contact dermatitis (with transdermal system), blurred vision or other changes in vision, contact sensitization (with transdermal system), convulsions, muscle cramps, Tourette's syndrome, toxic psychosis, or weight loss

General Dosing Information

To reduce the occurrence of insomnia, the last dose of methylphenidate prompt-release tablets for each day should be administered before 6 p.m.

If paradoxical aggravation of symptoms or other adverse events occur, the dosage should be reduced, or, if necessary the drug should be discontinued. If improvement is not observed after appropriate dosage adjustment over a one month period the drug should be discontinued.

Concerta brand methylphenidate brand extended-release tablets have biologically inert components of the tablet that remain intact during gastrointestinal transit and are eliminated in the stool as a tablet shell along with insoluble core components.

When symptoms of attention-deficit hyperactivity disorder are controlled in children, dosage reduction or interruption in therapy may be possible during weekends and school holidays and at other times when the child is under less stress. However, some children may require year-round daily dosing.

Prolonged use of methylphenidate may result in psychological or physical dependence.

When the medication is to be discontinued following high-dose and/or long-term administration, the dosage should be reduced gradually in order to reduce the occurrence of withdrawal symptoms.

Transdermal systems

It is recommended that methylphenidate transdermal patches be applied to the hip area 2 hours before an effect is needed and should be removed 9 hours after application.

Methylphenidate transdermal patches may be removed earlier than 9 hours if a shorter duration of effect is desired or late day side effects appear. Plasma concentrations generally begin declining when the patch is removed. However, absorption may continue for several hours. Individualization of wear time may help manage some of the side effects caused by methylphenidate. If aggravation of symptoms or other adverse events occur, the dosage or wear time should be reduced, or, if necessary, the drug should be discontinued. Residual methylphenidate remains in used patches when worn as recommended.

Diet/Nutrition

Ritalin™ and Ritalin-SR™ brands of methylphenidate tablets should be taken with or after a meal or snack. This will reduce the occurrence of nausea and stomach pain.

Concerta™ brand of methylphenidate extended-release tablets may be administered with or without food, and should be given once daily in the morning.

Metadate® CD brand of methylphenidate extended-release capsules should be administered in the morning, before breakfast. The capsules should be swallowed whole with the aid of liquids and must not be opened, crushed or chewed.

Note: Following the administration of Metadate® CD, the presence of a high fat meal delays the early peak level by one hour. Plasma levels then rise rapidly following the food-induced delay in absorption. A high-fat meal increases the maximum concentration (C_{max}) by 30% and the total concentration (AUC) by 17%.

Oral Dosage Forms

METHYLPHENIDATE HYDROCHLORIDE EXTENDED-RELEASE CAPSULES USP

Usual adult and adolescent dose

For attention-deficit hyperactivity disorder—

Oral, initially 20 mg once a day in the morning, before breakfast. Dosage may be adjusted weekly in 10 to 20 mg increments to a maximum of 60 mg once daily in the morning, before breakfast.

Usual adult prescribing limits

60 mg per day

Usual pediatric dose

For attention-deficit hyperactivity disorder—

Children younger than 6 years of age—

Children up to 6 years of age: Safety and efficacy have not been established.

Children 6 years of age and over—

Children over 6 years of age: Oral, initially 20 mg once a day in the morning, before breakfast. Dosage may be adjusted weekly in 20 mg increments to a maximum of 60 mg once daily in the morning, before breakfast.

Usual pediatric prescribing limits

60 mg

Strength(s) usually available

U.S.—

Note: Metadate CD is an extended-release capsule comprised of both immediate-release (IR) and extended-release (ER) beads such that 30% of the dose (6 mg) is provided by the IR component and 70% of the dose (14 mg) is provided by the ER component.

20 mg (Rx) [*Metadate® CD* (dibutyl sebacate; ethylcellulose aqueous dispersion; FD&C Blue No. 2; polyethylene glycol; gelatin; hydroxypropylmethylcellulose; povidone; sugar spheres)].

10 mg [*Ritalin LA®* (ammonio methacrylate copolymer; black iron oxide; gelatin; methacrylic acid copolymer; polyethylene glycol; red iron oxide; sugar spheres; talc; titanium dioxide; triethyl citrate; yellow iron oxide)].

20 mg [*Ritalin LA®* (ammonio methacrylate copolymer; gelatin; methacrylic acid copolymer; polyethylene glycol; red iron oxide; sugar spheres; talc; titanium dioxide; triethyl citrate)].

30 mg [*Ritalin LA®* (ammonio methacrylate copolymer; gelatin; methacrylic acid copolymer; polyethylene glycol; red iron oxide; sugar spheres; talc; titanium dioxide; triethyl citrate; yellow iron oxide)].

40 mg [*Ritalin LA®* (ammonio methacrylate copolymer; black iron oxide; gelatin; methacrylic acid copolymer; polyethylene glycol; red iron oxide; sugar spheres; talc; titanium dioxide; triethyl citrate; yellow iron oxide)].

Packaging and storage

Store at 25° C (77° F); excursions permitted between 15 and 30 °C (59 and 86°F)

METHYLPHENIDATE HYDROCHLORIDE TABLETS USP

Usual adult and adolescent dose

For narcolepsy or attention-deficit hyperactivity disorder—

Oral, 5 to 20 mg two or three times a day, preferably with or after meals.

Usual adult prescribing limits

90 mg per day.

Usual pediatric dose

Attention-deficit hyperactivity disorder—

Children up to 6 years of age: Dosage has not been established.

Children 6 years of age and older: Oral, initially 5 mg two times a day, with or after breakfast and lunch, the dosage being increased as needed and tolerated by 5 to 10 mg per day at one-week intervals.

Note: If improvement in condition does not occur after appropriate dosage adjustment over a one-month period, it is recommended that the medication be discontinued.

Usual pediatric prescribing limits

60 mg per day.

Strength(s) usually available

U.S.—

5 mg (Rx) [*Ritalin*].

10 mg (Rx) [*Ritalin* (scored)].

20 mg (Rx) [*Ritalin* (scored)].

Canada—

10 mg (Rx) [*PMS-Methylphenidate* (scored); *Riphenidate; Ritalin* (scored)].

20 mg (Rx) [*PMS-Methylphenidate* (scored); *Riphenidate; Ritalin* (scored)].

Packaging and storage

Store below 30 °C (86 °F), preferably between 15 and 30 °C (59 and 86 °F), protected from light, unless otherwise specified by manufacturer. Store in a tight container.

Auxiliary labeling

- May cause drowsiness.

Note

Controlled substance in the U.S. and Canada.

METHYLPHENIDATE HYDROCHLORIDE EXTENDED-RELEASE TABLETS USP

Usual adult and adolescent dose

Methylphenidate extended-release tablets have a duration of action of eight hours. They may be used in place of prompt-release methylphenidate tablets in patients whose dosage over eight hours with prompt-release tablets corresponds to the available strength of extended-release tablets.

Usual pediatric dose

Children up to 6 years of age: Dosage has not been established.

Children 6 years of age and older: See *Usual adult and adolescent dose.*

Strength(s) usually available

U.S.—

20 mg (Rx) [*Ritalin-SR*].

Canada—

20 mg (Rx) [*Ritalin SR*].

Packaging and storage

Store below 30 °C (86 °F), preferably between 15 and 30 °C (59 and 86 °F), protected from light and moisture, unless otherwise specified by manufacturer. Store in a tight container.

Auxiliary labeling
• Swallow tablets whole.
• May cause drowsiness.

Note
Controlled substance in the U.S. and Canada.

METHYLPHENIDATE HYDROCHLORIDE EXTENDED-RELEASE TABLETS USP ONCE DAILY

Usual adult and adolescent dose
Attention Deficit Hyperactivity Disorder (ADHD)—
For patients 13 years of age or older not currently taking methylphenidate, or who are currently taking other stimulants: Oral, initially 18 mg once daily in the morning. Dosage may be increased as needed and tolerated in weekly increments of 18 mg, to a maximum dose of 72 mg per day (not to exceed 2 mg per kg per day).
For patients currently taking methylphenidate prompt-release tablets or extended-release tablets USP (e.g., Ritalin-SR):

Previous Dosage of Methylphenidate prompt-release or extended-release USP tablets	Initial Dose of Concerta brand of Methylphenidate extended-release Tablets
5 mg Methylphenidate prompt-release tablets two or three times daily or 20 mg Methylphenidate extended release tablets USP once daily	18 mg once daily, in the morning
10 mg Methylphenidate prompt-release tablets two or three times daily or 40 mg Methylphenidate extended release tablets USP once daily	36 mg once daily, in the morning
15 mg Methylphenidate prompt-release tablets two or three times daily or 60 mg Methylphenidate extended release tablets USP once daily	54 mg once daily, in the morning

Usual adult and adolescent prescribing limits
Initial conversion dosage should not exceed 54 mg a day. After conversion, dosage may be adjusted to a maximum of 72 mg a day (not to exceed 2mg per kg per day)

Usual pediatric dose
Children up to 6 years of age: Dosage has not been established.
For children 6 to 12 years of age not currently taking methylphenidate, or who are currently taking other stimulants: Oral, initially 18 mg once daily in the morning. Dosage may be increased as needed and tolerated in weekly increments of 18 mg, to a maximum dose of 54 mg per day
For patients currently taking methylphenidate prompt-release tablets or extended-release tablets USP (e.g., Ritalin-SR):

Previous Dosage of Methylphenidate prompt-release or extended-release USP tablets	Initial Dose of Concerta brand of Methylphenidate extended-release Tablets
5 mg Methylphenidate prompt-release tablets two or three times daily or 20 mg Methylphenidate extended release tablets USP once daily	18 mg once daily, in the morning
10 mg Methylphenidate prompt-release tablets two or three times daily or 40 mg Methylphenidate extended release tablets USP once daily	36 mg once daily, in the morning
15 mg Methylphenidate prompt-release tablets two or three times daily or 60 mg Methylphenidate extended release tablets USP once daily	54 mg once daily, in the morning

Usual pediatric prescribing limits
54 mg per day

Strength(s) usually available
U.S.—
18 mg (Rx) [*Concerta* (butylated hydroxytoluene; carnauba wax; cellulose acetate; hydroxypropyl methylcellulose; lactose; phosphoric acid; poloaxmer; polyethylene glycol; polyethylene oxides; sodium chloride; stearic acid; succinic acid; synthetic iron oxides; titanium dioxide; triacetin)].
27 mg (Rx) [*Concerta* (butylated hydroxytoluene; carnauba wax; cellulose acetate; hydroxypropyl methylcellulose; lactose; phosphoric acid; poloaxmer; polyethylene glycol; polyethylene oxides; sodium chloride; stearic acid; succinic acid; synthetic iron oxides; titanium dioxide; triacetin)].
36 mg (Rx) [*Concerta* (butylated hydroxytoluene; carnauba wax; cellulose acetate; hydroxypropyl methylcellulose; lactose; phosphoric acid; poloaxmer; polyethylene glycol; polyethylene oxides; sodium chloride; stearic acid; succinic acid; synthetic iron oxides; titanium dioxide; triacetin)].
54 mg (Rx) [*Concerta* (butylated hydroxytoluene; carnauba wax; cellulose acetate; hydroxypropyl methylcellulose; lactose; phosphoric acid; poloaxmer; polyethylene glycol; polyethylene oxides; sodium chloride; stearic acid; succinic acid; synthetic iron oxides; titanium dioxide; triacetin)].
Canada—
Not commercially available.

Packaging and storage
Store at 25 °C (77 °F), with excursions permitted to 15 and 30 °C (59 and 86 °F). Protect from light and moisture.

Auxiliary labeling
• Swallow tablets whole; Do not crush or chew
• May cause blurred vision
• Take in the morning
• May cause drowsiness.

Note
Controlled substance in the U.S.

METHYLPHENIDATE HYDROCHLORIDE TRANSDERMAL SYSTEMS USP

Usual adult and adolescent dose
Attention deficit hyperactivity disorder (ADHD)—
[2]Transdermal, dosage should be titrated to effect. The recommended dose titration schedule is shown in the table below. Dose titration, final dosage, and wear time should be individualized according to the needs and response of the patient.

Methylphenidate Transdermal System – Recommended Titration Schedule (Patients New to Methylphenidate)

	Upward titration, if response is not maximized			
	Week 1	Week 2	Week 3	Week 4
Patch size	12.5 cm²	18.75 cm²	25 cm²	37.5 cm²
Methylphenidate content per patch	27.5 mg	41.3 mg	55 mg	82.5 mg
Delivered dose*	10 mg	15 mg	20 mg	30 mg
Delivery rate*	(1.1 mg/hr)*	(1.6 mg/hr)*	(2.2 mg/hr)*	(3.3 mg/hr)*

Note: *Nominal in vivo delivery rate in pediatric subjects aged 6 to 12 when applied to the hip, based on a 9-hour wear period.

Patients converting from another formulation of methylphenidate should follow the above titration schedule due to differences in bioavailability of methylphenidate transdermal systems compared to other products.

Usual pediatric dose
Children up to 6 years of age: Dosage has not been established.
Children 6 years of age and older: See *Usual adult and adolescent dose.*

Strength(s) usually available
U.S.—
27.5 mg per patch (Rx) [*Daytrana* (acrylic adhesive; silicone adhesive)].
41.3 mg per patch (Rx) [*Daytrana* (acrylic adhesive; silicone adhesive)].
55 mg per patch (Rx) [*Daytrana* (acrylic adhesive; silicone adhesive)].
82.5 mg per patch (Rx) [*Daytrana* (acrylic adhesive; silicone adhesive)].

Packaging and storage
Store below 25 °C (77 °F); excursions permitted to 15 to 30 °C (59 to 86 °F). Do not store patches unpouched.

Stability
Once the tray is opened, use contents within 2 months. Apply the patch immediately upon removal from the protective pouch.

Auxiliary labeling
• May cause dizziness or drowsiness.
• Do not exceed prescribed dose.
• Apply to dry, clean, hairless area of skin. Use a different application area each time.
• Dispose properly by removing and folding sticky sides together. Discard away from children and pets.

Note
Controlled substance in the U.S. and Canada.

Revised: 04/26/2006
Developed: 08/15/1995

METHYLPREDNISOLONE—See *Corticosteroids—Glucocorticoid Effects (Systemic)*

METHYLTESTOSTERONE—See *Androgens (Systemic)*

METIPRANOLOL—See *Beta-adrenergic Blocking Agents (Ophthalmic)*

METOCLOPRAMIDE Systemic

VA CLASSIFICATION (Primary/Secondary): AU300/GA609

Commonly used brand name(s): *Apo-Metoclop; Metoclopramide omega; Nu-Metoclopramide; PMS-Metoclopramide; Reglan.*

Note: For a listing of dosage forms and brand names by country availability, see *Dosage Forms* section(s).

Category

Dopaminergic blocking agent; gastrointestinal emptying (delayed) adjunct; peristaltic stimulant; antiemetic.

Indications

Note: Bracketed information in the *Indications* section refers to uses that are not included in U.S. product labeling.

Accepted

Radiography, gastrointestinal, adjunct and
Intubation, intestinal—Metoclopramide injection is indicated to facilitate intestinal intubation in adults and children, and to stimulate gastric emptying and intestinal transit of barium in cases where delayed emptying interferes with radiological examinations of stomach or small intestine.

Gastroparesis (treatment)[1]—Metoclopramide is indicated for the relief of symptoms of acute and recurrent diabetic gastroparesis.

Nausea and vomiting, cancer chemotherapy-induced (prophylaxis)—Metoclopramide injection is indicated in high doses for the prevention of nausea and vomiting associated with emetogenic cancer chemotherapy.

Some clinicians may prefer ondansetron to high-dose metoclopramide for prophylaxis of cancer chemotherapy-induced nausea and vomiting because ondansetron is less toxic, and in some studies, has been proven more effective than high-dose metoclopramide.

Nausea and vomiting, postoperative (prophylaxis)—Metoclopramide is indicated for the prophylaxis of postoperative nausea and vomiting in cases where nasogastric suction is undesirable.

Reflux, gastroesophageal (treatment)[1]—Oral metoclopramide is indicated in adults for the symptomatic short-term treatment of heartburn and reflux esophagitis due to delayed gastric emptying. [In infants, it is used in the treatment of chronic vomiting and recurrent bronchopulmonary manifestations associated with gastroesophageal reflux.]

[Nausea and vomiting, postoperative, drug-related (treatment)]—Metoclopramide is used in the treatment of drug-related postoperative nausea and vomiting.

[Gastric emptying, slow (treatment)] or
[Gastric stasis, in preterm infants (treatment)]—Metoclopramide is used for correcting the slow gastric emptying in postvagotomy stasis, in idiopathic stasis, and in various collagen diseases such as scleroderma. In addition, it is used for persistent functional feeding intolerance and gastric stasis in preterm infants.

[Pneumonitis, aspiration (prophylaxis)][1]—Metoclopramide is used prior to general anesthesia to promote gastric emptying and reduce the risk of aspiration, especially in emergency surgery, cesarean sections, or delivery.

[Headache, vascular (treatment adjunct)][1]—Metoclopramide is used to counteract the gastric stasis and nausea associated with migraine, and to promote the absorption of orally administered analgesics given in the treatment of migraine.

[Hiccups, persistent (treatment)][1]—Metoclopramide is used in the control of persistent hiccups.

[Metoclopramide has been used in the treatment of lactation deficiency; however, it has generally been replaced by more effective medications.]

[1]Not included in Canadian product labeling.

Pharmacology/Pharmacokinetics

Physicochemical characteristics

pKa—0.6 and 9.3.

Mechanism of action/Effect

Dopaminergic blocking agents—Gastrointestinal emptying (delayed) adjunct; peristaltic stimulant: Exact mechanism of action is unknown; however, it is believed that metoclopramide inhibits gastric smooth muscle relaxation produced by dopamine, thus enhancing cholinergic responses of the gastrointestinal smooth muscle. Accelerates intestinal transit and gastric emptying by preventing relaxation of gastric body and increasing the phasic activity of antrum. At the same time, this action is accompanied by relaxation of the upper small intestine, resulting in an improved coordination between the body and antrum of the stomach and the upper small intestine. Decreases reflux into the esophagus by increasing the resting pressure of the lower esophageal sphincter and improves acid clearance from the esophagus by increasing amplitude of esophageal peristaltic contractions.

Antiemetic—Dopamine antagonist action raises the threshold of activity in the chemoreceptor trigger zone and decreases the input from afferent visceral nerves. High doses of metoclopramide have been found to antagonize 5-hydroxytryptamine (5-HT) receptors in the peripheral nervous system in animals.

Other actions/effects

Metoclopramide stimulates prolactin secretion and causes a transient increase in circulating aldosterone levels, which may be associated with transient fluid retention.

Absorption

Rapid.

Protein binding

Approximately 30%.

Biotransformation

Hepatic.

Half-life

4 to 6 hours.

Onset of action

Intramuscular—10 to 15 minutes.
Intravenous—1 to 3 minutes.
Oral—30 to 60 minutes.

Time to peak serum concentrations

1 to 2 hours after a single oral dose.

Duration of action

1 to 2 hours.

Elimination

Renal; approximately 85% of an oral dose appears in the urine within 72 hours as unchanged drug and sulfate and glucuronide conjugates.

Precautions to Consider

Cross-sensitivity and/or related problems

Patients sensitive to procaine and procainamide may be sensitive to this medication also.

Mutagenicity/Tumorigenicity

An Ames mutagenicity test performed on metoclopramide was negative.

Dopaminergic blocking medications produce an elevation in prolactin concentrations, which persists during long-term administration. Tissue culture experiments indicate that approximately one third of human breast cancers are prolactin-dependent *in vitro* , a factor of potential importance if the prescription of these medications is contemplated in a patient with a previously detected breast cancer. Although disturbances such as galactorrhea, amenorrhea, gynecomastia, and impotence have been reported, the clinical significance of elevated serum prolactin concentrations is unknown for most patients. An increase in mammary neoplasms has been found in rodents after long-term administration of dopaminergic blocking medications. However, neither clinical studies nor epidemiologic studies conducted to date have shown an association between long-term administration of these medications and mammary tumorigenesis; the available evidence is considered too limited to be conclusive at this time.

Pregnancy/Reproduction

Fertility—Studies in rats, mice, and rabbits at doses from 12 to 250 times the human dose have shown that metoclopramide does not impair fertility.

Pregnancy—Extensive studies in humans have not been done.

Studies in animals have not shown that metoclopramide causes adverse effects in the fetus.

FDA Pregnancy Category B.

Breast-feeding
Problems in humans have not been documented; however, risk-benefit must be considered since metoclopramide is distributed into breast milk.

Pediatrics
Safety and effectiveness in pediatric patients have not been established.
Extrapyramidal effects, especially dystonic reactions, of metoclopramide are more likely to occur in children shortly after initiation of therapy, and usually with doses higher than 0.5 mg per kg of body weight (mg/kg) per day. Methemoglobinemia has been reported in premature and full-term neonates receiving metoclopramide intramuscularly at a dose of 1 to 2 mg/kg a day for 3 days or more.
Care should be exercised; metoclopramide's prolonged clearance in neonates may produce excessive serum concentrations. In addition neonates have reduced levels of NADH-cytochrome b_5 reductase which make neonates more susceptible to methemoglobinema.

Geriatrics
Extrapyramidal effects, especially parkinsonism and tardive dyskinesia, of metoclopramide are more likely to occur in elderly patients following usual or high doses over a long period of time. Geriatric patients should therefore receive the lowest possible dose of metoclopramide that is effective. If parkinsonian-like symptoms develop, metoclopramide should be discontinued before initiating any specific anti-parkinsonian agents.
Sedation has been reported in metoclopramide users. In the elderly sedation may cause confusion and and manifest as over-sedation.

Drug interactions and/or related problems
The following drug interactions and/or related problems have been selected on the basis of their potential clinical significance (possible mechanism in parentheses where appropriate)—not necessarily inclusive (» = major clinical significance):

Note: Only specific interactions between metoclopramide and other oral medications have been identified in this monograph. However, because of increased gastrointestinal motility and decreased gastric emptying time caused by metoclopramide, absorption of oral medications from the stomach may be decreased, while absorption from the small intestine may be enhanced.

Combinations containing any of the following medications, depending on the amount present, may also interact with this medication.

Acetaminophen, or
Tetracycline
(concurrent use may increase rate and/or extent of absorption from the small intestine)

» Alcohol
(concurrent use may increase the central nervous system [CNS] depressant effects of either alcohol or metoclopramide; concurrent use also may accelerate gastric emptying of alcohol, thus possibly increasing its rate and extent of absorption from the small intestine)

Anticholinergics or other medications with anticholinergic activity (see *Appendix II*) or
Opioid-containing medications
(concurrent use may antagonize the effects of metoclopramide on gastrointestinal motility)

Apomorphine
(prior administration of metoclopramide may decrease the emetic response to apomorphine; also, concurrent use may potentiate the CNS depressant effects of either apomorphine or metoclopramide)

Bromocriptine
(metoclopramide may increase serum prolactin concentrations and interfere with effects of bromocriptine; dosage adjustment of bromocriptine may be necessary)

Cimetidine
(concurrent use may decrease the effect of cimetidine due to decreased absorption)

» CNS depression-producing medications, other (see *Appendix II*)
(concurrent use may increase the sedative effects of either these medications or metoclopramide)

Cyclosporine
(the decrease in gastric emptying time caused by metoclopramide may increase the bioavailability of cyclosporine; monitoring of cyclosporine concentrations may be necessary)

Digoxin
(concurrent use may decrease absorption of digoxin from stomach; dosage adjustment of digoxin may be necessary)

Extrapyramidal reaction-causing medications (see *Appendix II*)
(concurrent use with metoclopramide may increase the frequency and severity of extrapyramidal effects)

Hepatotoxic medications (see *Appendix II*)
(concurrent use with metoclopramide may increase the risk of hepatotoxicity)

Levodopa
(metoclopramide has been reported to decrease the effectiveness of levodopa with concurrent use)

Mexiletine
(concurrent use with metoclopramide may accelerate absorption of mexiletine)

Monoamine oxidase (MAO) inhibitors, including furazolidine and procarbazine
(metoclopramide releases catecholamines in patients with essential hypertension and should be used cautiously, if at all, in patients receiving MAO inhibitors)

Pergolide
(dopamine antagonists such as metoclopramide may decrease the effectiveness of pergolide)

Succinylcholine
(metoclopramide has been reported to prolong succinylcholine block; dosage reduction of succinylcholine may be necessary with concurrent use)

Laboratory value alterations
The following have been selected on the basis of their potential clinical significance (possible effect in parentheses where appropriate)—not necessarily inclusive (» = major clinical significance).

With diagnostic test results
Gonadorelin test
(concurrent use with metoclopramide may blunt the response to gonadorelin by increasing serum prolactin concentrations)

Hepatic function test
(results may be altered)

With physiology/laboratory test values
Aldosterone and
Prolactin, serum
(concentrations may be increased)

Medical considerations/Contraindications
The medical considerations/contraindications included have been selected on the basis of their potential clinical significance (reasons given in parentheses where appropriate)—not necessarily inclusive (» = major clinical significance).

Except under special circumstances, this medication should not be used when the following medical problems exist:

» Epilepsy
(severity and frequency of seizures or extrapyramidal effects may be increased)

» Gastrointestinal hemorrhage, mechanical obstruction, or perforation
(stimulation of gastrointestinal motility may aggravate condition)

» Hypersensitivity to metoclopramide, procaine, or procainamide

» Pheochromocytoma
(may cause hypertensive crisis)

Risk-benefit should be considered when the following medical problems exist:

Asthma
(administration of metoclopramide may increase risk of bronchospasm)

Cirrhosis, or
Congestive heart failure
(patients may be at risk for developing fluid retention and volume overload)

Depression, mental
(condition may be exacerbated)

Hypertension
(administration of intravenous metoclopramide may worsen condition due to release of catecholamines)

NADH-cytochrome $b_5$reductase deficiency
(administration of metoclopramide may increase risk of developing methemoglobinemia and/or sulfhemoglobinemia)

Parkinson's disease
(symptoms may be exacerbated)

» Renal failure, severe, chronic
(risk of extrapyramidal effects may be increased; reduced dosage is recommended)

Patient monitoring
The following may be especially important in patient monitoring (other tests may be warranted in some patients, depending on condition; » = major clinical significance):

Blood glucose levels
(exogenously administered insulin may begin to act before food has left the stomach leading to hypoglycemia; insulin dosage or timing of dosage may require adjustment)

Side/Adverse Effects

Note: Methemoglobinemia has been reported in premature and full-term neonates receiving metoclopramide at a dose of 1 to 4 mg per kg of body weight (mg/kg) a day for 1 to 3 days or more.

The following side/adverse effects have been selected on the basis of their potential clinical significance (possible signs and symptoms in parentheses where appropriate)—not necessarily inclusive:

Those indicating need for medical attention

Incidence rare

Agranulocytosis (chills; fever; sore throat; general feeling of tiredness or weakness); ***cardiovascular effects, specifically hypotension*** (dizziness or fainting); ***hypertension*** (dizziness; severe or continuing headaches; increase in blood pressure); ***tachycardia*** (fast or irregular heartbeat); ***extrapyramidal effects, dystonic*** (muscle spasms of face, neck, and back; tic-like or twitching movements; twisting movements of body; inability to move eyes; weakness of arms and legs); ***extrapyramidal effects, parkinsonian*** (difficulty in speaking or swallowing; loss of balance control; mask-like face; shuffling walk; stiffness of arms or legs; trembling and shaking of hands and fingers); ***hepatotoxicity*** (abdominal pain or tenderness; clay colored stools; dark urine; decreased appetite; fever; headache; itching; loss of appetite; nausea and vomiting; skin rash; swelling of feet or lower legs; unusual tiredness or weakness; yellow eyes or skin); ***neuroleptic malignant syndrome (NMS)*** (convulsions; difficulty in breathing; fast heartbeat; high fever; high or low blood pressure; increased sweating; loss of bladder control; severe muscle stiffness; unusually pale skin; tiredness); ***tardive dyskinesia*** (lip smacking or puckering; puffing of cheeks; rapid or worm-like movements of tongue; uncontrolled chewing movements; uncontrolled movements of arms and legs)—usually occurs after at least one year of continuous treatment and may persist after discontinuation of metoclopramide

Note: *Extrapyramidal effects* may occur at therapeutic doses in any age group. However, they occur more frequently in children and young adults, and at the higher doses used in prophylaxis of vomiting due to cancer chemotherapy. *Dystonic* reactions may start within minutes after start of intravenous therapy and disappear within 24 hours after discontinuation of metoclopramide. Onset of *parkinsonian* symptoms may vary from a few weeks to several months after initiation of therapy; symptoms are reversible upon discontinuation of metoclopramide.

With high doses

Agitation (unusual nervousness, restlessness, or irritability); ***panic-like sensation; restless legs syndrome*** (aching or discomfort in lower legs or sensation of crawling in legs)

Note: These effects may occur within minutes of receiving high doses of metoclopramide and may last for 2 to 24 hours.

Those indicating need for medical attention only if they continue or are bothersome

Incidence more frequent

Diarrhea—with high doses; ***drowsiness; restlessness; unusual tiredness or weakness***

Incidence less frequent or rare

Breast tenderness and swelling; changes in menstruation; constipation; dizziness; headache; impotence (loss in sexual ability, desire, drive, or performance; decreased interest in sexual intercourse; inability to have or keep an erection); ***incontinence*** (loss of bladder control); ***insomnia*** (trouble in sleeping); ***mental depression; prolactin stimulation*** (increased flow of breast milk); ***nausea; skin rash; urinary frequency*** (increased need to urinate; passing urine more often); ***unusual dryness of mouth; unusual irritability***

Overdose

For specific information on the agents used in the management of metoclopramide overdose, see:
- *Diphenhydramine* in *Antihistamines (Systemic)* monograph; and/or
- *Methylene Blue (Systemic)* monograph.

For more information on the management of overdose or unintentional ingestion, **contact a Poison Control Center** (see *Poison Control Center Listing*).

Clinical effects of overdose

Symptoms are self-limiting and usually disappear within 24 hours.

The following have been selected on the basis of their potential clinical significance (possible signs and symptoms in parentheses where appropriate)—not necessarily inclusive:

Confusion; drowsiness, severe; extrapyramidal effects, severe; seizures

Treatment of overdose

To decrease absorption—
Dialysis is not likely to be an effective method of drug removal in overdose situations; hemodialysis and continuous ambulatory peritoneal dialysis do not remove significant amounts of metoclopramide.

Specific treatment—
Anticholinergic or antiparkinson drugs or antihistamines with anticholinergic properties (50 mg of diphenhydramine administered intramuscularly in adults and 1 mg per kg of body weight [mg/kg] intramuscularly or intravenously in infants and children) to help in controlling the extrapyramidal reactions.

Methylene blue (1 to 2 mg/kg of a 1% solution injected intravenously over a 5-minute period) is used to reverse methemoglobinemia resulting from metoclopramide administration in premature and full-term infants.

Supportive care—
Patients in whom intentional overdose is confirmed or suspected should be referred for psychiatric consultation.

Patient Consultation

As an aid to patient consultation, refer to *Advice for the Patient, Metoclopramide (Systemic).*

In providing consultation, consider emphasizing the following selected information (» = major clinical significance):

Before using this medication

» Conditions affecting use, especially:
Sensitivity to metoclopramide, procaine, or procainamide
Breast-feeding—Distributed into breast milk
Use in children—Extrapyramidal effects more likely; increased risk of methemoglobinemia in premature and full-term infants
Use in the elderly—Extrapyramidal effects more likely
Other medications, especially acetaminophen, alcohol and CNS depressants, tetracycline
Other medical problems, especially epilepsy; gastrointestinal bleeding, mechanical obstruction, or perforation; pheochromocytoma; or severe renal function impairment

Proper use of this medication

» Taking 30 minutes before meals and at bedtime (for oral dosage forms)
» Not taking more medication than the amount prescribed
» Proper administration of metoclopramide oral solution (concentrate): Mix with liquid or semi-solid food, such as water, juices, soda or soda-like beverages, applesauce, and puddings
» Proper dosing
Missed dose: Using as soon as possible; not using if almost time for next dose
» Proper storage

Precautions while using this medication

» Avoiding use of alcohol or other CNS depressants
» Caution if drowsiness occurs

Side/adverse effects

Signs of potential side effects, especially agranulocytosis, cardiovascular effects, extrapyramidal effects, hepatotoxicity, neuroleptic malignant syndrome (NMS), and tardive dyskinesia

General Dosing Information

In patients with severe renal function impairment (i.e., creatinine clearance < 40 mL per minute), the normally prescribed dose should be reduced by 50%, since adverse effects are more likely to be exacerbated.

For parenteral dosage forms only

Intravenous injections of metoclopramide should be made *slowly* over a 1- to 2-minute period, since a transient but intense feeling of anxiety and restlessness followed by drowsiness may occur with rapid administration.

Intravenous infusion should be made *slowly* over a period of not less than 15 minutes. Metoclopramide injection may be diluted for intravenous infusion with 50 mL of 5% dextrose in water, sodium chloride injection, 5% dextrose in 0.45% sodium chloride, Ringer's injection, or lactated Ringer's injection.

For treatment of adverse effects and/or overdose
Recommended treatment for metoclopramide's adverse effects and/or overdose includes:
• Anticholinergic or antiparkinson drugs or antihistamines with anticholinergic properties (50 mg of diphenhydramine administered intramuscularly in adults and 1 mg per kg of body weight [mg/kg] intramuscularly or intravenously in infants and children) to help in controlling the extrapyramidal reactions.
• Methylene blue (1 to 2 mg/kg of a 1% solution injected intravenously over a 5-minute period) is used to reverse methemoglobinemia resulting from metoclopramide administration in premature and full-term infants.

Oral Dosage Forms

Note: Bracketed uses in the *Dosage Forms* section refer to categories of use and/or indications that are not included in U.S. product labeling.

The dosing and strengths of the dosage forms available are expressed in terms of metoclopramide base.

METOCLOPRAMIDE ORAL SOLUTION USP

Usual adult and adolescent dose
Treatment of diabetic gastroparesis[1]—
Oral, 10 mg (base) thirty minutes before symptoms are likely to occur or before each meal and at bedtime, up to four times a day.

Note: In the initial treatment of diabetic gastroparesis, the parenteral route of administration is recommended if severe symptoms are present. Therapy may begin at 10 mg (base) administered intramuscularly or intravenously three or four times a day, the dose adjusted as needed.

Treatment of gastroesophageal reflux[1]—
Oral, 10 to 15 mg (base) thirty minutes before symptoms are likely to occur or before each meal and at bedtime, up to four times a day.

Note: Intermittent symptoms may be treated by taking 20 mg of metoclopramide prior to the provoking situation.

[Treatment of hiccups][1]—
Oral, 10 to 20 mg (base) four times a day for seven days. An initial dose of 10 mg intramuscularly may be given if necessary.

Note: In patients with renal function impairment whose creatinine clearance is less than 40 mL per minute, initial dosage should be reduced by approximately one half.

Usual adult and adolescent prescribing limits
500 mcg (0.5 mg) per kg of body weight per day.

Usual pediatric dose
Gastrointestinal emptying (delayed) adjunct or
Peristaltic stimulant—
Oral, 0.1 to 0.2 mg per kg of body weight per dose, given thirty minutes before meals and at bedtime.

Strength(s) usually available
U.S.—
5 mg (base) per 5 mL (Rx) [*Reglan;* GENERIC].
Canada—
5 mg (base) per 5 mL (Rx) [*PMS-Metoclopramide*].

Packaging and storage
Store between 20 and 25 °C (68 and 77 °F), in a tight container, unless otherwise specified by manufacturer. Protect from light. Protect from freezing.

Auxiliary labeling
• May cause drowsiness.
• Avoid alcoholic beverages.

METOCLOPRAMIDE HYDROCHLORIDE ORAL SOLUTION (CONCENTRATE)

Usual adult and adolescent dose
See *Metoclopramide Oral Solution USP*.

Usual adult and adolescent prescribing limits
See *Metoclopramide Oral Solution USP*.

Usual pediatric dose
See *Metoclopramide Oral Solution USP*.

Strength(s) usually available
U.S.—
Note: Not commercially available.
Canada—
Not commercially available.

Packaging and storage
Store between 15 and 30 °C (59 and 86 °F), in a tight container, unless otherwise specified by manufacturer. Protect from light. Protect from freezing.

Preparation of dosage form
Each dose should be mixed with liquid or semi-solid food such as water, juices, soda or soda-like beverages, applesauce, or puddings.

Auxiliary labeling
• Dilute before use.
• May cause drowsiness.
• Avoid alcoholic beverages.

METOCLOPRAMIDE TABLETS USP

Usual adult and adolescent dose
See *Metoclopramide Oral Solution USP*.

Usual adult and adolescent prescribing limits
See *Metoclopramide Oral Solution USP*.

Usual pediatric dose
See *Metoclopramide Oral Solution USP*.

Usual geriatric dose
See *Metoclopramide Oral Solution USP*.

Strength(s) usually available
U.S.—
5 mg (Rx) [*Reglan* (scored); GENERIC].
10 mg (Rx) [*Reglan* (scored); GENERIC].
Canada—
5 mg (Rx) [*Apo-Metoclop; Nu-Metoclopramide; PMS-Metoclopramide;* GENERIC].
10 mg (Rx) [*Apo-Metoclop; Nu-Metoclopramide* (scored); *PMS-Metoclopramide;* GENERIC].

Packaging and storage
Store between 20 and 25 °C (68 and 77 °F), unless otherwise specified by manufacturer. Store in a tight, light-resistant container.

Auxiliary labeling
• May cause drowsiness.
• Avoid alcoholic beverages.

Parenteral Dosage Forms

Note: Bracketed uses in the *Dosage Forms* section refer to categories of use and/or indications that are not included in U.S. product labeling.

METOCLOPRAMIDE INJECTION USP

Usual adult and adolescent dose
Gastrointestinal emptying (delayed) adjunct or
Peristaltic stimulant—
Intravenous, 10 mg as a single dose.
[Treatment of hiccups][1]—
Intramuscular, 10 mg initially, followed by oral metoclopramide at a dose of 10 to 20 mg four times a day for seven days.
Antiemetic: For prevention of cancer chemotherapy-induced emesis—
Intravenous infusion, 2 mg per kg of body weight, administered thirty minutes before cisplatin or other highly emetogenic chemotherapeutic agent; may be repeated as needed every two or three hours.

Note: For prevention of emesis induced by chemotherapeutic agents with low emetic potential—Intravenous infusion, 1 mg per kg of body weight.

Continuous intravenous infusion, 3 mg per kg of body weight before chemotherapy, followed by 0.5 mg per kg of body weight per hour for eight hours.
Antiemetic: For prevention of postoperative emesis—
Intramuscular, 10 to 20 mg near the end of surgery.

Usual pediatric dose
Antiemetic—For prevention of cancer chemotherapy-induced emesis or
Gastrointestinal emptying (delayed) adjunct or
Peristaltic stimulant—
Intravenous, 1 mg per kg of body weight as a single dose. May be repeated one time after sixty minutes.

Note: To reduce the chance of increased adverse reactions, dosages should not exceed 2 mg per kg of body weight. Some clinicians recommend concurrent therapy with diphenhydramine at an intravenous dose of 1 mg per kg of body weight 15 minutes prior to metoclopramide infusion to limit side effects that may occur with doses of less than 2 mg per kg of body weight.

Strength(s) usually available
U.S.—
5 mg per mL (Rx) [*Reglan;* GENERIC].

Canada—
5 mg per mL (Rx) [*Metoclopramide omega;* GENERIC].

Packaging and storage

Store between 15 and 30 °C (59 and 86 °F), unless otherwise specified by manufacturer. Protect from light (if injection does not contain an antioxidant).

Preparation of dosage form

Doses of Metoclopramide Injection USP in excess of 10 mg may be mixed with 50 mL of 0.9% sodium chloride injection, 5% dextrose injection, 5% dextrose in 0.45% sodium chloride injection, Ringer's injection, or lactated Ringer's injection.

Stability

Unused portion should be discarded.

Dilutions of metoclopramide injection may be stored for up to 48 hours after preparation if protected from light, or 24 hours if not protected from light.

Dilutions of metoclopramide and 0.9% sodium chloride may be stored frozen for up to 4 weeks after preparation.

Incompatibilities

Metoclopramide injection is incompatible with calcium gluconate, cephalothin sodium, chloramphenicol sodium, cisplatin, erythromycin lactobionate, furosemide, methotrexate, penicillin G potassium, and sodium bicarbonate.

[1]Not included in Canadian product labeling.

Revised: 04/02/2004

METOLAZONE—See *Diuretics, Thiazide (Systemic)*

METOPROLOL—See *Beta-adrenergic Blocking Agents (Systemic)*

METRONIDAZOLE Systemic

VA CLASSIFICATION (Primary/Secondary): AM900/AP109; AP200; GA900

Commonly used brand name(s): *Apo-Metronidazole; Flagyl; Flagyl ER; Flagyl I.V.; Flagyl I.V. RTU; Metric 21; Metro I.V.; Novonidazol; Protostat; Trikacide.*

Note: For a listing of dosage forms and brand names by country availability, see *Dosage Forms* section(s).

Category

Antibacterial (systemic); antiprotozoal; bowel disease (inflammatory) suppressant; anthelmintic (systemic).

Indications

Note: Bracketed information in the *Indications* section refers to uses that are not included in U.S. product labeling.

Accepted

Amebiasis, extraintestinal (treatment)—Metronidazole is indicated in the treatment of extraintestinal amebiasis, including amebic liver abscess, caused by *Entamoeba histolytica.* When used in the treatment of invasive amebiasis, metronidazole should be administered concurrently or sequentially with a luminal amebicide (e.g., iodoquinol, paromomycin, tetracycline, diloxanide furoate). When used in the treatment of amebic liver abscesses, metronidazole therapy does not obviate the need for aspiration of the abscess.

Amebiasis, intestinal (treatment)—Oral metronidazole is indicated in the treatment of acute intestinal amebiasis caused by *Entamoeba histolytica.* Metronidazole may not eradicate intestinal amebic infections, requiring treatment with a luminal amebicide.

Bone and joint infections (treatment)—Metronidazole is indicated in the treatment of bone and joint infections caused by *Bacteroides* species, including the *B. fragilis* group (*B. fragilis, B. distasonis, B. ovatus, B. thetaiotaomicron, B. vulgatus*).

Brain abscess (treatment)—Metronidazole is indicated in the treatment of brain abscess caused by *Bacteroides* species, including the *B. fragilis* group.

Central nervous system (CNS) infections (treatment)—Metronidazole is indicated in the treatment of CNS infections, including meningitis, caused by *Bacteroides* species, including the *B. fragilis* group.

Endocarditis, bacterial (treatment)—Metronidazole is indicated in the treatment of endocarditis caused by *Bacteroides* species, including the *B. fragilis* group.

Intra-abdominal infections (treatment)—Metronidazole is indicated in the treatment of intra-abdominal infections, including peritonitis, intra-abdominal abscess, and liver abscess, caused by *Bacteroides* species, including the *B. fragilis* group, *Clostridium* species, *Eubacterium* species, *Peptococcus* species, and *Peptostreptococcus* species.

Pelvic infections, female (treatment)—Metronidazole is indicated in the treatment of female pelvic infections, including endometritis, endomyometritis, tubo-ovarian abscess, and postsurgical vaginal cuff infections, caused by *Bacteroides* species, including the *B. fragilis* group, *Clostridium* species, *Peptococcus* species, and *Peptostreptococcus* species.

Perioperative infections, colorectal (prophylaxis)—Intravenous metronidazole is indicated for the prophylaxis of perioperative infections during colorectal surgery.

Pneumonia, *Bacteroides* species (treatment)—Metronidazole is indicated in the treatment of lower respiratory tract infections, including pneumonia, empyema, and lung abscess, caused by *Bacteroides* species, including the *B. fragilis* group.

Septicemia, bacterial (treatment)—Metronidazole is indicated in the treatment of bacterial septicemia caused by *Bacteroides* species, including the *B. fragilis* group, and *Clostridium* species.

Skin and soft tissue infections (treatment)—Metronidazole is indicated in the treatment of skin and soft tissue infections caused by *Bacteroides* species, including the *B. fragilis* group, *Clostridium* species, *Fusobacterium* species, *Peptococcus* species, and *Peptostreptococcus* species.

Trichomoniasis (treatment)—Oral metronidazole is indicated in the treatment of symptomatic and asymptomatic trichomoniasis, in males and females, caused by *Trichomonas vaginalis.*

Vaginosis, bacterial (treatment)—Oral metronidazole (extended release formulation) is indicated in the treatment of bacterial vaginosis caused by *Gardnerella vaginalis, Mobiluncus* spp, *mycoplasma hominis* and anaerobes (*Peptostreptococcus* spp and *Bacteroides* spp).

[Balantidiasis (treatment)][1]—Metronidazole is used in the treatment of *Balantidium coli* infection.

[Bowel disease, inflammatory (treatment)][1]—Metronidazole is used in the treatment of inflammatory bowel disease.

[Colitis, antibiotic-associated (treatment)][1]—Metronidazole is used in the treatment of antibiotic-associated diarrhea and colitis caused by *C. difficile.*

[Dracunculiasis (treatment)][1]—Metronidazole is used in the treatment of dracunculiasis (guinea worm infection) caused by *Dracunculus medinensis.* It decreases the inflammation around the ulcer, increasing the ease of removing the worm.

[Gastritis, *Helicobacter pylori*–associated (treatment adjunct)][1] or
[Ulcer, duodenal, *Helicobacter pylori*–associated (treatment adjunct)][1]—Some studies indicate that metronidazole may be effective, in combination with bismuth subsalicylate or colloidal bismuth subcitrate, and other oral antibiotic therapy, such as ampicillin or amoxicillin, in the treatment of *Helicobacter pylori*–associated gastritis and duodenal ulcer. However, metronidazole resistance may occur, especially in patients who have been previously exposed to metronidazole.

[Giardiasis (treatment)][1]—Oral metronidazole is used in the treatment of giardiasis caused by *Giardia lamblia.*

[Periodontal infections (treatment)][1]—Metronidazole is used in the treatment of periodontal infections caused by *Bacteroides* species.

Not all species or strains of a particular organism may be equally susceptible to metronidazole.

Unaccepted

Metronidazole is not effective against facultative anaerobes, obligate aerobes, *Propionibacterium acnes, Actinomyces* species, or *Candida albicans.*

[1]Not included in Canadian product labeling.

Pharmacology/Pharmacokinetics

Physicochemical characteristics

Molecular weight—
Metronidazole: 171.16.
Metronidazole hydrochloride: 207.62.

Mechanism of action/Effect
Antibacterial (systemic); antiprotozoal—Microbicidal; active against most obligate anaerobic bacteria and protozoa by undergoing intracellular chemical reduction via mechanisms unique to anaerobic metabolism. Reduced metronidazole, which is cytotoxic but short-lived, interacts with DNA to cause a loss of helical structure, strand breakage, and resultant inhibition of nucleic acid synthesis and cell death.

Absorption
Well absorbed orally; bioavailability at least 80%.

Distribution
Distributed to saliva, bile, seminal fluid, breast milk, bone, liver and liver abscesses, lungs, and vaginal secretions; crosses the placenta and blood-brain barrier, also.

Vol_D—
- In adults: Approximately 0.55 L/kg.
- In neonates: 0.54–0.81 L/kg.

Protein binding
Low (<20%).

Biotransformation
Hepatic; metabolized primarily by side-chain oxidation and glucuronide conjugation to 2-hydroxymethyl (also active) and other metabolites.

Half-life
In adults—
- Normal liver function: 8 hours (range, 6 to 12 hours).
- Alcoholic liver disease: 18 hours (range, 10 to 29 hours).

In neonates—
- 28 to 30 weeks gestational age: Approximately 75 hours.
- 32 to 35 weeks gestational age: Approximately 35 hours.
- 36 to 40 weeks gestational age: Approximately 25 hours.

Time to peak serum concentration:
1 to 2 hours (oral).

Peak serum concentration
Peak serum concentrations following a 250-mg, 500-mg, and 2-gram oral dose are approximately 6, 12, and 40 mcg/mL, respectively.

At recommended intravenous doses, peak steady-state serum concentrations are approximately 25 mcg/mL; trough concentrations are approximately 18 mcg/mL.

Elimination
Renal—60 to 80%; of this amount, approximately 20% excreted unchanged in urine. Renal clearance approximately 10 mL/min/1.73 M^2.

Fecal—6 to 15%; inactive metabolites also present in feces.

In dialysis—
- Hemodialysis: Metronidazole and primary metabolites rapidly removed from the blood by hemodialysis (half-life shortened to approximately 2.6 hours).
- Peritoneal dialysis: Metronidazole is not significantly removed by peritoneal dialysis.

Precautions to Consider

Carcinogenicity/Tumorigenicity
Metronidazole has been shown to be carcinogenic in a number of studies in mice. Pulmonary tumorigenesis has been reported in six studies in mice, including one study in which the animals were dosed on an intermittent schedule (every four weeks). Malignant hepatic tumors have also been reported in male mice given very high doses (approximately 500 mg/kg/day). Malignant lymphomas have been reported in one lifetime feeding study in mice.

Metronidazole has also been shown to be carcinogenic in rats. Several long-term, oral-dosing studies in rats have shown that metronidazole causes a statistically significant increase in the incidence of various neoplasms, especially mammary and hepatic tumors, in female rats.

Two lifetime tumorigenicity studies in hamsters have given negative results.

Metronidazole has not been shown to be carcinogenic or tumorigenic in humans.

Mutagenicity
Studies have shown that metronidazole is mutagenic in bacteria and fungi, although this has not been confirmed in mammals.

Pregnancy/Reproduction
Pregnancy—

Metronidazole crosses the placenta and enters the fetal circulation rapidly. Adequate and well-controlled studies in humans have not been done. Studies in rats, given doses of up to 5 times the human dose, have not shown that metronidazole causes impaired fertility or birth defects in the fetus. Metronidazole, administered intraperitoneally to pregnant mice at approximately the human dose, has been shown to cause fetotoxicity. When administered orally, no fetotoxicity was seen in pregnant mice. However, the use of metronidazole in the treatment of trichomoniasis is not recommended during the first trimester. If metronidazole is used during the second and third trimesters for trichomoniasis, it is recommended that its use be limited to those patients whose symptoms are not controlled by local palliative treatment. Also, the 1-day course of therapy should not be used since this results in higher maternal and fetal serum concentrations.

Studies in rats given doses of up to 5 times the usual human dose have not shown that metronidazole causes impaired fertility or birth defects in the fetus. Metronidazole, administered intraperitoneally to pregnant mice at approximately the human dose, has been shown to cause fetotoxicity. When metronidazole was administered orally, no fetotoxicity was seen in pregnant mice.

FDA Pregnancy Category B.

Breast-feeding
Metronidazole is distributed into breast milk; concentrations are similar to those found in the maternal plasma. Use is not recommended in nursing mothers since some studies in rats and mice have shown that metronidazole is carcinogenic and may cause adverse effects in the infant. However, use in the treatment of anaerobic bacterial infections or a short course of treatment with metronidazole for amebiasis, severe periodontal infections, or trichomoniasis may be necessary in nursing mothers. During treatment with metronidazole, the breast milk should be expressed and discarded. Breast-feeding may be resumed 24 to 48 hours after treatment is completed.

Pediatrics
When used for the treatment of anaerobic infections and amebiasis, metronidazole has not demonstrated any pediatrics-specific problems that would limit its usefulness in children.

Geriatrics
No information is available on the relationship of age to the effects of metronidazole in geriatric patients. However, elderly patients are more likely to have an age-related decrease in hepatic function, which may require an adjustment in dosage in patients receiving metronidazole.

Dental
Metronidazole may cause dry mouth, an unpleasant or sharp metallic taste, and alteration of taste sensation. Dry mouth may contribute to the development of caries, periodontal disease, oral candidiasis, and discomfort.

Drug interactions and/or related problems
The following drug interactions and/or related problems have been selected on the basis of their potential clinical significance (possible mechanism in parentheses where appropriate)—not necessarily inclusive (» = major clinical significance):

Note: Combinations containing any of the following medications, depending on the amount present, may also interact with this medication.

» Alcohol
(it is recommended that metronidazole not be used concurrently with, or for at least 3 days following, ingestion of alcohol; accumulation of acetaldehyde by interference with the oxidation of alcohol may occur, resulting in disulfiram-like effects such as abdominal cramps, nausea, vomiting, headache, or flushing; in addition, modifications in the taste of alcoholic beverages have been reported during concurrent use)

» Anticoagulants, coumarin- or indandione-derivative
(effects may be potentiated when these agents are used concurrently with metronidazole, because of inhibition of enzymatic metabolism of anticoagulants; periodic prothrombin time determinations may be required during therapy to determine if dosage adjustments of anticoagulants are necessary)

Cimetidine
(hepatic metabolism of metronidazole may be decreased when metronidazole and cimetidine are used concurrently, possibly resulting in delayed elimination and increased serum metronidazole concentrations; monitoring of serum concentrations as a guide to dosage is recommended since dosage adjustments of metronidazole may be necessary during and after cimetidine therapy)

» Disulfiram
(it is recommended that metronidazole not be used concurrently with, or for 2 weeks following, disulfiram in alcoholic patients; such use may result in confusion and psychotic reactions because of combined toxicity)

» Lithium
(lithium concentrations may increase when metronidazole therapy is introduced; serum lithium and serum creatinine levels should be monitored several days after beginning metronidazole in order to detect impending lithium intoxication)

Neurotoxic medications, other (See *Appendix II*)
(concurrent use of metronidazole with other neurotoxic medications may increase the potential for neurotoxicity)

Phenobarbital
(phenobarbital may induce microsomal liver enzymes, increasing metronidazole's metabolism and resulting in a decrease in half-life and plasma concentration)

Phenytoin
(metronidazole may impair the clearance of phenytoin, increasing phenytoin's plasma concentration)

Laboratory value alterations

The following have been selected on the basis of their potential clinical significance (possible effect in parentheses where appropriate)—not necessarily inclusive (» = major clinical significance).

With physiology/laboratory test values
Alanine aminotransferase (ALT [SGPT]), serum and
Aspartate aminotransferase (AST [SGOT]), serum and
Hexokinase glucose and
Lactate dehydrogenase (LDH) and
Triglycerides
(metronidazole has a high absorbance at the wavelength at which nicotinamide-adenine dinucleotide [NADH] is determined; therefore, elevated liver enzyme concentrations may appear to be suppressed by metronidazole when measured by continuous-flow methods based on endpoint decrease in reduced NADH; unusually low liver enzyme concentrations, including zero values, have been reported)

Medical considerations/Contraindications

The medical considerations/contraindications included have been selected on the basis of their potential clinical significance (reasons given in parentheses where appropriate)—not necessarily inclusive (» = major clinical significance).

Risk-benefit should be considered when the following medical problems exist:

» Active organic disease of the CNS, including epilepsy
(metronidazole may cause CNS toxicity, including seizures with high doses, and peripheral neuropathy)

» Blood dyscrasias, or history of
(metronidazole may cause leukopenia)

Cardiac function impairment
(parenteral dosage forms—because of sodium content)

» Hepatic function impairment, severe
(metabolized in the liver; hepatic dysfunction may lead to decreased plasma clearance and accumulation of metronidazole and its metabolites; dosage may need to be reduced with severe hepatic function impairment)

Hypersensitivity to metronidazole

» Known or previously unrecognized candidiasis
(metronidazole may cause more prominent symptoms)

Patient monitoring

The following may be especially important in patient monitoring (other tests may be warranted in some patients, depending on condition; » = major clinical significance):

For giardiasis
» Stool examinations
(3 stool examinations, taken several days apart, beginning 3 to 4 weeks following treatment are recommended if symptoms persist; however, in some successfully treated patients, the lactose intolerance brought on by the infection may persist for a period of some weeks or months, mimicking the symptoms of giardiasis; in cases of treatment failure, alternate drugs may be used)

Side/Adverse Effects

The following side/adverse effects have been selected on the basis of their potential clinical significance (possible signs and symptoms in parentheses where appropriate)—not necessarily inclusive:

Those indicating need for medical attention

Incidence less frequent
Peripheral neuropathy (numbness, tingling, pain, or weakness in hands or feet)—usually with high doses or prolonged use; ***seizures***—usually with high doses

Incidence rare
CNS toxicity (ataxia—clumsiness or unsteadiness; encephalopathy—mood or other mental changes); ***hypersensitivity*** (skin rash, hives, redness, or itching); ***leukopenia*** (sore throat and fever); ***pancreatitis*** (severe abdominal and back pain; anorexia; nausea and vomiting); ***thrombocytopenia*** (unusual bleeding or bruising; black, tarry stools; blood in urine or stools; pinpoint red spots on skin)—reversible; ***thrombophlebitis*** (pain, tenderness, redness, or swelling at site of injection); ***Urinary tract effects*** (frequent or painful urination; inability to control urine flow; sense of pelvic pressure); ***vaginal candidiasis*** (any vaginal irritation, discharge, or dryness not present before therapy)

Those indicating need for medical attention only if they continue or are bothersome

Incidence more frequent
CNS effects (dizziness or light-headedness; headache); ***gastrointestinal disturbance*** (diarrhea; loss of appetite; nausea or vomiting; stomach pain or cramps)

Incidence less frequent or rare
Change in taste sensation; dryness of mouth; unpleasant or sharp metallic taste

Those not indicating need for medical attention

Incidence less frequent or rare
Dark urine

Overdose

For more information on the management of overdose or unintentional ingestion, **contact a poison control center** (see *Poison Control Center Listing*).

Clinical effects of overdose

The following effects have been selected on the basis of their potential clinical significance (possible signs and symptoms in parentheses where appropriate)—not necessarily inclusive:
Ataxia; nausea and vomiting; peripheral neuropathy; seizures

Treatment of overdose

Since there is no specific antidote, treatment for metronidazole overdose should be symptomatic and supportive. Patients in whom intentional overdose is confirmed or suspected should be referred for psychiatric consultation.

Patient Consultation

As an aid to patient consultation, refer to *Advice for the Patient, Metronidazole (Systemic)*.

In providing consultation, consider emphasizing the following selected information (» = major clinical significance):

Before using this medication

» Conditions affecting use, especially:
Hypersensitivity to metronidazole
Pregnancy—Metronidazole crosses the placenta; use is not recommended during the first trimester of pregnancy
Breast-feeding—Metronidazole is distributed into breast milk; metronidazole is not recommended during breast-feeding
Dental—Metronidazole may cause dry mouth, an unpleasant or sharp metallic taste, and alteration of taste sensation
Other medications, especially alcohol, coumarin- or indandione-derivative anticoagulants, disulfiram, or lithium
Other medical problems, especially active organic disease of the CNS, a history of blood dyscrasias, known or previously unrecognized candidiasis, or severe hepatic function impairment

Proper use of this medication

Taking with meals or a snack to minimize gastrointestinal irritation
Taking extended-release formulation on an empty stomach to maximize dosage form characteristics
» Compliance with full course of therapy
» Importance of not missing doses and taking at evenly spaced times
» Proper dosing
Missed dose: Taking as soon as possible; not taking if almost time for next dose; not doubling doses
» Proper storage

Precautions while using this medication

Follow-up visit to physician after treatment for giardiasis to ensure that infection has been eradicated.
Checking with physician if no improvement within a few days
» Avoiding use of alcoholic beverages or other alcohol-containing preparations while taking and for at least 3 days after discontinuing this medication
Possible dryness of mouth; using sugarless candy or gum, ice, or saliva substitute for relief; checking with dentist if dry mouth continues for more than 2 weeks
» Caution if dizziness or light-headedness occurs
Prevention of reinfection in trichomoniasis; possible need for concurrent treatment of male sexual partner and use of a condom

Side/adverse effects

Signs of potential side effects, especially CNS toxicity, hypersensitivity, leukopenia, pancreatitis, peripheral neuropathy, seizures, thrombocytopenia, thrombophlebitis, urinary tract effects and vaginal candidiasis.

Dark urine may be alarming to patient although medically insignificant

General Dosing Information

Patients with severely impaired hepatic function metabolize metronidazole slowly. Close monitoring for toxicity, as well as reduction in dose, may be required.

Anuric patients do not generally require a reduction in dose since metabolites of metronidazole may be rapidly removed by hemodialysis. Also, reduced renal function does not significantly affect single-dose pharmacokinetics of metronidazole.

Patients with candidiasis may present with more prominent symptoms during metronidazole therapy, requiring treatment with a candidacidal agent.

For oral dosage forms only

Metronidazole may be taken with meals or a snack to lessen gastrointestinal irritation.

The extended–release formulation of metronidazole should be taken on an empty stomach, at least one hour before or two hours after meals, in order to ensure maximal performance of the extended–release characteristics.

When metronidazole is used in the treatment of trichomoniasis, sexual partners should receive concurrent therapy since asymptomatic trichomoniasis in the male partner is a frequent source of reinfection in the female. The male partner should be advised to use a condom for the duration of treatment.

For parenteral dosage forms only

Parenteral metronidazole should be administered by slow intravenous infusion only, either continuously or intermittently over a 1-hour period.

If metronidazole is administered concurrently with a primary intravenous solution, the primary solution should be discontinued while metronidazole is being infused.

Serum metronidazole concentrations may be lower in patients whose gastric secretions are removed by continuous nasogastric aspiration, since metronidazole may be removed in the gastric aspirate.

Oral Dosage Forms

Note: Bracketed uses in the *Dosage Forms* section refer to categories of use and/or indications that are not included in U.S. product labeling.

Note: The dosing and dosage forms available are expressed in terms of metronidazole base.

METRONIDAZOLE CAPSULES

Usual adult and adolescent dose

Antibacterial (systemic)—

Anaerobic infections: Oral, 7.5 mg (base) per kg of body weight, up to a maximum of 1 gram, every six hours for seven days or longer.

[Bowel disease, inflammatory][1]: Oral, 500 mg (base) four times a day.

[Colitis, antibiotic-associated][1]: Oral, 500 mg (base) three or four times a day.

[Gastritis, *Helicobacter pylori*–associated (treatment adjunct)][1] or [Ulcer, duodenal, *Helicobacter pylori*–associated (treatment adjunct)][1]—Oral, 500 mg (base) three times a day, in conjunction with bismuth subsalicylate or colloidal bismuth subcitrate and other oral antibiotic therapy, such as ampicillin or amoxicillin, for one to two weeks.

[Vaginosis, bacterial][1]: Oral, 500 mg (base) two times a day for seven days.

Antiprotozoal—

Amebiasis: Oral, 500 to 750 mg (base) three times a day for five to ten days.

Amebic liver abscess: Oral, 500 to 750 mg (base) three times a day for five to ten days.

[Balantidiasis][1]: Oral, 750 mg (base) three times a day for five or six days.

[Giardiasis][1]: Oral, 2 grams (base) once a day for three days; or 250 mg three times a day for five to seven days.

Trichomoniasis: Oral, 2 grams (base) as a single dose; 1 gram two times a day for one day; 375 mg two times a day for seven days; or 250 mg three times a day for seven days.

Anthelmintic (systemic)—

[Dracunculiasis][1]: Oral, 250 mg (base) three times a day for ten days.

Usual adult prescribing limits

Antibacterial (systemic)—

Up to a maximum of 4 grams (base) daily.

Usual pediatric dose

Antibacterial (systemic)—

Anaerobic infections[1]: Oral, 7.5 mg (base) per kg of body weight every six hours, or 10 mg per kg of body weight every eight hours.

Antiprotozoal—

Amebiasis: Oral, 11.6 to 16.7 mg (base) per kg of body weight three times a day for ten days.

[Balantidiasis][1]: Oral, 11.6 to 16.7 mg (base) per kg of body weight three times a day for five days.

[Giardiasis][1]: Oral, 5 mg (base) per kg of body weight three times a day for five to seven days.

Trichomoniasis: Oral, 5 mg (base) per kg of body weight three times a day for seven days.

Anthelmintic (systemic)—

[Dracunculiasis][1]: Oral, 8.3 mg (base) per kg of body weight, up to a maximum of 250 mg, three times a day for ten days.

Strength(s) usually available

U.S.—

375 mg (base) (Rx) [*Flagyl* (Black iron oxide; corn starch; D&C Yellow No. 10; FD&C Green No.3; gelatin; magnesium stearate; titanium dioxide)].

Canada—

500 mg (base) (Rx) [*Flagyl* (sodium 5.47 mg); *Trikacide*].

Packaging and storage

Store below 40 °C (104 °F), preferably between 15 and 30 °C (59 and 86 °F), in a well-closed container, unless otherwise specified by manufacturer. Store in a light-resistant container.

Auxiliary labeling

- Avoid alcoholic beverages.
- May cause dizziness.
- Continue medicine for full time of treatment.

METRONIDAZOLE TABLETS USP

Usual adult and adolescent dose

See *Metronidazole Capsules*.

Usual adult prescribing limits

See *Metronidazole Capsules*.

Usual pediatric dose

See *Metronidazole Capsules*.

Strength(s) usually available

U.S.—

250 mg (base) (Rx) [*Flagyl; Metric 21; Protostat* (scored; lactose)].

500 mg (base) (Rx) [*Flagyl; Protostat* (scored; lactose)].

Canada—

250 mg (base) (Rx) [*Apo-Metronidazole; Flagyl* (sodium 3.1 mg); *Novonidazol* (scored; sodium 2.2 mg); *Trikacide*].

Packaging and storage

Store in a dry place at 25 °C (77 °F); excursions permitted between 15 and 30 °C (59 and 86 °F), unless otherwise specified by manufacturer. Store in a well-closed, light-resistant container.

Preparation of dosage form

For patients who cannot take oral solids—According to the primary manufacturer, the tablets may be crushed and suspended in Cherry Syrup NF to prepare a pediatric dosage form. The recommended concentration per 5 mL is the dose calculated for a particular pediatric patient. The suspension is stable for 30 days if stored at ambient room temperature or refrigerated. Dispense with "shake well" instructions.

Auxiliary labeling

- Avoid alcoholic beverages.
- May cause dizziness.
- Continue medicine for full time of treatment.

METRONIDAZOLE EXTENDED RELEASE TABLETS

Usual adult and adolescent dose

Antibacterial (systemic)—

Vaginosis, bacterial: Oral, 750 mg (base) once a day for seven days.

Usual pediatric dose

Safety and efficacy have not been established.

Strength(s) usually available

U.S.—

750 mg (base) [*Flagyl ER* (FD&C Blue No.2 Aluminum Lake; hydroxypropyl methylcellulose; lactose; magnesium stearate; poly (meth) acrylic acid ester copolymers; polyethylene glycol; polysorbate 80; silicon dioxide; simethicone emulsion; talc; titanium dioxide)].

Packaging and storage
Store in a dry place at 25 °C (77 °F); excursions permitted between 15 and 30 °C (59 and 86 °F), unless otherwise specified by manufacturer. Store in a well-closed, light-resistant container.

Auxiliary labeling
- Avoid alcoholic beverages.
- Continue medicine for full time of treatment.
- Take on an empty stomach, at least one hour before or two hours after meals.

Parenteral Dosage Forms
Note: Bracketed uses in the *Dosage Forms* section refer to categories of use and/or indications that are not included in U.S. product labeling.

Note: The dosing and dosage forms available are expressed in terms of metronidazole base.

METRONIDAZOLE INJECTION USP
Usual adult and adolescent dose
Antibacterial (systemic)—

Anaerobic infections: Intravenous infusion, 15 mg (base) per kg of body weight initially, then 7.5 mg per kg of body weight, up to a maximum of 1 gram, every six hours for seven days or longer.

Perioperative infections, colonic (prophylaxis): Intravenous infusion, 15 mg (base) per kg of body weight one hour prior to the start of surgery; and 7.5 mg per kg of body weight six and twelve hours after the initial dose.

[Antiprotozoal—Amebiasis][1]—

Intravenous infusion, 500 to 750 mg (base) every eight hours for five to ten days.

Usual adult prescribing limits
Antibacterial (systemic)—

Up to a maximum of 4 grams (base) daily.

Usual pediatric dose
[Anaerobic infections][1]—

Preterm infants: Intravenous infusion, 15 mg per kg of body weight (base) as an initial dose, then 7.5 mg per kg of body weight every twelve hours starting 48 hours after the initial dose.

Term infants:Intravenous infusion, 15 mg (base) per kg of body weight as an initial dose, then 7.5 mg per kg of body weight every twelve hours starting 24 hours after the initial dose.

Infants greater than 7 days of age and children:Intravenous infusion, 15 mg (base) per kg of body weight as an initial dose, then 7.5 mg per kg of body weight every six hours.

Strength(s) usually available
U.S.—

500 mg in 100 mL (base) (Rx) [*Flagyl I.V. RTU* (sodium 14 mEq); *Metro I.V.* (sodium 13.5 mEq); GENERIC].

Canada—

500 mg in 100 mL (base) (Rx) [*Flagyl;* GENERIC].

Packaging and storage
Store below 40 °C (104 °F), preferably between 15 and 30 °C (59 and 86 °F), unless otherwise specified by manufacturer. Protect from light during storage. Protect from freezing.

Incompatibilities
Intravenous admixtures of metronidazole and other medications are not recommended.

Additional information
Metronidazole Injection USP is an isotonic (297 to 310 mOsm per liter), ready-to-use solution, requiring no dilution or buffering prior to administration.

Metronidazole Injection USP in prefilled plastic minibags should not be used in series connections. This may result in air embolism because of residual air (approximately 15 mL), which may be drawn from the primary plastic bag before administration of the infusion from the secondary plastic bag is completed.

METRONIDAZOLE HYDROCHLORIDE FOR INJECTION
Usual adult and adolescent dose
See *Metronidazole Injection USP*.

Usual adult prescribing limits
See *Metronidazole Injection USP*.

Usual pediatric dose
See *Metronidazole Injection USP*.

Strength(s) usually available
U.S.—

500 mg (base) (Rx) [*Flagyl I.V.* (sodium 5 mEq)].

Canada—

Not commercially available.

Packaging and storage
Prior to reconstitution, store below 30 °C (86 °F), in a light-resistant container, unless otherwise specified by manufacturer.

Preparation of dosage form
Metronidazole hydrochloride for injection must not be given by direct intravenous injection since the initial dilution has an extremely low pH (0.5 to 2.0). It must be diluted further and neutralized prior to administration.

To prepare initial dilution for intravenous infusion, add 4.4 mL of sterile water for injection, bacteriostatic water for injection, 0.9% sodium chloride injection, or bacteriostatic sodium chloride injection to each 500-mg vial to provide a concentration of 100 mg per mL (pH 0.5 to 2.0). The resulting solution should be further diluted in 100 mL of 0.9% sodium chloride injection, 5% dextrose injection, or lactated Ringer's injection. The final dilution must be neutralized with approximately 5 mEq of sodium bicarbonate injection per 500 mg of metronidazole (final pH 6 to 7). Since carbon dioxide gas is produced during neutralization, it may be necessary to relieve the pressure in the final container. The final concentration should not exceed 8 mg per mL since neutralization decreases the solubility of metronidazole and precipitation may occur.

Stability
After reconstitution, solutions retain their potency for 96 hours if stored below 30 °C (86 °F) in room light. Diluted and neutralized solutions retain their potency for 24 hours.

Do not refrigerate neutralized solutions since precipitation may occur.

Incompatibilities
Do not use with aluminum needles or hubs.

Intravenous admixtures of metronidazole with other medications are not recommended.

[1]Not included in Canadian product labeling.

Revised: 04/06/2001

METRONIDAZOLE Topical
VA CLASSIFICATION (Primary): DE752

Commonly used brand name(s): *MetroCream; MetroGel; MetroLotion.*

Note: For a listing of dosage forms and brand names by country availability, see *Dosage Forms* section(s).

Category
Antirosacea agent (topical).

Indications
Note: Bracketed information in the *Indications* section refers to uses that are not included in U.S. product labeling.

Accepted
Rosacea (treatment)—Topical metronidazole is indicated [as a primary agent] in the treatment of the inflammatory papules, pustules, and erythema of rosacea (acne rosacea; "adult acne").

Unaccepted
Topical metronidazole is not effective against the accompanying telangiectasias seen in rosacea patients.

Pharmacology/Pharmacokinetics
Physicochemical characteristics
Chemical Group—Nitroimidazole

Molecular weight—171.16.

Mechanism of action/Effect
Unknown, but apparently not due to an antiparasitic effect on the mite *Demodex folliculorum*, found in hair follicles and sebaceous secretions, or to any effect on sebum production. Topical metronidazole may have an antioxidant effect. It has been shown to significantly reduce the concentrations of neutrophil-generated reactive oxygen species, hydroxyl radicals and hydrogen peroxide, which are potent oxidants capable of causing tissue injury at the site of inflammation. Topical metronidazole may also have an effect on neutrophil cellular functions, which is partly attributable to its direct anti-inflammatory effect.

Absorption
Minimal; only trace amounts found in the serum following topical application of a 0.75% gel.

Distribution
Absorbed metronidazole crosses the placenta and the blood-brain barrier.

Peak serum concentration
Minimal; up to 66 nanograms per mL following application of 1 gram of gel (equivalent to 7.5 mg of metronidazole) to the face of rosacea patients. Serum concentrations were reported to be undetectable in some patients.

Precautions to Consider

Cross-sensitivity and/or related problems
Patients sensitive to parabens may be sensitive to topical formulations of metronidazole also since they contain methyl- and propylparabens.

Patients sensitive to imidazole preparations such as clotrimazole and tioconazole also may be sensitive to metronidazole.

Carcinogenicity/Tumorigenicity
Carcinogenicity studies have not been done using topical formulations of metronidazole.

A number of studies using chronic, oral administration of metronidazole in mice and rats have shown that metronidazole is carcinogenic and tumorigenic. However, metronidazole has not been shown to be carcinogenic or tumorigenic in humans (See *Metronidazole [Systemic]*).

Mutagenicity
Studies have shown that metronidazole is mutagenic in bacteria and fungi. A dose-related increase in the frequency of micronuclei was observed after intraperitoneal injection in mice. Also, an increase in chromosomal aberrations was reported in patients with Crohn's disease who were administered 200 to 1200 mg of metronidazole per day for 1 to 24 months. However, no increase in chromosomal aberrations was seen in the circulating human lymphocytes of patients treated for 8 months.

Pregnancy/Reproduction
Fertility—Adequate and well-controlled studies using topical metronidazole in humans have not been done. However, studies using oral metronidazole in rats or mice have not shown that metronidazole causes impaired fertility.

Pregnancy—Absorbed metronidazole crosses the placenta and enters the fetal circulation rapidly. Adequate and well-controlled studies using topical metronidazole in humans have not been done.

Studies using oral metronidazole in rats and mice have not shown that metronidazole causes adverse effects in the fetus.

FDA Pregnancy Category B.

Breast-feeding
Metronidazole, applied topically, is minimally absorbed. Only trace amounts appear in the serum following topical application. Therefore, topical metronidazole is unlikely to be distributed into breast milk in significant amounts since the topical dose is small. In addition, it is unlikely that the nursing infant would absorb significant amounts of metronidazole or that it would cause serious problems in the nursing infant.

Pediatrics
Safety and efficacy have not been established. Since rosacea is considered primarily an adult-onset disease, topical metronidazole is not indicated in the treatment of pediatric patients.

Geriatrics
No information is available on the relationship of age to the effects of topical metronidazole in geriatric patients.

Medical considerations/Contraindications
The medical considerations/contraindications included have been selected on the basis of their potential clinical significance (reasons given in parentheses where appropriate)—not necessarily inclusive (» = major clinical significance).

Risk-benefit should be considered when the following medical problems exist:

Blood dyscrasias, or history of
(caution is recommended because metronidazole is a nitroimidazole)

Sensitivity to topical metronidazole

Side/Adverse Effects
Note: Because metronidazole is minimally absorbed, with only trace amounts appearing in the serum following topical application, those side/adverse effects reported with systemic use of metronidazole have not been reported with topical use of the medication.

If local irritation occurs, topical metronidazole should be applied less frequently or discontinued.

The following side/adverse effects have been selected on the basis of their potential clinical significance (possible signs and symptoms in parentheses where appropriate)—not necessarily inclusive:

Those indicating need for medical attention only if they continue or are bothersome
Incidence less frequent

Dry skin; redness or other signs of skin irritation not present before therapy; stinging or burning of the skin; watering of eyes

Incidence rare

Metallic taste in the mouth; nausea; tingling or numbness of extremities

Patient Consultation
As an aid to patient consultation, refer to *Advice for the Patient, Metronidazole (Topical).*

In providing consultation, consider emphasizing the following selected information (» = major clinical significance):

Before using this medication
» Conditions affecting use, especially:
Sensitivity to topical metronidazole, methyl- and propylparabens, or imidazole preparations
Pregnancy—Absorbed metronidazole crosses the placenta and enters fetal circulation rapidly

Proper use of this medication
» Not using medication in or near the eyes; tearing may occur
Washing eyes out immediately with large amounts of cool tap water if medication gets into eyes; checking with physician if eyes continue to burn or are painful
Before applying, thoroughly washing affected area(s) with a mild, nonirritating cleanser, rinsing well, and gently patting dry

To use
After washing affected area(s), applying medication with fingertips; washing medication off hands afterward
» Importance of applying medication to entire affected area
» Compliance with full course of therapy, which may take 9 weeks or longer
» Proper dosing
Missed dose: Applying as soon as possible; not applying if almost time for next dose
» Proper storage

Precautions while using this medication
Checking with physician if no improvement within 3 weeks; may take up to 9 weeks before full therapeutic benefit is seen

Possibility of stinging or burning of the skin after application; checking with physician if irritation continues

Using only "oil-free" cosmetics to avoid worsening rosacea

General Dosing Information
Before this medication is applied, the affected area(s) should be washed thoroughly with a mild, nonirritating cleanser, rinsed well, and gently patted dry.

After washing the affected area(s), a thin film of the medication should be applied and rubbed into the entire affected area.

Topical metronidazole should not be used in or near the eyes. Tearing has been reported when the medication is applied too close to the eyes.

If local irritation occurs, topical metronidazole should be applied less frequently or discontinued.

Topical Dosage Forms

METRONIDAZOLE CREAM

Usual adult dose
Rosacea—
Topical, to the affected area(s) two times a day, morning and evening, [for nine weeks].

Usual pediatric dose
Safety and efficacy have not been established. Since rosacea is considered primarily an adult-onset disease, topical metronidazole is not needed in the treatment of pediatric patients.

Strength(s) usually available
U.S.—
7.5 mg per gram (0.75%) (Rx) [*MetroCream* (emulsifying wax; sorbitol solution; glycerin; isopropyl palmitate; benzyl alcohol; lactic acid and/or sodium hydroxide; purified water)].

Canada—
7.5 mg per gram (0.75%) (Rx) [*MetroCream* (emulsifying wax; sorbitol solution; glycerin; isopropyl palmitate; benzyl alcohol; lactic acid and/or sodium hydroxide; purified water)].

Packaging and storage
Store between 15 and 30 °C (59 and 86 °F), in a well-closed container, unless otherwise specified by manufacturer. Protect from freezing.

Auxiliary labeling
- For external use only.
- Continue medication for full time of treatment.

Additional information
Patients may use cosmetics after application of metronidazole cream.

METRONIDAZOLE GEL USP

Usual adult dose
See *Metronidazole Cream.*

Usual pediatric dose
See *Metronidazole Cream.*

Strength(s) usually available
U.S.—
7.5 mg per gram (0.75%) (Rx) [*MetroGel* (purified water; methylparaben; propylparaben; propylene glycol; carbomer 940; sodium hydroxide; edetate disodium)].

Canada—
7.5 mg per gram (0.75%) (Rx) [*MetroGel* (methylparaben; propylparaben; purified water; propylene glycol; carbomer 940; edetate disodium; sodium hydroxide)].

Packaging and storage
Store between 15 and 30 °C (59 and 86 °F), in a well-closed container, unless otherwise specified by manufacturer. Protect from freezing.

Auxiliary labeling
- For external use only.
- Continue medication for full time of treatment.

Additional information
Metronidazole gel is an aqueous, nongreasy, invisible, and nonstaining preparation.

Patients may use cosmetics after application of metronidazole gel.

METRONIDAZOLE LOTION

Usual adult dose
See *Metronidazole Cream.*

Usual pediatric dose
See *Metronidazole Cream.*

Strength(s) usually available
U.S.—
7.5 mg per gram (0.75%) (Rx) [*MetroLotion* (benzyl alcohol; carbomer 941; cyclomethicone; glycerin; glyceryl stearate; light mineral oil; PEG-100 stearate; polyethylene glycol 400; potassium sorbate; purified water; steareth-21; stearyl alcohol; sodium hydroxide and/or lactic acid)].

Canada—
Not commercially available.

Packaging and storage
Store at controlled room temperature 20–25 °C (68–77 °F). Protect from freezing.

Auxiliary labeling
- For external use only.
- Continue medication for full time of treatment.

Additional information
Patients may use cosmetics after waiting not less than 5 minutes for the metronidazole lotion to dry.

Selected Bibliography

Bleicher PA, Charles HJ, Sober AJ. Topical metronidazole therapy for rosacea. Arch Dermatol 1987 May; 123: 609-14.

Aronson IK, Rumsfield JA, West DP, Alexander J, Fischer JH, Paloucek FP. Evaluation of topical metronidazole gel in acne rosacea. Drug Intell Clin Pharm 1987 Apr; 21: 348-51.

Nielsen PG. Metronidazole treatment in rosacea. Int J Dermatol 1988 Jan-Feb; 27: 1-5.

Revised: 12/22/1999

METRONIDAZOLE Vaginal

VA CLASSIFICATION (Primary): GU301

Commonly used brand name(s): *Flagyl; MetroGel-Vaginal; Nidagel.*

Note: For a listing of dosage forms and brand names by country availability, see *Dosage Forms* section(s).

Category
Anti-infective (vaginal).

Indications
Note: Bracketed information in the *Indications* section refers to uses that are not included in U.S. product labeling.

Accepted
Vaginosis, bacterial (treatment)—Vaginal metronidazole is indicated in the local treatment of bacterial vaginosis (previously known as *Haemophilus* vaginitis, *Gardnerella* vaginitis, nonspecific vaginitis, *Corynebacterium* vaginitis, or anaerobic vaginosis).

There are only limited clinical data regarding metronidazole gel's efficacy in treating bacterial vaginosis during pregnancy.

[Trichomoniasis (treatment)]—Metronidazole vaginal tablets and vaginal cream are indicated in the local treatment of trichomoniasis.

Not all species or strains of a particular organism may be equally susceptible to metronidazole.

Unaccepted
Vaginal metronidazole is not effective against aerobic or facultative anaerobic bacteria, or in the treatment of vulvovaginitis caused by *Chlamydia trachomatis, Neisseria gonorrhoeae, Candida albicans*, or *Herpes simplex* virus. Metronidazole vaginal gel has not been proven to be clinically effective in the treatment of *Trichomonas vaginalis.*

Pharmacology/Pharmacokinetics

Physicochemical characteristics
Chemical Group—Imidazole.

Molecular weight—171.16.

Mechanism of action/Effect
The exact mechanism of action has not been completely established. Metronidazole is thought to be microbicidal against most obligate anaerobic bacteria and protozoa. To be active, it must undergo intracellular chemical reduction via mechanisms unique to anaerobic metabolism. The short-lived reduced forms are cytotoxic and interact with DNA to cause a loss of helical structure and strand breakage resulting in inhibition of nucleic acid synthesis and cell death.

Note: Metronidazole permits natural vaginal flora recovery because it has little effect on *Lactobacillus sp.*

Other actions/effects
Metronidazole may produce a local antioxidant and anti-inflammatory effect on inflamed tissue by affecting neutrophil function.

Absorption
Vaginal cream or

Vaginal tablets—Approximately 20% of the administered dose of metronidazole (500 mg) is absorbed systemically, producing plasma concentrations approximately 12% of that resulting from a single 500-mg oral dose. The rate of absorption is less predictable with the vaginal tablets than with the cream.

Vaginal gel—Approximately 56% of the administered dose of metronidazole (37.5 mg) is absorbed systemically, producing plasma concentrations approximately 2% of that resulting from a single 500-mg oral dose.

Distribution
Systemically absorbed metronidazole may be distributed into breast milk and to most tissues. It crosses the blood-brain barrier and placenta.

Protein binding
Low (< 20%).

Biotransformation
Systemically absorbed metronidazole is metabolized primarily by side-chain oxidation by the hepatic cytochrome P450 enzyme system to two active metabolites, 1-[2-hydroxyethyl]-2-hydroxymethyl-5-nitroimidazole and 1-acetic acid-2-methyl-5-nitroimidazole. The hydroxylated metabolite is approximately 30% as potent as the parent compound while the acetic acid metabolite is 5% as potent. Small amounts of other metabolites (including glucuronide and sulfide conjugates) are also formed.

Half-life

Elimination (determined with systemic administration)—Normal hepatic function: 8 hours (range, 6 to 12 hours) for unchanged metronidazole.

Time to peak serum concentration:

Vaginal cream—11 hours.
Vaginal gel—6 to 12 hours.
Vaginal tablet—20 hours.

Peak serum concentration

Vaginal cream—1.86 mg per liter (mg/L) (10.87 micromole/L).

Vaginal gel—0.152 to 0.368 mg/L (0.89 to 2.15 micromole/L).

Vaginal tablet—1.89 mg/L (11.04 micromole/L).

Elimination

Renal—60 to 80% of a systemic dose; of this amount, approximately 20% is excreted unchanged.

Fecal—6 to 15% of a systemic dose.

Precautions to Consider

Note: Some of the following information relates to the oral formulation. Depending on the vaginal product's strength and formulation, the vaginal administration of metronidazole may yield 2 to 12% of the blood concentrations achieved after a single 500-mg oral dose. The possibility of systemic effects may need to be considered until further studies quantify the degree of clinical significance.

Carcinogenicity

Carcinogenicity studies have not been done using vaginal formulations of metronidazole. Systemic metronidazole has not been shown to be carcinogenic in humans.

Systemic metronidazole has been shown to be carcinogenic in a number of studies in mice and rats, including a study in which it produced malignant lymphomas in mice.

Tumorigenicity

Tumorigenicity studies have not been done using vaginal formulations of metronidazole. Systemic metronidazole has not been shown to be tumorigenic in humans.

Pulmonary tumorigenesis has been reported in six studies in mice, including a study in which the animals were dosed every 4 weeks. Malignant hepatic tumors have also been reported in male mice given very high doses (approximately 500 mg per kg of body weight [mg/kg] per day). Several long-term oral-dose studies in rats have shown that metronidazole causes a statistically significant increase in the incidence of various neoplasms, especially mammary and hepatic tumors in female rats. Two lifetime tumorigenicity studies in hamsters using oral formulations have given negative results.

Mutagenicity

Studies have shown that metronidazole is mutagenic in bacteria and fungi, although this has not been confirmed in mammals.

Pregnancy/Reproduction

Fertility—No evidence of impaired fertility was found in mice.

Pregnancy—Metronidazole crosses the placenta, entering the fetal circulation rapidly. Adequate and well-controlled studies in humans have not been done.

Tumorigenicity has been demonstrated in animal studies, which may suggest that metronidazole should be withheld during pregnancy until more clinical data regarding vaginal administration are available.

A small study reported that intrauterine deaths resulted when metronidazole was administered intraperitoneally to pregnant mice in doses comparable to the oral human dose. No fetotoxicity or teratogenicity occurred with orally administered metronidazole.

FDA Pregnancy Category B.

Breast-feeding

Metronidazole is distributed into breast milk; concentrations are similar to those found in the maternal plasma. Use in nursing mothers is not recommended. The theoretical risk is based on tumorigenicity studies in animals; human data have not supported this. Also, metronidazole may change the taste of the breast milk. If a nursing mother is treated with metronidazole, the breast milk may be expressed and discarded and breast-feeding resumed 24 to 48 hours after treatment is completed.

Pediatrics

No information is available on the relationship of age to the effects of vaginal metronidazole in pediatric patients.

Geriatrics

No information is available on the relationship of age to the effects of vaginal metronidazole in geriatric patients. However, elderly patients are more likely to have an age-related decrease in hepatic function, which may affect metronidazole elimination.

Drug interactions and/or related problems

The following drug interactions and/or related problems have been selected on the basis of their potential clinical significance (possible mechanism in parentheses where appropriate)—not necessarily inclusive (» = major clinical significance):

Note: Combinations containing any of the following medications, depending on the amount present, may also interact with this medication.

» Alcohol
(caution in concurrent use with vaginal metronidazole and for at least 1 day following completion of treatment is advisable because systemic metronidazole may interfere with the oxidation of alcohol; such use may result in disulfiram-like effects such as abdominal cramps, nausea, vomiting, headache, or flushing of the face from acetaldehyde accumulation; changes in the taste of alcoholic beverages also have been reported during concurrent use)

» Anticoagulants, coumarin- or indandione-derivative
(anticoagulant effects may be potentiated when these agents are used concurrently with metronidazole because of inhibition of enzymatic metabolism of anticoagulants; periodic prothrombin time determinations may be required during and following concurrent therapy to determine if dosage adjustments of anticoagulants are necessary)

Cimetidine
(hepatic metabolism of metronidazole may be decreased when metronidazole and cimetidine are used concurrently, possibly resulting in delayed elimination and increased serum metronidazole concentrations)

» Disulfiram
(it is recommended that metronidazole not be used concurrently with, or for 2 weeks following, disulfiram in alcoholic patients; such use may result in confusion and psychotic reactions because of combined toxicity)

Lithium
(concurrent use of systemic metronidazole with lithium has resulted in decreased renal clearance of lithium and lithium toxicity; adjustments of lithium dosage may be required)

Neurotoxic medications, other (see *Appendix II*)
(concurrent use of systemic metronidazole with other neurotoxic medications may increase the potential for neurotoxicity)

Phenytoin
(systemic metronidazole may impair the metabolism of phenytoin by inhibiting microsomal enzymes and increasing phenytoin's plasma concentration; the extent to which intravaginal metronidazole affects phenytoin is not presently known)

Laboratory value alterations

The following have been selected on the basis of their potential clinical significance (possible effect in parentheses where appropriate)—not necessarily inclusive (» = major clinical significance).

With diagnostic test results
Alanine aminotransferase (ALT [SGPT]) and
Aspartate aminotransferase (AST [SGOT]) and
Hexokinase glucose and
Lactate dehydrogenase (LDH) and
Triglycerides
(metronidazole has a high absorbance at the wavelength at which nicotinamide-adenine dinucleotide [NADH] is determined; therefore, falsely low values may occur when these substances are measured by continuous-flow methods based on endpoint decrease in reduced NADH)

White blood cell count
(may be increased or decreased)

Medical considerations/Contraindications

The medical considerations/contraindications included have been selected on the basis of their potential clinical significance (reasons given in parentheses where appropriate)—not necessarily inclusive (» = major clinical significance).

Risk-benefit should be considered when the following medical problems exist:

» Epilepsy or
» Other neurologic disease
(systemic metronidazole has caused CNS toxicity, including seizures and peripheral neuropathy)

» Hepatic function impairment, severe
(metronidazole is metabolized in the liver; hepatic function impairment may lead to decreased plasma clearance and accumulation of metronidazole and its metabolites and increased risk of side

effects; dosage may need to be reduced in patients with severe hepatic function impairment)

Hypersensitivity to metronidazole

Leukopenia, or history of
(oral metronidazole has caused leukopenia; the possibility should be considered that vaginal metronidazole may induce or exacerbate leukopenia, especially with prolonged or multiple courses of therapy)

Patient monitoring

The following may be especially important in patient monitoring (other tests may be warranted in some patients, depending on condition; » = major clinical significance):

Leukocyte count, total and differential
(determinations recommended when metronidazole is used for longer than 10 days or if a second course of therapy is needed)

Side/Adverse Effects

Note: Convulsions, peripheral neuropathy, and ataxia have been reported rarely with systemic administration of metronidazole. The possibility should be considered that these effects may also occur with vaginal administration, especially with the higher-potency formulations available in Canada or with prolonged use. If neurological symptoms occur, the medication should be discontinued. Severe symptoms may require immediate medical attention.

The incidences of side effects listed below are those reported in studies with the 0.75% gel. Although specific information about the incidence of side effects with the vaginal tablet or vaginal cream is not available, it is possible that some adverse effects could occur more frequently with these higher-potency formulations than with the gel. Also, the possibility of systemic effects may need to be considered since vaginal administration of metronidazole may yield 2 to 12% of the blood concentrations achieved after a single oral 500-mg dose.

The following side/adverse effects have been selected on the basis of their potential clinical significance (possible signs and symptoms in parentheses where appropriate)—not necessarily inclusive:

Those indicating need for medical attention

Incidence more frequent

Candida cervicitis or vaginitis (itching in the vagina; pain during sexual intercourse; thick, white vaginal discharge without odor or with mild odor)—incidence 6 to 15%

Incidence less frequent

Abdominal cramping or pain—incidence 3.4%; ***burning or irritation of penis of sexual partner; burning or increased frequency of urination; vulvitis*** (itching, stinging or redness of genital area)

Those indicating need for medical attention only if they continue or are bothersome

Incidence less frequent

Altered taste sensation including metallic taste; CNS effects (dizziness or lightheadedness; headache); ***dryness of mouth; furry tongue; gastrointestinal disturbances*** (diarrhea, nausea or vomiting); ***loss of appetite***

Those not indicating need for medical attention

Incidence less frequent

Dark urine

Those indicating possible need for medical attention if they occur after medication is discontinued

Vaginal candidiasis (itching of the vagina or outside genitals; pain during sexual intercourse; thick, white vaginal discharge without odor or with mild odor)

Patient Consultation

As an aid to patient consultation, refer to *Advice for the Patient, Metronidazole (Vaginal).*

In providing consultation, consider emphasizing the following selected information (» = major clinical significance):

Before using this medication

» Conditions affecting use, especially:
Sensitivity to metronidazole
Pregnancy—Metronidazole crosses the placenta; discussing use of medicine with physician before using during pregnancy
Breast-feeding—Metronidazole is distributed into breast milk and is not recommended during breast-feeding
Other medications, especially alcohol, coumarin- or indandione-derivative anticoagulants, or disulfiram
Other medical problems, especially epilepsy or other neurologic disease or severe hepatic function impairment

Proper use of this medication

» Washing hands immediately before and after vaginal administration
Avoiding getting medication into the eyes; washing with large amounts of cool tap water immediately if medication does get into eyes; checking with physician if eyes continue to be painful
Reading patient directions carefully before use

Proper administration technique
Following directions regarding filling the applicator, insertion technique, and cleaning the applicator after each use

For cream or gel dosage forms
Puncturing metal tamper-resistant seal on tube with top of cap

For vaginal tablet dosage form
Placing vaginal tablet into the applicator, immersing exposed tablet in tap water for a few seconds before vaginal insertion to facilitate disintegration

» Compliance with full course of therapy, even during menstruation
» Proper dosing
Missed dose: Inserting as soon as possible; not inserting if almost time for next dose
» Proper storage

Precautions while using this medication

Checking with physician if no improvement within a few days

Follow-up visit to physician after treatment for bacterial vaginosis to ensure that infection has been eradicated

» Avoiding use of alcoholic beverages or other alcohol-containing preparations while using and for at least 1 day after discontinuing this medication

» Caution if dizziness or lightheadedness occurs

Protecting clothing because of possible soiling with vaginal metronidazole; avoiding use of tampons

» Using hygienic measures to cure infection and prevent reinfection, e.g., wearing freshly washed cotton panties instead of synthetic panties

» Sexual abstinence is recommended during treatment to prevent cross-infection, reinfection, or dilution of the dose. If this recommendation is not followed, use of the vaginal cream and vaginal tablets should be avoided with latex contraceptive devices, such as cervical caps, condoms, or diaphragms, since these products contain oils that damage latex

For trichomoniasis:
» Using condoms to prevent reinfection with trichomoniasis after treatment; possible need for concurrent treatment of male partner for trichomoniasis

Side/adverse effects

Signs of potential side effects, especially candida cervicitis or vaginitis, abdominal cramping or pain, burning or irritation of penis of sexual partner, increased frequency of urination, vulvitis, altered taste sensation, CNS effects, dryness of mouth, furry tongue, gastrointestinal disturbances, loss of appetite
Dark urine may be alarming to patient although medically insignificant
Possibility of vaginal candidiasis occurring after medication has been discontinued

General Dosing Information

If sensitization or irritation occurs, treatment with vaginal metronidazole should be discontinued.

The cream and the vaginal tablet (but not the gel) may contain oils that may damage latex contraceptive devices, such as cervical caps, condoms, or diaphragms, and reduce their efficacy.

Vaginal applicators should be used with caution after the sixth month of pregnancy.

If there is no response to therapy, the presence of pathogens unresponsive to metronidazole should be ruled out by potassium hydroxide (KOH) wet mounts before a second course of therapy is initiated.

In treating bacterial vaginosis, concurrent treatment of the male partner generally is unnecessary.

In treating trichomoniasis, both sexual partners should receive metronidazole therapy concurrently since asymptomatic trichomoniasis in the male partner is a frequent source of reinfection in the female.

Vaginal Dosage Forms

Note: Bracketed uses in the *Dosage Forms* section refer to categories of use and/or indications that are not included in U.S. product labeling.

METRONIDAZOLE VAGINAL CREAM

Usual adult and adolescent dose

Bacterial vaginosis or

[Trichomoniasis]—

Intravaginal, 500 mg (one applicatorful) one or two times a day for ten or twenty consecutive days.

Usual pediatric dose

Safety and efficacy have not been established.

Strength(s) usually available

U.S.—

Not commercially available.

Canada—

10% w/w (Rx) [*Flagyl* (methylparaben; propylparaben)].

Packaging and storage

Store below 40 °C (104 °F), preferably between 15 and 30 °C (59 and 86 °F), unless otherwise specified by manufacturer. Protect from freezing.

Auxiliary labeling

- May cause dizziness.
- Continue medicine for full time of treatment.
- For vaginal use only.
- Avoid alcoholic beverages.

Note

Include patient package insert (PPI) when dispensing.

METRONIDAZOLE VAGINAL GEL

Usual adult and adolescent dose

Bacterial vaginosis—

Intravaginal, 37.5 mg (one applicatorful) one or two times a day for five days.

Usual pediatric dose

Safety and efficacy have not been established.

Strength(s) usually available

U.S.—

0.75% (Rx) [*MetroGel-Vaginal* (EDTA; methylparaben; propylparaben; propylene glycol)].

Canada—

0.75% (Rx) [*Nidagel* (EDTA; methylparaben; propylparaben; propylene glycol)].

Packaging and storage

Store below 40 °C (104 °F), preferably between 15 and 30 °C (59 and 86 °F), unless otherwise specified by manufacturer. Protect from freezing. Keep out of reach of children.

Auxiliary labeling

- May cause dizziness.
- Continue medicine for full time of treatment.
- For vaginal use only.
- Avoid alcoholic beverages.

Note

Include patient package insert (PPI) when dispensing.

METRONIDAZOLE VAGINAL TABLETS

Usual adult and adolescent dose

Bacterial vaginosis or

[Trichomoniasis]—

Intravaginal, 500 mg placed high into the vagina every night for ten or twenty consecutive days.

Usual pediatric dose

Safety and efficacy have not been established.

Strength(s) usually available

U.S.—

Not commercially available.

Canada—

500 mg (Rx) [*Flagyl*].

Packaging and storage

Store below 40 °C (104 °F), preferably between 15 and 30 °C (59 and 86 °F), unless otherwise specified by manufacturer. Protect from light.

Auxiliary labeling

- May cause dizziness.
- Continue medicine for full time of treatment.
- For vaginal use only.
- Avoid alcoholic beverages.

Note

Include patient package insert (PPI) when dispensing.

Patient should be instructed on technique for placement including immersing the vaginal tablet (in applicator) in tap water for a few seconds before insertion to facilitate disintegration.

Selected Bibliography

Alper MM, Barwin N, McLean WM, et al. Systemic absorption of metronidazole by the vaginal route. Obstet Gynecol 1985 Jun; 65(6): 781-4.

Hillier SL, Lipinski C, Briseldene A, et al. Efficacy of intravaginal 0.75% metronidazole gel for the treatment of bacterial vaginosis. Obstet Gynecol 1993 June; 81(6): 963-7.

Revised: 08/13/1998

MEZLOCILLIN—See *Penicillins (Systemic)*

MICAFUNGIN Systemic†

VA CLASSIFICATION (Primary): AM700

Commonly used brand name(s): *Mycamine*.

Note: For a listing of dosage forms and brand names by country availability, see *Dosage Forms* section(s).

†Not commercially available in Canada.

Category

Antifungal (systemic).

Indications

General Considerations

Micafungin is active *in vitro* against. *Candida albicans, C. glabrata, C. krusei, C. parapsilosis*, and *C. tropicalis*.

In vivo micafungin has shown activity in both mucosal and disseminated murine models of candidiasis.

Accepted

Candidiasis, esophageal (treatment)—Micafungin is indicated for the treatment of patients with esophageal candidiasis.

Candidiasis, (prophylaxis)—Micafungin is indicated for the prevention of *Candida* infections in patients undergoing hematopoietic stem cell transplantation.

Unaccepted

The efficacy of micafungin against infections caused by fungi other than *Candida* has not been established.

Pharmacology/Pharmacokinetics

Physicochemical characteristics

Source—Micafungin sodium is a semisynthetic lipopeptide (echinocandin) synthesized by a chemical modification of a fermentation product of *Coleophoma empetri* F-11899.

Molecular weight—Micafungin sodium: 1292.26.

Solubility—Micafungin sodium is freely soluble in water, isotonic sodium chloride solution, *N,N*-dimethylformamide and dimethylsulfoxide, slightly soluble in methyl alcohol, and practically insoluble in acetonitrile, ethyl alcohol (95%), acetone, diethyl ether and *n*-hexane.

pH—Between 5-7 for reconstituted solution

Mechanism of action/Effect

Micafungin inhibits the synthesis of (1,3)-beta-D-glucan, an essential component of the fungal cell wall.

Absorption

- AUC_{0-24}: HIV positive patients with esophageal candidiasis: 54 ± 13 mcg h/mL following 50 mg dose; 115 ± 25 mcg h/mL following 100 mg dose; 167±40 mcg h/mL following 150 mg dose.
- AUC_{0-24}: Hematopoietic stem cell transplant patients: 234 ± 34 mcg h/mL following a 3 mg/kg dose; 339 ± 72 mcg h/mL following a 4 mg/kg dose; 479 ± 157 mcg h/mL following a 6 mg/kg dose; 663 ± 212 mcg h/mL following a 8 mg/kg dose.
- In healthy volunteers the ratio of metabolite to parent exposure (AUC):
- M-1, 150 mg/day: 6 to 11%.
- M-2, 150 mg/day: 1 to 2%.
- M-5, 150 mg/day: 6 to 2%.

Distribution

Volume of distribution (Vol_D)—Terminal phase: 0.39 ± 0.11 L/kg body weight in adult patients with esophageal candidiasis given doses of 50 mg to 150 mg.

Protein binding

Very high (>99%); predominantly to albumin

Biotransformation

Micafungin is metabolized to M-1 by arylsulfatase, with further metabolism to M-2 by catechol-*O*-methyltransferase. M-5 is formed by hydroxylation at the side chain of micafungin and catalyzed by cytochrome CYP450 isozymes.

In vitro micafungin is a substrate and a weak inhibitor of CYP3A.

In vivo hydroxylation by CYP3A is not a major pathway for micafungin.

Half-life

• HIV positive patients with esophageal candidiasis: 15.6 ± 2.8 following 50 mg dose; 16.9 ± 4.4 mcg/mL following 100 mg dose; 15.2 ± 2.2 mcg/mL following 150 mg dose.

• Hematopoietic stem cell transplant patients: 14 ± 1.4 mcg/mL following a 3 mg/kg dose; 14.2 ± 3.2 mcg/mL following a 4 mg/kg dose; 14.9 ± 2.6 mcg/mL following a 6 mg/kg dose; 17.2 ± 2.3 mcg/mL following a 8 mg/kg dose.

Peak Serum Concentration

• HIV positive patients with esophageal candidiasis: 5.1 ± 1 mcg/mL following 50 mg dose; 10.1 ± 2.6 mcg/mL following 100 mg dose; 16.4 ± 6.5 mcg/mL following 150 mg dose.

• Hematopoietic stem cell transplant patients: 21.1 ± 2.84 mcg/mL following a 3 mg/kg dose; 29.2 ± 6.2 mcg/mL following a 4 mg/kg dose; 38.4 ± 6.9 mcg/mL following a 6 mg/kg dose; 60.8 ± 26.9 mcg/mL following a 8 mg/kg dose.

Elimination

Renal and fecal recovery accounted for 82.5% of the administered dose. However fecal is the major route of elimination (total radioactivity at 28 days was 71.0% of the administered dose).

In hemodialysis, micafungin is highly protein bound and not dialyzable.

Precautions to Consider

Carcinogenicity

No life-time studies have been done in animals to evaluate the carcinogenic potential of micafungin.

Mutagenicity

Micafungin sodium showed no evidence of mutagenic or clastogenic effects in *in vitro* and *in vivo* tests including bacterial reversion, chromosomal aberration, and the intravenous mouse micronucleus test.

Pregnancy/Reproduction

Fertility—No impairment of fertility was seen in animal studies with micafungin sodium. However, intravenous administration of micafungin to male rats at or above 10 mg/kg for 9 weeks showed vacuolation of the epididymal ductal epithelial cells. Higher doses resulted in higher epididymis weights and reduced numbers of sperm cells.

Seminiferous tubular atrophy and decreased sperm was observed in studies done in dogs given intravenous doses of micafungin at 10 and 32 mg/kg for 39-weeks.

Pregnancy—Adequate and well controlled studies in humans have not been done. Studies in animals have shown that micafungin causes adverse effects in the fetus. Since animal studies are not always predictive of human response, micafungin should be used during pregnancy only if clearly needed.

Micafungin crosses the placenta. Pregnant rabbits given intravenous doses of micafungin at 32 mg/kg resulted in visceral abnormalities and abortion. Visceral abnormalities included abnormal lobation of the lung, levocardia, retrocaval ureter, anomalous right subclavian artery, and dilatation of the ureter.

FDA Pregnancy Category C

Breast-feeding

Micafungin is distributed into the milk of lactating rats. It is not known whether micafungin is distributed in human milk. Caution should be exercised when micafungin is administered to a nursing woman.

Pediatrics

No information is available on the relationship of age to the effects of micafungin in the pediatric population. Safety and efficacy have not been established.

Geriatrics

Appropriate studies performed to date have not demonstrated geriatrics-specific problems that would limit the usefulness of micafungin in the elderly. However, some elderly patients may be more sensitive to the effects of micafungin.

Pharmacogenetics

Micafungin AUC was approximately 23% greater in women than in men due to smaller body weight, following 14 daily doses of 150 mg in healthy volunteers.

Micafungin AUC was 26% greater in Japanese compared with blacks due to smaller body weight, following 14 daily doses of 150 mg in healthy volunteers.

Drug interactions and/or related problems

The following drug interactions and/or related problems have been selected on the basis of their potential clinical significance (possible mechanism in parentheses where appropriate)—not necessarily inclusive (» = major clinical significance):

Note: Combinations containing any of the following medications, depending on the amount present, may also interact with this medication.

» Nifedipine
(concomitant administration with micafungin increased nifedipine AUC by 18% and C_{max} by 42%; patients should be monitored for nifedipine toxicity and dosage should be reduced if necessary)

» Sirolimus
(concomitant administration with micafungin increased sirolimus AUC by 21%; patients should be monitored for sirolimus toxicity and dosage should be reduced if necessary)

Laboratory value alterations

The following have been selected on the basis of their potential clinical significance (possible effect in parentheses where appropriate)—not necessarily inclusive (» = major clinical significance).

With physiology/laboratory test values

» Alanine aminotransferase or
» Alkaline phosphatase, blood or
» Aspartate aminotransferase
(values may be increased)

» Creatinine, blood or
» Lactate dehydrogenase, blood or
» Urea, blood
(concentrations may be increased)

Medical considerations/Contraindications

The medical considerations/contraindications included have been selected on the basis of their potential clinical significance (reasons given in parentheses where appropriate)—not necessarily inclusive (» = major clinical significance).

Except under special circumstances, this medication should not be used when the following medical problem exists:

» Hypersensitivity to micafungin or to any component of the product

Risk-benefit should be considered when the following medical problem exists:

Hepatic function impairment, moderate or severe
(AUC and C_{max} values were 22% lower in patients with moderate hepatic impairment; studies in patients with severe hepatic impairment have not been done)

Patient monitoring

The following may be especially important in patient monitoring (other tests may be warranted in some patients, depending on condition; » = major clinical significance):

» Hematological effects
(patients who develop hemolysis or hemolytic anemia should be closely monitored for the risk/benefit of continuing micafungin therapy.)

» Hepatic effects
(patients who develop abnormal liver function tests during micafungin therapy should be monitored for evidence of worsening hepatic function and evaluated for the risk/benefit of continuing micafungin therapy.)

» Renal function impairment
(elevations in BUN and creatinine have been reported; patients who develop abnormal renal function tests while receiving micafungin therapy should be monitored for worsening renal function)

Side/Adverse Effects

The following side/adverse effects have been selected on the basis of their potential clinical significance (possible signs and symptoms in parentheses where appropriate)—not necessarily inclusive:

Those indicating need for medical attention

Incidence less frequent

Abnormal liver function test results (lab results that show problems with liver); ***hypokalemia*** (convulsions; decreased urine; dry mouth; irregular heartbeat; increased thirst; loss of appetite; mood changes;

muscle pain or cramps; nausea or vomiting; numbness or tingling in hands, feet, or lips; shortness of breath; unusual tiredness or weakness); ***hypomagnesemia*** (drowsiness; loss of appetite; mood or mental changes; muscle spasms [tetany] or twitching; seizures; nausea or vomiting; trembling; unusual tiredness or weakness); ***hypophosphatemia*** (bone pain; convulsions; loss of appetite; trouble breathing; unusual tiredness or weakness); ***leukopenia*** (black, tarry stools; chest pain; chills; cough; fever; painful or difficult urination; shortness of breath; sore throat; sores, ulcers, or white spots on lips or in mouth; swollen glands; unusual bleeding or bruising; unusual tiredness or weakness); ***lymphopenia*** (fever or chills; cough or hoarseness; lower back or side pain; painful or difficult urination); ***neutropenia*** (black, tarry, stools; chills; cough; fever; lower back or side pain; painful or difficult urination; pale skin; shortness of breath; sore throat; ulcers, sores, or white spots in mouth; unusual bleeding or bruising; unusual tiredness or weakness)

Incidence rare

Anemia (pale skin; troubled breathing with exertion; unusual bleeding or bruising; unusual tiredness or weakness); ***febrile neutropenia*** (black, tarry stools; chills; cough; fever; lower back or side pain; painful or difficult urination; pale skin; shortness of breath; sore throat; ulcers, sores, or white spots in mouth; unusual bleeding or bruising; unusual tiredness or weakness); ***hypertension*** (blurred vision; dizziness; nervousness; headache; pounding in the ears; slow or fast heartbeat); ***hypocalcemia*** (abdominal cramps; confusion; convulsions; difficulty in breathing; irregular heartbeats; mood or mental changes; muscle cramps in hands, arms, feet, legs, or face; numbness and tingling around the mouth, fingertips, or feet; shortness of breath; tremor); ***thrombocytopenia*** (black, tarry stools; bleeding gums; blood in urine or stools; pinpoint red spots on skin; unusual bleeding or bruising)

Incidence unknown

Anaphylactoid reaction (cough; difficulty swallowing; dizziness; fast heartbeat; hives; itching; puffiness or swelling of the eyelids or around the eyes, face, lips or tongue; shortness of breath; skin rash; tightness in chest; unusual tiredness or weakness; wheezing); ***hypersensitivity*** (difficulty in breathing or swallowing; fast heartbeat; shortness of breath; skin itching; rash, or redness; swelling of face, throat, or tongue); ***shock*** (cold clammy skin; confusion; dizziness; lightheadedness; fast, weak pulse; sweating; wheezing)

Observed during postmarketing trials

Acute renal failure (agitation; coma; confusion; decreased urine output; depression; dizziness; headache; hostility; irritability; lethargy; muscle twitching; nausea; rapid weight gain; seizures; stupor; swelling of face, ankles, or hands; unusual tiredness or weakness); ***hepatic function impairment*** (abdominal or stomach pain; chills; light-colored stools; dark urine; diarrhea; dizziness; fever; headache; itching; loss of appetite; nausea; rash; unpleasant breath odor; unusual tiredness or weakness; vomiting of blood; yellow eyes or skin); ***hemolytic anemia*** (back, leg, or stomach pains; bleeding gums; chills; dark urine; difficulty breathing; fatigue; fever; general body swelling; headache; loss of appetite; nausea or vomiting; nosebleeds; pale skin; sore throat; yellowing of the eyes or skin); ***hepatocellular damage*** (fever; stomach pain; yellow eyes or skin); ***renal impairment*** (lower back/side pain; decreased frequency/amount of urine; bloody urine; increased thirst; loss of appetite; nausea; vomiting; unusual tiredness or weakness; swelling of face, fingers, lower legs; weight gain; troubled breathing; increased blood pressure); ***white blood cell count decreased***

Those indicating need for medical attention only if they continue or are bothersome

Incidence less frequent

Abdominal pain (stomach pain); ***diarrhea; headache; hyperbilirubinemia*** (yellow eyes or skin); ***infusion site inflammation; nausea; phlebitis*** (bluish color changes in skin color; pain; tenderness; swelling of foot or leg); ***pyrexia*** (fever); ***rash; rigors*** (feeling unusually cold; shivering); ***vomiting***

Incidence rare

Appetite decreased; dizziness; dysgeusia (loss of taste; change in taste); ***dyspepsia*** (acid or sour stomach; belching; heartburn; indigestion; stomach discomfort upset or pain); ***flushing*** (feeling of warmth; redness of the face, neck, arms and occasionally upper chest); ***injection site pain; pruritus*** (itching skin); ***somnolence*** (sleepiness or unusual drowsiness); ***upper abdominal pain*** (upper stomach pain)

Overdose

For more information on the management of overdose or unintentional ingestion, **contact a poison control center** (see *Poison Control Center Listing*).

Treatment of overdose

There is no known specific antidote to micafungin. Treatment is generally symptomatic and supportive.

To enhance elimination—

Micafungin is highly protein bound and, therefore, not dialyzable.

Supportive care—

Patients in whom intentional overdose is confirmed or suspected should be referred for psychiatric consultation.

Patient Consultation

As an aid to patient consultation, refer to *Advice for the Patient, Micafungin (Systemic)*.

In providing consultation, consider emphasizing the following selected information (» = major clinical significance):

Before using this medication

» Conditions affecting use, especially:

Hypersensitivity to micafungin or any ingredients in the formulation

Pregnancy—Should be used during pregnancy only if clearly needed

Breast-feeding—Caution should be exercised when micafungin is administered to a nursing woman

Use in children—Safety and efficacy have not been established

Other medications, especially nifedipine or sirolimus

Other medical problems, especially hematological effects, hepatic effects, hepatic function impairment or renal function impairment

Proper use of this medication

» Proper dosing

Missed dose: Taking as soon as possible; not taking if almost time for next scheduled dose; not doubling doses

» Proper storage

Side/adverse effects

Signs of potential side effects, especially abnormal liver function test results, acute renal failure, anaphylactoid reaction, anemia, febrile neutropenia, hemolytic anemia, hepatic function impairment, hepatocellular damage, hypersensitivity, hypertension, hypocalcemia, hypokalemia, hypomagnesemia, hypophosphatemia, leukopenia, lymphopenia, neutropenia, renal impairment, shock, thrombocytopenia or white blood cell count decreased

General Dosing Information

Aseptic technique should be strictly observed in handling of materials for reconstitution and dilution since micafungin contains no preservative or bacterial agent.

An existing intravenous line should be flushed with 0.9% Sodium Chloride Injection, USP, prior to micafungin infusion.

No loading dose is required; 85% of the steady-state concentration is achieved after three daily doses.

Micafungin should be administered by slow intravenous infusion over a period of 1 hour.

Parenteral Dosage Forms

MICAFUNGIN SODIUM

Usual adult dose

Candidiasis, esophageal—

Intravenous infusion, 150 mg daily dose for approximately 15 days (range 10 to 30 days).

Candida, prophylaxis—

Intravenous infusion, 50 mg daily dose for approximately 19 days (range 6 to 51 days).

Note: For patients with renal impairment: no dosage adjustment is necessary.

Following hemodialysis: no supplementary dosing.

For patients with moderate hepatic impairment: no dosage adjustment is necessary; use of micafungin has not been studied in patients with severe hepatic insufficiency.

Usual pediatric dose

Safety and efficacy have not been established.

Usual geriatric dose

See *Usual adult dose*.

Strength(s) usually available

U.S.—

50 mg (Rx) [*Mycamine* (citric acid; lactose; sodium hydroxide)].

Packaging and storage
Store lyophilized cake/powder at 25° C (77° F), excursions permitted to 15° to 30°C (59° to 86°F).
Store the reconstituted product in the original vial at 25 °C (77° F) for up to 24 hours.
Store diluted infusion solution at 25° C (77° F) for up to 24 hours. Protect from light.

Preparation of dosage form
• To reconstitute micafungin, aseptically add 5 mL of 0.9% Sodium Chloride Injection into the vial.
• Visually inspect for particulate matter and discoloration. Do not use if there is any precipitation or foreign matter.
• Gently dissolve by swirling the vial. **Do not vigorously shake the vial.**
• Protect the diluted solution from light; however, it is not necessary to cover the infusion drip container or tubing.

For prophylaxis of Candida infections:
• Add 50 mg micafungin reconstituted solution (5 mL) into 100 mL of 0.9% Sodium Chloride Injection, USP.

For the treatment of esophageal candidiasis:
• Add 150 mg micafungin reconstituted solution (15 mL) into 100 mL of 0.9% Sodium Chloride Injection, USP.

Incompatibilities
Micafungin should not be mixed or co-infused with other medications. A precipitation has been shown to occur with other commonly used medications.

Auxiliary labeling
• Do not shake. Rotate vial gently.
• For single use only. Discard unused drug.

Caution
Micafungin is preservative-free. Do not use if solution is cloudy or has precipitated. Visually inspect the reconstituted solution prior to infusion.

Developed: 04/14/2005

MICONAZOLE—See *Antifungals, Azole (Vaginal), Miconazole (Systemic), Miconazole (Topical)*

MIDAZOLAM Systemic

VA CLASSIFICATION (Primary/Secondary): CN302/CN400; CN206

Note: Controlled substance classification
U.S.: Schedule IV

Commonly used brand name(s): *Versed*.

Note: For a listing of dosage forms and brand names by country availability, see *Dosage Forms* section(s).

Category
Sedative-hypnotic; anesthetic, general, adjunct; anesthetic, local, adjunct; anticonvulsant.

Indications
Note: Bracketed information in the *Indications* section refers to uses that are not included in U.S. product labeling.

WARNING: Midazolam should be used only in hospital or ambulatory care settings, including physicians' and dentists' offices, that provide for continuous monitoring of respiratory and cardiac function; also, flumazenil, resuscitative drugs and age- and size-appropriate resuscitative equipment, and personnel trained in their use, should be immediately available. Midazolam has been associated with respiratory depression and respiratory arrest, especially when used concomitantly with opioid analgesics for conscious sedation or when rapidly administered intravenously, and when used orally for sedation in non-critical care settings; in some cases, death or hypoxic encephalopathy has occurred

Accepted
Sedation and amnesia—Midazolam is indicated for preoperative sedation (induction of sleepiness or drowsiness and relief of apprehension) and to impair memory of perioperative events.

Sedation, conscious—Midazolam, used either alone or in conjunction with a narcotic, is indicated to produce sedation, anxiolysis, and amnesia prior to short diagnostic procedures or endoscopic procedures, such as bronchoscopy, gastroscopy, cystoscopy, coronary angiography, cardiac catheterization, and [direct-current cardioversion].

Midazolam also is indicated for sedation, anxiolysis, and amnesia prior to certain dental and minor surgical[1] procedures. This medication may be preferable to diazepam for intravenous sedation because of its faster onset of action, more consistent anterograde amnesia, and virtual lack of venous complications.

Sedation—Midazolam is indicated for the sedation of patients in intensive care settings, including intubated patients receiving mechanical ventilation.

Anesthesia, general, adjunct—Midazolam is indicated for induction of general anesthesia prior to administration of other anesthetic agents. It may be used in conjunction with narcotic premedication, thereby achieving induction of anesthesia within a relatively narrow dose range and in a short period of time. It may also be used for intravenous supplementation of nitrous oxide and oxygen (balanced anesthesia) for short surgical procedures; however, the recovery time may be prolonged compared to that of thiopental. The use of midazolam in longer surgical procedures has not been studied.

[Anesthesia, local, adjunct][1]—Midazolam is indicated as an adjunct to local or regional anesthesia for some diagnostic and therapeutic procedures. It may be used for sedation of healthy patients receiving subarachnoid or epidural anesthesia.

[Status epilepticus (treatment)][1]—Midazolam is indicated for the treatment of status epilepticus in adults and children, including children with refractory status epilepticus, treated with a benzodiazepine, phenobarbital or phenytoin. Midazolam treatment by intranasal and buccal/sublingual routes is indicated for prolonged seizures (including status epilepticus) when parenteral administration is not feasible.

[1]Not included in Canadian product labeling.

Pharmacology/Pharmacokinetics

Physicochemical characteristics
Molecular weight—362.24.
pKa—Midazolam base: 6.

Mechanism of action/Effect
Midazolam is a relatively short-acting benzodiazepine central nervous system (CNS) depressant. Its effects on the CNS are dependent on the dose administered, the route of administration, and whether it is used concomitantly with other medications.

Midazolam has anxiolytic, hypnotic, anticonvulsant, muscle relaxant, and anterograde amnestic effects, which are characteristic of benzodiazepines.

Although the exact mechanisms of the actions of benzodiazepines have not been completely established, it has been postulated that the actions of benzodiazepines are mediated through the inhibitory neurotransmitter gamma-aminobutyric acid (GABA), which is one of the major inhibitory neurotransmitters in the brain. Benzodiazepines are believed to increase the activity of GABA, thereby calming the patient, relaxing skeletal muscles, and, in high doses, producing sleep.

Benzodiazepines act as agonists at the benzodiazepine receptors, which have been shown to form a component of the benzodiazepine-GABA receptor-chloride ionophore complex. Most anxiolytics appear to act through at least one component of this complex to enhance the inhibitory action of GABA. Other actions of benzodiazepines, such as sedative, anticonvulsant, and muscle relaxant effects, may be mediated through a similar mechanism, although different receptor subtypes may be involved.

The hypnotic effect of midazolam appears to be related to GABA accumulation and occupation of the benzodiazepine receptor. Midazolam has a relatively high affinity (about twice that of diazepam) for the benzodiazepine receptor. It is believed that there are separate benzodiazepine and GABA receptors coupled to a common ionophore (chloride) channel, and that occupation of both receptors produces membrane hyperpolarization and neuronal inhibition. Midazolam interferes with reuptake of GABA, thereby causing accumulation of GABA. Also, it is postulated that the action of midazolam in induction of anesthesia involves excess GABA at neuronal synapses.

The site and mechanism of the amnestic action of midazolam are not known; however, the degree of amnesia usually, but not always, parallels the degree of drowsiness produced by midazolam.

Other actions/effects
Midazolam causes a moderate decrease in cerebrospinal fluid pressure (lumbar puncture measurements), similar to that produced by thiopental, when it is used for induction of anesthesia in patients without intracranial lesions.

In intracranial surgical patients with normal intracranial pressure but decreased compliance (subarachnoid screw measurements), midazolam attenuates the increase in intracranial pressure due to intubation to a degree comparable to that of thiopental.

Studies have shown that intraocular pressure is lowered moderately when midazolam is used for induction of anesthesia in patients without eye disease; studies have not been done in patients with glaucoma. Midazolam, like other benzodiazepines, may have anticholinergic effects on patients with glaucoma (angle-closure, acute).

Respiratory depression is produced; however, the respiratory depressant effect of midazolam is dose-related.

The cardiovascular effects of midazolam appear to be minimal. Cardiac hemodynamic studies have shown midazolam to cause a slight to moderate decrease in mean arterial pressure, cardiac output, stroke volume, and systemic vascular resistance when used for induction of anesthesia. In a study comparing the systemic vascular effects of midazolam and lorazepam in patients on cardiopulmonary bypass, midazolam was more effective than lorazepam in attenuating the increase in systemic vascular resistance accompanying cardiopulmonary bypass. Midazolam may cause slow heart rates (less than 65 per minute) to rise slightly, especially in patients taking propranolol for angina; it may cause faster heart rates (e.g., 85 per minute) to slow slightly.

Absorption

Mean absolute bioavailability of midazolam following intramuscular administration is greater than 90%. Mean absolute bioavailability of midazolam following oral administration is about 36%.

Distribution

Widely distributed in the body, including the cerebrospinal fluid and brain. The volume of distribution (Vol_D) usually averages between 1 and 3.1 (range, 0.95 to 6.6) liters per kg of body weight in the majority of patients.

Note: In patients with congestive heart failure—A twofold to threefold increase in Vol_D has been shown in a small group of patients, following a single intravenous dose of 5 mg.

In obese patients—Significant increase in Vol_D because of greatly enhanced distribution of midazolam into peripheral adipose tissue.

Protein binding

Plasma—Very high, 97% in healthy individuals and 93.5% in patients with renal failure.

Biotransformation

Rapidly metabolized by cytochrome P450 3A4 enzymes to 1-hydroxymethyl midazolam and 4-hydroxymidazolam. These metabolites may have some pharmacologic activity but less than that of the parent compound.

Half-life

Distribution—

15 minutes.

Elimination—

Midazolam: Approximately 2.5 (range, 1 to 5; rarely up to 12.3) hours in healthy patients.

Note: In patients with congestive heart failure—A twofold to threefold increase in elimination half-life has been shown in a small group of patients; however, total body clearance appeared to remain unchanged.

In patients with chronic renal failure—Elimination half-life does not appear to be significantly altered.

In obese patients—Because of greatly enhanced distribution of midazolam into peripheral adipose tissue, the elimination half-life is prolonged but there is no change in total body clearance.

In pediatric patients—The weight-adjusted clearance of midazolam in pediatric patients older than 1 year of age is the same as or higher than in adult patients. Clearance is slower and the terminal elimination half-life is longer (6.5 to 12 hours) in critically ill neonates as compared with those rates in other pediatric patients or adult patients.

1-Hydroxymethyl midazolam and 4-hydroxymidazolam: Elimination half-life is similar to that of midazolam.

Onset of action

Sedation—

Intramuscular: Within 15 minutes.

Intravenous: Within 1.5 to 5 minutes.

Oral: Within 30 minutes.

Anesthesia, induction—

Intravenous: With narcotic premedication—Approximately 0.75 to 1.5 minutes.

Without narcotic premedication—2 to 2.5 minutes.

Amnesia—

Intramuscular: In one study—30 minutes after administration, no recall shown in 73% of patients; 60 minutes after administration, no recall shown in 40% of patients.

Intravenous: For sedation in endoscopy studies—71% of patients had no recall of introduction of endoscope and 82% of patients had no recall of withdrawal of endoscope.

Note: Time of onset is affected by total dose administered and whether narcotic premedication is used concurrently.

Rapid onset of action after intravenous administration is due to the high lipophilicity of midazolam at physiologic pH.

Peak serum concentration

The peak serum concentration achieved with intramuscular administration of midazolam is about one half that achieved with intravenous administration. The mean peak serum concentration achieved with oral administration of 1 mg per kg of body weight of midazolam to pediatric patients 2 to 12 years of age was 201 ± 101 nanograms per mL.

Time to peak effect

Intramuscular—15 to 60 minutes. The time to attain peak effect may be longer in geriatric patients.

Duration of action

The relatively short duration of action of midazolam is due in part to its very high metabolic clearance and rapid rate of elimination. The termination of action after single doses is caused by both distribution into peripheral tissues and metabolic transformation.

The duration of the amnestic action appears to be directly dose-related.

Time to recovery

Usually within 2 hours, but may take up to 6 hours.

Note: Patients who receive midazolam usually recover at a slower rate than patients who receive thiopental.

Elimination

Renal; following intravenous administration, less than 0.03% of dose is excreted in urine as unchanged drug; 1-hydroxymethyl midazolam and 4-hydroxymidazolam metabolites are excreted in the urine as glucuronide conjugates.

Note: Elimination following intramuscular or oral administration is comparable to that following intravenous administration.

Precautions to Consider

Cross-sensitivity and/or related problems

Patients sensitive to other benzodiazepines may be sensitive to this medication also.

Carcinogenicity/Tumorigenicity

In 2-year studies in mice, midazolam was administered with the diet in doses of 1, 9, and 80 mg per kg of body weight (mg/kg) per day. At doses of 80 mg/kg per day, midazolam greatly increased the incidence of hepatic tumors in female mice and caused a small but significant increase in benign thyroid follicular cell tumors in male mice. These tumors occurred after chronic administration of midazolam, whereas only a single dose or several doses are usually used in humans. When midazolam was administered at doses of 9 mg/kg per day (25 times a human dose of 0.35 mg/kg per day), there was no increase in the incidence of tumors.

Mutagenicity

Midazolam was shown to have no mutagenic activity in *Salmonella typhimurium* (5 bacterial strains), Chinese hamster lung cells (V79), human lymphocytes, or in the micronucleus test in mice.

Pregnancy/Reproduction

Fertility—A reproduction study in male and female rats did not show midazolam to cause any impairment of fertility when given at doses up to 10 times the human intravenous dose of 0.35 mg/kg.

Pregnancy—Midazolam crosses the placenta. Since chlordiazepoxide and diazepam have been reported to increase the risk of congenital malformations when used during the first trimester of pregnancy, midazolam may be associated with this increased risk also.

Segment II teratology studies in rabbits and rats did not show midazolam to cause teratogenic effects when the medication was administered in doses 5 to 10 times the human dose of 0.35 mg/kg. In addition, studies in rats did not show midazolam to cause any adverse effects during gestation and lactation when administered at doses approximately 10 times the human dose of 0.35 mg/kg.

FDA Pregnancy Category D.

Labor and delivery—In humans, measurable concentrations of midazolam have been found in maternal venous serum, umbilical venous and arterial serum, and amniotic fluid, indicating placental transfer of the medication. Following intramuscular administration of 0.05 mg/kg of midazolam, both the venous and umbilical arterial serum concentrations were lower than maternal concentrations.

Labor and delivery—Midazolam was compared with thiopental for rapid-sequence intubation in women delivering babies by cesarean section. The neonates whose mothers received midazolam were more likely than the neonates whose mothers received thiopental to require tracheal intubation. In a second similar study, neonates whose mothers received midazolam were more likely to experience hypothermia and reduced body tone as compared with neonates whose mothers received thiopental. Additionally, midazolam is usually not recommended for induction of anesthesia prior to cesarean section because of the secondary CNS depressant effects on the neonate. Administration of other benzodiazepines during the last weeks of pregnancy has caused neonatal CNS depression.

Labor and delivery—Also, use of benzodiazepines just prior to or during labor may cause neonatal flaccidity.

Breast-feeding

Midazolam is distributed into breast milk. Midazolam received in the breast milk by neonates may be eliminated slowly because of their immature organ function. Neonates may be more susceptible to respiratory depression than older pediatric patients are.

Pediatrics

The weight-adjusted clearance of midazolam in pediatric patients older than 1 year of age is the same as or higher than in adult patients. Clearance is slower and the terminal elimination half-life is longer in critically ill neonates than in other pediatric patients or adult patients.

Neonates are more likely than other pediatric patients or adult patients to experience respiratory depression following administration of midazolam.

Midazolam injection contains benzyl alcohol. Administration of excessive amounts of benzyl alcohol to neonates has been associated with toxicity, including death. Although midazolam administered to neonates in the recommended doses does not contain amounts of benzyl alcohol associated with toxicity, the total load of benzyl alcohol from all sources must be considered. The 1-mg-per-mL and the 5-mg-per-mL vials of midazolam contain equal amounts of benzyl alcohol. The amount of benzyl alcohol the neonates receive may be decreased by diluting the 5-mg-per-mL vials to prepare neonatal dosages.

Geriatrics

The clearance of midazolam is reduced in geriatric patients as compared with that in younger adults.

When midazolam is used intravenously to produce sedation, anxiolysis, and amnesia in patients 60 years of age and older, debilitated, and/or chronically ill, dosage increments should be smaller and the rate of injection slower than in younger adults because the risk of underventilation or apnea is greater and the time to peak effect may be longer in older patients. Also, if concomitant CNS depressant premedication is used, the dose of midazolam should be reduced by at least 50%.

When midazolam is used for induction of anesthesia, patients older than 55 years of age, whether premedicated or not, usually require lower doses.

Also, time to complete recovery after midazolam administration for the induction of anesthesia may be prolonged in the elderly.

In addition, elderly patients are more likely to have age-related chronic renal failure, which may require reduction of dosage in patients receiving midazolam.

Drug interactions and/or related problems

The following drug interactions and/or related problems have been selected on the basis of their potential clinical significance (possible mechanism in parentheses where appropriate)—not necessarily inclusive (» = major clinical significance):

Note: Combinations containing any of the following medications, depending on the amount present, may also interact with this medication.

» Alcohol or

» CNS depression-producing medications, other, including those commonly used for preanesthetic medication or induction or supplementation of anesthesia (see *Appendix II*)
(concurrent use may increase the CNS depressant, respiratory depressant, and hypotensive effects of either these medications or midazolam; decrease dosage requirements of either these medications or midazolam; and prolong recovery from anesthesia; midazolam dosage may be reduced by at least 50% in elderly or debilitated patients receiving other CNS depression-producing medications)
(when midazolam is used as an intramuscular premedication prior to use of thiopental as an induction agent, a reduction in thiopental dosage of about 15% may be required)
(severe hypotension may occur in neonates receiving a continuous infusion of midazolam followed by a rapid injection of fentanyl)

Cimetidine or
Clarithromycin or
Diltiazem or
Erythromycin or
Fluconazole or
Indinavir or
Itraconazole or
Ketoconazole or
Ritonavir or
Roxithromycin or
» Saquinavir or
Verapamil or
Cytochrome P450 3A4 inhibitors, other (see *Appendix II*)
(inhibition of the cytochrome P450 3A4 enzyme system may cause a decrease in the metabolism of midazolam, which may result in delayed elimination and increased blood concentration; interaction with cytochrome P450 3A4 inhibitors is more likely when midazolam is administered orally than when it is administered parenterally)

Grapefruit or
Grapefruit juice
(decreased metabolism of midazolam, with resulting increased blood concentrations of midazolam, may occur; there may be an increased risk of toxicity; because this interaction occurs in large part in the gut wall, it is more likely when midazolam is administered orally than when it is administered parenterally)

Hypotension-producing medications, other (see *Appendix II*)
(hypotensive effects may be potentiated when these medications are used concurrently with midazolam; patients should be monitored for excessive fall in blood pressure during and following concurrent use)

Rifampin or
Cytochrome P450 3A4 inducers, other (see *Appendix II*)
(induction of the cytochrome P450 3A4 enzyme system may cause an increase in the metabolism of midazolam, which may result in its accelerated elimination and decreased blood concentration; the interaction is more likely when midazolam is administered orally than when it is administered parenterally)

Medical considerations/Contraindications

The medical considerations/contraindications included have been selected on the basis of their potential clinical significance (reasons given in parentheses where appropriate)—not necessarily inclusive (» = major clinical significance).

Except under special circumstances, this medication should not be used when the following medical problem exists:

» Allergy to midazolam, history of

Risk-benefit should be considered when the following medical problems exist:

Alcohol intoxication, acute, with depressed vital signs
(potential additive CNS depression)

Coma or
Shock
(hypnotic or hypotensive effects may be intensified or prolonged)

Congestive heart failure
(possible twofold to threefold increase in elimination half-life and a 40% increase in the volume of distribution)

» Glaucoma, angle-closure, acute
(midazolam, like other benzodiazepines, may have anticholinergic effect)

Hepatic function impairment
(midazolam is metabolized by the liver; in one study, patients with cirrhosis of the liver had reduced clearance and a longer elimination half-life of midazolam than healthy control subjects)

» Myasthenia gravis or
Neuromuscular disorders, other, such as muscular dystrophies and myotonias
(condition may be exacerbated)

Obesity
(midazolam's elimination half-life may be prolonged and volume of distribution may be increased)

» Pulmonary disease, obstructive, chronic, severe or
» Pulmonary insufficiency, acute
(midazolam has respiratory depressant effects; sedation and respiratory depression may be prolonged; patients with chronic obstructive pulmonary disease are unusually sensitive to the respiratory depressant effects of midazolam)

Renal failure, chronic
(peak concentration of midazolam may be higher in these patients than in healthy patients; induction of anesthesia may occur more rapidly, and recovery may be prolonged)

Hypersensitivity to other benzodiazepines

Caution is recommended in geriatric or debilitated patients and in higher-risk surgical patients, whether premedicated or not, because they may require lower doses for induction of anesthesia; caution should be used when intravenous midazolam is administered to patients with uncompensated acute illnesses, such as electrolyte disturbances

Also, caution should be used in ophthalmology patients during surgery because some patients may be confused or disoriented if they awaken during the procedure. This is especially important in patients with an open globe for cataract surgery or in patients for whom movement might be critical

Patient monitoring

The following may be especially important in patient monitoring (other tests may be warranted in some patients, depending on condition; » = major clinical significance):

» Blood oxygenation (pulse oximetry) and
» Blood pressure and
» Respiratory status and
» Vital signs, other
(it is recommended that patients be monitored continuously; when midazolam is used by non-anesthesiologists to produce deep sedation for surgical or diagnostic procedures, it is recommended that the patient be monitored continuously by someone not involved in conducting the surgical or diagnostic procedure; patients should be monitored for early signs of hypoventilation or apnea)

Note: Various organizations, including the American Society of Anesthesiologists (ASA) and the American Academy of Pediatrics (AAP), have established guidelines for pre-, intra-, and post-procedural care, evaluation, and monitoring of patients receiving sedation for diagnostic and therapeutic procedures. The level of monitoring should be appropriate to the level of sedation and the procedure being performed. When midazolam is used for light sedation (i.e., the patient is able to tolerate unpleasant procedures without cardiorespiratory compromise and is able to respond purposefully to verbal commands) by non-anesthesiologists, the American Society of Anesthesiologists recommends that a designated individual, other than the person performing the procedure, be present to monitor the patient. That designated person would be permitted to assist with other minor, interruptible tasks. However, when midazolam is used to produce deep sedation, the patient should be monitored continuously by someone not involved in conducting the surgical or diagnostic procedure. For deeply sedated patients, the person monitoring the patient should not assist with other tasks, even if the tasks are minor and interruptible.

Side/Adverse Effects

Note: The most frequent side/adverse effects of midazolam during anesthesia and surgery include decreased tidal volume and/or respiratory rate (in 23.3% of patients following intravenous administration and in 10.8% of patients following intramuscular administration) and apnea (in 15.4% of patients following intravenous administration). In addition, variations in blood pressure and pulse rate may occur.

Serious cardiorespiratory side/adverse effects have occurred primarily in older, chronically ill patients, with concomitant administration of other cardiorespiratory depressants (such as opioid [narcotic] analgesics) and with rapid administration of midazolam; these side/adverse effects have included respiratory depression, apnea, respiratory arrest, and/or cardiac arrest, sometimes resulting in death. Patients undergoing procedures involving the upper airway (e.g., upper endoscopy or dental procedures) are more likely than patients undergoing other types of procedures to experience respiratory depression, apnea, and respiratory arrest.

Midazolam administered intravenously has been associated with respiratory depression and respiratory arrest, especially when used concomitantly with opioid analgesics for conscious sedation or when rapidly administered; in some cases, death or hypoxic encephalopathy has occurred.

Midazolam administered orally has been associated with respiratory depression and respiratory arrest, especially when used for sedation in noncritical care settings.

Impairment of psychomotor skills may occur following midazolam sedation or anesthesia and may persist for varying lengths of time, depending upon the combination of medications and total dosages administered. Possible adverse effects on the patient's ability to drive or perform other tasks requiring alertness and coordination should be kept in mind when midazolam is administered for an outpatient procedure. It is recommended that patients not operate hazardous machinery or a motor vehicle until the effects of midazolam, such as drowsiness and amnesia, have subsided or until the day after anesthesia and surgery, whichever period of time is longer.

The following side/adverse effects have been selected on the basis of their potential clinical significance (possible signs and symptoms in parentheses where appropriate)—not necessarily inclusive:

Those indicating need for medical attention

Incidence more frequent

Apnea; hypotension—especially in patients premedicated with narcotic; ***respiratory depression***

Incidence rare—< 1%, primarily following intravenous administration

Emergence delirium; hyperventilation; irregular or fast heartbeat; muscle tremor; phlebitis; skin rash, hives, or itching; uncontrolled or jerky movements of body; unusual excitement, irritability, or restlessness; wheezing or difficulty in breathing

Note: *Muscle tremor, uncontrolled or jerky movements of body, unusual excitement, irritability, or restlessness* possibly are due to inadequate or excessive dosing or improper administration of medication; also, the possibility of cerebral hypoxia or paradoxical reaction should be considered.

Those indicating need for medical attention only if they continue or are bothersome

Incidence more frequent

Hiccups; pain at intramuscular injection site; pain during intravenous injection; tenderness at intravenous injection site

Incidence less frequent or rare

Blurred vision or other changes in vision; coughing; dizziness, lightheadedness, or feeling faint; drowsiness, prolonged; headache; lumps or hardness at injection site; muscle stiffness at intramuscular injection site; nausea; numbness, tingling, pain, or weakness in hands or feet; redness at injection site; vomiting

Overdose

For specific information on the agents used in the management of midazolam overdose, see:

- *Flumazenil (Systemic)* monograph; and/or
- *Sympathomimetic Agents—Cardiovascular Use (Parenteral-Systemic)* monograph.

For more information on the management of overdose or unintentional ingestion, **contact a Poison Control Center** (see *Poison Control Center Listing).*

Clinical effects of overdose

The following effects have been selected on the basis of their potential clinical significance (possible signs and symptoms in parentheses where appropriate)—not necessarily inclusive:

Acute

Cardiovascular depression; respiratory depression

Treatment of overdose

To enhance elimination—
It is not known if peritoneal dialysis, forced diuresis, or hemodialysis is useful in the treatment of midazolam overdose.

Specific treatment—
Administering flumazenil. See the package insert or the *Flumazenil (Systemic)* monograph for specific dosing guidelines for the use of this product.
For hypotension: Treatment may include intravenous fluid therapy, repositioning, vasopressors (if indicated), and other appropriate countermeasures.

Monitoring—
Monitoring of respiration, pulse rate, and blood pressure.

Supportive care—
General supportive measures.
Maintenance of a patent airway and support of ventilation.

Patient Consultation

As an aid to patient consultation, refer to *Advice for the Patient, Midazolam (Systemic).*

Note: The capacity of midazolam to cause anterograde amnesia should be considered when providing consultation to patients. Patients counseled after receiving midazolam may not remember being counseled.

In providing consultation, consider emphasizing the following selected information (» = major clinical significance):

Before receiving this medication

» Conditions affecting use, especially:

Hypersensitivity to midazolam or other benzodiazepines

In 2-year studies in mice, chronic administration of midazolam at doses of 80 mg per kg of body weight (mg/kg) per day greatly increased incidence of hepatic tumors in female mice and caused a small but significant increase in benign thyroid follicular cell tumors in male mice

Pregnancy—Risk of congenital malformations may be increased when midazolam is used during first trimester

Labor and delivery—Midazolam usually is not recommended for induction of anesthesia prior to cesarean section because of secondary CNS depressant effects on neonate; use of benzodiazepines just prior to or during labor may cause neonatal flaccidity

Breast-feeding—Midazolam is distributed into human breast milk; neonates may have difficulty eliminating the midazolam received in breast milk; neonates may experience respiratory depression after receiving midazolam in breast milk

Use in children—Critically ill neonates have reduced clearance of midazolam, and they are more likely than older pediatric patients or adult patients to experience respiratory depression after receiving midazolam; midazolam contains benzyl alcohol; excessive amounts of benzyl alcohol can cause toxicity in neonates

Pediatric patients may require a higher dose of midazolam on a weight-adjusted basis than required for adult patients

Use in the elderly—When midazolam is used intravenously to produce sedation, anxiolysis, and amnesia in patients 60 years of age and older, dosage increments should be smaller and the rate of injection slower than in younger adults because risk of underventilation or apnea is greater and the time to peak effect may be longer in older patients; if concomitant CNS depressant premedication is used, dosage of midazolam should be reduced by at least 50%; time to complete recovery after midazolam administration for induction of anesthesia may be prolonged in the elderly

Other medications, especially alcohol or other CNS depression-producing medications, or saquinavir

Other medical problems, especially myasthenia gravis, severe chronic obstructive pulmonary disease, or acute pulmonary insufficiency

Precautions after receiving this medication

» Possibility of psychomotor impairment following use of midazolam; using caution in driving or performing other tasks requiring alertness and coordination until the effects of midazolam have subsided or until the day after receiving midazolam, whichever period of time is longer

» Avoiding use of alcohol or other CNS depressants within 24 hours after receiving midazolam, except as directed by doctor

General Dosing Information

Midazolam has been shown to be three to four times as potent per mg as diazepam.

The dosage of midazolam must be individualized for each patient. Lower doses are usually required for elderly, debilitated, or high-risk surgical patients and for neonates. The dosage of midazolam should be adjusted according to the type and amount of premedication used. Additionally, the dose requirement of midazolam of each patient may vary. The dose always should be individualized and titrated slowly. The doses given in *Usual adult and adolescent dose* and *Usual pediatric dose* should be regarded as general guidelines only.

Midazolam should be used only in hospital or ambulatory care settings, including physicians' and dentists' offices, that provide for continuous monitoring of respiratory and cardiac function.

Prior to administration of midazolam, flumazenil, age- and size-appropriate resuscitative equipment, oxygen, and skilled personnel for the maintenance of a patent airway and support of ventilation must be immediately available. When midazolam is used to produce deep sedation for surgical or diagnostic procedures, it is recommended that the patient be monitored continuously by someone not involved in conducting the surgical or diagnostic procedure.

Midazolam should be administered intravenously as an induction agent only by a person trained in general anesthesia and should be used for conscious sedation only when a person skilled in maintaining a patent airway and supporting ventilation is present, because of possible respiratory depression.

When midazolam is administered intravenously for conscious sedation, it should be injected slowly in multiple small injections to attain the desired effect; it should not be administered by rapid or single bolus intravenous injection, because of the risk of respiratory depression and/or arrest, especially in elderly or debilitated patients. Three to five minutes should elapse between each small injection, so the full effect of the injection can be assessed before another injection is administered.

To facilitate slower intravenous injection of midazolam, the 1-mg-per-mL solution or dilution of the 1-mg-per-mL or 5-mg-per-mL solution is recommended.

During intravenous administration of midazolam, patients should be monitored continuously for early signs of underventilation or apnea, which can lead to hypoxia/cardiac arrest unless effective countermeasures are immediately taken. Also, monitoring of vital signs should be continued during the recovery period. In one case series, respiratory arrest occurred in patients 30 to 120 minutes after administration of midazolam. Patients should be monitored for several hours following use of midazolam.

Adult and pediatric patients undergoing procedures involving the upper airway (e.g., upper endoscopy or dental procedures) are more likely than patients undergoing other types of procedures to experience respiratory depression, apnea, and respiratory arrest when midazolam is used.

Caution should be taken to avoid intra-arterial injection because adverse effects of intra-arterial administration of intravenous midazolam in humans are not known. Extravasation should also be avoided.

Midazolam contains benzyl alcohol and so may not be administered by the intrathecal or epidural routes.

Administration of excessive amounts of benzyl alcohol to neonates has been associated with toxicity, including death. Although midazolam administered to neonates in the recommended doses does not contain amounts of benzyl alcohol associated with toxicity, the total load of benzyl alcohol from all sources must be considered. The 1-mg-per-mL and the 5-mg-per-mL vials of midazolam contain equal amounts of benzyl alcohol. The amount of benzyl alcohol may be decreased for neonatal patients by diluting the 5-mg-per-mL vials to prepare neonatal dosages.

When midazolam is administered intramuscularly, it is recommended that the medication be injected deep into a large muscle mass.

When midazolam is used for peroral endoscopic procedures, a topical anesthetic agent and the availability of necessary countermeasures are recommended because an increase in cough reflex and laryngospasm may occur.

When midazolam is used for bronchoscopic procedures, a narcotic premedication is recommended.

Midazolam may produce partial or complete impairment of recall for up to several hours, depending on the dose.

Although midazolam is approved by the Food and Drug Administration (FDA) for administration by the intramuscular, intravenous, and oral routes only, the intranasal, buccal,rectal, and sublingual routes are sometimes used in pediatric patients. The 5-mg-per-mL midazolam injection has been used intranasally and sublingually for preoperative sedation and amnesia and sedation, anxiolysis, and amnesia prior to diagnostic or short therapeutic procedures by placing midazolam into a small syringe (with the needle removed) and administering it intranasally or sublingually. The midazolam 5-mg-per-mL injection has also been used intranasally and buccally for treatment of seizures. In one study, pediatric patients receiving intranasal midazolam were more likely to cry and cried longer than pediatric patients receiving the drug sublingually.

Oral midazolam should not be mixed in any other liquid prior to ingestion.

Patients receiving midazolam for sedation in the intensive care unit also may require appropriate analgesia. Administration of an opioid analgesic in addition to midazolam will reduce the dose requirement for midazolam.

Abrupt discontinuation of long-term midazolam therapy may result in precipitation of symptoms of withdrawal. Midazolam should be tapered gradually if it has been administered for more than a few days.

Diet/Nutrition
Bioavailability of orally administered midazolam may be increased by ingestion of grapefruit or grapefruit juice, resulting in higher blood concentrations of midazolam.

Oral Dosage Forms

Note: The dosing and dosage forms available are expressed in terms of midazolam base.

MIDAZOLAM HYDROCHLORIDE ORAL SOLUTION

Usual pediatric dose
Sedation, preoperative, and amnesia or
Sedation, conscious (sedation, anxiolysis, and amnesia)—
Infants and children 6 months of age and older: Oral, 0.25 to 0.5 mg (base) per kg of body weight thirty to forty-five minutes prior to induction of anesthesia or to the diagnostic or therapeutic procedure. Younger (6 months to 6 years of age) and less cooperative children may need higher doses (i.e., up to 1 mg per kg of body weight). Lower doses (i.e., 0.25 mg per kg of body weight) may be sufficient for older and more cooperative patients.

Usual pediatric prescribing limits
15 to 20 mg.
Note: When midazolam is administered concomitantly with narcotic analgesics or other CNS depressants or to patients having cardiac or respiratory compromise or higher risk surgical patients, the dosage of midazolam should be reduced.

Strength(s) usually available
U.S.—
2 mg (base) per mL (Rx) [*Versed* (sorbitol; glycerin; citric acid anhydrous; sodium citrate; sodium benzoate; sodium saccharin; edetate disodium; FD&C Red #33)].
Canada—
Dosage form not commercially available.

Packaging and storage
Store in a tight, light-resistant container.
Store between 15 and 30 °C (59 and 86 °F), preferably at 25 °C (77 °F).

Auxiliary labeling
- Protect from light.
- Take by mouth only (use oral dispenser included with medication).

Note
Include patient package insert and oral dispenser when dispensing.

Parenteral Dosage Forms

Note: Bracketed uses in the *Dosage Forms* section refer to categories of use and/or indications that are not included in U.S. product labeling.
The dosing and dosage forms available are expressed in terms of midazolam base.

MIDAZOLAM HYDROCHLORIDE INJECTION

Usual adult dose
Sedation, preoperative, and amnesia—
Patients younger than 60 years of age—
American Society of Anesthesiologists (ASA) I or II (good-risk surgical patients):
Intramuscular, 70 to 80 mcg (0.07 to 0.08 mg) (base) per kg of body weight, approximately thirty to sixty minutes before surgery.
ASA III or IV (patients with severe systemic disease or debilitation):
Intramuscular, 20 to 50 mcg (0.02 to 0.05 mg) (base) per kg of body weight, approximately thirty to sixty minutes before surgery.
Patients 60 years of age and older—
Intramuscular, 20 to 50 mcg (0.02 to 0.05 mg) (base) per kg of body weight, approximately thirty to sixty minutes before surgery.
Note: Lower doses may be sufficient in elderly or debilitated patients.
Midazolam may be administered concurrently with atropine or scopolamine hydrochloride and reduced doses of narcotics. Observe patients for signs of cardiorespiratory depression.
Sedation, conscious (sedation, anxiolysis, and amnesia)—
Unpremedicated patients younger than 60 years of age—
Intravenous, initially no more than 2.5 mg (base), administered slowly over a period of at least two minutes, immediately prior to the procedure; after an additional two or more minutes to allow for clinical effect, dosage may be further titrated in small increments of the initial dose (with intervals of two or more minutes being allowed after each increment) to the desired effect. A total dose of more than 5 mg is not usually necessary. Additional maintenance doses may be administered, if necessary, in increments of 25% of initial dose to maintain desired level of sedation.
Note: When midazolam is administered concomitantly with narcotic analgesics or other CNS depressants, the dosage of midazolam should be reduced by approximately 30%.
The desired endpoint for conscious sedation can usually be attained within three to six minutes, depending on the total dose administered and whether or not narcotic premedication is used concomitantly.
The therapeutic dosage range between sedation and unconsciousness or disorientation appears to be narrower than for other benzodiazepines (e.g., diazepam, lorazepam).
Unpremedicated patients 60 years of age and older, and debilitated or chronically ill patients—
Intravenous, initially no more than 1.5 mg (base), administered slowly over a period of at least two minutes, immediately prior to procedure; after an additional two or more minutes to allow for clinical effect, dosage may be further titrated, if necessary, but the rate of administration should not exceed 1 mg over a two-minute period (intervals of two or more minutes should be allowed each time). A total dose of more than 3.5 mg is not usually necessary. Additional maintenance doses may be administered, if necessary, in increments of 25% of initial dose to maintain desired level of sedation.
Note: When midazolam is administered concomitantly with narcotic analgesics or other CNS depressants, the dosage of midazolam should be reduced by 50%.
Also, dosage increments should be smaller and the rate of injection slower because the danger of underventilation or apnea is greater in elderly patients and patients with chronic disease states or decreased pulmonary reserve; also, it may take longer to achieve the peak effect in these patients.
The desired endpoint for conscious sedation can usually be attained within three to six minutes, depending on the total dose administered and whether or not narcotic premedication is used concomitantly.
The therapeutic dosage range between sedation and unconsciousness or disorientation appears to be narrower than for other benzodiazepines (e.g., diazepam, lorazepam).
Anesthesia, general, adjunct (prior to administration of other general anesthetics)—
Unpremedicated patients—
Up to 55 years of age—Intravenous, initially 300 to 350 mcg (0.3 to 0.35 mg) (base) per kg of body weight, administered over a period of five to thirty seconds and allowing two minutes for effect.
Note: If necessary to complete induction, additional doses may be given in increments of about 25% of initial dose, or inhalation general anesthetics may be used.
Up to 600 mcg (0.6 mg) (base) per kg of body weight as a total dose may be used for induction, if necessary; however, larger doses may prolong recovery.
55 years of age and older—ASA I or II (good-risk surgical patients): Intravenous, initially 150 to 300 mcg (0.15 to 0.3 mg) (base) per kg of body weight, administered over a period of twenty to thirty seconds.
ASA III or IV (patients with severe systemic disease or debilitation): Intravenous, initially 150 to 250 mcg (0.15 to 0.25 mg) (base) per kg of body weight, administered over a period of twenty to thirty seconds.
Premedicated (sedative or narcotic) patients—
Up to 55 years of age—Intravenous, 150 to 350 mcg (0.15 to 0.35 mg) (base) per kg of body weight, administered over a period of twenty to thirty seconds and allowing two minutes for effect. A dose of 250 mcg (0.25 mg) per kg of body weight is usually sufficient.
55 years of age and older—ASA I or II: Intravenous, initially 200 mcg (0.2 mg) (base) per kg of body weight.
ASA III or IV: Intravenous, 150 mcg (0.15 mg) (base) per kg of body weight may be sufficient.

Note: When sedative or, especially, narcotic premedication has been administered, the recommended dose range of midazolam is 150 to 350 mcg (0.15 to 0.35 mg) (base) per kg of body weight.

Additional doses may be given in increments of about 25% of induction dose in response to signs of lightening anesthesia, repeated as necessary.

Narcotic premedications frequently used include: fentanyl (1.5 to 2 mcg [0.0015 to 0.002 mg] per kg of body weight intravenously five minutes before induction); morphine (up to 150 mcg [0.15 mg] per kg of body weight intramuscularly, the dosage being individualized); meperidine (up to 1 mg per kg of body weight intramuscularly, the dosage being individualized); and fentanyl citrate and droperidol combination (0.02 mL per kg of body weight intramuscularly).

Sedative premedications frequently used include: hydroxyzine pamoate (100 mg orally) and secobarbital sodium (200 mg orally).

Premedications should be administered at least thirty to sixty minutes prior to midazolam induction, with the exception of narcotic analgesics (e.g., fentanyl), which should be administered two to five minutes before induction.

Sedation in critical care settings—

Intravenous infusion, 20 to 100 mcg (0.02 to 0.1 mg) (base) per kg of body weight per hour, initially, then titrated to the desired level of sedation. If a loading dose is needed, 10 to 50 mcg (0.01 to 0.05 mg) per kg of body weight may be administered over several minutes prior to initiation of the continuous infusion. This dose may be repeated at 10-15 minute intervals until adequate sedation is achieved.

[Anesthetic, local, adjunct (epidural or axillary block)][1]—

Intravenous, 30 to 60 mcg (0.03 to 0.06 mg) (base) per kg of body weight, the dosage being slowly titrated.

Note: Individual response to midazolam is variable. The infusion rate should be titrated to the desired level of sedation, taking into account the patient's age, clinical status and current medications. In general, midazolam should be infused at the lowest rate that produces the desired level of sedation. Assessment of sedation should be performed at regular intervals and the midazolam infusion rate adjusted up or down by 25% to 50% of the initial infusion rate so as to assure adequate titration of sedation level. Larger adjustments or even a small incremental dose may be necessary if rapid changes in the level of sedation are indicated. In addition, the infusion rate should be decreased by 10% to 25% every few hours to find the minimum effective infusion rate. Finding the minimum effective infusion rate decreases the potential accumulation of midazolam and provides for the most rapid recovery once the infusion is terminated.

[Status epilepticus (treatment)][1]—

Intravenous, 0.125 mg per kg of body weight followed by a 3 mg per hour continuous infusion.

Intramuscular, 0.2 mg per kg of body weight.

Note: Buccal, 10 mg.

Patients weighing 50 kg or greater: Intranasal, 50 mg.

Patients weighing less than 50 kg: Intranasal, 25 mg.

Usual pediatric dose

Sedation, preoperative, and amnesia or
Sedation, conscious (sedation, anxiolysis, and amnesia)—

Infants up to 6 months of age—

The dose is not clearly established because there is variability in when pediatric patients progress from neonatal to infant physiology in terms of their abilities to tolerate, metabolize, and eliminate midazolam. Pediatric patients up to 6 months of age are especially vulnerable to airway obstruction and hypoventilation. Titration with small increments and careful monitoring are especially important when midazolam is used in pediatric patients up to 6 months of age.

Infants and children 6 months to 5 years of age—

Intravenously by intermittent injection, 50 to 100 mcg (0.05 to 0.1 mg) (base) per kg of body weight; sometimes up to 600 mcg (0.6 mg) per kg of body weight may be necessary, but usually no more than a total of 6 mg is needed to reach the desired endpoint.

Intramuscular, 100 to 150 mcg (0.1 to 0.15 mg) (base) per kg of body weight. Doses of up to 500 mcg (0.5 mg) per kg of body weight have been used for deep sedation.

Children 6 to 12 years of age—

Intravenously by intermittent injection, 25 to 50 mcg (0.025 to 0.05 mg) (base) per kg of body weight; sometimes up to 400 mcg (0.4 mg) per kg of body weight may be necessary, but usually no more than a total of 10 mg is needed to reach the desired endpoint.

Intramuscular, 100 to 150 mcg (0.1 to 0.15 mg) (base) per kg of body weight. Doses of up to 500 mcg (0.5 mg) per kg of body weight have been used for deep sedation.

Adolescents 12 to 16 years of age—

See *Usual adult dose*. Some adolescents may require higher doses than adults, but usually no more than a total of 10 mg is needed to reach the desired endpoint.

Note: In obese pediatric patients, the dose should be calculated based on ideal body weight.

Anesthesia, general, adjunct (prior to administration of other general anesthetics)—

Infants up to 6 months of age—

The dose is not clearly established because there is variability in when pediatric patients progress from neonatal to infant physiology in terms of their abilities to tolerate, metabolize, and eliminate midazolam. Pediatric patients up to 6 months of age are especially vulnerable to airway obstruction and hypoventilation. Titration with small increments and careful monitoring are especially important when midazolam is used in pediatric patients up to 6 months of age.

Infants and children 6 months to 5 years of age—

Intravenously by intermittent injection, 50 to 100 mcg (0.05 to 0.1 mg) (base) per kg of body weight; sometimes up to 600 mcg (0.6 mg) per kg of body weight may be necessary, but usually no more than a total of 6 mg is needed to reach the desired endpoint.

Children 6 to 12 years of age—

Intravenously by intermittent injection, 25 to 50 mcg (0.025 to 0.05 mg) (base) per kg of body weight; sometimes up to 400 mcg (0.4 mg) per kg of body weight may be necessary, but usually no more than a total of 10 mg is needed to reach the desired endpoint.

Adolescents 12 to 16 years of age—

See *Usual adult dose*. Some adolescents may require higher doses than adults, but usually no more than a total of 10 mg is needed to reach the desired endpoint.

Sedation in critical care settings—

Neonates up to 32 weeks gestation—

Intravenous infusion in patients whose trachea is intubated, 30 mcg (0.03 mg) (base) per kg of body weight per hour.

Note: Intravenous loading doses should not be administered to neonatal patients.

Neonates 32 weeks gestation and older—

Intravenous infusion in patients whose trachea is intubated, 60 mcg (0.06 mg) (base) per kg of body weight per hour.

Note: Intravenous loading doses should not be administered to neonatal patients.

Infants and children—

Intravenous infusion in patients whose trachea is intubated, initially, 60 to 120 mcg (0.06 to 0.12 mg) (base) per kg of body weight per hour, then titrated to desired effect. An intravenous loading dose of 50 to 200 mcg (0.05 to 0.2 mg) per kg of body weight administered over at least two to three minutes can be used prior to initiation of the continuous infusion.

Note: The rate of infusion can be increased or decreased (generally by 25% of the initial or subsequent infusion rate) as required, or supplemental intravenous doses of midazolam can be administered to increase or maintain the desired effect. Frequent assessment at regular intervals using standard pain/sedation scales is recommended.

[Status epilepticus (treatment)][1]—

Intravenous, 0.15 to 0.2 mg per kg of body weight bolus followed by a 1 to 5 mcg per kg of body weight per minute continuous infusion.

Intramuscular, 0.2 mg per kg of body weight.

Note: Intranasal, 0.2 mg per kg of body weight.

Strength(s) usually available

U.S.—

1 mg (base) per mL (Rx) [*Versed* (benzyl alcohol 1%; disodium edetate 0.01%; sodium chloride 0.8%)].

5 mg (base) per mL (Rx) [*Versed* (benzyl alcohol 1%; disodium edetate 0.01%; sodium chloride 0.8%)].

Canada—

1 mg (base) per mL (Rx) [*Versed* (benzyl alcohol 10.45 mg; disodium edetate 0.1 mg; sodium chloride 8 mg)].

5 mg (base) per mL (Rx) [*Versed* (benzyl alcohol 10.45 mg; disodium edetate 0.1 mg; sodium chloride 8 mg)].

Packaging and storage
Store between 15 and 30 °C (59 and 86 °F), unless otherwise specified by manufacturer. Protect from freezing.

Preparation of dosage form
Midazolam injection is compatible with 5% dextrose in water, 0.9% sodium chloride, and lactated Ringer's solution.

Midazolam injection may be mixed in same syringe with frequently used premedicants, such as morphine sulfate, meperidine hydrochloride, atropine sulfate, or scopolamine hydrobromide.

Stability
Midazolam injection should not be used if it contains a precipitate or is discolored.

When midazolam injection is mixed in the same syringe with frequently used premedicants, such as morphine sulfate, meperidine hydrochloride, atropine sulfate, or scopolamine hydrobromide, the solution is stable for 30 minutes.

When midazolam injection is diluted in 5% dextrose in water or 0.9% sodium chloride, the solution is stable for 24 hours; if mixed with lactated Ringer's solution (Hartmann's solution), the solution should be used within 4 hours.

Note
Controlled substance in the U.S.

---

[1]Not included in Canadian product labeling.

Revised: 01/14/2002

MIDODRINE Systemic

VA CLASSIFICATION (Primary): CV900

Commonly used brand name(s): *ProAmatine*.

Note: For a listing of dosage forms and brand names by country availability, see *Dosage Forms* section(s).

Category
Antihypotensive, idiopathic orthostatic; vasopressor.

Indications
Note: Bracketed information in the *Indications* section refers to uses that are not included in U.S. product labeling.

Accepted
Hypotension (treatment)—Midodrine is indicated for the treatment of symptomatic orthostatic hypotension. Midodrine should be used in patients who are considerably impaired and for whom standard clinical care, including nonpharmacologic treatment (such as support stockings), fluid expansion, and lifestyle changes, has not been successful.

[Hypotension, intradialytic (treatment)][1]—Midodrine is indicated for the treatment of hypotension in patients who are undergoing hemodialysis.

[Hypotension, secondary, psychotropic agent-induced (treatment)][1]—Midodrine is indicated for the treatment of hypotension induced by the use of psychotropic agents.

[Hypotension, secondary, infection-related (treatment)][1]—Midodrine is indicated for the treatment of infection-related hypotension in pediatric patients.

---

[1]Not included in Canadian product labeling.

Pharmacology/Pharmacokinetics

Physicochemical characteristics
Molecular weight—290.7.

pH—3.5 to 5.5 (5% aqueous solution).

pKa—7.8 (0.3% aqueous solution).

Solubility—

Water: Soluble.

Methanol: Sparingly soluble.

Mechanism of action/Effect
Midodrine is a prodrug for desglymidodrine, the active metabolite. Desglymidodrine, an alpha$_1$-agonist, increases blood pressure and vascular tone by stimulating the alpha-adrenergic receptors of the arteriolar and venous vasculature. It does not stimulate cardiac beta-adrenergic receptors. Desglymidodrine does not have effects on the central nervous system because it diffuses poorly across the blood-brain barrier. Desglymidodrine increases standing, sitting, and supine systolic and diastolic blood pressure in patients with orthostatic hypotension of various etiologies.

Other actions/effects
Desglymidodrine may have a bradycardiac effect, primarily due to vagal reflex.

Absorption
Rapidly absorbed. Absolute bioavailability of desglymidodrine is 93% and is not affected by food. The amount of desglymidodrine formed after oral or intravenous administration is about the same.

Protein binding
Not significant for midodrine or desglymidodrine.

Biotransformation
Studies have not been done. Deglycination of midodrine to desglymidodrine occurs in various tissues. Both midodrine and desglymidodrine are metabolized in part by the liver.

Half-life
Elimination—

Midodrine—Approximately 25 minutes.

Desglymidodrine—3 to 4 hours.

Time to peak concentration
Midodrine—30 minutes.

Desglymidodrine—1 to 2 hours.

Duration of action
Approximately 2 to 3 hours after a 10-mg dose.

Elimination
Desglymidodrine—Renal: Approximately 80% by active renal tubular secretion.

In dialysis—

Desglymidodrine is dialyzable.

Precautions to Consider

Carcinogenicity
No evidence of carcinogenicity was found in long-term studies in rats and mice given daily doses of 3 to 4 times the maximum recommended human dose (MRHD) on a mg per square meter of body surface area (mg/m^2) basis.

Mutagenicity
No evidence of mutagenicity was found in investigational studies.

Pregnancy/Reproduction
Fertility—No impaired fertility was observed in the dominant lethal assay in male mice. No other fertility studies have been done.

Pregnancy—Adequate and well-controlled studies in humans have not been done.

Reproduction studies in rats and rabbits given doses 13 and 7 times the maximum recommended human dose, respectively, on a mg/m^2 basis showed an increased rate of embryo resorption and reduced fetal body weight. Fetal survival in rabbits was also decreased at doses of 7 times the maximum recommended human dose. No teratogenic effects were observed in studies in rats and rabbits.

FDA Pregnancy Category C.

Breast-feeding
It is not known whether midodrine is distributed into breast milk. However, problems in humans have not been documented.

Pediatrics
A study performed in 120 patients 6 months to 12 years of age has not demonstrated pediatrics-specific problems that would limit the usefulness of midodrine in children.

Geriatrics
Studies performed in patients 65 years of age and older have not demonstrated geriatrics-specific problems that would limit the usefulness of midodrine in the elderly. Serum concentrations of midodrine and desglymidodrine in patients 65 years of age and older are similar to those of patients younger than 65.

Drug interactions and/or related problems
The following drug interactions and/or related problems have been selected on the basis of their potential clinical significance (possible mechanism in parentheses where appropriate)—not necessarily inclusive (» = major clinical significance):

Note: Combinations containing any of the following medications, depending on the amount present, may also interact with this medication.

Alpha-adrenergic blocking agents, such as:
Doxazosin
Prazosin
Terazosin
(concurrent use may antagonize the antihypotensive effects of midodrine)

Bradycardia-causing medications, such as:
Beta-adrenergic blocking agents
» Digitalis glycosides
(concurrent use may have additive bradycardiac effects; digitalis glycosides may exacerbate or precipitate atrioventricular [AV] block or arrhythmia)

Medications eliminated by active renal tubular secretion, such as:
Cimetidine
Flecainide
Metformin
Procainamide
Quinidine
Ranitidine
Triamterene
(concurrent use may interfere with renal clearance of these medications or of desglymidodrine because of competition for active renal tubular secretion)

» Sodium-retaining corticosteroids, such as fludrocortisone
(concurrent use may increase sodium retention and cause supine hypertension; decreasing salt intake prior to initiation of midodrine therapy or reducing the dose of the corticosteroid may minimize this effect)

» Vasoconstricting medications, such as:
Dihydroergotamine
Ephedrine
Phenylephrine
Phenylpropanolamine
Pseudoephedrine
(effects on blood pressure may be additive with concurrent use; blood pressure should be monitored carefully)

Medical considerations/Contraindications

The medical considerations/contraindications included have been selected on the basis of their potential clinical significance (reasons given in parentheses where appropriate)—not necessarily inclusive (» = major clinical significance).

Except under special circumstances, this medication should not be used when the following medical problems exist:

» Cardiac disease, severe or
» Hypertension, supine, persistent and excessive or
» Pheochromocytoma or
» Thyrotoxicosis
(increases in blood pressure due to midodrine therapy may aggravate these conditions)

» Renal function impairment, acute
(decreased elimination may increase serum concentrations of desglymidodrine)

» Urinary retention
(condition may be exacerbated because of the action of desglymidodrine on the alpha-adrenergic receptors of the bladder neck)

Risk-benefit should be considered when the following medical problems exist:

Hepatic function impairment
(metabolism of midodrine and desglymidodrine may be decreased)

Renal function impairment
(elimination of desglymidodrine may be decreased; renal function should be assessed prior to midodrine therapy)

Sensitivity to midodrine

Visual problems, diabetes-associated or
Visual problems, history of
(increases in blood pressure from midodrine therapy may aggravate this condition, particularly with concurrent use of fludrocortisone, a corticosteroid known to cause an increase in intraocular pressure and glaucoma)

Patient monitoring

The following may be especially important in patient monitoring (other tests may be warranted in some patients, depending on condition; » = major clinical significance):

Blood pressure measurements
(supine and sitting blood pressure should be monitored during midodrine therapy)

Hepatic function determinations and
Renal function determinations
(because desglymidodrine is metabolized by the liver and eliminated by the kidneys, it may be necessary to evaluate renal and hepatic function prior to initiation of and during midodrine therapy)

Side/Adverse Effects

The following side/adverse effects have been selected on the basis of their potential clinical significance (possible signs and symptoms in parentheses where appropriate)—not necessarily inclusive:

Those indicating need for medical attention

Incidence more frequent

Hypertension, supine (blurred vision; cardiac awareness; headache; pounding in the ears)

Note: *Supine hypertension* is the most serious adverse effect that may occur with midodrine therapy. In clinical trials, patients experienced both sitting and supine hypertension. Approximately 13.4% of patients administered 10 mg of midodrine experienced systolic blood pressures of about 200 mm Hg. This was most commonly seen in patients with relatively elevated systolic blood pressures prior to treatment.

Incidence rare

Bradycardia (fainting; increased dizziness; slow pulse)

Those indicating need for medical attention only if they continue or are bothersome

Incidence more frequent

Burning, itching, or prickling of the scalp; chills; piloerection (goosebumps); ***urinary frequency, retention, or urgency***

Incidence less frequent

Anxiety or nervousness; confusion; dry mouth; flushing of face or vasodilation; headache or feeling of pressure in the head; skin rash

Incidence rare

Backache; canker sores; dizziness; dry skin; gastrointestinal effects, including flatulence; gastrointestinal distress; heartburn; and nausea; insomnia (trouble in sleeping); ***leg cramps; pain or sensitivity of skin to touch; somnolence*** (drowsiness); ***visual field defects; weakness***

Overdose

For specific information on the agents used in the management of midodrine overdose, see the *Phentolamine (Systemic)* monograph.

For more information on the management of overdose or unintentional ingestion, **contact a Poison Control Center** (see *Poison Control Center Listing*).

Clinical effects of overdose

The following effects have been selected on the basis of their potential clinical significance (possible signs and symptoms in parentheses where appropriate)—not necessarily inclusive:

Acute and chronic

Hypertension (blurred vision; cardiac awareness; headache; pounding in the ears); ***piloerection*** (goosebumps); ***sensation of coldness; urinary retention***

Treatment of overdose

To decrease absorption—Emesis may be induced.

Specific treatment—Administration of alpha-sympatholytic medications, such as phentolamine.

Supportive care—Patients in whom intentional overdose is confirmed or suspected should be referred for psychiatric consultation.

Patient Consultation

As an aid to patient consultation, refer to *Advice for the Patient, Midodrine (Systemic)*.

In providing consultation, consider emphasizing the following selected information (» = major clinical significance):

Before using this medication

» Conditions affecting use, especially:
Sensitivity to midodrine
Other medications, especially digitalis glycosides, sodium-retaining corticosteroids, or vasoconstricting medications
Other medical problems, especially acute renal function impairment, persistent and excessive supine hypertension, pheochromocytoma, severe cardiac disease, thyrotoxicosis, or urinary retention

Proper use of this medication

» Not taking last daily dose after the evening meal or less than 3 to 4 hours before bedtime

» Not taking dose if patient will be supine for any length of time

» Proper dosing

Missed dose: Taking as soon as possible; not taking if almost time for next dose; not doubling doses

» Proper storage

Precautions while using this medication

Not taking other medications, especially nonprescription sympathomimetic agents, unless discussed with physician

Side/adverse effects

Signs of potential side effects, especially supine hypertension and bradycardia

General Dosing Information

After initial treatment, midodrine should be continued only in patients who have significant symptomatic improvement.

It is not recommended that midodrine be used in patients with initial supine systolic pressure above 180 mm Hg.

For treatment of adverse effects

To control supine hypertension, it may be helpful for the patient to avoid becoming fully supine, such as by sleeping with the head of the bed elevated. If supine hypertension persists, midodrine should be discontinued.

Oral Dosage Forms

Note: Bracketed uses in the *Dosage Forms* section refer to categories of use and/or indications that are not included in U.S. product labeling.

MIDODRINE HYDROCHLORIDE TABLETS

Usual adult dose

Hypotension, idiopathic orthostatic (treatment)—

Oral, 10 mg three times a day in approximately four-hour intervals during the daytime hours, taken shortly before or upon rising in the morning, at midday, and in the late afternoon (not later than six p.m.). Doses may be administered in three-hour intervals, if necessary, to control symptoms. However, midodrine should not be administered more frequently than in three-hour intervals and should not be administered after the evening meal or less than four hours before bedtime.

Note: Single doses up to 20 mg are associated with severe and persistent systolic supine hypertension, occurring in 45% of patients.

An initial dose of 2.5 mg is recommended for patients with abnormal renal function.

[Hypotension, intradialytic][1]—

Oral, 5 to 10 mg thirty minutes prior to hemodialysis.

[Hypotension, secondary, psychotropic agent-induced][1]—

Oral, 6.7 to 15 mg per day.

Usual adult prescribing limits

Doses greater than 30 mg have been tolerated, but their safety and efficacy have not been studied or established.

Usual pediatric dose

[Hypotension, secondary, infection-related][1]—

Infants up to 6 months of age: Safety and efficacy have not been established.

Infants and children 6 months of age or older: Oral, 0.06 mg per kg of body weight.

Strength(s) usually available

U.S.—

2.5 mg (Rx) [*ProAmatine*].

5 mg (Rx) [*ProAmatine*].

Packaging and storage

Store between 15 and 25 °C (59 and 77 °F), unless otherwise specified by manufacturer.

Auxiliary labeling

- Do not take other medicines without your doctor's advice.

---

[1]Not included in Canadian product labeling.

Revised: 01/30/2001
Developed: 04/02/1997

MIFEPRISTONE Systemic

VA CLASSIFICATION (Primary): HS109

Commonly used brand name(s): *Mifeprex*.

Another commonly used name is RU 486.

Note: For a listing of dosage forms and brand names by country availability, see *Dosage Forms* section(s).

Category

Abortifacient.

Indications

Accepted

Abortion—Mifepristone is indicated in combination with misoprostol for the medical termination of intrauterine pregnancy of 49 days' duration or less.

Pharmacology/Pharmacokinetics

Physicochemical characteristics

Molecular weight—429.6.

Mechanism of action/Effect

Mifepristone competitively inhibits the actions of progesterone at progesterone-receptor sites, resulting in termination of pregnancy. The combination of mifepristone and misoprostol causes expulsion of the products of conception through decidual necrosis, myometrial contractions, and cervical softening.

Absorption

The absolute bioavailability of oral mifepristone is 69%.

Protein binding

Very high (98%); predominantly to albumin and alpha 1–acid glycoprotein.

Biotransformation

Hepatic, by Cytochrome P450 3A4 isoenzyme to the N-monodemethylated metabolite (RU 42 633); RU 42 698, which results from the loss of two methyl groups from position 11 beta; and RU 42 698, which results from terminal hydroxylation of the 17–propynyl chain.

Half-life

Terminal—18 hours; begins slowly and becomes more rapid with time.

Time to peak concentration

90 minutes after a 600 mg oral dose.

Peak plasma concentration:

1.98 mg/L following a single 600 mg oral dose.

Elimination

Fecal; 83% of a 600 mg dose over 11 days.

Renal; 9% of a 600 mg dose over 11 days.

Precautions to Consider

Carcinogenicity

Studies in humans or animals have not been done.

Mutagenicity

Mifepristone was not found to be mutagenic in multiple assays, including the Ames test, *Saccharomyces cerevisiae* D4 cell conversion test, and *Schizosaccharomyces pompe* P1 cell forward mutation test. No positive results were noted during tests designed to induce chromosomal damage, including induction of chromosome aberrations in CHO cells, induction of genetic damage in V79 Chinese hamster lung cells, and the mouse micronucleus assay.

Pregnancy/Reproduction

Fertility—Mifepristone necessarily disrupts the estrus cycle, however, it did not appear to have an effect on long term fertility in rats given 0.3 mg per kg per day orally. Administration of up to 100 mg per kg did not affect the future reproductive capabilities of rats given the drug on the day after birth. In one study, rats given mifepristone 1 mg every other day as neonates were noted to have oviduct and ovary malformations, delayed male puberty, deficient male sexual behavior, reduced testicular size, and lowered ejaculation frequency.

Pregnancy—Mifepristone is used to terminate intrauterine pregnancy and has no other use during pregnancy.

Other prostaglandins, including misoprostol, have been reported to be teratogenic in human beings. Skull defects, cranial nerve palsies, delayed growth, delayed psychomotor development, facial malformation, and limb defects have been reported following exposure to prostaglandins in the first trimester.

Mifepristone administration at doses equivalent to one-sixth the normal human exposure to rabbits resulted in skull deformities, but studies in mice and rats have revealed no teratogenic effects.

Breast-feeding

It is unknown whether mifepristone is distributed into breast milk. Because the effects of mifepristone on infants are unknown, women who are breast-feeding should consult their healthcare provider to decide if they should discard their breast milk for a few days following administration of mifepristone and misoprostol.

Pediatrics

No information is available. Safety and efficacy have not been established.

Geriatrics

There is no appropriate use of mifepristone in the geriatric population.

Drug interactions and/or related problems

The following drug interactions and/or related problems have been selected on the basis of their potential clinical significance (possible mechanism in parentheses where appropriate)—not necessarily inclusive (» = major clinical significance):

Note: Combinations containing any of the following medications, depending on the amount present, may also interact with this medication.

» Anticoagulant therapy
(excessive bleeding may occur)

» Corticosteroid therapy, long-term, concurrent

» Cytochrome P450 enzyme inducers, including:
Carbamazepine
Dexamethasone
Phenobarbital
Phenytoin
Rifampin
St. John's Wort
(although specific interaction studies have not been performed, it is likely the metabolism of mifepristone will be induced, resulting in decreased serum levels of mifepristone)

» Cytochrome P450 enzyme inhibitors, including:
Erythromycin
Grapefruit juice
Itraconazole
Ketoconazole
(although specific interaction studies have not been performed, it is likely the metabolism of mifepristone will be inhibited, resulting in increased serum levels of mifepristone)

Laboratory value alterations

The following have been selected on the basis of their potential clinical significance (possible effect in parentheses where appropriate)—not necessarily inclusive (» = major clinical significance).
Alanine aminotransferase (ALT [SGPT]) or
Alkaline phosphatase or
Aspartate aminotransferase (AST [SGOT]) or
Gamma-glutamyltransferase (GT)
(rare reports of significant changes of these serum enzymes)

Medical considerations/Contraindications

The medical considerations/contraindications included have been selected on the basis of their potential clinical significance (reasons given in parentheses where appropriate)—not necessarily inclusive (» = major clinical significance).

Except under special circumstances, this medication should not be used when the following medical problems exist:

» Hemorrhagic disorder
(excessive bleeding may occur)

» Adrenal failure, chronic

» Ectopic pregnancy or
» Undiagnosed adnexal mass
(treatment procedure will not terminate ectopic pregnancy)

» Hypersensitivity to mifepristone, misoprostol or other prostaglandins

» Intrauterine device (IUD)
(IUD must be removed prior to initiation of treatment procedure)

» Porphyria, inherited

Risk-benefit should be considered when the following medical problems exist:

Anemia, severe or
Hemostatic disorders or
Hypocoagulability
(mifepristone causes heavy bleeding in a small portion of users, care should be exercised)

Chronic medical conditions such as:
Cardiovascular disease or
Hypertension or
Hepatic disease or
Respiratory disease or
Renal disease or
Diabetes mellitus, insulin-dependent or
Women older than 35 years of age who smoke (10 or more cigarettes per day)
(should be treated with caution because no safety and efficacy data available)

Patient monitoring

The following may be especially important in patient monitoring (other tests may be warranted in some patients, depending on condition; » = major clinical significance):

Clinical examination or
Ultrasonagraphic scan
(should occur 14 days after mifepristone administration to confirm termination of pregnancy and assess bleeding; pregnancy test for HCG may not be reliable at this time)

» Ectopic pregnancy
(should be monitored; could have an undiagnosed ectopic pregnancy since some expected symptoms of medical abortion may be similar to those of ruptured ectopic pregnancy; may have been missed even if patient had ultrasonography prior to being prescribed mifepristone)

Hematocrit and
Hemoglobin concentration and
Red blood cell count (RBC)
(mifepristone caused hemoglobin decreases greater than 2 gm/deciliter in clinical trials)

» Infection and sepsis
(cases of serious bacterial infection, including very rare cases of fatal septic shock, have been reported; patient should be monitored for sustained fever ≥ 100.4 °F, severe abdominal pain, or pelvic tenderness in the days following medical abortion; atypical presentations including significant leukocytosis, tachycardia or hemoconcentration can also occur)

» Vaginal bleeding
(monitor and counsel to seek immediate medical attention for prolonged heavy vaginal bleeding [i.e., soaking through two thick full-size sanitary pads per hour for two consecutive hours]; may be sign of incomplete abortion or other complications and prompt medical or surgical intervention may be needed to prevent development of hypovolemic shock)

Side/Adverse Effects

Although no causal relationship has been established, serious bacterial infections (e.g. *Clostridium sordellii*), including five very rare cases of fatal septic shock, have have been reported following use of mifepristone. Infection may present without fever, bacteremia, or significant findings on pelvic examination.

The following side/adverse effects have been selected on the basis of their potential clinical significance (possible signs and symptoms in parentheses where appropriate)—not necessarily inclusive:

Those indicating need for medical attention

Incidence less frequent

Decrease in hemoglobin concentration (unusual tiredness or weakness)—occurred at a rate of 6% in French trials only; ***uterine hemorrhage*** (excessively heavy vaginal bleeding)

Incidence not determined—Observed during clinical practice, estimates of frequency can not be determined

Infection, systemic bacterial (fever or chills; cough or hoarseness; lower back or side pain; painful or difficult urination); ***myocardial infarction*** (chest pain or discomfort; pain or discomfort in arms, jaw, back or neck; shortness of breath; nausea; sweating; vomiting); ***pregnancy, ruptured ectopic*** (sudden increase in abdominal or shoulder pain; unusual or large amount of vaginal bleeding; pale, cold clammy skin; confusion; dizziness, lightheadedness; fast, weak pulse; sweating)

Those indicating need for medical attention only if they continue or are bothersome

Incidence more frequent

Abdominal pain or uterine cramping; back pain; diarrhea; dizziness; fatigue (unusual tiredness or weakness); ***headache; nausea and vomiting***

Incidence less frequent

Anemia (pale skin; troubled breathing, exertional; unusual bleeding or bruising; unusual tiredness or weakness); ***anxiety; asthenia*** (lack or loss of strength); ***dyspepsia*** (acid or sour stomach; belching; heartburn; indigestion; stomach discomfort, upset, or pain); ***fever; insomnia*** (sleeplessness or trouble sleeping); ***leg pain; leukorrhea*** (increased clear or white vaginal discharge); ***rigors*** (shaking chills); ***sinusitis*** (pain or tenderness around eyes and cheekbones; fever; stuffy or runny nose; headache; cough; shortness of breath or troubled breathing; tightness of chest or wheezing); ***syncope*** (fainting or lightheadedness when getting up from a lying or sitting position); ***vaginitis*** (itching of the vagina or genital area; pain during sexual intercourse; thick, white vaginal discharge with no odor or with a mild odor); ***viral infection*** (chills; cough or hoarseness fever; cold; flu-like symptoms)

Overdose

For more information on the management of overdose or unintentional ingestion, **contact a poison control center** (see *Poison Control Center Listing*).

Treatment of overdose

There is no known specific antidote to mifepristone. Treatment is generally symptomatic and supportive.

Patients ingesting a massive overdose should be closely observed for signs of adrenal failure.

Patients in whom intentional overdose is confirmed or suspected should be referred for psychiatric consultation.

Patient Consultation

As an aid to patient consultation, refer to *Advice for the Patient, Mifepristone (Systemic)*.

In providing consultation, consider emphasizing the following selected information (» = major clinical significance):

Before using this medication

» Conditions affecting use, especially:

Hypersensitivity to mifepristone, misoprostol or other prostaglandins

Pregnancy—Increased risk of fetal malformation if treatment procedure is not successful in terminating pregnancy

Breast-feeding—Should consult with healthcare provider to decide if breast milk should be discarded for a few days following administration of this medication

Other medications, especially anticoagulants, corticosteroids, hepatic enzyme inducers, hepatic enzyme inhibitors

Other medical problems, especially adrenal failure, hemorrhagic disorders, ectopic pregnancy or undiagnosed adnexal masses, intrauterine devices in place, porphyria (inherited),

Proper use of this medication

Patient monitoring especially for signs of ruptured ectopic pregnancies.

» Proper dosing

Precautions while using this medication

» Importance of seeking immediate medical attention if prolonged heavy vaginal bleeding (soaking through two thick full-size sanitary pads per hour for two consecutive hours) is experienced

» Importance if checking with doctor right away if symptoms of infection or sepsis (i.e., sustained fever ≥ 100.4°F, severe abdominal pain, prolonged heavy bleeding, syncope, tachycardia, weakness, nausea, vomiting, diarrhea, or pelvic tenderness) occur

Follow Up

Three visits to physician, including follow-up visit 14 days after mifepristone administration

Advisability of surgical termination if medical abortion is not successful

Side/adverse effects

Signs of potential side effects, especially decrease in hemoglobin concentration or uterine hemorrhage

Signs of potential side effects observed during clinical practice, especially, myocardial infarction, ruptured ectopic pregnancy, or systemic bacterial infection

General Dosing Information

Patients receiving mifepristone should be under supervision of a physician who has read and understood the prescribing information.

Patients may only receive mifepristone directly from a physician's office which has registered with the manufacturer and has signed the Prescribers Agreement. The drug is not available through pharmacies.

Prescribers should make sure that patients receive and have an opportunity to discuss the Medication Guide and Patient Agreement.

Mifepristone use requires the same preventive measures as those taken prior to and during surgical abortion to prevent rhesus immunization.

Treatment with mifepristone and misoprostol to terminate pregnancy requires 3 office visits by the patient.

Treatment protocol is:

- Day One—Mifepristone is administered to the patient in physician's office.
- Day Three—Unless expulsion of products of conception has already occurred, misoprostol is administered to the patient in the physician's office.
- Day Fourteen—Patient returns for clinical exam to verify termination of pregnancy.

Although there is no clinical evidence, the effectiveness of mifepristone may be lower if misoprostol is administered more than two days after mifepristone administration.

Surgical termination of the pregnancy is recommended following medical abortion treatment failure due to the risk of fetal malformation with prostaglandins.

Another pregnancy can occur following termination of pregnancy and before normal menses resumes. Patient should be advised that contraception can be initiated after pregnancy termination is confirmed or before she resumes sexual intercourse.

Oral Dosage Forms

MIFEPRISTONE TABLETS

Usual adult dose

Abortifacient—

Oral, 600 mg (three 200 mg tablets) as a single dose on day one, followed on day three by 400 mcg (two 200 mcg tablets) of misoprostol as a single dose, if abortion has not yet occurred.

Usual pediatric dose

Safety and efficacy have not been established.

Usual geriatric dose

Safety and efficacy have not been established.

Strength(s) usually available

U.S.—

200 mg (Rx) [*Mifeprex* (colloidal silica anhydrous; corn starch; magnesium stearate; microcrystalline cellulose; povidone)].

Packaging and storage

Store at 25 °C (77 °F), in a tight container. Protect from light.

Additional information

Tablets are packaged in a blister package containing 3 tablets, supplied in individual cartons.

Product is not available through pharmacies.

Revised: 09/14/2005
Developed: 10/13/2000

MIGLITOL Systemic †

VA CLASSIFICATION (Primary): HS504

Commonly used brand name(s): *Glyset*.

Note: For a listing of dosage forms and brand names by country availability, see *Dosage Forms* section(s).

†Not commercially available in Canada.

Category

Antidiabetic agent.

Indications

Accepted

Diabetes, type 2 (treatment)—Miglitol is indicated as an adjunct to diet in the treatment of patients with type 2 diabetes (previously referred to as non-insulin-dependent diabetes mellitus [NIDDM]) whose blood glucose cannot be controlled by diet alone. Miglitol may be used as monotherapy or in combination with a sulfonylurea antidiabetic agent.

Pharmacology/Pharmacokinetics

Physicochemical characteristics

Source—Miglitol is derived from desoxynojirimycin.
Molecular weight—207.2.
pKa—5.9.

Mechanism of action/Effect
By reversibly inhibiting α-glucoside hydrolase enzymes which are located in the brush border of the small intestine, miglitol delays the hydrolysis of ingested complex sugars. By slowing the breakdown of oligosaccharides and disaccharides into monosaccharides, this action slows the absorption of glucose into the bloodstream and thus reduces postprandial hyperglycemia. Unlike other antihyperglycemic agents such as sulfonylureas, miglitol does not enhance insulin secretion.

Other actions/effects
Miglitol and sulfonylureas can be used together, creating an additive antihyperglycemic effect. This medication combination has additional effects as the miglitol will decrease the insulinotropic and weight-increasing effects of sulfonylureas.

Miglitol has minor inhibitory activity against lactase but is not expected to cause lactose intolerance.

Absorption
Absorption of miglitol is saturable at high doses with 25 mg being completely absorbed while a 100-mg dose is only 50-70% absorbed.

No evidence exists to show that systemic absorption of miglitol adds to its therapeutic effect.

Distribution
Distribution is thought to occur in the extracellular fluid, with a volume of distribution of 0.18 L per kg. A very small amount of miglitol is excreted into human breast milk, 0.02% of a 100-mg maternal dose

Protein binding
Very low (less than 4%).

Biotransformation
Miglitol is not metabolized. No metabolites have been detected in the feces, plasma, or urine of humans or any animal species studied.

Half-life
Elimination—
2 hours.

Onset of action
Research has shown significant reductions in postprandial plasma glucose after 1 hour since administration.

Time to peak concentration
Peak concentration is generally reached in 2 to 3 hours.

Elimination
Renal—Unchanged miglitol is eliminated renally. Over 95% of a 25-mg dose is recovered in the urine within 24 hours. However, at higher doses, the cumulative recovery of miglitol is somewhat lower because of incomplete bioavailability.

Precautions to Consider

Carcinogenicity
No evidence of carcinogenicity was noted in mice administered oral doses of up to 500 mg per kg of body weight (mg/kg) (corresponding to greater than five times the human exposure based on area under the plasma concentration-time curve [AUC]) for 21 months, or in rats administered oral doses corresponding to the maximum human exposure based on AUC for 24 months.

Mutagenicity
In vitro studies including the bacterial mutagenesis (Ames) assay and the eukaryotic forward mutation assay (CHO/HGPRT) showed that miglitol was non-mutagenic. In addition, the *in vivo* mouse micronucleus test and dominant lethal assay indicated that miglitol was non-mutagenic.

Pregnancy/Reproduction
Fertility—A fertility study in Wistar rats treated with an oral miglitol dose of 300 mg per kg of body weight (approximately 8 times the maximum human exposure based on body surface area) did not indicate a negative effect on fertility or reproduction.

Pregnancy—Adequate and well-controlled studies have not been done in humans.

Studies in rats and rabbits administered doses of 50, 150, and 450 mg/kg (corresponding to approximately 1.5, 4, and 12 times the maximum recommended human exposure based on body surface area) and 10, 45, and 200 mg/kg (corresponding to approximately 0.5, 3, and 10 times the human exposure), respectively, failed to reveal evidence of fetal malformation attributable to miglitol. However, a dose of 450 mg/kg in a rat study caused a slight but significant reduction in fetal weight, and a dose of 200 mg/kg in a rabbit study caused a slight reduction in fetal weight, delayed ossification of the fetal skeleton, and an increase in the percentage of nonviable fetuses. In addition, in a perinatal study in rats, an increase in stillborn progeny was noted at a dose of 300 mg/kg.

FDA Pregnancy Category B.

Breast-feeding
Miglitol is distributed into human breast milk to a very small degree (0.02% of 100-mg maternal dose) but problems in humans have not been documented. Although the nursing infant is exposed to a small percentage of the drug (approximately 0.4% of the maternal dose), miglitol is not recommended for a nursing woman.

Pediatrics
Appropriate studies on the relationship of age to the effects of miglitol have not been performed in the pediatric population. Safety and efficacy have not been established.

Geriatrics
Appropriate studies performed to date have not demonstrated geriatrics-specific problems that would limit the usefulness of miglitol in the elderly.

Pharmacogenetics
No significant difference in the pharmacokinetics of miglitol was observed between elderly men and women.

Pharmacokinetic studies demonstrated similar results in Caucasian and Japanese subjects. A pharmacodynamic response study comparing healthy Black and Caucasian subjects indicated similar glucose and insulin responses to a single 50-mg miglitol dose.

Drug interactions and/or related problems
The following drug interactions and/or related problems have been selected on the basis of their potential clinical significance (possible mechanism in parentheses where appropriate)—not necessarily inclusive (» = major clinical significance):

Note: Combinations containing any of the following medications, depending on the amount present, may also interact with this medication.

» Digestive enzyme preparations, such as amylase or pancreatin or
» Intestinal adsorbents, such as charcoal
(may reduce the effect of miglitol; concomitant use should be avoided)

» Propranolol or
» Ranitidine
(in volunteer studies, miglitol was shown to reduce the bioavailability of propranolol by 40% and of ranitidine by 60%)

Laboratory value alterations
The following have been selected on the basis of their potential clinical significance (possible effect in parentheses where appropriate)—not necessarily inclusive (» = major clinical significance).

With physiology/laboratory test values
Iron, serum
(low serum iron occurred in 9.2% of patients treated with miglitol although hemoglobin or other hematologic factors were not reduced)

Medical considerations/Contraindications
The medical considerations/contraindications included have been selected on the basis of their potential clinical significance (reasons given in parentheses where appropriate)—not necessarily inclusive (» = major clinical significance).

Except under special circumstances, this medication should not be used when the following medical problems exist:

» Diabetic ketoacidosis

Intestinal disorders, including:
» Chronic conditions associated with marked disorders of digestion or absorption
» Colonic ulceration
» Conditions that may be adversely affected by increased intestinal gas formation
» Inflammatory bowel disease
» Obstructive intestinal disease, or predisposition to

Risk-benefit should be considered when the following medical problems exist:

» Renal function impairment
(miglitol is excreted primarily by the kidneys; therefore, accumulation is expected in patients with renal function impairment; plasma concentrations of miglitol following a 25-mg dose administered three times a day were more than two times higher in patients with creatinine clearances less than 25 mL per minute [mL/min] than in patients with creatinine clearances greater than 60 mL/min; dosage adjustment to correct increased plasma concentrations is not feasible because miglitol acts locally; although long-term studies have not been conducted in patients with severe

renal function impairment [serum creatinine greater than 2 mg per dL], use of miglitol in these patients is not recommended)

» Hypersensitivity to miglitol

Patient monitoring

The following may be especially important in patient monitoring (other tests may be warranted in some patients, depending on condition; » = major clinical significance):

» Creatinine clearance
(monitor to check renal function)

» Glucose concentrations, blood
(one-hour postprandial concentrations are recommended during treatment initiation and dose titration to determine the minimum effective dose; periodic monitoring is recommended thereafter to assess therapeutic response)

» Glycosylated hemoglobin determinations
(recommended at 3-month intervals for monitoring of long-term glycemic control)

Side/Adverse Effects

Note: When administered alone, miglitol is not expected to cause hypoglycemia. However, sulfonylureas may cause hypoglycemia and, although not observed in clinical trials, miglitol given in combination with a sulfonylurea may increase the hypoglycemic potential of the sulfonylurea.

The following side/adverse effects have been selected on the basis of their potential clinical significance (possible signs and symptoms in parentheses where appropriate)—not necessarily inclusive:

Those indicating need for medical attention only if they continue or are bothersome

Incidence more frequent

Abdominal pain (stomach or abdomen pain); ***diarrhea*** (increase in bowel movements; loose stools; soft stools); ***flatulence*** (bloated full feeling; excess air or gas in stomach or intestines; passing gas)

Note: In clinical trials, the occurrence of *abdominal pain* and *diarrhea* usually diminished with continued treatment.

Incidence less frequent

Skin rash

Note: In clinical trials, *skin rash* usually was transient.

Overdose

For more information on the management of overdose or unintentional ingestion, **contact a poison control center** (see *Poison Control Center Listing*).

Clinical effects of overdose

Note: Overdose of miglitol would not be expected to cause serious systemic reactions because it produces no extraintestinal side effects.

The following effects have been selected on the basis of their potential clinical significance (possible signs and symptoms in parentheses where appropriate)—not necessarily inclusive:

Abdominal discomfort (stomach cramps or pain); ***diarrhea*** (increase in bowel movements; loose stools; soft stools); ***flatulence*** (bloated full feeling; excess air or gas in stomach or intestines; passing gas)

Treatment of overdose

There is no known specific antidote to miglitol. Treatment is generally symptomatic and supportive.

Patients in whom intentional overdose is confirmed or suspected should be referred for psychiatric consultation.

Patient Consultation

As an aid to patient consultation, refer to *Advice for the Patient, Miglitol (Systemic)*.

In providing consultation, consider emphasizing the following selected information (» = major clinical significance):

Before using this medication

» Conditions affecting use, especially:
Hypersensitivity to miglitol
Breast-feeding—Miglitol is distributed into human breast milk to a very small degree (0.02% of 100 mg maternal dose) but problems in humans have not been documented. Although the nursing infant is exposed to a small percentage of the drug (approximately 0.4% of the maternal dose), miglitol is not recommended for a nursing woman.
Other medications, especially activated charcoal, digestive enzymes, propranolol or ranitidine.
Other medical problems, especially chronic intestinal disease, diabetic ketoacidosis, inflammatory bowel disease or renal function impairment.

Proper use of this medication

» Importance of adherence to recommended regimens for diet, exercise, and glucose monitoring

» Taking medication at the beginning of each main meal

» Proper dosing
Missed dose: If meal completed without having taken medication: Skipping missed dose; taking next dose with next meal; not doubling doses

Proper storage

Precautions while using this medication

» Regular visits to physician to check progress

» *Carefully following special instructions of health care team:*
Discussing use of alcohol and tobacco
Not taking other medications unless discussed with physician
Getting counseling for family members to help the patient with diabetes; also, special counseling for pregnancy planning and contraception
Making travel plans that include readiness for diabetic emergencies and eating meals at the usual times, even with changing time zones

» Preparing for and understanding what to do in case of diabetic emergency; carrying medical history and current medication list and wearing medical identification

» Recognizing symptoms of hypoglycemia: anxiety; behavior change similar to drunkenness; blurred vision; cold sweats; coma; confusion; cool, pale skin; difficulty in concentrating; drowsiness; excessive hunger; fast heartbeat; headache (continuing); nausea; nervousness; nightmares; restless sleep; seizures; shakiness; slurred speech; and unusual tiredness or weakness

» Recognizing what brings on symptoms of hypoglycemia, such as delaying or missing a meal or snack; drinking significant amounts of alcohol; exercising more than usual; having an illness, including vomiting or diarrhea; taking certain medications; or using other antidiabetic medication

» Knowing what to do if symptoms of hypoglycemia occur, such as ingesting a source of glucose (not sucrose) or, if severe, injecting glucagon

» Recognizing symptoms of hyperglycemia and ketoacidosis: blurred vision; drowsiness; dry mouth; flushed, dry skin; fruit-like breath odor; increased urination (frequency and volume); ketones in urine; loss of appetite; somnolence (sleepiness); stomachache, nausea, or vomiting; tiredness; troubled breathing (rapid and deep); unconsciousness; and unusual thirst

» Recognizing what brings on symptoms of hyperglycemia, such as exercising less than usual, having a fever or infection, not taking enough or skipping a dose of antidiabetic medication, or overeating or not following meal plan

» Knowing what to do if symptoms of hyperglycemia occur, such as checking blood glucose and contacting a member of the health care team

General Dosing Information

Temporary insulin therapy may be needed if a diabetic patient is stressed by such factors as fever, trauma, infection, or surgery.

For treatment of adverse effects

Although not seen in clinical trials, miglitol, combined with sulfonylurea, may induce hypoglycemia. For treatment of mild to moderate hypoglycemia, oral glucose (dextrose) rather than sucrose should be given to patient because miglitol inhibits hydrolysis of sucrose to glucose and fructose. For treatment of severe hypoglycemia, an intravenous glucose infusion or a glucagon injection may be needed.

Oral Dosage Forms

MIGLITOL TABLETS

Usual adult dose

Type 2 diabetes—
Oral, initially 25 mg three times a day at the start (with the first bite) of each main meal. Dosage may be increased after four to eight weeks to 50 mg three times a day, then after twelve weeks, if necessary, to 100 mg three times a day.

Note: To decrease the occurrence of gastrointestinal side effects, some patients may require an initial dosage of 25 mg once a day with a gradual increase to three times a day.

If an increase in dosage to 100 mg three times a day fails to produce a further reduction in postprandial glucose concentration or glycosylated hemoglobin determination, consideration should be given to lowering the dose.

Usual adult prescribing limits
100 mg 3 times daily.

Usual pediatric dose
Safety and efficacy have not been established.

Usual geriatric dose
See *Usual adult dose.*

Strength(s) usually available
U.S.—
25 mg (Rx) [*Glyset* (hydroxypropyl methylcellulose; magnesium stearate; microcrystalline cellulose; polyethylene glycol; polysorbate 80; starch; titanium dioxide)].
50 mg (Rx) [*Glyset* (hydroxypropyl methylcellulose; magnesium stearate; microcrystalline cellulose; polyethylene glycol; polysorbate 80; starch; titanium dioxide)].
100 mg (Rx) [*Glyset* (hydroxypropyl methylcellulose; magnesium stearate; microcrystalline cellulose; polyethylene glycol; polysorbate 80; starch; titanium dioxide)].

Canada—
Not commercially available.

Packaging and storage
Store below 40 °C (104 °F), preferably between 15 and 30 °C (59 and 86 °F).

Auxiliary labeling
- Take with food.
- Keep out of reach of children.

Developed: 11/09/2000

MIGLUSTAT Systemic†

VA CLASSIFICATION (Primary): HS452
Commonly used brand name(s): *Zavesca.*
Note: For a listing of dosage forms and brand names by country availability, see *Dosage Forms* section(s).

†Not commercially available in Canada.

Category
Substrate reduction therapy.

Indications
Accepted
Gaucher disease, type 1 mild to moderate (treatment)—Miglustat is indicated for treatment of mild to moderate type 1 Gaucher disease in adults for whom enzyme replacement therapy is not a therapeutic option (e.g., due to constraints such as allergy, hypersensitivity, or poor venous access).

Pharmacology/Pharmacokinetics
Physicochemical characteristics
Source—Synthetic analogue of D-glucose.
Chemical Group—N-alkylated imino sugar
Molecular weight—219.28.
Solubility—Highly soluble in water.

Mechanism of action/Effect
Miglustat functions as a competitive and reversible inhibitor of the enzyme glucosylceramide synthase, the initial enzyme in a series of reactions which results in the synthesis of most glycosphingolipids. The goal of treatment with miglustat is to reduce the rate of glycosphingolipid biosynthesis so that the amount of glycosphingolipid substrate is reduced to a level which allows the residual activity of the deficient glucocerebrosidase enzyme to be more effective (substrate reduction therapy). *In vitro* and *in vivo* studies have shown that miglustat can reduce the synthesis of glucosylceramide-based glycosphingolipids. In clinical trials, miglustat improved liver and spleen volume, as well as hemoglobin concentration and platelet count.

Absorption
Mean oral bioavailability: 97%

Distribution
Vol_D: 83 to 105 liters; indicating that miglustat distributes into extravascular tissues

Protein binding
Does not bind to plasma proteins

Biotransformation
There is no evidence that miglustat is metabolized in humans.

Half-life
6 to 7 hours

Time to peak concentration
T_{max}—2 to 2.5 hours
Delayed 2 hours when administered with food

Elimination
Majority of drug is excreted unchanged in the urine; renal impairment has a significant effect on the pharmacokinetics of miglustat resulting in increased systemic exposure of miglustat

Special populations
Renal insufficiency: Limited data indicates that the clearance of miglustat decreases 40% in mild, 60% in moderate and 70% in severe renal impairment; dose should be decreased based on creatinine clearance

Hepatic insufficiency: No studies have been done since miglustat is not metabolized in the human liver

Race: Ethnic differences have not been evaluated in Gaucher patients; however, apparent oral clearance in patients of Ashkenazi Jewish descent was not statistically significant to that in others, based on a cross study analysis

Precautions to Consider
Carcinogenicity
Long term studies in animals to evaluate the carcinogenic potential of miglustat have not been conducted.

Mutagenicity
Miglustat was not mutagenic or clastogenic in a battery of *in vitro* and *in vivo* assays including the bacterial reverse mutation (Ames), chromosomal aberration (in human lymphocytes), gene mutation in mammalian cells (Chinese hamster ovary), and mouse micronucleus assays.

Pregnancy/Reproduction
Fertility—Male rats, given miglustat 20 mg per kg per day (systemic exposure less than then human therapeutic systemic exposure based on body surface area comparisons, mg per m^2) oral gavage 14 days prior to mating, had decreased spermatogenesis with altered sperm morphology and motility and decreased fertility. Decreased spermatogenesis was reversible following 6 weeks of drug withdrawal. At higher doses of 60 mg per kg per day (2 times the human therapeutic systemic exposure based on body surface area comparison, mg per m^2) resulted in seminiferous tubule and testicular atrophy/degeneration.

Female rats were given oral gavage doses of 20, 60, 180 mg per kg per day beginning 14 days before mating and continuing through gestation. Effects observed at 20 mg per kg per day (systemic exposure less than the human therapeutic systemic exposure, based on body surface area) included decreased corpora lutea, increased postimplantation loss, and decreased live births.

Pregnancy—Miglustat is contraindicated in women who are pregnant or who may become pregnant. Risk-benefit must be carefully considered and the patient should be apprised of the potential hazard to the fetus.

Miglustat may cause fetal harm when administered to pregnant women. In female rats given miglustat by oral gavage at doses of 20, 60, 180 mg per kg per day beginning 14 days before mating and continuing through gestation day 17 (organogenesis), decreased live births including complete litter loss and decreased fetal weight was observed in the mid and high dose groups (systemic exposures ≥ 2 times the human therapeutic systemic exposure based on body surface area comparison). In pregnant rats given miglustat by oral gavage at doses of 20, 60, 180 mg per kg per day from gestation day 6 through lactation (postpartum day 20), dystocia and delayed parturition were observed in the mid- and high-dose groups (systemic exposure ≥ 2 times the human therapeutic systemic exposure, based on body surface area comparison), in addition decreased live births and pup body weights were observed at ≥ 20 mg per kg per day (systemic exposures less than the human therapeutic systemic exposure, based on body surface area comparison).

In pregnant rabbits given miglustat by oral gavage at doses of 15, 30, and 45 mg per kg per day during gestation days 6 to 18 (organogenesis), maternal death and decreased body weight gain were observed at 15 mg per kg per day (systemic exposures less than the human therapeutic systemic exposure, based on body surface area comparisons).

FDA Pregnancy Category X

Labor and delivery—Studies in pregnant rats exposed to miglustat during gestation through lactation are associated with dystocia and delayed parturition at systemic exposure 2 times the human therapeutic systemic exposure, based on body surface area comparisons.

Breast-feeding

It is not known whether miglustat is distributed into human breast milk. Because many drugs are distributed into human breast milk and because of the serious potential for adverse reactions in nursing infants from miglustat, it should not be used in nursing mothers unless the potential benefit justifies the potential risk to the infant. A decision should be made whether to discontinue nursing or discontinue taking the drug, taking into account the importance of the drug to the mother.

Pediatrics

Appropriate studies on the relationship of age to the effect of miglustat have not been done in the pediatric population. Safety and effectiveness have not been established in patients under the age of 18. The effects of miglustat on growth and development in children have not been evaluated.

Geriatrics

Appropriate studies on the relationship of age to the effects of miglustat have not been performed in the geriatric population. Clinical studies of miglustat did not include sufficient numbers of patients aged 65 and over to determine whether they respond differently than younger patients. Other reported clinical experience has not identified differences in responses between elderly and younger patients. In general, dose selection for elderly patients should be cautious, usually starting at the low end of the dosing range, reflecting the greater frequency of decreased hepatic, renal, and cardiac function and of concomitant disease or other drug therapy.

Pharmacogenetics

There were no statistically significant gender differences in miglustat pharmacokinetics, based on pooled data analysis.

Drug interactions and/or related problems

The following drug interactions and/or related problems have been selected on the basis of their potential clinical significance (possible mechanism in parentheses where appropriate)—not necessarily inclusive (» = major clinical significance):

Note: Miglustat does not inhibit or induce various substrates of cytochrome P450 enzymes; consequently significant interactions are unlikely with drugs that are substrates of cytochrome P450 enzymes.

Concomitant therapy with loperamide during clinical trials did not appear to significantly alter the pharmacokinetics of miglustat.

Note: Combinations containing any of the following medications, depending on the amount present, may also interact with this medication.

Imiglucerase
(coadministration of miglustat and imiglucerase appeared to increase the clearance of imiglucerase by 70%, these results are not conclusive because of the small number of subjects studied and because patients took variable doses of imiglucerase; combination therapy with imiglucerase and miglustat is not indicated)

Medical considerations/Contraindications

The medical considerations/contraindications included have been selected on the basis of their potential clinical significance (reasons given in parentheses where appropriate)—not necessarily inclusive (» = major clinical significance).

Except under special circumstances, this medication should not be used when the following medical problem exists:

Hypersensitivity to miglustat or any of the components of the medicine

» Gaucher disease, type 1 severe
(safety and efficacy of miglustat have not been established in patients with severe type 1 Gaucher disease; defined as hemoglobin concentration below 9 g per dL or a platelet count below 50 x10^9 per L or active bone disease)

Risk-benefit should be considered when the following medical problems exist:

» Renal insufficiency
(miglustat is substantially excreted by the kidney and the risk of adverse reactions may be increased in patients with impaired renal function; dose reductions are recommended for patients with mild to moderate renal impairment; use in patients with severe renal impairment is not recommended)

Patient monitoring

The following may be especially important in patient monitoring (other tests may be warranted in some patients, depending on condition; » = major clinical significance):

Diarrhea and
Weight loss
(incidence of diarrhea was noted to decrease over time and resulted in an increased use of anti-diarrheal medicines; patients may need to be instructed to avoid high carbohydrate content foods during treatment if they present with diarrhea)

» Neurological examination
(all patients undergoing treatment should have baseline and repeat neurological evaluations at approximately 6 month intervals; patients who develop symptoms such as numbness and tingling should have a careful reassessment of the risk/benefit of miglustat therapy and cessation of treatment may be considered)

Tremor
(approximately 30% of patients have reported tremor or exacerbation of existing tremor on treatment; usually began within the first month and in many cases resolved between 1 to 3 months during treatment; dose reduction may ameliorate the tremor within days but discontinuation may be required)

Side/Adverse Effects

Approximately 30% of patients have reported tremor or exacerbation of existing tremor on treatment. These tremors were described as an exaggerated physiological tremor of the hands. Tremor usually began within the first month of therapy and in many cases resolved between 1 to 3 months during treatment. Dose reduction may ameliorate the tremor within days but discontinuation with treatment may sometimes be required.

Cases of peripheral neuropathy have been reported in patients treated with miglustat. Patients who develop symptoms such as numbness and tingling should have a careful re-assessment of the risk/benefit of miglustat therapy and cessation of treatment may be considered.

Diarrhea and weight loss were common in clinical studies of patients treated with miglustat, approximately 85% and 65% of treated patients, respectively, reporting these conditions. Diarrhea appears to be the result of the disaccharidase inhibitory activity of miglustat, with a resultant osmotic diarrhea. It is unclear if weight loss results from diarrhea and associated gastrointestinal complaints, a decrease in food intake, or a combination of these or other factors. The incidence of diarrhea was noted to decrease over time with continued miglustat treatment, and was noted to result in an increase in the use of antidiarrheal medications, most commonly loperamide. Patients may be instructed to avoid a high carbohydrate content foods during treatment with miglustat if they present with diarrhea. The incidence of weight loss was most evident in the first 12 months of treatment.

Miglustat therapy may be less effective in patients previously treated with enzyme replacement therapy.

The following side/adverse effects have been selected on the basis of their potential clinical significance (possible signs and symptoms in parentheses where appropriate)—not necessarily inclusive:

Those indicating need for medical attention

Incidence more frequent

Paresthesia (burning, crawling, itching, numbness, prickling, "pins and needles", or tingling feelings); ***thrombocytopenia*** (black, tarry stools; bleeding gums; blood in urine or stools; pinpoint red spots on skin; unusual bleeding or bruising)

Incidence unknown

Peripheral neuropathy (burning, numbness, tingling, or painful sensations; weakness in arms, hands, legs, or feet; unsteadiness or awkwardness); ***tremor*** (trembling or shaking of hands or feet; shakiness in legs, arms, hands, feet)

Those indicating need for medical attention only if they continue or are bothersome

Incidence more frequent

Abdominal distention (swelling of abdominal or stomach area; full or bloated feeling or pressure in the stomach)—with and without gas; ***abdominal pain*** (stomach pain); ***anorexia*** (loss of appetite; weight loss); ***back pain; bloating*** (swelling); ***cramps; constipation*** (difficulty having a bowel movement (stool)); ***diarrhea; dizziness; dry mouth; dyspepsia*** (acid or sour stomach; belching; heartburn; indigestion; stomach discomfort, upset or pain); ***epigastric pain*** (pain or discomfort in chest, upper stomach, or throat; heartburn)—not food related; ***flatulence*** (bloated, full feeling; excess air or gas in stomach or intestines; passing gas); ***headache; heaviness in limbs; leg cramps; memory loss; menstrual disorder*** (menstrual changes); ***nausea;***

unsteady gait; visual disturbances (change in vision); ***vomiting; weakness***—generalized; ***weight decrease***

Overdose

For more information on the management of overdose or unintentional ingestion, **contact a poison control center** (see *Poison Control Center Listing*).

In the clinical development program for miglustat, no patient experienced an overdose of study drug. However, miglustat has been administered at doses of up to 3,000 mg per day (approximately 10 times the recommended starting dose administered to Gaucher patients) for up to six months in human immunodeficiency virus (HIV)-positive patients. Adverse events observed in the HIV studies included granulocytopenia, dizziness, and paresthesia. Leukopenia and neutropenia have been also observed in a similar group of patients receiving 800 mg per day or above.

Patient Consultation

As an aid to patient consultation, refer to *Advice for the Patient, Miglustat (Systemic)*.

In providing consultation, consider emphasizing the following selected information (» = major clinical significance):

Before using this medication

» Conditions affecting use, especially:
  Hypersensitivity to miglustat or any excipient
  Pregnancy—Miglustat should not be used during pregnancy
  Breast-feeding—Miglustat should not be used in nursing women
  Other medical problems, especially severe, type 1 gaucher disease and renal impairment (moderate to severe)

Proper use of this medication

» Proper dosing
  Importance of taking doses three times a day at regular intervals
  Missed dose: Taking as soon as possible; not taking if almost time for next scheduled dose; not doubling doses
» Proper storage

Precautions while using this medication

Regular visits to physician check progress; importance of regular neurological exams

Understanding diarrhea, gastrointestinal complaints, and weight loss are common side effects

Importance of adhering to dietary instructions for patients with diarrhea; low carbohydrate content diets

» Promptly reporting any numbness, pain, tingling, pain, or burning in the hands and feet

» Promptly reporting the development of a tremor or the worsening of an existing tremor

Importance of using contraception; Male patients should maintain reliable contraceptive measures during treatment and three months beyond cessation of therapy

Importance of discussing pregnancy with doctor and understanding risks and benefits

Side/adverse effects

Signs of potential side effects, especially paresthesia, peripheral neuropathy, thrombocytopenia, tremor

General Dosing Information

For oral dosing forms:

Therapy should be directed by physicians knowledgeable in the management of patients with Gaucher disease.

Treatment with miglustat as monotherapy at a starting dose of 100 mg three times a daily (dosing range 100 mg once daily to 200 mg three times daily) in adult type 1 Gaucher disease patients who were either treatment naive or who had not taken enzyme replacement therapy in the previous 6 months resulted in decreases in liver and spleen volume after 12 months of treatment, and increases in platelet counts and hemoglobin concentration after 24 months of treatment. However, in adult type 1 Gaucher disease patients who had been treated with enzyme replacement therapy for at least 2 years, switching to miglustat as monotherapy was associated with decreases in platelet counts after discontinuation of enzyme replacement therapy. Platelet counts also declined after disinclination of enzyme replacement therapy in patients treated with combination therapy.

Men and women should use effective birth control during treatment with miglustat. Until further information is available, it is advised that before seeking to conceive, male patients should cease miglustat and maintain reliable contraceptive methods for 3 months thereafter.

Patients should be informed of the potential risks and benefits of miglustat therapy and of alternative modes of therapy.

Diet/Nutrition

Miglustat may be taken with or without food. Capsules should be swallowed whole with water.

Oral Dosage Forms

MIGLUSTAT CAPSULES

Usual adult dose

Gaucher disease—
  Oral, 100 mg administered three times a day at regular intervals. It may be necessary to reduce the dose to one 100 mg capsule once or twice a day in some patients who experience adverse effects.

Note: • Mild renal impairment (adjusted creatinine clearance 50 to 70 mL per min per 1.73 m²)—Starting dose is 100 mg twice a day
  • Moderate renal impairment (adjusted creatinine clearance 30 to 50 mL per min per 1.73 m²)—Starting dose is 100 mg once a day

Severe renal impairment (adjusted creatinine clearance < 30 mL per min per 1.73 m²)—Use is not recommended

Usual pediatric dose

Safety and efficacy have not been established in patients under the age of 18.

Usual geriatric dose

See *Usual adult dose;* dose selection should be done with caution

Strength(s) usually available

U.S.—
  100 mg (Rx) [*Zavesca* (sodium starch glycollate; povidone (K30); magnesium stearate)].

Canada—
  Not commercially available

Packaging and storage

Store between 20 to 25 °C (68 to 77 °F). Brief exposure to 15 to 30ºC (59 to 86ºF) is permitted.

Auxiliary labeling

• This medication could be harmful if you are pregnant or breast-feeding. Consult your pharmacist if you are pregnant, plan to become pregnant, or if you are breast-feeding.

Developed: 03/01/2004

MILK-BASED ENTERAL NUTRITION FORMULAS—See *Enteral Nutrition Formulas (Systemic)*

MINERAL OIL—See *Laxatives (Local)*

MINOCYCLINE—See *Tetracyclines (Systemic)*

MINOXIDIL Systemic

VA CLASSIFICATION (Primary): CV409

Commonly used brand name(s): *Loniten*.

Note: For a listing of dosage forms and brand names by country availability, see *Dosage Forms* section(s).

Category

Antihypertensive.

Indications

Accepted

Hypertension (treatment)—Minoxidil is indicated for treatment of hypertension.

Because of its serious side effects, minoxidil is not considered to be a primary agent in the treatment of essential hypertension. It is recommended for use only in patients with symptomatic or organ-damaging hypertension not responsive to other treatment.

For additional information on initial therapeutic guidelines related to the treatment of hypertension, see *Appendix III*.

Unaccepted

Use of extemporaneous topical preparations from minoxidil oral tablets is not recommended for treatment of male pattern baldness because there is lack of data on the best formulation and the risks associated with possible systemic absorption. A topical product is commercially available for this indication.

Pharmacology/Pharmacokinetics

Physicochemical characteristics

Molecular weight—209.25.
pKa—Approximately 4.6.

Mechanism of action/Effect

The exact cellular mechanism of antihypertensive action is unknown. The predominant effect of minoxidil is direct vasodilation of arterioles with little effect on veins. It reduces peripheral resistance and causes a reflex increase in heart rate and cardiac output.

Absorption

At least 90% absorbed from the gastrointestinal tract.

Biotransformation

Hepatic, at least 90%; metabolites have much less pharmacologic activity than minoxidil.

Half-life

Drug and metabolites—4.2 hours; not altered in impaired renal function.

Onset of action

30 minutes.

Time to peak concentration

1 hour.

Time to peak effect

Single dose—2 to 3 hours.

Multiple doses—Maximum blood pressure response with continued use usually occurs within 3 to 7 days (patients receiving the largest doses respond in the shortest period of time and vice versa).

Duration of action

Usually 24 to 48 hours; up to 75 hours in some patients.

Elimination

Fecal—3% (may be increased to up to 20% in severe renal function impairment).
Renal—97%, mostly as metabolites.
In dialysis—Removable by hemodialysis; however, this does not rapidly reverse the pharmacologic effect.

Precautions to Consider

Carcinogenicity

Twenty-two-month studies in rats at doses 15 times the human dose revealed no evidence of tumorigenicity.

Mutagenicity

In Ames test, no evidence of mutagenicity was found.

Pregnancy/Reproduction

Fertility—A reduction in conception rate occurred in rats receiving minoxidil at doses 5 times the human dose.

Pregnancy—Minoxidil crosses the placenta. Studies in humans have not been done. However, hypertrichosis has been reported in newborns following maternal minoxidil administration.

Studies in rats and rabbits did not reveal teratogenic effects; however, there was an increased incidence of fetal resorptions in rabbits given minoxidil at 5 times the human dose.

FDA Pregnancy Category C.

Breast-feeding

Minoxidil passes into breast milk. However, problems in humans have not been documented.

Pediatrics

Appropriate studies on the relationship of age to the effects of minoxidil have not been performed in the pediatric population. However, pediatrics-specific problems that would limit the usefulness of this medication in children are not expected.

Geriatrics

Although appropriate studies on the relationship of age to the effects of minoxidil have not been performed in the geriatric population, the elderly may be more sensitive to the hypotensive effects. In addition, the risk of minoxidil-induced hypothermia may be increased in elderly patients. Elderly patients are also more likely to have age-related renal function impairment, which may require reduction of dosage in patients receiving minoxidil.

Drug interactions and/or related problems

The following drug interactions and/or related problems have been selected on the basis of their potential clinical significance (possible mechanism in parentheses where appropriate)—not necessarily inclusive (» = major clinical significance):

Note: Combinations containing any of the following medications, depending on the amount present, may also interact with this medication.

» Antihypertensives, potent parenteral, such as diazoxide or nitroprusside or
» Guanethidine or
» Nitrates
(concurrent use with minoxidil may result in a severe, additive hypotensive effect; patients should be continuously observed for excessive fall in blood pressure for several hours after concurrent administration of potent peripheral antihypertensives or nitrates; concurrent use with guanethidine is not recommended)

Anti-inflammatory drugs, nonsteroidal (NSAIDs), especially indomethacin
(may reduce antihypertensive effects of minoxidil; indomethacin, and possibly other NSAIDs, may antagonize the antihypertensive effect by inhibiting renal prostaglandin synthesis and/or by causing sodium and fluid retention; the patient should be carefully monitored to confirm that the desired effect is being obtained)

Hypotension-producing medications, other (see *Appendix II*)
(hypotensive effects may be potentiated when these medications are used concurrently with minoxidil)
(although some antihypertensive and/or diuretic combinations are used for therapeutic advantage, dosage adjustments may be necessary during concurrent use)

Sympathomimetics
(may reduce antihypertensive effects of minoxidil; the patient should be carefully monitored to confirm that the desired effect is being obtained)

Laboratory value alterations

The following have been selected on the basis of their potential clinical significance (possible effect in parentheses where appropriate)—not necessarily inclusive (» = major clinical significance).

With physiology/laboratory test values

Alkaline phosphatase concentrations, serum and
Plasma renin activity (PRA) and
Sodium concentrations, serum
(may be increased)

Blood urea nitrogen (BUN) and
Creatinine
(serum concentrations may be increased initially, but decline to pretreatment levels with continued treatment)

Erythrocyte count and
Hematocrit and
Hemoglobin concentrations
(may be decreased as a result of hemodilution; usually recover to pretreatment levels with continued treatment)

Medical considerations/Contraindications

The medical considerations/contraindications included have been selected on the basis of their potential clinical significance (reasons given in parentheses where appropriate)—not necessarily inclusive (» = major clinical significance).

Risk-benefit should be considered when the following medical problems exist:

Cerebrovascular disease or accident or
Myocardial infarction
(a reduction in arterial pressure caused by minoxidil may further limit blood flow to the ischemic area)

» Congestive heart failure not due to hypertension
(may be exacerbated secondary to fluid retention caused by minoxidil)

» Coronary insufficiency, including angina pectoris
(may be exacerbated)

» Pericardial effusion
(minoxidil may aggravate this condition)

» Pheochromocytoma
(use may stimulate release of catecholamines from the tumor)

» Renal function impairment
(reduced elimination; lower doses may be required)

Sensitivity to minoxidil

Patient monitoring

The following may be especially important in patient monitoring (other tests may be warranted in some patients, depending on condition; » = major clinical significance):

» Blood pressure measurements
(recommended at periodic intervals in patients being treated for hypertension; selected patients may be trained to perform blood pressure measurements at home and report the results at regular physician visits)

» Weight measurements
(daily weight measurements by the patient are recommended to detect excessive sodium and water retention)

Side/Adverse Effects

Note: Minoxidil has been shown to cause severe myocardial toxicity in dogs. However, this effect has not been observed in other animals or in humans at this time, although nonspecific electrocardiogram (ECG) changes are commonly seen, pericardial effusion (sometimes progressing to cardiac tamponade) occurs in about 3% of patients, and pericarditis has been reported.

The following side/adverse effects have been selected on the basis of their potential clinical significance (possible signs and symptoms in parentheses where appropriate)—not necessarily inclusive:

Those indicating need for medical attention

Incidence more frequent

Reflex sympathetic activation (fast or irregular heartbeat; flushing or redness of skin); ***sodium and water retention*** (bloating; swelling of feet or lower legs; rapid weight gain of more than 5 pounds [2 kg] in adults or 2 pounds [1 kg] in children)

Incidence less frequent

Angina, new or exacerbated, or pericarditis (chest pain)

Incidence rare

Allergic reaction or Stevens-Johnson syndrome (skin rash and itching)

With long-term use

Paresthesia (numbness or tingling of hands, feet, or face); ***pericardial effusion or pulmonary hypertension*** (shortness of breath)

Those indicating need for medical attention only if they continue or are bothersome

Incidence more frequent—occurs in most patients

Hypertrichosis (excessive hair growth, usually on face, arms, and back)

Note: *Hypertrichosis* usually develops within 3 to 6 weeks after initiation of minoxidil therapy, and return to pretreatment appearance occurs approximately 1 to 6 months after the medication is withdrawn. The increased hair growth may be extensive and may be especially disturbing to women and children; various depilatory methods may help.

Incidence less frequent or rare

Breast tenderness in males and females; vasodilation (headache)

Overdose

For more information on the management of overdose or unintentional ingestion, **contact a Poison Control Center** (see *Poison Control Center Listing*).

Treatment of overdose

Administration of intravenous sodium chloride injection is recommended to maintain blood pressure and facilitate urine formation.

Sympathomimetics such as norepinephrine or epinephrine should be avoided because of the risk of excessive cardiac stimulation.

Hypotension may be treated with phenylephrine, vasopressin, or dopamine, but they are recommended only if lack of perfusion of a vital organ occurs.

Patient Consultation

As an aid to patient consultation, refer to *Advice for the Patient, Minoxidil (Systemic)*.

In providing consultation, consider emphasizing the following selected information (» = major clinical significance):

Before using this medication

» Conditions affecting use, especially:
Sensitivity to minoxidil
Pregnancy—Decreased conception and increased resorption in animals; hypertrichosis reported in newborns
Breast-feeding—Passes into breast milk
Other medications, especially guanethidine or nitrates
Other medical problems, especially congestive heart failure, coronary insufficiency, pericardial effusion, pheochromocytoma, or renal function impairment

Proper use of this medication

Possible need for control of weight and diet, especially sodium intake
» Patient may not experience symptoms of hypertension; importance of taking medication even if feeling well
» Does not cure, but helps control hypertension; possible need for lifelong therapy; serious consequences of untreated hypertension
Compliance with therapy; taking medication at the same time(s) each day to maintain the therapeutic effect
Caution in taking combination therapy; taking each drug at the right time
» Proper dosing
Missed dose: Taking as soon as remembered if within a few hours; not taking if forgotten until next day; not doubling doses
» Proper storage

Precautions while using this medication

Making regular visits to physician to check progress
» Checking resting pulse as directed; checking with physician if an increase of 20 or more beats per minute above normal occurs
» Checking weight daily; weight gain of 2 to 3 lb (approximately 1 kg) in adults is normal and is usually lost with continued treatment; checking with physician if rapid weight gain of more than 5 lb (2 lb in children) or signs of fluid retention occur
» Not taking other medications, especially nonprescription sympathomimetics, unless discussed with physician

Side/adverse effects

Probability of hypertrichosis, which is reversible when medication is withdrawn
Signs of potential side effects, especially sodium and water retention, reflex sympathetic activation, angina, pericarditis, allergic reaction, Stevens-Johnson syndrome, paresthesia, and pulmonary hypertension

General Dosing Information

Sodium and water retention occurs rapidly in almost all patients receiving minoxidil and is difficult to control. Concomitant use of a diuretic (usually a loop diuretic) is recommended to prevent serious fluid accumulation and possible development of tolerance due to expansion of plasma volume.

Reflex tachycardia also occurs very commonly and may be less pronounced if a beta-adrenergic blocking agent or other sympathetic nervous system suppressant is used concurrently. The usual dose of beta-adrenergic blocker recommended is the equivalent of 80 to 160 mg of propranolol a day in divided doses. If beta-adrenergic blocking agents cannot be used, methyldopa in a dose of 250 to 750 mg twice a day may be substituted. Some investigators have used clonidine in a dose of 100 to 200 mcg (0.1 to 0.2 mg) twice a day.

If pericardial effusion occurs and does not respond to therapeutic measures, it is recommended that minoxidil therapy be withdrawn.

Because a few cases of rebound hypertension have been reported following abrupt withdrawal of minoxidil, caution is recommended when discontinuing the medication.

Oral Dosage Forms

MINOXIDIL TABLETS USP

Usual adult and adolescent dose

Antihypertensive—
Initial: Oral, 5 mg a day as a single dose or as two divided doses, the dosage being adjusted in 100% increments as required (i.e., up to 10, 20, 40 mg, etc.).
Maintenance: Oral, 10 to 40 mg a day, as a single dose or in divided daily doses.
For severe hypertension—Oral, 0.1 to 0.2 mg per kg of body weight per dose.

Note: It is recommended that an interval of at least three days be allowed between each dosage adjustment, in order for the full effect of each dose to be obtained. In some patients, dosage adjustment may be made every six hours with careful monitoring.
Geriatric patients may be more sensitive to effects of the usual adult dose.

Usual adult prescribing limits

100 mg a day.

Usual pediatric dose

Antihypertensive—

Children up to 12 years of age—

Initial—Oral, 200 mcg (0.2 mg) per kg of body weight a day as a single dose or as two divided doses, the dosage being adjusted as required (i.e., in increments of 100, 150, 200 mcg per kg of body weight, etc.), up to 50 mg a day.

Maintenance—Oral, 250 mcg (0.25 mg) to 1 mg per kg of body weight a day, as a single dose or in divided daily doses, up to 50 mg a day.

Children over 12 years of age—

See *Usual adult and adolescent dose.*

Note: It is recommended that an interval of at least three days be allowed between each dosage adjustment, in order for the full effect of each dose to be obtained. When more rapid control of blood pressure is required, dosage adjustment may be made every six hours with careful monitoring.

Strength(s) usually available

U.S.—

2.5 mg (Rx) [*Loniten* (scored); GENERIC (scored)].

10 mg (Rx) [*Loniten* (scored); GENERIC (scored)].

Canada—

2.5 mg (Rx) [*Loniten* (scored)].

10 mg (Rx) [*Loniten* (scored)].

Packaging and storage

Store below 40 °C (104 °F), preferably between 15 and 30 °C (59 and 86 °F) unless otherwise specified by manufacturer. Store in a tight container.

Auxiliary labeling

- Do not take other medicines without your doctor's advice.

Note

Check refill frequency to determine compliance in hypertensive patients.

Selected Bibliography

The fifth report of the Joint National Committee on Detection, Evaluation, and Treatment of High Blood Pressure (JNC V). Arch Intern Med 1993; 153(2): 154-83.

Revised: 11/17/2004

MINOXIDIL Topical

VA CLASSIFICATION (Primary): DE900

Commonly used brand name(s): *Apo-Gain; Gen-Minoxidil; Minoxigaine; Rogaine; Rogaine Extra Strength For Men; Rogaine For Men; Rogaine For Women.*

Note: For a listing of dosage forms and brand names by country availability, see *Dosage Forms* section(s).

Category

Hair growth stimulant, alopecia androgenetica, topical.

Indications

Accepted

Alopecia androgenetica (treatment)—Minoxidil topical solution is indicated for treatment of alopecia androgenetica (also called male pattern baldness in men) in both adult males and females for the 2% strength and in adult males only for the 5% strength. Alopecia androgenetica is expressed in males as baldness of the vertex of the scalp and/or as frontal hair recession. In females, it is expressed as diffuse hair loss or thinning in the frontoparietal areas. Topical minoxidil is less likely to be effective in men with predominantly frontal hair loss than in patients with the other forms of alopecia androgenetica.

Acceptance not established

There are *insufficient data* to show that 2% minoxidil is effective in the treatment of alopecia areata.

Pharmacology/Pharmacokinetics

Physicochemical characteristics

Molecular weight—209.25.

pKa—4.6.

Mechanism of action/Effect

Topical minoxidil stimulates hair growth in some persons with alopecia androgenetica. The mechanism by which minoxidil stimulates hair growth is not established, but possible mechanisms include increased cutaneous blood flow as a result of vasodilation, stimulation of resting hair follicles (telogen phase) into active growth (anagen phase), and stimulation of hair follicle cells.

Other actions/effects

Most studies have not found changes in blood pressure. In one report of 30 patients using 3% topical minoxidil for 15 months, seven normotensive patients absorbed a sufficient amount of minoxidil to decrease their systolic blood pressure by 60 mm of mercury and their diastolic blood pressure by 24 mm of mercury. The patients were asymptomatic and tachycardia did not occur. Systemically absorbed oral minoxidil may cause peripheral arterial vasodilation, reduced peripheral resistance, a reflex increase in heart rate and cardiac output, and fluid retention.

Absorption

Low percutaneous absorption; 1.6 to 3.9% of the total applied topical dose is absorbed systemically; however, absorption may increase if medication is applied to inflamed skin. Applying a 5-microliter-per-squared-centimeter dose to the entire scalp is expected to yield a systemic dose of 1.2 mg for the 1% topical solution of minoxidil and 2.7 mg for the 5% solution of minoxidil. Applying a 1 or 2% topical concentration of minoxidil to up to 50% of the scalp is unlikely to cause systemic side effects, since the average absorbed dose is less than 1.2 mg of minoxidil.

Onset of action

At least 4 months with twice-daily applications for the 2% strength, and 2 months for the 5% strength (although in some patients effect still takes 4 months).

Duration of action

In one study with continuous treatment using topical minoxidil for alopecia androgenetica, hair regrowth tended to peak at one year, with a slow decline in regrowth over subsequent years. Even so, after 4½ to 5 years of treatment, there were still more nonvellus hairs than there were at the beginning of the treatment.

New hair growth achieved during therapy may be expected to be lost 3 to 4 months after withdrawal of minoxidil, and progressive hair loss will resume.

Elimination

Renal—Approximately 95% of systemically absorbed minoxidil is eliminated within 4 days.

Precautions to Consider

Carcinogenicity

A 1-year study of minoxidil applied topically in rats and rabbits showed no evidence of carcinogenicity.

Mutagenicity

Minoxidil was not found to be mutagenic in the Salmonella (Ames) test, the DNA damage/alkaline elution assay, or the rat micronucleus test.

Pregnancy/Reproduction

Fertility—There was a dose-dependent decreased conception rate in male and female rats given 1 or 5 times the maximum recommended oral antihypertensive human dose.

Pregnancy—Adequate and well-controlled studies in humans have not been done.

With oral administration of minoxidil, no teratogenic effects occurred in rats or rabbits, but there was evidence of increased fetal resorption in rabbits (but not rats) at 5 times the maximum recommended antihypertensive human dose.

Labor and delivery—The effects of minoxidil on labor or delivery are unknown.

Breast-feeding

Orally administered minoxidil is distributed into breast milk. It is not known whether topical minoxidil is distributed into breast milk. However, because of the potential for adverse effects, topical minoxidil should not be administered to women who are breast-feeding.

Pediatrics

No information is available on the relationship of age to the effects of topical minoxidil in pediatric patients. Safety and efficacy have not been established for pediatric patients up to 18 years of age. Use in infants is not recommended.

Geriatrics

No information is available on the relationship of age to the effects of this medication in geriatric patients. Safety and efficacy have not been established in patients older than 65 years of age.

Older patients up to 65 years of age have not demonstrated geriatric-specific problems that would limit the usefulness of topical minoxidil; however, the best results are shown in younger patients with a short history of hair loss.

Drug interactions and/or related problems

The following drug interactions and/or related problems have been selected on the basis of their potential clinical significance (possible mechanism in parentheses where appropriate)—not necessarily inclusive (» = major clinical significance):

Note: Combinations containing any of the following medications, depending on the amount present, may also interact with this medication.

» Corticosteroids, topical or
» Petrolatum, topical or
» Retinoids, topical
(concurrent use on the same area may enhance cutaneous absorption of topical minoxidil because of increased stratum corneum permeability and is not recommended; in one patient, concurrent use of a topical retinoid on the same area as topical minoxidil caused a lesion consisting of granulation tissue similar to pyogenic granuloma)

Guanethidine
(concurrent use may increase the chance of orthostatic hypotension)

Medical considerations/Contraindications

The medical considerations/contraindications included have been selected on the basis of their potential clinical significance (reasons given in parentheses where appropriate)—not necessarily inclusive (» = major clinical significance).

Risk-benefit should be considered when the following medical problems exist:

Allergy to minoxidil or propylene glycol

Cardiovascular disease or
Hypertension
(patients with these conditions were excluded from the clinical trials of topical minoxidil because of the potential that adverse systemic effects could occur for the rare patient who might receive significant systemic absorption from its use; although their deaths were not attributable to topical minoxidil treatment, unexplained sudden death occurred in two patients with underlying undetected, untreated cardiovascular conditions who used topical minoxidil)

Skin irritation or abrasion, including scalp psoriasis or severe sunburn
(systemic absorption may be increased)

Patient monitoring

The following may be especially important in patient monitoring (other tests may be warranted in some patients, depending on condition; » = major clinical significance):

Blood pressure and
Heart rate and
Weight
(if a patient's history indicates a potential problem, determinations are recommended prior to initiation of therapy and at periodic intervals during therapy to check for possible systemic effects; if systemic effects occur, it is recommended that minoxidil be discontinued; minimal effects on blood pressure are expected in normotensive patients)

Side/Adverse Effects

Note: Although their deaths were not attributed to topical minoxidil therapy, sudden death has been reported in two patients treated with topical minoxidil who had underlying cardiovascular conditions—one patient had undetected Wolff-Parkinson-White syndrome and the other patient had untreated hypertension and cardiosclerotic cardiovascular disease.

The following side/adverse effects have been selected on the basis of their potential clinical significance (possible signs and symptoms in parentheses where appropriate)—not necessarily inclusive:

Those indicating need for medical attention

Incidence less frequent
Contact dermatitis (itching or skin rash)

Incidence rare
Allergic reaction (reddened skin; skin rash; swelling of face); ***alopecia, increased*** (increased hair loss); ***burning of scalp; folliculitis*** (acne; inflammation or soreness at root of hair)—at site of application

Signs and symptoms of systemic absorption—rare
Chest pain; fast or irregular heartbeat; headache; hypotension—usually not symptomatic; ***lightheadedness; neuritis*** (numbness or tingling of hands, feet, or face); ***reflex hypertension; sexual dysfunction*** (decrease of sexual ability or desire); ***sodium and water retention*** (swelling of face, hands, feet, or lower legs; rapid weight gain); ***vasodilation*** (flushing; headache); ***visual disturbances, including decreased visual acuity*** (blurred vision or other changes in vision)

Note: Signs and symptoms of toxicity resulting from systemic absorption are unlikely unless a patient applies minoxidil too frequently to a large surface area (such as that occurring in a woman who had alopecia totalis) or unless the product is ingested orally (as was the case of one man attempting suicide by consuming topical minoxidil).

Overdose

For specific information on the agents used in the management of oral ingestion of topical minoxidil overdose, see:
- *Phenylephrine* or *Dopamine* in *Sympathomimetic Agents—Cardiovascular Use (Parenteral-Systemic)* monograph; and/or
- *Vasopressin (Systemic)* monograph.

For more information on the management of overdose or unintentional ingestion, **contact a Poison Control Center** (see *Poison Control Center Listing*).

Clinical effects of overdose

The following effects have been selected on the basis of their potential clinical significance (possible signs and symptoms in parentheses where appropriate)—not necessarily inclusive:

Chest pain; fast or irregular heartbeat; hypotension—usually not symptomatic; ***neuritis*** (numbness or tingling of hands, feet, or face); ***reflex hypertension; sodium and water retention*** (swelling of face, hands, feet, or lower legs; rapid weight gain); ***vasodilation*** (flushing; headache)

Treatment of overdose

If systemic toxicity occurs as a result of overdose by oral ingestion of topical minoxidil, treatment may include the following:

To enhance elimination—Hemodialysis. Minoxidil and its metabolites are hemodialyzable.

Specific treatment—Hypotension may be treated with phenylephrine, angiotensin II, vasopressin, or dopamine, but these medications are recommended only if lack of perfusion of a vital organ occurs. Sympathomimetic medications, such as norepinephrine or epinephrine, should be avoided because of the risk of excessive cardiac stimulation.

Supportive care—Administration of intravenous sodium chloride injection is recommended to maintain blood pressure and facilitate urine formation. Patients in whom intentional overdose is known or suspected should be referred for psychiatric consultation.

Patient Consultation

As an aid to patient consultation, refer to *Advice for the Patient, Minoxidil (Topical)*.

In providing consultation, consider emphasizing the following selected information (» = major clinical significance):

Before using this medication

» Conditions affecting use, especially:
Allergy to minoxidil or propylene glycol (an inactive component of the preparation)
Pregnancy—Animal studies using oral minoxidil have shown problems during pregnancy, but not birth defects
Breast-feeding—Not recommended, since medication may cause problems in nursing babies
Other medications, especially topical corticosteroids, petrolatum, or retinoids

Proper use of this medication

Reading patient instructions carefully
» Keeping away from fire or flame.
» Not using more medication or more frequently than prescribed; not applying to other parts of body; risk of adverse systemic effects with excessive use
» Not using other skin products on treated skin; hair colorings, hair permanents, and hair relaxers may be used during the course of minoxidil therapy, but minoxidil should be washed from scalp before

their use; avoid using minoxidil 24 hours before and after hair products are applied, and do not double doses to make up for these missed minoxidil doses

Proper administration technique—Applying to affected area of dry scalp, beginning at the center of the balding area; not shampooing hair for 4 hours after minoxidil application

Method of application depends on applicator used (spray, extended spray tip, dropper, and/or rub-on assembly)

Washing hands immediately after application to remove any medication that may be on them

Allowing full drying for 2 to 4 hours; minoxidil can stain clothing, hats, or bed linens if not allowed to fully dry; however, not using hairdryer to speed drying, since this could decrease efficacy of the medication by removing product from the hair or scalp

Avoiding transfer of medication to other parts of body or onto bed linens by allowing complete drying of medication before retiring

Checking with physician before applying to abraded, irritated, or sunburned scalp

» Avoiding contact with eyes, nose, or mouth; flushing area with large amounts of cool tap water if accidental contact occurs; avoiding inhalation of pump spray

» Proper dosing

Missed dose: Using as soon as remembered if within a few hours; not using if almost time for next dose; not doubling amount used

» Proper storage

Precautions while using this medication

Regular visits to physician to check progress

Telling physician if itching, burning, or redness occurs after application; if reaction is severe, washing minoxidil off and checking with physician before using again

Hair loss may continue for 2 weeks after initiating minoxidil therapy, but if it continues, patient should discuss continuation of medication with physician. If hair growth does not increase in 4 months, patient should discuss continuation of medication with physician

Side/adverse effects

Signs of potential side effects, especially contact dermatitis, allergic reaction, burning of scalp, folliculitis, increased alopecia, and systemic absorption (chest pain, fast or irregular heartbeat, hypotension, lightheadedness, neuritis, reflex hypertension, sexual dysfunction, sodium and water retention, vasodilation, and visual disturbances, including decreased visual acuity)

General Dosing Information

If systemic effects occur, topical minoxidil should be discontinued and the patient should be seen by a physician.

Females are advised not to use the 5% solution because it does not work any better in females than the 2% solution and has caused excessive or unusual facial hair growth in females. Minoxidil will not work in males or females who experience hair loss caused by endocrine or nutritional problems or caused by skin damage that can occur from scarring, burns, or severe hair grooming methods, such as hair loss from ponytails or cornrowing. Minoxidil will not work for sudden or patchy hair loss.

If dermatologic reactions occur, it is recommended that discontinuation of topical minoxidil therapy be considered. Patients should not apply minoxidil if skin is red, infected, irritated, or painful.

Hair loss may continue for 2 weeks after initiation of minoxidil therapy, but if it continues past 2 weeks, patient should notify physician. If hair growth has not improved in 4 months of therapy, patient should reconsider continuing the use of topical minoxidil.

Patient should be instructed about proper administration of topical minoxidil, including the avoidance of inhaling the spray mist. In the event of accidental contact with sensitive areas (eye, abraded skin, mucous membranes), the sensitive area that is burning or irritated should be washed with copious amounts of cool water. Application should be restricted to the thinning or balding area of the scalp, and hands should be washed afterwards to avoid inadvertent translocation of minoxidil to inappropriate areas of the body. Waiting 2 to 4 hours for the minoxidil to dry before retiring is also recommended to avoid translocation of medication and to avoid rubbing it off inadvertently onto bed linens. Minoxidil may stain bed linens, hats, or clothing if it has not fully dried.

Topical minoxidil should be applied to the dry skin of the scalp. A hairdryer should not be used after application, as it might interfere with the efficacy of minoxidil. At least 4 hours should be allowed after minoxidil application before shampooing.

Hair colorings, hair permanents, and hair relaxers may be used with topical minoxidil; however, to avoid skin irritation, patient should wash minoxidil from scalp first before having hair treatments, avoid using minoxidil 24 hours before and 24 hours after having chemical treatments, and avoid making up missed doses by using more minoxidil when treatment is reinitiated.

Topical Dosage Forms

MINOXIDIL TOPICAL SOLUTION

Usual adult dose

Hair growth stimulant—

Adults up to 65 years of age: Topical, to the scalp, 1 mL two times a day.

Adults 65 years of age and older: Use and dose have not been established.

Note: The same dose is used regardless of the size of the area being treated.

Usual pediatric dose

Hair growth stimulant—

Infants: Use is not recommended.

Children up to 18 years of age: Use and dose have not been established.

Strength(s) usually available

U.S.—

2% (20 mg per mL) (OTC) [*Rogaine For Men* (alcohol 60% v/v; propylene glycol; water); *Rogaine For Women* (alcohol 60% v/v; propylene glycol; water); GENERIC].

5% (50 mg per mL) (OTC) [*Rogaine Extra Strength For Men* (alcohol 30% v/v; propylene glycol 50% v/v; water)].

Canada—

2% (20 mg per mL) (Rx) [*Apo-Gain* (alcohol 63%; propylene glycol; water); *Gen-Minoxidil* (alcohol; propylene glycol; water); *Minoxigaine* (alcohol 63%; propylene glycol; water); *Rogaine* (alcohol 63%)].

Note: Packaging may include spray, extended spray, dropper, and/or rub-on tips for application.

Packaging and storage

Store between 15 and 30 °C (59 and 86 °F), unless otherwise specified by manufacturer. Store in a tight container. Protect from light. Protect from freezing.

Auxiliary labeling

- For external use only.
- Flammable: Keep away from fire or flame.

Selected Bibliography

Rumsfield JA, West DP, Fiedler-Weiss VC, et al. Topical minoxidil therapy for hair regrowth. Clin Pharm 1987 May; 6(5): 386-92.

Clissold SP, Heel RC. Topical minoxidil. A preliminary review of its pharmacodynamic properties and therapeutic efficacy in alopecia areata and alopecia androgenetica [review]. Drugs 1987 Feb; 33(2): 107-22.

Revised: 11/18/2003

MIRTAZAPINE Systemic

VA CLASSIFICATION (Primary): CN609

Commonly used brand name(s): *Remeron; Remeron SolTab.*

Note: For a listing of dosage forms and brand names by country availability, see *Dosage Forms* section(s).

Category

Antidepressant.

Indications

Accepted

Depressive disorder, major (treatment)—Mirtazapine is indicated for the treatment of depression. The effectiveness of using mirtazapine for longer than 6 weeks has not been evaluated in controlled trials.

Pharmacology/Pharmacokinetics

Physicochemical characteristics

Chemical Group—Piperazinoazepine. Mirtazapine has a tetracyclic structure. It is structurally unrelated to selective serotonin reuptake inhibitors, tricyclic antidepressants, or monoamine oxidase inhibitors.

Molecular weight—265.36.

Solubility—Slightly soluble in water.

Mechanism of action/Effect

The exact mechanism of action is unknown. Evidence indicates that mirtazapine may enhance central noradrenergic and serotonergic activity, possibly through its antagonist activity at central presynaptic alpha$_2$-adrenergic inhibitory autoreceptors and heteroreceptors. Mirtazapine shows no significant affinity for serotonin 5-HT$_{1A}$ or 5-HT$_{1B}$ receptors.

Other actions/effects

Mirtazapine is a potent antagonist at serotonin 5-HT$_2$ and 5-HT$_3$ receptors, and a moderate antagonist at muscarinic receptors. Mirtazapine produces sedative effects due to potent histamine H$_1$ receptor antagonism, and orthostatic hypotension due to moderate peripheral alpha$_1$-adrenergic receptor antagonism.

Absorption

Rapid and complete; however, due to first-pass metabolism, absolute bioavailability is about 50%. The rate and extent of mirtazapine absorption are minimally affected by food.

Protein binding

High (85%).

Biotransformation

Mirtazapine is extensively metabolized after oral administration by demethylation and hydroxylation followed by glucuronide conjugation. *In vitro* testing indicates that cytochrome P450 2D6 (CYP2D6) and cytochrome P450 1A2 (CYP1A2) are involved in formation of the 8-hydroxy metabolite of mirtazapine, and cytochrome P450 3A (CYP3A) is responsible for the formation of the *N*-desmethyl and *N*-oxide metabolites. Several metabolites possess pharmacological activity, but plasma levels are very low.

Half-life

Elimination—

About 20 to 40 hours across age and gender subgroups. In females of all ages, the elimination half-life is significantly longer than in males (mean 37 hours versus 26 hours).

The half-life of the (−)-enantiomer is about twice that of the (+)-enantiomer.

Time to peak concentration

About 2 hours.

Steady-state plasma concentration

Attained within 5 days. Dose and plasma levels are linearly related over a dose range of 15 to 80 mg. Because of the difference in elimination half-life, the plasma level of the (−)-enantiomer is about three times as high as the plasma level of the (+)-enantiomer.

Elimination

Renal—

75%.

Fecal—

15%.

Precautions to Consider

Carcinogenicity/Tumorigenicity

Carcinogenicity studies in mice given doses of 2, 20, and 200 mg per kg of body weight per day (mg/kg/day), which is up to 20 times the maximum recommended human dose (MRHD) of 45 mg per day (mg/day) on a mg per square meter of body surface area (mg/m^2) basis, found an increase in hepatocellular adenomas and carcinomas in male mice in the high dose group. Carcinogenicity studies in rats given doses of 2, 20, and 60 mg/kg/day, which is up to 12 times the MRHD on a mg/m^2 basis, found an increase in hepatocellular adenomas in females at the middle and high doses, and an increase in hepatocellular tumors and thyroid follicular adenomas/cystadenomas and carcinomas in males at the high dose. These effects may have been mediated by nongenotoxic mechanisms, the relevance of which to humans is unknown.

Mutagenicity

Mirtazapine had no mutagenic or clastogenic effects, and did not induce general DNA damage based on the Ames test, the *in vitro* gene mutation assay in Chinese hamster V 79 cells, the *in vitro* sister chromatid exchange assay in cultured rabbit lymphocytes, the *in vivo* bone marrow micronucleus test in rats, and the unscheduled DNA synthesis assay in HeLa cells.

Pregnancy/Reproduction

Fertility—When given mirtazapine doses that were three or more times the MRHD of 45 mg/day on a mg/m^2 basis, rats showed disrupted estrous cycling. Also, in rats given mirtazapine doses that were 20 times the MRHD on a mg/m^2 basis, preimplantation fetal losses occurred. Mating and conception in rats were not affected by mirtazapine.

Pregnancy—Adequate and well-controlled studies in humans have not been done.

Studies in pregnant rats and rabbits given mirtazapine doses of up to 20 and 17 times the MRHD on a mg/m^2 basis, respectively, showed no teratogenic effects. However, in rats receiving 20 times the MRHD on a mg/m^2 basis, there were an increase in postimplantation fetal losses, a decrease in pup birth weights, and an increase in pup deaths during the first 3 days of lactation. The cause of these deaths is unknown.

FDA Pregnancy Category C.

Labor and delivery—The effect of mirtazapine on labor and delivery is unknown.

Breast-feeding

It is not known whether mirtazapine is distributed into breast milk.

Pediatrics

Safety and efficacy have not been established.

Antidepressants increase the risk of suicidal thinking and behavior (suicidality) in children and adolescents with major depressive disorder (MDD) and other psychiatric disorders. Anyone considering the use of mirtazapine or any other antidepressant in a child or adolescent must balance this risk with the clinical need.

Pooled analyses of short-term placebo controlled trials of nine antidepressant drugs in children and adolescents with MDD, obsessive compulsive disorder, or other psychiatric disorders have revealed a greater risk of adverse events representing suicidality during the first few months of treatment in those receiving antidepressants.

Geriatrics

No geriatrics-specific problems that would limit the usefulness of mirtazapine in the elderly were seen in studies that included elderly subjects. However, mirtazapine clearance was reduced by 40% in elderly males, and by 10% in elderly females as compared with younger males and younger females, respectively. Also, elderly patients are more likely to have age-related renal function impairment, which may decrease mirtazapine clearance.

Pharmacogenetics

Mirtazapine exhibits a longer half-life in females than in males across all age groups. The mean elimination half-life was found to be 37 hours in females, and 26 hours in males. Also, in elderly females, mirtazapine clearance was reduced by 10%, while in elderly males clearance was reduced by 40%. However, responsiveness to mirtazapine therapy showed no age or gender differences, and initial dosing recommendations are the same for all adult patients.

Dental

Prolonged use of mirtazapine may decrease or inhibit salivary flow, thus contributing to the development of caries, periodontal disease, oral candidiasis, and discomfort.

Drug interactions and/or related problems

The following drug interactions and/or related problems have been selected on the basis of their potential clinical significance (possible mechanism in parentheses where appropriate)—not necessarily inclusive (» = major clinical significance):

Note: Combinations containing any of the following medications, depending on the amount present, may also interact with this medication.

» Alcohol or

» CNS depression-producing medications, other (see *Appendix II*)
(CNS depressant effects of these medications and mirtazapine are additive; concurrent use is not recommended)

Antihypertensive medications
(hypotensive effect of these medications or mirtazapine may be enhanced)

Enzyme inducers, hepatic, cytochrome P450 (see *Appendix II*) or
Enzyme inhibitors, hepatic, various (see *Appendix II*)
(*in vitro* studies have shown mirtazapine to be a substrate for cytochrome P450 isoenzymes CYP2D6, CYP1A2, and CYP3A4; metabolism and pharmacokinetics of mirtazapine may be affected by induction or inhibition of these isoenzymes)

» Monoamine oxidase (MAO) inhibitors, including furazolidone, procarbazine, and selegiline
(serious, sometimes fatal reactions have occurred in patients taking MAO inhibitors in combination with, or soon after discontinuing, other antidepressant medications; symptoms have included autonomic instability with rapid fluctuation of vital signs, diaphoresis, dizziness, flushing, hyperthermia, mental status changes ranging from agitation to coma, myoclonus, nausea, rigidity, seizures, tremor, and vomiting; although there is no experience with the combination in humans, use of mirtazapine concurrently with an MAO inhibitor, or within 14 days of discontinuing therapy with an

MAO inhibitor is **contraindicated**; also, MAO inhibitor therapy should not be initiated within 14 days of the discontinuation of mirtazapine)

Laboratory value alterations

The following have been selected on the basis of their potential clinical significance (possible effect in parentheses where appropriate)—not necessarily inclusive (» = major clinical significance).

With physiology/laboratory test values

Alanine aminotransferase (ALT [SGPT])
(during premarketing studies, increases in ALT [SGPT] to ≥ three times the upper limit of normal were seen in 2% of patients receiving mirtazapine as compared with 0.3% of patients receiving placebo; while these increases were clinically significant, and led to discontinuation of mirtazapine in some patients, most of these patients did not develop signs or symptoms of decreased hepatic function; in some patients, ALT [SGPT] levels returned to normal with continued use of mirtazapine)

Cholesterol, total
(during premarketing studies, increases in nonfasting cholesterol to ≥ 20% above the upper limits of normal were seen in 15% of patients receiving mirtazapine as compared with 7% of patients receiving placebo)

Triglycerides, serum
(during premarketing studies, increases in nonfasting triglyceride to ≥ 500 mg per deciliter were seen in 6% of patients receiving mirtazapine as compared with 3% of patients receiving placebo)

Medical considerations/Contraindications

The medical considerations/contraindications included have been selected on the basis of their potential clinical significance (reasons given in parentheses where appropriate)—not necessarily inclusive (» = major clinical significance).

Except under special circumstances, this medication should not be used when the following medical problem exists:

» Hypersensitivity to mirtazapine

Risk-benefit should be considered when the following medical problems exist:

Cardiovascular or cerebrovascular disease that could be exacerbated by hypotension, such as history of myocardial infarction, angina, or ischemic stroke or

Conditions that would predispose patients to hypotension, such as dehydration or hypovolemia
(mirtazapine showed a significant orthostatic hypotensive effect in early trials with normal volunteers; however, during premarketing studies, this effect was seen less frequently in depressed patients)

Drug abuse or dependence, or history of
(patients with a history of drug abuse should be observed closely for signs of misuse or abuse of mirtazapine, as with any new central nervous system [CNS] drug)

» Hepatic function impairment
(significant alanine aminotransferase [ALT (SPGT)] elevations [≥ three times the upper limit of normal] occurred in some patients with normal liver function while they were receiving mirtazapine in premarketing studies; most of these patients did not develop signs or symptoms of decreased hepatic function, but the increases in ALT [SGPT] levels led to discontinuation of mirtazapine in some patients; in other patients, ALT [SGPT] levels returned to normal with continued use of mirtazapine; mirtazapine should be used with caution in patients with impaired hepatic function)
(clearance of a single 15-mg oral dose of mirtazapine was reduced by 30% in patients with hepatic function impairment as compared with clearance in patients with normal hepatic function)

Mania or hypomania, or history of
(mania or hypomania has occurred rarely in patients treated with mirtazapine)

Phenylketonuria (PKU)
(*Remeron SolTab* brand of mirtazapine oral disintegrating tablets contains aspartame, which is metabolized to phenylalanine)

Renal function impairment
(the clearance of a single 15-mg oral dose of mirtazapine was reduced by about 30% in patients with moderate renal function impairment [glomerular filtration rate (GFR) = 11 to 39 mL per minute per 1.73 square meters of body surface area (mL/min/1.73m^2)], and by about 50% in patients with severe renal function impairment [GFR < 10 mL/min/1.73m^2])

Seizures, history of
(one patient experienced a seizure during premarketing clinical trials of mirtazapine; there are no controlled studies of mirtazapine use in patients who have a history of seizures)

Patient monitoring

The following may be especially important in patient monitoring (other tests may be warranted in some patients, depending on condition; » = major clinical significance):

Absolute neutrophil count (ANC)
(should be performed periodically during treatment, especially if patient develops signs and symptoms associated with agranulocytosis)

Careful supervision of depressed patients including those with:
Abnormal behaviors (i.e., agitation, panic attacks, hostility) or
Clinical worsening of their depression or
Suicidal ideation and behavior (suicidality)
(recommended especially during early treatment phase before peak effectiveness of mirtazapine is achieved or at the time of increases or decreases in dose; prescribing the smallest number of tablets necessary for good patient management is recommended to decrease the risk of overdose; consideration should be given to changing the therapeutic regimen, including possibly discontinuing the medicine, in patients whose depression is persistently worse or whose emergent suicidality or other symptoms are severe, abrupt in onset, or were not part of the patient's presenting symptoms)

Side/Adverse Effects

The following side/adverse effects have been selected on the basis of their potential clinical significance (possible signs and symptoms in parentheses where appropriate)—not necessarily inclusive:

Those indicating need for medical attention

Incidence less frequent

Dyspnea (shortness of breath); ***edema*** (swelling); ***flu-like symptoms; hyperkinesia*** (increased movement); ***hypokinesia*** (decreased movement); ***mood or mental changes, including abnormal thinking; agitation; anxiety; apathy; and confusion; skin rash***

Incidence rare

Agranulocytosis or neutropenia (chills; fever; sore throat; sores in mouth)—may be asymptomatic; ***facial edema*** (swelling of face); ***impotence*** (decreased sexual ability); ***menstrual changes*** (painful menstruation; absence of menstruation); ***mood or mental changes, including delusions; depersonalization; emotional lability; hallucinations; hostility; and mania; seizures***

Note: Use of mirtazapine was associated with *agranulocytosis* in two, and severe *neutropenia* in one of 2796 patients treated in premarketing clinical studies. Recovery occurred in all three patients after mirtazapine was discontinued. Mirtazapine treatment should be discontinued in any patient who develops fever, sore throat, stomatitis, or other signs of infection and who has a low white blood cell (WBC) count. The patient should then be closely monitored.

Those indicating need for medical attention only if they continue or are bothersome

Incidence more frequent

Constipation; dizziness; drowsiness; dryness of mouth; increased appetite; weight gain

Note: *Weight gain* led to discontinuation of mirtazapine treatment in 8% of patients enrolled in U.S. premarketing studies.

Incidence less frequent

Abdominal pain; abnormal dreams; asthenia (weakness); ***back pain; hyperesthesia*** (increased sensitivity to touch); ***hypotension*** (low blood pressure); ***increased thirst; myalgia*** (pain in muscles); ***nausea; orthostatic hypotension*** (dizziness or fainting when getting up suddenly from a sitting or lying position); ***tremor*** (trembling or shaking); ***urinary frequency*** (increased need to urinate); ***vertigo*** (sense of constant movement of self or surroundings); ***vomiting***

Overdose

For specific information on the agents used in the management of mirtazapine overdose, see the *Charcoal, Activated (Oral-Local)* monograph.

For more information on the management of overdose or unintentional ingestion, **contact a poison control center** (see *Poison Control Center Listing*).

Clinical effects of overdose

The following effects have been selected on the basis of their potential clinical significance (possible signs and symptoms in parentheses where appropriate)—not necessarily inclusive:

Acute
Disorientation; drowsiness; impaired memory; tachycardia (fast heartbeat)

Note: Experience with mirtazapine overdose is very limited.

Treatment of overdose

Note: The possibility of multiple drug involvement should be considered in managing overdose.
There is no specific antidote for mirtazapine. General measures used in the treatment of overdose with any antidepressant should be employed.

Monitoring—Monitoring of cardiac and vital signs is recommended.

Supportive care—Establish and maintain an airway, oxygenation and ventilation. Employ general symptomatic and supportive measures. Patients in whom intentional overdose is confirmed or suspected should be referred for psychiatric consultation.

Patient Consultation

As an aid to patient consultation, refer to *Advice for the Patient, Mirtazapine (Systemic)*.

In providing consultation, consider emphasizing the following selected information (» = major clinical significance):

Before using this medication

» Conditions affecting use, especially:
Because of Food and Drug Administration [FDA] reports of the occurrence of suicidality in clinical trials for various antidepressant drugs in pediatric patients with major depressive disorder [MDD], mirtazapine must be used with caution in treating pediatric patients for MDD.
Use in the elderly—Elderly patients, especially males, may have reduced clearance
Dental—Possible dryness of mouth; using sugarless candy or gum, ice, or saliva substitute for relief; checking with physician or dentist if dry mouth continues for more than 2 weeks
Contraindicated medications—Monoamine oxidase (MAO) inhibitors
Other medications, especially alcohol or CNS depression-producing medications
Other medical problems, especially hypersensitivity to mirtazapine or hepatic function impairment

Proper use of this medication

Taking with or without food, as directed by physician
» Proper dosing
» Proper storage

Precautions while using this medication

» Not using concurrently or within 14 days of discontinuing therapy with an MAO inhibitor; not beginning MAO inhibitor therapy within 14 days of discontinuing therapy with mirtazapine
» Avoiding use of alcohol or other CNS depression-producing medications
Regular visits to physician to check progress during therapy
» Checking with physician immediately if any symptoms of infection, especially fever, chills, sore throat, or mucus membrane ulcerations, occur
» Possible drowsiness, impairment of judgement, thinking, or motor skills; caution when driving, using machinery, or doing other jobs requiring alertness
Possible orthostatic hypotension; getting up slowly from a lying or sitting position

Side/adverse effects

Signs of potential side effects, especially dyspnea, edema, flu-like symptoms, hyperkinesia, hypokinesia, mood or mental changes, skin rash, agranulocytosis or neutropenia, facial edema, impotence, menstrual changes, and seizures

General Dosing Information

Any symptoms of infection, especially flu-like symptoms, such as fever, chills, or sore throat, or mucous membrane ulcerations, occurring during mirtazapine treatment should be reported to the physician immediately. The patient should be evaluated for possible agranulocytosis.

Long-term efficacy of mirtazapine has not been evaluated in controlled trials, and its usefulness as long-term therapy for an individual patient should be evaluated periodically.

Remeron brand of oral disintegrating tablets is a freeze-dried formulation of mirtazapine which rapidly disintegrates on the tongue and does not require water to aid dissolution or swallowing.

Oral disintegrating tablets may contain aspartame, which is metabolized to phenylalanine. This substance must be used with caution in patients with phenylketonuria.

Diet/Nutrition

Food has a minimal effect on mirtazapine absorption.

Oral Dosage Forms

MIRTAZAPINE TABLETS

Usual adult dose

Antidepressant—
Oral, initially 15 mg once a day, preferably in the evening prior to sleep. The dose may be increased, as needed and tolerated, at intervals of not less than one to two weeks.

Note: Plasma mirtazapine levels may be higher in elderly patients and in patients with moderate to severe renal or hepatic function impairment than in younger adults without renal or hepatic function impairment because of decreased clearance.

Usual adult prescribing limits

Up to 45 mg a day.

Usual pediatric dose

Safety and efficacy have not been established.

Usual geriatric dose

See *Usual adult dose*.

Strength(s) usually available

U.S.—
15 mg (Rx) [*Remeron* (scored; corn starch; hydroxypropyl cellulose; magnesium stearate; colloidal silicon dioxide; lactose)].
30 mg (Rx) [*Remeron* (scored; corn starch; hydroxypropyl cellulose; magnesium stearate; colloidal silicon dioxide; lactose)].

Packaging and storage

Store between 20 and 25 °C (68 and 77 °F), unless otherwise specified by manufacturer.

Auxiliary labeling

- Avoid alcoholic beverages.
- May cause dizziness or drowsiness.

MIRTAZAPINE ORAL DISINTEGRATING TABLETS

Usual adult dose

See *Mirtazapine tablets*

Usual adult prescribing limits

See *Mirtazapine Tablets*

Usual pediatric dose

See *Mirtazapine Tablets*

Usual geriatric dose

See *Mirtazapine Tablets*.

Strength(s) usually available

U.S.—
15 mg (Rx) [*Remeron SolTab* (mannitol; granular mannitol; crospovidone; sodium bicarbonate; citric acid; microcrystalline cellulose; aspartame; magnesium stearate; orange flavor)].
30 mg (Rx) [*Remeron SolTab* (scored; mannitol; granular mannitol; crospovidone; sodium bicarbonate; citric acid; microcrystalline cellulose; aspartame; magnesium stearate; orange flavor)].
45 mg (Rx) [*Remeron SolTab* (mannitol; granular mannitol; crospovidone; sodium bicarbonate; citric acid; microcrystalline cellulose; aspartame; magnesium stearate; orange flavor)].

Packaging and storage

Store at 25 °C (77 °F), unless otherwise specified by manufacturer.

Auxiliary labeling

- Avoid alcoholic beverages.
- May cause dizziness or drowsiness.

Note

Remeron brand of oral disintegrating tablets contains aspartame, which is metabolized to phenylalanine and must be used with caution in patients with phenylketonuria.

Additional information

Proper handling/administration—With dry hands, peel back the foil backing of one blister. Do not attempt to push the oral disintegrating tablet through the foil backing. Gently remove the tablet and place it immediately on top of the tongue. It will dissolve in seconds, and should then be swallowed with saliva.

Revised: 01/25/2005
Developed: 02/26/1997

MISOPROSTOL Systemic

VA CLASSIFICATION (Primary): HS200

Commonly used brand name(s): *Cytotec*.

Note: For a listing of dosage forms and brand names by country availability, see *Dosage Forms* section(s).

Category

Gastric mucosa protectant; antiulcer agent.

Indications

Note: Bracketed information in the *Indications* section refers to uses that are not included in U.S. product labeling.

General Considerations

General considerations for use in pregnancy

Misoprostol is a prostaglandin E_1 analogue. Although not approved for use in pregnancy by the Food and Drug Administration (FDA), misoprostol is widely used to treat certain obstetrical and gynecologic conditions because of its uterotonic and cervical-ripening actions. The results of over 200 studies involving more than 16,000 women have demonstrated that misoprostol is a safe and effective agent as well as "one of the most important medications in obstetrical practice". Misoprostol is useful for therapeutic abortion in the first and second trimesters, cervical ripening, and induction of labor.

Complete abortion was achieved in 94.6% of women with gestational age up to 63 days using a regimen of 600 micrograms (mcg) of misoprostol by mouth forty-eight hours after 200 mg of mifepristone by mouth. Significantly higher rate of complete abortion was found in women with gestational age up to 49 days compared to those with gestational age up to 63 days given either 600 or 200 mg of mifepristone followed forty-eight hours later by 600 mcg of misoprostol. Similarly, successful rate over 98% was reported in studies using the regimen of oral mifepristone 600 mg and vaginal misoprostol 800 mcg thirty-six to forty-eight hours later in women with pregnancy up to 56 or 63 days of duration. Reducing the dose of mifepristone to 200 mg by mouth followed by 800 mcg of misoprostol vaginally forty-eight hours later achieved complete medical abortion in 97 to 98% of the subjects with up to 56 days of pregnancy and 96% in the group of 57 to 63 days of pregnancy.

The rate of abortion within forty-eight hours was 87.2 and 89.2%, respectively, when misoprostol was administered intravaginally at a dose of 200 mcg either every six or every twelve hours to women seeking termination of pregnancy at 12 to 22 weeks' gestation. Increasing the dose of misoprostol (600 mcg every twelve hours) resulted in similar abortion rate (89.5% within 48 hours), but with more side effects.

An alternative regimen for termination of pregnancy in the second trimester is to administer vaginal misoprostol 36 to 48 hours after oral mifepristone. When women with pregnancy between 14 to 20 weeks of gestation were given 200 mcg of misoprostol vaginally thirty-six to forty-eight hours after a dose of 200 mg of mifepristone orally, significant difference was shown in the median induction-abortion interval, the percentage of women aborting within 24 hours, and the median amount of misoprostol used compared with those receiving the same dose of misoprostol orally. The successful abortion rate was even higher in women receiving 600 mg of oral mifepristone, followed by a loading dose of 600 mcg of vaginal misoprostol, and then 400 mcg of either oral or vaginal misoprostol every three hours (for a maximum of five doses).

Misoprostol, when used for cervical ripening and induction of labor, resulted in shorter first stage, shorter induction-to-vaginal delivery interval, decreased incidence of oxytocin augmentation, and decreased total units of oxytocin used. In studies compared vaginal misoprostol with dinoprostone and/or oxytocin, misoprostol is superior to dinoprostone and/or oxytocin for cervical ripening and labor induction. Significant difference in causing cervical ripening, inducing labor, shortening the duration of labor, and decreasing the need for oxytocin augmentation was found in patients receiving misoprostol. Misoprostol also results in significantly shorter induction-to-vaginal delivery interval, significant difference in the median change of the Bishop score, and significant higher numbers of vaginal delivery within 24 to 36 hours compared with dinoprostone and/or oxytocin.

The studied treatment regimens for medical abortion in the first trimester (a 63 days' gestation) were oral 200 to 600 mg of mifepristone followed thirty-six to forty-eight hours later by a single dose of 400 to 600 mcg of misoprostol administered orally or 800 mcg of misoprostol administered vaginally. Reducing the dose of mifepristone to 200 mg did not affect efficacy.

The dosing regimen used for medical termination of pregnancy in the second trimester is vaginal 200 to 400 mcg of misoprostol every twelve hours or 400 mcg of misoprostol every six hours. Alternatively, vaginal 200 to 400 mcg every three hours (for a maximum of five doses) thirty-six to forty-eight hours after oral administration of 200 to 600 mg of mifepristone has been used. A loading dose of 600 to 800 mcg of misoprostol vaginally may be used to increase efficacy.

The recommended dose of misoprostol for cervical ripening and induction of labor is vaginal 25 mcg every three to six hours as an initial dose. A maximum of 4 to 8 doses within 24 hours may be given, if needed, or until active labor occurs. Using higher doses of misoprostol may increase its efficacy; however, uterine hyperstimulation and other adverse maternal and fetal outcomes were associated with higher doses (> 25 mcg) or more frequent dosing intervals (< every 3 to 6 hours).

It is not recommended to use misoprostol for cervical ripening or inducing labor in patients with previous cesarean delivery or prior major uterine surgery because of the adverse maternal and fetal outcomes, especially uterine rupture. Grand multiparity also appears to be a relative risk factor for uterine rupture; therefore, misoprostol is not recommended in these patients either.

Currently, there is insufficient clinical evidence to support the safety or efficacy of misoprostol used in patients with multifetal gestations or suspected fetal macrosomia.

Misoprostol also has been investigated in the prevention of postpartum hemorrhage, using either the oral or rectal route of administration, and compared with placebo or other oxytocics. Results of most of these studies show a trend toward less postpartum hemorrhage with misoprostol, suggesting that it might be effective for this indication without causing serious side effects. These studies, however, failed to reveal a significant statistical difference regarding blood loss. Recent studies indicated misoprostol is comparable to standard oxytocics.

Accepted

[Abortion, therapeutic (treatment)][1]—Misoprostol when either orally or vaginally administered, is indicated in combination use with mifepristone for the medical termination of intrauterine pregnancy of 63 days' duration or less.

[Abortion, second trimester (treatment)][1]—Misoprostol when vaginally administered, is indicated for the medical termination of intrauterine pregnancy in the second trimester.

[Cervical ripening][1]—Prior to induction of labor when medically or obstetrically indicated, misoprostol administered vaginally is used to initiate or continue ripening an unfavorable cervix in pregnant patients at or near term.

[Hemorrhage, postpartum (prophylaxis)][1]—Misoprostol is used as an alternative agent in reducing the incidence of postpartum hemorrhage, especially in situations in which oxytocin and other uterotonic drugs are not available.

[Labor, induction of][1]—Misoprostol administered vaginally is used for induction of labor at or near term.

Ulcer, gastric, nonsteroidal anti-inflammatory drug–induced (prophylaxis)—Misoprostol is indicated for the prevention of gastric ulcer associated with the use of nonsteroidal anti-inflammatory drugs (NSAIDs), including aspirin, in patients at high risk of complications from gastric ulcer, such as the elderly, and in patients with concomitant disease or patients at high risk of developing gastric ulceration, such as those with a history of ulcer.

[Ulcer, gastric, nonsteroidal anti-inflammatory drug–induced (treatment)]—Misoprostol is indicated for the treatment of gastric ulcer associated with the use of nonsteroidal anti-inflammatory drugs (NSAIDs).

[Ulcer, duodenal (treatment)]—Misoprostol is indicated in the short-term treatment of duodenal ulcer caused by peptic ulcer disease (PUD).

[1]Not included in Canadian product labeling.

Pharmacology/Pharmacokinetics

Physicochemical characteristics

Chemical Group—Synthetic prostaglandin E_1 analog.

Molecular weight—382.54.

Mechanism of action/Effect

Cytoprotective—Misoprostol enhances natural gastromucosal defense mechanisms and healing in acid-related disorders, probably by increasing production of gastric mucus and mucosal secretion of bicarbonate.

Antisecretory—Misoprostol inhibits basal and nocturnal gastric acid secretion by direct action on the parietal cells; also inhibits gastric acid secretion stimulated by food, coffee, histamine, and pentagastrin. It decreases pepsin secretion under basal, but not histamine, stimulation. Misoprostol has no significant effect on fasting or postprandial gastrin or intrinsic factor output.

Other actions/effects

Misoprostol may produce uterine contractions, bleeding, and expulsion of the products of conception.

Absorption

Rapidly absorbed following oral administration. Maximal plasma concentrations of misoprostol acid, the primary biologically active metabolite, are decreased when the dose is taken with food. Total availability of misoprostol acid is reduced by the concomitant use of antacid, but this effect does not appear to be clinically important.

Distribution

Volume of distribution (Vol_D) of misoprostol acid—40 L.

Protein binding

High (approximately 85%).

Biotransformation

Rapidly de-esterified to misoprostol acid. The de-esterified metabolite undergoes further metabolism by beta and omega oxidation; oxidation is followed by reduction of the ketone to yield prostaglandin F analogs.

Half-life

Terminal (misoprostol acid)—20 to 40 minutes.

Time to peak concentration

Misoprostol acid—12 ± 3 minutes.
IV administration—20 minutes (0.34 hour)
Oral administration—25 minutes (0.42 hour)

Peak serum concentration

IV administration—470.5 pg/mL
Oral administration—206.5 pg/mL

Time to steady-state concentration

Plasma steady-state concentrations of misoprostol acid were achieved within 2 days in multiple-dose studies.

Duration of action

3 to 6 hours.

Elimination

Renal (64 to 73% of the oral dose is excreted within the first 24 hours; 56% within the first 8 hours).
Fecal (15% of the oral dose is excreted within the first 24 hours).

Precautions to Consider

Cross-sensitivity and/or related problems

Patients sensitive to other prostaglandins or prostaglandin analogs may be sensitive to misoprostol also.

Carcinogenicity/Mutagenicity

Animal studies have not shown misoprostol to be carcinogenic or mutagenic.

Pregnancy/Reproduction

Fertility—Administration of misoprostol to breeding male and female rats at doses 6.25 times to 625 times the maximum recommended human therapeutic dose, produced dose-related pre- and post-implantation losses and a significant decrease in the number of live pups born at the highest dose. These findings suggest the possibility of a general adverse effect on fertility in males and females.

Pregnancy—**Misoprostol is contraindicated for use in pregnant women to reduce the risk of ulcers induced by non-steroidal anti-inflammatory drugs (NSAID's)**. Studies in humans have shown that misoprostol causes an increase in the frequency and intensity of uterine contractions. Misoprostol administration also has been associated with a higher incidence of uterine bleeding and expulsion of uterine contents. Miscarriages caused by misoprostol are likely to be incomplete, resulting in very serious medical complications, sometimes requiring hospitalization and surgery, and possibly causing infertility.

Research studies and clinical evidence have demonstrated that misoprostol is a safe and effective agent to treat certain off-labeled obstetrical and gynecologic conditions. It has been widely accepted and used for therapeutic abortion in the first and second trimesters, cervical ripening, and induction of labor. Misoprostol is also used as an alternative agent in reducing the incidence of postpartum hemorrhage, especially in situations in which oxytocin and other uterotonic drugs are not available. See *General Considerations* in *Indications* section.

FDA Pregnancy Category X.

Patients of childbearing potential may use misoprostol if nonsteroidal anti-inflammatory drug (NSAID) therapy is required and patient is at high risk of complications from gastric ulcers associated with the use of NSAIDs, or is at high risk of developing gastric ulceration. Such patients must comply with effective contraceptive measures, must have had a negative serum pregnancy test within 2 weeks prior to initiation of therapy, and must start misoprostol therapy only on the second or third day of the next normal menstrual period.

Labor and Delivery

Misoprostol can induce or augment uterine contractions. Vaginal administration of misoprostol, outside of its approved indication, has been used as a cervical ripening agent for the induction of labor and for treatment of serious postpartum hemorrhage in the presence of uterine atony. A major adverse effect of the obstetrical use of misoprostol is hyperstimulation of the uterus which may progress to uterine tetany with marked impairment of uteroplacental blood flow, uterine rupture (requiring surgical repair, hysterectomy, and/or salpingo-oophorectomy), or amniotic fluid embolism. Pelvic pain, retained placenta, severe genital bleeding, shock, fetal bradycardia, and fetal and maternal death have been reported with the use of misoprostol. There may be an increased risk of uterine tachysystole, uterine rupture, meconium passage, meconium staining of amniotic fluid and Cesarean delivery due to uterine hyperstimulation with the use of higher doses of misoprostol, including the manufactured 100 mcg tablet. The risk of uterine rupture increases with advancing gestational ages and with prior uterine surgery, including Cesarean delivery. Uterine rupture has been reported when misoprostol was administered in pregnant women to induce labor or to induce an abortion beyond the eighth week of pregnancy. The effect of misoprostol on later growth, development, and functional maturation of the child when misoprostol is used for cervical ripening ro induction of labor have not been established. Information on misoprostol's effect on the need for forceps delivery or other intervention is unknown.

Breast-feeding

It is unlikely that misoprostol is distributed into breast milk since it is rapidly metabolized throughout the body. However, it is not known if the active metabolite, misoprostol acid, is distributed into breast milk. Therefore, administration of misoprostol to nursing women is not recommended because of the potential distribution of misoprostol acid, which could cause significant diarrhea in the nursing infant.

Pediatrics

Appropriate studies on the relationship of age to the effects of misoprostol have not been performed in patients up to 18 years of age. Safety and efficacy have not been established.

Geriatrics

Studies performed in approximately 500 ulcer patients 65 years of age or older have not demonstrated geriatrics-specific problems that would limit the usefulness of misoprostol in the elderly.

Drug interactions and/or related problems

The following drug interactions and/or related problems have been selected on the basis of their potential clinical significance (possible mechanism in parentheses where appropriate)—not necessarily inclusive (» = major clinical significance):

Note: Combinations containing any of the following medications, depending on the amount present, may also interact with this medication.

Magnesium-containing antacids
(concurrent use with misoprostol may aggravate misoprostol-induced diarrhea)

Medical considerations/Contraindications

The medical considerations/contraindications included have been selected on the basis of their potential clinical significance (reasons given in parentheses where appropriate)—not necessarily inclusive (» = major clinical significance).

Risk-benefit should be considered when the following medical problems exist:

Cerebral vascular disease or
Coronary artery disease
(although the effect has not been reported with misoprostol, prostaglandins and prostaglandin analogs have been reported to cause hypotension via peripheral vasodilation, thus increasing the risk of severe complications in these conditions)

Epilepsy
(although the effect has not been reported with misoprostol, prostaglandins and prostaglandin analogs have been reported to cause epileptic seizures when given by routes other than oral; it is recommended that misoprostol be used in epileptics only when their condition is adequately controlled)

Inflammatory bowel disease
(diarrhea may be exacerbated, leading to dehydration; careful monitoring is recommended)

Sensitivity to prostaglandins or prostaglandin analogs

Side/Adverse Effects

The following side/adverse effects have been selected on the basis of their potential clinical significance (possible signs and symptoms in parentheses where appropriate)—not necessarily inclusive:

Those indicating need for medical attention only if they continue or are bothersome

Incidence more frequent

Abdominal or stomach pain, mild; diarrhea

Note: *Diarrhea* is dose-related. It usually develops early in the course of therapy and is self-limiting, often resolving after 8 days. However, rare instances of profound diarrhea leading to severe dehydration have been reported, and some patients have required discontinuation of misoprostol because of continuing severe diarrhea.

Incidence less frequent or rare

Constipation; dyspepsia (heartburn, indigestion, or acid stomach); ***flatulence*** (gas); ***headache; nausea and/or vomiting; uterine stimulation*** (cramps in lower abdomen or stomach area); ***vaginal bleeding***

Overdose

The toxic dose in humans has not been determined. Cumulative total daily doses of 1600 mcg have been tolerated with only gastrointestinal disturbances.

For more information on the management of overdose or unintentional ingestion, **contact a Poison Control Center** (see *Poison Control Center Listing).*

Clinical effects of overdose

The following effects have been selected on the basis of their potential clinical significance (possible signs and symptoms in parentheses where appropriate)—not necessarily inclusive:

Abdominal pain; bradycardia (slow heartbeat); ***convulsions*** (seizures); ***diarrhea; dyspnea*** (troubled breathing); ***fever; hypotension*** (low blood pressure); ***palpitations*** (fast or pounding heartbeat); ***sedation*** (drowsiness); ***seizures; tremor***

Treatment of overdose

There is no specific treatment for misoprostol overdose. Treatment should be symptomatic, and general supportive care is indicated.

Elimination—It is not known if misoprostol acid is dialyzable. However, misoprostol is metabolized like a fatty acid, so it is unlikely that dialysis would be appropriate treatment for overdosage.

Supportive care—Patients in whom intentional overdose is confirmed or suspected should be referred for psychiatric consultation.

Patient Consultation

As an aid to patient consultation, refer to *Advice for the Patient, Misoprostol (Systemic).*

In providing consultation, consider emphasizing the following selected information (» = major clinical significance):

Before using this medication

» Conditions affecting use, especially:
- Sensitivity to prostaglandins or prostaglandin analogs
- Pregnancy—Contraindicated during pregnancy for the treatment of NSAID-induced stomach ulcers, because of risk of miscarriage; patients of childbearing potential must take measures to assure they are not pregnant prior to therapy and to prevent pregnancy during therapy
- Breast-feeding—Not recommended because of possibility of causing diarrhea in nursing infant

Proper use of this medication

Taking with or after meals and at bedtime

» Proper dosing

Missed dose: Taking as soon as possible; not taking if almost time for next dose; not doubling doses

» Proper storage

Precautions while using this medication

» Stopping medication and checking with physician immediately if pregnancy is suspected

Consulting physician if diarrhea develops and continues for more than a week

Side/adverse effects

Signs of potential side effects, especially continuing and severe diarrhea, stomach pain, constipation, dyspepsia, flatulence, headache, nausea and/or vomiting, uterine stimulation, vaginal bleeding

General Dosing Information

Misoprostol therapy should be started at the onset of treatment with nonsteroidal anti-inflammatory drugs (NSAIDs), and continued for the duration of NSAID therapy.

Misoprostol should be taken with or after meals and at bedtime, for maximum effectiveness.

If required, antacids may be administered before or after misoprostol for the relief of pain. However, magnesium-containing antacids are not recommended since they may aggravate misoprostol-induced diarrhea.

Misoprostol has not been shown to have an effect on gastrointestinal pain or discomfort; caution should be used when relying on symptomatology as the sole diagnostic and follow-up procedure.

For treatment of duodenal ulcer

Therapy with misoprostol should continue for a total of 4 weeks unless healing has been documented by endoscopic examination. If necessary, treatment may continue for an additional 4 weeks if ulcers have not fully healed after the initial 4 weeks.

Treatment of side and adverse effects

Diarrhea—Taking with food or milk will lessen adverse effects such as loose stools, diarrhea, and abdominal cramping. The incidence of diarrhea can be minimized by reducing the dose of misoprostol,administering after meals and at bedtime and by avoiding coadministration with magnesium containing antacids.

Oral Dosage Forms

Note: Bracketed uses in the *Dosage Forms* section refer to categories of use and/or indications that are not included in U.S. product labeling.

MISOPROSTOL TABLETS

Usual adult dose

[Abortion][1]—

Oral, 400 mcg (two 200-mcg tablets) as a single dose on day three (forty-eight hours after oral administration of 200 to 600 mg of mifepristone), if abortion has not yet occurred.

Alternative regimen: Vaginal, 800 mcg (four 200-mcg tablets) as a single dose on day three (forty-eight hours after oral administration of 200 to 600 mg of mifepristone), if abortion has not yet occurred.

[Abortion, second trimester][1]—

Intravaginal, 200 to 400 mcg of misoprostol every twelve hours or 400 mcg of misoprostol every six hours placed into the posterior fornix of the vaginal canal.

Alternative regimen: Intravaginal, 200 to 400 mcg every three hours (for a maximum of five doses) thirty-six to forty-eight hours after oral administration of 200 to 600 mg of mifepristone. A loading dose of 600 to 800 mcg of misoprostol vaginally may be used to increase efficacy.

Note: The duration of pregnancies and the criteria for performing therapeutic abortion varies widely in the second trimester. Moreover, the uterus becomes more sensitive to uterotonic agents such as misoprostol with increasing gestational age. Therefore, a wide range of doses has been used for abortion in the second trimester; higher doses may be needed early in the second trimester, and reduced doses may be used in the late stage of second trimester.

[Cervical ripening or][1]
[Induction of labor][1]—

Intravaginal, 25 mcg (one quarter of 100-mcg tablets) as an initial dose placed into the posterior fornix of the vaginal canal every three to six hours. A maximum of four to eight doses within twenty-four hours may be given, if needed, or until active labor occurs. The dose may be increased to 50 mcg every six hours in some situations

Note: Oxytocin should not be administered less than 4 hours after the last misoprostol dose

Fetal heart rate and uterine activity should be continuously monitored in a hospital setting in patients receiving misoprostol for cervical ripening and induction of labor

[Prevention of postpartum hemorrhage][1]—

Oral, 400 to 600 mcg immediately following delivery of the child.

Alternative regimen: Rectal, 400 to 600 mcg immediately following delivery of the child

Prevention of nonsteroidal anti-inflammatory drug–induced gastric ulcer—

Oral, 200 mcg (0.2 mg) four times a day with foodor 400 mcg (0.4 mg) two times a day with food.

[Treatment of nonsteroidal anti-inflammatory drug–induced gastric ulcer]—

Oral, 400 mcg (0.4 mg) to 800 mcg (0.8 mg) a day in divided doses, taken immediately after a meal or with food or milk. When appropriate should be taken simultaneously with nonsteroidal anti-inflammatory drugs (NSAIDs).

[Treatment of duodenal ulcer]—

Oral, 800 mcg (0.8 mg) a day in two or four divided doses (200 mcg four times a day or 400 mcg two times a day), for four weeks, taken with food. If necessary, treatment may be continued for additional four weeks if ulcers have not fully healed after the initial four-week treatment.

Note: The last dose of the day should be taken at bedtime with food.

Dose may be reduced to 100 mcg (0.1 mg) in those patients sensitive to higher doses.

Patients with renal impairment do not routinely require dosage adjustments. However, in patients with renal failure, a starting dose of 100 mcg (0.1 mg) is recommended.

Usual pediatric and adolescent dose
Dosage has not been established.

Usual geriatric dose
See *Usual adult dose*.

Note: Dosage may need to be reduced if usual dose is not tolerated.

Strength(s) usually available
U.S.—

0.1 mg (Rx) [*Cytotec* (scored)].

0.2 mg (Rx) [*Cytotec* (scored)].

Canada—

Note: Dispense with patient insert.

0.1 mg (Rx) [*Cytotec*].

0.2 mg (Rx) [*Cytotec* (scored)].

Packaging and storage
Store at or below 25 °C (77 °F), in a well-closed container, unless otherwise specified by manufacturer. Protect from light, moisture and humidity.

Auxiliary labeling
- Take with food or milk.
- Continue medicine for full time of treatment.
- Do not give medication to any other persons.

[1]Not included in Canadian product labeling.

Selected Bibliography
Jones J, Baily R. Misoprostol: a prostaglandin E_1 analog with antisecretory and cytoprotective properties. DICP 1989; 23: 276-81.

Knodell RG, et al. Stress-related mucosal damage: critical evaluation of potential new therapeutic agents. Pharmacotherapy 1987; 7(6 Pt 2): 104S-109S.

Garris RE, Kirkwood CF. Misoprostol: a prostaglandin E_1 analogue. Clin Pharm 1989; 8: 627-41.

Revised: 09/25/2002

MITOMYCIN Systemic

VA CLASSIFICATION (Primary/Secondary): AN200/DE600

Commonly used brand name(s): *Mutamycin*.

Another commonly used name is mitomycin-C.

Note: For a listing of dosage forms and brand names by country availability, see *Dosage Forms* section(s).

Category
Antineoplastic.

Indications
Note: Bracketed information in the *Indications* section refers to uses that are not included in U.S. product labeling.

Accepted
Carcinoma, gastric (treatment)

[Carcinoma, esophageal (treatment)][1]

Carcinoma, pancreatic (treatment)

[Carcinoma, anal (treatment)][1]

[Carcinoma, colorectal (treatment)]

[Carcinoma, breast (treatment)][1]

[Carcinoma, head and neck (treatment)][1]

[Carcinoma, biliary (treatment)][1]

[Carcinoma, lung, non-small cell (treatment)][1]

[Carcinoma, cervical (treatment)][1]—Mitomycin is indicated, in combination with other agents, for palliative treatment of adenocarcinoma of the stomach or pancreas unresponsive to surgery and/or radiotherapy. Mitomycin is also used for treatment of anal or esophageal carcinomas, adenocarcinoma of the colon or breast; some head and neck tumors; and advanced biliary, non-small-cell lung, and cervical squamous cell carcinomas.

[Carcinoma, bladder (treatment)]—Mitomycin is used for topical treatment of superficial transitional cell carcinoma of the urinary bladder.

[Leukemia, chronic myelocytic (treatment)][1]—Mitomycin is used for treatment of chronic myelocytic leukemia.

[1]Not included in Canadian product labeling.

Pharmacology/Pharmacokinetics
Physicochemical characteristics
Molecular weight—334.34.

Mechanism of action/Effect
Mitomycin is classified as an antibiotic but is not useful as an antimicrobial agent because of its toxicity. Mitomycin is cell cycle-phase nonspecific, although it is most active in the G and S phases of cell division. After enzyme activation in the tissues, it functions as a bifunctional or trifunctional alkylating agent. Mitomycin causes cross-linking of DNA and inhibits DNA synthesis and, to a lesser extent, also inhibits RNA and protein synthesis.

Distribution
Does not cross the blood-brain barrier.

Biotransformation
Hepatic (primarily); some in other tissues.

Half-life
Initial, following 30-mg bolus injection—17 minutes.

Elimination
Renal (10% unchanged); the percentage of a dose excreted in urine increases with increasing doses due to saturation of metabolic pathways at relatively low doses.

Precautions to Consider
Carcinogenicity/Mutagenicity
Secondary malignancies are potential delayed effects of many antineoplastic agents, although it is not clear whether the effect is related to their mutagenic or immunosuppressive action. The effect of dose and duration of therapy is also unknown, although risk seems to increase with long-term use. Although information is limited, available data seem to indicate that the carcinogenic risk is greatest with the alkylating agents.

Mitomycin is carcinogenic in rats and mice.

Pregnancy/Reproduction
Fertility—Gonadal suppression, resulting in amenorrhea or azoospermia, may occur in patients taking antineoplastic therapy, especially with the alkylating agents. In general, these effects appear to be related to dose and length of therapy and may be irreversible. Prediction of the degree of testicular or ovarian function impairment is complicated by the common use of combinations of several antineoplastics, which makes it difficult to assess the effects of individual agents. The effects of mitomycin on fertility are not known.

Pregnancy—First trimester: It is usually recommended that use of antineoplastics, especially combination chemotherapy, be avoided whenever possible, especially during the first trimester. Although information is limited because of the relatively few instances of antineoplastic administration during pregnancy, the mutagenic, teratogenic, and carcinogenic potential of these medications must be considered.

Other hazards to the fetus include adverse reactions seen in adults.

In general, use of a contraceptive is recommended during cytotoxic drug therapy.

Mitomycin is reported to cause teratogenicity in animals.

Breast-feeding
Although very little information is available regarding distribution of antineoplastic agents into breast milk, breast-feeding is not recommended while mitomycin is being administered because of the risks to the infant (adverse effects, mutagenicity, carcinogenicity).

Pediatrics
Appropriate studies on the relationship of age to the effects of mitomycin have not been performed in the pediatric population. However, pedi-

atrics-specific problems that would limit the usefulness of this medication in children are not expected.

Geriatrics

No information is available on the relationship of age to the effects of mitomycin in geriatric patients. However, elderly patients are more likely to have age-related renal function impairment, which may require caution in patients receiving mitomycin.

Dental

The bone marrow depressant effects of mitomycin may result in an increased incidence of microbial infection, delayed healing, and gingival bleeding. Dental work, whenever possible, should be completed prior to initiation of therapy or deferred until blood counts have returned to normal. Patients should be instructed in proper oral hygiene during treatment, including caution in use of regular toothbrushes, dental floss, and toothpicks.

Mitomycin may also cause stomatitis associated with considerable discomfort.

Drug interactions and/or related problems

The following drug interactions and/or related problems have been selected on the basis of their potential clinical significance (possible mechanism in parentheses where appropriate)—not necessarily inclusive (» = major clinical significance):

Note: Combinations containing any of the following medications, depending on the amount present, may also interact with this medication.

Blood dyscrasia-causing medications (see *Appendix II*)
(leukopenic and/or thrombocytopenic effects of mitomycin may be increased with concurrent or recent therapy if these medications cause the same effects; dosage adjustment of mitomycin, if necessary, should be based on blood counts)

» Bone marrow depressants, other (see *Appendix II*) or
Radiation therapy
(additive bone marrow depression may occur; dosage reduction may be required when two or more bone marrow depressants, including radiation, are used concurrently or consecutively)

Doxorubicin
(concurrent use may result in increased cardiotoxicity; it is recommended that the total dose of doxorubicin not exceed 450 mg per square meter of body surface)

Vaccines, killed virus
(because normal defense mechanisms may be suppressed by mitomycin therapy, the patient's antibody response to the vaccine may be decreased. The interval between discontinuation of medications that cause immunosuppression and restoration of the patient's ability to respond to the vaccine depends on the intensity and type of immunosuppression-causing medication used, the underlying disease, and other factors; estimates vary from 3 months to 1 year)

» Vaccines, live virus
(because normal defense mechanisms may be suppressed by mitomycin therapy, concurrent use with a live virus vaccine may potentiate the replication of the vaccine virus, may increase the side/adverse effects of the vaccine virus, and/or may decrease the patient's antibody response to the vaccine; immunization of these patients should be undertaken only with extreme caution after careful review of the patient's hematologic status and only with the knowledge and consent of the physician managing the mitomycin therapy. The interval between discontinuation of medications that cause immunosuppression and restoration of the patient's ability to respond to the vaccine depends on the intensity and type of immunosuppression-causing medication used, the underlying disease, and other factors; estimates vary from 3 months to 1 year. Patients with leukemia in remission should not receive live virus vaccine until at least 3 months after their last chemotherapy. Immunization with oral poliovirus vaccine should also be postponed in persons in close contact with the patient, especially family members)

Laboratory value alterations

The following have been selected on the basis of their potential clinical significance (possible effect in parentheses where appropriate)—not necessarily inclusive (» = major clinical significance).

With physiology/laboratory test values
Blood urea nitrogen (BUN) and
Creatinine, serum
(concentrations may be increased, indicating renal toxicity)

Medical considerations/Contraindications

The medical considerations/contraindications included have been selected on the basis of their potential clinical significance (reasons given in parentheses where appropriate)—not necessarily inclusive (» = major clinical significance).

Risk-benefit should be considered when the following medical problems exist:

» Bone marrow depression
» Chickenpox, existing or recent (including recent exposure) or
» Herpes zoster
(risk of severe generalized disease)
» Coagulation disorders
» Infection
» Renal function impairment
(use is not recommended in patients with a serum creatinine greater than 1.7 mg per 100 mL)
Sensitivity to mitomycin
» Caution should be used also in patients who have received previous cytotoxic drug therapy or radiation therapy.

Patient monitoring

» Blood urea nitrogen (BUN) concentrations and
» Creatinine concentrations, serum
(recommended prior to initiation of therapy and at periodic intervals during therapy; frequency varies according to clinical state, agent, dose, and other agents being used concurrently)
» Hematocrit or hemoglobin and
» Leukocyte count, total and, if appropriate, differential and
» Observation for fragmented red blood cells on peripheral blood smears and
» Platelet count
(determinations recommended prior to initiation of therapy and at periodic intervals during therapy; frequency varies according to clinical state, agent, dose, and other agents being used concurrently)

Note: It is recommended that renal and hematologic function be followed during and for at least 8 weeks after mitomycin therapy, especially in patients receiving doses of 60 mg or more, to detect possible hemolytic-uremic syndrome or bone marrow depression.

Side/Adverse Effects

Note: Many "side effects" of antineoplastic therapy are unavoidable and represent the medication's pharmacologic action. Some of these (for example, leukopenia and thrombocytopenia) are actually used as parameters to aid in individual dosage titration.

The following side/adverse effects have been selected on the basis of their potential clinical significance (possible signs and symptoms in parentheses where appropriate)—not necessarily inclusive:

Those indicating need for medical attention

Incidence more frequent

Leukopenia (fever or chills; cough or hoarseness; lower back or side pain; painful or difficult urination)—usually asymptomatic; ***thrombocytopenia*** (unusual bleeding or bruising; black, tarry stools; blood in urine or stools; pinpoint red spots on skin)—usually asymptomatic

Note: *Leukopenia and thrombocytopenia* occur up to 8 weeks after initiation of therapy (average, 4 weeks), and counts return to normal within 10 weeks after therapy is stopped, although in about 25% of episodes counts do not recover. Severity of bone marrow depression varies and determines subsequent dosage of mitomycin.

Incidence less frequent

Pneumopathy (cough; shortness of breath); ***renal toxicity*** (blood in urine; decreased urination; shortness of breath; swelling of feet or lower legs); ***stomatitis*** (sores in mouth and on lips)

Note: *Pneumopathy* usually occurs after several doses; it can be severe and may be life-threatening.

Renal toxicity has included a hemolytic-uremic syndrome (consisting of microangiopathic hemolytic anemia [hematocrit 25% or less], irreversible renal failure, thrombocytopenia [platelet count less than 100,000], and less frequently, pulmonary hypertension, neurologic abnormalities, and hypertension), which is fatal in greater than 50% of cases. Renal failure without hemolysis has also been reported. The syndrome may occur at any time during therapy with mitomycin, alone or in combination with other chemotherapy. Use of blood product transfusions may exacerbate the symptoms in some patients. Incidence appears to be greatest in patients receiving doses of mitomycin of 60 mg or greater.

Incidence rare

Bloody vomit; thrombophlebitis or cellulitis (redness or pain, especially at site of injection)—caused by extravasation

Note: Extravasation may also occur without accompanying burning or stinging. Delayed erythema and ulceration have occurred weeks to months after mitomycin administration, at or distant from the injection site.

Those indicating need for medical attention only if they continue or are bothersome

Incidence more frequent

Loss of appetite; nausea and vomiting

Note: *Nausea and vomiting* usually occur within 1 to 2 hours; vomiting usually stops in 3 to 4 hours, while nausea may persist for 2 or 3 days.

Incidence less frequent

Numbness or tingling in fingers and toes; purple-colored bands on nails—occur with repeated doses; ***skin rash; unusual tiredness or weakness***—may last several days to 3 weeks

Those not indicating need for medical attention

Incidence less frequent

Loss of hair

Those indicating the need for medical attention if they occur after medication is discontinued

Bone marrow depression (black, tarry stools; blood in urine or stools; cough or hoarseness; fever or chills; lower back or side pain; painful or difficult urination; pinpoint red spots on skin; unusual bleeding or bruising); ***possible hemolytic-uremic syndrome*** (blood in urine, decreased urination, shortness of breath, swelling of feet or lower legs); ***delayed skin reaction*** (red or painful skin)

Note: Cumulative *myelosuppression* may occur with repeated doses.

Patient Consultation

As an aid to patient consultation, refer to *Advice for the Patient, Mitomycin (Systemic).*

As an aid to patient consultation, consider emphasizing the following selected information (» = major clinical significance):

Before using this medication

» Conditions affecting use, especially:
- Sensitivity to mitomycin
- Pregnancy—Use not recommended because of mutagenic, teratogenic, and carcinogenic potential; advisability of using contraception; telling physician immediately if pregnancy is suspected
- Breast-feeding—Not recommended because of risk of serious side effects
- Other medications, especially other bone marrow depressants or previous cytotoxic drug or radiation therapy
- Other medical problems, especially chickenpox, coagulation disorders, herpes zoster, other infections, or renal function impairment

Proper use of this medication

Caution in taking combination therapy; taking each medication at the right time

Frequency of nausea and vomiting; importance of continuing medication despite stomach upset

» Proper dosing

Precautions while using this medication

» Importance of close monitoring by physician

» Avoiding immunizations unless approved by physician; other persons in patient's household should avoid immunizations with oral poliovirus vaccine; avoiding persons who have taken oral poliovirus vaccine or wearing a protective mask that covers nose and mouth

Caution if bone marrow depression occurs:

» Avoiding exposure to persons with infections, especially during periods of low blood counts; checking with physician immediately if fever or chills, cough or hoarseness, lower back or side pain, or painful or difficult urination occurs

» Checking with physician immediately if unusual bleeding or bruising; black, tarry stools; blood in urine or stools; or pinpoint red spots on skin occur

Caution in use of regular toothbrush, dental floss, or toothpick; physician, dentist, or nurse may suggest alternatives; checking with physician before having dental work done

Not touching eyes or inside of nose unless hands washed immediately before

Using caution to avoid accidental cuts with use of sharp objects such as safety razor or fingernail or toenail cutters

Avoiding contact sports or other situations where bruising or injury could occur

» Possibility of local tissue injury and scarring if infiltration of intravenous solution occurs or as delayed reaction; telling doctor or nurse right away about redness, pain, or swelling at injection or any other site

Side/adverse effects

Importance of discussing possible effects, including cancer, with physician

Signs of potential side effects, especially leukopenia, thrombocytopenia, pneumopathy, renal toxicity, stomatitis, bloody vomit, thrombophlebitis, or cellulitis caused by extravasation

Physician or nurse can help in dealing with side effects

Possibility of hair loss; should return after treatment has ended

General Dosing Information

Patients receiving mitomycin should be under supervision of a physician experienced in cancer chemotherapy.

A variety of dosage schedules and regimens of mitomycin in combination with other antitumor agents are used. The prescriber may consult the medical literature as well as the manufacturer's literature in choosing a specific dosage.

Mitomycin is usually administered intravenously via a functioning intravenous catheter.

Care must be taken to avoid extravasation during intravenous administration because of the risk of severe ulceration and necrosis. Extravasation may occur with or without an accompanying stinging or burning sensation and even if there is adequate blood return when the injection needle is aspirated. Delayed erythema and ulceration occurring either at or distant from the injection site have been reported weeks to months following mitomycin administration, even when no evidence of extravasation was observed during administration. Skin grafting has been required in some of the cases.

Mitomycin must not be administered intramuscularly or subcutaneously because it will cause local tissue necrosis.

Mitomycin has also been administered intra-arterially (for example, into hepatic artery) for treatment of some tumors.

Dosage of mitomycin subsequent to the initial course should be adjusted to meet the individual requirements of each patient, on the basis of hematological response of the patient to the previous dose. An additional course of mitomycin should be given only after circulating blood elements have returned to acceptable levels (leukocytes above 3000 per cubic millimeter and platelets above 75,000 per cubic millimeter).

Patients who have not responded after two courses of mitomycin are unlikely to show a response.

Special precautions are recommended in patients who develop thrombocytopenia as a result of administration of mitomycin. These may include extreme care in performing invasive procedures; regular inspection of intravenous sites, skin (including perirectal area), and mucous membrane surfaces for signs of bleeding or bruising; limiting frequency of venipuncture and avoiding intramuscular injections; testing urine, emesis, stool, and secretions for occult blood; care in use of regular toothbrushes, dental floss, toothpicks, safety razors, and fingernail and toenail cutters; avoiding constipation; and using caution to prevent falls and other injuries. Such patients should avoid alcohol and any aspirin intake because of the risk of gastrointestinal bleeding. Platelet transfusions may be required.

Patients who develop leukopenia should be observed carefully for signs of infection. Antibiotic support may be required. In neutropenic patients who develop fever, broad-spectrum antibiotic coverage should be initiated empirically, pending bacterial cultures and appropriate diagnostic tests.

Topical bladder instillations with 20 to 40 mg of mitomycin in a strength of 1 mg per mL in distilled water, which is retained for as long as possible (usually 2 to 3 hours), are used once weekly for 8 procedures per course in the treatment of small bladder papillomas.

Safety considerations for handling this medication

There is limited but increasing evidence and concern that personnel involved in preparation and administration of parenteral antineoplastics may be at some risk because of the potential mutagenicity, teratogenicity, and/or carcinogenicity of these agents, although the actual risk is unknown. USP advisory panels recommend cautious handling both in preparation and disposal of antineoplastic agents. Precautions that have been suggested include:

- Use of a biological containment cabinet during reconstitution and dilution of parenteral medications and wearing of disposable surgical gloves and masks.
- Use of proper technique to prevent contamination of the medication, work area, and operator during transfer between containers (including proper training of personnel in this technique).
- Cautious and proper disposal of needles, syringes, vials, ampuls, and unused medication.

A number of medical centers have developed detailed guidelines for handling of antineoplastic agents.

Combination chemotherapy

Mitomycin may be used in combination with other agents in various regimens. As a result, incidence and/or severity of side effects may be altered and different dosages (usually reduced) may be used.

Parenteral Dosage Forms

Note: Bracketed uses in the *Dosage Forms* section refer to categories of use and/or indications that are not included in U.S. product labeling.

MITOMYCIN FOR INJECTION USP

Usual adult and adolescent dose

Carcinoma, gastric or
Carcinoma, pancreatic or
[Carcinoma, colorectal]—
Intravenous, 20 mg per square meter of body surface area as a single dose repeated every six to eight weeks.
A suggested dosage adjustment schedule for subsequent doses is:

Nadir after Prior Dose (cells per cubic millimeter)		Percentage of Prior Dose to Be Given
Leukocytes	Platelets	
>4000	>100,000	100
3000–3999	75,000–99,999	100
2000–2999	25,000–74,999	70
<2000	<25,000	50

Usual adult prescribing limits

Doses greater than 20 mg per square meter of body surface area appear to be no more effective than lower doses and increase the risk of toxicity.

Usual pediatric dose

See *Usual adult and adolescent dose.*

Strength(s) usually available

U.S.—
5 mg (Rx) [*Mutamycin* (mannitol 10 mg)].
20 mg (Rx) [*Mutamycin* (mannitol 20 mg)].
40 mg (Rx) [*Mutamycin* (mannitol 80 mg)].

Canada—
5 mg (Rx) [*Mutamycin* (mannitol 10 mg)].
20 mg (Rx) [*Mutamycin* (mannitol 20 mg)].
40 mg (Rx) [*Mutamycin* (mannitol 80 mg)].

Packaging and storage

Store below 40 °C (104 °F), preferably between 15 and 30 °C (59 and 86 °F), unless otherwise specified by manufacturer. Protect from light.

Preparation of dosage form

Mitomycin for Injection USP is reconstituted for intravenous use by adding 10 mL (5-mg vial), 40 mL (10-mg vial), or 80 mL (40-mg vial) of sterile water for injection to the vial and shaking to dissolve, allowing to stand at room temperature if necessary until solution occurs; a blue-gray solution is produced.

Reconstituted solutions may be further diluted with 5% dextrose injection, 0.9% sodium chloride injection, or sodium lactate injection for administration by intravenous infusion.

Stability

Reconstituted solutions of mitomycin are stable for 14 days refrigerated or 7 days at room temperature, when protected from light. When further diluted for administration by intravenous infusion, reconstituted solutions are stable for 3 hours in 5% dextrose injection, 12 hours in 0.9% sodium chloride injection, or 24 hours in sodium lactate injection at room temperature.

Revised: 09/27/1997

MITOTANE Systemic

VA CLASSIFICATION (Primary/Secondary): AN900/HS900

Commonly used brand name(s): *Lysodren.*

Another commonly used name is o,p′-DDD.

Note: For a listing of dosage forms and brand names by country availability, see *Dosage Forms* section(s).

Category

Antineoplastic; antiadrenal.

Indications

Note: Bracketed information in the *Indications* section refers to uses that are not included in U.S. product labeling.

Accepted

Carcinoma, adrenocortical (treatment)—Mitotane is indicated in the treatment of inoperable functional and nonfunctional adrenocortical carcinoma.

[Cushing's syndrome (treatment)][1]—Mitotane is used in the treatment of Cushing's syndrome.

[1]Not included in Canadian product labeling.

Pharmacology/Pharmacokinetics

Physicochemical characteristics

Molecular weight—320.05.

Mechanism of action/Effect

Mitotane apparently suppresses the activity of the adrenal cortex. Mechanism of cytotoxic action is unknown, but may be related to adrenal suppression.

Absorption

Approximately 35 to 40% absorbed from the gastrointestinal tract.

Distribution

To all body tissues; stored in fat; small amount (as metabolite) crosses blood-brain barrier.

Biotransformation

Hepatic and renal, to water-soluble metabolite.

Half-life

18 to 159 days.

Onset of action

Reduced concentrations of 17-hydroxycorticosteroid usually occur within 2 or 3 days after initiation of therapy; tumor response may occur within 6 weeks.

Time to peak plasma concentration

3 to 5 hours.

Elimination

Renal, 10 to 25% (as metabolite); bile, 1 to 17% (as metabolite). Measurable plasma concentrations persist for 6 to 9 weeks after withdrawal of mitotane.

Precautions to Consider

Carcinogenicity/Mutagenicity

Studies have not been done.

Pregnancy/Reproduction

Pregnancy—Studies have not been done in either animals or humans. Problems in humans have not been documented. However, caution is recommended, especially during the first trimester.

FDA Pregnancy Category C.

Breast-feeding

It is not known whether mitotane is distributed into breast milk. However, problems in humans have not been documented.

Pediatrics

Appropriate studies with mitotane have not been performed in the pediatric population. However, pediatrics-specific problems that would limit the usefulness of this medication in children are not expected.

Geriatrics

No geriatrics-specific information is available on the use of mitotane in geriatric patients.

Drug interactions and/or related problems

The following drug interactions and/or related problems have been selected on the basis of their potential clinical significance (possible mechanism in parentheses where appropriate)—not necessarily inclusive (» = major clinical significance):

Note: Combinations containing any of the following medications, depending on the amount present, may also interact with this medication.

» Central nervous system (CNS) depression-producing medications (see *Appendix II*)
(concurrent use may produce additive CNS depressant effects)

Corticosteroids, glucocorticoid and mineralocorticoid
(higher dosage may be required to treat adrenal insufficiency since mitotane alters metabolism of these steroids)

Corticotropin (ACTH)
(mitotane may inhibit the adrenal response to ACTH; this may interfere with the therapeutic response to ACTH)

Laboratory value alterations

The following have been selected on the basis of their potential clinical significance (possible effect in parentheses where appropriate)—not necessarily inclusive (» = major clinical significance).

With physiology/laboratory test values

Plasma cortisol concentrations and
Urinary 17-hydroxycorticosteroid concentrations
(may be decreased as a result of adrenocortical inhibition)

Protein-bound iodine (PBI) concentrations
(may be decreased as a result of mitotane binding to thyroid-binding globulin)

Serum uric acid concentrations
(may be decreased)

Medical considerations/Contraindications

The medical considerations/contraindications included have been selected on the basis of their potential clinical significance (reasons given in parentheses where appropriate)—not necessarily inclusive (» = major clinical significance).

Risk-benefit should be considered when the following medical problems exist:

» Hepatic function impairment other than metastatic lesion of the adrenal cortex
(reduced metabolism and possible accumulation; reduction in dosage may be required)

» Infection

Sensitivity to mitotane

Patient monitoring

The following may be especially important in patient monitoring (other tests may be warranted in some patients, depending on condition; » = major clinical significance):

Neurological assessments
(recommended at periodic intervals in patients receiving mitotane for longer than 2 years)

» 8 a.m. plasma cortisol concentrations or

» 24-hour urinary 17-hydroxycorticosteroid concentrations
(recommended at periodic intervals to aid in assessing clinical response and to determine if steroid supplement therapy is necessary)

Side/Adverse Effects

The following side/adverse effects have been selected on the basis of their potential clinical significance (possible signs and symptoms in parentheses where appropriate)—not necessarily inclusive:

Those indicating need for medical attention

Incidence more frequent—40 to 80%

Adrenocortical insufficiency (darkening of skin; diarrhea; dizziness; drowsiness; loss of appetite; mental depression; nausea and vomiting; skin rash; unusual tiredness)

Incidence less frequent

Double vision; hemorrhagic cystitis (blood in urine); ***lens opacity or toxic retinopathy*** (blurred vision)

Incidence rare

Allergic reaction (shortness of breath; wheezing)

Those indicating need for medical attention only if they continue or are bothersome

Incidence less frequent

Aching muscles; fever; flushing or redness of skin; muscle twitching; orthostatic hypotension (dizziness or lightheadedness when getting up from a lying or sitting position)

Patient Consultation

As an aid to patient consultation, refer to *Advice for the Patient, Mitotane (Systemic)*.

In providing consultation, consider emphasizing the following selected information (» = major clinical significance):

Before using this medication

» Conditions affecting use, especially:
Sensitivity to mitotane
Pregnancy—Caution is recommended, especially during the first trimester
Other medications, especially CNS depressants
Other medical problems, especially hepatic function impairment other than metastatic lesion of the adrenal cortex or infection

Proper use of this medication

» Importance of not taking more or less medication than the amount prescribed

» Checking with physician before discontinuing medication because of risk of adrenal suppression

» Proper dosing
Missed dose: Taking as soon as possible; not taking if almost time for next dose; not doubling doses; checking with physician

» Proper storage

Precautions while using this medication

» Importance of close monitoring by the physician
Carrying medical identification card

» Caution in taking alcohol or other CNS depressants

» Caution if dizziness or drowsiness occurs, especially if driving, using machines, or doing other things that require alertness

» Checking with physician immediately if injury, infection, or other illness occurs, because of the risk of adrenal insufficiency; physician may prescribe steroid supplement

Side/adverse effects

Signs of potential side effects, especially adrenocortical insufficiency, double vision, hemorrhagic cystitis, lens opacity, toxic retinopathy, and allergic reaction

General Dosing Information

Patients receiving mitotane should be under supervision of a physician experienced in cancer chemotherapy.

Initial treatment often occurs in the hospital until dosage is stabilized.

Dosage must be adjusted to the maximum dose tolerated to meet the individual requirements of each patient, based on appearance of adverse reactions and improvement in clinical response.

Glucocorticoid therapy is usually required in patients being treated with mitotane; mineralocorticoid therapy may also be required, especially with prolonged therapy. Because metabolism of exogenous corticosteroids may be altered in patients receiving mitotane, higher than normal replacement doses may be required. Steroid therapy may have to be continued after mitotane is withdrawn, until adrenocortical function returns to normal.

Continuous treatment with the maximum tolerated dosage of mitotane appears to be more effective than intermittent courses.

Duration of treatment depends on clinical response. Only 10% of patients showing no response after 3 months of treatment at the maximum tolerated dosage will show a response to continued therapy.

It is recommended that mitotane be temporarily withdrawn immediately following shock or severe trauma and that steroids be administered, because adrenal suppression may prevent the normal response to stress.

Oral Dosage Forms

Note: Bracketed uses in the *Dosage Forms* section refer to categories of use and/or indications that are not included in U.S. product labeling.

MITOTANE TABLETS USP

Usual adult dose

Carcinoma, adrenocortical—
Initial: Oral, 2 to 6 grams per day in three or four divided doses; the dosage may be increased until adverse reactions occur.

Note: The maximum tolerated dosage may vary from 2 to 16 grams per day, with an average dosage of 9 to 10 grams per day.

[Cushing's syndrome][1]—
Initial: Oral, 3 to 6 grams per day in three or four divided doses.
Maintenance: Oral, 0.5 to 4 grams per day in divided doses.

Usual pediatric dose

Carcinoma, adrenocortical—
Oral, 100 to 500 mcg (0.1 to 0.5 mg) per kg of body weight; or initially, 1 to 2 grams per day in divided doses, the dosage being gradually increased to 5 to 7 grams per day.

Strength(s) usually available

U.S.—
500 mg (Rx) [*Lysodren* (scored)].

Canada—
500 mg (Rx) [*Lysodren* (scored)].

Packaging and storage

Store below 40 °C (104 °F), preferably between 15 and 30 °C (59 and 86 °F), unless otherwise specified by the manufacturer. Store in a tight, light-resistant container.

Auxiliary labeling
- May cause drowsiness.

[1]Not included in Canadian product labeling.

Revised: 10/29/2003

MITOXANTRONE Systemic

VA CLASSIFICATION (Primary): AN900

Commonly used brand name(s): *Novantrone*.

Note: For a listing of dosage forms and brand names by country availability, see *Dosage Forms* section(s).

Category

Antineoplastic.

Indications

Note: Bracketed information in the *Indications* section refers to uses that are not included in U.S. product labeling.

Accepted

Cancer, prostate, advanced hormone-refractory (treatment)[1]—Mitoxantrone, in combination with corticosteroids, is indicated as initial palliative treatment of patients with pain related to advanced hormone-refractory prostate cancer.

[Hepatoma (treatment)]—Mitoxantrone is indicated for the treatment of hepatoma in adults.

Leukemia, acute nonlymphocytic (treatment)—Mitoxantrone is indicated, in combination with other agents, for the treatment of acute nonlymphocytic (including myelocytic, promyelocytic, monocytic, and erythroid) leukemia in adults.

Multiple sclerosis (treatment)[1]—Mitoxantrone is indicated for reducing neurologic disability and/or the frequency of clinical relapses in patients with secondary (chronic) progressive, progressive relapsing, or worsening relapsing-remitting multiple sclerosis.

[Leukemia, acute lymphocytic (treatment)]—Mitoxantrone is used for the treatment of recurrent acute lymphocytic leukemia in adults.

[Carcinoma, breast (treatment)]—Mitoxantrone is indicated, alone or in combination with other agents, for treatment of breast carcinoma, including locally advanced and metastatic disease.

[Lymphomas, non-Hodgkin's (treatment)]—Mitoxantrone is used for treatment of non-Hodgkin's lymphomas.

Acceptance not established

Use of mitoxantrone for the treatment of acute lymphoblastic leukemia has not been established, due to insufficient data.

Unaccepted

Mitoxantrone is not indicated in treatment of patients with primary progressive multiple sclerosis.

[1]Not included in Canadian product labeling.

Pharmacology/Pharmacokinetics

Physicochemical characteristics

Molecular weight—517.41.

Mechanism of action/Effect

Mitoxantrone appears to be most active in the late S phase of cell division, but is not cycle phase–specific. Although the exact mechanism of action is unknown, evidence seems to indicate involvement of two effects—binding to DNA by intercalation between base pairs, and a nonintercalative electrostatic interaction—resulting in inhibition of DNA and RNA synthesis.

Other actions/effects

Also has antiviral, antibacterial, antiprotozoal, and immunosuppressant effects.

Distribution

Rapid and extensive; largest concentrations are in the thyroid, liver, heart, and red blood cells.

Protein binding

High (78%).

Biotransformation

Hepatic.

Half-life

Mean, 5.8 days (range, 2.3–13.0 days).

Elimination

Biliary/fecal, up to 25% in 5 days.

Renal, 6-11% (65% unchanged).

Extensive tissue uptake and binding accounts for most of a dose, which is then thought to be gradually released.

In dialysis—Because of extensive tissue binding, unlikely to be significantly removed by hemodialysis or peritoneal dialysis.

Precautions to Consider

Carcinogenicity

Secondary malignancies are potential delayed effects of many antineoplastic agents, although it is not clear whether the effect is related to their mutagenic or immunosuppressive action. The effect of dose and duration of therapy is also unknown, although the risk seems to increase with long-term use. Although information is limited, available data seem to indicate that the carcinogenic risk is greatest with the alkylating agents.

Mutagenicity

Mitoxantrone may cause chromosomal aberrations in animals and is mutagenic in bacterial systems. It has been reported to cause DNA damage and sister chromatid exchanges *in vitro* .

Pregnancy/Reproduction

Fertility—Gonadal suppression, resulting in amenorrhea or azoospermia, may occur in patients taking antineoplastic therapy, especially with the alkylating agents. In general, these effects appear to be related to dose and length of therapy and may be irreversible. Prediction of the degree of testicular or ovarian function impairment is complicated by the common use of combinations of several antineoplastics, which makes it difficult to assess the effects of individual agents.

Pregnancy—Adequate and well-controlled studies in humans have not been done.

First trimester: It is usually recommended that use of antineoplastics, especially combination chemotherapy, be avoided whenever possible, especially during the first trimester. Although information is limited because of the relatively few instances of antineoplastic administration during pregnancy, the mutagenic, teratogenic, and carcinogenic potential of these medications must be considered.

Other hazards to the fetus include adverse reactions seen in adults.

In general, use of a contraceptive is recommended during cytotoxic drug therapy.

Studies in rats found an increased incidence of low fetal birth weight and retarded development of the fetal kidney, and studies in rabbits found an increased incidence of premature delivery. Mitoxantrone was not found to be teratogenic in rabbits.

FDA Pregnancy Category D.

Breast-feeding

Although very little information is available regarding distribution of antineoplastic agents into breast milk, breast-feeding is not recommended while mitoxantrone is being administered because of the risks to the infant (adverse effects, mutagenicity, carcinogenicity). It is not known whether mitoxantrone is distributed into breast milk.

Pediatrics

Appropriate studies on the relationship of age to the effects of mitoxantrone have not been performed in the pediatric population.

Geriatrics

Appropriate studies on the relationship of age to the effects of mitoxantrone have not been performed in the geriatric population. However, no geriatrics-specific problems have been documented to date.

Dental

The bone marrow depressant effects of mitoxantrone may result in an increased incidence of microbial infection, delayed healing, and gingival bleeding. Dental work, whenever possible, should be completed prior to initiation of therapy or deferred until blood counts have returned to normal. Patients should be instructed in proper oral hygiene during treatment, including caution in use of regular toothbrushes, dental floss, and toothpicks.

Mitoxantrone also causes stomatitis or mucositis, which may be associated with considerable discomfort.

Drug interactions and/or related problems

The following drug interactions and/or related problems have been selected on the basis of their potential clinical significance (possible

mechanism in parentheses where appropriate)—not necessarily inclusive (» = major clinical significance):

Note: Combinations containing any of the following medications, depending on the amount present, may also interact with this medication.

Allopurinol or
Colchicine or
» Probenecid or
» Sulfinpyrazone
(mitoxantrone may raise the concentration of blood uric acid; dosage adjustment of antigout medications may be necessary to control hyperuricemia and gout; allopurinol may be preferred to prevent or reverse mitoxantrone-induced hyperuricemia because of risk of uric acid nephropathy with uricosuric antigout agents)

Blood dyscrasia-causing medications (See *Appendix II*)
(leukopenic and/or thrombocytopenic effects of mitoxantrone may be increased with concurrent or recent therapy if these medications cause the same effects; dosage adjustment of mitoxantrone, if necessary, should be based on blood counts)

» Bone marrow depressants, other (See *Appendix II*) or
Radiation therapy
(additive bone marrow depression may occur; dosage reduction may be required when two or more bone marrow depressants, including radiation, are used concurrently or consecutively)

Daunorubicin or
Doxorubicin or
Radiation therapy to mediastinal area
(use of mitoxantrone in a patient who has previously received any of these increases the risk of cardiotoxicity)

Vaccines, killed virus
(because normal defense mechanisms may be suppressed by mitoxantrone therapy, the patient's antibody response to the vaccine may be decreased. The interval between discontinuation of medications that cause immunosuppression and restoration of the patient's ability to respond to the vaccine depends on the intensity and type of immunosuppression-causing medication used, the underlying disease, and other factors; estimates vary from 3 months to 1 year)

» Vaccines, live virus
(because normal defense mechanisms may be suppressed by mitoxantrone therapy, concurrent use with a live virus vaccine may potentiate the replication of the vaccine virus, may increase the side/adverse effects of the vaccine virus, and/or may decrease the patient's antibody response to the vaccine; immunization of these patients should be undertaken only with extreme caution after careful review of the patient's hematologic status and only with the knowledge and consent of the physician managing the mitoxantrone therapy. The interval between discontinuation of medications that cause immunosuppression and restoration of the patient's ability to respond to the vaccine depends on the intensity and type of immunosuppression-causing medication used, the underlying disease, and other factors; estimates vary from 3 months to 1 year. Patients with leukemia in remission should not receive live virus vaccine until at least 3 months after their last chemotherapy. Immunization with oral poliovirus vaccine should also be postponed in persons in close contact with the patient, especially family members)

Laboratory value alterations

The following have been selected on the basis of their potential clinical significance (possible effect in parentheses where appropriate)—not necessarily inclusive (» = major clinical significance).

With physiology/laboratory test values
Alanine aminotransferase (ALT [SGPT]) values, serum and
Aspartate aminotransferase (AST [SGOT]) values, serum and
Bilirubin concentrations, serum
(may be increased, indicating hepatotoxicity)

Uric acid
(concentrations in blood and urine may be increased)

Medical considerations/Contraindications

The medical considerations/contraindications included have been selected on the basis of their potential clinical significance (reasons given in parentheses where appropriate)—not necessarily inclusive (» = major clinical significance).

Risk-benefit should be considered when the following medical problems exist:

» Bone marrow depression
» Chickenpox, existing or recent (including recent exposure) or
» Herpes zoster
(risk of severe generalized disease)

Gout, history of or
Urate renal stones, history of
(risk of hyperuricemia)

» Heart disease
(increased risk of cardiotoxicity)

Hepatic function impairment, severe
(mitoxantrone clearance may be reduced; dosage adjustment may be necessary)

» Infection

Sensitivity to mitoxantrone

» Caution should be used also in patients with inadequate bone marrow reserves due to previous cytotoxic drug or radiation therapy.

Patient monitoring

The following may be especially important in patient monitoring (other tests may be warranted in some patients, depending on condition; » = major clinical significance):

Alanine aminotransferase (ALT [SGPT]) values, serum and
Aspartate aminotransferase (AST [SGOT]) values, serum and
Bilirubin concentrations, serum and
Lactate dehydrogenase (LDH) values, serum
(determinations recommended prior to initiation of therapy and at periodic intervals during therapy; frequency varies according to clinical state, agent, dose, and other agents being used concurrently)

» Chest x-ray and
» Echocardiography and
Electrocardiogram (ECG) studies and
» Radionuclide angiography determination of ejection fraction
(recommended prior to initiation of therapy and at periodic intervals during therapy)

» Hematocrit or hemoglobin and
» Leukocyte count, total and, if appropriate, differential and
» Platelet count
(determinations recommended prior to initiation of therapy and at periodic intervals during therapy; frequency varies according to clinical state, agent, dose, and other agents being used concurrently)

Uric acid concentrations, serum
(recommended prior to initiation of therapy and at periodic intervals during therapy)

Side/Adverse Effects

Note: Many "side effects" of antineoplastic therapy are unavoidable and represent the medication's pharmacologic action. Some of these (for example, leukopenia and thrombocytopenia) are actually used as parameters to aid in individual dosage titration.

Cardiotoxicity has been reported, including decreased left ventricular ejection fraction, congestive heart failure, ECG changes, arrhythmias such as tachycardia, and, rarely, myocardial infarction. The risk of cardiotoxicity seems to be increased at cumulative mitoxantrone doses exceeding 140 mg per square meter of body surface (100 mg per square meter of body surface in patients with risk factors such as previous treatment with anthracyclines or mediastinal radiation or existing heart disease).

The following side/adverse effects have been selected on the basis of their potential clinical significance (possible signs and symptoms in parentheses where appropriate)—not necessarily inclusive:

Those indicating need for medical attention

Incidence more frequent

Cough or shortness of breath; gastrointestinal bleeding (black, tarry stools); ***leukopenia or infection*** (fever or chills; cough or hoarseness; lower back or side pain; painful or difficult urination)—usually asymptomatic; ***stomach pain; stomatitis or mucositis*** (sores in mouth and on lips)

Note: *Cough or shortness of breath* may be associated with congestive heart failure.

In *leukopenia*, the nadir of the leukocyte count usually occurs within 10 days and usually recovers within 21 days.

Stomatitis or mucositis usually occurs within 1 week after the start of treatment.

Incidence less frequent

Arrhythmias (fast or irregular heartbeat); ***congestive heart failure*** (swelling of feet and lower legs); ***conjunctivitis*** (sore, red eyes); ***jaundice*** (yellow eyes or skin); ***renal failure*** (decrease in urination); ***sei-***

zures; thrombocytopenia (unusual bleeding or bruising; black, tarry stools; blood in urine or stools; pinpoint red spots on skin)—usually asymptomatic

Incidence rare

Allergic reaction, possible (skin rash); ***extravasation*** (blue skin at site of injection, pain or redness at site of injection); ***local irritation or phlebitis*** (pain or redness at site of injection)

Note: Tissue necrosis has been reported in only a few cases after *extravasation.*

Those indicating need for medical attention only if they continue or are bothersome

Incidence more frequent

Amenorrhea (irregular menstrual periods; stopping of menstrual bleeding); ***asthenia; aphthosis*** (oral bleeding); ***constipation; cutaneous mycosis; diarrhea; headache; menorrhagia*** (longer or heavier menstrual periods); ***nausea and vomiting; pharyngitis*** (body aches or pain; congestion; cough; dryness or soreness of throat; fever; runny nose; tender, swollen glands in neck); ***rhinitis*** (stuffy, runny nose; sneezing); ***upper respiratory tract infection; urinary tract infection***

Note: *Nausea and vomiting* are usually mild to moderate.

Those not indicating need for medical attention

Incidence more frequent

Blue-green urine; loss of hair

Incidence less frequent

Blue color in whites of eyes

Patient Consultation

As an aid to patient consultation, refer to *Advice for the Patient, Mitoxantrone (Systemic).*

In providing consultation, consider emphasizing the following selected information (» = major clinical significance):

Before using this medication

» Conditions affecting use, especially:

Sensitivity to mitoxantrone

Pregnancy—Use not recommended because of mutagenic, teratogenic, and carcinogenic potential; advisability of using contraception; telling physician immediately if pregnancy is suspected

Breast-feeding—Not recommended because of risk of serious side effects

Other medications, especially other bone marrow depressants, probenecid, or sulfinpyrazone

Other medical problems, especially chickenpox, herpes zoster, heart disease, or other infection

Proper use of this medication

Caution in taking combination therapy; taking each medication at the right time

Importance of ample fluid intake and subsequent increase in urine output to aid in excretion of uric acid

Frequency of nausea and vomiting; importance of continuing medication despite stomach upset

» Proper dosing

Precautions while using this medication

» Importance of close monitoring by the physician

» Avoiding immunizations unless approved by physician; other persons in patient's household should avoid immunizations with oral poliovirus vaccine; avoiding persons who have taken oral poliovirus vaccine or wearing a protective mask that covers nose and mouth

Caution if bone marrow depression occurs:

» Avoiding exposure to persons with infections, especially during periods of low blood counts; checking with physician immediately if fever or chills, cough or hoarseness, lower back or side pain, or painful or difficult urination occurs

» Checking with physician immediately if unusual bleeding or bruising; black, tarry stools; blood in urine or stools; or pinpoint red spots on skin occur

Caution in use of regular toothbrush, dental floss, or toothpick; physician, dentist, or nurse may suggest alternatives; checking with physician before having dental work done

Not touching eyes or inside of nose unless hands washed immediately before

Using caution to avoid accidental cuts with use of sharp objects such as safety razor or fingernail or toenail cutters

Avoiding contact sports or other situations where bruising or injury could occur

Side/adverse effects

Importance of discussing possible effects with physician

Signs of potential side effects, especially cough, shortness of breath, gastrointestinal bleeding, leukopenia, infection, stomach pain, stomatitis, mucositis, arrhythmias, congestive heart failure, conjunctivitis, jaundice, renal failure, seizures, thrombocytopenia, allergic reaction, extravasation, local irritation, and phlebitis

Physician or nurse can help in dealing with side effects

Urine may have blue-green color and whites of eyes may have a blue color during treatment

Possibility of hair loss; normal hair growth should return after treatment has ended

General Dosing Information

Patients receiving mitoxantrone should be under supervision of a physician experienced in cancer chemotherapy.

A variety of dosage schedules of mitoxantrone, alone or in combination with other antitumor agents, are used. The prescriber may consult the medical literature as well as the manufacturer's literature in choosing a specific dosage.

Dosage must be adjusted to meet the individual requirements of each patient, on the basis of clinical response and appearance or severity of toxicity.

Mitoxantrone hydrochloride injection should not be administered intrathecally; paralysis has occurred after administration by this route. Safety of administration by any route other than the intravenous route has not been established.

Mitoxantrone hydrochloride concentrate for injection must be diluted prior to intravenous administration.

An additional course of mitoxantrone should be given only after toxic hematological effects from the first course have subsided.

Although mitoxantrone is nonvesicant and does not usually cause a severe local reaction, if extravasation occurs during intravenous administration, the injection and infusion should be stopped immediately and resumed, completing the dose, in another vein.

Development of uric acid nephropathy in patients with leukemia or lymphoma may be prevented by adequate oral hydration and, in some cases, administration of allopurinol. Alkalinization of urine may be necessary if serum uric acid concentrations are elevated.

Special precautions are recommended in patients who develop thrombocytopenia as a result of administration of mitoxantrone. These may include extreme care in performing invasive procedures; regular inspection of intravenous sites, skin (including perirectal area), and mucous membrane surfaces for signs of bleeding or bruising; limiting frequency of venipuncture and avoiding intramuscular injections; testing urine, emesis, stool, and secretions for occult blood; care in use of regular toothbrushes, dental floss, toothpicks, safety razors, and fingernail and toenail cutters; avoiding constipation; and using caution to prevent falls and other injuries. Such patients should avoid alcohol and any aspirin intake because of the risk of gastrointestinal bleeding. Platelet transfusions may be required.

Patients who develop leukopenia should be observed carefully for signs of infection. Antibiotic support may be required. In neutropenic patients who develop fever, broad-spectrum antibiotic coverage should be initiated empirically, pending bacterial cultures and appropriate diagnostic tests.

Safety considerations for handling this medication

There is limited but increasing evidence and concern that personnel involved in preparation and administration of parenteral antineoplastics may be at some risk because of the potential mutagenicity, teratogenicity, and/or carcinogenicity of these agents, although the actual risk is unknown. USP advisory panels recommend cautious handling both in preparation and disposal of antineoplastic agents. Precautions that have been suggested include:

- Use of a biological containment cabinet during reconstitution and dilution of parenteral medications and wearing of disposable surgical gloves and masks.
- Use of proper technique to prevent contamination of the medication, work area, and operator during transfer between containers (including proper training of personnel in this technique).
- Cautious and proper disposal of needles, syringes, vials, ampuls, and unused medication.

A number of medical centers have developed detailed guidelines for handling of antineoplastic agents.

Parenteral Dosage Forms

Note: Bracketed uses in the *Dosage Forms* section refer to categories of use and/or indications that are not included in U.S. product labeling.

MITOXANTRONE FOR INJECTION CONCENTRATE USP

Note: Although Mitoxantrone for Injection Concentrate USP is available as the hydrochloride salt, dosing and strengths are expressed in terms of the base.

Usual adult dose

Cancer, prostate, advanced hormone-refractory[1]—

Intravenous infusion, over a short period of time, 12 to 14 mg (base) per square meter of body surface area every twenty-one days

Multiple sclerosis[1]—

Intravenous infusion, over 5 to 15 minutes, 12 mg (base) per square meter of body surface area every 3 months.

Leukemia, acute nonlymphocytic—

Initial—

Intravenous infusion (introduced slowly into the tubing of a freely running intravenous infusion of 0.9% sodium chloride injection or 5% dextrose injection over a period of not less than 3 minutes), 12 mg (base) per square meter of body surface area daily on days 1 to 3, in combination with 100 mg of cytarabine (cytosine arabinoside) per square meter of body surface area daily given as a continuous twenty-four hour intravenous infusion on days 1 to 7.

Note: If response to the initial course is inadequate, a second induction course at the same dosage may be given.

If severe or life-threatening nonhematologic toxicity occurs during the first induction course, it is recommended that the second course not be administered until the toxicity has resolved.

Maintenance—

Intravenous infusion (introduced slowly into the tubing of a freely running intravenous infusion of 0.9% sodium chloride injection or 5% dextrose injection over a period of not less than 3 minutes), 12 mg (base) per square meter of body surface area daily on days 1 and 2, in combination with 100 mg of cytarabine (cytosine arabinoside) per square meter of body surface area daily given as a continuous twenty-four hour intravenous infusion on days 1 to 5.

Note: The maintenance or consolidation course should not be initiated until leukocyte and platelet counts have returned to pretreatment levels. The maintenance course is usually given approximately six weeks after the first induction course. A second consolidation course may be given four weeks after the first.

[Carcinoma, breast] or
[Hepatoma]or
[Lymphomas, non-Hodgkin's]—

Intravenous infusion (introduced slowly into the tubing of a freely running intravenous infusion of 0.9% sodium chloride injection or 5% dextrose injection over a period of not less than three minutes), 14 mg (base) per square meter of body surface area every twenty-one days.

Note: A lower initial dose (12 mg [base] per square meter of body surface area is recommended in patients with inadequate bone marrow reserves. Each subsequent dose should not be given until leukocyte and platelet counts have recovered after the previous dose; dosage reduction may be necessary if severe bone marrow depression occurs.

Usual pediatric dose

Dosage has not been established.

Strength(s) usually available

U.S.—

2 mg (base) per mL (10-, 12.5-, and 15-mL vials) (Rx) [*Novantrone*].

Canada—

2 mg (base) per mL (10- and 12.5-mL vials) (Rx) [*Novantrone*].

Packaging and storage

Store between 15 and 25 °C (59 and 77 °F). Protect from freezing.

Preparation of dosage form

Mitoxantrone for Injection Concentrate USP must be diluted for administration by intravenous infusion. The dose of mitoxantrone for injection concentrate should be diluted to at least 50 mL in 0.9% sodium chloride injection or 5% dextrose injection.

Stability

Mitoxantrone for Injection Concentrate USP contains no preservative. Unused portions of solution prepared for intravenous infusion should be discarded. After penetration of the stopper, remaining portions of undiluted mitoxantrone for injection concentrate may be stored for no longer than 7 days at room temperature (15 to 25 °C [59 to 77 °F]) or 14 days in the refrigerator.

Incompatibilities

Mitoxantrone should not be mixed with heparin, since a precipitate may form.

Note

Any mitoxantrone solution that comes in contact with the skin or mucosa should be washed off thoroughly with warm water.

[1]Not included in Canadian product labeling.

Revised: 11/28/2000

MODAFINIL Systemic

VA CLASSIFICATION (Primary): CN809

Note: Controlled substance classification

U.S.: Schedule IV

Commonly used brand name(s): *Provigil*.

Note: For a listing of dosage forms and brand names by country availability, see *Dosage Forms* section(s).

Category

Central nervous system (CNS) stimulant.

Indications

Accepted

Narcolepsy (treatment)—Modafinil is indicated to improve wakefulness in patients with excessive daytime sleepiness associated with narcolepsy, obstructive sleep apnea/hyponea (OSAHS), or shift work sleep disorder (SWSD). In OSAHS, modafinil is indicated as an adjunct to standard treatment. Continuing efficacy beyond 9 weeks has not been evaluated in placebo-controlled trials.

Pharmacology/Pharmacokinetics

Physicochemical characteristics

Molecular weight—273.36.

Solubility—Practically insoluble in water.

Mechanism of action/Effect

The mechanism of action of modafinil is uncertain. The pharmacological profile of modafinil differs from that of sympathomimetic amines. The CNS-activating actions of modafinil, methylphenidate, and amphetamine were studied in cats given doses of each medication that produced equivalent wakefulness. CNS-activation with methylphenidate and with amphetamine was widespread; however, CNS-activation with modafinil occurred in discrete brain regions, suggesting a more specific wakefulness-promoting effect with modafinil. Modafinil does not show alpha-adrenergic agonist activity *in vitro* or in animal studies; however, the wakefulness induced by modafinil can be attenuated by prazosin, an $alpha_1$-adrenergic antagonist. Modafinil does not bind to norepinephrine, serotonin, dopamine, gamma-aminobutyric acid (GABA), adenosine, histamine H_3, melatonin, or benzodiazepine receptors, nor does it inhibit monoamine oxidase (MAO)-B or phosphodiesterases II through V.

Modafinil is a racemic compound. Animal studies showed no pharmacological differences between the two enantiomers; human studies have not been conducted.

Other actions/effects

Modafinil produces alterations in mood, perception, thinking, and feelings that are typical of other CNS stimulants and is reinforcing in primate self-administration tests of abuse potential. Also, modafinil blocks dopamine reuptake *in vitro*.

There is *in vitro* evidence that modafinil induces cytochrome P450 1A2 (CYP1A2), CYP2B6, and CYP3A4 to a small degree and in a concentration-dependent manner. However, *in vivo* evidence of enzyme induction by modafinil exists only for CYP3A4.

Modafinil is a reversible inhibitor of CYP2C19 in humans and shows CYP2C9-inhibiting activity in *in vitro* studies.

Absorption
Rapid. Absolute bioavailability is unknown. Food may delay absorption but does not affect bioavailability.

Distribution
Vol_D—Large; about 0.9 L per kg of body weight.

Protein binding
Moderate (60%); primarily to albumin.

Biotransformation
Hepatic. Modafinil undergoes hydrolytic deamidation, *S*-oxidation, aromatic ring hydroxylation, and glucuronide conjugation, forming inactive metabolites. Decreases in plasma trough concentrations of about 20% were seen after 9 weeks of modafinil administration at doses of 400 mg per day in human subjects, indicating some autoinduction of metabolism. The isoenzyme CYP3A4 is involved in modafinil metabolism.

In nine patients with cirrhosis of the liver (stages B, B+, C, and C+ by the Child criteria), oral clearance of modafinil was reduced by about 60% and steady-state concentration was doubled compared with values from patients with normal hepatic function.

Half-life
Elimination—
Effectively, about 15 hours after multiple dosing; the elimination half-life of the levo-isomer is about three times that of the dextro-isomer.

Time to peak plasma concentration
2 to 4 hours.

Time to steady-state plasma concentration
2 to 4 days.

Peak serum concentration
At steady-state with a dosage of 400 mg per day, peak serum concentration is 40 micromoles per L.

Elimination
Primarily renal, < 10% as unchanged modafinil. After administration of a radiolabeled dose to human subjects, 80% and 1% of the administered dose were recovered in the urine and the feces, respectively, over 11 days. Severe renal failure (creatinine clearance ≤ 20 mL per minute) had no effect on the pharmacokinetics of modafinil after administration of a single 200-mg dose; however, exposure to an inactive metabolite (modafinil acid) was increased ninefold.

Precautions to Consider

Cross-sensitivity and/or related problems
Patients who have had left ventricular hypertrophy or clinically significant, symptomatic mitral valve prolapse in association with the use of other CNS stimulant medications may experience similar effects with the use of modafinil.

Carcinogenicity/Tumorigenicity/Mutagenicity
Modafinil showed no evidence of being carcinogenic, tumorigenic, or mutagenic in rodent studies or in *in vitro* testing. However, dosage in one rodent study was insufficient to fully evaluate the carcinogenicity of modafinil.

Pregnancy/Reproduction
Fertility—No effect on fertility was seen when male and female rats were administered modafinil in doses of 4.8 times the maximum recommended human dose (MRHD) on a mg per square meter of body surface area (mg/m^2) basis prior to and throughout mating and gestation. However, dosage may have been insufficient and sample size may have been too small to fully evaluate the effect of modafinil on fertility.

Pregnancy—Adequate and well-controlled studies in humans have not been done. Modafinil may decrease the effectiveness of steroidal contraceptives during concurrent use and for 1 month after discontinuation of modafinil, making pregnancy more likely unless alternate forms of contraception are employed.

Offspring of rats given modafinil in oral doses of 200 mg per kg per day (10 times the MRHD on a mg/m^2 basis) during fetal organogenesis exhibited hydronephrosis and skeletal variations. Also, the number of resorptions was increased. Maternal toxicity was not seen. No effect was seen in the offspring of rats given an oral dose of 100 mg per kg per day (5 times the MRHD on a mg/m^2 basis). No embryotoxicity was seen in the offspring of rabbits given modafinil in oral doses of 100 mg per kg per day (10 times the MRHD on a mg/m^2 basis) during fetal organogenesis. However, animal studies were insufficient to ensure a comprehensive evaluation of modafinil's effects in pregnancy.

FDA Pregnancy Category C.

Labor and delivery—The effect of modafinil on labor and delivery in humans has not been systematically evaluated.

Breast-feeding
It is not known whether modafinil or its metabolites are distributed into human breast milk.

Pediatrics
No information is available on the relationship of age to the effects of modafinil in pediatric patients. Safety and efficacy in children younger than 16 years of age have not been established.

Geriatrics
Appropriate studies on the relationship of age to the effects of modafinil have not been performed in the geriatric population. Small pharmacokinetic studies indicate that modafinil clearance may be reduced in geriatric patients by about 20%. However, in 15 patients older than 65 years of age who participated in clinical trials, the incidence of adverse effects was similar to that in other age groups.

Pharmacogenetics
In patients who are deficient in CYP2D6 activity, plasma concentrations of CYP2D6 substrates that have an ancillary metabolic pathway involving CYP2C19 (e.g., clomipramine, desipramine) may be increased due to CYP2C19 inhibition by modafinil.

Drug interactions and/or related problems
The following drug interactions and/or related problems have been selected on the basis of their potential clinical significance (possible mechanism in parentheses where appropriate)—not necessarily inclusive (» = major clinical significance):

Note: Combinations containing any of the following medications, depending on the amount present, may also interact with this medication.

Alcohol
(the effects of alcohol use in patients receiving modafinil are unknown; avoiding drinking alcohol is recommended)

» Antidepressants, tricyclic
(although a brief trial in healthy volunteers showed no effect on the pharmacokinetics of either medication, one patient receiving modafinil in a clinical trial had increased plasma concentrations of clomipramine and its active metabolite desmethylclomipramine with concurrent use; the clearance of medications that are metabolized primarily by cytochrome P450 2D6 [CYP2D6] but that have an ancillary metabolic pathway involving CYP2C19, such as some tricyclic antidepressants, including clomipramine and desipramine, may be reduced with concurrent modafinil use in patients who are poor metabolizers of CYP2D6 substrates)

» CNS stimulation-producing medications, other (see *Appendix II*)
(additive CNS stimulation may occur, causing nervousness, irritability, insomnia, or possibly seizures or cardiac arrhythmias; close observation is recommended during concurrent use with modafinil)
(the absorption of modafinil may be delayed by approximately 1 hour when coadministered with methylphenidate or dextroamphetamine, although the extent of absorption and the disposition of both agents are unchanged)

Inducers of CYP3A4, such as:
Carbamazepine or
Phenobarbital or
Rifampin
(plasma concentrations of modafinil may be decreased)

Inhibitors of CYP3A4, such as:
Itraconazole or
Ketoconazole
(plasma concentrations of modafinil may be increased)

» Monoamine oxidase (MAO) inhibitors, including furazolidone, procarbazine, and selegiline
(studies have not been done; caution is advised during concomitant use of modafinil and an MAO inhibitor)

» Substrates of CYP2C9, such as:
Phenytoin or
Warfarin
(*in vitro*, modafinil suppresses CYP2C9 activity in human hepatocytes in a concentration-related manner; increased concentrations of these medications may occur; patient monitoring is advised during concomitant use of modafinil and CYP2C9 substrates)

» Substrates of CYP2C19, such as:
Diazepam or
Mephenytoin or
Propranolol
(modafinil reversibly inhibits the activity of CYP2C19; metabolism of medications that are largely metabolized by CYP2C19 may be

reduced during concurrent modafinil treatment; dosages of these medications may need to be reduced)

» Substrates of CYP3A4, other, such as:
Cyclosporine or
Steroidal contraceptives or
Theophylline
(modafinil modestly induces CYP3A4, which may lead to decreased plasma concentrations of concomitantly administered medications that are metabolized by this isoenzyme)
(cyclosporine concentrations were reduced by 50% in a transplant patient after 1 month of concomitant therapy with 200 mg per day of modafinil)
(nonsteroidal contraceptive methods should be used during and for 1 month after discontinuation of modafinil use)

Laboratory value alterations

The following have been selected on the basis of their potential clinical significance (possible effect in parentheses where appropriate)—not necessarily inclusive (» = major clinical significance).

With physiology/laboratory test values
Eosinophil counts
(abnormally high eosinophil counts occurred in about 2% of patients during premarketing studies of modafinil; however, elevations were clinically insignificant)
Alkaline phosphatase (AP) or
Gamma-glutamyltransferase (GGT) plasma concentrations
(increased AP and GGT concentrations occurred in patients receiving modafinil in premarketing studies; elevations were clinically insignificant but were outside of the normal range in about 1% of patients; however, GGT concentrations appeared to increase over time in subjects receiving modafinil in trials that were of 9 weeks duration)
(no changes were seen in other measures of hepatic function)

Medical considerations/Contraindications

The medical considerations/contraindications included have been selected on the basis of their potential clinical significance (reasons given in parentheses where appropriate)—not necessarily inclusive (» = major clinical significance).

Risk-benefit should be considered when the following medical problems exist:
Angina, unstable or
Myocardial infarction, recent history of
(experience with modafinil in patients with these conditions is limited; caution is recommended)
» Clinically significant manifestations of mitral valve prolapse in association with use of other CNS stimulants, history of or
» Left ventricular hypertrophy in association with use of other CNS stimulants, history of
(the risk of developing similar effects with modafinil use may be increased; use of modafinil is not recommended)
» Hepatic function impairment (severe)
(clearance of modafinil is reduced; dosage reductions of 50% are recommended)
Hypertension
(use of modafinil in patients with hypertension has not been systematically evaluated; monitoring of blood pressure is recommended)
» Psychosis, history of
(multiple doses of 600 mg per day of modafinil, in association with sleep deprivation, induced ideas of reference, paranoid delusions, and auditory hallucinations in one healthy male volunteer; modafinil should be used with caution in patients with a history of psychosis)
Renal function impairment (severe)
(although exposure to modafinil was unaffected, exposure to modafinil acid, a metabolite of modafinil, was increased ninefold in patients with creatinine clearance ≤ 20 mL per minute compared with patients with normal renal function; the safety of exposure to high concentrations of modafinil acid is unknown)
Sensitivity to modafinil

Patient monitoring

The following may be especially important in patient monitoring (other tests may be warranted in some patients, depending on condition; » = major clinical significance):

Assessment of amount and frequency of modafinil use
(studies designed to measure abuse potential indicate that modafinil produces psychoactive and euphoric effects and feelings consistent with other scheduled CNS stimulants; patients should be monitored at periodic intervals for signs of abuse or misuse of modafinil, such as dosage escalation or drug-seeking behavior)
Prothrombin time
(more frequent monitoring of prothrombin time is advisable whenever modafinil is coadministered with warfarin)

Side/Adverse Effects

The following side/adverse effects have been selected on the basis of their potential clinical significance (possible signs and symptoms in parentheses where appropriate)—not necessarily inclusive:

Those indicating need for medical attention

Incidence less frequent
Ataxia (clumsiness or unsteadiness); ***cardiac arrhythmia, hypotension, or hypertension*** (dizziness or fainting); ***chest pain; CNS effects, including amnesia*** (problems with memory); ***confusion; emotional lability*** (rapidly changing moods); ***or mental depression; chills or fever; dyskinesia, oro-facial*** (uncontrolled movements of the face, mouth, or tongue); ***hyperglycemia*** (increased thirst; increased urination); ***pharyngitis*** (sore throat); ***shortness of breath; urinary retention*** (trouble in urinating); ***vision changes; including abnormal vision; or amblyopia*** (blurred vision or other changes in vision)

Those indicating need for medical attention only if they continue or are bothersome

Incidence more frequent
Anxiety; headache—may be dose-related; ***insomnia*** (trouble in sleeping); ***nausea; nervousness***

Incidence less frequent
Anorexia (decrease in appetite); ***back pain; constipation*** (difficulty having a bowel movement (stool)); ***diarrhea; dizziness; dryness of mouth; dryness of skin; dyspepsia*** (acid or sour stomach; belching; heartburn; indigestion; stomach discomfort upset or pain); ***edema*** (swelling); ***eosinophilia*** (black, tarry stools; chest pain; chills; cough; fever; painful or difficult urination; shortness of breath; sore throat sores; ulcers or white spots on lips or in mouth swollen glands unusual bleeding or bruising unusual tiredness or weakness); ***epistaxis*** (bloody nose); ***flu syndrome*** (chills; cough; diarrhea; fever; general feeling of discomfort or illness; headache; joint pain; loss of appetite; muscle aches and pains); ***hypertonia*** (muscle stiffness); ***increased thirst; rhinitis*** (stuffy or runny nose); ***paresthesia*** (tingling, burning, or prickling sensations in the skin); ***taste perversion; tremor*** (trembling or shaking); ***vasodilation*** (headache; flushing or redness of skin); ***vertigo*** (dizziness or lightheadedness; feeling of constant movement of self or surroundings; sensation of spinning); ***vomiting***

Those indicating possible abuse of modafinil and the need for medical attention

Psychosis (severe mental illness, similar to schizophrenia)—after repeated, high-dose use

Overdose

For more information on the management of overdose or unintentional ingestion, **contact a Poison Control Center** (see *Poison Control Center Listing*).

Clinical effects of overdose

Note: Two patients who took modafinil doses of ≥ 4000 mg displayed non-life-threatening adverse effects and were fully recovered by the next day. In 151 instances of ingestion of ≥ 1000 mg of modafinil, no unexpected effects or specific organ toxicities were seen.

The following effects have been selected on the basis of their potential clinical significance (possible signs and symptoms in parentheses where appropriate)—not necessarily inclusive:

Acute
Agitation or excitation; increased blood pressure; increased heart rate; insomnia (trouble in sleeping)

Treatment of overdose

There is no specific antidote to modafinil. Treatment is primarily symptomatic and supportive.

To decrease absorption—Emesis or gastric lavage may be employed in the absence of contraindications to these measures.

Monitoring—Cardiovascular function should be monitored.

Supportive care—Patients in whom intentional overdose is confirmed or suspected should be referred for psychiatric consultation.

Note: There is no evidence that dialysis or manipulation of urinary pH will enhance the elimination of modafinil.

Patient Consultation

As an aid to patient consultation, refer to *Advice for the Patient, Modafinil (Systemic).*

In providing consultation, consider emphasizing the following selected information (» = major clinical significance):

Before using this medication

» Conditions affecting use, especially:
Sensitivity to other CNS stimulants
Pharmacogenetics—In patients with CYP2D6 deficiency, decreased clearance of CYP2D6 substrates that have ancillary metabolism via CYP2C19
Other medications, especially other CNS stimulation-producing medications; monoamine oxidase inhibitors; or substrates of CYP2C9, CYP2C19, or CYP3A4
Other medical problems, especially severe hepatic function impairment, history of left ventricular hypertrophy or clinically significant manifestations of mitral valve prolapse in association with use of other CNS stimulants, or history of psychosis

Proper use of this medication

» Taking only as directed by physician because of habit-forming potential

» Proper dosing
Missed dose: Taking if remembered before 12:00 noon; skipping if remembered later to avoid interference with nighttime sleep; returning to regular dosing schedule; not doubling doses

» Proper storage

Precautions while using this medication

Regular visits to physician to check progress of therapy

» Not increasing dose if medication becomes less effective; checking with physician

» Using alternative to steroidal contraceptives during and for 1 month after discontinuing modafinil therapy because of possible decreased efficacy of steroidal contraceptives

» Possible impairment of judgment, thinking, motor skills, or vision; not driving, using machines, or engaging in other potentially dangerous activities until effects of medication are known

» Checking with physician if dependence on modafinil is suspected

» Checking with physician before discontinuing after long-term or high-dose therapy; tapering of dosage may be required

Side/adverse effects

Signs of potential side effects, especially ataxia; cardiac arrhythmia, hypotension, or hypertension; CNS effects, including amnesia, confusion, emotional lability, mental depression; chills or fever; oro-facial dyskinesia; hyperglycemia; pharyngitis; shortness of breath; urinary retention; and vision changes, including abnormal vision or amblyopia
Possible psychosis with modafinil abuse

General Dosing Information

Female patients with child-bearing potential should be advised to use non-steroidal contraception during and for 1 month following modafinil use.

Patients should be advised to notify physician immediately of any signs or symptoms of an allergic reaction, such as skin rash or hives, that develop during modafinil therapy.

Placebo-controlled trials to determine the efficacy of modafinil beyond 9 weeks have not been conducted. Patients who receive long-term modafinil therapy should be evaluated periodically to determine the continuing effectiveness of the medication.

Prolonged or high-dose use of modafinil may result in psychological or physical dependence.

After long-term use, modafinil should be withdrawn gradually to avoid the possibility of withdrawal symptoms.

Oral Dosage Forms

MODAFINIL TABLETS

Usual adult dose

Narcolepsy—
Oral, 200 mg once a day.

Note: Patients with narcolepsy and obstructive sleep apnea/hyponea should take modafinil as a single dose in the morning.
Patients with shift work sleep disorder should take modafinil 1 hour prior to the start of their work shift.

Note: Doses of 400 mg once a day are well tolerated, but have not shown greater efficacy than doses of 200 mg once a day.
Patients with severe hepatic function impairment should receive one half of the dosage recommended for patients with normal hepatic function.

Usual adult prescribing limits

400 mg per day.

Usual pediatric dose

Narcolepsy—
Safety and efficacy in children up to 16 years of age have not been established.

Usual geriatric dose

Narcolepsy—
See *Usual adult dose.*

Note: Reduced doses should be considered in geriatric patients because of possible reduced elimination of modafinil.

Strength(s) usually available

U.S.—
100 mg (Rx) [*Provigil* (lactose; corn starch; magnesium silicate; croscarmellose sodium; povidone; magnesium stearate; talc)].
200 mg (Rx) [*Provigil* (scored; lactose; corn starch; magnesium silicate; croscarmellose sodium; povidone; magnesium stearate; talc)].

Packaging and storage

Store between 20 and 25 °C (68 and 77 °F), unless otherwise specified by manufacturer.

Auxiliary labeling

- May cause dizziness or blurred vision.
- May interfere with the effectiveness of birth control pills or implants.

Revised: 11/16/2004
Developed: 03/10/1999

MODULAR ENTERAL NUTRITION FORMULAS—
See *Enteral Nutrition Formulas (Systemic)*

MOEXIPRIL—See *Angiotensin-converting Enzyme (ACE) Inhibitors (Systemic)*

MOEXIPRIL Systemic†

VA CLASSIFICATION (Primary/Secondary): CV800/CV409; CV900
Commonly used brand name(s): *Univasc.*

Note: For a listing of dosage forms and brand names by country availability, see *Dosage Forms* section(s).

†Not commercially available in Canada.

Category

Antihypertensive.

Indications

Accepted

Hypertension (treatment)—Moexipril is indicated, alone or in combination with a thiazide diuretic, in the treatment of hypertension.
For additional information on initial therapeutic guidelines related to the treatment of hypertension, see *Appendix III.*

Pharmacology/Pharmacokinetics

Physicochemical characteristics

Molecular weight—
Moexipril hydrochloride: 535.04.
Moexiprilat: 470.53.

Mechanism of action/Effect

Moexipril is a nonsulfhydryl-containing angiotensin-converting enzyme (ACE) inhibitor. It is a prodrug for moexiprilat, the active metabolite. Moexiprilat lowers blood pressure by competitively inhibiting ACE activity. ACE catalyzes the conversion of angiotensin I to angiotensin II. Angiotensin II, a vasoconstrictor, stimulates aldosterone secretion by the adrenal cortex and directly suppresses renin release. Inhibition of ACE decreases angiotensin II formation, resulting in reduced peripheral arterial resistance, increased plasma renin activity, and decreased aldosterone secretion. The decrease in aldosterone secretion results in diuresis and natriuresis and a slight increase in serum potassium concentrations.

Other actions/effects

ACE is also known as kininase II, an enzyme that degrades bradykinin. After ACE inhibition, local kinin concentrations may increase and the formation of prostaglandins may be enhanced. Both bradykinin and prostaglandins have local vasodilatory effects that may contribute to moexipril's antihypertensive effects.

Absorption

Incompletely absorbed. Bioavailability of moexipril is approximately 13% and is significantly affected by food, which reduces the peak plasma concentration (C_{max}) and area under the plasma concentration-time curve (AUC). An open, randomized, crossover trial found that bioavailability of moexipril was reduced by 40% when administered with food. Food appears to decrease the rate of absorption more than the extent of absorption. The decrease in bioavailability may not be clinically significant, especially during long-term dosing.

Distribution

Vol_D of moexiprilat—183 L.

Protein binding

Moexiprilat—Moderate (50%).

Biotransformation

Moexipril—Rapidly converted to moexiprilat, the active metabolite. Conversion to the active metabolite is thought to require carboxyesterases and is likely to occur in organs or tissues, other than the gastrointestinal tract, in which carboxyesterases occur. The liver is thought to be one site of conversion, but not the primary site.

Half-life

Elimination:
- Moexipril—
  - Approximately 1 hour.
- Moexiprilat—
  - 2 to 9 hours.
  - Effective elimination half-life: Approximately 12 hours.

Onset of action

Approximately 1 hour.

Time to peak concentration

Moexipril—1.5 hours.
Moexiprilat—3 to 4 hours.

Elimination

Fecal—53% (52% as moexiprilat and 1% as moexipril).
Renal—13% (1% as moexipril, 7% as moexiprilat, and 5% as other metabolites).
In dialysis—It is not known whether moexipril is dialyzable.

Precautions to Consider

Cross-sensitivity and/or related problems

Patients hypersensitive to other angiotensin-converting enzyme (ACE) inhibitors may also be hypersensitive to moexipril.

Carcinogenicity

No evidence of carcinogenicity was found in long-term studies in mice and rats at doses up to 14 or 27.3 times the maximum recommended human dose (MRHD) on a mg per square meter of body surface area (mg/m²) basis.

Mutagenicity

No evidence of mutagenicity was found in the Ames test and microbial reverse mutation assay, with and without activation, or in an *in vivo* nucleus anomaly test. However, at a 20-hour harvest time, increased chromosomal aberration frequency in Chinese hamster ovary cells was detected under metabolic activation conditions.

Pregnancy/Reproduction

Fertility—No evidence of impaired fertility, reproductive toxicity, or teratogenicity was detected in reproduction studies performed in rabbits and rats at doses up to 0.7 and 90.9 times the MRHD, respectively, on a mg/m² basis.

Pregnancy—ACE inhibitors, including moexipril, can cause fetal and neonatal morbidity and mortality when administered to pregnant women during the second and third trimesters. Moexipril should be discontinued as soon as possible when pregnancy is detected unless no alternative therapy can be used. In the latter instance, serial ultrasound examinations should be performed to assess the intra-amniotic environment. If oligohydramnios is observed, moexipril should be discontinued unless it is considered lifesaving for the mother. Perinatal diagnostics, such as contraction-stress testing (CST), a non-stress test (NST), or biophysical profiling (BPP) may also be appropriate during the applicable week of pregnancy. Oligohydramnios may not appear until after the fetus has sustained irreversible damage.

Fetal exposure to ACE inhibitors limited to the first trimester is not associated with fetal or neonatal morbidity. Fetal exposure to ACE inhibitors during the second and third trimesters can cause hypotension, renal failure, anuria, skull hypoplasia, and death in the fetus or neonate. Maternal oligohydramnios, which may result from decreased fetal renal function, has been reported, and has been associated with fetal limb contractures, craniofacial deformation, and hypoplastic lung development. Prematurity, intrauterine growth retardation, and patent ductus arteriosus have also been reported, although the relationship of these occurrences to drug exposure is not clear.

Infants exposed *in utero* to moexipril should be closely observed for hypotension, oliguria, and hyperkalemia. Oliguria should be treated with support of blood pressure and renal perfusion.

Embryotoxic, fetotoxic, or teratogenic effects were not observed in rats or rabbits given up to 90.9 and 0.7 times the MRHD, respectively, on a mg/m² basis.

FDA Pregnancy Category C (first trimester).
FDA Pregnancy Category D (second and third trimesters).

Breast-feeding

It is not known whether moexipril is distributed into breast milk. However, problems in humans have not been documented.

Pediatrics

No information is available on the relationship of age to the effects of moexipril in pediatric patients. Safety and efficacy have not been established.

Geriatrics

Use of moexipril in a limited number of patients 65 years of age and over (33% of patients in clinical studies) has not demonstrated geriatrics-specific problems that would limit the usefulness of moexipril in the elderly. However, moexipril plasma concentrations are slightly higher and renal clearance is reduced in these patients as compared with younger individuals.

Pharmacogenetics

Black hypertensive patients may be less responsive to the antihypertensive effects of moexipril, possibly because these patients may have low-renin hypertension. Black patients also may have a greater risk of developing ACE inhibitor-induced angioedema, or may have more severe angioedema, than white patients.

Surgical

It is recommended that ACE inhibitors be withheld before surgery because of reports of abnormal responses to the induction of anesthesia and poor tolerance of hypovolemia with concurrent administration of ACE inhibitors.

Drug interactions and/or related problems

The following drug interactions and/or related problems have been selected on the basis of their potential clinical significance (possible mechanism in parentheses where appropriate)—not necessarily inclusive (» = major clinical significance):

Note: Combinations containing any of the following medications, depending on the amount present, may also interact with this medication.

Alcohol
(use with ACE inhibitors may produce postural hypotensive effects shortly after drinking alcohol, especially when initiating ACE inhibitor therapy)

Allopurinol
(concurrent use with another ACE inhibitor, captopril, has been reported to cause hypersensitivity reactions in two cases; however, the basis for this interaction cannot be determined)

Antacids that contain both aluminum and magnesium
(concurrent use with another ACE inhibitor, captopril, has resulted in reduced bioavailability)

Anti-inflammatory drugs, nonsteroidal (NSAIDs)
(concurrent and, especially, long-term use of NSAIDs can decrease the effectiveness of ACE inhibitors, presumably by counteracting the effect of ACE inhibitor–stimulated prostaglandin biosynthesis; concurrent use in patients with low renal perfusion can lead to further renal deterioration)

Digoxin
(pharmacokinetic interactions have not been reported with concurrent use of moexipril; however, increases in serum digoxin concentrations have been reported with concurrent use of another ACE inhibitor, captopril)

» Diuretics or
Hypotension-producing medications, other (see *Appendix II*)
(concurrent use may produce additive hypotensive effects, especially when initiating moexipril therapy; if diuretics are used concurrently, withdrawal of diuretic therapy for several days, reducing the initial dose of moexipril, or cautiously increasing salt intake before initiation of moexipril therapy may minimize hypotensive effects)

» Diuretics, potassium-sparing or
» Potassium-containing medications or
» Potassium supplements or substances containing high concentrations of potassium or
» Salt substitutes that contain substantial amounts of potassium
(concurrent use may lead to further increases in serum potassium; caution and monitoring of serum potassium concentrations are recommended)

Lithium
(increases in serum lithium concentrations and symptoms of lithium toxicity have been reported during concurrent use with ACE inhibitors; caution and frequent monitoring of serum lithium concentrations are recommended)

Sympathomimetics
(concurrent use of these agents may counteract the antihypertensive effects of moexipril; the patient should be carefully monitored to confirm that the desired therapeutic effect is obtained)

Laboratory value alterations

The following have been selected on the basis of their potential clinical significance (possible effect in parentheses where appropriate)—not necessarily inclusive (» = major clinical significance).

With physiology/laboratory test values

Alkaline phosphatase, serum and
Bilirubin, serum and
Transaminases, serum
(significant increases may be a sign of ACE inhibitor-associated hepatotoxicity)

Antinuclear antibody (ANA) titer
(a positive ANA titer has been associated rarely with use of other ACE inhibitors, although it has not been associated with moexipril)

Blood urea nitrogen (BUN) and
Creatinine, serum
(concentrations may be transiently increased, especially in patients who are currently taking diuretics and in patients with renal function impairment)

Potassium, serum
(concentrations may be increased secondary to reduced circulating aldosterone concentrations, especially in patients with renal function impairment and/or diabetes mellitus)

Protein, urine
(protein in urine has been reported with use of other ACE inhibitors; however, ACE inhibitors may have a beneficial antiproteinuric effect in patients with renal diseases associated with proteinuria, such as diabetic nephropathy)

Uric acid, serum
(concentration increases have been reported)

Medical considerations/Contraindications

The medical considerations/contraindications included have been selected on the basis of their potential clinical significance (reasons given in parentheses where appropriate)—not necessarily inclusive (» = major clinical significance).

Except under special circumstances, this medication should not be used when the following medical problems exist:

» Angioedema, history of, related to previous ACE inhibitor therapy
(increased risk for development of moexipril-related angioedema)

» Hypersensitivity to moexipril

Risk-benefit should be considered when the following medical problems exist:

» Angioedema, hereditary or
» Angioedema, idiopathic, history of
(increased risk for development of angioedema)

Aortic stenosis or
Cerebrovascular disease or
Ischemic heart disease
(reduction in blood pressure from ACE inhibitor therapy could result in cerebrovascular accident or myocardial infarction)

Collagen-vascular disease, such as systemic lupus erythematosus (SLE) or scleroderma
(increased risk for development of neutropenia or agranulocytosis with ACE inhibitor therapy)

Congestive heart failure
(ACE inhibitor therapy may interfere with the compensatory mechanisms of the renin-angiotensin-aldosterone system in heart failure patients. The glomerular filtration rate [GFR] may be further reduced in patients with poor renal perfusion, leading to oliguria and/or progressive azotemia and, possibly, acute renal failure and/or death)

» Dehydration (sodium or volume depletion due to excessive perspiration, vomiting, diarrhea, prolonged diuretic therapy, dialysis, or dietary salt restriction)
(increased risk of symptomatic hypotension; sodium-depleted patients, usually as a result of diuretic therapy, are at increased risk of developing ACE inhibitor-induced acute renal dysfunction and/or failure. Renal insufficiency caused by ACE inhibition is, in nearly all cases, reversible after discontinuing the ACE inhibitor)

Diabetes mellitus
(increased risk of hyperkalemia; increased insulin sensitivity and/or increased glucose tolerance has been reported in diabetic patients receiving ACE inhibitors)

» Dialysis with high-flux membranes or
Low-density lipoprotein apheresis with dextran sulfate absorption
(anaphylactoid reactions have been reported in patients undergoing these procedures who are concurrently taking an ACE inhibitor)

Hepatic function impairment
(peak plasma concentration [C_{max}] and area under the plasma concentration-time curve [AUC] may be increased for moexipril; C_{max} may be decreased and AUC may be increased for moexiprilat)

» Hymenoptera venom desensitizing treatment
(life-threatening anaphylactoid reactions have been reported in two patients undergoing desensitizing treatment with hymenoptera venom while receiving ACE inhibitors)

» Hyperkalemia
(further increases in serum potassium concentrations may occur secondary to decreased aldosterone secretion)

» Renal artery stenosis, bilateral or in a single kidney or
» Renal function impairment
(plasma concentrations of moexipril and moexiprilat may be increased due to decreased elimination; increased risk of agranulocytosis and neutropenia, hyperkalemia, and ACE inhibitor-induced acute renal insufficiency and/or failure; increases in blood urea nitrogen [BUN] and serum creatinine may occur, especially in those patients pretreated with a diuretic; renal function should be monitored during the first few weeks of moexipril therapy; dosage adjustment and/or discontinuation of the diuretic may be necessary)

Patient monitoring

The following may be especially important in patient monitoring (other tests may be warranted in some patients, depending on condition; » = major clinical significance):

» Blood pressure measurements
(antihypertensive effect of moexipril may diminish towards the end of the dosing interval; blood pressure measurements should be taken just before dosing to adjust the dose of moexipril according to the patient's response)

Leukocyte count
(determinations recommended periodically in patients at risk for neutropenia, particularly those with renal function impairment and/or a collagen-vascular disease)

Potassium, serum
(determinations recommended periodically, especially in patients concurrently receiving potassium supplements or potassium-sparing diuretics)

Renal function
(determinations recommended during the first few weeks of therapy in patients with renal function impairment)

Side/Adverse Effects

The following side/adverse effects have been selected on the basis of their potential clinical significance (possible signs and symptoms in parentheses where appropriate)—not necessarily inclusive:

Note: *Asymptomatic acute renal insufficiency* has occurred in patients taking ACE inhibitors. In clinical trials, increases in serum creatinine concentrations to at least 140% of baseline occurred in 1% of patients treated with moexipril and in 2% of patients treated with moexipril and hydrochlorothiazide. These hypertensive patients had no apparent pre-existing renal disease. Acute renal insufficiency is usually reversible after discontinuing the ACE inhibitor.

Those indicating need for medical attention

Incidence less frequent

Hypotension (lightheadedness or fainting)—especially during the first few days of therapy or in sodium- or volume-depleted patients as a result of prolonged diuretic therapy, dialysis, diarrhea, dietary salt restriction, or vomiting; ***skin rash***

Incidence rare

Anemia, hemolytic (bleeding gums, nosebleeds, or pale skin); ***angioedema of the face, extremities, lips, tongue, glottis, and/or larynx*** (hoarseness; sudden trouble in swallowing or breathing; swelling of face, mouth, hands, or feet); ***chest pain; hepatotoxicity*** (yellow eyes or skin); ***hyperkalemia*** (confusion; irregular heartbeat; nervousness; numbness or tingling of hands, feet, or lips; shortness of breath or trouble breathing; weakness or heaviness of legs); ***neutropenia or agranulocytosis*** (chills; fever; sore throat); ***pancreatitis*** (bloating or pain of the stomach; fever; nausea; vomiting); ***peripheral edema*** (swelling of ankles, feet, or legs)

Note: *Angioedema* involving the tongue, glottis, or larynx may cause airway obstruction, which could be fatal. Angioedema may develop at any time during angiotensin-converting enzyme (ACE) inhibitor therapy. In placebo-controlled trials, symptoms suggestive of angioedema or facial edema were reported in less than 0.5% of patients treated with moexipril. None of the cases was life-threatening. Black patients may have an increased risk of developing ACE inhibitor-induced angioedema or may have more severe angioedema. In cases of angioedema, moexipril therapy should be discontinued and the patient carefully observed until the swelling resolves.

Hepatotoxicity has been reported rarely in patients receiving ACE inhibitors. The syndrome begins with cholestatic jaundice and progresses to fulminant hepatic necrosis and sometimes death. The mechanism of this effect is not fully understood. Patients who develop jaundice or significant elevations of hepatic enzymes should discontinue therapy with moexipril and receive appropriate medical follow-up.

ACE inhibitor-associated *neutropenia or agranulocytosis* and bone marrow depression have been reported. These conditions have occurred rarely in patients with uncomplicated hypertension, but more frequently in hypertensive patients with renal function impairment, especially if a collagen-vascular disease, such as systemic lupus erythematosus or scleroderma, exists.

Those indicating need for medical attention only if they continue or are bothersome

Incidence more frequent

Cough, dry, persistent*; *dizziness; flushing

Note: In clinical trials, persistent, nonproductive *cough* was reported in 6.1% of moexipril-treated patients versus 2.2% of patients given placebo. The mechanism of this effect is probably the inhibition of endogenous bradykinin degradation. Cough usually resolves following discontinuation of moexipril therapy.

Incidence less frequent

Diarrhea; dry mouth; fatigue (unusual tiredness); ***headache; loss of taste; myalgia*** (muscle pain); ***nausea; palpitations*** (heartbeat sensations); ***photosensitivity*** (increased sensitivity to the sun); ***pruritus*** (itching); ***unusual sweating***

Overdose

For more information on the management of overdose or unintentional ingestion, **contact a Poison Control Center** (see *Poison Control Center Listing*).

Clinical effects of overdose

The following effects have been selected on the basis of their potential clinical significance (possible signs and symptoms in parentheses where appropriate)—not necessarily inclusive:

Acute and chronic

Hypotension (dizziness, lightheadedness or fainting)

Treatment of overdose

Symptomatic and supportive; may include volume expansion for correction of hypotension and monitoring of renal function and serum potassium.

Patient Consultation

In providing consultation, consider emphasizing the following selected information (» = major clinical significance):

Before using this medication

» Conditions affecting use, especially:

Hypersensitivity to moexipril or other angiotensin-converting enzyme (ACE) inhibitors

Pregnancy—ACE inhibitor-associated fetal and neonatal morbidity and mortality have been reported in humans; moexipril should be discontinued as soon as possible when pregnancy is detected

Other medications, especially diuretics (particularly potassium-sparing), potassium-containing medications or substances, potassium supplements, or salt substitutes

Other medical problems, especially angioedema, history of, idiopathic, or hereditary; dehydration (sodium or volume depletion); dialysis with high-flux membranes; hymenoptera venom desensitizing treatment; hyperkalemia; renal artery stenosis; or renal function impairment

Surgical—Withholding moexipril before surgery because of possible interaction with anesthesia induction and risk of hypovolemia

Proper use of this medication

Taking medication at the same time each day to maintain the therapeutic effect of moexipril

Taking medication 1 hour before a meal

» Compliance with therapy; treatment period may be indefinite and necessary to prevent more serious consequences of hypertension; not stopping therapy without consulting physician

» Proper dosing

Missed dose: Taking as soon as possible; not taking if almost time for next dose; not doubling doses

» Proper storage

Precautions while using this medication

Regular visits to physician to check progress

Notifying physician immediately if pregnancy is suspected

» Not taking other medications, especially nonprescription sympathomimetics, potassium-containing salt substitutes, or potassium supplements, unless discussed with physician

Caution when driving or doing other things requiring alertness, because of possible dizziness, especially after the initial dose of moexipril and in patients concurrently taking diuretics

Reporting any signs of infection (chills, fever, or sore throat) to physician because of risk of neutropenia

Reporting any signs of facial or extremity swelling and difficulty in swallowing or breathing because of risk of angioedema

To prevent dehydration and hypotension, checking with physician if severe nausea, vomiting, or diarrhea occurs and continues

Caution when exercising or during hot weather because of the risk of dehydration and hypotension due to reduced fluid volume

Avoiding alcoholic beverages because of increased risk of additive hypotensive effect

Caution if any kind of surgery (including dental surgery) or emergency treatment is required

Side/adverse effects

Signs of potential side effects, especially hypotension, skin rash, hemolytic anemia, angioedema, chest pain, hepatotoxicity, hyperkalemia, neutropenia or agranulocytosis, pancreatitis, and peripheral edema

General Dosing Information

Dosage must be adjusted to meet the individual requirements of each patient, on the basis of clinical response.

Black hypertensive patients may be less responsive to the antihypertensive effects of moexipril, possibly because these patients may have low-renin hypertension.

The antihypertensive effect of moexipril may diminish towards the end of the dosing period. If blood pressure is not controlled, it may be necessary to divide the dose into a twice-daily regimen or increase the dose, as appropriate.

For treatment of adverse effects

For angioedema with swelling confined to the face and lips, treatment other than withdrawal of the medication is usually not necessary, although antihistamines may relieve the symptoms.

Treatment of angioedema involving the tongue, glottis, or larynx may include the following:
- Withdrawal of the angiotensin-converting enzyme (ACE) inhibitor and close observation of the patient to ensure full resolution of the symptoms.
- Subcutaneous epinephrine.
- Intravenous antihistamines, such as chlorpheniramine or diphenhydramine.
- Intravenous corticosteroids.

Note: The exact mechanism of angioedema is not known, but it may involve ACE inhibitor-induced inhibition of bradykinin degradation and not immunoglobulin E (IgE). Therefore, administration of epinephrine, antihistamines, and corticosteroids may not be effective in severe cases of angioedema and it may be necessary to ensure an open airway.

Oral Dosage Forms

MOEXIPRIL HYDROCHLORIDE TABLETS

Usual adult dose

Antihypertensive—

Oral, initially 7.5 mg once a day, taken one hour before a meal.

The recommended dose range is 7.5 to 30 mg a day, taken one hour before a meal. Dose may be taken once a day or divided into two doses.

Note: It is recommended that diuretic therapy be withdrawn two to three days before moexipril therapy is initiated to reduce the likelihood of hypotension. If hypertension is not controlled by moexipril alone, the diuretic may be reinstated. If diuretic therapy cannot be discontinued, an initial moexipril dose of 3.75 mg, given under medical supervision, is recommended until the blood pressure has stabilized.

An initial dose of 3.75 mg once a day is recommended for patients with a creatinine clearance ≤ forty mL/min. Dosage may be cautiously titrated upward to a maximum daily dose of 15 mg.

Usual adult prescribing limits

Antihypertensive—

30 mg per day; 15 mg per day for patients with a creatinine clearance ≤ forty mL/min. Doses above 60 mg per day have not been studied.

Usual pediatric dose

Safety and efficacy have not been established.

Strength(s) usually available

U.S.—

7.5 mg (Rx) [*Univasc* (scored; lactose)].

15 mg (Rx) [*Univasc* (scored)].

Canada—

Not commercially available.

Packaging and storage

Store at controlled room temperature, between 20 and 25 °C (68 and 77 °F) in a tightly closed container, unless otherwise specified by manufacturer. Protect from excessive moisture.

Auxiliary labeling

- Do not take other medicines without your doctor's advice.

Developed: 08/19/1997

MOMETASONE—See *Corticosteroids (Nasal), Corticosteroids (Topical)*

MOMETASONE Inhalation-Local

VA CLASSIFICATION (Primary/Secondary): RE110/RE190

Commonly used brand name(s): *Asmanex Twisthaler.*

Note: For a listing of dosage forms and brand names by country availability, see *Dosage Forms* section(s).

Category

Anti-inflammatory (inhalation); antiasthmatic.

Indications

Accepted

Asthma, chronic (treatment)—Mometasone furoate inhalation powder is indicated for the maintenance treatment of asthma as prophylactic therapy in patients 12 years of age and older; mometasone furoate inhalation powder is also indicated for asthma patients who require oral corticosteroid therapy, where adding mometasone furoate inhalation therapy may reduce or eliminate the need for oral corticosteroids.

Unaccepted

Mometasone furoate inhalation powder is not indicated for the relief of acute bronchospasm.

Mometasone furoate inhalation powder is not indicated in the primary treatment of status asthmaticus or other acute episodes of asthma where intensive measures are required.

Pharmacology/Pharmacokinetics

Physicochemical characteristics

Molecular weight—Mometasone furoate: 521.44.

Mechanism of action/Effect

The precise mechanism by which corticosteroids affect asthma is not known. Corticosteroids have been shown to have a wide range of effects on multiple cell types (e.g., eosinophils, lymphocytes, macrophages, mast cells, and neutrophils) and mediators (e.g., histamine, eicosanoids, cytokines, and leukotrienes) involved in inflammation and the asthma response.

In a study of 15 asthmatic patients receiving 50 or 100 mcg of mometasone furoate inhalation powder to placebo twice daily for two weeks, mometasone furoate inhalation powder reduced airway reactivity to adenosine monophosphate. In another study, pretreatment with mometasone furoate inhalation powder for 5 days attenuated the early and late phase reactions following inhaled allergen challenge and also reduced allergen-induced hyperresponsiveness to methacholine. Mometasone furoate inhalation powder was also shown to attenuate the increase in inflammatory cells in induced sputum following allergen and methacholine challenge.

Absorption

Using an assay with a lower quantitation limit (LOQ) of 50 picograms per mL, mometasone furoate inhalation powder was virtually undetectable in plasma.

Plasma concentrations of unchanged mometasone furoate inhalation powder were shown to be very low compared to the total radioactivity.

Bioavailability is less than 1%.

Distribution

Volume of distribution (Vol_D): 152 L following intravenous administration

Protein binding

Very high (98 to 99%) in a concentration of 5 to 500 μg per mL

Biotransformation

Hepatic—Mometasone furoate undergoes extensive metabolism to multiple metabolites. CYP3A4 plays a primary role in the metabolism of mometasone furoate.

Half-life

Following intravenous administration, the mean terminal half-life of mometasone furoate is approximately 5 hours.

Time to peak concentration

1 to 2.5 hours

Peak plasma concentration

94 to 114 pcg per mL

Time to peak effect

1 to 2 weeks or longer after starting treatment

Elimination

Fecal—Following an inhaled dose, 74% of the radioactivity is excreted within 7 days.

Renal—Following an inhaled dose, 8% of the radioactivity is excreted within 7 days.

Precautions to Consider

Carcinogenicity

There was no statistically significant increase in the incidence of tumors in Sprague Dawley rats given an inhalation dose of 67 mcg per kg of body weight (mcg/kg) of mometasone furoate (approximately eight times the maximum recommended daily [MRD] inhalation dose in adult humans on an AUC basis) in a 2-year carcinogenicity study.

Also, there was no statistically significant increase in the incidence of tumors in Swiss CD-1 mice given an inhalation dose of 160 mcg/kg of mometasone furoate (approximately ten times the MRD inhalation dose in adult humans on an AUC basis) in a 19–month carcinogenicity study.

Mutagenicity

Mometasone furoate produced an increase in chromosome aberrations *in vitro* in Chinese hamster ovary cell assay. Mometasone furoate was not mutagenic in the mouse-lymphoma assay and the *Salmonella* / *Escherichia coli* /mammalian microsome mutation assay, a Chinese hamster lung cell (CHL) chromosomal-aberrations assay, an *in vivo* mouse bone marrow erythrocyte-micronucleus assay, a rat bone marrow chromosomal-aberration assay, and the mouse male germ cell chromosomal-aberration assay. Mometasone furoate did not induce unscheduled DNA synthesis *in vivo* in rat hepatocytes.

Pregnancy/Reproduction

Fertility—In rats, impairment of fertility did not occur when mometasone furoate was given in subcutaneous doses of up to 15 mcg/kg (approximately 6 times the MRD inhalation dose in adults on an AUC basis).

Pregnancy—Adequate and well-controlled studies in humans have not been done. Mometasone furoate increased fetal malformations when administered to pregnant mice, rats, and rabbits. Corticosteroids, including inhalation mometasone furoate, should be used during pregnancy only if the potential benefits justify the potential risk to the fetus.

In mice, mometasone furoate caused cleft palate when given in subcutaneous doses of 60 mcg per kg and above (less than the MRD intranasal dose in adult humans on a mcg/m^2 basis). Fetal survival was reduced at 180 mcg per kg (approximately equal to the MRD inhalation dose in adults).

In rabbits, mometasone furoate was teratogenic and caused flexed front paws, gallbladder agenesis, umbilical hernia, and hydrocephaly when given in a topical dermal dose of 150 mcg/kg (approximately 3 times the MRD inhalation dose in adult humans on a mcg/m^2 basis). Mometasone furoate given orally increased resorptions and caused cleft palate and/or head malformations at 700 mcg per kg (less than the MRD inhalation dose in adults on an AUC basis). Most liters were aborted or resorbed following a 2800 mcg per kg dose (approximately 2 times the MRD inhalation dose in adults on an AUC basis).

In rats, mometasone furoate produced umbilical hernia when given in a topical dermal dose of 600 mcg/kg (approximately 6 times the MRD inhalation dose in adult humans on a mcg/m^2 basis). At a dose of 300 mcg/kg (approximately 3 times the MRD inhalation dose in adult humans on a mcg/m^2 basis), delayed ossification was observed. Subcutaneous doses of 15 mcg per kg mometasone (approximately 6 times the MRD inhalation dose in adults on an AUC basis) throughout pregnancy or during the later stages of pregnancy caused prolonged and difficult labor and reduced the number of live births, birth weight and early pup survival.

FDA Pregnancy Category C

Postpartum—

Infants born to women receiving corticosteroids should be carefully monitored since hypoadrenalism may occur.

Breast-feeding

It is not known whether mometasone furoate is distributed into breast milk. However, since other corticosteroids are distributed into breast milk, caution should be used when inhalation mometasone furoate is administered to women who are breast-feeding.

Pediatrics

Safety and efficacy in children less than 12 years of age have not been established. Infants born to mothers receiving corticosteroids during pregnancy should be monitored for hypoadrenalism. Mometasone furoate inhalation powder may cause a reduction in growth velocity when administered to pediatric patients. The potential effects of prolonged treatment on growth velocity should be weighed against clinical benefits obtained and the risks associated with alternative therapies.

Geriatrics

No information is available on the relationship of age to the effects of mometasone inhalation powder in geriatric patients.

Drug interactions and/or related problems

The following drug interactions and/or related problems have been selected on the basis of their potential clinical significance (possible mechanism in parentheses where appropriate)—not necessarily inclusive (» = major clinical significance):

Note: Combinations containing any of the following medications, depending on the amount present, may also interact with this medication.

Anticonvulsants or
Corticosteroids
(may reduce bone mass)

Ketoconazole
(may increase plasma levels of mometasone furoate during concomitant dosing)

Medical considerations/Contraindications

The medical considerations/contraindications included have been selected on the basis of their potential clinical significance (reasons given in parentheses where appropriate)—not necessarily inclusive (» = major clinical significance).

Except under special circumstances, this medication should not be used when the following medical problem exists:

» Hypersensitivity to mometasone furoate or any of its components

Risk-benefit should be considered when the following medical problems exist:

Cataracts or
Glaucoma or
Intraocular pressure increased
(may be associated with the development of cataracts and/or glaucoma and also rarely may increase intraocular pressure)

Hepatic impairment
(may increase mometasone plasma concentrations)

Immobilization, prolonged or
Osteoporosis, family history
(may increase the risk of decreased bone mineral content)

» Infections, systemic, fungal, bacterial, parasitic or viral, untreated
(corticosteroids may mask the infection; in addition, some infections, such as chickenpox or measles, may have a more serious course in patients on immunosuppressant doses of corticosteroids; exposure to these viruses may warrant prophylaxis and/or treatment with immunoglobulins or antiviral agents)

» Ocular herpes simplex
(corticosteroids may make this condition worse)

» Tuberculosis, latent or active, of respiratory tract
(corticosteroids may mask or activate the infection)

Patient monitoring

The following may be especially important in patient monitoring (other tests may be warranted in some patients, depending on condition; » = major clinical significance):

» Adrenal response
(particular care should be taken in observing patients postoperatively or during periods of stress for evidence of inadequate adrenal response)

» Corticosteroid effects, systemic
(patients should be observed carefully for any evidence of systemic corticosteroid effects)

Growth in children
(stadiometry should be used routinely to monitor the growth of children 12 years of age and older)

Side/Adverse Effects

Note: Some clinically important cases of growth suppression have been reported for orally inhaled corticosteroids. See also *Pediatrics* section.

Rarely, systemic corticosteroid effects such as hypercorticism and adrenal suppression may occur, especially with the use of higher doses.

Note: Patients should be instructed to contact their physician immediately when episodes of asthma that are not responsive to bronchodilators occur during the course of treatment with the mometasone inhaler. During such episodes, patients may require therapy with oral corticosteroids.

Note: It is possible that systemic corticosteroid effects such as hypercorticism, reduced bone mineral density and adrenal suppression may occur in a small number of patients, particularly at higher doses. If such changes occur, the mometasone inhaler dose should be reduced slowly, consistent with accepted procedures for management of asthma symptoms and for tapering of systemic steroids.

The following side/adverse effects have been selected on the basis of their potential clinical significance (possible signs and symptoms in parentheses where appropriate)—not necessarily inclusive:

Those indicating need for medical attention

Incidence more frequent

Pharyngitis (body aches or pain; congestion; cough; dryness or soreness of throat; fever; hoarseness; runny nose; tender, swollen glands in neck; trouble in swallowing; voice changes); ***sinusitis*** (stuffy or runny nose or headache); ***upper respiratory tract infection*** (cold or flu-like symptoms)

Incidence less frequent

Gastroenteritis (abdominal or stomach pain; diarrhea loss of appetite; nausea; weakness); ***infection*** (fever or chills; cough or hoarseness; lower back or side pain; painful or difficult urination); ***urinary tract infection*** (bladder pain; bloody or cloudy urine; difficult, burning, or painful urination; frequent urge to urinate; lower back or side pain)

Incidence rare

Nasal or oral candidiasis (white patches inside nose or mouth)

Those indicating need for medical attention only if they continue or are bothersome

Incidence more frequent

Allergic rhinitis (unexplained runny nose or sneezing); ***arthralgia*** (pain in joints; muscle pain or stiffness; difficulty in moving); ***depression*** (discouragement; feeling sad or empty; irritability; lack of appetite; loss of interest or pleasure; tiredness; trouble concentrating; trouble sleeping); ***dysmenorrhea*** (increased abdominal pain and cramping during menstrual periods); ***dyspepsia*** (stomach discomfort following meals; upset stomach); ***fatigue; headache; musculoskeletal pain; nasal burning and irritation; sinus congestion*** (stuffy nose; headache)

Incidence less frequent

Abdominal pain; accidental injury; anorexia (loss of appetite; weight loss); ***back pain; earache; epistaxis*** (bloody mucus or unexplained nosebleeds); ***flatulence; flu-like symptoms*** (chills; cough; diarrhea; fever; general feeling of discomfort or illness; headache; joint pain; loss of appetite; muscle aches and pains; nausea; runny nose; shivering; sore throat; sweating; trouble sleeping; unusual tiredness or weakness; vomiting); ***insect bite; insomnia*** (sleeplessness; trouble sleeping; unable to sleep); ***menstrual disorder*** (menstrual changes); ***myalgia*** (joint pain; swollen joints; muscle aching or cramping; muscle pains or stiffness; difficulty in moving); ***nausea; pain; post-procedure pain; respiratory disorder*** (chest congestion); ***skin laceration; throat dry; vomiting***

Overdose

For more information on the management of overdose or unintentional ingestion, **contact a poison control center** (see *Poison Control Center Listing*).

Treatment of overdose

For acute overdose—Because of low systemic bioavailability of mometasone inhalation powder, and an absence of acute drug-related systemic findings in clinical studies, acute overdose with mometasone inhalation powder is unlikely to require any therapy other than observation.

For chronic overdose—Chronic overdosage with mometasone inhalation powder may result in signs or symptoms of hypercorticism.

Supportive care—

Treatment should be symptomatic and supportive. Patients in whom intentional overdose is confirmed or suspected should be referred for psychiatric consultation.

Patient Consultation

As an aid to patient consultation, refer to *Advice for the Patient, Mometasone (Inhalation-Local)*.

In providing consultation, consider emphasizing the following selected information (» = major clinical significance):

Before using this medication

» Conditions affecting use, especially:

Hypersensitivity to mometasone or anhydrous lactose

Breast-feeding—Cautious use in nursing women because other corticosteroids pass into breast milk

Use in children—Chronic use may stunt growth; monitoring of growth is important; exposure to chickenpox or measles should be avoided

Other medical problems, especially tuberculosis, ocular herpes simplex virus, or bacterial, parasitic, fungal, or systemic viral infections

Proper use of this medication

» Not using to relieve acute asthma attacks; continuing use of mometasone even if using other medications for asthma attack

» Importance of not using more than the amount prescribed

» Compliance with therapy by using every day in regularly spaced doses

Rinsing mouth with water after each dose; not swallowing rinse water

Proper administration technique for inhaler

» Reading patient instructions carefully; checking frequently with health care professional for proper use of inhaler

» Recording the date the foil pouch was opened on the cap label

» Not using inhaler more than 45 days after opening foil pouch or when the dose counter reads "00"

» Proper dosing

» Proper storage

Precautions while using this medication

» Checking with physician in the following circumstances:

Periods of unusual stress

A severe asthma attack occurs

Asthma symptoms do not improve or condition worsens

Exposure to chickenpox or measles occurs

Carrying medical identification stating that supplemental systemic corticosteroid therapy may be required in emergency situations, periods of unusual stress, or acute asthma attack

» Caution if any kind of surgery or emergency treatment is required; informing health care professional that inhalation corticosteroid is being used

Side/adverse effects

Signs of potential side effects, especially adrenal suppression, gastroenteritis, hypercorticism, infection, musculoskeletal pain, nasal or oral candidiasis, pharyngitis, sinusitis, upper respiratory tract infection

General Dosing Information

Mometasone furoate inhalation powder should be used at regular intervals to increase its effectiveness.

Caution is recommended when patients are transferred from systemic corticosteroids to inhaled mometasone because deaths due to adrenal insufficiency have occurred in asthmatic patients during and after transfer from systemic corticosteroids to less systemically available inhaled corticosteroids. After withdrawal from systemic corticosteroids, several months are required for recovery of hypothalamic-pituitary-adrenal (HPA) function. Patients who have been maintained on the equivalent of 20 mg or more of prednisone per day may be most susceptible, particularly when their systemic corticosteroids have been almost completely withdrawn. During this period of HPA suppression, patients may exhibit signs and symptoms of adrenal insufficiency when exposed to trauma, surgery, infection (particularly gastroenteritis), or other conditions associated with severe electrolyte loss. In recommended doses, mometasone by inhalation may control asthma symptoms during these episodes but supplies lower-than-normal physiological amounts of glucocorticoid systemically and does not provide the mineralocorticoid activity necessary for coping with these emergencies. During periods of stress or if a severe asthma attack occurs, patients who have been withdrawn from systemic corticosteroids should be instructed to immediately resume oral corticosteroids in large doses and to contact their physician for further instructions. These patients should also be instructed to carry a warning card indicating that they may need systemic corticosteroids during periods of stress or if a severe asthma attack occurs.

For patients currently receiving chronic oral corticosteroid therapy, prednisone should be reduced no faster than 2.5 mg per day on a weekly basis, beginning after at least 1 week of mometasone therapy. Patients should be carefully monitored for signs of asthma instability, including serial objective measures of air flow, and for signs of adrenal insufficiency. Once prednisone reduction is complete, the dosage of mometasone should be reduced to the lowest effective dose.

Maximum benefit may not be achieved for 1 to 2 weeks or longer after starting treatment.

It is desirable to titrate to the lowest effective dose once asthma stability is achieved.

Caution is recommended if a systemic corticosteroid is replaced with a less systemically available inhaled corticosteroid, such as mometasone, since adrenal insufficiency may occur.

Treatment of Adverse Effects

If bronchospasm, with an immediate increase in wheezing, occurs after dosing, it should be treated immediately with a fast-acting inhaled bronchodilator. It is recommended that treatment with inhaled mometasone be discontinued and alternative therapy instituted.

Patients who are on medications that suppress the immune system are more susceptible to infections; therefore, children or adults using mometasone who have not had diseases such as chickenpox or measles should avoid exposure. If the patient is exposed to chickenpox, prophylaxis with varicella zoster immune globulin (VZIG) may be indicated. If the patient is exposed to measles, prophylaxis with intramuscular pooled immune globulin (IG) may be indicated. If chickenpox develops, treatment with antiviral agents may be considered.

If oropharyngeal candidiasis develops, it should be treated with appropriate local or systemic antifungal therapy while still continuing with mometasone furoate inhalation powder.

Oral Dosage Forms

MOMETASONE FUROATE INHALATION POWDER

Usual adult dose

Asthma (treatment)—
Oral, dose is based on previous therapy.
Previous asthma therapy consisting of bronchodilators alone: 220 mcg once daily in the evening.
Previous asthma therapy consisting of inhaled corticosteroids alone: 220 mcg once daily in the evening.
Previous asthma therapy consisting of oral corticosteroids: 440 mcg twice daily.

Usual adult prescribing limits

Previous asthma therapy consisting of bronchodilators alone: 440 mcg once daily or 220 mcg twice daily.

Previous asthma therapy consisting of inhaled corticosteroids alone: 440 mcg once daily or 220 mcg twice daily.

Previous asthma therapy consisting of oral corticosteroids: 880 mcg.

Usual pediatric dose

Asthma (treatment)—
Children less than 12 years of age: Safety and efficacy have not been established.
Children 12 years of age and older: See *Usual adult dose.*

Usual pediatric prescribing limits

Children 12 years of age and older: See *Usual adult prescribing limits.*

Usual geriatric dose

See *Usual adult dose.*

Usual geriatric prescribing limits

See *Usual adult prescribing limits.*

Strength(s) usually available

U.S.—
220 mcg, which delivers 200 mcg mometasone furoate (Rx) [*Asmanex Twisthaler* (anhydrous lactose)].

Note: This product delivers 14, 30, 60, or 120 inhalation units. It is comprised of an assembled plastic cap-activated dosing mechanism with dose counter and a protective foil pouch. Discard the inhaler 45 days after opening the foil pouch or when the dose counter reads "00", whichever comes first.

Packaging and storage

Store at 25 °C (77 °F), excursions permitted between 15° and 30°C (59° and 86°F). Protect from moisture.

Note: Include patient instructions when dispensing.
Demonstrate administration technique.
Patients should be instructed to inhale rapidly and deeply.

Developed: 06/10/2005

MONOMERIC (ELEMENTAL) ENTERAL NUTRITION FORMULAS—See *Enteral Nutrition Formulas (Systemic)*

MONTELUKAST Systemic

VA CLASSIFICATION (Primary): RE180

Commonly used brand name(s): *Singulair.*

Note: For a listing of dosage forms and brand names by country availability, see *Dosage Forms* section(s).

Category

Antiasthmatic (leukotriene receptor antagonist); antiallergic (leukotriene receptor antagonist).

Indications

Accepted

Asthma, bronchial, chronic (prophylaxis and treatment)—Montelukast is indicated for prophylaxis and chronic treatment of asthma in adults and pediatric patients 12 months of age and older.

Rhinitis, seasonal allergic (treatment)—Montelukast is indicated for the relief of symptoms of seasonal allergic rhinitis in adults and pediatric patients 2 years of age and older.

Unaccepted

Montelukast is not indicated for treatment of bronchospasm in acute asthma attacks, including status asthmaticus.

Pharmacology/Pharmacokinetics

Physicochemical characteristics

Molecular weight—608.18.

Solubility—Freely soluble in ethanol, methanol, and water and practically insoluble in acetonitrile.

Mechanism of action/Effect

Montelukast inhibits bronchoconstriction due to antigen challenge. Montelukast is a selective leukotriene receptor antagonist of the cysteinyl leukotriene $CysLT_1$ receptor. The cysteinyl leukotrienes (LTC_4, LTD_4, LTE_4) are products of arachidonic acid metabolism that are released from various cells, including mast cells and eosinophils. They bind to cysteinyl leukotriene receptors (CysLT) found in the human airway. Binding of cysteinyl leukotrienes to leukotriene receptors has been correlated with the pathophysiology of asthma, including airway edema, smooth muscle contraction, and altered cellular activity associated with the inflammatory process, factors that contribute to the signs and symptoms of asthma. Montelukast binding to the $CysLT_1$ receptor is high-affinity and selective, preferring the $CysLT_1$ receptor to other pharmacologically important airway receptors, such as the prostanoid, cholinergic, or beta-adrenergic receptor. Montelukast inhibits physiologic actions of LTD_4 at the $CysLT_1$ receptors, without any agonist activity.

Absorption

Rapid.

For the 10-mg tablets—Mean oral bioavailability is 64%. Bioavailability is not affected by a standard meal in the morning.

For the 5-mg chewable tablet—Mean oral bioavailability is 73% in the fasted state versus 63% when administered with a standard meal in the morning.

For the 4-mg oral granule formulation—A high fat meal in the morning did not effect the AUC of montelukast. However, the meal decreased C_{max} by 35%.

Distribution

Steady-state volume of distribution averages 8 to 11 liters.

Protein binding

Plasma proteins—Very high (more than 99%).

Biotransformation

Hepatic, extensive. Involves cytochrome P450 3A4 and 2C9.

Half-life

Range, 2.7 to 5.5 hours in healthy young adults.

Onset of action

In clinical trials, the treatment effect was achieved after the first dose.

Time to peak concentration

10-mg tablet—3 to 4 hours.
5-mg chewable tablet—2 to 2.5 hours.
4-mg oral granule formulation—1.3 to 3.3 hours. A high fat meal prolonged T_{max} to 3.5 to 9.3 hours.

Peak plasma concentration

The peak plasma concentration is not affected by administration with a standard meal in the morning.

Duration of action

Single dose—24 hours.

Note: There was no rebound worsening of asthma following withdrawal of montelukast after 12 weeks of therapy.

Elimination

Biliary/fecal, 86%.
Renal, less than 0.2%.
Plasma clearance averages 45 mL per minute in healthy adults.
In dialysis—
It is not known whether montelukast is removable by peritoneal dialysis or hemodialysis.

Note: The pharmacokinetics of montelukast are nearly linear at doses of up to 50 mg.

Precautions to Consider

Carcinogenicity

A 2-year study in Sprague Dawley rats at oral (gavage) doses of up to 200 mg per kg of body weight per day (mg/kg/day) (approximately 160 and 190 times the maximum recommended daily oral dose in adults and children, respectively, on a mg per square meter of body surface area basis) and a 92-week study in mice at oral doses of up to 100 mg/kg/day (approximately 40 and 50 times the maximum recommended daily oral dose in adults and children, respectively, on a mg per square meter of body surface area basis) found no evidence of carcinogenicity or tumorigenicity.

Mutagenicity
Montelukast was not found to be mutagenic or clastogenic in the microbial mutagenesis assay, the V-79 mammalian cell mutagenesis assay, the alkaline elution assay in rat hepatocytes, the chromosomal aberration assay in Chinese hamster ovary cells, and the *in vivo* mouse bone marrow chromosomal aberration assay.

Pregnancy/Reproduction
Fertility—A reduction in fertility was seen in female rats on oral doses of montelukast of 200 mg/kg (approximately 160 times the maximum recommended daily oral dose in adults, on a mg per square meter of body surface area basis). However, no effects on fertility were seen in female rats on oral doses of montelukast of 100 mg/kg (approximately 80 times the maximum recommended daily oral dose in adults, on a mg per square meter of body surface area basis). No reduction in fertility was seen in male rats at oral doses of up to 800 mg/kg (approximately 650 times the maximum recommended daily oral dose in adults, on a mg per square meter of body surface area basis).

Pregnancy—Adequate and well-controlled studies in humans have not been done.

Studies in rats at oral doses of up to 400 mg/kg/day (approximately 320 times the maximum recommended daily oral dose in adults on a mg per square meter of body surface area basis) and in rabbits at oral doses of up to 300 mg/kg/day (approximately 490 times the maximum recommended daily oral dose in adults on a mg per square meter of body surface area basis) found no evidence of teratogenicity. Montelukast crosses the placenta in rats and rabbits.

Risk-benefit should be considered before use of montelukast during pregnancy.

FDA Pregnancy Category B.

Note: To facilitate monitoring of fetal outcomes of pregnant women exposed to montelukast, healthcare providers are encouraged to register patients by calling the Pregnancy Registry for *Singulair* at (800) 986–8999.

Breast-feeding
It is not known whether montelukast is distributed into breast milk in humans. However, it is distributed into breast milk in rats. Risk-benefit should be considered before breast-feeding during treatment with montelukast.

Pediatrics
Safety and efficacy have not been established in infants younger than 12 months of age. Oral granules are recommended for use in infants 12 to 23 months of age. Oral granules or chewable tablets are recommended for use in children 2 to 5 years of age. Chewable tablets are recommended for children 6 years of age and older.

Adolescents
The pharmacokinetics of the 10-mg tablet are similar in adolescents 15 years of age and older and young adults; the pharmacokinetics of the 5-mg chewable tablet in children 6 to 14 years of age are similar to those of the 10-mg tablet in adults. The 5-mg chewable tablet is recommended for children 6 to 14 years of age and the 10-mg tablet is recommended for adolescents 15 years of age and older.

Geriatrics
The pharmacokinetics and oral bioavailability of montelukast are similar in elderly and younger adults. The plasma half-life is slightly longer in the elderly, but no dosage adjustment is necessary.

No information is available comparing the use of montelukast in elderly patients with its use in younger adults. However, a small percentage of the patients in clinical trials were 65 years of age and over, and no differences in efficacy or adverse effects were observed.

Drug interactions and/or related problems
The following drug interactions and/or related problems have been selected on the basis of their potential clinical significance (possible mechanism in parentheses where appropriate)—not necessarily inclusive (» = major clinical significance):

Note: Although studies have not been done, because of the potential for interactions, monitoring is recommended during concurrent use with potent cytochrome P450 enzyme inducers, such as rifampin.

Studies have not found that montelukast causes significant changes in the pharmacokinetics of theophylline, warfarin, immunoreactive digoxin, terfenadine, fexofenadine, oral contraceptives containing norethindrone 1 mg and ethinyl estradiol 35 mcg, prednisone, or prednisolone.

Combinations containing any of the following medications, depending on the amount present, may also interact with this medication.

Phenobarbital
(concurrent use results in significant decreases [approximately 40%] in the area under the curve [AUC] for montelukast, as a result of induction of hepatic metabolism; however, no dosage adjustment is necessary)

Laboratory value alterations
The following have been selected on the basis of their potential clinical significance (possible effect in parentheses where appropriate)—not necessarily inclusive (» = major clinical significance).

With physiology/laboratory test values

Alanine aminotransferase (ALT [SGPT]) and
Aspartate aminotransferase (AST [SGOT])
(serum values may infrequently be increased)

Eosinophils
(mean peripheral eosinophils may be increased by approximately 13 to 15% from baseline)

Medical considerations/Contraindications
The medical considerations/contraindications included have been selected on the basis of their potential clinical significance (reasons given in parentheses where appropriate)—not necessarily inclusive (» = major clinical significance).

Except under special circumstances, this medication should not be used when the following medical problem exists:

» Hypersensitivity to montelukast or any component of this product

Risk-benefit should be considered when the following medical problems exist:

Hepatic function impairment
(metabolism of montelukast may be decreased in patients with mild to moderate hepatic function impairment and clinical evidence of cirrhosis; half-life may be slightly prolonged [to a mean of 7.4 hours]; however, dosage adjustment is not necessary; montelukast has not been evaluated in patients with severe hepatic function impairment)

» Hypersensitivity to aspirin
(avoidance of aspirin or NSAIDs; montelukast has not been shown to truncate bronchoconstrictor response to aspirin or other NSAIDs in aspirin-sensitive asthmatic patients)

Phenylketonuria (PKU)
(montelukast chewable tablets contains aspartame, which is metabolized to phenylalanine)

Side/Adverse Effects
Note: Systemic eosinophilia has occurred rarely in patients taking montelukast, sometimes presenting with the clinical features of vasculitis consistent with Churg-Strauss syndrome, a condition that is often treated with systemic corticosteroid therapy. These events have usually, but not always, occurred in association with the reduction of oral corticosteroid therapy. It is recommended that physicians be alert for signs of eosinophilia, vasculitic rash, worsening of pulmonary symptoms, cardiac complications, and/or neuropathy in these patients. A causal association between montelukast and these underlying conditions has not been established.

The following side/adverse effects have been selected on the basis of their potential clinical significance (possible signs and symptoms in parentheses where appropriate)—not necessarily inclusive:

Those indicating need for medical attention
Incidence less frequent

Elevated hepatic enzymes (asymptomatic)

Note: *Elevated hepatic enzymes* include alanine aminotransferase (ALT [SGPT]) and aspartate aminotransferase (AST [SGOT]).

Incidence rare

Pyuria (pus in the urine)

Incidence not determined—Observed during clinical practice; estimates of frequency can not be determined

Aggressive behavior (attack; assault; force); ***agitation*** (anxiety; nervousness; restlessness; irritability; dry mouth; shortness of breath; hyperventilation; trouble sleeping; irregular heartbeats; shaking); ***Anaphylaxis*** (cough; difficulty swallowing; dizziness; fast heartbeat; hives; itching; puffiness or swelling of the eyelids or around the eyes, face, lips or tongue; shortness of breath; skin rash; tightness in chest; unusual tiredness or weakness; wheezing); ***angioedema*** (large, hive-like swelling on face, eyelids, lips, tongue, throat, hands, legs, feet, sex organs); ***cholestatic hepatitis*** (abdominal or stomach pain; chills; clay-colored stools; dark urine; diarrhea; dizziness; fever; headache; itching; loss of appetite; nausea; rash; unpleasant breath odor; unusual tiredness or weakness; vomiting of blood; yellow eyes or skin); ***hallucinations*** (seeing, hearing, or feeling things that are not there); ***hepatic eosinophilic infiltration*** (dark urine; general tiredness and weakness; light-colored stools; nausea and vomiting; upper right abdominal pain; yellow eyes and skin); ***palpitations*** (fast, irregular, pounding, or racing heartbeat or pulse); ***pancreatitis*** (bloating; chills; constipation; darkened urine; fast heartbeat; fever; indigestion; loss of appetite; nausea; pains in stomach, side, or abdomen, possibly radiating to the back; vomiting; yellow eyes or skin); ***pruritus*** (itching skin); ***seizures*** (convulsions, muscle spasm or jerking of all extremities; sudden loss of consciousness; loss of bladder control); ***urticaria*** (hives or welts; itching; redness of skin; skin rash)

Those indicating need for medical attention only if they continue or are bothersome

Incidence more frequent

Headache

Incidence less frequent

Abdominal or stomach pain; asthenia or fatigue (weakness or unusual tiredness); ***cough; dental pain; dizziness; dyspepsia*** (heartburn); ***fever; gastroenteritis, infectious*** (abdominal or stomach pain); ***nasal congestion*** (stuffy nose); ***skin rash***

Incidence not determined—Observed during clinical practice; estimates of frequency can not be determined

Arthralgia (pain in joints; muscle pain or stiffness; difficulty in moving); ***bruising*** (large, flat, blue or purplish patches in the skin); ***diarrhea; dream abnormalities; drowsiness*** (sleepiness); ***edema*** (swelling); ***increased bleeding tendency; insomnia*** (sleeplessness; trouble sleeping; unable to sleep); ***irritability; myalgia*** (joint pain; swollen joints; muscle aching or cramping; muscle pains or stiffness; difficulty in moving); ***nausea; paraesthesia/hypoesthesia*** (burning, crawling, itching, numbness, prickling, "pins and needles", or tingling feelings); ***restlessness; vomiting***

Overdose

Clinical effects of overdose

The following effects have been selected on the basis of their potential clinical significance (possible signs and symptoms in parentheses where appropriate)—no necessarily inclusive:

Abdominal pain; hyperkinesia (increase in body movements); ***mydriasis*** (bigger, dilated, or enlarged pupils [black part of eye]; increased sensitivity of eyes to light); ***somnolence*** (sleepiness or unusual drowsiness); ***thirst***

Note: There have been reports of acute overdosage in pediatric patients in post-marketing experience and clinical studies of up to at least 150 mg per day with montelukast.

No adverse experiences were reported in the majority of overdosage reports.

Treatment of overdose

Treatment may include removal of unabsorbed material from the gastrointestinal tract, clinical monitoring, and supportive therapy if required.

It is not known if montelukast can be removed by peritoneal dialysis or hemodialysis.

Patients in whom intentional overdose is confirmed or suspected should be referred for psychiatric consultation.

Patient Consultation

As an aid to patient consultation, refer to *Advice for the Patient, Montelukast (Systemic).*

In providing consultation, consider emphasizing the following selected information (» = major clinical significance):

Before using this medication

» Conditions affecting use, especially:
- Hypersensitivity to montelukast or any component of the product
- Pregnancy—Healthcare providers encouraged to register pregnant patients taking montelukast by calling Pregnancy Registry at (800) 986–8999
- Breast-feeding—Risk-benefit should be considered
- Use in children—Safety and efficacy not established in infants younger than 12 months of age
- Other medical problems, especially hypersensitivity to aspirin

Proper use of this medication

» Importance of not using this medicine to treat acute asthma symptoms
» Proper dosing
Missed dose: Taking as soon as remembered; not taking if almost time for next dose; not doubling doses
» Proper storage

Precautions while using this medication

» Compliance with therapy; using every day, even during symptom-free periods
» Importance of not discontinuing montelukast without discussing with physician
» Checking with physician if condition becomes worse
» Importance of not discontinuing any concurrent antiasthmatic medication without physician's advice

Side/adverse effects

Signs of potential side effects, especially pus in the urine

Signs of potential side effects observed during clinical practice, especially aggressive behavior, agitation, anaphylaxis, angioedema, cholestatic hepatitis, hallucinations, hepatic eosinophilic infiltration, palpitations, pancreatitis, pruritus, rash, seizures, or urticaria

General Dosing Information

Montelukast should be taken once daily. For *asthma*, dose should be taken in the evening. For *seasonal allergic rhinitis*, time of administration may be individualized to suit patient needs.

Patients with both asthma and seasonal allergic rhinitis should take only one tablet daily in the evening.

Patients should be instructed to have appropriate rescue treatment available while being treated with montelukast. Therapy with montelukast may be continued during acute exacerbations of asthma.

Montelukast should not be abruptly substituted for inhaled or oral corticosteroids. If appropriate, the dose of corticosteroids should be tapered gradually under medical supervision. Rarely, the reduction of systemic corticosteroids in patients on another leukotriene antagonist has been followed by the occurrence of eosinophilia, vasculitic rash, worsening pulmonary symptoms, cardiac complications, and/or neuropathy sometimes presenting as Churg-Strauss syndrome, a systemic eosinophilic vasculitis. A causal relationship between this phenomenon and leukotriene receptor antagonism has not been established and the problem was not observed during clinical trials with montelukast. However, caution and appropriate clinical monitoring is recommended when systemic corticosteroid dose reduction is considered in patients receiving montelukast.

Montelukast should not be used as monotherapy for the treatment or management of exercise-induced bronchospasm. The patient should be instructed to continue with the usual regimen of an inhaled beta-agonist for prophylaxis of exercise-induced bronchospasm and to have a short-acting inhaled beta-agonist available for rescue treatment.

Montelukast chewable tablets contain aspartame, which is metabolized to phenylalanine. This substance must be used with caution in patients with phenylketonuria.

Diet/Nutrition

Montelukast oral granules can be administered without regard to time of meals.

Oral Dosage Forms

MONTELUKAST SODIUM TABLETS

Note: Oral granules are recommended for use in infants 12 to 23 months of age. Oral granules or chewable tablets are recommended for use in children 2 to 5 years of age. Chewable tablets are recommended for children 6 to 14 years of age and tablets are recommended for use in children 15 years of age and over and in adults.

Usual adult and adolescent dose

Asthma, bronchial, chronic and
Rhinitis, seasonal allergic (treatment)—
Oral, 10 mg once a day.

Usual pediatric dose

Asthma, bronchial, chronic and
Rhinitis, seasonal allergic (treatment)—
- Infants younger than 12 months of age: Safety and efficacy have not been established.
- Infants 12 to 23 months: See *Montelukast Sodium Oral Granules*
- Children 2 to 5 years of age: See *Montelukast Sodium Chewable Tablets* or *Montelukast Sodium Oral Granules*
- Children 6 to 14 years of age: See *Montelukast Sodium Chewable Tablets.*
- Children 15 years of age and over: See *Usual adult and adolescent dose.*

Usual geriatric dose
Asthma, bronchial, chronic and
Rhinitis, seasonal allergic (treatment)—
See *Usual adult and adolescent dose.*

Strength(s) usually available
U.S.—
10 mg (Rx) [*Singulair* (lactose monohydrate)].
Note: This product contains 10.4 mg of montelukast sodium, which is equivalent to 10 mg of the free acid.

Packaging and storage
Store between 15 and 30 °C (59 and 86 °F). Protect from light. Protect from moisture.

MONTELUKAST SODIUM CHEWABLE TABLETS

Note: Oral granules are recommended for use in infants 12 to 23 months of age. Oral granules or chewable tablets are recommended for use in children 2 to 5 years of age. Chewable tablets are recommended for children 6 to 14 years of age and tablets are recommended for use in children 15 years of age and over and in adults.

Usual adult and adolescent dose
Asthma, bronchial, chronic and
Rhinitis, seasonal allergic (treatment)—
See *Montelukast Sodium Tablets.*

Usual pediatric dose
Asthma, bronchial, chronic and
Rhinitis, seasonal allergic (treatment)—
Infants younger than 12 months of age: Safety and efficacy have not been established.
Infants 12 to 23 months of age: See *Montelukast Sodium Oral Granules*
Children 2 to 5 years of age: Oral, 4 mg once a day or see *Montelukast Sodium Oral Granules.*
Children 6 to 14 years of age: Oral, 5 mg once a day.
Children 15 years of age and over: See *Montelukast Sodium Tablets.*

Usual geriatric dose
Asthma, bronchial, chronic and
Rhinitis, seasonal allergic (treatment)—
See *Montelukast Sodium Tablets.*

Strength(s) usually available
U.S.—
4 mg (Rx) [*Singulair* (mannitol; microcrystalline cellulose; hydroxypropyl cellulose; red ferric oxide; croscarmellose sodium; cherry flavor; aspartame; magnesium stearate)].
5 mg (Rx) [*Singulair* (aspartame [contains 0.842 mg of phenylalanine]; mannitol; microcrystalline cellulose; croscarmellose sodium; hydroxypropyl cellulose; cherry flavor; magnesium stearate; red iron oxide)].
Note: This product contains either 4.2 mg or 5.2 mg of montelukast sodium which is equivalent to 4 mg or 5 mg, respectively of the free acid.

Packaging and storage
Store between 15 and 30 °C (59 and 86 °F). Protect from light. Protect from moisture.

Auxiliary labeling
• This medication can be taken with or without food.

Caution
Montelukast chewable tablets contains aspartame, which is metabolized to phenylalanine and must be used with caution in patients with phenylketonuria.

MONTELUKAST SODIUM ORAL GRANULES

Note: Oral granules are recommended for use in infants 12 to 23 months of age. Oral granules or chewable tablets are recommended for use in children 2 to 5 years of age. Chewable tablets are recommended for children 6 to 14 years of age and tablets are recommended for use in children 15 years of age and over and in adults.

Usual adult and adolescent dose
Asthma, bronchial, chronic and
Rhinitis, seasonal allergic (treatment)—
See *Montelukast Sodium Tablets*

Usual pediatric dose
Asthma, bronchial, chronic and
Rhinitis, seasonal allergic (treatment)—
Infants younger than 12 months of age: Safety and efficacy have not been established.
Infants 12 to 23 months of age: Oral, 4 mg (one packet) once a day.
Children 2 to 5 years of age: Oral, 4 mg (one packet) once a day or see *Montelukast Sodium Chewable Tablets.*
Children 6 to 14 years of age: See *Montelukast Sodium Chewable Tablets.*
Children 15 years of age and over: See *Montelukast Sodium Tablets.*

Usual geriatric dose
Asthma, bronchial, chronic—
See *Montelukast Sodium Tablets.*

Strength(s) usually available
U.S.—
4 mg (Rx) [*Singulair* (mannitol; hydroxypropyl cellulose; magnesium stearate)].
Note: This product contains 4.2 mg of montelukast sodium which is equivalent to 4 mg of the free acid.

Packaging and storage
Store at 25 °C (77 °F), excursions permitted to 15 to 30 °C (59 to 86 °F). Protect from moisture and light.

Stability
Based on stability studies, only applesauce, carrots, rice or ice cream should be used if mixing montelukast oral granules with spoonful of food for administration. Packet of oral granules should not be opened until ready to use. After opening packet, full dose must be administered within 15 minutes. If mixed with food, montelukast must not be stored for future use. Discard any unused portion.

Auxiliary labeling
• Do not dilute

Additional information
Montelukast oral granules can be administered either directly in the mouth or mixed with a spoonful of cold or room temperature soft foods (e.g., applesauce, carrots, rice or ice cream).

Revised: 11/09/2004
Developed: 08/12/1998

MORPHINE—See *Opioid (Narcotic) Analgesics (Systemic)*

MOXIFLOXACIN—See *Fluoroquinolones (Systemic)*

MOXIFLOXACIN Ophthalmic†

VA CLASSIFICATION (Primary): OP201

Commonly used brand name(s): *Vigamox.*

Note: For a listing of dosage forms and brand names by country availability, see *Dosage Forms* section(s).

†Not commercially available in Canada.

Category

Antibacterial (ophthalmic).

Indications

Accepted

Bacterial conjunctivitis (treatment)—Moxifloxacin solution is indicated for the treatment of bacterial conjunctivitis caused by susceptible strains of the following organisms: *Corynebacterium species, Micrococcus luteus, Staphylococcus aureus, Staphylococcus epidermidis, Staphylococcus haemolyticus, Staphylococcus hominis, Staphylococcus warneri, Streptococcus pneumoniae, Streptococcus viridans group* (aerobic gram-positive microorganisms), *Acinetobacter lwoffii, Haemophilus influenzae, Haemophilus parainfluenzae* (aerobic gram-negative microorganisms), *Chlamydia trachomatis* (other microorganisms).

Pharmacology/Pharmacokinetics

Physicochemical characteristics

Chemical Group—Quinolone
pH—Approximately 6.8

Mechanism of action/Effect

Moxifloxacin is an 8-methoxy fluoroquinolone with a diazabicyclononyl ring at the C7 position. The antibacterial action of moxifloxacin results from inhibition of the topoisomerase II (DNA gyrase) and topoisomerase IV. DNA gyrase is an essential enzyme that is involved in the replication, transcription and repair of bacterial DNA. Topoisomerase IV is an enzyme known to play a key role in the partitioning of the chromosomal DNA during bacterial cell division. The mechanism of action for quinolones, including moxifloxacin, is different from that of macrolides, aminoglycosides, or tetracyclines. Therefore, moxifloxacin may be active against pathogens that are resistant to these antibiotics and these antibiotics may be active against pathogens that are resistant to moxifloxacin. There is no cross-resistance between moxifloxacin and the aforementioned classes of antibiotics. Cross resistance has been observed between systemic moxifloxacin and some other quinolones. *In vitro* resistance to moxifloxacin develops via multiple-step mutations. Resistance to moxifloxacin occurs *in vitro* at a general frequency of between 1.8×10^{-9} to $< 1 \times 10^{-11}$ for Gram-positive bacteria.

Absorption
AUC: 45 ng/mL/hr

The AUC values were 1,000 times lower than the mean AUC reported after max therapeutic 400 mg oral doses of moxifloxacin.

Half-life
Plasma: 13 hours

Peak plasma concentration:
Steady-state C_{max}: 2.7 ng/mL

C_{max} values were 1,600 times lower than the mean C_{max} reported after therapeutic 400 mg oral doses of moxifloxacin.

Precautions to Consider

Cross-sensitivity and/or related problems
Patients allergic to one quinolone may be allergic to other quinolones, including moxifloxacin

Carcinogenicity/Mutagenicity
Long-term studies in animals to determine the carcinogenic potential of moxifloxacin have not been performed. However, in an accelerated study with initiators and promoters, moxifloxacin was not carcinogenic in rats following up to 38 weeks of oral dosing at 500 mg/kg/day (approximately 21,700 times the highest recommended total daily human ophthalmic dose for a 50 kg person, on a mg/kg basis).

Moxifloxacin was not mutagenic in four bacterial strains used in the Ames *Salmonella* reversion assay. As with other quinolones, the positive response observed with moxifloxacin in strain TA 102 using the same assay may be due to the inhibition of DNA gyrase. Moxifloxacin was not mutagenic in the CHO/HGPRT mammalian cell gene mutation assay. An equivocal result was obtained in the same assay when v79 cells were used. Moxifloxacin was clastogenic in the v79 chromosome aberration assay, but it did not induce unscheduled DNA synthesis in cultured rat hepatocytes. There was no evidence of genotoxicity *in vivo* in a micronucleus test or a dominant lethal test in mice.

Pregnancy/Reproduction
Fertility—Moxifloxacin had no effect on fertility in male and female rats at oral doses as high as 500 mg/kg/day, approximately 21,700 times the highest recommended total daily human ophthalmic dose. At 500 mg/kg orally there were slight effects on sperm morphology (head-tail separation) in male rats and on the estrous cycle in female rats.

Pregnancy—Adequate and well-controlled studies in pregnant women have not been done. Moxifloxacin solution should be used during pregnancy only if the potential benefit justifies the potential risk to the fetus.

Moxifloxacin was not teratogenic when administered to pregnant rats during organogenesis at oral doses as high as 500 mg/kg/day (approximately 21,700 times the highest recommended total daily human ophthalmic dose); however, decreased fetal body weights and slightly delayed fetal skeletal development were observed. There was no evidence of teratogenicity when pregnant Cynomolgus monkeys were given oral doses as high as 100 mg/kg/day (approximately 4,300 times the highest recommended total daily human ophthalmic dose). An increased incidence of smaller fetuses was observed at 100 mg/kg/day.

FDA Pregnancy Category C

Breast-feeding
It is not known whether moxifloxacin is distributed into human milk, however it can be presumed that some will be present. Caution should be exercised when moxifloxacin solution is administered to a nursing mother.

Pediatrics
Appropriate studies on the relationship of age to the effects of moxifloxacin have not been performed in the pediatric population. The safety and effectiveness of moxifloxacin solution in infants below 1 year of age have not been established.

There is no evidence that the ophthalmic administration of moxifloxacin has any effect on weight bearing joints, even though oral administration of some quinolones has been shown to cause arthropathy in immature animals.

Geriatrics
Appropriate studies on the relationship of age to the effects of moxifloxacin have not been performed in the geriatric population. No geriatrics specific problems have been reported to date and no overall differences in safety and effectiveness have been observed between elderly and younger patients.

Drug interactions and/or related problems
The following drug interactions and/or related problems have been selected on the basis of their potential clinical significance (possible mechanism in parentheses where appropriate)—not necessarily inclusive (» = major clinical significance):

Drug-drug interaction studies have not been conducted with moxifloxacin solution. *In vitro* studies indicate that moxifloxacin does not inhibit CYP3A4, CYP2D6, CYP2C9, CYP2C19, or CYP1A2 indicating that moxifloxacin is unlikely to alter the pharmacokinetics of drugs metabolized by these cytochrome P450 isozymes.

Medical considerations/Contraindications
The medical considerations/contraindications included have been selected on the basis of their potential clinical significance (reasons given in parentheses where appropriate)—not necessarily inclusive (» = major clinical significance).

Except under special circumstances, this medication should not be used when the following medical problem exists:

» Moxifloxacin solution is contraindicated in patients with a history of hypersensitivity to moxifloxacin, to other quinolones, or to any of the components in this medication.

Side/Adverse Effects
The following side/adverse effects have been selected on the basis of their potential clinical significance (possible signs and symptoms in parentheses where appropriate)—not necessarily inclusive:

In patients receiving systemically administered quinolones, including moxifloxacin, serious and occasionally fatal hypersensitivity (anaphylactic) reactions have been reported, some following the first dose. Some reactions were accompanied by cardiovascular collapse, loss of consciousness, angioedema (including laryngeal, pharyngeal or facial edema), airway obstruction, dyspnea, urticaria, and itching. If an allergic reaction to moxifloxacin occurs, discontinue use of the drug. Serious acute hypersensitivity reactions may require immediate emergency treatment. Oxygen and airway management should be administered as clinically indicated.

Those indicating need for medical attention
Incidence unknown

Hypersensitivity reactions (fainting or loss of consciousness; fast or irregular breathing; swelling of eyes or eyelids; trouble in breathing; tightness in chest, and/or wheezing; skin rash; itching)

Those indicating need for medical attention only if they continue or are bothersome
Incidence more frequent

Conjunctivitis (redness; pain; swelling of eye, eyelid, or inner lining of eyelid; burning, dry or itching eyes; discharge; excessive tearing); ***decreased visual acuity*** (decreased vision); ***dry eye; keratitis*** (eye redness, irritation, or pain); ***ocular discomfort*** (pain in eye); ***ocular hyperemia*** (redness of eye); ***ocular pain; ocular pruritus*** (itching of the eye); ***subconjunctival hemorrhage*** (decreased vision or any change in vision); ***tearing***

Incidence less frequent

Fever; increased cough; infection (fever or chills; cough or hoarseness; lower back or side pain; painful or difficult urination); ***otitis media*** (decreased hearing; fever; general body discomfort; rubbing or pulling of the ears (in children); and vomiting and diarrhea (in infants); sore throat); ***pharyngitis*** (body aches or pain; congestion; cough; dryness or soreness of throat; fever; hoarseness; runny nose; tender, swollen glands in neck; trouble in swallowing; voice changes); ***rash; rhinitis*** (runny nose)

Overdose
For more information on the management of overdose or unintentional ingestion, **contact a poison control center** (see *Poison Control Center Listing*).

Patient Consultation
As an aid to patient consultation, refer to *Advice for the Patient, Moxifloxacin (Systemic).*

In providing consultation, consider emphasizing the following selected information (» = major clinical significance):

Before using this medication

» Conditions affecting use, especially:

Hypersensitivity to moxifloxacin, to other quinolones, or to other components in this medication.

Pregnancy—Use is not recommended in pregnant women

Breast-feeding—Use is not recommended in nursing mothers

Use in children—Safety and efficacy have not been established in pediatric patients under one year of age.

Drug-drug interaction studies have not been conducted.

Proper use of this medication

» Proper dosing

Missed dose: Using as soon as possible; not using if almost time for next scheduled dose; not doubling doses

Proper storage

Preventing contamination: Not touching applicator tip to any surface, or the eye.

Not wearing contact lenses if signs and symptoms of bacterial conjunctivitis are present.

Precautions while using this medication

Potential for allergic reaction. Discontinue immediately and contact your doctor at the first sign of a rash or allergic reaction.

General Dosing Information

For ophthalmic dosing forms:

Not for injection. Moxifloxacin solution should not be injected subconjunctivally, nor should it be introduced directly into the anterior chamber of the eye.

As with other anti-infectives, prolonged use may result in overgrowth of non-susceptible organisms, including fungi. If superinfection occurs, discontinue use and institute alternative therapy. Whenever clinical judgment dictates, the patient should be examined with the aid of magnification, such as slit-lamp biomicroscopy, and, where appropriate, fluorescein staining. Patients should be advised not to wear contact lenses if they have signs and symptoms of bacterial conjunctivitis.

Avoid contaminating the applicator tip with material from the eye, fingers or other source.

Systemically administered quinolones, including moxifloxacin, have been associated with hypersensitivity reactions, even following a single dose. Discontinue use immediately and contact your physician at the first sign of a rash or allergic reaction.

Treatment of adverse events

If an allergic reaction to moxifloxacin occurs, discontinue use of the drug. Serious acute hypersensitivity reactions may require immediate emergency treatment. Oxygen and airway management should be administered as clinically indicated.

Ophthalmic Dosage Forms

MOXIFLOXACIN HYDROCHLORIDE OPHTHALMIC SOLUTION

Usual adult dose

Bacterial conjunctivitis—

Topical, to the conjunctiva, one drop three times a day in the affected eye for 7 days.

Usual pediatric dose

See *Usual adult dose* for pediatric patients one year of age and older.

Usual geriatric dose

See *Usual adult dose.*

Strength(s) usually available

U.S.—

0.05% (5 mg base (Rx) [*Vigamox* (may also contain hydrochloric acid/sodium hydroxide; boric acid; sodium chloride; purified water)].

Canada—

Not commercially available.

Packaging and storage

Store at 2°C to 25°C (36°F to 77°F).

Auxiliary labeling

- For the eye
- Do not touch or contaminate the tip of the container
- Keep out of reach of children
- Continue medicine for full time of treatment

Developed: 04/14/2004

MUMPS VIRUS VACCINE LIVE Systemic

VA CLASSIFICATION (Primary): IM100

Note: This monograph is specific for the sterile lyophilized preparation of the Jeryl Lynn (B level) strain of mumps virus grown in cell cultures of chick embryo.

Commonly used brand name(s): *Mumpsvax*.

Note: For a listing of dosage forms and brand names by country availability, see *Dosage Forms* section(s).

Category

Immunizing agent (active).

Indications

General Considerations

Persons generally can be considered immune to mumps only if they have documentation of adequate immunization with mumps vaccine on or after their first birthdays, if they have laboratory evidence of mumps immunity, or if they have a physician's diagnosis of mumps infection.

Most individuals born before 1957 can generally be considered immune to mumps because of probable previous infection. However, birth before 1957 provides only presumptive evidence of immunity, mumps can occur in some persons born before 1957.

Although serologic tests may be conducted to determine the susceptibility of persons with unknown immunity, studies have not indicated an increased risk of adverse reactions from live mumps vaccinations in persons already immune to mumps.

The combined measles, mumps, and rubella virus vaccine live should be used for vaccinating individuals who are likely to be susceptible to more than one of these viruses, unless otherwise contraindicated.

Children vaccinated with mumps virus vaccine live at less than 12 months of age should be revaccinated. Based on available evidence, there is no reason to routinely revaccinate persons who were vaccinated originally when 12 months of age or older. However, persons should be revaccinated if there is evidence to suggest that the initial immunization was ineffective.

Accepted

Mumps (prophylaxis)—Mumps virus vaccine live is indicated for immunization against mumps. The main objective of mumps immunization is to prevent complications, such as orchitis, which may occur in up to 20% of postpubescent and adult males infected with mumps virus, and meningoencephalitis, which may occur in up to 15% of persons infected with mumps virus. In addition, mumps infection during the first trimester of pregnancy may increase the rate of spontaneous abortion.

Unless otherwise contraindicated, all susceptible persons 12 months of age or older should be immunized against mumps, including:

- Children 12 months of age and older. All children 12 months of age and older should receive mumps virus vaccine live, preferably as the combined measles, mumps, and rubella virus vaccine live, as part of the routine childhood immunization schedule. Infants less than 12 months of age may retain maternal mumps-neutralizing antibodies that may interfere with the immune response to mumps virus vaccine live. Therefore, children vaccinated when less than 12 months of age should be revaccinated.
- International travelers. Persons without evidence of mumps immunity who travel abroad should be vaccinated against mumps because mumps is endemic throughout most of the world. These persons should receive either a single-antigen vaccine or a combined-antigen vaccine as appropriate prior to international travel. However, the combined measles, mumps, and rubella virus vaccine live is preferred for persons likely to be susceptible to more than one of these viruses; if a single-antigen mumps vaccine is not readily available, travelers should receive measles, mumps, and rubella virus vaccine live regardless of their immune status to measles and rubella.

Pharmacology/Pharmacokinetics

Mechanism of action/Effect

Following subcutaneous injection, mumps vaccine produces a modified, noncommunicable mumps infection and provides active immunity to mumps.

Protective effect

A single injection of the vaccine has been shown to induce mumps-neutralizing antibodies in approximately 97% of susceptible children and approximately 93% of susceptible adults. The pattern of antibody response closely resembles that observed following natural mumps.

Duration of protective effect

Although the antibody level following mumps virus vaccination is significantly lower than that attained following natural infection, it provides long lasting protection against the disease. Vaccine-induced antibody levels have been shown to persist for at least 15 years with a rate of decline comparable to that seen in natural infection. If the pattern of comparable immunity continues, permanent immunity following vaccination may be expected. Continued surveillance will be required to demonstrate this.

Precautions to Consider

Note: In the past, persons with a history of anaphylactic reaction following egg ingestion were considered to be at increased risk for serious reactions after receipt of mumps-containing vaccines, which are produced in chick embryo fibroblasts. Protocols requiring caution were developed for skin testing and vaccinating these persons. However, the predictive value of such skin testing and the need for special protocols when vaccinating egg-allergic persons with mumps-containing vaccines is uncertain. The results of recent studies suggest that anaphylactic reactions to mumps-containing vaccines are not associated with hypersensitivity to egg antigens but with some other component of the vaccines. The risk for serious allergic reaction to these vaccines in egg-allergic patients is extremely low, and skin testing is not necessarily predictive of vaccine hypersensitivity.

Pregnancy/Reproduction

Pregnancy—Although mumps virus vaccine live has been shown to infect the placenta and fetus, there is no evidence that it causes congenital malformations in humans. However, because of the theoretical risk of fetal damage, it is important to avoid giving live virus vaccines to pregnant women. Live mumps vaccine, when combined with rubella virus vaccine live, should not be administered to women known to be pregnant or who are considering becoming pregnant within the next 3 months. Women vaccinated with monovalent mumps virus vaccine live should avoid becoming pregnant for 30 days after the vaccination. Routine precautions for vaccinating postpubertal women include asking if they are or may be pregnant, excluding those who say they are, and explaining the theoretical risk to those who plan to receive the vaccine.

Studies have not been done in animals.

FDA Pregnancy Category C.

Breast-feeding

It is not known whether mumps virus vaccine live is distributed into breast milk. However, problems in humans have not been documented.

Pediatrics

Mumps vaccination is a part of routine childhood immunization. Therefore, children 12 months of age and older should receive the combined measles, mumps, and rubella virus vaccine instead of a single-antigen vaccine. Children who received monovalent mumps virus vaccine live rather than combined measles, mumps, and rubella virus vaccine live on or after their first birthdays also should receive a primary dose of measles and rubella virus vaccines. The American Academy of Pediatrics (AAP) and the Advisory Committee on Immunization Practices (ACIP) recommend that all children receive a second dose of measles-containing vaccine (preferably as the combined measles, mumps, and rubella virus vaccine live). Doses of the combined measles, mumps, and rubella virus vaccine live or other measles-containing vaccines should be separated by at least 1 month.

Children with end-stage renal disease receiving maintenance hemodialysis have a degree of immunosuppression that reduces their response to vaccination. One small trial showed that only 50% of these vaccinated children developed mumps antibodies. Therefore, it may be necessary to monitor postvaccination antibody levels in children with end-stage renal disease, and to revaccinate those children who have failed to demonstrate seroconversion.

Drug interactions and/or related problems

The following drug interactions and/or related problems have been selected on the basis of their potential clinical significance (possible mechanism in parentheses where appropriate)—not necessarily inclusive (» = major clinical significance):

Note: Combinations containing any of the following medications, depending on the amount present, may also interact with this medication.

Blood products or
Immune globulins
(concurrent administration with mumps virus vaccine live may interfere with the patient's immune response to the virus because of the possibility of antibodies to mumps virus in these products. Mumps virus vaccine live should be administered at least 14 days before, or more than 3 months after, administration of blood products or immune globulins)

» Corticosteroids or
» Immunosuppressive agents or
» Radiation therapy
(because normal defense mechanisms are suppressed, concurrent use with mumps virus vaccine live may potentiate the replication of the vaccine virus, may increase the side/adverse effects of the vaccine virus, and/or may decrease the patient's antibody response to mumps virus vaccine live. The interval between discontinuation of medications that cause immunosuppression and restoration of the patient's ability to respond to mumps virus vaccine live depends on the intensity and type of immunosuppression-causing medication used, the underlying disease, and other factors; estimates vary from 3 months to 1 year. Patients with leukemia in remission should not receive mumps virus vaccine live until at least 3 months after their last chemotherapy. This precaution does not apply to corticosteroids used as replacement therapy, for short-term [less than 2 weeks] systemic therapy, or by other routes of administration that do not cause immunosuppression)

Live virus vaccines, other
(data are lacking on impairment of antibody responses to rubella, measles, mumps, or oral poliovirus vaccine [OPV] when these vaccines are administered on different days within 1 month of each other; however, OPV and measles, mumps, and rubella virus vaccine live [or its individual component vaccines] can be administered at any time before, with, or after each other, if indicated)

Laboratory value alterations

The following have been selected on the basis of their potential clinical significance (possible effect in parentheses where appropriate)—not necessarily inclusive (» = major clinical significance).

With diagnostic test results
Tuberculin skin test
(short-term suppression of tuberculin skin test results lasting several weeks may occur, which may yield false-negative results; if required, tuberculin skin tests should be administered before, simultaneously with, or at least 4 to 6 weeks after administration of mumps virus vaccine live)

Medical considerations/Contraindications

The medical considerations/contraindications included have been selected on the basis of their potential clinical significance (reasons given in parentheses where appropriate)—not necessarily inclusive (» = major clinical significance).

Except under special circumstances, this medication should not be used when the following medical problems exist:

» Febrile illness, severe
(the decision to administer or delay vaccination because of current or recent febrile illness depends largely on the cause of the illness and the severity of symptoms; minor illnesses, such as upper respiratory infection, do not preclude administration of the vaccine; for persons whose compliance with medical care cannot be assured, every opportunity should be taken to provide appropriate vaccination)
(children with moderate or severe febrile illnesses can be vaccinated as soon as they have recovered from the acute phase of the illness; this wait avoids superimposing adverse effects of vaccination on the underlying illness or mistakenly attributing a manifestation of the underlying illness to the vaccine; routine physical examinations or measurements of temperatures are not prerequisites for vaccinating infants and children who appear to be in good health; asking the parent or guardian if the child is ill, postponing vaccination for children with moderate or severe febrile illnesses, and vaccinating those without contraindications are appropriate procedures in childhood immunization programs)

» Immune deficiency conditions, congenital or hereditary, family history of, or

» Immune deficiency conditions, primary or acquired
(replications of live vaccine viruses can be enhanced in persons with immunodeficiency diseases and in persons with immunosuppression, as occurs with leukemia, lymphoma, generalized malignancy, or therapy with alkylating agents, antimetabolites, radiation, or large doses of corticosteroids)
(patients with leukemia in remission who have not received chemotherapy for at least 3 months may receive live-virus vaccines; the exact amount of systemically absorbed corticosteroids and the duration of administration needed to suppress the immune system of an otherwise healthy child are not well defined; most experts agree that short term [i.e., less than 2 weeks], low- to moderate-dose corticosteroid therapy, or long-term alternate-day treatment with short-acting preparations, maintenance physiologic doses [replacement therapy], or administration of corticosteroids topically [skin or eyes], by aerosol, or by intra-articular, bursal, or tendon injection usually does not contraindicate administration of live virus vaccine; although a theoretical concern has been raised, no evidence of increased severe reactions to live vaccines has been reported among persons receiving corticosteroid therapy by aerosol, and such therapy is not in itself a reason to delay vaccination)
(the immunosuppressive effects of corticosteroid treatment vary with its dosage, but many clinicians consider a dose equivalent to either 2 mg per kg of body weight (mg/kg) or a total of 20 mg per day of prednisone sufficiently immunosuppressive to raise concern about the safety of vaccination with live virus vaccines; corticosteroids used in greater-than-physiologic doses also can reduce the immune response to vaccines; physicians should wait at least 3 months after discontinuation of therapy to administer a live-virus vaccine in patients who have received systemically absorbed high doses of corticosteroids for ≥ 2 weeks)

Risk-benefit should be considered when the following medical problems exist:

Allergy to neomycin
(patients allergic to systemic or topical neomycin may be allergic to the mumps virus vaccine live because each 0.5-mL vaccine dose contains approximately 25 mcg of neomycin, which is used in the production of the vaccine to prevent bacterial overgrowth in the viral culture. A history of hypersensitivity reactions, such as delayed-type allergic reaction (contact dermatitis) to neomycin, generally does not preclude immunization. However, a history of anaphylaxis due to topically or systemically administered neomycin precludes immunization with this vaccine)

Allergy to gelatin
(patients allergic to gelatin also may be allergic to mumps virus vaccine live, since gelatin is used as a stabilizer in the production of the vaccine The literature records a single case report of a person with an anaphylactic sensitivity to gelatin having an anaphylactic reaction after receipt of the combined measles, mumps, and rubella virus vaccine licensed in the U.S; similar cases have been reported in Japan. Therefore, such persons should be vaccinated with the combined measles, mumps and rubella virus vaccine and its component vaccines with extreme caution)

Thrombocytopenia or vaccine-associated thrombocytopenia
(persons who experienced thrombocytopenia with the first dose of vaccine may develop thrombocytopenia with additional doses. These persons should be tested serologically to determine the need for additional doses of vaccine. The risk-benefit ratio should be evaluated before vaccination is considered in such cases)

Sensitivity to mumps virus vaccine live

Side/Adverse Effects

Note: In field trials before licensure, illness did not occur more frequently in vaccinees than in unvaccinated controls. Illnesses reported following mumps virus vaccination have been mainly episodes of parotitis and low-grade fever. Allergic reactions including rash, pruritus, and purpura have been temporally associated with mumps vaccination, but are uncommon and usually mild and of brief duration. The reported occurrence of encephalitis within 30 days of receipt of a mumps-containing vaccine (0.4 instances per million doses) was not greater than the observed background incidence rate of central nervous system (CNS) dysfunction in the general population. No association has been established between mumps virus vaccination and pancreatic damage or subsequent development of diabetes mellitus.

The following side/adverse effects have been selected on the basis of their potential clinical significance (possible signs and symptoms in parentheses where appropriate)—not necessarily inclusive:

Those indicating need for medical attention

Incidence rare

Anaphylactic reaction (difficulty in breathing or swallowing; hives; itching, especially of feet or hands; reddening of skin, especially around ears; swelling of eyes, face, or inside of nose; unusual tiredness or weakness, sudden and severe); ***encephalitis or meningoencephalitis*** (confusion; severe or continuing headache; irritability; stiff neck; or vomiting); ***fever over 39.4 °C (103 °F); orchitis in postpubescent and adult males*** (pain, tenderness, or swelling in testicles and scrotum); ***thrombocytopenic purpura*** (bruising or purple spots on skin)

Those indicating need for medical attention only if they continue or are bothersome

Incidence more frequent

Burning or stinging at injection site—due to acid pH of vaccine

Incidence less frequent or rare

Delayed-type, cell-mediated, allergic reaction (itching, swelling, redness, tenderness or hard lump at place of injection); ***fever of 37.7 °C (100 °F) or less; parotitis*** (swollen glands on side of face or neck); ***skin rash***

Patient Consultation

As an aid to patient consultation, refer to *Advice for the Patient, Mumps Virus Vaccine Live (Systemic).*

In providing consultation, consider emphasizing the following selected information (» = major clinical significance):

Before receiving this vaccine

» Conditions affecting use, especially:
Sensitivity to mumps virus vaccine live or allergy to gelatin or neomycin
Pregnancy—Use of mumps virus vaccine live during pregnancy or pregnancy within 30 days of immunization is not recommended
Use in children—Use is not recommended for infants up to 12 months of age
Other medications, especially immunosuppressive agents or radiation therapy
Other medical problems, especially severe febrile illness; primary or acquired immune deficiency conditions; or family history of congenital or hereditary immune deficiency conditions

Proper use of this medication

Waiting at least 14 days after receiving vaccine before receiving blood products or immune globulins
Waiting at least 3 months after administration of blood products or immune globulins before receiving vaccine
» Proper dosing

Precautions after receiving this vaccine

» Not becoming pregnant for 3 months after receiving rubella and mumps virus vaccine live or 30 days after receiving monovalent mumps virus vaccine live without first checking with physician, because of possible problems during pregnancy
Checking with physician before receiving tuberculin skin test within 4 to 6 weeks of this vaccine, since the results of the test may be affected by mumps vaccine

Side/adverse effects

Signs of potential side effects, especially anaphylactic reaction, encephalitis or meningoencephalitis, fever over 39.4 °C, orchitis in postpubescent and adult males, or thrombocytopenic purpura

General Dosing Information

The American Academy of Pediatrics (AAP) and the Advisory Committee on Immunization Practices (ACIP) recommend that all children 12 to 15 months of age receive two doses of measles, mumps, and rubella virus vaccine live. Children who received monovalent mumps virus vaccine live rather than the combined measles, mumps, and rubella virus vaccine live on or after their first birthdays also should receive a primary dose of measles and rubella virus vaccines. Doses of the combined measles, mumps, and rubella virus vaccine live or other measles-containing vaccines should be separated by at least 1 month.

The dosage of mumps vaccine is the same for both children and adults.

When sterilizing syringes before vaccination, care should be taken to avoid preservatives, antiseptics, detergents, and disinfectants, since the vaccine virus is easily inactivated by these substances.

To prevent inactivation of the vaccine, it is recommended that only the diluent provided by the manufacturer be used.

A 25-gauge, 5/8th-inch needle is recommended for administration of the vaccine.

Mumps vaccine is administered subcutaneously. While not routinely recommended, intramuscular administration is considered effective and safe also. The vaccine should not be injected intravenously.

Although measles, mumps, and rubella vaccines are commercially available as a combination vaccine (measles, mumps, and rubella virus vaccine live) and, as such, are administered as a single injection, the commercially available individual vaccines should not be mixed in the same syringe or administered at the same body site.

ACIP continues to recommend measles, mumps, and rubella virus vaccine live for human immunodeficiency virus (HIV)-infected persons without evidence of immunity to these viruses. Because the immunologic response to both live and killed antigen vaccines may decrease as HIV disease progresses, vaccination early in the course of HIV infection may be more likely to induce an immune response. Therefore, HIV-infected infants without severe immunosuppression should receive measles, mumps, and rubella virus vaccine live as soon as possible upon reaching their first birthday. Evaluation and testing of asymptomatic persons to identify HIV infection are not necessary before deciding to administer measles, mumps, and rubella virus vaccine live.

In general, simultaneous administration of the most widely used live and inactivated vaccines does not impair antibody responses or increase rates of adverse effects. Vaccines recommended for administration at 12 to 15 months of age can be administered at either one or two visits. There are equivalent antibody responses and no clinically significant increases in frequency of adverse events when diphtheria toxoid, tetanus toxoid, and pertussis vaccine (DTP); measles, mumps, and rubella virus vaccine live; oral poliovirus vaccine (OPV) or inactivated poliovirus vaccine (IPV); and *Haemophilus influenzae* type b conjugate vaccine (HbCV) are administered either simultaneously at different sites or at separate times. If a child might not be brought back for future vaccinations, all vaccines (including DTP [or DTaP]; measles, mumps, and rubella virus vaccine live; OPV [or IPV]; varicella; HbCV; and hepatitis B vaccines) may be administered simultaneously, as appropriate to the child's age and previous vaccination status.

For treatment of adverse effects

Recommended treatment includes:

- For mild hypersensitivity reaction—Administering antihistamines, and, if necessary, corticosteroids.
- For severe hypersensitivity or anaphylactic reaction—Administering epinephrine. Antihistamines or corticosteroids also may be administered as required.

Parenteral Dosage Forms

MUMPS VIRUS VACCINE LIVE (FOR INJECTION) USP

Usual adult and adolescent dose

Immunizing agent (active)—

Subcutaneous, 0.5 mL, preferably into the outer aspect of the upper arm.

Usual pediatric dose

Immunizing agent (active)—

Infants up to 12 months of age: Use is not recommended.

Infants and children 12 months of age and older: See *Usual adult and adolescent dose*.

Strength(s) usually available

U.S.—

Not less than the equivalent of 20,000 median tissue culture infective doses [$TCID_{50}$] of the U.S. Reference Mumps Virus in each 0.5-mL dose (Rx) [*Mumpsvax* (neomycin 25 mcg)].

Canada—

Not less than the equivalent of 5000 median tissue culture infective doses [$TCID_{50}$] of the U.S. Reference Mumps Virus in each 0.5-mL dose (Rx) [*Mumpsvax* (neomycin 17.5 mcg)].

Packaging and storage

Store the lyophilized form of the vaccine, the diluent, and the reconstituted form of the vaccine between 2 and 8 °C (36 and 46 °F), unless otherwise specified by the manufacturer.

Alternatively, the diluent for the single-dose vials only may be stored between 15 and 30 °C (59 and 86 °F).

Protect both the lyophilized form and the reconstituted form of the vaccine from light.

Preparation of dosage form

To reconstitute, use only the diluent provided by the manufacturer, since it is free of preservatives or other substances that might inactivate the vaccine.

Single-dose vial—Withdraw the entire volume of diluent (approximately 0.5 mL) into the syringe. Inject all the diluent in the syringe into the vial of lyophilized vaccine and agitate to mix thoroughly. Withdraw the entire contents into the syringe and inject the total volume of restored vaccine subcutaneously.

10-dose vial (in U.S., available only to government agencies/institutions)—Withdraw the entire contents (7 mL) of the diluent vial into the syringe to be used for reconstitution. Inject all of the diluent in the syringe into the 10-dose vial of lyophilized vaccine and agitate to mix thoroughly. The 10-dose container can be used with either syringes or a jet injector. Since the vaccine and diluent do not contain preservatives, special care should be taken to prevent contamination of the multiple-dose vial of vaccine. In addition, the vial should be stored properly until the reconstituted vaccine is used. Discard unused vaccine after 8 hours.

50-dose vial (in U.S., available only to government agencies/institutions)—Withdraw the entire contents (30 mL) of the diluent vial into the syringe to be used for reconstitution. Inject all of the diluent in the syringe into the 50-dose vial of lyophilized vaccine and agitate to mix thoroughly. The 50-dose container is designed to be used only with a jet injector. Since the vaccine and diluent do not contain preservatives, special care should be taken to prevent contamination of the multiple-dose vial of vaccine. In addition, the vial should be stored properly until the reconstituted vaccine is used. Discard unused vaccine after 8 hours.

Stability

Both the lyophilized and reconstituted vaccine should be stored between 2 and 8 °C (36 and 46 °F) and protected from light. Improper storage and protection may inactivate the virus.

Use the reconstituted vaccine as soon as possible. Discard unused reconstituted vaccine after 8 hours.

The reconstituted vaccine is clear yellow. It should not be used if it is discolored.

Incompatibilities

Preservatives or other substances may inactivate the vaccine; therefore, only the diluent supplied by the manufacturer should be used for reconstitution.

A sterile syringe free of preservatives, antiseptics, disinfectants, and detergents should be used for each injection and/or reconstitution of the vaccine because these substances may inactivate the live virus vaccine.

Auxiliary labeling

- Protect from light.
- Store in refrigerator.
- Discard reconstituted vaccine if not used within 8 hours.

Note

The date and time of reconstitution should be indicated on the vial if the reconstituted vaccine is not used at once.

Revised: 07/23/1997

MUPIROCIN Nasal

VA CLASSIFICATION (Primary): NT900

Commonly used brand name(s): *Bactroban Nasal*.

Note: For a listing of dosage forms and brand names by country availability, see *Dosage Forms* section(s).

Category

Antibacterial (nasal).

Indications

Accepted

Staphylococcus aureus, methicillin-resistant (treatment)—Intranasal mupirocin calcium is indicated for the eradication of nasal colonization with methicillin-resistant *S. aureus* in adult patients and health care workers as part of a comprehensive infection control program to reduce the risk of infection among patients at high risk of methicillin-resistant *S. aureus* infection during institutional outbreaks of infections with this pathogen.

In clinical trials, more than 90% of persons treated with intranasal mupirocin had eradication of nasal colonization 2 to 4 days after completion of therapy, as compared with 5 to 30% of persons administered the vehicle only. In one study, recolonization in approximately 30% of patients was reported within 4 weeks after completion of therapy as compared with 85 to 100% cases of recolonization with administration of the vehicle only.

Acceptance not established

There are insufficient data to establish that intranasal mupirocin calcium is safe and effective as part of an intervention program to prevent autoinfection of high-risk patients from their own nasal colonization with *S. aureus*.

There are insufficient data to recommend use of intranasal mupirocin calcium for general prophylaxis of any infection in any patient population.

Unaccepted

The safety and efficacy of using intranasal mupirocin calcium for more than 5 days have not been established. There are no human clinical or animal data to support the use of this product for more than 5 days or in ways not described in this monograph.

Pharmacology/Pharmacokinetics

Physicochemical characteristics

Source—Produced by fermentation of *Pseudomonas fluorescens*.

Molecular weight—
Mupirocin calcium: 1075.36.
Mupirocin free acid: 500.6.

Mechanism of action/Effect

Mupirocin inhibits bacterial protein synthesis by reversibly and specifically binding to bacterial isoleucyl transfer-RNA synthetase. Because of this process, mupirocin does not demonstrate *in vitro* cross-resistance with other classes of antimicrobial agents.

The type of mupirocin resistance that may occur appears to result from the production of a modified isoleucyl transfer-RNA synthetase. High-level plasmid-mediated resistance (minimum inhibitory concentration [MIC] > 1024 mcg per mL) has been reported in some strains of *Staphylococcus aureus* and coagulase-negative staphylococci.

Mupirocin is bactericidal at concentrations achieved by topical intranasal administration. However, the minimum bactericidal concentration (MBC) against relevant intranasal pathogens is generally eightfold to thirtyfold higher than the MIC. In addition, mupirocin is highly protein-bound, and the effect of nasal secretions on the MIC of intranasal mupirocin has not been determined.

Mupirocin has been shown to be active against most strains of methicillin-resistant *S. aureus*, both *in vitro* and in clinical studies of the eradication of nasal colonization.

Absorption

Repeated intranasal applications of 0.2 gram of mupirocin calcium ointment three times a day for 3 days to five adult males resulted in no evidence of systemic absorption of mupirocin. For up to 72 hours after the nasal applications, concentrations of mupirocin in urine and of monic acid in urine and serum were below the limits of determination of the assay. The lower detectable limits of the assay were 50 nanograms per mL of mupirocin in urine, 75 nanograms per mL of monic acid in urine, and 10 nanograms per mL of monic acid in serum. Extrapolation of the detectable limit of the urine assay for monic acid yields a mean of 3.3% (range, 1.2 to 5.1%) of the applied dose that could possibly be absorbed systemically from the nasal mucosa of adults.

Protein binding

Very high (> 97%).

Biotransformation

Mupirocin is rapidly metabolized following intravenous or oral administration. The principal metabolite is monic acid, which has no antibacterial activity.

Half-life

A study of seven men who were administered intravenous mupirocin reported an elimination half-life of 20 to 40 minutes for mupirocin and 30 to 80 minutes for monic acid.

Elimination

Predominately renal as monic acid after intravenous administration of mupirocin.

Precautions to Consider

Carcinogenicity

Long-term animal studies have not been done.

Mutagenicity

The following *in vitro* or *in vivo* tests, using either mupirocin calcium or mupirocin sodium, did not show any mutagenic potential: rat primary hepatocyte unscheduled DNA synthesis, sediment analysis for DNA strand breaks, *Salmonella* reversion test (Ames); *Escherichia coli* mutation assay, metaphase analysis of human lymphocytes, mouse lymphoma assay, and bone marrow micronuclei assay in mice.

Pregnancy/Reproduction

Fertility—No evidence of impaired fertility was found in reproductive studies in rats administered mupirocin sodium subcutaneously at doses that were comparable (on a mg-per-square-meter [mg/m^2] basis) to up to 40 times the human intranasal dose of approximately 20 mg of mupirocin per day.

Pregnancy—Adequate and well-controlled studies in humans have not been done.

No evidence of harm to the fetus was found in reproductive studies in rats and rabbits administered mupirocin (salt not disclosed) subcutaneously at doses that were comparable (on a mg-per-square-meter [mg/m^2] basis) to up to 65 and 130 times, respectively, the human intranasal dose of approximately 20 mg of mupirocin per day.

FDA Pregnancy Category B.

Breast-feeding

It is not known whether mupirocin is distributed into breast milk. However, problems in humans have not been documented.

Pediatrics

Safety and efficacy have not been established. Appropriate studies on the relationship of age to the effects of mupirocin have not been performed in children up to 12 years of age. However, a report of a pharmacokinetic study in neonates and premature infants indicated that significant systemic absorption occurred following administration of intranasal mupirocin.

Geriatrics

Appropriate studies on the relationship of age to the effects of mupirocin have not been performed in the geriatric population. However, no geriatrics-specific problems have been documented to date.

Drug interactions and/or related problems

The following drug interactions and/or related problems have been selected on the basis of their potential clinical significance (possible mechanism in parentheses where appropriate)—not necessarily inclusive (» = major clinical significance):

Note: Combinations containing any of the following medications, depending on the amount present, may also interact with this medication.

» Intranasal products, other
(concurrent use of mupirocin with other intranasal products has not been studied and is not recommended until studies are done)

Medical considerations/Contraindications

The medical considerations/contraindications included have been selected on the basis of their potential clinical significance (reasons given in parentheses where appropriate)—not necessarily inclusive (» = major clinical significance).

Except under special circumstances, this medication should not be used when the following medical problem exists:

» Sensitivity to mupirocin

Side/Adverse Effects

The following side/adverse effects have been selected on the basis of their potential clinical significance (possible signs and symptoms in parentheses where appropriate)—not necessarily inclusive:

Those indicating need for medical attention

Incidence less frequent

Cough; respiratory disorder, including upper respiratory tract congestion (chest congestion)

Incidence rare

Ear pain

Those indicating need for medical attention only if they continue or are bothersome

Incidence more frequent

Headache

Incidence less frequent or rare

Burning or stinging in the nose; pharyngitis (sore throat); ***pruritus*** (itching); ***rhinitis*** (stuffy or runny nose); ***taste perversion*** (change in taste)

Overdose

There was no evidence of systemic absorption following repeated intranasal applications of mupirocin calcium in adults. (See *Absorption*.) In addition, intravenous infusions of 252 mg of mupirocin and single oral doses of 500 mg of mupirocin have been well tolerated in adults.

Patient Consultation

As an aid to patient consultation, refer to *Advice for the Patient, Mupirocin (Nasal)*.

In providing consultation, consider emphasizing the following selected information (» = major clinical significance):

Before using this medication

» Conditions affecting use, especially:
 Sensitivity to mupirocin
 Use in children—Safety and efficacy have not been established in children up to 12 years of age; in addition, a report of a pharmacokinetic study in neonates and premature infants indicated that significant systemic absorption occurred following administration of intranasal mupirocin
 Other medications, especially other intranasal products

Proper use of this medication

» Proper administration: First washing hands; applying approximately one half of the ointment from single-use tube directly from tube into nostril; applying the remainder of ointment directly into other nostril; closing nostrils by pressing sides of nose together and then releasing them repeatedly for approximately 1 minute to help spread medication throughout inside of nostrils; another method is pressing sides of nose together and gently massaging nose; being careful not to touch eyes; discarding tube after using; washing hands afterwards to remove any medication that may be on them

» Proper dosing
 Missed dose: Using as soon as possible; not using if almost time for next dose; not doubling doses

» Proper storage

Precautions while using this medication

» Keeping medication away from eyes; medication may cause severe burning and tearing of eyes that may last days or weeks; contacting physician if this occurs

» Not using any other medication in your nose without checking with physician

» Discontinuing medication and checking with physician if severe nasal irritation occurs

Side/adverse effects

Signs of potential side effects, especially cough; respiratory disorder, including upper respiratory tract congestion; and ear pain

General Dosing Information

The single-use tube should not be reused, but should be discarded immediately after use.

If sensitization or a severe local irritation develops, treatment with mupirocin should be discontinued.

Patients should be cautioned to keep mupirocin away from the eyes. Under test conditions, application of mupirocin nasal ointment to the eye caused severe symptoms, such as burning and tearing, that resolved over days to weeks.

Nasal Dosage Forms

MUPIROCIN CALCIUM NASAL OINTMENT

Usual adult and adolescent dose

Antibacterial, nasal—
 Intranasal, approximately one half of the ointment from a single-use tube applied into each nostril two times a day (morning and evening) for five days.

Usual adult and adolescent prescribing limits

Five days of twice-daily treatment.

Usual pediatric dose

Antibacterial, nasal—
 Children up to 12 years of age: Safety has not been established.
 Children 12 years of age and older: See *Usual adult and adolescent dose*.

Usual geriatric dose

Antibacterial, nasal—
 See *Usual adult and adolescent dose*.

Strength(s) usually available

U.S.—
 2% (Rx) [*Bactroban Nasal* (2.15% w/w mupirocin calcium equivalent to 2% mupirocin free acid; paraffin; glycerin esters mixture [Softisan 649])].

Packaging and storage

Store at or below 25 °C (77 °F). Protect from freezing.

Auxiliary labeling

- For the nose.
- Keep away from eyes.

Developed: 11/04/1997

MUPIROCIN Topical

VA CLASSIFICATION (Primary): DE101

Commonly used brand name(s): *Bactroban*.

Other commonly used names are pseudomonic acid and pseudomonic acid A.

Note: For a listing of dosage forms and brand names by country availability, see *Dosage Forms* section(s).

Category

Antibacterial (topical).

Indications

Note: Bracketed information in the *Indications* section refers to uses that are not included in U.S. product labeling.

Accepted

Impetigo (treatment)—Mupirocin ointment is indicated [alone as a primary agent] in the topical treatment of [localized] impetigo caused by *Staphylococcus aureus* and beta-hemolytic streptococci, including *Streptococcus pyogenes*.

[However, some USP medical experts prefer systemic antibacterials in the treatment of most cases of impetigo.]

[Eczema, infected (treatment)] or
[Folliculitis (treatment)][1]—Mupirocin is used as a primary agent in the topical treatment of localized infected eczema and folliculitis caused by *S. aureus*.

[Skin infections, bacterial, minor (prophylaxis)]—Mupirocin is used in the topical prophylaxis of minor bacterial skin infections.

Skin lesions, secondarily infected, traumatic (treatment)—Mupirocin cream is indicated for the treatment of secondarily infected traumatic skin lesions (up to 10 cm in length or 100 cm^2 in area) due to susceptible strains of *Staphylococcus aureus* and *Streptococcus pyogenes*.

Not all species or strains of a particular organism may be susceptible to mupirocin.

Unaccepted

Mupirocin is not effective against *Enterobacteriaceae, Pseudomonas aeruginosa*, or fungi.

[1]Not included in Canadian product labeling.

Pharmacology/Pharmacokinetics

Physicochemical characteristics

Source—Produced by fermentation of *Pseudomonas fluorescens*.

Chemical Group—Structurally unrelated to other systemic or topical antibacterials.

Molecular weight—500.63.

Mechanism of action/Effect

The mechanism of action is not completely understood. Mupirocin is bacteriostatic at low concentrations and bactericidal at high concentrations. This agent reversibly and specifically binds to bacterial isoleucyl transfer RNA synthetase, thereby inhibiting bacterial protein and RNA synthesis. DNA synthesis and cell wall formation are affected to a lesser extent.

Absorption

Virtually no systemic absorption (< 1.1 nanograms per mL of whole blood) following application to lower arm of normal males with occlusion for 24 hours.

Precautions to Consider

Pregnancy/Reproduction

Fertility—Adequate and well-controlled studies in humans have not been done.

Studies in rats and rabbits given oral, subcutaneous, and intramuscular doses of up to 100 times the human topical dose, have not shown that mupirocin causes impaired fertility.

Pregnancy—Adequate and well-controlled studies in humans have not been done.

Studies in rats and rabbits given oral, subcutaneous, and intramuscular doses of up to 100 times the human topical dose, have not shown that mupirocin causes adverse effects in the fetus.

FDA Pregnancy Category B.

Breast-feeding
It is not known whether mupirocin is distributed into breast milk. However, problems in humans have not been documented. Mupirocin is unlikely to be distributed into breast milk in significant amounts since virtually no systemic absorption occurs following topical administration.

Pediatrics
The safety and effectiveness of *Bactroban Cream* have not been established in children up to 3 months of age.

The safety and effectiveness of *Bactroban Ointment* have not been established in children up to 2 months of age.

Geriatrics
In two studies, 30 patients over 65 years old were treated with *Bactroban Cream* and no overall difference in the efficacy or safety was observed.

Medical considerations/Contraindications
The medical considerations/contraindications included have been selected on the basis of their potential clinical significance (reasons given in parentheses where appropriate)—not necessarily inclusive (» = major clinical significance).

Risk-benefit should be considered when the following medical problem exists:

Sensitivity to mupirocin

Side/Adverse Effects

Note: The polyethylene glycol vehicle in mupirocin ointment may irritate broken skin or mucous membranes.

When mupirocin ointment is applied to extensive open wounds or burns, the possibility of absorption of the polyethylene glycol vehicle, resulting in serious renal toxicity, should be considered.

Mupirocin ointment has not been reported to cause contact sensitization or photosensitivity reactions.

The following side/adverse effects have been selected on the basis of their potential clinical significance (possible signs and symptoms in parentheses where appropriate)—not necessarily inclusive:

Those indicating need for medical attention only if they continue or are bothersome
Incidence less frequent

Dry skin; skin burning, itching, pain, rash, redness, stinging, or swelling; headache; nausea

Incidence rare

Abdominal pain; dizziness; secondary wound infection; ulcerative stomatitis (sores in mouth or on lips)

Patient Consultation

As an aid to patient consultation, refer to *Advice for the Patient, Mupirocin (Topical).*

In providing consultation, consider emphasizing the following selected information (» = major clinical significance):

Proper use of this medication
» Not for ophthalmic use

To use

Before applying, washing affected area(s) with soap and water and drying thoroughly; applying small amount and rubbing in gently

After applying, covering treated area(s) with gauze dressing if desired

» Compliance with full course of therapy

» Proper dosing

Missed dose: Applying as soon as possible; not applying if almost time for next dose

» Proper storage

Precautions while using this medication
Checking with physician or pharmacist if no improvement within 3 to 5 days

General Dosing Information

Topical mupirocin is not for ophthalmic use.

The treated area(s) may be covered with a gauze dressing if desired.

When mupirocin ointment is applied to extensive open wounds or burns, the possibility of absorption of the polyethylene glycol vehicle, resulting in serious renal toxicity, should be considered.

If skin irritation or hypersensitivity develops, treatment with mupirocin ointment should be discontinued.

Patients not showing a clinical response within 3 to 5 days of treatment should be re-evaluated.

Topical Dosage Forms

Note: Bracketed uses in the *Dosage Forms* section refer to categories of use and/or indications that are not included in U.S. product labeling.

MUPIROCIN OINTMENT USP

Usual adult and adolescent dose
Impetigo or

[Eczema, infected] or

[Folliculitis][1]—

Topical, to the affected area(s), three times a day.

Usual pediatric dose
Impetigo—

Children up to 2 months of age: Safety and efficacy have not been established.

Children 2 months to 16 years of age: See *Usual adult and adolescent dose.*

Strength(s) usually available
U.S.—

2% (Rx) [*Bactroban* (polyethylene glycol [PEG] 400; PEG 3350)].

Canada—

2% (OTC) [*Bactroban* (polyethylene glycol [PEG] 400; PEG 3350)].

Packaging and storage
Store between 15 and 30 °C (59 and 86 °F), in a well-closed container, unless otherwise specified by manufacturer. Protect from freezing.

Auxiliary labeling
- For external use only.
- Continue medicine for full time of treatment.

Note
Mupirocin ointment is available in a bland, water-miscible ointment base.

MUPIROCIN CALCIUM CREAM 2%

Usual adult and adolescent dose
Secondarily infected traumatic skin lesion—

Topical, the affected area(s), three times a day for 10 days.

Usual pediatric dose
Secondarily infected traumatic skin lesion—

Children up to 3 months of age: Safety and efficacy have not been established.

Children 3 months to 16 years of age: See *Usual adult and adolescent dose.*

Strength(s) usually available
U.S.—

2% (Rx) [*Bactroban* (benzyl alcohol; cetomacrogol 1000; cetyl alcohol; mineral oil; phenoxyethanol; purified water; stearyl alcohol; xanthan gum)].

Packaging and storage
Store at or below 25° C (77° F). Protect from freezing

Auxiliary labeling
- For external use only.
- Continue medicine for full time of treatment.

Note
Mupirocin cream is available in an oil and water-based emulsion.

[1]Not included in Canadian product labeling.

Selected Bibliography

Rumsfield J. West DP, Aronson IK. Topical mupirocin in the treatment of bacterial skin infections. Drug Intell Clin Pharm 1988 Dec; 20: 943-8.

Parenti MA, Hartfield SM, Leyden JJ. Mupirocin: a topical antibiotic with a unique structure and mechanism of action. Clin Pharm 1987 Oct; 6: 761-70.

Revised: 06/11/2001

MUROMONAB-CD3 Systemic

VA CLASSIFICATION (Primary): IM403

Commonly used brand name(s): *Orthoclone OKT3.*

Note: For a listing of dosage forms and brand names by country availability, see *Dosage Forms* section(s).

Category

Monoclonal antibody; immunosuppressant.

Indications

Accepted

Transplant rejection, organ (treatment)—Muromonab-CD3 is indicated, usually in combination with azathioprine, cyclosporine, and/or corticosteroids, for treatment of acute rejection of renal transplants (allografts). It is also indicated for treatment of steroid-resistant acute rejection of hepatic and cardiac transplants.

Pharmacology/Pharmacokinetics

Mechanism of action/Effect

Muromonab-CD3, a murine monoclonal antibody, reacts with a T3 (CD3) molecule that is linked to an antigen receptor on the surface membrane of human T lymphocytes and thereby blocks both the generation and function of the T cells in response to antigenic challenge. Initially, binding of muromonab-CD3 to T lymphocytes leads to early activation of T cells and subsequent cytokine release; however, ultimately, T cell functions are blocked. Muromonab-CD3 does not cause myelosuppression.

Onset of action

Number of circulating CD3 positive T cells is reduced within minutes after administration.

Time to steady-state serum trough concentration

3 days.

Steady-state trough serum concentration

With dose of 5 mg per day—0.9 mcg per mL.

Duration of action

Number of circulating CD3 positive T cells returns to pretreatment levels, and T cell function returns to normal, within 1 week after muromonab-CD3 is withdrawn.

Precautions to Consider

Cross-sensitivity and/or related problems

Patients sensitive to any product of murine (mouse) origin may also be sensitive to muromonab-CD3. Muromonab-CD3 may induce human anti-mouse antibody production and hypersensitivity in patients.

Carcinogenicity

Studies have not been done in either animals or humans; however, suppression of cell-mediated immunity in organ transplant patients is associated with an increased risk of benign and malignant lymphoproliferative disorders, lymphomas, and skin cancers. Lymphomas have developed in humans treated with muromonab-CD3. Other infrequently reported neoplasms have included multiple myeloma, leukemia, breast carcinoma, adenocarcinoma, cholangiocarcinoma, and recurrences of pre-existing hepatoma and renal cell carcinoma.

Pregnancy/Reproduction

Pregnancy—Studies have not been done in humans. However, muromonab-CD3 is an immunoglobulin G (IgG) antibody that may cross the human placenta; the effect of cytokine release and immunosuppression on the fetus is unknown.

Studies have not been done in animals.

FDA Pregnancy Category C.

Breast-feeding

Problems in humans have not been documented. However, breast-feeding is generally not recommended while muromonab-CD3 is being administered because of the potential risks to the infant (adverse effects, carcinogenicity). It is not known whether muromonab-CD3 is distributed into breast milk.

Pediatrics

Appropriate studies on the relationship of age to the effects of muromonab-CD3 have not been performed in the pediatric population. Muromonab-CD3 has been used in children, with appropriate dosage adjustments. Small children may be at increased risk of dehydration as a result of gastrointestinal fluid loss from diarrhea and/or vomiting with the cytokine release syndrome. The risk of long-term adverse cognitive sequelae to high fever, seizures, central nervous system (CNS) infections, aseptic meningitis, etc., is unknown.

Geriatrics

No information is available on the relationship of age to the effects of muromonab-CD3 in geriatric patients.

Dental

The immunosuppressant effects of muromonab-CD3 may result in an increased incidence of microbial infection and delayed healing. Dental work, whenever possible, should be completed prior to initiation of therapy and undertaken only with great caution during therapy. Patients should be instructed in proper oral hygiene during treatment, including caution in use of regular toothbrushes, dental floss, and toothpicks.

Drug interactions and/or related problems

The following drug interactions and/or related problems have been selected on the basis of their potential clinical significance (possible mechanism in parentheses where appropriate)—not necessarily inclusive (» = major clinical significance):

» Immunosuppressant agents, other, such as:
  Azathioprine
  Chlorambucil
  Corticosteroids, glucocorticoid
  Cyclophosphamide
  Cyclosporine
  Cytarabine
  Mercaptopurine
  Tacrolimus
  (although muromonab-CD3 is often administered in conjunction with azathioprine, cyclosporine, and/or corticosteroids, concurrent use may increase the risk of infection and development of lymphoproliferative disorders; reduced dosage of corticosteroids and azathioprine is recommended when muromonab-CD3 therapy is begun; continued use of cyclosporine or tacrolimus is recommended only with extreme caution and in reduced dosage because of the increased incidence of lymphoproliferative disorders when muromonab-CD3 is added to tacrolimus-based or cyclosporine-based regimens)
  (concurrent use of other immunosuppressant agents with muromonab-CD3 has been shown to alter the time course of anti-mouse antibody development as well as the specificity [idiotypic, isotypic, allotypic] of the antibodies formed)

Indomethacin
  (concurrent use may cause an increased risk of encephalopathy)

Vaccines, killed virus
  (because normal defense mechanisms may be suppressed by muromonab-CD3 therapy, the patient's antibody response to the vaccine may be decreased. The interval between discontinuation of medications that cause immunosuppression and restoration of the patient's ability to respond to the vaccine depends on the intensity and type of immunosuppression-causing medication used, the underlying disease, and other factors; estimates vary from 3 months to 1 year)

» Vaccines, live virus
  (because normal defense mechanisms may be suppressed by muromonab-CD3 therapy, concurrent use with a live virus vaccine may potentiate the replication of the vaccine virus, may increase the side/adverse effects of the vaccine virus, and/or may decrease the patient's antibody response to the vaccine; immunization of these patients should be undertaken only with extreme caution after careful review of the patient's immunologic status and only with the knowledge and consent of the physician managing the muromonab-CD3 therapy. The interval between discontinuation of medications that cause immunosuppression and restoration of the patient's ability to respond to the vaccine depends on the intensity and type of immunosuppression-causing medication used, the underlying disease, and other factors; estimates vary from 3 months to 1 year. Immunization with oral poliovirus vaccine should also be postponed in persons in close contact with the patient, especially family members)

Laboratory value alterations

The following have been selected on the basis of their potential clinical significance (possible effect in parentheses where appropriate)—not necessarily inclusive (» = major clinical significance).

With physiology/laboratory test values
Hepatic transaminase
(serum values may be increased transiently after the first few doses of muromonab-CD3)

Medical considerations/Contraindications

The medical considerations/contraindications included have been selected on the basis of their potential clinical significance (reasons given in parentheses where appropriate)—not necessarily inclusive (» = major clinical significance).

Except under special circumstances, this medication should not be used when the following medical problems exist:

» Anti-mouse antibody titre of 1:1000 or more
(increased risk of hypersensitivity to muromonab-CD3)
» Fever greater than 37.8 °C (100 °F)
(should be lowered by antipyretics, after infection has been ruled out, before administration of muromonab-CD3)
» Fluid overload, as seen on chest x-ray or as a weight gain of greater than 3% within 1 week before administration is planned or
» Heart failure, uncompensated
(risk of severe and potentially fatal pulmonary edema)

Risk-benefit should be considered when the following medical problems exist:

» Angina, unstable or
» Cerebrovascular disease or
» Chronic obstructive pulmonary disease or
» Heart failure of any etiology or
» Intravascular volume overload or depletion of any etiology (e.g., excessive dialysis, recent intensive diuresis, blood loss, etc.) or
» Ischemic heart disease, symptomatic or
» Myocardial infarction, recent or
» Neuropathy, advanced symptomatic or
» Pulmonary edema of any etiology or
» Seizures, history of or
» Septic shock or
» Vascular disease, advanced symptomatic
(increased risk of serious complications from cytokine release syndrome; condition should be corrected or stabilized prior to initiation of muromonab-CD3 therapy)
» Chickenpox, existing or recent (including recent exposure) or
» Herpes zoster
(risk of severe generalized disease)
» Infection
Sensitivity to muromonab-CD3
Thrombosis, history of
(arterial or venous thromboses of allografts and other vascular beds [e.g., heart, lungs, brain, bowel] have been reported in patients treated with muromonab-CD3)

Patient monitoring

The following may be especially important in patient monitoring (other tests may be warranted in some patients, depending on condition; » = major clinical significance):

Note: Recommended targets are fewer than 25 CD3-positive T cells per cubic millimeter or muromonab-CD3 concentrations of 800 nanograms per mL or more.

» Assay for circulating T cells expressing the CD3 antigen or
» Muromonab-CD3 concentrations, plasma, as determined by enzyme-linked immunosorbent assay (ELISA)
(recommended at periodic intervals during therapy to assess efficacy)
Blood counts, complete, including differential and leukocytes and
Platelet counts
(recommended at periodic intervals during therapy)
» Body temperature determinations
(recommended prior to administration and at frequent intervals for several hours after administration, especially with the first two doses)
Hepatic function determinations, including serum transaminase and alkaline phosphatase values and bilirubin concentrations and
Renal function determinations, including blood urea nitrogen and serum creatinine concentrations
(recommended at periodic intervals during therapy)

Side/Adverse Effects

Note: Neutralizing antibodies, primarily of the IgG class, have been detected in most patients during or following the second week of muromonab-CD3 therapy and may potentially reduce subsequent effectiveness by blocking the ability of muromonab-CD3 to bind to the CD3 antigen on T lymphocytes. Development of neutralizing antibodies has been linked to reappearance of CD3 positive T cells prior to withdrawal of muromonab-CD3.

The following side/adverse effects have been selected on the basis of their potential clinical significance (possible signs and symptoms in parentheses where appropriate)—not necessarily inclusive:

Those indicating need for medical attention

Incidence more frequent

Cytokine release syndrome, mild (diarrhea; dizziness or faintness; fever and chills; headache; malaise [general feeling of discomfort or illness]; muscle or joint pain; nausea and vomiting)

Note: Symptoms of the *cytokine release syndrome* occur in most patients, usually 30 minutes to 48 hours after the first dose, and last several hours; both frequency and severity seem to decrease with each subsequent dose; fever and chills occurring later may be due to infection; cytokine release syndrome may also occur with dosage increases or resumption of dosing after a period of withdrawal.

Incidence less frequent

Anaphylaxis (rapid or irregular heartbeat; shortness of breath or wheezing; swelling of face or throat); ***or hypersensitivity*** (itching or tingling; skin rash); ***blood dyscrasias, including aplastic anemia*** (shortness of breath, troubled breathing, wheezing, or tightness in chest; sores, ulcers, or white spots on lips or in mouth; swollen or painful glands; unusual bleeding or bruising); ***neutropenia*** (usually asymptomatic; rarely, fever or chills; cough or hoarseness; lower back or side pain; painful or difficult urination); ***and thrombocytopenia*** (usually asymptomatic; rarely, unusual bleeding or bruising; black, tarry stools; blood in urine or stools; pinpoint red spots on skin); ***cytokine release syndrome, severe*** (chest pain; rapid or irregular heartbeat; shortness of breath or wheezing; trembling and shaking of hands; weakness); ***hearing loss; impaired vision; neurologic or neuropsychiatric reactions, including aseptic meningitis syndrome*** (fever; headache; stiff neck; unusual sensitivity of eyes to light; and seizures); ***encephalopathy*** (confusion; hallucinations; unusual tiredness; coma); ***headache; seizures***—some resulting in death

Note: *Anaphylactic reactions*, which are serious and occasionally fatal, usually occur within 10 minutes after a dose, and may be difficult to differentiate from the *cytokine release syndrome*. Such reactions may include cardiovascular collapse, cardiorespiratory arrest, loss of consciousness, hypotension/shock, tachycardia, tingling, angioedema (including laryngeal, pharyngeal, or facial edema), airway obstruction, bronchospasm, dyspnea, urticaria, and pruritus.

Symptoms of the *cytokine release syndrome* occur in most patients, usually 30 minutes to 48 hours after the first dose, and last several hours; both frequency and severity seem to decrease with each subsequent dose; fever and chills occurring later may be due to infection; *cytokine release syndrome* may also occur with dosage increases or resumption of dosing after a period of withdrawal.

Cardiorespiratory findings with the *cytokine release syndrome* may include tachypnea; respiratory distress, failure, or arrest; cardiovascular collapse; cardiac arrest; myocardial infarction; tachycardia; hypertension; hemodynamic instability; hypotension including profound shock; heart failure; cardiogenic and noncardiogenic pulmonary edema; adult respiratory distress syndrome; hypoxemia; apnea; and arrhythmias. Of these, severe, potentially fatal pulmonary edema is the most serious.

An acute and transient decline in the glomerular filtration rate and diminished urine output, manifested as an increase in the serum creatinine concentration, may occur as a result of *cytokine release*, and may lead to reversible renal function impairment.

Neuropsychiatric reactions may be caused partly by T cell activation resulting in systemic release of cytokines.

Neurologic signs and symptoms are usually reversible, even with continued treatment, but are sometimes irreversible.

Symptoms of *aseptic meningitis syndrome* usually occur within the first 3 days of therapy. Examination of cerebrospinal fluid may show leukocytosis, elevated protein, or reduced glucose concentrations.

Those indicating possible need for medical attention if they occur after medication is discontinued

Infection (fever and chills)

Note: During the first month after transplantation, patients are at risk of reinfection from infections existing prior to transplantation, infection received from organisms infecting the donor organ, and the usual postoperative (intravenous line–related, wound, or nosocomial pneumonia) infections. After the first month, transplantation patients receiving immunosuppressive therapy are at increased risk of infection with cytomegalovirus (CMV), Epstein-Barre virus (EBV), and herpes simplex virus (HSV). EBV infection can contribute to lymphoproliferative disorders. Clinically significant infections can occur with any microorganism.

Overdose

For more information on the management of overdose, **contact a Poison Control Center** (see *Poison Control Center Listing*).

Clinical effects of overdose

Acute

Chills; diarrhea; edema (swelling in feet and/or legs); ***fever; myalgia*** (muscle pain); ***pulmonary edema*** (shortness of breath); ***renal failure*** (greatly increased or decreased frequency of urination or amount of urine; increased thirst; loss of appetite; nausea; vomiting); ***vomiting***

Treatment of overdose

Treatment of overdose with muromonab-CD3 is symptomatic and supportive.

Patient Consultation

As an aid to patient consultation, refer to *Advice for the Patient, Muromonab-CD3 (Systemic)*.

In providing consultation, consider emphasizing the following selected information (» = major clinical significance):

Before using this medication

» Conditions affecting use, especially:

Sensitivity to muromonab-CD3

Pregnancy—May cross placenta; risk of adverse effects unknown

Breast-feeding—Not recommended because of risk of serious side effects

Use in children—Possible increased risk of dehydration as a result of diarrhea and/or vomiting associated with cytokine release syndrome

Other medications, especially other immunosuppressants

Other medical problems, especially angina, cerebrovascular disease, chickenpox, chronic obstructive pulmonary disease, fever, heart failure, herpes zoster, infection, ischemic heart disease, myocardial infarction, neuropathy, pulmonary edema, seizures, or vascular disease

Proper use of this medication

» Proper dosing

Precautions while using this medication

» Importance of close monitoring by physician

» Avoiding immunizations unless approved by physician; other persons in patient's household should avoid immunizations with oral poliovirus vaccine; avoiding persons who have taken oral poliovirus vaccine or wearing a protective mask that covers nose and mouth

Avoiding exposure to persons with bacterial infections; telling physician if signs of bacterial infection occur

» Possible cytokine release syndrome, which should be reduced after second and subsequent doses; telling doctor or nurse immediately if symptoms of angioedema, cardiac effects, or pulmonary edema occur

Side/adverse effects

Signs of potential side effects, especially cytokine release syndrome, anaphylaxis or hypersensitivity, blood dyscrasias (e.g., aplastic anemia, neutropenia, thrombocytopenia), hearing loss, impaired vision, and neurologic or neuropsychiatric reactions (e.g., encephalopathy, headache, seizures)

General Dosing Information

Patients receiving muromonab-CD3 should be under supervision of a physician experienced in immunosuppressive therapy.

It is recommended that equipment and medications necessary for cardiopulmonary resuscitation be immediately available during administration of each dose of muromonab-CD3.

Muromonab-CD3 should be administered by intravenous push over a period of less than 1 minute.

Acetaminophen, antihistamines, and/or corticosteroids may be used to reduce or treat early reactions. Patient temperature should be maintained below 37.8 °C (100 °F) at administration of each dose. Administration of high-dose corticosteroids (e.g., 8 mg per kg of body weight of methylprednisolone administered intravenously) is recommended 1 to 4 hours prior to the first dose of muromonab-CD3.

Dosage reduction of other immunosuppressive therapy is recommended when muromonab-CD3 therapy is begun. Dosage should be returned to maintenance levels approximately 3 days before muromonab-CD3 therapy is completed.

Initiation of anti-infective prophylaxis may be warranted in patients at high risk for infection or viral-induced lymphoproliferative disorders. If an infection develops, it must be treated promptly; withdrawal of muromonab-CD3 may be necessary.

For treatment of adverse effects

Intensive treatment with oxygen, intravenous fluids, corticosteroids, pressor amines, antihistamines, intubation, etc., may be required for serious manifestations of the cytokine release syndrome.

Subcutaneous aqueous epinephrine (0.3 to 0.5 mL of the 1:1000 dilution), along with other resuscitative measures, may be required for severe anaphylaxis.

Parenteral Dosage Forms

MUROMONAB-CD3 INJECTION

Usual adult and adolescent dose

Transplant rejection, organ (treatment)—

Intravenous (rapid), 5 mg a day for ten to fourteen days.

Note: Intravenous administration of methylprednisolone sodium succinate (8 mg per kg of body weight) one to four hours prior to the first dose of muromonab-CD3 is recommended to reduce the incidence and severity of the cytokine release syndrome.

Usual pediatric dose

Transplant rejection, organ (treatment)—

Children less than 12 years of age: Intravenous (rapid), 100 mcg (0.1 mg) per kg of body weight a day for ten to fourteen days.

Strength(s) usually available

U.S.—

1 mg per mL (Rx) [*Orthoclone OKT3* (polysorbate 80)].

Canada—

1 mg per mL (Rx) [*Orthoclone OKT3*].

Packaging and storage

Store between 2 and 8 °C (36 and 46 °F), unless otherwise specified by manufacturer. Protect from freezing.

Preparation of dosage form

Sterile muromonab-CD3 is prepared for intravenous administration by drawing the solution into a syringe through a low protein–binding 0.2 or 0.22 micrometer filter, then discarding the filter and attaching an appropriate needle.

Stability

Because the product contains no bacteriostatic agent, muromonab-CD3 injection should be used immediately after the ampul is opened and any unused portion should be discarded. In addition, muromonab-CD3 injection, like other protein solutions, may develop a few fine translucent particles, which have not been shown to affect potency.

Incompatibilities

Muromonab-CD3 should not be administered by intravenous infusion or in conjunction with other drug solutions.

Auxiliary labeling

- Do not shake.

Revised: 06/01/1999

MYCOPHENOLATE Systemic

VA CLASSIFICATION (Primary): IM403

Commonly used brand name(s): *CellCept*.

Note: For a listing of dosage forms and brand names by country availability, see *Dosage Forms* section(s).

Category

Immunosuppressant.

Indications

Accepted

Transplant rejection, organ (prophylaxis adjunct)—Mycophenolate is indicated for the prophylaxis of organ rejection in patients receiving allogeneic renal, cardiac, or hepatic transplants. Mycophenolate should be used concomitantly with cyclosporine and corticosteroids.

[Lupus nephritis (treatment)][1]—Mycophenolate is indicated for the treatment of lupus nephritis.

Acceptance not established

Mycophenolate has been used as an adjunct in the treatment of myasthenia gravis, including in patients whose conditions are refractory to other immunosuppressant agents or who are steroid-dependent. However, no consensus was reached among USP Expert Committee members with regard to the safety and efficacy of mycophenolate for this indication. Although some committee members advocated using mycophenolate to treat myasthenia gravis, lack of randomized, controlled trials and insufficient safety and efficacy data precluded others from supporting acceptance of this indication.

---

[1]Not included in Canadian product labeling.

Pharmacology/Pharmacokinetics

Physicochemical characteristics

Molecular weight—Mycophenolate mofetil: 433.5.

pKa—

- Morpholino group: 5.6.
- Phenolic group: 8.5.

Mechanism of action/Effect

Mycophenolate mofetil inhibits immunologically mediated inflammatory responses in animal models and inhibits tumor development and prolongs survival in murine tumor transplant models. As a potent, selective, noncompetitive, and reversible inhibitor of inosine monophosphate dehydrogenase (IMPDH), mycophenolic acid (MPA), the active metabolite, inhibits the *de novo* synthesis pathway of guanosine nucleotides without being incorporated into DNA. Because T and B lymphocytes are critically dependent for their proliferation on *de novo* synthesis of purines, while other cell types can utilize salvage pathways, MPA has potent cytostatic effects on lymphocytes. MPA inhibits proliferative responses of T and B lymphocytes to both mitogenic and allospecific stimulation. The addition of guanosine or deoxyguanosine reverses the cytostatic effects of MPA on lymphocytes. MPA also suppresses antibody formation by B lymphocytes. MPA prevents the glycosylation of lymphocyte and monocyte glycoproteins that are involved in intercellular adhesion of these cells to endothelial cells, and may inhibit recruitment of leukocytes into sites of inflammation and graft rejection. Mycophenolate mofetil does not inhibit the early events in the activation of human peripheral blood mononuclear cells, such as the production of interleukin-1 and interleukin-2, but does block the coupling of these events to DNA synthesis and proliferation.

Absorption

Rapid and extensive after oral administration. Mean absolute bioavailability in 12 healthy volunteers was 94%.

Observations that a secondary peak in plasma MPA concentrations occurs 6 to 12 hours after a dose and that concurrent administration of cholestyramine results in an approximately 40% decrease in MPA concentrations suggest that enterohepatic recirculation is involved.

Food had no effect on the extent of absorption of mycophenolate when administered at doses of 1.5 grams two times a day; however, the maximum plasma concentrations of MPA were decreased by 40% in the presence of food.

Distribution

Mean apparent volume of distribution—In healthy volunteers: Approximately 3.6 and 4 liters per kg of body weight (L/kg), following intravenous and oral administration, respectively. Studies comparing mean blood to plasma ratios of radioactivity concentrations indicate that MPA and mycophenolic acid glucuronide (MPAG), the phenolic glucuronide metabolite, do not extensively distribute into the cellular fractions of blood.

Protein binding

To plasma albumin—High (97% for MPA at clinically relevant concentrations, and 82% for MPAG at concentration ranges normally seen in stable renal transplant patients). At higher MPAG concentrations (e.g., in patients with renal impairment or delayed graft function), binding of MPA may be decreased as a result of competition between MPA and MPAG for binding sites.

Biotransformation

Mycophenolate mofetil is hydrolyzed presystemically and completely to MPA, the active metabolite, which is then metabolized primarily by glucuronyl transferase to MPAG, the inactive phenolic glucuronide; other metabolites include those of the 2-hydroxyethyl-morpholino moiety. Evidence suggests that enterohepatic recirculation contributes to MPA plasma concentrations.

Plasma clearance is approximately 193 mL per minute after oral administration and 177 mL per minute after intravenous administration.

Half-life

For MPA—Mean apparent: Approximately 17.9 hours after oral administration and 16.6 hours after intravenous administration.

Time to peak plasma concentration

Adults—

- Cardiac transplant:
  - Early (day before hospital discharge post–cardiac transplant)—Approximately 1.8 hours.
  - Late (more than 6 months post–cardiac transplant)—1.1 hours.
- Renal transplant:
  - Early (less than 40 days post–renal transplant)—Approximately 1.31 hours.
  - Late (more than 3 months post–renal transplant)—0.9 hour.

Children (based on limited data 21 days post–renal transplant)—

- 3 months to 6 years of age: Approximately 1.25 hours.
- 6 to 12 years of age: 0.5 hour.
- 12 to 18 years of age: 0.5 to approximately 1.1 hours (dose-related).

Peak plasma concentration

Adults—

- Cardiac transplant:
  - Early (day before hospital discharge post–cardiac transplant)—Approximately 11.5 mcg per mL (mcg/mL).
  - Late (more than 6 months post–cardiac transplant)—20 mcg/mL.
- Renal transplant:
  - Early (less than 40 days post–renal transplant)—Approximately 8.16 and 13.5 mcg/mL in studies of multiple doses of 1 and 1.5 grams, respectively, two times a day.
  - Late (more than 3 months post–renal transplant)—Approximately 24.1 mcg/mL in studies of multiple doses of 1.5 grams two times a day.
  - Note: In single-dose studies in patients with chronic or severe renal insufficiency, increased plasma concentrations of mycophenolate mofetil metabolites (75% increase in MPA and 3- to 6-fold increase in MPAG) have been observed.

Children (based on limited data 21 days post–renal transplant)—

- 3 months to 6 years of age:
  - At doses of 15 mg per kg of body weight (mg/kg) two times a day—Approximately 3.7 mcg/mL.
- 6 to 12 years of age:
  - At doses of 15 mg/kg two times a day—Approximately 13.5 mcg/mL.
- 12 to 18 years of age:
  - At doses of 15 mg/kg two times a day—Approximately 13.2 mcg/mL.
  - At doses of 23 mg/kg two times a day—Approximately 11.5 mcg/mL.

Elimination

Renal—93% (less than 1% as MPA; 87% as MPAG). Renal clearance occurs by renal tubular secretion and glomerular filtration.

Fecal—6%.

In dialysis—MPA and MPAG usually are not removed by hemodialysis, although small amounts of MPAG are removed at high plasma MPAG concentrations (greater than 100 mcg per mL).

Precautions to Consider

Carcinogenicity/Tumorigenicity

No evidence of tumorigenicity was found in carcinogenicity studies in mice and rats given daily oral doses of up to 180 mg per kg of body weight (mg/kg) and 15 mg/kg, respectively, for 104 weeks. In mice, the highest dose tested was 0.5 times the recommended clinical dose (2 grams per day) when corrected for differences in body surface area (BSA); in rats the highest dose was 0.08 times the recommended clinical dose when corrected for BSA. Although lower than the doses given to patients, these doses were considered adequate to evaluate potential risk to humans.

Suppression of cell-mediated immunity in organ transplant patients is associated with an increased risk of benign and malignant lymphoproliferative disorders, lymphomas, and skin cancers. Lymphomas have developed in humans treated with mycophenolate, although a definite causal relationship has not been established. Other neoplasms have been reported infrequently.

Mutagenicity
No evidence of genotoxicity, with or without metabolic activation, was found in the bacterial mutation assay, the yeast mitotic gene conversion assay, the mouse micronucleus aberration assay, or the Chinese hamster ovary cell (CHO) chromosomal aberration assay.

Pregnancy/Reproduction
Fertility—Studies in male rats at oral doses of up to 20 mg/kg a day (0.1 times the recommended clinical dose when corrected for BSA) found no effect on fertility. A study in female rats at oral doses of 4.5 mg/kg a day (0.02 times the recommended clinical dose when corrected for BSA) found no effect on fertility or reproductive parameters in the dams or in the offspring.

Pregnancy—Adequate and well-controlled studies in humans have not been done. However, because of the teratogenic effects of mycophenolate observed in animals, it is recommended that women, including those women with a history of infertility (unless the result of hysterectomy), use two reliable forms of contraception simultaneously before, during, and for 6 weeks after discontinuing mycophenolate therapy. Mycophenolate should not be initiated in women of childbearing potential without a negative serum or urine pregnancy test with a sensitivity of at least 50 million International Units (mIU) per mL obtained within 1 week prior to beginning therapy.

A study in female rats at oral doses of 4.5 mg/kg a day (0.02 times the recommended clinical dose when corrected for BSA) found that mycophenolate caused malformations (primarily of the head and eyes) in the first generation offspring in the absence of maternal toxicity. Studies in rats and rabbits at oral doses of 6 mg/kg a day and 90 mg/kg a day (equivalent to 0.03 and 0.92 times the recommended clinical dose when corrected for BSA), respectively, found fetal resorptions and malformations in the absence of maternal toxicity.

FDA Pregnancy Category C.

Breast-feeding
It is not known whether mycophenolate is distributed into breast milk in humans. Because many drugs are distributed into human milk, and because of the potential for serious adverse reactions in nursing infants from mycophenolate, a decision should be made whether to discontinue nursing or to discontinue the drug, taking into account the importance of the drug to the mother.

However, studies in rats treated with mycophenolate have shown mycophenolic acid (MPA) to be distributed into milk.

Pediatrics
Renal transplant—Appropriate studies performed to date have not demonstrated pediatrics-specific problems that would limit the usefulness of mycophenolate in children following renal transplantation.

Cardiac or hepatic transplants—No information is available on the relationship of age to the effects of this medication in pediatric patients receiving allogeneic cardiac or hepatic transplants. Safety and efficacy have not been established.

Geriatrics
No information is available on the relationship of age to the effects of mycophenolate in geriatric patients. In general, dose selection should be cautious reflecting the greater frequency of decreased hepatic, renal or cardiac function and of concomitant or other drug therapy. Elderly patients may be at an increased risk of adverse reactions compared with younger individuals.

Dental
The immunosuppressive effects of mycophenolate may result in an increased incidence of certain microbial infections and delayed healing. Dental work, whenever possible, should be completed prior to initiation of therapy and undertaken with caution during therapy. Patients should be instructed in proper oral hygiene.

Drug interactions and/or related problems
The following drug interactions and/or related problems have been selected on the basis of their potential clinical significance (possible mechanism in parentheses where appropriate)—not necessarily inclusive (» = major clinical significance):

Note: Combinations containing any of the following medications, depending on the amount present, may also interact with this medication.

Acyclovir or
Valacyclovir or
Ganciclovir or
Valganciclovir
(in the presence of renal impairment, acyclovir or its prodrug [e.g., valacyclovir] or ganciclovir or its prodrug [e.g., valganciclovir] may compete with MPAG for tubular secretion, thus further increasing plasma concentrations of each; renally impaired patients should be monitored carefully with coadministration)

» Azathioprine
(concomitant administration not recommended due to both having potential to cause bone marrow depression and concomitant use has not been studied clinically)

Antacids, magnesium- or aluminum hydroxide–containing
(concurrent administration may result in decreased absorption of mycophenolate; simultaneous administration is not recommended)

Cholestyramine
(plasma concentrations of MPA may be decreased as a result of interruption of enterohepatic recirculation of MPAG possibly caused by intestinal binding with cholestyramine; caution with concomitant use because of potential to reduce mycophenolate efficacy)

Medications that alter gastrointestinal flora
(may disrupt enterohepatic circulation; interference with MPAG hydrolysis may result in less MPA available for absorption)

» Immunosuppressants, other, such as:
Antithymocyte globulin
Chlorambucil
Corticosteroids, glucocorticoid
Cyclophosphamide
Cyclosporine
Mercaptopurine
Muromonab-CD3
Tacrolimus
(increased risk of development of lymphomas and other malignancies of the skin or increased susceptibility to infection due to increased intensity and duration of immunosuppression)

Oral contraceptives
(concomitant use significantly decreased levonorgestrol AUC; recommended coadministration with caution and consideration of additional birth control methods)

Probenecid or
Medications that undergo renal tubular secretion
(probenecid may inhibit renal tubular secretion and, therefore, increase plasma concentrations of the metabolites of mycophenolate; other medications known to undergo renal tubular secretion may also compete with MPAG to raise plasma concentrations of either drug undergoing tubular secretion)

Trimethoprim/sulfamethoxazole
(concomitant use decreased AUC and C_{max} of mycophenolate)

Vaccines, live attenuated
(use should be avoided during mycophenolate treatment; vaccinations may be less effective during this time)

Laboratory value alterations
The following have been selected on the basis of their potential clinical significance (possible effect in parentheses where appropriate)—not necessarily inclusive (» = major clinical significance).

With physiology/laboratory test values

Alanine aminotransferase (ALT [SGPT]) and
Alkaline phosphatase and
Aspartate aminotransferase (AST [SGOT])
(values may be increased)

Calcium and
Phosphate and
Potassium, serum
(concentrations may be increased or decreased)

Chloride, serum
(concentration may be decreased)

Cholesterol, serum
(values may be increased)

Creatinine, serum
(concentration may be increased)

Glucose, blood
(concentration may be increased or decreased)

Leukocytes (neutrophils [WBC])
(blood counts may be increased or decreased)

Medical considerations/Contraindications

The medical considerations/contraindications included have been selected on the basis of their potential clinical significance (reasons given in parentheses where appropriate)—not necessarily inclusive (» = major clinical significance).

Except under special circumstances, this medication should not be used when the following medical problem exists:

» Hypersensitivity to mycophenolate mofetil, mycophenolic acid or any component of the drug product

» Hypersensitivity to polysorbate 80 (TWEEN)

Risk-benefit should be considered when the following medical problems exist:

Delayed renal graft function, posttransplant
(increased MPAG concentrations reported, as well as increased incidence of some adverse events [anemia, thrombocytopenia, hyperkalemia], as compared with patients without delayed graft function; observation, but not dosage reduction, is recommended)

» Digestive system disease, active
(risk of gastrointestinal ulceration, hemorrhage, or perforation, possibly associated with mycophenolate administration; should be administered with caution)

Hereditary deficiency of hypoxanthine-guanine phosphoribosyl-transferase (HGPRT) such as
Kelley-Seegmiller syndrome or
Lesch-Nyhan
(on theoretical grounds, because mycophenolate is an inosine monophosphate dehydrogensase [IMPDH] inhibitor, it should be avoided in patients with these rare conditions)

» Phenylketonuria (PKU)
(Cellcept brand of oral suspension contains aspartame, which is metabolized to phenylalanine; care should be taken if administered to patients with PKU)

» Renal function impairment, severe
(reduced elimination; mycophenolate doses should not be greater than 1 gram twice per day and patients should be carefully observed)

Patient monitoring

The following may be especially important in patient monitoring (other tests may be warranted in some patients, depending on condition; » = major clinical significance):

» Complete blood count (CBC)
(recommended weekly during the first month of therapy, twice a month for the second and third months of treatment, and then once a month through the remainder of the first year)

Side/Adverse Effects

The following side/adverse effects have been selected on the basis of their potential clinical significance (possible signs and symptoms in parentheses where appropriate)—not necessarily inclusive:

Those indicating need for medical attention

Incidence more frequent

Anemia—asymptomatic; ***chest pain; cough, increased***—more common in patients receiving mycophenolate for cardiac transplantation than in patients receiving mycophenolate for renal transplantation; ***dyspnea*** (shortness of breath)—more common in patients receiving mycophenolate for cardiac transplantation than in patients receiving mycophenolate for renal transplantation; ***hematuria*** (blood in urine); ***hypertension***—asymptomatic; ***leukopenia (neutropenia) or infection*** (fever or chills, cough or hoarseness, lower back or side pain, painful or difficult urination); ***peripheral edema*** (swelling of feet or lower legs)

Note: *Neutropenia* occurs most frequently 31 to 180 days posttransplant. Incidence of fatal infections or sepsis (usually cytomegalovirus [CMV] viremia) in three controlled studies was similar (less than 2%) between patients receiving mycophenolate and those receiving control therapy in combination with other immunosuppressants.

Incidence less frequent

Arrhythmia (irregular heartbeat); ***arthralgia*** (joint pain); ***colitis*** (abdominal pain)—sometimes caused by cytomegalovirus; ***gastrointestinal hemorrhage*** (bloody vomit); ***gingival hyperplasia*** (enlarged gums); ***gingivitis*** (red, inflamed, bleeding gums); ***myalgia*** (muscle pain); ***neutropenia, severe; oral moniliasis*** (white patches on mouth, tongue, or throat); ***pancreatitis*** (abdominal pain); ***stomatitis*** (sores inside mouth); ***thrombocytopenia*** (unusual bleeding or bruising; black, tarry stools; blood in urine or stools; pinpoint red spots on skin)—usually asymptomatic; ***tremor*** (trembling or shaking of hands or feet)

Note: *Severe neutropenia* is defined as an absolute neutrophil count (ANC) of less than 500 cells per microliter.

Incidence not determined—Observed during clinical practice; estimates of frequency cannot be determined

Infectious endocarditis (chest pain or discomfort; chills; fever; heart murmur; shortness of breath); ***interstitial lung disorder*** (cough; difficult breathing; fever; shortness of breath); ***intestinal villous atrophy*** (abdominal pain; abdominal distention; chronic or occasional diarrhea; stools that float, are foul smelling or "fatty"); ***meningitis*** (severe headache; drowsiness; confusion; stiff neck and/or back; general feeling of illness or nausea); ***mycobacterial infection, atypical*** (fever or chills; cough or hoarseness; lower back or side pain; painful or difficult urination); ***pulmonary fibrosis*** (fever; cough; shortness of breath); ***respiratory failure*** (blue lips, fingernails, or skin; difficult or troubled breathing; irregular, fast or slow, or shallow breathing; shortness of breath); ***tuberculosis*** (chest pain; cough; coughing or spitting up blood; difficulty in breathing; sore throat; muscle aches; night sweats; sudden high fever or low-grade fever for months; unusual tiredness)

Those indicating need for medical attention only if they continue or are bothersome

Incidence more frequent

Abdominal or stomach pain; constipation or diarrhea; dyspepsia (heartburn); ***headache; nausea; vomiting; weakness***

Incidence less frequent

Acne; dizziness; insomnia (trouble in sleeping); ***skin rash***

Overdose

For more information on the management of overdose or unintentional ingestion, **contact a Poison Control Center** (see *Poison Control Center Listing*).

Clinical effects of overdose

The experience with overdose of mycophenolate in humans is very limited. The events received from reports of overdose fall within the known safety profile of the drug.

With limited experience in clinical trials, cardiac and hepatic transplant patients given doses of 4 or 5 grams per day appeared to have a higher rate of gastrointestinal intolerance including nausea, vomiting, and/or diarrhea, and occasional hematologic abnormalities, principally neutropenia, leading to dose reduction or discontinuation compared with patients taking 3 grams per day or less.

Treatment of overdose

Mycophenolic acid (MPA) and the phenolic glucuronide of MPA (MPAG) are unusually not removed by hemodialysis. However, at high MPAG concentrations (>100 mcg per mL), MPAG is removed in small amounts.

By increasing excretion of the drug, MPA can be removed by bile acid sequestrants, such as cholestyramine.

Patient Consultation

As an aid to patient consultation, refer to *Advice for the Patient, Mycophenolate (Systemic)*. In providing consultation, consider emphasizing the following selected information (» = major clinical significance):

Before using this medication

» Conditions affecting use, especially:

Hypersensitivity to mycophenolate mofetil, mycophenolic acid or any component of the drug product

Pregnancy—Causes birth defects in animals; two forms of effective birth control recommended before, during, and for 6 weeks after discontinuing mycophenolate

Breast-feeding—Mycophenolate is distributed into milk of lactating rats; risk/benefit considerations due to potential for adverse effects

Use in children—Renal transplant—Safety and efficacy established in children greater than 3 months
Cardiac or hepatic transplants—Safety and efficacy not established in children

Use in the elderly—Dose selection should be cautious

Dental—Dental work should be completed prior to initiation of therapy whenever possible

Other medications, especially azathioprine or other immunosuppressants

Other medical problems, especially active digestive system disease, phenylketonuria, or renal function impairment

Proper use of this medication

Taking on empty stomach

Importance of reading and adhering to patient information leaflet

For oral suspension—Using oral dispenser provided to measure proper dose

» Proper dosing

Importance of not using more or less medication than the amount prescribed

Getting into the habit of taking at the same time each day

» Checking with physician before discontinuing or changing medication

Swallowing capsule or tablet whole

Missed dose: Taking as soon as possible; not taking if almost time for next dose; not doubling doses

» Proper storage

Precautions while using this medication

» Importance of close monitoring by physician

Maintaining good dental hygiene and seeing dentist regularly for teeth cleaning

Avoiding contact with people with colds or other infections

» Handling medicine with caution and avoiding inhalation or direct contact with skin or mucous membranes due to possible teratogenic effects

» Disposing of constituted oral suspension after 60 days

Side/adverse effects

Signs of potential side effects, especially anemia, chest pain, increased cough, dyspnea, hematuria, hypertension, leukopenia or infection, peripheral edema, arrhythmia, arthralgia, colitis, gastrointestinal hemorrhage, gingival hyperplasia, gingivitis, myalgia, severe neutropenia, oral moniliasis, pancreatitis, stomatitis, thrombocytopenia, and tremor

Signs of potential side effects observed during clinical practice, especially infectious endocarditis, interstitial lung disorder, intestinal villous atrophy, meningitis, mycobacterial infection (atypical), pulmonary fibrosis, respiratory failure, or tuberculosis

General Dosing Information

Patients receiving mycophenolate should be under the supervision of a physician experienced in immunosuppressive therapy.

If neutropenia (absolute neutrophil count [ANC] less than 1300 cells per microliter) develops, dosage reduction or interruption of mycophenolate therapy, along with appropriate diagnostic tests, is recommended.

Mycophenolate oral suspension may contain aspartame, which is metabolized to phenylalanine. Therefore, care should be taken if mycophenolate oral suspension is administered to patients with phenylketonuria (PKU).

Diet/Nutrition

Administration of the oral dosage forms on an empty stomach is recommended.

For parenteral dosage form

It is recommended that the parenteral dosage form be used only in patients unable to take mycophenolate orally for prophylaxis of transplant rejection. Mycophenolate should not be administered intravenously for more than 14 days.

Mycophenolate for injection should be administered by slow intravenous infusion over a period of no less than 2 hours by either a peripheral or central vein catheter. Mycophenolate for injection should not be administered by rapid intravenous injection.

Mycophenolate for injection should be diluted to a concentration of 6 mg per mL prior to infusion.

Safety considerations for handling this medication

Because there is evidence in animal models that mycophenolate is teratogenic, the tablets of mycophenolate should not be crushed and the capsules of mycophenolate should not be opened or crushed. Inhalation or direct contact with skin or mucous membranes of the powder contained in mycophenolate capsules and oral suspension (before or after reconstitution) should be avoided. Contact of mycophenolate solution with the skin should be avoided. If contact with the skin occurs, the affected skin should be washed thoroughly with soap and water. If contact of mycophenolate occurs with the eyes, the eyes should be rinsed thoroughly with water.

If a spill occurs, wipe up using paper towels wetted with water to remove spilled powder or suspension. Caution should be exercised in the handling and preparation of solutions of intravenous mycophenolate.

The manufacturer does not make any recommendations regarding the use of a biological containment cabinet or the wearing of disposable surgical gloves during reconstitution and dilution of mycophenolate for injection.

Oral Dosage Forms

Note: Dosage and strength are expressed in terms of the mofetil ester.

MYCOPHENOLATE MOFETIL CAPSULES

Usual adult dose

Transplant rejection, prophylaxis—

Cardiac—

Oral, 1.5 grams two times a day as soon as possible following cardiac transplant surgery, in combination with cyclosporine and corticosteroids.

Renal—

Oral, 1 gram two times a day as soon as possible following renal transplant surgery, in combination with cyclosporine and corticosteroids.

Note: In patients with severe chronic renal function impairment who are beyond the immediate posttransplant period, doses greater than 1 gram twice a day should be avoided, and patients should be observed carefully.

Hepatic—

Oral, 1.5 grams two times a day given as soon as possible following hepatic transplantation surgery, in combination with cyclosporine and corticosteroids.

[Lupus nephritis]—

Oral, 0.5 to 1 gram two times a day.

Usual pediatric dose

Transplant rejection, prophylaxis—

Cardiac—

Safety and efficacy have not been established.

Renal—

Less than 3 months of age—Safety and efficacy have not been established.

Patients with a body surface area 1.25 m^2 to 1.5 m^2—Oral, 750 mg twice daily (1.5 gram daily dose).

Patients with a body surface area >1.5 m^2—Oral, 1 gram twice daily (2 gram daily dose).

Hepatic—

Safety and efficacy have not been established.

Usual geriatric dose

See *Usual adult dose*.

Strength(s) usually available

U.S.—

250 mg (Rx) [*CellCept*].

Packaging and storage

Store between 15 and 30 °C (59 and 86 °F). Protect from light.

Auxiliary labeling

- Take on empty stomach.
- Swallow capsule whole. Do not open or crush.

Note

Because of potential teratogenicity, mycophenolate capsules should not be opened or crushed. Great care should be taken to prevent inhalation of mycophenolate powder and exposure of the skin to it. Any powder that comes in contact with the skin or mucosae should be washed off thoroughly with soap and water (eyes should be rinsed with plain water).

MYCOPHENOLATE MOFETIL FOR SUSPENSION

Usual adult dose

See *Mycophenolate Mofetil Capsules*. If required, mycophenolate oral suspension can be administered via a nasogastric tube with a minimum size of 8 French (minimum 1.7 mm interior diameter).

Usual pediatric dose

Transplant rejection, prophylaxis—

Cardiac—

Safety and efficacy have not been established.

Renal—

Less than 3 months of age—Safety and efficacy have not been established.

3 months to 18 years of age—Oral, 600 mg per m^2 administered twice daily.

If required, mycophenolate oral suspension can be administered via a nasogastric tube with a minimum size of 8 French (minimum 1.7 mm interior diameter).

Hepatic—
Safety and efficacy have not been established.

Usual pediatric prescribing limits
Renal transplant—Up to a maximum daily dose of 2 grams per 10 mL

Usual geriatric dose
See *Mycophenolate Mofetil Capsules.*

Strength(s) usually available
U.S.—

Note: *CellCept* oral suspension contains aspartame, a source of phenylalanine (0.56 mg phenylalanine per mL suspension).

200 mg per mL (Rx) [*CellCept* (citric acid anhydrous; colloidal silicon dioxide; methylparaben; mixed fruit flavor; sodium citrate dihydrate; sorbitol; soybean lecithin; xanthan gum)].

Packaging and storage
Store dry powder at 25 °C (77 °F); excursions permitted between to 15 to 30 °C (59 to 86 °F).
Store reconstituted suspension at 25 °C (77 °F); excursions permitted between to 15 to 30 °C (59 to 86 °F) up to 60 days. Storage in a refrigerator at 2 to 8 °C (36 to 46 °F) is acceptable. Do not freeze.

Preparation of dosage form
Mycophenolate powder for oral suspension should be constituted by the pharmacist prior to dispensing to the patient as follows:
• Tap the closed bottle several times to loosen powder.
• Measure 94 mL water in a graduated cylinder.
• Add approximately half the total amount of water for constitution to the bottle and shake the closed bottle well for about 1 minute.
• Add the remainder of water and shake closed bottle well again for about 1 minute.
• Remove child-resistant cap and push bottle adapter into neck of bottle.
• Close bottle with child-resistant cap tightly. This will assure the proper seating of the bottle adapter in the bottle and child-resistant status of cap.
Mycophenolate oral suspension should not be mixed with any other medication.
The constituted oral suspension should be dispensed with a patient instruction sheet and oral dispensers. Writing the expiration date of the constituted suspension on the bottle label is recommended (60 days following constitution).

Stability
The shelf-life of the constituted suspension is 60 days. Any unused portion should be discarded after 60 days after reconstitution.

Auxiliary labeling
• Take on empty stomach.
• Discard unused drug after 60 days

Caution
Because of teratogenic effects of mycophenolate demonstrated in rats and rabbits, care should be taken to avoid inhalation or direct contact with skin or mucous membranes of the dry powder or the constituted suspension. If contact occurs, wash thoroughly with soap and water and rinse eyes with water.

MYCOPHENOLATE MOFETIL TABLETS

Usual adult dose
See *Mycophenolate Mofetil Capsules.*

Usual pediatric dose
See *Mycophenolate Mofetil Capsules.*

Usual geriatric dose
See *Mycophenolate Mofetil Capsules.*

Strength(s) usually available
U.S.—
500 mg (Rx) [*CellCept* (film-coated)].

Packaging and storage
Store between 15 and 30 °C (59 and 86 °F). Protect from light.

Auxiliary labeling
• Take on empty stomach.
• Swallow tablet whole. Do not crush.

Note
Because of potential teratogenicity, mycophenolate tablets should not be crushed.

Parenteral Dosage Forms

Note: Dosage and strength are expressed in terms of the mofetil ester.

MYCOPHENOLATE MOFETIL HYDROCHLORIDE FOR INJECTION

Usual adult dose
Transplant rejection, prophylaxis—
Cardiac—
Intravenous infusion, 1.5 grams two times a day (over no less than 2 hours) as soon as possible following cardiac transplant surgery, in combination with cyclosporine and corticosteroids. The first dose of mycophenolate should be infused within twenty-four hours after transplantation surgery.

Renal—
Intravenous infusion, 1 gram two times a day (over 2 hours) as soon as possible following renal transplant surgery, in combination with cyclosporine and corticosteroids. The first dose of mycophenolate should be infused within twenty-four hours after transplantation surgery.

Hepatic—
Intravenous infusion, 1 gram two times a day (over no less than 2 hours) as soon as possible following hepatic transplantation, in combination with cyclosporine and corticosteroids.

Usual pediatric dose
Safety and efficacy have not been established.

Usual geriatric dose
Transplant rejection, prophylaxis—
Hepatic: Intravenous infusion, 1 gram two times a day

Strength(s) usually available
U.S.—
500 mg (Rx) [*CellCept* (lyophilized powder; citric acid 5 mg; polysorbate 80 [TWEEN] 25 mg)].

Packaging and storage
Vials containing unreconstituted lyophilized mycophenolate and reconstituted solutions of mycophenolate should be stored between 15 and 30 °C (59 and 86 °F), preferably at 25 °C (77 °F).

Preparation of dosage form
• Two vials of mycophenolate for injection are used to prepare each 1-gram dose, and three vials of mycophenolate for injection are used to prepare each 1.5-gram dose. The manufacturer of *CellCept* recommends administration of a solution containing 6 mg of mycophenolate per mL (mg/mL).
• Each vial of mycophenolate for injection should be reconstituted with 14 mL of 5% dextrose injection, resulting in about 15 mL of solution.
• The vials should be gently agitated to dissolve the mycophenolate powder.
• To prepare a 1-gram dose of mycophenolate, the diluted contents of two vials should be withdrawn and further diluted in 140 mL of 5% dextrose injection. To prepare a 1.5-gram dose of mycophenolate, the diluted contents of three vials should be withdrawn and further diluted in 210 mL of 5% dextrose injection.
Mycophenolate for injection does not contain an antimicrobial preservative. Aseptic technique should be used when diluting mycophenolate for injection.

Stability
Because mycophenolate for injection does not contain an antimicrobial preservative, the manufacturer recommends administration of mycophenolate solution within 6 hours of dilution of the lyophilized powder. The labeling does not give information on the stability of the solution.
The prepared solution should be inspected for particulate matter and discoloration before administration to the patient and should be discarded if particulate matter or discoloration is present.

Incompatibilities
Mycophenolate is not compatible with any intravenous infusion solutions except 5% dextrose injection. Mycophenolate should not be infused concurrently with other drugs or intravenous infusion solutions in the same intravenous catheter.

---

[1]Not included in Canadian product labeling.

Revised: 04/13/2006

NABUMETONE—See *Anti-inflammatory Drugs, Nonsteroidal (Systemic)*

NADOLOL—See *Beta-adrenergic Blocking Agents (Systemic)*

NAFCILLIN—See *Penicillins (Systemic)*

NALBUPHINE—See *Opioid (Narcotic) Analgesics (Systemic)*

NALTREXONE Systemic

VA CLASSIFICATION (Primary/Secondary): AD800/AD100

Commonly used brand name(s): *ReVia; Vivitrol.*

Note: For a listing of dosage forms and brand names by country availability, see *Dosage Forms* section(s).

Category

Opioid (narcotic) antagonist; opioid (narcotic) abuse therapy adjunct; alcohol abuse therapy adjunct.

Indications

Accepted

Opioid (narcotic) drug use, illicit (treatment adjunct)—Naltrexone tablets are indicated as an adjunct to other measures, including psychological and social counseling, in the treatment of detoxified, formerly opioid-dependent individuals. Naltrexone assists in maintaining an opioid-free state in these individuals; however, an unequivocally beneficial effect on recidivism rates has not been demonstrated.

Alcoholism (treatment)—Naltrexone tablets and extended-release injectable suspension are indicated as an adjunct to other measures, including psychological and social counseling, in the treatment of alcohol dependence.

Unaccepted

Naltrexone is *not* effective in treating dependency on cocaine or other nonopioid drugs.

Pharmacology/Pharmacokinetics

Physicochemical characteristics

Molecular weight—Naltrexone: 341.41.

Mechanism of action/Effect

Naltrexone binds to opioid receptors in the central nervous system (CNS) and competitively inhibits the actions of opioid drugs (both pure agonists and agonist/antagonists) and endogenous opioids. Naltrexone markedly attenuates or completely blocks opioid-induced euphoria and physical dependence; with continued use it may therefore reduce the patient's craving for opioid drugs. Naltrexone may be more effective in blocking the subjective effects (such as euphoria) than the objective effects (such as respiratory depression or miosis) of opioids.

The mechanism of action whereby naltrexone reduces alcohol craving and consumption is not completely understood. Naltrexone may attenuate alcohol-induced euphoria, thereby reducing the patient's craving for alcohol.

Other actions/effects

Naltrexone precipitates withdrawal symptoms in individuals who are physically dependent on opioid drugs. It also blocks the therapeutic (e.g., analgesic, antidiarrheal, and antitussive) actions of opioids. Although naltrexone has few if any actions other than opioid blockade, it produces some pupillary constriction via an unknown mechanism.

Absorption

Rapid and almost complete.

Protein binding

Low (21%).

Biotransformation

Hepatic; approximately 98% of a dose is metabolized. Naltrexone is subject to extensive first-pass hepatic metabolism. The major metabolite, 6-beta-naltrexol, has opioid antagonist activity and may contribute to the therapeutic effect.

Half-life

Elimination—
- Naltrexone: Approximately 4 hours; independent of dose.
- 6-Beta-naltrexol: Approximately 13 hours; independent of dose.

Time to peak concentration

For both naltrexone and 6-beta-naltrexol—1 hour; independent of dose.

Peak serum concentration

Following a single 50-mg dose—
- Naltrexone: 8.6 nanograms per mL.
- 6-Beta-naltrexol: 99.3 nanograms per mL.

Note: Naltrexone and 6-beta-naltrexol do not accumulate with long-term administration of 100 mg of naltrexone a day.

Duration of action

Dose-dependent; as determined by blockade of the effects of 25 mg of intravenously administered heroin—
- 50-mg dose: 24 hours.
- 100-mg dose: 48 hours.
- 150-mg dose: 72 hours.

Elimination

Primarily renal; 60% of a dose is excreted in the urine within 48 hours. Less than 2% of a dose is excreted in the urine as unchanged naltrexone; about 43% of a dose is excreted as unchanged or conjugated 6-beta-naltrexol.

Precautions to Consider

Carcinogenicity/Tumorigenicity

Studies in rats have shown that naltrexone caused small increases in the numbers of mesotheliomas in males and tumors of vascular origin in both sexes. However, only the incidence of vascular tumors in females (4%) exceeded the maximum (2%) reported in historical control groups.

Mutagenicity

Naltrexone produced weakly positive findings in the *Drosophila* recessive lethal assay and in nonspecific DNA repair tests with *E. coli*. However, no positive findings were reported in 20 other tests using bacterial, mammalian, and tissue culture systems. The significance of these findings is not known.

Pregnancy/Reproduction

Fertility—Studies in rats given doses of 100 mg per kg (approximately 100 times the human therapeutic dose) have shown that naltrexone causes a significant increase in pseudopregnancy and a decrease in the pregnancy rate of mated females. The relevance of these findings to humans is not known.

Pregnancy—Adequate and well-controlled studies in humans have not been done.

Naltrexone has been shown to have embryocidal and fetotoxic effects in rats (doses of 30 times the human dose equivalent prior to and throughout gestation) and rabbits (doses of 60 times the human dose equivalent during the period of organogenesis).

FDA Pregnancy Category C.

Breast-feeding

It is not known whether naltrexone is distributed into breast milk. However, problems in humans have not been documented.

Pediatrics

Appropriate studies on the relationship of age to the effects of naltrexone have not been performed in the pediatric population. However, no pediatrics-specific problems have been documented.

Geriatrics

Appropriate studies on the relationship of age to the effects of naltrexone have not been performed in the geriatric population. However, no geriatrics-specific problems have been documented.

Drug interactions and/or related problems

The following drug interactions and/or related problems have been selected on the basis of their potential clinical significance (possible mechanism in parentheses where appropriate)—not necessarily inclusive (» = major clinical significance):

Note: Combinations containing any of the following medications also interact with this medication.

Hepatotoxic medications (see *Appendix II*)
(additive hepatotoxicity may occur)

» Opioid (narcotic) medications
(administration of naltrexone to a patient physically dependent on opioid drugs will precipitate withdrawal symptoms; symptoms may appear within 5 minutes of naltrexone administration, persist for up to 48 hours, and be difficult to reverse; opioid-dependent pa-

tients should be detoxified before treatment with naltrexone; a naloxone challenge test usually is administered before naltrexone therapy is started to verify abstinence [see *General Dosing Information*])

(naltrexone blocks the therapeutic effects of opioids [i.e., analgesic, antidiarrheal, and antitussive]; naltrexone therapy should not be initiated in patients receiving these agents for therapeutic purposes; also, patients receiving naltrexone should be advised to use alternative medications when necessary)

(administration of increased doses of opioids to override naltrexone-induced blockade of opioid receptors may result in increased and more prolonged respiratory depression and/or circulatory collapse)

(naltrexone should be discontinued several days prior to elective surgery if administration of an opioid medication prior to, during, or following surgery is unavoidable)

(the efficacy of naltrexone in antagonizing opioid effects not mediated via opioid receptors [i.e., those which may be caused by histamine release, such as facial swelling, itching, generalized erythema, hives, and, to some extent, hypotension] has not been fully determined; naltrexone may not antagonize these effects completely)

Thioridazine

(lethargy and somnolence have been reported rarely when patients taking thioridazine have begun naltrexone therapy)

Laboratory value alterations

The following have been selected on the basis of their potential clinical significance (possible effect in parentheses where appropriate)—not necessarily inclusive (» = major clinical significance).

With physiology/laboratory test values

Serum transaminase (ALT [SGPT]; AST [SGOT]) activity

(excessive doses of naltrexone may cause hepatocellular damage in a dose-dependent manner; elevation of serum transaminase activity may occur; although mild abnormalities occur frequently in patients with alcohol or drug addiction, and are not necessarily related to naltrexone-induced hepatotoxicity, significant abnormalities indicative of the medication's hepatotoxic potential have occurred in subjects receiving about five times the recommended daily dose; in one placebo-controlled study, 5 of 26 subjects developed elevations of serum transaminases 3 to 19 times the baseline value; the abnormalities were reversible upon discontinuation of naltrexone, and symptomatic hepatotoxicity with clinical use has not been reported)

Medical considerations/Contraindications

The medical considerations/contraindications included have been selected on the basis of their potential clinical significance (reasons given in parentheses where appropriate)—not necessarily inclusive (» = major clinical significance).

Except under special circumstances, this medication should not be used when the following medical problems exist:

» Allergic reaction to naltrexone, history of

» Dependence on opioid drugs, current, as demonstrated by presence of withdrawal symptoms, detection of opioid drugs in urine, or failure to pass naloxone challenge test
(naltrexone will precipitate or exacerbate withdrawal symptoms)

» Hepatic failure or

» Hepatitis, acute
(increased risk of hepatotoxicity)

Risk-benefit should be considered when the following medical problems exist:

» Hepatic disease, current or recent history of, excluding mild liver function abnormalities known to be associated with opioid or alcohol dependence
(increased risk of hepatotoxicity; naltrexone may cause hepatocellular damage in a dose-dependent manner)

For injectable naltrexone

Coagulation disorder (e.g., hemophilia and severe hepatic failure) or Thrombocytopenia
(naltrexone intramuscular injection should be administered with caution)

Patient monitoring

The following may be especially important in patient monitoring (other tests may be warranted in some patients, depending on condition; » = major clinical significance):

» Hepatic function tests
(recommended prior to initiation of therapy to detect hepatic injury and/or to determine baseline values, then periodically thereafter; naltrexone should be discontinued if significant abnormalities occur)

Side/Adverse Effects

The following side/adverse effects have been selected on the basis of their potential clinical significance (possible signs and symptoms in parentheses where appropriate)—not necessarily inclusive:

Those indicating need for medical attention

Incidence less frequent

Skin rash

Incidence rare

Blurred vision or aching, burning, or swollen eyes; chest pain; confusion; discomfort while urinating and/or frequent urination; edema (swelling of face, fingers, feet, or lower legs; weight gain); ***fever; gastrointestinal ulceration*** (abdominal or stomach pain, severe); ***hallucinations; increased blood pressure; itching; mental depression or other mood or mental changes; ringing or buzzing in ears; shortness of breath***

Those indicating need for medical attention only if they continue or are bothersome

Incidence more frequent

Abdominal cramping or pain, mild to moderate; anxiety, nervousness, restlessness, and/or trouble in sleeping; headache; joint or muscle pain; nausea or vomiting; unusual tiredness

Incidence less frequent or rare

Chills; constipation; cough; diarrhea; dizziness; fast or pounding heartbeat; hoarseness; injection site reaction (bleeding, blistering, burning, coldness, discoloration of skin, feeling of pressure, hives, infection, inflammation, itching, lumps, numbness, pain, rash, redness, scarring, soreness, stinging, swelling, tenderness, tingling, ulceration, or warmth at site); ***increased thirst; irritability; loss of appetite; runny or stuffy nose; sexual problems in males; sinus problems; sneezing; sore throat***

Note: In some individuals, *loss of appetite* has led to substantial weight loss requiring discontinuation of therapy.

Some of the above-listed side/adverse effects are identical to symptoms of *opioid withdrawal* (see list below). Several of them, such as *abdominal pain, anxiety, joint or muscle pain, nausea or vomiting,* and *unusual tiredness,* may lessen or disappear during continued use. It has been suggested that such effects may be mild withdrawal symptoms in some patients.

Those indicating possible withdrawal in patients physically dependent on opioid drugs

Note: These side effects may occur within 5 minutes after administration of naltrexone and may persist for up to 48 hours.

Abdominal or stomach cramps; anxiety, nervousness, restlessness, or irritability; diarrhea; fast heartbeat; fever, continuing runny nose, or sneezing; gooseflesh; increased sweating; increased yawning; joint or muscle pain; loss of appetite; nausea or vomiting; shivering or trembling; trouble in sleeping; weakness

Overdose

For more information on the management of overdose or unintentional ingestion, **contact a Poison Control Center** (see *Poison Control Center Listing*).

Treatment of overdose

Clinical experience with overdose is lacking. It is recommended that the patient be closely monitored and the observed symptoms treated as required.

Patient Consultation

As an aid to patient consultation, refer to *Advice for the Patient, Naltrexone (Systemic).*

In providing consultation, consider emphasizing the following selected information (» = major clinical significance):

Before using this medication

» Conditions affecting use, especially:

Allergic reaction to naltrexone, history of

Other medications, especially opioids

Other medical problems, especially hepatic failure; hepatitis, acute; or other hepatic disease

Proper use of this medication

» Importance of taking or receiving each dose as scheduled

» Not administering to a patient who is actively drinking at time of initial naltrexone injection

» Proper dosing

For tablets: If dosing schedule is—

One tablet every day—

Taking as soon as possible; not taking if not remembered until the next day; not doubling the next day's dose

One tablet every weekday and two tablets on Saturday—

If weekday dose missed—Following missed dose directions as for one tablet every day

If Saturday dose missed—Taking two tablets as soon as possible if remembered the same day, or taking one tablet if not remembered until Sunday, then returning to regular dosing schedule on Monday

Two tablets every other day—

Taking two tablets as soon as remembered, skipping a day, then continuing every other day; or

Taking two tablets as soon as possible if remembered the same day, or taking one tablet if not remembered until the next day, then returning to the regular dosing schedule

Two tablets on Monday and Wednesday and three tablets on Friday—

If Monday or Wednesday dose missed—Taking two tablets as soon as possible if remembered the same day, or taking one tablet if not remembered until the next day, then returning to the regular dosing schedule

If Friday dose missed—Taking three tablets as soon as possible if remembered the same day; taking two tablets if not remembered until Saturday or one tablet if not remembered until Sunday; returning to the regular dosing schedule on Monday

Three tablets every three days—

Taking three tablets as soon as remembered, skipping two days, then continuing every three days; or

Taking three tablets as soon as possible if remembered the same day; taking two tablets if not remembered until the next day, or one tablet if not remembered until the following day, then returning to the regular dosing schedule

For intramuscular injection: Receiving next dose as soon as possible

» Proper storage

Precautions while using this medication

» Regular visits to physician or clinic; blood tests may be needed to detect possible hepatotoxicity

» Importance of compliance with all components of a comprehensive treatment program, including attending counseling sessions and/or support group meetings; naltrexone is intended only as an aid to other forms of therapy that discourage return to alcohol or opioid use

» Not attempting to overcome effects of naltrexone by taking opioids; such attempts may lead to coma or death; therapy with naltrexone may lead to increased sensitivity to the effects of narcotics

» Not using opioid medications to relieve pain, diarrhea, or cough because naltrexone also prevents therapeutic effects of opioids

» Not taking naltrexone to perform activities (for example, driving) while under the influence of alcohol

Informing patient that once naltrexone is injected into the body, it is not possible to remove it

» Never sharing medication with others, especially those dependent on opioids

» Notifying all physicians, dentists, and pharmacists of use of naltrexone

» Carrying identification card indicating use of medication

» Contacting doctor if skin reaction including pain, tenderness, induration, and pruritus, at injection site worsens, especially if no improvement after one month

Advising patient that mild nausea may occur following initial naltrexone injection and should subside within a few days with less likelihood of nausea in subsequent injections

Side/adverse effects

Signs of potential side effects, especially skin rash; blurred vision or aching, burning, or swollen eyes; chest pain; confusion; discomfort while urinating and/or frequent urination; edema; fever; gastrointestinal ulceration; hallucinations; itching; mental depression or other mood or mental changes; ringing or buzzing in ears; shortness of breath

General Dosing Information

When naltrexone is used as adjunct therapy to treat opioid (narcotic) abuse, naltrexone therapy should not be initiated until the patient has been completely detoxified, is free of withdrawal symptoms, and has remained opioid-free for 7 to 10 days (following use of a relatively short-acting opioid such as heroin) or longer (following use of a longer-acting opioid such as methadone). Abstinence should be verified by examination of the urine for opioids and/or a naloxone challenge test.

Clonidine or methadone may be used to prevent or attenuate withdrawal symptoms during detoxification; however, if methadone is used, initiation of naltrexone therapy must be delayed until there is no risk of precipitating withdrawal symptoms.

The naloxone challenge test should not be administered if withdrawal symptoms are present or the patient's urine contains opioids. Naloxone may be administered intravenously or subcutaneously. If the intravenous route is used, an initial dose of 200 mcg (0.2 mg) should be administered and the patient observed for 30 seconds for withdrawal symptoms; if none occurs, an additional 600 mcg (0.6 mg) of naloxone should be administered and the patient observed for 20 minutes. If the subcutaneous route is used, 800 mcg (0.8 mg) of naloxone should be administered and the patient observed for 20 minutes for withdrawal symptoms. If withdrawal symptoms occur, the naloxone challenge should be repeated at 24-hour intervals until absence of opioid dependence is confirmed.

It is recommended that naltrexone therapy be initiated with a low dose (e.g., 25 mg), which may be increased to 50 mg a day if no signs or symptoms of withdrawal occur. Alternatives to daily administration include several maintenance dosing regimens permitting administration of higher doses every second or third day on an occasional or regular basis (e.g., over weekends). It has been suggested that less frequent dosing, scheduled to suit the individual patient, may improve compliance. The alternative dosing schedules have not been studied in the treatment of alcoholism.

In emergency situations requiring an opioid analgesic, naltrexone's effects can be overcome by administering sufficiently high doses of the analgesic. It is recommended that a rapidly acting analgesic with minimal potential for respiratory depression be administered in doses carefully titrated to the needs of the patient. Since high doses of analgesic are required, the risk of adverse effects, including severe, prolonged respiratory depression and circulatory collapse, is greatly increased. Therefore, such treatment must be carried out in a hospital setting, where the patient can be carefully monitored by trained personnel. Some patients on naltrexone therapy may be sensitive to low doses of opioids. In these patients, adverse effects may occur even with low doses of opioids.

Naltrexone does not cause physical or psychological dependence.

Tolerance to the opioid-blocking action of naltrexone has not been reported.

Long-term success with naltrexone-based regimens for the treatment of alcoholism or opioid drug dependence has not been established. Compliance may be improved if the medication is administered as a component of an integrated program including psychosocial therapy.

For parenteral dosage form

Naltrexone for extended-release intramuscular injection must be administered by a healthcare professional.

Naltrexone should NOT be administered intravenously.

Patients should not be actively drinking at the time of initial naltrexone administration.

Pretreatment with oral naltrexone is not required before using injectable naltrexone.

No data have been systematically collected pertaining to a switch from oral naltrexone to injectable naltrexone.

There are no data regarding reinitiating treatment in patients previously treated with injectable naltrexone.

For treatment of adverse effects

Precipitation of withdrawal symptoms in physically dependent patients: Symptoms may be very difficult to reverse. It is recommended that the patient be monitored closely and treated for observed symptoms as required.

Oral Dosage Forms

NALTREXONE HYDROCHLORIDE TABLETS

Usual adult dose

Opioid (narcotic) drug use, illicit (treatment adjunct)—

Initial—

Oral, 25 mg for the first dose; an additional 25 mg may be given one hour later if no withdrawal symptoms occur.

Maintenance—
Oral, 50 mg every twenty-four hours. Alternatively, the weekly dose of 350 mg may be administered using an intermittent dosing schedule, such as:
Oral, 50 mg every twenty-four hours on weekdays and 100 mg on Saturday; or
Oral, 100 mg every forty-eight hours; or
Oral, 100 mg every Monday and Wednesday and 150 mg on Friday; or
Oral, 150 mg every seventy-two hours.

Alcoholism (treatment)—
Oral, 50 mg every twenty-four hours for up to twelve weeks.

Usual pediatric dose

Dosage in patients up to 18 years of age has not been established.

Strength(s) usually available

U.S.—
50 mg (Rx) [*ReVia* (scored; lactose; microcrystalline cellulose; crospovidone; colloidal silicon dioxide; magnesium stearate; hydroxypropyl methylcellulose; titanium dioxide; polyethylene glycol; polysorbate 80; yellow iron oxide; red iron oxide); GENERIC].

Canada—
50 mg (Rx) [*ReVia* (scored; lactose monohydrate; microcrystalline cellulose; crospovidone; colloidal silicon dioxide; magnesium stearate; microcrystalline methylcellulose; Pale Yellow Opadry® YS-1–6378–G)].

Packaging and storage

Store below 40 °C (104 °F), preferably between 15 and 30 °C (59 and 86 °F), in a tight, light-resistant container, unless otherwise specified by manufacturer.

Parenteral Dosage Forms

NALTREXONE HYDROCHLORIDE FOR EXTENDED-RELEASE INJECTABLE SUSPENSION

Usual adult dose

Alcoholism (treatment)—
Intramuscular, recommended dose of 380 mg every 4 weeks or once a month administered by a health care professional as a gluteal IM injection, alternating buttocks, using the kit components provided.

Usual pediatric dose

Safety and efficacy have not been established in the pediatric population.

Strength(s) usually available

U.S.—
380 mg naltrexone microspheres (Rx) [*Vivitrol* (single-use kit; 4-mL vial diluent containing: carboxymethylcellulose sodium salt; polysorbate 20; sodium chloride; water for injection)].

Packaging and storage

Store the entire dose pack in the refrigerator between 2 and 8 °C (36 and 46 °F) or unrefrigerated for no more than 7 days prior to administration at temperatures not exceeding 25 °C (77 °F). Protect from freezing.

Preparation of dosage form

Naltrexone should be prepared for suspension only with the diluent supplied in the dose kit and must be administered with the needle in the dose kit. All components (i.e., the microspheres, diluent, preparation needle, and an administration needle with safety device) are required to administer naltrexone. An extra administration needle is provided in case of clogging. The components in the dose kit should not be substituted with any other components.

Stability

Naltrexone should be visually inspected for particulate matter and discoloration prior to administration. A properly mixed suspension will be milky white, will not contain clumps, and will move freely down the wall of the vial. If not, discard contents of the vial.

Auxiliary labeling

Keep out of reach of children.

Revised: 05/23/2006

NANDROLONE—See *Anabolic Steroids (Systemic)*

NAPROXEN—See *Anti-inflammatory Drugs, Nonsteroidal (Systemic)*

NARATRIPTAN Systemic

VA CLASSIFICATION (Primary): CN105
Commonly used brand name(s): *Amerge*.
Note: For a listing of dosage forms and brand names by country availability, see *Dosage Forms* section(s).

Category

Antimigraine agent.

Indications

General Considerations

Naratriptan should only be prescribed for patients who have an established clear diagnosis of migraine.

Accepted

Headache, migraine (treatment)—Naratriptan is indicated to relieve (abort) acute migraine headaches (with or without aura).

Unaccepted

Naratriptan is not recommended for treatment of basilar artery migraine or hemiplegic migraine.

Naratriptan is not recommended for treatment of cluster headaches. Efficacy and safety of naratriptan in these conditions have not been established.

Pharmacology/Pharmacokinetics

Physicochemical characteristics

Molecular weight—371.93.

Mechanism of action/Effect

Naratriptan's mechanism of action has not been established. It is thought that agonist activity at the 5-hydroxytryptamine $(5\text{-HT})_{1D}$ and 5-HT_{1B} receptor subtypes provides relief of headaches. Naratriptan is a highly selective agonist at these receptor subtypes; it has no significant activity at 5-HT_2, 5-HT_3, or 5-HT_4 receptor subtypes or at adrenergic, dopaminergic, histamine, muscarinic, or benzodiazepine receptors. It has been proposed that constriction of cerebral blood vessels resulting from $5\text{-HT}_{1D/1B}$ receptor stimulation reduces the pulsation that may be responsible for the pain of migraine headaches. It has also been proposed that naratriptan may relieve migraine headaches by decreasing the release of pro-inflammatory neuropeptides.

Absorption

Oral—Rapid; bioavailability is 70%. The rate and extent of the absorption of naratriptan are not affected by administration with food. The rate of absorption is slower during a migraine attack.

Protein binding

Low (28 to 31%), at plasma concentrations of 50 to 1000 nanograms per mL (nanograms/mL).

Biotransformation

Hepatic. *In vitro* studies indicate that naratriptan is metabolized by cytochrome P450 isoenzymes into inactive metabolites.

Half-life

Approximately 6 hours.

Time to peak concentration

Within 2 to 3 hours (3 to 4 hours during a migraine attack).

Elimination

Renal—80% (50% of the dose as unchanged; 30% as metabolites).

Precautions to Consider

Carcinogenicity/Tumorigenicity

Lifetime carcinogenicity studies were done in mice and rats receiving naratriptan by oral gavage. In mice receiving doses of 200 mg per kg of body weight (mg/kg) per day (reflects an area under the plasma concentration-time curve [AUC] exposure of 110 times the exposure in humans receiving the maximum recommended human dose [MRHD]), no evidence of tumorigenicity was found. Two studies were done in rats, one receiving a standard diet and the other a nitrate-supplemented diet. Rats receiving the standard and nitrate-supplemented diet with doses of naratriptan 5, 20, and 90 mg/kg per day reflected plasma concentration AUC exposures of 7, 40, and 236 times the MRHD and 7, 29, 180 times the MRHD at week 13, respectively. There was an increase in the incidence of thyroid follicular hyperplasia and thyroid follicular adenomas in high-dosed male rats in both studies. However, there was only an increase in thyroid follicular hyperplasia in the high-dosed female rats. Also, in the standard and nitrate supplement studies, the exposure to achieve the no-effect dose for thyroid tumors was 40 and 29 times the MRHD, respectively. In the standard study, there was an increase in the incidence of the benign c-cell adenomas in the thyroid of the high-dosed male rats. The incidence of benign lymphocytic thymoma was increased in all of the females in the nitrate-supplemented diet study.

Mutagenicity

Naratriptan demonstrated no mutagenic effects in the Ames test or in the *in vitro* thymidine locus mouse lymphoma gene mutation assays. There was no evidence of clastogenic activity in the *in vitro* human lymphocyte assay or in the *in vivo* mouse micronucleus cytogenetics assay. A mutagenic product (WHO nitrosation assay) is formed *in vitro* from nitrosated naratriptan, and has been found in stomachs of rats receiving a nitrate-supplemented diet. It was not determined in the two rat studies whether the nitrosated product is systemically absorbed. However, no changes were found in the stomachs of the rats.

Pregnancy/Reproduction

Fertility—A reproductive toxicity study in male and female rats receiving doses of naratriptan up to 10, 60, 170, or 340 mg/kg per day (AUC exposure approximately 11, 70, 230, and 470 times the MRHD) found a treatment-related decrease in the number of females exhibiting normal estrous cycles at doses of 170 mg/kg per day or greater. In female rats receiving doses up to 60 mg/kg per day or greater, an increase in preimplantation loss was observed. In the high-dose group males, testicular and/or epididymal atrophy along with spermatozoa depletion resulted in reduced mating success. Also, the preimplantation loss in females may have been due to the testicular and/or epididymal atrophy. However, the exposures achieved at approximately 11, 70, and 230 times the MRHD of naratriptan resulted in no preimplantation loss, anestrus, and testicular effects, respectively.

A study in rats receiving 10, 60, or 340 mg/kg per day for 6 months found changes in the female reproductive tract including atrophic or cystic ovaries at the highest dose. However, in rats receiving 60 mg/kg per day (85 times the MRHD) of naratriptan, no effect was observed.

Pregnancy—Adequate and well-controlled trials have not been done in pregnant women.

In a reproductive toxicity study, rats and rabbits receiving oral doses of naratriptan equivalent to maternal plasma exposure of 11, 70, and 230 times the MRHD had evidence of developmental toxicity, such as embryo lethality, fetal abnormalities, pup mortality, and offspring growth retardation.

In pregnant rats doses of naratriptan of up to 10, 60, or 340 mg/kg per day (maternal plasma exposures [AUC] approximately 11, 70, and 470 times the MRHD, respectively) given during the organogenesis period resulted in an increase in dose-related embryonic death. The increased incidence of embryo lethality was statistically significant at the highest dose only. However, the incidence of fetal structural variations, such as incomplete or irregular ossification of skull bones, sternebrae, and ribs were increased at all the doses. The highest dose was found to be maternally toxic, which resulted in a lower than normal maternal weight gain during gestation.

In pregnant Dutch rabbits receiving doses of naratriptan of up to 1, 5, or 30 mg/kg per day (approximately 4, 20, and 120 times the MRHD on a mg per square meter of body surface area [mg/m²] basis, respectively), during the organogenesis period, an increase in incidences of fused sternebrae at the highest dose was observed. In addition, at all the doses there was evidence of an increase in embryonic death, and fetal variations, such as major blood vessel variations, incomplete skeletal ossification, and supernumerary ribs. The highest dose in this study was also found to be maternally toxic, which resulted in a lower maternal weight gain during gestation. A study in pregnant New Zealand white rabbits, during the organogenesis period, receiving naratriptan doses of 1, 5, or 30 mg/kg (maternal exposure approximately 2.5, 19, and 140 times the MRHD) per day found decreased fetal weights and increased incidences of fetal skeletal variations at all doses. In contrast with the Dutch rabbits, the maternal weight gain in the New Zealand white rabbits was lower at doses of naratriptan of 5 mg/kg or greater.

In female rats receiving 10, 60, 340 mg/kg doses of naratriptan during late gestation and lactation, behavioral impairment, such as tremors, was observed. At doses of 60 mg/kg per day or greater of naratriptan, a decrease in offspring viability and growth was observed. However, maternal toxicity occurred only at the highest doses. The maternal exposure achieved at approximately 11 times the MRHD of naratriptan did not cause any developmental effects.

FDA Pregnancy Category C.

Breast-feeding

It is not known whether naratriptan is distributed into human breast milk. Naratriptan is distributed into the milk of lactating rats.

Pediatrics

No information is available on the relationship of age to the effects of naratriptan in pediatric patients. Safety and efficacy have not been established.

Adolescents

In clinical trials, 300 children 12 to 17 years of age have been treated with naratriptan (0.25- to 1.5-mg doses); adverse effects were similar to those occurring in patients older than 17 years of age. However, the safety and efficacy of naratriptan in children up to 18 years of age have not been established.

Geriatrics

Use of naratriptan in elderly patients is not recommended.

Drug interactions and/or related problems

The following drug interactions and/or related problems have been selected on the basis of their potential clinical significance (possible mechanism in parentheses where appropriate)—not necessarily inclusive (» = major clinical significance):

Note: Combinations containing any of the following medications, depending on the amount present, may also interact with this medication.

Dihydroergotamine or
Ergotamine or
Methysergide or
Other 5-hydroxytryptamine ($5HT_1$) agonists such as:
Sumatriptan or
Zolmitriptan
(a delay of 24 hours between administration of dihydroergotamine, ergotamine, methysergide, or other $5HT_1$ and naratriptan is recommended because of the possibility of additive and/or prolonged vasoconstriction)

Serotonergics (see *Appendix II*), such as:
Fluoxetine
Fluvoxamine
Paroxetine
Sertraline
(concurrent use may result in weakness, hyperreflexia, and incoordination; monitoring is recommended)

Medical considerations/Contraindications

The medical considerations/contraindications included have been selected on the basis of their potential clinical significance (reasons given in parentheses where appropriate)—not necessarily inclusive (» = major clinical significance).

Except under special circumstances, this medication should not be used when the following medical problems exist:

» Coronary artery disease, especially:
Angina pectoris
Myocardial infarction, history of
Myocardial ischemia, silent, documented
Prinzmetal's angina or

» Other conditions in which coronary vasoconstriction would be detrimental
(naratriptan may cause coronary vasospasms)

» Hypertension, uncontrolled
(may be exacerbated)

» Peripheral vascular disease, including:
Ischemic bowel disease
(may be exacerbated)

Risk-benefit should be considered when the following medical problems exist:

» Cerebrovascular accident, history of
($5HT_1$ agonists may precipitate a cerebrovascular syndrome; caution should be used when administering to patients at risk for cerebrovascular events)

» Coronary artery disease, predisposition to
(naratriptan may cause serious coronary adverse effects; patients in whom coronary artery disease is a possibility on the basis of age or the presence of other risk factors, such as diabetes, hypercholesterolemia, obesity, a strong family history of coronary artery disease, or tobacco smoking should be evaluated for the presence of cardiovascular disease before naratriptan is prescribed; even after a satisfactory evaluation, the advisability of administering the patient's first dose under medical supervision should be considered)

» Hepatic function impairment, severe or
» Renal function impairment, severe
(studies have shown a decrease in naratriptan clearance in patients with moderate hepatic and renal impairment; caution is rec-

ommended; a dosage adjustment is recommended in patients with severe hepatic and renal impairment)

» Hypersensitivity to naratriptan

» Hypertension, controlled
(may precipitate an increase in systolic and diastolic pressure)

Patient monitoring
The following may be especially important in patient monitoring (other tests may be warranted in some patients, depending on condition; » = major clinical significance):

Electrocardiogram (ECG)
(monitoring is recommended for long-term intermittent users of naratriptan)

Side/Adverse Effects
The following side/adverse effects have been selected on the basis of their potential clinical significance (possible signs and symptoms in parentheses where appropriate)—not necessarily inclusive:

Those indicating need for medical attention
Incidence more frequent
Chest pain, severe; heaviness, tightness, or pressure in chest, throat, and/or neck; paresthesias (sensation of burning, warmth or heat, numbness, tightness, or tingling)

Incidence less frequent or rare
Arrythmias (irregular heartbeat); ***bradycardia*** (slow heartbeat); ***convulsions; decreased blood pressure; increased blood pressure***

Those indicating need for medical attention only if they continue or are bothersome
Incidence more frequent
Dizziness; drowsiness; malaise (increased tiredness); ***nausea and/or vomiting***

Incidence less frequent
Anxiety; arthralgia (joint pain); ***blurred vision; chills and/or fever; constipation; diarrhea; gastroenteritis*** (diarrhea; nausea; stomach pain); ***increased thirst; muscle or joint stiffness, tightness, or rigidity; muscle pain or spasms; palpitations*** (pounding heartbeat); ***polyuria*** (sudden, large increase in frequency and quantity of urine); ***pruritus*** (itching of the skin); ***sleep disorders*** (difficulty sleeping); ***skin rash; stomach discomfort and/or pain; syncope*** (fainting); ***tremors*** (trembling or shaking of hands or feet)

Incidence rare
Acne; anemia (unusual tiredness or weakness); ***bone or skeletal pain; confusion; eye problems, including dry eyes; eye pain and/or discomfort; fluid imbalance; mood or mental changes, including agitation; hallucinations; and panic disorders; restlessness; taste perversion*** (change in taste sensation)

Overdose
For more information on the management of overdose or unintentional ingestion, **contact a Poison Control Center** (see *Poison Control Center Listing*).

Clinical effects of overdose
The following effects have been selected on the basis of their potential clinical significance (possible signs and symptoms in parentheses where appropriate)—not necessarily inclusive:

Acute and/or chronic
Increased blood pressure; lightheadedness; loss of coordination; tension in neck; tiredness

Treatment of overdose
Monitoring—
Electrocardiogram (ECG) monitoring should be performed in patients who present with symptoms of chest pain or other symptoms consistent with angina.
Patients should be monitored for at least 24 hours after an overdose of naratriptan.

Supportive care—
Maintaining an open airway and breathing, maintaining proper fluid and electrolyte balance and/or correcting hypertension. Patients in whom intentional overdose is confirmed or suspected should be referred for psychiatric consultation.

Patient Consultation
As an aid to patient consultation, refer to *Advice for the Patient, Naratriptan—(Systemic)*.

In providing consultation, consider emphasizing the following» selected information (» = major clinical significance):

Before using this medication
» Conditions affecting use, especially:
Hypersensitivity to naratriptan
Use in the elderly—Use is not recommended
Other medical problems, especially cerebrovascular accident (history of), coronary artery disease, predisposition to coronary artery disease, or other conditions that may be adversely affected by coronary artery constriction, hepatic function impairment (severe), peripheral vascular disease, renal function impairment (severe), hypertension

Proper use of this medication
» Not administering if atypical headache symptoms are present; checking with physician instead
Administering after onset of headache pain
Additional benefit may be obtained if the patient lies down in a quiet, dark room after administering medication
» Not taking additional doses if first dose does not provide substantial relief; taking alternate medication as previously advised by physician, then checking with physician as soon as possible
» Taking additional doses, if needed, for return of migraine headache after initial relief was obtained, provided that prescribed limits (quantity used and frequency of administration) are not exceeded
» Compliance with prophylactic therapy, if prescribed
» Proper dosing
» Proper storage

Precautions while using this medication
Avoiding alcohol, which aggravates headache

» Caution when driving or doing anything else requiring alertness because of possible drowsiness, dizziness, lightheadedness, impairment of physical or mental abilities

Side/adverse effects
Signs of potential side effects, especially chest pain, severe; heaviness, tightness, or pressure in chest and/or neck; paresthesias; upper respiratory tract infection; arrythmias; hypertension; bradycardia; and convulsions

Oral Dosage Forms

NARATRIPTAN HYDROCHLORIDE TABLETS
Note: The dosing and strengths of the dosage form available are expressed in terms of naratriptan base (not the hydrochloride salt).

Usual adult dose
Antimigraine agent—
Oral, 1 or 2.5 mg (base) as a single dose. If necessary, additional doses may be taken at intervals of at least four hours.
A starting dose of less than 2.5 mg is recommended for patients with mild to moderate hepatic or renal impairment.

Usual adult prescribing limits
5 mg in twenty-four hours.
2.5 mg in patients with mild or moderate hepatic or renal impairment.

Usual pediatric dose
Safety and efficacy have not been established in children up to 18 years of age.

Usual geriatric dose
Use is not recommended.

Strength(s) usually available
U.S.—
1 mg (base) (Rx) [*Amerge* (croscarmellose sodium; hydroxypropyl methylcellulose; lactose; magnesium stearate; microcrystalline cellulose; triacetin; titanium dioxide; iron oxide yellow; indigo carmine aluminum lake (FD&C Blue No. 2))].
2.5 mg (base) (Rx) [*Amerge* (croscarmellose sodium; hydroxypropyl methylcellulose; lactose; magnesium stearate; microcrystalline cellulose; triacetin; titanium dioxide; iron oxide yellow; indigo carmine aluminum lake (FD&C Blue No. 2))].

Packaging and storage
Store below 25 °C (77 °F).

Auxiliary labeling
• Take with a full glass of water.

Developed: 07/07/1998

NATALIZUMAB Systemic†

VA CLASSIFICATION (Primary/Secondary): CN900 /IM409

Commonly used brand name(s): *Tysabri*.

Note: For a listing of dosage forms and brand names by country availability, see *Dosage Forms* section(s).

†Not commercially available in Canada.

Category

Multiple sclerosis (MS) therapy agent; biologic response modifier.

Indications

Accepted

Multiple sclerosis (treatment)—is indicated as monotherapy for the treatment of patients with relapsing forms of multiple sclerosis to delay the accumulation of physical disability and reduce the frequency of clinical exacerbations. The safety and efficacy of natalizumab beyond two years are unknown.

Natalizumab is recommended for patients who have had an inadequate response to, or are unable to tolerate, alternate multiple sclerosis therapies.

Acceptance not established

Safety and efficacy in patients with chronic progressive multiple sclerosis have not been established.

Pharmacology/Pharmacokinetics

Physicochemical characteristics

Source—Natalizumab is a recombinant humanized IgG4-kappa monoclonal antibody produced in murine myeloma cells.

Chemical Group—Natalizumab contains human framework regions and the complementarity-determining regions of a murine antibody that binds to alpha 4-integrin.

Molecular weight—Natalizumab: 149 kilodaltons.

Mechanism of action/Effect

The specific mechanism of natalizumab in patients with multiple sclerosis has not been fully defined.

Natalizumab is a recombinant IgG4kappa monoclonal antibody against alpha4 integrins, expressed on the surface of all leukocytes except neutrophils. Binding of alpha4 integrins results in inhibition of adhesion of leukocytes to their counter-receptors. Specifically, natalizumab binds to the alpha4-subunit of alpha4beta1 integrin and alpha4beta7 integrin. Vascular-cell adhesion molecule-1 (VCAM-1) and mucosal addressin-cell adhesion molecule-1 (MadCAM-1) are receptors for the alpha4 family on integrins. Disruption of these molecular interactions prevents transmigration of leukocytes across the endothelium into inflamed parenchymal tissue.

The effect of natalizumab in multiple sclerosis may be secondary to the blockade of the interaction of alpha4beta1-integrin expressed by inflammatory cells with VCAM-1 on vascular endothelial cells, and with connecting segment-1 (CS-1) and/or osteopontin expressed by parenchymal cells in the brain. The result of these molecular interactions may inhibit further recruitment and inflammatory activity of activated immune cells.

In an animal model of multiple sclerosis, repeated administration of natalizumab reduced leukocyte migration into brain parenchyma and reduced plaque formation detected by magnetic resonance imaging (MRI). The clinical significance of these findings to humans is unknown.

Distribution

Volume of distribution (Vol_D)—5.7 ± 1.9 L

Half-life

11 ± 4 days following repeat intravenous administration of a 300 mg dose.

Time to steady-state concentration

Approximately 24 weeks after every 4 weeks of dosing

Peak serum concentration

110 ± 52 mcg/mL following repeat intravenous administration of a 300 mg dose.

Steady state trough concentration

Ranged from 23 to 29 mcg/mL over the dosing period.

Elimination

Clearance—16 ± 5 mL/hour.

Note: Natalizumab clearance increased less than proportionally with body weight (a 43% increase in body weight resulted in a 32% increase in clearance).

The presence of persistent anti-natalizumab antibodies increased natalizumab clearance approximately 3-fold.

Precautions to Consider

Tumorigenicity

Natalizumab showed no effects on *in vitro* assays of an alpha4-integrin positive tumor line proliferation/cytotoxicity or demonstrated no increase in tumor growth rates or metastasis from natalizumab treatment in SCID and nude mice with two alpha4-integrin positive tumor lines.

Mutagenicity

No clastogenic or mutagenic effects were revealed in the Ames or human chromosomal aberration assays.

Pregnancy/Reproduction

Fertility—Studies in female guinea pigs given doses of 30 mg/kg showed a reduction in fertility and 47% reductions in pregnancy rate. No reductions were seen at doses 10 mg/kg (2.3-fold the clinical dose). Implantations were seen in only 36% of animals having corpora lutea in the 30 mg/kg group versus (66-72%) in the other groups. Natalizumab did not affect male fertility at doses up to 7-fold the clinical dose.

Pregnancy—Adequate and well controlled studies in humans have not been done. Because animal reproduction studies are not always predictive of human response, natalizumab should be used during pregnancy only if clearly needed. If a woman becomes pregnant while taking natalizumab, discontinuation of natalizumab should be considered.

If a woman becomes pregnant while taking natlizumab, enrolling her in the TYSABRI® Pregnancy Exposure Registry should be considered (1-800-456-2255).

Studies done in monkeys and guinea pigs found no evidence of teratogenic effects at doses up to 30 mg/kg (7 times the human clinical dose based on a body weight comparison). A small reduction in pup survival was noted at post-natal day 14 in comparison to controls in female guinea pigs exposed to natalizumab during the second half of pregnancy. In one study monkeys treated with 30 mg/kg of natalizumab during pregnancy revealed an increase in the number of abortions (33% vs 17% in controls). However no effects on abortion rates were noted during any other study. When pregnant dams exposed to approximately 7-fold the clinical dose, fetal serum levels at the time of delivery were approximately 35% of the maternal serum natalizumab levels. Pregnant monkeys treated with 2.3-fold the clinical dose demonstrated natalizumab-related changes in the fetus. These changes included mild anemia, reduced platelet count, increased spleen weights, and reduced liver and thymus weights associated with increased splenic extramedullary hematopoiesis, thymic atrophy, and decreased hepatic hematopoiesis. Offspring of mothers treated with natalizumab at 7-fold the clinical dose also demonstrated reduced platelet counts, however the effect was reversed upon clearance of natalizumab. There was no evidence of anemia in these offspring.

FDA Pregnancy Category C

Breast-feeding

It is not known whether natalizumab is distributed into human milk. Because many drugs and immunoglobulins are distributed in human milk and because the potential for serious adverse reactions is unknown, a decision should be made whether to discontinue nursing or natalizumab taking into account the importance of therapy to the mother.

Pediatrics

Safety and effectiveness of natalizumab in pediatric multiple sclerosis patients below 18 years of age have not been established.

Natalizumab is not indicated for use in pediatric patients.

Geriatrics

No information is available on the relationship of age to the effects of natalizumab in geriatric patients.

Drug interactions and/or related problems

The following drug interactions and/or related problems have been selected on the basis of their potential clinical significance (possible mechanism in parentheses where appropriate)—not necessarily inclusive (» = major clinical significance):

Note: Combinations containing any of the following medications, depending on the amount present, may also interact with this medication.

» Antineoplastic agents or

» Immunomodulating agents or
» Immunosuppressant agents
(concomitant use may further increase risk of infections; safety and efficacy of combination use not established)

Interferon beta-1a
(reduces natalizumab clearance by approximately 30%, however no dosage adjustment of natalizumab is necessary to maintain safety)

Vaccines
(no data available on effects of vaccination concomitant with natalizumab; no data available on secondary transmission of infection by live vaccines in patients receiving natalizumab)

Laboratory value alterations

The following have been selected on the basis of their potential clinical significance (possible effect in parentheses where appropriate)—not necessarily inclusive (» = major clinical significance).

With physiology/laboratory test values
Basophils or
Eosinophils or
Lymphocytes or
Monocytes or
Red blood cells, nucleated
(increases have been observed during treatment with natalizumab, however levels are reversible returning to baseline within 16 weeks after the last dose)

Medical considerations/Contraindications

The medical considerations/contraindications included have been selected on the basis of their potential clinical significance (reasons given in parentheses where appropriate)—not necessarily inclusive (» = major clinical significance).

Except under special circumstances, this medication should not be used when the following medical problem exists:

» Compromised immune system function
(should NOT be used due to increased risk of PML)

» Hypersensitivity to natalizumab or any of its components

» Progressive multifocal leukoencephalopathy (PML), past or current
(contraindicated in patients who have or have had PML)

Risk-benefit should be considered when the following medical problems exist:

» Hepatic insufficiency or
» Renal insufficiency
(use with caution; patients with hepatic or renal insufficiency have not been studied.)

Patient monitoring

The following may be especially important in patient monitoring (other tests may be warranted in some patients, depending on condition; » = major clinical significance):

» Signs and symptoms of progressive multifocal leukoencephalopathy (PML)
(natalizumab dosing should be withheld immediately at first sign or symptoms suggestive of PML)
(for diagnosis, an evaluation that includes a gadolinium-enhanced magnetic resonance imaging [MRI] scan of the brain, and when indicated, cerebrospinal fluid analysis for JC viral DNA)

Side/Adverse Effects

The following side/adverse effects have been selected on the basis of their potential clinical significance (possible signs and symptoms in parentheses where appropriate)—not necessarily inclusive:

Those indicating need for medical attention

Incidence more frequent

Allergic reaction (cough; difficulty swallowing; dizziness; fast heartbeat; hives; itching; puffiness or swelling of the eyelids or around the eyes, face, lips or tongue; shortness of breath; skin rash; tightness in chest; unusual tiredness or weakness; wheezing); ***immunogenicity*** (body produces substance that can bind to drug making it less effective or cause side effects); ***infusion -related reaction*** (dizziness fever or chills; facial swelling; headache; nausea or vomiting; shortness of breath; skin rash; weakness)

Incidence rare

Cholelithiasis (abdominal fullness; gaseous abdominal pain; recurrent fever; yellow eyes or skin); ***depression including; suicidal ideation*** (thoughts of killing oneself; changes in behavior); ***hypersensitivity reactions including; anaphylaxis/anaphylactoid reactions*** (cough; difficulty swallowing; dizziness; fast heartbeat; hives; itching; puffiness or swelling of the eyelids or around the eyes, face, lips or tongue; shortness of breath; skin rash; tightness in chest; unusual tiredness or weakness; wheezing); ***chest pain; dizziness; dyspnea*** (shortness of breath, difficult or labored breathing; tightness in chest; wheezing); ***fever; flushing*** (feeling of warmth; redness of the face, neck, arms and occasionally, upper chest); ***hypotension*** (blurred vision; confusion; dizziness; faintness, or lightheadedness when getting up from a lying or sitting position suddenly; sweating; unusual tiredness or weakness); ***nausea; pruritus*** (itching skin); ***rash; rigors*** (feeling unusually cold; shivering); ***urticaria*** (hives or welts; itching redness of skin; skin rash); ***pneumonia*** (chest pain; cough; fever or chills; sneezing; shortness of breath; sore throat; troubled breathing; tightness in chest; wheezing)

Incidence unknown

Progressive multifocal leukoencephalopathy (PML) (back pain; blurred vision; confusion; convulsions; dizziness; drowsiness; fever; headache; unusual tiredness or weakness)

Those indicating need for medical attention only if they continue or are bothersome

Incidence more frequent

Abdominal discomfort (stomach soreness or discomfort); ***abnormal liver function test*** (lab results that show problems with liver); ***arthralgia*** (pain in joints; muscle pain or stiffness; difficulty in moving); ***depression*** (discouragement; feeling sad or empty; irritability; lack of appetite; loss of interest or pleasure; tiredness; trouble concentrating; trouble sleeping); ***dermatitis*** (blistering, crusting, irritation, itching, or reddening of skin; cracked, dry, scaly skin; swelling); ***dysmenorrhea*** (pain; cramps; heavy bleeding); ***fatigue*** (unusual tiredness or weakness); ***gastroenteritis*** (abdominal or stomach pain; diarrhea; loss of appetite; nausea; weakness); ***headache; irregular menstruation; tonsillitis*** (congestion, fever, sore throat, swollen glands); ***upper respiratory tract infection*** (cough; fever; sneezing sore throat); ***urinary frequency*** (increased need to urinate; passing urine more often); ***urinary tract infection*** (bladder pain; bloody or cloudy urine; difficult, burning, or painful urination; frequent urge to urinate; lower back or side pain); ***urinary urgency*** (frequent strong or increased urge to urinate); ***vaginitis*** (itching of the vagina or genital area; pain during sexual intercourse; thick, white vaginal discharge with no odor or with a mild odor)

Incidence less frequent

Amenorrhea (absent, missed, or irregular menstrual periods; stopping of menstrual bleeding); ***chest discomfort; local bleeding; syncope*** (fainting); ***tremor*** (trembling or shaking of hands or feet; shakiness in legs, arms, hands, feet)

Overdose

For more information on the management of overdose or unintentional ingestion, **contact a poison control center** (see *Poison Control Center Listing*).

Treatment of overdose

Supportive care—
There is no known specific antidote to natalizumab. Treatment is generally symptomatic and supportive.
Patients in whom intentional overdose is confirmed or suspected should be referred for psychiatric consultation.

Patient Consultation

As an aid to patient consultation, refer to *Advice for the Patient, Natalizumab (Systemic)*.

In providing consultation, consider emphasizing the following selected information (» = major clinical significance):

Before using this medication

» Conditions affecting use, especially:
Hypersensitivity to natalizumab or any of its components
Pregnancy—Risk benefit considerations; if pregnancy occurs while taking natalizumab, discontinuation should be considered
Breast-feeding—Risk benefit considerations due to unknown potential for adverse effects
Use in children—Not indicated for use in pediatric patients.
Other medications, especially antineoplastic agents, immunomodulating agents, orimmunosuppressive agents
Other medical problems, especially compromised immune system function, past or current progressive multifocal leukoencephalopathy (PML), hepatic insufficiency or renal insufficiency

Proper use of this medication

» Importance of mandatory registration in the TOUCH™ program for prescribers, infusion centers, and pharmacies and enrollment of patients meeting all requirements of the program prior to natalizumab use

» Obtaining an MRI scan prior to initiating natalizumab therapy

» Proper dosing
Asking your doctor what to do.
Proper storage

Precautions while using

» Monitoring patient for any signs or symptoms suggestive of progressive multifocal leukoencephalopathy (PML)

» Reporting any signs or symptoms consistent with a hypersensitivity reaction right away

» Avoiding immunizations unless approved by physician.

Side/adverse effects

Signs of potential side effects, especially allergic reaction, immunogenicity, cholelithiasis, depression including suicidal ideation; hypersensitivity reactions including anaphylaxis/anaphylactoid reactions, chest pain, dizziness, dyspnea, fever, flushing, hypotension, nausea, pruritus, rash, rigors, urticaria; pneumonia or progressive multifocal leukoencephalopathy (PML)

General Dosing Information

Because of the risk of progressive multifocal leukoencephalopathy (PML) which could lead to death or severe disability, *natalizumab is made available to prescribers, infusion center and pharmacies registered with a special restricted distribution program called the TOUCH™ Prescribing Program*. Additionally natalizumab may only be administered to patients who are enrolled in and meet all the conditions of the TOUCH™ program. For more information contact the TOUCH™ Prescribing Program at 1-800-456-2255 or see the package insert for TYSABRI®.

An MRI scan should be obtained prior to initiating therapy with natalizumab. The MRI may be helpful in differentiating subsequent multiple sclerosis symptoms from PML.

Natalizumab should be administered as an IV infusion over approximately one hour.

Natalizumab infusion should not be administered as an IV push or bolus injection.

Patients should be observed during the infusion and for 1 hour after the infusion is complete.

The infusion should be discontinued upon the first observation of any signs or symptoms consistent with a hypersensitivity-type reaction, and not re-treating patients who have experienced a hypersensitivity reaction.

If the presence of persistent antibodies is suspected, antibody tested should be performed. Antibodies detected within the first 6 months of treatment may be transient and disappear with continued dosing. Testing should be repeated at 3 months after the initial positive result to confirm that antibodies are persistent. Prescribers should then assess risk benefit of continued natalizumab use in a patient with persistent antibodies.

Patients who become persistently positive for antibodies to natalizumab may be more likely to have an infusion-related reaction than those who are antibody-negative.

Filtration devices should not be used during administration.

Other medications should not be injected into infusion side ports or mixing other medications with natalizumab.

Parenteral Dosage Forms

NATALIZUMAB FOR INJECTION

Usual adult dose

Multiple sclerosis (treatment)—
Intravenous infusion, recommended 300 mg over approximately one hour every four weeks.

Usual adult prescribing limits

Maximum amount of natalizumab that can be safely administered not determined; safety of doses greater than 300 mg not adequately evaluated

Usual pediatric dose

Natalizumab is not indicated for use in pediatric patients.

Usual geriatric dose

See *Usual adult dose.*

Strength(s) usually available

U.S.—
300 mg natalizumab [*Tysabri* (preservative-free, single-use vial; 123 mg sodium chloride; 17 mg sodium phosphate, monobasic, monohydrate; 7.24 mg sodium phosphate, dibasic, heptahydrate; 3 mg polysorbate 80; in water for injection)].

Packaging and storage

Store between 2 and 8 °C (36 and 46 °F). Do not shake or freeze. Protect from light.

Preparation of dosage form

Each vial of natalizumab is intended for single use only. Prior to dilution and administration inspect the natalizumab vial for particulate material, the color should be clear to slightly opalescent. If discolored or visible particulates are observed, the vial must not be used. To prepare the solution, withdraw 15 mL of the natalizumab concentrate using aseptic technique. Inject the natalizumab concentrate into 100 mL of 0.9% Sodium Chloride Injection, USP. No other IV diluents may be used to prepare the natalizumab solution. Gently invert to mix. Do not shake. Again visually inspect the solution for particulate matter. Following dilution of natalizumab, infuse immediately or refrigerate at 2 to 8 °C, and use within 8 hours. If stored at 2 to 8 °C, allow the solution to reach room temperature before infusion.

After infusion is complete, flush with 0.9% Sodium Chloride Injection, USP. See the manufacturer's package insert for instructions.

Stability

Natalizumab contains no preservatives and should be used immediately after dilution or can be stored at 2 to 8 °C, and be used within 8 hours. Natalizumab should not be used beyond the expiration date stamped on the carton or vial.

Auxiliary labeling

- Do not shake.
- Do not freeze.
- For single dose only. Discard unused drug.

Revised: 07/29/2006
Developed: 01/31/2005

NATEGLINIDE Systemic

VA CLASSIFICATION (Primary): HS509

Commonly used brand name(s): *Starlix.*

Note: For a listing of dosage forms and brand names by country availability, see *Dosage Forms* section(s).

Category

Antidiabetic agent.

Indications

Accepted

Diabetes, type 2 (treatment)—Nateglinide is indicated as monotherapy to lower blood glucose concentrations in patients with type 2 diabetes (previously referred to as non-insulin-dependent diabetes mellitus [NIDDM]) whose hyperglycemia cannot be controlled by diet and exercise. It also is indicated in combination with metformin or a thiazolidinedione in patients whose hyperglycemia cannot be controlled by metformin alone or after a therapeutic response to a thiazolidinedione. In such patients, nateglinide should be added to, but not substituted for, a regimen that includes metformin or a thiazolidinedione.

Nateglinide is not recommended for use as monotherapy in patients who have been chronically treated with other antidiabetic agents. Patients whose hyperglycemia cannot be controlled with glyburide or other insulin secretagogues should not be switched to nateglinide. Nateglinide also should not be added to the regimen that includes an insulin secretagogue.

Pharmacology/Pharmacokinetics

Physicochemical characteristics

Molecular weight—317.43.

Solubility—Freely soluble in methanol, ethanol, and chloroform; soluble in ether; sparingly soluble in acetonitrile and octanol; practically insoluble in water.

Mechanism of action/Effect

Nateglinide lowers blood glucose concentrations by stimulating the release of insulin from functioning beta cells of pancreatic islet tissue. Nateglinide interacts with the adenosine triphosphate (ATP)-sensitive potassium channel on pancreatic beta cells. The subsequent depolarization of the beta cell opens the calcium channel, producing calcium influx and insulin secretion.

Absorption
Rapidly absorbed following oral administration prior to a meal. Administration with or after a meal results in a decrease in the peak plasma concentration (C_{max}), and a delay in the time to reach the C_{max} (T_{max}). However, there is no change in the area under the plasma concentration-time curve (AUC).

Distribution
Absolute bioavailability is approximately 73%. Following intravenous administration to healthy volunteers, the steady-state volume of distribution (Vol_D) was approximately 10 L.

Nataglinide has a low affinity for heart and skeletal muscle tissue.

Protein binding
Very high (98%); primarily to serum albumin and to a lesser extent to alpha 1–acid glycoprotein.

Biotransformation
Metabolism is via hydroxylation followed by glucuronidation. The major metabolites have less antidiabetic activity than nateglinide, but the isoprene minor metabolite has antidiabetic activity comparable to that of nateglinide.

Cytochrome P450 isoenzymes CYP2C9 and CYP3A4 have been shown *in vitro* to be involved in the metabolism of nateglinide.

Half-life
Elimination—1.5 hours.

Onset of action
20 minutes.

Time to peak concentration
1 hour.

Duration of action
4 hours.

Elimination
Renal, 83% (75% within 6 hours after dosing). Approximately 16% excreted as parent compound.

Fecal, approximately 10%.

Precautions to Consider

Carcinogenicity/Tumorigenicity
No evidence of carcinogenicity or tumorigenicity was found in a 2-year study in which Sprague-Dawley rats were administered nateglinide orally at doses up to 900 mg per kg of body weight (mg/kg) per day (equivalent to 30 to 40 times the human therapeutic exposure following doses of 120 mg 3 times a day before meals) or in a 2-year study in which B6C3F1 mice were administered nateglinide orally at doses up to 400 mg/kg per day (equivalent to 10 to 30 times the human therapeutic exposure following doses of 120 mg 3 times a day before meals).

Mutagenicity
No evidence of mutagenicity was found following the *in vitro* Ames test, mouse lymphoma assay, chromosome aberration assay in Chinese hamster lung cells, or in the *in vivo* mouse micronucleus test.

Pregnancy/Reproduction
Fertility—Fertility was unaffected by administration of nateglinide to rats at doses up to 600 mg/kg (approximately 16 times the human therapeutic exposure following doses of 120 mg 3 times a day before meals).

Pregnancy—Adequate and well-controlled studies have not been done in humans. Nateglinide should not be used during pregnancy.

No evidence of teratogenicity was found in rats administered doses up to 1000 mg/kg (approximately 60 times the human therapeutic exposure following doses of 120 mg 3 times a day before meals). However, adverse embryonic development and an increased incidence of gallbladder agenesis or small gallbladder were observed in rabbits administered doses of 500 mg/kg (approximately 40 times the human therapeutic exposure following doses of 120 mg 3 times a day before meals).

FDA Pregnancy Category C.

Labor and delivery—The effect of nateglinide on labor and delivery in humans is not known.

Breast-feeding
It is not known whether nateglinide is distributed into human breast milk. However, studies have shown that nateglinide is distributed into the milk of lactating rats. Nateglinide should not be administered to nursing mothers.

Pediatrics
No information is available on the relationship of age to the effects of nateglinide in pediatric patients. Safety and efficacy have not been established.

Geriatrics
Appropriate studies performed to date have not demonstrated geriatrics-specific problems that would limit the usefulness of nateglinide in the elderly. However, elderly patients may be more susceptible to hypoglycemia and greater sensitivity of some older individuals to nateglinide therapy cannot be ruled out.

Drug interactions and/or related problems
The following drug interactions and/or related problems have been selected on the basis of their potential clinical significance (possible mechanism in parentheses where appropriate)—not necessarily inclusive (» = major clinical significance):

Note: Combinations containing any of the following medications, depending on the amount present, may also interact with this medication.

Anti-inflammatory drugs, nonsteroidal (NSAIDs) or
Beta-adrenergic blocking agents, nonselective or
Monoamine oxidase (MAO) inhibitors or
Salicylates
(these medications may potentiate the hypoglycemic action of nateglinide or other oral antidiabetic agents; glycemic control should be monitored closely when these medications are either administered to or withdrawn from patients taking nateglinide)

» Beta-adrenergic blocking agents
(these medications may blunt some of the symptoms of hypoglycemia, making detection of this condition more difficult)

Corticosteroids or
Diuretics, thiazide or
Sympathomimetic agents or
Thyroid hormones
(these medications may reduce the hypoglycemic action of nateglinide or other oral antidiabetic agents; glycemic control should be monitored closely when these medications are either administered to or withdrawn from patients taking nateglinide)

Laboratory value alterations
The following have been selected on the basis of their potential clinical significance (possible effect in parentheses where appropriate)—not necessarily inclusive (» = major clinical significance).

With physiology/laboratory test values
Uric acid
(in clinical trials, concentrations were slightly increased in patients who received nateglinide alone, nateglinide in combination with metformin, metformin alone, and glyburide alone; the clinical significance of this finding is unknown)

Medical considerations/Contraindications
The medical considerations/contraindications included have been selected on the basis of their potential clinical significance (reasons given in parentheses where appropriate)—not necessarily inclusive (» = major clinical significance).

Except under special circumstances, this medication should not be used when the following medical problems exist:

» Diabetic ketoacidosis or
» Type 1 diabetes
(these conditions should be treated with insulin)

» Hypersensitivity to nateglinide or any components of the formulation

Risk-benefit should be considered when the following medical problems exist:

Adrenal or pituitary insufficiency or
Malnourishment or
Renal impairment, severe
(patients with these conditions are more susceptible to hypoglycemia due to the glucose lowering effect of nateglinide treatment)

Alcohol ingestion or
Insufficient caloric intake, acute or chronic or
Strenuous physical exercise—May increase the risk of hypoglycemia

Fever or
Infection or
Surgery or
Trauma
(transient loss of glycemic control may accompany these conditions; insulin therapy may be needed)

Hepatic function impairment
(area under the plasma concentration-time curve [AUC] and peak plasma concentration [C_{max}] were increased by 30% in nondiabetic

volunteers who had mild hepatic function impairment compared with healthy volunteers; however, studies have not been done in patients with moderate to severe hepatic disease; caution is recommended in patients with chronic hepatic disease)

» Neuropathy, autonomic
(some of the symptoms of hypoglycemia may be blunted, making detection more difficult)

Patient monitoring

The following may be especially important in patient monitoring (other tests may be warranted in some patients, depending on condition; » = major clinical significance):

» Glucose concentrations, blood and
» Glycosylated hemoglobin (HbA_{1C}) values
(recommended periodically to assess the response to therapy)

Side/Adverse Effects

The following side/adverse effects have been selected on the basis of their potential clinical significance (possible signs and symptoms in parentheses where appropriate)—not necessarily inclusive:

Those indicating need for medical attention

Incidence less frequent

Hypoglycemia (anxiety; behavior change similar to drunkenness; blurred vision; cold sweats; coma; confusion; cool, pale skin; difficulty in concentrating; drowsiness; excessive hunger; fast heartbeat; headache; nausea; nervousness; nightmares; restless sleep; seizures; shakiness; slurred speech; unusual tiredness or weakness)

Incidence not determined—Observed during clinical practice; estimates of frequency can not be determined

Hypersensitivity reactions such as; rash; itching; urticaria (hives or welts; itching; redness of skin; skin rash)

Those indicating need for medical attention only if they continue or are bothersome

Incidence more frequent

Upper respiratory infection (cough; runny or stuffy nose; sore throat)

Incidence less frequent

Arthropathy (joint pain; swelling in joints); ***back pain; dizziness; flu symptoms*** (abdominal pain; chills; cough; headache; pain in joints or muscles; runny nose; sneezing; sore throat)

Overdose

For more information on the management of overdose or unintentional ingestion, **contact a poison control center** (see *Poison Control Center Listing*).

There have been no instances of overdose with nateglinide in clinical trials.

Clinical effects of overdose

The following effects have been selected on the basis of their potential clinical significance (possible signs and symptoms in parentheses where appropriate)—not necessarily inclusive:

Hypoglycemia (anxiety; behavior change similar to drunkenness; blurred vision; cold sweats; coma; confusion; cool, pale skin; difficulty in concentrating; drowsiness; excessive hunger; fast heartbeat; headache; nausea; nervousness; nightmares; restless sleep; seizures; shakiness; slurred speech; unusual tiredness or weakness)

Treatment of overdose

To enhance elimination—

Dialysis is not expected to be effective since nateglinide is highly protein-bound.

Specific treatment—

Mild hypoglycemic symptoms without loss of consciousness or other neurological symptoms may require only oral glucose, dose adjustment, or adjusted timing of meals.

More severe hypoglycemic reactions involving neurological symptoms should be treated with intravenous glucose.

Patient Consultation

As an aid to patient consultation, refer to *Advice for the Patient, Nateglinide (Systemic)*.

In providing consultation, consider emphasizing the following selected information (» = major clinical significance):

Before using this medication

» Conditions affecting use, especially:
Pregnancy—Should not be used during pregnancy
Breast-feeding—Should not be administered to a nursing woman
Use in the elderly—Elderly patients may be more susceptible to hypoglycemia
Other medications, especially beta-adrenergic blocking agents
Other medical problems, especially autonomic neuropathy, diabetic ketoacidosis, or type 1 diabetes

Proper use of this medication

» Importance of adherence to recommended regimens for diet, exercise, and glucose monitoring

» Taking medication 1 to 30 minutes before each meal; skipping dose if meal is skipped

» Taking medication even when not feeling ill; possibility of having to take antidiabetic medication for the rest of life to prevent or delay complications of diabetes

» Proper dosing
Missed dose: Taking before next main meal; not doubling doses; not taking if corresponding meal was skipped

Proper storage

Precautions while using this medication

» Regular visits to physician

» *Carefully following special instructions of health care team:*
Discussing use of alcohol
Not taking other medications unless discussed with physician
Getting counseling for family members to help the patient with diabetes; also, special counseling for pregnancy planning and contraception
Making travel plans that include readiness for diabetic emergencies and eating meals at the usual times, even with changing time zones

» Preparing for and understanding what to do in case of diabetic emergency; carrying medical history and current medication list and wearing medical identification

» Recognizing what brings on symptoms of hypoglycemia, such as using other antidiabetic medication; delaying or missing a meal; exercising more than usual; drinking significant amounts of alcohol; or illness, including vomiting or diarrhea

» Recognizing symptoms of hypoglycemia: anxiety; behavior change similar to drunkenness; blurred vision; cold sweats; confusion; cool, pale skin; difficulty in concentrating; drowsiness; excessive hunger; fast heartbeat; headache; nausea; nervousness; nightmares; restless sleep; shakiness; slurred speech; and unusual tiredness or weakness

» Knowing what to do if symptoms of hypoglycemia occur, such as eating glucose tablets or gel, corn syrup, honey, or sugar cubes; drinking fruit juice, nondiet soft drink, or sugar dissolved in water; or getting emergency medical assistance if symptoms are severe

» Recognizing what brings on symptoms of hyperglycemia, such as not taking enough antidiabetic medication, skipping a dose of antidiabetic medication, overeating or not following meal plan, having a fever or infection, or exercising less than usual

» Recognizing symptoms of hyperglycemia and ketoacidosis: blurred vision; drowsiness; dry mouth; flushed, dry skin; fruit-like breath odor; increased urination (frequency and volume); ketones in urine; loss of appetite; stomachache, nausea, or vomiting; tiredness; troubled breathing (rapid and deep); unconsciousness; and unusual thirst

» Knowing what to do if symptoms of hyperglycemia occur, such as checking blood glucose and contacting a member of the health care team

Side/adverse effects

Sign of potential side effects, especially hypoglycemia

Signs of potential side effects observed during clinical practice, especially hypersensitivity reactions such as a rash, itching, and urticaria

General Dosing Information

Secondary failure of nateglinide may occur over time.

Diet/Nutrition

Nateglinide should be taken 1 to 30 minutes before a meal. Taking nateglinide before a meal reduces the risk of hypoglycemia.

Taking nateglinide with or after a meal results in a decrease in the peak plasma concentration (C_{max}) and a delay in the time to reach C_{max} (T_{max}).

When a meal is skipped, the scheduled dose of nateglinide also should be skipped to reduce the risk of hypoglycemia.

Oral Dosage Forms

NATEGLINIDE TABLETS

Usual adult dose

Antidiabetic agent—

As monotherapy or in combination with metformin: Oral, 120 mg three times a day before meals. A dose of 60 mg three times a day alone or in combination with metformin or a thiazolidinedione before meals may be used in patients who are close to their target glycosylated hemoglobin (HbA_{1c}) values at the time of initiation of nateglinide.

Usual pediatric dose

Antidiabetic agent—

Safety and efficacy have not been established.

Usual geriatric dose

See *Usual adult dose.*

Strength(s) usually available

U.S.—

60 mg (Rx) [*Starlix* (colloidal silicon dioxide; croscarmellose sodium; hydroxypropyl methylcellulose; iron oxides [red or yellow]; lactose monohydrate; magnesium stearate; microcrystalline cellulose; polyethylene glycol; povidone; talc; titanium dioxide)].

120 mg [*Starlix* (colloidal silicon dioxide; croscarmellose sodium; hydroxypropyl methylcellulose; iron oxides [red or yellow]; lactose monohydrate; magnesium stearate; microcrystalline cellulose; polyethylene glycol; povidone; talc; titanium dioxide)].

Packaging and storage

Store at 25°C (77° F); excursions permitted between 15 and 30 °C (59 and 86 °F). Dispense in a tight container.

Revised: 08/10/2004
Developed: 05/29/2001

NEDOCROMIL Inhalation-Local

VA CLASSIFICATION (Primary/Secondary): RE110/RE190

Commonly used brand name(s): *Tilade.*

Note: For a listing of dosage forms and brand names by country availability, see *Dosage Forms* section(s).

Category

Anti-inflammatory, nonsteroidal (inhalation); asthma prophylactic; antiallergic (inhalation).

Indications

Note: Bracketed information in the *Indications* section refers to indications that are not included in U.S. product labeling.

Accepted

Asthma, bronchial (prophylaxis)—Nedocromil is indicated for prevention of airway inflammation and bronchoconstriction in patients with bronchial asthma who require daily therapy. It may be used alone as primary therapy or with other asthma medications, such as bronchodilators and/or corticosteroids. In mild or moderate asthma, nedocromil may be used instead of corticosteroids, inhaled or systemic.

[Bronchospasm (prophylaxis)]—Nedocromil is indicated for prevention of bronchospasm in patients with reversible obstructive airways disease. It may be used regularly or occasionally just prior to an anticipated exposure to such provocation as inhaled allergens, exercise, cold air, or atmospheric pollutants.

Unaccepted

Nedocromil is not a bronchodilator and, therefore, is not indicated for the reversal or relief of acute bronchospasm, especially in status asthmaticus.

Pharmacology/Pharmacokinetics

Physicochemical characteristics

Chemical Group—Pyranoquinoline.
Molecular weight—415.31.
pKa—2.

Mechanism of action/Effect

Nedocromil inhibits activation and release of inflammatory mediators from a variety of cell types in the lumen and mucosa of the bronchial tree. These mediators, which include the leukotrienes, histamine, and prostaglandins, are preformed or derived from arachidonic acid metabolism through the lipoxygenase and cyclo-oxygenase pathways. A range of human cells associated with asthma, such as eosinophils, neutrophils, macrophages, monocytes, mast cells, and platelets, may be involved. Nedocromil exhibits specific anti-inflammatory properties when administered directly to the bronchial mucosa. It has demonstrated a significant inhibitory effect on allergen-induced early and late asthmatic reactions and on bronchial hyperresponsiveness. Nedocromil may also affect sensory nerves in the lung. The mechanism of action of nedocromil may be due partly to inhibition of axon reflexes and release of sensory neuropeptides, such as substance P, neurokinin A, and calcitonin-gene–related peptides. The result is inhibition of bradykinin-induced bronchoconstriction. Nedocromil does not possess any bronchodilator, antihistamine, or corticosteroid activity. At recommended doses, inhaled nedocromil has no known systemic activity.

Absorption

The extent of absorption is about 7 to 9% of a single inhaled dose of 3.5 to 4 mg and 17% of multiple inhaled doses, with absorption largely from the respiratory tract.

Gastrointestinal tract—Although most of an inhaled dose of nedocromil is subsequently swallowed, only 2 to 3% of it is absorbed from the gastrointestinal tract.

Respiratory tract—5 to 6% of an inhaled dose of nedocromil is absorbed slowly from the respiratory tract.

Distribution

Distributed into plasma. With repeated dosing, nedocromil seems to exert a residual effect that allows for twice-a-day dosing for some patients.

Protein binding

Approximately 89% is reversibly bound to plasma proteins when plasma concentrations range between 0.5 and 50 mcg/mL.

Biotransformation

Nedocromil is not metabolized.

Half-life

Approximately 1.5 to 3.3 hours.

Onset of action

Nedocromil has been shown to prevent bronchospasm when administered up to 30 minutes before exposure to a chemical irritant, an allergen, or exercise.

When nedocromil is used as maintenance therapy, clinical improvement in symptoms and lung function usually occurs within 2 to 4 weeks of the beginning of treatment. In some patients, improvement of symptoms can occur within a few days.

Time to peak concentration

Following single-dose or multiple-dose inhalation—In asthmatic patients: 5 to 90 minutes.

Peak serum concentration

Following single-dose or multiple-dose inhalation—In asthmatic patients: 2.8 nanograms per mL.

Duration of action

When a single dose is administered prior to an allergen challenge, nedocromil inhibits the late reactions of bronchoconstriction occurring 6 to 12 hours after provocation.

Elimination

Rapidly excreted as unchanged drug, in the bile and urine.

Precautions to Consider

Cross-sensitivity and/or related problems

Patients sensitive to fluorocarbons may be sensitive to the fluorocarbons, dichlorotetrafluoroethane and dichlorodifluoromethane, contained in this preparation.

Carcinogenicity/Mutagenicity

Various animal studies and *in vitro* studies using human cells showed no evidence of mutagenic or carcinogenic potential.

Pregnancy/Reproduction

Fertility—The results of fertility studies of nedocromil in rats and mice showed no effect on male or female fertility.

Pregnancy—Adequate and well controlled studies in humans have not been done.

In reproduction studies in rats and mice, small amounts of nedocromil crossed the placenta but did not cause teratogenic or embryotoxic effects.

FDA Pregnancy Category B.

Breast-feeding

It is not known whether nedocromil is distributed into human breast milk. However, problems in humans have not been documented. In animal studies, small amounts of nedocromil were distributed into milk but did not cause adverse effects.

Pediatrics

Appropriate studies have been performed in children 6 years of age and older, although data regarding use of nedocromil in treatment of childhood asthma remain limited to date. These studies have not demonstrated pediatrics-specific problems that would limit the usefulness of nedocromil in children. The types and frequency of side effects associated with nedocromil use in children were similar to those observed in adults.

Nedocromil appeared to offset the increase of symptoms of asthma when used in pediatric patients who experience seasonal exacerbations of asthma.

Geriatrics

No information is available on the relationship of age to the effects of nedocromil in geriatric patients.

Drug interactions and/or related problems

The following drug interactions and/or related problems have been selected on the basis of their potential clinical significance (possible mechanism in parentheses where appropriate)—not necessarily inclusive (» = major clinical significance):

Note: Nedocromil has not shown an increase in frequency of adverse reactions or lab abnormalities with concomittant use of other antiasthma medications, such as inhaled or oral bronchodilators, or inhaled corticosteriods; however, no formal drug interaction studies have been conducted.

Medical considerations/Contraindications

The medical considerations/contraindications included have been selected on the basis of their potential clinical significance (reasons given in parentheses where appropriate)—not necessarily inclusive (» = major clinical significance).

Risk-benefit should be considered when the following medical problem exists:

Sensitivity to nedocromil

Side/Adverse Effects

The following side/adverse effects have been selected on the basis of their potential clinical significance (possible signs and symptoms in parentheses where appropriate)—not necessarily inclusive:

Those indicating need for medical attention

Incidence less frequent

Abdominal pain; bronchospasm, increased (increased wheezing, tightness in chest, or difficulty in breathing)—may be due to sensitivity to nedocromil or fluorocarbon propellants

Incidence rare

Arthritis (pain, stiffness, or swelling of joints); ***neutropenia or leukopenia*** (signs of infection, such as fever, sore throat, body aches, or chills)

Those indicating need for medical attention only if they continue or are bothersome

Incidence less frequent—(about 4 to 7%)

Cough; headache; nausea or vomiting; rhinitis (runny or stuffy nose); ***throat irritation***

Incidence rare

Sensation of warmth; tremor

Those not indicating need for medical attention

Incidence more frequent—(about 12% or more)

Unpleasant taste after inhalation

Overdose

Clinical effects of overdose

Overdosage of necrodomil is unlikely to result in any clinical manifestations which would require more than the observation of the patient and discontinuation of the medication where appropriate.

Patient Consultation

As an aid to patient consultation, refer to *Advice for the Patient, Nedocromil (Inhalation)*.

In providing consultation, consider emphasizing the following selected information (» = major clinical significance):

Before using this medication

» Conditions affecting use, especially:
  Sensitivity to nedocromil

Proper use of this medication

» Helps prevent, but does not relieve, acute attacks of asthma or bronchospasm

Reading patient instructions carefully before using

Using metered dose inhaler; checking periodically with doctor, nurse, or pharmacist for proper use of inhaler to prevent incorrect dosage

Priming inhaler with three actuations before using for the first time or if inhaler has not been used for more than seven days

Proper administration technique

» Proper dosing

Importance of not increasing or decreasing dose without physician's supervision

Proper administration technique if spacer device used

Proper cleaning procedure for inhaler

Missed dose: If used regularly, using as soon as possible; using any remaining doses for that day at regularly spaced intervals

» Proper storage

Importance of storing canister at room temperature before use for best results

Keeping out of the reach of children

For patients on scheduled dosing regimen

» Compliance with therapy; 2 to 4 weeks usually required for maximum therapeutic benefit after the beginning of nedocromil therapy

Precautions while using this medication

» Checking with physician if symptoms do not improve within 2 to 4 weeks; checking with physician immediately if condition becomes worse

» Importance of not discontinuing any concurrent antiasthmatic medication without physician's advice

Gargling or rinsing mouth after inhalation to relieve throat irritation and unpleasant taste

Side/adverse effects

Signs of potential side effects, especially abdominal pain, increased bronchospasm, arthritis, or neutropenia or leukopenia

General Dosing Information

In maintenance therapy, nedocromil must be used regularly, even during symptom-free periods, to achieve benefit.

It is essential that patients be properly instructed in the use of the inhaler, and that the correct method be reinforced periodically.

A decrease in severity of clinical symptoms or in the need for concomitant therapy is a sign of improvement that usually will be evident in the first 2 to 4 weeks of therapy if patient responds to nedocromil therapy.

After a patient becomes stabilized on nedocromil, the frequency of administration may be slowly decreased to a frequency that maintains freedom from exacerbations of asthma. The frequency of administration is usually no less than twice a day.

When nedocromil is added to an existing regimen of bronchodilators and/or inhaled or systemic corticosteroids, a reduction in dosage of the corticosteroid or bronchodilator may be achieved in some patients. However, the reduction should be gradual and under close medical supervision to avoid an exacerbation of asthma, since nedocromil has a very limited capacity to effectively substitute for inhaled or systemic corticosteroids.

Nedocromil therapy should be continued during acute exacerbations, unless the patient becomes intolerant to the use of inhaled dosage forms.

When nedocromil is added to as-needed usage of beta$_2$-adrenergic bronchodilators, symptom control and pulmonary function improve after approximately 2 weeks of therapy.

Studies were conducted comparing both two-times-a-day and four-times-a-day nedocromil dosing regimens. The medication was found to be more effective when used four times a day; however, if good control of symptoms has been maintained on the four-times-daily regimen, a less frequent dosing schedule may be considered.

Nedocromil inhaler requires priming with three actuations before the initial use and when the inhaler has not been used for more than 7 days.

For treatment of adverse effects

Recommended treatment consists of the following:

- Discontinue nedocromil and substitute alternative therapy if bronchospasm occurs after administration of nedocromil.

Inhalation Dosage Forms

Note: Bracketed uses in the *Dosage Forms* section refer to categories of use and/or indications that are not included in U.S. product labeling.

NEDOCROMIL INHALATION AEROSOL

Usual adult and adolescent dose

Asthma, bronchial (prophylaxis)—

Oral inhalation, 3.5 or 4 mg (2 inhalations) four times a day at regular intervals. Dosage frequency may be reduced to three times a day and then two times a day when patient's asthma is under good control.

[Bronchospasm (prophylaxis)]—

Oral inhalation, 4 mg (2 inhalations) as a single dose up to thirty minutes before exercise or exposure to any precipitating factor.

Usual adult prescribing limits

14 mg or 16 mg of nedocromil per twenty-four-hour period (2 inhalations four times daily at evenly spaced intervals).

Note: If the patient's asthma is well-controlled, as demonstrated by the absence of serious exacerbations and only occasional use of inhaled or oral beta$_2$-adrenergic bronchodilators, a less frequent dosing schedule may be effective.

Usual pediatric dose

Children up to 6 years of age: Safety and efficacy have not been established.

Children 6 years of age and older: See *Usual adult and adolescent dose.*

Usual geriatric dose

See *Usual adult and adolescent dose.*

Strength(s) usually available

U.S.—

Note: Each 16.2 gm canister contains 210 gm of nedocromil and provides 104 actuations. Use of the inhaler should not exceed 104 actuations as the dose may be inaccurate for subsequent doses.

1.75 mg per metered spray (Rx) [*Tilade*].

Canada—

2 mg per metered spray (Rx) [*Tilade*].

Note: Each 17 mL canister contains 112 actuations.

In Canada, metered dose inhalers are labeled according to the amount of nedocromil delivered at the valve; in the U.S., metered dose inhalers are labeled according to the amount of nedocromil delivered at the mouthpiece or actuator. Therefore, 2 mg of nedocromil delivered at the valve is equivalent to 1.75 mg delivered at the mouthpiece.

Packaging and storage

Store between 2 and 30 °C (36 and 86 °F), unless otherwise specified by manufacturer. Protect from freezing.

Canister contents are under pressure, therefore the canister should not be punctured, incinerated, or placed near sources of heat. The product should not be exposed to temperatures above 49 °C (120 °F).

Auxiliary labeling

- For oral inhalation only.
- Shake well before using.
- Store away from heat and direct sunlight.
- Do not use with other mouthpieces.

Note

Include patient instructions when dispensing.

Demonstrate inhalation technique to patient when dispensing.

Additional information

This product contains dichlorotetrafluoroethane and dichlorodifluoromethane, substances that harm public health and the environment by destroying ozone in the upper atmosphere.

Selected Bibliography

Parish RC, Miller LJ. Nedocromil sodium. Ann Pharmacother 1993; 27: 599-606.

Brogden RN, Sorkin EM. Nedocromil sodium. An updated review of its pharmacological properties and therapeutic efficacy in asthma. Drugs 1993; 45(5): 693-715.

Revised: 06/14/1999

NEDOCROMIL Ophthalmic

VA CLASSIFICATION (Primary): OP801

Commonly used brand name(s): *Alocril.*

Note: For a listing of dosage forms and brand names by country availability, see *Dosage Forms* section(s).

Category

Mast cell stabilizer (ophthalmic); antiallergic (ophthalmic).

Indications

Accepted

Conjunctivitis, allergic (treatment)—Nedocromil ophthalmic solution is indicated for the treatment of itching associated with allergic conjunctivitis.

Pharmacology/Pharmacokinetics

Physicochemical characteristics

Molecular weight—415.30.

pH—4.0 to 5.5

Mechanism of action/Effect

Nedocromil sodium is a mast cell stabilizer and inhibits the release of mediators from cells involved in hypersensitivity reactions. Decreased chemotaxis and decreased activation of eosinophils have been demonstrated.

Other actions/effects

In vitro studies showed that nedocromil sodium inhibits histamine release from a population of mast cells having been defined as belonging to the mucosal sub-type and β-glucuronide release from macrophages.

Absorption

Low—less than 4% of the total dose was systemically absorbed following multiple doses of a 2% ophthalmic solution.

Absorption is mainly through the nasolacrimal duct rather than through the conjunctiva.

Biotransformation

Nedocromil sodium is not metabolized.

Elimination

Urine—70%

Feces—30%

Precautions to Consider

Carcinogenicity/Mutagenicity

A 2 year inhalation carcinogenicity study of nedocromil sodium at a dose of 24 mg/kg/day (approximately 400 times the maximum recommended human daily ocular dose on a mg/kg basis) in Wistar rats showed no carcinogenic potential.

Nedocromil sodium showed no mutagenic potential in the Ames Salmonella/microsome plate assay, mitotic gene conversion in *Saccharomyces cerevisiae*, mouse lymphoma forward mutation and mouse micronucleus assay.

Pregnancy/Reproduction

Fertility—Reproduction and fertility studies in mice and rats showed no effects on male and female fertility at a subcutaneous dose of 100 mg/kg/day (more than 1600 times the maximum recommended human daily ocular dose on a mg/kg basis).

Pregnancy—Reproduction in mice, rats and rabbits using a subcutaneous dose of 100 mg/kg/day (more than 1600 times the maximum recommended human daily ocular dose on a mg/kg basis) revealed no evidence of teratogenicity or harm to fetus due to nedocromil sodium. There are, however, no adequate and well-controlled studies in pregnant women.

FDA Pregnancy Category B

Breast-feeding

It is not known whether nedocromil is distributed into human breast milk.

Pediatrics

Safety and effectiveness in children below the age of 3 years have not been established.

Geriatrics

No overall differences in safety or effectiveness have been observed between elderly and younger patients.

Medical considerations/Contraindications

The medical considerations/contraindications included have been selected on the basis of their potential clinical significance (reasons given in parentheses where appropriate)—not necessarily inclusive (» = major clinical significance).

Risk-benefit should be considered when the following medical problems exist:

» Sensitivity to nedocromil

Side/Adverse Effects

The following side/adverse effects have been selected on the basis of their potential clinical significance (possible signs and symptoms in parentheses where appropriate)—not necessarily inclusive:

Those indicating need for medical attention only if they continue or are bothersome

Incidence more frequent

Headache—40%; ***nasal congestion*** (stuffy nose)—10 to 30%; ***ocular burning, irritation and stinging***—10 to 30%; ***unpleasant taste***—10 to 30%; ***asthma*** (cough; difficulty breathing; noisy breathing; shortness of breath; tightness in chest; wheezing)—1 to 10%; ***conjunctivitis*** (redness, pain, swelling of eye, eyelid, or inner lining of eyelid; burning, dry or itching eyes; discharge; excessive tearing)—1 to 10%; ***eye redness***—1 to 10%; ***photophobia*** (blurred vision; change in color vision; difficulty seeing at night; increased sensitivity of eyes to sunlight)—1 to 10%; ***rhinitis*** (stuffy nose; runny nose; sneezing)—1 to 10%

Patient Consultation

As an aid to patient consultation, refer to *Advice for the Patient, Nedocromil (Ophthalmic).*

In providing consultation, consider emphasizing the following selected information (» = major clinical significance):

Proper use of this medication

» Proper dosing

Missed dose: Using as soon as possible; not using if almost time for next scheduled dose; not doubling doses

Proper storage

Precautions while using this medication

Users of contact lenses should refrain from wearing lenses while exhibiting the signs and symptoms of allergic conjunctivitis

Side/adverse effects

Signs of potential side effects, especially headache, ocular burning, stinging and irritation, unpleasant taste and nasal congestion.

General Dosing Information

For ophthalmic dosing forms:

Treatment should be continued throughout the period of exposure (i.e. pollen season) or until exposure to the offending allergen is terminated.

Ophthalmic Dosage Forms

NEDOCROMIL SODIUM OPHTHALMIC SOLUTION

Usual adult dose

Conjunctivitis, allergic—

Topical, to the conjunctiva, 1 or 2 drops in each eye twice daily.

Note: Nedocromil ophthalmic solution should be used at regular intervals.

Usual pediatric dose

See *Usual adult dose.*

Usual geriatric dose

See *Usual adult dose.*

Strength(s) usually available

U.S.—

2% nedocromil sodium (Rx) [*Alocril* (benzalkonium chloride 0.01%; edetate disodium 0.05%)].

Packaging and storage

Store between 2 and 25 °C (36 and 77 °F). Keep tightly closed.

Auxiliary labeling

- For the eye.

Revised: 08/07/2000

Developed: 03/28/2000

NELFINAVIR Systemic

VA CLASSIFICATION (Primary): AM830

Commonly used brand name(s): *Viracept.*

Another commonly used name is NFV

Note: For a listing of dosage forms and brand names by country availability, see *Dosage Forms* section(s).

Category

Antiviral (systemic).

Indications

General Considerations

Nelfinavir is a human immunodeficiency virus (HIV) protease inhibitor. Cross-resistance between nelfinavir and reverse transcriptase inhibitors is unlikely because different enzyme targets are involved. Clinical HIV isolates exhibiting zidovudine or pyridinone resistance retain *in vitro* susceptibility to nelfinavir. The potential for cross-resistance between nelfinavir and other protease inhibitors has not been fully explored. A clinical HIV isolate exhibiting reduced susceptibility to saquinavir (sevenfold) did not show reduced susceptibility to nelfinavir. However, several isolates exhibiting ritonavir resistance (eight- to one hundred thirteenfold) were also less sensitive to nelfinavir (five- to fortyfold). Therapy with nelfinavir (ranging from 2 to 52 weeks) is associated with reduced sensitivity to nelfinavir, ranging from a five- to a ninety-threefold loss of sensitivity in *in vitro* phenotypic assays. The most frequent site of mutation associated with reduced nelfinavir sensitivity is codon 30. After 12 to 16 weeks of therapy, the incidence of mutation at this site was 56% in patients receiving nelfinavir monotherapy and 6% in patients receiving triple therapy with nelfinavir, lamivudine, and zidovudine. The clinical relevance of phenotypic and genotypic changes in the virus associated with nelfinavir therapy has not been established.

Accepted

Human immunodeficiency virus (HIV) infection (treatment)—Nelfinavir in combination with other antiretrovirals is indicated in the treatment of HIV infection when antiretroviral therapy is warranted.

Pharmacology/Pharmacokinetics

Note: No substantial differences were observed between the pharmacokinetic properties of nelfinavir in healthy volunteers and in patients infected with human immunodeficiency virus (HIV).

Physicochemical characteristics

Molecular weight—

Nelfinavir: 567.79.

Nelfinavir mesylate: 663.9.

Mechanism of action/Effect

Nelfinavir inhibits HIV type 1 protease. HIV protease cleaves the viral precursor proteins gag and pol, which are required to produce mature, infectious virus particles. Inhibition of HIV protease results in the production of immature, noninfectious virus particles.

Absorption

Maximum plasma concentration and area under the plasma concentration-time curve (AUC) values were two to three times higher under fed conditions than under fasting conditions.

Distribution

Apparent Vol_D—2 to 7 liters per kilogram.

Protein binding

Very high (> 98%).

Biotransformation

Following a single oral 750-mg dose, 82 to 86% of the total plasma nelfinavir remains unchanged; one major and several minor metabolites are found in plasma; the major oxidative metabolite has *in vitro* antiviral activity comparable to that of the parent drug. Nelfinavir is metabolized *in vitro* by multiple cytochrome P450 isoforms, including CYP3A.

Half-life

Terminal half-life in plasma—3.5 to 5 hours.

Time to peak concentration

Following single and multiple oral doses of 500 to 750 mg with food—2 to 4 hours.

Peak plasma concentration

Following multiple dosing with 750 mg three times a day for 28 days (steady state)—Average, 3 to 4 mcg per mL.

Elimination

Fecal—87% of an oral 750-mg dose is recovered in feces; 22% of this portion consists of unchanged nelfinavir, while 78% of this portion consists of numerous oxidative metabolites.

Renal—1 to 2% of an oral 750-mg dose is recovered in urine; unchanged nelfinavir is the major component.

Precautions to Consider

Carcinogenicity

Studies in mice and rats were conducted with nelfinavir at oral doses up to 1000 mg per kg per day. No evidence of a tumorigenic effect was noted in mice at systemic exposures up to 9-fold those measured in humans at the recommended therapeutic dose (750 mg TID or 1250 mg BID). In rats, thyroid follicular cell adenomas and carcinomas were increased in males at 300 mg per kg per day and higher in females at 1000 mg per kg per day. Systemic exposures at 300 and 1000 mg per kg per day were 1-fold to 3-fold, respectively, those measured in humans at the recommended therapeutic dose. Repeated administration of nelfinavir to rats produced effects consistent with hepatic microsomal enzyme induction and increased thyroid hormone disposition; these effects predispose rats, but not humans, to thyroid follicular cell neoplasms.

Mutagenicity

Nelfinavir is not mutagenic *in vitro* in the Ames test, the mouse lymphoma assay, or in human lymphocytes, or *in vivo* in the rat micronucleus assay.

Pregnancy/Reproduction

Fertility—Nelfinavir did not affect mating or fertility in male or female rats; reproductive performance of offspring born to female rats that had been exposed to nelfinavir from midpregnancy through lactation also was not affected.

Pregnancy—Adequate and well-controlled studies have not been done in humans.

In pregnant rats, nelfinavir was not maternally toxic when administered in doses that resulted in systemic exposure (based on the steady-state area under the plasma concentration-time curve [AUC]) comparable to that observed in humans receiving the recommended therapeutic dose. Exposure of female rats to nelfinavir from midpregnancy through lactation had no effect on the survival, growth, or development of the offspring to weaning. In pregnant rabbits, fetal development was not affected by administration of nelfinavir at doses up to the level at which a slight decrease in maternal body weight was observed; however, even at the highest dose evaluated, systemic exposure in rabbits was significantly lower than comparable human exposure.

FDA Pregnancy Category B.

Breast-feeding

It is not known whether nelfinavir is distributed into breast milk. However, the U.S. Public Health Service Centers for Disease Control and Prevention advises HIV-infected women not to breast-feed, to avoid postnatal transmission of HIV to an uninfected child.

Nelfinavir is distributed into milk in rats.

Pediatrics

Nelfinavir has been studied in one open-label, uncontrolled trial in pediatric patients ranging from 2 to 13 years of age; the adverse event profile observed during the pediatric clinical trial with nelfinavir was similar to that observed in adult patients.

Response rates in pediatric patients less than 2 years of age appear to be poorer than in those patients 2 years of age or older.

Geriatrics

No information is available on the relationship of age to the effects of nelfinavir in geriatric patients.

Drug interactions and/or related problems

The following drug interactions and/or related problems have been selected on the basis of their potential clinical significance (possible mechanism in parentheses where appropriate)—not necessarily inclusive (» = major clinical significance):

Note: Based on known metabolic profiles of these agents, clinically significant medication interactions are not expected between nelfinavir and azithromycin, clarithromycin, dapsone, erythromycin, fluconazole, itraconazole, or sulfamethoxazole/trimethoprim.

It is recommended that nelfinavir be taken with food, and that didanosine be taken on an empty stomach. Therefore, nelfinavir should be taken more than 2 hours before or 1 hour after didanosine is taken.

Combinations containing any of the following medications, depending on the amount present, may also interact with this medication.

» Amiodarone or
» Astemizole or
» Cisapride or
» Ergot derivatives or
» Midazolam or
» Pimozide
» Quinidine or
» Terfenadine or
» Triazolam
(use is contraindicated)

Azithromycin
(close monitoring for known side effects such as liver enzyme abnormalities and hearing impairment is warranted)

Calcium channel blocking agents, dihydropyridine
(may increase plasma concentrations of calcium channel blocking agents)

Carbamazepine or
Phenobarbital or
Phenytoin
(concurrent use may cause a decrease in the plasma concentration of nelfinavir and phenytoin)

Delavirdine or
Nevirapine
(safety and efficacy has not been established for these combinations)

Didanosine
(didanosine requires food while nelfinavir should be given on an empty stomach; therefore, didanosine should be taken one hour before or two hours after nelfinavir)

» Fluticasone
(concurrent use may cause an increase in the plasma concentration of fluticasone; use with caution; consider alternatives to fluticasone)

HMG-CoA Reductase Inhibitors including:
Atorvastatin or
» Lovastatin or
» Simvastatin
(atorvastatin levels may rise when combined with nelfinavir; consider using lowest possible dose of atorvastatin or a different HMG-CoA reductase inhibitor)
(lovastatin and simvastatin may increase the potential for serious adverse effects when combined with nelfinavir)

» Immunosuppressants including:
Cyclosporine or
Sirolimus or
Tacrolimus
(nelfinavir may increase the plasma concentrations of these drugs)

Indinavir
(concurrent use causes an 83% increase in the AUC of nelfinavir; the AUC for indinavir increases by 51%; the safety of this combination has not been established)

Ketoconazole
(concurrent use causes a 35% increase in the AUC of nelfinavir; no dose adjustment is needed)

Lamivudine
(concurrent use causes a 10% increase in the AUC of lamivudine)

Methadone
(the plasma concentration of methadone may be decreased; may need to increase methadone dose)

Oral contraceptives, such as:
» Ethinyl estradiol
(concurrent administration with nelfinavir causes a decrease in the plasma concentrations of ethinyl estradiol; alternative or additional contraceptive measures should be used)

» Rifabutin
(concurrent use causes a 32% decrease in the AUC of nelfinavir; the AUC for rifabutin increases by 207%; it is recommended that the dose of rifabutin be reduced to one-half the usual dose when administered concurrently with nelfinavir)

» Rifampin
(concurrent use causes an 82% decrease in the AUC of nelfinavir; concurrent use is not recommended)

Ritonavir
(concurrent use causes a 152% increase in the AUC of nelfinavir; the safety of this combination has not been established)

Saquinavir
(concurrent use causes an 18% increase in the AUC of nelfinavir; the AUC for saquinavir increases by 392%; the safety of this combination has not been established)

» Sildenafil
(dose should not exceed 25mg in 48 hour period)

» St. John's Wort (hypericum perforatum)
(may lead to loss of virologic response and possible resistance to nelfinavir or other coadministered antiretroviral agents)

» Trazodone
(concurrent use of trazodone and nelfinavir may increase plasma concentrations of trazodone; should be used with caution and a lower dose of trazodone should be considered)

Zidovudine
(concurrent use causes a 35% decrease in the AUC of zidovudine; no dose adjustments are needed)

Laboratory value alterations

The following have been selected on the basis of their potential clinical significance (possible effect in parentheses where appropriate)—not necessarily inclusive (» = major clinical significance).

With physiology/laboratory test values
Leukopenia
Neutropenia
(nelfinavir may lead to these conditions in pediatric patients)

Medical considerations/Contraindications

The medical considerations/contraindications included have been selected on the basis of their potential clinical significance (reasons given in parentheses where appropriate)—not necessarily inclusive (» = major clinical significance).

Except under special circumstances, this medication should not be used when the following medical problems exist:

» Hypersensitivity to nelfinavir

Risk-benefit should be considered when the following medical problem exists:

» Diabetes mellitus or
» Hyperglycemia
(new onset diabetes mellitus, exacerbation of pre-existing diabetes mellitus and hyperglycemia have been reported during post-marketing surveillance)

» Hemophilia
(increased bleeding including spontaneous skin hematomas and hemarthrosis, have been reported in patients with hemophilia type A and B treated with protease inhibitors)

» Hepatic impairment
(nelfinavir is metabolized primarily by the liver; caution should be exercised when administering nelfinavir to patients with hepatic impairment)

Phenylketonuria
(the oral powder form of nelfinavir contains 11.2 grams of phenylalanine per gram of powder)

Patient monitoring

The following may be especially important in patient monitoring (other tests may be warranted in some patients, depending on condition; » = major clinical significance):

Blood glucose determinations
(development of hyperglycemia or diabetes may be associated with the use of protease inhibitors; close monitoring of patient glucose concentrations is recommended; new cases of diabetes or hyperglycemia that might be associated with use of protease inhibitors should be reported to the FDA or the pharmaceutical manufacturer)

Infection
(Immune reconstitution syndrome has been reported in patients treated with combination antiretroviral therapy including nelfinavir. During the initial phase of combination antiretroviral treatment, patients whose immune system responds may develop an inflammatory response to indolent or residual opportunistic infections.)

Side/Adverse Effects

Note: There have been reports of increased bleeding, including spontaneous skin hematomas and hemarthrosis, in HIV-infected patients with hemophilia type A or B who are receiving protease inhibitor therapy. A causal relationship has not been established.

The following side/adverse effects have been selected on the basis of their potential clinical significance (possible signs and symptoms in parentheses where appropriate)—not necessarily inclusive:

Those indicating need for medical attention

Diabetes, or hyperglycemia (dry or itchy skin; fatigue; hunger, increased; thirst, increased; unexplained weight loss; urination, increased); ***ketoacidosis*** (confusion; dehydration; fruity mouth odor; nausea; vomiting; weight loss)

Incidence not determined and indicating the need for medical attention—Observed during clinical practice; estimates of frequency cannot be determined

Bilirubinemia; bronchospasm (cough; difficulty breathing; noisy breathing; shortness of breath; tightness in chest; wheezing); ***fever; jaundice*** (chills; clay-colored stools; dark urine; dizziness; fever; headache; itching; loss of appetite; nausea; abdominal or stomach pain; area rash; unpleasant breath odor; unusual tiredness or weakness; vomiting of blood; yellow eyes or skin); ***metabolic acidosis*** (confusion; drowsiness; muscle tremors; nausea; rapid, deep breathing; restlessness; stomach cramps; unusual tiredness or weakness); ***QTc prolongation*** (irregular heartbeat; recurrent fainting); ***torsades de pointes*** (chest pain or discomfort; irregular or slow heart rate; fainting; shortness of breath)

Those indicating need for medical attention only if they continue or are bothersome

Incidence more frequent

Diarrhea; fat redistribution

Incidence less frequent

Flatulence (intestinal gas); ***nausea; skin rash***

Overdose

For specific information on the agents used in the management of Nelfinavir overdose, see:

- *Charcoal, Activated (Oral-Local)* monograph.

For more information on the management of overdose or unintentional ingestion, **contact a Poison Control Center** (see *Poison Control Center Listing*).

Treatment of overdose

There is no specific antidote for overdose with nelfinavir.

To decrease absorption—Emesis or gastric lavage may be used. Activated charcoal may be used to aid removal of unabsorbed nelfinavir.

Dialysis is unlikely to significantly remove drug from the blood because nelfinavir is highly protein bound.

Supportive care—Patients in whom intentional overdose is confirmed or suspected should be referred for psychiatric consultation.

Patient Consultation

As an aid to patient consultation, refer to *Advice for the Patient, Nelfinavir (Systemic)*.

In providing consultation, consider emphasizing the following selected information (» = major clinical significance):

Before using this medication

» Conditions affecting use, especially:
Hypersensitivity to nelfinavir
Breast-feeding—Not recommended for HIV-infected mothers
Use in children—Safety and efficacy have not been established in children up to 2 years of age
Other medications, especially amiodarone, astemizole, cisapride, cyclosporine, ergot derivatives, ethinyl estradiol, fluticasone, lovastatin, midazolam, norethindrone, quinidine, rifabutin, rifampin, sildenafil, simvastatin, sirolimus, St. John's Wort, tacrolimus, terfenadine, and triazolam
Other medical problems, especially diabetes mellitus, hyperglycemia, hemophilia, hepatic impairment

Proper use of this medication

» Importance of taking nelfinavir with food
» Importance of not taking more medication than prescribed
» Compliance with full course of therapy
» Importance of not missing doses and of taking at evenly spaced times
Not sharing medication with others
» Proper dosing
Missed dose: Taking as soon as possible; not taking if almost time for next dose; not doubling doses
» Proper storage

Precautions while using this medication

» Not taking any other medications (prescription or nonprescription) without first consulting your physician

Taking nelfinavir more than 2 hours before or 1 hour after taking didanosine

» Using alternate or additional contraceptive measures if oral contraceptives are taken during nelfinavir therapy

» Regular visits to physician for blood tests and monitoring of blood glucose concentrations

Side/adverse effects

Signs of potential side effects, especially bilirubinemia, bronchospasm, fever, jaundice metabolic acidosis, QTc prolongation, torsades de pointes, diabetes, hyperglycemia and ketoacidosis

General Dosing Information

Diet/Nutrition

For optimal absorption, nelfinavir should be taken with food.

The oral powder form of nelfinavir contains 11.2 grams of phenylalanine per gram of powder.

For treatment of adverse effects

Recommended treatment consists of the following:

- Diarrhea may be controlled with nonprescription medications that slow gastrointestinal motility, such as loperamide.

Oral Dosage Forms

Note: The dosing and strength of dosing forms available are expressed in terms of nelfinavir base (not the mesylate salt).

NELFINAVIR MESYLATE ORAL POWDER

Note: Nelfinavir Mesylate Oral Powder contains 11.2 grams of phenylalanine per gram of powder.

Usual adult and adolescent dose

The oral powder usually is used only in children. See *Nelfinavir Mesylate Tablets*.

Usual pediatric dose

Human immunodeficiency virus (HIV) infection—

Children 2 to 13 years of age: Oral, 45 to 55 mg per kg twice daily or 25 to 35 mg per kg three times daily.

Children up to 2 years of age: Dosage has not been established.

Usual pediatric prescribing limits

Should not exceed the adult maximum dose of 2500 mg per day

Strength(s) usually available

U.S.—

50 mg (base) per gram (Rx) [*Viracept* (phenylalanine, 11.2 mg per gram)].

Packaging and storage

Store at 15 to 30 °C (59 to 86 °F), unless otherwise specified by manufacturer.

Preparation of dosage form

The oral powder form of nelfinavir may be mixed with a small amount of water, milk, formula, soy formula, soy milk, or dietary supplements. Acidic foods or juices (e.g., apple juice, applesauce, orange juice) are not recommended because the combination may result in a bitter taste. The oral powder should not be reconstituted with water in its original container. Once mixed, the entire contents must be consumed to obtain the full dose.

Stability

Once reconstituted, nelfinavir should be taken within 6 hours.

Auxiliary labeling

- Take with food.

NELFINAVIR MESYLATE TABLETS

Usual adult and adolescent dose

Human immunodeficiency virus (HIV) infection—

Oral, 1250 mg twice daily or 750 mg three times a day with food in combination with nucleoside analogs.

Note: Patients unable to swallow the 250 mg or the 650 mg tablets may dissolve the tablets in a small amount of water.

Usual adult and adolescent prescribing limits

2500 mg per day

Usual pediatric dose

See *Nelfinavir Mesylate Oral Powder*.

Usual geriatric dose

See *Usual adult and adolescent dose*.

Strength(s) usually available

U.S.—

250 mg (base) (Rx) [*Viracept*].

625 mg (base) (Rx) [*Viracept*].

Packaging and storage

Store at 15 to 30 °C (59 to 86 °F), unless otherwise specified by manufacturer.

Auxiliary labeling

- Take with food.

Revised: 10/11/2005
Developed: 08/05/1998

NEOMYCIN—See *Aminoglycosides (Systemic), Neomycin (Ophthalmic), Neomycin (Oral-Local), Neomycin (Topical)*

NEOMYCIN AND POLYMYXIN B Topical

VA CLASSIFICATION (Primary): DE101

Commonly used brand name(s): *Neosporin Cream*.

NOTE: The *Neomycin and Polymyxin B (Topical)* monograph is maintained on the *USP DI* electronic data base. A copy of the most recent revision of the complete monograph can be accessed on the *USP DI* Updates Online website. See the front cover of book for details on accessing the site.

For information on the specific components of this combination, see the *USP DI* monographs for *Neomycin (Topical)*.

The information that follows is selectively abstracted from the complete monograph and is provided to facilitate drug use review and patient counseling.

Note: For a listing of dosage forms and brand names by country availability, see *Dosage Forms* section(s).

Category

Antibacterial (topical).

Indications

Note: Bracketed information in the *Indications* section refers to uses that are not included in U.S. product labeling.

Accepted

Skin infections, bacterial, minor (prophylaxis)—Neomycin and polymyxin B combination is indicated in the topical prophylaxis of superficial skin infections caused by susceptible organisms in minor abrasions, burns, and cuts.

[Ulcer, dermal (treatment)]—Neomycin and polymyxin B combination is used in the topical treatment of dermal ulcer.

Not all species or strains of a particular organism may be susceptible to neomycin and polymyxin B combination.

Patient Consultation

As an aid to patient consultation, refer to *Advice for the Patient, Neomycin and Polymyxin B (Topical)*.

In providing consultation, consider emphasizing the following selected information (» = major clinical significance):

Before using this medication

» Conditions affecting use, especially:

Sensitivity to aminoglycosides, polymyxins, or parabens

Proper use of this medication

» Not using on deep wounds, puncture wounds, animal bites, serious burns, or raw areas without checking with physician or pharmacist

» Not for ophthalmic use

To use

Before applying, washing affected area(s) with soap and water, and drying thoroughly

Applying small amount of medication to affected area(s) and rubbing in gently

After applying, covering treated area(s) with gauze dressing if desired

» Not using for longer than 1 week or on extensive areas of the body unless directed by physician; may increase the possibility of side effects

» Compliance with full course of therapy

» Proper dosing

Missed dose: Applying as soon as possible; not applying if almost time for next dose

» Proper storage

Precautions while using this medication

Checking with physician or pharmacist if no improvement within 1 week

Side/adverse effects
Signs of potential side effects, especially hypersensitivity and ototoxicity

Topical Dosage Forms

NEOMYCIN AND POLYMYXIN B SULFATES CREAM USP

Usual adult and adolescent dose
Skin infections, bacterial, minor (prophylaxis)—
Topical, to the affected area(s), one to three times a day.

Usual pediatric dose
Skin infections, bacterial, minor (prophylaxis)—
Children up to 2 years of age: Dosage has not been established.
Children 2 years of age and over: See *Usual adult and adolescent dose*.

Strength(s) usually available
U.S.—
3.5 mg of neomycin (base) and 10,000 Units of polymyxin B (base) per gram (OTC) [*Neosporin Cream* (methylparaben 0.25%; propylene glycol)].
Canada—
Note: In Canada, *Neosporin* cream also contains gramicidin.
Not commercially available.

Auxiliary labeling
- For external use only.
- Continue medication for full time of treatment.

Revised: 06/09/1994

NEOMYCIN, POLYMYXIN B, AND BACITRACIN Ophthalmic

VA CLASSIFICATION (Primary): OP201

Commonly used brand name(s): *Ak-Spore Ophthalmic Ointment; Neocidin Ophthalmic Ointment; Neosporin Ophthalmic Ointment; Neotal; Ocu-Spor-B; Ocusporin; Ocutricin Ophthalmic Ointment; Ophthalmic; Spectro-Sporin; Triple Antibiotic.*

Note: For a listing of dosage forms and brand names by country availability, see *Dosage Forms* section(s).

Category

Antibacterial (ophthalmic).

Indications

Note: Bracketed information in the *Indications* section refers to uses that are not included in U.S. product labeling.

Accepted
Ocular infections (treatment)—Ophthalmic neomycin, polymyxin B, and bacitracin combination is indicated in the short-term treatment of superficial external ocular infections caused by susceptible organisms.
[Blepharitis, bacterial (treatment)]
[Blepharoconjunctivitis (treatment)]
[Conjunctivitis, bacterial (treatment)]
[Keratitis, bacterial (treatment)]or
[Keratoconjunctivitis, bacterial (treatment)]—Ophthalmic neomycin, polymyxin B, and bacitracin combination is used in the treatment of bacterial blepharitis, blepharoconjunctivitis, bacterial conjunctivitis, bacterial keratitis, and bacterial keratoconjunctivitis.

Note: Long-term treatment with this medication is rarely indicated.
Not all species or strains of a particular organism may be susceptible to neomycin, polymyxin B, and bacitracin combination.

Pharmacology/Pharmacokinetics

Physicochemical characteristics
Source—
Neomycin: Derived from *Streptomyces fradiae*.
Polymyxin B: Derived from polymyxin B_1 and polymyxin B_2, which are produced by the growth of *Bacillus polymyxa*.
Bacitracin: Derived from a mixture of related antibiotics (mainly bacitracin A), which are produced by the growth of *Bacillus subtilis* ssp. *licheniformis*.

Chemical Group—
Neomycin: Aminoglycosides.
Polymyxin B: Polypeptides.
Bacitracin: Cyclic polypeptides.

Mechanism of action/Effect
Neomycin—See *Neomycin (Ophthalmic)*.
Polymyxin B is bactericidal and active against *Pseudomonas aeruginosa* and other gram-negative bacteria. It is a surface-active basic polypeptide that binds to anionic phospholipid sites in bacterial cytoplasmic membranes, disrupts membrane structure, and alters membrane permeability to allow leakage of intracellular contents. Its action is antagonized by calcium and magnesium.
Bacitracin, a polypeptide antibiotic, is usually bactericidal against gram-positive organisms. It acts within the bacterial cell membrane and interferes with bacterial cell wall synthesis by binding to and inhibiting the dephosphorylation of a membrane-bound lipid pyrophosphate. Pyrophosphate is the precursor of a carrier molecule, undecaprenyl phosphate, which is involved in peptidoglycan polymerization.

Absorption
Neomycin and polymyxin B—May be absorbed following topical application to the eye if tissue damage is present.
Bacitracin—Not significantly absorbed.

Precautions to Consider

Cross-sensitivity and/or related problems
Patients sensitive to one aminoglycoside or polymyxin may be sensitive to other aminoglycosides or polymyxins also.

Pregnancy/Reproduction
Pregnancy—Problems in humans have not been documented.

Breast-feeding
Problems in humans have not been documented.

Pediatrics
Appropriate studies on the relationship of age to the effects of neomycin, polymyxin B, and bacitracin combination have not been performed in the pediatric population. However, no pediatrics-specific problems have been documented to date.

Geriatrics
Appropriate studies on the relationship of age to the effects of neomycin, polymyxin B, and bacitracin combination have not been performed in the geriatric population. However, no geriatrics-specific problems have been documented to date.

Medical considerations/Contraindications
The medical considerations/contraindications included have been selected on the basis of their potential clinical significance (reasons given in parentheses where appropriate)—not necessarily inclusive (» = major clinical significance).

Risk-benefit should be considered when the following medical problem exists:
Sensitivity to neomycin, polymyxin B, or bacitracin

Side/Adverse Effects

The following side/adverse effects have been selected on the basis of their potential clinical significance (possible signs and symptoms in parentheses where appropriate)—not necessarily inclusive:

Those indicating need for medical attention
Incidence more frequent
Hypersensitivity (itching, rash, redness, swelling, or other sign of irritation not present before therapy)

Those not indicating need for medical attention
Blurred vision, from the ointment

Patient Consultation

As an aid to patient consultation, refer to *Advice for the Patient, Neomycin, Polymyxin B, and Bacitracin (Ophthalmic)*.
In providing consultation, consider emphasizing the following selected information (» = major clinical significance):

Before using this medication
» Conditions affecting use, especially:
Sensitivity to neomycin, polymyxin B, or bacitracin or to any related antibiotic, such as amikacin, colistimethate, colistin, gentamicin, kanamycin, netilmicin, paromomycin, streptomycin, or tobramycin

Proper use of this medication
Proper administration technique for ophthalmic ointment
» Compliance with full course of therapy

» Proper dosing
 Missed dose: Applying as soon as possible; not applying if almost time for next dose
» Proper storage

Precautions while using this medication
 Checking with physician if no improvement within a few days

Side/adverse effects
 Blurred vision may occur for a few minutes after application of ophthalmic ointments
 Signs of potential side effects, especially hypersensitivity

Ophthalmic Dosage Forms

NEOMYCIN AND POLYMYXIN B SULFATES AND BACITRACIN ZINC OPHTHALMIC OINTMENT USP

Usual adult and adolescent dose
Ophthalmic antibacterial—Topical, to the conjunctiva, a thin strip (approximately 1 cm) of ointment every three to four hours for seven to ten days.

Usual pediatric dose
See *Usual adult and adolescent dose.*

Strength(s) usually available
U.S.—
 3.5 mg of neomycin (base), 5,000 Units of polymyxin B (base), and 400 Units of bacitracin zinc per gram (Rx) [*Neotal; Triple Antibiotic*].
 3.5 mg of neomycin (base), 10,000 Units of polymyxin B (base), and 400 Units of bacitracin zinc per gram (Rx) [*Ak-Spore Ophthalmic Ointment; Neocidin Ophthalmic Ointment; Neosporin Ophthalmic Ointment; Ocu-Spor-B; Ocusporin; Ocutricin Ophthalmic Ointment; Ophthalmic; Spectro-Sporin;* GENERIC].
Canada—
 3.5 mg of neomycin (base), 10,000 Units of polymyxin B (base), and 400 Units of bacitracin zinc per gram (Rx) [*Neosporin Ophthalmic Ointment*].

Packaging and storage
Store below 40 °C (104 °F), preferably between 15 and 30 °C (59 and 86 °F), unless otherwise specified by manufacturer. Store in a collapsible ophthalmic ointment tube. Protect from freezing.

Auxiliary labeling
- For the eye.
- Continue medicine for full time of treatment.

Revised: 05/24/1995

NEOMYCIN, POLYMYXIN B, AND BACITRACIN Topical

VA CLASSIFICATION (Primary): DE101

Commonly used brand name(s): *Bactine First Aid Antibiotic; Foille; Mycitracin; Neosporin Maximum Strength Ointment; Neosporin Ointment; Topisporin.*

NOTE: The *Neomycin, Polymyxin B, and Bacitracin (Topical)* monograph is maintained on the *USP DI* electronic data base. A copy of the most recent revision of the complete monograph can be accessed on the *USP DI* Updates Online website. See the front cover of book for details on accessing the site.
 For information on the specific components of this combination, see the *USP DI* monographs for *Neomycin (Topical).*
 The information that follows is selectively abstracted from the complete monograph and is provided to facilitate drug use review and patient counseling.

Note: For a listing of dosage forms and brand names by country availability, see *Dosage Forms* section(s).

Category
Antibacterial (topical).

Indications
Note: Bracketed information in the *Indications* section refers to uses that are not included in U.S. product labeling.

Accepted
Skin infections, bacterial, minor (prophylaxis)—Topical neomycin, polymyxin B, and bacitracin combination is indicated in the prophylaxis of superficial skin infections caused by susceptible organisms in minor abrasions, burns, and cuts.
[Skin infections, bacterial, minor (treatment)] or
[Ulcer, dermal (treatment)]—Topical neomycin, polymyxin B, and bacitracin combination is used in the treatment of minor bacterial skin infections and dermal ulcer.
 Not all species or strains of a particular organism may be susceptible to neomycin, polymyxin B, and bacitracin combination.

Unaccepted
Neomycin is not effective against *Pseudomonas aeruginosa.*

Patient Consultation
As an aid to patient consultation, refer to *Advice for the Patient, Neomycin, Polymyxin B, and Bacitracin (Topical).*
In providing consultation, consider emphasizing the following selected information (» = major clinical significance):

Before using this medication
» Conditions affecting use, especially:
 Sensitivity to aminoglycosides or polymyxins

Proper use of this medication
 Not using on deep or puncture wounds, serious burns, or raw areas unless directed by physician
 Not for ophthalmic use
 Before applying, washing affected area with soap and water, and drying thoroughly
 After applying, covering treated area with gauze dressing if desired
» Compliance with full course of therapy
» Proper dosing
 Missed dose: Applying as soon as possible; not applying if almost time for next dose
» Proper storage

Precautions while using this medication
 Checking with physician or pharmacist if no improvement within 1 week

Side/adverse effects
 Signs of side effects, especially hypersensitivity and ototoxicity

Topical Dosage Forms

NEOMYCIN AND POLYMYXIN B SULFATES AND BACITRACIN OINTMENT USP

Usual adult and adolescent dose
Antibacterial—
 Topical, to the skin, two to five times a day.

Usual pediatric dose
See *Usual adult and adolescent dose.*

Strength(s) usually available
U.S.—
 3.5 mg of neomycin (base), 5000 Units of polymyxin B (base), and 400 Units of bacitracin per gram (OTC) [GENERIC].
 3.5 mg of neomycin (base), 5000 Units of polymyxin B (base), and 500 Units of bacitracin per gram (OTC) [*Bactine First Aid Antibiotic; Foille; Mycitracin;* GENERIC].
Canada—
 Not commercially available.

Auxiliary labeling
- For external use only.
- Continue medication for full time of treatment.

NEOMYCIN AND POLYMYXIN B SULFATES AND BACITRACIN ZINC OINTMENT USP

Usual adult and adolescent dose
See *Neomycin and Polymyxin B Sulfates and Bacitracin Ointment USP.*

Usual pediatric dose
See *Neomycin and Polymyxin B Sulfates and Bacitracin Ointment USP.*

Strength(s) usually available
U.S.—
 3.5 mg of neomycin (base), 5000 Units of polymyxin B (base), and 400 Units of bacitracin zinc per gram (OTC) [*Neosporin Ointment; Topisporin;* GENERIC].
 3.5 mg of neomycin (base), 10,000 Units of polymyxin B (base), and 500 Units of bacitracin zinc per gram (OTC) [*Neosporin Maximum Strength Ointment*].
Canada—
 3.5 mg of neomycin (base), 5000 Units of polymyxin B (base), and 400 Units of bacitracin zinc per gram (Rx) [GENERIC].

Auxiliary labeling
- For external use only.
- Continue medication for full time of treatment.

Revised: 07/25/1994

NEOMYCIN, POLYMYXIN B, AND GRAMICIDIN Ophthalmic

VA CLASSIFICATION (Primary): OP201

Commonly used brand name(s): *Ak-Spore Ophthalmic Solution; Neocidin Ophthalmic Solution; Neosporin Ophthalmic Solution; Ocu-Spor-G; Ocutricin Ophthalmic Solution; P.N. Ophthalmic; Tri-Ophthalmic; Tribiotic; Triple Antibiotic.*

Note: For a listing of dosage forms and brand names by country availability, see *Dosage Forms* section(s).

Category

Antibacterial (ophthalmic).

Indications

Note: Bracketed information in the *Indications* section refers to uses that are not included in U.S. product labeling.

Accepted

Ocular infections (treatment)—Ophthalmic neomycin, polymyxin B, and gramicidin combination is indicated in the treatment of short-term superficial external ocular infections caused by susceptible organisms.

[Blepharitis, bacterial (treatment)]
[Blepharoconjunctivitis (treatment)] or
[Conjunctivitis, bacterial (treatment)]—Ophthalmic neomycin, polymyxin B, and gramicidin combination is indicated for the treatment of bacterial blepharitis, blepharoconjunctivitis, and bacterial conjunctivitis.

Note: Not all species or strains of a particular organism may be susceptible to neomycin, polymyxin B, and gramicidin combination.

Pharmacology/Pharmacokinetics

Physicochemical characteristics

Source—
Neomycin: Derived from *Streptomyces fradiae.*
Polymyxin B: Derived from polymyxin B_1 and polymyxin B_2, which are produced by the growth of *Bacillus polymyxa.*
Gramicidin: Mixture of three pairs of antibacterial substances (gramicidin A, B, and C), which are produced by the growth of *Bacillus brevis.*

Chemical Group—
Neomycin: Aminoglycosides.
Polymyxin B: Polypeptides.
Gramicidin: Polypeptides.

Mechanism of action/Effect

Neomycin—See *Neomycin (Ophthalmic).*
Polymyxin B—See *Neomycin, Polymyxin B, and Bacitracin (Ophthalmic).*
Gramicidin acts as a cationic detergent by altering the permeability of bacterial cytoplasmic membranes, with resultant changes in the intracellular cation content, especially potassium.

Note: Gramicidin, which has activity against gram-positive cocci and some *Neisseria,* is considered to be bactericidal, but may be bacteriostatic depending on the susceptibility of the organism. It is inactivated by serum and body fluids and is only effective topically. It should not be used systemically since it is very toxic and is a potent hemolytic.

Absorption

Neomycin; polymyxin B—May be absorbed following topical application to the eye if tissue damage is present.
Gramicidin—Not significantly absorbed.

Precautions to Consider

Cross-sensitivity and/or related problems

Patients sensitive to one aminoglycoside or polymyxin may be sensitive to other aminoglycosides or polymyxins also.

Pregnancy/Reproduction

Pregnancy—Problems in humans have not been documented.

Breast-feeding

Problems in humans have not been documented.

Pediatrics

Appropriate studies on the relationship of age to the effects of neomycin, polymyxin B, and gramicidin combination have not been performed in the pediatric population. However, no pediatrics-specific problems have been documented to date.

Geriatrics

Appropriate studies on the relationship of age to the effects of neomycin, polymyxin B, and gramicidin combination have not been performed in the geriatric population. However, no geriatrics-specific problems have been documented to date.

Medical considerations/Contraindications

The medical considerations/contraindications included have been selected on the basis of their potential clinical significance (reasons given in parentheses where appropriate)—not necessarily inclusive (» = major clinical significance).

Risk-benefit should be considered when the following medical problem exists:
Sensitivity to neomycin, polymyxin B, or gramicidin

Side/Adverse Effects

For neomycin, dose-related punctate staining of the cornea has occurred.
The following side/adverse effects have been selected on the basis of their potential clinical significance (possible signs and symptoms in parentheses where appropriate)—not necessarily inclusive:

Those indicating need for medical attention

Incidence more frequent
Hypersensitivity (itching, rash, redness, swelling, or other sign of irritation in or around the eye not present before therapy)

Those indicating need for medical attention only if they continue or are bothersome

Incidence less frequent
Burning or stinging of the eye

Patient Consultation

As an aid to patient consultation, refer to *Advice for the Patient, Neomycin, Polymyxin B, and Gramicidin (Ophthalmic).*

In providing consultation, consider emphasizing the following selected information (» = major clinical significance):

Before using this medication

» Conditions affecting use, especially:
Sensitivity to neomycin, polymyxin B, or gramicidin or to any related antibiotic, such as amikacin, colistimethate, colistin, gentamicin, kanamycin, netilmicin, paromomycin, streptomycin, or tobramycin

Proper use of this medication

Proper administration technique for ophthalmic solution
» Compliance with full course of therapy
» Proper dosing
Missed dose: Applying as soon as possible; not applying if almost time for next dose
» Proper storage

Precautions while using this medication

Checking with physician if no improvement within a few days

Side/adverse effects

Signs of potential side effects, especially hypersensitivity

General Dosing Information

Although some manufacturers recommend a dose of 2 drops of an ophthalmic solution at appropriate intervals, the conjunctival sac will usually hold only 1 drop.

Ophthalmic Dosage Forms

NEOMYCIN AND POLYMYXIN B SULFATES AND GRAMICIDIN OPHTHALMIC SOLUTION USP

Usual adult and adolescent dose

Antibacterial, ophthalmic—
Acute infections: Topical, to the conjunctiva, 1 drop every 15 to 30 minutes initially, the frequency being reduced gradually depending on patient response.
Other infections: Topical, to the conjunctiva, 1 drop two to four times a day, or more frequently, for seven to ten days.

Usual pediatric dose

See *Usual adult and adolescent dose.*

Strength(s) usually available

U.S.—

1.75 mg of neomycin (base), 10,000 Units of polymyxin B (base), and 25 mcg (0.025 mg) of gramicidin per mL (Rx) [*Ak-Spore Ophthalmic Solution* (alcohol 0.5%; thimerosal 0.001%); *Neocidin Ophthalmic Solution; Neosporin Ophthalmic Solution* (alcohol 0.5%; thimerosal 0.001%); *Ocu-Spor-G; Ocutricin Ophthalmic Solution; P.N. Ophthalmic; Tribiotic; Tri-Ophthalmic; Triple Antibiotic;* GENERIC].

Canada—

1.75 mg of neomycin (base), 10,000 Units of polymyxin B (base), and 25 mcg (0.025 mg) of gramicidin per mL (Rx) [*Neosporin Ophthalmic Solution* (alcohol 0.5%, benzalkonium chloride)].

Packaging and storage

Store below 40 °C (104 °F), preferably between 15 and 30 °C (59 and 86 °F), unless otherwise specified by manufacturer. Store in a tight container. Protect from freezing.

Auxiliary labeling

- For the eye.
- Continue medicine for full time of treatment.

Revised: 10/16/1998

NEOMYCIN, POLYMYXIN B, AND HYDROCORTISONE Ophthalmic

VA CLASSIFICATION (Primary): OP350

Commonly used brand name(s): *Ak-Spore H.C. Ophthalmic Suspension; Cortisporin Eye/Ear Suspension; Cortisporin Ophthalmic Suspension.*

Note: For a listing of dosage forms and brand names by country availability, see *Dosage Forms* section(s).

Category

Anti-inflammatory (steroidal), ophthalmic; corticosteroid (ophthalmic); antibacterial (ophthalmic).

Indications

Accepted

Inflammation, ocular (treatment) and

Ocular infections, superficial (treatment)—Ophthalmic neomycin, polymyxin B, and hydrocortisone combination is indicated for steroid-responsive inflammatory ocular conditions for which a corticosteroid is indicated and where bacterial infection or a risk of bacterial infection exists. Ocular corticosteroids are indicated in inflammatory conditions of the palpebral and bulbar conjunctiva, cornea, and anterior segment of the globe where the inherent risk of corticosteroid use in certain infective conjunctivitides is accepted to obtain a reduction in edema and inflammation. They are also indicated in chronic anterior uveitis and corneal injury from chemical, radiation, or thermal burns, or from penetration of foreign bodies. The use of a combination medication containing an antibacterial component is indicated where the risk of infection is high or where there is an expectation that potentially dangerous numbers of bacteria will be present in the eye. Ophthalmic neomycin, polymyxin B, and hydrocortisone combination is active against the following common bacterial eye pathogens: *Staphylococcus aureus, Escherichia coli, Haemophilus influenzae, Klebsiella* species, *Enterobacter (Aerobacter)* species, *Neisseria* species, and *Pseudomonas aeruginosa*.

Note: Not all species or strains of a particular organism may be susceptible to neomycin and polymyxin B.

Unaccepted

Neomycin, polymyxin B, and hydrocortisone combination is not effective against *Serratia marcescens* or streptococci, including *Streptococcus pneumoniae*.

Pharmacology/Pharmacokinetics

Physicochemical characteristics

Source—

Neomycin: Derived from *Streptomyces fradiae*.

Polymyxin B: Derived from polymyxin B_1 and polymyxin B_2, which are produced by the growth of *Bacillus polymyxa*.

Chemical Group—

Neomycin: Aminoglycosides.

Polymyxin B: Polypeptides.

Hydrocortisone: Corticosteroids.

Molecular weight—Hydrocortisone: 362.47.

Mechanism of action/Effect

Neomycin—See *Neomycin (Ophthalmic)*.

Polymyxin B—See *Neomycin, Polymyxin B, and Bacitracin (Ophthalmic)*.

Hydrocortisone—See *Corticosteroids (Ophthalmic)*.

Absorption

Neomycin; polymyxin B—May be absorbed following topical application to the eye if tissue damage is present.

Hydrocortisone—May be absorbed following topical application to the eye.

Precautions to Consider

Cross-sensitivity and/or related problems

Patients sensitive to one aminoglycoside or polymyxin may be sensitive to other aminoglycosides or polymyxins also.

Carcinogenicity

Neomycin—*In vitro* treatment of cultured human lymphocytes with neomycin caused increased frequency of chromosome aberrations at the highest concentrations (80 mg per mL) tested. However, the effects of neomycin on carcinogenesis in humans are not known.

Polymyxin B—Long-term studies in animals to evaluate carcinogenic potential have not been conducted with polymyxin B sulfate.

Corticosteroids—Long-term studies in animals (rats, rabbits, mice) showed no evidence of carcinogenicity attributable to oral administration of corticosteroids. Long-term animal studies have not been performed to evaluate the carcinogenic potential of topical corticosteroids.

Mutagenicity

Neomycin—*In vitro* treatment of cultured human lymphocytes with neomycin increased the frequency of chromosome aberrations at the highest concentrations (80 mg per mL) tested. However, no mutagenic effect of neomycin in humans is known.

Polymyxin B—Long-term studies in animals to evaluate its mutagenic potential have not been conducted with polymyxin B sulfate.

Corticosteroids—Long-term studies in animals (rats, rabbits, mice) showed no evidence of mutagenicity attributable to oral administration of corticosteroids. Studies to determine mutagenicity of topical hydrocortisone have revealed negative results.

Pregnancy/Reproduction

Fertility—Polymyxin B—Polymyxin B has been reported to impair the motility of equine sperm, but its effects on human male or female fertility are unknown.

Corticosteroids—Long-term animal studies have not been performed to evaluate the effect of topical corticosteroids on fertility.

Pregnancy—Adequate and well-controlled studies in humans have not been done for ophthalmic neomycin, polymyxin B, and hydrocortisone combination. Ophthalmic corticosteroids should be used during pregnancy only if potential benefit justifies potential risk to the fetus.

Topical corticosteroids have been shown to be teratogenic in rabbits at concentrations of 0.5% on days 6 to 18 of gestation, and in mice at a concentration of 15% on days 10 to 13 of gestation.

FDA Pregnancy Category C.

Breast-feeding

Systemically administered corticosteroids appear in human milk and can suppress growth, interfere with endogenous corticosteroid production, or cause other untoward effects. However, it is not known whether topical administration of corticosteroids can result in sufficient systemic absorption to produce detectable quantities in human milk. Problems in humans have not been documented. Because of the potential for serious adverse reactions in nursing infants from this ophthalmic corticosteroid, a decision should be made whether to discontinue nursing or to discontinue the drug, taking into account the importance of the drug to the mother.

Pediatrics

Appropriate studies on the relationship of age to the effects of ophthalmic neomycin, polymyxin B, and hydrocortisone combination have not been performed in the pediatric population. Safety and efficacy have not been established.

Geriatrics

Appropriate studies on the relationship of age to the effects of ophthalmic neomycin, polymyxin B, and hydrocortisone combination have not been performed in the geriatric population. However, no geriatrics-specific problems have been documented to date.

Medical considerations/Contraindications

The medical considerations/contraindications included have been selected on the basis of their potential clinical significance (reasons

given in parentheses where appropriate)—not necessarily inclusive (» = major clinical significance).

Except under special circumstances, this medication should not be used when the following medical problem exists:

» Epithelial herpes simplex keratitis (dendritic keratitis) or
» Fungal diseases of ocular structures or
» Mycobacterial infection of the eye or
» Other viral diseases of the cornea and conjunctiva or
» Vaccinia or
Varicella

» Hypersensitivity to neomycin, polymyxin B, hydrocortisone, or any of its components (some products may contain the preservatives, thimerosal or benzalkonium chloride)

Risk-benefit should be considered when the following medical problems exist:

For hydrocortisone

Cataract surgery
(use of corticosteroids after cataract surgery may delay healing and increase the incidence of filtering blebs)

Glaucoma
(corticosteroids should be used with caution in the presence of glaucoma)

» Herpes simplex keratitis
(may exacerbate severity of condition; great caution required)

For neomycin and/or polymyxin B

Blepharitis, acute, purulent
Conjunctivitis, acute, purulent

Patient monitoring

The following may be especially important in patient monitoring (other tests may be warranted in some patients, depending on condition; » = major clinical significance):

Fluorescein staining and
Slit lamp biomicroscopy
(initial prescription and renewal of medication beyond 20 mL should be made by physician only after examination of patient; if signs and symptoms fail to improve after 2 days, patient should be re-evaluated)

Fungal cultures
(consideration of possibility of corneal fungal infections after prolonged corticosteroid dosing; fungal cultures should be taken when appropriate)

Intraocular pressure monitoring
(may be required if medication is used for 10 days or longer)

Ophthalmologic examinations
(may be required at periodic intervals for patients on long-term therapy [more than 6 weeks], since chronic therapy may cause posterior subcapsular cataracts, especially in children; may cause increased intraocular pressure and glaucoma; and may enhance the establishment of secondary ocular infections)

Side/Adverse Effects

Note: The prolonged use of corticosteroids may result in ocular hypertension and/or glaucoma, with damage to the optic nerve, defects in visual acuity and fields of vision, and in posterior subcapsular cataract formation. Prolonged use also may suppress the host immune response, thereby increasing the hazard of secondary ocular infections. In the diseases that cause thinning of the cornea or sclera, perforations have occurred with the use of topical corticosteroids. In acute purulent conditions of the eye, corticosteroids may mask infection or enhance exisiting infection.

Topical antibiotics, particularly neomycin sulfate, may cause cutaneous sensitization. The exact incidence of hypersensitivity reactions (primarily skin rash) due to topical antibiotics is not known. The manifestations of sensitization to topical antibiotics are usually itching, reddening, and edema of the conjunctiva and eyelid. A sensitization reaction may also manifest as a failure to heal.

The following side/adverse effects have been selected on the basis of their potential clinical significance (possible signs and symptoms in parentheses where appropriate)—not necessarily inclusive:

Those indicating need for medical attention

Incidence more frequent

Hypersensitivity (itching, rash, redness, swelling, or other sign of irritation not present before therapy)

Incidence rare

Allergic reaction, specifically anaphylaxis (severe shortness of breath or trouble breathing; sudden, severe decrease in blood pressure; swelling around face); ***delayed healing of eye infection; glaucoma; ocular hypertension; optic nerve damage; posterior subcapsular cataract; visual acuity defects; and/or visual field defects*** (blurred vision or other change in vision)

Those indicating need for medical attention only if they continue or are bothersome

Incidence less frequent

Burning or stinging when applying medication

Patient Consultation

As an aid to patient consultation, refer to *Advice for the Patient, Neomycin, Polymyxin B, and Hydrocortisone (Ophthalmic)*.

In providing consultation, consider emphasizing the following selected information (» = major clinical significance):

Before using this medication

» Conditions affecting use, especially:
Hypersensitivity to neomycin, polymyxin B, or hydrocortisone or to any component of the product or any related antibiotic, such as amikacin, colistimethate, colistin, gentamicin, kanamycin, netilmicin, paromomycin, streptomycin, or tobramycin
Pregnancy—Risk benefit consideration
Breast-feeding—Risk benefit consideration due to potential for serious adverse reactions in nursing infants
Other medical problems, especially dendritic keratitis; fungal diseases of ocular structures; herpes simplex keratitis; mycobacterial infection of the eye;; or vaccinia, varicella, or other viral disease of the cornea or conjunctiva

Proper use of this medication

Proper administration technique for ophthalmic suspension
» Avoiding allowing the tip of dispensing container to contact eye, eyelid, fingers, or any other surface
» Compliance with full course of therapy
» Proper dosing
Missed dose: Applying as soon as possible; not applying if almost time for next dose
» Checking with physician before using leftover medication on other eye problems
» Proper storage

Precautions while using this medication

Need for ophthalmologic examinations at regular intervals during therapy lasting 10 or more days

Checking with physician if no improvement within a few days or if condition gets worse or rash/allergic reaction develops

Importance of use of this medicine by one person to avoid spreading infection

Side/adverse effects

Signs of potential side effects, especially hypersensitivity; allergic reaction, specifically anaphylaxis; delayed healing of eye infection; glaucoma; ocular hypertension; optic nerve damage; posterior subcapsular cataract; visual acuity defects; visual field defects

General Dosing Information

Although some manufacturers recommend a dose of 2 drops of an ophthalmic solution at appropriate intervals, the conjunctival sac will usually hold only 1 drop.

Ophthalmic neomycin, polymyxin B, and hydrocortisone should not be injected into the eye.

One dispenser bottle of medication contains 7.5 mL (10 mL in Canada). It is recommended that not more than 20 mL of medication should be prescribed initially, and the prescription should not be refilled without further evaluation of the condition.

Ophthalmic Dosage Forms

NEOMYCIN AND POLYMYXIN B SULFATES AND HYDROCORTISONE OPHTHALMIC SUSPENSION USP

Note: The dosing and strengths of the dosage forms available are expressed in terms of neomycin base.

Usual adult and adolescent dose

Inflammation, ocular (treatment) or
Ocular infections, superficial (treatment)—
Topical, to the conjunctiva, one or two drops every three to four hours depending on the severity of the condition. The medication may be used more frequently if necessary.

Usual pediatric dose

Safety and efficacy have not been established.

Strength(s) usually available

U.S.—

3.5 mg of neomycin (base), 10,000 Units of polymyxin B (base), and 10 mg of hydrocortisone per mL 1% (Rx) [*Ak-Spore H.C. Ophthalmic Suspension; Cortisporin Ophthalmic Suspension* (thimerosal 0.001%; cetyl alcohol; glyceryl monostearate; mineral oil; polyoxyl 40 stearate; propylene glycol; water for injection; sulfuric acid); GENERIC].

Canada—

3.5 mg of neomycin (base), 10,000 Units of polymyxin B sulfate, and 10 mg of hydrocortisone per mL 1% (Rx) [*Cortisporin Eye/Ear Suspension* (benzalkonium chloride; cetyl alcohol; glyceryl monostearate; mineral oil; polyoxyethylene stearate; propylene glycol; sulfuric acid; water for injection)].

Packaging and storage

Store at 15 to 25 °C (59 and 77 °F), unless otherwise specified by manufacturer. Store in a tight container. Protect from freezing.

Auxiliary labeling

- For the eye.
- Shake well.
- Do not touch or contaminate the tip of the container
- Keep in the original container. Close container tightly after use
- Keep out of reach of children
- Continue medicine for full time of treatment.

Note: One dispenser bottle of medication contains 7.5 mL (10 mL in Canada). It is recommended that not more than 20 mL of medication should be prescribed initially, and the prescription should not be refilled without further evaluation of the condition.

Revised: 02/15/2005

NEOMYCIN, POLYMYXIN B, AND HYDROCORTISONE Otic

VA CLASSIFICATION (Primary): OT250

Commonly used brand name(s): *AK-Spore HC Otic; Antibiotic Ear; Cort-Biotic; Cortatrigen Ear; Cortatrigen Modified Ear Drops; Cortisporin; Cortomycin; Drotic; Ear-Eze; LazerSporin-C; Masporin Otic; Octicair; Octigen; Otic-Care; Otic-Care Ear; Otimar; Otisan; Otocidin; Otocort; Pediotic; UAD Otic.*

Note: For a listing of dosage forms and brand names by country availability, see *Dosage Forms* section(s).

Category

Antibacterial-corticosteroid (otic).

Indications

Note: Bracketed information in the *Indications* section refers to uses that are not included in U.S. product labeling.

Accepted

Ear canal infections, external (treatment) or
Mastoidectomy cavity infections (treatment)—Otic neomycin, polymyxin B, and hydrocortisone combination is indicated in the treatment of external ear canal infections and mastoidectomy cavity infections caused by susceptible organisms.

[Otitis media, chronic suppurative (treatment)][1]—Otic neomycin, polymyxin B, and hydrocortisone combination is used in the treatment of chronic suppurative otitis media.

Not all species or strains of a particular organism may be susceptible to neomycin and polymyxin B.

[1]Not included in Canadian product labeling.

Pharmacology/Pharmacokinetics

Physicochemical characteristics

Source—

Neomycin: Derived from *Streptomyces fradiae.*

Polymyxin B: Derived from polymyxin B_1 and polymyxin B_2, which are produced by the growth of *Bacillus polymyxa.*

Chemical Group—

Neomycin: Aminoglycosides.

Polymyxin B: Polypeptides.

Hydrocortisone: Corticosteroids.

Molecular weight—Hydrocortisone: 362.47.

Mechanism of action/Effect

Neomycin—See *Neomycin (Ophthalmic).*

Polymyxin B—See *Neomycin, Polymyxin B, and Bacitracin (Ophthalmic).*

Hydrocortisone—See *Corticosteroids (Otic).*

Absorption

Neomycin; polymyxin B; hydrocortisone—May be absorbed following topical application to the ear if the eardrum is perforated or tissue damage is present.

Precautions to Consider

Cross-sensitivity and/or related problems

Patients sensitive to one aminoglycoside or polymyxin may be sensitive to other aminoglycosides or polymyxins also.

Carcinogenicity

Long-term studies in animals (rats, rabbits, mice) given oral corticosteroids showed no carcinogenicity.

Pregnancy/Reproduction

Pregnancy—Adequate and well-controlled studies in humans have not been done for otic neomycin, polymyxin B, and hydrocortisone combination.

Topical corticosteroids have been shown to be teratogenic in rabbits when applied at concentrations of 0.5% on days 6 to 18 of gestation and in mice when applied at a concentration of 15% on days 10 to 13 of gestation.

FDA Pregnancy Category C.

Breast-feeding

Oral hydrocortisone is distributed into breast milk. It is not known if otic neomycin, polymyxin B, and hydrocortisone combination is distributed into breast milk. However, problems in humans have not been documented.

Pediatrics

Appropriate studies on the relationship of age to the effects of otic neomycin, polymyxin B, and hydrocortisone combination have not been performed in the pediatric population. However, no pediatrics-specific problems have been documented to date.

Geriatrics

Appropriate studies on the relationship of age to the effects of otic neomycin, polymyxin B, and hydrocortisone combination have not been performed in the geriatric population. However, no geriatrics-specific problems have been documented to date.

Medical considerations/Contraindications

The medical considerations/contraindications included have been selected on the basis of their potential clinical significance (reasons given in parentheses where appropriate)—not necessarily inclusive (» = major clinical significance).

Risk-benefit should be considered when the following medical problems exist:

Sensitivity to aminoglycosides, polymyxins, or sulfites

For hydrocortisone

» Bullous myringitis
» Herpes simplex
» Herpes zoster oticus
» Tubercular or fungal infections of the ear
» Vaccinia, varicella, or other viral disease of the ear

For neomycin and/or polymyxin B

Otitis media, chronic or
Perforated eardrum
(possibility of ototoxicity)

Side/Adverse Effects

The following side/adverse effects have been selected on the basis of their potential clinical significance (possible signs and symptoms in parentheses where appropriate)—not necessarily inclusive:

Those indicating need for medical attention

Incidence more frequent

Hypersensitivity (itching, skin rash, redness, swelling, or other sign of irritation in or around the ear not present before therapy)

Patient Consultation

As an aid to patient consultation, refer to *Advice for the Patient, Neomycin, Polymyxin B, and Hydrocortisone (Otic).*

In providing consultation, consider emphasizing the following selected information (» = major clinical significance):

Before using this medication

» Conditions affecting use, especially:

Sensitivity to aminoglycosides, polymyxins, or sulfites

Pregnancy—Topical corticosteroids have been shown to be teratogenic in rabbits and mice

Proper use of this medication

Proper administration technique for otic solution and suspension
» Compliance with full course of therapy
» Proper dosing
Missed dose: Applying as soon as possible; not applying if almost time for next dose
» Not using longer than 10 days unless otherwise directed by physician
» Proper storage

Precautions while using this medication

Checking with physician if no improvement within 1 week

Side/adverse effects

Signs of potential side effects, especially hypersensitivity

General Dosing Information

This medication may be warmed, but not above body temperature, prior to administration.

A cotton wick may be placed in the ear canal and then saturated with the suspension. The wick should be kept moist by adding suspension every 4 to 8 hours and it should be replaced at least once daily.

Therapy should not be continued for more than 10 days.

If infection has not improved within 1 week, condition should be re-evaluated.

Otic Dosage Forms

Note: Bracketed uses in the *Dosage Forms* section refer to categories of use and/or indications that are not included in U.S. product labeling.

NEOMYCIN AND POLYMYXIN B SULFATES AND HYDROCORTISONE OTIC SOLUTION USP

Usual adult and adolescent dose

Ear canal infections, external—
Topical, to the ear canal, 4 drops three or four times a day.
Mastoidectomy cavity infections or
[Otitis media, chronic suppurative][1]—
Topical, to the mastoidectomy cavity or ear canal, 4 to 10 drops every six to eight hours.

Note: In the treatment of mastoidectomy cavity infections, the dose depends on the size of the mastoidectomy cavity. Some cavities may require up to 1 or 2 dropperfuls of otic solution or suspension in adults.

Usual pediatric dose

Ear canal infections, external—
Topical, to the ear canal, 3 drops three or four times a day.
Mastoidectomy cavity infections—
Topical, to the mastoidectomy cavity, 4 or 5 drops every six to eight hours.

Note: In the treatment of mastoidectomy cavity infections, the dose depends on the size of the mastoidectomy cavity.

[Otitis media, chronic suppurative][1]—
Topical, to the ear canal, 2 to 5 drops every six to eight hours.

Strength(s) usually available

U.S.—
3.5 mg of neomycin (base), 10,000 Units of polymyxin B (base), and 10 mg of hydrocortisone per mL (Rx) [*AK-Spore HC Otic* (potassium metabisulfite; propylene glycol; glycerin); *Antibiotic Ear; Cortatrigen Modified Ear Drops* (potassium metabisulfite; propylene glycol; glycerin); *Cort-Biotic; Cortisporin* (potassium metabisulfite 0.1%; cupric sulfate; glycerin; hydrochloric acid; propylene glycol); *Drotic* (potassium metabisulfite; propylene glycol; glycerin); *Ear-Eze* (potassium metabisulfite; propylene glycol; glycerin); *LazerSporin-C; Masporin Otic; Octicair* (potassium metabisulfite; propylene glycol; glycerin); *Octigen; Otic-Care* (glycerin; hydrochloric acid; propylene glycol; potassium metabisulfite); *Otic-Care Ear* (glycerin; hydrochloric acid; propylene glycol; potassium metabisulfite); *Otimar; Otocidin; Otocort;* GENERIC].

Canada—
3.5 mg of neomycin (base), 10,000 Units of polymyxin B (base), and 10 mg of hydrocortisone per mL (Rx) [*Cortisporin* (benzalkonium chloride)].

Packaging and storage

Store below 40 °C (104 °F), preferably between 15 and 30 °C (59 and 86 °F), unless otherwise specified by manufacturer. Store in a tight, light-resistant container. Protect from freezing.

Auxiliary labeling

- For the ear.
- Continue medicine for full time of treatment.

NEOMYCIN AND POLYMYXIN B SULFATES AND HYDROCORTISONE OTIC SUSPENSION USP

Usual adult and adolescent dose

Ear canal infections, external—
Topical, to the ear canal, 4 drops three or four times a day.
Mastoidectomy cavity infections; or
[Otitis media, chronic suppurative][1]—
Topical, to the mastoidectomy cavity or ear canal, 4 to 10 drops every six to eight hours.

Note: In the treatment of mastoidectomy cavity infections, the dose depends on the size of the mastoidectomy cavity. Some cavities may require up to 1 or 2 dropperfuls of otic solution or suspension in adults.

Usual pediatric dose

Ear canal infections, external—
Topical, to the ear canal, 3 drops three or four times a day.
Mastoidectomy cavity infections—
Topical, to the mastoidectomy cavity, 4 or 5 drops every six to eight hours.

Note: In the treatment of mastoidectomy cavity infections, the dose depends on the size of the mastoidectomy cavity.

[Otitis media, chronic suppurative][1]—
Topical, to the ear canal, 2 to 5 drops every six to eight hours.

Strength(s) usually available

U.S.—
3.5 mg of neomycin (base), 10,000 Units of polymyxin B (base), and 10 mg of hydrocortisone per mL (Rx) [*AK-Spore HC Otic* (cetyl alcohol; propylene glycol; polysorbate 80; thimerosal); *Antibiotic Ear; Cortatrigen Ear* (cetyl alcohol; propylene glycol; polysorbate 80; thimerosal); *Cort-Biotic; Cortisporin* (thimerosal 0.01%; cetyl alcohol; propylene glycol; polysorbate 80); *Cortomycin; Masporin Otic; Octigen; Otic-Care* (cetyl alcohol; polyoxyl 40 stearate; polysorbate 80; propylene glycol; sulfuric acid; benzalkonium chloride); *Otic-Care Ear* (cetyl alcohol; propylene glycol; polysorbate 80; thimerosal); *Otimar; Otisan; Otocort; Pediotic* (thimerosal 0.001%; cetyl alcohol; glyceryl monostearate; mineral oil; polyoxyl 40 stearate; propylene glycol); *UAD Otic;* GENERIC].

Canada—
3.5 mg of neomycin (base), 10,000 Units of polymyxin B (base), and 10 mg of hydrocortisone per mL (Rx) [*Cortisporin* (benzalkonium chloride)].

Packaging and storage

Store below 40 °C (104 °F), preferably between 15 and 30 °C (59 and 86 °F), unless otherwise specified by manufacturer. Store in a tight, light-resistant container. Protect from freezing.

Auxiliary labeling

- Shake well.
- For the ear.
- Continue medicine for full time of treatment.

[1]Not included in Canadian product labeling.

Revised: 06/02/1995

NEOSTIGMINE—See *Antimyasthenics (Systemic)*

NEPAFENAC Ophthalmic†

VA CLASSIFICATION (Primary): OP302

Commonly used brand name(s): *Nevanac.*

Note: For a listing of dosage forms and brand names by country availability, see *Dosage Forms* section(s).

†Not commercially available in Canada.

Category

Anti-inflammatory, nonsteroidal, ophthalmic.

Indications

Accepted

Inflammation, ocular (treatment)—Nepafenac ophthalmic suspension is indicated for the treatment of pain and inflammation associated with cataract surgery.

Pharmacology/Pharmacokinetics

Physicochemical characteristics

Molecular weight—Nepafenac: 254.28.
pH—Approximately 7.4.
Osmolality—305 mOsmol/kg.

Mechanism of action/Effect

Nepafenac ophthalmic is a nonsteroidal anti-inflammatory and analgesic prodrug. Nepafenac penetrates the cornea and is converted by ocular tissue hydrolases to amfenac, a nonsteroidal anti-inflammatory drug (NSAID). NSAIDs inhibit the activity of the enzyme cyclooxygenase in ocular tissues, resulting in decreased prostaglandin production.

Other actions/effects

Clinical studies indicate that perioperative use of nepafenac does not significantly affect intraocular pressure; however, changes in intraocular pressure may occur following cataract surgery.

Peak plasma concentration

The mean steady state C_{max} for nepafenac and amfenac were 0.31 +/- 0.104 ng/mL and 0.422 +/- 0.121 ng/mL following ocular administration.

Pharmacogenetics

Studies done in healthy subjects revealed no significant gender differences in steady-state pharmacokinetics of amfenac following three-times daily dosing of nepafenac.

Precautions to Consider

Cross-sensitivity and/or related problems

Individuals sensitive to acetylsalicylic acid, phenylacetic acid derivatives, and other nonsteroidal anti-inflammatory agents may be sensitive to nepafenac ophthalmic.

Carcinogenicity

Nepafenac has not been evaluated in long-term carcinogenicity studies.

Mutagenicity

Increased chromosomal aberrations were observed in Chinese hamster ovary cells exposed *in vitro* to nepafenac suspension. Nepafenac was not mutagenic in the Ames assay or in the mouse lymphoma forward mutation assay. No increase in the formation of micronucleated polychromatic erythrocytes *in vivo* in the mouse micronucleus assay in the bone marrow of mice following oral doses of nepafenac up to 5000 mg/kg was observed.

Pregnancy/Reproduction

Fertility—No impairment of fertility was observed in male and female rats when nepafenac was orally administered at doses of 3 mg/kg (approximately 90 and 380 times the plasma exposure to nepafenac and metabolite, amfenac).

Pregnancy—Nepafenac crosses the placenta in rats. Adequate and well controlled studies in humans have not been done. Because animal reproduction studies are not always predictive of human response, nepafenac should be used during pregnancy only if the potential benefit justifies the potential risk to the fetus. Because of the known effects of prostaglandin biosynthesis inhibiting drugs on the fetal cardiovascular system (closure of the ductus arterious), the use of nepafenac ophthalmic suspension during late pregnancy should be avoided.

Studies done in rabbits and rats given doses of nepafenac up to 10 mg/kg/day revealed no evidence of teratogenicity, despite the induction of maternal toxicity. In rats maternally toxic doses ≥ 10 mg/kg were associated with dystocia, increased post-implantation loss, reduced fetal weights and growth, and reduce fetal survival.

FDA Pregnancy Category C

Breast-feeding

Nepafenac ophthalmic is distributed into the milk of lactating rats. It is not known whether this drug is distributed in human milk. Because many drugs are distributed in human milk, caution should be exercised when nepafenac is administered to a nursing woman.

Pediatrics

The safety and effectiveness of nepafenac ophthalmic in pediatric patients under 10 years of age have not been established.

Geriatrics

Appropriate studies performed to date have not demonstrated geriatrics-specific problems that would limit the usefulness of nepafenac in the elderly.

Drug interactions and/or related problems

The following drug interactions and/or related problems have been selected on the basis of their potential clinical significance (possible mechanism in parentheses where appropriate)—not necessarily inclusive (» = major clinical significance):

Note: Combinations containing any of the following medications, depending on the amount present, may also interact with this medication.

Medications that prolong bleeding time
(may increase risk of bleeding)

Other topical NSAIDs or
Topical steroids
(may increase potential for healing problems)

Medical considerations/Contraindications

The medical considerations/contraindications included have been selected on the basis of their potential clinical significance (reasons given in parentheses where appropriate)—not necessarily inclusive (» = major clinical significance).

Except under special circumstances, this medication should not be used when the following medical problem exists:

» Hypersensitivity to nepafenac ophthalmic or to any ingredients in the formulation or to other NSAIDs

Risk-benefit should be considered when the following medical problems exist:

Complicated ocular surgeries or
Corneal denervation or
Corneal epithelial defects or
Diabetes mellitus or
Ocular surface diseases or
Rheumatoid arthritis or
Repeat ocular surgeries within a short period of time
(caution; postmarketing experience suggests an increased risk for corneal adverse events which may be sight threatening)

» Bleeding tendencies
(caution; may increase risk of bleeding)

» Contact lenses, use of
(nepafenac ophthalmic should not be administered while wearing contact lenses)

Patient monitoring

The following may be especially important in patient monitoring (other tests may be warranted in some patients, depending on condition; » = major clinical significance):

» Corneal health, including
Corneal erosion or
Corneal perforation or
Corneal thinning or
Corneal ulceration or
Epithelial breakdown
(may result in keratitis; closely monitor; if evidence of corneal epithelial breakdown, discontinue immediately, events may be sight threatening)

Side/Adverse Effects

The following side/adverse effects have been selected on the basis of their potential clinical significance (possible signs and symptoms in parentheses where appropriate)—not necessarily inclusive:

Those indicating need for medical attention

Incidence less frequent

Vitreous detachment (seeing flashes or sparks of light; seeing floating spots before the eyes, or a veil or curtain appearing across part of vision)

Those indicating need for medical attention only if they continue or are bothersome

Incidence more frequent

Foreign body sensation (feeling of having something in the eye); ***increase in intraocular pressure*** (blurred vision; change in vision; loss of vision); ***sticky sensation of eyelids; visual acuity decrease*** (decrease in vision)

Incidence less frequent

Conjunctival edema (swelling and/or redness of eye and lining of eyelid); ***corneal edema*** (swelling of the eye); ***dry eye; headache; hypertension*** (blurred vision; dizziness; nervousness; headache; pounding in the ears; slow or fast heartbeat); ***lid margin crusting***

(crusting in corner of eye); ***nausea; ocular discomfort*** (pain in eye); ***ocular hyperemia*** (redness of eye); ***ocular pain*** (eye pain); ***ocular pruritus*** (eye itching); ***photophobia*** (blurred vision; change in color vision; difficulty seeing at night; increased sensitivity of eyes to sunlight); ***sinusitis*** (pain or tenderness around eyes and cheekbone; fever; stuffy or runny nose; headache; cough; shortness of breath or troubled breathing; tightness of chest or wheezing); ***tearing; vomiting***

Overdose

For more information on the management of overdose or unintentional ingestion, **contact a poison control center** (see *Poison Control Center Listing*).

Treatment of overdose

There is no known specific antidote to nepafenac. Treatment is generally symptomatic and supportive.

Supportive care—

Patients in whom intentional overdose is confirmed or suspected should be referred for psychiatric consultation.

Patient Consultation

As an aid to patient consultation, refer to *Advice for the Patient, Nepafenac (Ophthalmic)*.

In providing consultation, consider emphasizing the following selected information (» = major clinical significance):

Before using this medication

» Conditions affecting use, especially:

Hypersensitivity to nepafenac or to any ingredients in its formulation or to other NSAIDs

Pregnancy—Should be administered to a pregnant woman only if clearly needed

Breast-feeding—Caution should be exercised when administering this drug to a nursing woman.

Use in children—Safety and efficacy have not been established in pediatric patients below the age of 10 years.

Proper use of this medication

Proper administration technique

» Proper dosing

Missed dose: Using as soon as possible; not using if almost time for next scheduled dose; not doubling doses

» Proper storage

Precautions while using this medication

» Nepafenac ophthalmic solution should not be used while wearing contact lenses

Side/adverse effects

Signs of potential side effects, especially vitreous detachment

General Dosing Information

Nepafenac ophthalmic may be administered in conjunction with other topical ophthalmic medications such as beta-blockers, carbonic anhydrase inhibitors, alpha-agonists, cycloplegics, and mydriatics.

Using for more than 1 day prior to surgery and/or beyond 14 days post surgery may increase patient risk and severity of corneal adverse effects.

Ocularly applied nonsteroidal anti-inflammatory drugs may cause increased bleeding of ocular tissues (including hyphemas) in conjunction with ocular surgery.

Ophthalmic Dosage Forms

NEPAFENAC OPHTHALMIC SOLUTION

Usual adult dose

Anti-inflammatory, nonsteroidal, ophthalmic—

Topical, to the conjunctiva, one drop to the affected eye(s) three times daily beginning 1 day prior to cataract surgery, continued on the day of surgery and two weeks postoperative.

Usual pediatric dose

Safety and efficacy have not been established in pediatric patients below the age of 10 years.

Usual geriatric dose

See *Usual adult dose*.

Strength(s) usually available

U.S.—

0.1% (Rx) [*Nevanac* (mannitol; carbomer 974P; sodium chloride; tyloxapol; edetate disodium benzalkonium chloride; sodium hydroxide; hydrochloric acid; purified water)].

Packaging and storage

Store between 2 and 25 °C (36 and 77 °F).

Auxiliary labeling

- For the eye
- Shake well

Developed: 09/23/2005

NESIRITIDE Systemic

VA CLASSIFICATION (Primary): CV900

Commonly used brand name(s): *Natrecor*.

Note: For a listing of dosage forms and brand names by country availability, see *Dosage Forms* section(s).

Category

Cardiotonic.

Indications

Accepted

Heart failure, congestive (treatment)—Nesiritide is indicated for the intravenous treatment of patients with acutely decompensated congestive heart failure who have dyspnea at rest or with minimal activity. In this population, the use of nesiritide reduced pulmonary capillary wedge pressure and improved dyspnea.

Pharmacology/Pharmacokinetics

Physicochemical characteristics

Source—Nesiritide is a sterile, purified preparation of human B-type natriuretic peptide (hBNP) manufactured from *Escherichia coli* using recombinant DNA technology. It has the same 32–amino acid sequence as the endogenous peptide, which is produced by the ventricular myocardium.

Molecular weight—3464 grams per mole.

Mechanism of action/Effect

Human BNP increases intracellular concentrations of guanosine 3′5′-cyclic monophosphate (cGMP) and smooth muscle cell relaxation by binding to the particulate guanylate cyclase receptor of vascular smooth muscle and endothelial cells. Cyclic GMP serves as a second messenger to dilate veins and arteries. In human studies in patients with heart failure, nesiritide has been shown to reduce pulmonary capillary wedge pressure (in a dose-dependent manner) and systemic arterial pressure.

Absorption

Administration of nesiritide exhibits biphasic disposition from the plasma.

Distribution

Volume of distribution of the central compartment (V_C): 0.073 L per kg.

Volume of distribution at steady state (V_{SS}): 0.19 L per kg.

Half-life

Mean terminal elimination half-life is approximately 18 minutes.

Elimination

Nesiritide is cleared via three independent mechanisms. They are:

- Cellular internalization and lysosomal proteolysis after binding to cell surface clearance receptors.
- Proteolytic cleavage by endopeptidases, such as neutral endopeptidase, which are present on the vascular lumenal surface.
- Renal filtration.

Precautions to Consider

Carcinogenicity and Tumorigenicity

Long-term studies in animals have not been performed.

Mutagenicity

Nesiritide did not increase the frequency of mutations when used in an *in vitro* bacterial cell assay, the Ames test. No other genotoxicity studies were performed.

Pregnancy/Reproduction

Fertility—Long-term studies in animals have not been performed to evaluate the effect on fertility.

Pregnancy—Studies have not been done in humans. Nesiritide should be used during pregnancy only if the potential benefit justifies any possible risk to the fetus.

Studies have not been done in animals.

FDA Pregnancy Category C.

Breast-feeding

It is not known whether nesiritide is distributed into human breast milk. Therefore, caution should be exercised when nesiritide is administered to a nursing woman.

Pediatrics

No information is available on the relationship of age to the effects of nesiritide in the pediatric population. Safety and efficacy have not been established.

Geriatrics

Appropriate studies performed to date have not demonstrated geriatrics-specific problems that would limit the usefulness of nesiritide in the elderly. In clinical studies, no overall differences in effectiveness or response were observed. However, some elderly patients may be more sensitive to the effects of nesiritide than younger patients.

Drug interactions and/or related problems

The following drug interactions and/or related problems have been selected on the basis of their potential clinical significance (possible mechanism in parentheses where appropriate)—not necessarily inclusive (» = major clinical significance):

Note: Combinations containing any of the following medications, depending on the amount present, may also interact with this medication.

» Angiotensin-converting enzyme (ACE) inhibitors, oral
(concomitant use may cause an increase in symptomatic hypotension)

Laboratory value alterations

The following have been selected on the basis of their potential clinical significance (possible effect in parentheses where appropriate)—not necessarily inclusive (» = major clinical significance).

With physiology/laboratory test values
Creatinine, serum
(values may be increased to 0.5 mg per dL above baseline or higher)

Medical considerations/Contraindications

The medical considerations/contraindications included have been selected on the basis of their potential clinical significance (reasons given in parentheses where appropriate)—not necessarily inclusive (» = major clinical significance).

Except under special circumstances, this medication should not be used when the following medical problems exist:

» Cardiomyopathy, restrictive or obstructive or
» Conditions in which cardiac output is dependent upon venous return or
» Pericardial tamponade or
» Pericarditis, constrictive or
» Valvular stenosis, significant
(use of nesiritide is not recommended)
» Hypersensitivity to nesiritide or any of its components
» Low cardiac filling pressures, suspected or known
(nesiritide should be avoided in these patients)
» Shock, cardiogenic or
» Systolic blood pressure less than 90 mm Hg
(nesiritide should not be used as primary therapy for these patients)

Risk-benefit should be considered when the following medical problems exist:

Heart failure, severe
(patients with renal function dependent on the activity of the renin-angiotensin-aldosterone system who are also in severe heart failure may develop azotemia if treated with nesiritide)
» Systolic blood pressure between 90 and 100 mm Hg
(risk of symptomatic hypotension may be increased; nesiritide should be used with caution)

Patient monitoring

The following may be especially important in patient monitoring (other tests may be warranted in some patients, depending on condition; » = major clinical significance):

Allergic reaction or
Untoward reaction
(patients should always be monitored following the parenteral administration of protein pharmaceuticals or *E. coli*-derived products)
Blood pressure
(nesiritide should only be administered in settings where blood pressure can be monitored closely; the dose should be reduced or the medication may be discontinued in patients who develop hypotension)

Side/Adverse Effects

The following side/adverse effects have been selected on the basis of their potential clinical significance (possible signs and symptoms in parentheses where appropriate)—not necessarily inclusive:

Those indicating need for medical attention

Incidence more frequent
Hypotension, asymptomatic

Incidence less frequent
Angina pectoris (chest pain or discomfort; chest tightness; shortness of breath); ***apnea*** (bluish lips or skin; difficulty in breathing); ***atrial fibrillation*** (fast or irregular heartbeat; dizziness; fainting); ***AV node conduction abnormalities; bradycardia*** (slow or irregular heartbeat; lightheadedness; dizziness or fainting; unusual tiredness or weakness); ***hypotension, symptomatic*** (cool, clammy skin; dizziness; lightheadedness; weakness); ***ventricular extrasystoles*** (fast or irregular heartbeat); ***ventricular tachycardia*** (fast heartbeat)

Those indicating need for medical attention only if they continue or are bothersome

Incidence more frequent
Headache

Incidence less frequent
Abdominal pain; amblyopia (blurred, or impaired vision); ***anemia*** (pale skin; troubled breathing; unusual bleeding or bruising; unusual tiredness or weakness); ***anxiety; back pain; catheter pain; confusion; cough, increased; cramps of the leg; dizziness; fever; hemoptysis*** (coughing or spitting up blood); ***injection site reaction; insomnia*** (sleeplessness); ***nausea; paresthesia*** (burning, crawling, itching, numbness, prickling, "pins and needles", or tingling feelings on the skin); ***pruritus*** (itching skin); ***rash; somnolence*** (sleepiness or unusual drowsiness); ***sweating; tremor; vomiting***

Overdose

For more information on the management of overdose or unintentional ingestion, **contact a poison control center** (see *Poison Control Center Listing*).

No data are available with respect to overdosage in humans. The expected reaction would be excessive hypotension.

Treatment of overdose

Treatment should be symptomatic and supportive.

Patient Consultation

As an aid to patient consultation, refer to *Advice for the Patient, Nesiritide (Systemic)*.

In providing consultation, consider emphasizing the following selected information (» = major clinical significance):

Before using this medication

» Conditions affecting use, especially:
Hypersensitivity to nesiritide or any of its components
Pregnancy—Should be used during pregnancy only if potential benefit justifies possible risk
Breast-feeding—Caution should be exercised when nesiritide is administered to a nursing woman.
Other medications, especially oral angiotensin-converting enzyme (ACE) inhibitors
Other medical problems, especially cardiogenic shock, conditions in which cardiac output is dependent upon venous return, constrictive pericarditis, low cardiac filling pressure, pericardial tamponade, restrictive or obstructive cardiomyopathy, significant valvular stenosis, or systolic blood pressure less than 90 mm Hg

Proper use of this medication

» Importance of physician drawing the nesiritide bolus from the prepared infusion bag.
» Importance of physician not initiating nesiritide at a dose that is above the recommended dose.
» Proper dosing

Side/adverse effects

Signs of potential side effects, especially asymptomatic hypotension, angina pectoris, apnea, atrial fibrillation, AV node conduction abnormalities, bradycardia, symptomatic hypotension, ventricular extrasystoles, and ventricular tachycardia

General Dosing Information

The IV tubing should be primed with an infusion of 25 mL prior to connecting to the patient's vascular access port and prior to administering the bolus or starting the infusion.

In a clinical trial, there was limited experience with increasing the dose of nesiritide above the recommended dose. In 23 patients, all of who had central hemodynamic monitoring, the infusion dose of nesiritide was increased by 0.005 mcg per kg per minute (preceded by a bolus of 1 mcg per kg), no more frequently than every 3 hours up to a maximum dose of 0.03 mcg per kg per minute. Nesiritide should not be titrated at frequent intervals.

For treatment of adverse effects

If hypotension should occur, the dose of nesiritide should be reduced or the medication may be discontinued. Administration of intravenous fluids, changes in body position, or other measures to increase blood pressure may be instituted, as needed. Hypotension may last for up to several hours, therefore, the patient should be closely observed before restarting the medication.

Parenteral Dosage Forms

NESIRITIDE FOR INJECTION

Usual adult dose

Cardiotonic—

Intravenous, 2 mcg per kg of body weight administered as a **intravenous direct that must be drawn from the prepared infusion bag** over approximately sixty seconds followed by a continuous infusion at a dose of 0.01 mcg per kg of body weight per minute.

Step 1: Administration of the IV direct—Withdraw the appropriate intravenous, direct volume as indicated on the table from the nesiritide infusion bag and administer over approximately 60 seconds through an IV port in the tubing.

- Bolus Volume (mL) = Patient Weight (kg)/3

Patient Weight (kg)	Volume of IV, Direct (mL = kg/3)
60	20
70	23.3
80	26.7
90	30
100	33.3
110	36.7

Step 2: Administration of the Continuous Infusion—Immediately following the administration of the bolus, infuse nesiritide at a flow rate of 0.1 mL per kg per hour. This will deliver a nesiritide dose of 0.01 mcg per kg per minute. To calculate the infusion flow rate to deliver a 0.01 mcg per kg per minute dose, use the following formula and table:

- Infusion flow Rate (mL/hr) = Patient Weight (kg) x 0.1

Patient Weight (kg)	Infusion Flow Rate (mL/hr)
60	6
70	7
80	8
90	9
100	10
110	11

Adult prescribing limits

Nesiritide should not be initiated at a dose that is higher than the recommended dose of a 2 mcg per kg bolus followed by an infusion of 0.01 mcg per kg per minute.

Usual pediatric dose

Safety and efficacy have not been established.

Usual geriatric dose

See *Usual adult dose*.

Strength(s) usually available

U.S.—

1.5 mg (Rx) [*Natrecor* (preservative-free; citric acid monohydrate 2.1 mg; mannitol 20 mg; sodium citrate dihydrate 2.94 mg)].

Packaging and storage

Store between 20 and 25 °C (68 and 77 °F), excursions permitted to 15 to 30 °C (59 to 86 °F), or refrigerated between 2 and 8 °C (36 and 46 °F). Keep in carton until time of use.

Preparation of dosage form

Add 5 mL of diluent removed from a pre-filled 250-mL plastic IV bag to one 1.5-mg vial of nesiritide. Recommended preservative-free diluents are: 5% percent dextrose injection, 0.9% sodium chloride injection, 5% dextrose and 0.45% sodium chloride injection, or 5% dextrose and 0.2% sodium chloride injection. Gently rock but do not shake the contents of the vial to ensure complete reconstitution. Withdraw the entire contents of the reconstituted nesiritide vial and add the reconstituted nesiritide to the 250-mL plastic IV bag and invert the bag several times to ensure complete mixing. The resulting solution will have a concentration of approximately 6 mcg per mL.

Stability

Nesiritide reconstituted solution can be stored at room temperature or it may be refrigerated up to 24 hours. The reconstituted solution should be inspected visually for particulate matter and discoloration prior to administration, whenever solution and container permit.

Incompatibilities

Nesiritide is chemically and/or physically incompatible with injectable formulations of bumetanide, enalaprilat, ethacrynate sodium, furosemide, heparin, hydralazine, and insulin. These drugs should not be administered with nesiritide through the same intravenous catheter.

The preservative, sodium metabisulfite, also is incompatible with nesiritide. Injectable drugs that contain this preservative should not be administered with nesiritide through the same infusion line.

Nesiritide binds to heparin. Therefore, heparin-coated catheters should not be used for administration because the amount of nesiritide delivered to the patient may be decreased. Heparin infusions should be administered through a separate catheter.

Auxiliary labeling

- For single dose only. Discard unused drug after 24 hours.

Revised: 08/24/2004
Developed: 10/09/2001

NETILMICIN—See *Aminoglycosides (Systemic)*

NEUROMUSCULAR BLOCKING AGENTS Systemic

This monograph includes information on the following: 1) Atracurium Besylate; 2) Cisatracurium; 3) Doxacurium; 4) Gallamine; 5) Mivacurium; 6) Pancuronium; 7) Rapacuronium#; 8) Rocuronium; 9) Succinylcholine; 10) Tubocurarine; 11) Vecuronium.

Note: See also the individual *Cisatracurium (Systemic)*, *Doxacurium (Systemic)*, *Mivacurium (Systemic)*,, *Rapacuronium* and *Rocuronium (Systemic)* monographs.

INN:

Atracurium Besylate—Atracurium besilate
Succinylcholine—Suxamethonium

VA CLASSIFICATION (Primary/Secondary):

Atracurium—MS300
Cisatracurium—MS300
Doxacurium—MS300
Gallamine—MS300
Mivacurium—MS300
Pancuronium—MS300
#Rapacuronium—MS300
Rocuronium—MS300
Succinylcholine—MS300
Tubocurarine—MS300/DX900
Vecuronium—MS300

Commonly used brand name(s): *Anectine*[9]; *Flaxedil*[4]; *Mivacron*[5]; *Nimbex*[2]; *Norcuron*[11]; *Nuromax*[3]; *Pavulon*[6]; *Quelicin*[9]; *Sucostrin*[9]; *Tracrium*[1]; *Zemuron*[8].

Other commonly used names are: Atracurium besilate [Atracurium Besylate]; Curare [Tubocurarine]; and Suxamethonium [Succinylcholine]

Note: For a listing of dosage forms and brand names by country availability, see *Dosage Forms* section(s).

#Rapacuronium was voluntarily withdrawn from the market on 03/2001

Category

Neuromuscular blocking paralyzing agent

Note: Depolarizing neuromuscular blocking agent—Succinylcholine.

Nondepolarizing neuromuscular blocking agent—Atracurium, cisatracurium, doxacurium, gallamine, mivacurium, pancuronium, rapacuronium, rocuronium, tubocurarine, vecuronium.

Note: Rapacuronium was voluntarily withdrawn from the market on 03/2001

Indications

Note: Bracketed information in the *Indications* section refers to uses that are not included in U.S. product labeling.

Accepted

Skeletal muscle paralysis—The neuromuscular blocking agents are indicated as adjuncts to anesthesia to induce skeletal muscle relaxation and to facilitate the management of patients undergoing mechanical ventilation.

Generally, a relatively short-acting nondepolarizing neuromuscular blocking agent or a single dose of the depolarizing neuromuscular blocking agent succinylcholine is used to facilitate endotracheal intubation. Continuous infusion of succinylcholine may be used for short surgical procedures requiring muscle relaxation. Nondepolarizing neuromuscular blocking agents, or, less commonly, succinylcholine administered by continuous infusion, are used for surgical procedures requiring an intermediate or prolonged duration of muscle relaxant action and to facilitate controlled ventilation.

Convulsions (treatment)—[Atracurium][1], [gallamine], [pancuronium][1], [succinylcholine], tubocurarine, and [vecuronium][1] are indicated to reduce the intensity of muscle contractions of pharmacologically or electrically induced convulsions. Succinylcholine is generally preferred because of its short duration of action.

[Neuromuscular blocking agents are also used to decrease the muscular manifestations of persistent convulsions associated with toxic reactions to other medications.][1]

Myasthenia gravis (diagnosis)—Tubocurarine is indicated as a diagnostic aid for myasthenia gravis when the results of tests with neostigmine or edrophonium are inconclusive.

[1]Not included in Canadian product labeling.

Pharmacology/Pharmacokinetics

See *Table 1*, page 2087.
See *Table 2*, page 2088.

Physicochemical characteristics

Molecular weight—

- Atracurium besylate: 1243.51.
- Cisatracurium besylate: 1243.5.
- Doxacurium chloride: 1106.14.
- Gallamine triethiodide: 891.54.
- Mivacurium chloride: 1100.18.
- Pancuronium bromide: 732.68.
- Rapacuronium bromide: 677.78.

Note: Rapacuronium was voluntarily withdrawn from the market on 03/2001

- Rocuronium bromide: 609.7.
- Succinylcholine chloride: 361.31.
- Tubocurarine chloride: 771.74.
- Vecuronium bromide: 637.75.

Mechanism of action/Effect

Neuromuscular blocking agents produce skeletal muscle paralysis by blocking neural transmission at the myoneural junction. The paralysis is selective initially and usually appears in the following muscles consecutively: levator muscles of eyelids, muscles of mastication, limb muscles, abdominal muscles, muscles of the glottis, and finally, the intercostal muscles and the diaphragm. Neuromuscular blocking agents have no known effect on consciousness or the pain threshold.

Depolarizing neuromuscular blocking agents compete with acetylcholine for the cholinergic receptors of the motor end plate and, like acetylcholine, combine with these receptors to produce depolarization; however, because of their high affinity for the cholinergic receptors and their resistance to acetylcholinesterase, they produce a more prolonged depolarization than does acetylcholine. This results initially in transient muscle contractions, usually visible as fasciculations, followed by inhibition of neuromuscular transmission. This type of neuromuscular block is not antagonized, and may even be enhanced, by anticholinesterase agents.

With prolonged or repeated use of depolarizing neuromuscular blocking agents, neuromuscular blockade resembling a nondepolarization block may be produced, resulting in prolonged respiratory depression or apnea.

Nondepolarizing neuromuscular blocking agents inhibit neuromuscular transmission by competing with acetylcholine for the cholinergic receptors of the motor end plate, thereby reducing the response of the end plate to acetylcholine. This type of neuromuscular block is usually antagonized by anticholinesterase agents.

Other actions/effects

Tubocurarine and, to a lesser extent, atracurium, mivacurium, and succinylcholine may cause histamine release. Cisatracurium, doxacurium, and aminosteroid neuromuscular blockers such as gallamine, pancuronium, rapacuronium, rocuronium, and vecuronium are least likely to cause histamine release.

Note: Rapacuronium was voluntarily withdrawn from the market on 03/2001Gallamine and pancuronium also have vagolytic activity.

Gallamine, and to a lesser extent, pancuronium, cause sympathetic stimulation.

Tubocurarine can also cause ganglionic blockade.

Succinylcholine may cause vagal stimulation.

Precautions to Consider

Cross-sensitivity and/or related problems

Patients sensitive to bromides may be sensitive to the bromide salts of pancuronium rapacuronium, rocuronium, or vecuronium also.

Note: Rapacuronium was voluntarily removed from the market on 03/2001

Patients sensitive to iodine or iodides may be sensitive to the iodide salt of gallamine also.

Mutagenicity

Atracurium—Mutagenic activity was observed in the mouse lymphoma assay under conditions in which more than 80% of the treated cells were killed, i.e., a relatively strong effect with concentrations of 80 and 100 mcg per mL in the absence of metabolic activation and a much weaker effect with concentrations of 1.2 mg per mL or higher in the presence of metabolic activation. However, mutagenic activity has not been demonstrated in the Ames test or in a rat bone marrow cytogenicity assay.

Cisatracurium—Positive results occurred in the mouse lymphoma assay, both in the presence and absence of exogenous metabolic activation (rat liver S-9). In the absence of metabolic activation, cisatracurium was positive at *in vitro* concentrations of 40 micrograms per mL (mcg/mL) or higher. In the presence of S-9, cisatracurium was mutagenic at a concentration of 300 mcg/mL, but not at lower or higher concentrations. No mutagenicity was found in the Ames *Salmonella* mutation test, a rat bone marrow cytogenic assay, or an *in vitro* human lymphocyte cytogenic assay.

Doxacurium—No mutagenicity was detected in the Ames *Salmonella* assay, mouse lymphoma assay, and human lymphocyte assay. However, statistically significant increases in the incidence of structural abnormalities, relative to vehicle controls, occurred in the *in vivo* rat bone marrow cytogenic assay in male rats receiving 0.1 mg per kg of body weight (mg/kg) (0.625 mg per square meter of body surface area [mg/m^2]) when the animals were sacrificed 6 hours, but not 24 or 48 hours, after administration. Structural abnormalities also occurred in female rats administered 0.2 mg/kg (1.25 mg/m^2) when the animals were sacrificed 24 hours, but not 6 or 48 hours, after administration. Abnormalities did not occur in male or female rats receiving 0.3 mg/kg (1.875 mg/m^2) at any time after administration. Because of the lack of a dose-dependent effect, the likelihood that the abnormalities found in this study were treatment-related or are clinically significant is low.

Mivacurium—Mivacurium displayed no mutagenicity in the Ames *Salmonella* test, the mouse lymphoma assay, the human lymphocyte assay, or the *in vivo* rat bone marrow cytogenetic assay.

Rapacuronium—No mutagenic effects were observed in either the Ames test or the Mouse Lymphoma cell assay. No chromosomal abnormalities were induced in mammalian cell cultures.

Note: Rapacuronium was voluntarily removed from the market on 03/2001

Pregnancy/Reproduction

Pregnancy—*Atracurium:* Adequate and well-controlled studies have not been done in humans. However, studies in rabbits (doses of 0.15 mg per kg of body weight [mg/kg] once a day or 0.1 mg/kg twice a day on Day 6 through Day 18 of gestation) have shown that atracurium causes visceral and skeletal anomalies. Also, postimplantation losses were greater in the group given 0.15 mg/kg once daily than in controls.

FDA Pregnancy Category C.

Cisatracurium: Adequate and well-controlled studies have not been done in humans. No maternal or fetal toxicity or teratogenicity was found in studies in nonventilated rats receiving maximum subparalyzing doses of 4 mg/kg subcutaneously (equivalent to eight times the intravenous human ED_{95} [dose required to produce 95% suppression of the twitch response to peripheral nerve stimulation]) or in ventilated rats receiving paralyzing doses of 0.5 or 1 mg/kg intravenously (equivalent to 10 or 20 times the intravenous human ED_{95}, respectively)

FDA Pregnancy Category B.

Doxacurium: Adequate and well-controlled studies have not been done in pregnant women. No maternal or fetal toxicity or teratogenicity was found in animal studies performed in nonventilated mice and rats receiving subcutaneous injections of subparalyzing doses.

FDA Pregnancy Category C.

Gallamine: Problems in humans have not been documented. However, it has been determined that gallamine crosses the placenta.

Mivacurium: Adequate and well-controlled studies have not been done in pregnant women. However, the possibility of a prolonged response should be considered, because plasma cholinesterase activity may be reduced during pregnancy. In animal studies, no maternal or fetal toxicity or teratogenicity occurred with subcutaneous administration of maximal subparalyzing doses to nonventilated pregnant rats or mice.

FDA Pregnancy Category C.

Pancuronium: Studies have not been done in either animals or humans. However, problems in humans have not been documented.

FDA Pregnancy Category C.

Rapacuronium: Rapacuronium crosses the placenta. There are no adequate, well-controlled studies in humans. In animal studies, no teratogenic effects were observed in rabbits or rats at doses up to 3 mg/kg per day and 2.25 mg/kg per day (0.3 and 0.1 times the maximum recommended human intravenous dose for adults on a mg/m² basis), respectively. Post-implantation loss in rabbits and fetotoxicity in rats were observed at 0.1 times the maximum recommended human intravenous dose for adults on a mg/m² basis.

FDA Pregnancy Category C

Note: Rapacuronium was voluntarily withdrawn from the market on 03/2001.

Rocuronium: Rocuronium crosses the placenta. Adequate and well-controlled studies in humans have not been done. No teratogenic effects were seen in a teratogenicity study in rats at dosages of 0.3 mg per kg of body weight (mg/kg).

FDA Pregnancy Category B.

Succinylcholine: Studies have not been done in humans. However, succinylcholine has been shown to cause intrauterine growth retardation and limb deformities resembling clubfoot when administered to the rat fetus between the 16th and 19th days of gestation or when injected in chick embryos from the 5th to 15th days of incubation.

FDA Pregnancy Category C.

Tubocurarine: Although adequate and well-controlled studies have not been done in humans, it has been determined that tubocurarine crosses the placenta. In animal studies, intramuscular injection of tubocurarine into the intercapsular region of the rat fetus on the 16th and 19th days of gestation caused growth retardation (incidence 21 to 23%) and limb deformity (incidence 7 to 8%), respectively. Tubocurarine has also caused growth retardation and limb deformities when injected into chick embryos from the 5th to the 15th day of incubation.

Tubocurarine may cause congenital fetal contractures if large and repeated doses are administered during the early months of pregnancy, possibly by immobilizing the fetus at the time of joint formation.

FDA Pregnancy Category C.

Vecuronium: Vecuronium crosses the placenta. Studies have not been done in either animals or humans.

FDA Pregnancy Category C.

Labor and delivery—Atracurium has been shown to cross the placenta in small quantities following administration to pregnant women for delivery by cesarean section. Although no adverse effects in the neonates were reported with atracurium, tubocurarine has been reported to cause diminished skeletal muscle activity leading to respiratory difficulty in the newborn when large and repeated doses are given near delivery. The possibility of neonatal respiratory depression or reduced skeletal muscle activity should be considered when any of these agents is used near delivery.

Labor and delivery—*Cisatracurium:* Use of cisatracurium during labor, vaginal delivery, or cesarean section has not been studied in humans. Whether administration to the mother may affect the fetus has not been determined. However, potentiation of neuromuscular blockade may occur if magnesium salts are used for management of toxemia of pregnancy.

Labor and delivery—*Doxacurium:* Doxacurium has not been studied in obstetrics (labor, vaginal delivery, or cesarean section). Doxacurium is not recommended for cesarean section because its duration of action exceeds the expected duration of the surgical procedure.

Labor and delivery—*Rapacuronium:* Rapacuronium was administered in doses of 2.5 mg/kg to 15 patients for rapid sequence induction of anesthesia for Cesarean section. Patients also received thiopental at doses of 4 to 6 mg/kg. No neonates had APGAR scores below 6 at five minutes after birth. Measurable venous umbilical concentrations of rapacuronium and the 3–hydroxymetabolite indicate that maternal/fetal transfer of the drug occurs during delivery

Note: Rapacuronium was voluntarily withdrawn from the market on 03/2001.

Labor and delivery—*Rocuronium:* Rocuronium was administered in doses of 0.6 mg/kg to 55 patients for rapid-sequence induction of anesthesia for cesarean section. Patients were also given thiopental at doses of 4 to 6 mg/kg. Anesthesia was maintained with isoflurane and nitrous oxide in oxygen. No neonate had an Apgar score below seven at 5 minutes after birth. Neonatal blood (umbilical venous) concentrations of rocuronium were 18% of maternal levels. Intubating conditions were poor or inadequate at 1 minute in four patients receiving 4 mg/kg of thiopental. Increasing the thiopental dose to 6 mg/kg improved intubating conditions; however, increasing the thiopental dose to improve intubating conditions is controversial and is not recommended due to an increased chance of central nervous system (CNS) depression in the neonate. Rocuronium is not recommended for rapid-sequence induction in cesarean section patients

Breast-feeding

It is not known whether neuromuscular blocking agents are distributed into breast milk. However, problems in humans have not been documented.

Pediatrics

Note: Many multi-dose vials of neuromuscular blocking agents contain benzyl alcohol. Administration of excessive doses of benzyl alcohol to neonates has been associated with neurologic and other complications.

Atracurium, gallamine, and tubocurarine: Neonates up to 1 month of age may be more sensitive to the effects of nondepolarizing neuromuscular blocking agents. Older infants are more sensitive than children to the effects of nondepolarizing neuromuscular blocking agents.

Cisatracurium: Appropriate studies on the relationship of age to the effects of cisatracurium in children 2 to 12 years of age have shown that the ED_{95} of cisatracurium is lower, the onset of action is faster, the duration of action is shorter, and recovery time after administration of a reversal agent is more rapid than in adults. However, pediatrics-specific adverse effects or other problems that would limit the use of cisatracurium in children have not been documented.

Doxacurium: Doxacurium has been studied in a limited number of infants and children up to 2 years of age. A study that included fifteen infants up to 11 months of age found that the ED_{50} and ED_{75} of doxacurium in infants are about one half those observed in children 3 to 10 years of age. Children ages 2 to 12 years are less sensitive to the effects of doxacurium than are adults or infants. Higher doses (on a mcg/kg basis) are required to achieve comparable levels of neuromuscular blockade. Even with higher doses, the onset of action, the duration of clinical effect (time for the twitch response to peripheral stimulation to return to 25% of the control value), and the recovery index (time for the spontaneous recovery from 25% to 75% of the twitch response to peripheral stimulation) are all significantly shorter in children than in adults.

There may be a high incidence of myopathy in pediatric patients who receive doxacurium to facilitate mechanical ventilation in intensive care units. In a trial in fourteen pediatric patients 6 months to 10 years of age who received doxacurium in intensive care units for 4.7 to 12.3 days, prolonged recovery was observed in over 40% of the patients.

Mivacurium: Appropriate studies on the relationship of age to the effects of mivacurium in patients up to 2 years of age have not shown that mivacurium causes different, or more severe, adverse effects in infants than in children or adults. No significant difference in the potency of a single dose of mivacurium was found between infants less than 6 months of age, infants 6 to 12 months of age, and older children during halothane anesthesia. The effective infusion rate of mivacurium is similar in infants and children

Pancuronium: The prolonged use of pancuronium to facilitate mechanical ventilation in neonates has been associated with myopathy. Some premature neonates administered pancuronium for emergency anesthesia and surgery subsequently developed methemoglobinemia. The cause of the methemoglobinemia has not been established.

Rapacuronium: Rapacuronium was studied in 384 pediatric patients under halothane anesthesia, aged 1 month to 12 years, in clinical trials Compared with adults, children exhibit increased clearance of rapacuronium 3 mg/kg.

Note: Rapacuronium was voluntarily withdrawn from the market on 03/2001.

Rocuronium: Appropriate studies on the relationship of age to the effects of rocuronium have not been performed in infants up to 3 months of age. Rocuronium was studied in 228 pediatric patients 3 months to 12 years of age in preapproval clinical trials. When halothane anesthesia was used without atropine pretreatment, a high incidence of tachycardia (exceeding 30% over baseline) was observed in patients given 0.6 to 0.8 mg/kg of rocuronium. A smaller, transient increase in heart rate was observed in another study of pediatric patients. Compared with adults, children have increased clearance of rocuronium. Compared with older children, infants have a longer duration of paralysis after an intubating dose of rocuronium. Some pediatric patients have experienced tachycardia, increased blood pressure, and resistance to neuromuscular blockade when phenylephrine nose drops were administered after rocuronium.

Succinylcholine: Hyperkalemic rhabdomyolysis resulting in cardiac arrest and death has occurred in apparently healthy pediatric patients after administration of succinylcholine. The adverse events occurred in pediatric patients with previously undiagnosed skeletal muscle myopathy (e.g., Duchenne's muscular dystrophy). Because it is not possible to predict when a pediatric patient may experience a serious adverse reaction, it is recommended that the use of succinylcholine be restricted to emergency situations or other situations where the immediate securing of the airway is needed (e.g., laryngospasm).

Vecuronium: Pediatric patients 7 weeks to 1 year of age are more sensitive to the effects of vecuronium (on a mg-per-kg basis) than are adults. Recovery time may be 1½ times that of adults.

Geriatrics

Although appropriate studies with neuromuscular blocking agents have not been performed in the geriatric population, geriatrics-specific problems that would limit the usefulness of these medications in the elderly are not expected. However, elderly patients are more likely to have age-related renal function impairment, which may decrease the rate of clearance of*gallamine, pancuronium, succinylcholine, tubocurarine,* or *vecuronium*from the body and thereby prolong their effects

Appropriate studies performed to date have not demonstrated geriatrics-specific problems that would limit the usefulness of *cisatracurium, doxacurium, mivacurium, rapacuronium* or *rocuronium*in the elderly

Note: Rapacuronium was voluntarily withdrawn from the market on 03/2001.

Drug interactions and/or related problems

The following drug interactions and/or related problems have been selected on the basis of their potential clinical significance (possible mechanism in parentheses where appropriate)—not necessarily inclusive (» = major clinical significance):

See *Table 3,* page 2089.

Laboratory value alterations

The following have been selected on the basis of their potential clinical significance (possible effect in parentheses where appropriate)—not necessarily inclusive (» = major clinical significance).

With physiology/laboratory test values

Succinylcholine

Serum potassium concentrations

(may be increased; increase may cause cardiac arrest or arrhythmias in patients with severe trauma, burns, or neurologic disorders; this effect may persist for several weeks or months after the initial trauma)

Medical considerations/Contraindications

The medical considerations/contraindications included have been selected on the basis of their potential clinical significance (reasons given in parentheses where appropriate)—not necessarily inclusive (» = major clinical significance).

See *Table 4,* page 2091.

Side/Adverse Effects

See *Table 5,* page 2093.

Note: Overdose of the neuromuscular blocking agents may result in prolonged respiratory depression or apnea and cardiovascular collapse.

Overdose

For specific information on the agents used in the management of a neuromuscular blocking agent overdose, see:

- *Atropine* in
- *Anticholinergics/Antispasmodics (Systemic)* monograph;
- *Edrophonium (Systemic)* monograph;
- *Neostigmine* in
- *Antimyasthenics (Systemic)* monograph; and/or
- *Pyridostigmine* in
- *Antimyasthenics (Systemic)* monograph.

For more information on the management of overdose or unintentional ingestion, **contact a Poison Control Center** (see *Poison Control Center Listing).*

Clinical effects of overdose

The following effects have been selected on the basis of their potential clinical significance (possible signs and symptoms in parentheses where appropriate)—not necessarily inclusive:

Acute

Apnea; hypotension, severe; paralysis, prolonged; shock

Treatment of overdose

Specific treatment—

Administering anticholinesterase agents, such as edrophonium, neostigmine, or pyridostigmine, to antagonize the action of the nondepolarizing neuromuscular blocking agents. It is recommended that atropine or another suitable anticholinergic agent be administered prior to or concurrently with the antagonist to counteract its cholinergic side effects.

The depolarization block produced by succinylcholine is not antagonized by anticholinesterase agents such as edrophonium, neostigmine, and pyridostigmine. However, if succinylcholine has been administered over a prolonged period of time and the characteristic depolarization block has gradually changed to a nondepolarization block, as determined with a peripheral nerve stimulator, small doses of the anticholinesterase agent may be tried as an antagonist. If an anticholinesterase agent is used as an antagonist, it is recommended that atropine be administered prior to or concurrently with the antagonist to counteract its cholinergic side effects. Patients should be closely observed for at least 1 hour after reversal of nondepolarization block for possible return of muscle relaxation.

The antagonists are merely adjuncts to, and are not to be substituted for, the institution of measures to ensure adequate ventilation. Ventilatory assistance must be continued until the patient can maintain an adequate ventilatory exchange unassisted.

Monitoring—

Determining the nature and degree of the neuromuscular blockade, using a peripheral nerve stimulator.

Supportive care—

For apnea or prolonged paralysis—maintaining an adequate airway and administering manual or mechanical ventilation. Artificial respiration should be continued until complete recovery of normal respiration is assured.

For severe hypotension or shock—administering fluids and vasopressors as needed to treat

General Dosing Information

Neuromuscular blocking agents have no known effect on consciousness or the pain threshold; therefore, when used as an adjunct to surgery, the neuromuscular blocking agent should always be used with adequate anesthesia.

Since neuromuscular blocking agents may cause respiratory depression, they should be used only by those individuals experienced in the techniques of tracheal intubation, artificial respiration, and the administration of oxygen under positive pressure; facilities for these procedures should be immediately available.

The stated doses are intended as a guideline. Actual dosage must be individualized. To minimize the risk of overdosage, it is recommended that a peripheral nerve stimulator be used to monitor response to the neuromuscular blocking agents.

When nondepolarizing neuromuscular blocking agents are administered concurrently with potent general anesthetics such as enflurane, ether, isoflurane, methoxyflurane, or cyclopropane, the dosage of vecuronium should be decreased by 15%, and that of the other neuromuscular blocking agents should be reduced by 33 to 50%, or as determined with a peripheral nerve stimulator. Halothane causes less potentiation of neuromuscular blockade than either enflurane or isoflurane; therefore, a smaller reduction in the dosage of the neuromuscular blocking agent may be considered.

ATRACURIUM

Summary of Differences

Pharmacology/pharmacokinetics:
Mechanism of action/effect:
A nondepolarizing neuromuscular blocking agent.
Action is usually antagonized by anticholinesterase agents.
Other actions/effects:
May cause histamine release.
Protein-binding:
High.
Biotransformation:
In plasma, by ester hydrolysis and by Hofmann elimination; independent of hepatic or renal function or plasma pseudocholinesterase activity.
Half-life:
Distribution: 2–3.4 minutes.
Elimination: 20 minutes.
Onset of action:
Initial effect within 2 minutes; intubation conditions in 2–2.5 minutes.
Time to peak effect:
1.7–10 (average 3–5) minutes.
Duration of peak effect:
20–35 minutes (balanced anesthesia); not changed by repeated dosing, provided that recovery from the prior dose begins before subsequent doses are given.
Time to recovery:
From time of injection (balanced anesthesia):
25% of twitch response achieved in 35–45 minutes and 95% of twitch response achieved in 60–70 minutes.
From beginning of recovery:
Balanced anesthesia—95% of twitch response achieved in 30 minutes.
Inhalation anesthesia—95% of twitch response achieved in 40 minutes.
Elimination:
Renal and biliary; less than 10% of the quantity excreted via the biliary route as unchanged atracurium.
Precautions:
Pregnancy:
Teratogenic and embryotoxic effects have been demonstrated in rabbits.
Has been shown to cross the human placenta.
Drug interactions and/or related problems:
May increase incidence and severity of bradycardia and hypotension when used together with opioid analgesics; also, histamine release may be additive to that induced by many opioids.
Use with digitalis glycosides not reported to cause cardiac arrhythmias or other undesirable cardiac effects.
Effects may be enhanced or prolonged in patients receiving chronic lithium therapy.
Effects not prolonged by cholinesterase inhibitors or hexafluorenium.
Alkaline solutions such as barbiturate injections should not be mixed in the same syringe, or administered simultaneously through the same intravenous needle, with atracurium. Alkaline solutions may change the pH of the acidic atracurium solution, resulting in inactivation of atracurium or precipitation of a free acid.
Serious side effects with concurrent use of methotrimeprazine have not been reported.
Additive effects with physostigmine have not been reported.
Medical considerations/contraindications:
Lower risk of problems than with gallamine or pancuronium if used in patients with cardiac conditions in which tachycardia would be undesirable.
Efficacy not reduced by hepatic function impairment.
Caution required in patients with pre-existing hypotension.
Effects not prolonged in patients with renal function impairment or shock.
Side/adverse effects:
Moderate risk of side effects associated with histamine release.
More likely than neuromuscular blocking agents with steroidal structure or doxacurium, but less likely than mivacurium or tubocurarine, to cause flushing of skin.
Hives and laryngospasm have been reported.

Additional Dosing Information

See also *General Dosing Information.*

Atracurium must be administered intravenously because intramuscular injection may cause tissue irritation and because there are no clinical data to support intramuscular administration.

A reduction in dosage and rate of administration is recommended for patients in whom histamine release may be hazardous. Also, patients with neuromuscular disease, severe electrolyte disorders, or carcinomatosis should receive lower doses because of potential enhancement of neuromuscular blockade or difficulties with reversal.

Bradycardia occurring during atracurium administration may be treated by intravenous administration of atropine.

The duration of effect is prolonged in obese patients when atracurium is dosed based on total body weight. One researcher recommends reducing the dose of atracurium by 2.3 mg for each 10 kg total body weight over 70 kg to avoid a prolonged effect.

Parenteral Dosage Forms

ATRACURIUM BESYLATE INJECTION

Usual adult and adolescent dose

Skeletal muscle paralysis
Initial—
Intravenous, 400 to 500 mcg (0.4 to 0.5 mg) per kg of body weight; or
For patients in whom histamine release might be hazardous—
Intravenous, 300 to 400 mcg (0.3 to 0.4 mg) per kg of body weight, administered slowly or in divided doses over a period of one minute.
For administration after steady-state enflurane or isoflurane anesthesia has been established—
Intravenous, 250 to 350 mcg (0.25 to 0.35 mg) per kg of body weight, or approximately one-third less than the usual initial dose. Halothane causes less potentiation of neuromuscular blockade; therefore, a smaller reduction in atracurium dosage may be considered.
After succinylcholine-assisted endotracheal intubation under balanced anesthesia—
Intravenous, 300 to 400 mcg (0.3 to 0.4 mg) per kg of body weight. If a potent inhalation anesthetic is being administered, even lower doses may be required. The effects of succinylcholine, as determined using a peripheral nerve stimulator, should be permitted to subside prior to administration of atracurium.
Supplemental—
Intravenous, 80 to 100 mcg (0.08 to 0.1 mg) per kg of body weight twenty to forty-five minutes following the initial dose, then every fifteen to twenty-five minutes or as required by clinical conditions; or
Intravenous infusion (initiated after recovery from the effects of an initial intravenous dose of 300 to 500 mcg [0.3 to 0.5 mg]—
Balanced anesthesia—
9 to 10 mcg (0.009 to 0.01 mg) per kg of body weight per minute until the desired degree of neuromuscular blockade is re-established, after which the rate of infusion may be adjusted according to clinical requirements and patient response. Most patients require 5 to 9 mcg (0.005 to 0.009 mg) per kg of body weight per minute, although some may require as little as 2 mcg (0.002 mg) per kg of body weight per minute and others may require as much as 15 mcg (0.015 mg) per kg of body weight per minute.
After steady-state enflurane or isoflurane anesthesia has been established—
The required rate of infusion may be reduced by approximately 33%. A smaller reduction in the rate of infusion may be considered for patients anesthetized with halothane.
For cardiopulmonary bypass procedures in which hypothermia is induced—
The required rate of infusion may be reduced by approximately 50%.

Usual pediatric dose

Neonates up to 1 month of age—
Dosage has not been established.
Children 1 month to 2 years of age (under halothane anesthesia)—
Intravenous, 300 to 400 mcg (0.3 to 0.4 mg) per kg of body weight, initially.
Children 2 years of age and over—
See *Usual adult and adolescent dose.*

Note: Maintenance doses may be required somewhat more frequently than in adults.

Strength(s) usually available

U.S.—
10 mg per mL (Rx) [*Tracrium* (benzyl alcohol [multiple-dose vials only]); GENERIC].

Canada—

10 mg per mL (Rx) [*Tracrium;* GENERIC].

Packaging and storage

Store between 2 and 8 °C (36 and 46 °F), unless otherwise specified by manufacturer. Protect from freezing.

Preparation of dosage form

For intravenous infusion—Atracurium besylate injection may be diluted with 0.9% sodium chloride injection, 5% dextrose injection, or 5% dextrose in 0.9% sodium chloride injection. Lactated Ringer's injection should *not* be used (see *Incompatibilities,* below). A solution prepared by adding 2 mL of atracurium besylate injection (10 mg per mL) to 98 mL of diluent contains 200 mcg (0.2 mg) of atracurium besylate per mL; a solution prepared by adding 5 mL of atracurium besylate injection (10 mg per mL) to 95 mL of diluent contains 500 mcg (0.5 mg) per mL.

Stability

Intravenous infusion solutions prepared with 5% dextrose injection, 0.9% sodium chloride injection, or 5% dextrose in 0.9% sodium chloride injection may be stored in a refrigerator or at room temperature for up to 24 hours without significant loss of potency. Unused portions of such solutions should be discarded after 24 hours.

Atracurium besylate injection should be used within 14 days if stored at room temperature (25 °C [77 °F]), even if later refrigerated.

Incompatibilities

Alkaline solutions such as barbiturate injections should not be mixed in the same syringe, or administered simultaneously through the same intravenous needle, with atracurium. Alkaline solutions may change the pH of the acidic atracurium solution, resulting in inactivation of atracurium or precipitation of a free acid.

Spontaneous degradation of atracurium has been shown to occur more rapidly when the medication is diluted with lactated Ringer's injection than when the medication is diluted with 0.9% sodium chloride injection. Therefore, it is recommended that lactated Ringer's injection not be used to prepare intravenous infusion solutions containing atracurium.

CISATRACURIUM

Summary of Differences

Note: See *Cisatracurium (Systemic)* single drug monograph for specific information

CISATRACURIUM INJECTION

Strength(s) usually available

U.S.—

2 mg (base) per mL (Rx) [*Nimbex* (benzenesulfonic acid; benzyl alcohol 0.9% [10-mL multiple-dose vial only])].

10 mg (base) per mL (Rx) [*Nimbex* (benzenesulfonic acid)].

Canada—

2 mg (base) per mL (Rx) [*Nimbex* (benzenesulfonic acid; benzyl alcohol 0.9% [10-mL multiple-dose vial only])].

10 mg (base) per mL (Rx) [*Nimbex* (benzenesulfonic acid)].

Note: The 10-mg-per-mL strength is intended only for preparing intravenous infusions for adults to be used in the intensive care unit. The 10-mg-per-mL vials contain benzyl alcohol and should not be used to prepare infusions for neonates.

DOXACURIUM

Summary of Differences

Note: See *Doxacurium (Systemic)* single drug monograph for specific information

DOXACURIUM CHLORIDE INJECTION

Strength(s) usually available

U.S.—

1 mg per mL (Rx) [*Nuromax* (0.9% benzyl alcohol)].

Canada—

1 mg per mL (Rx) [*Nuromax* (0.9% benzyl alcohol)].

GALLAMINE

Summary of Differences

Pharmacology/pharmacokinetics:

Mechanism of action/effect:

A nondepolarizing neuromuscular blocking agent.

Action is usually antagonized by anticholinesterase agents.

Other actions/effects:

Has vagolytic activity.

Less likely than most other neuromuscular blocking agents to cause histamine release.

Biotransformation:

Essentially none.

Half-life:

Distribution: 16 minutes.

Elimination: 150 minutes.

Onset of action:

Initial effect within 1–2 minutes.

Time to peak effect:

3–5 minutes.

Duration of peak effect:

15–30 minutes; increased by repeated dosing.

Elimination:

Renal, almost completely as unchanged gallamine.

Precautions:

Cross-sensitivity and/or related problems:

Cross-sensitivity may occur in patients sensitive to iodine or iodides.

Drug interactions and/or related problems:

Vagolytic activity may decrease risk of opioid analgesic-induced bradycardia and/or hypotension, but may increase risk of tachycardia and/or hypertension in some patients.

Use with digitalis glycosides not reported to cause cardiac arrhythmias or other undesirable cardiac effects.

Effects may be enhanced or prolonged by beta-adrenergic blocking agents.

Medical considerations/contraindications:

More likely than most other neuromuscular blocking agents to cause problems in patients with cardiac conditions in which tachycardia would be undesirable.

Less likely than other neuromuscular blocking agents to cause problems in patients for whom histamine release would be hazardous.

Caution required in patients with pre-existing hypertension.

Prolongation of effects in patients with renal function impairment or shock more likely and/or more severe than with other neuromuscular blocking agents.

Side/adverse effects:

Side effects caused by histamine release have not been reported.

More likely than other neuromuscular blocking agents to cause hypertension and/or tachycardia.

Additional Dosing Information

See also *General Dosing Information.*

In usual doses, gallamine has a slightly shorter duration of action than tubocurarine; however, in very large doses, its duration of action may be longer.

Parenteral Dosage Forms

GALLAMINE TRIETHIODIDE INJECTION USP

Usual adult and adolescent dose

Skeletal muscle paralysis

Surgery—

Initially 1 mg per kg of body weight, not to exceed 80 mg per dose; then 500 mcg (0.5 mg) to 1 mg per kg of body weight after an interval of fifty to sixty minutes, if necessary, for prolonged procedures.

Convulsions (treatment), electrically induced—

Intravenous, 40 to 60 mg

Note: A dose of 1 mg per kg of body weight produces a 50% reduction in respiratory minute volume; a dose of 1.5 mg per kg of body weight produces a 75% reduction in respiratory minute volume.

Usual pediatric dose

Intravenous, 2 mg per kg of body weight. A dose of 4 mg per kg of body weight is sometimes used in pediatric patients to provide good intubating conditions in one to two minutes. An increase in heart rate to over one hundred and fifty beats per minute should be anticipated when a dose of 4 mg per kg of body weight is administered.

Note: Caution in use is recommended, especially for patients weighing less than 5 kg.

Strength(s) usually available
U.S.—
20 mg per mL (Rx) [*Flaxedil* (edetate disodium; sodium bisulfite)].
Canada—
20 mg per mL (Rx) [*Flaxedil* (potassium metabisulfite 1 mg per mL; sodium sulfite 2 mg per mL)].

Packaging and storage
Store below 40 °C (104 °F), preferably between 15 and 30 °C (59 and 86 °F), unless otherwise specified by manufacturer. Protect from light. Protect from freezing.

MIVACURIUM

Summary of Differences

Note: See *Mivacurium (Systemic)* single drug monograph for specific information.

MIVACURIUM INJECTION

Strength(s) usually available
U.S.—
2 mg per mL (Rx) [*Mivacron*].
Canada—
2 mg per mL (Rx) [*Mivacron*].

PANCURONIUM

Summary of Differences

Pharmacology/pharmacokinetics:
Mechanism of action/effect:
A nondepolarizing neuromuscular blocking agent.
Action is usually antagonized by anticholinesterase agents.
Other actions/effects:
Has vagolytic activity.
Less likely than most other neuromuscular blocking agents to cause histamine release.
Protein-binding:
Very low.
Biotransformation:
Hepatic, in small quantities.
Half-life:
Distribution: 10–13 minutes.
Elimination: 114–116 minutes.
Onset of action:
Initial effect within 1 minute; intubation conditions in 2–3 minutes.
Time to peak effect:
3–4.5 minutes, depending on dose.
Duration of peak effect:
35–45 minutes; increased by repeated dosing.
Time to recovery:
From time of injection: 90% of twitch response achieved in <60 minutes.
Elimination:
Renal (about 80% as unchanged pancuronium); about 10% biliary (up to 10% as unchanged pancuronium).
Precautions:
Cross-sensitivity and/or related problems:
Cross-sensitivity may occur in patients sensitive to bromides.
Pediatrics:
The prolonged use of pancuronium to facilitate mechanical ventilation in neonates has been associated with myopathy. Some premature neonates administered pancuronium for emergency anesthesia and surgery subsequently developed methemoglobinemia. The cause of the methemoglobinemia has not been established.
Drug interactions and/or related problems:
Vagolytic activity may decrease risk of opioid analgesic-induced bradycardia and/or hypotension, but may increase risk of tachycardia and/or hypertension in some patients.
Use with digitalis glycosides may cause cardiac arrhythmias or other undesirable cardiac effects.
Effects may be enhanced or prolonged by beta-adrenergic blocking agents.
Effects may be enhanced or prolonged in patients receiving chronic lithium therapy.
Effects not prolonged by cholinesterase inhibitors or hexafluorenium.
Serious side effects with concurrent use of methotrimeprazine have not been reported.
Additive effects with physostigmine have not been reported.
Effects may be decreased by hydrocortisone or prednisone.
Medical considerations/contraindications:
More likely than most other neuromuscular blocking agents to cause problems in patients with cardiac conditions in which tachycardia would be undesirable.
Caution required in patients for whom histamine release would be hazardous.
Effects may be prolonged by hepatic function impairment.
Effects may be prolonged by renal function impairment, but to a lesser extent than for gallamine.
Side/adverse effects:
Relatively low risk of side effects associated with histamine release.
May cause itching of skin more frequently than other neuromuscular blocking agents.
Excessive salivation has been reported.

Additional Dosing Information

See also *General Dosing Information.*

Pancuronium is approximately 5 times as potent as tubocurarine.

Parenteral Dosage Forms

PANCURONIUM BROMIDE INJECTION

Usual adult and adolescent dose
Initial—
Intravenous, 40 to 100 mcg (0.04 to 0.1 mg) per kg of body weight. Incremental doses starting at 10 mcg (0.01 mg) per kg of body weight may then be administered, generally every twenty to sixty minutes, the dosage being adjusted as needed.
For administration after steady-state enflurane or isoflurane anesthesia has been established and/or after succinylcholine-assisted endotracheal intubation—
Intravenous, 40 mcg (0.04 mg) per kg of body weight, initially, then adjusted according to patient response.
For endotracheal intubation—
Intravenous, 60 to 100 mcg (0.06 to 0.1 mg) per kg of body weight.

Usual pediatric dose
Neonates up to 1 month of age—
Dosage must be individualized by the physician. Dosage may be based on the patient's response to a test dose of 20 mcg (0.02 mg) per kg of body weight.
Children 1 month of age and over—
See *Usual adult and adolescent dose.*

Strength(s) usually available
U.S.—
1 mg per mL (Rx) [*Pavulon* (benzyl alcohol)].
2 mg per mL (Rx) [*Pavulon* (benzyl alcohol)].
Canada—
1 mg per mL (Rx) [*Pavulon*].
2 mg per mL (Rx) [*Pavulon*].

Packaging and storage
Store between 2 and 8 °C (36 and 46 °F), unless otherwise specified by manufacturer. Protect from freezing.

RAPACURONIUM

Summary of Differences

Note: See *Rapacuronium (Systemic)* single drug monograph for specific information

Note: Rapacuronium was voluntarily withdrawn from the market on 03/2001

RAPACURONIUM BROMIDE FOR INJECTION

Strength(s) usually available
U.S.—

Note: Rapacuronium bromide was voluntarily withdrawn from the United States market by the manufacturer (Organon, Inc.) on March 27, 2001.
Not commercially available

ROCURONIUM

Summary of Differences

Note: See *Rocuronium (Systemic)* single drug monograph for specific information

ROCURONIUM BROMIDE FOR INJECTION

Strength(s) usually available

U.S.—
 10 mg/mL (Rx) [*Zemuron*].

Canada—
 10 mg/mL (Rx) [*Zemuron*].

SUCCINYLCHOLINE

Summary of Differences

Pharmacology/pharmacokinetics:

Mechanism of action/effect:
 A depolarizing neuromuscular blocking agent.
 Action not antagonized by anticholinesterase agents.

Other actions/effects:
 May cause histamine release.

Biotransformation:
 In plasma; rapidly hydrolyzed by pseudocholinesterase.

Onset of action:
 Intravenous: Initial effect within 0.5–1 minute.
 Intramuscular: Initial effect within 3 minutes.

Time to peak effect:
 Intravenous: 1–2 minutes.

Duration of peak effect:
 Intravenous: 4 to 6 minutes.
 Intramuscular: 10–30 minutes.

Elimination:
 Renal; about 10% as unchanged succinylcholine.

Precautions:

Pediatrics:
 Pediatric patients are especially susceptible to succinylcholine-induced myoglobinemia, myoglobinuria, and cardiac effects. Hyperkalemic rhabdomyolysis resulting in cardiac arrest and death has occurred in apparently healthy pediatric patients after administration of succinylcholine. The adverse events occurred in pediatric patients with previously undiagnosed skeletal muscle myopathy (e.g., Duchenne's muscular dystrophy). Because it is not possible to predict when a pediatric patient may experience a serious adverse reaction, it is recommended that the use of succinylcholine be restricted to emergency situations or other situations where the immediate securing of the airway is needed (e.g., laryngospasm).

Drug interactions and/or related problems:
 May increase incidence and severity of bradycardia and hypotension when used together with opioid analgesics; also, histamine release may be additive to that induced by many opioids.
 Potentiation of effect by hydrocarbon inhalation anesthetics less than for nondepolarizing neuromuscular blocking agents.
 Effects not enhanced or prolonged by beta-adrenergic blocking agents.
 Effects not reversed by calcium salts.
 Effects prolonged by cholinesterase inhibitors or hexafluorenium.
 Use with digitalis glycosides may cause cardiac arrhythmias or other undesirable cardiac effects.
 Effects may be enhanced or prolonged in patients receiving chronic lithium therapy.
 Serious side effects with concurrent use of methotrimeprazine have been reported.
 Additive effects with physostigmine have been reported.
 Effects may be enhanced by potassium-depleting medications.

Laboratory value alterations:
 Serum potassium concentration may be increased. Carbon dioxide production and oxygen consumption may be increased transiently.

Medical considerations/contraindications:
 Succinylcholine is contraindicated in patients with skeletal muscle myopathies. Additionally, succinylcholine should not be used in patients with major burn injury, severe trauma, extensive denervation of skeletal muscle, or upper neuron injury. Use of succinylcholine in these patients may result in dangerous hyperkalemia. Cardiac arrest has occurred when succinylcholine was used in patients with these conditions.
 Caution required in patients with cardiovascular function impairment.
 Effects may be prolonged in patients with renal function impairment, but to a lesser extent than for gallamine.

Caution also required in:
 Conditions that may lead to low plasma pseudocholinesterase activity (severe anemia, dehydration, exposure to neurotoxic insecticides or other cholinesterase inhibitors, severe hepatic disease or cirrhosis, malnutrition, pregnancy, recessive hereditary trait).
 Conditions that may be adversely affected by increase in intraocular pressure (open eye injury, glaucoma, ocular surgery).
 Fractures or muscle spasm.
 Malignant hyperthermia, history of in patient or close relative.

Side/adverse effects:
 Moderate risk of side effects associated with histamine release.
 More likely than other neuromuscular blocking agents to cause bradycardia or cardiac arrhythmias.
 Increased intraocular pressure, malignant hyperthermia, rhabdomyolysis leading to myoglobinemia and myoglobinuria, postoperative muscle pains and stiffness, and excessive salivation have been reported.

Additional Dosing Information

See also *General Dosing Information*.

Succinylcholine is usually administered intravenously but may be administered intramuscularly if necessary.

When administered intramuscularly, the injection should be deep and high into the deltoid muscle.

An initial test dose of 10 mg may be administered to determine the sensitivity of the patient and recovery time.

Patients with low levels of pseudocholinesterase activity will require reduced doses, because they are unusually sensitive to the effects of succinylcholine.

If low pseudocholinesterase activity is suspected, a test dose of 5 to 10 mg may be administered.

Premedication with atropine or scopolamine is recommended to prevent excessive salivation.

To reduce the severity of muscle fasciculations, a small dose of a nondepolarizing agent may be administered prior to administration of succinylcholine.

Following administration, succinylcholine may cause transient bradycardia accompanied by hypotension, cardiac arrhythmias, and possibly a short period of sinus arrest due to vagal stimulation, especially with repeated administration and in children. These effects may be inhibited by prior administration of atropine or thiopental sodium.

Succinylcholine may cause myoglobinemia and myoglobinuria, especially in children. Administration of small doses of tubocurarine prior to succinylcholine has been shown to decrease the incidence of myoglobinuria.

Repeated doses of succinylcholine may result in tachyphylaxis.

Succinylcholine produces transient increase in the resting tension of muscles at the time neuromuscular transmission is blocked in normal people. This may be detected as an increase in jaw tension in some children anesthetized with potent inhalation agents.

Parenteral Dosage Forms

SUCCINYLCHOLINE CHLORIDE INJECTION USP

Usual adult and adolescent dose

For short surgical procedures—
 Intravenous, usually 600 mcg (0.6 mg) (range 300 mcg [0.3 mg] to 1.1 mg) per kg of body weight, initially. Repeated doses may be administered, if necessary, calculated on the basis of response to the first dose.
 Intramuscular, 3 to 4 mg per kg of body weight, not to exceed a total dose of 150 mg.

For prolonged surgical procedures—
 Intravenous, initially 600 mcg (0.6 mg) to 1.1 mg per kg of body weight; subsequent doses to be individualized for maintaining degree of relaxation required.

Note: Administration of repeated fractional doses is generally not recommended because of possible tachyphylaxis and prolonged apnea; continuous infusion is preferred for prolonged surgical procedures.

Intravenous infusion, as a 0.1 to 0.2% solution in 5% dextrose injection, sodium chloride injection, or other appropriate diluent, administered at a rate of 500 mcg (0.5 mg) to 10 mg per minute, depending on patient response and degree of relaxation required, for up to one hour.

Note: When succinylcholine is administered by infusion, careful monitoring of neuromuscular function with a peripheral nerve stimulator is recommended to avoid overdose and to detect development of a nondepolarizing block.

Electroshock therapy—

Intravenous, 10 to 30 mg administered approximately one minute before the shock, although dosage must be individualized according to the size and physical condition of the patient.

Intramuscular, up to 2.5 mg per kg of body weight, not to exceed a total dose of 150 mg.

Usual pediatric dose

Endotracheal intubation—

Intramuscular, up to 2.5 mg per kg of body weight, not to exceed a total dose of 150 mg.

Intravenous, 1 to 2 mg per kg of body weight. Repeated doses may be administered, if necessary, calculated on the basis of response to the first dose.

Note: Administration of succinylcholine by continuous intravenous infusion is considered to be unsafe in neonates and children because of the risk of malignant hyperpyrexia.

Strength(s) usually available

U.S.—

20 mg per mL (Rx) [*Anectine* (methylparaben); *Quelicin* (methylparaben; propylparaben); *Sucostrin* (methylparaben; propylparaben)].

50 mg per mL (Rx) [*Quelicin*].

Canada—

20 mg per mL (Rx) [*Quelicin* (methylparaben; propylparaben)].

100 mg per mL (Rx) [*Quelicin*].

Packaging and storage

Store between 2 and 8 °C (36 and 46 °F). Protect from freezing.

Stability

Do not use if the solution is not absolutely clear.

Only freshly prepared solutions of succinylcholine should be used.

The stability of diluted solutions may vary, depending on the specific product. See the manufacturer's prescribing information for product-specific information.

Succinylcholine is rapidly hydrolyzed, quickly loses potency, and may cause formation of a precipitate when mixed with alkaline solutions of other medications. Therefore, succinylcholine should not be mixed in the same syringe or administered simultaneously through the same needle with solutions of short-acting barbiturates such as thiopental sodium or other medications that have an alkaline pH. It should be injected separately.

SUCCINYLCHOLINE CHLORIDE STERILE USP

Note: Because succinylcholine chloride sterile is not commercially available in the U.S. or Canada, the bracketed uses and the use of the superscript 1 in this section reflect the lack of labeled (approved) indications for this medication in these countries.

Usual adult and adolescent dose

[Intravenous infusion, as a 0.1 to 0.2% solution in 5% dextrose injection][1], sodium chloride injection, or other appropriate diluent, administered at a rate of 500 mcg (0.5 mg) to 10 mg per minute, depending on patient response and degree of relaxation required, for up to one hour.

Note: When succinylcholine is administered by infusion, careful monitoring of neuromuscular function with a peripheral nerve stimulator is recommended to avoid overdose and to detect development of a nondepolarizing block.

Usual pediatric dose

Use of succinylcholine by continuous intravenous infusion is not recommended, because of the risk of malignant hyperpyrexia.

Strength(s) usually available

U.S.—

Not commercially available.

Canada—

Not commercially available.

Packaging and storage

Prior to reconstitution, store below 40 °C (104 °F), preferably between 15 and 30 °C (59 and 86 °F), unless otherwise specified by manufacturer.

Preparation of dosage form

For intravenous infusion, sterile succinylcholine chloride may be dissolved in 0.9% sodium chloride injection, 5% dextrose injection, or other appropriate infusion solution.

Stability

Only freshly prepared solutions of succinylcholine should be used.

The reconstituted solution should be used within 24 hours.

Succinylcholine is rapidly hydrolyzed, quickly loses potency, and may cause formation of a precipitate when mixed with alkaline solutions of other medications. Therefore, succinylcholine should not be mixed in the same syringe or administered simultaneously through the same needle with solutions of short-acting barbiturates such as thiopental sodium or other medications that have an alkaline pH. It should be injected separately.

[1]Not included in Canadian product labeling.

TUBOCURARINE

Summary of Differences

Indications:

Also indicated as a diagnostic aid for myasthenia gravis.

Pharmacology/pharmacokinetics:

Mechanism of action/effect:

A nondepolarizing neuromuscular blocking agent.

Action is usually antagonized by anticholinesterase agents.

Other actions/effects:

Most likely of the neuromuscular blocking agents to cause histamine release.

Protein-binding:

Moderate.

Biotransformation:

Hepatic.

Half-life:

Distribution: 4.8–6.4 minutes.

Elimination: 84–120 minutes.

Onset of action:

Intravenous: Initial effect within 1 minute.

Intramuscular: Initial effect within 15–25 minutes.

Time to peak effect:

Intravenous: 2–5 minutes.

Duration of peak effect:

20–40 minutes; increased with repeated dosing.

Time to recovery:

From time of injection: 50% of twitch response achieved in 50 minutes and 95% of twitch response achieved in 74–90 minutes.

Elimination:

Renal (about 40% as unchanged tubocurarine) and biliary (about 12% as unchanged tubocurarine).

Precautions:

Pregnancy:

May cause congenital fetal contractures if large and repeated doses are administered during the early months of pregnancy.

Also, diminished skeletal muscle activity of the newborn may occur if large and repeated doses are administered near delivery.

Drug interactions and/or related problems:

May increase incidence and severity of bradycardia and hypotension when used together with opioid analgesics; also, histamine release may be additive to that induced by many opioids.

Use with digitalis glycosides not reported to cause cardiac arrhythmias or other undesirable cardiac effects.

Effects not prolonged by cholinesterase inhibitors or hexafluorenium.

Effects may be prolonged or enhanced by calcium salts.

Serious side effects with concurrent use of methotrimeprazine have not been reported.

Additive effects with physostigmine have not been reported.

Medical considerations/contraindications:

Caution required in patients with cardiovascular function impairment.

Effects may be reduced by hepatic function impairment.

Caution required in patients with pre-existing hypotension.

Effects may be prolonged in patients with renal function impairment or shock, but to a lesser extent than for gallamine.

Side/adverse effects:

Relatively high risk of side effects associated with histamine release.

Decrease in blood pressure occurs more frequently than with other neuromuscular blocking agents.

Additional Dosing Information

See also *General Dosing Information*.

Tubocurarine is usually administered intravenously as a sustained injection over a period of 1 to 1.5 minutes. It may also be administered intramuscularly, if necessary, but is slowly and irregularly absorbed.

Rapid intravenous injection and/or large doses of tubocurarine may cause an increased release of histamine, resulting in hypotension and in decreased respiratory capacity due to bronchospasm combined with drug-induced paralysis of the respiratory muscles. Hypotension may also occur because of ganglionic blockade or as a complication of positive pressure respiration.

Parenteral Dosage Forms

TUBOCURARINE CHLORIDE INJECTION USP

Usual adult and adolescent dose

Skeletal muscle paralysis—

Adjunct to surgical anesthesia—

Intramuscular or intravenous, 6 to 9 mg initially, then 3 to 4.5 mg in three to five minutes if necessary. For prolonged procedures, supplemental doses of 3 mg may be administered.

Note: Dosage may generally be calculated on the basis of 157 mcg (0.157 mg) per kg of body weight.

Aid to controlled respiration—

Intravenous, initially 16.5 mcg (0.0165 mg) per kg of body weight, the subsequent doses being adjusted as needed.

Electroshock therapy—

Intravenous, 157 mcg (0.157 mg) per kg of body weight, administered over a period of thirty to ninety seconds.

Note: Initially, a dose of 3 mg less than the calculated total dose should be used.

Diagnostic aid (myasthenia gravis)—

Intravenous, 4 to 33 mcg (0.004 to 0.033 mg) per kg of body weight.

Note: It is recommended that the test be terminated within two to three minutes by intravenous injection of 1.5 mg of neostigmine, since the marked exaggeration of myasthenia gravis symptoms may result in prolonged respiratory paralysis.

Usual pediatric dose

Skeletal muscle paralysis

Adjunct to surgical anesthesia—

Neonates up to 4 weeks of age—Intravenous, 250 to 500 mcg (0.25 to 0.5 mg) per kg of body weight initially; then subsequent doses in increments of one-fifth or one-sixth of the initial doses, if necessary.

Infants and children—Intravenous, 500 mcg (0.5 mg) per kg of body weight.

Strength(s) usually available

U.S.—

3 mg (20 Units) per mL (Rx).

Canada—

3 mg (20 Units) per mL (Rx).

Packaging and storage

Store below 40 °C (104 °F), preferably between 15 and 30 °C (59 and 86 °F), unless otherwise specified by manufacturer. Protect from freezing.

Stability

When tubocurarine is mixed with a barbiturate solution such as methohexital sodium or thiopental sodium, a precipitate may form because of the high pH of the barbiturate solution. Each medication should be given in a separate syringe.

VECURONIUM

Summary of Differences

Pharmacology/pharmacokinetics:

Mechanism of action/effect:

A nondepolarizing neuromuscular blocking agent.

Action is usually antagonized by anticholinesterase agents.

Other actions/effects:

Less likely than most other neuromuscular blocking agents to cause histamine release.

Protein-binding:

Moderate to high.

Biotransformation:

Hepatic; only 5–10% of a dose is metabolized. One metabolite has some neuromuscular blocking activity.

Half-life:

Distribution: 4 minutes.

Elimination: 65 to 75 minutes.

Onset of action:

Initial effect within 1 minute; intubation conditions in 2.5–3 minutes.

Time to peak effect:

3–5 minutes.

Duration of peak effect:

25–30 minutes (balanced anesthesia); not changed by repeated dosing, provided that recovery from the prior dose begins before subsequent doses are given.

Time to recovery:

From time of injection (balanced anesthesia): 25% of twitch response achieved in 25–40 minutes and 95% of twitch response achieved in 45–65 minutes.

Elimination:

Biliary (25–50% of a dose) and renal (3–35% of a dose).

Precautions:

Cross-sensitivity and/or related problems:

Cross-sensitivity may occur in patients sensitive to bromides.

Pregnancy/reproduction:

Has been shown to cross the human placenta.

Pediatrics:

Patients 7 weeks to 1 year of age are more sensitive to the effects of vecuronium than are adults; recovery time may be 1½ times that of adults. The dose of vecuronium preventing skeletal muscle movement in response to a surgical skin incision in 95% of patients (ED_{95}) is about 45 to 50 mcg per kg of body weight in neonates and infants, 82 mcg per kg of body weight for children 5 to 7 years of age, and 55 mcg per kg of body weight for adolescents 13 to 16 years of age. Similar age-related differences in continuous infusion requirements have been observed such that it could be expected that the infusion rate required for a child 5 years of age may be twice that of an adult.

Drug interactions and/or related problems:

May increase incidence and severity of bradycardia and hypotension when used together with opioid analgesics.

Use with digitalis glycosides not reported to cause cardiac arrhythmias or other undesirable cardiac effects.

Effects not prolonged by cholinesterase inhibitors or hexafluorenium.

Serious side effects with concurrent use of methotrimeprazine have not been reported.

Additive effects with physostigmine have not been reported.

Medical considerations/contraindications:

Caution required in patients with cardiovascular function impairment.

Effects may be prolonged by hepatic function impairment.

Side/adverse effects:

Relatively low risk of side effects caused by histamine release.

Long-term use in the intensive care unit to facilitate mechanical ventilation has been associated with prolonged paralysis and skeletal muscle weakness.

Additional Dosing Information

See also *General Dosing Information.*

Vecuronium is to be administered by intravenous injection only.

Parenteral Dosage Forms

VECURONIUM BROMIDE FOR INJECTION

Usual adult and adolescent dose

Initial—

For intubation—

Intravenous, 80 to 100 mcg (0.08 to 0.1 mg) per kg of body weight.

For administration after the patient has been anesthetized with enflurane or isoflurane (i.e., more than 5 minutes after anesthesia has been instituted or after steady state has been achieved)—

Intravenous, 60 to 85 mcg (0.06 to 0.085 mg) per kg of body weight, or approximately 15% less than the usual initial dose.

For administration after succinylcholine-assisted endotracheal intubation—

Intravenous, 40 to 60 mcg (0.04 to 0.06 mg) per kg of body weight under inhalation anesthesia, or 50 to 60 mcg (0.05 to 0.06 mg) per kg of body weight under balanced anesthesia. The effects of succinylcholine, as determined with a peripheral nerve stimulator, should be permitted to subside prior to administration of vecuronium.

Note: If larger initial doses are required by the individual patient, initial doses ranging from 150 to 280 mcg (0.15 to 0.28 mg) per kg of body weight have been administered during surgery with halothane anesthesia without adverse effects on the cardiovascular system occurring, provided that adequate ventilation was maintained.

Supplemental—

Intravenous, 10 to 15 mcg (0.01 to 0.015 mg) per kg of body weight, administered twenty-five to forty minutes following the initial dose, then every twelve to fifteen minutes or as required by clinical conditions; or

Intravenous infusion (initiated after recovery from the effects of an initial intravenous dose of 80 to 100 mcg per kg of body weight has begun): 1 mcg (0.001 mg) per kg of body weight per minute, initially, then adjusted according to clinical requirements and patient response. Average infusion rates may range from 0.8 to 1.2 mcg (0.0008 to 0.0012 mg) per kg of body weight per minute.

After steady-state enflurane or isoflurane anesthesia has been established—

The required rate of infusion may be reduced by 25 to 60%. This reduction may not be required for patients anesthetized with halothane.

Usual pediatric dose

Neonates—

Dosage has not been established.

Patients 7 weeks to 1 year of age—

Dosage must be individualized. Pediatric patients 7 weeks to 1 year of age are more sensitive to the effects of vecuronium than adults and recovery time may be 1½ times that of adults.

Patients 1 to 10 years of age—

Dosage must be individualized. Pediatric patients 1 to 10 years of age may require a slightly higher initial dose and slightly more frequent supplemental doses than adults.

Patients 10 years of age and older—

Initial—

See *Usual adult and adolescent dose.*

Supplemental—

Intravenous—See *Usual adult and adolescent dose.*

Intravenous infusion—Dosage has not been established.

Strength(s) usually available

U.S.—

10 mg (Rx) [*Norcuron* (lyophylized; citric acid anhydrous 20.75 mg; mannitol 97 mg; sodium phosphate dibasic anhydrous 16.25 mg)].

20 mg (Rx) [*Norcuron* (citric acid anhydrous 41.5 mg; mannitol 194 mg; sodium phosphate dibasic anhydrous 32.5 mg)].

Canada—

10 mg (Rx) [*Norcuron*].

20 mg (Rx).

Packaging and storage

Prior to reconstitution, store between 15 and 30 °C (59 and 86 °F), protected from light, unless otherwise specified by manufacturer.

Preparation of dosage form

Reconstitute using bacteriostatic water for injection (provided by the manufacturer in some packages of vecuronium bromide for injection) or another compatible intravenous solution, such as 5% dextrose injection, 0.9% sodium chloride injection, 5% dextrose in sodium chloride injection, or lactated Ringer's injection. For direct intravenous injection, the medication is generally reconstituted using 5 or 10 mL of diluent. For intravenous infusion, the medication is diluted to a convenient concentration, such as 10 or 20 mg per 100 mL of infusion solution.

Stability

After reconstitution with bacteriostatic water for injection, the solution may be stored at room temperature or in a refrigerator; it should be used within 5 days. After reconstitution with other compatible intravenous solutions, the solution should be stored in a refrigerator and used within 24 hours. Reconstituted solutions are intended to be used only once; unused portions should be discarded.

Incompatibilities

Alkaline solutions such as barbiturate injections should not be mixed in the same syringe, or administered simultaneously through the same intravenous needle, with vecuronium.

Revised: 11/08/2001

Table 1. Pharmacology/Pharmacokinetics

Drug	Protein Binding	Biotransformation	Half-life Distribution/ Elimination (min)	Elimination Primary (% excreted unchanged)/Secondary (% excreted unchanged)
Depolarizing				
Succinylcholine	—	In plasma, by pseudocholinesterase*	—	Renal (about 10)
Nondepolarizing				
Atracurium	High	In plasma†	2–3.4/20	Renal and biliary (<10)
Gallamine	—	Essentially none	16/150	Renal (almost 100)
Pancuronium	Very low	Hepatic (in small quantities)	10–13/89–161	Renal (about 80)/10% biliary (up to 10)
Tubocurarine	Moderate§	Hepatic	4.8–6.4/84–120	Renal (about 40)/biliary (12)
Vecuronium	Moderate to high#	Hepatic**	4/65–75††	25–50% Biliary within 42 hr/3–35% renal within 24 hr‡‡

*Hydrolyzed rapidly to succinylmonocholine (a weak nondepolarizing neuromuscular blocking agent that is one-twentieth as potent as succinylcholine), then more slowly to succinic acid and choline.

†Metabolized by ester hydrolysis catalyzed by nonspecific esterases and by Hofmann elimination, a nonenzymatic chemical process that occurs at plasma pH; is independent of hepatic or renal function or plasma pseudocholinesterase activity.

§With plasma concentrations of 5 to 50 mcg/mL.

#With doses of 40 to 100 mcg per kg of body weight.

**Only 5 to 10% of a dose is metabolized. However, one metabolite, 3-deacetyl vecuronium, has been shown in animal studies to have neuromuscular blocking activity that is 50% as potent as that of vecuronium.

††May be decreased to 35 to 40 minutes in late pregnancy and prolonged in patients with cirrhosis or cholestasis.

‡‡Up to 25% of a dose may be excreted in bile, and up to 10% of a dose may be excreted in urine, as 3-deacetyl vecuronium.

Table 2. Pharmacology/Pharmacokinetics*

Drug	Initial Dose (mg/kg)	Onset of Initial Action (Time to Intubation Conditions) (min)	Time to Peak Effect (min)	Duration of Peak Effect (min)/Effect of Repeated Dosing	Time to Recovery in min (% of twitch response attained)
Depolarizing					
Succinylcholine					
Intramuscular	3–4	Up to 3	—	10–30†	—
Intravenous	0.3–1	0.5–1	1–2	4–10†	
Nondepolarizing					
Atracurium					
Intravenous	0.4–0.5	Within 2 (2–2.5)	3–5 (range 1.7–10)	20–35 under balanced anesthesia/no change‡	From time of injection—balanced anesthesia‡: 35–45 (25); 60–70 (95) From beginning of recovery§—balanced anesthesia: 30 (95) inhalation anesthesia: 40 (95)
Gallamine					
Intravenous	1	1–2	3–5	15–30/increased#	—
Pancuronium					
Intravenous	0.04 0.06 0.08	Within 0.75 (2–3) 0.5	4.5— Within 3	—/increased# 35–45/increased#—/increased#	From time of injection#: <60 (90)——
Tubocurarine					
Intramuscular	0.1–0.3	15–25		—	—
Intravenous	0.1–0.3	Within 1	2–5	20–40/ increased#	From time of injection: 50 (50); 74–90 (95)
Vecuronium					
Intravenous	0.08–0.1	1 (2.5–3)	3–5	25–30 under balanced anesthesia/ no change‡	From time of injection—balanced anesthesia‡: 25–40 (25); 45–65 (95)

*Onset of initial action and of effective skeletal muscle relaxation (peak effect) are dose-dependent and decrease with increasing doses. Duration of effective skeletal muscle relaxation and time to recovery are also dose-dependent and increase with increasing doses. Other factors, especially administration of hydrocarbon inhalation anesthetics or other potentiating medications, also influence the duration of effective skeletal muscle relaxation and time to recovery.

†Duration of action and time to recovery with succinylcholine may be increased when plasma pseudocholinesterase activity is decreased.

‡The duration of peak effect and time to recovery with atracurium or vecuronium are not affected by repeated administration of recommended maintenance doses, provided that recovery from the effects of the previous dose begins prior to administration of a subsequent dose.

§Once recovery begins, the rate of recovery is independent of atracurium dosage; however, it is affected by the type of anesthesia administered.

#Following a single dose, the action of the medication is terminated by redistribution into inactive sites. However, following multiple doses, the inactive sites of uptake become saturated, and factors of degradation and/or elimination then directly influence the duration of action and time to recovery.

Table 3. Drug Interactions and/or Related Problems

Note: Combinations containing any of the following medications, depending on the amount present, may also interact with this medication.	Depolarizing: *I*=Succinylcholine	Nondepolarizing: *II*=Atracurium, *III*=Gallamine		*IV*=Pancuronium, *V*=Tubocurarine, *VI*=Vecuronium		
	I	*II*	*III*	*IV*	*V*	*VI*
» Aminoglycosides, possibly including oral neomycin (if significant quantities are absorbed in patients with renal function impairment), or » Anesthetics, parenteral-local (large doses leading to significant plasma concentrations) or » Capreomycin or » Citrate-anticoagulated blood (massive transfusions) or » Clindamycin or Lidocaine (intravenous doses > 5 mg per kg) or » Lincomycin or » Polymyxins or Procaine (intravenous) or Trimethaphan (large doses) (neuromuscular blocking activity of these medications may be additive to that of neuromuscular blocking agents)*	✓	✓	✓	✓	✓	✓

Table 3. Drug Interactions and/or Related Problems *(continued)*

Note: Combinations containing any of the following medications, depending on the amount present, may also interact with this medication.	Depolarizing	Nondepolarizing				
	I=Succinylcholine	*II*=Atracurium *III*=Gallamine		*IV*=Pancuronium *V*=Tubocurarine *VI*=Vecuronium		
	I	*II*	*III*	*IV*	*V*	*VI*
Analgesics, opioid (narcotic), especially those commonly used as adjuncts to anesthesia (central respiratory depressant effects of opioid analgesics may be additive to the respiratory depressant effects of neuromuscular blocking agents)*	✓	✓	✓	✓	✓	✓
(high doses of sufentanil may reduce the initial dosage requirements for a nondepolarizing neuromuscular blocking agent; it is recommended that a peripheral nerve stimulator be used to determine dosage)		✓	✓	✓	✓	✓
(concurrent use of a neuromuscular blocking agent prevents or reverses muscle rigidity induced by sufficiently high doses of most opioid analgesics, especially alfentanil, fentanyl, or sufentanil)	✓	✓	✓	✓	✓	✓
(gallamine and pancuronium, because of their vagolytic activity, may decrease the risk of opioid analgesic-induced bradycardia or hypotension [especially in patients receiving chronic therapy with beta-adrenergic blocking agents and/or vasodilators for treatment of coronary artery disease], but may also increase the risk of tachycardia or hypertension in some patients)			✓	✓		
(a nonvagolytic neuromuscular blocking agent will not decrease the risk of opioid analgesic-induced bradycardia or hypotension; in some patients [especially patients with compromised cardiac function and/or those receiving a beta-adrenergic blocking agent preoperatively], the incidence and/or severity of these effects may be increased)	✓	✓			✓	✓
(histamine release induced by tubocurarine or, to a lesser extent, atracurium or succinylcholine, may be additive to that induced by many opioid analgesics [except alfentanil, fentanyl, and sufentanil, which do not cause histamine release], leading to increased risk of hypotension; administration of histamine [both H_1 and H_2] receptor–blocking agents may prevent or reduce this effect)	✓	✓			✓	
Anesthetics, hydrocarbon inhalation, such as: Chloroform Cyclopropane Enflurane Ether Halothane Isoflurane Methoxyflurane Trichloroethylene (concurrent use with succinylcholine may increase the potential for malignant hyperthermia; also, repeated concurrent use may enhance the initial transient bradycardia produced by succinylcholine)	✓					
(neuromuscular blocking activity of inhalation anesthetics, especially enflurane or isoflurane, may be additive to that of the nondepolarizing neuromuscular blocking agents; dosage of vecuronium should be reduced by 15%, and dosage of other neuromuscular blocking agents should be reduced by ⅓ to ½ of the usual dose or as determined with a peripheral nerve stimulator)*		✓	✓	✓	✓	✓
(halogenated hydrocarbon anesthetics may also potentiate succinylcholine-induced neuromuscular blockade, but to a lesser extent than they potentiate the effects of nondepolarizing neuromuscular blocking agents)*	✓					
Antimyasthenics or Edrophonium (these agents may antagonize the effects of nondepolarizing neuromuscular blocking agents; parenteral neostigmine or pyridostigmine are indicated to reverse neuromuscular blockade following surgery; although the usefulness of edrophonium for this purpose has been considered to be limited because of its brief duration of action, recent studies indicate that edrophonium is equivalent to neostigmine in reversing the effects of tubocurarine)		✓	✓	✓	✓	✓
(these agents may prolong phase I block when used concurrently with succinylcholine*; however, if succinylcholine has been used for a prolonged period of time and the depolarization block has changed to a nondepolarization block, edrophonium, neostigmine, or pyridostigmine may reverse the nondepolarization block)	✓					
(neuromuscular blocking agents may antagonize the effects of antimyasthenics on skeletal muscle; temporary dosage adjustment may be required to control symptoms of myasthenia gravis following surgery)	✓	✓	✓	✓	✓	✓

Table 3. Drug Interactions and/or Related Problems *(continued)*

Note: Combinations containing any of the following medications, depending on the amount present, may also interact with this medication.	Depolarizing *I*=Succinylcholine	Nondepolarizing *II*=Atracurium *III*=Gallamine		*IV*=Pancuronium *V*=Tubocurarine *VI*=Vecuronium		
	I	*II*	*III*	*IV*	*V*	*VI*
Beta-adrenergic blocking agents (concurrent use may enhance or prolong the blockade of the nondepolarizing neuromuscular blocking agents)*			✓	✓	✓	
Calcium salts (calcium salts usually reverse the effects of nondepolarizing neuromuscular blocking agents)		✓	✓	✓	✓	✓
(concurrent use has been reported to enhance or prolong the neuromuscular blocking action of tubocurarine)*					✓	
» Cholinesterase inhibitors, especially echothiophate, demecarium, and isoflurophate, or Cyclophosphamide or » Insecticides, neurotoxic, exposure to, possibly including large quantities of topical malathion, or Phenelzine or Thiotepa (may decrease plasma concentrations or activity of pseudocholinesterase, the enzyme that metabolizes succinylcholine, thereby enhancing the neuromuscular blockade of succinylcholine; effects of echothiophate, demecarium, or isoflurophate may persist for weeks or months after the cholinesterase inhibitor has been discontinued)*	✓					
» Digitalis glycosides (cardiac effects may be increased when digitalis glycosides are used concurrently with succinylcholine and, to a lesser extent, with pancuronium, possibly resulting in cardiac arrhythmias)	✓			✓		
Doxapram (the residual effects of neuromuscular blocking agents may be masked temporarily by doxapram when it is used post-anesthesia)	✓	✓	✓	✓	✓	✓
Hexafluorenium (concurrent use may prolong the action of succinylcholine and may minimize or prevent the muscle fasciculations and pain that may occur when succinylcholine is used alone; however, concurrent use may increase the potential for development of a dual block)*	✓					
Lithium (chronic therapy) (concurrent use may enhance or prolong the neuromuscular blockade of atracurium, succinylcholine, or pancuronium)*	✓	✓		✓		
Magnesium salts, parenteral, or » Procainamide or » Quinidine (concurrent use may enhance the blockade of the neuromuscular blocking agents)*	✓	✓	✓	✓	✓	✓
Methotrimeprazine (concurrent use with succinylcholine may cause tachycardia, a fall in blood pressure, CNS stimulation and delirium, and an aggravation of extrapyramidal effects)	✓					
Neuromuscular blocking agents, depolarizing (prior administration may enhance the blockade of nondepolarizing neuromuscular blocking agents; if a depolarizing agent is used before a nondepolarizing agent, administration of the nondepolarizing agent should be delayed until the effects of the depolarizing agent have decreased)		✓	✓	✓	✓	✓
Neuromuscular blocking agents, nondepolarizing (concurrent use may enhance the blockade of depolarizing neuromuscular blocking agents if they have been administered over a prolonged period of time and the depolarized block has gradually changed to a nondepolarized block)	✓					
(concurrent use of pancuronium and another nondepolarizing neuromuscular blocking agent may substantially reduce the required dose of both medications)		✓		✓	✓	✓
» Physostigmine (concurrent use with succinylcholine is not recommended since high doses of physostigmine may cause muscle fasciculation and ultimately, a depolarization block, which may be additive to that produced by succinylcholine)	✓					

Table 3. Drug Interactions and/or Related Problems *(continued)*

Note: Combinations containing any of the following medications, depending on the amount present, may also interact with this medication.	Depolarizing	Nondepolarizing				
	I=Succinylcholine	*II*=Atracurium *III*=Gallamine		*IV*=Pancuronium *V*=Tubocurarine *VI*=Vecuronium		
	I	*II*	*III*	*IV*	*V*	*VI*
Potassium-depleting medications, such as: Amphotericin B Bumetanide Carbonic anhydrase inhibitors Corticosteroids, glucocorticoid, especially with significant mineralocorticoid activity Corticosteroids, mineralocorticoid Corticotropin, chronic therapeutic use Ethacrynic acid Furosemide Indapamide Thiazide diuretics (hypokalemia induced by these medications may enhance the blockade of nondepolarizing neuromuscular blocking agents; serum potassium determinations and correction of serum potassium concentration may be necessary prior to administration of nondepolarizing neuromuscular blocking agents)*		✓	✓	✓	✓	✓
(hydrocortisone and prednisone have also been reported to decrease the efficacy of pancuronium by an unknown mechanism; increased dosage of pancuronium or use of an alternate neuromuscular blocking agent may be necessary)				✓		

*Increased or prolonged respiratory depression or paralysis (apnea) may occur but is of minor clinical significance while the patient is being mechanically ventilated. However, caution and careful monitoring of the patient are recommended during and following concurrent or sequential use, especially if there is a possibility of incomplete reversal of neuromuscular blockade postoperatively.

Table 4. Medical considerations/Contraindications

Note: A blank space usually signifies lack of information; it is not necessarily an indication that a given medical problem is of no concern. However, the pharmacologic similarity of the nondepolarizing neuromuscular blocking agents may suggest that if caution is required in particular medical problems for one agent, then it may be required for the others as well.

The medical considerations/contraindications included have been selected on the basis of their potential clinical significance (reasons given in parentheses where appropriate)—not necessarily inclusive (» = major clinical significance).	Depolarizing	Nondepolarizing				
	I=Succinylcholine	*II*=Atracurium *III*=Gallamine		*IV*=Pancuronium *V*=Tubocurarine *VI*=Vecuronium		
	I	*II*	*III*	*IV*	*V*	*VI*
Allergic reaction to the neuromuscular blocker considered for use, history of	✓	✓	✓	✓	✓	✓
» Burns, severe, or Digitalis toxicity or in patients recently digitalized or » Neuromuscular disease, degenerative or dystrophic, or Paraplegia or Purpura fulminans or » Spinal cord injury or » Trauma, severe (succinylcholine is contraindicated in patients with skeletal muscle myopathies, major burn injury, severe trauma, extensive denervation of skeletal muscle, or upper neuron injury; use of succinylcholine in these patients may result in dangerous hyperkalemia; serious cardiac arrhythmias including cardiac arrest have occurred when succinylcholine was used in patients with these conditions as a result of increased serum potassium concentrations)	✓					
Carcinoma, bronchogenic (action of neuromuscular blocking agent may be enhanced)	✓	✓	✓	✓	✓	✓
Cardiac conditions in which tachycardia would be undesirable (gallamine and pancuronium may cause tachycardia)			✓	✓		
Cardiovascular function impairment	✓				✓	✓
Conditions in which histamine release would be hazardous (these neuromuscular blocking agents may cause histamine release)	✓	✓		✓	✓	✓

Table 4. Medical considerations/Contraindications *(continued)*

Note: A blank space usually signifies lack of information; it is not necessarily an indication that a given medical problem is of no concern. However, the pharmacologic similarity of the nondepolarizing neuromuscular blocking agents may suggest that if caution is required in particular medical problems for one agent, then it may be required for the others as well.

The medical considerations/contraindications included have been selected on the basis of their potential clinical significance (reasons given in parentheses where appropriate)—not necessarily inclusive (» = major clinical significance).	Depolarizing	Nondepolarizing				
	I=Succinylcholine	*II*=Atracurium *III*=Gallamine		*IV*=Pancuronium *V*=Tubocurarine *VI*=Vecuronium		
	I	*II*	*III*	*IV*	*V*	*VI*
Conditions in which low levels of plasma pseudocholinesterase activity may exist, such as: Anemia, severe Dehydration Exposure to neurotoxic insecticides or other cholinesterase inhibitors Hepatic disease, severe, or cirrhosis Malnutrition Pregnancy Recessive hereditary trait (prolonged respiratory depression or apnea may occur)	✓					
Dehydration or Electrolyte or acid-base imbalance (action of neuromuscular blocking agent may be altered)	✓	✓	✓	✓	✓	✓
Eye injury, open, or Glaucoma or Ocular surgery (succinylcholine may increase intraocular pressure)	✓					
Fractures or muscle spasm (initial muscle fasciculations may cause additional trauma)	✓					
Hepatic function impairment (patients may have decreased levels of pseudocholinesterase activity, possibly resulting in prolonged respiratory depression or apnea) (effect of panuronium or tubocurarine may be reduced) (effect of vecuronium may be prolonged)	✓			✓	✓	✓
Hyperkalemia, preexisting (may be exacerbated by succinylcholine-induced increases in serum potassium concentration)	✓					
Hypertension (gallamine may increase blood pressure)			✓			
Hyperthermia (intensity and duration of action of depolarizing agents may be decreased and that of nondepolarizing agents may be increased)	✓		✓	✓	✓	
Hypotension (rapid IV administration and/or large doses of atracurium or tubocurarine may cause hypotension)		✓			✓	
Hypothermia (intensity and/or duration of action of succinylcholine and atracurium may be increased and that of gallamine, pancuronium, and tubocurarine may be decreased)	✓	✓	✓	✓	✓	
» Malignant hyperthermia, history of in patient or close relative, or suspected predisposition to (may be induced by succinylcholine)	✓					
Myasthenia gravis, except when tubocurarine is used as a diagnostic agent	✓	✓	✓	✓	✓	✓
Pulmonary function impairment or Respiratory depression (risk of additive respiratory depression)	✓	✓	✓	✓	✓	✓
Renal function impairment (eliminated by kidneys; prolonged neuromuscular blockade may occur)	✓			✓	✓	
» Renal function impairment (eliminated by kidneys primarily as unchanged drug; prolonged neuromuscular blockade may occur)			✓			
» Shock (action of gallamine may be prolonged)			✓			
Shock (action of tubocurarine may be prolonged)					✓	

Table 5. Side/Adverse Effects*

Note: A blank space usually signifies lack of information; it is not necessarily an indication that a given medical problem is of no concern. However, the pharmacologic similarity of the nondepolarizing neuromuscular blocking agents may suggest that if caution is required in particular medical problems for one agent, then it may be required for the others as well.

The following side/adverse effects have been selected on the basis of their potential clinical significance (possible signs and symptoms in parentheses where appropriate)—not necessarily inclusive:	Depolarizing	Nondepolarizing				
	I=Succinylcholine	*II*=Atracurium *III*=Gallamine		*IV*=Pancuronium *V*=Tubocurarine *VI*=Vecuronium		
	I	*II*	*III*	*IV*	*V*	*VI*
Medical attention needed						
Anaphylactic, anaphylactoid, or other hypersensitivity reaction	R	R	R	R	R	R
Bradycardia	L†	R‡	U	U	R	R‡
Bronchospasm	R§	R§	U	R§	R§	R§
Cardiac arrhythmias	L†	U	U	U	R	U
Circulatory depression or collapse—may occur in overdose	R§	R§	U	R§	R§	R§
Decreased blood pressure—may reach hypotensive levels; with usual doses of tubocurarine, or larger-than-recommended doses of atracurium, may be caused by ganglionic blockade; may also occur as a complication of high-dose positive pressure respiration	R†§	L§	U	R§	M§	R§
Edema	R§	R§	U	R§	R§	R§
Erythema	R§	R§	U	R§	R§	R§
Flushing of skin	R§	M§	U	R§	R§	R§
Hives	U	R	U	U	U	U
Increased blood pressure—may reach hypertensive levels; with gallamine or pancuronium, may be caused by vagolytic activity	R†	L	M	L	U	U
Increased intraocular pressure—possibly caused by contraction of extraocular muscle; occurs immediately after injection and during the fasciculation phase	M	U	U	U	U	U
Laryngospasm	U	R	U	U	U	U
Malignant hyperthermic crisis	R	U	U	U	U	U
Myoglobinemia and myoglobinuria caused by rhabdomyolysis—especially in children; may lead to myoglobinuric acute renal failure	R	U	U	U	U	U
Tachycardia—with gallamine, occurs after doses of 500 mcg (0.5 mg) per kg of body weight and reaches a maximum within 3 minutes, then declines gradually to the control level; with gallamine and pancuronium, may be due to vagolytic activity	L†§	L§	M	L§	R§	R§
Medical attention needed only if continuing or bothersome						
Itching of skin	R§	R§	U	L§	R§	R§
Muscle pain and stiffness, postoperative—possibly caused by muscle fasciculations that occur immediately following injection; incidence may vary from 10% in patients maintained on bed rest for 1 day to 70% in ambulatory patients; symptoms usually appear 12 to 24 hours following administration and last for several hours to a few days	M	—	—	—	—	—
Salivation, excessive	L	U	U	L	U	U
Skin rash	R§	R§	U	L§	R§	R§

*Differences in frequency of occurrence may reflect either lack of clinical-use data or actual pharmacologic distinctions among agents (although their pharmacologic similarity suggests that side effects occurring with one may occur with the others). M=more frequent; L=less frequent; R=rare; U=unknown.

†Succinylcholine may cause transient bradycardia accompanied by hypotension, cardiac arrhythmias, and possibly a short period of sinus arrest due to increased vagal stimulation, especially with repeated administration and in children. Following these effects, tachycardia and hypertension may occur due to asphyxial pressor response and mild sympathetic ganglion stimulation.

‡Atracurium and vecuronium have little or no direct effect on heart rate; bradycardia may occur because these medications do not counteract the bradycardia caused by other medications (e.g., anesthetics, opioid analgesics) or vagal stimulation.

§May be caused by histamine release, especially following rapid intravenous injection and/or large doses, or an overdose. The risk of clinically significant histamine release is highest with tubocurarine; moderate with atracurium, or succinylcholine; relatively low with pancuronium or vecuronium; and least with gallamine.

NEVIRAPINE Systemic

VA CLASSIFICATION (Primary): AM840

Commonly used brand name(s): *Viramune*.

Another commonly used name is NVP

Note: For a listing of dosage forms and brand names by country availability, see *Dosage Forms* section(s).

Category

Antiviral (Systemic).

Indications

Note: Bracketed information in the *Indications* section refers to uses that are not included in U.S. product labeling.

General Considerations

There is a strong association between the minimum plasma human immunodeficiency virus (HIV) RNA achieved in the first months of antiretroviral treatment and subsequent clinical response. CD4 cell counts are independently predictive of response. Therefore, antiretroviral treatment should be guided by monitoring the laboratory parameters of plasma HIV RNA and CD4 cell count, as well as the clinical condition of the patient.

Drug resistance testing is necessary to identify which mutations are selected by nevirapine-containing regimens. Drug resistance testing should be considered for all patients presenting with symptomatic acute HIV infection or other evidence documenting infection within several months of presentation, particularly if the source patient was taking antiretroviral medications (see *Patient monitoring*).

Accepted

Human immunodeficiency virus type 1 (HIV-1) infection (treatment)—Nevirapine is indicated, in combination with other antiretroviral agents, for the treatment of HIV-1 infection. Drug-resistant HIV emerges rapidly and uniformly when nevirapine is administered as monotherapy. Therefore, nevirapine should always be administered in combination with at least two other antiretroviral agents when it is used for the treatment of HIV-1 infection.

Based on serious and life-threatening hepatotoxicity observed in controlled and uncontrolled studies, nevirapine should not be initiated in adult females with CD4+ cell counts greater than 250 cells/mm³ or in adult males with CD4+ cell counts greater than 400 cells/mm³ unless the benefit outweighs the risk.

The 15-day lead-in period with nevirapine 200 mg daily dosing has been demonstrated to reduce the frequency of rash.

[Mother-to-child transmission of HIV-1 infection (prophylaxis)][1]—Nevirapine is indicated for the prevention of mother-to-child transmission of HIV-1 infection.

Note: The administration of single dose nevirapine to the mother intrapartum and to the infant postpartum effectively reduces vertical transmission of HIV-1 and is less costly and easier to administer than other antiretroviral regimens. However, mutations conferring resistance to nevirapine could be observed after a single dose even with a low level of viral replication. Therefore, in the U.S. the use of nevirapine for the prevention of mother-to-child transmission of HIV-1 infection should be restricted to previously untreated women with HIV infection who present in labor; however, in developing countries nevirapine may be considered as one of several strategies in the prevention of mother-to-child transmission of HIV-1 infection.

[1]Not included in Canadian product labeling.

Pharmacology/Pharmacokinetics

Note: Pharmacokinetic parameters in pregnant women receiving intrapartum nevirapine were similar though somewhat more variable than in nonpregnant adults, possibly due to incomplete drug absorption associated with impaired gastrointestinal function during labor.

Physicochemical characteristics

Chemical Group—Nevirapine is structurally a member of the dipyridodiazepinone chemical class of compounds.

Molecular weight—266.3.

Mechanism of action/Effect

Nevirapine is a nonnucleoside reverse transcriptase inhibitor (NNRTI) of human immunodeficiency virus-1 (HIV-1). Nevirapine binds directly to reverse transcriptase (RT) and blocks RNA-dependent and DNA-dependent polymerase activities by causing disruption of the enzyme's catalytic site. The activity of nevirapine does not compete with template or nucleoside triphosphates. HIV-2 RT and eukaryotic DNA polymerases are not inhibited by nevirapine.

The relationship between *in vitro* susceptibility of HIV-1 to nevirapine and the inhibition of HIV-1 replication in humans has not been established. The *in vitro* antiviral activity of nevirapine was measured in peripheral blood mononuclear cells, monocyte derived macrophages, lymphoblastoid cell lines. The 50% inhibitory concentration (IC_{50}) ranged from 10-100 nM against laboratory and clinical isolates HIV-1. In cell cultures, nevirapine demonstrated additive to synergistic activity against HIV in drug combination regimens with zidovudine, didanosine, stavudine, lamivudine, saquinavir, and indinavir.

Absorption

Nevirapine is readily absorbed (> 90%) after oral administration in healthy volunteers and in adults with HIV-1 infection. Absolute bioavailability in 12 healthy adults following single-dose administration was 93% for a 50-mg tablet and 91% for a 50-mg oral suspension. When nevirapine was administered to 24 healthy adults with either a high-fat breakfast or an antacid, the extent of absorption was comparable to that seen under fasting conditions

Distribution

Widely distributed. Nevirapine is highly lipophilic and essentially is nonionized at physiologic pH. Nevirapine readily crosses the placenta and is distributed into breast milk. Nevirapine concentrations in the cerebrospinal fluid (CSF) were 45% of the concentrations in plasma, which is a ratio that is approximately equal to the fraction not bound to plasma protein.

Vol_D—1.21 ± 0.09 L per kg.

Protein binding

Moderate; nevirapine is about 60% bound to plasma proteins in the plasma concentration range of 1-10 mcg/mL.

Biotransformation

In vivo studies in humans and *in vitro* studies with human liver microsomes have shown that nevirapine is extensively biotransformed via cytochrome P450 oxidative metabolism to several hydroxylated metabolites. *In vitro* studies with human liver microsomes suggest that oxidative metabolism of nevirapine is mediated primarily by cytochrome P450 isozymes from the CYP3A family, although other isozymes may have a secondary role.

Half-life

Approximately 45 hours after a single dose, and 25 to 30 hours following multiple dosing with 200 to 400 mg per day.

Time to peak concentration

4 hours after a single 200-mg dose.

Peak serum concentration

2 micrograms per mL after a single 200-mg dose.

Elimination

Renal; approximately 91% of a radiolabeled dose was recovered in the urine, with > 80% of that made up of glucuronide conjugates of hydroxylated metabolites. Less than 5% of the recovered radiolabeled dose was made up of the parent drug.

Fecal; approximately 10% of a radiolabeled dose was recovered in the feces.

Nevirapine has been shown to be an inducer of hepatic cytochrome P450 metabolic enzymes. The pharmacokinetics of autoinduction are characterized by by an approximately 1.5 to 2 fold increase in the apparent oral clearance of nevirapine as treatment continues from a single dose to two to four weeks of dosing with 200 to 400 mg/day. Autoinduction also results in a corresponding decrease in the terminal phase half life of nevirapine in plasma from approximately 45 hours (single dose) to approximately 25 to 30 hours following multiple dosing with 200 to 400 mg/day.

Precautions to Consider

Carcinogenicity

Long-term carcinogenicity studies in mice and rats were carried out with nevirapine. Mice were dosed with 0, 50, 375 or 750 mg/kg/day for two years. Hepatocellular adenomas and carcinomas were increased at all doses in males and at the two high doses in females. In studies in which rats were administered nevirapine at doses of 0, 3.5, 17.5 or 35 mg/kg/day for two years, an increase in hepatocellular adenomas was seen in males at all doses and in females at the high dose. The systemic exposure (based on AUCs) at all doses in the two animal studies were lower than that measured in humans at the 200 mg bid dose. The mechanism of the carcinogenic potential is unknown. However, in genetic toxicology assays, nevirapine showed no evidence of mutagenic or clastogenic activity in a battery of *in vitro* and *in vivo* studies. These included microbial assays for gene mutation (Ames: Salmonella strains and E. *coli*), mammalian cell gene mutation assay (CHO/HGPRT), cytogenetic assays using a Chinese hamster ovary cell line and a mouse bone marrow micronucleus assay following oral administration. Given the lack of genotoxic activity of nevirapine, the relevance to humans of hepatocellular neoplasms in nevirapine treated mice and rats is not known.

Pregnancy/Reproduction

Fertility—Evidence of impaired fertility was seen in female rats at doses providing systemic exposure (based on the area under the plasma concentration-time curve [AUC]) approximately equivalent to that attained with the recommended clinical dose of nevirapine.

In reproductive toxicology studies, evidence of impaired fertility was seen in female rats at doses providing systemic exposure, based on AUC, approximately equivalent to that provided with the recommended clinical dose of nevirapine.

Pregnancy—Nevirapine crosses the placenta and achieves neonatal blood concentrations comparable to that in the mother (cord-to-maternal blood ratio approximately 0.9).

There are no adequate and well-controlled studies in pregnant women. Nevirapine should be used during pregnancy only if the potential benefit justifies the potential risk to the fetus. Severe hepatic events, including fatalities, have been reported in pregnant women receiving chronic nevirapine therapy as part of combination treatment of HIV infection. It is unclear if pregnancy augments the already increased risk observed in non-pregnant women.

Teratogenic effects of nevirapine have not been observed in reproductive studies with rats and rabbits. In rats, however, a significant decrease in fetal weight occurred at doses producing systemic concentrations approximately 50% higher than human therapeutic exposure.

Note: It is strongly recommended that physicians who are treating HIV-infected pregnant women and their newborns report cases of prenatal exposure to antiretroviral drugs to the Antiretroviral Pregnancy Registry. The Antiretroviral Pregnancy Registry is an epidemiological project to collect observational, nonexperimental data on antiretroviral exposure during pregnancy for the purpose of assessing the potential teratogenicity of these drugs. Registry data will be used to supplement animal toxicology studies and assist physicians in weighing the potential risks and benefits of treatment for individual patients. Physicians should register patients by calling (800)-258-4263.

FDA Pregnancy Category C.

Breast-feeding

The Centers for Disease Control and Prevention recommend that HIV-infected mothers not breast-feed their infants to avoid risking postnatal transmission of HIV. Nevirapine is distributed into breast milk. The median concentration in four breast milk samples obtained from three women during the first week after delivery was approximately 76% (range 54 to 104%) of serum levels. To prevent postnatal transmission of HIV infection and the potential for serious adverse reactions in nursing infants, mothers in developed countries should not breast feed; however, this approach cannot be recommended in developing countries since the problem is more complicated.

Pediatrics

In children, nevirapine elimination accelerates during the first years of life, reaching a maximum at around 2 years of age, followed by a gradual decline during the rest of childhood.

The Pediatric AIDS Clinical Trials Group Protocol 250 Team (PACTG 250) evaluated the safety and pharmacokinetics of nevirapine, administered to infants as a single 2 mg/kg dose at age 48 to 72 hours. No adverse effects were seen. Nevirapine elimination was prolonged in the infants, and this regimen maintained serum concentrations associated with antiviral activity in the infants for the first week of life (see also *Pregnancy*).

Granulocytopenia was more commonly observed in children receiving both zidovudine and nevirapine.

Geriatrics

Nevirapine pharmacokinetics do not appear to change with age in HIV-1 infected adults (range 18 to 68 years); however, nevirapine has not been extensively evaluated in patients older than 55 years of age.

Clinical studies of nevirapine did not include sufficient numbers of subjects aged 65 and older to determine whether elderly subjects respond differently from younger subjects. In general, dose selection for an elderly patient should be cautious, reflecting the greater frequency of decreased hepatic, renal or cardiac function, and of concomitant disease or other drug therapy.

Pharmacogenetics

Women appear to be at higher risk than men of developing rash with nevirapine.

Drug interactions and/or related problems

The following drug interactions and/or related problems have been selected on the basis of their potential clinical significance (possible mechanism in parentheses where appropriate)—not necessarily inclusive (» = major clinical significance):

Note: Nevirapine is both metabolized by and induces the activity of cytochrome P450 isoenzymes (CYP3A and CYP2B6), with maximal induction occurring within 2 to 4 weeks of initiating multiple-dose therapy. The induction of CYP3A by nevirapine may result in lower plasma concentrations of concurrently administered drugs that are extensively metabolized by CYP3A.

Note: Combinations containing any of the following medications, depending on the amount present, may also interact with this medication.

Amprenavir or
Indinavir or
» Lopinavir/ritonavir or
Nelfinavir or
Saquinavir
(caution is required when nevirapine is concurrently administered with a protease inhibitor, as the plasma concentrations of the protease inhibitors may be reduced to subtherapeutic concentrations due to increased hepatic metabolism by nevirapine)
(nevirapine decreases the AUC and C_{max} of indinavir and saquinavir; in contrast, protease inhibitors do not appear to affect the pharmacokinetics of nevirapine)
(the appropriate doses for indinavir, nelfinavir, or saquinavir used in combination with nevirapine have not been established)
(a dose increase of lopinavir/ritonavir is recommended in combination with nevirapine)

Antiarrhythmics, such as
Amiodarone or
Disopyramide or
Lidocaine
(should be used with caution due to potential drug interaction; plasma concentrations may be decreased by co-administration with nevirapine; dose adjustment of co-administered drug may be needed due to possible decrease in clinical effect)

Anticonvulsants, such as
Carbamazepine or
Clonazepam or
Ethosuximide
(should be used with caution due to potential drug interaction; plasma concentrations may be decreased by co-administration with nevirapine; dose adjustment of co-administered drug may be needed due to possible decrease in clinical effect)

Antifungals, such as
Itraconazole
(should be used with caution due to potential drug interaction; plasma concentrations may be decreased by co-administration with nevirapine; dose adjustment of co-administered drug may be needed due to possible decrease in clinical effect)

» Antithrombotics, such as
» Warfarin
(potential for increases in coagulation; frequent monitoring of anticoagulation levels is recommended)

Calcium channel blockers, such as
Diltiazem or
Nifedipine or
Verapamil
(should be used with caution due to potential drug interaction; plasma concentrations may be decreased by co-administration with nevirapine; dose adjustment of co-administered drug may be needed due to possible decrease in clinical effect)

Cancer chemotherapy, such as
Cyclophosphamide
(should be used with caution due to potential drug interaction; plasma concentrations may be decreased by co-administration with nevirapine; dose adjustment of co-administered drug may be needed due to possible decrease in clinical effect)

» Clarithromycin
(clarithromycin exposure was significantly decreased by nevirapine; however, 14-OH metabolite concentrations were increased; because clarithromycin active metabolite has reduced activity against *Mycobacterium avium-intracellulare complex*, overall activity against this pathogen may be altered; alternatives to clarithromycin, such as azithromycin, should be considered)

» Contraceptives, estrogen-containing, oral or
Ethinyl estradiol or
Norethindrone
(The AUC values of oral contraceptives are reduced in the presence of nevirapine; nevirapine decreased plasma levels of ethinyl estradiol and norethindrone therefore, oral contraceptives and other hormonal methods of birth control should not be used as the primary means of contraception when nevirapine is prescribed to women of childbearing potential; an alternate method of contraception is recommended)

Efavirenz
(AUC, C_{max} and C_{min} are decreased; appropriate doses for this combination are not established)

Ergot alkaloids, such as
Ergotamine
(should be used with caution due to potential drug interaction; plasma concentrations may be decreased by co-administration with nevirapine; dose adjustment of co-administered drug may be needed due to possible decrease in clinical effect)

» Fluconazole
» Ketoconazole
(concurrent use of fluconazole should be done with caution because of the risk of increased exposure to nevirapine; patients

should be monitored closely for nevirapine-associated adverse events)

(concurrent use of ketoconazole with nevirapine results in significantly reduced plasma concentrations of ketoconazole; concurrent use is not recommended)

Immunosuppressants, such as
Cyclosporin
Tacrolimus
Sirolimus

(should be used with caution due to potential drug interaction; plasma concentrations may be decreased by co-administration with nevirapine; dose adjustment of co-administered drug may be needed due to possible decrease in clinical effect)

» Methadone

(nevirapine may decrease plasma concentrations of methadone by increasing its hepatic metabolism; narcotic withdrawal syndrome has been reported in patients treated with nevirapine and methadone concurrently; methadone-maintained patients beginning nevirapine therapy should be monitored for evidence of withdrawal and methadone dose should be adjusted accordingly)

Motility agents, such as
Cisapride

(should be used with caution due to potential drug interaction; plasma concentrations may be decreased by co-administration with nevirapine; dose adjustment of co-administered drug may be needed due to possible decrease in clinical effect)

Opiate agonists, such as
Fentanyl

(should be used with caution due to potential drug interaction; plasma concentrations may be decreased by co-administration with nevirapine; dose adjustment of co-administered drug may be needed due to possible decrease in clinical effect)

» Prednisone

(concurrent use with nevirapine results in increased incidence and severity of rash in the first 6 weeks of nevirapine therapy; concurrent use is not recommended; use of prednisone to prevent nevirapine-associated rash is not recommended)

» Rifabutin

(rifabutin accelerates the metabolism of nonnucleoside reverse transcriptase inhibitors (NNRTIs), such as nevirapine through induction of hepatic P450 cytochrome isoenzymes, resulting in subtherapeutic levels of nevirapine; in addition nevirapine retards the metabolism of rifabutin, resulting in increased serum levels of rifabutin; a dosage adjustment may be required when rifabutin is administered with nevirapine)

» Rifampin

(rifampin accelerates the metabolism of NNRTIs, such as nevirapine through induction of hepatic P450 cytochrome isoenzymes, resulting in subtherapeutic levels of nevirapine; in addition nevirapine retards the metabolism of rifampin, resulting in increased serum levels of rifampin and the likelihood of increased toxicity; data are insufficient to assess whether dose adjustments are necessary when rifampin is coadministered with nevirapine; concurrent use of nevirapine with rifampin is not recommended; consider rifabutin instead)

» St. John's wort

(concurrent use of St. John's wort [*hypericum perforatum*] or St. John's wort containing products with nevirapine is expected to substantially decrease nevirapine concentrations and may result in suboptimal levels of nevirapine and lead to loss of virologic response and possible resistance to nevirapine; concurrent use is not recommended)

Zidovudine

(AUC and C_{max} of zidovudine are decreased; should be used with caution)

Laboratory value alterations

The following have been selected on the basis of their potential clinical significance (possible effect in parentheses where appropriate)—not necessarily inclusive (» = major clinical significance).

With physiology/laboratory test values
» Alanine aminotransferase (ALT [SGPT]), serum and
» Alkaline phosphatase, serum and
Amylase and
» Aspartate aminotransferase (AST [SGOT]), serum and
» Bilirubin, serum and
» Gamma glutamyl transferase (GGT)

(values may be increased)

Hemoglobin and
Platelets and
Neutrophils and

(values may be decreased)

Mean corpuscular volume (MCV)

(values may be increased)

Medical considerations/Contraindications

The medical considerations/contraindications included have been selected on the basis of their potential clinical significance (reasons given in parentheses where appropriate)—not necessarily inclusive (» = major clinical significance).

Except under special circumstances, this medication should not be used when the following medical problem exists:

» Hepatic function impairment, severe

(nevirapine is hepatotoxic and extensively metabolized by the liver; it is associated with a significant incidence of hepatotoxicity, usually occurring in the initial month of therapy; because increased nevirapine levels and nevirapine accumulation may be observed in patients with serious liver disease, nevirapine should not be administered to patients with severe hepatic impairment.)

» Hypersensitivity to nevirapine or any of the compounds in the tablet or the oral suspension

Risk-benefit should be considered when the following medical problems exist:

Hepatic function impairment, moderate

(it is not clear whether a dose adjustment is needed for patients with mild to moderate hepatic impairment, because multiple dose pharmacokinetic data are not available for this population; patients with moderate hepatic impairment and ascites may be at risk of accumulating nevirapine in the systemic circulation; caution should be exercised when nevirapine is administered to patients with moderate hepatic impairment; increased ALT or AST at the start of antiretroviral therapy are associated with a greater risk of adverse hepatic events)

Hepatitis B or C

(co-infection with hepatitis B or C at the start of antiretroviral therapy are associated with a greater risk of adverse hepatic events)

Renal function impairment

(nevirapine metabolites are extensively eliminated by the kidney; although no studies have been done, nevirapine should be used with caution in patients with renal function impairment)

Patient monitoring

The following may be especially important in patient monitoring (other tests may be warranted in some patients, depending on condition; » = major clinical significance):

Note: **The first 18 weeks of therapy with nevirapine are a critical period during which intensive monitoring of patients is required to detect potentially life-threatening hepatic events and skin reactions. The optimal frequency of monitoring during this time period has not been established. Some experts recommend clinical and laboratory monitoring more often than once per month, and in particular, would include monitoring of liver function tests at baseline, prior to dose escalation and at two weeks post-dose escalation. After the initial 18-week period, frequent clinical and laboratory monitoring should continue throughout nevirapine treatment. In addition, the 14-day lead-in period with nevirapine 200 mg daily dosing has been demonstrated to reduce the frequency of rash.**

Note: Severe, life-threatening, and in some cases fatal hepatotoxicity, including fulminant and cholestatic hepatitis, hepatic necrosis and hepatic failure, has been reported in patients treated with nevirapine; in some cases, patients presented with non-specific prodromal signs or symptoms of hepatitis and progressed to hepatic failure; these events are often associated with rash.

Women, and patients with higher CD4 counts, are at increased risk of these hepatic events; women with CD4 counts >250 cells/mm^3, including pregnant women receiving chronic treatment for HIV infection, are at considerably higher risk of these events; patients with signs or symptoms of hepatitis must discontinue nevirapine and seek medical evaluation immediately; patients with increased AST or ALT levels at the start of antiretroviral therapy are associated with a greater risk of hepatic adverse events (see *Side/Adverse Effects*)

» Alanine aminotransferase (ALT [SGPT]), serum and
» Alkaline phosphatase, serum and
» Aspartate aminotransferase (AST [SGOT]), serum and
» Bilirubin, serum

(intensive clinical and laboratory monitoring, including liver function tests, is essential at baseline and during the first 18

weeks of therapy; monitoring should continue at frequent intervals thereafter)

(liver function tests should be performed **immediately** if a patient experiences signs or symptoms suggestive of hepatitis and/or hypersensitivity reaction; liver function tests should also be obtained for all patients who develop a rash in the first 18 weeks of treatment)

(physicians and patients should be vigilant for the appearance of signs or symptoms of hepatitis, such as fatigue, malaise, anorexia, nausea, jaundice, bilirubinuria, acholic stools, liver tenderness or hepatomegaly; the diagnosis of hepatotoxicity should be considered in this setting, even if liver function tests are initially normal or alternative diagnoses are possible)

» Drug-resistance tests

(drug resistance testing [genotype or phenotype] is necessary to identify which mutations are selected by nevirapine-containing regimens; drug resistance testing [genotype or phenotype] should be considered for all patients presenting with symptomatic acute HIV infection or other evidence documenting infection within several months of presentation, particularly if the source patient was taking antiretroviral medications.)

(drug-resistant HIV may be transmitted heterosexually either before or during pregnancy; a study of nevirapine prophylaxis showed that the K103M mutation could be selected following a single dose of nevirapine; therefore, it is recommended that resistance testing be performed on maternal HIV, particularly when there has been prior antiretroviral exposure or when prevalence of resistant HIV in the community is high.)

» Human immunodeficiency virus (HIV) RNA, plasma and
» CD4 lymphocyte count

(there is a strong association between the minimum HIV RNA achieved in the first months of antiretroviral treatment and subsequent clinical response; CD4 cell counts are independently predictive of response; therefore, antiretroviral treatment should be guided by monitoring the laboratory parameters of plasma HIV RNA and CD4 cell count; treatment should not be initiated in adult females with CD4+ cell counts greater than 250 cells/mm^3 or in adult males with CD4+ cell counts greater than 400 cells/mm^3)

Note: Severe, life-threatening skin reactions, including fatal cases, have occurred in patients treated with nevirapine. These have included cases of Stevens-Johnson syndrome, toxic epidermal necrolysis, and hypersensitivity reactions characterized by rash, constitutional findings, and organ dysfunction (see *Side/Adverse Effects*).

» Skin reactions

(monitor for skin reactions or rash intensively during the first 12 to 18 weeks of treatment and frequently thereafter; treatment should be discontinued if a reaction is discovered)

(These reactions can include, but are not limited to, severe rash or rash accompanied by fever, general malaise, fatigue, muscle or joint aches, blisters, oral lesions, conjunctivitis, facial edema, and/or hepatitis, eosinophilia, granulocytopenia, lymphadenopathy, and renal dysfunction. Patients developing signs or symptoms of severe skin reactions or hypersensitivity reactions must permanently discontinue nevirapine and seek medical evaluation immediately. Nevirapine should not be restarted following severe skin rash or hypersensitivity reaction. Some of the risk factors for developing serious cutaneous reactions include failure to follow the initial dosing of 200 mg daily during the 14-day lead-in period and delay in stopping the nevirapine treatment after the onset of the initial symptoms.)

Side/Adverse Effects

Note: **Severe, life-threatening, and fatal cases of hepatotoxicity including fulminant and cholestatic hepatitis, hepatic necrosis and hepatic failure, and skin reactions have been reported among human immunodeficiency virus (HIV)-infected patients treated with nevirapine. Hepatotoxicity, which was all attributable to nevirapine has been reported at the 8th Conference on Retroviruses and Opportunistic Infections.**

In clinical trials, the risk of hepatic events regardless of severity was greatest in the first 6 weeks of therapy. The risk continued to be greater in the nevirapine groups compared to controls through 18 weeks of treatment. However, hepatic events may occur at any time during treatment. In some cases, patients presented with nonspecific, prodromal signs or symptoms of fatigue, malaise, anorexia, nausea, jaundice, liver tenderness or hepatomegaly, with or without initially abnormal serum transaminase levels. Some of these events have progressed to hepatic failure with transaminase elevation, with or without hyperbilirubinemia, prolonged partial thromboplastin time, or eosinophilia. Rash and fever accompanied some of these hepatic events. Patients with signs or symptoms of hepatitis must be advised to discontinue nevirapine and immediately seek medical evaluation, which should include liver function tests. The patients at greatest risk of hepatic events, including potentially fatal events, are women with high CD4 counts. Increased AST or ALT levels and/or co-infection with hepatitis B or C at the start of antiretroviral therapy are associated with a greater risk of hepatic adverse events. In general, women have a three fold higher risk than men for symptomatic, often rash-associated, hepatic events (5.8% versus 2.2%), and patients with higher CD4 counts at initiation of nevirapine therapy are at higher risk for symptomatic hepatic events with nevirapine. In a retrospective review, women with CD4 counts >250 cells/mm^3 had a 12 fold higher risk of symptomatic hepatic adverse events compared to women with CD4 counts <250 cells/mm^3 (11.0% versus 0.9%). An increased risk was observed in men with CD4 counts >400 cells/mm^3 (6.3% versus 2.3% for men with CD4 counts <400 cells/mm^3).

Severe, life-threatening skin reactions, including fatal cases, have occurred in patients treated with nevirapine. These have included cases of Stevens-Johnson syndrome, toxic epidermal necrolysis, and hypersensitivity reactions characterized by rash, constitutional findings, and organ dysfunction. These reactions can include, but are not limited to, severe rash or rash accompanied by fever, general malaise, fatigue, muscle or joint aches, blisters, oral lesions, conjunctivitis, facial edema, and/or hepatitis, eosinophilia, granulocytopenia, lymphadenopathy, and renal dysfunction. Patients developing signs or symptoms of severe skin reactions or hypersensitivity reactions must permanently discontinue nevirapine and seek medical evaluation immediately. Nevirapine should not be restarted following severe skin rash or hypersensitivity reaction. Some of the risk factors for developing serious cutaneous reactions include failure to follow the initial dosing of 200 mg daily during the 14-day lead-in period and delay in stopping the nevirapine treatment after the onset of the initial symptoms. If patients present with a suspected nevirapine-associated rash, liver function tests should be performed. Patients with rash-associated AST or ALT elevations should be permanently discontinued from nevirapine.

It is essential that patients be monitored intensively during the first 18 weeks of therapy with nevirapine to detect potentially life-threatening hepatotoxicity or skin reactions. The greatest risk of severe rash or hepatic events (often associated with rash) occurs in the first 6 weeks of therapy. However, the risk of any hepatic event, with or without rash, continues past this period and monitoring should continue at frequent intervals. In some cases, hepatic injury has progressed despite discontinuation of treatment. Nevirapine should not be restarted following severe hepatic, skin or hypersensitivity reactions. In addition, the 14-day lead-in period with nevirapine 200 mg daily dosing must be strictly followed.

The most common clinical toxicity of nevirapine is rash. Severe or life-threatening rash occurred in approximately 2% of nevirapine-treated patients, most frequently within the first 6 weeks of therapy. Rashes are usually mild to moderate, maculopapular erythematous cutaneous eruptions, with or without pruritus, located on the trunk, face and extremities. Women tend to be at higher risk for development of nevirapine associated rash.

Patients with hepatotoxicity may have gastrointestinal symptoms or rash; however, most are asymptomatic.

Serious hepatotoxicity (including liver failure requiring transplantation in one instance) has been also reported in a small number of individuals receiving nevirapine as part of a combination regimen for post-exposure prophylaxis (an unapproved use) of nosocomial or sexual HIV exposure.

In September 2000, two cases of life-threatening hepatotoxicity were reported in health-care workers taking nevirapine for post-exposure prophylaxis after occupational HIV exposure. In the first case, a female health-care worker required liver transplantation after developing fulminant hepatitis and end-stage hepatic failure while taking nevirapine, zidovudine, and lamivudine as post-exposure prophylaxis following a needlestick injury. In the second case, a male physician was hospitalized with life-threatening fulminant hepatitis while taking nevirapine, zidovudine, and lamivudine as post-exposure prophylaxis following a mucous membrane exposure.

The Food and Drug Administration (FDA) received reports of 22 cases of serious adverse reactions related to nevirapine taken for post-exposure prophylaxis from 03/97 to 09/00, including the two case reports of fulminant hepatitis. These reactions included hepatotoxicity, skin reaction, and rhabdomyolysis. Many of these patients apparently did not take the phase-in dose of 200 mg two times a day for 2 weeks, but took the full 400 mg a day from the start.

To characterize nevirapine-associated post-exposure prophylaxis toxicity, the Centers for Disease Control and Prevention (CDC) and the FDA reviewed MedWatch reports of serious adverse reactions in persons taking nevirapine for post-exposure prophylaxis.

The U.S. Public Health Service first recommended post-exposure prophylaxis after certain occupational exposures to HIV in 1996. These recommendations, updated in 1998, are being revised to include other antiretroviral agents that have been approved by FDA for use in HIV-infected persons. Nevirapine is not recommended for basic or expanded post-exposure prophylaxis regimens. However, data on the safe and effective use of single-dose nevirapine for the prevention of perinatal HIV transmission and a theoretical advantage of more rapid activity have prompted clinicians to include nevirapine in post-exposure prophylaxis regimens following HIV exposures.

In the HIV post-exposure prophylaxis registry, which collected data on occupational HIV post-exposure prophylaxis use from October 1995 through March 1999, six cases of serious adverse reactions related to post-exposure prophylaxis were reported among 492 registered participants; a severe skin reaction occurred in one of 11 health-care workers taking a regimen that included nevirapine.

Because most occupational HIV exposures do not result in transmission of HIV, health care providers considering prescribing post-exposure prophylaxis for exposed persons must balance the risk for HIV transmission represented by the exposure and the exposure source against the potential toxicity of the specific agent(s) used. In many circumstances, the risks associated with nevirapine as part of a post-exposure prophylaxis regimen outweigh the anticipated benefits.

However, no serious toxicity has been reported in women or infants receiving two-dose nevirapine (the HIVNET 012 regimen) for prevention of perinatal transmission of HIV. Combination antiretroviral regimens containing nevirapine may be used in HIV-infected persons after weighing the risks and benefits and monitoring adverse reactions.

The redistribution or accumulation of body fat, including central obesity, dorsocervical fat enlargement (buffalo hump), peripheral wasting, breast enlargement, and "cushingoid appearance" have been reported in patients receiving antiretroviral therapy. A causal relationship has not been confirmed.

The following side/adverse effects have been selected on the basis of their potential clinical significance (possible signs and symptoms in parentheses where appropriate)—not necessarily inclusive:

Those indicating need for medical attention

Note: Clinical practice has shown that the most serious adverse reactions with nevirapine are clinical hepatitis/hepatic failure, Stevens-Johnson Syndrome, toxic epidermal necrolysis, and hypersensitivity reactions. Clinical hypersensitivity reactions may be isolated or associated with signs of hypersensitivity which may include severe rash, or rash accompanied by fever, general malaise, fatigue, muscle or joint aches, blisters, oral lesions, conjunctivitis, facial edema, and/or hepatitis, eosinophilia, granulocytopenia, lymphadenopathy, and renal dysfunction.

Incidence more frequent

Granulocytopenia (chills, fever, or sore throat)—occurs more frequently in children; ***hepatitis and hepatic failure*** (dark urine; general tiredness and weakness; light-colored stools; nausea and vomiting; upper right abdominal pain; yellow eyes and skin)—including cholestatic hepatitis, infectious hepatitis, hepatic failure, and/or LFT abnormalities with clinical symptoms; ***skin rash*** (blistering, peeling, loosening of skin; chills; cough; diarrhea; fever; itching; joint or muscle pain; red irritated eyes; red skin lesions, often with a purple center; sore throat; sores, ulcers, or white spots in mouth or on lips; unusual tiredness or weakness)—including erythema multiforme, exfoliative dermatitis, necrosis requiring surgery, Stevens-Johnson syndrome, and/or toxic epidermal necrolysis

Note: Severe, life-threatening hypersensitivity skin reactions, including *Stevens-Johnson syndrome*, have been reported in HIV-infected individuals receiving nevirapine for treatment, usually during the first 6 weeks of therapy

Note: Nevirapine has the most common treatment limiting side effect of *rash*. Severe or life-threatening rash has been observed in 2% of patients taking nevirapine in clinical trials, women tend to be at higher risk for rash development. In a multicenter, retrospective cohort study of all patients who received nevirapine over a 5-year period, severe rash was noted in 9 of 95 women and 3 of 263 men. Women were more likely to discontinue nevirapine therapy because of rash. After adjusting for age and baseline CD4 cell count in multivariate analysis, women had a 7-fold increase in risk for severe rash and were 3.5 times more likely to discontinue nevirapine therapy The rashes typically occur within the first 6 weeks of therapy, and are usually mild to moderate (grade 1 rash 14.8% incidence), maculopapular erythematous cutaneous eruptions, with or without pruritus, located on the trunk, face, and extremities.

Incidence less frequent

Fever; hepatitis prodromal symptoms (loss of appetite; nausea; unusual tiredness or weakness; vomiting); ***hepatotoxicity*** (dark urine; yellow skin or eyes)

Note: *Fever*, in the absence of any apparent cause, is a significant predictor for the development of rash in patients receiving nevirapine. This has not been reported with use of the HIVNET 012 two-dose nevirapine regimen.

Incidence rare

Arthralgia (joint pain); ***myalgia*** (muscle pain); ***paresthesia*** (tingling, burning, or prickly sensations); ***peripheral neuropathy*** (pain, numbness, or tingling of hands, arms, legs, or feet); ***somnolence*** (sleepiness or unusual drowsiness); ***ulcerative stomatitis*** (sores or ulcers in the mouth)

Incidence not determined—Observed during clinical practice; estimates of frequency cannot be determined

Allergic reactions (fainting or loss of consciousness; fast or irregular breathing; swelling of eyes or eyelids; trouble in breathing; tightness in chest and/or wheezing; skin rash; itching)—including anaphylaxis, angioedema, bullous eruptions, ulcerative stomatitis and/or urticaria; ***anemia*** (pale skin; troubled breathing with exertion; unusual bleeding or bruising; unusual tiredness or weakness); ***eosinophilia*** (black, tarry stools; chest pain; chills; cough; fever; painful or difficult urination; shortness of breath; sore throat; sores, ulcers, or white spots on lips or in mouth; swollen glands; unusual bleeding); ***fulminant and cholestatic hepatitis; hepatic necrosis; hypersensitivity reactions with rash***—may also include one or more of the following:lymphadenopathy, renal dysfunction, hepatitis, eosinophilia, granulocytopenia; also can be associated with constitutional findings such as fever, blistering, oral lesions, conjunctivitis, facial edema, muscle or joint aches, general malaise, fatigue or significant hepatic abnormalities; ***jaundice*** (chills; clay-colored stools; dark urine; dizziness; fever; headache; itching; loss of appetite; nausea; abdominal or stomach pain; area rash; unpleasant breath odor; unusual tiredness or weakness; vomiting of blood; yellow eyes or skin); ***neutropenia*** (chills; cough; fever; sore throat; sores, ulcers, or white spots on lips or in mouth; swollen glands)

Those indicating need for medical attention only if they continue or are bothersome

Incidence more frequent

Gastrointestinal effects (abdominal or stomach pain; diarrhea; nausea); ***fatigue*** (unusual tiredness or weakness); ***headache***

Incidence not determined—Observed during clinical practice; estimates of frequency cannot be determined

Drug withdrawal; redistribution/accumulation of body fat; vomiting

Overdose

For more information on the management of overdose or unintentional ingestion, **contact a poison control center** (see *Poison Control Center Listing*).

Note: Cases of nevirapine overdosage ranging from 800 to 1800 mg per day for up to 15 days have been reported.

Clinical effects of overdose

The following effects have been selected on the basis of their potential clinical significance (possible signs and symptoms in parentheses where appropriate)—not necessarily inclusive:

Edema (bloating or swelling of face, hands, lower legs, and/or feet); ***erythema nodosum*** (fever; pain in ankles or knees; painful, red lumps under the skin, mostly on the legs); ***fatigue*** (unusual tiredness or weakness); ***fever; headache; insomnia*** (trouble sleeping); ***nausea; pulmonary infiltrates*** (cough; chest pain; unusual tiredness or weakness); ***rash; vertigo*** (dizziness; sense of constant movement of self or surroundings); ***vomiting; weight decrease***

Treatment of overdose

There is no known antidote for nevirapine overdose; however, all side effects may subside following discontinuation of nevirapine treatment.

Patient Consultation

As an aid to patient consultation, refer to *Advice for the Patient, Nevirapine (Systemic)*.

In providing consultation, consider emphasizing the following selected information (» = major clinical significance)

Before using this medication

» Conditions affecting use, especially:
  Hypersensitivity to nevirapine
  Pregnancy—Nevirapine crosses the placenta; nevirapine has been shown to decrease perinatal transmission of HIV
  Breast-feeding—Nevirapine is distributed into breast milk; breast-feeding is not recommended in HIV-infected mothers because of the risk of passing HIV to the infant and the potential for serious adverse reactions in nursing infants
  Use in children—Granulocytopenia occurs more frequently in children
  Pharmacogenetics—Greater incidence of rash in women
  Other medications, especially estrogen or progestin-containing contraceptives, clarithromycin, fluconazole, ketoconazole, lopinavir/ritonavir, methadone, prednisone, rifabutin, rifampin, St. John's wort or warfarin
  Other medical problems, especially severe hepatic function impairment

Proper use of this medication

Nevirapine may be taken with or without food
Importance of reading patient package insert with each new prescription and each refill
» Importance of not taking more medication than prescribed; importance of not discontinuing nevirapine without checking with physician
» Compliance with full course of therapy
» Importance of not missing doses and taking doses at evenly spaced times
Not sharing medication with others
» Proper dosing especially with oral suspension, rinsing the dose cup and administering the rinse to the patient.
Missed dose: Taking as soon as possible; not taking if almost time for next dose; not doubling doses
» Proper storage

Precautions while using this medication

» Because nevirapine interacts with so many medications, not taking any other medications (prescription or nonprescription) without first consulting your physician
» Regular visits to physician for blood tests
» Using an additional method of contraception if taking estrogen or progestin containing contraceptives concurrently
» Patient monitoring especially CD4 lymphocyte count, drug resistance, liver function, plasma HIV RNA levels and skin reactions.
» The first 18 weeks of therapy are a critical period during which intensive monitoring of patients is required to detect potentially life-threatening hepatic events and skin reactions
» Being aware that nevirapine therapy does not reduce the risk of transmitting HIV to others through sexual contact or contamination through blood.

Side/adverse effects

Signs of potential side effects, especially, arthralgia, fever, granulocytopenia, hepatitis and hepatic failure, myalgia, paresthesia, peripheral neuropathy, skin rash including erythema multiforme, exfoliative dermatitis, necrosis, Stevens-Johnson syndrome and toxic epidermal necrolysis, somnolence and ulcerative stomatitis.
(Signs of potential side effects observed during clinical practice, especially allergic reactions, anemia, eosinophilia, fulminant and cholestatic hepatitis, hepatic necrosis, hypersensitivity reactions including hepatitis, eosinophilia, granulocytopenia, lymphadenopathy and renal dysfunction, jaundice and neutropenia; also can be associated with constitutional findings such as fever, blistering, oral lesions, conjunctivitis, facial edema, muscle or joint aches, general malaise, fatigue or significant hepatic abnormalities)

General Dosing Information

The first 18 weeks of therapy with nevirapine are a critical period during which intensive monitoring of patients is required to detect potentially life threatening hepatic events and skin reactions.

Drug-resistant HIV emerges rapidly and uniformly when nevirapine is administered as monotherapy. Mutations conferring resistance to nevirapine could be observed after a single dose even with a low level of viral replication. Therefore, nevirapine should always be administered in combination with at least one other antiretroviral agent. Resistance to nevirapine usually confers resistance to other nonnucleoside reverse transcriptase inhibitors (NNRTIs) [efavirenz and delavirdine]. Thus this is "class resistance". However, nevirapine is indicated as a monotherapy for the prevention of mother-to-child transmission of HIV-1 infection.

Although significantly more hepatotoxicity was observed among nevirapine users, due to greater time on nevirapine, only CD4 cell increase was independently associated with severe hepatotoxicity. Since the incidence of severe hepatotoxicity was not increased in patients with chronic hepatitis C virus (HCV) or hepatitis B virus (HBV) infection, nevirapine therapy should not be withheld from patients with chronic viral hepatitis.

Patients at greatest risk of hepatic events, including potentially fatal events, are women with CD4 counts greater than 250 cells/mm^3. In general, women have a three-fold higher risk than men for symptomatic, often rash-associated, hepatic events (5.8% versus 2.2%), and patients with higher CD4 counts at initiation of nevirapine therapy are at higher risk for symptomatic hepatic events with nevirapine. In a retrospective review, women with CD4 counts >250 cells/mm^3 had a 12–fold higher risk of symptomatic hepatic adverse events compared to women with CD4 counts <250 cells/mm^3 (11.0% versus 0.9%). An increased risk was observed in men with CD4 counts >400 cells/mm^3 (6.3% versus 2.3% for men with CD4 counts <400 cells/mm^3).

Nevirapine therapy should be interrupted in patients who develop moderate or severe liver function test abnormalities. Therapy may be restarted with a 14-day period of 200 mg per day before increasing the dose to 400 mg per day when liver function tests return to baseline. Nevirapine should be discontinued permanently if moderate or severe liver function test abnormalities recur. If clinical hepatitis occurs, nevirapine should be permanently discontinued and not restarted after recovery. In some cases, hepatic injury progresses despite discontinuation of treatment.

Nevirapine may be administered with or without food.

Nevirapine should be discontinued if patients experience severe rash or rash accompanied by constitutional findings. Patients experiencing rash during the 14–day lead in period of 200 mg per day (4 mg per kg per day in pediatric patients) should not have their nevirapine dose increased until the rash has resolved.

If clinical hepatitis occurs, nevirapine should be permanently discontinued and not restarted until after recovery.

Patients who interrupt nevirapine therapy for more than 7 days should restart dosing with 200 mg once a day for the first 14 days, then increase the dose to 200 mg twice a day.

Administer the entire measured dose of suspension using an oral dosing syringe (recommended especially for volumes of 5 mL or less) or a dosing cup. If a dosing cup is used, rinse thoroughly with water and administer the rinse to the patient.

The duration of clinical benefit from antiretroviral therapy may be limited. Patients receiving nevirapine or any other antiretroviral therapy may continue to develop opportunistic infections and other complications of HIV infection, and therefore should remain under close clinical observation by physicians experienced in the treatment of patients with associated HIV diseases.

When administering nevirapine as part of an antiretroviral regimen, the complete product information for each therapeutic component should be consulted before initiation of treatment

Oral Dosage Forms

NEVIRAPINE HEMIHYDRATE ORAL SUSPENSION

Note: Dose and strength are expressed in terms of nevirapine base.

Usual adult dose

Human immunodeficiency virus (HIV) infection (treatment)—
  Oral, 200 mg (base) once a day for the first fourteen days, (this lead-in period should be used because it has been found to lessen the frequency of rash) then 200 mg two times a day, in combination with other antiretroviral agents.
  Dialysis patients: An additional 200 mg dose of nevirapine should be given following each dialysis treatment.For patients with renal impairment not on dialysis (CrCl ≥ 20 mL/min) dose not require dosing adjustment.
  Note: Nevirapine should not be initiated in adult females with CD4+ cell counts greater than 250 cells/mm^3 or in adult males with

CD4+ cell counts greater than 400 cells/mm^3 unless the benefit outweighs the risk.

A dose increase to 533/133 mg of lopinavir and ritinavir twice daily with food is recommended for patients receiving concomitant therapy with nevirapine.

[Mother-to-child transmission of HIV-1 infection (prophylaxis)][1]—

Oral, a single 200 mg dose at the onset of labor to an HIV-1-infected woman.

Note: Nevirapine elimination is prolonged in pregnant women during labor and in newborns. A regimen of a single 200-mg oral dose administered to the mother during labor and a single 2 mg/kg dose administered to the newborn at 48 to 72 hours after birth maintains serum nevirapine concentrations above 100 mcg/L (10 times the *in vitro* 50% inhibitory concentration against wild-type HIV-1) throughout the first week of life. This limited regimen has been shown to be extremely well tolerated and to reduce mother-to-child transmission by nearly 50% in mothers and infants receiving no other antiretrovirals. There are few data describing the safety and pharmacokinetics of nevirapine during long term use in pregnancy.

Usual adult dosing limits
400 mg (base) per day.

Usual pediatric dose
Human immunodeficiency virus (HIV) infection (treatment)—

Infants 2 months and children up to 8 years of age: Oral, 4 mg (base) per kg of body weight once a day for fourteen days, then 7 mg per kg of body weight two times a day, in combination with other antiretroviral agents.

Children 8 years of age and older: Oral, 4 mg (base) per kg of body weight once a day for fourteen days, then 4 mg per kg of body weight two times a day, in combination with other antiretroviral agents.

Note: In children, nevirapine elimination accelerates during the first years of life, reaching a maximum at around 2 years of age, followed by a gradual decline during the rest of childhood. Alternatively, children may receive 150 mg/m^2 across all ages, once daily for the first 2 weeks of therapy followed by the same dose twice daily.

[Mother-to-child transmission of HIV-1 infection (prophylaxis)][1]—

Oral, a single 2 mg/kg dose within 72 hours of birth.

Usual pediatric dosing limits
400 mg (base) per day.

Strength(s) usually available
U.S.—

50 mg (base) per 5 mL (in 240-mL bottles) (Rx) [*Viramune* (methylparaben; propylparaben; sorbitol; sucrose)].

Canada—

Not commercially available.

Packaging and storage
Store at 25 °C (77 °F); excursions permitted to 15 - 30 °C (59 - 86 °F)

Auxiliary labeling
Please read patients information enclosed.• You should take this medicine exactly as prescribed. Do not skip or discontinue unless directed.
- Ask you doctor or pharmacist before using non prescription drugs.
- Does not require refrigeration.
- Shake gently prior to administration
- Keep out of reach of children

NEVIRAPINE TABLETS

Usual adult dose
See *Nevirapine Hemihydrate Oral Suspension.*

Usual adult dosing limits
See *Nevirapine Hemihydrate Oral Suspension.*

Usual pediatric dose
See *Nevirapine Hemihydrate Oral Suspension.*

Usual pediatric dosing limits
See *Nevirapine Hemihydrate Oral Suspension.*

Strength(s) usually available
U.S.—

200 mg (Rx) [*Viramune* (lactose monohydrate)].

Canada—

200 mg (Rx) [*Viramune* (lactosemonohydrate)].

Packaging and storage
Store at 25 °C (77 °F); excursions permitted to 15 - 30 °C (59 - 86 °F)

Auxiliary labeling
Please read patients information enclosed.• You should take this medicine exactly as prescribed. Do not skip or discontinue unless directed.
- Ask you doctor or pharmacist before using non prescription drugs.
- Keep out of reach of children

[1]Not included in Canadian product labeling.

Revised: 02/14/2005

NIACIN Systemic

This monograph includes information on the following: 1) Niacin; 2) Niacinamide.

INN:

Niacin—Nicotinic acid
Niacinamide—Nicotinamide

VA CLASSIFICATION (Primary/Secondary): VT130/CV359

Commonly used brand name(s): *Niacor[1]; Niaspan[1]; Nicolar[1]; Nicotinex Elixir[1]; Novo-Niacin[1]; Slo-Niacin[1]*.

Other commonly used names are: Nicotinamide [Niacinamide] Nicotinic acid [Niacin] Vitamin B_3 [Niacin; Niacinamide]

Note: For a listing of dosage forms and brand names by country availability, see *Dosage Forms* section(s).

Category

Note: Niacin and niacinamide (vitamin B_3) are water-soluble vitamins.
Nutritional supplement (vitamin)—Niacin; Niacinamide.
Antihyperlipidemic—Niacin

Indications

Accepted

Niacin deficiency (prophylaxis and treatment)—Niacin and niacinamide are indicated for prevention and treatment of vitamin B_3 deficiency states. Vitamin B_3 deficiency may occur as a result of inadequate nutrition or intestinal malabsorption but does not occur in healthy individuals receiving an adequate balanced diet. Simple nutritional deficiency of individual B vitamins is rare since dietary inadequacy usually results in multiple deficiencies. For prophylaxis of niacin deficiency, dietary improvement, rather than supplementation, is advisable. For treatment of niacin deficiency, supplementation is preferred.

Deficiency of niacin may lead to pellagra.

Recommended intakes may be increased and/or supplementation may be necessary in the following persons or conditions (based on documented niacin deficiency):

Diabetes mellitus
Fever, chronic
Gastrectomy
Hartnup disease
Hepatic-biliary tract disease—cirrhosis
Hyperthyroidism
Infection, chronic
Intestinal diseases—celiac disease, persistent diarrhea, tropical sprue, regional enteritis
Malabsorption syndromes associated with pancreatic insufficiency
Malignancy
Oropharyngeal lesions
Stress, continuing

Some unusual diets (e.g., reducing diets that drastically restrict food selection) may not supply minimum daily requirements of niacin. Supplementation is necessary in patients receiving total parenteral nutrition (TPN) or undergoing rapid weight loss or in those with malnutrition, because of inadequate dietary intake.

Recommended intakes for all vitamins and most minerals are increased during pregnancy. Many physicians recommend that pregnant women receive multivitamin and mineral supplements, especially those pregnant women who do not consume an adequate diet and those in high-risk categories (i.e., women carrying more than one fetus, heavy cigarette smokers, and alcohol and drug abusers). However, taking excessive amounts of a multivitamin and mineral supplement may be harmful to the mother and/or fetus and should be avoided.

Recommended intakes for all vitamins and most minerals are increased during breast-feeding.

Hyperlipidemia (treatment)—Niacin (but not niacinamide) is also indicated in the treatment of hyperlipidemia. Niacin is recommended for use only in patients with primary hyperlipidemia (type IIa, IIb, III, IV, or V hyperlipoproteinemia) and a significant risk of coronary artery disease who have not responded to other measures alone. It is one of the drugs of first choice for initiating therapy to reduce low density lipoprotein (LDL)–cholesterol concentrations and triglycerides, and to increase high density lipoprotein (HDL)–cholesterol concentrations.

Studies have suggested that control of elevated cholesterol and triglycerides may not lessen the danger of cardiovascular disease and mortality, although incidence of nonfatal myocardial infarctions may be decreased.

For additional information on initial therapeutic guidelines related to the treatment of hyperlipidemia, see *Appendix III*.

Unaccepted

Niacin is not useful for treatment of schizophrenia and other mental disorders not related to niacin deficiency. Niacin also has not been proven effective for treatment of acne, alcohol dependence, drug-induced hallucinations, hyperkinesis, leprosy, livedoid vasculitis, peripheral vascular disease, motion sickness, or for prevention of heart attacks.

Pharmacology/Pharmacokinetics

Physicochemical characteristics

Molecular weight—
- Niacin: 123.11.
- Niacinamide: 122.13.

pKa—
- Niacin: 4.85.
- Niacinamide: 0.5 and 3.35.

Mechanism of action/Effect

Nutritional supplement—Niacin, after conversion to niacinamide, is a component of two coenzymes, nicotinamide adenine dinucleotide (NAD) and nicotinamide adenine dinucleotide phosphate (NADP), which are necessary for tissue respiration; glycogenolysis; and lipid, amino acid, protein, and purine metabolism.

Antihyperlipidemic—Niacin, in gram doses, lowers total cholesterol (TC), low-density lipoprotein cholesterol (LDL-C), and triglyceride (TG) concentrations by inhibiting the synthesis of very low density lipoproteins (VLDL), which are precursors to the formation of low-density lipoproteins, the principal carrier of blood cholesterol.

Other actions/effects

Niacin (but not niacinamide) causes direct peripheral vasodilation.

Absorption

The B vitamins, including niacin and niacinamide, are readily absorbed from the gastrointestinal tract, except in malabsorption syndromes.

Niacin extended-release—rapidly absorbed; 60 to 76% of oral dose

To maximize bioavailability, administer niacin extended-release with a low-fat meal or snack

Biotransformation

Hepatic. Dietary tryptophan is converted by intestinal bacteria to niacin and niacinamide (about 60 mg of tryptophan is equivalent to 1 mg of niacin). Niacin is also converted to niacinamide as needed.

Niacin extended-release—The pharmacokinetic profile of niacin is complicated due to rapid and extensive first-pass metabolism. One pathway is through a conjugation step with glycine to form nicotinuric acid (NUA). NUA is excreted in the urine and a small amount may be metabolized back to niacin. The other pathway results in the formation of nicotinamide adenine dinucleotide (NAD). Nicotinamide is further metabolized to at least N-methylnicotinamide (MNA) and nicotinamide-N-oxide (NNO). MNA is further metabolized to N-methyl-2-pyridone-5-carboxamide (2PY) and N-methyl-4-pyridone-5-carboxamide (4PY).

Half-life

Elimination—Approximately 45 minutes.

Onset of action

Reduced cholesterol concentrations—Oral: Several days.

Reduced triglyceride concentrations—Oral: Several hours.

Time to peak concentration

Oral—45 minutes.

Niacin extended-release—4 to 5 hours depending on dose administered

Peak plasma concentrations

Niacin extended-release—
- 2 x 500 mg: 0.6 microgram per mL
- 2 x 750 mg: 4.9 micrograms per mL
- 2 x 1000 mg: 15.5 micrograms per mL

Elimination

Renal (almost entirely as metabolites). Excess beyond daily needs is excreted, largely unchanged, in urine.

Niacin extended-release—
- Following single and multiple doses: 60 to 76% of the dose is recovered in urine as niacin and metabolites
- Following multiple doses: up to 12% is recovered unchanged

The ratio of metabolites recovered in urine is dose dependent.

Precautions to Consider

Carcinogenicity

Niacin was not carcinogenic when administered to mice for a lifetime as a 1% solution in drinking water. The mice received 6 to 8 times a human dose of 3000 milligrams per day on a milligrams per square meter basis. No studies have been conducted with niacin extended-release.

Mutagenicity

Niacin was negative for mutagenicity in the Ames test. No studies have been conducted with niacin extended-release.

Pregnancy/Reproduction

Pregnancy—Problems in humans have not been documented with intake of normal daily recommended amounts.

Adequate and well-controlled studies in humans and animals have not been done at doses typically used for lipid disorders.

If a women receiving niacin extended-release for primary hypercholesterolemia (Types IIa or IIb) becomes pregnant, the drug should be discontinued. If a woman being treated with niacin extended-release for hypertriglyceridemia (Types IV or V) conceives, the benefits and risks of continued therapy should be assessed per individual.

Niacin extended-release—FDA Pregnancy Category C

Breast-feeding

Problems in humans have not been documented with intake of normal daily recommended amounts.

It is not know whether niacin extended-release is distributed into breast milk. However, niacin has been reported to be distributed in human milk. Because of the potential for serious adverse reactions in nursing infants from lipid-altering doses of nicotinic acid, a decision should be made whether to discontinue nursing or to discontinue therapy, taking into account the importance of therapy to the mother.

Pediatrics

Problems in pediatrics have not been documented with intake of normal daily recommended amounts. Appropriate studies of niacin as an antihyperlipidemic have not been performed in the pediatric population. However, use of niacin as an antihyperlipidemic in children under 2 years of age is not recommended since cholesterol is required for normal development.

Niacin extended-release—No studies have been conducted in patients under 21 years of age.

Geriatrics

Problems in geriatrics have not been documented with intake of normal daily recommended amounts.

Pharmacogenetics

Niacin extended-release—Following administration of niacin extended-release, steady state plasma concentrations are higher in women than in men, with the magnitude of difference varying with dose and metabolite. Gender differences in plasma levels may be due to gender-specific differences in metabolic rate or volume of distribution. Studies suggest that women have a greater hypolipidemic response than men at equivalent doses of niacin extended-release.

Drug interactions and/or related problems

The following drug interactions and/or related problems have been selected on the basis of their potential clinical significance (possible mechanism in parentheses where appropriate)—not necessarily inclusive (» = major clinical significance):

» Alcohol
(niacin extended-release and concomitant alcohol may result in increased adverse effects, such as flushing and pruritus)

» Anticoagulants
(caution should be used with concomitant use with niacin extended-release; prothrombin time and platelet count monitoring is recommended)

» Antihypertensives
(niacin may potentiate the effects of ganglionic blocking agents and vasoactive therapy resulting in postural hypotension)

Aspirin
(concomitant use may decrease the metabolic clearance of nicotinic acid)

» Bile acid sequestrants
(as great an interval as possible should elapse between the ingestion of bile acid-binding resins and the administration of niacin)

Chenodiol or
Ursodiol
(effect may be decreased when chenodiol or ursodiol is used concurrently with antihyperlipidemics, which tend to increase cholesterol saturation of bile)

» HMG-CoA reductase inhibitors
(concurrent use with niacin may be associated with an increased risk of rhabdomyolysis and acute renal failure; combined therapy with lovastatin, pravastatin, or simvastatin should include careful monitoring for symptoms of myopathy or rhabdomyolysis)

» Vasoactive drugs, such as:
Adrenergic blocking agents or
Calcium channel blockers, or
Nitrates
(caution should be used when niacin extended-release is used in patients with unstable angina or in the acute phase of myocardial infarction, especially patients also receiving vasoactive drugs; may result in increased risk of hypotension)

Vitamins, or
Other supplements containing niacin or related compounds such as nicotinamide
(may potentiate the adverse effects of niacin extended-release)

Laboratory value alterations

The following have been selected on the basis of their potential clinical significance (possible effect in parentheses where appropriate)—not necessarily inclusive (» = major clinical significance).

Note: Usually occur only with large doses.

With diagnostic test results
Niacin may produce fluorescent substances and falsely elevated results
Urine glucose determinations using cupric sulfate (Benedict's reagent)
(niacin may produce false-positive reactions)

With physiology/laboratory test values
Amylase, and
Bilirubin, total, and
Glucose, fasting, and
Lactate dehydrogenase activity, serum and
Transaminase activity, serum
(may be increased)

Phosphorus concentrations, serum
(dose-related reductions in phosphorus levels are associated with the use of niacin extended-release; monitor periodically, especially in patients at risk for hypophosphatemia)

Platelet count reduction
(niacin extended-release has been associated with dose-related reductions in platelet counts)

Prothrombin time, increased
(niacin extended-release increases prothrombin time; patients undergoing surgery should be carefully evaluated)

Uric acid concentrations in blood
(may be increased by large doses of niacin)

Medical considerations/Contraindications

The medical considerations/contraindications included have been selected on the basis of their potential clinical significance (reasons given in parentheses where appropriate)—not necessarily inclusive (» = major clinical significance).

Except under special circumstances, this medication should not be used when the following medical problems exists:

Note: These medical problems are contraindications for niacin extended-release due to the higher doses used to treat hyperlipidemia. These medical problems are relative contraindications (risk-benefit) for niacin used for prophylaxis and treatment of niacin deficiency.

» Arterial bleeding
(niacin extended-release is contraindicated in patients with arterial bleeding)

» Hepatic dysfunction, active or
» Transaminases, serum, unexplained elevations
(niacin extended-release is contraindicated in patients with significant or unexplained hepatic dysfunction)

Hypersensitivity to niacin or niacinamide

» Peptic ulcer disease, active
(niacin extended-release is contraindicated in patients with active peptic ulcer disease)

Risk-benefit should be considered when the following medical problems exist:

» Arterial bleeding or hemorrhage or
Glaucoma
(these conditions may be exacerbated)

» Diabetes mellitus
(large doses of niacin may cause impaired glucose tolerance; adjustment of diet and/or hypoglycemic therapy may be necessary)

Gout
(large doses may cause hyperuricemia)

» Hepatic disease
(large doses may cause hepatic damage)

» Hepatobiliary disease, history of or
Jaundice, history of
(patients with a past history of these medical problems should be closely observed during niacin extended-release therapy; frequent monitoring of liver function tests and blood glucose is recommended)

Hypotension
(may worsen due to vasodilating effects of niacin)

» Peptic ulcer
(large doses may activate peptic ulcer)

Renal dysfunction
(caution is advised when niacin extended-release is used in patients with renal dysfunction; increased drug exposure may result due to decreased renal elimination of niacin and metabolites)

Patient monitoring

The following may be especially important in patient monitoring (other tests may be warranted in some patients, depending on condition; » = major clinical significance):

Cholesterol concentrations, serum
(determinations recommended at periodic intervals during antihyperlipidemic therapy)

Glucose concentrations, blood and
Hepatic function determinations and
Uric acid concentrations
(determinations recommended at periodic intervals in patients receiving high doses of niacin or niacinamide for prolonged periods)

Phosphorus concentrations, serum
(periodic monitoring in patients at risk for hypophosphatemia)

Platelet counts, and
Prothrombin time
(periodic monitoring during niacin extended-release therapy; monitor closely in patients on concomitant niacin extended-release and anticoagulant)

Side/Adverse Effects

Note: Flushing and pruritus may be reduced with the extended-release dosage form of niacin. Spontaneous reports suggest that flushing may also be accompanied by symptoms of dizziness, tachycardia, palpitations, shortness of breath, sweating, chills, and/or edema, which in rare cases may lead to syncope.

The following side/adverse effects have been selected on the basis of their potential clinical significance (possible signs and symptoms in parentheses where appropriate)—not necessarily inclusive:

Those indicating need for medical attention

Incidence rare
Allergic reaction, anaphylactic (skin rash or itching; wheezing)—after intravenous administration

With long-term use of extended-release niacin
Hepatotoxicity or cholestasis (darkening of urine; light gray-colored stools; loss of appetite; severe stomach pain; yellow eyes or skin)

Those indicating need for medical attention only if they continue or are bothersome

Incidence less frequent—with niacin only
Feeling of warmth; flushing or redness of skin, especially on face and neck; headache; pain, abdominal; rash; rhinitis (stuffy nose; runny nose; sneezing)

With high oral doses
Cardiac arrhythmias (unusually fast, slow, or irregular heartbeat); ***diarrhea; dizziness or faintness; dryness of skin or eyes; hyper-***

glycemia (frequent urination or unusual thirst)—may occasionally be fatal; ***hyperuricemia*** (joint pain; side, lower back, or stomach pain; swelling of feet or lower legs); ***myalgia*** (fever; muscle aching or cramping; unusual tiredness or weakness); ***nausea or vomiting; peptic ulcer, aggravation of*** (stomach pain); ***pruritus*** (itching of skin)—may be severe

Note: Rarely, along with markedly elevated creatine kinase (CK) concentrations, fever, muscle aching or cramping, or unusual tiredness or weakness may be symptoms of myositis or rhabdomyolysis; incidence may be increased in patients treated concurrently with lovastatin, pravastatin, or simvastatin.

Patient Consultation

As an aid to patient consultation, refer to *Advice for the Patient, Niacin (Vitamin B_3) (Systemic)* or *Niacin—For High Cholesterol (Systemic)*.

In providing consultation, consider emphasizing the following selected information (» = major clinical significance):

Description of use

Description should include function in the body, signs of deficiency, and unproven uses

Importance of diet

For use as a vitamin supplement

Importance of proper nutrition; supplement may be needed because of inadequate dietary intake

Food sources of niacin; effects of processing

Not using vitamins as substitute for balanced diet

Recommended daily intake for niacin

Before using this medication

For use as a vitamin supplement

See *Indications* for conditions and medications affecting requirements.

For use as an antihyperlipidemic (niacin only)

Importance of diet, exercise, and weight reduction to control hyperlipidemia.

» Conditions affecting use, especially:

Hypersensitivity to niacin or niacinamide

Pregnancy—Women that become pregnant while receiving niacin for primary hypercholesterolemia (Types IIa and IIb) should discontinue drug therapy.

Women who conceive while receiving niacin for hypertriglyceridemia (Types IV or V) should consider the benefits and risks of continued therapy; decisions should be made on an individual basis.

Niacin extended-release—FDA Pregnancy Category C

Breast-feeding—Niacin has been reported to be distributed in human breast milk. Due to the potential risks of serious adverse reactions in nursing infants, a decision should be made whether to discontinue nursing or to discontinue drug therapy, taking into account the importance of the drug to the mother.

Use in children—Not recommended as antihyperlipidemic in children under 2 years of age since cholesterol is required for normal development

Niacin extended-release—Safety and efficacy have not been established for patients under 21 years of age.

Niacin extended-release—Other medications, especially alcohol, anticoagulants, antihypertensives, bile acid sequesterants, HMG-CoA reductase inhibitors, or vasoactive drugs,

Other medical problems, especially arterial bleeding or hemorrhage, diabetes mellitus, hepatic disease, or peptic ulcer

Proper use of this medication

Possibility of stomach upset; taking with meals or milk; checking with physician if stomach upset continues

Proper administration of extended-release dosage forms: Swallowing whole without crushing, breaking, or chewing; contents of capsule may be mixed with jam or jelly and swallowed without chewing

For use as an antihyperlipidemic (niacin only)

» Niacin extended-release should be taken at bedtime, after a low-fat snack.

» To avoid or minimize flushing: take aspirin (approximately 30 minutes prior to niacin extended-release) or a non-steroidal anti-inflammatory drug before administration;. avoid ingestion of alcohol or hot drinks around the time of niacin extended-release administration

» Take this medication exactly as your doctor ordered. If you stop taking this medication for any period of time, contact your doctor prior to restarting therapy.

» Importance adherence to recommended regimens for diet and exercise.

Niacin does not cure the condition but instead helps control it

» Proper storage

» Proper dosing

Missed dose: For use as a vitamin supplement—No cause for concern because of length of time necessary for depletion; remembering to take as directed

For use as an antihyperlipidemic (niacin only)—If you miss a dose of this medicine, skip the missed dose and go back to your regular dosing schedule. Do not double doses.

Precautions while using this medication

Caution if dizziness or faintness occurs

For use as an antihyperlipidemic (niacin only):

» Importance of close monitoring by physician to check progress

» Checking with physician before discontinuing medication; blood lipid concentrations may increase significantly

Notify physician when taking vitamins or other nutritional supplements containing niacin or related compounds such as nicotinamide.

(Notify physician if diabetic patient notices changes in blood glucose.)

Side/adverse effects

Signs of potential side effects, especially anaphylactic reaction with injection only; hepatotoxicity or cholestasis with high doses of extended-release niacin

General Dosing Information

For use as a vitamin supplement—

Dosages of niacin and niacinamide as vitamin supplements are equal; some clinicians prefer niacinamide because of its lack of vasodilating effect.

Because of the infrequency of single B vitamin deficiencies, combinations are commonly administered. Many commercial combinations of B vitamins are available.

When used for treatment of pellagra, niacin or niacinamide is usually given in combination with 5 mg each of thiamine, riboflavin, and pyridoxine.

For use as an antihyperlipidemic (niacin only)—

For patients switching from immediate-release niacin to niacin extended-release, therapy with niacin extended-release should be initiated with low doses and the dose should be titrated to the desired therapeutic response.

If therapy is discontinued for an extended period, reinstitution of therapy should include a titration phase.

If lipid response to niacin extended-release alone is insufficient, or if higher doses are not well tolerated, patients may benefit from combination therapy with bile acid binding resin or an HMG-CoA reductase inhibitor.

Extended-release dosage forms should not be broken, crushed or chewed. For product specific information, check the manufacturer's product information.

For parenteral dosage forms only—

In most cases, parenteral administration is indicated only when oral administration is not acceptable (for example, in nausea, vomiting, and preoperative and postoperative conditions) or possible (for example, in malabsorption syndromes or following gastric resection).

When administered intravenously, niacin or niacinamide should be given at a rate not exceeding 2 mg per minute.

Diet/Nutrition

For use as a vitamin supplement—

Niacin or niacinamide may be taken with meals or milk if nausea, vomiting, or diarrhea occurs. A physician should be consulted if stomach upset continues.

Recommended dietary intakes for niacin are defined differently worldwide.

For U.S.—

The Recommended Dietary Allowances (RDAs) for vitamins and minerals are determined by the Food and Nutrition Board of the National Research Council and are intended to provide adequate nutrition in most healthy persons under usual environmental stresses. In addition, a different designation may be used by the FDA for food and dietary supplement labeling purposes, as with Daily Value (DV). DVs replace the previous labeling terminology United States Recommended Daily Allowances (USRDAs).

For Canada—

Recommended Nutrient Intakes (RNIs) for vitamins, minerals, and protein are determined by Health and Welfare Canada and provide recommended amounts of a specific nutrient while minimizing the risk of chronic diseases.

Daily recommended intakes for niacin are generally defined as follows:

Persons	U.S. (mg)	Canada (mg)
Infants and children		
Birth to 3 years of age	5–9	4–9
4 to 6 years of age	12	13
7 to 10 years of age	13	14–18
Adolescent and adult males	15–20	14–23
Adolescent and adult females	13–15	14–16
Pregnant females	17	14–16
Breast-feeding females	20	14–16

These are usually provided by adequate diets.

Best dietary sources of niacin include meats, eggs, and milk and dairy products; dietary tryptophan (from protein) is converted to niacin. There is little loss of niacin from foods with ordinary cooking.

For use as an antihyperlipidemic (niacin only)—
Importance of diet, exercise, and weight reduction to control hyperlipidemia.

Bioequivalence information

Equivalent doses of niacin extended release should not be substituted for sustained-release (modified-release, timed-released) niacin preparations or immediate-released (crystalline) niacin.

Niacin extended release tablet strengths are not interchangable.

For treatment of adverse effects

Tolerance to the vasodilating and gastrointestinal effects of niacin usually occurs within 2 weeks.

The severe flushing, pruritus, and gastrointestinal effects may be minimized by starting therapy with a low dose and increasing the dosage gradually, and by taking niacin with meals or milk.

Persistent flushing may sometimes be controlled with 300 mg of aspirin taken 30 minutes before each niacin dose.

NIACIN

Oral Dosage Forms

NIACIN EXTENDED-RELEASE CAPSULES

Note: Dose-related hepatotoxicity may be more prevalent with high doses of the extended-release dosage form of niacin.
Flushing and pruritus may be reduced with the extended-release dosage form of niacin.

Usual adult and adolescent dose

Antihyperlipidemic—
Initial: Oral, 1 gram three times a day, the dosage being increased in increments of 500 mg a day every two to four weeks as needed.
Note: Some clinicians may begin with 500 mg per day and gradually increase the dosage to 4 grams a day.
Maintenance: Oral, 1 to 2 grams three times a day.

Deficiency (prophylaxis)—
Oral, amount based on normal daily recommended intakes:

Persons	U.S. (mg)	Canada (mg)
Adolescent and adult males	15–20	14–23
Adolescent and adult females	13–15	14–16
Pregnant females	17	14–16
Breast-feeding females	20	14–16

Deficiency (treatment)—
Treatment dose is individualized by prescriber based on severity of deficiency.

Usual adult prescribing limits

Oral, 6 grams a day.

Usual pediatric dose

Dosage form is not recommended for use in children.

Strength(s) usually available

U.S.—
125 mg (OTC) [GENERIC].
250 mg [GENERIC].
400 mg [GENERIC].
500 mg [GENERIC].

Canada—
Not commercially available.

Note: For use as a dietary supplement, some strengths of these niacin preparations may exceed the dosage range recommended by USP DI Advisory Panels based on the amount necessary to meet normal nutritional needs.

Packaging and storage

Store below 40 °C (104 °F), preferably between 15 and 30 °C (59 and 86 °F), in a well-closed container, unless otherwise specified by manufacturer.

Auxiliary labeling

- Swallow capsules whole.
- Take with meals or milk.

Note

Contents of capsule may be mixed with jelly or jam and swallowed without chewing.

NIACIN ORAL SOLUTION

Usual adult and adolescent dose

Antihyperlipidemic—
Initial: Oral, 1 gram three times a day, the dosage being increased in increments of 500 mg a day every two to four weeks as needed.
Maintenance: Oral, 1 to 2 grams three times a day.

Deficiency (prophylaxis or treatment)—
See *Niacin Extended-release Capsules.*

Usual adult prescribing limits

Oral, 6 grams a day.

Usual pediatric dose

Deficiency (prophylaxis)—
Oral, amount based on normal daily recommended intakes:

Persons	U.S. (mg)	Canada (mg)
Infants and children		
Birth to 3 years of age	5–9	4–9
4 to 6 years of age	12	13
7 to 10 years of age	13	14–18

Deficiency (treatment)—
Treatment dose is individualized by prescriber based on severity of deficiency.

Strength(s) usually available

U.S.—
50 mg per 5 mL (OTC) [*Nicotinex Elixir* (alcohol 14%)].

Canada—
Not commercially available.

Note: For use as a dietary supplement, the strength of this niacin preparation may exceed the dosage range recommended by USP DI Advisory Panels based on the amount necessary to meet normal nutritional needs.

Packaging and storage

Store below 40 °C (104 °F), preferably between 15 and 30 °C (59 and 86 °F), in a tight container, unless otherwise specified by manufacturer. Protect from freezing.

Auxiliary labeling

- Take with meals or milk.

NIACIN TABLETS USP

Usual adult and adolescent dose

Antihyperlipidemic—
Initial: Oral, 1 gram three times a day, the dosage being increased in increments of 500 mg a day every two to four weeks as needed.
Note: Some clinicians may begin with 100 mg per day and gradually increase the dosage to 4 grams per day.
Maintenance: Oral, 1 to 2 grams three times a day.

Deficiency (prophylaxis or treatment)—
See *Niacin Extended-release Capsules.*

Usual adult prescribing limits

Oral, 6 grams a day.

Usual pediatric dose

Deficiency (prophylaxis or treatment)—
See *Niacin Oral Solution.*

Strength(s) usually available

U.S.—
25 mg (OTC) [GENERIC].
50 mg (OTC) [GENERIC].
100 mg (OTC) [GENERIC].
125 mg (OTC) [GENERIC].
250 mg (OTC) [GENERIC].
400 mg (OTC) [GENERIC].
500 mg [*Niacor* (scored); *Nicolar* (scored; tartrazine); GENERIC].

Canada—
50 mg (OTC) [*Novo-Niacin;* GENERIC].
100 mg (OTC) [GENERIC].
500 mg (OTC) [GENERIC].

Note: For use as a dietary supplement, some strengths of these niacin preparations may exceed the dosage range recommended by USP DI Advisory Panels based on the amount necessary to meet normal nutritional needs.

Packaging and storage

Store below 40 °C (104 °F), preferably between 15 and 30 °C (59 and 86 °F), unless otherwise specified by manufacturer. Store in a well-closed container.

Auxiliary labeling

- Take with meals or milk.

NIACIN EXTENDED-RELEASE TABLETS

Note: Dose-related hepatotoxicity may be more prevalent with high doses of the extended-release dosage form.

Flushing and pruritus may be reduced with the extended-release dosage form of niacin.

Usual adult and adolescent dose

Antihyperlipidemic—

Initial: Oral, 500 milligrams once daily at bedtime for 1 to 4 weeks. If dose is tolerated and response is inadequate, the dose may be increased to 1000 milligrams (2 x 500 milligrams) once daily at bedtime.

Note: One manufacturer of an OTC niacin extended-release tablet recommends not to exceed 500 milligrams daily without the direction of a physician.

Maintenance: Oral, 1 to 2 grams three times a day. Dose is titrated to optimal effect that is well tolerated.

Note: Some clinicians may use a maintenance dose of 500 mg to 1 gram two to three times a day.

One manufacturer has a titration schedule. The daily dose should not increase by more than 500 milligrams in any 4-week period. The recommended maintenance dose is 1000 milligrams (two 500 milligram tablets) to 2000 milligrams (two 1000 milligram tablets OR four 500 milligram tablets) once daily at bedtime.

Deficiency (prophylaxis and treatment)—
See *Niacin Extended-release Capsules.*

Usual adult prescribing limits

Oral, 6 grams a day.
Niaspan®—Oral, 2000 milligrams a day.

Usual pediatric dose

Dosage form is not recommended for use in children.

Strength(s) usually available

U.S.—
250 mg [*Slo-Niacin* (scored); GENERIC].
500 mg [*Niaspan* (unscored); *Slo-Niacin* (scored); GENERIC].
750 mg [*Niaspan* (unscored); *Slo-Niacin* (scored); GENERIC].
1000 mg [*Niaspan* (unscored); GENERIC].
1000 mg (OTC) [GENERIC].

Canada—
500 mg (OTC) [GENERIC].

Note: For use as a dietary supplement, some strengths of these niacin preparations may exceed the dosage range recommended by USP DI Advisory Panels based on the amount necessary to meet normal nutritional needs.

Packaging and storage

Store below 40 °C (104 °F), preferably between 15 and 30 °C (59 and 86 °F), in a well-closed container, unless otherwise specified by manufacturer.

Note: Niaspan—Store at room temperature, (20 to 25 °C (68 to 77 °F)

Auxiliary labeling

- Swallow tablets whole.
- Take with meals or milk.

Note

If tablets are scored, they may be broken, but not crushed or chewed, before swallowing.

Parenteral Dosage Forms

NIACIN INJECTION USP

Usual adult and adolescent dose

Deficiency (prophylaxis)—
Intravenous infusion, as part of total parenteral nutrition solutions, the specific amount determined by individual patient need.

Deficiency (treatment)—
Intramuscular, 50 to 100 mg five or more times a day.
Intravenous (slow), 25 to 100 mg two or more times a day.

Usual pediatric dose

Deficiency (prophylaxis)—
Intravenous infusion, as part of total parenteral nutrition solutions, the specific amount determined by individual patient need.

Deficiency (treatment)—
Intravenous (slow), up to 300 mg a day.

Strength(s) usually available

U.S.—
100 mg per mL (Rx) [GENERIC].

Canada—
Not commercially available.

Packaging and storage

Store below 40 °C (104 °F), preferably between 15 and 30 °C (59 and 86 °F), unless otherwise specified by manufacturer. Protect from freezing.

Preparation of dosage form

For administration by the intravenous route, niacin injection should be diluted to a strength of 2 mg per mL or added to 500 mL of sodium chloride injection and administered at a rate not exceeding 2 mg per minute.

NIACINAMIDE

Oral Dosage Forms

NIACINAMIDE TABLETS USP

Usual adult and adolescent dose

Deficiency (prophylaxis)—
Oral, amount based on normal daily recommended intakes:

Persons	U.S. (mg)	Canada (mg)
Adolescent and adult males	15–20	14–23
Adolescent and adult females	13–15	14–16
Pregnant females	17	14–16
Breast-feeding females	20	14–16

Deficiency (treatment)—
Treatment dose is individualized by prescriber based on severity of deficiency.

Usual pediatric dose

Deficiency (prophylaxis)—
Oral, amount based on normal daily recommended intakes:

Persons	U.S. (mg)	Canada (mg)
Infants and children		
Birth to 3 years of age	5–9	4–9
4 to 6 years of age	12	13
7 to 10 years of age	13	14–18

Deficiency (treatment)—
Treatment dose is individualized by prescriber based on severity of deficiency.

Strength(s) usually available

U.S.—
50 mg (OTC) [GENERIC].
100 mg (OTC) [GENERIC].
125 mg (OTC) [GENERIC].
250 mg (OTC) [GENERIC].
500 mg (Rx/OTC) [GENERIC].

Canada—
100 mg (OTC) [GENERIC].
500 mg (OTC) [GENERIC].

Note: For use as a dietary supplement, some strengths of these niacinamide preparations may exceed the dosage range recommended by USP DI Advisory Panels based on the amount necessary to meet normal nutritional needs.

Packaging and storage

Store below 40 °C (104 °F), preferably between 15 and 30 °C (59 and 86 °F), unless otherwise specified by manufacturer. Store in a tight container.

Parenteral Dosage Forms

NIACINAMIDE INJECTION USP

Usual adult and adolescent dose

Deficiency (prophylaxis)—
Intravenous infusion, as part of total parenteral nutrition solutions, the specific amount determined by individual patient need.

Deficiency (treatment)—
Intramuscular, 50 to 100 mg five or more times a day.
Intravenous (slow), 25 to 100 mg two or more times a day.

Usual pediatric dose

Deficiency (prophylaxis)—
Intravenous infusion, as part of total parenteral nutrition solutions, the specific amount determined by individual patient need.

Deficiency (treatment)—
Intravenous (slow), up to 300 mg a day.

Strength(s) usually available

U.S.—
100 mg per mL (Rx) [GENERIC].

Canada—
Not commercially available.

Packaging and storage

Store below 40 °C (104 °F), preferably between 15 and 30 °C (59 and 86 °F), unless otherwise specified by manufacturer. Protect from freezing.

Revised: 06/04/2003

NIACIN AND LOVASTATIN
Systemic

VA CLASSIFICATION (Primary): CV359

Commonly used brand name(s): *Advicor*.

NOTE: The *Niacin and Lovastatin (Systemic)* monograph is maintained on the *USP DI* electronic database. A copy of the most recent revision of the complete monograph can be accessed on the *USP DI* Updates Online website. See the front cover of book for details on accessing the site. The information that follows is selectively abstracted from the complete monograph and is provided to facilitate drug use review and patient counseling.

Note: For a listing of dosage forms and brand names by country availability, see *Dosage Forms* section(s).

Category

Antihyperlipidemic.

Indications

Accepted

Hyperlipidemia (treatment)—Niacin extended-release and lovastatin combination therapy is indicated for treatment of primary hypercholesterolemia (heterozygous familial and nonfamilial) and mixed dyslipidemia (Frederickson Types IIa and IIb) in patients who require further triglyceride lowering or HDL raising effects and have been previously treated with lovastatin and may benefit from having niacin added to their regimen, or in patients who require further LDL lowering effects and have been previously treated with niacin and may benefit from having lovastatin added to their regimen.

Note: Initial medical therapy should be started with a single agent. If a particular single agent is not effective, treatment with another single agent may be appropriate before resorting to combination therapy.

Unaccepted

Niacin extended-release and lovastatin combination therapy is not indicated for initial treatment of primary hypercholesterolemia and mixed dyslipidemia.

Patient Consultation

As an aid to patient consultation, refer to *Advice for the Patient, Niacin and Lovastatin (Systemic)*.

In providing consultation, consider emphasizing the following selected information (» = major clinical significance):

Before using this medication

» Not using niacin extended-release and lovastatin combination therapy until your body has adjusted to each of the individual medicines

» Conditions affecting use, especially:
Hypersensitivity to niacin, lovastatin or any component of this medication.
Pregnancy—Contraindicated during pregnancy or in women planning to become pregnant in the near future.
Breast-feeding—Contraindicated in women who are breast-feeding
Pharmacogenetics—Niacin plasma concentrations are generally higher in women than in men, however this does not warrant dose adjustment
Dental—Notifying dentist that patient is being treated with niacin extended-release and lovastatin combination
Surgical—Patients undergoing elective major surgery or having acute medical or surgical conditions should have their treatment with niacin extended-release and lovastatin combination stopped a few days before their surgery or when any major acute medical or surgical condition supervenes
Other medications, especially alcohol-large quantities, antihypertensive agents, clarithromycin, clofibrate, coumarin anticoagulants, cyclosporine, erythromycin, fenofibrate, gemfibrozil, grapefruit juice (> 1 quart per day), HIV protease inhibitors, itraconazole, ketoconazole, nefazodone, and vitamins or supplements containing niacin or related compounds such as nicotinamide
Other medical problems, especially active peptic ulcer disease, acute hepatic disease, arterial bleeding, hepatic dysfunction, hypersensitivity to niacin or lovastatin, persistent elevations in serum transaminases, women who are pregnant and in lactating mothers
Laboratory value alterations especially catecholamine fluorometry, urine glucose tests, and creatine kinase.

Proper use of this medication

Patient monitoring especially lipid profile, liver function tests, glucose monitoring in diabetic patients, serum creatine kinase, phosphorus monitoring, platelet monitoring, and prothrombin time.
Not crushing, breaking, or chewing tablets
Taking at bedtime with a low-fat snack. Not drinking grapefruit juice around the time medicine is taken. Not drinking more than one quart of grapefruit juice daily while being treated with medicine
Flushing may occur and may last several hours. Avoiding alcohol or hot drinks may reduce effect. Flushing should lessen after several weeks
» Proper dosing
Missed dose: Taking as soon as possible; not taking if almost time for next dose; do not double dose. If medicine not taken for more than seven days, not taking until checking with doctor about need to reduce dose
» Proper storage

Precautions while using this medication

Notifying physician immediately if pregnancy is suspected because of possible harm to the fetus
Notifying physician immediately if unexplained dark-colored urine, a fever, muscle cramps or spasms, muscle pain or stiffness, or feeling very tired or weak. These symptoms may indicate rhabdomyolysis.
Diabetics: Medicine may affect blood sugar levels.

Side/adverse effects

Signs of potential side effects, especially abdominal pain, asthenia, flushing, generalized pain or back pain, hyperglycemia, infection, myalgia, myopathy, and rhabdomyolysis.

Oral Dosage Forms

NIACIN EXTENDED RELEASE AND LOVASTATIN TABLETS

Usual adult dose

Antihyperlipidemia—
Before initiating treatment with niacin extended-release and lovastatin combination product, titration and stabilization with the following single-entity products should be accomplished:
—*If the patient has previously been receiving any niacin product other than Niaspan brand of niacin extended-release tablets*: The other product should be discontinued and the patient started on Niaspan using the recommended Niaspan titration schedule, which begins at 500 mg at bedtime. Dosage adjustment increases

should not be more than 500 mg every 4 weeks up to a maximum of 2000 mg. After the dose of Niaspan has been stabilized, the patient may be switched directly to a niacin-equivalent dose of the combination product.

—*If the patient has previously been receiving Niaspan brand of niacin extended-release tablets*: The dose of Niaspan should be stabilized and then the patient may be switched directly to a niacin-equivalent dose of the combination product.

—*If the patient has previously been receiving Mevaco, brand of lovastatin tablets*: The dose of Mevacor should be stabilized and then Niaspan brand of niacin extended-release tablets, should be added to the regimen. Once the Niaspan dose has also been stabilized, the patient may be switched to a niacin-equivalent dose of the combination product.

The lowest dose of the combination product of niacin extended-release and lovastatin is 500 mg / 20 mg, respectively, at bedtime, with a low fat snack. Dosage adjustments should be made at intervals of 4 weeks or more and the dose should not be increased by more than 500 mg based on the niacin-extended release component of the combination product.

Note: If the niacin extended-release and lovastatin combination product is discontinued for more than 7 days, reinstitution of therapy should begin with the lowest dose of the combination product.

Usual adult prescribing limits

A daily dose of niacin extended-release and lovastatin combination greater than 2000 mg / 40 mg, respectively, is not recommended.

Usual pediatric dose

Safety and efficacy have not been established. Because pediatric patients are not likely to benefit from cholesterol lowering for at least a decade and because experience with this drug or its active ingredients is limited, treatment of pediatric patient with niacin extended-release and lovastatin combination is not recommended.

Usual geriatric dose

See *Usual adult dose*.

Strength(s) usually available

U.S.—

500 mg of niacin extended-release and 20 mg of lovastatin (Rx) [*Advicor* (hydroxypropyl methylcellulose, povidone, stearic acid, polyethylene glycol, titanium, dioxide, polysorbate 80.)].

750 mg of niacin extended-release and 20 mg of lovastatin (Rx) [*Advicor* (hydroxypropyl methylcellulose, povidone, stearic acid, polyethylene glycol, titanium, dioxide, polysorbate 80.)].

1000 mg of niacin extended-release and 20 mg of lovastatin (Rx) [*Advicor* (hydroxypropyl methylcellulose, povidone, stearic acid, polyethylene glycol, titanium, dioxide, polysorbate 80.)].

Canada—

Not commercially available

Auxiliary labeling

- Avoid alcohol while on this medication.
- Grapefruit and grapefruit juice should not be taken with this medication.
- Take with food
- Take at bedtime
- Swallow whole. Do not crush or chew
- Harmful if pregnant or breast-feeding
- Ask before using non-prescription drugs

Revised: 07/18/2003
Developed: 09/03/2002

NIACINAMIDE—See *Niacin (Systemic)*

NICARDIPINE—See *Calcium Channel Blocking Agents (Systemic)*

NICOTINE Inhalation-Systemic

VA CLASSIFICATION (Primary): AD600

Commonly used brand name(s): *Nicotrol Inhaler*.

Note: For a listing of dosage forms and brand names by country availability, see *Dosage Forms* section(s).

Category

Smoking cessation adjunct.

Indications

Accepted

Nicotine dependence (treatment adjunct)—The nicotine inhaler is indicated as a temporary aid for cigarette smokers who want to give up smoking. It serves as an alternative source of nicotine and provides relief of nicotine withdrawal symptoms in nicotine-dependent individuals who are acutely withdrawing from cigarette smoking. It is recommended that the nicotine inhaler be used in conjunction with a comprehensive behavioral smoking cessation program.

Pharmacology/Pharmacokinetics

Physicochemical characteristics

Source—Tobacco plant.
Molecular weight—162.23.
pKa—At 15 °C (59 °F): pKa_1—7.84; pKa_2—3.04.
Solubility—Freely soluble in water.
Partition coefficient—15:1 at pH 7.

Mechanism of action/Effect

Nicotine acts as an agonist at the nicotinic-cholinergic receptors in the autonomic ganglia, adrenal medulla, neuromuscular junctions, and brain. Nicotine's positive reinforcing properties are believed to be the result of the release of neurotransmitters including acetylcholine, beta-endorphin, dopamine, norepinephrine, serotonin, and others that mediate pleasure, arousal, mood, appetite, and other desirable psychological states.

Other actions/effects

Cardiovascular effects include peripheral vasoconstriction, tachycardia, and elevated blood pressure.

Absorption

Nicotine is absorbed rapidly through the mucous membranes and respiratory tract, and slowly through the buccal mucosa.

The high, rapid rise and decline in nicotine plasma concentrations that occur with cigarette smoking do not occur with the use of the nicotine inhaler.

Distribution

Most of the nicotine released from the inhaler is deposited in the mouth. Less than 5% of a dose reaches the lower respiratory tract.

Nicotine is distributed into breast milk; the milk-to-plasma ratio average is 2.9:1.

The volume of distribution following intravenous administration is approximately 2 to 3 L per kg.

Protein binding

Very low (< 5%).

Biotransformation

Primarily hepatic; also metabolized in the kidneys and lungs. More than 20 metabolites have been identified; all are less active than the parent compound. The primary urinary metabolites are cotinine, which comprises 15% of a dose; and trans-3-hydroxycotinine, which comprises 45% of a dose.

Half-life

Elimination—

Nicotine: 1 to 2 hours.
Cotinine: 15 to 20 hours.

Time to peak concentration

Within 15 minutes of the end of an inhalation.

Peak plasma concentration (at steady-state)

Following an intensive inhalation regimen (80 deep inhalations over 20 minutes) every hour for 10 hours—

At 20 °C (68 °F): 22.5 nanograms per mL (nanograms/mL), range 11.1 to 40.4 nanograms/mL.

At 30 °C (86 °F): 29.7 nanograms/mL, range 17.6 to 47.2 nanograms/mL.

At 40 °C (104 °F): 34 nanograms/mL, range 24.1 to 48.6 nanograms/mL.

Following as-needed use—

6 to 8 nanograms/mL (approximately one third the concentration achieved with cigarette smoking).

Elimination

Renal, approximately 10% excreted unchanged; up to 30% may be excreted in acidified urine (pH < 5) and with a high urine flow rate. The average plasma clearance is approximately 1.2 L per minute in a healthy adult smoker.

Precautions to Consider

Carcinogenicity
Nicotine does not appear to be carcinogenic in laboratory animals. Inconclusive evidence suggests that its metabolite, cotinine, may be carcinogenic in rats.

Tumorigenicity
When given in conjunction with tumor initiators, nicotine and its metabolites increased the incidence of tumors in hamsters and rats.

Mutagenicity
Neither nicotine nor its metabolite, cotinine, was shown to be mutagenic in the Ames *Salmonella* test. Nicotine induced reparable DNA damage in an *Escherichia coli* test system and was shown to be genotoxic in Chinese hamster ovary cells.

Pregnancy/Reproduction
Fertility—In rats and rabbits, nicotine caused a reduction in DNA synthesis, resulting in delayed or inhibited implantation. Rats treated with nicotine during the time of gestation have produced decreased litter sizes.

Pregnancy—The nicotine inhaler is not recommended for use during pregnancy and should be used only if the likelihood of smoking cessation justifies the potential risk in pregnant patients who continue to smoke. Pregnant smokers should be encouraged to attempt smoking cessation using educational and behavioral interventions before using pharmacological measures. Cigarette smoking may cause low birth weight, increased risk of spontaneous abortion, and increased perinatal mortality. Spontaneous abortion during nicotine replacement therapy has been reported and possibly may be due to the nicotine.

Studies in pregnant rhesus monkeys have shown that nicotine administered intravenously reduced maternal uterine blood flow and produced acidosis, hypercarbia, and hypotension in the fetus. Nicotine administered intravenously to pregnant ewes reduced breathing movements in the fetal lamb. Teratogenicity has been demonstrated in the offspring of mice given toxic doses (25 mg per kg of body weight) of nicotine.

FDA Pregnancy Category D.

Labor—The nicotine inhaler is not recommended for use during labor because its effect on the mother and fetus is not known.

Delivery—The nicotine inhaler is not recommended for use during delivery.

Breast-feeding
Nicotine is distributed into breast milk. The ability of infants to clear nicotine via hepatic first-pass metabolism is probably lowest at birth. Nicotine concentrations in breast milk may be expected to be lower with the nicotine inhaler than with cigarette smoking. The risk of exposing the infant to nicotine from the inhaler should be weighed against the risk associated with exposing the infant to nicotine from continued smoking by the mother.

Pediatrics
Small amounts of nicotine can cause poisoning in children. Even used nicotine inhaler cartridges contain enough nicotine to cause serious harm in children. The cartridges also are small enough to cause choking if they are swallowed.

Safety and efficacy in children younger than 18 years of age have not been established. However, there are no specific medical problems that would limit the usefulness of the nicotine inhaler in adolescent smokers. The nicotine inhaler may be used in older adolescents only if the potential benefit justifies the potential risk.

Geriatrics
One hundred thirty-two patients 60 years of age or older have participated in clinical trials, and geriatrics-specific problems that would limit the usefulness of this medication in the elderly are not expected. However, elderly patients are more likely to have cardiac function impairment, which may require caution in patients receiving the nicotine inhaler.

Drug interactions and/or related problems
The following drug interactions and/or related problems have been selected on the basis of their potential clinical significance (possible mechanism in parentheses where appropriate)—not necessarily inclusive (» = major clinical significance):

Note: Combinations containing any of the following medications, depending on the amount present, may also interact with this medication.

» Antidepressants, tricyclic or
» Theophylline
(smoking cessation, with or without nicotine replacement, may alter the pharmacokinetics of these agents; dosage adjustment may be necessary)

Medical considerations/Contraindications
The medical considerations/contraindications included have been selected on the basis of their potential clinical significance (reasons given in parentheses where appropriate)—not necessarily inclusive (» = major clinical significance).

Except under special circumstances, this medication should not be used when the following medical problems exist:

» Allergy or hypersensitivity to nicotine or to menthol

» Angina pectoris, severe or worsening or
» Cardiac arrhythmias, life-threatening or
» Myocardial infarction, recent
(use is not recommended)

Risk-benefit should be considered when the following medical problems exist:

Angina pectoris or
Cardiac arrhythmias or
Myocardial infarction, history of or
Vasospastic disease, such as:
Buerger's disease
Prinzmetal's angina
Raynaud's phenomena
(patients should be evaluated carefully before beginning therapy with the nicotine inhaler)

» Asthma or
» Chronic obstructive pulmonary disease (COPD)
(use of the nicotine inhaler has not been studied in patients with these conditions; however, nicotine is an airway irritant and may cause bronchospasm; other forms of nicotine replacement may be preferable in patients with severe bronchospastic airway disease, but if the nicotine inhaler is used, caution is recommended)

Diabetes mellitus, type 1 or
Hyperthyroidism or
Pheochromocytoma
(nicotine causes release of catecholamines from the adrenal medulla; caution is recommended)

Hepatic function impairment
(nicotine is extensively metabolized in the liver, and its total system clearance is dependent upon hepatic blood flow; therefore, reduced clearance should be anticipated)

» Hypertension, accelerated
(risk of progression to malignant hypertension is increased; caution is recommended)

Peptic ulcer disease, active
(nicotine delays healing; caution is recommended)

Side/Adverse Effects
The following side/adverse effects have been selected on the basis of their potential clinical significance (possible signs and symptoms in parentheses where appropriate)—not necessarily inclusive:

Those indicating need for medical attention
Incidence less frequent

Allergic reaction (fever with or without chills; headache; nausea with or without vomiting; runny nose; shortness of breath, tightness in chest, trouble in breathing, or wheezing; skin rash, itching, or hives; tearing of eyes); ***fast or irregular heartbeat***

Note: If *fast or irregular heartbeat* occurs, use of the nicotine inhaler should be discontinued.

Those indicating need for medical attention only if they continue or are bothersome
Incidence more frequent

Coughing—incidence 32%; ***dyspepsia*** (indigestion)—incidence 18%; ***headache***—incidence 26%; ***mouth and throat irritation***—incidence 40%; ***rhinitis*** (stuffy nose)—incidence 23%

Note: The frequency of *coughing* and *mouth and throat irritation* decreases with continued use.

Incidence less frequent

Back pain; change in taste; diarrhea; fever; flatulence (passing of gas); ***flu-like symptoms; hiccups; nausea; nicotine withdrawal*** (anxiety; dizziness; feelings of drug dependence; mental depression; pain in muscles; trouble in sleeping; unusual tiredness or weakness); ***pain, general; pain in jaw and neck; paresthesias*** (sensation of burning, numbness, tightness, tingling, warmth or heat); ***sinusitis*** (stuffy nose); ***tooth disorders***

Overdose

For specific information on the agents used in the management of nicotine overdose, see:

- *Atropine* in *Anticholinergics/Antispasmodics (Systemic)* monograph;
- *Barbiturates (Systemic)* monograph;
- *Charcoal, Activated (Oral-Local)* monograph;
- *Lorazepam* in *Benzodiazepines (Systemic)* monograph; and/or
- *Sympathomimetic Agents—Cardiovascular Use (Parenteral-Systemic)* monograph.

For more information on the management of overdose or unintentional ingestion, **contact a Poison Control Center** (see *Poison Control Center Listing*).

The minimum lethal oral dose of nicotine for adults is reported to be 40 to 60 mg.

Clinical effects of overdose

The following effects have been selected on the basis of their potential—clinical significance (possible signs and symptoms in parentheses where appropriate) not necessarily inclusive:

Abdominal pain; bradycardia; cold sweat; confusion; death—due to respiratory paralysis or cardiac failure; ***diarrhea; disturbed hearing and vision; dizziness; extreme exhaustion***—with large overdoses; ***headache; hypotension***—with large overdoses; ***nausea; pale skin; respiratory failure***—with large overdoses; ***salivation; seizures***—at lethal doses; ***tremors; vomiting; weakness***

Treatment of overdose

To decrease absorptionFollowing ingestion of a nicotine inhaler cartridge, activated charcoal should be administered (via nasogastric tube if the patient is unconscious). A saline cathartic or sorbitol may be added to the first dose of activated charcoal. Repeated doses of charcoal should be administered as long as the cartridge remains in the gastrointestinal tract because it will continue to release nicotine. The cartridge may be visualized using a radiograph.

Supportive care—

Administration of lorazepam or barbiturates for seizures, and atropine for excess bronchial secretions, diarrhea, bradycardia, or hypotension; respiratory support for respiratory failure; vigorous fluid support for hypotension and cardiovascular collapse. Vasopressors may be administered if hypotension does not respond to atropine and fluids. Patients in whom intentional overdose is confirmed or suspected should be referred for psychiatric consultation.

Patient Consultation

As an aid to patient consultation, refer to *Advice for the Patient, Nicotine (Inhalation-Systemic)*.

In providing consultation, consider emphasizing the following selected information (» = major clinical significance):

Before using this medication

» Conditions affecting use, especially:

Allergy or hypersensitivity to nicotine or to menthol

Pregnancy—Use is not recommended; spontaneous abortions have been reported; use only if likelihood of smoking cessation justifies the potential risk in pregnant patients who continue to smoke

Breast-feeding—Distributed into breast milk

Use in children—A small amount of nicotine from a nicotine inhaler cartridge can cause poisoning in children; cartridge also can cause choking if swallowed

Other medications, especially theophylline or tricyclic antidepressants

Other medical problems, especially accelerated hypertension, asthma, chronic obstructive pulmonary disease (COPD), life-threatening cardiac arrhythmias, recent myocardial infarction, or severe or worsening angina pectoris

Proper use of this medication

» Reading patient directions carefully before using

Using the nicotine inhaler at or above room temperature (60 °F [16 °C]) because cold temperatures decrease the amount of nicotine inhaled

» Participating in a comprehensive behavioral smoking cessation program

Gradually reducing use of the nicotine inhaler by keeping a tally of, and steadily reducing, daily usage or setting a planned date for stopping use

» Proper dosing

» Proper storage

Precautions while using this medication

» Not smoking during treatment with the nicotine inhaler

» Not using the nicotine inhaler for longer than 6 months

» Not using the nicotine inhaler during pregnancy

» Prevention of unintentional ingestion of nicotine by children or pets to prevent poisoning or choking

Side/adverse effects

Signs of potential side effects, especially allergic reaction and fast or irregular heartbeat

General Dosing Information

It must be emphasized that smoking should be stopped upon initiation of therapy. Continued smoking while using the nicotine inhaler may cause adverse effects as a result of peak nicotine concentrations higher than concentrations found after smoking alone.

If a patient is unable to stop smoking by the fourth week of therapy, treatment should be discontinued because the patient is unlikely to quit on that attempt.

The safety and efficacy of the use of the nicotine inhaler for longer than 6 months has not been evaluated and is not recommended.

To minimize the risk of becoming dependent on the nicotine inhaler, gradual withdrawal from therapy should begin after 3 months of use. Suggested strategies include keeping a tally of, and steadily reducing, daily usage or setting a planned date for stopping use of the nicotine inhaler.

Inhalation Dosage Forms

NICOTINE FOR INHALATION

Usual adult and adolescent dose

Smoking cessation adjunct—

Oral inhalation, initially 6 to 16 cartridges (24 to 64 mg) per day for up to twelve weeks followed by a gradual reduction in dosage over a period of up to twelve weeks.

Note: An inhalation regimen consisting of frequent, continuous puffing for 20 minutes is recommended.

Usual adult and adolescent prescribing limits

16 cartridges per day.

Usual pediatric dose

Safety and efficacy have not been established.

Strength(s) usually available

U.S.—

10 mg (4 mg delivered) per cartridge in a kit containing 42 cartridges (Rx) [*Nicotrol Inhaler*].

Packaging and storage

Store below 30 °C (86 °F). Protect from light.

Auxiliary labeling

- For oral inhalation only.
- Include patient information when dispensing.

Developed: 07/06/1998

NICOTINE Nasal

VA CLASSIFICATION (Primary): AD600

Commonly used brand name(s): *Nicotrol NS*.

Note: For a listing of dosage forms and brand names by country availability, see *Dosage Forms* section(s).

Category

Smoking cessation adjunct.

Indications

Accepted

Nicotine dependence (treatment adjunct)—Nicotine nasal spray is indicated as a temporary aid for cigarette smokers who want to give up smoking. It serves as an alternate source of nicotine and provides relief from nicotine withdrawal symptoms in nicotine-dependent individuals acutely withdrawing from cigarette smoking. It is recommended that nicotine nasal spray be used in conjunction with a comprehensive behavioral smoking cessation program.

Pharmacology/Pharmacokinetics

Physicochemical characteristics

Source—Tobacco plant.
Molecular weight—162.23.
pH—7.
pKa—At 15 °C (59 °F): pKa_1—7.84; pKa_2—3.04.
Solubility—Freely soluble in water.

Mechanism of action/Effect

Nicotine acts as an agonist at the nicotine receptors in the autonomic ganglia, adrenal medulla, neuromuscular junctions, and brain. Nicotine's positive reinforcing properties are believed to be the result of the release of neurotransmitters including acetylcholine, beta-endorphin, dopamine, norepinephrine, serotonin, and others that mediate pleasure, arousal, mood, appetite, and other desirable psychological states.

Other actions/effects

Cardiovascular effects include peripheral vasoconstriction, tachycardia, and elevated blood pressure.

Absorption

Nicotine is absorbed rapidly through the mucous membranes and respiratory tract.

Following administration of two sprays, one in each nostril, approximately 53% enters the systemic circulation.

Distribution

Nicotine is distributed into breast milk; the milk-to-plasma ratio average is 2.9:1.

The volume of distribution following intravenous administration is approximately 2 to 3 L per kg.

Protein binding

Very low (< 5%).

Biotransformation

Primarily hepatic; also metabolized in the kidneys and lungs. More than 20 metabolites have been identified; all are less active than the parent compound. The primary urinary metabolites are cotinine, which comprises 15% of a dose; and trans-3-hydroxycotinine, which comprises 45% of a dose.

Half-life

Elimination—
- Nicotine: 1 to 3 hours.
- Cotinine: 15 to 20 hours.

Absorption—
- Nicotine: Approximately 3 minutes.

Time to peak concentration

4 to 15 minutes.

Peak arterial plasma concentration

5 to 15 nanograms per mL. However, individual plasma nicotine concentrations following administration of nicotine nasal spray may vary widely.

Elimination

Renal, approximately 10% excreted unchanged; up to 30% may be excreted in acidified urine (pH < 5) or with a high urine flow rate. The average plasma clearance is approximately 1.2 L per minute in a healthy adult smoker.

Precautions to Consider

Carcinogenicity

Nicotine does not appear to be carcinogenic in laboratory animals. Inconclusive evidence suggests that cotinine may be carcinogenic in rats.

Tumorigenicity

When given in conjunction with tumor initiators, nicotine and its metabolites increased the incidence of tumors in hamsters and rats.

Mutagenicity

Neither nicotine nor its metabolite, cotinine, was shown to be mutagenic in the Ames *Salmonella* test. Nicotine induced reparable DNA damage in an *Escherichia coli* test system and was shown to be genotoxic in Chinese hamster ovary cells.

Pregnancy/Reproduction

Fertility—In rats and rabbits, nicotine caused a reduction in DNA synthesis, resulting in delayed or inhibited implantation. Rats treated with nicotine during the time of gestation have produced decreased litter sizes.

Pregnancy—Nicotine replacement therapy is not recommended for use during pregnancy and should be used only if the likelihood of smoking cessation justifies the potential risk in pregnant patients who continue to smoke. Pregnant smokers should be encouraged to attempt smoking cessation using educational and behavioral interventions before using pharmacological measures.

Cigarette smoking may cause low birth weight, increased risk of spontaneous abortion, and increased perinatal mortality. Spontaneous abortion during nicotine replacement therapy has been reported, and possibly may be due to the nicotine.

Studies in pregnant rhesus monkeys have shown that nicotine administered intravenously produces acidosis, hypercarbia, and hypotension in the fetus. Nicotine administered intravenously to pregnant ewes reduced breathing movements in the fetal lamb. Teratogenicity has been demonstrated in offspring of mice given toxic doses of nicotine.

FDA Pregnancy Category D.

Labor—Nicotine nasal spray is not recommended for use during labor because its effect on the mother and fetus is not known.

Delivery—Nicotine nasal spray is not recommended for use during delivery.

Breast-feeding

Nicotine is distributed into breast milk. The ability of infants to clear nicotine via hepatic first-pass metabolism is probably lowest at birth. Nicotine concentrations in breast milk may be expected to be lower with nicotine nasal spray than with cigarette smoking. The risk of exposing the infant to nicotine from the nasal spray should be weighed against the risk associated with exposing the infant to nicotine from continued smoking by the mother.

Pediatrics

The amount of nicotine that is tolerated by adult smokers can cause poisoning in children. Use in children is not recommended.

Geriatrics

Appropriate studies on the relationship of age to the effects of nicotine nasal spray have not been performed in the geriatric population. However, 41 patients 60 years of age and older participated in clinical trials, and geriatrics-specific problems that would limit the usefulness of this medication in the elderly are not expected.

Drug interactions and/or related problems

The following drug interactions and/or related problems have been selected on the basis of their potential clinical significance (possible mechanism in parentheses where appropriate)—not necessarily inclusive (» = major clinical significance):

Note: Combinations containing any of the following medications, depending on the amount present, may also interact with this medication.

Acetaminophen or
» Beta-adrenergic blocking agents, such as propranolol or
Caffeine or
Imipramine or
Oxazepam or
Pentazocine or
» Theophylline
(smoking cessation may increase the therapeutic effects of these agents by decreasing metabolism; a decrease in dosage may be necessary)

» Insulin
(smoking cessation may increase the therapeutic effects of insulin by increasing absorption; a decrease in dosage may be necessary)

Nasal decongestants, topical, such as xylometazoline
(concurrent use by patients with rhinitis may prolong the time to peak nicotine concentration by approximately 40%)

Medical considerations/Contraindications

The medical considerations/contraindications included have been selected on the basis of their potential clinical significance (reasons given in parentheses where appropriate)—not necessarily inclusive (» = major clinical significance).

Except under special circumstances, this medication should not be used when the following medical problems exist:

» Allergy or hypersensitivity to nicotine or any component of the nasal spray
» Angina pectoris, severe or worsening or
» Cardiac arrhythmias, life-threatening or
» Myocardial infarction, recent
(use is not recommended)
» Chronic nasal disorders, such as:
Allergy
Polyps, nasal
Rhinitis

Sinusitis
(safety and efficacy have not been established; use is not recommended)

Risk-benefit should be considered when the following medical problems exist:

Angina pectoris or
Cardiac arrhythmias or
Myocardial infarction, history of or
Vasospastic disease, such as:
Buerger's disease
Prinzmetal's angina
Raynaud's phenomena
(patients should be evaluated carefully before beginning therapy with nicotine nasal spray)

Common cold or
Rhinitis, acute
(extent of absorption may be reduced by approximately 10%; peak plasma concentration may be reduced by approximately 20%, and time to peak concentration may be prolonged by approximately 30% in patients with rhinitis)

Diabetes, type 1 or
Hyperthyroidism or
Pheochromocytoma
(nicotine causes release of catecholamines from the adrenal medulla; caution is recommended)

Hepatic function impairment
(nicotine is extensively metabolized in the liver, and its total system clearance is dependent upon blood flow; therefore, reduced clearance should be anticipated)

» Hypertension, accelerated
(risk of progression to malignant hypertension is increased by cigarette smoking; caution is recommended)

Peptic ulcer disease, active
(nicotine delays healing; caution is recommended)

Side/Adverse Effects

The following side/adverse effects have been selected on the basis of their potential clinical significance (possible signs and symptoms in parentheses where appropriate)—not necessarily inclusive:

Those indicating need for medical attention

Incidence more frequent

Feelings of physical dependence—incidence 32%; ***pain in joints; shortness of breath; swelling of gums, mouth, or tongue; tightness in chest; tingling in arms, legs, hands, or feet***

Incidence less frequent

Confusion; fast or irregular heartbeat; nasal blister or ulcer; numbness of nose or mouth; pain in muscles; paresthesias of nose, mouth, or head (burning, tingling, or prickly sensations); ***pharyngitis*** (difficulty in swallowing; dryness or pain in throat)

Note: If *fast or irregular heartbeat* occurs, use of nicotine nasal spray should be discontinued.

Incidence rare

Amnesia; bronchitis; bronchospasm; difficulty in speaking; edema (swelling of feet or lower legs); ***migraine headache; purpura*** (blood-containing blisters on skin); ***skin rash***

Those indicating need for medical attention only if they continue or are bothersome

Incidence more frequent

Back pain; constipation; cough; headache; indigestion; nasal irritation, moderate or severe—incidence 94%; ***nausea; runny nose; sneezing; throat irritation; watery eyes***

Note: The severity of *nasal irritation* usually declines with continued use.

Incidence less frequent

Abdominal pain; acne; burning or irritation in eyes; change in sense of smell, transient; change in sense of taste, transient; dysmenorrhea or menstrual disorders; earache; flatulence; flushing of face; gum problems; hoarseness; itching; nasal congestion; nosebleed, transient; sinus irritation

Incidence rare

Changes in vision; diarrhea; dryness of mouth; hiccups; increased sputum production

Overdose

For specific information on the agents used in the management of nicotine overdose, see:

- *Atropine* in *Anticholinergics/Antispasmodics (Systemic)* monograph;
- *Barbiturates (Systemic)* monograph;
- *Lorazepam* in *Benzodiazepines (Systemic)* monograph; and/or
- *Sympathomimetic Agents—Cardiovascular Use (Parenteral-Systemic)* monograph.

For more information on the management of overdose or unintentional ingestion, **contact a Poison Control Center** (see *Poison Control Center Listing*).

The minimum lethal oral dose of nicotine for adults is reported to be 40 to 60 mg.

Clinical effects of overdose

The following effects have been selected on the basis of their potential clinical significance (possible signs and symptoms in parentheses where appropriate)—not necessarily inclusive:

Abdominal pain; bradycardia; cold sweat; confusion; death—due to respiratory paralysis or cardiac failure; ***diarrhea; disturbed hearing and vision; dizziness; excessive salivation; extreme exhaustion; fast or irregular heartbeat; headache; hypotension; nausea; pale skin; seizures***—at lethal doses; ***tremors; vomiting; weakness***

Treatment of overdose

To decrease absorption—
Following eye contact: Flushing the eyes with a gentle stream of water for 20 minutes.

Supportive care—
Administration of lorazepam or barbiturates for seizures, and atropine for excess bronchial secretions, diarrhea, bradycardia, or hypotension; respiratory support for respiratory failure; vigorous fluid support for hypotension and cardiovascular collapse. Vasopressors may be administered if hypotension does not respond to atropine and fluids. Patients in whom intentional overdose is confirmed or suspected should be referred for psychiatric consultation.

Patient Consultation

As an aid to patient consultation, refer to *Advice for the Patient, Nicotine (Nasal)*.

In providing consultation, consider emphasizing the following selected information (» = major clinical significance):

Before using this medication

» Conditions affecting use, especially:
Allergy or hypersensitivity to nicotine or any component of the nasal spray
Pregnancy—Not recommended during pregnancy; spontaneous abortions have been reported; use only if likelihood of smoking cessation justifies the potential risk in pregnant patients who continue to smoke
Breast-feeding—Distributed into breast milk
Use in children—Use is not recommended
Other medications, especially beta-adrenergic blocking agents, insulin, or theophylline
Other medical problems, especially angina pectoris, severe or worsening; cardiac arrhythmias, life-threatening; chronic nasal disorders; hypertension, accelerated; or myocardial infarction, recent

Proper use of this medication

» Reading patient instructions carefully before using
» Participating in a comprehensive behavioral smoking cessation program
Tapering off use of nicotine nasal spray by using only one half of a dose at a time, skipping doses by not medicating every hour, keeping tally of and steadily reducing daily usage, or setting date for stopping use of nicotine nasal spray
» Proper dosing
» Proper storage

Precautions while using this medication

» Not recommended for use by nonsmokers because of potential for addiction
» Continuing use of nicotine nasal spray for at least 1 week to adapt to the irritant effects of the spray; contacting physician if irritant effects do not lessen after 1 week
» Avoiding contact of nicotine nasal spray with skin, mouth, eyes, and ears
» Not using nicotine nasal spray for longer than 3 months
» Not using nicotine nasal spray during pregnancy
» Prevention of unintentional ingestion of nicotine nasal spray by children or pets to prevent poisoning

Side/adverse effects

Signs of potential side effects, especially feelings of physical dependence; pain in joints; shortness of breath; swelling of gums, mouth, or tongue; tightness in chest; tingling in arms, legs, hands, or feet; confusion; fast or irregular heartbeat; nasal blister or ulcer; numbness of nose or mouth; pain in muscles; paresthesias of nose, mouth, or head; pharyngitis; amnesia; bronchitis; bronchospasm; difficulty in speaking; edema; migraine headache; purpura; and skin rash

General Dosing Information

The necessity for immediate cessation of smoking upon initiation of therapy must be emphasized. Continued smoking while using nicotine nasal spray may cause adverse effects as a result of peak nicotine concentrations higher than concentrations found after smoking alone.

If a patient is unable to stop smoking by the fourth week of therapy, treatment should be discontinued because the patient is unlikely to quit on that attempt.

Because of the risk of addiction, nicotine nasal spray should not be used by nonsmokers.

No optimal strategy for tapering off use of nicotine nasal spray was found during clinical trials. However, suggested strategies include using only one half of a dose at a time, skipping doses by not medicating every hour, keeping a tally of and steadily reducing daily usage, or setting a planned date for stopping use of nicotine nasal spray.

Safety considerations for handling this medication

If even a small amount of nicotine nasal spray comes into contact with the skin, mouth, eyes, or ears, the affected area should be immediately rinsed with water only.

Nasal Dosage Forms

NICOTINE NASAL SOLUTION

Usual adult dose

Smoking cessation adjunct—

Intranasal, initially 1 or 2 mg per hour. Dosage then should be individualized based upon degree of nicotine dependence and occurrence of symptoms of nicotine excess.

Note: One mg of nicotine is delivered by two sprays, one in each nostril.

Usual adult prescribing limits

The minimum recommended dose is 8 mg per day. The maximum recommended dose is 5 mg per hour or 40 mg per day. The maximum recommended duration of therapy is three months.

Usual pediatric dose

Use is not recommended.

Strength(s) usually available

U.S.—

0.5 mg per 50 microliter metered spray (Rx) [*Nicotrol NS* (disodium phosphate; sodium dihydrogen phosphate; citric acid; methylparaben; propylparaben; edetate disodium; sodium chloride; polysorbate 80; aroma; water)].

Packaging and storage

Store below 30 °C (86 °F), unless otherwise specified by manufacturer.

Auxiliary labeling

- For the nose.
- Include patient information when dispensing.

Revised: 08/05/1998

NICOTINE Systemic

VA CLASSIFICATION (Primary): AD600

Commonly used brand name(s): *Commit; Habitrol; NicoDerm CQ; Nicoderm; Nicorette; Nicorette Plus; Nicotrol; Prostep.*

Note: For a listing of dosage forms and brand names by country availability, see *Dosage Forms* section(s).

Category

Smoking cessation adjunct.

Indications

Accepted

Nicotine dependence (treatment adjunct)—Nicotine replacement therapy products (e.g. chewing gum, lozenges, transdermal systems) are indicated as temporary aids for the cigarette smoker who wants to give up smoking. They serve as alternative sources of nicotine and provide relief of nicotine withdrawal symptoms in nicotine-dependent individuals who are acutely withdrawing from cigarette smoking.

It is recommended that nicotine replacement therapy be used in conjunction with comprehensive behavior modification programs that include education, counseling, and psychological support.

Generally, smokers who have a strong physical nicotine dependence are more likely to benefit from the use of these nicotine products. Smoking withdrawal effects such as irritability, drowsiness, fatigue, headache, and nicotine craving are lessened with their use.

Acceptance not established

Nicotine, in conjunction with a 5-aminosalicylic acid compound or other conventional maintenance therapy, has been used in the treatment of ulcerative colitis to ameliorate the condition and relieve symptoms but not induce remission in nonsmoking patients with mild to moderate ulcerative colitis. However, there are insufficient data to support the safety and efficacy of nicotine for this use. (Evidence rating: I)

Nicotine, in conjunction with an antipsychotic such as haloperidol, has been used in the treatment of Gilles de la Tourette's syndrome to decrease the severity and frequency of tics and vocalizations of Tourette's syndrome. However, there are insufficient data to support the safety and efficacy of nicotine for this use. (Evidence rating: II)

Pharmacology/Pharmacokinetics

Physicochemical characteristics

Source—Tobacco plant.

Molecular weight—Nicotine: 162.24.

pKa—

pKa_1: 7.84.

pKa_2: 3.04.

Mechanism of action/Effect

Smoking cessation adjunct—

Nicotine acts as an agonist at the nicotinic cholinergic receptors at the autonomic ganglia, in the adrenal medulla, at neuromuscular junctions, and in the brain. Nicotine's positive reinforcing properties are believed to be the result of the release of neurotransmitters including acetylcholine, beta-endorphin, dopamine, norepinephrine, serotonin, and others that mediate pleasure, arousal, elevated mood, appetite, and other desirable psychological states.

When the gum is chewed, nicotine is displaced from polacrilex by alkaline saliva.

Other actions/effects

Has actions on the chemoreceptors of the aortic and carotid bodies, resulting in reflex vasoconstriction, tachycardia, elevated blood pressure, and stimulation of respiration.

Stimulates sympathetic ganglia and adrenal medulla, causing release of catecholamines, resulting in direct sympathomimetic effects on the heart and peripheral vasculature.

Has actions that tend to reduce blood pressure and heart rate. In low concentrations, stimulates certain chemoreceptors in the pulmonary and coronary circulation, leading to reflex bradycardia and hypotension.

Causes release of antidiuretic hormone (ADH) by stimulation of hypothalamus.

Stimulation of emetic chemoreceptor trigger zone of medulla oblongata and vagal reflex activation may result in vomiting.

Parasympathetic stimulation increases tone and motor activity of the gastrointestinal tract, leading to nausea, vomiting, and occasionally diarrhea.

Effects of nicotine on exocrine glands cause an initial stimulation followed by inhibition of salivary and bronchial secretions.

Action on the central nervous system (CNS) may result in respiratory failure due to both central paralysis and peripheral blockade of muscles of respiration.

Absorption

Chewing gum—

Buccal mucosa: Absorption enhanced by buffering of gum to pH 8.5; rate of absorption is slower than from lungs during smoking.

Stomach: Not absorbed in significant amounts when gum is swallowed because of poor release of nicotine from gum in acidic pH of stomach.

Transdermal systems—

Skin: Well absorbed.

Distribution

Nicotine passes into and accumulates in breast milk. The milk-to-plasma ratio average is 2.9:1.

The volume of distribution following intravenous administration is approximately 2 to 3 L per kg of body weight.

Protein binding
Very low (< 5%).

Biotransformation
Primarily hepatic; smaller amounts are metabolized in the kidneys and lungs. More than 20 metabolites have been identified. All are believed to be less active than the parent compound. Cotinine is the primary metabolite.

Half-life
Following intravenous administration—
Nicotine: 1 to 2 hours.
Cotinine: 15 to 20 hours.
Following removal of the transdermal system, due to continued absorption from the skin depot—
3 to 4 hours.

Time to peak concentration
Chewing gum—
15 to 30 minutes after start of chewing.
Transdermal systems—
4 to 12 hours after application.

Peak plasma concentration
Chewing gum (following a single piece of gum chewed for 30 minutes)—
5 or 10 nanograms per mL (nanograms/mL) with a 2- or 4-mg piece of gum, respectively.
Transdermal systems—
Following application of the 14-mg-per-day system: 6 to 16 nanograms/mL.
Following application of the 21-mg-per-day system: 13 to 19 nanograms/mL.
Following application of the 22-mg-per-day system: 7 to 31 nanograms/mL.

Elimination
Renal, 10 to 20% unchanged; up to 30% may be excreted unchanged in acidified urine (pH < 5) or with high urine flow rates.

Precautions to Consider

Carcinogenicity
Nicotine does not appear to be carcinogenic in laboratory animals. Inconclusive evidence suggests that cotinine, an oxidized metabolite, may be carcinogenic in rats.

Tumorigenicity
When given in combination with tumor initiators, nicotine and its metabolites increased the incidence of tumors in hamsters and rats.

Mutagenicity
Neither nicotine nor its metabolite, cotinine, was shown to be mutagenic in the Ames *Salmonella* test. Nicotine induced reparable DNA damage in an *Escherichia coli* test system. Nicotine was shown to be genotoxic in Chinese hamster ovary cells.

Pregnancy/Reproduction
Fertility—Impaired fertility has been demonstrated in mice following administration of nicotine. In addition, implantation was delayed or inhibited in rats and rabbits by reduction in DNA synthesis that appears to be caused by nicotine. Rats treated with nicotine during the time of gestation have produced decreased litter sizes.

Pregnancy—Nicotine replacement therapy is not recommended during pregnancy and should be used only if the likelihood of smoking cessation outweighs the potential risks that continued smoking poses to the fetus. Pregnant smokers should be encouraged to attempt smoking cessation using education and behavioral interventions before using pharmacological measures.

Cigarette smoking may cause low birth weight, increased risk of spontaneous abortion, and increased perinatal mortality. Spontaneous abortion during nicotine replacement therapy has been reported, and possibly may be due to the nicotine.

Studies in pregnant rhesus monkeys have shown that nicotine administered intravenously decreases uterine blood flow and produces acidosis, hypercarbia, and hypotension in the fetus. A study in sheep has shown that nicotine at a dose of 0.25 mg per kg of body weight administered intravenously to the ewe resulted in reduced breathing movements in the fetal lamb. Teratogenicity has been demonstrated in offspring of mice given toxic doses of nicotine.

Nicotine chewing gum—FDA Pregnancy Category C.

Nicotine transdermal systems—FDA Pregnancy Category D.

Breast-feeding
Nicotine is distributed into and accumulates in breast milk and is not recommended for use by breast-feeding women.

Pediatrics
Appropriate studies on the relationship of age to the effects of nicotine have not been performed in children up to 18 years of age. Safety and efficacy have not been established.

Small amounts of nicotine can cause serious harm in children. Even nicotine transdermal systems that have been used still contain enough nicotine to cause toxicity in children.

Adolescents
Appropriate studies on the relationship of age to the effects of nicotine have not been performed in adolescents up to 18 years of age. However, no specific problems in nicotine-dependent adolescents have been documented to date. Nicotine replacement therapy should be considered only when there is clear evidence of nicotine dependence and a desire to quit smoking.

Geriatrics
Studies performed in a limited number of patients 60 years of age or older have not demonstrated geriatrics-specific problems that would limit the usefulness of nicotine in the elderly.

Dental
When used over an extended period of time, nicotine gum may cause severe occlusal stress because its viscosity is heavier than that of ordinary chewing gum. Nicotine gum can cause loosening of inlays or fillings, can stick to dentures, and can cause damage to oral mucosa and natural teeth. The use of hard sugarless candy between doses of gum is recommended to help provide oral stimulation required by some patients. Also, some temporomandibular joint dysfunction and pain have been associated with excessive chewing.

Drug interactions and/or related problems
The following drug interactions and/or related problems have been selected on the basis of their potential clinical significance (possible mechanism in parentheses where appropriate)—not necessarily inclusive (» = major clinical significance):

Note: Combinations containing any of the following medications, depending on the amount present, may also be affected by cessation of smoking.

Acetaminophen or
» Bronchodilators, xanthine-derivative, except dyphylline or
Caffeine or
Imipramine or
Oxazepam or
Pentazocine or
» Propoxyphene or
» Propranolol, and possibly other beta-adrenergic blocking agents
(smoking cessation may increase therapeutic effects of these agents by decreasing metabolism, thereby increasing serum concentrations; a decrease in dosage may be necessary)

» Alpha-adrenergic blocking agents, such as labetalol and prazosin
(smoking cessation may increase the therapeutic effects of these agents as a result of the decrease in circulating catecholamines; a decrease in dosage may be necessary)

» Insulin
(smoking cessation and concurrent therapy with nicotine chewing gum, transdermal systems, or other smoking deterrents, such as lobeline sulfate and silver acetate, may increase the therapeutic effects of insulin by increasing absorption, thereby increasing serum concentrations; a decrease in insulin dosage may be necessary when a patient with diabetes who is taking insulin suddenly stops smoking)

» Sympathomimetic agents, such as isoproterenol and phenylephrine
(smoking cessation may decrease the therapeutic effects of these agents as a result of the decrease in circulating catecholamines; an increase in dosage may be necessary)

Medical considerations/Contraindications
The medical considerations/contraindications included have been selected on the basis of their potential clinical significance (reasons given in parentheses where appropriate)—not necessarily inclusive (» = major clinical significance).

Except under special circumstances, this medication should not be used when the following medical problems exist:

» Angina pectoris, severe or
» Cardiac arrhythmias, life-threatening or
» Cerebrovascular accident, recent or
» Post–myocardial infarction
(may be exacerbated by action on heart of catecholamines released from adrenal medulla)

Risk-benefit should be considered when the following medical problems exist:

Angina pectoris or

Cardiac arrhythmias or
Diabetes, type 1 or
» Hypertension or
Hyperthyroidism or
Myocardial infarction, history of or
Pheochromocytoma or
Vasospastic diseases, such as Buerger's disease and Prinzmetal's (or variant) angina
(increases in blood pressure, heart rate, and plasma glucose concentrations may result from effects of nicotine-induced catecholamine release)
(risk of progression to malignant hypertension in patients with accelerated hypertension)

Peptic ulcer disease, active
(nicotine delays healing; caution is recommended)

Sensitivity to nicotine or to any component of the product

For the chewing gum only (in addition to the above)
Dental problems or
Temporomandibular joint (TMJ) disorder
(injury to teeth or aggravation of TMJ may result from mechanical effects of chewing gum)
Esophagitis, history of or
Inflammation of mouth or throat
(may be exacerbated)

For the transdermal systems only (in addition to the above)
Skin diseases, such as atopic or eczematous dermatitis
(transdermal systems may be irritating)

Patient monitoring

The following may be especially important in patient monitoring (other tests may be warranted in some patients, depending on condition; » = major clinical significance):

» Evaluation of progress of smoking cessation
(recommended periodically during therapy to assess therapeutic efficacy of nicotine replacement products and to re-evaluate their use)

Side/Adverse Effects

Note: Side effects are dose-dependent; extremely high doses can produce toxic symptoms, even in nicotine-tolerant individuals.

The following side/adverse effects have been selected on the basis of their potential clinical significance (possible signs and symptoms in parentheses where appropriate)—not necessarily inclusive:

Those indicating need for medical attention

Incidence more frequent
For chewing gum only
Injury or irritation to mouth, teeth, or dental work
Note: Nicotine gum is stickier and of heavier viscosity than ordinary gum, making it harder to chew.

Incidence less frequent
For all nicotine replacement products
Hypertension

Incidence rare
For all nicotine replacement products
Fast or irregular heartbeat; hypersensitivity reactions, local or generalized, including edema (swelling); ***erythema*** (redness); ***pruritus*** (itching); ***rash; or urticaria*** (hives)
Note: If *fast or irregular heartbeat* or *hypersensitivity reactions* occur, use of nicotine replacement products should be discontinued. Further exposure in patients who have experienced a hypersensitivity reaction could result in serious allergic reactions to all forms of nicotine, including cigarettes.

Those indicating need for medical attention only if they continue or are bothersome

Incidence more frequent
For all nicotine replacement products
Headache, mild; increased appetite
For chewing gum only
Belching—may be minimized by modifying chewing technique; ***increased watering of mouth, mild; jaw muscle ache; sore mouth or throat***
For transdermal systems only
Erythema, pruritus, and/or burning at site of application (redness, itching, and/or burning)—usually subsides within 24 hours
Note: If *erythema, pruritus, or burning at site of application* is severe or persists, use of nicotine transdermal systems should be discontinued.

Incidence less frequent or rare
For all nicotine replacement products
Change in sense of taste; coughing, increased; dizziness or lightheadedness, mild; drowsiness; dryness of mouth; dysmenorrhea (menstrual pain); ***gastrointestinal effects, such as abdominal or stomach pain; constipation; diarrhea; flatulence*** (passing of gas); ***indigestion, mild; loss of appetite; and nausea or vomiting; muscle or joint pain; sweating, increased; trouble in sleeping or abnormal dreams; unusual irritability or nervousness***
Note: If *trouble in sleeping or abnormal dreams* occur when the transdermal system is worn for 24 hours, it should be taken off at bedtime (after approximately 16 hours) and replaced upon arising the next day.
For chewing gum only
Hiccups; hoarseness
For lozenge only
Heartburn (pain in the chest below the breastbone; belching; feeling of indigestion); ***hiccups***

Overdose

For specific information on the agents used in the management of nicotine overdose, see:
- *Atropine* in *Anticholinergics/Antispasmodics (Systemic)* monograph;
- *Barbiturates (Systemic)* monograph;
- *Charcoal, Activated (Oral-Local)* monograph;
- *Ipecac (Oral-Local)* monograph;
- *Lorazepam* in *Benzodiazepines (Systemic)* monograph; and/or
- *Sympathomimetic Agents—Cardiovascular Use (Parenteral-Systemic)* monograph.

For more information on the management of overdose or unintentional ingestion, **contact a Poison Control Center** (see *Poison Control Center Listing*).

The minimum lethal oral dose of nicotine for adults is reported to be 40 to 60 mg.

Overdose may occur if many pieces of gum are chewed simultaneously or in rapid succession. Overdose also may occur if several transdermal systems are worn simultaneously. Absorption may be reduced by the early nausea and vomiting known to occur with excessive nicotine intake. If gum is swallowed without chewing, nicotine will not be released or absorbed in significant amounts because of the acid pH of the stomach.

Clinical effects of overdose

The following effects have been selected on the basis of their potential clinical significance (possible signs and symptoms in parentheses where appropriate)—not necessarily inclusive:

Early effects of overdose (in possible order of occurrence)
Nausea and/or vomiting; increased watering of mouth, severe; abdominal pain, severe; diarrhea, severe; pale skin; cold sweat; headache, severe; dizziness, severe; disturbed hearing and vision; tremor; confusion; weakness, severe

Late effects of overdose (in possible order of occurrence)
Extreme exhaustion; fainting; hypotension; difficulty in breathing, severe; fast, weak, or irregular pulse; seizures; death—due to respiratory paralysis or cardiac failure

Treatment of overdose

For chewing gum only—
To decrease absorption: In a conscious patient, if emesis has not occurred, vomiting may be induced with ipecac syrup. In an unconscious patient, a clear airway must be secured and ventilatory support may be required. Gastric lavage may be performed followed by administration of a suspension of activated charcoal that is to be left in the stomach.
To enhance elimination: A saline cathartic will hasten the gastrointestinal passage of the gum.

For transdermal systems only—
To decrease absorption: Remove the patch and flush the skin surface with water and dry. Do not use soap because it may increase nicotine absorption. If the patch has been ingested, administer activated charcoal. In an unconscious patient, the airway should be secured before administering activated charcoal via a nasogastric tube. Repeated doses of charcoal should be administered as long as the patch remains in the gastrointestinal tract because it will continue to release nicotine.
To enhance elimination: A saline cathartic or sorbitol may be added to the first dose of activated charcoal to speed passage of the patch.

For all nicotine replacement products—
Supportive care: Administration of anticonvulsants such as lorazepam or barbiturates for seizures, and atropine for excessive bronchial secretions or diarrhea; respiratory support for respiratory failure; intensive fluid support for hypotension and cardiovascular collapse. Vasopressors may be administered if hypotension does not respond to atropine and fluids. Patients in whom intentional overdose is confirmed or suspected should be referred for psychiatric consultation.

Patient Consultation

As an aid to patient consultation, refer to *Advice for the Patient, Nicotine (Systemic).*

In providing consultation, consider emphasizing the following selected information (» = major clinical significance):

Before using this medication

» Conditions affecting use, especially:
Sensitivity to nicotine or to any component of the product
Pregnancy—Not recommended during pregnancy; spontaneous abortions have been reported; use only if the likelihood of smoking cessation outweighs the potential risks that continued smoking poses to the fetus
Breast-feeding—Distributed into and accumulates in breast milk
Use in children—Small amounts of nicotine can cause serious harm in children
Dental—Chewing gum may cause severe occlusive stress resulting in damage to teeth, dentures, or dental work
Other medications, especially alpha-adrenergic blocking agents, insulin, propoxyphene, propranolol, sympathomimetic agents, or xanthine-derivative bronchodilators (except dyphylline)
Other medical problems, especially severe angina pectoris, life-threatening cardiac arrhythmias, recent cerebrovascular accident, hypertension, or post-myocardial infarction state

Proper use of this medication

Proper administration of the chewing gum
» Reading patient instructions carefully before using
» Using as directed on the label; participating in a behavioral modification program to increase likelihood of success in quitting
» Using gum only when there is an urge to smoke; chewing gum slowly and intermittently (chewing it several times, then "parking" it between cheek and gums; chewing again after tingling sensation subsides) for 30 minutes
» Not chewing too fast, not chewing more than one piece of gum at a time, and not chewing more than one piece within an hour, to avoid adverse effects or overdose
» Not drinking acidic beverages, such as citrus juices, coffee, soft drinks, or tea within 15 minutes before or while chewing gum

Compliance with chewing gum therapy
» Reducing number of pieces chewed each day over a 2- to 3-month period
» Importance of carrying gum at all times during therapy
Using hard sugarless candy between doses of gum to help alleviate urge to smoke between doses of chewing gum

Proper administration of lozenge
» Reading patient instructions carefully before using
» Using as directed on the label; participating in a behavioral modification program to increase likelihood of success in quitting
» Stop all smoking when beginning therapy with nicotine replacement lozenge.
» Do not eat or drink for 15 miuntes before using nicotine replacement lozenge.
» Suck on the lozenge slowly until it dissolves. Do not bite or chew the lozenge like a hard candy. Do not swallow the lozenge.
» Stop using the lozenges after 12 weeks.
» Do not use nicotine replacement lozenges if you continue to smoke, chew tobacco, use snuff or any other product containing nicotine, such as nicotine gum or patch.

Compliance with lozenge therapy
» Reducing number of lozenges used each day over a 2- to 3-month period
» Importance of carrying lozenges at all times during therapy

Proper administration of the transdermal systems
» Reading patient instructions carefully before using
» Participating in a behavioral modification program to increase likelihood of success in quitting
» Keeping patch in sealed pouch until ready to apply to skin
» Not trimming or cutting patch
Applying to clean, dry skin area on upper arm or torso free of oil, hair, scars, cuts, burns, or irritation
Pressing the patch firmly in place with palm for about 10 seconds; making sure there is good contact, especially around edges
Keeping patch in place even during showering, bathing, or swimming; replacing patches that have fallen off
» Washing hands with plain water after handling patches; soap will enhance transdermal absorption of nicotine
» Alternating application sites; not keeping patch on for more than 24 hours because it loses strength and may irritate the skin
Folding used patches in half with adhesive sides together, and replacing in protective pouch or aluminum foil; disposing of patch carefully, out of reach of children or pets
Getting into the habit of changing patch at the same time each day to help increase compliance
Removing the patch during strenuous exercise to prevent increased nicotine plasma concentrations
Removing the 24-hour patch at bedtime (after 16 hours) if you begin having abnormal dreams or disturbed sleep and putting a new patch on upon awakening the next day
» Proper dosing
» Proper storage

Precautions while using this medication

» Not smoking during treatment with nicotine replacement products
» Not using nicotine replacement products during pregnancy
» Preventing accidental ingestion of nicotine replacement products by children or pets to avoid poisoning

For the chewing gum only:
» Not chewing more than 24 pieces of gum a day
» Not using gum for longer than 12 weeks to avoid physical dependence; consulting physician if need for gum continues after 12 weeks
» Discontinuing use and consulting physician or dentist if excessive sticking to dental work occurs; gum may damage dental work or dentures

For the lozenge only:
» Not using more than 20 lozenges a day
» Not using lozenge for longer than 12 weeks; consulting physician if need for lozenge continues after 12 weeks

For the transdermal systems only:
» Calling physician and not applying new patch if evidence of allergic reaction; knowing that allergic reaction to nicotine patch could cause reaction to use of cigarettes or other products containing nicotine
» Not using patches for longer than 12 weeks; consulting physician if need for patch continues after 12 weeks

Side/adverse effects

Signs of potential side effects, especially injury or irritation to mouth, teeth, or dental work (with gum only); hypertension; fast or irregular heartbeat; and hypersensitivity reactions

General Dosing Information

The necessity of immediate cessation of smoking upon initiation of therapy must be emphasized. Continued smoking while using nicotine replacement products may cause adverse effects as a result of peak nicotine concentrations higher than those found after smoking alone.

For chewing gum only

When there is an urge to smoke, one piece of gum is chewed very slowly and intermittently (chewing it several times, then "parking" it between the cheek and gums; chewing again after the tingling sensation subsides) for about 30 minutes until most of the nicotine is released.

The amount of nicotine released depends on the rate of chewing and the amount of time the saliva is in contact with the resin.

No liquids, especially acidic beverages, should be consumed within 15 minutes before or while chewing a piece of gum because a decrease in the pH of the mouth may interfere with the absorption of nicotine.

The use of nicotine polacrilex for longer than 6 months may be an indication that this medication is being used as a substitute source of nicotine to maintain nicotine dependence. However, while the use of nicotine replacement products is preferable to a return to smoking, these products should be continued beyond 6 months only if the patient believes that discontinuation of replacement therapy will definitely result in an immediate resumption of smoking.

For lozenge only

Avoid eating or drinking for 15 minutes before using the lozenge. Effectiveness of lozenge may be reduced by some beverages.

Suck on the lozenge slowly until it dissolves. Do not chew it or bite it like a hard candy. Do not swallow the lozenge.

Stop using the lozenge after 12 weeks. The patient should talk to their healthcare professional if they still feel the need to use the lozenge.

Do not continue to smoke, chew tobacco, use snuff or any other product containing nicotine (e.g., nicotine gum or patch).

For transdermal systems only

If a patient is unable to stop smoking by the fourth week of therapy, treatment should be discontinued, as the patient is unlikely to quit on that attempt.

It is recommended that nicotine transdermal systems be removed during, and a new system applied following, strenuous exercise. If left on, nicotine plasma concentrations may be increased as a result of increased absorption of nicotine from the skin depot, increased skin temperature, and increased cutaneous vasodilation and perfusion.

The use of nicotine transdermal systems for longer than 12 weeks in patients who have stopped smoking has not been evaluated and is not recommended.

Most manufacturers supply supportive instructional materials and provide telephone information accessible by patients.

Oral Dosage Forms

NICOTINE POLACRILEX GUM USP

Usual adult and adolescent dose

Smoking cessation adjunct—

Patients smoking fewer than twenty-five cigarettes a day, use the 2-mg strength.

Patients smoking twenty-five or more cigarettes a day, use the 4-mg strength.

Weeks one to six—Oral, one piece of chewing gum every one to two hours.

Weeks seven to nine—Oral, one piece of chewing gum every two to four hours.

Weeks ten to twelve—Oral, one piece of chewing gum every four to eight hours.

Note: Patients should use at least nine pieces of chewing gum daily during the first six weeks of therapy.

Usual adult prescribing limits

Twenty-four pieces of chewing gum a day.

Usual pediatric dose

Safety and efficacy have not been established.

Usual geriatric dose

See *Usual adult and adolescent dose.*

Strength(s) usually available

U.S.—

2 mg (OTC) [*Nicorette* (flavors; glycerin; gum base; sodium bicarbonate; sodium carbonate; sorbitol)].

4 mg (OTC) [*Nicorette* (flavors; glycerin; gum base; sodium carbonate; sorbitol; D&C Yellow No. 10)].

Canada—

2 mg (OTC) [*Nicorette* (gum; menthol; magnesium oxide; peppermint oil; sodium bicarbonate; sodium carbonate; xylitol)].

4 mg (Rx) [*Nicorette Plus* (gum; magnesium oxide; menthol; peppermint oil; sodium carbonate; xylitol; D&C Yellow No. 10)].

Packaging and storage

Store between 15 and 30 °C (59 and 86 °F), unless otherwise specified by manufacturer. Protect from light.

Auxiliary labeling

- Chew slowly.
- Do not chew more than 24 pieces in one day.

NICOTINE POLACRILEX LOZENGES

Usual adult and adolescent dose

Smoking cessation adjunct—

Patients who smoke their first cigarette within 30 minutes of waking up should take/use the 4 mg strength.

Patients who smoke their first cigarette after 30 minutes of waking up should take/use the 2 mg strength.

Weeks one to six—Oral, suck one lozenge every one to two hours.

Weeks seven to nine—Oral, suck one lozenge every two to four hours.

Weeks ten to twelve—Oral, suck one lozenge every four to eight hours.

Usual adult prescribing limits

Twenty lozenges a day.

Usual pediatric dose

Safety and efficacy have not been established in children up to 18 years of age.

Usual geriatric dose

See *Usual adult and adolescent dose.*

Strength(s) usually available

U.S.—

Note: Lozenges are sugar-free.

2 mg (OTC) [*Commit*].

4 mg (OTC) [*Commit*].

Canada—

Not commercially available.

Packaging and storage

Store between 15 and 30 °C (59 and 86 °F) unless otherwise specified by manufacturer. Protect from light.

Auxiliary labeling

- Dissolve slowly in mouth
- Do not swallow whole.
- Keep out of reach of children and pets.
- Please read the patient information leaflet enclosed.

Topical Dosage Forms

NICOTINE TRANSDERMAL SYSTEM USP

Usual adult and adolescent dose

Smoking cessation adjunct; depending on the product—

Patients weighing more than 100 pounds (45 kg), smoking more than ten cigarettes a day, and without cardiovascular disease—

Sixteen-hour system: Topical, to intact skin:

Nicotrol: One 15-mg system applied for sixteen hours per day for six weeks. Alternatively, one 15-mg system applied for sixteen hours per day for eight weeks. Patients who have successfully abstained from smoking for eight weeks should have their dose reduced to one 10-mg system applied for sixteen hours per day for two weeks. The dosage should be further reduced to one 5-mg system applied for sixteen hours per day for two weeks.

Twenty-four-hour system: Topical, to intact skin:

Habitrol: Initially one 21-mg system per day for three to eight weeks. Patients who have successfully abstained from smoking should have their dose reduced to one 14-mg system per day for the next two to four weeks. The dosage should be further reduced to one 7-mg system per day for the following two to four weeks.

Nicoderm, NicoDerm CQ, or generic: Initially one 21-mg system per day for six weeks. Patients who have successfully abstained from smoking should have their dose reduced to one 14-mg system per day for two weeks. The dosage should be further reduced to one 7-mg system per day for two weeks.

Prostep: Initially one 22-mg system per day for four to eight weeks. Patients who have successfully abstained from smoking should have their dose reduced to one 11-mg system per day for two to four weeks.

Patients weighing less than 100 pounds (45 kg), smoking fewer than ten cigarettes a day, or with cardiovascular disease—

Sixteen-hour system: Topical, to intact skin:

Nicotrol: One 15-mg system applied for sixteen hours per day for six weeks.

Twenty-four-hour system: Topical, to intact skin:

Habitrol: Initially one 14-mg system per day for four to eight weeks. Patients who have successfully abstained from smoking should have their dose reduced to one 7-mg system per day for the next two to four weeks.

Nicoderm, NicoDerm CQ, or generic: Initially one 14-mg system per day for six weeks. Patients who have successfully abstained from smoking should have their dose reduced to one 7-mg system per day for two to four weeks.

Prostep: One 11-mg system per day for four to eight weeks.

Usual pediatric dose

Safety and efficacy have not been established.

Usual geriatric dose

See *Usual adult and adolescent dose.*

Strength(s) usually available

U.S.—

16-hour System:

15 mg (OTC) [*Nicotrol*].

24-hour Systems:

7 mg (OTC) [*NicoDerm CQ;* GENERIC].

14 mg (OTC) [*NicoDerm CQ;* GENERIC].

21 mg (OTC) [*NicoDerm CQ;* GENERIC].

Canada—
- 16-hour Systems:
  - 5 mg (OTC) [*Nicotrol*].
  - 10 mg (OTC) [*Nicotrol*].
  - 15 mg (OTC) [*Nicotrol*].
- 24-hour Systems:
  - 7 mg (OTC) [*Nicoderm*].
  - 7 mg (OTC) [*Habitrol*].
  - 11 mg (OTC) [*Prostep*].
  - 14 mg (OTC) [*Nicoderm*].
  - 14 mg (OTC) [*Habitrol*].
  - 21 mg (OTC) [*Nicoderm*].
  - 21 mg (OTC) [*Habitrol*].
  - 22 mg (OTC) [*Prostep*].

Note: Nicotine transdermal systems are designed to release a constant, controlled dose of nicotine over the period during which they are applied to the skin. Systems are labeled by the dose actually absorbed by the patient, not by the total nicotine content.

Packaging and storage
Store between 15 and 30 °C (59 and 86 °F), unless otherwise specified by manufacturer. Store in the intact, light-resistant pouch. Because nicotine is volatile, the system may lose strength if removed from pouch prematurely.

Auxiliary labeling
- For external use only.
- Follow the manufacturer's directions carefully.

Revised: 04/21/2003

NIFEDIPINE—See *Calcium Channel Blocking Agents (Systemic)*

NILUTAMIDE—See *Antiandrogens, Nonsteroidal (Systemic)*

NIMODIPINE—See *Calcium Channel Blocking Agents (Systemic)*

NISOLDIPINE Systemic

VA CLASSIFICATION (Primary/Secondary): CV200/CV409

Commonly used brand name(s): *Sular*.

Note: For a listing of dosage forms and brand names by country availability, see *Dosage Forms* section(s).

Category
Antihypertensive.

Indications

Accepted
Hypertension (treatment)—Nisoldipine is indicated for the treatment of hypertension. It may be used alone or in combination with other antihypertensive agents.

For additional information on initial therapeutic guidelines related to the treatment of hypertension, see *Appendix III*.

Pharmacology/Pharmacokinetics

Physicochemical characteristics
Molecular weight—388.4.

Mechanism of action/Effect
Nisoldipine is a dihydropyridine calcium channel blocking agent. Nisoldipine inhibits the influx of calcium ions across cellular membranes in vascular smooth muscle; this action results in arterial vasodilation. Vascular resistance and, consequently, blood pressure are thereby reduced and this also leads to a mild or transient increase in heart rate. Because nisoldipine is more selective for calcium channels in vascular smooth muscle than in cardiac muscle, vasodilation occurs mainly in coronary and peripheral arteries. *In vitro,* nisoldipine also has a negative inotropic effect, but this effect has not been seen in patients receiving the drug. Nisoldipine has no clinically important chronotropic effects and no significant electrocardiographic effects.

Absorption
Absolute bioavailability of nisoldipine (from the extended-release dosage form) is about 5%. Metabolism of nisoldipine occurs in the gut wall (which is partially the reason for its low bioavailability) and decreases from the proximal to the distal parts of the intestine. Food with a high fat content increases the bioavailability of the extended-release formulation of nisoldipine, resulting in an increase in the peak plasma concentration (C_{max}) of up to 300%; however, the area under the plasma concentration-time curve (AUC) is decreased by about 25%. This phenomenon appears to be specific for the extended-release formulation (the only formulation currently available) and is thought to be due to increased release of nisoldipine proximally. Therefore, it is recommended that the extended-release form of nisoldipine not be taken with a high-fat meal. Grapefruit juice has been shown to interfere with the metabolism of nisoldipine, causing approximately a mean threefold increase in C_{max} and approximately a mean twofold increase in the AUC. It is recommended that nisoldipine not be administered with grapefruit juice.

Protein binding
Very high (> 99%).

Biotransformation
Nisoldipine is metabolized extensively and undergoes metabolism primarily by hydroxylation of the isobutyl ester. Although five major urinary metabolites have been identified, only one in plasma is considered to be active (with an activity of about 10% of the parent compound) and appears in plasma at concentrations approximately equal to that of the parent compound. Nisoldipine is believed to be metabolized by the cytochrome P450 enzyme system, although the specific enzyme responsible for nisoldipine metabolism has not been identified. It should be noted, however, that the cytochrome P450 3A4 enzyme is responsible for the metabolism of other dihydropyridines.

Half-life
Elimination—

Extended-release dosage form (postabsorption clearance): Range, 7 to 12 hours.

Time to peak concentration
Extended-release dosage form: 6 to 12 hours after dosing.

Elimination
Renal—60 to 80%, primarily as metabolites.

In dialysis—

Nisoldipine is highly protein bound and does not appear to be removable by dialysis.

Precautions to Consider

Cross-sensitivity and/or related problems
Patients hypersensitive to other dihydropyridine calcium channel blocking agents may also be hypersensitive to nisoldipine.

Carcinogenicity
A study in male mice given a mean dose of 163 mg per kg of body weight (mg/kg) per day of nisoldipine showed an increased frequency of stomach papilloma. This dose represents 16 times the maximum recommended human dose (MRHD) of 60 mg per day on a mg per square meter of body surface area (mg/m^2) basis. No evidence of stomach neoplasia was observed at lower doses (up to 58 mg/kg per day).

Tumorigenicity
No evidence of tumorigenicity was observed in male and female rats given mean daily dietary doses of nisoldipine of up to 82 and 111 mg/kg for up to 24 months, or in female mice given mean doses of nisoldipine of up to 217 mg/kg per day for up to 21 months. In male and female rats, these doses represent 16 and 19 times the MRHD on a mg/m^2 basis, respectively. In female mice, these doses represent 20 times the MRHD on a mg/m^2 basis.

Mutagenicity
Nisoldipine was negative for genotoxicity in the Ames test and the CHO/HGRPT assay for mutagenicity. Nisoldipine was negative for clastogenicity in the *in vivo* mouse micronucleus test and in the *in vitro* CHO cell test for clastogenicity.

Pregnancy/Reproduction
Fertility—No effect on fertility was seen when nisoldipine was given to male and female rats at doses of up to 30 mg/kg per day. This dose represents approximately five times the MRHD on a mg/m^2 basis.

Pregnancy—Adequate and well-controlled studies in pregnant women have not been done. Nisoldipine should be used in pregnancy only if the potential benefit outweighs the potential risk to the fetus. Neither teratogenicity nor fetotoxicity was seen at doses of nisoldipine that were not maternally toxic. Fetotoxicity was seen in rats and rabbits given maternally-toxic doses (as determined by reduced maternal body weight gain) of nisoldipine. In pregnant rats, increased fetal resorption (postimplantation loss) was observed at nisoldipine doses of 100 mg/kg per day and decreased fetal weight was observed at nisoldipine doses of both 30 and 100 mg/kg per day. These doses are about 5 and 16 times the MRHD, respectively, on a mg/m² basis. Decreased fetal and placental weights were observed in pregnant rabbits given nisoldipine doses of 30 mg/kg per day. This dose represents approximately 10 times the MRHD on a mg/m² basis. A study in which pregnant monkeys (both treated and control) had high rates of abortion and mortality showed forelimb and vertebral abnormalities (not previously seen in control monkeys of the same strain) in the only surviving fetus of the monkeys treated with 100 mg/kg of nisoldipine per day. This dose represents approximately 30 times the MRHD on a mg/m² basis.

FDA Pregnancy Category C.

Breast-feeding

It is not known whether nisoldipine is distributed into breast milk. Nisoldipine is not recommended in mothers who are breast-feeding.

Pediatrics

No information is available on the relationship of age to the effects of nisoldipine in pediatric patients. Safety and efficacy have not been established.

Geriatrics

Elderly patients have been reported to have twofold to threefold higher plasma concentrations (peak plasma concentration [C_{max}] and area under the plasma concentration-time curve [AUC]) than do younger subjects.

Drug interactions and/or related problems

The following drug interactions and/or related problems have been selected on the basis of their potential clinical significance (possible mechanism in parentheses where appropriate)—not necessarily inclusive (» = major clinical significance):

Note: Combinations containing any of the following medications, depending on the amount present, may also interact with this medication.

Beta-adrenergic blocking agents
(concurrent use of propranolol with a commercially unavailable immediate-release form of nisoldipine has been reported to blunt the mild increase in heart rate caused by nisoldipine; additionally, the blood pressure-lowering effect of nisoldipine may be additive when used concurrently)

Cimetidine
(concurrent use with cimetidine has resulted in a 30 to 45% increase in the area under the plasma concentration-time curve [AUC] and peak plasma concentration [C_{max}] of nisoldipine)

» Grapefruit juice
(concurrent use with grapefruit juice has been reported to significantly increase the bioavailability of nisoldipine. In a study with 12 subjects, administration of nisoldipine with grapefruit juice resulted in a mean increase in C_{max} of 300% and a mean increase in AUC of 200%, but increases as high as 700% and 500%, respectively, also occurred; grapefruit juice or other grapefruit products should not be taken before or after administration of nisoldipine)

Quinidine
(concurrent use with quinidine has resulted in a 26% decrease in the AUC of nisoldipine)

Ranitidine
(concurrent use with ranitidine has resulted in a 15 to 20% decrease in the AUC of nisoldipine)

Medical considerations/Contraindications

The medical considerations/contraindications included have been selected on the basis of their potential clinical significance (reasons given in parentheses where appropriate)—not necessarily inclusive (» = major clinical significance).

Except under special circumstances, this medication should not be used when the following medical problem exists:

» Hypersensitivity to nisoldipine or other dihydropyridine calcium channel blocking agents

Risk-benefit should be considered when the following medical problems exist:

» Coronary artery disease
(initiating therapy or increasing the dosage of a calcium channel blocking agent in these patients [and particularly in patients with severe obstructive coronary artery disease] has been rarely associated with an increase in the frequency, duration, and/or severity of angina, or an acute myocardial infarction; in clinical studies, these effects occurred in 1.5% of patients treated with nisoldipine and in 0.9% of patients given placebo)

Congestive heart failure
(although nisoldipine has not been shown to have a negative inotropic effect in patients with New York Heart Association (NYHA) Class II, III, or IV heart failure, it should be used with caution in these patients and in patients with impaired ventricular function)

Hepatic function impairment
(plasma concentrations of nisoldipine have increased fivefold in patients with cirrhosis; lower starting and maintenance doses of nisoldipine are recommended in these patients)

Patient monitoring

The following may be especially important in patient monitoring (other tests may be warranted in some patients, depending on condition; » = major clinical significance):

» Blood pressure measurements
(blood pressure should be carefully monitored during initial administration of nisoldipine and during dosage increases, particularly in patients currently taking medications that lower blood pressure, in elderly patients, and in patients with impaired hepatic function)

Side/Adverse Effects

The following side/adverse effects have been selected on the basis of their potential clinical significance (possible signs and symptoms in parentheses where appropriate)—not necessarily inclusive:

Those indicating need for medical attention

Incidence more frequent

Edema, peripheral (swelling of ankles, feet, and lower legs)—incidence is 22% and is dose-related

Incidence less frequent

Chest pain; hypotension (dizziness, lightheadedness, or fainting); ***rash***

Note: Excessive *hypotension* can occur during initial titration or at the time of an increase in the dosage of nisoldipine.

Incidence rare

Hypersensitivity reaction, which may include angioedema (swelling of the arms, face, legs, lips, tongue, and/or throat); ***shortness of breath; tachycardia*** (fast heart rate); ***chest tightness; hypotension*** (dizziness, lightheadedness, or fainting); ***and/or rash***

Those indicating need for medical attention only if they continue or are bothersome

Incidence more frequent

Headache—incidence 22% (placebo, 15%)

Incidence less frequent

Dizziness; nausea; pharyngitis (hoarseness; sore throat); ***palpitations*** (heartbeat sensations); ***sinusitis*** (headache; stuffy nose)

Overdose

For more information on the management of overdose or unintentional ingestion, **contact a Poison Control Center** (see *Poison Control Center Listing*).

Treatment of overdose

No information is available on the clinical effects of overdose with nisoldipine.

For cardiovascular support—May include elevation of extremities, careful administration of intravenous calcium, vasopressors, and/or fluids.

To enhance elimination—Because nisoldipine is highly protein bound, it is not likely to be removed by dialysis; however, plasmapheresis may be beneficial.

Monitoring—Cardiovascular and respiratory functions should be monitored.

Supportive care—Patients in whom intentional overdose is confirmed or suspected should be referred for psychiatric consultation.

Patient Consultation

As an aid to patient consultation, refer to *Advice for the Patient, Nisoldipine (Systemic)*.

In providing consultation, consider emphasizing the following selected information (» = major clinical significance):

Before using this medication

» Conditions affecting use, especially:
Hypersensitivity to nisoldipine or other dihydropyridine calcium channel blocking agents
Pregnancy—Administration not recommended unless potential benefit outweighs the potential risk

Breast-feeding—Not known if distributed into breast milk; not recommended in nursing mothers

Use in the elderly—Elderly patients may have two-fold to three-fold higher plasma concentrations than younger subjects

Other medications or substances, especially grapefruit juice

Other medical problems, especially coronary artery disease

Proper use of this medication

Compliance with therapy; taking medication at the same time each day to maintain the therapeutic effect

» Swallowing tablet whole without dividing, chewing, or crushing

» Nisoldipine should not be taken with a high-fat meal or with grapefruit juice or other grapefruit products because of the risk of an increase in the bioavailability of nisoldipine

» Proper dosing

Missed dose: Taking as soon as possible; not taking if almost time for next scheduled dose; not doubling doses

» Proper storage

Precautions while using this medication

» Visiting the physician regularly to check progress

» Caution when driving or doing other things requiring alertness because of possible dizziness, lightheadedness, or fainting

Side/adverse effects

Signs of potential side effects, especially peripheral edema, chest pain, hypotension, rash, and a hypersensitivity reaction which may include angioedema, shortness of breath, tachycardia, and/or chest tightness

General Dosing Information

Administration of nisoldipine with a high-fat meal should be avoided to prevent the significant increase in peak nisoldipine plasma concentration (C_{max}) that may result with that combination. Likewise, grapefruit juice and grapefruit products should not be taken before or after administration of nisoldipine in order to avoid significant increases in C_{max} and the area under the plasma concentration-time curve (AUC).

Oral Dosage Forms

NISOLDIPINE EXTENDED-RELEASE TABLETS

Usual adult dose

Hypertension—

Oral, initially 20 mg once daily. The dose may be increased in 10 mg increments per week, or longer intervals, until blood pressure is controlled. The usual maintenance dosage is 20 to 40 mg once daily.

Patients older than 65 years of age and patients with impaired hepatic function should receive an initial dose of 10 mg daily. Lower maintenance doses should be used in patients with hepatic function impairment.

Usual adult prescribing limits

60 mg once daily.

Usual pediatric dose

Safety and efficacy have not been established

Strength(s) usually available

U.S.—

10 mg (Rx) [*Sular* (hydroxypropylcellulose; lactose; corn starch; crospovidone; microcrystalline cellulose; sodium lauryl sulfate; povidone; magnesium stearate; hydroxypropylmethylcellulose; polyethylene glycol; ferric oxide; titanium dioxide)].

20 mg (Rx) [*Sular* (hydroxypropylcellulose; lactose; corn starch; crospovidone; microcrystalline cellulose; sodium lauryl sulfate; povidone; magnesium stearate; hydroxypropylmethylcellulose; polyethylene glycol; ferric oxide; titanium dioxide)].

30 mg (Rx) [*Sular* (hydroxypropylcellulose; lactose; corn starch; crospovidone; microcrystalline cellulose; sodium lauryl sulfate; povidone; magnesium stearate; hydroxypropylmethylcellulose; polyethylene glycol; ferric oxide; titanium dioxide)].

40 mg (Rx) [*Sular* (hydroxypropylcellulose; lactose; corn starch; crospovidone; microcrystalline cellulose; sodium lauryl sulfate; povidone; magnesium stearate; hydroxypropylmethylcellulose; polyethylene glycol; ferric oxide; titanium dioxide)].

Packaging and storage

Store below 30 °C (86 °F). Protect from light and moisture. Dispense in tight, light-resistant containers.

Auxiliary labeling

- Do not take other medicines without your doctor's advice.
- Swallow tablets whole. Do not break, crush, or chew.

Developed: 01/04/1999

NITAZOXANIDE Systemic†

VA CLASSIFICATION (Primary): AP109

Commonly used brand name(s): *Alinia*.

Note: For a listing of dosage forms and brand names by country availability, see *Dosage Forms* section(s).

†Not commercially available in Canada.

Category

Antiprotozoal.

Indications

Note: Bracketed information in the *Indications* section refers to uses that are not included in U.S. product labeling.

General Considerations

Nitazoxanide and its metabolite, tizoxanide, are active *in vitro* in inhibiting the growth of trophozoites of *Giardia lamblia* and sporozoites and oocysts of *Cryptosporidium parvum*.

Accepted

Diarrhea (treatment)—Nitazoxanide is indicated for the treatment of diarrhea caused by *Cryptosporidium parvum* in pediatric patients between 1 and 11 years of age. Nitazoxanide is also indicated for the treatment of diarrhea caused by *Giardia lamblia*.

[Parasitic infections, intestinal (treatment)]—Nitazoxanide is indicated for the treatment of intestinal parasitic infections caused by *Ancylostoma duodenale, Ascaris lumbricoides, Balantidium coli, Blastocystis hominis, Cyclospora cayetanensis, Entamoeba histolytica/E. dispar, Enterobius vermicularis, Hymenolepis nana, Isospora belli, Taenia saginata*, or *Trichuris trichiura*.

Unaccepted

HIV-infected or Immunodeficient Patients—Nitazoxanide tablets and oral suspension have not been studied for the treatment of diarrhea caused by *Giardia lamblia* in HIV-infected or immunodeficient patients. Nitazoxanide tablets and oral suspension have not been shown to be superior to placebo for the treatment of diarrhea caused by *Cryptosporidium parvum* in HIV-infected or immunodeficient patients.

Pharmacology/Pharmacokinetics

Physicochemical characteristics

Source—Synthetic antiprotozoal agent.

Molecular weight—307.3.

Solubility—Poorly soluble in ethanol, practically insoluble in water.

Mechanism of action/Effect

The antiprotozoal activity is believed to be due to the interference with the pyruvate:ferredoxin oxireductase (PFOR) enzyme-dependent electron transfer reaction which is essential to anaerobic energy metabolism. Studies have shown that the PFOR enzyme from *Giardia lamblia* directly reduces nitazoxanide by transfer of electrons in the absence of ferredoxin. The DNA-derived PFOR protein sequence of *Cryptosporidium parvum* appears to be similar to that of *Giardia lamblia*. Interference with the PFOR enzyme-dependent electron transfer reaction may not be the only pathway by which nitazoxanide exhibits antiprotozoal activity.

Absorption

AUC (in mcg hr per mL), oral suspension, child (1 to 11 years), single dose with food: 11.7 to 13.5 for tizoxanide; 16.9 to 19 for tizoxanide glucuronide

AUC (in mcg hr per mL), tablet, adult ($\geq$ 12 years), single dose with food: 39.5 to 41.9 for tizoxanide; 46.5 to 63 for tizoxanide glucuronide

The relative bioavailability of the suspension compared to the tablet was 70%. When administered with food the AUC and C_{max} increased by two-fold and 50%, respectively, for the tablet and 45 to 50% and $\leq$ 10%, respectively, for the oral suspension.

Protein binding
Very High (greater than 99%); bound to proteins

Biotransformation
Rapidly hydrolyzed to an active metabolite, tizoxanide (desacetyl-nitazoxanide); followed by conjugation, primarily by glucuronidation to tizoxanide glucuronide.

Time to peak concentration
Maximum plasma concentrations of tizoxanide and tizoxanide glucuronide: 1 to 4 hours

Peak plasma concentration:
C_{max} (mcg/mL), oral suspension, child (1 to 11 years), single dose with food: 3 to 3.11 for tizoxanide; 2.84 to 3.64 for tizoxanide glucuronide

C_{max} (mcg/mL), tablet, adult ($\geq$ 12 years), single dose with food: 9.1 to 10.6 for tizoxanide; 7.3 to 10.5 for tizoxanide glucuronide

Elimination
Renal: approximately 33% as Tizoxanide and tizoxanide glucuronide
Fecal: approximately 66% as Tizoxanide
Biliary: Tizoxanide and tizoxanide glucuronide

Precautions to Consider

Carcinogenicity
Long-term carcinogenicity studies have not been conducted.

Mutagenicity
Nitazoxanide was not genotoxic in the Chinese hamster ovary (CHO) cell chromosomal aberration assay or the mouse micronucleus assay. Nitazoxanide was genotoxic in one tester strain in the Ames bacterial mutagenicity assay.

Pregnancy/Reproduction
Fertility—No evidence of impaired fertility was found in rats or rabbits.

Pregnancy—Adequate and well controlled studies in humans have not been done.

Studies in animals have not shown that nitazoxanide causes adverse effects in the fetus.

FDA Pregnancy Category B

Breast-feeding
It is not known whether nitazoxanide is distributed in human milk. Because many drugs are distributed in human milk, caution should be exercised when nitazoxanide is administered to a nursing woman.

Pediatrics
Safety and efficacy of nitazoxanide oral suspension have not been established in pediatric patients less than one year of age.

A single nitazoxanide tablet contains a greater amount of nitazoxanide than is recommended for pediatric dosing and should not be used in pediatric patients 11 years and younger.

Geriatrics
Although appropriate studies on the relationship of age to the effects of nitazoxanide have not been performed in the geriatric population, no geriatrics-specific problems have been documented. However, the greater frequency of decreased hepatic, renal, or cardiac function, and of concomitant disease or other drug therapy in elderly patients should be considered.

Drug interactions and/or related problems
The following drug interactions and/or related problems have been selected on the basis of their potential clinical significance (possible mechanism in parentheses where appropriate)—not necessarily inclusive (» = major clinical significance):

Note: Combinations containing any of the following medications, depending on the amount present, may also interact with this medication.

Caution should be used when administering nitazoxanide concurrently with other highly plasma protein-bound drugs with narrow therapeutic indices, as competition for binding sites may occur.

Laboratory value alterations
The following have been selected on the basis of their potential clinical significance (possible effect in parentheses where appropriate)—not necessarily inclusive (» = major clinical significance).

With physiology/laboratory test values

Alanine aminotransferase (ALT [SGPT])
Creatinine
(levels may be increased)

Medical considerations/Contraindications
The medical considerations/contraindications included have been selected on the basis of their potential clinical significance (reasons given in parentheses where appropriate)—not necessarily inclusive (» = major clinical significance).

Except under special circumstances, this medication should not be used when the following medical problem exists:

» Hypersensitivity to nitazoxanide

Risk-benefit should be considered when the following medical problems exist:

Biliary disease or
Hepatic disease or
Renal disease
(the effects of nitazoxanide on these conditions have not been studied; caution is recommended)

» Diabetes mellitus
(the oral suspension contains 1.48 grams of sucrose per 5 mL; diabetic patients or their care givers should monitor the effect on blood glucose and modify hypoglycemic therapy appropriately)

» HIV positive patients or
» Immunocompromised patients
(Safety and effectiveness have not been established in HIV positive or immunodeficient patients.)

Side/Adverse Effects
The following side/adverse effects have been selected on the basis of their potential clinical significance (possible signs and symptoms in parentheses where appropriate)—not necessarily inclusive:

Those indicating need for medical attention only if they continue or are bothersome
Incidence more frequent

Abdominal pain (stomach pain)

Incidence less frequent

Diarrhea; headache; vomiting

Incidence rare

Anorexia (loss of appetite; weight loss); ***appetite increase; discolored urine; dizziness; enlarged salivary glands; eye discoloration***—pale yellow; ***fever; flatulence*** (bloated full feeling; excess air or gas in stomach or intestines; passing gas); ***infection; malaise*** (general feeling of discomfort or illness; unusual tiredness or weakness); ***nausea; pruritus*** (itching skin); ***rhinitis*** (stuffy nose; runny nose; sneezing); ***sweating***

Overdose
For more information on the management of overdose or unintentional ingestion, **contact a poison control center** (see *Poison Control Center Listing*).

Clinical effects of overdose
Single oral doses of up to 4000 mg nitazoxanide in a tablet formulation have been administered to healthy adult volunteers without significant adverse effects.

Treatment of overdose
To decrease absorption—
Emptying the stomach with gastric lavage may be appropriate soon after oral administration.

Specific treatment—
There is no specific antidote. Treatment is symptomatic and supportive.
Patients should be carefully observed following an overdose of nitazoxanide.

Supportive care—
Treatment should be primarily symptomatic and supportive.
Patients in whom intentional overdose is confirmed or suspected should be referred for psychiatric consultation.

Patient Consultation
As an aid to patient consultation, refer to *Advice for the Patient, Nitazoxanide (Systemic)*.

In providing consultation, consider emphasizing the following selected information (» = major clinical significance):

Before using this medication
» Conditions affecting use, especially:
Hypersensitivity to nitazoxanide
Pregnancy—FDA Pregnancy Category B

Use in children—Safety and effectiveness of nitazoxanide oral suspension in pediatric patients less than one year of age have not been established. A single nitazoxanide tablet contains a greater amount of nitazoxanide than is recommended for pediatric dosing and should not be used in patients 11 years or younger.

Use in the elderly—Appropriate studies in the elderly have not been done. Caution is advised due to age-related decreases in hepatic, renal, or cardiac function.

Other medications, especially highly plasma protein-bound drugs with narrow therapeutic indices (competition for binding sites may occur)

Other medical conditions, especially diabetes mellitus (suspension contains sucrose), HIV positive patients, or immunocompromised patients

Proper use of this medication

Taking with meals

Shaking oral suspension well before each dose

Importance of using a calibrated oral syringe or spoon to accurately measure each dose.

Discarding any unused portion of reconstituted oral suspension after 7 days

» Proper dosing

Missed dose: Take as soon as possible; not taking if almost time for next dose; not doubling doses

» Proper storage

Side/adverse effects

Signs of potential side effects, especially discolored urine

General Dosing Information

Diabetic patients and their caregivers should be aware that the oral suspension contains 1.48 grams of sucrose per 5 mL.

Diet/Nutrition

Nitazoxanide should be taken with food.

Oral Dosage Forms

Note: Bracketed uses in the *Dosage Forms* section refer to categories of use and/or indications that are not included in U.S. product labeling.

NITAZOXANIDE FOR ORAL SUSPENSION

Usual adult and adolescent dose

Diarrhea caused by *Cryptosporidium parvum*—

Safety and efficacy have not been established in children older than 11 years of age or in adults.

Note: Safety and efficacy have not been established in HIV-positive or immunodeficient patients.

Diarrhea caused by *Giardia lamblia*—

Oral, 500mg every 12 hours with food for 3 days.

Note: Safety and efficacy have not been established in HIV-positive or immunodeficient patients.

[Intestinal parasitic infections]—

Oral, 500 mg every 12 hours for 3 days.

Usual pediatric dose

Diarrhea—

Infants less than one year of age: Safety and efficacy have not been established.

Children 12 to 47 months of age: Oral, 100 mg every 12 hours for 3 days.

Children 4 to 11 years of age: Oral, 200 mg every 12 hours for 3 days.

Children 12 years of age or older: See *Usual adult and adolescent dose*.

[Intestinal parasitic infections]—

Infants less than one year of age: Safety and efficacy have not been established.

Children 12 to 47 months of age: Oral, 100 mg every 12 hours for 3 days.

Children 4 to 11 years of age: Oral, 200 mg every 12 hours for 3 days.

Children 12 years of age or older: See *Usual adult and adolescent dose*.

Strength(s) usually available

U.S.—

100 mg per 5 mL (when reconstituted according to manufacturer's instructions) (Rx) [*Alinia* (available in a 60-mL bottle; sodium benzoate; sucrose; xanthan gum; microcrystalline cellulose and carboxymethylcellulose sodium; anhydrous citric acid; sodium citrate dihydrate; acacia gum; sugar syrup; FD&C Red #40; natural strawberry flavoring)].

Canada—

Not commercially available.

Packaging and storage

Store the unsuspended powder and the reconstituted oral suspension at 25 °C; excursions permitted to 15 and 30 °C (59 and 86 °F). Store the reconstituted solution in a tightly-closed container.

Preparation of dosage form

To prepare nitazoxanide for oral suspension, tap bottle until all powder flows freely, add approximately half of the total 48-mL of water required for reconstitution and shake vigorously to suspend powder. Add remainder of water and again shake vigorously.

Stability

The reconstituted oral suspension may be stored for 7 days.

Auxiliary labeling

- Shake well before each administration.
- Take with food.
- Discard any unused portion after 7 days.

Additional information

The oral suspension is pink and strawberry flavored.

NITAZOXANIDE TABLETS

Usual adult and adolescent dose

Diarrhea caused by *Giardia lamblia*—

Oral, one tablet every 12 hours with food for 3 days.

Note: Safety and efficacy have not been established in HIV-positive or immunodeficient patients.

[Intestinal parasitic infections]—

Oral, 500 mg every 12 hours for 3 days.

Usual pediatric dose

Diarrhea—

Oral tablet should not be used in pediatric patients 11 years or younger.

[Intestinal parasitic infections]—

Infants less than one year of age: Safety and efficacy have not been established.

Children 1 to 11 years of age: Oral tablet should not be used in pediatric patients 11 years or younger.

Children 12 years of age or older: See *Usual adult and adolescent dose*.

Strength(s) usually available

U.S.—

500 mg (Rx) [*Alinia* (maize starch; pregelatinized corn starch; hydroxypropyl methylcellulose; sucrose; sodium starch glycolate; talc; magnesium stearate; soy lecithin; polyvinyl alcohol; xanthan gum; titanium dioxide; FD&C Yellow No. 10 aluminum lake; FD&C Yellow No. 6 aluminum lake; FD&C Blue No. 2 aluminum lake)].

Canada—

Not commercially available.

Packaging and storage

Store tablets at 25 °C; excursions permitted to 15 and 30 °C (59 and 86 °F).

Auxiliary labeling

- Take with food.

Revised: 10/26/2004
Developed: 04/07/2003

NITISINONE Systemic†

VA CLASSIFICATION (Primary): HS452

Commonly used brand name(s): *Orfadin*.

Note: For a listing of dosage forms and brand names by country availability, see *Dosage Forms* section(s).

†Not commercially available in Canada.

Category

Tyrosine degradation inhibitor.

Indications

Accepted

Hereditary tyrosinemia type 1 [HT-1] (treatment adjunct)—Nitisinone is indicated as an adjunct to dietary restriction of tyrosine and phenylalanine in the treatment of hereditary tyrosinemia type 1.

Pharmacology/Pharmacokinetics

Physicochemical characteristics

Molecular weight—329.23.

Solubility—Nitisinone is practically insoluble in water, soluble in 2M sodium hydroxide and in methanol, and sparingly soluble in alcohol.

Mechanism of action/Effect

Nitisinone is a competitive inhibitor (although nitisinone binds so tightly as to functionally be non-competitive) of 4-hydroxyphenyl-pyruvate dioxygenase, an enzyme upstream of fumarylacetoacetate hydrolyase [FAH] in the tyrosine catabolic pathway. By inhibiting the normal catabolism of tyrosine in patients with hereditary tyrosinemia type 1 [HT-1], nitisinone prevents the accumulation of the catabolic intermediates maleylacetoacetate and fumarylacetoacetate. In patients with HT-1, these catabolic intermediates are converted to the toxic metabolites succinylacetone and succinylacetoacetate, which are responsible for the observed liver and kidney toxicity. Succinylacetone can also inhibit the porphyrin synthesis pathway leading to the accumulation of 5-aminolevulinate, a neurotoxin responsible for the porphyric crises characteristic of HT-1.

Plasma concentration

Capsule and liquid formulations are bioequivalent in both the plasma concentration and C_{max}

The effects of food on the pharmacokinetics of nitisinone has not been studied.

Half-life

Terminal—54 hours

Time to peak concentration

Oral administration as a capsule—3 hours

Oral administration as a liquid—15 minutes

Precautions to Consider

Carcinogenicity

Studies to determine the carcinogenic potential of nitisinone have not been done in animals.

Mutagenicity

Nitisinone was not mutagenic in the Ames test.

Pregnancy/Reproduction

Pregnancy—Adequate reproductive toxicity studies have not been conducted with nitisinone. It is not known if nitisinone can produce harm to the fetus if administered to pregnant women. Nitisinone should only be given to a pregnant woman if clearly needed.

In rats given 100 mg per kg per day, (12 times the recommended clinical dose based on relative body surface area), reduced litter size, decreased pup weight at birth and decreased survival of pups after birth was demonstrated.

FDA Pregnancy Category C

Breast-feeding

It is not known whether nitisinone is distributed into human breast milk. However, rats exposed to nitisinone via breast milk showed signs of ocular toxicity and lower body weight, which suggests that nitisinone is distributed into the breast milk of rats.

Pediatrics

Appropriate studies performed to date in patients from birth to 21.7 years of age (median age 9 months) have not demonstrated pediatrics-specific problems that would limit the usefulness of nitisinone in children. HT-1 is presently a disease of the pediatric population.

Geriatrics

No information is available on the relationship of age to the effects of nitisinone in geriatric patients. However, elderly patients are more likely to have an age-related decrease in hepatic, renal, or cardiac function, which may require cautious dosage selection starting at the low end of the dosing range.

Pharmacogenetics

The effects of gender and race on the pharmacokinetics of nitisinone have not been studied.

Drug interactions and/or related problems

No drug-drug interaction studies have been conducted with nitisinone.

Laboratory value alterations

The following have been selected on the basis of their potential clinical significance (possible effect in parentheses where appropriate)—not necessarily inclusive (» = major clinical significance).

With physiology/laboratory test values

Hepatic enzymes

(may be elevated)

Medical considerations/Contraindications

No contraindicated medical conditions have been reported in product information for nitisinone.

Patient monitoring

The following may be especially important in patient monitoring (other tests may be warranted in some patients, depending on condition; » = major clinical significance):

» Hepatic function, including

Alpha-fetoprotein, serum

(regular liver monitoring by imaging (ultrasound, computerized tomography, magnetic resonance imaging) and laboratory tests, including serum alpha-fetoprotein concentration is recommended; an increase in serum alpha-fetoprotein concentration may be a sign of inadequate treatment, and an exponential increase in serum alfa-fetoprotein or signs of nodules in the liver should be promptly evaluated for potential liver neoplasia)

» Phosphate, serum

(should be measured as a screening test for patients with renal involvement at risk of secondary hypophosphatemia and rickets.)

» Platelet count and

White blood cell count

(platelet and white blood cell count should be monitored regularly during nitisinone therapy because of the risk of transient thrombocytopenia and leukopenia.)

» Succinylacetone, urine

(monitoring is recommended to guide nitisinone dosage adjustments)

» Tyrosine, plasma

(plasma tyrosine levels should be kept below 500 micromoles per liter in order to avoid toxic effects to the eyes, skin and nervous system.)

Side/Adverse Effects

The following side/adverse effects have been selected on the basis of their potential clinical significance (possible signs and symptoms in parentheses where appropriate)—not necessarily inclusive:

Those indicating need for medical attention

Incidence more frequent

Liver failure (headache; stomach pain; vomiting; dark-colored urine; general feeling of tiredness or weakness; light-colored stools; yellow eyes or skin); ***neoplasm, hepatic*** (bloated abdomen; dull, achy, upper abdominal pain; loss of appetite; unexplained weight loss)

Incidence less frequent

Blepharitis (redness, swelling, and/or itching of eyelid); ***cataracts*** (blindness; blurred vision; decreased vision); ***conjunctivitis*** (redness, pain, swelling of eye, eyelid, or inner lining of eyelid burning; dry or itching eyes; drainage from eyes, excessive tearing from eyes); ***corneal opacity*** (blindness; blurred vision; decreased vision); ***dermatitis, exfoliative*** (blisters on skin; chills; fever; general feeling of discomfort or illness; red, thickened, or scaly skin; swollen and/or painful glands; unusual bruising); ***dry skin; epistaxis*** (bloody nose; unexplained nosebleeds); ***eye pain; keratitis*** (irritation or inflammation of eye); ***leukopenia*** (black, sticky stools; chest pain or discomfort; chills; cough; fever; painful or difficult urination; shortness of breath; sore throat; sores, ulcers, or white spots on lips or in mouth; swollen glands; unusual bleeding or bruising; unusual tiredness or weakness); ***photophobia*** (blurred vision; change in color vision; difficulty seeing at night; increased sensitivity of eyes to sunlight); ***porphyria*** (darkening of urine; fluid-filled skin blisters; itching of the skin; light-colored stools; sensitivity to the sun; skin thinness; yellow eyes or skin); ***pruritus*** (itching skin); ***rash, maculopapular*** (rash with flat lesions or small raised lesions on the skin); ***thrombocytopenia*** (black, tarry stools; blood in urine or stools; pinpoint red spots on skin; unusual bleeding or bruising)

Incidence rare

Brain tumor (change in personality; changes in vision; confusion; headache; problems with walking or talking; seizures; vomiting; weakness); ***bronchitis*** (cough producing mucus; difficulty breathing; shortness of breath; tightness in chest; wheezing); ***cyanosis*** (bluish color of fingernails, lips, skin, palms, or nail beds); ***dehydration*** (confusion; decreased urination; dizziness; dry mouth; fainting; increase in heart rate; lightheadedness; rapid breathing; sunken eyes; thirst; unusual tiredness or weakness; wrinkled skin); ***enanthema*** (skin rash found mostly on mucous membranes such as eyes and mouth); ***encephalopathy*** (agitation; back pain; blurred vision; coma; confusion; dizziness; drowsiness; fever; headache; irritability; mood or mental changes; seeing things that are not there; seizures; stiff neck; unusual tiredness or weakness; vomiting); ***fracture, pathologic*** (pain or swelling in arms or legs without any injury); ***gastroenteritis*** (abdominal or stomach pain; diarrhea; loss of appetite; nausea; weakness); ***hemorrhage, gastrointestinal*** (black, tarry stools; bloody stools; vomiting of blood or material that looks like coffee grounds); ***hepatic function disorder*** (dark urine; light-colored stools; loss of appetite; nausea and vomiting; unusual tiredness; yellow eyes or skin; fever with or without chills; stomach pain); ***hyperkinesia*** (increase in body movements); ***hypoglycemia*** (anxiety; chills; cold sweats; cool, pale skin; headache; increased hunger; nausea; nervousness; shakiness); ***infection; liver enlargement*** (full feeling in upper abdomen; pain in upper abdomen); ***melena*** (bloody or black, tarry stools); ***otitis*** (earache; redness or swelling in ear); ***respiratory insufficiency*** (pale or blue lips, fingernails, or skin; difficult or troubled breathing; irregular, fast or slow, or shallow breathing; shortness of breath); ***seizures; septicemia*** (chills; confusion; dizziness; lightheadedness; fainting; fast heartbeat; fever; rapid, shallow breathing); ***thirst, increased***

Those indicating need for medical attention only if they continue or are bothersome

Incidence less frequent or rare

Abdominal pain; alopecia (hair loss; thinning of hair); ***amenorrhea*** (absent, missed, or irregular menstrual periods; stopping of menstrual bleeding); ***diarrhea; gastritis*** (burning feeling in chest or stomach; tenderness in stomach area; stomach upset; indigestion); ***headache; nervousness; somnolence*** (sleepiness or unusual drowsiness); ***tooth discoloration***

Overdose

For more information on the management of overdose or unintentional ingestion, **contact a poison control center** (see *Poison Control Center Listing*).

Accidental ingestion of nitisinone by individuals eating normal diets not restricted in tyrosine and phenylalanine will result in elevated tyrosine levels. In volunteers given a single 1 mg per kg dose of nitisinone, the plasma tyrosine level reached a maximum of 1200 micromoles per liter from 48 to 120 hours after dosing. After a washout period of 14 days, the mean value of plasma tyrosine was still 808 micromoles per liter. Fasted samples obtained several weeks later showed tyrosine levels back to normal. Nitisinone was generally well tolerated in these studies. There were no reports of changes in vital signs or laboratory data of any clinical significance. There was one report of sensitivity to sunlight.

Treatment of overdose

No information is available about specific treatment for an overdose of nitisinone. Restriction of tyrosine and phenylalanine in the diet should limit toxicity associated with tyrosinemia.

Monitoring—

Monitor for potential adverse events.

Supportive care—

Treatment should be symptomatic and supportive.

Patients in whom intentional overdose is confirmed or suspected should be referred for psychiatric consultation.

Patient Consultation

As an aid to patient consultation, refer to *Advice for the Patient, Nitisinone (Systemic)*.

In providing consultation, consider emphasizing the following selected information (» = major clinical significance):

Proper use of this medication

» Taking at least one hour before a meal

» For young children, opening capsules and suspending contents in a small amount of water, formula or apple sauce immediately before use.

» Proper dosing

Missed dose: Taking as soon as possible; not taking if almost time for next dose; not doubling doses

» Proper storage: Keeping capsules refrigerated

Precautions while using this medication

» Importance of maintaining a dietary restriction of tyrosine and phenylalanine while taking nitisinone.

» Reporting unexplained eye symptoms, rash, jaundice or excessive bleeding to the prescribing physician immediately.

» Regular visits to physician to check progress during therapy.

» Importance of keeping scheduled appointments with nutritionist

» Possible eye photosensitivity; wearing sunglasses that block ultraviolet light.

Side/adverse effects

Signs of potential side effects, especially liver failure, hepatic neoplasm, blepharitis, cataracts, conjunctivitis, corneal opacity, exfoliative dermatitis, dry skin, epistaxis, eye pain, keratitis, leukopenia, photophobia, porphyria, maculopapular rash, thrombocytopenia, brain tumor, bronchitis, cyanosis, dehydration, enanthema, encephalopathy, pathologic fracture, gastroenteritis, gastrointestinal hemorrhage, hepatic function disorder, hyperkinesia, hypoglycemia, infection, liver enlargement, melena, otitis, pruritus, respiratory insufficiency, seizures, septicemia, and increased thirst.

General Dosing Information

Treatment with nitisinone should be initiated by a physician experienced in the treatment of hereditary tyrosinemia type 1.

Slit-lamp examination of the eyes should be performed before initiation of nitisinone treatment and at regular intervals (every year) during treatment.

Patients who develop photophobia, eye pain, or signs of inflammation such as redness, swelling or burning of the eyes during treatment with nitisinone should undergo slit-lamp re-examination and immediate measurement of the plasma tyrosine concentration.

Nitisinone dosage should not be adjusted in order to lower the plasma tyrosine concentration, since the HT-1 metabolic defect may result in deterioration of the patient's clinical condition.

Patients and their caregivers should be advised to immediately report unexplained eye symptoms, rash, jaundice or excessive bleeding.

Diet/Nutrition

A more restricted diet should be implemented if the plasma tyrosine level is above 500 micromoles per liter.

Patients and their caregivers should be advised of the need to maintain dietary restriction of tyrosine and phenylalanine when taking nitisinone to treat hereditary tyrosinemia type 1.

A nutritionist skilled in managing children with inborn errors of metabolism should be employed to design a low-protein diet deficient in tyrosine and phenylalanine.

Since the effect of food is unknown, nitisinone should be taken at least one hour before a meal.

Oral Dosage Forms

NITISINONE CAPSULES

Usual adult dose

Tyrosine degradation inhibitor—

Oral, 1 mg per kg of body weight per day as a recommended initial dose divided for morning and evening administration. The total dose may be split unevenly in order to limit the total number of capsules given at each administration.

Note: The dose of nitisinone should be adjusted in each patient.—Nitisinone treatment should lead to normalized porphyrin metabolism (i.e., normal erythrocyte PBG-synthase activity and urine 5-ALA). Succinylacetone should not be detectable in urine or plasma. If the biochemical parameters (except plasma succinylacetone) are not normalized within one month after start of nitisinone treatment, the dose should be increased to 1.5 mg per kg of body weight per day. For plasma succinylacetone, it may take up to three months before the level is normalized after the start of nitisinone treatment. A dose of 2 mg per kg of body weight per day may be needed once liver function has improved.

Usual adult and adolescent prescribing limits

Initial: 1 mg per kg of body weight per day divided in a morning and afternoon dose

Maintenance: Up to 2 mg per kg of body weight per day

Usual pediatric dose

See *Usual adult and adolescent dose*.

Usual pediatric prescribing limits

See *Usual adult prescribing limits*

Strength(s) usually available

U.S.—

2 mg (Rx) [*Orfadin* (pregelatinized starch)].

5 mg (Rx) [*Orfadin* (pregelatinized starch)].

10 mg (Rx) [*Orfadin* (pregelatinized starch)].

Canada—

Not commercially available.

Packaging and storage

Store between 2 and 8 °C (36 and 46 °F).

Preparation of dosage form

For patients who cannot take oral solids—

For young children, capsules may be opened and the contents suspended in a small amount of water, formula, or apple sauce immediately before use.

Auxiliary labeling

- Keep refrigerated
- Take on an empty stomach, 1 hour before or 2 to 3 hours after eating

Revised: 06/12/2002
Developed: 04/18/2002

NITRATES Systemic

This monograph includes information on the following: 1) Isosorbide Dinitrate; 2) Isosorbide Mononitrate; 3) Nitroglycerin.

VA CLASSIFICATION (Primary/Secondary):

Isosorbide dinitrate—CV250/CV900
Isosorbide mononitrate—CV250
Nitroglycerin—CV250/CV402; CV900

Commonly used brand name(s): *Apo-ISDN*[1]; *Cedocard-SR*[1]; *Coradur*[1]; *Coronex*[1]; *Deponit*[3]; *Dilatrate-SR*[1]; *IMDUR*[2]; *ISDN*[1]; *ISMO*[2]; *Isordil*[1]; *Isordil Tembids*[1]; *Isordil Titradose*[1]; *Minitran*[3]; *Monoket*[2]; *Nitro-Bid*[3]; *Nitro-Bid IV*[3]; *Nitro-Dur*[3]; *Nitrocot*[3]; *Nitrodisc*[3]; *Nitrogard*[3]; *Nitroglyn E-R*[3]; *Nitroject*[3]; *Nitrol*[3]; *Nitrolingual*[3]; *Nitrong SR*[3]; *Nitro-par*[3]; *Nitrostat*[3]; *Nitro-time*[3]; *Sorbitrate*[1]; *Transderm-Nitro*[3]; *Tridil*[3].

Another commonly used name is: Glyceryl trinitrate [Nitroglycerin].

Note: For a listing of dosage forms and brand names by country availability, see *Dosage Forms* section(s).

Category

Note: All of the nitrates have similar pharmacologic actions; however, clinical uses among specific agents may vary because of actual pharmacokinetic differences, availability of specific testing, and/or availability of clinical-use data.

Antianginal—Isosorbide Dinitrate; Isosorbide Mononitrate; Nitroglycerin.
Antihypertensive—Nitroglycerin Injection.
Vasodilator, congestive heart failure—Isosorbide Dinitrate; Nitroglycerin

Indications

Note: Bracketed information in the *Indications* section refers to uses that are not included in U.S. product labeling.

See *Table 1*, page 2131.

Accepted

Angina pectoris, acute (treatment)—The sublingual, lingual, and extended-release buccal[1] dosage forms of nitroglycerin and the sublingual[1] and chewable dosage forms of isosorbide dinitrate are indicated for the relief of pain of an acute episode of angina pectoris due to coronary artery disease. Sublingual or lingual nitroglycerin is preferred; isosorbide dinitrate should be used in patients intolerant of or unresponsive to nitroglycerin. Sublingual isosorbide dinitrate[1] or sublingual or lingual nitroglycerin may be administered to relieve acute anginal attacks that may occur while the patient is on oral prophylactic therapy.

Angina pectoris, acute (prophylaxis)—The sublingual, lingual[1], and extended-release buccal dosage forms of nitroglycerin and the sublingual or chewable dosage forms of isosorbide dinitrate are indicated for prophylaxis of acute angina attacks in situations (such as stress or exertion) likely to provoke such attacks.

Angina pectoris, chronic (treatment)—The regular, chewable, sublingual, and extended-release oral dosage forms of isosorbide dinitrate; the regular and extended-release oral dosage forms of isosorbide mononitrate; and the extended-release oral and buccal dosage forms of nitroglycerin are indicated for the prophylaxis and long-term treatment of angina pectoris due to coronary artery disease, but not in the treatment of acute anginal attacks (except for chewable isosorbide dinitrate and buccal nitroglycerin). Rapid first-pass hepatic destruction of nitroglycerin may increase the dosage requirements of the oral extended-release capsules and tablets in the prophylaxis and treatment of angina.

Nitroglycerin injection is indicated in the treatment of unstable angina pectoris in patients who have not responded to recommended doses of other organic nitrates and/or a beta-blocker.

Nitroglycerin ointment and nitroglycerin transdermal systems are indicated for the prophylaxis and long-term treatment of angina pectoris but are not indicated for the relief of an acute angina episode.

Hypertension (treatment) or
Hypotension, controlled—Nitroglycerin injection is indicated for blood pressure control during certain surgical procedures and for controlled hypotension during surgery to reduce bleeding into the surgical field.

Myocardial infarction (treatment adjunct) or
Congestive heart failure (treatment)—Nitroglycerin injection is indicated in the adjunctive therapy for congestive heart failure associated or not associated with acute myocardial infarction. (Treatment of congestive heart failure not associated with acute myocardial infarction is not included in Canadian product labeling.) [Sublingual][1], [lingual][1], and [topical][1] nitroglycerin and; [regular oral][1], [chewable], and [sublingual][1] isosorbide dinitrate are also being used for treatment of congestive heart failure, whether or not it is associated with acute myocardial infarction. In general, the oral extended-release dosage forms are not recommended because the effects are difficult to terminate if excessive hypotension or tachycardia develops, although these dosage forms may be acceptable once the patient is stabilized.

[Anal fissures, chronic (treatment)][1]—Topical nitroglycerin is indicated for the treatment of chronic anal fissures.

[1]Not included in Canadian product labeling.

Pharmacology/Pharmacokinetics

Physicochemical characteristics

Molecular weight—

Isosorbide dinitrate: 236.14.
Isosorbide mononitrate: 191.14.
Nitroglycerin: 227.09.

Mechanism of action/Effect

Antianginal or cardiac load–reducing agent—Not specifically known but thought to cause a reduction of myocardial oxygen demand. This is attributed to a reduction in left ventricular preload and afterload because of venous (predominantly) and arterial dilation with a more efficient redistribution of blood flow within the myocardium.

Antihypertensive—Peripheral vasodilation.

Absorption

Isosorbide dinitrate—Bioavailability is 59% after sublingual administration and 22% after oral administration.

Isosorbide mononitrate—Nearly 100%.

Protein binding

Nitroglycerin—Moderate (60%).
Isosorbide mononitrate—Very low (< 4%).

Biotransformation

Hepatic (very rapid and nearly complete) and in blood (enzymatically). Oral dosage forms undergo extensive first-pass metabolism.

Half-life

Isosorbide dinitrate—

Sublingual: 60 minutes.
Oral: 4 hours.

Isosorbide mononitrate—

5 hours.

Nitroglycerin—

1 to 4 minutes.

Onset of action

Note: Although information is limited, pharmacokinetics of sublingual tablets administered buccally are probably similar to those after sublingual administration.

Isosorbide dinitrate—

Oral tablets: 15 to 40 minutes.
Chewable tablets: 2 to 5 minutes.
Extended-release capsules and tablets: 30 minutes.
Sublingual tablets: 2 to 5 minutes.

Isosorbide mononitrate—

Oral tablets: 1 hour.

Nitroglycerin—
Buccal tablets: 3 minutes.
Lingual aerosol: 2 to 4 minutes.
Intravenous infusion: Immediate.
Sublingual tablets: 1 to 3 minutes.
Ointment: Within 30 minutes.
Transdermal systems: Within 30 minutes.

Duration of action

Note: Although information is limited, pharmacokinetics of sublingual tablets administered buccally are probably similar to those after sublingual administration.

Isosorbide dinitrate—
Oral tablets: 4 to 6 hours.
Chewable tablets: 1 to 2 hours.
Extended-release capsules and tablets: 12 hours.
Sublingual tablets: 1 to 2 hours.

Nitroglycerin—
Buccal extended-release tablets: Approximately 5 hours.
Extended-release capsules and tablets: 8 to 12 hours.
Intravenous infusion: Several minutes (dose-dependent).
Sublingual tablets: 30 to 60 minutes.
Ointment: 4 to 8 hours.
Transdermal systems: 8 to 24 hours.

Elimination

Renal (after nearly total metabolism).

Precautions to Consider

Cross-sensitivity and/or related problems

Patients sensitive to one nitrate may be sensitive to other nitrates also, although the reaction is rare.

Patients sensitive to nitrites may be sensitive to nitrates also, although the reaction is rare.

Carcinogenicity

Studies with isosorbide dinitrate or nitroglycerin have not been done. Studies in mice given oral isosorbide mononitrate at doses of up to 900 mg per kg of body weight (mg/kg) per day (102 times the human exposure comparing body surface area) did not reveal evidence of carcinogenicity.

Pregnancy/Reproduction

Fertility—*Isosorbide dinitrate:* Studies in rats given isosorbide dinitrate at doses of 25 or 100 mg/kg per day found no impairment of fertility.

Isosorbide mononitrate: No adverse effect on fertility was observed in male and female rats given isosorbide mononitrate at doses of up to 500 mg/kg per day (125 times the human exposure comparing body surface area).

Pregnancy—Adequate and well-controlled studies in humans have not been done.

Studies in rabbits given isosorbide dinitrate in oral doses of 35 and 150 times the maximum daily recommended human dose have shown a dose-related increase in embryotoxicity. Administration of isosorbide mononitrate to rats at doses of 500 mg/kg per day (125 times the human exposure comparing body surface area) was associated with increased rates of prolonged gestation, prolonged parturition, stillbirths and neonatal death, and decreases in birth weight, live litter size, and pup survival. No evidence of developmental abnormalities, fetal abnormalities, or other effects on reproductive performance was observed in rats and rabbits given isosorbide mononitrate at doses of 250 mg/kg per day.

FDA Pregnancy Category C.

Breast-feeding

It is not known whether nitrates are distributed into breast milk. However, problems in humans have not been documented.

Pediatrics

Appropriate studies on the relationship of age to the effects of nitrates have not been performed in the pediatric population.

Geriatrics

Appropriate studies on the relationship of age to the effects of nitrates have not been performed in the geriatric population. However, elderly patients may be more sensitive to the hypotensive effects of nitrates. In addition, elderly patients are more likely to have age-related renal function impairment, which may require caution in patients receiving nitrates.

Drug interactions and/or related problems

The following drug interactions and/or related problems have been selected on the basis of their potential clinical significance (possible mechanism in parentheses where appropriate)—not necessarily inclusive (» = major clinical significance):

Note: Combinations containing any of the following medications, depending on the amount present, may also interact with this medication.

Acetylcholine or
Histamine or
Norepinephrine (levarterenol)
(effects of these medications may be decreased when they are used concurrently with nitrates)

» Alcohol, moderate or excessive amounts or
» Antihypertensives or
Hypotension-producing medications, other (see *Appendix II*) or
Opioid (narcotic) analgesics or
» Vasodilators, other
(concurrent use may intensify the orthostatic hypotensive effects of nitrates; dosage adjustments may be necessary)

Heparin
(the anticoagulant effect of heparin may be decreased in patients receiving nitroglycerin via intravenous infusion; adjustment of heparin dosage may be required to maintain the desired degree of anticoagulation during and following administration of a nitroglycerin infusion)

Phosphodiesterase inhibitors including
» Sildenafil or
» Tadalafil or
» Vardenafil
(sildenafil, tadalafil, and vardenafil can potentiate the hypotensive effects of nitrates and its use in patients who are concurrently using nitrates in any form is **contraindicated**; deaths have been reported with concurrent use; if a patient treated with these erectile dysfunction drugs needs a rapidly effective nitrate [e.g., in case of an acute angina pectoris attack], the patient must be hospitalized immediately)

Sympathomimetics
(concurrent use may reduce the antianginal effects of nitrates)
(nitrates may counteract the pressor effect of sympathomimetics, possibly resulting in hypotension)

Laboratory value alterations

The following have been selected on the basis of their potential clinical significance (possible effect in parentheses where appropriate)—not necessarily inclusive (» = major clinical significance).

With diagnostic test results
Serum cholesterol determinations by the Zlatkis-Zak color reaction method
(may be falsely decreased)

With physiology/laboratory test values
Methemoglobin concentrations in blood
(may be increased by excessive doses of nitrates)
Urine catecholamine concentrations (epinephrine and norepinephrine) and
Urine vanillylmandelic acid (VMA) concentrations
(may be markedly increased by nitroglycerin)

Medical considerations/Contraindications

The medical considerations/contraindications included have been selected on the basis of their potential clinical significance (reasons given in parentheses where appropriate)—not necessarily inclusive (» = major clinical significance).

Except under special circumstances, this medication should not be used when the following medical problems exist:

For all nitrates
» Hypersensitivity to any nitrates or nitrites or any component of the nitrate prescribed

For nitroglycerin injection only
» Cerebral hemorrhage or
» Head trauma, recent
(nitroglycerin may increase cerebrospinal fluid pressure)
» Pericardial tamponade
» Pericarditis, constrictive

Risk-benefit should be considered when the following medical problems exist:

For all nitrates
» Anemia, severe
» Cerebral hemorrhage or
» Head trauma, recent
(nitrates may increase cerebrospinal fluid pressure)
» Glaucoma
(nitrates may increase intraocular pressure)

Hepatic function impairment, severe
(increased risk of methemoglobinemia)
» Hyperthyroidism
Hypertrophic cardiomyopathy
(angina may be aggravated)
Hypotension, with low systolic pressure
(may be aggravated, accompanied by paradoxical bradycardia and increased angina pectoris)
» Myocardial infarction, recent
(risk of hypotension and tachycardia, which may aggravate ischemia)
Renal function impairment, severe

For oral dosage forms only (in addition to the above)
Gastrointestinal hypermotility or
Malabsorption syndrome
(use of extended-release dosage forms should be avoided because they may not dissolve and may be excreted intact)

For nitroglycerin injection only (in addition to the above)
» Hypovolemia
(risk of producing severe hypotension and shock; should be corrected prior to use of nitroglycerin)
» Normal or low pulmonary capillary wedge pressure
(patients may be unusually sensitive to hypotensive effects)

Patient monitoring

The following may be especially important in patient monitoring (other tests may be warranted in some patients, depending on condition; » = major clinical significance):

Blood pressure determinations and
Heart rate determinations
(recommended at periodic intervals in patients using nitrates regularly to aid in dosage adjustment)

Side/Adverse Effects

The following side/adverse effects have been selected on the basis of their potential clinical significance (possible signs and symptoms in parentheses where appropriate)—not necessarily inclusive:

Those indicating need for medical attention

Incidence rare
Blurred vision; dryness of mouth; headache, severe or prolonged; skin rash

Those indicating need for medical attention only if they continue or are bothersome

Incidence more frequent—dose-related
Flushing of face and neck; headache; nausea or vomiting; orthostatic hypotension (dizziness or lightheadedness, especially when getting up from a lying or sitting position); ***restlessness; tachycardia*** (fast heartbeat)

Incidence less frequent
Sore, reddened skin—topical nitroglycerin dosage forms

Overdose

For more information on the management of overdose or unintentional ingestion, **contact a Poison Control Center** (see *Poison Control Center Listing*).

Clinical effects of overdose

The following effects have been selected on the basis of their potential clinical significance (possible signs and symptoms in parentheses where appropriate)—not necessarily inclusive:

Signs and symptoms of overdose (in order of occurrence)
Bluish-colored lips, fingernails, or palms of hands; dizziness, extreme, or fainting; feeling of extreme pressure in head; shortness of breath; unusual tiredness or weakness; weak and fast heartbeat; fever; convulsions

Note: Cyanosis may occur at blood methemoglobin concentrations of 1.5 grams per 100 mL. More pronounced signs of methemoglobinemia (pressure in head, tiredness or weakness, shortness of breath) occur at concentrations of 20 to 50 grams per 100 mL.

Treatment of overdose

Any remaining nitroglycerin should be removed (e.g., ointment, transdermal system). Buccal or sublingual tablets should be removed and the gum wiped clean at the site of insertion.

If excessive hypotension occurs, elevate the legs to aid venous return.

The rapid metabolism of nitroglycerin usually makes additional measures unnecessary. However, if additional correction of severe hypotension is required, administration of an intravenous alpha-adrenergic agonist such as methoxamine or phenylephrine may be considered; epinephrine should be avoided since it aggravates the shock-like reaction.

Methemoglobin concentrations in blood should be monitored and methemoglobinemia treated with high-flow oxygen and intravenous methylene blue.

Patient Consultation

See *Table 2,* page 2131.

General Dosing Information

Dosage must be adjusted to the needs and tolerance of the individual patient. Dosage requirements may be increased by a worsening of the patient's condition or a loss of medication potency.

Tolerance to the pharmacologic and therapeutic effects of nitrate medications may occur. Nitrate tolerance manifests as a decrease in patient response to the nitrate or as a need for progressively higher doses to maintain therapeutic effect. The development of nitrate tolerance may occur with any nitrate dosage form that maintains continuous medication blood levels. Tolerance can be managed by adjustments in dosing strategy. Intermittent nitrate therapy appears to be effective. An optimal nitrate-free period of at least 8 to 12 hours appears to be effective in preventing attenuation of nitrate effect. Careful monitoring is recommended to make sure that the desired therapeutic effect is being maintained.

Nitrate therapy should be discontinued if blurred vision or dry mouth continues or is severe.

When this medication is to be discontinued following high-dose or long-term administration, dosage should be reduced gradually to prevent possible withdrawal rebound angina.

For oral dosage forms only

There have been reports of patients finding intact or partially dissolved extended-release isosorbide dinitrate tablets in the stool. Some patients may benefit by a change from the extended-release tablet to the extended-release capsule or the regular oral tablet and an increase in dosage to an effective level for each individual patient.

For buccal extended-release nitroglycerin tablets or sublingual tablets administered buccally only

The tablet should be placed between upper lip and gum (above the incisors) or between cheek and upper gum, and allowed to dissolve in place. Tablet placement sites may be alternated as patient desires.

The dissolution time of the buccal extended-release tablet may vary from 3 to 5 hours in most patients. The dissolution rate is increased when the tablet is touched with the tongue or the patient drinks hot liquids. The buccal extended-release tablet utilizes an inert polymer vehicle which enables a metered nitroglycerin release not affected by pH, food, or drink (placement is suggested behind the upper lip if food and drink are to be taken during dosing).

Use at bedtime is not recommended because of the risk of aspiration.

Sublingual isosorbide dinitrate and nitroglycerin tablets may also be administered buccally. Although information is limited, onset and duration of action are probably similar to sublingual dosing.

Diet/Nutrition

The regular oral dosage forms of this medication should preferably be taken with a glass of water on an empty stomach (either 1 hour before or 2 hours after meals) for faster absorption.

ISOSORBIDE DINITRATE

Oral Dosage Forms

ISOSORBIDE DINITRATE EXTENDED-RELEASE CAPSULES USP

Usual adult dose
Antianginal—
Oral, 40 to 80 mg every eight to twelve hours.

Usual pediatric dose
Dosage has not been established.

Strength(s) usually available
U.S.—
40 mg (Rx) [*Dilatrate-SR; Isordil Tembids;* GENERIC].
Canada—
Not commercially available.

Packaging and storage
Store below 40 °C (104 °F), preferably between 15 and 30 °C (59 and 86 °F), unless otherwise specified by manufacturer. Store in a well-closed container.

Stability
Loss of potency is accelerated by exposure to heat and moisture.

Auxiliary labeling
- Caution with alcoholic beverages.
- Swallow capsules whole.
- Store in a cool, dry place.

ISOSORBIDE DINITRATE TABLETS USP

Usual adult dose
Antianginal—
Oral, 5 to 20 mg every six hours, the dosage being adjusted as needed and tolerated. The dosage range is 5 to 40 mg four times a day, with the usual dosage range being 20 to 40 mg four times a day.

Usual pediatric dose
Dosage has not been established.

Strength(s) usually available
U.S.—
2.5 mg (Rx) [GENERIC].
5 mg (Rx) [*ISDN; Isordil Titradose; Sorbitrate;* GENERIC].
10 mg (Rx) [*ISDN; Isordil Titradose; Sorbitrate;* GENERIC].
20 mg (Rx) [*ISDN; Isordil Titradose; Sorbitrate;* GENERIC].
30 mg (Rx) [*Isordil Titradose; Sorbitrate;* GENERIC].
40 mg (Rx) [*Isordil Titradose; Sorbitrate;* GENERIC].
Canada—
10 mg (Rx) [*Apo-ISDN; Coronex; Isordil Titradose;* GENERIC].
30 mg (Rx) [*Apo-ISDN; Coronex; Isordil Titradose;* GENERIC].

Packaging and storage
Store below 40 °C (104 °F), preferably between 15 and 30 °C (59 and 86 °F), unless otherwise specified by manufacturer. Store in a well-closed container.

Stability
Loss of potency is accelerated by exposure to heat and moisture.

Auxiliary labeling
- Caution with alcoholic beverages.
- Store in a cool, dry place.

ISOSORBIDE DINITRATE CHEWABLE TABLETS USP

Usual adult dose
Antianginal—
Oral, 5 mg chewed well every two to three hours, the dosage being adjusted as needed and tolerated.

Note: Chewed tablet is to be held in mouth for one or two minutes to allow time for absorption through buccal tissues.

Usual pediatric dose
Dosage has not been established.

Strength(s) usually available
U.S.—
5 mg (Rx) [*Sorbitrate*].
10 mg (Rx) [*Sorbitrate*].
Canada—
Not commercially available.

Packaging and storage
Store below 40 °C (104 °F), preferably between 15 and 30 °C (59 and 86 °F), unless otherwise specified by manufacturer. Store in a well-closed container.

Stability
Loss of potency is accelerated by exposure to heat and moisture.

Auxiliary labeling
- Caution with alcoholic beverages.
- Chew well before swallowing.
- Store in a cool, dry place.

Note
Chewable tablets up to 10 mg each are exempt from child-resistant container regulations.

ISOSORBIDE DINITRATE EXTENDED-RELEASE TABLETS USP

Usual adult dose
Antianginal—
Oral, 20 to 80 mg every eight to twelve hours.

Usual pediatric dose
Dosage has not been established.

Strength(s) usually available
U.S.—
40 mg (Rx) [*Isordil Tembids;* GENERIC].
Canada—
20 mg (Rx) [*Cedocard-SR; Coradur;* GENERIC].
40 mg (Rx) [*Cedocard-SR*].

Packaging and storage
Store below 40 °C (104 °F), preferably between 15 and 30 °C (59 and 86 °F), unless otherwise specified by manufacturer. Store in a well-closed container.

Stability
Loss of potency is accelerated by exposure to heat and moisture.

Auxiliary labeling
- Caution with alcoholic beverages.
- Swallow tablets whole.
- Store in a cool, dry place.

Sublingual Dosage Forms

ISOSORBIDE DINITRATE SUBLINGUAL TABLETS USP

Usual adult dose
Antianginal—
Sublingual or buccal, 2.5 to 5 mg every two to three hours as needed.

Usual pediatric dose
Dosage has not been established.

Strength(s) usually available
U.S.—
2.5 mg (Rx) [*Isordil; Sorbitrate;* GENERIC].
5 mg (Rx) [*Isordil; Sorbitrate;* GENERIC].
10 mg (Rx) [*Isordil;* GENERIC].
Canada—
5 mg (Rx) [*Apo-ISDN; Coronex; Isordil;* GENERIC].

Packaging and storage
Store below 40 °C (104 °F), preferably between 15 and 30 °C (59 and 86 °F), unless otherwise specified by manufacturer. Store in a well-closed container.

Stability
Loss of potency is accelerated by exposure to heat and moisture.

Auxiliary labeling
- Caution with alcoholic beverages.
- Dissolve tablets under tongue.
- Store in a cool, dry place.

Note
Do not dispense sublingual tablets in child-resistant containers. Sublingual tablets up to 10 mg each are exempt from child-resistant container regulations.

ISOSORBIDE MONONITRATE

Summary of Differences

Pharmacology/pharmacokinetics:
Protein binding—Very low.
Half-life—5 hours.

Oral Dosage Form

ISOSORBIDE MONONITRATE TABLETS

Usual adult dose
Antianginal—
Oral, 20 mg two times a day, with the two doses given seven hours apart.

Note: An initial dose of 5 mg may be appropriate for patients of particularly small stature; the dosage being increased to at least 10 mg by the second or third day of therapy.

Usual pediatric dose
Safety and efficacy have not been established.

Strength(s) usually available
U.S.—
10 mg (Rx) [*Monoket* (scored)].
20 mg (Rx) [*ISMO; Monoket* (scored)].
Canada—
20 mg (Rx) [*ISMO*].

Packaging and storage
Store below 40 °C (104 °F), preferably between 15 and 30 °C (59 and 86 °F) in a tight container, unless otherwise specified by manufacturer.

Stability
Loss of potency is accelerated by exposure to heat and moisture.

Auxiliary labeling
- Caution with alcoholic beverages.
- Store in a cool, dry place.

ISOSORBIDE MONONITRATE EXTENDED-RELEASE TABLETS

Usual adult dose
Antianginal—
Oral, 30 or 60 mg once a day, the dosage being increased after several days to 120 mg once a day, as needed and tolerated. Rarely, 240 mg once a day may be needed.

Usual pediatric dose
Safety and efficacy have not been established.

Strength(s) usually available
U.S.—
30 mg (Rx) [*IMDUR* (scored)].
60 mg (Rx) [*IMDUR* (scored)].
120 mg (Rx) [*IMDUR* (scored)].
Canada—
60 mg (Rx) [*IMDUR* (scored)].

Packaging and storage
Store between 2 and 30 °C (36 and 86 °F) in a tight container.

Stability
Loss of potency is accelerated by exposure to heat and moisture.

Auxiliary labeling
- Caution with alcoholic beverages.
- Store in a cool, dry place.
- Do not crush or chew.

NITROGLYCERIN

Summary of Differences
Category:
Antihypertensive; cardiac load–reducing agent.
Indications:
Hypertension (parenteral dosage form); hypotension, controlled (parenteral dosage form); acute myocardial infarction; congestive heart failure.
Pharmacology/pharmacokinetics:
Half-life—1 to 4 minutes.
Precautions:
Medical considerations/contraindications—Contraindicated in increased intracranial pressure, constrictive pericarditis (parenteral dosage form); caution needed in hypovolemia or severe hepatic or renal function impairment (parenteral dosage form).

Additional Dosing Information
See also *General Dosing Information.*

For sublingual tablets only
Judging the ability of a sublingual tablet to relieve angina by the presence of a tingling or burning sensation after a tablet has been dissolved under the tongue is not completely reliable since some patients may be unable to detect these effects. Newer, stabilized sublingual nitroglycerin tablets are making such potency testing less useful, since the stabilized tablets may be less likely to produce these detectable effects.

Nitroglycerin tablets should maintain their potency through the expiration date on the bottle, provided the cap is tightly replaced after each use and proper storage instructions are adhered to.

A supplementary stainless steel container has been developed and approved for temporary storage of small quantities of nitroglycerin tablets. The pendant-type container on a chain, which can be worn around the patient's neck, is intended to provide a convenient source of nitroglycerin for emergency use.

For intravenous infusion form only
Special nitroglycerin infusion sets made of non-PVC plastic cause minimal absorption; therefore, nearly all the calculated dose will be delivered to the patient. When these sets are used, *dosage instructions should be followed with care,* as changing from a standard set (PVC) to a special set (non-PVC) may result in excessive nitroglycerin dosage unless allowances are made for the difference in the amount of nitroglycerin actually delivered to the patient.

For ointment dosage form only
The dose should be individualized starting with ½ to 1 inch of ointment as squeezed from the tube and then increasing the dose by ½ inch at each application until the desired clinical effect and the greatest asymptomatic decrease in resting blood pressure occur. The largest dose that does not cause symptomatic hypotension is used as the patient's individualized dose.

The ointment is applied with the dose-measuring application papers supplied with the medicine. The ointment is squeezed onto the measuring scale printed on the paper. The paper is then used to spread the ointment onto the skin in a thin, even layer, covering an area (at least 2 by 3 inches) of the same size at each dose without rubbing or massage.

The site of ointment application may be the non-hairy skin of the chest, stomach, front of the thighs, or any other accessible area of clean, dry skin. Application to the chest is commonly preferred since the patient also benefits psychologically from applying medication to the area where the pain is experienced.

For transdermal dosage forms only
Application should preferably be made at the same time each day (after removal of the previous system) to areas of clean, dry, hairless skin on the chest, inner side of the upper arm, or shoulders; application to extremities below the knee or elbow should be avoided. Skin areas with extensive scarring, calluses, or irritation should also be avoided. Application sites should be varied to avoid causing skin irritation.

All available transdermal systems provide therapeutic effects within 30 minutes and sustain the required plasma concentration of nitroglycerin for 8 to 24 hours.

The transdermal units *should not* be cut or trimmed in an attempt to adjust dosage.

A new dosage unit should be applied if the first becomes loosened or falls off.

Removal of the transdermal unit before defibrillation or cardioversion is recommended because of the potential for altered electrical conductivity and enhanced risk of arcing associated with use of defibrillators.

Buccal Dosage Forms

NITROGLYCERIN EXTENDED-RELEASE BUCCAL TABLETS

Usual adult dose
Antianginal—
Buccal, 1 mg dissolved in place on the oral mucosa every five hours during waking hours, the dosage being increased by frequency and/or strength as required.

Usual pediatric dose
Dosage has not been established.

Strength(s) usually available
U.S.—
1 mg (Rx) [*Nitrogard*].
2 mg (Rx) [*Nitrogard*].
2.5 mg (Rx) [*Nitrogard*].
3 mg (Rx) [*Nitrogard*].
5 mg (Rx) [*Nitrogard*].
Canada—
Not commercially available.

Packaging and storage
Store between 15 and 30 °C (59 and 86 °F), unless otherwise specified by manufacturer. Store in a glass container with a tight screw cap.

Stability
Loss of potency is accelerated by exposure to heat and moisture.

Auxiliary labeling
- Caution with alcoholic beverages.
- Dissolve tablet between lip or cheek and upper gum.
- Do not chew or swallow.
- Keep in original container, tightly closed.
- Store in a cool, dry place.

Lingual Dosage Forms

NITROGLYCERIN LINGUAL AEROSOL

Usual adult dose
Antianginal—
On or under the tongue, 1 or 2 metered doses (400 or 800 mcg [0.4 or 0.8 mg]) repeated at five-minute intervals as needed for relief of angina attack.

Note: If relief is not obtained after a total of 3 metered doses in a fifteen-minute period, the physician should be contacted or the patient taken to a hospital.

Usual adult prescribing limits
1.2 mg per day.

Usual pediatric dose
Dosage has not been established.

Strength(s) usually available
U.S.—
400 mcg (0.4 mg) per metered dose (Rx) (Rx) [*Nitrolingual*].
Canada—
Not commercially available.

Packaging and storage
Store below 40 °C (104 °F), preferably between 15 and 30 °C (59 and 86 °F), unless otherwise specified by manufacturer. Protect from freezing.

Auxiliary labeling
- Do not shake.
- Caution with alcoholic beverages.
- Store in a cool place.

Oral Dosage Forms

NITROGLYCERIN EXTENDED-RELEASE CAPSULES

Usual adult dose
Antianginal—
Oral, 2.5, 6.5, or 9 mg every twelve hours, the dosage being increased to every eight hours if needed and tolerated.

Usual pediatric dose
Dosage has not been established.

Strength(s) usually available
U.S.—
2.5 mg (Rx) [*Nitrocot; Nitroglyn E-R; Nitro-par; Nitro-time;* GENERIC].
6.5 mg (Rx) [*Nitroglyn E-R; Nitro-par; Nitro-time;* GENERIC].
9 mg (Rx) [*Nitroglyn E-R; Nitro-par; Nitro-time;* GENERIC].
Canada—
Not commercially available.

Packaging and storage
Store between 15 and 30 °C (59 and 86 °F), unless otherwise specified by manufacturer. Store in a container with a tight screw cap.

Stability
Loss of potency is accelerated by exposure to heat and moisture.

Auxiliary labeling
- Caution with alcoholic beverages.
- Swallow capsules whole.
- Keep container tightly closed.
- Store in a cool, dry place.

NITROGLYCERIN EXTENDED-RELEASE TABLETS

Usual adult dose
Antianginal—
Oral, 2.6 or 6.5 mg every twelve hours, the dosage being increased to every eight hours as needed and tolerated.

Usual pediatric dose
Dosage has not been established.

Strength(s) usually available
U.S.—
2.6 mg (Rx) [GENERIC].
6.5 mg (Rx) [GENERIC].
Canada—
2.6 mg (Rx) [*Nitrong SR*].

Packaging and storage
Store between 15 and 30 °C (59 and 86 °F), unless otherwise specified by manufacturer. Store in a glass container with a tight screw cap.

Stability
Loss of potency is accelerated by exposure to heat and moisture.

Auxiliary labeling
- Caution with alcoholic beverages.
- Swallow tablets whole.
- Keep container tightly closed.
- Store in a cool, dry place.

Parenteral Dosage Forms

NITROGLYCERIN INJECTION USP

Usual adult dose
Antianginal or
Antihypertensive or
Cardiac load–reducing agent—
Intravenous infusion, initially administered at a rate of 5 mcg (0.005 mg) per minute, the dosage being increased by increments of 5 mcg per minute at three- to five-minute intervals until an effect is obtained or until the rate is 20 mcg (0.02 mg) per minute. If no effect is obtained at 20 mcg per minute, the dosage may be increased further by increments of 10 mcg (0.01 mg) per minute at the same time intervals, and later increased by increments of 20 mcg (0.02 mg) per minute if necessary to obtain an effect. The dosage increments should be reduced and the time interval between dosage increases lengthened when a partial effect is observed, to attain the desired response cautiously.

Note: Close attention must be given to manufacturers" instructions for dilution, dosage, and administration because concentrations and/or volume per vial of nitroglycerin may differ among the several products available from different manufacturers.

Stated dosage is based on use of special, non-polyvinylchloride (non-PVC) intravenous infusion sets. Dosage requirements may vary when standard intravenous infusion sets of polyvinyl chloride (PVC) are used. Continuous concurrent monitoring of blood pressure and heart rate in *all patients* must be performed to establish the correct effective dose.

To achieve optimal control of dosage and effects, it is recommended that nitroglycerin be administered intravenously by means of an infusion pump, a micro-drip regulator, or a similar device to allow precise adjustment of the flow rate.

Standard intravenous infusion sets made of PVC plastic may unpredictably absorb 40 to 80% of the nitroglycerin from a diluted solution for infusion.

Some intravenous filters may also absorb nitroglycerin, but the effect is variable; since nitroglycerin dosage is titrated according to response, no precaution is necessary.

Extra caution should be observed when non-PVC infusion sets are used to administer intravenous nitroglycerin. Some infusion pumps—
- When turned off may not completely stop the flow of infusion solution with these non-PVC sets.
- May not accurately deliver the infusion solution at low rates of flow.
- Require extension sets and other connecting equipment made of PVC, thus partially negating the advantage of the non-PVC infusion set.

Close monitoring of patient hemodynamic response is required. All infusion pumps should be tested with the infusion set being used to ensure accurate delivery of nitroglycerin at low flow rates and complete interruption of flow when the set is turned off.

Usual adult prescribing limits
No fixed maximum dose established. Dosage is titrated to individual patient response beginning with small doses (to which hypersensitive patients may respond).

Usual pediatric dose
Dosage has not been established.

Strength(s) usually available
U.S.—
5 mg per mL (Rx) [*Nitro-Bid IV; Tridil;* GENERIC].
Canada—
1 mg per mL (Rx) [*Nitroject*].
5 mg per mL (Rx) [*Nitroject; Tridil;* GENERIC].

Packaging and storage
Store between 15 and 30 °C (59 and 86 °F), unless otherwise specified by manufacturer. Protect from light. Protect from freezing.

Preparation of dosage form
- *Not for direct intravenous injection.*
- Must be diluted prior to infusion. Dilution may be in 5% dextrose injection or 0.9% sodium chloride injection, followed by thorough mixing. Dilution and storage of nitroglycerin injection should be made only in glass parenteral solution bottles, to avoid absorption of nitroglycerin into plastic containers.
- *Must not be admixed with other medications.*

Stability
It is recommended that diluted solutions of nitroglycerin not be kept or used longer than 24 hours, unless otherwise specified by the manufacturer. Solution is *not* explosive either before or after dilution.

Note
Manufacturer's package information must be checked for dilution, administration, and dosage because of product differences.

Some products contain substantial amounts of propylene glycol or ethanol.

Sublingual Dosage Forms

NITROGLYCERIN TABLETS (SUBLINGUAL) USP

Usual adult dose

Antianginal—

Sublingual or buccal, 300 to 600 mcg (0.3 to 0.6 mg) repeated at five-minute intervals as needed for relief of angina attack.

Note: If relief is not obtained after a total of 3 tablets used over a fifteen-minute period, the physician should be contacted or the patient taken to a hospital.

Usual adult prescribing limits

10 mg per day.

Usual pediatric dose

Dosage has not been established.

Strength(s) usually available

U.S.—

300 mcg (0.3 mg) (Rx) [*Nitrostat;* GENERIC].
400 mcg (0.4 mg) (Rx) [*Nitrostat;* GENERIC].
600 mcg (0.6 mg) (Rx) [*Nitrostat;* GENERIC].

Canada—

300 mcg (0.3 mg) (Rx) [*Nitrostat;* GENERIC].
600 mcg (0.6 mg) (Rx) [*Nitrostat;* GENERIC].

Packaging and storage

Store between 15 and 30 °C (59 and 86 °F), unless otherwise specified by manufacturer. Store in original container with tight metal screw cap.

Stability

Loss of potency through volatilization of nitroglycerin from tablets is accelerated by exposure to air, heat, and moisture. After the bottle is opened, stabilized tablets will maintain potency through the expiration date provided the bottle cap is replaced tightly after each use.

Auxiliary labeling

- Caution with alcoholic beverages.
- Dissolve tablets under tongue.
- Keep in original container, tightly closed.
- Store in a cool, dry place.

Note

Do not dispense sublingual nitroglycerin tablets in child-resistant containers.

Suggest to the patient that the cotton be removed from the container *before* the tablets are required for angina attack.

USP requires that sublingual forms of nitroglycerin be dispensed in the original unopened manufacturer's container.

Sublingual nitroglycerin tablets should not be placed in containers with other medications.

Topical Dosage Forms

NITROGLYCERIN OINTMENT USP

Usual adult dose

Antianginal—

Topical, to the skin, 15 to 30 mg of nitroglycerin (contained in 2.5 to 5 cm [1 to 2 inches] of ointment as squeezed from the tube) every eight hours during the day and at bedtime. If angina occurs between doses, frequency of application may be increased to every six hours.

Note: Ointment is applied in a thin, even layer covering an area of the same size (measuring at least 2 by 3 inches) at each use, but is not to be rubbed or massaged into the skin.

[Chronic anal fissures (treatment)][1]—

Topical, twice daily.

Usual adult prescribing limits

75 mg of nitroglycerin (contained in 12.5 cm [5 inches] of ointment as squeezed from the tube) per application. Rarely, application as frequently as every four hours may be necessary.

Usual pediatric dose

Dosage has not been established.

Strength(s) usually available

U.S.—

2% (Rx) [*Nitro-Bid; Nitrol;* GENERIC].

Canada—

2% (Rx) [*Nitrol*].

Packaging and storage

Store between 15 and 30 °C (59 and 86 °F), unless otherwise specified by manufacturer. Store in a tight container.

Auxiliary labeling

- Caution with alcoholic beverages.
- For external use only.
- Store in a cool place.
- Keep tightly closed.

Note

Dispense ointment in original manufacturer's tube together with patient instructions and dose-measuring papers.

NITROGLYCERIN TRANSDERMAL SYSTEM

Usual adult dose

Antianginal—

Topical, to the intact skin, 1 transdermal dosage system, delivering the smallest available dose of nitroglycerin in its dosage series, every twenty-four hours. Dosage adjustments may be made by changing to the next larger dosage system in the series or to a combination of systems.

Note: To prevent tolerance, it is recommended that the patch be left on only 12 to 14 hours a day, with a patch-off period of 10 to 12 hours before the next daily patch is applied.

Usual pediatric dose

Dosage has not been established.

Strength(s) usually available

U.S.—

Dose of nitroglycerin delivered per hour:

0.1 mg (Rx) [*Minitran; Nitro-Dur; Transderm-Nitro*].
0.2 mg (Rx) [*Deponit; Minitran; Nitrodisc; Nitro-Dur; Transderm-Nitro;* GENERIC].
0.3 mg (Rx) [*Nitrodisc; Nitro-Dur*].
0.4 mg (Rx) [*Deponit; Minitran; Nitrodisc; Nitro-Dur; Transderm-Nitro;* GENERIC].
0.6 mg (Rx) [*Minitran; Nitro-Dur; Transderm-Nitro;* GENERIC].
0.8 mg (Rx) [*Nitro-Dur; Transderm-Nitro,* GENERIC].

Canada—

Dose of nitroglycerin delivered per hour:

0.2 mg (Rx) [*Minitran; Nitro-Dur; Transderm-Nitro*].
0.3 mg (Rx) [*Nitro-Dur*].
0.4 mg (Rx) [*Minitran; Nitro-Dur; Transderm-Nitro*].
0.6 mg (Rx) [*Minitran; Nitro-Dur; Transderm-Nitro*].
0.8 mg (Rx) [*Minitran; Nitro-Dur; Transderm-Nitro*].

Packaging and storage

Store between 15 and 30 °C (59 and 86 °F), unless otherwise specified by manufacturer.

Auxiliary labeling

- Caution with alcoholic beverages.
- For external use only.
- Store in a cool place.

Note

Include patient instructions when dispensing.

[1]Not included in Canadian product labeling.

Revised: 10/14/2004

Table 1. Indications

Legend:
I=Angina pectoris, acute (treatment)
II=Angina pectoris, acute (prophylaxis)
III=Angina pectoris, chronic (treatment)
IV=Hypertension (treatment); or Hypotension, controlled
V=Myocardial infarction (treatment adjunct)
VI=Congestive heart failure (treatment)

	I	II	III	IV	V	VI
Isosorbide dinitrate:						
Oral Tablets, regular			✓		[✓]1	[✓]1
Extended-release capsules or tablets			✓			
Chewable tablets	✓	✓	✓		[✓]	[✓]
Sublingual	✓1	✓	✓		[✓]1	[✓]1
Isosorbide mononitrate: Oral Tablets, regular			✓			
Nitroglycerin: Buccal, extended-release	✓1	✓	✓			
Lingual, aerosol	✓	✓1			[✓]1	[✓]1
Oral, extended-release			✓			
Parenteral			✓	✓	✓	✓
Sublingual	✓	✓			[✓]1	[✓]1
Topical Ointment			✓		[✓]1	[✓]1
Transdermal systems			✓		[✓]	[✓]

1Not included in Canadian product labeling

Table 2. Patient Consultation

As an aid to patient consultation, refer to *Advice for the Patient, Nitrates—Lingual Aerosol (Systemic)*, *Nitrates—Oral (Systemic)*, *Nitrates—Sublingual, Chewable, or Buccal (Systemic)*, or *Nitrates—Topical (Systemic)*.
Consider advising the patient on the following:

Legend:
Buccal: **I**=Extended-release nitroglycerin
Lingual: **II**=Aerosol nitroglycerin
Oral: **III**=Regular; **IV**=Chewable; **V**=Extended-release
Sublingual: **VI**=Isosorbide dinitrate; **VII**=Nitroglycerin
Topical: **VIII**=Nitroglycerin ointment; **IX**=Transdermal nitroglycerin

	Buccal	Lingual	Oral			Sublingual		Topical	
	I	II	III	IV	V	VI	VII	VIII	IX
Before using this medication									
» Conditions affecting use, especially: Hypersensitivity to the nitrate or any component of the product prescribed, any nitrate or nitrite	✓	✓	✓	✓	✓	✓	✓	✓	✓
Use in the elderly—May have increased sensitivity to hypotensive effects	✓	✓	✓	✓	✓	✓	✓	✓	✓
Other medications, especially antihypertensives, moderate or excessive amounts of alcohol, other vasodilators, sildenafil, or vardenafilSildenafil and vardenafil are **contraindicated** for concomitant use with any nitrate	✓	✓	✓	✓	✓	✓	✓	✓	✓
Other medical problems, especially cerebral hemorrhage, constrictive pericarditis, glaucoma, hyperthyroidism, hypovolemia, normal or low pulmonary capillary wedge pressure, pericardial tamponade, recent head trauma, or recent myocardial infarction	✓	✓	✓	✓	✓	✓	✓	✓	✓
Proper use of this medication » Compliance with therapy	✓	✓	✓	✓	✓	✓	✓	✓	✓
» Reading patient instructions carefully		✓						✓	✓
Proper administration: » Regular tablet or extended-release capsule or tablet—Taking with full glass of water on empty stomach			✓		✓				
» Buccal— Placing under upper lip (above incisors) against gum or between cheek and upper gum; placing between upper lip (above incisors) and gum if food or drink to be taken within 3 to 5 hours; patients with dentures may place anywhere between cheek and gum	✓					✓	✓		
Touching with tongue or drinking hot liquids may increase rate of dissolution	✓					✓	✓		
Bedtime use not recommended because of risk of aspiration	✓					✓	✓		
Replacing tablet if inadvertently swallowed	✓					✓	✓		
Not using chewing tobacco while tablet in place	✓								
» Chewable tablet—Chewing well and holding in mouth for approximately 2 minutes				✓					
» Lingual aerosol— Removing plastic cover; not shaking container		✓							
Holding container vertically and spraying onto or under tongue; not inhaling spray		✓							
Closing mouth after each spray; not swallowing immediately		✓							

Table 2. Patient Consultation *(continued)*

As an aid to patient consultation, refer to *Advice for the Patient, Nitrates—Lingual Aerosol (Systemic), Nitrates—Oral (Systemic), Nitrates—Sublingual, Chewable, or Buccal (Systemic),* or *Nitrates—Topical (Systemic).* Consider advising the patient on the following:	Buccal	Lingual	Oral			Sublingual		Topical	
	Legend: I=Extended-release nitroglycerin	II=Aerosol nitroglycerin	III=Regular IV=Chewable V=Extended-release			VI=Isosorbide dinitrate VII=Nitroglycerin		VIII=Nitroglycerin ointment IX=Transdermal nitroglycerin	
	I	**II**	**III**	**IV**	**V**	**VI**	**VII**	**VIII**	**IX**
» Sublingual tablet—Placing under the tongue; avoiding eating, drinking, smoking, or using chewing tobacco while tablet is dissolving						✓	✓		
» Ointment—Cleansing skin before applying; measuring; using applicator; spreading evenly over same size of skin area in each application; not rubbing into skin; applying to skin free of hair, in different areas; proper application of occlusive dressing, if ordered								✓	
Transdermal—Not trimming or cutting patch; applying to clean, dry skin free of hair, scars, cuts, or irritation (after removal of previous system); replacing systems that have loosened or fallen off; alternating application sites									✓
» Not chewing, crushing, or swallowing	✓					✓	✓		
» Not breaking, crushing, or chewing before swallowing					✓				
For use in treating acute angina attacks									
» Sitting down and using medication at first sign of angina attack; caution if dizziness or faintness occurs	✓	✓		✓		✓	✓		
Remaining calm until medicine has opportunity to work	✓	✓		✓		✓	✓		
» Relief usually occurs within 5 minutes—	✓	✓		✓		✓	✓		
Dose may be repeated if pain not relieved in 5 to 10 minutes; calling physician or going to emergency room if angina pain not relieved by 3 doses in 15 minutes		✓		✓		✓	✓		
Not repeating dose; using sublingual nitroglycerin and calling physician or going to emergency room if angina pain not relieved in 15 minutes	✓								
For use in preventing angina									
» This dosage form does not relieve angina attacks but rather prevents them (exceptions are chewable and sublingual isosorbide dinitrate)			✓	✓	✓			✓	✓
Using 5 to 10 minutes prior to anticipated stress to prevent attack	✓	✓		✓		✓	✓		
Missed dose:									
Taking/using as soon as possible unless next scheduled dose is within:									✓
—2 hours (exception is oral extended-release);	✓		✓	✓		✓	✓	✓	
—6 hours (for oral extended-release);					✓				
Returning to regular dosing schedule; not doubling doses	✓		✓	✓	✓	✓	✓	✓	✓
» Proper storage	✓	✓	✓	✓	✓	✓	✓	✓	✓
Protecting from freezing		✓							
Not puncturing, breaking, or burning aerosol container		✓							
Storing in cool place, tightly closed								✓	
Lack of reliability of flushing or headache as test of potency							✓		
» Keeping sublingual nitroglycerin in original glass, screw-cap bottle (unless using special nitroglycerin container) with cotton plug removed; avoiding handling tablets; capping quickly and tightly after each use; not storing in same container as other medications; not carrying close to body or in auto glove compartment; not storing in refrigerator or bathroom medicine cabinet							✓		
Precautions while using this medication									
» Not taking sildenafil, tadalafil, or vardenafil while taking this medication because excessive hypotension and possibly death can occur. *If a patient is treated with these drugs for erectile dysfunction and needs a rapidly effective nitrate as in the case of an acute angina pectoris attack, the patient must be hospitalized immediately.*	✓	✓	✓	✓	✓	✓	✓	✓	✓
» Checking with physician before discontinuing medication; gradual dosage reduction may be needed	✓	✓	✓	✓	✓	✓	✓	✓	✓
» Caution when getting up suddenly from a lying or sitting position	✓	✓	✓	✓	✓	✓	✓	✓	✓
» Caution in using alcohol, while standing for long periods or exercising, and during hot weather because of enhanced orthostatic hypotensive effects	✓	✓	✓	✓	✓	✓	✓	✓	✓
» Headache as a common effect; should decrease with continuing therapy; checking with physician if continuing or severe	✓	✓	✓	✓	✓	✓	✓	✓	✓
Notifying physician if undigested extended-release tablets are found in stools (for isosorbide dinitrate only)					✓				
Side/adverse effects									
Signs of potential side effects, especially blurred vision, dryness of mouth, severe or prolonged headache, and skin rash	✓	✓	✓	✓	✓	✓	✓	✓	✓

NITRAZEPAM—See *Benzodiazepines (Systemic)*

NITROFURANTOIN Systemic

VA CLASSIFICATION (Primary): AM600

Commonly used brand name(s): *Apo-Nitrofurantoin; Furadantin; Macrobid; Macrodantin; Novo-Furantoin.*

Note: For a listing of dosage forms and brand names by country availability, see *Dosage Forms* section(s).

Category

Antibacterial (systemic).

Indications

Accepted

Urinary tract infections, bacterial (treatment)—Nitrofurantoin is indicated in the treatment of urinary tract infections caused by susceptible strains of *Escherichia coli*, enterococci, *Staphylococcus aureus*, *Staphylococcus saprophyticus*, *Klebsiella* species, *Enterobacter* species, and *Proteus* species.

Urinary tract infections, bacterial (prophylaxis)—Nitrofurantoin is used in the prophylaxis or long-term suppression of urinary tract infections.

Not all species or strains of a particular organism may be susceptible to nitrofurantoin. Some strains of *Enterobacter* or *Klebsiella* species are resistant to nitrofurantoin. Nitrofurantoin is not active against most strains of *Proteus* or *Serratia* species. Nitrofurantoin has no activity against *Pseudomonas* species.

Unaccepted

Nitrofurantoin is not indicated for the treatment of pyelonephritis or perinephric abscesses.

Nitrofurantoin is not indicated for the treatment of any systemic infection or for prostatitis.

Pharmacology/Pharmacokinetics

Physicochemical characteristics

Molecular weight—238.16.

Mechanism of action/Effect

Nitrofurantoin, a synthetic, broad-spectrum, weakly acidic antibacterial, is generally bactericidal at therapeutic concentrations. Therapeutic concentrations are achieved only in the urine. The mechanism of antimicrobial action is unique among antibacterials. Nitrofurantoin is reduced by bacterial flavoproteins to reactive intermediates, which inactivate or alter bacterial ribosomal proteins and other macromolecules. These inactivations or alterations of bacterial ribosomal proteins and macromolecules cause the inhibition of vital biochemical processes of aerobic energy metabolism and the syntheses of bacterial deoxyribonucleic acid (DNA), ribonucleic acid (RNA), cell wall, and protein. The fact that nitrofurantoin interferes with a variety of bacterial processes may explain the lack of acquired bacterial resistance to nitrofurantoin. The multiple and simultaneous mutations of the target macromolecules that would be required to achieve resistance would probably be lethal to the bacteria.

Absorption

Microcrystalline—Rapidly and completely absorbed in the small intestine.

Macrocrystalline—More slowly absorbed and usually causes less gastrointestinal irritation.

The presence of food can increase the bioavailability of both forms of nitrofurantoin; this also increases the duration of therapeutic urinary concentrations.

The monohydrate forms a gel matrix upon exposure to gastric and intestinal fluids that releases nitrofurantoin over time.

Distribution

High concentrations are achieved in urine and the kidneys; serum concentrations are very low; crosses the placenta and blood-brain barrier.

Protein binding

Moderate (60%).

Biotransformation

Approximately two thirds of the drug is rapidly metabolized and inactivated in most body tissues, including the liver.

Half-life

0.3 to 1 hour.

Elimination

Renal—Primarily excreted by glomerular filtration with some tubular secretion and reabsorption; 30 to 40% rapidly excreted unchanged; the macrocrystalline form is excreted more slowly; active drug accumulates in patients with impaired renal function and may reach toxic concentrations.

Biliary—May also be excreted in the bile.

In dialysis—Nitrofurantoin is dialyzable.

Precautions to Consider

Cross-sensitivity and/or related problems

Patients hypersensitive to one nitrofuran may be hypersensitive to other nitrofurans also.

Carcinogenicity

Nitrofurantoin, given as 0.3% of the diet to female Holtzman rats for up to 44.5 weeks or given as 0.1% to 0.187% of the diet to female Sprague-Dawley rats for 75 weeks, has not been shown to be carcinogenic. No evidence of carcinogenicity was found in 2 chronic rodent bioassays in male and female Sprague-Dawley rats and 2 chronic bioassays in Swiss mice and in BDF_1 mice. Increased incidences of tubular adenomas, benign mixed tumors, and granulosa cell tumors of the ovary were seen in female $B6C3F_1$ mice. There was an increased incidence of uncommon kidney tubular cell neoplasms, osteosarcomas, and neoplasms of the subcutaneous tissue in male F344/N rats. Lung papillary adenomas of unknown significance were observed in the F1 generation of pregnant mice given 75 mg per kg of body weight (mg/kg) of nitrofurantoin by subcutaneous injection.

Mutagenicity

Nitrofurantoin has induced point mutations in certain strains of *Salmonella typhimurium* and forward mutations in L5178Y mouse lymphoma cells. It has also induced increased numbers of sister chromatid exchanges and chromosomal aberrations in Chinese hamster ovary cells but not in human cells in culture. Results of the sex-linked recessive lethal assay in *Drosophila* were negative after oral or parenteral administration of nitrofurantoin. The medication did not induce heritable mutation in the rodent models examined.

Pregnancy/Reproduction

Fertility—Nitrofurantoin, given in high doses in rats, has been shown to cause temporary spermatogenic arrest, which was reversible upon discontinuation of the medication. Nitrofurantoin, in doses of 10 mg/kg per day or greater, may produce slight to moderate spermatogenic arrest, with decreased sperm counts, in human males.

Pregnancy—Nitrofurantoin crosses the placenta. Use is contraindicated in pregnancy at term and during labor and delivery, or when the onset of labor is imminent, because of the possibility of hemolytic anemia due to immature erythrocyte enzyme systems in the fetus.

Reproduction studies have been performed in rabbits and rats given doses up to 6 times the human dose; these studies have revealed no evidence of impaired fertility or harm to the fetus due to nitrofurantoin. In a single study conducted in mice given 68 times the human dose (based on mg/kg administered to the dam), growth retardation and a low incidence of minor and common malformations were observed. However, fetal malformations were not observed at 25 times the human dose.

In one published transplacental carcinogenicity study, nitrofurantoin has been shown to induce lung papillary adenomas in the F1 generation mice at doses 19 times the human dose on a mg/kg per body weight basis.

FDA Pregnancy Category B.

Breast-feeding

Nitrofurantoin is distributed into breast milk in trace amounts. Hemolytic anemia may occur, especially in glucose-6-phosphate dehydrogenase (G6PD)–deficient infants.

Pediatrics

Use of nitrofurantoin is contraindicated in infants up to 1 month of age because of the possibility of hemolytic anemia due to immature erythrocyte enzyme systems. The safety and efficacy of the formulation combining the macrocrystalline and monohydrate forms of nitrofurantoin have not been established in children up to 12 years of age.

Geriatrics

No information is available on the relationship of age to the effects of nitrofurantoin in geriatric patients. However, elderly patients are more likely to have an age-related decrease in renal function, which may require a decrease in dosage or change in medication. Side effects, such as acute pneumonitis and peripheral neuropathy, may also occur more frequently in elderly patients.

Drug interactions and/or related problems

The following drug interactions and/or related problems have been selected on the basis of their potential clinical significance (possible mechanism in parentheses where appropriate)—not necessarily inclusive (» = major clinical significance):

Note: Combinations containing any of the following medications, depending on the amount present, may also interact with this medication.

» Hemolytics, other (see *Appendix II*)
(concurrent use with nitrofurantoin may increase the potential for toxic side effects)

Hepatotoxic medications, other (see *Appendix II*)
(concurrent use of nitrofurantoin with other hepatotoxic medications may increase the potential for hepatotoxicity)

Magnesium trisilicate
(magnesium trisilicate reduces both the rate and extent of absorption of nitrofurantoin, probably by adsorption of nitrofurantoin to its surface)

Nalidixic acid
(nitrofurantoin interferes with the therapeutic effects of nalidixic acid)

» Neurotoxic medications, other (see *Appendix II*)
(concurrent use of nitrofurantoin with other neurotoxic medications may increase the potential for neurotoxicity)

» Probenecid or
» Sulfinpyrazone
(these medications may inhibit renal tubular secretion of nitrofurantoin, resulting in increased serum concentrations and/or toxicity, prolonged elimination half-life, and reduced urinary concentrations and effectiveness; dosage adjustment of probenecid may be necessary)

Laboratory value alterations

The following have been selected on the basis of their potential clinical significance (possible effect in parentheses where appropriate)—not necessarily inclusive (» = major clinical significance).

With diagnostic test results

Glucose, urine
(nitrofurantoin may produce metabolites in the urine that may give false-positive results with copper sulfate reduction tests, such as *Benedict's* solution or *Fehling's* solution; nitrofurantoin does not interfere with the glucose enzymatic test)

With physiology/laboratory test values

Alanine aminotransferase (ALT [SGPT]), serum, or
Aspartate aminotransferase (AST [SGOT]), serum, or
Phosphorus, serum
(values may be increased)

Hemoglobin
(may be decreased)

Medical considerations/Contraindications

The medical considerations/contraindications included have been selected on the basis of their potential clinical significance (reasons given in parentheses where appropriate)—not necessarily inclusive (» = major clinical significance).

Risk-benefit should be considered when the following medical problems exist:

Anemia or
Debilitating disease or
Diabetes mellitus or
Electrolyte imbalance or
Vitamin B deficiency
(these conditions may predispose the patient to peripheral neuropathy from nitrofurantoin)

» Glucose-6-phosphate dehydrogenase (G6PD) deficiency
(hemolysis may occur in patients with G6PD deficiency who take nitrofurantoin)

Hypersensitivity to nitrofurans

» Neuropathy, peripheral
(nitrofurantoin may cause peripheral neuropathy)

» Pulmonary disease
(nitrofurantoin may cause acute, subacute, and chronic pulmonary reactions, including pneumonitis)

» Renal function impairment
(because nitrofurantoin is excreted through the kidneys, it is recommended that nitrofurantoin not be given to patients with a creatinine clearance of less than 60 mL per minute [1.00 mL per second]; nitrofurantoin loses its effectiveness in patients with renal function impairment, and toxic effects are increased)

Patient monitoring

The following may be especially important in patient monitoring (other tests may be warranted in some patients, depending on condition; » = major clinical significance):

Hepatic function determinations
(may be required periodically during long-term therapy to detect changes in hepatic function; if hepatitis occurs, nitrofurantoin should be discontinued immediately and appropriate measures taken)

» Pulmonary function determinations
(may be required periodically during long-term therapy if pulmonary reactions [e.g., diffuse interstitial pneumonitis, pulmonary fibrosis] occur; if pulmonary reactions occur, nitrofurantoin should be discontinued and appropriate measures taken)

Renal function determinations
(may be required in patients who receive long-term therapy to determine if changes in renal function have occurred)

Side/Adverse Effects

Note: Acute pneumonitis is more common in the elderly; symptoms usually occur within the first week of therapy. Acute pulmonary reactions are often manifested by fever, chills, cough, chest pain, dyspnea, pulmonary infiltration with consolidation or pleural effusion on radiograph, and eosinophilia. The pneumonitis is often reversible with discontinuation of the drug; corticosteroids may be beneficial in severe cases. Chronic pulmonary reactions, including diffuse interstitial pneumonitis and fibrosis, are insidious in onset and are more likely to occur in patients who have been on nitrofurantoin therapy for at least 6 months. The severity of chronic pulmonary reactions and their degree of resolution appear to be related to the duration of continued nitrofurantoin therapy after the first clinical signs appear. Pulmonary function may be permanently impaired even after the drug has been stopped, especially if pulmonary reactions are not recognized early. In subacute pulmonary reactions, recovery may require several months after termination of nitrofurantoin treatment. If nitrofurantoin therapy is continued, the symptoms may become more severe. Changes in ECG, such as nonspecific ST/T wave changes or bundle branch block, have been associated with pulmonary reactions.

Peripheral neuropathy is an ascending sensorimotor neuropathy, which may be progressive if the drug is not discontinued immediately. Peripheral neuropathy occurs more frequently in patients with renal dysfunction and in the elderly; however, it also occurs in patients with normal renal function who have received nitrofurantoin for prolonged periods of time. Demyelination and degeneration of both sensory and motor nerves occur. Nitrofurantoin should be stopped at the first signs of neuritis.

Superinfections with *Pseudomonas* or *Candida* can sometimes occur during treatment with nitrofurantoin. These superinfections have been limited to the genitourinary tract.

The following side/adverse effects have been selected on the basis of their potential clinical significance (possible signs and symptoms in parentheses where appropriate)—not necessarily inclusive:

Those indicating need for medical attention

Incidence more frequent

Hypersensitivity reactions including anaphylaxis (shortness of breath; swelling of face; changes in facial skin color); ***angioedema*** (sudden trouble in swallowing or breathing; swelling of face, mouth, hands, or feet; hoarseness); ***arthralgia*** (joint pain); ***chills; drug fever*** (fever, shortly after onset of therapy); ***maculopapular, erythematous, or eczematous eruptions*** (skin rash); ***myalgia*** (muscle pain); ***pruritus*** (itching); ***and urticaria*** (hives); ***pneumonitis*** (chest pain; chills; cough; fever; general feeling of discomfort or illness; troubled breathing)

Incidence less frequent

Hematologic reactions, specifically granulocytopenia (sore throat and fever); ***leukopenia*** (sore throat and fever); ***megaloblastic anemia*** (unusual tiredness or weakness); ***or thrombocytopenia*** (rarely, unusual bleeding or bruising; black, tarry stools; blood in urine or stools; pinpoint red spots on skin); ***neurotoxicity*** (dizziness; drowsiness; headache; unusual tiredness or weakness); ***peripheral neu-***

ropathy (burning, numbness, tingling, or painful sensations; weakness in arms, hands, legs, or feet)

Incidence rare

Aplastic anemia (shortness of breath, troubled breathing, wheezing, or tightness in chest; sores, ulcers, or white spots on lips or in mouth; swollen or painful glands; unusual bleeding or bruising); ***benign intracranial hypertension*** (loss of appetite; headache; vomiting; visual changes; bulging fontanel in infants); ***cyanosis*** (bluish color of skin)—secondary to methemoglobinemia; ***hemolytic anemia*** (pale skin; unusual tiredness or weakness); ***hepatotoxicity, including hepatitis, cholestatic jaundice, chronic active hepatitis, and hepatic necrosis*** (yellow eyes or skin; darkening of urine; itching; abdominal or stomach pain, continuing; pale stools or black, tarry stools; headache, continuing; general feeling of discomfort or illness; unpleasant breath odor, continuing; vomiting of blood); ***optic neuritis*** (blurred vision or loss of vision, with or without eye pain); ***pancreatitis*** (severe stomach pain with nausea or vomiting); ***pseudomembranous colitis*** (abdominal or stomach cramps or pain, severe; diarrhea, watery and severe, which may also be bloody; fever); ***psychological disturbances, such as confusion; mental depression; and psychotic reactions*** (mood or mental changes); ***severe skin reactions, including exfoliative dermatitis, erythema multiforme, and Stevens-Johnson syndrome*** (blistering, peeling, or loosening of skin and mucous membranes; fever; general feeling of discomfort or illness; red, thickened, or scaly skin; red skin lesions, often with a purple center)

Those indicating need for medical attention only if they continue or are bothersome

Incidence more frequent

Gastrointestinal disturbances (abdominal or stomach pain or upset; diarrhea; gas; loss of appetite; nausea or vomiting); ***headache***

Those not indicating need for medical attention

Rust-yellow to brown discoloration of urine; transient alopecia (loss of hair, temporary)

Those indicating the need for medical attention if they occur after medication is discontinued

Pseudomembranous colitis (abdominal or stomach cramps or pain, severe; diarrhea, watery and severe, which may also be bloody; fever)

Overdose

For more information on the management of overdose or unintentional ingestion, **contact a Poison Control Center** (see *Poison Control Center Listing*).

Treatment of overdose

Recommended treatment consists of the following:

To decrease absorption—Induction of emesis if vomiting has not already occurred.

Specific treatment—Maintaining a high fluid intake to promote urinary excretion of nitrofurantoin. Nitrofurantoin is removable from the circulation by dialysis.

Supportive care—Patients in whom intentional overdose is known or suspected should be referred for psychiatric consultation.

Patient Consultation

As an aid to patient consultation, refer to *Advice for the Patient, Nitrofurantoin (Systemic).*

In providing consultation, consider emphasizing the following selected information (» = major clinical significance):

Before using this medication

» Conditions affecting use, especially:
- Hypersensitivity to nitrofurans
- Pregnancy—Nitrofurantoin is contraindicated at term and during labor and delivery because of the possibility of hemolytic anemia in the fetus
- Breast-feeding—Not recommended since hemolytic anemia may occur in G6PD-deficient infants
- Use in children—Nitrofurantoin is contraindicated in infants up to 1 month of age because of the possibility of hemolytic anemia
- Use in the elderly—Side effects, such as acute pneumonitis and peripheral neuropathy, may occur more frequently in elderly patients
- Other medications, especially other hemolytics, other neurotoxic medications, probenecid, or sulfinpyrazone
- Other medical problems, especially G6PD deficiency, peripheral neuropathy, pulmonary disease, or renal function impairment

Proper use of this medication

» Not giving to infants up to 1 month of age

Taking with food or milk

Proper administration technique for oral liquid
- Shaking well before each dose
- Using a specially marked measuring spoon or other device
- May be mixed with water, milk, fruit juices, or infants' formulas

Proper administration technique for extended-release tablets
- Swallowing tablet whole; not breaking, crushing, or chewing before swallowing

» Compliance with full course of therapy

» Proper dosage

Missed dose: Taking as soon as possible; not taking if almost time for next dose; not doubling doses

» Proper storage

Precautions while using this medication

Regular visits to physician to check progress if on long-term therapy

Checking with physician if no improvement within a few days

» Patients with diabetes: False-positive reactions with copper sulfate urine glucose tests may occur

Side/adverse effects

Rust-yellow to brown discoloration of urine may be alarming to patient although medically insignificant

Signs of potential side effects, especially hypersensitivity reactions, including angioedema, maculopapular, erythematous, or eczematous eruptions, pruritus, urticaria, anaphylaxis, arthralgia, myalgia, drug fever, and chills; pneumonitis; hematologic reactions, specifically granulocytopenia, leukopenia, megaloblastic anemia, or thrombocytopenia; neurotoxicity; peripheral neuropathy; aplastic anemia; benign intracranial hypertension; cyanosis; hemolytic anemia, hepatotoxicity, including hepatitis, cholestatic jaundice, chronic active hepatitis, and hepatic necrosis; optic neuritis; pancreatitis; pseudomembranous colitis; psychological disturbances, such as confusion, mental depression, and psychotic reactions; severe skin reactions, including exfoliative dermatitis, erythema multiforme, and Stevens-Johnson syndrome

General Dosing Information

Nitrofurantoin should preferably be taken with food or milk. This minimizes gastrointestinal irritation, delays and increases absorption of both the macrocrystalline and microcrystalline forms, increases the peak concentration of the macrocrystalline form, and prolongs the duration of therapeutic concentrations in the urine.

Nitrofurantoin therapy should be continued for seven days or for at least three days after the sterility of the urine is obtained. An infection that continues indicates a need for re-evaluation.

Patients on long-term suppressive therapy require a reduction in dose.

Patients with impaired renal function (creatinine clearance less than 60 mL per minute [1.00 mL per second]) should not receive nitrofurantoin since increased toxicity due to possible accumulation of toxic metabolites may occur. Also, nitrofurantoin is ineffective in patients whose creatinine clearance is less than 40 mL per minute.

Due to the lack of broad tissue distribution, many patients treated with nitrofurantoin are predisposed to the persistence or reappearance of bacteriuria. Urine specimens for culture and susceptibility testing should be obtained both before and after completion of treatment with nitrofurantoin; if persistence or reappearance of bacteriuria occurs, other therapeutic agents with broad tissue distribution should be considered.

For treatment of adverse effects

For antibiotic-associated pseudomembranous colitis (AAPMC):

Some patients may develop AAPMC, caused by *Clostridium difficile* toxin, during or following administration of nitrofurantoin. Mild cases may respond to discontinuation of the drug alone. Moderate to severe cases may require fluid, electrolyte, and protein replacement. In cases not responding to the above measures or in more severe cases, treatment with an antibacterial medication effective against AAPMC may be necessary.

Oral Dosage Forms

NITROFURANTOIN CAPSULES USP

Usual adult and adolescent dose

Antibacterial—

Oral, 50 to 100 mg every six hours. Most uncomplicated infections caused by susceptible bacteria are adequately treated with 50 mg three times a day.

Urinary tract infections, bacterial (prophylaxis)—Oral, 50 to 100 mg once a day at bedtime.

Usual adult prescribing limits
Up to 600 mg daily; or up to 10 mg per kg of body weight daily.

Usual pediatric dose
Antibacterial—
Infants up to 1 month of age: Use is contraindicated because of the possibility of hemolytic anemia due to immature erythrocyte enzyme systems.
Infants and children 1 month of age and older: Oral, 0.75 to 1.75 mg per kg of body weight every six hours.Therapeutic doses up to 10 mg per kg of body weight daily in four evenly divided doses have been used.
Urinary tract infections, bacterial (prophylaxis):
Infants up to 1 month of age—Use is contraindicated because of the possibility of hemolytic anemia due to immature erythrocyte enzyme systems.
Infants and children 1 month of age and older—Oral, 1 mg per kg of body weight once a day at bedtime. Alternatively, the dose may be given in two divided doses.

Strength(s) usually available
U.S.—
25 mg (Rx) [*Macrodantin* (macrocrystalline); GENERIC (macrocrystalline)].
50 mg (Rx) [*Macrodantin* (macrocrystalline); GENERIC (macrocrystalline and microcrystalline)].
100 mg (Rx) [*Macrodantin* (macrocrystalline); GENERIC (macrocrystalline and microcrystalline)].
Canada—
25 mg (Rx) [*Macrodantin* (macrocrystalline)].
50 mg (Rx) [*Macrodantin* (macrocrystalline); *Novo-Furantoin;* GENERIC].
100 mg (Rx) [*Macrodantin* (macrocrystalline); *Novo-Furantoin;* GENERIC].

Packaging and storage
Store below 40 °C (104 °F), preferably between 15 and 30 °C (59 and 86 °F), unless otherwise specified by manufacturer. Store in a tight, light-resistant container.

Auxiliary labeling
- Continue medicine for full time of treatment.
- Take with food or milk.
- May discolor urine.

NITROFURANTOIN EXTENDED-RELEASE CAPSULES

Usual adult and adolescent dose
Antibacterial—
Oral, 100 mg every twelve hours for seven days.

Usual pediatric dose
Antibacterial—
Children up to 12 years of age: Safety and efficacy have not been established.
Children 12 years of age and older: See *Usual adult dose.*

Strength(s) usually available
U.S.—
100 mg (Rx) [*Macrobid* (macrocrystalline 25 mg; monohydrate 75 mg)].
Canada—
100 mg (Rx) [*Macrobid* (macrocrystalline 25 mg; monohydrate 75 mg)].

Packaging and storage
Store below 40 °C (104 °F), preferably between 15 and 30 °C (59 and 86 °F), unless otherwise specified by manufacturer. Store in a tight, light-resistant container.

Auxiliary labeling
- Continue medicine for full time of treatment.
- Take with food or milk.
- May discolor urine.

NITROFURANTOIN ORAL SUSPENSION USP

Usual adult and adolescent dose
See *Nitrofurantoin Capsules USP.*

Usual adult prescribing limits
See *Nitrofurantoin Capsules USP.*

Usual pediatric dose
See *Nitrofurantoin Capsules USP.*

Strength(s) usually available
U.S.—
25 mg per 5 mL (Rx) [*Furadantin* (methylparaben; propylparaben; saccharin; sorbitol)].
Canada—
Not commercially available.

Packaging and storage
Store between 20 and 25 °C (68 and 77 °F). Store in a tight, light-resistant container. Protect from freezing.

Incompatibilities
Nitrofurantoin and its solutions are discolored by alkalis and by exposure to strong light and decompose upon contact with metals other than stainless steel or aluminum.

Auxiliary labeling
- Shake well.
- Continue medicine for full time of treatment.
- Take with food or milk.
- May discolor urine.

Note
Dispense in amber bottles.
When dispensing, include a calibrated liquid-measuring device.

Additional information
The oral suspension dosage form is readily miscible with water, milk, fruit juices, or infants' formulas.

NITROFURANTOIN TABLETS USP

Usual adult and adolescent dose
See *Nitrofurantoin Capsules USP.*

Usual adult prescribing limits
See *Nitrofurantoin Capsules USP.*

Usual pediatric dose
See *Nitrofurantoin Capsules USP.*

Strength(s) usually available
U.S.—
50 mg (Rx) [GENERIC].
100 mg (Rx) [GENERIC].
Canada—
50 mg (Rx) [*Apo-Nitrofurantoin*].
100 mg (Rx) [*Apo-Nitrofurantoin*].

Packaging and storage
Store below 40 °C (104 °F), preferably between 15 and 30 °C (59 and 86 °F), unless otherwise specified by manufacturer. Store in a tight, light-resistant container.

Incompatibilities
Nitrofurantoin and its solutions are discolored by alkalis and by exposure to strong light and decompose upon contact with metals other than stainless steel or aluminum.

Auxiliary labeling
- Continue medicine for full time of treatment.
- Take with food or milk.
- May discolor urine.

Note
Dispense in amber bottles.

Revised: 06/14/1999

NITROGLYCERIN—See *Nitrates (Systemic)*

NITROPRUSSIDE Systemic

VA CLASSIFICATION (Primary/Secondary): CV402/CV500; CV900; AD900

Commonly used brand name(s): *Nipride; Nitropress.*

Note: For a listing of dosage forms and brand names by country availability, see *Dosage Forms* section(s).

Category

Antihypertensive; vasodilator, congestive heart failure; myocardial infarction therapy adjunct; antidote (to ergot alkaloid poisoning).

Indications

Note: Bracketed information in the *Indications* section refers to uses that are not included in U.S. product labeling.

Accepted

Congestive heart failure (treatment)[1]—Nitroprusside is indicated for the management of acute congestive heart failure.

Hypertension (treatment)—Nitroprusside is indicated for the immediate reduction of blood pressure of patients in hypertensive crisis.

For additional information on initial therapeutic guidelines related to the treatment of hypertension, see *Appendix III.*

Hypotension, controlled (induction and maintenance)—Nitroprusside is indicated for producing controlled hypotension during surgery to reduce bleeding into the surgical field.

[Hypertension, paroxysmal, in surgery for pheochromocytoma (treatment)][1]—Nitroprusside is used to control paroxysmal hypertension prior to and during surgery for pheochromocytoma.

[Myocardial infarction (treatment adjunct)][1]—Use of nitroprusside to reduce afterload is also recommended in patients with acute myocardial infarction who are hypertensive with persistent chest pain or left ventricular failure.

[Valvular regurgitation (treatment adjunct)][1]—Nitroprusside is also used as an adjunct to standard treatment of aortic or mitral regurgitation prior to surgical intervention.

[Toxicity, ergot alkaloid (treatment)][1]—Nitroprusside is also used for treatment of peripheral vasospasm caused by ergot alkaloid overdose.

Acceptance not established

Studies and case reports suggest that nitroprusside may be used for the treatment of *pulmonary hypertension in pediatric patients.* However, data are insufficient to establish safety and efficacy of nitroprusside for this indication.

Unaccepted

Nitroprusside should *not* be used in the treatment of compensatory hypertension (such as in arteriovenous shunt or coarctation of the aorta).

[1]Not included in Canadian product labeling.

Pharmacology/Pharmacokinetics

Physicochemical characteristics

Molecular weight—297.95.

Mechanism of action/Effect

Antihypertensive—Hypertension or controlled hypotension: Causes vasodilation by a direct effect on arterial and venous smooth muscle, with no effect on uterine or duodenal smooth muscle or on myocardial contractility; regional distribution of blood flow is only marginally affected. Reduces peripheral resistance and has a variable effect on cardiac output. Is more active on veins than arteries (but less markedly so than nitroglycerin). Increases renin activity.

Vasodilator, congestive heart failure—Beneficial effects in congestive heart failure are due to decreased systemic resistance, preload and afterload reduction, and improved cardiac output.

Myocardial infarction therapy adjunct—The effect of nitroprusside on ischemic myocardial areas is not totally known. It dilates coronary arteries. The medication reportedly reduces myocardial oxygen consumption and relieves persistent chest pain but has also been found to aggravate ischemia by redistributing blood flow away from ischemic myocardium.

Valvular regurgitation therapy adjunct—In the treatment of valvular regurgitation, nitroprusside reduces aortic and left ventricular impedance.

Antidote (to ergot alkaloid poisoning)—Causes vasodilation.

Other actions/effects

Slightly increases heart rate. Decreases platelet aggregation.

Biotransformation

By intraerythrocytic reaction with hemoglobin to produce cyanmethemoglobin and cyanide ion. Exogenous cyanide is sequestered by erythrocyte methemoglobin as cyanmethemoglobin until intraerythrocytic methemoglobin is saturated. Some cyanide ion is eliminated from the body as expired hydrogen cyanide, but most is enzymatically converted to thiocyanate, which is eliminated in the urine; this reaction requires a hepatic mitochondrial enzyme, rhodanase (thiosulfate-cyanide sulfur transferase), and a sulfur donor, especially thiosulfate, cystine, and cysteine. Cyanide not removed by any of these methods binds to mitochondrial cytochromes and prevents oxidative metabolism; cells either are forced to provide for their energy needs via anaerobic pathways, generating lactic acid, or die hypoxic deaths.

Cyanide is normally found in serum and is derived from dietary substrates and tobacco smoke. Normal cyanide ion concentrations in packed erythrocytes are less than 1 micromole per liter (25 mg per liter); these concentrations are doubled in heavy smokers.

At healthy steady state, less than 1% of hemoglobin is in the form of methemoglobin. Nitroprusside metabolism leads to methemoglobin formation either through dissociation of cyanmethemoglobin formed in the original reaction of nitroprusside with hemoglobin or by direct oxidation of hemoglobin by the released nitroso group. A patient with normal red-cell mass and normal methemoglobin concentrations can buffer about 175 mcg of cyanide ion per kg of body weight (mcg/kg), corresponding to a little less than 500 mcg/kg of infused sodium nitroprusside.

Thiosulfate is a normal constituent of serum, produced by cysteine. Normal physiological concentrations of 0.1 millimole per liter (11 mg per liter) are approximately double in children and in adults who are not eating. When thiosulfate is being supplied only by normal physiologic mechanisms, conversion of cyanide ion to thiocyanate generally occurs at about 1 mcg/kg per minute. This rate of cyanide clearance corresponds to steady-state processing of a sodium nitroprusside infusion of slightly more than 2 mcg/kg per minute. Cyanide begins to accumulate when sodium nitroprusside infusions exceed this rate.

Half-life

Nitroprusside—Circulatory: About 2 minutes.
Thiosulfate—After intravenous infusion: About 20 minutes.
Thiocyanate—About 3 days; may be doubled or tripled in renal failure.

Onset of action

Hypotensive—Within 1 to 2 minutes after start of an adequate infusion.

Time to peak effect

Hypotensive—Almost immediate.

Duration of action

Hypotensive—1 to 10 minutes after infusion is stopped.

Elimination

Thiocyanate and infused thiosulfate—Renal.

Precautions to Consider

Carcinogenicity/Mutagenicity

Studies have not been done in either animals or humans.

Pregnancy/Reproduction

Pregnancy—Adequate and well-controlled studies in humans have not been done. Birth of a stillborn infant without any obvious anomalies was reported after one woman was given nitroprusside to control gestational hypertension; however, cyanide concentrations in the infant's liver were well below usual toxic levels and the mother demonstrated no cyanide toxicity.

Teratogenicity studies in laboratory animals have not been done. In three studies in pregnant ewes, nitroprusside was shown to cross the placenta; fetal cyanide levels were dose-related to maternal levels; fatal cyanide levels could be produced in fetuses by using high rates of nitroprusside administration to the pregnant ewes.

FDA Pregnancy Category C.

Breast-feeding

It is not known whether nitroprusside is excreted in breast milk. Problems in humans have not been documented.

Pediatrics

Appropriate studies on the relationship of age to the effects of nitroprusside have not been performed in the pediatric population. However, pediatrics-specific problems that would limit the usefulness of this medication in children are not expected.

Geriatrics

Although appropriate studies on the relationship of age to the effects of nitroprusside have not been performed in the geriatric population, the elderly may be more sensitive to the hypotensive effects. In addition, elderly patients are more likely to have age-related renal function impairment, which may require caution in patients receiving nitroprusside.

Drug interactions and/or related problems

The following drug interactions and/or related problems have been selected on the basis of their potential clinical significance (possible mechanism in parentheses where appropriate)—not necessarily inclusive (» = major clinical significance):

Note: Combinations containing any of the following medications, depending on the amount present, may also interact with this medication.

Dobutamine
(concurrent use with nitroprusside may result in a higher cardiac output and a lower pulmonary wedge pressure)

Hypotension-producing medications, other (see *Appendix II*)
(concurrent use may result in increased hypotensive effects which may be severe; dosage adjustment based on careful blood pressure monitoring is recommended)

Sympathomimetics
(hypotensive effects of nitroprusside may be reduced when it is used concurrently with sympathomimetics)

Laboratory value alterations

The following have been selected on the basis of their potential clinical significance (possible effect in parentheses where appropriate)—not necessarily inclusive (» = major clinical significance).

With physiology/laboratory test values

Bicarbonate concentrations, blood and
PCO_2 and
pH
(may be decreased, indicating metabolic acidosis, during cyanide toxicity; however, may not be present until an hour or more after toxic cyanide concentrations are reached)

Cyanide, serum
(concentrations increased with excessive rate of nitroprusside infusion; except at low nitroprusside infusion rates [less than 2 mcg per kg of body weight (mcg/kg) per minute] or with brief use, concentrations produced are significant, potentially reaching toxic or lethal levels; venous blood appears bright red because of hyperoxemia)

Lactate, arterial blood
(concentrations may be increased in overdose, indicating metabolic acidosis, during cyanide toxicity; however, may not be present until an hour or more after toxic cyanide concentrations are reached)

Methemoglobin, blood
(concentrations may rarely be increased if amount of nitroprusside administered exceeds rate at which back-conversion of methemoglobin to hemoglobin can occur; blood appears chocolate brown, without color change on exposure to air)

Oxygen, venous blood
(concentrations increased in cyanide toxicity; venous blood appears bright red)

Thiocyanate, serum
(concentrations increased as a result of cyanide enzymatic reaction with thiosulfate; with prolonged infusions, the steady-state concentration is increased with increased infusion rate)

Medical considerations/Contraindications

The medical considerations/contraindications included have been selected on the basis of their potential clinical significance (reasons given in parentheses where appropriate)—not necessarily inclusive (» = major clinical significance).

Risk-benefit should be considered when the following medical problems exist:

Anemia—for use in producing controlled hypotension during anesthesia only; patient's capacity to compensate may be diminished; should be corrected prior to use of nitroprusside

» Cerebrovascular or coronary artery insufficiency
(reduced tolerance of hypotension)

» Encephalopathy or other conditions where intracranial pressure is elevated
(intracranial pressure may be further increased; nitroprusside should be used only with extreme caution)

» Hepatic function impairment
(hepatic enzyme is involved in metabolism of nitroprusside)

Hypothyroidism
(thiocyanate, one of the metabolic products of nitroprusside, inhibits both uptake and binding of iodine)

Hypovolemia—for use in producing controlled hypotension during anesthesia only; patient's capacity to compensate may be diminished; should be corrected prior to use of nitroprusside

» Leber's hereditary optic atrophy or
» Tobacco amblyopia
(deficiency or absence of enzyme [rhodanase] needed for metabolism of nitroprusside)

Pulmonary function impairment
(aggravation of hypoxemia)

» Renal function impairment
(reduced excretion of thiocyanate)

Sensitivity to nitroprusside

» Vitamin B_{12} deficiency
(related to metabolism)

Patient monitoring

The following may be especially important in patient monitoring (other tests may be warranted in some patients, depending on condition; » = major clinical significance):

Acid-base balance and
Oxygen concentrations, venous
(may indicate metabolic acidosis resulting from cyanide toxicity; however, because measurable effects may be delayed an hour or more after toxic cyanide concentrations are reached, these values should not be used to decide when to treat for cyanide toxicity)

» Blood pressure determinations
(should be made continuously, either with a continually reinflated sphygmomanometer or, preferably, an intra-arterial pressure sensor)
(pulmonary artery diastolic or wedge pressure determinations may be required in patients with acute myocardial infarction)

Cyanide concentrations, serum
(may be determined; however, not particularly useful because the cyanide assay is technically difficult and cyanide concentrations in body fluids other than packed red cells are difficult to interpret)

Methemoglobin concentrations, blood
(recommended in patients who have received more than 10 mg of nitroprusside per kg of body weight and who exhibit signs of impaired oxygen delivery despite adequate cardiac output and adequate arterial pO_2)

Thiocyanate concentrations, serum
(recommended at daily intervals in patients receiving prolonged nitroprusside infusions at a rate greater than 3 mcg per kg of body weight [mcg/kg] per minute [1 mcg/kg per minute in anuric patients]; should not exceed 1 millimole per liter)

For congestive heart failure

Invasive hemodynamic monitoring and
Urine output
(recommended to guide titration of infusion rate)

Side/Adverse Effects

Note: A severe rebound hypertension has been reported after discontinuation of an infusion used to produce controlled hypotension during surgery.

The following side/adverse effects have been selected on the basis of their potential clinical significance (possible signs and symptoms in parentheses where appropriate)—not necessarily inclusive:

Those indicating need for medical attention

Signs and/or symptoms of excessively rapid fall in blood pressure (appear to be related to rate of administration rather than total dose)

Abdominal pain (stomach pain); ***dizziness; excessive sweating; headache; muscle twitching; nervousness or anxiety; restlessness; retching; tachycardia, reflex***

Note: Excessive *hypotension*, sometimes to levels low enough to compromise perfusion of vital organs, may be produced by small transient excesses in the infusion rate. Excessively rapid decreases in blood pressure can lead to irreversible ischemic injuries or death if patients are not properly monitored.

Signs and/or symptoms of thiocyanate toxicity

Ataxia; blurred vision; delirium; dizziness; headache; loss of consciousness; nausea and vomiting; shortness of breath; tinnitus (ringing in ears)

Note: Mild neurotoxicity (*tinnitus, miosis, hyperreflexia*) occurs at serum thiocyanate concentrations of 1 millimole per liter (60 mg per liter). Thiocyanate toxicity becomes life-threatening at serum concentrations of 200 mg per liter.

Signs and/or symptoms of cyanide toxicity

Absence of reflexes; coma; distant heart sounds; hypotension; imperceptible pulse; metabolic acidosis; pink color; very shallow breathing; widely dilated pupils

Note: Nitroprusside infusion rates greater than 2 mcg per kg of body weight (mcg/kg) per minute generate cyanide ion faster than the body can normally eliminate it (administration of thiosulfate greatly increases the body's capacity for cyanide elimination). The capacity of methemoglobin to buffer cyanide is exhausted from about 500 mcg/kg of nitroprusside (the amount administered in less than an hour at a rate of 10 mcg/kg per minute). Above this level, toxic effects of cyanide may be rapid, serious, and lethal.

Elevated cyanide concentrations, metabolic acidosis, and marked clinical deterioration have occasionally been reported in patients given infusions at recommended rates for only a few hours (in one case, for only 35 minutes).

Incidence less frequent or rare

Flushing; hypothyroidism; ileus; increased intracranial pressure; methemoglobinemia—concentrations greater than 10%; ***pain or redness at site of injection; skin rash***

Note: *Hypothyroidism*—Thiocyanate interferes with iodine uptake by the thyroid.

Methemoglobinemia is usually rare, because the back-conversion process returning methemoglobin to hemoglobin is normally rapid. Even in patients congenitally incapable of back-converting methemoglobin, a cumulative dose of 10 mg of nitroprusside per kg of body weight (mg/kg) (e.g., given at a rate of 10 mcg/kg per minute for 16 hours) would be required to produce 10% methemoglobinemia.

General Dosing Information

Nitroprusside should be administered *only* by intravenous infusion by means of an infusion pump, preferably a volumetric pump.

It is recommended that patients receiving nitroprusside be in a setting with available equipment and personnel to allow blood pressure to be monitored continuously.

Care should be taken to avoid extravasation because of possible irritation.

Larger than ordinary doses may be required for hypotensive anesthesia in young, vigorous males.

It is recommended that administration of nitroprusside be discontinued immediately if administration of 10 mcg (0.01 mg) (sodium nitroprusside dihydrate) per kg of body weight per minute for 10 minutes does not produce adequate reduction of blood pressure.

Concurrent administration of sodium thiosulfate (at 5 to 10 times the rate of sodium nitroprusside administration) may reduce the risk of cyanide toxicity by increasing the rate of cyanide conversion. However, it has not been extensively studied, and in one study appeared to potentiate nitroprusside's hypotensive effect. Caution is necessary to avoid prolonged or high doses of sodium nitroprusside with sodium thiosulfate, which could lead to thiocyanate toxicity and hypovolemia.

Apparent tolerance has occurred occasionally. Although a correlation between tachyphylaxis and concomitant cyanide toxicity has been proposed, no correlation has been demonstrated.

For use in treatment of hypertension

It is recommended that oral antihypertensive therapy be instituted while the patient is receiving nitroprusside and that nitroprusside be withdrawn as soon as the patient has stabilized. Patients receiving concomitant antihypertensive medication require lower doses of nitroprusside.

For use in treatment of congestive heart failure

Addition of a potent inotropic medication such as dopamine or dobutamine may be useful when doses of nitroprusside that are effective in restoring pump function in left ventricular congestive heart failure cause excessive hypotension.

For treatment of adverse effects/overdose

For methemoglobinemia

- Intravenous administration of methylene blue in a dose of 1 to 2 mg per kg of body weight (mg/kg) given over several minutes. Extreme caution is necessary in patients likely to have substantial amounts of cyanide bound to methemoglobin as cyanmethemoglobin.

For excessive hypotension

- Slowing or discontinuation of infusion; symptoms disappear quickly (within 1 to 10 minutes). Placement of the patient in the Trendelenberg position to maximize venous return may be helpful.

For thiocyanate toxicity

- Hemodialysis; clearance rates during dialysis can approach the blood flow rate of the dialyzer.

For cyanide toxicity

- Discontinuation of nitroprusside administration. Because metabolic acidosis may not be evident until more than an hour after the appearance of dangerous cyanide concentrations, laboratory test results should not be awaited; treatment should be initiated with reasonable suspicion of cyanide toxicity.
- Intravenous administration of sodium nitrite (as a 3% solution), in a dose of 4 to 6 mg/kg over 2 to 4 minutes. Sodium nitrite provides a buffer for cyanide by converting as much hemoglobin into methemoglobin as the patient can safely tolerate; this dose can be expected to convert about 10% of the patient's hemoglobin, and this level of methemoglobinemia is not associated with any known hazards. Sodium nitrite infusion may cause transient vasodilation and hypotension, which should be managed as necessary. Amyl nitrite inhalations may be used in environments where intravenous administration of sodium nitrite may be delayed.
- Immediately following sodium nitrite infusion, intravenous infusion of sodium thiosulfate in a sufficient amount to convert the cyanide into thiocyanate. The recommended dose of sodium thiosulfate is 150 to 200 mg/kg; a typical adult dose is 50 mL of a 25% solution (sodium thiosulfate is also available as a 50% solution). Thiocyanate concentrations will be raised in acutely cyanide-toxic patients, but not to a dangerous level.
- Hemodialysis is not effective in removing cyanide.
- If necessary, the nitrite/thiosulfate regimen may be repeated, at half the original doses, after 2 hours.

Parenteral Dosage Forms

SODIUM NITROPRUSSIDE STERILE

Usual adult and adolescent dose

Antihypertensive—

Intravenous infusion, initially, 0.3 mcg (0.0003 mg) (sodium nitroprusside dihydrate) per kg of body weight per minute, adjusted every few minutes according to response; usual dose is 3 mcg (0.003 mg) per kg of body weight per minute.

Note: Geriatric patients may be more sensitive to the usual adult dose of nitroprusside.

Usual adult prescribing limits

10 mcg (0.01 mg) per kg of body weight per minute for a maximum period of 10 minutes, or a total dose of 3.5 mg per kg of body weight (500 mcg [0.5 mg] per kg of body weight during short-term infusions such as in controlled hypotension during surgery). To keep the steady-state thiocyanate concentration below 1 millimole per liter, the rate of a prolonged infusion should be no more than 3 mcg per kg of body weight per minute (1 mcg per kg of body weight per minute in anuric patients).

Usual pediatric dose

Antihypertensive—

See *Usual adult and adolescent dose.*

For severe hypertension—Intravenous infusion, 0.53 to 10 micrograms per kg of body weight per minute.

Strength(s) usually available

U.S.—

50 mg (sodium nitroprusside dihydrate) (Rx) [*Nitropress;* GENERIC].

Canada—

50 mg (sodium nitroprusside dihydrate) (Rx) [*Nipride*].

Packaging and storage

Store below 40 °C (104 °F), preferably between 15 and 30 °C (59 and 86 °F), unless otherwise specified by manufacturer. Protect from light.

Preparation of dosage form

Nitroprusside is prepared for intravenous infusion by dissolving the contents of a 50-mg vial in 2.3 mL of 5% dextrose injection only and shaking gently to dissolve. The reconstituted solution must be diluted further in 250 to 1000 mL of 5% dextrose injection to achieve the desired concentration and the container is wrapped in a supplied opaque sleeve, aluminum foil, or other opaque material to protect it from light (it is not necessary to wrap the infusion drip chamber or the tubing).

Stability

Solutions of nitroprusside should be freshly prepared and any unused portion discarded. A freshly prepared solution has a slight brownish tint and should be discarded if the color is dark brown, orange, or blue.

It is recommended that solutions of nitroprusside not be kept or used longer than 24 hours, unless otherwise specified by the manufacturer.

No other medications should be added to infusion fluid containing nitroprusside.

Sodium nitroprusside solution is rapidly degraded by trace contaminants, often with resulting color changes. A change in color to blue, green, or bright red indicates reaction of nitroprusside ion with another substance, and the solution must be replaced and discarded.

Sodium nitroprusside solution is sensitive to certain wavelengths of light and therefore must be protected from light. After preparation of the medication, the container should be promptly wrapped in the supplied opaque sleeve, aluminum foil, or other opaque material (it is not necessary to wrap the infusion drip chamber or the tubing).

Selected Bibliography

Kreye VAW. Sodium nitroprusside. In: Scriabine A, ed. Pharmacology of antihypertensive drugs. New York: Raven Press, 1980: 373-96.

Gaskins JD, Holt RJ, Kessler C. Comparative review of intravenous nitroglycerin and nitroprusside sodium. Hosp Form 1982 Jul; 928-34.

Revised: 11/17/2004

NITROUS OXIDE—See *Anesthetics, Inhalation (Systemic)*

NIZATIDINE—See *Histamine H_2-receptor Antagonists (Systemic)*

NONOXYNOL 9—See *Spermacides (Vaginal)*

NORELGESTROMIN AND ETHINYL ESTRADIOL Systemic†

VA CLASSIFICATION (Primary): HS104

Commonly used brand name(s): *Ortho Evra.*

Note: For a listing of dosage forms and brand names by country availability, see *Dosage Forms* section(s).

†Not commercially available in Canada.

Category

Contraceptive, systemic.

Indications

Accepted

Pregnancy, prevention of—Norelgestromin and ethinyl estradiol combination is indicated for the prevention of pregnancy.

Unaccepted

Norelgestromin and ethinyl estradiol combination is not indicated for use in emergency contraception.

Norelgestromin and ethinyl estradiol combination should not be used to induce withdrawal bleeding as a test for pregnancy, nor should it be used during pregnancy to treat threatened or habitual abortion.

Pharmacology/Pharmacokinetics

Physicochemical characteristics

Molecular weight—

Norelgestromin: 327.47.

Ethinyl estradiol: 296.41.

Mechanism of action/Effect

Contraceptive, systemic—norelgestromin and ethinyl estradiol combination acts by suppression of gonadotropins. The primary mechanism of this action is inhibition of ovulation. Other alterations include changes in the cervical mucus (which increase the difficulty of sperm entry into the uterus) and the endometrium (which reduce the likelihood of implantation).

Absorption

Following transdermal application, both norelgestromin and ethinyl estradiol appear rapidly in the serum.

The absorption of norelgestromin and ethinyl estradiol following transdermal application was studied under conditions encountered in a health club (sauna, whirlpool, and treadmill) and in a cold water bath. The results indicated that for norelgestromin there were no significant treatment effects on steady state concentrations or area under the curve when compared to normal wear. For ethinyl estradiol, slight increases were observed due to sauna, whirlpool and treadmill, however, the steady state concentration values following these treatments were within the reference range. There was no significant effect of cold water on these parameters.

Protein binding

Norelgestromin—very high (greater than 97%); serum albumin.

Ethinyl estradiol—extensively bound to serum albumin.

Biotransformation

Hepatic metabolism of norelgestromin occurs and metabolites include norgestrel and various hydroxylated and conjugated metabolites. Ethinyl estradiol is also metabolized to various hydroxylated products and their glucuronide and sulfate conjugates.

Half-life

Elimination—

- Norelgestromin—28 hours
- Ethinyl estradiol—17 hours

Time to peak concentration

Following transdermal application a serum plateau is reached by approximately 48 hours.

Duration of action

Steady state serum levels are maintained throughout the wear period.

The patch can maintain serum concentrations of norelgestromin and ethinyl estradiol in the target range for 9 full days.

Elimination

The metabolites of norelgestromin and ethinyl estradiol are eliminated by renal and fecal pathways.

Post therapy return of hypothalamic pituitary ovarian function

Follicle stimulating hormone (FSH), luteinizing hormone (LH), and estradiol mean values, though suppressed during therapy, returned to near baseline values during the 6 weeks post therapy.

Precautions to Consider

Carcinogenicity

No carcinogenicity studies have been conducted with norelgestromin in humans

Bridging studies done previously for oral norelgestromin and ethinyl estradiol combination in rats and monkeys were exposed to 16 and 8 times the human exposure, respectively, supported the approval.

Mutagenicity

Norelgestromin was tested in several *in vitro* mutagenicity assays and in one *in vivo* rat micronucleus assay and was found to have no genotoxic potential.

Pregnancy/Reproduction

Pregnancy—Norelgestromin was tested for its reproductive toxicity in a developmental toxicity study in rabbits using the subcutaneous route of administration. Doses of 0, 1, 2, 4 and 6 mg per kg of body weight were administered daily on gestation days 7 through 19. These doses gave systemic exposure of approximately 25 to 125 times the human exposure with norelgestromin and ethinyl estradiol combination. Malformations reported were paw hyperflexion at 4 and 6 mg per kg and paw hyperextension and cleft palate at 6 mg per kg.

Since the immediate postpartum period is also associated with an increased risk of thromboembolism, hormonal contraceptives should be started no earlier than four weeks after delivery in women who elect not to breast feed.

Norelgestromin and ethinyl estradiol transdermal system should be discontinued if pregnancy is confirmed. However, studies do not indicate a teratogenic effect when oral contraceptives are taken inadvertently during pregnancy.

FDA Pregnancy Category X

Breast-feeding

It is not known whether norelgestromin and ethinyl estradiol combination is distributed into human breast milk. However, small amounts of combination hormonal contraceptive steroids have been identified in the milk of nursing mothers and a few adverse effects on the child have been reported, including jaundice and breast enlargement. In addition, combination hormonal contraceptives given in the postpartum period may interfere with lactation by decreasing the quantity and quality of breast milk. Long-term follow-up of infants whose mothers used combination hormonal contraceptives while breast feeding has shown no deleterious effects. However, the nursing mother should be advised not to use norelgestromin and ethinyl estradiol combination, but to use other forms of contraception, until she has completely weaned her child.

Pediatrics

No information is available on the relationship of age to the effects of norelgestromin and ethinyl estradiol combination in the pediatric population. Use of the product before menarche is not indicated, and the safety and efficacy have not been established.

Adolescents

Safety and efficacy of norelgestromin and ethinyl estradiol combination have been established in women of reproductive age. Safety and efficacy are expected to be the same for post-pubertal adolescents under the age of 16 and for users 16 years and older. Use of the product before menarche is not indicated.

Geriatrics

No information is available on the relationship of age to the effects of norelgestromin and ethinyl estradiol combination in geriatric patients over the age of 65. Norelgestromin and ethinyl estradiol combination is not indicated in this population.

Drug interactions and/or related problems

The following drug interactions and/or related problems have been selected on the basis of their potential clinical significance (possible mechanism in parentheses where appropriate)—not necessarily inclusive (» = major clinical significance):

Note: Combinations containing any of the following medications, depending on the amount present, may also interact with this medication.

Acetaminophen
(may increase plasma ethinyl estradiollevels when administered with oral contraceptives possibly by inhibition of conjugation; co-administration with oral contraceptives may also causedecreased plasma concentrations of acetaminophen.)

» Ampicillin or
» Barbiturates or
» Carbamazepine or
» Felbamate or
» Griseofulvin or
» Oxcarbazepine or
» Phenylbutazone or
» Phenytoin or
» Rifampin or
» Topiramate
(contraceptive effectiveness may be reduced when hormonal contraceptives are co-administered with some antibiotics, antifungals, anticonvulsants, and other drugs that increase metabolism of contraceptive steroids. This could result in unintended pregnancy or breakthrough bleeding.)

» Anti-HIV protease inhibitors
(significant increases and decreases in the mean AUC of the estrogen and progestin have been noted when co-administered with oral combination hormonal contraceptives. The safety and efficacy of oral contraceptive products may be affected and it is unknown whether this applies to transdermal administration, but healthcare professionals should refer to the individual anti-HIV protease inhibitors for more information.)

Ascorbic acid or
Atorvastatin or
CYP 3A4 inhibitors such as itraconazole or ketoconazole
(may increase plasma hormone levels.)

Clofibric acid or
Morphine or
Salicylic acid or
Temazepam or
(increased clearance of these drugs has been noted when administered with oral contraceptives.)

» Cyclosporine or
» Prednisolone or
» Theophylline
(increased plasma concentrations of cyclosporine, prednisolone and theophylline have been reported with concomitant administration of oral contraceptives.)

» Smoking, tobacco
(cigarette smoking increases the risk of serious side effects from hormonal contraceptive use. The risk increases with age and with heavy smoking [15 or more cigarettes per day] and is quite marked in women over 35 years of age. Smoking in combination with oral contraceptive use has been shown to substantially increase the incidence of myocardial infarctions and mortality rates associated with circulatory disease, especially in women 35 years of age or older.)

» St. John's Wort (Hypericum perforatum)
(may induce hepatic enzymes (cyctochrome P450) and p-glycoprotein transporter and may reduce the effectiveness of contraceptive steroids or result in breakthrough bleeding.)

Tetracycline
(contraceptive effectiveness may be reduced when co-administered with tetracycline. However, in a pharmacokinetic drug interaction study, oral administration of tetracycline HCl 500 mg four times a day for 3 days prior to and 7 days during wear of the norelgestromin and ethinyl estradiol patch did not significantly affect the pharmacokinetics of norelgestromin and ethinyl estradiol.)

Laboratory value alterations

The following have been selected on the basis of their potential clinical significance (possible effect in parentheses where appropriate)—not necessarily inclusive (» = major clinical significance).

With physiology/laboratory test values
» Antithrombin III or
» Glucose tolerance
(may be decreased)

Binding proteins
(may be elevated in the serum.)

» Clotting factors VII, VIII, IX, X or
» Norepinephrine-induced platelet aggregability or
» Prothrombin time
(may be increased)

» Serum folate levels
(may be depressed by hormonal contraceptive therapy.)

Sex hormone binding globulins [SHBG]
(are increased and result in elevated levels of total circulating endogenous sex steroids and corticoids; however, free or biologically active levels either decrease or remain unchanged.)

Thyroid binding globulin [TBG]
(may be increased, leading to increased circulating total thyroid hormone, as measured by protein-bound iodine, T4 by column or by radioimmunoassay. Free T3 resin uptake is decreased, reflecting the elevated TBG.)

Triglycerides
(may be increased and levels of various other lipids and lipoproteins may be affected.)

Medical considerations/Contraindications

The medical considerations/contraindications included have been selected on the basis of their potential clinical significance (reasons given in parentheses where appropriate)—not necessarily inclusive (» = major clinical significance).

Except under special circumstances, this medication should not be used when the following medical problem exists:

» Breast cancer, known or suspected, or
» Breast cancer, personal history of
(women who currently have or have had breast cancer should not use hormonal contraceptives because breast cancer is usually a hormonally sensitive tumor. Numerous epidemiological studies give conflicting reports on the relationship between breast cancer and combination oral contraceptive use. Some studies show an increased risk in having breast cancer diagnosed among current users and recent users of hormonal contraceptives, while others show that the risk appears to decrease over time after discontin-

uation. No consistent relationships have been found with dose or type of steroid. Some studies have found a small increase in risk for women who first use hormonal contraceptives before age 20. However, most studies show a similar pattern of risk regardless of a woman's reproductive history or her family breast cancer history. Since most of these studies used oral hormonal contraceptives, it is not known whether norelgestromin and ethinyl estradiol transdermal system is distinct from oral contraceptives in this regard.)

» Carcinoma of the endometrium or
» Estrogen-dependent neoplasia, known or suspected
(some studies suggest that combination oral contraceptive use has been associated with an increase in the risk of cervical intraepithelial neoplasia in some populations of women. However, there continues to be controversy about the extent to which such findings may be due to differences in sexual behavior and other factors. In spite of many studies of the relationship between oral contraceptive use and cervical cancer, a cause-and-effect relationship has not been established. It is not known whether norelgestromin and ethinyl estradiol transdermal system is distinct from oral contraceptives in this regard.)

» Cholestatic jaundice of pregnancy or
» Jaundice with prior hormonal contraceptive use

» Cerebrovascular disease, current or past history, or
» Coronary artery disease, current or past history
(hormonal contraceptives have been shown to increase both the relative and attributable risks of cerebrovascular events, such as thrombotic and hemorrhagic strokes; this risk is greatest among women over 35 years of age who are hypertensive and also smoke.In a large study, the relative risk of thrombotic stroke has been shown to range from 3 for normotensive users to 14 for users with severe hypertension. The relative risk of hemorrhagic stroke is reported to be 1.2 for nonsmokers who used hormonal contraceptives, 2.6 for smokers who did not use hormonal contraceptives, 7.6 for smokers who used hormonal contraceptives, 1.8 for normotensive users and 25.7 for users with severe hypertension.)

(norelgestromin and ethinyl estradiol should be discontinued or strictly avoided if any cardiovascular or cerebrovascular accidents occur.)

(a positive association has been observed between the amount of estrogen and progestin in hormonal contraceptives and the risk of vascular disease. A decline in serum high-density lipoproteins (HDL) has been reported with many progestinal agents which may increase the incidence of ischemic heart disease. However, because estrogens increase HDL cholesterol, the net effect of a hormonal contraceptive depends on the balance achieved between doses of estrogen and progestin and the activity of the progestin used in the contraceptives. It is unknown whether norelgestromin and ethinyl estradiol is distinct from other combination hormonal contraceptives with regard to the occurrence of venous and arterial thrombosis.)

» Diabetes with vascular involvement
(hormonal contraceptives have been shown to cause a decrease in glucose tolerance in some users)

(progestins are known to cause glucose intolerance, while estrogens may create a state of hyperinsulinemia. In a 6-cycle clinical trial with norelgestromin and ethinyl estradiol, there were no clinically significant changes in fasting blood glucose from baseline to end of treatment. In non-diabetic women, combination hormonal contraceptives appear to have no effect on fasting blood glucose.)

» Vaginal bleeding, abnormal, undiagnosed
(malignancy should be ruled out in cases of abnormal vaginal bleeding. Breakthrough bleeding and spotting are sometimes encountered in women using norelgestromin and ethinyl estradiol. Nonhormonal causes should be considered and adequate diagnostic measures should be taken to rule out malignancy, other pathology, or pregnancy. Some women may encounter amenorrhea or oligomenorrhea after discontinuation of hormonal contraceptive use, especially when such a condition was pre-existent.)

» Headaches with focal neurological symptoms
(the onset or exacerbation of migraine headache or the development of headache with a new pattern that is recurrent, persistent or severe requires discontinuation of norelgestromin and ethinyl estradiol and evaluation of the cause.)

» Hepatic adenomas or
» Hepatic carcinomas
(benign hepatic adenomas are associated with hormonal contraceptive use, although the incidence of benign tumors is rare in the United States. Rupture of benign, hepatic adenomas may cause death through intra-abdominal hemorrhage. Indirect calculations have estimated the attributable risk to be in the range of 3.3 cases/100,000 for users, a risk that increases after four or more years of use, especially with hormonal contraceptives containing 50 micrograms or more of estrogen.)

(studies have shown an increased risk of developing hepatocellular carcinoma in long term oral contraceptive users, however, these cancers are extremely rare in the United States. It is unknown if norelgestromin and ethinyl estradiol transdermal system is distinct form oral contraceptives in this regard.)

» Hepatocellular disease, acute or chronic, with abnormal liver function
(the hormones in norelgestromin and ethinyl estradiol may be poorly metabolized in patients with impaired liver function.)

» Hypersensitivity to norelgestromin and ethinyl estradiol combination or any of it components

» Hypertension, severe
(women with significant hypertension should not be started on hormonal contraception. Women with a history of hypertension or hypertension-related diseases, or renal disease should be encouraged to use another method of contraception. If women elect to use norelgestromin and ethinyl estradiol, they should be monitored closely and if a clinically significant elevation of blood pressure occurs, therapy should be discontinued.)

» Surgery, major, with prolonged immobilization
(a two to four-fold increase in the relative risk of post-operative thromboembolic complications has been reported with the use of hormonal contraceptives. The relative risk of venous thrombosis in women who have predisposing conditions is twice that of women without such medical conditions. If feasible, hormonal contraceptives should be discontinued at least four weeks prior to and for two weeks after elective surgery of a type associated with an increase in risk of thromboembolism and during and following prolonged immobilization.)

» Thrombophlebitis, current or past history, or
» Thromboembolic disorders, current or past history
(an increased risk of thromboembolic and thrombotic disease associated with the use of hormonal contraceptives is well established. Case control studies have found the relative risk of users compared to nonusers to be 3 for the first episode of superficial venous thrombosis, 4 to 11 for deep vein thrombosis or pulmonary embolism, and 1.5 to 6 for women with predisposing conditions for venous thromboembolic disease. The risk of thromboembolic disease associated with hormonal contraceptives is not related to length of use and disappears after treatment is discontinued.)

» Valvular heart disease with complications

Risk-benefit should be considered when the following medical problems exist:

Depression
(women with a history of depression should be carefully observed and norelgestromin and ethinyl estradiol combination should be discontinued if significant depression occurs. Women who become significantly depressed while using combination hormonal contraceptives should stop the medication and use another method of contraception in an attempt to determine whether the symptom is drug related.)

Gallbladder disease
(combination hormonal contraceptives such as norelgestromin and ethinyl estradiol may worsen existing gallbladder disease and may accelerate the development of this disease in previously asymptomatic women. Women with a history of combination hormonal contraceptive-related cholestasis are more likely to have the condition recur with subsequent combination hormonal contraceptive use.)

Hypertension
(an increase in blood pressure has been reported in women taking hormonal contraceptives and this increase is more likely in older hormonal contraceptive users and with extended duration of use. For most women, elevated blood pressure will return to normal after stopping hormonal contraceptive use.)

Liver function
(if jaundice develops in any woman using norelgestromin and ethinyl estradiol combination, the medication should be discontinued. The hormones in norelgestromin and ethinyl estradiol combination may be poorly metabolized in women with impaired liver function.)

Myocardial infarction
(an increased risk of myocardial infarction has been attributed to hormonal contraceptive use. This risk is primarily in smokers or women with other underlying risk factors for coronary artery disease such as hypertension, hypercholesterolemia, morbid obesity and diabetes. There is some evidence that the risk of myocardial infarction associated with hormonal contraceptives is lower when the progestin has minimal androgenic activity than when the activity is greater. The relative risk of heart attack for current hormonal contraceptive users has been estimated to be two to six compared to non-users. The risk is very low under the age of 30. In a study in the United States, the risk of developing myocardial infarction after discontinuing combination hormonal contraceptives persists for at least 9 years for women 40–49 years of age who had used combination hormonal contraceptives for five or more years, but this increased risk was not demonstrated in other age groups.)

» Obesity
(results from clinical trials indicate that transdermal norelgestromin and ethinyl estradiol may be less effective in women with body weight greater than or equal to 198 pounds (90 kilograms) than in women with lower body weights.)

Patient monitoring

The following may be especially important in patient monitoring (other tests may be warranted in some patients, depending on condition; » = major clinical significance):

Contact lenses
(contact lens wearers who develop visual changes or changes in lens tolerance should be assessed by an ophthalmologist.)

Fluid retention
(careful monitoring is required in patients with conditions which might be aggravated by fluid retention.)

Glucose, blood
(careful monitoring is recommended in prediabetic and diabetic women who are taking combination hormonal contraceptives.)

Lipid profile, serum
(routine assessment is needed for women who are being treated for hyperlipidemias; some progestins may elevate LDL levels and may render the control of hyperlipidemias more difficult.A small proportion of women will have persistent hypertriglyceridemia while taking hormonal contraceptives.)

» Physical examination and follow-up
(women using norelgestromin and ethinyl estradiol combination should have annual medical evaluations and physical examinations. Special attention should be given to blood pressure, breasts, abdomen and pelvic organs, including cervical cytology and relevant laboratory tests. In case of undiagnosed, persistent or recurrent abnormal vaginal bleeding, appropriate measures should be conducted to rule out malignancy or other pathology. Women with a strong family history of breast cancer or who have breast nodules should be monitored with particular care.)

Side/Adverse Effects

Note: Cigarette smoking increases the risk of serious cardiovascular side effects from hormonal contraceptive use. This risk increases with age and with heavy smoking (15 or more cigarettes per day) and is quite marked in women over 35 years of age. Women who use hormonal contraceptives, including norelgestromin and ethinyl estradiol combination, should be strongly advised not to smoke.

Note: The use of combination hormonal contraceptives is associated with increased risks of several serious conditions including myocardial infarction, thromboembolism, stroke, hepatic neoplasia and gallbladder disease, although the risk of serious morbidity or mortality is very small in healthy women without underlying risk factors. The risk of morbidity and mortality increased significantly in the presence of other underlying risk factors such as hypertension, hyperlipidemias, obesity and diabetes.

The following side/adverse effects have been selected on the basis of their potential clinical significance (possible signs and symptoms in parentheses where appropriate)—not necessarily inclusive:

Those indicating need for medical attention

Incidence more frequent

Upper respiratory infection (body aches or pain; chills; cough; difficulty in breathing; ear congestion; fever; headache; loss of voice; nasal congestion; runny nose; sneezing; sore throat; unusual tiredness or weakness)

Incidence not determined—Rate of incidence is not included in the product information

Note: An increased risk of the following serious adverse reactions has been associated with the use of combination hormonal contraceptives:

Arterial thromboembolism (difficulty breathing; pain in chest, groin, or legs, especially the calves; slurred speech; sudden headache; sudden loss of coordination; sudden, severe weakness or numbness in arm or leg; sudden, unexplained shortness of breath; vision changes); ***cerebral hemorrhage*** (blurred vision; headache sudden and severe; inability to speak; seizures; slurred speech; temporary blindness; weakness in arm and/or leg on one side of the body, sudden and severe); ***cerebral thrombosis*** (confusion; numbness of hands); ***cholestatic jaundice*** (abdominal or stomach pain; chills; light-colored stools; dark urine; diarrhea; dizziness; fever; headache; itching; loss of appetite; nausea; rash; unpleasant breath odor; unusual tiredness or weakness; vomiting of blood; yellow eyes or skin); ***gallbladder disease*** (pain in abdomen); ***hepatic adenomas or benign liver tumors*** (swelling, pain, or tenderness in upper abdominal area); ***hypertension*** (blurred vision; dizziness; nervousness; headache; pounding in the ears; slow or fast heartbeat); ***myocardial infarction*** (chest pain or discomfort; nausea; pain or discomfort in arms, jaw, back or neck; shortness of breath; sweating); ***pulmonary embolism*** (anxiety; chest pain; cough; dizziness or lightheadedness; fainting; fast heartbeat; sudden shortness of breath or troubled breathing); ***thrombophlebitis and venous thrombosis with or without embolism*** (changes in skin color, pain, tenderness, or swelling of foot or leg); ***mesenteric thrombosis*** (pain in lower abdomen); ***retinal thrombosis*** (change in vision; eye pain)

Note: There is evidence of an association between the following conditions and the use of combination hormonal contraceptives:

Those indicating need for medical attention only if they continue or are bothersome

Incidence more frequent

Application site reaction (burning; itching; redness; skin rash; swelling; or soreness at patch site); ***breast symptoms*** (pain; soreness; swelling; or discharge from the breast or breasts); ***cramps, menstrual; headache; nausea; pain, abdominal***

Incidence not determined—Rate of incidence is not included in the product information

Note: The following adverse reactions have been reported in users of combination hormonal contraceptives and are believed to be drug-related:

Amenorrhea (absent missed or irregular menstrual periods; stopping of menstrual bleeding); ***bleeding, breakthrough*** (unusual vaginal bleeding); ***breast changes*** (tenderness or enlargement of the breasts); ***secretion from the breasts; candidiasis, vaginal*** (itching of the vagina or outside genitals; pain during sexual intercourse; thick, white curd-like vaginal discharge without odor or with mild odor); ***cervical erosion, change in*** (light vaginal bleeding between periods and after intercourse); ***cervical secretion, change in*** (change in amount of vaginal discharge; bloody vaginal discharge); ***corneal curvature, steepening of*** (vision changes); ***edema*** (swelling); ***gastrointestinal symptoms*** (abdominal cramps; bloating); ***infertility, temporary after discontinuation of treatment*** (trouble getting pregnant); ***intolerance to contact lenses; lactation, diminution in when given immediately postpartum*** (decreased amount of breast milk); ***melasma which may persist*** (brown, blotchy spots on exposed skin); ***menstrual flow, change in; mental depression*** (discouragement; feeling sad or empty; irritability; lack of appetite; loss of interest or pleasure; tiredness; trouble concentrating; trouble sleeping); ***migraine*** (headache, severe and throbbing); ***rash; spotting*** (light vaginal bleeding between regular menstrual periods); ***tolerance to carbohydrates, reduced*** (blurred vision; dry mouth; increased hunger or thirst; increased urination); ***vomiting; weight, increase or decrease in***

Overdose

For more information on the management of overdose or unintentional ingestion, **contact a poison control center** (see *Poison Control Center Listing*).

Note: No serious ill effects have been reported following accidental ingestion of large doses of hormonal contraceptives.

Clinical effects of overdose

The following effects have been selected on the basis of their potential clinical significance (possible signs and symptoms in parentheses where appropriate)—not necessarily inclusive:

Nausea; vomiting; withdrawal bleeding—in females

Treatment of overdose

If overdose is suspected, the transdermal system should be removed and symptomatic treatment should be administered.

Supportive care—

Patients in whom intentional overdose is confirmed or suspected should be referred for psychiatric consultation.

Patient Consultation

As an aid to patient consultation, refer to *Advice for the Patient, Norelgestromin and Ethinyl Estradiol (Systemic).*

In providing consultation, consider emphasizing the following selected information (» = major clinical significance):

Before using this medication

» Conditions affecting use, especially:

Hypersensitivity to norelgestromin and ethinyl estradiol combination or any of its components.

Pregnancy—Not recommended for use during pregnancy

Breast-feeding—It is not known whether norelgestromin and ethinyl estradiol combination is distributed into human breast milk. However, small amounts of combination hormonal contraceptive steroids have been identified in the milk of nursing mothers and a few adverse effects on the child have been reported, including jaundice and breast enlargement.

Use in adolescents—Safety and efficacy of norelgestromin and ethinyl estradiol combination have been established in women of reproductive age. Safety and efficacy are expected to be the same for post-pubertal adolescents under the age of 16 and for users 16 years and older. Use of the product before menarche is not indicated.

Other medications, especially ampicillin, anti-HIV protease inhibitors, barbiturates, carbamazepine, cyclosporine, felbamate, griseofulvin, oxcarbazepine, phenylbutazone, phenytoin, prednisolone, rifampin, tobacco (smoking), St. John's Wort (hypericum perforatum), theophylline, or topiramate.

Other medical problems, especially breast cancer (known, suspected or personal history of), carcinoma of the endometrium or estrogen-dependent neoplasia (known or suspected), cholestatic jaundice (of pregnancy) or jaundice (with prior hormonal contraceptive use), cerebrovascular disease (current or past history), coronary artery disease (current or past history), diabetes (with vascular involvement), headaches (with focal neurological symptoms), hepatic adenomas, hepatic carcinomas, hepatocellular disease (acute, chronic, with abnormal liver function), hypertension (severe), obesity, surgery (major, with prolonged immobilization), thrombophlebitis (current or history of), thromboembolic disorders (current or history of), vaginal bleeding (abnormal, undiagnosed) or valvular heart disease (with complications).

Proper use of this medication

» Reading patient package insert carefully

» Use of additional form of birth control for first 7 days

» Proper transdermal patch application

» Compliance with therapy; applying each new patch on the same day of the week

» Proper dosing

Missed doses for the monophasic cycle—

Forgetting to apply the first patch of a new patch cycle (Week One/Day 1)—applying the patch as soon as remembered and using back-up contraception for the first week of the new cycle. This will result in a new patch start day.

Forgetting to change the patch in the middle of the patch cycle (Week Two/Day 8 or Week Three/Day 15) for one or two days—applying a new patch immediately; applying the next patch on the usual day. No back-up contraception is needed.

Forgetting to change the patch in the middle of the patch cycle (Week Two/Day 8 or Week Three/Day 15) for more than two days—stopping the current contraceptive cycle and starting a new four-week cycle immediately by putting on a new patch; using back-up contraception for the first week of the new cycle.

Forgetting to remove the patch at the end of the patch cycle (Week Four/Day 22)—taking it off as soon as remembered; starting the next cycle on the usual day. No back-up contraception is needed.

Proper storage

Precautions while using this medication

» Regular visits to physician at least every 6 to 12 months to check progress

» Caution if medical or dental surgery or emergency treatment is required—increased risk of thrombotic complications

» Body weight greater than or equal to 198 pounds (90 kilograms) may cause norelgestromin and ethinyl estradiol to be less effective

» Physiology and Laboratory test alterations especially Antithrombin III, factors VII, VIII, IX or X, glucose tolerance, norepinephrine-induced platelet aggregability, prothrombin time, and serum folate levels. If scheduled for laboratory tests, telling physician if using contraceptive transdermal patch.

What to expect and do if vaginal bleeding occurs

What to expect and do if a menstrual period is missed; contacting health professional if two menstrual periods are missed

» Stopping medication immediately and checking with physician if pregnancy is suspected

Not refilling an old prescription for contraceptives without having a physical examination by physician, especially after a pregnancy

May be a choking hazard if ingested by small children

Side/adverse effects

Signs of potential side effects, especially upper respiratory infection, arterial thromboembolism, cerebral hemorrhage, cerebral thrombosis, cholestatic jaundice, gallbladder disease, hepatic adenomas or benign liver tumors, hypertension, myocardial infarction, pulmonary embolism, thrombophlebitis and venous thrombosis with or without embolism, mesenteric thrombosis, retinal thrombosis.

General Dosing Information

The transdermal system should be kept in its protective packaging until it is used. It should be applied to clean, dry, intact, healthy skin on the buttock, abdomen, upper outer arm or upper torso, in a place where it won't be rubbed by tight clothing. It should not be placed on skin that is red, irritated or cut, nor should it be placed on the breasts.

To prevent interference with the adhesive properties of the transdermal system, no make-up, creams, lotions, powders or other topical products should be applied to the skin area where the patch is or will be placed. The system should be pressed firmly in place with the palm of the hand for 10 seconds, making sure that the edges stick well. The patch should be checked daily to make sure it is sticking.

The patch is worn for seven days. On Day 8, the patch is removed and a new one is applied immediately. The used patch still contains active hormones and should be carefully folded in half so that it sticks to itself before throwing it away.

A new patch is applied for Week Two (Day 8) and again for Week Three (Day 15). Every new patch should be applied on the same day of the week. Each new patch should be applied to a new spot on the skin, although they may be kept within the same anatomic area. Week Four is patch-free and withdrawal bleeding is expected to occur during this time.

The next four-week cycle is started by applying a new patch on the day after Day 28, no matter when the menstrual period begins or ends. Under no circumstances should there be more than a seven-day patch-free interval between patch cycles.

If the transdermal system is partially or completely detached for less than one day, the woman should try to reapply it to the same place or replace it with a new patch immediately. No back-up contraception is needed. If the transdermal system is partially or completely detached for more than one day the woman may not be protected from pregnancy. She should stop the current contraceptive cycle and start a new cycle immediately by applying a new patch. Back-up contraception must be used for the first week of the new cycle.

A patch should not be re-applied if it is no longer sticky, if it has become stuck to itself or another surface, if it has other material stuck to it or if it has previously become loose or fallen off. If a patch cannot be re-applied, a new patch should be applied immediately. Supplemental adhesives or wraps should not be used to hold the patch in place.

If a woman wishes to change her Patch Change Day she should complete her current cycle, removing the third patch on the correct day. During the patch-free week, she may select an earlier Patch Change Day by applying a new patch on the desired day. In no case should there be more than 7 consecutive patch-free days.

When switching from an oral contraceptive, treatment with norelgestromin and ethinyl estradiol combination should begin on the first day of withdrawal bleeding. If there is no withdrawal bleeding within 5 days of the last active tablet, pregnancy must be ruled out. If therapy starts later than the first day of withdrawal bleeding, a non-hormonal contraceptive should be used concurrently for 7 days. If more than 7 days elapse after taking the last active oral contraceptive tablet, the possibility of ovulation and conception should be considered.

For use after childbirth, women who elect not to breast-feed should start contraceptive therapy with norelgestromin and ethinyl estradiol combination no sooner than 4 weeks after childbirth. If a woman begins using norelgestromin and ethinyl estradiol combination postpartum, and has not yet had a menstrual period, the possibility of ovulation and conception should be considered, and she should use an additional method of contraception for the first seven days.

After an abortion or miscarriage that occurs in the first trimester, norelgestromin and ethinyl estradiol combination may be started immediately and no back-up contraception is needed. If use is not started within 5 days following a first trimester abortion, the woman should follow the instructions for a woman starting norelgestromin and ethinyl estradiol combination for the first time. She should be advised to use a non-hormonal contraceptive method in the meantime. Norelgestromin and ethinyl estradiol combination should be started no earlier than 4 weeks after a second trimester abortion or miscarriage. When used postpartum or postabortion, the increased risk of thromboembolic disease must be considered.

In the event of breakthrough bleeding or spotting, treatment should be continued. If breakthrough bleeding persists longer then a few cycles, a cause other than norelgestromin and ethinyl estradiol combination should be considered. In the event of no withdrawal bleeding, occurring during the patch free week, treatment should be resumed on the next scheduled Change Day. If norelgestromin and ethinyl estradiol combination is used correctly, the absence of withdrawal bleeding is not necessarily an indication of pregnancy. However, the possibility of pregnancy should be considered, especially if absence of withdrawal bleeding occurs in 2 consecutive cycles.

If patch use results in uncomfortable irritation, the patch may be removed and a new patch may be applied to a different location until the next Change Day. Only one patch should be worn at a time.

Ectopic as well as intrauterine pregnancy may occur in contraceptive failure.

Patients should be counseled that this product does not protect against HIV infection (AIDS) and other sexually transmitted diseases.

Transdermal Dosage Forms

NORELGESTROMIN AND ETHINYL ESTRADIOL TRANSDERMAL SYSTEM

Usual adult and adolescent dose

Contraceptive—

Transdermal, one transdermal system to be applied and kept in place for one week and replaced weekly for three weeks with a new transdermal system. Every new patch should be applied on the same day of the week. During week four, a transdermal system is not used and withdrawal bleeding is expected to occur. Each transdermal system delivers 150 micrograms of norelgestromin and 20 micrograms of ethinyl estradiol into the bloodstream per 24 hours.This level of transdermal release of ethinyl estradiol results in exposure to ethinyl estradiol greater than that produced by an oral contraceptive product containing 20 micrograms or ethinyl estradiol.

Note: With a Sunday start schedule, the patient should apply her first patch on the first Sunday after the onset of menstruation. If the patient's menstrual period begins on a Sunday, she should apply her first patch that same day.

With a First Day Start schedule, the patient should apply her first patch during the first 24 hours of her menstrual period.

Usual adult prescribing limits

One transdermal system per week

Usual pediatric dose

Safety and efficacy have not been established.

Usual geriatric dose

Norelgestromin and ethinyl estradiol combination has not been studied in women over 65 years of age and is not indicated in this population

Strength(s) usually available

U.S.—

150 mcg of norelgestromin and 20 mcg of ethinyl estradiol delivered per day (a total of 6 mg of norelgestromin and 0.75 mg of ethinyl estradiol per 20 square centimeters [cm^2] (Rx) [*Ortho Evra* (polysobutylene/polybutene adhesive; crospovidone; non-woven polyester fabric; lauryl lactate; polyethylene terephthalate film; polydimethylsiloxane coating)].

Canada—

Not commercially available.

Packaging and storage

Store at 25 °C (77 °F); excursions permitted to 15 to 30 °C (59 to 86 °F).Store patches in their protective pouches. Do not store in the refrigerator or freezer.

Auxiliary labeling

- Do not freeze.
- Do not refrigerate.

Revised: 11/29/2005
Developed: 04/15/2002

NOREPINEPHRINE—See *Sympathomimetic Agents—Cardiovascular Use (Parenteral-Systemic)*

NORETHINDRONE—See *Progestins (Systemic)*

NORFLOXACIN—See *Fluoroquinolones (Systemic), Norfloxacin (Ophthalmic)*

NORGESTREL—See *Progestins (Systemic)*

NORTRIPTYLINE—See *Antidepressants, Tricyclic (Systemic)*

NYSTATIN Oral-Local

VA CLASSIFICATION (Primary): AM700

Commonly used brand name(s): *Mycostatin; Nadostine; Nilstat; Nystex; PMS Nystatin.*

Note: For a listing of dosage forms and brand names by country availability, see *Dosage Forms* section(s).

Category

Antifungal (oral-local).

Indications

Note: Bracketed information in the *Indications* section refers to uses that are not included in U.S. product labeling.

Accepted

Candidiasis, oropharyngeal (treatment)—Nystatin lozenges (pastilles), nystatin oral suspension, and nystatin for oral suspension are indicated in the local treatment of fungal infections of the oral cavity caused by *Candida albicans* and other *Candida* species.

[Candidiasis, oropharyngeal (prophylaxis)]—Nystatin oral suspension, lozenges (pastilles), and nystatin for oral suspension are used in the prophylaxis of oropharyngeal candidiasis.

Not all species or strains of a particular organism may be susceptible to nystatin.

Unaccepted
Nystatin is not indicated in the treatment of systemic fungal infections since it is not absorbed from the gastrointestinal tract.

USP medical experts do not recommend nystatin oral tablets for any indication.

Pharmacology/Pharmacokinetics

Mechanism of action/Effect
Binds to sterols in the fungal cell membrane, resulting in the cell membrane's inability to function as a selective barrier, thus allowing loss of essential cellular constituents.

Absorption
Not absorbed from the gastrointestinal tract.

Saliva concentrations
Saliva concentrations of nystatin are maintained above those required *in vitro* to inhibit the growth of clinically significant *Candida* species for approximately 2 hours after the start of oral dissolution of 2 nystatin lozenges (400,000 units).

Elimination
Fecal. Orally administered nystatin is excreted almost entirely as unchanged drug.

Precautions to Consider

Carcinogenicity/Mutagenicity
Studies have not been done to evaluate the carcinogenic or mutagenic potential of nystatin.

Pregnancy/Reproduction
Fertility—Studies have not been done to evaluate the effect of nystatin on fertility in either males or females.

Pregnancy—Studies in humans have not shown that nystatin causes adverse effects on the fetus.

Breast-feeding
It is not known whether oral nystatin is excreted in breast milk. However, problems in humans have not been documented.

Pediatrics
Use of nystatin lozenges is not recommended in infants and children up to 5 years of age since this age group may not be capable of using the lozenges or tablets safely. However, no pediatrics-specific problems have been documented to date with nystatin oral suspension.

Geriatrics
No information is available on the relationship of age to the effects of oral nystatin in geriatric patients.

Dental
Patients with full or partial dentures who have symptomatic oral candidiasis may need to soak their dentures nightly in reconstituted nystatin for oral suspension to eliminate *Candida* species from the dentures. In rare cases when this does not eliminate the fungus, it may be necessary to have new dentures made.

Medical considerations/Contraindications
The medical considerations/contraindications included have been selected on the basis of their potential clinical significance (reasons given in parentheses where appropriate)—not necessarily inclusive (» = major clinical significance).

Risk-benefit should be considered when the following medical problem exists:

Intolerance to nystatin

Side/Adverse Effects
The following side/adverse effects have been selected on the basis of their potential clinical significance (possible signs and symptoms in parentheses where appropriate)—not necessarily inclusive:

Those indicating need for medical attention only if they continue or are bothersome
Incidence less frequent

Gastrointestinal disturbances (diarrhea; nausea or vomiting; stomach pain)

Patient Consultation
As an aid to patient consultation, refer to *Advice for the Patient, Nystatin (Oral).*

In providing consultation, consider emphasizing the following selected information (» = major clinical significance):

Before using this medication
» Conditions affecting use, especially:

Intolerance to nystatin

Use in children—Nystatin lozenges or tablets are not recommended in infants and children up to 5 years of age since this age group may not be capable of using the lozenges or tablets safely

Proper use of this medication
Proper administration technique for dry powder, lozenges, and oral suspension

» Compliance with full course of therapy

» Proper dosing

Missed dose: Taking as soon as possible; not taking if almost time for next dose; not doubling doses

» Proper storage

Side/adverse effects
Signs of potential side effects, especially gastrointestinal disturbance

General Dosing Information
The oral suspension should be administered by placing ½ of the dose in each side of the mouth. The patient should hold the suspension in the mouth or swish it throughout the mouth for as long as possible, then gargle and swallow.

Lozenges (pastilles) should be allowed to dissolve slowly and completely in the mouth. They should not be chewed or swallowed whole.

To prevent relapse, therapy should be continued for 48 hours after symptoms have disappeared and the cultures have returned to normal.

Oral Dosage Forms

NYSTATIN LOZENGES (PASTILLES)

Usual adult and adolescent dose
Candidiasis—

Oral, as a lozenge dissolved slowly and completely in the mouth, 200,000 to 400,000 Units four or five times a day for up to fourteen days.

Usual pediatric dose
Candidiasis—

Infants and children up to 5 years of age: Use is not recommended since this age group may not be capable of using the lozenges safely.

Children 5 years of age and over: See *Usual adult and adolescent dose.*

Strength(s) usually available
U.S.—

200,000 Units (Rx) [*Mycostatin*].

Canada—

Not commercially available.

Packaging and storage
Store between 2 and 8 °C (36 and 46 °F), in a well-closed container, unless otherwise specified by manufacturer.

Auxiliary labeling
- Refrigerate.
- Dissolve slowly in mouth.
- Continue medicine for full time of treatment.

NYSTATIN ORAL SUSPENSION USP

Usual adult and adolescent dose
Candidiasis—

Oral, 400,000 to 600,000 Units four times a day.

Usual pediatric dose
Candidiasis—

Premature and low-birth-weight infants: Oral, 100,000 Units four times a day.

Older infants: Oral, 200,000 Units four times a day.

Children: See *Usual adult and adolescent dose.*

Strength(s) usually available
U.S.—

100,000 Units per mL (Rx) [*Mycostatin; Nilstat; Nystex;* GENERIC].

Canada—

100,000 Units per mL (Rx) [*Mycostatin; Nadostine; Nilstat; PMS Nystatin*].

Packaging and storage
Store below 40 °C (104 °F), preferably between 15 and 30 °C (59 and 86 °F), unless otherwise specified by manufacturer. Store in a tight, light-resistant container. Protect from freezing.

Auxiliary labeling
- Shake well.
- Continue medicine for full time of treatment.

Note
When dispensing, include a calibrated liquid-measuring device.

NYSTATIN FOR ORAL SUSPENSION USP

Usual adult and adolescent dose
See *Nystatin Oral Suspension USP*.

Usual pediatric dose
See *Nystatin Oral Suspension USP*.

Strength(s) usually available
U.S.—
50,000,000 Units (Rx) [GENERIC].
150,000,000 Units (Rx) [GENERIC].
500,000,000 Units (Rx) [GENERIC].
1,000,000,000 Units (Rx) [*Nilstat;* GENERIC].
2,000,000,000 Units (Rx) [*Nilstat;* GENERIC].
5,000,000,000 Units (Rx) [GENERIC].
10,000,000,000 Units (Rx) [GENERIC].
Canada—
Note: One-eighth (1/8) teaspoonful of nystatin for oral suspension is approximately equal to 500,000 units.
1,000,000,000 Units (Rx) [*Nilstat*].
2,000,000,000 Units (Rx) [*Nilstat*].

Packaging and storage
Prior to reconstitution, store below 40 °C (104 °F), preferably between 15 and 30 °C (59 and 86 °F), unless otherwise specified by manufacturer. Store in a tight container.

Preparation of dosage form
Add 1/8 teaspoonful (approximately 500,000 Units) of dry powder to approximately 120 mL of water. Stir well.

Stability
After mixing, suspension should be used immediately since nystatin for oral suspension contains no preservatives.

Auxiliary labeling
- Dissolve in water immediately before taking.
- Continue medicine for full time of treatment.

Note
Explain administration technique.

NYSTATIN TABLETS USP

Usual adult and adolescent dose
Candidiasis—
Oral, 500,000 to l,000,000 Units three times a day.

Usual pediatric dose
Candidiasis—
Infants and children up to 5 years of age: Use is not recommended since this age group may not be capable of using the tablet safely.
Children 5 years of age and over: Oral, 500,000 Units four times a day.

Strength(s) usually available
U.S.—
500,000 Units (Rx) [*Mycostatin* (film-coated); *Nilstat* (film-coated); GENERIC].
Canada—
500,000 Units (Rx) [*Mycostatin* (film-coated); *Nadostine* (film-coated); *Nilstat* (film-coated)].

Packaging and storage
Store below 40 °C (104 °F), preferably between 15 and 30 °C (59 and 86 °F), unless otherwise specified by manufacturer. Store in a tight, light-resistant container.

Auxiliary labeling
- Continue medicine for full time of treatment.

Revised: 04/14/1995

NYSTATIN Topical

VA CLASSIFICATION (Primary): DE102

Commonly used brand name(s): *Mycostatin; Nadostine; Nilstat; Nyaderm; Nystex; Nystop; Pedi-Dri.*

Note: For a listing of dosage forms and brand names by country availability, see *Dosage Forms* section(s).

Category

Antifungal (topical).

Indications

Note: Bracketed information in the *Indications* section refers to uses that are not included in U.S. product labeling.

Accepted
Candidiasis, cutaneous (treatment) or
Candidiasis, mucocutaneous (treatment)—Topical nystatin is indicated in the treatment of cutaneous and mucocutaneous mycotic infections caused by *Candida (Monilia) albicans* and other *Candida* species.
[Tinea barbae (treatment)] or
[Tinea capitis (treatment)]—Topical nystatin is used in the treatment of tinea barbae and tinea capitis.

Not all species or strains of a particular organism may be susceptible to nystatin.

Pharmacology/Pharmacokinetics

Physicochemical characteristics
Chemical Group—Polyene.
Molecular weight—926.13.

Mechanism of action/Effect
Nystatin is both fungistatic and fungicidal *in vitro* . Topical nystatin binds to sterols in the fungal cell membrane, resulting in the cell membrane's inability to function as a selective barrier, allowing loss of essential intracellular constituents.

Absorption
Not absorbed following topical application to intact skin or mucous membranes.

Precautions to Consider

Pregnancy/Reproduction
Pregnancy—Problems in humans have not been documented.

Breast-feeding
It is not known whether topically applied nystatin is distributed into breast milk. However, problems in humans have not been documented.

Pediatrics
Appropriate studies on the relationship of age to the effects of topical nystatin have not been performed in the pediatric population. However, no pediatrics-specific problems have been documented to date. When this medication is used in the treatment of candidiasis, occlusive dressings (e.g., tight-fitting diaper, plastic pants) should be avoided since they provide conditions that favor growth of yeast and release of its irritating endotoxin.

Geriatrics
No information is available on the relationship of age to the effects of topical nystatin in geriatric patients.

Medical considerations/Contraindications
The medical considerations/contraindications included have been selected on the basis of their potential clinical significance (reasons given in parentheses where appropriate)—not necessarily inclusive (» = major clinical significance).

Risk-benefit should be considered when the following medical problem exists:
Hypersensitivity to nystatin

Side/Adverse Effects

The following side/adverse effects have been selected on the basis of their potential clinical significance (possible signs and symptoms in parentheses where appropriate)—not necessarily inclusive:

Those indicating need for medical attention
Skin irritation not present before therapy

Patient Consultation

As an aid to patient consultation, refer to *Advice for the Patient, Nystatin (Topical)*.

In providing consultation, consider emphasizing the following selected information (» = major clinical significance):

Before using this medication

» Conditions affecting use, especially:
Hypersensitivity to nystatin

Proper use of this medication

Not for ophthalmic use
Applying sufficient medication to cover affected area
Proper administration technique for topical powder
» Not applying occlusive dressing over this medication unless directed to do so by physician; avoiding tight-fitting diapers and plastic pants on diaper area of children
» Compliance with full course of therapy
» Proper dosing
Missed dose: Applying as soon as possible
» Proper storage

Side/adverse effects

Signs of potential side effects, especially skin irritation not present before therapy

General Dosing Information

The cream is usually preferred to the ointment for candidiasis involving intertriginous areas. However, very moist lesions involving intertriginous areas are usually best treated with the topical powder.

For fungal infection of the feet, the powder should be dusted freely on the feet as well as in the shoes and socks.

Nystatin does not stain the skin or mucous membrane.

Nystatin does not exhibit activity against bacteria.

Symptomatic relief usually occurs within 24 to 72 hours following initiation of therapy.

Therapy for a period of 2 weeks is usually sufficient, but more prolonged treatment may be necessary.

When this medication is used in the treatment of candidiasis, occlusive dressings should be avoided since they provide conditions that favor growth of yeast and release of its irritating endotoxin. An oleaginous ointment, a thin film of polyethylene, a bandage, a tight-fitting diaper, plastic pants, or tape may constitute an occlusive dressing.

Topical Dosage Forms

NYSTATIN CREAM USP

Usual adult and adolescent dose

Candidiasis—
Topical, to the skin, two times a day.

Usual pediatric dose

See *Usual adult and adolescent dose.*

Strength(s) usually available

U.S.—
100,000 USP Nystatin Units per gram (Rx) [*Mycostatin* (aluminum hydroxide concentrated wet gel; cetearyl alcohol; ceteareth-20; glyceryl monostearate; polyethylene glycol monostearate; propylene glycol; simethicone; sorbic acid; sorbitol solution; titanium dioxide; white petrolatum); *Nilstat; Nystex;* GENERIC].

Canada—
100,000 Units per gram (OTC) [*Mycostatin; Nadostine; Nilstat; Nyaderm*].

Packaging and storage

Store below 40 °C (104 °F), preferably between 15 and 30 °C (59 and 86 °F), in a collapsible tube, or in other tight container. Protect from freezing.

Auxiliary labeling

- For external use only.
- Continue medication for full time of treatment.

NYSTATIN OINTMENT USP

Usual adult and adolescent dose

See *Nystatin Cream USP*.

Usual pediatric dose

See *Nystatin Cream USP*.

Strength(s) usually available

U.S.—
100,000 USP Nystatin Units per gram (Rx) [*Nilstat; Nystex* (mineral oil; polyethylene); GENERIC].

Canada—
100,000 Units per gram (OTC) [*Mycostatin; Nadostine; Nilstat; Nyaderm*].

Packaging and storage

Store in a well-closed container, preferably between 15 and 30 °C (59 and 86 °F). Protect from freezing.

Auxiliary labeling

- For external use only.
- Continue medication for full time of treatment.

NYSTATIN TOPICAL POWDER USP

Usual adult and adolescent dose

Topical, to the skin, two or three times a day.

Usual pediatric dose

See *Usual adult and adolescent dose.*

Strength(s) usually available

U.S.—
100,000 USP Nystatin Units per gram (Rx) [*Mycostatin* (talc); *Nystop* (talc); *Pedi-Dri* (aluminum chlorhydroxide; corn starch; kaolin; perfume; silica)].

Canada—
100,000 Units per gram (OTC) [*Mycostatin*].

Packaging and storage

Store in a well-closed container below 40 °C (104 °F), preferably between 15 and 30 °C (59 and 86 °F), unless otherwise specified by manufacturer.

Auxiliary labeling

- For external use only.
- Keep container tightly closed.
- Continue medication for full time of treatment.

Revised: 02/05/1999

NYSTATIN Vaginal

VA CLASSIFICATION (Primary): GU302

Commonly used brand name(s): *Mycostatin; Nadostine; Nilstat; Nyaderm.*

Note: For a listing of dosage forms and brand names by country availability, see *Dosage Forms* section(s).

Category

Antifungal (vaginal).

Indications

Note: Bracketed information in the *Indications* section refers to uses that are not included in U.S. product labeling.

Accepted

Candidiasis, vulvovaginal (treatment)—Vaginal nystatin is indicated in the local treatment of vulvovaginal candidiasis caused by *Candida albicans* and other *Candida* species.

[Candidiasis, oropharyngeal (treatment)]—Nystatin vaginal tablets are used as lozenges to treat oropharyngeal candidiasis since their slow dissolution rate provides prolonged oral contact.

Not all species or strains of a particular organism may be susceptible to nystatin.

Unaccepted

Nystatin is not effective against *Trichomonas vaginalis* or *Gardnerella vaginalis (Haemophilus vaginalis)*.

Pharmacology/Pharmacokinetics

Physicochemical characteristics

Source—Derived from *Streptomyces noursei.*
Chemical Group—Polyene antifungal.

Mechanism of action/Effect

Binds to sterols in the fungal cell membrane, resulting in the cell membrane's inability to function as a selective barrier, which allows loss of essential cellular constituents.

Precautions to Consider

Carcinogenicity/Mutagenicity

Long-term studies in animals have not been done to evaluate the carcinogenic or mutagenic potential of nystatin.

Pregnancy/Reproduction

Fertility—Long-term studies in animals have not been done to evaluate the effect of nystatin on fertility in females.

Pregnancy—Studies in animals have not been done. However, studies in humans have not shown that nystatin causes adverse effects on the fetus.

FDA Pregnancy Category A.

Breast-feeding

It is not known whether vaginal nystatin is distributed into breast milk. However, problems in humans have not been documented.

Pediatrics

No information is available on the relationship of age to the effects of vaginal nystatin in pediatric patients.

Geriatrics

No information is available on the relationship of age to the effects of vaginal nystatin in geriatric patients.

Medical considerations/Contraindications

The medical considerations/contraindications included have been selected on the basis of their potential clinical significance (reasons given in parentheses where appropriate)—not necessarily inclusive (» = major clinical significance).

Risk-benefit should be considered when the following medical problem exists:
Sensitivity to nystatin

Side/Adverse Effects

The following side/adverse effects have been selected on the basis of their potential clinical significance (possible signs and symptoms in parentheses where appropriate)—not necessarily inclusive:

Those indicating need for medical attention

Incidence rare
Vaginal irritation not present before therapy (vaginal burning or itching)

Patient Consultation

As an aid to patient consultation, refer to *Advice for the Patient, Nystatin (Vaginal).*

In providing consultation, consider emphasizing the following selected information (» = major clinical significance):

Before using this medication

» Conditions affecting use, especially:
Sensitivity to nystatin

Proper use of this medication

Reading patient instructions before using medication
Using applicator cautiously during pregnancy
Using medication during menstual periods if they start during treatment period
» Compliance with full course of therapy
» Proper dosing
Missed dose: Inserting as soon as possible; not inserting if almost time for next dose
» Proper storage

Precautions while using this medication

» Using hygienic measures to control sources of infection or reinfection
Checking with physician about douching or intercourse during therapy
Protection of clothing because of possible vaginal drainage

Side/adverse effects

Signs of potential side effects, especially vaginal irritation not present before therapy

General Dosing Information

Therapy for a period of 2 weeks is usually sufficient, but more prolonged treatment may be necessary. Treatment of resistent infections may be supplemented with oral products.

To prevent thrush in the newborn, it is suggested that nystatin vaginal tablets be administered to pregnant patients with vulvovaginal candidiasis in a dosage of 100,000 to 200,000 Units daily for 3 to 6 weeks prior to delivery.

Vaginal Dosage Forms

NYSTATIN VAGINAL CREAM

Usual adult and adolescent dose

Antifungal—
Intravaginal, 1 (100,000-Unit) applicatorful one or two times a day for two weeks; or 1 (500,000-Unit) applicatorful once daily.

Note: For severe infections, the dose of 500,000-Units of vaginal cream may be increased to every 12 hours.

Usual pediatric dose

Dosage has not been established.

Strength(s) usually available

U.S.—
Not commercially available.

Canada—
25,000 Units per gram (100,000 Units per applicatorful) (Rx) [*Mycostatin; Nadostine; Nyaderm*].
100,000 Units per gram (500,000 Units per applicatorful) (Rx) [*Nilstat*].

Packaging and storage

Store below 40 °C (104 °F), preferably between 15 and 30 °C (59 and 86 °F), unless otherwise specified by manufacturer. Store in a tight, light-resistant container.

Auxiliary labeling

- Continue medicine for full time of treatment.
- For vaginal use only.

Note

Include patient instructions when dispensing.

Explain administration technique.

NYSTATIN VAGINAL TABLETS USP

Usual adult and adolescent dose

Antifungal—
Intravaginal, 100,000 Units one or two times a day for two weeks.

Usual pediatric dose

Dosage has not been established.

Strength(s) usually available

U.S.—
100,000 Units (Rx) [GENERIC].

Canada—
100,000 Units (Rx) [*Mycostatin; Nadostine; Nilstat*].

Packaging and storage

Store below 40 °C (104 °F), preferably between 15 and 30 °C (59 and 86 °F), unless otherwise specified by manufacturer. Store in a tight, light-resistant container.

Note: Some manufacturers recommend storage in a refrigerator.

Auxiliary labeling

- Continue medicine for full time of treatment.
- For vaginal use only.
- Refrigerate.

Note

Include patient instructions when dispensing.

Explain administration technique (for use as oral lozenge).

Revised: 08/11/1998

NYSTATIN AND TRIAMCINOLONE
Topical

VA CLASSIFICATION (Primary): DE250

Commonly used brand name(s): *Dermacomb; Myco II; Myco-Triacet II; Mycobiotic II; Mycogen II; Mycolog II; Mykacet; Mykacet II; Mytrex; Tristatin II.*

NOTE: The *Nystatin and Triamcinolone (Topical)* monograph is maintained on the *USP DI* electronic data base. A copy of the most recent revision of the complete monograph can be accessed on the *USP DI* Updates Online website. See the front cover of book for details on accessing the site.

For information on the specific components of this combination, see the *USP DI* monographs for *Corticosteroids (Topical)* and *Nystatin (Topical).*

The information that follows is selectively abstracted from the complete monograph and is provided to facilitate drug use review and patient counseling.

Note: For a listing of dosage forms and brand names by country availability, see *Dosage Forms* section(s).

Category
Antifungal-corticosteroid (topical).

Indications
Note: Bracketed information in the *Indications* section refers to uses that are not included in U.S. product labeling.

Accepted
Candidiasis, cutaneous (treatment)—Nystatin and triamcinolone combination is indicated as a secondary agent in the topical treatment of cutaneous candidiasis, [accompanied by inflammation], caused by *Candida albicans (Monilia albicans)* and other *Candida* species.

The use of nystatin and triamcinolone combination has been shown to provide greater benefit than nystatin alone during the first few days of treatment [or for as long as inflammation persists. After this time, USP medical experts recommend the use of plain nystatin or other topical antifungal agents. Also, nystatin and triamcinolone combination is recommended only for short-term (less than 2 weeks) treatment of inflammatory candidiasis confined to limited areas of the skin].

Not all species or strains of a particular organism may be susceptible to nystatin.

Unaccepted
Nystatin and triamcinolone combination is not recommended in the treatment of mucocutaneous candidiasis. In addition, nystatin is not effective against bacteria, protozoa, trichomonads, or viruses.

Patient Consultation
As an aid to patient consultation, refer to *Advice for the Patient, Nystatin and Triamcinolone (Topical).*

In providing consultation, consider emphasizing the following selected information (» = major clinical significance):

Before using this medication
» Conditions affecting use, especially:
- Sensitivity to nystatin or corticosteroids
- Pregnancy—Topical corticosteroids may be systemically absorbed; potent corticosteroids have been shown to be teratogenic in animals following topical application
- Breast-feeding—Systemic corticosteroids are distributed into breast-milk and may cause growth suppression in the infant; topical corticosteroids may be systemically absorbed
- Use in children—Children may absorb a proportionately larger amount of topical corticosteroid than adults, making them more susceptible to HPA axis suppression and Cushing's syndrome
- Other medical problems, especially Herpes simplex; tubercular infections of the skin; vaccinia, eczema vaccinatum, varicella, or other viral infections of the skin

Proper use of this medication
» Not for ophthalmic use

» Checking with physician before using medication on other skin problems

Applying a thin layer of medication to affected area and rubbing in gently and thoroughly

» Not applying occlusive dressing over this medication unless directed to do so by physician; wearing loose-fitting clothing when using on inguinal area; avoiding tight-fitting diapers and plastic pants on diaper area of children

» Compliance with full course of therapy; not using more often or longer than directed by physician; excessive use on thin skin areas may result in skin atrophy and stretch marks

» Proper dosing

Missed dose: Applying as soon as possible; not applying if almost time for next dose

» Proper storage

Precautions while using this medication
» Using hygienic measures to cure infection or prevent reinfection; keeping affected area as cool and dry as possible

Checking with physician if no improvement within 2 or 3 weeks

» May be more likely to cause systemic toxicity in children; chronic use may interfere with growth and development also; having children closely monitored by their physician

» Diabetics: May rarely cause hyperglycemia and glucosuria; checking with physician before changing diet or dosage of antidiabetic medication

Side/adverse effects
Side effects more likely to occur in children

Signs of potential side effects, especially hypersensitivity; acne or oily skin; increased hair growth especially on the face; increased loss of hair, especially on the scalp; reddish purple lines on arms, face, legs, trunk, or groins; skin atrophy

Topical Dosage Forms

NYSTATIN AND TRIAMCINOLONE ACETONIDE CREAM USP

Usual adult and adolescent dose

Antifungal—

Topical, to the skin, two times a day, morning and evening.

Usual pediatric dose

See *Usual adult and adolescent dose.*

Strength(s) usually available

U.S.—

100,000 Units of nystatin and 1 mg of triamcinolone acetonide per gram [*Dermacomb; Myco II; Mycobiotic II; Mycogen II; Mycolog II; Myco-Triacet II; Mykacet II; Mytrex; Tristatin II*; GENERIC].

Canada—

Not commercially available.

Auxiliary labeling
- For external use only.
- Continue medication for full time of treatment.
- Do not use in or around the eyes.

NYSTATIN AND TRIAMCINOLONE ACETONIDE OINTMENT USP

Usual adult and adolescent dose

Antifungal—

Topical, to the skin, two or three times a day.

Usual pediatric dose

See *Usual adult and adolescent dose.*

Strength(s) usually available

U.S.—

100,000 Units of nystatin and 1 mg of triamcinolone acetonide per gram [*Myco II; Mycobiotic II; Mycogen II; Mycolog II; Myco-Triacet II; Mykacet; Mytrex; Tristatin II*; GENERIC].

Canada—

Not commercially available.

Auxiliary labeling
- For external use only.
- Continue medication for full time of treatment.
- Do not use in or around the eyes.

Revised: 08/15/1994

OCTOXYNOL 9—See *Spermacides (Vaginal)*

OCTREOTIDE Systemic

VA CLASSIFICATION (Primary/Secondary): GA208/BL116; CV900; HS900

Commonly used brand name(s): *Sandostatin; Sandostatin LAR Depot.*

Note: For a listing of dosage forms and brand names by country availability, see *Dosage Forms* section(s).

Category

Antidiarrheal (gastrointestinal tumor; acquired immunodeficiency syndrome [AIDS]); growth hormone suppressant (acromegaly); antihemorrhagic (bleeding gastroesophageal varices); antihypotensive (carcinoid crisis); antihypoglycemic (pancreatic tumor).

Indications

Note: Bracketed information in the *Indications* section refers to uses that are not included in U.S. product labeling.

Accepted

Tumors, gastrointestinal (treatment adjunct)—Octreotide is indicated for palliative management of gastrointestinal endocrine tumors, such as:

Carcinoid tumors—To suppress or inhibit the associated severe diarrhea and facial flushing episodes.

Vasoactive intestinal polypeptide–secreting tumors (VIPomas)—For the treatment of the profuse watery diarrhea associated with VIPomas.

Acromegaly (treatment)—Octreotide is indicated to suppress secretion of growth hormone from pituitary tumors and decrease blood concentrations of insulin-like growth factor-I (IGF-I; somatomedin C) in patients with acromegaly who have not optimally responded to or cannot be treated with surgical resection or pituitary irradiation or have been unable to tolerate bromocriptine. Octreotide may be used as adjunctive therapy with irradiation to help relieve symptoms of acromegaly and possibly slow the rate of tumor growth.

[Pancreatic surgery, complications of (prophylaxis)]—Octreotide is indicated to reduce the incidence and severity of the postoperative complications of high-risk pancreatic surgery. These complications may include abscess formation and subsequent sepsis, acute pancreatitis, pancreatic fistula, and peripancreatic fluid collection.

[Varices, gastroesophageal, bleeding (treatment)]—Octreotide, with an appropriate adjunctive therapeutic intervention such as sclerotherapy, is indicated to control bleeding and early rebleeding and to reduce transfusion requirements in patients with bleeding gastroesophageal varices associated with cirrhosis. Octreotide has been shown to improve the 5-day survival rate in these patients.

[Hypotension (treatment)][1]—Octreotide is indicated to reverse life-threatening hypotension due to carcinoid crisis during induction of anesthesia.

[Tumors, pancreatic (treatment adjunct)][1]—Octreotide is indicated for use as palliative treatment of the symptoms resulting from hyperinsulinemia from severe refractory metastatic insulinoma.

[Diarrhea, acquired immunodeficiency syndrome (AIDS)-associated (treatment)][1]—Octreotide is indicated in AIDS patients with severe secretory diarrhea who have failed to respond to antimicrobial or antimotility agents.

[Diarrhea, chemotherapy-induced (treatment)][1]—Octreotide is indicated for the treatment of chemotherapy-induced diarrhea.

Acceptance not established

Use of octreotide for the treatment of hepatocellular carcinoma has not been established, due to insufficient reliable data supporting efficacy.

[1]Not included in Canadian product labeling.

Pharmacology/Pharmacokinetics

Physicochemical characteristics

Molecular weight—Octreotide (base): 1019.26.

pH—4 to 4.6.

Mechanism of action/Effect

Gastrointestinal tumors—The action of octreotide is similar to that of naturally occurring somatostatin, but with a prolonged duration. Like the naturally occurring hormone, octreotide suppresses secretion of serotonin and the gastroenteropancreatic peptides including gastrin, motilin, and secretin, stimulates fluid and electrolyte absorption from the gastrointestinal tract, and prolongs intestinal transit time. It blocks the carcinoid flush, decreases circulating concentrations of serotonin metabolite 5-hydroxyindoleacetic acid (5-HIAA), and controls other symptoms associated with the carcinoid syndrome.

Acromegaly—Octreotide suppresses secretion of growth hormone and insulin-like growth factor-I (IGF-I; somatomedin C).

Prophylaxis of complications of high-risk pancreatic surgery—Complications of high-risk pancreatic surgery, such as abscess formation and subsequent sepsis, acute pancreatitis, pancreatic fistula, and peripancreatic fluid collection, occur as a result of fluid leaking from the pancreatic remnant into the surrounding tissues. This fluid contains digestive enzymes that cause inflammation and destruction of the surrounding intestinal organs and vessels. When administered perioperatively, octreotide suppresses secretion of pancreatic fluid.

Bleeding gastroesophageal varices—The exact mechanism of action is unknown but is believed to be related to the suppression of vasoactive gastrointestinal hormones and exertion of a direct vasomotor effect on the splanchnic vessels, resulting in a reduction of splanchnic blood flow.

Other actions/effects

Octreotide suppresses secretion of glucagon, insulin, and thyroid stimulating hormone, and suppresses the luteinizing hormone response to gonadotropin-releasing hormone. Octreotide also inhibits gallbladder contractions and decreases bile secretion.

Absorption

Immediate-release dosage form—Absorbed rapidly and completely from the injection site.

Protein binding

In patients with acromegaly—Moderate (41.2%).

In all other patients—High (65%, to lipoproteins and to a lesser extent to albumin).

Half-life

Immediate-release dosage form—
- Elimination:
  - Subcutaneous—
    - 1.7 hours.
  - Intravenous—
    - Alpha phase: Approximately 10 minutes.
    - Beta phase: Approximately 90 minutes.

May be increased in elderly patients (by up to 46%) and in patients with renal function impairment requiring dialysis.

Time to peak concentration

Immediate-release dosage form—Approximately 30 minutes.
- Long-acting dosage form—
  - Initial: 60 minutes.
  - Plateau: 2 to 3 weeks.

Peak serum concentration

Immediate-release dosage form—
- 5.2 nanograms/mL with a 100-mcg dose.

Long-acting dosage form—
- Initial: 0.03 nanogram/mL/mg.
- Plateau: 0.07 nanogram/mL/mg.

Duration of action

Immediate-release dosage form—Up to 12 hours (depending on the type of tumor).

Elimination

Renal (32% of dose).

Precautions to Consider

Carcinogenicity

Injection site tumors in patients treated with octreotide for up to 5 years have not been reported.

Mice treated subcutaneously for 85 to 99 weeks at doses up to 2000 mcg per kg of body weight per day (8 times the human exposure based on body surface area) demonstrated no carcinogenic potential.

In a 116-week study, rats given the highest dose level of 1250 mcg per kg of body weight per day (10 times the human exposure based on body surface area) subcutaneously showed a 27% and 12% incidence of injection site sarcomas or squamous cell carcinomas in males and females, respectively, compared with an 8 to 10% incidence in the vehicle-controlled group. The increased incidence of injection site tumors was most probably caused by irritation and the rat's high sensitivity to repeated injections at the same site. Rotating injections sites would prevent chronic irritation in humans.

Female rats treated with 1250 mcg per kg of body weight per day had a 15% incidence of uterine adenocarcinomas compared with 7% and 0% in saline-control and vehicle-control females, respectively. The presence of endometritis along with the absence of corpora lutea, the reduction in mammary fibroadenomas, and the presence of uterine dilatation suggest that the uterine tumors were associated with estrogen dominance in the aged female rats which does not occur in humans.

Mutagenicity
No mutagenic potential of octreotide has been demonstrated in studies in laboratory animals.

Pregnancy/Reproduction
Fertility—Studies in rats at doses of up to 1000 mcg per kg of body weight (seven times the human exposure based on body surface area) a day have not shown that octreotide causes impaired fertility.

Pregnancy—Adequate and well-controlled studies in humans have not been done. Because animal reproduction studies are not always predictive of human response, this drug should be used during pregnancy only if clearly needed.

Studies in rats and rabbits at doses of up to 30 times the maximum human dose have not shown that octreotide causes adverse effects in the fetus.

FDA Pregnancy Category B.

Breast-feeding
It is not known whether octreotide is distributed into breast milk. Because many drugs are distributed into human milk, caution should be exercised when octreotide is administered to a nursing woman.

Pediatrics
Appropriate studies with immediate-release octreotide have not been performed in the pediatric population. One to 10 mcg per kg of body weight, given to children as young as 1 month old, were well tolerated in children with congenital hyperinsulinism. One case in which an infant (a case of nesidioblastosis) suffered a seizure while undergoing octreotide therapy was thought to be unrelated to octreotide administration. A single death has been reported in a male 16 months of age with enterocutaneous fistula who developed sudden abdominal pain and increased nasogastric drainage and died 8 hours after receiving a single 100-mcg subcutaneous dose of octreotide.

Safety and efficacy of long-acting octreotide in pediatric patients have not been established.

Geriatrics
Appropriate studies on the relationship of age to the effects of octreotide have not been performed in the geriatric population. However, studies performed to date in patients as old as 83 years of age have not demonstrated geriatrics-specific problems that would limit the usefulness of this medication in the elderly. In general, dose selection for an elderly patient should be cautious, usually starting at the low end of the dosing range, reflecting the greater frequency of decreased hepatic, renal, or cardiac function, and of concomitant disease or other drug therapy.

Drug interactions and/or related problems
The following drug interactions and/or related problems have been selected on the basis of their potential clinical significance (possible mechanism in parentheses where appropriate)—not necessarily inclusive (» = major clinical significance):

Note: Combinations containing any of the following medications, depending on the amount present, may also interact with this medication.

» Antidiabetic agents, sulfonylurea or
» Diazoxide, oral or
» Glucagon or
» Growth hormone or
» Insulin or
» Oral glycemic agents
(use of these medications during octreotide therapy may result in hypoglycemia or hyperglycemia; patient monitoring and dosage adjustment of these medications may be necessary)

Beta-adrenergic blocking agents
(because of the bradycardic effect of octreotide, dosage adjustment may be required)

Bromocriptine or
Drugs metabolized by cytochrome CYP3A4 or
Quinidine or
Terfenadine
(concomitant administration of these medicines and octreotide may increase the availability of these medicines; caution should be used)

Calcium channel blocking agents or
Electrolyte balance agents or
Fluid balance agents
(dosage of these drugs may need to be adjusted when used concomitantly with octreotide)

» Cyclosporine
(may decrease blood levels of cyclosporine and result in transplant rejection)

Laboratory value alterations
The following have been selected on the basis of their potential clinical significance (possible effect in parentheses where appropriate)—not necessarily inclusive (» = major clinical significance).

With diagnostic test results

Schilling test
(abnormal results have been seen)

With physiology/laboratory test values

Alanine aminotransferase (ALT [SGPT]) and
Alkaline phosphatase and
Aspartate aminotransferase (AST [SGOT]) and
Gamma-glutamyltransferase (GGT), serum
(values may be increased if hyperbilirubinemia develops)

Electrocardiogram
(changes such as QT prolongation, axis shifts, early repolarization, low voltage, R/S transition, R-wave progression, and nonspecific ST-T wave changes have been seen in patients with acromegaly)

Thyroid hormones
(serum concentration of thyroxine [T_4] may be decreased; hypothyroidism occurred in one clinical trial patient [with a carcinoid tumor] after 19 months of receiving 1.5 mg of octreotide daily)

Vitamin B_{12}, serum
(concentrations may be decreased)

Zinc, serum
(concentrations may increase excessively in patients receiving total parenteral nutrition [TPN] when fluid loss is corrected)

Medical considerations/Contraindications
The medical considerations/contraindications included have been selected on the basis of their potential clinical significance (reasons given in parentheses where appropriate)—not necessarily inclusive (» = major clinical significance).

Except under special circumstances, this medication should not be used when the following medical problem exists:

» Sensitivity to octreotide or any of its components

Risk-benefit should be considered when the following medical problems exist:

» Diabetes mellitus
(therapy used to control glycemic states may need to be adjusted)

» Gallbladder disease or gallstones, or history of
(increased risk of cholelithiasis possibly due to alteration of fat absorption and decrease in gallbladder motility caused by octreotide)

» Renal function impairment, severe
(half-life of octreotide may be increased; dosage adjustment may be necessary)

Patient monitoring
The following may be especially important in patient monitoring (other tests may be warranted in some patients, depending on condition; » = major clinical significance):

Carotene, serum concentrations and
Fecal fat, quantitative
(octreotide therapy may alter absorption of dietary fats; periodic 72-hour fecal fat and serum carotene determinations are recommended to assess possible aggravation of fat malabsorption)

Glucose
(measurement of blood concentrations is recommended at the beginning of octreotide therapy and at each change of dosage if clinical signs of increase or decrease occur)

» Growth hormone
(recommended at 1- to 4-hour intervals for 8 to 12 hours following a dose of immediate-release octreotide and at 6-month intervals thereafter to assess response in patients with acromegaly; after transfer to the long-acting dosage form, monitoring is recommended at 3-month intervals)

» 5-hydroxyindoleacetic acid (5-HIAA), quantitative, urine and
Serotonin and
Substance P, plasma
(periodic determinations are recommended during therapy in patients with carcinoid tumors to assess patient response)

Insulin-like growth factor-I (IGF-I; somatomedin C)
(an alternative to measurement of growth hormone; may be measured one time 2 weeks after immediate-release octreotide initia-

tion or change of dosage and at 6-month intervals thereafter to assess response in patients with acromegaly; after transfer to the long-acting dosage form, monitoring is recommended at 3-month intervals)

Thyroid function determinations
(baseline and periodic thyroid function tests using total and free serum thyroxine [T_4] are recommended during chronic therapy)

» Ultrasonograms
(therapy with octreotide, as with the natural hormone somatostatin, may be associated with cholelithiasis, presumably due to an alteration of fat absorption and possibly to decreased motility of the gallbladder; baseline and periodic ultrasonograms may be required to assess the presence of gallstones)

Vasoactive intestinal polypeptide (VIP)
(periodic determinations are recommended in patients with VIP-secreting tumors [VIPomas] to assess patient response)

Vitamin B_{12}, serum
(periodic determinations are recommended during chronic therapy)

Zinc, serum
(periodic determinations are recommended in patients receiving TPN)

Side/Adverse Effects

Note: Isolated reports of hepatic dysfunctions associated with octreotide administration include acute hepatitis without cholestasis, slow development of hyperbilirubinemia, and gallstone formation and/or biliary sludge. The risk of gallstone formation and/or biliary sludge increases with long-term therapy, which usually is required in the treatment of acromegaly.

Development of antibodies has been seen in up to 25% of patients treated with octreotide. In most of these cases, therapeutic response to octreotide has not been affected. However, in two patients with acromegaly, the duration of growth hormone suppression following an injection of immediate-release octreotide was doubled as compared with that in patients without antibodies.

The following side/adverse effects have been selected on the basis of their potential clinical significance (possible signs and symptoms in parentheses where appropriate)—not necessarily inclusive:

Those indicating need for medical attention

Incidence more frequent

Arrhythmias (irregular heartbeat)—incidence 9% in patients with acromegaly, 3% in patients with carcinoid tumors; ***bradycardia*** (slow heartbeat)—incidence 25% in patients with acromegaly, 19% in patients with carcinoid tumors; ***goiter*** (changes in menstrual periods; decreased sexual ability in males; dry, puffy skin; feeling cold; swelling of front part of neck; weight gain)—incidence 9% in patients with acromegaly; incidence 0% in patients without acromegaly; ***hypothyroidism*** (constipation; depressed mood; dry skin and hair; feeling cold; hair loss; hoarseness or husky voice; muscle cramps and stiffness; slowed heartbeat; weight gain; unusual tiredness or weakness)—incidence 12% in patients with acromegaly

Note: Hypothyroidism has only been reported in several isolated patients without acromegaly.

Incidence less frequent or rare

Hyperglycemia (blurred vision; drowsiness; dry mouth; flushed, dry skin; fruit-like breath odor; increased urination [frequency and volume]; ketones in urine; loss of appetite; stomachache, nausea, or vomiting; tiredness; troubled breathing [rapid and deep]; unconsciousness; unusual thirst); ***hypoglycemia*** (anxiety; behavior change similar to drunkenness; blurred vision; cold sweats; coma; confusion; cool, pale skin; difficulty in concentrating; drowsiness; excessive hunger; fast heartbeat; headache; nausea; nervousness; nightmares; restless sleep; seizures; shakiness; slurred speech; unusual tiredness or weakness); ***pancreatitis, acute*** (abdominal pain or distension; nausea; vomiting)

Note: Octreotide therapy is occasionally associated with mild transient *hypoglycemia* or *hyperglycemia* due to an alteration in the balance between the counterregulatory hormones, insulin, glucagon, and growth hormone.

Acute pancreatitis generally is seen within the first hours or days of octreotide administration and resolves when therapy is discontinued.

Those indicating need for medical attention only if they continue or are bothersome

Incidence more frequent

Gastrointestinal symptoms (abdominal or stomach pain or discomfort; constipation; diarrhea; flatulence; nausea and vomiting); ***headache; pain, stinging, tingling, or burning sensation at injection site, with redness and swelling***

Note: *Gastrointestinal symptoms* usually are self-limiting and usually are resolved after 2 to 3 weeks of therapy. In rare instances, gastrointestinal side effects may resemble acute intestinal obstruction, with progressive abdominal distension, severe epigastric pain, abdominal tenderness and guarding.

Incidence less frequent or rare

Alopecia; backache; blurred vision; cold symptoms (runny nose; sore throat); ***depression*** (discouragement; feeling sad or empty; irritability; lack of appetite; loss of interest or pleasure; tiredness; trouble concentrating; trouble sleeping); ***dizziness or lightheadedness; edema*** (swelling of feet or lower legs); ***fat malabsorption*** (stools that float, foul smelling and fatty in appearance); ***fatigue; fever; flu symptoms*** (chills; cough; diarrhea; fever; general feeling of discomfort or illness; headache; joint pain; loss of appetite; muscle aches and pains; nausea; runny nose; shivering; sore throat; sweating; trouble sleeping; unusual tiredness or weakness; vomiting); ***joint pain; pollakiuria*** (frequent urination usually with very small amounts of urine); ***pruritus*** (itching skin); ***redness or flushing of face; unusual weakness; urinary tract infection*** (bladder pain; bloody or cloudy urine; difficult, burning, or painful urination; frequent urge to urinate; lower back or side pain); ***visual disturbance*** (blurred or loss of vision; disturbed color perception; night blindness; double vision; tunnel vision; halos around lights; overbright appearance of lights)

Overdose

For more information on the management of overdose or unintentional ingestion, **contact a Poison Control Center** (see *Poison Control Center Listing*).

Clinical effects of overdose

The following effects have been selected on the basis of their potential clinical significance (possible signs and symptoms in parentheses where appropriate)—not necessarily inclusive:

Abdominal cramps; decrease in heart rate; diarrhea; dizziness; empty feeling in stomach; flushing of face; nausea

Treatment of overdose

Supportive care—Recommended treatment consists of temporary withdrawal of octreotide and symptomatic treatment of the clinical effects.

Patient Consultation

As an aid to patient consultation, refer to *Advice for the Patient, Octreotide (Systemic)*.

In providing consultation, consider emphasizing the following selected information (» = major clinical significance):

Before using this medication

» Conditions affecting use, especially:
Sensitivity to octreotide or any of its components
Use in the elderly—Dose selection should be cautious
Other medications, especially cyclosporine, glucagon, growth hormone, insulin, oral diazoxide, oral glycemic agents, or sulfonylurea antidiabetic agents
Other medical problems, especially diabetes mellitus, gallbladder disease or gallstones, or severe renal impairment

Proper use of this medication

» Taking medication only as directed by physician
» Reading directions in starter kit before using
» Carefully selecting and rotating injection sites
Allowing medication to reach room temperature if pain, stinging, tingling, or burning sensation occurs upon injection
» Safe handling and disposal of needles and syringes; not reusing needles and syringes
» Proper dosing
Missed dose: Long-acting dosage form—Contacting physician
Immediate-release dosage form—Using as soon as possible unless almost time for next dose, then going back to regular dosing schedule; not doubling doses
» Proper storage

Precautions while using this medication

» Importance of close monitoring by physician

Side/adverse effects

Signs of potential side effects, especially arrhythmias, bradycardia, goiter, hyperglycemia, hypoglycemia, hypothyroidism, and acute pancreatitis

General Dosing Information

Preferred sites for subcutaneous administration of octreotide injection (immediate-release dosage form) are the hip, thigh, and abdomen.

Octreotide suspension (long-acting dosage form) is recommended for intragluteal administration only. Injection into the deltoid muscle causes significant discomfort at the site. Intravenous or subcutaneous administration is not recommended.

Multiple injections at the same injection site within short periods of time are not recommended. This is to avoid irritating the area.

Local reactions at the injection site may be minimized by allowing the medication to reach room temperature before injection and by administering slowly.

Periodic exacerbation of symptoms may occur despite good overall control. During these times, if the patient is receiving octreotide injection, the dosage should be adjusted. If the patient is receiving octreotide suspension, octreotide injection, at the previous dosage, should be administered concurrently with octreotide suspension until symptoms are again controlled. Administration of octreotide injection may then be discontinued.

For gastrointestinal tumors

When initiating therapy with octreotide suspension, octreotide injection, at the current dosage, should be administered concurrently for at least 2 weeks (up to 4 weeks may be required in some patients) to allow octreotide suspension to reach therapeutic concentrations. Failure to do so may result in exacerbation of symptoms.

For acromegaly

If after 3 months there is no significant decrease in growth hormone concentration and no appreciable improvement in clinical symptoms, octreotide therapy should be discontinued.

Octreotide therapy should be withheld for approximately 8 weeks each year from patients who have received irradiation, to assess disease activity. During this time, if growth hormone or insulin-like growth factor-I (IGF-I) concentration increases or if clinical signs and symptoms recur, octreotide therapy should be reinstated.

Diet/Nutrition

To avoid the occurrence of gastrointestinal side effects, injections of octreotide should be scheduled between meals and at bedtime.

Parenteral Dosage Forms

Note: Bracketed uses in the *Dosage Forms* section refer to categories of use and/or indications that are not included in U.S. product labeling.

OCTREOTIDE ACETATE FOR INJECTABLE SUSPENSION

Usual adult and adolescent dose

Gastrointestinal tumors—

Patients not currently receiving octreotide—To ascertain responsiveness to octreotide, it is recommended that therapy be initiated and maintained for at least two weeks with the immediate-release dosage form (see *Octreotide Acetate Injection*).

Patients currently receiving octreotide injection: Intragluteal, 20 mg every four weeks for two months. Dosage may then be increased to 30 mg every four weeks or decreased to 10 mg every four weeks, based on patient response.

Note: Administration of octreotide injection at the current dosage should be maintained for at least two weeks to allow octreotide suspension to reach therapeutic concentrations.

Acromegaly—

Patients not currently receiving octreotide—

To ascertain responsiveness to octreotide, it is recommended that therapy be initiated and maintained for at least two weeks with the immediate-release dosage form (see *Octreotide Acetate Injection*).

Patients currently receiving octreotide injection—

Intragluteal, 20 mg every four weeks for three months. Dosage should then be titrated based on the following criteria:

If growth hormone concentrations are less than 2.5 nanograms per mL, IGF-I concentrations are normal, and clinical symptoms are controlled—Intragluteal, 20 mg every four weeks.

If growth hormone concentrations are greater than 2.5 nanograms per mL, IFG-I concentrations are elevated, and/or clinical symptoms are uncontrolled—Intragluteal, 30 mg every four weeks.

If growth hormone concentrations are less than or equal to 1 nanogram per mL, IFG-I concentrations are normal and clinical symptoms are controlled—Intragluteal, 10 mg every four weeks.

If growth hormone concentrations, IGF-I concentrations, and clinical symptoms are not controlled with 30 mg—Intragluteal, 40 mg every four weeks.

Note: Administration at dosing intervals greater than every four weeks is not recommended; efficacy at this schedule has not been determined.

Because of the increase in the half-life of octreotide, patients with renal failure requiring dialysis may need an adjustment in the dosage.

Usual adult prescribing limits

Gastrointestinal tumors—30 mg every four weeks.

Acromegaly—40 mg every four weeks.

Usual pediatric dose

Safety and efficacy have not been established.

Usual geriatric dose

See *Usual adult and adolescent dose*.

Note: Because of the significant increase in the half-life of octreotide and the decrease in clearance seen in geriatric patients, dosage adjustment may be required.

Strength(s) usually available

U.S.—

10 mg (base) per vial (Rx) [*Sandostatin LAR Depot*].

20 mg (base) per vial (Rx) [*Sandostatin LAR Depot*].

30 mg (base) per vial (Rx) [*Sandostatin LAR Depot*].

Canada—

Not commercially available.

Packaging and storage

Store at 2 to 8 °C (36 to 46 °F), unless otherwise specified by manufacturer. Protect from light.

Note: Octreotide for injectable suspension vial and diluent should be taken from the refrigerator 30 to 60 minutes before administration to allow them to warm to room temperature.

Preparation of dosage form

The manufacturer's instructions for preparation should be followed.

Stability

Octreotide suspension should be administered immediately after preparation.

Auxiliary labeling

- Refrigerate.

Note

Injection sites should be rotated.

OCTREOTIDE ACETATE INJECTION

Usual adult and adolescent dose

Gastrointestinal tumors—

Subcutaneous, 50 mcg initially, administered two or three times a day, the dose being increased gradually according to patient tolerance and response. The following dosages are recommended for specific tumors:

Carcinoid tumors:

Initial: Subcutaneous, 100 to 600 mcg per day, administered in two to four divided doses, for the first two weeks of therapy.

Maintenance: Subcutaneous, 50 to 1500 mcg per day. In clinical trials, the median maintenance dosage was 450 mcg per day.

Vasoactive intestinal polypeptide–secreting tumors (VIPomas): Subcutaneous, 200 to 300 mcg per day, administered in two to four divided doses, for the first two weeks of therapy. Dosage may then be increased based on patient response.

Acromegaly—

Subcutaneous or intravenous, initially 50 mcg three times a day. Dosage is titrated every two weeks as needed, according to IGF-I concentrations, to a dose of 100 to 200 mcg three times a day; or, for rapid titration, dosage increase may be based on multiple serum growth hormone concentrations taken at one- to four-hour intervals over eight to twelve hours. Doses of up to 500 mcg three times a day have been used rarely.

Note: Octreotide injection may be administered subcutaneously (the preferred route) or intravenously. To help prevent pain at the injection site, octreotide should be given in the smallest volume needed to achieve the proper dose. In emergencies, intravenous injections may be used cautiously.

If an increase in dose fails to provide additional benefit, the dose should be reduced.

[Complications of pancreatic surgery (prophylaxis of)]—

Subcutaneous, 100 mcg three times a day for seven days beginning on the day of surgery at least one hour before laparotomy.

[Bleeding gastroesophageal varices]—
Intravenous infusion, 25 mcg per hour for forty-eight hours. Infusion should continue for up to five days in patients at high risk for rebleeding.

[Pancreatic tumors][1]—
Subcutaneous, 50 to 150 mcg initially, administered two times a day thirty minutes before meals, the dose being increased gradually according to patient tolerance and response.

[Acquired immunodeficiency syndrome (AIDS)-associated diarrhea][1]—
Subcutaneous, 100 to 1800 mcg per day.

[Chemotherapy–induced diarrhea][1]—
Subcutaneous, 100 to 150 mcg three times a day as a starting dose. Dosage may be increased up to 2000 mcg three times a day if needed. Treatment may last three to five days or until diarrhea resolves.

Usual adult prescribing limits

Acromegaly—1500 mcg daily.

Usual pediatric dose

Gastrointestinal tumors—
Subcutaneous, 1 to 10 mcg per kg of body weight per day.

Usual geriatric dose

See *Usual adult and adolescent dose*.

Note: Because of the significant increase in the half-life of octreotide and the decrease in clearance seen in geriatric patients, dosage adjustment may be required.

Strength(s) usually available

U.S.—

Note: The 50 mcg per mL, 100 mcg per mL, and 500 mcg per mL strengths are packaged as single-use ampuls; the remaining strengths are packaged as multiple-dose vials.

50 mcg per mL (Rx) [*Sandostatin*].
100 mcg per mL (Rx) [*Sandostatin*].
200 mcg per mL (Rx) [*Sandostatin*].
500 mcg per mL (Rx) [*Sandostatin*].
1000 mcg per mL (Rx) [*Sandostatin*].

Canada—

Note: The 50 mcg per mL, 100 mcg per mL, and 500 mcg per mL strengths are packaged as single-use ampuls; the 200 mcg per mL strength is packaged as a multiple-dose vial.

50 mcg per mL (Rx) [*Sandostatin*].
100 mcg per mL (Rx) [*Sandostatin*].
200 mcg per mL (Rx) [*Sandostatin*].
500 mcg per mL (Rx) [*Sandostatin*].

Packaging and storage

Octreotide may be stored at room temperature protected from light for up to 14 days. However, for prolonged periods, store at 2 to 8 °C (36 to 46 °F), unless otherwise specified by manufacturer. Protect from freezing. Protect from light.

Note: Solution should be allowed to warm to room temperature before administration. Do not warm artificially before injection. Single-use ampuls should be opened just prior to use and any unused portion discarded.

Preparation of dosage form

Octreotide is stable when diluted in 50 to 200 mL of either sterile 0.9% sodium chloride injection or 5% dextrose injection. The diluted solution can be infused intravenously over a 15- to 30-minute period or administered via a direct intravenous injection over a 3-minute period. In emergencies, rapid intravenous injections may be used cautiously.

Stability

If protected from light, octreotide injection is stable at room temperature, preferably between 15 and 30 °C (59 and 86 °F), for 14 days. When diluted in 0.9% sodium chloride injection, octreotide injection is stable at room temperature for 24 hours. Octreotide should not be used if it is discolored or if particulate matter forms in the solution.

Incompatibilities

Octreotide is not compatible with fat emulsions or with total parenteral nutrition (TPN) solutions because decreased efficacy may result if glycosyloctreotide conjugates form.

Note

Subcutaneous injection sites should be rotated.

[1]Not included in Canadian product labeling.

Revised: 12/21/2005

OCTYL METHOXYCINNAMATE—See *Sunscreen Agents (Topical)*

OCTYL SALICYLATE—See *Sunscreen Agents (Topical)*

OFLOXACIN—See *Fluoroquinolones (Systemic)*, *Ofloxacin (Ophthalmic)*

OFLOXACIN Ophthalmic

VA CLASSIFICATION (Primary): OP201

Commonly used brand name(s): *Ocuflox*.

Note: For a listing of dosage forms and brand names by country availability, see *Dosage Forms* section(s).

Category

Antibacterial (ophthalmic).

Indications

Accepted

Conjunctivitis, bacterial (treatment)—Ophthalmic ofloxacin is indicated in the treatment of conjunctivitis caused by susceptible strains of *Enterobacter cloacae*, *Haemophilus influenzae*, *Proteus mirabilis*, *Pseudomonas aeruginosa*, *Staphylococcus aureus*, *Staphylococcus epidermidis*, and *Streptococcus pneumoniae*.

Not all species or strains of a particular organism may be susceptible to ofloxacin.

Corneal ulcers, bacterial (treatment)[1]—Ophthalmic ofloxacin is indicated in the treatment of corneal ulcers caused by susceptible strains of *Propionibacterium acnes*, *P. aeruginosa*, *Serratia marcescens*, *S. aureus*, *S. epidermidis*, and *S. pneumoniae*.

Efficacy for *S. marcescens* was studied in less than ten infections.

[1]Not included in Canadian product labeling.

Pharmacology/Pharmacokinetics

Physicochemical characteristics

Chemical Group—Fluoroquinolone.
Molecular weight—361.37.
pH—6.4 (range 6.0 to 6.8).
Osmolarity—300 mOsmol per kilogram.

Mechanism of action/Effect

Ofloxacin's bactericidal action results from interference with the enzyme, DNA gyrase, which is needed for synthesis of bacterial DNA.

Absorption

In one study in which ophthalmic ofloxacin was administered 4 times a day for 10½ days, the maximum plasma concentration was approximately 1.9 nanograms per mL.

Elimination

Excreted in the urine, primarily as unchanged drug.

Precautions to Consider

Cross-sensitivity and/or related problems

Patients sensitive to fluoroquinolones or their derivatives, such as cinoxacin, ciprofloxacin, enoxacin, lomefloxacin, nalidixic acid, or norfloxacin, may be sensitive to ofloxacin also.

Carcinogenicity

Studies to determine the carcinogenic potential of ofloxacin have not been done.

Mutagenicity

Ofloxacin was mutagenic in the unscheduled DNA synthesis (UDS) test using rat hepatocytes and in the mouse lymphoma assay. However, ofloxacin was not mutagenic in the UDS assay using human fibroblasts, the Ames test, *in vitro* and *in vivo* cytogenic assay, sister chromatid exchange assay (Chinese hamster and human cell lines), dominant lethal assay, or mouse micronucleus assay.

Pregnancy/Reproduction

Fertility—In studies in rats, ofloxacin did not affect male or female fertility when given orally in doses of up to 360 mg per kg of body weight (mg/kg) per day.

Pregnancy—Adequate and well-controlled studies have not been done in humans.

Studies using ophthalmic ofloxacin have not been done in animals. However, systemic doses below 810 mg/kg per day in rats and below 160 mg/kg per day in rabbits were not shown to be teratogenic. Doses of 810 mg/kg per day in rats resulted in decreased fetal body weight and minor fetal skeletal variations; rabbits given doses of 160 mg/kg per day showed an increase in fetal mortality.

In addition, although systemic ofloxacin has been shown to cause arthropathy in immature animals, ophthalmic ofloxacin has not caused arthropathy or had any other effect on weight-bearing joints in immature animals.

FDA Pregnancy Category C.

Labor—Studies in rats given systemic doses of ofloxacin of up to 360 mg/kg per day during late gestation showed no adverse effect of the medication on labor.

Delivery—Studies in rats given systemic doses of ofloxacin of up to 360 mg/kg per day during late gestation showed no adverse effect of the medication on delivery.

Breast-feeding

It is not known whether ophthalmic ofloxacin is distributed into breast milk. An orally administered dose of 200 mg of ofloxacin in nursing women resulted in concentrations of ofloxacin in the milk that were similar to its concentrations in plasma. However, for ophthalmic ofloxacin, the dose is much smaller and the plasma concentration is much lower than those of oral ofloxacin.

Pediatrics

Appropriate studies on the relationship of age to the effects of ophthalmic ofloxacin have not been performed in children up to 1 year of age. Safety and efficacy have not been established.

Although ofloxacin and other quinolones cause arthropathy in immature animals after oral administration, ophthalmic ofloxacin administered to immature animals did not cause arthropathy. In addition, there is no evidence that the ophthalmic dosage form has any effect on the weight-bearing joints.

Geriatrics

Appropriate studies on the relationship of age to the effects of ophthalmic ofloxacin have not been performed in the geriatric population. However, no geriatrics-specific problems have been documented to date.

Drug interactions and/or related problems

Drug interaction studies have not been performed with the ophthalmic dosage form of ofloxacin. However, it is known that systemic ofloxacin may elevate plasma concentrations of theophylline, interfere with the metabolism of caffeine, and enhance the clinical effects of warfarin. Systemic ofloxacin has also been associated with a transient elevation of serum creatinine in patients who received cyclosporine.

Medical considerations/Contraindications

The medical considerations/contraindications included have been selected on the basis of their potential clinical significance (reasons given in parentheses where appropriate)—not necessarily inclusive (» = major clinical significance).

Except under special circumstances, this medication should not be used when the following medical problem exists:

» Sensitivity to ofloxacin or other fluoroquinolones or their derivatives

Side/Adverse Effects

Note: An incident of Stevens-Johnson syndrome that progressed to toxic epidermal necrolysis was reported in a patient who was receiving topical ophthalmic ofloxacin. Systemic quinolones, including ofloxacin, have been associated with serious and occasionally fatal hypersensitivity reactions, some of which involved cardiovascular collapse, loss of consciousness, angioedema (including laryngeal, pharyngeal, or facial edema), airway obstruction, dyspnea, urticaria, and itching. Prolonged use of anti-infectives, including ofloxacin, may result in the overgrowth of nonsusceptible organisms, including fungi.

The following side/adverse effects have been selected on the basis of their potential clinical significance (possible signs and symptoms in parentheses where appropriate)—not necessarily inclusive:

Those indicating need for medical attention

Incidence rare

Dizziness; hypersensitivity reactions (itching, rash, or hives; swelling of face or lips; tightness in chest or wheezing; troubled breathing); ***periocular or facial edema*** (swelling or puffiness of eye or face)

Those indicating need for medical attention only if they continue or are bothersome

Incidence more frequent

Burning of eye

Incidence less frequent

Blurred vision; chemical conjunctivitis or keratitis (redness, irritation, or itching of eye, eyelid, or inner lining of eyelid); ***eye pain; foreign body sensation*** (feeling of something in the eye); ***photophobia*** (increased sensitivity of eye to light); ***stinging, redness, itching, tearing, or dryness of eye***

Patient Consultation

As an aid to patient consultation, refer to *Advice for the Patient, Ofloxacin (Ophthalmic).*

In providing consultation, consider emphasizing the following selected information (» = major clinical significance):

Before using this medication

» Conditions affecting use, especially:

Sensitivity to ofloxacin or other fluoroquinolones or their derivatives

Pregnancy—Studies using ophthalmic ofloxacin have not been done; however, studies in animals given very high doses of systemic ofloxacin have shown fetotoxicity

Breast-feeding—Oral ofloxacin is distributed into breast milk; it is not known whether ophthalmic ofloxacin is distributed into breast milk

Use in children—Safety and efficacy have not been established in infants up to 1 year of age

Proper use of this medication

Proper administration technique

» Compliance with full course of therapy

» Proper dosing

Missed dose: Applying as soon as possible; not applying if almost time for next dose

» Proper storage

Precautions while using this medication

Checking with physician if no improvement within 7 days

» Discontinuing use of ofloxacin and contacting physician if rash or allergic reaction occurs

Possible photophobic reactions; wearing sunglasses and avoiding prolonged exposure to bright light

Side/adverse effects

Signs of potential side effects, especially dizziness, hypersensitivity reactions, and periocular or facial edema

General Dosing Information

Ofloxacin ophthalmic solution is not for injection into the eye.

Although some manufacturers recommend doses of 2 drops of ophthalmic solutions at appropriate intervals, the conjunctival sac usually holds less than 1 drop.

If hypersensitivity develops, therapy with ophthalmic ofloxacin should be discontinued.

For treatment of adverse effects

Recommended treatment consists of the following:

- For mild hypersensitivity reaction—Administering antihistamines and, if necessary, glucocorticoids.
- For severe hypersensitivity or anaphylactic reaction—Administering epinephrine. Oxygen and airway management, including intubation, should be administered if clinically appropriate. Antihistamines and/or glucocorticoids may also be administered as required.
- For superinfection—Ophthalmic ofloxacin should be discontinued and an alternative therapy started. If clinically appropriate, the eye should be examined with the aid of magnification, such as slit lamp biomicroscopy, and, if appropriate, fluorescein staining.

Ophthalmic Dosage Forms

OFLOXACIN OPHTHALMIC SOLUTION

Usual adult and adolescent dose

Bacterial conjunctivitis—

Topical, to the conjunctiva, 1 drop in affected eye every two to four hours, while patient is awake, for two days; then, 1 drop four times a day for up to five more days.

Bacterial corneal ulcers—

Topical, to the conjunctiva, 1 drop in affected eye every thirty minutes, while patient is awake, and 1 drop four to six hours after retiring, for two days; then, 1 drop every hour while awake for up to seven more days; then, 1 drop four times a day from the seventh, eighth, or ninth day through treatment completion.

Usual pediatric dose

Bacterial conjunctivitis—

Infants up to 1 year of age: Safety and efficacy have not been established.

Children 1 year of age and older: See *Usual adult and adolescent dose.*

Bacterial corneal ulcers—

Infants up to 1 year of age: Safety and efficacy have not been established.

Children 1 year of age and older: See *Usual adult and adolescent dose.*

Strength(s) usually available

U.S.—

0.3% (Rx) [*Ocuflox* (benzalkonium chloride 0.005%; sodium chloride; hydrochloric acid; sodium hydroxide)].

Canada—

0.3% (Rx) [*Ocuflox* (benzalkonium chloride 0.005%; sodium chloride; hydrochloric acid; sodium hydroxide)].

Packaging and storage

Store between 15 and 25 °C (59 and 77 °F), unless otherwise specified by manufacturer.

Auxiliary labeling

- For the eye.

Selected Bibliography

Gwon A. Topical ofloxacin compared with gentamicin in the treatment of external ocular infection. Ofloxacin Study Group. Br J Ophthalmol 1992 Dec; 76(12): 714-8.

Gwon A. Ofloxacin vs tobramycin for the treatment of external ocular infection. Ofloxacin Study Group II. Arch Ophthalmol 1992 Sep; 110(9): 1234-7.

Borrmann L, Tang-Liu DD, Kann J, et al. Ofloxacin in human serum, urine, and tear film after topical application. Cornea 1992 May; 11(3): 226-30.

Revised: 09/22/1998

OFLOXACIN Otic

VA CLASSIFICATION (Primary): OT101

Commonly used brand name(s): *Floxin Otic.*

Note: For a listing of dosage forms and brand names by country availability, see *Dosage Forms* section(s).

Category

Antibacterial (otic).

Indications

Accepted

Otitis externa (treatment)

Otitis media, acute (treatment) or

Otitis media, chronic suppurative (treatment)—Otic ofloxacin is indicated for the treatment of otitis externa (in adults and children 1 year of age and older) caused by *Staphylococcus aureus* and *Pseudomonas aeruginosa.* In addition, otic ofloxacin is indicated for treatment of acute otitis media (in children 1 to 12 years of age with tympanostomy tubes) due to *Staphylococcus aureus, Streptococcus pneumoniae, Haemophilus influenzae, Moraxella catarrhalis,* and *Pseudomonas aeruginosa.* Otic ofloxacin is also indicated for treatment of chronic suppurative otitis media (in adults and children 12 years of age and older with perforated tympanic membranes) due to *Staphylococcus aureus, Proteus mirabilis,* and *Pseudomonas aeruginosa.*

Pharmacology/Pharmacokinetics

Physicochemical characteristics

Chemical Group—Fluoroquinolone.

Molecular weight—361.38.

pH—6.5.

Mechanism of action/Effect

Bactericidal; ofloxacin acts intracellularly by inhibiting DNA gyrase. DNA gyrase is an essential bacterial enzyme that is a critical catalyst in the replication, transcription, deactivation, and repair of bacterial DNA.

Absorption

In two single-dose studies in adults with tympanostomy tubes, with and without otorrhea, mean serum ofloxacin concentrations were low after otic administration of a 0.3% ofloxacin solution (4.1 nanograms per mL [n=3] and 5.4 nanograms per mL [n=5], respectively). In a study in adults with perforated tympanic membranes, the maximum serum ofloxacin concentration after otic administration of a 0.3% solution was 10 nanograms per mL. Concentrations of ofloxacin in the middle ear mucosa of adult patients with perforated tympanic membranes (detectable in 11 of 16 subjects) varied widely, ranging from 1.2 to 602 micrograms per gram after otic administration of a 0.3% solution. Concentrations of ofloxacin in otorrhea were found to be high (389 to 2850 micrograms per gram) 30 minutes after otic administration of a 0.3% solution to 13 subjects with chronic suppurative otitis media and perforated tympanic membranes; however, this measurement does not necessarily reflect the exposure of the middle ear to ofloxacin.

Precautions to Consider

Cross-sensitivity and/or related problems

Patients sensitive to systemic ofloxacin or to other quinolones or their derivatives may be sensitive to otic ofloxacin also.

Carcinogenicity

Long-term studies have not been done.

Mutagenicity

Ofloxacin was not found to be mutagenic in the Ames test, the sister chromatid exchange assay (Chinese hamster and human cell lines), the unscheduled DNA synthesis (UDS) assay using human fibroblasts, the dominant lethal assay, or the mouse micronucleus assay. However, ofloxacin was positive in the rat hepatocyte UDS assay and in the mouse lymphoma assay.

Pregnancy/Reproduction

Fertility—Studies in male and female rats administered oral doses of ofloxacin of up to 360 mg per kg of body weight (mg/kg) per day (over 1000 times the maximum recommended clinical dose in humans, based on body surface area, assuming total absorption from the ear of a patient treated with ofloxacin otic solution twice a day) found no effect on reproductive performance.

Pregnancy—Adequate and well-controlled studies in humans have not been done.

Studies in rats and rabbits administered oral doses of ofloxacin of 810 mg/kg per day and 160 mg/kg per day, respectively, found an embryocidal effect. These doses produced decreased fetal body weights and increased fetal mortality in rats and rabbits, respectively. Minor fetal skeletal variations were reported in rats administered oral doses of ofloxacin of 810 mg/kg per day. No teratogenic effects have been shown in pregnant rats and rabbits administered oral doses of ofloxacin as high as 810 mg/kg per day and 160 mg/kg per day, respectively. No adverse effects on the developing embryo or fetus have been found at doses relevant to the amount of ofloxacin that would be delivered topically to the ear at the recommended clinical doses. In addition, studies in rats administered oral doses of ofloxacin of up to 360 mg/kg per day during late gestation found no adverse effects on late fetal development, labor, delivery, lactation, neonatal viability, or growth of the newborn.

It is recommended that risk-benefit be considered before use of ofloxacin otic solution in pregnant women.

FDA Pregnancy Category C.

Breast-feeding

It is not known whether ofloxacin is distributed into human breast milk following topical otic administration. Administration of a single 200-mg oral dose in nursing women has been shown to produce an ofloxacin concentration in breast milk similar to that in plasma. Because of the potential for serious adverse reactions from ofloxacin in nursing infants, risk-benefit should be considered before making a decision about either continuing nursing or using the medication.

Pediatrics

A study of audiometric parameters in 30 pediatric patients treated with otic ofloxacin found no changes in hearing function. Safety and efficacy in children 1 year of age and older have been demonstrated. However, safety and efficacy in children younger than 1 year of age have not been established.

Although systemically administered quinolones, including ofloxacin, have been shown to cause arthropathy in immature animals, a study in which 0.3% ofloxacin otic solution was administered in the middle ear of young growing guinea pigs for 1 month found no systemic effects, quinolone-induced lesions, erosions of the cartilage in weight-bearing joints, or other signs of arthropathy.

Geriatrics
No information is available on the relationship of age to the effects of otic ofloxacin in geriatric patients.

Medical considerations/Contraindications
The medical considerations/contraindications included have been selected on the basis of their potential clinical significance (reasons given in parentheses where appropriate)—not necessarily inclusive (» = major clinical significance).

Except under special circumstances, this medication should not be used when the following medical problem exists:
» Sensitivity to ofloxacin or other quinolones or their derivatives (serious and occasionally fatal hypersensitivity [anaphylactic] reactions have been reported following systemic use of quinolones, including ofloxacin)

Side/Adverse Effects

Note: Systemic administration of quinolones, including ofloxacin, at doses much higher than those given or absorbed by the otic route, has resulted in lesions or erosions of the cartilage in weight-bearing joints and other signs of arthropathy in immature animals of various species. However, a study in which 0.3% ofloxacin otic solution was administered in the middle ear of young growing guinea pigs for 1 month found no systemic effects, quinolone-induced lesions, erosions of the cartilage in weight-bearing joints, or other signs of arthropathy.

Serious and occasionally fatal hypersensitivity (anaphylactic) reactions have been reported with systemic administration of ofloxacin and other quinolones, some following the first dose. In some cases, the reactions were accompanied by cardiovascular collapse, loss of consciousness, angioedema (including laryngeal, pharyngeal, or facial edema), airway obstruction, dyspnea, urticaria, and itching. If an allergic reaction to otic ofloxacin is suspected, it is recommended that the medication be stopped.

The following side/adverse effects have been selected on the basis of their potential clinical significance (possible signs and symptoms in parentheses where appropriate)—not necessarily inclusive:

Those indicating need for medical attention
Incidence less frequent
Application site reaction (burning, itching, redness, skin rash, swelling, or other sign of irritation not present before use of this medicine); ***dizziness or vertigo***

Incidence rare
Fever; headache; otorrhagia (bleeding from the ear); ***pharyngitis*** (sore throat); ***rhinitis or sinusitis*** (runny or stuffy nose); ***tachycardia*** (fast heartbeat); ***tinnitus*** (ringing in the ear)

Those indicating need for medical attention only if they continue or are bothersome
Incidence less frequent
Change in taste; earache; numbness or tingling

Patient Consultation

As an aid to patient consultation, refer to *Advice for the Patient, Ofloxacin (Otic)*.

In providing consultation, consider emphasizing the following selected information (» = major clinical significance):

Before using this medication
» Conditions affecting use, especially:
Sensitivity to ofloxacin or other quinolones or their derivatives
Pregnancy—Studies with otic ofloxacin have not been done; because of the embryocidal and fetotoxic effects of large systemic doses in animals, risk-benefit should be considered before using during pregnancy; however, ofloxacin has not been shown to cause problems when given in doses comparable to doses administered by the otic route
Breast-feeding—It is not known whether otic ofloxacin is distributed into breast milk; however, oral ofloxacin is distributed into breast milk
Use in children—Safety and efficacy have not been established in children up to 1 year of age

Proper use of this medication
» Reading patient medication guide before using eardrops; checking with physician if patient has questions
» Proper administration technique; not touching applicator tip to any surface, including the ear, in order to avoid contamination
» Compliance with full course of therapy
» Proper dosing
Missed dose: Using as soon as possible; not using if almost time for next dose
» Proper storage

Precautions while using this medication
Checking with physician if no improvement within a few days

» Discontinuing medication and checking with physician immediately at the first sign of a rash or allergic reaction

Side/adverse effects
Signs of potential side effects, especially application site reaction, dizziness or vertigo, fever, headache, otorrhagia, pharyngitis, rhinitis or sinusitis, tachycardia, and tinnitus

General Dosing Information

It is recommended that the bottle be held in the hand for 1 or 2 minutes before use to warm the solution; this will help prevent the dizziness that may occur following instillation of a cold solution into the ear. The patient should lie with the affected ear up for instillation of the drops and hold this position for 5 minutes after instillation. This procedure may then be repeated for the opposite ear, if necessary.

As with other antiinfectives, prolonged use may lead to overgrowth of nonsusceptible organisms, including fungi. It is recommended that cultures be obtained if the infection has not improved after 1 week, to aid in selection of further treatment.

If otorrhea persists after a full course of therapy, or occurs two or more times during a period of 6 months, it is recommended that further evaluation be undertaken to exclude underlying conditions, such as cholesteatoma, foreign body, or tumor.

Because of the serious anaphylactic reaction that has been reported with systemic ofloxacin, it is recommended that otic ofloxacin be discontinued at the first sign of an allergic reaction. Emergency medical treatment, including oxygen and airway management, including intubation, may be needed for serious acute hypersensitivity reactions.

Ofloxacin otic solution is not for ophthalmic use or for injection.

Otic Dosage Forms

OFLOXACIN OTIC SOLUTION

Usual adult and adolescent dose
Otitis externa—
Topical, to the ear canal, 10 drops in the affected ear two times a day for ten days.
Otitis media, chronic suppurative (in patients with perforated tympanic membranes)—
Topical, to the ear canal, 10 drops in the affected ear two times a day for fourteen days. It is recommended that the tragus be pumped four times during instillation, by pushing inward, to facilitate penetration of the solution into the middle ear.

Usual pediatric dose
Otitis externa—
Children 12 years of age and older: See *Usual adult and adolescent dose*.
Children 1 to 12 years of age: Topical, to the ear canal, 5 drops in the affected ear two times a day for ten days.
Children younger than 1 year of age: Safety and efficacy have not been established.
Otitis media, acute (in pediatric patients with tympanostomy tubes)—
Children 1 to 12 years of age: Topical, to the ear canal, 5 drops in the affected ear two times a day for ten days. It is recommended that the tragus be pumped four times during instillation, by pushing inward, to facilitate penetration of the solution into the middle ear.
Children younger than 1 year of age: Safety and efficacy have not been established.

Strength(s) usually available
U.S.—
0.3% (Rx) [*Floxin Otic* (benzalkonium chloride 0.0025%; sodium chloride 0.9%; hydrochloric acid; sodium hydroxide)].

Packaging and storage
Store between 15 and 25 °C (59 and 77 °F).

Auxiliary labeling
- For the ear.
- Continue medicine for full time of treatment.

Revised: 08/27/1998

OLANZAPINE Systemic†

VA CLASSIFICATION (Primary): CN709

Commonly used brand name(s): *Zyprexa; Zyprexa Intramuscular; Zyprexa Zydis.*

Note: For a listing of dosage forms and brand names by country availability, see *Dosage Forms* section(s).

†Not commercially available in Canada.

Category

Antipsychotic.

Indications

Accepted

Agitation associated with schizophrenia and bipolar I mania (treatment)—Olanzapine intramuscular is indicated for the treatment of agitation associated with schizophrenia and bipolar I mania. "Psychomotor agitation" is defined in DSM-IV criteria for Bipolar I Disorder as "excessive motor activity associated with a feeling of inner tension." Patients experiencing agitation often manifest behaviors that interfere with their diagnosis and care, e.g., threatening behaviors, escalating or urgently distressing behavior, or self-exhausting behavior, leading clinicians to the use of intramuscular antipsychotic medications to achieve immediate control of the agitation.

Bipolar disorder (treatment)—Oral olanzapine is indicated for the treatment of acute mixed or manic episodes associated with Bipolar I Disorder. The combination of oral olanzapine with lithium or valproate is indicated for the short-term treatment of acute manic episodes associated with Bipolar I Disorder.

Schizophrenia (treatment)—Oral olanzapine is indicated for the treatment of schizophrenia.

Unaccepted

Olanzapine is not approved for the treatment of patients with dementia-related psychosis.

Olanzapine is not approved for the treatment of behavioral symptoms in elderly patients with dementia.

Pharmacology/Pharmacokinetics

Physicochemical characteristics

Chemical Group—Thienobenzodiazepine.

Molecular weight—312.44.

Solubility—Practically insoluble in water.

Mechanism of action/Effect

The exact mechanism of action of olanzapine, as with other drugs having efficacy in schizophrenia, is unknown. However, this effect may be mediated through a combination of dopamine and serotonin 5-HT_2 antagonism. Olanzapine is a selective monoaminergic antagonist with a strong affinity for serotonin 5-HT_{2A} and 5-HT_{2C} receptors, and dopamine D_1, D_2, D_3, and D_4 receptors.

The mechanism of action of olanzapine in the treatment of acute manic episodes associated with Bipolar I Disorder is unknown.

Olanzapine binds weakly to gamma-aminobutyric acid type A ($GABA_A$), benzodiazepine (BZD), and beta-adrenergic receptors.

Olanzapine's high affinity binding to, and antagonism of, muscarinic M_1, M_2, M_3, M_4, and M_5 receptors may explain its anticholinergic effects. Olanzapine also binds with high affinity to histamine H_1 and alpha$_1$-adrenergic receptors. Antagonism of histamine H_1 and alpha$_1$-adrenergic receptors may be responsible for the occurrence of somnolence and orthostatic hypotension, respectively, seen with olanzapine use.

Other actions/effects

A modest elevation in prolactin levels persists during chronic olanzapine administration, probably due to antagonism of dopamine D_2 receptors. The clinical significance of elevated prolactin levels is unknown for most patients, although such effects as galactorrhea, amenorrhea, gynecomastia, and impotence have been reported in patients receiving prolactin-elevating medications. Also, studies have found approximately one third of human breast cancers to be prolactin-dependent *in vitro*.

Absorption

Well absorbed; however, 40% of the absorbed drug is metabolized before reaching systemic circulation. The rate and extent of olanzapine absorption are unaffected by food. Oral bioavailability of olanzapine was not affected by single doses of cimetidine (800 mg) or aluminum- and magnesium-containing antacids.

Distribution

Extensively distributed throughout the body, with a volume of distribution of approximately 1000 L.

Protein binding

High (93%); primarily to albumin and alpha$_1$-acid glycoprotein.

Biotransformation

Olanzapine is metabolized primarily through oxidation mediated by cytochrome P450 (CYP) enzymes and by direct glucuronidation. *In vitro* studies suggest that oxidation is mediated by cytochrome P450 isozymes IA_2 (CYP1A2) and IID_6 (CYP2D6), and by the flavin-containing monooxygenase system. However, studies in subjects who are deficient in CYP2D6 indicate that CYP2D6-mediated metabolism is a minor pathway of olanzapine metabolism.

The two major metabolites, 10-*N*-glucuronide and 4′-*N*-desmethyl olanzapine, are not pharmacologically active at the plasma levels achieved during normal therapeutic olanzapine dosing.

A study in six patients with clinically significant cirrhosis revealed little effect of hepatic function impairment on the pharmacokinetics of olanzapine.

Half-life

Elimination—

Mean, 30 hours; range, 21 to 54 hours. Mean apparent plasma clearance is 25 L per hour (L/hr); range, 12 to 47 L/hr.

Time to peak concentration

Peak plasma concentration of olanzapine occurs approximately 6 hours following oral administration. Kinetics are linear over the therapeutic dosage range. Following olanzapine intramuscular administration, peak plasma concentrations occur within 15 to 45 minutes.

Time to steady-state plasma concentration

Steady-state plasma concentration of olanzapine, which is approximately twice the concentration seen after a single dose, is achieved in about 1 week with once-a-day dosing.

Peak serum concentration

A 5-mg dose of intramuscular olanzapine for injection produces a maximum plasma concentration approximately 5 times higher than that produced by a 5-mg dose of oral olanzapine.

Elimination

Renal—

Approximately 57% of an administered dose is renally excreted, 7% as unchanged drug. Pharmacokinetics of olanzapine were similar in patients with severe renal function impairment and in patients with normal renal function. Pharmacokinetics of the metabolites of olanzapine were not studied in patients with renal function impairment.

Fecal—

Approximately 30% of an administered dose.

In dialysis—

Olanzapine is not removed by dialysis.

Precautions to Consider

Carcinogenicity/Tumorigenicity

In carcinogenicity studies, significant increases in the incidence of mammary gland adenomas and adenocarcinomas occurred in female mice receiving 0.5 times the maximum recommended human daily dose (MRHD) of 20 mg per day of olanzapine on a mg per square meter of body surface area (mg/m²) basis and in female rats receiving two times the MRHD of olanzapine on a mg/m² basis. A toxicity study in rats showed prolactin levels to be elevated up to fourfold at the same doses of olanzapine that were used in the carcinogenicity studies. The increased incidence of mammary gland neoplasms found in rodents after chronic administration of antipsychotic drugs is considered to be prolactin mediated. Drugs that antagonize dopamine D_2 receptors, including olanzapine, are associated with increased prolactin levels in humans. Because studies have found approximately one third of human breast cancers to be prolactin-dependent *in vitro*, this prolactin level elevation may be of importance when considering use of these medications in patients with previously detected breast cancers. However, there has been no association shown between chronic administration of medications that elevate prolactin levels and tumorigenesis in either epidemiological or clinical studies to date. Current evidence is too limited to be conclusive.

Two carcinogenicity studies were conducted in which mice received olanzapine for 78 weeks at doses ranging from 0.06 to 5 times the MRHD on a mg/m² basis (0.8 to 5 times the MRHD in one study, and 0.06 to 2 times the MRHD in the other study). In one of these studies, a significant increase in the incidence of liver hemangiomas and hemangiosarcomas was seen in female mice dosed at two times the MRHD. In the other study, this increased incidence of liver hemangiomas and hemangiosarcomas was not seen, but early mortality was increased in male mice receiving five times the MRHD.

Mutagenicity

Olanzapine demonstrated no mutagenic potential in the following tests: Ames reverse mutation test, *in vivo* micronucleus test in mice, the chromosomal aberration test in Chinese hamster ovary cells, unscheduled DNA synthesis test in rat hepatocytes, induction of forward mutation test in mouse lymphoma cells, or *in vivo* sister chromatid exchange test in bone marrow of Chinese hamsters.

Pregnancy/Reproduction

Fertility—The mating performance, but not the fertility, of male rats was impaired during administration of olanzapine at doses that were 11 times the maximum recommended human daily dose (MRHD) of 20 mg per day on a mg per square meter of body surface area (mg/m^2) basis. The impairment of mating performance was reversed with discontinuation of olanzapine administration. Studies in female rats indicate that olanzapine may produce a delay in ovulation. When olanzapine was administered at doses that were 1.5 times the MRHD on a mg/m^2 basis, female rats showed a decrease in fertility. At doses that were 2.5 times the MRHD on a mg/m^2 basis, female rats showed an increased precoital period, and a reduced mating index.

Pregnancy—Adequate and well-controlled studies in humans have not been done.

Olanzapine should be used during pregnancy only if the potential benefit justifies the potential risk to the fetus.

Of seven pregnancies that occurred during clinical trials with olanzapine, two resulted in normal births, one resulted in neonatal death due to a cardiovascular defect, three ended in therapeutic abortions, and one ended in spontaneous abortion.

Olanzapine crosses the placenta in rats. No evidence of teratogenicity was seen in rats administered olanzapine at doses up to nine times the MRHD on a mg/m^2 basis, or in rabbits administered olanzapine at doses up to 30 times the MRHD on a mg/m^2 basis. At the maximum doses in these studies, early fetal resorptions and increased numbers of nonviable fetuses were observed in rats, and increased fetal resorptions and decreased fetal weight were observed in rabbits. The maximum dose used in the rabbit study was considered to be maternally toxic. Also, in rats, gestation was prolonged at a dose that was five times the MRHD on a mg/m^2 basis.

FDA Pregnancy Category C.

Labor and delivery—The effect of olanzapine on labor and delivery in humans is unknown. Olanzapine did not affect parturition in rats.

Breast-feeding

It is not known whether olanzapine is distributed into human breast milk. However, olanzapine is distributed into the milk of rats, and use in nursing mothers is not recommended.

Pediatrics

No information is available on the relationship of age to the effects of olanzapine in pediatric patients. Safety and efficacy have not been established in patients up to 18 years of age.

Geriatrics

No geriatrics-specific problems that would limit the usefulness of olanzapine in the elderly were seen in studies that included elderly subjects. However, the mean elimination half-life was found to be about 1.5 times greater in elderly subjects than in younger subjects in one study.

According to an FDA Public Health Advisory, olanzapine is not approved for the treatment of behavioral symptoms in elderly patients with dementia. Clinical studies of olanzapine and other atypical antipsychotic drugs for treatment of behavioral symptoms in the elderly with dementia have shown a higher death rate associated with their use compared to patients receiving a placebo. Causes of death varied, but most seemed to be either heart-related (i.e., heart failure or sudden death) or from infections (i.e., pneumonia).

Studies in patients with various psychiatric symptoms in association with Alzheimer's disease have suggested that there may be a different tolerability profile in this population compared to younger patients with schizophrenia. As with other CNS-active drugs, olanzapine should be used with caution in elderly patients with dementia. A lower starting dose for any geriatric patient should be considered due to the presence of factors that might decrease pharmacokinetic clearance or increase the pharmacodynamic response to olanzapine.

Pharmacogenetics

Olanzapine clearance is approximately 30% lower in females than in males. However, no differences in adverse effects or efficacy were seen in clinical studies, and dosage adjustments based on gender are not recommended.

Comparisons of pharmacokinetic data from studies conducted in Japan with data from studies conducted in the U.S. indicate a twofold higher exposure to olanzapine in Japanese subjects when doses are equivalent. However, no clinically significant differences in safety or efficacy were seen when comparisons were made among Caucasian, African-descent, and pooled Asian and Hispanic patient groups. Dosage adjustments based on race are not recommended.

Drug interactions and/or related problems

The following drug interactions and/or related problems have been selected on the basis of their potential clinical significance (possible mechanism in parentheses where appropriate)—not necessarily inclusive (» = major clinical significance):

Note: *In vitro* studies indicate that olanzapine has little potential to inhibit CYP1A2, CYP2C9, CYP2C19, CYP2D6, or CYP3A. Therefore, olanzapine is not expected to interfere with the metabolism of medications that are metabolized by these enzymes.

Combinations containing any of the following medications, depending on the amount present, may also interact with this medication.

Agents that induce CYP1A2 or glucuronyl transferase enzymes, such as carbamazepine, omeprazole, or rifampin
(olanzapine clearance may be increased; carbamazepine therapy at a dose of 200 mg two times a day increased olanzapine clearance by about 50%)

Agents that inhibit CYP1A2, such as fluvoxamine
(olanzapine clearance may be decreased, although, because multiple enzymes are involved in olanzapine metabolism, the effect of inhibiting one isozyme may not be significant)

» Alcohol or
» Central nervous system (CNS) depression-producing medications, other (See *Appendix II*) or
» Diazepam
(additive CNS depressant effects may occur; orthostatic hypotension may be potentiated)

» Anticholinergics, other (See *Appendix II*)
(anticholinergic effects of either these medications or olanzapine may be increased; disruption of the body's ability to reduce core temperature may be a special consideration)

Antihypertensive agents
(hypotensive effects of these medications or olanzapine may be enhanced)

Dopamine agonists or
Levodopa
(effects of these medications may be antagonized by olanzapine)

Fluoxetine
(causes a small increase in the maximum concentration of olanzapine and a small decrease in olanzapine clearance; compared to the overall variability between individuals, the magnitude of impact of this factor is small; dose modification is not routinely recommended)

» Hepatotoxic medications (See *Appendix II*)
(asymptomatic but clinically significant alanine aminotransferase [ALT (SGPT)] value increases occurred in about 2% of patients in premarketing studies of olanzapine; about 1% of patients discontinued olanzapine treatment due to increased transaminase levels; caution is recommended when olanzapine is used concurrently with hepatotoxic medications)

Lorazepam
(additive effect of somnolence with co-administration of intramuscular lorazepam and intramuscular olanzapine for injection compared to either drug alone)

Smoking, cigarette
(olanzapine clearance is increased by about 40%)

Laboratory value alterations

The following have been selected on the basis of their potential clinical significance (possible effect in parentheses where appropriate)—not necessarily inclusive (» = major clinical significance).

With physiology/laboratory test values

Alanine aminotransferase (ALT [SGPT]) values and
Aspartate transaminase (AST [SGOT]) values and
Gamma-glutamyl transpeptidase (GGT) values
(in premarketing studies, about 2% of patients with baseline ALT [SGPT] values ≤ 90 international units per L [IU/L] had ALT value increases to > 200 IU/L during treatment with olanzapine; none of these patients experienced symptoms of liver function impairment, and in most the ALT value returned to normal with continued olanzapine treatment; asymptomatic increases in AST and GGT were seen also; about 1% of patients in clinical trials discontinued olanzapine treatment due to increased transaminase values)

Blood glucose
(patients with a diagnosis of or risk factors for diabetes mellitus should undergo fasting blood glucose testing at the beginning of treatment and periodically during treatment)

Creatinine phosphokinase, serum
(elevated levels may be a sign of a potentially fatal symptom complex sometimes referred to as Neuroleptic Malignant Syndrome (NMS) which has been associated with administration of antipsychotic drugs, including olanzapine)

Myoglobulin, urine
(presence in the urine may be a sign of NMS)

Prolactin concentration, serum
(sustained elevations occur during olanzapine therapy)

Medical considerations/Contraindications

The medical considerations/contraindications included have been selected on the basis of their potential clinical significance (reasons given in parentheses where appropriate)—not necessarily inclusive (» = major clinical significance).

Except under special circumstances, this medication should not be used when the following medical problem exists:

» Hypersensitivity to olanzapine

Risk-benefit should be considered when the following medical problems exist:

Aspiration pneumonia, increased risk of
(should be used cautiously in these patients)

» Alzheimer's dementia
(dysphagia associated with olanzapine use may increase risk of aspiration pneumonia; possible increased risk of seizures because of lowered seizure threshold with Alzheimer's dementia)

» Breast cancer, or history of
(prolactin-dependent breast cancers may be exacerbated)

» Cardiovascular disease, including:
Conduction abnormalities or
Heart failure or
Myocardial infarction or ischemia, or history of, or
» Cerebrovascular disease or
» Conditions that would predispose to hypotension, including:
Dehydration or
Hypovolemia
(orthostatic hypotension may be exacerbated, or may exacerbate preexisting cardiovascular or cerebrovascular conditions)
(dehydration may predispose to increased core body temperature, and antipsychotic medications may disrupt the body's ability to lower core body temperature, thus increasing the risk of heatstroke)

Conditions which may contribute to an elevation in core body temperature, such as
Exposure to extreme heat or
Strenuous exercise
(appropriate care is advised; disruption of the body's ability to reduce core body temperature has been attributed to antipsychotic agents)

Dementia
(may increase occurrence of cerebrovascular adverse events (CVAE) such as stroke and transient ischemic attacks including fatalities; patients and/or caregivers should be instructed to report signs of CVAEs such as weakness, numbness, and problems with speech or vision)

» Diabetes mellitus or
» Risk factors for diabetes mellitus such as
Obesity or
Family history of diabetes
(increased risk of treatment-emergent hyperglycemia-related adverse events including ketoacidosis, hyperosmolar coma, or death in patients treated with atypical antipsychotics including olanzapine; patients should be monitored carefully)

Drug abuse or dependence, history of
(patients should be observed closely for signs of misuse or abuse of olanzapine, as with any new CNS medication)

» Glaucoma, narrow angle or
» Paralytic ileus, history of, or
» Prostatic hypertrophy, clinically significant
(may be exacerbated due to cholinergic antagonism by olanzapine)

» Hepatic function impairment or
» Pre-existing conditions associated with limited hepatic functional reserve
(in premarketing studies, about 1% of patients discontinued olanzapine treatment due to increased transaminase levels; transaminase levels should be assessed periodically in patients with significant hepatic disease)

Seizures, or history of
(seizures occurred rarely in premarketing studies of olanzapine; it is recommended that olanzapine be used with caution in patients with a history of seizures or a decreased seizure threshold)

Patient monitoring

The following may be especially important in patient monitoring (other tests may be warranted in some patients, depending on condition; » = major clinical significance):

Alanine aminotransferase (ALT [SGPT]) values and
Aspartate transaminase (AST [SGOT]) values
(recommended periodically in patients with significant hepatic disease)

Careful supervision of patients with suicidal tendencies
(recommended in high-risk patients, since the possibility of a suicide attempt is inherent in schizophrenia and in bipolar disorder)

Hyperglycemia
(all patients should be monitored for symptoms of hyperglycemia including polydipsia, polyuria, polyphagia, and weakness; patients developing symptoms should undergo fasting blood glucose testing)

Side/Adverse Effects

Note: Disturbances of body temperature regulation have been associated with use of other antipsychotic agents. Caution is advised in administering olanzapine to patients who will be experiencing conditions that may contribute to an elevation in core body temperature, such as strenuous exercise, exposure to extreme heat, or dehydration.

The neuroleptic malignant syndrome (NMS) has been associated with the use of other antipsychotic agents. NMS is a potentially fatal symptom complex that may include hyperpyrexia, muscle rigidity, altered mental status, and autonomic instability seen as irregular pulse or blood pressure, tachycardia, diaphoresis, and cardiac dysrhythmia. Elevated creatine kinase, myoglobinuria (rhabdomyolysis), and acute renal failure also may occur. Differential diagnosis should exclude serious medical illnesses, such as pneumonia or systemic infection presenting in conjunction with extrapyramidal effects, as well as central anticholinergic toxicity, heatstroke, drug fever, and primary CNS pathology.

The following side/adverse effects have been selected on the basis of their potential clinical significance (possible signs and symptoms in parentheses where appropriate)—not necessarily inclusive:

Those indicating need for medical attention

Incidence more frequent

Agitation; akathisia (restlessness or need to keep moving); ***extrapyramidal effects, Parkinsonism*** (difficulty in speaking or swallowing; stiffness of arms or legs; trembling or shaking of hands and fingers); ***personality disorder*** (nonaggressive objectionable behavior)

Note: *Akathisia* and *extrapyramidal effects* are dose-related.

Incidence less frequent

Accidental injury; chest pain; dyskinesia (twitching, twisting, uncontrolled repetitive movements of tongue, lips, face, arms, or legs); ***dyskinetic events including; buccoglossal syndrome; choreoathetosis*** (restlessness or agitation; uncontrolled jerking or twisting movements of hands, arms, or legs; uncontrolled movements of lips, tongue, or cheeks); ***extrapyramidal effects, dystonic*** (inability to move eyes; muscle spasms of face, neck, and back; twitching movements); ***fever; flu-like symptoms; hypertension*** (blurred vision; dizziness; nervousness; headache; pounding in the ears; slow or fast heartbeat); ***mood or mental changes, including amnesia; anxiety; euphoria; hostility; and nervousness; peripheral edema*** (swelling of feet or ankles); ***residual effects including; movement disorder*** (unusual or incomplete body or facial movements); ***myoclonus*** (muscle twitching or jerking; rhythmic movement of muscles); ***twitching; tardive dyskinesia*** (lip smacking or puckering; puffing of cheeks; rapid or worm-like movements of tongue; uncontrolled chewing movements; uncontrolled movements of arms and legs); ***vaginitis*** (itching of the vagina or genital area; pain during sexual intercourse; thick, white vaginal discharge with no odor or with a mild odor)

Note: *Tardive dyskinesia* occurs more frequently in elderly patients, especially elderly women. The risk of developing the syndrome, and of experiencing irreversible effects, appears to increase with treatment duration and total cumulative dose, although it may develop at any time during antipsychotic therapy. There is no known treatment for tardive dyskinesia, although partial or complete remission may occur when the antipsychotic medication is withdrawn. Alternatively, the antipsychotic medication may suppress the signs of the syndrome, masking the underlying process. For these reasons, olanzapine should be used only in those patients with chronic illness that is responsive to antipsychotic medication, and for whom potentially less harmful treatments are unavailable or inappropriate. Also, the smallest effective dose of olanzapine should be used and the need for continuing treatment should be assessed periodically.

Incidence rare

Dyspnea (trouble in breathing); ***facial edema*** (swelling of face); ***menstrual changes; skin rash; ventricular extrasystoles*** (extra heartbeat); ***water intoxication*** (confusion; mental or physical sluggishness)

Incidence not determined—Observed during clinical practice, estimates of frequency can not be determined

Anaphylactoid reaction (cough; difficulty swallowing; dizziness; fast heartbeat; hives; itching; puffiness or swelling of the eyelids or around the eyes, face, lips or tongue; shortness of breath; skin rash; tightness in chest; unusual tiredness or weakness; wheezing); ***angioedema*** (large, hive-like swelling on face, eyelids, lips, tongue, throat, hands, legs, feet, sex organs); ***diabetic coma; pancreatitis*** (bloating; chills; constipation; darkened urine; fast heartbeat; fever; indigestion; loss of appetite; nausea; pains in stomach, side, or abdomen, possibly radiating to the back; vomiting; yellow eyes or skin); ***priapism*** (painful or prolonged erection of the penis); ***pruritus*** (itching skin); ***urticaria*** (hives or welts; itching; redness of skin; skin rash)

Those indicating need for medical attention only if they continue or are bothersome

Incidence more frequent

Abnormal gait (change in walking and balance, clumsiness, or unsteadiness); ***amblyopia*** (problems with vision); ***asthenia*** (weakness); ***constipation; dizziness; drowsiness; dry mouth; dyspepsia*** (acid or sour stomach; belching; heartburn; indigestion; stomach discomfort, upset, or pain); ***headache; increased weight; postural hypotension*** (dizziness or fainting when getting up suddenly from a lying or sitting position); ***rhinitis*** (runny nose); ***somnolence*** (sleepiness or unusual drowsiness); ***speech disorder*** (difficulty in speaking); ***tremor*** (trembling or shaking)

Note: *Asthenia, drowsiness, dry mouth,* and *tremor* are dose-related. *Postural hypotension* is most likely to occur during the initial dose-titration period.

During premarketing long-term continuation treatment with olanzapine (median exposure 238 days), 56% of patients had *weight gain* > 7% of their baseline weight. The average weight gain was 5.4 kg.

Incidence less frequent

Abdominal pain; abnormal vision (changes in vision); ***acne*** (blemishes on the skin; pimples); ***apathy*** (lack of feeling or emotion; uncaring); ***articulation impairment*** (speaking unclearly); ***confusion*** (mood or mental changes); ***dry skin; dysmenorrhea*** (pain; cramps; heavy bleeding); ***edema*** (swelling); ***extremity pain (other than joint)*** (pain in arms or legs); ***hypertonia*** (tightness of muscles); ***hypotension*** (low blood pressure); ***increased appetite; increased cough; increased salivation*** (watering of mouth); ***insomnia*** (trouble in sleeping); ***joint pain; nausea; paresthesia*** (burning, crawling, itching, numbness, prickling, "pins and needles", or tingling feelings); ***pharyngitis*** (sore throat); ***stuttering; sweating; tachycardia*** (fast heartbeat); ***thirst; urinary incontinence*** (trouble in controlling urine); ***vomiting; weight loss***

Note: *Nausea* is dose related.

Incidence rare

Decreased libido (decrease in sexual desire); ***diplopia*** (double vision); ***palpitation*** (awareness of heartbeat); ***photosensitivity*** (increased sensitivity of skin to sunlight)

Overdose

For specific information on the agents used in the management of olanzapine overdose, see:

- *Charcoal, Activated (Oral-Local)* monograph; and
- *Sympathomimetic Agents—Cardiovascular Use (Parenteral-Systemic)*

For more information on the management of overdose or unintentional ingestion, **contact a Poison Control Center** (see *Poison Control Center Listing*).

Clinical effects of overdose

The following effects have been selected on the basis of their potential clinical significance (possible signs and symptoms in parentheses where appropriate)—not necessarily inclusive:

Acute

Note: During premarketing trials, 67 cases of acute overdosage with olanzapine were identified. The highest reported ingestion was 300 mg. The only symptoms reported in this patient were drowsiness and slurred speech. Among overdose patients who were evaluated in hospitals, none showed changes in laboratory analyses or electrocardiograms (ECG), and vital signs were usually within normal limits.

Treatment of overdose

Multiple drug involvement should be considered. There is no specific antidote to olanzapine.

To decrease absorption—Gastric lavage, after intubation if patient is unconscious, and administration of activated charcoal with a laxative should be considered. Activated charcoal has been shown to reduce absorption of olanzapine, and may be of use since olanzapine does not reach peak plasma levels for approximately 6 hours following ingestion. The risk of aspiration with induction of emesis may be increased by possible obtundation, seizures, or dystonic reaction of the head and neck.

Specific treatment—Hypotension and circulatory collapse may be treated with intravenous fluids and/or sympathomimetic agents. Because of olanzapine-induced alpha blockade, sympathomimetics with beta agonist activity such as epinephrine and dopamine may worsen hypotension and should not be used.

Monitoring—Continuous ECG monitoring should be employed to detect possible arrhythmias. Close medical supervision should continue until patient recovers.

Supportive care—Airway should be established and maintained to ensure adequate oxygenation and ventilation which may include intubation. Patients in whom intentional overdose is confirmed or suspected should be referred for psychiatric consultation.

Note: Olanzapine is not removed by dialysis.

Patient Consultation

As an aid to patient consultation, refer to *Advice for the Patient, Olanzapine (Systemic).*

In providing consultation, consider emphasizing the following selected information (» = major clinical significance)

Before using this medication

» Conditions affecting use, especially:

Carcinogenicity/Tumorigenicity—Increase in mammary gland neoplasias seen in animal studies; sustained prolactin level elevations with olanzapine use; one third of human breast cancers are prolactin-dependent *in vitro;* no association between chronic administration of prolactin level–increasing antipsychotic medications and tumorigenesis seen in epidemiological or clinical studies in humans; evidence inconclusive

Pregnancy—Seven pregnancies occurring during clinical trials ended in two normal births, one neonatal death due to cardiovascular defect, one spontaneous abortion, three therapeutic abortions; should be used during pregnancy only if potential benefit justifies potential risk to the fetus

Breast-feeding—Distributed into the milk of rats; use in nursing mothers not recommended

Use in children—Safety and efficacy have not been established in patients up to 18 years of age.

Use in the elderly—Should be used with caution in elderly patients with dementia; lower starting dose for any geriatric patient should be considered; not approved for the treatment of behavioral disorders in elderly patients with dementia; associated with a higher death rate

Dental—Possible dryness of mouth

Other medications, especially alcohol, anticholinergics, CNS depression-producing medications, diazepam, or hepatotoxic medications

Other medical problems, especially hypersensitivity to olanzapine, Alzheimer's dementia, breast cancer, cardiovascular disease, cerebrovascular disease, conditions that would predispose to hypotension, diabetes mellitus or risk factors for diabetes mellitus, glaucoma, hepatic function impairment, pre-existing conditions associated with limited hepatic functional reserve, paralytic ileus, or prostatic hypertrophy

Proper use of this medication

Compliance with therapy; not taking more or less medicine than prescribed

» Importance of caregivers contacting doctor and not giving this medicine for treatment of behavioral problems in elderly patients with dementia

Taking with or without food, on a full or empty stomach, as directed by physician

» Proper dosing

» Proper storage

Precautions while using this medication

Possible drowsiness, impaired judgement, thinking, motor skills, or vision; caution when driving, operating machinery, or doing jobs requiring alertness, coordination, or clear vision

Possible orthostatic hypotension; rising slowly from a sitting or lying position

Possible impairment of ability to regulate core body temperature; avoiding overheating and dehydration

Avoiding use of alcoholic beverages; not taking other CNS depressants unless prescribed by physician

Telling your doctor about all medications you are taking; prescription and nonprescription.

Side/adverse effects

Signs of potential side effects, especially agitation, akathesia, extrapyramidal effects, Parkinsonism, personality disorder, accidental injury, chest pain, dyskinesia, dyskinetic events, dystonic extrapyramidal effects, fever, flu-like symptoms, hypertension, mood or mental changes, peripheral edema, residual effects, tardive dyskinesia, vaginitis, dyspnea, facial edema, menstrual changes, skin rash, ventricular extrasystoles, and water intoxication

Signs of potential side effects observed during clinical practice, especially anaphylactoid reaction, angioedema, diabetic coma, pancreatitis, priapism, pruritus, and urticaria

General Dosing Information

Since the possibility of suicide is inherent in schizophrenia, patients should not have access to large quantities of olanzapine. To reduce the risk of overdose, the patient should be supplied with the smallest quantity of medication necessary for satisfactory patient management.

Olanzapine may induce orthostatic hypotension associated with dizziness, tachycardia, and in some patients, syncope, especially during the initial dose-titration. For oral olanzapine therapy, the risk of orthostatic hypotension and syncope may be minimized by initiating therapy with 5 mg once per day. A more gradual titration to the target dose should be considered if hypotension occurs. For intramuscular olanzapine for injection therapy, patients should remain recumbent if drowsy or dizzy after injection until examination has indicated that they are not experiencing postural hypotension and/or bradycardia.

Phenylketonurics—Olanzapine orally disintegrating tablets contain phenylalanine.

Diet/Nutrition

Olanzapine may be taken without regard to food.

Bioequivalence information

Olanzapine tablets and orally disintegrating tablets dosage forms are bioequivalent

For treatment of adverse effects

Neuroleptic malignant syndrome (NMS)—Recommended treatment consists of the following:

- *Discontinuing olanzapine and other drugs not essential to current therapy.*
- Providing intensive symptomatic treatment and medical monitoring.
- Treating any concomitant serious medical problems for which specific treatments are available.
- After recovery, giving careful consideration to the reintroduction of antipsychotic drug therapy in patients with severe psychosis requiring treatment, because of possible recurrence of NMS; closely monitoring patients in whom antipsychotic drug therapy is reintroduced after recovery from NMS.

Tardive dyskinesia—There is no known effective treatment. If signs and symptoms of tardive dyskinesia appear, discontinuation of olanzapine treatment should be considered if clinically feasible. To minimize the occurrence of tardive dyskinesia, chronic antipsychotic treatment should be in the smallest effective dose for the shortest duration necessary to produce a satisfactory clinical response.

Oral Dosage Forms

OLANZAPINE TABLETS

Usual adult dose

Bipolar disorder—

Olanzapine monotherapy—Oral, general starting dose of 10 to 15 mg once per day without regard to meals. If indicated, dosage adjustments should generally occur at intervals of not less than 24 hours with recommended dose increments/decrements of 5 mg per day.

Olanzapine in combination with lithium or valproate—Oral, general starting dose of 10 mg once per day without regard to meals.

Note: Dosing in special populations—Recommended starting dose is 5 mg in patients who are debilitated, who have a predisposition to hypotensive reactions, who otherwise exhibit a combination of factors that may result in slower metabolism of olanzapine (e.g., nonsmoking female patients 65 years of age or older) or who may be more pharmacodynamically sensitive to olanzapine. When indicated, dose escalation should be performed with caution in these patients.

Schizophrenia—

Oral, initially 5 to 10 mg once a day, with a target dose of 10 mg once a day within several days. Dosage may then be adjusted as needed and tolerated at increments or decrements of 5 mg a day, at intervals of not less than one week.

Note: Dosing in special populations—See note for special populations under *Usual adult dose* for bipolar disorder.

Usual adult prescribing limits

20 mg a day.

Usual pediatric dose

Bipolar disorder and Schizophrenia—

Safety and efficacy in children up to 18 years of age have not been established.

Usual geriatric dose

Bipolar disorder and Schizophrenia—

See *Usual adult dose.*

Usual geriatric prescribing limits

See *Usual adult prescribing limits.*

Strength(s) usually available

U.S.—

2.5 mg (Rx) [*Zyprexa* (carnauba wax; color mixture white; crospovidone; FD&C Blue No. 2 Aluminum Lake; hydroxypropyl cellulose; hypromellose; lactose; magnesium stearate; microcrystalline cellulose; titanium dioxide)].

5 mg (Rx) [*Zyprexa* (carnauba wax; color mixture white; crospovidone; FD&C Blue No. 2 Aluminum Lake; hydroxypropyl cellulose; hypromellose; lactose; magnesium stearate; microcrystalline cellulose; titanium dioxide)].

7.5 mg (Rx) [*Zyprexa* (carnauba wax; color mixture white; crospovidone; FD&C Blue No. 2 Aluminum Lake; hydroxypropyl cellulose; hypromellose; lactose; magnesium stearate; microcrystalline cellulose)].

10 mg (Rx) [*Zyprexa* (carnauba wax; color mixture white; crospovidone; FD&C Blue No. 2 Aluminum Lake; hydroxypropyl cellulose; hypromellose; lactose; magnesium stearate; microcrystalline cellulose)].

15 mg (Rx) [*Zyprexa* (carnauba wax; color mixture white; crospovidone; FD&C Blue No. 2 Aluminum Lake; hydroxypropyl cellulose; hypromellose; lactose; magnesium stearate; microcrystalline cellulose; titanium dioxide; FD&C Blue No. 2 Aluminum Lake)].

20 mg (Rx) [*Zyprexa* (carnauba wax; color mixture white; crospovidone; FD&C Blue No. 2 Aluminum Lake; hydroxypropyl cellulose; hypromellose; lactose; magnesium stearate; microcrystalline cellulose; titanium dioxide; synthetic red iron oxide)].

5 mg (Rx) [*Zyprexa Zydis* (orally disintegrating tablet; gelatin; mannitol; aspartame; sodium methyl paraben; sodium propyl paraben; phenylalanine 0.34 mg)].

10 mg (Rx) [*Zyprexa Zydis* (orally disintegrating tablet; gelatin; mannitol; aspartame; sodium methyl paraben; sodium propyl paraben; phenylalanine 0.45 mg)].

15 mg (Rx) [*Zyprexa Zydis* (orally disintegrating tablet; gelatin; mannitol; aspartame; sodium methyl paraben; sodium propyl paraben; phenylalanine 0.67 mg)].

20 mg (Rx) [*Zyprexa Zydis* (orally disintegrating tablet; gelatin; mannitol; aspartame; sodium methyl paraben; sodium propyl paraben; phenylalanine 0.9 mg)].

Packaging and storage
Store between 20 and 25 °C (68 and 77 °F), unless otherwise specified by manufacturer. Protect from light and moisture.

Auxiliary labeling
- Avoid alcoholic beverages.
- May cause drowsiness. Be careful while driving or operating machinery. Use caution until you become familiar with its effects
- Tell your doctor about all medications you are taking; prescription and nonprescription.
- Protect from light

Parenteral Dosage Forms

OLANZAPINE FOR INJECTION

Usual adult dose
Agitation associated with schizophrenia or bipolar mania—

Intramuscular, recommended initial dose of 10 mg. A lower dose of 5 or 7.5 mg may be considered when clinical factors warrant. Subsequent doses up to 10 mg may be given following the initial dose if agitation persists. Efficacy of repeated doses of intramuscular olanzapine for injection in agitated patients has not been evaluated. Safety has also not been evaluated for total daily doses greater than 30 mg, or 10 mg injections given more frequently than 2 hours after the initial dose, and 4 hours after the second dose. If ongoing olanzapine therapy is clinically indicated, oral olanzapine may be initiated in a range of 5 to 20 mg per day as soon as clinically appropriate. See *Olanzapine Tablets* for oral dosing.

Note: A lower dose of 2.5 mg per injections should be considered for patients who otherwise might be debilitated, be predisposed to hypotensive reactions, or be more pharmacodynamically sensitive to olanzapine.

Usual pediatric dose
Safety and efficacy in children up to 18 years of age have not been established.

Usual geriatric dose
Intramuscular, dose of 5 mg per injection should be considered.

Strength(s) usually available
U.S.—

10 mg (Rx) [*Zyprexa Intramuscular* (50 mg lactose monohydrate; 3.5 mg tartaric acid; aspartame; may contain hydrochloric acid to adjust pH; may contain sodium hydroxide to adjust pH)].

Packaging and storage
Store at controlled room temperature between 20 and 25°C (68° to 77°F) before reconstitution. Reconstituted solution may be stored at controlled room temperature for up to 1 hour if necessary. Protect from light. Do not freeze.

Preparation of dosage form
Dissolve the contents of the vial using 2.1 mL sterile water for injection to provide a solution containing approximately 5 mg per mL of olanzapine. The resulting solution should appear clear and yellow. Olanzapine reconstituted with sterile water for injection should be used immediately (within 1 hour) after reconstitution. The reconstituted solution should be inspected visually for particulate matter and discoloration prior to administration. The following provides injection volumes for delivering various doses of reconstituted intramuscular olanzapine for injection:
- 10-mg dose—total contents of vial
- 7.5-mg dose—1.5 mL
- 5-mg dose—1 mL
- 2.5-mg dose—0.5 mL

Auxiliary labeling
- For intramuscular (I.M.) use only.
- Tell your doctor about all medications you are taking; prescription and nonprescription.
- Do not freeze
- Protect from light
- For single dose only. Discard unused drug.

Revised: 04/18/2005

OLMESARTAN Systemic†

VA CLASSIFICATION (Primary): CV805

Commonly used brand name(s): *Benicar.*

Note: For a listing of dosage forms and brand names by country availability, see *Dosage Forms* section(s).

†Not commercially available in Canada.

Category
Antihypertensive.

Indications

Accepted
Hypertension (treatment)—Olmesartan is indicated for treatment of hypertension and may be used alone or in combination with other antihypertensive agents.

For additional information on initial therapeutic guidelines related to the treatment of hypertension, see *Appendix III.*

Pharmacology/Pharmacokinetics

Physicochemical characteristics
Molecular weight—Olmesartan medoxomil: 558.59.

Solubility—Olmesartan medoxomil is practically insoluble in water and sparingly soluble in methanol.

Mechanism of action/Effect
Antihypertensive—Olmesartan blocks the vasoconstrictor effects of angiotensin II by selectively blocking the binding of angiotensin II to the AT_1 receptor in vascular smooth muscle. Angiotensin II is formed from angiotensin I in a reaction catalyzed by angiotensin converting enzyme (ACE, kininase II). Angiotensin II is the principal pressor agent of the renin-angiotensin system, with effects that include vasoconstriction, stimulation of synthesis and release of aldosterone, cardiac stimulation and renal reabsorption of sodium. Olmesartan's action is independent of the pathways for angiotensin II synthesis. An AT_2 receptor is also found in many tissues, but this receptor is not known to be associated with cardiovascular homeostasis. Olmesartan has more than a 12,500-fold greater affinity for the AT_1 rather than the AT_2 receptor. Blockade of the angiotensin II receptor inhibits the negative regulatory feedback of angiotensin II on renin secretion, but the resulting increased plasma renin activity and circulating angiotensin II levels do not overcome the effect of olmesartan on blood pressure.

Other actions/effects
In addition to to inhibiting the biosynthesis of angiotensin II from angiotensin I, ACE inhibitors also inhibit the degradation of of bradykinin, a reaction also catalyzed by ACE. Because olmesartan does not inhibit ACE (kininase II), it does not affect the response of bradykinin. It is unknown whether this difference has clinical relevance.

Absorption
Absolute bioavailability of olmesartan from the administered prodrug, olmesartan medoxomil, is approximately 26%. Food does not affect the bioavailability of olmesartan.

Distribution
Volume of distribution (Vol_D)—approximately 17 liters

Protein binding
Very high (99%) to plasma proteins and does not penetrate red blood cells

The protein binding is constant at plasma olmesartan concentrations well above the range achieved with recommended doses.

Biotransformation
Olmesartan medoxomil is rapidly and completely bioactivated by ester hydrolysis to olmesartan during absorption from the gastrointestinal tract. There is virtually no further metabolism of olmesartan.

Elimination
Approximately 13 hours

Time to peak plasma concentration
1 to 2 hours

Steady state concentration
Olmesartan shows linear pharmacokinetics with steady-state levels being achieved within 3 to 5 days and no accumulation in plasma occurring following once-daily dosing.

Elimination
Total plasma clearance—1.3 L/hour

Renal clearance—0.6 L/hour

Renal—Approximately 35 to 50%
Fecal (biliary)—Approximately 50 to 65%
In dialysis—The pharmacokinetics of olmesartan in patients undergoing hemodialysis has not been studied.

Pharmacodynamics

Olmesartan medoxomil doses of 2.5 to 40 mg inhibit the pressor effects of angiotensin I infusion. The duration of the inhibitory effect was related to dose, with doses of olmesartan medoxomil >40 mg giving >90% inhibition at 24 hours.

Plasma concentrations of angiotensin I and angiotensin II and plasma renin activity (PRA) increase after single and repeated administration of olmesartan to healthy subjects and hypertensive patients. Repeated administration of up to 80 mg olmesartan had minimal influence on aldosterone levels and no effect on serum potassium.

Precautions to Consider

Carcinogenicity

Olmesartan was not carcinogenic when administered by dietary administration to rats for up to 2 years. Additionally, two carcinogenicity studies conducted in mice, a 6-month gavage study in the p53 Knockout mouse and a 6-month dietary administration study in the Hras2 transgenic mouse, revealed no evidence of a carcinogenic effect of olmesartan.

Mutagenicity

Olmesartan tested negative in the *in vitro* Syrian hamster embryo cell transformation assay and showed no evidence of genetic toxicity in the Ames test for bacterial mutagenicity. However, olmesartan was shown to induce chromosomal aberrations in cultured cells *in vitro* . It also tested positive for thymidine kinase mutations in the *in vitro* mouse lymphoma assay. At oral doses of up to 2000 mg per kg of body weight, olmesartan medoxomil tested negative *in vivo* for mutations in the MutaMouse intestine and kidney, for DNA damage in the rat kidney (comet assay) and for clastogenicity in mouse bone marrow (micronucleus test).

Pregnancy/Reproduction

Fertility—Fertility of rats was unaffected by the administration of olmesartan medoxomil at high dose levels of 1000 mg per kg of body weight per day (240 times the maximum recommended human dose) when the starting dose was given 2 weeks (female) or 9 weeks (male) prior to mating.

Pregnancy—When pregnancy is detected, olmesartan should be discontinued as soon as possible. On rare occasions (less often than once in every thousand pregnancies), no alternative therapy can be found. In these cases, the patient should be apprised of the potential hazards and serial ultrasound examinations should be performed to assess the intra-amniotic environment.

Because olmesartan acts directly on the renin-angiotensin system, it can cause fetal and neonatal morbidity and death when administered to pregnant women. Several dozen cases have been reported in the world literature of patients who were taking angiotensin converting enzyme (ACE) inhibitors.

Fetal exposure to drugs that act directly on the renin-angiotensin system during the second and third trimesters has been associated with fetal and neonatal injury, including hypotension, neonatal skull hypoplasia, anuria, reversible or irreversible renal failure and death. Oligohydramnios has also been reported, possibly resulting from decreased fetal function, and may cause fetal limb contractures, craniofacial deformation and hypoplastic lung development. If oligohydramnios is observed, olmesartan should be discontinued unless it is considered lifesaving for the mother. Oligohydramnios may not appear until after the fetus has sustained irreversible damage. In addition, prematurity, intrauterine growth retardation and patent ductus arteriosus have also been reported, although it is not clear whether these occurrences were due to exposure to the drug. When limited to the first trimester, exposure to olmesartan does not appear to be associated with these adverse effects. However, mothers who were exposed to this drug during the first trimester should be informed.

Infants exposed *in utero* to angiotensin II receptor antagonists should be observed closely for hypotension, oliguria, and hyperkalemia. Oliguria should be treated with support of blood pressure and renal perfusion. Dialysis or exchange transfusion may be necessary to reverse hypotension and/or substitute for disordered renal function.

No clinical experience with the use of olmesartan in pregnant women is available. When olmesartan was administered orally at high doses to pregnant rats or pregnant rabbits, no teratogenic effects were observed. However, in rats, significant decreases in pup birth weight and weight gain were observed at doses ≥1.6 mg per kg of body weight per day, and delays in developmental milestones and dose-dependent increases in the incidence of dilation of the renal pelvis were observed at doses ≥8 mg per kg of body weight per day. The no observed effect dose for developmental toxicity in rats is 0.3 mg per kg of body weight per day, about one-tenth the maximum recommended human dose (MRHD) of 40 mg per day.

FDA Pregnancy Category C (first trimester)

FDA Pregnancy Category D (second and third trimesters)

Breast-feeding

It is not known whether olmesartan is distributed into breast milk. However, olmesartan is distributed at low concentration in the milk of lactating rats. Because of the potential for adverse effects on the nursing infant, a decision should be made whether to discontinue nursing or discontinue the drug, taking into account the importance of the drug to the mother.

Pediatrics

Safety and effectiveness in pediatric patients have not been established. The pharmacokinetics of olmesartan have not been studied in patients younger than 18 years of age. Infants exposed *in utero* to angiotensin II receptor antagonists should be observed closely for hypotension, oliguria, and hyperkalemia. Oliguria should be treated with support of blood pressure and renal perfusion. Dialysis or exchange transfusion may be necessary to reverse hypotension and/or substitute for disordered renal function. See *Pregnancy* section.

Geriatrics

In pharmacokinetics studies of olmesartan in the patients 65 years of age and older, maximum plasma concentrations of olmesartan were similar in young adults and the elderly. Modest accumulation of olmesartan was observed in the elderly with repeated dosing. AUC was 33% higher in elderly patients and there was a reduction in renal clearance (CL_R) of approximately 30%. No overall differences in safety or effectiveness were observed between elderly patients and younger patients. However, greater sensitivity in older patients cannot be ruled out.

Pharmacogenetics

Minor differences were observed in the pharmacokinetics of olmesartan in women compared to men with AUC and C_{max} being 10 to 15% higher in women than in men. The antihypertensive effect of olmesartan was similar in men and women. However, black patients showed a smaller response to the antihypertensive effect of olmesartan, as has been seen with other ACE inhibitors, angiotensin receptor blockers and beta-blockers.

Drug interactions and/or related problems

The following drug interactions and/or related problems have been selected on the basis of their potential clinical significance (possible mechanism in parentheses where appropriate)—not necessarily inclusive (» = major clinical significance):

Note: Clinically significant medication interactions are not expected between olmesartan and digoxin, warfarin, antacids [$Al(OH)_3$/ $Mg(OH)_2$], or drugs that inhibit, induce, or are metabolized by cytochrome P450 enzymes.

Note: Combinations containing any of the following medications, depending on the amount present, may also interact with this medication.

» Diuretics
(concurrent use with olmesartan may have additive hypotensive effects, especially in volume-depleted and/or salt-depleted patients)

Laboratory value alterations

The following have been selected on the basis of their potential clinical significance (possible effect in parentheses where appropriate)—not necessarily inclusive (» = major clinical significance).

With physiology/laboratory test values

Bilirubin, serum and
Liver enzymes
(may elevate serum bilirubin and liver enzymes)

Blood urea nitrogen (BUN) and
Creatinine, serum
(increases in BUN and serum creatinine, including creatinine phosphokinase, have been reported in patients with unilateral or bilateral renal artery stenosis who were treated with angiotensin-converting enzyme (ACE) inhibitors, there has been no long-term use of olmesartan and patients with this condition, but similar results may be expected)

Hematocrit and hemoglobin levels
(small decreases of 0.3 volume percent and 0.3 g per dL, respectively, were observed)

Medical considerations/Contraindications

The medical considerations/contraindications included have been selected on the basis of their potential clinical significance (reasons given in parentheses where appropriate)—not necessarily inclusive (» = major clinical significance).

Except under special circumstances, this medication should not be used when the following medical problem exists:

» Hypersensitivity to olmesartan or any component of the product

Risk-benefit should be considered when the following medical problems exist:

» Congestive heart failure, severe
(treatment with ACE inhibitors and angiotensin receptor antagonists has been associated with oliguria, azotemia, acute renal failure and/or death)

Hepatic impairment, moderate
(may increase C_{max} of olmesartan; may increase AUC of olmesartan by about 60%)

Renal artery stenosis, unilateral or bilateral or
» Renal function impairment
(increases in serum creatinine or BUN concentrations in patients with renal artery stenosis who were treated with ACE inhibitors and similar results may be anticipated with olmesartan; may elevate serum concentrations of olmesartan with the AUC approximately tripled in patients with severe renal impairment (creatinine clearance <20 mL per min); changes in renal function as a result of inhibiting the renin-angiotensin-aldosterone system have been associated with oliguria, progressive azotemia, acute renal failure and/or death in susceptible patients)

Salt depletion or
Volume depletion
(may increase the risk of symptomatic hypotension; close medical supervision recommended; lower starting dose consideration should be given)

Patient monitoring

The following may be especially important in patient monitoring (other tests may be warranted in some patients, depending on condition; » = major clinical significance):

» Blood pressure measurements
(periodic monitoring to individualize dose to the patient's response)

Side/Adverse Effects

The following side/adverse effects have been selected on the basis of their potential clinical significance (possible signs and symptoms in parentheses where appropriate)—not necessarily inclusive:

Those indicating need for medical attention

Incidence less frequent

Bronchitis (cough producing mucus; difficulty breathing; shortness of breath; tightness in chest; wheezing); ***hematuria*** (blood in urine); ***upper respiratory tract infection*** (ear congestion; nasal congestion; chills; cough, fever, sneezing, or sore throat; body aches or pain; headache; loss of voice; runny nose; unusual tiredness or weakness; difficulty in breathing)

Incidence rare

Hyperlipemia (large amount of fat in the blood); ***hyperuricemia*** (joint pain, stiffness, or swelling; lower back, side, or stomach pain; swelling of feet or lower legs); ***tachycardia*** (fast, pounding, or irregular heartbeat or pulse); ***urinary tract infection*** (bladder pain; bloody or cloudy urine; difficult, burning, or painful urination; frequent urge to urinate; lower back or side pain)

Frequency unknown

Hypotension (blurred vision; confusion; dizziness, faintness, or lightheadedness when getting up from a lying or sitting position suddenly; sweating; unusual tiredness or weakness)

Incidence not determined—Observed during clinical practice; estimates of frequency can not be determined

Angioedema (large, hive-like swelling on face, eyelids, lips, tongue, throat, hands, legs, feet, sex organs); ***rhabdomyolysis*** (dark-colored urine; fever; muscle cramps or spasms; muscle pain or stiffness; unusual tiredness or weakness)

Those indicating need for medical attention only if they continue or are bothersome

Incidence less frequent

Back pain; diarrhea; dizziness; headache; hyperglycemia (abdominal pain; blurred vision; dry mouth; fatigue; flushed, dry skin; fruit-like breath odor; increased hunger; increased thirst; increased urination; nausea; sweating; troubled breathing; unexplained weight loss; vomiting); ***hypertriglyceridemia; influenza-like symptoms*** (chills; cough; diarrhea; fever; general feeling of discomfort or illness; headache; joint pain; loss of appetite; muscle aches and pains; nausea; runny nose; shivering; sore throat; sweating; trouble sleeping; unusual tiredness or weakness; vomiting); ***pharyngitis*** (body aches or pain; congestion; cough; dryness or soreness of throat; fever; hoarseness; runny nose; tender, swollen glands in neck; trouble in swallowing; voice changes); ***rhinitis*** (stuffy nose; runny nose; sneezing); ***sinusitis*** (pain or tenderness around eyes and cheekbones; fever; stuffy or runny nose; headache; cough; shortness of breath or troubled breathing; tightness of chest or wheezing)

Incidence rare

Abdominal pain (stomach pain); ***arthralgia*** (pain in joints; muscle pain or stiffness; difficulty in moving); ***chest pain; arthritis*** (pain, swelling, or redness in joints; muscle pain or stiffness; difficulty in moving); ***cough; dyspepsia*** (acid or sour stomach; belching; heartburn; indigestion; stomach discomfort, upset, or pain); ***facial edema*** (swelling or puffiness of face); ***fatigue*** (unusual tiredness or weakness); ***gastroenteritis*** (abdominal or stomach pain; diarrhea; loss of appetite; nausea; weakness); ***hypercholesterolemia; insomnia*** (sleeplessness; trouble sleeping; unable to sleep); ***myalgia*** (joint pain; swollen joints; muscle aching or cramping; muscle pains or stiffness; difficulty in moving); ***nausea; pain; peripheral edema*** (bloating or swelling of face, arms, hands, lower legs, or feet; rapid weight gain; tingling of hands or feet; unusual weight gain or loss); ***rash; skeletal pain; vertigo*** (dizziness or lightheadedness; feeling of constant movement of self or surroundings; sensation of spinning)

Overdose

For more information on the management of overdose or unintentional ingestion, **contact a poison control center** (see *Poison Control Center Listing*).

Clinical effects of overdose

The following effects have been selected on the basis of their potential clinical significance (possible signs and symptoms in parentheses where appropriate)—not necessarily inclusive:

Bradycardia (chest pain or discomfort; lightheadedness; dizziness or fainting; shortness of breath; slow or irregular heartbeat; unusual tiredness)—could be encountered if parasympathetic (vagal) stimulation occurs; ***hypotension*** (blurred vision; confusion; dizziness, faintness, or lightheadedness when getting up from a lying or sitting position suddenly; sweating; unusual tiredness or weakness); ***tachycardia*** (fast, pounding, or irregular heartbeat or pulse)

Treatment of overdose

There is no specific antidote to olmesartan. Treatment is generally symptomatic and supportive.

To enhance elimination—
The dialyzability of olmesartan is unknown.
Dialysis is not expected to be effective because of the high degree of protein binding (99%).

Monitoring—
Monitor blood pressure.

Supportive care—
Treatment should be symptomatic and supportive.
Correct symptomatic hypotension.
Patients in whom intentional overdose is confirmed or suspected should be referred for psychiatric consultation.

Patient Consultation

As an aid to patient consultation, refer to *Advice for the Patient, Olmesartan (Systemic)*.

In providing consultation, consider emphasizing the following selected information (» = major clinical significance):

Before using this medication

» Conditions affecting use, especially:
Hypersensitivity to olmesartan or any components of the product
Pregnancy—Fetal exposure to drugs that act directly on the renin-angiotensin system during the second and third trimesters has been associated with fetal and neonatal injury, including hypotension, neonatal skull hypoplasia, anuria, reversible or irreversible renal failure and death. When pregnancy is detected, olmesartan should be discontinued as soon as possible.
Breast-feeding—Because of the potential for adverse effects on the nursing infant, olmesartan is not recommended for nursing mothers.
Use in the elderly—Elderly patients may experience greater sensitivity to the effects of olmesartan.
Pharmacogenetics—The antihypertensive effect of olmesartan was similar in men and women. However, black patients showed a smaller response to the antihypertensive effect of

olmesartan, as has been seen with other ACE inhibitors, angiotensin receptor blockers and beta-blockers.
Other medications, especially diuretics
Other medical problems, especially renal function impairment and severe congestive heart failure

Proper use of this medication

» Proper dosing
Missed dose: Taking as soon as possible; not taking if almost time for next scheduled dose; not doubling doses
» Proper storage

Precautions while using this medication

» Notifying physician immediately if pregnancy is suspected because of possibility of fetal or neonatal injury and/or death

Regular visits to physician to check progress and monitor blood pressure

Not taking other medications without consulting the physician

Side/adverse effects

Signs of potential side effects, especially bronchitis, hematuria, upper respiratory tract infection, hyperlipemia, hyperuricemia, tachycardia, urinary tract infection, and hypotension
Signs of potential side effects observed during clinical practice, especially angioedema and rhabdomyolysis

General Dosing Information

If blood pressure is not controlled by olmesartan alone, a diuretic may be added. Olmesartan may be administered with other antihypertensive agents.

Diet/Nutrition

Olmesartan may be administered with or without food.

For treatment of adverse effects

Treatment of symptomatic hypotension—placing patient in the supine position and, if necessary, administering an intravenous infusion of normal saline

Oral Dosage Forms

OLMESARTAN MEDOXOMIL TABLETS

Usual adult dose

Hypertension—
Oral, initially 20 mg once daily as monotherapy in patients who are not volume-contracted, prescribed and monitored by a physician. For patients requiring a further reduction in blood pressure after two weeks of therapy, the dose may be increased to the maximum of 40 mg once daily. Twice-daily dosing offers no advantage over the same total dose given once daily

Note: A lower starting dose should be given consideration in patients with possible depletion of intravascular volume.

Usual adult prescribing limits

40 mg per day

Usual pediatric dose

Safety and efficacy have not been established.

Usual geriatric dose

See *Usual adult dose*.

Usual geriatric prescribing limits

See *Usual adult prescribing limits*.

Strength(s) usually available

U.S.—
5 mg (Rx) [*Benicar* (hydroxypropylcellulose; lactose; low-substituted hydroxypropylcellulose; magnesium stearate; microcrystalline cellulose; talc; titanium dioxide; yellow iron oxide)].
20 mg (Rx) [*Benicar* (hydroxypropylcellulose; lactose; low-substituted hydroxypropylcellulose; magnesium stearate; microcrystalline cellulose; talc; titanium dioxide)].
40 mg (Rx) [*Benicar* (hydroxypropylcellulose; lactose; low-substituted hydroxypropylcellulose; magnesium stearate; microcrystalline cellulose; talc; titanium dioxide)].

Packaging and storage

Store between 20 and 25 °C (68 and 77 °F)

Revised: 01/31/2005
Developed: 12/26/2002

OLMESARTAN AND HYDROCHLOROTHIAZIDE Systemic

VA CLASSIFICATION (Primary): CV408
Commonly used brand name(s): *Benicar HCT*.
Note: For a listing of dosage forms and brand names by country availability, see *Dosage Forms* section(s).

Category

Antihypertensive.

Indications

Accepted

Hypertension (treatment)—Olmesartan and hydrochlorothiazide combination is indicated for the treatment of hypertension.

For additional information on initial therapeutic guidelines related to the treatment of hypertension, see *Appendix III*.

Unaccepted

Fixed-dosage combinations are generally not recommended for initial therapy and are useful for subsequent therapy only when the proportion of the component agents corresponds to the dose of the individual agents, as determined by titration. The fixed combination is indicated for initial therapy when the hypertension is severe enough that the value of achieving prompt blood pressure control exceeds the risk of initiating combination therapy in these patients.

Pharmacology/Pharmacokinetics

Physicochemical characteristics

Molecular weight—
Olmesartan medoxomil—558.6.
Hydrochlorothiazide—297.7.
Solubility—
Olmesartan medoxomil—insoluble in water, sparingly soluble in methanol.
Hydrochlorothiazide—slightly soluble in water, freely soluble in sodium hydroxide.

Mechanism of action/Effect

Olmesartan medoxomil—Blocks the vasoconstrictor effects of angiotensin II by selectively blocking the binding of angiotensin II to the AT_1 receptor in vascular smooth muscle
Hydrochlorothiazide—Thiazides affect the renal tubular mechanisms of electrolyte reabsorption, directly increasing excretion of sodium and chloride in approximately equivalent amounts.

Absorption

Bioavailability: Olmesartan medoxomil—26%

Olmesartan medoxomil

Volume of distribution (Vol_D)—17 L

Protein binding

Olmesartan medoxomil—Very high (99%)

Half-life

Olmesartan medoxomil—13 hours
Hydrochlorothiazide—5.6 to 14.8 hours

Onset of action

Hydrochlorothiazide—2 hours

Time to peak concentration

Olmesartan medoxomil—1 to 2 hours

Time to steady state concentration

Olmesartan medoxomil—3 to 5 days

Elimination

Olmesartan medoxomil—
Renal—35 to 50% (0.6 L per hour)
Fecal—50 to 65%
Plasma clearance—1.3 L per hour
Hydrochlorothiazide—
Renal—61% eliminated unchanged in 24 hours

Precautions to Consider

Carcinogenicity

No carcinogenicity studies have been conducted with olmesartan medoxomil and hydrochlorothiazide combination.

Olmesartan medoxomil—Olmesartan medoxomil was not carcinogenic when administered by dietary administration to rats for up to 2 years. Additionally, two carcinogenicity studies conducted in mice, a 6-month gavage study in the p53 Knockout mouse and a 6-month dietary administration study in the Hras2 transgenic mouse, revealed no evidence of a carcinogenic effect of olmesartan medoxomil.

Hydrochlorothiazide—No evidence of carcinogenicity was found in two-year feeding studies at doses of up to approximately 600 mg/kg per day in female mice and 100 mg/kg per day in male and female rats. However, evidence was equivocal for hepatocarcinogenicity in male mice.

Mutagenicity

Olmesartan medoxomil and hydrochlorothiazide combination was negative in the *Salmonella-Escherichia coli*/mammalian microsome reverse mutation test up to the maximum recommended plate concentration for the standard assays. Positive responses were seen in tests for clastogenic activity in the *in vitro* Chinese hamster lung (CHL) chromosomal aberration assay. However, no synergism in clastogenic activity was detected between olmesartan medoxomil and hydrochlorothiazide. Olmesartan medoxomil and hydrochlorothiazide combination tested negative in the *in vivo* mouse bone marrow erythrocyte micronucleus assay at doses of up to 3144 mg per kg

Olmesartan medoxomil—Olmesartan medoxomil tested negative in the *in vitro* Syrian hamster embryo cell transformation assay and showed no evidence of genetic toxicity in the Ames test for bacterial mutagenicity. However, olmesartan medoxomil was shown to induce chromosomal aberrations in cultured cells *in vitro* . It also tested positive for thymidine kinase mutations in the *in vitro* mouse lymphoma assay. At oral doses of up to 2000 mg per kg of body weight, olmesartan medoxomil tested negative *in vivo* for mutations in the MutaMouse intestine and kidney, for DNA damage in the rat kidney (comet assay) and for clastogenicity in mouse bone marrow (micronucleus test).

Hydrochlorothiazide—Positive test results were obtained in the *in vitro* CHO Sister Chromatid Exchange (clastogenicity) and in the Mouse Lymphoma Cell (mutagenicity) assays at hydrochlorothiazide concentrations from 43 to 1300 mcg per mL, and in the *Aspergillus nidulans* non-disjunction assay at an unspecified concentration. Other mutagenicity tests were negative.

Pregnancy/Reproduction

Fertility—No studies of fertility have been conducted on the combination of olmesartan medoxomil and hydrochlorothiazide.

Olmesartan medoxomil: Fertility of rats was unaffected by the administration of olmesartan medoxomil at high dose levels of 1000 mg per kg of body weight per day (240 times the maximum recommended human dose) when the starting dose was given 2 weeks (female) or 9 weeks (male) prior to mating.

Hydrochlorothiazide: Hydrochlorothiazide did not produce adverse effects on the fertility of mice and rats of either sex at doses up to 100 mg/kg and 4 mg/kg, respectively.

Pregnancy—Medications affecting the renin-angiotensin system, such as olmesartan, can cause fetal and neonatal morbidity and mortality when administered to pregnant women. Olmesartan and hydrochlorothiazide combination should be discontinued as soon as possible when pregnancy is detected.

Fetal exposure to medications affecting the renin-angiotensin system during the second and third trimesters of pregnancy have been associated with hypotension, neonatal skull hypoplasia, anuria, renal failure, and even death in the newborn. Maternal oligohydramnios has also been reported, probably reflecting decreasing fetal renal function. Oligohydramnios in this setting has been associated with fetal limb contractures, craniofacial deformation, and hypoplastic lung development. Prematurity, intrauterine growth retardation, and patent ductus arteriosus also have been reported. However, it is not clear that these occurrences were related to drug exposure.

It is recommended that infants exposed *in utero* to olmesartan and hydrochlorothiazide combination be closely observed for hypotension, oliguria, and hyperkalemia. Oliguria should be treated with support of blood pressure and renal perfusion. If oligohydramnios is observed, olmesartan and hydrochlorothiazide combination should be discontinued unless it is considered lifesaving for the mother. Oligohydramnios, however, may not appear until after the fetus has sustained irreversible damage.

There is no clinical experience with the use of olmesartan and hydrochlorothiazide combination in pregnant women. No teratogenic effects were observed in pregnant mice or rats given 1625 mg per kg per day. However, the pregnant rats did experience decreased fetal body weights.

Olmesartan: Passes across the placenta in rats.

Hydrochlorothiazide: Thiazide diuretics cross the placenta and appear in cord blood. There is a risk of fetal or neonatal jaundice, thrombocytopenia, and possibly other adverse effects.

FDA Pregnancy Category C (first trimester) and D (second and third trimesters)

Breast-feeding

It is not known whether olmesartan is distributed into breast milk. However, olmesartan is distributed at low concentrations in the milk of lactating rats. Because of the potential for adverse effects on the nursing infant, a decision should be made whether to discontinue nursing or discontinue the drug, taking into account the importance of the drug to the mother.

Hydrochlorothiazide is distributed into breast milk. A decision should be made whether to discontinue nursing or discontinue the drug, taking into account the importance of the drug to the mother and the potential for adverse effects on the nursing infant.

Pediatrics

No information is available on the relationship of age to the effects of olmesartan and hydrochlorothiazide combination in pediatric patients. Safety and efficacy have not been established.

Geriatrics

Studies of olmesartan and hydrochlorothiazide combination have included a limited number of patients 65 years of age and over. No geriatrics-specific problems that would limit the usefulness of olmesartan and hydrochlorothiazide combination in the elderly have been identified. Dose selection for an elderly patient should be cautious, usually starting at the low end of the dosing range, reflecting the greater frequency of decreased hepatic, renal, or cardiac function, and of concomitant disease or other drug therapy. Modest accumulation of olmesartan was seen with repeated dosing. The risk of toxic reactions to olmesartan and hydrochlorothiazide may be greater in patients with impaired renal function because this drug is known to be substantially excreted by the kidney.

Pharmacogenetics

Max concentration and AUC were 10 to 15% higher in women than in men.

In clinical trials, the antihypertensive effects of olmesartan were lower in black patients.

Drug interactions and/or related problems

The following drug interactions and/or related problems have been selected on the basis of their potential clinical significance (possible mechanism in parentheses where appropriate)—not necessarily inclusive (» = major clinical significance):

Note: Combinations containing any of the following medications, depending on the amount present, may also interact with this medication.

Alcohol or
Analgesics, narcotic or
Barbiturates
(concurrent administration with olmesartan and hydrochlorothiazide combination may potentiate orthostatic hypotension)

Antidiabetic agents or
Insulin
(hydrochlorothiazide may increase blood glucose concentrations; dosage adjustment of the antidiabetic medication may be necessary)

Anti-inflammatory drugs, nonsteroidal (NSAIDs)
(may antagonize the diuretic, natriuretic, and antihypertensive effects of hydrochlorothiazide; patients should be carefully monitored to confirm that the desired effect is being obtained)

Cholestyramine or
Colestipol
(cholestyramine or colestipol may inhibit gastrointestinal absorption of hydrochlorothiazide by up to 85% and 43%, respectively)

Corticosteroids or
ACTH
(concurrent use with hydrochlorothiazide may intensify electrolyte depletion, particularly hypokalemia)

Hypotension-producing medications, other (See *Appendix II*)
(concurrent use with olmesartan and hydrochlorothiazide combination may produce additive hypotensive effects)

» Lithium
(concurrent use with olmesartan and hydrochlorothiazide combination is not recommended; hydrochlorothiazide may reduce the renal clearance of lithium and increase the risk of lithium toxicity)

Skeletal muscle relaxants
(possible increased responsiveness to the muscle relaxant)

Sympathomimetics, such as norepinephrine
(olmesartan and hydrochlorothiazide combination may decrease the response to sympathomimetic agents)

Laboratory value alterations

The following have been selected on the basis of their potential clinical significance (possible effect in parentheses where appropriate)—not necessarily inclusive (» = major clinical significance).

With physiology/laboratory test values

Alanine aminotransferase (ALT [SGPT]), serum or
Aspartate aminotransferase (AST [SGOT]), serum or
Gamma glutamyl transferase (GGT), serum
(concentrations may be increased)

Blood urea nitrogen (BUN) or
Creatinine, serum
(may be increased by more than 50%)

Calcium, serum
(concentrations may be increased)

Cholesterol and
Triglycerides
(serum concentrations may be increased)

Magnesium, serum
(concentrations may be decreased)

Phosphokinase
(may be increased)

Potassium, serum
(concentrations may be increased or decreased, especially with brisk diuresis, when cirrhosis is present, or after prolonged therapy)

Medical considerations/Contraindications

The medical considerations/contraindications included have been selected on the basis of their potential clinical significance (reasons given in parentheses where appropriate)—not necessarily inclusive (» = major clinical significance).

Except under special circumstances, this medication should not be used when the following medical problem exists:

» Anuria
(not recommended due to the hydrochlorothiazide component)

» Hypersensitivity to sulfonamide drugs or to any component of this product

Risk-benefit should be considered when the following medical problems exist:

Hepatic impairment or
Liver disease, progressive or
Renal impairment
(may elevate concentration of olmesartan in the body)

Hyperglycemia or
Diabetes mellitus
(condition may be exacerbated by thiazide therapy; dosage adjustments of insulin or oral hypoglycemic agents may be required)

Hyperuricemia or
Gout
(condition may be exacerbated by thiazide therapy)

Renal impairment
(may precipitate azotemia; discontinuation of treatment should be considered if severe renal impairment becomes evident)

Sympathectomy
(may increase the antihypertensive effects of this medicine)

Systemic lupus erythematosus
(thiazide diuretics may exacerbate this condition)

Volume depleted or salt depleted patients

Patient monitoring

The following may be especially important in patient monitoring (other tests may be warranted in some patients, depending on condition; » = major clinical significance):

Electrolytes, serum
Electrolytes, urine
(periodic determinations of serum fluids and electrolytes to detect possible electrolyte imbalance should be performed at appropriate intervals; serum and urine determinations are important when the patient is vomiting; signs may include hyponatremia, hypochloremic alkalosis and hypokalemia)

Side/Adverse Effects

The following side/adverse effects have been selected on the basis of their potential clinical significance (possible signs and symptoms in parentheses where appropriate)—not necessarily inclusive:

Note: Lightheadedness may occur, especially during the first days of therapy. Patients should report this to the prescribing physician.

Those indicating need for medical attention only if they continue or are bothersome

Incidence more frequent

Dizziness; upper respiratory tract infection (chest pain; chills; cough; ear congestion or pain; fever; head congestion; hoarseness or other voice changes; nasal congestion; runny nose; sneezing; sore throat)

Incidence less frequent

Hyperuricemia (joint pain, stiffness, or swelling; lower back, side, or stomach pain; swelling of feet or lower legs); ***nausea***

Incidence unknown

Abdominal pain; arthralgia (joint pain; muscle pain or stiffness; difficulty in moving); ***arthritis*** (pain, swelling, or redness in joints; muscle pain or stiffness; difficulty in moving); ***azotemia*** (bloody or cloudy urine; pain in lower back or side; thirst; dry mouth; dizziness); ***back pain; chest pain; creatine phosphokinase increased; cough; diarrhea; dyspepsia*** (acid or sour stomach; belching; heartburn; indigestion; stomach discomfort upset or pain); ***electrolyte imbalance*** (confusion; irregular heartbeat; muscle cramps or pain; numbness, tingling, pain, or weakness in hands or feet; seizures; trembling; unusual tiredness or weakness; weakness and heaviness of legs); ***facial edema*** (swelling or puffiness of face); ***gastroenteritis*** (abdominal or stomach pain; diarrhea; loss of appetite; nausea; weakness); ***hematuria*** (blood in urine); ***hyperglycemia*** (abdominal pain; blurred vision; dry mouth; fatigue; flushed, dry skin; fruit-like breath odor; increased hunger; increased thirst; increased urination; nausea; sweating; troubled breathing; unexplained weight loss; vomiting); ***hyperkalemia*** (abdominal pain; confusion; irregular heartbeat; nausea or vomiting; nervousness; numbness or tingling in hands, feet, or lips; shortness of breath; difficult breathing; weakness or heaviness of legs); ***hyperlipidemia*** (large amount of fat in the blood); ***hypokalemia*** (convulsions; decreased urine; dry mouth; irregular heartbeat; increased thirst; loss of appetite; mood changes; muscle pain or cramps; nausea or vomiting; numbness or tingling in hands, feet, or lips; shortness of breath; unusual tiredness or weakness); ***lightheadedness; myalgia*** (joint pain; swollen joints; muscle aching or cramping; muscle pains or stiffness; difficulty in moving); ***oliguria*** (decrease in amount of urine); ***peripheral edema*** (bloating or swelling of face, arms, hands, lower legs, or feet; rapid weight gain; tingling of hands or feet; unusual weight gain or loss); ***postural hypotension*** (chills; cold sweats; confusion; dizziness, faintness, or lightheadedness when getting up from lying or sitting position); ***rash; syncope*** (fainting); ***vertigo*** (dizziness or lightheadedness; feeling of constant movement of self or surroundings; sensation of spinning)

Overdose

For more information on the management of overdose or unintentional ingestion, **contact a poison control center** (see *Poison Control Center Listing*).

Clinical effects of overdose

The following effects have been selected on the basis of their potential clinical significance (possible signs and symptoms in parentheses where appropriate)—not necessarily inclusive:

Bradycardia due to vagal stimulation; dehydration; electrolyte depletion; hypotension; tachycardia

Treatment of overdose

Symptomatic and supportive.

Patient Consultation

As an aid to patient consultation, refer to *Advice for the Patient, Olmesartan and Hydrochlorothiazide (Systemic)*.

In providing consultation, consider emphasizing the following selected information (» = major clinical significance):

Before using this medication

» Conditions affecting use, especially:

Hypersensitivity to sulfonamide drugs or to any component of this product

Pregnancy—Not recommended for use during pregnancy; can cause fetal and neonatal morbidity and mortality

Breast-feeding—Hydrochlorothiazide is distributed into breast milk.

Other medications, especially lithium

Other medical problems, especially anuria, hepatic function impairment, renal artery stenosis, or renal function impairment

Proper use of this medication

Possible need for control of weight and diet, especially sodium intake; risks associated with sodium depletion; not taking salt substitutes or using low-salt milk unless approved by physician

» Patient may not experience symptoms of hypertension; importance of taking medication even if feeling well

» Does not cure, but helps control, hypertension; possible need for life-long therapy; checking with physician before discontinuing medication; serious consequences of untreated hypertension

» Proper dosing

Missed dose: Taking as soon as possible; not taking if almost time for next dose; not doubling doses

» Proper storage

Precautions while using this medication

» Notifying physician immediately if pregnancy is suspected

Making regular visits to physician to check progress

» Not taking other medications, especially nonprescription sympathomimetics, unless discussed with physician

To prevent dehydration and hypotension, checking with physician if severe nausea, vomiting, or diarrhea occurs and continues

Caution when exercising or during hot weather because of the risk of dehydration and hypotension due to reduced fluid volume

» Caution in using alcohol because of the risk of dehydration and hypotension due to reduced fluid volume

Diabetics: May increase blood sugar levels

Side/adverse effects

Signs of potential side effects, especially dizziness, electrolyte imbalance, or upper respiratory tract infection.

General Dosing Information

For oral dosing forms:

Inadequate fluid intake, excessive perspiration, diarrhea or vomiting can lead to an excessive fall in blood pressure.

Olmesartan and hydrochlorothiazide combination is recommended for therapy only after dosage titration with the individual components.

Oral Dosage Forms

OLMESARTAN MEDOXOMIL AND HYDROCHLOROTHIAZIDE TABLETS

Usual adult dose

Antihypertensive—

Oral, 1 tablet (20 mg/12.5 mg) once daily. May be increased after 2 weeks to 40 mg olmesartan medoxomil component once per day

Usual adult prescribing limits

Olmesartan medoxomil component—Doses above 40 mg do not appear to have greater effect. Twice-daily dosing offers no advantage over the same total dose given once daily.

Usual pediatric dose

Safety and efficacy have not been established in pediatric patients.

Usual geriatric dose

See *Usual adult dose*.

Usual geriatric prescribing limits

See *Usual adult prescribing limits*.

Strength(s) usually available

U.S.—

20 mg of olmesartan medoxomil and 12.5 mg of hydrochlorothiazide (Rx) [*Benicar HCT* (hydroxypropylcellulose; hypromellose; lactose; low-substituted hydroxypopylcellulose; magnesium stearate; mycrocrystalline cellulose; red iron oxide; talc; titanium dioxide; yellow iron oxide)].

40 mg of olmesartan medoxomil and 12.5 mg of hydrochlorothiazide (Rx) [*Benicar HCT* (hydroxypropylcellulose; hypromellose; lactose; low-substituted hydroxypopylcellulose; magnesium stearate; mycrocrystalline cellulose; red iron oxide; talc; titanium dioxide; yellow iron oxide)].

40 mg of olmesartan medoxomil and 25 mg of hydrochlorothiazide (Rx) [*Benicar HCT* (hydroxypropylcellulose; hypromellose; lactose; low-substituted hydroxypopylcellulose; magnesium stearate; mycrocrystalline cellulose; red iron oxide; talc; titanium dioxide; yellow iron oxide)].

Packaging and storage

Store between 20 and 25 °C (68 and 77 °F)

Developed: 08/05/2005

OLOPATADINE Ophthalmic

VA CLASSIFICATION (Primary): OP801

Commonly used brand name(s): *Patanol*.

Note: For a listing of dosage forms and brand names by country availability, see *Dosage Forms* section(s).

Category

Antihistaminic (H_1-receptor), ophthalmic; mast cell stabilizer, ophthalmic; antiallergic, ophthalmic.

Indications

Accepted

Conjunctivitis, allergic (treatment)—Ophthalmic olopatadine is indicated for temporary prevention of itching of the eye due to allergic conjunctivitis.

Pharmacology/Pharmacokinetics

Physicochemical characteristics

Molecular weight—Olopatadine hydrochloride: 373.88.

pH—approximately 7

Osmolality—approximately 300 mOsm per kg

Mechanism of action/Effect

Olopatadine is a relatively selective histamine H_1-receptor antagonist that inhibits the type 1 immediate hypersensitivity reaction *in vivo* and *in vitro*. Olopatadine also inhibits the release of histamine from mast cells. Olopatadine does not affect alpha-adrenergic, dopamine, muscarinic types 1 and 2, or serotonin receptors.

Absorption

Ophthalmic use of olopatadine usually does not produce measurable plasma concentrations. Two studies in normal volunteers (total 24 subjects) administered olopatadine 0.15% ophthalmic solution in each eye once every 12 hours for 2 weeks found that plasma concentrations were generally below the quantitative limit of the assay (less than 0.5 nanograms per mL). Samples in which olopatadine was quantifiable were typically those taken within 2 hours of dosing and contained plasma concentrations ranging from 0.5 to 1.3 nanograms per mL.

Biotransformation

The mono-desmethyl and the *N*-oxide metabolites have been detected at low concentrations in the urine.

Half-life

Elimination—

Plasma: Approximately 3 hours.

Elimination

Renal (60 to 70% as unchanged drug). Also, low concentrations of 2 metabolites (mono-desmethyl and *N*-oxide) have been detected in the urine.

Precautions to Consider

Carcinogenicity

Studies in mice and rats given oral doses of olopatadine of up to 500 and 200 mg per kg of body weight (mg/kg) per day, respectively, which (based on a 40 microliter drop size and a 50 kg person) were 150,000 and 50,000 times, respectively, the maximum recommended ocular human dose (MROHD), found no evidence of carcinogenicity.

Mutagenicity

Olopatadine was not found to be mutagenic in an *in vitro* bacterial reverse mutation (Ames) test, an *in vitro* mammalian chromosome aberration assay, or an *in vivo* mouse micronucleus test.

Pregnancy/Reproduction

Fertility—Studies in male and female rats given oral doses of olopatadine that were 100,000 times the MROHD level found a slight decrease in the fertility index and a reduced implantation rate. No effects on fertility were observed at doses of 15,000 times the MROHD.

Pregnancy—Adequate and well-controlled studies in humans have not been done. Because animal studies are not always predictive of human responses, this drug should be used in pregnant women only if the potential benefit to the mother justifies the potential risk to the embryo or fetus.

Olopatadine was not found to be teratogenic in rats or rabbits. However, studies in rats given doses of 600 mg/kg per day (150,000 times the MROHD) and in rabbits given doses of 400 mg/kg per day (100,000 times the MROHD) during organogenesis resulted in a decrease in live fetuses and a decrease in fetal weight. In addition, rates treated with 600 mg/kg per day during late gestation through the lactation period showed a decreased in neonatal survival and body weight.

FDA Pregnancy Category C.

Breast-feeding

It is not known whether ophthalmic olopatadine is absorbed in sufficient quantities to be distributed into human breast milk. However, it has been found in the milk of nursing rats following oral administration. Caution should be exercised when ophthalmic olopatadine is administered to a nursing mother.

Pediatrics

Safety and efficacy in children up to 3 years of age have not been established.

Geriatrics

No information is available on the relationship of age to the effects of ophthalmic olopatadine in geriatric patients.

Medical considerations/Contraindications

The medical considerations/contraindications included have been selected on the basis of their potential clinical significance (reasons given in parentheses where appropriate)—not necessarily inclusive (» = major clinical significance).

Except under special circumstances, this medication should not be used when the following medical problem exists:

» Hypersensitivity to olopatadine or any component of the product including benzalkonium chloride (may be used as a preservative)

Side/Adverse Effects

The following side/adverse effects have been selected on the basis of their potential clinical significance (possible signs and symptoms in parentheses where appropriate)—not necessarily inclusive:

Those indicating need for medical attention only if they continue or are bothersome

Incidence more frequent

Cold-like symptoms, such as sore throat and runny nose; headache; pharyngitis (sore throat)

Incidence less frequent

Asthenia (unusual tiredness or weakness); ***back pain; blurred vision; burning, dryness, itching, or stinging of the eye; change in taste; feeling of something in the eye; flu syndrome*** (chills; cough; diarrhea; fever; general feeling of discomfort or illness; headache; joint pain; loss of appetite; muscle aches and pains; nausea; runny nose; shivering; sore throat; sweating; trouble sleeping; unusual tiredness or weakness; vomiting); ***hyperemia*** (redness of eye or inside of eyelid); ***increased cough; keratitis*** (eye redness, irritation, or pain); ***lid edema*** (swelling of eyelid); ***nausea; pain; rhinitis*** (stuffy or runny nose); ***sinusitis*** (headache or runny nose)

Patient Consultation

As an aid to patient consultation, refer to *Advice for the Patient, Olopatadine (Ophthalmic)*.

In providing consultation, consider emphasizing the following selected information (» = major clinical significance):

Before using this medication

» Conditions affecting use, especially:

Hypersensitivity to olopatadine or any component of the product including benzalkonium chloride (preservative)

Pregnancy—Risk-benefit should be considered

Breast-feeding—Caution should be exercised when administering to nursing woman

Use in children—Safety and efficacy not established below 3 years of age

Proper use of this medication

Not using for contact lens related irritation

Not inserting contact lens if eye is red

Removing contact lenses prior to administration; waiting at least 10 minutes after administration before reinserting lenses only if eyes are not red

» Proper administration; using a second drop if necessary; not touching applicator tip to any surface; keeping container tightly closed

» Proper dosing

Missed dose: Using as soon as possible; not using if almost time for next dose; using next dose at regularly scheduled time; not doubling doses

» Proper storage

Precautions while using this medication

» Checking with physician if symptoms do not improve or if condition worsens

Side/adverse effects

Signs of potential side effects, especially conjunctivitis, hypersensitivity, or infection

General Dosing Information

Patients should be advised to not wear contact lens if their eye is red.

Olopatadine should not be used to treat contact lens related irritation. Olopatadine contains benzalkonium chloride as a preservative, which may be absorbed by contact lenses. Contact lenses should be removed prior to administration of olopatadine. Patients whose eyes are not red should be instructed to wait at least ten minutes after instilling olopatadine before they insert their contact lenses.

Although some manufacturers recommend a dose of 2 drops of an ophthalmic solution at appropriate intervals, the conjunctival sac usually will hold 1 drop or less.

Ophthalmic Dosage Forms

Note: The dosing and strength of the dosage form available are expressed in terms of olopatadine base.

OLOPATADINE HYDROCHLORIDE OPHTHALMIC SOLUTION

Usual adult and adolescent dose

Allergic conjunctivitis—

Topical, to the conjunctiva, 1 drop (0.1% solution) in each affected eye two times a day, separated by an interval of at least six to eight hours or 1 drop (0.2% solution) in each affected eye once a day.

Usual pediatric dose

Allergic conjunctivitis—

Children up to 3 years of age: Safety and efficacy have not been established.

Children 3 years of age and older: See *Usual adult and adolescent dose*.

Strength(s) usually available

U.S.—

0.1% (1 mg olopatadine [base] per mL) (Rx) [*Patanol* (benzalkonium chloride 0.01%; dibasic sodium phosphate; sodium chloride; hydrochloric acid/sodium hydroxide; purified water)].

0.2% (base) (Rx) [GENERIC (povidone; dibasic sodium phosphate; sodium chloride; edetate disodium; benzalkonium chloride 0.01% [preservative]; hydrochloric acid/sodium hydroxide [adjust pH]; purified water)].

Packaging and storage

For 0.1% solution: Store between 4 and 30 °C (39 and 86 °F). Keep bottle tightly closed when not in use.

For 0.2% solution: Store between 2 and 25 °C (36 and 77 °F). Keep bottle tightly closed when not in use.

Auxiliary labeling

- For the eye.
- Do not touch or contaminate the tip of the container.

Revised: 08/05/2005

OMALIZUMAB Systemic†

VA CLASSIFICATION (Primary): RE190

Commonly used brand name(s): *Xolair*.

Note: For a listing of dosage forms and brand names by country availability, see *Dosage Forms* section(s).

†Not commercially available in Canada.

Category

Antiasthmatic; Monoclonal antibody.

Indications

Accepted

Asthma, persistent, moderate to severe (prophylaxis)—Omalizumab is indicated for adults and adolescents (12 years of age and above) with moderate to severe persistent asthma who have a positive skin test or in vitro reactivity to a perennial aeroallergen and whose symptoms are inadequately controlled with inhaled corticosteroids.

Unaccepted
Omalizumab is not indicated to treat acute asthma exacerbations and should not be used for treatment of acute bronchospasm of status asthmaticus.

Pharmacology/Pharmacokinetics

Physicochemical characteristics
Source—Omalizumab is produced by a Chinese hamster ovary cell suspension culture in a nutrient medium containing the antibiotic gentamicin. Gentamicin is not detectable in the final product.

Molecular weight—149 kilodaltons.

Mechanism of action/Effect
Omalizumab inhibits the binding of IgE to the high-affinity IgE receptor (Fc[epsiv]RI) on the surface of mast cells and basophils. Reduction in surface-bound IgE on Fc[epsiv]RI-bearing cells limits the degree of release of mediators of the allergic response. Treatment with omalizumab also reduces the number of Fc[epsiv]RI receptors on basophils in atopic patients.

Absorption
Slow; Absolute bioavailability: 62%

Distribution
Vol_D: 78 ± 32 mL/kg

Half-life
Serum elimination half-life: 26 days

Time to peak concentration
Peak serum concentrations: 7 to 8 days

Elimination
Clearance of omalizumab involves IgG clearance processes as well as clearance via specific binding and complex formation with its target ligand, IgE. Liver elimination of IgG includes degradation in the liver reticuloendothelial system (RES) and endothelial cells. Intact IgG is also excreted in bile. In studies with mice and monkeys, omalizumab: IgE complexes were eliminated by interactions with Fc receptors within the RES at rates that were generally faster than IgG clearance. In asthma patients the apparent clearance averages 2.4 ± 1.1 mL/kg/day. In addition, doubling body weight approximately doubled apparent clearance.

Precautions to Consider

Carcinogenicity/Mutagenicity
No long-term studies have been performed in animals to evaluate the carcinogenic potential of omalizumab. No evidence of mutagenic activity was observed in Ames tests using six different strains of bacteria with and without metabolic activation at omalizumab concentrations up to 5000 mcg/mL.

Pregnancy/Reproduction
Fertility—The effects of omalizumab on male and female fertility have been assessed in cynomolgus monkey studies. Administration of omalizumab at doses up to and including 75 mg/kg/week did not elicit reproductive toxicity in male cynomolgus monkeys and did not inhibit reproductive capability, including implantation, in female cynomolgus monkeys. These doses provide a 2- to 16-fold safety factor based on total dose and 2- to 5-fold safety factor based on AUC over the range of adult clinical doses.

Pregnancy—Adequate and well-controlled studies of omalizumab in pregnant women have not been done. Because animal reproduction studies are not always predictive of human response, omalizumab should be used during pregnancy only if clearly needed. IgG molecules are known to cross the placental barrier.

Reproduction studies in cynomolgus monkeys have been conducted with omalizumab. Subcutaneous doses up to 75 mg/kg (12-fold the maximum clinical dose) of omalizumab did not elicit maternal toxicity, embryotoxicity, or teratogenicity when administered throughout organogenesis and did not elicit adverse effects on fetal or neonatal growth when administered throughout late gestation, delivery, and nursing.

FDA Pregnancy Category B

Breast-feeding
It is not known whether omalizumab is distributed into breast milk. However, IgG is distributed in human milk and therefore it is expected that omalizumab will be present in human milk. The potential for omalizumab absorption or harm to the infant are unknown; caution should be exercised when administering omalizumab to a nursing woman.

The excretion of omalizumab in milk was evaluated in female cynomolgus monkeys receiving subcutaneous doses of 75 mg/kg/week. Neonatal plasma levels of omalizumab after in utero exposure and 28 days of nursing were between 11% and 94% of the maternal plasma level. Milk levels of omalizumab were 1.5% of maternal blood concentration.

Pediatrics
Appropriate studies have not been performed on the relationship of age to the effects of omalizumab in the pediatric population. Safety and effectiveness in pediatric patients below the age of 12 have not been established.

Geriatrics
Appropriate studies performed to date have not demonstrated geriatrics-specific problems that would limit the use of omalizumab in the elderly. In clinical trials 134 patients 65 years of age or older were treated with omalizumab. Although there were no apparent age-related differences observed in these studies, the number of patients aged 65 and over is not sufficient to determine whether they respond differently from younger patients.

Drug interactions and/or related problems
The following drug interactions and/or related problems have been selected on the basis of their potential clinical significance (possible mechanism in parentheses where appropriate)—not necessarily inclusive (» = major clinical significance):

Note: No formal drug interaction studies have been performed with omalizumab. The concomitant use of omalizumab and allergen immunotherapy has not been evaluated.

Laboratory value alterations
The following have been selected on the basis of their potential clinical significance (possible effect in parentheses where appropriate)—not necessarily inclusive (» = major clinical significance).

With physiology/laboratory test values

Serum IgE

(Serum total IgE levels increase following administration of omalizumab due to formation of omalizumab:IgE complexes. Elevated serum total IgE levels may persist for up to 1 year following discontinuation of omalizumab. Serum total IgE levels obtained less than 1 year following discontinuation may not reflect steady state free IgE levels and should not be used to reassess the dosing regimen.)

Medical considerations/Contraindications
The medical considerations/contraindications included have been selected on the basis of their potential clinical significance (reasons given in parentheses where appropriate)—not necessarily inclusive (» = major clinical significance).

Except under special circumstances, this medication should not be used when the following medical problem exists:

» Hypersensitivity to omalizumab or any of its ingredients

Patient monitoring
The following may be especially important in patient monitoring (other tests may be warranted in some patients, depending on condition; » = major clinical significance):

» Anaphylaxis

(Anaphylaxis has occurred within 2 hours of the first or subsequent administration of omalizumab in 3 [< 0.1%] patients without other identifiable allergic triggers. These events included urticaria and throat and/or tongue edema. Patients should be observed after injection of omalizumab, and medications for the treatment of severe hypersensitivity reactions including anaphylaxis should be available. If a severe hypersensitivity reaction to omalizumab occurs, therapy should be discontinued.)

Malignancy

(Malignant neoplasms were observed in 20 of 4127 [0.5%] omalizumab-treated patients compared with 5 of 2236 [0.2%] control patients in clinical studies of asthma and other allergic disorders. The observed malignancies in omalizumab-treated patients were a variety of types, with breast, non-melanoma skin, prostate, melanoma, and parotid occurring more than once, and five other types occurring once each. The majority of patients were observed for less than 1 year. The impact of longer exposure to omalizumab or use in patients at higher risk for malignancy [e.g., elderly, current smokers] is not known.)

Side/Adverse Effects
The following side/adverse effects have been selected on the basis of their potential clinical significance (possible signs and symptoms in parentheses where appropriate)—not necessarily inclusive:

The most serious adverse reactions occurring in clinical studies with omalizumab are malignancies and anaphylaxis. The observed incidence of malignancy among omalizumab-treated patients (0.5%) was numerically higher than among patients in control groups (0.2%). Anaphylactic reactions were rare but temporally associated with omalizumab administration.

Those indicating need for medical attention

Incidence rare

Anaphylaxis (cough; difficulty swallowing; dizziness; fast heartbeat; hives; itching; puffiness or swelling of the eyelids or around the eyes, face, lips or tongue; shortness of breath; skin rash; tightness in chest; unusual tiredness or weakness; wheezing); ***malignant neoplasm***—various types

Those indicating need for medical attention only if they continue or are bothersome

Incidence more frequent

Arthralgia (muscle or joint pain); ***headache; injection site reaction*** (bleeding; blistering; burning; coldness; discoloration of skin; feeling of pressure; hives; infection; inflammation; itching; lumps; numbness; pain; rash; redness; scarring; soreness; stinging; swelling; tenderness; tingling; ulceration; warmth); ***leg pain; pain; pharyngitis*** (body aches or pain; congestion; cough; dryness or soreness of throat; fever; hoarseness; runny nose; tender, swollen glands in neck; trouble in swallowing; voice changes); ***sinusitis*** (pain or tenderness around eyes and cheekbones; fever; stuffy or runny nose; headache; cough; shortness of breath or troubled breathing; tightness of chest or wheezing); ***upper respiratory tract infection*** (cough; sore throat); ***viral infections*** (chills; cough or hoarseness; fever; cold or flu-like symptoms)

Incidence less frequent or rare

Arm pain; dermatitis (blistering, crusting, irritation, itching, or reddening of skin; cracked, dry, scaly skin; swelling); ***dizziness; earache; fatigue*** (unusual tiredness or weakness); ***immunogenicity*** (body produces substances that can bind to drug making it less effective or cause side effects); ***pruritus*** (itching skin)

Overdose

For more information on the management of overdose or unintentional ingestion, **contact a poison control center** (see *Poison Control Center Listing*).

The maximum tolerated dose of omalizumab has not been determined. Single intravenous doses of up to 4000 mg have been administered to patients without evidence of dose-limiting toxicities. The highest cumulative dose administered to patients was 44,000 mg over a 20-week period, which was not associated with toxicities.

Patient Consultation

As an aid to patient consultation, refer to *Advice for the Patient, Omalizumab (Systemic)*.

In providing consultation, consider emphasizing the following selected information (» = major clinical significance):

Before using this medication

» Conditions affecting use, especially:
Hypersensitivity to omalizumab
Use in children—Safety and effectiveness in pediatric patients below the age of 12 have not been established.
No formal drug interaction studies have been performed with omalizumab.

Proper use of this medication

» Proper dosing
A blood test before starting treatment and your weight will determine your dose
» Importance of remaining in the clinic or healthcare facility the entire observation period determined by your doctor
» Omalizumab should not be used for the treatment of acute bronchospasm or status asthmaticus
Proper storage

Precautions while using this medication

Asthma may not immediately improve

Discontinuation of treatment can result in asthma symptoms returning

Knowing signs and symptoms of anaphylaxis and getting immediate medical attention

Do not suddenly stop taking or change your dose of your inhaled steroids or other asthma medicine you are taking unless your doctor tells you to do so.

Side/adverse effects

Signs of potential side effects, especially anaphylaxis and malignant neoplasms

General Dosing Information

For parenteral dosing forms

Omalizumab has not been shown to alleviate asthma exacerbations acutely and should not be used for the treatment of acute bronchospasm or status asthmaticus.

Systemic or inhaled corticosteroids should not be abruptly discontinued upon initiation of omalizumab therapy. Decreases in corticosteroids should be performed under the direct supervision of a physician and may need to be performed gradually.

Patients receiving omalizumab should be told not to decrease the dose of, or stop taking any other asthma medications unless otherwise instructed by their physician. Patients should be told that they may not see immediate improvement in their asthma after beginning omalizumab therapy.

Treatment of adverse effects

An observation period of the patient is recommended and medications for the treatment of severe hypersensitivity reactions, including anaphylaxis should be available.

Parenteral Dosage Forms

OMALIZUMAB FOR INJECTION

Usual adult dose

Asthma, persistent, moderate to severe (prophylaxis)—
Subcutaneous, 150 to 375 mg every 2 or 4 weeks.
Doses (mg) and dosing frequency are determined by serum total IgE level (IU/mL), measured before the start of treatment, and body weight (kg). Doses of more than 150 mg are divided among more than one injection site to limit injections to not more than 150 mg per site.
Total IgE levels are elevated during treatment and remain elevated for up to one year after the discontinuation of treatment. Therefore, re-testing of IgE levels during omalizumab treatment cannot be used as a guide for dose determination. Dose determination after treatment interruptions lasting less than 1 year should be based on serum IgE levels obtained at the initial dose determination. Total serum IgE levels may be re-tested for dose determination if treatment with omalizumab has been interrupted for one year or more. Doses should be adjusted for significant changes in body weight.

Table A: ADMINISTRATION EVERY 4 WEEKS—

	30-60 kg	> 60-70 kg	> 70-90 kg	> 90-150 kg
≥30-100 IU/mL	150	150	150	300
> 100-200 IU/mL	300	300	300	See Table B
> 200-300 IU/mL	300	See Table B	See Table B	See Table B
> 300-400 IU/mL	See Table B	See Table B	See Table B	See Table B
> 400-500 IU/mL	See Table B	See Table B	See Table B	See Table B
> 500-600 IU/mL	See Table B	See Table B	See Table B	See Table B

Table B: ADMINISTRATION EVERY 2 WEEKS—

	30-60 kg	> 60-70 kg	> 70-90 kg	> 90-150 kg
≥30-100 IU/mL	See Table A	See Table A	See Table A	See Table A
> 100-200 IU/mL	See Table A	See Table A	See Table A	225
> 200-300 IU/mL	See Table A	225	225	300
> 300-400 IU/mL	225	225	300	Do not dose
> 400-500 IU/mL	300	300	375	Do not dose
> 500-600 IU/mL	300	375	Do not dose	Do not dose
> 600-700 IU/mL	375	Do not dose	Do not dose	Do not dose

Usual pediatric dose

See *Usual adult dose* for pediatric patients 12 years of age and older.

Usual geriatric dose

See *Usual adult dose.*

Strength(s) usually available

U.S.—
202.5 mg (Rx) [*Xolair* (sucrose; L-histidine hydrochloride monohydrate; L-histidine; polysorbate 20)].

Canada—
Not commercially available

Packaging and storage

Omalizumab should be shipped at controlled ambient temperature (<30°C [<86°F]). Omalizumab should be stored under refrigerated conditions 2-8°C (36-46°F). Do not use beyond the expiration date stamped on carton.

Reconstituted omalizumab vials should be protected from direct sunlight.

Preparation of dosage form

The lyophilized product takes 15-20 minutes to dissolve. The fully reconstituted product will appear clear or slightly opalescent and may have a few small bubbles or foam around the edge of the vial. The reconstituted product is somewhat viscous; in order to obtain the full 1.2 mL dose, ALL OF THE PRODUCT MUST BE WITHDRAWN from the vial before expelling any air or excess solution from the syringe.

Draw 1.4 mL of Sterile Water for Injection, USP into a 3-cc syringe equipped with a 1-inch, 18-gauge needle.

Place the vial upright on a flat surface and using standard aseptic technique, insert the needle and inject the Sterile Water for Injection, USP directly onto the product.

Keeping the vial upright, gently swirl the upright vial for approximately 1 minute to evenly wet the powder. Do not shake.

Gently swirl the vial for 5-10 seconds approximately every 5 minutes in order to dissolve any remaining solids. There should be no visible gel-like particles in the solution. Do not use if foreign particles are present. Some vials may take longer than 20 minutes to dissolve completely. If this is the case, repeat until there are no visible gel-like particles in the solution. It is acceptable to have small bubbles or foam around the edge of the vial. Do not use if the contents of the vial do not dissolve completely by 40 minutes.

Invert the vial for 15 seconds in order to allow the solution to drain toward the stopper. Using a new 3-cc syringe equipped with a 1-inch, 18-gauge needle, insert the needle into the inverted vial. Position the needle tip at the very bottom of the solution in the vial stopper when drawing the solution into the syringe. Before removing the needle from the vial, pull the plunger all the way back to the end of the syringe barrel in order to remove all of the solution from the inverted vial.

Replace the 18-gauge needle with a 25-gauge needle for subcutaneous injection.

Expel air, large bubbles, and any excess solution in order to obtain the required 1.2 mL dose. A thin layer of small bubbles may remain at the top of the solution in the syringe.

Number of injections and the total volume injected can be found in the table below. There is a 1.2 mL maximum delivered volume per vial.

Dose (mg)	Number of Injections	Total Volume Injected (mL)
150	1	1.2
225	2	1.8
300	2	2.4
375	3	3.0

Stability

Omalizumab is for single use only and contains no preservatives. The solution should be used for subcutaneous administration within 8 hours following reconstitution when stored in the vial at 2-8ºC (36-46ºF), or within 4 hours of reconstitution when stored at room temperature.

Auxiliary labeling

- For subcutaneous (SC) use only.

Additional information

A vial delivers 1.2 mL (150 mg) of omalizumab.

Because the solution is slightly viscous, the injection may take 5-10 seconds to administer.

Developed: 04/07/2004

OMEGA-3-ACID ETHYL ESTERS Systemic†

VA CLASSIFICATION (Primary): CV359

Commonly used brand name(s): *Omacor*.

Note: For a listing of dosage forms and brand names by country availability, see *Dosage Forms* section(s).

†Not commercially available in Canada.

Category

Antihyperlipidemic.

Indications

Accepted

Hypertriglyceridemia (treatment)—Omega-3-acid ethyl esters is indicated as an adjunct to diet to reduce very high (≥ 500 mg/dL) triglyceride (TG) levels in adult patients.

Pharmacology/Pharmacokinetics

Physicochemical characteristics

Source—Omega-3-acid ethyl esters is predominately a combination of ethyl esters of eicosapentaenoic acid (EPA) and docosahexaenoic acid (DHA).

Molecular weight—
EPA ethyl ester: 330.51.
DHA ethyl ester: 356.55.

Mechanism of action/Effect

Although the mechanism of action for omega-3-acid ethyl esters is not completely understood, possible mechanisms of action include inhibition of acyl CoA:1,2-diacylglycerol acyltransferase and increased peroxisomal β-oxidation in the liver. Omega-3-acid ethyl ester may reduce the synthesis of triglycerides in the liver because EPA and DHA are poor substrates for the enzymes responsible for TG synthesis and they inhibit esterification of other fatty acids.

Absorption

EPA and DHA were absorbed when administered as ethyl ester orally in both healthy volunteers and patients with hypertriglyceridemia. However, omega-3-acids administered as ethyl esters induced significant dose-dependent increases in serum phospholipid EPA. Increases in DHA content were less marked and not dose-dependent. Uptake of EPA and DHA into phospholipids in patients given omega-3-acid ethyl esters was independent of age (< 49 years vs. ≥ 49 years), however females have greater uptake of EPA into serum phospholipids than males.

Precautions to Consider

Cross-sensitivity and/or related problems

Omega-3-acid ethyl esters should be used with caution in patients with known sensitivity or allergy to fish.

Carcinogenicity

Carcinogenicity studies done in male rats given oral doses of 100, 600, 2000 mg/kg/day for 101 weeks and in female rats given the same doses for 89 weeks showed no evidence of increase incidence of tumors. Standard lifetime carcinogenicity studies have not been done in mice.

Mutagenicity

No evidence of mutagenicity or clastogenicity was found in *in vitro* tests, with and without metabolic activation, including the Ames test with *Salmonella typhimurium* and *Escherichia coli*, the chromosomal aberration assay in Chinese hamster lung cells or human lymphocytes, or in the *in vivo* mouse micronucleus test.

Pregnancy/Reproduction

Fertility—No adverse effects on fertility were observed in studies in rats given doses up to 2000 mg/kg/day (5 times the human systemic exposure following an oral dose of 4 g/day based on body surface area comparison). Male rats were treated for 10 weeks prior to mating and female rats were treated 2 weeks prior to and throughout mating, gestation and lactation.

Pregnancy—Adequate and well controlled studies in humans have not been done. Omega-3-acids should be used during pregnancy only if the potential benefit justifies the potential risk to the fetus.

Studies in animals have shown that omega-3-acid ethyl esters have been shown to have an embryocidal effect in pregnant rats when given doses resulting in exposures 7 times the recommended human dose of 4 g/day based on a body surface area comparison. However no adverse effects were seen in the high dose group given 200 mg/kg/day (5 times the recommended human dose of 4 g/day based on a body surface area comparison) when given to pregnant rats from gestation day 14 through lactation day 21. No adverse effects were observed in female rats given doses (5 times the recommended human dose of 4 g/day based on a body surface area comparison) prior to mating, and through gestation and lactation or in pregnant rats given doses up to 6000 mg/kg/day (14 times the recommended human dose of 4 g/day based on a body surface area comparison) from gestation day 6 through 15.

Studies done in pregnant rabbits given oral doses (2 times the recommended human dose of 4 g/day based on a body surface area comparison) from gestation day 7 through 19 revealed no adverse effects in fetuses. However rabbits given higher doses (4 times the recommended human dose of 4 g/day based on a body surface area comparison) did show evidence of maternal toxicity.

FDA Pregnancy Category C

Breast-feeding

It is not known whether omega-3-acid ethyl esters are distributed into breast milk. Because many drugs are distributed into breast milk, caution should be exercised when omega-3-acid ethyl esters are administered to a nursing woman.

Pediatrics
Safety and effectiveness in pediatric patients under 18 years of age have not been established.

Geriatrics
Appropriate studies performed to date have not demonstrated geriatrics-specific problems that would limit the usefulness of omega-3-acid ethyl esters in the elderly.

Drug interactions and/or related problems
The following drug interactions and/or related problems have been selected on the basis of their potential clinical significance (possible mechanism in parentheses where appropriate)—not necessarily inclusive (» = major clinical significance):

Note: Combinations containing any of the following medications, depending on the amount present, may also interact with this medication.

» Anticoagulants
(prolongation of bleeding time may occur; monitor bleeding time periodically when anticoagulants are used concurrently with omega-3-acid ethyl esters.)

» Beta blockers or
» Estrogens or
» Thiazides
(medications known to exacerbate hypertriglyceridemia (HTG) should be discontinued or changed before considering TG-lowering drug therapy.)

Laboratory value alterations
The following have been selected on the basis of their potential clinical significance (possible effect in parentheses where appropriate)—not necessarily inclusive (» = major clinical significance).

With diagnostic test results
Transaminases, serum
(increases in ALT levels without concurrent increases in AST levels have been observed)

Medical considerations/Contraindications
The medical considerations/contraindications included have been selected on the basis of their potential clinical significance (reasons given in parentheses where appropriate)—not necessarily inclusive (» = major clinical significance).

Except under special circumstances, this medication should not be used when the following medical problem exists:

» Hypersensitivity to omega-3-acid ethyl esters or any component of the medication

Patient monitoring
The following may be especially important in patient monitoring (other tests may be warranted in some patients, depending on condition; » = major clinical significance):

Alanine aminotransferase (ALT) levels
(monitor periodically during treatment with omega-3-acid ethyl esters)

» Low-density lipoprotein cholesterol (LDL-C)
(treatment to reduce very high TG levels may result in elevations in LDL-C and non LDL-C; patients should be monitored to ensure that LDL-C levels do not increase excessively)

Prolongation of bleeding time
(patients receiving treatment with both omega-3-acid ethyl esters and anticoagulants should be monitored periodically)

» TG levels
(periodic testing during therapy should be performed to measure patients' TG levels and therapy withdrawn in patients who do not have an adequate response after 2 months of treatment)

Side/Adverse Effects
The following side/adverse effects have been selected on the basis of their potential clinical significance (possible signs and symptoms in parentheses where appropriate)—not necessarily inclusive:

Those indicating need for medical attention
Incidence less frequent

Angina pectoris (arm, back or jaw pain; chest pain or discomfort; chest tightness or heaviness; fast or irregular heartbeat; shortness of breath; sweating; nausea); ***dyspnea*** (shortness of breath; difficult or labored breathing; tightness in chest; wheezing)

Those indicating need for medical attention only if they continue or are bothersome
Incidence less frequent

Back pain; eructation (belching; bloated full feeling; excess air or gas in stomach); ***flu syndrome*** (chills; cough; diarrhea; fever; general feeling of discomfort or illness; headache; joint pain; loss of appetite; muscle aches and pains; nausea; runny nose; shivering sore throat; sweating; trouble sleeping; unusual tiredness or weakness; vomiting); ***infection*** (fever or chills; cough or hoarseness; lower back or side pain; painful or difficult urination); ***pain; rash; taste perversion*** (change in taste bad unusual or unpleasant (after)taste)

Overdose
For more information on the management of overdose or unintentional ingestion, **contact a poison control center** (see *Poison Control Center Listing*).

Treatment of overdose
There is no known specific antidote to omega-3-acid ethyl esters. Treatment is generally symptomatic and supportive.

Supportive care—
Patients in whom intentional overdose is confirmed or suspected should be referred for psychiatric consultation.

Patient Consultation
As an aid to patient consultation, refer to *Advice for the Patient, Omega-3-Acid Ethyl Esters (Systemic).*

In providing consultation, consider emphasizing the following selected information (» = major clinical significance):

Before using this medication
» Conditions affecting use, especially:
Hypersensitivity to omega-3-acid ethyl esters or any component of the medication
Pregnancy—Adequate and well controlled studies in humans have not been done. Omega-3-acids should be used during pregnancy only if the potential benefit justifies the potential risk to the fetus.
Breast-feeding—It is not known whether omega-3-acid ethyl esters are distributed into breast milk. Because many drugs are distributed into breast milk, caution should be exercised when omega-3-acid ethyl esters are administered to a nursing woman.
Use in children—Safety and effectiveness in pediatric patients under 18 years of age have not been established.

Proper use of this medication
Compliance with therapy; taking medication at the same time each day to maintain the antihyperlipidemic effect
Compliance with prescribed diet during treatment
» Proper dosing
Missed dose: Taking as soon as possible; not taking if almost time for next scheduled dose; not doubling doses
» Proper storage

Precautions while using this medication
Regular visits to physician to check progress
Not using alcohol excessively because elevations of liver enzymes may occur

Side/adverse effects
Signs of potential side effects, especially angina pectoris or dyspnea

General Dosing Information
Prior to starting omega-3-acid ethyl esters therapy, secondary causes for hyperlipidemia, such as poorly controlled diabetes mellitus, hypothyroidism, and alcoholism should be excluded and a laboratory test performed to measure triglycerides (TG).

Medication known to exacerbate HTG (such as beta blockers, thiazides, and estrogens) should be discontinued or changed before considering TG-lowering drug therapy.

The importance of advising patients that the use of lipid-regulating agents dose not reduce the importance of adhering to diet.

Diet/Nutrition
May be taken with meals.

Prior to treatment with omega-3-acid ethyl esters, control of hypertriglyceridemia with diet, exercise, weight reduction in obese patients, and treatment of underlying medical problems should be attempted. The patient should be placed on a standard cholesterol-lowering diet before receiving omega-3-acid ethyl esters and should continue on this diet during treatment with omega-3-acid ethyl esters.

For additional information on initial therapeutic guidelines related to the treatment of hyperlipidemia, see *Appendix III*.

Oral Dosage Forms
OMEGA-3-ACID ETHYL ESTERS CAPSULES
Usual adult dose
Antitriglyceridemic—
Oral, 4 grams per day. The daily dose may be taken as a single 4-g dose (4 capsules) or as two 2-g doses (2 capsules given twice daily).

Note: Patients should be placed on an appropriate lipid lowering diet before receiving treatment with omega-3-acid ethyl esters and then continue the diet throughout treatment.

Usual pediatric dose
Safety and efficacy have not been established.

Usual geriatric dose
See *Usual adult dose.*

Strength(s) usually available
U.S.—

1 g (Rx) [*Omacor* (α-tocopherol [in a carrier of partially hydrogenated vegetable oils including soybean oil] and gelatin; glycerol; purified water)].

Packaging and storage
Store at 25 °C (77 °F); excursions permitted to 15° to 30 °C (59° to 86 °F). Protect from freezing.

Auxiliary labeling
- Keep out of reach of children.
- Do not freeze.

Developed: 01/18/2005

OMEPRAZOLE Systemic

VA CLASSIFICATION (Primary): GA304

Commonly used brand name(s): *Losec; Prilosec; Zegerid.*

Note: For a listing of dosage forms and brand names by country availability, see *Dosage Forms* section(s).

Category
Gastric acid pump inhibitor; antiulcer agent.

Indications
Note: Bracketed information in the *Indications* section refers to uses that are not included in U.S. product labeling.

Accepted
Dyspepsia (treatment)—Omeprazole is indicated for the treatment of a complex of symptoms which may be caused by any of the conditions where a reduction in gastric acid secretion is required (e.g., duodenal ulcer, gastric ulcer, nonsteroidal anti-inflammatory drugs [NSAID]–associated gastric and duodenal ulcer, reflux esophagitis, gastroesophageal reflux disease [GERD]) or when no identifiable organic cause is found (i.e., functional dyspepsia)

Gastroesophageal reflux disease [GERD] (prophylaxis and treatment)—Omeprazole is indicated for the treatment of heartburn and other symptoms associated with gastroesophageal reflux disease. Omeprazole is indicated for the short-term treatment of erosive esophagitis (associated with GERD) that has been diagnosed by endoscopy. Omeprazole also is indicated to maintain healing of erosive esophagitis.

Hypersecretory conditions, gastric (treatment)
Zollinger-Ellison syndrome (treatment)
Mastocytosis, systemic (treatment) or
Adenoma, multiple endocrine (treatment)—Omeprazole is indicated for the long-term treatment of pathologic gastric hypersecretion associated with Zollinger-Ellison syndrome (alone or as part of multiple endocrine neoplasia Type-1), systemic mastocytosis, and multiple endocrine adenoma.

Ulcer, peptic (treatment)
Ulcer, duodenal (treatment)—Omeprazole is indicated for the short-term treatment of active duodenal ulcer and active benign gastric ulcer.

Ulcer, peptic, *Helicobacter pylori*–associated (treatment adjunct)—Omeprazole is indicated in combination with clarithromycin [and amoxicillin or metronidazole] for the treatment of duodenal and gastric ulcer associated with *H. pylori* infection. Eradication of *H. pylori* has been shown to reduce the risk of ulcer recurrence.

Upper gastrointestinal hemorrhage (prophylaxis)—Omeprazole is indicated for the reduction of risk of upper gastrointestinal bleeding in critically ill patients.

[Ulcer, peptic, nonsteroidal anti-inflammatory drug–induced (treatment)]—Omeprazole is indicated for the treatment of duodenal or gastric ulcers associated with the use of nonsteroidal anti-inflammatory drugs (NSAIDs).

Pharmacology/Pharmacokinetics

Physicochemical characteristics
Chemical Group—Substituted benzimidazole
Molecular weight—345.42.
pKa—4 and 8.8.
Solubility—Freely soluble in ethanol and methanol; slightly soluble in acetone and isopropanol and very slightly soluble in water.

Mechanism of action/Effect
Omeprazole is a selective and irreversible proton pump inhibitor. Omeprazole suppresses gastric acid secretion by specific inhibition of the hydrogen–potassium adenosinetriphosphatase (H^+, K^+-ATPase) enzyme system found at the secretory surface of parietal cells. It inhibits the final transport of hydrogen ions (via exchange with potassium ions) into the gastric lumen. Since the H^+, K^+-ATPase enzyme system is regarded as the acid (proton) pump of the gastric mucosa, omeprazole is known as a gastric acid pump inhibitor. The inhibitory effect is dose-related. Omeprazole inhibits both basal and stimulated acid secretion irrespective of the stimulus.

Omeprazole does not have anticholinergic or histamine H_2-receptor antagonist properties.

Other actions/effects
Omeprazole has demonstrated antimicrobial activity *in vitro* against *Helicobacter pylori*, by selective inhibition of *H. pylori* urease, which is necessary for gastric colonization.

Omeprazole has the ability to inhibit the hepatic cytochrome P450 mixed function oxidase system.

Absorption
Rapid.

Absolute bioavailability is about 30 to 40% at doses of twenty to forty milligrams, due in large part to presystemic metabolism. Bioavailability in patients with chronic hepatic disease is about 100%, reflecting decreased first-pass effect. Bioavailability in healthy elderly volunteers was 76%, as compared with 58% in young volunteers.

AUC for powder for oral suspension—1446 ng*hr per mL

When omeprazole powder for oral suspension is given one hour after a meal, AUC is reduced by 24% compared to administration prior to a meal.

Distribution
Distributed in tissue, particularly gastric parietal cells.

Protein binding
Very high (approximately 95%, bound to albumin and $alpha_1$-acid glycoprotein).

Biotransformation
Hepatic, extensive. Omeprazole is subject to saturable, first-pass metabolism, and is completely and rapidly metabolized by the hepatic P450 (CYP) enzyme system.

Half-life
Plasma—

Normal hepatic function: 30 minutes to 1 hour.
Chronic hepatic disease: 3 hours.

Onset of action
Within one hour.

Time to peak concentration
Within 30 minutes to 3.5 hours.

Peak plasma concentration:
C_{max}—902 ng per mL for powder for oral suspension on day 7 of 20-mg once-daily dosing

When omeprazole powder for oral suspension is given one hour after a meal, C_{max} is reduced by 63% compared to administration prior to a meal.

Time to peak effect
Within 2 hours.

Duration of action
Up to 72 hours or more (96 hours required for full restoration of acid production).

Elimination
Renal—70 to 77%. No unchanged omeprazole was detected in urine. Two metabolites eliminated in urine have been identified as hydroxyomeprazole and the corresponding carboxylic acid.

Fecal—18 to 23%; significant biliary elimination of omeprazole metabolites

Total body clearance—500 to 600 mL per minute

In dialysis—Not readily dialyzable, because of extensive protein binding.

Precautions to Consider

Carcinogenicity/Tumorigenicity/Mutagenicity

In two 2-year studies in rats, omeprazole, given in doses corresponding to 4 to 352 times the human dose, caused end-life gastric carcinoid tumors and enterochromaffin-like (ECL) cell hyperplasia in a dose-related manner in both male and female animals. Incidence was markedly higher in female rats, which had higher blood levels of omeprazole. These ECL cell changes have been shown to be caused by high levels of gastrin (or hypergastrinemia). Pronounced acid inhibition at extremely high doses of gastric acid pump inhibitors or H_2-receptor antagonists results in the same feedback elevation of gastrin and subsequent ECL cell changes of the stomach. Gastric carcinoids seldom occur in the untreated rat. Additionally, ECL cell hyperplasia was present in all treated groups of both sexes. In one of the studies, female rats were treated with about 2.8 times the human dose of 40 mg per day based on body surface area for one year, then followed for an additional year without the drug. No carcinoids were seen in these rats. An increased incidence of treatment-related ECL cell hyperplasia was observed at the end of one year. By the second year, the difference was much smaller but still showed more hyperplasia in the treated group. An unusual primary malignant tumor in the stomach was seen in one rat. No similar tumor was seen in male or female rats treated for two years. For this strain of rat no similar tumor has been noted historically, but a finding involving only one tumor is difficult to interpret.

In a 52-week study in Sprague-Dawley rats, brain astrocytomas were found in a small number of males that received omeprazole about 0.2 to 6.4 times the human dose of 20 mg per day, based on body surface area. No astrocytomas were observed in female rats in this study. In a 2-year carcinogenicity study in Sprague-Dawley rats, no astrocytomas were found in males or females at a high dose about 57 times the human dose. A 78-week mouse carcinogenicity study of omeprazole did not show increased tumor occurrence, but the study was not conclusive. A 26-week p53 (±) transgenic mouse carcinogenicity study was negative.

Omeprazole was not mutagenic in the Ames test, in an *in vitro* mouse lymphoma cell assay, and in an *in vivo* rat liver DNA damage assay. A mouse micronucleus test at 625 and 6250 times the human dose gave a positive result for clastogenic effects, as did an *in vivo* bone marrow chromosome aberration test and an *in vitro* human lymphocyte chromosomal aberration assay. A second mouse micronucleus test at 2000 times the human dose, but with different (suboptimal) sampling times, was negative.

Pregnancy/Reproduction

Fertility—In a rat fertility and general reproductive performance test, omeprazole, in a dose 35 to 345 times the human dose, was not toxic or deleterious to the reproductive performance of parental animals.

Pregnancy—Adequate and well-controlled studies in humans have not been done. Sporadic instances of congenital abnormalities in infants born to women who received omeprazole during pregnancy have been reported. Omeprazole should be used during pregnancy only if the potential benefit to pregnant women justifies the potential risk to the fetus.

An expert review of published data on experiences with omeprazole use during pregnancy by the Teratogen Information System [TERIS] concluded that therapeutic doses during pregnancy are unlikely to pose a substantial teratogenic risk (the quantity and quality of data were assessed as fair).

Several studies have reported no apparent adverse short term effects on the infant when single dose oral or intravenous omeprazole was administered to over 200 pregnant women as premedication for cesarean section under general anesthesia.

Studies in pregnant rats did not show omeprazole to have any teratogenic potential at doses 345 times the human dose. Omeprazole produced dose-related increases in embryo-lethality, fetal resorptions, and pregnancy disruptions in rabbits receiving 17 to 172 times the human dose. In rats, dose-related embryo/fetal toxicity and postnatal developmental toxicity were observed in offspring resulting from parents treated with 35 to 345 times the human dose.

Note: The powder for oral suspension formulation of omeprazole contains sodium bicarbonate. Chronic use of sodium bicarbonate may lead to systemic alkalosis and increased sodium intake can produce edema and weight increase. There are no adequate and well-controlled studies in pregnant women. Therefore, risk-benefit should be considered.

FDA Pregnancy Category C.

Breast-feeding

Omeprazole has been shown to be distributed into human milk following oral administration of 20 mg. The peak concentration of omeprazole in breast milk was less than 7% of the peak serum concentration which corresponds to 0.004 mg of omeprazole per 200 mL of breast milk. In rats, omeprazole administration during late gestation and lactation at doses about 2.8 to 28 times the 40 mg per day human dose based on body surface area resulted in decreased weight gain in pups. Because omeprazole is distributed into human milk with the potential for serious adverse reaction in nursing infants, and because of the potential for tumorigenicity shown in rat carcinogenicity studies, a decision should be made to discontinue nursing or to discontinue the drug, taking into account the importance of the drug to the mother.

Note: In addition, sodium bicarbonate which is present in the powder for oral suspension formulation should be used with caution in nursing mothers.

Pediatrics

Appropriate studies on the relationship of age to the effects of omeprazole have not been performed in the pediatric population. Safety and efficacy have not been established in patients less than 18 years of age.

Geriatrics

No information is available on the relationship of age to the effects of omeprazole in geriatric patients. However, a somewhat decreased rate of elimination and an increased bioavailability are more likely to occur in geriatric patients taking omeprazole. Greater sensitivity of some older individuals can not be ruled out; however, no dosage adjustment is necessary in the elderly.

Pharmacogenetics

Pharmacokinetic studies in Asian subjects receiving single 20-mg doses of omeprazole showed an approximately fourfold increase in the area under the plasma concentration-time curve (AUC) as compared to Caucasian subjects. Dosage adjustments should be considered for Asian patients, especially for prophylaxis of recurrence of erosive esophagitis.

Drug interactions and/or related problems

The following drug interactions and/or related problems have been selected on the basis of their potential clinical significance (possible mechanism in parentheses where appropriate)—not necessarily inclusive (» = major clinical significance):

Note: Only specific interactions between omeprazole and other medications have been identified in this monograph. However, omeprazole, by increasing gastric pH, has the potential to affect the bioavailability of any medication for which absorption is pH-dependent. Also, omeprazole may prevent the degradation of acid-labile drugs.

In addition, because of omeprazole's ability to inhibit hepatic microsomal drug metabolism, elimination of other medications that require hepatic metabolism via the cytochrome P450 system or that are highly extracted by the liver may be decreased during concurrent use with omeprazole.

Combinations containing any of the following medications, depending on the amount present, may also interact with this medication.

Ampicillin esters
Iron salts or
Itraconazole or
Ketoconazole
(omeprazole may increase gastrointestinal pH; concurrent use with omeprazole may result in a reduction in absorption of ampicillin esters, iron salts, itraconazole, or ketoconazole)

» Anticoagulants, coumarin- or indandione-derivative or
» Diazepam or
» Phenytoin or
» Warfarin
(inhibition of the cytochrome P450 enzyme system by omeprazole, especially in high doses, may cause a decrease in the hepatic metabolism of these medications, which may result in delayed elimination and increased blood concentrations, when these medications are used concurrently with omeprazole)
(monitoring of blood concentrations, or prothrombin time for anticoagulants, is recommended as a guide to dosage since dosage adjustment of these medications may be necessary during and after omeprazole therapy to prevent bleeding due to anticoagulant potentiation)

Benzodiazepines or
Cyclosporine or
Disulfiram
(clinical reports of interaction with these drugs metabolized via the cytochrome P-450 system; patients should be monitored to determine necessity of dose adjustments)

Bone marrow depressants (see *Appendix II*)
(concurrent use of omeprazole with these medications may increase the leukopenic and/or thrombocytopenic effects of both these medications; if concurrent use is required, close observation for toxic effects should be considered)

Clarithromycin
(concomitant use has resulted in plasma level increases of omeprazole, clarithromycin, and 14-hydroxy-clarithromycin)

Laboratory value alterations

The following have been selected on the basis of their potential clinical significance (possible effect in parentheses where appropriate)—not necessarily inclusive (» = major clinical significance).

With physiology/laboratory test values
Alanine aminotransferase (ALT [SGPT]) and
Alkaline phosphatase and
Aspartate aminotransferase (AST [SGOT])
(serum values may be increased)

Gastrin, serum
(concentrations will increase during the first 1 to 2 weeks of omeprazole therapy and return to normal after the medication is discontinued; this increase is probably due to the inhibition of acid secretion, which eliminates the negative feedback effect of acid on gastrin secretion; in addition to stimulating gastric acid secretion, gastrin promotes the growth and proliferation of endocrine or enterochromaffin-like [ECL] cells in the gastric mucosa)

Medical considerations/Contraindications

The medical considerations/contraindications included have been selected on the basis of their potential clinical significance (reasons given in parentheses where appropriate)—not necessarily inclusive (» = major clinical significance).

Except under special circumstances, this medication should not be used when the following medical problem exists:

» Hypersensitivity to omeprazole or any of its components

Risk-benefit should be considered when the following medical problems exist:

» Hepatic disease, chronic, current or history of
(dosage reduction may be required due to increased half-life in chronic hepatic disease)

Side/Adverse Effects

Note: Gastric fundic gland polyps have occurred rarely in patients receiving omeprazole; these appear to be benign and reversible upon discontinuance of omeprazole.

Gastroduodenal carcinoids have been reported in patients with Zollinger-Ellison syndrome who have received long-term omeprazole therapy. These carcinoids are believed to be a manifestation of the underlying syndrome, which is known to be associated with such tumors.

Atrophic gastritis has been noted occasionally in gastric corpus biopsies from patient receiving long-term omeprazole therapy.

Overt liver disease has occurred rarely, and included hepatocellular, cholestatic, or mixed hepatitis, liver necrosis (sometimes fatal), hepatic failure (sometimes fatal), and hepatic encephalopathy.

The following side/adverse effects have been selected on the basis of their potential clinical significance (possible signs and symptoms in parentheses where appropriate)—not necessarily inclusive:

Those indicating need for medical attention

Incidence rare

Generalized skin reactions, including toxic epidermal necrolysis (blisters; chills; fever; general feeling of discomfort or illness; muscle aches; red or irritated eyes; redness, tenderness, itching, burning, or peeling of skin; sore throat; sores or ulcers on lips or in mouth)—sometimes fatal; ***Stevens-Johnson syndrome*** (bleeding or crusting sores on lips; chills; fever; muscle cramps; pain; skin rash or itching; sore throat; sores, ulcers, or white spots on lips, in mouth, or on genitals); ***or erythema multiforme*** (blisters on palms of hands and soles of feet; fever; general feeling of discomfort or illness; joint pain; redness of skin); ***hematologic abnormalities, specifically anemia*** (unusual tiredness or weakness); ***agranulocytosis*** (chills; fever; sore throat; unusual tiredness or weakness)—sometimes fatal; ***hemolytic anemia*** (back, leg, or stomach pain; loss of appetite; unusual tiredness or weakness); ***leukocytosis*** (sore throat and fever); ***neutropenia*** (continuing ulcers or sores in mouth); ***pancytopenia or thrombocytopenia*** (unusual bleeding or bruising); ***hematuria*** (bloody urine); ***proteinuria*** (cloudy urine); ***urinary tract infection*** (bloody or cloudy urine; difficult, burning, or painful urination; frequent urge to urinate)

Those indicating need for medical attention only if they continue or are bothersome

Incidence more frequent

Abdominal pain or colic

Incidence less frequent

Asthenia (muscle pain; unusual tiredness); ***back pain; central nervous system (CNS) disturbances, specifically dizziness; headache; somnolence*** (unusual drowsiness); ***or unusual tiredness; chest pain; cough; gastrointestinal disturbances, specifically acid regurgitation*** (heartburn); ***constipation; diarrhea or loose stools; flatulence*** (gas); ***or nausea and vomiting; skin rash or itching; upper respiratory infection (URI)*** (ear congestion; nasal congestion; chills; cough, fever, sneezing, or sore throat; body aches or pain; headache; loss of voice; runny nose; unusual tiredness or weakness; difficulty in breathing)

Overdose

For more information on the management of overdose or unintentional ingestion, **contact a Poison Control Center** (see *Poison Control Center Listing*).

Clinical effects of overdose

The following effects have been selected on the basis of their potential clinical significance (possible signs and symptoms in parentheses where appropriate)—not necessarily inclusive:

Blurred vision; confusion; diaphoresis (increased sweating); ***drowsiness; dryness of mouth; flushing; headache; malaise*** (general feeling of discomfort or illness); ***nausea; tachycardia*** (fast or irregular heartbeat); ***vomiting***

Note: Additionally, sodium bicarbonate (present in omeprazole powder for oral suspension) overdose may cause hypocalcemia, hypokalemia, hypernatremia, and seizures.

Treatment of overdose

Since there is no specific antidote for overdose with omeprazole, treatment should be symptomatic and supportive. Due to extensive protein binding, omeprazole is not readily dialyzable. Patients in whom intentional overdose is confirmed or suspected should be referred for psychiatric consultation.

Patient Consultation

As an aid to patient consultation, refer to *Advice for the Patient, Omeprazole (Systemic).*

In providing consultation, consider emphasizing the following selected information (» = major clinical significance):

Before using this medication

» Conditions affecting use, especially:
Hypersensitivity to omeprazole or any of its components
Pregnancy—Reports of congenital defects; risk-benefit must be considered
Breast-feeding—Distributed into breast milk; may cause potentially serious adverse effects in nursing infants; risk-benefit considerations
Use in children—Safety and efficacy not established
Use in the elderly—No dosage adjustments necessary; greater sensitivity can not be ruled out
Other medications, especially anticoagulants, diazepam, phenytoin or warfarin
Other medical problems, especially chronic hepatic disease or history of or hypersensitivity to omeprazole or any of its components.

Proper use of this medication

Taking the capsule form of this medication immediately before a meal, preferably the morning meal

Taking the powder for oral suspension form of this medication on an empty stomach at least one hour prior to a meal.

If receiving the powder for oral suspension form of this medication through a nasogastric or orogastric tube, suspending enteral feeding approximately 3 hours before and 1 hour after administration of this medication

May take antacids for relief of pain, unless otherwise instructed by physician

Swallowing capsule form of this medication whole; not crushing, breaking, chewing, or opening the capsule

» Using only water and not other liquids or foods to dilute powder for oral suspension.

» Importance of telling physician of medical conditions such as metabolic alkalosis, hypocalcemia, Bartter's syndrome, hypokalemia, respiratory alkalosis, or other conditions affected by the use of sodium bicarbonate. Omeprazole powder for oral suspension contains sodium bicarbonate and it is contraindicated in patients with metabolic alkalosis and hypocalcemia.

» Compliance with full course of therapy

» Proper dosing

Missed dose: Taking as soon as possible; not taking if almost time for next dose; not doubling doses

» Proper storage

Precautions while using this medication

» Regular visits to physician to check progress

Side/adverse effects

Signs of potential side effects, especially generalized skin reactions, hematologic abnormalities, hematuria, proteinuria, and urinary tract infection

General Dosing Information

Omeprazole capsules should be swallowed whole, and not chewed or crushed. Omeprazole magnesium tablets also should be swallowed whole.

Omeprazole powder for oral suspension contains 1680 mg (20 mEq) of sodium bicarbonate. Sodium bicarbonate is contraindicated in patients with metabolic alkalosis and hypocalcemia. Sodium bicarbonate should be used with caution in patients with Bartter's syndrome, hypokalemia, and respiratory alkalosis or nursing mothers. Long-term administration of bicarbonate with calcium or milk can cause milk-alkali syndrome.

Symptomatic response to omeprazole therapy does not preclude the presence of gastric malignancy.

In patients who initially had grades 3 or 4 erosive esophagitis for maintenance after healing, 20 mg daily of omeprazole was effective, while 10 mg did not demonstrate effectiveness

For therapy of dyspepsia, omeprazole usually is used for 4 weeks. If after 2 weeks of treatment the patient does not respond to therapy, or there is an early clinical indication of a lack of efficacy, the patient should be thoroughly investigated in order to rule out organic disease. If there are indications of a clinical response following the initial 2 weeks of treatment, omeprazole may be continued for an additional 2 weeks.

Efficacy of omeprazole used for longer than 8 weeks in patients with GERD or erosive esophagitis has not been established. For therapy of gastrointestinal reflux disease, omeprazole usually is used for short-term (4- to 8-week) courses; however, additional 4- to 8-week courses of treatment may be considered if there is recurrence of severe or symptomatic gastroesophageal reflux poorly responsive to customary medical treatment. Controlled studies of omeprazole used as maintenance therapy to prevent erosive esophagitis recurrence have not been conducted beyond 12 months, although a limited number of patients have received continuous maintenance treatment for up to 6 years. Dosage adjustments should be considered for Asian patients, especially for prophylaxis of erosive esophagitis recurrence, since pharmacokinetic studies in Asian subjects receiving single 20-mg doses of omeprazole showed an approximately fourfold increase in the area under the plasma concentration-time curve (AUC) as compared to Caucasian subjects.

Omeprazole may be taken with antacids.

Initial titration of doses and subsequent dosage adjustment of omeprazole is recommended in the long-term treatment of pathological hypersecretory conditions (e.g., Zollinger-Ellison syndrome, systemic mastocytosis, multiple endocrine adenomas). Doses of up to 120 mg three times a day have been administered. Patients may require at least one increase in dose per year. If the daily dose is greater than 80 mg, it should be administered in divided doses. Zollinger-Ellison syndrome has been treated continuously with omeprazole for more than 5 years.

Diet/Nutrition

Omeprazole *capsules* should be taken immediately before meals. Omeprazole magnesium *tablets* may be taken with food or on an empty stomach. Omeprazole *powder for oral solution* should be taken on an empty stomach one hour before a meal. For patients receiving continuous nasogastric or orogastric tube feeding, enteral feeding should be suspended approximately 3 hours before and 1 hour after administration of omeprazole *powder for oral solution.*

Bioequivalence information

Omeprazole capsules and omeprazole magnesium tablets are not bioequivalent.

Oral Dosage Forms

Note: Dosing recommendations vary between dosage forms; please check the appropriate section for dosage form–specific dosing recommendations.

OMEPRAZOLE DELAYED-RELEASE CAPSULES

Usual adult dose

Gastroesophageal reflux disease (treatment)—

Oral, 20 mg once a day for four to eight weeks.

Note: A dosage of 40 mg once a day has been used for esophagitis associated with gastroesophageal reflux disease refractory to other treatment regimens.

Erosive esophagitis (prophylaxis)—

Oral, 20 mg once a day.

Gastric hypersecretory conditions (e.g., Zollinger-Ellison syndrome, systemic mastocytosis, multiple endocrine adenomas)—

Oral, 60 mg once a day, the dosage being adjusted as needed, and therapy continued for as long as clinically indicated. Doses of up to 120 mg three times a day have been used. If the total daily dose is greater than 80 mg, it should be administered in divided doses.

Duodenal ulcer—

Oral, 20 mg once a day.

Note: The dosage can be increased to 40 mg once a day for duodenal ulcer refractory to other treatment regimens.

Gastric ulcer (treatment)—

Oral, 40 mg once a day for four to eight weeks.

Peptic ulcer associated with *Helicobacter pylori* infection—

Oral, omeprazole 40 mg once a day before breakfast taken in combination with clarithromycin 500 mg three times a day for the first fourteen days. For days 15 through 28, further treatment with omeprazole 20 mg once a day before breakfast follows.

Usual pediatric dose

Safety and efficacy have not been established.

Strength(s) usually available

U.S.—

10 mg (Rx) [*Prilosec*].

20 mg (Rx) [*Prilosec*].

40 mg (Rx) [*Prilosec*].

Canada—

Not commercially available.

Packaging and storage

Store between 15 and 30 °C (59 and 86 °F), in a tight container, unless otherwise specified by manufacturer. Protect from light.

Auxiliary labeling

- Take before meals.
- Swallow capsules whole.

OMEPRAZOLE MAGNESIUM DELAYED-RELEASE TABLETS

Note: The dosing and dosage forms of omeprazole magnesium are expressed in terms of omeprazole base.

Usual adult dose

Dyspepsia (treatment)—

Oral, 20 mg once a day for four weeks. Some patients respond adequately to a dose of 10 mg once a day.

Gastroesophageal reflux disease (treatment)—

Oral, 20 mg once a day for the relief of heartburn and regurgitation. Further investigation is needed if symptom control in not achieved after four weeks of treatment. Some patients respond adequately to a dose of 10 mg once a day. In patients requiring maintenance therapy, doses of 10 mg once a day have been used. For the treatment of reflux esophagitis, 20 mg once a day is recommended. The dosage may be increased to 40 mg once a day for esophagitis refractory to other treatment regimens. In patients requiring maintenance therapy, doses of 10 mg once a day have been used. If reflux esophagitis recurs, the dose may be increased to 20 or 40 mg once a day.

Gastric hypersecretory conditions (e.g., Zollinger-Ellison syndrome, systemic mastocytosis, multiple endocrine adenomas)—

Oral, 60 mg once a day, the dosage being adjusted as needed, and therapy continued for as long as clinically indicated. Doses of up to 120 mg three times a day have been used. If the total daily dose is greater than 80 mg, it should be administered in divided doses and given two times a day.

Duodenal ulcer—

Oral, 20 mg once a day. For patients not healed after the initial course of therapy (healing usually occurs within two weeks), an additional two weeks of treatment is needed. The dosage may be increased to 20 to 40 mg once a day for duodenal ulcer refractory to other treatment regimens. In patients requiring maintenance therapy, doses of 10 mg once a day, increased to 20 to 40 mg once a day as needed, have been used.

Gastric ulcer (treatment)—
Oral, 20 mg once a day. For patients not healed after the initial course of therapy (healing usually occurs within four weeks), an additional four weeks of treatment is needed. The dosage may be increased to 40 mg once a day for gastric ulcer refractory to other treatment regimens. In patients requiring maintenance therapy, doses of 20 mg once a day, increased to 40 mg once a day as needed, have been used.

Peptic ulcer associated with *H. pylori* infection—
Oral, triple therapy regimens of omeprazole 20 mg, plus clarithromycin 500 mg, plus amoxicillin 1000 mg or omeprazole 20 mg, plus clarithromycin 250 mg, plus metronidazole 500 mg, in which all three medications are taken twice a day for seven days. These regimens are followed by further treatment with omeprazole, 20 mg once a day for up to three weeks for active duodenal ulcer, and 20 to 40 mg once a day for up to twelve weeks for active gastric ulcer.

Peptic ulcer, nonsteroidal anti-inflammatory drug–induced (treatment)—
Oral, 20 mg once a day. For patients not healed after the initial course of therapy (healing usually occurs within four weeks), an additional four weeks of treatment is needed. In patients requiring maintenance therapy, doses of 20 mg once a day for up to six months have been used.

Usual pediatric dose
Safety and efficacy have not been established.

Usual geriatric dose
See *Usual adult dose*. The daily dose should not exceed 20 mg.

Strength(s) usually available
U.S.—
Not commercially available.

Canada—
10 mg (base) (Rx) [*Losec*].
20 mg (base) (Rx) [*Losec*].

Packaging and storage
Store between 15 and 30 °C (59 and 86 °F), in a tight container, unless otherwise specified by manufacturer. Protect from moisture and humidity.

Auxiliary labeling
• Swallow tablets whole.

OMEPRAZOLE FOR SUSPENSION

Usual adult dose
Ulcer, duodenal (treatment)—
Oral, 20 mg once per day for four weeks. Most patients heal within four weeks. Some patients may require an additional four weeks of therapy.

Ulcer, peptic (treatment)—
Oral, 40 mg once per day for 4 to 8 weeks.

Gastroesophageal reflux disease (treatment)—
No esophageal lesions: Oral, 20 mg once a day for up to four weeks
With erosive esophagitis and accompanying symptoms: Oral, 20 mg once per day for four to eight weeks.
Maintenance of healing of erosive esophagitis: 20 mg once per day

Upper gastrointestinal hemorrhage (prophylaxis)—
Oral, Loading dose first day: 40 mg initially, followed by 40 mg after 6 to 8 hours. Maintenance after first day: 40 mg once daily for up to 14 days. The use of omeprazole in critically ill patients beyond 14 days has not been evaluated.

Usual pediatric dose
Safety and efficacy have not been established.

Usual geriatric dose
See *Usual adult dose*. The daily dose should not exceed 20 mg.

Strength(s) usually available
U.S.—
20 mg (Rx) [*Zegerid* (single-dose packets; sodium bicarbonate; sucrose; sucralose; xanthan gum; xylitol; flavorings)].
40 mg (Rx) [*Zegerid* (single-dose packets; sodium bicarbonate; sucrose; sucralose; xanthan gum; xylitol; flavorings)].

Packaging and storage
Store at 25 °C (68 to 77 °F) excursions permitted to 15 to 30 °C (59 to 86 °F)

Preparation of dosage form
Empty 20-mg unit dose packet contents into a small cup containing 2 tablespoons of water. ***Do not use other liquids or foods.*** Stir well and drink immediately. Refill cup with water and drink

For administration through a nasogastric or orogastric tube, the suspension should be constituted with approximately 20 mL of water. ***Do not use other liquids or foods.*** Stir well and administer immediately. An appropriately-sized syringe should be used to instill the suspension in the tube. The suspension should be washed through the tube with 20 mL of water.

Auxiliary labeling
• Dissolve in water before use

Additional information
Omeprazole powder for oral suspension contains 460 mg sodium per dose in the form of sodium bicarbonate. This should be taken into account for patients on a sodium-restricted diet.

Revised: 06/09/2005

ONDANSETRON Systemic

VA CLASSIFICATION (Primary): GA605
Commonly used brand name(s): *Zofran; Zofran ODT.*

Note: For a listing of dosage forms and brand names by country availability, see *Dosage Forms* section(s).

Category
Antiemetic.

Indications

General Considerations
Ondansetron is not a drug that stimulates gastric or intestinal peristalsis. It should not be used instead of nasogastric suction.

Accepted
Nausea and vomiting, cancer chemotherapy-induced (prophylaxis)—Ondansetron is indicated for the prevention of nausea and vomiting associated with initial and repeat courses of moderately or highly emetogenic cancer chemotherapy, including high-dose cisplatin ≥50 mg per m².

Studies done to date comparing ondansetron to high-dose metoclopramide have shown ondansetron to be more effective in preventing nausea and vomiting induced by emetogenic chemotherapy agents during the acute phase lasting 24 hours after the start of chemotherapy.

The combination of ondansetron plus dexamethasone has been shown to provide better emetic control over cisplatin-induced emesis than ondansetron alone.

Nausea and vomiting, postoperative (prophylaxis)—Ondansetron is indicated for the prevention of postoperative nausea and vomiting. Patients at greatest risk of developing postoperative nausea and vomiting include patients who have previously experienced postoperative nausea, patients predisposed to motion sickness, and patients with high levels of preoperative anxiety. The incidence of postoperative nausea and vomiting is also higher in women and children than in men and adults, respectively. Routine prophylaxis is not recommended for patients in whom there is little expectation that postoperative nausea and vomiting will occur, except in cases in which the stress of vomiting may damage the operation site.

Nausea and vomiting, radiotherapy-induced (prophylaxis)—Ondansetron tablets and oral solution are indicated for the prevention of nausea and vomiting associated with radiotherapy in patients receiving total body irradiation, or single high-dose fraction or daily fractions to the abdomen.

Unaccepted
Ondansetron is not effective in preventing motion-induced nausea and vomiting.

Pharmacology/Pharmacokinetics

Physicochemical characteristics
Molecular weight—293.4 (ODT orally disintegrating tablets) and 365.9 (oral tablets and solution).

pH—Injection: 3.3 to 4.

Mechanism of action/Effect
Antiemetic—Ondansetron is a competitive, highly selective antagonist of 5-hydroxytryptamine (serotonin) subtype 3 (5-HT_3) receptors. 5-HT_3 receptors are present peripherally on vagal nerve terminals and centrally in the area postrema of the brain. It is not certain whether ondansetron's action is mediated peripherally, centrally, or both. Cytotoxic drugs and radiation appear to damage gastrointestinal mucosa, causing the release of serotonin from the enterochromaffin cells of the gastrointestinal tract. Stimulation of 5-HT_3 receptors causes transmis-

sion of sensory signals to the vomiting center via vagal afferent fibers to induce vomiting. By binding to 5-HT_3 receptors, ondansetron blocks vomiting mediated by serotonin release.

Ondansetron has no dopamine-receptor antagonist activity.

Other actions/effects

Multiple oral doses or multiday intravenous doses of ondansetron administered to healthy volunteers slowed colonic transit time. However, following single intravenous doses of 0.15 mg of ondansetron per kg of body weight (mg/kg), no effects were observed on esophageal motility, gastric motility, lower esophageal sphincter pressure, small intestine transit time, or plasma prolactin concentrations.

Absorption

Ondansetron is well absorbed after oral administration and undergoes limited first-pass metabolism. The extent and rate of ondansetron's absorption following a single oral dose is greater in women than in men. However, it is not known if this difference is clinically significant. Mean bioavailability, in healthy subjects, following a single 8-mg oral dose is approximately 56%.

Distribution

The volume of distribution (Vol_D) in healthy young males following administration of 8 mg of ondansetron as an intravenous infusion over 5 minutes was about 160 L. Patients 4 to 12 years of age reportedly have a Vol_D somewhat larger than do adults.

Thirty-six percent of circulating ondansetron is distributed into erythrocytes.

Protein binding

High (70 to 76%).

Biotransformation

Hepatic; extensive. Primarily hydroxylation, followed by glucuronide or sulfate conjugation.

Half-life

The mean elimination half-life in adult cancer patients is 5.7 hours. Elderly patients tend to have an increased elimination half-life, while most pediatric patients less than 15 years of age have shorter mean terminal half-lives (range, 2.5 to 3 hours) than patients older than 15 years of age. Adults with mild to moderate hepatic impairment had a mean half-life of 11.6 hours, while those with severe hepatic impairment had a mean half-life prolonged to 20.6 hours.

A study performed in normal volunteers to evaluate the pharmacokinetics of a single 4-mg dose of ondansetron administered as a 5-minute intravenous infusion and as a single intramuscular injection showed that the mean elimination half-life was not affected by route of administration.

Peak plasma concentration

Following administration of a single intravenous dose of 0.15 mg/kg to healthy volunteers, peak plasma concentrations of 102 to 106 nanograms per mL were observed in those from 19 to 74 years of age, and 170 nanograms per mL in those ≥ 75 years of age. Mean peak plasma concentrations in volunteers who received a single 4-mg dose of ondansetron via a 5-minute intravenous infusion or as a single intramuscular injection were 42.9 nanograms/mL at 10 minutes following the infusion, and 31.9 nanograms/mL at 41 minutes after intramuscular injection.

Following administration of a single oral dose of 8 mg of ondansetron to healthy volunteers:

Age group (years)	Gender	Peak plasma concentration (nanograms per mL)
19–40	M	26.2
	F	42.7
61–74	M	24.1
	F	52.4
≥75	M	37
	F	46.1

The higher plasma concentrations in females may be attributed to slower clearance, smaller apparent Vol_D (adjusted for weight), and higher absolute bioavailability in females than in males.

Elimination

Predominantly hepatic; less than 5% of an intravenous dose of ondansetron is recovered unchanged in the urine.

Following administration of a single intravenous dose of 0.15 mg/kg to healthy volunteers, plasma clearance values were 0.381 liters per hour per kg of body weight (L/hr/kg) in subjects 9 to 40 years of age, 0.319 L/hr/kg in subjects 61 to 74 years of age, and 0.262 L/hr/kg in subjects ≥ 75 years of age.

Elderly patients tended to have lower clearance values than did younger adults, while most pediatric patients 4 to 12 years of age had greater clearance values than adults.

Precautions to Consider

Cross-sensitivity and/or related problems

Patients sensitive to other selective 5-HT_3 receptor antagonists may also be sensitive to ondansetron.

Carcinogenicity

Carcinogenic effects were not seen in 2-year studies in rats and mice given ondansetron orally in doses up to 10 and 30 mg per kg of body weight (mg/kg) per day, respectively.

Mutagenicity

Standard tests showed no mutagenic activity of ondansetron.

Pregnancy/Reproduction

Fertility—Ondansetron had no effect on the fertility or reproductive performance of male and female rats when given in oral doses up to 15 mg/kg per day.

Pregnancy—Adequate and well-controlled studies in humans have not been done. Because animal reproduction studies are not always predictive of human response, this drug should be used during pregnancy only if clearly needed.

Studies in pregnant rats and rabbits given intravenous doses of up to 4 mg/kg per day, and oral doses of up to 15 and 30 mg/kg per day, respectively, have not shown that ondansetron causes adverse effects in the fetus.

FDA Pregnancy Category B.

Breast-feeding

It is not known whether ondansetron is distributed into human breast milk. However, ondansetron is distributed into the milk of rats. Because many drugs are distributed in human milk, caution should be exercised when ondansetron is administered to a nursing woman.

Pediatrics

Studies performed to date that included cancer patients 6 months to 18 years of age and postoperative patients 1 month to 12 years of age have not demonstrated pediatrics-specific problems that would limit the usefulness of ondansetron in children. However, the clearance of ondansetron in pediatric patients 1 to 4 months of age is slower and the half-life is about 2.5-fold longer than patients who are greater than 4 months to 24 months of age. As a precaution, it is recommended that patients less than 4 months of age receiving this drug be closely monitored.

Geriatrics

Studies performed to date that included cancer patients over 65 years of age have not demonstrated geriatrics-specific problems that would limit the usefulness of ondansetron in the elderly.

Drug interactions and/or related problems

The following drug interactions and/or related problems have been selected on the basis of their potential clinical significance (possible mechanism in parentheses where appropriate)—not necessarily inclusive (» = major clinical significance):

Carbamazepine or
Phenytoin or
Rifampicin
(concomitant use significantly increased ondansetron clearance and decreased ondansetron blood concentrations; no dose adjustments necessary)

Enzyme inducers, hepatic, cytochrome P450 (see *Appendix II*) or
Enzyme inhibitors, hepatic, various (see *Appendix II*)
(because ondansetron is metabolized by hepatic cytochrome P450 enzymes, inducers or inhibitors of these enzymes potentially may alter its clearance and half-life; ondansetron does not appear to induce or inhibit the cytochrome P450 enzyme system of the liver)

Tramadol
(two small studies indicate that ondansetron may be associated with increase in patient controlled administration of tramadol)

Laboratory value alterations

The following have been selected on the basis of their potential clinical significance (possible effect in parentheses where appropriate)—not necessarily inclusive (» = major clinical significance).

With physiology/laboratory test values
Alanine aminotransferase (ALT [SGPT]) and
Aspartate aminotransferase (AST [SGOT])
(values may be increased; increases reportedly are transient and unrelated to dose or duration of therapy)

Bilirubin, serum
(concentrations may be increased; increases reportedly are transient and unrelated to dose or duration of therapy)

Medical considerations/Contraindications

The medical considerations/contraindications included have been selected on the basis of their potential clinical significance (reasons given in parentheses where appropriate)—not necessarily inclusive (» = major clinical significance).

Except under special circumstances, this medication should not be used when the following medical problem exists:

» Hypersensitivity to ondansetron or any component of the product or to other selective 5-HT_3 receptor antagonists

Risk-benefit should be considered when the following medical problems exist:

Hepatic function impairment
(use of ondansetron may result in increases in hepatic enzymes; in patients with severe hepatic insufficiency, ondansetron clearance is reduced, plasma half-life is increased, and bioavailability approaches 100%; dosage adjustments are needed)

Phenylketonuria (PKU)
(*Zofran* brand of ondansetron oral disintegrating tablets contains aspartame, which is metabolized to phenylalanine)

Surgery, abdominal
(use of ondansetron may mask a progressive ileus and/or gastric distension)

Side/Adverse Effects

Note: Since ondansetron is used in conjunction with cancer chemotherapeutic agents, it is difficult to attribute some side effects, such as diarrhea and fever, to ondansetron alone.

Signs and symptoms consistent with extrapyramidal effects have been reported in a very small number of patients receiving ondansetron; however, a causal relationship has not been established.

The following side/adverse effects have been selected on the basis of their potential clinical significance (possible signs and symptoms in parentheses where appropriate)—not necessarily inclusive:

Those indicating need for medical attention

Incidence rare

Anaphylaxis (hypotension; skin rash, hives, and/or itching; troubled breathing); ***bronchospasm*** (shortness of breath, tightness in chest, troubled breathing, or wheezing); ***chest pain; injection-site reactions*** (pain, redness, and burning at site of injection)

Incidence not determined—Observed during clinical practice of oral and injectable formulations; estimates of frequency can not be determined

Angioedema (large, hive-like swelling on face, eyelids, lips, tongue, throat, hands, legs, feet, sex organs); ***cardiopulmonary arrest*** (no pulse or blood pressure; no breathing; unconscious; heart stops); ***dystonic reactions*** (inability to move eyes; increased blinking or spasms of eyelid; sticking out of tongue; trouble in breathing, speaking, or swallowing; uncontrolled twisting movements of neck, trunk, arms, or legs; unusual facial expressions; weakness of arms and legs); ***hypersensitivity reaction*** (difficulty in breathing or swallowing; fast heartbeat; shortness of breath; skin itching, rash, or redness; swelling of face, throat, or tongue); ***hypotension*** (blurred vision; confusion; dizziness, faintness, or lightheadedness when getting up from a lying or sitting position suddenly; sweating; unusual tiredness or weakness); ***laryngeal edema*** (coughing; difficulty in breathing; difficulty in swallowing; hoarseness; shortness of breath; slow or irregular breathing; tightness in chest; wheezing); ***laryngospasm*** (shortness of breath; trouble in breathing; tightness in chest; wheezing); ***liver enzyme abnormalities*** (lab results that show problems with liver); ***oculogyric crisis*** (fixed position of the eye); ***shock*** (cold clammy skin; confusion; dizziness; lightheadedness; fast, weak pulse; sweating; wheezing); ***shortness of breath; stridor*** (noisy breathing); ***urticaria*** (hives or welts; itching; redness of skin; skin rash)

Incidence not determined—Observed during clinical practice of injectable formulations; estimates of frequency can not be determined

Arrhythmias (dizziness; fainting; fast, slow, or irregular heartbeat); ***atrial fibrillation*** (fast or irregular heartbeat; dizziness; fainting); ***bradycardia*** (chest pain or discomfort; lightheadedness, dizziness or fainting; shortness of breath; slow or irregular heartbeat; unusual tiredness); ***electrocardiographic alterations; palpitations*** (irregular heartbeat); ***premature ventricular contractions*** (chest pain or discomfort; shortness of breath; weakness; lightheadedness; irregular heartbeat); ***second-degree heart block*** (chest pain or discomfort; decreased or irregular heartbeat; pain in neck, back, or jaw; shortness of breath; weakness); ***ST segment depression; supraventricular tachycardia*** (fainting; fast, pounding, or irregular heartbeat or pulse; palpitations); ***syncope*** (fainting); ***ventricular tachycardia*** (fainting; fast, pounding, or irregular heartbeat or pulse; palpitations)

Those indicating need for medical attention only if they continue or are bothersome

Incidence more frequent

Constipation; diarrhea; fever; headache

Incidence less frequent or rare

Abdominal pain or stomach cramps; cold sensation (feeling cold); ***dizziness or lightheadedness; drowsiness; dryness of mouth; paresthesias*** (burning, tingling, or prickling sensations); ***pruritus*** (itching); ***skin rash; unusual tiredness or weakness***

Overdose

For information on the management of overdose or unintentional ingestion, **contact a Poison Control Center** (see *Poison Control Center Listing*).

Clinical effects of overdose

Individual doses as large as 145 mg and total daily dosages as large as 252 mg have been administered intravenously without significant adverse events.

Hypotension and faintness occurred in a patient who ingested 48 mg of oral ondansetron. Sudden blindness (amaurosis) of 2 to 3 minutes' duration plus severe constipation occurred in another patient who was administered a single dose of 72 mg of ondansetron intravenously. A vasovagal episode with transient second-degree heart block was observed in another patient following the infusion of 32 mg of ondansetron over a 4-minute period. In all cases, the events resolved completely.

Treatment of overdose

There is no specific antidote for ondansetron overdose.

Supportive care—Patients should be managed with appropriate supportive therapy. Patients in whom intentional overdose is confirmed or suspected should be referred for psychiatric evaluation.

Patient Consultation

As an aid to patient consultation, refer to *Advice for the Patient, Ondansetron (Systemic)*.

In providing consultation, consider emphasizing the following selected information (» = major clinical significance):

Before using this medication

» Conditions affecting use, especially:
Hypersensitivity to ondansetron or any component of the product or to other selective 5-HT_3 receptor antagonists
Use in children—Safety/efficacy established in patients 1 month of age and older for prevention of post-operative nausea and vomiting; 6 months of age and older for chemo-induced nausea and vomiting; close monitoring recommended for patients less than 4 months of age receiving ondansetron

Proper use of this medication

Taking additional oral dose if vomiting occurs within 30 minutes after a dose; checking with doctor if vomiting persists
Proper handling/administration of the oral disintegrating tablets
Importance of diluting vials of ondansetron injection except for administration for postoperative nausea and vomiting
Not diluting flexible plastic containers of ondansetron for injection
» Proper dosing
Missed dose: Taking missed dose as soon as possible if nausea or vomiting occurs
» Proper storage

Side/adverse effects

Signs of potential side effects, especially anaphylaxis, bronchospasm, chest pain, or injection-site reactions
Signs of potential side effects observed during clinical practice of oral and injectable formulations, especially angioedema, cardiopulmonary arrest, dystonic reactions, hypersensitivity reaction, hypotension, laryngeal edema, laryngospasm, liver enzyme abnormalities, oculogyric crisis, shock, shortness of breath, stridor, or urticaria
Signs of potential side effects observed during clinical practice of injectable formulations, especially arrhythmias, atrial fibrillation, bradycardia, electrocardiographic alterations, palpitations, premature ventricular contractions, second-degree heart block, ST segment depression, supraventricular tachycardia, syncope, or ventricular tachycardia

General Dosing Information

For prophylaxis against nausea and vomiting induced by *highly* emetogenic chemotherapeutic agents, the parenteral form of ondansetron is recommended. The oral forms of ondansetron are indicated for the prevention of nausea and vomiting induced by *moderately* emetogenic-chemotherapeutic agents.

Zofran brand of oral disintegrating tablets is a freeze-dried formulation of ondansetron that rapidly disintegrates on the tongue and does not require water to aid dissolution or swallowing.

Oral disintegrating tablets may contain aspartame, which is metabolized to phenylalanine. This substance must be used with caution in patients with phenylketonuria.

The use of ondansetron in patients with chemotherapy-induced nausea and vomiting or in patients following abdominal surgery may mask a progressive ileus and/or gastric distension.

Bioequivalence information

Ondansetron oral solution or orally disintegrating tablets in 4-mg and 8-mg doses are bioequivalent to corresponding doses of ondansetron tablets and may be used interchangeably. One 24-mg ondansetron tablet is bioequivalent to and interchangeable with three 8-mg ondansetron tablets.

Oral Dosage Forms

ONDANSETRON HYDROCHLORIDE ORAL SOLUTION

Usual adult and adolescent dose

Nausea and vomiting, moderately emetogenic cancer chemotherapy-induced (prophylaxis)—
- Initial: Oral, 8 mg thirty minutes prior to chemotherapy.
- Post-chemotherapy: Oral, 8 mg eight hours after the initial dose, followed by 8 mg every twelve hours for one to two days.

Nausea and vomiting, postoperative (prophylaxis)—
- Oral, 16 mg one hour prior to induction of anesthesia.

Nausea and vomiting, radiotherapy-induced (prophylaxis)—
- Initial: Oral, 8 mg one to two hours prior to radiotherapy.
- Post-radiotherapy: Oral, 8 mg every eight hours.

Note: In patients with hepatic function impairment, the maximum recommended dose of ondansetron is 8 mg a day.

In patients with renal function impairment, no dosage adjustment is needed. There is no experience beyond first-day administration of ondansetron.

Usual pediatric dose

Nausea and vomiting, moderately emetogenic cancer chemotherapy-induced (prophylaxis)—
- Children up to 4 years of age—
  - Dosage has not been established.
- Children 4 to 11 years of age—
  - Initial—Oral, 4 mg thirty minutes prior to chemotherapy.
  - Post-chemotherapy—Oral, 4 mg four and eight hours after the initial dose, followed by 4 mg every eight hours for one to two days.
- Children 12 years of age and older—
  - See *Usual adult and adolescent dose*.

Nausea and vomiting, postoperative (prophylaxis) or
Nausea and vomiting, radiotherapy-induced (prophylaxis)—
- Dosage has not been established.

Usual geriatric dose

See *Usual adult and adolescent dose*.

Strength(s) usually available

U.S.—
- 4 mg (base) per 5 mL (Rx) [*Zofran* (strawberry flavored; sorbitol; citric acid anhydrous; sodium benzoate; sodium citrate)].

Canada—
- 4 mg per 5 mL (Rx) [*Zofran* (strawberry flavored; sorbitol; citric acid anhydrous; sodium benzoate; sodium citrate dihydrate)].

Packaging and storage

Store between 15 and 30 °C (59 and 86 °F), unless otherwise specified by manufacturer. Protect from light. Store bottles upright in cartons.

ONDANSETRON HYDROCHLORIDE TABLETS

Usual adult and adolescent dose

See *Ondansetron Hydrochloride Oral Solution* or

Nausea and vomiting, highly emetogenic cancer chemotherapy-induced (prophylaxis)—
- Oral, recommended single 24-mg tablet administered 30 minutes before the start of single-day chemotherapy, including cisplatin $\geq$50 mg per m^2.
- Multi-day, single-dose administration of ondansetron tablets has not been studied.

Usual pediatric dose

See *Ondansetron Hydrochloride Oral Solution*.

There is no experience with the use of 24-mg ondansetron tablets in pediatric patients.

Usual geriatric dose

See *Ondansetron Hydrochloride Oral Solution*.

Strength(s) usually available

U.S.—
- 4 mg (base) (Rx) [*Zofran* (lactose; microcrystalline cellulose; pregelatinized starch; hydroxypropyl methylcellulose; magnesium stearate; titanium dioxide; sodium benzoate)].
- 8 mg (base) (Rx) [*Zofran* (lactose; microcrystalline cellulose; pregelatinized starch; hydroxypropyl methylcellulose; magnesium stearate; titanium dioxide; iron oxide)].
- 24 mg base (Rx) [*Zofran* (lactose; microcrystalline cellulose; pregelatinized starch; hypromellose; magnesium stearate; titanium dioxide; triacetin; iron oxide red)].

Canada—
- 4 mg (Rx) [*Zofran* (lactose; microcrystalline cellulose; pregelatinized starch; magnesium stearate; methyl hydroxypropyl cellulose; Opadry yellow; Opaspray yellow [containing titanium dioxide and iron oxide yellow])].
- 8 mg (Rx) [*Zofran* (lactose; microcrystalline cellulose; pregelatinized starch; magnesium stearate; methyl hydroxypropyl cellulose; Opadry yellow; Opaspray yellow [containing titanium dioxide and iron oxide yellow])].

Packaging and storage

Store between 2 and 30 °C (36 and 86 °F), unless otherwise specified by manufacturer. Protect from light.

ONDANSETRON ORAL DISINTEGRATING TABLETS

Note: *Zofran* brand of oral disintegrating tablets is a freeze-dried formulation of ondansetron which rapidly disintegrates on the tongue and does not require water to aid dissolution or swallowing.

Usual adult and adolescent dose

See *Ondansetron Hydrochloride Oral Solution*.

Usual pediatric dose

See *Ondansetron Hydrochloride Oral Solution*.

Usual geriatric dose

See *Ondansetron Hydrochloride Oral Solution*.

Strength(s) usually available

U.S.—
- 4 mg (base) (Rx) [*Zofran ODT* (aspartame [< 0.03 mg]; gelatin; mannitol; methylparaben sodium; propylparaben sodium; strawberry flavor)].
- 8 mg (base) (Rx) [*Zofran* (aspartame [< 0.03 mg]; gelatin; mannitol; methylparaben sodium; propylparaben sodium; strawberry flavor)].

Canada—
- Not commercially available.

Packaging and storage

Store between 2 and 30 °C (36 and 86 °F), unless otherwise specified by manufacturer. Protect from light.

Caution

Zofran brand of oral disintegrating tablets contains aspartame, which is metabolized to phenylalanine and must be used with caution in patients with phenylketonuria.

Additional information

Proper handling/administration—With dry hands, peel back the foil backing of one blister. Do not attempt to push the oral disintegrating tablet through the foil backing. Gently remove the tablet and place it immediately on top of the tongue. It will dissolve in seconds, and should then be swallowed with saliva.

Parenteral Dosage Forms

ONDANSETRON HYDROCHLORIDE INJECTION

Usual adult dose

Nausea and vomiting, cancer chemotherapy-induced (prophylaxis)—
- Intravenous, 32 mg administered over fifteen minutes beginning thirty minutes prior to chemotherapy. Alternatively, three doses of 150 mcg (0.15 mg) per kg of body weight, each administered over fifteen minutes, with the initial dose beginning thirty minutes prior to chemotherapy, and subsequent doses administered four and eight hours after the first dose. Or, 8 mg administered over fifteen minutes beginning thirty minutes prior to chemotherapy, followed immediately by a continuous infusion of 1 mg per hour for up to twenty-four hours.

Nausea and vomiting, postoperative (prophylaxis)—
Intravenous, 4 mg administered undiluted over not less than thirty seconds and preferably over two to five minutes, beginning immediately prior to induction of anesthesia, or postoperatively if the patient experiences nausea and/or vomiting occurring shortly after surgery. Alternatively, 4 mg may be administered undiluted as a single intramuscular injection.

Note: Vial: Ondansetron injection **requires no dilution for administration for postoperative nausea and vomiting**.

Note: In patients with severe hepatic function impairment (Child-Pugh score of 10 or greater), the maximum recommended dose of ondansetron is 8 mg a day, infused over 15 minutes beginning 30 minutes before the start of emetogenic chemotherapy. There is no experience beyond first-day administration of ondansetron.

In patients with renal function impairment, no dosage adjustment is needed. There is no experience beyond first-day administration of ondansetron.

Usual pediatric dose

Nausea and vomiting, cancer chemotherapy-induced (prophylaxis)—
Children up to 6 months of age: Dosage has not been established.
Children 6 months to 18 years of age: Intravenous, three doses of 150 mcg (0.15 mg) per kg of body weight, each administered over fifteen minutes, with the initial dose beginning thirty minutes prior to chemotherapy, and subsequent doses administered four and eight hours after the first dose. Alternatively, 3 to 5 mg per square meter of body surface area administered over fifteen minutes beginning immediately prior to chemotherapy, followed after therapy by oral ondansetron 4 mg every eight hours for up to five days.

Nausea and vomiting, postoperative (prophylaxis)—
Children up to 1 month of age: Dosage has not been established.
Children 1 month to 12 years of age: Intravenous, a single dose of 100 mcg (0.1 mg) per kg of body weight for those weighing 40 kg or less, or a single 4-mg dose for those weighing more than 40 kg, administered over not less than thirty seconds and preferably over two to five minutes.

Usual geriatric dose

See *Usual adult dose*.

Strength(s) usually available

U.S.—
2 mg (base) per mL (Rx) [*Zofran* (sodium chloride; citric acid monohydrate 0.5 mg; sodium citrate dihydrate 0.25 mg; [may contain methylparaben 1.2 mg, propylparaben 0.15 mg])].
32 mg (base) per 50 mL (premixed) (Rx) [*Zofran* (preservative-free; dextrose 2500 mg; citric acid 26 mg; sodium citrate 11.5 mg)].

Canada—
2 mg per mL (Rx) [*Zofran*].

Packaging and storage

Store between 2 and 30 °C (36 and 86 °F), unless otherwise specified by manufacturer. Protect from light. Avoid excessive heat. Do not freeze.

Preparation of dosage form

Vial: Dilute before use (except for administration for postoperative nausea and vomiting). Ondansetron should be diluted in 50 mL of 5% Dextrose Injection of 0.9% Sodium Chloride Injection before administration.

Flexible Plastic Container: Requires no dilution. See manufacturer's instructions for use. Ondansetron injection premixed in flexible plastic containers is to be administered by IV drip infusion only. *Do not use flexible plastic container in series connections.*

Stability

Intravenous infusions of ondansetron retain their potency for 48 hours at room temperature under normal lighting after dilution with 5% dextrose injection, dextrose and sodium chloride injections, 0.9% sodium chloride injection, and 3% sodium chloride injection.

Parenteral drug products should be inspected visually for particulate matter and discoloration before administration whenever solution and container permit.

Although ondansetron injection is chemically and physically stable when diluted as recommended, sterile precautions should be observed because diluents generally do not contain preservative. After dilution, do not use beyond 24 hours.

Incompatibilities

The following medications may be incompatible with ondansetron and should be avoided in admixtures: acyclovir, allopurinol, aminophylline, amphotericin B, ampicillin, ampicillin and sulbactam, amsacrine, cefepime, cefoperazone, furosemide, ganciclovir, lorazepam, methylprednisolone, mezlocillin, piperacillin, and sargramostim. In addition, alkaline solutions and fluorouracil in concentrations greater than 0.8 mg per mL have been shown to be physically incompatible with ondansetron. In particular, this applies to alkaline solutions as a precipitate may form. If used with a primary IV fluid system, the primary solution should be discontinued during ondansetron injection premixed infusion.

Caution

Occasionally, ondansetron precipitates at the stopper/vial interface in vials stored upright. If a precipitate is observed, resolubilize by shaking the vial vigorously. Potency and stability are not affected.

Selected Bibliography

Markham A, Sorkin EM. Ondansetron: an update of its therapeutic use in chemotherapy-induced and postoperative nausea and vomiting. Drugs 1993; 45: 931-52.

Revised: 04/12/2005

OPIOID (NARCOTIC) ANALGESICS Systemic

Note: PALLADONE (hydromorphone hydrochloride, extended release capsules) was suspended from the market by Purdue Pharma in July 2005. Drinking alcohol while taking PALLADONE may cause rapid release of hydromorphone and high drug levels in the body. High drug levels of hydromorphone may have serious effects, including depressed breathing, lack of breathing, coma, and death.

This monograph includes information on the following: 1) Anileridine*; 2) Butorphanol†; 3) Codeine; 4) Hydrocodone‡*; 5) Hydromorphone; 6) Levorphanol; 7) Meperidine; 8) Methadone; 9) Morphine; 10) Nalbuphine; 11) Opium; 12) Oxycodone; 13) Oxymorphone; 14) Pentazocine; 15) Propoxyphene.

Note: See also individual *Buprenorphine (Systemic)* and *Dezocine (Systemic)* monographs.

See also *Fentanyl Derivatives (Systemic)* for information on alfentanil, fentanyl, and sufentanil.

INN:
Meperidine—Pethidine
Propoxyphene—Dextropropoxyphene

VA CLASSIFICATION (Primary/Secondary):
Anileridine—CN101/CN206
Butorphanol—CN101/CN206
Codeine
Oral—CN101/RE301; GA400
Parenteral—CN101/GA400
Hydrocodone—CN101/RE301
Hydromorphone
Oral—CN101/RE301
Parenteral—CN101/CN206; RE301
Rectal—CN101
Levorphanol
Oral—CN101
Parenteral—CN101/CN206
Meperidine
Oral—CN101
Parenteral—CN101/CN206
Methadone—CN101/AD900; RE301
Morphine
Oral—CN101/RE301; GA400
Parenteral—CN101/CN206; RE301; GA400
Rectal—CN101/RE301
Nalbuphine—CN101/CN206
Opium
Oral—GA400/CN101
Parenteral—CN101
Oxycodone—CN101
Oxymorphone
Parenteral—CN101/CN206
Rectal—CN101
Pentazocine
Oral—CN101
Parenteral—CN101/CN206
Propoxyphene—CN101

Drug	U.S.	Canada
Anileridine		N
Butorphanol	II	††
Codeine	II	N
Hydrocodone	‡‡	N
Hydromorphone	II	N
Levorphanol	II	N
Meperidine	II	N
Methadone	II	N§§
Morphine	II	N
Nalbuphine	**	C
Opium	II	N
Oxycodone	II	N
Oxymorphone	II	N
Pentazocine	IV	N
Propoxyphene	IV	N

Commonly used brand name(s): *642*[15]; *AVINZA*[9]; *Astramorph PF*[9]; *Cotanal-65*[15]; *Darvon*[15]; *Darvon-N*[15]; *Demerol*[7]; *Dilaudid*[5]; *Dilaudid-5*[5]; *Dilaudid-HP*[5]; *Dolophine*[8]; *Duramorph*[9]; *Epimorph*[9]; *Hycodan*[4]; *Hydrostat IR*[5]; *Kadian*[9]; *Leritine*[1]; *Levo-Dromoran*[6]; *M S Contin*[9]; *M-Eslon*[9]; *M.O.S*[9]; *M.O.S.-S.R*[9]; *MS IR*[9]; *MSIR*[9]; *MS/L*[9]; *MS/L Concentrate*[9]; *MS/S*[9]; *MS`IR*[9]; *Methadose*[8]; *Morphine Extra-Forte*[9]; *Morphine Forte*[9]; *Morphine H.P*[9]; *Morphitec*[9]; *Nubain*[10]; *Numorphan*[13]; *OMS Concentrate*[9]; *Oramorph SR*[9]; *OxyContin*[12]; *PMS-Hydromorphone*[5]; *PMS-Hydromorphone Syrup*[5]; *PP-Cap*[15]; *Pantopon*[11]; *Paveral*[3]; *RMS Uniserts*[9]; *Rescudose*[9]; *Robidone*[4]; *Roxanol*[9]; *Roxanol 100*[9]; *Roxanol UD*[9]; *Roxicodone*[12]; *Roxicodone Intensol*[12]; *Stadol*[2]; *Statex*[9]; *Statex Drops*[9]; *Supeudol*[12]; *Talwin*[14]; *Talwin-Nx*[14].

Other commonly used names are: Dextropropoxyphene [Propoxyphene], Dihydromorphinone [Hydromorphone], Laudanum [Opium Tincture], Levorphan [Levorphanol], Pethidine [Meperidine], Papaveretum [Opium (Parenteral)]

Note: For a listing of dosage forms and brand names by country availability, see *Dosage Forms* section(s).

*Not commercially available in U.S.

†Not commercially available in Canada.

‡Commercially available in the U.S. only in combination with other active ingredients. See *Cough/Cold Combinations (Systemic)*, *Opioid (Narcotic) Analgesics and Acetaminophen (Systemic)*, and *Opioid (Narcotic) Analgesics and Aspirin (Systemic)*.

**Not a controlled substance in the U.S.

††Not commercially available in Canada.

‡‡Commercially available in the U.S. only in combination with other active ingredients.

§§Available in Canada only through practitioners authorized to treat opioid addicts.

Category

Note: All of the opioid analgesics have similar pharmacologic actions; however, clinical uses among specific agents may vary because of actual pharmacokinetic differences, differences in potential for causing adverse effects, lack of specific testing, and/or lack of clinical-use data.

Analgesic—Anileridine; Butorphanol; Codeine; Hydrocodone; Hydromorphone; Levorphanol; Meperidine; Methadone; Morphine; Nalbuphine; Opium; Oxycodone; Oxymorphone; Pentazocine; Propoxyphene

Note: Butorphanol, nalbuphine, and pentazocine are opioid agonist/antagonist analgesics; the other agents in this group are opioid agonist analgesics.

Anesthesia adjunct (opioid analgesic)—Parenteral dosage forms only: Butorphanol; Hydromorphone; Levorphanol; Meperidine; Morphine; Nalbuphine; Oxymorphone; Pentazocine

Note: For other opioids used primarily as anesthesia adjuncts, see *Fentanyl Derivatives (Systemic)*.

Antidiarrheal—Codeine; Morphine; Opium Tincture

Note: For other opioids used only as antidiarrheals, see individual monograph listings for *Difenoxin and Atropine, Diphenoxylate and Atropine, Loperamide,* and *Paregoric.*

Antitussive—Codeine (oral dosage forms only); Hydrocodone; Hydromorphone; Methadone; Morphine

Note: For use of hydromorphone as an antitussive, see *Cough-Cold Combinations (Systemic)—Hydromorphone and Guaifenesin*.

Suppressant (narcotic abstinence syndrome)—Methadone; Opium Tincture.

Pulmonary edema therapy adjunct—Morphine

Indications

Note: PALLADONE (hydromorphone hydrochloride, extended release capsules) was suspended from the market by Purdue Pharma in July 2005.

Note: Bracketed information in the *Indications* section refers to uses that are not included in U.S. product labeling.

Accepted

Pain (treatment)—Morphine, methadone, and parenteral opium are indicated for relief of severe pain; codeine and propoxyphene are indicated for relief of mild to moderate pain; and the other opioid analgesics are indicated for relief of moderate to severe pain. Oxycodone extended-release tablets are indicated for relief of moderate to severe pain when a continuous, around-the-clock analgesic is needed for an extended period of time. Hydromorphone extended-release capsules are indicated for the management of **persistent**, moderate to severe pain in patients requiring continuous, around-the-clock analgesia with a high potency opioid for an extended period of time (e.g., weeks to months or longer).

Epidural or intrathecal administration of small doses of opioid analgesics may provide prolonged pain relief. Although administration via these routes may decrease the risk of some side/adverse effects, respiratory depression may occur. Solutions containing a preservative must *not* be used. Only morphine sulfate is currently commercially available in a dosage form that is FDA–approved for administration via these routes.

For relief of pain due to acute myocardial infarction, morphine is usually considered the drug of choice. Butorphanol and pentazocine are less desirable than other opioid analgesics for this purpose because they have cardiovascular effects that tend to increase cardiac work. Although nalbuphine has not been reported to adversely affect cardiovascular function in patients with acute myocardial infarction (and may be less likely than morphine to cause hypotension), its effects in patients with severely compromised cardiac function caused by acute myocardial infarction have not been fully determined. Therefore, these agents should be used with caution in such patients.

Parenterally administered opioid analgesics (except for methadone) are indicated to provide obstetrical analgesia.

Controlled clinical studies have shown that intrathecal, but not epidural, administration of opioid analgesics provides adequate relief of labor pain. Only a preservative-free solution should be used. Morphine sulfate is the only opioid analgesic currently commercially available in a dosage form that is FDA–approved for administration via these routes.

Anesthesia, general or local, adjunct—Parenteral dosage forms of butorphanol, [hydromorphone], levorphanol, meperidine, morphine, nalbuphine, oxymorphone, and pentazocine are indicated to supplement general, regional, or local anesthesia. During surgery, they are often used in conjunction with other agents, such as a combination of an ultrashort-acting barbiturate, a neuromuscular blocking agent, and an inhalation anesthetic (usually nitrous oxide), for the maintenance of "balanced" anesthesia.

Parenteral dosage forms of most opioid analgesics are indicated to provide analgesic, antianxiety, and sedative effects as presurgical medication. However, other medications, such as benzodiazepines, are more commonly used if the patient is not in pain.

Diarrhea (treatment)—[Codeine][1], [morphine], and opium tincture are indicated for treatment of diarrhea. In diarrhea caused by poisoning, these agents should not be used until the toxic material has been eliminated from the gastrointestinal tract.

Cough (treatment)—Although only codeine (oral dosage forms), hydrocodone, and hydromorphone are indicated as antitussives, all opioid analgesics depress the cough reflex. Meperidine, oxymorphone, and propoxyphene have relatively less antitussive activity than other opioid analgesics, especially in low or moderate doses.

[Methadone and morphine are sometimes used as antitussives when severe pain is present and coughing cannot be relieved by other means.]

Opioid (narcotic) abstinence syndrome (prophylaxis and treatment); or Opioid (narcotic) drug use, illicit (treatment)—Methadone is indicated as a suppressant to permit detoxification. Oral methadone is also indicated as maintenance therapy to discourage addicts from returning to illicit use of other opioid drugs.

Edema, pulmonary, acute (treatment adjunct)—Morphine is indicated as adjunctive therapy in the treatment of acute pulmonary edema secondary to left ventricular failure.

Oxymorphone is also FDA–approved as an adjunct in the treatment of acute pulmonary edema. However, oxymorphone is rarely if ever used for this indication; morphine is the preferred medication.

[Opioid (narcotic) dependence, neonatal (treatment)]—Opium tincture is used in diluted form in the treatment of neonatal opioid dependence.

[Pain, during mechanical ventilation, neonatal (treatment)]—Intravenous administration of morphine is indicated for control of pain during mechanical ventilation in neonates.

[Pain, postoperative, neonatal (treatment)]—Intravenous administration of morphine is indicated for control of postoperative pain in neonates.

Unaccepted

Methadone is not recommended for obstetrical analgesia because its long duration of action increases the risk of neonatal respiratory depression.

Oxycodone extended-release tablets are not intended for use as a "prn" (as needed) analgesic. Oxycodone extended-release tablets are not for use in the immediate post-operative period (the first 12–24 hours) unless the patient was receiving the drug prior to surgery. It is not used for mild pain or for pain not expected to last for an extended period of time.

Hydromorphone extended-release capsules are not intended to be used as the first opioid product prescribed for a patient, in patients who require opioid analgesia for a short period of time, or for use as a "prn" (as needed) analgesic.

---

[1]Not included in Canadian product labeling.

Pharmacology/Pharmacokinetics

See *Table 1,* page 2208.

See *Table 2,* page 2209.

Physicochemical characteristics

Molecular weight—
- Anileridine: 352.46.
- Butorphanol tartrate: 477.55.
- Codeine phosphate: 406.37 (hemihydrate); 397.36 (anhydrous).
- Codeine sulfate: 750.86 (trihydrate); 696.81 (anhydrous).
- Hydrocodone bitartrate: 494.50 (hydrate); 449.46 (anhydrous).
- Hydromorphone hydrochloride: 321.80.
- Levorphanol tartrate: 443.49 (dihydrate); 407.46 (anhydrous).
- Meperidine hydrochloride: 283.80.
- Methadone hydrochloride: 345.91.
- Morphine sulfate: 758.83 (pentahydrate); 668.76 (anhydrous).
- Nalbuphine hydrochloride: 393.91.
- Oxycodone hydrochloride: 351.83.
- Oxymorphone hydrochloride: 337.80.
- Pentazocine hydrochloride: 321.89.
- Pentazocine lactate: 375.51.
- Propoxyphene hydrochloride: 375.94.
- Propoxyphene napsylate: 565.72 (monohydrate); 547.71 (anhydrous).

Mechanism of action/Effect

Opioid analgesics bind with stereospecific receptors at many sites within the central nervous system (CNS) to alter processes affecting both the perception of pain and the emotional response to pain. Although the precise sites and mechanisms of action have not been fully determined, alterations in release of various neurotransmitters from afferent nerves sensitive to painful stimuli may be partially responsible for the analgesic effects. When these medications are used as adjuncts to anesthesia, analgesic actions may provide dose-related protection against hemodynamic responses to surgical stress.

It has been proposed that there are multiple subtypes of opioid receptors, each mediating various therapeutic and/or side effects of opioid drugs. The actions of an opioid analgesic may therefore depend upon its binding affinity for each type of receptor and on whether it acts as a full agonist or a partial agonist or is inactive at each type of receptor.

At least two types of opioid receptors (mu and kappa) mediate analgesia. A third type of receptor (sigma) may not mediate analgesia; actions at this receptor may produce the subjective and psychotomimetic effects characteristic of pentazocine and, to a lesser extent, butorphanol and nalbuphine. Morphine and other opioid agonists exert their agonist activity primarily at the mu receptor, whereas buprenorphine, nalbuphine, and pentazocine exert agonist activity at the kappa and sigma receptors. Mu receptors are widely distributed throughout the CNS, especially in the limbic system (frontal cortex, temporal cortex, amygdala, and hippocampus), thalamus, striatum, hypothalamus, and midbrain as well as laminae I, II, IV, and V of the dorsal horn in the spinal cord. Kappa receptors are localized primarily in the spinal cord and in the cerebral cortex.

Nalbuphine and pentazocine may displace opioids having only agonist activity from their receptor binding sites and competitively inhibit their actions. The medications may therefore precipitate withdrawal symptoms in patients who are physically dependent on such agonists. Butorphanol appears to have no significant antagonist activity at the mu receptor; in some studies, it failed to produce withdrawal symptoms in patients physically dependent on morphine. However, butorphanol does not substitute for mu-receptor agonists sufficiently to prevent or attenuate withdrawal symptoms caused by abrupt discontinuation of these agonists in physically dependent patients. Also, opioid agonist/antagonist drugs share several pharmacologic actions that differ from those of opioids having only agonist activity; i.e., different respiratory depressant, subjective, psychotomimetic, and hemodynamic effects; lower dependence liability; and reduced severity of withdrawal symptoms produced when they are discontinued after prolonged use.

Antidiarrheal—
- Act locally and possibly centrally to alter intestinal motility.

Antitussive—
- Suppress the cough reflex by a direct central action, probably in the medulla or pons.

Suppressant (narcotic abstinence syndrome)—
- Substitute for other opioid drugs when administered orally and prevent or attenuate withdrawal symptoms during detoxification. Withdrawal symptoms that may occur when the substituted opioid is discontinued are usually greatly reduced in severity. With continued administration, methadone may produce cross-tolerance to the euphoric effects of other opioid drugs, thereby reducing the patient's desire for such drugs.

Biotransformation

Hepatic; also in intestinal mucosa.

Precautions to Consider

Pregnancy/Reproduction

Pregnancy—Risk-benefit must be considered because opioid analgesics cross the placenta. Regular use during pregnancy may cause physical dependence in the fetus, leading to withdrawal symptoms (convulsions, irritability, excessive crying, tremors, hyperactive reflexes, fever, vomiting, diarrhea, sneezing, and yawning) in the neonate. Use of methadone by pregnant women participating in methadone maintenance programs has also been associated with fetal distress *in utero* and low birth weight.

For butorphanol, nalbuphine, pentazocine, and propoxyphene: Although studies in humans have not been done, studies in animals have not shown that these agents cause adverse effects on fetal development (Pentazocine and naloxone tablets—FDA Pregnancy Category C).

For codeine, hydrocodone, hydromorphone, morphine, and opium: Although teratogenic effects in humans have not been documented, controlled studies have not been done. Studies in animals have shown codeine (single dose of 100 mg per kg) to cause delayed ossification in mice and (in doses of 120 mg per kg) increased resorptions in rats, and hydrocodone, hydromorphone, and morphine to be teratogenic in very high doses (FDA Pregnancy Category C).

For anileridine, levorphanol, meperidine, methadone, oxycodone, and oxymorphone: Although teratogenic effects in humans have not been documented, controlled studies have not been done.

Labor and delivery—Opioid analgesics, including epidurally or intrathecally administered opioids, readily enter the fetal circulation when used during labor and may cause respiratory depression in the neonate, especially the premature neonate. These agents should be used with caution, if at all, during the delivery of a premature infant. Methadone is not recommended for obstetrical analgesia because its long duration of action increases the risk of neonatal respiratory depression. Also, morphine, hydromorphone, codeine, and possibly other opioids may prolong labor. Intrathecal administration of up to 1 mg of morphine sulfate has little effect on the first stage of labor but may prolong the second stage of labor.

Labor and delivery—Oral hydromorphone extended-release capsules should not be initiated prior to or during labor or in the immediate postpartum period. Women who are taking opioids during pregnancy should not be withdrawn abruptly during labor and delivery. Their current dose of medication should be maintained since abrupt withdrawal can precipitate delivery. Neonates whose mothers have been taking hydromorphone chronically may exhibit withdrawal symptoms and/or respiratory depression in the post-delivery period.

Breast-feeding

Problems in humans with most opioid analgesics have not been documented. Butorphanol, codeine, meperidine, methadone, morphine, and propoxyphene are distributed into breast milk. Information concerning the distribution of other opioid analgesics into breast milk is lacking. With usual analgesic doses, concentrations of those drugs known to be distributed into breast milk are generally low. However, risk-benefit must be considered when methadone is administered to a nursing mother in a methadone maintenance program because use of maintenance doses may cause physical dependence in the infant.

Pediatrics

Children up to 2 years of age may be more susceptible to the effects, especially the respiratory depressant effects, of these medications.

Paradoxical excitation is especially likely to occur in pediatric patients receiving opioid analgesics.

Oral hydromorphone extended-release capsules: Safety and effectiveness have not been established in patients younger than 18 years of age.

Geriatrics

Geriatric patients may be more susceptible to the effects, especially the respiratory depressant effects, of these medications. Also, geriatric patients are more likely to have prostatic hypertrophy or obstruction and age-related renal function impairment, and are therefore more likely to be adversely affected by opioid-induced urinary retention. In addition, geriatric patients may metabolize or eliminate these medications more slowly than younger adults. Lower doses or longer dosing intervals than those usually recommended for adults may be required, and are usually therapeutically effective, for these patients.

Dental

Opioid analgesics may decrease or inhibit salivary flow, thus contributing to the development of caries, periodontal disease, oral candidiasis, and discomfort.

Drug interactions and/or related problems

The following drug interactions and/or related problems have been selected on the basis of their potential clinical significance (possible mechanism in parentheses where appropriate)—not necessarily inclusive (» = major clinical significance):

Note: PALLADONE (hydromorphone hydrochloride, extended release capsules) was suspended from the market by Purdue Pharma in July 2005. Drinking alcohol while taking PALLADONE may cause rapid release of hydromorphone and high drug levels in the body. High drug levels of hydromorphone may have serious effects, including depressed breathing, lack of breathing, coma, and death.

See *Table 3*, page 2210.

Laboratory value alterations

The following have been selected on the basis of their potential clinical significance (possible effect in parentheses where appropriate)—not necessarily inclusive (» = major clinical significance).

With diagnostic test results

Gastric emptying studies
(opioid analgesics delay gastric emptying, thereby invalidating test results)

Hepatobiliary imaging using technetium Tc 99m disofenin
(delivery of technetium Tc 99m disofenin to the small bowel may be prevented because opioid analgesics [except for butorphanol] may cause constriction of the sphincter of Oddi and increased biliary tract pressure; these actions result in delayed visualization and thus resemble obstruction of the common bile duct)

With physiology/laboratory test values

Amylase, serum
(may be increased)

Cerebrospinal fluid (CSF) pressure
(may be increased; effect is secondary to respiratory depression–induced carbon dioxide retention)

Plasma amylase activity and
Plasma lipase activity
(may be increased because opioid analgesics [except butorphanol] can cause contractions of the sphincter of Oddi and increased biliary tract pressure; the diagnostic utility of determinations of these enzymes may be compromised for up to 24 hours after the medication has been given)

Serum alanine aminotransferase (ALT [SGPT]) and
Serum alkaline phosphatase and
Serum aspartate aminotransferase (AST [SGOT]) and
Serum bilirubin and
Serum lactate dehydrogenase (LDH)
(activity may be increased in patients receiving propoxyphene)

Medical considerations/Contraindications

The medical considerations/contraindications included have been selected on the basis of their potential clinical significance (reasons given in parentheses where appropriate)—not necessarily inclusive (» = major clinical significance).

Except under special circumstances, this medication should not be used when the following medical problems exist:

For hydromorphone and oxycodone

» Paralytic ileus, suspected or known
(hydromorphone and oxycodone are **contraindicated** in the setting of this condition)

For all opioid analgesic usage

» Asthma, acute attack or
» Bronchial asthma, severe or
» Hypercarbia or
» Respiratory depression, acute
(contraindicated in these patients in unmonitored settings or the absence of resuscitative equipment)

Biliary tract disease or
Pancreatitis, acute
(may cause spasm of the sphincter of oddi, use with caution)

» Blood volume, depleted
» Circulatory shock
(may cause severe hypotension)

» Diarrhea associated with pseudomembranous colitis caused by cephalosporins, lincomycins (possibly including topical clindamycin), or penicillins or
» Diarrhea caused by poisoning, until toxic material has been eliminated from gastrointestinal tract
(opioid analgesics may slow elimination of toxic material, thereby worsening and/or prolonging the diarrhea)

» Hypersensitivity to opioid analgesic considered for use or any of its components

For epidural or intrathecal administration

» Any condition that precludes epidural or intrathecal administration, such as:
» Coagulation defects caused by anticoagulant therapy or hematologic disorders
(trauma to a blood vessel during administration may result in uncontrollable CNS or soft tissue hemorrhage)

» Infection at or near site of administration
(risk of spreading the infection into the CNS)

Risk-benefit should be considered when the following medical problems exist:

For all opioid analgesics

Abdominal conditions, acute
(diagnosis or clinical course may be obscured)

Addison's disease
Cardiac arrhythmias or
Convulsions, history of
(may be induced or exacerbated by opioids; meperidine and propoxyphene may be especially likely to induce or exacerbate convulsions; with meperidine, the proconvulsant activity of its metabolite normeperidine may be responsible)

Drug abuse or dependence, current or history of, including alcoholism, or
Emotional instability or
Suicidal ideation or attempts
(patient predisposition to drug abuse)

Gallbladder disease or gallstones
(opioids [except butorphanol] may cause biliary contraction)

Gastrointestinal tract surgery, recent
(opioids may alter gastrointestinal motility)

Head injury or
Increased intracranial pressure, pre-existing or
Intracranial lesions
(risk of respiratory depression and further elevation of cerebrospinal fluid pressure is increased; also, opioids may cause sedation and pupillary changes that may obscure clinical course of head injury)

Hepatic function impairment
(opioids metabolized in liver)

Hypothyroidism
(risk of respiratory depression and prolonged CNS depression is greatly increased)

» Inflammatory bowel disease, severe
(risk of toxic megacolon may be increased, especially with repeated dosing)

Kyphoscoliosis with respiratory depression
(opioids should be given with caution)

Prostatic hypertrophy or obstruction or
Urethral stricture or
Urinary tract surgery, recent
(opioids may cause urinary retention)

Myxedema
(opioids should be given with caution)

Renal function impairment
(increased risk of convulsions [with meperidine] or other adverse effects because opioids and/or their metabolites excreted primarily via kidneys; also, opioids may cause urinary retention)

» Respiratory impairment or disease, chronic
(opioids may decrease respiratory drive and increase airway resistance in patients with these conditions)

Toxic psychosis
(caution should be used when given with opioids)

Caution is also advised in administration to very young, elderly, or very ill or debilitated patients, who may be more sensitive to the effects, especially the respiratory depressant effects, of these medications.

For butorphanol, nalbuphine, or pentazocine only (in addition to those medical problems listed above)

Dependence on opioid agonist analgesics, current
(nalbuphine and pentazocine may precipitate, and butorphanol does not prevent occurrence of, withdrawal symptoms)

Hypertension
(butorphanol may increase blood pressure in these patients when used as presurgical medication)

» Myocardial infarction, acute
(pentazocine and butorphanol may increase cardiac work; effects of nalbuphine in patients with severely compromised cardiac function have not been fully evaluated)

For epidural or intrathecal administration (in addition to those medical problems listed above as applying to all opioid analgesics)

Dependence on opioid analgesics, current
(low doses of opioids administered via epidural or intrathecal injection will not prevent withdrawal symptoms from occurring in a physically dependent patient)

Patient monitoring

The following may be especially important in patient monitoring (other tests may be warranted in some patients, depending on condition; » = major clinical significance):

Bowel motility
(monitor for decreased bowel motility in postoperative patients receiving opioids)

» Respiratory function
(monitoring recommended for at least 24 hours following epidural or intrathecal injection because delayed respiratory depression may occur up to 24 hours after administration via these routes)

Side/Adverse Effects

See *Table 4*, page 2213.

Note: Physical dependence, with or without psychological dependence, may occur with chronic administration of opioid analgesics; an abstinence syndrome may occur when these drugs are discontinued. Specific withdrawal symptoms that may occur, and their severity, depend upon the specific drug used, the abruptness of withdrawal, and the degree to which dependence has developed. Butorphanol, nalbuphine, and pentazocine have lower dependence liability and potential for abuse than opioid agonists; codeine and propoxyphene have lower dependence liability and potential for abuse than other agonists because of their comparatively lower potency with usual doses.

Epidural or intrathecal administration does not eliminate the risk of severe side effects common to systemic opioid analgesics. Respiratory depression may occur shortly after administration because of direct venous redistribution to the respiratory centers in the CNS. Also, delayed respiratory depression may occur up to 24 hours after administration, possibly as the result of rostral spread of the medication. Intrathecal administration and/or injection into thoracic sites are more likely to cause respiratory depression than epidural administration and/or injection into lumbar sites.

Following epidural or intrathecal administration of morphine, urinary retention occurs very frequently (incidence about 90% in males and somewhat lower in females) and may persist for 10 to 20 hours following injection. Catheterization may be required. Also, dose-related generalized pruritus occurs frequently. Excessive sedation is uncommon, and loss of motor, sensory, or sympathetic function does not occur.

Those indicating possible withdrawal and the need for medical attention if they occur after medication is discontinued

Body aches; diarrhea; fast heartbeat; fever, runny nose, or sneezing; gooseflesh; increased sweating; increased yawning; loss of appetite; nausea or vomiting; nervousness, restlessness, or irritability; shivering or trembling; stomach cramps; trouble in sleeping; unusually large pupils; weakness

Note: *The signs and symptoms of withdrawal* listed above are characteristic of the abstinence syndrome produced by abrupt discontinuation of mu-receptor agonists such as morphine. The milder abstinence syndrome produced by abrupt discontinuation of opioids having mixed agonist/antagonist activity may also include some of these signs and symptoms.

It has been proposed that adverse effects (such as tachycardia, hypertension, hyperpnea, hyperalgesia, nausea, and vomiting) occurring (rarely) after naloxone is administered for postoperative reversal of opioid effects following a lengthy surgical procedure may be manifestations of an induced abstinence syndrome in acutely dependent individuals. However, other symptoms more commonly associated with an opioid withdrawal syndrome have not been reported.

Overdose

For specific information on the agents used in the management of opioid (narcotic) analgesics overdose, see:
- *Naloxone (Systemic)* monograph.

For more information on the management of overdose or unintentional ingestion, **contact a Poison Control Center** (see *Poison Control Center Listing*).

Clinical effects of overdose

The following effects have been selected on the basis of their potential clinical significance (possible signs and symptoms in parentheses where appropriate)—not necessarily inclusive:

Acute and chronic
Cold, clammy skin; confusion; convulsions; dizziness, severe; drowsiness, severe; low blood pressure; nervousness or restlessness, severe; pinpoint pupils of eyes; slow heartbeat; slow or troubled breathing; unconsciousness; weakness, severe

Note: *Convulsions* are more likely to occur with meperidine or propoxyphene than with other opioids.

Treatment of overdose

To decrease absorption—Emptying the stomach via induction of emesis or gastric lavage (if the opioid was taken orally). However, treatment of respiratory depression or other potentially life-threatening adverse effects must take precedence.

Specific treatment—Administering the opioid antagonist naloxone. However, larger doses of naloxone may be required for treatment of overdose with butorphanol, nalbuphine, pentazocine, or propoxyphene. Naloxone injections may be repeated at two- to three-minute intervals as needed. The fact that naloxone may also antagonize the analgesic actions of opioid analgesics and may precipitate withdrawal symptoms in physically dependent patients must be kept in mind. For reversal of postoperative opioid depression, dosage of naloxone must be carefully titrated to avoid interference with control of postoperative pain or causing other adverse effects; hypertension and tachycardia, sometimes resulting in left ventricular failure and pulmonary edema, have occurred following naloxone administration in these circumstances (especially in cardiac patients). See the package insert or *Naloxone (Systemic)* for specific dosing guidelines for use of this product.

Monitoring—Continuing to monitor the patient (mandatory because the duration of action of the opioid analgesic may exceed that of the antagonist) and administering additional naloxone as needed. Alternatively, initial treatment may be followed by continuous intravenous infusion of naloxone, with the rate of infusion being adjusted according to patient response.

Supportive care—Establishing adequate respiratory exchange through provision of a patent airway and institution of assisted or controlled respiration. Administering intravenous fluids and/or vasopressors and using other supportive measures as needed. Patients in whom intentional overdose is confirmed or suspected should be referred for psychiatric consultation.

Patient Consultation

Note: PALLADONE (hydromorphone hydrochloride, extended release capsules) was suspended from the market by Purdue Pharma in July 2005. Drinking alcohol while taking PALLADONE may cause rapid release of hydromorphone and high drug levels in the body. High drug levels of hydromorphone may have serious effects, including depressed breathing, lack of breathing, coma, and death.

As an aid to patient consultation, refer to *Advice for the Patient, Narcotic Analgesics—For Pain Relief (Systemic), Narcotic Analgesics—For*

Surgery and Obstetrics (Systemic), and *Opium Preparations (Systemic).*

In providing consultation, consider emphasizing the following selected information (» = major clinical significance):

Before using this medication

» Conditions affecting use, especially:

Sensitivity to the opioid considered for use, history of

Pregnancy—Opioids cross the placenta; regular use by pregnant women may cause physical dependence in the fetus and withdrawal symptoms in the neonate

Breast-feeding—Butorphanol, codeine, meperidine, methadone, morphine, and propoxyphene are known to be distributed into breast milk; high-dose methadone may cause dependence in nursing infants

Use in children—Children up to 2 years of age are more susceptible to the effects of opioids, especially respiratory depression; also, children may be more likely to experience paradoxical CNS excitation during therapy

Hydromorphone extended-release capsules are not recommended for children younger than 18 years of age.

Use in the elderly—Geriatric patients are more susceptible to the effects of opioids, especially respiratory depression

Dental—May cause dryness of mouth, which can lead to caries, periodontal disease, oral candidiasis, and discomfort

Other medications, especially alcohol or other CNS depressants, monoamine oxidase inhibitors, naltrexone, rifampin, and zidovudine

Other medical problems, especially diarrhea caused by antibiotics or poisoning, asthma or other respiratory problems, paralytic ileus, suspected or known, depleted blood volume, circulatory shock, and severe inflammatory bowel disease

Proper use of this medication

Proper administration of

» Injections (if dispensed to the patient for home use)

» Meperidine syrup—Mixing with ½ glass (4 ounces) of water to lessen numbing effect in mouth and throat

» Methadone oral concentrate—Diluting with water to at least 1 ounce before taking, unless premixed at a methadone treatment center

» Methadone dispersible tablets—Must be dissolved in water or fruit juice before taking

Morphine oral liquid—May be mixed with fruit juice to improve taste

» Hydromorphone extended-release capsules, morphine extended-release tablets, and oxycodone extended-release tablets—Swallowing tablets whole; not breaking, crushing, or chewing

» Morphine extended-release capsules for once daily administration—Swallowing tablets whole (not chewing, crushing, or dissolving) or opening capsule and sprinkling entire bead contents on a small amount of applesauce immediately prior to ingestion and not chewing, crushing, or dissolving the capsule beads due to risk of acute overdose

Suppository dosage forms—Proper administration technique

Proper administration of opium tincture

Medication may be diluted in water, which will cause it to turn milky

Taking with food or meals if gastrointestinal irritation occurs

» Importance of not taking more medication than the amount prescribed because of danger of overdose and habit-forming potential

» Not increasing dose if medication is less effective after a few weeks; checking with physician

Missed dose: If on scheduled dosing, taking as soon as possible; not taking if almost time for next dose; not doubling doses

» Proper storage

Precautions while using this medication

Regular visits to physician to check progress during long-term therapy

» Read the instructions for the patient, if available.

Talk to you doctor if pain persists or worsens while taking this medicine.

This medicine should be protected from theft or misuse in the work or home environment.

» Avoiding use of alcoholic beverages or other CNS depressants during therapy, unless prescribed or otherwise approved by physician

» Caution if dizziness, drowsiness, lightheadedness, or false sense of well-being occurs

» Caution when getting up suddenly from a lying or sitting position

Lying down if nausea or vomiting, or dizziness or lightheadedness occurs

Need to inform physician or dentist of use of medication if any kind of surgery (including dental surgery) or emergency treatment is required

Possible dryness of mouth; using sugarless gum or candy, ice, or saliva substitute for relief; checking with dentist if dry mouth continues for more than 2 weeks

» Checking with physician before discontinuing medication after prolonged use of high doses; gradual dosage reduction may be necessary to avoid withdrawal symptoms

» Suspected overdose: Getting emergency help at once

For opium tincture when used as antidiarrheal only:

» Consulting physician if diarrhea continues and/or fever develops

Side/adverse effects

Signs of potential side effects, especially respiratory depression or impairment; allergic reactions; confusion, convulsions, hallucinations, mental depression, or other signs of CNS toxicity; hepatotoxicity; hypertension; and paradoxical CNS excitation, especially in children

General Dosing Information

These medications may suppress respiration, especially in very young, elderly, very ill, or debilitated patients and those with respiratory problems. Lower doses may be required for these patients. However, elderly patients may also be more sensitive to the analgesic effects of these medications so that lower doses or an increased dosing interval may be sufficient to provide effective analgesia.

Dosage and dosing intervals should be individualized on the basis of the potency and duration of action of the specific drug used, the severity of pain, the condition of the patient, other medications given concurrently, and patient response.

Concurrent administration of a nonopioid analgesic (such as aspirin or other salicylates, other nonsteroidal anti-inflammatory analgesics, or acetaminophen) with opioid analgesics provides additive analgesia and may permit lower doses of the opioid analgesic to be utilized.

Some clinicians recommend that patients in severe chronic pain receive opioid analgesics on a fixed dosage schedule so that they remain free of pain rather than on an as needed basis after pain recurs. The medication should be given orally if possible.

Tolerance to many of the effects of these medications may develop with repeated administration. The first sign of tolerance is usually a decrease in the duration of adequate analgesia. Tolerance to the respiratory depressant effects of opioid analgesics develops concurrently with tolerance to their analgesic effects. Careful adjustment of dosage as required to provide adequate analgesia is not likely to increase the risk of respiratory depression. Patients who become tolerant to one of these agents may be partially cross-tolerant to the others. However, when an alternate opioid analgesic is substituted for one to which tolerance has developed, it is recommended that one-half of the equianalgesic dose of the new medication be used initially. Dosage of the new medication may then be adjusted as necessary.

Psychological and physical dependence may occur with chronic administration of opioid analgesics, including epidurally or intrathecally administered opioid analgesics; an abstinence syndrome may occur when these drugs are discontinued. Physical dependence in patients receiving prolonged therapy for severe chronic pain rarely leads to true addiction, i.e., a desire to continue taking the drug (for its euphoric effect) after it is no longer required for treatment. Fear of causing addiction should not result in failure to provide adequate pain relief, although caution is advised if patient predisposition toward drug abuse is known or strongly suspected. Gradual withdrawal may minimize the development of withdrawal symptoms following prolonged use.

For parenteral dosage forms only

Rapid intravenous injection of most opioid analgesics has caused anaphylactoid reactions, severe respiratory depression, hypotension, peripheral circulatory collapse, and cardiac arrest. It is recommended that when an opioid analgesic must be given intravenously, dosage should be reduced and a dilute solution should be injected slowly over a period of several minutes. An opioid antagonist and equipment for artificial ventilation should be available.

When an opioid analgesic is administered parenterally, the patient usually should be lying down and should remain recumbent for a period of time to minimize side effects such as hypotension, dizziness, lightheadedness, nausea, and vomiting. If these side effects occur in an ambulatory patient, they may be relieved if the patient lies down.

In patients with shock, impaired perfusion may prevent complete absorption following intramuscular or subcutaneous injection. Repeated administration may result in overdose due to an excessive amount suddenly being absorbed when circulation is restored.

Opioid analgesics may not provide sufficient analgesia to prevent or overcome hemodynamic responses to surgical stress when used as the sole intravenous supplement to nitrous oxide for the maintenance of balanced anesthesia. Concurrent use of other medications, such as a benzodiazepine, an ultrashort-acting barbiturate, or a potent hydrocarbon inhalation anesthetic, may be required.

Epidural or intrathecal administration of opioid analgesics should be performed only by physicians experienced in these techniques. Solutions containing a preservative must *not* be injected via these routes. *Resuscitative equipment and medications should be immediately available for management of respiratory depression or other complications that may arise from inadvertent intrathecal or intravascular administration.* Also, facilities for adequate monitoring of the patient's respiratory status must be available.

For epidural or intrathecal administration, injection into the lumbar area may be preferred because of the increased risk of respiratory depression with injection into the thoracic area. Also, the epidural route is preferred, whenever possible, because of the increased risk of respiratory depression with intrathecal administration.

Prior to epidural administration, proper placement of the needle or catheter in the epidural space must be verified. Aspiration to check for blood in the cerebrospinal fluid may be performed; however, the fact that intravascular administration is possible even when aspiration for blood is negative must be kept in mind. Alternatively, administration of 5 mL (3 mL for obstetrical patients) of preservative-free 1.5% lidocaine hydrochloride with epinephrine 1:200,000 injection may be used to verify placement in the epidural space. Tachycardia occurring after injection of the test medication indicates that the medication has entered the circulation; sudden onset of segmental anesthesia indicates that the medication has been administered intrathecally.

Following epidural or intrathecal injection of an opioid analgesic, administration of low doses of naloxone via continuous intravenous infusion for 24 hours may decrease the incidence of potential side effects without interfering with the analgesic effectiveness of the medication.

ANILERIDINE

Summary of Differences

Pharmacology/pharmacokinetics:
- Equivalence—
  - 75 mg via oral administration therapeutically equivalent to 10 mg of intramuscular morphine.
- Biotransformation—
  - Metabolized mostly in the liver.
- Onset of action—
  - Oral: 15 minutes
- Duration of action—
  - 2 or 3 hours
- Excretion—
  - Very little is excreted in the urine.

Oral dosage forms

ANILERIDINE HYDROCHLORIDE TABLETS USP

Usual adult dose

Analgesic—
- Oral, 25 to 50 mg (base) every 6 hours as needed.

Usual pediatric dose

Analgesic—
- Dosage in patients up to 12 years of age has not been established.

Strength(s) usually available

U.S.—
- Not commercially available.

Canada—
- 25 mg (base) (Rx) [*Leritine*].

Packaging and storage

Store between 15 and 30 °C (59 and 86 °F). Protect from light.

Note: Controlled substance in Canada.

BUTORPHANOL

Summary of Differences

Indications:
- Caution required when used as analgesic to relieve pain due to acute myocardial infarction because of cardiovascular effects that tend to increase cardiac work.

Pharmacology/pharmacokinetics:
- Mechanism of action/effect—
  - An opioid agonist/antagonist analgesic.
  - Agonist: Has agonist activity at the kappa and sigma receptors.
  - Antagonist: Probably has no direct antagonist activity at the mu receptor; antagonist effects may result from failure to substitute for mu receptor agonists sufficiently to prevent or attenuate withdrawal symptoms in physically dependent patients.
- Equivalence—
  - 2 mg via intramuscular injection therapeutically equivalent to 10 mg of intramuscular morphine.
- Protein binding—
  - High.
- Half-life—
  - 2.5–4 hours.
- Onset of action—
  - Intramuscular: 10–30 minutes.
  - Intravenous: 2–3 minutes.
- Time to peak concentration—
  - 0.5–1 hour.
- Peak plasma concentration—
  - 2.2 nanograms/mL.
- Time to peak effect—
  - Intramuscular: 30–60 minutes.
  - Intravenous: 30 minutes.
- Duration of action (nontolerant patients only; decreases as tolerance develops during chronic therapy)—
  - Intramuscular: 3–4 hours.
  - Intravenous: 2–4 hours.
- Elimination—
  - 72% Renal, < 5% as unchanged buprenorphine; 15% biliary.

Precautions:
- Laboratory value alterations—
  - Does not interfere with hepatobiliary imaging.
  - Does not increase plasma amylase or lipase activity.
- Medical considerations/contraindications—
  - Caution not required in gallbladder disease or gallstones.
  - Also, should be used with caution in patients physically dependent on opioid agonists, in hypertensive patients (when used preoperatively), and in patients with acute myocardial infarction.

Side/adverse effects:
- Less likely to cause constipation than most other opioids.
- Biliary spasm has not been reported.
- Rarely, may cause subjective and psychotomimetic effects characteristic of sigma receptor agonists.
- Has lower dependence liability than opioid agonists.
- Withdrawal symptoms less severe than those produced by opioid agonist analgesics.

Parenteral Dosage Forms

BUTORPHANOL TARTRATE INJECTION USP

Usual adult dose

Analgesic—
- Intramuscular, 1 to 4 mg (usually 2 mg) every three to four hours as needed.
- Intravenous, 500 mcg (0.5 mg) to 2 mg (usually 1 mg) every three to four hours as needed.

Anesthesia adjunct—
- Preoperative—
  - Intravenous, usually 2 mg sixty to ninety minutes prior to surgery, although dosage must be individualized.
- Balanced anesthesia—
  - Intravenous, initially 1 to 4 mg, followed by supplemental doses of 500 mcg (0.5 mg) to 1 mg as needed.

  Note: Dosage must be individualized. Supplemental doses of up to 60 mcg (0.06 mg) per kg of body weight may be necessary in some patients.

  The total quantity of butorphanol required during surgery usually ranges between 60 and 180 mcg (0.06 and 0.18 mg) per kg of body weight.

Usual pediatric dose

Dosage in patients up to 18 years of age has not been established.

Strength(s) usually available

U.S.—
- With preservative (benzethonium chloride 0.1 mg/mL):
  - 2 mg per mL (Rx) [*Stadol*].
- Without preservative:
  - 1 mg per mL (Rx) [*Stadol*].
  - 2 mg per mL (Rx) [*Stadol*].

Canada—
- Not commercially available.

Packaging and storage

Store between 15 and 30 °C (59 and 86 °F), unless otherwise specified by manufacturer. Protect from light. Protect from freezing.

Auxiliary labeling
- May cause drowsiness.
- Avoid alcoholic beverages.

Note
Controlled substance in the U.S.

CODEINE

Summary of Differences

Indications:
Oral dosage forms also indicated as antitussive.
Also, used as antidiarrheal.
Pharmacology/pharmacokinetics:
Mechanism of action/effect—
An opioid agonist analgesic; exerts agonist activity primarily at the mu receptor, but with usual doses is relatively weak.
Equivalence—
120 mg via intramuscular injection or 200 mg via oral administration therapeutically equivalent to 10 mg of intramuscular morphine.
Protein binding—
Very low.
Half-life—
2.5–4 hours.
Biotransformation—
Hepatic; about 10% demethylated to morphine.
Onset of action—
Analgesic:
Intramuscular—10–30 minutes.
Subcutaneous—10–30 minutes.
Oral—30–45 minutes.
Time to peak effect—
Analgesic:
Intramuscular—30–60 minutes.
Oral—1–2 hours.
Duration of action—
Analgesic (in nontolerant patients only; decreases as tolerance develops during chronic therapy): Intramuscular, subcutaneous, or oral—4 hours.
Antitussive: Oral—4–6 hours.
Elimination—
Renal, 5–15% as unchanged codeine and 10% as unchanged or conjugated morphine.
Side/adverse effects:
More likely than most other opioids to cause constipation, especially during chronic therapy.
Has lower dependence liability than most other opioid agonists.
Withdrawal symptoms less severe than those produced by stronger opioid agonist analgesics.

Additional Dosing Information

See also *General Dosing Information.*

For parenteral dosage forms only

Local tissue irritation, pain, and induration may occur with repeated subcutaneous injection.

Oral Dosage Forms

Note: Bracketed uses in the *Dosage Forms* section refer to categories of use and/or indications that are not included in U.S. product labeling.

CODEINE PHOSPHATE ORAL SOLUTION

Usual adult dose
Analgesic—
Oral, 15 to 60 mg (usually 30 mg) every three to six hours as needed.
[Antidiarrheal][1]—
Oral, 30 mg up to four times a day.
Antitussive—
Oral, 10 to 20 mg every four to six hours.

Usual adult prescribing limits
Antitussive—
Up to 120 mg in twenty-four hours.

Usual pediatric dose
Analgesic—
Premature infants: Use is not recommended.
Newborn infants: Dosage has not been established.
Infants and children: Oral, 500 mcg (0.5 mg) per kg of body weight or 15 mg per square meter of body surface every four to six hours as needed.
[Antidiarrheal][1]—
Oral, 500 mcg (0.5 mg) per kg of body weight up to four times a day.
Antitussive—
Children up to 2 years of age—
Use is not recommended.
Children 2 to 5 years of age—
Oral, 1 mg per kg of body weight per day, administered in four equal divided doses, or for
Children 2 years of age (average body weight 12 kg)—Oral, 3 mg every four to six hours, not to exceed 12 mg per day.
Children 3 years of age (average body weight 14 kg)—Oral, 3.5 mg every four to six hours, not to exceed 14 mg per day.
Children 4 years of age (average body weight 16 kg)—Oral, 4 mg every four to six hours, not to exceed 16 mg per day.
Children 5 years of age (average body weight 18 kg)—Oral, 4.5 mg every four to six hours, not to exceed 18 mg per day.
Children 6 to 12 years of age—
Oral, 5 to 10 mg every four to six hours, not to exceed 60 mg per day.

Note: Use of a calibrated measure is recommended to prevent possible overdosage in children up to 6 years of age.

Strength(s) usually available
U.S.—
15 mg per 5 mL (Rx).
Canada—
10 mg per mL (Rx) [*Paveral*].

Packaging and storage
Store below 40 °C (104 °F), preferably between 15 and 30 °C (59 and 86 °F), in a tight, light-resistant container, unless otherwise specified by manufacturer. Protect from freezing.

Auxiliary labeling
- May cause drowsiness.
- Avoid alcoholic beverages.
- May be habit-forming.

Note
Controlled substance in both the U.S. and Canada.

CODEINE PHOSPHATE TABLETS USP

Usual adult dose
Analgesic—
Oral, 15 to 60 mg (usually 30 mg) every three to six hours as needed.
[Antidiarrheal][1]—
Oral, 30 mg up to four times a day.
Antitussive—
Oral, 10 to 20 mg every four to six hours.

Usual adult prescribing limits
Antitussive—
Up to 120 mg in twenty-four hours.

Usual pediatric dose
Analgesic—
Premature infants: Use is not recommended.
Newborn infants: Dosage has not been established.
Infants and children: Oral, 500 mcg (0.5 mg) per kg of body weight or 15 mg per square meter of body surface every four to six hours as needed.
[Antidiarrheal][1]—
Oral, 500 mcg (0.5 mg) per kg of body weight up to four times a day.
Antitussive—
Children up to 2 years of age—
Use is not recommended.
Children 2 to 5 years of age—
Oral, 1 mg per kg of body weight per day, administered in four equal divided doses, or for
Children 2 years of age (average body weight 12 kg)—Oral, 3 mg every four to six hours, not to exceed 12 mg per day.
Children 3 years of age (average body weight 14 kg)—Oral, 3.5 mg every four to six hours, not to exceed 14 mg per day.
Children 4 years of age (average body weight 16 kg)—Oral, 4 mg every four to six hours, not to exceed 16 mg per day.
Children 5 years of age (average body weight 18 kg)—Oral, 4.5 mg every four to six hours, not to exceed 18 mg per day.
Children 6 to 12 years of age—
Oral, 5 to 10 mg every four to six hours, not to exceed 60 mg per day.

Strength(s) usually available
U.S.—
30 mg (Rx) [GENERIC].
60 mg (Rx) [GENERIC].
Canada—
15 mg (Rx) [GENERIC].
30 mg (Rx) [GENERIC].

Note: Strengths of commercially available tablets do not correspond to recommended antitussive doses.

Packaging and storage
Store below 40 °C (104 °F), preferably between 15 and 30 °C (59 and 86 °F). Store in a well-closed, light-resistant container.

Auxiliary labeling
- May cause drowsiness.
- Avoid alcoholic beverages.
- May be habit-forming.

Note
Controlled substance in both the U.S. and Canada.

CODEINE SULFATE TABLETS USP

Usual adult dose
Analgesic—
Oral, 15 to 60 mg (usually 30 mg) every three to six hours as needed.
[Antidiarrheal]—
Oral, 30 mg up to four times a day.
Antitussive—
Oral, 10 to 20 mg every four to six hours.

Usual pediatric dose
Analgesic—
Premature infants: Use is not recommended.
Newborn infants: Dosage has not been established.
Infants and children: Oral, 500 mcg (0.5 mg) per kg of body weight or 15 mg per square meter of body surface every four to six hours as needed.
[Antidiarrheal]—
Oral, 500 mcg (0.5 mg) per kg of body weight up to four times a day.
Antitussive—
Children up to 2 years of age—
Use is not recommended.
Children 2 to 5 years of age—
Oral, 1 mg per kg of body weight per day, administered in four equal divided doses, or for
Children 2 years of age (average body weight 12 kg)—Oral, 3 mg every four to six hours, not to exceed 12 mg per day.
Children 3 years of age (average body weight 14 kg)—Oral, 3.5 mg every four to six hours, not to exceed 14 mg per day.
Children 4 years of age (average body weight 16 kg)—Oral, 4 mg every four to six hours, not to exceed 16 mg per day.
Children 5 years of age (average body weight 18 kg)—Oral, 4.5 mg every four to six hours, not to exceed 18 mg per day.
Children 6 to 12 years of age—
Oral, 5 to 10 mg every four to six hours, not to exceed 60 mg per day.

Strength(s) usually available
U.S.—
15 mg (Rx) [GENERIC].
30 mg (Rx) [GENERIC].
60 mg (Rx) [GENERIC].
Canada—
Not commercially available.

Note: Strengths of commercially available tablets do not correspond to recommended antitussive doses.

Packaging and storage
Store below 40 °C (104 °F), preferably between 15 and 30 °C (59 and 86 °F). Store in a well-closed container.

Auxiliary labeling
- May cause drowsiness.
- Avoid alcoholic beverages.
- May be habit-forming.

Parenteral Dosage Forms

CODEINE PHOSPHATE INJECTION USP

Usual adult dose
Analgesic—
Intramuscular, intravenous, or subcutaneous, 15 to 60 mg (usually 30 mg) every four to six hours as needed.

Usual pediatric dose
Analgesic—
Premature infants: Use is not recommended.
Newborn infants: Dosage has not been established.
Infants and children: Intramuscular or subcutaneous, 500 mcg (0.5 mg) per kg of body weight or 15 mg per square meter of body surface every four to six hours as needed.

Strength(s) usually available
U.S.—
With preservative:
30 mg per mL (Rx) [GENERIC].
60 mg per mL (Rx) [GENERIC].
Canada—
30 mg per mL (Rx) [GENERIC].
60 mg per mL (Rx) [GENERIC].

Packaging and storage
Store below 40 °C (104 °F), preferably between 15 and 30 °C (59 and 86 °F), unless otherwise specified by manufacturer. Protect from light. Protect from freezing.

Auxiliary labeling
- May cause drowsiness.
- Avoid alcoholic beverages.
- May be habit-forming.

Note
Controlled substance in both the U.S. and Canada.

CODEINE PHOSPHATE SOLUBLE TABLETS

Usual adult dose
Analgesic—
Intramuscular or subcutaneous, 15 to 60 mg (usually 30 mg) every four to six hours as needed.

Usual pediatric dose
Analgesic—
Premature infants: Use is not recommended.
Newborn infants: Dosage has not been established.
Infants and children: Intramuscular or subcutaneous, 500 mcg (0.5 mg) per kg of body weight or 15 mg per square meter of body surface every four to six hours as needed.

Strength(s) usually available
U.S.—
30 mg (Rx) [GENERIC].
60 mg (Rx) [GENERIC].
Canada—
Not commercially available.

Packaging and storage
Store between 15 and 30 °C (59 and 86 °F), in a tight, light-resistant container, unless otherwise specified by manufacturer.

Preparation of dosage form
For parenteral administration—Dissolve the required number of tablets in a suitable volume of sterile water for injection, then filter through a 0.22-micron membrane filter.

Auxiliary labeling
- May cause drowsiness.
- Avoid alcoholic beverages.
- May be habit-forming.

Note
Controlled substance in the U.S.

CODEINE SULFATE SOLUBLE TABLETS

Usual adult dose
Analgesic—
Intramuscular or subcutaneous, 15 to 60 mg (usually 30 mg) every four to six hours as needed.

Usual pediatric dose
Analgesic—
Premature infants: Use is not recommended.
Newborn infants: Dosage has not been established.
Infants and children: Intramuscular or subcutaneous, 500 mcg (0.5 mg) per kg of body weight or 15 mg per square meter of body surface every four to six hours as needed.

Strength(s) usually available
U.S.—
30 mg (Rx) [GENERIC].
60 mg (Rx) [GENERIC].
Canada—
Not commercially available.

Packaging and storage
Store between 15 and 30 °C (59 and 86 °F), in a tight, light-resistant container, unless otherwise specified by manufacturer.

Preparation of dosage form
For parenteral administration—Dissolve the required number of tablets in a suitable volume of sterile water for injection, then filter through a 0.22–micron membrane filter.

Auxiliary labeling
- May cause drowsiness.
- Avoid alcoholic beverages.
- May be habit-forming.

Note
Controlled substance in the U.S.

[1]Not included in Canadian product labeling.

HYDROCODONE

Summary of Differences

Indications:
Also, indicated as an antitussive.
Pharmacology/pharmacokinetics—
Mechanism of action/effect—
An opioid agonist analgesic; exerts agonist activity primarily at the mu receptor.
Half-life—
3.8 hours.
Onset of action—
Analgesic: Oral 10–30 minutes.
Time to peak effect—
Analgesic: Oral 30–60 minutes.
Duration of action—
Analgesic (nontolerant patients only; decreases as tolerance develops during chronic therapy): Oral—4–6 hours.
Antitussive: Oral—4–6 hours.
Elimination—
Renal.
Side/adverse effects:
More likely than most other opioids to cause side effects associated with histamine release.

Oral Dosage Forms

HYDROCODONE BITARTRATE SYRUP

Usual adult dose
Antitussive—
Oral, 5 mg every four to six hours as needed.

Usual pediatric dose
Dosage has not been established.

Strength(s) usually available
U.S.—
Not commercially available.
Canada—
5 mg per 5 mL (Rx) [*Hycodan* (sucrose); *Robidone* (alcohol 3.2%; sugar)].

Note: In Canada, *Hycodan* contains only hydrocodone bitartrate; in the U.S., *Hycodan* contains homatropine in addition to hydrocodone bitartrate.

Packaging and storage
Store below 40 °C (104 °F), preferably between 15 and 30 °C (59 and 86 °F), in a well-closed container, unless otherwise specified by manufacturer. Protect from freezing.

Auxiliary labeling
- May cause drowsiness.
- Avoid alcoholic beverages.
- May be habit-forming.

Note
Controlled substance in Canada.

HYDROCODONE BITARTRATE TABLETS USP

Usual adult dose
Analgesic—
Oral, 5 to 10 mg every four to six hours as needed.
Antitussive—
Oral, 5 mg every four to six hours as needed.

Usual pediatric dose
Analgesic—
Oral, 150 mcg (0.15 mg) per kg of body weight every six hours as needed.

Strength(s) usually available
U.S.—
Not commercially available.
Canada—
5 mg (Rx) [*Hycodan* (scored; lactose)].

Note: In Canada, *Hycodan* contains only hydrocodone bitartrate; in the U.S., *Hycodan* contains homatropine in addition to hydrocodone bitartrate.

Packaging and storage
Store below 40 °C (104 °F), preferably between 15 and 30 °C (59 and 86 °F). Store in a tight, light-resistant container.

Auxiliary labeling
- May cause drowsiness.
- Avoid alcoholic beverages.
- May be habit-forming.

Note
Controlled substance in Canada.

HYDROMORPHONE

Summary of Differences

Indications:
Also, indicated as an antitussive; see also *Cough/Cold Combinations (Systemic)—Hydromorphone and Guaifenesin.*
Pharmacology/pharmacokinetics:
Mechanism of action/effect—
An opioid agonist analgesic; exerts agonist activity primarily at the mu receptor.
Equivalence—
1.5 mg via intramuscular injection, 7.5 mg via oral administration, or 3 mg via rectal administration therapeutically equivalent to 10 mg of intramuscular morphine.
The once daily dose of hydromorphone extended-release capsule is equivalent to the same total daily dose of immediate-release hydromorphone given in divided doses every 6 hours based on AUC in healthy human subjects.
Half-life—
Intravenous: approximately 3 hours.
Oral, extended-release capsule, mean: approximately 18 hours
Oral, immediate-release: 2.6–4 hours.
Onset of action—
Intramuscular: 15 minutes.
Intravenous: 10–15 minutes.
Oral, extended-release capsule: approximately 1 hour
Oral, immediate-release: 30 minutes.
Subcutaneous: 15 minutes.
Time to peak effect—
Intramuscular: 30–60 minutes.
Intravenous: 15–30 minutes.
Oral: 90–120 minutes.
Subcutaneous: 30–90 minutes.
Time to steady-state—
Oral, extended-release capsule: within 2 to 3 days.
Duration of action (nontolerant patients only; decreases as tolerance develops during chronic therapy)—
Intramuscular: 4–5 hours.
Intravenous: 2–3 hours.
Oral, extended-release capsule: greater than 24 hours
Oral, immediate-release: 4 hours.
Subcutaneous: 4 hours.
Elimination—
Renal.

Oral Dosage Forms

HYDROMORPHONE HYDROCHLORIDE EXTENDED-RELEASE CAPSULES

Usual adult dose
Analgesic (opioid tolerant patients only)—
Oral, 12 to 32 mg given once a day. Dosage must be individualized based on the patient's opioid requirement. Patients selected for therapy are those already receiving opioid therapy, who have demonstrated opioid tolerance, and who require a minimum total daily

dose of opiate medication equivalent to 12 mg of oral hydromorphone. Patients considered opioid tolerant are those who are taking at least 60 mg oral morphine per day, or at least 30 mg oral oxycodone per day, or at least 8 mg oral hydromorphone per day. See manufacturer's instructions for additional dosing information.

Note: Over estimating the dose of this medication when converting patients from another opioid medication can result in fatal overdose with the first dose.

Hepatic impairment, severe: Use not recommended. Use has not been studied in patients with severe hepatic impairment.

Hepatic impairment, mild to moderate: Use with caution. Careful initial dose selection and observation is recommended in patients with mild to moderate hepatic impairment.

Renal impairment, mild to moderate: Use with caution. The plasma concentration of hydromorphone were slightly higher in patients with mild to moderate renal impairment compared to subjects with normal renal function, based on calculated creatinine clearance. Dosages should be adjusted according to the clinical situation.

Usual pediatric dose

The safety and effectiveness have not been established in patients younger than 18 years.

Usual geriatric dose

See also *Usual adult dose.*

Note: Dosages should be adjusted according to the clinical situation. As with all opioids, the starting dose should be reduced to 33% to 50% of the usual dosage in debilitated patients. Respiratory depression is the primary hazard in elderly or debilitated patients following a large initial dose in nontolerant patients or when opioids are given in conjunction with other agents that depress respiration.

Strength(s) usually available

U.S.—

Note: PALLADONE (hydromorphone hydrochloride, extended release capsules) was suspended from the market by Purdue Pharma in July 2005. Drinking alcohol while taking PALLADONE may cause rapid release of hydromorphone and high drug levels in the body. High drug levels of hydromorphone may have serious effects, including depressed breathing, lack of breathing, coma, and death.

Canada—

Note: Purdue Pharma has not shipped any PALLADONE XL (hydromorphone hydrochloride, extended release capsules) to Canada since December 2004.

Auxiliary labeling

- Swallow whole. Do not crush or chew.
- May cause drowsiness. Be careful while driving or operating machinery. Use caution until you become familiar with its effects.
- Avoid alcohol while on this medication.
- You should take this medication exactly as prescribed. Do not skip or discontinue unless directed.
- Ask your doctor or pharmacist before using nonprescription drugs.
- Please read patient information leaflet enclosed.
- This medication may be habit forming.
- Keep out of the reach of children.

Note

Controlled substance in the U.S.

Additional information

The extended-release capsules are for use only in opioid-tolerant patients.

HYDROMORPHONE HYDROCHLORIDE ORAL SOLUTION

Usual adult dose

Analgesic—

Oral, 2.5 to 10 mg every three to six hours, depending on the severity of pain and patient tolerance.

Usual pediatric dose

Dosage must be individualized by physician, depending on the severity of pain and the patient's age, size, and opioid tolerance.

Strength(s) usually available

U.S.—

5 mg per 5 mL [*Dilaudid-5*].

Canada—

5 mg per 5 mL [*Dilaudid* (sucrose); *PMS-Hydromorphone Syrup*].

HYDROMORPHONE HYDROCHLORIDE TABLETS USP

Usual adult dose

Analgesic—

Oral, 2 mg every three to six hours as needed.

Note: Dosage may be increased to 4 mg or more every four to six hours, depending on the severity of pain and patient tolerance.

Usual pediatric dose

Dosage must be individualized by physician, depending on the severity of pain and the patient's age, size, and opioid tolerance.

Strength(s) usually available

U.S.—

1 mg (Rx) [*Hydrostat IR*].
2 mg (Rx) [*Dilaudid* (lactose); *Hydrostat IR;* GENERIC].
3 mg (Rx) [*Hydrostat IR*].
4 mg (Rx) [*Dilaudid* (lactose); *Hydrostat IR;* GENERIC].
8 mg (Rx) [*Dilaudid*].

Canada—

1 mg (Rx) [*Dilaudid; PMS-Hydromorphone*].
2 mg (Rx) [*Dilaudid; PMS-Hydromorphone;* GENERIC].
4 mg (Rx) [*Dilaudid; PMS-Hydromorphone;* GENERIC].
8 mg (Rx) [*Dilaudid; PMS-Hydromorphone*].

Packaging and storage

Store below 40 °C (104 °F), preferably between 15 and 30 °C (59 and 86 °F), unless otherwise specified by manufacturer. Store in a tight, light-resistant container.

Auxiliary labeling

- May cause drowsiness.
- Avoid alcoholic beverages.
- May be habit-forming.

Note

Controlled substance in both the U.S. and Canada.

Parenteral Dosage Forms

HYDROMORPHONE HYDROCHLORIDE INJECTION USP

Usual adult dose

Analgesic—

Intramuscular or subcutaneous, 1 to 2 mg every three to six hours as needed; may be increased to 3 or 4 mg every four to six hours if pain is severe.

Note: For opioid-tolerant patients requiring high-dose therapy, the 10-mg-per-mL concentration may be substituted for lower strengths of hydromorphone hydrochloride injection or for other opioid analgesics. Dosage must be individualized, depending on the severity of pain, opioid requirements at the time therapy with the high-potency injection is initiated, and patient response. Although patients who have become tolerant to another opioid may be at least partially cross-tolerant to hydromorphone also, it is recommended that one-half of the equianalgesic dose of hydromorphone be used initially, then adjusted as necessary.

Intravenous, 500 mcg (0.5 mg) to 1 mg every three hours as needed; administered slowly.

Usual pediatric dose

Dosage must be individualized by physician on the basis of patient's age and size.

Strength(s) usually available

U.S.—

With preservatives:
1 mg per mL (Rx) [GENERIC].
2 mg per mL (Rx) [*Dilaudid* (methylparaben and propylparaben); GENERIC].
3 mg per mL (Rx) [GENERIC].
4 mg per mL (Rx) [GENERIC].

Without preservative:
1 mg per mL (Rx) [*Dilaudid*].
2 mg per mL (Rx) [*Dilaudid*].
4 mg per mL (Rx) [*Dilaudid*].
10 mg per mL (Rx) [*Dilaudid-HP*].

Canada—

Without preservative:
2 mg per mL (Rx) [*Dilaudid*].
10 mg per mL (Rx) [*Dilaudid-HP*].

Packaging and storage

Store below 40 °C (104 °F), preferably between 15 and 30 °C (59 and 86 °F), unless otherwise specified by manufacturer. Protect from light. Protect from freezing.

Auxiliary labeling
- May cause drowsiness.
- Avoid alcoholic beverages.
- May be habit-forming.

Note
Controlled substance in both the U.S. and Canada.

Rectal Dosage Forms

HYDROMORPHONE HYDROCHLORIDE SUPPOSITORIES

Usual adult dose
Analgesic—
Rectal, 3 mg every four to eight hours as needed.

Usual pediatric dose
Dosage has not been established.

Strength(s) usually available
U.S.—
3 mg (Rx) [*Dilaudid*].
Canada—
3 mg (Rx) [*Dilaudid; PMS-Hydromorphone*].

Packaging and storage
Store between 2 and 8 °C (36 and 46 °F), in a well-closed container, unless otherwise specified by manufacturer. Protect from freezing.

Auxiliary labeling
- May cause drowsiness.
- Avoid alcoholic beverages.
- May be habit-forming.
- Store in refrigerator.

Note
Controlled substance in both the U.S. and Canada.

LEVORPHANOL

Summary of Differences
Pharmacology/pharmacokinetics:
Mechanism of action/effect—
An opioid agonist analgesic; exerts agonist activity primarily at the mu receptor.
Equivalence—
2 mg via intramuscular injection or 4 mg via oral administration therapeutically equivalent to 10 mg of intramuscular morphine.
Protein binding—
Moderate.
Onset of action—
Oral: 10–60 minutes.
Time to peak effect—
Intramuscular: 60 minutes.
Intravenous: Within 20 minutes.
Oral: 90–120 minutes.
Subcutaneous: 60–90 minutes.
Duration of action (nontolerant patients only; duration decreases as tolerance develops during chronic therapy)—
Intramuscular, intravenous, oral, or subcutaneous: 4–5 hours.
Elimination—
Renal.

Oral Dosage Forms

LEVORPHANOL TARTRATE TABLETS USP

Usual adult dose
Analgesic—
Oral, 2 mg; may be increased to 3 or 4 mg if pain is severe.

Usual pediatric dose
Dosage must be individualized by physician on the basis of patient's age and size.

Strength(s) usually available
U.S.—
2 mg (Rx) [*Levo-Dromoran* (scored; lactose); GENERIC].
Canada—
2 mg (Rx) [*Levo-Dromoran* (scored; lactose)].

Packaging and storage
Store between 15 and 30 °C (59 and 86 °F), in a light-resistant container, unless otherwise specified by manufacturer. Store in a well-closed container.

Auxiliary labeling
- May cause drowsiness.
- Avoid alcoholic beverages.
- May be habit-forming.

Note
Controlled substance in both the U.S. and Canada.

Parenteral Dosage Forms

LEVORPHANOL TARTRATE INJECTION USP

Usual adult dose
Analgesic—
Subcutaneous, 2 mg; may be increased to 3 mg if pain is severe.

Note: The medication may also be given intravenously.
For preoperative analgesia—Subcutaneous, 1 to 2 mg ninety minutes prior to surgery.

Usual pediatric dose
Dosage must be individualized by physician on the basis of patient's age and size.

Strength(s) usually available
U.S.—
With preservatives:
2 mg per mL (Rx) [*Levo-Dromoran* (methylparaben and propylparaben [1-mL ampuls]; or 0.45% phenol [10-mL vials])].
Canada—
With preservatives:
2 mg per mL (Rx) [*Levo-Dromoran* (0.45% phenol)].

Packaging and storage
Store below 40 °C (104 °F), preferably between 15 and 30 °C (59 and 86 °F), unless otherwise specified by manufacturer. Protect from freezing.

Auxiliary labeling
- May cause drowsiness.
- Avoid alcoholic beverages.
- May be habit-forming.

Note
Controlled substance in both the U.S. and Canada.

MEPERIDINE

Summary of Differences
Pharmacology/pharmacokinetics:
Mechanism of action/effect—
An opioid agonist analgesic; exerts agonist activity primarily at the mu receptor.
Equivalence—
75 mg via intramuscular injection or 300 mg via oral administration therapeutically equivalent to 10 mg of intramuscular morphine.
Protein binding—
High.
Half-life—
2.4–4 hours.
Biotransformation—
Metabolized to normeperidine, which is active and toxic.
Onset of action—
Intramuscular: 10–15 minutes.
Intravenous: 1 minute.
Oral: 15 minutes.
Subcutaneous: 10–15 minutes.
Time to peak effect—
Intramuscular: 30–50 minutes.
Intravenous: 5–7 minutes.
Oral: 60–90 minutes.
Subcutaneous: 30–50 minutes.
Duration of action (nontolerant patients only; decreases as tolerance develops during chronic therapy)—
Intramuscular, intravenous, oral, or subcutaneous: 2–4 hours.
Elimination—
Renal, 5% as unchanged meperidine.
Precautions:
Drug interactions and/or related problems—
May increase effects of coumarin- or indandione-derivative anticoagulants.
Contraindicated in patients who have received a monoamine oxidase (MAO) inhibitor within past 14–21 days; concurrent use has produced serious, sometimes fatal, reactions.

Concurrent use with amphetamines, which have some MAO-inhibiting activity, not recommended because of risk of serious reactions similar to those reported with other MAO inhibitors.

Side/adverse effects:

More likely than most other opioids to cause side effects associated with histamine release, convulsions, or constipation.

Additional Dosing Information

See also *General Dosing Information.*

For oral dosage forms only

The syrup may be diluted with half glass (120 mL) of water to prevent a slight topical anesthetic effect on the mucous membranes.

For parenteral dosage forms only

Intramuscular administration is preferred when repeated doses are required. Repeated subcutaneous administration causes local tissue irritation and induration.

Inadvertent injection around a nerve trunk may cause sensory-motor paralysis, which is usually, but not always, transitory.

Oral Dosage Forms

MEPERIDINE HYDROCHLORIDE SYRUP USP

Usual adult dose

Analgesic—

Oral, 50 to 150 mg (usually 100 mg) every three to four hours as needed.

Usual pediatric dose

Analgesic—

Oral, 1.1 to 1.76 mg per kg of body weight, not to exceed 100 mg, every three to four hours as needed. Use of a calibrated measure is recommended to prevent possible overdosage in children up to 6 years of age.

Strength(s) usually available

U.S.—

50 mg per 5 mL (Rx) [*Demerol* (glucose; saccharin sodium); GENERIC].

Canada—

Not commercially available.

Packaging and storage

Store below 40 °C (104 °F), preferably between 15 and 30 °C (59 and 86 °F). Store in a tight, light-resistant container. Protect from freezing.

Auxiliary labeling

- May cause drowsiness.
- Avoid alcoholic beverages.
- May be habit-forming.

Note

Controlled substance in the U.S.

MEPERIDINE HYDROCHLORIDE TABLETS USP

Usual adult dose

Analgesic—

Oral, 50 to 150 mg (usually 100 mg) every three to four hours as needed.

Usual pediatric dose

Analgesic—

Oral, 1.1 to 1.76 mg per kg of body weight, not to exceed 100 mg, every three to four hours as needed.

Strength(s) usually available

U.S.—

50 mg (Rx) [*Demerol;* GENERIC].

100 mg (Rx) [*Demerol;* GENERIC].

Canada—

50 mg (Rx) [*Demerol* (scored)].

Packaging and storage

Store below 40 °C (104 °F), preferably between 15 and 30 °C (59 and 86 °F). Store in a well-closed, light-resistant container.

Auxiliary labeling

- May cause drowsiness.
- Avoid alcoholic beverages.
- May be habit-forming.

Note

Controlled substance in both the U.S. and Canada.

Parenteral Dosage Forms

MEPERIDINE HYDROCHLORIDE INJECTION USP

Usual adult dose

Analgesic—

Intramuscular (preferred) or subcutaneous, 50 to 150 mg (usually 100 mg) every three to four hours as needed.

Intravenous infusion, 15 to 35 mg per hour as required, administered using an infusion pump.

Note: Dosage must be adjusted according to the severity of pain and patient response.

Obstetrical analgesia: Intramuscular (preferred) or subcutaneous, 50 to 100 mg administered when pains become regular. May be repeated at one- to three-hour intervals as needed.

Anesthesia adjunct—

Preoperative: Intramuscular (preferred) or subcutaneous, 50 to 100 mg thirty to ninety minutes prior to anesthesia.

Intravenous, by repeated slow injection of fractional doses of a solution diluted to 10 mg per mL.

Intravenous infusion, as a solution diluted to 1 mg per mL.

Note: Dosage must be titrated to the needs of the patient, depending on the premedication given, the type of anesthesia, and the nature and duration of the surgical procedure.

Usual pediatric dose

Analgesic—

Intramuscular (preferred) or subcutaneous, 1.1 to 1.76 mg per kg of body weight, not to exceed 100 mg, every three to four hours as needed.

Preoperative—

Intramuscular (preferred) or subcutaneous, 1 to 2.2 mg per kg of body weight, not to exceed 100 mg, thirty to ninety minutes prior to anesthesia.

Strength(s) usually available

U.S.—

Note: In addition to being available in single- or multiple-dose units containing the concentrations listed above, *Demerol* is available in single-dose ampuls that contain 0.5, 1.5, or 2 mL of the 50 mg per mL concentration (providing 25, 75, or 100 mg of meperidine hydrochloride, respectively).

With preservative:

25 mg per mL (Rx) [GENERIC].

50 mg per mL (Rx) [*Demerol* (metacresol); GENERIC].

75 mg per mL (Rx) [GENERIC].

100 mg per mL (Rx) [*Demerol* (metacresol); GENERIC].

Without preservative:

10 mg per mL (Rx) [GENERIC].

25 mg per mL (Rx) [*Demerol;* GENERIC].

50 mg per mL (Rx) [*Demerol;* GENERIC].

75 mg per mL (Rx) [*Demerol;* GENERIC].

100 mg per mL (Rx) [*Demerol;* GENERIC].

Canada—

With preservative:

50 mg per mL (Rx) [*Demerol* (metacresol)].

100 mg per mL (Rx) [*Demerol* (metacresol)].

Without preservative:

10 mg per mL (Rx) [GENERIC].

25 mg per mL (Rx) [GENERIC].

50 mg per mL (Rx) [*Demerol;* GENERIC].

75 mg per mL (Rx) [*Demerol;* GENERIC].

100 mg per mL (Rx) [*Demerol;* GENERIC].

Packaging and storage

Store below 40 °C (104 °F), preferably between 15 and 30 °C (59 and 86 °F), unless otherwise specified by manufacturer. Protect from light. Protect from freezing.

Incompatibilities

Solutions of meperidine are chemically incompatible with aminophylline, barbiturates, heparin, iodides, methicillin, phenytoin, sodium bicarbonate, sulfadiazine, and sulfisoxazole.

Auxiliary labeling

- May cause drowsiness.
- Avoid alcoholic beverages.
- May be habit-forming.

Note

Controlled substance in both the U.S. and Canada.

METHADONE

Summary of Differences

Note: In the U.S., methadone may be dispensed for treatment of opioid addiction only through treatment programs that have been approved by the Food and Drug Administration (FDA), Drug Enforcement Administration (DEA), and designated state authorities. Use of methadone in such programs is subject to treatment requirements stipulated in the Code of Federal Regulations.

In Canada, methadone is a controlled substance (Classification N). It is available only through physicians who have received special authorization to prescribe the medication for treatment of opioid addiction.

Indications:
- Also, indicated as narcotic abstinence syndrome suppressant.
- Also, used as antitussive.
- Not recommended for obstetrical analgesia.

Pharmacology/pharmacokinetics:
- Mechanism of action/effect—
  - An opioid agonist analgesic; exerts agonist activity primarily at the mu receptor.
- Equivalence—
  - 10 mg via intramuscular injection or 20 mg via oral administration therapeutically equivalent to 10 mg of intramuscular morphine.
- Protein binding—
  - High.
- Half-life—
  - 15–25 hours; increases with repeated administration.
- Onset of action—
  - Intramuscular: 10–20 minutes.
  - Oral: 30–60 minutes.
- Time to peak effect—
  - Intramuscular: 1–2 hours.
  - Intravenous: 15–30 minutes.
  - Oral: 1.5–2 hours.
- Duration of action (in nontolerant patients, may increase considerably with chronic use because of accumulation of methadone or active metabolites; may then decrease as tolerance develops during chronic therapy)—
  - Intramuscular: 4–5 hours.
  - Intravenous: 3–4 hours.
  - Oral: 4–6 hours.
- Elimination—
  - Primarily renal (rate increased in acidic urine); also some biliary elimination.

Precautions:
- Drug interactions and/or related problems—
  - Urinary acidifiers may increase methadone elimination, thereby reducing the plasma concentration; withdrawal symptoms may occur in some physically dependent patients.
  - Phenytoin or rifampin may increase methadone metabolism and precipitate withdrawal symptoms in physically dependent patients.

Side/adverse effects:
- May be more likely than most other opioids to cause constipation.

Additional Dosing Information

See also *General Dosing Information.*

U.S. Federal regulations permit methadone to be used in detoxification and maintenance treatment programs for opioid addiction. Short-term (up to 30 days) or long-term (up to 180 days) detoxification programs use methadone to alleviate adverse physiological or psychological consequences of withdrawal from illicit opioids, with dosage gradually being decreased until a drug-free state is achieved. After 180 days, patients who have not achieved a drug-free state are considered to be receiving maintenance treatment. Patients 18 years of age or older may also be enrolled directly into a maintenance program without first attempting detoxification. In maintenance treatment programs, relatively stable doses of opioid are given on a continuing basis as a substitute for illicit opioids.

Detoxification and comprehensive maintenance programs must include a full range of medical and rehabilitative services in addition to opioid administration. However, patients who are awaiting admission to a comprehensive maintenance program may receive up to 120 days of interim maintenance treatment, which consists only of opioid administration and needed medical services.

Oral administration is preferred for detoxification and mandatory for maintenance.

For parenteral dosage forms only

Intramuscular administration is recommended when repeated doses are required. Repeated subcutaneous administration causes local tissue irritation and induration.

Oral Dosage Forms

METHADONE HYDROCHLORIDE ORAL CONCENTRATE USP

Usual adult dose

Analgesic—
- Oral, 5 to 20 mg every four to eight hours. Dosage may be increased or the interval between doses decreased if pain is very severe or if the patient becomes tolerant to the medication.

Suppressant (narcotic abstinence syndrome)—
- Detoxification: Oral, 15 to 40 mg once a day or as needed to control observed withdrawal symptoms; dosage to be reduced at one- or two-day intervals according to patient response.
- Maintenance: Dosage must be individualized.

Usual adult prescribing limits

Up to 120 mg per day.

Usual pediatric dose

Analgesic—
- Dosage must be individualized by physician on the basis of patient's age and size. Use of a calibrated measure is recommended to prevent possible overdosage in children up to 6 years of age.

Suppressant (narcotic abstinence syndrome)—
- Dosage must be individualized by physician according to the needs of the specific patient. Dosage must not exceed 120 mg per day.
- Note: Patients younger than 18 years of age may be admitted to methadone maintenance programs only after two documented attempts at short-term (up to thirty days) detoxification or drug-free treatment have failed. A one-week waiting period is required between a detoxification attempt and admission to a methadone maintenance program. A parent, legal guardian, or other responsible adult designated by the State authority must complete and sign a consent to treatment form for all such minors.

Strength(s) usually available

U.S.—
- 10 mg per mL (Rx) [*Methadose;* GENERIC].

Packaging and storage

Store between 15 and 30 °C (59 and 86 °F). Store in a tight container. Protect from light. Protect from freezing.

Preparation of dosage form

Each dose must be diluted with water or another liquid before administration. For use in the treatment of chronic pain, each dose should be diluted to at least 30 mL. U.S. Federal regulations stipulate that the oral concentrate be diluted with water or other suitable liquid before being administered to a patient undergoing treatment for opioid addiction. It is recommended that each dose be diluted to 90 mL or more as a deterrent to misuse by injection. Treatment centers that dispense both methadone and levomethadyl (which must also be dispensed as a diluted liquid) should use liquids of different colors for preparing each medication, so that they can be readily distinguished from each other.

Auxiliary labeling
- May cause drowsiness.
- Avoid alcoholic beverages.
- May be habit-forming.

Note

Controlled substance in the U.S.

When preparing the label, indicate that the medication must be diluted with water or another liquid to 30 mL or more prior to administration.

If the concentrate is being taken home, make sure the patient understands the dilution requirements.

METHADONE HYDROCHLORIDE ORAL SOLUTION USP

Usual adult dose

Analgesic—
- Oral, 5 to 20 mg every four to eight hours. Dosage may be increased or the interval between doses decreased if pain is very severe or if the patient becomes tolerant to the medication.

Usual pediatric dose

Analgesic—
- Dosage must be individualized by physician on the basis of patient's age and size. Use of a calibrated measure is recommended to prevent possible overdosage in children up to 6 years of age.

Strength(s) usually available
U.S.—
5 mg per 5 mL (Rx) [GENERIC].
10 mg per 5 mL (Rx) [GENERIC].
Canada—
Not commercially available.

Packaging and storage
Store between 15 and 30 °C (59 and 86 °F). Store in a tight container. Protect from light. Protect from freezing.

Auxiliary labeling
- May cause drowsiness.
- Avoid alcoholic beverages.
- May be habit-forming.

Note
Controlled substance in the U.S.

METHADONE HYDROCHLORIDE TABLETS USP

Usual adult dose
Analgesic—
Oral, 2.5 to 10 mg every three to four hours as needed initially. For chronic use, dose and dosing interval to be adjusted according to patient response.

Usual pediatric dose
Analgesic—
Dosage must be individualized by physician on the basis of patient's age and size.

Strength(s) usually available
U.S.—
5 mg (Rx) [*Dolophine* (lactose; sucrose); *Methadose;* GENERIC].
10 mg (Rx) [*Dolophine* (lactose; sucrose); *Methadose;* GENERIC].
Canada—
Not commercially available.

Packaging and storage
Store below 40 °C (104 °F), preferably between 15 and 30 °C (59 and 86 °F). Store in a well-closed container.

Auxiliary labeling
- May cause drowsiness.
- Avoid alcoholic beverages.
- May be habit-forming.

Note
Controlled substance in the U.S.

METHADONE HYDROCHLORIDE TABLETS (DISPERSIBLE) USP

Usual adult dose
Suppressant (narcotic abstinence syndrome)—
Detoxification: Oral, 15 to 40 mg once a day or as needed to control observed withdrawal symptoms; dosage to be reduced at one- or two-day intervals according to patient response.
Maintenance: Dosage must be individualized.

Usual adult prescribing limits
Up to 120 mg per day.

Usual pediatric dose
Suppressant (narcotic abstinence syndrome)—
Dosage must be individualized by physician according to the needs of the specific patient. Dosage must not exceed 120 mg per day.

Note: Patients younger than 18 years of age may be admitted to methadone maintenance programs only after two documented attempts at short-term (up to thirty days) detoxification or drug-free treatment have failed. A one-week waiting period is required between a detoxification attempt and admission to a methadone maintenance program. A parent, legal guardian, or other responsible adult designated by the State authority must complete and sign a consent to treatment form for all such minors.

Strength(s) usually available
U.S.—
40 mg (Rx) [*Methadose;* GENERIC].

Packaging and storage
Store between 15 and 30 °C (59 and 86 °F). Store in a well-closed container.

Preparation of dosage form
U.S. Federal regulations stipulate that the tablets must be dispersed in water or other suitable liquid before being administered to the patient. Treatment centers that dispense both methadone and levomethadyl (which must also be dispensed as a diluted liquid) should use liquids of different colors for preparing each medication, so that they can be readily distinguished from each other. The dispersible tablets have been formulated with insoluble excipients as a deterrent to misuse of the medication by injection.

Auxiliary labeling
- May cause drowsiness.
- Avoid alcoholic beverages.
- May be habit-forming.

Note
Controlled substance in the U.S.

Parenteral Dosage Forms

METHADONE HYDROCHLORIDE INJECTION USP

Usual adult dose
Analgesic—
Intramuscular or subcutaneous, 2.5 to 10 mg every three to four hours as needed.
Suppressant (narcotic abstinence syndrome)—
For detoxification only: Intramuscular or subcutaneous, 15 to 40 mg once a day or as needed to control observed withdrawal symptoms; dosage to be reduced at one- or two-day intervals according to patient response.

Note: Parenteral administration in a detoxification regimen is recommended only for patients unable to take medication orally.

Usual pediatric dose
Analgesic—
Dosage must be individualized by physician on the basis of patient's age and size

Strength(s) usually available
U.S.—
With preservative:
10 mg per mL (Rx) [*Dolophine* (chlorobutanol)].
Without preservative:
10 mg per mL (Rx) [*Dolophine*].

Packaging and storage
Store below 40 °C (104 °F), preferably between 15 and 30 °C (59 and 86 °F), in a light-resistant container. Protect from freezing.

Auxiliary labeling
- May cause drowsiness.
- Avoid alcoholic beverages.
- May be habit-forming.

Note
Controlled substance in the U.S.

MORPHINE

Summary of Differences

Indications:
Drug of choice to relieve pain due to acute myocardial infarction.
Also, indicated as adjunctive therapy in the treatment of acute pulmonary edema secondary to left ventricular failure.
Also, used as antitussive.
Pharmacology/pharmacokinetics:
Mechanism of action/effect—
An opioid agonist analgesic; exerts agonist activity primarily at the mu receptor.
Equivalence—
60 mg via oral administration therapeutically equivalent to 10 mg intramuscularly; however, with chronic use on a fixed schedule may decrease to 20–30 mg.
Protein binding—
Low.
Half-life—
2–3 hours.
Onset of action—
Epidural: 15–60 minutes.
Intramuscular: 10–30 minutes.
Intrathecal: 15–60 minutes.
Rectal: 20–60 minutes.
Subcutaneous: 10–30 minutes.
Time to peak effect—
Intramuscular: 30–60 minutes.
Intravenous: 20 minutes.
Oral (immediate-release dosage forms): 1–2 hours.
Subcutaneous: 50–90 minutes.

Duration of action (nontolerant patients only; may decrease as tolerance develops during chronic therapy)—
Epidural: Up to 24 hours.
Intramuscular: 4–5 hours.
Intrathecal: Up to 24 hours.
Intravenous: 4–5 hours.
Oral: 4–5 hours with immediate-release dosage forms; 8 or 12 hours (depending on specific product) with extended-release dosage forms.
Subcutaneous: 4–5 hours.
Elimination—
85% Renal, 9–12% as unchanged morphine; 7–10% biliary.
Precautions:
Drug interactions and/or related problems—
May decrease clearance of zidovudine; toxicity of either or both medications may be potentiated.
Side/adverse effects:
More likely than most other opioids to cause constipation and to produce symptoms associated with histamine release.

Additional Dosing Information

See also *General Dosing Information.*

For oral dosage forms only

The oral dosage forms are recommended for administration via a fixed dosage schedule to patients with severe, chronic pain. However, low doses of an immediate-release oral dosage form may be used on an as-needed basis to relieve "breakthrough" pain that occurs during chronic treatment with an extended-release dosage form.

Periodic attempts should be made to reduce the dosage after an initial response has been achieved and maintained for at least 3 days.

The oral liquid may be diluted in a glass of fruit juice just prior to ingestion, if desired, to improve the taste.

The extended-release tablets are to be swallowed whole. They should not be broken, crushed, or chewed.

For parenteral dosage forms only

Intramuscular administration is recommended when repeated doses are required. Repeated subcutaneous administration causes local tissue irritation, pain, and induration.

The 25- or 50-mg-per-mL concentration of morphine sulfate injection available in Canada may be administered undiluted to opioid-tolerant patients requiring high-dose therapy. The 25-mg-per-mL concentration of morphine sulfate injection available in the U.S. is intended only for the preparation of intravenous infusion solutions and is not to be administered via other parenteral routes.

Bioequivalence information

Bioavailability or bioequivalence problems among different brands of Morphine Sulfate Tablets (immediate-release) and different brands of Morphine Sulfate Oral Solution have not been documented.

Morphine Sulfate Extended-release Capsules (available in Canada) should not be interchanged with other extended-release dosage forms containing morphine hydrochloride or morphine sulfate. Bioavailability or bioequivalence studies comparing the products have not been done.

Oral Dosage Forms

MORPHINE HYDROCHLORIDE SYRUP

Usual adult dose

Analgesic—
Chronic pain: Dosage and dosing interval must be individualized by the physician according to the severity of pain and patient response. Initial oral doses of 10 to 30 mg every four hours are recommended by most manufacturers of oral morphine products. However, some patients receiving the medication via the recommended fixed dosing schedule may respond to lower doses, while others have required 75 mg or more.

Usual pediatric dose

Analgesic—
Dosage must be individualized by the physician according to the severity of pain as well as on the basis of the patient's age and size. Use of calibrated measure is recommended to prevent possible overdosage in children up to 6 years of age.

Strength(s) usually available

U.S.—
Not commercially available.
Canada—
1 mg per mL (Rx) [*Morphitec* (alcohol 5%; tartrazine); *M.O.S*].
5 mg per mL (Rx) [*Morphitec* (alcohol 5%; tartrazine); *M.O.S*].
10 mg per mL (Rx) [*Morphitec* (alcohol 5%; tartrazine); *M.O.S*].
20 mg per mL (Rx) [*Morphitec* (alcohol 5%; tartrazine); *M.O.S*].
50 mg per mL (Rx) [*M.O.S*].

Packaging and storage

Store below 40 °C (104 °F), preferably between 15 and 30 °C (59 and 86 °F), in a well-closed container, unless otherwise specified by manufacturer. Protect from freezing.

Auxiliary labeling

- May cause drowsiness.
- Avoid alcoholic beverages.
- May be habit-forming.

Note

Controlled substance in Canada.

MORPHINE HYDROCHLORIDE TABLETS

Usual adult dose

Analgesic—
Chronic pain: Dosage and dosing interval must be individualized by the physician according to the severity of pain and patient response. Initial oral doses of 10 to 30 mg every four hours are recommended by most manufacturers of oral morphine products. However, some patients receiving the medication via the recommended fixed dosing schedule may respond to lower doses, while others have required 75 mg or more.

Usual pediatric dose

Analgesic—
Dosage must be individualized by the physician according to the severity of pain as well as on the basis of the patient's age and size.

Strength(s) usually available

U.S.—
Not commercially available.
Canada—
10 mg (Rx) [*M.O.S*].
20 mg (Rx) [*M.O.S*].
40 mg (Rx) [*M.O.S*].
60 mg (Rx) [*M.O.S*].

Packaging and storage

Store below 40 °C (104 °F), preferably between 15 and 30 °C (59 and 86 °F), in a well-closed container, unless otherwise specified by manufacturer. Protect from freezing.

Auxiliary labeling

- May cause drowsiness.
- Avoid alcoholic beverages.
- May be habit-forming.

Note

Controlled substance in Canada.

MORPHINE HYDROCHLORIDE EXTENDED-RELEASE TABLETS

Usual adult dose

Analgesic—
Chronic pain: Dosage must be individualized by the physician according to the severity of pain and patient response.

Usual pediatric dose

Dosage has not been established.

Strength(s) usually available

U.S.—
Not commercially available.
Canada—
30 mg (Rx) [*M.O.S.-S.R*].
60 mg (Rx) [*M.O.S.-S.R*].

Packaging and storage

Store below 40 °C (104 °F), preferably between 15 and 30 °C (59 and 86 °F), in a well-closed container, unless otherwise specified by manufacturer.

Auxiliary labeling

- Swallow tablets whole.
- May cause drowsiness.
- Avoid alcoholic beverages.
- May be habit-forming.

Note: Controlled substance in Canada.

MORPHINE SULFATE CAPSULES

Usual adult dose

Analgesic—
Chronic pain: Dosage and dosing interval must be individualized by the physician according to the severity of pain and patient re-

sponse. Initial oral doses of 10 to 30 mg every four hours are recommended by most manufacturers of oral morphine products. However, some patients receiving the medication via the recommended fixed dosing schedule may respond to lower doses, while others have required 75 mg or more.

Usual pediatric dose

Analgesic—

Dosage must be individualized by the physician according to the severity of pain as well as on the basis of the patient's age and size.

Strength(s) usually available

U.S.—

15 mg (Rx) [*MSIR*].
30 mg (Rx) [*MSIR*].

Canada—

Not commercially available.

MORPHINE SULFATE EXTENDED-RELEASE CAPSULES

Note: The extended-release capsule dosage form has not been evaluated for bioequivalence with other extended-release dosage forms containing morphine hydrochloride or morphine sulfate and should not be interchanged with them.

Usual adult dose

Analgesic—

Chronic pain: Oral, administer dose every twelve to twenty-four hours.

Note: Dosage must be individualized by the physician according to the severity of pain and patient response.

Note: Patients being transferred from other opioid analgesics or other morphine dosage forms to the morphine sulfate extended-release capsules should receive a total daily dose of oral morphine sulfate equivalent to the established total daily dose of previously administered medication, administered in divided doses at twelve-hour or twenty-four-hour intervals. The manufacturers' prescribing information contains recommendations for calculating equivalent dosage.

Usual adult prescribing limits

AVINZA extended-release capsules must be limited to a maximum daily dose of 1600 mg per day. Doses of over 1600 mg per day contain a quantity of fumaric acid that has not been demonstrated to be safe, and which may result in serious renal toxicity.

Usual pediatric dose

Dosage has not been established.

Strength(s) usually available

U.S.—

Note: ***AVINZA*capsules are indicated for once daily administration and are to be swallowed whole or the contents of the capsules sprinkled on applesauce. The capsule beads are not to be chewed, crushed, or dissolved due to the risk of rapid release and absorption of a potentially fatal dose of morphine.**

30 mg (Rx) [*AVINZA* (ammonio-methacrylate copolymers; fumaric acid; povidone; sodium lauryl sulfate; sugar starch spheres; talc; black ink; gelatin; titanium dioxide; D&C yellow No. 10)].
60 mg (Rx) [*AVINZA* (ammonio-methacrylate copolymers; fumaric acid; povidone; sodium lauryl sulfate; sugar starch spheres; talc; black ink; gelatin; titanium dioxide; FD&C green No. 3)].
90 mg (Rx) [*AVINZA* (ammonio-methacrylate copolymers; fumaric acid; povidone; sodium lauryl sulfate; sugar starch spheres; talc; black ink; gelatin; titanium dioxide; FD&C red No. 40)].
120 mg (Rx) [*AVINZA* (ammonio-methacrylate copolymers; fumaric acid; povidone; sodium lauryl sulfate; sugar starch spheres; talc; black ink; gelatin; titanium dioxide; FD&C red No. 3; FD&C blue No. 1)].
20 mg (Rx) [*Kadian*].
50 mg (Rx) [*Kadian*].
100 mg (Rx) [*Kadian*].

Canada—

Note: The M-Eslon product has not been compared to any slow-release morphine preparation on the Canadian market, and is therefore not interchangeable.

10 mg (Rx) [*M-Eslon*].
20 mg (Rx) [*Kadian*].
30 mg (Rx) [*M-Eslon*].
50 mg (Rx) [*Kadian*].
60 mg (Rx) [*M-Eslon*].
100 mg (Rx) [*Kadian; M-Eslon*].

Packaging and storage

Store between 15 and 30 °C (59 and 86 °F).

Auxiliary labeling

- Swallow whole. Do not crush or chew.
- May cause drowsiness.
- Avoid alcoholic beverages.
- May be habit-forming.
- Caution: Federal law prohibits the transfer of this drug to any person other than the patient for whom it was prescribed.

Note

Controlled substance in U.S. and Canada.

Additional information

The 60-, 90-, and 120-mg extended-release capsules are for use only in opioid-tolerant patients.

MORPHINE SULFATE ORAL SOLUTION

Note: Bioavailability or bioequivalence problems among different brands of Morphine Sulfate Oral Solution have not been documented.

Usual adult dose

Analgesic—

Chronic pain: Dosage and dosing interval must be individualized by the physician according to the severity of pain and patient response. Initial oral doses of 10 to 30 mg every four hours are recommended by most manufacturers of oral morphine products. However, some patients receiving the medication via the recommended fixed dosing schedule may respond to lower doses, while others have required 75 mg or more.

Usual pediatric dose

Analgesic—

Dosage must be individualized by the physician according to the severity of pain as well as on the basis of the patient's age and size. Use of calibrated measure is recommended to prevent possible overdosage in children up to 6 years of age.

Strength(s) usually available

U.S.—

10 mg per 2.5 mL (unit dose) (Rx) [*Rescudose; Roxanol UD*].
10 mg per 5 mL (Rx) [*MSIR* (sucrose); *MS/L;* GENERIC].
20 mg per 5 mL (Rx) [*MSIR; Roxanol UD;* GENERIC].
20 mg per mL (Rx) [*MSIR; MS/L Concentrate; OMS Concentrate; Roxanol*].
30 mg per 1.5 mL (Rx) [*Roxanol UD*].
100 mg per 5 mL (Rx) [*Roxanol 100*].

Canada—

2 mg per mL (Rx) [GENERIC].
4 mg per mL (Rx) [GENERIC].
20 mg per mL (Rx) [*Statex Drops*].
50 mg per mL (Rx) [*Statex Drops*].

Packaging and storage

Store between 15 and 30 °C (59 and 86 °F), in a tight, light-resistant container, unless otherwise specified by manufacturer. Protect from freezing.

Auxiliary labeling

- May cause drowsiness.
- Avoid alcoholic beverages.
- May be habit-forming.

Note

Controlled substance in both the U.S. and Canada.

MORPHINE SULFATE SYRUP

Usual adult dose

Analgesic—

Chronic pain: Dosage and dosing interval must be individualized by the physician according to the severity of pain and patient response. Initial oral doses of 10 to 30 mg every four hours are recommended by most manufacturers of oral morphine products. However, some patients receiving the medication via the recommended fixed dosing schedule may respond to lower doses, while others have required 75 mg or more.

Usual pediatric dose

Analgesic—

Dosage must be individualized by the physician according to the severity of pain as well as on the basis of the patient's age and size.

Strength(s) usually available

U.S.—

Not commercially available.

Canada—

1 mg per mL (Rx) [*Statex*].
5 mg per mL (Rx) [*Statex*].
10 mg per mL (Rx) [*Statex*].

Packaging and storage
Store below 40 °C (104 °F), preferably between 15 and 30 °C (59 and 86 °F), in a well-closed container, unless otherwise specified by manufacturer. Protect from freezing.

Auxiliary labeling
- May cause drowsiness.
- Avoid alcoholic beverages.
- May be habit-forming.

Note
Controlled substance in Canada.

MORPHINE SULFATE TABLETS
Note: Bioavailability or bioequivalence problems among different brands of Morphine Sulfate Tablets have not been documented.

Usual adult dose
Analgesic—
Chronic pain: Dosage and dosing interval must be individualized by the physician according to the severity of pain and patient response. Initial oral doses of 10 to 30 mg every four hours are recommended by most manufacturers of oral morphine products. However, some patients receiving the medication via the recommended fixed dosing schedule may respond to lower doses, while others have required 75 mg or more.

Usual pediatric dose
Analgesic—
Chronic pain: Dosage must be individualized by the physician according to the severity of pain as well as on the basis of the patient's age and size.

Strength(s) usually available
U.S.—
15 mg (Rx) [*MSIR* (scored); GENERIC].
30 mg (Rx) [*MSIR* (scored); GENERIC].
Canada—
5 mg (Rx) [*MS·IR* (scored); *Statex* (scored)].
10 mg (Rx) [*MS·IR* (scored); *Statex* (scored)].
15 mg (Rx) [GENERIC].
20 mg (Rx) [*MS·IR* (scored)].
25 mg (Rx) [*Statex* (scored)].
30 mg (Rx) [*MS·IR* (scored); GENERIC].
50 mg (Rx) [*Statex* (scored)].

Packaging and storage
Store below 40 °C (104 °F), preferably between 15 and 30 °C (59 and 86 °F), in a well-closed container, unless otherwise specified by manufacturer.

Auxiliary labeling
- May cause drowsiness.
- Avoid alcoholic beverages.
- May be habit-forming.

Note
Controlled substance in both the U.S. and Canada.

MORPHINE SULFATE EXTENDED-RELEASE TABLETS
Usual adult dose
Analgesic—
Chronic pain: Oral, 30 mg every twelve hours, initially, with dosage and dosing interval then being adjusted according to the requirements of the individual patient.

Note: Patients being transferred from other opioid analgesics or other morphine dosage forms to the morphine sulfate extended-release tablets should receive a total daily dose of oral morphine sulfate equivalent to the established total daily dose of previously administered medication, administered in divided doses at twelve-hour intervals. The manufacturers' prescribing information contains recommendations for calculating equivalent dosage.

Usual pediatric dose
Dosage has not been established.

Strength(s) usually available
U.S.—
15 mg (Rx) [*M S Contin;* GENERIC].
30 mg (Rx) [*M S Contin; Oramorph SR;* GENERIC].
60 mg (Rx) [*M S Contin; Oramorph SR;* GENERIC].
100 mg (Rx) [*M S Contin; Oramorph SR;* GENERIC].
200 mg (Rx) [*M S Contin*].
Canada—
15 mg (Rx) [*M S Contin*].
30 mg (Rx) [*M S Contin; Oramorph SR*].
60 mg (Rx) [*M S Contin; Oramorph SR*].
100 mg (Rx) [*M S Contin; Oramorph SR*].
200 mg (Rx) [*M S Contin* (scored)].

Packaging and storage
Store below 40 °C (104 °F), preferably between 15 and 30 °C (59 and 86 °F), in a well-closed container, unless otherwise specified by manufacturer.

Auxiliary labeling
- Swallow tablets whole.
- May cause drowsiness.
- Avoid alcoholic beverages.
- May be habit-forming.

Note
Controlled substance in both the U.S. and Canada.

Parenteral Dosage Forms
MORPHINE SULFATE INJECTION USP
Usual adult dose
Analgesic—
Intramuscular or subcutaneous, 5 to 20 mg (usually 10 mg, initially) every four hours as needed. For severe, chronic pain the medication may also be administered by subcutaneous infusion, using a portable pump, at a rate titrated to the requirements and response of the individual patient.

Note: The recommendation of an initial 10-mg dose is based on a 70-kg person.
In Canada, the 25- or 50-mg-per-mL concentration may be substituted for lower strengths of morphine sulfate injection or for other opioid analgesics in opioid-tolerant patients requiring high-dose therapy. Dosage must be individualized, depending on the severity of pain, opioid requirements at the time therapy with the high-potency injection is initiated, and patient response. Although patients who have become tolerant to another opioid may be at least partially cross-tolerant to morphine also, it is recommended that one-half of the equianalgesic dose of morphine be used initially, then adjusted as necessary.

Intravenous, 4 to 10 mg diluted in 4 to 5 mL of sterile water for injection, administered slowly. For severe, chronic pain the medication may also be administered via intravenous infusion at a rate titrated to the requirements and response of the individual patient.

Epidural (in the lumbar region), 5 mg.

Note: If adequate pain relief is not achieved within one hour, incremental doses of 1 to 2 mg may be administered at intervals sufficient to assess effectiveness, up to a maximum of 10 mg per twenty-four hours.

Intrathecal, 200 mcg (0.2 mg) to 1 mg as a single dose.

Note: Clinical experience with repeated intrathecal injections is limited. Therefore, repeated administration via this route is not recommended. Alternate routes of administration should be considered for treating recurrent or chronic pain.

Usual pediatric dose
Analgesic—
Subcutaneous, 100 to 200 mcg (0.1 to 0.2 mg) per kg of body weight every four hours as needed, not to exceed 15 mg per dose.
Intravenous, 50 to 100 mcg (0.05 to 0.1 mg) per kg of body weight, administered very slowly.
[Mechanical ventilation]—
Neonates—
Intravenous, 50 mcg per kg of body weight (mcg/kg) as an initial loading bolus over thirty minutes to one hour followed by continuous infusion of 10 to 30 mcg/kg per hour and titrated to the requirements and response of the individual patient.
Preoperative—
Intramuscular, 50 to 100 mcg (0.05 to 0.1 mg) per kg of body weight, not to exceed 10 mg per dose.
[Postoperative]—
Neonates—
Intravenous, 50 mcg per kg of body weight (mcg/kg) as an initial loading dose followed by continuous infusion of 15 mcg/kg per hour and titrated to the requirements and response of the individual patient.

Strength(s) usually available
U.S.—
With preservative:
1 mg per mL (Rx) [GENERIC].
2 mg per mL (Rx) [GENERIC].
4 mg per mL (Rx) [GENERIC].
5 mg per mL (Rx) [GENERIC].
8 mg per mL (Rx) [GENERIC].
10 mg per mL (Rx) [GENERIC].
15 mg per mL (Rx) [GENERIC].

25 mg per mL (Rx) [GENERIC].
50 mg per mL (Rx) [GENERIC].
Without preservative:
500 mcg (0.5 mg) per mL (Rx) [*Astramorph PF; Duramorph;* GENERIC].
1 mg per mL (Rx) [*Astramorph PF; Duramorph;* GENERIC].
50 mg per mL (Rx) [GENERIC].

Canada—
With preservative:
1 mg per mL (Rx) [GENERIC].
2 mg per mL (Rx) [GENERIC].
5 mg per mL (Rx) [GENERIC].
10 mg per mL (Rx) [GENERIC].
15 mg per mL (Rx) [GENERIC].
25 mg per mL (Rx) [*Morphine Forte*].
50 mg per mL (Rx) [*Morphine Extra-Forte*].
Without preservative:
500 mcg (0.5 mg) per mL (Rx) [*Epimorph;* GENERIC].
1 mg per mL (Rx) [*Epimorph;* GENERIC].
2 mg per mL (Rx) [GENERIC].
25 mg per mL (Rx) [*Morphine H.P;* GENERIC].
50 mg per mL (Rx) [*Morphine H.P;* GENERIC].

Packaging and storage

Store below 40 °C (104 °F), preferably between 15 and 30 °C (59 and 86 °F), unless otherwise specified by manufacturer. Protect from light. Protect from freezing.

Stability

Do not autoclave the preservative-free injection.

Unused portion of preservative-free injection must be discarded.

Incompatibilities

Morphine Sulfate Injection USP is incompatible with soluble barbiturates.

Auxiliary labeling

- May cause drowsiness.
- Avoid alcoholic beverages.
- May be habit-forming.

Note

Controlled substance in both the U.S. and Canada.

MORPHINE SULFATE SOLUBLE TABLETS

Usual adult dose

Analgesic—
Intramuscular or subcutaneous, 5 to 20 mg (usually 10 mg, initially) every four hours as needed.

Note: The recommendation of an initial 10-mg dose is based on a 70-kg person.

Usual pediatric dose

Analgesic—
Subcutaneous, 100 to 200 mcg (0.1 to 0.2 mg) per kg of body weight every four hours as needed, not to exceed 15 mg per dose.

Strength(s) usually available

U.S.—
10 mg (Rx) [GENERIC].
15 mg (Rx) [GENERIC].
30 mg (Rx) [GENERIC].

Canada—
Not commercially available.

Packaging and storage

Store between 15 and 30 °C (59 and 86 °F), in a tight, light-resistant container, unless otherwise specified by manufacturer.

Preparation of dosage form

For parenteral administration—Dissolve the required number of tablets in a suitable volume of sterile water for injection, then filter through a 0.22–micron membrane filter.

Auxiliary labeling

- May cause drowsiness.
- Avoid alcoholic beverages.
- May be habit-forming.

Note

Controlled substance in the U.S.

Rectal Dosage Forms

MORPHINE HYDROCHLORIDE SUPPOSITORIES

Usual adult dose

Analgesic—
Rectal, 20 to 30 mg every four to six hours.

Usual pediatric dose

Analgesic—
Dosage must be individualized by the physician according to the severity of pain as well as on the basis of the patient's age and size.

Strength(s) usually available

U.S.—
Not commercially available.

Canada—
10 mg (Rx) [*M.O.S*].
20 mg (Rx) [*M.O.S*].
30 mg (Rx) [*M.O.S*].

Packaging and storage

Store below 40 °C (104 °F), preferably between 15 and 30 °C (59 and 86 °F), in a well-closed container, unless otherwise specified by manufacturer. Protect from freezing.

Auxiliary labeling

- May cause drowsiness.
- Avoid alcoholic beverages.
- May be habit-forming.

Note

Controlled substance in Canada.

MORPHINE SULFATE SUPPOSITORIES

Usual adult dose

Analgesic—
Rectal, 10 to 30 mg every four hours or as required.

Note: Dosage must be individualized according to the severity of pain and the response of the patient.

Usual pediatric dose

Analgesic—
Dosage must be individualized by physician on the basis of the patient's age and size.

Strength(s) usually available

U.S.—
5 mg (Rx) [*MS/S; RMS Uniserts; Roxanol;* GENERIC].
10 mg (Rx) [*MS/S; RMS Uniserts; Roxanol;* GENERIC].
20 mg (Rx) [*MS/S; RMS Uniserts; Roxanol;* GENERIC].
30 mg (Rx) [*MS/S; RMS Uniserts; Roxanol;* GENERIC].

Canada—
5 mg (Rx) [*Statex*].
10 mg (Rx) [*MS IR; Statex*].
20 mg (Rx) [*MS IR; Statex*].
30 mg (Rx) [*MS IR; Statex*].

Packaging and storage

Store between 15 and 30 °C (59 and 86 °F), in a well-closed container, unless otherwise specified by manufacturer. Protect from freezing.

Auxiliary labeling

- May cause drowsiness.
- Avoid alcoholic beverages.
- May be habit-forming.

Note

Controlled substance in both the U.S. and Canada.

NALBUPHINE

Summary of Differences

Indications:
Caution required when used as analgesic to relieve pain in patients with severely compromised cardiac function; cardiovascular effects in these patients have not been fully evaluated.

Pharmacology/pharmacokinetics—
Mechanism of action/effect—
An opioid agonist/antagonist analgesic.
Agonist: Has agonist activity at the kappa and sigma receptors.
Antagonist: Has antagonist activity at the mu receptor; may precipitate withdrawal symptoms in patients who are physically dependent on mu receptor agonists.

Equivalence—
10 mg via intramuscular injection therapeutically equivalent to 10 mg of intramuscular morphine.

Half-life—
5 hours.

Onset of action—
Intramuscular: Within 15 minutes.
Intravenous: 2–3 minutes.
Subcutaneous: Within 15 minutes.

Time to peak concentration—
Intramuscular: 0.5 hour.
Peak plasma concentration—
48 nanograms per mL.
Time to peak effect—
Intramuscular: 60 minutes.
Intravenous: 30 minutes.
Duration of action (nontolerant patients only; decreases as tolerance develops during chronic therapy)—
Intramuscular: 3–6 hours.
Intravenous: 3–4 hours.
Subcutaneous: 3–6 hours.
Elimination—
Renal.

Precautions:
Drug interactions and/or related problems—
May antagonize effects of mu receptor agonists.
Medical considerations/contraindications—
Should be used with caution in patients who are physically dependent on opioid agonists.

Side/adverse effects:
Rarely, may cause subjective and psychotomimetic effects characteristic of sigma receptor agonists.
Respiratory depression subject to a "ceiling effect," after which the depth of respiratory depression does not increase with dose.
More likely than most other opioid analgesics to produce symptoms associated with histamine release.
Has lower dependence liability than opioid agonists.
Withdrawal symptoms less severe than those produced by opioid agonist analgesics.

Parenteral Dosage Forms

NALBUPHINE HYDROCHLORIDE INJECTION

Usual adult dose

Analgesic—
Intramuscular, intravenous, or subcutaneous, 10 mg every three to six hours as needed.

Note: The usual adult dose is based on a 70-kg person.

Anesthesia adjunct (balanced anesthesia)—
Initial: Intravenous, 300 mcg (0.3 mg) to 3 mg per kg of body weight, administered over a ten- to fifteen-minute period.
Supplemental: Intravenous, 250 to 500 mcg (0.25 to 0.5 mg) per kg of body weight, as required.

Usual adult prescribing limits

For nontolerant patients—
Up to 20 mg as a single dose and up to 160 mg as a total daily dose.

Usual pediatric dose

Dosage has not been established.

Strength(s) usually available

U.S.—
With preservatives:
10 mg per mL (Rx) [*Nubain* (methylparaben; propylparaben; sodium metabisulfite); GENERIC].
20 mg per mL (Rx) [*Nubain* (methylparaben; propylparaben; sodium metabisulfite); GENERIC].
Without preservatives:
10 mg per mL (Rx) [*Nubain*].
20 mg per mL (Rx) [*Nubain*].

Canada—
With preservatives:
10 mg per mL (Rx) [*Nubain* (methylparaben; propylparaben; sodium metabisulfite)].
20 mg per mL (Rx) [*Nubain* (methylparaben; propylparaben; sodium metabisulfite)].

Packaging and storage

Store between 15 and 30 °C (59 and 86 °F), unless otherwise specified by manufacturer. Protect from light. Protect from freezing.

Auxiliary labeling

- May cause drowsiness.
- Avoid alcoholic beverages.

Note

Controlled substance in Canada.

OPIUM

Summary of Differences

Indications:
Oral dosage form—
Indicated as antidiarrheal.
Also, used as narcotic abstinence syndrome suppressant in neonates.

Pharmacology/pharmacokinetics:
Mechanism of action/effect—
An opioid agonist analgesic; has agonist activity primarily at the mu receptor.
Equivalence—
13.3 mg parenterally is therapeutically equivalent to 10 mg of intramuscular morphine.
Elimination—
Renal and biliary.

Additional Dosing Information

See also *General Dosing Information.*

The effects of opium preparations are due primarily to the morphine component.

For oral dosage form only

Alteration of intestinal motility in patients with traveler's diarrhea may result in prolonged fever by slowing expulsion of infectious organisms that penetrate intestinal mucosa (for example, *Shigella, Salmonella,* and certain strains of *Escherichia coli*).

Opium may produce fluid retention in the bowel, which may mask dehydration and electrolyte depletion caused by severe diarrhea, especially in young children. Patients with severe or prolonged diarrhea should be monitored for signs of dehydration or electrolyte imbalance, and corrective therapy administered as required.

To reduce the risk of toxic megacolon in patients with acute inflammatory bowel disease, treatment with opium tincture should be discontinued promptly if abdominal distention or other gastrointestinal symptoms occur.

Tolerance to the antidiarrheal effects of opium tincture may develop with prolonged use.

Following prolonged administration of high doses, opium tincture should be withdrawn gradually in order to reduce the possibility of withdrawal symptoms.

Many clinicians have recommended use of diluted opium tincture instead of paregoric in the treatment of neonatal narcotic dependence, because of the risks associated with two of the components of the paregoric formulation. Opium tincture is diluted to produce the same concentration of morphine as paregoric and may be administered every 3 hours, with gradual withdrawal over 2 to 4 weeks when symptoms are controlled.

For parenteral dosage form only

This formulation contains all of the alkaloids of opium as the hydrochlorides.

Oral Dosage Forms

OPIUM TINCTURE (Laudanum) USP

Usual adult dose

Antidiarrheal—
Oral, 0.3 to 1 mL (usually 0.6 mL) (the equivalent of morphine—3 to 10 mg) four times a day.

Usual adult prescribing limits

A single dose of 1 mL, or a total of 6 mL within twenty-four hours.

Usual pediatric dose

Dosage has not been established.

Strength(s) usually available

U.S.—
10% of opium (the equivalent of 900 mg to 1.1 grams of anhydrous morphine per 100 mL) (Rx) [GENERIC (alcohol 17–21%)].

Canada—
10% of opium (the equivalent of 900 mg to 1.1 grams of anhydrous morphine per 100 mL) (Rx) [GENERIC (alcohol 17–21%)].

Packaging and storage

Store below 40 °C (104 °F), preferably between 15 and 30 °C (59 and 86 °F), unless otherwise specified by manufacturer. Store in a tight, light-resistant container. Avoid exposure to direct sunlight and excessive heat. Protect from freezing.

Auxiliary labeling
- May cause drowsiness.
- Avoid alcoholic beverages.
- Do not take other medicines without your doctor's advice.
- Keep out of reach of children.
- May be habit-forming.

Note

Caution—Be careful not to confuse opium tincture with camphorated tincture of opium (paregoric).

Controlled substance in both the U.S. and Canada.

Refrigeration is not recommended because decreased solubility and precipitation of some of the ingredients may occur. If this occurs, the preparation must be discarded.

Parenteral Dosage Forms

OPIUM ALKALOIDS HYDROCHLORIDES INJECTION (Papaveretum)

Usual adult dose

Analgesic—

Intramuscular or subcutaneous, 5 to 20 mg every four to five hours as needed.

Usual pediatric dose

Dosage has not been established.

Strength(s) usually available

U.S.—

Not commercially available.

Canada—

With preservatives:

20 mg, as hydrochlorides of opium alkaloids, per mL (Rx) [*Pantopon* (methylparaben; propylparaben)].

Note: Contains 10 mg of anhydrous morphine per mL.

Packaging and storage

Store between 15 and 30 °C (59 and 86 °F), unless otherwise specified by manufacturer. Protect from freezing.

Auxiliary labeling
- May cause drowsiness.
- Avoid alcoholic beverages.
- May be habit-forming.

Note

Controlled substance in Canada.

OXYCODONE

Summary of Differences

Indications:

Oxycodone extended-release tablets are indicated for relief of moderate to severe pain when a continuous, around-the-clock analgesic is needed for an extended period of time. Oxycodone extended-release tablets are not intended for use as a "prn" (as needed) analgesic. It's not for use in the immediate post-operative period (the first 12–24 hours), unless the patient was receiving the drug prior to surgery. Oxycodone extended-release tablets are not used for mild pain or for pain not expected to last for an extended period of time.

Pharmacology/pharmacokinetics:

Mechanism of action/effect—

An opioid agonist analgesic; has agonist activity primarily at the mu receptor.

Equivalence—

30 mg via oral administration therapeutically equivalent to 10 mg of intramuscular morphine.

Half-life—

2–3 hours.

Time to peak effect—

Oral: 1 hour.

Duration of action (nontolerant patients only; duration decreases as tolerance develops during chronic therapy)—

Oral: 3–4 hours.

Elimination—

Renal.

Oral Dosage Forms

OXYCODONE HYDROCHLORIDE ORAL SOLUTION USP

Usual adult dose

Analgesic—

Oral, 5 mg every three to six hours as needed; may be increased if severe pain is present.

Usual pediatric dose

Dosage must be individualized by physician on the basis of patient's age and size. Use of calibrated measure is recommended to prevent possible overdosage in children up to 6 years of age.

Strength(s) usually available

U.S.—

5 mg per 5 mL (Rx) [*Roxicodone* (alcohol 7–9%)].
20 mg per mL (Rx) [*Roxicodone Intensol*].

Canada—

Not commercially available.

Packaging and storage

Store between 15 and 30 °C (59 and 86 °F), unless otherwise specified by manufacturer. Store in a tight, light-resistant container. Protect from freezing.

Auxiliary labeling
- May cause drowsiness.
- Avoid alcoholic beverages.
- May be habit-forming.

Note

Controlled substance in the U.S.

OXYCODONE HYDROCHLORIDE TABLETS USP

Usual adult dose

Analgesic—

Oral, 5 to 15 mg every 4 to 6 hours as needed; may be increased if severe pain is present.

Usual pediatric dose

Dosage must be individualized by physician on the basis of patient's age and size.

Strength(s) usually available

U.S.—

15 mg (Rx) [*Roxicodone* (scored)].
30 mg (Rx) [*Roxicodone* (scored)].

Canada—

5 mg (Rx) [*Supeudol*].
10 mg (Rx) [*Supeudol*].

Packaging and storage

Store below 40 °C (104 °F), preferably between 15 and 30 °C (59 and 86 °F). Store in a tight, light-resistant container.

Auxiliary labeling
- May cause drowsiness.
- Avoid alcoholic beverages.
- May be habit-forming.

Note

Controlled substance in both the U.S. and Canada.

OXYCODONE HYDROCHLORIDE EXTENDED-RELEASE TABLETS

Usual adult dose

Analgesic—

Oral, administer dose every twelve hours.

Note: Dosage must be individualized by the physician according to the severity of pain and patient response.

Oxycodone extended-release tablets are not intended for use as a "prn" (as needed) analgesic.

The 80-mg and 160-mg dose should be used in opioid tolerant patients only. Fatal respiratory depression may occur in patients who have not previously received opioids.

Note: The 160 mg tablet is comparable to two 80 mg tablets when taken on an empty stomach. With a high fat meal, however, there is a greater peak plasma concentration following one 160 mg tablet. Dietary caution should be taken when patients are initially titrated to the 160 mg tablets.

Note: Tablets are to be swallowed whole and are not to be broken, chewed, or crushed. Taking broken, chewed, or crushed tablets increases the rate of absorption and may lead to a potentially fatal dose.

Usual pediatric dose

Safety and efficacy have not been established.

Strength(s) usually available
U.S.—
10 mg (Rx) [*OxyContin*].
20 mg (Rx) [*OxyContin*].
40 mg (Rx) [*OxyContin*].
80 mg (Rx) [*OxyContin*].
160 mg (Rx) [*OxyContin*].
Canada—
10 mg (Rx) [*OxyContin*].
20 mg (Rx) [*OxyContin*].
40 mg (Rx) [*OxyContin*].
80 mg (Rx) [*OxyContin*].

Packaging and storage
Store below 40 °C (104 °F), preferably between 15 and 30 °C (59 and 86 °F). Store in a tight, light-resistant container.

Auxiliary labeling
- May cause drowsiness.
- Avoid alcoholic beverages.
- May be habit-forming.

Note
Controlled substance in both the U.S. and Canada.

Rectal Dosage Forms

OXYCODONE HYDROCHLORIDE SUPPOSITORIES

Usual adult dose
Analgesic—
Rectal, 10 to 40 mg three or four times a day.

Usual pediatric dose
Dosage must be individualized by physician on the basis of patient's age and size.

Strength(s) usually available
U.S.—
Not commercially available.
Canada—
10 mg (Rx) [*Supeudol*].
20 mg (Rx) [*Supeudol*].

Packaging and storage
Store between 2 and 8 °C (36 and 46 °F), in a well-closed container, unless otherwise specified by manufacturer. Protect from freezing.

Auxiliary labeling
- May cause drowsiness.
- Avoid alcoholic beverages.
- May be habit-forming.
- Store in refrigerator. Protect from freezing.

Note
Controlled substance in Canada.

OXYMORPHONE

Summary of Differences

Indications:
FDA-approved, but rarely if ever used, as adjunctive therapy in the treatment of acute pulmonary edema secondary to left ventricular failure.
Pharmacology/pharmacokinetics:
Mechanism of action/effect—
An opioid agonist analgesic; has agonist activity primarily at the mu receptor.
Equivalence—
1 mg via intramuscular injection or 10 mg rectally therapeutically equivalent to 10 mg of intramuscular morphine.
Onset of action—
Intramuscular: 10–15 minutes.
Intravenous: 5–10 minutes.
Subcutaneous: 10–20 minutes.
Rectal: 15–30 minutes.
Time to peak effect—
Intramuscular: 30–90 minutes.
Intravenous: 15–30 minutes.
Rectal: 2 hours.
Duration of action (nontolerant patients only; duration decreases as tolerance develops during chronic therapy)—
Intramuscular: 3–6 hours.
Intravenous: 3–4 hours.
Subcutaneous: 3–6 hours.
Rectal: 3–6 hours.
Elimination—
Renal.

Parenteral Dosage Forms

OXYMORPHONE HYDROCHLORIDE INJECTION USP

Usual adult dose
Analgesic—
Intramuscular or subcutaneous, 1 to 1.5 mg every three to six hours as needed.
Intravenous, 500 mcg (0.5 mg).
Note: Doses may be cautiously increased, if necessary, if pain is severe.
For obstetrical analgesia—Intramuscular, 500 mcg (0.5 mg) to 1 mg.

Usual pediatric dose
Dosage has not been established.

Strength(s) usually available
U.S.—
With preservatives:
1 mg per mL (Rx) [*Numorphan* (methylparaben; propylparaben)].
1.5 mg per mL (Rx) [*Numorphan* (methylparaben; propylparaben)].
Canada—
With preservatives:
1.5 mg per mL (Rx) [*Numorphan* (methylparaben; propylparaben)].

Packaging and storage
Store below 40 °C (104 °F), preferably between 15 and 30 °C (59 and 86 °F), unless otherwise specified by manufacturer. Protect from light. Protect from freezing.

Auxiliary labeling
- May cause drowsiness.
- Avoid alcoholic beverages.
- May be habit-forming.

Note
Controlled substance in both the U.S. and Canada.

Rectal Dosage Forms

OXYMORPHONE HYDROCHLORIDE SUPPOSITORIES USP

Usual adult dose
Analgesic—
Rectal, 5 mg every four to six hours as needed.

Usual pediatric dose
Dosage has not been established.

Strength(s) usually available
U.S.—
5 mg (Rx) [*Numorphan*].
Canada—
5 mg (Rx) [*Numorphan*].

Packaging and storage
Store between 2 and 8 °C (36 and 46 °F), in a well-closed container. Protect from freezing.

Auxiliary labeling
- May cause drowsiness.
- Avoid alcoholic beverages.
- May be habit-forming.
- Store in refrigerator. Protect from freezing.

Note
Controlled substance in both the U.S. and Canada.

PENTAZOCINE

Summary of Differences

Indications:
Less desirable than morphine or other opioid agonist analgesics for relief of pain due to acute myocardial infarction because of cardiovascular effects that tend to increase cardiac work.
Pharmacology/pharmacokinetics:
Mechanism of action/effect—
An opioid agonist/antagonist analgesic.
Agonist: Has agonist activity at the kappa and sigma receptors.

Antagonist: Has antagonist activity at the mu receptor; may precipitate withdrawal symptoms in patients who are physically dependent on mu receptor agonists.

Equivalence—

60 mg via intramuscular injection or 180 mg via oral administration therapeutically equivalent to 10 mg of intramuscular morphine.

Protein binding—

Moderate.

Half-life—

2–3 hours.

Onset of action—

Intramuscular: 15–20 minutes.
Intravenous: 2–3 minutes.
Oral: 15–30 minutes.
Subcutaneous: 15–20 minutes.

Time to peak effect—

Intramuscular: 30–60 minutes.
Intravenous: 15–30 minutes.
Oral: 60–90 minutes.
Subcutaneous: 30–60 minutes.

Duration of action (nontolerant patients only; decreases as tolerance develops during chronic therapy)—

Intramuscular: 2–3 hours.
Intravenous: 2–3 hours.
Oral: 3 hours.
Subcutaneous: 2–3 hours.

Elimination—

Renal, 5–23% as unchanged pentazocine, and biliary.

Precautions:

Drug interactions and/or related problems—

May antagonize the effects of mu receptor agonists.

Medical considerations/contraindications—

Must be used with caution in patients physically dependent on opioid agonists and in patients with acute myocardial infarction.

Side/adverse effects:

Although occurs rarely, more likely than butorphanol or nalbuphine to cause subjective and psychotomimetic effects characteristic of sigma receptor agonists.

Respiratory depression subject to a "ceiling effect," after which the depth of respiratory depression does not increase with dose.

Has lower dependence liability than opioid agonists.

Withdrawal symptoms less severe than those produced by opioid agonist analgesics.

Additional Dosing Information

See also *General Dosing Information.*

The naloxone present in the pentazocine and naloxone dosage formulation has no pharmacologic activity when administered orally. If the product is misused by injection, the naloxone antagonizes the effects of pentazocine. Also, injection of the medication will precipitate withdrawal symptoms if the patient is physically dependent on an opioid agonist.

For long-term administration, the oral form of the medication is preferred. If the parenteral form is used instead, dosage should be reduced gradually when the medication is to be discontinued to reduce the risk of withdrawal symptoms.

The extent to which pentazocine may produce withdrawal symptoms in patients who are physically dependent on opioid analgesics depends upon the dose of pentazocine, the specific opioid drug involved, and the degree to which physical dependence has developed.

For parenteral dosage forms only

Intravenous or intramuscular administration is recommended, especially when repeated doses are required. Subcutaneous administration may lead to severe tissue damage at the injection site. When the intramuscular route is used, rotation of injection sites is essential to prevent tissue damage.

Oral Dosage Forms

PENTAZOCINE HYDROCHLORIDE TABLETS USP

Usual adult dose

Analgesic—

Oral, 50 mg of pentazocine (base) every three to four hours as needed. The dose may be increased to 100 mg (base) if necessary, but total daily dosage should not exceed 600 mg (base).

Usual adult prescribing limits

Analgesic—

Up to 600 mg of pentazocine (base) per day.

Usual pediatric dose

Dosage has not been established.

Strength(s) usually available

U.S.—

Not commercially available.

Canada—

50 mg (base) (Rx) [*Talwin* (scored; sulfites)].

Packaging and storage

Store below 40 °C (104 °F), preferably between 15 and 30 °C (59 and 86 °F), unless otherwise specified by manufacturer. Store in a tight, light-resistant container.

Auxiliary labeling

- May cause drowsiness.
- Avoid alcoholic beverages.
- May be habit-forming.

Note

Controlled substance in Canada.

PENTAZOCINE AND NALOXONE HYDROCHLORIDES TABLETS USP

Usual adult dose

Analgesic—

Oral, 50 mg of pentazocine (base) every three to four hours as needed. The dose may be increased to 100 mg (base) if necessary, but total daily dosage should not exceed 600 mg (base).

Usual adult prescribing limits

Analgesic—

Up to 600 mg of pentazocine (base) per day.

Usual pediatric dose

Dosage has not been established.

Strength(s) usually available

U.S.—

50 mg (base), with 500 mcg (0.5 mg) of naloxone hydrochloride (Rx) [*Talwin-Nx* (scored)].

Canada—

Not commercially available.

Packaging and storage

Store below 40 °C (104 °F), preferably between 15 and 30 °C (59 and 86 °F), unless otherwise specified by manufacturer. Store in a tight, light-resistant container.

Auxiliary labeling

- May cause drowsiness.
- Avoid alcoholic beverages.
- May be habit-forming.

Note

Controlled substance in the U.S.

Parenteral Dosage Forms

PENTAZOCINE LACTATE INJECTION USP

Usual adult dose

Analgesic—

Intramuscular, intravenous, or subcutaneous, 30 mg (base) every three to four hours as needed.

Obstetrical analgesia—

Intramuscular, 30 mg (base) as a single dose; or

Intravenous, 20 mg (base) administered when contractions become regular and repeated two or three times at two- to three-hour intervals as needed.

Usual adult prescribing limits

Up to 360 mg (base) daily.

As a single dose, up to 30 mg (base) intravenously or 60 mg (base) intramuscularly.

Usual pediatric dose

Dosage has not been established.

Strength(s) usually available

U.S.—

With preservative:

30 mg (base) per mL (Rx) [*Talwin* (acetone sodium bisulfite; methylparaben)].

Without preservative:

30 mg (base) per mL (Rx) [*Talwin* (may contain acetone sodium bisulfite)].

Canada—

Without preservative:

30 mg (base) per mL (Rx) [*Talwin*].

Packaging and storage
Store below 40 °C (104 °F), preferably between 15 and 30 °C (59 and 86 °F), unless otherwise specified by manufacturer. Protect from freezing.

Incompatibilities
Precipitation will occur if a soluble barbiturate is mixed in the same syringe as pentazocine.

Auxiliary labeling
- May cause drowsiness.
- Avoid alcoholic beverages.
- May be habit-forming.

Note
Controlled substance in both the U.S. and Canada.

PROPOXYPHENE

Summary of Differences

Pharmacology/pharmacokinetics:
Mechanism of action/effect—
An opioid agonist analgesic; has agonist activity at the mu receptor.
Equivalence—
Dose therapeutically equivalent to 10 mg of intramuscular morphine too toxic to administer.
Protein binding—
High.
Biotransformation—
Metabolite norpropoxyphene is toxic.
Half-life—
Propoxyphene: 6–12 hours.
Norpropoxyphene: 30–36 hours.
Onset of action—
Oral: 15–60 minutes.
Time to peak concentration—
Oral: 2–2.5 hours.
Peak plasma concentration—
0.05–0.1 mcg per mL.
Time to peak effect—
Oral: 2 hours.
Duration of action (nontolerant patients only; decreases as tolerance develops during chronic therapy)—
Oral: 4–6 hours.
Elimination—
Renal, < 10% as unchanged propoxyphene; biliary.
Precautions:
Drug interactions and/or related problems—
Risk of convulsions if overdose of propoxyphene administered to amphetamine-treated patients.
May increase effects of coumarin- or indandione-derivative anticoagulants.
Concurrent use with carbamazepine not recommended because may decrease carbamazepine metabolism, leading to increased risk of toxicity.
Effects may be decreased in patients who smoke because tobacco smoking increases propoxyphene metabolism.
Laboratory value alterations—
May elevate levels of enzymes in liver function tests.
Side/adverse effects:
May be more likely than most opioid analgesics to cause convulsions.
Hepatotoxicity has been reported.
Has lower dependence liability than other opioid agonists.
Withdrawal symptoms less severe than those produced by stronger opioid agonist analgesics.

Additional Dosing Information

See also *General Dosing Information.*

100 mg of propoxyphene napsylate are equivalent to 65 mg of propoxyphene hydrochloride.

Oral Dosage Forms

PROPOXYPHENE HYDROCHLORIDE CAPSULES USP

Usual adult dose
Analgesic—
Oral, 65 mg every four hours as needed.

Usual adult prescribing limits
Up to 390 mg daily.

Usual pediatric dose
Dosage has not been established.

Strength(s) usually available
U.S.—
65 mg (Rx) [*Cotanal-65; Darvon; PP-Cap;* GENERIC].
Canada—
Not commercially available.

Packaging and storage
Store below 40 °C (104 °F), preferably between 15 and 30 °C (59 and 86 °F). Store in a tight container.

Auxiliary labeling
- May cause drowsiness.
- Avoid alcoholic beverages.
- May be habit-forming.

Note
Controlled substance in both the U.S. and Canada.

PROPOXYPHENE HYDROCHLORIDE TABLETS

Usual adult dose
Analgesic—
Oral, 65 mg every four hours as needed.

Usual adult prescribing limits
Analgesic—
Oral, up to 390 mg daily.

Usual pediatric dose
Dosage has not been established.

Strength(s) usually available
U.S.—
Not commercially available.
Canada—
65 mg (Rx) [*642* (scored)].

Packaging and storage
Store below 40 °C (104 °F), preferably between 15 and 30 °C (59 and 86 °F), in a well-closed container, unless otherwise specified by manufacturer.

Auxiliary labeling
- May cause drowsiness.
- Avoid alcoholic beverages.
- May be habit-forming.

Note
Controlled substance in Canada.

PROPOXYPHENE NAPSYLATE CAPSULES

Usual adult dose
Analgesic—
Oral, 100 mg every four hours as needed.

Usual adult prescribing limits
Analgesic—
Up to 600 mg daily.

Usual pediatric dose
Dosage has not been established.

Strength(s) usually available
U.S.—
Not commercially available.
Canada—
100 mg (Rx) [*Darvon-N*].

Packaging and storage
Store below 40 °C (104 °F), preferably between 15 and 30 °C (59 and 86 °F), unless otherwise specified by manufacturer. Store in a tight container.

Auxiliary labeling
- May cause drowsiness.
- Avoid alcoholic beverages.
- May be habit-forming.

Note
Controlled substance in Canada.

PROPOXYPHENE NAPSYLATE ORAL SUSPENSION USP

Usual adult dose
Analgesic—
Oral, 100 mg every four hours as needed.

Usual adult prescribing limits
Analgesic—
Up to 600 mg daily.

Usual pediatric dose
Dosage has not been established.

Strength(s) usually available
U.S.—
50 mg per 5 mL (Rx) [*Darvon-N* (butylparaben; methylparaben; propylparaben; saccharin; sucrose)].

Canada—
Not commercially available.

Packaging and storage
Store below 40 °C (104 °F), preferably between 15 and 30 °C (59 and 86 °F), unless otherwise specified by manufacturer. Store in a tight container. Protect from light. Protect from freezing.

Auxiliary labeling
- Shake well.
- May cause drowsiness.
- Avoid alcoholic beverages.
- May be habit-forming.

Note
Controlled substance in the U.S.

PROPOXYPHENE NAPSYLATE TABLETS USP

Usual adult dose
Analgesic—
Oral, 100 mg every four hours as needed.

Usual adult prescribing limits
Analgesic—
Up to 600 mg daily.

Usual pediatric dose
Dosage has not been established.

Strength(s) usually available
U.S.—
100 mg (Rx) [*Darvon-N;* GENERIC].

Canada—
Not commercially available.

Packaging and storage
Store below 40 °C (104 °F), preferably between 15 and 30 °C (59 and 86 °F), unless otherwise specified by manufacturer. Store in a tight container.

Auxiliary labeling
- May cause drowsiness.
- Avoid alcoholic beverages.
- May be habit-forming.

Note
Controlled substance in the U.S.

Revised: 08/11/2005

Table 1. Pharmacology/Pharmacokinetics

Drug	Protein Binding	Half-life (hr)*	Elimination: Primary (% excreted unchanged)†	Elimination: Secondary
Butorphanol	High	2.5–4	72% Renal (<5)	15% Biliary
Codeine‡	Very low	2.5–4	Renal (5–15); 10% as unchanged or conjugated morphine	
Hydrocodone		3.8	Renal	
Hydromorphone		2.6–4	Renal	
Levorphanol	Moderate		Renal	
Meperidine§	High	2.4–4	Renal (5)	
Methadone#	High	15–25; increases with repeated administration	Renal; rate increased in acidic urine	Biliary
Morphine	Low	2–3	85% Renal (9–12)	7–10% Biliary
Nalbuphine		5	Renal	
Opium			Renal	Biliary
Oxycodone		2–3	Renal	
Oxymorphone			Renal	
Pentazocine	Moderate	2–3	Renal (5–23)	Biliary
Propoxyphene**	High	6–12 (propoxyphene) 30–36 (norpropoxyphene)	Renal (<10)	Biliary

*Half-life may be increased in geriatric patients because of decreased clearance rate. Also, significant increases have been reported in patients with hepatic cirrhosis for meperidine (6 to 7 hr), morphine, and pentazocine.

†All opioid analgesics are excreted primarily as metabolites.

‡About 10% of a dose is demethylated to morphine, which may contribute to the therapeutic actions.

§Metabolite normeperidine is active and toxic (having central nervous system (CNS) excitatory [proconvulsant] activity) and accumulates in patients with renal function impairment.

#Some metabolites are active; drug and/or metabolites may accumulate with repeated administration.

**Metabolite norpropoxyphene may be toxic; it is not known whether this metabolite has analgesic activity.

Table 2. Pharmacology/Pharmacokinetics

Drug and Route*	Equivalence†	Time to Peak Concentration (hr)	Peak Plasma Concentration	Therapeutic Effects		
				Onset of Analgesic Action (min)	Peak Analgesic Effect (min)	Duration of Action Analgesic (hr)‡/Antitussive (hr)
Anileridine						
Oral	75			15		2–3
Butorphanol						
IM	2	0.5–1	2.2 nanograms§/mL	10–30	30–60	3–4
IV				2–3	30	2–4
Codeine						
Oral	200			30–45	60–120	4/4–6
IM	120			10–30	30–60	4
SC				10–30		4
Hydrocodone						
Oral				10–30	30–60	4–6/4–6
Hydromorphone						
Oral	7.5			30	90–120	4
IM	1.5			15	30–60	4–5
IV				10–15	15–30	2–3
SC				15	30–90	4
Rectal	3					
Levorphanol						
Oral	4			10–60	90–120	4–5
IM	2				60	4–5
IV					Within 20	4–5
SC					60–90	4–5
Meperidine						
Oral	300			15	60–90	2–4
IM	75			10–15	30–50	2–4
IV				1	5–7	2–4
SC				10–15	30–50	2–4
Methadone						
Oral	20			30–60	90–120	4–6#
IM	10			10–20	60–120	4–5#
IV					15–30	3–4#
Morphine						
Oral	60**					
Extended-release tablets						8–12
Other oral dosage forms				Slower than IM	60–120	4–5
IM	10			10–30	30–60	4–5
IV					20	4–5
SC				10–30	50–90	4–5
Epidural				15–60		Up to 24
Intrathecal				15–60		Up to 24
Rectal				20–60		
Nalbuphine						
IM	10	0.5	48 nanograms§/mL	Within 15	60	3–6
IV				2–3	30	3–4
SC				Within 15		3–6
Opium						
Parenteral	13.3					
Oxycodone						
Oral	30				60	3–4
Oxymorphone						
IM	1			10–15	30–90	3–6
IV				5–10	15–30	3–4
SC				10–20		3–6
Rectal	10			15–30	120	3–6
Pentazocine						
Oral	180			15–30	60–90	3
IM	60			15–20	30–60	2–3
IV				2–3	15–30	2–3
SC				15–20	30–60	2–3
Propoxyphene						
Oral	††	2–2.5	0.05–0.1 mcg/mL	15–60	120	4–6

*IM=Intramuscular; IV=Intravenous; SC=Subcutaneous.

†Dose in mg therapeutically equivalent to a 10-mg intramuscular dose of morphine.

‡In nontolerant patients only. The first sign of tolerance is usually a decrease in the duration of adequate analgesia. Also, may be increased in geriatric patients because of decreased clearance rate.

§Nanograms.

#Increases with repeated dosing because of accumulation of drug and/or active metabolites.

**For single doses or occasional use only; with chronic dosing on a fixed schedule, may decrease to 20 or 30 mg.

††Dose equivalent to 10 mg of morphine would be too toxic to administer. Values reported under *time to peak concentration* and *peak plasma concentration* were determined following a 65-mg dose of propoxyphene hydrochloride or a 100-mg dose of propoxyphene napsylate.

Table 3. Drug Interactions and/or Related Problems

Note: Combinations containing any of the following medications, depending on the amount present, may also interact with this medication.	Agonist											Agonist/Antagonist		
	Legend: I=Codeine II=Hydrocodone III=Hydromorphone IV=Levorphanol				V=Meperidine VI=Methadone VII=Morphine			VIII=Opium IX=Oxycodone X=Oxymorphone XI=Propoxyphene				XII=Butorphanol XIII=Nalbuphine XIV=Pentazocine		
	I	*II*	*III*	*IV*	*V*	*VI*	*VII*	*VIII*	*IX*	*X*	*XI*	*XII*	*XIII*	*XIV*
Acidifiers, urinary, such as: Ammonium chloride Ascorbic acid Potassium or sodium phosphate (acidification of the urine by these medications increases methadone excretion, resulting in decreased methadone plasma concentrations; high doses of urinary acidifiers, such as several grams daily of ammonium chloride, may cause withdrawal symptoms in patients who are dependent on methadone)						✓								
» Alcohol or » CNS depression-producing medications, other (See *Appendix II*) (concurrent use with opioid analgesics may result in increased CNS depressant, respiratory depressant, and hypotensive effects; caution is recommended and dosage of one or both agents should be reduced. In addition, some phenothiazines increase, while others decrease, the effects of opioid analgesics used as adjuncts to anesthesia)	✓	✓	✓	✓	✓	✓	✓	✓	✓	✓	✓	✓	✓	✓
(concurrent use with other CNS depressants having habituation potential may increase the risk of habituation)	✓	✓	✓	✓	✓	✓	✓	✓	✓	✓	✓	✓	✓	✓
Amphetamines (amphetamines may potentiate the analgesic effects of meperidine; however, concurrent use of the 2 medications is not recommended because the monoamine oxidase inhibiting effect of amphetamines may increase the risk of hypotension, severe respiratory depression, coma, convulsions, hyperpyrexia, vascular collapse, and death)					✓									
(an overdose of propoxyphene may potentiate the CNS stimulating effects of amphetamines; fatal convulsions can result)											✓			
Anticholinergics or other medications with anticholinergic activity (See *Appendix II*) (concurrent use with opioid analgesics may result in increased risk of severe constipation, which may lead to paralytic ileus, and/or urinary retention)	✓	✓	✓	✓	✓	✓	✓	✓	✓	✓	✓	✓	✓	✓
Anticoagulants, coumarin- or indandione-derivative (meperidine and propoxyphene have been reported to increase the effects of these anticoagulants; although clinical significance has not been established, the possibility should be considered that adjustment of anticoagulant dosage based on prothrombin time determinations may be necessary during and following concurrent use)					✓						✓			
Antidiarrheals, antiperistaltic, such as: Difenoxin and atropine Diphenoxylate and atropine Kaolin, pectin, belladonna alkaloids, and opium Loperamide Opium tincture Paregoric (concurrent use with an opioid analgesic may increase the risk of severe constipation as well as central nervous system [CNS] depression)	✓	✓	✓	✓	✓	✓	✓	✓	✓	✓	✓	✓	✓	✓

Antihypertensives, especially ganglionic blockers such as guanadrel, guanethidine, and mecamylamine, or Diuretics or Hypotension-producing medications, other (See *Appendix II)* (hypotensive effects of these medications may be potentiated when used concurrently with opioid analgesics, leading to increased risk of orthostatic hypotension; patients should be monitored during concurrent use)	✓	✓	✓	✓	✓	✓	✓	✓	✓	✓	✓	✓	✓	✓
» Buprenorphine (buprenorphine is a partial mu-receptor agonist with high affinity for, and a slow rate of dissociation from, the mu receptor; if administered prior to another opioid agonist, it may reduce the therapeutic effects of the other opioid; in one study in opioid addicts receiving chronic administration of 8 mg of buprenorphine per day, the effects of large doses [up to 120 mg] of morphine were blocked during buprenorphine therapy and for at least 30 hours following the last dose of buprenorphine)	✓	✓	✓	✓	✓	✓	✓	✓	✓	✓				
(buprenorphine may also have some antagonist activity at the kappa receptor; the possibility should be considered that it may also reduce the therapeutic effects of subsequently administered butorphanol, nalbuphine, or pentazocine)												✓	✓	✓
(buprenorphine antagonizes the respiratory depressant effects of large doses of previously administered mu-receptor agonists; however, additive respiratory depression may occur if buprenorphine is administered in conjunction with low doses of other mu-receptor agonists or with kappa-receptor agonists)	✓	✓	✓	✓	✓	✓	✓	✓	✓	✓	✓	✓	✓	✓
(buprenorphine may precipitate withdrawal symptoms in physically dependent patients who are chronically receiving potent mu-receptor agonists; however, because of its partial agonist activity, buprenorphine may partially suppress spontaneous withdrawal symptoms caused by abrupt discontinuation of these agonists)		✓	✓	✓	✓	✓	✓	✓	✓	✓				
» Carbamazepine (concurrent use with propoxyphene may result in decreased carbamazepine metabolism and lead to increased carbamazepine blood concentration and toxicity; concurrent use is not recommended)											✓			
Hydroxyzine (concurrent use with opioid analgesics may result in increased analgesia as well as increased CNS depressant and hypotensive effects)	✓	✓	✓	✓	✓	✓	✓	✓	✓	✓	✓	✓	✓	✓
Metoclopramide (opioid analgesics may antagonize the effects of metoclopramide on gastrointestinal motility)	✓	✓	✓	✓	✓	✓	✓	✓	✓	✓	✓	✓	✓	✓
» Monoamine oxidase (MAO) inhibitors, including furazolidone, pargyline, and procarbazine (concurrent use with meperidine has resulted in unpredictable, severe, and sometimes fatal reactions, including immediate excitation, sweating, rigidity, and severe hypertension, or, in some patients, hypotension, severe respiratory depression, coma, seizures, hyperpyrexia, and cardiovascular collapse; meperidine is contraindicated in patients who have received an MAO inhibitor within 14 to 21 days)					✓									
(other opioid analgesics may be used cautiously and in reduced dosage in patients receiving MAO inhibitors; however, it is recommended that a small test dose [¼ of the usual dose] or several small incremental test doses over a period of several hours first be administered to permit observation of any interaction)	✓	✓	✓	✓		✓	✓	✓	✓	✓	✓	✓	✓	✓
Naloxone (antagonizes the analgesic, CNS, and respiratory depressant effects of opioid analgesics; however, larger doses may be required to reverse the effects of butorphanol, nalbuphine, pentazocine, or propoxyphene than are needed to reverse the effects of other opioids; also, because naloxone may precipitate withdrawal symptoms in physically dependent patients, dosage of naloxone should be carefully titrated when used to treat opioid overdosage in dependent patients)	✓	✓	✓	✓	✓	✓	✓	✓	✓	✓	✓	✓	✓	✓

Table 3. Drug Interactions and/or Related Problems *(continued)*

Note: Combinations containing any of the following medications, depending on the amount present, may also interact with this medication.	Agonist											Agonist/Antagonist		
	Legend: I=Codeine II=Hydrocodone III=Hydromorphone IV=Levorphanol				V=Meperidine VI=Methadone VII=Morphine			VIII=Opium IX=Oxycodone X=Oxymorphone XI=Propoxyphene				XII=Butorphanol XIII=Nalbuphine XIV=Pentazocine		
	I	*II*	*III*	*IV*	*V*	*VI*	*VII*	*VIII*	*IX*	*X*	*XI*	*XII*	*XIII*	*XIV*
» Naltrexone (administration of naltrexone to a patient physically dependent on opioid drugs will precipitate withdrawal symptoms; symptoms may appear within 5 minutes of naltrexone administration, persist for up to 48 hours, and be difficult to reverse)	✓	✓	✓	✓	✓	✓	✓	✓	✓	✓	✓	✓	✓	✓
(naltrexone blocks the therapeutic effects of opioids [i.e., analgesic, antidiarrheal, and antitussive]; naltrexone therapy should not be initiated in patients receiving these agents for therapeutic purposes; also, patients receiving naltrexone should be advised to use alternative medications when necessary)	✓	✓	✓	✓	✓	✓	✓	✓	✓	✓	✓	✓	✓	✓
(administration of increased doses of opioids to override naltrexone blockade of opioid receptors may result in increased and prolonged respiratory depression and/or circulatory collapse)	✓	✓	✓	✓	✓	✓	✓	✓	✓	✓	✓	✓	✓	✓
(naltrexone should be discontinued several days prior to elective surgery if administration of an opioid prior to, during, or following surgery is unavoidable)	✓	✓	✓	✓	✓	✓	✓	✓	✓	✓	✓	✓	✓	✓
(the efficacy of naltrexone in antagonizing opioid effects not mediated via opioid receptors [i.e., those that may be caused by histamine release, such as facial swelling, itching, generalized erythema, hives, and, to some extent, hypotension] has not been fully determined; naltrexone may not antagonize these effects completely)	✓	✓	✓	✓	✓	✓	✓	✓	✓	✓	✓	✓	✓	✓
Neuromuscular blocking agents and possibly other medications having some neuromuscular blocking activity (respiratory depressant effects of neuromuscular blockade may be additive to central respiratory depressant effects of opioid analgesics; increased or prolonged respiratory depression [apnea] or paralysis may occur but is of minor clinical significance if the patient is being mechanically ventilated; however, caution and careful monitoring of the patient are recommended during and following concurrent or sequential use, especially if there is a possibility of incomplete reversal of neuromuscular blockade postoperatively)	✓	✓	✓	✓	✓	✓	✓	✓	✓	✓	✓	✓	✓	✓
Nicotine chewing gum or Other smoking deterrents or Smoking, tobacco, or cessation of (tobacco smoking may increase the metabolism of propoxyphene leading to decreased therapeutic effects; also, smoking cessation by a patient receiving propoxyphene chronically may increase its effects)											✓			
Opioid agonist analgesics, including alfentanil, fentanyl, and sufentanil (additive CNS depressant, respiratory depressant, and hypotensive effects may occur if two or more opioid agonist analgesics are used concurrently)	✓	✓	✓	✓	✓	✓	✓	✓	✓	✓	✓			
(pentazocine and nalbuphine may partially antagonize the analgesic and CNS depressant effects of opioid agonists)													✓	✓
(in patients who are not physically dependent on opioid agonists, concurrent use of butorphanol, nalbuphine, or pentazocine may result in additive side effects)												✓	✓	✓
(in patients who are physically dependent on opioid agonists, nalbuphine and pentazocine may precipitate, and butorphanol will not prevent or attenuate, withdrawal symptoms)												✓	✓	✓
Phenytoin, chronic use of, or » Rifampin (these medications may increase methadone metabolism, probably via induction of hepatic microsomal enzyme activity, and may precipitate withdrawal symptoms in patients being treated for opioid dependence; methadone dosage adjustments may be necessary when phenytoin or rifampin therapy is initiated or discontinued)						✓								
» Zidovudine (morphine may competitively inhibit the hepatic glucuronidation and decrease the clearance of zidovudine; concurrent use should be avoided because the toxicity of either or both of these medications may be potentiated)							✓							

Table 4. Side/Adverse Effects*

The following side/adverse effects have been selected on the basis of their potential clinical significance (possible signs and symptoms in parentheses where appropriate)—not necessarily inclusive:

Legend:
I=Butorphanol
II=Codeine
III=Hydrocodone
IV=Hydromorphone
V=Levorphanol
VI =Meperidine
VII=Methadone
VIII=Morphine
IX=Nalbuphine
X=Opium
XI=Oxycodone
XII=Oxymorphone
XIII=Pentazocine
XIV=Propoxyphene

	I	II	III	IV	V	VI	VII	VIII	IX	X	XI	XII	XIII	XIV
Medical attention needed														
Allergic reaction (skin rash, hives, and/or itching†; swelling of face)	R (<1%)	L	R	R	R	R	R	L	L	R	R	R	L	L
Atelectasis; bronchospastic allergic reaction; laryngeal edema, allergic; laryngospasm, allergic; or respiratory depression‡ (shortness of breath, slow or irregular breathing, troubled breathing)	R (<1%)	L	L	L	L	L	L	L	R (<1%)	R	R	L	L	U
CNS stimulation, paradoxical (unusual excitement or restlessness)—especially in children	R	L	R	R	R	R	R	R	R	R	R	R	R	R
Confusion§—may include delusions and feelings of depersonalization or unreality	R (<1%)	L	L	L	L	L	L	L	R (<1%)	L	R	L	R	R
Convulsions	U	R	R	U	U	L	U	U	U	U	U	U	R	L
Fast, slow, or pounding heartbeat	R (<1%)	L	L	L	L	L	L	L	R (<1%)	R	U	L	L	U
Hallucinations§	R (<1%)	R	R	R	R	R	R	R	R (<1%)	R	R	R	R	U
Hepatotoxicity (dark urine, pale stools, yellow eyes or skin)	U	U	U	U	U	U	U	U	U	U	U	U	U	R
Histamine release (decreased blood pressure, fast heartbeat, increased sweating, redness or flushing of face, wheezing or troubled breathing)	L	L	M	L	R	M	M	M	M	L	L	L	L	L
Increased blood pressure	R (<1%)	U	R	U	U	U	U	U	R	(U)	U	U	L	R
Mental depression	R (<1%)	R	R	R	R	R	R	R	R (<1%)	R	R	R	R	R
Muscle rigidity, especially in muscles of respiration—with large doses	U	R	R	U	U	U	U	R	U	U	U	U	U	R
Paralytic ileus or toxic megacolon (severe constipation, bloating, nausea, stomach cramps or pain, vomiting)—in patients with inflammatory bowel disease	R	R	R	R	R	R	R	R	R	R	R	R	R	R
Ringing or buzzing in the ears	R	U	R	U	U	U	U	U	U	U	U	U	R	L
Trembling or uncontrolled muscle movements	U	R	R	L	U	L	U	L	U	L	U	U	R	L
Medical attention needed only if continuing or bothersome														
Antidiuretic effect (decreased urination)	L	L	L	L	L	L	L	L	R (<1%)	L	L	L	L	L
Biliary spasm (stomach cramps or pain)	U	R	R	L	L	L	L (<1%)	L	R (<1%)	R	U	L	R	R
Blurred or double vision or other changes in vision	R (<1%)	L	L	L	L	L	L	L	R (<1%)	L	U	L	L	L
Constipation	R	M	L	L	L	M	M	M	U	R	L	L	L	L

Table 4. Side/Adverse Effects* *(continued)*

The following side/adverse effects have been selected on the basis of their potential clinical significance (possible signs and symptoms in parentheses where appropriate)—not necessarily inclusive:

Legend: I=Butorphanol; II=Codeine; III=Hydrocodone; IV=Hydromorphone; V=Levorphanol; VI=Meperidine; VII=Methadone; VIII=Morphine; IX=Nalbuphine; X=Opium; XI=Oxycodone; XII=Oxymorphone; XIII=Pentazocine; XIV=Propoxyphene

Side/adverse effect	I	II	III	IV	V	VI	VII	VIII	IX	X	XI	XII	XIII	XIV
Dizziness, feeling faint, or lightheadedness—especially in ambulatory patients.	L	L	M	M	M	M	M	M	L	M	M	M	L	M
Drowsiness	M (40%)	M	M	M	M	M	M	M	M (36%)	M	M	M	M	M
Dry mouth	R (<1%)	L	L	L	L	L	L	L	L (4%)	L	L	L	L	L
False sense of well-being	R (<1%)	L	L	L	U	L	L	L	R (<1%)	L	U	L	M	L
Gastrointestinal irritation (stomach cramps or pain)	R	R	R	L	L	L	L	L	R	R	U	L	R	R
General feeling of discomfort or illness§	L	L	L	L	L	L	L	L	R (<1%)	L	L	L	L	L
Headache	L (3%)	L	L	L	L	L	L	L	L (3%)	L	L	L	L	L
Hypotension (dizziness, feeling faint, lightheadedness, unusual tiredness or weakness)—although hypotension may occur in recumbent patients, orthostatic hypotension commonly occurs in ambulatory patients	L	L	M	M	M	M	M	M	L	M	M	M	L	M
Loss of appetite	L	L	L	M	L	L	L	L	L	R	U	R	R	R
Nausea or vomiting—occurs more frequently in ambulatory patients; are more frequent with initial doses, and are less likely to occur with subsequent doses	L (6%)	L	L	L	M	M	M	M	L (6%)	R	M	M	M	M
Nervousness or restlessness§	R (<1%)	L	L	L	L	L	L	L	R (<1%)	L	L	L	L	L
Nightmares or unusual dreams§	R (<1%)	R	R	U	U	L	U	U	R (<1%)	U	U	U	L	L
Redness, swelling, pain, or burning at site of injection	R	L	—	L	L	L	R	L	L	L	—	L	L	—
Unusual tiredness or weakness	L	L	M	M	M	M	M	M	L	M	M	M	L	M
Ureteral spasm (difficult or painful urination, frequent urge to urinate)	L	L	L	L	L	L	L	L	R (<1%)	L	L	L	L	L
Trouble in sleeping	R	R	R	R	R	R	L	R	R	R	R	R	R	R

*Differences in frequency of occurrence may reflect either lack of clinical-use data or actual pharmacologic distinctions among agents (although their pharmacologic similarity suggests that side effects occurring with one may occur with the others). M = more frequent; L = less frequent; R = rare; U = unknown.

†*Generalized or facial pruritus* may represent an opioid-induced dysesthesia rather than an allergic reaction, especially following epidural or intrathecal administration, and requires medical attention only if bothersome to the patient.

‡*Respiratory depression* induced by butorphanol, nalbuphine, and pentazocine differs from that due to other opioid analgesics in that the depth of respiratory depression is not increased with higher doses (ceiling effect); however, with butorphanol the duration of respiratory depression is increased with higher doses.

§Although these effects may occur with large doses of any opioid analgesic, with butorphanol, nalbuphine, and pentazocine they may be part of a group of subjective and psychotomimetic effects characteristic of opioids having sigma-receptor activity. These effects include *confusion, delusions, feelings of depersonalization or unreality, hallucinations* (usually visual), *dysphoria, nightmares, and nervousness or anxiety.* These effects generally occur with large doses of these drugs; although they occur rarely with any of them, they may be most likely to occur with pentazocine.

OPIOID (NARCOTIC) ANALGESICS AND ACETAMINOPHEN Systemic

This monograph includes information on the following: 1) Acetaminophen and Codeine; 2) Dihydrocodeine and Acetaminophen; 3) Hydrocodone and Acetaminophen; 4) Oxycodone and Acetaminophen; 5) Pentazocine and Acetaminophen; 6) Propoxyphene and Acetaminophen.

PEN:
Acetaminophen and Codeine—Co-codAPAP
Hydrocodone and Acetaminophen—Co-hycodAPAP
Oxycodone and Acetaminophen—Co-oxycodAPAP
Propoxyphene napsylate and Acetaminophen—Co-proxAPAP

INN:
Acetaminophen—Paracetamol
Propoxyphene—Dextropropoxyphene

VA CLASSIFICATION (Primary): CN101

Note: Controlled substances in the U.S. and Canada as follows:

Drug	U.S.	Canada
Acetaminophen and Codeine		
Capsules; Tablets	III	N
Oral solution	IV	N
Oral suspension	IV	**
Dihydrocodeine and Acetaminophen	III	**
Hydrocodone and Acetaminophen	III	**
Oxycodone and Acetaminophen	II	N
Pentazocine and Acetaminophen	IV	**
Propoxyphene and Acetaminophen	IV	**

**Not commercially available in Canada.

Commonly used brand name(s): *Acet Codeine 30*[1]; *Acet Codeine 60*[1]; *Acet-2*[1]; *Acet-3*[1]; *Allay*[3]; *Anexsia 5/500*[3]; *Anexsia 7.5/650*[3]; *Anolor DH 5*[3]; *Atasol-15*[1]; *Atasol-30*[1]; *Atasol-8*[1]; *Bancap-HC*[3]; *Capital with Codeine*[1]; *Cetaphen Extra Strength with Codeine*[1]; *Cetaphen with Codeine*[1]; *Co-Gesic*[3]; *Cotabs*[1]; *DHC plus*[2]; *Darvocet-N 100*[6]; *Darvocet-N 50*[6]; *Dolacet*[3]; *Dolagesic*[3]; *Duocet*[3]; *E-Lor*[6]; *EZ III*[1]; *Empracet-30*[1]; *Empracet-60*[1]; *Emtec-30*[1]; *Endocet*[4]; *Exdol-8*[1]; *HY-PHEN*[3]; *Hyco-Pap*[3]; *Hycomed*[3]; *Hydrocet*[3]; *Hydrogesic*[3]; *Lenoltec with Codeine No.1*[1]; *Lenoltec with Codeine No.2*[1]; *Lenoltec with Codeine No.3*[1]; *Lenoltec with Codeine No.4*[1]; *Lorcet 10/650*[3]; *Lorcet Plus*[3]; *Lorcet-HD*[3]; *Lortab*[3]; *Lortab 10/500*[3]; *Lortab 2.5/500*[3]; *Lortab 5/500*[3]; *Lortab 7.5/500*[3]; *Margesic #3*[1]; *Margesic-H*[3]; *Novo-Gesic C15*[1]; *Novo-Gesic C30*[1]; *Novo-Gesic C8*[1]; *Oncet*[3]; *Oxycocet*[4]; *PMS-Acetaminophen with Codeine*[1]; *Panacet 5/500*[3]; *Panlor*[3]; *Percocet*[4]; *Percocet 10/650*[4]; *Percocet 2.5/325*[4]; *Percocet 5/325*[4]; *Percocet 7.5/500*[4]; *Percocet-Demi*[4]; *Phenaphen with Codeine No. 3*[1]; *Phenaphen with Codeine No.4*[1]; *Polygesic*[3]; *Propacet 100*[6]; *Pyregesic-C*[1]; *Roxicet*[4]; *Roxicet 5/500*[4]; *Roxilox*[4]; *Stagesic*[3]; *T-Gesic*[3]; *Talacen*[5]; *Triatec-30*[1]; *Triatec-8*[1]; *Triatec-8 Strong*[1]; *Tylenol with Codeine Elixir*[1]; *Tylenol with Codeine No.1*[1]; *Tylenol with Codeine No.1 Forte*[1]; *Tylenol with Codeine No.2*[1]; *Tylenol with Codeine No.3*[1]; *Tylenol with Codeine No.4*[1]; *Tylox*[4]; *Ugesic*[3]; *Vanacet*[3]; *Vendone*[3]; *Vicodin*[3]; *Vicodin ES*[3]; *Wygesic*[6]; *Zydone*[3].

Other commonly used names are: APAP with codeine [Acetaminophen and Codeine], Co-codAPAP [Acetaminophen and Codeine], Co-hycodAPAP [Hydrocodone and Acetaminophen], Co-oxycodAPAP [Oxycodone and Acetaminophen], Co-proxAPAP [Propoxyphene napsylate and Acetaminophen], Drocode and Acetaminophen [Dihydrocodeine and Acetaminophen], Hydrocodone with APAP [Hydrocodone and Acetaminophen], Oxycodone with APAP [Oxycodone and Acetaminophen], Propoxyphene with APAP [Propoxyphene and Acetaminophen]

NOTE: The *Opioid (Narcotic) Analgesics and Acetaminophen (Systemic)* monograph is maintained on the *USP DI* electronic data base. A copy of the most recent revision of the complete monograph can be accessed on the *USP DI* Updates Online website. See the front cover of book for details on accessing the site.

For information on the specific components of this combination, see the *USP DI* monographs for *Acetaminophen (Systemic)* and *Opioid (Narcotic) Analgesics (Systemic)*.

The information that follows is selectively abstracted from the complete monograph and is provided to facilitate drug use review and patient counseling.

Note: For a listing of dosage forms and brand names by country availability, see *Dosage Forms* section(s).

Category

Analgesic

Note: Opioid agonist analgesics—Codeine, Dihydrocodeine, Hydrocodone, Oxycodone, and Propoxyphene.
Opioid agonist/antagonist analgesic—Pentazocine.

Indications

Accepted

Pain (treatment)—Indicated for the symptomatic relief of:

Mild to moderate pain—Pentazocine and acetaminophen; propoxyphene and acetaminophen.

Mild to severe pain (depending on the dose of codeine)—Acetaminophen and codeine.

Moderate to moderately severe pain—Dihydrocodeine and acetaminophen; hydrocodone and acetaminophen; oxycodone and acetaminophen.

[1]Not included in Canadian product labeling.

Patient Consultation

As an aid to patient consultation, refer to *Advice for the Patient, Narcotic Analgesics and Acetaminophen (Systemic).*

In providing consultation, consider emphasizing the following selected information (» = major clinical significance):

Before using this medication

» Conditions affecting use, especially:
- Sensitivity to acetaminophen or to opioid analgesic considered for use, history of
- Pregnancy—Acetaminophen and opioid analgesics cross the placenta; regular use of opioids by pregnant women may cause physical dependence in the fetus and withdrawal symptoms in the neonate
- Breast-feeding—Acetaminophen, codeine, and propoxyphene are distributed into breast milk
- Use in children—Children up to 2 years of age are more susceptible to the effects of opioids, especially respiratory depression; also, children may be more likely to experience paradoxical CNS excitation during therapy
- Use in the elderly—Geriatric patients are more susceptible to the effects of opioids, especially respiratory depression
- Other medications, especially alcohol or other CNS depressants, monoamine oxidase inhibitors, tricyclic antidepressants, zidovudine, and naltrexone
- Other medical problems, especially alcoholism (active or in remission), diarrhea caused by antibiotics or poisoning, asthma or other respiratory problems, hepatic disease, viral hepatitis, and severe inflammatory bowel disease

Proper use of this medication

» Importance of not taking more medication than the amount prescribed because of danger of overdose and habit-forming potential of opioid analgesics; also, acetaminophen may cause liver damage with long-term or high-dose use

» Not increasing dose if medication is less effective after a few weeks; checking with physician

Missed dose (if on scheduled dosing): Taking as soon as possible; not taking if almost time for next dose; not doubling doses

» Proper storage

Precautions while using this medication

Regular visits to physician to check progress during long-term or high-dose therapy

» Caution if other medications containing opioid analgesics or acetaminophen are used

» Avoiding use of alcohol or other central nervous system (CNS) depressants during therapy unless prescribed or otherwise approved by physician

Checking with your physician if you consume three or more alcohol-containing beverages per day; acetaminophen may increase the risk of liver damage

Not regularly taking aspirin or other salicylates or other nonsteroidal anti-inflammatory drugs concurrently, unless directed by physician or dentist

» Caution if dizziness, drowsiness, lightheadedness, or false sense of well-being occurs

Caution when getting up suddenly from a lying or sitting position

Lying down if nausea or vomiting, or dizziness or lightheadedness occurs

Caution if any kind of surgery (including dental surgery) or emergency treatment is required

Possible dryness of mouth; using sugarless gum or candy, ice, or saliva substitute for relief; checking with dentist if dry mouth continues for more than 2 weeks

» Checking with physician before discontinuing medication after prolonged use of high doses; gradual dosage reduction may be necessary to avoid withdrawal symptoms

» Suspected overdose: Getting emergency help at once

Side/adverse effects

Signs of potential side effects, especially respiratory depression or impairment; allergic reactions; confusion, convulsions, hallucinations, mental depression, or other signs of CNS toxicity; agranulocytosis; hepatotoxicity; hypertension; paradoxical CNS excitation, especially in children; renal function impairment; and thrombocytopenia

ACETAMINOPHEN AND CODEINE

Summary of Differences

Category:
Codeine is an opioid agonist analgesic.

Indications:
Indicated for relief of mild to severe pain, depending on the dose of codeine.

Pharmacology/pharmacokinetics: For orally administered codeine:
Mechanism of action/effect: An opioid agonist analgesic; exerts agonist activity primarily at the mu receptor, but with usual doses is relatively weak.
Equivalence: 200 mg therapeutically equivalent to 10 mg of intramuscular morphine.
Protein binding: Very low.
Half-life: 2.5–4 hours
Biotransformation: Hepatic; about 10% demethylated to morphine.
Onset of action: 30–45 minutes.
Time to peak effect: 1–2 hours.
Duration of action (nontolerant patients only; decreases as tolerance develops during chronic therapy): 4 hours.
Elimination: Renal, 5–15% as unchanged codeine and 10% as unchanged or conjugated morphine.

Precautions:
Pregnancy—Codeine has been shown to cause delayed ossification in mice and increased resorptions in rats.
Breast-feeding—Codeine is distributed into breast milk.

Side/adverse effects:
Codeine is more likely than most other opioids to cause constipation, especially during chronic therapy.
Codeine has lower dependence liability and potential for abuse than most other opioid agonists with usual doses.
Withdrawal symptoms produced by codeine are less severe than those produced by stronger opioid agonist analgesics.

Oral Dosage Forms

ACETAMINOPHEN AND CODEINE PHOSPHATE CAPSULES USP

Usual adult dose

Analgesic—
Oral, 1 or 2 capsules containing 325 mg of acetaminophen and 30 mg of codeine phosphate every four hours as needed; or
Oral, 1 capsule containing 325 mg of acetaminophen and 60 mg of codeine phosphate every four hours as needed.

Usual pediatric dose

Dosage must be individualized by the physician.

Strength(s) usually available

U.S.—
325 mg of acetaminophen and 30 mg of codeine phosphate (Rx) [*Phenaphen with Codeine No. 3* (D&C Yellow #10; edible ink; FD&C Blue #1; FD&C Yellow #6; gelatin; magnesium stearate; sodium starch glycolate; stearic acid)].
325 mg of acetaminophen and 60 mg of codeine phosphate (Rx) [*Phenaphen with Codeine No.4* (lactose; cornstarch; D&C Yellow #10; edible ink; FD&C Green #3 or Blue #1; FD&C Yellow 6; gelatin; magnesium stearate; sodium starch glycolate; stearic acid)].

Canada—
Note: In Canada, *Phenaphen with Codeine* contains phenobarbital, aspirin, and codeine. See *Barbiturates and Analgesics (Systemic)*.
Not commercially available.

Auxiliary labeling
- May cause drowsiness.
- Avoid alcoholic beverages.
- May be habit-forming.

ACETAMINOPHEN AND CODEINE PHOSPHATE ORAL SOLUTION USP

Usual adult dose

Analgesic—
Oral, 15 mL every four hours, as needed.

Usual pediatric dose

Analgesic—
Children up to 3 years of age: Dosage has not been established.
Children 3 to 7 years of age: Oral, 5 mL three or four times a day, as needed.
Children 7 to 12 years of age: Oral, 10 mL three or four times a day, as needed.

Strength(s) usually available

U.S.—
120 mg of acetaminophen and 12 mg of codeine phosphate, per 5 mL (Rx) [*Tylenol with Codeine Elixir* (alcohol 7%); GENERIC].

Canada—
160 mg of acetaminophen and 8 mg of codeine phosphate, per 5 mL (Rx) [*PMS-Acetaminophen with Codeine* (alcohol 7%); *Tylenol with Codeine Elixir* (alcohol 7%)].

Auxiliary labeling
- May cause drowsiness.
- Avoid alcoholic beverages.
- May be habit-forming.

ACETAMINOPHEN AND CODEINE PHOSPHATE ORAL SUSPENSION USP

Usual adult dose

See *Acetaminophen and Codeine Phosphate Oral Solution USP*.

Usual pediatric dose

See *Acetaminophen and Codeine Phosphate Oral Solution USP*.

Strength(s) usually available

U.S.—
120 mg of acetaminophen and 12 mg of codeine phosphate, per 5 mL (Rx) [*Capital with Codeine*].

Canada—
Not commercially available.

Auxiliary labeling
- May cause drowsiness.
- Avoid alcoholic beverages.
- Shake well.
- May be habit-forming.

ACETAMINOPHEN AND CODEINE PHOSPHATE TABLETS USP

Usual adult dose

Analgesic—
Oral, 1 or 2 tablets containing 300 mg of acetaminophen and 15 or 30 mg of codeine phosphate every four hours as needed; or
Oral, 1 tablet containing 300 mg of acetaminophen and 60 mg of codeine phosphate every four hours as needed; or
Oral, 1 tablet containing 650 mg of acetaminophen and 30 mg of codeine phosphate every four hours as needed.

Usual pediatric dose

Dosage must be individualized by the physician.

Strength(s) usually available

U.S.—
300 mg of acetaminophen and 15 mg of codeine phosphate (Rx) [*Tylenol with Codeine No.2* (sodium metabisulfite); GENERIC].
300 mg of acetaminophen and 30 mg of codeine phosphate (Rx) [*Pyregesic-C; Tylenol with Codeine No.3* (sodium metabisulfite); GENERIC].
300 mg of acetaminophen and 60 mg of codeine phosphate (Rx) [*Tylenol with Codeine No.4* (sodium metabisulfite); GENERIC].
650 mg of acetaminophen and 30 mg of codeine phosphate (Rx) [*EZ III; Margesic #3*].

Canada—
300 mg of acetaminophen and 30 mg of codeine phosphate (Rx) [*Acet Codeine 30* (scored); *Empracet-30* (scored); *Emtec-30; Triatec-30*].
300 mg of acetaminophen and 60 mg of codeine phosphate (Rx) [*Acet Codeine 60* (scored); *Empracet-60; Lenoltec with Codeine No.4; Tylenol with Codeine No.4*].

Auxiliary labeling
- May cause drowsiness.
- Avoid alcoholic beverages.
- May be habit-forming.

ACETAMINOPHEN, CODEINE PHOSPHATE, AND CAFFEINE TABLETS

Usual adult dose

Analgesic—
Oral, 1 or 2 tablets every four hours as needed.

Usual pediatric dose

Dosage must be individualized by the physician.

Strength(s) usually available

U.S.—
Not commercially available.

Canada—
300 mg of acetaminophen, 8 mg of codeine phosphate, and 15 mg of caffeine (OTC) [*Lenoltec with Codeine No.1; Novo-Gesic C8; Tylenol with Codeine No.1;* GENERIC (may be scored)].
300 mg of acetaminophen, 8 mg of codeine phosphate, and 30 mg of caffeine citrate (OTC) [*Exdol-8* (scored)].
300 mg of acetaminophen, 15 mg of codeine phosphate, and 15 mg of caffeine (Rx) [*Acet-2* (scored); *Lenoltec with Codeine No.2; Novo-Gesic C15* (scored); *Tylenol with Codeine No.2*].
300 mg of acetaminophen, 30 mg of codeine phosphate, and 15 mg of caffeine (Rx) [*Acet-3* (scored); *Lenoltec with Codeine No.3; Novo-Gesic C30* (scored); *Tylenol with Codeine No.3*].
325 mg of acetaminophen, 8 mg of codeine phosphate, and 15 mg of caffeine (OTC) [*Cetaphen with Codeine*].
325 mg of acetaminophen, 8 mg of codeine phosphate, and 30 mg of caffeine citrate (OTC) [*Atasol-8* (scored); *Cotabs; Triatec-8*].
325 mg of acetaminophen, 15 mg of codeine phosphate, and 30 mg of caffeine citrate (Rx) [*Atasol-15* (scored)].
325 mg of acetaminophen, 30 mg of codeine phosphate, and 30 mg of caffeine citrate (Rx) [*Atasol-30* (scored)].
500 mg of acetaminophen, 8 mg of codeine phosphate, and 15 mg of caffeine (OTC) [*Cetaphen Extra Strength with Codeine; Tylenol with Codeine No.1 Forte;* GENERIC].
500 mg of acetaminophen, 8 mg of codeine phosphate, and 30 mg of caffeine citrate (OTC) [*Triatec-8 Strong*].

Auxiliary labeling
- May cause drowsiness.
- Avoid alcoholic beverages.
- May be habit-forming.

DIHYDROCODEINE AND ACETAMINOPHEN

Summary of Differences

Category:
Dihydrocodeine is an opioid agonist analgesic.

Indications:
Indicated for relief of moderate to moderately severe pain.

Oral Dosage Forms

DIHYDROCODEINE BITARTRATE, ACETAMINOPHEN, AND CAFFEINE CAPSULES

Usual adult dose

Analgesic—
Oral, 2 capsules every four hours.

Usual pediatric dose

Dosage has not been established.

Strength(s) usually available

U.S.—
16 mg of dihydrocodeine bitartrate, 356.4 mg of acetaminophen, and 30 mg of caffeine (Rx) [*DHC plus* (croscarmellose sodium; FD&C Blue #1; FD&C Green #3; gelatin; silica gel; silicon dioxide; sodium lauryl sulfate; cornstarch; titanium dioxide; zinc stearate)].

Canada—
Not commercially available.

Auxiliary labeling
- May cause drowsiness.
- Avoid alcoholic beverages.
- May be habit-forming.

HYDROCODONE AND ACETAMINOPHEN

Summary of Differences

Category:
Hydrocodone is an opioid agonist analgesic.

Indications:
Indicated for relief of moderate to moderately severe pain.

Pharmacology/pharmacokinetics: For orally administered hydrocodone:
Mechanism of action/effect: An opioid agonist analgesic; exerts agonist activity primarily at the mu receptor.
Half-life: 3.8 hours
Onset of action: 10–30 minutes.
Time to peak effect: 30–60 minutes.
Duration of action (nontolerant patients only; decreases as tolerance develops during chronic therapy): 4–6 hours.

Precautions:
Pregnancy—Hydrocodone teratogenic in animals in very high doses.
Breast-feeding—Not known whether hydrocodone is distributed into breast milk.

Side/adverse effects:
Hydrocodone is more likely than most other opioids to cause side effects associated with histamine release.

Oral Dosage Forms

HYDROCODONE BITARTRATE AND ACETAMINOPHEN CAPSULES

Usual adult dose

Analgesic—
Oral, one capsule every four to six hours, as needed. Dosage may be increased to two capsules every six hours if necessary.

Usual adult prescribing limits

Analgesic—
Eight capsules per 24 hours.

Usual pediatric dose

Dosage has not been established.

Strength(s) usually available

U.S.—
5 mg of hydrocodone bitartrate and 500 mg of acetaminophen (Rx) [*Allay; Anolor DH 5; Bancap-HC; Dolacet; Dolagesic; Hycomed; Hyco-Pap; Hydrocet; Hydrogesic; Lorcet-HD; Margesic-H; Panlor; Polygesic; Stagesic; T-Gesic; Ugesic; Vendone; Zydone* (FD&C Yellow 6); GENERIC].

Canada—
Not commercially available.

Auxiliary labeling
- May cause drowsiness.
- Avoid alcoholic beverages.
- May be habit-forming.

HYDROCODONE BITARTRATE AND ACETAMINOPHEN ORAL SOLUTION

Usual adult dose

Analgesic—
Oral, 5 to 15 mL every four to six hours as needed.

Usual pediatric dose

Dosage has not been established.

Strength(s) usually available

U.S.—
2.5 mg of hydrocodone bitartrate and 167 mg of acetaminophen per 5 mL (Rx) [*Lortab* (alcohol 7%; citric acid; ethyl maltol; glycerin, methylparaben; propylene glycol; propylparaben; saccharin sodium; sorbitol solution; sucrose; D&C Yellow #10; FD&C Yellow #6)].

Canada—
Not commercially available.

Auxiliary labeling
- May cause drowsiness.
- Avoid alcoholic beverages.
- May be habit-forming.

HYDROCODONE BITARTRATE AND ACETAMINOPHEN TABLETS USP

Usual adult dose

Analgesic—
Oral, 1 or 2 tablets containing 2.5 mg of hydrocodone bitartrate and 500 mg of acetaminophen every four to six hours; or

Oral, 1 tablet containing 5 mg of hydrocodone bitartrate and 500 mg of acetaminophen every four to six hours as needed, with dosage being increased to 2 tablets every six hours if necessary; or
Oral, 1 tablet containing 7.5 mg of hydrocodone bitartrate and 650 mg of acetaminophen every four to six hours as needed, with dosage being increased to 2 tablets every six hours if necessary; or
Oral, 1 tablet containing 7.5 mg of hydrocodone bitartrate and 750 mg of acetaminophen every four to six hours as needed; or
Oral, 1 tablet containing 10 mg of hydrocodone bitartrate and 650 mg of acetaminophen every four to six hours as needed.

Usual adult prescribing limits
Up to 40 mg of hydrocodone bitartrate and 4 grams of acetaminophen in twenty-four hours.

Usual pediatric dose
Dosage has not been established.

Strength(s) usually available
U.S.—
2.5 mg of hydrocodone bitartrate and 500 mg of acetaminophen (Rx) [*Lortab 2.5/500* (scored); GENERIC].
5 mg of hydrocodone bitartrate and 500 mg of acetaminophen (Rx) [*Anexsia 5/500* (scored); *Co-Gesic* (scored); *Duocet* (scored); *HY-PHEN* (scored); *Lortab 5/500* (scored); *Oncet; Panacet 5/500* (scored); *Vanacet; Vicodin* (scored); GENERIC].
7.5 mg of hydrocodone bitartrate and 500 mg of acetaminophen (Rx) [*Lortab 7.5/500* (scored); GENERIC].
7.5 mg of hydrocodone bitartrate and 650 mg of acetaminophen (Rx) [*Anexsia 7.5/650* (scored); *Lorcet Plus* (scored); GENERIC].
7.5 mg of hydrocodone bitartrate and 750 mg of acetaminophen (Rx) [*Vicodin ES* (scored); GENERIC].
10 mg of hydrocodone bitartrate and 500 mg of acetaminophen (Rx) [*Lortab 10/500* (scored; colloidal silicon dioxide; croscarmellose sodium; crospovidone; microcrystalline cellulose; povidone; pregelatinized starch; stearic acid; FD&C Red #27 Lake; FD&C Red #30 Lake)].
10 mg of hydrocodone bitartrate and 650 mg of acetaminophen (Rx) [*Lorcet 10/650* (scored; colloidal silicon dioxide; croscarmellose sodium; crospovidone; microcrystalline cellulose; povidone; pregelatinized starch; stearic acid; FD&C Blue #1 Lake)].
Canada—
Not commercially available.

Auxiliary labeling
- May cause drowsiness.
- Avoid alcoholic beverages.
- May be habit-forming.

OXYCODONE AND ACETAMINOPHEN

Summary of Differences

Category:
Oxycodone is an opioid agonist analgesic.
Indications:
Indicated for relief of moderate to moderately severe pain.
Pharmacology/pharmacokinetics: For orally administered oxycodone:
Mechanism of action/effect: An opioid agonist analgesic. Has agonist activity primarily at the mu receptor.
Equivalence: 30 mg via oral administration therapeutically equivalent to 10 mg of intramuscular morphine.
Half-life: 2–3 hours
Time to peak effect: 1 hour.
Duration of action (nontolerant patients only; duration decreases as tolerance develops during chronic therapy): 3–4 hours.
Elimination: Renal.
Precautions:
Breast-feeding—Not known whether oxycodone is distributed into breast milk.

Oral Dosage Forms

OXYCODONE AND ACETAMINOPHEN CAPSULES USP

Usual adult dose
Analgesic—
Oral, 1 capsule every four to six hours as needed.

Usual pediatric dose
Dosage has not been established.

Strength(s) usually available
U.S.—
5 mg of oxycodone hydrochloride and 500 mg of acetaminophen (Rx) [*Roxilox; Tylox* (sodium metabisulfite); GENERIC].
Canada—
Not commercially available.

Auxiliary labeling
- May cause drowsiness.
- Avoid alcoholic beverages.
- May be habit-forming.

OXYCODONE AND ACETAMINOPHEN ORAL SOLUTION

Usual adult dose
Analgesic—
Oral, 5 mL every four to six hours as needed.

Usual pediatric dose
Dosage has not been established.

Strength(s) usually available
U.S.—
5 mg of oxycodone hydrochloride and 325 mg of acetaminophen per 5 mL (Rx) [*Roxicet* (alcohol 0.4%; edetic acid; saccharin)].
Canada—
Not commercially available.

Auxiliary labeling
- May cause drowsiness.
- Avoid alcoholic beverages.
- May be habit-forming.

OXYCODONE AND ACETAMINOPHEN TABLETS USP

Usual adult dose
Oral, 1 to 2 tablets every four to six hours as needed.

Usual pediatric dose
Dosage has not been established.

Strength(s) usually available
U.S.—
2.5 mg of oxycodone hydrochloride and 325 mg of acetaminophen [*Percocet 2.5/325* (colloidal silicon dioxide; croscarmellose sodium; crospovidone; microcrystalline cellulose; povidone; pregelatinized corn starch; stearic acid)].
5 mg of oxycodone hydrochloride and 325 mg of acetaminophen (Rx) [*Endocet; Percocet 5/325* (scored; colloidal silicon dioxide; croscarmellose sodium; crospovidone); *Roxicet* (scored); GENERIC].
5 mg of oxycodone hydrochloride and 500 mg of acetaminophen (Rx) [*Roxicet 5/500* (scored); GENERIC].
7.5 mg of oxycodone hydrochloride and 500 mg of acetaminophen [*Percocet 7.5/500* (colloidal silicon dioxide; croscarmellose sodium; crospovidone; microcrystalline cellulose; povidone; pregelatinized corn starch; stearic acid)].
10 mg of oxycodone hydrochloride and 650 mg of acetaminophen [*Percocet 10/650* (colloidal silicon dioxide; croscarmellose sodium; crospovidone; microcrystalline cellulose; povidone; pregelatinized corn starch; stearic acid)].
Canada—
2.5 mg of oxycodone hydrochloride and 325 mg of acetaminophen (Rx) [*Percocet-Demi* (double-scored)].
5 mg of oxycodone hydrochloride and 325 mg of acetaminophen (Rx) [*Endocet* (scored); *Oxycocet* (scored); *Percocet* (scored); *Roxicet* (scored)].

Auxiliary labeling
- May cause drowsiness.
- Avoid alcoholic beverages.
- May be habit-forming.

PENTAZOCINE AND ACETAMINOPHEN

Summary of Differences

Category:
Pentazocine is an opioid agonist/antagonist analgesic.
Indications:
Indicated for relief of moderate pain.
Pharmacology/pharmacokinetics: For orally administered pentazocine:
Mechanism of action/effect: An opioid agonist/antagonist analgesic.
Agonist—Has agonist activity at the kappa and sigma receptors.
Antagonist—Has antagonist activity at the mu receptor; may precipitate withdrawal symptoms in patients who are physically dependent on mu receptor agonists.
Equivalence: 180 mg therapeutically equivalent to 10 mg of intramuscular morphine.
Protein binding: Moderate.
Half-life: 2–3 hours
Onset of action: 15–30 minutes.

Time to peak effect: 60–90 minutes.
Duration of action (nontolerant patients only; decreases as tolerance develops during chronic therapy): 3 hours.
Elimination—Renal, 5–23% as unchanged pentazocine, and biliary.

Precautions:
Pregnancy—Studies in animals have not shown that pentazocine causes adverse effects on the fetus.
Breast-feeding—Not known whether pentazocine is distributed into breast milk.
Drug interactions and/or related problems—
May partially antagonize effects of opioid agonist analgesics.
May cause withdrawal symptoms if given to a patient physically dependent on an opioid agonist.
Medical considerations/contraindications—
Precaution in patients who are physically dependent on an opioid agonist.
Precaution in patients with acute myocardial infarction.

Side/adverse effects:
Although effects occur rarely, pentazocine more likely than butorphanol or nalbuphine to cause subjective and psychotomimetic effects characteristic of sigma receptor agonists.
Respiratory depression subject to a "ceiling effect," after which the depth of respiratory depression does not increase with dose.
Pentazocine has less dependence liability and potential for abuse than opioid agonists.
Pentazocine produces withdrawal symptoms that are less severe than those produced by opioid agonist analgesics.

Oral Dosage Forms

PENTAZOCINE HYDROCHLORIDE AND ACETAMINOPHEN TABLETS

Usual adult dose
Analgesic—
Oral, 1 tablet every four hours.

Usual adult prescribing limits
Up to 6 tablets daily.

Usual pediatric dose
Dosage has not been established.

Strength(s) usually available
U.S.—
650 mg of acetaminophen and 25 mg of pentazocine base (Rx) [*Talacen* (scored; colloidal silicon dioxide; FD&C Blue #1; gelatin; microcrystalline cellulose; potassium sorbate; pregelatinized starch; sodium lauryl sulfate; sodium metabisulfite; sodium starch glycolate; stearic acid)].
Canada—
Not commercially available.

Auxiliary labeling
- May cause drowsiness.
- Avoid alcoholic beverages.
- May be habit-forming.

PROPOXYPHENE AND ACETAMINOPHEN

Summary of Differences

Category:
Propoxyphene is an opioid agonist analgesic.

Indications:
Indicated for relief of mild to moderate pain.

Pharmacology/pharmacokinetics: For orally administered propoxyphene:
Mechanism of action/effect: An opioid agonist analgesic; has agonist activity primarily at the mu receptor.
Equivalence: Dose therapeutically equivalent to 10 mg of intramuscular morphine too toxic to administer.
Protein binding: High.
Biotransformation: Metabolite norpropoxyphene is toxic.
Half-life:
Propoxyphene—6–12 hours
Norpropoxyphene—30–36 hours
Onset of action: 15–60 minutes.
Time to peak concentration: 2–2.5 hours.
Peak plasma concentration: 0.05–0.1 mcg per mL.
Time to peak effect: 2 hours.
Duration of action (nontolerant patients only; decreases as tolerance develops during chronic therapy): 4–6 hours.
Elimination: Renal, $<$ 10% as unchanged propoxyphene; biliary.

Precautions:
Pregnancy—Studies in animals have not shown that propoxyphene causes adverse effects on the fetus.
Breast-feeding—Propoxyphene is distributed into breast milk.
Drug interactions and/or related problems—Risk of convulsions if overdose of propoxyphene administered to amphetamine-treated patients.
May increase effects of coumarin- or indanedione-derivative anticoagulants.
Concurrent use with carbamazepine not recommended because may decrease carbamazepine metabolism, leading to increased risk of toxicity.
Laboratory value alterations—May cause liver function test abnormalities.

Side/adverse effects:
Propoxyphene may be more likely than most opioid analgesics to cause convulsions.
Hepatotoxicity has been reported with propoxyphene.
Propoxyphene has less dependence liability and potential for abuse than other opioid agonists with usual doses.
Propoxyphene produces withdrawal symptoms that are less severe than those produced by stronger opioid agonist analgesics.

Oral Dosage Forms

PROPOXYPHENE HYDROCHLORIDE AND ACETAMINOPHEN TABLETS USP

Usual adult dose
Analgesic—
Oral, 1 tablet every four hours, as needed.

Usual pediatric dose
Dosage has not been established.

Strength(s) usually available
U.S.—
65 mg of propoxyphene hydrochloride and 650 mg of acetaminophen (Rx) [*E-Lor*; *Wygesic* (scored); GENERIC].
Canada—
Not commercially available.

Auxiliary labeling
- May cause drowsiness.
- Avoid alcoholic beverages.
- May be habit-forming.

PROPOXYPHENE NAPSYLATE AND ACETAMINOPHEN TABLETS USP

Usual adult dose
Analgesic—
Oral, 2 tablets containing 50 mg of propoxyphene napsylate and 325 mg of acetaminophen every four hours, as needed; or
Oral, 1 tablet containing 100 mg of propoxyphene napsylate and 650 mg of acetaminophen every four hours, as needed.

Usual pediatric dose
Dosage has not been established.

Strength(s) usually available
U.S.—
50 mg of propoxyphene napsylate and 325 mg of acetaminophen (Rx) [*Darvocet-N 50*; GENERIC].
100 mg of propoxyphene napsylate and 650 mg of acetaminophen (Rx) [*Darvocet-N 100* (cellulose; cornstarch; FD&C Yellow #6; magnesium stearate; stearic acid; titanium dioxide); *Propacet 100*; GENERIC].
Canada—
Not commercially available.

Auxiliary labeling
- May cause drowsiness.
- Avoid alcoholic beverages.
- May be habit-forming.

Revised: 05/21/2001

OPIOID (NARCOTIC) ANALGESICS AND ASPIRIN Systemic

This monograph includes information on the following: 1) Aspirin and Codeine; 2) Aspirin and Codeine, Buffered; 3) Aspirin and Dihydrocodeine; 4) Hydrocodone and Aspirin; 5) Oxycodone and Aspirin; 6) Pentazocine and Aspirin; 7) Propoxyphene and Aspirin.

PEN: Aspirin and Codeine—Co-codaprin

INN: Propoxyphene—Dextropropoxyphene

VA CLASSIFICATION (Primary): CN101

Note: Controlled substances in the U.S. and Canada as follows:

Drug	U.S.	Canada
Aspirin and Codeine	III	N
Aspirin and Codeine, Buffered	III	N
Aspirin and Dihydrocodeine	III	**
Hydrocodone and Aspirin	III	**
Oxycodone and Aspirin	II	N
Pentazocine and Aspirin	IV	**
Propoxyphene and Aspirin	IV	N

**Not available in Canada.

Commonly used brand name(s): *222[1]; 282[1]; 292[1]; 692[7]; Anacin with Codeine[1]; C2 Buffered with Codeine[2]; C2 with Codeine[1]; Damason-P[4]; Darvon Compound-65[7]; Darvon-N Compound[7]; Darvon-N with A.S.A.[7]; Empirin with Codeine No.3[1]; Empirin with Codeine No.4[1]; Endodan[5]; Lortab ASA[4]; Novo-AC and C[1]; Oxycodan[5]; PC-Cap[7]; Panasal 5/500[4]; Percodan[5]; Percodan-Demi[5]; Propoxyphene Compound-65[7]; Roxiprin[5]; Synalgos-DC[3]; Talwin Compound[6]*.

Other commonly used names are: A.C.&C [ASA‡, Codeine, and Caffeine] AC and C [ASA‡, Codeine, and Caffeine] Dihydrocodeine Compound [Aspirin and Dihydrocodeine] Drocode and aspirin [Aspirin and Dihydrocodeine] Propoxyphene Hydrochloride Compound [Propoxyphene, Aspirin, and Caffeine]

NOTE: The *Opioid (Narcotic) Analgesics and Aspirin (Systemic)* monograph is maintained on the *USP DI* electronic data base. A copy of the most recent revision of the complete monograph can be accessed on the *USP DI* Updates Online website. See the front cover of book for details on accessing the site.

For information on the specific components of this combination, see the *USP DI* monographs for *Opioid (Narcotic) Analgesics (Systemic)* and *Salicylates (Systemic)*.

The information that follows is selectively abstracted from the complete monograph and is provided to facilitate drug use review and patient counseling. **Aspirin** is a brand name in Canada; acetylsalicylic acid is the generic name. ASA, a commonly used designation for aspirin (or acetylsalicylic acid) in both the U.S. and Canada, is the term used in Canadian product labeling.

Note: For a listing of dosage forms and brand names by country availability, see *Dosage Forms* section(s).

Category

Analgesic

Note: Opioid agonist analgesics—Codeine, dihydrocodeine, hydrocodone, oxycodone, and propoxyphene.

Opioid agonist/antagonist analgesic—Pentazocine.

Indications

Accepted

Pain (treatment)—Indicated for symptomatic relief of:

Mild to severe pain (depending on the dose of codeine)
(Aspirin and codeine; buffered aspirin and codeine.)

Mild to moderate pain
(Propoxyphene and aspirin.)

Moderate pain
(Pentazocine and aspirin.)

Moderate to moderately severe pain
(Aspirin and dihydrocodeine; oxycodone and aspirin.)

Moderate to severe pain
(Hydrocodone and aspirin.)

[1]Not included in Canadian product labeling.

Patient Consultation

As an aid to patient consultation, refer to *Advice for the Patient, Narcotic Analgesics and Aspirin (Systemic)*.

In providing consultation, consider emphasizing the following selected information (» = major clinical significance):

Before using this medication

» Conditions affecting use, especially:

Sensitivity to the opioid considered for use, to aspirin, or to nonsteroidal anti-inflammatory drugs (NSAIDs), history of

Pregnancy—Aspirin and opioid analgesics cross the placenta; high-dose chronic use or abuse of aspirin in the third trimester may be hazardous to the mother as well as the fetus and/or neonate, causing heart problems in fetus or neonate and/or bleeding in mother, fetus, or neonate; high-dose chronic use or abuse may also prolong and complicate labor and delivery; also, regular use of opioids by pregnant women may cause physical dependence in the fetus and withdrawal symptoms in the neonate; not taking aspirin during the third trimester unless prescribed by physician

Breast-feeding—Aspirin, codeine, and propoxyphene are distributed into breast milk

Use in children and in teenagers—Checking with physician before giving to children or teenagers with symptoms of acute febrile illness, especially influenza or varicella, because of the risk of Reye's syndrome; also, increased susceptibility to aspirin toxicity in children, especially with fever and dehydration; also, children up to 2 years of age are more susceptible to the effects of opioids, especially respiratory depression; in addition, children may be more likely to experience opioid-induced paradoxical CNS excitation during therapy

Use in the elderly—Increased risk of aspirin toxicity and of opioid-induced adverse effects, especially respiratory depression

Other medications, especially alcohol or other CNS depressants, anticoagulants, antidiabetic agents (oral), those cephalosporins that may cause hypoprothrombinemia, methotrexate, monoamine oxidase inhibitors, naltrexone, nonsteroidal anti-inflammatory drugs (NSAIDs), platelet aggregation inhibitors, plicamycin, probenecid, sulfinpyrazone, urinary alkalizers, valproic acid, vancomycin, and zidovudine

Other medical problems, especially coagulation or platelet function disorders, diarrhea caused by antibiotics or poisoning, asthma or other respiratory problems, and gastrointestinal problems such as ulceration or erosive gastritis (especially a bleeding ulcer) or other severe inflammatory bowel disease

Proper use of this medication

» Taking with food or a full glass (240 mL) of water to minimize stomach irritation

» Not taking medication if it has a strong vinegar-like odor

» Importance of not taking more medication than the amount prescribed because of danger of overdose of aspirin or opioid analgesics and habit-forming potential of opioid analgesics

» Not increasing dose if medication seems less effective after a few weeks; checking with physician instead

» Proper dosing

Missed dose (if on scheduled dosing): Taking as soon as possible; not taking if almost time for next dose; not doubling doses

» Proper storage

Precautions while using this medication

Regular visits to physician to check progress during long-term therapy

» Caution if other medications containing aspirin or other salicylates or opioid analgesics are used

» Avoiding use of alcohol or other central nervous system (CNS) depressants during therapy unless prescribed or otherwise approved by physician; also, alcohol consumption may increase risk of aspirin-induced stomach problems

Not taking acetaminophen or ibuprofen or other NSAIDs concurrently for more than a few days unless directed by physician or dentist

» Caution if dizziness, drowsiness, lightheadedness, or false sense of well-being occurs

Caution when getting up suddenly from a lying or sitting position

Lying down if nausea or vomiting, or dizziness or lightheadedness occurs

Need to inform physician or dentist of use of medication if any kind of surgery (including dental surgery) or emergency treatment is required

Caution if any kind of surgery is required; aspirin should be discontinued 5 days prior to surgery unless otherwise directed by physician or dentist

Checking with pharmacist before using the buffered formulation (available in Canada) with any other oral medication; antacids in the formulation may interfere with absorption of many oral medications

(Diabetics: Aspirin may cause false urine sugar test results with prolonged use of 8 or more 325-mg (5-grain), or 4 or more 650-mg (10-grain), doses per day)

(Possible dryness of mouth; using sugarless gum or candy, ice, or saliva substitute for relief; checking with dentist if dry mouth continues for more than 2 weeks)

» Checking with physician before discontinuing medication after prolonged use of high doses; gradual dosage reduction may be necessary to avoid withdrawal symptoms

» Suspected overdose: Getting emergency help at once

Side/adverse effects

Signs of potential side effects, especially respiratory depression or impairment; allergic reactions; confusion, convulsions, hallucinations, mental depression, or other signs of CNS toxicity; gastrointestinal toxicity; hepatotoxicity; hypertension, and paradoxical CNS excitation, especially in children

ASPIRIN AND CODEINE

Summary of Differences

Category:
Codeine is an opioid agonist analgesic.

Indications:
Indicated for relief of mild to severe pain, depending on the dose of codeine.

Pharmacology/pharmacokinetics: For orally administered codeine:
Mechanism of action/effect: An opioid agonist analgesic; exerts agonist activity primarily at the mu receptor, but with usual doses is relatively weak.
Equivalence: 200 mg therapeutically equivalent to 10 mg of intramuscular morphine.
Protein binding: Very low.
Half-life: 2.5–4 hours.
Biotransformation: Hepatic; about 10% demethylated to morphine.
Onset of action: 30–45 minutes.
Time to peak effect: 1–2 hours.
Duration of action (nontolerant patients only; decreases as tolerance develops during chronic therapy): 4 hours.
Elimination: Renal, 5–15% as unchanged codeine and 10% as unchanged or conjugated morphine.

Precautions:
Pregnancy—Codeine has been shown to cause delayed ossification in mice and increased resorptions in rats.
Breast-feeding—Codeine is distributed into breast milk.

Side/adverse effects:
Codeine is more likely than most other opioids to cause constipation, especially during chronic therapy.
Codeine has lower dependence liability and potential for abuse than most other opioid agonists with usual doses.
Withdrawal symptoms produced by codeine are less severe than those produced by stronger opioid agonist analgesics.

Oral Dosage Forms

ASPIRIN AND CODEINE PHOSPHATE TABLETS USP

Usual adult dose
Oral, 1 or 2 tablets every four hours as needed.

Usual pediatric dose
Dosage has not been established.

Strength(s) usually available
U.S.—
325 mg of aspirin and 15 mg of codeine phosphate (Rx) [GENERIC].
325 mg of aspirin and 30 mg of codeine phosphate (Rx) [*Empirin with Codeine No.3;* GENERIC].
325 mg of aspirin and 60 mg of codeine phosphate (Rx) [*Empirin with Codeine No.4;* GENERIC].
Canada—
Not commercially available.

Auxiliary labeling
- May cause drowsiness.
- Avoid alcoholic beverages.
- Take with food or with a full glass of water.
- May be habit-forming.

ASPIRIN, CODEINE PHOSPHATE, AND CAFFEINE TABLETS USP

Usual adult dose
Analgesic—
Oral, 1 or 2 tablets every four hours as needed.

Usual pediatric dose
Dosage has not been established.

Strength(s) usually available
U.S.—
Not commercially available.
Canada—
Note: 30 mg of caffeine citrate are equivalent to 15 mg of caffeine base.
325 mg of ASA, 8 mg of codeine phosphate, and 15 mg of caffeine (OTC) [*C2 with Codeine;* GENERIC].
325 mg of ASA, 8 mg of codeine phosphate, and 32 mg of caffeine (OTC) [*Anacin with Codeine*].
375 mg of ASA, 8 mg of codeine phosphate, and 30 mg of caffeine (OTC) [GENERIC].
375 mg of ASA, 8 mg of codeine phosphate, and 30 mg of caffeine citrate (OTC) [*222* (double-scored)].
375 mg of ASA, 15 mg of codeine phosphate, and 30 mg of caffeine citrate (Rx) [*282* (scored)].
375 mg of ASA, 30 mg of codeine phosphate, and 30 mg of caffeine citrate (Rx) [*292* (scored)].
400 mg of ASA, 8 mg of codeine phosphate, and 15 mg of caffeine (OTC) [*Novo-AC and C*].
500 mg of ASA, 8 mg of codeine phosphate, and 15 mg of caffeine (OTC) [GENERIC].

Auxiliary labeling
- May cause drowsiness.
- Avoid alcoholic beverages.
- Take with food or with a full glass of water.
- May be habit-forming.

ASPIRIN AND CODEINE, BUFFERED

Summary of Differences

Category:
Codeine is an opioid agonist analgesic.

Indications:
Indicated for relief of mild to severe pain, depending on the dose of codeine.

Pharmacology/pharmacokinetics: For orally administered codeine:
Mechanism of action/effect: An opioid agonist analgesic; exerts agonist activity primarily at the mu receptor, but with usual doses is relatively weak.
Equivalence: 200 mg therapeutically equivalent to 10 mg of intramuscular morphine.
Protein binding: Very low.
Half-life: 2.5–4 hours.
Biotransformation: Hepatic; about 10% demethylated to morphine.
Onset of action: 30–45 minutes.
Time to peak effect: 1–2 hours.
Duration of action (nontolerant patients only; decreases as tolerance develops during chronic therapy): 4 hours.
Elimination: Renal, 5–15% as unchanged codeine and 10% as unchanged or conjugated morphine.

Precautions:
Pregnancy—Codeine has been shown to cause delayed ossification in mice and increased resorptions in rats.
Breast-feeding—Codeine is distributed into breast milk.
Drug interactions and/or related problems—Antacids present as buffering agents may decrease absorption of many orally administered medications; antacids generally should be taken 1 to 2 hours before or after other orally administered medications, although intervals of 3 to 8 hours between antacid ingestion and administration of specific agents (i.e., fluoroquinolone antibiotics, ketoconazole, and oral tetracyclines) have been recommended.

Side/adverse effects:
Codeine is more likely than most other opioids to cause constipation, especially during chronic therapy.
Codeine has lower dependence liability and potential for abuse than most other opioid agonists with usual doses.
Withdrawal symptoms produced by codeine are less severe than those produced by stronger opioid agonist analgesics.

Oral Dosage Forms

ASPIRIN, CODEINE PHOSPHATE, CAFFEINE, ALUMINA, AND MAGNESIA TABLETS

Usual adult dose

Analgesic—
Oral, 1 or 2 tablets every four hours as needed.

Usual pediatric dose

Dosage has not been established.

Strength(s) usually available

U.S.—
Not commercially available.

Canada—
325 mg of ASA, 8 mg of codeine phosphate, and 15 mg of caffeine, with 35 mg of aluminum hydroxide and 70 mg of magnesium hydroxide (OTC) [*C2 Buffered with Codeine*].

Auxiliary labeling

- May cause drowsiness.
- Avoid alcoholic beverages.
- Take with food or with a full glass of water.
- May be habit-forming.

ASPIRIN AND DIHYDROCODEINE

Summary of Differences

Category:
Dihydrocodeine is an opioid agonist analgesic.

Indications:
Indicated for relief of moderate to moderately severe pain.

Oral Dosage Forms

ASPIRIN, CAFFEINE, AND DIHYDROCODEINE BITARTRATE CAPSULES USP

Usual adult dose

Analgesic—
Oral, 2 capsules every four hours as needed.

Usual pediatric dose

Dosage has not been established.

Strength(s) usually available

U.S.—
356.4 mg of aspirin, 30 mg of caffeine, and 16 mg of dihydrocodeine bitartrate (Rx) [*Synalgos-DC*].

Canada—
Not commercially available.

Auxiliary labeling

- May cause drowsiness.
- Avoid alcoholic beverages.
- Take with food or with a full glass of water.
- May be habit-forming.

HYDROCODONE AND ASPIRIN

Summary of Differences

Category:
Hydrocodone is an opioid agonist analgesic.

Indications:
Indicated for relief of moderate to severe pain.

Pharmacology/pharmacokinetics: For orally administered hydrocodone:
Mechanism of action/effect: An opioid agonist analgesic; exerts agonist activity primarily at the mu receptor.
Half-life: 3.8 hours.
Onset of action: 10–30 minutes.
Time to peak effect: 30–60 minutes.
Duration of action (nontolerant patients only; decreases as tolerance develops during chronic therapy): 4–6 hours.

Precautions:
Pregnancy—Hydrocodone teratogenic in animals in very high doses.
Breast-feeding—Not known whether hydrocodone is distributed into breast milk.

Side/adverse effects:
Hydrocodone is more likely than most other opioids to cause side effects associated with histamine release.

Oral Dosage Forms

HYDROCODONE BITARTRATE AND ASPIRIN TABLETS

Usual adult dose

Analgesic—
Oral, 1 or 2 tablets every four to six hours as needed.

Usual pediatric dose

Dosage has not been established.

Strength(s) usually available

U.S.—
5 mg of hydrocodone bitartrate and 500 mg of aspirin (Rx) [*Damason-P; Lortab ASA; Panasal 5/500*].

Canada—
Not commercially available.

Auxiliary labeling

- May cause drowsiness.
- Avoid alcoholic beverages.
- Take with food or with a full glass of water.
- May be habit-forming.

OXYCODONE AND ASPIRIN

Summary of Differences

Category:
Oxycodone is an opioid agonist analgesic.

Indications:
Indicated for relief of moderate to moderately severe pain.

Pharmacology/pharmacokinetics: For orally administered oxycodone:
Mechanism of action/effect: An opioid agonist analgesic; has agonist activity primarily at the mu receptor.
Equivalence: 30 mg via oral administration therapeutically equivalent to 10 mg of intramuscular morphine.
Half-life: 2–3 hours.
Time to peak effect: 1 hour.
Duration of action (nontolerant patients only; duration decreases as tolerance develops during chronic therapy): 3–4 hours.
Elimination: Renal.

Precautions:
Breast-feeding—Not known whether oxycodone is distributed into breast milk.

Oral Dosage Forms

OXYCODONE AND ASPIRIN TABLETS USP

Usual adult dose

Analgesic—
Oral, 1 or 2 half-strength tablets or 1 full-strength tablet, every four to six hours as needed. Dosage may be increased if necessary for severe pain.

Usual pediatric dose

Analgesic—
Children up to 6 years of age—Use is not recommended.
Children 6 to 12 years of age—Oral, ¼ half-strength tablet every six hours as needed.
Children 12 years of age and over—Oral, ½ half-strength tablet every six hours as needed.

Strength(s) usually available

U.S.—
Half-strength: 2.25 mg of oxycodone hydrochloride and 190 mcg (0.19 mg) of oxycodone terephthalate, with 325 mg of aspirin (Rx) [*Percodan-Demi* (scored)].
Full-strength: 4.5 mg of oxycodone hydrochloride and 380 mcg (0.38 mg) of oxycodone terephthalate, with 325 mg of aspirin (Rx) [*Endodan; Percodan* (scored); *Roxiprin;* GENERIC].

Canada—
Half-strength: 2.5 mg of oxycodone hydrochloride and 325 mg of ASA (Rx) [*Percodan-Demi* (scored)].
Full-strength: 5 mg of oxycodone hydrochloride and 325 mg of ASA (Rx) [*Endodan* (scored); *Oxycodan* (scored); *Percodan* (scored)].

Auxiliary labeling

- May cause drowsiness.
- Avoid alcoholic beverages.
- Take with food or with a full glass of water.
- May be habit-forming.

PENTAZOCINE AND ASPIRIN

Summary of Differences

Category:
Pentazocine is an opioid agonist/antagonist analgesic.
Indications:
Indicated for relief of moderate pain.
Pharmacology/pharmacokinetics: For orally administered pentazocine:
Mechanism of action/effect: An opioid agonist/antagonist analgesic.
Agonist—Has agonist activity at the kappa and sigma receptors.
Antagonist—Has antagonist activity at the mu receptor; may precipitate withdrawal symptoms in patients who are physically dependent on mu-receptor agonists.
Equivalence: 180 mg therapeutically equivalent to 10 mg of intramuscular morphine.
Protein binding: Moderate.
Half-life: 2–3 hours
Onset of action: 15–30 minutes.
Time to peak effect: 60–90 minutes.
Duration of action (nontolerant patients only; decreases as tolerance develops during chronic therapy): 3 hours.
Elimination: Renal, 5–23% as unchanged pentazocine, and biliary.
Precautions:
Pregnancy—Studies in animals have not shown that pentazocine causes adverse effects in the fetus.
Breast-feeding—Not known whether pentazocine is distributed into breast milk.
Drug interactions and/or related problems—
May partially antagonize effects of opioid agonist analgesics.
May cause withdrawal symptoms if given to a patient physically dependent on an opioid agonist.
Medical considerations/contraindications—
Precaution in patients who are physically dependent on an opioid agonist.
Precaution in patients with acute myocardial infarction.
Side/adverse effects:
Although effects occur rarely, pentazocine more likely than butorphanol or nalbuphine to cause subjective and psychotomimetic effects characteristic of sigma receptor agonists.
Respiratory depression subject to a “ceiling effect”, after which the depth of respiratory depression does not increase with dose.
Pentazocine has less dependence liability and potential for abuse than opioid agonists.
Pentazocine produces withdrawal symptoms that are less severe than those produced by opioid agonist analgesics.

Oral Dosage Forms

PENTAZOCINE HYDROCHLORIDE AND ASPIRIN TABLETS USP

Usual adult dose
Analgesic—
Oral, 2 tablets three or four times a day as needed.

Usual pediatric dose
Dosage has not been established.

Strength(s) usually available
U.S.—
12.5 mg of pentazocine (base) and 325 mg of aspirin (Rx) [*Talwin Compound*].
Canada—
Not commercially available.

Auxiliary labeling
- May cause drowsiness.
- Avoid alcoholic beverages.
- Take with food or with a full glass of water.
- May be habit-forming.

PROPOXYPHENE AND ASPIRIN

Summary of Differences

Category:
Propoxyphene is an opioid agonist analgesic.
Indications:
Indicated for relief of mild to moderate pain.
Pharmacology/pharmacokinetics: For orally administered propoxyphene:
Mechanism of action/effect: An opioid agonist analgesic; has agonist activity primarily at the mu receptor.
Equivalence: Dose therapeutically equivalent to 10 mg of intramuscular morphine too toxic to administer.
Protein binding: High.
Biotransformation: Metabolite norpropoxyphene is toxic.
Half-life:
Propoxyphene—6–12 hours.
Norpropoxyphene—30–36 hours.
Onset of action: 15–60 minutes.
Time to peak concentration: 2–2.5 hours.
Peak plasma concentration: 0.05–0.1 mcg per mL.
Time to peak effect: 2 hours.
Duration of action (nontolerant patients only; decreases as tolerance develops during chronic therapy): 4–6 hours.
Elimination: Renal, <10% as unchanged propoxyphene; biliary.
Precautions:
Pregnancy—Studies in animals have not shown that propoxyphene causes adverse effects in the fetus.
Breast-feeding—Propoxyphene is distributed into breast milk.
Drug interactions and/or related problems—
Risk of convulsions if overdose of propoxyphene administered to amphetamine-treated patients.
May increase effects of coumarin- or indandione-derivative anticoagulants.
Concurrent use with carbamazepine not recommended because may decrease carbamazepine metabolism, leading to increased risk of toxicity.
Laboratory value alterations—May cause liver function test abnormalities.
Side/adverse effects:
Propoxyphene may be more likely than most opioid analgesics to cause convulsions.
Hepatotoxicity has been reported with propoxyphene.
Propoxyphene has less dependence liability and potential for abuse than other opioid agonists with usual doses.
Propoxyphene produces withdrawal symptoms that are less severe than those produced by stronger opioid agonist analgesics.

Oral Dosage Forms

PROPOXYPHENE HYDROCHLORIDE, ASPIRIN, AND CAFFEINE CAPSULES USP

Usual adult dose
Oral, 1 capsule every four hours, as needed.

Usual adult prescribing limits
Up to 390 mg of propoxyphene hydrochloride a day.

Usual pediatric dose
Dosage has not been established.

Strength(s) usually available
U.S.—
65 mg of propoxyphene hydrochloride, 389 mg of aspirin, and 32.4 mg of caffeine (Rx) [*Darvon Compound-65; PC-Cap; Propoxyphene Compound-65;* GENERIC].
Canada—
Not commercially available.

Auxiliary labeling
- May cause drowsiness.
- Avoid alcoholic beverages.
- Take with food or with a full glass of water.
- May be habit-forming.

PROPOXYPHENE HYDROCHLORIDE, ASPIRIN, AND CAFFEINE TABLETS

Usual adult dose
Analgesic—
Oral, 1 tablet every four hours, as needed.

Usual adult prescribing limits
Up to 390 mg of propoxyphene hydrochloride a day.

Usual pediatric dose
Dosage has not been established.

Strength(s) usually available

U.S.—
Not commercially available.

Canada—
65 mg of propoxyphene hydrochloride, 375 mg of ASA, and 30 mg of caffeine (Rx) [*692* (scored)].

Auxiliary labeling

- May cause drowsiness.
- Avoid alcoholic beverages.
- Take with food or with a full glass of water.
- May be habit-forming.

PROPOXYPHENE NAPSYLATE AND ASPIRIN CAPSULES

Usual adult dose

Analgesic—
Oral, 1 capsule every four hours, as needed.

Usual adult prescribing limits

Up to 600 mg of propoxyphene napsylate a day.

Usual pediatric dose

Dosage has not been established.

Strength(s) usually available

U.S.—
Not commercially available.

Canada—
100 mg of propoxyphene napsylate and 325 mg of ASA (Rx) [*Darvon-N with A.S.A.*].

Auxiliary labeling

- May cause drowsiness.
- Avoid alcoholic beverages.
- Take with food or with a full glass of water.
- May be habit-forming.

PROPOXYPHENE NAPSYLATE, ASPIRIN, AND CAFFEINE CAPSULES

Usual adult dose

Analgesic—
Oral, 1 capsule every four hours, as needed.

Usual adult prescribing limits

Up to 600 mg of propoxyphene napsylate a day.

Usual pediatric dose

Dosage has not been established.

Strength(s) usually available

U.S.—
Not commercially available.

Canada—
100 mg of propoxyphene napsylate, 375 mg of ASA, and 30 mg of caffeine (Rx) [*Darvon-N Compound*].

Auxiliary labeling

- May cause drowsiness.
- Avoid alcoholic beverages.
- Take with food or with a full glass of water.
- May be habit-forming.

Revised: 06/14/2000

OPIUM—See *Opioid (Narcotic) Analgesics (Systemic)*

ORAL REHYDRATION SALTS—See *Carbohydrates and Electrolytes (Systemic)*

ORLISTAT Oral-Local†

VA CLASSIFICATION (Primary): HS452

Commonly used brand name(s): *Xenical*.

Note: For a listing of dosage forms and brand names by country availability, see *Dosage Forms* section(s).

†Not commercially available in Canada.

Category

Lipase inhibitor.

Indications

Accepted

Obesity, exogenous (treatment)—Orlistat is indicated for the management of obesity in persons with an initial body mass index (BMI) ≥ 30 kg per square meter of body surface area (kg/m^2), or a BMI ≥ 27 kg/m^2 when other risk factors (such as hypertension, diabetes, or dyslipidemia) are present. Orlistat should be used in conjunction with a reduced-calorie diet for management of obesity, including weight loss, weight maintenance, and reduction of the risk of weight gain following previous weight loss. Weight loss has been observed within 2 weeks of initiation of orlistat therapy.

Although the long-term effects of orlistat on morbidity and mortality associated with obesity have not been established, observational epidemiologic studies suggest that weight loss, if maintained, may produce health benefits for obese patients who have or are at risk of developing weight-related comorbidities, including cardiovascular disease, type 2 diabetes, certain forms of cancer, gallstones, and certain respiratory disorders.

Acceptance not established

Although orlistat is used in obese type 2 diabetes patients, there is insufficient data to show that orlistat is beneficial as primary treatment of *type 2 diabetes*.

Pharmacology/Pharmacokinetics

Physicochemical characteristics

Molecular weight—495.7.

Solubility—Freely soluble in chloroform; very soluble in methanol and ethanol; practically insoluble in water..

Mechanism of action/Effect

Orlistat is a reversible inhibitor of intestinal lipases. In the lumen of the stomach and intestine, it bonds covalently with active serine residues of gastric and pancreatic lipases, making them unavailable to hydrolyze dietary triglycerides into absorbable fatty acids and monoglycerides. Because undigested triglycerides are not absorbed, a calorie deficit may occur, having a positive effect on weight control. Systemic absorption is minimal and is not needed for activity.

At therapeutic doses, orlistat inhibits dietary fat absorption by approximately 30%.

Other actions/effects

Postprandial, cholecystokinin plasma concentrations were decreased after multiple doses of orlistat in two studies; however, two other studies have shown no difference from placebo. No clinically significant changes in gallbladder motility, bile composition or lithogenicity, or colonic cell proliferation rate, and no clinically significant reductions of gastric emptying time or gastric acidity were observed. In addition, no effects on plasma triglyceride levels or systemic lipases were observed.

Time to protective effect

Weight loss has been observed within 2 weeks of initiation of therapy.

Absorption

Systemic absorption of orlistat is minimal.

Protein binding

Very high (>99%).

Biotransformation

Believed to occur mainly within the gastrointestinal wall to form relatively inactive metabolites.

Half-life

1 to 2 hours.

Elimination
Biliary, fecal—97% (83% as unchanged drug).

Precautions to Consider

Carcinogenicity
Carcinogenicity studies in rats and mice showed no carcinogenic potential for orlistat at doses equivalent to 38 and 46 times the human daily dose calculated on an area under the concentration-time curve (AUC) basis of total drug-related material.

Mutagenicity
Orlistat showed no detectable mutagenic or genotoxic activity in the Ames test, a mammalian forward mutation assay, an *in vitro* clastogenesis assay in peripheral human lymphocytes, an unscheduled DNA synthesis assay in rat hepatocytes in culture, and an *in vivo* mouse micronucleus test.

Pregnancy/Reproduction
Fertility—There were no observable effects on fertility or reproduction in rats given doses of 400 mg per kg (mg/kg) per day (equivalent to 12 times the human dose on a mg per square meter of body surface area [mg/m^2] basis).

Pregnancy—Adequate and well-controlled studies in humans have not been done. Orlistat is not recommended for use during pregnancy

Rats and rabbits given doses up to 800 mg/kg per day showed no embryotoxicity or teratogenicity. This dose is 23 and 47 times the daily human dose calculated on a mg/m^2 basis for rats and rabbits, respectively. The incidence of dilated cerebral ventricles was increased in mid- and high-dose groups (6 and 23 times the daily human dose on a mg/m^2 basis) of the rat teratology study. However, this finding was not reproduced in subsequent, similar studies.

FDA Pregnancy Category B.

Breast-feeding
It is not known whether orlistat is distributed into human breast milk.

Pediatrics
Appropriate studies on the relationship of age to the effects of orlistat have not been performed in the pediatric population. Safety and efficacy have not been established.

Geriatrics
No information is available on the relationship of age to the effects of orlistat in geriatric patients.

Drug interactions and/or related problems
The following drug interactions and/or related problems have been selected on the basis of their potential clinical significance (possible mechanism in parentheses where appropriate)—not necessarily inclusive (» = major clinical significance):

Note: Drug-drug interaction studies indicated that orlistat had no effect on the pharmacokinetics and/or pharmacodynamics of alcohol, digoxin, glyburide, nifedipine (extended-release tablets), oral contraceptives, phenytoin, or warfarin. Alcohol did not affect the pharmacodynamics of orlistat.

Combinations containing any of the following medications, depending on the amount present, may also interact with this medication.

» Fat-soluble vitamins and analogues
(in a pharmacokinetic interaction study, concomitant administration of orlistat reduced the absorption of a vitamin E acetate supplement by approximately 60% and a beta-carotene supplement by approximately 30%; the effect on the absorption of supplemental vitamin D, vitamin A, and nutritionally-derived vitamin K is not known)

Pravastatin
(in a study of hypercholesterolemic subjects, the bioavailability and lipid-lowering effects of pravastatin were increased by coadministration of orlistat.)

Cyclosporine
(preliminary data indicate that cyclosporine plasma concentrations may be reduced when orlistat is co-administered with cyclosporine; therefore, cyclosporine should be taken at least 2 hours before or after orlistat is administered; monitoring frequency of cyclosporine concentrations should be increased in patients on orlistat therapy)

» Warfarin
(vitamin K status may be decreased with orlistat; patients on chronic warfarin therapy should be monitored closely for changes in coagulation parameters)

Laboratory value alterations
The following have been selected on the basis of their potential clinical significance (possible effect in parentheses where appropriate)—not necessarily inclusive (» = major clinical significance).

With physiology/laboratory test values
Oxalate, urine (increased levels may occur)

Medical considerations/Contraindications
The medical considerations/contraindications included have been selected on the basis of their potential clinical significance (reasons given in parentheses where appropriate)—not necessarily inclusive (» = major clinical significance).

Except under special circumstances, this medication should not be used when the following medical problems exist:

» Chronic malabsorption

» Cholestasis

Risk-benefit should be considered when the following medical problems exist:

Anorexia nervosa or
Bulimia
(increased risk of misuse)

» History of hyperoxaluria or calcium oxalate nephrolithiasis
(increased risk of nephrolithiasis)

Sensitivity to orlistat

Side/Adverse Effects

Note: Side effects caused by orlistat usually disappear within 2 to 3 days of discontinuing the medication.

The following side/adverse effects have been selected on the basis of their potential clinical significance (possible signs and symptoms in parentheses where appropriate)—not necessarily inclusive:

Those indicating need for medical attention
Incidence more frequent
Influenza-like symptoms (fever; chills; headache; bodyache); ***upper respiratory tract infection*** (runny nose; nasal congestion; sneezing; sore throat; cough; fever)

Incidence less frequent
Lower respiratory tract infection (cough; troubled breathing; tightness in chest; wheezing); ***tooth or gingival disorder*** (tooth or gum problems)

Incidence rare
infectious diarrhea (contagious diarrhea); ***otitis*** (change in hearing; earache; pain in ear); ***urinary tract infection*** (bloody or cloudy urine; difficult or painful urination; frequent urge to urinate)

Those indicating need for medical attention only if they continue or are bothersome
Incidence more frequent
Abdominal pain; gastrointestinal symptoms, including; fatty/oily stool (oily bowel movements); ***fecal incontinence*** (inability to hold bowel movement); ***fecal urgency*** (immediate need to have bowel movement); ***flatus with discharge*** (gas with leaky bowel movements); ***increased defecation*** (increase in bowel movements); ***oily evacuation*** (oily bowel movements); ***oily spotting*** (oily spotting of underclothes); ***headache***

Incidence less frequent
Anxiety; back pain; menstrual irregularities (menstrual changes); ***rectal pain or discomfort***

Incidence rare
Arthritis (joint pain); ***dizziness; dryness of skin; fatigue*** (unusual tiredness or weakness); ***insomnia*** (trouble in sleeping); ***myalgia*** (muscle pain); ***nausea; skin rash; vomiting***

Overdose
For more information on the management of overdose or unintentional ingestion, **contact a poison control center** (see *Poison Control Center Listing*).

Clinical effects of overdose
Doses of up to 400 mg three times a day for 15 days have produced no significant adverse effects.

Treatment of overdose
Observe for 24 hours. Systemic effects attributable to the lipase-inhibiting properties of orlistat are expected to be rapidly reversible.

Patients in whom intentional overdose is confirmed or suspected should be referred for psychiatric consultation.

Patient Consultation

As an aid to patient consultation, refer to *Advice for the Patient, Orlistat (Oral-Local)*.

In providing consultation, consider emphasizing the following selected information (» = major clinical significance):

Importance of diet

» Using with a nutritionally balanced, calorie-restricted diet containing no more than 30% of calories as fat

Before using this medication

» Conditions affecting use, especially:
- Pregnancy—Not recommended for use during pregnancy
- Breast-feeding—Not known if orlistat is excreted in human milk
- Other medications, especially warfarin
- Other medical problems, especially chronic malabsorption, cholestasis, history of hyperoxaluria or calcium oxalate nephrolithiasis

Proper use of this medication

» Taking with meals or within 1 hour of eating; omitting dose if a meal is missed or contains no fat

Importance of adhering to diet with less than 30% of calories as fat

Taking daily multivitamin supplement (that includes fat-soluble vitamins) at least 2 hours before or after orlistat

» Proper dosing

Missed dose: Skipping missed dose; continuing on regular schedule with next dose; not doubling doses

» Proper storage

Precautions while using this medication

» Regular visits to physician to check progress of therapy

For patients with diabetes: Improved metabolic control resulting from weight loss may require a reduction in oral hypoglycemic medication or insulin dose

» Medication may cause troublesome gastrointestinal effects, including oily spotting, flatus with discharge, fecal urgency, increased defecation, and fecal incontinence

Side/adverse effects

Signs of potential side effects, especially influenza-like symptoms; upper respiratory infection; lower respiratory infection; tooth or gingival disorder; infectious diarrhea; otitis; and urinary tract infection

General Dosing Information

Organic causes of obesity, such as hypothyroidism, should be excluded before orlistat therapy is started.

Orlistat should be taken during fat-containing meals or up to 1 hour after the meal. Doses in excess of 360 mg per day have not been shown to provide additional benefit.

Weight loss has been observed within 2 weeks of initiation of therapy.

Weight loss induced by orlistat may be accompanied by improved metabolic control in patients with diabetes, requiring reduction of hypoglycemic medication or insulin dose.

Diet/Nutrition

Orlistat therapy should be used in conjunction with a nutritionally balanced, reduced-calorie diet that contains no more than 30% of calories as fat. Higher fat levels increase the likelihood of side effects. The daily intake of fat, protein, and carbohydrate should be distributed over three main meals. If a meal is occasionally missed or contains no fat, the dose of orlistat should be omitted.

Because orlistat reduces absorption of some fat-soluble vitamins and beta-carotene, patients should take a daily multivitamin supplement containing fat-soluble vitamins to prevent deficiency. The supplement should be taken at least 2 hours before or after the administration of orlistat.

Oral Dosage Forms:

ORLISTAT CAPSULES

Usual adult dose

Obesity management—

Oral, 120 mg three times a day, with each fat-containing meal. The dose should be taken during fat-containing meals or up to 1 hour after the meal.

Note: Doses in excess of 360 mg a day have not been shown to provide additional benefit.

Usual adult prescribing limits

360 mg a day.

Usual pediatric dose

Safety and efficacy have not been established.

Strength(s) usually available

U.S.—

120 mg (Rx) [*Xenical* (microcrystalline cellulose; sodium starch glycolate; sodium lauryl sulfate; povidone; talc)].

Packaging and storage

Store at 25 °C (77 °F); excursions permitted to 15° to 30°C (59° to 86°F). Store in a well-closed container.

Revised: 06/28/2002
Developed: 11/22/1999

ORPHENADRINE—See *Skeletal Muscle Relaxants (Systemic)*

OSELTAMIVIR Systemic

VA CLASSIFICATION (Primary): AM890

Commonly used brand name(s): *Tamiflu*.

Note: For a listing of dosage forms and brand names by country availability, see *Dosage Forms* section(s).

Category

Antiviral (Systemic).

Indications

General Considerations

Oseltamivir is not a substitute for early vaccination on an annual basis as recommended by the Centers for Disease Control's Immunization Practices Advisory Committee.

Resistance—

Decreased neuraminidase susceptibility of influenza virus to oseltamivir carboxylate was demonstrated in 1.3% (4 out of 301 isolates) of adult and adolescent patients treated in clinical studies. In similar studies with pediatric patients aged 1 to 12 years, 8.6% (9 out of 105) of patients showed decreased neuraminidase susceptibility of influenza to oseltamivir carboxylate. The active site of neuraminidase showed specific mutation in genotypic analysis. No studies were performed to determine the role of alterations in the viral hemagglutinin.

In vitro studies demonstrate the development of reduced susceptibility of influenza A virus in the presence of increasing concentrations of oseltamivir carboxylate. Genetic analysis showed reduced susceptibility and is associated with mutations that result in amino acid changes in the viral neuraminidase or viral hemagglutinin or both.

Cross-resistance—

Genotypic analysis demonstrates similar mutations in the viral neuraminidase from clinical isolates between oseltamivir-induced and zanamivir-resistant virus. An estimation of incidence of oseltamivir resistance and possible cross-resistance to zanamivir in clinical isolates cannot be made due to limitations in the assays available.

Accepted

Influenza (treatment)—Oseltamivir is indicated for the treatment of uncomplicated acute illness due to influenza infection in patients 1 year and older who have been symptomatic for no more than 2 days.

Influenza (prophylaxis)—Oseltamivir is indicated for the prophylaxis of influenza in patients 1 year and older.

According to the Canadian manufacturer, oseltamivir is indicated for the prevention of influenza illness in adults and adolescents 13 years and older following close contact with an infected individual (the index case). The decision to administer oseltamivir for prophylaxis to close contacts should be based on the knowledge that influenza is circulating in the area and the index case demonstrates characteristic symptoms of influenza.

Acceptance not established

There is no evidence for efficacy of oseltamivir in any illness caused by agents other than influenza viruses Types A and B.

Efficacy of oseltamivir in patients who begin treatment after 40 hours of symptoms has not been established.

Efficacy of oseltamivir in the treatment of subjects with chronic cardiac disease and/or respiratory disease has not been established.

Efficacy of oseltamivir for treatment or prophylaxis has not been established in immunocompromised patients.

Pharmacology/Pharmacokinetics

Physicochemical characteristics

Molecular weight—

Oseltamivir free base: 312.4.

Oseltamivir phosphate: 410.4.

Mechanism of action/Effect

Oseltamivir is an inhibitor of influenza virus neuraminidase, possibly altering particle aggregation and release.

Absorption

Oral oseltamivir phosphate is readily absorbed then extensively converted to oseltamivir carboxylate, the active form, predominantly by hepatic esterases. At least 75% of an oral dose reaches the systemic circulation as oseltamivir carboxylate. Less than 5% of an oral dose reaches the systemic circulation as oseltamivir phosphate.

Distribution

Oseltamivir carboxylate—Volume of distribution is 23 to 26 liters following intravenous administration in 24 subjects

Protein binding

Oseltamivir phosphate–Moderate (42%)

Oseltamivir carboxylate–Very low (< 3%)

Biotransformation

Hepatic; Oseltamivir, ethyl ester prodrug, undergoes extensive hydrolysis to the active ester form, oseltamivir carboxylate.

Half-life

Elimination–1 to 3 hours for oseltamivir and 6 to 10 hours for oseltamivir carboxylate.

Peak serum concentration

Results after multiple doses of 75 milligrams twice daily of oseltamivir phosphate:

Oseltamivir phosphate–65.2 nanograms/milliliter (ng/mL)

Oseltamivir carboxylate–348 ng/mL

Time to peak effect

24 hours for a significant reduction in viral titers after initiation of oral treatment after inoculation with experimental influenza virus.

Elimination

Renal–Oseltamivir carboxylate is extensively eliminated by renal excretion (> 99%).

Renal clearance (18.8 L/hr) exceeds glomerular filtration rate (7.5 L/hr), indicating that tubular secretion occurs.

Fecal–Elimination of an oral radiolabeled dose is < 20% in the feces.

Precautions to Consider

Carcinogenicity

Long-term tests with oseltamivir are underway and have not yet been completed. However, a 26-week dermal carcinogenicity study of oseltamivir carboxylate in which FVB/Tg./AC transgenic mice were dosed at 40, 140, 400 or 780 mg per kg of body weight per day was negative.

Mutagenicity

Oseltamivir was non-mutagenic in the Ames test and the human lymphocyte chromosome assay with and without enzymatic activation and negative in the mouse micronucleus test. It was found to be positive in a Syrian Hamster Embryo (SHE) cell transformation test. Oseltamivir carboxylate was non-mutagenic in the AMES test and the L5178Y mouse lymphoma assay with and without enzymatic activation and negative in the SHE cell transformation test.

Pregnancy/Reproduction

Fertility—Doses of oseltamivir administered to female rats 2 weeks before mating, during mating and until Day 6 of pregnancy were 50, 250, and 1500 milligrams/kilogram per day. Doses of oseltamivir were administered to male rats 4 weeks before mating, during, and for 2 weeks after mating. Oseltamivir lacked an effect on fertility, mating performance, or early embryonic development at any dose level. The highest dose was approximately 100 times the human systemic exposure (area under the concentration curve 0 to 24 hours) of oseltamivir carboxylate.

Pregnancy—Adequate and well-controlled studies in humans have not been done. In a rat study, minimal maternal toxicity was reported with 1500 milligrams/kilogram (mg/kg) per day orally and no maternal toxicities were reported with 50 and 250 mg/kg per day orally. In a rabbit study, slight and marked maternal toxicities were observed, respectively, with 150 and 500 mg/kg per day and no maternal toxicities with 50 mg/kg per day. In the rat and rabbit study there was a dose-dependent increase in the incidence rates of a variety of minor skeleton abnormalities and variants in the exposed offspring. However, the individual incidence rate of each skeletal abnormality or variant remained within the background rates of occurrence in the species studied. Oseltamivir should be used during pregnancy only if the potential benefit justifies the potential risk to the fetus.

FDA Pregnancy Category C

Breast-feeding

It is not known whether oseltamivir is distributed into human breast milk. Oseltamivir and oseltamivir carboxylate are distributed into the milk of lactating rats. Oseltamivir should be used only if the potential benefit for the lactating mother justifies the potential risk to the breast-fed infant.

Pediatrics

Appropriate studies performed to date have not demonstrated pediatrics-specific problems that would limit the usefulness of oseltamivir in children 1 year of age and greater. Safety and efficacy have not been established in children less than 1 year of age.

Geriatrics

Appropriate studies performed to date have not demonstrated geriatric-specific problems that would limit the usefulness of oseltamivir in the elderly.

Drug interactions and/or related problems

The following drug interactions and/or related problems have been selected on the basis of their potential clinical significance (possible mechanism in parentheses where appropriate)—not necessarily inclusive (» = major clinical significance):

» Probenecid
(concomitant administration results in an approximate two-fold increase in the active metabolite due to a decrease in active anionic tubular secretion in the kidney)

Medical considerations/Contraindications

The medical considerations/contraindications included have been selected on the basis of their potential clinical significance (reasons given in parentheses where appropriate)—not necessarily inclusive (» = major clinical significance).

Except under special circumstances, this medication should not be used when the following medical problem exists:

» Hypersensitivity to oseltamivir or any component of the formulation

Risk-benefit should be considered when the following medical problems exist:

Cardiac disease, chronic or
Illness caused by agents other than influenza viruses Types A or B or
Respiratory disease
(efficacy has not been established)

Hepatic impairment
(safety and pharmacokinetics have not been evaluated)

» Renal function impairment
(safety has not been established in patients with renal failure, creatinine clearance below 10 milliliters/minute (mL/min); dosage adjustment is recommended in patients with a creatinine clearance of less than 30 mL/min)

Severe or unstable medical condition
(safety and efficacy not established in the treatment of influenza in patients with any medical condition which might require hospitalization)

Side/Adverse Effects

The following side/adverse effects have been selected on the basis of their potential clinical significance (possible signs and symptoms in parentheses where appropriate)—not necessarily inclusive:

Those indicating need for medical attention

Incidence less frequent

Bronchitis (phlegm producing cough; wheezing)

Incidence rare

Angina, unstable (arm, back or jaw pain; chest pain or discomfort; chest tightness or heaviness; fast or irregular heartbeat; shortness of breath); ***humerus fracture; peritonsillar abscess*** (sore throat, tender glands of jaw and throat, facial swelling, drooling, headache, fever, hoarseness); ***pseudomembranous colitis*** (abdominal or stomach cramps; pain; bloating; abdominal tenderness; diarrhea, watery and severe, which may also be bloody; fever; increased thirst; nausea or vomiting; unusual tiredness or weakness; unusual weight loss)

Incidence not determined—Observed during clinical practice; estimates of frequency can not be determined

Allergy (dizziness; fast heartbeat; shortness of breath; skin rash or itching over the entire body; sweating; weakness; wheezing); ***anaphylactic/anaphylactoid reactions*** (cough; difficulty swallowing; dizziness; fast heartbeat; hives; itching, puffiness or swelling of the eyelids or around the eyes, face, lips or tongue; shortness of breath; skin rash; tightness in chest; unusual tiredness or weakness; wheezing); ***arrhythmia*** (dizziness; fainting; fast, slow, or irregular heartbeat); ***erythema multiforme*** (blistering, peeling, loosening of skin; chills; cough; diarrhea; fever; itching; joint or muscle pain; red irritated eyes; sore throat; sores, ulcers, or white spots in mouth or on lips; unusual tiredness or weakness); ***hepatitis*** (dark urine; general tiredness and weakness; light-colored stools; nausea and vomiting; upper right abdominal pain; yellow eyes and skin); ***seizure*** (convulsions; muscle spasm or jerking of all extremities; sudden loss of consciousness; loss of bladder control); ***Stevens-Johnson syndrome*** (blistering, peeling, loosening of skin; chills; cough; diarrhea; itching; joint or muscle pain; red irritated eyes; red skin lesions, often with a purple center; sore throat; sores, ulcers, or white spots in mouth or on lips; unusual tiredness or weakness); ***swelling of the face or tongue; toxic epidermal necrolysis*** (blistering, peeling, loosening of skin; chills; cough; diarrhea; itching; joint or muscle pain; red irritated eyes; red skin lesions, often with a purple center; sore throat; sores, ulcers, or white spots in mouth or on lips; unusual tiredness or weakness); ***urticaria*** (hives or welts; itching; redness of skin; skin rash)

Those indicating need for medical attention only if they continue or are bothersome

Incidence more frequent

Diarrhea; nausea; vomiting—Onset of nausea was predominately after the first dose and usually resolved within 1 to 2 days with continued dosing.

Incidence less frequent

Abdominal pain; conjunctivitis (redness, pain, swelling of eye, eyelid, or inner lining of eyelid; burning, dry or itching eyes; discharge; excessive tearing)—primarily in pediatric patients; ***cough; dizziness; ear disorder***—primarily in pediatric patients; ***epistaxis*** (bloody nose; unexplained nosebleeds)—primarily in pediatric patients; ***fatigue; headache; insomnia*** (trouble in sleeping)

Incidence rare

Anemia (pale skin; troubled breathing with exertion; unusual bleeding or bruising; unusual tiredness or weakness); ***pneumonia*** (chest pain; cough; fever or chills; sneezing; shortness of breath; sore throat; troubled breathing; tightness in chest; wheezing); ***pyrexia*** (fever)

Incidence not determined—Observed during clinical practice; estimates of frequency can not be determined

Aggravation of diabetes (blurred vision; dry mouth; fatigue; flushed, dry skin; fruit-like breath odor; increased hunger; increased thirst; increased urination; loss of consciousness; nausea; stomachache; sweating; troubled breathing; unexplained weight loss; vomiting); ***confusion*** (mood or mental changes); ***dermatitis*** (blistering, crusting, irritation, itching, or reddening of skin; cracked, dry, scaly skin; swelling); ***eczema*** (skin rash encrusted, scaly and oozing); ***rash***

Overdose

For more information on the management of overdose or unintentional ingestion, **contact a poison control center** (see *Poison Control Center Listing*).

Clinical effects of overdose

Single doses of up to 1000 mg of oseltamivir have been associated with nausea and/or vomiting.

Treatment of overdose

To enhance elimination—There is no data available on removal of oseltamivir or oseltamivir carboxylate by hemodialysis or hemoperfusion; however, greater than 99% of oseltamivir carboxylate is eliminated by renal excretion.

Specific treatment—Treatment is symptomatic. No specific antidote is available.

Supportive care—Patients in whom intentional overdose is confirmed or suspected should be referred for psychiatric consultation.

Patient Consultation

As an aid to patient consultation, refer to *Advice for the Patient, Oseltamivir (Systemic)*.

In providing consultation, consider emphasizing the following selected information (» = major clinical significance):

Before using this medication

» Conditions affecting use, especially:
- Hypersensitivity to oseltamivir or any component of the formulation
- Other medications, especially probenecid.
- Other medical problems, especially renal function impairment

Proper use of this medication

Importance of informing patient that oseltamivir is not a substitute for early influenza vaccination on an annual basis as recommended by the Centers for Disease Control

Supplying patient information about oseltamivir

» For patients taking oseltamivir for treatment of influenza infection: Importance of taking medication within 2 days after onset of symptoms; taking medication either with food or on an empty stomach; however, taking with food may lessen the occurrence of stomach upset; compliance with full 5-day course of therapy

For patients taking oseltamivir for prevention of influenza infection: Importance of taking medication within 2 days after exposure to influenza virus; taking medication either with food or on an empty stomach; however, taking with food may lessen the occurrence of stomach upset; taking medication for at least 10 days

For patients taking oral suspension dosage form: Proper administration technique; not using after expiration date

» Proper dosing

Missed dose: Taking as soon as remembered, except if it is near the next dose (within 2 hours); not doubling the dose; informing doctor about missed doses.

» Proper storage

Precautions while using this medication

Checking with physician if no improvement after finishing medication.

Side/adverse effects

» Signs of potential side effects, especially bronchitis, humerus fracture, peritonsillar abscess, pseudomembranous colitis, or unstable angina

Signs of potential side effects observed during clinical practice, especially allergy, anaphylactic/anaphylactoid reactions, arrhythmia, erythema multiforme, hepatitis, seizure, Stevens-Johnson syndrome, swelling of the face or tongue, toxic epidermal necrolysis, or urticaria

General Dosing Information

For influenza treatment: Oseltamivir must be started within 2 days after the onset of signs and symptoms of influenza (weakness, headache, fever, cough, and sore throat). Oseltamivir may be taken with or without food. Tolerability may be enhanced in some patients when taken with food.

For influenza prophylaxis: Oseltamivir must be started within 2 days after exposure to person infected with influenza. Oseltamivir may be taken with or without food. Tolerability may be enhanced in some patients when taken with food.

For oral suspension—An oral dosing dispenser with 30 mg, 45 mg, and 60 mg graduations is provided with the oral suspension. The 75 mg dose can be measure using a combination of 30 mg and 45 mg. The pharmacist should recommend the use of this dispenser. However, if this dispenser is lost or damaged, another dosing syringe or other device may be used to administer the following volumes:
- 2.5 mL (½ teaspoon [tsp]) for children ≤15 kg
- 3.8 mL (¾ tsp) for >15 to 23 kg
- 5 mL (1 tsp) for >23 to 40 kg
- 6.2 mL (1¼ tsp) for >40 kg

Oral Dosage Forms

Note: The available dosage form contains oseltamivir phosphate, but dosage and strength are expressed in terms of the base.

OSELTAMIVIR PHOSPHATE CAPSULES

Usual adult and adolescent (≥13 years) dose

Influenza (treatment)—

Oral, 75 milligrams (mg) two times a day for 5 days. Oseltamivir should be initiated within 2 days of onset of influenza symptoms.

For adult patients who cannot swallow a capsule—See *Oseltamivir Phosphate for Oral Suspension*

Note: Renal Impairment: In patients with a creatinine clearance between 10 and 30 mL/min the recommended dose is 75 mg once daily for 5 days. Use of oseltamivir in patients with renal failure (creatinine clearance below 10 mL/min) has not been studied. No recommended dose regimens are available for patients having routine hemodialysis and continuous peritoneal dialysis treatment with end-stage renal disease.

Influenza (prophylaxis)—

Oral, 75 mg once a day for at least 10 days following close contact with an infected individual. Oseltamivir should be initiated within 2 days of influenza exposure. Recommended dose for prophylaxis during a community outbreak of influenza is 75 mg once a day. Duration of protection lasts as long as dosing is continued.

Note: Renal Impairment: In patients with a creatinine clearance between 10 and 30 mL/min, the recommended dose is 75 mg once every other day. No recommended dose regimens are available for patients having routine hemodialysis and continuous peritoneal dialysis treatment with end-stage renal disease.

Usual adult and adolescent prescribing limits

Safety and efficacy have been demonstrated for up to 6 weeks.

Usual pediatric dose

Children less than 1 year of age—Safety and efficacy have not been established.

Children 1 year of age and older—See *Oseltamivir Phosphate for Oral Suspension*

Usual geriatric dose

See *Usual adult dose*

Strength(s) usually available

U.S.—

75 mg (Rx) [*Tamiflu* (croscarmellose sodium; ethanol; gelatin; povidone K 30; pregelatinized starch; purified water; sodium stearyl fumarate; talc; titanium dioxide; black iron oxide; red iron oxide; yellow iron oxide; FD & C Blue #2 (imprint on capsule))].

Canada—

75 mg (Rx) [*Tamiflu* (corn starch; croscarmellose sodium; gelatin; iron oxides; povidone K 30; sodium stearyl fumarate; talc; titanium dioxide)].

Packaging and storage

Store at 25 °C (77 °F); excursions permitted to 15 to 30 °C (59 to 86 °F).

Auxiliary labeling

- Continue medication for full time of treatment

OSELTAMIVIR PHOSPHATE FOR ORAL SUSPENSION

Usual adult dose

See *Oseltamivir Phosphate Capsules*.

Usual pediatric dose

Influenza (treatment)—

For infants and children 1 year of age or older or adult patients who cannot swallow a capsule:

Body weight in kg	Body weight in lbs	Recommended dose for 5 days	Number of bottles needed to obtain the recommended dose
≤15 kg	≤33 lbs	30 mg twice daily	1
>15 kg to 23 kg	>33 lbs to 51 lbs	45 mg twice daily	2
>23 kg to 40 kg	>51 lbs to 88 lbs	60 mg twice daily	2
>40 kg	>88 lbs	75 mg twice daily	3

Oseltamivir therapy should begin within 2 days of exposure.

Note: In patients with a creatinine clearance between 10 and 30 mL per minute, the recommended dose is 75 mg once a day for five days. No recommended dosing regimens are available for patients with end-stage renal disease who are undergoing routine hemodialysis or continuous peritoneal dialysis.

Influenza (prophylaxis)[1]—

For infants and children 1 year of age or older following close contact with an infected individual:

Body weight in kg	Body weight in lbs	Recommended dose for 10 days	Number of bottles needed to obtain the recommended dose
≤15 kg	≤33 lbs	30 mg once daily	1
>15 kg to 23 kg	>33 lbs to 51 lbs	45 mg once daily	2
>23 kg to 40 kg	>51 lbs to 88 lbs	60 mg once daily	2
>40 kg	>88 lbs	75 mg once daily	3

Oseltamivir therapy should begin within 2 days of exposure.

Note: In patients with a creatinine clearance between 10 and 30 mL per minute, the recommended dose is 30 mg oral suspension once per day. No recommended dosing regimens are available for patients with end-stage renal disease who are undergoing routine hemodialysis or continuous peritoneal dialysis.

Usual pediatric limits

Prophylaxis in children 1 to 12 years of age following close contact with an infected individual has not been evaluated for longer than 10 days duration.

Usual geriatric dose

See *Oseltamivir Phosphate Capsules*

Strength(s) usually available

U.S.—

12 mg per mL (Rx) [*Tamiflu* (xanthan gum; monosodium citrate; sodium benzoate; sorbitol; saccharin sodium; titanium dioxide; tutti-frutti flavoring)].

Canada—

Not commercially available.

Packaging and storage

Prior to reconstitution, store between 15 and 30 °C (59 and 86 °F). After reconstitution, store the suspension between 15 and 30 °C (59 and 86 °F) or refrigerated between 2 and 8 °C (36 and 46 °F). Protect from freezing.

Preparation of dosage form

It is recommended that the oral suspension be reconstituted as follows by the pharmacist prior to dispensing to the patient:

- Tap the closed bottle several times to loosen the powder.
- Measure 23 mL of water in a graduated cylinder.
- Add the total amount of water for reconstitution to the bottle and shake the closed bottle well for 15 seconds.
- Remove the child-resistant cap and push the bottle adapter into the neck of the bottle.
- Close the bottle with the child-resistant cap tightly. This will assure the proper seating of the bottle adapter in the bottle and the child-resistant status of the cap.

Stability

After reconstitution, the oral suspension should be used within 10 days.

Auxiliary labeling

- Refrigerate - Do not freeze.
- Shake well before using.
- Take by mouth only (use oral dispenser included with medication).

Note

Include patient package insert and oral dispenser when dispensing.

[1]Not included in Canadian product labeling.

Revised: 01/12/2006
Developed: 01/13/2000

OXACILLIN—See *Penicillins (Systemic)*

OXALIPLATIN Systemic†

VA CLASSIFICATION (Primary): AN900

Commonly used brand name(s): *Eloxatin*.

Note: For a listing of dosage forms and brand names by country availability, see *Dosage Forms* section(s).

†Not commercially available in Canada.

Category

Antineoplastic.

Indications

Note: Bracketed information in the *Indications* section refers to uses that are not included in U.S. product labeling.

Accepted

Carcinoma, colon (treatment adjuvant)—Oxaliplatin is indicated for use in combination with infusional 5-fluorouracil/leucovorin (5-FU/LV) for the adjuvant treatment of stage III cancer patients who have undergone complete resection of the primary tumor. The indication is based on an improvement in disease-free survival, with no demonstrated benefit in overall survival after a median follow up of 4 years.

Carcinoma, colorectal (treatment)—Oxaliplatin is indicated for use in combination with infusional 5–fluorouracil/leucovorin (5–FU/LV) for the treatment of advanced carcinoma of the colon or rectum.

Oxaliplatin is also indicated, [in combination with 5–FU/LV or capecitabine, for the first-line treatment of nonresectable, advanced, or metastatic colon or rectal carcinoma.][1] Prior adjuvant or palliative 5–FU-based chemotherapy and radiation therapy are permitted.

[Colon cancer, stage II, adjuvant treatment in combination with 5-fluorouracil/leucovorin]—Trial results from oxaliplatin-fluorouracil regimens in the adjuvant setting of colon cancer are clearly positive. Both the MOSAIC (FOLFOX; infusional-fluorouracil (5-FU)/leucovorin (LCV) plus oxaliplatin) and the NSABP C-07 (FLOX; bolus 5-FU/LCV plus oxaliplatin) trials improved 3-year disease free survival (DFS) in patients with stage II and stage III colon cancer. The FOLFOX regimen in the MOSAIC trial also showed durability of DFS at 4 years. Grade 3/4 diarrhea on the FLOX regimen (38%) was substantially greater than with FOLFOX (4%); this is consistent with the known significant degree of diarrhea on the weekly 5-FU bolus schedule.

[Gastric carcinoma, advanced/metastatic]—Oxaliplatin in combination with irinotecan or fluorouracil with leucovorin or folinic acid has demonstrated activity in the treatment of advanced/metastatic gastric carcinoma. The average overall survival was 7.3 to 10 months in 4 phase II clinical trials. Three trials reported average time to progression in the range of 5.2 to 5.5 months. Oxaliplatin/5-FU based regimens do not appear to greatly increase median survival, but appear to be comparable to other 5-FU-based regimens with regards to symptom relief in this population. Oxaliplatin-based regimens may result in slightly less severe toxicity - all trials reported leukopenia or neutropenia, grade 1/2 nausea and vomiting, and neuropathy.

Acceptance not established

Use of oxaliplatin for the treatment of pancreatic carcinoma has not been established, due to insufficient data supporting efficacy. Awaiting results of phase III comparison of gemcitabine in combination with oxaliplatin (GEMOX) vs. gemcitabine alone, in this patient population.

[1]Not included in Canadian product labeling.

Pharmacology/Pharmacokinetics

Physicochemical characteristics

Molecular weight—397.3.

Solubility—Oxaliplatin is slightly soluble in water at 6 milligrams per milliliter, very slightly soluble in methanol, and practically insoluble in ethanol and acetone.

Mechanism of action/Effect

Oxaliplatin undergoes nonenzymatic conversion in physiologic solutions to active derivatives via displacement of the labile oxalate ligand. Several transient reactive species are formed, including monoaquo and diaquo diaminocyclohexane (DACH) platinum, which covalently bind with macromolecules. Both inter- and intra-strand Pt-DNA crosslinks are formed. Crosslinks are formed between the *N7* positions of two adjacent guanines (GG), adjacent adenine-guanines (AG), and guanines separated by an intervening nucleotide (GNG). These crosslinks inhibit DNA replication and transcription. Cytotoxicity is cell-cycle nonspecific.

Other actions/effects

In vivo studies have shown antitumor activity of oxaliplatin against colon carcinoma. In combination with 5-fluorouracil (5-FU), oxaliplatin exhibits *in vitro* and *in vivo* antiproliferative activity greater than either compound alone in several tumor models [HT29 (colon), GR (mammary), and L1210 (leukemia)].

Absorption

Interpatient and intrapatient variability in ultrafilterable platinum exposure (AUC_{0-48}) assessed over 3 cycles was moderate to low (23% to 6%, respectively).

Note: AUC_{0-48hr} of platinum in the plasma ultrafiltrate increases as renal function decreases. The AUC_{0-48hr} of platinum in patients with mild (creatinine clearance, CL_{cr} 50 to 80 milliliters per minute), moderate (CL_{cr} 30 to <50 milliliters per minute) and severe renal (CL_{cr} <30 milliliters per minute) impairment is increased by about 60, 140 and 190%, respectively, compared to patients with normal renal function (CL_{cr} >80 milliliters per minute).

Distribution

Volume of distribution (Vol_D)—440 liters, following 2-hour intravenous infusion of oxaliplatin; approximately 15% of platinum is present in the systemic circulation; remaining 85% is rapidly distributed into tissues or eliminated in the urine.

Protein binding

Very high (greater than 90%), irreversible plasma protein binding, primarily to albumin and gamma-globulins; binding is irreversible and accumulates (approximately 2-fold) in erythrocytes.

Biotransformation

Oxaliplatin undergoes rapid and extensive nonenzymatic biotransformation. The reactive oxaliplatin derivatives are present as a fraction of the unbound platinum in plasma ultrafiltrate. Up to 17 platinum containing derivatives have been observed in plasma ultrafiltrate including several cytotoxic species and a number of noncytotoxic conjugated species. There is no evidence of cytochrome P450-mediated metabolism *in vitro* .

Half-life

Following oxaliplatin administration the decline of ultrafilterable platinum levels is triphasic.

Alpha phase (distribution)—0.43 hours.

Beta phase (distribution)—16.8 hours.

Gamma phase (terminal)—391 hours.

Peak plasma concentration

Ultrafilterable platinum C_{max} was 0.814 micrograms per milliliter following a single 2-hour intravenous infusion dose of 85 milligrams per square meter.

Elimination

Renal (after 5 days)—major route; approximately 54%.

Fecal (after 5 days)—approximately 2%.

Clearance—10 to 17 liters per hour; similar to or exceeded the average human glomerular filtration rate (GFR; 7.5 liters per hour).

Note: Renal clearance of ultrafilterable platinum is significantly correlated with GFR.

Precautions to Consider

Cross-sensitivity and/or related problems

Contraindicated in patients with a history of known allergy to oxaliplatin or other platinum compounds. Allergic reactions can occur within minutes of administration. Drug related deaths associated with platinum compounds from this reaction have been reported.

Carcinogenicity

Long-term animal studies have not been performed to evaluate the carcinogenic potential of oxaliplatin.

Mutagenicity

Oxaliplatin was not mutagenic to bacteria (Ames test) but was mutagenic to mammalian cells *in vitro* (L5178Y mouse lymphoma assay). It was clastogenic both *in vitro* (chromosome aberration in human lymphocytes) and *in vivo* (mouse bone marrow micronucleus assay).

Pregnancy/Reproduction

Fertility—In dogs, testicular damage, characterized by degeneration, hypoplasia, and atrophy has been observed after administration of 0.75 mg per kg per day for 5 days every 28 days for three cycles (canine dose represents approximately one-sixth the recommended human dose on a body surface area basis).

The pregnancy rate was not affected when male rats given three cycles of oxaliplatin were mated with female rats given less than one-seventh the recommended human dose on a body surface area basis for two cycles. Oxaliplatin caused developmental mortality and delayed growth of baby rats in this fertility study.

Pregnancy—Oxaliplatin may cause fetal harm when administered to a pregnant women. Women of childbearing potential should be advised to avoid becoming pregnant while receiving treatment with oxaliplatin. If the patient does become pregnant while receiving oxaliplatin, the patient should be apprised of the potential hazard to the fetus.

Oxaliplatin caused developmental mortality (administered gestation days 6 to 10 or 11 to 16) and adversely affected fetal growth (administered gestation days 6 to 10) of baby rats when pregnant rats were administered less than one-tenth the recommended human dose based on body surface area during gestation.

FDA Pregnancy Category D

Breast-feeding

It is not known if oxaliplatin or its derivatives are excreted in human milk. However, due to the potential serious adverse reactions in nursing infants, a decision should be made whether to discontinue nursing or delay the use of the drug, taking into account the importance of the drug to the mother.

Pediatrics

No information is available on the relationship of age to the effects of oxaliplatin in the pediatric population. Safety and efficacy have not been established.

Geriatrics

Appropriate studies on the relationship of age to the effects of oxaliplatin have been performed in the geriatric population.

The rates of overall adverse events, were similar to different age groups. The incidence of diarrhea, dehydration, hypokalemia, leukopenia, fatigue, and syncope were higher in patients 65 years of age and older.

Drug interactions and/or related problems

The following drug interactions and/or related problems have been selected on the basis of their potential clinical significance (possible mechanism in parentheses where appropriate)—not necessarily inclusive (» = major clinical significance):

Anticoagulants
(according to postmarketing experience, prolongation of prothrombin time and of INR in patients with concomitant use)

» Bone marrow depressants, other (see *Appendix II*) or
Radiation therapy
(additive bone marrow depression and gastrointestinal adverse eventsmay occur when two or more bone marrow depressants, including radiation, are used concurrently or consecutively)

5-Fluorouracil (5-FU)
(5-FU plasma concentrations are increased approximately 20% with concomitant oxaliplatin doses of 130 mg per m^2 body surface area administered every 3 weeks. No pharmacokinetic interaction is seen with concomitant doses of 85 mg per m^2 body surface area of oxaliplatin administered every 2 weeks.)

Nephrotoxic medications, other (see *Appendix II*) or
Ototoxic medications, other (see *Appendix II*)
(concurrent and/or sequential administration may increase the potential for ototoxicity and nephrotoxicity)

Vaccines, killed virus
(because normal defense mechanisms may be suppressed by oxaliplatin therapy, the patient's antibody response to the vaccine may be decreased. The interval between discontinuation of medications that cause immunosuppression and restoration of the patient's ability to respond to the vaccine depends on the intensity and type of immunosuppression-causing medication used, the underlying disease, and other factors; estimates vary from 3 months to 1 year)

» Vaccines, live virus
(because normal defense mechanisms may be suppressed by oxaliplatin therapy, concurrent use with a live virus vaccine may potentiate the replication of the vaccine virus, may increase the side/adverse effects of the vaccine virus, and/or may decrease the patient's antibody response to the vaccine; immunization of these patients should be undertaken only with extreme caution after careful review of the patient's hematologic status and only with the knowledge and consent of the physician managing the oxaliplatin therapy. The interval between discontinuation of medications that cause immunosuppression and restoration of the patient's ability to respond to the vaccine depends on the intensity and type of immunosuppression-causing medication used, the underlying disease, and other factors; estimates vary from 3 months to 1 year. In addition, immunization with oral poliovirus vaccine should be postponed in persons in close contact with the patient, especially family members)

Laboratory value alterations

The following have been selected on the basis of their potential clinical significance (possible effect in parentheses where appropriate)—not necessarily inclusive (» = major clinical significance).

With physiologic/laboratory test values
Alanine aminotransferase (ALT [SGPT]) or
Aspartate aminotransferase (AST [SGOT]) or
Bilirubin
(increased values occurred in ≥ 5% of patients based on laboratory values and NCI CTC grade 3/4)

» Serum creatinine
(elevations in serum creatinine occurred in 10% of patients in clinical trial; the incidence of Grade 3/4 elevations in serum creatinine in the oxaliplatin and infusional 5–FU/LV combination arm was 1%)

Medical considerations/Contraindications

The medical considerations/contraindications included have been selected on the basis of their potential clinical significance (reasons given in parentheses where appropriate)—not necessarily inclusive (» = major clinical significance).

Except under special circumstances, this medication should not be used when the following medical problem exists:

» Hypersensitivity to oxaliplatin or other platinum compounds
(drug related deaths associated with platinum compounds from allergic reactions have been reported.)

Risk-benefit should be considered when the following medical problems exist:

» Renal function impairment
(use with caution; platinum is primarily eliminated renally)

Patient monitoring

The following may be especially important in patient monitoring (other tests may be warranted in some patients, depending on condition; » = major clinical significance):

Laboratory testing such as:
Alanine aminotransferase (ALT [SGPT]) and
Aspartate aminotransferase (AST [SGOT]) and
Bilirubin, serum and
Creatinine, serum and
Hemoglobin and
Platelet count and
White blood cell count with differential
(standard monitoring is recommended before each oxaliplatin cycle; patients should be monitored for signs of low blood cell counts and should report fever, persistent diarrhea or evidence of infection)

» Neuropathy and neurotoxicity evaluation
(patients should be evaluated for neuropathy and neurotoxicity prior to subsequent oxaliplatin therapy cycles)

» Pulmonary toxicity
(patients should be monitored for unexplained respiratory symptoms such as nonproductive cough, dyspnea, crackles, or radiological pulmonary infiltrates; oxaliplatin should be discontinued until interstitial lung disease or pulmonary fibrosis can be excluded)

Side/Adverse Effects

Neurologic effects, both acute, reversible effects and persistent neurosensory toxicity are expected side effects of oxaliplatin. Neurosensory toxicity may be precipitated or exacerbated by exposure to cold or cold objects.

Acute, reversible, primarily peripheral, sensory neuropathy may occur within hours of oxaliplatin infusion or one to two days of dosing. This neuropathy usually resolves within 14 days and frequently recurs with subsequent dosing. Symptoms may include transient paresthesia, dysesthesia, and hypoesthesia in the hands, feet, perioral area, or throat. Symptoms may be triggered by exposure to cold temperature or cold objects. Mucositis prophylaxis (ice) should be avoided during the infusion of oxaliplatin. Jaw spasm, abnormal tongue sensation, dysarthria, eye pain, and feeling of chest pressure have also been reported.

In 1 to 2% of patients an acute syndrome of pharyngolaryngeal dysesthesia was observed. Symptoms may include subjective sensations of dysphagia or dyspnea, without any laryngospasm or bronchospasm.

Persistent (greater than 14 days), primarily peripheral, sensory neuropathy that is usually characterized by paresthesias, dysethesias, hypoesthesias, but may also include deficits in proprioception that can interfere with daily activities, such as writing, buttoning, swallowing, and difficulty walking. These symptoms may improve in some patients when oxaliplatin is discontinued.

The following side/adverse effects have been selected on the basis of their potential clinical significance (possible signs and symptoms in parentheses where appropriate)—not necessarily inclusive:

Note: Concomitant administration with 5-Fluorouracil may alter the frequency of occurrence of the following side effects.

Those indicating need for medical attention

Incidence more frequent

Anemia (pale skin; troubled breathing with exertion; unusual bleeding or bruising; unusual tiredness or weakness); ***arthralgia*** (pain in joints; muscle pain or stiffness; difficulty in moving); ***chest pain; cough, persistent; dehydration*** (confusion; decreased urination; dizziness; dry mouth; fainting; increase in heart rate; lightheadedness; rapid breathing; sunken eyes; thirst; unusual tiredness or weakness; wrinkled skin); ***dyspnea*** (difficult breathing); ***edema*** (swelling); ***hand-foot syndrome*** (blistering, peeling, redness, and/or swelling of palms of hands or bottoms of feet; numbness, pain, tingling, or unusual sensations in palms of hands or bottoms of feet); ***injection site reaction*** (bleeding, blistering, burning, coldness, discoloration of skin; feeling of pressure; hives; infection; inflammation; itching; lumps; numbness; pain; rash; redness; scarring; soreness; stinging; swelling; tenderness; tingling; ulceration; warmth)—including extravasation; ***leukopenia or neutropenia*** (black, tarry stools; chest pain; chills; cough; fever; painful or difficult urination; shortness of breath; sore throat; sores, ulcers, or white spots on lips or in mouth; swollen glands; unusual bleeding or bruising; unusual tiredness or weakness); ***neuropathy*** (abnormal tongue sensation; burning, prickling, itching, or tingling of skin; difficulty in articulating words; difficulty breathing; difficulty performing daily activities such as writing, buttoning, swallowing or walking; difficulty swallowing; eye pain; jaw spasm; numbness, decreased feeling, or pain in the hands, feet, around mouth, or throat; pressure in chest; sensation of pins and needles, stabbing pain)—two types: acute, reversible, primarily peripheral, sensory neuropathy or persistent (greater than 14 days), primarily peripheral, sensory neuropathy; ***stomatitis*** (swelling or inflammation of the mouth); ***thrombocytopenia*** (black, tarry stools; bleeding gums; blood in urine or stools; pinpoint red spots on skin; unusual bleeding or bruising); ***thromboembolism*** (pain in chest, groin, or legs, especially the calves; difficulty breathing; severe, sudden headache; slurred speech; sudden, unexplained shortness of breath; sudden loss of coordination; sudden, severe weakness or numbness in arm or leg; vision changes)

Note: Extravasation may result in local pain and inflammation, that may be severe and lead to complications, including necrosis.

Incidence less frequent

Allergic reaction (cough; difficulty swallowing; dizziness; fast heartbeat; hives; itching; puffiness or swelling of the eyelids or around the eyes, face, lips or tongue; shortness of breath; skin rash; tightness in chest; unusual tiredness or weakness; wheezing); ***hypokalemia*** (convulsions; decreased urine; dry mouth; irregular heartbeat; increased thirst; loss of appetite; mood changes; muscle pain or cramps; nausea or vomiting; numbness or tingling in hands, feet, or lips; shortness of breath; unusual tiredness or weakness)

Incidence rare

Pulmonary fibrosis (fever; cough; shortness of breath)

Incidence not determined—Observed during post-marketing experience; estimates of frequency can not be determined

Anaphylactic shock (cough; difficulty swallowing; dizziness; fast heartbeat; hives; itching; puffiness or swelling of the eyelids or around the eyes, face, lips or tongue; shortness of breath; skin rash; tightness in chest; unusual tiredness or weakness; wheezing); ***angioedema*** (large, hive-like swelling on face, eyelids, lips, tongue, throat, hands, legs, feet, sex organs); ***colitis including*** (stomach cramps; tenderness; pain; watery or bloody diarrhea; fever); ***clostridium difficile diarrhea*** (severe abdominal or stomach cramps and pain; abdominal tenderness; watery and severe diarrhea, which may also be bloody; fever); ***cranial nerve palsies*** (weakness of the muscles in your face); ***deafness; decreased visual acuity*** (decrease in vision); ***diarrhea, severe; dysarthria*** (trouble in speaking; slurred speech; changes in patterns and rhythms of speech); ***fasciculations*** (twitches of the muscle visible under the skin); ***hemolytic uremic syndrome*** (black, tarry, stools; stomach pain; blood in urine; fever; increased or decreased urination; pinpoint red spots on skin; swelling of face, fingers, feet, or lower legs; unusual bleeding or bruising; unusual tiredness or weakness; yellow eyes or skin); ***hepatic veno-occlusive disease*** (bloated abdomen; pain and fullness in right upper abdomen; weight gain; yellow eyes and skin); ***ileus*** (abdominal pain; severe constipation; severe vomiting); ***immuno-allergic hemolytic anemia*** (back, leg, or stomach pains; bleeding gums; chills; dark urine; difficulty breathing; fatigue; fever; general body swelling; headache; loss of appetite; nausea or vomiting; nosebleeds; pale skin; sore throat; yellowing of the eyes or skin); ***immuno-allergic thrombocytopenia*** (black, tarry stools; bleeding gums; blood in urine or stools; pinpoint red spots on skin; unusual bleeding or bruising); ***intestinal obstruction*** (abdominal pain; severe constipation; nausea; vomiting); ***Lhermitte's sign*** (an electric shock-like sensation that moves down the back and into the legs following a bending movement of the neck); ***loss of deep tendon reflexes; metabolic acidosis*** (confusion; drowsiness; muscle tremors; nausea; rapid, deep breathing; restlessness; stomach cramps; unusual tiredness or weakness); ***optic neuritis*** (blindness; blue-yellow color blindness; blurred vision; decreased vision; eye pain); ***pancreatitis*** (bloating; chills; constipation; darkened urine; fast heartbeat; fever; indigestion; loss of appetite; nausea; pains in stomach, side, or abdomen, possibly radiating to the back; vomiting; yellow eyes or skin); ***visual field disturbance*** (blurred vision; decrease or change in vision)

Those indicating need for medical attention only if they continue or are bothersome

Incidence more frequent

Abdominal pain; anorexia (loss of appetite; weight loss); ***back pain; constipation; diarrhea; dizziness; dyspepsia*** (acid or sour stomach; belching; heartburn; indigestion; stomach discomfort, upset or pain); ***fatigue*** (unusual tiredness or weakness); ***fever; headache; insomnia*** (sleeplessness; trouble sleeping; unable to sleep); ***nausea; rhinitis*** (stuffy nose; runny nose; sneezing); ***rigors*** (feeling unusually cold shivering); ***upper respiratory infection*** (ear congestion; nasal congestion; chills; cough; fever; sneezing, or sore throat; body aches or pain; headache; loss of voice; runny nose; unusual tiredness or weakness; difficulty in breathing); ***vomiting***

Incidence less frequent

Dysuria (difficult or painful urination; burning while urinating); ***epistaxis*** (bloody nose); ***flatulence*** (bloated, full feeling; excess air or gas in stomach or intestines; passing gas); ***flushing*** (feeling of warmth; redness of the face, neck, arms and occasionally, upper chest); ***gastroesophageal reflux*** (heartburn; vomiting); ***hiccup; lacrimation, abnormal*** (unusual tearing of eyes); ***mucositis*** (cracked lips; diarrhea; difficulty in swallowing; sores, ulcers, or white spots on lips, tongue, or inside mouth); ***peripheral edema*** (bloating or swelling of face, arms, hands, lower legs, or feet; rapid weight gain; tingling of hands or feet unusual; weight gain or loss); ***pharyngitis*** (body aches or pain; congestion; cough; dryness or soreness of throat; fever; hoarseness; runny nose; tender, swollen glands in neck; trouble in swallowing; voice changes); ***rash; taste perversion*** (change in taste; bad, unusual or unpleasant (after) taste)

Those not indicating need for medical attention

Incidence less frequent

Alopecia (hair loss; thinning of hair)

Overdose

For more information on the management of overdose or unintentional ingestion, **contact a poison control center** (see *Poison Control Center Listing).*

Clinical effects of overdose

The following effects have been selected on the basis of their potential clinical significance (possible signs and symptoms in parentheses where appropriate)—not necessarily inclusive:

Chest pain; bradycardia (chest pain or discomfort; dizziness or fainting; lightheadedness; shortness of breath; slow or irregular heartbeat; unusual tiredness); ***diarrhea; dyspnea*** (difficulty breathing); ***dysesthesia*** (lack of sensation); ***myelosuppression*** (black, tarry stools; blood in urine or stools; cough or hoarseness; difficult urination; fever or chills; lower back or side pain painful; pinpoint red spots on skin; unusual bleeding or bruising); ***neurotoxicity*** (agitation; coma; confusion; disorientation; dizziness; involuntary, rapid, rhythmic movement of the eyes; lack of coordination; lethargy; muscle twitching; paralysis; severe weakness; seizures; slurred speech; tremors); ***paresthesia*** (burning, prickling, itching, or tingling of skin); ***respiratory failure; thrombocytopenia*** (black, tarry stools; bleeding gums; blood in urine or stools; pinpoint red spots on skin; unusual bleeding or bruising); ***vomiting, profuse; wheezing***

Treatment of overdose

Specific treatment—

There is no known antidote for oxaliplatin

See the package insert or *Parenteral dosage forms, Oxaliplatin (Systemic)* for specific dosing guidelines for use of this product.

Supportive care—

Inpatient supportive care should be given, including hydration, electrolyte support, and platelet transfusion.

Patients in whom intentional overdose is confirmed or suspected should be referred for psychiatric consultation.

Patient Consultation

As an aid to patient consultation, refer to *Advice for the Patient, Oxaliplatin (Systemic).*

In providing consultation, consider emphasizing the following selected information (» = major clinical significance):

Before using this medication

» Conditions affecting use, especially:

Hypersensitivity to oxaliplatin or other platinum compounds

Pregnancy—Use not recommended during pregnancy because it may cause fetal harm; advising woman of childbearing potential to avoid becoming pregnant while receiving treatment with oxaliplatin; apprising patient of potential hazard to the fetus; reporting suspected pregnancy to the physician immediately

Breast-feeding—Use of oxaliplatin has potential serious adverse reactions in nursing infants; decision should be made whether to discontinue nursing or delay the use of the drug, taking into account the importance of oxaliplatin to the mother

Use in the elderly—The incidence of some adverse effects are higher in patients ≥ 65. No dose modifications recommended.

Other medical problems, especially renal function impairment

Proper use of this medication

Frequency of severe nausea and vomiting; importance of continuing treatment regimen as directed by physician despite stomach upset

Monitoring patient for signs of neuropathy or pulmonary toxicity; performing standard laboratory monitoring.

» Proper dosing, especially dose modifications for neurotoxicity, gastrointestinal or hematologic toxicity.

Proper storage

Precautions while using this medication

» Importance of close monitoring by a qualified physician experienced in the use of cancer chemotherapeutic agents

» Avoiding immunizations unless approved by physician; other persons in patient's household should avoid immunizations with oral poliovirus vaccine; avoiding persons who have taken oral poliovirus vaccine or wearing a protective mask that covers nose and mouth

Caution if bone marrow depression occurs:

» Avoiding exposure to persons with infections, especially during periods of low blood counts; checking with physician immediately if fever or chills, cough or hoarseness, lower back or side pain, or painful or difficult urination occurs

» Checking with your healthcare professional immediately if you have persistent vomiting, diarrhea, dehydration, cough or difficulty breathing

» Checking with healthcare professional immediately if unusual bleeding or bruising; black, tarry stools; blood in urine or stools; or pinpoint red spots on skin occur

» Checking with your healthcare professional immediately if you notice any redness, pain, or swelling in the area you are receiving your medicine.

To reduce precipitation or exacerbation of persistent neurosensory toxicity, avoid cold drinks, the use of ice cubes in drinks, cold temperatures, and cold objects. Cover your skin if you must go outside in cold temperatures. Do not put ice or ice packs on your body. Do not breathe deeply when exposed to cold air. Do not take things from the freezer or refrigerator without wearing gloves. Do not run the air conditioner at high levels in the house or in the car in hot weather.

Caution in use of regular toothbrush, dental floss, or toothpick; physician, dentist, or nurse may suggest alternatives; checking with physician before having dental work done

Not touching eyes or inside of nose unless hands washed immediately before

Using caution to avoid accidental cuts with use of sharp objects such as safety razor or fingernail or toenail cutters

Avoiding contact sports or other situations where bruising or injury could occur

» Possibility of local tissue injury and scarring if infiltration of intravenous solution occurs; telling doctor or nurse right away about redness, pain, or swelling at injection site

Side/adverse effects

Importance of discussing expected side effects of oxaliplatin, especially its neurologic effects, with physician. Avoiding cold drinks, the use of ice, and covering skin before going out in cold temperatures to lessen neurologic effects.

Signs of potential side effects, especially anemia, arthralgia, chest pain, dehydration, dyspnea, edema, hand-foot syndrome, hypokalemia, injection site reaction, leukopenia, neutropenia, neuropathy, persistent cough, pulmonary fibrosis, stomatitis, thrombocytopenia, thromboembolism.

Signs of potential side effects observed during post-marketing experience, especially anaphylactic shock, angioedema, colitis (including clostridium difficile diarrhea), cranial nerve palsies, deafness, severe diarrhea, decreased visual acuity, dysarthria, fasciculations, hemolytic uremic syndrome, hepatic veno-occlusive disease, ileus, immuno-allergic hemolytic anemia, immuno-allergic thrombocytopenia, intestinal obstruction, Lhermitte's sign, loss of deep tendon reflexes, metabolic acidosis, optic neuritis, pancreatitis, or visual field disturbance.

General Dosing Information

Oxaliplatin should be administered under the supervision of a qualified physician experienced in the use of cancer chemotherapeutic agents. Appropriate management of therapy and complications is possible only when adequate diagnostic and treatment facilities are readily available.

The administration of oxaliplatin does not require prehydration.

Premedication with antiemetics, including 5-HT_3 blockers with or without dexamethasone, is recommended.

Oxaliplatin extravasation may result in local pain and inflammation that may be severe and lead to complications, including necrosis.

The oxaliplatin infusion line should be flushed with 5% dextrose injection prior to administration of any concomitant medication.

Diet/Nutrition

The use of ice, cold drinks, cold objects and the exposure of skin to the cold should be avoided during the infusion of oxaliplatin because cold temperature can exacerbate acute neurological symptoms.

Safety considerations for handling this medication

Care should be exercised in the handling and preparation of infusion solutions prepared from oxaliplatin including: the use of gloves, washing the skin immediately and thoroughly with soap and water if a solution of oxaliplatin contacts the skin, and flushing the mucous membranes thoroughly with water if contact with oxaliplatin occurs.

There is limited but increasing evidence and concern that personnel involved in preparation and administration of parenteral antineoplastics may be at some risk because of the potential mutagenicity, teratogenicity, and/or carcinogenicity of these agents, although the actual risk is unknown. USP advisory panels recommend cautious handling both in preparation and disposal of antineoplastic agents. Precautions that have been suggested include:

- Use of a biological containment cabinet during reconstitution and dilution of parenteral medications and wearing of disposable surgical gloves and masks.
- Use of proper technique to prevent contamination of the medication, work area, and operator during transfer between containers (including proper training of personnel in this technique).
- Cautious and proper disposal of needles, syringes, vials, ampuls, and unused medication.

A number of medical centers have developed detailed guidelines for handling of antineoplastic agents.

Combination chemotherapy

Oxaliplatin is used as part of a treatment regimen that also includes 5-fluorouracil and leucovorin. As a result, incidence and/or severity of side effects may be altered by the use of 5-fluorouracil and leucovorin as part of the regimen.

For treatment of adverse effects

In patients with anaphylactic-like reactions to oxaliplatin, the use of epinephrine, corticosteroids, and antihistamines have been employed to alleviate symptoms.

For patients with persistent Grade 3 neurosensory events, discontinuing therapy should be considered. The infusional 5–FU/LV regimen need not be altered.

Prolongation of infusion time for oxaliplatin from 2 hours to 6 hours decreases the C_{max} by an estimated 32% and may mitigate acute toxicities. The infusion time for infusional 5-FU and leucovorin do not need to be changed.

Parenteral Dosage Forms

Note: Bracketed uses in the *Dosage Forms* section refer to categories of use and/or indications that are not included in U.S. product labeling.

OXALIPLATIN INJECTION

Usual adult dose

Carcinoma, colon, stage III—

The recommended dose schedule for oxaliplatin given every two weeks for 12 cycles (total of 6 months) as follows:

- Day 1: Intravenous, 85 mg per m² in 250 to 500 mL 5% dextrose in water and leucovorin 200 mg per m² in 5% dextrose in water both given over 120 minutes at the same time in separate bags using a Y-line, followed by 5-fluorouracil 400 mg per m² IV bolus given over 2 to 4 minutes, followed by 5-fluorouracil 600 mg per m² IV infusion in 500 mL 5% dextrose in water (recommended) as a 22-hour continuous infusion.
- Day 2: Intravenous, leucovorin 200 mg per m² given over 120 minutes, followed by 5-fluorouracil 400 mg per m² IV bolus given over 2 to 4 minutes, followed by 5-fluorouracil 600 mg per m² IV infusion in 500 mL 5% dextrose in water (recommended) as a 22-hour continuous infusion.

For 5-fluorouracil dosing information, see *Fluorouracil (Systemic)* and for leucovorin dosing information, see *Leucovorin (Systemic)*.

Note: For patients who experience persistent Grade 2 neurosensory events that do not resolve, a dose reduction of oxaliplatin to 75 mg per m² should be considered. The infusional 5-FU/LV part of the regimen does not need to be altered. For patients who experience persistent Grade 3 neurosensory events, discontinuing therapy should be considered.

For patients following recovery from grade 3/4 gastrointestinal (despite prophylactic treatment) or grade 3/4 hematologic toxicity, a dose reduction of oxaliplatin to 75 mg per m² and infusional 5-FU to 300 mg per m² bolus and 500 mg per m² 22-hour infusion is recommended. The next dose should be delayed until: neutrophils ≥ 1.5 x 10⁹ per L and platelets ≥ 75 x 10⁹ per L.

Carcinoma, colorectal, advanced—

The recommended dose schedule for oxaliplatin given every two weeks is as follows:

- Day 1: Intravenous, 85 mg per m² in 250 to 500 mL 5% dextrose in water and leucovorin 200 mg per m² in 5% dextrose in water both given over 120 minutes at the same time in separate bags using a Y-line, followed by 5-fluorouracil 400 mg per m² IV bolus given over 2 to 4 minutes, followed by 5-fluorouracil 600 mg per m² IV infusion in 500 mL 5% dextrose in water (recommended) as a 22-hour continuous infusion.
- Day 2: Intravenous, leucovorin 200 mg per m² given over 120 minutes, followed by 5-fluorouracil 400 mg per m² IV bolus given over 2 to 4 minutes, followed by 5-fluorouracil 600 mg per m² IV infusion in 500 mL 5% dextrose in water (recommended) as a 22-hour continuous infusion.

For 5-fluorouracil dosing information, see *Fluorouracil (Systemic)* and for leucovorin dosing information, see *Leucovorin (Systemic)*.

Note: For patients who experience persistent Grade 2 neurosensory events that do not resolve, a dose reduction of oxaliplatin to 65 mg per m² should be considered. The infusional 5-FU/LV part of the regimen does not need to be altered.

For patients following recovery from grade 3/4 gastrointestinal (despite prophylactic treatment) or grade 3/4 hematologic toxicity, a dose reduction of oxaliplatin to 65 mg per m² and infusional 5-FU by 20% (300 mg per m² bolus and 500 mg per m² 22-hour infusion) is recommended.The next dose should be delayed until: neutrophils ≥ 1.5 x 10⁹ per L and platelets ≥ 75 x 10⁹ per L.

Because several doses and regimens using oxaliplatin as *[first-line treatment]*[1] of colorectal carcinoma, are showing activity, no individual dose/regimen is listed here. Consult the medical literature and/or experts in the field of oncology for information on dosage.

Usual pediatric dose

Safety and efficacy have not been established.

Usual geriatric dose

See *Usual adult dose.*

Strength(s) usually available

U.S.—

Note: *Eloxatin* was available as lyophilized powder for injection prior to January 2005.

50 mg single-use vial with gray elstomeric stopper (sterile, preservative-free, aqueous solution of 5 mg/mL) (Rx) [*Eloxatin* (water for injection, USP)].

100 mg single-use vial with gray elstomeric stopper (sterile, preservative-free, aqueous solution of 5 mg/mL) (Rx) [*Eloxatin* (water for injection, USP)].

Canada—

Not commercially available

Packaging and storage

Store at 25°C (77°F), excursions permitted to 15 to 30°C (59 to 86°F), unless otherwise specified by manufacturer. Do not freeze and protect from light the concentrated solution. Keep in original outer carton.

Preparation of dosage form

Note: *A final dilution must never be performed with a sodium chloride solution or other chloride-containing solutions*

The solution must be further diluted in an infusion solution of 250 to 500 mL of 5% Dextrose Injection, USP. See the manufacturer's package insert for instructions.

This product should be visually inspected for particulate matter prior to administration. Samples containing visible particulates should not be used.

Stability

After dilution with 250 to 500 mL of 5% dextrose injection, the shelf life is 6 hours at room temperature [20 to 25°C (68 to 77°F)] or up to 24 hours under refrigeration at 2 to 8°C (36 to 46°F).After final dilution, protection from light is not required.

Incompatibilities

Oxaliplatin is incompatible in solution with alkaline medications or media (such as basic solutions of 5-fluorouracil) and must not be mixed with these or administered simultaneously through the same infusion line. **The infusion line should be flushed with D5W prior to administration of any concomitant medication.**

Do not use needles or intravenous administration sets containing aluminum parts that may come in contact with oxaliplatin to prepare or mix the drug. Aluminum has been reported to cause degradation of platinum compounds.

Auxiliary labeling

- Caution: Chemotherapy. Handle and dispose of properly
- Do not freeze
- Protect from light

[1]Not included in Canadian product labeling.

Revised: 03/29/2006
Developed: 01/30/2003

OXANDROLONE—See *Anabolic Steroids (Systemic)*

OXAPROZIN—See *Anti-inflammatory Drugs, Nonsteroidal (Systemic)*

OXAZEPAM—See *Benzodiazepines (Systemic)*

OXCARBAZEPINE Systemic†

INN: Oxcarbazepine

VA CLASSIFICATION (Primary): CN400

Commonly used brand name(s): *Trileptal.*

Some other commonly used names are: GP47680.

Note: For a listing of dosage forms and brand names by country availability, see *Dosage Forms* section(s).

†Not commercially available in Canada.

Category

Anticonvulsant.

Indications

Accepted

Epilepsy, partial seizures (treatment)—Oxcarbazepine is indicated for monotherapeutic or adjunctive therapeutic use in the treatment of partial seizures in adults and children ages 4 to 16 with epilepsy.

Pharmacology/Pharmacokinetics

Physicochemical characteristics

Molecular weight—252.27.

Solubility—Oxcarbazepine is slightly soluble in acetone, chloroform, dichloromethane, and methanol. It is practically insoluble in ethanol, ether, and water.

Mechanism of action/Effect

The exact mechanism by which oxcarbazepine exerts its anticonvulsant effect is unknown. It is known that the pharmacological activity of oxcarbazepine occurs primarily through its 10–monohydroxy metabolite (MHD). *In vitro* studies indicate an MHD-induced blockade of voltage-sensitive sodium channels, resulting in stabilization of hyperexcited neuronal membranes, inhibition of repetitive neuronal discharges, and diminution of propagation of synaptic impulses.

Absorption

Oxcarbazepine is completely absorbed.

Food does not alter the rate and extent of absorption of oxcarbazepine.

Distribution

The apparent volume of distribution of the pharmacologically active 10–monohydroxy metabolite (MHD) is 49 liters.

Oxcarbazepine and MHD are distributed to breast milk.

Protein binding

Moderate (40%). Oxcarbazepine binds predominantly to serum albumin. Neither oxcarbazepine nor its 10–monohydroxy metabolite binds with alpha-1–acid blycoprotein.

Biotransformation

Oxcarbazepine undergoes rapid and extensive hepatic metabolism to its 10–monohydroxy metabolite (MHD). MHD is further metabolized by conjugation with glucuronic acid.

Note: Autoinduction has not been observed with oxcarbazepine.

Half-life

Oxcarbazepine—2 hours

10–monohydroxy metabolite—9 hours

Note: In patients with renal function impairment with a creatinine clearance < 30 mL per minute, the half-life of MHD is prolonged to 19 hours, with a two-fold increase in the area under the concentration-time curve (AUC).

Time to peak concentration

Median of 4.5 hours

Elimination

Renal—greater than 95%, with more than 99% of the dose excreted in the form of metabolites.

Fecal—less than 4%.

Precautions to Consider

Cross-sensitivity and/or related problems

Approximately 25 to 30% of patients with hypersensitivity reactions to carbamazepine can be expected to react similarly to oxcarbazepine. Patients should be questioned particularly regarding any prior experience with carbamazepine before prescribing oxcarbazepine.

Carcinogenicity/Tumorigenicity/Mutagenicity

In several 2-year carcinogenicity studies, oxcarbazepine was administered orally at doses of up to 100 mg per kg of body weight (mg/kg) a day in mice and 250 mg/kg to rats, and the pharmacologically active 10–monohydroxy metabolite (MHD) was administered orally to rats at doses up to 600 mg/kg/day. A dose-related increased incidence of hepatocellular adenomas was observed in mice receiving oxcarbazepine doses ≥ 70 mg/kg/day. The incidence of hepatocellular carcinomas was increased in female rats receiving oxcarbazepine at doses ≥ 25 mg/kg/day (approximately 10% of the maximum recommended human dose [MRHD] on a mg per square meter of body surface area [mg/m^2] basis), while the incidences of hepatocellular adenomas and/or carcinomas were increased in male and female rats receiving MHD 600 mg/kg/day (2.4 times the MRHD) and MHD 250 mg/kg/day or more (MRHD equivalent). An increase was seen in the incidence of benign testicular cell tumors in rats receiving oxcarbazepine ≥ 250 mg/kg/day and in the incidence of granular cell tumors of the cervix and vagina in rats receiving MHD 600 mg/kg/day.

Mutagenicity

Oxcarbazepine increased mutation frequencies in 1 of 5 bacterial strains during *in vitro* Ames testing. Chromosomal aberrations and polyploidy were produced in the Chinese hamster ovary assay *in vitro* by both oxcarbazepine and its 10–monohydroxy metabolite (MHD), in the absence of metabolic activation. MHD was negative in the Ames test, and no mutagenic or clastogenic activity was found with either oxcarbazepine or MHD in V79 Chinese hamster cells *in vitro* . Oxcarbazepine and MHD were both negative for clastogenic or aneugenic effects (micronucleus formation) in an *in vivo* rat bone marrow assay.

Pregnancy/Reproduction

Fertility—Rats administered MHD in doses of 50, 150, or 450 mg/kg prior to and during mating and the early stages of gestation experienced disruptions of estrous cyclicity, reductions in the numbers of corpus luteums and implantations, and produced fewer live embryos at the highest dose level (approximately 2 times the MRHD, on a mg/m^{2}basis).

Pregnancy—Adequate and well-controlled studies of oxcarbazepine in pregnant women have not been performed.

Reproduction studies in pregnant rats given oral oxcarbazepine (30, 300, or 1000 mg/kg) throughout the organogenesis stage of pregnancy revealed increased incidences of craniofacial, cardiovascular, and skeletal fetal malformations at intermediate and high doses (approximately 1.2 and 4 times the maximum recommended human dose, respectively). When female rats were dosed with oxcarbazepine (25, 50, or 150 mg/kg) during the latter stage of gestation and throughout lactation, a persistent reduction in body weights and behavior activity levels was observed in offspring exposed to the highest dose level. Similar reductions in offspring weights were observed at the highest dose in rats administered 25, 50, or 250 mg/kg of the 10–monohydroxy metabolite of oxcarbazepine during the latter stage of gestation and throughout lactation

Increased incidence in embryofetal mortality was observed in pregnant rats receiving 1000 mg/kg, and in pregnant rabbits receiving 200 mg/kg.

Note: Oxcarbazepine has a close structural relationship to carbamazepine, a known human teratogen. Although well-controlled clinical studies in pregnant women are lacking, it is likely that oxcarbazepine is teratogenic in humans, and should be used in pregnancy only if the potential benefits justify the potential associated fetal risk.

FDA Pregnancy Category C

Labor and delivery—The effect of oxcarbazepine on labor and delivery has not been studied.

Breast-feeding

Oxcarbazepine and its pharmacologically active 10–monohydroxy metabolite are distributed into human breast milk. Both medications exhibited a milk-to-plasma concentration ratio of 0.5. Because of the potential for serious adverse reactions to oxcarbazepine in nursing infants, a decision should be made about whether to discontinue nursing or to discontinue the drug in nursing women, taking into account the importance of the drug to the mother.

Pediatrics

Appropriate studies performed to date have not demonstrated pediatrics-specific problems that would limit the usefulness of oxcarbazepine in children. Clearance of oxcarbazepine in children less than 8 years of age is 30 to 40 % greater than that in older children and adults; higher maintenance dosing may be required.

Geriatrics

Due to age-related changes in creatinine clearance, the maximum plasma concentration and area under the concentration-time curve (AUC) values of the 10–monohydroxy metabolite of oxcarbazepine were 30 to 60% higher in older volunteers (60 to 82 years of age) as compared with younger volunteers (18 to 32 years of age).

No information is available on the relationship of age to the effects of oxcarbazepine in geriatric patients. However, elderly patients are more likely to have age-related impairments in renal function, resulting in the need for dosing adjustments.

Drug interactions and/or related problems

The following drug interactions and/or related problems have been selected on the basis of their potential clinical significance (possible mechanism in parentheses where appropriate)—not necessarily inclusive (» = major clinical significance):

Note: Other anticonvulsants that induce cytochrome P450 enzymes can decrease plasma concentrations of oxcarbazepine and its active 10-monohydroxy metabolite, MHD. Oxcarbazepine can inhibit CYP2C19, and induce CYP3A4/5; inhibition of CYP3A4/5 occurred at high concentrations, and is thought unlikely to be of clinical significance. Oxcarbazepine and MHD induce a subgroup of the cytochrome P450 3A family, CYP3A4 and CYP3A5, resulting in increased metabolism and lower plasma concentrations of medications broken down via this route. Inhibition of CYP2C19 may increase concentrations of MHD by 22%, and oxcarbazepine by 47%. Oxcarbazepine and MHD have little or no capacity to inhibit

CYP1A2, CYP2A6, CYP2C9, CYP2D6, CYP2E1, CYP4A9, and CYP4A11.

Combinations containing any of the following medications, depending on the amount present, may also interact with this medication.

» Alcohol or
» CNS depression-producing medications, other (see *Appendix II*)
(Additive sedative effects may occur)

Anticonvulsants, including
» Carbamazepine
» Phenobarbital
» Phenytoin
» Valproic acid
(Antiepileptic agents that are cytochrome P450 inducers have decreased plasma concentrations of oxcarbazepine and its 10–monohydroxy metabolite (MHD).)
(Oxcarbazepine and MHD may increase the concentration of phenobarbital by about 14%; at oxcarbazepine doses above 1200 mg a day, phenytoin concentrations may be increased by about 40%)

» Oral contraceptives
(Oxcarbazepine and MHD induce cytochrome enzymes CYP3A4 and CYP3A5, causing lower plasma concentrations of hormonal oral contraceptives and decreasing their effectiveness; use of additional non-hormonal forms of contraception is recommended)

» Dihydropyridine calcium channel antagonists, including
» Felodipine
» Verapamil
(Oxcarbazepine and MHD induce cytochrome enzymes CYP3A4 and CYP3A5, causing lower plasma concentrations of dihydropyridine calcium channel blockers)

Laboratory value alterations

The following have been selected on the basis of their potential clinical significance (possible effect in parentheses where appropriate)—not necessarily inclusive (» = major clinical significance).

With physiology/laboratory test values

Serum sodium
(Serum sodium has declined to below 125 mmol/liter in patients treated with oxcarbazepine)

Thyroid function
(T4 levels were observed to decline during clinical trials of oxcarbazepine, without alteration of T3 or TSH levels)

Note: Abnormal liver function test results have been reported in post-marketing surveillance.

Medical considerations/Contraindications

The medical considerations/contraindications included have been selected on the basis of their potential clinical significance (reasons given in parentheses where appropriate)—not necessarily inclusive (» = major clinical significance).

Except under special circumstances, this medication should not be used when the following medical problem exists:

» Previous allergic reaction to oxcarbazepine or to any of its metabolites

Risk-benefit should be considered when the following medical problems exist:

» Hypersensitivity to oxcarbazepine or to any of its components

» Prior hypersensitivity reaction to carbamazepine
(clinical trials have revealed that 25 to 30% of patients with previous allergic reactions to carbamazepine will experience hypersensitivity reactions to oxcarbazepine; patients with this condition should ordinarily be treated with oxcarbazepine only if the potential benefit justifies the potential risk)

» Hyponatremia
(Condition may be exacerbated)

Renal function impairment
(Excretion decreased in patients with a creatinine clearance < 30 mL per minute; dosage reductions may be needed)

Patient monitoring

The following may be especially important in patient monitoring (other tests may be warranted in some patients, depending on condition; » = major clinical significance):

» Serum sodium level
(Clinically significant hyponatremia has developed during oxcarbazepine use; this has generally occurred within the first 3 months of initiating therapy, although onset of serum sodium level decline below 125 mmol/liter has occurred more than a year after first dosing.)

Side/Adverse Effects

Serious dermatological reactions, including Stevens-Johnson syndrome and toxic epidermal necrolysis, have been reported in both children and adults in association with oxcarbazepine use. Such serious skin reactions may be life-threatening, and some patients have required hospitalization with very rare reports of fatal outcome. Recurrence of the serious skin reactions following re-challenge with oxcarbazepine has also been reported. If a patient develops a skin reaction while taking oxcarbazepine, considerations should be given to discontinuing oxcarbazepine use and prescribing another antiepileptic medication.

There have been post-marketing reports of multi-organ hypersensitivity occurring in close temporal association to the initiation of oxcarbazepine therapy in adult and pediatric patients. Although there have been a limited number of reports, many of these cases resulted in hospitalization and some were considered life threatening. Signs and symptoms included fever and rash associated with other organ involvement. Other associated symptoms included lymphadenopathy, hepatitis, liver function test abnormalities, hematological abnormalities (e.g., eosinophilia, thrombocytopenia, neutropenia), pruritus, nephritis, oliguria, hepato-renal syndrome, arthralgia and asthenia. If a multi-organ hypersensitivity reaction is suspected, oxcarbazepine should be discontinued and an alternative treatment started.

Use of oxcarbazepine has been associated with central nervous system related adverse events including: 1) cognitive symptoms such as psychomotor slowing, difficulty with concentration, and speech or language problems, 2) somnolence or fatigue, and 3) coordination abnormalities, including ataxia and gait disturbances.

The following side/adverse effects have been selected on the basis of their potential clinical significance (possible signs and symptoms in parentheses where appropriate)—not necessarily inclusive:

Those indicating need for medical attention

Incidence more frequent

Ataxia or abnormal gait (change in walking and balance; clumsiness or unsteadiness); ***abnormal vision, diplopia, or nystagmus*** (change in vision; double vision; uncontrolled back-and-forth and/or rolling eye movements); ***dizziness; emotional lability*** (crying; false sense of well-being; mental depression); ***upper respiratory tract infection*** (cough; fever; sneezing; or sore throat); ***vertigo*** (feeling of constant movement of self or surroundings; sensation of spinning)

Incidence less frequent

Abnormal accommodation (blurred vision; change in near or distance vision; difficulty in focusing); ***abnormal EEG*** (episodes of confusion; unusual feelings); ***bronchitis*** (cough; shortness of breath; troubled breathing; tightness in chest; wheezing); ***bruising; fever; hyponatremia*** (agitation; loss of consciousness; confusion; convulsions; decreased urination; dizziness; fast or irregular heartbeat; increased thirst; muscle cramps); ***hypotension*** (blurred vision; confusion; dizziness, faintness or light-headedness when getting up from a lying or sitting position; unusual tiredness or weakness); ***neurotoxicity, especially abnormal coordination*** (awkwardness; trembling or shaking of arms, legs, hands, or feet; trouble in walking); ***abnormal thinking*** (confusion; disorientation); ***aggravated convulsions; amnesia*** (memory loss); ***dysmetria*** (poor control in body movements—for example, when reaching or stepping); ***frequent falls; pharyngitis*** (congestion; cough; hoarseness; sore throat); ***sinusitis*** (fever; headache; pain or tenderness around eyes or cheekbones; stuffy or runny nose); ***skin rash; thirst, increased; urinary tract infection*** (bloody or cloudy urine; pain or burning while urinating; frequent urge to urinate); ***vaginitis*** (itching of the vagina, with or without white vaginal discharge); ***viral or other infections*** (fever; general feeling of illness)

Incidence rare

Agitation (anxiety; nervousness; irritability; restlessness); ***confusion; edema in legs*** (swelling of the legs); ***erythema multiforme*** (sores, ulcers, or white spots in mouth or on lips; muscle pain, cramps, or weakness); ***gastritis*** (burning feeling in chest or stomach; stomach upset); ***hypoesthesia*** (decreased response to stimulation); ***lymphadenopathy*** (swollen glands); ***multiorgan hypersensitivity disorders, characterized by; skin rash; fever; eosinophilia*** (fever); ***arthralgia*** (joint pain); ***purpura*** (purple spots on skin); ***rectal hemorrhage*** (rectal bleeding); ***Stevens-Johnson syndrome*** (redness, blistering, peeling, or loosening of skin; fever; hives or itching; bleeding or crusting sores on lips; sore throat; chills; muscle or joint pain; unusual tiredness or weakness; chest pain); ***toxic epidermal necrolysis*** (fever; muscle pain; skin rash; sore throat)

Those indicating need for medical attention only if they continue or are bothersome

Incidence more frequent

Abdominal pain; fatigue (unusual tiredness or weakness); ***headache; nausea; rhinitis*** (runny nose; stuffy nose; sneezing); ***somnolence*** (sleepiness or unusual drowsiness); ***tremor; vomiting***

Incidence less frequent

Abnormal feeling (general feeling of illness); ***acne; back pain; chest pain; constipation; cough; diarrhea; dryness of mouth; dyspepsia*** (acid or sour stomach; belching; heartburn); ***epistaxis*** (bloody nose); ***hot flashes*** (feeling of warmth and redness of the face, neck, arms and occasionally chest); ***insomnia*** (trouble in sleeping); ***micturition disturbance*** (increased urination); ***muscle weakness; nervousness; speech disorder*** (difficulty in speaking); ***sweating, increased; taste perversion*** (change in your sense of taste)

Overdose

For more information on the management of overdose or unintentional ingestion, **contact a poison control center** (see *Poison Control Center Listing*).

Treatment of overdose

To decrease absorption—

Absorption may be minimized by gastric lavage and/or administration of activated charcoal

Specific treatment—

There is no specific antidote currently available for oxcarbazepine overdose. Symptomatic and supportive treatment has enabled the recovery from overdose by all cases reported to date

Supportive care—

Patients in whom intentional overdose is confirmed or suspected should be referred for psychiatric consultation.

Patient Consultation

As an aid to patient consultation, refer to *Advice for the Patient, Oxcarbazepine (Systemic)*.

In providing consultation, consider emphasizing the following selected information (» = major clinical significance):

Before using this medication

» Conditions affecting use, especially:

Hypersensitivity to oxcarbazepine or any of its components or prior hypersensitivity reactions to carbamazepine, a structurally similar anticonvulsant.

Carcinogenicity/Tumorigenicity/Mutagenicity—Shown to be carcinogenic and mutagenic in animal studies

Pregnancy—Should only be used in pregnancy if the potential benefits justify the associated risk to the fetus.

Breast-feeding—Oxcarbazepine and its pharmacologically active 10–monohydroxy metabolite are distributed into human breast milk. Risk/benefit should be considered.

Use in children—Children below 2 years of age have not been studied

Use in the elderly—Elderly patients may require dosing adjustments due to age-related reductions in creatinine clearance.

Other medications, especially carbamazepine, felodipine, oral contraceptives, phenobarbital, phenytoin, valproic acid, or verapamil

Other medical problems, especially prior hypersensitivity response to carbamazepine, hyponatremia, or renal function impairment.

Proper use of this medication

Proper administration of oral suspension: Shaking well and using dosing syringe to administer prescribed amount

» Proper dosing

Missed dose: Taking as soon as possible; not taking if almost time for next scheduled dose; notifying physician if missing 2 or more doses; not doubling doses

» Proper storage

Precautions while using this medication

» Regular visits to physician to check progress of therapy

» Caution when using alcoholic beverages or other drugs that could enhance the sedating effects of oxcarbazepine

» Consulting physician immediately in the event of a skin reaction; advising patients that serious skin reactions have been reported in association with oxcarbazepine use

» Instructing patient to report fever associated with rash or swollen glands (organ system involvement) to physician immediately

» Use of supplemental non-hormonal forms of contraception in addition to oral hormonal contraceptive agents

» Checking with physician before discontinuing medication; gradual dose reduction is usually needed to maintain seizure control

» Possible drowsiness, dizziness, blurred or double-vision, light-headedness, weakness, or muscular incoordination: Caution when driving, using machines, or performing other work that requires alertness

» Caution when getting up suddenly from a lying or sitting position

Side/adverse effects

Signs of potential side effects, especially ataxia or abnormal gait, abnormal vision (including diplopia or nystagmus), dizziness, emotional lability, upper respiratory tract infection, vertigo, abnormal accommodation, abnormal EEG, bronchitis, bruising, fever, hyponatremia, hypotension, neurotoxicity (especially abnormal coordination, abnormal thinking, aggravated convulsions, amnesia, dysmetria, or frequent falls), pharyngitis, sinusitis, skin rash, increased thirst, urinary tract infection, vaginitis, viral or other infections, agitation, confusion, edema in legs, erythema multiforme, gastritis, hypoesthesia, lymphadenopathy, multiorgan hypersensitivity disorders, purpura, rectal hemorrhage, Stevens-Johnson syndrome, or toxic epidermal necrolysis

Signs of potential side effects observed during clinical practice, especially multi-organ hypersensitivity disorders

General Dosing Information

For oral dosing forms:

Patients receiving concomitant therapy with other antiepileptic drugs should have plasma levels of these drugs monitored during the period of oxcarbazepine introduction and titration.

Although older children (8 years of age and older) and adults share similarities in the pharmacokinetics of oxcarbazepine, younger children (less than 8 years of age) have 30 to 40% greater clearances compared with older children and adults, and may require higher maintenance dosing.

Anticonvulsant medications should be withdrawn gradually to minimize the potential for increased seizure frequency.

Diet/Nutrition

Oxcarbazepine may be taken with or without food.

Bioequivalence information

Oxcarbazepine oral suspension and tablets may be interchanged at equal doses.

Oral Dosage Forms

OXCARBAZEPINE ORAL SUSPENSION

Usual adult dose

See *Oxcarbazepine Tablets*.

Usual pediatric dose

See *Oxcarbazepine Tablets*.

Usual geriatric dose

See *Oxcarbazepine Tablets*.

Strength(s) usually available

U.S.—

300 mg per 5 mL (Rx) [*Trileptal* (ascorbic acid; dispersible cellulose; ethanol; macrogol stearate; methyl parahydroxybenzoate; propylene glycol; propyl parahydroxybenzoate; purified water; sodium saccharin; sorbic acid; sorbitol; yellow-plum-lemon aroma)].

Packaging and storage

Store at 25 °C (77 °F); excursions permitted to 15 to 30 °C (59 to 86 °F).

Preparation of dosage form

Before using oxcarbazepine oral suspension:

- Shake the bottle well and prepare the dose immediately afterwards.
- Withdraw the prescribed amount of oral suspension from the bottle using the oral dosing syringe supplied.
- Mix the oral suspension in a small glass of water just prior to administration or swallow directly from the syringe.
- After each use, close the bottle and rinse the syringe with warm water and allow it to dry thoroughly.

Auxiliary labeling

- This drug alone or with alcohol may cause drowsiness. Use care when driving or operating machinery.
- Keep out of reach of children.

OXCARBAZEPINE TABLETS

Usual adult dose

Anticonvulsant—

Adjunctive therapy—

Oral, initially 300 mg two times a day. The dosage may be increased, as needed and tolerated, by a maximum of 600 mg a day at intervals of one week. The recommended daily dose is 1200 mg.

Note: Doses above 1200 mg a day showed somewhat greater effectiveness in controlled trials, but most patients were unable to tolerate higher doses due to adverse effects.

Patients should be closely observed during the initiation of oxcarbazepine, and plasma concentrations of concomitant antiepileptic agents should be monitored.

Conversion to monotherapy—

Oral, initially 300 mg two times a day. Dose reductions of concomitant anticonvulsants should be initiated simultaneously. The dosage of oxcarbazepine may be increased, as needed and tolerated, by a maximum of 600 mg a day at intervals of one week, to achieve the recommended daily dose of 2400 mg. The maximum dose of oxcarbazepine should be reached over 2 to 4 weeks, while the concomitant anticonvulsants should be completely withdrawn over 3 to 6 weeks.

Note: Close observation of the patient is necessary during this transition period to monotherapy.

Initiation of monotherapy—

Oral, initially 300 mg two times a day. The dosage may be increased, as needed and tolerated, by 300 mg a day at intervals of 3 days, until the total daily dose reaches 1200 mg.

Note: In patients with renal function impairments (creatinine clearance < 30 mL per minute), oxcarbazepine should be started at one-half the usual initiation dose, and increased slowly to reach the desired clinical response.

Usual adult prescribing limits

2400 mg a day.

Usual pediatric dose

Anticonvulsant (adjunctive therapy)—

Children 4 to 16 years of age

Adjunctive therapy

Initial—Oral, 8 to 10 mg per kg of body weight per day, given in equally divided, two times a day doses. The total initial dose should not exceed 600 mg per day.

The target maintenance dose is dependent upon the patient's weight:

20 to 29 kg—900 mg a day.
29.1 to 39 kg—1200 mg a day.
Above 39 kg—1800 mg a day.

Note: Achievement of the target maintenance dose of oxcarbazepine should occur over 2 weeks.

Conversion to monotherapy

Oral, initially 8 to 10 mg per kg of body weight per day, given in equally divided, two times a day doses, while simultaneously initiating the reduction of the dose of the concomitant antiepileptic drugs. The dosage of oxcarbazepine may be increased, as needed and tolerated, by a maximum increment of 10 mg per kg of body weight per day at intervals of one week, to achieve the recommended daily maintenance dose by weight shown in the table below. The concomitant anticonvulsants should be completely withdrawn over 3 to 6 weeks.

Weight in kg	From dose (mg/day)	To dose (mg/day)
20	600	900
25	900	1200
30	900	1200
35	900	1500
40	900	1500
45	1200	1500
50	1200	1800
55	1200	1800
60	1200	2100
65	1200	2100
70	1500	2100

Note: Close observation of the patient is necessary during this transition period to monotherapy.

Initiation of monotherapy

Oral, initially 8 to 10 mg per kg of body weight per day given in equally divided, two times a day doses. The dose should be increased, by 5 mg per kg of body weight per day at intervals of 3 days, until the total daily dose reaches the recommended daily dose.

Children up to 2 years of ageSafety and efficacy have not been established.

Usual pediatric prescribing limits

2100 mg per day.

Usual geriatric dose

See *Usual adult dose*.

Usual geriatric prescribing limits

See *Usual adult prescribing limits*.

Strength(s) usually available

U.S.—

150 mg (Rx) [*Trileptal* (double-scored; film coated)].
300 mg (Rx) [*Trileptal* (double-scored; film coated)].
600 mg (Rx) [*Trileptal* (double-scored; film coated)].

Packaging and storage

Store at 25°C (77°F); excursions permitted between 15°C and 30°C (59°F and 86 °F), in a tight container.

Auxiliary labeling

- May cause drowsiness.
- Avoid alcoholic beverages.

Revised: 06/07/2005
Developed: 05/12/2000

OXICONAZOLE Topical

VA CLASSIFICATION (Primary): DE102

Commonly used brand name(s): *Oxistat; Oxizole*.

Note: For a listing of dosage forms and brand names by country availability, see *Dosage Forms* section(s).

Category

Antifungal (topical).

Indications

Accepted

Tinea corporis (treatment)[1]
Tinea cruris (treatment)[1] or
Tinea pedis (treatment)—Oxiconazole is indicated in the topical treatment of tinea corporis (ringworm of the body), tinea cruris (ringworm of the groin; jock itch), and tinea pedis (ringworm of the foot; athlete's foot) caused by *Trichophyton rubrum*, *T. mentagrophytes*, and *Epidermophyton floccosum*.

Tinea (pityriasis) versicolor (treatment)[1]—Oxiconazole (cream only) is indicated in the topical treatment of tinea (pityriasis) versicolor (ringworm of the trunk) caused by *Malassezia furfur*.

[1]Not included in Canadian product labeling.

Pharmacology/Pharmacokinetics

Physicochemical characteristics

Molecular weight—Oxiconazole nitrate: 492.15.

Mechanism of action/Effect

Inhibits ergosterol biosynthesis, which is necessary for fungal cellular membrane integrity.

Absorption

Low—Systemic absorption.

Elimination

Less than 0.3% of a topically applied dose of oxiconazole cream (2.5 mg per square cm of body surface area) was recovered in the urine up to 5 days after application of the cream formulation.

Precautions to Consider

Carcinogenicity

No studies have been done.

Mutagenicity

No evidence of mutagenic effect was found in 2 mutation assays (Ames test and Chinese hamster V79 *in vitro* cell mutation assay) and in 2 cytogenetic assays (human peripheral blood lymphocyte *in vitro* chromosome aberration assay and *in vivo* micronucleus assay in mice).

Pregnancy/Reproduction

Fertility—Fertility was not impaired in female rats given oral doses of 3 mg per kg of body weight (mg/kg) a day and in male rats given 15 mg/kg a day. However, rats given higher oral doses than those listed above exhibited reduced sperm counts, extended estrous cycles, and decreased mating frequency.

Pregnancy—Adequate and well-controlled studies in humans have not been done.

Teratogenic studies in rabbits, rats, and mice given oral doses of 100, 150, and 200 mg/kg a day, respectively, have not shown that oxiconazole causes adverse effects on the fetus.

FDA Pregnancy Category B.

Breast-feeding

Topical oxiconazole is distributed into breast milk. Problems in humans have not been documented.

Pediatrics

Appropriate studies performed with oxiconazole cream to date have not demonstrated pediatric-specific problems that would limit the usefulness of oxiconazole cream in children. However, the indications for which oxiconazole cream has been shown to be effective rarely occur in children below the age of 12.

Geriatrics

Appropriate studies on the relationship of age to the effects of topical oxiconazole have not been performed in the geriatric population. However, no geriatrics-specific problems have been documented to date.

Medical considerations/Contraindications

The medical considerations/contraindications included have been selected on the basis of their potential clinical significance (reasons given in parentheses where appropriate)—not necessarily inclusive (» = major clinical significance).

Risk-benefit should be considered when the following medical problem exists:

Sensitivity to oxiconazole

Side/Adverse Effects

The following side/adverse effects have been selected on the basis of their potential clinical significance (possible signs and symptoms in parentheses where appropriate)—not necessarily inclusive:

Those indicating need for medical attention

Incidence less frequent

Burning and pruritus (itching)—not present before use of this medicine

Incidence rare

Contact dermatitis, allergic (blistering, burning, crusting, dryness, or flaking of skin; itching; scaling; severe redness, soreness, or swelling of skin); ***folliculitis*** (burning, itching, and pain in hairy areas; pus at root of hair); ***skin irritation***—not present before use of this medicine

Those indicating need for medical attention only if they continue or are bothersome

Incidence less frequent or rare

Pain; skin rash; stinging; tingling

Overdose

For more information on the management of overdose or unintentional ingestion, **contact a poison control center** (see *Poison Control Center Listing*).

Clinical effects of overdose

Overdoses in humans have not been reported. An animal toxicology study demonstrated 3 deaths and severe dermal inflammation after 5% oxiconazole cream was applied at a rate of 1gram per kg of body weight over approximately 10% of the body surface area of rats for 35 days.

Patient Consultation

As an aid to patient consultation, refer to *Advice for the Patient, Oxiconazole (Topical)*.

In providing consultation, consider emphasizing the following selected information (» = major clinical significance):

Before using this medication

» Conditions affecting use, especially:
Sensitivity to oxiconazole
Breast-feeding—Distributed into breast milk

Proper use of this medication

Applying sufficient medication to cover affected and surrounding areas, and rubbing in gently

» Avoiding contact with the eyes, nose mouth, and other mucous membranes; not using in vagina

Wash hands after application to affected areas.

» Compliance with full course of therapy; fungal infections may require prolonged therapy

» Proper dosing

Missed dose: Applying as soon as possible; not applying if almost time for next dose

» Proper storage

Precautions while using this medication

Checking with physician if no improvement occurs within 2 to 4 weeks

» Using hygienic measures to cure infection and prevent reinfection:

For tinea cruris:

Avoiding underwear that is tight-fitting or made from synthetic materials; wearing loose-fitting cotton underwear instead

Using a bland, absorbent powder or an antifungal powder on the skin; using the powder between administration times for oxiconazole

For tinea pedis:

Carefully drying feet, especially between toes, after bathing

Avoiding socks made from wool or synthetic materials; wearing clean, cotton socks and changing them each day or more often if feet perspire excessively

Wearing sandals or well-ventilated shoes

Using bland, absorbent powder or an antifungal powder between toes, on feet, and in socks and shoes 1 or 2 times a day; using the powder between administration times for oxiconazole

Side/adverse effects

Signs of potential side effects, especially burning and pruritus, allergic contact dermatitis, folliculitis, and skin irritation.

General Dosing Information

To reduce the possibility of recurrence, tinea corporis, tinea cruris, and tinea (pityriasis) versicolor should be treated for at least 2 weeks; tinea pedis should be treated for at least 4 weeks.

Hypopigmented or hyperpigmented patches of the skin due to tinea versicolor may not readily resolve following successful therapy. Resolution may take months, depending on individual skin type and incidental sun exposure. Ringworm of the trunk (tinea versicolor) may recur because the causative organism is part of the normal skin flora

Topical Dosage Forms

Note: The dosing and strength of the dosage forms available are expressed in terms of oxiconazole base.

OXICONAZOLE NITRATE CREAM

Usual adult and adolescent dose

Tinea pedis
Tinea corporis[1]
Tinea cruris[1]—
Topical, to the skin and surrounding areas, one to two times a day.

Tinea (pityriasis) versicolor[1]—
Topical, to the skin and surrounding areas, once daily.

Usual pediatric dose

See *Usual adult and adolescent dose*.

Strength(s) usually available

U.S.—
1% (base) (Rx) [*Oxistat*].

Canada—
1% (base) (OTC) [*Oxizole*].

Packaging and storage

Store between 15 and 30 °C (59 and 86 °F), unless otherwise specified by manufacturer.

Auxiliary labeling

- For external use only.
- Continue medicine for full time of treatment.

OXICONAZOLE NITRATE LOTION

Usual adult and adolescent dose

Tinea pedis
Tinea corporis[1]
Tinea cruris[1]—
Topical, to the skin and surrounding areas, one to two times a day.

Usual pediatric dose
See *Usual adult and adolescent dose.*

Strength(s) usually available
U.S.—

1% (base) (Rx) [*Oxistat*].

Canada—

1% (base) (OTC) [*Oxizole*].

Packaging and storage
Store between 15 and 30 °C (59 and 86 °F), unless otherwise specified by manufacturer.

Auxiliary labeling
- Shake well
- For external use only.
- Continue medicine for full time of treatment.

[1]Not included in Canadian product labeling.

Selected Bibliography

Cleary JD, et al. Imidazoles and triazoles in antifungal therapy. DICP Ann Pharmacother (USA) 1990; 24(2): 148-52.

Jegasothy BV, Pakes GE. Oxiconazole nitrate: pharmacology, efficacy, and safety of a new imidazole antifungal agent. Clin Ther 1991 Jan-Feb; 13(1): 126-41.

Revised: 03/15/2000

OXPRENOLOL—See *Beta-adrenergic Blocking Agents (Systemic)*

OXTRIPHYLLINE—See *Bronchodilators, Theophylline (Systemic)*

OXYBUTYNIN Systemic

VA CLASSIFICATION (Primary): GU201

Commonly used brand name(s): *Ditropan; Ditropan XL*.

Note: For a listing of dosage forms and brand names by country availability, see *Dosage Forms* section(s).

Category
Antispasmodic (urinary tract).

Indications

Accepted
Urologic disorders, symptoms of (treatment) and

Irritative voiding, symptoms of (treatment)—Oxybutynin is indicated for the relief of symptoms associated with voiding, such as frequent urination, urgency, urge incontinence, nocturia, and incontinence in patients with uninhibited neurogenic bladder contractions and in those patients with reflex neurogenic bladder.

Unaccepted
Oxybutynin has been used as an antispasmodic in the symptomatic treatment of gastrointestinal disorders; however, its effectiveness has not been established.

Pharmacology/Pharmacokinetics

Physicochemical characteristics
Molecular weight—393.9.

pKa—6.96.

Mechanism of action/Effect
Exerts direct antispasmodic effect on smooth muscle and inhibits the action of acetylcholine at postganglionic cholinergic sites, thus increasing bladder capacity and delaying the initial desire to void by reducing the number of motor impulses reaching the detrusor muscle. It does not block acetylcholine effects at skeletal myoneural junctions or at autonomic ganglia; neither does it have effect on the smooth muscle of blood vessels.

Other actions/effects
Oxybutynin has also shown (in animal studies) moderate antihistaminic, some local anesthetic, mild analgesic, and very low mydriatic and antisialagogue activity.

Absorption
Rapidly absorbed from gastrointestinal tract.

$AUC_{(0-48)}$: Extended release tablets, 18.4 ng hr/mL for R-oxybutynin, 34.2 ng hr/mL for S-oxybutynin

AUC_{inf}: Extended release tablets, 21.3 ng hr/mL for R-oxybutynin, 39.5 ng hr/mL for S-oxybutynin

Pediatrics: AUC: Extended release tablets, 12.8 ng hr/mL for R-oxybutynin, 23.7 for S-oxybutynin

Distribution
Volume of distribution (Vol_D—Extended release tablets, 193 L after intravenous administration

Biotransformation
Hepatic, primarily by CYP3A4; metabolic products include phenylcyclohexylglycolic acid and desethyloxybutynin.

Half-life
Extended release tablets: 13.2 hours for R-oxybutynin, 12.4 hours for S-oxybutynin

Onset of action
30 minutes to 1 hour.

Time to peak concentration
Extended release tablets: Adults, 12.7 hours for R-oxybutynin, 11.8 hours for S-oxybutynin. Pediatrics, 5 hours

Peak plasma concentration
Extended release tablets: Adults, 1 ng per mL for R-oxybutynin, 1.8 ng per L for S-oxybutynin. Pediatrics, 0.7 ng/mL for R-oxybutynin, 1.3 ng/mL for S-oxybutynin

Time to peak effect
3 to 6 hours.

Duration of action
6 to 10 hours (antispasmodic effect).

Elimination
Primarily renal.

Precautions to Consider

Carcinogenicity
A 24–month study in rats at dosages of up to 50 times the maximum human exposure based on surface area showed no evidence of carcinogenicity.

Mutagenicity
No evidence of mutagenicity has been found in studies on several test systems.

Pregnancy/Reproduction
Fertility—Reproduction studies in the hamster, rabbit, rat, and mouse have not shown oxybutynin to impair fertility.

Pregnancy—Adequate and well-controlled studies in humans have not been done.

Reproduction studies in the hamster, rabbit, rat, and mouse have not shown oxybutynin to harm the fetus.

FDA Pregnancy Category B.

Breast-feeding
Problems in humans have not been documented. However, oxybutynin may inhibit lactation.

Pediatrics
Appropriate studies on the relationship of age to the effects of oxybutynin have not been performed in children up to 5 years of age.

Oxybutynin extended release tablets should not be administered to children who can not swallow the tablet whole without chewing, dividing or crushing it

Geriatrics
Geriatric patients may be more sensitive than younger adults to the anticholinergic effects of oxybutynin.

Oxybutynin may also exacerbate underlying disease states in these patients.

Dental
Prolonged use of oxybutynin may decrease or inhibit salivary flow, thus contributing to the development of caries, periodontal disease, oral candidiasis, and discomfort.

Drug interactions and/or related problems
The following drug interactions and/or related problems have been selected on the basis of their potential clinical significance (possible

mechanism in parentheses where appropriate)—not necessarily inclusive (» = major clinical significance):

Note: Combinations containing any of the following medications, depending on the amount present, may also interact with this medication.

» Anticholinergics or other medications with anticholinergic activity (See *Appendix II*)
(concurrent use may intensify the anticholinergic effects of oxybutynin)

Central nervous system (CNS) depression-producing medications, other (See *Appendix II*)
(concurrent use may increase the sedative effects of either these medications or oxybutynin)

CYP3A4 inhibitors, such as:
Antimycotic agents:
» Ketoconazole or
Itraconazole or
Miconazole or
Macrolide antibiotics:
Clarithromycin or
Erythromycin
(may alter oxybutynin mean pharmacokinetic parameters; caution is advised when CYP3A4 inhibitors are co-administered with oxybutynin)

Medical considerations/Contraindications

The medical considerations/contraindications included have been selected on the basis of their potential clinical significance (reasons given in parentheses where appropriate)—not necessarily inclusive (» = major clinical significance).

Except under special circumstances, this medication should not be used when the following medical problem exists:

» Gastrointestinal tract obstructive disease as in achalasia and pyloroduodenal stenosis
(decrease in motility and tone may occur, resulting in obstruction and gastric retention)

» Glaucoma, angle-closure, or predisposition to
(possible mydriatic effect of oxybutynin resulting in increased intraocular pressure may precipitate an acute attack of angle-closure glaucoma)

» Hemorrhage, acute, with unstable cardiovascular status
(increase in heart rate may be undesirable)

Hypersensitivity to oxybutynin

» Intestinal atony in the elderly or debilitated patient or
» Paralytic ileus
(use of oxybutynin may lead to obstruction)

Megacolon or
Megacolon, toxic
(use is contraindicated)

» Myasthenia gravis
(oxybutynin may aggravate condition because of inhibition of acetylcholine action)

» Ulcerative colitis, severe
(large doses may suppress intestinal motility and may cause paralytic ileus; also, use may precipitate or aggravate the serious complication of toxic megacolon)

» Uropathy, obstructive, such as bladder neck obstruction due to prostatic hypertrophy
(urinary retention may be precipitated or aggravated)

Risk-benefit should be considered when the following medical problems exist:

» Cardiac disease, especially mitral stenosis, cardiac arrhythmias, congestive heart failure, coronary heart disease or
(increase in heart rate may be undesirable)

Hepatic function impairment
(decreased metabolism of oxybutynin)

» Hernia, hiatal, associated with reflux esophagitis or
Hypertension
(may be aggravated)

Hyperthyroidism
(characterized by tachycardia, which may be increased)

Neuropathy, autonomic
(urinary retention and cycloplegia may be aggravated)

» Prostatic hypertrophy, nonobstructive
(reduction in tone of urinary bladder may lead to complete urinary retention)

Renal function impairment
(decreased excretion may increase the risk of side effects)

Sensitivity to oxybutynin

» Tachycardia
(may be increased)

Toxemia of pregnancy
(hypertension may be aggravated)

» Urinary retention or
(urinary retention may be precipitated or aggravated)

Xerostomia
(prolonged use may further reduce limited salivary flow)

Caution in use is also recommended in patients over 40 years of age because of danger of precipitating undiagnosed glaucoma.

In patients with diarrhea the possibility of intestinal obstruction should be excluded before oxybutynin is administered.

Patient monitoring

The following may be especially important in patient monitoring (other tests may be warranted in some patients, depending on condition; » = major clinical significance):

Cystometry
(recommended at periodic intervals to evaluate response to therapy)

Side/Adverse Effects

Note: When oxybutynin is given to patients where the environmental temperature is high, there is risk of a rapid increase in body temperature because of suppression of sweat gland activity.

The following side/adverse effects have been selected on the basis of their potential clinical significance (possible signs and symptoms in parentheses where appropriate)—not necessarily inclusive:

Those indicating need for medical attention

Incidence rare

Allergic reaction (skin rash or hives); ***increased intraocular pressure*** (eye pain)

Incidence not determined—Observed during clinical practice; estimates of frequency can not be determined

Cardiac arrhythmia (dizziness; fainting; fast, slow, or irregular heartbeat)

Those indicating need for medical attention only if they continue or are bothersome

Incidence more frequent

Constipation; decreased sweating; diarrhea; dizziness; drowsiness; dryness of eyes mouth, nose, and throat; dyspepsia (acid or sour stomach; belching; heartburn; indigestion; stomach discomfort, upset or pain); ***rhinitis*** (stuffy nose; runny nose; sneezing)

Incidence less frequent or rare

Decreased flow of breast milk; decreased saliva secretion (difficulty in swallowing); ***decreased sexual ability; difficult urination; difficulty in accommodation*** (blurred vision); ***headache; mydriatic effect*** (increased sensitivity of eyes to light); ***nausea or vomiting; palpitations*** (fast, irregular, pounding, or racing heartbeat or pulse); ***trouble in sleeping; unusual tiredness or weakness; vasodilation*** (feeling of warmth or heat; flushing or redness of skin, especially on face and neck; headache; feeling faint, dizzy, or light-headedness; sweating)

Incidence not determined—Observed during clinical practice; estimates of frequency cannot be determined

Convulsions (seizures); ***hallucinations*** (seeing, hearing, or feeling things that are not there); ***impotence*** (loss in sexual ability, desire, drive, or performance; decreased interest in sexual intercourse; inability to have or keep an erection); ***peripheral edema*** (bloating or swelling of face, arms, hands, lower legs, or feet; rapid weight gain; tingling of hands or feet; unusual weight gain or loss); ***tachycardia*** (fast, pounding, or irregular heartbeat or pulse)

Overdose

For specific information on the agents used in the management of oxybutynin overdose, see:

- *Physostigmine (Systemic)* monograph

For more information on the management of overdose or unintentional ingestion, **contact a Poison Control Center** (see *Poison Control Center Listing*).

Clinical effects of overdose

The following effects have been selected on the basis of their potential clinical significance (possible signs and symptoms in parentheses where appropriate)—not necessarily inclusive:

Clumsiness or unsteadiness; confusion; convulsions; dizziness; severe drowsiness; fast heartbeat; fever; flushing or redness of

face; hallucinations; respiratory depression (shortness of breath or troubled breathing); ***unusual excitement, nervousness, restlessness, or irritability***

Treatment of overdose

To decrease absorption—
Consider administration of activated charcoal.

Specific treatment—
Consider a diagnostic trial with physostigmine.

Supportive care—
In the event of respiratory depression, starting and maintaining artificial respiration. Treating fever symptomatically with ice packs or alcohol sponging.

Patient Consultation

As an aid to patient consultation, refer to *Advice for the Patient, Oxybutynin (Systemic).*

In providing consultation, consider emphasizing the following selected information (» = major clinical significance):

Before using this medication

» Conditions affecting use, especially:
Hypersensitivity to oxybutynin
Breast-feeding—Oxybutynin may inhibit lactation
Use in the elderly—Increased sensitivity to anticholinergic effects
Dental—Possible development of dental problems because of decreased salivary flow
Other medications, especially other anticholinergics or ketoconazole
Other medical problems, especially cardiac diseases, glaucoma, hemorrhage, hiatal hernia, intestinal atony, myasthenia gravis, paralytic ileus, prostatic hypertrophy, megacolon, obstruction in gastrointestinal or urinary tract, tachycardia, ulcerative colitis, urinary retention

Proper use of this medication

Taking medication on an empty stomach with water, or with food or milk to reduce gastric irritation
Extended release tablets should be swallowed whole.
» Importance of not taking more medication than the amount prescribed
» Proper dosing
Missed dose: Taking as soon as possible; if almost time for next dose, not taking at all; not doubling doses
» Proper storage

Precautions while using this medication

» Avoiding use of alcohol or other CNS depressants
Possible increased sensitivity of eyes to light
» Caution if drowsiness or blurred vision occurs
» Caution during exercise and hot weather; overheating may result in heat stroke
Possible dryness of mouth, nose, and throat; using sugarless gum or candy, ice, or saliva substitute for relief of dry mouth; checking with physician or dentist if dry mouth continues for more than 2 weeks
The extended release tablet shell may be removed from your body and visible in your stool.

Side/adverse effects

Signs of potential side effects, especially allergic reaction or increased intraocular pressure

General Dosing Information

Oxybutynin may be taken on an empty stomach with water; however, if gastric irritation occurs it may be taken with food or milk.

Cystometry and other appropriate diagnostic procedures should precede treatment with oxybutynin.

If urinary tract infection is present, appropriate antibacterial therapy should be administered.

Oral Dosage Forms

OXYBUTYNIN CHLORIDE SYRUP USP

Usual adult and adolescent dose

Antispasmodic (urinary tract)—
Oral, 5 mg two or three times a day, the dosage being adjusted as needed and tolerated.

Usual adult prescribing limits

Antispasmodic (urinary tract)—
Oral, 5 mg four times a day or 20 mg daily.

Usual pediatric dose

Antispasmodic (urinary tract)—
Children up to 5 years of age: Dosage has not been established.
Children 5 years of age and over: Oral, 5 mg two times a day

Usual pediatric prescribing limit

Antispasmodic (urinary tract)—
Oral, 5 mg three times a day

Usual geriatric dose

See *Usual adult and adolescent dose.*

Note: Geriatric patients may be more sensitive to the effects of the usual adult dose.

Strength(s) usually available

U.S.—
5 mg per 5 mL (Rx) [*Ditropan* (methylparaben; sucrose); GENERIC].

Canada—
5 mg per 5 mL (Rx) [*Ditropan* (methylparaben; sucrose)].

Packaging and storage

Store at controlled room temperature 15 to 30 °C (59 and 86 °F), unless otherwise specified by manufacturer. Store in a tight, light-resistant container. Protect from freezing.

Auxiliary labeling

- May cause drowsiness or blurred vision.

OXYBUTYNIN CHLORIDE TABLETS USP

Usual adult and adolescent dose

See *Oxybutynin Chloride Syrup USP.*

Usual adult prescribing limits

See *Oxybutynin Chloride Syrup USP.*

Usual pediatric dose

See *Oxybutynin Chloride Syrup USP.*

Usual pediatric prescribing limit

See *Oxybutynin Chloride Syrup USP.*

Usual geriatric dose

See *Oxybutynin Chloride Syrup USP.*

Note: Geriatric patients may be more sensitive to the effects of the usual adult dose.

Strength(s) usually available

U.S.—
5 mg (Rx) [*Ditropan* (scored); GENERIC].

Canada—
5 mg (Rx) [*Ditropan* (scored)].

Packaging and storage

Store at controlled room temperature 15 to 30 °C (59 and 86 °F), unless otherwise specified by manufacturer. Store in a tight, light-resistant container.

Auxiliary labeling

- May cause drowsiness or blurred vision.

OXYBUTYNIN CHLORIDE EXTENDED RELEASE TABLETS USP

Usual adult and adolescent dose

Antispasmodic (urinary tract)—
Oral, 5 mg to 10 mg once daily, the dosage may be adjusted in 5–mg intervals on a weekly basis to achieve a balance of efficacy and tolerability

Usual adult prescribing limits

Antispasmodic (urinary tract)—
30 mg per day

Usual pediatric dose

Antispasmodic (urinary tract)—
Children up to 6 years of age: Dosage has not been established; Children 6 years of age and over: Oral,.5 mg once daily, dosage may be adjusted in 5–mg increments to achieve a balance of efficacy and tolerability

Usual pediatric prescribing limits

Antispasmodic (urinary tract)—
20 mg per day

Usual geriatric dose

See *Usual adult and adolescent dose*

Note: Geriatric patients may be more sensitive to the effects of the usual adult dose.

Strength(s) usually available

U.S.—
5 mg (Rx) [*Ditropan* (acetate; butylated hydroxy toluene; cellulose acetate; hypromellose; lactose; magnesium stearate; polyethylene

glycol; polyethylene oxide; polysorbate 80; sodium chloride; synthetic iron oxides; titanium dioxide); GENERIC].

10 mg (Rx) [*Ditropan* (acetate; butylated hydorxy toluene; cellulose acetate; hypromellose; lactose; magnesium stearate; polyethylene glycol; polyethylene oxide; polysorbate 80; sodium chloride; synthetic iron oxides; titanium dioxide); GENERIC].

15 mg (Rx) [*Ditropan* (acetate; butylated hydorxy toluene; cellulose acetate; hypromellose; lactose; magnesium stearate; polyethylene glycol; polyethylene oxide; polysorbate 80; sodium chloride; synthetic iron oxides; titanium dioxide); GENERIC].

Canada—

5 mg (Rx) [*Ditropan XL* (scored)].

10 mg (Rx) [*Ditropan XL* (scored)].

Packaging and storage

Store at 25°C (77 °F), excursions permitted 15 to 30 °C (59 and 86 °F). Protect from moisture and humidity.

Auxiliary labeling

- May cause drowsiness or blurred vision.

Revised: 10/27/2004

OXYCODONE—See *Opioid (Narcotic) Analgesics (Systemic)*

OXYMETAZOLINE Ophthalmic

VA CLASSIFICATION (Primary): OP802

Commonly used brand name(s): *OcuClear; Visine L.R.*

Note: For a listing of dosage forms and brand names by country availability, see *Dosage Forms* section(s).

Category

Decongestant (ophthalmic).

Indications

Accepted

Ocular redness (treatment)—Oxymetazoline is indicated for the temporary relief of redness associated with minor irritations of the eye, such as those caused by pollen-related allergies, colds, dust, smog, wind, swimming, or wearing contact lenses.

Pharmacology/Pharmacokinetics

Physicochemical characteristics

Molecular weight—260.37.

Mechanism of action/Effect

Oxymetazoline is a direct-acting sympathomimetic amine. It acts on alpha-adrenergic receptors in the arterioles of the conjunctiva to produce vasoconstriction, resulting in decreased conjunctival congestion.

Onset of action

Within 5 minutes.

Duration of action

Approximately 6 hours.

Precautions to Consider

Cross-sensitivity and/or related problems

Patients sensitive to other ophthalmic sympathomimetics may be sensitive to this medication also.

Pregnancy/Reproduction

Pregnancy—Oxymetazoline may be systemically absorbed.

Studies have not been done in humans or animals.

Breast-feeding

Problems in humans have not been documented; however, oxymetazoline may be systemically absorbed.

Pediatrics

Check with physician before using oxymetazoline ophthalmic solution in children up to 6 years of age. Eye redness in children can occur with illnesses, such as allergies, fevers, colds, and measles, that may require medical attention.

Geriatrics

Appropriate studies on the relationship of age to the effects of oxymetazoline have not been performed in the geriatric population. However, no geriatrics-specific problems have been documented to date.

Drug interactions and/or related problems

The following drug interactions and/or related problems have been selected on the basis of their potential clinical significance (possible mechanism in parentheses where appropriate)—not necessarily inclusive (» = major clinical significance):

Antidepressants, tricyclic or
Maprotiline
(if significant systemic absorption of ophthalmic oxymetazoline occurs, concurrent use may potentiate the pressor effect of oxymetazoline)

Medical considerations/Contraindications

The medical considerations/contraindications included have been selected on the basis of their potential clinical significance (reasons given in parentheses where appropriate)—not necessarily inclusive (» = major clinical significance).

Risk-benefit should be considered when the following medical problems exist:

Coronary artery disease or
Heart disease, including angina or
Hypertension
(if significant systemic absorption of ophthalmic oxymetazoline occurs, condition may be exacerbated due to drug-induced cardiovascular effects)

Eye disease, infection, or injury
(may mask symptoms and delay treatment)

Glaucoma, narrow-angle, or predisposition to
(may precipitate an attack by dilating pupil)

Hyperthyroidism
(may exacerbate existing tachycardia or elevated blood pressure)

Sensitivity to oxymetazoline

Side/Adverse Effects

Note: Excessive dosage and/or prolonged use may cause increased irritation of the conjunctiva. Prolonged use may also cause reactive hyperemia.

The following side/adverse effects have been selected on the basis of their potential clinical significance (possible signs and symptoms in parentheses where appropriate)—not necessarily inclusive:

Those indicating need for medical attention

With excessive dosage and/or prolonged use
Hyperemia, reactive (increase in irritation or redness of eyes)

Symptoms of systemic absorption
Fast, irregular, or pounding heartbeat; headache or lightheadedness; nervousness; trembling; trouble in sleeping

Patient Consultation

As an aid to patient consultation, refer to *Advice for the Patient, Oxymetazoline (Ophthalmic)*.

In providing consultation, consider emphasizing the following selected information (» = major clinical significance):

Before using this medication

» Conditions affecting use, especially:
Sensitivity to oxymetazoline or any other eye decongestant
Use in children—Checking with physician before using medication in children up to 6 years of age; eye redness in children can occur with illnesses, such as allergies, fevers, colds, and measles, that may require medical attention

Proper use of this medication

Not using if solution becomes cloudy or changes color
Proper administration technique
Preventing contamination: Not touching applicator tip to any surface and keeping container tightly closed

» Importance of not using more medication than the amount recommended and not using for more than 72 hours, unless directed to do so by physician; overuse may increase eye irritation and the chance of side effects

» Proper dosing

» Proper storage

Precautions while using this medication

» Stopping medication and checking with physician if eye pain or change in vision occurs or if redness or irritation continues, gets worse, or lasts for more than 72 hours

Side/adverse effects

Side effects usually are rare when medication is used for short periods of time at low doses

Signs of potential side effects, especially reactive hyperemia or symptoms of systemic absorption

General Dosing Information

Treatment should not be continued for more than 72 hours unless otherwise directed by physician.

Although the manufacturer recommends that patients remove soft contact lenses before using oxymetazoline ophthalmic solution, USP medical experts do not believe this precaution is necessary unless the patient has corneal epithelial problems. No significant problems have been documented with ophthalmic solutions containing 0.03% or less of benzalkonium chloride as a preservative when they are used as eye drops in patients with no significant corneal surface problem.

Ophthalmic Dosage Forms

OXYMETAZOLINE HYDROCHLORIDE OPHTHALMIC SOLUTION USP

Usual adult and adolescent dose

Topical, to the conjunctiva, 1 drop of a 0.025% solution every six hours as needed, or as directed by physician.

Usual pediatric dose

Children up to 6 years of age—Dosage must be individualized by physician.

Children 6 years of age and older—See *Usual adult and adolescent dose.*

Strength(s) usually available

U.S.—

0.025% (OTC) [*Visine L.R.* (boric acid; edetate disodium; sodium borate; sodium chloride)].

Canada—

0.025% (OTC) [*OcuClear* (boric acid; disodium edetate; hydrochloric acid and/or sodium hydroxide; sodium chloride)].

Packaging and storage

Store between 15 and 30 °C (59 and 86 °F), unless otherwise specified by manufacturer. Store in a tight container. Protect from freezing.

Stability

Do not use if solution contains a precipitate or changes color.

Auxiliary labeling

- For the eye.
- Keep container tightly closed.

Revised: 08/13/1998

OXYMETHOLONE—See *Anabolic Steroids (Systemic)*

OXYMORPHONE—See *Opioid (Narcotic) Analgesics (Systemic)*

OXYTETRACYCLINE—See *Tetracyclines (Systemic)*

OXYTOCIN Systemic

VA CLASSIFICATION (Primary/Secondary): GU600/DX900; HS900

Commonly used brand name(s): *Pitocin; Syntocinon.*

Note: For a listing of dosage forms and brand names by country availability, see *Dosage Forms* section(s).

Category

Oxytocic—Oxytocin.

Antihemorrhagic (postpartum and postabortal uterine bleeding)—Oxytocin Injection.

Lactation stimulant—Oxytocin Nasal Solution.

Diagnostic aid (utero-placental insufficiency; placental reserve)—Oxytocin Injection

Indications

Note: Bracketed information in the *Indications* section refers to uses that are not included in U.S. product labeling.

Accepted

Labor, medical induction of or

Labor, augmentation of or

Abortion, incomplete (treatment)—Parenterally administered oxytocin is indicated for induction and augmentation of labor. Parenteral oxytocin is also indicated for management of incomplete abortion. Oxytocin is sometimes used in combination with prostaglandins.

Abortion, therapeutic—Parenterally administered oxytocin is indicated for performance of therapeutic abortion. Oxytocin is sometimes used in combination with hypertonic sodium chloride, urea, or prostaglandins.

Hemorrhage, postabortion (treatment)

Hemorrhage, postpartum (treatment)—Oxytocin is indicated in the management of postabortion and postpartum bleeding or hemorrhage.

Lactation deficiency (treatment)—Intranasally administered oxytocin is indicated for stimulation of impaired milk ejection (lack of let-down). Nasal oxytocin is recommended for short-term use, generally during the first week postpartum.

[Fetal distress (diagnosis)][1] or

[Utero-placental insufficiency (diagnosis)][1]—Oxytocin is administered parenterally to assess fetal-placental respiratory capabilities in high-risk pregnancies. This is also referred to as the oxytocin challenge test.

---

[1]Not included in Canadian product labeling.

Pharmacology/Pharmacokinetics

Physicochemical characteristics

Source—Synthetically produced pituitary hormone.

Molecular weight—1007.19.

Mechanism of action/Effect

Uterine—

The uterine myometrium contains receptors specific to oxytocin. Oxytocin stimulates contraction of uterine smooth muscle by increasing intracellular calcium concentrations, thus mimicking contractions of normal, spontaneous labor and transiently impeding uterine blood flow. Amplitude and duration of uterine contractions are increased, leading to dilation and effacement of the cervix. The number of oxytocin receptors and, therefore, uterine response to oxytocin increases gradually throughout pregnancy, reaching its peak at term.

For diagnosis of fetal distress and utero-placental insufficiency: By comparing baseline and oxytocin-induced fetal heart rate patterns and uterine contraction patterns, the oxytocin challenge test may aid in determining if there is adequate placental reserve for continuation of a high-risk pregnancy. The occurrence of a fetal heart rate pattern exhibiting late decelerations with administration of oxytocin may indicate utero-placental insufficiency.

Lactation—

Stimulates smooth muscle to facilitate ejection of milk from breasts. Oxytocin does not increase milk production.

Absorption

Rapidly absorbed through nasal mucous membranes; may be erratic.

Protein binding

Low (30%).

Biotransformation

Enzymatic hydrolysis, primarily by tissue oxytocinase. Oxytocinase is also found in placental tissue and plasma.

Half-life

1 to 6 minutes (decreased in late pregnancy and lactation).

Onset of action

Nasal—Within a few minutes.

Intramuscular—3 to 5 minutes.

Intravenous—Immediate.

Duration of action

Nasal—20 minutes.

Intramuscular—2 to 3 hours.

Intravenous—Uterine activity generally subsides within one hour.

Elimination

Only small amounts are excreted unchanged.

Precautions to Consider

Carcinogenicity/Mutagenicity

No animal or human studies have been conducted to evaluate the carcinogenic or mutagenic potential of oxytocin.

Pregnancy/Reproduction

Pregnancy—

For augmentation or stimulation of labor—

Oxytocin is not indicated for use in the first trimester of pregnancy, other than for the treatment of incomplete abortion or therapeutic abortion.

Animal reproductive studies have not been conducted.

For stimulation of lactation—

Not recommended for use during pregnancy because its use may result in contractions and abortion.

FDA Pregnancy Category X.

Labor and delivery—Based on extensive clinical use and known pharmacologic properties of oxytocin, it is not expected to cause an increased risk of fetal abnormalities when used as indicated. Because of maternal and fetal risks, oxytocin must be administered with caution. It has been reported to cause fetal bradycardia, neonatal retinal hemorrhage, and neonatal jaundice, in addition to maternal effects.

Labor and delivery—Fetal deaths due to various causes have reportedly been associated with the parenteral use of oxytocics for induction or augmentation of labor.

Labor and delivery—Excessive dosage or administration of oxytocin to hypersensitive patients may cause uterine hypertonicity with spasm and tetanic contraction or uterine rupture. Abruptio placentae, impaired uterine blood flow, amniotic fluid embolism, and fetal trauma including cardiac arrhythmias, intracranial hemorrhage, and asphyxia may occur as a result.

Labor and delivery—Oxytocin may inhibit, rather than promote, expulsion of the placenta and increase the risk of hemorrhage and infection.

Breast-feeding

For stimulation of milk ejection—Problems in humans have not been documented. Only minimal amounts pass into breast milk.

Drug interactions and/or related problems

The following drug interactions and/or related problems have been selected on the basis of their potential clinical significance (possible mechanism in parentheses where appropriate)—not necessarily inclusive (» = major clinical significance):

Note: Combinations containing any of the following medications, depending on the amount present, may also interact with this medication.

Anesthetics, hydrocarbon inhalation, such as
Cyclopropane
Enflurane
Halothane
Isoflurane

(cyclopropane anesthesia may lessen tachycardia but worsen hypotension caused by oxytocin; maternal sinus bradycardia and abnormal atrioventricular rhythms have been reported with concurrent use, although the correlation is controversial)

(enflurane [concentrations > 1.5%], halothane [concentrations > 1%], and possibly isoflurane produce a dose-dependent decrease in the uterine response to oxytocics and may abolish the response if sufficient concentrations [> 3% of enflurane] are administered; uterine hemorrhage may result)

Caudal block anesthesia with a vasoconstrictor or
Vasopressors

(concurrent use with oxytocin may potentiate the pressor effect of the sympathomimetic pressor amines with possible severe hypertension and rupture of cerebral blood vessels)

(severe hypertension has been reported when oxytocin was given 3 to 4 hours after caudal block anesthesia with a vasoconstrictor)

» Sodium chloride, intra-amniotic for abortion or
» Urea, intra-amniotic for abortion or
» Oxytocics, other

(concurrent use with oxytocin may result in uterine hypertonus, possibly causing uterine rupture or cervical laceration, especially in the absence of adequate cervical dilation; although combinations are sometimes used for therapeutic advantage, patient should be monitored closely during concurrent use; when used as an adjunct to abortifacients, it is recommended that oxytocin not be administered until the oxytocic effect of the abortifacient has subsided, to reduce the risk of uterine rupture and cervical laceration; water intoxication may also occur in patients given oxytocin following the use of intra-amniotic hypertonic saline for abortion)

Laboratory value alterations

The following have been selected on the basis of their potential clinical significance (possible effect in parentheses where appropriate)—not necessarily inclusive (» = major clinical significance).

With physiology/laboratory test values

Bilirubin, neonatal serum concentrations

(neonatal jaundice has been reported, although it is not clear whether jaundice is due to oxytocin or labor process itself)

Chloride and
Sodium

(antidiuretic effect of oxytocin may cause reduced maternal serum concentrations and water intoxication)

Medical considerations/Contraindications

The medical considerations/contraindications included have been selected on the basis of their potential clinical significance (reasons given in parentheses where appropriate)—not necessarily inclusive (» = major clinical significance).

Except under special circumstances, this medication should not be used when the following medical problems exist:

For all indications

» Allergy to oxytocin, history of

For augmentation or induction of labor

» Absolute contraindications to vaginal delivery
» Hypertonic uterine patterns

Risk-benefit should be considered when the following medical problems exist:

For all indications, except for stimulation of lactation

Cardiac disease, especially involving fixed cardiac output or
Hypertension or
Renal function impairment

(increased susceptibility to fluid overload, arrhythmia, or hypotension and reflex tachycardia; reduction in dosage is recommended)

Exaggerated response to oxytocin or other oxytocics, history of

(excessive dosage or administration of oxytocin to hypersensitive patients may cause uterine hypertonicity with spasm and tetanic contraction, which can lead to uterine rupture, cervical lacerations, abruptio placentae, impaired uterine blood flow, amniotic fluid embolism, and fetal trauma including cardiac arrhythmias, intracranial hemorrhage, and asphyxia)

For augmentation or induction of labor only, in addition to those problems listed above

» Relative contraindications to vaginal delivery
» Uterine inertia

(*prolonged use* of oxytocin is not recommended; in cases of uterine inertia, it is recommended that oxytocin be administered for no longer than 6 to 8 hours)

Patient monitoring

The following may be especially important in patient monitoring (other tests may be warranted in some patients, depending on condition; » = major clinical significance):

Acid-base equilibrium determinations, fetal and
Contractions—frequency, duration, and force of and
Fetal heart rate monitoring, continuous and
Heart rate and blood pressure determinations, maternal and
Uterine tone, resting

(recommended at frequent intervals during labor and delivery)

Fluid intake and output determinations

(recommended to reduce the risk of water intoxication, especially during prolonged administration of oxytocin)

Side/Adverse Effects

The following side/adverse effects have been selected on the basis of their potential clinical significance (possible signs and symptoms in parentheses where appropriate)—not necessarily inclusive:

Those indicating need for medical attention

Incidence rare

With nasal use

Psychotic reaction—one case reported; ***seizures***—one case reported; ***unexpected uterine bleeding or contractions***

With parenteral use

Afibrinogenemia or pelvic hematoma or postpartum hemorrhage (increased or continuing vaginal bleeding); ***allergy or*** (skin rash or itching; hives); ***generalized anaphylaxis*** (difficulty in breathing; skin rash or itching; hives); ***cardiac arrhythmias or premature ventricular contractions*** (fast or irregular heartbeat); ***hypotension*** (weakness; dizziness); ***followed by hypertension and*** (continuing or severe headache); ***reflexive tachycardia*** (fast heartbeat); ***uterine rupture*** (increased or continuing vaginal bleeding; severe pelvic or abdominal pain); ***water intoxication*** (seizures; coma; confusion; continuing headache; rapid weight gain)

Note: Fatal *allergic reactions* have occurred with the use of oxytocin.

Hypotension may be caused by administration of large doses or rapid intravenous infusion.

Maternal death due to *uterine rupture* has been reported to be associated with the parenteral administration of oxytocics for the induction or augmentation of labor.

Because of its slight antidiuretic effect, prolonged intravenous administration of oxytocin (usually in doses of 40 to 50 milliunits or more per minute) with large volumes of fluid may produce severe *water intoxication.* Maternal deaths due to hypertensive episodes and subarachnoid hemorrhage have been reported.

Those indicating need for medical attention only if they continue or are bothersome

Incidence rare

With parenteral use

Nausea; vomiting

With nasal use

Lacrimation (tearing of the eyes); ***nasal irritation; rhinorrhea*** (runny nose)

Patient Consultation

As an aid to patient consultation, refer to *Advice for the Patient, Oxytocin (Systemic).*

In providing consultation, consider emphasizing the following selected information (» = major clinical significance):

Before using this medication

» Conditions affecting use, especially:
Allergy to oxytocin

Proper use of this medication

For intranasal use only
Proper administration
» Proper dosing

Precautions while using this medication

Possible therapeutic failure of nasal spray when used as lactation stimulant

Side/adverse effects

Signs of potential side effects, especially:
(For parenteral use—Water intoxication, afibrinogenemia, pelvic hematoma, postpartum hemorrhage, anaphylaxis, allergy, cardiac arrhythmias, premature ventricular contractions, hypotension, and uterine rupture)
(For nasal use—Unexpected uterine bleeding or contractions, psychotic reaction, and seizures)

General Dosing Information

Patients receiving oxytocin should be hospitalized and under the supervision of a physician experienced in its use.

Therapeutic failure frequently occurs with the administration of nasal spray for stimulation of lactation.

For parenteral dosage forms only

Oxytocin must be diluted and administered by intravenous infusion for induction or stimulation of labor. Intramuscular administration of oxytocin is not recommended for induction or stimulation of labor, since intramuscular administration is difficult to regulate and may lead to uterine hyperactivity and fetal distress.

It is recommended that oxytocin infusion be administered intravenously by means of an infusion pump, a microdrip regulator, or a similar device to allow precise adjustment of the flow rate.

Dosage must be adjusted to meet the individual requirements of each patient, on the basis of maternal and fetal response.

Oxytocin should not be used simultaneously by more than one route.

For treatment of adverse effects

Oxytocin infusion should be discontinued or the rate of infusion decreased at the first sign of uterine hyperactivity or fetal distress. Supportive care, including administration of oxygen to the mother, is also recommended.

Nasal Dosage Forms

OXYTOCIN NASAL SOLUTION USP

Usual adult dose

Lactation stimulant—

Intranasal, 1 spray into one or both nostrils two to three minutes before nursing or pumping of breasts.

Strength(s) usually available

U.S.—

40 Units per mL (Rx) [*Syntocinon*].

Canada—

40 Units per mL (Rx) [*Syntocinon*].

Packaging and storage

Store below 40 °C (104 °F), preferably between 15 and 30 °C (59 and 86 °F), unless otherwise specified by manufacturer.

Parenteral Dosage Forms

Note: Bracketed uses in the *Dosage Forms* section refer to categories of use and/or indications that are not included in U.S. product labeling.

OXYTOCIN INJECTION USP

Usual adult dose

Augmentation or
Induction of labor—

Intravenous infusion, initially no more than 0.5 to 2 milliunits per minute, increased every fifteen to sixty minutes in increments of 1 to 2 milliunits per minute until adequate uterine activity is established, up to 20 milliunits per minute (usually 2 to 5 milliunits per minute). Occasionally, doses higher than 20 milliunits per minute may be required.

The infusion rate may be reduced by similar increments, once labor is established.

Abortion, incomplete (treatment) or
Abortion, therapeutic—

Intravenous infusion, 10 Units at a rate of 20 to 40 milliunits per minute.

Hemorrhage, postpartum (treatment)—

Intravenous infusion, 10 Units at a rate of 20 to 40 milliunits per minute following delivery of the infant(s) and preferably the placenta(s).

Intramuscular, 10 Units after delivery of the placenta(s).

Hemorrhage, postabortion (treatment)—

Intravenous infusion, 10 Units at a rate of 20 to 100 milliunits per minute.

[Utero-placental insufficiency (diagnosis)][1]—

Intravenous infusion, initially 0.5 milliunits per minute, doubled every twenty minutes as necessary to the effective dose (usually 5 to 6 milliunits per minute). When three moderate uterine contractions (duration of forty to sixty seconds) occur in one ten-minute interval, the infusion is discontinued and baseline and oxytocin-induced fetal heart rate and uterine contraction patterns are compared.

Strength(s) usually available

U.S.—

10 Units per mL (Rx) [*Pitocin; Syntocinon;* GENERIC].

Canada—

5 Units per mL (Rx) [*Syntocinon*].
10 Units per mL (Rx) [*Syntocinon*].

Packaging and storage

Store below 40 °C (104 °F), preferably between 15 and 30 °C (59 and 86 °F), unless otherwise specified by manufacturer. Protect from freezing.

Preparation of dosage form

For augmentation or induction of labor—Using standard aseptic technique, add 10 units of Oxytocin Injection USP to 1000 mL of normal saline (0.9% sodium chloride injection), lactated Ringer's solution, or other nonhydrating diluent. Final solution concentration is 10 milliunits per mL.

For control of postabortion or postpartum uterine bleeding—Using standard aseptic technique, add 10 to 40 units of Oxytocin Injection USP to 1000 mL of a nonhydrating diluent. Final solution concentration is 10 to 40 milliunits per mL.

[1]Not included in Canadian product labeling.

Revised: 06/30/1994

PACLITAXEL Systemic

VA CLASSIFICATION (Primary): AN900

Commonly used brand name(s): *Taxol*.

Note: For a listing of dosage forms and brand names by country availability, see *Dosage Forms* section(s).

Category

Antineoplastic.

Indications

Note: Bracketed information in the *Indications* section refers to uses that are not included in U.S. product labeling.

Accepted

Carcinoma, ovarian, epithelial (treatment)—Paclitaxel is indicated as first-line and subsequent therapy for treatment of advanced ovarian carcinoma. When used as first-line therapy, paclitaxel is indicated in combination with cisplatin.

Paclitaxel is indicated, in combination with carboplatin or cisplatin, for the [treatment of fallopian tube and peritoneal carcinomas, of ovarian origin][1].

Carcinoma, breast, node–positive (treatment adjunct)[1]—Paclitaxel is indicated for the adjuvant treatment of node–positive breast cancer when administered sequentially to standard doxorubicin–containing combination chemotherapy.

[Carcinoma, breast (treatment, first-line)][1]—Paclitaxel is indicated as first line therapy, as a single agent or in combination with other chemotherapeutic agents, for treatment of metastatic breast carcinoma (Evidence rating: IA). First-line therapy with paclitaxel, in combination with carboplatin, is indicated for treatment of locally advanced and/or metastatic breast carcinoma. Traztuzumab may be added to this combination, in HER2/neu positive patients.

Carcinoma, breast (treatment, salvage)—Paclitaxel is indicated for treatment of metastatic breast carcinoma after failure of combination chemotherapy or at relapse within 6 months of adjuvant chemotherapy. Prior therapy should have included an anthracycline unless clinically contraindicated.[1]

Kaposi's sarcoma, acquired immunodeficiency syndrome (AIDS)-associated (treatment)[1]—Paclitaxel is indicated for second-line treatment of AIDS-associated Kaposi's sarcoma.

Carcinoma, lung, non-small cell (treatment)—Paclitaxel is indicated, in combination with cisplatin, for first-line treatment of non-small cell lung carcinoma in patients who are not candidates for radiation therapy or potentially curative surgery.

[Carcinoma, bladder (treatment)][1] or

[Carcinoma, head and neck (treatment)][1]—Paclitaxel is indicated for treatment of transitional cell bladder carcinoma (Evidence rating: IIID) and head and neck carcinoma (Evidence rating: IIID).

[Carcinoma, cervical (treatment)][1]

[Carcinoma, esophageal (treatment)][1] or

[Carcinoma, endometrial (treatment)][1]—Paclitaxel is considered reasonable medical therapy at some point in the management of cervical carcinoma (Evidence rating: IIID), esophageal carcinoma (Evidence rating: IIID), and endometrial carcinoma (Evidence rating: IIID).

[Carcinoma, lung, small cell (treatment)][1]—Paclitaxel is indicated for treatment of small cell lung carcinoma.

[Carcinoma, prostate (treatment)][1]—Paclitaxel, in combination therapy, is considered reasonable medical therapy at some point in the management of hormone-refractory prostate carcinoma (Evidence rating: IIID).

[Carcinoma, gastric (treatment)][1]—Paclitaxel, in combination therapy, is considered reasonable medical therapy at some point in the management of advanced gastric carcinoma (Evidence rating: IIID).

[Carcinoma, unknown primary site (treatment)][1]—Paclitaxel is indicated for the first-line treatment of carcinoma of unknown primary site (CUPS), as part of a combination regimen with carboplatin and etoposide. There was not a clear consensus by the USP medical experts. Some of the experts are hesitant about the use of this regimen and suggest that individual case factors (e.g. metastatic sites, disease factors, patient characteristics, etc.) be considered when choosing an appropriate treatment.

[Tumors, germ cell, testicular (treatment)][1]—Paclitaxel is indicated for the treatment of testicular germ cell tumors, alone or in combination with other agents (e.g., cisplatin, ifosfamide, etoposide), in patients with disease refractory to cisplatin-based chemotherapy.

Acceptance not established

Use of paclitaxel for the treatment of malignant melanoma has not been established, due to insufficient data supporting efficacy. Additional studies, of sufficient size, confirming antitumor activity (comparative to dacarbazine) with fully published and peer-reviewed data are needed.

[1]Not included in Canadian product labeling.

Pharmacology/Pharmacokinetics

Note: Pharmacokinetic studies were conducted in adult cancer patients who received paclitaxel in single doses of 15 to 135 mg per square meter of body surface area (mg/m^2) given by 1-hour infusions (15 patients), 30 to 275 mg/m^2 given by 6-hour infusions (36 patients), and 200 to 275 mg/m^2 given by 24-hour infusions (54 patients). Pharmacokinetic studies were also conducted in ovarian cancer patients who received single doses of 135 mg/m^2 given by 3-hour infusions (seven patients), 135 mg/m^2 given by 24-hour infusions (two patients), 175 mg/m^2 given by 3-hour infusions (five patients), and 175 mg/m^2 given by 24-hour infusions (four patients).

Physicochemical characteristics

Source—Semi-synthetic. Obtained from *Taxus baccata*..

Chemical Group—Paclitaxel is a diterpenoid taxane.

Molecular weight—853.93.

Mechanism of action/Effect

Paclitaxel belongs to the class of medications known as antimicrotubule agents. It promotes the assembly of microtubules from tubulin dimers and stabilizes microtubules by preventing depolymerization. This stability results in the inhibition of the normal dynamic reorganization of the microtubule network that is essential for vital interphase and mitotic cellular functions. In addition, paclitaxel induces abnormal arrays or "bundles" of microtubules throughout the cell cycle and multiple asters of microtubules during mitosis.

Other actions/effects

Paclitaxel enhances the cytotoxic effects of ionizing radiation *in vitro* .

Distribution

The mean steady-state volume of distribution (Vol_D) ranged from 227 to 688 liters per square meter of body surface area following single doses of 135 and 175 mg/m^2 given over 24 hours. Similar Vol_D were obtained following single doses of 15 to 135 mg/m^2 given over 1 hour and single doses of 30 to 275 mg/m^2 given over 6 hours. This indicates extensive extravascular distribution and/or tissue binding.

The mean area under the plasma concentration-time curve (AUC) (24-hour infusion) was 6300 and 7993 nanograms per hour per mL for doses of 135 and 175 mg/m^2, respectively. The mean maximum plasma concentration following a 24-hour infusion of paclitaxel was 195 and 365 nanograms per mL for doses of 135 and 175 mg/m^2, respectively.

The mean AUC (3-hour infusion) was 7952 and 15,007 nanograms per hour per mL for doses of 135 and 175 mg/m^2, respectively. The mean maximum plasma concentration following a 3-hour infusion of paclitaxel was 2170 and 3650 nanograms per mL for doses of 135 and 175 mg/m^2, respectively.

Protein binding

Very high (89 to 98%).

Biotransformation

Hepatic. Metabolized via the cytochrome P450 isoenzyme CYP2C8 to one major metabolite (6-alpha-hydroxypaclitaxel), and via the cytochrome P450 isoenzyme CYP3A4 to two minor metabolites (3-para-hydroxypaclitaxel and 6-alpha,3″-para-dihydroxypaclitaxel).

Half-life

Terminal—Mean (standard deviation): Range 5.3 (4.6) to 17.4 (4.7) hours, following 1-hour and 6-hour infusions at doses of 15 to 275 mg per square meter of body surface area.

Elimination

Not completely understood. Mean (standard deviation) values for urinary recovery of unchanged drug following 1-, 6-, and 24-hour infusions at doses of 15 to 275 mg per square meter of body surface area ranged from 1.3% (0.5%) to 12.6% (16.2%) of the dose, indicating extensive nonrenal clearance. High concentrations of paclitaxel and its metabolites have been reported in the bile.

The decline in plasma concentrations is biphasic; the initial rapid decline represents distribution to the peripheral compartment and significant elimination. The later phase is due, in part, to a relatively slow efflux from the peripheral compartment.

Mean values for total body clearance were 21.7 and 23.8 liters per hour per square meter of body surface area, following single doses of 135 and 175 mg/m^2 given by 24-hour infusions, respectively. Clearance values following single doses of 135 and 175 mg/m² given by 3-hour infusions were 17.7 and 12.2 liters per hour per square meter of body surface area, respectively.

Precautions to Consider

Cross-sensitivity and/or related problems

Patients sensitive to polyoxyethylated castor oil may be sensitive to paclitaxel also, since the injection contains a polyoxyethylated castor oil vehicle.

Carcinogenicity

Studies with paclitaxel have not been done.

Secondary malignancies are potential delayed effects of many antineoplastic agents, although it is not clear whether the effect is related to their mutagenic or immunosuppressive action. The effect of dose and duration of therapy is also unknown, although risk seems to increase with long-term use.

Mutagenicity

Paclitaxel is mutagenic in *in vitro* (chromosome aberrations in human lymphocytes) and in *in vivo* (micronucleus test in mice) mammalian test systems. However, it was not mutagenic in the Ames test or the CHO/HGPRT gene mutation assay.

Pregnancy/Reproduction

Fertility—Studies in rats at doses of 1 mg per kg of body weight (mg/kg) (6 mg per square meter of body surface area) found that paclitaxel reduced fertility.

Pregnancy—Adequate and well-controlled studies in humans have not been done.

First trimester: It is usually recommended that use of antineoplastics, especially combination chemotherapy, be avoided whenever possible, especially during the first trimester. Although information is limited because of the relatively few instances of antineoplastic administration during pregnancy, the mutagenic, teratogenic, and carcinogenic potential of these medications must be considered.

Other hazards to the fetus include adverse reactions seen in adults.

In general, use of contraception is recommended during cytotoxic drug therapy.

Paclitaxel was found to cause maternal and embryo-fetal toxicity in rabbits at intravenous doses of 3 mg/kg (33 mg per square meter of body surface area) given during organogenesis. In rats and rabbits, paclitaxel was found to cause abortions, decreased corpora lutea, a decrease in implantations and live fetuses, and increased resorptions and embryo-fetal deaths. No gross external, soft tissue, or skeletal alterations occurred.

FDA Pregnancy Category D.

Breast-feeding

Although very little information is available regarding distribution of antineoplastic agents into breast milk, breast-feeding is not recommended during chemotherapy because of the potential risks to the infant (adverse effects, mutagenicity, carcinogenicity). It is not known whether paclitaxel is distributed into breast milk.

Pediatrics

No information is available on the relationship of age to the effects of paclitaxel in pediatric patients, although phase I studies in children have been reported. Safety and efficacy have not been established.

Geriatrics

One retrospective study on the relationship of age to the effects of paclitaxel found no difference in dose intensity achieved in elderly patients.

Dental

The bone marrow depressant effects of paclitaxel may result in an increased incidence of microbial infection, delayed healing, and gingival bleeding. Dental work, whenever possible, should be completed prior to initiation of therapy or deferred until blood counts have returned to normal. Patients should be instructed in proper oral hygiene during treatment, including caution in use of regular toothbrushes, dental floss, and toothpicks.

Paclitaxel also may cause mucositis, which is usually mild but which at high doses may be associated with considerable discomfort.

Drug interactions and/or related problems

The following drug interactions and/or related problems have been selected on the basis of their potential clinical significance (possible mechanism in parentheses where appropriate)—not necessarily inclusive (» = *major clinical significance*):

Note: Combinations containing any of the following medications, depending on the amount present, may also interact with this medication.

Blood dyscrasia-causing medications (see *Appendix II*)
(leukopenic and/or thrombocytopenic effects of paclitaxel may be increased with concurrent or recent therapy if these medications cause the same effects; dosage adjustment of paclitaxel, if necessary, should be based on blood counts)

» Bone marrow depressants, other (see *Appendix II*) or
Radiation therapy
(additive bone marrow depression may occur; dosage reduction may be required when two or more bone marrow depressants, including radiation, are used concurrently or consecutively)
(severity of paclitaxel-induced neutropenia may be related to the extent of prior myelotoxic therapy)
(in one Phase I study, administration of cisplatin before paclitaxel, rather than after, was found to reduce paclitaxel clearance by approximately 25%)

Vaccines, killed virus
(because normal defense mechanisms may be suppressed by paclitaxel therapy, the patient's antibody response to the vaccine may be decreased. The interval between discontinuation of medications that cause immunosuppression and restoration of the patient's ability to respond to the vaccine depends on the intensity and type of immunosuppression-causing medication used, the underlying disease, and other factors; estimates vary from 3 months to 1 year)

» Vaccines, live virus
(because normal defense mechanisms may be suppressed by paclitaxel therapy, concurrent use with a live virus vaccine may potentiate the replication of the vaccine virus, may increase the side/adverse effects of the vaccine virus, and/or may decrease the patient's antibody response to the vaccine; immunization of these patients should be undertaken only with extreme caution after careful review of the patient's hematologic status and only with the knowledge and consent of the physician managing the paclitaxel therapy. The interval between discontinuation of medications that cause immunosuppression and restoration of the patient's ability to respond to the vaccine depends on the intensity and type of immunosuppression-causing medication used, the underlying disease, and other factors; estimates vary from 3 months to 1 year. In addition, immunization with oral poliovirus vaccine should be postponed in persons in close contact with the patient, especially family members)

Laboratory value alterations

The following have been selected on the basis of their potential clinical significance (possible effect in parentheses where appropriate)—not necessarily inclusive (» = major clinical significance).

With physiology/laboratory test values
Alkaline phosphatase values, serum and
Aspartate aminotransferase (AST [SGOT]) values, serum and
Bilirubin concentrations, serum
(may be increased transiently; elevations of alkaline phosphatase and bilirubin may be dose-related)

Triglycerides
(elevations in serum concentrations have been reported)

Medical considerations/Contraindications

The medical considerations/contraindications included have been selected on the basis of their potential clinical significance (reasons given in parentheses where appropriate)—not necessarily inclusive (» = major clinical significance).

Risk-benefit should be considered when the following medical problems exist:

» Bone marrow depression
(will be increased; it is recommended that paclitaxel not be administered to patients with solid tumors when baseline neutrophil counts are lower than 1500 cells per cubic millimeter, and that subsequent doses not be administered until neutrophil counts have returned to greater than 1500 cells per cubic millimeter and platelet counts to greater than 100,000 cells per cubic millimeter or to baseline values; it is also recommended that paclitaxel not be administered to patients with AIDS-associated Kaposi's sarcoma when baseline neutrophil counts are lower than 1000 cells per cubic millimeter)

Cardiac function impairment, including:
Angina
» Cardiac conduction abnormalities
Congestive heart failure, history of
Myocardial infarction within the past 6 months
(the patient's ability to tolerate the cardiovascular side effects of paclitaxel may be reduced)

» Chickenpox, existing or recent (including recent exposure) or
» Herpes zoster
(risk of severe generalized disease)
» Infection
» Sensitivity to paclitaxel
» Caution should be used also in patients who have had previous cytotoxic drug therapy or radiation therapy

Patient monitoring

The following may be especially important in patient monitoring (other tests may be warranted in some patients, depending on condition; » = major clinical significance):

» Hematocrit or hemoglobin and
» Leukocyte count, total and, if appropriate, differential and
» Platelet count
(determinations recommended prior to initiation of therapy and at periodic intervals during therapy; frequency varies according to clinical state, agent, dose, and other agents being used concurrently)
» Vital signs
(recommended frequently, especially during the first hour of paclitaxel infusion)

Side/Adverse Effects

Note: Neutropenia is the major dose-limiting effect.

The following side/adverse effects have been selected on the basis of their potential clinical significance (possible signs and symptoms in parentheses where appropriate)—not necessarily inclusive:

Those indicating need for medical attention

Incidence more frequent

Anemia (unusual tiredness or weakness)—usually asymptomatic; ***hypersensitivity reaction*** (flushing of face; skin rash or itching; shortness of breath; rarely [with proper premedication], severe shortness of breath; severe skin reaction); ***leukopenia or neutropenia, with or without infection*** (fever or chills; cough or hoarseness; lower back or side pain; painful or difficult urination); ***thrombocytopenia*** (unusual bleeding or bruising; black, tarry stools; blood in urine or stools; pinpoint red spots on skin)—usually asymptomatic

Note: Incidence and severity of *anemia* seem to increase with increasing exposure to paclitaxel.

With proper premedication, *hypersensitivity reactions* are usually mild (flushing of face, skin rash, shortness of breath). However, severe reactions (hypotension requiring treatment, dyspnea requiring bronchodilators, angioedema or generalized urticaria, chest pain) can occur, even with premedication, and necessitate immediate discontinuation of paclitaxel and aggressive symptomatic therapy. Severe symptoms usually occur within the first 10 minutes of paclitaxel infusion, after the first or second dose of paclitaxel. A fatal reaction occurred in a patient who was not premedicated. In general, it is recommended that paclitaxel not be readministered to patients who have experienced a severe hypersensitivity reaction. However, in patients with objective tumor responses and without other options to paclitaxel therapy, re-treatment may be attempted with extreme caution and aggressive premedication by experienced practitioners.

Severe *neutropenia* (neutrophil count below 500 cells per cubic millimeter) is common but only infrequently persists for more than 7 days. The nadir of the neutrophil counts usually occurs at approximately day 11 of paclitaxel therapy; in general, neutropenia is rapidly reversible, with recovery by day 15 to 21. Cumulative neutropenia does not occur. The most common infections associated with neutropenia are urinary tract infections, upper respiratory infections, and sepsis. Fatalities have occurred from neutropenia-related sepsis.

In *thrombocytopenia,* the nadir of the platelet counts usually occurs at approximately day 8 or 9 of paclitaxel therapy. Platelet counts generally do not fall below 100,000 cells per cubic millimeter. Hemorrhagic episodes may also be disease-related.

Incidence less frequent

Cardiovascular effects, including bradycardia; hypotension; or abnormal electrocardiogram (ECG)—usually asymptomatic; ***elevated serum hepatic enzymes***—asymptomatic

Note: *Cardiovascular effects* have also included more severe atrioventricular (AV) blocks, occasionally resulting in third-degree block requiring cardiac pacing. Atypical chest pains and a fatal myocardial infarction have also occurred, as well as asymptomatic bundle branch block and transient ventricular tachycardia, although the exact relationship to paclitaxel is unknown.

Incidence rare

Extravasation, with phlebitis or cellulitis (pain or redness at site of injection); ***mucositis*** (sores in mouth and on lips)

Note: Oropharyngeal *mucositis* is dose-related; it is infrequent or mild at usual recommended doses and usually resolves 5 to 7 days following treatment. However, esophageal and intestinal epithelial necrosis and ulceration have been reported.

Those indicating need for medical attention only if they continue or are bothersome

Incidence more frequent

Arthralgias or myalgias (pain in joints or muscles, especially in arms or legs); ***diarrhea; nausea and vomiting; peripheral neuropathy, including mild paresthesia*** (numbness, burning, or tingling in hands or feet)

Note: *Arthralgias or myalgias* usually begin 2 to 3 days after treatment and resolve within 5 days. Pain is usually relieved by analgesics, but occasionally may be severe enough to require narcotics.

Nausea and vomiting are usually mild or moderate.

Incidence and severity of *peripheral neuropathy* are dose-related; at usual doses, a sensory neuropathy in a glove-and-stocking distribution occurs. Only rarely is withdrawal of paclitaxel necessary. Symptoms usually appear after multiple doses and improve or resolve within several months after paclitaxel is discontinued. High doses (over 250 mg per square meter of body surface area) may cause dose-limiting motor and autonomic dysfunction, especially in patients with pre-existing neuropathies, beginning as early as 24 to 72 hours after treatment.

Those not indicating need for medical attention

Incidence more frequent

Alopecia (loss of hair)

Note: Complete loss of hair (including scalp hair, eyebrows, eyelashes, and pubic hair) occurs in almost all patients between days 14 and 21, but is reversible after therapy has ended.

Patient Consultation

As an aid to patient consultation, refer to *Advice for the Patient, Paclitaxel (Systemic).*

In providing consultation, consider emphasizing the following selected information (» = major clinical significance):

Before using this medication

» Conditions affecting use, especially:
Sensitivity to paclitaxel
Pregnancy—Use not recommended because of mutagenic, teratogenic, and carcinogenic potential; advisability of using contraception; telling physician immediately if pregnancy is suspected
Breast-feeding—Not recommended because of risk of serious side effects
Other medications, especially other bone marrow depressants, or other cytotoxic drugs or radiation therapy
Other medical problems, especially cardiac conduction abnormalities, chickenpox, herpes zoster, or infection

Proper use of this medication

Frequency of nausea and vomiting; importance of continuing medication despite stomach upset
» Proper dosing

Precautions while using this medication

» Importance of close monitoring by the physician
» Avoiding immunizations unless approved by physician; other persons in patient's household should avoid immunizations with oral poliovirus vaccine; avoiding other persons who have taken oral poliovirus vaccine or wearing a protective mask that covers nose and mouth

Caution if bone marrow depression occurs:

» Avoiding exposure to persons with infections, especially during periods of low blood counts; checking with physician immediately if fever or chills, cough or hoarseness, lower back or side pain, or painful or difficult urination occurs
» Checking with physician immediately if unusual bleeding or bruising; black, tarry stools; blood in urine or stools; or pinpoint red spots on skin occur

Caution in use of regular toothbrush, dental floss, or toothpick; physician, dentist, or nurse may suggest alternatives; checking with physician before having dental work done

Not touching eyes or inside of nose unless hands are washed immediately before

Using caution to avoid accidental cuts with use of sharp objects such as safety razor or fingernail or toenail cutters

Avoiding contact sports or other situations where bruising or injury could occur

Side/adverse effects

May cause adverse effects such as blood problems; importance of discussing possible effects with physician

Signs of potential side effects, especially hypersensitivity reaction, leukopenia or neutropenia, thrombocytopenia, extravasation, and mucositis

Asymptomatic side effects, including anemia, thrombocytopenia, cardiovascular effects, and elevated hepatic enzymes

Physician or nurse can help in dealing with side effects

Possibility of hair loss; normal hair growth should return after treatment has ended

General Dosing Information

Patients receiving paclitaxel should be under supervision of a physician experienced in cancer chemotherapy.

A variety of dosage schedules and regimens of paclitaxel, alone or in combination with other antitumor agents, are used. The prescriber may consult the medical literature as well as the manufacturer's literature in choosing a specific dosage.

It is recommended that patients receiving paclitaxel be under continuous observation for at least the first 30 minutes of the infusion and at frequent intervals after that. Equipment and medications (including epinephrine and oxygen) necessary for treatment of a possible anaphylactic reaction should be immediately available during each administration of paclitaxel.

Paclitaxel concentrate for injection must be diluted before administration by intravenous infusion.

The needle should be carefully positioned in the vein to avoid extravasation and resulting phlebitis and cellulitis.

In order to prevent severe hypersensitivity reactions, it is recommended that all patients be premedicated with corticosteroids (such as dexamethasone), diphenhydramine, and histamine H_2-receptor antagonists (such as cimetidine or ranitidine) (see *Parenteral Dosage Forms* for specific dosing).

Mild hypersensitivity symptoms (flushing, skin reactions, dyspnea, hypotension, tachycardia) do not require interruption of paclitaxel therapy. However, severe reactions (hypotension requiring treatment, dyspnea requiring bronchodilators, angioedema, or generalized urticaria) require immediate withdrawal of paclitaxel and aggressive symptomatic therapy. It is generally recommended that paclitaxel administration not be repeated in patients who have experienced severe hypersensitivity reactions to the medication. However, in patients with objective tumor responses and without other options to paclitaxel therapy, re-treatment may be attempted with extreme caution and aggressive premedication by experienced practitioners.

If severe peripheral neuropathy occurs, it is recommended that subsequent dosage of paclitaxel be reduced by 20%.

If significant cardiac conduction abnormalities occur during administration of paclitaxel, appropriate therapy is recommended, along with continuous cardiac monitoring during subsequent paclitaxel administration.

If severe neutropenia (neutrophil counts of less than 500 cells per cubic millimeter for 7 days or more) occurs during a course of paclitaxel, it is recommended that the paclitaxel dose for subsequent courses be reduced by 20%.

Patients who develop leukopenia should be observed carefully for signs of infection. Antibiotic support may be required. In neutropenic patients who develop fever, broad-spectrum antibiotic coverage should be initiated empirically, pending bacterial cultures and appropriate diagnostic tests. Patients with advanced acquired immunodeficiency syndrome (AIDS) may require concomitant administration of a hematopoietic growth factor such as granulocyte colony stimulating factor (G-CSF).

Special precautions are recommended in patients who develop thrombocytopenia as a result of administration of paclitaxel. These may include extreme care in performing invasive procedures; regular inspection of intravenous sites, skin (including perirectal area), and mucous membrane surfaces for signs of bleeding or bruising; limiting frequency of venipuncture and avoiding intramuscular injections; testing urine, emesis, stool, and secretions for occult blood; care in use of regular toothbrushes, dental floss, toothpicks, safety razors, and fingernail and toenail cutters; avoiding constipation; and using caution to prevent falls and other injuries. Such patients should avoid alcohol and aspirin intake because of the risk of gastrointestinal bleeding. Platelet transfusions may be required.

Safety considerations for handling this medication

There is limited but increasing evidence and concern that personnel involved in preparation and administration of parenteral antineoplastics may be at some risk because of the potential mutagenicity, teratogenicity, and/or carcinogenicity of these agents, although the actual risk is unknown. USP advisory panels recommend cautious handling both in preparation and disposal of antineoplastic agents. Precautions that have been suggested include:

- Use of a biological containment cabinet during reconstitution and dilution of parenteral medications and wearing of disposable surgical gloves and masks.
- Use of proper technique to prevent contamination of the medication, work area, and operator during transfer between containers (including proper training of personnel in this technique).
- Cautious and proper disposal of needles, syringes, vials, ampuls, and unused medication.

A number of medical centers have developed detailed guidelines for handling of antineoplastic agents.

Parenteral Dosage Forms

Note: Bracketed uses in the *Dosage Forms* section refer to categories of use and/or indications that are not included in U.S. product labeling.

PACLITAXEL CONCENTRATE FOR INJECTION

Usual adult dose

Ovarian carcinoma—

For previously *untreated* patients: Intravenous (as a twenty–four hour infusion), 135 mg per square meter of body surface area, followed by cisplatin 75 mg per square meter of body surface area, repeated every twenty-one days. (Canadian product labeling recommends a dose of 175 mg per square meter of body surface area, followed by cisplatin 75 mg per square meter of body surface area, as a three-hour intravenous infusion, repeated every twenty-one days).

For previously *treated* patients: Intravenous (as a three or twenty-four-hour infusion), 135 or 175 mg per square meter of body surface area, repeated every twenty-one days. (Canadian product labeling recommends a dose of 175 mg per square meter of body surface area as a three- or twenty-four-hour intravenous infusion, repeated every twenty-one days.)

For the treatment of [fallopian tube and peritoneal carcinomas of ovarian origin][1], patients have benefited from intravenous doses of paclitaxel 135 to 175 mg/m^2 (by 3–hour infusion), in combination with carboplatin AUC 5 to 6, every 21 days, for 5 to 9 treatment cycles. Duration of paclitaxel infusion may be adjusted from 1 hour to 24 hours, depending on toxicity.

Patients have also benefited from intravenous doses of paclitaxel 135 to 175 mg/m^2 (by 3–hour infusion), in combination with cisplatin 50 to 75 mg/m^2, every 21 to 28 days. Duration of paclitaxel infusion may be increased to 24 hours, depending on toxicity.

Breast carcinoma—

Intravenous (as a three- or twenty-four-hour infusion), 175 mg per square meter of body surface area, repeated every twenty-one days. Because several doses and regimens using paclitaxel in combination with carboplatin (and trastuzumab in HER2/neu positive disease) are showing activity, no individual dose/regimen for first-line therapy is listed here. Consult the medical literature and/or experts in the field of oncology for information on dosage.

Breast carcinoma, node-positive[1]—

Intravenous (as a three-hour infusion), 175 mg per square meter of body surface area, repeated every twenty–one days for four courses administered sequentially to doxorubicin–containing combination chemotherapy.

AIDS-associated Kaposi's sarcoma[1]—

Intravenous (as a three- or twenty-four-hour infusion), 135 mg per square meter of body surface area, repeated every twenty-one days or

Intravenous (as a three- or twenty-four-hour infusion), 100 mg per square meter of body surface area, repeated every fourteen days.

Carcinoma, lung, non-small cell—

Intravenous (as a twenty-four-hour infusion), 135 mg per square meter of body surface area followed by cisplatin 75 mg per square meter of body surface area, repeated every twenty-one days (Canadian product labeling recommends a dose of 175 mg per square meter of body surface area as a three-hour intravenous infusion, followed by cisplatin, repeated every twenty-one days.).

[Carcinoma, bladder][1] or
[Carcinoma, head and neck][1] or
[Carcinoma, cervical][1] or
[Carcinoma, esophageal][1] or
[Carcinoma, endometrial][1] or
[Carcinoma, lung, small cell][1] or
[Carcinoma, prostate][1] or
[Carcinoma, gastric][1]—

Consult medical literature and manufacturer's literature for specific dosage.

[Carcinoma, unknown primary site][1]—

Patients have benefited from a 1-hour intravenous infusion of 200 mg/m², on day 1 of a 21-day treatment cycle, combined with intravenous carboplatin and oral etoposide, for 4 to 8 cycles.

[Tumors, germ cell, testicular][1]—

Patients have benefited from intravenous doses of 175–250 mg/m², by 3- to 24-hour infusion, every 21 days. The shorter infusion time is equally effective and less troublesome for the patient.

Note: To prevent severe hypersensitivity reactions, all patients should be premedicated with corticosteroids (e.g., dexamethasone 20 mg orally or intravenously [patients with solid tumors] or dexamethasone 10 mg orally [patients with AIDS-associated Kaposi's sarcoma] approximately twelve and six hours prior to paclitaxel administration); diphenhydramine (e.g., 50 mg intravenously, thirty to sixty minutes prior to paclitaxel) or its equivalent; and cimetidine (e.g., 300 mg intravenously, thirty to sixty minutes prior to paclitaxel), ranitidine (e.g., 50 mg intravenously, thirty to sixty minutes prior to paclitaxel), or famotidine (e.g., 20 mg intravenously, thirty to sixty minutes prior to paclitaxel).

Contact of paclitaxel with plasticized polyvinyl chloride (PVC) equipment or devices must be avoided because of the risk of patient exposure to the plasticizer DEHP (di-[2-ethylhexyl]phthalate), which may be leached from PVC infusion bags or sets. Paclitaxel solutions should be diluted and stored in glass or polypropylene bottles or in plastic bags (polypropylene, polyolefin) and administered through polyethylene-lined administration sets.

Paclitaxel intravenous infusion should be administered through an in-line filter with a microporous membrane not greater than 0.22 microns. Use of filter devices that incorporate short inlet and outlet PVC-coated tubing has not resulted in significant leaching of DEHP. Frequent changing of filters (e.g., every twelve hours) may be necessary because of clogging during the infusion.

Usual pediatric dose
Safety and efficacy in pediatric patients have not been established.

Strength(s) usually available
U.S.—

6 mg per mL (5-, 16.7-, and 50-mL multidose vials) (Rx) [*Taxol* (polyoxyethylated castor oil 527 mg per mL; dehydrated alcohol USP 49.7% v/v)].

Canada—

6 mg per mL (single-dose vials) (Rx) [*Taxol* (polyoxyethylated castor oil 527 mg per mL; dehydrated alcohol USP 49.7% v/v)].

Packaging and storage
Store between 20 and 25 °C (68 and 77 °F), unless otherwise specified by the manufacturer. Not adversely affected by freezing.

Preparation of dosage form
Paclitaxel concentrate for injection must be diluted before administration.

Paclitaxel concentrate for injection is prepared for administration by intravenous infusion by diluting it to a concentration of 0.3 to 1.2 mg per mL in 5% dextrose injection, 0.9% sodium chloride injection, or 5% dextrose in Ringer's injection.

Note: Diluted solutions of paclitaxel may show haziness, which is attributed to the formulation vehicle.

Stability
Diluted solutions of paclitaxel are physically and chemically stable for up to 27 hours at ambient room temperature (approximately 25 °C [77 °F]) and room lighting conditions.

Auxiliary labeling
- Must be diluted prior to administration.

Note
If paclitaxel solution contacts the skin, the skin should be washed immediately and thoroughly with soap and water. If paclitaxel contacts mucous membranes, thorough flushing with water is recommended.

[1]Not included in Canadian product labeling.

Revised: 09/11/2003

PACLITAXEL PROTEIN-BOUND Systemic†

VA CLASSIFICATION (Primary): AN900

Commonly used brand name(s): *Abraxane*.

Note: For a listing of dosage forms and brand names by country availability, see *Dosage Forms* section(s).

†Not commercially available in Canada.

Category
Antineoplastic.

Indications

Accepted
Carcinoma, breast (treatment)—Paclitaxel protein-bound particles for injectable suspension is indicated for the treatment of breast cancer after failure of combination chemotherapy for metastatic disease or relapse within 6 months of adjuvant chemotherapy. Prior therapy should have included an anthracycline unless clinically contraindicated.

Pharmacology/Pharmacokinetics

Physicochemical characteristics
Source—Paclitaxel is a natural product obtained from *Taxus* media.

Molecular weight—Paclitaxel: 853.91.

Solubility—Paclitaxel is highly lipophilic, insoluble in water.

Mechanism of action/Effect
Paclitaxel belongs to the class of medications known as antimicrotubule agents. It promotes the assembly of microtubules from tubulin dimers and stabilizes microtubules by preventing depolymerization. This stability results in the inhibition of the normal dynamic reorganization of the microtubule network that is essential for vital interphase and mitotic cellular functions. In addition, paclitaxel induces abnormal arrays or "bundles" of microtubules throughout the cell cycle and multiple asters of microtubules during mitosis.

Absorption
The AUCs were dose proportional over 80 to 375 mg/m².

Distribution
Volume of distribution (Vol_D)—632 L/m².

The volume of distribution of paclitaxel protein-bound administered over 30 minutes was 53% higher than 175 mg/m² paclitaxel injection over 3 hours.

Protein binding
Very high (89 to 98%) to human serum proteins.

Biotransformation
Metabolized by CYP2C8 to 6α-hydroxypaclitaxel and to two minor metabolites, 3′-*p*-hydroxypaclitaxel and 6α, 3′-*p*-dihydroxypaclitaxel, by CYP3A4.

Half-life
Terminal—About 27 hours.

Peak serum concentration
Following the recommended dose of 260 mg/m², the maximum concentration of paclitaxel was 18741 ng/mL.

Elimination
Urinary: 4% unchanged drug; less than 1% as metabolites 6α-hydroxypaclitaxel and 3′-*p*-hydroxypaclitaxel.

Fecal: approximately 20% of the total dose.

Clearance: 15 L/hr/m². The clearance of 260 mg/m² paclitaxel protein-bound administered over 30 minutes was 43% larger than 175 mg/m² paclitaxel injection over 3 hours.

Precautions to Consider

Cross-sensitivity and/or related problems

Carcinogenicity
The carcinogenic potential of paclitaxel protein-bound has not been evaluated.

Mutagenicity
Paclitaxel is mutagenic in *in vitro* (chromosome aberrations in human lymphocytes) and in *in vivo* (micronucleus test in mice) mammalian test systems. However, it was not mutagenic in the Ames test or the CHO/HGPRT gene mutation assay.

Pregnancy/Reproduction

Fertility—Men should be advised not to father a child while receiving treatment with paclitaxel protein-bound particles.

Studies done in male rats given 42 mg/m² on a weekly basis for 11 weeks prior to mating with untreated females resulted in significantly reduced fertility, decreased pregnancy and increased loss of embryos in mated females. A low incidence of skeletal and soft tissue fetal anomalies were observed at doses of 3 and 12 mg/m²/week. Testicular atrophy/degeneration has also been observed in single dose toxicology studies in rodents given paclitaxel protein-bound particles at 54 mg/m² and dogs at 175 mg/m².

Pregnancy—Adequate and well-controlled studies in pregnant women have not been done.

Risk benefit must be carefully considered when this medication is required in life-threatening situations or in serious diseases for which other medicines cannot be used or are ineffective. If this drug is used during pregnancy or if the patient becomes pregnant while receiving this drug, the patient should be apprised to the potential hazard to the fetus. Women of childbearing potential should be advised to avoid becoming pregnant while receiving treatment with paclitaxel protein-bound particles.

Studies done in rats given paclitaxel protein-bound particles at doses of 6 mg/m² on gestation days 7 to 17 revealed embryo-and fetotoxicity, indicated by intrauterine mortality, increased resorptions, reduced number of litters and live fetuses, reduction in fetal body weight and increased in fetal anomalies. Fetal anomalies included soft tissue and skeletal malformations, such as eye bulge, folded retina, microphthalmia, and dilation of brain ventricles. A lower incidence if soft tissue and skeletal malformations were revealed at 3 mg/m².

FDA Pregnancy Category D

Breast-feeding

It is not known whether paclitaxel protein-bound is distributed into breast milk. Because many drugs are distributed in human milk and because of the potential for serious adverse reactions in the nursing infant, it is recommended that nursing be discontinued when receiving paclitaxel protein-bound particles.

Following intravenous administration of carbon-14 labeled paclitaxel to rats on days 9 to 10 postpartum, concentrations of radioactivity in milk were higher than in plasma and declined in parallel with plasma concentrations.

Pediatrics

Safety and effectiveness of paclitaxel protein-bound in pediatric patients have not been evaluated.

Geriatrics

Appropriate studies performed to date have not demonstrated geriatric-specific problems that would limit the usefulness of paclitaxel protein-bound in the elderly.

Drug interactions and/or related problems

The following drug interactions and/or related problems have been selected on the basis of their potential clinical significance (possible mechanism in parentheses where appropriate)—not necessarily inclusive (» = major clinical significance):

Note: Combinations containing any of the following medications, depending on the amount present, may also interact with this medication.

No formal drug interaction studies have been conducted.

CYP2C8, substrates or inhibitors, or
CYP3A4, substrates or inhibitors such as
Indinavir or
Nelfinavir or
Ritonavir or
Saquinavir
(in the absence of formal drug interaction studies, caution should be exercised with concomitant administration with paclitaxel protein-bound particles)

Laboratory value alterations

The following have been selected on the basis of their potential clinical significance (possible effect in parentheses where appropriate)—not necessarily inclusive (» = major clinical significance).

With physiology/laboratory test values
Alkaline phosphatase values, serum or
Aspartate aminotransferase (AST [SGOT]) values, serum or
Bilirubin concentrations, serum or
Creatinine, serum or
GGT
(may be increased)

Medical considerations/Contraindications

The medical considerations/contraindications included have been selected on the basis of their potential clinical significance (reasons given in parentheses where appropriate)—not necessarily inclusive (» = major clinical significance).

Except under special circumstances, this medication should not be used when the following medical problem exists:

» Hypersensitivity to paclitaxel protein-bound particles

» Bone marrow depression
(should not be administered to patients with baseline neutrophil counts of less that 1,500 cells/mm³; frequent monitoring of blood counts should be instituted during treatment and patients should not be retreated with subsequent cycles of paclitaxel protein-bound particles until neutrophils recover to a level greater than 1,500 cells/mm³ and platelets recover to a level greater than 100,000 cells/mm³)

Risk-benefit should be considered when the following medical problems exist:

Hepatic function impairment or
Renal function impairment
(the effect of hepatic or renal dysfunction on the disposition of paclitaxel protein-bound has not been investigated)

» Neuropathy, grade 3
(if grade 3 sensory neuropathy develops, treatment should be withheld until resolution to grade 1 or 2 followed by a dose reduction for all subsequent courses of paclitaxel protein-bound particles)

Patient monitoring

The following may be especially important in patient monitoring (other tests may be warranted in some patients, depending on condition; » = major clinical significance):

» Extravasation
(closely monitor infusion site for possible infiltration during drug administration)

» Peripheral blood cell counts
(monitor for the occurrence of myelotoxicity in all patients receiving paclitaxel protein-bound particles; frequent monitoring of blood counts should be instituted during treatment and patients should not be retreated with subsequent cycles of paclitaxel protein-bound particles until neutrophils recover to a level greater than 1,500 cells/mm³ and platelets recover to a level greater than 100,000 cells/mm³; if severe neutropenia [less than 500 cells/mm³ for seven days or more] a dose reduction for subsequent courses of therapy is recommended)

Side/Adverse Effects

The following side/adverse effects have been selected on the basis of their potential clinical significance (possible signs and symptoms in parentheses where appropriate)—not necessarily inclusive:

Note: Paclitaxel protein-bound contains human albumin, a derivative of human blood. A theoretical risk for transmission of Creutzfeldt-Jacob Disease (CJD) is considered extremely remote.

Those indicating need for medical attention

Incidence more frequent

Anemia (pale skin; troubled breathing with exertion; unusual bleeding or bruising; unusual tiredness or weakness); ***infections including; oral candidiasis*** (sore mouth or tongue; white patches in mouth and/or on tongue); ***pneumonia*** (chest pain; cough; fever or chills; sneezing; shortness of breath; sore throat; troubled breathing; tightness in chest; wheezing); ***respiratory tract infection*** (cough; fever; sneezing; sore throat); ***neutropenia*** (black, tarry stools; chills; cough; fever; lower back or side pain; painful or difficult urination; pale skin; shortness of breath; sore throat ulcers; sores, or white spots in mouth unusual bleeding or bruising; unusual tiredness or weakness); ***sensory neuropathy*** (blurred or double vision; loss of taste)

Incidence less frequent

Bleeding; cardiovascular events, including; abnormal electrocardiogram (ECG); bradycardia (chest pain or discomfort; lightheadedness, dizziness or fainting; shortness of breath; slow or irregular heartbeat; unusual tiredness); ***cardiac arrest*** (stopping of heart; no blood pressure or pulse; unconsciousness); ***chest pain; hypertension; hypotension*** (blurred vision; confusion; dizziness, faintness, or lightheadedness when getting up from a lying or sitting position suddenly; sweating; unusual tiredness or weakness); ***pulmonary thromboembolism*** (pain in chest, groin, or legs, especially the calves; difficulty breathing; severe, sudden headache; slurred speech; sudden, unexplained shortness of breath; sudden loss of coordination; sudden, severe weakness or numbness in arm or leg; vision changes); ***pulmonary emboli*** (anxiety; chest pain; cough; fainting; fast heartbeat; sudden shortness of breath or troubled breathing; dizziness or lightheadedness); ***supraventricular tachycardia*** (fainting; fast, pounding, or irregular heartbeat or pulse; palpitations); ***thrombosis*** (tenderness, pain, swelling, warmth, skin discoloration, and prominent superficial veins over affected area); ***febrile neutropenia*** (black, tarry stools; chills; cough; fever; lower back or side pain; painful or difficult urination; pale skin; shortness of breath; sore throat; ulcers, sores, or white spots in mouth; unusual bleeding or bruising; unusual tiredness or weakness); ***hypersensitivity*** (difficulty in breathing or swallowing; fast heartbeat; shortness of breath; skin itching, rash, or redness swelling of face, throat, or tongue); ***neuropathy*** (burning, tingling, numbness or pain in the hands, arms, feet, or legs; sensation of pins and needles; stabbing pain); ***thrombocytopenia*** (black, tarry stools; bleeding gums; blood in urine or stools; pinpoint red spots on skin; unusual bleeding or bruising)

Incidence rare

Cerebrovascular attacks (stroke) (confusion; difficulty in speaking; slow speech; inability to speak; inability to move arms, legs, or facial muscles; double vision; headache); ***interstitial pneumonia*** (cough; difficult breathing; fever; shortness of breath); ***lung fibrosis*** (shortness of breath; chest pain or tightness); ***pneumothorax*** (sudden onset of severe breathing; difficulty severe pain in chest); ***transient ischemic attack*** (confusion; numbness or tingling in face, arms or legs; trouble speaking, thinking or walking; headache)

Those indicating need for medical attention only if they continue or are bothersome

Incidence more frequent

Alopecia (loss of hair); ***arthralgia/myalgia*** (pain in joints, muscle pain or stiffness difficulty in moving); ***asthenia*** (lack or loss of strength); ***cough; diarrhea; dyspnea*** (shortness of breath difficult or labored breathing tightness in chest wheezing); ***edema*** (swelling); ***mucositis*** (cracked lips; diarrhea; difficulty in swallowing; sores, ulcers, or white spots on lips, tongue, or inside mouth); ***nausea; vomiting***

Incidence less frequent

Injection site reaction (bleeding, blistering, burning, coldness, discoloration of skin, feeling of pressure, hives, infection, inflammation, itching, lumps, numbness, pain, rash, redness, scarring, soreness, stinging, swelling, tenderness, tingling, ulceration, or warmth at site of injection)

Incidence rare

Nail changes

Observed during clinical trials

Ocular/visual disturbances (blurred or loss of vision; disturbed color perception; night blindness; double vision; tunnel vision; halos around lights; overbright appearance of lights)

Overdose

For more information on the management of overdose or unintentional ingestion, **contact a poison control center** (see *Poison Control Center Listing*).

Clinical effects of overdose

The following effects have been selected on the basis of their potential clinical significance (possible signs and symptoms in parentheses where appropriate)—not necessarily inclusive:

Bone marrow suppression (chest pain; chills; cough or hoarseness; fever; lower back or side pain; painful or difficult urination; shortness of breath; sores, ulcers, or white spots on lips or in mouth; swollen glands; unusual bleeding or bruising; unusual tiredness or weakness); ***mucositis*** (cracked lips; diarrhea; difficulty in swallowing; sores, ulcers, or white spots on lips, tongue, or inside mouth); ***sensory neurotoxicity*** (blurred or double vision; loss of taste)

Treatment of overdose

There is no known specific antidote to paclitaxel protein-bound particles. Treatment is generally symptomatic and supportive.

Supportive care—

Patients in whom intentional overdose is confirmed or suspected should be referred for psychiatric consultation.

Patient Consultation

As an aid to patient consultation, refer to *Advice for the Patient, Paclitaxel Protein-Bound.*

In providing consultation, consider emphasizing the following selected information (» = major clinical significance):

Before using this medication

» Conditions affecting use, especially:

Hypersensitivity to paclitaxel protein-bound

Pregnancy—Use not recommended because of mutagenic, teratogenic, and carcinogenic potential; advisability of using contraception; telling physician immediately if pregnancy is suspected

Breast-feeding—Not recommended because of risk of serious side effects

Other medical problems, especially bone marrow depression or neuropathy

Proper use of this medication

» Proper dosing

Proper storage

Precautions while using this medication

» Importance of close monitoring by the physician

» Men receiving paclitaxel protein-bound should **NOT** father a child

Caution if bone marrow depression occurs:

» Avoiding exposure to persons with infections, especially during periods of low blood counts; checking with physician immediately if fever or chills, cough or hoarseness, lower back or side pain, or painful or difficult urination occurs

» Checking with physician immediately if unusual bleeding or bruising; black, tarry stools; blood in urine or stools; or pinpoint red spots on skin occur

Caution in use of regular toothbrush, dental floss, or toothpick; physician, dentist, or nurse may suggest alternatives; checking with physician before having dental work done

Not touching eyes or inside of nose unless hands are washed immediately before

Using caution to avoid accidental cuts with use of sharp objects such as safety razor or fingernail or toenail cutters

Avoiding contact sports or other situations where bruising or injury could occur

Side/adverse effects

Signs of potential side effects, especially anemia, bleeding, cardiovascular events, including abnormal electrocardiogram (ECG), bradycardia, cardiac arrest, chest pain, hypertension, hypotension, pulmonary thromboembolism, pulmonary emboli, supraventricular tachycardia, thrombosis; cerebrovascular attacks (stroke), febrile neutropenia, hypersensitivity, infections including oral candidiasis, pneumonia, respiratory tract infection, or neutropenia; interstitial pneumonia, lung fibrosis, neuropathy, pneumothorax, thrombocytopenia, or transient ischemic attack

General Dosing Information

Patients receiving paclitaxel protein-bound particles should be under the supervision of a physician experienced in cancer chemotherapy. Appropriate management of complications is possible only when adequate diagnostic and treatment facilities are readily available.

To avoid errors, read the entire preparation instructions prior to reconstitution.

Premedication to prevent hypersensitivity reactions are not required prior to the administration of paclitaxel protein-bound particles.

Limiting the infusion of paclitaxel protein-bound particles to 30 minutes, reduces the likelihood of infusion-related reactions.

Specialized DEHP-free solution containers or administration sets are not necessary to prepare or administer paclitaxel protein-bound particles.

Use of an in-line filter is not recommended.

Visually inspect for particulate matter and discoloration prior to administration.

Safety considerations for handling this medication

There is limited but increasing evidence and concern that personnel involved in preparation and administration of parenteral antineoplastics may be at some risk because of the potential mutagenicity, teratogenicity, and/or carcinogenicity of these agents, although the actual risk is unknown. USP advisory panels recommend cautious handling both in preparation and disposal of antineoplastic agents. Precautions that have been suggested include:

- Use of a biological containment cabinet during reconstitution and dilution of parenteral medications and wearing of disposable surgical gloves and masks.
- Use of proper technique to prevent contamination of the medication, work area, and operator during transfer between containers (including proper training of personnel in this technique).
- Cautious and proper disposal of needles, syringes, vials, ampuls, and unused medication.

A number of medical centers have developed detailed guidelines for handling of antineoplastic agents.

Parenteral Dosage Forms

PACLITAXEL PROTEIN-BOUND FOR INJECTION

Usual adult dose

Breast carcinoma—

Intravenous, 260 mg/m^2 administered over 30 minutes every 3 weeks.

Note: For patients with severe neutropenia (neutrophil <500 cells/mm^3 for a week or longer) or severe neuropathy: Dosage should be

220 mg/m² for subsequent courses. For recurrences of severe neutropenia or severe sensory neuropathy additional reductions to 180 mg/m².

For grade 3 neuropathy: Hold treatment until resolution to grade 1 or 2 and reduce the dose for all subsequent courses.

For patients with hepatic impairment: The dose for patients with bilirubin greater than 1.5 mg/dL is not known.

Usual pediatric dose
Safety and efficacy have not been established.

Usual geriatric dose
See *Usual adult dose.*

Strength(s) usually available
U.S.—

5 mg per mL vial (single-use vials) (Rx) [*Abraxane* (human albumin)].

Packaging and storage
Store between 20 and 25 °C (68 and 77 °F), in original carton to protect from light.

Preparation of dosage form
Paclitaxel protein-bound particle concentrate for injection must be diluted before administration.

- Aseptically, reconstitute each vial by slowly injecting 20 mL of 0.9% Sodium Chloride Injection, USP onto the inside wall of the vial over a minimum of one minute. DO NOT INJECT sodium chloride directly on to the lyophilized cake. This will cause foaming.
- After the injection is complete, allow the vial to sit for a minimum of 5 minutes to ensure proper wetting of the lyophilized cake.
- Gently swirl and/or invert the vial slowly for 2 minutes or until the cake has completely dissolved.
- If foaming or clumping occurs, let sit for at least 15 minutes until foam resides.
- Visually inspect for particulate matter and discoloration prior to administration. The reconstituted solution should be milky and homogenous without visible particles. If particulate matter or settling exist, gently invert the vial to ensure complete resuspension prior to use. However, **discard** the reconstituted suspension if particulates are observed.
- Calculate the exact total dosing volume of 5 mg/mL suspension required.
- Inject the appropriate amount of reconstituted solution into an empty, sterile, polyvinyl chloride (PVC) type IV bag.

Stability
Unopened vials of paclitaxel protein-bound particles are stable until the date indicated on the package when stored between 20 and 25 °C (68 and 77 °F), in the original package. Reconstituted solutions should be used immediately, but may be placed back in the original carton and refrigerated at 2 to 8 °C (36 to 46 °F) for a maximum of 8 hours if necessary.
Neither freezing nor refrigeration adversely affect the stability.
The suspension for infusion prepared as recommended in an infusion bag is stable at ambient temperature and lighting conditions for up to 8 hours.

Auxiliary labeling
- Caution: Chemotherapy. Handle and dispose of properly.

Caution
Paclitaxel protein-bound particles is a cytotoxic anticancer drug and requires caution when handling. The use of gloves is recommended.

Note
If paclitaxel solution contacts the skin, the skin should be washed immediately and thoroughly with soap and water. If paclitaxel contacts mucous membranes, thorough flushing with water is recommended.

Developed: 10/24/2005

PADIMATE O—See *Sunscreen Agents (Topical)*

PALIFERMIN Systemic†

VA CLASSIFICATION (Primary): AN700

Commonly used brand name(s): *Kepivance*.

Note: For a listing of dosage forms and brand names by country availability, see *Dosage Forms* section(s).

†Not commercially available in Canada.

Category
Antineoplastic adjunct; cytoprotective agent.

Indications
Note: Bracketed information in the *Indications* section refers to uses that are not included in U.S. product labeling.

Accepted
Mucositis, myelotoxic therapy induced—Palifermin is indicated to decrease the incidence and duration of severe oral mucositis in patients with hematologic malignancies receiving myelotoxic therapy requiring hematopoietic stem cell support.

Unaccepted
The safety and efficacy of palifermin have not been established in patients with nonhematologic malignancies.

Pharmacology/Pharmacokinetics

Physicochemical characteristics
Source—Palifermin is a human keratinocyte growth factor (KGF) produced by recombinant DNA technology in *Escherichia coli (E. Coli).*
Molecular weight—Palifermin: 16.3 kilodalton.
Solubility—Water soluble.
pH (reconstituted solution)—6.5

Mechanism of action/Effect
Keratinocyte growth factor (KGF) is an endogenous protein that binds to the KGF receptor, which has been reported to result in proliferation, differentiation, and migration of epithelial cells. The KGF receptor has been reported to be present on epithelial cells found in the tongue, buccal mucosa, esophagus, stomach, intestine, salivary gland, lung, liver, pancreas, kidney, bladder, mammary gland, skin (hair follicles and sebaceous gland), and the lens of the eye. The KGF receptor has not been found on cells of the hematopoietic lineage. Endogenous KGF receptor is produced by mesenchymal cells and is upregulated in response to epithelial tissue injury.

Distribution
Volume of distribution (Vol_D)—Steady state: 2 fold higher in cancer patients compared with healthy controls following a single 60 mcg/kg dose of palifermin.

Half-life
Elimination—4.5 hours (range 3.3 to 5.7 hours); similar between healthy subjects and cancer patients.

Elimination
Clearance—2 to 4 times higher in cancer patients compared with healthy subjects.

Precautions to Consider

Carcinogenicity
The carcinogenic potential of palifermin has not been evaluated in long-term animal studies.

Mutagenicity
No clastogenic or mutagenic potential was observed in the Ames or mammalian chromosomal aberration assays; however, such studies are generally not informative for biological products.

Pregnancy/Reproduction
Fertility—Studies done in male and female rats given daily intravenous doses up to 100 mcg/kg/day prior to and during mating revealed no effects on reproductive performance, fertility, and sperm assessment. Systemic toxicity, decreased epididymal sperm counts, and increased post-implantation loss were observed at doses ≥ 300 mcg/kg/day. Increased pre-implantation loss and a decreased fertility index were observed at palifermin doses of 1000 mcg/kg/day.

Pregnancy—Adequate and well controlled studies in pregnant women have not been done. Palifermin should be used during pregnancy only if the potential benefit to the mother justifies the potential risk to the fetus.

Studies in rabbits given doses 2.5 times the human dose and rats given 8 times the human dose have shown palifermin to be embryotoxic. Pregnant rabbits given IV doses of palifermin ≥ 150 mcg/kg/day from days 6 to 18 of gestation increased post-implantation loss and decreased fetal body weights. Treatment with these doses was also associated with maternal toxicity. No evidence of developmental toxicity was observed at doses up to 60 mcg/kg/day. Pregnant rats given IV doses of palifermin ≥ 500 mcg/kg/day from days 6 to 17 or 19 of gestation, increased post-implantation loss, decreased fetal body weights and/or increased skeletal variations. Treatment with these doses was also associated with maternal toxicity. No evidence of developmental toxicity was observed at doses up to 300 mcg/kg/day.

FDA Pregnancy Category C

Breast-feeding

It is not known whether palifermin is distributed in human milk. Because many drugs are distributed in human milk, caution should be exercised when palifermin is administered to a nursing woman.

Pediatrics

Safety and effectiveness of palifermin in pediatric patients have not been established.

Geriatrics

No information is available on the relationship of age to the effects of palifermin in geriatric patients.

Pharmacogenetics

No gender-related differences were observed in the pharmacokinetics of palifermin at doses ≤ 60 mcg/kg.

Drug interactions and/or related problems

The following drug interactions and/or related problems have been selected on the basis of their potential clinical significance (possible mechanism in parentheses where appropriate)—not necessarily inclusive (» = major clinical significance):

Note: Combinations containing any of the following medications, depending on the amount present, may also interact with this medication.

» Chemotherapy, myelotoxic
(should not be administered within 24 hours before, during infusion of, or within 24 hours after administration of myelotoxic chemotherapy; may increase severity and duration of oral mucositis)

Heparin
(palifermin has been shown to bind to heparin in vitro; if heparin is used to maintain an IV line, saline should be used to rinse the line prior to and after palifermin administration)

Laboratory value alterations

The following have been selected on the basis of their potential clinical significance (possible effect in parentheses where appropriate)—not necessarily inclusive (» = major clinical significance).

With physiology/laboratory test values

Amylase, serum
Lipase, serum
Protein, urine
(levels may increase)

Medical considerations/Contraindications

The medical considerations/contraindications included have been selected on the basis of their potential clinical significance (reasons given in parentheses where appropriate)—not necessarily inclusive (» = major clinical significance).

Except under special circumstances, this medication should not be used when the following medical problem exists:

» Hypersensitivity to *E. coli*-derived proteins, palifermin or any of its components

Risk-benefit should be considered when the following medical problems exist:

Non-hematologic malignancies
(palifermin has been shown to enhance the growth of human epithelial tumor cell lines in vitro and to increase the rate of tumor cell line growth in a human carcinoma xenograft)

Side/Adverse Effects

The following side/adverse effects have been selected on the basis of their potential clinical significance (possible signs and symptoms in parentheses where appropriate)—not necessarily inclusive:

Those indicating need for medical attention

Incidence rare

Skin rash, severe

Those indicating need for medical attention only if they continue or are bothersome

Incidence more frequent

Arthralgia (pain in joints; muscle pain or stiffness; difficulty in moving); ***dysesthesias including; hyperesthesia*** (increased sensitivity to pain; increased sensitivity to touch; tingling in the hands and feet); ***hypoesthesia*** (burning, crawling, itching, numbness, prickling, "pins and needles", or tingling feelings); ***paresthesias*** (burning, crawling, itching, numbness, prickling, "pins and needles", or tingling feelings); ***elevated serum lipase; elevated serum amylase; edema*** (swelling); ***erythema*** (flushing, redness of skin; unusually warm skin); ***fever; hypertension*** (blurred vision; dizziness; nervousness; headache; pounding in the ears; slow or fast heartbeat); ***pain; pruritus*** (itching skin); ***rash; taste altered*** (change in taste; bad unusual or unpleasant (after) taste); ***tongue discoloration; tongue thickening***

Incidence unknown

Immunogenicity (body produces substance that can bind to drug making it less effective or cause side effects)

Overdose

For more information on the management of overdose or unintentional ingestion, **contact a poison control center** (see *Poison Control Center Listing*).

Clinical effects of overdose

Five of 14 patients receiving six doses of 80 mcg/kg/day, administered intravenously over two weeks (three doses preceding and three doses following myeloablative chemotherapy/TBI) experienced severe or serious adverse events. These events were consistent with those observed at the recommended dose but generally more severe.

Treatment of overdose

There is no known specific antidote to palifermin. Treatment is generally symptomatic and supportive.

Supportive care—
Patients in whom intentional overdose is confirmed or suspected should be referred for psychiatric consultation.

Patient Consultation

As an aid to patient consultation, refer to *Advice for the Patient, Palifermin (Systemic)*.

In providing consultation, consider emphasizing the following selected information (» = major clinical significance):

Before using this medication

» Conditions affecting use, especially:
Hypersensitivity to *E. coli*-derived proteins, palifermin or any of its components
Pregnancy—Should be used during pregnancy only if the potential benefit to the mother justifies the potential risk to the fetus
Breast-feeding—Because many drugs are distributed in human milk, caution should be exercised when palifermin is administered to a nursing woman
Use in children—Safety and effectiveness have not been established.
Other medications, especially myelotoxic chemotherapy

Proper use of this medication

» The importance of reporting any adverse effects to your doctor
» Proper dosing
» Proper storage

Precautions while using this medication

» Informing patients of the evidence of tumor growth and cell stimulation in cell culture and in animal models of non-hematopoietic human tumors.

Side/adverse effects

Signs of potential side effects, especially severe skin rash

General Dosing Information

Palifermin should be administered by intravenous bolus infection.

Not using palifermin beyond the date stamped on the vial.

Parenteral Dosage Forms

Note: Bracketed information in the *Indications* section refers to uses that are not included in U.S. product labeling.

PALIFERMIN FOR INJECTION

Usual adult dose

Mucositis, myelotoxic therapy induced—
Intravenous bolus injection, 60 mg/kg/day, 3 consecutive days prior to and 3 consecutive days after myelotoxic therapy for a total of 6 doses.

Note: For pre-myelotoxic therapy: The first 3 doses should be administered prior to myelotoxic therapy, with the third dose 24 to 48 hours before myelotoxic therapy.

For post-myelotoxic therapy: The last 3 doses should be administered post-myelotic therapy; the first of these doses should be administered after, but on the same day of hematopoietic stem cell infusion and, at least 4 days after the most recent administration of palifermin.

Usual pediatric dose

Safety and effectiveness of palifermin in pediatric patients have not been established.

Usual geriatric dose

See *Usual adult dose.*

Strength(s) usually available

U.S.—

6.25 mg of palifermin (Rx) [*Kepivance* (L-histidine; mannitol; polysorbate; sucrose)].

Packaging and storage

Store between 2 and 8 °C (36 and 46 °F), in its container. Protect from light.

Preparation of dosage form

Palifermin lyophilized powder should be aseptically reconstituted with 1.2 mL Sterile Water for Injection USP to yield a final concentration of 5 mg/mL. The contents should be swirled gently during dissolution. **Do not shake or vigorously agitate the vial;** dissolution takes less than 3 minutes. Visually inspect the solution for discoloration and particular matter before administration. The reconstitution solution should be clear and colorless. If discoloration or particulate matter is observed, palifermin should not be used. **Do not filter** the reconstituted solution during preparation or administration.

The reconstituted solution contains no preservatives and is intended for single use only.

Stability

Following reconstitution, it is recommended that the product be used immediately; however, it may be stored refrigerated in its carton at 2 and 8 °C (36 and 46 °F) for up to 24 hours. If refrigerated, palifermin may be allowed to reach room temperature for a maximum of 1 hour but should be protected from light. Discard any left at room temperature for more that 1 hour.

Do not freeze the reconstituted solution.

Incompatibilities

Palifermin has been shown to bind to heparin *in vitro* . If heparin is used to maintain an IV line, saline should be used to rinse the line prior to and after palifermin administration.

Auxiliary labeling

- Do not shake.
- Protect from light.

Developed: 05/10/2005

PALIVIZUMAB Systemic

VA CLASSIFICATION (Primary): IM402

Commonly used brand name(s): *Synagis.*

Note: For a listing of dosage forms and brand names by country availability, see *Dosage Forms* section(s).

Category

Immunizing agent (passive).

Indications

Accepted

Respiratory syncytial virus infection (prophylaxis)—Palivizumab is indicated for the prevention of serious lower respiratory tract infection caused by respiratory syncytial virus (RSV) in pediatric patients at high risk of RSV disease. Safety and efficacy were established in infants and children with bronchopulmonary dysplasia (BPD), infants with a history of premature birth (gestation ≤ 35 weeks), and children with hemodynamically significant congenital heart disease [CHD].

Note: The safety and efficacy of palivizumab have not been demonstrated for treatment of established RSV disease.

Pharmacology/Pharmacokinetics

Physicochemical characteristics

Source—Palivizumab is a humanized monoclonal antibody (IgG1k) produced by recombinant DNA technology, directed to an epitope in the A antigenic site of the F protein of respiratory syncytial virus (RSV). It is a composite of 95% human and 5% murine antibody sequences. Palivizumab is supplied as a sterile lyophilized product.

Molecular weight—Approximately 148,000 Daltons.

Mechanism of action/Effect

Palivizumab exhibits neutralizing and fusion-inhibitory activity against RSV. These activities inhibit RSV replication in laboratory experiments. Although resistant RSV strains may be isolated in laboratory studies, a panel of 57 clinical RSV isolates were all neutralized by palivizumab.

Palivizumab serum concentrations of ≥ 40 mcg/mL have been shown to reduce pulmonary RSV replication in the cotton rat model of RSV infection by 100-fold.

The *in vivo* neutralizing activity of palivizumab was assessed in a randomized, placebo-controlled study of 35 pediatric patients tracheally intubated because of RSV disease. In these patients, palivizumab significantly reduced the quantity of RSV in the lower respiratory tract compared with that in control patients.

Protective effect

The safety and efficacy of palivizumab were assessed in a randomized, double blind, placebo controlled trial (IMpact-RSV Trial) of RSV disease prophylaxis among high-risk pediatric patients. This trial, conducted at 139 centers in the U.S., Canada, and the United Kingdom (U.K.), studied patients ≤ 24 months of age with bronchopulmonary dysplasia (BPD) and patients with premature birth (gestation ≤ 35 weeks) who were ≤ 6 months of age at study entry. Patients with uncorrected congenital heart disease were excluded from enrollment. In this trial, 500 patients were randomized to receive five monthly placebo injections and 1002 patients were randomized to receive five monthly injections of 15 mg per kg (mg/kg) of palivizumab. Subjects were randomized into the study for 28 days, and were followed for safety and efficacy for 150 days. Ninety-nine percent of all subjects completed the study and 93% received all five injections. The primary end point was the incidence of RSV hospitalization.

RSV hospitalization occurred among 53 of 500 (10.6%) patients in the placebo group and 48 of 1002 (4.8%) patients in the palivizumab group, a difference of 55%. The lower rate of RSV hospitalization was observed both in patients enrolled with a diagnosis of BPD and in patients enrolled with a diagnosis of prematurity without BPD. The lower rate of RSV hospitalization was observed throughout the course of the RSV season.

Among secondary end points, the incidence of intensive care unit (ICU) admission during hospitalization for RSV infection was lower among subjects receiving palivizumab (1.3%) than among those receiving placebo (3%), but there was no difference in the mean duration of ICU care. Overall, the data do not suggest that RSV illness was less severe among patients who received palivizumab and who required hospitalization due to RSV infection. Palivizumab did not alter the incidence and mean duration of hospitalization from non-RSV respiratory illness or the incidence of otitis media.

Half-life

Adults—18 days.

Children younger than 24 months of age—20 days.

Precautions to Consider

Carcinogenicity

Carcinogenicity studies have not been performed with palivizumab.

Tumorigenicity

Tumorigenicity studies have not been performed with palivizumab.

Mutagenicity

Mutagenicity studies have not been performed.

Pregnancy/Reproduction

Fertility—Reproductive toxicity studies have not been performed with palivizumab.

Pregnancy—Palivizumab is not indicated for adult usage and animal reproduction studies have not been conducted. It is also not known whether palivizumab can cause fetal harm when administered to a pregnant woman or could affect reproductive capacity.

FDA Pregnancy Category C.

Breast-feeding

Problems in humans have not been documented.

Pediatrics

Safety and efficacy have been established in infants with bronchopulmonary dysplasia (BPD), infants with a history of premature birth (gestation ≤ 35 weeks), and children with hemodynamically significant congenital heart disease [CHD].

Geriatrics

No information is available on the relationship of age to the effects of palivizumab in geriatric patients. However, palivizumab is not indicated for adult usage.

Laboratory value alterations

The following have been selected on the basis of their potential clinical significance (possible effect in parentheses where appropriate)—not necessarily inclusive (» = major clinical significance).

With physiology/laboratory test values

Aspartate aminotransferase (AST [SGOT])
(increases have been reported)

Medical considerations/Contraindications

The medical considerations/contraindications included have been selected on the basis of their potential clinical significance (reasons given in parentheses where appropriate)—not necessarily inclusive (» = major clinical significance).

Except under special circumstances, this medication should not be used when the following medical problem exists:

» Hypersensitivity to palivizumab
(palivizumab should not be used in pediatric patients with a history of severe prior reaction to palivizumab or other components of the product)

Risk-benefit should be considered when the following medical problems exist:

Coagulation disorder or
Thrombocytopenia
(as with any intramuscular injection, palivizumab should be given with caution to patients with these conditions)

Side/Adverse Effects

Note: In the combined pediatric prophylaxis studies of pediatric patients with BPD, prematurity or congenital heart failure [CHD] involving 1148 subjects receiving placebo and 1641 subjects receiving palivizumab, the proportions of subjects in the placebo and palivizumab groups who experienced any adverse effect or any serious adverse effect were similar.

Based on post-marketing experience, rare severe acute hypersensitivity reactions have been reported on initial or subsequent exposure. Very rare cases of anaphylaxis have also been reported following re-exposure. None of the hypersensitivity reactions were fatal. The relationship between these reactions and the development of antibodies to palivizumab is unknown.

Limited information from post-marketing reports suggests that, within a single RSV season, adverse events after a sixth or greater dose of palivizumab are similar in character and frequency to those after the initial five doses.

The following side/adverse effects have been selected on the basis of their potential clinical significance (possible signs and symptoms in parentheses where appropriate)—not necessarily inclusive:

Those indicating need for medical attention

Incidence more frequent

Cyanosis (bluish color of fingernails, lips, skin, palms, or nail beds)—in congenital heart disease patients; ***fever; otitis media*** (ringing or buzzing in the ears); ***skin rash; upper respiratory tract infection*** (difficulty in breathing)

Incidence less frequent or rare

Arrhythmia (dizziness, fainting, fast, slow, or irregular heartbeat)—in congenital heart disease patients; ***gastroenteritis*** (abdominal or stomach pain, diarrhea, loss of appetite, nausea, weakness); ***hernia*** (abdominal pain, lump in abdomen)

Incidence not determined—Observed during clinical practice, estimates of frequency cannot be determined

Anaphylaxis or acute hypersensitivity including: angioedema (large, hive-like swelling on face, eyelids, lips, tongue, throat, hands, legs, feet, sex organs); ***dyspnea*** (shortness of breath, difficult or labored breathing, tightness in chest wheezing); ***hypotonia*** (unusual weak feeling, loss of strength or energy, muscle pain or weakness); ***pruritus*** (itching skin); ***respiratory failure*** (blue lips, fingernails, or skin, difficult or troubled breathing, irregular, fast or slow, or shallow breathing, shortness of breath); ***unresponsiveness; urticaria*** (hives or welts, itching, redness of skin, skin rash)

Those indicating need for medical attention only if they continue or are bothersome

Less frequent or rare

Cough; diarrhea; rhinitis (stuffy nose, runny nose, sneezing); ***vomiting; wheezing***

Overdose

No data from clinical studies are available on overdosage. No toxicity was observed in rabbits administered a single intramuscular or subcutaneous injection of palivizumab at a dose of 50 mg/kg.

Patient Consultation

As an aid to patient consultation, refer to *Advice for the Patient, Palivizumab (Systemic)*.

In providing consultation, consider emphasizing the following selected information (» = major clinical significance):

Before using this medication

» Conditions affecting use, especially:
Other medical problems, especially hypersensitivity to palivizumab

Proper use of this medication

» Importance of contacting healthcare professional immediately if symptoms of an allergic reaction occur

» Importance of **not** shaking the vial prior to administration

» Administering intramuscular (IM) injection within 6 hours after reconstitution and discarding any unused portion

» Proper dosing
Proper storage

Side/adverse effects

Signs of potential side effects, especially cyanosis (in congenital heart disease patients), fever, otitis media, skin rash, and upper respiratory tract infection, arrhythmia (in congenital heart disease patients), gastroenteritis, or hernia

Signs of potential side effects observed during clinical practice, especially anaphylaxis or acute hypersensitivity, angioedema, dyspnea, hypotonia, pruritus, respiratory failure, unresponsiveness, or urticaria

General Dosing Information

In post-marketing experience, rare severe acute hypersensitivity reactions have been reported on initial or subsequent exposure. Very rare cases of anaphylaxis have also been reported following re-exposure. If a severe hypersensitivity reaction occurs, palivizumab therapy should be permanently discontinued. If milder hypersensitivity reactions occur, caution should be used on readministration of palivizumab

The recommended dose of palivizumab is 15 mg/kg of body weight. Palivizumab should be administered intramuscularly, preferably in the anterolateral aspect of the thigh. The gluteal muscle should not be used routinely as an injection site because of the risk of damage to the sciatic nerve. Injection volumes over 1 mL should be given as a divided dose.

Patients, including those who develop a respiratory syncytial virus (RSV) infection, should receive monthly doses throughout the RSV season. The first dose should be administered prior to commencement of the RSV season. In the northern hemisphere, the RSV season typically commences in November and lasts through April, but it may begin earlier or persist later in certain communities.

Sterile disposable syringes and needles should be used to prevent the transmission of hepatitis viruses or other infectious agents from one person to another. Syringes and needles should not be reused

Palivizumab serum levels are decreased after cardio-pulmonary bypass. Patients undergoing cardio-pulmonary bypass should receive a dose of palivizumab as soon as possible after the cardio-pulmonary bypass procedure, even if sooner than a month from the previous dose. Thereafter, doses should be administered monthly.

For treatment of adverse effects

Recommended treatment consists of the following:

- **For severe hypersensitivity or anaphylactic reaction—Administering epinephrine and providing supportive care as required.**

Parenteral Dosage Forms

PALIVIZUMAB INJECTION

Usual adult and adolescent dose

Use is not recommended.

Usual pediatric dose

Respiratory syncytial virus infection (prophylaxis)—
Intramuscular, 15 mg per kg of body weight per month.

Strength(s) usually available

U.S.—

50 mg palivizumab per vial (Rx) [*Synagis* (preservative-free; 47 mM histidine; 3 mM glycine; 5.6% mannitol)].

100 mg palivizumab per vial (Rx) [*Synagis* (preservative-free; 47 mM histidine; 3 mM glycine; 5.6% mannitol)].

Canada—

50 mg palivizumab per vial (Rx) [*Synagis*].

100 mg palivizumab per vial (Rx) [*Synagis*].

Packaging and storage

Store between 2 and 8 °C (36 and 46 °F), in its original container, unless otherwise specified by manufacturer.

Preparation of dosage form

To reconstitute, remove the tab portion of the vial cap and clean the rubber stopper with 70% ethanol or equivalent.

Slowly add 1 mL of sterile water for injection to a 100 mg vial. The vial should be gently swirled for 30 seconds to avoid foaming. **Do not shake vial.**

Reconstituted palivizumab should stand at room temperature for a minimum of 20 minutes until the solution clarifies.

Reconstituted palivizumab should be inspected visually for particulate matter and discoloration. Solution should be discarded if not clear or slightly opalescent

Reconstituted palivizumab does not contain preservative and should be administered within 6 hours of reconstitution.

Auxiliary labeling

- For intramuscular (IM) use only
- For single dose only. Discard unused drug.
- Do not shake
- Do not freeze.

Revised: 04/22/2004
Developed: 08/11/1998

PALONOSETRON Systemic†

VA CLASSIFICATION (Primary): GA605

Commonly used brand name(s): *Aloxi*.

Note: For a listing of dosage forms and brand names by country availability, see *Dosage Forms* section(s).

†Not commercially available in Canada.

Category

Antiemetic.

Indications

Note: Bracketed information in the *Indications* section refers to uses that are not included in U.S. product labeling.

Accepted

Nausea and vomiting, acute, cancer chemotherapy-induced (prophylaxis)—Palonosetron is indicated for the prevention of acute nausea and vomiting associated with initial and repeat courses of moderately and highly emetogenic cancer chemotherapy.

Nausea and vomiting, delayed, cancer chemotherapy-induced (prophylaxis)—Palonosetron is indicated for the prevention of delayed nausea and vomiting associated with initial and repeat courses of moderately emetogenic cancer chemotherapy.

Pharmacology/Pharmacokinetics

Physicochemical characteristics

Chemical Group—Selective serotonin 5-HT_3 receptor antagonist

Molecular weight—332.87 (palonosetron hydrochloride).

Solubility—

Freely soluble in water.
Soluble in propylene glycol.
Slightly soluble in ethanol and 2-propanol.

pH—4.5 to 5.5

Mechanism of action/Effect

Palonosetron is a selective 5-HT_3 receptor antagonist with a strong binding affinity for this receptor and little or no affinity for other receptors. 5-HT_3 receptors are located on the nerve terminals of the vagus in the periphery and centrally in the chemoreceptor trigger zone of the area postrema. It is thought that chemotherapeutic agents produce nausea and vomiting by releasing serotonin from the enterochromaffin cells of the small intestine and that the released serotonin then activates 5-HT_3 receptors located on vagal afferents to initiate the vomiting reflex.

Absorption

Mean AUC, IV, single dose, 3 mcg/kg: 35.8 ± 20.9 ng hr per mL

Distribution

Volume of Distribution (Vol_D) 5.8 to 10.8 L/kg

Protein binding

62%; bound to plasma proteins

Biotransformation

50% metabolized to form two primary metabolites: N-oxide-palonosetron and 6-S-hydroxy-palonosetron; 5-HT_3 receptor antagonist activity of metabolites is less than 1% of palonosetron

CYP2D6 and to a lesser extent, CYP3A and CYP1A2 are involved in the metabolism of palonosetron suggested by in vitro metabolism studies; clinical pharmacokinetic parameters were not significantly different between poor and extensive metabolizers of CYP2D6 substrates

Half-life

Elimination, mean: approximately 40 hours

Peak plasma concentration:

IV, single dose, 3 mcg/kg: 5.6 ± 5.5 nanograms per mL

Elimination

Renal (IV single dose, 10 mcg/kg); approximately 80% recovered in the urine within 144 hours; 40% unchanged palonosetron

Renal clearance: 66.5 ± 18.2 mL per hr per kg

Total body clearance: 160 ± 35 mL per hr per kg

In dialysis: unlikely to be of benefit due to large volume of distribution

Precautions to Consider

Cross-sensitivity and/or related problems

Patients sensitive to other selective 5-HT_3 receptor antagonists may also be sensitive to palonosetron.

Carcinogenicity

In a 104–week carcinogenicity study in rats, male and female rats were treated with oral doses of 15, 30, and 60 mg per kg per day and 15, 45, and 90 mg per kg per day, respectively. The highest doses produced a systemic exposure to palonosetron of 137 and 308 times the recommended dose. Treatment with palonosetron produced increased incidences of adrenal benign pheochromocytoma and combined benign and malignant adenoma and carcinoma and pituitary adenoma in male rats. In female rats, it produced hepatocellular adenoma and carcinoma and increased the incidence of thyroid C-cell adenoma and combined adenoma and carcinoma.

Tumorigenicity

In a 104–week carcinogenicity study in mice, animals were treated with oral doses of palonosetron at 10, 30, and 60 mg per kg per day. Treatment with palonosetron was not tumorigenic.

Mutagenicity

Palonosetron was not genotoxic in the Ames test, the Chinese hamster ovarian cell forward mutation test, the ex vivo hepatocyte unscheduled DNA synthesis (UDS) test or the mouse micronucleus test. It was, however, positive for clastogenic effects in the Chinese hamster ovarian cell chromosomal aberration test.

Pregnancy/Reproduction

Fertility—No effect on fertility was seen in studies in male and female rats and rabbits.

Pregnancy—Adequate and well controlled studies in humans have not been done. Studies in animals have not shown that palonosetron causes adverse effects.

FDA Pregnancy Category B

Labor and delivery—Adequate and well controlled studies in humans have not been done.

Breast-feeding

It is not known if palonosetron is distributed in breast milk. Due to the potential for serious adverse reactions in nursing infants, a decision should be made whether to discontinue nursing or discontinue the drug.

Pediatrics

Safety and effectiveness in patients below the age of 18 years have not been established.

Geriatrics

Appropriate studies performed to date have not demonstrated geriatrics-specific problems that would limit the usefulness of palonosetron in the elderly. However, greater sensitivity in some older individuals cannot be ruled out. No dose adjustments or special monitoring are required for geriatric patients.

Pharmacogenetics

Total body clearance was 25% higher in Japanese subjects compared to caucasians, however, no dose adjustment is required.

Drug interactions and/or related problems

The following drug interactions and/or related problems have been selected on the basis of their potential clinical significance (possible mechanism in parentheses where appropriate)—not necessarily inclusive (» = major clinical significance):

Note: Combinations containing any of the following medications, depending on the amount present, may also interact with this medication.

Anthracycline, cumulative high dose or
Antiarrhythmic drugs or

Diuretics
(palonosetron should be used with caution in patients taking these medicines because they may lead to the prolongation of cardiac conduction times, especially the QTc interval)

Laboratory value alterations

The following have been selected on the basis of their potential clinical significance (possible effect in parentheses where appropriate)—not necessarily inclusive (» = major clinical significance).

With physiology/laboratory test values
Alanine aminotransferase (ALT [SGPT]), serum or
Aspartate aminotransferase (AST [SGOT]) or
Bilirubin
(may exhibit transient asymptomatic increases)

Medical considerations/Contraindications

The medical considerations/contraindications included have been selected on the basis of their potential clinical significance (reasons given in parentheses where appropriate)—not necessarily inclusive (» = major clinical significance).

Except under special circumstances, this medication should not be used when the following medical problem exists:

» Hypersensitivity to palonosetron or any of its components, or other selective 5-HT_3 receptor antagonists.

Risk-benefit should be considered when the following medical problems exist:

» Cardiac conduction intervals prolonged or
» QTc interval prolonged, have or may develop
Electrolyte abnormalities or
Hypokalemia or
Hypomagnesemia
(palonosetron should be administered with caution in these patients)

Renal impairment, severe
(may increase total systemic exposure by up to 28%; dosage adjustment is not necessary)

Side/Adverse Effects

The following side/adverse effects have been selected on the basis of their potential clinical significance (possible signs and symptoms in parentheses where appropriate)—not necessarily inclusive:

Those indicating need for medical attention only if they continue or are bothersome

Incidence more frequent

Constipation (difficulty having a bowel movement (stool)); ***headache***

Incidence less frequent

Anxiety (fear; nervousness); ***bradycardia*** (chest pain or discomfort; lightheadedness; dizziness; fainting; shortness of breath; slow or irregular heartbeat; unusual tiredness); ***diarrhea; dizziness; hyperkalemia*** (abdominal pain; confusion; irregular heartbeat; nausea or vomiting; nervousness; numbness or tingling in hands, feet, or lips; shortness of breath; difficult breathing; weakness or heaviness of legs); ***hypotension*** (blurred vision; confusion; dizziness, faintness, or lightheadedness when getting up from a lying or sitting position suddenly; sweating; unusual tiredness or weakness); ***tachycardia*** (fast, pounding, or irregular heartbeat or pulse); ***weakness***

Incidence rare

Abdominal pain; allergic dermatitis (raised red swellings on the skin, the buttocks, legs or ankles; large, flat, blue or purplish patches in the skin; painful knees and ankles; fever; stomach pain; bloody or black, tarry stools; blood in urine); ***amblyopia*** (blurred vision; change in vision; impaired vision); ***anorexia*** (loss of appetite; weight loss); ***appetite decrease; arthralgia*** (joint pain); ***dry mouth; dyspepsia*** (acid or sour stomach; belching; heartburn; indigestion; stomach discomfort upset or pain); ***electrolyte fluctuations*** (confusion; irregular heartbeat; muscle cramps or pain; numbness, tingling, pain, or weakness in hands or feet; seizures; trembling; unusual tiredness or weakness; weakness and heaviness of legs); ***euphoric mood*** (happy); ***extrasystoles*** (extra heartbeats); ***eye irritation*** (red, sore eyes); ***fatigue*** (tired); ***fever; flatulence*** (bloated full feeling; excess air or gas in stomach or intestines; passing gas); ***flu-like syndrome*** (chills; cough; diarrhea; fever; general feeling of discomfort or illness; headache; joint pain; loss of appetite; muscle aches and pains; nausea; runny nose; shivering; sore throat; sweating; trouble sleeping; unusual tiredness or weakness; vomiting); ***glycosuria*** (sugar in the urine); ***hiccups; hot flash*** (feeling of warmth; redness of the face, neck, arms and occasionally, upper chest; sudden sweating); ***hyperglycemia*** (abdominal pain; blurred vision; dry mouth; fatigue; flushed, dry skin; fruit-like breath odor; increased hunger; increased thirst; increased urination; nausea; sweating; troubled breathing; unexplained weight loss; vomiting); ***hypersomnia*** (unusually deep sleep; unusually long duration of sleep); ***hypertension*** (blurred vision; dizziness; nervousness; headache; pounding in the ears; slow or fast heartbeat); ***insomnia*** (excessive sleeping); ***metabolic acidosis*** (confusion; drowsiness; muscle tremors; nausea rapid; deep breathing; restlessness; stomach cramps; unusual tiredness; weakness); ***motion sickness*** (nausea); ***myocardial ischemia*** (chest pain or discomfort; nausea; pain or discomfort in arms, jaw, back or neck; shortness of breath; sweating; vomiting); ***paresthesia*** (burning, crawling, itching, numbness, prickling, "pins and needles", or tingling feelings); ***QT prolongation*** (irregular heartbeat; recurrent fainting); ***rash; sinus arrhythmia*** (fast or irregular heartbeat); ***sinus tachycardia*** (fast or irregular heartbeat); ***somnolence*** (sleepiness or unusual drowsiness); ***supraventricular extrasystoles*** (rapid or irregular heartbeat); ***tinnitus*** (continuing ringing or buzzing; unexplained noise in ears; hearing loss); ***urinary retention*** (decrease in urine volume; decrease in frequency of urination; difficulty in passing urine; [dribbling] painful urination); ***vein discoloration; vein distention*** (swelling or protruding veins)

Overdose

For more information on the management of overdose or unintentional ingestion, **contact a poison control center** (see *Poison Control Center Listing*).

Clinical effects of overdose

The following effects have been selected on the basis of their potential clinical significance (possible signs and symptoms in parentheses where appropriate)—not necessarily inclusive:

Collapse; convulsions (seizures); ***cyanosis*** (bluish color of fingernails, lips, skin, palms, or nail beds); ***gasping*** (gasping to breathe); ***pallor*** (paleness of skin)

Treatment of overdose

To enhance elimination—
Dialysis is unlikely to be an effective treatment

Specific treatment—
There is no known antidote to palonosetron.

Supportive care—
Treatment should be symptomatic and supportive.
Patients in whom intentional overdose is confirmed or suspected should be referred for psychiatric consultation.

Patient Consultation

As an aid to patient consultation, refer to *Advice for the Patient, Palonosetron (Parenteral)*.

In providing consultation, consider emphasizing the following selected information (» = major clinical significance):

Before using this medication

» Conditions affecting use, especially:
Hypersensitivity to palonosetron or any of its components, or other selective 5-HT_3 receptor antagonists.
Pregnancy—Adequate and well controlled studies in humans have not been done. Studies in animals have not shown that palonosetron causes adverse effects.
FDA Pregnancy Category B
Breast-feeding—It is not known if palonosetron is distributed in breast milk. Due to the potential for serious adverse reactions in nursing infants, a decision should be made whether to discontinue nursing or discontinue the drug.
Use in children—Safety and effectiveness in patients below the age of 18 years have not been established.
Use in the elderly—Appropriate studies performed to date have not demonstrated geriatrics-specific problems that would limit the usefulness of palonosetron in the elderly. However, greater sensitivity in some older individuals cannot be ruled out.
Other medical problems, especially kidney problems and irregular heartbeats.

Proper use of this medication

» Proper dosing
» Proper storage

General Dosing Information

For parenteral dosing forms:

Palonosetron should be infused over 30 seconds.

The infusion line should be flushed with normal saline before and after administration.

This product should be inspected visually for particulate matter and discoloration before administration whenever possible.

Parenteral Dosage Forms

Note: Bracketed information in the *Indications* section refers to uses that are not included in U.S. *product* labeling.

PALONOSETRON HYDROCHLORIDE INJECTION

Usual adult dose

Antiemetic—

Intravenous, direct (over 30 seconds), 0.25 mg (base) as a single dose approximately 30 minutes before the start of chemotherapy.

Usual adult prescribing limits

Repeated dosing of palonosetron within a seven day interval is not recommended.

Usual pediatric dose

Safety and efficacy have not been established.

Usual geriatric dose

See *Usual adult dose.*

Usual geriatric prescribing limits

See *Usual adult prescribing limits.*

Strength(s) usually available

U.S.—

0.25 mg (free base) in 5 mL (Rx) [*Aloxi* (mannitol; disodium edetate; citrate; water)].

Packaging and storage

Store between 20 and 25 °C (68 and 77 °F), in a tight container (excursions permitted to 15–30 °C (59 and 86 °F)). Protect from freezing. Protect from light.

Developed: 05/24/2004

PAMIDRONATE Systemic

VA CLASSIFICATION (Primary/Secondary): HS302/HS303

Commonly used brand name(s): *Aredia.*

Another commonly used name is APD.

Note: For a listing of dosage forms and brand names by country availability, see *Dosage Forms* section(s).

Category

Bone resorption inhibitor; antihypercalcemic.

Indications

Note: Bracketed information in the *Indications* section refers to uses that are not included in the U.S. product labeling.

Accepted

Hypercalcemia, associated with neoplasms (treatment)—Pamidronate disodium is indicated for the treatment of hypercalcemia of malignancy, with or without bone metastases, that is inadequately managed by oral hydration alone. It is used with saline hydration and may be used with loop diuretics.

Metastases, osteolytic (treatment adjunct)—Pamidronate is used in the treatment of osteolytic bone metastases sometimes found with breast cancer and myeloma.

Paget's disease of bone (treatment)—Pamidronate is indicated in the treatment of symptomatic Paget's disease (osteitis deformans), characterized by abnormal and accelerated bone metabolism in one or more bones. Signs and symptoms may include bone pain, deformity, and/or fractures; increased concentrations of serum alkaline phosphatase and/or urinary hydroxyproline; neurologic disorders associated with skull lesions and spinal deformities; and elevated cardiac output and other vascular disorders associated with increased vascularity of bones.

[Osteogenesis imperfecta (treatment)][1]—Pamidronate disodium is indicated in the treatment of osteogenesis imperfecta in pediatric patients.

Unaccepted

The safety and efficacy of pamidronate disodium in the treatment of hypercalcemia associated with hyperparathyroidism or other non tumor-related conditions have not been established.

[1]Not included in Canadian product labeling.

Pharmacology/Pharmacokinetics

Physicochemical characteristics

Chemical Group—Bisphosphate; an analog of pyrophosphate

Molecular weight—369.11.

Solubility—Soluble in water and in 2 N sodium hydroxide, sparingly soluble in 0.1 N hydrochloric acid and in 0.1 N acetic acid, and practically insoluble in organic solvents.

pH—

6.0 to 7.4 when vial is reconstituted with sterile water for injection, USP, according to the manufacturer's instructions

Approximately 8.3 (1% solution of pamidronate disodium in distilled water)

Mechanism of action/Effect

Pamidronate inhibits bone resorption and is believed to accomplish this by several mechanisms. It adsorbs onto the surface of hydroxyapatite crystals in mineralized bone matrix, thus reducing the solubility of the mineralized matrix and rendering it more resistant to osteoclastic resorption. By impairing attachment of osteoclast precursors to mineralized matrix, pamidronate blocks their transformation into mature, functioning osteoclasts.

Hypercalcemia of malignancy—Bone resorption is increased in the presence of neoplastic tissue. Pamidronate inhibits abnormal bone resorption and reduces the flow of calcium from the resorbing bone into the blood, effectively decreasing total and ionized serum calcium. When kidney function is adequate for the fluid load, hydration with saline increases urine output and the use of loop diuretics increases the rate of calcium excretion.

Paget's disease—Pamidronate reduces the rate of bone turnover, by an initial blocking of bone resorption, resulting in decreases in serum alkaline phosphatase (reflecting decreased bone formation) and decreases in urinary hydroxyproline excretion (reflecting decreased bone resorption, i.e., breakdown of collagen).

Osteolytic metastases—Osteolytic metastases result from accelerated bone resorption induced by the tumor via an activation of osteoclasts. By inhibiting bone resorption, pamidronate may reduce morbidity of bone metastases from breast cancer and myeloma.

Distribution

In cancer patients, 45 to 53% of an intravenous dose of 60 mg infused over 24 hours is adsorbed to bone preferentially in areas of high turnover.

The calculated mean ± SD body retention of pamidronate is 54 ± 16% of the dose over 120 hours based on pharmacokinetic data collected from cancer patients who had minimal or no bony involvement given an intravenous infusion of 30, 60, or 90 mg of pamidronate over 4 hours or 90 mg of pamidronate given over 24 hours. Accumulation in bone is not capacity limited and is dependent on the cumulative dose.

Protein binding

Moderate (approximately 54%); bound to human serum proteins.

Binding increases to approximately 5 mmol when exogenous 95% calcium is added to human plasma.

Biotransformation

Pamidronate is not metabolized.

Half-life

Alpha—1.6 hours.

Beta—27.2 hours.

Onset of action

Decreases in serum calcium concentrations are observed within 24 to 48 hours after pamidronate administration.

Peak serum concentration

AUC—

In patients with hepatic impairment, the mean AUC was 39.7% higher, however this increase in AUC is not considered to be clinically relevant.

In cancer patients with renal impairment ($Cr_{CL} < 30$ milliliters per minute) and at risk for bone metastases, the mean plasma AUC is doubled. Dosage adjustment does not appear to be necessary in these patients using recommended dose schedule.

Peak plasma concentration:—

Approximately 10 nmol per mL when infused intravenously at 60 mg over one hour.

Note: Hepatically impaired patients receiving a single 90 milligram dose of pamidronate infused over 4 hours exhibited a 28.6% higher peak plasma concentration (C_{max}) value.

Time to peak effect

Maximum lowering of serum calcium concentrations occurs by 3 to 7 days after pamidronate administration.

Elimination

The apparent total plasma clearance is about 180 milliliters per minute.

Elimination is exclusively renal. Following administration of 30, 60, or 90 milligrams of pamidronate over 4 hours or 90 mg of pamidronate over 24 hours, an overall mean ± SD of 46 ± 16% of the drug was eliminated unchanged in the urine within 120 hours.

Mean ± SD total clearance and renal clearance were 107 ± 50 milliliters per minute and 49 ± 28 milliliters per minute, respectively.

Urinary elimination rate decreases with decreasing creatine clearance. Cumulative urinary elimination is linearly related to dose.

Precautions to Consider

Cross-sensitivity and/or related problems

Patients sensitive to any bisphosphonate may also be sensitive to pamidronate.

Carcinogenicity

A 104-week carcinogenicity study with daily oral pamidronate administration in rats found a positive dose-response relationship for benign adrenal pheochromocytoma in males. The condition was observed in females, but was not statistically significant. Another 80-week study in mice found that daily oral pamidronate administration was not carcinogenic.

Mutagenicity

Pamidronate was nonmutagenic in the Ames test, *Salmonella* and *Escherichia*/liver-microsome test, nucleus-anomaly test, sister-chromatid-exchange study, point-mutation test, and micronucleus test in the rat.

Pregnancy/Reproduction

Fertility—In rats, decreased fertility occurred in first-generation offspring of parents who had received 150 mg of oral pamidronate per kg of body weight (mg/kg). This occurred only when animals were mated with members of the same dose group.

Pregnancy—Adequate and well-controlled studies have not been done in pregnant women.

Oral doses of 60 and 150 mg/kg of body weight a day increased the length of gestation and parturition in rats and increased pup mortality. Oral doses of 25 to 150 mg/kg a day during gestation failed to demonstrate any teratogenic, fetotoxic, or embryotoxic effects in rats or rabbits. Studies conducted in young rats have reported the disruption of dental dentine formation following bisphosphonates administration. Intravenous studies conducted in rats and rabbits determined that pamidronate produces maternal toxicity and embryo/fetal effects when given during organogenesis. Since it has been shown that pamidronate can have these effects in rats and rabbits, it should not be given to women during pregnancy. If the patient becomes pregnant while taking this drug, she should be apprised of the potential harm to the fetus. Women of childbearing potential should be advised to avoid becoming pregnant.

FDA Pregnancy Category D.

Breast-feeding

It is not known if pamidronate is distributed into human breast milk. Pamidronate has been reported to distribute into the milk of lactating rats. Lactating women treated with pamidronate should be advised **not** to breast feed their infant.

Pediatrics

No information is available on the relationship of age to the effects of pamidronate in pediatric patients. Safety and efficacy have not been established.

Geriatrics

Appropriate studies have not been performed in the geriatric population. However, elderly patients may be more prone to overhydration when treated with parenteral pamidronate in conjunction with hydration therapy. Careful monitoring of fluid and electrolyte status or infusing pamidronate in a smaller volume of fluid is recommended.

Drug interactions and/or related problems

The following drug interactions and/or related problems have been selected on the basis of their potential clinical significance (possible mechanism in parentheses where appropriate)—not necessarily inclusive (» = major clinical significance):

Note: Combinations containing any of the following, depending on the amount present, may also interact with this medication.

» Calcium-containing preparations or
» Vitamin D, including calcifediol and calcitriol
(concurrent use may antagonize the effects of pamidronate in the treatment of hypercalcemia)

» Nephrotoxic medications, other (See *Appendix II*) or
(caution is advised when these medications are used with pamidronate; may increase the potential for nephrotoxicity)

Medical considerations/Contraindications

The medical considerations/contraindications included have been selected on the basis of their potential clinical significance (reasons given in parentheses where appropriate)—not necessarily inclusive (» = major clinical significance).

Except under special circumstances, this medication should not be used when the following medical problem exists:

» Hypersensitivity to pamidronate, to any of its components, or to other bisphosphonates.

Risk-benefit should be considered when the following medical problems exist:

Anemia, or
Leukopenia, or
Thrombocytopenia
(careful monitoring with pamidronate treatment when these conditions exist)

» Cardiac failure
(overhydration should be avoided when pamidronate is used in patients with cardiac failure; infusing pamidronate in a smaller volume of fluid is recommended)

» Renal function impairment when serum creatinine is 5 mg per dL or greater
(pamidronate is excreted via the kidneys; use of pamidronate in patients with renal function impairment may require a lower dose and slower rate of infusion)

Patient monitoring

The following may be especially important in patient monitoring (other tests may be warranted in some patients, depending on condition; » = major clinical significance):

Alkaline phosphatase concentrations serum
(determinations recommended periodically during therapy for Paget's disease as a marker for disease activity)

Calcium, serum and
Electrolytes, serum and
Magnesium, serum and
Phosphate, serum and
Potassium, serum
(determinations recommended periodically during therapy; some clinicians recommend monitoring serum magnesium and potassium concentrations only with concurrent diuretic use; serum ionized calcium concentrations are preferable to determine free and bound calcium, but may not be available from a reliable lab)

Complete blood count with differential and
Hematocrit and
Hemoglobin
(determinations recommended periodically during therapy, especially for patients who develop fever during pamidronate use; patients with pre-existing anemia, leukopenia, or thrombocytopenia should be carefully monitored for the first 2 weeks of therapy)

Note: In patients receiving pamidronate for bone metastases who show evidence of deterioration in renal function, treatment should be withheld until renal function returns to baseline.

Renal deterioration was defined in a clinical study as follows:increase of 0.5 mg per dL for patients with normal baseline creatinineincrease of 1 mg per dL for patients with abnormal baseline creatinine

Treatment was resumed only when the creatinine returned to within 10% of the baseline value.

Creatinine, serum and
Renal function
(determinations recommended prior to each treatment)
(if there is deterioration of renal function during pamidronate therapy, the infusion should be discontinued)
(if serum creatinine exceeds 5 mg per dL, risk-benefit of continued treatment or reduction of dosage should be considered)

Fluid balance
Daily weights
Urine output
(follow carefully for dehydration and overhydration▱tients should be hydrated adequately throughout treatment with pamidronate, but overhydration should be avoided, especially in patients who have potential for cardiac failure)

Side/Adverse Effects

Note: Fluid overload, hypokalemia, hypomagnesemia, and hypophosphatemia may occur due to concurrent fluid and diuretic use.

The following side/adverse effects have been selected on the basis of their potential clinical significance (possible signs and symptoms in parentheses where appropriate)—not necessarily inclusive:

Those indicating need for medical attention

Incidence more frequent

Atrial fibrillation (fast or irregular heartbeat; dizziness; fainting); ***fluid overload*** (decrease in amount of urine; noisy, rattling breathing; shortness of breath; swelling of fingers, hands, feet, or lower legs; troubled breathing at rest; weight gain); ***gastrointestinal hemorrhage*** (black, tarry stools; bloody stools; vomiting of blood or material that looks like coffee grounds); ***hypertension*** (blurred vision; dizziness; nervousness; headache; pounding in the ears; slow or fast heartbeat); ***hypocalcemia*** (abdominal cramps; confusion; muscle spasms) ; ***hypokalemia*** (convulsions; decreased urine; dry mouth; irregular heartbeat; increased thirst; loss of appetite; mood changes; muscle pain or cramps; nausea or vomiting; numbness or tingling in hands, feet, or lips; shortness of breath; unusual tiredness or weakness); ***hypomagnesemia*** (drowsiness; loss of appetite; mood or mental changes; muscle spasms [tetany] or twitching; seizures; nausea or vomiting; trembling; unusual tiredness or weakness); ***leukopenia or lymphopenia*** (fever, chills, or sore throat); ***metastases*** (spread of cancer); ***pleural effusion*** (chest pain; shortness of breath); ***syncope*** (fainting); ***tachycardia*** (fast, pounding, or irregular heartbeat or pulse); ***thrombocytopenia*** (black, tarry stools; bleeding gums; blood in urine or stools; pinpoint red spots on skin; unusual bleeding or bruising)

Note: *Hypocalcemia* occurs less frequently when doses of 60 mg, rather than 90 mg, are used.

Incidence less frequent

Atrial flutter (fast or irregular heartbeat; dizziness; fainting); ***cardiac failure*** (chest pain or discomfort; dilated neck veins; extreme fatigue; irregular breathing; irregular heartbeat; shortness of breath; swelling of face, fingers, feet, or lower legs; weight gain; wheezing); ***edema*** (swelling); ***neutropenia*** (black, tarry, stools; chills; cough; fever; lower back or side pain; painful or difficult urination; pale skin; shortness of breath; sore throat; ulcers, sores, or white spots in mouth; unusual bleeding or bruising; unusual tiredness or weakness)

Incidence rare

Episcleritis (eye redness; mild eye pain or discomfort); ***iritis*** (sensitivity to light; tearing; throbbing pain); ***scleritis*** (eye redness; eye tenderness; decreased vision; increased tearing; sensitivity to light; severe eye pain); ***uveitis*** (eye pain; tearing; sensitivity of eye to light; redness of eye; blurred vision or other change in vision)

Incidence not determined

Anaphylactic shock (cough; difficulty swallowing; dizziness; fast heartbeat; hives; itching; puffiness or swelling of the eyelids or around the eyes, face, lips or tongue; shortness of breath; skin rash; tightness in chest; unusual tiredness or weakness; wheezing); ***angioedema*** (large, hive-like swelling on face, eyelids, lips, tongue, throat, hands, legs, feet, sex organs); ***hypotension*** (blurred vision; confusion; dizziness, faintness, or lightheadedness when getting up from a lying or sitting position suddenly; sweating; unusual tiredness or weakness)

Those indicating need for medical attention only if they continue or are bothersome

Incidence more frequent

Abdominal pain; anemia (pale skin; troubled breathing with exertion; unusual bleeding or bruising; unusual tiredness or weakness); ***anorexia*** (loss of appetite; weight loss); ***anxiety*** (fear; nervousness); ***arthralgia*** (pain in joints; muscle pain or stiffness; difficulty in moving); ***arthrosis*** (degenerative disease of the joint); ***asthenia*** (lack or loss of strength); ***bone pain; constipation; cough; diarrhea; dyspepsia*** (acid or sour stomach; belching; heartburn; indigestion; stomach discomfort, upset or pain); ***dyspnea*** (shortness of breath; difficult or labored breathing; tightness in chest; wheezing); ***fatigue*** (unusual tiredness or weakness); ***Fever, transient***—at higher doses; ***granulocytopenia*** (fever; chills; cough; sore throat; ulcers, sores, or white spots in mouth; shortness of breath; unusual tiredness or weakness); ***headache; hyperthyroidism*** (nervousness; sensitivity to heat; sweating; trouble sleeping; weight loss); ***hypophosphatemia*** (bone pain; convulsions; loss of appetite; trouble breathing; unusual tiredness or weakness); ***influenza-like symptoms*** (chills; cough; diarrhea; fever; general feeling of discomfort or illness; headache; joint pain; loss of appetite; muscle aches and pains; nausea; runny nose; shivering; sore throat; sweating; trouble sleeping; unusual tiredness or weakness; vomiting); ***insomnia*** (sleeplessness; trouble sleeping; unable to sleep); ***malaise*** (general feeling of discomfort or illness; unusual tiredness or weakness); ***moniliasis*** (skin rash; cracks in skin at the corners of mouth; soreness or redness around fingernails and toenails); ***myalgia*** (joint pain; swollen joints; muscle aching or cramping; muscle pains or stiffness; difficulty in moving); ***nausea***—at higher doses; ***pain, unspecified; pain and swelling at injection site***—at higher doses; ***rales*** (small clicking, bubbling, or rattling sounds in the lung when listening with a stethoscope); ***rhinitis*** (stuffy nose; runny nose; sneezing); ***sinusitis*** (pain or tenderness around eyes and cheekbones; fever; stuffy or runny nose; headache; cough; shortness of breath or troubled breathing; tightness of chest or wheezing); ***somnolence*** (sleepiness or unusual drowsiness); ***upper respiratory infection*** (ear congestion; nasal congestion; chills; cough, fever, sneezing, or sore throat; body aches or pain; headache; loss of voice; runny nose; unusual tiredness or weakness; difficulty in breathing); ***urinary tract infection*** (bladder pain; bloody or cloudy urine; difficult, burning, or painful urination; frequent urge to urinate; lower back or side pain); ***vomiting***

Incidence less frequent

Muscle stiffness; psychosis (feeling that others can hear your thoughts; feeling that others are watching you or controlling your behavior; feeling, seeing, or hearing things that are not there; severe mood or mental changes; unusual behavior); ***rigors*** (feeling unusually cold; shivering); ***stomatitis*** (swelling or inflammation of the mouth); ***uremia*** (ammonia-like breath odor; loss of appetite; nausea or vomiting; weight loss)

Overdose

For specific information on the agents used in the management of pamidronate overdose, see:

- *Calcium Supplements (Systemic)* monograph.

For more information on the management of overdose or unintentional ingestion, **contact a Poison Control Center** (see *Poison Control Center Listing*).

Treatment of overdose

Specific treatment—Hypocalcemia resulting from overdose should be treated with intravenous calcium.

Patient Consultation

As an aid to patient consultation, refer to *Advice for the Patient, Pamidronate (Systemic)*.

In providing consultation, consider emphasizing the following selected information (» = major clinical significance):

Before using this medication

» Conditions affecting use, especially:

Hypersensitivity to pamidronate or other bisphosphonates

Pregnancy—FDA Pregnancy Category D

Breast-feeding—Lactating women requiring pamidronate therapy should be advised not to breast feed their infant.

Use in children—Safety and efficacy have not been established.

Use in the elderly—Elderly patients may be more prone to overhydration when treated with pamidronate in conjunction with hydration therapy

Other medications, especially calcium- and vitamin D–containing preparations or other kidney impairing or damaging medications

Other medical problems, especially cardiac failure and renal function impairment

Proper use of this medication

» Proper dosing

Precautions while using this medication

Importance of close monitoring by physician

May cause drowsiness

For patients with hypercalcemia:

Possible need for calcium and vitamin D restriction, including calcifediol and calcitriol

Side/adverse effects

Signs of potential adverse effects, especially atrial fibrillation, atrial flutter, cardiac failure, edema, episcleritis, fluid overload, gastrointestinal hemorrhage, hypertension, hypocalcemia, hypokalemia, hypomagnesemia, iritis, leukopenia, lymphopenia, metastases, neutropenia, pleural effusion, scleritis, syncope, tachycardia, thrombocytopenia and uveitis.

(Signs of potential side effects observed during clinical practice, especially anaphylactic shock, angioedema and hypotension.)

General Dosing Information

The U.S. product manufacturer recommends that the daily dose of pamidronate be reconstituted and diluted in 0.45% or 0.9% sodium chloride or 5% dextrose injection. The Canadian products should be reconstituted and diluted in 0.9% sodium chloride or 5% dextrose injection. The volume of fluid and the duration of the infusion varies with use. In

Canada, the recommended infusion rate should not exceed 60 mg per hour (1 mg per minute), and the concentration of pamidronate infusion should never exceed 90 mg per 250 mL.

Pamidronate must never be given as a direct intravenous injection. It should be diluted and administered as a slow intravenous infusion. Regardless of the volume of solution in which pamidronate is diluted, slow intravenous infusion is absolutely necessary for safety.

Single doses of pamidronate should not exceed 90 milligrams and the duration of intravenous infusion should be no less than 2 hours.

All parenteral products should be visually inspected for particulate matter and discoloration prior to administration. Any solution found to have particulate matter or discoloration should be discarded.

Pamidronate should be given in a single intravenous solution and line separate from all other drugs.

Fluid overload, hypokalemia, hypomagnesemia, and hypophosphatemia may occur due to concurrent fluid and diuretic use.

Parenteral Dosage Forms

Note: Bracketed information in the *General Route of Administration* section refers to uses that are not included in U.S. product labeling.

PAMIDRONATE DISODIUM FOR INJECTION

Usual adult dose

Hypercalcemia, associated with neoplasms—

Intravenous infusion, 60 to 90 mg diluted in 1000 mL of sterile 0.45% or 0.9% sodium chloride or 5% dextrose, given as a single-dose over two to twenty-four hours for corrected serum calcium of approximately 12 to 13.5 mg per dL.

Note: Patients with renal failure or mild hypercalcemia may receive 30 mg of pamidronate over a period of four to twenty-four hours. Longer infusions (greater than 2 hours) may reduce risk for renal toxicity.

Patients with more severe hypercalcemia (corrected serum calcium greater than 13.5 mg per dL) may receive 90 mg of pamidronate over a period of two to twenty-four hours. Retreatment with pamidronate may be considered if hypercalcemia recurs; however, seven days should elapse before retreatment.

In Canada, the recommended total dose of pamidronate for a treatment course depends upon initial plasma calcium concentrations (uncorrected):

- Up to 3 mmol per L (up to 12 mg%): Intravenous infusion, 30 mg of pamidronate diluted in 125 mL of sterile 0.9% sodium chloride or 5% dextrose in water
- 3 to 3.5 mmol per L (12 to 14 mg%): Intravenous infusion, 30 mg of pamidronate diluted in 125 mL of sterile 0.9% sodium chloride or 5% dextrose in water or 60 mg of pamidronate diluted in 250 mL of sterile 0.9% sodium chloride or 5% dextrose in water
- 3.5 to 4 mmol per L (14 to 16 mg%): Intravenous infusion, 60 mg of pamidronate diluted in 250 mL of sterile 0.9% sodium chloride or 5% dextrose in water or 90 mg of pamidronate diluted in 500 mL of sterile 0.9% sodium chloride or 5% dextrose in water
- greater than 4 mmol per L (greater than 16 mg%): Intravenous infusion, 90 mg of pamidronate diluted in 500 mL of sterile 0.9% sodium chloride or 5% dextrose in water

The infusion rate should not exceed 22.5 mg per hour. Repeat infusion of pamidronate may be given if hypercalcemia recurs or if plasma calcium does not decrease within 2 days.

Osteolytic metastases (treatment adjunct)—

- In breast cancer: Intravenous infusion, 90 mg diluted in 250 mL of sterile 0.45% or 0.9% sodium chloride or 5% dextrose in water over a period of two hours once every three or four weeks
- In myeloma: Intravenous infusion, 90 mg diluted in 500 mL of sterile 0.45% or 0.9% sodium chloride or 5% dextrose in water over a period of four hours once a month.

Note: In Canada, the recommended solutions for dilution are sterile 0.9% sodium chloride or 5% dextrose in water.

Paget's disease of bone (treatment)—

Intravenous infusion, 30 mg diluted in 500 mL of sterile 0.45% or 0.9% sodium chloride or 5% dextrose in water over a period of four hours each day for 3 consecutive days.

Note: Some clinicians have found that a single dose of 60 to 90 mg is effective in some cases.

In Canada, the recommended total dose of pamidronate for a treatment course is 180 to 210 mg administered according to one of the treatment regimens below:

- Regimen 1: Intravenous infusion of 30 mg diluted in 250 to 500 mL of sterile 0.9% sodium chloride or 5% dextrose in water given at 15 mg per hour once weekly for 6 weeks for a total dose of 180 mg pamidronate or intravenous infusion of 60 mg diluted in 250 to 500 mL of sterile 0.9% sodium chloride or 5% dextrose in water given at 15 mg per hour once every second week for 3 treatments resulting in a total dose of 180 mg pamidronate
- Regimen 2: Intravenous infusion of 30 mg diluted in 250 to 500 mL of sterile 0.9% sodium chloride or 5% dextrose in water given at 15 mg per hour on week 1, then intravenous infusion of 60 mg diluted in 500 mL of sterile 0.9% sodium chloride or 5% dextrose in water given at 15 mg per hour on weeks 3, 5, and 7 for a total dose of 210 mg pamidronate

Retreatment regimen may be repeated after 6 months until remission of disease is achieved and when relapse occurs: Intravenous infusion of 60 mg diluted in 500 mL of sterile 0.9% sodium chloride or 5% dextrose in water given at 15 mg per hour every second week for 3 infusions for a total dose of 180 mg of pamidronate.

Usual pediatric dose

[Osteogenesis imperfecta (treatment)][1]—

Intravenous infusion, 0.5 to 1.0 mg per kg of body weight per day administered over a period of four hours given in 3 day cycles repeated every 3-4 months.

Strength(s) usually available

U.S.—

30 mg per vial (Rx) [*Aredia* (lyophilized; mannitol); GENERIC].
30 mg in 10 mL (Rx) [GENERIC (solution; mannitol; water of injection)].
60 mg in 10 mL (Rx) [GENERIC (solution; mannitol; water of injection)].
90 mg per vial (Rx) [*Aredia* (lyophilized; mannitol); GENERIC].
90 mg in 10 mL (Rx) [GENERIC (solution; mannitol; water of injection)].

Canada—

30 mg per vial (Rx) [*Aredia* (lyophilized; mannitol; phosphoric acid)].
30 mg in 10 mL (Rx) [GENERIC (solution)].
60 mg in 10 mL (Rx) [GENERIC (solution)].
90 mg per vial (Rx) [*Aredia* (lyophilized; mannitol; phosphoric acid)].
90 mg in 10 mL (Rx) [GENERIC (solution)].

Packaging and storage

Do not store above 30°C (86 °F).

Reconstituted pamidronate may be stored under refrigeration at 2°C to 8°C (36 °F to 46 °F) for up to 24 hours from vial entry.

Preparation of dosage form

Each vial of lyophilized powder should be reconstituted with 10 mL of sterile water for injection. Make sure the powder is completely dissolved before the solution is withdrawn.

The daily dose (from reconstituted vial of lyophilized powder or from vial of solution) should then be diluted in an appropriate volume of sterile 0.45% or 0.9% sodium chloride or 5% dextrose injection.

In Canada, the daily dose should be diluted in an appropriate volume of sterile 0.9% sodium chloride or 5% dextrose injection.

See *Usual Adult Dose* for specific volume used based on therapeutic use.

Stability

The diluted infusion solution is stable for twenty-four hours at room temperature.

Incompatibilities

Pamidronate should not be mixed with calcium-containing infusion solutions, such as Ringer's solution.

Auxiliary labeling

- Keep out of reach of children
- May cause drowsiness. Be careful while driving or operating machinery. Use caution until you become familiar with its effects.

[1]Not included in Canadian product labeling.

Selected Bibliography

Product information: Aredia®, pamidronate disodium. Novartis Pharmaceuticals Corporation, East Hanover, NJ, (PI revised 7/2002) reviewed 3/2003.

Product information: Aredia®, pamidronate disodium. Novartis Pharmaceuticals Canada Inc., Dorval, Quebec, (PI revised 5/2001) reviewed 3/2003.

Revised: 12/18/2003

PANCRELIPASE Systemic

VA CLASSIFICATION (Primary/Secondary): HS451/GA500

Commonly used brand name(s): *Cotazym; Cotazym E.C.S. 20; Cotazym E.C.S. 8; Cotazym-65 B; Cotazym-S; Creon 10; Creon 20; Creon 5; Enzymase-16; Ilozyme; Ku-Zyme HP; LIPRAM 4500; LIPRAM-CR10; LIPRAM-CR20; LIPRAM-PN10; LIPRAM-PN16; LIPRAM-PN20; LIPRAM-UL12; LIPRAM-UL18; LIPRAM-UL20; Pancoate; Pancrease; Pancrease MT 10; Pancrease MT 16; Pancrease MT 20; Pancrease MT 4; Panokase; Protilase; Ultrase MT 12; Ultrase MT 20; Viokase; Zymase.*

Another commonly used name is lipancreatin.

Note: For a listing of dosage forms and brand names by country availability, see *Dosage Forms* section(s).

Category

Enzyme (pancreatic) replenisher; digestant; diagnostic aid (pancreatic function).

Indications

Note: Bracketed information in the *Indications* section refers to uses that are not included in U.S. product labeling.

Accepted

Pancreatic insufficiency (treatment)—Pancrelipase is indicated as a pancreatic enzyme supplement and replacement therapy in conditions where pancreatic enzymes are either absent or deficient, resulting in inadequate fat and carbohydrate digestion. Such conditions are usually due to chronic pancreatitis, pancreatectomy, cystic fibrosis, gastrointestinal bypass surgery (Billroth II and total), and ductal obstruction from neoplasm (of the pancreas or common bile duct).

Steatorrhea (treatment)—Indicated for treating steatorrhea associated with the postgastrectomy syndrome and bowel resection, and for decreasing malabsorption in these patients.

[Pancreatic insufficiency (diagnosis)][1]—Pancrelipase is used as a presumptive test for pancreatic function, especially in pancreatic insufficiency due to chronic pancreatitis.

Unaccepted

Pancrelipase is not effective in the treatment of gastrointestinal disorders unrelated to pancreatic enzyme insufficiency.

[1]Not included in Canadian product labeling.

Pharmacology/Pharmacokinetics

Mechanism of action/Effect

Proteolytic, amylolytic, and lipolytic enzymes in pancrelipase enhance the digestion of proteins, starches, and fats in the gastrointestinal tract, primarily in the duodenum and upper jejunum. The activity of pancrelipase is greater in neutral or faintly alkaline media. Pancrelipase has about 12 times the lipolytic activity, 4 times the proteolytic activity, and 4 times the amylolytic activity of pancreatin.

The efficacy of pancrelipase activity is dependent on how much of the enzyme reaches the small intestine. This can be influenced by the enzyme dose, the prevention of release of pancrelipase in the stomach, the microsphere size of the delayed-release product, and the pH at which the microsphere dissolves and releases the enzyme, with activity being greater at a neutral or alkaline pH.

Precautions to Consider

Cross-sensitivity and/or related problems

Patients sensitive to pancreatin or pork protein may be sensitive to this medication also.

Pregnancy/Reproduction

Pregnancy—Studies have not been done in humans.

Studies have not been done in animals.

FDA Pregnancy Category C.

Breast-feeding

It is not known whether pancrelipase is distributed into breast milk. However, problems in humans have not been documented.

Pediatrics

Appropriate studies on the relationship of age to the effects of pancrelipase have not been performed in children up to 6 months of age.

Geriatrics

Appropriate studies on the relationship of age to the effects of pancrelipase have not been performed in the geriatric population. However, geriatrics-specific problems that would limit the usefulness of this medication in the elderly are not expected.

Drug interactions and/or related problems

The following drug interactions and/or related problems have been selected on the basis of their potential clinical significance (possible mechanism in parentheses where appropriate)—not necessarily inclusive (» = major clinical significance):

Note: Combinations containing any of the following medications, depending on the amount present, may also interact with this medication.

Antacids, calcium carbonate–and/or magnesium hydroxide–containing
(concurrent administration of antacids may be required to prevent inactivation of pancrelipase [except the enteric-coated dosage forms] by gastric pepsin and acid pH; however, calcium carbonate–and/or magnesium hydroxide–containing antacids are not recommended since they may decrease the effectiveness of pancrelipase)

Iron, supplements or preparations
(iron absorption may be decreased when used concurrently with pancrelipase)

Laboratory value alterations

The following have been selected on the basis of their potential clinical significance (possible effect in parentheses where appropriate)—not necessarily inclusive (» = major clinical significance).

With physiology/laboratory test values

Uric acid
(blood and urine concentrations may be increased; ribonuclease present in pancreatic extracts catalyzes the formation of purine precursors of uric acid, thus increasing the risk of hyperuricosuria, especially with large doses of the purine-rich older formulations of pancrelipase)

Medical considerations/Contraindications

The medical considerations/contraindications included have been selected on the basis of their potential clinical significance (reasons given in parentheses where appropriate)—not necessarily inclusive (» = major clinical significance).

Except under special circumstances, this medication should not be used if the following medical problems exist:

» Pancreatitis, acute

» Sensitivity to pork protein, pancrelipase, or pancreatin

Side/Adverse Effects

The following side/adverse effects have been selected on the basis of their potential clinical significance (possible signs and symptoms in parentheses where appropriate)—not necessarily inclusive:

Those indicating need for medical attention

Incidence rare

Allergic reaction (skin rash or hives); ***irritation of the mouth***—induced by enzymatic digestion of mucous membranes when tablet dosage form is retained in mouth; ***sensitization*** (shortness of breath; stuffy nose; troubled breathing; wheezing; tightness in chest)—induced by repeated inadvertent inhalation of powder dosage form or the powder from opened capsules

With high doses

Gastrointestinal effects, specifically diarrhea; intestinal obstruction; nausea; stomach cramps or pain; hyperuricemia or hyperuricosuria (blood in urine; joint pain; swelling of feet or lower legs)—more frequent with extremely high doses of the purine-rich older formulations of pancrelipase

Note: There have been reports of gastrointestinal stricture requiring surgery in cystic fibrosis patients receiving high potency pancrelipase for 12 months or longer. The pathogenesis is unknown at this time. The U. S. Food and Drug Administration has issued a voluntary recall of pancrelipase products that contain greater than 20,000 Units of lipase.

Patient Consultation

As an aid to patient consultation, refer to *Advice for the Patient, Pancrelipase (Systemic).*

In providing consultation, consider emphasizing the following selected information (» = major clinical significance):

Before using this medication

» Conditions affecting use, especially:
Sensitivity to pork protein, pancrelipase, or pancreatin
Other medical problems, especially acute pancreatitis

Proper use of this medication

Taking dose before or with meals for maximum effectiveness
» Importance of following diet ordered by physician
» Not chewing tablets; swallowing them quickly with liquid to lessen potential for mouth irritation
Not chewing or crushing capsules containing enteric-coated spheres
» Proper dosing
Missed dose: Taking as soon as possible; not taking if almost time for next dose; not doubling doses
» Proper storage

Precautions while using this medication

Possible concurrent use with antacids that contain calcium carbonate and/or magnesium hydroxide

Not changing brands or dosage forms of pancrelipase without checking with physician

Possible sensitization resulting from repeated inhalation of powder, either from opened capsules or from powder dosage form

Side/adverse effects

Signs of potential side effects, especially allergic reaction, hyperuricemia or hyperuricosuria (with extremely high doses); gastrointestinal effects; irritation of mucous membranes; and respiratory problems (with inhalation of powder)

General Dosing Information

The destruction of pancrelipase's enzymes by gastric pepsin or their inactivation by acid pH may be prevented by the use of enteric-coated dosage forms, particularly the enteric-coated spheres. Or, if dosage forms of pancrelipase which are not enteric-coated are used, the gastric and duodenal pH may be raised instead by the concurrent administration of sodium bicarbonate, aluminum hydroxide, histamine H_2-receptor antagonists, misoprostol, or omeprazole (also, antacid, H_2-receptor antagonist, misoprostol, or omeprazole administration may be necessary in patients with deficient pancreatic bicarbonate secretion for the control of steatorrhea). An H_2-receptor antagonist administered with meals may be preferred instead of antacids, especially in patients with high rates of acid secretion.

Dosage should be individualized and determined by the degree of maldigestion and malabsorption, the fat content of the diet, and the enzyme activity of each preparation rather than by the weight of the extract. Ideally, a starting dose of 8,000 to 10,000 Units of lipase should be given with each meal.

To avoid irritation of the mouth, lips, and tongue, the tablets should not be chewed. Instead, the tablets should be swallowed quickly, preferably with some liquid, since proteolytic enzymes (trypsin and chymotrypsin) present in pancrelipase, when retained in the mouth may begin to digest the mucous membranes and cause ulcerations.

Retention of the tablet dosage form in the esophagus may occur in some patients with esophageal abnormalities or in patients taking the tablet in a recumbent position. To decrease the likelihood of mucous membrane digestion, 1 or 2 mouthfuls of solid food should be swallowed after each dose.

Diet/Nutrition

Pancrelipase should preferably be taken before or with meals for maximum effectiveness.

In pancreatic insufficiency, a high-calorie diet which is high in protein and low in fat is recommended. In severe cases, higher doses of pancrelipase and dietary adjustment may be necessary. Some clinicians recommend that cystic fibrosis patients consume a liberal fat diet along with an increase in pancelipase dosage to ensure adequate energy intake. Adequate hydration should be ensured at all times for patients taking pancreatic enzymes.

Capsule dosage forms may be opened and sprinkled on food for administration to young children. However, capsules containing the enteric-coated spheres should be taken with liquids or small amounts of soft foods (e.g., applesauce, gelatin) that have a pH less than 5.5 and that do not require chewing. The soft food should be swallowed immediately and followed with a glass of water or juice.

Bioequivalence information

The microsphere size of the delayed-release product, among other factors, determines how much of the enzyme reaches the small intestine. It has been found that some delayed-release pancrelipase products provide higher levels of enzyme activity than labeled. Since substitution of one manufacturer's delayed-release product for another may sometimes be accompanied by therapeutic failure, caution should be exercised in substituting.

Oral Dosage Forms

PANCRELIPASE CAPSULES USP

Usual adult and adolescent dose

Enzyme (pancreatic) replenisher and
Digestant—
Oral, 1 to 3 capsules before or with meals and snacks, the dosage being adjusted as needed and tolerated.

Usual pediatric dose

Enzyme (pancreatic) replenisher and
Digestant—
Oral, contents of 1 to 3 capsules with meals, the dosage being adjusted as needed and tolerated.

Usual geriatric dose

See *Usual adult and adolescent dose.*

Strength(s) usually available

U.S.—
8000 USP Units of lipase, 30,000 USP Units of protease, and 30,000 USP Units of amylase, per capsule (Rx) [*Cotazym* (calcium carbonate 25 mg); *Ku-Zyme HP*].

Canada—
8000 USP Units of lipase, 30,000 USP Units of protease, and 30,000 USP Units of amylase, per capsule (Rx) [*Cotazym; Cotazym-65 B* (bile salts 65 mg; cellulase 2 mg)].

Packaging and storage

Store below 25 °C (77 °F), in a tight container, unless otherwise specified by manufacturer. Store with a desiccant.

Auxiliary labeling

- Take before or with meals.
- If capsules are opened, do not inhale powder.

PANCRELIPASE DELAYED-RELEASE CAPSULES USP

Note: Substitution of one manufacturer's delayed-release product for another has resulted in therapeutic failure.

Usual adult and adolescent dose

Enzyme (pancreatic) replenisher and
Digestant—
Oral, 1 to 4 capsules (or 4000 to 20,000 units) before or with meals and snacks (for capsules containing the enteric-coated spheres), the dosage being adjusted as needed and tolerated. Initial starting dose should be determined by clinical experience.

Usual pediatric dose

Enzyme (pancreatic) replenisher and
Digestant—
Infants less than 6 months—Dosage has not been established
Infants 6 months to 1 year of age—Oral, 2000 units of lipase per meal.
Children 1 to 6 years of age—Oral, contents of 1 or 2 capsules (or 4000 to 8000 units) with meals, the dosage being adjusted as needed and tolerated.
Children 7 to 12 years of age—4000 to 12000 units (more if necessary)
Note: Initial starting dose should be determined by clinical experience. The assessment of the endpoints in children is aided by charting growth curves.
Children over 12 years of age—See *Usual adult and adolescent dose.*
Note: Contents of capsules containing the enteric-coated spheres should be taken with liquids or a small amount of soft foods with a pH less than 5.5 that do not require chewing. The soft food should be swallowed immediately without chewing and followed with a glass of water or juice to insure swallowing.

Usual geriatric dose

See *Usual adult and adolescent dose.*

Strength(s) usually available

U.S.—
4000 USP Units of lipase, 12,000 USP Units of protease, and 12,000 USP Units of amylase, per capsule (Rx) [*Pancrease MT 4*].
4000 USP Units of lipase, 25,000 USP Units of protease, and 20,000 USP Units of amylase, per capsule (Rx) [*Pancoate; Pancrease; Protilase;* GENERIC].

5000 USP Units of lipase, 20,000 USP Units of protease, and 20,000 USP Units of amylase, per capsule (Rx) [*Cotazym-S*].

5000 USP Units of lipase, 18,750 USP Units of protease, and 16,600 USP Units of amylase, per capsule (Rx) [*Creon 5*].

10,000 USP Units of lipase, 30,000 USP Units of protease, and 30,000 USP Units of amylase, per capsule (Rx) [*Pancrease MT 10*].

10,000 USP Units of lipase, 37,500 USP Units of protease, and 33,200 USP Units of amylase, per capsule (Rx) [*Creon 10*].

12,000 USP Units of lipase, 24,000 USP Units of protease, and 24,000 USP Units of amylase, per capsule (Rx) [*Zymase*].

12,000 USP Units of lipase; 39,000 USP Units of protease, and 39,000 USP Units of amylase, per capsule (Rx) [*Ultrase MT 12*].

16,000 USP Units of lipase, 48,000 USP Units of protease, and 48,000 USP Units of amylase, per capsule (Rx) [*Enzymase-16; Pancrease MT 16;* GENERIC].

20,000 USP Units of lipase, 44,000 USP Units of protease, and 56,000 USP Units of amylase, per capsule (Rx) [*Pancrease MT 20*].

20,000 USP Units of lipase, 65,000 USP Units of protease, and 65,000 USP Units of amylase, per capsule (Rx) [*Ultrase MT 20*].

20,000 USP Units of lipase, 75,000 USP Units of protease, and 66,400 USP Units of amylase, per capsule (Rx) [*Creon 20*].

4500 USP Units of lipase, 20,000 USP units of amylase, and 25,000 USP Units of protease per capsule (Rx) [*LIPRAM 4500* (capsules containing enteric coated delayed-release microspheres; diethyl phthalate; hydroxypropyl methylcellulose; hypromellose phthalate; polyethylene glycol; povidone)].

10,000 USP Units of lipase, 33,200 USP units of amylase, and 37,500 USP Units of protease per capsule (Rx) [*LIPRAM-CR10* (capsules containing enteric coated delayed-release microspheres; diethyl phthalate; hydroxypropyl methylcellulose; hypromellose phthalate; polyethylene glycol; povidone)].

10,000 USP Units of lipase, 30,000 USP units of amylase, and 30,000 USP Units of protease per capsule (Rx) [*LIPRAM-PN10* (capsules containing enteric coated delayed-release microspheres; diethyl phthalate; hydroxypropyl methylcellulose; hypromellose phthalate; polyethylene glycol; povidone)].

12,000 USP Units of lipase, 39,000 USP units of amylase, and 39,000 USP Units of protease per capsule (Rx) [*LIPRAM-UL12* (capsules containing enteric coated delayed-release microspheres; diethyl phthalate; hydroxypropyl methylcellulose; hypromellose phthalate; polyethylene glycol; povidone)].

20,000 USP Units of lipase, 56,000 USP units of amylase, and 44,000 USP Units of protease per capsule (Rx) [*LIPRAM-PN20* (capsules containing enteric coated delayed-release microspheres; diethyl phthalate; hydroxypropyl methylcellulose; hypromellose phthalate; polyethylene glycol; povidone)].

16,000 USP Units of lipase, 48,000 USP units of amylase, and 48,000 USP Units of protease per capsule (Rx) [*LIPRAM-PN16* (capsules containing enteric coated delayed-release microspheres; diethyl phthalate; hydroxypropyl methylcellulose; hypromellose phthalate; polyethylene glycol; povidone)].

18,000 USP Units of lipase, 58,500 USP units of amylase, and 58,500 USP Units of protease per capsule (Rx) [*LIPRAM-UL18* (capsules containing enteric coated delayed-release microspheres; diethyl phthalate; hydroxypropyl methylcellulose; hypromellose phthalate; polyethylene glycol; povidone)].

20,000 USP Units of lipase, 66,400 USP units of amylase, and 75,000 USP Units of protease per capsule (Rx) [*LIPRAM-CR20* (capsules containing enteric coated delayed-release microspheres; diethyl phthalate; hydroxypropyl methylcellulose; hypromellose phthalate; polyethylene glycol; povidone)].

20,000 USP Units of lipase, 65,000 USP units of amylase, and 65,000 USP Units of protease per capsule (Rx) [*LIPRAM-UL20* (capsules containing enteric coated delayed-release microspheres; diethyl phthalate; hydroxypropyl methylcellulose; hypromellose phthalate; polyethylene glycol; povidone)].

Canada—

4000 USP Units of lipase, 12,000 USP Units of protease, and 12,000 USP Units of amylase, per capsule (Rx) [*Pancrease MT 4*].

4000 USP Units of lipase, 25,000 USP Units of protease, and 20,000 USP Units of amylase, per capsule (Rx) [*Pancrease*].

8000 USP Units of lipase, 30,000 USP Units of protease, and 30,000 USP Units of amylase, per capsule (Rx) [*Cotazym E.C.S. 8*].

10,000 USP Units of lipase, 30,000 USP Units of protease, and 30,000 USP Units of amylase, per capsule (Rx) [*Pancrease MT 10*].

16,000 USP Units of lipase, 48,000 USP Units of protease, and 48,000 USP Units of amylase, per capsule (Rx) [*Pancrease MT 16*].

20,000 USP Units of lipase, 55,000 USP Units of protease, and 55,000 USP Units of amylase, per capsule (Rx) [*Cotazym E.C.S. 20*].

Packaging and storage

Store below 25 °C (77 °F), in a tight, light-resistant container, unless otherwise specified by manufacturer. Store with a desiccant.

Auxiliary labeling

- Take before or with meals (for capsules containing the enteric-coated spheres).
- Swallow whole. Do not chew or crush (for capsules containing the enteric-coated spheres only).
- Do not refrigerate.

PANCRELIPASE POWDER

Usual adult and adolescent dose

Enzyme (pancreatic) replenisher and Digestant—

Oral, 0.7 gram with meals and snacks, the dosage being adjusted as needed and tolerated.

Usual pediatric dose

Enzyme (pancreatic) replenisher and Digestant—

Oral, 0.7 gram with meals, the dosage being adjusted as needed and tolerated.

Usual geriatric dose

See *Usual adult and adolescent dose*.

Strength(s) usually available

U.S.—

16,800 USP Units of lipase, 70,000 USP Units of protease, and 70,000 USP Units of amylase, per 0.7 gram (Rx) [*Viokase*].

Canada—

Not commercially available.

Packaging and storage

Store below 25 °C (77 °F), unless otherwise specified by manufacturer.

Auxiliary labeling

- Take with meals.
- Do not inhale.

PANCRELIPASE TABLETS USP

Usual adult and adolescent dose

Enzyme (pancreatic) replenisher and Digestant—

Oral, 1 to 3 tablets before or with meals and snacks, the dosage being adjusted as needed and tolerated.

Usual pediatric dose

Enzyme (pancreatic) replenisher and Digestant—

Oral, 1 or 2 tablets with meals.

Usual geriatric dose

See *Usual adult and adolescent dose*.

Strength(s) usually available

U.S.—

8000 USP Units of lipase, 30,000 USP Units of protease, and 30,000 USP Units of amylase, per tablet (Rx) [*Panokase; Viokase*].

11,000 USP Units of lipase, 30,000 USP Units of protease, and 30,000 USP Units of amylase, per tablet (Rx) [*Ilozyme*].

Canada—

Not commercially available.

Packaging and storage

Store below 25 °C (77 °F), in a tight container, unless otherwise specified by manufacturer. Store with a desiccant.

Auxiliary labeling

- Take before or with meals.
- Swallow whole. Do not crush or chew.

Revised: 09/16/2004

PANCURONIUM—See *Neuromuscular Blocking Agents (Systemic)*

PANTOPRAZOLE Systemic

VA CLASSIFICATION (Primary): GA304

Commonly used brand name(s): *Pantoloc; Protonix; Protonix I.V.*

Note: For a listing of dosage forms and brand names by country availability, see *Dosage Forms* section(s).

Category

Gastric acid pump inhibitor; antiulcer agent.

Indications

Note: Bracketed information in the *Indications* section refers to uses that are not included in U.S. product labeling.

Accepted

Gastroesophageal reflux disease [GERD] (treatment)—Pantoprazole delayed-release tablets are indicated for the short-term (up to 8 weeks) treatment of heartburn and other symptoms associated with GERD. Pantoprazole for injection is indicated for the short-term (7 to 10 days) treatment in patients with GERD and a history of erosive esophagitis. Pantoprazole for injection is not indicated for initial treatment of GERD.

[Gastroesophageal reflux disease [GERD] (prophylaxis)]—Pantoprazole is indicated for the prevention of relapse in patients with reflux esophagitis.

Hypersecretory conditions, gastric (treatment)—Pantoprazole for injection is indicated for the treatment of pathological hypersecretory conditions associated with Zollinger-Ellison Syndrome or other neoplastic conditions.

[Ulcer, duodenal (treatment)]—Pantoprazole is indicated for short-term (up to 4 weeks) treatment for symptom relief and healing in patients with active duodenal ulcer.

[Ulcer, duodenal, *Helicobacter pylori*-associated (treatment)]—Pantoprazole, in combination with clarithromycin and either amoxicillin or metronidazole, is indicated for treatment of patients with an active duodenal ulcer who are *H. pylori* positive.

[Ulcer, gastric (treatment)]—Pantoprazole is indicated for short-term (up to 8 weeks) treatment in patients with active benign gastric ulcer.

Pharmacology/Pharmacokinetics

Physicochemical characteristics

Chemical Group—Substituted benzimidazole

Molecular weight—

Delayed-release tablets: 432.4.

For injection: 405.4.

pH—Reconstituted solution: 9 to 10.

Mechanism of action/Effect

Pantoprazole is a proton pump inhibitor. It accumulates in the acidic compartment of parietal cells and is converted to the active form, a sulfanilamide, which binds to hydrogen-potassium-ATP-ase at the secretory surface of gastric parietal cells. Inhibition of hydrogen-potassium-ATP-ase blocks the final step of gastric acid production, leading to inhibition of both basal and stimulated acid secretion. The duration of inhibition of acid secretion does not correlate with the much shorter elimination half-life of pantoprazole.

Other actions/effects

Pantoprazole reduced *in vitro* counts of *Helicobacter pylori* more than four times at pH 4 (no effect was obtained at pH 7). A minimum inhibitory concentration of 0.064 to 0.25 mg/mL (depending on *H. pylori* strain) was determined for pantoprazole, with significant decreases obtained as low as 0.016 mg/mL.

Absorption

Rapidly absorbed. However, absorption may be delayed up to 2 hours or more if pantoprazole is taken with food.

Bioavailability (oral)—77%.

Distribution

Vol_D—Following intravenous administration to extensive metabolizers: 0.17 L per kg (11 to 23.6 L).

Protein binding

Very high (98%); primarily to albumin.

Biotransformation

Hepatic, extensive. The major enzyme involved in the metabolism of pantoprazole is the polymorphically expressed cytochrome P450 isoform S-mephenytoin hydroxylase, also known as CYP2C19. The primary metabolite is the conjugate desmethylpantoprazole. Some patients who are deficient in this enzyme system will be slow metabolizers of pantoprazole. Patients who are slow metabolizers (3% of Caucasians or African-Americans; 17% to 23% of Asians) can produce plasma concentrations 5 times or more higher than patients with the enzyme present.

Half-life

Elimination—Following oral or intravenous administration: 1 hour.

The half-life of pantoprazole is prolonged (7 to 9 hours) in patients with cirrhosis of the liver and in genetically determined slow metabolizers (3.5 to 10 hours).

Onset of action

Fifty-one percent of gastric acid secretion was inhibited within 2.5 hours following an initial oral dose of 40 mg.

Time to peak concentration

Following an oral dose of 40 mg in extensive metabolizers with normal hepatic function—2.4 hours. When pantoprazole is taken with food, the time to peak concentration is variable and may be significantly increased.

Peak serum concentration

Following an oral dose of 40 mg in extensive metabolizers with normal hepatic function—2.4 mcg per mL (mcg/mL).

Following an intravenous dose of 40 mg administered over 15 minutes to extensive metabolizers with normal hepatic function—5.52 mcg/mL.

Time to peak effect

Oral—Acid secretion decreased by 85% on day 7 after administration of oral pantoprazole 40 mg.

Intravenous—Acid secretion decreased by 100% after 2 hours of 80 mg intravenous administration.

Duration of action

Oral—Acid secretion returns to normal levels without rebound hypersecretion within 1 week.

Intravenous—Acid secretion returns to normal levels after 24 hours.

Elimination

Renal—71%.

Fecal—18% (biliary excretion).

Dialysis removes insignificant amounts of pantoprazole.

Precautions to Consider

Carcinogenicity

A moderate increase in enterochromaffin-like (ECL) cell density was apparent after one year among 39 patients, the majority taking 40 to 80 mg pantoprazole for up to 5 years. ECL density appeared to plateau after 4 years.

ECL hyperplasia and ECL carcinoid were produced in male Sprague-Dawley (SD) rats at pantoprazole doses of ≥50 mg per kg daily and ≥0.5 mg per kg daily in female SD rats after 17 months, most likely due to elevated gastrin levels during chronic therapy. ECL-cell neoplasms did not occur over 24 months observations in mice receiving 5, 25, or 150 mg per kg daily.

Tumorigenicity

Pantoprazole doses ≥50 mg per kg caused a slight increased frequency of hepatocellular tumor in rats, while in female mice dose of 150 mg per kg also resulted in an increased frequency. However, in both animals, the incidence of hepatocellular tumor was within historical control ranges for the strains tested. The tumors were characterized as late-appearing and primarily benign. Exposure to these unusually large doses for prolonged periods is associated with enzyme induction in rodents, leading to hepatomegaly and centrilobular hypertrophy. These findings not associated with the lower clinical doses and are apparently not applicable to human exposure.

An increased incidence of thyroid tumor in rats, although within the historical ranges for the strain tested, was observed following exposure to pantoprazole 200 mg per kg daily. Pantoprazole-induced liver enzyme induction results in increased metabolism of thyroid hormone, leading in turn to increased production of TSH, with subsequent increased trophic changes within the thyroid gland. No similar effects have been observed in humans following exposure to usual clinical doses.

Mutagenicity

Pantoprazole was positive in the *in vitro* human lymphocyte chromosomal aberration assays, in one of two mouse micronucleus tests for clastogenic effects, and in the *in vitro* Chinese hamster ovarian cell/HGPRT forward mutation assay for mutagenic effects. Equivocal results were observed in the *in vivo* rat liver DNA covalent binding assay. Pantoprazole was negative in the *in vitro* Ames mutation assay, the *in vitro* unscheduled DNA synthesis (UDS) assay with rat hepatocytes, the *in vitro* AS 52/GPT mammalian cell-forward gene mutation assay, the *in vitro* thymidine kinase mutation test with mouse lymphoma L5178Y cells, the *in vivo* rat bone marrow cell chromosomal aberration assay, and a 26-week p53 +/- transgenic mouse carcinogenicity study.

Pregnancy/Reproduction

Fertility—Pantoprazole at oral doses up to 98 times and 88 times in male and female rats, respectively, was found to have no effect on fertility and reproductive performance.

Pregnancy—Adequate and well-controlled studies in humans have not been done.

Animal studies have demonstrated that pantoprazole crosses the placental barrier; however, no teratogenic effects were observed. Doses of 15 mg per kg resulted in delayed fetal skeletal development. Because animal reproduction studies are not always predictive of human response, this drug should be used during pregnancy only if clearly needed.

FDA Pregnancy Category B.

Breast-feeding

It is not known whether pantoprazole is distributed into human breast milk. However, pantoprazole or its metabolites are distributed into the milk of rats (maximally 0.02% of an administered dose is excreted in the breast milk). Because pantoprazole has been shown to cause tumorigenic effects in animals, a decision should be made as to whether nursing should be discontinued or the medication withdrawn, taking into account the importance of pantoprazole to the mother.

Pediatrics

Appropriate studies on the relationship of age to the effects of pantoprazole have not been performed in the pediatric population. Safety and efficacy have not been established.

Geriatrics

Appropriate studies performed to date have not demonstrated geriatrics-specific problems that would limit the usefulness of pantoprazole in the elderly. Efficacy and safety are similar to those reported for younger adults.

Pharmacogenetics

No differences in efficacy or safety between men and women are apparent.

Approximately 3% of Caucasians and African-Americans and between 17% and 23% of Asians have deficiency of the CYP2C19 hepatic enzyme system, resulting in slow metabolism. Although certain pharmacokinetic values such as half-life and serum concentrations of pantoprazole will be enhanced in these patients, no specific dose adjustments are recommended, and no differences in safety or efficacy are apparent.

Drug interactions and/or related problems

The following drug interactions and/or related problems have been selected on the basis of their potential clinical significance (possible mechanism in parentheses where appropriate)—not necessarily inclusive (» = major clinical significance):

Note: Pantoprazole, by increasing gastric pH, has the potential to affect the bioavailability of any medication for which absorption is pH-dependent. Also, pantoprazole may prevent the degradation of acid-labile drugs.

Pantoprazole, although metabolized by hepatic cytochrome P 450 systems, does not appear to either inhibit or induce cytochrome P 450 enzyme activity. To date, no clinically significant interactions have been noted for such commonly used drugs as diazepam, phenytoin, nifedipine, theophylline, digoxin, warfarin, or oral contraceptives.

Ampicillin esters or
Iron salts or
Ketoconazole
(pantoprazole causes prolonged inhibition of gastric acid secretion, and thereby may interfere with the absorption of these medications and others for which bioavailability is determined by gastric pH)

Other IV products containing edetate disodium (EDTA)
(caution should be used with coadministration since pantoprazole IV contains EDTA and may cause zinc deficiency)

» Warfarin
(postmarketing reports of increased INR and prothrombin time with concomitant use of proton pump inhibitors, including pantoprazole, and warfarin; may lead to abnormal bleeding and even death; patients treated concomitantly should be monitored for increases in INR and prothrombin time)

Laboratory value alterations

The following have been selected on the basis of their potential clinical significance (possible effect in parentheses where appropriate)—not necessarily inclusive (» = major clinical significance).

With physiology/laboratory test values

Alanine aminotransferase (ALT [SGPT])
(mild and sporadic increases may occur during treatment)

Cholesterol, serum and
Creatinine, serum and
Glucose, blood and
Lipoprotein
Uric acid, serum and/or urine
(concentrations may be increased)

Gastrin, serum
(a moderate increase in fasting serum gastrin concentration may occur during treatment)

Tetrahydrocannabinol (THC)
(reports of false-positive urine screening tests in patients receiving most proton pump inhibitors, including pantoprazole; an alternative confirmatory method should be considered to verify positive results)

Medical considerations/Contraindications

The medical considerations/contraindications included have been selected on the basis of their potential clinical significance (reasons given in parentheses where appropriate)—not necessarily inclusive (» = major clinical significance).

Except under special circumstances, this medication should not be used when the following medical problem exists:

» Hypersensitivity to pantoprazole or any component of the formulation

Risk-benefit should be considered when the following medical problems exist:

Hepatic function impairment
(modest accumulation of drug [≤ 21%] may occur following once-daily administration to patients with severe hepatic function impairment; this risk should be weighed against the potential for reduced acid control that may occur following every-other-day administration; no dosage adjustment is needed in patients with mild or moderate hepatic function impairment)

Zinc deficiency, or prone to
(IV product contains edetate disodium which is a potent chelator of metal ions including zinc; zinc supplementation should be considered in patients treated with pantoprazole IV who are prone to zinc deficiency)

Side/Adverse Effects

The following side/adverse effects have been selected on the basis of their potential clinical significance (possible signs and symptoms in parentheses where appropriate)—not necessarily inclusive:

Those indicating need for medical attention

Incidence less frequent or rare

Anaphylaxis (changes in facial skin color; fast or irregular breathing; puffiness or swelling of the eyelids or around the eyes; shortness of breath, troubled breathing, tightness in chest, and/or wheezing; skin rash, hives, and itching); ***angioedema*** (large, hive-like swellings on eyelids, face, lips, mouth, and/or tongue); ***chest pain***—occurs more frequently following intravenous administration; ***dyspnea*** (shortness of breath); ***erythema multiforme*** (pain in joints or muscles; itching or redness of skin; bull's eye–like lesion on skin); ***gastroenteritis*** (abdominal pain; anorexia; diarrhea; nausea; weakness); ***hyperglycemia*** (increased frequency and volume of urination; unusual thirst); ***infection; injection site reaction*** (bleeding; blistering; burning; coldness; discoloration of skin; feeling of pressure; hives; infection; inflammation; itching; lumps; numbness; pain; rash; redness; scarring; soreness; stinging; swelling; tenderness; tingling; ulceration; warmth); ***jaundice*** (yellow eyes or skin); ***optic neuropathy, anterior ischemic*** (loss of vision, sudden); ***pancreatitis*** (abdominal pain; nausea; vomiting); ***speech disorder; Stevens-Johnson syndrome*** (aching joints and muscles; blistering, loosening, peeling, or redness of skin; unusual tiredness or weakness); ***toxic epidermal necrolysis*** (itching or redness of skin; loosening and/or stripping off of top layer of skin; skin tenderness with burning); ***urinary tract infection*** (difficulty in urinating; frequent urge to urinate; painful urination)

Incidence not determined—Observed during clinical practice with pantoprazole IV; estimates of frequency can not be determined

Anterior ischemic optic neuropathy (blindness; blurred vision; decreased vision); ***hepatic failure*** (headache; stomach pain; continuing vomiting; dark-colored urine; general feeling of tiredness or weakness; light-colored stools; yellow eyes or skin); ***interstitial nephritis*** (bloody or cloudy urine; fever; skin rash; swelling of feet or lower legs; greatly decreased frequency of urination or amount of urine); ***pancytopenia*** (high fever; chills; unexplained bleeding or bruising; bloody, black, or tarry stools; pale skin; unusual tiredness or weakness; cough; shortness of breath; sores, ulcers, or white spots on lips or in mouth; swollen glands); ***rhabdomyolysis*** (dark-colored urine; fever; muscle cramps or spasms; muscle pain or stiffness; unusual tiredness or weakness)

Those indicating need for medical attention only if they continue or are bothersome

Incidence more frequent

Diarrhea—occurs less frequently following intravenous administration; *headache*—occurs less frequently following intravenous administration

Incidence less frequent or rare

Abdominal pain—occurs more frequently following intravenous administration; *anxiety; arthralgia* (pain in joints); *asthenia* (loss of energy or strength; weakness); *back pain; belching; blurred vision; bronchitis* (chills; cough; headache; hoarseness); *confusion; constipation; cough, increased; dizziness; dyspepsia* (indigestion); *flatulence; flu-like syndrome* (abdominal pain; chills; cough; headache; pain in joints or muscles; runny nose; sneezing; sore throat); *hypertonia* (muscle rigidity or stiffness); *hypokinesia* (difficulty in moving); *insomnia* (trouble in sleeping); *migraine headache; nausea; neck pain; pain; pharyngitis* (sore throat); *rectal disorders; rhinitis* (runny or stuffy nose); *salivation, increased; sinusitis* (aching, fullness, or tension in area of affected sinus; headache; runny nose); *skin rash or itching; tinnitus* (ringing or buzzing in the ears); *upper respiratory tract infection* (cough; runny or stuffy nose; sore throat); *vertigo* (dizziness; feeling of constant movement of self or surroundings; sensation of spinning); *vomiting*

Incidence not determined—Observed during clinical practice with pantoprazole IV; estimates of frequency can not be determined

Speech disorder (difficulty in speaking)

Overdose

For more information on the management of overdose or unintentional ingestion, **contact a poison control center** (see *Poison Control Center Listing*).

Clinical effects of overdose

No adverse effects were reported in single-agent overdose with pantoprazole in doses of 400 and 600 mg. Death following multi-agent ingestion was attributed to chloroquine and zopiclone rather than pantoprazole.

The following effects have been selected on the basis of their potential clinical significance (possible signs and symptoms in parentheses where appropriate)—not necessarily inclusive:

Limited human overdose data available with any proton pump inhibitors. Signs or symptoms of overdose may include:

Abdominal pain; blurred vision; confusion; headache; mild tachycardia (fast, pounding, or irregular heartbeat or pulse); *nausea and vomiting; somnolence* (sleepiness or unusual drowsiness); *vasodilation* (feeling of warmth or heat; flushing or redness of skin, especially on face and neck; headache; feeling faint, dizzy, or lightheaded; sweating)

Treatment of overdose

Decontamination—activated charcoal, gastric lavage.

Symptomatic and supportive—therapy as indicated.

Monitoring parameters—Cardiac monitoring and blood pressure evaluation with significant overdose. Monitor fluid status and electrolytes with prolonged vomiting.

Due to extensive protein binding, pantoprazole is not readily dialyzable.

Patients in whom intentional overdose is confirmed or suspected should be referred for psychiatric consultation.

Patient Consultation

As an aid to patient consultation, refer to *Advice for the Patient, Pantoprazole (Systemic)*.

In providing consultation, consider advising the patient on the following (» = major clinical significance):

Before using this medication

» Conditions affecting use, especially:

Hypersensitivity to pantoprazole or any component of the formulation

Pregnancy—Causes delayed fetal skeletal development in animal studies; should be used during pregnancy only if clearly needed

Breast-feeding—Distributed into milk in animal studies; may cause potentially serious adverse effects in nursing infants

Other medications, especially warfarin

Proper use of this medication

Taking the tablet in the morning, with or without food

» Swallowing tablet form of this medication whole without breaking, chewing, or crushing

Talking with doctor about zinc supplements if prone to zinc deficiency and taking the IV formulation of this medicine

Taking antacids for pain relief for several days until pantoprazole begins to relieve pain; unless otherwise instructed by physician

» Compliance with full course of therapy

» Proper dosing

Missed dose: Taking as soon as possible; not taking if almost time for next dose; not doubling doses

» Proper storage

Precautions while using this medication

» Regular visits to physician to check progress

Side/adverse effects

Signs of potential side effects, especially anaphylaxis, angioedema, chest pain, dyspnea, erythema multiforme, gastroenteritis, infection, injection site reaction (for intravenous dose), jaundice, optic neuropathy, pancreatitis, speech disorder, Stevens-Johnson syndrome, toxic epidermal necrolysis, and urinary tract infection

Signs of potential side effects observed during clinical practice of pantoprazole IV, especially anterior ischemic optic neuropathy, hepatic failure, interstitial nephritis, pancytopenia, or rhabdomyolysis

General Dosing Information

In the treatment of gastroesophageal reflux disease and gastric ulcer, relief of symptoms usually occurs within 2 weeks and healing within 4 weeks. Therapy should not exceed 8 weeks. Controlled studies of pantoprazole used as maintenance therapy to prevent reflux esophagitis recurrence have not been conducted beyond 12 months, although in a limited number of patients have received continuous maintenance treatment for up to 8 years. In the treatment of duodenal ulcer, relief of symptoms usually occurs within 1 week and healing within 2 weeks. Therapy should not exceed 4 weeks.

In the treatment of gastric hypersecretory conditions, transition form oral to IV and from IV to oral formulations of gastric acid inhibitors should be performed in such a manner to ensure continuity of effect of suppression of acid secretion. Patients with Zollinger-Ellison Syndrome may be vulnerable to serious clinical complications of increased acid productions even after a short period of loss of effective inhibition.

Parenteral routes of administration other than intravenous are not recommended.

Since pantoprazole is acid-labile, it is administered as an enteric-coated tablet to prevent gastric decomposition and to increase bioavailability. Tablets should be swallowed whole, and not split, chewed, or crushed.

Diet/Nutrition

Tablets may be taken before, during, or following the morning meal. Neither food nor antacids altered the bioavailability of pantoprazole.

Oral Dosage Forms

Note: Bracketed information in the *Dosage Forms* section refers to categories of use and/or indications that are not included in U.S. product labeling.

PANTOPRAZOLE SODIUM SESQUIHYDRATE DELAYED-RELEASE TABLETS

Usual adult dose

Gastroesophageal reflux disease (treatment)—

Oral, 40 mg per day for up to eight weeks. An additional eight-week course may be considered in patients who have not healed after four to eight weeks of treatment.

[Gastroesophageal reflux disease (prophylaxis)]—

Oral, 20 mg once a day in the morning. Dose can be increased to 40 mg once a day in the morning in the case of recurrence.

[Ulcer, duodenal, *H. pylori*-associated (treatment)]—

Oral, triple therapy regimens of pantoprazole 40 mg, plus clarithromycin 500 mg, plus either amoxicillin 1000 mg or metronidazole 500 mg, in which all three medications are taken two times a day for seven days.

[Ulcer, duodenal (treatment)]—

Oral, 40 mg per day for up to two weeks. An additional two–week course may be considered in patients who have not healed after two weeks of treatment.

[Ulcer, gastric (treatment)]—

Oral, 40 mg per day for up to four weeks. An additional four–week course may be considered in patients who have not healed after four weeks of treatment.

Usual pediatric dose

Safety and efficacy have not been established.

Usual geriatric dose
See *Usual adult dose.*

Strength(s) usually available
U.S.—
40 mg pantoprazole [equivalent to 45.1 mg of pantoprazole sodium sesquihydrate] (Rx) [*Protonix*].

Canada—
20 mg pantoprazole [equivalent to 22.6 mg of pantoprazole sodium sesquihydrate] (Rx) [*Pantoloc*].
40 mg pantoprazole [equivalent to 45.1 mg of pantoprazole sodium sesquihydrate] (Rx) [*Pantoloc*].

Packaging and storage
Store at 15 to 30° C (59 and 86° F).

Auxiliary labeling
- Swallow tablets whole. Do not break, chew, or crush.

Parenteral Dosage Forms

PANTOPRAZOLE SODIUM FOR INJECTION

Usual adult dose
Gastroesophageal reflux disease (treatment)—
Intravenous infusion, 40 mg at a rate of 3 mg (7 mL) per minute over approximately fifteen minutes each day for seven to ten days.

Hypersecretory conditions, gastric (treatment)—
Intravenous infusion, 80 mg at a rate of 3 mg (7 mL) per minute over approximately fifteen minutes every 12 hours. Dosing frequency can be adjusted to individual patient needs base on acid output measurements. In those patients needing a higher dose, 80 mg every 8 hours is expected to maintain acid output below 10 mEq per hour.

Note: Dosage adjustments are not necessary in patients with renal or hepatic impairment, or for patients undergoing hemodialysis.

Note: Treatment with pantoprazole should be discontinued as soon as the patient is able to resume taking pantoprazole delayed-release tablets.

Usual adult prescribing limits
Gastroesophageal reflux disease (treatment)—Safety and efficacy of use for more than ten days have not been established.

Hypersecretory conditions, gastric (treatment)—Daily doses higher than 240 mg or administered for more than 6 days have not been studied.

Note: For patients with hepatic impairment—Doses higher than 40 mg per day have not been studied.

Usual pediatric dose
Safety and efficacy have not been established.

Usual geriatric dose
See *Usual adult dose.*

Strength(s) usually available
U.S.—
40 mg (base) (Rx) [*Protonix I.V.*].

Packaging and storage
Store pantoprazole for injection vials at 20 to 25 °C (68 to 77 °F); excursions permitted to 15 to 30 °C (59 to 86 °F). Protect from light.

Preparation of dosage form
For fifteen minute infusion of 0.4 mg per mL—Pantoprazole should be reconstituted with 10 mL of 0.9% sodium chloride injection. This solution should then be further diluted (admixed) with 100 mL of 5% dextrose injection, 0.9% sodium chloride injection, or lactated Ringer's injection to produce a final concentration of approximately 0.4 mg per mL.

For fifteen minute infusion of 0.8 mg per mL—Each vial of pantoprazole should be reconstituted with 10 mL of 0.9% sodium chloride injection. The contents of the two vials should be combined and then further diluted (admixed) with 80 mL of 5% dextrose injection, 0.9% sodium chloride injection, or lactated Ringer's injection to a total volume of 100 mL with a final concentration of approximately 0.8 mg per mL.

For two minute infusion—Pantoprazole should be reconstituted with 10 mL of 0.9% sodium chloride injection, to a final concentration of 4 mg per mL.

Stability
Parenteral pantoprazole should be inspected visually for particulate matter and discoloration prior to and during administration whenever solution and container permit.

The reconstituted solution may be stored for up to 2 hours at room temperature prior to further dilution or to 2-minute intravenous infusion. The admixed solution may be stored for up to 22 hours at room temperature prior to administration. Both the reconstituted solution and the admixed solution do not need to be protected from light.

Incompatibilities
For Y-site administration of pantoprazole, midazolam hydrochloride has been shown to be incompatible; zinc-containing products may not be compatible. Administration of pantoprazole should be stopped immediately if precipitation or discoloration occurs.

Additional information
Pantoprazole for injection may be administered intravenously through a dedicated line or through a Y-site. The intravenous line should be flushed with 5% dextrose injection, 0.9% sodium chloride injection, or lactated Ringer's injection before and after administration of pantoprazole. When administered through a Y-site, pantoprazole is compatible with the solutions above.

Revised: 02/15/2005
Developed: 04/03/2000

PARAMETHADIONE—See *Anticonvulsants, Dione (Systemic)*

PARICALCITOL—See *Vitamin D and Analogs (Systemic)*

PARAXETINE Systemic

VA CLASSIFICATION (Primary/Secondary): CN603/CN900

Commonly used brand name(s): *Paxil; Paxil CR.*

Note: For a listing of dosage forms and brand names by country availability, see *Dosage Forms* section(s).

Category

Antianxiety agent; antidepressant; antiobsessional agent; antipanic agent; premenstrual dysphoric disorder (PMDD) therapy agent; posttraumatic stress disorder therapy agent.

Indications

Accepted
Depressive disorder, major (treatment)—Paroxetine and paroxetine controlled release are indicated for the treatment of major depressive disorder. Treatment of acute depressive episodes typically requires 6 to 12 months of antidepressant therapy. Patients with recurrent or chronic depression may require long-term treatment. Paroxetine has shown effective maintenance of antidepressant response for up to 52 weeks of treatment in a placebo-controlled trial.

Generalized anxiety disorder (treatment)—Paroxetine is indicated for the treatment of generalized anxiety disorder (GAD).

Obsessive-compulsive disorder (treatment)—Paroxetine is indicated for the treatment of obsessions and compulsions in patients with obsessive-compulsive disorder characterized by recurrent and persistent ideas, thoughts, impulses or images (obsessions) that are ego-dystonic and/or repetitive, purposeful and intentional behaviors (compulsions) that are recognized by the person as excessive or unreasonable. Paroxetine has shown effective relapse prevention for up to 6 months of treatment in a placebo-controlled trial.

Panic disorder (treatment)—Paroxetine and paroxetine controlled release are indicated for the treatment of panic disorder, with or without agoraphobia.

Premenstrual dysphoric disorder (treatment)—Paroxetine controlled release is indicated for the treatment of premenstrual dysphoric disorder (PMDD).

Posttraumatic stress disorder (treatment)—Paroxetine is indicated for the treatment of posttraumatic stress disorder (PTSD).

Social anxiety disorder (treatment)—Paroxetine and paroxetine controlled release are indicated for the treatment of social anxiety disorder or social phobia.

Unaccepted
Paroxetine is not approved for use in treating bipolar depression.

Pharmacology/Pharmacokinetics

Note: A wide range of intersubject variability has been observed in the pharmacokinetic parameters of paroxetine.

Physicochemical characteristics

Chemical Group—Phenylpiperidine. Chemically unrelated to other selective serotonin reuptake inhibitors (SSRIs), or to tricyclic, tetracyclic, or any other currently available antidepressants.

Molecular weight—
Paroxetine hydrochloride: 374.8.
Paroxetine base: 329.37.

Solubility—5.4 mg of paroxetine hydrochloride per mL water.

Mechanism of action/Effect

Paroxetine potently and selectively inhibits neuronal serotonin reuptake through antagonism of the serotonin transporter. Its antidepressant, antiobsessional, and antipanic activities are presumed to be linked to potentiation of serotonergic activity in the central nervous system (CNS). Paroxetine inhibits the active membrane transport mechanism for reuptake of serotonin, which increases concentration of the neurotransmitter at the synaptic cleft and prolongs its activity at synaptic receptor sites. Inhibition of serotonin reuptake also enhances serotonergic neurotransmission by reducing turnover of the neurotransmitter via a negative feedback mechanism. Paroxetine inhibits serotonin reuptake *in vitro* more selectively and more potently than do fluoxetine, sertraline, fluvoxamine, zimeldine, or clomipramine. Paroxetine very weakly inhibits reuptake of norepinephrine and dopamine.

Receptor binding studies have demonstrated that paroxetine does not interact directly with central neurotransmitter receptor sites, including alpha$_1$-, alpha$_2$-, or beta-adrenoreceptors, and dopamine D_2, serotonin (5-hydroxytryptamine) $5HT_1$ or $5HT_2$, or histamine H_1 receptors. Paroxetine has very weak affinity for the muscarinic-cholinergic receptor, and does not inhibit monoamine oxidase.

Other actions/effects

Paroxetine potently inhibits the P450 2D6 (CYP2D6) isoenzyme of the hepatic cytochrome P450 system. *In vitro* studies indicate that paroxetine is a very weak inhibitor of CYP3A4. This inhibition of isoenzyme CYP3A4 is not likely to be of clinical significance, and an *in vivo* study revealed no effect of paroxetine on the pharmacokinetics of terfenadine, a CYP3A4 substrate.

Paroxetine inhibits serotonin (5-HT) uptake by platelets as well as neurons.

At therapeutic doses, paroxetine does not significantly impair psychomotor function and exerts no significant effects on heart rate, blood pressure, or electrocardiogram (ECG) parameters. Also, paroxetine does not appear to induce epileptiform activity or to lower the seizure threshold.

Absorption

Paroxetine is well absorbed from both the suspension and tablet forms, with bioavailability for both dosage forms ranging from 50 to 100%. And, paroxetine is equally bioavailable from the oral suspension and tablet dosage forms. Bioavailability increases after multiple dosing due to partial saturation of first-pass metabolism. Absorption is not influenced by the presence of food, milk, or antacids.

Paroxetine extended-release tablets are designed to control the rate of medication release over 4 to 5 hours. These tablets have an enteric coating that delays the release of medication until the tablets have left the stomach.

Distribution

Paroxetine is extensively distributed into tissues, with only 1% remaining in the systemic circulation. The volume of distribution (Vol_D) is large due to the lipophilic nature of paroxetine; values ranging from 3 to 28 L per kg of body weight (L/kg) have been reported. Paroxetine is distributed into breast milk in concentrations similar to plasma concentrations.

Protein binding

Very high (95%). *In vitro*, protein binding of phenytoin and warfarin are not altered by paroxetine.

Biotransformation

Paroxetine undergoes extensive first-pass metabolism in the liver. At least 85% of a paroxetine dose is oxidized to a catechol intermediate that undergoes subsequent methylation and conjugation to clinically inactive glucuronide and sulfate metabolites.

Metabolism is accomplished in part by cytochrome P450 2D6 (CYP2D6); saturation of this enzyme at clinical doses appears to account for the nonlinear kinetics observed with increasing dose and duration of paroxetine treatment. The elderly may be more susceptible to the saturation of hepatic metabolic capacity, leading to conversion to nonlinear kinetics, which results in increased plasma concentrations of paroxetine at lower-than-usual doses.

Half-life

Elimination—
About 24 hours (range, 3 to 65 hours) in healthy adults. Due to partially saturable kinetics, the elimination half-life may be increased in the elderly. However, there is wide intersubject variability. Half-life is prolonged in patients with severe hepatic or renal function impairment.

Onset of action

Antidepressant effects—Within 1 to 4 weeks, with improvement in sleep parameters usually occurring in 1 to 2 weeks.

Antiobsessional and antipanic effects—May require several weeks to occur.

Time to peak concentration

Immediate-release: Range, 2 to 8 hours.
Extended-release: Range, 6 to 10 hours.

Time to steady-state serum concentration

Usually achieved in 7 to 14 days in most patients, although it may take considerably longer in some patients.

Concentration

Peak plasma—Following dosing at 30 mg a day for 30 days in healthy volunteers, peak paroxetine plasma concentrations (C_{max}) ranged from 8.6 to 105 mcg/L (0.02 to 0.28 micromoles per L). Peak plasma concentrations are subject to wide interpatient variability because of first-pass metabolism, and increase in a nonlinear fashion with increasing dose because of saturation of CYP2D6. Following dosing at 20 milligrams a day for 15 days in healthy young volunteers, the mean maximal plasma concentration was 41 nanograms per milliliter at steady state and peak plasma levels occurred within 3 to 7 hours.

Steady-state serum—In nonelderly depressed patients receiving long-term dosing of 20 to 50 mg of paroxetine a day, mean steady-state serum concentrations ranged from 48.7 to 117 mcg/L (0.13 to 0.31 micromoles per L). In 15 normal male subjects, steady-state area under the plasma concentration-time curve (AUC) was about eight times greater than was predicted from single-dose kinetics. Nonlinearity is thought to be the result of increased systemic availability due to reduced first-pass metabolism, rather than a decrease in systemic clearance. There appears to be no correlation between paroxetine plasma concentrations and clinical efficacy or incidence of adverse effects.

Mean plasma concentrations in patients with creatinine clearances below 30 mL per minute (mL/min) were fourfold greater than those in healthy volunteers. Mean plasma concentrations in patients with creatinine clearances of 30 to 60 mL/min and in patients with hepatic function impairment were twofold greater.

Elimination

Renal—
In the 10-day period following administration of 30 mg of a paroxetine solution, approximately 64% of the dose was excreted in the urine, of which 2% or less was the parent compound.

Fecal—
In the 10-day period following administration of 30 mg of a paroxetine solution, about 36% of the dose was excreted in the feces, of which unchanged paroxetine comprised less than 1%.

Precautions to Consider

Carcinogenicity

In 2-year carcinogenicity studies, a significantly greater number of male rats in the group receiving 3.9 times the maximum recommended human dose (MRHD) of 50 mg for major depressive disorder, social anxiety disorder, general anxiety disorder, and posttraumatic stress disorder (3.2 times the MRHD of 60 mg for obsessive-compulsive disorder) on a mg per square meter of body surface area (mg/m^2) basis exhibited reticulum cell sarcomas than did rats receiving lower doses. Also, there was a significantly increased linear trend across dose groups for occurrence of lymphoreticular tumors in male rats. Female rats were unaffected. In mice receiving up to 2.4 times the MRHD for major depressive disorder, social anxiety disorder, general anxiety disorder, and posttraumatic stress disorder (2 times the MRHD for obsessive-compulsive disorder) on a mg/m^2 basis, there was a dose-related increase in the number of tumors in mice, but no drug-related increase in the number of mice with tumors. The relevance of these findings to humans is not known.

Mutagenicity

Paroxetine demonstrated no genotoxic effects in a battery of five *in vitro* and two *in vivo* assays, including the bacterial mutation assay, mouse lymphoma mutation assay, unscheduled DNA synthesis assay, tests for cytogenetic aberrations *in vivo* in mouse bone marrow and *in vitro* in human lymphocytes, and a dominant lethal test in rats.

Pregnancy/Reproduction

Fertility—Rats administered paroxetine at doses 2.9 times the MRHD for major depressive disorder, social anxiety disorder, general anxiety disorder, and posttraumatic stress disorder (2.4 times the MRHD for obsessive-compulsive disorder) on a mg/m² basis had reduced pregnancy rates.

Irreversible reproductive tract lesions occurred in male rats in toxicity studies of 2 to 52 weeks duration. These lesions comprised atrophic changes in the seminiferous tubules of the testes with arrested spermatogenesis at doses 4.9 times the MRHD major depressive disorder, social anxiety disorder, and general anxiety disorder (4.1 times the MRHD for obsessive-compulsive disorder and panic disorder) on a mg/m² basis, and vacuolation of the epididymal tubular epithelium at doses 9.8 times the MRHD for major depressive disorder, social anxiety disorder, and general anxiety disorder (8.2 times the MRHD for obsessive-compulsive disorder and panic disorder) on a mg/m² basis.

Pregnancy—Epidemiological studies have shown that infants born to women who had paroxetine during their first trimester had an increased risk of cardiovascular malformations, primarily ventricular and atrial septal defects (VSDs and ASDs). Septal defects can be symptomatic requiring surgery or asymptomatic resolving spontaneously. If a patient becomes pregnant while taking paroxetine, she should be advised of the potential harm to the fetus. Unless the benefits of paroxetine justify continuing treatment, consideration should be given to either discontinuing paroxetine or switching to another antidepressant. For women who intend to become pregnant or who are in their first trimester, paroxetine should only be initiated after consideration of the other available treatment options.

In a study based on Swedish national registry data, infants of 6896 women exposed to antidepressants in early pregnancy (5123 to SSRIs, including 815 to paroxetine) were evaluated. Infants exposed to paroxetine had a significant 80% increased risk of cardiovascular malformations (primarily VSDs and ASDs) compared with the entire registry. The rate of cardiovascular malformations following early pregnancy paroxetine exposure compared with the entire registry population was doubled (2% vs. 1%). However, no increase in overall risk of congenital malformations was shown in these paroxetine exposed infants.

Another cohort study using US United Healthcare data evaluated 5956 infants of mothers given paroxetine or other antidepressants during the first trimester (815 given paroxetine). This study showed a nonsignificant 50% increased risk for cardiovascular malformations for paroxetine compared with other antidepressants. The prevalence of cardiovascular malformations was higher during the first trimester for paroxetine compared with other antidepressants (1.5% vs. 1%). Of the mothers dispensed paroxetine in the first trimester, 9 out of 12 infants with cardiovascular malformations had VSDs. A significant 80% increased risk for paroxetine compared with other antidepressants for overall major congenital malformations was shown. Prevalence of all congenital malformations following first trimester exposure was 4% for paroxetine compared with 2% for other antidepressants.

No evidence of teratogenic effects was revealed in rat and rabbit reproduction studies when rats and rabbits were given 8 times and 2 times the MRHD on a mg per m² basis, respectively. However, pup deaths in rats increased during the first 4 days of lactation when dosing occurred during the last trimester of gestation and continued through lactation. This effect occurred at a dose of approximately one-sixth the MRHD on a mg per m² basis. The no-effect dose was not determined and cause of these deaths is not known.

Non-teratogenic effects—When exposed to paroxetine and other selective serotonin reuptake inhibitors (SSRIs) or selective norepinephrine reuptake inhibitors (SNRIs) late in the third trimester, neonates have developed complications requiring prolonged hospitalization, respiratory support, and tube feeding and these can arise immediately upon delivery. Features consistent with a direct toxic effect of SSRIs and SNRIs or a drug discontinuation syndrome including respiratory distress, cyanosis, apnea, seizures, temperature instability, feeding difficulty, vomiting, hypoglycemia, hypotonia, hypertonia, hyperreflexia, tremor, jitteriness, irritability, and constant crying have been reported. In some cases, it should be noted that the clinical picture is consistent with serotonin syndrome. When treating a pregnant woman with paroxetine during the third trimester, the physician should carefully consider the potential risks and benefits of treatment. The physician may consider tapering paroxetine in the third trimester.

There are postmarketing reports of premature births in pregnant women exposed to paroxetine or other SSRIs.

FDA Pregnancy Category D

Labor and delivery—The effect of paroxetine on labor and delivery is not known.

Breast-feeding

Paroxetine is distributed into breast milk in concentrations similar to those found in plasma. Caution should be exercised when paroxetine is administered to a nursing woman and the infant should be closely monitored.

Pediatrics

Safety and efficacy have not been established. Paroxetine is not approved for use in treating any indications in the pediatric population.

Antidepressants increase the risk of suicidal thinking and behavior (suicidality) in children and adolescents with major depressive disorder (MDD) and other psychiatric disorders. Anyone considering the use of paroxetine or any other antidepressant in a child or adolescent must balance this risk with the clinical need.

Pooled analyses of short-term placebo controlled trials of nine antidepressant drugs in children and adolescents with MDD, obsessive compulsive disorder, or other psychiatric disorders have revealed a greater risk of adverse events representing suicidality during the first few months of treatment in those receiving antidepressants.

Geriatrics

There were no overall differences in adverse events between elderly and younger patients, and the effectiveness was similar in younger and older patients. In premarketing studies of paroxetine, 17% of the patients were 65 years of age or older. These studies showed that clearance is reduced in the elderly. And, paroxetine is associated with increased plasma levels and prolongation of the elimination half-life relative to younger adults. Reduced paroxetine dosage is recommended for elderly patients and the lowest daily dose of paroxetine which is associated with clinical efficacy should be initiated and maintained.

A controlled study of elderly patients with major depressive disorder demonstrated paroxetine controlled release to be safe and effective in the treatment of patients greater than 60 years of age with major depressive disorder.

Pharmacogenetics

Approximately 2 to 10% of the adult population are slow metabolizers of CYP2D6 substrates. These patients have a reduced ability to metabolize paroxetine and may be more likely to experience adverse effects. Paroxetine dosage reductions may be necessary in these patients.

Drug interactions and/or related problems

The following drug interactions and/or related problems have been selected on the basis of their potential clinical significance (possible mechanism in parentheses where appropriate)—not necessarily inclusive (» = major clinical significance):

Note: Paroxetine is a potent inhibitor of cytochrome P450 2D6 (CYP2D6), but a very weak inhibitor of CYP3A4. Caution should be exercised when paroxetine is coadministered with medications that are metabolized by CYP2D6, such as tricyclic antidepressants, phenothiazines (e.g., thioridazine), or type IC antiarrhythmics (e.g., encainide, flecainide, or propafenone), or medications that inhibit CYP2D6, such as quinidine. Dosage reductions of paroxetine and/or the other medication may be necessary. Interactions with medications metabolized by the CYP3A4 isoenzyme are unlikely.

At steady state with paroxetine, the CYP2D6 isoenzyme is saturated, and paroxetine metabolism is governed by other hepatic P450 enzymes, which appear to be nonsaturable. Interactions with hepatic enzyme inducers, hepatic enzyme inhibitors, and other medications that are metabolized by the hepatic P450 enzyme system, other than those listed below, have not been studied and the possibility of a significant interaction should be considered.

In vitro studies have shown little chance of paroxetine being displaced by other highly protein-bound agents; also, paroxetine is unlikely to displace other highly protein-bound medications. *In vivo*, however, the potential exists for displacement of one highly protein-bound medication by another; increased free concentrations of the displaced agent could result, increasing the likelihood of adverse effects.

Combinations containing any of the following medications, depending on the amount present, may also interact with this medication.

Alcohol
(although paroxetine has not been shown to alter alcohol metabolism and does not appear to potentiate cognitive and psychomotor effects of alcohol in normal subjects, concomitant use is not recommended)

» Antidepressants, tricyclic (TCAs)
(paroxetine may inhibit TCA metabolism, leading to increased TCA plasma concentrations, and possibly causing adverse effects; maximum plasma concentration, area under the plasma concentration-time curve, and elimination half-life of a single 100-mg dose of desipramine were increased twofold, fivefold, and threefold, respectively, in subjects at steady-state receiving 20 mg per day of paroxetine; plasma concentration of the TCA may need to be mon-

itored, and dosage reduction of either the TCA or paroxetine may be required)

» Aspirin or
» Nonsteroidal anti-inflammatory drugs [NSAIDs] or
» Other drugs that affect coagulation
(caution should be used; risk of bleeding associated with concomitant use)

» Atomoxetine
(concomitant use of paroxetine and atomoxetine may result in increase in increases in atomoxetine AUC; dosage reduction of atomoxetine is recommended)

Cimetidine
(in one study, steady-state plasma concentrations of paroxetine were increased by approximately 50% during concurrent administration of cimetidine; although the clinical significance of this interaction has not been definitively established, initial dosage reductions of paroxetine are not thought to be necessary, but subsequent dose titration should be based on clinical effects)

CYP2D6 substrates, such as
Flecainide or
Fluoxetine or
Phenothiazines or
Propafenone or
Quinidine or
Risperidone
(use with caution; concomitant use of paroxetine and other drugs metabolized by CYP2D6 may require lower doses of paroxetine or the other drug)

Digoxin
(mean digoxin area under the plasma concentration-time curve [AUC] decreased 15% in the presence of paroxetine; since there is little clinical experience with this combination, concurrent administration should be undertaken with caution)

Highly protein-bound drugs
(use with caution since paroxetine is highly bound to plasma proteins; concurrent use may cause increased free concentrations of the other highly protein-bound drug or paroxetine could be displaced by the other highly bound drug; may increase the risk of adverse events)

Lithium
(use with caution due to limited clinical experience and potential for serotonin syndrome)

Metoprolol
(concomitant use of paroxetine and metoprolol may result in severe hypotension; postmarketing case report)

» Moclobemide
(because of the potentially fatal effects of concomitant use of paroxetine and nonselective, irreversible monoamine oxidase [MAO] inhibitors, and the increased risk of development of the serotonin syndrome with concomitant use of paroxetine and the selective, reversible MAO-A inhibitor moclobemide, concurrent use is not recommended; allowing 3 to 7 days to elapse between discontinuing moclobemide and initiating paroxetine therapy, and allowing 2 weeks to elapse between discontinuing paroxetine and initiating moclobemide therapy is advised)

» Monoamine oxidase (MAO) inhibitors, including furazolidone, procarbazine, and selegiline
(concurrent use of MAO inhibitors with paroxetine may result in potentially fatal reactions, which may include confusion, agitation, restlessness, and gastrointestinal symptoms, or possibly hyperpyretic episodes, severe convulsions, hypertensive crises, or the serotonin syndrome; concurrent use is **contraindicated,** and at least 14 days should elapse between discontinuation of one medication and initiation of the other)

Phenobarbital or
Primidone
(primidone is partially metabolized to phenobarbital, which induces many cytochrome P450 enzymes; administration of either of these agents concomitantly with paroxetine may reduce the systemic availability of paroxetine; no initial dosage adjustments of paroxetine are recommended, but subsequent titration should be based on clinical effects)

Phenytoin
(concomitant administration with paroxetine may decrease the systemic availability of either agent; no initial dosage adjustments are recommended, but subsequent titration should be based on clinical effects)

(concomitant use of paroxetine and phenytoin may result in increased phenytoin concentrations; postmarketing case report)

» Pimozide
(concomitant administration with paroxetine may increase the systemic availability of pimozide; due to the narrow therapeutic index of pimozide and its known ability to prolong the QT interval, concomitant use of pimozide and paroxetine is **contraindicated**)

Procyclidine
(concurrent use may increase the systemic availability of procyclidine; if anticholinergic effects occur, the dosage of procyclidine should be reduced)

» Serotonergics or other medications or substances with serotonergic activity (see *Appendix II*)
(increased risk of developing the serotonin syndrome, a rare but potentially fatal hyperserotonergic state; symptoms typically occur shortly [hours to days] after the addition of a serotonergic agent, such as paroxetine, to a regimen that includes serotonin-enhancing drugs or an increase in dosage of a serotonergic agent; symptoms include agitation, diaphoresis, diarrhea, fever, hyperreflexia, incoordination, mental status changes [confusion, hypomania], myoclonus, shivering, or tremor; if recognized early, the syndrome usually resolves quickly upon withdrawal of the offending agents)

(concurrent use of tryptophan and paroxetine is not recommended)

Sumatriptan
(may increase the risk of adverse reactions; if concomitant therapy is clinically warranted, appropriate observation of the patient is advised)

» St. John's Wort
(may increase undesirable effects)

Theophylline
(elevated theophylline concentrations have been reported during concurrent use; monitoring of theophylline serum concentrations during concurrent use is recommended)

» Thioridazine
(may prolong the QTc interval, which is associated with serious ventricular arrythmias and sudden death; administration of paroxetine and thioridazine is **contraindicated**)

» Warfarin
(although paroxetine does not alter *in vitro* protein binding of warfarin, a pharmacodynamic interaction may exist that causes an increased bleeding diathesis despite unaltered prothrombin time; since there is little clinical experience and there is increased risk of bleeding, caution is advised when these agents are used concomitantly)

Laboratory value alterations

The following have been selected on the basis of their potential clinical significance (possible effect in parentheses where appropriate)—not necessarily inclusive (» = major clinical significance).

With physiology/laboratory test values
Hematocrit or
Hemoglobin or
White blood cell counts
(may be decreased)

Medical considerations/Contraindications

The medical considerations/contraindications included have been selected on the basis of their potential clinical significance (reasons given in parentheses where appropriate)—not necessarily inclusive (» = major clinical significance).

Except under special circumstances, this medication should not be used when the following medical problem exists:

» Hypersensitivity to paroxetine or any of the inactive ingredients
(contraindicated in these patients)

Risk-benefit should be considered when the following medical problems exist:

» Bipolar disorder or risk of
(may increase likelihood of precipitation of a mixed/manic episode in these patients; prior to initiating paroxetine treatment, patient should be adequately screened to determine if they are at risk for bipolar disorder; such screening should include a detailed psychiatric history, including a family history of suicide, bipolar disorder, and depression.)

Diseases affecting metabolism or hemodynamic responses
(caution is advisable)

Epilepsy or

Seizures, history of
(as with other antidepressants, paroxetine should be introduced with caution; if seizures develop, paroxetine should be discontinued)

» Hepatic function impairment, severe
(paroxetine plasma concentrations and elimination half-life are increased; initial dosage should be reduced, starting at 10 mg once a day, and intervals between dosage increases should be lengthened)

Mania, history of
(activation of hypomania or mania has been reported in depressed patients treated with paroxetine)

Myocardial infarction, recent history of, or
Heart disease, unstable
(paroxetine has not been evaluated in patients with these conditions; caution is advised)

Narrow angle glaucoma
(caution should be used; mydriasis has been reported with paroxetine therapy and can cause acute angle closure in patients with this condition)

Neurological impairment, including developmental delay
(risk of seizures may be increased)

» Renal function impairment, severe
(in patients with creatinine clearance < 30 mL per minute [mL/min] and in patients with creatinine clearance between 30 and 60 mL/min, mean plasma paroxetine concentrations were four and two times, respectively, the plasma concentrations seen in healthy volunteers; initial dosage should be reduced, starting at 10 mg once a day, and intervals between dosage increases should be lengthened)

Patient monitoring

The following may be especially important in patient monitoring (other tests may be warranted in some patients, depending on condition; » = major clinical significance):

Careful supervision of patients including those with:
Abnormal behaviors (i.e., agitation, panic attacks, hostility) or
Clinical worsening of their depression or
Suicidal ideation and behavior (suicidality)
(recommended especially during early treatment phase before peak effectiveness of paroxetine is achieved or at the time of increases or decreases in dose; prescribing the smallest number of tablets necessary for good patient management is recommended to decrease risk of overdose; consideration should be given to changing the therapeutic regimen, including possibly discontinuing the medicine, in patients whose depression is persistently worse or whose emergent suicidality or other symptoms are severe, abrupt in onset, or were not part of the patient's presenting symptoms)

» Symptoms associated with discontinuation
(patients should be monitored for symptoms upon discontinuation; a gradual reduction in dose rather than abrupt cessation is recommended whenever possible; previously prescribed dose may be considered if intolerable symptoms occur following a decrease in the dose or upon discontinuation of treatment)

Side/Adverse Effects

Note: Side effects are usually mild and transient, with evidence of dose-dependency for some of the most common adverse effects. In addition, there is evidence of adaptation with continuing therapy (over 4 to 6 weeks) to some effects, such as nausea and dizziness.

Although changes in sexual desire, sexual performance and sexual satisfaction often occur as manifestations of a psychiatric disorder, they may also be a consequence of pharmacologic treatment. In particular, some evidence suggests that selective serotonin reuptake inhibitors (SSRIs) can cause such untoward sexual experiences

The following side/adverse effects have been selected on the basis of their potential clinical significance (possible signs and symptoms in parentheses where appropriate)—not necessarily inclusive:

Those indicating need for medical attention

Incidence less frequent

Agitation; chest pain; myalgia, myasthenia, or myopathy (muscle pain or weakness); ***palpitation*** (fast or irregular heartbeat); ***postural hypotension*** (chills; cold sweats; confusion; dizziness, faintness, or lightheadedness when getting up from lying or sitting position); ***respiratory disorder*** (chest congestion; difficulty in breathing); ***skin rash; tachycardia*** (fast, pounding, or irregular heartbeat or pulse)

Incidence rare

Abnormal bleeding (red or purple patches on skin); ***extrapyramidal symptoms; including akinesia or hypokinesia*** (absence of or decrease in body movements); ***dyskinesia*** (unusual or incomplete body movements); ***dystonia*** (unusual or sudden body or facial movements; inability to move eyes); ***and dysarthria*** (difficulty in speaking); ***hyponatremia*** (confusion; drowsiness; dryness of mouth; increased thirst; lack of energy; seizures); ***mania or hypomania*** (talking, feeling, and acting with excitement and activity you cannot control); ***mydriasis*** (bigger, dilated, or enlarged pupils [black part of eye]; increased sensitivity of eyes to light); ***seizures; serotonin syndrome*** (diarrhea; fever; increased sweating; mood or behavior changes; overactive reflexes; racing heartbeat; restlessness; shivering or shaking)

Note: Reports of *abnormal bleeding* have included published case reports documenting the occurrence of bleeding episodes in patients treated with psychotropic agents that interfere with serotonin reuptake. Additional epidemiological studies have confirmed the association between use of psychotropic agents that interfere with serotonin reuptake and the occurrence of upper gastrointestinal bleeding. In both studies, concurrent use of a nonsteroidal anti-inflammatory drug [NSAID] or aspirin potentiated the risk of bleeding. Although these studies focused on upper gastrointestinal bleeding, it is possible that bleeding at other sites would be similarly potentiated..

Hyponatremia has been reported mostly in elderly patients, some of whom were taking diuretics or were otherwise volume-depleted.

Activation of *mania/hypomania* occurred in about 1% of unipolar and in about 2% of a subset of bipolar patients during premarketing testing.

The *serotonin syndrome* is most likely to occur shortly (within hours to days) after a paroxetine dosage increase or the addition of another serotonergic agent to the patient's regimen. The syndrome may include cardiac arrhythmias, coma, disseminated intravascular coagulation, hypertension or hypotension, renal failure, respiratory failure, seizures, or severe hyperthermia.

Incidence not determined—Observed during clinical practice; estimates of frequency can not be determined

Agranulocytosis (cough or hoarseness; fever with or without chills; general feeling of tiredness or weakness; lower back or side pain; painful or difficult urination; sore throat; sores, ulcers, or white spots on lips or in mouth; unusual bleeding or bruising); ***akathisia*** (inability to sit still; need to keep moving; restlessness); ***anaphylaxis*** (cough; difficulty swallowing; dizziness; fast heartbeat; hives; itching; puffiness or swelling of the eyelids or around the eyes, face, lips or tongue; shortness of breath; skin rash; tightness in chest; unusual tiredness or weakness; wheezing); ***aplastic anemia*** (chest pain; chills; cough; fever; headache; shortness of breath; sores, ulcers, or white spots on lips or in mouth; swollen or painful glands; tightness in chest; unusual bleeding or bruising; unusual tiredness or weakness; wheezing); ***alveolitis, allergic*** (cough; shortness of breath; troubled breathing); ***bradykinesia*** (slow movement; slow reflexes); ***bone marrow aplasia*** (chest pain; chills; cough or hoarseness; fever; lower back or side pain; painful or difficult urination; shortness of breath; sores, ulcers, or white spots on lips or in mouth; swollen glands; unusual bleeding or bruising; unusual tiredness or weakness); ***cogwheel rigidity*** (incremental or ratchet-like movement of muscle; rigid or stiff muscles; muscle discomfort); ***eclampsia*** (seizure or coma late in pregnancy); ***galactorrhea*** (unexpected or excess milk flow from breasts); ***Guillain-Barre syndrome*** (sudden numbness and weakness in the arms and legs; inability to move arms and legs); ***hematopoiesis, impaired*** (unusual or decreased blood cell production); ***hemolytic anemia*** (back, leg, or stomach pains; bleeding gums; chills; dark urine; difficulty breathing; fatigue; fever; general body swelling; headache; loss of appetite; nausea or vomiting; nosebleeds; pale skin; sore throat; yellowing of the eyes or skin); ***Henoch-Schonlein purpura*** (raised red swellings on the skin, the buttocks, legs or ankles; large, flat, blue or purplish patches in the skin; painful knees and ankles; fever; stomach pain; bloody or black, tarry stools; blood in urine); ***hypertonia*** (excessive muscle tone; muscle tension or tightness; muscle stiffness); ***laryngismus*** (spasm of throat); ***liver function tests, elevated*** (lab results that show problems with liver); ***neuroleptic malignant syndrome*** (convulsions; difficulty in breathing; fast heartbeat; high fever; high or low blood pressure; increased sweating; loss of bladder control; severe muscle stiffness; unusually pale skin; tiredness); ***oculogyric crisis*** (fixed position of eye); ***optic neuritis*** (blindness; blue-yellow color blindness; blurred vision; decreased vision; eye pain); ***pancreatitis, acute*** (bloating; chills; constipation; darkened urine; fast heartbeat; fever; indigestion; loss of appetite; nausea; pains in stomach, side, or abdomen, possibly radiating to the back; vomiting; yellow eyes or skin); ***pancytopenia*** (high fever; chills; unexplained bleeding or bruising; bloody, black, or tarry stools; pale skin; unusual tiredness or weakness; cough; shortness of breath; sores, ulcers, or white spots on lips or in mouth; swollen glands); ***porphyria*** (darkening of urine or dark urine; fluid-filled skin blisters; itching of the skin; light-colored stools; sensitivity to the sun; skin thinness; yellow eyes or skin); ***priapism*** (painful or prolonged erection of the penis); ***prolactinemia*** (swelling of breasts or unusual milk production); ***pulmonary hypertension*** (shortness of breath); ***renal failure, acute*** (lower back/side pain; decreased frequency/amount of urine; bloody urine; increased thirst; loss of appetite; nausea; vomiting; unusual tiredness or weakness; swelling of face, fingers, lower legs; weight gain; troubled breathing; increased blood pressure); ***status epilepticus*** (epileptic seizure that will not stop); ***syndrome of inappropriate antidiuretic hormone (SIADH)*** (agitation; coma; confusion; decreased urine output; depression; dizziness; headache; hostility; irritability; lethargy; muscle twitching; nausea; rapid weight gain; seizures; stupor; swelling of face, ankles, or hands; unusual tiredness or weakness); ***thrombocytopenia*** (black, tarry stools; bleeding gums; blood in urine or stools; pinpoint red spots on skin; unusual bleeding or bruising); ***torsade de pointes*** (chest pain or discomfort; irregular or slow heart rate; fainting; shortness of breath); ***toxic epidermal necrolysis*** (blistering, peeling, loosening of skin; chills; cough; diarrhea; itching; joint or muscle pain; red irritated eyes; red skin lesions, often with a purple center; sore throat; sores, ulcers, or white spots in mouth or on lips; unusual tiredness or weakness); ***trismus*** (difficulty opening the mouth; lockjaw; muscle spasm, especially of neck and back); ***vasculitic syndrome*** (redness, soreness or itching skin; fever; sores, welting or blisters); ***ventricular fibrillation*** (fainting; fast, slow, or irregular heartbeat; shortness of breath; unusual tiredness or weakness); ***ventricular tachycardia*** (fainting; fast, pounding, or irregular heartbeat or pulse; palpitations)

Those indicating need for medical attention only if they continue or are bothersome

Incidence more frequent

Abdominal pain; asthenia (unusual tiredness or weakness); ***constipation; decreased appetite; diarrhea; dizziness; drowsiness; dryness of mouth; dyspepsia*** (acid or sour stomach; belching; heartburn; indigestion; stomach discomfort, upset or pain); ***flatulence*** (bloated, full feeling; excess air or gas in stomach or intestines; passing gas); ***headache; infection*** (fever or chills; cough or hoarseness; lower back or side pain; painful or difficult urination); ***insomnia*** (trouble in sleeping); ***libido, decreased*** (decreased sexual desire); ***nausea; nervousness; sexual dysfunction, especially ejaculatory disturbances, impotence or anorgasmia*** (decreased sexual ability); ***sweating; sinusitis*** (pain or tenderness around eyes and cheekbones; fever; stuffy or runny nose; headache; cough; shortness of breath or troubled breathing; tightness of chest or wheezing); ***somnolence*** (sleepiness or unusual drowsiness); ***trauma; tremor*** (trembling or shaking); ***urinary frequency or retention*** (problems in urinating); ***urinary disorder*** (trouble in urinating); ***vomiting***

Note: *Dryness of mouth* is probably due to a direct effect on the serotonin system rather than cholinergic blockade.

Incidence less frequent

Abnormal accommodation (blurred vision; change in near or distance vision; difficulty in focusing eyes); ***abnormal dreams; abnormal vision*** (changes in vision); ***allergic reaction, seasonal*** (itching, pain, redness, or swelling of eye or eyelid; watering of eyes; troubled breathing or wheezing; severe skin rash or hives; flushing; headache; fever; chills; runny nose; increased sensitivity to sunlight; joint pain; swollen glands); ***amnesia*** (loss of memory; problems with memory); ***anxiety; appetite, increased; arthralgia*** (pain in joints; muscle pain or stiffness; difficulty in moving); ***back pain; blurred vision; bronchitis*** (cough producing mucus; difficulty breathing; shortness of breath; tightness in chest; wheezing); ***chills; concentration impaired; confusion; cough increased; depersonalization*** (feeling of unreality; sense of detachment from self or body.); ***depression*** (discouragement, feeling sad or empty; irritability; lack of appetite; loss of interest or pleasure; tiredness; trouble concentrating; trouble sleeping); ***drugged feeling; dysmenorrhea*** (pain; cramps; heavy bleeding); ***eczema*** (skin rash encrusted, scaly and oozing); ***emotion, lack of; fever; hyperkinesia*** (increase in body movements); ***hypertension*** (blurred vision; dizziness; nervousness; headache; pounding in the ears; slow or fast heartbeat); ***menstrual disorder*** (menstrual changes); ***migraine*** (headache, severe and throbbing); ***myoclonus*** (muscle twitching or jerking; rhythmic movement of muscles); ***oropharynx disorder*** (lump in throat; tightness in throat); ***pain; paresthesia*** (tingling, burning, or prickling sensations); ***pharyngitis*** (body aches or pain; congestion; cough; dryness or soreness of throat; fever; hoarseness; runny nose; tender, swollen glands in neck; trouble in swallowing; voice changes); ***rhinitis*** (stuffy nose; runny nose sneezing); ***skin photosensitivity*** (increased sensitivity of skin to sunlight; itching; redness or other discoloration of skin; severe sunburn; skin rash); ***taste perversion*** (change in sense of taste); ***tooth disorder*** (problems with tooth); ***urinary tract infection*** (bladder pain; bloody or cloudy urine; difficult, burning, or painful urination; frequent urge to urinate; lower back or side pain); ***vaginitis*** (itching of the vagina or genital area; pain during sexual intercourse; thick, white vaginal discharge with no odor or with a mild odor); ***vasodilation*** (feeling of warmth or heat; flushing or redness of skin, especially on face and neck; headache; feeling faint, dizzy, or light-headedness; sweating); ***weight loss or gain; yawn***

Note: Paroxetine may cause less *weight loss* than fluoxetine or sertraline; also, it may cause less *weight gain* than imipramine, especially in females. Long-term paroxetine treatment may cause *increased appetite* and *weight gain*.

Those indicating the need for medical attention if they occur after medication is discontinued

Agitation, confusion, or restlessness; anxiety (fear; nervousness); ***diarrhea; dizziness, vertigo, or lightheadedness; dysphoric mood*** (feeling unwell or unhappy); ***electric shock sensations; emotional lability*** (crying; depersonalization; dysphoria; euphoria; mental depression; paranoia; quick to react or overreact emotionally; rapidly changing moods); ***headache; hypomania*** (actions that are out of control; irritability; nervousness; talking, feeling, and acting with excitement); ***increased sweating; insomnia*** (trouble in sleeping); ***irritability; lethargy*** (unusual drowsiness, dullness, tiredness, weakness or feeling of sluggishness); ***migraine-like visual disturbances*** (vision changes); ***myalgia*** (muscle pain); ***nausea or vomiting; paresthesia*** (burning, crawling, itching, numbness, prickling, "pins and needles", or tingling feelings); ***rhinorrhea*** (runny nose); ***sleep disturbances, including abnormal dreams*** (trouble in sleeping); ***tremor*** (trembling or shaking); ***unusual tiredness or weakness***

Note: Discontinuation symptoms, if they occur, usually start 1 to 4 days after stopping paroxetine; however, some patients may experience effects immediately. Instances of withdrawal symptoms occurring in patients after paroxetine dosage was tapered over 7 to 10 days have been reported. Although most effects are generally mild and transient, some patients may experience more severe symptoms.

Dose reduction of paroxetine at various doses has also been found to be associated with the appearance of new symptoms including: agitation, anxiety, confusion, dizziness, dysphoric mood, emotional lability, headache, hypomania, insomnia, irritability, lethargy, and sensory disturbances (including shock-like electrical sensations).

Overdose

For specific information on the agents used in the management of paroxetine overdose, see *Charcoal, Activated (Oral-Local)* monograph.

For more information on the management of overdose or unintentional ingestion, **contact a poison control center** (see *Poison Control Center Listing*).

Clinical effects of overdose

The following effects have been selected on the basis of their potential clinical significance (possible signs and symptoms in parentheses where appropriate)—not necessarily inclusive:

Dilated pupils (large pupils); ***dizziness; drowsiness; dryness of mouth; flushing of face; irritability; nausea; sinus tachycardia*** (racing heartbeat); ***tremor*** (trembling or shaking); ***vomiting***

Treatment of overdose

There is no specific antidote for paroxetine. Treatment is essentially symptomatic and supportive.

To decrease absorption—Decontaminating gastrointestinal tract by, gastric lavage, followed by administration of 20 to 30 grams of activated charcoal every 4 to 6 hours during the first 24 to 48 hours following ingestion.

Monitoring—Taking an electrocardiogram (ECG) and monitoring cardiac function if there is any sign of abnormality. Monitoring vital signs.

Supportive care—Establishing and monitoring airway. Patients in whom intentional overdose is confirmed or suspected should be referred for psychiatric consultation.

Note: Due to the large volume of distribution of paroxetine, forced diuresis, hemodialysis, hemoperfusion, or exchange transfusions are not likely to be of benefit.

If a tricyclic antidepressant has been coingested, the tricyclic toxicity may be prolonged due to inhibition of metabolism by paroxetine.

Patient Consultation

As an aid to patient consultation, refer to *Advice for the Patient, Paroxetine (Systemic)*.

In providing consultation, consider emphasizing the following selected information (» = major clinical significance):

Before using this medication

» Conditions affecting use, especially:

Pregnancy—May cause fetal harm. Notify your doctor if you become pregnant or if you plan to become pregnant during therapy. Risk benefit considerations including other available treatment options

Complications including prolonged hospitalization, respiratory support and tube feeding in neonates exposed to paroxetine and other SSRIs late in the third trimester; physician should carefully consider potential risks and benefits when treating a pregnant woman in her third trimester

FDA Pregnancy Category D

Breast-feeding—Distributed into breast milk. Tell your doctor if you are breast-feeding an infant.

Use in children—Safety and efficacy of paroxetine in pediatric patients have not been established. Preliminary data suggests an excess of occurrence of suicidal ideation and suicide attempts in clinical trials for various antidepressant drugs, including paroxetine, in pediatric patients with major depressive disorder.

Use in the elderly—Paroxetine is associated with increased plasma levels and prolongation of the elimination half-life relative to younger adults. There were no overall differences in adverse events between elderly and younger patients, and the effectiveness was similar in younger and older patients.

Contraindicated medications—Monoamine oxidase (MAO) inhibitors, pimozide, thioridazine

Other medications, especially aspirin, atomoxetine, moclobemide, nonsteroidal anti-inflammatory drugs, serotonergics or other medications or substances with serotonergic activity, St. John's wort, tricyclic antidepressants, and warfarin or other drugs that affect coagulation

Other medical problems, especially bipolar disorder or risk of, hypersensitivity to paroxetine or any of the inactive ingredients or severe hepatic or renal function impairment

Proper use of this medication

» Compliance with therapy; not taking more or less medicine than prescribed

Taking with or without food, on a full or empty stomach, as directed by physician

» Four or more weeks of therapy may be required before antidepressant effects are achieved; antiobsessional and antipanic effects may require several weeks to achieve

For patients taking oral suspension dosage form—Shaking well before measuring dose; measuring dose with a calibrated measuring device

For patients taking extended-release tablet dosage form—Swallowing tablet whole; not chewing or crushing

» Proper dosing

Missed dose: Taking as soon as possible; continuing on regular schedule with next dose; not doubling doses

» Proper storage

Precautions while using this medication

Regular visits to physician to check progress of therapy

Checking with physician before discontinuing medication

» Importance of patient tapering off of the medication as directed by the physician

» Importance of patient or caregiver notifying physician immediately if any signs of abnormal behavior, worsening depression or suicidality occur

» Not taking paroxetine within 2 weeks of taking a monoamine oxidase (MAO) inhibitor; not starting an MAO inhibitor within 2 weeks of discontinuing paroxetine

Avoiding use of alcoholic beverages

» Possible blurred vision, drowsiness, impairment of judgment, thinking, or motor skills; caution when driving or doing jobs requiring alertness until effects of medication are known

Side/adverse effects

Signs of potential side effects, especially agitation; chest pain; myalgia, myasthenia, or myopathy; palpitation; postural hypotension; respiratory disorder; skin rash; tachycardia; abnormal bleeding; extrapyramidal symptoms; hyponatremia; mania or hypomania; mydriasis; seizures; serotonin syndrome

(Signs of potential side effects observed during clinical practice, especially agranulocytosis; akathisia; anaphylaxis; aplastic anemia; allergic alveolitis; bradykinesia; bone marrow aplasia; cogwheel rigidity; eclampsia; galactorrhea; Guillain-Barre syndrome; impaired hematopoiesis; hemolytic anemia; Henoch-Schonlein purpura; hypertonia; laryngismus; elevated liver function tests; neuroleptic malignant syndrome; oculogyric crisis; optic neuritis; acute pancreatitis; pancytopenia; porphyria; priapism; prolactinemia; pulmonary hypertension; acute renal failure; status epilepticus; syndrome of inappropriate antidiuretic hormone (SIADH); thrombocytopenia; torsade de pointes; toxic epidermal necrolysis; trismus; vasculitic syndrome; ventricular fibrillation; or ventricular tachycardia)

Signs of discontinuation symptoms, especially agitation, anxiety, confusion, dizziness, dysphoric mood, emotional lability, headache, hypomania, insomnia, irritability, lethargy, and sensory disturbances (including shock-like electrical sensations).

General Dosing Information

Paroxetine may be administered once daily, usually in the morning, to diminish sleep disturbances and other adverse effects.

Potentially suicidal patients, particularly those who may use alcohol excessively, should not have access to large quantities of this medication. Some clinicians recommend that the patient have immediate access to the smallest total amount of medication necessary for satisfactory patient management.

Patients should be periodically reassessed to determine the need for continued treatment and dosage adjustments should be made to maintain the patient on the lowest effective dosage.

Abrupt discontinuation of paroxetine may result in discontinuation symptoms. It is not known whether tapering the dose will prevent or reduce discontinuation symptoms. Patients should be monitored for discontinuation symptoms, regardless of the indication for which paroxetine was prescribed. If intolerable symptoms occur following a decrease in dose or upon discontinuation of treatment, then resuming the previously prescribed dose may be considered. Subsequently the physician may continue decreasing the dose, but at a more gradual rate.

Diet/Nutrition

Paroxetine may be taken with or without food. Some clinicians advise their patients to take this medication with food to lessen gastrointestinal side effects.

For treatment of adverse effects

Serotonin syndrome—Serotonergic medications should be discontinued. Treatment is essentially symptomatic and supportive. The nonspecific serotonergic receptor antagonists cyproheptadine and methysergide have been reported to be of some use in shortening the duration of the syndrome.

Oral Dosage Forms

PAROXETINE HYDROCHLORIDE ORAL SUSPENSION

Note: The dosing and strength of the available dosage forms are expressed in terms of paroxetine base (not the hydrochloride salt).

Usual adult dose

Antianxiety, general or
Antidepressant or
Antiobsessional agent or
Posttraumatic stress disorder treatment—

Oral, initially 20 mg (base) once a day, usually in the morning. The dosage may be increased, as needed and tolerated, by 10 mg a day at intervals of at least seven days.

Antianxiety social—

Oral, initially 20 mg (base) once daily, usually in the morning

Antipanic agent—

Oral, initially 10 mg (base) once a day, usually in the morning. The dosage may be increased, as needed and tolerated, by 10 mg a day at intervals of at least seven days.

Note: For most patients, 20 mg a day is the optimal dosage for treatment of depression, social anxiety disorder, generalized anxiety disorder, and posttraumatic stress disorder. For treatment of obsessive-compulsive disorder and panic disorder, 40 mg a day is the recommended dosage.

For all indications, debilitated patients and patients with severe renal or hepatic function impairment should receive an initial dosage of 10 mg (base) a day, with upward titration as needed, up to a maximum of 40 mg a day. Longer intervals should be allowed between dosage increases in patients with renal or hepatic function impairment.

Usual adult prescribing limits

Antidepressant or
Generalized anxiety disorder or
Posttraumatic stress disorder treatment—
50 mg (base) per day.

Antianxiety agent or
Antiobsessional agent or
Antipanic agent—
60 mg (base) per day.

Antianxiety, social—
20 mg (base) per day

Note: For all indications, debilitated patients and patients with severe renal or hepatic function impairment, dosage should not exceed 40 mg per day.

Usual pediatric dose

Safety and efficacy have not been established.

Usual geriatric dose

Antianxiety
Antidepressant or
Antiobsessional agent or
Antipanic agent or
Posttraumatic stress disorder treatment—
Oral, initially 10 mg (base) once a day, usually in the morning. The dosage may be increased as needed and tolerated.

Usual geriatric prescribing limits

Antianxiety or
Antidepressant or
Antiobsessional agent or
Antipanic agent or
Posttraumatic stress disorder treatment—
40 mg (base) a day.

Strength(s) usually available

U.S.—

10 mg (base) per 5 mL (Rx) [*Paxil* (citric acid anhydrate; FD&C Yellow No. 6; flavorings; glycerin; methylparaben; microcrystalline cellulose; polacrilin potassium; propylparaben; propylene glycol; simethicone emulsion USP; sodium citrate dihydrate; sodium saccharin; sorbitol)].

Canada—

Not commercially available.

Packaging and storage

Store at or below 25 °C (77 °F), unless otherwise specified by manufacturer.

Auxiliary labeling

- Avoid alcoholic beverages.
- May cause drowsiness.
- Shake well before using.

Additional information

Paroxetine hydrochloride oral suspension is orange flavored.

PAROXETINE HYDROCHLORIDE TABLETS

Note: The dosing and strength of the available dosage forms are expressed in terms of paroxetine base (not the hydrochloride salt).

Usual adult dose

See *Paroxetine Hydrochloride Oral Suspension*

Usual adult prescribing limits

See *Paroxetine Hydrochloride Oral Suspension*

Usual pediatric dose

See *Paroxetine Hydrochloride Oral Suspension*

Usual geriatric dose

See *Paroxetine Hydrochloride Oral Suspension*

Usual geriatric prescribing limits

See *Paroxetine Hydrochloride Oral Suspension*

Strength(s) usually available

U.S.—

10 mg (base) (Rx) [*Paxil* (dibasic calcium phosphate dihydrate; hypromellose; magnesium stearate; polyethylene glycols; polysorbate 80; sodium starch glycolate; titanium dioxide; D&C Red No. 30; and/or D&C Yellow No. 10; and/or FD&C Blue No. 2; and/or FD&C Yellow No. 6); GENERIC].

20 mg (base) (Rx) [*Paxil* (scored; dibasic calcium phosphate dihydrate; hypromellose; magnesium stearate; polyethylene glycols; polysorbate 80; sodium starch glycolate; titanium dioxide; D&C Red No. 30; and/or D&C Yellow No. 10; and/or FD&C Blue No. 2; and/or FD&C Yellow No. 6); GENERIC].

30 mg (base) (Rx) [*Paxil* (dibasic calcium phosphate dihydrate; hypromellose; magnesium stearate; polyethylene glycols; polysorbate 80; sodium starch glycolate; titanium dioxide; D&C Red No. 30; and/or D&C Yellow No. 10; and/or FD&C Blue No. 2; and/or FD&C Yellow No. 6); GENERIC].

40 mg (base) (Rx) [*Paxil* (dibasic calcium phosphate dihydrate; hypromellose; magnesium stearate; polyethylene glycols; polysorbate 80; sodium starch glycolate; titanium dioxide; D&C Red No. 30; and/or D&C Yellow No. 10; and/or FD&C Blue No. 2; and/or FD&C Yellow No. 6); GENERIC].

Canada—

10 mg (base) (Rx) [*Paxil* (scored; dibasic calcium phosphate dihydrate USP; sodium starch glycolate NF; hydroxypropyl methylcellulose; hypromellose; polyethelene glycols; polysorbate 80; titanium dioxide; D&C Yellow No. 10 aluminum lake; and/or FD&C Blue No. 2 aluminum lake; and/or FD&C Yellow No. 6 aluminum lake)].

20 mg (base) (Rx) [*Paxil* (scored; dibasic calcium phosphate dihydrate USP; sodium starch glycolate NF; hydroxypropyl methylcellulose; hypromellose; magnesium stearate NF; polyethelene glycols; polysorbate 80; titanium dioxide; D&C Yellow No. 10 aluminum lake; and/or FD&C Blue No. 2 aluminum lake; and/or FD&C Yellow No. 6 aluminum lake)].

30 mg (base) (Rx) [*Paxil* (dibasic calcium phosphate dihydrate USP; sodium starch glycolate NF; hydroxypropyl methylcellulose; hypromellose; magnesium stearate NF; polyethelene glycols; polysorbate 80; titanium dioxide; D&C Yellow No. 10 aluminum lake; and/or FD&C Blue No. 2 aluminum lake; and/or FD&C Yellow No. 6 aluminum lake)].

Packaging and storage

Store between 15 and 30 °C (59 and 86 °F), unless otherwise specified by manufacturer.

Auxiliary labeling

- Avoid alcoholic beverages.
- May cause drowsiness.

PAROXETINE HYDROCHLORIDE EXTENDED-RELEASE TABLETS

Usual adult dose

Antidepressant—
Oral, initially 25 milligrams (mg) once a day, usually in the morning. The dosage may be increased, as needed and tolerated, by 12.5 mg a day at intervals of at least seven days.

Antipanic agent or
Premenstrual dysphoric disorder or
Social anxiety disorder—
Oral, initially 12.5 milligrams (mg) once a day, usually in the morning. The dosage may be increased, as needed and tolerated, by 12.5 mg a day at intervals of at least seven days.

Note: Debilitated patients and patients with severe renal or hepatic function impairment should receive an initial dosage of 12.5 mg a day, with upward titration as needed, to a maximum of 50 mg a day.

Usual adult prescribing limits

Antidepressant—
62.5 milligrams a day.

Antipanic agent—
75 milligrams a day.

Premenstrual dysphoric disorder—
25 milligrams a day.

Social anxiety disorder—
37.5 milligrams a day.

Usual pediatric dose

Safety and efficacy have not been established.

Usual geriatric dose

For antidepressant, antipanic disorder, or social anxiety disorder: *See Usual adult dose.*

Usual geriatric prescribing limits

Antidepressant—
50 milligrams a day.

Antipanic—
50 milligrams a day

Social anxiety disorder—
See Usual adult prescribing limits

Strength(s) usually available

U.S.—

12.5 milligrams (Rx) [*Paxil CR* (hypromellose; polyvinylpyrrolidone; lactose monohydrate; magnesium stearate; colloidal silicon dioxide; glyceryl behenate; methacrylic acid copolymer type C; sodium lauryl sulfate; polysorbate 80; talc; triethyl citrate; yellow ferric oxide and/or red ferric oxide and/or D&C Red No. 30 and/or D&C Yellow No. 6 and/or D&C Yellow No. 10 and/or FD&C Blue No. 2)].

25 milligrams (Rx) [*Paxil CR* (hypromellose; polyvinylpyrrolidone; lactose monohydrate; magnesium stearate; colloidal silicon dioxide; glyceryl behenate; methacrylic acid copolymer type C; sodium lauryl sulfate; polysorbate 80; talc; triethyl citrate; yellow ferric oxide and/or red ferric oxide and/or D&C Red No. 30 and/or D&C Yellow No. 6 and/or D&C Yellow No. 10 and/or FD&C Blue No. 2)].

37.5 milligrams (Rx) [*Paxil CR* (hypromellose; polyvinylpyrrolidone; lactose monohydrate; magnesium stearate; colloidal silicon dioxide; glyceryl behenate; methacrylic acid copolymer type C; sodium lauryl sulfate; polysorbate 80; talc; triethyl citrate; yellow ferric oxide and/or red ferric oxide and/or D&C Red No. 30 and/or D&C Yellow No. 6 and/or D&C Yellow No. 10 and/or FD&C Blue No. 2)].

Canada—

12.5 milligrams (Rx) [*Paxil CR* (hypromellose; polyvinylpyrrolidone; lactose monohydrate; magnesium stearate; colloidal silicon dioxide; glyceryl behenate; methacrylic acid copolymer type C; sodium lauryl sulfate; polysorbate 80; talc; triethyl citrate; yellow ferric oxide and/or red ferric oxide and/or D&C Red No. 30 and/or D&C Yellow No. 6 and/or D&C Yellow No. 10 and/or FD&C Blue No. 2)].

25 milligrams (Rx) [*Paxil CR* (hypromellose; polyvinylpyrrolidone; lactose monohydrate; magnesium stearate; colloidal silicon dioxide; glyceryl behenate; methacrylic acid copolymer type C; sodium lauryl sulfate; polysorbate 80; talc; triethyl citrate; yellow ferric oxide and/or red ferric oxide and/or D&C Red No. 30 and/or D&C Yellow No. 6 and/or D&C Yellow No. 10 and/or FD&C Blue No. 2)].

Packaging and storage
Store at or below 25 °C (77 °F).

Auxiliary labeling
- Avoid alcoholic beverages.
- May cause drowsiness. Be careful when driving or operating machinery. Use caution until you become familiar with its effects
- Swallow whole. Do not crush or chew the tablets.

Selected Bibliography

Albers LJ, Reist C, Helmeste D, et al. Paroxetine shifts imipramine metabolism. Psychiatry Res 1996; 59: 189-96.

Cohen LJ, DeVane CL. Clinical implications of antidepressant pharmacokinetics and pharmacogenetics. Ann Pharmacother 1996 Dec; 30: 1471-80.

Product Information: Paxil®, paroxetine, GlaxoSmithKline, Research Triangle Park, NC. (Revised 10/2003) reviewed 11/2003

Product Information: Paxil®, paroxetine, GlaxoSmithKline, Mississauga, Ontario. (Revised 08/2003) reviewed 11/2003

Product Information: Paxil CR™, paroxetine, GlaxoSmithKline, Research Triangle Park, NC. (Revised 10/2003) reviewed 11/2003

Revised: 12/30/2005
Developed: 11/02/1999

PEGASPARGASE Systemic†

VA CLASSIFICATION (Primary): AN900

Commonly used brand name(s): *Oncaspar.*

Another commonly used name is PEG-L-asparaginase.

Note: For a listing of dosage forms and brand names by country availability, see *Dosage Forms* section(s).

†Not commercially available in Canada.

Category
Antineoplastic.

Indications

Accepted
Acute lymphoblastic leukemia (ALL) (treatment)—Pegaspargase is indicated as a component of a multi-agent chemotherapeutic regimen for the treatment of patients with ALL and hypersensitivity to the native forms of L-asparaginase.

Acute lymphoblastic leukemia (first-line treatment)—Pegaspargase is indicated as a component of a multi-agent chemotherapeutic regimen for the first line treatment of patients with ALL.

Pharmacology/Pharmacokinetics

Physicochemical characteristics
Source—Pegaspargase is a modified version of the enzyme L-asparaginase. L-asparaginase is modified by covalently conjugating units of monomethoxypolyethylene glycol (PEG), which has a molecular weight of 5000, to the enzyme, forming the active ingredient PEG-L-asparaginase. The L-asparaginase used in the manufacture of pegaspargase is derived from *Escherichia coli.* Monomethoxypolyethylene glycol covalently linked with L-asparaginase decreases antigenicity and extends the plasma half-life, allowing lower doses and less frequent administration.

Mechanism of action/Effect
The growth of malignant and normal cells depends on the availability of specific nutrients and cofactors required for protein synthesis. Some nutrients can be synthesized within the cell, whereas others, such as essential amino acids, require exogenous sources. L-asparagine is a nonessential amino acid synthesized by the transamination of L-aspartic acid by a reaction catalyzed by the enzyme L-asparagine synthetase. The ability to synthesize asparagine is notably lacking in malignancies of lymphoid origin; therefore, leukemic cells are dependent on an exogenous source of asparagine for survival. Asparaginase catalyzes the conversion of L-asparagine to aspartic acid and ammonia. The enzyme does not enter cells; instead, it degrades circulating asparagine to aspartic acid, which cannot be converted to asparagine by the leukemic cells. Rapid depletion of asparagine, which results from treatment with the enzyme L-asparaginase, kills the leukemic cells. Normal cells, however, are less affected by the rapid depletion due to their ability to synthesize asparagine. This therapeutic approach is based on a specific metabolic defect in some leukemic cells that do not produce asparagine synthetase.

In animal studies, pegaspargase is more effective than L-asparaginase when administered at the same dose. One unit of pegaspargase was as effective as 5 units of *E. coli* L-asparaginase in one tumor type and nearly twice as active as L-asparaginase in another tumor type. In studies of animals with non-Hodgkin's lymphoma, pegaspargase in doses of 10 to 30 International Units per kg (IU/kg) was as effective as L-asparaginase 400 IU/kg, and caused fewer side effects.

Half-life
L-asparaginase levels are detectable for at least 15 days after intravenous treatment with pegaspargase. After a single intramuscular injection of pegaspargase (2500 International Units per square meter of body surface area [IU/m^2]) in children, the half-life was 5.73 days as compared with 1.24 days after *E. coli* L-asparaginase (25,000 IU/m^2) and 0.65 days after *Erwina* L-asparaginase (25,000 IU/m^2).

Among adults treated with pegaspargase 2500 IU/m^2 every 2 weeks, the half-life was 3.24 days in patients previously hypersensitive to L-asparaginase and 5.69 days in nonhypersensitive patients.

Peak serum concentration
Found in the lymph at about 20% of the concentration in plasma.

Elimination
The metabolic fate and method of elimination of pegaspargase are unknown. Little is excreted in the urine. In one study, the results of serum and urine enzyme-linked immunoadsorbent assay (ELISA) suggest that pegaspargase activity and protein are cleared by mechanisms other than urinary excretion. Possible mechanisms that are consistent with the results of this study include proteolysis of the enzyme and/or removal by an organ other than the kidneys. Although previous reports suggest this may not be the case, pegaspargase may be metabolized by the liver, excreted in the bile, or filtered from the plasma by the reticuloendothelial system.

Precautions to Consider

Cross-sensitivity and/or related problems
Patients who are allergic to native forms of L-asparaginase may also be allergic to pegaspargase. During clinical trials, approximately 18% of patients experienced hypersensitivity reactions to pegaspargase. Sixty-five percent of the patients who had reactions previously experienced hypersensitivity reaction to *Escherichia coli* asparaginase. The other 35% had no prior hypersensitivity reaction to native asparaginase. Since these trials included patients who had previous hypersensitivity reactions to the native asparaginase, the possibility exists that cross-sensitivity played a role in the reported reactions. Documentation of cross-sensitivity between *E. coli* and *Erwina* asparaginase in leukemic children exists in which 33% of patients experiencing a reaction to *E. coli* asparaginase also become hypersensitive to *Erwina* asparaginase. Therefore, this phenomenon should also be considered as a possible factor when reviewing the incidence of reported hypersensitivity reactions to pegaspargase.

Carcinogenicity
Long-term studies in animals have not been done.

Mutagenicity
Pegaspargase did not exhibit a mutagenic effect when tested against *Salmonella typhimurium* strains in the Ames mutagenicity assay.

Pregnancy/Reproduction
Fertility—Studies on the effects of pegaspargase on fertility have not been done.

Pregnancy—Studies have not been done in humans. However, pegaspargase should be avoided during pregnancy unless it is clearly needed.

Studies have not been done in animals.

FDA Pregnancy Category C.

Breast-feeding
It is not known whether pegaspargase is distributed into breast milk. However, because of the potential for serious adverse reactions due to pegaspargase in nursing infants, a decision should be made to either discontinue nursing or discontinue the medication, taking into account the importance of the medication to the welfare of the mother.

Pediatrics
Infants up to 1 year of age—Safety and efficacy have not been established.

Children 1 to 9 years of age—Safety and efficacy have been established.

Pediatric patients treated with pegaspargase had a somewhat lower incidence of known L-asparaginase toxicities, except for hypersensitivity reactions, than the adult patients treated with pegaspargase.

Geriatrics
No information is available on the relationship of age to the effects of pegaspargase in geriatric patients.

Dental
The leukopenic and thrombocytopenic effects of pegaspargase may result in an increased incidence of certain microbial infections of the mouth, delayed healing, and gingival bleeding. If leukopenia or thrombocytopenia occurs, dental work should be deferred until blood counts have returned to normal. Patients should be instructed in proper oral hygiene, including caution in use of regular toothbrushes, dental floss, and toothpicks.

Drug interactions and/or related problems
The following drug interactions and/or related problems have been selected on the basis of their potential clinical significance (possible mechanism in parentheses where appropriate)—not necessarily inclusive (» = major clinical significance):

Note: Combinations containing any of the following medications, depending on the amount present, may also interact with this medication.

» Anti-inflammatory drugs, nonsteroidal (NSAIDs) or
» Aspirin or
» Dipyridamole or
» Heparin or
» Warfarin
(patients treated with pegaspargase are at increased risk of bleeding complications, especially when administered concomitantly with agents with anticoagulant properties; imbalances in coagulation factors have been noted with the use of pegaspargase, predisposing the patient to bleeding and/or thrombosis; caution should be used when administering any concurrent anticoagulant therapy; it has also been suggested that blood coagulation factor XIII participates in the cross-linking between fibrins and between fibrin and asparaginase)

Blood-dyscrasia causing medications (see *Appendix II*)
(leukopenic and/or thrombocytopenic effects of pegaspargase may be increased with concurrent or recent therapy if these medications cause the same effects; dosage adjustment of pegaspargase, if necessary, should be based on blood counts)

» Bone marrow depressants, other (see *Appendix II*)
Radiation therapy
(additive bone marrow depression, including severe dermatitis and/or mucositis, may occur; dosage reduction may be required when two or more bone marrow depressants, including radiation, are used concurrently or consecutively)

Hepatotoxic medications, other (see *Appendix II*)
(concurrent use may increase the risk of toxicity)

Methotrexate
(pegaspargase antagonizes the effects of methotrexate [antifolate] when given before methotrexate administration; however, if pegaspargase is given 24 hours after methotrexate, the action of the antifolate is abbreviated at that point and patients can tolerate large doses of methotrexate)

Vaccines, killed virus
(because normal defense mechanisms may be suppressed by pegaspargase therapy, the patient's antibody response to the vaccine may be decreased. The interval between discontinuation of medications that cause immunosuppression and restoration of the patient's ability to respond to the vaccine depends on the intensity and type of immunosuppression-causing medication used, the underlying disease, and other factors; estimates vary from 3 months to 1 year)

» Vaccines, live virus
(because normal defense mechanisms may be suppressed by pegaspargase therapy, concurrent use with a live virus vaccine may potentiate the replication of the vaccine virus, may increase the side/adverse effects of the vaccine virus, and/or may decrease the patient's antibody response to the vaccine; immunization of these patients should be undertaken only with extreme caution after careful review of the patient's hematologic status and only with the knowledge and consent of the physician managing the pegaspargase therapy. The interval between discontinuation of medications that cause immunosuppression and restoration of the patient's ability to respond to the vaccine depends on the intensity and type of immunosuppression-causing medication used, the underlying disease, and other factors; estimates vary from 3 months to 1 year. Patients with leukemia in remission should not receive live virus vaccine until at least 3 months after their last chemotherapy. In addition, immunization with oral poliovirus vaccine should be postponed in persons in close contact with the patient, especially family members)

Laboratory value alterations
The following have been selected on the basis of their potential clinical significance (possible effect in parentheses where appropriate)—not necessarily inclusive (» = major clinical significance).

With physiology/laboratory test values
» Alanine aminotransferase (ALT [SGPT]) and
» Alkaline phosphatase and
» Amylase, serum and
» Aspartate aminotransferase (AST [SGOT]) and
» Bilirubin, serum concentrations and
» Blood urea nitrogen (BUN) and
» Glucose, serum and
» Uric acid, serum concentrations
(values may be increased)

» Prothrombin time
(may be prolonged)

Medical considerations/Contraindications
The medical considerations/contraindications included have been selected on the basis of their potential clinical significance (reasons given in parentheses where appropriate)—not necessarily inclusive (» = major clinical significance).

Except under special circumstances, this medication should not be used when the following medical problems exist:

» Allergy to pegaspargase

» Bleeding disorders, associated with previous asparaginase therapy
(pegaspargase should not be used in patients who have experienced significant hemorrhagic events associated with prior asparaginase therapy [all preparations])

» Pancreatitis, or history of
(pegaspargase should not be used in patients with active pancreatitis or a history of pancreatitis)

» Thrombosis with prior L-asparaginase therapy

Risk-benefit should be considered when the following medical problems exist:

» Anticoagulant therapy, or
» Bleeding disorders, history of
(may cause platelet dysfunction and hemorrhage)

» Chickenpox, existing or recent (including recent exposure) or
» Herpes zoster
(risk of severe generalized disease)

» Diabetes mellitus
(increased risk of hyperglycemia)

» Hepatic function impairment
(impaired metabolism of pegaspargase may result in fatty changes in the liver and liver failure)

» Tumor cell infiltration of the bone marrow

» Caution should be used also in patients with inadequate bone marrow reserves due to previous cytotoxic drug or radiation therapy

Patient monitoring

The following may be especially important in patient monitoring (other tests may be warranted in some patients, depending on condition; » = major clinical significance):

» Amylase, concentrations, serum
(recommended at periodic intervals throughout therapy to detect early evidence of pancreatitis)

Blood counts, complete, including differential and leukocytes and platelet counts and

Glucose, blood, concentrations and

Hepatic function determinations, including serum transaminase and alkaline phosphatase values and bilirubin concentrations
(recommended at periodic intervals throughout therapy)

Side/Adverse Effects

Note: In studies, adult patients treated with pegaspargase had a higher incidence of adverse reactions than children. The exception was hypersensitivity reactions, which occurred more frequently in children.

Anaphylactic-type reactions have been described in three cancer patients receiving intravenous pegaspargase administered over 1 hour every 2 weeks. In two of these patients, anaphylaxis occurred after the second (500 International Units per square meter of body surface area [IU/m^2]) and third (2000 IU/m^2) doses, respectively. A sudden disappearance of plasma asparaginase preceded both reactions. Anti-asparaginase antibodies were seen in one of the patients, and this patient previously had developed a mild allergic reaction to the native enzyme. The second patient, who did not possess anti-asparaginase antibodies, had not previously received native asparaginase. The third patient, who developed bronchospasm following the first dose, had not received native asparaginase previously and had normal enzyme levels with no antibodies present. These results suggest that a sudden disappearance of plasma enzyme levels may predispose patients to hypersensitivity reactions during subsequent pegaspargase administration.

Some investigators described significant reduction in plasma asparaginase activity despite continued administration of *Escherichia coli* asparaginase. The investigators attributed this reduction in enzyme activity to specific immune globulin G (IgG) antibodies (anti-L-asparaginase antibodies) that destroy the enzyme and/or enhance its clearance. This has been referred to as "silent hypersensitivity," as it can occur prior to, or in the absence of, an observable clinical hypersensitivity reaction.

Hepatotoxicity occurs in most patients to some degree. It is manifested by decreases in serum albumin and serum lipoprotein levels, and increases in liver transaminase levels. Biopsy specimens and autopsies have shown fatty changes in the liver. Liver toxicity can be dose-limiting, but function generally returns to normal after the medication is discontinued.

Neurotoxicity may occur in some patients. L-asparaginase breaks down L-asparagine into aspartic acid and ammonia, and L-glutamine into L-glutamic acid. Central nervous system changes may result from a high level of ammonia in the blood or from a lack of L-asparagine or L-glutamine in the brain. These changes are characterized by confusion and, rarely, stupor, coma, or death. Neurotoxicity is less common in children.

The following side/adverse effects have been selected on the basis of their potential clinical significance (possible signs and symptoms in parentheses where appropriate)—not necessarily inclusive:

Those indicating need for medical attention

Incidence more frequent

Allergic reaction (skin rash); ***coagulopathy*** (unusual bleeding or bruising); ***hyperglycemia*** (blurry vision; dry mouth and skin; fatigue; increased need to urinate; increased hunger or thirst; unexplained weight loss)—requiring insulin therapy; ***liver damage; pancreatitis*** (abdominal or stomach pain; constipation; nausea; vomiting)

Incidence less frequent

Anaphylactic reaction (difficulty in breathing or swallowing; hives; itching, especially of hands or feet; reddening of the skin, especially around ears; swelling of eyes, face, or inside of nose; unusual tiredness or weakness, sudden and severe); ***central nervous system (CNS) thrombosis*** (seizures; headache; muscle weakness; loss of coordination; visual disturbances); ***hyperbilirubinemia*** (yellow eyes or skin)

Incidence rare

Leukopenia, septicemia, thrombocytopenia, or bone marrow depression (black, tarry stools; blood in urine; cough or hoarseness; fever or chills; lower back or side pain; painful or difficult urination; pinpoint red spots on skin; unusual bleeding or bruising)

Incidence unknown

Glucose intolerance (faintness; nausea; skin paleness; sweating); ***sagittal sinus thrombosis*** (headache; confusion; nausea and vomiting; numbness or tingling in arms or legs); ***thrombosis*** (tenderness, pain, swelling, warmth, skin discoloration, and prominent superficial veins over affected area)

Those indicating need for medical attention only if they continue or are bothersome

Incidence more frequent

Fever; malaise (general feeling of discomfort or illness); ***nausea and vomiting***

Incidence less frequent

Anorexia (lack of appetite); ***arthralgia or myalgia*** (pain in joints or muscles); ***convulsions*** (seizures); ***hypoglycemia*** (anxiety; behavior change similar to drunkenness; blurred vision; cold sweats; confusion; cool pale skin; difficulty in concentrating; drowsiness; excessive hunger; fast heartbeat; headache; nausea; nervousness; nightmares; restless sleep; shakiness; slurred speech; unusual tiredness or weakness); ***hypoproteinemia; hypotension reaction*** (severe tiredness or weakness); ***pain at place of injection; tachycardia*** (fast heartbeat)

Patient Consultation

As an aid to patient consultation, refer to *Advice for the Patient, Pegaspargase (Systemic).*

In providing consultation, consider emphasizing the following selected information (» = major clinical significance):

Before using this medication

» Conditions affecting use, especially:

Sensitivity to pegaspargase

Pregnancy—Use is not recommended; women of childbearing age should be advised to avoid pregnancy during treatment

Breast-feeding—Use is not recommended because of the potential for serious adverse effects in nursing infants

Use in children—Safety and efficacy have not been established in infants up to 1 year of age.

Dental—Patients who develop blood dyscrasias may be at increased risk of microbial infections of the mouth, delayed healing, and gingival bleeding

Other medications, especially nonsteroidal anti-inflammatory drugs (NSAIDs), aspirin, dipyridamole, heparin, other bone marrow depressants, or warfarin

Other medical problems, especially allergy to pegaspargase; anticoagulant therapy; bleeding disorders associated with previous asparaginase therapy; chickenpox; diabetes mellitus; hepatic function impairment; herpes zoster; history of bleeding disorders; pancreatitis or history of; thrombosis with prior L-asparaginase therapy; or tumor cell infiltration of the bone marrow

Proper use of this medication

Caution in taking combination therapy; taking each medication at the right time

Importance of ample fluid intake and subsequent increase in urine output to aid in excretion of uric acid

Frequency of nausea and vomiting; importance of continuing medication despite stomach upset

» Proper dosing

Precautions while using this medication

» Importance of close monitoring by the physician

» Avoiding immunizations unless approved by physician; other persons in patient's household should avoid immunizations with oral poliovirus vaccine; avoiding persons who have taken oral poliovirus vaccine or wearing a protective mask that covers nose and mouth

Caution if bone marrow depression occurs:

» Avoiding exposure to persons with infections, especially during periods of low blood counts; checking with physician immediately if fever or chills, cough or hoarseness, lower back or side pain, or painful or difficult urination occurs

» Checking with physician immediately if unusual bleeding or bruising; black, tarry stools; blood in urine or stools; or pinpoint red spots on skin occur

Caution in use of regular toothbrush, dental floss, or toothpick; physician, dentist, or nurse may suggest alternatives; checking with physician before having dental work done

Not touching eyes or inside of nose unless hands washed immediately before

Using caution to avoid accidental cuts with use of sharp objects such as safety razor or fingernail or toenail cutters

Avoiding contact sports or other situations where bruising or injury could occur

» Possibility of local tissue injury and scarring if infiltration of intravenous solution occurs; telling doctor or nurse right away about redness, pain, or swelling at injection site

Side/adverse effects

Signs of potential side effects, especially allergic reaction, coagulopathy, hyperglycemia, liver damage, pancreatitis, anaphylactic reaction, central nervous system (CNS) thrombosis, hyperbilirubinemia, leukopenia, septicemia, thrombocytopenia, bone marrow depression, glucose intolerance, sagittal sinus thrombosis, or thrombosis

General Dosing Information

Hypersensitivity reactions to pegaspargase, including life-threatening anaphylaxis, may occur during therapy. Therefore, appropriate precautions should be taken prior to pegaspargase administration to prevent allergic or other unwanted reactions, especially in patients with known hypersensitivity to the other forms of L-asparaginase. Precautions should include a review of the patient's history regarding possible sensitivity and the ready availability of epinephrine 1:1000, oxygen, intravenous corticosteroids, and other appropriate agents used for control of immediate allergic reactions. All patients should be observed for 1 hour after pegaspargase administration. Delayed hypersensitivity (more than 1 hour after administration) is possible, however, reactions are more likely to occur within 1 hour of administration.

The National Cancer Institute has developed Common Toxicity Criteria that can be used by health care providers to classify the severity of hypersensitivity reactions. These criteria are:

- Grade 1 or mild hypersensitivity reactions (transient rash).
- Grade 2 or moderate hypersensitivity reactions (mild bronchospasm).
- Grade 3 or severe hypersensitivity reactions (moderate bronchospasm and/or serum sickness).
- Grade 4 or life-threatening hypersensitivity reactions (hypotension and/or anaphylaxis).

Grade 2–4 reactions are considered dose-limiting and require discontinuation of asparaginase therapy.

Pegaspargase should be given under the supervision of an individual who is qualified by training and experience to administer cancer chemotherapeutic agents.

When administered intravenously, a solution of pegaspargase in water for injection or 0.9% sodium chloride injection should be given over a period of 1 to 2 hours in 100 mL of 0.9% sodium chloride injection or 5% dextrose injection, through an infusion that is already running. When pegaspargase is given intramuscularly, no more than 2 mL of a solution in sodium chloride injection should be injected at a single site. If the volume to be administered is greater than 2 mL, multiple injection sites should be used.

As a component of selected multiple agent regimens, the recommended dose of pegaspargase is 2500 International Units per square meter of body surface area (IU/m^2) every 14 days by either the intramuscular or intravenous route of administration. However, the preferred route of administration is the intramuscular route because of the lower incidence of hepatotoxicity, coagulopathy, and gastrointestinal and renal disorders as compared with the intravenous route of administration.

Pegaspargase, like native L-asparaginase, is used generally in combination with other chemotherapeutic agents, such as vincristine, methotrexate, cytarabine, daunorubicin, and doxorubicin. Multidrug chemotherapy now can cure about 70% of children and about 40% of adults with acute lymphoblastic leukemia. The usual drugs of choice for initial treatment ("induction") are vincristine, prednisone, and asparaginase with or without daunorubicin or doxorubicin, which produce a remission in more than 95% of children and about 75% of adults.

The use of pegaspargase as the sole induction agent should be undertaken only in an unusual situation in which a combined regimen, using other chemotherapeutic agents such as vincristine, methotrexate, cytarabine, daunorubicin, or doxorubicin, is inappropriate because of toxicity or other specific patient-related factors, or in patients refractory to other therapy. When pegaspargase is to be used as the sole induction agent, the recommended dosage regimen is also 2500 IU/m^2 every 14 days.

Recurrence of childhood acute lymphoblastic leukemia occurs in about 30 to 50% of patients and indicates irresistible progression of the disease. While systemic (i.e., hematologic) relapse is due to drug resistance of leukemic cells, pharmacologic barriers may be responsible for local relapses such as meningeal involvement, leukemic ophthalmopathy or testicular infiltration. L-asparaginase seems to be an important component of drug combinations for reinduction therapy for systemic relapse. Following reinduction therapy, modification of continuation therapy is necessary.

Local relapses require local treatment, i.e., radiotherapy and intrathecal administration of chemotherapy. Local relapse is almost always followed by hematologic relapse; therefore, intensification of systemic therapy is also recommended. Prevention of these relapses is much more important and probably more successful than treatment.

Safety considerations for handling this medication

There is limited but increasing evidence and concern that personnel involved in preparation and administration of parenteral antineoplastic agents may be at some risk because of the potential mutagenicity, teratogenicity, and/or carcinogenicity of these agents, although the actual risk is unknown. USP advisory panels recommend cautious handling both in preparation and disposal of antineoplastic agents. Precautions that have been suggested include:

- Use of a biological containment cabinet during reconstitution and dilution of parenteral medications and wearing of disposable surgical gloves and masks.
- Use of proper technique to prevent contamination of the medication, work area, and operator during transfer between containers (including proper training of personnel in this technique).
- Cautious and proper disposal of needles, syringes, vials, ampuls, and unused medication.

A number of medical centers have developed detailed guidelines for handling of antineoplastic agents.

Pegaspargase may be a contact irritant, and therefore the solution must be handled and administered with care. Gloves are recommended. Inhalation of vapors and contact with skin or mucous membranes, especially those of the eyes, must be avoided.

For treatment of adverse effects

Recommended treatment consists of the following:

- For mild hypersensitivity reaction—Administering antihistamines, and, if necessary, corticosteroids.
- For severe hypersensitivity or anaphylactic reaction—Administering epinephrine. Antihistamines or corticosteroids may also be administered as required.

Parenteral Dosage Forms

PEGASPARGASE INJECTION

Usual adult and adolescent dose

Leukemia, acute lymphoblastic (treatment)—

Intramuscular or intravenous, 2500 International Units per square meter of body surface area administered no more frequently than every fourteen days.

Usual pediatric dose

See *Usual adult and adolescent dose*.

Strength(s) usually available

U.S.—

750 International Units (IU) per 5-mL vial (Rx) [*Oncaspar*].

Canada—

Not commercially available.

Packaging and storage

Store between 2 and 8 °C (36 and 46 °F), unless otherwise specified by the manufacturer. Protect from freezing.

Stability

Storage above or below the recommended temperature may reduce potency. Freezing destroys potency, and product should be discarded if freezing occurs.

- Use only one dose per vial; do not re-enter the vial. Discard unused portions. Do not save unused drug for later administration.
- Do not use if cloudy or if precipitate is present.
- Do not use if stored at room temperature for more than 48 hours.

Auxiliary labeling

- Avoid excessive agitation. Do not shake.
- Do not freeze; discard if freezing occurs.

Revised: 08/08/2006
Developed: 08/29/1997

PEGFILGRASTIM Systemic

VA CLASSIFICATION (Primary): BL400

Commonly used brand name(s): *Neulasta*™.

Note: For a listing of dosage forms and brand names by country availability, see *Dosage Forms* section(s).

Category

Hematopoietic stimulant; antineutropenic.

Indications

Accepted

Febrile neutropenia (prophylaxis)—Pegfilgrastim is indicated to decrease the incidence of infection, as manifested by febrile neutropenia, in patients with non-myeloid malignancies receiving myelosuppressive anti-cancer drugs associated with a clinically significant incidence of febrile neutropenia.

Pharmacology/Pharmacokinetics

Physicochemical characteristics

Source—A covalent conjugate of recombinant methionyl human G-CSF (Filgrastim) and monomethoxypolyethylene glycol. Filgrastim is derived from the bacterial fermentation of a strain of *Escherichia coli*.

Molecular weight—39 Kilodaltons.

Solubility—Soluble in water.

Mechanism of action/Effect

Pegfilgrastim is a Colony Stimulating Factor that acts on hematopoietic cells by binding to specific cell surface receptors thereby stimulating proliferation, differentiation, commitment, and end cell functional activation.

Half-life

15 to 80 hours after a subcutaneous injection.

Elimination

Clearance of pegfilgrastim decreases with increases in dose. This is attributed to neutrophil receptor binding. The concentration of pegfilgrastim declines rapidly at the onset of neutrophil recovery. In addition, the number of neutrophils and higher body weight resulted in higher systemic exposure to pegfilgrastim when doses were normalized for body weight.

Precautions to Consider

Carcinogenicity

In rats, no cancerous or precancerous lesions were noted in a toxicity study of six months duration given once weekly subcutaneous injections of up to 1000 mcg per kg of body weight of pegfilgrastim (approximately 23 times the recommended human dose).

The carcinogenic potential of pegfilgrastim has not been evaluated in long-term animal studies.

Mutagenicity

No mutagenesis studies were conducted with pegfilgrastim.

Pregnancy/Reproduction

Fertility—In rats, once weekly subcutaneous injections of 1000 mcg per kg of body weight had no affect on fertility, sperm assessment or reproductive performance.

Pregnancy—Studies in humans have not been done. However, pegfilgrastim should be used during pregnancy only if the potential benefit to the mother justifies the potential risk to the fetus.

Studies in rabbits using doses of 50 to 1000 mcg per kg of body weight per dose (4 to 80 fold higher, respectively than the recommended human dose) have shown that pegfilgrastim may cause decreased maternal food consumption and subsequent decreased maternal and fetal body weight, increased abortions, increased resorptions, and decreased number of live fetuses.

Studies in rats have shown that very low levels (< 0.5%) of pegfilgrastim crosses the placenta when subcutaneously administered. At doses of 1000 mcg per kg of body weight per dose every other day during the period of organogenesis there was no associated embryotoxic or fetotoxic outcomes, but there was an increased incidence of wavy ribs in fetuses.

FDA Pregnancy Category C.

Breast-feeding

It is not known whether pegfilgrastim is distributed into human breast milk. However, problems in humans have not been documented.

In rats doses up to 1000 mcg per kg of body weight per dose did not result in any effect on the growth and development of offspring when maternally administered through day 18 of lactation.

Pediatrics

No information is available on the relationship of age to the effects of pegfilgrastim in the pediatric population. Safety and efficacy have not been established.

The 6-mg fixed-dose single-use syringe formulation should not be used in infants, children, and smaller adolescents weighing less than 45 kg.

Geriatrics

In clinical studies, a small population of elderly patients (18% aged 65 and over and 3% aged 75 and over) showed no overall differences in safety or efficacy when compared to younger patients. Prospective studies on the relationship of age to the effects of pegfilgrastim have not been performed, and clinically relevant differences cannot be excluded.

Pharmacogenetics

No gender-related differences were observed in the pharmacokinetics of pegfilgrastim.

Drug interactions and/or related problems

The following drug interactions and/or related problems have been selected on the basis of their potential clinical significance (possible mechanism in parentheses where appropriate)—not necessarily inclusive (» = major clinical significance):

Note: Combinations containing any of the following medications, depending on the amount present, may also interact with this medication.

» Cytotoxic chemotherapy agents
(pegfilgrastim should not be administered in the period between 14 days before and 24 hours after administration of cytotoxic chemotherapy because of the increase in sensitivity of rapidly dividing myeloid cells to cytotoxic chemotherapy.)
(Pegfilgrastim has not been studied in patients receiving chemotherapy associated with delayed myelosuppression [e.g., nitrosoureas, mitomycin C])

Fluorouracil (5-FU) or other antimetabolites
(concomitant administration has not been evaluated in humans. Adverse effects have been documented in animals when pegfilgrastim was administered 0 to 3 days prior to use of 5-FU)

Lithium
(may potentiate the release of neutrophils; more frequent monitoring of neutrophil counts is recommended)

Radiation therapy
(pegfilgrastim use has not been studied in patients receiving radiation therapy)

Laboratory value alterations

The following have been selected on the basis of their potential clinical significance (possible effect in parentheses where appropriate)—not necessarily inclusive (» = major clinical significance).

With physiology/laboratory test values

Alkaline phosphatase or
Lactate dehydrogenase (LDH) or
Uric acid
(reversible elevations may be observed)

Note: In clinical trials the incidence of LDH elevation was 19%, alkaline phosphatase was 9%, and uric acid was 8%. Treatment intervention was not required.

White blood cells (WBC)
(counts greater than 100 x 10^9 per liter were observed in less than 1% of a population of 465 patients in clinical studies.)

Medical considerations/Contraindications

The medical considerations/contraindications included have been selected on the basis of their potential clinical significance (reasons given in parentheses where appropriate)—not necessarily inclusive (» = major clinical significance).

Except under special circumstances, this medication should not be used when the following medical problem exists:

» Hypersensitivity to *E coli*-derived proteins, pegfilgrastim, filgrastim, or any other components of this product

Risk-benefit should be considered when the following medical problems exist:

Hepatic insufficiency
(pharmacokinetic profile has not been assessed)

Myeloid malignancies and myelodysplasia
(the use of pegfilgrastim has not been studied in these conditions. The possibility that pegfilgrastim can act as a growth factor for any

tumor type cannot be excluded. The granulocyte colony stimulating factor receptor through which pegfilgrastim and Filgrastim act has been found on tumor cell lines, including some myeloid, T-lymphoid, lung, head and neck and bladder tumor cell lines.)

» Peripheral blood progenitor cell (PBPC) mobilization
(rare cases of splenic rupture have been reported following the administration of the parent compound, Filgrastim, for PBPC mobilization in both healthy donors and patients with cancer; some of these cases were fatal. Use of pegfilgrastim for PBPC mobilization has not been studied and therefore, is not recommended.)

Sepsis
(cases of adult respiratory distress syndrome have been reported in neutropenic patients with sepsis who received the parent compound, Filgrastim.)

» Sickle cell disease
(pegfilgrastim should only be used in patients with this condition after careful consideration of the potential risks and benefits; there has been one report of a fatality in a patient who received the parent compound, Filgrastim)

Patient monitoring

The following may be especially important in patient monitoring (other tests may be warranted in some patients, depending on condition; » = major clinical significance):

» Adult respiratory distress syndrome (ARDS)
(patients receiving pegfilgrastim who develop fever, lung infiltrates, or respiratory distress should be evaluated for the possibility of ARDS. In the event that ARDS occurs, pegfilgrastim treatment should be discontinued or withheld until resolution of problem.)

Hematocrit and
Platelet count
(patients hematologic status should be assessed before chemotherapy administration begins and should be regularly monitored throughout the course of chemotherapy)

Sickle cell crisis
(patients with sickle cell disease who receive pegfilgrastim should be kept well hydrated and monitored for the occurrence of sickle cell crisis)

» Spleen, enlarged or
» Splenic rupture
(rare cases of splenic rupture have been reported following the administration of the parent compound, Filgrastim, for PBPC mobilization in both healthy donors and patients with cancer; some of these cases were fatal; patients receiving pegfilgrastim who report left upper abdominal or shoulder tip pain should be monitored for these conditions)

Side/Adverse Effects

The following side/adverse effects have been selected on the basis of their potential clinical significance (possible signs and symptoms in parentheses where appropriate)—not necessarily inclusive:

Note: There is a potential for immunogenicity. The incidence has not been determined. In clinical trials a small population of patients developed binding antibodies to pegfilgrastim. However, these antibodies were not neutralizing. The detection of antibody formation is dependent on several factors such as the sensitivity and specificity of the assay, and may be influenced by sample handling, concomitant medications and underlying disease.

The parent compound, Filgrastim, rarely has been associated with allergic-type reactions including anaphylaxis, skin rash, and urticaria occurring on initial or subsequent treatment. Allergic reactions have been reported in post-marketing experience with pegfilgrastim.

Cytopenias have been reported in patients treated with other recombinant growth factors. A theoretical possibility exists that antibodies to pegfilgrastim may cross-react with endogenous granulocyte colony stimulating factor. However, immune-mediated neutropenia has not been observed in clinical studies with pegfilgrastim.

Those indicating need for medical attention

Incidence more frequent

Fever, neutropenic; granulocytopenia (chills; cough; fever; sore throat; ulcers; sores, or white spots in mouth)

Note: *Neutropenic fever* and *granulocytopenia* may be attributed to the underlying malignancy or cytotoxic chemotherapy.

Incidence rare

Adult respiratory distress syndrome (ARDS) (shortness of breath; tightness in chest; troubled breathing; wheezing); ***hypoxia*** (bluish lips or skin); ***spleen, ruptured or enlarged*** (pain, left upper abdominal or shoulder)

Note: Although not observed in patients who received pegfilgrastim, rare cases of *ARDS* have been reported with the parent compound, Filgrastim. If *ARDS* occurs, pegfilgrastim therapy should be discontinued or withheld until the condition is corrected. In addition, patients should be given appropriate medical therapy.

Rare cases of *splenic rupture* have been reported following the administration of pegfilgrastim. *Splenic rupture*, some cases resulting in death, has also been associated with filgrastim. Patients receiving pegfilgrastim who report left upper abdominal and/or shoulder tip pain should be evaluated for an enlarged spleen or splenic rupture.

Incidence not determined—Observed during clinical practice

Anaphylaxis (cough; difficulty swallowing; dizziness; fast heartbeat; hives, itching, puffiness or swelling of the eyelids or around the eyes, face, lips or tongue; shortness of breath; skin rash; tightness in chest; unusual tiredness or weakness; wheezing); ***skin rash; urticaria*** (hives or welts; itching; redness of skin; skin rash)

Those indicating need for medical attention only if they continue or are bothersome

Incidence more frequent

Abdominal pain; alopecia (hair loss; thinning of hair); ***anorexia*** (loss of appetite; weight loss); ***arthralgia*** (joint pain); ***asthenia*** (lack or loss of strength); ***bone pain; constipation; diarrhea; dizziness; dyspepsia*** (acid or sour stomach; belching; heartburn; indigestion; stomach discomfort, upset, or pain); ***edema, peripheral*** (swelling of hands, ankles, feet, or lower legs); ***fatigue; fever; headache; insomnia*** (trouble sleeping); ***mucositis*** (cracked lips; diarrhea; difficulty in swallowing; sores, ulcers, or white spots on lips, tongue, or inside mouth); ***myalgia*** (muscle soreness); ***nausea; skeletal pain; stomatitis*** (swelling or inflammation of the mouth); ***taste perversion*** (change in sense of taste); ***vomiting; weakness, generalized***

Note: With the exception of *medullary bone pain*, most of the side/adverse effects listed above were attributed by the investigators to the underlying malignancy or cytotoxic chemotherapy.

In clinical trials, *medullary bone pain* occurred at an incidence of 26% and was generally mild to moderate in severity. Approximately 12% of subjects required non-narcotic analgesics, and less than 6% of subjects required narcotic analgesics to alleviate the pain.

Incidence unknown

Immunogenicity (body produces substance that can bind to drug making it less effective or cause side effects)

Overdose

For more information on the management of overdose or unintentional ingestion, **contact a poison control center** (see *Poison Control Center Listing*).

The maximum amount of pegfilgrastim that can be safely administered in single or multiple doses has not been determined. In clinical trials, a single dose of 300 mcg per kg of body weight has been administered subcutaneously without serious adverse effects.

Treatment of overdose

Specific treatment—
Leukapheresis should be considered in the management of symptomatic individuals.

Patient Consultation

As an aid to patient consultation, refer to *Advice for the Patient, Pegfilgrastim (Systemic)*.

In providing consultation, consider emphasizing the following selected information (» = major clinical significance):

Before using this medication

» Conditions affecting use, especially:
Hypersensitivity to *E coli*-derived proteins, pegfilgrastim, Filgrastim, or any other components of this product
Other medications, especially cytotoxic chemotherapy agents
Other medical problems, especially peripheral blood progenitor cell (PBPC) mobilization or sickle cell disease

Proper use of this medication

» Proper dosing
Proper storage

Precautions while using this medication

» Regular visits to physician for blood count and other monitoring

» Importance of notifying physician if upper abdominal and/or shoulder tip pain occur

Side/adverse effects
Signs of potential side effects, especially neutropenic fever, granulocytopenia, adult respiratory distress syndrome, hypoxia, ruptured spleen, enlarged spleen, and bone pain
Signs of potential side effect observed during clinical practice, especially anaphylaxis, skin rash, and urticaria

General Dosing Information

For parenteral dosing forms:

Safety considerations for handling this medication
Following administration of pegfilgrastim from the prefilled syringe, the UltraSafe® Needle Guard should be activated to prevent accidental needle sticks. The prefilled syringe should be disposed of by placing the entire prefilled syringe with guard activated into an approved puncture proof container.

Parenteral Dosage Forms

PEGFILGRASTIM INJECTION

Usual adult dose
Neutropenia, chemotherapy-related—
Subcutaneous, 6 mg administered once per chemotherapy cycle.

Note: Pegfilgrastim should not be administered during the period between 14 days before and 24 hours after administration of cytotoxic chemotherapy.
No dosing adjustment is necessary for patients with renal dysfunction.
Pharmacokinetic profile in patients with hepatic insufficiency has not been assessed.

Usual pediatric dose
Neutropenia, chemotherapy-related—
Safety and efficacy have not been established.

Note: The 6-mg fixed dose formulation should not be used in infants, children, and smaller adolescents weighing less than 45 kg.

Usual geriatric dose
See *Usual adult dose.*

Strength(s) usually available
U.S.—
6 mg of pegfilgrastim (10 mg per mL) in a single-dose syringe (Rx) [*Neulasta*™ (acetate (0.35 mg); polysorbate 20 (0.02 mg); sodium (0.02 mg); sorbitol (30.0 mg); water for injection, USP)].
Canada—
10 mg per mL (Rx) [*Neulasta*].

Packaging and storage
Store refrigerated between 36 and 46 °F (2 and 8 °C), in their carton until time of use, to protect from light. Pegfilgrastim may reach room temperature for a maximum of 48 hours prior to injection and should be protected from light. Discard pegfilgrastim if left at room temperature longer than 48 hours. Protect from freezing. If freezing should occur, pegfilgrastim may be allowed to thaw in the refrigerator one time. If frozen a second time, pegfilgrastim should be discarded.

Preparation of dosage form
Pegfilgrastim should be visually inspected for discoloration and particulate matter before administration and should not be administered if particulates or discoloration are observed.
Avoid shaking.

Additional information
Discard if frozen more than once.

Revised: 11/02/2005
Developed: 04/28/2002

PEGINTERFERON ALFA-2A
Systemic

VA CLASSIFICATION (Primary): IM404

Commonly used brand name(s): *Pegasys.*

Note: For a listing of dosage forms and brand names by country availability, see *Dosage Forms* section(s).

Category

Biological response modifier.

Indications

Accepted
Chronic hepatitis B (treatment)—Peginterferon alfa-2a is indicated for the treatment of adult patients with HBeAg positive and HBeAg negative chronic hepatitis B who have compensated liver disease and evidence of viral replication and liver inflammation.
Chronic hepatitis C virus infection (treatment)—Peginterferon alfa-2a is indicated alone or in combination with ribavirin tablets (Copegus) for the treatment of adults with chronic hepatitis C virus infection who have compensated liver disease and have not been previously treated with interferon alpha.

Pharmacology/Pharmacokinetics

Physicochemical characteristics
Source—Synthetic. Peginterferon alfa-2a is a covalent conjugate of recombinant alfa-2a interferon with a single branched bis-monomethoxy polyethylene glycol (PEG) chain. Interferon alfa-2a is produced using recombinant DNA technology in which a cloned human leukocyte interferon gene is inserted into and expressed in Escherichia coli.
Molecular weight—60,000 daltons.

Mechanism of action/Effect
Interferons bind to specific receptors on the cell surface initiating intracellular signaling via a complex cascade of protein-protein interactions leading to rapid activation of gene transcription. Interferon-stimulated genes modulate many biological effects including the inhibition of viral replication in infected cells, inhibition of cell proliferation, and immunomodulation. Interferon alfa-2a stimulates the production of effector proteins such as serum neopterin and 2′5′ oligoadenylate synthetase.

Half-life
Terminal—80 hours (range 50 to 140 hours)

Time to peak concentration
72 and 96 hours

Peak serum concentration
Time to steady state concentration: 5 to 8 weeks with once weekly dosing.

Elimination
Mean systemic clearance: 94 mL/h; end stage renal disease patients have a 25% to 45% reduction in clearance.

Precautions to Consider

For information pertaining to the Precautions to Consider for ribavirin, a component of the peginterferon alfa-2a therapeutic and ribavirin combination treatment regimen, see *Ribavirin (Systemic).*

Carcinogenicity
Studies to determine the carcinogenic potential of peginterferon alfa-2a have not been done.

Mutagenicity
Peginterferon alfa-2a did not cause DNA damage when tested in the Ames bacterial mutagenicity assay and in the in vitro chromosomal aberration assay in human lymphocytes, either in the presence or the absence of metabolic activation.

Pregnancy/Reproduction
Fertility—Peginterferon alfa-2a may impair fertility in women. Prolonged menstrual cycles and/or amenorrhea were observed in female cynomolgus monkeys given subcutaneous injections of 600 mcg per kg of body weight per dose (7200 mcg per m^2 per dose) of peginterferon alfa-2a every other day for one month, at approximately 180 times the recommended weekly human dose for a 60 kg person (based on body surface area). Menstrual cycle irregularities were accompanied by both a decrease and delay in the peak 17β-estradiol and progesterone levels following administration of peginterferon alfa-2a to female monkeys. A return to normal menstrual rhythm followed cessation of treatment. Every other day dosing with 100 mcg per kg (1200 mcg per m^2) peginterferon alfa-2a (equivalent to approximately 30 times the recommended human dose) had no effects on cycle duration or reproductive hormone status.
The effects of peginterferon alfa-2a on male fertility have not been studied. However, no adverse effects on fertility were observed in male Rhesus monkeys treated with non-pegylated interferon alfa-2a for 5 months at doses up to 25 x 10^6 IU per kg of body weight per day.

Pregnancy—There are no adequate and well controlled studies of peginterferon alfa-2a in human women. Peginterferon alfa-2a should be used during pregnancy only if the potential benefit justifies the potential risk to the fetus. Peginterferon alfa-2a is recommended for use in women of childbearing potential only when they are using effective contraception during therapy.

Peginterferon alfa-2a has not been studied for its teratogenic effect. Non-pegylated interferon alfa-2a treatment of pregnant Rhesus monkeys at approximately 20 to 500 times the human weekly dose resulted in a statistically significant increase in abortions. No teratogenic effects were seen in offspring delivered at term. Peginterferon alfa-2a should be assumed to have abortifacient potential.

FDA Pregnancy Category C

Breast-feeding

It is not known if peginterferon alfa-2a is distributed into breast milk. Because of the potential for adverse reactions from the drug in nursing infants, a decision must be made whether to discontinue nursing or discontinue peginterferon alfa-2a treatment.

Pediatrics

No information is available on the relationship of age to the effects of peginterferon alfa-2a in the pediatric population. Safety and efficacy have not been established in patients less than 18 years of age

Peginterferon alfa-2a is contraindicated in neonates and infants because it contains benzyl alcohol. Benzyl alcohol is associated with an increased incidence of neurologic and other complications in neonates and infants which could be potentially fatal.

Geriatrics

Appropriate studies on the relationship of age to the effects of peginterferon alfa-2a have not been performed in the geriatric population. Dose selection should be done with caution. Elderly patients are more likely to have age related problems including adverse reactions related to alpha interferons, such as decreased renal function, CNS, cardiac, and systemic (flu-like) effects that may be more severe and caution should be exercised.

Pharmacogenetics

Gender: The pharmacokinetics of peginterferon alfa-2a are similar in males and females.

Race: African-Americans had lower response rates to peginterferon alfa-2a than Caucasians in clinical trials.

For information pertaining to the Medication Advisory Screening of ribavirin, a component of the peginterferon alfa-2a and ribavirin combination treatment regimen, see *Ribavirin (Systemic)*.

Drug interactions and/or related problems

The following drug interactions and/or related problems have been selected on the basis of their potential clinical significance (possible mechanism in parentheses where appropriate)—not necessarily inclusive (» = major clinical significance):

Note: Combinations containing any of the following medications, depending on the amount present, may also interact with this medication.

» Didanosine
([co-administration of ribavirin] and didanosine is not recommended; reports of hepatic failure, as well as peripheral neuropathy, pancreatitis and symptomatic hyperlactatemia/ lactic acidosis have been reported in clinical trials)

» Methadone
(study showed concomitant use associated with methadone levels 10 to 15% higher than baseline; significance of this unknown; patients should be monitored for the signs and symptoms of methadone toxicity)

» NRTIs
(hepatic decompensation [some fatal] were observed among CHC/HIV coinfected cirrhotic patients; patients receiving peginterferon alfa-2a/Ribavirin and NRTIs should be closely monitored for treatment associated toxicities; dose reductions or discontinuation of peginterferon alfa-2a, Ribavirin or both should also be considered if worsening toxicities are observed)

» Ribavirin
(extreme care must be taken to avoid pregnancy in female patients and female partners of male patients taking peginterferon alfa-2a and ribavirin co-therapy; women of childbearing potential and men must use two forms of effective contraception during treatment and for at least six months after co-therapy treatment has concluded)

» Theophylline
(inhibition of CYP3A4 led to an increase in theophylline AUC; theophylline serum levels should be monitored and appropriate dose adjustment considered)

Laboratory value alterations

The following have been selected on the basis of their potential clinical significance (possible effect in parentheses where appropriate)—not necessarily inclusive (» = major clinical significance).

With diagnostic test results

Thyroid function
(peginterferon alfa-2a treatment has been associated with development of hypothyroidism and hyperthyroidism.)

With physiology/laboratory test values

Alanine aminotransferase (ALT [SGPT]) serum
(less than 1% of patients had elevated ALT levels 5–to 10–fold above baseline during treatment; transient elevations of ALT up to 5–fold above baseline were observed but were not associated with the alteration of function of other liver function tests)

(25% and 27% of patients experienced elevations of 5 to 10x ULN and 12% and 18% had elevations of >10x ULN during treatment of HBeAg negative and HBeAg positive disease, respectively; ALT flares of 5 to 10% ULN occurred in 13% and 16% of patients, while ALT flares of >10x ULN occurred in 7% and 12% of patients in HBeAg negative and HBeAg positive disease, respectively, after discontinuation of therapy)

Lymphocytes
(decreases in lymphocytes are induced by interferon alfa therapy; lymphopenia was observed in 86% of patients receiving peginterferon alfa-2a alone, 5% had severe lymphopenia; median lymphocyte levels returned to pre-treatment levels after 4 to 12 weeks after cessation of therapy.)

Neutrophils
(decreases in neutrophil count below normal were observed in 95% of patients treated with peginterferon alfa-2a monotherapy or with peginterferon alfa-2a combination therapy with ribavirin; severe, life-threatening neutropenia occurred in 5% of the patients receiving either monotherapy or combination therapy; dose modifications may be needed; median neutrophil counts returned to pre-treatment levels 4 weeks after cessation of therapy)

Platelet counts
(platelet counts decreased in 52% of patients receiving peginterferon alfa-2a alone and 33% of patients treated with concomitant ribavirin; median platelet counts returned to pre-treatment levels 4 weeks after cessation of therapy)

Serum neutralizing antibodies
(9% of patients treated with peginterferon alfa-2a developed binding antibodies to interferon alfa–2a, 3% of patients developed low-titer neutralizing antibodies)

Triglyceride levels
(triglyceride levels are elevated in patients receiving alfa interferon therapy)

(In hepatitis C studies, hypothyroidism or hyperthyroidism requiring treatment, dose modification or discontinuation occurred in 4% and 1% of peginterferon alfa-2a treated patients and 4% and 2% of peginterferon alfa-2a and alfa interferon therapy.)

Medical considerations/Contraindications

The medical considerations/contraindications included have been selected on the basis of their potential clinical significance (reasons given in parentheses where appropriate)—not necessarily inclusive (» = major clinical significance).

Except under special circumstances, this medication should not be used when the following medical problem exists:

» Autoimmune hepatitis
(peginterferon alfa-2a is contraindicated in patients with autoimmune hepatitis)

» Bone marrow suppression
(bone marrow function may be depressed and may result in severe cytopenias; alfa interferons have rarely been associated with aplastic anemia)

» Coinfection with Hepatitis B virus (HBV) or
» Coinfection with Human immunodeficiency virus (HIV)
(safety and efficacy have not been established in hepatitis C patients coinfected with these viruses)

» Coinfection with Hepatitis C (HCV) or
» Coinfection with Human immunodeficiency virus (HIV)
(safety and efficacy have not been established in hepatitis B patients coinfected with these viruses)

» Diabetes mellitus or
» Hyperglycemia or
» Hyperthyroidism or
» Hypoglycemia or
» Hypothyroidism
(patients with these conditions at baseline who cannot be effectively treated by medication should not begin peginterferon alfa-2a therapy; patients who develop these conditions during treatment and cannot be controlled by medication may require a discontinuation of peginterferon alfa-2a.)

» Hepatic decompensation, before or during treatment
(peginterferon alfa-2a is contraindicated in patients with Child-Pugh class B and C)

» Hypersensitivity to peginterferon alfa-2a or any of its components

» Infections
(serious and severe bacterial infections, some fatal and some associated with neutropenia, have been observed in patients treated with alfa interferons; therapy should be discontinued in patients who develop severe infections and appropriate antibiotic therapy instituted)

» Liver transplant recipients or
» Other organ transplant recipients
(safety and efficacy have not been established in these patients)

» Mental depression, history of
(peginterferon alfa-2a should be used with extreme caution in patients with a history of depression; adverse events include aggressive behavior, psychoses, hallucinations, bipolar disorders, and mania; in severe cases therapy should be stopped immediately and psychiatric intervention instituted)

» Psychiatric illness, other
(life-threatening or fatal neuropsychiatric reactions may manifest including suicide, suicide ideation, depression, relapse of drug addiction and drug overdose; these may occur in patients with or without previous psychiatric illness)

» Pulmonary disorders, such as
» Bronchiolitis obliterans or
» Dyspnea or
» Interstitial pneumonitis and sarcoidosis or
» Pneumonia or
» Pulmonary infiltrates
(these conditions may be induced or aggravated by peginterferon alfa-2a therapy; treatment should be discontinued if persistent or unexplained pulmonary infiltrates or pulmonary function impairment occur)

» Renal impairment
(25% to 45% higher exposure to peginterferon alfa-2a is seen in patients with end stage renal disease undergoing hemodialysis; patients with impaired renal function signs and symptoms of interferon toxicity should be closely monitored; peginterferon should be used with caution in patients with creatinine clearance < 50 mL/min; dose reduction may be needed)

Risk-benefit should be considered when the following medical problems exist:

Autoimmune disorders such as
Interstitial nephritis or
Idiopathic thrombocytopenic purpura (ITP) or
Myositis or
Psoriasis or
Rheumatoid arthritis or
Systemic lupus erythematosus or
Thyroiditis
(development or exacerbation of condition may occur; peginterferon alfa-2a should be used with caution)

» Cardiac disease, pre-existing
(should be administered with caution; hypertension, supraventricular arrhythmias, chest pain, and myocardial infarction have been observed)

Hematologic abnormalities
(peginterferon alfa-2a treatment is associated with decreases in white blood cells, absolute neutrophil count, lymphocytes and platelet counts; often starting within first two weeks of treatment; dose reduction recommended; caution is advised in patients with baseline neutrophil count <1500 cells/mm^3, platelet count <90,000 cells/mm^3, or hemoglobin <10 grams/dL; therapy should be discontinued, at least temporarily, in patients who develop severe decreases in neutrophil and/or platelet counts)

Severe anemia, risk of
(caution should be exercised in initiating treatment in patients at risk of severe anemia, such as those with spherocytosis or history of gastrointestinal bleeding)

Patient monitoring

The following may be especially important in patient monitoring (other tests may be warranted in some patients, depending on condition; » = major clinical significance):

Alanine aminotransferase (ALT) or
Bilirubin serum
(dose reduction necessary with progressive ALT increases above baseline values; immediate discontinuation of therapy if ALT increases continue despite dose reduction or accompanied by increased bilirubin or evidence of hepatic decompensation)

» Blood cell counts, complete (CBC) including
» Hemoglobin
» Platelet count
White Blood Cell count
(should be obtained pre-treatment and monitored routinely during therapy)

» Colitis
(ulcerative, and hemorrhagic/ischemic colitis, sometimes fatal, have been observed within 12 weeks of starting alpha interferon treatment; peginterferon alfa-2a should be discontinued immediately if symptoms develop; colitis usually resolves within 1 to 3 weeks of discontinuation of therapy)

Blood glucose
(peginterferon alfa-2a therapy may need to be discontinued if hyperglycemia or hypoglycemia develops and can not be treated with medication)

Fever
(fever is commonly caused by peginterferon alfa-2a therapy, other causes of persistent fever must be ruled out, especially in patients with neutropenia)

» Hypersensitivity reactions
(severe acute hypersensitivity reactions including urticaria, angioedema and bronchoconstriction have been rarely observed; if such reactions occur therapy should be discontinued and appropriate medical therapy immediately instituted)

» Infections
(serious and severe bacterial infections, some fatal, have been observed in patients treated with alfa interferons; patients should be monitored for signs of infections as some can be associated with neutropenia; therapy should be discontinued in patients who develop severe infections and appropriate antibiotic therapy instituted)

Interferon toxicity
(for patients with end-stage renal disease requiring hemodialysis a dose reduction is recommended and signs and symptoms of interferon toxicity should be closely monitored)

» Neuropsychiatric monitoring
(all patients should be monitored for evidence of depression and other psychiatric symptoms; patients should be advised to report any sign or symptom of depression or suicidal ideation to their prescribing physician)

» Ophthalmologic exams
(patients should have an exam at baseline; and patients with preexisting conditions should have a periodic exams during treatment; if ocular symptoms develop patients should immediately receive an eye examination; treatment may need to be discontinued; decrease or loss of vision, retinopathy including macular edema, retinal artery or vein thrombosis, retinal hemorrhages and cotton wool spots, optic neuritis, and papilledema are induced or aggravated by alpha interferon treatment)

» Pancreatitis
(pancreatitis, sometimes fatal, has occurred during alpha interferon treatment; peginterferon alfa-2a should be suspended if symptoms or signs are found and should be discontinued if patient has a diagnosis of pancreatitis.)

» Pregnancy tests
(combination therapy of peginterferon alfa-2a and ribavirin should not be started unless a report of a negative pregnancy test has been obtained immediately prior to initiation of therapy; monthly pregnancy tests must be performed during combination therapy)

Thyroid stimulating hormone (TSH)
(peginterferon alfa-2a may need to be discontinued if thyroid dysfunction occurs that cannot be treated with medication)

Side/Adverse Effects

The following side/adverse effects have been selected on the basis of their potential clinical significance (possible signs and symptoms in parentheses where appropriate)—not necessarily inclusive:

Those indicating need for medical attention

Incidence more frequent

Depression (discouragement; feeling sad or empty; irritability; lack of appetite; loss of interest or pleasure; tiredness; trouble concentrating; trouble sleeping); ***neutropenia*** (black, tarry, stools; chills; cough; fever; lower back or side pain; painful or difficult urination; pale skin; shortness of breath; sore throat; ulcers, sores, or white spots in mouth; unusual bleeding or bruising; unusual tiredness or weakness); ***pyrexia*** (fever)

Incidence less frequent

Anemia (pale skin; troubled breathing with exertion; unusual bleeding or bruising; unusual tiredness or weakness); ***bacterial infection including; sepsis*** (chills; confusion; dizziness; lightheadedness; fainting; fast heartbeat; fever; rapid, shallow breathing); ***osteomyelitis*** (increase in bone pain); ***endocarditis*** (chest pain or discomfort; chills; fever; heart murmur; shortness of breath); ***pyelonephritis*** (chills; fever; frequent or painful urination; headache; stomach pain); ***pneumonia*** (chest pain; cough; fever or chills; sneezing; shortness of breath; sore throat; troubled breathing; tightness in chest; wheezing); ***hypersensitivity reactions*** (anaphylaxis; urticaria); ***hypothyroidism*** (constipation; depressed mood; dry skin and hair; feeling cold; hair loss; hoarseness or husky voice; muscle cramps and stiffness; slowed heartbeat; weight gain; unusual tiredness or weakness); ***lymphopenia*** (fever or chills; cough or hoarseness; lower back or side pain; painful or difficult urination); ***thrombocytopenia*** (black, tarry, stools; chills; cough; fever; lower back or side pain; pale skin; unusual bleeding or bruising; unusual tiredness or weakness)

Those indicating need for medical attention only if they continue or are bothersome

Incidence more frequent

Abdominal pain (stomach pain); ***alopecia*** (hair loss; thinning of hair); ***anorexia*** (loss of appetite; weight loss); ***arthralgia*** (muscle or joint pain); ***anxiety*** (fear; nervousness); ***back pain; concentration impairment; dermatitis*** (blistering, crusting, irritation, itching, or reddening of skin; cracked, dry, scaly skin; swelling); ***diarrhea; dizziness; dry mouth; fatigue/asthenia*** (loss of strength or energy; muscle pain or weakness); ***headache; injection site reaction*** (numbness; pain; rash; redness; scarring; soreness; stinging; swelling; tenderness; tingling; ulceration; warmth); ***insomnia*** (sleeplessness; trouble sleeping; unable to sleep); ***irritability; nausea; nervousness; myalgia*** (joint pain; swollen joints; muscle aching or cramping; muscle pains or stiffness; difficulty in moving); ***pain; pruritus*** (itching skin); ***rigors*** (feeling unusually cold; shivering); ***sweating, increased; vomiting***

Incidence less frequent

Blurred vision; cough; dry skin; dyspnea (shortness of breath; difficult or labored breathing; tightness in chest; wheezing); ***eczema; memory impairment*** (being forgetful); ***mood alteration; rash; weight loss***

Incidence rare

Dyspepsia (acid or sour stomach; belching; heartburn; indigestion; stomach discomfort, upset or pain)

Incidence not determined—Observed during clinical practice; estimates of frequency can not be determined

Hearing impairment (loss of hearing; changes in hearing); ***Hearing loss***

Overdose

For more information on the management of overdose or unintentional ingestion, **contact a poison control center** (see *Poison Control Center Listing*).

There is limited experience with overdosage. The maximum dose received by any patient was 7 times the intended dose of peginterferon alfa-2a (180 mcg per day for 7 days). There were no serious reactions attributed to overdosages. Weekly dosages of up to 630 mcg have been administered to patients with cancer. Dose-limiting toxicities were fatigue, elevated liver enzymes, neutropenia, and thrombocytopenia. There is no specific antidote for peginterferon alfa-2a. Hemodialysis and peritoneal dialysis are not effective.

Patient Consultation

As an aid to patient consultation, refer to *Advice for the Patient, Peginterferon Alfa-2a.*

For information pertaining to the Patient Consultation of ribavirin, a component of the peginterferon alfa-2a and ribavirin combination treatment regimen, see *Ribavirin (Systemic).*

In providing consultation, consider emphasizing the following selected information (» = major clinical significance):

Before using this medication

» Conditions affecting use, especially:

Hypersensitivity to peginterferon alfa-2a or any of its components

Pregnancy—Should be used during pregnancy only if the potential benefit justifies the risk to the fetus; effective contraception necessary for women of childbearing potential during peginterferon alfa-2a therapy

Breast-feeding—Decision must be made whether to discontinue nursing or discontinue treatment based on the potential for adverse reactions

Use in the elderly—Elderly patients are more likely to have age related problems that may be more severe; caution should be used

Other medications, especially didanosine, methadone, NRTIs, ribavirin or theophylline

Other medical problems, especially autoimmune hepatitis, bone marrow suppression, Coinfection with Human immunodeficiency virus (HIV) and Hepatitis B or Hepatitis C, diabetes mellitus, hepatic decompensation (before or during treatment), history of mental depression, hyperglycemia, hyperthyroidism, hypoglycemia, hyperthyroidism, infections, liver transplant recipients, other organ transplant recipients, other psychiatric illness, pre-existing cardiac disease, or renal impairment

Proper use of this medication

» Proper dosing

Missed dose: Taking as soon as possible; not taking if almost time for next scheduled dose; not doubling doses

» Proper storage

Precautions while using this medication

» Caution while driving or operating machinery until you are familiar with this drug's effects; may cause dizziness, confusion, somnolence, and fatigue

Side/adverse effects

Signs of potential side effects, especially anemia, bacterial infection, depression, hypersensitivity reactions, hypothyroidism, lymphopenia, neutropenia, pyrexia, and thrombocytopenia

General Dosing Information

For information pertaining to General Dosing Information for ribavirin, a component of the peginterferon alfa-2a and ribavirin combination treatment regimen, see *Ribavirin (Systemic).*

There are no safety and efficacy data on treatment for longer than 48 weeks. If the patient has not demonstrated an early virologic response after 12 to 24 weeks of therapy, consideration should be given to discontinuing therapy.

Peginterferon alfa-2a may be self-injected only if the physician determines that it is appropriate and the patient agrees to medical follow-up as necessary and training in proper injection technique has been provided. The patient must also be supplied with a puncture-resistant container for the disposal of used needles and syringes and cautioned against any reuse of any needles and syringes. The full container should be disposed of according to the directions provided by the physician.

Patients being treated with peginterferon alfa-2a in combination with ribavirin should be instructed to practice effective contraception during therapy and for 6 months post-therapy. The physician should be notified immediately in the event of a pregnancy.

It is unknown if therapy with peginterferon alfa-2a alone or in combination with ribavirin will prevent transmission of hepatitis C virus (HCV) infection to others or prevent cirrhosis, liver failure or liver cancer that might result from HCV infection.

Diet/Nutrition

The combination therapy of peginterferon alfa-2a and ribavirin should be taken with food.

For information pertaining to the Dosage Forms of ribavirin, a component of the peginterferon alfa-2a and ribavirin combination treatment regimen, see *Ribavirin (Systemic).*

Parenteral Dosage Forms

PEGINTERFERON ALFA-2A FOR INJECTION

Usual adult dose

Chronic hepatitis B virus infection (treatment)—

• General (for moderate to severe adverse reactions): Initial dose reduction to 135 mcg is generally adequate. In some cases, dose reduction to 90 mcg may be needed. After the adverse reaction improves, re-escalation of the dose may be considered.

• Renal insufficiency: In patients with end-stage renal disease requiring hemodialysis, dose reduction to 135 mcg peginterferon alfa-2a is recommended.

• Liver function: In patients with progressive ALT increases above baseline values, the dose of peginterferon alfa-2a should be reduced to 135 mcg. Discontinue if ALT increases continue to progress or are accompanied by increased bilirubin or hepatic decompensation.

• Hematological: In patients with an absolute neutrophil count (ANC) less than 750 per mm^3, the peginterferon alfa-2a dose should be reduced to 135 mcg. In patients with a platelet count less than 50,000 per mm^3, the dose should be reduced to 90 mcg. Discontinue peginterferon alfa-2a if ANC falls below 500 per mm^3 until values return to more than 1,000 mm^3. Peginterferon alfa-2a should also be discontinued if platelet count fall below 25, 000/mm^3

• Depression: In patients with mild depression, no dosing modifications are required. In patients with moderate depression, dosing should be reduced to 135 mcg; in some cases, a dose reduction to 90 mcg may be needed. Peginterferon alfa-2a should be discontinued if severe depression develops.

Peginterferon alfa-2a monotherapy—
Subcutaneous, 180 micrograms once weekly for 48 weeks administered in the abdomen or thigh.
Dosing modifications:

Genotype	Peginterferon Alfa-2a Dose	Ribavirin Dose	Duration
Genotype 1, 4	180 mcg	<75 kg =1000 mg	48 weeks
		≥75 kg =1200 mg	48 weeks
Genotype 2, 3	180 mcg	800 mg	24 weeks

Note: Since ribavirin absorption increased when administered with a meal, patients are advised to take ribavirin with food.

• Hemoglobin: Reduce only the ribavirin dose to 600 mg a day (one 200 mg tablet in the morning and two 200 mg tablets in the evening) if hemoglobin levels are less than 10g/dL in patients with no history of cardiac disease. Reduce only ribavirin dose to 600 mg a day (one 200 mg tablet in the morning and two 200 mg tablets in the evening) if hemoglobin levels are greater than or equal to 2g/dL, during any four week period treatment, in patients with a history of stable cardiac disease. Discontinue ribavirin if hemoglobin levels decrease to less than 8.5 g/dL in patients with no history of cardiac disease or if hemoglobin levels decrease to less than 12 g/dL in patients with a history of stable cardiac disease (despite four weeks at reduced dose). Once ribavirin has been withheld due to laboratory or clinical manifestation, an attempt may be made to restart ribavirin at 600 mg daily and further increase the dose to 800 mg daily upon physician's judgment. However, it is not recommended that ribavirin be increased to the original dose of 1000 mg or 1200 mg.

• Renal Impairment: Ribavirin should not be used in patients with creatinine clearance less than 50 mL/min.

Peginterferon alfa-2a in combination with ribavirin—
Peginterferon alfa-2a: Subcutaneous, 180 micrograms once weekly
Ribavirin: Oral, recommended dose and duration for peginterferon alfa-2a/ribavirin therapy based on viral genotypes as follows in the table below:
Dosing modifications:

Chronic hepatitis C virus infection (treatment)—

• General (for moderate to severe adverse reactions): Initial dose reduction to 135 mcg is generally adequate. In some cases, dose reduction to 90 mcg may be needed. After the adverse reaction improves, re-escalation of the dose may be considered.

• Renal insufficiency: In patients with end-stage renal disease requiring hemodialysis, dose reduction to 135 mcg peginterferon alfa-2a is recommended.

• Liver function: In patients with progressive ALT increases above baseline values, the dose of peginterferon alfa-2a should be reduced to 135 mcg. Discontinue if ALT increases continue to progress or are accompanied by increased bilirubin or hepatic decompensation.

• Hematological: In patients with an absolute neutrophil count (ANC) less than 750 per mm^3, the peginterferon alfa-2a dose should be reduced to 135 mcg. In patients with a platelet count less than 50,000 per mm^3, the dose should be reduced to 90 mcg. Discontinue peginterferon alfa-2a if ANC falls below 500 per mm^3 until values return to more than 1,000 mm^3. Peginterferon alfa-2a should also be discontinued if platelet count fall below 25,000/mm.^{3}

• Depression: In patients with mild depression, no dosing modifications are required. In patients with moderate depression, dosing should be reduced to 135 mcg; in some cases, a dose reduction to 90 mcg may be needed. Peginterferon alfa-2a should be discontinued if severe depression develops.

Peginterferon alfa-2a monotherapy—
Subcutaneous, 180 micrograms once weekly for 48 weeks administered in the abdomen or thigh.
Dosing modifications:

Genotype	Peginterferon Alfa-2a Dose	Ribavirin Dose	Duration
Genotype 1, 4	180 mcg	<75 kg =1000 mg	48 weeks
		≥75 kg =1200 mg	48 weeks
Genotype 2, 3	180 mcg	800 mg	24 weeks

Note: Since ribavirin absorption increased when administered with a meal, patients are advised to take ribavirin with food.

Note: The peginterferon alfa-2a/ribavirin dose should be modified or discontinued if severe adverse reactions or laboratory abnormalities develop until the adverse reactions abate, if appropriate. If intolerance persists after dose adjustment, combination therapy should be discontinued.

Peginterferon alfa-2a in combination with ribavirin—
Peginterferon alfa-2a: Subcutaneous, 180 micrograms once weekly
Ribavirin: Oral, recommended dose and duration for peginterferon alfa-2a/ribavirin therapy based on viral genotypes as follows in the table below:

Usual pediatric dose

Safety and efficacy have not been established in patients less than 18 years of age.

Usual geriatric dose

Caution should be exercised in the use of peginterferon alfa-2a in adult patients 65 years of age or older due to the possible greater severity of adverse reactions and systemic effects in this population.

Strength(s) usually available

U.S.—
180 mcg of peginterferon alfa-2a per 1-mL vial (Rx) [*Pegasys* (package of one single-use vial and package of 4 single-use vials with 4 syringes available; 8 mg sodium chloride; 0.05 mg polysorbate 80; 10 mg benzyl alcohol; 2.62 mg sodium acetate trihydrate; 0.05 mg acetic acid)].

Canada—
Not commercially available.

Packaging and storage

Store in the refrigerator at 2 and 8°C (36 to 46 °F). Protect from light. Do not freeze or shake.

Stability

Vials are for single use only. Any unused portion should be discarded.

Auxiliary labeling

• For subcutaneous injection only
• Visually inspect vial for particulate matter and discoloration. Return vials with particulate matter or discoloration to the pharmacist.
• Drink plenty of water while taking this medication, especially during the initial stages.
• May cause dizziness, confusion, somnolence, and fatigue. Be careful while driving or operating machinery. Use caution until you become familiar with its effects.

Additional information

The peginterferon alfa-2a vials contain benzyl alcohol. Benzyl alcohol has been reported to be associated with an increased incidence of neurological and other complications in neonates and infants, which are sometimes fatal.

Revised: 08/11/2005
Developed: 12/17/2003

PEGINTERFERON ALFA-2B
Systemic

VA CLASSIFICATION (Primary): IM404

Commonly used brand name(s): *PEG-Intron*.

Note: For a listing of dosage forms and brand names by country availability, see *Dosage Forms* section(s).

Category

Biological response modifier.

Indications

Accepted

Hepatitis C, chronic (treatment)—Peginterferon alfa-2b is indicated for the treatment of chronic hepatitis C virus infection in adults with compensated liver disease who have not been previously treated with alpha interferon.

Pharmacology/Pharmacokinetics

Physicochemical characteristics

Source—Synthetic. Peginterferon alfa-2b is a covalent conjugate of recombinant alfa interferon with monomethoxy polyethylene glycol (PEG). It is manufactured by bacterial fermentation of a strain of *Escherichia coli* that bears a genetically engineered plasmid containing the gene for human interferon. The native gene was obtained from human leukocytes.

Molecular weight—
Interferon alfa-2b: 19,271 daltons.
Peginterferon alfa-2b: 31,000 daltons.

Specific activity—
Approximately 0.7×10^8 International Units (IU) per mg of protein.

Mechanism of action/Effect

The interferon alfa-2b moiety is responsible for the biological activity of peginterferon alfa-2b. Interferons exert their cellular activities by binding to specific membrane receptors on the cell surface. Through a complex sequence of intracellular events, peginterferon alfa-2b raises concentrations of effector proteins such as serum neopterin and 2′5′oligoadenylate synthetase, raises body temperature, and causes reversible decreases in leukocyte and platelet counts.

Half-life

Absorption—4.6 hours.
Elimination—Mean 40 hours (range 22 to 60 hours).

Time to peak concentration

15 to 44 hours.

Duration of action

48 to 72 hours.

Elimination

Renal—30%. Clearance may be reduced by one half in patients with renal function impairment (creatinine clearance < 50 mL per minute).

Precautions to Consider

Carcinogenicity

The carcinogenic potential of peginterferon alfa-2b has not been tested.

Mutagenicity

Peginterferon alfa-2b did not cause damage to DNA when tested in the standard battery of mutagenesis assays.

Pregnancy/Reproduction

Fertility—Reversible irregularities in cynomolgus monkey menstrual cycles were observed following subcutaneous injections of 4239 mcg per square meter of body surface area (mcg/m^2) every other day for one month (approximately 345 times the recommended weekly human dose based on body surface area). No effects on cycle duration or reproductive hormone status were seen following doses of 262 mcg/m^2 every other day (approximately 21 times the weekly human dose). Effects on male fertility have not been studied.

Pregnancy—Adequate and well-controlled studies in humans have not been done.

Non-pegylated interferon alfa-2b administered to *Macaca mulatta* (rhesus) monkeys at doses of 15 and 30 million International Units (IU) per kg of body weight (IU/kg) (equivalent to human doses of 5 and 10 million IU/kg based on body surface area) have been shown to have abortifacient effects. It should be expected that peginterferon alfa-2b also has abortifacient potential. Peginterferon alfa-2b is recommended for use in fertile women only when an effective contraceptive also is being used.

FDA Pregnancy Category C.

Breast-feeding

It is not known whether peginterferon alfa-2b is distributed in human breast milk. However, breast feeding is not recommended during therapy due to the potential risk to the infant.

Pediatrics

No information is available on the relationship of age to the effects of peginterferon alfa-2b in pediatric patients. Safety and efficacy in patients up to 18 years of age have not been established.

Geriatrics

Studies performed in a limited number of patients 65 years of age or older have not demonstrated geriatrics-specific problems that would limit the usefulness of peginterferon alfa-2b in the elderly. However, elderly patients are more likely to have age-related renal function impairment, which may require caution in patients receiving peginterferon alfa-2b.

Drug interactions and/or related problems

The following drug interactions and/or related problems have been selected on the basis of their potential clinical significance (possible mechanism in parentheses where appropriate)—not necessarily inclusive (» = major clinical significance):

Ribavirin
(safety and efficacy of concurrent use have not been established)

Laboratory value alterations

The following have been selected on the basis of their potential clinical significance (possible effect in parentheses where appropriate)—not necessarily inclusive (» = major clinical significance).

With physiology/laboratory test values
Alanine aminotransferase (ALT [SGPT])
(values increased two to five times above baseline in 10% of patients; however, increases were transient and were not associated with other changes in hepatic function)

» Neutrophil count and
» Platelet count
(may be severely decreased)

Thyroid stimulating hormone
(abnormal levels may develop)

Medical considerations/Contraindications

The medical considerations/contraindications included have been selected on the basis of their potential clinical significance (reasons given in parentheses where appropriate)—not necessarily inclusive (» = major clinical significance).

Except under special circumstances, this medication should not be used when the following medical problems exist:

» Autoimmune hepatitis

» Hepatic disease, decompensated
(studies on the use of peginterferon alfa−2b have not been done; use of peginterferon alfa−2b is not recommended in patients with decompensated hepatic disease; if symptoms [ascites, coagulopathy, decreased serum albumin, jaundice] occur, peginterferon alfa−2b therapy should be discontinued.)

Risk-benefit should be considered when the following medical problems exist:

» Autoimmune disorders, such as:
Interstitial nephritis
Psoriasis
Rheumatoid arthritis
Systemic lupus erythematosus
Thrombocytopenia
Thyroiditis
(these conditions may be exacerbated; caution is recommended)

» Cardiovascular disease
(caution is recommended; close monitoring also is recommended in patients with a history of arrhythmias or myocardial infarction)

» Diabetes mellitus or
» Hyperglycemia or
» Hyperthyroidism or
» Hypothyroidism
(these conditions may be aggravated; therapy with peginterferon alfa-2b should not be initiated in patients with these conditions who cannot be effectively treated by medication)

Human immunodeficiency virus (HIV) infection or
Transplant, liver or other organ, history of
(safety and efficacy in these patients have not been established)

Hypersensitivity to peginterferon alfa-2b or any of its components

» Psychiatric disorders
(extreme caution is recommended; neuropsychiatric events such as aggressive behavior, depression, homicidal ideation, relapse of drug addiction or overdose, suicidal ideation, and suicide have occurred during peginterferon alfa-2b therapy or follow-up in patients with and without previous psychiatric disorders)

» Pulmonary function impairment or
» Pulmonary infiltrates
(close monitoring of patients with these conditions is recommended)

» Renal function impairment
(close monitoring for signs and symptoms of toxicity is recommended; dosage adjustment may be required; clearance of peginterferon alfa-2b may be reduced by up to 50% in patients with creatinine clearances less than 50 mL per minute; caution is recommended in these patients)

Patient monitoring

The following may be especially important in patient monitoring (other tests may be warranted in some patients, depending on condition; » = major clinical significance):

Alanine aminotransferase (ALT [SGPT]) values and
Aspartate aminotransferase (AST [SGOT]) values and
Bilirubin concentrations, serum
(counts should be monitored prior to initiation of therapy, 2 weeks after initiation of therapy, and at periodic intervals during the 48 weeks of therapy, at the discretion of the physician)

» Complete blood count
(recommended prior to initiation of therapy and at periodic intervals during therapy)

Electrocardiogram (ECG)
(recommended prior to initiation of therapy and at periodic intervals during therapy in patients with cardiac disease, particularly those with a history of myocardial infarction or arrhythmias)

» Hepatitis C virus RNA, serum
(concentrations should be assessed after 24 weeks of therapy; if at that time concentrations are not below the limit of detection of the assay, consideration should be given to discontinuing therapy with peginterferon alfa-2b)

» Thyroid-stimulating hormone (TSH)
(serum concentrations should be monitored prior to initiation of therapy, at at 12-week intervals during the 48 weeks of therapy, at the discretion of the physician)

» Neuropsychiatric monitoring
(regular monitoring is recommended; if severe psychiatric disturbances occur, peginterferon alfa-2b therapy should be immediately discontinued and psychiatric intervention should be instituted)

Ophthalmic examination
(baseline examination is recommended, particularly in the presence of diabetes or hypertension)

Side/Adverse Effects

Note: Development of low-titer ($\leq$ 64) neutralizing antibodies has been reported. However, the clinical and pathological significance of the development of antibodies is not known as there was no effect on the clinical response of the medication or increased incidence of side or adverse effects during clinical trials.

The following side/adverse effects have been selected on the basis of their potential clinical significance (possible signs and symptoms in parentheses where appropriate)—not necessarily inclusive:

Those indicating need for medical attention

Incidence more frequent

Anxiety; depression; emotional lability (mood swings); ***fever; hemorrhagic or ulcerative colitis*** (abdominal pain; bloody diarrhea; fever); ***hepatomegaly*** (abdominal pain); ***infection, viral; insomnia*** (trouble in sleeping); ***irritability; neutropenia*** (chills or fever; cough or hoarseness; lower back or side pain; painful or difficult urination); ***pancreatitis*** (abdominal pain, continuing; nausea; vomiting); ***thrombocytopenia*** (black, tarry stools; blood in urine or stools; pinpoint red spots on skin; unusual bleeding or bruising)

Note: Therapy with peginterferon alfa-2b should be immediately discontinued in patients who develop *hemorrhagic or ulcerative colitis*. This condition usually resolves within 1 to 3 weeks after discontinuation of therapy.

Therapy with peginterferon alfa-2b should be suspended in patients in whom *pancreatitis* is suspected and discontinued in patients in whom it is confirmed.

Incidence less frequent

Hypothyroidism (constipation; drowsiness; dry hair and skin; menstrual disturbances; sensitivity to cold; unusual tiredness or weakness; weight gain)

Incidence rare

Aplastic anemia (headache; shortness of breath; unusual tiredness or weakness); ***arrhythmias*** (irregular heartbeat); ***cardiomyopathy*** (dizziness; palpitations; shortness of breath; vertigo); ***hypersensitivity reaction*** (anaphylaxis; angioedema; bronchoconstriction; urticaria); ***hyperthyroidism*** (diarrhea; fast or irregular heartbeat; insomnia; mood swings; muscle weakness; nervousness; restlessness; sensitivity to heat; sweating, excessive; tremors; warm, smooth, moist skin; weight loss); ***myocardial infarction*** (chest pain, severe; cool, pale skin; dizziness; nausea; shortness of breath; sweating); ***nephritis, interstitial*** (backache; fever; possibly decreased urine output); ***neuropsychiatric events, including aggressive behavior; homicidal ideation; relapse of drug addiction or overdose; suicidal ideation; suicide attempt; psoriasis*** (itching of skin); ***retinal ischemia or retinal vein thrombosis*** (decrease in vision; eye pain); ***rheumatoid arthritis*** (aching, pain, and/or stiffness in joints); ***systemic lupus erythematosus–like syndrome*** (abdominal pain; loss of appetite; pain in joints; sensitivity to sunlight; shortness of breath; skin rash; thick, scaly skin; unusual tiredness or weakness; weight loss); ***transient ischemic attack*** (difficulty speaking; numbness or loss of feeling in one or both limbs on the same side of the body; paralysis; weakness); ***urticaria*** (hives or skin rash; itching)

Note: Therapy with peginterferon alfa-2b should be immediately discontinued in patients who develop *hypersensitivity reactions*. Appropriate medical therapy should be instituted as soon as possible.

Those indicating need for medical attention only if they continue or are bothersome

Incidence more frequent

Abdominal pain; alopecia (hair loss); ***anorexia*** (loss of appetite); ***cough; diarrhea; dizziness; dry skin; dyspepsia*** (indigestion); ***fatigue; flu-like symptoms*** (abdominal pain; chills; cough; headache; pain in joints or muscles; runny nose; sneezing; sore throat); ***flushing of skin; headache; injection site reaction*** (bruising; irritation; itching); ***malaise; musculoskeletal pain; nausea; pharyngitis*** (sore throat); ***rigors*** (chills); ***sinusitis*** (aching, fullness, or tension in area of affected sinus; headache; runny nose); ***skin rash or itching; sweating, increased; vomiting; weight loss***

Note: *Flu-like symptoms* usually decrease in severity as therapy continues. Taking an antipyretic before peginterferon alfa-2b or taking peginterferon alfa-2b at bedtime may lessen the occurrence of these symptoms.

Incidence less frequent

Hypertonia (muscle rigidity or stiffness); ***pain at injection site***

Patient Consultation

As an aid to patient consultation, refer to *Advice for the Patient, Peginterferon Alfa-2b (Systemic)*.

In providing consultation, consider emphasizing the following selected information (» = major clinical significance):

Before using this medication

» Conditions affecting use, especially:
Hypersensitivity to peginterferon alfa-2b or any of its components
Pregnancy—Effective contraception is recommended for fertile females receiving peginterferon alfa-2b therapy
Breast-feeding—Breast-feeding is not recommended because of the potential risk to the nursing infant
Other medical problems, especially autoimmune disorders, autoimmune hepatitis, cardiovascular disease, decompensated hepatic disease, diabetes mellitus, hyperglycemia, hyperthyroidism, hypothyroidism, psychiatric disorders, pulmonary function impairment, pulmonary infiltrates, or renal function impairment

Proper use of this medication

» Compliance with therapy
» Reading patient directions carefully with regard to:
—Preparation of the injection
—Use of disposable syringes
—Proper administration technique
—Stability of the injection
» Proper dosing
Missed dose: Taking missed dose as soon as possible if remembered during same or next day, then going back to regular dosing schedule; checking with physician for instructions if missed dose is not remembered within first two days; not doubling doses or taking more than one dose within a week
» Proper storage

Precautions while using this medication

» Importance of close monitoring by the physician
» Checking with physician immediately if signs of mental depression, especially suicidal thoughts, occur

Side/adverse effects

Signs of potential side effects, especially anxiety, depression, emotional lability, fever, hemorrhagic or ulcerative colitis, hepatomegaly, viral infection, insomnia, irritability, neutropenia, pancreatitis, thrombocytopenia, hypothyroidism, aplastic anemia, arrhythmias, cardiomyopathy, hypersensitivity reaction, hyperthyroidism, myocardial infarction, interstitial nephritis, neuropsychiatric events, psoriasis, retinal ischemia or retinal vein thrombosis, rheumatoid arthritis, systemic lupus erythematosus–like syndrome, transient ischemic attack, and urticaria
Possibility of some hair loss

General Dosing Information

Patients receiving peginterferon alfa-2b should be under the supervision of a physician who is experienced in immunomodulatory therapy.

There are no data supporting use of peginterferon alfa-2b for more than 48 weeks, or in cases of relapse.

If it is determined that peginterferon alfa-2b can be used outside of the physician's office, the person who will be administering the injections should be instructed in proper aseptic technique for reconstitution and injection, and in proper disposal of syringes and needles. If the patient is to self-administer peginterferon alfa-2b, the physical ability of that patient to self-inject subcutaneously should be assessed.

It is recommended that the patient be well-hydrated, especially during initiation of peginterferon alfa-2b therapy.

Parenteral Dosage Forms

PEGINTERFERON ALFA-2B FOR INJECTION

Usual adult dose

Hepatitis C, chronic—

Patients weighing 37 to 45 kg: Subcutaneous, 40 mcg once a week (on the same day) for one year.

Patients weighing 46 to 56 kg: Subcutaneous, 50 mcg once a week (on the same day) for one year.

Patients weighing 57 to 72 kg: Subcutaneous, 64 mcg once a week (on the same day) for one year.

Patients weighing 73 to 88 kg: Subcutaneous, 80 mcg once a week (on the same day) for one year.

Patients weighing 89 to 106 kg: Subcutaneous, 96 mcg once a week (on the same day) for one year.

Patients weighing 107 to 136 kg: Subcutaneous, 120 mcg once a week (on the same day) for one year.

Patients weighing 137 to 160 kg: Subcutaneous, 150 mcg once a week (on the same day) for one year.

Note: Dosage should be decreased by one half in patients who develop a serious adverse reaction during therapy or who have neutrophil counts less than 0.75×10^9 cells per liter or platelet counts less than 80×10^9 cells per liter. Therapy should be permanently discontinued in patients in whom adverse reactions persist or recur after dosage reduction and in patients with neutrophil counts less than 0.5×10^9 cells per liter or platelet counts less than 50×10^9 cells per liter.

Usual pediatric dose

Hepatitis C, chronic—

Safety and efficacy have not been established.

Usual geriatric dose

See *Usual adult dose.*

Strength(s) usually available

U.S.—

74 mcg (Rx) [*PEG-Intron* (dibasic sodium phosphate anhydrous 1.11 mg; monobasic sodium phosphate dihydrate 1.11 mg; sucrose 59.2 mg; polysorbate 80 0.074 mg)].

118 mcg (Rx) [*PEG-Intron* (dibasic sodium phosphate anhydrous 1.11 mg; monobasic sodium phosphate dihydrate 1.11 mg; sucrose 59.2 mg; polysorbate 80 0.074 mg)].

177.6 mcg (Rx) [*PEG-Intron* (dibasic sodium phosphate anhydrous 1.11 mg; monobasic sodium phosphate dihydrate 1.11 mg; sucrose 59.2 mg; polysorbate 80 0.074 mg)].

222 mcg (Rx) [*PEG-Intron* (dibasic sodium phosphate anhydrous 1.11 mg; monobasic sodium phosphate dihydrate 1.11 mg; sucrose 59.2 mg; polysorbate 80 0.074 mg)].

Packaging and storage

Store lyophilized powder at 25 °C (77 °F), excursions between 15 and 30 °C (59 and 86 °F) permitted. Following reconstitution with supplied diluent, solution may be stored between 2 and 8 °C (36 and 46 °F) for up to 24 hours. Do not freeze.

Preparation of dosage form

Peginterferon alfa-2b should be reconstituted with 0.7 mL of the supplied diluent. No other diluents or solutions should be used. The vial should then be gently swirled until the powder has completely dissolved. Following reconstitution, the final concentrations are 100 mcg per milliliter (mcg/mL), 160 mcg/mL, 240 mcg/mL, and 300 mcg/mL for the 74-mcg, 118.4-mcg, 177.6-mcg, and 222-mcg vials, respectively.

Developed: 06/12/2001

PEGVISOMANT Systemic†

VA CLASSIFICATION (Primary): HS900

Commonly used brand name(s): *Somavert.*

Note: For a listing of dosage forms and brand names by country availability, see *Dosage Forms* section(s).

†Not commercially available in Canada.

Category

Growth hormone suppressant (acromegaly).

Indications

Accepted

Acromegaly, (treatment)—Pegvisomant is indicated for the treatment of acromegaly in patients who have an inadequate response to surgery and/or radiation therapy and /or other medical therapies, or for whom these therapies are not appropriate. The goal with this treatment is to normalize serum IGF-I levels.

Pharmacology/Pharmacokinetics

Physicochemical characteristics

Source—Pegvisomant is a protein of (rDNA origin) synthesized by a specific strain of *Escherichia coli* bacteria that has been genetically modified by the addition of a plasmid that carries a gene for growth hormone receptor antagonist.

Molecular weight—

Pegvisomant (protein): 21,998 daltons.

PEG portion of pegvisomant: approximately 5000 daltons.

The predominant molecular weights of pegvisomant (covalently bound to 4 to 6 PEG/protein molecules) are approximately 42,000, 47,000, and 52,000 daltons.

Mechanism of action/Effect

Pegvisomant selectively binds to growth hormone (GH) receptors on cell surfaces, where it blocks the binding of endogenous GH, and thus interferes with GH signal transduction. Inhibition of GH action results in decreased serum concentrations of insulin-like growth factor-I (IGF-I), as well as other GH-responsive proteins, including IGF binding protein-3 (IGFBP-3), and the acid-labile subunit (ALS).

Other actions/effects

Radiolabeled pegvisomant does not cross the blood-brain barrier in rats. There is no available data to demonstrate drug-abuse potential or psychological dependence with pegvisomant.

Absorption

The mean extent of absorption of a 20 mg subcutaneous dose is 57%, relative to a 10 mg intravenous dose.

Distribution

Volume of distribution (Vol_D)—7 L (12% coefficient of variation), suggesting that pegvisomant does not distribute extensively into tissues.

Half-life

Elimination (serum)—approximately 6 days following either single or multiple doses.

Time to peak serum concentration

Following subcutaneous administration—33 to 77 hours

Elimination

Systemic clearance (estimated mean)—36 to 28 mL per hour following subcutaneous doses of 10 to 20 mg per day.

Clearance following multiple doses is lower than following a single dose.

The pegvisomant molecule has covalently bound polyethylene glycol polymers in order to reduce the clearance rate.

Clearance was found to increase with body weight.

Less than 1% of the administered dose is recovered in the urine over 96 hours.

Therapeutic plasma concentrations

Mean ± SEM serum concentrations following 12 weeks of therapy with daily doses of 10, 15 and 20 mg were 6600 ± 1330; 16,000 ± 2200; and 27,000 ± 3100 ng per mL, respectively

Precautions to Consider

Cross-sensitivity and/or related problems

The stopper on the vial of pegvisomant contains latex. which may cause an allergic reaction.

Carcinogenicity

Standard two-year rodent bioassays with pegvisomant have not been done

Mutagenicity

Pegvisomant was not mutagenic in the Ames assay or clastogenic in the *in vitro* chromosomal aberration test in human lymphocytes.

Pregnancy/Reproduction

Fertility—Studies in female rabbits given subcutaneous doses up to 10 mg per kg per day (10 times the maximum human therapeutic exposure based on body surface area, mg per m²) had no effect on fertility or reproductive performance.

Pregnancy—Early embryonic development and teratology studies in pregnant rabbits given subcutaneous doses of 1, 3 and 10 mg per kg per day revealed no evidence of teratogenic effects associated with pegvisomant treatment during organogenesis. However at the 10 mg per kg per day dose (10 times the maximum human therapeutic dose based on body surface area) a slight increase in post-implantation loss was observed in both studies.

Since there are no adequate and well controlled studies in humans, and animal studies are not always predictive of human response, pegvisomant should only be administered during pregnancy if clearly needed.

FDA Pregnancy Category B

Breast-feeding

It is not known whether pegvisomant is distributed into human breast milk. However, because many drugs are distributed into breast milk caution should be exercised when administering pegvisomant to a nursing women.

Pediatrics

Safety and effectiveness of pegvisomant in pediatric patients have not been established.

Geriatrics

No information is available on the relationship of age to the effects of pegvisomant in geriatric patients. However elderly patients are more likely to have age-related medical problems such as renal function impairment, which may require caution, and starting at the low end of the dosing range.

Pharmacogenetics

A population pharmacokinetic analysis was done and found no gender effect on the pharmacokinetics of pegvisomant.

The effect of race on the pharmacokinetics of pegvisomant has not been studied.

Drug interactions and/or related problems

The following drug interactions and/or related problems have been selected on the basis of their potential clinical significance (possible mechanism in parentheses where appropriate)—not necessarily inclusive (» = major clinical significance):

Note: Combinations containing any of the following medications, depending on the amount present, may also interact with this medication.

» Hypoglycemic agents, or
» Insulin
(concomitant use with pegvisomant may require a dose reduction; growth hormone (GH) opposes the effects of insulin on carbohydrate metabolism by decreasing insulin sensitivity, thus glucose tolerance may be increased)

» Opioids
(may require higher serum concentrations of pegvisomant to achieve appropriate IGF-I suppression)

Laboratory value alterations

The following have been selected on the basis of their potential clinical significance (possible effect in parentheses where appropriate)—not necessarily inclusive (» = major clinical significance).

With diagnostic test results

» Glucose tolerance test
(glucose tolerance may be increased)

With physiology/laboratory test values

» Growth hormone (GH) levels
(pegvisomant is structurally similar to GH, which causes it to cross react in GH assays; since serum concentrations of pegvisomant are 100 to 1000 times higher in patients undergoing pegvisomant therapy than endogenous GH serum levels seen in patients with acromegaly, GH assays will over estimate true GH levels; therefore, monitoring and dose adjustments should only be based on serum IGF-I levels)

Medical considerations/Contraindications

The medical considerations/contraindications included have been selected on the basis of their potential clinical significance (reasons given in parentheses where appropriate)—not necessarily inclusive (» = major clinical significance).

Except under special circumstances, this medication should not be used when the following medical problem exists:

» Hypersensitivity to pegvisomant or any of its components

Risk-benefit should be considered when the following medical problems exist:

Diabetes mellitus
(growth hormone may cause decreasing insulin sensitivity; adjustment of insulin dosage may be needed)

Hepatic function impairment
(patients with baseline transaminases elevated more than 3 times the upper limit of normal should not be treated with pegvisomant)

Renal insufficiency
(studies have not been done in patients with renal insufficiency)

Patient monitoring

The following may be especially important in patient monitoring (other tests may be warranted in some patients, depending on condition; » = major clinical significance):

Glucose, serum
(patients should be carefully monitored for hypoglycemia and doses of anti-diabetic drugs reduced as necessary)

» Growth hormone deficiency
(patients should be carefully observed for clinical signs and symptoms of a GH deficient state despite the presence of elevated GH concentrations)

» IGF-I levels, serum
(serum IGF-I concentrations should be monitored four to six weeks after therapy is initiated or any dose adjustments are made and at least every six months after IGF-I levels have normalized)

» Liver tests, serum
(should be monitored; pegvisomant should be discontinued if liver injury is confirmed or if transaminase elevations at least 3 times the upper limit of normal [ULN] with any increase in serum total bilirubin or transaminase elevations at least 5 times ULN)

» Tumors that secrete growth hormone
(should be carefully monitored with periodic imaging scans of the sella turcica; tumors may expand causing serious complications)

Side/Adverse Effects

The following side/adverse effects have been selected on the basis of their potential clinical significance (possible signs and symptoms in parentheses where appropriate)—not necessarily inclusive:

Immunogenicity—development of low titer non-neutralizing anti-GH antibodies occurred in approximately 17% of the patients during premarketing clinical studies. Although these antibodies did not impact the efficacy of pegvisomant, the long term clinical significance of these antibodies is not known.

Those indicating need for medical attention

Incidence more frequent

Abnormal liver function tests (lab results that show problems with liver); ***chest pain; infection*** (fever or chills; cough or hoarseness; lower back or side pain; painful or difficult urination); ***injection site reaction*** (Bleeding, blistering, burning, coldness, discoloration of skin; feeling of pressure; hives; infection; inflammation; itching; lumps)

Those indicating need for medical attention only if they continue or are bothersome

Incidence more frequent

Accidental injury; back pain; diarrhea; dizziness; flu syndrome (chills; cough; diarrhea; fever; general feeling of discomfort or illness; headache; joint pain; loss of appetite; muscle aches and pains; nausea; runny nose; shivering; sore throat; sweating; trouble sleeping; unusual tiredness or weakness; vomiting); ***hypertension*** (blurred vision; dizziness; nervousness; headache; pounding in the ears; slow or fast heartbeat); ***nausea; pain; paresthesia*** (burning, crawling, itching, numbness, prickling, "pins and needles", or tingling feelings); ***peripheral edema*** (bloating or swelling of face, arms, hands, lower legs, or feet; rapid weight gain; tingling of hands or feet; unusual weight gain or loss); ***sinusitis*** (pain or tenderness around eyes and cheekbones; fever; stuffy or runny nose; headache; cough; shortness of breath or troubled breathing; tightness of chest or wheezing)

Overdose

For more information on the management of overdose or unintentional ingestion, **contact a poison control center** (see *Poison Control Center Listing*).

Clinical effects of overdose

The following effects have been selected on the basis of their potential clinical significance (possible signs and symptoms in parentheses where appropriate)—not necessarily inclusive:

Fatigue (unusual tiredness or weakness)

Treatment of overdose

There is no known specific antidote to pegvisomant. Treatment is generally symptomatic and supportive.

In case of overdose, administration of pegvisomant should be discontinued and not resumed until IGF-I levels return to within or above the normal range.

Supportive care—
Patients in whom intentional overdose is confirmed or suspected should be referred for psychiatric consultation.

Patient Consultation

As an aid to patient consultation, refer to *Advice for the Patient, Pegvisomant (Systemic)*.

In providing consultation, consider emphasizing the following selected information (» = major clinical significance):

Before using this medication

» Conditions affecting use, especially:
  Hypersensitivity to pegvisomant or any of its components
  The stopper on the vial of pegvisomant contains latex which may cause an allergic reaction
  Pregnancy—Use is not generally recommended
  Other medications, especially hypoglycemic agents, insulin, or opioids

Proper use of this medication

» Taking within six hours of reconstitution
» Not using if the solution is discolored or cloudy
» Proper dosing
  Missed dose: Taking as soon as possible; not taking if almost time for next scheduled dose; not doubling doses
» Proper storage

Precautions while using this medication

» Telling physician if allergy to latex exists

Side/adverse effects

Signs of potential side effects, especially abnormal liver function tests, chest pain, infection, or injection site reaction

General Dosing Information

The goal of pegvisomant therapy is to achieve and maintain serum IGF-I concentrations within the age adjusted normal range and to alleviate the signs and symptoms of acromegaly.

Titration of dosing should be based on IGF-I levels. After the patient has begun daily subcutaneous injections of 10 mg of pegvisomant, serum IGF-I concentrations should be measured every four to six weeks. At this time the dosage should be adjusted in 5 mg increments if the IGF-I levels are still elevated, or 5 mg decrements if the IGF-I levels are below the normal range.

It is unknown if increased dosing would benefit patients who remain symptomatic while achieving normalized IGF-I levels.

Parenteral Dosage Forms

PEGVISOMANT FOR INJECTION

Usual adult dose

Growth hormone suppressant—
  Subcutaneous, 40 mg loading dose under physician supervision; 10 mg daily, patient administered

Usual adult prescribing limits

Up to 30 mg per day (maximum maintenance dose)

Usual pediatric dose

Safety and efficacy have not been established

Usual geriatric dose

See *Usual adult dose*.

Note: Dose selection should be cautious, usually at the low end of the dosing range

Strength(s) usually available

U.S.—
  10 mg of pegvisomant protein (equivalent to 21 mg pegvisomant) (Rx) [*Somavert* (glycine; mannitol; sodium phosphate dibasic anhydrous; sodium phosphate monobasic monohydrate; sterile water)].
  15 mg of pegvisomant protein (equivalent to 32 mg pegvisomant) (Rx) [*Somavert* (glycine; mannitol; sodium phosphate dibasic anhydrous; sodium phosphate monobasic monohydrate; sterile water)].
  20 mg of pegvisomant protein (equivalent to 43 mg pegvisomant) (Rx) [*Somavert* (glycine; mannitol; sodium phosphate dibasic anhydrous; sodium phosphate monobasic monohydrate; sterile water)].

Packaging and storage

Store between 2 and 8°C (36 and 46°F). Protect from freezing.

Preparation of dosage form

Each vial of pegvisomant should be reconstituted in 1 mL of the diluent provided in the package. To prepare the solution withdraw 1 mL of the solution (sterile water for injection, USP) and inject it into the vial of pegvisomant aiming the stream of liquid at the side of the glass wall. Hold the vial between the palms of both hands and gently roll to dissolve the powder. The vial should not be shaken. Discard the diluent vial containing the remaining water for injection. Visually inspect for particulate matter and discoloration prior to administration, if the solution is cloudy, do not inject it. Only one dose should be administered from each vial and should be administered within six hours after reconstitution. See the manufacturer's package insert for instructions.

Stability

After reconstitution, pegvisomant should be administered within six hours.

Auxiliary labeling

- Refrigerate—Do not freeze
- Dissolve in water before use
- Do not shake

Developed: 11/26/2003

PEMETREXED Systemic†

VA CLASSIFICATION (Primary): AN300

Commonly used brand name(s): *Alimta*.

Note: For a listing of dosage forms and brand names by country availability, see *Dosage Forms* section(s).

†Not commercially available in Canada.

Category

Antineoplastic.

Indications

Accepted

Mesothelioma, pleural (treatment)—Pemetrexed is indicated, in combination with cisplatin, for the treatment of patients with malignant pleural mesothelioma whose disease is unresectable or who are otherwise not candidates for curative surgery.

Carcinoma, lung, non-small cell (treatment)—Pemetrexed is indicated for the treatment of patients with locally advanced or metastatic non-small cell lung cancer (NSCLC) after prior chemotherapy.
  Effectiveness of pemetrexed in second-line NSCLC was based on the surrogate endpoint, response rate. There are no controlled trials demonstrating a clinical benefit, such as a favorable survival effect or improvement of disease-related symptoms.

Pharmacology/Pharmacokinetics

Physicochemical characteristics

Molecular weight—597.49.

Mechanism of action/Effect

Pemetrexed is an antifolate containing the pyrrolopyrimidine-based nucleus that exerts its antineoplastic activity by disrupting folate-dependent metabolic processes essential for cell replication. *In vitro* studies have shown that pemetrexed inhibits thymidylate synthase (TS), dihydrofolate reductase (DHFR), and glycinamide ribonucleotide formyltransferase (GARFT), all folate-dependent enzymes involved in the de novo biosynthesis of thymidine and purine nucleotides. Pemetrexed is transported into cells by both the reduced folate carrier and membrane folate binding protein transport systems. Once in the cell, pemetrexed is converted to polyglutamate forms by the enzyme folyl polyglutamate synthase. The polyglutamate forms are retained in cells and are inhibitors of TS and GARFT. Polyglutamation is a time- and concentration-dependent process that occurs in tumor cells and, to a lesser extent, in normal tissues. Polyglutamated metabolites have an increased intracellular half-life resulting in prolonged drug action in malignant cells. Preclinical studies have shown that pemetrexed inhibits the *in vitro* growth of mesothelioma cell lines (MSTO-211H, NCI-H2052). Studies with the MSTO-211H mesothelioma cell line showed synergistic effects when pemetrexed was combined concurrently with cisplatin. Absolute neutrophil counts (ANC) following single-agent administration of pemetrexed to patients not receiving folic acid and vitamin B12 supplementation were characterized using population pharmacodynamic analyses. Severity of hematologic toxicity, as measured by the depth of the ANC nadir, is inversely proportional to the systemic exposure of pemetrexed. It was also observed that lower ANC nadirs occurred in patients with elevated baseline cystathionine or homocysteine concentrations. The levels of these substances can be reduced by folic acid and vitamin B12 supplementation. There is no cumulative effect of pemetrexed exposure on ANC nadir over multiple treatment cycles.

Absorption

The total systemic clearance of pemetrexed is 91.8 mL per min in patients with normal renal function (creatinine clearance of 90 mL per min). The clearance decreases, and exposure (AUC) increases, as renal function decreases. Pemetrexed total systemic exposure (AUC) and maximum plasma concentration (C_{max}) increase proportionally with dose.

Distribution
Vol_D—16.1 liters

Protein binding
81% bound to plasma proteins; binding is not affected by degree of renal impairment

Half-life
Elimination—3.5 hours

Time to peak concentration
Time to ANC nadir with pemetrexed systemic exposure (AUC), varied between 8 to 9.6 days over a range of exposures from 38.3 to 316.8 μg per hr per mL. Return to baseline ANC occurred 4.2 to 7.5 days after the nadir over the same range of exposures.

Elimination
Pemetrexed is not metabolized to an appreciable extent and is primarily eliminated in the urine, with 70% to 90% of the dose recovered unchanged within the first 24 hours following administration.

Total systemic clearance, normal renal function (creatinine clearance of 90 mL/minute): 91.8 mL/minute

Special Populations
Gender—The pharmacokinetics of pemetrexed were not different in male and female patients.

Race—The pharmacokinetics of pemetrexed were similar in Caucasians and patients of African descent. Insufficient data are available to compare pharmacokinetics for other ethnic groups.

Hepatic Insufficiency—There was no effect of elevated AST (SGOT), ALT (SGPT), or total bilirubin on the pharmacokinetics of pemetrexed. However, studies of hepatically impaired patients have not been conducted.

Renal Insufficiency—Pharmacokinetic analyses of pemetrexed included 127 patients with reduced renal function. Plasma clearance of pemetrexed in the presence of cisplatin decreases as renal function decreases, with increase in systemic exposure. Patients with creatinine clearances of 45, 50, and 80 mL/min had 65%, 54%, and 13% increases, respectively in pemetrexed total systemic exposure (AUC) compared to patients with creatinine clearance of 100 mL per min.

Precautions to Consider

Carcinogenicity/Tumorigenicity/ Mutagenicity
No carcinogenicity studies have been conducted with pemetrexed. Pemetrexed was clastogenic in the *in vivo* micronucleus assay in mouse bone marrow but was not mutagenic in multiple *in vitro* tests (Ames assay, CHO cell assay).

Pregnancy/Reproduction
Fertility—Pemetrexed administered at i.v. doses of 0.1 mg/kg/day or greater to male mice (about 1/1666 the recommended human dose on a mg/m^2 basis) resulted in reduced fertility, hypospermia, and testicular atrophy.

Pregnancy—There are no studies of pemetrexed in pregnant women. Patients should be advised to avoid becoming pregnant. If pemetrexed is used during pregnancy, or if the patient becomes pregnant while taking pemetrexed, the patient should be apprised of the potential hazard to the fetus.

Pemetrexed may cause fetal harm when administered to a pregnant woman. Pemetrexed was fetotoxic and teratogenic in mice at i.v. doses of 0.2 mg/kg (0.6 mg/m^2) or 5 mg/kg (15 mg/m^2) when given on gestation days 6 through 15. Pemetrexed caused fetal malformations (incomplete ossification of talus and skull bone) at 0.2 mg/kg (about 1/833 the recommended i.v. human dose on a mg/m^2 basis), and cleft palate at 5 mg/kg (about 1/33 the recommended i.v. human dose on a mg/m^2 basis). Embryotoxicity was characterized by increased embryo-fetal deaths and reduced litter sizes.

FDA Pregnancy Category D

Breast-feeding
It is not known whether pemetrexed or its metabolites are distributed into human milk. Because many drugs are distributed in human milk, and because of the potential for serious adverse reactions in nursing infants from pemetrexed, it is recommended that nursing be discontinued if the mother is treated with pemetrexed.

Pediatrics
The safety and effectiveness of pemetrexed in pediatric patients have not been established.

Geriatrics
No information is available on the relationship of age to the effects of pemetrexed in geriatric patients. However, no geriatrics specific problems have been documented to date.

Pharmacogenetics
Dose adjustments based on gender other than those recommended for all patients have not been necessary.

Dental
The bone marrow depressant effects of pemetrexed may result in an increased incidence of microbial infection, delayed healing, and gingival bleeding. Dental work, whenever possible, should be completed prior to initiation of therapy or deferred until blood counts have returned to normal. Patients should be instructed in proper oral hygiene during treatment, including caution in use of regular toothbrushes, dental floss, and toothpicks.

Drug interactions and/or related problems
The following drug interactions and/or related problems have been selected on the basis of their potential clinical significance (possible mechanism in parentheses where appropriate)—not necessarily inclusive (» = major clinical significance):

Note: Combinations containing any of the following medications, depending on the amount present, may also interact with this medication.

Aspirin
(does not affect the pharmacokinetics of pemetrexed when administered in low to moderate doses [325 mg every 6 hours]; the effect of greater doses of aspirin on pemetrexed pharmacokinetics is unknown.)

» Bone marrow depressants, other (see *Appendix II*) or
Radiation therapy
(additive bone marrow depression may occur; dosage reduction may be required when two or more bone marrow depressants, including radiation, are used concurrently or consecutively.)

Ibuprofen
(daily ibuprofen doses of 400 mg qid reduce pemetrexed's clearance by about 20% [and increase AUC by 20%] in patients with normal renal function; the effect of greater doses of ibuprofen on pemetrexed pharmacokinetics is unknown.)
(ibuprofen [400 mg qid] can be administered with pemetrexed in patients with normal renal function [creatinine clearance ≥80 mL/min]; caution should be used when administering ibuprofen concurrently with pemetrexed to patients with mild to moderate renal insufficiency [creatinine clearance from 45 to 79 mL/min].)

Nephrotoxic drugs (see *Appendix II*)
(pemetrexed is primarily eliminated unchanged renally as a result of glomerular filtration and tubular secretion; concomitant administration of nephrotoxic drugs could result in delayed clearance of pemetrexed)

Non-steroidal anti-inflammatory drugs (NSAIDs)
(patients with mild to moderate renal insufficiency should avoid taking NSAIDs with short elimination half-lives for a period of 2 days before, the day of, and 2 days following administration of pemetrexed.)
(in the absence of data regarding potential interaction between pemetrexed and NSAIDs with longer half-lives, all patients taking these NSAIDs should interrupt dosing for at least 5 days before, the day of, and 2 days following pemetrexed administration; if concomitant administration of an NSAID is necessary, patients should be monitored closely for toxicity, especially myelosuppression, renal, and gastrointestinal toxicity.)

Probenecid or
Other substances that are tubularly secreted
(concomitant administration could potentially result in delayed clearance of pemetrexed.)

Vaccines, killed virus
(normal defense mechanisms may be suppressed by pemetrexed therapy and the patient's antibody response to the vaccine may be decreased. The interval between discontinuation of medications that cause immunosuppression and restoration of the patient's ability to respond to the vaccine depends on the intensity and type of immunosuppression-causing medication used, the underlying disease, and other factors; estimates vary from 3 months to 1 year)

» Vaccines, live virus
(normal defense mechanisms may be suppressed by pemetrexed therapy, concurrent use with a live virus vaccine may potentiate the replication of the vaccine virus, may increase the side/adverse

effects of the vaccine virus, and/or may decrease the patient's antibody response to the vaccine; immunization of these patients should be undertaken only with extreme caution after careful review of the patient's hematologic status and only with the knowledge and consent of the physician managing the pemetrexed therapy. The interval between discontinuation of medications that cause immunosuppression and restoration of the patient's ability to respond to the vaccine depends on the intensity and type of immunosuppression-causing medication used, the underlying disease, and other factors; estimates vary from 3 months to 1 year. Patients with leukemia in remission should not receive live virus vaccine until at least 3 months after their last chemotherapy. Immunization with oral poliovirus vaccine should also be postponed in persons in close contact with the patient, especially family members)

Laboratory value alterations

The following have been selected on the basis of their potential clinical significance (possible effect in parentheses where appropriate)—not necessarily inclusive (» = major clinical significance).

With physiology/laboratory test values

Alanine aminotransferase (ALT [SGPT]), serum and
Aspartate aminotransferase (AST [SGOT]), serum
(values may be increased with pemetrexed therapy)

Creatinine
(levels may be elevated)

Medical considerations/Contraindications

The medical considerations/contraindications included have been selected on the basis of their potential clinical significance (reasons given in parentheses where appropriate)—not necessarily inclusive (» = major clinical significance).

Except under special circumstances, this medication should not be used when the following medical problem exists:

Hypersensitivity to pemetrexed or any component of the formulation

» Renal function, impaired
(pemetrexed is primarily eliminated unchanged by renal excretion; pemetrexed should not be administered to patients whose creatine clearance is less than 45 mL per min; insufficient numbers of patients have been studied with creatine clearance less than 45 mL per min to give a dose recommendation; no dosage adjustment is needed in patients with creatine clearance ≥ 45 mL per min.)
(decreased renal function will result in reduced clearance and greater exposure (AUC) to pemetrexed compared with patients with normal renal function.)

Risk-benefit should be considered when the following medical problems exist:

Third space fluid, such as
Ascites or
Pleural effusion
(effect of third space fluid, such as pleural effusion and ascites is unknown; in patients with clinically significant third space fluid, consideration should be given to draining the effusion prior to pemetrexed administration.)

Patient monitoring

The following may be especially important in patient monitoring (other tests may be warranted in some patients, depending on condition; » = major clinical significance):

» Complete blood counts, including
Platelet counts

Chemistry tests
(chemistry tests to evaluate renal and hepatic function should be performed on all patients; patients should be monitored for nadir and recovery, which were tested in the clinical study before each dose and on days 8 and 15 of each cycle; patients should not begin a new cycle of treatment unless the ANC is ≥1500 cells/mm^3, the platelet count is ≥100,000 cells/mm^3, and creatinine clearance is ≥45 mL/min.)

Concomitant NSAID administration
(if concomitant administration of an NSAID is necessary, patients should be monitored closely for toxicity, especially myelosuppression, renal, and gastrointestinal toxicity.)

Side/Adverse Effects

Pemetrexed should be administered under the supervision of a qualified physician experienced in the use of antineoplastic agents. Appropriate management of complications is possible only when adequate diagnostic and treatment facilities are readily available. Treatment-related adverse events of pemetrexed seen in clinical trials have been reversible. Skin rash has been reported more frequently in patients not pretreated with a corticosteroid in clinical trials. Pretreatment with dexamethasone (or equivalent) reduces the incidence and severity of cutaneous reaction

The following side/adverse effects have been selected on the basis of their potential clinical significance (possible signs and symptoms in parentheses where appropriate)—not necessarily inclusive:

Those indicating need for medical attention

Incidence more frequent

Anemia (pale skin; troubled breathing with exertion; unusual bleeding or bruising; unusual tiredness or weakness); ***infection with grade 3 or 4 neutropenia*** (black, tarry stools; chills; cough; fever; lower back or side pain; painful or difficult urination; pale skin; shortness of breath; sore throat; ulcers, sores, or white spots in mouth; unusual bleeding or bruising; unusual tiredness or weakness); ***leukopenia*** (black, tarry stools; chest pain; chills; cough; fever; painful or difficult urination; shortness of breath; sore throat; sores, ulcers, or white spots on lips or in mouth; swollen glands; unusual bleeding or bruising; unusual tiredness or weakness); ***neutropenia*** (black, tarry, stools; chills; cough; fever; lower back or side pain; painful or difficult urination; pale skin; shortness of breath; sore throat; ulcers, sores, or white spots in mouth; unusual bleeding or bruising; unusual tiredness or weakness); ***thrombocytopenia*** (black, tarry stools; bleeding gums; blood in urine or stools; pinpoint red spots on skin; unusual bleeding or bruising); ***thrombosis/embolism*** (severe headaches of sudden onset sudden; loss of coordination; pains in chest, groin, or legs, especially calves of legs; sudden onset of shortness of breath for no apparent reason; sudden onset of slurred speech; sudden vision changes)

Incidence less frequent

Allergic reaction/hypersensitivity (fainting or loss of consciousness; fast or irregular breathing; swelling of eyes or eyelids; trouble in breathing; tightness in chest, and/or wheezing; skin rash; itching); ***febrile neutropenia*** (black, tarry stools; chills; cough; fever; lower back or side pain; painful or difficult urination; pale skin; shortness of breath; sore throat; ulcers, sores, or white spots in mouth; unusual bleeding or bruising; unusual tiredness or weakness); ***infection/febrile neutropenia, other*** (black, tarry stools; chills; cough; fever; lower back or side pain; painful or difficult urination; pale skin; shortness of breath; sore throat; ulcers, sores, or white spots in mouth; unusual bleeding or bruising; unusual tiredness or weakness); ***renal failure*** (lower back/side pain; decreased frequency/amount of urine; bloody urine; increased thirst; loss of appetite; nausea; vomiting; unusual tiredness or weakness; swelling of face, fingers, lower legs; weight gain; troubled breathing; increased blood pressure)

Those indicating need for medical attention only if they continue or are bothersome

Incidence more frequent

Alopecia (hair loss; thinning of hair); ***anorexia*** (loss of appetite; weight loss); ***arthralgia*** (pain in joints; muscle pain or stiffness; difficulty in moving); ***chest pain; constipation*** (difficulty having a bowel movement (stool)); ***diarrhea without colostomy; dehydration*** (confusion; decreased urination; dizziness; dry mouth; fainting; increase in heart rate; lightheadedness; rapid breathing; sunken eyes; thirst; unusual tiredness or weakness; wrinkled skin); ***depression*** (discouragement; feeling sad or empty; irritability; lack of appetite; loss of interest or pleasure; tiredness; trouble concentrating; trouble sleeping); ***desquamation*** (peeling of skin); ***dysphagia*** (difficulty swallowing); ***dyspnea*** (shortness of breath; difficult or labored breathing; tightness in chest; wheezing); ***edema*** (swelling); ***esophagitis*** (difficulty in swallowing; pain or burning in throat; chest pain; heartburn; vomiting; sores, ulcers, or white spots on lips or tongue or inside the mouth); ***fatigue*** (unusual tiredness or weakness); ***fever; infection*** (fever or chills; cough or hoarseness; lower back or side pain; painful or difficult urination)—without neutropenia; ***mood alteration; nausea; myalgia*** (joint pain; swollen joints; muscle aching or cramping; muscle pains or stiffness; difficulty in moving); ***neuropathy*** (burning, tingling, numbness or pain in the hands, arms, feet, or legs; sensation of pins and needles; stabbing pain); ***odynophagia*** (pain produced by swallowing); ***pharyngitis*** (stuffy or runny nose; muscle aches; unusual tiredness or weakness; fever; sore throat; headache); ***rash; stomatitis*** (swelling or inflammation of the mouth); ***vomiting***

Overdose

For more information on the management of overdose or unintentional ingestion, **contact a poison control center** (see *Poison Control Center Listing*).

There have been few cases of pemetrexed overdose. Reported toxicities included neutropenia, anemia, thrombocytopenia, mucositis, and rash. Anticipated complications of overdose include bone marrow suppression as manifested by neutropenia, thrombocytopenia, and anemia. In addition, infection with or without fever, diarrhea, and mucositis may be seen. If an overdose occurs, general supportive measures should be instituted as deemed necessary by the treating physician. In clinical trials, leucovorin was permitted for CTC Grade 4 leukopenia lasting ≥3 days, CTC Grade 4 neutropenia lasting ≥3 days, and immediately for CTC Grade 4 thrombocytopenia, bleeding associated with Grade 3 thrombocytopenia, or Grade 3 or 4 mucositis. The following intravenous doses and schedules of leucovorin were recommended for intravenous use: 100 mg/m^2, intravenously once, followed by leucovorin, 50 mg/m^2, intravenously every 6 hours for 8 days. The ability of pemetrexed to be dialyzed is unknown.

Treatment of overdose

Supportive care—

Patients in whom intentional overdose is confirmed or suspected should be referred for psychiatric consultation.

Patient Consultation

As an aid to patient consultation, refer to *Advice for the Patient, Pemetrexed (Systemic)*.

In providing consultation, consider emphasizing the following selected information (» = major clinical significance):

Before using this medication

» Conditions affecting use, especially:

Hypersensitivity to pemetrexed or to any ingredient used in the formulation

Pregnancy—Not recommended for use during pregnancy; may cause fetal harm when administered to pregnant women; telling physician immediately if pregnancy is suspected.

Breast-feeding—It is recommended that nursing be discontinued

Use in children—Safety and efficacy have not been established

Other medications, especially non-steroidal anti-inflammatory drugs (NSAIDs)

Other medical problems, especially impaired renal function

Proper use of this medication

» Proper dosing

Taking corticosteroid during treatment

Folic acid and vitamin B_{12} supplementation during treatment

Importance of regular blood tests

Proper storage

Precautions while using this medication

Importance of regular visits to physician; dose may be adjusted or treatment delayed based on general condition

» Checking with physician immediately if fever or chills, diarrhea or mouth sores occur

Obtaining medicine to help control stomach upset, nausea, vomiting, and diarrhea

Knowing signs and symptoms of low blood cell counts

Checking with physician if rash or fatigue persists or if they are severe; checking with physician if severe tiredness or weakness occurs

Understanding that weight loss and loss of appetite are common side effects; importance of talking with physician if this is a problem

Caution if bone marrow depression occurs:

» You may get redness or sores on your lips, mouth, or throat. Talk with your doctor about proper mouth and throat care.

» Avoiding immunizations unless approved by physician; other persons in patients household should avoid immunizations with oral poliovirus vaccine, avoiding other persons who have taken oral poliovirus vaccine or wearing a protective mask that covers nose and mouth.

» Avoiding exposure to persons with infections, especially during periods of low blood counts; checking with physician immediately if fever or chills, cough or hoarseness, lower back or side pain, or painful or difficult urination occurs

» Checking with physician immediately if unusual bleeding or bruising; black, tarry stools; blood in urine or stools; or pinpoint red spots on skin occur

Caution in use of regular toothbrush, dental floss, or toothpick; physician, dentist, or nurse may suggest alternatives; checking with physician before having dental work done

Not touching eyes or inside of nose unless hands washed immediately before

Using caution to avoid accidental cuts with use of sharp objects such as safety razor or fingernail or toenail cutters

Avoiding contact sports or other situations where bruising or injury could occur

Side/adverse effects

Signs of potential side effects, especially allergic reactions/hypersensitivity, anemia, febrile neutropenia, infection/febrile neutropenia (other), infection with grade 2 or 3 neutropenia, leukopenia, neutropenia, renal failure, thrombocytopenia, thrombosis/embolism

General Dosing Information

For parenteral dosing forms:

Pemetrexed should be administered under the supervision of a qualified physician experienced in the use of antineoplastic agents.

Pemetrexed can suppress bone marrow function, manifested by neutropenia, thrombocytopenia, and anemia; myelosuppression is usually the dose-limiting toxicity. Dose reductions for subsequent cycles are based on nadir ANC, platelet count, and maximum nonhematologic toxicity seen in the previous cycle.

Patients treated with pemetrexed must be instructed to take folic acid and vitamin B_{12} as a prophylactic measure to reduce treatment-related hematologic and GI toxicity. In clinical studies, less overall toxicity and reductions in Grade 3/4 hematologic and nonhematologic toxicities such as neutropenia, febrile neutropenia, and infection with Grade 3/4 neutropenia were reported when pretreatment with folic acid and vitamin B_{12} was administered.

As with other potentially toxic anticancer agents, care should be exercised in the handling and preparation of infusion solutions of pemetrexed. The use of gloves is recommended. If a solution of pemetrexed contacts the skin, wash the skin immediately and thoroughly with soap and water. If pemetrexed contacts the mucous membranes, flush thoroughly with water. Several published guidelines for handling and disposal of anticancer agents are available. There is no general agreement that all of the procedures recommended in the guidelines are necessary or appropriate.

Pemetrexed is not a vesicant. There is no specific antidote for extravasation of pemetrexed. To date, there have been few reported cases of pemetrexed extravasation, which were not assessed as serious by the investigator. Pemetrexed extravasation should be managed with local standard practice for extravasation as with other non-vesicants.

Parenteral Dosage Forms

PEMETREXED DISODIUM FOR INJECTION

Usual adult dose

Malignant pleural mesothelioma—

Intravenous infusion, 500 mg per square meter administered as an intravenous infusion over 10 minutes on Day 1 of each 21-day cycle. The recommended dose of cisplatin is 75 mg per square meter infused over 2 hours beginning approximately 30 minutes after the end of pemetrexed administration. Patients should receive hydration consistent with local practice prior to and/or after receiving cisplatin. See cisplatin package insert for more information.

Carcinoma, lung, non-small cell (treatment)—

Intravenous infusion, 500 mg per square meter administered as an intravenous infusion over 10 minutes on Day 1 of each 21-day cycle.

Premedication Regimen—

Corticosteroid: Skin rash has been reported more frequently in patients not pretreated with a corticosteroid. Pretreatment with dexamethasone (or equivalent) reduces the incidence and severity of cutaneous reaction. In clinical trials, dexamethasone 4 mg was given by mouth twice daily the day before, the day of, and the day after pemetrexed administration.

Premedication Regimen—

Vitamin Supplementation: To reduce toxicity, patients treated with pemetrexed must be instructed to take a low-dose oral folic acid preparation or multivitamin with folic acid on a daily basis. At least 5 daily doses of folic acid must be taken during the 7-day period preceding the first dose of pemetrexed; and dosing should continue during the full course of therapy and for 21 days after the last dose of pemetrexed. Patients must also receive one (1) intramuscular injection of vitamin B12 during the week preceding the first dose of pemetrexed and every 3 cycles thereafter. Subsequent vitamin B12 injections may be given the same day as pemetrexed. In clinical trials, the dose of folic acid studied ranged from 350 to 1000 mcg, and the dose of vitamin B12 was 1000 mcg. The most commonly used dose of oral folic acid in clinical trials was 400 mcg.

Dose Reduction Recommendations—Dose adjustments at the start of a subsequent cycle should be based on nadir hematologic counts or maximum nonhematologic toxicity from the preceding cycle of therapy. Treatment may be delayed to allow sufficient time for recovery. Upon recovery, patients should be retreated using the guidelines below.—

Hematologic Toxicities: Dose reduction for pemetrexed (single-agent or in combination) and cisplatin-hematologic toxicities

Hematologic Toxicity Associated with pemetrexed (single-agent or in combination) and cisplatin	Dose reduction
Nadir ANC <500/mm³ and nadir platelets ≥50,000/mm³	75% of previous dose (both drugs)
Nadir platelets <50,000/mm³ regardless of nadir ANC	50% of previous dose (both drugs)

Non-Hematologic Toxicities: If patients develop nonhematologic toxicities (excluding neurotoxicity) ≥Grade 3 (except Grade 3 transaminase elevations), pemetrexed (as a single-agent or in combination) should be withheld until resolution to less than or equal to the patient's pre-therapy value. Treatment should be resumed according to guidelines below

Non-Hematologic Toxicity (excluding neurotoxicity)	Dose Reduction of Pemetrexed (mg/m²)	Dose Reduction of Cisplatin (mg/m²)
Any Grade 3 or 4 toxicities except mucositis	75% of previous dose	75% of previous dose
Any diarrhea requiring hospitalization	75% of previous dose	75% of previous dose
Grade 3 or 4 mucositis	50% of previous dose	100% of previous dose

Neurotoxicity: In the event of neurotoxicity, the recommended dose adjustments for pemetrexed (as a single-agent or in combination) and cisplatin are described in below. Patients should discontinue therapy if Grade 3 or 4 neurotoxicity is experienced.

Neurotoxicity CTC Grade	Dose Reduction of Pemetrexed (mg/m²)	Dose Reduction of Cisplatin (mg/m²)
0-1	100% of previous dose	100% of previous dose
2	100% of previous dose	50% of previous dose

Note: Pemetrexed therapy should be discontinued if a patient experiences any hematologic or nonhematologic Grade 3 or 4 toxicity after 2 dose reductions (except Grade 3 transaminase elevations) or immediately if Grade 3 or 4 neurotoxicity is observed.

Note: Renally Impaired Patients—In clinical studies, patients with creatinine clearance ≥ 45 mL/min required no dose adjustments other than those recommended for all patients. Insufficient numbers of patients with creatinine clearance below 45 mL/min have been treated to make dosage recommendations for this group of patients. Therefore, pemetrexed should not be administered to patients whose creatinine clearance is <45 mL/min using the standard Cockcroft and Gault formula (below) or GFR measured by Tc99m-DPTA serum clearance method:

Males: [140 − Age in years] × Actual Body Weight (kg)/ 72 × Serum Creatinine (mg/dL) = mL/min

Females: Estimated creatinine clearance for males × 0.85

Caution should be exercised when administering pemetrexed concurrently with NSAIDs to patients whose creatinine clearance is <80 mL/min

Note: Hepatically Impaired Patients—Pemetrexed is not extensively metabolized by the liver. Dose adjustments based on hepatic impairment experienced during treatment with pemetrexed are provided in the table above for non-hematologic toxicities.

Usual pediatric dose
Safety and efficacy have not been established.

Usual geriatric dose
See *Usual adult dose.*

Strength(s) usually available
U.S.—

500 mg base (Rx) [*Alimta* (mannitol; hydrochloric acid and/or sodium hydroxide)].

Canada—

Not commercially available

Packaging and storage
Stored at 25°C (77°F); excursions permitted to 15-30°C (59-86°F); Pemetrexed is not light sensitive.

Preparation of dosage form
Preparation for Intravenous Infusion Administration

- Use aseptic technique during the reconstitution and further dilution of pemetrexed for intravenous infusion administration.
- Calculate the dose and the number of pemetrexed vials needed. Each vial contains 500 mg of pemetrexed. The vial contains an excess of pemetrexed to facilitate delivery of label amount
- Reconstitute 500-mg vials with 20 mL of 0.9% Sodium Chloride Injection (preservative free) to give a solution containing 25 mg/mL pemetrexed. Gently swirl each vial until the powder is completely dissolved. The resulting solution is clear and ranges in color from colorless to yellow or green-yellow without adversely affecting product quality. The pH of the reconstituted pemetrexed solution is between 6.6 and 7.8. FURTHER DILUTION IS REQUIRED.
- Parenteral drug products should be inspected visually for particulate matter and discoloration prior to administration. If particulate matter is observed, do not administer.
- The appropriate volume of reconstituted pemetrexed solution should be further diluted to 100 mL with 0.9% Sodium Chloride Injection (preservative free) and administered as an intravenous infusion over 10 minutes.
- When prepared as directed, reconstitution and infusion solutions of pemetrexed contain no antimicrobial preservatives. Discard any unused portion. Reconstitution and further dilution prior to intravenous infusion is only recommended with 0.9% Sodium Chloride Injection (preservative free). Pemetrexed is physically incompatible with diluents containing calcium, including Lactated Ringer's Injection, USP and Ringer's Injection, USP and therefore these should not be used. Coadministration of pemetrexed with other drugs and diluents has not been studied, and therefore is not recommended.

Stability
Chemical and physical stability of reconstituted and infusion solutions of pemetrexed were demonstrated for up to 24 hours following initial reconstitution, when stored at refrigerated or ambient room temperature and lighting.

Incompatibilities
Pemetrexed is physically incompatible with diluents containing calcium, including Lactated Ringer's Injection, USP and Ringer's Injection.

Coadministration of pemetrexed with other drugs and diluents has not been studied and is not recommended.

Auxiliary labeling
- For intravenous infusion only.
- Caution: Chemotherapy. Handle and Dispose of Properly.
- You may need a vitamin supplement when using this medication. Ask your pharmacist or doctor.

Note
As with other potentially toxic anticancer agents, care should be exercised in the handling and preparation of infusion solutions of pemetrexed.

Revised: 11/03/2004
Developed: 04/07/2004

PEMIROLAST Ophthalmic†

USA: Pemirolast Potassium

INN: Pemirolast

JAN: Pemirolast

VA CLASSIFICATION (Primary): OP801

Commonly used brand name(s): *Alamast.*

Note: For a listing of dosage forms and brand names by country availability, see *Dosage Forms* section(s).

†Not commercially available in Canada.

Category
Mast cell stabilizer (ophthalmic); Antiallergic (ophthalmic).

Indications

Accepted
Conjunctivitis, allergic (prophylaxis)—Pemirolast ophthalmic solution is indicated for the prophylaxis of itching of the eye associated with allergic conjunctivitis.

Pharmacology/Pharmacokinetics

Physicochemical characteristics
Molecular weight—Pemirolast: 266.3.

Solubility—Freely soluble in water.

pH—8.0.

Mechanism of action/Effect
Pemirolast is a mast cell stabilizer and inhibits the release of inflammatory mediators from cells associated with Type I immediate hypersensitivity reactions. The drug has been observed to block antigen-stimulated calcium ion influx into mast cells. Pemirolast also inhibits the chemotaxis of eosinophils into ocular tissue, and prevents inflammatory mediator release from human eosinophils.

Biotransformation
Liver—Extent unknown.

Half-life
Elimination—Mean of 4.5 hours.

Onset of action
Up to 4 weeks.

Time to peak concentration
Mean of 0.42 hours.

Peak serum concentration
A mean peak plasma level of 4.7 ng/mL occurred after 2 weeks of administration.

Elimination
Renal, 84 to 90% of dose eliminated within 24 hours; about 10 to 15% of the dose was excreted unchanged.

Precautions to Consider

Carcinogenicity/Mutagenicity
Pemirolast was neither clastogenic nor mutagenic when studied in a series of bacterial and mammalian gene mutation and chromosomal injury tests *in vitro* . Additional *in vivo studies* in rats did not reveal clastogenesis after exposure to pemirolast.

Pregnancy/Reproduction
Fertility—Pemirolast did not affect mating and fertility in rats exposed to oral doses of up to 250 mg/kg (approximately 20,000 times the recommended human dose).

Pregnancy—There are no adequate and well-controlled studies in pregnant women. However, when given to rats at oral doses of 250 mg/kg or more (approximately 20,000 times the recommended human dose), pemirolast caused increased incidences of interventricular septal defect, fetuses with wavy rib, splitting of thoracic vertebrae, thymic remnant in the neck, and reduced numbers of ossified sternebrae, sacral and caudal vertebrae, and metatarsi. The incidence of renal pelvis/ureteral dilation was also increased in the fetuses and neonates of rats given oral doses of 400 mg/kg (approximately 30,000 times the recommended human dose), during pregnancy. Teratogenicity was not observed in rabbits exposed to oral doses of up to 150 mg/kg (approximately 12,000 times the recommended human dose).

An increase was observed in the incidence of pre- and post-implantation losses, as well as in the number of embryo/fetal survival failures, decreased neonatal body weight, and delays in neonatal development in rats exposed to oral doses of pemirolast 400 mg/kg. Reductions in the number of corpus lutea, the number of implantations, and the number of live fetuses was observed in the F_1 generation of rats descendent from F_0 dams given oral doses of pemirolast 250 mg/kg or more during late gestation and lactation periods.

FDA Pregnancy Category C

Breast-feeding
It is not known whether pemirolast is distributed into human breast milk. However, pemirolast is distributed in the milk of lactating rats at concentrations higher than those in plasma. Caution should be exercised when pemirolast is administered to nursing women. Problems in humans have not been established.

Pediatrics
The safety and effectiveness of pemirolast has not been established for children below the age of 3 years.

Geriatrics
No information is available on the relationship of age to the effects of pemirolast in geriatric patients.

Medical considerations/Contraindications
The medical considerations/contraindications included have been selected on the basis of their potential clinical significance (reasons given in parentheses where appropriate)—not necessarily inclusive (» = major clinical significance).

Except under special circumstances, this medication should not be used when the following medical problem exists:

» Sensitivity to pemirolast

Risk-benefit should be considered when the following medical problems exist:

Contact lens-related irritation
(Pemirolast should not be used to treat the symptoms of contact lens-related irritation.)

Side/Adverse Effects
The following side/adverse effects have been selected on the basis of their potential clinical significance (possible signs and symptoms in parentheses where appropriate)—not necessarily inclusive:

Those indicating need for medical attention
Incidence less frequent

Bronchitis (cough, producing mucus; difficulty breathing; tightness in chest); ***dysmenorrhea*** (increased stomach pain and cramping; painful menstrual bleeding); ***sinusitis*** (headache; pain and tenderness around eyes and cheekbones; runny or stuffy nose)

Those indicating need for medical attention only if they continue or are bothersome
Incidence more frequent

Cold/flu symptoms (chills; cough; fever; headache; runny or stuffy nose; sneezing; sore throat); ***headache***

Incidence less frequent

Allergy (itching; redness; eyelid swelling); ***back pain; cough; fever; foreign body sensation in eye; burning, dryness, and discomfort of eye*** (burning sensation in eye; eye discomfort; dryness of eyes); ***sneezing and nasal congestion*** (stuffy nose)

Overdose
For more information on the management of overdose or unintentional ingestion, **contact a poison control center** (see *Poison Control Center Listing*).

No information is available regarding the occurrence of overdose with ophthalmic preparations of pemirolast.

Patient Consultation
As an aid to patient consultation, refer to *Advice for the Patient, Pemirolast (Ophthalmic)*.

In providing consultation, consider emphasizing the following selected information (» = major clinical significance):

Before using this medication
» Conditions affecting use, especially:
Sensitivity to pemirolast
Use in children—The safety and effectiveness of pemirolast in children below the age of 3 years have not been established.

Proper use of this medication
» To prevent contamination of the medicine dropper tip and solution, not touching eyelids or the surrounding areas with the dropper tip; keeping the bottle tightly closed when not in use

» Proper dosing
Missed dose: Applying it as soon as possible; not using if almost time for next dose; using next dose at regularly scheduled time; not doubling doses

Proper storage

Precautions while using this medication
» Possible absorption by soft contact lenses of preservative used with pemirolast ophthalmic solution; for patients whose eyes are not red, and who wear contact lenses, waiting at least 10 minutes after applying pemirolast ophthalmic solution before they insert contact lenses

Side/adverse effects
Signs of potential side effects, especially bronchitis, dysmenorrhea, or sinusitis

General Dosing Information
Symptomatic response to treatment (decreased itching) may occur within a few days, yet may require up to 4 weeks of therapy.

Pemirolast is intended for topical ophthalmic use only. It should not be used orally or for injection.

Ophthalmic Dosage Form

PEMIROLAST POTASSIUM OPHTHALMIC SOLUTION

Usual adult dose
Conjunctivitis, allergic—
Topical, to the conjunctiva of the eye, 1 or 2 drops in each affected eye four times daily.

Usual pediatric dose

Conjunctivitis, allergic—
Children older than 3 years of age: See *Usual adult dose.*
Children up to 3 years of age: Safety and efficacy have not been established.

Usual geriatric dose

See *Usual adult dose.*

Strength(s) usually available

U.S.—
0.1% (Rx) [*Alamast* (10 mg per 10 mL bottle; lauralalkonium chloride 0.005%)].

Packaging and storage

Store between 15 and 25 °C (59 and 77 °F), in a tight container.

Auxiliary labeling

- For the eye.
- Keep tightly closed

Developed: 04/26/2000

PENBUTOLOL—See *Beta-adrenergic Blocking Agents (Systemic)*

PENCICLOVIR Topical

VA CLASSIFICATION (Primary): DE103

Commonly used brand name(s): *Denavir.*

Note: For a listing of dosage forms and brand names by country availability, see *Dosage Forms* section(s).

Category

Antiviral (topical).

Indications

General Considerations

Penciclovir is an antiviral agent used to treat infections caused by herpes viruses. Penciclovir has *in vitro* inhibitory activity against herpes simplex virus types 1 and 2 (HSV-1 and HSV-2).

Accepted

Herpes labialis (treatment)—Topical penciclovir is indicated in the treatment of recurrent herpes labialis (cold sores) in adults.

Pharmacology/Pharmacokinetics

Physicochemical characteristics

Chemical Group—9-[4-hydroxy-3-(hydroxymethyl) butyl]guanine.

Molecular weight—253.26.

Solubility—At 20 °C 0.2 mg/mL in methanol; 1.3 mg/mL in propylene glycol; and 1.7 mg/mL in water; in aqueous buffer (pH 2) the solubility is 10 mg/mL.

Partition coefficient—In *n*-octanol/water at pH 7.5 penciclovir has a partition coefficient of 0.024 (logP = −1.62).

Mechanism of action/Effect

Penciclovir is phosphorylated by the enzyme thymidine kinase to a monophosphate form. The monophosphate is converted to penciclovir triphosphate by cellular phosphokinases. Studies show that penciclovir triphosphate inhibits herpes simplex virus polymerase competitively with deoxyguanosine triphosphate. This effect selectively inhibits herpes viral DNA synthesis and replication.

Absorption

Measurable concentrations of penciclovir have not been detected in plasma or urine following daily topical application in healthy male volunteers. Male volunteers were given doses approximately 67 times the estimated recommended clinical dose.

Systemic absorption of penciclovir following topical administration has not been studied in patients younger than 18 years of age.

Precautions to Consider

Carcinogenicity

A 2-year study in mice and rats given famciclovir (the oral prodrug of penciclovir) in doses of 600 mg per kg of body weight (mg/kg) per day showed an increased incidence of mammary adenocarcinoma in female rats. This dose is approximately 395 times the maximum theoretical human exposure to penciclovir following application of the topical product, based on 24-hour area under the plasma concentration-time curve (AUC) comparisons.

A 2-year study in mice and rats given famciclovir in doses of up to 240 mg/kg per day found no increase of tumor incidence among male rats or in male and female mice at doses of up to 600 mg/kg per day. These doses are approximately 190 times and 100 times, respectively, the maximum theoretical human AUC for penciclovir.

Mutagenicity

In vitro studies found that penciclovir did not cause an increase in gene mutation in the Ames test or in unscheduled DNA repair in mammalian HeLaS3 cells. An increase in clastogenic response was seen with penciclovir in the mouse lymphoma cell assay and in human lymphocytes.

In vivo studies showed an increase in micronuclei in mouse bone marrow following intravenous administration of penciclovir at doses greater than or equal to 500 mg/kg, which is approximately 810 times the maximum recommended human dose.

Pregnancy/Reproduction

Fertility—Adequate and well controlled studies on the effects of topical penciclovir have not been done in humans. Intravenous administration of penciclovir at doses of 160 mg/kg per day and 100 mg/kg per day resulted in testicular toxicity in rats and dogs.

Pregnancy—Adequate and well-controlled studies have not been done in humans.

Studies done in rats and rabbits given intravenous doses of 80 mg/kg per day and 60 mg/kg per day, respectively, have shown no adverse effect on the course and outcome of pregnancy or on fetal development. The body surface area doses were 260 and 355 times, respectively, the maximum recommended human dose following topical application of penciclovir cream.

FDA Pregnancy Category B.

Breast-feeding

It is not known whether penciclovir is distributed into breast milk after topical application.

However, penciclovir was distributed into the milk of lactating rats at concentrations higher than those seen in plasma following oral administration of famciclovir (the oral prodrug of penciclovir).

Pediatrics

No information is available on the relationship of age to the effects of penciclovir in pediatric patients. Safety and efficacy have not been established.

Geriatrics

In patients 65 years of age and older, the adverse events profile was comparable to that observed in younger patients.

Medical considerations/Contraindications

The medical considerations/contraindications included have been selected on the basis of their potential clinical significance (reasons given in parentheses where appropriate)—not necessarily inclusive (» = major clinical significance).

Except under special circumstances, this medication should not be used when the following problem exists:

» Immune deficiency conditions in patients who are immunocompromised
(the effect of penciclovir has not been established)

Risk-benefit should be considered when the following medical problem exists:

Sensitivity to penciclovir or other components of the formulation

Side/Adverse Effects

The following side/adverse effects have been selected on the basis of their potential clinical significance (possible signs and symptoms in parentheses where appropriate)—not necessarily inclusive:

Those indicating need for medical attention

Incidence rare
Application site reaction

Those indicating need for medical attention only if they continue or are bothersome

Incidence more frequent
Headache—incidence 5.3%

Incidence less frequent
Hypoesthesia (abnormally decreased sensitivity, particularly to touch); ***skin rash, erythematous*** (redness of the skin); ***taste perversion*** (change in sense of taste)

Overdose

For more information on the management of overdose or unintentional ingestion, **contact a Poison Control Center** (see *Poison Control Center Listing*).

There is no information on overdose. Penciclovir is poorly absorbed following oral administration. Adverse reactions related to penciclovir ingestion are unlikely.

Patient Consultation

As an aid to patient consultation, refer to *Advice for the Patient, Penciclovir (Topical)*.

In providing consultation, consider emphasizing the following selected information (» = major clinical significance):

Before using this medication

» Conditions affecting use, especially:
  Sensitivity to penciclovir or other components of the formulation
  Other medical problems, especially immune deficiency conditions

Proper use of this medication

» Using only on herpes labialis on the lips and face
» Beginning as early as possible at the first signs of symptoms (during the prodrome stage or when lesion appears)
» Avoiding application in or near the eyes
» Avoiding application to mucous membranes or within oral cavity
» Proper dosing
  Missed dose: Applying as soon as possible; not applying if almost time for next dose
» Proper storage

Side/adverse effects

Signs of potential side effects, especially application site reaction

General Dosing Information

Penciclovir cream is for external use only. Contact with eyes and mucous membranes should be avoided.

The effect of penciclovir has not been established in immunocompromised patients.

Topical Dosage Forms

PENCICLOVIR CREAM

Usual adult dose

Antiviral—
Topical, to cold sores every two hours during waking hours for four days.

Usual pediatric dose

Safety and efficacy have not been established.

Usual geriatric dose

See *Usual adult dose*.

Strength(s) usually available

U.S.—
1% (10 mg per gram) (Rx) [*Denavir* (cetomacrogol 1000 BP; cetostearyl alcohol; mineral oil; propylene glycol; purified water; white petrolatum)].

Packaging and storage

Store at or below 30 °C (86 °F). Protect from freezing.

Auxiliary labeling

- For external use only.
- Do not use in eyes.
- Continue medicine for full time of treatment.

Revised: 08/12/1998
Developed: 11/12/1997

PENICILLAMINE Systemic

VA CLASSIFICATION (Primary/Secondary): MS109/GU900; AD300

Commonly used brand name(s): *Cuprimine; Depen*.

Note: For a listing of dosage forms and brand names by country availability, see *Dosage Forms* section(s).

Category

Chelating agent; antirheumatic (disease-modifying); antiurolithic (cystine calculi); antidote (to heavy metals).

Indications

Note: Bracketed information in the *Indications* section refers to uses that are not included in U.S. product labeling.

Accepted

Wilson's disease (treatment)—Penicillamine is indicated in the treatment of symptomatic patients (those with tissue damage due to deposition of excessive copper in various tissues) and as prophylaxis against the development of tissue damage in asymptomatic patients.

Arthritis, rheumatoid (treatment);
[Felty's syndrome (treatment)][1] or
[Vasculitis, rheumatoid (treatment)][1]—Penicillamine is indicated in the treatment of patients with severe, active rheumatoid arthritis [including Felty's syndrome or rheumatoid vasculitis] who have not responded to other therapy.

Cystinuria (treatment) or
Renal calculi, cystine, recurrence (prophylaxis)—Penicillamine is indicated in the treatment of patients with excessive urinary cystine concentration and/or recurrent cystine stone formation who have not responded to or will not comply with other prophylactic measures.

[Toxicity, heavy metal (treatment)]—Penicillamine is less effective than other chelating agents (edetate calcium disodium or dimercaprol) for the treatment of severe lead poisoning. It is used as adjunctive treatment following initial therapy with another chelating agent. It may also be used as sole therapy in the treatment of asymptomatic patients with moderately elevated blood concentrations of lead. Penicillamine is also used in the treatment of poisoning due to other heavy metals, including mercury.

Unaccepted

Penicillamine is not effective in treating ankylosing spondylitis or psoriatic arthritis.

[1]Not included in Canadian product labeling.

Pharmacology/Pharmacokinetics

Physicochemical characteristics

Molecular weight—149.22.

Mechanism of action/Effect

Chelating agent—
Penicillamine chelates mercury, lead, copper, iron, and probably other heavy metals to form stable, soluble complexes that are readily excreted in the urine.

Antirheumatic—
The mechanism of action of penicillamine in rheumatoid arthritis is not known, but may involve improvement of lymphocyte function. It markedly reduces IgM rheumatoid factor and immune complexes in serum and synovial fluid, but does not significantly lower absolute concentrations of serum immunoglobulins. *In vitro,* penicillamine depresses T-cell but not B-cell activity. However, the relationship of these effects to the activity of penicillamine in rheumatoid arthritis is not known.

Antiurolithic (cystine calculi)—
Penicillamine combines chemically with cystine (cysteine–cysteine disulfide) to form penicillamine–cysteine disulfide, which is more soluble than cystine and is readily excreted. As a result, urinary cystine concentrations are lowered and the formation of cystine calculi is prevented. With prolonged treatment, existing cystine calculi may be gradually dissolved.

Antidote (to heavy metals)—
See *Chelating agent* above.

Biotransformation

Hepatic.

Onset of action

Wilson's disease—1 to 3 months.
Rheumatoid arthritis—2 to 3 months.

Elimination

Renal and fecal.

Precautions to Consider

Cross-sensitivity and/or related problems

Patients who have had a previous allergy to penicillin may theoretically have cross-reactivity to penicillamine. However, trace amounts of penicillin have been eliminated since penicillamine is being produced synthetically rather than as a degradation product of penicillin.

Carcinogenicity

Long-term animal carcinogenicity studies with penicillamine have not been done. However, in one study in autoimmune disease–prone NZB Hybrid mice receiving 400 mg per kg of body weight (mg/kg) intraperitoneally 5 days a week for 6 months, 5 of 10 of the animals tested developed lymphocytic leukemia.

Mutagenicity

In the Ames test, penicillamine is directly mutagenic to *S. typhimurium* strain TA92. Mutagenicity is enhanced by kidney postmitochondrial subcellular fraction 9. In Chinese hamster V79 cells, penicillamine does not induce gene mutations. In cultivated mammalian cells, penicillamine induces sister-chromatid exchanges and chromosome aberrations.

Pregnancy/Reproduction

Fertility— No studies are available on the effect of penicillamine on fertility.

Pregnancy— Penicillamine can cause fetal harm when administered to pregnant women. There are no controlled studies on the use of penicillamine in pregnant women. Normal outcomes have been reported as well as characteristic congenital cutis laxa and associated birth defects have been reported in infants born of mothers who received therapy with penicillamine during pregnancy. Penicillamine should be used in women of child bearing potential only when the expected benefits outweigh the possible hazards. Women of child bearing potential should be informed of this risk and advised to report any missed menstrual periods or other indications of possible pregnancy to their healthcare provider.

In rheumatoid arthritis: It is recommended that penicillamine not be used in pregnant women with rheumatoid arthritis.

In cystinuria: It is recommended that penicillamine be avoided if possible in pregnant patients with cystinuria.

In Wilson's disease: Although birth defects have not been reported in infants of women receiving penicillamine for Wilson's disease, it is recommended that the daily dose be limited to 750 mg. Also, if cesarean section is planned, it is recommended that the daily dose be limited to 250 mg during the last 6 weeks of pregnancy and following surgery until wound healing is complete.

Studies in animals have shown that penicillamine causes skeletal defects, cleft palates, and an increased number of resorptions when administered to rats in doses six times the maximum recommended human dose.

FDA Pregnancy Category D

Breast-feeding

No studies are available in animals or humans on whether penicillamine is distributed into breast milk. Women receiving penicillamine should not breast feed their infants.

Pediatrics

Appropriate studies with penicillamine have not been performed in the pediatric population. Efficacy for treatment of juvenile arthritis has not been established. However, pediatrics-specific problems that would limit the usefulness of this medication for other indications in children are not expected.

Geriatrics

Adequate and well-controlled studies have not been done. Clinical trials in limited subjects aged 65 years and over suggest greater risk in the elderly for overall skin rash and abnormality of taste. Dose selection for an elderly patient should be cautious due to the greater frequency of decreased hepatic, renal, or cardiac function, and of concomitant disease or other drugs. Careful monitoring of renal function is recommended.

Dental

The leukopenic and thrombocytopenic effects of penicillamine may result in an increased incidence of microbial infection, delayed healing, and gingival bleeding. If leukopenia or thrombocytopenia occurs, dental work should be delayed until blood counts have returned to normal, and patients should be instructed in proper oral hygiene, including caution in use of regular toothbrushes, dental floss, and toothpicks.

Penicillamine may cause oral ulcerations, which in some cases have the appearance of aphthous stomatitis, and, rarely, cheilosis, glossitis, or gingivostomatitis.

Surgical

Consider a reduction in dosage to 250 mg per day when surgery is contemplated because of the effects of penicillamine on collagen and elastin. The full dose given before surgery may be resumed when wound healing is complete.

Drug interactions and/or related problems

The following drug interactions and/or related problems have been selected on the basis of their potential clinical significance (possible mechanism in parentheses where appropriate)—not necessarily inclusive (» = major clinical significance):

Note: Combinations containing any of the following medications, depending on the amount present, may also interact with this medication.

4-Aminoquinolines or
Bone marrow depressants (See *Appendix II*) or
» Gold compounds or
Immunosuppressants, except glucocorticoids or
» Phenylbutazone
(concurrent use with penicillamine may increase the potential for serious hematologic and/or renal adverse reactions; concurrent use with gold compounds or phenylbutazone is not recommended)
(concurrent use with 4-aminoquinolines may also increase the risk of severe dermatologic reactions)

Iron supplements
(concurrent use may decrease the effects of penicillamine; if necessary, iron may be administered in short courses, but a period of 2 hours should elapse between administration of penicillamine and of iron)

Pyridoxine
(penicillamine may cause anemia or peripheral neuritis by acting as a pyridoxine antagonist or increasing renal excretion of pyridoxine; requirements for pyridoxine may be increased during penicillamine therapy)

Laboratory value alterations

The following have been selected on the basis of their potential clinical significance (possible effect in parentheses where appropriate)—not necessarily inclusive (» = major clinical significance).

With physiology/laboratory test values

Renal imaging using technetium Tc 99m gluceptate
(penicillamine may cause transchelation of technetium Tc 99m gluceptate to a compound excreted through the hepatobiliary system, resulting in gallbladder visualization; gallbladder visualization may mimic abnormal kidney localization on posterior views of renal images)

Medical considerations/Contraindications

The medical considerations/contraindications included have been selected on the basis of their potential clinical significance (reasons given in parentheses where appropriate)—not necessarily inclusive (» = major clinical significance).

Risk-benefit should be considered when the following medical problems exist:

» Agranulocytosis or aplastic anemia, penicillamine-related, history of
(risk of recurrence)

Hypersensitivity to penicillamine, history of

In rheumatoid arthritis patients

Renal function impairment, current or history of
(increased risk of adverse renal effects)

Patient monitoring

The following may be especially important in patient monitoring (other tests may be warranted in some patients, depending on condition; » = major clinical significance):

Blood cell counts, white and differential and
Hemoglobin determinations and
Platelet counts, direct and
Urinalyses, especially for protein and cells
(recommended at least every 2 weeks during the first 5 months of therapy, then monthly thereafter during therapy; however, more frequent testing of blood cell count and urinalyses may be advisable during the first 6 weeks of therapy and for several weeks following an increase in maintenance dosage)

Hepatic function determinations
(recommended every 6 months for the duration of therapy; in Wilson's disease, recommended every 3 months at least during the first year of therapy)

In cystinuria

X-ray for renal calculi
(recommended annually during therapy since cystine stones may form rapidly, sometimes within 6 months)

In rheumatoid arthritis

Urinary protein determinations, 24-hour
(recommended at 1- to 2-week intervals for those patients who develop moderate degrees of proteinuria)

In Wilson's disease
Urinary copper analyses, 24-hour
(recommended prior to and soon after initiation of therapy to determine optimal dosage; during continued therapy, recommended approximately every 3 months; urine specimens must be collected in copper-free glassware)

Side/Adverse Effects

The following side/adverse effects have been selected on the basis of their potential clinical significance (possible signs and symptoms in parentheses where appropriate)—not necessarily inclusive:

Those indicating need for medical attention

Incidence more frequent

Allergic reaction (fever; joint pain; skin rash, hives, and/or itching; swelling of lymph glands); ***fever***—drug-induced; ***pemphigus foliaceus or vulgaris*** (lesions on the face, neck, scalp, and/or trunk); ***stomatitis*** (ulcers, sores, or white spots on lips or in mouth)

Incidence less frequent

Agranulocytosis (sore throat and fever with or without chills; sores, ulcers, or white spots on lips or in mouth); ***aplastic anemia*** (shortness of breath, troubled breathing, tightness in chest, and/or wheezing; sores, ulcers, or white spots on lips or in mouth; swollen and/or painful glands; unusual bleeding or bruising; unusual tiredness or weakness); ***glomerulopathy, possible impending*** (bloody or cloudy urine; swelling of face, feet, or lower legs; weight gain)—glomerulopathy may progress to nephrotic syndrome; ***hemolytic anemia*** (troubled breathing, exertional; unusual tiredness or weakness); ***leukopenia*** (usually asymptomatic; fever or chills; cough or hoarseness; lower back or side pain; painful or difficult urination)—rarely; ***thrombocytopenia*** (usually asymptomatic; rarely, unusual bleeding or bruising; black, tarry stools; blood in urine or stools; pinpoint red spots on skin)

Incidence rare

Bronchiolitis, obstructive (coughing, wheezing, or shortness of breath); ***dermatitis, exfoliative*** (fever with or without chills; red, thickened, or scaly skin; swollen and/or painful glands; unusual bruising); ***Goodpasture's syndrome*** (difficulty in breathing, spitting blood, unusual tiredness or weakness); ***jaundice, cholestatic*** (dark urine, itching, pale stools, yellow eyes or skin); ***myasthenia gravis syndrome*** (difficulty in breathing, chewing, talking, or swallowing; double vision; muscle weakness); ***necrolysis, toxic epidermal*** (redness, tenderness, itching, burning, or peeling of skin; sore throat; fever with or without chills; red or irritated eyes); ***neuritis, optic*** (eye pain, blurred vision, or any change in vision)—may be caused by pyridoxine deficiency; ***pancreatitis or peptic ulcer reactivation*** (abdominal or stomach pain, severe); ***ringing or buzzing in ears; systemic lupus erythematosus (SLE)–like syndrome*** (skin rash, hives, and/or itching; blisters on skin; chest pain; general feeling of discomfort or illness; joint pain)

Those indicating need for medical attention only if continuing or bothersome

Incidence more frequent

Diarrhea; lessening or loss of sense of taste; loss of appetite; nausea or vomiting; stomach pain, mild

Patient Consultation

As an aid to patient consultation, refer to *Advice for the Patient, Penicillamine (Systemic).*

In providing consultation, consider emphasizing the following selected information (» = major clinical significance):

Before using this medication

» Conditions affecting use, especially:
- Hypersensitivity to penicillamine or penicillin, history of
- Pregnancy—Has been reported to cause birth defects in humans
- Breast-feeding—Mothers taking penicillamine should not breast feed their infants.
- Use in the elderly—Increased risk of hematologic toxicity, skin rash and abnormality of taste
- Other medications, especially gold compounds and phenylbutazone
- Other medical problems, especially a history of penicillamine-induced agranulocytosis or aplastic anemia

Proper use of this medication

For patients with cystinuria
- Taking medication on an empty stomach
- Importance of high fluid intake, especially at night
- Possible need for low-methionine diet

For patients with rheumatoid arthritis
- Taking medication on an empty stomach
- Improvement in condition may require 2 to 3 months of therapy

For patients with Wilson's disease
- Taking medication on an empty stomach
- Possible need for low-copper diet
- Improvement in condition may require 1 to 3 months of therapy

For patients with lead poisoning
- Taking medication on an empty stomach

For all patients

» Compliance with therapy; checking with physician before discontinuing medication since interruption of therapy may cause sensitivity reactions when therapy is reinstituted

» Proper dosing
Missed dose: If dosing schedule is—
- Once a day: Taking as soon as possible; not taking if not remembered until next day; not doubling doses
- Two times a day: Taking as soon as possible; not taking if almost time for next dose; not doubling doses
- More than two times a day: Taking if remembered within an hour; not taking if not remembered until later; not doubling doses

» Proper storage

Precautions while using this medication

Regular visits to physician to check progress during therapy

Caution in use of regular toothbrush, dental floss, or toothpick; physician, dentist, or nurse may suggest alternatives; checking with physician before having dental work done.

Caution if any kind of surgery (including dental surgery) is required because of the effects of penicillamine on collagen and elastin

Avoiding concurrent use of iron-containing medications; for treatment of iron deficiency short courses of iron supplementation may be given—two hours should elapse between administration of penicillamine and iron

» Contact your healthcare provider if you have fever, sore throat, chills, bruising, or bleeding.

» Contact your healthcare provider if you have difficulty breathing or an unexplained cough.

Side/adverse effects

Signs of potential side effects, especially allergic reactions, fever (drug-induced), pemphigus foliaceus or vulgaris, stomatitis, blood dyscrasias, glomerulopathy, obstructive bronchiolitis, exfoliative dermatitis, Goodpasture's syndrome, jaundice, myasthenia gravis syndrome, toxic epidermal necrolysis, optic neuritis, pancreatitis, peptic ulcer reactivation, ringing or buzzing in ears, and SLE-like syndrome

General Dosing Information

Penicillamine therapy should be continued on a daily basis because interruptions for even a few days may cause sensitivity reactions following reinstitution of therapy.

If surgery is necessary during penicillamine therapy, the dosage should be reduced to 250 mg daily because of the effects on collagen and elastin. Reinstitution of full therapy should be delayed until wound healing is complete.

In the treatment of cystinuria or Wilson's disease, a daily dose of 250 mg may be administered, with the dosage being increased gradually to the optimum dosage if the patient cannot tolerate the usual initial dose of penicillamine. This may also help to reduce the incidence of adverse reactions.

Patients with rheumatoid arthritis (whose nutrition is impaired), cystinuria, or Wilson's disease should be given 25 mg of pyridoxine daily during therapy because penicillamine increases the intake requirement for this vitamin.

Impairment of sense of taste may occur with penicillamine therapy. Except for patients with Wilson's disease, normal taste acuity may be restored while therapy with penicillamine is continued by administering 5 to 10 mg of copper daily (5 to 10 drops of a 4% cupric sulfate solution may be administered in fruit juice two times a day).

If the patient develops a drug-induced fever, therapy should be temporarily discontinued.

If the patient develops pemphigus vulgaris or foliaceus, therapy should be discontinued. Treatment with high-dose corticosteroids, alone or with an immunosuppressant, is recommended.

If therapy is interrupted for any reason, it should be reinstituted with a small dosage, which is gradually increased until full dosage is achieved.

In cystinuria

Penicillamine should be given on an empty stomach (at least 1 hour before meals or 2 hours after meals) and at least 1 hour apart from any other medication, food, or milk.

The daily dosage of penicillamine may range from 1 to 4 grams.

The dosage of penicillamine should be based on measurements of urinary cystine excretion. Urinary cystine excretion should be maintained at less than 100 mg daily in patients with a history of renal calculi and/or pain, or at 100 to 200 mg daily in patients without a history of renal calculi.

If administration in four equally divided doses is not possible, the larger dose should be given at bedtime; or, if the occurrence of side effects requires dosage reduction, the bedtime dose should be one of the doses retained.

To help prevent the formation of cystine stones, a high fluid intake is recommended. The patient should drink 500 mL of water at bedtime and another 500 mL once during the night when the urine is more concentrated and more acidic than during the day. Usually the greater the fluid intake, the lower the required dose of penicillamine.

A diet low in methionine may be necessary to minimize cystine production. This diet is not recommended in growing children or during pregnancy because of its low protein content.

In lead poisoning

Penicillamine should be administered on an empty stomach, 2 hours before meals or at least 3 hours after meals.

In rheumatoid arthritis

Penicillamine should be given on an empty stomach (at least 1 hour before meals or 2 hours after meals) and at least 1 hour apart from any other medication, food, or milk in order to achieve maximum absorption and to reduce the possibility of inactivation by metal binding.

Dosage up to 500 mg per day may be given as a single dose. Dosage above 500 mg per day should be administered in divided doses.

During initial therapy, if the dosage has been increased up to 1 to 1.5 grams of penicillamine per day and after 3 to 4 months there is still no improvement in the patient's condition, the medication should be discontinued.

The maintenance dosage of penicillamine may need adjustment during the course of treatment. Changes in maintenance dosage levels may not be noticed clinically or in the erythrocytic sedimentation rate until 2 or 3 months after each dosage adjustment.

For those patients who require an increase in the maintenance dosage to achieve maximal disease suppression after the first 6 to 9 months of therapy, the daily dosage may be increased by 125 or 250 mg per day at 3-month intervals up to 1.5 grams per day.

In Wilson's disease

Dosage of penicillamine should be determined by measurements of urinary copper excretion to achieve and maintain a negative copper balance.

Penicillamine should be administered on an empty stomach (30 minutes to 1 hour before meals and at least 2 hours after the evening meal).

The dosage may be increased as indicated by urinary copper analyses, but dosage greater than 2 grams daily is usually not necessary.

In conjunction with penicillamine therapy, a low-copper diet of less than 2 mg daily should be maintained. Such a diet should exclude, most importantly, chocolate, nuts, shellfish, mushrooms, liver, molasses, broccoli, and cereals enriched with copper. Distilled or demineralized water should be used if the patient's drinking water contains more than 100 mcg (0.1 mg) of copper per liter.

Sulfurated potash (10 to 40 mg) may be administered with meals to minimize absorption of copper (capsules of sulfurated potash may be prepared by using light magnesium oxide as a diluent).

Oral Dosage Forms

Note: Bracketed uses in the *Dosage Forms* section refer to categories of use and/or indications that are not included in U.S. product labeling.

PENICILLAMINE CAPSULES USP

Usual adult and adolescent dose

Chelating agent—
Oral, 250 mg four times a day.

Antirheumatic—
Oral, initially 125 or 250 mg once a day as a single dose, the dosage being increased, if necessary and tolerated, by adding 125 or 250 mg per day at two- to three-month intervals up to a maximum of 1.5 grams per day.

Note: Some clinicians recommend a maximum dose of 1 gram per day in rheumatoid arthritis.

Antiurolithic—
Oral, 500 mg four times a day.

[Antidote (to heavy metals)]—
Oral, 500 mg to 1.5 grams per day for one to two months.

Usual pediatric dose

Chelating agent—
Infants older than 6 months of age and young children: Oral, 250 mg as a single dose administered in fruit juice.
Older children: See *Usual adult and adolescent dose*.

Antirheumatic—
Efficacy and dosage have not been established.

Antiurolithic—
Oral, 7.5 mg per kg of body weight four times a day.

[Antidote (to heavy metals)]—
Oral, 30 to 40 mg per kg of body weight or 600 to 750 mg per square meter of body surface per day for one to six months.

Usual geriatric dose

Oral, initially 125 mg per day. Dosage may be increased, if necessary and tolerated, by adding 125 mg per day at two- to three-month intervals, up to a maximum of 750 mg per day.

Strength(s) usually available

U.S.—
125 mg (Rx) [*Cuprimine* (lactose)].
250 mg (Rx) [*Cuprimine* (lactose)].

Canada—
125 mg (Rx) [*Cuprimine* (lactose)].
250 mg (Rx) [*Cuprimine* (lactose)].

Packaging and storage

Store below 40 °C (104 °F), preferably between 15 and 30 °C (59 and 86 °F), unless otherwise specified by manufacturer. Store in a tight container.

Auxiliary labeling

- Take on an empty stomach.

PENICILLAMINE TABLETS USP

Usual adult and adolescent dose

Chelating agent—
Oral, 250 mg four times a day.

Antirheumatic—
Oral, initially 125 or 250 mg once a day as a single dose, the dosage being increased, if necessary and tolerated, by adding 125 or 250 mg per day at two- to three-month intervals up to a maximum of 1.5 grams per day.

Note: Some clinicians recommend a maximum dose of 1 gram per day in rheumatoid arthritis.

Antiurolithic—
Oral, 500 mg four times a day.

[Antidote (to heavy metals)]—
Oral, 500 mg to 1.5 grams per day for one to two months.

Usual pediatric dose

Chelating agent—
Infants older than 6 months of age and young children: Oral, 250 mg as a single dose administered in fruit juice.
Older children: See *Usual adult and adolescent dose*.

Antirheumatic—
Dosage has not been established.

Antiurolithic—
Oral, 7.5 mg per kg of body weight four times a day.

[Antidote (to heavy metals)]—
Oral, 30 to 40 mg per kg of body weight or 600 to 750 mg per square meter of body surface per day for one to six months.

Usual geriatric dose

Oral, initially 125 mg per day. Dosage may be increased, if necessary and tolerated, by adding 125 mg per day at two- to three-month intervals, up to a maximum of 750 mg per day.

Strength(s) usually available

U.S.—
250 mg (Rx) [*Depen* (scored; lactose)].

Canada—
250 mg (Rx) [*Depen* (scored; lactose)].

Packaging and storage

Store below 40 °C (104 °F), preferably between 15 and 30 °C (59 and 86 °F), unless otherwise specified by manufacturer. Store in a tight container.

Auxiliary labeling

- Take on an empty stomach.

Revised: 01/20/2005

PENICILLIN G—See *Penicillins (Systemic)*

PENICILLIN V—See *Penicillins (Systemic)*

PENICILLINS Systemic

This monograph includes information on the following: 1) Amoxicillin; 2) Ampicillin; 3) Bacampicillin; 4) Carbenicillin; 5) Cloxacillin; 6) Dicloxacillin†; 7) Flucloxacillin*; 8) Methicillin†; 9) Mezlocillin†; 10) Nafcillin; 11) Oxacillin†; 12) Penicillin G; 13) Penicillin V; 14) Piperacillin; 15) Pivampicillin*; 16) Pivmecillinam*; 17) Ticarcillin.

INN:

Amoxicillin—Amoxicilline
Carbenicillin indanyl sodium—Carindacillin
Methicillin—Meticillin
Penicillin G benzathine—Benzathine benzylpenicillin
Penicillin V—Phenoxymethylpenicillin

BAN:

Amoxicillin—Amoxycillin
Carbenicillin indanyl sodium—Carindacillin
Penicillin G benzathine—Benzathine penicillin
Penicillin G procaine—Procaine penicillin
Penicillin V—Phenoxymethylpenicillin

VA CLASSIFICATION (Primary):

Amoxicillin—AM112
Ampicillin—AM112
Bacampicillin—AM112
Carbenicillin—AM114
Cloxacillin—AM113
Dicloxacillin—AM113
Flucloxacillin—AM113
Methicillin—AM113
Mezlocillin—AM114
Nafcillin—AM113
Oxacillin—AM113
Penicillin G—AM111
Penicillin V—AM111
Piperacillin—AM114
Pivampicillin—AM112
Pivmecillinam—AM112
Ticarcillin—AM114

Commonly used brand name(s): *Amoxil*[1]; *Ampicin*[2]; *Apo-Amoxi*[1]; *Apo-Ampi*[2]; *Apo-Cloxi*[5]; *Apo-Pen VK*[13]; *Ayercillin*[12]; *Bactocill*[11]; *Beepen-VK*[13]; *Betapen-VK*[13]; *Bicillin L-A*[12]; *Cloxapen*[5]; *Crysticillin 300 A.S.*[12]; *Dycill*[6]; *Dynapen*[6]; *Fluclox*[7]; *Geocillin*[4]; *Geopen*[4]; *Geopen Oral*[4]; *Ledercillin VK*[13]; *Megacillin*[12]; *Mezlin*[9]; *Nadopen-V*[13]; *Nadopen-V 200*[13]; *Nadopen-V 400*[13]; *Nafcil*[10]; *Nallpen*[10]; *Novamoxin*[1]; *Novo-Ampicillin*[2]; *Novo-Cloxin*[5]; *Novo-Pen-VK*[13]; *Nu-Amoxi*[1]; *Nu-Ampi*[2]; *Nu-Cloxi*[5]; *Nu-Pen-VK*[13]; *Omnipen*[2]; *Omnipen-N*[2]; *Orbenin*[5]; *PVF*[13]; *PVF K*[13]; *Pathocil*[6]; *Pen Vee*[13]; *Pen Vee K*[13]; *Pen-Vee*[13]; *Penbritin*[2]; *Penglobe*[3]; *Pentids*[12]; *Permapen*[12]; *Pfizerpen*[12]; *Pfizerpen-AS*[12]; *Pipracil*[14]; *Polycillin*[2]; *Polycillin-N*[2]; *Polymox*[1]; *Pondocillin*[15]; *Principen*[2]; *Prostaphlin*[11]; *Pyopen*[4]; *Selexid*[16]; *Spectrobid*[3]; *Staphcillin*[8]; *Tegopen*[5]; *Ticar*[17]; *Totacillin*[2]; *Totacillin-N*[2]; *Trimox*[1]; *Unipen*[10]; *V-Cillin K*[13]; *Veetids*[13]; *Wycillin*[12]; *Wymox*[1].

Note: For a listing of dosage forms and brand names by country availability, see *Dosage Forms* section(s).

*Not commercially available in U.S.
†Not commercially available in Canada.

Category

Antibacterial (systemic).

Indications

Note: Bracketed information in the *Indications* section refers to uses that are not included in U.S. product labeling.

General Considerations

Penicillins can be classified into four broad categories, each covering a different spectrum of activity. The natural penicillins (penicillin G and penicillin V) have activity against many gram-positive organisms, gram-negative cocci, and some other gram-negative organisms. The aminopenicillins (ampicillin, amoxicillin, bacampicillin, and pivampicillin) have activity against penicillin-sensitive gram-positive bacteria, as well as *Escherichia coli*, *Proteus mirabilis*, *Salmonella* sp., *Shigella* sp., and *Haemophilus influenzae*. The antistaphylococcal penicillins (cloxacillin, dicloxacillin, flucloxacillin, methicillin, nafcillin, and oxacillin) are also active against beta-lactamase-producing staphylococci. The antipseudomonal penicillins (carbenicillin, mezlocillin, piperacillin, and ticarcillin) have less activity against gram-positive organisms than the natural penicillins or aminopenicillins; however, unlike the other penicillins, these penicillins are active against some gram-negative bacilli, including *Pseudomonas aeruginosa*.

Resistance to penicillins is thought to be due to 3 main mechanisms. The first is alteration of the antibiotic target sites' penicillin-binding proteins (PBPs); the second is inactivation of the penicillin by bacterially produced enzymes (beta-lactamases); and the third is decreased permeability of the cell wall to penicillins. Of these 3 mechanisms, production of beta-lactamase is the most common and the most important.

The spectrums of activity of penicillin G and penicillin V include *Staphylococcus* and *Streptococcus* species. However, most strains of *Staphylococcus aureus* and *Staphyloccus epidermidis* produce beta-lactamases, which destroy these penicillins. A small proportion of community-acquired strains (5 to 15%) of *S. aureus* remains susceptible to penicillin G. Penicillin G also has activity against the gram-negative cocci, *Neisseria meningitidis* and *Neisseria gonorrhoeae*. However, resistance to penicillin G by beta-lactamase-producing *N. gonorrhoeae* has become a widespread problem in many parts of the world. Penicillin G is more active than penicillin V against *Haemophilus* and *Neisseria* species. Some other organisms for which penicillin G has good activity include *Actinomyces israelii*, *Bacillus anthracis*, oropharyngeal *Bacteroides* species, *Borrelia burgdorferi*, *Clostridium* sp., *Corynebacterium diphtheriae*, *Erysipelothrix rhusiopathiae*, *Listeria monocytogenes*, *Spirillium minor*, *Streptobacillus moniliformis*, and *Treponema pallidum*.

The aminopenicillins have activity against *H. influenzae*, *E. coli*, *P. mirabilis*, and *Salmonella* and some *Shigella* species, while also retaining activity against penicillin-sensitive gram-positive bacteria. However, many Enterobacteriaceae, *H. influenzae*, *Salmonella* and *Shigella* species are resistant to these penicillins because of beta-lactamase production by these organisms. Bacampicillin and pivampicillin are esters of ampicillin that are hydrolyzed during absorption to liberate ampicillin; this results in increased bioavailability and serum concentrations of ampicillin. Amoxicillin has the same *in vitro* activity as ampicillin, although amoxicillin has slightly better activity against *Enterococcus faecalis*, *E. coli*, and *Salmonella* sp.

The antistaphylococcal penicillins were developed to treat beta-lactamase-producing staphylococci. These penicillins are active against both penicillin-sensitive and penicillin-resistant staphylococci, as well as *Streptococcus pyogenes* and *Streptococcus pneumoniae*. However, they are less potent than penicillin G against penicillin-sensitive bacteria, and they have very little activity against *Enterococcus faecalis* and gram-negative organisms. Nafcillin has more intrinsic activity than methicillin against staphylococci and streptococci. The mechanism of methicillin-resistant *S. aureus* is not due to beta-lactamase production by the organism, but results from an alteration of penicillin-binding proteins. Methicillin-resistant staphylococci are also resistant to the other penicillins in this category.

The antipseudomonal penicillins are active against a wide variety of gram-negative bacteria, including *P. aeruginosa*, *Enterobacter*, *Morganella*, and *Providencia* species. These penicillins are less active than ampicillin against streptococci and enterococci; however, their activity against non-beta-lactamase-producing *Haemophilus*, *N. meningitidis*, and *N. gonorrhoeae* is similar to that of ampicillin. These agents are also destroyed by beta-lactamases produced by gram-positive and some gram-negative organisms. Ticarcillin is 2 to 4 times more active than carbenicillin against *P. aeruginosa*. Mezlocillin has a spectrum of activity similar to that of carbenicillin and ticarcillin; however, mezlocillin has better activity against non-beta-lactamase-producing strains of *Klebsiella*, *H. influenzae*, and *Bacteroides fragilis*. Piperacillin has excellent activity against streptococci, *Neisseria*, and *Haemophilus* species and is the most active penicillin against *P. aeruginosa*.

Another penicillin, which does not neatly fit into any of these four categories, is pivmecillinam. Pivmecillinam is hydrolyzed during absorption to liberate the active agent, mecillinam. Mecillinam has poor activity against gram-positive organisms, *Haemophilus*, and *Neisseria* species; however, it has very good activity against many gram-negative bacteria, including *E. coli*, many *Klebsiella*, *Enterobacter*, and *Citrobacter* species. It has variable activity against *Proteus* sp. and does not inhibit *P. aeruginosa* or anaerobes, such as *B. fragilis* or *Clostridium* species.

Accepted

Actinomycosis (treatment)—Penicillin G (parenteral) and [penicillin V][1] are indicated in the treatment of actinomycosis caused by *Actinomyces* sp.

Anthrax (treatment)—Penicillin G (parenteral), [penicillin V][1], and penicillin G procaine are indicated in the treatment of anthrax caused by *B. anthracis*.

Arthritis, gonococcal (treatment)—Penicillin G (parenteral) is indicated in the treatment of infective arthritis caused by susceptible strains of *N. gonorrhoeae*.

Bejel (treatment)—Penicillin G benzathine and penicillin G procaine are indicated in the treatment of bejel caused by *Treponema pallidum endemicum*.

Bone and joint infections (treatment)—Carbenicillin (parenteral), cloxacillin (parenteral), [methicillin][1], [nafcillin (parenteral)][1], [oxacillin (parenteral)][1], [penicillin G (parenteral)][1], and piperacillin are indicated in the treatment of bone and joint infections caused by susceptible organisms.

Bronchitis, bacterial exacerbations (treatment)—Amoxicillin, ampicillin, bacampicillin, cloxacillin (oral), dicloxacillin, penicillin V, and pivampicillin are indicated in the treatment of bronchitis caused by susceptible organisms.

Diphtheria (prophylaxis)—Penicillin G (parenteral), [penicillin G benzathine][1], penicillin G procaine, and penicillin V are indicated in the prophylaxis of diphtheria, caused by *C. diphtheriae*, as an adjunct to antitoxin.

Endocarditis, bacterial (prophylaxis)—[Amoxicillin][1], [ampicillin][1], penicillin G (parenteral), and penicillin V are indicated in the prophylaxis of bacterial endocarditis caused by susceptible organisms.

Endocarditis, bacterial (treatment)—Ampicillin (parenteral), carbenicillin (parenteral), cloxacillin (parenteral), [methicillin][1], [nafcillin (parenteral)][1], [oxacillin (parenteral)], [penicillin G (parenteral)][1] and penicillin G procaine are indicated in the treatment of bacterial endocarditis caused by susceptible organisms.

Erysipelas (treatment)—Penicillin G (parenteral), penicillin V, and penicillin G procaine are indicated in the treatment of erysipelas caused by susceptible strains of group A streptococci.

Erysipeloid (treatment)—Penicillin G (parenteral), [penicillin V][1], [penicillin G benzathine][1], and [penicillin G procaine][1] are indicated in the treatment of erysipeloid, including endocarditis and septicemia, caused by *E. rhusiopathiae*.

Gingivitis, acute, necrotizing, ulcerative (treatment)—Penicillin G (oral and parenteral), penicillin V, and penicillin G procaine are indicated in the treatment of acute, necrotizing, ulcerative gingivitis, also called Vincent's angina or "trench mouth," a pharyngeal and tonsillar infection caused by anaerobes and spirochetes.

Gonorrhea, endocervical and urethral, uncomplicated (treatment)—Amoxicillin, in combination with probenecid, and [penicillin G (parenteral)][1] are indicated in the treatment of gonorrhea caused by susceptible strains of *N. gonorrhoeae*. However, because of resistance to penicillin, other agents, such as ceftriaxone, cefixime, or ciprofloxacin, are considered to be first-line agents.

Intra-abdominal infections (treatment)—Carbenicillin (parenteral), mezlocillin, [penicillin G (parenteral)][1], piperacillin, and ticarcillin are indicated in the treatment of intra-abdominal infections caused by susceptible organisms.

Listeriosis (treatment)—[Ampicillin (parenteral)][1] and penicillin G (parenteral) are indicated in the treatment of listeriosis caused by *L. monocytogenes*.

Meningitis, bacterial (treatment)—Ampicillin (parenteral), carbenicillin (parenteral), [nafcillin (parenteral)][1], [oxacillin (parenteral)][1], penicillin G (parenteral), [piperacillin][1], and [ticarcillin][1] are indicated in the treatment of bacterial meningitis caused by susceptible organisms.

Otitis media, acute (treatment)—Amoxicillin, ampicillin, bacampicillin, penicillin G procaine, penicillin G (oral), penicillin V, and pivampicillin are indicated in the treatment of acute otitis media caused by susceptible organisms.

Pasteurella multocida infections (treatment)—[Ampicillin (parenteral)][1], penicillin G (parenteral), and [penicillin V][1] are indicated in the treatment of infections caused by *P. multocida*.

Pelvic infections, female (treatment)—[Carbenicillin (parenteral)][1], mezlocillin, piperacillin, and ticarcillin are indicated in the treatment of female pelvic infections caused by susceptible organisms.

Pericarditis, bacterial (treatment)—Penicillin G (parenteral), penicillin G procaine, and [nafcillin (parenteral)][1] are indicated in the treatment of bacterial pericarditis caused by susceptible organisms.

Pharyngitis, bacterial (treatment)—Amoxicillin, ampicillin, bacampicillin, cloxacillin (oral), dicloxacillin, flucloxacillin, penicillin G benzathine, pencillin G (oral), penicillin V, and pivampicillin are indicated in the treatment of bacterial pharyngitis caused by susceptible organisms.

Pinta (treatment)—Penicillin G benzathine and penicillin G procaine are indicated in the treatment of pinta caused by *Treponema carateum*.

Pneumonia, bacterial (treatment)—Amoxicillin, ampicillin, bacampicillin, carbenicillin (parenteral), cloxacillin, dicloxacillin, mezlocillin, penicillin G (parenteral), penicillin G procaine, piperacillin, and ticarcillin are indicated in the treatment of bacterial pneumonia caused by susceptible organisms.

Prostatitis (treatment)—Carbenicillin (oral) is indicated in the treatment of prostatitis caused by susceptible organisms.

Rat-bite fever (treatment)—Penicillin G (parenteral), penicillin G procaine, and [penicillin V][1] are indicated in the treatment of rat-bite fever caused by *S. moniliformis* or *S. minor*.

Rheumatic fever (prophylaxis)—Penicillin V, and penicillin G benzathine are indicated in the prophylaxis of rheumatic fever caused by group A streptococci.

Scarlet fever (treatment)—Penicillin V penicillin G procaine, and [penicillin G (parenteral)][1] are indicated in the treatment of scarlet fever caused by group A streptococci.

Septicemia, bacterial (treatment)—Ampicillin (parenteral), carbenicillin (parenteral), cloxacillin (parenteral), methicillin, mezlocillin, nafcillin (parenteral), oxacillin (parenteral), penicillin G (parenteral), penicillin G procaine, piperacillin, and ticarcillin are indicated in the treatment of bacterial septicemia caused by susceptible organisms.

Sinusitis (treatment)—Amoxicillin, ampicillin, bacampicillin, cloxacillin, flucloxacillin, methicillin, nafcillin, oxacillin, and penicillin V are indicated in the treatment of sinusitis caused by susceptible organisms.

Skin and soft tissue infections (treatment)—Carbenicillin (parenteral), cloxacillin, dicloxacillin, flucloxacillin, methicillin, mezlocillin, nafcillin, oxacillin, penicillin G procaine, [penicillin G (parenteral)][1], penicillin V, piperacillin, pivampicillin, and ticarcillin are indicated in the treatment of skin and soft tissue infections caused by susceptible organisms.

Syphilis (treatment)—Penicillin G benzathine is indicated in the treatment of primary, secondary, and early and late latent syphilis. Penicillin G (parenteral) and penicillin G procaine, in combination with probenecid, are indicated in the treatment of tertiary syphilis. Penicillin G (parenteral) is indicated in the treatment of neurosyphilis. Penicillin G benzathine fails to achieve adequate concentrations in the cerebrospinal fluid.

Tetanus (treatment)—Penicillin G (parenteral) is indicated in the treatment of the infecting organism in tetanus, *Clostridium tetani*.

Ulcer, duodenal, associated with *Helicobacter pylori* (treatment)[1]—Amoxicillin is indicated as part of a triple antibiotic therapy, in combination with clarithromycin and lansoprazole, for patients who are infected with *H. pylori* and have duodenal ulcer disease (either active or a 1-year history of a duodenal ulcer) to eradicate the organism and thereby reduce the risk of ulcer recurrence.

Amoxicillin also is indicated as part of a dual antibiotic therapy, in combination with lansoprazole, in patients who are infected with *H. pylori* and have duodenal ulcer disease (either active or a 1-year history of a duodenal ulcer) when the patient is either intolerant or allergic to clarithromycin or when clarithromycin resistance is suspected or confirmed.

See *Clarithromycin (Systemic)* and *Lansoprazole (Systemic)* monographs for additional information pertaining to these medications.

Urinary tract infections, bacterial (treatment)—Amoxicillin, ampicillin, bacampicillin, carbenicillin (oral and parenteral), mezlocillin, piperacillin, pivampicillin, pivmecillinam, and ticarcillin are indicated in the treatment of bacterial urinary tract infections caused by susceptible organisms.

Yaws (treatment)—Penicillin G benzathine, penicillin G procaine, and [penicillin G (parenteral)] are indicated in the treatment of yaws caused by *Treponema pallidum pertenue*.

[Chlamydial infections in pregnant women (treatment)][1]—Amoxicillin and ampicillin are used in the treatment of chlamydial infections in pregnant women who cannot tolerate erythromycin.

[Gas gangrene infections (treatment)][1]—Penicillin G (parenteral) is used in the treatment of gas gangrene caused by *Clostridium* sp.

[Gastritis, *Helicobacter pylori*-associated (treatment adjunct)][1] or
[Ulcer, peptic, *Helicobacter pylori*-associated (treatment adjunct)][1]—Amoxicillin is used, in combination with metronidazole and bismuth subsalicylate, in the treatment of gastritis and peptic ulcer disease caused by *H. pylori*.

[Leptospirosis (treatment)][1]—Ampicillin (parenteral) and penicillin G (parenteral) are used in the treatment of leptospirosis caused by *Leptospira* sp.

[Lyme disease (treatment)][1]—Amoxicillin and penicillin V are used in the treatment of early Lyme disease, caused by *B. burgdorferi*. Amoxicillin, in combination with probenecid, and penicillin G (parenteral) are used to treat more advanced stages of Lyme disease, including mild neurological manifestations, cardiac manifestations, and arthritis.

[Typhoid fever (treatment)][1]—Amoxicillin and ampicillin are used in the treatment of typhoid fever caused by *Salmonella typhi*.

Unaccepted

For carbenicillin (oral)—

Since effective serum concentrations are not achieved with oral carbenicillin, it is indicated only for urinary tract infections and prostatitis.

For nafcillin (oral)—

The oral absorption of nafcillin is erratic and the resulting serum concentrations are low; therefore, use of oral nafcillin is not recommended.

For penicillin G benzathine (parenteral)—

Parenteral penicillin G benzathine is not indicated for the treatment of meningitis or neurosyphilis because it fails to achieve adequate concentrations in the cerebrospinal fluid (CSF).

For penicillin G (oral)—

Because of the low serum concentrations achieved with oral penicillin G, it is not indicated for the treatment of severe infections.

---

[1]Not included in Canadian product labeling.

Pharmacology/Pharmacokinetics

See *Table 1*, page 2325.

See *Table 2*, page 2326.

Physicochemical characteristics

Chemical Group—

- Amoxicillin: Aminopenicillin
- Ampicillin: Aminopenicillin
- Bacampicillin: Aminopenicillin
- Carbenicillin: Carboxypenicillin
- Cloxacillin: Isoxazolyl penicillin
- Dicloxacillin: Isoxazolyl penicillin
- Flucloxacillin: Isoxazolyl penicillin
- Mezlocillin: Acylureidopenicillin
- Oxacillin: Isoxazolyl penicillin
- Piperacillin: Acylureidopenicillin
- Pivampicillin: Aminopenicillin
- Ticarcillin: Carboxypenicillin

Molecular weight—

- Amoxicillin: 419.45.
- Ampicillin: 349.40.
- Ampicillin sodium: 371.39.
- Bacampicillin hydrochloride: 501.98.
- Carbenicillin disodium: 422.36.
- Carbenicillin indanyl sodium: 516.54.
- Cloxacillin sodium: 475.88.
- Dicloxacillin sodium: 510.32.
- Flucloxacillin: 453.87.
- Methicillin sodium: 420.41.
- Mezlocillin sodium: 561.56.
- Nafcillin sodium: 454.47.
- Oxacillin sodium: 441.43.
- Penicillin G benzathine: 981.19.
- Penicillin G potassium: 372.48.
- Penicillin G procaine: 588.72.
- Penicillin G sodium: 356.37.
- Penicillin V potassium: 388.48.
- Piperacillin sodium: 539.54.
- Pivampicillin hydrochloride: 500.01.
- Pivmecillinam: 439.57.
- Ticarcillin disodium: 428.38.

Mechanism of action/Effect

Bactericidal; inhibit bacterial cell wall synthesis. Action is dependent on the ability of penicillins to reach and bind penicillin-binding proteins (PBPs) located on the inner membrane of the bacterial cell wall. PBPs (which include transpeptidases, carboxypeptidases, and endopeptidases) are enzymes that are involved in the terminal stages of assembling the bacterial cell wall and in reshaping the cell wall during growth and division. Penicillins bind to, and inactivate, PBPs, resulting in the weakening of the bacterial cell wall and lysis.

Distribution

Penicillins are widely distributed to most tissues and body fluids, including peritoneal fluid, blister fluid, urine (high concentrations), pleural fluid, middle ear fluid, intestinal mucosa, bone, gallbladder, lung, female reproductive tissues, and bile. Distribution into the cerebrospinal fluid (CSF) is low in subjects with noninflamed meninges, as is penetration into purulent bronchial secretions.

Penicillins also cross the placenta and are distributed into breast milk.

Biotransformation

Hepatic metabolism accounts for less than 30% of the biotransformation of most penicillins, with the exception of nafcillin and oxacillin.

Bacampicillin—A prodrug of ampicillin; bacampicillin is hydrolyzed by esterases in the intestinal wall during absorption to produce ampicillin. Bacampicillin provides earlier and higher peak concentrations of ampicillin than administration of ampicillin does.

Carbenicillin indanyl sodium—After absorption, carbenicillin indanyl sodium is rapidly converted to carbenicillin by hydrolysis of the ester linkage.

Penicillin G benzathine (intramuscular)—Slowly released from the intramuscular injection site and hydrolyzed to penicillin G, resulting in serum concentrations that are much lower but much more prolonged than other parenteral penicillins.

Penicillin G procaine—Dissolves slowly at the site of injection, giving a plateau-type blood level at 4 hours, which falls slowly over the next 15 to 20 hours.

Pivampicillin—A prodrug of ampicillin, which is converted during absorption to ampicillin, formaldehyde, and pivalic acid, by non-specific esterases in most body tissues. Pivampicillin provides earlier and higher peak concentrations of ampicillin than administration of ampicillin does.

Pivmecillinam—A prodrug of mecillinam, which is converted during absorption to mecillinam, formaldehyde, and pivalic acid, by nonspecific esterases in most body tissues.

Elimination

Primarily renal (glomerular filtration and tubular secretion).

Hepatic metabolism accounts for less than 30% of the elimination of most penicillins, with the exception of nafcillin and oxacillin.

Biliary—Some penicillins, such as ampicillin, mezlocillin, nafcillin, penicillin G, piperacillin, and pivmecillinam, may be excreted in the bile in high concentrations. Approximately 10% of cloxacillin, dicloxacillin, flucloxacillin, and oxacillin is recovered in the bile.

Precautions to Consider

Cross-sensitivity and/or related problems

Patients allergic to one penicillin may be allergic to other penicillins also.

Patients allergic to cephalosporins or cephamycins may be allergic to penicillins also. Patients allergic to procaine or other ester-type local anesthetics may also be allergic to sterile penicillin G procaine suspension, which is an equimolar compound of procaine and penicillin G.

Carcinogenicity

Amoxicillin, ampicillin, bacampicillin, cloxacillin, dicloxacillin, methicillin, nafcillin, oxacillin, penicillin G, penicillin V—Long-term studies have not been performed in animals.

Carbenicillin—Long-term studies have not been performed in animals. Rats given 25 to 100 mg per kg of body weight (mg/kg) per day of carbenicillin for 18 months developed mild liver pathology (bile duct hyperplasia) at all dose levels, but there was no evidence of drug-related neoplasia.

Mutagenicity

Amoxicillin, ampicillin, bacampicillin, cloxacillin, dicloxacillin, methicillin, nafcillin, oxacillin, penicillin G, penicillin V—Long-term studies have not been performed in animals.

Pregnancy/Reproduction

Fertility—*Amoxicillin:* Studies in mice and rats at doses up to 10 times the human dose of amoxicillin revealed no evidence of impaired fertility.

Bacampicillin: Studies in mice and rats given doses of up to 750 mg/kg (more than 25 times the usual human dose) showed no evidence of impaired fertility. Also, bacampicillin had no effect on the reproductive organs of rats or dogs receiving daily oral doses of up to 800 and 650 mg, respectively, for 6 months.

Carbenicillin: Administration of carbenicillin at doses of up to 1000 mg/kg had no apparent effect on the fertility or reproductive performance of rats.

Cloxacillin, dicloxacillin, methicillin, nafcillin, oxacillin, penicillin G, penicillin V: Reproductive studies performed in the mouse, rat, and rabbit given these penicillins have revealed no evidence of impaired fertility.

Mezlocillin: Studies in mice and rats given doses up to twice the usual human dose have not shown that mezlocillin impairs fertility.

Piperacillin: Studies in mice and rats given doses up to 4 times the human dose of piperacillin have shown no evidence of impaired fertility.

Ticarcillin: Reproductive studies done in mice and rats given ticarcillin have revealed no evidence of impaired fertility.

Pregnancy—Penicillins cross the placenta. Adequate and well-controlled studies in humans have not been done to determine whether penicillins are teratogenic; however, penicillins are widely used in pregnant women and problems have not been documented.

Amoxicillin: Studies in mice and rats at doses up to 10 times the human dose of amoxicillin revealed no evidence of harm to the fetus.

FDA Pregnancy Category B.

Ampicillin: Studies in animals given doses several times the human dose have revealed no evidence of adverse effects in the fetus.

FDA Pregnancy Category B.

Bacampicillin: Studies in mice and rats given doses of up to 750 mg/kg (more than 25 times the usual human dose) have not shown that bacampicillin causes adverse effects in the fetus.

FDA Pregnancy Category B.

Carbenicillin: Reproductive studies using doses of 500 or 1000 mg/kg in rats, 200 mg/kg in mice, and 500 mg/kg in monkeys showed no harm to the fetus.

FDA Pregnancy Category B.

Cloxacillin, dicloxacillin, methicillin, nafcillin, oxacillin, penicillin G, penicillin V: Reproductive studies performed in the mouse, rat, and rabbit given these penicillins have revealed no evidence of impaired fertility or harm to the fetus.

FDA Pregnancy Category B.

Flucloxacillin, pivampicillin, pivmecillinam: Safety during pregnancy has not been established.

Mezlocillin: Studies in mice and rats given doses up to twice the usual human dose have not shown that mezlocillin causes adverse effects in the fetus.

FDA Pregnancy Category B.

Piperacillin: Studies in mice and rats given doses up to 4 times the usual human dose have not shown that piperacillin causes adverse effects in the fetus.

FDA Pregnancy Category B.

Ticarcillin: Reproductive studies done in mice and rats given ticarcillin have not shown that ticarcillin causes adverse effects in the fetus.

FDA Pregnancy Category B.

Breast-feeding

Penicillins are distributed into breast milk, some in low concentrations. Although significant problems in humans have not been documented, the use of penicillins by nursing mothers may lead to sensitization, diarrhea, candidiasis, and skin rash in the infant.

Pediatrics

Many penicillins have been used in pediatric patients and no pediatrics-specific problems have been documented to date. However, the incompletely developed renal function of neonates and young infants may delay the excretion of renally eliminated penicillins.

Because pivampicillin and pivmecillinam have been associated with a decrease in serum carnitine, it is recommended that these penicillins be avoided in children less than 3 months of age.

The 200-mg and the 400-mg chewable tablets of amoxicillin contain 1.8 mg and 3.6 mg phenylalanine, respectively, produced through the metabolism of aspartame. These dosage forms should be used with caution, if at all, in patients with phenylketonuria. The other strengths and dosage forms of amoxicillin do not contain phenylalanine.

Geriatrics

Penicillins have been used in geriatric patients and no geriatrics-specific problems have been documented to date. However, elderly patients are more likely to have age-related renal function impairment, which may require an adjustment in dosage in patients receiving penicillins.

Dental

Prolonged use of penicillins may lead to the development of oral candidiasis.

Drug interactions and/or related problems

The following drug interactions and/or related problems have been selected on the basis of their potential clinical significance (possible mechanism in parentheses where appropriate)—not necessarily inclusive (» = major clinical significance):

Note: Combinations containing any of the following medications, depending on the amount present, may also interact with this medication.

Allopurinol
(concurrent use with ampicillin or bacampicillin may significantly increase the possibility of skin rash, especially in hyperuricemic patients; however, it has not been established that allopurinol, rather than the presence of hyperuricemia, is responsible for this effect)

» Aminoglycosides
(mixing penicillins with aminoglycosides *in vitro* has resulted in substantial mutual inactivation; if these groups of antibacterials are to be administered concurrently, they should be administered at separate sites at least 1 hour apart)

» Angiotensin-converting enzyme (ACE) inhibitors or
» Diuretics, potassium-sparing or
» Potassium-containing medications, other or
» Potassium supplements
(concurrent administration of these medications with parenteral penicillin G potassium may promote serum potassium accumulation with possible resultant hyperkalemia, especially in patients with renal insufficiency; concurrent administration with ACE inhibitors may result in hyperkalemia since reduction of aldosterone production induced by ACE inhibitors may lead to elevation of serum potassium)

» Anticoagulants, coumarin- or indandione-derivative or
» Heparin or
» Thrombolytic agents
(concurrent use of these medications with high-dose parenteral carbenicillin, piperacillin, or ticarcillin may increase the risk of hemorrhage because these penicillins inhibit platelet aggregation; patients should be monitored carefully for signs of bleeding; concurrent use of these penicillins with thrombolytic agents may increase the risk of severe hemorrhage and is not recommended)

» Anti-inflammatory drugs, nonsteroidal (NSAIDs), especially aspirin or
Diflunisal, very high doses or
Other salicylates or
» Platelet aggregation inhibitors, other (see *Appendix II*) or
» Sulfinpyrazone
(concurrent use of these medications with high-dose parenteral carbenicillin, piperacillin, or ticarcillin may increase the risk of hemorrhage because of additive inhibition of platelet function; in addition, hypoprothrombinemia induced by large doses of salicylates and the gastrointestinal ulcerative or hemorrhagic potential of NSAIDs, salicylates, or sulfinpyrazone may also increase the risk of hemorrhage when these medications are used concurrently with these penicillins)

Chloramphenicol or
Erythromycins or
Sulfonamides or
Tetracyclines
(since bacteriostatic drugs may interfere with the bactericidal effect of penicillins in the treatment of meningitis or in other situations in which a rapid bactericidal effect is necessary, it is best to avoid concurrent therapy; however, chloramphenicol and ampicillin are sometimes administered concurrently to pediatric patients)

» Cholestyramine or
» Colestipol
(may impair absorption of oral penicillin G when used concurrently; patients should be advised to take oral penicillin G and these medications several hours apart)

» Contraceptives, estrogen-containing, oral
(there have been case reports of reduced oral contraceptive effectiveness in women taking ampicillin, amoxicillin, and penicillin V, resulting in unplanned pregnancy. This is thought to be due to a reduction in enterohepatic circulation of estrogens. Although the association is weak, patients should be advised of this information and given the option to use an alternate or additional method of contraception while taking any of these penicillins)

Disulfiram
(metabolism of the ester moiety of bacampicillin yields acetaldehyde and ethanol, which are later converted to acetaldehyde; furthermore, since disulfiram blocks the hepatic conversion of acetaldehyde to nontoxic compounds, concurrent use with bacampicillin may result in nausea, vomiting, confusion, and cardiovascular abnormalities)

Hepatotoxic medications, other (see *Appendix II*)
(concurrent use of other hepatotoxic medications with cloxacillin, dicloxacillin, flucloxacillin, mezlocillin, nafcillin, oxacillin, or piperacillin may increase the potential for hepatotoxicity)

» Methotrexate
(concurrent use with penicillins has resulted in decreased clearance of methotrexate and in methotrexate toxicity; this is thought to be due to competition for renal tubular secretion; patients should be closely monitored; leucovorin doses may need to be increased and administered for longer periods of time)

» Probenecid
(probenecid decreases renal tubular secretion of penicillins when used concurrently; this effect results in increased and prolonged serum concentrations, prolonged elimination half-life, and increased risk of toxicity. Penicillins and probenecid are often used concurrently to treat sexually transmitted diseases [STDs] or other infections in which high and/or prolonged antibiotic serum and tissue concentrations are required)

Laboratory value alterations

The following have been selected on the basis of their potential clinical significance (possible effect in parentheses where appropriate)—not necessarily inclusive (» = major clinical significance).

With diagnostic test results

» Glucose, urine
(high urinary concentrations of a penicillin may produce false-positive or falsely elevated test results with copper sulfate tests [Benedict's, *Clinitest*, or Fehling's]; glucose enzymatic tests [*Clinistix* or *Testape*] are not affected)

Direct antiglobulin (Coombs') tests
(false-positive result may occur during therapy with any penicillin)

Protein, urine
(high urinary concentrations of mezlocillin or ticarcillin may produce false-positive protein reactions [pseudoproteinuria] with the sulfosalicylic acid and boiling test, the acetic acid test, the biuret reaction, and the nitric acid test; bromophenol blue reagent test strips [*Multi-stix*] are reportedly unaffected)

With physiology/laboratory test values

Alanine aminotransferase (ALT [SGPT]) and
Alkaline phosphatase and
Aspartate aminotransferase (AST [SGOT]) and
Lactate dehydrogenase (LDH), serum
(values may be increased)

Bilirubin, serum
(an increase has been associated with mezlocillin, piperacillin, and ticarcillin)

Blood urea nitrogen (BUN) and
Creatinine, serum
(an increase has been associated with flucloxacillin, mezlocillin, and piperacillin)

Estradiol or
Estriol, total conjugated or
Estriol-glucuronide or
Estrone, conjugated
(concentrations may be transiently decreased in pregnant women following administration of ampicillin and bacampicillin)

» Partial thromboplastin time (PTT) and
» Prothrombin time (PT)
(an increase has been associated with intravenous carbenicillin, piperacillin, and ticarcillin)

Potassium, serum
(hyperkalemia may occur following administration of large doses of parenteral penicillin G potassium because of high potassium content; hypokalemia may occur following administration of parenteral carbenicillin, mezlocillin, piperacillin, or ticarcillin, which may act as a nonreabsorbable anion in the distal renal tubules; this may cause an increase in pH and result in increased urinary potassium loss; the risk of hypokalemia increases with use of larger doses)

Sodium, serum
(hypernatremia may occur following administration of large doses of parenteral carbenicillin, mezlocillin, penicillin G sodium, or ticarcillin because of the high sodium content of these medications)

Uric acid, serum
(flucloxacillin may transiently decrease the serum uric acid concentration in some patients)

White blood cell count
(leukopenia or neutropenia is associated with the use of all penicillins; the effect is more likely to occur with prolonged therapy and severe hepatic function impairment)

Medical considerations/Contraindications

The medical considerations/contraindications included have been selected on the basis of their potential clinical significance (reasons given in parentheses where appropriate)—not necessarily inclusive (» = major clinical significance).

Except under special circumstances, this medication should not be used when the following medical problem exists:

» Allergy to penicillins

Risk-benefit should be considered when the following medical problems exist:

Allergy, general, history of sensitivity to multiple allergens

» Bleeding disorders, history of
(some penicillins, especially carbenicillin, piperacillin, and ticarcillin, may cause platelet dysfunction and hemorrhage)

Carnitine deficiency
(pivampicillin and pivmecillinam may reduce serum carnitine concentrations by increasing the urinary excretion of carnitine; use of these penicillins is not recommended in patients with carnitine deficiency or in infants up to 3 months of age)

» Congestive heart failure (CHF) or
Hypertension
(the sodium content of high doses of parenteral carbenicillin and ticarcillin should be considered in patients who require sodium restriction)

» Cystic fibrosis
(patients with cystic fibrosis may be at increased risk of fever and skin rash when given piperacillin)

» Gastrointestinal disease, history of, especially antibiotic-associated colitis
(penicillins may cause pseudomembranous colitis)

» Mononucleosis, infectious
(a morbilliform skin rash may occur in a high percentage [43 to 100%] of patients taking ampicillin, bacampicillin, or pivampicillin)

» Phenylketonuria
(the 200-mg and the 400-mg chewable tablets of amoxicillin and clavulanate contain aspartame, which is metabolized to phenylalanine, and may be hazardous to patients with phenylketonuria)

» Renal function impairment
(because most penicillins are excreted through the kidneys, a reduction in dosage, or increase in dosing interval, is recommended in patients with renal function impairment; also, the sodium content of high doses of parenteral carbenicillin and ticarcillin, and the potassium content of high doses of penicillin G potassium, should be considered in patients with severe renal function impairment)

Patient monitoring

The following may be especially important in patient monitoring (other tests may be warranted in some patients, depending on condition; » = major clinical significance):

For carbenicillin (parenteral), piperacillin, ticarcillin

» Partial thromboplastin time (PTT) and
» Prothrombin time (PT)
(may be required prior to and during prolonged therapy in patients with renal function impairment who are receiving high doses since hemorrhagic manifestations may occur, although this effect is rare)

» Potassium, serum or
» Sodium, serum
(determinations may be required periodically in patients with low potassium reserves and in patients receiving cytotoxic medications or diuretics who are also receiving high doses since hypokalemia may occur; also, because of the high sodium content of these medications, hypernatremia may occur)

For methicillin

» Renal function determinations
(may be required during prolonged therapy since methicillin may cause interstitial nephritis in up to 33% of patients treated with methicillin for more than 10 days)

For mezlocillin

Potassium, serum
(may be required periodically during prolonged therapy in patients receiving high doses since hypokalemia may occur)

For penicillin G (parenteral)

Potassium, serum or
» Sodium, serum
(may be required periodically during therapy in patients receiving high doses of penicillin G potassium or penicillin G sodium since hyperkalemia or hypernatremia may occur; very high doses of penicillin G potassium may cause severe or fatal hyperkalemia; very high doses of penicillin G sodium may cause congestive heart failure)

For all penicillins (if Clostridium difficile colitis occurs)

» Stool cytotoxin assays
(enzyme immunoassay of stool samples for the presence of *C. difficile* toxins may be required prior to treatment of patients with antibiotic-associated colitis to document the presence of *C. difficile* toxins; however, *C. difficile* and its toxins may persist following treatment with oral vancomycin, metronidazole, or cholestyramine,

despite clinical improvement; follow-up cultures and toxin assays are not recommended if clinical improvement is complete)

Side/Adverse Effects

Note: In clinical trials using combination therapy with amoxicillin plus clarithromycin and lansoprazole, or amoxicillin plus lansoprazole, no adverse reactions specific to these drug combinations were observed. Adverse reactions that have occurred have been limited to those previously reported with amoxicillin, clarithromycin, or lansoprazole. The side effects most commonly reported with the amoxicillin and lansoprazole combination were diarrhea and headache; the side effects most commonly reported with amoxicillin, clarithromycin, and lansoprazole combination were diarrhea, headache, and taste perversion. See *Clarithromycin (Systemic)* and *Lansoprazole (Systemic)* monographs for additional information pertaining to these medications.

The following side/adverse effects have been selected on the basis of their potential clinical significance (possible signs and symptoms in parentheses where appropriate)—not necessarily inclusive:

Those indicating need for medical attention

Incidence less frequent

Allergic reactions, specifically anaphylaxis (fast or irregular breathing; puffiness or swelling around face; shortness of breath; sudden, severe decrease in blood pressure); ***exfoliative dermatitis*** (red, scaly skin); ***serum sickness-like reactions*** (skin rash; joint pain; fever); ***skin rash, hives, or itching***

Incidence rare

Clostridium difficile colitis (severe abdominal or stomach cramps and pain; abdominal tenderness; watery and severe diarrhea, which may also be bloody; fever); ***hepatotoxicity*** (fever; nausea and vomiting; yellow eyes or skin); ***interstitial nephritis*** (fever; possibly decreased urine output; skin rash); ***leukopenia or neutropenia*** (sore throat and fever); ***mental disturbances*** (anxiety; confusion; agitation or combativeness; depression; seizures; hallucinations; expressed fear of impending death); ***pain at site of injection; platelet dysfunction or thrombocytopenia*** (unusual bleeding or bruising); ***seizures***

Note: *Hepatotoxicity* has been associated with several penicillins, especially cloxacillin, dicloxacillin, flucloxacillin, and oxacillin; however, flucloxacillin appears to have a very high association with cholestatic jaundice, especially in older patients and those receiving flucloxacillin for more than 14 days. Also, one small study found HIV-infected patients to be more susceptible to oxacillin-hepatotoxicity (81%) than HIV-negative patients (4.5%).

Interstitial nephritis is seen primarily with methicillin, and to a lesser degree with nafcillin and oxacillin, but may occur with any penicillin.

Mental disturbances are toxic reactions to the procaine content of penicillin G procaine; this reaction may be seen in patients who receive a large single dose of the medication, as in the treatment of gonorrhea.

Platelet dysfunction is primarily associated with carbenicillin, piperacillin, and ticarcillin; it may be more pronounced in patients with renal insufficiency due to the prolongation of the penicillin's half-life and uremic platelet dysfunction.

Clostridium difficile colitis may occur up to several weeks after discontinuation of these medications.

Seizures are more likely to occur in patients receiving high doses of a penicillin and/or patients with severe renal function impairment.

Those indicating need for medical attention only if they continue or are bothersome

Incidence more frequent

Gastrointestinal reactions (mild diarrhea; nausea or vomiting); ***headache; oral candidiasis*** (sore mouth or tongue; white patches in mouth and/or on tongue); ***vaginal candidiasis*** (vaginal itching and discharge)

Overdose

For more information on the management of overdose or unintentional ingestion, **contact a Poison Control Center** (see *Poison Control Center Listing*).

Treatment of overdose

Specific treatment—Hemodialysis may aid in the removal of penicillins from the blood.

Supportive care—Since there is no specific antidote, treatment of penicillin overdose should be symptomatic and supportive. Patients in whom intentional overdose is known or suspected should be referred for psychiatric consultation.

Patient Consultation

As an aid to patient consultation, refer to *Advice for the Patient, Penicillins (Systemic).*

In providing consultation, consider emphasizing the following selected information (» = major clinical significance):

Before using this medication

» Conditions affecting use, especially:

Allergy to penicillins, cephalosporins, or cephamycins

Pregnancy—Penicillins cross the placenta

Breast-feeding—Penicillins are distributed into breast milk

Use in children—Neonates and young infants may have reduced elimination of renally eliminated penicillins due to incompletely developed renal function; aspartame-containing amoxicillin products should be used with caution, if at all, in patients with phenylketonuria

Other medications, especially aminoglycosides; angiotensin-converting enzyme inhibitors; cholestyramine; colestipol; coumarin- or indandione-derivative anticoagulants; estrogen-containing oral contraceptives; heparin; methotrexate; nonsteroidal anti-inflammatory drugs (NSAIDs), especially aspirin; other platelet aggregation inhibitors; other potassium-containing medications; potassium-sparing diuretics; potassium supplements; probenecid; sulfinpyrazone; or thrombolytic agents

Other medical problems, especially a history of bleeding disorders; congestive heart failure; cystic fibrosis; active or history of gastrointestinal disease, especially antibiotic-associated colitis; infectious mononucleosis; phenylketonuria; or renal function impairment

Proper use of this medication

Taking on an empty stomach (for ampicillin, bacampicillin oral suspension, carbenicillin, cloxacillin, dicloxacillin, flucloxacillin, nafcillin, oxacillin, penicillin G)

Taking on a full or empty stomach (for amoxicillin, bacampicillin tablets, penicillin V, pivampicillin, pivmecillinam)

Taking amoxicillin suspension straight or mixed with formulas, milk, fruit juice, water, ginger ale, or other cold drinks; taking immediately after mixing; drinking full dose

Not drinking acidic fruit juices or other acidic beverages within 1 hour of taking oral penicillin G

Proper administration technique for oral liquids and/or pediatric drops

Not using after expiration date

» Compliance with full course of therapy, especially in streptococcal infections

» Importance of not missing doses and taking at evenly spaced times

» Proper dosing

Missed dose: Taking as soon as possible; not taking if almost time for next dose; not doubling doses

» Proper storage

Precautions while using this medication

Checking with physician if no improvement within a few days

» For severe diarrhea, checking with physician before taking any antidiarrheals; for mild diarrhea, kaolin- or attapulgite-containing antidiarrheals may be used, but antiperistaltic antidiarrheals should be avoided; checking with physician or pharmacist if mild diarrhea continues or worsens

» Possibly using an alternate or additional method of contraception if taking estrogen-containing oral contraceptives concurrently, especially with ampicillin, amoxicillin, or penicillin V

» Diabetic patients: False-positive reactions with copper sulfate urine glucose tests may occur

Possible interference with diagnostic tests

Side/adverse effects

Signs of potential side effects, especially allergic reactions, *Clostridium difficile* colitis, hepatotoxicity, interstitial nephritis, leukopenia or neutropenia, mental disturbances, pain at site of injection, platelet dysfunction or thrombocytopenia, and seizures

General Dosing Information

Therapy should be continued for at least 10 days in Group A beta-hemolytic streptococcal infections to help prevent the occurrence of acute rheumatic fever.

For oral dosage forms only

Penicillins, except amoxicillin, bacampicillin hydrochloride tablets, penicillin V, pivampicillin, and pivmecillinam, should preferably be taken with a full glass (240 mL) of water on an empty stomach (either 1 hour before or 2 hours after meals) to obtain optimum serum and/or urine concentrations. Amoxicillin, bacampicillin hydrochloride tablets, penicillin V, pivampicillin, and pivmecillinam may be taken on a full or empty stomach.

For treatment of adverse effects

Serious anaphylactoid reactions require immediate emergency treatment, which consists of the following:

- Parenteral epinephrine.
- Oxygen.
- Intravenous corticosteroids.
- Airway management (including intubation).

For *Clostridium difficile* colitis—

- Some patients may develop *Clostridium difficile* colitis during or following administration of penicillins.
- *C. difficile* colitis may result in severe watery diarrhea, which may occur during therapy or up to several weeks after therapy is discontinued. If diarrhea occurs, administration of antiperistaltic antidiarrheals (e.g., opioids, diphenoxylate and atropine combination, loperamide, paregoric) is not recommended since they may delay the removal of toxins from the colon, thereby prolonging and/or worsening the condition.
- Mild cases may respond to discontinuation of the medication alone. Moderate to severe cases may require fluid, electrolyte, and protein replacement.
- In cases not responding to the above measures or in more severe cases, oral doses of vancomycin, metronidazole, or cholestyramine may be used. Oral vancomycin is effective in doses of 125 mg every 6 hours for 5 to 10 days. The dose of metronidazole is 250 to 500 mg every 8 hours and the dose of cholestyramine is 4 grams four times a day. Recurrences, which occur in approximately 25% of patients treated with vancomycin or metronidazole, may be treated with a second course of these medications.
- Cholestyramine resin has been shown to bind *C. difficile* toxin *in vitro*. If cholestyramine resin is administered in conjunction with oral vancomycin, the medications should be administered several hours apart since the resin has been shown to bind oral vancomycin also.

AMOXICILLIN

Summary of Differences

Category:
  Aminopenicillin.

Pharmacology/pharmacokinetics:
  High oral absorption (75 to 90%).

Precautions:
  Pediatrics—Patients with phenylketonuria should be aware that the 200-mg and the 400-mg chewable tablets contain 1.8 mg and 3.6 mg phenylalanine, respectively, as a component of aspartame. Other dosage forms and strengths do not contain aspartame.
  Drug interactions and/or related problems—May also interact with oral contraceptives.
  Medical considerations/Contraindications—Caution also needed in infectious mononucleosis. The amoxicillin products containing aspartame (200-mg and 400-mg chewable tablets) are hazardous to patients with phenylketonuria.

Additional Dosing Information

Patients with impaired renal function do not generally require a reduction in dose unless the impairment is severe. Patients whose renal function impairment is severe (glomerular filtration rate of < 30 mL per minute) should not receive the 875-mg tablet.

The 200-mg and the 400-mg chewable tablets contain phenylalanine.

For oral dosage forms only

Amoxicillin may be taken on a full or empty stomach.

Amoxicillin may be taken with formulas, milk, fruit juice, water, ginger ale, or other cold drinks.

Oral Dosage Forms

Note: Bracketed uses in the *Dosage Forms* section refer to categories of use and/or indications that are not included in U.S. product labeling.

AMOXICILLIN CAPSULES USP

Usual adult dose

Antibacterial—

Ear, nose, and throat infections: Mild or moderate—Oral, 500 mg every twelve hours or 250 mg every eight hours. Severe—Oral, 875 mg every twelve hours or 500 mg every eight hours.

Lower respiratory tract infections: Mild, moderate, or severe—Oral, 875 mg every twelve hours or 500 mg every eight hours.

Skin or skin structure infections: Mild or moderate—Oral, 500 mg every twelve hours or 250 mg every eight hours. Severe—Oral, 875 mg every twelve hours or 500 mg every eight hours.

Genitourinary tract infections: Mild or moderate—Oral, 500 mg every twelve hours or 250 mg every eight hours. Severe—Oral, 875 mg every twelve hours or 500 mg every eight hours.

Gonorrhea, acute uncomplicated (anogenital and urethral infections): Oral, 3 grams as a single dose.

Endocarditis, bacterial (prophylaxis): Oral, 3 grams one hour before the procedure, then 1.5 grams six hours after the initial dose.

Duodenal ulcer, *Helicobacter pylori*–associated[1]: Triple antibiotic therapy: Oral, 1000 mg amoxicillin with 500 mg clarithromycin and 30 mg lansoprazole two times a day at twelve-hour intervals for fourteen days. Dual antibiotic therapy: Oral, 1000 mg amoxicillin with 30 mg lansoprazole three times a day at eight-hour intervals for fourteen days.

[Chlamydia, treatment in pregnant women][1]: Oral, 500 mg every eight hours for seven to ten days.

[Gastritis, *Helicobacter pylori*][1] or
[Ulcer, peptic, *Helicobacter pylori*][1]: Oral, 500 mg four times a day; or 750 mg three times a day.

[Lyme disease][1]: Oral, 250 to 500 mg three or four times a day for three to four weeks. Duration of therapy is based on clinical response. Treatment failures have occurred and retreatment may be necessary.

Patients with severe renal function impairment require an adjustment in dosage as follows:

Patients with a glomerular filtration rate of 10-30 mL per minute—Oral, 500 mg or 250 mg every twelve hours, depending on the severity of the infection.

Patients with a glomerular filtration rate of < 10 mL per minute—Oral, 500 mg or 250 mg every twenty-four hours, depending on the severity of the infection.

Patients on hemodialysis—Oral, 500 mg or 250 mg every twenty-four hours, depending on the severity of the infection. An additional dose should be administered both during and at the end of the dialysis session.

Note: Patients with severe renal function impairment (glomerular filtration rate of < 30 mL per minute) should not receive the 875-mg tablet.

Usual adult prescribing limits

4.5 grams a day.

Usual pediatric dose

Antibacterial—

Gonorrhea, endocervical and urethral, uncomplicated: Oral, 50 mg per kg of body weight and 25 mg of probenecid per kg of body weight simultaneously as a single dose in prepubertal children. However, probenecid is not recommended in children under 2 years of age.

Duodenal ulcer, *Helicobactor pylori* –associated[1]: Safety and efficacy have not been established for pediatric or adolescent patients.

[Lyme disease][1]: Oral, 6.7 to 13.3 mg per kg of body weight every eight hours for ten to thirty days. Duration of therapy is based on clinical response. Treatment failures have occurred and retreatment may be necessary.

For all other indications: Infants and children up to 40 kg of body weight, see *Amoxicillin for Oral Suspension USP*.

Children 40 kg of body weight and over—See *Usual adult dose*.

Strength(s) usually available

U.S.—
  250 mg (Rx) [*Amoxil; Trimox; Wymox;* GENERIC].
  500 mg (Rx) [*Amoxil; Trimox; Wymox;* GENERIC].

Canada—
  250 mg (Rx) [*Amoxil; Apo-Amoxi; Novamoxin; Nu-Amoxi*].
  500 mg (Rx) [*Amoxil; Apo-Amoxi; Novamoxin; Nu-Amoxi*].

Packaging and storage

Store between 15 and 30 °C (59 and 86 °F). Store in a tight container.

Auxiliary labeling

- Continue medication for full time of treatment.

AMOXICILLIN FOR ORAL SUSPENSION USP

Usual adult dose

See *Amoxicillin Capsules USP*.

Usual adult prescribing limits

See *Amoxicillin Capsules USP*.

Usual pediatric dose

Antibacterial—

Neonates and infants up to 3 months of age: Oral, not more than 30 mg per kg of body weight per day in divided doses every twelve hours.

Infants 3 months of age and older and children weighing less than 40 kg:

Ear, nose, and throat infections—Mild or moderate: Oral, 20 mg per kg of body weight per day in divided doses every eight hours or 25 mg per kg of body weight per day in divided doses every twelve hours. Severe: Oral, 40 mg per kg of body weight per day in divided doses every eight hours or 45 mg per kg of body weight per day in divided doses every twelve hours.

Lower respiratory tract infections—Mild, moderate, or severe: Oral, 40 mg per kg of body weight per day in divided doses every eight hours or 45 mg per kg of body weight per day in divided doses every twelve hours.

Skin or skin structure infections—Mild or moderate: Oral, 20 mg per kg of body weight per day in divided doses every eight hours or 25 mg per kg of body weight per day in divided doses every twelve hours. Severe: Oral, 40 mg per kg of body weight per day in divided doses every eight hours or 45 mg per kg of body weight per day in divided doses every twelve hours.

Genitourinary tract infections—Mild or moderate: Oral, 20 mg per kg of body weight per day in divided doses every eight hours or 25 mg per kg of body weight per day in divided doses every twelve hours. Severe: Oral, 40 mg per kg of body weight per day in divided doses every eight hours or 45 mg per kg of body weight per day in divided doses every twelve hours.

Gonorrhea, acute uncomplicated (anogenital or urethral) infections—Oral, 50 mg per kg of body weight and 25 mg of probenecid per kg of body weight simultaneously as a single dose in prepubertal children. However, probenecid is not recommended in children under 2 years of age.

Duodenal ulcer, *Helicobactor pylori*–associated[1]—Safety and efficacy have not been established for pediatric or adolescent patients.

Children 40 kg of body weight and over—See *Usual adult dose*.

Strength(s) usually available

U.S.—

50 mg per mL (when reconstituted according to manufacturer's instructions) (Rx) [*Amoxil; Trimox; Polymox*].

125 mg per 5 mL (when reconstituted according to manufacturer's instructions) (Rx) [*Amoxil; Polymox; Trimox; Wymox;* GENERIC].

200 mg per 5 mL (when reconstituted according to manufacturer's instructions) (Rx) [*Amoxil*].

250 mg per 5 mL (when reconstituted according to manufacturer's instructions) (Rx) [*Amoxil; Polymox; Trimox; Wymox;* GENERIC].

400 mg per 5 mL (when reconstituted according to manufacturer's instructions) (Rx) [*Amoxil*].

Canada—

50 mg per mL (when reconstituted according to manufacturer's instructions) (Rx) [*Amoxil*].

125 mg per 5 mL (when reconstituted according to manufacturer's instructions) (Rx) [*Amoxil; Apo-Amoxi; Novamoxin; Nu-Amoxi*].

250 mg per 5 mL (when reconstituted according to manufacturer's instructions) (Rx) [*Amoxil; Apo-Amoxi; Novamoxin; Nu-Amoxi*].

Packaging and storage

Prior to reconstitution, store between 15 and 30 °C (59 and 86 °F). Store in a tight container.

Stability

After reconstitution, suspensions retain their potency for up to 14 days at room temperature or for up to 14 days if refrigerated, depending on the manufacturer.

Note: Some manufacturers prefer refrigerated storage.

Auxiliary labeling

- Refrigerate.
- Shake well.
- Continue medication for full time of treatment.
- Beyond-use date.
- Take by mouth only (pediatric drops).

Note

Explain administration technique for pediatric drops (50 mg per mL).

When dispensing, include a calibrated liquid-measuring device.

AMOXICILLIN TABLETS

Usual adult dose

See *Amoxicillin Capsules USP*.

Usual adult prescribing limits

See *Amoxicillin Capsules USP*.

Usual pediatric dose

See *Amoxicillin Capsules USP*.

Strength(s) usually available

U.S.—

500 mg (Rx) [*Amoxil*].

875 mg (Rx) [*Amoxil*].

Canada—

Not commercially available.

Packaging and storage

Store at or below 25 °C (77 °F).

Auxiliary labeling

- Continue medication for full time of treatment.

AMOXICILLIN TABLETS (CHEWABLE) USP

Usual adult dose

See *Amoxicillin Capsules USP*.

Usual adult prescribing limits

See *Amoxicillin Capsules USP*.

Usual pediatric dose

See *Amoxicillin Capsules USP*.

Strength(s) usually available

U.S.—

125 mg (Rx) [*Amoxil*].

200 mg (Rx) [*Amoxil* (aspartame [containing 1.8 mg phenylalanine])].

250 mg (Rx) [*Amoxil;* GENERIC].

400 mg (Rx) [*Amoxil* (aspartame [containing 3.6 mg phenylalanine])].

Canada—

125 mg (Rx) [*Amoxil*].

250 mg (Rx) [*Amoxil*].

Packaging and storage

Store between 15 and 30 °C (59 and 86 °F). Store in a tight container.

Auxiliary labeling

- Should be chewed or crushed.
- Continue medication for full time of treatment.

[1]Not included in Canadian product labeling.

AMPICILLIN

Summary of Differences

Category:

Aminopenicillin.

Precautions:

Drug interactions and/or related problems—Also interacts with allopurinol and oral contraceptives.

Medical considerations/contraindications—Caution also needed in infectious mononucleosis.

Additional Dosing Information

Patients with impaired renal function do not generally require a reduction in dose unless the impairment is severe.

Oral Dosage Forms

Note: Bracketed uses in the *Dosage Forms* section refer to categories of use and/or indications that are not included in U.S. product labeling.

AMPICILLIN CAPSULES USP

Usual adult and adolescent dose

Antibacterial—

Oral, 250 to 500 mg every six hours.

[Typhoid fever][1]: Oral, 25 mg per kg of body weight every six hours.

Usual adult prescribing limits

4 grams a day.

Usual pediatric dose

Antibacterial—

Infants and children up to 20 kg of body weight: A product of suitable strength is not available for infants and children up to 20 kg of body weight. See *Ampicillin for Oral Suspension USP*.

Children 20 kg of body weight and over: See *Usual adult and adolescent dose*.

Strength(s) usually available

U.S.—

250 mg (Rx) [*Omnipen; Principen; Totacillin;* GENERIC].

500 mg (Rx) [*Omnipen; Principen; Totacillin;* GENERIC].

Canada—

250 mg (Rx) [*Apo-Ampi; Novo-Ampicillin; Nu-Ampi; Penbritin*].

500 mg (Rx) [*Apo-Ampi; Novo-Ampicillin; Nu-Ampi; Penbritin*].

Packaging and storage

Store below 40 °C (104 °F), preferably between 15 and 30 °C (59 and 86 °F), unless otherwise specified by manufacturer. Store in a tight container.

Auxiliary labeling

- Continue medication for full time of treatment.
- Take on empty stomach.

AMPICILLIN FOR ORAL SUSPENSION USP

Usual adult and adolescent dose

See *Ampicillin Capsules USP*.

Usual adult prescribing limits

See *Ampicillin Capsules USP*.

Usual pediatric dose

Antibacterial—

Infants and children up to 20 kg of body weight: Oral, 12.5 to 25 mg per kg of body weight every six hours; or 16.7 to 33.3 mg per kg of body weight every eight hours

Children 20 kg of body weight and over: See *Usual adult and adolescent dose*.

Strength(s) usually available

U.S.—

100 mg per mL (Rx) [*Polycillin*].

125 mg per 5 mL (Rx) [*Omnipen; Polycillin; Principen; Totacillin;* GENERIC].

250 mg per 5 mL (Rx) [*Omnipen; Polycillin; Principen; Totacillin;* GENERIC].

500 mg per 5 mL (Rx) [*Polycillin*].

Canada—

125 mg per 5 mL (Rx) [*Apo-Ampi; Novo-Ampicillin; Nu-Ampi*].

250 mg per 5 mL (Rx) [*Apo-Ampi; Novo-Ampicillin; Nu-Ampi; Penbritin*].

Packaging and storage

Prior to reconstitution, store below 40 °C (104 °F), preferably between 15 and 30 °C (59 and 86 °F), unless otherwise specified by manufacturer. Store in a tight container.

Stability

After reconstitution, suspensions retain their potency for 7 days at room temperature or for 14 days if refrigerated, depending on manufacturer.

Auxiliary labeling

- Refrigerate.
- Shake well.
- Continue medication for full time of treatment.
- Beyond-use date.
- Take by mouth only (pediatric drops).
- Take on empty stomach.

Note

Explain administration technique for pediatric drops (100 mg per mL).

When dispensing, include a calibrated liquid-measuring device.

Parenteral Dosage Forms

Note: Bracketed uses in the *Dosage Forms* section refer to categories of use and/or indications that are not included in U.S. product labeling.

Note: The dosing and strengths of the dosage forms available are expressed in terms of ampicillin base (not the sodium salt).

AMPICILLIN SODIUM STERILE USP

Usual adult and adolescent dose

Antibacterial—

Intramuscular or intravenous, 250 to 500 mg (base) every six hours.

Endocarditis, bacterial

Meningitis, bacterial or

Septicemia, bacterial: Intramuscular or intravenous, 1 to 2 grams (base) every three to four hours.

Listeriosis: Intramuscular or intravenous, 50 mg per kg of body weight every six hours.

[Leptospirosis][1]: Intramuscular or intravenous, 500 mg to 1 gram every six hours.

[Typhoid fever][1]: Intramuscular or intravenous, 25 mg per kg of body weight every six hours.

Usual adult prescribing limits

14 grams a day.

Usual pediatric dose

Antibacterial—

Meningitis, bacterial—

Neonates up to 2 kg of body weight—Intramuscular or intravenous, 25 to 50 mg per kg of body weight every twelve hours during the first week of life, then 50 mg per kg of body weight every eight hours thereafter.

Neonates 2 kg of body weight and over—Intramuscular or intravenous, 50 mg per kg of body weight every eight hours during the first week of life, then 50 mg per kg of body weight every six hours thereafter.

For all other indications—

Infants up to 20 kg of body weight—Intramuscular or intravenous, 12.5 mg (base) per kg of body weight every six hours.

Infants and children 20 kg of body weight and over—See *Usual adult and adolescent dose*.

Strength(s) usually available

U.S.—

125 mg (base) (Rx) [*Omnipen-N; Polycillin-N;* GENERIC].

250 mg (base) (Rx) [*Omnipen-N; Polycillin-N; Totacillin-N;* GENERIC].

500 mg (base) (Rx) [*Omnipen-N; Polycillin-N; Totacillin-N;* GENERIC].

1 gram (base) (Rx) [*Omnipen-N; Polycillin-N; Totacillin-N;* GENERIC].

2 grams (base) (Rx) [*Omnipen-N; Polycillin-N; Totacillin-N;* GENERIC].

10 grams (base) (Rx) [*Omnipen-N; Polycillin-N;* GENERIC].

Canada—

125 mg (base) (Rx) [*Ampicin; Penbritin*].

250 mg (base) (Rx) [*Ampicin; Penbritin*].

500 mg (base) (Rx) [*Ampicin; Penbritin*].

1 gram (base) (Rx) [*Ampicin; Penbritin*].

2 grams (base) (Rx) [*Ampicin; Penbritin*].

Packaging and storage

Prior to reconstitution, store below 40 °C (104 °F), preferably between 15 and 30 °C (59 and 86 °F), unless otherwise specified by manufacturer. Protect the reconstituted solution from freezing.

Preparation of dosage form

To prepare initial dilution for intramuscular use, depending on the manufacturer, add 0.9 to 1.2 mL of sterile water for injection or bacteriostatic water for injection to each 125-mg vial, 0.9 to 1.9 mL of diluent to each 250-mg vial, 1.2 to 1.8 mL of diluent to each 500-mg vial, 2.4 to 7.4 mL of diluent to each 1-gram vial, and 6.8 mL of diluent to each 2-gram vial.

To prepare initial dilution for direct intermittent intravenous use, add 5 mL of sterile water for injection or bacteriostatic water for injection to each 125-, 250-, or 500-mg vial or at least 7.4 to 10 mL of diluent to each 1- or 2-gram vial. The resulting solution should be administered slowly over a 3- to 5-minute period for each 125- to 500-mg dose or over a 10- to 15-minute period for each 1- to 2-gram dose. More rapid administration may result in convulsive seizures.

Intravenous infusions of sterile ampicillin sodium should be administered in a suitable diluent in a concentration not exceeding 30 mg per mL (see manufacturer's package insert).

For reconstitution of pharmacy bulk vials or piggyback infusion bottles, see manufacturer's labeling for instructions.

Stability

After reconstitution for intramuscular or direct intravenous use, solutions retain their potency for 1 hour.

After reconstitution for intravenous infusion, solutions in concentrations up to 30 mg per mL retain at least 90% of their potency for 2 to 8 hours at room temperature or for up to 72 hours if refrigerated in suitable diluents (see manufacturer's package insert).

Concentrated solutions (100 mg per mL) prepared from pharmacy bulk vials retain their potency for 2 hours at room temperature or for 4 hours if refrigerated.

Diluted solutions (20 mg per mL or less) in 5% dextrose injection retain their potency for 2 hours at room temperature or for 3 hours if refrigerated.

Incompatibilities

Extemporaneous admixtures of beta-lactam antibacterials (penicillins and cephalosporins) and aminoglycosides may result in substantial mutual inactivation. If these groups of antibacterials are administered concurrently, they should be administered in separate sites at least 1 hour apart. Do not mix them in the same intravenous bag, bottle, or tubing.

When aminoglycosides and penicillins are administered separately by different routes, a reduction in aminoglycoside serum concentration may occur. Usually this is clinically significant only in patients with severely impaired renal function when the excretion of both medications is delayed.

Additional information

The sodium content is approximately 3.4 mEq (3.4 mmol) per gram of ampicillin, depending on the manufacturer. This must be considered in patients on a restricted sodium intake when calculating total daily sodium intake.

---

[1]Not included in Canadian product labeling.

BACAMPICILLIN

Summary of Differences

Category:

Aminopenicillin.

Pharmacology/pharmacokinetics:
    Hydrolyzed to ampicillin during absorption.
Precautions:
    Drug interactions and/or related problems—Also interacts with allopurinol and disulfiram.
    Medical considerations/contraindications—Caution also needed in infectious mononucleosis.

Additional Dosing Information

Bacampicillin is stable in the presence of gastric acid. Also, food does not delay or reduce absorption of bacampicillin hydrochloride tablets. Therefore, the tablets may be taken on a full or empty stomach. However, bacampicillin hydrochloride oral suspension should preferably be taken with a full glass (240 mL) of water on an empty stomach (either 1 hour before or 2 hours after meals) to obtain optimum serum and/or urine concentrations.

Patients with impaired renal function do not generally require a reduction in dose unless the impairment is severe. The serum half-life increases when the creatinine clearance is below 30 mL per minute (0.50 mL per second).

Oral Dosage Forms

Note: The dosing and strengths of the dosage forms available are expressed in terms of bacampicillin hydrochloride (not the base).

BACAMPICILLIN HYDROCHLORIDE FOR ORAL SUSPENSION USP

Usual adult and adolescent dose
Antibacterial—
    Oral, 400 to 800 mg every twelve hours.

Usual adult prescribing limits
3.2 grams a day.

Usual pediatric dose
Antibacterial—
    Oral, 12.5 to 25 mg per kg of body weight every twelve hours.

Strength(s) usually available
U.S.—
Note: 125 mg of bacampicillin hydrochloride are equivalent to 87.5 mg of ampicillin.
    125 mg per 5 mL (Rx) [*Spectrobid*].
Canada—
    Not commercially available.

Packaging and storage
Prior to reconstitution, store below 40 °C (104 °F), preferably between 15 and 30 °C (59 and 86 °F), unless otherwise specified by manufacturer. Store in a tight container.

Stability
After reconstitution, suspensions retain their potency for 10 days if refrigerated.

Auxiliary labeling
- Refrigerate.
- Shake well.
- Continue medication for full time of treatment.
- Beyond-use date.
- Take on empty stomach.

Note
When dispensing, include a calibrated liquid-measuring device.

BACAMPICILLIN HYDROCHLORIDE TABLETS USP

Usual adult and adolescent dose
See *Bacampicillin Hydrochloride for Oral Suspension USP*.

Usual adult prescribing limits
See *Bacampicillin Hydrochloride for Oral Suspension USP*.

Usual pediatric dose
Infants and children up to 25 kg of body weight—Use of the tablets is not recommended. See *Bacampicillin Hydrochloride for Oral Suspension USP*.
Children 25 kg of body weight and over—See *Usual adult and adolescent dose*.

Strength(s) usually available
U.S.—
    400 mg (Rx) [*Spectrobid*].
Canada—
    400 mg (Rx) [*Penglobe* (scored)].
    800 mg (Rx) [*Penglobe* (scored)].
Note: 400 mg of bacampicillin hydrochloride are equivalent to 280 mg of ampicillin.

Packaging and storage
Store below 40 °C (104 °F), preferably between 15 and 30 °C (59 and 86 °F), unless otherwise specified by manufacturer. Store in a tight container.

Auxiliary labeling
- Continue medication for full time of treatment.

CARBENICILLIN

Summary of Differences

Category:
    Antipseudomonal penicillin.
Pharmacology/pharmacokinetics:
    Renal elimination of oral carbenicillin is approximately 36%, and 75 to 95% for intravenous carbenicillin.
Precautions:
    Drug interactions and/or related problems—Parenteral carbenicillin also interacts with anticoagulants and other medications that affect blood clotting.
    Laboratory value alterations—May increase bleeding time; may also cause hypernatremia.
    Medical considerations/contraindications—Caution in patients with a history of bleeding disorders, congestive heart failure, or hypertension.
    Patient monitoring—Bleeding time and serum potassium and sodium determinations may be required (parenteral only).

Additional Dosing Information

For oral dosage forms only
Patients with severely impaired renal function (creatinine clearance less than 10 mL per minute) will not achieve therapeutic urine concentrations of carbenicillin.

For parenteral dosage forms only
Intramuscular injections should not exceed 2 grams in each site.
Intermittent infusions may be administered over a 30- to 40-minute period.
Patients with impaired renal function may require a reduction in dose and should be observed for hemorrhagic complications.

Oral Dosage Forms

Note: The dosing and strengths of the dosage forms available are expressed in terms of carbenicillin indanyl sodium (not the base).

CARBENICILLIN INDANYL SODIUM TABLETS USP

Usual adult and adolescent dose
Antibacterial—
    Oral, 500 mg to 1 gram every six hours.

Usual pediatric dose
Dosage has not been established.

Strength(s) usually available
U.S.—
    500 mg (Rx) [*Geocillin*].
Canada—
    500 mg (Rx) [*Geopen Oral*].
Note: 500 mg of carbenicillin indanyl sodium are equivalent to 382 mg of carbenicillin and 118 mg of indanyl sodium.

Packaging and storage
Store below 40 °C (104 °F), preferably between 15 and 30 °C (59 and 86 °F), unless otherwise specified by manufacturer. Store in a tight container.

Auxiliary labeling
- Continue medication for full time of treatment.

Parenteral Dosage Forms

Note: The dosing and strengths of the dosage forms available are expressed in terms of carbenicillin disodium (not the base).

CARBENICILLIN DISODIUM STERILE USP

Usual adult and adolescent dose
Antibacterial—
    Intramuscular or intravenous, 50 to 83.3 mg per kg of body weight every four hours.
    Urinary tract infections: Intramuscular or intravenous, 1 to 2 grams every six hours; or up to 50 mg per kg of body weight every six hours.

Usual adult prescribing limits
Up to 40 grams a day.

Usual pediatric dose

Antibacterial—

Neonates up to 2 kg of body weight: Intramuscular or intravenous, 75 mg per kg of body weight every twelve hours during the first week of life; followed by 75 mg per kg of body weight every eight hours thereafter.

Neonates 2 kg of body weight and over: Intramuscular or intravenous, 75 mg per kg of body weight every eight hours during the first week of life; followed by 75 mg per kg of body weight every six hours thereafter.

Older infants and children: Intramuscular or intravenous, 25 to 75 mg per kg of body weight every six hours; or 16.7 to 50 mg per kg of body weight every four hours.

Strength(s) usually available

U.S.—

1 gram (Rx) [*Geopen*].
2 grams (Rx) [*Geopen*].
5 grams (Rx) [*Geopen*].
10 grams (Rx) [*Geopen*].
30 grams (Rx) [*Geopen*].

Canada—

1 gram (Rx) [*Pyopen*].
5 grams (Rx) [*Pyopen*].

Packaging and storage

Prior to reconstitution, store below 40 °C (104 °F), preferably between 15 and 30 °C (59 and 86 °F), unless otherwise specified by manufacturer.

Preparation of dosage form

To prepare initial dilution for intramuscular use, depending on the manufacturer, add 2 to 3.6 mL of sterile water for injection or bacteriostatic water for injection (preserved with 0.9% benzyl alcohol) to each 1-gram vial, 4 to 7.2 mL of diluent to each 2-gram vial, and 7 to 17 mL of diluent to each 5-gram vial. Lidocaine hydrochloride injection 0.5% (without epinephrine) may also be used as a diluent for intramuscular use.

To prepare initial dilution for direct intravenous use, reconstitute as directed above for intramuscular use. Each gram of carbenicillin should be further diluted with the addition of not less than 5 mL of diluent. The resulting solution should be administered as slowly as possible to avoid vein irritation.

For reconstitution of pharmacy bulk vials or piggyback infusion bottles, see manufacturer's labeling for instructions.

Caution—Use of diluents containing benzyl alcohol is not recommended for preparation of medications for use in neonates. A fatal toxic syndrome consisting of metabolic acidosis, CNS depression, respiratory problems, renal failure, hypotension, and possibly seizures and intracranial hemorrhages has been associated with this use.

Stability

After reconstitution for intramuscular or direct intravenous use, solutions retain their potency for 24 hours at room temperature or for 72 hours if refrigerated.

Intravenous infusions in suitable diluents (see manufacturer's package insert), concentrated solutions (200 mg per mL), or diluted solutions (10 to 100 mg per mL) prepared from pharmacy bulk vials retain their potency for 24 hours at room temperature or for 72 hours if refrigerated.

Incompatibilities

Extemporaneous admixtures of beta-lactam antibacterials (penicillins and cephalosporins) and aminoglycosides may result in substantial mutual inactivation. If these groups of antibacterials are administered concurrently, they should be administered in separate sites at least 1 hour apart. Do not mix them in the same intravenous bag, bottle, or tubing.

When aminoglycosides and penicillins are administered separately by different routes, a reduction in aminoglycoside serum concentration may occur. Usually this is clinically significant only in patients with severely impaired renal function when the excretion of both medications is delayed.

Additional information

The sodium content is approximately 4.7 to 5.3 mEq (4.7 to 5.3 mmol), but may be as high as 6.5 mEq (6.5 mmol), per gram of carbenicillin. This must be considered in patients on a restricted sodium intake when calculating total daily sodium intake.

CLOXACILLIN

Summary of Differences

Category: Penicillinase-resistant penicillin.

Pharmacology/pharmacokinetics: Very high plasma protein binding (95%).

Precautions: Drug interactions and/or related problems—May interact with other hepatotoxic medications.

Side/adverse effects: May be an increased risk of hepatotoxicity.

Additional Dosing Information

Patients with impaired renal function do not generally require a reduction in dose unless the impairment is severe.

Cloxacillin should be taken on an empty stomach, preferably 1 hour before meals.

Oral Dosage Forms

Note: The dosing and strengths of the dosage forms available are expressed in terms of cloxacillin base (not the sodium salt).

CLOXACILLIN SODIUM CAPSULES USP

Usual adult and adolescent dose

Antibacterial—

Oral, 250 to 500 mg (base) every six hours.

Usual adult prescribing limits

6 grams (base) a day.

Usual pediatric dose

Antibacterial—

Infants and children up to 20 kg of body weight: Oral, 6.25 to 12.5 mg (base) per kg of body weight every six hours.

Children 20 kg of body weight and over: See *Usual adult and adolescent dose.*

Strength(s) usually available

U.S.—

250 mg (base) (Rx) [*Cloxapen;* GENERIC].
500 mg (base) (Rx) [*Cloxapen;* GENERIC].

Canada—

250 mg (base) (Rx) [*Apo-Cloxi; Novo-Cloxin; Nu-Cloxi; Orbenin*].
500 mg (base) (Rx) [*Apo-Cloxi; Novo-Cloxin; Nu-Cloxi; Orbenin*].

Packaging and storage

Store below 40 °C (104 °F), preferably between 15 and 30 °C (59 and 86 °F), unless otherwise specified by manufacturer. Store in a tight container.

Auxiliary labeling

- Continue medication for full time of treatment.
- Take on empty stomach.

CLOXACILLIN SODIUM FOR ORAL SOLUTION USP

Usual adult and adolescent dose

See *Cloxacillin Sodium Capsules USP.*

Usual adult prescribing limits

See *Cloxacillin Sodium Capsules USP.*

Usual pediatric dose

See *Cloxacillin Sodium Capsules USP.*

Strength(s) usually available

U.S.—

125 mg per 5 mL (base) (Rx) [*Tegopen;* GENERIC].

Canada—

125 mg per 5 mL (base) (Rx) [*Apo-Cloxi; Novo-Cloxin; Nu-Cloxi; Orbenin*].

Packaging and storage

Prior to reconstitution, store below 40 °C (104 °F), preferably between 15 and 30 °C (59 and 86 °F), unless otherwise specified by manufacturer. Store in a tight container.

Stability

After reconstitution, solutions retain their potency for 14 days if refrigerated.

Auxiliary labeling

- Refrigerate.
- Continue medication for full time of treatment.
- Beyond-use date.
- Take on empty stomach.

Note

When dispensing, include a calibrated liquid-measuring device.

Parenteral Dosage Forms

Note: The dosing and dosage forms available are expressed in terms of cloxacillin base (not the sodium salt).

CLOXACILLIN SODIUM INJECTION

Usual adult and adolescent dose

Antibacterial—

Intravenous, 250 to 500 mg (base) every six hours.

Usual adult prescribing limits
6 grams (base) a day.

Usual pediatric dose
Antibacterial—
Infants and children up to 20 kg of body weight: Intravenous, 6.25 to 12.5 mg (base) per kg of body weight every six hours.
Children 20 kg of body weight and over: See *Usual adult and adolescent dose.*

Note: Cystic fibrosis patients: Intravenous, 25 mg (base) per kg of body weight every six hours.

Strength(s) usually available
U.S.—
Not commercially available.
Canada—
250 mg (base) (Rx) [*Orbenin; Tegopen*].
500 mg (base) (Rx) [*Orbenin; Tegopen*].
2 grams (base) (Rx) [*Orbenin; Tegopen*].

Packaging and storage
Prior to reconstitution, store between 15 and 30 °C (59 and 86 °F), unless otherwise specified by manufacturer.

Preparation of dosage form
To prepare for intramuscular injection, add 1.9 mL or 1.7 mL of sterile water for injection to each 250 mg or 500 mg vial, respectively, and shake to dissolve.
To prepare for intravenous injection, add 4.9 mL, 4.8 mL, or 6.8 mL of sterile water for injection to each 250 mg, 500 mg, or 2 gram vial, respectively, and shake to dissolve.
For direct intravenous use, the resulting solution should be administered slowly over a 2- to 4-minute period.
For intermittent intravenous use, the resulting solution should be further diluted with a suitable diluent (see manufacturer's package insert). It may be administered over a 30- to 40-minute period.

Stability
After reconstitution with suitable diluents (see manufacturer's package insert), solutions retain their potency for 24 hours at controlled room temperature (25 °C [77 °F]), or 72 hours if refrigerated.

Incompatibilities
Extemporaneous admixtures of beta-lactam antibacterials (penicillins and cephalosporins) and aminoglycosides may result in substantial mutual inactivation. If these groups of antibacterials are administered concurrently, they should be administered in separate sites at least 1 hour apart. Do not mix them in the same intravenous bag, bottle, or tubing.
When aminoglycosides and penicillins are administered separately by different routes, a reduction in aminoglycoside serum concentration may occur. Usually this is clinically significant only in patients with severely impaired renal function when the excretion of both medications is delayed.

DICLOXACILLIN

Summary of Differences

Category: Penicillinase-resistant penicillin.
Pharmacology/pharmacokinetics: Very high plasma protein binding (95 to 98%).
Precautions: Drug interactions and/or related problems—May react with other hepatotoxic medications.
Side/adverse effects: May be an increased risk of hepatotoxicity.

Additional Dosing Information

Patients with impaired renal function do not generally require a reduction in dose unless the impairment is severe.

Dicloxacillin should be taken on an empty stomach, preferably 1 hour before meals.

Oral Dosage Forms

Note: The dosing and strengths of the dosage forms available are expressed in terms of dicloxacillin base (not the sodium salt).

DICLOXACILLIN SODIUM CAPSULES USP

Usual adult and adolescent dose
Antibacterial—
Oral, 125 to 250 mg (base) every six hours.

Usual adult prescribing limits
6 grams (base) a day.

Usual pediatric dose
Antibacterial—
Infants and children up to 40 kg of body weight: Oral, 3.125 to 6.25 mg (base) per kg of body weight every six hours.
Children 40 kg of body weight and over: See *Usual adult and adolescent dose.*

Note: Cystic fibrosis patients: Oral, 12.5 to 25 mg (base) per kg of body weight every six hours.

Strength(s) usually available
U.S.—
125 mg (base) (Rx) [*Dynapen*].
250 mg (base) (Rx) [*Dycill; Dynapen; Pathocil;* GENERIC].
500 mg (base) (Rx) [*Dycill; Dynapen; Pathocil;* GENERIC].
Canada—
Not commercially available.

Packaging and storage
Store below 40 °C (104 °F), preferably between 15 and 30 °C (59 and 86 °F), unless otherwise specified by manufacturer. Store in a tight container.

Auxiliary labeling
- Continue medication for full time of treatment.
- Take on empty stomach.

DICLOXACILLIN SODIUM FOR ORAL SUSPENSION USP

Usual adult and adolescent dose
See *Dicloxacillin Sodium Capsules USP*.

Usual adult prescribing limits
See *Dicloxacillin Sodium Capsules USP*.

Usual pediatric dose
See *Dicloxacillin Sodium Capsules USP*.

Strength(s) usually available
U.S.—
62.5 mg per 5 mL (base) (Rx) [*Dynapen; Pathocil*].
Canada—
Not commercially available.

Packaging and storage
Prior to reconstitution, store below 40 °C (104 °F), preferably between 15 and 30 °C (59 and 86 °F), unless otherwise specified by manufacturer. Store in a tight container.

Stability
After reconstitution, suspensions retain their potency for 7 days at room temperature or for 14 days if refrigerated.

Auxiliary labeling
- Refrigerate.
- Shake well.
- Continue medication for full time of treatment.
- Beyond-use date.
- Take on empty stomach.

Note
When dispensing, include a calibrated liquid-measuring device.

FLUCLOXACILLIN

Summary of Differences

Category:
Penicillinase-resistant penicillin.
Pharmacology/pharmacokinetics:
Very high plasma protein binding (94%).
Precautions:
Drug interactions and/or related problems—May react with other hepatotoxic medications.
Laboratory value alterations—May transiently decrease the serum uric acid concentration in some patients.
Side/adverse effects:
May be an increased risk of cholestatic jaundice.

Additional Dosing Information

Patients with impaired renal function do not generally require a reduction in dose unless the impairment is severe.

Flucloxacillin should be taken on an empty stomach, preferably 1 hour before meals.

Oral Dosage Forms

Note: The dosing and strengths of the dosage forms available are expressed in terms of flucloxacillin sodium (not the base).

FLUCLOXACILLIN SODIUM CAPSULES

Usual adult and adolescent dose

Antibacterial—
Oral, 250 to 500 mg every six hours.

Usual pediatric dose

Antibacterial—
Children less than 12 years of age and up to 40 kg of body weight: Oral, 125 to 250 mg every six hours; or 6.25 to 12.5 mg per kg of body weight every six hours
Infants up to 6 months of age: Oral, 6.25 mg per kg of body weight every six hours.

Strength(s) usually available

U.S.—
Not commercially available.
Canada—
250 mg (Rx) [*Fluclox*].
500 mg (Rx) [*Fluclox*].

Packaging and storage

Store between 15 and 30 °C (59 and 86 °F). Store in a tight container.

Auxiliary labeling

- Continue medication for full time of treatment.
- Take on empty stomach.

FLUCLOXACILLIN FOR ORAL SUSPENSION USP

Usual adult and adolescent dose

See *Flucloxacillin Sodium Capsules*.

Usual pediatric dose

See *Flucloxacillin Sodium Capsules*.

Strength(s) usually available

U.S.—
Not commercially available.
Canada—
125 mg per 5 mL (Rx) [*Fluclox*].
250 mg per 5 mL (Rx) [*Fluclox*].

Packaging and storage

Prior to reconstitution, store between 15 and 30 °C (59 and 86 °F). Store in a tight container.

Stability

After reconstitution, the suspension retains its potency for 7 days when refrigerated.

Auxiliary labeling

- Refrigerate.
- Shake well.
- Continue medication for full time of treatment.
- Beyond-use date.
- Take on empty stomach.

Note

When dispensing, include a calibrated liquid-measuring device.

METHICILLIN

Summary of Differences

Category: Penicillinase-resistant penicillin.
Precautions: Patient monitoring—Renal function determinations may be required because of interstitial nephritis.
Side/adverse effects—May be increased risk of interstitial nephritis.

Additional Dosing Information

Methicillin sodium for injection should be administered by deep intragluteal injection or by intravenous injection only.

Patients with impaired renal function require a reduction in dose.

Parenteral Dosage Forms

Note: The dosing and strengths of the dosage forms available are expressed in terms of methicillin sodium (not the base).

METHICILLIN SODIUM FOR INJECTION USP

Usual adult and adolescent dose

Antibacterial—
Intramuscular, 1 gram every four to six hours.
Intravenous, 1 gram every six hours.

Usual adult prescribing limits

24 grams a day.

Usual pediatric dose

Antibacterial—
Meningitis, bacterial—
Neonates up to 2 kg of body weight—Intramuscular or intravenous, 25 to 50 mg per kg of body weight every twelve hours during the first week of life, then 50 mg per kg of body weight every eight hours thereafter.
Neonates 2 kg of body weight and over—Intramuscular or intravenous, 50 mg per kg of body weight every eight hours during the first week of life, then 50 mg per kg of body weight every six hours thereafter.
For all other indications—
Infants and children up to 40 kg of body weight—Intramuscular or intravenous, 25 mg per kg of body weight every six hours.
Children 40 kg of body weight and over—See *Usual adult and adolescent dose*.

Note: Cystic fibrosis patients—Intramuscular or intravenous, 50 mg per kg of body weight every six hours.

Strength(s) usually available

U.S.—
1 gram (Rx) [*Staphcillin*].
4 grams (Rx) [*Staphcillin*].
6 grams (Rx) [*Staphcillin*].
10 grams (Rx) [*Staphcillin*].
Canada—
Not commercially available.

Packaging and storage

Prior to reconstitution, store between 15 and 30 °C (59 and 86 °F).

Preparation of dosage form

To prepare initial dilution for intramuscular use, add 1.5 mL of sterile water for injection or 0.9% sodium chloride injection to each 1-gram vial, 5.7 mL of diluent to each 4-gram vial, and 8.6 mL of diluent to each 6-gram vial to provide a concentration of 500 mg per mL.

To prepare initial dilution for direct intravenous use, reconstitute as directed above for intramuscular use. Each mL (500 mg) of the resulting solution should be further diluted in 25 mL of 0.9% sodium chloride injection and administered at the rate of 10 mL per minute.

For reconstitution of pharmacy bulk vials or piggyback infusion bottles, see manufacturer's labeling for instructions.

Stability

After reconstitution for intramuscular use, solutions retain their potency for 24 hours at room temperature or for 4 days if refrigerated.

After reconstitution for intravenous use, solutions in concentrations of 2 to 20 mg per mL retain at least 90% of their potency for 8 hours at room temperature in suitable diluents (see manufacturer's package insert).

Incompatibilities

Extemporaneous admixtures of beta-lactam antibacterials (penicillins and cephalosporins) and aminoglycosides may result in substantial mutual inactivation. If these groups of antibacterials are administered concurrently, they should be administered in separate sites at least 1 hour apart. Do not mix them in the same intravenous bag, bottle, or tubing.

When aminoglycosides and penicillins are administered separately by different routes, a reduction in aminoglycoside serum concentration may occur. Usually this is clinically significant only in patients with severely impaired renal function when the excretion of both medications is delayed.

Extemporaneous admixtures of other drugs with methicillin sodium for injection are not recommended.

Additional information

The total sodium content is approximately 2.24 mEq (2.24 mmol) per gram of methicillin sodium. This must be considered in patients on a restricted sodium intake when calculating total daily sodium intake.

MEZLOCILLIN

Summary of Differences

Category:
Antipseudomonal penicillin.
Precautions:
Drug interactions and/or related problems—May also interact with other hepatotoxic medications.
Laboratory value alterations—May produce false-positive protein reactions with various urine protein tests.
Patient monitoring—Serum potassium determinations may be required.

Additional Dosing Information

Intramuscular injections should not exceed 2 grams in each site.

Adults with impaired renal function may require a reduction in dose as follows:

Creatinine Clearance (mL/min)/(mL/sec)	Dose
> 30/0.50	See *Usual adult and adolescent dose*
10–30/0.17–0.50	1.5 to 3 grams every 6 to 8 hours
< 10/0.17	1.5 to 2 grams every 8 hours
Hemodialysis patients	3 to 4 grams after each dialysis, then every 12 hours
Peritoneal dialysis patients	3 grams every 12 hours

Parenteral Dosage Forms

Note: The dosing and strengths of the dosage forms available are expressed in terms of mezlocillin sodium (not the base).

MEZLOCILLIN SODIUM STERILE USP

Usual adult and adolescent dose

Antibacterial—

Intramuscular or intravenous, 33.3 to 58.3 mg per kg of body weight every four hours; 50 to 87.5 mg per kg of body weight every six hours; or 3 to 4 grams every four to six hours.

Urinary tract infections, complicated: Intravenous, 37.5 to 50 mg per kg of body weight every six hours; or 3 grams every six hours.

Urinary tract infections, uncomplicated: Intramuscular or intravenous, 25 to 31.25 mg per kg of body weight every six hours; or 1.5 to 2 grams every six hours.

Usual adult prescribing limits

24 grams a day.

Usual pediatric dose

Antibacterial—

Neonates up to 2 kg of body weight: Intramuscular or intravenous, 50 to 75 mg per kg of body weight every twelve hours during the first week of life, then 50 mg per kg of body weight every eight hours thereafter.

Neonates 2 kg of body weight and over: Intramuscular or intravenous, 50 mg per kg of body weight every eight hours during the first week of life, then 50 mg per kg of body weight every six hours thereafter.

Infants over 1 month of age and children up to 12 years of age: Intramuscular or intravenous, 50 mg per kg of body weight every four hours.

Strength(s) usually available

U.S.—

1 gram (Rx) [*Mezlin*].
2 grams (Rx) [*Mezlin*].
3 grams (Rx) [*Mezlin*].
4 grams (Rx) [*Mezlin*].
20 grams (Rx) [*Mezlin*].

Canada—

Not commercially available.

Packaging and storage

Prior to reconstitution, store below 30 °C (86 °F). After reconstitution, if precipitation occurs during refrigeration, the solution may be warmed to 37 °C (98.6 °F) for 20 minutes in a water bath, and shaken well.

Preparation of dosage form

To prepare initial dilution for intramuscular use, add 3 to 4 mL of sterile water for injection or 0.5 or 1% lidocaine hydrochloride injection (without epinephrine) to each 1-gram vial and shake vigorously.

The resulting solution should be administered slowly over a 12- to 15-second period to minimize discomfort.

To prepare initial dilution for intravenous use, add at least 10 mL of sterile water for injection, 5% dextrose injection, or 0.9% sodium chloride injection to each 1-gram vial and shake vigorously. For direct intravenous use, the resulting solution should be administered slowly over a 3- to 5-minute period to minimize vein irritation. The concentration should not exceed 10% (100 mg per mL).

For intermittent intravenous use, the resulting solution should be further diluted in 50 to 100 mL of a suitable diluent (see manufacturer's package insert). It may be administered over a 30-minute period by direct infusion or by a Y-type hook-up.

For reconstitution of piggyback infusion bottles, see manufacturer's labeling for instructions. If the Y-type or piggyback method of administration is used, the primary infusion should be temporarily discontinued during infusion of mezlocillin.

Stability

After reconstitution with suitable diluents (see manufacturer's package insert), solutions at concentrations of 10 and 100 mg per mL retain at least 90% of their potency for 24 to 72 hours at controlled room temperature (15 to 30 °C [59 to 86 °F]) or for 1 to 7 days if refrigerated.

After reconstitution with sterile water for injection, 0.9% sodium chloride injection, or 5% dextrose injection, solutions at concentrations of up to 100 mg per mL retain their potency for 4 weeks when frozen at −12 °C (10 °F).

After reconstitution with sterile water for injection, 0.9% sodium chloride injection, or 0.5 or 1% lidocaine hydrochloride injection (without epinephrine), solutions at concentrations of up to 250 mg per mL retain their potency for 24 hours at room temperature.

Solutions range from clear and colorless to pale yellow in color. However, the powder and reconstituted solution may darken slightly during storage; this darkening does not affect their potency.

Incompatibilities

Extemporaneous admixtures of beta-lactam antibacterials (penicillins and cephalosporins) and aminoglycosides may result in substantial mutual inactivation. If these groups of antibacterials are administered concurrently, they should be administered in separate sites at least 1 hour apart. Do not mix them in the same intravenous bag, bottle, or tubing.

When aminoglycosides and penicillins are administered separately by different routes, a reduction in aminoglycoside serum concentration may occur. Usually this is clinically significant only in patients with severely impaired renal function when the excretion of both medications is delayed.

Additional information

The sodium content is approximately 1.9 mEq (43 mg) per gram of mezlocillin. This must be considered in patients on a restricted sodium intake when calculating total daily sodium intake.

NAFCILLIN

Summary of Differences

Category:
Penicillinase-resistant penicillin.

Pharmacology/pharmacokinetics:
Oral absorption—Erratic and poor.
Protein binding—High (90%).
Hepatic biotransformation—High (60–70%).

Precautions:
Drug interactions and/or related problems—
May also interact with other hepatotoxic medications.

Side/adverse effects:
May be an increased risk of interstitial nephritis.

Additional Dosing Information

Nafcillin sodium for injection should be administered by deep intragluteal injection or by intravenous injection only.

Oral Dosage Forms

Note: The dosing and strengths of the dosage forms available are expressed in terms of nafcillin base (not the sodium salt).

NAFCILLIN SODIUM CAPSULES USP

Usual adult and adolescent dose

Antibacterial—

Oral, 250 mg to 1 gram (base) every four to six hours.

Usual adult prescribing limits

6 grams (base) daily.

Usual pediatric dose

Antibacterial—

Pharyngitis, bacterial—
Oral, 250 mg (base) every eight hours.

For all other indications—
Neonates—Oral, 10 mg (base) per kg of body weight every six to eight hours.
Older infants and children—Oral, 6.25 to 12.5 mg (base) per kg of body weight every six hours.

Strength(s) usually available

U.S.—

250 mg (base) (Rx) [*Unipen*].

Canada—

Not commercially available.

Packaging and storage

Store below 40 °C (104 °F), preferably between 15 and 30 °C (59 and 86 °F), unless otherwise specified by manufacturer. Store in a tight container.

Auxiliary labeling

- Continue medication for full time of treatment.
- Take on empty stomach.

NAFCILLIN SODIUM TABLETS USP

Usual adult and adolescent dose

See *Nafcillin Sodium Capsules USP*.

Usual adult prescribing limits

See *Nafcillin Sodium Capsules USP*.

Usual pediatric dose

See *Nafcillin Sodium Capsules USP*.

Strength(s) usually available

U.S.—

500 mg (base) (Rx) [*Unipen*].

Canada—

Not commercially available.

Packaging and storage

Store below 40 °C (104 °F), preferably between 15 and 30 °C (59 and 86 °F), unless otherwise specified by manufacturer. Store in a tight, light-resistant container.

Auxiliary labeling

- Continue medication for full time of treatment.
- Take on empty stomach.

Parenteral Dosage Forms

Note: The dosing and strengths of the dosage forms available are expressed in terms of nafcillin base (not the sodium salt).

NAFCILLIN SODIUM FOR INJECTION USP

Usual adult and adolescent dose

Antibacterial—

Bone and joint infections
Endocarditis, bacterial
Meningitis, bacterial or
Pericarditis, bacterial: Intravenous, 1.5 to 2 grams every four to six hours.

For all other indications: Intramuscular, 500 mg (base) every four to six hours. Intravenous, 500 mg to 1.5 grams (base) every four hours.

Usual adult prescribing limits

Intramuscular—Up to 12 grams (base) a day.
Intravenous—Up to 20 grams (base) a day.

Usual pediatric dose

Antibacterial—

Meningitis, bacterial—

Neonates up to 2 kg of body weight:

Intramuscular or intravenous, 25 to 50 mg per kg of body weight every twelve hours during the first week of life, then 50 mg per kg of body weight every eight hours thereafter.

Neonates 2 kg of body weight and over:

Intramuscular or intravenous, 50 mg per kg of body weight every eight hours during the first week of life, then 50 mg per kg of body weight every six hours thereafter.

For all other indications—

Neonates:

Intramuscular, 10 mg (base) per kg of body weight every twelve hours.

Intravenous, 10 to 20 mg (base) per kg of body weight every four hours; or 20 to 40 mg per kg of body weight every eight hours.

Older infants and children:

Intramuscular, 25 mg (base) per kg of body weight every twelve hours.

Intravenous, 10 to 20 mg (base) per kg of body weight every four hours; or 20 to 40 mg per kg of body weight every eight hours.

Strength(s) usually available

U.S.—

500 mg (base) (Rx) [*Nafcil; Nallpen;* GENERIC].
1 gram (base) (Rx) [*Nafcil; Nallpen; Unipen;* GENERIC].
2 grams (base) (Rx) [*Nafcil; Nallpen; Unipen;* GENERIC].
10 grams (base) (Rx) [*Nafcil; Nallpen; Unipen;* GENERIC].

Canada—

500 mg (base) (Rx) [*Unipen*].

Packaging and storage

Prior to reconstitution, store below 40 °C (104 °F), preferably between 15 and 30 °C (59 and 86 °F), unless otherwise specified by manufacturer.

Preparation of dosage form

To prepare initial dilution for intramuscular use, depending on the manufacturer, add 1.7 to 1.8 mL of sterile water for injection or bacteriostatic water for injection to each 500-mg vial, 3.4 mL of diluent to each 1-gram vial, or 6.6 to 6.8 mL of diluent to each 2-gram vial to provide 250 mg (base) per mL.

To prepare initial dilution for direct intravenous use, reconstitute as directed above for intramuscular use. The resulting solution should be further diluted in 15 to 30 mL of sterile water for injection or 0.9% sodium chloride injection and administered over a 5- to 10-minute period.

For reconstitution of pharmacy bulk vials or piggyback infusion bottles, see manufacturer's labeling for instructions.

Intravenous infusions of nafcillin sodium for injection should be administered in suitable diluents (see manufacturer's package insert) in a concentration of 2 to 40 mg per mL. Infusions should be administered over at least a 30- to 60-minute period to avoid vein irritation.

Stability

After reconstitution for intramuscular use, solutions retain their potency for 3 days at room temperature or for 7 days if refrigerated, depending on the manufacturer.

After reconstitution for intravenous use, solutions in concentrations of 2 to 40 mg per mL retain at least 90% of their potency for 24 hours at room temperature or for 96 hours if refrigerated (depending on the manufacturer) in suitable diluents (see manufacturer's package insert).

Concentrated solutions (100 mg per mL) prepared from pharmacy bulk vials retain their potency for 8 hours at room temperature or for 48 hours if refrigerated.

Concentrated solutions (250 mg per mL) retain their potency for 3 days at room temperature or for 7 days if refrigerated or frozen.

Incompatibilities

Extemporaneous admixtures of beta-lactam antibacterials (penicillins and cephalosporins) and aminoglycosides may result in substantial mutual inactivation. If these groups of antibacterials are administered concurrently, they should be administered in separate sites at least 1 hour apart. Do not mix them in the same intravenous bag, bottle, or tubing.

When aminoglycosides and penicillins are administered separately by different routes, a reduction in aminoglycoside serum concentration may occur. Usually this is clinically significant only in patients with severely impaired renal function when the excretion of both medications is delayed.

Additional information

The total sodium content is approximately 2.9 mEq (2.9 mmol) per gram of nafcillin. This must be considered in patients on a restricted sodium intake when calculating total daily sodium intake.

OXACILLIN

Summary of Differences

Category: Penicillinase-resistant penicillin.
Pharmacology/pharmacokinetics: High plasma protein binding (90%).
Precautions: Drug interactions and/or related problems—May also interact with other hepatotoxic medications.
Side/adverse effects: May be an increased risk of hepatotoxicity and interstitial nephritis.

Additional Dosing Information

Patients with impaired renal function do not generally require a reduction in dose.

Oral Dosage Forms

Note: The dosing and strengths of the dosage forms available are expressed in terms of oxacillin base (not the sodium salt).

OXACILLIN SODIUM CAPSULES USP

Usual adult and adolescent dose

Antibacterial—

Oral, 500 mg to 1 gram (base) every four to six hours.

Usual adult prescribing limits

6 grams (base) a day.

Usual pediatric dose
Antibacterial—
Children up to 40 kg of body weight: Oral, 12.5 to 25 mg (base) per kg of body weight every six hours.
Children 40 kg of body weight and over: See *Usual adult and adolescent dose.*

Strength(s) usually available
U.S.—
250 mg (base) (Rx) [*Bactocill; Prostaphlin;* GENERIC].
500 mg (base) (Rx) [*Bactocill; Prostaphlin;* GENERIC].
Canada—
Not commercially available.

Packaging and storage
Store between 15 and 30 °C (59 and 86 °F). Store in a tight container.

Auxiliary labeling
- Continue medication for full time of treatment.
- Take on empty stomach.

OXACILLIN SODIUM FOR ORAL SOLUTION USP

Usual adult and adolescent dose
See *Oxacillin Sodium Capsules USP.*

Usual adult prescribing limits
See *Oxacillin Sodium Capsules USP.*

Usual pediatric dose
See *Oxacillin Sodium Capsules USP.*

Strength(s) usually available
U.S.—
250 mg per 5 mL (base) (Rx) [*Prostaphlin;* GENERIC].
Canada—
Not commercially available.

Packaging and storage
Prior to reconstitution, store between 15 and 30 °C (59 and 86 °F). Store in a tight container.

Stability
After reconstitution, solutions retain their potency for 7 days at room temperature or for 14 days if refrigerated.

Auxiliary labeling
- Refrigerate.
- Continue medication for full time of treatment.
- Beyond-use date.
- Take on empty stomach.

Note
When dispensing, include a calibrated liquid-measuring device.

Parenteral Dosage Forms

OXACILLIN SODIUM FOR INJECTION USP

Usual adult and adolescent dose
Antibacterial—
Intramuscular or intravenous, 250 mg to 1 gram (base) every four to six hours.
Meningitis, bacterial: Intravenous, 1.5 to 2 grams every four hours.

Usual pediatric dose
Antibacterial—
Meningitis, bacterial—
Neonates up to 2 kg of body weight—Intramuscular or intravenous, 25 to 50 mg per kg of body weight every twelve hours during the first week of life, then 50 mg per kg of body weight every eight hours thereafter.
Neonates 2 kg of body weight and over—Intramuscular or intravenous, 50 mg per kg of body weight every eight hours during the first week of life, then 50 mg per kg of body weight every six hours thereafter.
For all other indications—
Premature infants and neonates—Intramuscular or intravenous, 6.25 mg (base) every six hours.
Children up to 40 kg of body weight—Intramuscular or intravenous, 12.5 to 25 mg (base) per kg of body weight every six hours; or 16.7 mg per kg of body weight every four hours.
Children 40 kg of body weight and over—See *Usual adult and adolescent dose.*

Strength(s) usually available
U.S.—
250 mg (base) (Rx) [*Prostaphlin*].
500 mg (base) (Rx) [*Bactocill; Prostaphlin;* GENERIC].
1 gram (base) (Rx) [*Bactocill; Prostaphlin;* GENERIC].
2 grams (base) (Rx) [*Bactocill; Prostaphlin;* GENERIC].
4 grams (base) (Rx) [*Bactocill; Prostaphlin*].
10 grams (base) (Rx) [*Bactocill; Prostaphlin;* GENERIC].
Canada—
Not commercially available.

Packaging and storage
Prior to reconstitution, store between 15 and 30 °C (59 and 86 °F).

Preparation of dosage form
To prepare initial dilution for intramuscular use, depending on the manufacturer, add 1.4 mL of sterile water for injection to each 250-mg vial, 2.7 to 2.8 mL of diluent to each 500-mg vial, 5.7 mL of diluent to each 1-gram vial, 11.4 to 11.5 mL of diluent to each 2-gram vial, and 21.8 to 23 mL of diluent to each 4-gram vial to provide a concentration of 250 mg per 1.5 mL.
To prepare initial dilution for direct intravenous use, add 5 mL of sterile water for injection or 0.9% sodium chloride injection to each 250- or 500-mg vial, 10 mL of diluent to each 1-gram vial, 20 mL of diluent to each 2-gram vial, and 40 mL of diluent to each 4-gram vial. The resulting solution should be administered slowly over a 10-minute period.
Intravenous infusions of oxacillin sodium for injection should be administered in a suitable diluent in a concentration of up to 40 mg per mL (see manufacturer's package insert).
For reconstitution of pharmacy bulk vials, piggyback infusion bottles, and dual-compartment vials, see manufacturer's labeling for instructions.

Stability
After reconstitution for intramuscular use, solutions retain their potency for 4 days at room temperature or for 7 days if refrigerated.
Concentrated solutions (100 mg per mL) prepared from pharmacy bulk vials retain their potency for 48 hours at room temperature or for 7 days if refrigerated.
Diluted solutions (up to 40 mg per mL) retain their potency for 72 hours at room temperature, for 7 days if refrigerated, or for 30 days if frozen.
Solutions (10 to 50 mg per mL) prepared from piggyback infusion bottles retain their potency for 24 hours at room temperature.

Incompatibilities
Extemporaneous admixtures of beta-lactam antibacterials (penicillins and cephalosporins) and aminoglycosides may result in substantial mutual inactivation. If these groups of antibacterials are administered concurrently, they should be administered in separate sites at least 1 hour apart. Do not mix them in the same intravenous bag, bottle, or tubing.
When aminoglycosides and penicillins are administered separately by different routes, a reduction in aminoglycoside serum concentration may occur. Usually this is clinically significant only in patients with severely impaired renal function when the excretion of both medications is delayed.

Additional information
The total sodium content (derived from dibasic sodium phosphate buffer and oxacillin sodium) is approximately 2.8 to 3.1 mEq (64 to 71 mg) per gram of oxacillin. This must be considered in patients on a restricted sodium intake when calculating total daily sodium intake.

PENICILLIN G

Summary of Differences

Category:
Natural penicillin.
Pharmacology/pharmacokinetics:
Oral absorption low (15 to 30%).
Time to peak serum concentration—
Benzathine salt: 24 hours.
Procaine salt: 4 hours.
Precautions:
Cross-sensitivity and/or related problems—
Cross-sensitivity with other ester-type local anesthetics may also occur with administration of penicillin G procaine.
Drug interactions and/or related problems—
Use of angiotensin-converting enzyme (ACE) inhibitors, potassium-sparing diuretics, other potassium-containing medications, or potassium supplements with parenteral penicillin G potassium may promote hyperkalemia; also oral penicillin G may interact with cholestyramine and colestipol.
Patient monitoring—
Serum potassium or sodium determinations may be required (parenteral only).
Side/adverse effects:
May be an increased risk of mental disturbances with administration of penicillin G procaine.

Additional Dosing Information

Patients with impaired renal function do not generally require a reduction in dose unless the impairment is severe.

For oral dosage forms only

Oral administration of penicillin G commonly results in low serum concentrations. Therefore, severe infections should not be treated with oral penicillin during the acute stage.

Penicillin G is an acid-labile penicillin; therefore, concurrent administration with acidic fruit juices and other acidic beverages should be avoided.

Oral Dosage Forms

Note: The dosing and strengths of the dosage forms available are expressed in terms of penicillin G benzathine (not the base).

PENICILLIN G BENZATHINE SUSPENSION

Usual adult and adolescent dose

Antibacterial—

Oral, 200,000 to 500,000 Units (125 to 312 mg) every four to six hours.

Continuous prophylaxis of streptococcal infections in patients with a history of rheumatic heart disease: Oral, 200,000 to 250,000 Units (125 to 156 mg) every twelve hours.

Usual adult prescribing limits

2,000,000 Units a day.

Usual pediatric dose

Antibacterial—

Infants and children up to 12 years of age: Oral, 4167 to 15,000 Units per kg of body weight every four hours; 6250 to 22,500 Units per kg of body weight every six hours; or 8333 to 30,000 Units per kg of body weight every eight hours.

Children 12 years of age and older: See *Usual adult and adolescent dose*.

Strength(s) usually available

U.S.—

Not commercially available.

Canada—

250,000 Units (156 mg) per 5 mL (Rx) [*Megacillin*].
500,000 Units (312 mg) per 5 mL (Rx) [*Megacillin*].

Packaging and storage

Store between 15 and 30 °C (59 and 86 °F), unless otherwise specified by manufacturer.

Stability

The reconstituted suspension may be stored at room temperature until the labeled expiration date.

Auxiliary labeling

- Continue medication for full time of treatment.
- Take on empty stomach.
- Beyond-use date.

PENICILLIN G POTASSIUM FOR ORAL SOLUTION USP

Usual adult and adolescent dose

See *Penicillin G Benzathine Suspension*.

Usual adult prescribing limits

See *Penicillin G Benzathine Suspension*.

Usual pediatric dose

See *Penicillin G Benzathine Suspension*.

Strength(s) usually available

U.S.—

400,000 Units (250 mg) per 5 mL (Rx) [GENERIC].

Canada—

Not commercially available.

Packaging and storage

Prior to reconstitution, store below 40 °C (104 °F), preferably between 15 and 30 °C (59 and 86 °F), unless otherwise specified by manufacturer. Store in a tight container.

Stability

After reconstitution, solutions retain their potency for 14 days if refrigerated.

Auxiliary labeling

- Refrigerate.
- Continue medication for full time of treatment.
- Beyond-use date.
- Take on empty stomach.

Note

When dispensing, include a calibrated liquid-measuring device.

PENICILLIN G POTASSIUM TABLETS USP

Usual adult and adolescent dose

See *Penicillin G Benzathine Suspension*.

Usual adult prescribing limits

See *Penicillin G Benzathine Suspension*.

Usual pediatric dose

See *Penicillin G Benzathine Suspension*.

Strength(s) usually available

U.S.—

200,000 Units (125 mg) (Rx) [GENERIC].
250,000 Units (156 mg) (Rx) [GENERIC].
400,000 Units (250 mg) (Rx) [*Pentids;* GENERIC].
800,000 Units (500 mg) (Rx) [GENERIC].

Canada—

500,000 Units (312 mg) (Rx) [*Megacillin* (scored)].

Packaging and storage

Store below 40 °C (104 °F), preferably between 15 and 30 °C (59 and 86 °F), unless otherwise specified by manufacturer. Store in a tight container.

Auxiliary labeling

- Continue medication for full time of treatment.
- Take on empty stomach.

Parenteral Dosage Forms

Note: Bracketed uses in the *Dosage Forms* section refer to categories of use and/or indications that are not included in U.S. product labeling.

Note: The dosing and strengths of the dosage forms available are expressed in terms of penicillin G salt (not the base).

STERILE PENICILLIN G BENZATHINE SUSPENSION USP

Usual adult and adolescent dose

Antibacterial—

Bejel
Pinta or
Yaws: Intramuscular, 1,200,000 Units as a single dose.

Continuous prophylaxis of streptococcal infections in patients with a history of rheumatic heart disease: Intramuscular, 1,200,000 Units every three to four weeks.

Pharyngitis, streptococcal: Intramuscular, 1,200,000 Units as a single dose.

Syphilis (primary, secondary, and early latent): Intramuscular, 2,400,000 Units as a single dose.

Syphilis (tertiary and late latent, excluding neurosyphilis): Intramuscular, 2,400,000 Units once a week for three weeks.

Usual adult prescribing limits

2,400,000 Units a day.

Usual pediatric dose

Antibacterial—

Pharyngitis, group A streptococcal—

Infants and children up to 27.3 kg of body weight—Intramuscular, 300,000 to 600,000 Units as a single dose.

Children 27.3 kg of body weight and over—Intramuscular, 900,000 Units as a single dose.

Rheumatic fever (prophylaxis)—

Intramuscular, 1,200,000 Units every two or three weeks.

Syphilis (primary, secondary, and early latent)—

Intramuscular, 50,000 Units per kg of body weight, up to 2,400,000 Units, as a single dose.

Syphilis (late latent or latent of unknown duration)—

Intramuscular, 50,000 Units per kg of body weight once a week for three weeks.

Strength(s) usually available

U.S.—

600,000 Units in 1 mL (Rx) [*Bicillin L-A; Permapen*].
1,200,000 Units in 2 mL (Rx) [*Bicillin L-A*].
2,400,000 Units in 4 mL (Rx) [*Bicillin L-A*].
3,000,000 Units in 10 mL (Rx) [*Bicillin L-A*].

Canada—

1,200,000 Units in 2 mL (Rx) [*Bicillin L-A*].

Packaging and storage

Store between 2 and 8 °C (36 and 46 °F).

Additional information

For deep intramuscular use only. Do not administer intravenously, intra-arterially, subcutaneously, by fat-layer injection, or into or near a nerve. Intravenous injection may cause embolic or toxic reactions. Intra-arterial injection may cause extensive necrosis of the extremity or organ, especially in children. Subcutaneous and fat-layer injection may cause pain and induration. Injection into or near a nerve may result in permanent neurological damage.

Injection of penicillin G benzathine should be made at a slow, steady rate to prevent blockage of the needle because of the high concentration of suspended material.

Intramuscular administration of penicillin G benzathine results in much lower and more prolonged serum concentrations than those attained with other parenteral penicillins.

PENICILLIN G POTASSIUM FOR INJECTION USP

Usual adult and adolescent dose

Antibacterial—

Intramuscular or intravenous, 1,000,000 to 5,000,000 Units every four to six hours.

Actinomycosis: Intramuscular or intravenous, 10,000,000 to 20,000,000 Units a day for two to six weeks.

Anthrax: Intramuscular or intravenous, 2,000,000 Units every six hours.

Clostridial infections: Intramuscular or intravenous, 20,000,000 Units a day.

Erysipelas: Intramuscular or intravenous, 600,000 to 2,000,000 Units every six hours.

Erysipeloid endocarditis: Intramuscular or intravenous, 12,000,000 to 20,000,000 Units a day.

Listeriosis: Intramuscular or intravenous, 300,000 Units per kg of body weight a day.

Meningitis, bacterial: Intramuscular or intravenous, 50,000 Units per kg of body weight every four hours; or 24,000,000 Units daily divided every two to four hours.

Neurosyphilis: Intravenous, 2,000,000 to 4,000,000 Units every four hours for ten to fourteen days.

Pasteurella multocida septicemia and meningitis: Intramuscular or intravenous, 4,000,000 to 6,000,000 Units a day.

Pericarditis, bacterial: Intramuscular or intravenous, 20,000,000 to 30,000,000 Units a day for four to six weeks.

Rat-bite fever: Intramuscular or intravenous, 20,000,000 Units a day.

[Leptospirosis][1]: Intramuscular or intravenous, 1,500,000 Units every six hours.

[Lyme disease][1]: Intravenous, 20,000,000 to 24,000,000 Units a day for two to three weeks. Duration of therapy is based on clinical response. Treatment failures have occurred and retreatment may be necessary.

Usual adult prescribing limits

80,000,000 Units a day.

Usual pediatric dose

Antibacterial—

Listeriosis in neonates—

500,000 to 1,000,000 Units daily.

Meningitis, bacterial—

Neonates up to 2 kg of body weight—Intramuscular or intravenous, 25,000 to 50,000 Units per kg of body weight every twelve hours during the first week of life, then 50,000 Units per kg of body weight every eight hours thereafter.

Neonates 2 kg of body weight and over—Intramuscular or intravenous, 50,000 Units per kg of body weight every eight hours during the first week of life, then 50,000 Units per kg of body weight every six hours thereafter.

Syphilis, congenital—

Intramuscular or intravenous, 50,000 Units per kg of body weight every twelve hours for the first week of life, then 50,000 Units per kg of body weight every eight hours for the next ten to fourteen days.

[Lyme disease][1]—

Intravenous, 250,000 to 400,000 Units per kg of body weight daily for two to three weeks. Duration of therapy is based on clinical response. Treatment failures have occurred and retreatment may be necessary.

For all other indications—

Premature and full-term neonates—Intramuscular or intravenous, 30,000 Units per kg of body weight every twelve hours.

Older infants and children—Intramuscular or intravenous, 8333 to 16,667 Units per kg of body weight every four hours; or 12,500 to 25,000 Units per kg of body weight every six hours.

Strength(s) usually available

U.S.—

1,000,000 Units (Rx) [GENERIC].
5,000,000 Units (Rx) [*Pfizerpen;* GENERIC].
10,000,000 Units (Rx) [GENERIC].
20,000,000 Units (Rx) [*Pfizerpen;* GENERIC].

Canada—

1,000,000 Units (Rx) [GENERIC].
5,000,000 Units (Rx) [GENERIC].
10,000,000 Units (Rx) [GENERIC].

Packaging and storage

Prior to reconstitution, store below 40 °C (104 °F), preferably between 15 and 30 °C (59 and 86 °F), unless otherwise specified by manufacturer.

Preparation of dosage form

To prepare initial dilution for intramuscular or intravenous use, see manufacturer's labeling for instructions.

To prepare for further dilution for intravenous use, see manufacturer's labeling for instructions.

Stability

After reconstitution, solutions retain their potency for 24 hours at room temperature or for 7 days if refrigerated.

Incompatibilities

Penicillin G potassium is rapidly inactivated by oxidizing and reducing agents, such as alcohols and glycols.

Extemporaneous admixtures of beta-lactam antibacterials (penicillins and cephalosporins) and aminoglycosides may result in substantial mutual inactivation. If these groups of antibacterials are administered concurrently, they should be administered in separate sites at least 1 hour apart. Do not mix them in the same intravenous bag, bottle, or tubing.

When aminoglycosides and penicillins are administered separately by different routes, a reduction in aminoglycoside serum concentration may occur. Usually this is clinically significant only in patients with severely impaired renal function when the excretion of both medications is delayed.

Additional information

Daily doses of 10,000,000 Units or more should be administered by slow intravenous infusion or by intermittent piggyback infusion because of possible electrolyte imbalance.

The potassium content and sodium content (derived from sodium citrate buffer) of penicillin G potassium for injection are approximately 1.7 mEq (66.3 mg) and 0.3 mEq (6.9 mg) per 1,000,000 Units of penicillin G, respectively. The sodium content must be considered in patients on a restricted sodium intake when calculating total daily sodium intake.

STERILE PENICILLIN G PROCAINE SUSPENSION USP

Usual adult and adolescent dose

Antibacterial—

Intramuscular, 600,000 to 1,200,000 Units a day.

Diphtheria: Intramuscular, 300,000 to 600,000 Units a day as adjunctive therapy to diphtheria antitoxin.

Neurosyphilis: Intramuscular, 2,400,000 Units a day, and 500 mg of probenecid orally four times a day, for ten to fourteen days.

Rat-bite fever: Intramuscular, 600,000 Units every twelve hours for ten to fourteen days.

Usual pediatric dose

Antibacterial—

Syphilis, congenital: Intramuscular, 50,000 Units per kg of body weight a day for ten to fourteen days.

Strength(s) usually available

U.S.—

600,000 Units in 1 mL (Rx) [*Wycillin*].
1,200,000 Units in 2 mL (Rx) [*Wycillin*].
2,400,000 Units in 4 mL (Rx) [*Wycillin*].
3,000,000 Units in 10 mL (Rx) [*Crysticillin 300 A.S.; Pfizerpen-AS*].

Canada—

3,000,000 Units per 10 mL (Rx) [*Ayercillin* (propylparaben 0.013%)].
5,000,000 Units per 10 mL (base) (Rx) [*Wycillin*].

Packaging and storage

Store between 2 and 8 °C (36 and 46 °F).

Additional information

For deep intramuscular use only. Do not administer intravenously, intra-arterially, or into or near a nerve. Intravenous injection may cause embolic or toxic reactions. Intra-arterial injection may cause extensive necrosis of the extremity or organ, especially in children.

Some patients may experience immediate toxic reactions to procaine, especially when administered in large single doses. These reactions, usually transient, may be characterized by anxiety, confusion, agitation or combativeness, depression, seizures, hallucinations, or expressed fear of impending death.

PENICILLIN G SODIUM FOR INJECTION USP

Usual adult and adolescent dose
See *Penicillin G Potassium for Injection USP*.

Usual adult prescribing limits
See *Penicillin G Potassium for Injection USP*.

Usual pediatric dose
See *Penicillin G Potassium for Injection USP*.

Strength(s) usually available
U.S.—
5,000,000 Units (Rx) [GENERIC].
Canada—
1,000,000 Units (Rx) [GENERIC].
5,000,000 Units (Rx) [GENERIC].
10,000,000 Units (Rx) [GENERIC].

Packaging and storage
Prior to reconstitution, store below 40 °C (104 °F), preferably between 15 and 30 °C (59 and 86 °F), unless otherwise specified by manufacturer.

Preparation of dosage form
To prepare initial dilution for intramuscular or intravenous use, see manufacturer's labeling for instructions.

Stability
After reconstitution, solutions retain their potency for 24 hours at room temperature or for 7 days if refrigerated.

Incompatibilities
Penicillin G sodium is rapidly inactivated by acids, alkalies, and oxidizing agents and in carbohydrate solutions at alkaline pH.
Extemporaneous admixtures of beta-lactam antibacterials (penicillins and cephalosporins) and aminoglycosides may result in substantial mutual inactivation. If these groups of antibacterials are administered concurrently, they should be administered in separate sites at least 1 hour apart. Do not mix them in the same intravenous bag, bottle, or tubing.
When aminoglycosides and penicillins are administered separately by different routes, a reduction in aminoglycoside serum concentration may occur. Usually this is clinically significant only in patients with severely impaired renal function when the excretion of both medications is delayed.

Additional information
Daily doses of 10,000,000 Units or more should be administered by slow intravenous infusion to avoid causing possible electrolyte imbalance.
The sodium content is approximately 2 mEq (2 mmol) per million Units of penicillin G. This must be considered in patients on a restricted sodium intake when calculating total daily sodium intake.

---

[1]Not included in Canadian product labeling.

PENICILLIN V

Summary of Differences

Category: Penicillin G–related natural penicillin.
Precautions: Drug interactions and/or related problems—Also interacts with oral contraceptives.

Additional Dosing Information

Penicillin V may be taken on a full or empty stomach.
Patients with impaired renal function do not generally require a reduction in dose unless the impairment is severe.

Oral Dosage Forms

Note: Bracketed uses in the *Dosage Forms* section refer to categories of use and/or indications that are not included in U.S. product labeling.

Note: The dosing and strengths of the dosage forms available are expressed in terms of penicillin V salt (not the base).

PENICILLIN V BENZATHINE SUSPENSION

Usual adult and adolescent dose
Antibacterial—
Oral, 200,000 to 500,000 Units every six to eight hours.
Continuous prophylaxis of streptococcal infections in patients with a history of rheumatic heart disease: Oral, 200,000 Units every twelve hours.

Usual pediatric dose
Antibacterial—
Infants and children up 60 kg of body weight: Oral, 100,000 to 250,000 Units every six to eight hours.
Children 60 kg of body weight and over: See *Usual adult and adolescent dose*.

Strength(s) usually available
U.S.—
Not commercially available.
Canada—
250,000 Units (156 mg) per 5 mL (Rx) [*PVF*].
300,000 Units (180 mg) per 5 mL (Rx) [*Pen-Vee*].
500,000 Units (300 mg) per 5 mL (Rx) [*Pen-Vee; PVF*].

Packaging and storage
Prior to reconstitution, store below 40 °C (104 °F), preferably between 15 and 30 °C (59 and 86 °F), unless otherwise specified by manufacturer. Store in a tight container.

Stability
Store at room temperature.

Auxiliary labeling
- Continue medication for full time of treatment.
- Beyond-use date.

Note
When dispensing, include a calibrated liquid-measuring device.

PENICILLIN V POTASSIUM FOR ORAL SOLUTION USP

Usual adult and adolescent dose
Antibacterial—
Oral, 125 to 500 mg (200,000 to 800,000 Units) every six to eight hours.
Continuous prophylaxis of streptococcal infections in patients with a history of rheumatic heart disease: Oral, 125 to 250 mg (200,000 to 400,000 Units) every twelve hours.
Erysipelas: Oral, 500 mg every six hours.
Erysipeloid, uncomplicated: Oral, 250 mg every six hours for five to ten days.
Gingivitis, acute, necrotizing, ulcerative: Oral, 500 mg every six hours.
*Pasteurella*infections: Oral, 500 mg every six hours for ten to fourteen days.
Rat-bite fever: Oral, 500 mg every six hours for fourteen days.
[Lyme disease][1]: Oral, 250 to 500 mg three or four times a day for three to four weeks. Duration of therapy is based on clinical response. Treatment failures have occurred and retreatment may be necessary.

Usual adult prescribing limits
7.2 grams (11,520,000 Units) a day.

Usual pediatric dose
Antibacterial—
[Lyme disease][1]—
Oral, 5 to 12.5 mg per kg of body weight four times a day for three to four weeks. Duration of therapy is based on clinical response. Treatment failures have occurred and retreatment may be necessary.

For all other indications—
Infants and children up to 12 years of age—Oral, 2.5 to 8.3 mg (4167 to 13,280 Units) per kg of body weight every four hours; 3.75 to 12.5 mg (6250 to 20,000 Units) per kg of body weight every six hours; or 5 to 16.7 mg (8333 to 26,720 Units) per kg of body weight every eight hours.
Children 12 years of age and older—See *Usual adult and adolescent dose*.

Strength(s) usually available
U.S.—
125 mg (200,000 Units) per 5 mL (Rx) [*Beepen-VK; Betapen-VK; Ledercillin VK; Pen Vee K; Veetids;* GENERIC].
250 mg (400,000 Units) per 5 mL (Rx) [*Beepen-VK; Betapen-VK; Ledercillin VK; Pen Vee K; V-Cillin K; Veetids;* GENERIC].
Canada—
125 mg (200,000 Units) per 5 mL (Rx) [*Apo-Pen VK; Nadopen-V 200; V-Cillin K*].
250 mg (400,000 Units) per 5 mL (Rx) [*Nadopen-V 400; V-Cillin K*].
300 mg (500,000 Units) per 5 mL (Rx) [*Apo-Pen VK; Novo-Pen-VK*].

Packaging and storage
Prior to reconstitution, store below 40 °C (104 °F), preferably between 15 and 30 °C (59 and 86 °F), unless otherwise specified by manufacturer. Store in a tight container.

Stability
After reconstitution, solutions retain their potency for 14 days if refrigerated.

Auxiliary labeling
- Refrigerate.
- Continue medication for full time of treatment.
- Beyond-use date.
- Shake well.

Note
When dispensing, include a calibrated liquid-measuring device.

PENICILLIN V POTASSIUM TABLETS USP

Usual adult and adolescent dose
See *Penicillin V Potassium for Oral Solution USP.*

Usual adult prescribing limits
See *Penicillin V Potassium for Oral Solution USP.*

Usual pediatric dose
See *Penicillin V Potassium for Oral Solution USP.*

Strength(s) usually available
U.S.—

250 mg (400,000 Units) (Rx) [*Beepen-VK; Ledercillin VK; Pen Vee K; V-Cillin K; Veetids;* GENERIC].

500 mg (800,000 Units) (Rx) [*Beepen-VK; Ledercillin VK; Pen Vee K; V-Cillin K; Veetids;* GENERIC].

Canada—

250 mg (400,000 Units) (Rx) [*Ledercillin VK* (scored); *V-Cillin K*].

300 mg (500,000 Units) (Rx) [*Apo-Pen VK; Nadopen-V* (scored); *Novo-Pen-VK; Nu-Pen-VK; Pen Vee* (scored); *PVF K* (scored)].

500 mg (800,000 Units) (Rx) [*Ledercillin VK*].

Packaging and storage
Store below 40 °C (104 °F), preferably between 15 and 30 °C (59 and 86 °F), unless otherwise specified by manufacturer. Store in a tight container.

Auxiliary labeling
- Continue medication for full time of treatment.

[1]Not included in Canadian product labeling.

PIPERACILLIN

Summary of Differences
Category:

Antipseudomonal penicillin.

Precautions:

Drug interactions and/or related problems—Also interacts with anticoagulants and other medications that affect blood clotting, and other hepatotoxic medications.

Laboratory value alterations—May increase bleeding time.

Medical considerations/contraindications—Caution in patients with a history of bleeding disorders and cystic fibrosis.

Patient monitoring—Serum potassium and sodium determinations may be required.

Additional Dosing Information
Intramuscular injections should not exceed 2 grams in each site.

Adults with impaired renal function may require a reduction in dose as follows:

Creatinine Clearance (mL/min)/(mL/sec)	Dose (base)
> 40/0.67	See *Usual adult and adolescent dose*
20–40/0.33–0.67	3 to 4 grams every 8 hours
<20/0.33	3 to 4 grams every 12 hours
Hemodialysis patients	1 gram after each dialysis, then 2 grams every 8 hours

Parenteral Dosage Forms
Note: The dosing and strengths of the dosage forms available are expressed in terms of piperacillin base (not the sodium salt).

PIPERACILLIN SODIUM STERILE USP

Usual adult and adolescent dose
Antibacterial—

Intramuscular or intravenous, 3 to 4 grams (base) every four to six hours.

Meningitis, bacterial: Intravenous, 4 grams every four hours; or 75 mg per kg of body weight every six hours.

Urinary tract infections, complicated: Intravenous, 3 to 4 grams (base) every six to eight hours.

Urinary tract infections, uncomplicated: Intramuscular or intravenous, 1.5 to 2 grams (base) every six hours or 3 to 4 grams every twelve hours.

Usual adult prescribing limits
24 grams (base) a day.

Usual pediatric dose
Antibacterial—

Meningitis, bacterial—

Neonates up to 2 kg of body weight—Intramuscular or intravenous, 50 mg per kg of body weight every twelve hours during the first week of life, then 50 mg per kg of body weight every eight hours thereafter.

Neonates 2 kg of body weight and over—Intramuscular or intravenous, 50 mg per kg of body weight every eight hours during the first week of life, then 50 mg per kg of body weight every six hours thereafter.

For all other indications—

Infants and children under 12 years of age—Dosage has not been established.

Children 12 years of age and older—See *Usual adult and adolescent dose.*

Note: Cystic fibrosis patients—Intravenous, 350 to 450 mg per kg of body weight daily.

Strength(s) usually available
U.S.—

2 grams (base) (Rx) [*Pipracil*].

3 grams (base) (Rx) [*Pipracil*].

4 grams (base) (Rx) [*Pipracil*].

40 grams (base) (Rx) [*Pipracil*].

Canada—

2 grams (base) (Rx) [*Pipracil*].

3 grams (base) (Rx) [*Pipracil*].

4 grams (base) (Rx) [*Pipracil*].

Packaging and storage
Prior to reconstitution, store below 40 °C (104 °F), preferably between 15 and 30 °C (59 and 86 °F), unless otherwise specified by manufacturer.

Preparation of dosage form
To prepare initial dilution for intramuscular use, add 4 mL of sterile water for injection or 0.5 or 1% lidocaine hydrochloride injection (without epinephrine) to each 2-gram vial, 6 mL of diluent to each 3-gram vial, and 7.8 mL of diluent to each 4-gram vial to provide a concentration of 1 gram (base) per 2.5 mL.

To prepare initial dilution for intravenous use, add at least 5 mL of a suitable diluent (see manufacturer's package insert) for each gram of piperacillin and shake well until dissolved. For direct intravenous use, the resulting solution should be administered slowly over a 3- to 5-minute period. For intermittent intravenous use, the resulting solution should be further diluted with a suitable diluent (see manufacturer's package insert) to at least 50 mL. It should be administered over approximately a 20- to 30-minute period.

For reconstitution of pharmacy bulk vials or piggyback infusion bottles, see manufacturer's labeling for instructions.

Stability
After reconstitution with suitable diluents (see manufacturer's package insert), solutions retain their potency for 24 hours at controlled room temperature, 7 days if refrigerated, or 1 month if frozen at −15 °C (5 °F).

Incompatibilities
Because of chemical instability, piperacillin should not be used for intravenous admixtures with solutions containing *only* sodium bicarbonate.

Extemporaneous admixtures of beta-lactam antibacterials (penicillins and cephalosporins) and aminoglycosides may result in substantial mutual inactivation. If these groups of antibacterials are administered concurrently, they should be administered in separate sites at least 1 hour apart. Do not mix them in the same intravenous bag, bottle, or tubing.

When aminoglycosides and penicillins are administered separately by different routes, a reduction in aminoglycoside serum concentration may occur. Usually this is clinically significant only in patients with severely impaired renal function when the excretion of both medications is delayed.

Additional information
The sodium content is approximately 1.98 mEq (45.5 mg) per gram of piperacillin. This must be considered in patients on a restricted sodium intake when calculating total daily sodium intake.

PIVAMPICILLIN

Summary of Differences

Category: Aminopenicillin.

Pharmacology/pharmacokinetics: Converted to ampicillin during absorption.

Pediatrics: Should be avoided in children up to 3 months of age since pivampicillin decreases serum carnitine concentrations.

Precautions: Medical considerations/contraindications—Caution in patients with carnitine deficiency.

Additional Dosing Information

Patients with impaired renal function do not generally require a reduction in dose unless the impairment is severe.

Pivampicillin may be taken on a full or empty stomach.

Oral Dosage Forms

Note: The dosing and strengths of the dosage forms available are expressed in terms of pivampicillin (not the ampicillin base).

PIVAMPICILLIN FOR ORAL SUSPENSION USP

Usual adult and adolescent dose

Antibacterial—

Oral, 525 to 1050 mg two times a day.

Usual pediatric dose

Antibacterial—

Infants 3 to 12 months of age: Oral, 20 to 30 mg per kg of body weight two times a day.

Children 1 to 3 years of age: Oral, 175 mg two times a day.

Children 4 to 6 years of age: Oral, 262.5 mg two times a day.

Children 7 to 10 years of age: Oral, 350 mg two times a day

Children 10 years of age and older: See *Usual adult and adolescent dose.*

Strength(s) usually available

U.S.—

Not commercially available.

Canada—

35 mg per mL (Rx) [*Pondocillin*].

Note: 35 mg of pivampicillin are equivalent to 26.4 mg of ampicillin.

Packaging and storage

Prior to reconstitution, store between 15 and 30 °C (59 and 86 °F). Store in a tight container.

Auxiliary labeling

- Shake well.
- Continue medication for full time of treatment.
- Beyond-use date.

Note

When dispensing, include a calibrated liquid-measuring device.

PIVAMPICILLIN TABLETS

Usual adult and adolescent dose

Antibacterial—

Oral, 500 mg to 1 gram two times a day.

Usual pediatric dose

Antibacterial—

Children 10 years of age and over: See *Usual adult and adolescent dose.*

Children up to 10 years of age: A product of suitable strength is not available for infants and children up to 10 years of age. See *Pivampicillin for Oral Suspension USP.*

Strength(s) usually available

U.S.—

Not commercially available.

Canada—

500 mg (Rx) [*Pondocillin*].

Note: 500 mg of pivampicillin are equivalent to 377 mg of ampicillin.

Packaging and storage

Store between 15 and 30 °C (59 and 86 °F). Store in a tight container.

Auxiliary labeling

- Continue medication for full time of treatment.

PIVMECILLINAM

Summary of Differences

Category: Aminopenicillin.

Pharmacology/pharmacokinetics: Converted to mecillinam during absorption.

Pediatrics: Should be avoided in children up to 3 months of age since pivmecillinam decreases serum carnitine concentrations.

Precautions: Medical considerations/contraindications—Caution in patients with carnitine deficiency.

Additional Dosing Information

Patients with impaired renal function do not generally require a reduction in dose unless the impairment is severe.

Pivmecillinam may be taken on a full or empty stomach.

Oral Dosage Forms

Note: The dosing and strengths of the dosage forms available are expressed in terms of pivmecillinam hydrochloride (not the mecillinam base).

PIVMECILLINAM HYDROCHLORIDE TABLETS

Usual adult and adolescent dose

Antibacterial—

Oral, 200 mg two to four times a day for three days.

Usual pediatric dose

Antibacterial—

Children up to 40 kg of body weight: Dosage has not been established.

Children 40 kg of body weight and over: See *Usual adult and adolescent dose.*

Strength(s) usually available

U.S.—

Not commercially available.

Canada—

200 mg (Rx) [*Selexid*].

Note: 200 mg of pivmecillinam hydrochloride is equivalent to 137 mg of mecillinam.

Packaging and storage

Store between 15 and 30 °C (59 and 86 °F). Store in a tight container.

Auxiliary labeling

- Continue medication for full time of treatment.

TICARCILLIN

Summary of Differences

Category:

Antipseudomonal penicillin.

Precautions:

Drug interactions and/or related problems—Also interacts with anticoagulants and other medications that affect blood clotting.

Laboratory value alterations—May increase bleeding time and may cause false-positive protein reaction for various urine protein tests.

Medical considerations/contraindications—Caution in patients with a history of bleeding disorders, and congestive heart failure or hypertension.

Patient monitoring—Bleeding time and serum potassium and sodium determinations may be required.

Additional Dosing Information

Intramuscular injections should not exceed 2 grams in each site.

Patients with impaired renal function should be observed for hemorrhagic complications.

Note: After an initial intravenous loading dose of 3 grams (base), adults with impaired renal function may require a reduction in dose as follows:

Creatinine Clearance (mL/min)/(mL/sec)	Dose (base)
> 60/1	3 grams every 4 hours
30–60/0.5–1	2 grams every 4 hours
10–30/0.17–0.5	2 grams every 8 hours
<10/0.17	2 grams every 12 hours
<10 with impaired hepatic function	2 grams every 24 hours
Hemodialysis	2 grams every 12 hours plus 3 grams after dialysis
Peritoneal dialysis	3 grams every 12 hours

Parenteral Dosage Forms

Note: The dosing and strengths of the dosage forms available are expressed in terms of ticarcillin base (not the sodium salt).

TICARCILLIN DISODIUM STERILE USP

Usual adult and adolescent dose

Antibacterial—

Intravenous infusion, 3 grams (base) every four hours; or 4 grams every six hours.

Meningitis, bacterial: Intravenous infusion, 75 mg per kg of body weight every six hours.

Urinary tract infections, complicated: Intravenous infusion, 3 grams (base) every six hours.

Urinary tract infections, uncomplicated: Intramuscular or intravenous, 1 gram (base) every six hours.

Usual adult prescribing limits

24 grams a day.

Usual pediatric dose

Antibacterial—

Neonates up to 2 kg of body weight—

Intramuscular or intravenous, 75 mg per kg of body weight every twelve hours during the first week of life; followed by 75 mg per kg of body weight every eight hours thereafter.

Neonates 2 kg of body weight and over—

Intramuscular or intravenous, 75 mg per kg of body weight every eight hours during the first week of life; followed by 75 mg per kg of body weight every six hours thereafter.

Children up to 40 kg of body weight—

Intravenous infusion, 33.3 to 50 mg (base) per kg of body weight every four hours; or 50 to 75 mg per kg of body weight every six hours.

Urinary tract infections, bacterial (complicated)—Intravenous infusion, 25 to 33.3 mg (base) per kg of body weight every four hours; or 37.5 to 50 mg per kg of body weight every six hours.

Urinary tract infections, bacterial (uncomplicated)—Intramuscular or intravenous, 12.5 to 25 mg (base) per kg of body weight every six hours; or 16.7 to 33.3 mg per kg of body weight every eight hours.

Children 40 kg of body weight and over—

See *Usual adult and adolescent dose.*

Strength(s) usually available

U.S.—

1 gram (base) (Rx) [*Ticar*].
3 grams (base) (Rx) [*Ticar*].
6 grams (base) (Rx) [*Ticar*].
20 grams (base) (Rx) [*Ticar*].
30 grams (base) (Rx) [*Ticar*].

Canada—

1 gram (base) (Rx) [*Ticar*].
3 grams (base) (Rx) [*Ticar*].
6 grams (base) (Rx) [*Ticar*].
20 grams (base) (Rx) [*Ticar*].

Packaging and storage

Prior to reconstitution, store below 40 °C (104 °F), preferably between 15 and 30 °C (59 and 86 °F), unless otherwise specified by manufacturer.

Preparation of dosage form

To prepare initial dilution for intramuscular use, add 2 mL of sterile water for injection, 1% lidocaine hydrochloride injection (without epinephrine), or sodium chloride injection to each 1-gram vial to provide a concentration of 1 gram per 2.6 mL.

To prepare initial dilution for direct intravenous use, add at least 4 mL of 5% dextrose, 0.9% sodium chloride, or lactated Ringer's injection to each 1-gram vial. Each gram of ticarcillin may be further diluted if desired. The resulting solution should be administered as slowly as possible to avoid vein irritation.

Intermittent infusions may be administered over a 30-minute to 2-hour period in adults. In neonates, intermittent infusions may be administered over a 10- to 20-minute period.

For reconstitution of pharmacy bulk vials or piggyback infusion bottles, see manufacturer's labeling for instructions.

Stability

After reconstitution for intramuscular use, solutions retain their potency for 12 hours at room temperature or for 24 hours if refrigerated.

After reconstitution for intravenous use, solutions in concentrations of 10 to 50 mg per mL retain at least 90% of their potency for 48 to 72 hours at room temperature or for 14 days if refrigerated in suitable diluents (see manufacturer's package insert).

If frozen after reconstitution with sterile water for injection, 0.9% sodium chloride injection, 5% dextrose injection, Ringer's injection, or lactated Ringer's injection, solutions in concentrations up to 100 mg per mL retain their potency up to 30 days at −18 °C (0 °F). Once thawed, solutions must be used within 24 hours.

Incompatibilities

Extemporaneous admixtures of beta-lactam antibacterials (penicillins and cephalosporins) and aminoglycosides may result in substantial mutual inactivation. If these groups of antibacterials are administered concurrently, they should be administered in separate sites at least 1 hour apart. Do not mix them in the same intravenous bag, bottle, or tubing.

When aminoglycosides and penicillins are administered separately by different routes, a reduction in aminoglycoside serum concentration may occur. Usually this is clinically significant only in patients with severely impaired renal function when the excretion of both medications is delayed.

Additional information

The sodium content is approximately 5.2 mEq (5.2 mmol), but may be as high as 6.5 mEq (6.5 mmol), per gram of ticarcillin. This must be considered in patients on a restricted sodium intake when calculating total daily sodium intake.

Revised: 06/11/1999

Table 1. Pharmacology/Pharmacokinetics

Drug	Oral Absorption (%)	Time to Peak Serum Concentration (hr)	Peak Serum Concentration		Half-life (hr)		
			Dose	mcg/mL	Creatinine Clearance > 50 mL/min (0.83 mL/sec)	Creatinine Clearance 10–30 mL/min (0.17–0.83 mL/sec)	Creatinine Clearance < 10 mL/min (0.17 mL/sec)
Amoxicillin	75–90	1–2 (oral)	250 mg (oral)	3.5–5	1	4.5	12.6
Ampicillin	35–50	1.5–2 (oral) 1 (IM)*	500 mg (oral) 500 mg (IM) 500 mg (IV)*	3–6 7–14 12–29	1–1.5	3.4	19
Bacampicillin	35–50†	0.5–1† (oral)	400 mg (oral)	7.9†	1†	4.5†	12.6†
Carbenicillin	30	0.5–1 (oral and IM)	500 mg (oral) 1 gram (IM) 2 grams (IV)	6.5 20 241	1–1.5	9.6	18.2
Cloxacillin	50	1–2 (oral)	500 mg (oral) 500 mg (IM)	8 16	0.5–1		2.5
Dicloxacillin	37–50	0.5–1 (oral)	125 mg (oral)	4.7	0.5–1		1.8
Flucloxacillin	30–50	1 (oral)	250 mg (oral)	6–10	0.7–1.3		

Table 1. Pharmacology/Pharmacokinetics *(continued)*

Drug	Oral Absorption (%)	Time to Peak Serum Concentration (hr)	Peak Serum Concentration		Half-life (hr)		
			Dose	mcg/mL	Creatinine Clearance > 50 mL/min (0.83 mL/sec)	Creatinine Clearance 10–30 mL/min (0.17–0.83 mL/sec)	Creatinine Clearance < 10 mL/min (0.17 mL/sec)
Methicillin		0.5–1 (IM)	1 gram (IM) 1 gram (IV)	12 60	0.3–1		4
Mezlocillin		0.5–1 (IM)	1 gram (IM) 4 grams (IV)	35–45 254	0.8–1.1	2	2.6
Nafcillin	Erratic; poor	1–2 (oral) 0.5–1 (IM)	1 gram (IM)	7.6	0.5–1.5	1.9	2.1
Oxacillin	30–35	0.5–1 (oral and IM)	500 mg (oral) 500 mg (IM)	5–7 15	0.4–0.7		0.8
Penicillin G (Oral) (IV) Benzathine (IM) Procaine (IM)	15–30	1–2 24 4	3,200,000 units (IV) 300,000 units (IM)	2.2–17 0.03–0.05	0.5–0.7		4.1
Penicillin V	60–73	0.5–1 (oral)	250 mg (oral)	2–3	0.5–1		4.1
Piperacillin		0.5 (IM)	4 grams (IV)	412	0.6–1.2	2	2.8
Pivampicillin	35–50†	1† (oral)	500 mg (oral)	13†	1†		
Pivmecillinam	Poor‡	0.5–1.5‡ (oral)	200 mg (oral)	3.3‡	1‡		
Ticarcillin		0.5–1 (IM)	3 grams (IV)	190	1–1.2	5.2	8.9

*IV=intravenous; IM=intramuscular.
†As ampicillin.
‡As mecillinam.

Table 2. Pharmacology/Pharmacokinetics

Drug	Protein Binding (%)	Hepatic Biotransformation (%)	Renal Elimination (% unchanged)	Vol_D (L/kg)	Removal by Hemodialysis
Amoxicillin	Low (20)	10	60–75	0.36	Yes
Ampicillin	Low (20)	10	75–90	0.29	Yes
Bacampicillin	Low (18–20)*	10*	70–75*	0.29*	Yes
Carbenicillin	Moderate (50)	0–2	36 (oral) 75–95 (intravenous)	0.12	Yes
Cloxacillin	Very high (95)	20	30–60	0.11	No
Dicloxacillin	Very high (95–98)	10	50–70	0.08	No
Flucloxacillin	Very high (94)		50–65		No
Methicillin	Low to moderate (40)	10	60–80	0.36	No
Mezlocillin	Low to moderate (16–42)	20–30	55–60	0.23	Yes
Nafcillin	High (90)	60–70	11–30	1.1	No
Oxacillin	High (90–94)	45	55–60	0.4	No
Penicillin G (Oral) (Parenteral) Benzathine (IM) Procaine	Moderate (60)	20	20 60–90	0.5–0.7	Yes
Penicillin V	High (80)	55	20–40	0.5	Yes
Piperacillin	Low (16)	20–30	60–80	0.23	Yes†
Pivampicillin	Low (20)*	10*	25–30*		
Pivmecillinam	Low (5–10)‡		60–80‡		Yes§
Ticarcillin	Moderate (45–60)	15	60–80	0.16	Yes

*As ampicillin.
†Hemodialysis removes 30–50% of piperacillin in 4 hours.
‡As mecillinam.
§Hemodialysis removes 50–70% of pivmecillinam in 4 hours.

PENICILLINS AND BETA-LACTAMASE INHIBITORS Systemic

This monograph includes information on the following: 1) Amoxicillin and Clavulanate; 2) Ampicillin and Sulbactam†; 3) Piperacillin and Tazobactam; 4) Ticarcillin and Clavulanate.

INN: Amoxicillin—Amoxicilline

BAN: Amoxicillin—Amoxycillin

VA CLASSIFICATION (Primary):

Amoxicillin and Clavulanate—AM112
Ampicillin and Sulbactam—AM112
Piperacillin and Tazobactam—AM114
Ticarcillin and Clavulanate—AM114

Commonly used brand name(s): *Augmentin*[1]; *Clavulin-125F*[1]; *Clavulin-250*[1]; *Clavulin-250F*[1]; *Clavulin-500F*[1]; *Tazocin*[3]; *Timentin*[4]; *Unasyn*[2]; *Zosyn*[3].

Note: For a listing of dosage forms and brand names by country availability, see *Dosage Forms* section(s).

†Not commercially available in Canada.

Category

Antibacterial (systemic).

Indications

Note: Bracketed information in the *Indications* section refers to uses that are not included in U.S. product labeling.

General Considerations

Ampicillin and amoxicillin have activity against *Haemophilus influenzae*, *Escherichia coli*, and *Salmonella* and *Shigella* species, and also retain activity against penicillin-sensitive gram-positive bacteria. However, many Enterobacteriaceae and *H. influenzae* are resistant as a result of beta-lactamase production. Amoxicillin has the same spectrum of activity as ampicillin, although amoxicillin has slightly better activity against *Enterococcus faecalis*, *E. coli*, and *Salmonella* sp., and slightly less activity against *Shigella* sp.

Ticarcillin combines the gram-negative spectrum of ampicillin with activity against most species of *Enterobacter*, *Providencia*, and *Morganella* sp. It also has some activity against *Pseudomonas aeruginosa* and some indole-positive *Proteus* sp.

Piperacillin is more active than ticarcillin against *P. aeruginosa* and *Klebsiella* sp., but has activity similar to that of ticarcillin against most other gram-negative bacteria. Piperacillin also inhibits *Pseudomonas cepacia*, *Pseudomonas maltophilia*, and *Pseudomonas fluorescens*.

Resistance to penicillins is thought to be due to three main mechanisms. The first is alteration of the antibiotic target sites' penicillin-binding proteins (PBPs); the second is inactivation of the penicillin by bacterially produced enzymes (beta-lactamases); and the third is decreased permeability of the cell wall to penicillins. Of these three mechanisms, production of beta-lactamase is the most common and the most important.

When combined with a penicillin, beta-lactamase inhibitors, which include clavulanic acid (clavulanate), sulbactam, and tazobactam, have effectively extended the penicillin's spectrum of activity. Like penicillins, the beta-lactamase inhibitors are beta-lactam compounds; however, they have minimal intrinsic antibacterial activity. Instead of being hydrolyzed by beta-lactamases, they irreversibly bind to these enzymes, thereby protecting the penicillin from hydrolysis ('suicide' inhibition). Beta-lactamase inhibitors only work when a beta-lactamase enzyme is present. They will not alter the susceptibility of organisms inherently resistant to the penicillin; nor will they alter resistance patterns due to other causes, e.g., alteration of the penicillin-binding proteins (PBPs) (the mechanism of resistance for methicillin-resistant staphylococci).

Clavulanate, sulbactam, and tazobactam are irreversible inhibitors of a wide variety of plasmid-mediated and some chromosomally mediated bacterial beta-lactamases. Clavulanate and tazobactam are highly active, and sulbactam is moderately active, against transferable plasmid-mediated beta-lactamases. The inhibitory effect on chromosomally mediated type I enzymes is variable. Any beta-lactam agent, including beta-lactamase inhibitors and penicillins, may induce beta-lactamase production. Therefore, organisms such as *Enterobacter*, *Serratia*, *Morganella*, and *Pseudomonas* species may produce more beta-lactamase enzyme when they are exposed to a penicillin or a beta-lactamase inhibitor. Clavulanate is a moderate inducer of the chromosomal enzymes in these organisms; sulbactam and tazobactam are weaker inducers. Also, if the complex with the beta-lactamase inhibitor is not stable, regeneration of the beta-lactamase may occur. If so, the enzyme must be repeatedly inactivated for inhibition to be maintained. It is also easier to protect a beta-lactam antibiotic against organisms that produce a small amount of enzyme than it is to protect against organisms producing a large amount.

All three beta-lactamase inhibitors inactivate staphylococcal penicillinase. Beta-lactamase inhibitors inactivate the chromosomally mediated beta-lactamases of *Proteus vulgaris* and *Bacteroides* sp., and the class IV beta-lactamases present in some *Klebsiella* sp. Resistance in *H. influenzae* and *Neisseria gonorrhoeae* that produce TEM beta-lactamases is rare since these organisms produce only a small quantity of enzyme and are very permeable to the inhibitor.

Clavulanate is a potent inhibitor of plasmid-mediated enzymes, most commonly found in Enterobacteriaceae. However, all beta-lactamases are not equally susceptible. The class I beta-lactamases of the Richmond-Sykes classification are often resistant, including beta-lactamases typically produced by *Enterobacter*, *Citrobacter*, and *Serratia* species, and *P. aeruginosa*. Clavulanic acid is available as a combined product with both amoxicillin and ticarcillin, resulting in products with broad-spectrum antibacterial activity against beta-lactamase-producing strains of *E. coli*, *H. influenzae*, *Moraxella (Branhamella) catarrhalis*, many *Klebsiella* sp., most *Bacteroides* sp., *Staphylococcus aureus*, and *Staphylococcus epidermidis*, except methicillin-resistant staphylococcal strains. Combining ticarcillin with clavulanic acid increases the activity of ticarcillin to include 60 to 80% of ticarcillin-resistant strains of Enterobacteriaceae and all beta-lactamase-producing strains of *S. aureus*, *H. influenzae*, and *Bacteroides* sp. No increase in activity is provided against *P. aeruginosa*.

Sulbactam also inhibits many beta-lactamases, including those produced by *Bacteroides*, *Haemophilus*, and *Klebsiella* sp., and *N. gonorrhoeae*, but it appears to be less potent than clavulanic acid against several beta-lactamases, including staphylococcal beta-lactamases, TEM-type enzymes, especially strains of *E. coli* and other pathogens producing TEM-1 and TEM-2 beta-lactamases, and the beta-lactamases typically present in *Bacteroides fragilis*.

Tazobactam also has a broad spectrum of activity, and appears to be at least as effective as clavulanic acid against a wide variety of beta-lactamases. Tazobactam may have greater activity than clavulanate against some Enterobacteriaceae class I chromosomally mediated beta-lactamases, such as those of *Morganella morganii*, *E. coli*, *Klebsiella pneumoniae*, *Citrobacter diversus*, *Proteus mirabilis*, *Providencia stuartii*, and *P. aeruginosa*. Both tazobactam and clavulanate have greater activity against these organisms than sulbactam has. The piperacillin and tazobactam combination also has good activity against staphylococci, streptococci, *H. influenzae*, *Moraxella catarrhalis*, *Enterococcus faecalis*, and *Listeria monocytogenes*. Greater resistance was seen with *Enterococcus faecium*, *Enterobacter* sp., *Citrobacter freundii*, *Serratia* sp., and *Xanthomonas maltophilia*.

Accepted

Bone and joint infections (treatment)—Ticarcillin and clavulanate combination and [ampicillin and sulbactam combination][1] are indicated in the treatment of bone and joint infections caused by susceptible organisms.

Intra-abdominal infections (treatment)—Ampicillin and sulbactam combination, piperacillin and tazobactam combination, and ticarcillin and clavulanate combination are indicated in the treatment of intra-abdominal infections caused by susceptible organisms.

Otitis media, acute (treatment)—Amoxicillin and clavulanate combination is indicated in the treatment of acute otitis media caused by susceptible organisms.

Pelvic infections, female (treatment)—Ampicillin and sulbactam combination, piperacillin and tazobactam combination, and ticarcillin and clavulanate combination are indicated in the treatment of female pelvic infections caused by susceptible organisms.

Pneumonia, bacterial (treatment)—Amoxicillin and clavulanate combination, piperacillin and tazobactam combination, and ticarcillin and clavulanate combination are indicated in the treatment of bacterial pneumonia caused by susceptible organisms.

Pneumonia, nosocomial (treatment)—Piperacillin and tazobactam combination is indicated in the treatment of nosocomial pneumonia caused by susceptible organisms.

Septicemia, bacterial (treatment)—Ticarcillin and clavulanate combination and [piperacillin and tazobactam combination][1] are indicated in the treatment of bacterial septicemia caused by susceptible organisms.

Sinusitis (treatment)—Amoxicillin and clavulanate combination is indicated in the treatment of sinusitis caused by susceptible organisms.

Skin and soft tissue infections (treatment)—Amoxicillin and clavulanate combination, ampicillin and sulbactam combination, piperacillin and tazobactam combination, and ticarcillin and clavulanate combination are indicated in the treatment of skin and soft tissue infections caused by susceptible organisms.

Urinary tract infections, bacterial (treatment)—Amoxicillin and clavulanate combination and ticarcillin and clavulanate combination are indicated in the treatment of bacterial urinary tract infections caused by susceptible organisms.

[Bronchitis (treatment)][1]—Amoxicillin and clavulanate combination is used in the treatment of bronchitis caused by susceptible organisms.

[Chancroid (treatment)][1]—Amoxicillin and clavulanate combination is used in the treatment of chancroid caused by *Haemophilus ducreyi*.

[Gonorrhea, endocervical and urethral (treatment)][1]—Ampicillin and sulbactam combination is used in the treatment of uncomplicated endocervical and urethral gonorrhea caused by *Neisseria gonorrhoeae*.

[Perioperative infection prophylaxis for colorectal surgery, abdominal hysterectomy, and high-risk cesarean section]—Ticarcillin and clavulanate combination is used prophylactically to help prevent perioperative infections that may result from colorectal surgery, abdominal hysterectomy, and high-risk cesarean section; however, other agents (i.e., cefazolin for hysterectomy and high-risk cesarean section, and neomycin plus erythromycin base for colorectal surgery) are preferred for use as perioperative prophylaxis in these procedures.

Unaccepted

Piperacillin and tazobactam combination should not be used for the treatment of complicated urinary tract infections because of inadequate efficacy at the usual dose (3.375 grams every six hours).

---

[1]Not included in Canadian product labeling.

Pharmacology/Pharmacokinetics

Physicochemical characteristics

Source—
- Clavulanate: Naturally occurring compound produced by *Streptomyces clavuligerus*.
- Sulbactam: Synthetic penicillanic acid sulfone.
- Tazobactam: Analog of sulbactam.

Chemical Group—
- Amoxicillin: Aminopenicillin.
- Ampicillin: Aminopenicillin.
- Piperacillin: Acylureidopenicillin.
- Ticarcillin: Carboxypenicillin.

Molecular weight—
- Amoxicillin: 419.46.
- Ampicillin sodium: 371.39.
- Clavulanate potassium: 237.25.
- Piperacillin sodium: 539.55.
- Sulbactam sodium: 255.23.
- Tazobactam sodium: 322.28.
- Ticarcillin disodium: 428.4.

Mechanism of action/Effect

Penicillins—Bactericidal; inhibit bacterial cell wall synthesis. Action is dependent on the ability of penicillins to reach and bind penicillin-binding proteins (PBPs) located on the inner membrane of the bacterial cell wall. PBPs (which include transpeptidases, carboxypeptidases, and endopeptidases) are enzymes that are involved in the terminal stages of assembling the bacterial cell wall and in reshaping the cell wall during growth and division. Penicillins bind to, and inactivate, PBPs, resulting in the weakening of the bacterial cell wall and lysis.

Beta-lactamase inhibitors—Act by irreversibly binding to the beta-lactamase enzyme, preventing hydrolysis of the beta-lactam ring of the penicillin. The inhibitor first forms a noncovalent complex, which is fully reversible, with a beta-lactam agent. Beta-lactamase inhibitors then act by recognizing the serine residue at the active site of the beta-lactamase enzyme. The structure of the inhibitor is opened and a covalent acyl-enzyme complex is formed with the serine residue. This prevents the beta-lactamase enzyme from hydrolyzing the penicillin and the liberation of the beta-lactamase enzyme.

Absorption

Amoxicillin and clavulanate are both well absorbed after oral administration and are stable in the presence of gastric acid. This combination product may be given without regard to meals; however, the absorption of clavulanate is greater when taken with food than in a fasting state. Oral bioavailability of amoxicillin and clavulanic acid is approximately 90% and 75%, respectively. Orally administered sulbactam is poorly absorbed.

Distribution

The penicillins and beta-lactamase inhibitors are widely distributed to most tissues and body fluids, including peritoneal fluid, blister fluid, urine (high concentrations), pleural fluid, middle ear fluid, intestinal mucosa, bone, gallbladder, lung, female reproductive tissues, and bile. Distribution into the cerebrospinal fluid (CSF) is low in subjects with noninflamed meninges, as is penetration into purulent bronchial secretions.

Penicillins also cross the placenta and are distributed into breast milk.

Volume of distribution (Vol_D)—
- Amoxicillin: 0.36 L/kg.
- Ampicillin: 0.29 L/kg.
- Piperacillin: 0.23 L/kg.
- Ticarcillin: 0.16 L/kg.

Protein binding

Amoxicillin—Low (17 to 20%).
Ampicillin—Low (20 to 28%).
Clavulanic acid—Low (22 to 30%).
Piperacillin—Low (Approximately 16 to 30%).
Sulbactam—Moderate (38%).
Tazobactam—Low (Approximately 30%).
Ticarcillin—Moderate (45 to 60%).

Biotransformation

Hepatic—
- Amoxicillin: Approximately 10% of a dose is metabolized.
- Ampicillin: Approximately 10% of a dose is metabolized to inactive penicilloic acid.
- Clavulanic acid: Less than 50% of a dose is metabolized.
- Piperacillin: Metabolized to the desethyl metabolite, which has minor activity.
- Sulbactam: Less than 25% of a dose is metabolized.
- Tazobactam: Metabolized to a single, inactive metabolite.
- Ticarcillin: Less than 15% of a dose is metabolized.

Half-life

Normal renal function—
- Amoxicillin: Approximately 1.3 hours.
- Ampicillin: Approximately 1 hour.
- Clavulanic acid: Approximately 1 hour.
- Piperacillin: 0.7 to 1.2 hours.
- Sulbactam: Approximately 1 hour.
- Tazobactam: 0.7 to 1.2 hours.
- Ticarcillin: to 1.2 hours.

Impaired renal function (severe)—
- Amoxicillin: Approximately 12 hours.
- Ampicillin: 9 to 19 hours.
- Clavulanate: Approximately 3 hours.
- Piperacillin: 1.4 to 2.8 hours.
- Sulbactam: Approximately 9 hours.
- Tazobactam: 2.8 to 4.8 hours.
- Ticarcillin: Approximately 9 hours.

Time to peak serum concentration

Amoxicillin and clavulanic acid combination—1 to 2 hours.
Ampicillin and sulbactam combination—End of infusion.
Piperacillin and tazobactam combination—End of infusion.
Ticarcillin and clavulanate combination—End of infusion.

Peak serum concentration

Amoxicillin and clavulanic acid combination—
- Chewable tablets and oral suspension: Approximately 6.9 mcg per mL (mcg/mL) amoxicillin and 1.6 mcg/mL clavulanic acid after an oral dose of 250 mg amoxicillin and 62.5 mg clavulanic acid.
- Tablets (film-coated): Approximately 4.4 to 4.7 mcg/mL amoxicillin and 2.3 to 2.5 mcg/mL clavulanic acid after an oral dose of 250 mg amoxicillin and 125 mg clavulanic acid.

Ampicillin and sulbactam combination—
- Intramuscular: Approximately 8 to 35 mcg/mL ampicillin and 6 to 25 mcg/mL sulbactam following an intramuscular dose of 1.5 grams (1 gram of ampicillin and 500 mg of sulbactam).
- Intravenous: Approximately 40 to 70 mcg/mL ampicillin and 20 to 40 mcg/mL sulbactam following an intravenous dose of 1.5 grams (1 gram of ampicillin and 500 mg of sulbactam).

Piperacillin and tazobactam combination—
- Approximately 242 mcg/mL piperacillin and 24 mcg/mL tazobactam following an intravenous dose of 3.375 grams (3 grams of piperacillin and 0.375 gram of sulbactam).

Ticarcillin and clavulanic acid combination—
- Approximately 330 mcg/mL ticarcillin and 8 mcg/mL clavulanic acid following an intravenous dose of 3.1 grams (3 grams of ticarcillin and 0.1 gram of clavulanic acid).

Elimination

Primarily renal (glomerular filtration and tubular secretion)—

Amoxicillin and clavulanic acid combination:

50 to 78%, and 25 to 40% of an administered dose of amoxicillin and clavulanic acid, respectively, are excreted unchanged in the urine within the first 6 hours after administration.

Ampicillin and sulbactam combination:

75 to 85% of an administered dose of both ampicillin and sulbactam is excreted unchanged in the urine within the first 8 hours after administration.

Piperacillin and tazobactam combination:

Approximately 68% and 80% of an administered dose of piperacillin and tazobactam, respectively, are excreted unchanged in the urine.

Ticarcillin and clavulanic acid combination:

60 to 70%, and 35 to 45% of an administered dose of ticarcillin and clavulanic acid, respectively, are excreted unchanged in the urine within the first 6 hours after administration.

Biliary—

Ampicillin and sulbactam:

Less than 1%.

Piperacillin and tazobactam combination:

Less than 2%.

In dialysis—

Hemodialysis:

Hemodialysis removes amoxicillin, ampicillin, clavulanate, piperacillin, sulbactam, tazobactam, and ticarcillin from the blood.

Piperacillin and tazobactam combination—30 to 40% of an administered dose is removed, plus an additional 5% of the tazobactam dose as the metabolite.

Peritoneal dialysis:

Piperacillin and tazobactam combination—6 to 21% of an administered dose is removed, plus an additional 16% of the tazobactam dose as the metabolite.

Precautions to Consider

Cross-sensitivity and/or related problems

Patients allergic to one penicillin may be allergic to other penicillins also.

Patients allergic to cephalosporins, cephamycins, or beta-lactamase inhibitors may be allergic to penicillin and beta-lactamase inhibitor combinations also.

Carcinogenicity

Long-term carcinogenicity studies in animals have not been done on any of the penicillin and beta-lactamase inhibitor combinations.

Mutagenicity

Amoxicillin and clavulanic acid combination—The mutagenic potential of amoxicillin and clavulanic acid combination was studied *in vitro* with an Ames test, a human lymphocyte cytogenetic assay, a yeast test, and a mouse lymphoma forward mutation assay, and *in vivo* with mouse micronucleus tests and a dominant lethal test. All results were negative with the exception of the *in vitro* mouse lymphoma assay, in which weak activity was found at very high, cytotoxic concentrations.

Ampicillin and sulbactam combination—Long-term studies in animals have not been done to evaluate the mutagenic potential of this combination.

Piperacillin and tazobactam combination—Microbial mutagenicity studies with piperacillin and tazobactam combination at concentrations of up to 14.84 and 1.86 mcg, respectively, per plate were negative. Negative results were also found in the unscheduled DNA synthesis (UDS) test at concentrations of up to 5689 and 711 mcg per mL (mcg/mL), respectively, in the mammalian point mutation (Chinese hamster ovary cell HPRT) assay at concentrations of up to 8000 and 1000 mcg/mL, respectively, and in the mammalian cell (BALB/c-3T3) transformation assay at concentrations of up to 8 and 1 mcg/mL, respectively. *In vivo*, piperacillin and tazobactam combination did not induce chromosomal aberrations in rats administered intravenous doses of 1500 and 187.5 mg per kg of body weight (mg/kg), respectively; this dose is similar to the maximum recommended human daily dose based on mg per square meter of body surface area (mg/m^2).

Ticarcillin and clavulanic acid combination—Studies performed *in vitro* and *in vivo* did not indicate a potential for mutagenicity.

Pregnancy/Reproduction

Fertility—*Amoxicillin and clavulanic acid combination:* Studies in rats given doses of up to 5.7 times the usual human dose (dosed with a 2:1 ratio formulation of amoxicillin:clavulanate) have not shown that amoxicillin and clavulanate combination impairs fertility.

Ampicillin and sulbactam combination: Studies in mice, rats, and rabbits given doses of up to 10 times the human dose have not shown that ampicillin and sulbactam combination adversely affects fertility.

Piperacillin and tazobactam combination: Reproduction studies in rats revealed no evidence of impaired fertility when piperacillin and tazobactam combination was administered at doses similar to the maximum recommended human daily dose based on body surface area (mg/m^2). There was also no evidence of impaired fertility when tazobactam was administered at doses of up to three times the maximum recommended human daily dose based on body surface area (mg/m^2).

Ticarcillin and clavulanic acid combination: Studies in rats given daily doses of up to 1050 mg/kg have not shown that ticarcillin and clavulanate combination impairs fertility.

Pregnancy—Penicillins cross the placenta. Clavulanic acid also crosses the placenta. Adequate and well-controlled studies in humans have not been done; however, problems in humans have not been documented.

Amoxicillin and clavulanate combination: Studies in rats and mice given oral dosages of up to 1200 mg per kg of body weight per day, equivalent to 7200 and 4080 mg per square meter of body surface area per day, respectively (4.9 and 2.8 times the maximum human oral dose, based on body surface area), caused no adverse effects in the fetus.

FDA Pregnancy Category B.

Ampicillin and sulbactam combination: Studies in mice, rats, and rabbits given doses of up to 10 times the human dose have not shown that ampicillin and sulbactam combination causes adverse effects in the fetus.

FDA Pregnancy Category B.

Piperacillin and tazobactam combination: Teratology studies performed in mice and rats given piperacillin and tazobactam combination at doses one to two times, respectively, the human dose based on body surface area (mg/m^2) revealed no evidence of harm to the fetus. In addition, no evidence of harm to the fetus was found when tazobactam was administered to mice and rats at doses of up to 6 and 14 times the human dose, respectively, based on body surface area (mg/m^2). Tazobactam crosses the placenta in mice; concentrations in the fetus are 10% or less of those found in maternal plasma.

FDA Pregnancy Category B.

Ticarcillin and clavulanate combination: Studies in rats given daily doses of up to 1050 mg/kg have not shown that ticarcillin and clavulanate combination causes adverse effects in the fetus.

FDA Pregnancy Category B.

Labor and delivery—*Amoxicillin and clavulanate combination and ampicillin and sulbactam combination:* Oral ampicillin class antibiotics generally are poorly absorbed during labor. Studies in guinea pigs have shown that intravenous administration of ampicillin decreased the uterine tone, the frequency of contractions, the height of contractions, and the duration of contractions. However, it is not known whether the use of these medications in humans during labor or delivery has any immediate or delayed adverse effects on the fetus, prolongs the duration of labor, or increases the likelihood that forceps delivery or other obstetrical intervention or resuscitation of the newborn will be necessary.

Breast-feeding

Penicillins and sulbactam are distributed into breast milk in low concentrations; it is not known whether clavulanic acid and tazobactam are distributed into breast milk. Although significant problems in humans have not been documented, the use of penicillins by nursing mothers may lead to sensitization, diarrhea, candidiasis, and skin rash in the infant.

Pediatrics

Many penicillins have been used in pediatric patients, and no pediatrics-specific problems have been documented to date. However, the incompletely developed renal function of neonates and young infants may delay the excretion of renally eliminated penicillins.

Amoxicillin and clavulanate combination: The 200-mg and the 400-mg chewable tablets contain 2.1 mg and 4.2 mg phenylalanine, respectively, produced through the metabolism of aspartame. The 200-mg-per-5 mL and the 400-mg-per-5 mL strengths of the oral suspension contain 7 mg of phenylalanine per 5 mL. These dosage forms should be used with caution, if at all, in patients with phenylketonuria. The other strengths and dosage forms of amoxicillin and clavulanate combination do not contain phenylalanine.

Piperacillin and tazobactam combination: Although safety and efficacy have not been established in pediatric patients, the results of one study found the clearance and elimination half-life to be increased in infants < 6 months of age. Piperacillin and tazobactam combination had no effect on bilirubin-albumin binding *in vitro* .

Geriatrics

Penicillins have been used in geriatric patients and no geriatrics-specific problems have been documented to date. However, elderly patients are more likely to have an age-related decrease in renal function, which may require an adjustment in dosage in patients receiving penicillins.

Dental

Prolonged use of penicillins may lead to the development of oral candidiasis.

Drug interactions and/or related problems

The following drug interactions and/or related problems have been selected on the basis of their potential clinical significance (possible mechanism in parentheses where appropriate)—not necessarily inclusive (» = major clinical significance):

Note: Combinations containing any of the following medications, depending on the amount present, may also interact with this medication.

Allopurinol
(concurrent use with ampicillin may significantly increase the possibility of skin rash, especially in hyperuricemic patients; however, it has not been established that allopurinol, rather than the presence of hyperuricemia, is responsible for this effect)

Aminoglycosides
(concurrent administration of piperacillin and tazobactam combination with tobramycin decreased the urinary recovery of tobramycin by 38%; concurrent administration of tobramycin and ticarcillin resulted in a decrease in serum tobramycin concentration by 11%)

» Anticoagulants, coumarin- or indanedione-derivative or
» Heparin or
» Thrombolytic agents
(concurrent use of these medications with high-dose piperacillin or ticarcillin may increase the risk of hemorrhage because these penicillins inhibit platelet aggregation; patients should be monitored carefully for signs of bleeding; concurrent use of piperacillin or ticarcillin with thrombolytic agents may increase the risk of severe hemorrhage and is not recommended; increases in prothrombin time have been reported in patients taking amoxicillin and clavulanate combination concurrently with anticoagulants)

» Anti-inflammatory drugs, nonsteroidal (NSAIDs), especially aspirin or Diflunisal, very high doses or
Other salicylates or
» Platelet aggregation inhibitors, other (see *Appendix II*) or
» Sulfinpyrazone
(concurrent use of these medications with high-dose piperacillin or ticarcillin may increase the risk of hemorrhage because of additive inhibition of platelet function; in addition, hypoprothrombinemia induced by large doses of salicylates and the gastrointestinal ulcerative or hemorrhagic potential of NSAIDs, salicylates, or sulfinpyrazone may also increase the risk of hemorrhage when these medicines are used concurrently with piperacillin or ticarcillin)

Chloramphenicol or
Erythromycins or
Sulfonamides or
Tetracyclines
(since bacteriostatic drugs may interfere with the bactericidal effect of penicillins in the treatment of meningitis or in other situations in which a rapid bactericidal effect is necessary, it is best to avoid concurrent therapy; however, chloramphenicol and ampicillin are sometimes administered concurrently in pediatric patients)

» Oral contraceptives
(as with other broad spectrum antibiotics, penicillins and beta-lactamase inhibitors may decrease the efficacy of oral contraceptives)

» Probenecid
(probenecid decreases renal tubular secretion of penicillins, sulbactam, and tazobactam [but not clavulanic acid, which is cleared primarily by glomerular filtration] when used concurrently; this effect results in increased and more prolonged serum concentrations, prolonged elimination half-life [half-life of piperacillin increased by 21%, that of tazobactam by 71%, and that of sulbactam by 40%], and increased risk of toxicity. Penicillins and probenecid are often used concurrently to treat sexually transmitted diseases [STDs] or other infections in which high and/or prolonged antibiotic serum and tissue concentrations are required)

Vecuronium or
Nondepolarizing muscle relaxants, other
(concurrent use with piperacillin and tazobactam combination may prolong neuromuscular blockade)

Laboratory value alterations

The following have been selected on the basis of their potential clinical significance (possible effect in parentheses where appropriate)—not necessarily inclusive (» = major clinical significance).

With diagnostic test results

» Glucose, urine
(high urinary concentrations of a penicillin may produce false-positive or falsely elevated test results with copper-reduction tests [Benedict's, *Clinitest*, or Fehling's]; glucose enzymatic tests [*Clinistix* or *Testape*] are not affected)

Direct antiglobulin (Coombs') tests
(false-positive result may occur during therapy with any penicillin)

Protein, urine
(high urinary concentrations of piperacillin or ticarcillin may produce false-positive protein reactions [pseudoproteinuria] with the sulfosalicylic acid and boiling test, the acetic acid test, the biuret reaction, and the nitric acid test; bromophenol blue reagent test strips [*Multi-stix*] are reportedly unaffected)

With physiology/laboratory test values

Alanine aminotransferase (ALT [SGPT]) and
Alkaline phosphatase and
Aspartate aminotransferase (AST [SGOT]) and
Lactate dehydrogenase (LDH), serum
(values may be increased)

Bilirubin, serum
(concentrations may be increased)

Blood urea nitrogen (BUN) and
Creatinine, serum
(increased concentrations have been associated with ampicillin and sulbactam, piperacillin, and ticarcillin)

Estradiol or
Estriol, total conjugated or
Estriol-glucuronide or
Estrone, conjugated
(concentrations may be decreased transiently in pregnant women following administration of amoxicillin and ampicillin)

Hematocrit or
Hemoglobin concentrations
(may be decreased with the piperacillin and tazobactam combination)

» Partial thromboplastin time (PTT) and
» Prothrombin time (PT)
(an increase has been associated with piperacillin and ticarcillin)

Potassium, serum
(hypokalemia may occur following administration of piperacillin or ticarcillin, either of which may act as a nonreabsorbable anion in the distal renal tubules; this may cause an increase in pH and result in increased urinary potassium loss; the risk of hypokalemia increases with use of larger doses)

Sodium, serum
(hypernatremia may occur following administration of large doses of ticarcillin because of the medication's high sodium content)

Uric acid, serum
(ticarcillin may transiently decrease the serum concentration in some patients)

White blood count
(leukopenia or neutropenia is associated with the use of all penicillins; the effect is more likely to occur with prolonged therapy and severe hepatic function impairment)

Medical considerations/Contraindications

The medical considerations/contraindications included have been selected on the basis of their potential clinical significance (reasons given in parentheses where appropriate)—not necessarily inclusive (» = major clinical significance).

Except under special circumstances, these medications should not be used when the following medical problems exist:

» Allergy to penicillins or beta-lactamase inhibitors
» Cholestatic jaundice, amoxicillin and clavulanate combination–associated, history of or
» Hepatic dysfunction, amoxicillin and clavulanate combination–associated, history of
(severe heptotoxicity resulting in death has occurred with the amoxicillin and clavulanate combination, usually associated with serious underlying diseases or concomitant medications)

Risk-benefit should be considered when the following medical problems exist:

Allergy, general, history of, such as asthma, eczema, hay fever, hives
(serious hypersensitivity reactions are more likely to occur in patients with sensitivity to multiple allergens)

» Allergy to cephalosporins

» Bleeding disorders, history of
(some penicillins, especially piperacillin and ticarcillin, may cause platelet dysfunction and hemorrhage)

» Congestive heart failure (CHF) or
Hypertension
(the sodium content of the parenteral dosage forms of penicillins and beta-lactamase combinations should be considered in patients who require sodium restriction)

» Cystic fibrosis
(patients with cystic fibrosis may be at increased risk for fever and skin rash when given piperacillin)

» Gastrointestinal disease, active or a history of, especially antibiotic-associated colitis
(penicillins may cause pseudomembranous colitis)

» Hepatic dysfunction
(the amoxicillin and clavulanate combination may exacerbate hepatic dysfunction and should be used with caution in these patients; heptotoxicity with this combination is usually reversible; however, rare cases have resulted in death)

» Mononucleosis, infectious
(a morbilliform skin rash may occur in a high percentage of patients taking ampicillin)

» Phenylketonuria
(the 200-mg-per-5 mL and the 400-mg-per-5 mL formulations, as well as the 200-mg and the 400-mg chewable tablets, of amoxicillin and clavulanate combination contain aspartame, which is metabolized to phenylalanine, and may be hazardous to patients with phenylketonuria)

» Renal function impairment
(because most penicillins are excreted through the kidneys, a reduction in dosage, or an increase in dosing interval, is recommended in patients with renal function impairment; also, the sodium content of high doses of ticarcillin should be considered in patients with severe renal function impairment)

Patient monitoring

The following may be especially important in patient monitoring (other tests may be warranted in some patients, depending on condition; » = major clinical significance):

For amoxicillin and clavulanate combination and ticarcillin and clavulanate
Hepatic function and
Renal function
(periodic monitoring is advisable during prolonged therapy)

For amoxicillin and clavulanate combination, piperacillin and tazobactam combination, and ticarcillin and clavulanate combination
Hematopoietic function
(periodic monitoring is advisable during prolonged therapy)

For piperacillin and tazobactam combination and ticarcillin and clavulanate combination
» Partial thromboplastin time (PTT) and
» Prothrombin time (PT)
(may be required prior to and during prolonged therapy in patients with renal function impairment who are receiving high doses, since hemorrhagic manifestations may occur, although the effect is rare)
Potassium, serum
(determinations may be required periodically during therapy in patients with low potassium reserves and in patients receiving cytotoxic medications or diuretics, since hypokalemia may occur)

For all penicillin and beta-lactamase inhibitor combinations (if Clostridium difficile colitis occurs)
» Stool toxin assays
(enzyme immunoassay of stool samples for the presence of *C. difficile* toxins may be required prior to treatment of patients with antibiotic-associated colitis to document the presence of *C. difficile* toxins; however, *C. difficile* and its toxins may persist following treatment with oral vancomycin, metronidazole, or cholestyramine, despite clinical improvement; follow-up cultures and toxin assays are not recommended if clinical improvement is complete)

Side/Adverse Effects

The following side/adverse effects have been selected on the basis of their potential clinical significance (possible signs and symptoms in parentheses where appropriate)—not necessarily inclusive:

Those indicating need for medical attention

Incidence less frequent
Allergic reactions, specifically anaphylaxis (fast or irregular breathing; puffiness or swelling around face; shortness of breath; sudden, severe decrease in blood pressure); ***elevated liver function tests; oral candidiasis*** (sore mouth or tongue; white patches in mouth and/or on tongue); ***serum sickness-like reactions*** (skin rash; joint pain; fever); ***skin rash, hives, or itching***; ***thrombophlebitis*** (pain, redness, and swelling at site of injection); ***vaginal candidiasis*** (vaginal itching and discharge)

Incidence rare
Chest pain; clostridium difficile colitis (severe abdominal or stomach cramps and pain; abdominal tenderness; watery and severe diarrhea, which may also be bloody; fever); ***dysuria or urinary retention*** (trouble in urinating); ***edema*** (swelling of face, fingers, lower legs, or feet; weight gain); ***erythema multiforme or Stevens-Johnson syndrome*** (blistering, peeling, or loosening of skin and mucous membranes; fever; malaise [general feeling of illness or discomfort; red skin lesions, often with a purple center); ***hepatic dysfunction, including cholestatic hepatitis*** (abdominal pain; nausea or vomiting; yellow eyes or skin); ***glossitis*** (redness, swelling, or soreness of tongue); ***leukopenia or neutropenia*** (sore throat and fever); ***platelet dysfunction*** (unusual bleeding or bruising); ***proteinuria or pyuria*** (cloudy urine); ***seizures; toxic epidermal necrolysis*** (blistering, peeling, loosening of skin; chills; cough; diarrhea; itching; joint or muscle pain; red, irritated eyes; red skin lesions, often with a purple center; sore throat; sores, ulcers, or white spots in mouth or on lips; unusual tiredness or weakness)

Note: *Platelet dysfunction* is primarily associated with piperacillin and ticarcillin.

Clotridium difficile colitis may occur up to several weeks after discontinuation of these medications.

Seizures are more likely to occur in patients receiving high doses of a penicillin and/or patients with severe renal function impairment.

Those indicating need for medical attention only if they continue or are bothersome

Incidence more frequent
Gastrointestinal reactions (gas; mild diarrhea; nausea or vomiting; stomach pain; swelling of abdomen); ***headache***

Incidence rare
Chills; epistaxis (nosebleed); ***fatigue*** (unusual tiredness or weakness); ***malaise*** (general feeling of discomfort or illness); ***prolonged muscle relaxation***—with piperacillin and tazobactam combination

Overdose

For specific information on the agents used in the management of penicillins and beta-lactamase inhibitors overdose, see:
- *Barbiturates (Systemic)* monograph and/or
- Diazepam in *Benzodiazepines (Systemic)* monograph.

For more information on the management of overdose or unintentional ingestion, **contact a Poison Control Center** (see *Poison Control Center Listing*).

Treatment of overdose

Since there is no specific antidote, treatment of penicillin overdose should be symptomatic and supportive.

If motor excitability or convulsions occur, general supportive measures, including the administration of anticonvulsive agents (e.g., diazepam or barbiturates) may be considered.

Specific treatment—Hemodialysis may aid in the removal of penicillins from the blood.

Supportive care—Patients in whom intentional overdose is confirmed or suspected should be referred for psychiatric consultation.

Patient Consultation

As an aid to patient consultation, refer to *Advice for the Patient, Penicillins and Beta-lactamase Inhibitors (Systemic)*.

In providing consultation, consider emphasizing the following selected information (» = major clinical significance):

Before using this medication

» Conditions affecting use, especially:
Allergy to penicillins, cephalosporins, cephamycins, or beta-lactamase inhibitors
Pregnancy—Penicillins and clavulanic acid cross the placenta
Breast-feeding—Penicillins and sulbactam are distributed into breast milk.
Use in children—Neonates and young infants may have reduced elimination of renally eliminated penicillins due to incompletely developed renal function; aspartame-containing amoxicillin and clavulanate combination products should be used with caution, if at all, in patients with phenylketonuria
Other medications, especially aminoglycosides; coumarin- or indanedione-derivative anticoagulants; heparin; nonsteroidal

anti-inflammatory drugs (NSAIDs), especially aspirin; oral contraceptives; other platelet aggregation inhibitors; probenecid; sulfinpyrazone; or thrombolytic agents

Other medical problems, especially a history of bleeding disorders; cholestatic jaundice; congestive heart failure; cystic fibrosis; active or history of gastrointestinal disease, especially antibiotic-associated colitis; hepatic dysfunction; infectious mononucleosis; phenylketonuria; or renal function impairment

Proper use of this medication

Taking amoxicillin and clavulanate combination on a full or empty stomach; administration with food may decrease the incidence of gastrointestinal side effects (diarrhea, nausea, and vomiting)

Proper administration technique for oral liquids: Using a specially marked measuring spoon or other device to measure each dose

Not using after expiration date

Chewing or crushing chewable tablets before swallowing

» Importance of taking at evenly spaced times and not missing doses

» Proper dosing

Missed dose: Taking as soon as possible; not taking if almost time for next dose; not doubling doses

» Proper storage

Precautions while using this medication

Checking with physician if no improvement within a few days or if symptoms become worse

» For severe diarrhea, checking with physician before taking any antidiarrheals; for mild diarrhea, kaolin- or attapulgite-containing, but not other, antidiarrheals may be tried; checking with physician or pharmacist if mild diarrhea continues or worsens

» Patients with diabetes: False-positive reactions with copper sulfate urine glucose tests may occur, especially with amoxicillin and clavulanate, ampicillin and sulbactam, and piperacillin and tazobactam combinations

Possible interference with diagnostic tests

Side/adverse effects

Signs of potential side effects, especially allergic reactions; oral candidiasis; serum sickness-like reactions; skin rash, hives, or itching; thrombophlebitis; vaginal candidiasis; chest pain; clostridium difficile colitis; dysuria or urinary retention; edema; erythema multiforme or Stevens-Johnson syndrome; hepatic dysfunction; glossitis; leukopenia or neutropenia; platelet dysfunction; and seizures

General Dosing Information

As with other antibacterials, the possiblility of superinfection with mycotic or bacterial pathogens should be kept in mind during therapy with a penicillin and beta-lactamase inhibitor combination. If superinfection occurs, the penicillin and beta-lactamase inhibitor combination should be discontinued and appropriate treatment instituted.

Appropriate culture and susceptibility tests should be performed before treatment with a penicillin and beta-lactamase inhibitor combination in order to isolate and identify the organism(s) causing infection and determine their susceptibility to antimicrobials. Once the results of culture and antimicrobial testing are known, therapy should be adjusted as appropriate.

There are insufficient data to support the use of ticarcillin and clavulanate combination in the treatment of septicemia or infections in pediatric patients when the suspected or proven pathogen is *Haemophilus influenzae* type b.

For oral dosage forms only

Amoxicillin and clavulanate combination may be taken on a full or empty stomach. Administration with food may decrease the incidence of gastrointestinal side effects (diarrhea, nausea, and vomiting).

For treatment of adverse effects

Serious anaphylactoid reactions require immediate emergency treatment, which consists of the following:

- Parenteral epinephrine.
- Oxygen.
- Intravenous corticosteroids.
- Airway management (including intubation).

For *Clostridium difficile* colitis—

• Some patients may develop *C. difficile* colitis during or following administration of penicillins.

• *C. difficile* colitis may result in severe watery diarrhea, which may occur during therapy or up to several weeks after therapy is discontinued. If diarrhea occurs, administration of antiperistaltic antidiarrheals (e.g., opioids, diphenoxylate and atropine combination, loperamide, paregoric) is not recommended since they may delay the removal of toxins from the colon, thereby prolonging and/or worsening the condition.

• Mild cases may respond to discontinuation of the medication alone. Moderate to severe cases may require fluid, electrolyte, and protein replacement.

• In cases not responding to the above measures or in more severe cases, oral doses of vancomycin, metronidazole, or cholestyramine may be used. Oral vancomycin is effective in doses of 125 mg every 6 hours for 5 to 10 days. The dose of metronidazole is 250 to 500 mg every 8 hours, and the dose of cholestyramine is 4 grams four times a day. Recurrences, which occur in approximately 25% of patients treated with vancomycin or metronidazole, may be treated with a second course of these medications.

• Cholestyramine resin has been shown to bind *C. difficile* toxin *in vitro* . If cholestyramine resin is administered in conjunction with oral vancomycin, the medications should be administered several hours apart since the resin has been shown to bind oral vancomycin also.

AMOXICILLIN AND CLAVULANATE

Summary of Differences

Precautions:

Pediatrics—Patients with phenylketonuria should be aware that the 200-mg and the 400-mg chewable tablets contain 2.1 mg and 4.2 mg phenylalanine, respectively, as a component of aspartame. The 200-mg-per-5-mL and the 400-mg-per-5-mL strengths of the oral suspension contain 7 mg of phenyalanine. Other dosage forms and strengths do not contain aspartame.

Drug interactions and/or related problems—Clavulanic acid does not interact with probenecid.

Laboratory value alterations—Amoxicillin may decrease total conjugated estriol, estriol-glucuronide, conjugated estrone, and estradiol concentrations in pregnant women.

Medical considerations/Contraindications—Hepatic dysfunction and phenylketonuria.

Patient monitoring—Periodic monitoring of hepatic function and renal function is advisable during prolonged therapy.

Additional Dosing Information

Amoxicillin and clavulanate combination may be taken on a full or empty stomach. However, clavulanate absorption is greater when administered at the beginning of a meal. Also, administration with food may decrease the incidence of gastrointestinal side effects (diarrhea, nausea, and vomiting).

Patients with hepatic impairment should be dosed with caution and hepatic function should be monitored at regular intervals.

Severe diarrhea has been reported less frequently when amoxicillin and clavulanate combination is dosed every twelve hours compared with every eight hours.

The 200-mg-per-5 mL and the 400-mg-per-5 mL formulations of amoxicillin and clavulanate oral suspension, as well as the 200-mg and the 400-mg chewable tablets, contain phenylalanine.

Amoxicillin and clavulanate 250-mg tablets and 250-mg chewable tablets do not contain the same amount of clavulanate. The 250-mg tablets contain 125 mg of clavulanate, and the 250-mg chewable tablets contain 62.5 mg of clavulanate. Therefore, these products should not be substituted for each other or used interchangeably. This is important to ensure that there is a sufficient concentration of clavulanate at the site of infection to inhibit the beta-lactamase that is present.

Because the 250-mg tablet and the 250-mg chewable tablet have different amoxicillin-to-clavulanic acid ratios, the 250-mg tablet should not be used in children who weigh less than 40 kg.

Since the 250-mg and the 500-mg strengths of amoxicillin and clavulanate combination tablets contain the same amount of clavulanate (125 mg), two 250-mg tablets are not equivalent to one 500-mg tablet.

Patients with impaired renal function generally do not require dosage reduction unless the renal impairment is severe. Adults and adolescents with severely impaired renal function may receive 500 mg or 250 mg with the dosing interval increased as follows:

Creatinine clearance (mL/min)/(mL/sec)	Dosing interval (hours)
$>$ 30/0.5	8
10–30/0.17–0.5	12
$<$ 10/$<$ 0.17	24

Patients on hemodialysis should receive 500 mg or 250 mg every 24 hours, depending on the severity of the infection. They should receive an additional dose both during and at the end of dialysis.

Patients with severe renal impairment (glomerular filtration rate $<$ 30 mL per minute) should not receive the 875-mg tablet.

Oral Dosage Forms

Note: Bracketed uses in the *Dosage Forms* section refer to categories of use and/or indications that are not included in U.S. product labeling.

AMOXICILLIN AND CLAVULANATE POTASSIUM FOR ORAL SUSPENSION USP

Usual adult and adolescent dose

Antibacterial—

Pneumonia and other severe infections—

Oral, 875 mg of amoxicillin and 125 mg of clavulanic acid every twelve hours or 500 mg of amoxicillin and 125 mg of clavulanic acid every eight hours.

Other infections—

Oral, 500 mg of amoxicillin and 125 mg of clavulanic acid every twelve hours or 250 mg of amoxicillin and 125 mg of clavulanic acid every eight hours.

Note: Adults who have difficulty swallowing may be given the 125-mg-per-5 mL or the 250-mg-per-5 mL formulation of oral suspension in place of the 500-mg tablet. The 200-mg-per-5 mL or the 400-mg-per-5 mL formulation of oral suspension may be used in place of the 875-mg tablet.

Usual pediatric dose

Antibacterial—

Dosage is based on the amoxicillin component.

Neonates and infants up to 12 weeks (3 months) of age—

Oral, 15 mg of amoxicillin per kg of body weight every twelve hours.

Note: Use of the formulation containing 125 mg of amoxicillin per 5 mL of oral suspension is recommended by the manufacturer since experience is limited with the 200-mg-per-5 mL formulation.

Infants 3 months of age and older and children up to 40 kg of body weight—

Otitis media, acute

Pneumonia

Sinusitis

Other severe infections—

Oral, 22.5 mg of amoxicillin per kg of body weight every twelve hours (using the formulation containing either 200 mg of amoxicillin per 5 mL or 400 mg of amoxicillin per 5 mL) or 13.3 mg of amoxicillin per kg of body weight every eight hours (using the formulation containing either 125 mg of amoxicillin per 5 mL or 250 mg of amoxicillin per 5 mL).

Less severe infections—Oral, 12.5 mg of amoxicillin per kg of body weight every twelve hours (using the formulation containing either 200 mg of amoxicillin per 5 mL or 400 mg of amoxicillin per 5 mL) or 6.7 mg of amoxicillin per kg of body weight every eight hours (using the formulation containing either 125 mg of amoxicillin per 5 mL or 250 mg of amoxicillin per 5 mL).

Children weighing more than 40 kg of body weight—

See *Usual adult and adolescent dose*.

Strength(s) usually available

U.S.—

125 mg of amoxicillin and 31.25 mg of clavulanic acid per 5 mL (when reconstituted according to manufacturer's instructions) (Rx) [*Augmentin*].

200 mg of amoxicillin and 28.5 mg of clavulanic acid per 5 mL (when reconstituted according to manufacturer's instructions) (Rx) [*Augmentin* (aspartame)].

250 mg of amoxicillin and 62.5 mg of clavulanic acid per 5 mL (when reconstituted according to manufacturer's instructions) (Rx) [*Augmentin*].

400 mg of amoxicillin and 57 mg of clavulanic acid per 5 mL (when reconstituted according to manufacturer's instructions) (Rx) [*Augmentin* (aspartame)].

Note: The amoxicillin and clavulanate combination products with 200 mg of amoxicillin per 5 mL of oral suspension and 400 mg of amoxicillin per 5 mL contain 7 mg of phenylalanine per 5 mL, as a component of aspartame.

Canada—

125 mg of amoxicillin and 31.25 mg of clavulanic acid per 5 mL (when reconstituted according to manufacturer's instructions) (Rx) [*Clavulin-125F*].

250 mg of amoxicillin and 62.5 mg of clavulanic acid per 5 mL (when reconstituted according to manufacturer's instructions) (Rx) [*Clavulin-250F*].

Packaging and storage

Prior to reconstitution, store at or below 25 °C (77 °F). Store in a tight container.

Stability

After reconstitution, suspensions retain their potency for 10 days if refrigerated.

Auxiliary labeling

- Refrigerate.
- Shake well.
- Continue medication for full time of treatment.
- Beyond-use date.

Note

When dispensing, include a calibrated liquid-measuring device.

AMOXICILLIN AND CLAVULANATE POTASSIUM TABLETS USP

Usual adult and adolescent dose

Antibacterial—

Pneumonia and other severe infections—

Oral, 875 mg of amoxicillin and 125 mg of clavulanic acid every twelve hours or 500 mg of amoxicillin and 125 mg of clavulanic acid every eight hours.

Other infections—

Oral, 500 mg of amoxicillin and 125 mg of clavulanic acid every twelve hours or 250 mg of amoxicillin and 125 mg of clavulanic acid every eight hours.

[Chancroid][1]—

Oral, 500 mg of amoxicillin and 125 mg of clavulanic acid, or 500 mg of amoxicillin and 250 mg of clavulanic acid every eight hours for three to seven days.

Usual pediatric dose

Antibacterial—

Infants and children up to 40 kg of body weight—

See *Amoxicillin and Clavulanate Potassium for Oral Suspension*.

Note: Because the 250-mg tablet and the 250-mg chewable tablet have different amoxicillin-to-clavulanic acid ratios, the 250-mg tablet should not be used in children who weigh less than 40 kg.

Children 40 kg of body weight and over—

See *Usual adult and adolescent dose*.

Strength(s) usually available

U.S.—

250 mg of amoxicillin and 125 mg of clavulanic acid (Rx) [*Augmentin*].

500 mg of amoxicillin and 125 mg of clavulanic acid (Rx) [*Augmentin*].

875 mg of amoxicillin and 125 mg of clauvulanic acid (Rx) [*Augmentin*].

Canada—

250 mg of amoxicillin and 125 mg of clavulanic acid (Rx) [*Clavulin-250*].

500 mg of amoxicillin and 125 mg of clavulanic acid (Rx) [*Clavulin-500F*].

Note: Two 250-mg tablets are not equivalent to one 500-mg tablet since both strengths contain equal amounts of clavulanate potassium.

Packaging and storage

Store at or below 25 °C (77 °F). Store in a tight container.

Auxiliary labeling

- Continue medication for full time of treatment.

AMOXICILLIN AND CLAVULANATE POTASSIUM TABLETS (CHEWABLE) USP

Usual adult and adolescent dose

See *Amoxicillin and Clavulanate Potassium for Oral Suspension*.

Usual pediatric dose

See *Amoxicillin and Clavulanate Potassium for Oral Suspension*.

Strength(s) usually available

U.S.—

125 mg of amoxicillin and 31.25 mg of clavulanic acid (Rx) [*Augmentin*].

200 mg of amoxicillin and 28.5 mg of clavulanic acid (Rx) [*Augmentin* (aspartame [containing 2.1 mg of phenylalanine])].

250 mg of amoxicillin and 62.5 mg of clavulanic acid (Rx) [*Augmentin*].

400 mg of amoxicillin and 57 mg of clavulanic acid (Rx) [*Augmentin* (aspartame [containing 4.2 mg of phenylalanine])].

Canada—

Not commercially available.

Packaging and storage

Store at or below 25 °C (77 °F) Store in a tight container.

Auxiliary labeling

- Should be chewed or crushed.
- Continue medication for full time of treatment.

[1]Not included in Canadian product labeling.

AMPICILLIN AND SULBACTAM

Summary of Differences

Precautions:

Drug interactions and/or related problems—Concurrent use with allopurinol may increase the risk of skin rash.

Laboratory value alterations—Ampicillin may decrease total conjugated estriol, estriol-glucuronide, conjugated estrone, and estradiol concentrations in pregnant women.

Medical considerations/contraindications—Use in patients with infectious mononucleosis may increase the risk of skin rash.

Additional Dosing Information

Ampicillin and sulbactam combination should be administered by deep intramuscular injection or by direct, slow intravenous injection over at least a 10- to 15-minute period. It may also be administered by intravenous infusion in 50 to 100 mL of a suitable diluent over a 15- to 30-minute period.

Adults with impaired renal function may require an increase in the dosing interval as follows:

Creatinine clearance (mL/min)/(mL/sec)	Dosing interval (hours)
≥ 30/0.5	6 to 8
15–29/0.25–0.48	12
5–14/0.08–0.23	24
< 5/0.08	48

Parenteral Dosage Forms

Note: Bracketed uses in the *Dosage Forms* section refer to categories of use and/or indications that are not included in U.S. product labeling.

AMPICILLIN SODIUM AND SULBACTAM SODIUM STERILE USP

Usual adult and adolescent dose

Antibacterial—

Intramuscular or intravenous, 1.5 to 3 grams (1 to 2 grams of ampicillin and 500 mg to 1 gram of sulbactam) every six hours.

[Gonorrhea:][1]—

Intramuscular, 1.5 grams (1 gram of ampicillin and 500 mg of sulbactam) as a single dose with 1 gram of oral probenecid.

Usual adult prescribing limits

4 grams of sulbactam daily.

Usual pediatric dose

Antibacterial—

Children up to 1 year of age: Safety and efficacy have not been established.

Children 1 to 12 years of age: Dosage has not been established. However, doses of 200 to 400 mg per kg of body weight of ampicillin and 100 to 200 mg per kg of body weight of sulbactam per day, administered in divided doses, have been used.

Strength(s) usually available

U.S.—

1.5 grams (1 gram of ampicillin and 500 mg of sulbactam) (Rx) [*Unasyn* (sodium 5 mEq [5 mmol])].

3 grams (2 grams of ampicillin and 1 gram of sulbactam) (Rx) [*Unasyn* (sodium 10 mEq [10 mmol])].

Canada—

Not commercially available.

Packaging and storage

Prior to reconstitution, store below 30 °C (86 °F), unless otherwise specified by manufacturer.

Preparation of dosage form

To prepare initial dilution for intramuscular use, add 3.2 mL of sterile water for injection or of 0.5 or 2% lidocaine hydrochloride injection (without epinephrine) to each 1.5-gram vial and 6.4 mL of diluent to each 3-gram vial to provide an ampicillin concentration of 250 mg per mL and a sulbactam concentration of 125 mg per mL.

To prepare initial dilution for direct intermittent intravenous use, add 3.2 mL of sterile water for injection to each 1.5-gram vial and 6.4 mL of diluent to each 3-gram vial to provide an ampicillin concentration of 250 mg per mL and a sulbactam concentration of 125 mg per mL. The resulting solution should be immediately diluted with a suitable diluent (see manufacturer's package insert) to a final ampicillin concentration of 2 to 30 mg per mL and a final sulbactam concentration of 1 to 15 mg per mL.

Solutions should be allowed to stand following dissolution, allowing any foaming to dissipate, in order to permit visual inspection for complete solubilization.

For reconstitution of piggyback infusion bottles or ADD-Vantage Vials®, consult manufacturer's labeling.

Stability

After reconstitution for intramuscular use, solutions retain their potency for 1 hour.

After reconstitution for intravenous infusion, solutions containing 30 mg of ampicillin and 15 mg of sulbactam per mL retain their potency for 8 hours at 25 °C (77 °F) or for 48 hours at 4 °C (39 °F) in sterile water for injection or 0.9% sodium chloride injection. Solutions containing 20 mg of ampicillin and 10 mg of sulbactam per mL retain their potency for 72 hours at 4 °C (39 °F) in sterile water for injection or 0.9% sodium chloride injection. Solutions containing 20 mg of ampicillin and 10 mg of sulbactam per mL retain their potency for 2 hours at 25 °C (77 °F) or for 4 hours at 4 °C (39 °F) in 5% dextrose injection. Solutions containing 2 mg of ampicillin and 1 mg of sulbactam per mL retain their potency for 4 hours at 25 °C (77 °F) in 5% dextrose injection. For stability in other diluents, consult manufacturer's package insert.

Solutions (250 mg of ampicillin and 125 mg of sulbactam per mL) may vary in color from pale yellow to yellow. Dilute solutions (up to 30 mg of ampicillin and 15 mg of sulbactam per mL) may vary in color from colorless to pale yellow.

Incompatibilities

Extemporaneous admixtures of beta-lactam antibacterials (penicillins) and aminoglycosides may result in substantial mutual inactivation. If these groups of antibacterials are administered concurrently, they should be administered at separate sites at least 1 hour apart. Do not mix them in the same intravenous bag, bottle, or tubing.

When aminoglycosides and penicillins are administered separately by different routes, a reduction in aminoglycoside serum concentration may occur. Usually this is clinically significant only in patients with severely impaired renal function in whom the excretion of both medications is delayed.

Additional information

The sodium content (derived from ampicillin sodium and sulbactam sodium) is approximately 5 mEq (5 mmol) per 1.5 grams (1 gram of ampicillin and 500 mg of sulbactam). This must be considered in patients on a restricted sodium intake when calculating total daily sodium intake.

[1]Not included in Canadian product labeling.

PIPERACILLIN AND TAZOBACTAM

Summary of Differences

Precautions:

Drug interactions and/or related problems—Piperacillin also interacts with anticoagulants and other medications that affect blood clotting.

Laboratory value alterations—May cause false-positive protein reaction in various urine protein tests; may decrease serum potassium concentrations; may increase prothrombin time and partial thromboplastin time.

Medical considerations/contraindications—Caution required in patients with history of bleeding problems; patients with cystic fibrosis may be at increased risk of fever and skin rash.

Side/adverse effects:

Increased risk of platelet dysfunction. Prolonged muscle relaxation may occur.

Additional Dosing Information

Piperacillin and tazobactam combination should be administered by intravenous infusion over a 30-minute period.

The half-life of piperacillin and tazobactam is increased by 25% and 18%, respectively, in patients with hepatic cirrhosis. However, this difference does not warrant an adjustment in dose.

Patients with nosocomial pneumonia should be treated with both piperacillin and tazobactam combination and an aminoglycoside antibiotic. If *Pseudomonas aeruginosa* is isolated from the patient, treatment with the aminoglycoside should continue. If *P. aeruginosa* is not isolated, the aminoglycoside may be discontinued if determined appropriate by the physician based upon the severity of the infection as well as the patient's clinical and bacteriological progress.

Patients with impaired renal function may require a reduction in dose and should be observed for hemorrhagic complications. Reductions in dose for adults and adolescents with impaired renal function are as follows:

Creatinine clearance (mL/min)/(mL/sec)	Dose/Dosing interval (piperacillin and tazobactam)
> 40/0.67	3.375 grams every 6 hours
20–40/0.33–0.67	2.25 grams every 6 hours
< 20/0.33	2.25 grams every 8 hours
Hemodialysis patients	2.25 grams every 8 hours and 0.75 gram after each dialysis

Note: If an aminoglycoside is being used concurrently with piperacillin and tazobactam combination, the dose of the aminoglycoside should be reduced in patients with renal function impairment according to the recommendations of the manufacturer.

Parenteral Dosage Forms

PIPERACILLIN SODIUM AND TAZOBACTAM SODIUM STERILE

Usual adult and adolescent dose

Antibacterial—

Nosocomial pneumonia: Intravenous infusion, 3.375 grams (3 grams of piperacillin and 0.375 grams of tazobactam) every four hours in addition to therapy with an aminoglycoside for seven to fourteen days.

Other infections: Intravenous infusion, 3.375 grams to 4.5 grams (3 to 4 grams of piperacillin and 0.375 to 0.5 grams of tazobactam) every six to eight hours for seven to ten days.

Usual pediatric dose

Antibacterial—

Infants and children up to 12 years of age: Dosage has not been established.

Children 12 years of age and older: See *Usual adult and adolescent dose*.

Strength(s) usually available

U.S.—

2.25 grams (2 grams of piperacillin and 0.25 grams of tazobactam) (Rx) [*Zosyn* (sodium 4.7 mEq [4.7 mmol])].

3.375 grams (3 grams of piperacillin and 0.375 grams of tazobactam) (Rx) [*Zosyn* (sodium 7.1 mEq [7.1 mmol])].

4.5 grams (4 grams of piperacillin and 0.5 grams of tazobactam) (Rx) [*Zosyn* (sodium 9.4 mEq [9.4 mmol])].

Canada—

2.25 grams (2 grams of piperacillin and 0.25 grams of tazobactam) (Rx) [*Tazocin* (sodium 4.7 mEq [4.7 mmol])].

3.375 grams (3 grams of piperacillin and 0.375 grams of tazobactam) (Rx) [*Tazocin* (sodium 7 mEq [7 mmol])].

4.5 grams (4 grams of piperacillin and 0.5 grams of tazobactam) (Rx) [*Tazocin* (sodium 9.4 mEq [9.4 mmol])].

Packaging and storage

Prior to reconstitution, store below 40 °C (104 °F), preferably between 15 and 30 °C (59 and 86 °F), unless otherwise specified by manufacturer.

Preparation of dosage form

To prepare initial dilution for intravenous use, add 5 mL of compatible reconstituion diluent per gram of piperacillin to each vial and shake well until dissolved. Compatible reconstitution diluents include the following: 0.9% Sodium chloride for injection, Sterile water for injection, Dextrose 5%, Bacteriostatic saline/parabens, Bacteriostatic water/parabens, Bacteriostatic saline/benzyl alcohol, Bacteriostatic water/benzyl alcohol. This solution should be further diluted to the desired final volume (50 to 150 mL) with compatible intravenous diluents. Compatible intravenous diluents include the following:

0.9% Sodium chloride for injection, Sterile water for injection, Dextrose 5%, Dextran 6% in saline

Note: The maximum recommended volume per dose of sterile water for injection is 50 mL.

Lactated Ringer's injection is *not* compatible with piperacillin and tazobactam combination.

The prepared solution should be inspected for particulate matter and discoloration prior to administration, whenever the solution and container permit.

For reconstitution of ADD-Vantage® vials, consult the manufacturer's labeling.

Stability

After reconstitution for intravenous use, solutions retain their potency for 24 hours at room temperature (21 to 24 °C [70 to 75 °F]) or for up to 7 days if refrigerated at 4 °C (39 °F).

Incompatibilities

Lactated Ringer's injection is *not* compatible with piperacillin and tazobactam combination.

Extemporaneous admixtures of beta-lactam antibacterials (penicillins) and aminoglycosides may result in substantial mutual inactivation. If these groups of antibacterials are administered concurrently, they should be administered in separate sites at least 1 hour apart. Do not mix them in the same intravenous bag, bottle, or tubing.

When aminoglycosides and penicillins are administered separately by different routes, a reduction in aminoglycoside serum concentration may occur. Usually this is clinically significant only in patients with severely impaired renal function in whom the excretion of both medications is delayed.

Additional information

The sodium content is approximately 2.35 mEq (2.35 mmol) per gram of piperacillin. This must be considered in patients on a restricted sodium intake when calculating total daily sodium intake.

PIPERACILLIN SODIUM AND TAZOBACTAM SODIUM INJECTION

Usual adult and adolescent dose

Antibacterial—

See *Piperacillin Sodium and Tazobactam Sodium Sterile*

Usual pediatric dose

Antibacterial—

See *Piperacillin Sodium and Tazobactam Sodium Sterile*

Strength(s) usually available

U.S.—

Note: The 2.25-gram and 3.375-gram strengths are available in 50-mL containers. The 4.5-gram strength is available in a 100-mL container.

2.25 grams (2 grams of piperacillin and 0.25 grams of tazobactam) (Rx) [*Zosyn* (sodium 5.7 mEq [5.7 mmol])].

3.375 grams (3 grams of piperacillin and 0.375 grams of tazobactam) (Rx) [*Zosyn* (sodium 8.6 mEq [8.6 mmol])].

4.5 grams (4 grams of piperacillin and 0.5 grams of tazobactam) (Rx) [*Zosyn* (sodium 11.4 mEq [11.4 mmol])].

Canada—

Not commercially available.

Packaging and storage

Store at or below −20 °C (−4 °F).

Incompatibilities

Extemporaneous admixtures of beta-lactam antibacterials (penicillins) and aminoglycosides may result in substantial mutual inactivation. If these groups of antibacterials are administered concurrently, they should be administered in separate sites at least 1 hour apart. Do not mix them in the same intravenous bag, bottle, or tubing.

When aminoglycosides and penicillins are administered separately by different routes, a reduction in aminoglycoside serum concentration may occur. Usually this is clinically significant only in patients with severely impaired renal function in whom the excretion of both medications is delayed.

Additional information

The sodium content is approximately 2.85 mEq (2.85 mmol) per gram of piperacillin. This must be considered in patients on a restricted sodium intake when calculating total daily sodium intake.

TICARCILLIN AND CLAVULANATE

Summary of Differences

Precautions:

Drug interactions and/or related problems—Ticarcillin interacts with anticoagulants and other medications that affect blood clotting; clavulanic acid does not interact with probenecid.

Laboratory value alterations—May cause false-positive protein reaction for various urine protein tests; may decrease serum potassium concentrations; may increase prothrombin time and partial thromboplastin time; may increase serum sodium concentrations; may decrease uric acid.

Medical considerations/contraindications—Caution required in patients with history of bleeding problems; caution also required in patients with congestive heart failure, hypertension, or renal function impairment because of sodium content.

Side/adverse effects:
Increased risk of platelet dysfunction.

Additional Dosing Information

Sterile ticarcillin disodium and clavulanate potassium and ticarcillin disodium and clavulanate potassium injection should be administered by intravenous infusion over a 30-minute period.

Based on *in vitro* synergism between ticarcillin and clavulanic acid combination and aminoglycoside antibiotics against *P. aeruginosa*, combined therapy has been successful, especially in patients who have impaired host defenses. When used in combination, both drugs should be used in their full therapeutic doses. When results of culture and susceptibility tests become available, antimicrobial therapy should be adjusted as appropriate.

In those patients in whom meningeal seeding from a distant infection site or in whom meningitis is suspected or documented, or in patients who require prophylaxis against central nervous system infection, an alternate agent with demonstrated clinical efficacy in this setting should be used instead of ticarcillin and clavulanate combination.

Patients with impaired renal function may require a reduction in dose and should be observed for hemorrhagic complications. After an initial loading dose of 3 grams of ticarcillin and 100 mg of clavulanic acid, adults with impaired renal function may require a reduction in dose as follows:

Creatinine clearance (mL/min)/(mL/sec)	Dose/Dosing interval
> 60/1	3.1 grams every 4 hours
30–60/0.5–1	2 grams every 4 hours
10–30/0.17–0.5	2 grams every 8 hours
< 10/0.17	2 grams every 12 hours
< 10 with hepatic dysfunction	2 grams every 24 hours
Peritoneal dialysis patients	3.1 grams every 12 hours
Hemodialysis patients	2 grams every 12 hours; and 3.1 grams after each dialysis

Parenteral Dosage Forms

Note: Bracketed uses in the *Dosage Forms* section refer to categories of use and/or indications that are not included in U.S. product labeling.

TICARCILLIN AND CLAVULANIC ACID FOR INJECTION USP

Usual adult

Antibacterial—
Adults 60 kg of body weight and over—
Gynecologic infections (treatment):
Moderate infection—Intravenous infusion, 50 mg of ticarcillin and 1.7 mg of clavulanic acid per kg of body weight every six hours.
Severe infection—Intravenous infusion, 50 mg of ticarcillin and 1.7 mg of clavulanic acid per kg of body weight every four hours.
Other infections (treatment): Intravenous infusion, 3 grams of ticarcillin and 100 mg of clavulanic acid every four to six hours.
Adults weighing less than 60 kg—
Gynecologic and other infections (treatment): Intravenous infusion, 50 mg of ticarcillin and 1.7 mg of clavulanic acid per kg of body weight every four to six hours.
[Surgical prophylaxis]: Intravenous infusion, 3 grams of ticarcillin and 100 mg of clavulanic acid one-half to one hour prior to the start of surgery, or (for cesarean section) as soon as the umbilical cord is clamped, then 3.1 grams (3 grams of ticarcillin and 100 mg of clavulanic acid) at four-hour intervals for a total of three doses.

Usual pediatric dose

Antibacterial—
Infants less than 1 month of age—
Dosage has not been established.
Infants and children 1 month to 12 years of age—
Intravenous infusion, 50 mg of ticarcillin and 1.7 mg of clavulanic acid per kg of body weight every four to six hours.
Note: Children with cystic fibrosis—Intravenous infusion, 350 to 450 mg of ticarcillin and 11.7 to 17 mg of clavulanic acid per kg of body weight a day in divided doses.
Children 12 years of age and older—
See *Usual adult and adolescent dose (Adults and adolescents up to 60 kg of body weight)*.

Strength(s) usually available

U.S.—
3.1 grams (3 grams of ticarcillin and 100 mg of clavulanic acid) (Rx) [*Timentin* (sodium 4.75 mEq [4.75 mmol] per gram)].
31 grams (30 grams of ticarcillin and 1 gram of clavulanic acid) (Rx) [*Timentin*].
Canada—
3.1 grams (3 grams of ticarcillin and 100 mg of clavulanic acid) (Rx) [*Timentin* (sodium 4.75 mEq [4.75 mmol] per gram)].
31 grams (30 grams of ticarcillin and 1 gram of clavulanic acid) (Rx) [*Timentin*].

Packaging and storage

Prior to reconstitution, store below 40 °C (104 °F), preferably between 15 and 30 °C (59 and 86 °F), unless otherwise specified by manufacturer.

Preparation of dosage form

To prepare initial dilution for direct intravenous use, add 13 mL of sterile water for injection or sodium chloride injection to each 3.1-gram vial to provide a ticarcillin concentration of approximately 200 mg per mL and a clavulanic acid concentration of approximately 6.7 mg per mL. The resulting solution should be further diluted to desired volume in sodium chloride injection, 5% dextrose injection, or lactated Ringer's injection and administered over a 30-minute period by direct infusion or through a Y-type intravenous infusion set.

Once reconstituted, the ticarcillin and clavulanate solution should be visually inspected for particulate matter prior to administration. If particulate matter is present, the solution should be discarded. The color of ticarcillin and clavulanate reconstituted solution normally ranges from light to dark yellow, depending on the concentration of the solution and the duration and temperature of storage.

For reconstitution of piggyback infusion bottles or pharmacy bulk vials, see manufacturer's labeling for instructions. If the Y-type method of administration is used, the primary infusion should be temporarily discontinued during infusion of ticarcillin and clavulanate combination.

Stability

After reconstitution for intravenous use, solutions containing 200 mg of ticarcillin per mL retain their potency for 6 hours at room temperature (21 to 24 °C [70 to 75 °F]) or for up to 72 hours if refrigerated at 4 °C (39 °F).

Solutions containing 10 to 100 mg of ticarcillin per mL in sodium chloride injection or lactated Ringer's injection retain their potency for 24 hours at room temperature (21 to 24 °C [70 to 75 °F]) or for 7 days if refrigerated at 4 °C (39 °F). Solutions containing 10 to 100 mg of ticarcillin per mL in 5% dextrose injection retain their potency for 24 hours at room temperature or for 3 days if refrigerated.

After reconstitution, solutions containing 100 mg of ticarcillin or less per mL in sodium chloride injection or lactated Ringer's injection may be frozen and stored for up to 30 days. Solutions in 5% dextrose injection may be frozen for 7 days. Thawed solutions should be used within 8 hours. Solutions should not be refrozen once they have been thawed.

Incompatibilities

Extemporaneous admixtures of beta-lactam antibacterials (penicillins) and aminoglycosides may result in substantial mutual inactivation. If these groups of antibacterials are administered concurrently, they should be administered in separate sites at least 1 hour apart. Do not mix them in the same intravenous bag, bottle, or tubing.

When aminoglycosides and penicillins are administered separately by different routes, a reduction in aminoglycoside serum concentration may occur. Usually this is clinically significant only in patients with severely impaired renal function in whom the excretion of both medications is delayed.

Sterile ticarcillin disodium and clavulanate potassium combination is incompatible with sodium bicarbonate.

Additional information

The sodium content is approximately 4.75 mEq (4.75 mmol) per gram of ticarcillin. This must be considered in patients on a restricted sodium intake when calculating total daily sodium intake.

The potassium content is approximately 0.15 mEq (6 mg) per 100 mg of clavulanic acid.

TICARCILLIN AND CLAVULANIC ACID INJECTION

Usual adult and adolescent dose

See *Sterile Ticarcillin Disodium and Clavulanate Potassium USP*.

Usual pediatric dose

See *Sterile Ticarcillin Disodium and Clavulanate Potassium USP*.

Strength(s) usually available

U.S.—
3.1 grams (3 grams of ticarcillin and 100 mg of clavulanic acid) in 100 mL (Rx) [*Timentin* (sodium 4.75 mEq [4.75 mmol] per gram)].

Canada—
Not commercially available.

Packaging and storage

Do not store above −10 °C (14 °F), unless otherwise specified by manufacturer.

Preparation of dosage form

Thaw container at room temperature before administration, making sure that all ice crystals have melted.

Minibags should not be used in series connections. Doing so may result in air embolism because of residual air being drawn from the primary container before administration of intravenous solution from the secondary container is complete.

Stability

Thawed solutions should be used within 8 hours. Once thawed, solutions should not be refrozen.

Incompatibilities

Extemporaneous admixtures of beta-lactam antibacterials (penicillins) and aminoglycosides may result in substantial mutual inactivation. If these groups of antibacterials are administered concurrently, they should be administered in separate sites at least 1 hour apart. Do not mix them in the same intravenous bag, bottle, or tubing.

When aminoglycosides and penicillins are administered separately by different routes, a reduction in aminoglycoside serum concentration may occur. Usually this is clinically significant only in patients with severely impaired renal function in whom the excretion of both medications is delayed.

Additional information

The sodium content is approximately 4.75 mEq (4.75 mmol) per gram of ticarcillin. This must be considered in patients on a restricted sodium intake when calculating total daily sodium intake.

The potassium content is approximately 0.15 mEq (6 mg) per 100 mg of clavulanic acid.

Revised: 12/12/2000

PENTAMIDINE Inhalation

VA CLASSIFICATION (Primary): AP109

Commonly used brand name(s): *NebuPent; Pentacarinat; Pneumopent.*

Note: For a listing of dosage forms and brand names by country availability, see *Dosage Forms* section(s).

Category

Antiprotozoal.

Indications

Note: Bracketed information in the *Indications* section refers to uses that are not included in U.S. product labeling.

Accepted

Pneumonia, *Pneumocystis carinii* (PCP) (prophylaxis)—Aerosolized pentamidine is indicated in both secondary prophylaxis (patients who have already had at least one episode of *Pneumocystis carinii* pneumonia), and primary prophylaxis (HIV-infected patients with a CD4 lymphocyte count less than or equal to 200 cells per cubic millimeter) of *Pneumocystis carinii* pneumonia.

[Pneumonia, *Pneumocystis carinii* (PCP) (treatment)][1]—Aerosolized pentamidine is used in the treatment of mild (A-a gradient < 30 mm Hg) *Pneumocystis carinii* pneumonia. However, preliminary studies have suggested that aerosolized pentamidine may be less effective than conventional systemic therapies; patients receiving this regimen should be followed closely for evidence of progressive disease.

[1]Not included in Canadian product labeling.

Pharmacology/Pharmacokinetics

Physicochemical characteristics

Molecular weight—340.42.

Mechanism of action/Effect

Not clearly defined; pentamidine may interfere with incorporation of nucleotides into RNA and DNA and may inhibit oxidative phosphorylation, resulting in inhibition of DNA, RNA, phospholipid, and protein biosynthesis; may also interfere with folate transformation.

Absorption

Systemic absorption of inhaled pentamidine is minimal, with serum pentamidine concentrations less than 20 nanograms per mL after a nebulized dose of 4 mg per kg in most cases (versus 612 nanograms per mL after a single intravenous dose of 4 mg per kg). Peak systemic absorption occurs at, or near, completion of inhalation therapy.

Distribution

Aerosolized pentamidine produces concentrations approximately 10 to 100 times higher in the lungs than would a comparable dose of intravenous pentamidine.

Elimination

Unknown; in one study, cumulative percentage of total dose renally excreted was 0.4% over a 72-hour period.

Precautions to Consider

Carcinogenicity/Mutagenicity

Pentamidine has not been shown to be mutagenic in Ames studies. Carcinogenicity studies have not been done.

Pregnancy/Reproduction

Fertility—Studies have not been done.

Pregnancy—Studies with aerosolized pentamidine have not been done in humans.

Studies with aerosolized pentamidine have not been done in animals. However, studies in rabbits have shown that systemic pentamidine was associated with an increased incidence of post-implantation losses and delayed fetal ossification.

FDA Pregnancy Category C.

Breast-feeding

It is not known whether pentamidine is distributed into breast milk.

Pediatrics

No information is available on the relationship of age to the effects of aerosolized pentamidine in pediatric patients. Safety and efficacy have not been established. However, if sulfamethoxazole and trimethoprim combination is not tolerated, aerosolized pentamidine is recommended for children 5 years of age and older.

Geriatrics

No information is available on the relationship of age to the effects of pentamidine in geriatric patients.

Dental

Pentamidine may cause a bitter or metallic taste, gingivitis, hypersalivation, or dry mouth.

Drug interactions and/or related problems

At this time, no clinically significant drug interactions and/or related problems have been documented in patients receiving prophylactic aerosolized pentamidine.

Medical considerations/Contraindications

The medical considerations/contraindications included have been selected on the basis of their potential clinical significance (reasons given in parentheses where appropriate)—not necessarily inclusive (» = major clinical significance).

Except under special circumstances, this medication should not be used when the following medical problem exists:

» Allergy to pentamidine
(aerosolized pentamidine is contraindicated in patients with a history of an anaphylactic reaction to inhaled or systemic pentamidine)

Risk-benefit should be considered when the following medical problem exists:

Asthma
(aerosolized pentamidine may induce acute bronchospasm, usually in patients with a history of asthma; this may be reduced by pretreatment with a bronchodilator)

Patient monitoring

At this time, there are no particular laboratory tests or monitoring parameters recommended routinely for patients receiving prophylactic aerosolized pentamidine. However, baseline parameters, including pulmonary function tests, serum amylase and lipase, may be obtained for the first treatment, and then followed as needed.

Side/Adverse Effects

Note: The prophylactic use of aerosolized pentamidine has a very low incidence of severe side effects. Many adverse reactions will be due to other medications, other concurrent infections, or the HIV disease itself, and may be difficult to differentiate.

Coughing and bronchospasm occur primarily in patients who are cigarette smokers and continue to smoke, or have an underlying pulmonary disease, such as asthma.

A number of cases of extrapulmonary pneumocystosis and pneumothorax have been reported in patients receiving aerosolized pentamidine. These are thought to be infectious complications due to subclinical, peripheral infection and poor systemic distribution of aerosolized pentamidine. Although the incidence is not known at this time, one study found that extrapulmonary pneumocystosis appears to occur more frequently in, but is not limited to, patients who have been diagnosed with AIDS for longer than 12 months. These patients usually have had prior episodes of *Pneumocystis carinii* pneumonia (PCP), often do not have concurrent pneumonia, are receiving concurrent zidovudine, and have had prolonged treatment with aerosolized pentamidine. It is suggested that use of zidovudine and prophylactic aerosolized pentamidine may allow for the emergence of extrapulmonary pneumocystosis.

The following side/adverse effects have been selected on the basis of their potential clinical significance (possible signs and symptoms in parentheses where appropriate)—not necessarily inclusive:

Those indicating need for medical attention

Incidence more frequent

Chest pain or congestion; coughing; dyspnea (difficulty in breathing); ***pharyngitis*** (burning pain, dryness, or sensation of lump in throat; difficulty in swallowing); ***skin rash; wheezing***

Incidence rare

Extrapulmonary pneumocystosis—most frequent sites include the spleen, liver, lymph nodes, and eyes; ***pancreatitis*** (nausea; pain in upper abdomen, possibly radiating to the back; vomiting)—may occur more frequently with prolonged use; ***pneumothorax*** (sudden onset of severe breathing difficulty; severe pain in chest)

Incidence rare—with daily treatment doses only

Hypoglycemia, mild (anxiety; chills; cold sweats; cool, pale skin; headache; increased hunger; nausea; nervousness; shakiness); ***renal insufficiency*** (decreased urination; loss of appetite; nausea; unusual tiredness)

Those not indicating need for medical attention

Incidence less frequent

Bitter or metallic taste

Patient Consultation

As an aid to patient consultation, refer to *Advice for the Patient, Pentamidine (Inhalation)*.

In providing consultation, consider emphasizing the following selected information (» = major clinical significance):

Before using this medication

» Conditions affecting use, especially:
Allergy to pentamidine

Proper use of this medication

Importance of receiving medication for full course of therapy and on regular schedule

» Proper dosing

Missed dose: Receiving therapy as soon as possible

Precautions while using this medication

If also using a bronchodilator inhaler, using about 5 to 10 minutes prior to aerosolized pentamidine

Possible bitter or metallic taste; dissolving a hard candy in mouth after administration of medication

Cigarette smokers who continue to smoke are more likely to experience coughing and bronchospasm during aerosolized pentamidine therapy

Side/adverse effects

Signs of potential side effects, especially chest pain or congestion, coughing, dyspnea, pharyngitis, skin rash, wheezing, extrapulmonary pneumocystosis, pancreatitis, pneumothorax, hypoglycemia, and renal insufficiency

A bitter or metallic taste may occur; however, it is medically insignificant

General Dosing Information

Coughing and bronchospasm occur primarily in cigarette smokers who continue to smoke, or patients with an underlying pulmonary disease, such as asthma. A higher incidence of coughing and bronchospasm may be related to larger particle sizes; however, these symptoms appear to occur most frequently due to an increased particle load with larger doses. Pretreatment with a bronchodilator, e.g., albuterol, metaproterenol, or terbutaline, helps to alleviate this problem and may improve pentamidine distribution in the lung.

It is important that as much medication as possible reach the upper lobes of the lungs, since upper lobe *P. carinii* pneumonia relapses have occurred in patients while they were receiving aerosolized pentamidine. There appears to be a more uniform distribution of aerosolized pentamidine in the lungs when it is administered to patients in a supine or recumbent position.

Before aerosolized pentamidine treatment is started, a tuberculin skin test, chest x-ray, and sputum culture, if possible, should be performed to rule out tuberculosis due to *Mycobacterium tuberculosis*. A tuberculin skin test alone may not be useful because false negative readings often occur in AIDS patients. The risk of active disease or reactivation of latent tuberculosis infection is more prevalent in HIV-infected people. Also, the risk of transmission of tuberculosis to health care workers or others in the vicinity may exist.

Health care workers are advised to administer aerosolized pentamidine in a well-ventilated room if possible. Although one study found the environmental levels of pentamidine in a treatment room to be low, long-term occupational studies have not been done and the risk has not been established. Of primary concern is the previously mentioned risk of transmission of tuberculosis or other respiratory pathogens via aerosols, as well as anecdotal reports of a reversible decrease in pulmonary function testing parameters and chemical conjunctivitis due to ocular exposure to aerosolized pentamidine.

Two types of nebulizers have been shown to be effective in decreasing the incidence of *P. carinii* pneumonia. Respirgard II is a jet nebulizer and is used with NebuPent and Pentacarinat; Fisoneb is an ultrasonic nebulizer and is used with Pneumopent. Jet nebulizers use a high-flow gas to shear liquid strands from a thin layer of solution. The liquid strands hit a baffle, creating a wide variety of particle sizes. Larger particles generally fall by gravity and get reincorporated into the solution. Ultrasonic nebulizers generate an ultrahigh frequency sound, creating a geyser from which particles are expelled. When the flow through the nebulizer is interrupted, as with tidal breathing, the smaller particles coalesce into larger particles. Because of this, measurements of output and particle size will vary with different operating conditions.

Particle size produced by the nebulizer is an important factor in the location of aerosol deposition. The optimal size for deposition in the alveoli, where *Pneumocystis carinii* pneumonia (PCP) causes damage, is 1 to 2 microns; the optimal size for tracheobronchial deposition is 4 to 7 microns. Many factors can affect and limit aerosol deposition into the alveoli, including inspiratory flowrates, frequency of respiration, breath-holding, tidal volumes, and airway narrowing from bronchospasm, emphysema, mucus, and PCP.

Because of the differences in nebulizers and the efficacy with which they deliver aerosolized pentamidine, the nebulizers should not be utilized interchangeably with the different dosing regimens. The two regimens shown to be effective are described below.

Inhalation Dosage Forms

Note: Bracketed uses in the *Dosage Forms* section refer to categories of use and/or indications that are not included in U.S. product labeling.

PENTAMIDINE ISETHIONATE FOR INHALATION SOLUTION

Usual adult and adolescent dose

Pneumonia, *Pneumocystis carinii*—

For *NebuPent* and *Pentacarinat* using the Respirgard II jet nebulizer—

Prophylaxis:

Oral inhalation, 300 mg every four weeks, administered via the Respirgard II nebulizer. The aerosol treatment should be continued over a period of approximately thirty to forty-five minutes, until the nebulizer chamber is empty.

Note: A prophylactic dose of 150 mg every two weeks, administered via the Respirgard II nebulizer, has also been used if the patient cannot tolerate a single monthly dose. One study found that although patients who received 300 mg monthly had a lower rate of PCP than those receiving 150 mg every two weeks, the difference was not significant.

[Treatment][1]:

Oral inhalation, 600 mg a day, administered via the Respirgard II nebulizer for twenty-one days. Continue the aerosol treatment over a period of approximately twenty-five to thirty minutes.

Note: The flow rate for the nebulizer should be 5 to 7 liters per minute from a 40- to 50-pounds-per-square-inch (PSI) air or oxygen source.

Low pressure compressors (<20 PSI) should not be used.

For *Pneumopent* using the Fisoneb ultrasonic nebulizer—
Loading dose (prophylaxis):
Oral inhalation, 60 mg, administered via the Fisoneb ultrasonic nebulizer, every twenty-four to seventy-two hours for a total of 5 doses over a two week period. The aerosol treatment should be continued over a period of approximately fifteen minutes, until the nebulizer chamber is empty.
Maintenance dose (prophylaxis):
Oral inhalation, 60 mg, administered via the Fisoneb ultrasonic nebulizer, every two weeks.
Note: The flow rate of the nebulizer should be set at the mid-flow mark.

Usual pediatric dose
Pneumonia, *Pneumocystis carinii*—
Prophylaxis: Dosage has not been established. However, 300 mg every four weeks has been used in children 5 years of age and older who cannot tolerate sulfamethoxazole and trimethoprim combination.

Strength(s) usually available
U.S.—
300 mg (Rx) [*NebuPent* (Respirgard II nebulizer)].
Canada—
60 mg (Rx) [*Pneumopent* (Fisoneb nebulizer)].
300 mg (Rx) [*Pentacarinat* (Respirgard II nebulizer)].

Packaging and storage
Prior to reconstitution, store between 15 and 30 °C (59 and 86 °F), unless otherwise specified by manufacturer.

Preparation of dosage form
For *NebuPent* and *Pentacarinat*—
To prepare pentamidine for oral inhalation *prophylaxis*, add 6 mL of sterile water for injection to each 300-mg vial of sterile pentamidine isethionate.
To prepare pentamidine for oral inhalation *treatment*, add 6 mL of sterile water for injection to 600 mg of sterile pentamidine isethionate.
For administration, place the entire reconstituted contents into the reservoir chamber of the Respirgard II nebulizer.

For *Pneumopent*—
To prepare for oral inhalation, remove the rubber stopper and put it aside, upside down, on a clean surface for later use. Add 3 to 5 mL of sterile water for inhalation or sterile water for injection to the vial. Do not use tap water and do not use normal saline. Replace the rubber stopper. The powder should dissolve immediately; if it does not, gently shake the vial to mix it. It should form a clear, colorless solution; if the solution is cloudy, do not use it.
For administration, place the entire reconstituted contents into the chamber of the Fisoneb ultrasonic nebulizer.

Stability
For *NebuPent*—
After reconstitution, solutions in concentrations of 93 mg per mL retain at least 90% of their potency for up to 4 months when frozen in plastic syringes at −20 °C. Do not defrost and refreeze.

For *Pentacarinat*—
Store unopened vials at room temperature; protect from light.
After reconstitution, solutions in concentrations of approximately 2 mg per mL are stable for up to 24 hours at room temperature.

For *Pneumopent*—
Store unopened vials at room temperature.
After reconstitution, solution may be stored for up to 24 hours at room temperature or up to 48 hours in a refrigerator. Do not freeze.

Incompatibilities
Reconstitution of pentamidine with saline solutions may cause pentamidine to precipitate out of solution.

Additional information
Pentamidine inhalation solution should not be mixed with any other medications.
Do not use the Respirgard II nebulizer to administer a bronchodilator.

[1]Not included in Canadian product labeling.

Selected Bibliography
Monk JP, Benfield P. Inhaled pentamidine. An overview of its pharmacological properties and a review of its therapeutic use in Pneumocystis carinii pneumonia. Drugs 1990; 39(5): 741-56.

Revised: 03/03/1992

PENTAZOCINE—See *Opioid (Narcotic) Analgesics (Systemic)*

PENTOBARBITAL—See *Barbiturates (Systemic)*

PENTOSAN Systemic

VA CLASSIFICATION (Primary): GU900

Commonly used brand name(s): *Elmiron.*

Note: For a listing of dosage forms and brand names by country availability, see *Dosage Forms* section(s).

Category
Anti-inflammatory, local (interstitial cystitis).

Indications
Accepted
Cystitis, interstitial (treatment)—Pentosan is indicated for the relief of bladder pain or discomfort associated with interstitial cystitis. It may improve symptoms such as urinary urgency and urinary frequency, including nocturia. Symptoms of interstitial cystitis exacerbate and remit, with days up to years between episodes.

In clinical trials, approximately one fourth to one third of patients receiving pentosan reported an improvement in bladder pain and discomfort after 3 months of therapy.

Pharmacology/Pharmacokinetics
Physicochemical characteristics
Molecular weight—4000 to 6000.

Mechanism of action/Effect
The exact mechanism of action is not known, but pentosan has been found to adhere to the bladder wall mucosal membrane, which may act as a buffer to prevent irritating solutes from reaching the cells.

Other actions/effects
Pentosan has anticoagulant (1/15 the activity of heparin) and fibrinolytic effects.

Absorption
Approximately 3% of different administered doses.

Distribution
Pentosan is distributed to the uroepithelium of the genitourinary tract, with lesser amounts found in the bone marrow, liver, lung, periosteum, skin, and spleen.

Biotransformation
Pentosan undergoes depolymerization in the kidney; 68% of the drug undergoes desulfation in the liver and the spleen 1 hour after intravenous administration; both depolymerization and desulfation can be saturated with continued dosing.

Half-life
Elimination—
Intravenous: 24 hours after a 40-mg dose.
Oral: 4.8 hours for the unchanged drug.

Elimination
Renal, 3.5% with a single dose; 11% with multiple doses, with 3% of that as the unchanged drug.

Precautions to Consider
Carcinogenicity
Studies to determine the carcinogenic potential of pentosan have not been done in humans or animals.

Mutagenicity
Pentosan was not clastogenic or mutagenic when tested in the mouse micronucleus test or the Ames test.

Pregnancy/Reproduction
Fertility—Reproductive studies in mice and rats using intravenous daily doses of 15 mg per kg of body weight (mg/kg) and in rabbits using 7.5 mg/kg (0.42 and 0.14 times the daily oral human doses of pentosan based on body surface area, respectively) did not reveal evidence of impaired fertility.

Pregnancy—Studies have not been done in humans.
Reproductive studies in mice and rats using intravenous daily doses of 15 mg/kg and in rabbits using 7.5 mg/kg (0.42 and 0.14 times the daily

oral human doses of pentosan based on body surface area, respectively) did not reveal any harm to the fetus. Direct *in vitro* bathing of cultured mouse embryos with pentosan at a concentration of 1 mg per mL may cause reversible limb bud abnormalities.

FDA Pregnancy Category B.

Breast-feeding
It is not known whether pentosan is distributed into breast milk.

Pediatrics
No information is available on the relationship of age to the effects of pentosan in pediatric patients. Safety and efficacy have not been established.

Geriatrics
Studies performed in patients with interstitial cystitis have not demonstrated geriatrics-specific problems that would limit the usefulness of pentosan in the elderly.

Drug interactions and/or related problems
The following drug interactions and/or related problems have been selected on the basis of their potential clinical significance (possible mechanism in parentheses where appropriate)—not necessarily inclusive (» = major clinical significance):

Note: Combinations containing any of the following medications, depending on the amount present, may also interact with this medication.

» Medications/therapies that increase the risk of hemorrhage, such as:
Alteplase, recombinant or
Anticoagulants, coumarin-derivative or
Aspirin, high dose or
Heparin or
Streptokinase
(concurrent use with pentosan may increase the risk of hemorrhage; patients should be monitored for signs of hemorrhage; if hemorrhage occurs, pentosan should be discontinued)

Laboratory value alterations
The following have been selected on the basis of their potential clinical significance (possible effect in parentheses where appropriate)—not necessarily inclusive (» = major clinical significance).

With physiology/laboratory test values
Alanine aminotransferase (ALT [SGPT]), serum and
Alkaline phosphatase, serum and
Aspartate aminotransferase (AST [SGOT]), serum and
Gamma-glutamyl transpeptidase, serum and
Lactate dehydrogenase, serum
(increases in values of up to 2.5 times the normal values have occurred in 1.2% of patients taking pentosan; increases usually appeared 3 to 12 months after initiation of therapy, and were not associated with jaundice or other clinical signs or symptoms; these increases were transient, remained unchanged, or, rarely, progressed with continued use)

Partial thromboplastin time (PTT) and
Prothrombin time (PT)
(increases have been reported in fewer than 1% of patients taking pentosan; however, PTT and PT were unaffected in one study using up to 1200 mg of pentosan a day for 8 days)

Medical considerations/Contraindications
The medical considerations/contraindications included have been selected on the basis of their potential clinical significance (reasons given in parentheses where appropriate)—not necessarily inclusive (» = major clinical significance).

Risk-benefit should be considered when the following medical problems exist:

» Any condition in which risk of hemorrhage is present, such as:
Aneurysms or
Diverticula or
Gastrointestinal ulceration or
Hemophilia or
Polyps or
Thrombocytopenia or thrombocytopenia, heparin-induced, history of
(since pentosan has weak anticoagulant activity, an additive effect may occur; patients with these conditions should be evaluated carefully before beginning pentosan therapy)

Hepatic insufficiency or
Spleen disorders
(since pentosan is desulfated by the liver and the spleen, bioavailability of the parent or active metabolites may be increased; pentosan should be used cautiously in patients with these conditions)

Sensitivity to pentosan, structurally related compounds, or excipients

Patient monitoring
The following may be especially important in patient monitoring (other tests may be warranted in some patients, depending on condition; » = major clinical significance):

Alanine aminotransferase (ALT [SGPT]), serum and
Aspartate aminotransferase (AST [SGOT]), serum
(determinations recommended every 6 months during treatment)

Side/Adverse Effects

The following side/adverse effects have been selected on the basis of their potential clinical significance (possible signs and symptoms in parentheses where appropriate)—not necessarily inclusive:

Those indicating need for medical attention
Incidence rare—incidence ≤ 1%
Allergic reaction (skin rash or hives); ***amblyopia*** (vision impairment); ***anemia*** (unusual tiredness and weakness); ***dyspnea*** (difficulty in breathing); ***ecchymosis*** (unusual bleeding or bruising); ***leukopenia*** (chills; fever; sore throat); ***thrombocytopenia*** (unusual bleeding or bruising)

Those indicating need for medical attention only if they continue or are bothersome
Incidence less frequent
Abdominal pain—incidence 2%; ***alopecia*** (hair loss)—incidence 4%; ***diarrhea***—incidence 4%; ***dizziness***—incidence 1%; ***dyspepsia*** (stomach upset)—incidence 2%; ***headache***—incidence 3%; ***nausea***—incidence 4%; ***skin rash***—incidence 3%

Note: *Alopecia* may begin within the first 4 weeks of treatment; 97% of reported cases were limited to a single area on the scalp.

Incidence rare—incidence ≤ 1%
Anorexia (loss of appetite); ***conjunctivitis*** (irritated or red eyes); ***constipation; epistaxis*** (nosebleed); ***esophagitis*** (difficulty in swallowing); ***flatulence*** (stomach gas); ***gastritis*** (stomach upset); ***gum hemorrhage*** (bleeding gums); ***heartburn; mouth ulcer*** (sores in mouth); ***pharyngitis*** (dryness of throat; pain upon swallowing); ***photosensitivity*** (increased sensitivity of skin to sunlight); ***pruritus*** (itching); ***rhinitis*** (runny nose); ***tinnitus*** (ringing in the ears); ***urticaria*** (skin rash); ***vomiting***

Overdose

For information on the management of overdose or unintentional ingestion, **contact a Poison Control Center** (see *Poison Control Center Listing*).

Treatment of overdose
To decrease absorption—Gastric lavage.

Supportive care—Patients in whom intentional overdose is confirmed or suspected should be referred for psychiatric consultation.

Patient Consultation

As an aid to patient consultation, refer to *Advice for the Patient, Pentosan (Systemic)*.

In providing consultation, consider emphasizing the following selected information (» = major clinical significance):

Before using this medication
» Conditions affecting use, especially:
Sensitivity to pentosan, structurally related compounds, or excipients
Other medications, especially alteplase, recombinant; anticoagulants, coumarin-derivative; aspirin, high dose; heparin; or streptokinase
Other medical problems, especially aneurysms, diverticula, gastrointestinal ulceration, hemophilia, polyps, or thrombocytopenia

Proper use of this medication
Taking on empty stomach with a full glass (8 ounces) of water 1 hour before or 2 hours after meals
May require up to 3 to 6 months of therapy to feel effects
» Proper dosing
Missed dose: Taking as soon as possible; not taking if almost time for next dose; not doubling doses
» Proper storage

Precautions while using this medication
» Possibility of increased bleeding time
Following any dietary instructions

Side/adverse effects
Signs of potential side effects, especially allergic reaction, amblyopia, anemia, dyspnea, ecchymosis, leukopenia, thrombocytopenia, and alopecia

General Dosing Information

The clinical value and risks of treatment for longer than 6 months are not known.

Diet/Nutrition

Pentosan should be taken with a full glass (8 ounces) of water at least 1 hour before or 2 hours after meals.

Some patients with interstitial cystitis may benefit by avoiding acidic foods and beverages such as alcohol, caffeinated and citrus beverages, chocolate, spices, and tomatoes. However, this recommendation is not universal; patients should avoid foods or beverages that aggravate their condition.

Oral Dosage Form

PENTOSAN POLYSULFATE SODIUM Capsules

Usual adult dose

Cystitis, interstitial (treatment)—

Oral, 100 mg three times a day. If there is no improvement and no side/adverse effects have been reported after three months, pentosan therapy may be continued for another three months.

Usual pediatric dose

Safety and efficacy have not been established.

Strength(s) usually available

U.S.—

100 mg (Rx) [*Elmiron*].

Canada—

100 mg (Rx) [*Elmiron*].

Packaging and storage

Store below 40 °C (104 °F), preferably between 15 and 30 °C (59 and 86 °F), unless otherwise specified by the manufacturer.

Auxiliary labeling

- Take on empty stomach.

Revised: 05/20/1998
Developed: 02/11/1998

PENTOSTATIN Systemic

VA CLASSIFICATION (Primary): AN900

Commonly used brand name(s): *Nipent*.

Other commonly used names are 2′-deoxycoformycin and 2′DCF.

Note: For a listing of dosage forms and brand names by country availability, see *Dosage Forms* section(s).

Category

Antineoplastic.

Indications

Accepted

Leukemia, hairy cell (treatment)—Pentostatin is indicated as a single agent for treatment of patients with active hairy cell leukemia who have not received previous treatment or who have not responded to treatment with alpha interferons. Active disease is defined by clinically significant anemia, neutropenia, thrombocytopenia, or disease-related symptoms.

[Leukemia, chronic lymphocytic (treatment)][1]—Pentostatin is indicated for the treatment of relapsed/refractory chronic lymphocytic leukemia, as a single agent.

[Leukemia, prolymphocytic (treatment)][1]—Pentostatin is indicated for the treatment of relapsed/refractory prolymphocytic leukemia, as a single agent.

[Lymphoma, cutaneous T-cell (treatment)][1]—Pentostatin is indicated for the treatment of advanced, relapsed/refractory cutaneous T-cell lymphomas (e.g., Sézary syndrome, mycosis fungoides), as a single agent.

Acceptance not established

There are insufficient data to establish the safety and efficacy of pentostatin for the prophylaxis of *graft-versus-host disease*.

Use of pentostatin for the treatment of non-Hodgkin's lymphomas has not been established, due to insufficient data supporting efficacy (e.g., undefined role in combination chemotherapy; needs phase III support).

[1]Not included in Canadian product labeling.

Pharmacology/Pharmacokinetics

Physicochemical characteristics

Source—Isolated from fermentation cultures of *Streptomyces antibioticus*.

Chemical Group—Pentostatin is a purine (deoxyinosine) analog.

Molecular weight—268.27.

Mechanism of action/Effect

Pentostatin is an antimetabolite. Its exact mechanism of action in hairy cell leukemia is unknown. Pentostatin is a potent transition state inhibitor of adenosine deaminase (ADA), the greatest activity of which is found in cells of the lymphoid system. T-cells have higher ADA activity than B-cells, and T-cell malignancies have higher activity than B-cell malignancies. The cytotoxicity that results from prevention of catabolism of adenosine or deoxyadenosine is thought to be due to elevated intracellular levels of dATP, which can block DNA synthesis through inhibition of ribonucleotide reductase. Inhibition of RNA synthesis may also contribute to the cytotoxic effect. Although pentostatin arrests cells in the G_1 or S phase of cell division, it is also reported to have cell cycle-phase nonspecific actions (including increased DNA strand breaks).

Other actions/effects

Pentostatin appears to have immunosuppressant activity; significant reductions in T- and B-cells occur during treatment and T4 reductions persist, sometimes for months or years, after treatment.

Distribution

Pentostatin crosses the blood-brain barrier; cerebrospinal fluid concentrations achieved are 10 to 12.5% of serum concentrations within 24 hours after a single dose.

Protein binding

Low (4%).

Biotransformation

Hepatic; however, only small amounts are metabolized.

Half-life

Distribution—

11 minutes (following a single dose of 4 mg per square meter of body surface area infused over 5 minutes). A range of 17 to 85 minutes has also been reported.

Terminal—

Normal: 5.7 hours (following a single dose of 4 mg per square meter of body surface area infused over 5 minutes). A range of 2.6 to 15 hours has been reported.

Renal function impairment (creatinine clearance less than 50 mL per minute): 18 hours.

Onset of action

Time to achieve response—Median 4.7 months (range 2.9 to 24.1 months).

Duration of action

Pharmacologic—Inhibition of ADA: More than 1 week after a single dose.

Elimination

Renal, 90%, as unchanged drug and metabolites as measured by adenosine deaminase inhibitory activity. In two small studies, 32 to 73% was recovered unchanged.

Precautions to Consider

Carcinogenicity

Secondary malignancies are potential delayed effects of many antineoplastic agents, although it is not clear whether the effect is related to their mutagenic or immunosuppressive action. The effect of dose and duration of therapy is also unknown, although risk seems to increase with long-term use. Although information is limited, available data seem to indicate that the carcinogenic risk is greatest with the alkylating agents.

Antimetabolites have been shown to be carcinogenic in animals and may be associated with an increased risk of development of secondary carcinomas in humans, although the risk appears to be less than with alkylating agents.

Lymphoid neoplasms have been reported in humans.

Studies with pentostatin in animals have not been done.

Mutagenicity

Pentostatin was not found to be mutagenic in several strains of *Salmonella typhimurium*, including TA-98, TA-1535, TA-1537, and TA-1538. When tested with strain TA-100, a repeatable statistically significant response trend was observed with and without metabolic activation. The response was 2.1- to 2.2-fold higher than the background at 10 mg/plate, the maximum possible drug concentration. Formulated pentostatin was clastogenic in the *in vivo* mouse bone marrow micronucleus assay at 20, 120, and 240 mg per kg of body weight (mg/kg). Pentostatin was nonmutagenic to V79 Chinese hamster lung cells at the hypoxanthine-guanine-phosphororibosyltransferase (HGPRT) locus exposed for 3 hours to concentrations of 1 to 3 mg per mL, with or without metabolic activation. Pentostatin did not significantly increase chromosomal aberrations in V79 Chinese hamster lung cells exposed for 3 hours to 1 to 3 mg per mL in the presence or absence of metabolic activation.

Pregnancy/Reproduction

Fertility—Gonadal suppression, resulting in amenorrhea or azoospermia, may occur in patients taking antineoplastic therapy, especially with the alkylating agents. In general, these effects appear to be related to dose and length of therapy and may be irreversible. Prediction of the degree of testicular or ovarian function impairment is complicated by the common use of combinations of several antineoplastics, which makes it difficult to assess the effects of individual agents. Fertility studies with pentostatin have not been done in animals; however, mild seminiferous tubular degeneration was observed in a 5-day intravenous toxicity study at doses of 1 and 4 mg/kg in dogs.

Pregnancy—Adequate and well-controlled studies in women have not been done.

First trimester: It is usually recommended that use of antineoplastics, especially combination chemotherapy, be avoided whenever possible, especially during the first trimester. Although information is limited because of the relatively few instances of antineoplastic administration during pregnancy, the mutagenic, teratogenic, and carcinogenic potential of these medications must be considered.

Other hazards to the fetus include adverse reactions seen in adults.

In general, use of contraception is recommended during cytotoxic drug therapy.

Studies in rats at intravenous doses of 0, 0.01, 0.1, or 0.75 mg/kg (0, 0.06, 0.6, or 4.5 mg per square meter of body surface area, respectively) per day on days 6 through 15 of gestation found drug-related maternal toxicity at doses of 0.1 and 0.75 mg/kg (0.6 and 4.5 mg per square meter of body surface area, respectively) per day. Teratogenic effects (increased incidence of various skeletal malformations) were observed at doses of 0.75 mg/kg (4.5 mg per square meter of body surface area) per day. In a dose range–finding study in rats at intravenous doses of 0, 0.05, 0.1, 0.5, 0.75, or 1 mg/kg (0, 0.3, 0.6, 3, 4.5, or 6 mg per square meter of body surface area, respectively) per day, on days 6 through 15 of gestation, fetal malformations were observed. These malformations included an omphalocele at 0.05 mg/kg (0.3 mg per square meter of body surface area), gastroschisis at 0.75 mg/kg and 1 mg/kg (4.5 and 6 mg per square meter of body surface area, respectively), and a flexure defect of the hindlimbs at 0.75 mg/kg (4.5 mg per square meter of body surface area). Pentostatin was also teratogenic in mice in single intraperitoneal doses of 2 mg/kg (6 mg per square meter of body surface area) on day 7 of gestation. Pentostatin was not teratogenic in rabbits at intravenous doses of 0, 0.005, 0.01, or 0.02 mg/kg (0, 0.015, 0.03, or 0.06 mg per square meter of body surface area, respectively) per day; however, maternal toxicity, abortions, early deliveries, and deaths occurred in all drug-treated groups.

FDA Pregnancy Category D.

Breast-feeding

Although very little information is available regarding distribution of antineoplastic agents into breast milk, breast-feeding is not recommended during chemotherapy because of the potential risks to the infant (adverse effects, mutagenicity, carcinogenicity). It is not known whether pentostatin is distributed into breast milk.

Pediatrics

No information is available on the relationship of age to the effects of pentostatin in pediatric patients. Safety and efficacy have not been established.

Geriatrics

Although appropriate studies on the relationship of age to the effects of pentostatin have not been performed in the geriatric population, clinical trials have included elderly patients and geriatrics-specific problems that would limit the usefulness of this medication in the elderly are not expected. However, elderly patients are more likely to have age-related renal function impairment, which may require caution in patients receiving pentostatin.

Dental

The bone marrow depressant effects of pentostatin may result in an increased incidence of microbial infection, delayed healing, and gingival bleeding. Dental work, whenever possible, should be completed prior to initiation of therapy or deferred until blood counts have returned to normal. Patients should be instructed in proper oral hygiene during treatment, including caution in use of regular toothbrushes, dental floss, and toothpicks.

Pentostatin also sometimes causes stomatitis that is associated with considerable discomfort.

Drug interactions and/or related problems

The following drug interactions and/or related problems have been selected on the basis of their potential clinical significance (possible mechanism in parentheses where appropriate)—not necessarily inclusive (» = major clinical significance):

Note: Combinations containing any of the following medications, depending on the amount present, may also interact with this medication.

Allopurinol or
Colchicine or
» Probenecid or
» Sulfinpyrazone
(pentostatin may raise the concentration of blood uric acid; dosage adjustment of antigout agents may be necessary to control hyperuricemia and gout; allopurinol may be preferred to prevent or reverse pentostatin-induced hyperuricemia because of risk of uric acid nephropathy with uricosuric antigout agents)
(one case has been reported in which a patient receiving both allopurinol and pentostatin developed a fatal hypersensitivity vasculitis, although a definite connection with the combination has not been established)

Blood dyscrasia-causing medications (see *Appendix II*)
(leukopenic and/or thrombocytopenic effects of pentostatin may be increased with concurrent or recent therapy if these medications cause the same effects; dosage adjustment of pentostatin, if necessary, should be based on blood counts)

» Bone marrow depressants, other (see *Appendix II*) or
Radiation therapy
(additive bone marrow depression may occur; dosage reduction may be required when two or more bone marrow depressants, including radiation, are used concurrently or consecutively)

Fludarabine
(concurrent use with pentostatin is not recommended because of a possible increased risk of fatal pulmonary toxicity)

Vaccines, killed virus
(because normal defense mechanisms may be suppressed by pentostatin therapy, the patient's antibody response to the vaccine may be decreased. The interval between discontinuation of medications that cause immunosuppression and restoration of the patient's ability to respond to the vaccine depends on the intensity and type of immunosuppression-causing medication used, the underlying disease, and other factors; estimates vary from 3 months to 1 year)

» Vaccines, live virus
(because normal defense mechanisms may be suppressed by pentostatin therapy, concurrent use with a live virus vaccine may potentiate the replication of the vaccine virus, may increase the side/adverse effects of the vaccine virus, and/or may decrease the patient's antibody response to the vaccine; immunization of these patients should be undertaken only with extreme caution after careful review of the patient's hematologic status and only with the knowledge and consent of the physician managing the pentostatin therapy. The interval between discontinuation of medications that cause immunosuppression and restoration of the patient's ability to respond to the vaccine depends on the intensity and type of immunosuppression-causing medication used, the underlying disease, and other factors; estimates vary from 3 months to 1 year. Patients with leukemia in remission should not receive live virus vaccine until at least 3 months after their last chemotherapy. In addition, immunization with oral poliovirus vaccine should be postponed in persons in close contact with the patient, especially family members)

Vidarabine
(biochemical studies have shown an enhancement of vidarabine's effects by pentostatin, which could result in an increase in adverse effects of each)

Carmustine and
Cyclophosphamide (high dose) and
Etoposide
(one study has shown that pentostatin, when used concurrently with these medications, as part of a high dose regimen prior to

bone marrow transplant resulted in acute pulmonary edema and hypotension, leading to death)

Laboratory value alterations

The following have been selected on the basis of their potential clinical significance (possible effect in parentheses where appropriate)—not necessarily inclusive (» = major clinical significance).

With physiology/laboratory test values

Alanine aminotransferase (ALT [SGPT]) and
Alkaline phosphatase and
Aspartate aminotransferase (AST [SGOT]) and
Lactate dehydrogenase (LDH)
(serum values are transiently increased in most patients)

Creatinine
(dose-related increases in serum concentrations may occur, indicating renal toxicity, but increases are usually minor and transient at recommended doses in patients with normal baseline renal function)

Uric acid concentrations in blood and urine
(may be increased)

Medical considerations/Contraindications

The medical considerations/contraindications included have been selected on the basis of their potential clinical significance (reasons given in parentheses where appropriate)—not necessarily inclusive (» = major clinical significance).

Risk-benefit should be considered when the following medical problems exist:

» Bone marrow depression

Cardiovascular function impairment, including coronary artery disease, congestive heart failure, hypertension
(adverse cardiac effects of pentostatin may be more likely to occur)

» Chickenpox, existing or recent (including recent exposure) or
» Herpes zoster
(risk of severe generalized disease)

Gout, history of or
Urate renal stones, history of
(risk of hyperuricemia)

» Infection
(pentostatin should be withheld until active infection is controlled)

» Renal function impairment
(reduced elimination; in patients with increased serum creatinine concentrations, pentostatin should be withheld and creatinine clearance determined)

» Sensitivity to pentostatin

» Caution should be used also in patients who have had previous cytotoxic drug therapy or radiation therapy.

Patient monitoring

The following may be especially important in patient monitoring (other tests may be warranted in some patients, depending on condition; » = major clinical significance):

» Creatinine clearance and/or

Creatinine concentrations, serum
(creatinine clearance and/or serum creatinine concentration determinations are recommended prior to initiation of therapy; serum creatinine concentration determinations are recommended before each dose and at other appropriate intervals during therapy)

» Hematocrit or hemoglobin and
» Leukocyte count, total and, if appropriate, differential and
» Platelet count
(determinations recommended prior to initiation of therapy and at periodic intervals during therapy, especially during early courses; frequency varies according to clinical state, agent, dose, and other agents being used concurrently)

Uric acid concentrations, serum
(determinations recommended prior to initiation of therapy and at periodic intervals during therapy; frequency varies according to clinical state, agent, dose, and other agents being used concurrently)

Side/Adverse Effects

Note: In patients with progressive hairy cell leukemia, neutropenia may worsen during the initial courses of pentostatin therapy.

Most side/adverse effects decrease in severity with continued treatment.

The following side/adverse effects have been selected on the basis of their potential clinical significance (possible signs and symptoms in parentheses where appropriate)—not necessarily inclusive:

Those indicating need for medical attention

Incidence more frequent

Allergic reaction (sudden skin rash or itching); ***anemia***—usually asymptomatic; ***central nervous system (CNS) toxicity*** (unusual tiredness; anxiety or nervousness; confusion; mental depression; numbness or tingling of hands or feet; sleepiness; trouble in sleeping); ***hepatic function impairment***—usually asymptomatic; ***leukopenia or infection*** (fever or chills; cough or hoarseness; lower back or side pain; painful or difficult urination); ***pain; thrombocytopenia*** (unusual bleeding or bruising; black, tarry stools; blood in urine or stools; pinpoint red spots on skin)—usually asymptomatic

Note: *Unusual tiredness* has been reported to increase with repeated weekly dosing and has been reduced by limiting pentostatin to three weekly doses or giving it every other week.

With high doses, *CNS toxicity* may lead to seizures, coma, and death.

Although hepatic enzyme elevations are usually transient, severe *hepatotoxicity* requiring withdrawal of pentostatin has been reported.

Severe *neutropenia* has occurred during early courses of treatment with pentostatin.

Infections may be bacterial, viral, or fungal, may occur even in the absence of leukopenia, and may be life-threatening.

Incidence less frequent—less than 10%

Cardiac effects, including angina and myocardial infarction, congestive heart failure, and acute arrhythmias (chest pain; swelling of feet or lower legs); ***changes in vision; keratoconjunctivitis*** (sore, red eyes); ***pulmonary toxicity, including bronchitis, dyspnea, epistaxis, lung edema, pneumonia, pharyngitis, rhinitis, or sinusitis*** (cough; nosebleed; shortness of breath); ***renal toxicity***—asymptomatic; seen as increases in serum creatinine; ***stomatitis*** (sores in mouth or on lips); ***stomach pain; thrombophlebitis*** (cramps in lower legs)

Note: *Cardiac effects* tend to occur in patients with preexisting cardiovascular conditions. Fatalities have occurred.

Keratoconjunctivitis is transient but may recur with subsequent doses.

Those indicating need for medical attention only if they continue or are bothersome

Incidence more frequent

Diarrhea; headache; loss of appetite; muscle pain; nausea and vomiting; skin rash

Note: Maculopapular *skin rashes* are occasionally severe and may worsen with continued treatment, necessitating withdrawal of pentostatin. *Herpes simplex* and *herpes zoster* infections may also occur. Inflammation of multiple actinic (solar) keratoses has been reported.

Incidence less frequent—less than 10%

Back pain; constipation; dry skin; flatulence (bloating or gas); ***flu-like syndrome*** (general feeling of discomfort or illness); ***itching; joint pain; weakness; weight loss***

Overdose

For more information on the management of overdose or unintentional ingestion, **contact a Poison Control Center** (see *Poison Control Center Listing*).

Treatment of overdose

Treatment consists of withdrawal of pentostatin and supportive therapy.

Patient Consultation

As an aid to patient consultation, refer to *Advice for the Patient, Pentostatin (Systemic)*.

In providing consultation, consider emphasizing the following selected information (» = major clinical significance):

Before using this medication

» Conditions affecting use, especially:
Sensitivity to pentostatin
Pregnancy—Use not recommended because of mutagenic, teratogenic, and carcinogenic potential; advisability of using contraception; telling physician immediately if pregnancy is suspected

Breast-feeding—Not recommended because of risk of serious side effects

Other medications, especially probenecid, sulfinpyrazone, other bone marrow depressants, or other cytotoxic drug or radiation therapy

Other medical problems, especially chickenpox, herpes zoster, renal function impairment, or infection

Proper use of this medication

Frequency of nausea and vomiting; importance of continuing medication despite stomach upset

» Proper dosing

Precautions while using this medication

» Importance of close monitoring by the physician

» Avoiding immunizations unless approved by physician; other persons in patient's household should avoid immunizations with oral poliovirus vaccine; avoiding other persons who have taken oral poliovirus vaccine or wearing a protective mask that covers nose and mouth

Caution if bone marrow depression occurs:

» Avoiding exposure to persons with infections, especially during periods of low blood counts; checking with physician immediately if fever or chills, cough or hoarseness, lower back or side pain, or painful or difficult urination occurs

» Checking with physician immediately if unusual bleeding or bruising; black, tarry stools; blood in urine or stools; or pinpoint red spots on skin occur

Caution in use of regular toothbrush, dental floss, or toothpick; physician, dentist, or nurse may suggest alternatives; checking with physician before having dental work done

Not touching eyes or inside of nose unless hands washed immediately before

Using caution to avoid accidental cuts with use of sharp objects such as safety razor or fingernail or toenail cutters

Avoiding contact sports or other situations where bruising or injury could occur

Side/adverse effects

May cause adverse effects such as blood problems; importance of discussing possible effects with physician

Signs of potential side effects, especially allergic reaction, CNS toxicity, leukopenia or infection, pain, thrombocytopenia, cardiac effects, changes in vision, keratoconjunctivitis, pulmonary toxicity, stomatitis, stomach pain, and thrombophlebitis

Asymptomatic side effects, including anemia, hepatic function impairment, thrombocytopenia, and renal function impairment

Physician or nurse can help in dealing with side effects

General Dosing Information

Patients receiving pentostatin should be under supervision of a physician experienced in cancer chemotherapy.

It is recommended that antiemetics be prescribed for 48 to 74 hours after pentostatin administration.

If CNS toxicity occurs, it is recommended that pentostatin be withheld or discontinued.

If severe skin rash occurs, it is recommended that pentostatin be withheld.

If elevated serum creatinine occurs, it is recommended that pentostatin be withheld and creatinine clearance determined. No recommendations are available for dosage adjustment in renal function impairment (creatinine clearance less than 60 mL per minute).

Development of uric acid nephropathy in patients with leukemia or lymphoma may be prevented by adequate oral hydration and, in some cases, administration of allopurinol. Alkalinization of urine may be necessary if serum uric acid concentrations are elevated.

Special precautions are recommended in patients who develop thrombocytopenia as a result of administration of pentostatin. These may include extreme care in performing invasive procedures; regular inspection of intravenous sites, skin (including perirectal area), and mucous membrane surfaces for signs of bleeding or bruising; limiting frequency of venipuncture and avoiding intramuscular injections; testing urine, emesis, stool, and secretions for occult blood; care in use of regular toothbrushes, dental floss, toothpicks, safety razors, and fingernail and toenail cutters; avoiding constipation; and using caution to prevent falls and other injuries. Such patients should avoid alcohol and aspirin intake because of the risk of gastrointestinal bleeding. Platelet transfusions may be required.

It is recommended that pentostatin be temporarily withheld if the absolute neutrophil count (ANC) falls below 200 cells per cubic millimeter in patients who had an initial count of greater than 500 cells per cubic millimeter. Treatment with pentostatin may be resumed when the ANC returns to pretreatment levels.

Patients who develop leukopenia should be observed carefully for signs of infection. Antibiotic support may be required. In neutropenic patients who develop fever, broad-spectrum antibiotic coverage should be initiated empirically, pending bacterial cultures and appropriate diagnostic tests.

If active infection occurs during pentostatin treatment, it is recommended that pentostatin be withheld until the infection is controlled.

Safety considerations for handling this medication

There is limited but increasing evidence and concern that personnel involved in preparation and administration of parenteral antineoplastics may be at some risk because of the potential mutagenicity, teratogenicity, and/or carcinogenicity of these agents, although the actual risk is unknown. USP advisory panels recommend cautious handling both in preparation and disposal of antineoplastic agents. Precautions that have been suggested include:

- Use of a biological containment cabinet during reconstitution and dilution of parenteral medications and wearing of disposable surgical gloves and masks.
- Use of proper technique to prevent contamination of the medication, work area, and operator during transfer between containers (including proper training of personnel in this technique).
- Cautious and proper disposal of needles, syringes, vials, ampuls, and unused medication.

A number of medical centers have developed detailed guidelines for handling of antineoplastic agents.

Parenteral Dosage Forms

PENTOSTATIN FOR INJECTION

Usual adult dose

Leukemia, hairy cell—

Intravenous (by rapid injection or diluted in a larger volume and given over twenty to thirty minutes), 4 mg per square meter of body surface area every other week.

Note: Hydration with 500 to 1000 mL of 5% dextrose in 0.45% sodium chloride injection or the equivalent before administration and 500 mL after administration is recommended.

Higher doses are not recommended because of the risk of renal, hepatic, pulmonary, and CNS toxicity.

It is recommended that pentostatin treatment be continued until two doses after a complete response is achieved. If the best response achieved is a partial response, it is recommended that pentostatin be discontinued after twelve months of treatment. If a complete or partial response is not achieved after six months of treatment, it is recommended that pentostatin be discontinued.

[Leukemia, chronic lymphocytic][1]

[Leukemia, prolymphocytic][1]

[Lymphoma, cutaneous T-cell][1]

Because several doses and regimens using pentostatin are showing activity, no individual doses/regimens are listed here. Consult the medical literature and/or experts in the field of oncology for information on dosage.

Usual pediatric dose

Safety and efficacy have not been established.

Strength(s) usually available

U.S.—

10 mg (Rx) [*Nipent* (mannitol 50 mg; sodium hydroxide or hydrochloric acid)].

Canada—

10 mg (Rx) [*Nipent* (mannitol 50 mg; sodium hydroxide or hydrochloric acid)].

Packaging and storage

Store between 2 and 8 °C (36 and 46 °F), unless otherwise specified by manufacturer.

Preparation of dosage form

Pentostatin for injection is prepared for intravenous use by aseptically adding 5 mL of sterile water for injection to the 10-mg vial, producing a solution containing 2 mg of pentostatin per mL.

Pentostatin solutions may be given intravenously by rapid injection or further diluted in 25 to 50 mL of 5% dextrose injection or 0.9% sodium chloride injection (producing a solution containing 0.33 mg per mL or 0.18 mg per mL, respectively) for administration by intravenous infusion.

Stability

Reconstituted solutions contain no preservative and should be used within 8 hours of reconstitution.

Note

The manufacturer recommends that spills and wastes be treated with 5% sodium hypochlorite solution prior to disposal.

[1]Not included in Canadian product labeling.

Selected Bibliography

Kane BJ, Kuhn JG, Roush MK. Pentostatin: an adenosine deaminase inhibitor for the treatment of hairy cell leukemia. Ann Pharmacother 1992; 26: 939-47.

Revised: 06/30/2003

PENTOXIFYLLINE Systemic

VA CLASSIFICATION (Primary): CV900

Commonly used brand name(s): *Trental.*

Another commonly used name is oxypentifylline.

Note: For a listing of dosage forms and brand names by country availability, see *Dosage Forms* section(s).

Category

Blood viscosity–reducing agent.

Indications

Note: Bracketed information in the *Indications* section refers to uses that are not included in U.S. product labeling.

Accepted

Vascular disease, peripheral (treatment)—Pentoxifylline is indicated to provide symptomatic relief of intermittent claudication [and other signs and symptoms, including trophic ulcers] associated with chronic occlusive arterial disorders of the limbs. Although pentoxifylline may improve function as well as provide symptomatic relief, it is not intended as a replacement for more definitive therapy that may be needed, such as surgical bypass procedures or removal of arterial obstructions.

Unaccepted

Pentoxifylline is used, in conjunction with other forms of treatment, to promote healing of stasis ulcers associated with venous insufficiency. However, further study is needed to determine the efficacy of the medication for this purpose.

Pharmacology/Pharmacokinetics

Physicochemical characteristics

Chemical Group—A dimethylxanthine derivative.
Molecular weight—278.31.
Solubility—Soluble in water and ethanol, sparingly soluble in toluene.

Mechanism of action/Effect

Pentoxifylline reduces blood viscosity and improves erythrocyte flexibility, microcirculatory flow, and tissue oxygen concentrations. Improvement in erythrocyte flexibility appears to be due to inhibition of phosphodiesterase and a resultant increase in cyclic AMP in red blood cells. Reduction of blood viscosity may be the result of decreased plasma fibrinogen concentrations and inhibition of red blood cell and platelet aggregation.

Absorption

The administration of pentoxifylline with food delays absorption and reduces peak plasma levels, but the extent of absorption is not affected. Pentoxifylline is rapidly and completely absorbed (greater than 95%) following oral administration, but undergoes extensive (60% to 70%) first-pass metabolism.

Protein binding

Bound to erythrocyte membrane.

Biotransformation

First by erythrocytes and then hepatic. Some metabolites are active.

Half-life

Unchanged drug—0.4 to 0.8 hours.
Metabolites—1 to 1.6 hours.

Onset of action

Multiple doses—2 to 4 weeks.

Time to peak concentration

Within 2 to 4 hours.

Elimination

Renal (as metabolites).
Fecal—Less than 4%.

Precautions to Consider

Cross-sensitivity and/or related problems

Patients sensitive to methylxanthines such as caffeine, theophylline, or theobromine may be sensitive to pentoxifylline also.

Carcinogenicity

Studies in mice given pentoxifylline at doses up to 24 times the maximum recommended human dose for 18 months found no evidence of carcinogenicity.

Tumorigenicity

Studies in rats given pentoxifylline at doses up to 24 times the maximum recommended human dose for 18 months, with a 6-month drug-free period, showed an increase in benign mammary fibroadenomas in females at the highest dose.

Mutagenicity

Pentoxifylline was not found to be mutagenic in Ames tests in the presence and absence of metabolic activation.

Pregnancy/Reproduction

Pregnancy—Adequate and well-controlled studies have not been done in humans.

Studies in rabbits and rats given up to about 10 and 25 times the maximum recommended human dose, respectively, have found an increased incidence of fetal resorptions in rats when pentoxifylline was given at the highest dose. No fetal malformations were observed.

FDA Pregnancy Category C.

Breast-feeding

Pentoxifylline and its metabolites are distributed into breast milk. Although problems in humans have not been documented, breast-feeding during treatment is not recommended because pentoxifylline may be tumorigenic (as demonstrated by the occurrence of benign mammary fibroadenomas in animal studies).

Pediatrics

No information is available on the relationship of age to the effects of pentoxifylline in pediatric patients. Safety and efficacy have not been established.

Geriatrics

Bioavailability of pentoxifylline may be increased and excretion decreased in the elderly, with resulting increased potential for toxicity. In addition, elderly patients are more likely to have age-related renal function impairment, which may require caution in patients receiving pentoxifylline.

Drug interactions and/or related problems

The following drug interactions and/or related problems have been selected on the basis of their potential clinical significance (possible mechanism in parentheses where appropriate)—not necessarily inclusive (» = major clinical significance):

Note: Combinations containing any of the following medications, depending on the amount present, may also interact with this medication.

Anticoagulants, coumarin- or indandione-derivative, or
Heparin or
Other medications that may interfere with blood clotting by interfering with platelet function and/or by causing hypoprothrombinemia, such as:
- Cefamandole
- Cefoperazone
- Cefotetan
- Plicamycin
- Valproic acid, or

Platelet aggregation inhibitors, other (See *Appendix II*), or
Thrombolytic agents
(pentoxifylline inhibits platelet aggregation and has also caused prolongation of prothrombin time and bleeding; concurrent use with any of these medications may increase the risk of bleeding because of additive interferences with blood clotting; caution, increased monitoring of the patient for any indication of bleeding, and, when applicable, more frequent monitoring of the prothrombin time are recommended)

Antihypertensives
(antihypertensive effects may be potentiated when these medications are used concurrently with pentoxifylline; dosage adjustments of the antihypertensive may be necessary)

Cimetidine
(cimetidine significantly increases the steady-state plasma concentration of pentoxifylline, which may increase the chance of side effects during concurrent use)

Smoking, tobacco
(although pentoxifylline is not a peripheral vasodilator, smoking may interfere with the therapeutic effect because nicotine constricts blood vessels, which may worsen the condition for which pentoxifylline is being used; avoidance of smoking is recommended)

Sympathomimetic agents or
Xanthines, other
(concurrent use with pentoxifylline may lead to excessive central nervous system [CNS] stimulation)

Medical considerations/Contraindications

The medical considerations/contraindications included have been selected on the basis of their potential clinical significance (reasons given in parentheses where appropriate)—not necessarily inclusive (» = major clinical significance).

Risk-benefit should be considered when the following medical problems exist:

» Any condition in which there is a risk of bleeding, especially recent cerebral or retinal hemorrhage, or
Bleeding, active
(pentoxifylline may cause or exacerbate bleeding; careful patient selection and monitoring of at risk patients via hematocrit and/or hemoglobin determinations are recommended)

Cerebrovascular disease or
Coronary artery disease
(angina, arrhythmia, and/or hypotension have occurred in some patients with these medical problems during treatment with pentoxifylline)

» Hepatic function impairment or
» Renal function impairment
(medication may accumulate; lower doses may be required; therapy may be inadvisable in patients with severe impairment; patients with mild to moderate impairment should be closely monitored)

Sensitivity to pentoxifylline or other methylxanthines

Side/Adverse Effects

The following side/adverse effects have been selected on the basis of their potential clinical significance (possible signs and symptoms in parentheses where appropriate)—not necessarily inclusive:

Those indicating need for medical attention

Incidence rare
Arrhythmias (irregular heartbeat); ***chest pain***

Those indicating need for medical attention only if they continue or are bothersome

Incidence less frequent—dose-related
Dizziness; headache; nausea or vomiting; stomach discomfort

Overdose

For more information on the management of overdose or unintentional ingestion, *contact a Poison Control Center* (see *Poison Control Center Listing*).

Clinical effects of overdose

The following effects have been selected on the basis of their potential clinical significance (possible signs and symptoms in parentheses where appropriate)—not necessarily inclusive:

Acute effects—in order of occurrence
Drowsiness; flushing; faintness; unusual excitement; convulsions

Treatment of overdose

To decrease absorption—Immediate evacuation of the stomach.

Supportive care—Symptomatic and supportive treatment, including respiratory support, maintenance of blood pressure, and control of convulsions.

Patient Consultation

As an aid to patient consultation, refer to *Advice for the Patient, Pentoxifylline (Systemic)*.

In providing consultation, consider emphasizing the following selected information (» = major clinical significance):

Before using this medication

» Conditions affecting use, especially:
Sensitivity to pentoxifylline or other methylxanthines

Breast-feeding—Passes into breast milk; breast-feeding may be inadvisable on the basis of tumorigenic effects in animal studies

Use in the elderly—Increased risk of side effects because of decreased clearance

Other medical problems, especially hepatic or renal function impairment or any condition in which there is a risk of bleeding

Proper use of this medication

Swallowing whole without crushing, breaking, or chewing
» Taking with meals and/or antacids to reduce gastrointestinal irritation
» Proper dosing
Missed dose: Taking as soon as possible; not taking if almost time for next dose; not doubling doses
» Proper storage

Precautions while using this medication

Checking with physician before discontinuing medication; pentoxifylline may take several weeks to work
Avoiding smoking (nicotine constricts blood vessels)

Side/adverse effects

Signs of potential side effects, especially arrhythmias and chest pain

General Dosing Information

Pentoxifylline should be administered with mealsand/or with antacids to reduce gastrointestinal irritation.

If patients develop dose-related gastrointestinal or central nervous system side effects the dose should be reduced to 400 milligrams twice daily. If side effects persist, pentoxifylline should be discontinued.

Oral Dosage Forms

PENTOXIFYLLINE EXTENDED-RELEASE TABLETS

Usual adult dose

Peripheral vascular disease—
Oral, 400 mg three times a day with mealsor antacids.

Note: Dosage should be reduced to 400 mg two times a day if gastrointestinal or CNS side effects occur.
Geriatric patients may be more sensitive to the effects of the usual adult dose.

Usual pediatric dose

Safety and efficacy have not been established.

Strength(s) usually available

U.S.—
400 mg (Rx) [*Trental* (FD&C Red No. 3; hypromellose USP; magnesium stearate NF; polyethylene glycol NF; povidone USP; talc; titanium dioxide USP; hydroxyethyl cellulose)].

Canada—
400 mg (Rx) [*Trental;* GENERIC].

Packaging and storage

Store below 40 °C (104 °F), preferably between 15 and 30 °C (59 and 86 °F), in a well-closed container, unless otherwise specified by manufacturer. Protect from light.

Auxiliary labeling

- Take with meals or food.
- Swallow tablets whole.

Selected Bibliography

Ward A & Clissold SP:Pentoxifylline. A review of its pharmacodynamic and pharmacokinetic properties, and its therapeutic efficacy. Drugs 1987; 34: 50-97.

Revised: 02/01/2006

PERGOLIDE Systemic

VA CLASSIFICATION (Primary): CN500

Commonly used brand name(s): *Permax*.

Note: For a listing of dosage forms and brand names by country availability, see *Dosage Forms* section(s).

Category

Antidyskinetic (dopamine agonist).

Indications

Accepted

Parkinsonism (treatment adjunct)—Pergolide is indicated, as an adjunct to levodopa or levodopa/carbidopa therapy, for treatment of the signs and symptoms of idiopathic or postencephalitic Parkinson's disease to allow achievement of symptomatic relief with lower doses of levodopa or levodopa/carbidopa.

[Restless legs syndrome (treatment)][1]—Pergolide is indicated for the treatment of restless legs syndrome.

[1]Not included in Canadian product labeling.

Pharmacology/Pharmacokinetics

Physicochemical characteristics

Chemical Group—Pergolide is a semisynthetic ergot alkaloid derivative

Molecular weight—410.59.

Mechanism of action/Effect

Pergolide is a potent dopamine receptor agonist that directly stimulates post-synaptic dopamine receptors (at both D_1 and D_2 receptor sites) in the nigrostriatal system. Unlike bromocriptine, but similar to apomorphine and lysuride, the postsynaptic dopamine agonist properties are independent of presynaptic dopamine synthesis or stores.

Other actions/effects

Inhibits secretion of prolactin; causes transient rise in serum concentration of growth hormone in normal patients while in patients with acromegaly it causes a decrease; causes decrease in serum concentrations of luteinizing hormone (LH).

Absorption

Significant amount may be absorbed (at present, data on systemic bioavailability is insufficient).

Protein binding

Very high (approximately 90%).

Elimination

Primarily renal (approximately 55% of a radionuclide labeled dose). However, approximately 5% is excreted via expired carbon dioxide.

Precautions to Consider

Cross-sensitivity and/or related problems

Patients sensitive to other ergot derivatives may be sensitive to this medication also.

Carcinogenicity

Uterine neoplasms in rats and mice, endometrial adenomas and carcinomas in rats, and endometrial sarcomas in mice, occurred with doses as high as 340 and 12 times (in mice and rats, respectively) the maximum human oral dose. It is believed that this was due to the high estrogen/progesterone ratio that may occur in rodents as a result of inhibition of prolactin secretion. Human data are not available.

Mutagenicity

Pergolide generated a weak mutagenic response in the mammalian cell-point-mutation assay (in cultured L5178Y cells); other assays, including a DNA repair assay, an Ames bacterial mutation assay, and a hamster bone chromosome alteration determination, generated a mutagenic-negative response. Human-related studies are currently unavailable.

Pregnancy/Reproduction

Fertility—In a single study of male and female mice, fertility was preserved at dosage levels 0.6 and 1.7 mg/kg/day, but was impaired at 5.6mg/kg/day. The relevance of this data to humans is currently unknown.

Pregnancy—Adequate and well-controlled studies in humans have not been done. In pre-market release studies of women treated with pergolide for endocrine disorders, congenital abnormalities were associated with 6 out of 39 pregnancies. Although a causal relationship has yet to be established, this drug should be used only with caution during pregnancy.

Reproduction studies in mice and rabbits with doses as high as 375 and 133 times, respectively, the maximum human dose administered in clinical trials (6 mg/day) have not shown that pergolide causes adverse effects on the fetus.

FDA Pregnancy Category B.

Breast-feeding

Pergolide may inhibit lactation. Excretion of pergolide in breast milk has not yet been confirmed. However, since human milk excretion occurs with many drugs, a decision should be made regarding the benefit/risk of continuing the drug, compared with that of continuing nursing by the mother.

Pediatrics

No published pediatrics-specific information is available. Safety and efficacy have not been established.

Geriatrics

Studies performed to date have not demonstrated geriatrics-specific problems that would limit the usefulness of pergolide in the elderly.

Dental

Pergolide may decrease or inhibit salivary flow, thus contributing to the development of caries, periodontal disease, oral candidiasis, and discomfort.

Drug interactions and/or related problems

The following drug interactions and/or related problems have been selected on the basis of their potential clinical significance (possible mechanism in parentheses where appropriate)—not necessarily inclusive (» = major clinical significance):

Note: Drugs known to affect protein binding should be used with caution, due to pergolide's preferential binding with plasma protein.

Combinations containing any of the following medications, depending on the amount present, may also interact with this medication.

Droperidol or
Haloperidol or
Loxapine or
Methyldopa or
Metoclopramide or
Molindone or
Papaverine or
Phenothiazines or
Reserpine or
Thioxanthenes
(dopamine antagonists may decrease the effectiveness of pergolide)

Hypotension-producing medications, other (See *Appendix II*)
(concurrent use may result in additive hypotensive effects)

Laboratory value alterations

The following have been selected on the basis of their potential clinical significance (possible effect in parentheses where appropriate)—not necessarily inclusive (» = major clinical significance).

With physiology/laboratory test values

Plasma growth hormone concentrations
(may be transiently increased in individuals with normal concentrations; paradoxically reduced in patients with acromegaly)

Medical considerations/Contraindications

The medical considerations/contraindications included have been selected on the basis of their potential clinical significance (reasons given in parentheses where appropriate)—not necessarily inclusive (» = major clinical significance).

Except under special circumstances, this medication should not be used when the following medical problem exists:

» Sensitivity to pergolide or other ergot alkaloids

Risk-benefit should be considered when the following medical problems exist:

Cardiac dysrhythmias
(increased risk of atrial premature contractions and sinus tachycardia)

Psychiatric disorders
(pre-existing states of confusion and hallucinations may be exacerbated)

Patient monitoring

The following may be especially important in patient monitoring (other tests may be warranted in some patients, depending on condition; » = major clinical significance):

» Blood pressure measurements
(pergolide commonly decreases or less frequently increases blood pressure)

Note: Specific laboratory tests are not deemed essential. Periodic, routine laboratory screenings are recommended.

Side/Adverse Effects

The following side/adverse effects have been selected on the basis of their potential clinical significance (possible signs and symptoms in parentheses where appropriate)—not necessarily inclusive:

Those indicating need for medical attention

Incidence more frequent

Anemia (unusual tiredness or weakness); ***CNS effects, including anxiety; confusion; dyskinesias*** (uncontrolled movements of the body, such as the face, tongue, arms, hands, head, and upper body);

hallucinations (seeing, hearing, or feeling things that are not there); ***insomnia*** (trouble in sleeping); ***urinary tract infection*** (bloody or cloudy urine; difficult or painful urination; frequent urge to urinate); ***visual disturbances, including diplopia*** (visual changes; double vision)

Incidence less frequent

Hypertension (dizziness; headache); ***peripheral edema*** (swelling in hands and legs.)

Incidence rare

Cerebrovascular hemorrhage (severe or continuing headache; seizures; vision changes, such as blurred vision or temporary blindness; sudden weakness); ***myocardial infarction*** (severe chest pain; fainting; fast heartbeat; increased sweating; continuing or severe nausea and vomiting; nervousness; unexplained shortness of breath; weakness); ***neuroleptic malignant syndrome (NMS)*** (difficult or unusually fast breathing [difficulty in breathing]; fast heartbeat or irregular pulse; high fever; high or low [irregular] blood pressure; increased sweating; loss of bladder control; severe muscle stiffness; seizures; unusual tiredness or weakness; unusually pale skin); ***serous inflammation and fibrosis, including pleuritis*** (chest pain; chills; dry cough; fever; troubled breathing); ***pleural infection*** (chest pain; cough; fever; troubled breathing); ***pleural fibrosis*** (chest pain; cough; shortness of breath); ***pericarditis*** (anxiety; chest pain; chills; cough; fever; troubled breathing; weakness); ***pericardial effusion*** (chest pain; troubled breathing); ***retroperitoneal fibrosis*** (abdominal pain or pressure; decrease in flow of urine; pain in side or lower back)

Note: *Neuroleptic malignant syndrome* has been associated with the rapid reduction, withdrawal, or change of dosage in pergolide, and in other anti-Parkinsonian drugs.

Those indicating need for medical attention only if they continue or are bothersome

Incidence more frequent

Dyspepsia (heartburn); ***constipation; dizziness; drowsiness; influenza-like symptoms*** (headache; muscle pain; runny nose; chest congestion); ***hypotension*** (dizziness or lightheadedness, especially when getting up from a lying or sitting position); ***lower back pain; nausea; rhinitis*** (runny or stuffy nose); ***weakness***

Note: Approximately 10% of patients experience *orthostatic hypotension* during initial treatment. Tolerance usually develops with gradual dosage titration.

Incidence less frequent

Diarrhea; dryness of mouth; facial edema (swelling of the face); ***anorexia*** (loss of appetite); ***vomiting***

Overdose

For specific information on the agents used in the management of pergolide overdose, see:

- *Charcoal, Activated (Oral-Local)* monograph; and/or
- *Phenothiazines (Systemic)* monograph.

For more information on the management of overdose or unintentional ingestion, **contact a Poison Control Center** (see *Poison Control Center Listing*).

Treatment of overdose

Treatment is symptomatic and supportive, with possible utilization of the following:

To decrease absorption—Administration of activated charcoal instead of or in addition to gastric emptying. Repeated doses of charcoal over time may expedite the elimination of ingested pergolide prior to absorption.

Specific treatment—Antiarrhythmic medication, if necessary. Phenothiazine or other neuroleptic agent, to treat CNS stimulation.

Monitoring—Monitoring of cardiac function.

Supportive care—Maintenance of arterial blood pressure, and protection of the patient's airway. Patients in whom intentional overdose is confirmed or suspected should be referred for psychiatric consultation.

Patient Consultation

As an aid to patient consultation, refer to *Advice for the Patient, Pergolide (Systemic)*.

In providing consultation, consider emphasizing the following selected information (» = major clinical significance):

Before using this medication

» Conditions affecting use, especially:
  Sensitivity to pergolide or other ergot alkaloids
  Breast-feeding—May prevent lactation in mothers who intend to breast-feed
  Dental—Reduced salivary flow may contribute to dental problems

Proper use of this medication

Taking with meals to reduce gastric effects
» Proper dosing
  Missed dose: Taking as soon as possible; not taking if almost time for next dose; not doubling doses
» Proper storage

Precautions while using this medication

Regular visits to physician to check progress
» Caution when driving or doing jobs requiring alertness, because of possible drowsiness or dizziness
  Dizziness may be more likely to occur after initial doses; taking first dose at bedtime or while lying down; getting up slowly from sitting or lying position
  Possible dryness of mouth; using sugarless gum or candy, ice, or saliva substitute for relief; checking with physician or dentist if dry mouth continues for more than 2 weeks
  Checking with physician before reducing dosage or discontinuing medication

Side/adverse effects

Signs of potential side effects, especially anemia, CNS effects, urinary tract infection, visual disturbances, hypertension, peripheral edema, cerebrovascular hemorrhage, myocardial infarction, neuroleptic malignant syndrome, and serous inflammation and fibrosis

General Dosing Information

Titrated dosage is necessary to achieve the individual therapeutic blood concentration requirements and to minimize the risk of side effects.

Nausea and dizziness associated with initiation of pergolide therapy usually resolve with continued therapy; however, incidence and severity of these side effects may be reduced with a decrease in pergolide dose. Dizziness and nausea may be better tolerated by administering the initial dose at bedtime or while lying down. Also, administration of pergolide with food may alleviate the nausea

Abrupt change in pergolide dosage (reduction or withdrawal) has been associated with a symptom complex similar to neuroleptic malignant syndrome. Caution should be exercised whenever a change is required in pergolide dosage.

Oral Dosage Forms

Note: The dosing and strengths of the dosage forms available are expressed in terms of pergolide base, not the mesylate salt.

PERGOLIDE MESYLATE TABLETS

Usual adult and adolescent dose

Parkinsonism—

Oral, 50 mcg (0.05 mg) (base) a day for the first two days; the dosage being increased gradually by 100 or 150 mcg (0.1 or 0.15 mg) (base) every third day over the next twelve days of therapy. Afterwards, the dose may be increased by 250 mcg (0.25 mg) (base) every third day until optimum therapeutic effect is achieved.

Note: Usually administered in divided doses three times a day.

During dosage titration of pergolide the concurrent dose of levodopa or levodopa/carbidopa may be decreased with caution according to clinical response.

Clinical studies have documented a mean pergolide dosage of 3 mg per day. Concurrent administration of levodopa/carbidopa averaged 650 mg/day. Efficacy of pergolide dosage in excess of 5 mg/day has not been systematically evaluated.

[Restless legs syndrome (treatment)][1]—

Oral, 50 mcg (0.05 mg) (base) a day given two hours before bedtime. Dosage may be increased by 0.05 mg daily until optimum therapeutic effect is achieved.

Usual adult prescribing limits

5 mg daily.

Usual pediatric dose

Safety and efficacy have not been established.

Usual geriatric dose

See *Usual adult and adolescent dose.*

Strength(s) usually available

U.S.—

50 mcg (0.05 mg) (base) (Rx) [*Permax* (scored; croscarmellose sodium; iron oxide; lactose; magnesium stearate; methionine; povidone)].

250 mcg (0.25 mg) (base) (Rx) [*Permax* (scored; croscarmellose sodium; iron oxide; lactose; magnesium stearate; povidone; FD&C Blue No. 2)].

1 mg (base) (Rx) [*Permax* (scored; croscarmellose sodium; iron oxide; lactose; magnesium stearate; povidone)].

Canada—

50 mcg (0.05 mg) (base) (Rx) [*Permax* (scored; croscarmellose sodium; iron oxide yellow; lactose; magnesium stearate; povidine; FD &C Blue No. 2 Aluminum Lake)].

250 mcg (0.25 mg) (base) (Rx) [*Permax* (scored; croscarmellose sodium; iron oxide yellow; lactose; l-methionine; magnesium stearate; povidine)].

1 mg (base) (Rx) [*Permax* (scored; croscarmellose sodium; iron oxide red pure; lactose; magnesium stearate; povidine)].

Packaging and storage
Store between 15 and 30 °C (59 and 86 °F), unless otherwise specified by manufacturer.

Auxiliary labeling
- May cause drowsiness.
- May cause dizziness

[1]Not included in Canadian product labeling.

Selected Bibliography
Lieberman AN, Goldstein M, Gopinathan G, et al. D_1 and D_2 agonists in Parkinson's disease. Can J Neurol Sci 1987 Aug; 14(3 Suppl): 466-73.

Lieberman AN, Gopinathan G, Neophytides A, et al. Management of levodopa failures: the use of dopamine agonists. Clin Neuropharmacol 1986; 9(Suppl 2): S9-21.

Factor SA, Sanchez-Ramos JR, Weiner WJ. Parkinson's disease: An open label trial of pergolide in patients failing bromocriptine therapy. J Neurol Neurosurg Psychiatry 1988 Apr; 51(4): 529-33.

Revised: 01/07/2003

PERICYAZINE—See *Phenothiazines (Systemic)*

PERINDOPRIL—See *Angiotensin-converting Enzyme (ACE) Inhibitors (Systemic)*

PERPHENAZINE—See *Phenothiazines (Systemic)*

PHENAZOPYRIDINE Systemic

VA CLASSIFICATION (Primary): GU100

Commonly used brand name(s): *Azo-Standard; Baridium; Eridium; Geridium; Phenazo; Phenazodine; Pyridiate; Pyridium; Urodine; Urogesic; Viridium.*

Note: For a listing of dosage forms and brand names by country availability, see *Dosage Forms* section(s).

Category
Analgesic (urinary).

Indications
Accepted
Urinary tract irritation (treatment)—Phenazopyridine is indicated for short-term use to relieve symptoms such as pain, burning, and urinary urgency and/or frequency caused by irritation of the lower urinary tract mucosa. The underlying cause of the irritation must be determined and treated (for example, antibacterial therapy for infection).

Pharmacology/Pharmacokinetics
Physicochemical characteristics
Chemical Group—Azo dye.

Molecular weight—249.70.

Mechanism of action/Effect
Exerts a topical analgesic or local anesthetic action on the urinary tract mucosa. The exact mechanism of action is unknown.

Biotransformation
Probably hepatic; also in other tissues. One of the metabolites is acetaminophen.

Elimination
Renal. Up to 90% of a dose is excreted within 24 hours, as unchanged drug and metabolites. About 18% of a dose is eliminated as acetaminophen. Up to 65% of a dose may be excreted unchanged.

Precautions to Consider
Carcinogenicity
Long-term administration of phenazopyridine has caused neoplasia of the large intestine in rats and neoplasia of the liver in mice. No association between use of the medication in humans and development of neoplasia has been reported; however, studies in humans have not been done.

Pregnancy/Reproduction
Fertility—Studies in rats with doses up to 50 mg per kg of body weight (mg/kg) per day have not shown evidence of impaired fertility.

Pregnancy—Adequate and well-controlled studies have not been done in humans.

Studies in rats with doses up to 50 mg/kg per day have not shown evidence of harm to the fetus.

FDA Pregnancy Category B.

Breast-feeding
It is not known whether phenazopyridine or any of its metabolites are distributed into breast milk. However, problems in humans have not been documented.

Pediatrics
Appropriate studies with phenazopyridine have not been performed in the pediatric population. However, no pediatrics-specific problems have been documented to date.

Geriatrics
Although appropriate studies with phenazopyridine have not been performed in the geriatric population, no geriatrics-specific problems have been documented to date. However, elderly patients are more likely to have age-related renal function impairment, which may increase the risk of accumulation and toxicity in patients receiving phenazopyridine.

Laboratory value alterations
The following have been selected on the basis of their potential clinical significance (possible effect in parentheses where appropriate)—not necessarily inclusive (» = major clinical significance).

With physiology/laboratory test values

Urinalyses based on color reaction or spectroscopy, for example:

Bilirubin, urine, determined via foam test, talc-disk–Fouchet spot test, or Franklin's tablet-Fouchet test methods

Glucose, urine, determined using glucose oxidase

17-Hydroxycorticosteroids, urine, determined via Glenn-Nelson method

Ketones, urine, determined using sodium nitroprusside or Gerhardt ferric chloride test

17-Ketosteroids, urine, determined via Haltorff Koch modification of Zimmerman reaction

Kidney function tested via phenolsulfonphthalein (PSP) excretion

Protein, urine, determined using bromophenol blue test reagent strips or nitric acid ring test

Urobilinogen, urine, determined using Ehrlich's reagent
(phenazopyridine may interfere with test results by causing discoloration of the urine)

Medical considerations/Contraindications
The medical considerations/contraindications included have been selected on the basis of their potential clinical significance (reasons given in parentheses where appropriate)—not necessarily inclusive (» = major clinical significance).

Except under special circumstances, this medication should not be used when the following medical problem exists:

Renal function impairment
(increased risk of accumulation and toxicity)

Risk-benefit should be considered when the following medical problems exist:

Allergic reaction to phenazopyridine, history of

» Glucose-6-phosphate dehydrogenase (G6PD) deficiency
(increased risk of severe hemolytic anemia)

Hepatitis
(increased risk of adverse effects)

Side/Adverse Effects
Note: In addition to the side effects reported below, an anaphylactoid-like reaction has been reported.

The following side/adverse effects have been selected on the basis of their potential clinical significance (possible signs and symptoms in parentheses where appropriate)—not necessarily inclusive:

Those indicating need for medical attention

Incidence rare

Anemia, hemolytic (troubled breathing, exertional; unusual tiredness or weakness); ***aseptic meningitis*** (fever; confusion)—reported in 1 patient; causal relationship verified via rechallenge; ***dermatitis, allergic*** (skin rash); ***hepatotoxicity*** (yellow eyes or skin); ***methemoglobinemia*** (blue or blue-purple discoloration of skin; shortness of breath); ***renal function impairment or failure*** (increased blood pressure; shortness of breath; troubled breathing; tightness in chest, and/or wheezing; sudden decrease in amount of urine; swelling of face, fingers, feet, and/or lower legs; thirst, continuing; unusual tiredness or weakness; weight gain)

Note: *Hemolytic anemia* or *methemoglobinemia* may be more likely with an overdose or if the medication is administered to patients with renal function impairment, but have also been reported with therapeutic doses in patients with normal renal function. Also, *hemolytic anemia* is especially likely to occur in patients with glucose-6-phosphate dehydrogenase deficiency.

Hepatotoxicity has been reported in conjunction with impaired renal excretion of the medication; however, yellowish discoloration of eyes or skin may also occur independently of hepatotoxicity, indicating accumulation. Permanent staining of soft contact lenses has also been reported.

Those indicating need for medical attention only if they continue or are bothersome

Incidence less frequent or rare

Dizziness; headache; indigestion; pruritus (itching of the skin); ***stomach cramps or pain***

Overdose

For more information on the management of overdose or unintentional ingestion, **contact a poison control center** (see *Poison Control Center Listing*).

Clinical effects of overdose

The following effects have been selected on the basis of their potential clinical significance (possible signs and symptoms in parentheses where appropriate)—not necessarily inclusive:

Anemia, hemolytic (troubled breathing, exertional; unusual tiredness or weakness); ***hepatotoxicity*** (yellow eyes or skin); ***methemoglobinemia*** (blue or blue-purple discoloration of skin; shortness of breath); ***renal function impairment or failure*** (increased blood pressure; shortness of breath; troubled breathing; tightness in chest, and/or wheezing; sudden decrease in amount of urine; swelling of face, fingers, feet, and/or lower legs; thirst, continuing; unusual tiredness or weakness; weight gain)

Treatment of overdose

Specific treatment

Methemoglobinemia will respond to methylene blue intravenous, 1 to 2 mg per kg of body weight or ascorbic acid oral, 100 to 200 mg. The resulting reduction in methemoglobinemia and cyanosis is an aid in diagnosing phenazopyridine overdose.

Patients in whom intentional overdose is confirmed or suspected should be referred for psychiatric consultation.

Patient Consultation

As an aid to patient consultation, refer to *Advice for the Patient, Phenazopyridine (Systemic)*.

In providing consultation, consider emphasizing the following selected information (» = major clinical significance):

Before using this medication

» Conditions affecting use, especially:
  Allergic reaction to phenazopyridine, history of
  Other medical problems, especially glucose-6-phosphate dehydrogenase (G6PD) deficiency

Proper use of this medication

Taking with or following food (a meal or a snack) to reduce gastric upset

» Not using any saved portion of medication in the future unless authorized by physician

» Proper dosing
  Missed dose: Taking as soon as possible; not taking if almost time for next dose; not doubling doses

» Proper storage

Precautions while using this medication

» Informing physician if symptoms worsen

» Medication causes urine to turn reddish orange and may stain clothing
  Not wearing soft contact lenses during therapy because of possible permanent staining
  Diabetics: May cause false urine sugar and urine ketone test results
  Possible interference with laboratory test results; notifying person in charge that medication is being used

Side/adverse effects

Signs of potential side effects, especially allergic dermatitis, aseptic meningitis, hemolytic anemia, hepatotoxicity, methemoglobinemia, and renal impairment or failure

General Dosing Information

This medication should be taken with or following food to lessen gastric irritation.

When phenazopyridine is used concurrently with an antibacterial agent in the treatment of a urinary tract infection, the duration of phenazopyridine therapy should not exceed 2 days. Adequate evidence that more prolonged phenazopyridine therapy provides greater therapeutic benefit than is achieved with the antibacterial agent alone is not available.

Oral Dosage Forms

PHENAZOPYRIDINE HYDROCHLORIDE TABLETS USP

Usual adult and adolescent dose

Analgesic (urinary)—
  Oral, 200 mg three times a day, with or following food.

  Note: When used in combination with an antibacterial agent for the treatment of urinary tract infection, length of phenazopyridine treatment should not exceed two days.

Usual pediatric dose

Analgesic (urinary)—
  Oral, 4 mg per kg of body weight three times a day, with food.

Strength(s) usually available

U.S.—
  100 mg (Rx) [*Azo-Standard; Baridium; Eridium; Geridium; Phenazodine; Pyridiate; Pyridium; Urodine; Urogesic;* GENERIC].
  200 mg (Rx) [*Geridium; Phenazodine; Pyridiate; Pyridium; Urodine; Viridium;* GENERIC].

Canada—
  100 mg (OTC) [*Phenazo; Pyridium*].
  200 mg (OTC) [*Phenazo; Pyridium*].

Packaging and storage

Store below 40 °C (104 °F), preferably between 15 and 30 °C (59 and 86 °F), unless otherwise specified by manufacturer. Store in a tight container.

Auxiliary labeling

- May discolor urine.
- Take with food.

Note

Stains on clothing may be removed with a 0.25% solution of sodium dithionate or sodium hydrosulfite.

Revised: 12/17/1999

PHENDIMETRAZINE—See *Appetite Suppressants (Systemic)*

PHENELZINE—See *Antidepressants, Monoamine Oxidase (MAO) Inhibitor (Systemic)*

PHENINDAMINE—See *Antihistamines (Systemic)*

PHENOBARBITAL—See *Barbiturates (Systemic)*

PHENOLPHTHALEIN—See *Laxatives (Local)*

PHENOTHIAZINES Systemic

This monograph includes information on the following: 1) Chlorpromazine; 2) Fluphenazine; 3) Mesoridazine; 4) Methotrimeprazine*; 5) Pericyazine*; 6) Perphenazine; 7) Pipotiazine*; 8) Prochlorperazine; 9) Promazine*; 10) Thioproperazine*; 11) Thioridazine; 12) Trifluoperazine; 13) Triflupromazine†.

INN:
- Methotrimeprazine—Levomepromazine
- Pericyazine—Periciazine

BAN:
- Pipotiazine—Pipothiazine
- Triflupromazine—Fluopromazine

JAN:
- Methotrimeprazine—Levomepromazine
- Pericyazine—Propericiazine

VA CLASSIFICATION (Primary/Secondary):
- Chlorpromazine—CN701/GA609; AU305; CN309; CN206
- Fluphenazine—CN701/CN103
- Mesoridazine—CN701
- Methotrimeprazine—CN701/CN103; CN309; GA609; CN206
- Pericyazine—CN701
- Perphenazine—CN701/GA609
- Pipotiazine—CN701
- Prochlorperazine—CN701/GA609
- Promazine—CN701
- Thioproperazine—CN701
- Thioridazine—CN701/AU305; CN309
- Trifluoperazine—CN701/GA609
- Triflupromazine—CN701/GA609

Commonly used brand name(s): *Apo-Fluphenazine*[2]; *Apo-Perphenazine*[6]; *Apo-Thioridazine*[11]; *Apo-Trifluoperazine*[12]; *Chlorpromanyl-20*[1]; *Chlorpromanyl-40*[1]; *Chlorpromazine Hydrochloride Intensol*[1]; *Compazine*[8]; *Compazine Spansule*[8]; *Largactil*[1]; *Largactil Liquid*[1]; *Largactil Oral Drops*[1]; *Majeptil*[10]; *Mellaril*[11]; *Mellaril Concentrate*[11]; *Mellaril-S*[11]; *Modecate*[2]; *Modecate Concentrate*[2]; *Moditen Enanthate*[2]; *Moditen HCl*[2]; *Neuleptil*[5]; *Novo-Chlorpromazine*[1]; *Novo-Ridazine*[11]; *Novo-Trifluzine*[12]; *Nozinan*[4]; *Nozinan Liquid*[4]; *Nozinan Oral Drops*[4]; *Nu-Prochlor*[8]; *PMS Fluphenazine*[2]; *PMS Perphenazine*[6]; *PMS Prochlorperazine*[8]; *PMS Thioridazine*[11]; *PMS Trifluoperazine*[12]; *Permitil*[2]; *Permitil Concentrate*[2]; *Piportil L$_4$*[7]; *Prolixin*[2]; *Prolixin Concentrate*[2]; *Prolixin Decanoate*[2]; *Prolixin Enanthate*[2]; *Serentil*[3]; *Serentil Concentrate*[3]; *Stelazine*[12]; *Stelazine Concentrate*[12]; *Stemetil*[8]; *Stemetil Liquid*[8]; *Thorazine*[1]; *Thorazine Spansule*[1]; *Trilafon*[6]; *Trilafon Concentrate*[6]; *Vesprin*[13].

Note: For a listing of dosage forms and brand names by country availability, see *Dosage Forms* section(s).

*Not commercially available in U.S.
†Not commercially available in Canada.

Category

Antipsychotic—Chlorpromazine; Fluphenazine; Mesoridazine; Methotrimeprazine; Perphenazine; Pipotiazine; Prochlorperazine; Promazine; Thioproperazine; Thioridazine; Trifluoperazine; Triflupromazine.
Antipsychotic adjunct—Pericyazine.
Antiemetic—Chlorpromazine; Methotrimeprazine; Perphenazine; Prochlorperazine; Trifluoperazine; Triflupromazine.
Analgesic—Methotrimeprazine.
Sedative—Chlorpromazine; Methotrimeprazine; Thioridazine.
Antidyskinetic (Huntington's chorea)—Chlorpromazine; Thioridazine.
Antineuralgia adjunct—Fluphenazine.
Anesthetic adjunct—Chlorpromazine; Methotrimeprazine (intravenous)

Indications

Note: Bracketed information in the *Indications* section refers to uses that are not included in U.S. product labeling.

Accepted

Psychotic disorders (treatment)—Chlorpromazine, fluphenazine, mesoridazine, methotrimeprazine, perphenazine, pipotiazine, prochlorperazine, promazine, thioproperazine, thioridazine, trifluoperazine, and triflupromazine are indicated in the management of manifestations of psychotic conditions. They are clearly effective in schizophrenia, and produce a quieting effect in hyperactive or excited psychotic patients.

Note: Thioridazine and mesoridazine are indicated for the management of schizophrenic patients who fail to respond adequately to treatment with other antipsychotic drugs. Due to the risk of significant, potentially life-threatening, proarrhythmic effects with thioridazine and mesoridazine treatment, it is strongly recommended that a patient be given at least 2 trials, each with a different antipsychotic drug product, at an adequate dose, and for an adequate duration.

Note: Mesoridazine has not been proven to be effective in the treatment of refractory schizophrenic patients, as it has not been evaluated in clinical trials.

Methotrimeprazine is used in elderly patients for the management of psychosis associated with dementia.

Chlorpromazine, methotrimeprazine, and thioproperazine are indicated in the management of manifestations of the manic phase of manic-depressive illness.

[Chlorpromazine], [fluphenazine], mesoridazine, [thioridazine], and [trifluoperazine] are used in the treatment of adults with severe behavior problems associated with psychotic disorders who show combativeness and/or explosive, hyperexcitable behavior that is out of proportion to the immediate provocation. Chlorpromazine, [mesoridazine], thioridazine, and [trifluoperazine] also are used in the treatment of children with severe behavior problems associated with psychotic disorders who show combativeness and/or explosive, hyperexcitable behavior that is out of proportion to the immediate provocation and in whom other approaches to management have failed.

Long-acting parenteral forms, fluphenazine decanoate and enanthate and pipotiazine palmitate, are indicated for the maintenance treatment of nonagitated patients with chronic schizophrenia who are stabilized with shorter-acting neuroleptics and who may benefit from transfer to a longer-acting drug.

Psychotic disorders (treatment adjunct)—Pericyazine is indicated as an adjunctive medication for the control of residual prevailing hostility, impulsivity, and aggressiveness in patients with psychoses.

Nausea and vomiting (treatment)—Prochlorperazine, chlorpromazine, methotrimeprazine, perphenazine, [trifluoperazine], and triflupromazine are indicated in the control of severe nausea and vomiting in selected patients, with prochlorperazine being superior to other phenothiazines.

Pain (treatment)—Methotrimeprazine is indicated for the relief of moderate to severe pain in nonambulatory patients, and for the production of obstetrical analgesia when respiratory depression should be avoided.

Sedation—Methotrimeprazine is indicated as a presurgical or obstetrical medication to produce sedation and somnolence.

Chlorpromazine is indicated for relief of apprehension and restlessness before surgery.

Anesthesia, general, adjunct—[Chlorpromazine] and intravenously-administered methotrimeprazine are indicated as adjuncts to anesthesia, to increase the effects of anesthetics. The dose of a barbiturate or narcotic should be reduced by at least one half when used with chlorpromazine or methotrimeprazine during surgery or labor.

Tetanus (treatment adjunct)[1]—Chlorpromazine is indicated, usually in conjunction with a barbiturate, for the treatment of tetanus.

Porphyria, acute, intermittent (treatment)[1]—Chlorpromazine is indicated in the treatment of acute intermittent porphyria.

[Chlorpromazine is also used for the treatment of migraine headaches][1].

Hiccups, intractable (treatment)—Chlorpromazine is indicated for the relief of intractable hiccups.

[Pain, neurogenic (treatment adjunct)][1]—Fluphenazine has been used as an adjunct to tricyclic antidepressant therapy for some chronic pain states, such as in patients trying to withdraw from narcotics, and in treatment of symptoms of diabetic neuropathy.

[Huntington's disease, choreiform movement of (treatment)][1]—Chlorpromazine and thioridazine are effective in reducing choreiform movement in Huntington's disease, and have been used as alternatives to haloperidol.

Behavior problems, severe (treatment)—[Chlorpromazine], [fluphenazine], mesoridazine, [thioridazine], and [trifluoperazine] may be used in the treatment of adults with severe behavior problems associated with neurologic disease other than Pretension's disease who show combativeness and/or explosive, hyperexcitable behavior that is out of proportion to the immediate provocation and in whom other approaches to management have failed.

Chlorpromazine, [mesoridazine], thioridazine, and [trifluoperazine] also may be used when other approaches to management have failed in the treatment of children with severe behavior problems associated with neurologic disease other than juvenile Pretension's disease and in the short-term treatment of hyperactive children who show excessive motor activity with accompanying conduct disorders such as impulsivity, mood lability, aggressiveness, short attention span, and poor frustration tolerance. Their use is acceptable only in children who are displaying combative, dangerous, or destructive behaviors.

In exceptional cases, thioridazine may be used in the short-term treatment of geriatric patients with multiple symptoms, such as anxiety, agitation, depressed mood, tension, sleep disturbances, and fears. However, because of the anticholinergic effects of thioridazine and the availability of safer antipsychotic medications, its use should be restricted to those patients in whom several other approaches to management have been tried and have failed.

Although prochlorperazine and trifluoperazine have been used in the treatment of nonpsychotic anxiety, they generally have been replaced by less potentially harmful agents. Their use for this indication may be acceptable only in unusual cases after several non-antipsychotic approaches to treatment have been tried and have failed and the potential benefit outweighs the risks associated with these drugs.

Thioridazine has been used in the short-term treatment of adult patients with moderate to severe mental depression with varying degrees of anxiety. However, this medication generally has been replaced by less potentially harmful agents and its use for this indication may be acceptable only in unusual cases after several other approaches to treatment have been tried and have failed.

[1]Not included in Canadian product labeling.

Pharmacology/Pharmacokinetics

Physicochemical characteristics

Chemical Group—

Aliphatic: Chlorpromazine; methotrimeprazine; promazine; triflupromazine

Piperazine: Fluphenazine; perphenazine; prochlorperazine; thioproperazine; trifluoperazine

Piperidine: Mesoridazine; pericyazine; pipotiazine; thioridazine

Molecular weight—

Chlorpromazine: 318.87.
Chlorpromazine hydrochloride: 355.33.
Fluphenazine decanoate: 591.8.
Fluphenazine enanthate: 549.70.
Fluphenazine hydrochloride: 510.45.
Mesoridazine besylate: 544.77.
Methotrimeprazine: 328.48.
Pericyazine: 365.50.
Perphenazine: 403.98.
Pipotiazine palmitate: 714.10.
Prochlorperazine: 373.95.
Prochlorperazine edisylate: 564.15.
Prochlorperazine maleate: 606.10.
Prochlorperazine mesylate: 566.2.
Promazine hydrochloride: 320.89.
Thioproperazine mesylate: 638.84.
Thioridazine: 370.59.
Thioridazine hydrochloride: 407.05.
Trifluoperazine hydrochloride: 480.43.
Triflupromazine: 352.43.
Triflupromazine hydrochloride: 388.89.

Mechanism of action/Effect

Antipsychotic—Thought to improve psychotic conditions by blocking postsynaptic dopamine D_2 receptors in the mesolimbic area of the brain and by producing alpha-adrenergic blockade.

Antiemetic—Phenothiazines act centrally to inhibit or block the dopamine D_2 receptors in the medullary chemoreceptor trigger zone (CTZ) and peripherally by blocking the vagus nerve in the gastrointestinal tract. The antiemetic effects of phenothiazines may be augmented by their anticholinergic, sedative, and antihistaminic effects.

Analgesic; sedative—Methotrimeprazine raises pain threshold and produces amnesia by suppression of sensory impulses. The alpha-adrenergic blocking effects of phenothiazines may produce sedation and tranquilization.

Other actions/effects

Drug	Action*				
	Legend: **I**=Antiemetic **II**=Anticholinergic **III**=Extrapyramidal **IV**=Hypotensive **V**=Sedative				
	I	**II**	**III**	**IV**	**V**
Aliphatic					
Chlorpromazine	S	S	W–M	S	S
Methotrimeprazine	S	M–S	W–M	S	S
Promazine	M	S	W	S	S
Triflupromazine	S	S	M	M	M–S
Piperazine					
Fluphenazine	W	W	S	W	W
Perphenazine	S	W–M	S	W	W–M
Prochlorperazine	S	W	S	W	W–M
Thioproperazine	W	W	S	W	W
Trifluoperazine	S	W	S	W	W
Piperidine					
Mesoridazine	W	M	W	M–S	S
Pericyazine	S	S	M	M	S
Pipotiazine	W	W	S	W	W
Thioridazine	W	M–S	W	M–S	M–S

*S=strong; M=moderate; W=weak

Blockade of dopaminergic and alpha-adrenergic receptors in the tuberoinfundibular system by phenothiazines alters the release of hypothalamic and pituitary (hypophyseal) hormones, leading to increases in prolactin concentrations that persist throughout treatment.

Electrocardiogram (ECG) changes that reflect abnormal cardiac repolarization, including prolongation of the QT_c interval, have been observed in patients taking phenothiazines. Sudden and unexpected deaths due to cardiac arrest have occurred in patients taking phenothiazines who previously had been found to have these ECG changes. Thioridazine is the phenothiazine most frequently involved in cases of sudden cardiac death.

The cough reflex–suppressant effect of phenothiazines may increase the risk of aspiration or asphyxia.

Phenothiazines lower the seizure threshold.

Absorption

Absorption may be erratic and peak plasma concentrations show large interindividual differences, possibly due to large interindividual differences in extent of first-pass metabolism.

Distribution

Phenothiazines have a large volume of distribution, readily cross the placenta, and are distributed into breast milk.

Protein binding

Very high (90% or more).

Biotransformation

Hepatic to active and inactive metabolites. Because parenteral administration bypasses first-pass metabolism, the proportions of parent drug and metabolites present in the circulation may differ with different routes of administration. Depending on the contributions of the parent drug and each metabolite to efficacy and/or adverse effects, these differences in proportion can result in differences in effects, leading the patient to experience the oral and parenteral dosage forms of the same medication differently.

Cytochrome P450 2D6 (CYP2D6) has been shown to be involved in the metabolism of perphenazine and thioridazine.

Mesoridazine is an active metabolite of thioridazine.

Onset of action

Antipsychotic effect—

Gradual (up to several weeks) and variable between patients.

Long-acting parenteral dosage forms—

Fluphenazine decanoate injection: Antipsychotic effects usually begin between 24 and 72 hours after administration and become significant within 48 to 96 hours.

Pipotiazine palmitate injection: Antipsychotic effects usually begin within the first 48 to 72 hours after administration and become significant within 1 week.

Time to peak effect

Antipsychotic effect—Approximately 4 to 7 days to achieve steady-state plasma concentrations with oral dosage forms, and 4 to 6 weeks with depot dosage forms; peak therapeutic effects may take from 6 weeks to 6 months.

Antipsychotic and antiemetic effects (perphenazine)—1 to 2 hours after intramuscular injection, maintained for an average of 6 hours.

Analgesic effect (methotrimeprazine)—Within 20 to 40 minutes after intramuscular injection, maintained for about 4 hours.

Elimination

Renal and biliary, with some enterohepatic recycling.

In dialysis—Phenothiazines are not successfully dialyzed because of their high protein binding and large volume of distribution.

Precautions to Consider

Cross-sensitivity and/or related problems

Patients sensitive to one phenothiazine may be sensitive to other phenothiazines also.

Tumorigenicity

Phenothiazines produce an elevation in prolactin concentrations, which persists throughout administration. Tissue culture experiments indicate that approximately one third of human breast cancers are prolactin-dependent *in vitro* , a factor of potential importance if the prescription of these medications is contemplated in a patient with a previously detected breast cancer. Although disturbances such as galactorrhea, amenorrhea, gynecomastia, and impotence have been reported, the clinical significance of elevated serum prolactin concentrations is unknown for most patients. An increase in mammary neoplasms has been found in rodents after chronic administration of antipsychotic medications. However, neither clinical studies nor epidemiologic studies conducted to date have shown an association between long-term administration of these medications and mammary tumorigenesis; the available evidence is considered too limited to be conclusive at this time.

Pregnancy/Reproduction

Fertility—Animal studies with several phenothiazines have shown a decrease in fertility.

Pregnancy—Phenothiazines are not recommended for use during pregnancy. Phenothiazines cross the placenta. Although adequate and well-controlled studies in humans have not been done, there have been reports of prolonged jaundice, hyporeflexia or hyperreflexia, and extrapyramidal effects in the neonates of mothers who received phenothiazines during pregnancy.

Chlorpromazine: Reproductive studies in rodents have shown a potential for embryotoxicity, increased neonatal mortality, and decreased performance of the offspring in administered tests. The possibility of permanent neurological damage in offspring of rodent mothers cannot be excluded.

Fluphenazine: Withdrawal effects, including severe rhinorrhea, vomiting, respiratory distress, and extrapyramidal effects, have been reported in neonates following *in utero* exposure to fluphenazine throughout gestation. Single injections of the decanoate dosage form during gestation in rabbits and rats revealed no teratogenic effects. However, in rabbits, a dose of 5.6 mg per kg of body weight (mg/kg) may have interfered with implantation and also may have contributed to delayed ossification in the fetuses.

Mesoridazine: Intrauterine resorptions were increased in rats and rabbits given 70 mg/kg and 125 mg/kg of mesoridazine, respectively. However, no drug-related teratology was seen.

Methotrimeprazine: Reproductive studies in animals and clinical experience have failed to show a teratogenic effect. However, a possible antifertility effect has been suggested since successive generations of animals administered methotrimeprazine have shown smaller litter sizes than those of controls.

Pericyazine: Reproductive studies in rats and rabbits failed to show a teratogenic effect. However, in the rats, which were administered pericyazine from 33 days precoitus throughout pregnancy and lactation, the average pairing-to-birth interval was lengthened, indicating a possible antifertility effect. In mice administered 5 to 15 mg/kg of pericyazine from 8 to 14 days postcoitus, increased fetal death and delayed ossification were seen.

Pipotiazine: No teratogenic effects were seen in reproductive studies in mice, rats, and rabbits. However, when pipotiazine was administered to rats (5 mg/kg and 15 mg/kg) and rabbits (10 mg/kg and 20 mg/kg) throughout pregnancy, fetal toxicity, increased fetal resorption, and inhibited intrauterine fetal growth were seen.

Thioridazine: Reproductive studies in animals and clinical experience have failed to show a teratogenic effect.

Trifluoperazine: Reproductive studies in rats given more than 600 times the human dose showed an increased incidence of malformations and reduced weight and litter size linked to maternal toxicity.

All phenothiazines—FDA pregnancy categories are not included in product labeling presently.

Breast-feeding

Phenothiazines are distributed into breast milk and may cause drowsiness or movement disorders in the nursing infant. Breast-feeding while receiving phenothiazines is not recommended.

Pediatrics

Children are prone to develop neuromuscular or extrapyramidal reactions, especially dystonias, and should be closely monitored while receiving therapeutic doses of phenothiazines. Children with acute illnesses, such as chickenpox, central nervous system (CNS) infections, measles, gastroenteritis, and dehydration, are especially at risk.

Geriatrics

Geriatric patients tend to develop higher plasma concentrations of phenothiazines. Therefore, these patients usually require lower initial dosage and a more gradual titration of dosage.

Elderly patients appear to be more prone to orthostatic hypotension and exhibit an increased sensitivity to the anticholinergic and sedative effects of phenothiazines. In addition, they are more prone to develop extrapyramidal side effects, such as tardive dyskinesia and parkinsonism.

It has been suggested that elderly patients receive half the usual adult dose. Patients with organic mental disorders or acute confusional states should initially receive one third to one half the usual adult dose, with the dose being increased no more frequently than every 2 or 3 days, preferably at intervals of 7 to 10 days, if possible. After clinical improvement occurs, periodic attempts should be made to discontinue medication.

Pharmacogenetics

Cytochrome P450 2D6 (CYP2D6) has been shown to be involved in the metabolism of perphenazine and thioridazine. Approximately 7% of the white population are poor metabolizers of CYP2D6 substrates due to genotype and have reduced clearance and higher plasma concentrations of these medications. Single-dose studies have shown plasma concentrations of perphenazine and thioridazine to be about four times higher in poor metabolizers than in extensive metabolizers. However, one study of perphenazine serum concentrations corrected for dose (C/dose) at steady-state showed less variation in perphenazine C/dose between poor metabolizers and extensive metabolizers (twofold) than between individual subjects (thirtyfold).

Dental

The peripheral anticholinergic effects of phenothiazines may decrease or inhibit salivary flow, especially in middle-aged or elderly patients, thus contributing to the development of caries, periodontal disease, oral candidiasis, and discomfort.

Extrapyramidal reactions induced by phenothiazines will result in increased motor activity of the head, face, and neck. Occlusal adjustments, bite registrations, and treatment for bruxism may be made less reliable.

The leukopenic and thrombocytopenic effects of phenothiazines may result in an increased incidence of microbial infection, delayed healing, and gingival bleeding. If leukopenia or thrombocytopenia occurs, dental work should be deferred until blood counts have returned to normal, and patients should be instructed in proper oral hygiene, including caution in use of regular toothbrushes, dental floss, and toothpicks.

Surgical

Patients receiving phenothiazines who must undergo surgery should be closely monitored for hypotension. Also, dosage reductions of anesthetics and other CNS depressants are recommended.

Drug interactions and/or related problems

The following drug interactions and/or related problems have been selected on the basis of their potential clinical significance (possible mechanism in parentheses where appropriate)—not necessarily inclusive (» = major clinical significance):

Note: The isoenzyme cytochrome P450 2D6 (CYP2D6) is involved in the metabolism of perphenazine, thioridazine, and possibly other phenothiazines. Concurrent use of inhibitors of CYP2D6 and phenothiazines may lead to increased phenothiazine plasma concentrations and increased risk of developing adverse effects, including changes in cardiac rhythm. Also, phenothiazine use may inhibit the metabolism of other medications that are metabolized by CYP2D6. Therefore, possible interactions between phenothiazines and medications that inhibit CYP2D6 or that are substrates of CYP2D6, other than those listed below, should be considered.

Combinations containing any of the following medications, depending on the amount present, may also interact with this medication.

» Alcohol or
» CNS depression-producing medications, other (see *Appendix II*)
(prolonged and intensified CNS and respiratory depression and increased hypotensive effects may occur during concurrent or sequential use; dosage reductions may be necessary, except that dosage of anticonvulsant medications should not be decreased)
(use of a high dose of barbiturate with mesoridazine has resulted in respiratory arrest)
(dosage of CNS depressants such as anesthetics, barbiturates, and narcotics should be reduced by 50 to 75% when used with a phenothiazine, except in the case of anticonvulsant use of a barbiturate)
(barbiturates and carbamazepine increase the metabolism of phenothiazines by induction of hepatic microsomal enzymes, thus decreasing plasma concentrations, and possibly the therapeutic effect, of the phenothiazine)
(alcohol may increase the risk of heatstroke in patients receiving phenothiazines)

Amantadine or
Anticholinergics or other medications with anticholinergic action (see *Appendix II*)
(anticholinergic side effects of these medications and/or phenothiazines may be intensified; the hyperpyretic effect of phenothiazines may be potentiated by the loss of sweating as a cooling mechanism, possibly leading to heatstroke, especially when environmental temperatures are high; because of increased risk of paralytic ileus due to decreased intestinal motility, patients should be advised to report occurrence of gastrointestinal problems)
(parenteral methotrimeprazine, used as preanesthetic medication, may be administered concurrently, but with caution, with lowered doses of atropine or scopolamine; tachycardia and a fall in blood pressure may occur, and CNS reactions, such as stimulation, delirium, and extrapyramidal reactions, may be aggravated)

Amphetamines
(stimulant effects may be decreased when amphetamines are used concurrently with phenothiazines since phenothiazines produce dopamine D_2 receptor blockade; also, the antipsychotic effectiveness of phenothiazines may be reduced)

Antacids, aluminum- or magnesium-containing or
Antidiarrheals, adsorbent
(ingestion of these medications within 2 hours of a phenothiazine may inhibit the absorption of an orally administered phenothiazine)

Anticoagulants, oral
(effects may be decreased by phenothiazines)

Anticonvulsants, including barbiturates
(phenothiazines may lower the seizure threshold; dosage adjustment of anticonvulsant medications may be necessary)
(phenothiazines may inhibit phenytoin metabolism, leading to phenytoin toxicity)

» Antidepressants, tricyclic or
» Fluoxetine or
» Fluvoxamine or
» Paroxetine or
» Maprotiline
(concurrent use may prolong and intensify the sedative and anticholinergic effects of either these medications or phenothiazines; plasma concentrations of antidepressants and/or phenothiazines may be increased by mutual inhibition of metabolism; the risk of neuroleptic malignant syndrome [NMS] may be increased; QT interval–prolonging effects of these medications and phenothiazines increase the risk of developing cardiac arrhythmias)

» Antithyroid agents
(concurrent use with phenothiazines may increase the risk of agranulocytosis)

Apomorphine
(prior ingestion of phenothiazine antiemetics may decrease the emetic response to apomorphine; also, the CNS depressant effects of phenothiazine antiemetics are additive to those of apomorphine and may induce dangerous respiratory depression, circulatory system effects, or prolonged sleep)

Appetite suppressants
(concurrent use with phenothiazines may antagonize the anorectic effect of appetite suppressants)

Beta-adrenergic blocking agents
(concurrent use of beta-blocking agents, possibly including ophthalmics, with phenothiazines may result in increased plasma concentrations of both medications because of inhibition of metabolism; this may result in additive hypotensive effects, irreversible retinopathy, cardiac arrhythmias, and tardive dyskinesia)
(increases in plasma levels of thioridazine and its metabolites of 50 to 400% and 80 to 300%, respectively, have been reported with concurrent propranolol use)

Bromocriptine
(increased serum prolactin concentrations induced by phenothiazines may interfere with effects of bromocriptine; dosage adjustments may be necessary)

Diuretics, thiazide
(concurrent use may potentiate orthostatic hypotension, hyponatremia, and water intoxication; alternate methods of hypertension control should be considered)

» Extrapyramidal reaction-causing medications, other (see *Appendix II*)
(concurrent use with phenothiazines may increase the severity and frequency of extrapyramidal effects)

Hepatotoxic medications, other (see *Appendix II*)
(concurrent use of phenothiazines with medications known to alter hepatic microsomal enzyme activity may result in an increased incidence of hepatotoxicity; patients, especially those on prolonged administration or with a history of liver disease, should be carefully monitored)

» Hypotension-producing medications, other (see *Appendix II*)
(concurrent use with phenothiazines may produce severe hypotension with postural syncope)
(the antihypertensive effect of guanethidine may be antagonized by phenothiazines)

» Levodopa
(antiparkinsonian effects of levodopa may be inhibited when it is used concurrently with phenothiazines because of blockade of dopamine receptors in the brain)

» Lithium
(an encephalopathic syndrome has been reported in a few patients receiving lithium concurrently with antipsychotic medications; symptoms have included weakness, lethargy, fever, tremulousness, confusion, extrapyramidal symptoms, and, in some cases, irreversible brain damage; patients receiving this combination should be monitored closely for evidence of neurological toxicity)
(concurrent use with chlorpromazine and possibly other phenothiazines may reduce gastrointestinal absorption of the phenothiazine, thereby decreasing its serum concentrations by as much as 40%; concurrent use may increase rate of renal excretion of lithium; extrapyramidal symptoms may be increased; also, nausea and vomiting, early indications of lithium toxicity, may be masked by the antiemetic effect of some phenothiazines)

» Metrizamide
(risk of having seizures is increased with intrathecal metrizamide administration; phenothiazines should be discontinued at least 48 hours before, and not resumed for at least 24 hours following, myelography)

Opioid (narcotic) analgesics
(in addition to increased CNS and respiratory depression, concurrent use with phenothiazines increases orthostatic hypotension and increases the risk of severe constipation, which may lead to paralytic ileus and/or urinary retention)

Ototoxic medications, especially ototoxic antibiotics (see *Appendix II*)
(phenothiazines may mask some symptoms of ototoxicity such as tinnitus, dizziness, or vertigo)

Paroxetine
(the CNS effects of perphenazine were shown to be increased in five subjects when paroxetine was added to perphenazine treatment; paroxetine may interfere with the metabolism of phenothiazines through inhibition of CYP2D6)

Photosensitizing medications, other
(concurrent use with phenothiazines may cause additive photosensitizing effects)
(in addition, concurrent use of systemic methoxsalen, trioxsalen, or tetracyclines with phenothiazines may potentiate intraocular photochemical damage to the choroid, retina, or lens)

» QT interval–prolonging medications, other, including:
Astemizole or
Cisapride or
Disopyramide or
Erythromycin or
Pimozide or

Probucol or
Procainamide or
Quinidine
(additive QT interval prolongation may increase the risk of developing cardiac arrhythmias)

Succinylcholine
(concurrent use with methotrimeprazine may cause tachycardia and a fall in blood pressure, CNS stimulation and delirium, and an aggravation of extrapyramidal effects)

Sympathomimetic agents for cardiovascular use, especially:

» Epinephrine
(the alpha-adrenergic blocking action of phenothiazines may reduce the pressor response to these medications and reduce their duration of action)
(sympathomimetics that stimulate both alpha- and beta-adrenergic receptors, such as epinephrine, may lead to hypotension and tachycardia when used with a phenothiazine, due to unopposed beta-adrenergic stimulation)

Laboratory value alterations

The following have been selected on the basis of their potential clinical significance (possible effect in parentheses where appropriate)—not necessarily inclusive (» = major clinical significance).

With diagnostic test results

Bilirubin tests, urine
(phenothiazine use may produce false-positive results due to the presence of metabolites in urine)

» Electrocardiogram (ECG) readings
(prolonged QT_c intervals, lowered and inverted T waves, and the appearance of waves that may be bifid T or U waves have been reported; ECG changes seem to be caused by altered repolarization and not by myocardial damage; however, deaths, presumably due to cardiac arrest, have occurred in patients who previously had shown these ECG changes during phenothiazine treatment; ECG changes and sudden death have been seen more frequently with thioridazine use than with use of other phenothiazines; the predictive utility of monitoring ECGs in patients taking phenothiazines is questionable)

Gonadorelin test for hypothalamic-pituitary gonadotropic function
(phenothiazines may blunt the response to gonadorelin by increasing serum prolactin concentrations)

Metyrapone test of hypothalamic-pituitary complex
(interference may be caused by reduction of adrenocorticotropic hormone [ACTH] secretion due to phenothiazine use)

Phenylketonuria (PKU) test
(phenothiazines may produce false-positive results)

Medical considerations/Contraindications

The medical considerations/contraindications included have been selected on the basis of their potential clinical significance (reasons given in parentheses where appropriate)—not necessarily inclusive (» = major clinical significance).

Except under special circumstances, this medicine should not be used when the following medical problems exist:

» Cardiovascular disease, severe hypertension or hypotension or
» CNS depression, severe or
» Comatose states or
» Congenital long QT syndrome or
» History of cardiac arrhythmias or
» Known genetic defect leading to reduced levels of activity of P450 2D6 isozyme activity
(may be exacerbated)

Risk-benefit should be considered when the following medical problems exist:

» Alcoholism, active
(CNS depression and hypotension may be potentiated; risk of heatstroke may be increased; chronic alcohol abusers may be predisposed to hepatotoxic reactions during phenothiazine therapy; dosage reduction may be necessary)

Angina pectoris
(pain may be increased if phenothiazine treatment leads to an increase in physical activity)

» Blood dyscrasias
(may be exacerbated; treatment may have to be discontinued)

» Brain damage, subcortical or
» Cerebral atherosclerosis, marked
(a severe hyperthermic reaction may occur, sometimes 14 to 16 hours after phenothiazine administration)

Breast cancer
(potentially higher risk of disease progression and possible increased resistance to endocrine and cytotoxic treatment, due to phenothiazine-induced prolactin secretion)

» Cardiac reserve deficiency, such as mitral insufficiency, severe or
» Cerebrovascular insufficiency or
» Pheochromocytoma or
» Renal insufficiency
(severe hypotension is more likely to occur)

Cardiovascular disease
(increased risk of hypotension and/or exacerbation of condition by phenothiazine-induced hypotension; ECG changes related to repolarization have been seen in some patients without cardiovascular disease who were taking phenothiazines; myocardial depression, cardiomegaly, congestive heart failure [CHF], and arrhythmias may be induced)

Conditions for which vomiting is a sign, such as:
Brain tumor
Drug overdose
Intestinal obstruction
» Reye's syndrome
(diagnosis may be obscured by the antiemetic effect of phenothiazines; less likely with thioridazine)
(increased risk of hepatotoxicity in children and adolescents with Reye's syndrome)

Glaucoma, or predisposition to
(may be potentiated by anticholinergic effects of phenothiazines)

» Hepatic function impairment
(phenothiazines can cause hepatic dysfunction)
(metabolism may be decreased; higher serum phenothiazine concentrations may increase CNS effects)
(patients with a history of hepatic encephalopathy due to cirrhosis have increased sensitivity to the CNS effects of phenothiazines)

Parkinson's disease
(potentiation of extrapyramidal effects)

Peptic ulcer or
Urinary retention
(may be exacerbated; phenothiazines have caused bladder paralysis in some patients)

Prostatic hypertrophy, symptomatic
(increased risk of urinary retention)

Respiratory disorders, chronic, especially in children
(may be potentiated due to CNS depressant effect of phenothiazines; also, cough-suppressant effects of phenothiazines may be especially problematic in these patients)

Seizure disorders, or history of
(seizures may be precipitated)

» Sensitivity to any phenothiazine, or history of
(may be potentiated upon re-exposure to any phenothiazine in patients with a history of phenothiazine-induced blood dyscrasias, jaundice, or skin reactions)

Sensitivity to parabens, sulfites, or tartrazine
(some dosage forms of phenothiazines contain parabens, sulfites, or tartrazine [FD&C Yellow No. 5])

Caution should also be used in geriatric, emaciated, and debilitated patients, who usually require a lower initial dose, and in patients who will be exposed to organophosphate or carbamate pesticides, extreme heat, or extreme cold.

Patient monitoring

The following may be especially important in patient monitoring (other tests may be warranted in some patients, depending on condition; » = major clinical significance):

» Abnormal-movement determinations and
» Careful observation for early signs of tardive dyskinesia
(recommended at periodic intervals, especially in the elderly and in patients on high-dose or long-term maintenance therapy; reduction of the phenothiazine dosage, if clinically feasible, will aid in the detection of tardive dyskinesia since the medication may mask the syndrome; since there is no known effective treatment, the phenothiazine should be discontinued, if possible, or the dosage should be reduced at earliest signs, usually fine, worm-like movements of the tongue, to stop further development)
(for institutionalized patients, recommended every 2 to 3 months during therapy using the abnormal involuntary movement scale [AIMS], and again at 8 to 12 weeks after therapy has been discontinued)

Blood cell counts and differential in patients with sore throat and fever or infections
(may be required during high-dose or prolonged therapy when symptoms of infection develop; agranulocytosis is most likely to occur between the 4th and 10th weeks of therapy; if significant cellular depression occurs, medication should be discontinued and appropriate therapy initiated; rechallenge in recovered patients will usually cause a recurrence of agranulocytosis; use of alternate neuroleptics, such as haloperidol or thioxanthenes, is recommended)

Blood pressure measurements
(recommended periodically to detect hypotension; fatal hypotension has occurred with phenothiazine use)

ECG, baseline measurement
(Patients being considered for treatment with thioridazine should have a baseline ECG performed. Patients with a QTc interval greater than 450 msec should not receive thioridazine. Periodic ECG's during thioridazine treatment may be useful and it should be discontinued in patients who are found to have a QTc interval over 500 msec)

Hepatic function determinations and
Urine tests for bilirubin and bile
(may be required at periodic intervals during prolonged therapy, or if jaundice or influenza-like symptoms occur, to detect liver function impairment; jaundice is most likely to occur between the 2nd and 4th weeks of therapy and is thought to be a sensitivity reaction; phenothiazine should be discontinued if bilirubinemia, bilirubinuria, or jaundice occurs)

Ophthalmologic examinations
(recommended, if possible, prior to initiation of phenothiazine therapy as a baseline; initial screening should include measurement of visual acuity with and without refraction, a color vision test to detect possible central defects, and, if feasible, a slit-lamp microscopy study of the fundus and examination of the visual fields. Tests may be required at periodic intervals [usually every 6 to 12 months] during high-dose or prolonged therapy, since deposition of particulate matter in the lens and cornea has occurred with some phenothiazines, especially thioridazine; therapy should be discontinued if corneal, retinal, or lens changes are noticed; blurred vision, defective color vision, and night blindness are early symptoms of pigmentary retinopathy and may be reversible if the phenothiazine is discontinued in the early stages)

Phenothiazine concentrations, serum
(although generally not useful in determining dosage, determinations may be useful when toxicity or poor response occurs, or when noncompliance is suspected)

» Potassium levels, serum
(patients being considered for thioridazine treatment should have a baseline serum potassium level measurement. Serum potassium should be normalized before starting treatment. Periodic serum potassium levels during thioridazine treatment may be useful)

Side/Adverse Effects

The following side/adverse effects have been selected on the basis of their potential clinical significance (possible signs and symptoms in parentheses where appropriate)—not necessarily inclusive:

Those indicating need for medical attention

Incidence more frequent

Akathisia (restlessness or need to keep moving); ***blurred vision associated with anticholinergic effect; dystonic extrapyramidal effects*** (muscle spasms of face, neck, body, arms, or legs, causing unusual postures or expressions on face; sticking out of tongue; tic-like or twitching movements; trouble in breathing, speaking, or swallowing; twisting movements of body; inability to move eyes); ***hypotension*** (fainting)—less common with the piperazine phenothiazines; ***ocular changes; including deposition of opaque material in lens and cornea; epithelial keratopathy; or pigmentary retinopathy*** (blurred vision; defective color vision; difficulty seeing at night); ***parkinsonian extrapyramidal effects*** (difficulty in speaking or swallowing; loss of balance control; mask-like face; shuffling walk; stiffness of arms or legs; trembling and shaking of hands and fingers); ***tardive dyskinesia*** (lip smacking or puckering; puffing of cheeks; rapid or worm-like movements of tongue; uncontrolled chewing movements; uncontrolled movements of arms or legs); ***or tardive dystonia*** (unusual facial expressions or body positions; increased blinking or spasms of eyelid; uncontrolled twisting movements of neck, trunk, arms, or legs)

Note: *Hypotension* is more frequent in the elderly and at the beginning of treatment, especially if high doses are used. Acute hypotensive crisis leading to cardiac arrest has occurred rarely.

Parkinsonian effects occur more frequently in the elderly, whereas *dystonias* occur more often in younger patients. Symptoms may be seen in the first few days of treatment or after prolonged treatment, and can recur after even a single dose. *Extrapyramidal effects* may be dose-related and may decrease with a decrease in dosage. The effects are more common with the piperazine phenothiazines.

Ocular changes occur more frequently with high-dose or long-term use of phenothiazines, which are absorbed by melanin in the uveal tract of the eye. The deposition of a phenothiazine in the eye eventually can lead to damage of the rods and cones and to blindness. These ocular changes occur more frequently with thioridazine than with other phenothiazines. Although the greatest risk occurs with thioridazine doses above 800 mg per day, there have been cases reported with use of lower doses of thioridazine.

Tardive dyskinesia is seen more frequently in elderly patients, patients with brain damage, and patients who have received long-term treatment with antipsychotic medications. However, it can occur in any patient after as few as 3 months of antipsychotic therapy. Tardive dyskinesia can be masked by antipsychotic medication and may become evident after discontinuation of the medication. The syndrome may be irreversible.

Incidence less frequent

Difficulty in urinating; photosensitivity (skin rash; severe sunburn); ***skin rash***—associated with contact dermatitis (with liquid products), other allergic reaction, or cholestatic jaundice

Incidence rare

Blood dyscrasias; including agranulocytosis; leukocytopenia; or thrombocytopenia (sore throat; fever; unusual bleeding or bruising; unusual tiredness or weakness)—more frequent with aliphatic phenothiazines, less frequent with piperazine phenothiazines; ***cholestatic jaundice*** (abdominal or stomach pains; aching muscles and joints; fever and chills; severe skin itching; yellow eyes or skin; fatigue; nausea, vomiting, or diarrhea); ***dark urine; fever, significant; melanosis*** (tanning or blue-gray discoloration of skin)—more common in females and with long-term, high-dose chlorpromazine or thioridazine therapy; ***neuroleptic malignant syndrome (NMS)*** (difficult or fast breathing; drooling; fast heartbeat; fever; high or low [irregular] blood pressure; impaired consciousness, ranging from confusion to coma; increased sweating; loss of bladder control; severe muscle stiffness; trembling or shaking; trouble in speaking or swallowing); ***obstipation or paralytic ileus*** (severe constipation); ***paradoxical effects; including aggravation of psychosis; agitation; bizarre dreams; excitement; and insomnia*** (trouble in sleeping); ***pneumonia*** (chest pain; shortness of breath)—may be asymptomatic; ***priapism*** (prolonged, painful, inappropriate penile erection); ***QT prolongation and torsades de pointes*** (irregular or slow heart rate; recurrent fainting; sudden death)—appears to be dose related; ***seizures***—more common in patients with a family history of seizures or febrile convulsions; ***systemic lupus erythematosus–like syndrome*** (fever; hair loss; headaches; increased sensitivity of skin to sunlight; joint pain; redness of hands; skin rash; sores in mouth; unusual tiredness or weakness); ***temperature regulation dysfunction; including heatstroke*** (hot dry skin; inability to sweat; muscle weakness; confusion); ***or hypothermia*** (clumsiness; confusion; drowsiness; muscle weakness; shivering)

Note: *Agranulocytosis* can develop within the first 3 months of treatment, with recovery within 1 to 2 weeks after medication is discontinued; may recur upon rechallenge in recovered patients.

Dark urine usually is caused by the presence of phenothiazine metabolites in the urine; however, because hepatic dysfunction has been associated with phenothiazines, this effect should be reported to the physician.

Significant fever not attributable to any other cause may represent an idiosyncratic reaction to the phenothiazine. Discontinuing the phenothiazine may be necessary.

Liver function tests may be abnormal without overt *jaundice.* Jaundice may appear about 2 weeks after severe pruritus and may progress to chronic active hepatitis. Discontinuing medication may be necessary.

Heatstroke, caused by phenothiazine-induced suppression of temperature regulation in the hypothalamus, may occur in environmental conditions of high heat and high humidity. The effectiveness of sweating as a cooling mechanism may be reduced by humid conditions and by the anticholinergic effects of phenothiazines or their combination with other anticholinergic medications, such as nonprescription cold medications or antihistamines. Adequate interior environmental temperature control (air-conditioning) must be maintained for institutionalized patients during hot weather because of the increased risk of heatstroke and neuroleptic malignant syndrome (NMS). Patients should be advised to stay in cool areas, to avoid exertion and dehydration, and not to take other anticholinergic medications. Phenothiazines may also cause *hypothermia* in cold weather, since the disruption of the thermoregulatory mechanisms results in a poikilothermic state.

Skin pigmentation changes in *melanosis* occur on exposed areas of the body and may fade after discontinuation of the phenothiazine.

NMS may occur at any time during neuroleptic therapy and is potentially fatal. It is most commonly seen within the first month of therapy, after the patient has switched from one neuroleptic to another, or after a dosage increase. Along with the overt signs of skeletal muscle rigidity, hyperthermia, autonomic dysfunction, and altered consciousness, differential diagnosis may reveal leukocytosis (9500 to 26,000 cells per cubic millimeter), elevated liver enzyme tests, and elevated creatine kinase (CK).

Those indicating need for medical attention only if they continue or are bothersome

Incidence more frequent

Anticholinergic effects (constipation; decreased sweating; dizziness [orthostatic hypotension]; drowsiness; dry mouth)—less frequent with piperazine phenothiazines; ***nasal congestion***

Note: Drowsiness usually diminishes during the first few weeks of treatment or with a reduction in dosage.

Incidence less frequent

Changes in menstrual period; decreased sexual ability; fever, mild, after intramuscular injection of a phenothiazine; hypertrophic papillae of the tongue (rough or "fuzzy" tongue); ***increased salivation*** (watering of mouth); ***photophobia*** (increased sensitivity of eyes to light); ***secretion of milk, unusual; swelling or pain in breasts; weight gain, unusual***

Those indicating need for medical attention if they occur after the medication is discontinued

Incidence more frequent

Tardive dyskinesia, persistent (lip smacking or puckering; puffing of cheeks; rapid or worm-like movements of tongue; uncontrolled chewing movements; uncontrolled movements of arms or legs); ***or tardive dystonia, persistent*** (muscle spasms of face, neck, body, arms, or legs causing unusual postures or expressions on face; sticking out of tongue; tic-like or twitching movements; trouble in breathing, speaking, or swallowing; twisting movements of body; inability to move eyes)

Incidence less frequent

Dizziness; nausea and vomiting; stomach pain; trembling of fingers and hands

Overdose

For specific information on the agents used in the management of phenothiazine overdose, see:

- *Benztropine* in *Antidyskinetics (Systemic)* monograph;
- *Charcoal, Activated (Oral-Local)* monograph;
- *Diazepam* in *Benzodiazepines (Systemic)* monograph;
- *Digitalis Glycosides (Systemic)* monograph;
- *Diphenhydramine* in *Antihistamines (Systemic)* monograph;
- *Norepinephrine* and/or *Phenylephrine* in *Sympathomimetic Agents—Cardiovascular Use (Parenteral-Systemic)* monograph; and/or
- *Phenytoin* in *Anticonvulsants, Hydantoin (Systemic)* monograph.

For more information on the management of overdose or unintentional ingestion, **contact a Poison Control Center** (see *Poison Control Center Listing*).

Clinical effects of overdose

Note: Toxic blood concentration ranges have not been established for the phenothiazines. However, for thioridazine, toxicity may begin at a blood concentration of 1 mg/dL and the lethal concentration range is thought to be 2 to 8 mg/dL.

The following effects have been selected on the basis of their potential clinical significance (possible signs and symptoms in parentheses where appropriate)—not necessarily inclusive:

Acute

Areflexia or hyperreflexia (loss of or increase in reflexes); ***blurred vision; cardiac toxicity; including cardiac arrhythmia; cardiac arrest; congestive heart failure; hypotension; shock; tachycardia; QRS changes; or ventricular fibrillation*** (fainting; fast, slow, or irregular heartbeat; shortness of breath; unusual tiredness or weakness); ***CNS toxicity; including agitation; confusion; convulsions***—may be followed by respiratory depression; ***disorientation; drowsiness, stupor, or coma; dilated pupils; dryness of mouth; hyperpyrexia*** (fever); ***or hypothermia*** (clumsiness; confusion; drowsiness; muscle weakness; shivering); ***muscle rigidity; pulmonary edema or respiratory depression*** (trouble in breathing); ***vomiting***

Treatment of overdose

Treatment is essentially symptomatic and supportive.

To decrease absorption—

Attempting early gastric lavage; avoiding induction of vomiting because potential phenothiazine-induced impaired consciousness or dystonic reactions of the head and neck may result in aspiration of vomitus.

Administering activated charcoal slurry repeatedly.

Administering saline cathartic, especially if extended-release dosage form has been ingested.

Specific treatment—

Controlling cardiac arrhythmias with intravenous phenytoin, 9 to 11 mg per kg of body weight (mg/kg).

Digitalizing for cardiac failure.

Treating hypotension with intravenous fluids and a vasopressor such as norepinephrine or phenylephrine (not using a vasopressor with mixed alpha and beta agonist activity, such as epinephrine, because it may cause paradoxical hypotension due to alpha blockade by phenothiazine).

Controlling convulsions with diazepam followed by phenytoin while monitoring ECG; avoiding barbiturates since they may potentiate respiratory and CNS depression.

Administering benztropine or diphenhydramine to manage acute parkinsonian effects that may occur.

Monitoring—

Monitoring CNS function.

Monitoring cardiovascular function for not less than 5 days.

Supportive care—

Maintaining respiratory function, including pharyngeal and tracheal suction to remove excess mucus, if necessary.

Maintaining body temperature.

Patients in whom intentional overdose is confirmed or suspected should be referred for psychiatric consultation.

Note: Dialysis of phenothiazines has not been successful.

If extended-release dosage form has been ingested, treatment should continue for as long as overdose signs and symptoms remain.

Patient may not show arousal for up to 48 hours even when supportive and counteractive measures are employed.

Phenothiazines are radiopaque and ingested tablets may be seen on roentgenogram.

Patient Consultation

As an aid to patient consultation, refer to *Advice for the Patient, Phenothiazines (Systemic)*.

In providing consultation, consider emphasizing the following selected information (» = major clinical significance):

Before using this medication

» Conditions affecting use, especially:

Sensitivity to any phenothiazine

Pregnancy—Not recommended for use during pregnancy because of reports of jaundice, hyporeflexia or hyperreflexia, and extrapyramidal symptoms in neonates

Breast-feeding—Distributed into breast milk; may cause drowsiness or movement disorders in the infant

Use in children—Children, especially those with acute illnesses, are more prone to extrapyramidal symptoms

Use in the elderly—Elderly patients are more likely to develop extrapyramidal, anticholinergic, hypotensive, and sedative effects; reduced dosage recommended

Dental—Phenothiazine-induced blood dyscrasias may result in infections, delayed healing, and bleeding; dry mouth may cause caries and candidiasis; increased motor activity of face, head, and neck may interfere with some dental procedures

Other medications, especially alcohol, antithyroid agents, other CNS depression-producing medications, epinephrine, other extrapyramidal reaction-causing medications, other hypotension-producing medications, levodopa, lithium, maprotiline, metrizamide, other QT interval–prolonging medications, or antidepressants, tricyclic or the following: fluoxetine, fluvoxamine, or paraoxetine

Other medical problems, especially active alcoholism, blood dyscrasias, brain damage, cardiovascular disease, severe CNS depression, cerebrovascular disease, congenital long QT syndrome, hepatic function impairment, history of cardiac arrhythmias, known genetic defect leading to reduced levels of activity of P450 2D6 isoenzyme activity, pheochromocytoma, renal insufficiency, or Reye's syndrome

Proper use of this medication

» *Proper administration of this medication*

For oral dosage forms

Taking with food, milk, or water to reduce stomach irritation

Diluting each dose of medication that comes in dropper bottle with a recommended beverage immediately prior to use

Swallowing the extended-release dosage form whole

For rectal dosage forms

Chilling suppository if too soft to insert

How to insert suppository

» Compliance with therapy; not taking more or less medication than prescribed

» Several weeks of therapy may be required to produce desired effects in treatment of mental or emotional conditions

» Proper dosing

Missed dose when dosing schedule is:

One dose a day—Taking as soon as possible if remembered the same day; skipping missed dose if not remembered until the next day; going back to regular dosing schedule; not doubling doses

More than one dose a day—Taking as soon as possible if within an hour or so of missed dose; skipping missed dose if not remembered until later; going back to regular dosing schedule; not doubling doses

» Proper storage

Precautions while using this medication

Regular visits to physician to check progress of therapy

» Checking with physician before discontinuing medication; gradual dosage reduction may be needed

Avoiding use of antacids or antidiarrheal medication within 2 hours of taking phenothiazine

» Avoiding use of alcoholic beverages or other CNS depressants during therapy

Avoiding the use of over-the-counter medications for colds or allergies to prevent increased anticholinergic effects and risk of developing heatstroke

Caution if any laboratory tests required; possible changes in ECG readings, and interference with gonadorelin, metyrapone, phenylketonurea, and urine bilirubin test results

» Caution if any kind of surgery, dental treatment, or emergency treatment is required; telling physician or dentist in charge about phenothiazine because of possible drug interactions or hypotension

» Possible drowsiness or blurred vision; caution when driving, using machines, or doing other things requiring alertness or accurate vision

» Possible dizziness or lightheadedness (orthostatic hypotension); caution when getting up suddenly from a lying or sitting position

» Possible heatstroke: Caution during exercise, hot weather, or when taking hot baths

Possible hypothermia: Caution during prolonged exposure to cold

» Possible dryness of mouth; using sugarless gum or candy, ice, or saliva substitute for relief; checking with physician or dentist if dry mouth continues for more than 2 weeks

» Possible skin photosensitivity; avoiding unprotected exposure to sun; using protective clothing; using a sunblock product that includes protection against both UVA-caused photosensitivity reactions and UVB-caused sunburn reactions; avoiding use of sunlamp, tanning bed, or tanning booth; checking with physician if severe reaction occurs

» Possible eye photosensitivity; wearing sunglasses that block ultraviolet light

» Avoiding getting liquid dosage form on skin or clothing; may cause skin irritation

» Observing precautions for 6 to 12 weeks with long-acting parenteral forms

Side/adverse effects

Side effects more likely to occur in the elderly

Signs of potential side effects, especially akathisia, blurred vision, dystonias, hypotension, ocular changes, parkinsonian effects, QT prolongation and torsades de pointes, tardive dyskinesia or tardive dystonia, difficulty in urinating, photosensitivity, skin rash, blood dyscrasias, cholestatic jaundice, dark urine, fever, melanosis, neuroleptic malignant syndrome, obstipation or paralytic ileus, paradoxical effects, pneumonia, priapism, seizures, systemic lupus erythematosus–like syndrome, temperature regulation dysfunction

» Stopping medication and notifying physician immediately if signs and symptoms of neuroleptic malignant syndrome appear, especially muscle rigidity, fever, difficult or fast breathing, drooling, fast heartbeat, impaired consciousness ranging from confusion to coma, increased sweating, loss of bladder control, trembling and shaking, trouble in speaking or swallowing

» Notifying physician immediately if early signs of tardive dyskinesia appear, such as fine worm-like movements of the tongue or other uncontrolled movements of the mouth, tongue, jaw, fingers, or arms and legs; dosage adjustment or discontinuation may be needed to prevent irreversibility

Stopping medication and notifying physician immediately if signs and symptoms of QT prolongation and torsades de pointes appear, such as irregular or slow heart rate and recurrent fainting.

Possibility of discontinuation symptoms

General Dosing Information

Dosage must be individualized by gradual adjustment from the lower dosage range. After a favorable psychiatric response is noted (within several days to several months), that dosage should be continued for 2 weeks to 6 months, then gradually decreased to the lowest level that will maintain an adequate clinical response.

When extended therapy is discontinued, a gradual reduction in phenothiazine dosage over several weeks is recommended, since abrupt withdrawal may cause some patients on high or long-term dosage to experience transient dyskinetic signs, nausea, vomiting, gastritis, trembling, and/or dizziness. The continuation of treatment with antidyskinetic medications for several weeks after discontinuing the phenothiazine may reduce these symptoms but can precipitate psychosis. Also, preliminary evidence suggests that gradual dosage reduction may decrease the relapse risk associated with discontinuation.

The antiemetic effect of some phenothiazines may mask signs of drug toxicity or obscure diagnosis of conditions for which the primary symptom is nausea. Phenothiazines have no antiemetic effect when nausea is a result of vestibular stimulation or local gastrointestinal irritation.

An antidyskinetic agent such as trihexyphenidyl or benztropine may be used concurrently to control phenothiazine-induced extrapyramidal symptoms. Generally, these agents should be used only when required (not prophylactically), and only for a few weeks to 2 or 3 months. However, 2 to 3 weeks of prophylaxis may be considered in selected patients who have a history of or several risk factors for dystonic reactions or who exhibit paranoia.

Avoid skin contact with liquid forms of phenothiazine medication; contact dermatitis has resulted.

For oral liquid dosage forms only

Mixing liquid dosage forms with carbamazepine suspension or ingesting liquid dosage forms with carbamazepine suspension can result in the formation of an orange, rubbery precipitate.

For parenteral dosage forms only

Because hypotension is a possible side effect of phenothiazines, parenteral administration should be used only in patients who are bedfast or for acute therapy in ambulatory patients who can be closely monitored. A possible exception may be those patients who are dose-stabilized on the long-acting injectable forms.

Intramuscular injections should be administered slowly and deeply into the upper outer quadrant of the buttock. Patient should remain lying down for at least ½ hour after injection to avoid possible hypotensive effects.

To prevent irritation at the site of intramuscular injection, the following are recommended: rotation of the injection sites, dilution of the phenothiazine injection with sodium chloride injection, and/or addition of 2% procaine.

Effects of the long-acting injectable forms may last for 6 to 12 weeks. The side effects information and precautions apply during this period of time.

The dose of the long-acting injectable forms should *not* be increased to prolong the dosing interval, because of the increased incidence of extrapyramidal reactions and other adverse effects at higher doses. Each patient must be carefully supervised to determine the optimal dosing interval and lowest effective dose, depending on patient's response, age, physical condition, symptoms, severity of illness, and drug history.

Geriatric and pediatric patients, especially those acutely ill or dehydrated, should be monitored very carefully during parenteral therapy because of a higher incidence of hypotensive and extrapyramidal reactions in these age groups.

Diet/Nutrition

The oral dosage forms of this medication may be taken with food or a full glass (240 mL) of water or milk, if necessary, to lessen stomach irritation.

Requirements for riboflavin may be increased in patients receiving phenothiazines.

For treatment of adverse effects

Neuroleptic malignant syndrome (NMS)—

Treatment is essentially symptomatic and supportive and may include the following

- *Discontinuing phenothiazine immediately.*
- Hyperthermia—Administering antipyretics (aspirin or acetaminophen); using cooling blanket.
- Dehydration—Restoring fluids and electrolytes.
- Cardiovascular instability—Monitoring blood pressure and cardiac rhythm closely. Use of sodium nitroprusside may allow vasodilation with subsequent heat loss from the skin in patients with less-dominant muscle rigidity.
- Hypoxia—Administering oxygen; considering airway insertion and assisted ventilation.
- Muscle rigidity—There is anecdotal evidence that administering dantrolene sodium (orally, 100 to 300 mg per day in divided doses or intravenously, 1.25 to 1.5 mg per kg of body weight [mg/kg]) for muscle relaxation, or administering amantadine (100 mg two times a day) or bromocriptine (5 mg three times a day) to restore balance of dopamine and acetylcholine at the receptor site, may be helpful in reducing the duration and/or mortality rate of NMS.
- If neuroleptics must be continued because of severe psychosis, rechallenge should consist of:
  —at least 5 days of neuroleptic abstinence before rechallenge.
  —a neuroleptic of a different class from the one causing NMS.
  —a low dose.
  —using a neuroleptic only for controlling the psychosis.
  —avoiding parenteral and extended-action dosage forms.

Parkinsonism—

Treatment may include:

- Reducing the antipsychotic dosage, if possible, for treatment of milder effects.
- Administering oral antiparkinsonian agents (of the anticholinergic type) such as trihexyphenidyl, 2 mg three times per day, or benztropine for treatment of more severe parkinsonism and acute motor restlessness; using sparingly, only when side effects appear, and then usually for no longer than 3 months. Observing caution to prevent hyperpyrexia with concomitant use of phenothiazines and other medications with anticholinergic action.
- In elderly patients, using amantadine, 100 to 200 mg at bedtime, to minimize severe anticholinergic effects that may occur with other antidyskinetics.

Restlessness (akathisia)—

Reduce antipsychotic dosage, if possible. May respond to antiparkinsonian drugs or propranolol, 30 to 80 mg per day; nadolol, 40 mg per day; lorazepam, 0.5 mg three times a day or 1 mg two times a day; or diazepam, 2 mg two or three times a day. May require substitution of a less potent neuroleptic or an atypical antipsychotic agent.

Dystonia—

Acute dystonic postures or oculogyric crisis may be relieved by parenteral administration of benztropine, 2 mg intramuscularly or intravenously; diphenhydramine, 50 mg intramuscularly; or diazepam, 5 to 7.5 mg intravenously, to be followed by oral antidyskinetic medication for 1 or 2 days to prevent recurrent dystonic episodes. Dosage adjustments of the phenothiazine may control these effects, and discontinuation of the phenothiazine may reverse severe symptoms.

Tardive dyskinesia or tardive dystonia—

No known effective treatment. Dosage of phenothiazine should be reduced or medication discontinued, if clinically feasible, at earliest signs of tardive dyskinesia or tardive dystonia to prevent possible irreversible effects.

Pruritus associated with cholestasis—

- Topical treatment may include:
  —Topical corticosteroids combined with cool-water compresses, aluminum acetate solution, or calamine lotion.
  —For widespread itching, baths containing colloidal oatmeal or baking soda (2 cups per tubful).
  —For severe itching, topical anesthetics containing 20% benzocaine or 5% lidocaine; however, itching may be relieved for only 30 to 60 minutes.
- Oral treatment may include:
  —Initially, diphenhydramine, cyproheptadine, or hydroxyzine.
  —Bile acid sequestrants or cholestyramine, but only when topical and oral antipruritic agents fail to control symptoms.
  —Supplementation with fat-soluble vitamins (A, D, E, K) for patients with protracted jaundice.
  —Resuming therapy with a nonphenothiazine neuroleptic, such as loxapine, thioxanthenes, or molindone.

CHLORPROMAZINE

Summary of Differences

Category:

Includes antiemetic, antidyskinetic (Huntington's chorea), anti-migraine headache, sedative, and anesthetic adjunct uses.

Indications:

Includes treatment of intractable hiccups and acute, intermittent porphyria. Includes adjunctive treatment of tetanus.

Pharmacology/pharmacokinetics:

Chemical group—
Aliphatic

Actions—
Antiemetic: Strong
Anticholinergic: Strong
Extrapyramidal: Weak to moderate
Hypotensive: Strong
Sedative: Strong

Side/adverse effects:

Greater risk of developing melanosis than with other phenothiazines.

Additional Dosing Information

See also *General Dosing Information*.

For intractable hiccups, initially, chlorpromazine is administered orally. If symptoms persist for 2 or 3 days, intramuscular administration is indicated, followed by slow intravenous infusion if hiccups continue.

For parenteral use

Chlorpromazine injection must not be administered subcutaneously, because it causes severe tissue necrosis.

For intramuscular injection, diluting chlorpromazine injection with sodium chloride injection and/or adding 2% procaine may prevent irritation at the injection site.

The intravenous route of administration is used only for severe hiccups, migraine headache, surgery, and tetanus.

Before intravenous injection, chlorpromazine hydrochloride injection should be diluted with sodium chloride injection.

Close monitoring of blood pressure for hypotension is necessary during parenteral administration.

Oral Dosage Forms

Note: The dosing and strengths of the dosage forms available are expressed in terms of chlorpromazine base (not the hydrochloride salt).

CHLORPROMAZINE HYDROCHLORIDE EXTENDED-RELEASE CAPSULES

Usual adult and adolescent dose

Psychotic disorders—

Oral, 30 to 300 mg (base) one to three times per day, the dosage being adjusted as needed and tolerated.

Note: Geriatric, emaciated, or debilitated patients usually require a lower initial dose and more gradual dosage titration than do younger and healthier patients.

Usual adult prescribing limits

1 gram (base) per day.

Note: Although sometimes doses are increased gradually to 2 grams or more per day for short periods, 1 gram or less usually is sufficient for extended therapy.

Usual pediatric dose

The extended-release dosage form is not recommended for use in children.

Strength(s) usually available

U.S.—

30 mg (base) (Rx) [*Thorazine Spansule* (benzyl alcohol; calcium sulfate; cetylpyridinium chloride; FD&C Yellow No. 6; gelatin; glyceryl distearate; glyceryl monostearate; iron oxide; povidone; silicon dioxide; sodium lauryl sulfate; starch; sucrose; titanium dioxide; wax)].

75 mg (base) (Rx) [*Thorazine Spansule* (benzyl alcohol; calcium sulfate; cetylpyridinium chloride; FD&C Yellow No. 6; gelatin; glyceryl distearate; glyceryl monostearate; iron oxide; povidone; silicon dioxide; sodium lauryl sulfate; starch; sucrose; titanium dioxide; wax)].

150 mg (base) (Rx) [*Thorazine Spansule* (benzyl alcohol; calcium sulfate; cetylpyridinium chloride; FD&C Yellow No. 6; gelatin; glyceryl distearate; glyceryl monostearate; iron oxide; povidone; silicon dioxide; sodium lauryl sulfate; starch; sucrose; titanium dioxide; wax)].

Canada—

Not commercially available.

Packaging and storage
Store between 15 and 30 °C (59 and 86 °F), in a tight, light-resistant container, unless otherwise specified by manufacturer.

Auxiliary labeling
- May cause drowsiness.
- Avoid alcoholic beverages.

Additional information
Upon ingestion of the extended-release capsule, an initial dose is released promptly and the remaining medication is released gradually over a prolonged period.

The extended-release capsule may be used for initial treatment when once-a-day dosing is desired, and it may be used to help decrease side effects when large doses are required.

CHLORPROMAZINE HYDROCHLORIDE ORAL CONCENTRATE USP

Usual adult and adolescent dose
Psychotic disorders—

Oral, 10 to 25 mg (base) two to four times per day, the dosage being increased by 20 to 50 mg per day every three or four days as needed and tolerated.

Nausea and vomiting—

Oral, 10 to 25 mg (base) every four to six hours, as needed, the dosage being increased as needed and tolerated.

Apprehension and restlessness, presurgical—

Oral, 25 to 50 mg (base) two to three hours before surgery.

Hiccups, intractable—

Oral, 25 to 50 mg (base) three or four times per day. Parenteral administration is required if symptoms persist for two to three days with oral administration. (See *Chlorpromazine Hydrochloride Injection USP*.)

Porphyria, acute, intermittent—

Oral, 25 to 50 mg (base) three or four times per day. In most patients, treatment may be discontinued after several weeks; however, some patients may require maintenance therapy.

Note: Geriatric, emaciated, or debilitated patients usually require a lower initial dose and more gradual dosage titration than do younger and healthier patients.

Usual adult prescribing limits
1 gram (base) per day.

Note: Although sometimes doses are increased gradually to 2 grams or more per day for short periods, 1 gram or less usually is sufficient for extended therapy.

Usual pediatric dose
Psychotic disorders or

Nausea and vomiting—

Children up to 6 months of age: Dosage has not been established.

Children 6 months to 12 years of age: Oral, 550 mcg (0.55 mg) (base) per kg of body weight or 15 mg per square meter of body surface area every four to six hours, the dosage being adjusted as needed and tolerated.

Apprehension and restlessness, presurgical—

Oral, 550 mcg (0.55 mg) (base) per kg of body weight or 15 mg per square meter of body surface area two to three hours before surgery.

Strength(s) usually available
U.S.—

30 mg (base) per mL (Rx) [*Chlorpromazine Hydrochloride Intensol* (alcohol 0.068%; sodium sulfite; sodium bisulfite); GENERIC].

100 mg (base) per mL (Rx) [*Chlorpromazine Hydrochloride Intensol* (alcohol 0.068%; sodium sulfite; sodium bisulfite); GENERIC].

Canada—

40 mg (base) per mL (Rx) [*Chlorpromanyl-40* (tartrazine [FD&C Yellow No. 5]; parabens; sulfites; sucrose); *Largactil Oral Drops* (alcohol 17.5% v/v; sucrose 200 mg/mL)].

Packaging and storage
Store between 15 and 30 °C (59 and 86 °F), in a tight container, unless otherwise specified by manufacturer. Protect from light. Protect from freezing.

Preparation of dosage form
Dilute each dose immediately before administration in 60 mL or more of coffee, tea, milk, tomato or fruit juice, water, simple syrup, orange syrup, soup, pudding, or carbonated beverage.

Use entire mixture immediately; do not save for later use.

Stability
A slight yellowing will not alter potency; however, do not use if markedly discolored or if a precipitate is present.

If chlorpromazine solutions are mixed with thiopental, atropine, or solutions with a pH out of the range of 4 to 5, a precipitate will form.

Auxiliary labeling
- May cause drowsiness.
- Avoid alcoholic beverages.
- Avoid contact with skin or clothing.
- Must be diluted before use.

Caution
Patients sensitive to sulfites may be sensitive to some chlorpromazine hydrochloride oral concentrate products because of the sulfite preservatives present.

Note
Avoid skin contact with liquid forms of this medication; contact dermatitis has resulted.

Explain dosage measurement and dilution to patient, if self-administered, or to caregiver; however, concentrate dosage form is intended for institutional use.

CHLORPROMAZINE HYDROCHLORIDE SYRUP USP

Usual adult and adolescent dose
See *Chlorpromazine Hydrochloride Oral Concentrate USP*.

Usual adult prescribing limits
See *Chlorpromazine Hydrochloride Oral Concentrate USP*.

Usual pediatric dose
See *Chlorpromazine Hydrochloride Oral Concentrate USP*.

Strength(s) usually available
U.S.—

10 mg (base) per 5 mL (Rx) [*Thorazine* (orange-custard flavored); GENERIC].

Canada—

25 mg (base) per 5 mL (Rx) [*Largactil Liquid* (alcohol 0.5% v/v; sucrose 3.9 grams per 5 mL)].

100 mg (base) per 5 mL (Rx) [*Chlorpromanyl-20* (tartrazine [FD&C Yellow No. 5]; parabens; sulfites; sucrose); *Largactil Liquid* (alcohol 0.5% [v/v]; sucrose 3.6 grams per 5 mL)].

Packaging and storage
Store below 25 °C (77 °F), unless otherwise specified by manufacturer. Store in a tight, light-resistant container. Protect from freezing.

Stability
A slight yellowing will not alter potency; however, do not use if markedly discolored or if a precipitate is present.

Auxiliary labeling
- May cause drowsiness.
- Avoid alcoholic beverages.
- Avoid contact with skin or clothing.

Caution
Patients sensitive to sulfites may be sensitive to some chlorpromazine hydrochloride syrup products because of the sulfite preservatives present.

Note
Avoid skin contact with liquid forms of this medication; contact dermatitis has resulted.

CHLORPROMAZINE HYDROCHLORIDE TABLETS USP

Usual adult and adolescent dose
See *Chlorpromazine Hydrochloride Oral Concentrate USP*.

Usual adult prescribing limits
See *Chlorpromazine Hydrochloride Oral Concentrate USP*.

Usual pediatric dose
See *Chlorpromazine Hydrochloride Oral Concentrate USP*.

Strength(s) usually available
U.S.—

10 mg (base) (Rx) [*Thorazine* (lactose; methylparaben; propylparaben); GENERIC].

25 mg (base) (Rx) [*Thorazine* (lactose; methylparaben; propylparaben); GENERIC].
50 mg (base) (Rx) [*Thorazine* (lactose; methylparaben; propylparaben); GENERIC].
100 mg (base) (Rx) [*Thorazine* (lactose; methylparaben; propylparaben); GENERIC].
200 mg (base) (Rx) [*Thorazine* (lactose; methylparaben; propylparaben); GENERIC].

Canada—
10 mg (base) (Rx) [*Largactil; Novo-Chlorpromazine*].
25 mg (base) (Rx) [*Largactil; Novo-Chlorpromazine;* GENERIC].
50 mg (base) (Rx) [*Largactil; Novo-Chlorpromazine;* GENERIC].
100 mg (base) (Rx) [*Largactil; Novo-Chlorpromazine;* GENERIC].
200 mg (base) (Rx) [*Largactil*].

Packaging and storage
Store below 40 °C (104 °F), preferably between 15 and 30 °C (59 and 86 °F), unless otherwise specified by manufacturer. Store in a well-closed, light-resistant container.

Auxiliary labeling
- May cause drowsiness.
- Avoid alcoholic beverages.

Parenteral Dosage Forms

Note: The dosing and strengths of the dosage forms available are expressed in terms of chlorpromazine base (not the hydrochloride salt).

CHLORPROMAZINE HYDROCHLORIDE INJECTION USP

Usual adult dose
Psychotic disorders (severe)—
Intramuscular, 25 to 50 mg (base), the dose being repeated in one hour if needed, and every three to twelve hours thereafter as needed and tolerated. The dosage may be increased gradually over several days as needed and tolerated.

Nausea and vomiting—
Intramuscular, initially, 25 mg (base) in a single dose; if the dose is well tolerated, 25 to 50 mg may be administered every three to four hours as needed and tolerated until vomiting stops.

Nausea and vomiting during surgery—
Intramuscular: 12.5 mg (base) in a single dose; if no hypotension occurs, the dose may be repeated in thirty minutes as needed and tolerated.
Intravenous: 2 mg (base), diluted to a concentration of 1 mg per mL with sodium chloride injection, every two minutes as needed and tolerated, up to a cumulative dose of 25 mg.

Apprehension and restlessness, presurgical—
Intramuscular, 12.5 to 25 mg (base) one to two hours before surgery.

Hiccups, intractable—
If hiccups persist after oral treatment, intramuscular: 25 to 50 mg (base) three or four times per day.
If hiccups persist after intramuscular treatment, intravenous infusion: 25 to 50 mg (base), diluted in 500 to 1000 mL sodium chloride injection, administered slowly while patient is lying down. Blood pressure should be monitored closely.

Porphyria, acute, intermittent[1]—
Intramuscular, 25 mg (base) every six to eight hours until patient can take oral therapy.

Tetanus[1]—
Intramuscular: 25 to 50 mg (base) three or four times per day; dose and frequency of administration may be increased gradually, based on patient's response.
Intravenous infusion: 25 to 50 mg (base), diluted to a concentration of not more than 1 mg per mL with sodium chloride injection, administered at a rate of 1 mg per minute.

[Migraine headache (treatment)][1]—
Migraines—Intramuscular, 25 to 50 mg (maximum 100 mg).
Migraines—Intravenous, 12.5 to 25 mg (or 0.1 mg per kg of body weight), the dose being repeated in thirty minutes as needed and tolerated.

Note: Geriatric, emaciated, or debilitated patients usually require a lower initial dose and more gradual dosage titration than do younger and healthier patients.

Usual adult prescribing limits
1 gram (base) per day.

Note: Although sometimes doses are increased gradually to 2 grams or more per day for short periods, 1 gram or less usually is sufficient for extended therapy.

Usual pediatric dose
Psychotic disorders or
Nausea and vomiting—
Children up to 6 months of age: Dosage has not been established.
Children 6 months to 12 years of age: Intramuscular, 550 mcg (0.55 mg) (base) per kg of body weight or 15 mg per square meter of body surface area every six to eight hours as needed.

Nausea and vomiting during surgery—
Children up to 6 months of age: Dosage has not been established.
Children 6 months to 12 years of age: Intramuscular, 275 mcg (0.275 mg) (base) per kg of body weight, the dose being repeated in thirty minutes as needed and tolerated. Intravenous infusion, 275 mcg (0.275 mg) (base) per kg of body weight, diluted to a concentration of 1 mg per mL with 0.9% sodium chloride injection, administered at a rate of no more than 1 mg every 2 minutes.

Apprehension and restlessness, presurgical—
Children up to 6 months of age: Dosage has not been established.
Children 6 months to 12 years of age: Intramuscular, 550 mcg (0.55 mg) (base) per kg of body weight one to two hours before surgery.

Tetanus[1]—
Children up to 6 months of age: Dosage has not been established.
Children 6 months to 12 years of age: Intramuscular, 550 mcg (0.55 mg) (base) per kg of body weight every six to eight hours. Intravenous infusion, 550 mcg (0.55 mg) (base) per kg of body weight, diluted to a concentration of not more than 1 mg per mL with 0.9% sodium chloride injection, administered at a rate of 1 mg per 2 minutes.

Usual pediatric prescribing limits
Children 6 months to 5 years of age (up to 23 kg [50 pounds])—40 mg per day.
Children 5 to 12 years of age (23 to 46 kg [50 to 101 pounds])—75 mg per day, except in unmanageable cases.

Strength(s) usually available
U.S.—
25 mg (base) per mL (Rx) [*Thorazine* (sulfite; vials: benzyl alcohol 2%); GENERIC].

Canada—
25 mg (base) per mL (Rx) [*Largactil* (sodium sulfite; potassium metabisulfite); GENERIC].

Packaging and storage
Store below 40 °C (104 °F), preferably between 15 and 30 °C (59 and 86 °F), unless otherwise specified by manufacturer. Protect from light. Protect from freezing.

Preparation of dosage form
To dilute chlorpromazine hydrochloride injection to 1 mg/mL for intravenous administration, mix 1 mL (25 mg) of chlorpromazine hydrochloride injection with 24 mL of sodium chloride injection.

Stability
A slight yellowing will not alter potency; however, do not use if markedly discolored or if a precipitate is present.

Incompatibilities
A precipitate will form if chlorpromazine hydrochloride injection is mixed with thiopental, atropine, or solutions not having a pH of 4 to 5. Mixing chlorpromazine hydrochloride injection with agents other than sodium chloride injection or 2% procaine in the syringe is not recommended.

Caution
Medications containing benzyl alcohol are not recommended for use in neonates (first 30 days of postnatal life). A fatal toxic syndrome consisting of metabolic acidosis, CNS depression, respiratory problems, renal failure, hypotension, and possibly seizures and intracranial hemorrhages has been associated with the use of diluents containing benzyl alcohol for preparation of medications for use in neonates.

Patients sensitive to sulfites may be sensitive to some chlorpromazine hydrochloride injection products because of the sulfite preservatives present.

Note
Avoid skin contact with liquid forms of this medication; contact dermatitis has resulted.

Rectal Dosage Forms

CHLORPROMAZINE SUPPOSITORIES USP

Usual adult and adolescent dose
Nausea and vomiting—
Rectal, 50 to 100 mg every six to eight hours as needed.

Note: Geriatric, emaciated, or debilitated patients usually require a lower initial dose and more gradual dosage titration than do younger and healthier patients.

Usual adult prescribing limits
400 mg per day.

Usual pediatric dose
Psychotic disorders or
Nausea and vomiting—
Children up to 6 months of age: Dosage has not been established.
Children 6 months to 12 years of age: Rectal, 1 mg per kg of body weight every six to eight hours as needed.

Note: The 100-mg suppository dosage form is not recommended for pediatric use.

Strength(s) usually available
U.S.—
25 mg (Rx) [*Thorazine* (glycerin; glyceryl monopalmitate; glyceryl monostearate; hydrogenated coconut oil fatty acids; hydrogenated palm kernel oil fatty acids)].
100 mg (Rx) [*Thorazine* (glycerin; glyceryl monopalmitate; glyceryl monostearate; hydrogenated coconut oil fatty acids; hydrogenated palm kernel oil fatty acids)].
Canada—
100 mg (Rx) [*Largactil*].

Packaging and storage
Store between 15 and 30 °C (59 and 86 °F). Store in a well-closed, light-resistant container.

Auxiliary labeling
- May cause drowsiness.
- Avoid alcoholic beverages.
- For rectal use only.

Note
Explain administration technique to patient, if self-administered, or to caregiver.

[1]Not included in Canadian product labeling.

FLUPHENAZINE

Summary of Differences
Category:
Includes use as antineuralgia adjunct in patients with chronic pain.
Pharmacology/pharmacokinetics:
Chemical group—
Piperazine
Actions—
Antiemetic: Weak
Anticholinergic: Weak
Extrapyramidal: Strong
Hypotensive: Weak
Sedative: Weak

Additional Dosing Information
See also *General Dosing Information.*

For long-acting parenteral dosage forms
A dry syringe and needle (at least 21 gauge) should be used, since use of a wet needle or syringe may cause the solution to become cloudy.
After the initial dose of the decanoate or enanthate extended-action injection, dosages and dosing intervals are determined by the patient's response.

Oral Dosage Forms

FLUPHENAZINE HYDROCHLORIDE ELIXIR USP

Usual adult and adolescent dose
Psychotic disorders—
Initial: Oral, 2.5 to 10 mg per day in divided doses every six to eight hours, the dosage being increased gradually as needed and tolerated.
Maintenance: Oral, 1 to 5 mg per day as a single dose or in divided doses.

Note: Emaciated or debilitated patients usually require a lower initial dosage (1 to 2.5 mg per day), and more gradual dosage titration than do healthier patients.

Usual adult prescribing limits
20 mg per day.

Usual pediatric dose
Psychotic disorders—
Oral, 250 to 750 mcg (0.25 to 0.75 mg) one to four times per day.

Usual geriatric dose
Psychotic disorders—
Oral, 1 to 2.5 mg per day, the dosage being increased gradually as needed and tolerated.

Strength(s) usually available
U.S.—
2.5 mg per 5 mL (0.5 mg per mL) (Rx) [*Prolixin* (alcohol 14% v/v; FD&C Yellow No. 6; flavors; glycerin; polysorbate 40; purified water; sodium benzoate; sucrose); GENERIC].
Canada—
2.5 mg per 5 mL (0.5 mg per mL) (Rx) [*PMS Fluphenazine;* GENERIC].

Packaging and storage
Store below 40 °C (104 °F), preferably between 15 and 30 °C (59 and 86 °F), unless otherwise specified by manufacturer. Store in a tight container. Protect from light. Protect from freezing.

Stability
Flavoring oils may separate from the solution upon standing, producing a wispy precipitate or globular material; however, potency is not affected. If precipitate is present, shake gently to redisperse the oils. Discard if solution fails to clear.

Auxiliary labeling
- May cause drowsiness.
- Avoid alcoholic beverages.
- Avoid contact with skin or clothing.
- Keep container tightly closed.

Note
Avoid skin contact with liquid forms of this medication; contact dermatitis has resulted.

Explain proper measurement of dose to patient, if self-administered, or to caregiver.

FLUPHENAZINE HYDROCHLORIDE ORAL SOLUTION USP

Usual adult and adolescent dose
See *Fluphenazine Hydrochloride Elixir USP.*

Usual adult prescribing limits
See *Fluphenazine Hydrochloride Elixir USP.*

Usual pediatric dose
See *Fluphenazine Hydrochloride Elixir USP.*

Usual geriatric dose
See *Fluphenazine Hydrochloride Elixir USP.*

Strength(s) usually available
U.S.—
5 mg per mL (Rx) [*Permitil Concentrate* (alcohol 1%); *Prolixin Concentrate* (alcohol 14%; sodium benzoate); GENERIC].
Canada—
Not commercially available.

Packaging and storage
Store below 40 °C (104 °F), preferably between 15 and 30 °C (59 and 86 °F), unless otherwise specified by manufacturer. Store in a tight container. Protect from light. Protect from freezing.

Preparation of dosage form
Dilute each dose just before using in at least 60 mL (2 fluid ounces) of water; homogenized milk; caffeine-free carbonated beverages; pineapple, apricot, prune, orange, tomato, or grapefruit juice; or V-8© juice.

Incompatibilities
Do not mix fluphenazine hydrochloride oral solution with beverages containing caffeine (coffee, cola), tannins (tea), or pectins (apple juice), because of physical incompatibility.

Auxiliary labeling
- May cause drowsiness.
- Avoid alcoholic beverages.
- Avoid contact with skin or clothing.
- Must be diluted before use.

Note
Avoid skin contact with liquid forms of this medication; contact dermatitis has resulted.

Explain dosage measurement and dilution to patient, if self-administered, or to caregiver.

FLUPHENAZINE HYDROCHLORIDE TABLETS USP

Usual adult and adolescent dose
See *Fluphenazine Hydrochloride Elixir USP.*

Usual adult prescribing limits
See *Fluphenazine Hydrochloride Elixir USP*.

Usual pediatric dose
See *Fluphenazine Hydrochloride Elixir USP*.

Usual geriatric dose
See *Fluphenazine Hydrochloride Elixir USP*.

Strength(s) usually available
U.S.—
- 1 mg (Rx) [*Prolixin;* GENERIC].
- 2.5 mg (Rx) [*Permitil* (scored; lactose); *Prolixin;* GENERIC].
- 5 mg (Rx) [*Permitil* (scored; lactose); *Prolixin* (tartrazine); GENERIC].
- 10 mg (Rx) [*Permitil* (scored; lactose); *Prolixin* (D&C Red No. 27; D&C Red No. 30); GENERIC].

Canada—
- 1 mg (Rx) [*Apo-Fluphenazine; PMS Fluphenazine*].
- 2 mg (Rx) [*Apo-Fluphenazine; PMS Fluphenazine*].
- 5 mg (Rx) [*Apo-Fluphenazine; PMS Fluphenazine*].
- 10 mg (Rx) [*Moditen HCl*].

Packaging and storage
Store below 40 °C (104 °F), preferably between 15 and 30 °C (59 and 86 °F), unless otherwise specified by manufacturer. Store in a tight, light-resistant container.

Auxiliary labeling
- May cause drowsiness.
- Avoid alcoholic beverages.

Parenteral Dosage Forms

FLUPHENAZINE DECANOATE INJECTION USP

Usual adult dose
Psychotic disorders—

Initial: Intramuscular or subcutaneous, 12.5 to 25 mg, the dose being repeated or increased every one to three weeks as needed and tolerated.

Maintenance: Intramuscular or subcutaneous, usually up to 50 mg every one to four weeks, as needed and tolerated.

Note: For doses greater than 50 mg, increases should be made cautiously in increments of 12.5 mg.

Patients who have had no previous exposure to phenothiazines or who are at high risk for adverse effects may begin fluphenazine therapy with a short-acting dosage form and change to the long-acting injection after response is established.

Usual adult prescribing limits
100 mg per dose.

Usual pediatric dose
Psychotic disorders—

Children 5 to 12 years of age: Intramuscular or subcutaneous, 3.125 to 12.5 mg, the dose being repeated every one to three weeks as needed and tolerated.

Children 12 years of age and older: Intramuscular or subcutaneous, initially 6.25 to 18.75 mg per week, the dose being increased to 12.5 to 25 mg and administered every one to three weeks as needed and tolerated.

Strength(s) usually available
U.S.—
- 25 mg per mL (Rx) [*Prolixin Decanoate* (sesame oil; benzyl alcohol 1.2% w/v); GENERIC].

Canada—
- 25 mg per mL (Rx) [*Modecate* (sesame oil; benzyl alcohol 1.5%); GENERIC].
- 100 mg per mL (Rx) [*Modecate Concentrate* (sesame oil; benzyl alcohol 1.5%); GENERIC].

Packaging and storage
Store below 40 °C (104 °F), preferably between 15 and 30 °C (59 and 86 °F), unless otherwise specified by manufacturer. Protect from light. Protect from freezing.

Caution
Medications containing benzyl alcohol are not recommended for use in neonates (first 30 days of postnatal life). A fatal toxic syndrome consisting of metabolic acidosis, CNS depression, respiratory problems, renal failure, hypotension, and possibly seizures and intracranial hemorrhages has been associated with the use of diluents containing benzyl alcohol for preparation of medications for use in neonates.

Note
Avoid skin contact with liquid forms of this medication; contact dermatitis has resulted.

Additional information
The onset of action of the initial dose is generally between 24 and 72 hours after administration, and antipsychotic effects become significant within 48 to 96 hours.

The effects of a single injection of fluphenazine decanoate usually last for 2 to 4 weeks, but may last for up to 6 weeks in some patients. The side effects information and precautions apply during this period of time.

The time to steady-state from a dosage change requires 6 to 12 weeks or longer.

FLUPHENAZINE ENANTHATE INJECTION USP

Usual adult and adolescent dose
Psychotic disorders—

Intramuscular or subcutaneous, initially, 25 mg every two weeks; the dose and dosing interval may be adjusted based on patient response.

Note: Patients who have had no previous exposure to phenothiazines or who are at high risk for adverse effects may begin fluphenazine therapy with a short-acting dosage form and change to the long-acting injection after response and dosage are established.

Although the usual dosage is 25 mg every two weeks, dosages have ranged from 12.5 to 100 mg every one to three weeks.

For doses greater than 50 mg, increases should be made cautiously in increments of 12.5 mg.

Usual adult prescribing limits
100 mg per dose.

Usual pediatric dose
Psychotic disorders—

Children up to 12 years of age: Dosage has not been established.

Children 12 years of age and older: See *Usual adult and adolescent dose.*

Strength(s) usually available
U.S.—
- 25 mg per mL (Rx) [*Prolixin Enanthate* (sesame oil; benzyl alcohol 1.5% w/v)].

Canada—
- 25 mg per mL (Rx) [*Moditen Enanthate* (sesame oil; benzyl alcohol 1.5% w/v)].

Packaging and storage
Store below 40 °C (104 °F), preferably between 15 and 30 °C (59 and 86 °F), unless otherwise specified by manufacturer. Protect from light. Protect from freezing.

Caution
Medications containing benzyl alcohol are not recommended for use in neonates (first 30 days of postnatal life). A fatal toxic syndrome consisting of metabolic acidosis, CNS depression, respiratory problems, renal failure, hypotension, and possibly seizures and intracranial hemorrhages has been associated with the use of diluents containing benzyl alcohol for preparation of medications for use in neonates.

Note
Avoid skin contact with liquid forms of this medication; contact dermatitis has resulted.

Additional information
The effects of a single dose of fluphenazine enanthate usually last for about 2 weeks, but may last for up to 6 weeks in some patients. The side effects information and precautions apply during this period of time.

FLUPHENAZINE HYDROCHLORIDE INJECTION USP

Usual adult and adolescent dose
Psychotic disorders—

Intramuscular, initially, 1.25 mg, the dose being adjusted and repeated as needed and tolerated to a total initial dosage of 2.5 to 10 mg per day administered in divided doses at six- to eight-hour intervals.

Note: Emaciated or debilitated patients usually require a lower initial dose (1 to 2.5 mg daily) and more gradual dosage titration than do healthier patients.

The parenteral dose of fluphenazine hydrochloride is usually about one third to one half the oral dose.

Usual adult prescribing limits
10 mg per day.

Usual pediatric dose
Psychotic disorders—

Children up to 12 years of age: Dosage has not been established.

Children 12 years of age and older: See *Usual adult and adolescent dose.*

Usual geriatric dose
Psychotic disorders—
Intramuscular, 1 to 2.5 mg per day, the dosage being increased gradually as needed and tolerated.

Strength(s) usually available
U.S.—
2.5 mg per mL (Rx) [*Prolixin* (pH 4.8 to 5.2; methylparaben 0.1%; propylparaben 0.01%; sodium chloride); GENERIC].
Canada—
10 mg per mL (Rx) [*PMS Fluphenazine*].

Packaging and storage
Store below 40 °C (104 °F), preferably between 15 and 30 °C (59 and 86 °F), unless otherwise specified by manufacturer. Protect from light. Protect from freezing.

Stability
A slight yellowing to a light amber color will not alter potency; however, do not use if markedly discolored or if a precipitate is present.

Note
Avoid skin contact with liquid forms of this medication; contact dermatitis has resulted.

MESORIDAZINE

Summary of Differences

Pharmacology/pharmacokinetics:
Chemical group—
Piperidine
Actions—
Antiemetic: Weak
Anticholinergic: Moderate
Extrapyramidal: Weak
Hypotensive: Moderate to strong
Sedative: Strong
Side/Adverse Effects—
Involved in Torsade de Pointes-type arrhythmias and sudden cardiac death more frequently than other phenothiazines.

Oral Dosage Forms

Note: The dosing and strengths of the dosage forms available are expressed in terms of mesoridazine base (not the besylate salt).

MESORIDAZINE BESYLATE ORAL SOLUTION USP

Usual adult and adolescent dose
Psychotic disorders—
Oral, starting dose—50 mg (base) three times per day, the dosage being adjusted as needed and tolerated.

Note: Geriatric, emaciated, or debilitated patients usually require a lower initial dose and more gradual dosage titration than do younger and healthier patients.

Usual adult prescribing limits
The usual optimum total daily dose range is 100 to 400 mg per day.

Usual pediatric dose
Psychotic disorders—
Children up to 12 years of age: Dosage has not been established.
Children 12 years of age and older: See *Usual adult and adolescent dose.*

Strength(s) usually available
U.S.—
25 mg (base) per mL (Rx) [*Serentil Concentrate* (alcohol 0.6% v/v; citric acid; FD&C Red No. 40; flavors; methylparaben; propylparaben; purified water; sodium citrate; sorbitol)].
Canada—
Not commercially available.

Packaging and storage
Store below 25 °C (77 °F). Store in a tight, light-resistant container. Protect from freezing.

Preparation of dosage form
Dilute each dose just before administration in distilled water, acidified tap water, orange juice, or grapefruit juice. The recommended dilution is 25 mg per 2 teaspoonfuls of diluent. Preparation and storage of bulk dilution is not recommended.

Auxiliary labeling
- May cause drowsiness.
- Avoid alcoholic beverages.
- Avoid contact with skin or clothing.
- Must be diluted before use.

Note
Avoid skin contact with liquid forms of this medication; contact dermatitis has resulted.

Explain dosage measurement and dilution to patient, if self-administered, or to caregiver.

MESORIDAZINE BESYLATE TABLETS USP

Usual adult and adolescent dose
See *Mesoridazine Besylate Oral Solution USP*.

Usual pediatric dose
See *Mesoridazine Besylate Oral Solution USP*.

Strength(s) usually available
U.S.—
10 mg (base) (Rx) [*Serentil* (acacia; carnauba wax; colloidal silicon dioxide; FD&C Red No. 40 aluminum lake; microcrystalline cellulose; povidone; sodium benzoate; stearic acid; sucrose; lactose; talc; titanium dioxide; starch; synthetic black iron oxide)].
25 mg (base) (Rx) [*Serentil* (acacia; carnauba wax; colloidal silicon dioxide; FD&C Red No. 40 aluminum lake; microcrystalline cellulose; povidone; sodium benzoate; stearic acid; sucrose; lactose; talc; titanium dioxide; synthetic black iron oxide)].
50 mg (base) (Rx) [*Serentil* (acacia; carnauba wax; colloidal silicon dioxide; FD&C Red No. 40 aluminum lake; microcrystalline cellulose; povidone; sodium benzoate; stearic acid; sucrose; lactose; talc; titanium dioxide; starch; gelatin; synthetic black iron oxide)].
100 mg (base) (Rx) [*Serentil* (acacia; carnauba wax; colloidal silicon dioxide; FD&C Red No. 40 aluminum lake; microcrystalline cellulose; povidone; sodium benzoate; stearic acid; sucrose; lactose; talc; titanium dioxide; starch; gelatin; synthetic black iron oxide)].
Canada—
10 mg (base) (Rx) [*Serentil* (corn starch; lactose)].
25 mg (base) (Rx) [*Serentil* (lactose)].
50 mg (base) (Rx) [*Serentil* (corn starch; lactose)].

Packaging and storage
Store below 30 °C (86 °F), unless otherwise specified by manufacturer. Store in a well-closed, light-resistant container.

Auxiliary labeling
- May cause drowsiness.
- Avoid alcoholic beverages.

Parenteral Dosage Forms

Note: The dosing and strengths of the dosage forms available are expressed in terms of mesoridazine base (not the besylate salt).

MESORIDAZINE BESYLATE INJECTION USP

Usual adult and adolescent dose
Psychotic disorders—
Intramuscular, 25 mg (base), the dose being repeated in one-half hour to one hour as needed and tolerated.

Note: The usual dosage range is 25 to 200 mg (base) per day.
Geriatric, emaciated, or debilitated patients usually require a lower initial dose and more gradual dosage titration than do younger and healthier patients.

Note: Because of possible hypotensive effects, reserve parenteral administration for bedfast patients or for acute ambulatory cases, and keep patient lying down for 30 minutes post-administration.

Usual adult prescribing limits
The usual optimum total daily dose range is 25 to 200 mg per day.

Usual pediatric dose
Psychotic disorders—
Children up to 12 years of age: Dosage has not been established.
Children 12 years of age and older: See *Usual adult and adolescent dose.*

Strength(s) usually available
U.S.—
25 mg (base) per mL (Rx) [*Serentil* (carbon dioxide gas; edetate disodium 0.5 mg; sodium chloride 7.2 mg; water for injection)].
Canada—
Not commercially available.

Packaging and storage
Store below 30 °C (86 °F), unless otherwise specified by manufacturer. Protect from light. Protect from freezing.

Stability
A slight yellowing will not alter potency; however, do not use if markedly discolored or if a precipitate is present.

Note
Avoid skin contact with liquid forms of this medication; contact dermatitis has resulted.

METHOTRIMEPRAZINE

Summary of Differences

Category:
Includes use as an analgesic, anesthetic adjunct, antiemetic, and sedative.

Indications:
Also indicated for relief of moderate to severe pain in nonambulatory patients, and for obstetrical pain and sedation when respiratory depression should be avoided; sedation and somnolence before surgery; adjunctive therapy in general anesthesia to increase effects of anesthetics.

Pharmacology/pharmacokinetics:
Chemical group—
Aliphatic
Actions—
Antiemetic: Strong
Anticholinergic: Moderate to strong
Extrapyramidal: Weak to moderate
Hypotensive: Strong
Sedative: Strong

Precautions:
Drug interactions and/or related problems—
Concurrent use with succinylcholine may cause tachycardia, a fall in blood pressure, CNS stimulation and delirium, and aggravation of extrapyramidal effects.

Oral Dosage Forms

Note: The dosing and strengths of the dosage forms available are expressed in terms of methotrimeprazine base (not the hydrochloride or maleate salts).

METHOTRIMEPRAZINE HYDROCHLORIDE ORAL SOLUTION

Usual adult and adolescent dose
Psychotic disorders or
Pain, severe—
Oral, initially, 50 to 75 mg (base) per day in two or three divided doses with meals, the dosage being increased gradually as needed and tolerated.

Note: If initial doses of 100 to 200 mg per day are required, the patient should be confined to bed for the first few days to prevent orthostatic hypotension.

Treatment of severe psychosis may require 1 gram or more per day.

Sedation or
Pain, moderate—
Oral, initially, 6 to 25 mg (base) per day in three divided doses with meals, the dosage being increased gradually as needed and tolerated.

Note: Daytime drowsiness may be decreased, if necessary, by dividing the daily dose unevenly and using lower doses during the day and higher doses at night.

Usual pediatric dose
Psychotic disorders or
Pain or
Sedation—
Oral, initially, 250 mcg (0.25 mg) (base) per kg of body weight per day in two or three divided doses with meals, the dosage being increased gradually as needed and tolerated.

Note: Dosage should not exceed 40 mg per day in children younger than twelve years of age.

Strength(s) usually available
U.S.—
Not commercially available.
Canada—
25 mg (base) per 5 mL (Rx) [*Nozinan Liquid* (alcohol 2%; sucrose 3.7 grams/5 mL)].
40 mg (base) per mL (Rx) [*Nozinan Oral Drops* (alcohol 16.5%; sucrose 200 mg/mL)].

Packaging and storage
Store below 40 °C (104 °F), preferably between 15 and 30 °C (59 and 86 °F), protected from light, unless otherwise specified by manufacturer. Protect from freezing.

Auxiliary labeling
- May cause drowsiness.
- Avoid alcoholic beverages.
- Avoid contact with skin or clothing.

Note
Avoid skin contact with liquid forms of this medication; contact dermatitis may result.

Additional information
Only enclosed calibrated dropper should be used for measuring doses of the 40 mg (base) per mL solution.

METHOTRIMEPRAZINE MALEATE TABLETS

Usual adult and adolescent dose
See *Methotrimeprazine Hydrochloride Oral Solution*.

Usual pediatric dose
See *Methotrimeprazine Hydrochloride Oral Solution*.

Strength(s) usually available
U.S.—
Not commercially available.
Canada—
2 mg (base) (Rx) [*Nozinan*].
5 mg (base) (Rx) [*Nozinan*].
25 mg (base) (Rx) [*Nozinan*].
50 mg (base) (Rx) [*Nozinan*].

Packaging and storage
Store below 40 °C (104 °F), preferably between 15 and 30 °C (59 and 86 °F), protected from light, unless otherwise specified by manufacturer.

Auxiliary labeling
- May cause drowsiness.
- Avoid alcoholic beverages.

Parenteral Dosage Forms

METHOTRIMEPRAZINE INJECTION USP

Usual adult and adolescent dose
Psychotic disorders, severe or
Pain, acute or intractable—
Intramuscular, initially, 10 to 20 mg every four to six hours, the dosage being increased as needed for pain and sedation.
Pain, obstetrical—
Intramuscular, initially, 15 to 20 mg, the dose being adjusted and repeated as needed.
Pain, postoperative—
Intramuscular, 2.5 to 7.5 mg immediately after surgery, the dose being adjusted and repeated every three to four hours as needed.

Note: After administration of the initial dose, the patient should be confined to bed or carefully supervised for at least 6 hours to prevent orthostatic hypotension, dizziness, or fainting.

Residual effects of anesthetic agents may be additive to the effects of methotrimeprazine.

Sedation, preanesthetic—
Intramuscular, 2 to 20 mg administered forty-five minutes to three hours before surgery.
Anesthesia adjunct during surgery or labor—
Intravenous infusion, 10 to 25 mg in 500 mL of 5% dextrose injection administered at a rate of 20 to 40 drops per minute.

Usual pediatric dose
Psychotic disorders, severe or
Pain—
Intramuscular, 62.5 to 125 mcg (0.062 to 0.125 mg) per kg of body weight per day in single or divided doses.
Anesthesia adjunct during surgery—
Intravenous infusion, 62.5 mcg (0.062 mg) per kg of body weight in 250 mL of 5% dextrose injection, administered at a rate of 20 to 40 drops per minute.

Usual geriatric dose
Pain—
Intramuscular, initially, 5 to 10 mg every four to six hours, the dosage being increased gradually as needed and tolerated.

Strength(s) usually available
U.S.—
Not commercially available.

Canada—

25 mg per mL (Rx) [*Nozinan* (sodium sulfite)].

Packaging and storage
Store below 40 °C (104 °F), preferably between 15 and 30 °C (59 and 86 °F), unless otherwise specified by manufacturer. Protect from light. Protect from freezing.

Incompatibilities
Methotrimeprazine should not be mixed in the same syringe with any drugs other than atropine sulfate or scopolamine hydrobromide.

Caution
Patients sensitive to sulfites may be sensitive to some methotrimeprazine injection products because of the sulfite preservatives present.

Note
Avoid skin contact with liquid forms of this medication; contact dermatitis may result.

PERICYAZINE

Summary of Differences
Indications:

Indicated as an adjunct in some patients with psychoses for the control of residual prevailing hostility, impulsivity, and aggressiveness.

Pharmacology/pharmacokinetics:

Chemical group—

Piperidine

Actions—

Antiemetic: Strong

Anticholinergic: Strong

Extrapyramidal: Moderate

Hypotensive: Moderate

Sedative: Strong

Oral Dosage Forms

PERICYAZINE CAPSULES

Usual adult dose
Psychotic disorders adjunct—

Initial: Oral, 5 mg in the morning and 10 mg in the evening; the dosage being adjusted as needed and tolerated.

Maintenance: Oral, 2.5 to 15 mg in the morning and 5 to 30 mg in the evening has been suggested; rarely will the dosage exceed 20 mg in the morning and 40 mg in the evening.

Usual pediatric dose
Psychotic disorders adjunct—

Children up to 5 years of age: Dosage has not been established.

Children 5 years of age and older: Oral, 2.5 to 10 mg in the morning and 5 to 30 mg in the evening as needed and tolerated.

Note: Dosage is approximately 1 to 3 mg per year of age per day.

Usual geriatric dose
Psychotic disorders adjunct—

Oral, initially 5 mg per day, the dosage being increased gradually as needed and tolerated; rarely will dosage exceed 30 mg per day.

Strength(s) usually available
U.S.—

Not commercially available.

Canada—

5 mg (Rx) [*Neuleptil*].

10 mg (Rx) [*Neuleptil*].

20 mg (Rx) [*Neuleptil*].

Packaging and storage
Store below 40 °C (104 °F), preferably between 15 and 30 °C (59 and 86 °F), protected from light, unless otherwise specified by manufacturer.

Auxiliary labeling
- May cause drowsiness.
- Avoid alcoholic beverages.

PERICYAZINE ORAL SOLUTION

Usual adult dose
See *Pericyazine Capsules*.

Usual pediatric dose
See *Pericyazine Capsules*.

Usual geriatric dose
See *Pericyazine Capsules*.

Strength(s) usually available
U.S.—

Not commercially available.

Canada—

10 mg per mL (Rx) [*Neuleptil* (alcohol 12% v/v; sucrose 250 mg/mL)].

Packaging and storage
Store below 40 °C (104 °F), preferably between 15 and 30 °C (59 and 86 °F), protected from light, unless otherwise specified by manufacturer.

Auxiliary labeling
- May cause drowsiness.
- Avoid alcoholic beverages.
- Avoid contact with skin or clothing.

Note
Avoid skin contact with liquid forms of this medication; contact dermatitis may result.

Additional information
Only enclosed calibrated dropper should be used for measuring dose.

PERPHENAZINE

Summary of Differences
Category:

Includes antiemetic use.

Pharmacology/pharmacokinetics:

Chemical group—

Piperazine

Actions—

Antiemetic: Strong

Anticholinergic: Weak to moderate

Extrapyramidal: Strong

Hypotensive: Weak

Sedative: Weak to moderate

Oral Dosage Forms

PERPHENAZINE ORAL SOLUTION USP

Usual adult and adolescent dose
Psychotic disorders (hospitalized patients)—

Oral, 8 to 16 mg two to four times per day, the dosage being adjusted as needed and tolerated.

Note: Geriatric, emaciated, or debilitated patients usually require a lower initial dose and more gradual dosage titration than do younger and healthier patients.

Adolescents usually require dosages at the lower end of the adult dosage range.

Usual adult prescribing limits
Psychotic disorders (hospitalized patients)—

64 mg per day.

Usual pediatric dose
Psychotic disorders—

Children up to 12 years of age: Dosage has not been established.

Children 12 years of age and older: See *Usual adult and adolescent dose*.

Strength(s) usually available
U.S.—

16 mg per 5 mL (Rx) [*Trilafon Concentrate*].

Canada—

16 mg per 5 mL (Rx) [*PMS Perphenazine*].

Packaging and storage
Store below 40 °C (104 °F), preferably between 15 and 30 °C (59 and 86 °F), unless otherwise specified by manufacturer. Store in a well-closed, light-resistant container. Protect from freezing.

Preparation of dosage form
Dilute each dose immediately before administration in water, salt solution, milk, tomato or fruit juice (except apple juice), soup, or a caffeine-free carbonated beverage. The recommended dilution is 2 fluid ounces (60 mL) of diluent for each teaspoonful (5 mL) of perphenazine oral solution.

Incompatibilities
Because of physical incompatibility, the oral solution should not be mixed with beverages containing caffeine or tannins (colas, coffee, or tea) or pectinates (apple juice).

Auxiliary labeling
- May cause drowsiness.
- Avoid alcoholic beverages.
- Avoid contact with skin or clothing.
- Must be diluted before use.

Note
Avoid skin contact with liquid forms of this medication; contact dermatitis has resulted.

Explain dosage measurement and dilution to patient, if self-administered, or to caregiver; however, the oral solution is intended primarily for institutional use.

PERPHENAZINE TABLETS USP

Usual adult and adolescent dose
Psychotic disorders—
Oral, 4 to 16 mg two to four times per day, the dosage being adjusted gradually as needed and tolerated.
Nausea and vomiting—
Oral, 8 to 16 mg per day in divided doses, the dosage being decreased as early as possible.

Note: Geriatric, emaciated, or debilitated patients usually require a lower initial dose and more gradual dosage titration than do younger and healthier patients.

Adolescents usually require dosages at the lower end of the adult dosage range.

Usual adult prescribing limits
Psychotic disorders—
Hospitalized patients: 64 mg per day.
Nonhospitalized patients: 24 mg per day for long-term use.
Nausea and vomiting—
24 mg per day.

Usual pediatric dose
Psychotic disorders or
Nausea and vomiting—
Children up to 12 years of age: Dosage has not been established.
Children 12 years of age and older: See *Usual adult and adolescent dose.*

Strength(s) usually available
U.S.—
2 mg (Rx) [*Trilafon* (butylparaben; lactose); GENERIC].
4 mg (Rx) [*Trilafon* (butylparaben; lactose); GENERIC].
8 mg (Rx) [*Trilafon* (butylparaben; lactose); GENERIC].
16 mg (Rx) [*Trilafon* (butylparaben; lactose); GENERIC].
Canada—
2 mg (Rx) [*Apo-Perphenazine;* GENERIC].
4 mg (Rx) [*Apo-Perphenazine;* GENERIC].
8 mg (Rx) [*Apo-Perphenazine;* GENERIC].
16 mg (Rx) [*Apo-Perphenazine;* GENERIC].

Packaging and storage
Store below 40 °C (104 °F), preferably between 15 and 30 °C (59 and 86 °F), unless otherwise specified by manufacturer. Store in a tight, light-resistant container.

Auxiliary labeling
- May cause drowsiness.
- Avoid alcoholic beverages.

Parenteral Dosage Forms

PERPHENAZINE INJECTION USP

Usual adult and adolescent dose
Psychotic disorders—
Intramuscular, initially 5 mg (in most patients) to 10 mg (in severely agitated patients). Dose may be adjusted, as needed and tolerated, and repeated every six hours until oral therapy is possible.
Nausea and vomiting—
Intramuscular, 5 to 10 mg as needed and tolerated for rapid control of severe vomiting.
Intravenous, up to 5 mg, diluted, as a slow-drip infusion (preferred in surgical patients) or up to 5 mg, diluted to 0.5 mg per mL with 0.9% sodium chloride injection, in fractional injections of up to 1 mg each, administered at intervals of not less than one to two minutes.

Note: Geriatric, emaciated, or debilitated patients usually require a lower initial dose and more gradual dosage titration than do younger and healthier patients.

For intramuscular administration, adolescents usually require dosages at the lower end of the adult dosage range.

Intravenous administration is recommended only for use in recumbent hospitalized adults when needed to control severe vomiting or violent retching during surgery.

In psychotic conditions, most patients are controlled and amenable to oral therapy within 24 to 48 hours.

Usual adult prescribing limits
Intramuscular administration, nonhospitalized patients: 15 mg per day.
Intramuscular administration, hospitalized patients: 30 mg per day.
Intravenous administration: 5 mg.

Usual pediatric dose
Psychotic disorders—
Children up to 12 years of age: Dosage has not been established.
Children 12 years of age and older: See *Usual adult and adolescent dose.*

Strength(s) usually available
U.S.—
5 mg per mL (Rx) [*Trilafon* (sodium bisulfite)].
Canada—
Not commercially available.

Packaging and storage
Store below 40 °C (104 °F), preferably between 15 and 30 °C (59 and 86 °F), unless otherwise specified by manufacturer. Protect from light. Protect from freezing.

Stability
A slight yellowing will not alter potency; however, do not use if markedly discolored or if a precipitate is present.

Caution
Patients sensitive to sulfites may be sensitive to some perphenazine injection products because of the sulfite preservatives present.

Note
Avoid skin contact with liquid forms of this medication; contact dermatitis has resulted.

PIPOTIAZINE

Summary of Differences

Indications:
For the control of residual prevailing hostility, impulsivity, and aggressiveness in psychotic patients already receiving antipsychotic medication.
Pharmacology/pharmacokinetics:
Chemical group—
Piperidine
Actions—
Antiemetic: Weak
Anticholinergic: Weak
Extrapyramidal: Strong
Hypotensive: Weak
Sedative: Weak

Additional Dosing Information

See also *General Dosing Information.*

A dry syringe and needle (at least 21-gauge) should be used, since use of a wet needle or syringe may cause the solution to become cloudy.

After the initial dose of pipotiazine palmitate extended-action injection, doses and dosing intervals are determined by the patient's response.

Parenteral Dosage Forms

PIPOTIAZINE PALMITATE INJECTION

Usual adult and adolescent dose
Psychotic disorders—
Intramuscular, initially 50 to 100 mg, the dose being increased in increments of 25 mg every two to three weeks, as needed and tolerated, usually up to a maintenance dose of 75 to 150 mg every four weeks.

Note: Geriatric patients usually require lower initial doses and, after initial titration, dosage should be reduced to the lowest effective maintenance dosage as soon as possible.

Usual pediatric dose
Children up to 12 years of age: Dosage has not been established.
Children 12 years of age and older: See *Usual adult and adolescent dose.*

Strength(s) usually available
U.S.—
Not commercially available.

Canada—
25 mg per mL (Rx) [*Piportil L_4* (sesame oil)].
50 mg per mL (Rx) [*Piportil L_4* (sesame oil)].

Packaging and storage
Store below 40 °C (104 °F), preferably between 15 and 30 °C (59 and 86 °F), protected from light, unless otherwise specified by manufacturer. Protect from freezing.

Note
Avoid skin contact with liquid forms of this medication; contact dermatitis may result.

Additional information
The onset of action is usually within the first 2 or 3 days after injection, and antipsychotic effects become significant within 1 week.
The effects of a single injection may last from 3 to 6 weeks, but adequate symptom control may be maintained with one injection every 4 weeks.

PROCHLORPERAZINE

Summary of Differences
Category:
Includes antiemetic use.
Pharmacology/pharmacokinetics:
Chemical group—
Piperazine
Actions—
Antiemetic: Strong
Anticholinergic: Weak
Extrapyramidal: Strong
Hypotensive: Weak
Sedative: Weak to moderate

Additional Dosing Information
See also *General Dosing Information.*
For parenteral dosage forms only
- Must be injected deeply into upper outer quadrant of the buttock.
- Subcutaneous administration is not recommended because of possible irritation at injection site.

Oral Dosage Forms
Note: The dosing and strengths of the dosage forms available are expressed in terms of prochlorperazine base (not the edisylate, maleate, or mesylate salts).

PROCHLORPERAZINE ORAL SOLUTION USP

Usual adult and adolescent dose
Psychotic disorders—
Oral, 5 to 10 mg (base) three or four times per day, the dosage being increased gradually every two to three days as needed and tolerated.
Nausea and vomiting—
Oral, 5 to 10 mg (base) three or four times per day.
Note: Geriatric, emaciated, or debilitated patients usually require a lower initial dose and more gradual dosage titration than do younger and healthier patients.

Usual adult prescribing limits
Psychotic disorders—
150 mg (base) per day.
Nausea and vomiting—
40 mg (base) per day.

Usual pediatric dose
Psychotic disorders—
Children up to 2 years of age or less than 9 kg of body weight: Dosage has not been established.
Children 2 to 12 years of age: Oral, 2.5 mg (base) two or three times per day, not to exceed 10 mg on the first day. Dosage may be increased based upon patient response.
Children 12 years of age and older: See *Usual adult and adolescent dose.*
Nausea and vomiting—
Children 9 to 14 kg of body weight: Oral, 2.5 mg (base) one or two times per day.
Children 14 to 18 kg of body weight: Oral, 2.5 mg (base) two or three times per day.
Children 18 to 39 kg of body weight: Oral, 2.5 mg (base) three times per day or 5 mg two times per day.

Usual pediatric prescribing limits
Psychotic disorders—
Children 2 to 6 years of age: 20 mg per day.
Children 6 to 12 years of age: 25 mg per day.
Nausea and vomiting—
Children 9 to 14 kg of body weight: 7.5 mg per day.
Children 14 to 18 kg of body weight: 10 mg per day.
Children 18 to 39 kg of body weight: 15 mg per day.

Strength(s) usually available
U.S.—
5 mg (base [as the edisylate salt]) per 5 mL (Rx) [*Compazine* (fruit-flavored; FD&C Yellow No. 6; flavors; polyoxyethylene polyoxypropylene glycol; sodium benzoate; sodium citrate; sucrose; water)].
Canada—
Not commercially available.

Packaging and storage
Store below 40 °C (104 °F), preferably between 15 and 30 °C (59 and 86 °F), unless otherwise specified by manufacturer. Store in a tight, light-resistant container. Protect from freezing.

Stability
A slight yellowing will not affect potency; however, do not use if markedly discolored or if a precipitate is present.

Auxiliary labeling
- May cause drowsiness.
- Avoid alcoholic beverages.
- Avoid contact with skin or clothing.

Note
Avoid skin contact with liquid forms of this medication; contact dermatitis has resulted.

PROCHLORPERAZINE MALEATE EXTENDED-RELEASE CAPSULES

Usual adult and adolescent dose
Psychotic disorders—
Dosage must be determined by physician.
Nausea and vomiting—
Oral, initially 15 mg (base) as a single dose in the morning or 10 mg every twelve hours, the dosage being increased as needed and tolerated.
Note: Geriatric, emaciated, or debilitated patients usually require a lower initial dose and more gradual dosage titration than do younger and healthier patients.

Usual adult prescribing limits
Psychotic disorders—
150 mg (base) per day.
Nausea and vomiting—
40 mg (base) per day.

Usual pediatric dose
The extended-release dosage form is not recommended for use in children.

Strength(s) usually available
U.S.—
10 mg (base) (Rx) [*Compazine Spansule* (benzyl alcohol; cetylpyridinium chloride; D&C Green No. 5; D&C Yellow No. 10; FD&C Blue No. 1; FD&C Red No. 40; FD&C Yellow No. 6; gelatin; glyceryl monostearate; sodium lauryl sulfate; starch; sucrose; wax)].
15 mg (base) (Rx) [*Compazine Spansule* (benzyl alcohol; cetylpyridinium chloride; D&C Green No. 5; D&C Yellow No. 10; FD&C Blue No. 1; FD&C Red No. 40; FD&C Yellow No. 6; gelatin; glyceryl monostearate; sodium lauryl sulfate; starch; sucrose; wax)].
Canada—
Not commercially available.

Packaging and storage
Store below 40 °C (104 °F), preferably between 15 and 30 °C (59 and 86 °F), in a well-closed container, unless otherwise specified by manufacturer. Protect from light.

Auxiliary labeling
- May cause drowsiness.
- Avoid alcoholic beverages.
- Swallow capsule whole.

Additional information
The extended-release capsule releases a dose of prochlorperazine promptly upon ingestion and releases the remainder of the medication over a prolonged period. Blood concentrations remain in the therapeutic range for 10 to 12 hours after a single dose.

PROCHLORPERAZINE MALEATE TABLETS USP

Usual adult and adolescent dose
See *Prochlorperazine Oral Solution USP*.

Usual adult prescribing limits
See *Prochlorperazine Oral Solution USP*.

Usual pediatric dose
See *Prochlorperazine Oral Solution USP*.

Note: The oral solution dosage form usually is preferred for use in children.

Usual pediatric prescribing limits
See *Prochlorperazine Oral Solution USP*.

Strength(s) usually available
U.S.—
5 mg (base) (Rx) [*Compazine* (lactose; sodium croscarmellose); GENERIC].
10 mg (base) (Rx) [*Compazine* (lactose; sodium croscarmellose); GENERIC].
Canada—
5 mg (base) (Rx) [*Nu-Prochlor; Stemetil*].
10 mg (base) (Rx) [*Nu-Prochlor; Stemetil*].

Packaging and storage
Store below 40 °C (104 °F), preferably between 15 and 30 °C (59 and 86 °F), unless otherwise specified by manufacturer. Store in a well-closed container. Protect from light.

Auxiliary labeling
- May cause drowsiness.
- Avoid alcoholic beverages.

PROCHLORPERAZINE MESYLATE ORAL SOLUTION

Usual adult and adolescent dose
See *Prochlorperazine Oral Solution USP*.

Usual adult prescribing limits
See *Prochlorperazine Oral Solution USP*.

Usual pediatric dose
See *Prochlorperazine Oral Solution USP*.

Usual pediatric prescribing limits
See *Prochlorperazine Oral Solution USP*.

Strength(s) usually available
U.S.—
Not commercially available.
Canada—
5 mg (base) per 5 mL (Rx) [*Stemetil Liquid* (sucrose 4 grams per 5 mL)].

Packaging and storage
Store below 40 °C (104 °F), preferably between 15 and 30 °C (59 and 86 °F), in a tight container, protected from light, unless otherwise specified by manufacturer. Protect from freezing.

Auxiliary labeling
- May cause drowsiness.
- Avoid alcoholic beverages.
- Avoid contact with skin or clothing.

Note
Avoid skin contact with liquid forms of this medication; contact dermatitis has resulted.

Parenteral Dosage Forms

Note: The dosing and strengths of the dosage forms available are expressed in terms of prochlorperazine base (not the edisylate or mesylate salts).

PROCHLORPERAZINE EDISYLATE INJECTION USP

Usual adult and adolescent dose
Psychotic disorders—
For immediate control of severely disturbed patients: Intramuscular, 10 to 20 mg (base); the dose may be repeated every two to four hours as needed, usually up to three or four doses. In resistant cases, the dose may be repeated every hour if needed.
Maintenance if prolonged parenteral administration is required: Intramuscular, 10 to 20 mg (base) every four to six hours.
Nausea and vomiting—
Intramuscular, 5 to 10 mg (base); the dose may be repeated every three to four hours, as needed.
Intravenous, 2.5 to 10 mg as a slow injection or infusion, at a rate not exceeding 5 mg per minute.

Note: For intravenous use, prochlorperazine edisylate injection may be administered undiluted or may be diluted in isotonic solution.

Single intravenous doses should not exceed 10 mg.

Nausea and vomiting in surgery—
Intramuscular, 5 to 10 mg (base) one to two hours before induction of anesthesia or during or after surgery to control acute symptoms; the dose may be repeated once in thirty minutes if needed.
Intravenous, 5 to 10 mg (base) administered as a slow injection or infusion (at a rate not exceeding 5 mg per minute) fifteen to thirty minutes before induction of anesthesia or during or after surgery to control acute symptoms; the dose may be repeated once if needed.

Note: For intravenous use, prochlorperazine edisylate injection may be administered undiluted or diluted in isotonic solution.

Single intravenous doses should not exceed 10 mg.

Note: Geriatric, emaciated, or debilitated patients usually require a lower initial dose and more gradual dosage titration than do younger and healthier patients.

Usual adult prescribing limits
Psychotic disorders—
200 mg (base) per day.
Nausea and vomiting—
40 mg (base) per day with no single intravenous dose exceeding 10 mg.

Usual pediatric dose
Psychotic disorders or
Nausea and vomiting—
Children up to 2 years of age or 9 kg of body weight: Dosage has not been established.
Children 2 to 12 years of age: Intramuscular, 132 mcg (0.132 mg) (base) per kg of body weight.
Children 12 years of age and older: See *Usual adult and adolescent dose*.

Note: Usually control is obtained with one dose, after which patient may be switched to an oral dosage form at the same or a higher dosage level.

Not recommended in pediatric surgery.

Usual pediatric prescribing limits
Children 2 to 6 years of age: 20 mg per day.
Children 6 to 12 years of age: 25 mg per day.

Strength(s) usually available
U.S.—
5 mg (base) per mL (Rx) [*Compazine* (sodium biphosphate 5 mg/mL; sodium tartrate 12 mg/mL; sodium saccharin 0.9 mg/mL; benzyl alcohol 0.75%); GENERIC].
Canada—
Not commercially available.

Packaging and storage
Store below 30 °C (86 °F), unless otherwise specified by manufacturer. Protect from light. Protect from freezing.

Preparation of dosage form
For intravenous administration, prochlorperazine edisylate injection may be diluted with isotonic solution or may be used undiluted.

Stability
A slight yellowing will not alter potency; however, do not use if markedly discolored or if a precipitate is present.

Incompatibilities
A white milky precipitate may form when prochlorperazine edisylate injection is mixed in the same syringe with a morphine sulfate injection that contains phenol.

Caution
Medications containing benzyl alcohol are not recommended for use in neonates (first 30 days of postnatal life). A fatal toxic syndrome consisting of metabolic acidosis, CNS depression, respiratory problems, renal failure, hypotension, and possibly seizures and intracranial hemorrhages has been associated with the use of diluents containing benzyl alcohol in preparation of medications for use in neonates.

Note
Avoid skin contact with liquid forms of this medication; contact dermatitis has resulted.

Subcutaneous administration is not recommended due to possible local irritation.

PROCHLORPERAZINE MESYLATE INJECTION

Usual adult and adolescent dose

Psychotic disorders—

For immediate control of severely disturbed patients: Intramuscular, 10 to 20 mg (base); the dose may be repeated every two to four hours as needed, usually up to three or four doses.

Maintenance if prolonged parenteral administration is required: Intramuscular, 10 to 20 mg (base) every four to six hours.

Nausea and vomiting—

Intramuscular, 5 to 10 mg (base); the dose may be repeated every three to four hours if needed.

Nausea and vomiting in surgery—

Intramuscular, 5 to 10 mg (base) one to two hours before induction of anesthesia or during or after surgery to control acute symptoms; the dose may be repeated once in thirty minutes and may be repeated every three to four hours to a total dose of 40 mg per day if needed.

Intravenous, 5 to 10 mg (base), administered (at a rate not exceeding 5 mg per minute) fifteen to thirty minutes before induction of anesthesia or during or after surgery to control acute symptoms; the dose may be repeated once if needed.

Intravenous infusion, 20 mg (base) in 1 liter of isotonic solution, administered during or after surgery.

Note: Geriatric, emaciated, or debilitated patients usually require a lower initial dose and more gradual dosage titration than do younger and healthier patients.

Usual adult prescribing limits

Psychotic disorders—

200 mg (base) per day.

Nausea and vomiting—

40 mg (base) per day.

Usual pediatric dose

Psychotic disorders or

Nausea and vomiting—

Children up to 2 years of age or less than 9 kg of body weight: Dosage has not been established.

Children 2 to 12 years of age: Intramuscular, 132 mcg (0.132 mg) (base) per kg of body weight, not exceeding 10 mg the first day, the dosage being increased thereafter as needed and tolerated.

Children 12 years of age and over: See *Usual adult and adolescent dose.*

Note: Usually control is obtained with one dose, after which patient may be switched to an oral dosage form at the same or at a higher dosage level.

Not recommended in pediatric surgery.

Usual pediatric prescribing limits

Children 2 to 6 years of age: 20 mg per day.

Children 6 to 12 years of age: 25 mg per day.

Strength(s) usually available

U.S.—

Not commercially available.

Canada—

5 mg (base) per mL (Rx) [*PMS Prochlorperazine; Stemetil* (sulfite); GENERIC].

Packaging and storage

Store below 40 °C (104 °F), preferably between 15 and 30 °C (59 and 86 °F), protected from light, unless otherwise specified by manufacturer. Protect from freezing.

Stability

A slight yellowing will not alter potency; however, do not use if markedly discolored or if a precipitate is present.

Caution

Patients sensitive to sulfites may be sensitive to some prochlorperazine products because of the sulfite preservatives present.

Note

Avoid skin contact with liquid forms of this medication; contact dermatitis has resulted.

Rectal Dosage Forms

PROCHLORPERAZINE SUPPOSITORIES USP

Usual adult and adolescent dose

Psychotic disorders—

Rectal, initially 10 mg three or four times per day; the dosage may be increased by 5 to 10 mg every two to three days as needed and tolerated.

Nausea and vomiting—

Rectal, 25 mg two times per day.

Note: Geriatric, emaciated, or debilitated patients usually require a lower initial dose and more gradual dosage titration than do younger and healthier patients.

Usual pediatric dose

Psychotic disorders—

Children 2 to 12 years of age: Rectal, initially 2.5 mg two or three times a day, not to exceed 10 mg on the first day; dosage may be increased based upon response.

Children 12 years of age and older: See *Usual adult and adolescent dose.*

Nausea and vomiting—

Children up to 2 years of age or less than 9 kg of body weight: Dosage has not been established.

Children 9 to 14 kg of body weight: Rectal, 2.5 mg one or two times per day.

Children 14 to 18 kg of body weight: Rectal, 2.5 mg two or three times per day.

Children 18 to 39 kg of body weight: Rectal, 2.5 mg three times per day or 5 mg two times per day.

Usual pediatric prescribing limits

Psychotic disorders—

Children 2 to 6 years of age: 20 mg per day.

Children 6 to 12 years of age: 25 mg per day.

Nausea and vomiting—

Children 9 to 14 kg of body weight: 7.5 mg per day.

Children 14 to 18 kg of body weight: 10 mg per day.

Children 18 to 39 kg of body weight: 15 mg per day.

Strength(s) usually available

U.S.—

2.5 mg (Rx) [*Compazine*].

5 mg (Rx) [*Compazine*].

25 mg (Rx) [*Compazine;* GENERIC].

Canada—

10 mg (Rx) [*Stemetil;* GENERIC].

Packaging and storage

Store between 15 and 30 °C (59 and 86 °F). Store in a tight container. Protect from light.

Auxiliary labeling

- May cause drowsiness.
- Avoid alcoholic beverages.
- For rectal use only.

Note

The 25-mg suppository is not recommended for use in children.

Explain administration technique to patient, if self-administered, or to caregiver.

PROMAZINE

Summary of Differences

Pharmacology/pharmacokinetics:

Chemical group—

Aliphatic

Actions—

Antiemetic: Moderate

Anticholinergic: Strong

Extrapyramidal: Weak

Hypotensive: Strong

Sedative: Strong

Parenteral Dosage Forms

PROMAZINE HYDROCHLORIDE INJECTION USP

Usual adult dose

Psychotic disorders—

Initial: Intramuscular, a single dose of 50 to 150 mg; dose may be adjusted and repeated after thirty minutes, if necessary, up to a cumulative dose of 300 mg.

Maintenance: Intramuscular, 10 to 200 mg every four to six hours may be used.

Note: Geriatric, emaciated, or debilitated patients usually require a lower initial dose and more gradual dosage titration than do younger and healthier patients.

Intravenous injection is not recommended generally, but may be used in severely agitated hospitalized patients. For intravenous use, dilute promazine hydrochloride injection to 25 mg or less per mL with 0.9% sodium chloride injection and administer slowly.

In acutely inebriated patients, the initial dose should not exceed 50 mg.

Usual adult prescribing limits
1 gram per day.

Note: Although doses sometimes are increased gradually to 2 grams or more per day for short periods, extended therapy with 1 gram or less per day usually is sufficient.

Usual pediatric dose
Psychotic disorders—
Children up to 12 years of age: Dosage has not been established.
Children 12 years of age and older: Intramuscular, 10 to 25 mg every four to six hours.

Strength(s) usually available
U.S.—
Not commercially available.
Canada—
50 mg per mL (Rx) [GENERIC].

Packaging and storage
Store below 40 °C (104 °F), preferably between 15 and 30 °C (59 and 86 °F), unless otherwise specified by manufacturer. Protect from light. Protect from freezing.

Stability
A slight yellowing will not alter potency; however, do not use if markedly discolored or if a precipitate is present.

Note
Avoid skin contact with liquid forms of this medication; contact dermatitis has resulted.

THIOPROPERAZINE

Summary of Differences

Pharmacology/pharmacokinetics:
Chemical group—
Piperazine
Actions—
Antiemetic: Weak
Anticholinergic: Weak
Extrapyramidal: Strong
Hypotensive: Weak
Sedative: Weak

Oral Dosage Forms

Note: The dosing and strengths of the dosage forms available are expressed in terms of thioproperazine base (not the mesylate salt).

THIOPROPERAZINE MESYLATE TABLETS

Usual adult and adolescent dose
Psychotic disorders—
Oral, initially 5 mg (base) per day, the dosage being adjusted gradually by 5 mg every two or three days as needed and tolerated.

Note: The usual effective dose is about 30 to 40 mg per day. In some patients, 90 mg or more per day may be necessary to control symptoms. Once symptoms are controlled, dosage should be reduced gradually to the lowest effective maintenance dose.

Usual pediatric dose
Psychotic disorders—
Children up to 3 years of age: Use is not recommended.
Children 3 to 11 years of age: Dosage has not been established.
Children 11 years of age and older: Oral, initially 1 to 3 mg (base) per day in a single dose or in divided doses; dosage may be increased every two to three days, as needed and tolerated.

Strength(s) usually available
U.S.—
Not commercially available.
Canada—
10 mg (base) (Rx) [*Majeptil* (scored)].

Packaging and storage
Store below 40 °C (104 °F), in a well-closed, light-resistant container, unless otherwise specified by manufacturer.

Auxiliary labeling
- May cause drowsiness.
- Avoid alcoholic beverages.

THIORIDAZINE

Summary of Differences

Category:
Includes sedative and antidyskinetic (Huntington's chorea) uses.
Pharmacology/pharmacokinetics:
Chemical group—
Piperidine
Actions—
Antiemetic: Weak
Anticholinergic: Moderate to strong
Extrapyramidal: Weak
Hypotensive: Moderate to strong
Sedative: Moderate to strong
Side/adverse effects:
More likely to cause pigmentary retinopathy than other phenothiazines.
Greater risk of developing melanosis than with other phenothiazines.
Involved in sudden cardiac death more frequently than other phenothiazines.

Oral Dosage Forms

THIORIDAZINE ORAL SUSPENSION USP

Note: The oral suspension dosage form contains thioridazine base, but the dosage and strength are expressed in equivalents of the hydrochloride salt.

Usual adult and adolescent dose
Psychotic disorders—
Initial: Oral, 50 to 100 mg (hydrochloride) one to three times per day, the dosage being adjusted gradually as needed and tolerated.
Maintenance: Oral, 50 to 200 mg (hydrochloride) two to four times per day.
Sedation—
Initial: Oral, 25 mg (hydrochloride) three times per day, the dosage being adjusted gradually as needed and tolerated.
Maintenance: Oral, 10 to 50 mg (hydrochloride) two to four times per day.

Note: Geriatric, emaciated, or debilitated patients usually require a lower initial dose and more gradual dosage titration than do younger and healthier patients.

Usual adult prescribing limits
Psychotic disorders—
800 mg (hydrochloride) per day.

Note: Dosages greater than 300 mg (hydrochloride) per day should be used only in severe neuropsychiatric conditions.

Sedation—
200 mg (hydrochloride) per day.

Usual pediatric dose
Psychotic disorders—
Children up to 2 years of age: Dosage has not been established.
Children 2 to 12 years of age: Oral, initially 10 to 25 mg (hydrochloride) two or three times per day, the dosage being adjusted gradually as needed and tolerated; the usual dosage range is 250 mcg (0.25 mg) to 3 mg per kg of body weight or 7.5 mg per square meter of body surface area four times per day.
Children 12 years of age and older: See *Usual adult and adolescent dose*.

Strength(s) usually available
U.S.—
25 mg (hydrochloride) per 5 mL (Rx) [*Mellaril-S* (buttermint flavor; carbomer 934; flavor; polysorbate 80; purified water; sodium hydroxide; sucrose)].
100 mg (hydrochloride) per 5 mL (Rx) [*Mellaril-S* (buttermint flavor; carbomer 934; flavor; polysorbate 80; purified water; sodium hydroxide; sucrose; D&C Yellow No. 10; FD&C Yellow No. 6)].
Canada—
10 mg (hydrochloride) per 5 mL (Rx) [*Mellaril; Novo-Ridazine*].

Packaging and storage
Store below 25 °C (77 °F) in a tight, light-resistant container. Protect from freezing.

Auxiliary labeling
- Shake well before using.
- May cause drowsiness.
- Avoid alcoholic beverages.
- Avoid contact with skin or clothing.

Note
Avoid skin contact with liquid forms of this medication; contact dermatitis has resulted.

THIORIDAZINE HYDROCHLORIDE ORAL SOLUTION USP

Usual adult and adolescent dose
See *Thioridazine Oral Suspension USP*.

Usual adult prescribing limits
See *Thioridazine Oral Suspension USP*.

Usual pediatric dose
See *Thioridazine Oral Suspension USP*.

Strength(s) usually available
U.S.—
30 mg per mL (Rx) [*Mellaril Concentrate* (alcohol 3%); GENERIC].
100 mg per mL (Rx) [*Mellaril Concentrate* (alcohol 4.2%); GENERIC].
Canada—
30 mg per mL (Rx) [*Mellaril* (alcohol 24.5 mg/mL; parabens); *PMS Thioridazine*].

Packaging and storage
Store between 15 and 30 °C (59 and 86 °F), unless otherwise specified by manufacturer. Store in a tight, light-resistant container. Protect from freezing.

Preparation of dosage form
Each dose must be diluted just before administration in a half glass (120 mL) of distilled water, acidified tap water, orange juice, or grapefruit juice.

Auxiliary labeling
- May cause drowsiness.
- Avoid alcoholic beverages.
- Avoid contact with skin or clothing.
- Must be diluted before use.

Note
Avoid skin contact with liquid forms of this medication; contact dermatitis has resulted.

Explain dosage measurement and dilution to patient, if self-administered, or to caregiver.

THIORIDAZINE HYDROCHLORIDE TABLETS USP

Usual adult and adolescent dose
See *Thioridazine Oral Suspension USP*.

Usual adult prescribing limits
See *Thioridazine Oral Suspension USP*.

Usual pediatric dose
See *Thioridazine Oral Suspension USP*.

Strength(s) usually available
U.S.—
10 mg (Rx) [*Mellaril;* GENERIC].
15 mg (Rx) [*Mellaril;* GENERIC].
25 mg (Rx) [*Mellaril;* GENERIC].
50 mg (Rx) [*Mellaril;* GENERIC].
100 mg (Rx) [*Mellaril;* GENERIC].
150 mg (Rx) [*Mellaril;* GENERIC].
200 mg (Rx) [*Mellaril;* GENERIC].
Canada—
10 mg (Rx) [*Apo-Thioridazine; Novo-Ridazine*].
25 mg (Rx) [*Apo-Thioridazine; Novo-Ridazine*].
50 mg (Rx) [*Apo-Thioridazine; Novo-Ridazine*].
100 mg (Rx) [*Apo-Thioridazine; Novo-Ridazine*].
200 mg (Rx) [*Novo-Ridazine*].

Packaging and storage
Store below 40 °C (104 °F), preferably between 15 and 30 °C (59 and 86 °F), unless otherwise specified by manufacturer. Store in a tight, light-resistant container.

Auxiliary labeling
- May cause drowsiness.
- Avoid alcoholic beverages.

TRIFLUOPERAZINE

Summary of Differences

Category:
Includes antiemetic use.

Pharmacology/pharmacokinetics:
Chemical group—
Piperazine
Actions—
Antiemetic: Strong
Anticholinergic: Weak
Extrapyramidal: Strong
Hypotensive: Weak
Sedative: Weak

Oral Dosage Forms

Note: Bracketed uses in the *Dosage Forms* section refer to categories of use and/or indications that are not included in U.S. product labeling.

The dosing and strengths of the dosage forms available are expressed in terms of trifluoperazine base (not the hydrochloride salt).

TRIFLUOPERAZINE HYDROCHLORIDE SYRUP USP

Usual adult and adolescent dose
Psychotic disorders—
Oral, initially 2 to 5 mg (base) one to two times per day, the dosage being increased gradually as needed and tolerated.
Note: The optimal dosage range is 15 to 20 mg per day for most patients.

[Nausea and vomiting]—
Oral, 1 to 2 mg (base) two times per day or as needed.

Note: Geriatric, emaciated, or debilitated patients usually require a lower initial dose and more gradual dosage titration than do younger and healthier patients.

Usual adult prescribing limits
Psychotic disorders—
40 mg (base) per day.

Usual pediatric dose
Psychotic disorders—
Children up to 6 years of age: Dosage has not been established.
Children 6 to 12 years of age: Oral, initially 1 mg (base) one or two times per day, the dosage being adjusted gradually as needed and tolerated.
Children 12 years of age and older: See *Usual adult and adolescent dose*.

Note: Most children 6 to 12 years of age will not need doses greater than 15 mg per day.

Strength(s) usually available
U.S.—
10 mg (base) per mL (Rx) [*Stelazine Concentrate* (banana-vanilla flavored; sulfite; sodium bisulfite; sucrose); GENERIC].
Canada—
10 mg (base) per mL (Rx) [*PMS Trifluoperazine*].

Packaging and storage
Store below 40 °C (104 °F), preferably between 15 and 30 °C (59 and 86 °F), in a tight, light-resistant container, unless otherwise specified by manufacturer. Protect from freezing.

Preparation of dosage form
Dilute each dose just before administration in 60 mL (2 fluid ounces) or more of milk, tomato or fruit juice, simple syrup, orange syrup, carbonated beverages, coffee, tea, water, pudding, or soup.

Auxiliary labeling
- May cause drowsiness.
- Avoid alcoholic beverages.
- Avoid contact with skin or clothing.
- Must be diluted before use.

Caution
Patients sensitive to sulfites may be sensitive to some trifluoperazine hydrochloride syrup products because of the sulfite preservatives present.

Note
Avoid skin contact with liquid forms of this medication; contact dermatitis has resulted.

Explain dosage measurement and dilution to patient, if self-administered, or to caregiver; however, the syrup is intended primarily for institutional use.

TRIFLUOPERAZINE HYDROCHLORIDE TABLETS USP

Usual adult and adolescent dose
See *Trifluoperazine Hydrochloride Syrup USP*.

Usual adult prescribing limits
See *Trifluoperazine Hydrochloride Syrup USP*.

Usual pediatric dose
See *Trifluoperazine Hydrochloride Syrup USP*.

Strength(s) usually available
U.S.—
1 mg (base) (Rx) [*Stelazine* (lactose); GENERIC].
2 mg (base) (Rx) [*Stelazine* (lactose); GENERIC].
5 mg (base) (Rx) [*Stelazine* (lactose); GENERIC].
10 mg (base) (Rx) [*Stelazine* (lactose); GENERIC].
Canada—
1 mg (base) (Rx) [*Apo-Trifluoperazine; Stelazine;* GENERIC].
2 mg (base) (Rx) [*Apo-Trifluoperazine; Novo-Trifluzine; Stelazine;* GENERIC].
5 mg (base) (Rx) [*Apo-Trifluoperazine; Novo-Trifluzine; Stelazine;* GENERIC].
10 mg (base) (Rx) [*Apo-Trifluoperazine; Novo-Trifluzine; Stelazine*].
20 mg (base) (Rx) [*Apo-Trifluoperazine;* GENERIC].

Packaging and storage
Store below 40 °C (104 °F), preferably between 15 and 30 °C (59 and 86 °F), unless otherwise specified by manufacturer. Store in a well-closed, light-resistant container.

Auxiliary labeling
- May cause drowsiness.
- Avoid alcoholic beverages.

Parenteral Dosage Forms

Note: The dosing and strengths of the dosage forms available are expressed in terms of trifluoperazine base (not the hydrochloride salt).

TRIFLUOPERAZINE HYDROCHLORIDE INJECTION USP

Usual adult and adolescent dose
Psychotic disorders—
Intramuscular, 1 to 2 mg (base) every four to six hours as needed.

Note: Geriatric, emaciated, or debilitated patients usually require a lower initial dose and more gradual dosage titration than do younger and healthier patients.

Usual adult prescribing limits
10 mg (base) per day, although most patients will not require more than 6 mg in twenty-four hours.

Usual pediatric dose
Psychotic disorders—
Children up to 6 years of age: Dosage has not been established.
Children 6 to 12 years of age: Intramuscular, 1 mg (base) one or two times per day.
Children 12 years of age and older: See *Usual adult and adolescent dose*.

Strength(s) usually available
U.S.—
2 mg (base) per mL (Rx) [*Stelazine* (benzyl alcohol 0.75%; sodium tartrate 4.75 mg/mL; sodium biphosphate 11.6 mg/mL; sodium saccharin 0.3 mg/mL)].
Canada—
Not commercially available.

Packaging and storage
Store below 40 °C (104 °F), preferably between 15 and 30 °C (59 and 86 °F), unless otherwise specified by manufacturer. Protect from light. Protect from freezing.

Stability
A slight yellowing will not alter potency; however, do not use if markedly discolored or if a precipitate is present.

Note
Avoid skin contact with liquid forms of this medication; contact dermatitis has resulted.

TRIFLUPROMAZINE

Summary of Differences

Category:
Includes antiemetic use.
Pharmacology/pharmacokinetics:
Chemical group—
Aliphatic
Actions—
Antiemetic: Strong
Anticholinergic: Strong
Extrapyramidal: Moderate
Hypotensive: Moderate
Sedative: Moderate to strong

Parenteral Dosage Forms

TRIFLUPROMAZINE HYDROCHLORIDE INJECTION USP

Usual adult and adolescent dose
Psychotic disorders—
Intramuscular, initially 60 mg; additional doses may be administered as needed.
Nausea and vomiting—
Intramuscular, 5 to 15 mg every four hours as needed.
Intravenous, 1 mg; additional doses may be administered as needed.

Note: Geriatric, emaciated, or debilitated patients usually require a lower initial dose and more gradual dosage titration than do younger and healthier patients.

Usual adult prescribing limits
Psychotic disorders—
Intramuscular, 150 mg per day.
Nausea and vomiting—
Intramuscular, 60 mg per day.
Intravenous, 3 mg per day.

Usual pediatric dose
Psychotic disorders or
Nausea and vomiting—
Children up to 2½ years of age: Dosage has not been established.
Children 2½ years of age and older: Intramuscular, 200 to 250 mcg (0.2 to 0.25 mg) per kg of body weight, not to exceed 10 mg per day.

Note: Intravenous administration is not recommended in children because of hypotension and rapid onset of severe extrapyramidal reactions.

Strength(s) usually available
U.S.—
10 mg per mL (Rx) [*Vesprin* (pH 3.5 to 5.2; benzyl alcohol 1.5% w/v; sodium chloride; sodium hydroxide and/or hydrochloric acid)].
20 mg per mL (Rx) [*Vesprin* (pH 3.5 to 5.2; benzyl alcohol 1.5% w/v; sodium chloride; sodium hydroxide and/or hydrochloric acid)].
Canada—
Not commercially available.

Packaging and storage
Store between 15 and 30 °C (59 and 86 °F), unless otherwise specified by manufacturer. Protect from light. Protect from freezing.

Stability
Normally, solution may appear clear to faintly yellowish-green. If it appears darker or otherwise discolored, or if a precipitate is present, do not use.

Caution
Medications containing benzyl alcohol are not recommended for use in neonates (first 30 days of postnatal life). A fatal toxic syndrome consisting of metabolic acidosis, CNS depression, respiratory problems, renal failure, hypotension, and possibly seizures and intracranial hemorrhages has been associated with the use of diluents containing benzyl alcohol for preparation of medications for use in neonates.

Note
Avoid skin contact with liquid forms of this medication; contact dermatitis has resulted.

Revised: 12/18/2003

PHENTERMINE—See *Appetite Suppressants (Systemic)*

PHENYLBENZIMIDAZOLE—See *Sunscreen Agents (Topical)*

PHENYLBUTAZONE—See *Anti-inflammatory Drugs, Nonsteroidal (Systemic)*

PHENYLEPHRINE—See *Phenylephrine (Nasal), Sympathomimetic Agents—Cardiovascular Use (Parenteral-Systemic)*

PHENYLEPHRINE Nasal

VA CLASSIFICATION (Primary): NT100

Commonly used brand name(s): *Alconefrin Nasal Drops 12; Alconefrin Nasal Drops 25; Alconefrin Nasal Drops 50; Alconefrin Nasal Spray 25; Doktors; Duration; Neo-Synephrine Nasal Drops; Neo-Synephrine Nasal Jelly; Neo-Synephrine Nasal Spray; Neo-Synephrine Pediatric Nasal Drops; Nostril Spray Pump; Nostril Spray Pump Mild; Rhinall; Rhinall-10 Children's Flavored Nose Drops; Vicks Sinex.*

NOTE: The *Phenylephrine (Nasal)* monograph is maintained on the *USP DI* electronic data base. A copy of the most recent revision of the complete monograph can be accessed on the *USP DI* Updates Online website. See the front cover of book for details on accessing the site.

The information that follows is selectively abstracted from the complete monograph and is provided to facilitate drug use review and patient counseling.

Note: For a listing of dosage forms and brand names by country availability, see *Dosage Forms* section(s).

Category

Decongestant (topical).

Indications

Note: Bracketed information in the *Indications* section refers to uses that are not included in U.S. product labeling.

Accepted

Congestion, nasal (treatment)—Nasal phenylephrine is indicated for the symptomatic relief of nasal congestion due to the common cold or hay fever, sinusitis, or other upper respiratory allergies.

[Congestion, sinus (treatment)]—Nasal phenylephrine is used for relief of sinus congestion.

Congestion, eustachian tube (treatment)—Nasal phenylephrine may be useful in the adjunctive therapy of middle ear infections by decreasing congestion around the eustachian ostia.

Patient Consultation

As an aid to patient consultation, refer to *Advice for the Patient, Phenylephrine (Nasal).*

In providing consultation, consider emphasizing the following selected information (» = major clinical significance):

Before using this medication

» Conditions affecting use, especially:
Sensitivity to phenylephrine or other nasal decongestants
Use in children—Children may be especially prone to systemic absorption of nasal phenylephrine and resulting side/adverse effects

Proper use of this medication

Proper administration technique

Preventing contamination:
Replacing cap right after use

For nasal drops
After using—Rinsing dropper with hot water and drying with clean tissue

For nasal spray
After using—Rinsing tip of spray bottle with hot water, taking care not to suck water into bottle, and drying with clean tissue

For nasal jelly
After using—Wiping tip of tube with clean, damp tissue

Preventing spread of infection: Not using container for more than one person

» Importance of not using more medication than the amount recommended

» Proper dosing
Missed dose: If on scheduled dosing regimen—Using right away if remembered within an hour or so; not using if remembered later; not doubling doses

» Proper storage

Side/adverse effects

Signs of potential side effects, especially rebound congestion and sympathomimetic systemic effects

Nasal Dosage Forms

PHENYLEPHRINE HYDROCHLORIDE NASAL JELLY USP

Usual adult and adolescent dose

Decongestant, topical—
Intranasal, a small quantity of a 0.5% jelly placed into each nostril and sniffed well back into the nasal passages every three or four hours as needed.

Usual pediatric dose

Pediatric strength not available.

Strength(s) usually available

U.S.—
0.5% (OTC) [*Neo-Synephrine Nasal Jelly*].

Canada—
Not commercially available.

Auxiliary labeling

- For the nose.

PHENYLEPHRINE HYDROCHLORIDE NASAL SOLUTION USP

Usual adult and adolescent dose

Decongestant, topical—
Intranasal, 2 or 3 drops or sprays of a 0.25 to 0.5% solution into each nostril every four hours as needed

Note: The nasal spray form of this medication is more effective and less likely to cause systemic absorption than is the drop form.

In cases of extreme nasal congestion, the 1% solution may be used initially.

Usual pediatric dose

Decongestant, topical—
Infants and children up to 2 years of age: Dosage must be individualized by physician.
Children 2 to 6 years of age: Intranasal, 2 or 3 drops of a 0.125 or 0.16% solution into each nostril every four hours as needed.
Children 6 to 12 years of age: Intranasal, 2 or 3 drops or sprays of a 0.25% solution into each nostril every four hours as needed.
Children 12 years of age and over: See *Usual adult and adolescent dose.*

Strength(s) usually available

U.S.—
0.125% (drops) (OTC) [*Neo-Synephrine Pediatric Nasal Drops*].
0.16% (drops) (OTC) [*Alconefrin Nasal Drops 12*].
0.2% (drops) (OTC) [*Rhinall-10 Children's Flavored Nose Drops*].
0.25% (drops) (OTC) [*Alconefrin Nasal Drops 25; Doktors; Neo-Synephrine Nasal Drops; Rhinall;* GENERIC].
0.25% (spray) (OTC) [*Alconefrin Nasal Spray 25; Doktors; Neo-Synephrine Nasal Spray; Nostril Spray Pump Mild; Rhinall*].
0.5% (drops) (OTC) [*Alconefrin Nasal Drops 50; Neo-Synephrine Nasal Drops*].
0.5% (spray) (OTC) [*Duration; Neo-Synephrine Nasal Spray; Nostril Spray Pump; Vicks Sinex;* GENERIC].
1% (drops) (OTC) [*Neo-Synephrine Nasal Drops*].
1% (spray) (OTC) [*Neo-Synephrine Nasal Spray;* GENERIC].

Canada—
0.25% (drops) (OTC) [*Neo-Synephrine Nasal Drops*].
0.25% (spray) (OTC) [*Neo-Synephrine Nasal Spray*].
0.5% (drops) (OTC) [*Neo-Synephrine Nasal Drops*].
0.5% (spray) (OTC) [*Neo-Synephrine Nasal Spray*].
1% (drops) (OTC) [*Neo-Synephrine Nasal Drops*].

Auxiliary labeling

- For the nose.

Revised: 05/16/1994

PHENYLEPHRINE Ophthalmic

VA CLASSIFICATION (Primary/Secondary): OP600/OP802; DX900

Commonly used brand name(s): *Ak-Dilate; Ak-Nefrin; Dilatair; Dionephrine; I-Phrine; Isopto Frin; Minims Phenylephrine; Mydfrin; Neo-Synephrine; Neofrin; Ocu-Phrin Sterile Eye Drops; Ocu-Phrin Sterile Ophthalmic Solution; Ocugestrin; Phenoptic; Prefrin Liquifilm; Relief Eye Drops for Red Eyes; Spersaphrine.*

Note: For a listing of dosage forms and brand names by country availability, see *Dosage Forms* section(s).

Category

Mydriatic; decongestant (ophthalmic); diagnostic aid (mydriatic).

Indications

Accepted

Note: The 2.5 and 10% phenylephrine ophthalmic solutions are indicated when rapid dilation of the pupil and reduction of congestion in the capillary bed are desired.

Uveitis with posterior synechiae (treatment) or
Synechiae, posterior (prophylaxis)—The 2.5 and 10% phenylephrine ophthalmic solutions are indicated in patients with uveitis when synechiae are present or may develop. The formation of synechiae may be prevented by concurrent use of either of these concentrations with atropine to produce wide dilation of the pupil; however, the vasoconstrictor effect of phenylephrine may be antagonistic to the increase of local blood flow in uveal inflammation.

Mydriasis, preoperative—The 2.5 and 10% phenylephrine ophthalmic solutions are indicated to produce dilation of the pupil prior to intraocular surgery.

Mydriasis, in diagnostic procedures—Refraction: Prior to determination of refractive errors, the 2.5% phenylephrine ophthalmic solution may be used effectively with homatropine, atropine, cyclopentolate, or tropicamide.

Ophthalmoscopy: The 2.5% phenylephrine ophthalmic solution is indicated to produce mydriasis for ophthalmoscopic examination.

Retinoscopy (shadow test): The 2.5% phenylephrine ophthalmic solution may be used alone when dilation of the pupil without cycloplegic action is desired for retinoscopy (shadow test).

Blanching test: The 2.5% phenylephrine ophthalmic solution is indicated for the blanching test. If blanching occurs, the congestion is superficial and probably does not indicate iritis.

Ocular redness (treatment)—The 0.12% phenylephrine ophthalmic solution is indicated to provide temporary relief of redness associated with minor eye irritations, such as those caused by hay fever, colds, dust, wind, swimming, sun, smog, smoke, or wearing contact lenses.

Pharmacology/Pharmacokinetics

Physicochemical characteristics

Molecular weight—203.67.

Mechanism of action/Effect

Phenylephrine is primarily a direct-acting sympathomimetic amine, which stimulates alpha-adrenergic receptors.

Mydriatic—
Phenylephrine acts on alpha-adrenergic receptors in the dilator muscle of the pupil, producing contraction.

Decongestant (ophthalmic)—
Phenylephrine acts on alpha-adrenergic receptors in the arterioles of the conjunctiva, producing constriction.

Time to peak effect

Mydriasis—
2.5% solution: 15 to 60 minutes.
10% solution: 10 to 90 minutes.

Duration of action

Mydriasis recovery time—
2.5% solution: 1 to 3 hours.
10% solution: 3 to 7 hours.

Precautions to Consider

Carcinogenicity

Long-term studies have not been done.

Pregnancy/Reproduction

Pregnancy—Studies have not been done in humans; however, ophthalmic phenylephrine may be systemically absorbed.

Studies have not been done in animals.

FDA Pregnancy Category C.

Breast-feeding

It is not known whether phenylephrine is distributed into breast milk and problems in humans have not been documented; however, ophthalmic phenylephrine may be systemically absorbed.

Pediatrics

The recommended dose should not be exceeded in pediatric patients, especially for the 2.5 and 10% solutions, since high doses of phenylephrine can increase blood pressure and cause irregular heartbeat. In addition, repeated use of 2.5 or 10% phenylephrine may result in rebound miosis and a reduced mydriatic effect. Moreover, the 10% phenylephrine solution is not recommended for use in infants, since a pronounced increase in blood pressure may occur. Also, the 2.5 and 10% concentrations are not recommended for use in low birth weight infants.

Geriatrics

Cardiovascular reactions, such as marked increase in blood pressure, syncope, myocardial infarction, tachycardia, arrhythmia, and fatal subarachnoid hemorrhage, have occurred primarily in elderly patients. In addition, repeated use of 2.5 or 10% phenylephrine, especially in older patients, may result in rebound miosis and a reduced mydriatic effect. Also, older patients may develop transient pigment floaters in the aqueous humor 40 to 45 minutes following administration of the 2.5 or 10% concentrations, the appearance of which may be similar to anterior uveitis or to a microscopic hyphema.

Drug interactions and/or related problems

The following drug interactions and/or related problems have been selected on the basis of their potential clinical significance (possible mechanism in parentheses where appropriate)—not necessarily inclusive (» = major clinical significance):

Note: Combinations containing any of the following medications, depending on the amount present, may also interact with this medication.

For 2.5 or 10% strengths only

Antidepressants, tricyclic or
Maprotiline or
Monoamine oxidase (MAO) inhibitors, including furazolidone, procarbazine, and selegiline
(if significant systemic absorption of ophthalmic phenylephrine occurs, concurrent use of these medications may potentiate the pressor effect of phenylephrine; in addition, if ophthalmic phenylephrine is administered during or within 21 days following the administration of MAO inhibitors, careful supervision with possible adjustment of dosage is recommended, since exaggerated adrenergic response may occur)

Guanadrel or
Guanethidine
(if significant systemic absorption of ophthalmic phenylephrine occurs, concurrent use of guanadrel or guanethidine may increase the mydriatic effect of phenylephrine; also, concurrent use may potentiate the pressor effect of phenylephrine, possibly resulting in hypertension and cardiac arrhythmias)

Medical considerations/Contraindications

The medical considerations/contraindications included have been selected on the basis of their potential clinical significance (reasons given in parentheses where appropriate)—not necessarily inclusive (» = major clinical significance).

Risk-benefit should be considered when the following medical problems exist:

For 2.5 or 10% strengths only

Arteriosclerotic changes, advanced
Cardiac disease
Diabetes mellitus
» Glaucoma, angle-closure, predisposition to
Hypertension
Idiopathic orthostatic hypotension
(a marked increase in blood pressure may occur)
Sensitivity to phenylephrine or sulfites

Side/Adverse Effects

The following side/adverse effects have been selected on the basis of their potential clinical significance (possible signs and symptoms in parentheses where appropriate)—not necessarily inclusive:

Those indicating need for medical attention

Incidence less frequent with 10% solution; incidence rare with 2.5% or weaker solution

Signs and symptoms of systemic absorption
Dizziness; fast, irregular, or pounding heartbeat; increase in blood pressure; increase in sweating; paleness; trembling

Those indicating need for medical attention only if they continue or are bothersome

Incidence more frequent with 2.5 or 10% solution
Burning or stinging of eyes; headache; browache; sensitivity of eyes to light; watering of eyes

Incidence less frequent
Eye irritation not present before therapy

Overdose

For specific information on the agents used in the management of phenylephrine ophthalmic overdose, see:

- *Phentolamine (Systemic)* monograph.

For more information on the management of overdose or unintentional ingestion, **contact a Poison Control Center** (see *Poison Control Center Listing*).

Treatment of overdose

Specific treatment—The hypertensive effects of phenylephrine may be treated with an alpha-adrenergic blocker, such as phentolamine 5 to 10 mg intravenously, repeated as necessary.

Patient Consultation

As an aid to patient consultation, refer to *Advice for the Patient, Phenylephrine (Ophthalmic)*.

In providing consultation, consider emphasizing the following selected information (» = major clinical significance):

Before using this medication

» Conditions affecting use, especially:
- Sensitivity to phenylephrine or to sulfites
- Use in children—May be especially sensitive to the effects of phenylephrine; also, the 10% strength is not recommended for use in infants, and the 2.5 and 10% strengths are not recommended for use in low birth weight infants
- Use in the elderly—Repeated use of 2.5 or 10% phenylephrine may increase the chance of side/adverse effects; also, cardiovascular reactions have occurred more often in elderly patients
- Other medical problems, especially, predisposition to angle-closure glaucoma

Proper use of this medication

Not using if solution turns brown or contains a precipitate
Proper administration technique
Preventing contamination: Not touching applicator tip to any surface; keeping container tightly closed
» Proper dosing
» Proper storage
For the 2.5 and 10% solutions
» Importance of not using more medication than the amount prescribed
Missed dose: Applying as soon as possible; not applying if almost time for next dose; applying next dose at regularly scheduled time

Precautions while using this medication

» Stopping medication and checking with physician if eye pain or change in vision occurs or if redness or irritation continues, gets worse, or lasts for more than 72 hours
For the 2.5 and 10% solutions:
» Medication may cause increased sensitivity of eyes to light; wearing sunglasses that block ultraviolet light to protect eyes from sunlight and other bright lights; checking with physician if this effect continues longer than 12 hours after discontinuation of medication

Side/adverse effects

Signs of potential side effects, especially systemic absorption

General Dosing Information

Although some manufacturers recommend a dose of 2 drops of an ophthalmic solution at appropriate intervals, the conjunctival sac will usually hold only 1 drop.

To avoid excessive systemic absorption, patient should apply digital pressure to the lacrimal sac during and for 2 or 3 minutes following instillation of medication.

Although some manufacturers recommend that patients not wear soft contact lenses during treatment with phenylephrine ophthalmic solution, USP medical experts do not believe this precaution is necessary unless the patient has corneal epithelial problems and the medication is to be used more often than once every 1 to 2 hours. No significant problems have been documented with ophthalmic solutions containing 0.03% or less of benzalkonium chloride as a preservative that are used in patients with no significant corneal surface problems.

For the 2.5 and 10% solutions

To prevent pain and subsequent lacrimation on administration, a suitable topical anesthetic may be applied a few minutes before use of phenylephrine solution.

The recommended dose should not be exceeded, especially in children and in individuals with high blood pressure or heart disease, since high doses of phenylephrine can increase blood pressure and cause irregular heartbeat.

Repeated use of phenylephrine, especially in older patients, may result in rebound miosis and a reduced mydriatic effect.

Ophthalmic Dosage Forms

PHENYLEPHRINE HYDROCHLORIDE OPHTHALMIC SOLUTION USP

Usual adult and adolescent dose

Mydriasis and vasoconstriction—
Topical, to the conjunctiva, 1 drop of a 2.5 or 10% solution, repeated in one hour if necessary.

Chronic mydriasis—
Topical, to the conjunctiva, 1 drop of a 2.5 or 10% solution two or three times a day.

Uveitis with posterior synechiae (treatment) or
Synechiae, posterior (prophylaxis)—
Topical, to the conjunctiva, 1 drop of a 2.5 or 10% solution, repeated in one hour if necessary, not to exceed three times a day. Treatment may be continued the following day, if necessary.

Note: Atropine sulfate and the application of hot compresses should also be used if indicated.

Mydriasis, preoperative—
Topical, to the conjunctiva, 1 drop of a 2.5 or 10% solution thirty to sixty minutes prior to surgery.

Mydriasis, in diagnostic procedures—
Refraction—
Topical, to the conjunctiva, 1 drop of a cycloplegic followed in five minutes by 1 drop of a 2.5% solution of phenylephrine. The need for additional drops of the cycloplegic, and the waiting period before adequate cycloplegia occurs, depend on the cycloplegic used.

Note: For a "one application method," the 2.5% solution may be used in combination with a cycloplegic for synergistic action.

Ophthalmoscopy—
Topical, to the conjunctiva, 1 drop of a 2.5% solution fifteen to thirty minutes prior to examination.

Retinoscopy (shadow test)—
Topical, to the conjunctiva, as a 2.5% solution.

Blanching test—
Topical, to the infected eye, 1 drop of a 2.5% solution.

Note: Eye should be examined for perilimbal blanching 5 minutes after application of phenylephrine.

Ocular redness (treatment)—
Topical, to the conjunctiva, 1 drop of a 0.12% solution every three or four hours as needed.

Usual pediatric dose

Mydriasis and vasoconstriction—
Topical, to the conjunctiva, 1 drop of a 2.5% solution, repeated in one hour if necessary.

Chronic mydriasis—
Topical, to the conjunctiva, 1 drop of a 2.5% solution two or three times a day.

Uveitis with posterior synechiae (treatment)—
Topical, to the conjunctiva, 1 drop of a 2.5% solution, repeated in one hour if necessary. Treatment may be continued the following day, if necessary.

Note: Atropine sulfate and application of hot compresses should also be used if indicated.

Mydriasis, preoperative—
Topical, to the conjunctiva, 1 drop of a 2.5% solution thirty to sixty minutes prior to surgery.

Mydriasis, in diagnostic procedures—
Refraction—
Topical, to the conjunctiva, 1 drop of a 1% solution of atropine, followed in ten to fifteen minutes by 1 drop of a 2.5% solution of phenylephrine and in five to ten minutes by a second drop of a 1% solution of atropine. In one to two hours, the eyes are ready for refraction.

Note: For a "one application method," the 2.5% solution of phenylephrine may be used in combination with a cycloplegic for synergistic action.

Ophthalmoscopy—
See *Usual adult and adolescent dose*.

Retinoscopy (shadow test)—
See *Usual adult and adolescent dose*.

Blanching test—
See *Usual adult and adolescent dose*.

Ocular redness (treatment)—
See *Usual adult and adolescent dose*.

Note: The 10% phenylephrine solution is not recommended for use in infants, since a pronounced increase in blood pressure may occur following instillation. Also, the 2.5 and 10% concentrations are not recommended for use in low birth weight infants.

Strength(s) usually available

U.S.—

0.12% (OTC) [*Ak-Nefrin; Isopto Frin; Ocu-Phrin Sterile Eye Drops; Prefrin Liquifilm* (polyvinyl alcohol 1.4%); *Relief Eye Drops for Red Eyes* (polyvinyl alcohol 1.4%); GENERIC].

2.5% (Rx) [*Ak-Dilate* (sodium bisulfite; benzalkonium chloride 0.01%); *Dilatair; I-Phrine; Mydfrin* (sodium bisulfite; benzalkonium chloride 0.01%; boric acid; edetate disodium; sodium hydroxide or hydrochloric acid); *Neofrin; Neo-Synephrine; Ocugestrin; Ocu-Phrin Sterile Ophthalmic Solution; Phenoptic;* GENERIC].

10% (Rx) [*Ak-Dilate* (sodium bisulfite; benzalkonium chloride 0.01%); *I-Phrine; Neofrin; Neo-Synephrine; Ocu-Phrin Sterile Ophthalmic Solution;* GENERIC].

Canada—

0.12% (OTC) [*Prefrin Liquifilm* (sodium bisulfite; polyvinyl alcohol 1.4%)].

2.5% (OTC) [*Ak-Dilate* (sodium bisulfite); *Dionephrine; Minims Phenylephrine; Mydfrin; Spersaphrine*].

10% (OTC) [*Minims Phenylephrine*].

Packaging and storage

Store below 40 °C (104 °F), preferably between 15 and 30 °C (59 and 86 °F), unless otherwise specified by manufacturer. Store in a tight, light-resistant container of not more than 15-mL size. Protect from freezing.

Stability

Prolonged exposure to air or strong light may cause oxidation and discoloration. Do not use if solution is brown or contains a precipitate.

Incompatibilities

Phenylephrine is chemically incompatible with the local anesthetic butacaine.

Auxiliary labeling

- For the eye.
- Keep container tightly closed.

Revised: 10/02/2000

PHENYTOIN—See *Anticonvulsants, Hydantoin (Systemic)*

PHYTONADIONE—See *Vitamin K (Systemic)*

PILOCARPINE Ophthalmic

VA CLASSIFICATION (Primary): OP118

Commonly used brand name(s): *Adsorbocarpine; Akarpine; Isopto Carpine; Minims Pilocarpine; Miocarpine; Ocu-Carpine; Ocusert Pilo-20; Ocusert Pilo-40; P.V. Carpine Liquifilm; Pilagan; Pilocar; Pilopine HS; Piloptic-1; Piloptic-2; Piloptic-3; Piloptic-4; Piloptic-6; Piloptic-½; Pilostat; Spersacarpine.*

Note: For a listing of dosage forms and brand names by country availability, see *Dosage Forms* section(s).

Category

Antiglaucoma agent (ophthalmic); miotic.

Indications

Accepted

Glaucoma, open-angle (treatment)—Pilocarpine is indicated primarily for the treatment of open-angle (chronic simple) glaucoma. It may be used in conjunction with a carbonic anhydrase inhibitor, epinephrine, timolol, fluorescein, or anesthetic, antibiotic, or anti-inflammatory steroid ophthalmic solutions.

Glaucoma, angle-closure (treatment)—Pilocarpine (hydrochloride or nitrate) ophthalmic solution is indicated for use alone or in combination with carbonic anhydrase inhibitors or hyperosmotic agents to lower intraocular pressure in the emergency treatment of acute angle-closure glaucoma prior to surgery or laser iridotomy. In addition, pilocarpine may be indicated for the treatment of chronic angle-closure glaucoma.

Glaucoma, angle-closure, *during* or *after* iridectomy (treatment)—Pilocarpine (hydrochloride or nitrate) ophthalmic solution may be indicated for the treatment of angle-closure glaucoma *during* or *after* iridectomy.

Glaucoma, secondary (treatment)—Pilocarpine may be indicated for the treatment of nonuveitic secondary glaucoma.

Miosis induction, postoperative or
Miosis induction, following ophthalmoscopy—Pilocarpine (hydrochloride or nitrate) ophthalmic solution is indicated to produce miosis in order to counteract the effects of cycloplegics and mydriatics following surgery or ophthalmoscopic examination.

Pharmacology/Pharmacokinetics

Physicochemical characteristics

Molecular weight—
Pilocarpine: 208.26.
Pilocarpine hydrochloride: 244.72.
Pilocarpine nitrate: 271.27.

Mechanism of action/Effect

Pilocarpine is a parasympathomimetic that directly stimulates cholinergic receptors. It produces contraction of the iris sphincter muscle, resulting in pupillary constriction (miosis); constriction of the ciliary muscle, resulting in increased accommodation; and reduction in intraocular pressure associated with an increase in the outflow and a decrease in the inflow of aqueous humor.

In chronic open-angle glaucoma, the exact mechanism by which miotics lower intraocular pressure is not precisely known; however, contraction of the ciliary muscle apparently opens the intertrabecular spaces and facilitates aqueous humor outflow. There is also a decrease in the rate of inflow of aqueous humor.

In angle-closure glaucoma, constriction of the pupil apparently pulls the iris away from the trabeculum, thereby relieving blockage of the trabecular meshwork.

Onset of action

Miosis—Solution (1%): Within 10 to 30 minutes.

Time to peak effect

Reduction in intraocular pressure—
Ocular system: 1.5 to 2 hours.
Solution: Within 75 minutes, depending on strength used.

Duration of action

Miosis—
Solution: About 4 to 8 hours.
Reduction in intraocular pressure—
Ocular system: 7 days.
Solution: 4 to 14 hours, depending on strength used.

Precautions to Consider

Carcinogenicity

No long-term studies have been done.

Pregnancy/Reproduction

Pregnancy—Studies have not been done in humans; however, ophthalmic pilocarpine may be systemically absorbed.

Studies have not been done in animals.

FDA Pregnancy Category C.

Breast-feeding

It is not known whether pilocarpine is distributed into breast milk and problems in humans have not been documented. However, ophthalmic pilocarpine may be systemically absorbed.

Pediatrics

Appropriate studies on the relationship of age to the effects of pilocarpine have not been performed in the pediatric population. However, no pediatrics-specific problems have been documented to date.

Geriatrics

Appropriate studies on the relationship of age to the effects of pilocarpine have not been performed in the geriatric population. However, no geriatrics-specific problems have been documented to date.

Drug interactions and/or related problems

The following drug interactions and/or related problems have been selected on the basis of their potential clinical significance (possible mechanism in parentheses where appropriate)—not necessarily inclusive (» = major clinical significance):

Belladonna alkaloids, ophthalmic or
Cyclopentolate
(concurrent use may interfere with the antiglaucoma action of pilocarpine; also, concurrent use with pilocarpine counteracts the

mydriatic effects of these medications; this anti-mydriatic effect may be used to therapeutic advantage)

Medical considerations/Contraindications

The medical considerations/contraindications included have been selected on the basis of their potential clinical significance (reasons given in parentheses where appropriate)—not necessarily inclusive (» = major clinical significance).

Risk-benefit should be considered when the following medical problems exist:

Asthma, bronchial

Infectious conjunctivitis or keratitis, acute—for ocular system dosage form only

» Iritis, acute, or other conditions in which pupillary constriction is undesirable

Retinal detachment, history of or predisposition to

Sensitivity to pilocarpine

Patient monitoring

The following may be especially important in patient monitoring (other tests may be warranted in some patients, depending on condition; » = major clinical significance):

Intraocular pressure determinations (recommended at periodic intervals during therapy)

Side/Adverse Effects

The following side/adverse effects have been selected on the basis of their potential clinical significance (possible signs and symptoms in parentheses where appropriate)—not necessarily inclusive:

Those indicating need for medical attention

Symptoms of systemic absorption

Increased sweating; muscle tremors; nausea, vomiting, or diarrhea; troubled breathing or wheezing; watering of mouth

Incidence less frequent or rare

Eye pain

Those indicating need for medical attention only if they continue or are bothersome

Incidence more frequent

Blurred vision or change in near or far vision; decrease in night vision

Incidence less frequent

Eye irritation; headache or browache

Overdose

For specific information on the agents used in the management of ophthalmic pilocarpine overdose, see:

- *Atropine* in *Anticholinergics/Antispasmodics (Systemic)* monograph.

For more information on the management of overdose or unintentional ingestion, **contact a Poison Control Center** (see *Poison Control Center Listing*).

Treatment of overdose

If accidental overdosage occurs in the eye, flushing the eye with water or normal saline.

If medication is accidentally ingested, inducing emesis or performing gastric lavage. Patients should be observed for signs of pilocarpine toxicity (i.e., unusual watering of mouth, unusual sweating, nausea, vomiting, and diarrhea); if these occur, therapy with anticholinergics, such as atropine, may be necessary.

Patient Consultation

As an aid to patient consultation, refer to *Advice for the Patient, Pilocarpine (Ophthalmic).*

In providing consultation, consider emphasizing the following selected information (» = major clinical significance):

Before using this medication

» Conditions affecting use, especially:
  Sensitivity to pilocarpine
  Other medical problems, especially acute iritis or other conditions in which pupillary constriction is undesirable

Proper use of this medication

Proper administration technique

Washing hands immediately after application to remove any medication that may be on them

» Importance of not using more medication than the amount prescribed

» Proper dosing

Missed dose:

For solution dosage form—Using as soon as possible; not using if almost time for next dose; using next dose at regularly scheduled time

For gel dosage form—Using as soon as possible; not using if not remembered until next day; using next dose at regularly scheduled time

For eye system dosage form—Replacing as soon as possible; inserting next eye system at regularly scheduled time

» Proper storage

For gel or solution dosage forms

Preventing contamination: Not touching applicator tip to any surface; keeping container tightly closed

For ocular system dosage form

Reading patient instructions carefully before using

Not using if damaged

Removing and replacing with new unit if too much medicine is being released

Precautions while using this medication

Regular visits to physician to check eye pressure during therapy

» Caution if blurred vision or change in near or far vision occurs, especially at night

Side/adverse effects

Signs of potential side effects, especially symptoms of systemic absorption or eye pain

General Dosing Information

Tolerance to pilocarpine may develop with prolonged use. Effectiveness may be restored by changing to another miotic for a short time and then resuming the original medication.

For the ocular system dosage form

The system should be placed in the eye at bedtime so that the pilocarpine-induced myopia may reach a stable level by morning.

Damaged or deformed systems should not be placed or retained in the eye. If a system is believed to be associated with an unexpected increase in action of the medication, it should be removed and replaced with a new system.

For the solution dosage forms

Although some manufacturers recommend a dose of 2 drops of an ophthalmic solution at appropriate intervals, the conjunctival sac will usually hold only 1 drop.

To avoid excessive systemic absorption, patient should press finger to the lacrimal sac during and for 1 or 2 minutes following instillation of the solution.

Although some manufacturers recommend that patients not wear soft contact lenses during treatment with pilocarpine ophthalmic solution, USP medical experts do not believe this precaution is necessary unless the patient has corneal epithelial problems and the medication is to be used more often than once every 1 to 2 hours. No significant problems have been documented with opththalmic solutions containing 0.03% or less of benzalkonium chloride as a preservative that are used in patients with no significant corneal surface problems.

Ophthalmic Dosage Forms

PILOCARPINE OCULAR SYSTEM USP

Usual adult and adolescent dose

Antiglaucoma agent (ophthalmic)—

Topical, to the conjunctiva, 1 ocular system delivering 20 or 40 mcg (0.02 or 0.04 mg) per hour, once every seven days.

Usual pediatric dose

Antiglaucoma agent (ophthalmic)—

Infants: Safety and efficacy have not been established.

Children: See *Usual adult and adolescent dose.*

Usual geriatric dose

See *Usual adult and adolescent dose.*

Strength(s) usually available

U.S.—

20 mcg (0.02 mg) per hour for seven days (Rx) [*Ocusert Pilo-20*].

40 mcg (0.04 mg) per hour for seven days (Rx) [*Ocusert Pilo-40*].

Canada—

20 mcg (0.02 mg) per hour for seven days (Rx) [*Ocusert Pilo-20*].

40 mcg (0.04 mg) per hour for seven days (Rx) [*Ocusert Pilo-40*].

Packaging and storage

Store between 2 and 8 °C (36 and 46 °F).

Auxiliary labeling
- For the eye.
- Refrigerate.

Note
Include patient instructions when dispensing.

PILOCARPINE HYDROCHLORIDE OPHTHALMIC GEL

Usual adult and adolescent dose
Antiglaucoma agent (ophthalmic)—
Topical, to the conjunctiva, approximately 1.5 cm (½-inch strip) of a 4% gel once a day at bedtime.

Usual pediatric dose
Antiglaucoma agent (ophthalmic)—
Safety and efficacy have not been established.

Usual geriatric dose
See *Usual adult and adolescent dose.*

Strength(s) usually available
U.S.—
4% (Rx) [*Pilopine HS*].
Canada—
4% (Rx) [*Pilopine HS*].

Packaging and storage
Store between 2 and 8 °C (36 and 46 °F), in a tight container, unless otherwise specified by manufacturer. Protect from freezing.

Stability
The 5-gram size requires refrigeration; the 3.5-gram size can be stored at room temperature.

Auxiliary labeling
- For the eye.
- Keep container tightly closed.

PILOCARPINE HYDROCHLORIDE OPHTHALMIC SOLUTION USP

Usual adult and adolescent dose
Antiglaucoma agent (ophthalmic)—
Chronic glaucoma—
Topical, to the conjunctiva, 1 drop of a 0.5 to 4% solution up to four times a day.

Acute angle-closure glaucoma—
Topical, to the conjunctiva, 1 drop of a 1 or 2% solution every five to ten minutes for three to six doses, then 1 drop every one to three hours until intraocular pressure is reduced.

Note: To possibly avoid a bilateral attack of angle-closure glaucoma, 1 drop of a 1 or 2% solution may be instilled in the unaffected eye every six to eight hours. However, more intensive treatment may precipitate an attack in the unaffected eye and should be avoided.

Miotic—
To counteract mydriatic effects of sympathomimetics—
Topical, to the conjunctiva, 1 drop of a 1% solution.
Prior to surgery for congenital glaucoma (goniotomy)—
Topical, to the conjunctiva, 1 drop of a 2% solution every four to six hours (usually for one or two doses) before surgery.
Prior to iridectomy—
Topical, to the conjunctiva, 1 drop of a 2% solution for four doses immediately before surgery.

Usual pediatric dose
See *Usual adult and adolescent dose.*

Note: For infants, the administration of solutions with strengths greater than 1% is not recommended.

Usual geriatric dose
See *Usual adult and adolescent dose.*

Strength(s) usually available
U.S.—
0.25% (Rx) [*Isopto Carpine;* GENERIC].
0.5% (Rx) [*Isopto Carpine; Ocu-Carpine; Pilocar; Piloptic-½; Pilostat;* GENERIC].
1% (Rx) [*Adsorbocarpine; Akarpine; Isopto Carpine; Ocu-Carpine; Pilocar; Piloptic-1; Pilostat;* GENERIC].
2% (Rx) [*Adsorbocarpine; Akarpine; Isopto Carpine; Ocu-Carpine; Pilocar; Piloptic-2; Pilostat;* GENERIC].
3% (Rx) [*Isopto Carpine; Ocu-Carpine; Pilocar; Piloptic-3; Pilostat;* GENERIC].
4% (Rx) [*Adsorbocarpine; Akarpine; Isopto Carpine; Ocu-Carpine; Pilocar; Piloptic-4; Pilostat;* GENERIC].
5% (Rx) [*Isopto Carpine; Ocu-Carpine;* GENERIC].
6% (Rx) [*Isopto Carpine; Ocu-Carpine; Pilocar; Piloptic-6; Pilostat;* GENERIC].
8% (Rx) [*Isopto Carpine;* GENERIC].
10% (Rx) [*Isopto Carpine*].
Canada—
0.5% (Rx) [*Isopto Carpine*].
1% (Rx) [*Isopto Carpine; Miocarpine; Pilostat; Spersacarpine*].
2% (Rx) [*Isopto Carpine; Miocarpine; Pilostat; Spersacarpine*].
4% (Rx) [*Isopto Carpine; Miocarpine; Pilostat; Spersacarpine*].
6% (Rx) [*Isopto Carpine; Miocarpine*].

Packaging and storage
Store below 40 °C (104 °F), preferably between 15 and 30 °C (59 and 86 °F), unless otherwise specified by manufacturer. Store in a tight container. Protect from freezing.

Auxiliary labeling
- For the eye.
- Keep container tightly closed.

PILOCARPINE NITRATE OPHTHALMIC SOLUTION USP

Usual adult and adolescent dose
Antiglaucoma agent (ophthalmic)—
Chronic glaucoma—
Topical, to the conjunctiva, 1 drop of a 1 to 4% solution two to four times a day.
Acute angle-closure glaucoma—
Topical, to the conjunctiva, 1 drop of a 1 or 2% solution every five to ten minutes for three to six doses, then 1 drop every one to three hours until intraocular pressure is reduced.

Note: To possibly avoid a bilateral attack of angle-closure glaucoma, 1 drop of a 1 or 2% solution may be instilled in the unaffected eye every six to eight hours. However, more intensive treatment may precipitate an attack in the unaffected eye and should be avoided.

Miotic—
To counteract mydriatic effects of sympathomimetics—
Topical, to the conjunctiva, 1 drop of a 1% solution.
Prior to surgery for congenital glaucoma (goniotomy)—
Topical, to the conjunctiva, 1 drop of a 2% solution every four to six hours (usually for one or two doses) before surgery.
Prior to iridectomy—
Topical, to the conjunctiva, 1 drop of a 2% solution for four doses immediately before surgery.

Usual pediatric dose
See *Usual adult and adolescent dose.*

Note: For infants, the administration of solutions with strengths greater than 1% is not recommended.

Usual geriatric dose
See *Usual adult and adolescent dose.*

Strength(s) usually available
U.S.—
1% (Rx) [*Pilagan*].
2% (Rx) [*Pilagan*].
4% (Rx) [*Pilagan*].
Canada—
1% (Rx) [*P.V. Carpine Liquifilm*].
2% (Rx) [*Minims Pilocarpine; P.V. Carpine Liquifilm*].
4% (Rx) [*Minims Pilocarpine; P.V. Carpine Liquifilm*].

Packaging and storage
Store below 40 °C (104 °F), preferably between 15 and 30 °C (59 and 86 °F), unless otherwise specified by manufacturer. Store in a tight, light-resistant container. Protect from freezing.

Auxiliary labeling
- For the eye.
- Keep container tightly closed.
- Shake well.

Revised: 06/21/1995

PIMECROLIMUS Topical

VA CLASSIFICATION (Primary): DE900

Commonly used brand name(s): *Elidel.*

Note: For a listing of dosage forms and brand names by country availability, see *Dosage Forms* section(s).

Category

Immunomodulator (topical).

Indications

Accepted

Dermatitis, atopic, mild to moderate, second-line (treatment)—Pimecrolimus cream is indicated as *second-line therapy* for the short-term and non-continuous chronic treatment of mild to moderate atopic dermatitis in non-immunocompromised patients 2 years of age and older, who have failed to respond adequately to other topical prescription treatments, or when those treatments are not advisable.

[Dermatitis, atopic, mild to moderate (treatment)][1]—Pimecrolimus cream is indicated for short-term use in children less than 2 years of age with mild to moderate atopic dermatitis.

Unaccepted

Studied have not evaluated the safety and efficacy of pimecrolimus in the treatment of clinically infected atopic dermatitis.

Pimecrolimus cream is not indicated for children younger than 2 years of age.

Long-term safety of topical calcineurin inhibitors, including pimecrolimus, has not been established.

The safety of pimecrolimus cream under occlusion, which may promote systemic exposure, has not been evaluated.

---

[1]Not included in Canadian product labeling.

Pharmacology/Pharmacokinetics

Physicochemical characteristics

Molecular weight—810.47.

Solubility—Pimecrolimus is soluble in methanol and ethanol and insoluble in water.

Mechanism of action/Effect

The mechanism of action of pimecrolimus in atopic dermatitis is not known. It has been demonstrated that pimecrolimus binds with high affinity to macrophilin-12 (FKBP-12) and inhibits the calcium-dependent phosphatase, calcineurin. As a consequence, it inhibits T cell activation by blocking the transcription of early cytokines. In particular, pimecrolimus inhibits at nanomolar concentrations Interleukin-2 and interferon gamma (Th1-type) and Interleukin-4 and Interleukin-10 (Th2-type) cytokine synthesis in human T cells. Also, pimecrolimus prevents the release of inflammatory cytokines and mediators from mast cells *in vitro* after stimulation by antigen/IgE.

Protein binding

High (74 to 87%)—plasma proteins

Biotransformation

Following the administration of a single oral radiolabeled dose of pimecrolimus, numerous circulating O-demethylation metabolites were seen. Studies with human liver microsomes indicate that pimecrolimus is metabolized *in vitro* by the CYP3A sub-family of metabolizing enzymes. No evidence of skin mediated drug metabolism was identified *in vivo* using the minipig or *in vitro* using stripped human skin.

Peak blood concentration:

Blood—Range from undetectable (less than 0.5 ng per mL) to less than 2 ng per mL.

Elimination

Following single oral radiolabeled administration—78.4% was recovered in the feces as metabolites. Less than 1% of the radioactivity found in the feces was due to unchanged pimecrolimus.

Precautions to Consider

Carcinogenicity/Tumorigenicity

A two year dermal carcinogenicity study in rats showed a statistically significant increase in the incidence of follicular cell adenoma of the thyroid in low, mid and high doses of pimecrolimus in male rats. Follicular cell adenoma of the thyroid was found at the lowest dose of 2 mg per kg of body weight per day. In an oral carcinogenicity study in male rats, no increase in the incidence of follicular cell adenoma was found at doses up to 10 mg per kg of body weight per day. Data from a recently conducted oral nine-month monkey study showed a dose-related increase in virus-associated lymphoma following administration of pimecrolimus. However, oral studies may not reflect continuous exposure or the same metabolic profile as the dermal route.

In a dermal carcinogenicity study in mice using pimecrolimus in an ethanolic solution, there was no increase noted in the incidence of neoplasms in the skin or other organs up to the highest dose of 4 mg per kg of body weight per day. However, in a 13 week repeat dose dermal toxicity study in mice using pimecrolimus in an ethanolic solution at a dose of 25 mg per kg of body weight per day lymphoproliferative changes, including lymphoma, were found. Lymphoproliferative changes were not found in this study at doses of 10 mg per kg of body weight per day. However, the latency time to lymphoma formation was shortened to 8 weeks after dermal administration of pimecrolimus dissolved in ethanol at a dose of 100 mg per kg of body weight per day.

In an oral (gavage) carcinogenicity study in mice, a significant increase in the incidence of lymphoma was noted in high dose male and female animals compared to vehicle control animals. Lymphomas were noted in the oral mouse carcinogenicity study at a dose of 45 mg per kg of body weight per day. No drug-related tumors were noted in this study at a dose of 15 mg per kg of body weight per day. In an oral (gavage) carcinogenicity study in rats, a significant increase in the incidence of benign thymoma was found in male and female rats treated with pimecrolimus at doses of 10 mg per kg of body weight per day compared to vehicle control animals. An increase in the incidence of benign thymoma was also noted in another oral (gavage) rat carcinogenicity study in 5 mg per kg of body weight per day pimecrolimus treated male rats compared to vehicle control treated male rats. No drug-related tumors were noted in the rat oral carcinogenicity study at a dose of 1 mg per kg of body weight per day in male animals.

In a 52-week dermal photo-carcinogenicity study, the median time to onset of skin tumor formation was decreased in hairless mice following chronic topical dosing with concurrent exposure to UV radiation with the vehicle cream alone. No additional effect on tumor development beyond the vehicle effect was noted with the addition of the active ingredient, pimecrolimus, to the vehicle cream.

A 39-week monkey toxicology test with doses of 15, 45, and 120 mg per kg of body weight per day showed a dose dependent increase in expression of immunosuppressive-related lymphoproliferative disorder (IRLD) associated with lymphocryptovirus (a monkey strain of virus related to human Epstein Barr virus). IRLD in monkeys mirrors what has been noted in human transplant patients after chronic systemic immunosuppressive therapy, post transplantation lymphoproliferative disease (PTLD), after treatment with chronic systemic immunosuppressive therapy. Both IRLD and PTLD can progress to lymphoma which is dependent on dose and duration of systemic immunosuppressive therapy. A dose dependent increase in opportunistic infections (a signal of systemic immunosuppression) was also noted in this study. IRLD occurred at the lowest dose of 15 mg/kg/day and a partial recovery from IRLD was noted upon cessation of dosing.

Mutagenicity

No evidence for a mutagenic or clastogenic potential for pimecrolimus was revealed in a battery of *in vitro* genotoxicity tests, including the Ames assay, mouse lymphoma L5178Y assay, and chromosome aberration test in V79 Chinese hamster cells and an *in vivo* mouse micronucleus test.

Pregnancy/Reproduction

Fertility—An oral fertility and embryofetal developmental study in rats revealed estrus cycle disturbances, post-implantation loss and reduction in litter size at the 45 mg per kg of body weight per day dose. No effect on fertility in female rats was noted at 10 mg per kg of body weight per day. No effect on fertility in male rats was noted at 45 mg per kg of body weight per day, which was the highest dose tested in this study.

A second oral fertility and embryofetal developmental study in rats showed reduced testicular and epididymal weights, reduced testicular sperm counts and motile sperm for males and estrus cycle disturbances, decreased corpora lutea, decreased implantations and viable fetuses for females at 45 mg/kg/day. No effect on fertility was noted at 10 mg/kg/day and 2 mg/kg/day for female and male rats, respectively.

Pregnancy—There are no adequate and well-controlled studies of topically administered pimecrolimus in pregnant women. Pimecrolimus should be used only if risk-benefit assessment indicates use during pregnancy.

Pimecrolimus crossed the placenta in oral rat and rabbit embryofetal developmental studies. In dermal embryofetal developmental studies, no maternal or fetal toxicity was observed in topical doses up to 10 mg per kg of body weight per day of 1% pimecrolimus cream in rats and rabbits, during the period of organogenesis.

A combined oral fertility and embryofetal developmental study was conducted in rats and an oral embryofetal developmental study was conducted in rabbits. Pimecrolimus was administered during the period of organogenesis up to doses of 45 mg per kg of body weight per day in rats and 20 mg per kg of body weight per day in rabbits. In the absence of maternal toxicity, indicators of embryofetal toxicity, such as, post-implantation loss and reduction of litter, were noted at 45 mg per kg of body weight per day in the oral fertility and embryofetal developmental study conducted in rats. No malformations in the fetuses were noted at 45 mg per kg of body weight per day in this study. No maternal toxicity, embryotoxicity or teratogenicity were noted in the oral rabbit embryofetal developmental toxicity study at 20 mg per kg of body weight per day, which was the highest dose tested in this study.

In an oral peri- and post-natal developmental study in rats, pimecrolimus was administered from gestational day 6 through lactational day 21 up to a dose level of 40 mg per kg of body weight per day. Only 2 of 22 females delivered live pups at the highest dose of 40 mg per kg of body weight per day. Postnatal survival, development of the F1 generation, their subsequent maturation and fertility were not affected at 10 mg per kg of body weight per day.

Pimecrolimus was transferred across the placenta in oral rat and rabbit embryofetal developmental studies.

FDA Pregnancy Category C

Breast-feeding

It is not known whether pimecrolimus is distributed into breast milk. Because of the potential for serious adverse reactions in nursing infants from pimecrolimus, a decision should be made whether to discontinue nursing or to discontinue the drug, taking into account the importance of the drug to the mother.

Pediatrics

Pimecrolimus cream is not indicated for use in children less than 2 years of age. The long-term safety and effect on the developing immune system are unknown.

Pimecrolimus is sometimes absorbed through the skin, though usually at very low amounts. Occasionally, children who have been treated with pimecrolimus have had measurable blood levels of the drug.

Geriatrics

Appropriate studies on the relationship of age to the effects of pimecrolimus have not been performed in the geriatric population. However, no geriatrics-specific problems have been documented to date.

Drug interactions and/or related problems

The following drug interactions and/or related problems have been selected on the basis of their potential clinical significance (possible mechanism in parentheses where appropriate)—not necessarily inclusive (» = major clinical significance):

Note: Potential interactions between pimecrolimus and other drugs, including immunizations, have not been systematically evaluated. Minimal systemic absorption of topically applied pimecrolimus should preclude the potential for significant interactions with other oral medications.

CYP3A inhibitors, such as:
Calcium channel blockers or
Cimetidine or
Erythromycin or
Fluconazole or
Itraconazole or
Ketoconazole
(patients with widespread and/or erythrodermic disease should use pimecrolimus with caution)

Medical considerations/Contraindications

The medical considerations/contraindications included have been selected on the basis of their potential clinical significance (reasons given in parentheses where appropriate)—not necessarily inclusive (» = major clinical significance).

Except under special circumstances, this medication should not be used when the following medical problem exists:

» Hypersensitivity to pimecrolimus or any of the components of the cream

» Immunocompromised patients
(should not be used in these patients)

» Infections, active cutaneous viral, or
» Infected atopic dermatitis
(pimecrolimus cream should not be applied topically to areas of active cutaneous viral infections or to clinically infected atopic dermatitis. Before commencing treatment with pimecrolimus infections at treatment sites should be cleared.)

» Netherton's syndrome
(potential for increased systemic absorption; use of pimecrolimus is not recommended)

» Pre-malignant skin conditions or
» Malignant skin conditions
(pimecrolimus use should be avoided; some malignant skin conditions, such as cutaneous T-cell lymphoma (CTCL), can present as dermatitis)

Risk-benefit should be considered when the following medical problems exist:

Eczema herpeticum (Kaposi's varicelliform eruption) or
Herpes simplex virus infection or
Varicella zoster virus infection (chicken pox or shingles)
(increased risk of superficial skin infections may be associated with these conditions)

Erythroderma, generalized
(safety and efficacy has not been established)

» Lymphadenopathy or
» Mononucleosis, acute infectious
(patients who develop lymphadenopathy while using pimecrolimus cream should have the etiology of their lymphadenopathy investigated; consider discontinuation of topical pimecrolimus if lymphadenopathy without a clear etiology develops or in the presence of acute infectious mononucleosis)
(in clinical studies there was a rare incidence (0.9%) of lymphadenopathy in patients which was usually related to ongoing infections and noted to resolve upon appropriate antibiotic therapy.)

Skin papilloma or
Warts
(discontinuation of pimecrolimus cream should be considered if there is a worsening of skin papillomas or they do not respond to therapy)

Patient monitoring

The following may be especially important in patient monitoring (other tests may be warranted in some patients, depending on condition; » = major clinical significance):

» Monitor for resolution of symptoms of atopic dermatitis and discontinue therapy; resume treatment at first signs of recurrence.

» If skin site reactions are severe or persists for more than 1 week consider discontinuation of therapy.

» Reevaluation at 6 weeks
(if no improvement in signs and symptoms of atopic dermatitis within 6 weeks, patients should be reexamined by healthcare provider for diagnosis confirmation)

Side/Adverse Effects

Although a causal relationship has not been established, rare cases of malignancy (e.g., skin and lymphoma) have been reported in patients treated with topical calcineurin inhibitors, including pimecrolimus cream.

Between December 2001 and 2004, the FDA had received 10 cases of postmarketing reports linking pimecrolimus with cancer-related adverse events. Four cases occurred in children, 3 of these in children less than 6 years of age, and the other 6 cases in adults. The most serious outcome was one hospitalization in an adult. All other cases reported nonserious outcomes.

Of the 10 postmarketing cases reporting cancer, 6 described cutaneous tumors, 1 described a lymph node/cutaneous tumor related event, and 3 others, unreported locations. Four cases described lymphomas; 5 cases described a variety of tumors, including basal cell carcinoma and squamous cell carcinoma; and 1 case described granulomatous lymphadenitis. Median time was 90 days after initiation of pimecrolimus treatment until diagnosis, with a 1 week to 300 day range. Two cases also reported a lymphadenopathy. Two cases were confounded: 1 with the presence of nodules prior to the basal cell carcinoma diagnosis; and another with a pre-existing condition associated with an increased risk for malignant transformation.

The potential for systemic immunosuppression is unknown and the role of pimecrolimus in the development of the cancer-related events in the individual postmarketing cases is also uncertain.

The following side/adverse effects have been selected on the basis of their potential clinical significance (possible signs and symptoms in parentheses where appropriate)—not necessarily inclusive:

Those indicating need for medical attention

Incidence more frequent

Application site reaction (burning; itching; redness; skin rash; swelling or soreness at site.); ***bronchitis*** (cough producing mucus; difficulty breathing; shortness of breath; tightness in chest; wheezing); ***ear infection*** (change in hearing; earache or pain in ear; ear drainage; fever); ***influenza*** (chills; cough; diarrhea; fever; general feeling of discomfort or illness; headache; joint pain; loss of appetite; muscle aches and pains; nausea; runny nose; shivering; sore throat; sweating; trouble sleeping; unusual tiredness or weakness; vomiting); ***gastroenteritis*** (abdominal or stomach pain; diarrhea; loss of appetite; nausea; weakness); ***pharyngitis streptococcal*** (body aches or pain; congestion; cough; dryness or soreness of throat; fever; hoarseness; runny nose; tender, swollen glands in neck; trouble in swallowing; voice changes); ***pyrexia*** (fever); ***skin infection*** (itching; pain; redness; swelling; tenderness; warmth on skin); ***tonsillitis*** (congestion; fever; sore throat; swollen glands); ***upper respiratory tract infection*** (ear congestion; nasal congestion; chills; cough; fever; sneezing, or sore throat; body aches or pain; headache; loss of voice; runny nose; unusual tiredness or weakness; difficulty in breathing); ***viral infection*** (chills; cough or hoarseness; fever; cold or flu-like symptoms)

Incidence less frequent

Asthma (cough; difficulty breathing; noisy breathing; shortness of breath; tightness in chest; wheezing); ***bacterial infection*** (chills; cough or hoarseness; fever; cold or flu-like symptoms); ***chickenpox*** (skin rash on face, scalp, or stomach); ***dyspnea*** (shortness of breath; difficult or labored breathing; tightness in chest; wheezing); ***herpes simplex dermatitis*** (blistering, crusting, irritation, itching, or reddening of skin; swelling; fever); ***hypersensitivity*** (fast heartbeat; fever; hives; itching; irritation; hoarseness; joint pain, stiffness or swelling; rash; redness of skin; shortness of breath; swelling of eyelids, face, lips, hands, or feet; tightness in chest; troubled breathing or swallowing; wheezing); ***infection, eye*** (blurred vision or other change in vision; eye pain; redness of eye; sensitivity of eye to light; tearing); ***laceration*** (tearing of skin); ***molluscum contagiosum*** (itchy, raised, round, smooth, skin-colored bumps found on just one area of the body; oozing, thick, white fluid); ***pneumonia*** (chest pain; cough; fever or chills; sneezing; shortness of breath; sore throat; troubled breathing; tightness in chest; wheezing); ***urticaria*** (hives or welts; itching; redness of skin; skin rash)

Incidence not determined—Observed during clinical practice; estimates of frequency can not be determined

Anaphylactic reaction (cough; difficulty swallowing; dizziness; fast heartbeat; hives, itching, puffiness or swelling of the eyelids or around the eyes, face, lips or tongue; shortness of breath; skin rash; tightness in chest; unusual tiredness or weakness; wheezing); ***angioneurotic edema*** (large, hive-like swelling on face, eyelids, lips, tongue, throat, hands, legs, feet, sex organs); ***basal cell carcinoma*** (sore that will not heal; growth or bump on skin); ***facial edema*** (swelling or puffiness of face); ***lymphomas*** (swollen glands; weight loss; general feeling of illness; black, tarry stools; yellow skin and eyes); ***malignant melanoma*** (new mole; change in size, shape or color of existing mole; mole that leaks fluid or bleeds); ***squamous cell carcinoma*** (small, red skin lesion, growth, or bump usually on face, ears, neck, hands or arms)

Those indicating need for medical attention only if they continue or are bothersome

Incidence more frequent

Application site burning; application site irritation; application site pruritus (itching skin at site); ***cough; diarrhea; folliculitis*** (burning, itching, and pain in hairy areas; pus at root of hair); ***headache; nasopharyngitis*** (stuffy or runny nose; muscle aches; unusual tiredness or weakness; fever; sore throat; headache); ***sore throat***

Incidence less frequent

Abdominal pain (stomach pain); ***acne*** (blemishes on the skin; pimples); ***application site erythema*** (flushing; redness of skin; unusually warm skin at site); ***arthralgias*** (pain in joints; muscle pain or stiffness; difficulty in moving); ***back pain; constipation*** (difficulty having a bowel movement (stool)); ***dysmenorrhea*** (pain; cramps; heavy bleeding); ***earache or otitis media*** (earache, redness or swelling in ear); ***epistaxis*** (bloody nose); ***herpes simplex*** (burning or stinging of skin; painful cold sores or blisters on lips, nose, eyes, or genitals); ***impetigo*** (bacterial skin infection); ***loose stools; nasal congestion*** (stuffy nose); ***nausea; rhinorrhea*** (runny nose); ***sinus congestion*** (stuffy nose; headache); ***sinusitis*** (pain or tenderness around eyes and cheekbone; fever; stuffy or runny nose; headache; cough; shortness of breath or troubled breathing; tightness of chest or wheezing); ***skin papilloma*** (lump or growth on skin); ***toothache; vomiting; wheezing*** (difficulty in breathing or troubled breathing)

Incidence not determined—Observed during clinical practice; estimates of frequency can not be determined

Flushing (feeling of warmth; redness of the face, neck, arms and occasionally, upper chest)—associated with alcohol use; ***ocular irritation*** (burning, stinging, itching, or mild discomfort of the eye)—after application of the cream to eyelids or near eyes

Overdose

For more information on the management of overdose or unintentional ingestion, **contact a poison control center** (see *Poison Control Center Listing*).

Treatment of overdose

No information is available about specific treatment for an overdose of pimecrolimus.

Supportive care—

Treatment should be symptomatic and supportive.

No incidents of accidental ingestion have been reported. If oral ingestion occurs, medical advice should be sought.

Patients in whom intentional overdose is confirmed or suspected should be referred for psychiatric consultation.

Patient Consultation

As an aid to patient consultation, refer to *Advice for the Patient, Pimecrolimus (Topical)*.

In providing consultation, consider emphasizing the following selected information (» = major clinical significance):

Before using this medication

» Conditions affecting use, especially:

Hypersensitivity to pimecrolimus or any of the components of the cream

Recently conducted monkey study showed dose-related increase in virus-associated lymphoma following oral pimecrolimus administration

Pregnancy—FDA Pregnancy Category C; should be used only if clearly needed during pregnancy; crosses the placenta in animals

Breast-feeding—Risk-benefit considerations

Not indicated in children less than 2 years of age; occasionally, children treated with pimecrolimus have had measurable blood levels of the drug

Other medical problems, especially active cutaneous viral infections, acute infectious mononucleosis, infected atopic dermatitis, immunocompromised patients, lymphadenopathy, Netherton's syndrome, pre-malignant skin conditions, or malignant skin conditions

Proper use of this medication

Using minimum amount of pimecrolimus needed to control patient's symptoms

» Using for short periods of time, not continuously and not using beyond one year of non-continuous use

Importance of seeing doctor for skin site reactions persisting more than one week

» Seeing healthcare provider for diagnosis confirmation if no improvement in signs and symptoms within 6 weeks

Clearing clinical infections at treatment sites before initiating topical pimecrolimus treatment

Washing hands after application if hands are not an area for treatment

» Proper dosing, especially no occlusive dressings

Missed dose: applying as soon as possible; not using if almost time for next scheduled dose; not doubling doses

Proper storage

Precautions while using this medication

» Importance of close monitoring by a physician

Reporting any adverse reactions to physician especially application site reactions and cutaneous infections

Not using pimecrolimus cream for any disorder other than that for which it was prescribed

» Minimizing or avoiding prolonged exposure to natural or artificial sunlight

Side/adverse effects

Signs of potential side effects, especially application site reaction, asthma, bacterial infection, bronchitis, chickenpox, dyspnea, ear infection, eye infection, hypersensitivity, gastroenteritis, herpes simplex dermatitis, influenza, laceration, molluscum contagiosum, pharyngitis streptococcal, pneumonia, pyrexia, skin infection, tonsillitis, upper respiratory tract infection, urticaria, or viral infection.

Signs observed during clinical practice, especially anaphylactic reaction, angioneurotic edema, basal cell carcinoma, facial edema, lymphomas, malignant melanoma, or squamous cell carcinoma

Between December 2001 and 2004, ten postmarketing reports linking pimecrolimus with cancer-related adverse events have been reported to the FDA with the most serious outcome being hospitalization of one adult and all other cases being nonserious.

General Dosing Information

Pimecrolimus cream is for external use only and should not be used ophthalmically.

The minimum amount of pimecrolimus needed to control the patient's symptoms should be used.

Pimecrolimus cream should not be used with occlusive dressings, which may promote systemic exposure and undue local irritation.

Patients using pimecrolimus cream should minimize or avoid prolonged natural or artificial sunlight exposure (tanning beds or UVA/B treatment).

Application is allowed on all skin surfaces, including the head, neck and intertriginous areas.

Patients should see a physician if an application site reaction is severe or persists for more than one week.

Therapy with pimecrolimus cream should be discontinued after signs and symptoms of atopic dermatitis have resolved.

If signs and symptoms (e.g., itch, rash, and redness) do not improve within 6 weeks, patients should be re-examined by their healthcare provider to confirm the diagnosis of atopic dermatitis.

The safety of pimecrolimus cream has not been established beyond one year of non-continuous use.

Topical Dosage Forms

PIMECROLIMUS CREAM

Usual adult dose

Atopic dermatitis—

Topical, 1% cream, apply a thin layer to the affected skin twice a day and rub in gently and completely. The patient or caregiver should stop using when signs and symptoms (e.g., itch, rash, and redness) resolve and should be instructed on what actions to take if symptoms recur.

Adult duration limits

6 weeks—If symptoms persist beyond 6 weeks the patient should be re-evaluated by their healthcare provider to confirm the diagnosis of atopic dermatitis.

Usual pediatric dose

Up to two years of age—Pimecrolimus cream is not indicated for use in children less than 2 years of age.

Two years of age and older—See *Usual adult dose*

Pediatric duration limits

Two years of age and older—See *Adult duration limits*

Usual geriatric dose

See *Usual adult dose.*

Geriatric duration limits

See *Adult duration limits*

Strength(s) usually available

U.S.—

1% (Rx) [*Elidel* (benzyl alcohol; cetyl alcohol; citric acid; mono- and di-glycerides; oleyl alcohol; propylene glycol; sodium cetostearyl sulphate; sodium hydroxide; stearyl alcohol; triglycerides; water)].

Packaging and storage

Store at 25 °C (77 °F); excursions permitted to 15 to 30 °C (59 to 86 °F). Do not freeze.

Auxiliary labeling

- Avoid extended exposure to sunlight or tanning beds while taking this drug
- External use only
- Use sparingly and rub well into affected areas

Revised: 03/27/2006
Developed: 11/05/2002

PIMOZIDE Systemic

VA CLASSIFICATION (Primary/Secondary): CN900/CN709

Commonly used brand name(s): *Orap*.

Note: For a listing of dosage forms and brand names by country availability, see *Dosage Forms* section(s).

Category

Antidyskinetic (Gilles de la Tourette's syndrome); antipsychotic.

Indications

Note: Bracketed information in the *Indications* section refers to uses that are not included in U.S. product labeling.

Accepted

Gilles de la Tourette's syndrome (treatment)[1]—Pimozide is indicated for the suppression of motor and vocal tics in patients with Tourette's disorder whose symptoms are severe and who cannot tolerate or have failed to respond satisfactorily to haloperidol.

[Psychotic disorders (treatment)]—Pimozide is used for maintenance therapy in the management of *chronic* schizophrenic patients *without* symptoms of excitement, agitation, or hyperactivity.

Unaccepted

Pimozide must not be used for simple tics or tics that are not associated with Tourette's disorder, because of the high risk of cardiovascular and extrapyramidal effects.

Pimozide is ineffective and should not be used for the management of patients with mania or acute schizophrenia.

[1]Not included in Canadian product labeling.

Pharmacology/Pharmacokinetics

Physicochemical characteristics

Chemical Group—A diphenylbutylpiperidine analog of butyrophenone and a derivative of the meperidine-like analgesics.

Molecular weight—461.56.

Solubility—Less than 0.01 mg per mL in water.

Mechanism of action/Effect

Pimozide's exact mechanism of action has not been established; however, pimozide is thought to block dopamine D_2 receptors in the central nervous system (CNS). Secondary changes in central dopamine function and metabolism, including increased brain turnover of dopamine, may contribute to both the therapeutic and the adverse effects of pimozide. Pimozide also appears to block voltage-operated calcium channels and to interact with opiate receptors, probably as an antagonist.

Pimozide is thought to have more specific dopamine receptor blocking activity and less alpha-adrenergic receptor antagonism than other neuroleptic agents. This results in less potential for inducing sedation and hypotension.

Other actions/effects

Electrocardiographic changes, including QT interval prolongation; flattening, notching, and inversion of the T wave; and the appearance of U waves have been observed with pimozide use.

Prolactin levels are elevated with antipsychotic drug therapy, probably due to antagonism of dopamine receptors. The clinical significance of elevated prolactin levels is unknown for most patients, although such effects as galactorrhea, amenorrhea, gynecomastia, and impotence have been reported in patients receiving prolactin-elevating medications. Also, studies have found approximately one third of human breast cancers to be prolactin-dependent *in vitro*.

Pimozide possesses anticholinergic activity and a substantial antiemetic effect.

Absorption

Approximately 50% absorbed after oral administration.

Biotransformation

Significant first-pass metabolism, primarily by *N*-dealkylation in the liver; *in vitro* data indicate that pimozide is metabolized, at least in part, by the cytochrome P450 3A (CYP3A) and CYP2D6 isoenzymes, producing two major metabolites of undetermined neuroleptic activity.

Half-life

Elimination—

Mean, 29 ± 10 hours in a single-dose study of healthy volunteers.

Mean, 55 ± 20 hours in a repeat-dose study of short duration in schizophrenic patients.

Mean, 111 ± 57 hours in a single-dose study of seven adults with Tourette's syndrome.

Mean, 66 ± 49 hours in a single-dose study of four male children, 6 to 13 years of age, with Tourette's syndrome.

Time to peak concentration

6 to 8 hours (range, 4 to 12 hours).

Elimination

Renal—

40 to 50% within one week in a single-dose study in healthy volunteers, mostly as metabolites.

Fecal—

20% within one week in a single-dose study in healthy volunteers, at least half as unchanged drug.

Precautions to Consider

Cross-sensitivity and/or related problems

Patients sensitive to neuroleptic agents such as haloperidol, loxapine, molindone, phenothiazines, or thioxanthenes may also be sensitive to pimozide.

Carcinogenicity

In a 24-month carcinogenicity study of rats receiving up to 50 times the maximum recommended human dose (MRHD), no increased incidence of tumors overall or at any site was observed in either sex. The meaning of these results is unclear because of the limited number of animals that survived the study.

Tumorigenicity

Studies in mice have shown that pimozide causes a dose-related increase in benign pituitary and mammary gland tumors. The mechanism of tumor induction is unknown, but may be related to elevated prolactin synthesis and release. The pituitary gland tumors, which developed in female mice only, developed as hyperplasia at doses approximating the human dose, and as adenoma at doses about 15 times the MRHD on a mg per kg of body weight (mg/kg) basis.

Mammary gland tumors increased in female mice treated with pimozide, which elevates serum prolactin concentrations. Prolactin concentrations increase in humans, also, with chronic administration of antipsychotic agents. Tissue culture experiments indicate that approximately one third of human breast cancers are prolactin-dependent *in vitro,* a factor of potential importance if the prescription of these drugs is contemplated in a patient with previously detected breast cancer or if the patient is young and chronic use of the medication is anticipated.

Mutagenicity

Pimozide did not have mutagenic activity in the Ames test with four bacterial test strains, in the mouse dominant lethal test, or in the micronucleus test in rats.

Pregnancy/Reproduction

Fertility—Studies in rats have shown prolonged estrus cycles and fewer pregnancies. These effects are thought to be due to an inhibition of or delay in implantation, which has also been observed in rodents administered other antipsychotic agents.

Pregnancy—Adequate and well-controlled studies in humans have not been done.

Studies in rats given doses eight times the maximum recommended human dose showed retarded fetal development. In rabbits, maternal toxicity, mortality, decreased weight gain, and embryotoxicity, including increased incidence of resorptions, were dose-related.

FDA Pregnancy Category C.

Breast-feeding

It is not known whether pimozide is distributed into breast milk. Problems in humans have not been documented, although there is potential for maternal mammary gland tumor formation and unknown cardiovascular effects in the infant.

Pediatrics

Because its use and safety have not been evaluated in other childhood disorders, pimozide currently is not recommended for use in children with conditions other than Tourette's disorder.

A gradual initiation of pimozide therapy in patients up to 12 years of age is recommended since information on safety and efficacy in this age group is very limited.

Children may be especially sensitive to the effects of pimozide.

Geriatrics

Geriatric patients tend to develop higher plasma concentrations because of changes in distribution due to decreases in lean body mass, total body water, and albumin, and often an increase in total body fat composition. These patients usually require a lower initial dosage and a more gradual dosage titration than do younger patients.

Elderly patients are more prone to the development of transient hypotension and exhibit an increased sensitivity to the anticholinergic and sedative effects of pimozide. Also, older patients tend to develop extrapyramidal side effects more frequently, especially parkinsonism and tardive dyskinesia.

Dental

The peripheral anticholinergic effects of pimozide may decrease or inhibit salivary flow, especially in middle-aged or elderly patients, thus contributing to the development of caries, periodontal disease, oral candidiasis, and discomfort.

Extrapyramidal reactions induced by pimozide will result in increased motor activity of the head, face, and neck. Occlusal adjustments, bite registrations, and treatment for bruxism may be made less reliable.

The blood dyscrasia-causing effects of pimozide may result in an increased incidence of microbial infection, delayed healing, and gingival bleeding. If leukopenia or thrombocytopenia occurs, dental work should be deferred until blood counts have returned to normal. Patients should be instructed in proper oral hygiene, including caution in use of regular toothbrushes, dental floss, and toothpicks.

Drug interactions and/or related problems

The following drug interactions and/or related problems have been selected on the basis of their potential clinical significance (possible mechanism in parentheses where appropriate)—not necessarily inclusive (» = major clinical significance):

Note: *In vitro* data indicate that pimozide is metabolized, at least in part, by the isoenzymes CYP3A, CYP2D6 and possibly CYP1A2. Possible interactions with medications that inhibit these isoenzymes, other than those listed below, should be considered.

Combinations containing any of the following medications, depending on the amount present, may also interact with this medication.

» Alcohol or
» CNS depression-producing medications, other (see *Appendix II*)
(concurrent use with pimozide may potentiate the CNS depressant effects of these medications)

» Amphetamines or
» Methylphenidate or
» Pemoline
(these medications may provoke tics; before therapy with pimozide is initiated, these medications should be withdrawn to determine the underlying cause of observed tics; pimozide is not indicated for the treatment of tics caused by other medications)
(pimozide may block the effects of amphetamines)

» Anticholinergics or other medications with anticholinergic activity (see *Appendix II*)
(concurrent use with pimozide may intensify anticholinergic effects, especially those of dry mouth, constipation, and unusual excitability, because of secondary anticholinergic effects of pimozide; symptoms of tardive dyskinesia may be worsened)

Anticonvulsants
(although there has been no primary documentation for a drug interaction with pimozide and anticonvulsants, the potential exists for a lowering of the convulsive threshold by pimozide; dosage adjustment of the anticonvulsant may be necessary when pimozide treatment is initiated or discontinued or when the dose is reduced)

Antidepressants, monoamine oxidase (MAO) inhibitor
(concurrent use may prolong and intensify the sedative, hypotensive, and anticholinergic effects of MAO inhibitors and pimozide)

» Azithromycin or
» Clarithromycin or
» Dirithromycin or
» Erythromycin or
» Troleandomycin
(concurrent use of pimozide with azithromycin, clarithromycin, dirithromycin, erythromycin, or troleandomycin is **contraindicated;** concurrent use of these medications may increase plasma concentrations of pimozide, due to inhibition of the P450 3A metabolic pathways by these macrolides; increased plasma concentrations of pimozide may result in cardiotoxic effects [prolongation of the QT interval and ventricular arrhythmias]; sudden deaths have occurred when clarithromycin was added to pimozide therapy, probably due to inhibition of pimozide metabolism by clarithromycin)

» Extrapyramidal reaction-causing medications, other (see *Appendix II*)
(concurrent use of these agents with pimozide may increase the anticholinergic, CNS depressant, and extrapyramidal effects of both medications)

Grapefruit juice
(concurrent use with pimozide may inhibit the metabolism of pimozide and increase its plasma concentration; increased pimozide concentrations may result in cardiotoxic effects [prolongation of the QT interval and ventricular arrhythmias])

» Human immunodeficiency virus (HIV) protease inhibitors, such as:
Indinavir or
Nelfinavir or
Ritonavir or
Saquinavir
(concurrent use of pimozide with indinavir, nelfinavir, ritonavir, or saquinavir is **contraindicated;** concurrent use of these medications may increase plasma concentrations of pimozide, because of inhibition of the P450 3A metabolic pathways by these antivirals; increased plasma concentrations of pimozide may result in cardiotoxic effects [prolongation of the QT interval and ventricular arrhythmias]; sudden deaths have occurred when another inhibitor of CYP3A enzymes was added to pimozide therapy, probably due to inhibition of pimozide metabolism)

» Itraconazole, or
» Ketoconazole
(concurrent use of pimozide with itraconazole or ketoconazole is **contraindicated;** concurrent use of these medications may increase plasma concentrations of pimozide, because of inhibition of the P450 3A metabolic pathways by these antifungals; increased plasma concentrations of pimozide may result in cardiotoxic effects [prolongation of the QT interval and ventricular arrhythmias]; sudden deaths have occurred when another inhibitor of CYP3A enzymes was added to pimozide therapy, probably due to inhibition of pimozide metabolism)

» Nefazodone or
» Zileuton
(concurrent use of pimozide with nefazodone or zileuton is **contraindicated;** concurrent use of these medications may increase plasma concentrations of pimozide, because of inhibition of the P450 3A metabolic pathways by these agents; increased plasma concentrations of pimozide may result in cardiotoxic effects [prolongation of the QT interval and ventricular arrhythmias]; sudden deaths have occurred when another inhibitor of CYP3A enzymes was added to pimozide therapy, probably due to inhibition of pimozide metabolism)

» QT interval–prolonging medications, other, such as:
Antidepressants, tricyclic or
Disopyramide or
Maprotiline or
Phenothiazines or
Probucol or
Procainamide or
Quinidine
(concurrent use of these agents with pimozide may potentiate cardiac arrhythmias through an additive prolongation of the QT interval; concurrent use is **contraindicated**)

Laboratory value alterations

The following have been selected on the basis of their potential clinical significance (possible effect in parentheses where appropriate)—not necessarily inclusive (» = major clinical significance).

With diagnostic test results
» Electrocardiogram [ECG]
(pimozide use may result in prolongation of the QT interval; flattening, notching, and inversion of the T-wave; and the appearance of U-waves)

Pregnancy tests, immunologic urine
(pimozide may produce false-positive results)

Medical considerations/Contraindications

The medical considerations/contraindications included have been selected on the basis of their potential clinical significance (reasons given in parentheses where appropriate)—not necessarily inclusive (» = major clinical significance).

Except under special circumstances, this medication should not be used when the following medical problems exist:
» Cardiac arrhythmias, history of or
» Long QT syndrome, congenital or acquired
(may be aggravated by use of pimozide, predisposing patients to ventricular arrhythmias)

» CNS depression, severe or
» Comatose states
(may be potentiated)

» Tics, motor or vocal, other than those caused by Tourette's disorder
(efficacy has not been established and risk of cardiovascular and extrapyramidal effects may outweigh potential benefit)

Risk-benefit should be considered when the following medical problems exist:
» Breast cancer, history of
(may be aggravated by increased serum prolactin concentrations)

Glaucoma, narrow angle or
Paralytic ileus, history of or
Prostatic hypertrophy, clinically significant
(condition may be exacerbated by secondary anticholinergic effects of pimozide)

Hepatic function impairment or
Renal function impairment
(metabolism and excretion of pimozide may be altered)

» Hypokalemia
(potassium deficiency, such as from diarrhea or use of diuretics, should be corrected before initiation of pimozide therapy because of risk of ventricular arrhythmias)

Seizures, or history of
(pimozide may lower seizure threshold; increased incidence of epileptic seizures has been reported)

Sensitivity to pimozide or other neuroleptics, such as haloperidol, loxapine, molindone, phenothiazines, or thioxanthenes

Patient monitoring

The following may be especially important in patient monitoring (other tests may be warranted in some patients, depending on condition; » = major clinical significance):

» Electrocardiogram [ECG]
(recommended at initiation of therapy as baseline, and periodically thereafter, especially during dosage adjustment; any indication of prolongation of the QTc interval beyond an absolute limit of 0.47 seconds in children, 0.52 seconds in adults, or more than 25% of the patient's original baseline should be considered a basis for stopping increase of dosage or for reducing dosage)

Careful observation for early signs of tardive dyskinesia, especially in the elderly or patients on high or extended maintenance dosage
(recommended at least every 3 months; since there is no known effective treatment if syndrome should develop, pimozide should be discontinued, if clinically feasible, at earliest signs, usually fine, worm-like movements of the tongue, to stop further development)

Careful observation for early signs of tardive dystonia
(recommended at periodic intervals; since there is no known effective treatment if syndrome should develop, pimozide should be discontinued, if clinically feasible, at the earliest signs)

Side/Adverse Effects

Note: Sudden, unexplained deaths have occurred in patients receiving pimozide, mainly at dosages above 10 mg a day. These deaths may be related to the prolonged QT interval associated with pimozide use.

The following side/adverse effects have been selected on the basis of their potential clinical significance (possible signs and symptoms in parentheses where appropriate)—not necessarily inclusive:

Those indicating need for medical attention

Incidence more frequent

Akathisia (restlessness or need to keep moving); ***arrhythmias, ventricular*** (dizziness or fainting; fast or irregular heartbeat)—seen on ECG as prolonged QT interval as well as lowered and inverted T-wave and S-T segment changes; ***extrapyramidal effects, parkinsonian*** (difficulty in speaking; loss of balance control; lack of facial expression; shuffling walk; slowed movements; stiffness of arms and legs; trembling and shaking of fingers and hands); ***mood or behavior changes; swelling or soreness of breasts***—less frequent in males; ***unusual secretion of milk***—rare in males

Note: In children, *akathisia* may appear to be a worsening of Tourette's syndrome symptoms and may improve with a decrease in dosage. *Mood or behavior changes* in children may occur as a dose-dependent dysphoria, which includes anxiety, crying spells, fearfulness, irritability, and social withdrawal.

Parkinsonian extrapyramidal effects often occur during the first few days of treatment and are usually mild to moderately severe. Although severe extrapyramidal effects have been reported to occur at relatively low doses, most are dose-related and may decrease in severity or disappear when dosage is reduced.

Incidence less frequent

Extrapyramidal effects, dystonic (difficulty in swallowing; inability to move eyes; muscle spasms, especially of the face, neck, or back; twisting movements of the body); ***menstrual changes; tardive dyskinesia*** (lip smacking or puckering; puffing of cheeks; rapid or worm-like movements of tongue; uncontrolled chewing movements; uncontrolled movements of arms and legs)

Note: Risk of developing *tardive dyskinesia* or of developing irreversible tardive dyskinesia may increase with long-term treatment and with total cumulative dose. The symptoms of tardive dyskinesia may be masked during therapy, but may appear after reduction of dose or withdrawal of pimozide. There is no known effective treatment. Careful observation during pimozide therapy for early signs of tardive dyskinesia and reduction of dosage or discontinuation of medication may prevent a more severe manifestation of the syndrome. Tardive dyskinesia is more prevalent among elderly patients, especially females, on high-dose therapy.

Incidence rare

Allergic reaction (skin rash and itching; swelling of face); ***blood dyscrasias*** (sore throat and fever; unusual bleeding or bruising); ***jaundice, obstructive*** (yellow eyes or skin); ***neuroleptic malignant syndrome (NMS)*** (convulsions; difficult or unusually fast breathing; fast heartbeat or irregular pulse; high fever; high or low [irregular] blood pressure; increased sweating; loss of bladder control; severe muscle stiffness); ***tardive dystonia*** (increased blinking or spasms of eyelid; unusual facial expressions or body positions; uncontrolled twisting movements of neck, trunk, arms, or legs)

Note: *NMS* is a potentially fatal symptom complex. Additional signs of NMS may include elevated creatine kinase (CK), myoglobinuria (rhabdomyolysis), and acute renal failure. NMS may occur at any time during neuroleptic therapy, but is more commonly seen soon after start of therapy, or after patient has switched from one neuroleptic to another, during combined therapy with another psychotropic medication, or after a dosage increase.

Those indicating need for medical attention only if they continue or are bothersome

Incidence more frequent

Blurred vision or other vision problems; constipation; drowsiness; dryness of mouth; hypotension, orthostatic (dizziness, lightheadedness, or fainting when getting up from a lying or sitting position); ***skin discoloration***

Note: *Orthostatic hypotension* is most common in elderly and debilitated patients for several hours after administration of pimozide.

Incidence less frequent

Asthenia (tiredness or weakness); ***decreased sexual ability; diarrhea; headache; loss of appetite and weight; mental depression; nausea and vomiting***

Those indicating the need for medical attention if they occur after the medication is discontinued

Dyskinesia, withdrawal emergent (lip smacking or puckering; puffing of cheeks; rapid or worm-like movements of tongue; uncontrolled chewing movements; uncontrolled movements of arms and legs)

Overdose

For specific information on the agents used in the management of pimozide overdose, see:

- *Albumin Human (Systemic)* monograph;
- *Benztropine* in *Antidyskinetics (Systemic)* monograph;
- *Diazepam* in *Benzodiazepines (Systemic)* monograph;
- *Diphenhydramine* in *Antihistamines (Systemic)* monograph;
- *Magnesium Sulfate (Systemic)* monograph; and/or
- *Metaraminol, Norepinephrine*, and/or *Phenylephrine* in *Sympathomimetic Agents–Cardiovascular Use (Parenteral-Systemic)* monograph.

For more information on the management of overdose or unintentional ingestion, **contact a Poison Control Center** (see *Poison Control Center Listing*).

Clinical effects of overdose

Note: The clinical effects of pimozide overdose are generally an exaggeration of adverse effects seen at therapeutic doses.

The following effects have been selected on the basis of their potential clinical significance (possible signs and symptoms in parentheses where appropriate)—not necessarily inclusive:

Acute

Coma; electrocardiogram (ECG) abnormalities; extrapyramidal reactions (muscle trembling, jerking, or stiffness; uncontrolled movements); ***hypotension*** (dizziness); ***respiratory depression*** (troubled breathing); ***seizures***

Treatment of overdose

Treatment is essentially symptomatic and supportive.

To decrease absorption—

Initiating gastric lavage. Induction of emesis is not advised, because of possible decreased seizure threshold and extrapyramidal reactions.

Specific treatment—

Counteracting hypotension and circulatory collapse with use of intravenous fluids, plasma, or concentrated albumin, and vasopressor agents such as norepinephrine, metaraminol, or phenylephrine. Epinephrine should *not* be used since it may cause paradoxical hypotension.

Administering intravenous diphenhydramine or benztropine to manage dystonias.

Administering diazepam to manage seizures.

Using magnesium sulfate followed by pacing and correction of electrolyte abnormalities if *torsades de pointes* develops.

Monitoring—

Immediately monitoring ECG and continuing until parameters are within normal range. Continuing monitoring ECG until parameters have remained within normal range for 24 hours in patients who develop *torsades de pointes.*

Observing patients for at least 4 days because of the long half-life of pimozide.

Supportive care—

Establishing a patent airway and mechanically assisting respiration, if necessary.

Patients in whom intentional overdose is confirmed or suspected should be referred for psychiatric consultation.

Patient Consultation

As an aid to patient consultation, refer to *Advice for the Patient, Pimozide (Systemic).*

In providing consultation, consider emphasizing the following selected information (» = major clinical significance):

Before using this medication

» Conditions affecting use, especially:

Sensitivity to pimozide or other neuroleptic agents

Pregnancy—Animal studies have shown fewer pregnancies; retarded fetal development; maternal toxicity; mortality; decreased weight gain; embryotoxicity; increased resorptions

Use in children—Not recommended for conditions other than Tourette's syndrome; therapy should be initiated gradually in patients up to 12 years of age; children may be more sensitive to effects of pimozide

Use in the elderly—Elderly patients are more likely to experience extrapyramidal, anticholinergic, hypotensive, and sedative effects; reduced dosage recommended

Dental—Dry mouth may cause caries, candidiasis, periodontal disease, and discomfort; increased motor activity of face, head, and neck may interfere with some dental procedures; pimozide-induced blood dyscrasias may result in infections, delayed healing, and bleeding

Contraindicated medications—Azithromycin, clarithromycin, dirithromycin, erythromycin, indinavir, itraconazole, ketoconazole, nefazodone, nelfinavir, ritonavir, saquinavir, troleandomycin, zileuton, or other QT interval-prolonging medications—

Other medications, especially alcohol, amphetamines, methylphenidate, other anticholinergic medications, other CNS depression-producing medications, other extrapyramidal reaction–producing medications, or pemoline

Other medical problems, especially cardiac arrhythmias, comatose states, congenital or acquired long QT syndrome, history of breast cancer, hypokalemia, severe CNS depression, or tics other than those caused by Tourette's disorder

Proper use of this medication

» Importance of not taking more medication than the amount prescribed because of cardiac effects

» Proper dosing

Missed dose: Skipping the missed dose and returning to regular dosing schedule; not doubling doses

» Proper storage

Precautions while using this medication

Regular visits to physician to check progress of therapy

» Not taking azithromycin, clarithromycin, dirithromycin, erythromycin, indinavir, itraconazole, ketoconazole, nefazodone, nelfinavir, ritonavir, saquinavir, troleandomycin, zileuton, or other QT interval–prolonging medications during pimozide therapy because of possible life-threatening cardiac arrhythmias

» Checking with physician before discontinuing medication; gradual dosage reduction may be needed

» Avoiding use of alcoholic beverages or other CNS depressants during therapy

Not taking with grapefruit juice

» Possible drowsiness, blurred vision, or muscle stiffness; caution when driving, using machinery, or doing other things requiring alertness, clear vision, and good muscle control

Possible dizziness or lightheadedness; avoiding getting up suddenly from a sitting or lying position

» Caution if any kind of surgery, dental treatment, or emergency surgery is required because of additive CNS–depressant effects of pimozide and medications used in these situations

Possible dryness of mouth; using sugarless gum or candy, ice, or saliva substitute for relief; checking with physician or dentist if dry mouth continues for more than 2 weeks

Side/adverse effects

Side effects are more likely in children and elderly or debilitated patients

» Stopping medication and notifying physician immediately if symptoms of neuroleptic malignant syndrome (NMS) appear

» Notifying physician as soon as possible if early symptoms of tardive dyskinesia appear

Possibility of withdrawal symptoms

Signs of potential side effects, especially akathisia, ventricular arrhythmias, parkinsonism, mood or behavior changes, swelling or soreness of breasts (less frequent in males), unusual secretion of milk (rare in males), dystonia, menstrual changes, tardive dyskinesia, allergic reaction, blood dyscrasias, obstructive jaundice, NMS, or tardive dystonia

General Dosing Information

Periodic attempts should be made to reduce the dosage of pimozide gradually to see whether tics persist at the level and extent first identified. In doing so, consideration should be given to the possibility that any increases in tic intensity and frequency may represent a transient withdrawal-related phenomenon rather than a return of disease symptoms. Two to three weeks should elapse before a final conclusion is reached that an increase in tic manifestations is a function of the underlying disease syndrome rather than a response to pimozide withdrawal. Also, spontaneous remission and fluctuating symptoms may occur in many patients, since pimozide's poor absorption and presystemic metabolism profile may result in highly variable absorption from day to day.

When discontinued, pimozide should be withdrawn gradually, over several weeks if possible, to minimize symptoms of withdrawal.

Sudden, unexpected deaths have occurred in patients taking high doses of pimozide, ie, doses greater than 10 milligrams. A possible mechanism was QT-interval prolongation resulting in ventricular arrhythmias.

Diet/Nutrition

Patients on pimozide therapy should avoid consumption of grapefruit juice, because it contains substances that may inhibit the metabolism of pimozide by CYP 3A enzymes.

For treatment of adverse reactions

Treatment is essentially symptomatic and supportive and may include the following:

- *Discontinuing pimozide immediately.*
- Hyperthermia—Administering antipyretics (aspirin or acetaminophen); using cooling blanket.
- Dehydration—Restoring fluids and electrolytes.
- Cardiovascular instability—Monitoring blood pressure and cardiac rhythm closely.
- Hypoxia—Administering oxygen; consider airway insertion and assisted ventilation.
- Muscle rigidity—Dantrolene sodium may be administered (100 to 300 mg per day in divided doses; 1.25 to 1.5 mg per kg of body weight [mg/kg], intravenously). Bromocriptine (5 to 7.5 mg every eight hours) has been used to reverse hyperpyrexia and muscle rigidity.

Neuroleptic malignant syndrome (NMS)—

Parkinsonism—

Many medical authorities advise that the only appropriate treatment of extrapyramidal symptoms is reduction of the antipsychotic dosage, if possible, to the lowest effective dose. Oral antidyskinetic agents, such as trihexyphenidyl (2 mg three times a day) or benztropine, may be effective in treating more severe parkinsonism and acute motor restlessness but are used sparingly, and then usually for no longer than 3 months. Extrapyramidal symptoms may reappear if both pimozide and the antidyskinetic agent are discontinued simultaneously. The antidyskinetic agent may have to be continued after pimozide is discontinued because of the different excretion rates of the medications. Milder effects may be treated by adjusting dosage.

Akathisia—

Restlessness may be treated with antiparkinsonian medications, or with propranolol (30 to 120 mg a day), nadolol (40 mg a day), pindolol (5 to 60 mg a day), lorazepam (1 or 2 mg two or three times a day), or diazepam (2 mg two or three times a day).

Dystonia—

Acute dystonic postures or oculogyric crisis may be relieved by parenteral administration of benztropine (2 mg intramuscularly), diphenhydramine (50 mg intramuscularly), or diazepam (5 to 7.5 mg intravenously), to be followed by oral antidyskinetic medication for one or two days to prevent recurrent dystonic episodes. These effects may be controlled by adjustments of pimozide dosage.

Tardive dyskinesia or tardive dystonia—

There is no known effective treatment. Dosage of pimozide should be lowered or medication discontinued, if clinically feasible, at earliest signs of tardive dyskinesia or tardive dystonia, to prevent irreversible effects.

Oral Dosage Forms

Note: Bracketed uses in the *Dosage Forms* section refer to categories of use and/or indications that are not included in U.S. product labeling.

PIMOZIDE TABLETS USP

Usual adult dose

Tourette's syndrome[1]—

Oral, initially, 1 to 2 mg a day in divided doses, the dosage being increased gradually as needed and tolerated.

Note: Elderly patients usually require a lower initial dosage and a more gradual dosage titration than do younger patients.

[Psychotic disorders]—

Oral, initially, 2 to 4 mg once a day, preferably in the morning, the dosage being increased as needed and tolerated by 2 to 4 mg a day at weekly intervals.

Note: The average maintenance dosage is 6 mg a day, with a usual range of 2 to 12 mg a day.

Elderly patients usually require a lower initial dosage and a more gradual dosage titration than do younger patients.

Usual adult prescribing limits

Tourette's syndrome[1]—

200 mcg (0.2 mg) per kg of body weight a day or 10 mg a day, whichever is less.

[Psychotic disorders]—

300 mcg (0.3 mg) per kg of body weight a day or 20 mg a day, whichever is less.

Note: Seizures and sudden unexpected deaths have occurred at dosages above 20 mg a day.

Usual pediatric dose

Tourette's syndrome[1]—

Children up to 12 years of age: Dosage has not been established.

Children 12 years of age and over: Oral, initially 50 mcg (0.05 mg) per kg of body weight, preferably as a single dose, the dosage being increased gradually as needed and tolerated.

Note: For children 2 years of age and over, some clinicians use an initial dosage of 1 mg a day, increased by 1 mg a day at intervals of seven to ten days, as needed and tolerated, until a significant decrease in tics is seen.

Usual pediatric prescribing limits

200 mcg (0.2 mg) per kg of body weight a day or 10 mg a day, whichever is less.

Strength(s) usually available

U.S.—

2 mg (Rx) [*Orap* (scored; calcium stearate; cellulose; lactose; corn starch)].

Canada—

1 mg (Rx) [*Orap* (scored)].

2 mg (Rx) [*Orap* (scored; calcium stearate; lactose; microcrystalline cellulose; corn starch)].

4 mg (Rx) [*Orap* (scored; calcium stearate; FD&C Blue No. 1; FD&C Yellow No. 5; lactose; microcrystalline cellulose; corn starch; tartrazine)].

10 mg (Rx) [*Orap* (scored; calcium stearate; FD&C Yellow No. 6; lactose; microcrystalline cellulose; corn starch)].

Packaging and storage

Store below 40 °C (104 °F), preferably between 15 and 30 °C (59 and 86 °F), unless otherwise specified by manufacturer. Store in a tight, light-resistant container.

Auxiliary labeling

- May cause drowsiness.
- Avoid alcoholic beverages.

[1]Not included in Canadian product labeling.

Revised: 11/24/1999

PINDOLOL—See *Beta-adrenergic Blocking Agents (Systemic)*

PIOGLITAZONE Systemic

VA CLASSIFICATION (Primary): HS505

Commonly used brand name(s): *Actos*.

Note: For a listing of dosage forms and brand names by country availability, see *Dosage Forms* section(s).

Category

Antidiabetic agent.

Indications

Accepted

Diabetes, type 2 (treatment)—Pioglitazone is indicated as adjunctive therapy to diet and exercise in the management of patients with type 2 diabetes mellitus (previously referred to as non-insulin-dependent diabetes mellitus [NIDDM]). Pioglitazone may be used as monotherapy or in combination with a sulfonylurea, metformin, or insulin when diet and exercise plus the single agent do not result in adequate glycemic control..

Pharmacology/Pharmacokinetics

Physicochemical characteristics

Chemical Group—Thiazolidinedione

Molecular weight—392.9 daltons.

Solubility—Soluble in N,N-dimethylformamide; slightly soluble in anhydrous ethanol; very slightly soluble in acetone and acetonitrile; practically insoluble in water; insoluble in ether.

Mechanism of action/Effect

Pioglitazone is a thiazolidinedione antidiabetic agent that is effective only in the presence of insulin. Its primary action is to decrease insulin resistance at peripheral sites and in the liver, resulting in increased insulin-dependent glucose disposal and decreased hepatic glucose output. These effects are accomplished through selective binding at the peroxisome proliferator–activated receptor-gamma (PPAR-gamma), which is found in adipose tissue, skeletal muscle, and the liver. Activation of these receptors modulates transcription of several insulin-responsive genes that control glucose and lipid metabolism.

Absorption

Rapid. Food slightly delays the time to achieve peak serum concentrations but does not alter the extent of absorption.

Distribution

Mean apparent volume of distribution (Vol_D)—.63L (0.22 to 1.04 L) per kg of body weight (following single-dose administration).

Protein binding

Very high (> 99%); in human serum, primarily to serum albumin. Metabolites are more than 98% bound to serum albumin.

Biotransformation

Pioglitazone is extensively metabolized in the liver to several active metabolites (Metabolite III - keto derivative, Metabolite IV - hydroxy derivative, and Metabolite II - hydroxy derivative). Cytochrome (CYP) P450 isoforms involved in the hepatic metabolism of pioglitazone are CYP2C8 and CYP3A4. The extrahepatic isoform, CYP1A1, is also involved in the metabolism of pioglitazone.

In *in vitro* studies, pioglitazone did not inhibit cytochrome P450.

Half-life

Serum—

Pioglitazone: 3 to 7 hours.

Total pioglitazone (pioglitazone plus active metabolites): 16 to 24 hours.

Time to peak concentration

2 hours; may be increased to 3 to 4 hours if taken with food.

Elimination

Biliary/fecal—It is assumed that most of a dose is excreted into bile as active drug or metabolites and is eliminated in the feces.

Renal—15% to 30%, primarily as metabolites and their conjugates; renal elimination of pioglitazone is negligible.

Apparent clearance—5 to 7 liters per hour.

Precautions to Consider

Carcinogenicity

During a 2-year carcinogenicity study conducted in male and female rats, no drug-induced tumors were observed except for benign and/or malignant transitional cell neoplasms of the urinary bladder. These were observed only in male rats at doses of 4 mg per kg of body weight (mg/kg) per day and above (approximately equal to the maximum recommended human oral dose based on mg per square meter of body surface area [mg/m^2]). Oral doses up to 63 mg/kg (approximately 14 times the maximum recommended human oral dose of 45 mg based on mg/m^2) were used in this study. Drug-induced tumors were not observed in any organ in male and female mice given oral doses up to 100 mg/kg per day (approximately 11 times the maximum recommended human oral dose based on mg/m^2).

Urinary tract tumors have been reported in rodents taking experimental drugs with dual PPAR alpha/gamma activity; however, pioglitazone is a selective agonist for PPAR gamma.

During clinical trials, no new cases of bladder tumors were detected in more than 1800 patients treated with pioglitazone. Abnormal urinary cytology was observed in 0.72% and 0.88% of patients treated with pioglitazone and placebo, respectively.

Mutagenicity

No evidence of mutagenicity was found in the Ames bacterial assay, a mammalian cell forward gene mutation assay, an *in vitro* cytogenetics assay, an unscheduled DNA synthesis assay, and an *in vivo* micronucleus assay.

Pregnancy/Reproduction

Fertility—Pioglitazone therapy may cause resumption of ovulation in premenopausal anovulatory patients with insulin resistance. As a result, these patients may be at an increased risk for pregnancy while taking pioglitazone. Therefore, adequate contraception in premenopausal women is recommended.

No evidence of impaired fertility was found in male and female rats given pioglitazone in oral dose of 40 mg/kg per day (approximately 9 times the maximum recommended human oral dose based on mg/m^2) throughout mating and gestation.

Pregnancy—It is recommended that insulin alone be used during pregnancy for maintenance of blood glucose concentrations that are as close to normal as possible. Abnormal maternal blood glucose concentrations have been associated with a higher incidence of congenital anomalies and increased neonatal morbidity and mortality.

Teratogenicity was not observed in rats treated with oral pioglitazone at doses of up to 80 mg/kg or in rabbits treated with up to 160 mg/kg during organogenesis (approximately 17 and 40 times the maximum recommended human oral dose based on mg/m^2, respectively). In rats treated with oral pioglitazone at doses of 10 mg/kg and above (approximately 2 times the maximum recommended human oral dose based on mg/m^2) during late gestation and lactation, delayed postnatal development was observed.

There are no adequate and well-controlled studies in pregnant women. Pioglitazone should be used during pregnancy only if the potential benefit justifies the potential risk to the fetus.

FDA Pregnancy Category C.

Breast-feeding

It is not known whether pioglitazone is distributed into human breast milk. However, it is distributed into the milk of lactating rats. Pioglitazone is not recommended for use by nursing mothers.

Pediatrics

Appropriate studies on the relationship of age to the effects of pioglitazone have not been performed in the pediatric population. Safety and efficacy have not been established.

Canadian manufacturer states that pioglitazone is not recommended for patients under 18 years of age.

Geriatrics

Placebo-controlled studies performed in approximately 500 patients 65 years of age or older have not demonstrated geriatrics-specific problems that would limit the use of pioglitazone in the elderly.

In a 24-week post-marketing study, overnight hospitalization for congestive heart failure was reported in 9.9% of patients on pioglitazone compared to 4.7% of patients on glyburide with a treatment difference observed from 6 weeks. This adverse event associated with pioglitazone was more marked in patients over 64 years of age.

Pharmacogenetics

No pharmacokinetic data is available among various ethnic groups.

In controlled clinical trials, the mean C_{max} and AUC values were increased 20% to 60% in females. Hemoglobin A_{1C} decreases from baseline were generally greater for females than for males. However, since therapy should be individualized for each patient to achieve glycemic control, no dose adjustment based on gender alone is recommended.

Drug interactions and/or related problems

The following drug interactions and/or related problems have been selected on the basis of their potential clinical significance (possible mechanism in parentheses where appropriate)—not necessarily inclusive (» = major clinical significance):

Note: Combinations containing any of the following medications, depending on the amount present, may also interact with this medication.

» Ketoconazole
(concurrent use may decrease metabolism of pioglitazone)

Midazolam
(concurrent administration may reduce midazolam serum concentrations)

Oral contraceptives, ethinylestradiol- and norethindrone-containing
(concurrent use may reduce plasma concentrations of both hormones)

Laboratory value alterations

The following have been selected on the basis of their potential clinical significance (possible effect in parentheses where appropriate)—not necessarily inclusive (» = major clinical significance).

With physiology/laboratory test values

Alanine aminotransferase (ALT [SGPT]) and
Aspartate aminotransferase (AST [SGOT])
(during controlled clinical trials, reversible elevations greater than three times the upper limit of normal were observed in 0.26% of pioglitazone-treated patients versus 0.25% of placebo-treated patients; however, ALT elevations were not clearly related to pioglitazone)

Cholesterol, total and
High-density lipoproteins (HDL) and
Low-density lipoproteins (LDL)
(during clinical trials, increases in HDL-C were observed in patients with lipid abnormalities; no consistent changes were observed in LDL-C and total cholesterol)

Creatine phosphokinase levels (CPK)
(during controlled clinical trials, sporadic, transient elevations in CPK levels were observed. They resolved without clinical sequel, and the relationship to pioglitazone therapy is unknown.)

Hematocrit and
Hemoglobin concentration
(during clinical trials, the mean hemoglobin concentration declined by 2% to 4% in patients treated with pioglitazone; decreases have been attributed to dilutional effects of increased plasma volume observed with pioglitazone)

Triglycerides
(during clinical trials, mean decreases in triglycerides were observed)

Medical considerations/Contraindications

The medical considerations/contraindications included have been selected on the basis of their potential clinical significance (reasons given in parentheses where appropriate)—not necessarily inclusive (» = major clinical significance).

Except under special circumstances, this medication should not be used when the following medical problems exist:

» Diabetes mellitus, type 1 or
» Diabetic ketoacidosis
(pioglitazone lowers plasma glucose concentrations only in the presence of insulin)

» Hepatic function impairment
(pioglitazone should not be started in patients with clinical evidence of active liver disease or in patients with an alanine aminotransferase value greater than 2.5 times the upper limit of normal)

» Hypersensitivity to pioglitazone

Risk-benefit should be considered when the following medical problem exists:

» Congestive heart failure
(use is not recommended in patients with New York Heart Association [NYHA] Class III and IV cardiac status because pioglitazone causes plasma volume expansion; pioglitazone should be initiated at the lowest approved dose in patients with NYHA Class II systolic heart failure; if dose escalation is necessary, dose should be increased gradually only after several months of treatment with careful monitoring for weight gain, edema, or signs of CHF exacerbation)

Edema
(should be used with caution in patients with edema)

Patient monitoring

The following may be especially important in patient monitoring (other tests may be warranted in some patients, depending on condition; » = major clinical significance):

» Cardiac status including:
CHF exacerbation signs and symptoms or
Edema or
Weight gain
(treatment should be discontinued if any deterioration in cardiac status occurs; if dose escalation is necessary in patients with NYHA Class II systolic heart failure, dose should be increased gradually only after several months of treatment with careful monitoring)

» Glucose concentrations, fasting blood
(regular monitoring recommended to assess therapeutic efficacy)

» Glycosylated hemoglobin determinations
(regular monitoring recommended to assess long-term glycemic control)

» Liver function tests
(recommended if the patient develops symptoms, such as abdominal pain, anorexia, dark urine, fatigue, nausea, or vomiting, that are suggestive of hepatic dysfunction)

» Transaminase values
(recommended prior to the start of therapy, every 2 months for the first year of therapy, and periodically thereafter; pioglitazone should not be initiated in patients exhibiting clinical evidence of active liver disease or ALT values greater than 2.5 times the upper limit of normal and should be discontinued if values become and remain greater than three times the upper limit of normal or if the patient develops jaundice)

Side/Adverse Effects

Note: Pioglitazone does not stimulate insulin secretion and, administered alone, is not expected to cause hypoglycemia. However, there is a potential for hypoglycemia when pioglitazone is administered in conjunction with insulin, metformin, or a sulfonylurea.

In all U.S. clinical trials, edema was more frequent after treatment with pioglitazone than placebo. The incidence of edema was 4.8% and 1.2% following treatment with pioglitazone and placebo, respectively. Edema occurred in 15.3% of patients who received combination therapy with insulin and pioglitazone versus 7% of patients who received combination therapy with insulin and placebo. In post-marketing experience, reports of initiation or worsening of edema have been received. Caution should be exercised when pioglitazone is administered to patients with edema.

In post-marketing experience with pioglitazone, cases of congestive heart failure have been reported in patients with and without previously known heart disease. In a 24-week post-marketing safety study comparing pioglitazone to glyburide in uncontrolled diabetic patients with NYHA Class II and III heart failure, overnight hospitalization for congestive heart failure was reported in 9.9% of patients on pioglitazone compared to 4.7% of patients on glyburide with a treatment difference observed from 6 weeks. CHF associated with pioglitazone was more marked in patients using insulin at baseline and in patients over 64 years of age. No difference in cardiovascular mortality between the treatment groups was observed.. Additional reports of hepatitis and hepatic enzyme elevations have also been received.

The following side/adverse effects have been selected on the basis of their potential clinical significance (possible signs and symptoms in parentheses where appropriate)—not necessarily inclusive:

Those indicating need for medical attention

Incidence more frequent

Congestive heart failure (chest pain; decreased urine output; dilated neck veins; extreme fatigue; irregular breathing; irregular heartbeat; shortness of breath; swelling of face, fingers, feet, or lower legs; tightness in chest; troubled breathing; weight gain; wheezing); ***tooth disorders***—incidence 5.3%

Incidence less frequent

Edema (swelling)—incidence 4.8% in monotherapy studies

Incidence unknown

Weight gain—mechanism of weight gain unclear but probably involves a combination of fluid retention and fat accumulation

Those indicating need for medical attention only if they continue or are bothersome

Incidence more frequent

Diabetes mellitus aggravated (blurred vision; dry mouth; fatigue; flushed, dry skin; fruit-like breath odor; increased hunger; increased thirst; increased urination; loss of consciousness; nausea; stomachache; sweating; troubled breathing; unexplained weight loss; vomiting)—incidence 5.1%; ***headache***—incidence 9.1%; ***myalgia*** (muscle soreness)—incidence 5.4%; ***pharyngitis*** (sore throat)—incidence 5.1%; ***sinusitis*** (runny or stuffy nose)—incidence 6.3%; ***upper respiratory tract infection*** (cough; fever; runny or stuffy nose; sore throat)—incidence 13.2%

Incidence less frequent

Anemia (pale skin; troubled breathing with exertion; unusual bleeding or bruising; unusual tiredness or weakness)—incidence 1.0%

Overdose

For more information on the management of overdose or unintentional ingestion, **contact a Poison Control Center** (see *Poison Control Center Listing*).

Clinical effects of overdose

During clinical trials, one patient took pioglitazone at a dose of 120 mg a day for 4 days followed by 180 mg for 7 days. The patient did not have any clinical symptoms during this period.

Patient Consultation

As an aid to patient consultation, refer to *Advice for the Patient, Pioglitazone (Systemic)*.

In providing consultation, consider emphasizing the following selected information (» = major clinical significance):

Before using this medication

» Conditions affecting use, especially:

Hypersensitivity to pioglitazone

Fertility—Adequate contraception recommended in premenopausal women due to possible ovulation in some premenopausal anovulatory women taking pioglitazone

Pregnancy—Use of insulin alone is recommended during pregnancy for maintenance of blood glucose concentrations as close to normal as possible

Breast-feeding—Not recommended for use by nursing mothers

Use in the elderly—In a post-marketing safety study, congestive heart failure requiring hospitalization was more marked in patients over 64 years of age.

Other medications, especially ketoconazole

Other medical problems, especially congestive heart failure, diabetic ketoacidosis, hepatic function impairment, or type 1 diabetes

Proper use of this medication

» Importance of adherence to recommended regimens for diet, exercise, and glucose monitoring

May be taken with or without food

» Proper dosing

Missed dose: Taking as soon as possible if remembered the same day; if dose is missed on one day, not doubling dose the following day

Precautions while using this medication

» Reporting symptoms, such as abdominal pain, anorexia, dark urine, fatigue, jaundice, nausea, or vomiting, that are suggestive of hepatic dysfunction to physician immediately

» Regular visits to physician to check progress and monitor liver function

» *Carefully following special instructions of health care team:*

Discussing use of alcohol

Not taking other medications unless discussed with physician

Getting counseling for family members to help the patient with diabetes; also, special counseling for pregnancy planning and contraception

Making travel plans that include readiness for diabetic emergencies and eating meals at the usual times, even with changing time zones

» Preparing for and understanding what to do in case of diabetic emergency; carrying medical history and current medication list and wearing medical identification

» Recognizing what brings on symptoms of hypoglycemia, such as using other antidiabetic medication; delaying or missing a meal; exercising more than usual; drinking significant amounts of alcohol; or illness, including vomiting or diarrhea

» Recognizing symptoms of hypoglycemia: anxiety; behavior change similar to drunkenness; blurred vision; cold sweats; confusion; cool, pale skin; difficulty in concentrating; drowsiness; excessive hunger; fast heartbeat; headache; nausea; nervousness; nightmares; restless sleep; shakiness; slurred speech; or unusual tiredness or weakness

» Knowing what to do if symptoms of hypoglycemia occur, such as eating glucose tablets or gel, corn syrup, honey, or sugar cubes; drinking fruit juice, nondiet soft drink, or sugar dissolved in water; or injecting glucagon if symptoms are severe

» Recognizing what brings on symptoms of hyperglycemia, such as not taking enough or skipping a dose of antidiabetic medication, overeating or not following meal plan, having a fever or infection, or exercising less than usual

» Recognizing symptoms of hyperglycemia and ketoacidosis: blurred vision; drowsiness; dry mouth; flushed, dry skin; fruit-like breath odor; increased urination (frequency and volume); ketones in urine; loss of appetite; stomachache, nausea, or vomiting; tiredness; troubled breathing (rapid and deep); unconsciousness; and unusual thirst

» Knowing what to do if symptoms of hyperglycemia occur, such as checking blood glucose and contacting a member of the health care team

» Recognizing symptoms and knowing what to do in the case of possible fluid retention which may lead to, or exacerbate, congestive heart failure

Side/adverse effects

Signs of potential side effects, especially congestive heart failure, edema, and tooth disorders

General Dosing Information

Management of type 2 diabetes should include nutritional counseling, weight reduction as needed, and exercise. These are not only important in the primary treatment of the disease but also to maintain the efficacy of the drug therapy.

The management of antidiabetic therapy should be individualized using HbA_{1C} which reflects glycemia over the past two to three months. It is recommended that patients be treated with pioglitazone for a period of time adequate to evaluate change in HbA_{1C} unless glycemic control deteriorates.

Pioglitazone should be initiated at the lowest approved dose if it is prescribed for patients with type 2 diabetes who have systolic heart failure (NYHA Class II). If subsequent dose escalation is necessary, the dose should be increased gradually only after several months of treatment with careful monitoring for weight gain, edema, or signs and symptoms of CHF exacerbation.

Diet/Nutrition

Food slightly delays the time to peak serum concentration but does not alter the extent of absorption. Pioglitazone may be taken without regard to meals.

Oral Dosage Forms

PIOGLITAZONE TABLETS

Usual adult dose

Antidiabetic agent—

As monotherapy—

Oral, initially 15 or 30 mg once daily without regard to meals. If the patient has an inadequate response to pioglitazone, the dose may be increased in increments up to 45 mg once daily. For patients not responding adequately to monotherapy, combination therapy should be considered.

Note: Dose adjustment in patients with renal insufficiency is not recommended.

In combination with insulin[1]—

Oral, initially 15 or 30 mg once daily without regard to meals. When pioglitazone is initiated, the current insulin dose can be continued; however, if hypoglycemia occurs or if the plasma glucose concentration is 100 mg/dL or less, the dose of insulin should be decreased by 10% to 25%.

In combination with metformin[1]—

Oral, initially 15 or 30 mg once daily without regard to meals. When pioglitazone is initiated, the current metformin dose can be continued. The metformin dose is unlikely to require adjustment due to hypoglycemia.

In combination with a sulfonylurea[1]—

Oral, initially 15 or 30 mg once daily without regard to meals. When pioglitazone is initiated, the current sulfonylurea dose can be continued; however, if hypoglycemia occurs, the dose of the sulfonylurea should be decreased.

Usual adult prescribing limits

45 mg of pioglitazone daily. Doses greater than 30 mg once daily for combination therapy have not been studied in clinical trials.

Usual pediatric dose

Safety and efficacy have not been established.

Usual geriatric dose

See *Usual adult dose*.

Strength(s) usually available

U.S.—

15 mg (Rx) [*Actos* (lactose monohydrate NF; hydroxypropylcellulose NF; carboxymethylcellulose calcium NF; magnesium stearate NF)].

30 mg (Rx) [*Actos* (lactose monohydrate NF; hydroxypropylcellulose NF; carboxymethylcellulose calcium NF; magnesium stearate NF)].

45 mg (Rx) [*Actos* (lactose monohydrate NF; hydroxypropylcellulose NF; carboxymethylcellulose calcium NF; magnesium stearate NF)].

Canada—

15 mg (Rx) [*Actos* (lactose monohydrate; hydroxypropylcellulose; carboxymethylcellulose calcium; magnesium stearate)].

30 mg (Rx) [*Actos* (lactose monohydrate; hydroxypropylcellulose; carboxymethylcellulose calcium; magnesium stearate)].

45 mg (Rx) [*Actos* (lactose monohydrate; hydroxypropylcellulose; carboxymethylcellulose calcium; magnesium stearate)].

Packaging and storage

Store at 25°C (77 °F). with excursions permitted to 15 and 30 °C (59 to 86°F). Store in a tightly closed container. Protect from moisture and humidity.

---

[1]Not included in Canadian product labeling.

Revised: 09/03/2004
Developed: 01/20/2000

PIPERACILLIN—See *Penicillins (Systemic)*

PIPOTIAZINE—See *Phenothiazines (Systemic)*

PIRBUTEROL—See *Bronchodilators, Adrenergic (Inhalation-Local)*

PIRENZEPINE—See *Anticholinergics/Antispasmodics (Systemic)*

PIROXICAM—See *Anti-inflammatory Drugs, Nonsteroidal (Systemic)*

PIVAMPICILLIN—See *Penicillins (Systemic)*

PIVMECILLINAM—See *Penicillins (Systemic)*

PNEUMOCOCCAL CONJUGATE VACCINE Systemic

VA CLASSIFICATION (Primary): IM100

Note: This monograph refers to the 7–valent conjugate vaccine (Diphtheria CRM_{197} protein conjugate) licensed in the U.S.

Commonly used brand name(s): *Prevnar*™.

Note: For a listing of dosage forms and brand names by country availability, see *Dosage Forms* section(s).

Category

Immunizing agent (active).

Indications

General Considerations

Streptococcus pneumoniae is a bacterial pathogen that causes invasive infections, such as bacteremia and meningitis, as well as pneumonia and upper respiratory tract infections, in adults and children worldwide.

In children older than 1 month, *S. pneumoniae* is the most common cause of invasive disease. Children in group child care have an increased risk of invasive pneumococcal disease. Pneumococcal meningitis in children between 1 and 23 months of age occurs at a rate of approximately 7 cases per 100,000 persons per year and has been associated with 8% mortality. Survivors may suffer neurological sequelae (25%) and hearing loss (32%).

Twenty to forty percent of cases of acute otitis media are associated with *S. pneumoniae*. The 7 serotypes contained in the pneumococcal 7–valent conjugate vaccine account for 60% of acute otitis media due to *S. pneumoniae*. Seventy percent of cases of community-acquired bacterial pneumonia are caused by *S. pneumoniae*. Approximately 80% of invasive pneumococcal disease in children under 6 years of age in the U.S. is attributable to the 7 serotypes of *S. pneumoniae* represented in the 7–valent conjugate vaccine.

Accepted

Pneumococcal disease (prophylaxis)—Pneumococcal 7–valent conjugate vaccine is indicated for active immunization of infants and toddlers against invasive disease caused by *S. pneumoniae* of capsular serotypes 4, 6B, 9V, 14, 18C, 19F, and 23F.

The vaccine is not intended for active infection.

The use of this vaccine does not replace the use of 23–valent pneumococcal polysaccharide vaccine in children >24 months of age with sickle cell disease, asplenia, HIV infection, chronic illness, or who are immunocompromised.

Pharmacology/Pharmacokinetics

Physicochemical characteristics

Source—The 7–valent conjugate vaccine contains the saccharides of the capsular antigens of the 7 *Streptococcus pneumoniae* serotypes 4, 6B, 9V, 14, 18C, 19F, and 23F, which cause 80% of invasive pneumococcal disease in children under 6 years of age in the U.S. Polysaccharides derived from the serotypes are purified and chemically activated to make saccharides, which are then conjugated to the protein carrier CRM_{197} to form the glycoconjugate. CRM_{197} is a nontoxic variant of diphtheria toxin isolated from cultures of *Corynebacterium diphtheriae*. The individual glycoconjugates are compounded to formulate the 7–valent conjugate vaccine, which provides 2 mcg of each saccharide of serotypes 4, 9V, 14, 18C, 19F, and 23F, and 4 mcg of serotype 6B per 0.5 mL dose. Each 0.5 mL dose also contains 20 mcg of CRM_{197} and 0.125 mg of aluminum as aluminum phosphate adjuvant.

Mechanism of action/Effect

The 7–valent conjugate vaccine induces functional antibodies to all vaccine serotypes, as measured by opsonophagocytosis following 3 doses.

Protective effect—

In a double-blind clinical trial, 37,816 infants were randomized to receive pneumococcal 7–valent conjugate vaccine or an investigational meningococcal group C conjugate vaccine (control) at 2, 4, 6 and 12 to 15 months of age. Per protocol analysis of the primary endpoint for efficacy included cases of pneumococcal disease due to serotypes represented in the 7–valent vaccine occurring 14 or more days after the third dose. At the time when 17 cases had occurred in the control group, no cases had occurred in the pneumococcal vaccine group. Preliminary efficacy data through an extended follow-up period to April, 1999 (4.5 years after the start of the study), showed 1 case in the pneumococcal vaccine group and 39 cases in the control group. Intent-to-treat analysis (including all cases among children who had received at least one dose of vaccine) showed similar efficacy: 3 cases in the pneumococcal vaccine group and 49 cases in the control group.

This vaccine does not protect against *S. pneumoniae* disease other than that caused by the 7 serotypes included in the vaccine, nor will it protect against other microorganisms that cause similar disease. It is not intended to replace the 23–valent vaccine in children > 24 months of age with sickle cell disease, asplenia, HIV infection, chronic illness or who are immunocompromised. It is also not recommended for use in adult populations.

Immunization with this vaccine does not substitute for routine diphtheria immunization.

Precautions to Consider

Carcinogenicity/Tumorigenicity/Mutagenicity

The pneumococcal 7–valent conjugate vaccine has not been evaluated for any carcinogenic or mutagenic potential.

Pregnancy/Reproduction
Fertility—This vaccine has not been evaluated for impairment of fertility.

Pregnancy—Studies have not been done in humans. The pneumococcal 7–valent conjugate vaccine is not recommended for use in pregnant women.

FDA Pregnancy Category C.

Breast-feeding
It is not known whether vaccine antigens or antibodies are distributed into breast milk. This vaccine is not recommended for use in nursing mothers.

Pediatrics
Infants younger than 6 weeks of age—The safety and effectiveness of this vaccine in children below the age of 6 weeks has not been established.

Infants born prematurely—Immune responses elicited by this vaccine in infants born prematurely have not been studied.

Children 7 months through 9 years of age—Immune responses of previously unvaccinated children in this age group to this vaccine appear to be comparable to responses of younger children.

Geriatrics
This vaccine is not recommended for use in adult populations and is not to be used as a substitute for the 23–valent pneumococcal polysaccharide vaccine in geriatric populations.

Drug interactions and/or related problems
The following drug interactions and/or related problems have been selected on the basis of their potential clinical significance (possible mechanism in parentheses where appropriate)—not necessarily inclusive (» = major clinical significance):

Note: Combinations containing any of the following medications, depending on the amount present, may also interact with this medication.

Anticoagulant therapy
(increased risk of bleeding with intramuscular injection)

Immunosuppressive agents
(impaired immunoresponsiveness may reduce the antibody response to immunization)

Medical considerations/Contraindications
The medical considerations/contraindications included have been selected on the basis of their potential clinical significance (reasons given in parentheses where appropriate)—not necessarily inclusive (» = major clinical significance).

Risk-benefit should be considered when the following medical problems exist:

Febrile illness, moderate to severe
(minor illnesses, such as a mild upper respiratory infection with or without low-grade fever, do not preclude administration of the vaccine)

Impaired immune responsiveness
(may reduce antibody response to active immunization)

Sensitivity to pneumococcal vaccine, including diptheria toxoid
(antigens of pneumococcal serotypes are conjugated to diptheria toxin)

Sensitivity to latex
(packaging contains dry natural rubber)

Thrombocytopenia or other coagulation disorder
(intramuscular administration may cause excessive bleeding)

Side/Adverse Effects
The following side/adverse effects have been selected on the basis of their potential clinical significance (possible signs and symptoms in parentheses where appropriate)—not necessarily inclusive:

Those indicating need for medical attention
Incidence less frequent

Fever over 39°C (102.2°F)

Incidence rare

Hypotonic-hyporesponsive episode (collapse or shock-like state)—3 cases reported; all received concurrent DTP vaccine; ***seizures*** (convulsions)

Those indicating need for medical attention only if they continue or are bothersome
Incidence more frequent

Decreased appetite; diarrhea (increase in bowel movements; loose stools; soft stools); ***drowsiness; fever of less than 39°C (102.2°F); irritability; redness, soreness, hard lump, swelling, or pain at injection site; restless sleep; vomiting***

Incidence less frequent

Skin rash or hives

Patient Consultation
As an aid to patient consultation, refer to *Advice for the Patient, Pneumococcal Conjugate Vaccine (Systemic)*.

In providing consultation, consider emphasizing the following selected information (» = major clinical significance):

Before using this medication
» Conditions affecting use, especially:

Sensitivity to pneumococcal vaccine components, including diphtheria toxoid and latex

Use in children—Safety and efficacy in infants below 6 weeks of age not established

Use in the elderly—Not recommended for use in adult populations

Proper use of this medication
» Proper dosing

Precautions after receiving this vaccine
» Notifying all patient's physicians that patient has received pneumococcal conjugate vaccine so that the information can be included in patient's medical records

Side/adverse effects
Signs of potential side effects, especially fever over 39 °C (102.2 °F), hypotonic-hyporesponsive episode, and seizures

General Dosing Information
Pneumococcal conjugate vaccine is usually well tolerated in infants. However, as with any biological, appropriate precautions should be taken prior to vaccine administration to prevent allergic or any other unwanted reactions. Precautions should include review of the patient's history regarding possible sensitivity and the ready availability of 1:1000 epinephrine injection and other appropriate agents used for control of immediate allergic reactions.

Pneumococcal conjugate is administered by intramuscular injection only. Care should be taken to prevent injection into or near a blood vessel or nerve.

A single dose is the same for all individuals; however, the number of doses depends on age at which the first dose is received.

Pneumococcal conjugate vaccine may be administered simultaneously with other vaccines (at separate sites). In clinical studies, pneumococcal conjugate vaccine has been administered with DTP-HbOC, DTaP and HbOC, OPV or IPV, Hep B vaccines, MMR, and varicella vaccine.

The use of pneumococcal conjugate vaccine does not replace the use of 23–valent pneumococcal polysaccharide vaccine in children over 24 months of age with sickle cell disease, HIV infection, chronic illness, or who are immunocompromised.

Parenteral Dosage Forms

PNEUMOCOCCAL CONJUGATE VACCINE INJECTION

Usual adult dose
Use of pneumococcal conjugate vaccine is not recommended in adults

Usual pediatric dose
Immunizing agent (active)—

Intramuscular, 0.5 mL, preferably in the anterolateral aspect of the thigh in infants or the deltoid muscle of the upper arm in toddlers and young children, according to the following dosing schedules:

Infants—

First dose—At 2 months of age.

Note: The vaccine series may be initiated as early as 6 weeks of age. The recommended dosing interval is 4 to 8 weeks.

Second dose—At 4 months of age.

Third dose—6 months of age.

Fourth dose—12 to 15 months of age.

Older infants and children—

Age 7 to 11 months at first dose—Two doses, two months apart, then a third dose after the 1–year birthday, separated from the second dose by at least 2 months.

Age 12 to 23 months—Two doses at least 2 months apart.

Age 24 months through 9 years—One dose.

Usual geriatric dose
Use of pneumococcal conjugate vaccine is not recommended in geriatric patients.

Strength(s) usually available

U.S.—

16 mcg total saccharide (2 mcg of each saccharide for serotypes 4, 9V, 14, 18C, 19F, and 23F, and 4 mcg of serotype 6B) and 20 mcg of diphtheria CRM_{197} protein (Rx) [*Prevnar*™ (single dose vials; 5 per package; 0.125 mg of aluminum per 0.5 mL dose as aluminum phosphate adjuvant)].

Packaging and storage

Store between 2 and 8°C (36 and 46 °F). Do not freeze.

Auxiliary labeling

- Shake the vial vigorously immediately before use in order to resuspend the contents.

Caution

The vaccine should not be used if it cannot be resuspended.

Additional information

After shaking, the vaccine is a homogeneous suspension.

Developed: 05/05/2000

PNEUMOCOCCAL VACCINE POLYVALENT Systemic

VA CLASSIFICATION (Primary): IM100

Note: This monograph refers to the 23-valent pneumococcal vaccine polyvalent licensed in the U.S. and Canada.

Commonly used brand name(s): *Pneumovax 23; Pnu-Imune 23.*

Note: For a listing of dosage forms and brand names by country availability, see *Dosage Forms* section(s).

Category

Immunizing agent (active).

Indications

General Considerations

Streptococcus pneumoniae is a bacterial pathogen that affects adults and children worldwide. It is a leading cause of illness in young children and causes illness and death among the elderly and persons who have certain underlying medical conditions.

The organism colonizes the upper respiratory tract and can cause the following types of illnesses:
- Disseminated invasive infections, including bacteremia and meningitis.
- Pneumonia and other lower respiratory tract infections.
- Upper respiratory infections, including otitis media and sinusitis.

Each year in the U.S., pneumococcal disease accounts for an estimated 3000 cases of meningitis, 50,000 cases of bacteremia, 500,000 cases of pneumonia, and 7 million cases of otitis media.

Children younger than 2 years of age and adults 65 years of age and older are at increased risk for pneumococcal infection. Persons who have certain underlying medical conditions also are at increased risk for developing pneumococcal infection or experiencing severe disease and complications. Adults at increased risk include those who are generally immunocompetent but who have chronic cardiovascular diseases (e.g., congestive heart failure or cardiomyopathy), chronic pulmonary diseases (e.g., chronic obstructive pulmonary disease [COPD] or emphysema), or chronic liver diseases (e.g., cirrhosis). Diabetes mellitus often is associated with cardiovascular or renal dysfunction, which increases the risk for severe pneumococcal illness. The incidence of pneumococcal infection is increased for persons who have liver disease as a result of alcohol abuse. Asthma has not been associated with an increased risk for pneumococcal disease, unless it occurs with chronic bronchitis, emphysema, or long-term use of systemic corticosteroids.

Persons with functional or anatomic asplenia (e.g., sickle cell disease or splenectomy) are at highest risk for pneumococcal infection, because this condition leads to reduced clearance of encapsulated bacteria from the blood stream. Children who have sickle cell disease or have had splenectomy are at increased risk for fulminant pneumococcal sepsis associated with high mortality.

The risk for pneumococcal infection is high for persons who have decreased responsiveness to polysaccharide antigens or an increased rate of decline in serum antibody concentrations as a result of:
- Immunosuppressive conditions (e.g., congenital immunodeficiency, human immunodeficiency virus [HIV] infection, leukemia, lymphoma, multiple myeloma, Hodgkin's disease, or generalized malignancy).
- Organ or bone marrow transplantation.
- Therapy with alkylating agents, antimetabolites, or systemic corticosteroids.
- Chronic renal failure or nephrotic syndrome.

S. pneumoniae is the most commonly identified bacterial pathogen that causes pneumonia in HIV-infected persons. In children, invasive pneumococcal disease often is the first clinical manifestation of HIV infection.

Most disease caused by *S. pneumoniae* in persons 2 years of age and older, including disease caused by strains with reduced antibiotic susceptibility, can be prevented by increasing the use of pneumococcal vaccine polyvalent among persons at increased risk for serious pneumococcal disease.

Because the indications for pneumococcal and influenza vaccines are similar, the time of administration of influenza vaccine, including mass vaccination at outpatient clinics, should be used as an opportunity to identify patients at risk for pneumococcal disease and vaccinate them with pneumococcal vaccine. However, influenza vaccine is administered once each year, whereas pneumococcal vaccine typically is administered only one time for persons in most groups (see *General Dosing Information*).

The use of pneumococcal polysaccharide vaccine consistently has been recommended by the Advisory Committee on Immunization Practices of the Centers for Disease Control and Prevention (CDC), the American Academy of Pediatrics (AAP), the American College of Physicians (ACP), and the American Academy of Family Physicians (AAFP). Most persons considered at risk for pneumococcal infection also should receive annual influenza vaccination.

Accepted

Pneumococcal disease (prophylaxis)—Pneumococcal vaccine polyvalent is indicated for immunization against pneumococcal disease caused by any of the 23 pneumococcal types included in the vaccine.

Unless otherwise contraindicated, all adults and children 2 years of age and older should be immunized against pneumococcal disease, especially:
- Persons 65 years of age and older. All persons 65 years of age and older should receive pneumococcal vaccine polyvalent, including previously unvaccinated persons and those who have not received the vaccine within 5 years and were younger than 65 years of age at the time of vaccination. All persons who have unknown vaccination status should receive one dose of pneumococcal vaccine polyvalent.
- Persons 2 to 64 years of age who have chronic illness. Persons 2 to 64 years of age who are at increased risk for pneumococcal disease or its complications if they become infected should be vaccinated. Persons at increased risk for severe disease include those with chronic illness such as chronic cardiovascular disease (e.g., congestive heart failure [CHF] or cardiomyopathies), chronic pulmonary disease (e.g., COPD or emphysema, but not asthma), diabetes mellitus, alcoholism, chronic liver disease (cirrhosis), or cerebrospinal fluid (CSF) leaks. Persons 50 to 64 years of age commonly have chronic illness, and 12% have pulmonary risk factors for invasive pneumococcal disease. Therefore, persons in this age group who have these risk factors should receive the vaccine. All persons at 50 years of age should have their overall vaccination status reviewed to determine whether they have risk factors that indicate a need for pneumococcal vaccination. Vaccination status also should be assessed during the adolescent immunization visit at 11 to 12 years of age.
- Persons 2 to 64 years of age who have functional or anatomic asplenia (e.g., sickle cell disease or splenectomy). Persons with such a condition should be informed that vaccination does not guarantee protection against fulminant pneumococcal disease, for which the case-fatality rate is 50 to 80%. Asplenic patients with unexplained fever or manifestations of sepsis should receive prompt medical attention, including evaluation and treatment for suspected bacteremia. Chemoprophylaxis also should be considered in these patients. When elective splenectomy is being planned, pneumococcal vaccine polyvalent should be administered at least 2 weeks before surgery.
- Persons 2 to 64 years of age who are living in special environments or social settings in which the risk for invasive pneumococcal disease or its complications is increased (e.g., Alaskan Natives and certain American Indian populations). In addition, because of reported outbreaks of pneumococcal disease, vaccination status should be assessed for residents of nursing homes and other long-term-care facil-

ities. Available data do not support routine pneumococcal vaccination of healthy children attending day care facilities. Recurrent upper respiratory tract diseases, including otitis media and sinusitis, are not specific indications for pneumococcal vaccination.

• Immunocompromised persons. Persons who have conditions associated with decreased immunologic function that increase the risk for severe pneumococcal disease or its complications should be vaccinated. Although the vaccine is not as effective for immunocompromised patients as it is for immunocompetent persons, the potential benefits and safety of the vaccine justify its use. Pneumococcal vaccine polyvalent is recommended for the following groups of immuncompromised persons 2 years of age and older:

—Persons with HIV infection, leukemia, lymphoma, Hodgkin's disease, multiple myeloma, generalized malignancy, chronic renal failure, and nephrotic syndrome.

—Persons with other conditions associated with immunosuppression (e.g., organ or bone marrow transplantation).

—Persons receiving immunosuppressive chemotherapy, including long-term systemic corticosteroids.

If earlier vaccination status is unknown, immunocompromised persons should be administered pneumococcal vaccine polyvalent.

Pharmacology/Pharmacokinetics

Physicochemical characteristics

Source—The currently available vaccines in the U.S. and Canada contain a mixture of purified capsular polysaccharides from the 23 most prevalent pneumococcal types responsible for 85 to 90% of serious pneumococcal disease. Each of the pneumococcal polysaccharide types is produced separately. The resultant 23 polysaccharides are separated from the cells, purified, and combined to give 25 mcg of each type per 0.5-mL dose of the final vaccine.

Other characteristics—

The U.S. nomenclature for these 23 types is: 1, 2, 3, 4, 5, 26, 51, 8, 9, 68, 34, 43, 12, 14, 54, 17, 56, 57, 19, 20, 22, 23, 70.

The Danish nomenclature for these 23 types is: 1, 2, 3, 4, 5, 6B, 7F, 8, 9N, 9V, 10A, 11A, 12F, 14, 15B, 17F, 18C, 19A, 19F, 20, 22F, 23F, 33F.

Mechanism of action/Effect

Pneumococcal capsular polysaccharide antigens induce type-specific antibodies that enhance opsonization, phagocytosis, and killing of pneumococci by leukocytes and other phagocytic cells.

Protective effect

The protective efficacy of pneumococcal vaccines containing 6 and 12 capsular polysaccharides was investigated in two controlled studies in gold miners in South Africa, in whom there is a high attack rate for pneumococcal pneumonia. Capsular type-specific attack rates for pneumococcal pneumonia were observed for the period from 2 weeks through about 1 year after vaccination. Protective efficacy for the vaccines containing 6 and 12 capsular polysaccharides was 76% and 92%, respectively, for the capsular types represented in the vaccines.

In similar studies using similar pneumococcal vaccines prepared for the National Institute of Allergy and Infectious Diseases, the reduction in pneumonia resulting from use of the capsular types contained in the vaccines was 79%. Reduction in type-specific pneumococcal bacteremia was 82%. A preliminary report suggests that in patients 2 years of age and older with sickle cell anemia and/or anatomical or functional asplenia, the vaccine is highly effective in preventing severe pneumococcal disease and bacteremia.

Time to protective effect

After vaccination, an antigen-specific antibody response, indicated by a twofold or greater rise in serotype-specific antibody, develops within 2 to 3 weeks in more than 80% of healthy adults; however, immune responses may not be consistent among all 23 serotypes in the vaccine.

Duration of protective effect

The duration of protective effect of the 23-valent pneumococcal vaccine polyvalent is unknown. However, in previous studies with other pneumococcal vaccines, it has been shown that antibody induced by the vaccine may persist for as long as 5 years. Type-specific antibody levels induced by the 14-valent pneumococcal vaccine have been observed to decline over a 42-month period but to remain significantly above prevaccination levels in almost all recipients who manifest an initial response. However, these quantitative measurements of antibodies do not account for the quality of the antibody being produced and the level of functional immune response. Tests measuring opsonophagocytic activity and the quality of antibodies produced (i.e., avidity for pneumococcal antigens) may be more relevant for evaluating response to pneumococcal vaccination.

Precautions to Consider

Pregnancy/Reproduction

Pregnancy—Studies have not been done in humans. No adverse consequences have been reported among newborns whose mothers inadvertently were vaccinated during pregnancy. However, if the vaccine is administered during pregnancy, it should be given after the first trimester and only to women at high risk for pneumococcal disease.

Studies have not been done in animals.

FDA Pregnancy Category C.

Breast-feeding

It is not known whether pneumococcal vaccine is distributed into breast milk. However, problems in humans have not been documented.

Pediatrics

Note: The incidence of bacteremia and meningitis due to *Streptococcus pneumoniae* is highest among preschool-age children, particularly among children younger than 2 years of age. *S. pneumoniae* is also the pathogen most commonly associated with acute otitis media, accounting for 20 to 48% of cases. Despite a critical need for a means to prevent pneumococcal disease among young children, effective vaccines are not available for children younger than 2 years of age.

The results of a multicenter study demonstrated that oral penicillin V (125 mg twice a day) given to infants and young children with sickle cell anemia reduced the incidence of severe bacteremia infection by 84% compared with a placebo control group. Therefore, daily penicillin prophylaxis for children with sickle cell anemia beginning before 2 months of age or earlier is recommended.

Infants and children younger than 2 years of age—Immunization is not recommended for infants and children younger than 2 years of age, since this age group may not show adequate response to many of the antigens, and antibody levels stimulated by the vaccine may not persist.

Children 2 years of age and older—Age-specific immune responses vary by serotype, and the response to some common pediatric pneumococcal serotypes (e.g., 6A and 14) is decreased in children 2 to 5 years of age. Other pediatrics-specific problems that would limit the usefulness of this vaccine in children 2 years of age and older are not expected.

Geriatrics

Appropriate studies on the relationship of age to the effects of pneumococcal vaccine have not been performed in the geriatric population. However, geriatrics-specific problems that would limit the usefulness of this vaccine in the elderly are not expected.

Drug interactions and/or related problems

The following drug interactions and/or related problems have been selected on the basis of their potential clinical significance (possible mechanism in parentheses where appropriate)—not necessarily inclusive (» = major clinical significance):

Note: Combinations containing any of the following medications, depending on the amount present, may also interact with this medication.

Immunosuppressive agents or
Radiation therapy
(because normal defense mechanisms are suppressed, the patient's antibody response to the pneumococcal vaccine may be decreased. If possible, persons who are to undergo therapy with medications that cause immunosuppression, including candidates for organ transplants, should receive the vaccine at least 10 days, and preferably more than 14 days, prior to receiving the immunosuppression-causing medication to receive the full immunizing effect of the vaccine. The precaution does not apply to corticosteroids used as replacement therapy, for short-term [less than 2 weeks] systemic therapy, or by other routes of administration that do not cause immunosuppression)
(patients with Hodgkin's disease should not receive the vaccine less than 2 weeks prior to, or during, immunosuppressive therapy, since some patients so immunized have exhibited postimmunization antibody levels below their preimmunization levels. In addition, patients with Hodgkin's disease who have received extensive chemotherapy and/or nodal irradiation should not receive the vaccine at all, since immunization of some intensively treated patients caused depression of pre-existing levels of antibody to some pneumococcal types)

Medical considerations/Contraindications

The medical considerations/contraindications included have been selected on the basis of their potential clinical significance (reasons

given in parentheses where appropriate)—not necessarily inclusive (» = major clinical significance).

Except under special circumstances, this medication should not be used when the following medical problems exist:

» Anaphylactic reaction or
» Arthus-type reaction, localized
(revaccination is contraindicated for persons who have experienced severe reaction to the initial dose)

Risk-benefit should be considered when the following medical problems exist:

Febrile illness, severe
(to avoid confusing manifestations of illness with possible side/adverse effects of vaccine; minor illnesses, such as upper respiratory infection, do not preclude administration of vaccine)

Sensitivity to pneumococcal vaccine

Sensitivity to thimerosal
(patients allergic to thimerosal may be allergic to the pneumococcal vaccine available in the U.S. because it may contain a small amount of thimerosal)

Thrombocytopenic purpura, idiopathic
(in one report, two stabilized patients experienced a relapse 2 to 14 days after vaccination; this relapse lasted up to 2 weeks)

Side/Adverse Effects

Note: No neurologic disorders (e.g., Guillain-Barré syndrome [GBS]) have been associated with administration of pneumococcal vaccine polyvalent. Although preliminary data have suggested that the pneumococcal vaccine polyvalent may cause transient increases in HIV replication, the importance of this occurrence is unknown. Pneumococcal vaccination has not been causally associated with death among vaccine recipients.

Early studies have indicated that local reactions (i.e., Arthus-type reactions) among adults receiving the second dose of 14-valent vaccine within 2 years after the first dose are more severe than those occurring after initial vaccination. However, subsequent studies have suggested that revaccination after intervals of 4 years or more is not associated with an increased incidence of side effects. Although severe local reactions may occur following a second dose of pneumococcal vaccine polyvalent, the rate of adverse reactions is not greater than the rate after the first dose. An evaluation of 1000 elderly patients who received a second dose of pneumococcal vaccine polyvalent indicated that they were not significantly more likely to be hospitalized in the 30 days after vaccination than were the approximately 66,000 persons who received their first dose of vaccine. No data are available to allow estimates of adverse reaction rates among persons who received more than two doses of pneumococcal vaccine.

The following side/adverse effects have been selected on the basis of their potential clinical significance (possible signs and symptoms in parentheses where appropriate)—not necessarily inclusive:

Those indicating need for medical attention

Incidence rare

Anaphylactic reaction (difficulty in breathing or swallowing; hives; itching, especially of soles or palms; reddening of skin, especially around ears; swelling of eyes, face, or inside of nose; unusual tiredness or weakness, sudden and severe); ***fever over 39 °C (102.2 °F)***

Those indicating need for medical attention only if they continue or are bothersome

Incidence more frequent

Redness, soreness, hard lump, swelling, or pain at injection site

Incidence less frequent or rare

Adenitis (swollen glands); ***arthralgia or myalgia*** (aches or pain in joints or muscles); ***asthenia*** (unusual tiredness or weakness); ***fever of 38.3 °C (101 °F) or less; malaise*** (vague feeling of bodily discomfort); ***skin rash***

Patient Consultation

As an aid to patient consultation, refer to *Advice for the Patient, Pneumococcal Vaccine Polyvalent (Systemic).*

In providing consultation, consider emphasizing the following selected information (» = major clinical significance):

Before receiving this vaccine

» Conditions affecting use, especially:
Sensitivity to pneumococcal vaccine or thimerosal
Pregnancy—Vaccine should be administered following the first trimester and only to women at high risk for pneumococcal disease
Use in children—Not recommended for infants and children younger than 2 years of age
Other medical problems, especially anaphylactic reaction or localized Arthus-type reaction

Proper use of this medication

» Proper dosing

Precautions after receiving this vaccine

» Notifying all patient's physicians that patient has received pneumococcal vaccine polyvalent 23 so that the information can be included in patient's medical records; the vaccine usually is administered only once

Side/adverse effects

Signs of potential side effects, especially anaphylactic reaction or fever over 39 °C (102.2 °F)

General Dosing Information

Pneumococcal vaccine polyvalent generally is considered safe based on the clinical experience in the U.S. However, severe systemic adverse effects (e.g., anaphylactic reactions) rarely have been reported among vaccine recipients. Therefore, appropriate precautions should be taken prior to pneumococcal vaccine polyvalent injection to prevent allergic or any other unwanted reactions. Precautions should include review of the patient's history regarding possible sensitivity and the ready availability of 1:1000 epinephrine injection and other appropriate agents used for control of immediate allergic reactions.

The dosage of pneumococcal vaccine polyvalent is the same for all persons—children and adults.

When sterilizing syringes before vaccination, care should be taken to avoid preservatives, antiseptics, detergents, and disinfectants, since the vaccine is easily inactivated by these substances.

Pneumococcal vaccine polyvalent is administered by subcutaneous or intramuscular injection. It is not recommended for intradermal injection, because it may cause severe local reactions. Also, intravenous administration is not recommended.

Persons with asymptomatic or symptomatic human immunodeficiency virus (HIV) infection should be vaccinated as soon as possible after their diagnosis is confirmed. Plasma HIV levels have been found to be transiently elevated after pneumococcal vaccination in some studies; other studies have not demonstrated such an elevation. However, no adverse effects of pneumococcal vaccination on patient survival have been detected. When cancer chemotherapy or other immunosuppressive therapy is being considered (e.g., for patients with Hodgkin's disease or those who undergo organ or bone marrow transplantation), the interval between vaccination and initiation of immunosuppressive therapy should be at least 2 weeks. Vaccination during chemotherapy or radiation therapy should be avoided.

Routine revaccination of immunocompetent persons previously unvaccinated with the 23-valent vaccine is not recommended. However, revaccination once is recommended for persons 2 years of age and older who are at highest risk for serious pneumococcal infection and those who are likely to have rapid decline in pneumococcal antibody levels, provided that 5 years have elapsed since receipt of the first dose of pneumococcal vaccine. Revaccination 3 years after the previous dose may be considered for children at highest risk for severe pneumococcal infection who would be 10 years of age or younger at the time of revaccination. These children include those with functional or anatomic asplenia (e.g., sickle cell disease or splenectomy) and those with conditions associated with rapid decline after initial vaccination (e.g., nephrotic syndrome, renal failure, or renal transplantation).

Persons at highest risk and those most likely to have rapid declines in antibody levels include persons with functional or anatomic asplenia, HIV infection, leukemia, lymphoma, Hodgkin's disease, multiple myeloma, generalized malignancy, chronic renal failure, nephrotic syndrome, or other conditions associated with immunosuppression (e.g., organ or bone marrow transplantation), and those receiving immunosuppressive chemotherapy (including long-term systemic corticosteroids). If vaccination status is unknown, patients in these categories should be administered pneumococcal vaccine.

Elderly persons 65 years of age and older should be administered a second dose of vaccine if they received the vaccine 5 years or more previously and were younger than 65 years of age at the time of primary vaccination. Elderly persons with unknown vaccination status should be administered one dose of pneumococcal vaccine.

Pneumococcal vaccine polyvalent, a polysaccharide vaccine, can be administered concurrently with other vaccines, using separate body sites, separate syringes, and the precautions that apply to each immunizing agent. No data indicate that administration of pneumococcal vaccine with measles, mumps, and rubella virus vaccine live, diphtheria toxoid, tetanus toxoid, and pertussis vaccine (DTP), poliovirus vaccines (oral [OPV], inactivated [IPV], or enhanced-potency inactivated [eIPV]), *Haemophilus influenzae* type b vaccine, hepatitis B vaccine, influenza virus vaccine, or other vaccines increases the severity of reactions or diminishes antibody response.

Patients who require antibiotic prophylaxis against pneumococcal infection should continue to receive antibiotic therapy after vaccination with pneumococcal vaccine.

For treatment of adverse effects

Recommended treatment includes

- For mild hypersensitivity reaction—Administering antihistamines, and, if necessary, corticosteroids.
- For severe hypersensitivity or anaphylactic reaction—Administering epinephrine. Antihistamines or corticosteroids may also be administered as required.

Parenteral Dosage Forms

PNEUMOCOCCAL VACCINE POLYVALENT INJECTION

Usual adult and adolescent dose

Immunizing agent (active)—

Intramuscular or subcutaneous, 0.5 mL, preferably into the outer aspect of the upper arm or into the lateral mid-thigh.

Usual pediatric dose

Immunizing agent (active)—

Infants and children up to 2 years of age: Use is not recommended, since this age group may not show adequate response to many of the antigens, and antibody levels stimulated by the vaccine may not persist.

Children 2 years of age and older: See *Usual adult and adolescent dose.*

Strength(s) usually available

U.S.—

25 mcg of polysaccharide from each of the 23 capsular types of pneumococci represented in the vaccine in each 0.5 mL dose (Rx) [*Pneumovax 23* (phenol 0.25%); *Pnu-Imune 23* (thimerosal 0.01%)].

Canada—

25 mcg of polysaccharide from each of the 23 capsular types of pneumococci represented in the vaccine in each 0.5 mL dose (Rx) [*Pneumovax 23* (phenol 0.25%)].

Packaging and storage

Store manufacturer-supplied filled syringes, unopened vials, and partially used vials of the vaccine between 2 and 8 °C (36 and 46 °F), unless otherwise specified by manufacturer. Protect from freezing.

Stability

The vaccine is a clear, colorless solution. It should not be used if it is discolored or contains a precipitate.

Incompatibilities

A sterile syringe free of preservatives, antiseptics, disinfectants, and detergents should be used for each injection because these substances may inactivate the vaccine.

Auxiliary labeling

- Store in refrigerator.

Selected Bibliography

Centers for Disease Control and Prevention (CDC). Recommendations of the Advisory Committee on Immunization Practices—prevention of pneumococcal disease. MMWR Morb Mortal Wkly Rep 1997; 46(RR-8): 1-24.

Revised: 02/02/1999

PODOFILOX Topical

BAN: Podophyllotoxin

VA CLASSIFICATION (Primary): DE500

Commonly used brand name(s): *Condylox.*

Another commonly used name is podophyllotoxin.

Note: For a listing of dosage forms and brand names by country availability, see *Dosage Forms* section(s).

Category

Antimitotic agent (topical).

Indications

Accepted

Condyloma acuminatum (treatment)—Podofilox is indicated for the treatment of condyloma acuminatum of the external genital areas; the gel, but not the solution, may be used for perianal warts. Neither the gel nor the solution should be used to treat warts on mucous membranes, including membranous areas of the urethra, rectum, and vagina.

Using a 3-day-on and 4-day-off treatment regimen of 0.5% podofilox solution for 2 to 4 weeks, 50% of patients (35 of 75 patients) showed clearing of up to 79% of their warts (412 of 524 warts); 35% of the warts reappeared in 60% of these patients. In two multicenter clinical studies using a 3-day-on and 4-day-off treatment regimen of 0.5% gel for 4 weeks, 25.6% of 106 patients and 38.4% of 176 patients showed complete clearing of their anogenital warts.

Pharmacology/Pharmacokinetics

Physicochemical characteristics

Source—Synthesized and purified from the plant families Coniferae (species of *Juniperus*) and Berberidaceae (species of *Podophyllum*).

Molecular weight—414.41.

Mechanism of action/Effect

The exact mechanism of action for podofilox is unknown. Podofilox is a potent mitotoxic agent that inhibits cell mitosis; cell division stops, other cellular processes are impaired, necrosis occurs, and the affected tissues gradually erode.

Absorption

Applying 0.05 mL of 0.5% podofilox solution topically to external genitals does not result in detectable serum concentrations; however, applying 0.1 to 1.5 mL results in systemic absorption. Multiple doses do not accumulate.

Half-life

Elimination—1 to 4.5 hours.

Time to peak concentration

Topically, 0.1 to 1.5 mL of 0.05% podofilox solution—1 to 2 hours.

Peak serum concentration

Topically, 0.1 to 1.5 mL of 0.05% podofilox solution—1 to 17 nanograms per mL.

Precautions to Consider

Carcinogenicity

Animal studies have not shown podofilox to be carcinogenic, including one study of podofilox topically administered to mice in doses of 0.04, 0.2, and 1 mg per kg of body weight (mg/kg) a day for 80 weeks.

Mutagenicity

Podofilox is not mutagenic according to the Ames plate reverse mutation assay (at concentrations up to 5 mg podofilox, with or without metabolic activation) and BALB/3T3 cells (at concentrations up to 0.008 micrograms per mL [mcg/mL] without metabolic activation and 12 mcg/mL with activation). Chromosome damage occurs at higher doses; 25 mg/kg (75 mg per square meter of body surface area) of podofilox caused disruption and breakage of chromosomes *in vivo* in the mouse micronucleus assay.

Pregnancy/Reproduction

Fertility—Problems in humans have not been documented.

Podofilox did not impair fertility in two generations of rats given daily topical doses of 0.2 mg/kg of body weight (1.18 mg per square meter of body surface area) (corresponding to the recommended human daily dose) during gametogenesis, mating, gestation, parturition, and lactation.

Pregnancy—Studies have not been done in humans; however, dose-related systemic absorption has occurred.

Podofilox was embryotoxic in rats that were given daily intraperitoneal doses of 5 mg/kg of body weight (29.5 mg per square meter of body surface area; corresponding to 19 times the maximum human recommended dose [MHRD]). It was not teratogenic in rats that were given daily topical doses of 0.21 mg/kg of body weight (2.95 mg per square meter of body surface area; corresponding to two times the MHRD) for 13 days.

FDA Pregnancy Category C.

Breast-feeding
It is not known if podofilox is distributed into breast milk; however, dose-related systemic absorption has occurred and the potential for serious adverse problems exists.

Pediatrics
Appropriate studies on the relationship of age to the effects of podofilox have not been performed in the pediatric population. Safety and efficacy have not been established.

Geriatrics
No information is available on the relationship of age to the effects of podofilox in geriatric patients.

Medical considerations/Contraindications
The medical considerations/contraindications included have been selected on the basis of their potential clinical significance (reasons given in parentheses where appropriate)—not necessarily inclusive (» = major clinical significance).

Risk-benefit should be considered when the following medical problem exists:
Sensitivity to podofilox

Side/Adverse Effects
The following side/adverse effects have been selected on the basis of their potential clinical significance (possible signs and symptoms in parentheses where appropriate)—not necessarily inclusive:

Those indicating need for medical attention
Incidence more frequent

Bleeding of skin, local—less than 5% for solution, 22.9% for gel; ***burning feeling of skin, local; dizziness***—less than 5% for solution only, indicating systemic absorption; ***phimosis*** (problems with foreskin of penis)—less than 5% for solution only; ***headache***—7% for gel only, indicating systemic absorption; ***hematuria*** (bloody urine)—less than 5% for solution only; ***inflammation of skin, local*** (redness or swelling of skin); ***itching of skin, local; malodor*** (bad odor)—less than 5% for solution only; ***pain during sexual intercourse***—less than 5% for solution only; ***pain of skin, local; scarring of skin***—less than 5% for solution only; ***skin erosion, local*** (skin ulcers); ***vesicle formation*** (blistering, crusting, or scabbing of treated skin); ***vomiting***—less than 5% for solution only, indicating systemic absorption

Note: Local *burning feeling of skin* (64% in males, 78% in females), *itching of skin* (50% in males, 65% in females), and *pain of skin* (50% in males, 72% in females) occur more frequently in females than in males. Severe reactions occur within the first 2 weeks of beginning treatment and, for the podofilox solution, are more frequent and severe in females than in males. *Inflammation of skin* (71% in males, 63% in females) occurs more frequently in males than females, and *skin ulcers* (67% in males and females) occur equally in both genders.

Those indicating need for medical attention only if they continue or are bothersome
Incidence more frequent

Desquamation, local (peeling of treated skin); ***chafing or dryness of skin, local; insomnia*** (trouble in sleeping)—less than 5% for solution only; ***soreness or tenderness of skin, local; stinging or tingling of skin, local***

Incidence less frequent

Discoloration of skin, local (changes in color of treated skin)—for gel only; ***skin rash***—for gel only

Overdose
For more information on the management of overdose or unintentional ingestion, **contact a Poison Control Center** (see *Poison Control Center Listing*).

Clinical effects of overdose
The following effects have been selected on the basis of their potential clinical significance (possible signs and symptoms in parentheses where appropriate)—not necessarily inclusive:

Signs of systemic absorption of topical administration—in order of appearance

Nausea; vomiting; diarrhea; bone marrow depression (chills; fever; sore throat; unusual bleeding or bruising); ***oral ulcers***

Note: *Bone marrow depression* occurred following 5 to 10 intravenous doses of 0.5 to 1 mg/kg a day, but was reversible.

Treatment of overdose
Treatment of systemic toxicity or accidental ingestion is essentially supportive.

To decrease absorption—Wash the skin free of any remaining drug.

Supportive care—Patients in whom intentional overdose is known or suspected should be referred for psychiatric consultation.

Patient Consultation
As an aid to patient consultation, refer to *Advice for the Patient, Podofilox (Topical)*.

In providing consultation, consider emphasizing the following selected information (» = major clinical significance):

Before using this medication
» Conditions affecting use, especially:
Sensitivity to podofilox

Proper use of this medication
» Carefully reading patient directions that come with medication before using

» Avoiding contact with eyes and mucous membranes, including mucous membranes of vagina, rectum, and urethra; if contact occurs, immediately flushing eyes with water for 15 minutes or thoroughly washing area of mucous membranes with water

» Importance of not using more medication than the amount prescribed or increasing the frequency to greater than 3 times a week or for more than 4 treatment cycles

» Not applying the medication to any other wart without discussing with the physician; not exceeding a total dose of 10 square centimeters

» Proper administration
Proper use of applicators; not reusing
Applying medication to approved wart area only
Washing medication off normal skin
Drying treated area before allowing it contact with normal skin
Washing hands and properly discarding applicator(s) after podofilox application

» Proper dosing
Missed dose: Applying as soon as possible, then returning to regular schedule

» Proper storage

Precautions while using this medication
Understanding that podofilox may not prevent wart recurrence or stop new warts from appearing

Contains alcohol and may be flammable; not using near heat, open flame, or while smoking

Side/adverse effects
Signs of potential side effects, especially bleeding of skin, local; burning feeling of skin, local; dizziness (solution only); phimosis (solution only); headache (gel only); hematuria (solution only); inflammation of skin, local; itching of skin, local; malodor (solution only); pain during sexual intercourse (solution only); pain of skin, local; scarring of skin (solution only); skin erosion; vesicle formation; and vomiting (solution only)

General Dosing Information
On advice of the health care professional, the patient should be able to identify the type of warts podofilox can and cannot be applied to and understand the correct method for applying podofilox. It is particularly important not to apply podofilox to squamous cell carcinomas.

If contact with eyes occurs, patient should wash eyes with a large amount of water and seek professional advice.

Hands should be washed before and after administering podofilox.

Area of treatment with podofilox should be completely dry before allowing treated skin to come in contact with normal skin.

Treatment with podofilox should be discontinued if response of wart to podofilox is unsatisfactory after four treatment cycles. Applying podofilox more frequently than recommended will not increase efficacy but can result in increasing the rate of local adverse effects or cause systemic absorption.

Topical Dosage Forms

PODOFILOX GEL

Usual adult dose
Condyloma acuminatum—

Topical, to external genital or perianal warts, two times a day for three consecutive days via applicator tip or finger, then treatment should be discontinued for four consecutive days and cycle repeated until there is no visible wart or for up to four treatment cycles. Treatment should be limited to ten square centimeters or less of wart tissue, and the amount applied should not exceed 0.5 grams of gel per day.

Usual adult prescribing limits
Safety and efficacy beyond four treatment cycles have not been established.

Usual pediatric dose
Condyloma acuminatum—
Safety and efficacy have not been established.

Strength(s) usually available
U.S.—
0.5% (Rx) [*Condylox* (alcohol; butylated hydroxytoluene; glycerin; hydroxypropyl cellulose; lactic acid; sodium lactate)].

Note: Packaging includes an applicator tip.

Packaging and storage
Store below 40 °C (104 °F), preferably between 15 and 30 °C (59 and 86 °F), unless otherwise specified by manufacturer.

Auxiliary labeling
- For external use only.
- Do not freeze.

Additional information
Podofilox gel is flammable; keep away from open flame.

PODOFILOX TOPICAL SOLUTION

Usual adult dose
Condyloma acuminatum—
Topical, to external genital warts, two times a day (every twelve hours) for three consecutive days via applicator tip, then treatment should be discontinued for four consecutive days and cycle repeated until there is no visible wart or for up to four treatment cycles. Treatment should be limited to ten square centimeters or less of wart tissue, and the amount applied should not exceed 0.5 mL of solution per day.

Usual adult prescribing limits
Safety and efficacy beyond four treatment cycles have not been established.

Usual pediatric dose
Condyloma acuminatum—
Safety and efficacy have not been established.

Strength(s) usually available
U.S.—
0.5% (Rx) [*Condylox* (alcohol—95%; lactic acid; sodium lactate)].

Packaging and storage
Store below 40 °C (104 °F), preferably between 15 and 30 °C (59 and 86 °F), unless otherwise specified by manufacturer.

Auxiliary labeling
- For external use only.
- Do not freeze.

Additional information
Podofilox is flammable; keep away from open flame.

Revised: 06/27/1998

PODOPHYLLUM Topical†

VA CLASSIFICATION (Primary): DE500

Commonly used brand name(s): *Podocon-25; Podofin.*

Note: For a listing of dosage forms and brand names by country availability, see *Dosage Forms* section(s).

†Not commercially available in Canada.

Category
Cytotoxic (topical).

Indications

General Considerations
Podophyllum contains a number of unidentified ingredients, and its activity may vary widely depending on the source of the material.

Accepted
Condyloma acuminatum (treatment)—Podophyllum is indicated for the treatment of condyloma acuminatum (venereal warts).

Epitheliomatosis, multiple superficial (treatment) or
Keratoses, pre-epitheliomatosis (treatment) or
Papilloma, of the larynx, juvenile (treatment)—Podophyllum is used in the treatment of multiple superficial epitheliomatosis, such as multiple superficial or infiltrating basal cell epithelioma, squamous cell epithelioma (prickle cell epithelioma), and basal-squamous cell epithelioma (mixed or transitional cell epithelioma); seborrheic, actinic, and roentgen ray keratoses; and juvenile papilloma of the larynx.

Unaccepted
Podophyllum has been used in the treatment of general types of verrucae, such as vulgaris (common warts), filiformis (filiform warts), plana (flat warts), and plantaris (plantar warts); however, it is much less effective in these types of warts than in venereal warts. Also, podophyllum therapy is less effective than other types of treatment for these warts.

Pharmacology/Pharmacokinetics

Physicochemical characteristics
Source—Dried resin from the roots and rhizomes of *Podophyllum peltatum* (mandrake or May apple plant), the North American variety; active constituents are lignans including podophyllotoxin (20%), alpha-peltatin (10%), and beta-peltatin (5%).

Mechanism of action/Effect
Podophyllum resin's major active constituent, podophyllotoxin, is a lipid-soluble compound that easily crosses cell membranes. Podophyllotoxin and its derivatives are potent cytotoxic agents that inhibit cell mitosis and deoxyribonucleic acid (DNA) synthesis in a manner similar to that of colchicine. Cell division is arrested, and other cellular processes are impaired, gradually resulting in the disruption of cells and erosion of the tissue.

Absorption
Topical podophyllum is systemically absorbed; absorption may be increased if podophyllum is applied to friable, bleeding, or recently biopsied warts.

Precautions to Consider

Cross-sensitivity and/or related problems
Patients sensitive to benzoin may be sensitive to this medication also because some preparations may contain tincture of benzoin.

Pregnancy/Reproduction
Pregnancy—Topical podophyllum is absorbed systemically and can cross the placenta. It should not be used during any phase of pregnancy, because of its teratogenic potential. Following oral administration during pregnancy, podophyllum has been reported to cause fetal abnormalities, such as skin tags on the ears and cheeks, limb malformations, and septal heart defects, as well as polyneuritis. Intrauterine death has occurred following topical application to vulval warts during the 32nd week of pregnancy. In one patient, minor fetal anomalies, including preauricular skin tags and a simian crease on the left hand, occurred following topical application during the 23rd, 24th, 25th, 28th, and 29th weeks of pregnancy.

Warts of the vaginal, perianal, or anal areas requiring treatment during pregnancy should be treated by alternative methods, such as electrodesiccation, diathermy, curettage, surgical excision, or cryosurgery with liquid nitrogen or dry ice.

Breast-feeding
Topical podophyllum is systemically absorbed. However, it is not known whether topical podophyllum is distributed into breast milk. Problems in humans have not been documented.

Pediatrics
Appropriate studies on the relationship of age to the effects of topical podophyllum have not been performed in the pediatric population. However, no pediatrics-specific problems have been documented to date.

Geriatrics
Appropriate studies on the relationship of age to the effects of topical podophyllum have not been performed in the geriatric population. However, no geriatrics-specific problems have been documented to date.

Laboratory value alterations
The following have been selected on the basis of their potential clinical significance (possible effect in parentheses where appropriate)—not necessarily inclusive (» = major clinical significance).

With physiology/laboratory test values
Alkaline phosphatase and
Aspartate aminotransferase (AST [SGOT]) and
Lactate dehydrogenase (LDH)
(serum values may be increased in association with renal failure and hepatotoxicity)

Medical considerations/Contraindications
The medical considerations/contraindications included have been selected on the basis of their potential clinical significance (reasons

given in parentheses where appropriate)—not necessarily inclusive (» = major clinical significance).

Risk-benefit should be considered when the following medical problems exist:

» Friable, bleeding, or recently biopsied warts (risk of systemic toxicity may be increased)

Sensitivity to podophyllum

Side/Adverse Effects

Note: Podophyllum resin topical solution is highly irritating to the eye and to mucous membranes in general.

Podophyllum can cause severe systemic toxicity, which may result from either topical application or ingestion. The toxic effects are usually reversible but have been fatal. Death can occur with ingestion of podophyllum in amounts as small as 300 mg.

Serious systemic toxicity has occurred following topical application of podophyllum to large areas or in excessive amounts, or when the medication was allowed to remain in contact with the skin or mucous membranes for a prolonged period of time.

The risk of systemic toxicity may be increased when podophyllum is applied to friable, bleeding, or recently biopsied warts, or when the medication is inadvertently applied to normal skin or mucous membranes surrounding the affected area(s).

Renal failure and hepatotoxicity have occurred following topical application of podophyllum.

Adverse effects on the nervous system may occur following topical application of podophyllum; these are usually delayed in onset and prolonged in duration.

Cerebral toxicity (manifested by altered sensorium ranging from mild confusion to coma) may occur following topical application of podophyllum and continue for 7 to 10 days during which the electroencephalogram (EEG) may show generalized slowing.

The following side/adverse effects have been selected on the basis of their potential clinical significance (possible signs and symptoms in parentheses where appropriate)—not necessarily inclusive:

Those indicating need for medical attention

Burning, redness, or other irritation of affected area; skin rash or itching—allergic reaction to benzoin, which may be present in some preparations

Overdose

For specific information on the agents used in the management of podophyllum overdose, see:

- *Charcoal, Activated (Oral-Local)* monograph.

For more information on the management of overdose or unintentional ingestion, **contact a Poison Control Center** (see *Poison Control Center Listing*).

Clinical effects of overdose

The following effects have been selected on the basis of their potential clinical significance (possible signs and symptoms in parentheses where appropriate)—not necessarily inclusive:

Initial symptoms of systemic toxicity

Abdominal or stomach pain; clumsiness or unsteadiness; confusion; decreased or loss of reflexes; diarrhea—sometimes severe and prolonged; ***excitement, irritability, or nervousness; hallucinations; leukopenia*** (sore throat and fever); ***muscle weakness; nausea or vomiting; thrombocytopenia*** (unusual bleeding or bruising)

Delayed symptoms of systemic toxicity

Autonomic neuropathy (difficult or painful urination; dizziness or lightheadedness, especially when getting up from a lying or sitting position; fast heartbeat); ***difficulty in breathing; drowsiness; paralytic ileus*** (constipation; nausea and vomiting; pain in upper abdomen or stomach, mild, dull, and continuing); ***peripheral neuropathy*** (numbness, tingling, pain, or weakness in hands or feet); ***seizures***

Note: If *peripheral neuropathy* occurs, it usually appears about 2 weeks after podophyllum application, may worsen progressively for up to 3 months, and may persist for up to 9 months or longer.

Treatment of overdose

Treatment of systemic toxicity or accidental ingestion is essentially supportive and may include the following:

To decrease absorption—If podophyllum is accidentally ingested and the patient is conscious, emesis should be immediately induced. If the patient is unconscious, gastric lavage should be performed. Activated charcoal may also be administered.

To enhance elimination—Charcoal hemoperfusion may be beneficial in life-threatening or deteriorating conditions.

Monitoring—Electrolytes, serum calcium, and hemoglobin concentrations should be closely monitored.

Supportive care—Intravenous therapy and respiratory support should be administered if necessary. Patients in whom intentional overdose is known or suspected should be referred for psychiatric consultation.

Patient Consultation

As an aid to patient consultation, refer to *Advice for the Patient, Podophyllum (Topical)*.

In providing consultation, consider emphasizing the following selected information (» = major clinical significance):

Before using this medication

» Conditions affecting use, especially:

Sensitivity to podophyllum or benzoin

Pregnancy—Podophyllum should not be used during pregnancy, because it is absorbed through the mother's skin

Breast-feeding—Podophyllum is absorbed through the mother's skin

Other medical problems, especially friable, bleeding, or recently biopsied warts, because of increased risk of systemic toxicity

Proper use of this medication

» Importance of keeping away from mouth; medication is poisonous

» Avoiding contact with the eyes and mucous membranes; if contact occurs, immediately flushing eyes with water for 15 minutes, and thoroughly washing skin with soap and water or (if preparation contains tincture of benzoin) swabbing it with rubbing alcohol

» Not using near heat, open flame, or while smoking

» Importance of not using more medication than the amount prescribed

» Not using on moles or birthmarks

» Not using on friable, bleeding, or recently biopsied warts

Proper administration

Preventing dissemination of podophyllum to uninvolved skin—Applying petrolatum around affected areas before applying podophyllum and/or applying talcum powder to treated area immediately after applying podophyllum

Using a toothpick or a cotton-tipped or glass applicator to apply medication

Applying one drop at a time, allowing time between drops for drying, until affected area is covered

Following application of podophyllum, allowing medication to remain on affected area for 1 to 6 hours as directed by physician; removing medication by thoroughly washing affected area with soap and water, or, if preparation contains tincture of benzoin, swabbing it with rubbing alcohol

Washing hands immediately after using medication

» Proper dosing

Missed dose: Applying as soon as possible

» Proper storage

Side/adverse effects

Signs of potential side effects, especially burning, redness, or other irritation of affected area; skin rash or itching; or initial or delayed symptoms of systemic toxicity

General Dosing Information

Some clinicians recommend that podophyllum be used only under medical supervision because of its potentially serious adverse effects.

Old, discolored, dried, or gritty preparations of podophyllum should not be used.

Podophyllum should not be applied to friable, bleeding, or recently biopsied warts, because systemic absorption of the medication may be increased.

Podophyllum should not be used on moles or birthmarks, since acute inflammation or ulceration may occur.

Podophyllum is most frequently used in a concentration of 25%; however, concentrations of 5 to 10% have been recommended for very large lesions (> 10 to 20 cm [2]) in order to minimize the risk of toxicity.

Also, to minimize the risk of toxicity, application of podophyllum should be limited to small areas of intact skin.

If podophyllum is to be self-administered, patients should be instructed to use the medication with great caution. It should be applied only to the affected areas, avoiding contact with normal tissue. This medication can cause severe erosive damage to normal skin.

If podophyllum accidentally comes in contact with normal tissue, it should be removed, preferably by thoroughly washing with soap and water, or, if the podophyllum preparation contains tincture of benzoin, swabbing with rubbing alcohol.

Great care should be taken to avoid contact with the eyes because podophyllum can cause corneal damage. If contact does occur, the eyes should be immediately and thoroughly flushed with water for 15 minutes.

To prevent dissemination of the medication to uninvolved skin, petrolatum may be applied to normal skin surrounding the affected areas prior to application of podophyllum and/or talcum powder may be applied to the treated area immediately following application of podophyllum.

A toothpick or a cotton-tipped or glass applicator should be used to apply the topical solution one drop at a time, until the affected area is covered. Sufficient time should be allowed between drops for drying.

For condyloma acuminatum

Following application of podophyllum, the medication should be allowed to remain on the affected area for a period of 1 to 6 hours as prescribed by the physician.

At the end of the treatment period, the medication should be removed, preferably by thoroughly washing with soap and water. Some clinicians recommend removing podophyllum preparations that contain tincture of benzoin by swabbing with rubbing alcohol; however, this may be more irritating than washing with soap and water.

A minimum of 7 days should elapse between treatments because of the risk of systemic toxicity. Treatment may be repeated at weekly intervals for up to 6 weeks; however, if a beneficial effect does not occur within 6 weeks, alternative therapy should be considered.

For multiple superficial epitheliomatosis or pre-epitheliomatosis keratoses

Before each subsequent application of the medication, the necrotic tissue should be removed by curettage or wiped away with gauze.

In response to treatment, the lesion usually sloughs off leaving a superficial ulcer and a moderate degree of dermatitis of the immediate surrounding tissue. When treatment is discontinued, the lesion may be dressed with a mild antiseptic ointment; healing usually occurs in a few days, except in very large lesions, which may take longer to heal.

Topical Dosage Forms

PODOPHYLLUM RESIN TOPICAL SOLUTION USP

Usual adult and adolescent dose

Condyloma acuminatum—

Topical, to the skin, as a 10 to 25% solution for a period of one to six hours; treatment may be repeated at one-week intervals for up to six weeks.

Multiple superficial epitheliomatosis or
Pre-epitheliomatosis keratoses—

Topical, to the skin, as a 25% solution once a day; treatment should be continued for several days following the initial slough.

Juvenile papilloma of the larynx—

Topical, to the lesion, as a 12.5% solution once a day. The intervals of treatment can be gradually increased as the lesions become smaller; however, applications at short intervals give the best results.

Usual pediatric dose

See *Usual adult and adolescent dose*.

Strength(s) usually available

U.S.—

25% (Rx) [*Podocon-25; Podofin*].

Note: Other strengths are currently not commercially available; compounding required for prescriptions.

Canada—

Podophyllum resin of the North American variety is not commercially available.

Packaging and storage

Store below 40 °C (104 °F), preferably between 15 and 30 °C (59 and 86 °F), unless otherwise specified by manufacturer. Store in a tight, light-resistant container. Protect from freezing.

Preparation of dosage form

For treatment of juvenile papilloma of the larynx, the 25% solution should be diluted with an equal volume of 95% alcohol to yield the 12.5% solution.

A 25% Podophyllum Resin Topical Solution USP may be prepared extemporaneously by mixing 25 grams of the alcohol-soluble extractive of podophyllum resin in alcohol and 10 grams of the alcohol-soluble extractive of benzoin in alcohol, and diluting with alcohol to make 100 mL.

The solution should be prepared with native North American podophyllum resin, rather than a mixture of North American and Indian resins, because the Indian resin is stronger and more irritating than the North American variety. Also, the resin should be free of guaiacium gum, which may be a sensitizer.

Other vehicles that may be used for preparation of podophyllum resin topical solution include mineral oil or collodion.

Stability

Exposure to light, air, and warmth may cause precipitation and darkening of the solution because of evaporation and decomposition; such solutions should be discarded.

Auxiliary labeling

- Poison.
- For external use only.
- Shake well.
- Keep container tightly closed.

Revised: 08/19/1997

POLIOVIRUS VACCINE INACTIVATED—See *Poliovirus Vaccine (Systemic)*

POLIOVIRUS VACCINE INACTIVATED ENHANCED POTENCY—See *Poliovirus Vaccine (Systemic)*

POLIOVIRUS VACCINE LIVE ORAL—See *Poliovirus Vaccine (Systemic)*

POLOXAMER 188—See *Laxatives (Local)*

POLYCARBOPHIL—See *Laxatives (Local)*

POLYETHYLENE GLYCOL AND ELECTROLYTES Local

VA CLASSIFICATION (Primary): GA209

Commonly used brand name(s):.

Note: For a listing of dosage forms and brand names by country availability, see *Dosage Forms* section(s).

Category

Evacuant (bowel).

Indications

Accepted

Bowel evacuation, preoperative, and

Bowel evacuation, pre-radiography—Polyethylene glycol (PEG) 3350 and electrolytes oral solution is indicated for bowel cleansing prior to gastrointestinal examination (e.g., colonoscopy, barium enema, intravenous pyelography) and colon surgery.

For double contrast barium enema, administration of the PEG-electrolyte solution alone has not been found to be an adequate method of bowel cleansing. PEG-electrolyte solution followed by oral administration of bisacodyl has been reported to achieve better removal of feces and correct degraded mucosal coating.

Pharmacology/Pharmacokinetics

Physicochemical characteristics

Molecular weight—

Potassium chloride: 74.55.
Sodium bicarbonate: 84.01.
Sodium chloride: 58.44.
Sodium sulfate: 322.20.

Osmolality—

280 mOsmol per kg of water.

Mechanism of action/Effect

Evacuant (bowel)—Cleansing of the bowel is achieved by fluid overload with the osmotically balanced PEG-electrolyte solution, which induces a liquid stool within a short period of time. The concentration of electrolytes in the solution causes no net absorption or secretion of ions; thus no significant changes in water or electrolyte balance occur.

Absorption

Negligible absorption from gastrointestinal tract.

Onset of action

30 to 60 minutes.

Elimination

Negligible renal excretion (<0.1%).

Precautions to Consider

Carcinogenicity/Mutagenicity

Studies to evaluate carcinogenic or mutagenic potential have not been performed.

Pregnancy/Reproduction

Pregnancy—Studies have not been done in humans.

Studies have not been done in animals.

FDA Pregnancy Category C.

Breast-feeding

It is not known whether PEG-electrolyte solution is distributed into breast milk. However, problems in humans have not been documented.

Pediatrics

Studies performed in children ranging in age from 6 months to 18 years have not demonstrated pediatrics-specific problems that would limit the usefulness of PEG-electrolyte solution in children.

Geriatrics

Appropriate studies performed to date have not demonstrated geriatrics-specific problems that would limit the usefulness of PEG-electrolyte solution in the elderly.

Drug interactions and/or related problems

The following drug interactions and/or related problems have been selected on the basis of their potential clinical significance (possible mechanism in parentheses where appropriate)—not necessarily inclusive (» = major clinical significance):

» Oral medications, other
(other oral medications administered within 1 hour of administration of PEG-electrolyte solution may be flushed from the gastrointestinal tract and not absorbed)

Laboratory value alterations

The following have been selected on the basis of their potential clinical significance (possible effect in parentheses where appropriate)—not necessarily inclusive (» = major clinical significance).

With diagnostic test results
Barium sulfate, rectal
(administration of PEG-electrolyte solution on the same day as a barium enema [either single or double contrast] may result in retained fluid and thus barium dilution and may prevent barium coating of the intestinal wall)

Medical considerations/Contraindications

The medical considerations/contraindications included have been selected on the basis of their potential clinical significance (reasons given in parentheses where appropriate)—not necessarily inclusive (» = major clinical significance).

Except under special circumstances, this medication should not be used when the following medical problems exist:

» Intestinal obstruction or
» Paralytic ileus or
» Perforated bowel or
» Toxic colitis or
» Toxic megacolon
(condition may be aggravated; colonic perforation may occur in patients with intestinal obstruction or toxic colitis)

Risk-benefit should be considered when the following medical problems exist:

Aspiration, predisposition to or
Impaired gag reflex or
Regurgitation, predisposition to or
Unconscious or semiconscious state
(administration via nasogastric tube may increase risk of complications)
Ulcerative colitis, severe
(condition may be aggravated)

Side/Adverse Effects

Note: Hypothermia was reported in one patient after ingestion of 5 liters of chilled PEG-electrolyte solution.

One patient experienced cardiac asystole after a large bowel movement following administration of PEG-electrolyte solution. Further studies are needed to establish a causal relationship.

The following side/adverse effects have been selected on the basis of their potential clinical significance (possible signs and symptoms in parentheses where appropriate)—not necessarily inclusive:

Those indicating need for medical attention

Incidence rare
Allergic reaction (skin rash)

Those indicating need for medical attention only if they continue or are bothersome

Incidence more frequent
Bloating; nausea

Incidence less frequent
Abdominal or stomach cramps; anal irritation; vomiting

Patient Consultation

As an aid to patient consultation, refer to *Advice for the Patient, Polyethylene Glycol and Electrolytes (Local).*

In providing consultation, consider emphasizing the following selected information (» = major clinical significance):

Before using this medication

» Conditions affecting use, especially:
Other oral medicines administered within 1 hour of solution
Other medical problems, especially intestinal obstruction, paralytic ileus, perforated bowel, toxic colitis, or toxic megacolon

Proper use of this medication

Special preparatory instructions may be given; patient should inquire in advance
» Taking solution exactly as directed for best test results
» Drinking all the solution for best results, unless otherwise directed by physician
» Fasting for at least 3 hours prior to ingestion of solution; clear liquids are allowed after ingestion of solution
Directions for the preparation of the powder dosage form
» Proper dosing
» Proper storage

Side/adverse effects

Signs of potential side effects, especially allergic reaction

General Dosing Information

Diet/Nutrition

Fasting is recommended for at least 3 hours prior to administration of the PEG-electrolyte solution.

The PEG-electrolyte solution may be administered on the morning of the examination, as long as enough time is allowed for the patient to drink the solution (3 hours) and for complete bowel evacuation (1 additional hour). If the patient is having a barium enema examination, the PEG-electrolyte solution should be administered early (e.g., 6 pm) the evening before the examination to permit proper mucosal coating by barium. No foods except clear liquids are allowed after administration of the solution.

Rapid drinking of each portion of the the PEG-electrolyte solution is recommended rather than drinking small amounts continuously.

Oral Dosage Forms

POLYETHYLENE GLYCOL 3350 AND ELECTROLYTES ORAL SOLUTION

Usual adult and adolescent dose

Bowel evacuant—
Oral, 240 mL every ten minutes, up to 4 L, or until the fecal discharge is clear and free of solid matter.

Note: May also be given via nasogastric tube at a rate of 20 to 30 mL per minute (1.2 to 1.8 L per hour).

Usual pediatric dose

Bowel evacuant—
Oral or by continuous nasogastric drip, 25 to 40 mL per kg of body weight per hour until the fecal discharge is clear and free of solid matter.

Usual geriatric dose

See *Usual adult and adolescent dose.*

Strength(s) usually available

U.S.—

Product	Content (mg/100 mL)				
	PEG 3350	NaCl	$NaHCO_3$	Na_2SO_4	KCl
U.S.—					
OCL (Rx)	6000	146	168	569	75
Canada—					
Peglyte (OTC)	5960	150	170	570	80

Packaging and storage

Store between 15 and 30 °C (59 and 86 °F). Store in a tight container.

Incompatibilities

The addition of flavoring agents, such as sugar, nutritional supplements, or other sweeteners, is *not* recommended. Such additives may change the osmolality of the solution; sucrose or glucose may cause fluid and electrolyte absorption. Additives may also predispose to colonic bacterial fermentation and formation of combustible gases.

POLYETHYLENE GLYCOL 3350 AND ELECTROLYTES FOR ORAL SOLUTION USP

Usual adult and adolescent dose

Bowel evacuant—

See *Polyethylene Glycol 3350 and Electrolytes Oral Solution*

Usual pediatric dose

Bowel evacuant—

See *Polyethylene Glycol 3350 and Electrolytes Oral Solution*

Usual geriatric dose

See *Polyethylene Glycol 3350 and Electrolytes Oral Solution.*

Strength(s) usually available

U.S.—

Product	Content (mg/100 mL)				
	PEG 3350	NaCl	$NaHCO_3$	Na_2SO_4	KCl
U.S.— *Co-Lav* (Rx) *Colovage* (Rx) *Colyte* (Rx) *Colyte-flavored* (Rx) *Colyte with Flavor Packs* (Rx) *Go-Evac* (Rx) *GoLYTELY* (Rx) *PEG-3350 & Electrolytes* (Rx)	6000	146	168	568	74.5
NuLYTELY (Rx) *NuLYTELY, Cherry Flavor* (Rx)	10500	280	143	—	37
Canada— *Colyte* (OTC) *GoLYTELY* (OTC) *Klean-Prep* (OTC)	6000	146	168	568	75
Peglyte (OTC)	6000	150	170	570	80

Packaging and storage

Store below 40 °C (104 °F), preferably between 15 and 30 °C (59 and 86 °F), unless otherwise specified by manufacturer. Store in a tight container.

Note: After reconstitution, solution should be refrigerated to improve palatability.

Preparation of dosage form

See manufacturer's package label for complete instructions on reconstitution.

Tap water must be used for reconstitution.

To assure that all ingredients have dissolved, solution must be shaken vigorously.

Stability

Reconstituted solution should be used within 48 hours. Unused portion should be discarded.

Incompatibilities

The addition of flavoring agents, such as sugar, nutritional supplements, or other sweeteners, is *not* recommended. Such additives may change the osmolality of the solution; sucrose or glucose may cause fluid and electrolyte absorption. Additives may also predispose to colonic bacterial fermentation and formation of combustible gases.

Revised: 08/29/2000

POLYMERIC ENTERAL NUTRITION FORMULAS See *Enteral Nutrition Formulas (Systemic)*

POLYTHIAZIDE—See *Diuretics, Thiazide (Systemic)*

POTASSIUM ACETATE—See *Potassium Supplements (Systemic)*

POTASSIUM AND SODIUM PHOSPHATES—See *Phosphates (Systemic)*

POTASSIUM BICARBONATE—See *Potassium Supplements (Systemic)*

POTASSIUM BICARBONATE AND POTASSIUM CHLORIDE—See *Potassium Supplements (Systemic)*

POTASSIUM BICARBONATE AND POTASSIUM CITRATE—See *Potassium Supplements (Systemic)*

POTASSIUM BITARTRATE AND SODIUM BICARBONATE—See *Laxatives (Local)*

POTASSIUM CHLORIDE—See *Potassium Supplements (Systemic)*

POTASSIUM CITRATE—See *Citrates (Systemic)*

POTASSIUM CITRATE AND CITRIC ACID—See *Citrates (Systemic)*

POTASSIUM CITRATE AND SODIUM CITRATE—See *Citrates (Systemic)*

POTASSIUM GLUCONATE—See *Potassium Supplements (Systemic)*

POTASSIUM GLUCONATE AND POTASSIUM CHLORIDE—See *Potassium Supplements (Systemic)*

POTASSIUM GLUCONATE AND POTASSIUM CITRATE—See *Potassium Supplements (Systemic)*

POTASSIUM PHOSPHATES—See *Phosphates (Systemic)*

PRAMIPEXOLE Systemic

VA CLASSIFICATION (Primary): CN500

Commonly used brand name(s): *Mirapex*.

Note: For a listing of dosage forms and brand names by country availability, see *Dosage Forms* section(s).

Category

Antidyskinetic (dopamine agonist).

Indications

Accepted

Parkinson's disease, idiopathic (treatment)—Pramipexole is indicated for treatment of the symptoms of idiopathic Parkinson's disease. Its efficacy has been demonstrated in patients with early Parkinson's disease, as well as in patients with advanced disease receiving concomitant levodopa therapy.

Pharmacology/Pharmacokinetics

Physicochemical characteristics

Molecular weight—302.27.

Mechanism of action/Effect

Pramipexole is a non-ergot dopamine agonist with high relative *in vitro* specificity and full intrinsic activity at the D_2 subfamily of dopamine receptors; it binds with higher affinity to D_3 than to D_2 or D_4 receptor subtypes. The relevance of this receptor specificity in Parkinson's disease is not known. Pramipexole's mechanism of action in the treatment of Parkinson's disease is not precisely known, but is believed to be related to its ability to stimulate dopamine receptors in the striatum. This theory is supported by electrophysiologic studies in animals that have demonstrated that pramipexole influences striatal neuronal firing rates via activation of dopamine receptors in the striatum and the substantia nigra, the site of neurons that send projections to the striatum.

Absorption

Rapid. Absolute bioavailability is greater than 90%, indicating that pramipexole is well absorbed and undergoes little presystemic metabolism. Food does not affect the extent of absorption.

Distribution

Extensive. Volume of distribution (Vol_D) is about 500 L. Pramipexole distributes into red blood cells, as indicated by an erythrocyte-to-plasma ratio of approximately 2.

Protein binding

Low (15%).

Biotransformation

No metabolites have been identified in plasma or urine.

Half-life

Elimination—

About 8 hours in young, healthy volunteers.

About 12 hours in elderly volunteers.

Time to peak concentration

Approximately 2 hours; the time to peak concentration is increased by about an hour if pramipexole is taken with a meal.

Steady state concentration

Pramipexole displays linear pharmacokinetics over the clinical dosage range. Steady-state concentrations are achieved within 2 days of dosing.

Elimination

Renal, with 90% of a pramipexole dose recovered in urine, almost all as unchanged drug. Nonrenal routes of elimination may contribute to a small extent. Renal clearance of pramipexole is approximately three times higher than the glomerular filtration rate, indicating secretion by the renal tubules, probably by the organic cationic transport system.

Pramipexole clearance is about 30% lower in females than in males. Most of this difference can be accounted for by differences in body weight, as there is no difference in half-life between females and males.

Pramipexole clearance may be reduced by about 30% in Parkinson's disease patients as compared with healthy elderly volunteers. Patients with Parkinson's disease appear to have reduced renal function, which may be related to the poorer general health of these patients. However, the pharmacokinetics of pramipexole are comparable between early and advanced Parkinson's disease patients.

Clearance of pramipexole decreases with age, most likely due to age-related reduction in renal function. Clearance was about 30% lower and half-life about 40% longer in elderly (65 years of age or older) volunteers as compared with that in younger (up to 40 years of age) volunteers.

Clearance of pramipexole was about 60% lower in patients with moderate impairment of renal function, and about 75% lower in patients with severe renal function impairment, as compared with clearance in healthy volunteers. Dosage reductions in these patients are recommended. Pramipexole clearance correlates well with creatinine clearance; thus, creatinine clearance can be used as a predictor of the extent of decrease in pramipexole clearance and can be used to guide dosage reductions. (See *Usual adult dose*.)

In dialysis—

A negligible amount of pramipexole is removed by dialysis; clearance is extremely low in dialysis patients.

Precautions to Consider

Carcinogenicity/Tumorigenicity

Two-year carcinogenicity studies with pramipexole conducted in mice and rats resulted in no significant increases in tumor occurrence.

Mutagenicity

Pramipexole was not mutagenic or clastogenic in a battery of assays, including the *in vitro* Ames assay, V79 gene mutation assay for HGPRT mutants, chromosomal aberration assay in Chinese hamster ovary cells, and *in vivo* mouse micronucleus assay.

Pregnancy/Reproduction

Fertility—In rat fertility studies, administration of pramipexole at a dose of 2.5 mg per kg of body weight (mg/kg) per day (5.4 times the highest clinical human dose on a mg per square meter of body surface area [mg/m²] basis), resulted in prolonged estrous cycles and inhibited implantation. These effects were associated with reductions in serum concentrations of prolactin, a hormone necessary for implantation and maintenance of early pregnancy in rats.

Pregnancy—Adequate and well-controlled studies have not been done in humans.

In animal studies, female rats that received pramipexole throughout pregnancy at a dose of 2.5 mg/kg of body weight (5.4 times the highest clinical human dose on a mg/m² basis) showed evidence of inhibited implantation. Administration of 1.5 mg of pramipexole per kg per day to pregnant rats during the period of organogenesis (gestation days 7 through 16) resulted in a high incidence of total resorption of embryos. These findings are thought to be due to the prolactin-lowering effects of pramipexole, since prolactin is necessary for implantation and maintenance of early pregnancy in rats (but not in rabbits or humans). Because of the pregnancy disruption and early embryonic loss in these studies, the teratogenic potential of pramipexole could not be adequately evaluated. Postnatal growth inhibition occurred in the offspring of rats treated with 0.5 mg pramipexole per kg per day (approximately equivalent to the highest human clinical dose on a mg/m² basis) or greater during the latter part of pregnancy and throughout lactation. In pregnant rabbits receiving up to 10 mg of pramipexole per kg per day during organogenesis, there was no evidence of adverse effects on embryo-fetal development.

FDA Pregnancy Category C.

Breast-feeding

It is not known whether pramipexole is distributed into breast milk. However, a radiolabeled single-dose study in lactating rats showed that drug-related materials were distributed into milk; concentrations of radioactivity in milk were three to six times greater than concentrations in plasma at equivalent time points.

Other studies have shown that pramipexole therapy has resulted in inhibition of prolactin secretion in humans and rats. Because of the potential for serious adverse reactions in the nursing infant, discontinuation of nursing or discontinuation of pramipexole is recommended.

Pediatrics

Appropriate studies on the relationship of age to the effects of pramipexole have not been performed in the pediatric population. Safety and efficacy have not been established.

Geriatrics

Pramipexole clearance was approximately 30% lower in subjects older than 65 years of age as compared with younger subjects because of an age-related reduction in renal function; this resulted in an increase in elimination half-life from approximately 8.5 hours to 12 hours.

In clinical studies, 38.7% of patients were older than 65 years of age. The relative risk of hallucination was increased in elderly patients. There were no other apparent differences in efficacy and safety of pramipexole between older and younger patients.

Drug interactions and/or related problems

The following drug interactions and/or related problems have been selected on the basis of their potential clinical significance (possible mechanism in parentheses where appropriate)—not necessarily inclusive (» = major clinical significance):

Note: Inhibitors of cytochrome P450 enzymes would not be expected to affect the elimination of pramipexole because pramipexole is not appreciably metabolized by these enzymes *in vivo* or *in vitro*. Pramipexole does not inhibit CYP enzymes CYP1A2, CYP2C9, CYP2C19, CYP2E1, or CYP3A4. Inhibition of CYP2D6 was not observed at pramipexole plasma concentrations following the highest recommended clinical dose (1.5 mg three times a day).

Combinations containing any of the following medications, depending on the amount present, may also interact with this medication.

» Carbidopa and levodopa combination or
» Levodopa
(concomitant administration with pramipexole may cause an increase in peak levodopa plasma concentration by about 40%, and a decrease in time to peak levodopa plasma concentration from 2.5 to 0.5 hours)
(pramipexole may potentiate the dopaminergic side effects of levodopa, causing or exacerbating preexisting dyskinesia; reducing levodopa dosage may ameliorate this effect)

Cimetidine
(by inhibiting renal tubular secretion of organic bases via the cationic transport system, cimetidine caused a 50% increase in the area under the plasma concentration-time curve [AUC] of pramipexole, as well as a 40% increase in the half-life of pramipexole in a small series of patients)

Dopamine antagonists, including:
Haloperidol
Metoclopramide
Phenothiazines
Thioxanthenes
(since pramipexole is a dopamine agonist, its actions may be diminished by dopamine antagonists)

Medications excreted by renal secretion, including:
Diltiazem
Quinidine
Quinine
Ranitidine
Triamterene
Verapamil
(coadministration of agents that are secreted via the cationic transport system decreases the clearance of pramipexole by about 20%; agents secreted via the anionic transport system have little effect on the clearance of pramipexole)

Medical considerations/Contraindications

The medical considerations/contraindications included have been selected on the basis of their potential clinical significance (reasons given in parentheses where appropriate)—not necessarily inclusive (» = major clinical significance).

Risk-benefit should be considered when the following medical problems exist:

Fibrotic complications from ergot-derived dopaminergic agents, history of
(condition may recur)

» Hallucinations
(condition may be exacerbated)

» Hypotension or
» Orthostatic hypotension
(condition may be exacerbated)

» Renal function impairment
(elimination may be impaired; dosage adjustments are necessary)

Retinal degeneration, or retinal problems
(studies in albino rats have shown retinal degeneration and loss of photoreceptor cells; although the significance of this effect in humans has not been established, disruption of disk shedding [a mechanism universally present in vertebrates] may be involved)

Sensitivity to pramipexole

Patient monitoring

The following may be especially important in patient monitoring (other tests may be warranted in some patients, depending on condition; » = major clinical significance):

Monitoring for symptoms of orthostatic hypotension
(particularly important during dose escalation)

Side/Adverse Effects

Note: Several cases have been reported of patients falling asleep without warning while engaged in daily living activities (including operation of a motor vehicle) after receiving pramipexole. A number of these events occurred as much as 1 year after initiation of pramipexole therapy.

Dopamine agonists appear to impair the systemic regulation of blood pressure, resulting in orthostatic hypotension, especially during dose escalation. In addition, patients with Parkinson's disease appear to have an impaired capacity to respond to an orthostatic challenge. Clear orthostatic effects were demonstrated in normal volunteers who received pramipexole. In clinical trials of pramipexole, however, incidence of clinically significant orthostatic hypotension was no greater in patients receiving the medication than in those patients receiving placebo. The explanation for this unexpected finding is not known; it may reflect a unique property of pramipexole, it may be the result of very careful dose titration, or it may be a factor of the patient selection criteria for the clinical trials, which excluded patients with active cardiovascular disease or significant baseline orthostatic hypotension.

Pramipexole may cause or exacerbate preexisting dyskinesia. It may also potentiate the dopaminergic side effects of levodopa. Dyskinesia may be ameliorated by reducing the concomitant dose of levodopa.

A case of rhabdomyolysis occurred in a 49-year-old male with advanced Parkinson's disease who received pramipexole. Symptoms resolved upon discontinuation of pramipexole.

Pathologic retinal changes consisting of degeneration and loss of photoreceptor cells were observed in albino rats given pramipexole in the premarketing carcinogenicity study. Retinal changes were not observed in albino mice, pigmented rats, monkeys, or minipigs. The potential significance of these effects for humans has not been established; however, this effect cannot be disregarded because it may involve disruption of disk shedding, a mechanism that is universally present in vertebrates.

A symptom complex (characterized by elevated temperature, muscular rigidity, altered consciousness, and autonomic instability) that resembles neuroleptic malignant syndrome and has no other obvious etiology has been reported in association with rapid dose reduction, withdrawal of, or changes in antiparkinsonian therapy. This effect was not observed during premarketing trials of pramipexole, but potentially could occur with the use of this dopaminergic agent.

Fibrotic complications, including retroperitoneal fibrosis, pulmonary infiltrates, pleural effusion, and pleural thickening, have been reported in some patients treated with ergot-derived dopaminergic agents. These complications may resolve upon discontinuation of the medication, but complete resolution does not always occur. Although these effects are believed to be associated with the ergoline structure of these compounds, it is not known if non–ergot-derived dopamine agonists such as pramipexole may produce similar adverse effects.

The following side/adverse effects have been selected on the basis of their potential clinical significance (possible signs and symptoms in parentheses where appropriate)—not necessarily inclusive:

Those indicating need for medical attention

Incidence more frequent

Asthenia (unusual tiredness or weakness); ***drowsiness; dyskinesia*** (twitching, twisting, or other unusual body movements); ***hallucinations*** (seeing, hearing, or feeling things that are not there)—higher risk in elderly patients; ***insomnia*** (trouble in sleeping); ***nausea; orthostatic hypotension*** (dizziness, lightheadedness, or fainting, especially when standing up)

Note: In the placebo-controlled premarketing trials conducted in patients with early Parkinson's disease, *hallucinations* were observed in 9% of patients receiving pramipexole, as compared with 2.6% of patients receiving placebo. In the placebo-controlled premarketing trials conducted in patients with advanced Parkinson's disease who were concomitantly receiving levodopa, 16.5% of patients reported hallucinations, as compared with 3.8% of patients receiving placebo. Age appears to increase the risk of hallucinations attributable to pramipexole. In the early Parkinson's disease patients in these studies, the incidence of hallucinations was 1.9 times higher in pramipexole patients than in placebo patients younger than 65 years of age, and 6.8 times higher than in placebo patients older than 65 years of age. In the advanced Parkinson's disease patients (who were receiving concomitant levodopa) in these studies, the incidence of hallucinations was 3.5 times higher than in placebo patients younger than 65 years of age, and 5.2 times higher than placebo in patients older than 65 years of age.

Incidence less frequent

Akathisia (restlessness or need to keep moving); ***amnesia*** (memory loss); ***confusion; diplopia or other eye or vision changes*** (double vision or other changes in vision); ***dysphagia*** (difficulty in swallowing); ***edema; falling asleep without warning; fever; frequent urination; muscle or joint pain; myasthenia*** (muscle weakness); ***paranoid reaction*** (fearfulness, suspiciousness, or other mental changes); ***pneumonia*** (cough; shortness of breath; troubled breathing; tightness in chest; wheezing)

Incidence rare

Abnormal thinking; chest pain; delusions (mood or mental changes); ***dizziness; dyspnea*** (troubled breathing); ***peripheral edema*** (swelling of arms or legs); ***urinary incontinence*** (loss of bladder control); ***urinary tract infection*** (bloody or cloudy urine; difficult, burning, or painful urination; frequent urge to urinate)

Those indicating need for medical attention only if they continue or are bothersome

Incidence more frequent

Constipation; dryness of mouth

Incidence less frequent

Abnormal dreams; anorexia (loss of appetite); ***decreased libido or impotence*** (decreased sexual drive or ability); ***increased sweating; malaise*** (general feeling of discomfort or illness); ***rhinitis*** (runny nose); ***skin problems, such as rash; weight loss***

Overdose

For information on the management of overdose or unintentional ingestion of pramipexole, **contact a Poison Control Center** (see *Poison Control Center Listing*).

Treatment of overdose

There is no known antidote for overdosage of a dopamine agonist.

To decrease absorption—Gastric lavage may be indicated.

Specific treatment—If signs of central nervous system (CNS) stimulation are present, a phenothiazine or butyrophenone neuroleptic agent may be indicated; however, the efficacy of such medications in reversing the effects of overdosage has not been assessed.

Monitoring—Electrocardiogram (ECG) monitoring may be indicated.

Supportive care—General supportive measures, including administration of intravenous fluids, may be indicated. Patients in whom intentional overdose is confirmed or suspected should be referred for psychiatric consultation.

Patient Consultation

As an aid to patient consultation, refer to *Advice for the Patient, Pramipexole (Systemic)*.

In providing consultation, consider emphasizing the following selected information (» = major clinical significance):

Before using this medication

» Conditions affecting use, especially:
- Sensitivity to pramipexole
- Pregnancy—Studies in rats showed evidence of inhibited implantation and a high incidence of total resorption of embryos
- Breast-feeding—Not recommended because of potential for serious adverse effects in the infant
- Use in the elderly—Age-related reductions in renal function may require dosage adjustments; also, increased risk of occurrence of hallucinations
- Other medications, especially carbidopa and/or levodopa
- Other medical problems, especially hallucinations, hypotension, orthostatic hypotension, or renal function impairment

Proper use of this medication

» Compliance with therapy; not taking more or less medicine than prescribed

» Proper dosing

Missed dose: Taking as soon as possible; not taking if almost time for next dose; not doubling doses

» Proper storage

Precautions while using this medication

» Regular visits to physician to check progress of therapy

» Checking with physician before discontinuing medication; gradual dosage reduction may be needed

» Possible drowsiness, dizziness, lightheadedness, vision problems, weakness, or muscular incoordination; caution when driving or doing jobs requiring alertness, clear vision, and coordination

» Possible falling asleep without warning while engaged in daily living activities such as driving a motor vehicle

» Caution when getting up suddenly from lying or sitting position

» Possible hallucinations, especially in older patients

Side/adverse effects

Signs of potential side effects, especially asthenia, drowsiness, dyskinesia, hallucinations, insomnia, nausea, orthostatic hypotension, akathisia, amnesia, confusion, diplopia or other eye or vision changes, dysphagia, edema, falling asleep without warning, fever, frequent urination, muscle or joint pain, myasthenia, paranoid reaction, pneumonia, abnormal thinking, chest pain, delusions, dizziness, dyspnea, peripheral edema, urinary incontinence, and urinary tract infection

General Dosing Information

Pramipexole doses should be titrated slowly in all patients. Dosage goal should be to achieve maximum therapeutic effect balanced against the principal side effects of dyskinesia, hallucinations, somnolence, and dry mouth.

When pramipexole is used in combination with levodopa, the dosage requirements of levodopa may be reduced. In one controlled study in advanced Parkinson's disease patients, the levodopa dosage was reduced by an average of 27% from baseline.

It is recommended that pramipexole be discontinued gradually over a period of 1 week. However, abrupt discontinuation has been uneventful in some studies.

Diet/Nutrition

Taking pramipexole with food may reduce the occurrence of nausea.

Oral Dosage Forms

PRAMIPEXOLE TABLETS

Note: In clinical studies, dosage was initiated at subtherapeutic doses to avoid intolerable adverse effects and orthostatic hypotension, and then gradually titrated upwards.

Usual adult dose

Parkinson's disease, idiopathic—

In patients with normal renal function:

Oral, initially 0.375 mg a day, administered in three divided doses. Dosages should be increased gradually at intervals of 5 to 7 days. A suggested schedule for titration follows:

Ascending Dosage Schedule of Pramipexole

Week	Dosage	Total Daily Dose
1	0.125 mg three times a day	0.375 mg
2	0.25 mg three times a day	0.75 mg
3	0.5 mg three times a day	1.5 mg
4	0.75 mg three times a day	2.25 mg
5	1 mg three times a day	3 mg
6	1.25 mg three times a day	3.75 mg
7	1.5 mg three times a day	4.5 mg

Maintenance: Pramipexole was effective and well tolerated over a dosage range of 1.5 to 4.5 mg a day (administered in divided doses three times a day) with or without concomitant levodopa. In one fixed-dose study in early Parkinson's disease patients, pramipexole doses of 3, 4.5, and 6 mg a day were not shown to provide any significant benefit beyond that achieved at a dose of 1.5 mg a day.

In patients with impaired renal function:

Pramipexole Dosage in Renal Impairment

Renal Status	Initial Dose	Maximum Dose
Normal to mild impairment (creatinine clearance > 60 mL/min)	0.125 mg three times a day	1.5 mg three times a day
Moderate impairment (creatinine clearance of 35 to 59 mL/min)	0.125 mg two times a day	1.5 mg two times a day
Severe impairment (creatinine clearance of 15 to 34 mL/min)	0.125 mg a day	1.5 mg a day
Very severe impairment (creatinine clearance less than 15 mL/min) and hemodialysis patients	Use of pramipexole has not been adequately studied in this patient population	

Usual pediatric dose
Safety and efficacy have not been established.

Strength(s) usually available
U.S.—
0.125 mg (Rx) [*Mirapex* (colloidal silicon dioxide; corn starch; magnesium stearate; mannitol; povidone)].
0.25 mg (Rx) [*Mirapex* (scored; colloidal silicon dioxide; corn starch; magnesium stearate; mannitol; povidone)].
1 mg (Rx) [*Mirapex* (scored; colloidal silicon dioxide; corn starch; magnesium stearate; mannitol; povidone)].
1.5 mg (Rx) [*Mirapex* (scored; colloidal silicon dioxide; corn starch; magnesium stearate; mannitol; povidone)].

Packaging and storage
Store between 20 and 25 °C (68 and 77 °F). Protect from light.

Auxiliary labeling
• May cause drowsiness.
• May cause dizziness.

Revised: 01/13/2000

PRAMLINTIDE Systemic†

VA CLASSIFICATION (Primary): HS509

Commonly used brand name(s): *Symlin.*

Note: For a listing of dosage forms and brand names by country availability, see *Dosage Forms* section(s).

†Not commercially available in Canada.

Category

Antidiabetic agent.

Indications

General Considerations

Proper patient selection is critical to safe and effective use of pramlintide. Before initiation of therapy, the patient's HbA1c, recent blood glucose monitoring data, history of insulin-induced hypoglycemia, current insulin regimen, and body weight should be reviewed. Pramlintide therapy should only be considered in patients with insulin-using type 2 or type 1 diabetes who fulfill the following criteria:
• have failed to achieve adequate glycemic control despite individualized insulin management;
• are receiving ongoing care under the guidance of a health care professional skilled in the use of insulin and supported by the services of diabetes educator(s).

Accepted

Diabetes, type 1 (treatment adjunct)—Pramlintide is indicated for Type 1 diabetes, as an adjunct treatment in patients who use mealtime insulin therapy and who have failed to achieve desired glucose control despite optimal insulin therapy.

Diabetes, type 2 (treatment adjunct)—Pramlintide is indicated for Type 2 diabetes, as an adjunct treatment in patients who use mealtime insulin therapy and who have failed to achieve desired glucose control despite optimal insulin therapy, with or without a concurrent sulfonylurea agent and/or metformin.

Pharmacology/Pharmacokinetics

Physicochemical characteristics

Molecular weight—Pramlintide acetate—3949.4.
Solubility—Pramlintide acetate is soluble in water.
pH—Pramlintide acetate: approximately 4

Mechanism of action/Effect

Pramlintide, by acting as an amylinomimetic agent, has the following effects:
• Modulation of gastric emptying—The gastric-emptying rate is an important determinant of the postprandial rise in plasma glucose. Pramlintide slows the rate at which food is released from the stomach to the small intestine following a meal and, thus, it reduces the initial postprandial increase in plasma glucose. This effect lasts for approximately 3 hours following administration and does not alter the net absorption of ingested carbohydrate or other nutrients.
• Prevention of the postprandial rise in plasma glucagon—In patients with diabetes, glucagon concentrations are abnormally elevated during the postprandial period, contributing to hyperglycemia. Pramlintide has been shown to decrease postprandial glucagon concentrations in insulin-using patients with diabetes.
• Satiety leading to decreased caloric intake and potential weight loss—Pramlintide administered prior to a meal has been shown to reduce total caloric intake. This effect appears to be independent of the nausea that can accompany pramlintide treatment.

Absorption

Bioavailability—approximately 30 to 40%

Protein binding

Moderate, approximately 60%

Biotransformation

Primarily by the kidneys; primary metabolite: des-lys pramlintide

Half-life

Approximately 48 minutes

Precautions to Consider

Carcinogenicity

No drug-induced tumors were observed in a two-year study conducted in CD-1 mice with doses of pramlintide 32, 67, and 159 times the exposure resulting from the maximum recommended human dose (MRHD) based on AUC. Another two-year study conducted in Sprague-Dawley rats with doses 3, 9, and 25 times the MRHD based on AUC resulted in no drug-induced tumors in any organ.

Mutagenicity

Pramlintide was not mutagenic in the Ames test and did not increase chromosomal aberration in the human lymphocytes assay. Pramlintide was not clastogenic in the *in vivo* mouse micronucleus test or in the chromosomal aberration assay utilizing Chinese hamster ovary cells.

Pregnancy/Reproduction

Fertility—Pramlintide administered at 8, 17, and 82 times the MRHD based on body surface area had no significant effects on fertility in male or female rates. The highest dose of 3 mg per kg of body weight per day resulted in dystocia in 8 of 12 female rats secondary to significant decreases in serum calcium levels.

Pregnancy—Adequate and well-controlled studies in humans have not been done. Because animal reproduction studies are not always predictive of human response, pramlintide should be used during pregnancy only if it is determined by the healthcare professional that the potential benefit justifies the potential risk to the fetus. Women with diabetes should be advised to inform their healthcare professional if they are pregnant or contemplating pregnancy.

Studies in perfused human placenta indicate that pramlintide has low potential to cross the maternal/fetal placental barrier.

Embryo fetal toxicity studies with pramlintide have been performed in rats and rabbits. Rats treated during organogenesis with 10 and 47 times the MRHD based on AUC resulted in increased congenital abnormalities (neural tube defect, cleft palate, exencephaly). Doses 9 times the MHRD based on AUC administered to pregnant rabbits had no adverse effects in embryofetal development.

FDA Pregnancy Category C

Breast-feeding

It is not known whether pramlintide is distributed into breast milk. Many drugs, including peptide drugs, are distributed into human milk. Therefore, pramlintide should be administered to nursing women only if it is determined by the healthcare professional that the potential benefit outweighs the potential risk to the infant.

Pediatrics

Safety and efficacy of pramlintide in pediatric patients have not been established.

Geriatrics

Appropriate studies performed to date have not demonstrated geriatrics-specific problems that would limit the usefulness of pramlintide in the elderly. However, greater sensitivity in some older individuals can not be ruled out. Both pramlintide and insulin regimens should be carefully managed to prevent an increased risk of severe hypoglycemia.

Drug interactions and/or related problems

The following drug interactions and/or related problems have been selected on the basis of their potential clinical significance (possible mechanism in parentheses where appropriate)—not necessarily inclusive (» = major clinical significance):

Note: Pramlintide has the potential to delay the absorption of concomitantly administered oral medications. When the rapid onset of a concomitant orally administered agent is a critical determinant of effectiveness (i.e., analgesics), the agent should be administered at least 1 hour prior to or 2 hours after pramlintide injection.

Combinations containing any of the following medications, depending on the amount present, may also interact with this medication.

ACE inhibitors or
Anti-diabetic products, oral or
Disopyramide or
Fibrates or
Fluoxetine or
MAO inhibitors or
Pentoxifylline or
Propoxyphene or
Salicylates or
Sulfonamide antibiotics
(may increase the blood glucose-lowering effect and susceptibility to hypoglycemia)

» Alpha-glucosidase inhibitors or
» Anticholinergic agents such as
Atropine or
» Other agents that slow intestinal absorption of nutrients or
» Other drugs that alter gastrointestinal motility
(concomitant use should not be considered due to the effects of pramlintide on gastric emptying)

Antihyperglycemic agents
(addition of any antihyperglycemic agent to an existing regimen of one or more antihyperglycemic agents [e.g., insulin, sulfonylurea] or other agents that can increase risk of hypoglycemia may necessitate further insulin dose adjustments and close blood glucose monitoring)

Beta-blockers or
Clonidine or
Guanethidine or
Reserpine
(use of these drugs may make early warning symptoms of hypoglycemia different or less pronounced)

Laboratory value alterations

The following have been selected on the basis of their potential clinical significance (possible effect in parentheses where appropriate)—not necessarily inclusive (» = major clinical significance).

With physiology/laboratory test values

HbA1c
(values may be increased or decreased indicating hyperglycemia or hypoglycemia)

Medical considerations/Contraindications

The medical considerations/contraindications included have been selected on the basis of their potential clinical significance (reasons given in parentheses where appropriate)—not necessarily inclusive (» = major clinical significance).

Except under special circumstances, this medication should not be used when the following medical problem exists:

» Gastroparesis, confirmed diagnosis
» HbA1c>9%
» Hypersensitivity to pramlintide or any of its components, including metacresol
» Hypoglycemia unawareness
» Hypoglycemia, severe and recurrent (requiring assistance during past 6 months)

Risk-benefit should be considered when the following medical problems exist:

» Hypoglycemia, insulin-induced, history of
(may increase risk or recurrence)

Patient monitoring

The following may be especially important in patient monitoring (other tests may be warranted in some patients, depending on condition; » = major clinical significance):

» Glucose monitoring
(frequent pre- and post-meal glucose monitoring combined with an initial 50% reduction in pre-meal doses of short-acting insulin to avoid increasing risk for insulin-induced severe hypoglycemia)

Side/Adverse Effects

Pramlintide alone does not cause hypoglycemia. However, pramlintide is indicated as an adjunct treatment in patients who use mealtime insulin therapy and co-administration of pramlintide with insulin can increase the risk of insulin-induced hypoglycemia, particularly in patients with type 1 diabetes.

The following side/adverse effects have been selected on the basis of their potential clinical significance (possible signs and symptoms in parentheses where appropriate)—not necessarily inclusive:

Those indicating need for medical attention

Incidence more frequent

Allergic reaction (cough; difficulty swallowing; dizziness; fast heartbeat; hives, itching, puffiness or swelling of the eyelids or around the eyes, face, lips or tongue; shortness of breath; skin rash; tightness in chest; unusual tiredness or weakness; wheezing); ***severe hypoglycemia*** (anxiety; blurred vision; chills; cold sweats; coma; confusion; cool pale skin; depression; dizziness; fast heartbeat; headache; increased hunger; nausea; nervousness; nightmares; seizures; shakiness; slurred speech; unusual tiredness or weakness)

Those indicating need for medical attention only if they continue or are bothersome

Incidence more frequent

Abdominal pain (stomach pain); ***anorexia*** (loss of appetite; weight loss); ***arthralgia*** (pain in joints; muscle pain or stiffness; difficulty in moving); ***coughing; dizziness; fatigue*** (unusual tiredness or weakness); ***headache; inflicted injury; nausea; vomiting***

Incidence less frequent

Pharyngitis (body aches or pain; congestion; cough; dryness or soreness of throat; fever; hoarseness; runny nose; tender, swollen glands in neck; trouble in swallowing; voice changes)

Overdose

For more information on the management of overdose or unintentional ingestion, **contact a poison control center** (see *Poison Control Center Listing*).

Single 10 mg doses of pramlintide (83 times the maximum dose of 120 mcg) were administered to three healthy volunteers. Severe nausea was reported in all three individuals and was associated with vomiting, diarrhea, vasodilation, and dizziness. No hypoglycemia was reported.

Treatment of overdose

Supportive care—
Pramlintide has a short half-life and in the case of overdose, supportive measures are indicated.

Patients in whom intentional overdose is confirmed or suspected should be referred for psychiatric consultation.

Patient Consultation

As an aid to patient consultation, refer to *Advice for the Patient, Pramlintide (Systemic)*.

In providing consultation, consider emphasizing the following selected information (» = major clinical significance):

Before using this medication

» Conditions affecting use, especially:
Hypersensitivity to pramlintide or any of its components, including metacresol
Pregnancy—Risk-benefit considerations; women with diabetes should inform their health care professionals if pregnant or contemplating pregnancy
Breast-feeding—Risk-benefit considerations
Use in children—Safety/efficacy not established
Use in the elderly—Careful management of pramlintide and insulin regimens to prevent an increased risk of severe hypoglycemia in the elderly
Other medications, especially alpha-glucosidase inhibitors, anitcholinergic agents, other agents that slow intestinal absorption of nutrients, or other drugs that alter gastrointestinal motility
Other medical problems, especially gastroparesis, confirmed diagnosis; HbA1c>9%; hypoglycemia unawareness; hypoglycemia, severe and recurrent (requiring assistance during past 6 months); or hypoglycemia, insulin-induced, history of

Proper use of this medication

» Importance of patient complying with current insulin regimen and with prescribed self-blood glucose monitoring while taking pramlintide
» Not mixing pramlintide and insulin and always giving as separate injections
» Proper dosing
Missed dose: Not giving an additional injection; not doubling doses
» Proper storage

Precautions while using this medication

» Regular visits to physician to check progress and monitor glucose levels
» Referring patients to the pramlintide patient guide for additional information

» Importance of advising patient and caregiver of symptoms of hypoglycemia and severe hypoglycemia including hunger, headache, sweating, tremor, irritability, difficulty concentrating, loss of consciousness, coma, or seizure

» Instructing patients on handling special situations such as intercurrent conditions (illness or stress), an inadequate or omitted insulin dose, inadvertent administration of increased insulin or pramlintide dose, inadequate food intake or missed meals

» Not driving or operating heavy machinery until the effects of pramlintide on blood sugar are known; discussing with doctor which activities should be avoided

» Importance of having fast-acting sugar such as hard candy, glucose tablets, juice or glucagon available to treat low blood sugar

Side/adverse effects

Signs of potential side effects, especially allergic reactions or severe hypoglycemia

General Dosing Information

Patients should NOT be considered for pramlintide therapy if they show poor compliance with current insulin regimen or with prescribed self-blood glucose monitoring.

When initiating therapy with pramlintide, initial insulin dose reduction is required in both type 1 and type 2 diabetes patients to reduce the risk of insulin-induced hypoglycemia. As this reduction in insulin can lead to glucose elevations, patients should be monitored at regular intervals to assess pramlintide tolerability and the effect on blood glucose, so that individualized insulin adjustments can be initiated.

Each pramlintide dose should be administered subcutaneously into the abdomen or thigh. Injection sites should be rotated so that the same site is not used repeatedly and should also be distinct from the site chosen for any concomitant insulin injection. Each pramlintide injection should be administered subcutaneously to the abdomen or thigh. Administration into the arm is not recommended due to variable absorption.

If pramlintide therapy is discontinued for any reason (e.g., surgery or illness), the same initiation protocol should be followed when pramlintide therapy is reinstituted.

If a pramlintide dose is missed, an additional injection should not be given.

Pramlintide therapy should be discontinued if any of the following occur: recurrent unexplained hypoglycemia that requires medical assistance; persistent clinically significant nausea; noncompliance with self-monitoring of blood glucose concentrations or with insulin dose adjustments or with scheduled health care professional contacts or recommended clinic visits.

Diet/Nutrition

Pramlintide should be administered subcutaneously immediately prior to each major meal (≥250 kcal or containing ≥30 g of carbohydrate).

Safety considerations for handling this medication

A new syringe and needle should always be used to give pramlintide and insulin injections.

Parenteral Dosage Forms

PRAMLINTIDE ACETATE INJECTION

Usual adult dose

Diabetes, type 1 (treatment adjunct)—

Subcutaneously, initial dose of 15 mcg immediately prior to major meals with 50% reduced preprandial, rapid-acting or short-acting insulin dosages, including fixed-mix insulins (70/30). Pramlintide dose may be increased to a maintenance dose of 30 mcg or 60 mcg as tolerated when no clinically significant nausea has occurred for at least 3 days. If significant nausea persists at the 45- or 60-mcg dose level, the pramlintide dose should be decreased to 30 mcg. If the 30-mcg dose is not tolerated; discontinuation of pramlintide should be considered.

Diabetes, type 2 (treatment adjunct)—

Subcutaneously, initial dose of 60 mcg immediately prior to major meals with 50% reduced preprandial, rapid-acting or short-acting insulin dosages, including fixed-mix insulins (70/30). Pramlintide dose may be increased to 120 mcg when no clinically significant nausea has occurred for 3 to 7 days.

Note: • Pramlintide and insulin dose adjustments should be made only as directed by the health care professional.

• Adjust insulin doses to optimize glycemic control once the target dose of pramlintide is achieved and nausea (if experienced) has subsided.

• Contact a health care professional skilled in the use of insulin to review pramlintide and insulin dose adjustments at least once a week until a target dose of pramlintide is achieved, pramlintide is well-tolerated, and blood glucose concentrations are stable.

• Contact a health care professional in the event of recurrent nausea or hypoglycemia. An increased frequency of mild to moderate hypoglycemia should be viewed as a warning sign of increased risk for severe hypoglycemia.

Note: For patients with moderate or severe renal impairment, dosing requirements for pramlintide are not altered. No studies have been done in dialysis patients.

Usual pediatric dose

Safety and efficacy have not been established in pediatric patients.

Usual geriatric dose

See *Usual adult dose*.

Strength(s) usually available

U.S.—

0.6 mg pramlintide acetate per mL (Rx) [*Symlin* (2.25 mg/mL metacresol as a preservative; D-mannitol as a tonicity modifier; acetic acid as a pH modifier; sodium acetate as a pH modifier)].

Packaging and storage

Unopened (not in-use) vials: Store between 2 and 8 °C (36 and 46 °F). Protect from light. Do not freeze. If vial has been frozen or overheated, it should be thrown away.

Opened (in-use) vials: Store refrigerated or at room temperature not greater than 25 °C (77 °F) for up to 28 days. Discard after 28 days.

Preparation of dosage form

To administer pramlintide from vials, use a U-100 insulin syringe (preferably a 0.3 mL [0.3 cc] size) for optimal accuracy. If using a syringe calibrated for use with U-100 insulin, use the table below to measure the microgram dosage in unit increments.

Dosage prescribed (mcg)	Increment using a U-100 syringe (Units)	Volume (cc or mL)
15	2.5	0.025
30	5	0.05
45	7.5	0.075
60	10	0.1
120	20	0.2

Pramlintide and insulin should always be administered as separate injections.

Pramlintide should not be mixed with any type of insulin.

Stability

Pramlintide should be inspected visually for particulate matter or discoloration prior to administration whenever the solution and the container permit.

Unopened refrigerated vials can be stored until the expiration date. Opened refrigerated or room temperature vials must be used within 28 days.

Auxiliary labeling

• For control of diabetes. Do not stop unless directed by a physician.

• This drug alone or with alcohol may cause drowsiness. Use care when driving or operating machinery.

• This is a diabetic patient.

Developed: 08/03/2005

PRAMOXINE—See *Anesthetics (Mucosal-Local), Anesthetics (Topical)*

PRAMOXINE AND MENTHOL—See *Anesthetics (Topical)*

PRAVASTATIN—See *HMG-CoA Reductase Inhibitors (Systemic)*

PRAZEPAM—See *Benzodiazepines (Systemic)*

PRAZOSIN Systemic

VA CLASSIFICATION (Primary/Secondary): CV150/CV409; CV900; AD900; GU900

Commonly used brand name(s): *Minipress*.

Note: For a listing of dosage forms and brand names by country availability, see *Dosage Forms* section(s).

Category

Antihypertensive; vasodilator, congestive heart failure; antidote (to ergot alkaloid poisoning); vasospastic therapy adjunct; benign prostatic hyperplasia therapy agent.

Indications

Note: Bracketed information in the *Indications* section refers to uses that are not included in U.S. product labeling.

Accepted

Hypertension (treatment)—Prazosin is indicated in the treatment of hypertension.

For additional information on initial therapeutic guidelines related to the treatment of hypertension, see *Appendix III*.

[Congestive heart failure (treatment)][1]—Prazosin may be used as an adjunct to digoxin and diuretics for the treatment of congestive heart failure. However, prazosin has not been shown to improve survival in these patients.

[Toxicity, ergot alkaloid (treatment)][1]—Prazosin is used for treatment of peripheral vasospasm caused by ergot alkaloid overdose.

[Pheochromocytoma (treatment)][1]—Prazosin is used for the management of hypertension associated with pheochromocytoma.

[Raynaud's phenomenon (treatment)][1]—Prazosin is used for treatment of Raynaud's phenomenon.

[Benign prostatic hyperplasia (BPH) (treatment)][1]—Prazosin is used for the treatment of urinary symptoms associated with benign prostatic hyperplasia. Prazosin has been shown to improve urinary flow and symptoms of BPH. However, the long-term effects of prazosin on the incidence of acute urinary obstruction or other complications of BPH or on the need for surgery have not yet been determined.

[1]Not included in Canadian product labeling.

Pharmacology/Pharmacokinetics

Physicochemical characteristics

Molecular weight—419.87.

pKa—6.5.

Mechanism of action/Effect

Prazosin is a selective alpha$_1$-adrenergic blocking agent. The alpha$_1$-adrenergic blocking action is thought to account primarily for its effects.

Hypertension—

Prazosin produces vasodilation and reduces peripheral resistance but generally has little effect on cardiac output. Antihypertensive effect is usually not accompanied by reflex tachycardia. There is little or no effect on renal blood flow or glomerular filtration rate.

Congestive heart failure—

Beneficial effects, resulting from vasodilation, are due to decreased systemic resistance, preload and afterload reduction, and resulting improved cardiac output.

Raynaud's phenomenon—

Therapeutic effect for vasospasm is due to inhibition of vasoconstriction by blocking of postsynaptic alpha$_1$ receptors.

Benign prostatic hyperplasia—

Relaxation of smooth muscle in the bladder neck, prostate, and prostate capsule produced by alpha$_1$-adrenergic blockade results in a reduction in urethral resistance and pressure, bladder outlet resistance, and urinary symptoms.

Other actions/effects

Prazosin may affect serum lipids. The most consistent changes observed are a decrease in levels of serum total cholesterol and low density lipoprotein (LDL) cholesterol. However, the implications of these changes are unclear.

Absorption

Well-absorbed from gastrointestinal tract; bioavailability is variable (50 to 85%).

Protein binding

Very high (97%; 20% to red blood cells).

Biotransformation

Primarily hepatic. Several metabolites have been identified in humans and animals (6-O-demethyl, 7-O-demethyl, 2-[1-piperazinyl]-4-amino-6,7-dimethoxyquinazoline, 2,4-diamino-6,7-dimethoxyquinazoline); in dog studies, three of the metabolites were shown to be responsible for approximately 10 to 25% of prazosin's hypotensive activity.

Half-life

2 to 3 hours; unchanged in renal function impairment, but may increase to more than double (6 to 8 hours) in congestive heart failure.

Onset of action

Hypertension—Within 30 to 90 minutes after a single dose.

Congestive heart failure—Rapid.

Time to peak concentration

1 to 3 hours.

Time to peak effect

Hypertension—

Single dose: 2 to 4 hours.

Multiple doses: Up to 3 to 4 weeks of therapy may be required for maximal therapeutic effect.

Congestive heart failure—

1 hour.

Duration of action

Hypertension—Single dose: 7 to 10 hours.

Congestive heart failure—6 hours.

Elimination

Primarily in bile and feces; 6 to 10% in urine. Excreted as unchanged drug (5 to 11%) and metabolites. Elimination of prazosin may be slower in patients with congestive heart failure than in normal subjects.

In dialysis—Not dialyzable.

Precautions to Consider

Cross-sensitivity and/or related problems

Patients sensitive to other quinazolines (doxazosin, terazosin) may also be sensitive to prazosin.

Carcinogenicity

An 18-month study in rats given prazosin at doses of more than 225 times the usual maximum recommended human dose of 20 mg per day did not demonstrate carcinogenic potential.

Mutagenicity

Prazosin was not mutagenic in *in vitro* genetic toxicology studies.

Pregnancy/Reproduction

Fertility—A study in male rats given subcutaneous injections of prazosin (1.4 mg per kg of body weight [mg/kg]) revealed reduced fertility manifested by a suppression of the fertilizing potential of spermatozoa.

A fertility and general reproductive performance study in male and female rats given prazosin at a dose of 75 mg/kg (225 times the usual maximum recommended human dose) demonstrated decreased fertility. However, when rats were given 25 mg/kg (75 times the usual maximum recommended human dose) decreased fertility was not seen.

Pregnancy—Adequate and well-controlled studies in humans have not been done. However, limited uncontrolled use of prazosin and a beta-blocking agent for the control of severe hypertension in 44 pregnant women revealed no drug-related fetal abnormalities or adverse effects. Also, use of prazosin during the last trimester in 8 pregnant women with hypertension produced no prolonged clinical problems. All infants were developing normally 6 to 30 months following delivery.

In rats given doses more than 225 times the usual maximum recommended human dose, prazosin has been shown to be associated with decreased litter weight at birth and at 1, 4, and 21 days of age. There was no evidence, however, of drug-related external, visceral, or skeletal abnormalities.

In pregnant rabbits and pregnant monkeys given doses of more than 225 times and 12 times the usual maximum recommended human dose, respectively, no drug-related external, visceral, or skeletal abnormalities were observed in the fetuses.

FDA Pregnancy Category C.

Breast-feeding

Prazosin is distributed into breast milk in small amounts.

Pediatrics

Appropriate studies on the relationship of age to the effects of prazosin have not been performed in the pediatric population. However, no pediatrics-specific problems have been documented to date.

Geriatrics

Although appropriate studies on the relationship of age to the effects of prazosin have not been performed in the geriatric population, geriatrics-specific problems are not expected to limit the usefulness of prazosin in the elderly. However, elderly patients may be more sensitive to the hypotensive effects and are more likely to have age-related renal function impairment, which may require lower prazosin doses. In addition, the risk of prazosin-induced hypothermia may be increased in elderly patients.

Drug interactions and/or related problems

The following drug interactions and/or related problems have been selected on the basis of their potential clinical significance (possible mechanism in parentheses where appropriate)—not necessarily inclusive (» = major clinical significance):

Note: Combinations containing any of the following medications, depending on the amount present, may also interact with this medication.

Anti-inflammatory drugs, nonsteroidal (NSAIDs), especially indomethacin
(antihypertensive effects of prazosin may be reduced when it is used concurrently with these agents; indomethacin, and possibly other NSAIDs, may antagonize the antihypertensive effect by inhibiting renal prostaglandin synthesis and/or by causing sodium and fluid retention; the patient should be carefully monitored to confirm that the desired effect is being obtained)

Hypotension-producing medications, other (see *Appendix II*)
(antihypertensive effects may be potentiated when these medications are used concurrently with prazosin; although some antihypertensive and/or diuretic combinations are frequently used to therapeutic advantage, dosage adjustments are necessary when these medications are used concurrently)

Sympathomimetics
(antihypertensive effects of prazosin may be reduced when it is used concurrently with these agents; the patient should be carefully monitored to confirm that the desired effect is being obtained)
(concurrent use of prazosin antagonizes the peripheral vasoconstriction produced by high doses of dopamine)
(concurrent use of prazosin may decrease the pressor response to ephedrine)
(concurrent use of prazosin may block the alpha-adrenergic effects of epinephrine, possibly resulting in severe hypotension and tachycardia)
(concurrent use of prazosin usually decreases, but does not reverse or completely block, the pressor effect of metaraminol)
(prior administration of prazosin may decrease the pressor effect and shorten the duration of action of methoxamine and phenylephrine)

Laboratory value alterations

The following have been selected on the basis of their potential clinical significance (possible effect in parentheses where appropriate)—not necessarily inclusive (» = major clinical significance).

With diagnostic test results
Vanillylmandelic acid (VMA), urinary
(concentrations may be increased; false positive results may occur in screening tests for pheochromocytoma)

Medical considerations/Contraindications

The medical considerations/contraindications included have been selected on the basis of their potential clinical significance (reasons given in parentheses where appropriate)—not necessarily inclusive (» = major clinical significance).

Risk-benefit should be considered when the following medical problems exist:

Angina pectoris
(may induce angina or aggravate pre-existing angina)

» Cardiac disease, severe
(prazosin is usually not used alone, although it may improve cardiac performance in some patients with severe refractory congestive heart failure)

Narcolepsy
(may exacerbate cataplexy; however, a clear cause-effect relationship has not been established)

Renal function impairment
(increased sensitivity to prazosin's effects; lower doses may be required)

Sensitivity to prazosin

Patient monitoring

The following may be especially important in patient monitoring (other tests may be warranted in some patients, depending on condition; » = major clinical significance):

» Blood pressure measurements
(recommended at periodic intervals in patients being treated for hypertension; selected patients may be trained to perform blood pressure measurements at home and report the results at regular physician visits)

Side/Adverse Effects

Note: A "first-dose orthostatic hypotensive reaction" sometimes occurs, most frequently 30 to 90 minutes after the initial dose of prazosin, and may be severe. Syncope or other postural symptoms, such as dizziness, may occur. Subsequent occurrence with dosage increases is also possible. Incidence appears to be dose-related; thus, it is important that therapy be initiated with the lowest possible dose. Patients who are volume-depleted or sodium-restricted may be more sensitive to the orthostatic hypotensive effects of prazosin, and the effect may be exaggerated after exercise.

Hypotensive side effects may be more likely to occur in geriatric patients.

The following side/adverse effects have been selected on the basis of their potential clinical significance (possible signs and symptoms in parentheses where appropriate)—not necessarily inclusive:

Those indicating need for medical attention

Incidence more frequent
Dizziness; orthostatic hypotension (dizziness or lightheadedness when getting up from a lying or sitting position; sudden fainting)

Incidence less frequent
Edema (swelling of feet or lower legs); ***palpitations*** (pounding heartbeat); ***urinary incontinence*** (loss of bladder control)

Incidence rare
Angina (chest pain); ***dyspnea*** (shortness of breath); ***priapism*** (painful, inappropriate erection of the penis, continuing)

Those indicating need for medical attention only if they continue or are bothersome

Incidence more frequent
Drowsiness; headache; malaise (lack of energy)

Incidence less frequent
Dryness of mouth; fatigue (unusual tiredness or weakness); ***nervousness***

Incidence rare
Nausea; urinary frequency (frequent urge to urinate)

Overdose

For more information on the management of overdose or unintentional ingestion, **contact a Poison Control Center** (see *Poison Control Center Listing*).

Treatment of overdose

Recommended treatment for prazosin overdose includes: Treatment of circulatory failure, either by placing the patient in the supine position and elevating the legs or by using additional measures if shock is present, is most important; volume expanders may be used to treat shock, followed, if necessary, by administration of a vasopressor; symptomatic, supportive treatment and monitoring of fluid and electrolyte status.

Patient Consultation

As an aid to patient consultation, refer to *Advice for the Patient, Prazosin (Systemic).*

In providing consultation, consider emphasizing the following selected information (» = major clinical significance):

Before using this medication

» Conditions affecting use, especially:
Sensitivity to quinazolines
Breast-feeding—Distributed into breast milk in small amounts
Use in the elderly—Increased sensitivity to hypotensive effects and increased risk of prazosin-induced hypothermia
Other medical problems, especially severe cardiac disease

Proper use of this medication

Compliance with therapy; taking medication at the same times each day to maintain the therapeutic effect
» Proper dosing
Missed dose: Taking as soon as possible; not taking if almost time for next dose; not doubling doses
» Proper storage

For use as an antihypertensive

Possible need for control of weight and diet, especially sodium intake

» Patient may not experience symptoms of hypertension; importance of taking medication even if feeling well

» Does not cure, but helps control hypertension; possible need for life-long therapy; serious consequences of untreated hypertension

For use in benign prostatic hyperplasia (BPH)

Relieves symptoms of BPH but does not change the size of the prostate; may not prevent the need for surgery in the future

Precautions while using this medication

Making regular visits to physician to check progress

» Caution if dizziness, lightheadedness, or sudden fainting occurs, especially after initial dose; taking first dose at bedtime

» Caution when getting up suddenly from a lying or sitting position

» Caution in using alcohol, while standing for long periods or exercising, and during hot weather because of enhanced orthostatic hypotensive effects

» Possibility of drowsiness

» Caution when driving or doing anything else requiring alertness because of possible drowsiness, dizziness, or lightheadedness

» Not taking other medications, especially nonprescription sympathomimetics, unless discussed with physician

Side/adverse effects

Signs of potential side effects, especially dizziness, orthostatic hypotension, edema, palpitations, urinary incontinence, angina, dyspnea, and priapism

General Dosing Information

Dosage of prazosin should be adjusted to meet the individual requirements of each patient, on the basis of blood pressure response.

Prazosin may be used alone or in combination with a thiazide diuretic or beta-adrenergic blocker, both of which reduce the tendency for sodium and water retention, although they also produce additive hypotension. If combination therapy is indicated, individual titration is required to ensure the lowest possible therapeutic dose of each drug.

In order to minimize the "first-dose orthostatic hypotensive reaction," an initial dose of 1 mg is recommended, with gradual increments as needed. Administration of the initial dose at bedtime is recommended, as well as the initial dose of each increment.

When a diuretic or other antihypertensive agent is added to prazosin therapy, the dose of prazosin should be reduced to 1 or 2 mg three times a day, followed by titration of dosage of the combination. When prazosin is added to existing diuretic or antihypertensive therapy, the dose of the other agent should be reduced and prazosin started at a dose of 0.5 or 1 mg two or three times a day.

Tolerance to the effects of prazosin may occur during treatment of congestive heart failure but usually not during treatment of hypertension. An early, transient (usually within the first few doses) blunting of hemodynamic effect may occur due to reflex activation of the sympathetic nervous system. The hemodynamic effect may spontaneously restore with uninterrupted therapy or the blunted effect may be overcome by temporarily interrupting prazosin therapy. A later apparent tolerance may result from fluid retention, requiring increased doses of diuretics; this effect may be minimized by increasing the dose of prazosin, temporarily interrupting prazosin therapy, or substituting another vasodilator.

Oral Dosage Forms

Note: Bracketed uses in the *Dosage Forms* section refer to categories of use and/or indications that are not included in U.S. product labeling.

PRAZOSIN HYDROCHLORIDE CAPSULES USP

Note: The dosing and strengths of the dosage forms available are expressed in terms of prazosin base (not the hydrochloride salt).

Usual adult dose

Antihypertensive—

Initial: Oral, 1 mg (base) two or three times a day.

Maintenance: Oral, adjusted gradually to meet individual requirements, most commonly 6 to 15 mg (base) a day in two or three divided doses.

[Toxicity, ergot alkaloid]—

Oral, 1 mg three times a day.

[Vasospastic therapy adjunct—Raynaud's phenomenon]—

Oral, 1 mg three times a day.

[Benign prostatic hyperplasia]—

Initial: Oral, 1 mg (base) two times a day.

Maintenance: Oral, 1 to 5 mg (base) two times a day.

Note: Geriatric patients may be more sensitive to the effects of the usual adult dose.

Usual adult prescribing limits

Daily doses higher than 20 mg (base) usually do not have increased efficacy, although some patients respond to up to 40 mg a day.

Usual pediatric dose

Antihypertensive—

Oral, 50 to 400 mcg (0.05 to 0.4 mg) (base) per kg of body weight per day in two or three divided doses. Single doses should not exceed 7 mg, and the total daily dose should not exceed 15 mg per day.

Strength(s) usually available

U.S.—

1 mg (base) (Rx) [*Minipress* (sucrose); GENERIC (sucrose)].

2 mg (base) (Rx) [*Minipress* (sucrose); GENERIC (sucrose)].

5 mg (base) (Rx) [*Minipress* (sucrose); GENERIC (sucrose)].

Canada—

Not commercially available.

Packaging and storage

Store below 40 °C (104 °F), preferably between 15 and 30 °C (59 and 86 °F), unless otherwise specified by manufacturer. Store in a well-closed, light-resistant container.

Auxiliary labeling

- Do not take other medicines without your doctor's advice.
- May cause dizziness.

Note

Check refill frequency to determine compliance in hypertensive patients.

PRAZOSIN HYDROCHLORIDE TABLETS

Note: The dosing and strengths of the dosage forms available are expressed in terms of prazosin base (not the hydrochloride salt).

Usual adult dose

Antihypertensive—

Initial: Oral, 500 mcg (0.5 mg) two or three times a day for at least 3 days. If tolerated, increase to 1 mg (base) two or three times a day for a further 3 days.

Maintenance: Oral, adjusted gradually to meet individual requirements, most commonly 6 to 15 mg (base) a day in two or three divided daily doses.

Toxicity, ergot alkaloid[1]—

Oral, 1 mg three times a day.

Vasospastic therapy adjunct—Raynaud's phenomenon[1]—

Oral, 1 mg three times a day.

Benign prostatic hyperplasia[1]—

Initial: Oral, 1 mg (base) two times a day.

Maintenance: Oral, 1 to 5 mg (base) two times a day.

Note: Geriatric patients may be more sensitive to the effects of the usual adult dose.

Usual adult prescribing limits

Daily doses higher than 20 mg (base) usually do not have increased efficacy, although some patients respond to up to 40 mg a day.

Usual pediatric dose

Antihypertensive—

See *Prazosin Hydrochloride Capsules USP*.

Strength(s) usually available

U.S.—

Not commercially available.

Canada—

1 mg (base) (Rx) [*Minipress* (scored); GENERIC].

2 mg (base) (Rx) [*Minipress* (scored); GENERIC].

5 mg (base) (Rx) [*Minipress* (scored); GENERIC].

Packaging and storage

Store below 40 °C (104 °F), preferably between 15 and 30 °C (59 and 86 °F), unless otherwise specified by manufacturer. Store in a well-closed, light-resistant container.

Auxiliary labeling

- Do not take other medicines without your doctor's advice.
- May cause dizziness.

Note

Check refill frequency to determine compliance in hypertensive patients.

[1]Not included in Canadian product labeling.

Selected Bibliography

The fifth report of the Joint National Committee on Detection, Evaluation, and Treatment of High Blood Pressure. Arch Intern Med 1993; 153: 154-83.

Revised: 08/19/1998

PREDNISOLONE—See *Corticosteroids—Glucocorticoid Effects (Systemic), Corticosteroids (Ophthalmic)*

PREDNISONE—See *Corticosteroids—Glucocorticoid Effects (Systemic)*

PREGABALIN Systemic

VA CLASSIFICATION (Primary/Secondary): CN900/CN400

Note: Controlled substance classification

U.S.: Schedule V

Canada: F

Commonly used brand name(s): *Lyrica.*

Note: For a listing of dosage forms and brand names by country availability, see *Dosage Forms* section(s).

Category

Antineuralgic; anticonvulsant.

Indications

Accepted

Neuralgia, post-herpetic (treatment)—Pregabalin is indicated for management of post-herpetic neuralgia.

Pain, peripheral neuropathy, diabetic (treatment)—Pregabalin is indicated for management of neuropathic pain associated with diabetic peripheral neuropathy.

Seizures, partial (treatment adjunctive)[1]—Pregabalin is indicated as adjunctive therapy for adult patients with partial onset seizures.

[1]Not included in Canadian product labeling.

Pharmacology/Pharmacokinetics

Physicochemical characteristics

Molecular weight—Pregabalin: 159.23.

pKa—

pK_{a1}: 4.2.

pK_{a2}: 10.6.

Solubility—Pregabalin is freely soluble in water and both basic and acidic aqueous solutions.

Partition coefficient—−1.35 at pH 7.4

Mechanism of action/Effect

The exact mechanism of action is unknown; however, pregabalin binds with high affinity to the $alpha_2$-delta site in central nervous tissue. Studies in animals suggest that binding to the $alpha_2$-delta subunit may be involved in pregabalin's antinociceptive and antiseizure effects. Pregabalin also reduces the calcium-dependent release of several neurotransmitters, possibly by modulation of calcium channel function.

Pregabalin is a structural derivative of the inhibitory neurotransmitter gamma-aminobutyric acid (GABA), but it does not bind directly to $GABA_A$, $GABA_B$, or benzodiazepine receptors, does not augment $GABA_A$ responses in cultured neurons, does not alter rat brain GABA concentration or have acute effects on GABA uptake or degradation. In cultured neurons, prolonged application of pregabalin increases the density of GABA transporter protein and increases the rate of functional GABA transport. Pregabalin does not block sodium channels, is not active at opiate receptors, and does not alter cyclooxygenase enzyme activity. It is inactive at serotonin and dopamine receptors and does not inhibit dopamine, serotonin, or noradrenaline.

Absorption

Well absorbed following oral administration. Pregabalin's oral bioavailability is ≥ 90%, independent of dose and the rate of absorption is decreased when given with food resulting in a decrease in C_{max} of approximately 25 to 30% and an increase in T_{max} to approximately 3 hours.

Distribution

Volume of distribution (Vol_D)—0.5 L/kg

Pregabalin crosses the blood brain barrier in mice, rats, and monkeys, crosses the placenta in rats, and is present in the milk of lactating rats.

Protein binding

Pregabalin does not bind to plasma protein.

Biotransformation

Pregabalin undergoes negligible metabolism in humans.

Half-life

Elimination—6.3 hours in subjects with normal renal function.

Plasma

Within 1.5 hours, following oral administration under fasting conditions.

Peak plasma concentration

Maximum plasma concentrations and AUC values increase linearly with regard to dose. Steady state is achieved within 24 to 48 hours following repeated administration.

Elimination

Renal: approximately 90% as unchanged drug, 0.9% as major metabolite N-methylated derivate of pregabalin.

Clearance: 67 to 80.9 mL/min in young healthy subjects.

In dialysis, pregabalin is effectively removed from plasma by hemodialysis.

Precautions to Consider

Carcinogenicity

Standard *in-vivo* lifetime carcinogenicity studies done revealed a high incidence of hemangiosarcoma in two different strains of mice.

Clinical studies done, comprising 6396 patient-years of exposure in patients >12 years of age found new or worsening tumors in 57 patients. However, without knowledge or background incidence and recurrence in similar populations not treated with pregabalin, it is not known whether the incidence seen is or is not affected by treatment.

No evidence of carcinogenicity was seen in two year studies done in rats given pregabalin at doses of 50, 150, or 450 mg/kg in males and 100, 300 or 900 mg/kg in females.

Mutagenicity

Pregabalin was not found to be mutagenic in bacteria or in mammalian cells *in vitro,* or clastogenic in mammalian systems *in vitro* and *in vivo,* and did not induce unscheduled DNA synthesis in mouse or rat hepatocytes.

Pregnancy/Reproduction

Fertility—Effects on male reproductive parameters have not been adequately studied. Clinical trials to assess the effect of pregabalin on sperm motility were conducted. Healthy young males were given pregabalin at 600 mg/day. After 3 months of treatment, the difference between placebo and pregabalin treated subjects in mean percent sperm with normal motility was <4% and neither group had a change from baseline of more than 2%.

Fertility studies done in male rats given oral doses of pregabalin (50 to 2500 mg/kg) prior to and during mating with untreated females revealed decreased sperm counts and sperm motility, increased sperm abnormalities, reduced fertility, increased preimplantation embryos loss, decreased litter size, decreased fetal body weights and increased incidence of fetal abnormalities. The effects on sperm and fertility were reversible and the no affect dose for male toxicity was approximately 3 times human exposure at the maximum recommended dose of 600 mg/day.

Adverse effects were also observed on testes and epididymides in male rats exposed to pregabalin at doses of 500 to 1250 mg/kg. The no effect dose in male rats was 250 mg/kg and was associated with plasma exposure approximately 8 times human exposure at the MRD.

Fertility studies done in female rats given oral doses of pregabalin (500, 1250, or 2500 mg/kg) prior to and during mating and early gestation disrupted estrous cyclicity and increased the number of days to mating at all doses. Embryolethality occurred at the highest dose and the low dose produced plasma exposure 9 times that in humans receiving the MRD. The no effect dose for females was not established.

Pregnancy—There are no adequate and well controlled studies in pregnant women. Pregabalin should be used during pregnancy only if the potential benefit justifies the potential risk to the fetus.

Studies done in rats and rabbits given pregabalin during pregnancy at doses that produced plasma pregabalin exposure ≥5 times human exposure at the MRD of 600 mg/day, showed increases of fetal structural abnormalities and other manifestations of developmental toxicity, including lethality, growth retardation, and nervous and reproductive system function impairment.

Pregnant rats given oral doses of pregabalin (500, 1250, or 2500 mg/kg) throughout organogenesis revealed increased incidences of specific skull alterations attributed to abnormally advanced ossification at ≥1250 mg/kg, and incidences of skeletal variations and retarded ossification were increased at all doses. Fetal body weights were decreased at the highest dose.

Pregnant rabbits given oral doses of pregabalin (500, 1250, or 2500 mg/kg) throughout organogenesis revealed decreased fetal body weights and increased incidences of skeletal malformations, visceral variations and retarded ossification at the highest dose. The no-effect dose for developmental toxicity in rabbits was associated with plasma exposure approximately 16 times human exposure at the MRD.

Studies done in female rats given pregabalin at doses of 50, 100, 250, 1250, or 2500 mg/kg throughout gestation and lactation revealed offspring growth reduction at ≥100 mg/kg, and decreased offspring survival at ≥250 mg/kg and 100% mortality at doses of ≥1250 mg/kg. When offspring were tested as adults, neurobehavioral abnormalities (decreased auditory startle responding) were observed at ≥250 mg/kg and reproductive impairment was seen at 1250 mg/kg. The no-effect dose for pre- and postnatal development toxicity in rats was 50 mg/kg and produce a plasma exposure approximately 2 times the human exposure at MRD.

FDA Pregnancy Category C

Labor and delivery—The effects of pregabalin on labor and delivery in pregnant women are unknown. Studies done in rats showed prolonged gestation and induced dystocia at exposure ≥50 times the mean human exposure at the maximum recommended clinical dose of 600 mg/day.

Breast-feeding
It is not known whether pregabalin is distributed into breast milk. However, pregabalin is distributed in the milk of rats. Because many drugs are distributed in human milk and because of the potential for tumorigenicity shown for pregabalin in animal studies, a decision should be made whether to discontinue nursing or to discontinue pregabalin, taking into account the importance of the drug to the mother.

Pediatrics
Safety and efficacy of pregabalin in pediatric patients have not been established.

Studies done with pregabalin in young rats given oral doses from 50 to 500 mg/kg from postnatal day 7 through sexual maturity produced neurobehavioral abnormalities and reproductive impairment. The neurobehavioral abnormalities persisted after cessation of dosing and is considered to represent long term effects. The low effect dose for developmental neurotoxicity and reproductive impairment was 50 mg/kg and is associated with pregabalin exposure equal to human exposure at the maximum recommended dose of 600 mg/day. A no-effect dose was not established.

Geriatrics
Appropriate studies to date have not demonstrated geriatrics-specific problems that would limit the usefulness of pregabalin in the elderly. However, elderly patients are more likely to have age-related renal function impairment, which may require a dosing reduction.

Pharmacogenetics
Pregabalin exposure associated with daily dose was similar between women and men.

The pharmacokinetics of pregabalin were not affected by race.

Drug interactions and/or related problems
The following drug interactions and/or related problems have been selected on the basis of their potential clinical significance (possible mechanism in parentheses where appropriate)—not necessarily inclusive (» = major clinical significance):

Note: Important pharmacokinetic interactions would be expected to occur between commonly used antiepileptic drugs and pregabalin.

Combinations containing any of the following medications, depending on the amount present, may also interact with this medication.

Alcohol or
Central nervous system (CNS) depression-producing medications, other (see *Appendix II*)
(concomitant treatment may increase CNS effects on cognitive and gross motor functioning; no clinically important effects on respiration were seen)

» Antidiabetic drugs such as
Thiazolidinedione
(caution; coadministering with pregabalin can cause weight gain and/or fluid retention, possibly exacerbating or leading to heart failure)

Laboratory value alterations
The following have been selected on the basis of their potential clinical significance (possible effect in parentheses where appropriate)—not necessarily inclusive (» = major clinical significance).

With physiology/laboratory test values

Creatine kinase
(levels may be elevated; pregabalin should be discontinued if myopathy is diagnosed or suspected or if markedly elevated creatine kinase levels occur)

Platelet count
(may be significantly decreased in 3% of pregabalin treated patients in controlled trials; no increase in bleeding related adverse events)

PR interval prolongation
(pregabalin has been associated with mild PR interval prolongation in clinical trial ECG data)

Medical considerations/Contraindications
The medical considerations/contraindications included have been selected on the basis of their potential clinical significance (reasons given in parentheses where appropriate)—not necessarily inclusive (» = major clinical significance).

Except under special circumstances, this medication should not be used when the following medical problem exists:

» Hypersensitivity to pregabalin or any of its components

Risk-benefit should be considered when the following medical problems exist:

» Congestive heart failure
(caution should be used when administering pregabalin)

» Diabetes mellitus
(pregabalin may increase weight gain; may increase risk factors for skin ulcerations)

» Renal function impairment
(dosage reduction is necessary; pregabalin clearance is proportional to creatinine clearance)

Patient monitoring
The following may be especially important in patient monitoring (other tests may be warranted in some patients, depending on condition; » = major clinical significance):

Skin integrity
(diabetic patients should be monitored for the development of skin ulcerations)

Side/Adverse Effects
The following side/adverse effects have been selected on the basis of their potential clinical significance (possible signs and symptoms in parentheses where appropriate)—not necessarily inclusive:

Those indicating need for medical attention
Incidence less frequent

Dyspnea (shortness of breath difficult or labored breathing tightness in chest wheezing)

Incidence rare

Allergic reaction (cough; difficulty swallowing; dizziness; fast heartbeat; hives; itching; puffiness or swelling of the eyelids or around the eyes, face, lips or tongue; shortness of breath; skin rash; tightness in chest; unusual tiredness or weakness; wheezing); ***Stevens-Johnson Syndrome*** (blistering, peeling, loosening of skin; chills; cough; diarrhea; itching; joint or muscle pain; red irritated eyes; red skin lesions, often with a purple center; sore throat; sores, ulcers, or white spots in mouth or on lips; unusual tiredness or weakness)

Those indicating need for medical attention only if they continue or are bothersome
Incidence more frequent

Abnormal gait (change in walking and balance, clumsiness, or unsteadiness); ***abnormal thinking*** (confusion; delusions; dementia); ***accidental injury; amnesia*** (loss of memory; problems with memory); ***ataxia*** (shakiness and unsteady walk; unsteadiness; trembling, or other problems with muscle control or coordination); ***blurred vision; blurry vision; confusion*** (mood or mental changes); ***constipation*** (difficulty having a bowel movement (stool)); ***dizziness; diplopia*** (double vision; seeing double); ***dry mouth; edema*** (swelling); ***headache; incoordination*** (lack of coordination); ***increased appetite; in-***

fection (fever or chills; cough or hoarseness; lower back or side pain; painful or difficult urination); ***neuropathy*** (burning, tingling, numbness or pain in the hands, arms, feet, or legs sensation of pins and needles stabbing pain); ***peripheral edema*** (bloating or swelling of face, arms, hands, lower legs, or feet; rapid weight gain; tingling of hands or feet; unusual weight gain or loss); ***somnolence*** (sleepiness or unusual drowsiness); ***speech disorder*** (difficulty in speaking); ***tremor*** (trembling or shaking of hands or feet; shakiness in legs, arms, hands, feet); ***weight gain***

Incidence less frequent

Abnormal vision (changes in vision); ***asthenia*** (cough; difficulty breathing; noisy breathing; shortness of breath; tightness in chest; wheezing); ***back pain; bronchitis*** (cough producing mucus difficulty breathing shortness of breath tightness in chest wheezing); ***chest pain; euphoria*** (false or unusual sense of well-being); ***eye disorder; facial edema*** (swelling or puffiness of face); ***flatulence*** (bloated full feeling; excess air or gas in stomach or intestines; passing gas); ***flu syndrome*** (chills; cough; diarrhea; fever; general feeling of discomfort or illness; headache; joint pain; loss of appetite; muscle aches and pains; nausea; runny nose; shivering; sore throat; sweating; trouble sleeping; unusual tiredness or weakness; vomiting); ***hypoglycemia*** (anxiety; blurred vision; chills; cold sweats; coma; confusion; cool pale skin; depression; dizziness; fast heartbeat; headache; increased hunger; nausea; nervousness; nightmares; seizures; shakiness; slurred speech; unusual tiredness or weakness); ***myasthenia*** (loss of strength or energy; muscle pain or weakness); ***myoclonus*** (muscle twitching or jerking rhythmic movement of muscles); ***pain; nervousness; nystagmus*** (uncontrolled eye movements); ***paresthesias*** (burning, crawling, itching, numbness, prickling, "pins and needles", or tingling feelings); ***twitching; urinary incontinence*** (loss of bladder control); ***vertigo*** (burning, tingling, numbness or pain in the hands, arms, feet, or legs; sensation of pins and needles; stabbing pain); ***visual field defects*** (blurred vision; decrease or change in vision); ***vomiting***

Overdose

For more information on the management of overdose or unintentional ingestion, **contact a poison control center** (see *Poison Control Center Listing*).

Treatment of overdose

There is no known specific antidote to pregabalin. Treatment is generally symptomatic and supportive.

To decrease absorption—

Emptying stomach by emesis or gastric lavage; usual precautions should be observed to maintain airway.

To enhance elimination—

Hemodialysis indicated by the patient's clinical state; patients with significant renal impairment may increase clearance of pregabalin approximately 50% in 4 hours.

Monitoring—

Monitoring of vital signs and observation of clinical status of the patient.

Supportive care—

Contacting a certified poison control center for up-to-date information on the management of overdose with pregabalin.

Patients in whom intentional overdose is confirmed or suspected should be referred for psychiatric consultation.

Patient Consultation

As an aid to patient consultation, refer to *Advice for the Patient, Pregabalin (Systemic)*.

In providing consultation, consider emphasizing the following selected information (» = major clinical significance):

Before using this medication

» Conditions affecting use, especially:

Hypersensitivity to pregabalin or any of its components

Pregnancy—Pregabalin should be used during pregnancy only if the benefit justifies the potential risk to the fetus.

Breast-feeding—Pregabalin is distributed in the milk of rats. It is not known whether pregabalin is distributed into breast milk.

Use in children—Safety and efficacy have not been established.

Use in the elderly—Elderly patients may be more likely to have age related renal function impairment, which may require a dosing reduction.

Other medications, especially antidiabetic drugs such as thiazolidinedione

Other medical problems, especially congestive heart failure or renal function impairment

Proper use of this medication

» Proper dosing

» Compliance with therapy; not taking more or less medicine than prescribed; not missing any doses

» Reading the patient information leaflet prior to beginning pregabalin therapy.

Pregabalin may be taken with or without food.

Missed dose: Taking as soon as possible; not taking if almost time for next scheduled dose; not doubling doses.

» Proper storage

Precautions while using this medication

» Regular visits to physician to check progress of therapy.

» Possible blurred or double vision, dizziness, drowsiness, impairment of thinking or motor skills; caution when driving or doing jobs requiring alertness.

» Discussing alcohol use or use of other CNS depressants with physician.

» Checking with physician before discontinuing medication.

» Checking with physician if changes in vision occur.

» Promptly reporting any unexplained muscle pain, tenderness, or weakness particularly if accompanied by malaise or fever.

» Notifying your physician if you become pregnant or if you plan to become pregnant during pregabalin therapy.

» Informing men of the possible risks of fathering a child during pregabalin therapy.

» Possible edema and weight gain.

» Reporting skin ulcerations to physicians.

Side/adverse effects

Signs of potential side effects, especially allergic reaction, dyspnea, or Stevens-Johnson Syndrome

General Dosing Information

Pregabalin oral clearance is consistent with age-related decreases in CLcr.

Patients should be informed to notify their physician if changes in vision occur. If visual disturbances persist, further assessment should be considered and more frequent assessments should be considered for patients routinely monitored for ocular conditions.

Patients may experience symptoms of insomnia, nausea, headache, and diarrhea following rapid or abrupt discontinuation of pregabalin.

Pregabalin should be tapered gradually over a minimum of 1 week rather than abrupt discontinuation.

Pregabalin should be withdrawn gradually to minimize the potential of increased seizure frequency in patients with seizure disorders.

As with any CNS active drug, patients should be carefully evaluated for a history of drug abuse and observed for signs of pregabalin misuse or abuse.

Oral Dosage Forms

PREGABALIN CAPSULES

Usual adult dose

Anticonvulsant, adjunctive treatment of partial seizures[1]—

Oral, 150 to 600 mg/day. The total daily dose should be divided and given two or three times a day (75 mg two times a day, or 50 mg three times a day). Based on individual response and tolerability the dose may be increased to a maximum dose of 600 mg/day.

Diabetic peripheral neuropathic pain—

Oral, 150 mg/day (50 mg three times a day) in patients with creatinine clearance of at least 60 mL/min. Dosage should begin at 50 mg three times a day (150 mg per day) and may be increased to 300 mg/day within 1 week based on efficacy and tolerability.

Postherpetic neuralgia—

Oral, 150 to 300 mg/day (75 to 150 mg two times and day, or 50 to 100 mg three times a day) in patients with creatine clearance of at least 60 mL/min. Dosage should begin at the low end of the range and may be increased to 300 mg/day within 1 week based on efficacy and tolerability. For patients who do not experience sufficient pain relief following 2 to 4 weeks of treatment with 300 mg/day and who are able to tolerate pregabalin: dosage may be increased to 600 mg/day (300 mg two times a day or 200 mg three times a day).

Note: For patients with renal function impairment:

—Creatinine clearance (CLcr) >60: 150, 300, 600 mg a day (as two or three divided doses).

—CLcr = 30-60 mL per minute: 75, 150, 300 mg/day (as two or three divided doses).

—CLcr = 15-30 mL per minute: 25-50, 75, 150 mg/day (as a single daily dose, or two divided doses).

—CLcr <15 mL per minute: 25, 25-50, 75 mg/day (as a single daily dose).

For patients undergoing hemodialysis, pregabalin daily dose should be adjusted based on renal function. In addition to the daily dose adjustment, a supplemental dose should be given immediately following every 4-hour hemodialysis treatment.

- Patients on the 25 mg single dose: one supplemental dose of 25 mg or 50 mg.
- Patients on the 25-50 mg single dose: one supplemental dose of 50 or 75 mg.
- Patients on the 75 mg single dose: one supplemental dose of 100 to 150 mg.

Usual adult prescribing limits
Up to 600 mg daily. Diabetic peripheral neuropathic pain: 300 mg per day.

Usual pediatric dose
Safety and efficacy of pregabalin in pediatric patients have not been established.

Usual geriatric dose
See *Usual adult dose.*

Usual geriatric prescribing limits
See *Usual adult prescribing limits*

Strength(s) usually available
U.S.—

25 mg (Rx) [*Lyrica* (black iron oxide; colloidal silicon dioxide; cornstarch; gelatin; lactose monohydrate; potassium hydroxide; propylene glycol; shellac; sodium lauryl sulfate; talc; titanium dioxide)].

50 mg (Rx) [*Lyrica* (black iron oxide; cornstarch; colloidal silicon dioxide; gelatin; lactose monohydrate; potassium hydroxide; propylene glycol; shellac; sodium lauryl sulfate; talc; titanium dioxide)].

75 mg (Rx) [*Lyrica* (black iron oxide; cornstarch; gelatin; lactose monohydrate; potassium hydroxide; propylene glycol; red iron oxide; shellac; talc; titanium dioxide)].

100 mg (Rx) [*Lyrica* (black iron oxide; cornstarch; gelatin; lactose monohydrate; potassium hydroxide; propylene glycol; red iron oxide; shellac; talc; titanium dioxide)].

150 mg (Rx) [*Lyrica* (black iron oxide; colloidal silicon dioxide; cornstarch; gelatin; lactose monohydrate; potassium hydroxide; propylene glycol; shellac; sodium lauryl sulfate; talc; titanium dioxide)].

200 mg (Rx) [*Lyrica* (black iron oxide; cornstarch; gelatin; lactose monohydrate; potassium hydroxide; propylene glycol; red iron oxide; shellac; talc; titanium dioxide)].

225 mg [*Lyrica* (black iron oxide; cornstarch; gelatin; lactose monohydrate; potassium hydroxide; propylene glycol; red iron oxide; shellac; talc; titanium dioxide)].

300 mg [*Lyrica* (black iron oxide; cornstarch; gelatin; lactose monohydrate; potassium hydroxide; propylene glycol; red iron oxide; shellac; talc; titanium dioxide)].

Canada—

25 mg (Rx) [*Lyrica* (black iron oxide; colloidal silicon dioxide; gelatin; lactose monohydrate; maize starch; potassium hydroxide; propylene glycol; shellac; sodium lauryl sulfate; talc; titanium dioxide)].

50 mg (Rx) [*Lyrica* (black iron oxide; colloidal silicon dioxide; gelatin; lactose monohydrate; maize starch; potassium hydroxide; propylene glycol; shellac; sodium lauryl sulfate; talc; titanium dioxide)].

75 mg (Rx) [*Lyrica* (black iron oxide; gelatin; lactose monohydrate; maize starch; potassium hydroxide; propylene glycol; red iron oxide; shellac; talc; titanium dioxide)].

150 mg (Rx) [*Lyrica* (black iron oxide; colloidal silicon dioxide; gelatin; lactose monohydrate; maize starch; potassium hydroxide; propylene glycol; shellac; sodium lauryl sulfate; talc; titanium dioxide)].

300 mg [*Lyrica* (black iron oxide; gelatin; lactose monohydrate; maize starch; potassium hydroxide; propylene glycol; red iron oxide; shellac; talc; titanium dioxide)].

Packaging and storage
Store at 25°C (77°F); excursions permitted to 15°C to 30°C (59°F to 86°F).

Auxiliary labeling
- May cause blurred vision.
- May cause drowsiness. Alcohol may intensify this effect.
- May cause drowsiness. Be careful while driving or operating machinery. Use caution until you become familiar with its effects.
- This medication can be taken with or without food.

Note
Pregabalin is a Schedule V controlled substance in the U.S. and Schedule F controlled substance in Canada.

[1]Not included in Canadian product labeling.

Developed: 11/14/2005

PRILOCAINE—See *Anesthetics (Parenteral-Local)*

PRIMIDONE Systemic

VA CLASSIFICATION (Primary): CN400

Commonly used brand name(s): *Apo-Primidone; Myidone; Mysoline; PMS Primidone; Sertan.*

Note: For a listing of dosage forms and brand names by country availability, see *Dosage Forms* section(s).

Category
Anticonvulsant.

Indications
Note: Bracketed information in the *Indications* section refers to uses that are not included in U.S. product labeling.

Accepted
Epilepsy (treatment)—Primidone, either alone or used concomitantly with other anticonvulsants, is indicated in the control of generalized tonic-clonic (grand mal), nocturnal myoclonic, complex partial (psychomotor), and simple partial (cortical focal) epileptic seizures.

[Essential tremor (treatment)][1]—Primidone is used in the treatment of essential (familial) tremor. Although propranolol is considered to be the treatment of choice for essential tremor, primidone provides effective treatment for some patients.

[1]Not included in Canadian product labeling.

Pharmacology/Pharmacokinetics

Physicochemical characteristics
Molecular weight—218.25.

Mechanism of action/Effect
Unknown, but anticonvulsant effects are thought to be due to the parent compound, primidone, as well as its two active metabolites, phenobarbital and phenylethylmalonamide (PEMA), whose actions may be synergistic.

Absorption
Rapid, usually complete with wide individual variation. Bioavailability—90 to 100% (indirect estimates).

Distribution
Primidone has a volume of distribution (V_D) of 0.64 to 0.86 liters per kg.

Primidone and its metabolites pass into breast milk, reaching a mean concentration of 75% of maternal steady-state serum levels.

Half-life
Primidone—3 to 23 hours.

Phenobarbital metabolite—75 to 126 hours.

PEMA metabolite—10 to 25 hours.

Time to peak concentration
Average 3 to 4 hours.

Therapeutic serum concentration
5 to 12 mcg of primidone per mL (mcg/mL) (23 to 55 mmol/L), which produces phenobarbital serum concentrations of 20 to 40 mcg/mL (86 to 172 mmol/L). Some clinicians have suggested that the optimal mean plasma primidone concentration is 12 mcg/mL with an associated mean derived phenobarbital concentration of 15 mcg/mL resulting in a primidone-to-phenobarbital ratio of 0.8; however, much variation occurs among patients.

	Protein Binding (%)	Biotransformation	Elimination (% unchanged)
Primidone	0–20	Hepatic; 2 active metabolites: phenobarbital (15–25%) and PEMA. PEMA is the major metabolite and less active than phenobarbital	Renal(64)
PEMA (metabolite)	Negligible	No further metabolism	Renal (6.6)
Phenobarbital (metabolite)	50	Hepatic (therapeutic doses of primidone produce therapeutic blood concentrations of phenobarbital)	Renal (5.1)

Precautions to Consider

Cross-sensitivity and/or related problems

Patients sensitive to barbiturates may be sensitive to this medication also.

Pregnancy/Reproduction

Pregnancy—Adequate and well-controlled studies in humans have not been done. However, reports have suggested an association between the use of other anticonvulsant drugs and an increased incidence of birth defects (fetal hydantoin syndrome) in newborns. Symptoms similar to fetal hydantoin syndrome, i.e., growth retardation, craniofacial and heart abnormalities, and hypoplasia of the fingernails and distal phalanges, have been shown to occur with primidone also.

Neonatal hemorrhage, with a coagulation defect resembling vitamin K deficiency, has been described in newborns whose mothers were taking primidone and other anticonvulsants. Risk may be reduced by administering water-soluble vitamin K prophylactically to the mother 1 month prior to and during delivery and also to the neonate, intramuscularly or subcutaneously, immediately after birth.

Breast-feeding

Primidone is distributed into breast milk in substantial amounts, and the use of primidone by nursing mothers may cause unusual drowsiness in the neonate.

Pediatrics

Some children may react to primidone with paradoxical excitement and restlessness.

Geriatrics

Unusual restlessness and excitement may sometimes occur as a paradoxical reaction in the elderly.

Drug interactions and/or related problems

The following drug interactions and/or related problems have been selected on the basis of their potential clinical significance (possible mechanism in parentheses where appropriate)—not necessarily inclusive (» = major clinical significance):

Note: Combinations containing any of the following medications, depending on the amount present, may also interact with this medication.

Although not all of the following interactions have been documented to pertain specifically to primidone, a potential exists for their occurrence because of the barbiturate metabolite of primidone.

Acetaminophen
(when acetaminophen in therapeutic doses is used concurrently in patients receiving chronic primidone therapy, its effects may be decreased because of increased metabolism resulting from induction of hepatic microsomal enzymes by the phenobarbital metabolite; also, risk of hepatotoxicity with single toxic doses or prolonged use of acetaminophen may be increased in chronic alcoholics or in patients regularly using hepatic-enzyme inducing agents)

» Adrenocorticoids, glucocorticoid and mineralocorticoid or
» Anticoagulants, coumarin- or indandione-derivative or
Antidepressants, tricyclic or
Chloramphenicol or
» Contraceptives, oral, estrogen-containing or
» Corticotropin (ACTH) or
Cyclosporine or
Dacarbazine or
Digitalis glycosides, with possible exception of digoxin or
Disopyramide or
Doxycycline or
Levothyroxine or
Metronidazole or
Mexiletine or
Quinidine
(concurrent use with primidone may decrease the effects of these medications because of increased metabolism resulting from induction of hepatic microsomal enzymes by the barbiturate metabolite; dosage increases may be necessary during and after primidone therapy)
(use of a nonhormonal method of birth control or a progestin-only oral contraceptive may be necessary during primidone therapy)
(also, concurrent use of tricyclic antidepressants with primidone may enhance central nervous system [CNS] depression, lower convulsive threshold, and decrease the effects of primidone; dosage adjustments may be necessary to control seizures)

» Alcohol or
» CNS depression-producing medications, other (See *Appendix II*)
(concurrent use may potentiate the CNS and respiratory depressant effects of either these medications or primidone; dosage adjustment of primidone may be necessary)

Amphetamines
(concurrent use may cause a delay in the intestinal absorption of the phenobarbital metabolite)

» Anticonvulsants, other
(concurrent use may cause a change in the pattern of epileptiform seizures because of altered medication metabolism; monitoring of plasma concentrations of both medications is recommended; dosage adjustments may be necessary)
(carbamazepine induces metabolism and decreases effects of primidone; monitoring of plasma concentrations is recommended as a guide to dosage if either medication is added or withdrawn from an existing regimen)
(concurrent use of valproic acid with primidone may cause higher serum concentrations of primidone leading to increased CNS depression and neurological toxicity because of protein binding displacement and reduced metabolism; half-life of valproic acid may be decreased; in addition, primidone may enhance valproic acid hepatotoxicity, presumably through the formation of hepatotoxic valproate metabolites; dosage adjustment of primidone may be necessary)

Carbonic anhydrase inhibitors
(osteopenia induced by primidone may be enhanced; it is recommended that patients receiving concurrent therapy be monitored for early signs of osteopenia and that the carbonic acid anhydrase inhibitor be discontinued and appropriate treatment initiated if necessary)

Cyclophosphamide
(concurrent use with primidone may induce microsomal metabolism to increase the formation of alkylating metabolites of cyclophosphamide, thereby reducing the half-life and increasing the leukopenic activity of cyclophosphamide)

Enflurane or
Halothane or
Methoxyflurane
(chronic use of primidone prior to anesthesia may increase anesthetic metabolism, leading to increased risk of hepatotoxicity)
(also, chronic use of primidone prior to anesthesia with methoxyflurane may increase formation of nephrotoxic metabolites, leading to increased risk of nephrotoxicity)

Fenoprofen
(concurrent use with primidone may decrease the elimination half-life of fenoprofen, possibly because of increased metabolism resulting from induction of hepatic microsomal enzyme activity; fenoprofen dosage adjustment may be required)

Folic acid
(requirements for folic acid may be increased in patients receiving anticonvulsant therapy)

Griseofulvin
(antifungal effects may be decreased when griseofulvin is used concurrently with primidone because of impaired absorption resulting in decreased serum concentrations; although the effect of decreased serum concentrations on therapeutic response has not been established, concurrent use preferably should be avoided)

Guanadrel or
Guanethidine
(concurrent use with primidone may aggravate orthostatic hypotension)

Haloperidol or
Loxapine or
Maprotiline or
Molindone or
Phenothiazines or
Thioxanthenes
(concurrent use may lower the seizure threshold because of altered metabolism; CNS depression may be increased; decreases in primidone dosage may be necessary)
(serum concentrations of neuroleptics may be significantly reduced when these medications are used concurrently with primidone because of increased metabolism)

Leucovorin
(large doses may counteract the anticonvulsant effects of primidone)

Methylphenidate
(concurrent use may increase serum concentrations of primidone because of metabolism inhibition, possibly resulting in toxicity; dosage adjustments may be necessary)

» Monoamine oxidase (MAO) inhibitors, including furazolidone, procarbazine, or selegiline
(concurrent use may prolong the effects of primidone because metabolism of the barbiturate metabolite may be inhibited; changes in the pattern of epileptiform seizures may occur; dosage adjustments of primidone may be necessary)

Phenobarbital
(although concurrent use with primidone is rarely indicated, since primidone is metabolized to phenobarbital, it may cause a change in the pattern of epileptiform seizures because of altered medication metabolism and also increase the sedative effect of either primidone or the barbiturate anticonvulsant; decreases in primidone dosage may be necessary)

Phenylbutazone
(concurrent use may decrease the efficacy of the phenobarbital metabolite of primidone by inducing hepatic microsomal enzymes and increasing its metabolism; also, hepatic enzyme inducers such as barbiturates may increase phenylbutazone metabolism and decrease its half-life)

Posterior pituitary
(concurrent use with primidone may increase the risk of cardiac arrhythmias and coronary insufficiency)

Rifampin
(concurrent use of rifampin with barbiturates may enhance the metabolism of hexobarbital by induction of hepatic microsomal enzymes, resulting in lower serum concentrations; there is conflicting data on rifampin's effect on phenobarbital blood levels; dosage adjustment may be required)

Vitamin D
(effects may be reduced by primidone, because of accelerated metabolism by hepatic microsomal enzyme induction; vitamin D supplementation may be required in patients on long-term primidone therapy to prevent osteomalacia, although rickets is rare)

Xanthines, such as:
Aminophylline
Caffeine
Oxtriphylline
Theophylline
(concurrent use with primidone, because of the barbiturate metabolite, may increase metabolism of the xanthines [except dyphylline] by induction of hepatic microsomal enzymes, resulting in increased theophylline clearance)

Laboratory value alterations

The following have been selected on the basis of their potential clinical significance (possible effect in parentheses where appropriate)—not necessarily inclusive (» = major clinical significance).

With diagnostic test results

Cyanocobalamin Co 57
(absorption of radioactive cyanocobalamin may be impaired by concurrent use of primidone)

Metyrapone test
(increased metabolism of metyrapone by an hepatic enzyme inducer such as primidone may decrease the response to metyrapone)

Phentolamine test
(primidone may cause a false-positive phentolamine test; it is recommended that all medications be withdrawn at least 24 hours, preferably 48 to 72 hours, prior to a phentolamine test)

With physiology/laboratory test values

Bilirubin concentrations, serum
(may be decreased in patients with congenital nonhemolytic unconjugated hyperbilirubinemia and in epileptics; this effect is presumably due to induction of glucuronyl transferase, the enzyme responsible for the conjugation of bilirubin)

Medical considerations/Contraindications

The medical considerations/contraindications included have been selected on the basis of their potential clinical significance (reasons given in parentheses where appropriate)—not necessarily inclusive (» = major clinical significance).

This medication should not be used when the following medical problem exists:

» Porphyria, acute intermittent or variegate, or history of
(barbiturate metabolite of primidone may aggravate symptoms of porphyria by inducing enzymes responsible for porphyrin synthesis)

Risk-benefit should be considered when the following medical problems exist:

Hepatic function impairment
(possible systemic accumulation of barbiturate metabolite)

Hyperkinesia
(may be precipitated or aggravated by primidone)

Renal function impairment
(possible systemic accumulation of barbiturate metabolite)

» Respiratory diseases such as asthma, emphysema, or those involving dyspnea or obstruction
(serious ventilatory depression may occur)

Sensitivity to primidone or barbiturates

Patient monitoring

The following may be especially important in patient monitoring (other tests may be warranted in some patients, depending on condition; » = major clinical significance):

Blood cell counts, complete and
Blood chemistry profiles
(manufacturer recommends that these tests be completed every 6 months)

Folate concentrations, serum
(determinations recommended periodically because of increased folate requirements of patients on long-term anticonvulsant therapy)

Phenobarbital concentrations, serum, and
Primidone concentrations, serum
(since phenobarbital is a major metabolite of primidone, serum concentrations of both may be required in some patients at periodic intervals to maintain maximum therapeutic efficacy)

Side/Adverse Effects

The following side/adverse effects have been selected on the basis of their potential clinical significance (possible signs and symptoms in parentheses where appropriate)—not necessarily inclusive:

Those indicating need for medical attention

Incidence less frequent

Paradoxical reaction (unusual excitement or restlessness)—especially in children and the elderly

Incidence rare

Anemia, megaloblastic (unusual tiredness or weakness); ***skin rash***

Note: *Megaloblastic anemia* may respond to folic acid without discontinuation of anticonvulsant therapy.

Signs of intolerance or overdose

Confusion; diplopia (double vision); ***nystagmus*** (continuous, uncontrolled back-and-forth and/or rolling eye movements); ***shortness of breath or troubled breathing***

Those indicating need for medical attention only if they continue or are bothersome

Incidence more frequent

Ataxia (clumsiness or unsteadiness); ***dizziness***

Incidence less frequent

Anorexia (loss of appetite); ***drowsiness; impotence*** (decreased sexual ability); ***mood or mental changes; nausea or vomiting***—usually decreases or disappears with continued use of medication

Patient Consultation

As an aid to patient consultation, refer to *Advice for the Patient, Primidone (Systemic)*.

In providing consultation, consider emphasizing the following selected information (» = major clinical significance):

Before using this medication

» Conditions affecting use, especially:

Sensitivity to primidone or barbiturates

Pregnancy—Abnormalities similar to fetal hydantoin syndrome may occur; neonatal hemorrhaging may occur at delivery

Breast-feeding—Distributed into breast milk, causing drowsiness in the baby

Use in children—Paradoxical excitement and restlessness may occur

Use in the elderly—Paradoxical excitement and restlessness may occur

Other medications, especially adrenocorticoids, anticoagulants, estrogens, estrogen-containing contraceptives, CNS depression-producing medications, other anticonvulsants, or monoamine oxidase inhibitors

Other medical problems, especially acute intermittent porphyria, or respiratory diseases

Proper use of this medication

» Compliance with therapy; taking every day in doses spaced as directed

» Proper dosing

Missed dose: Taking as soon as possible, unless within an hour of next scheduled dose; not doubling doses

» Proper storage

Precautions while using this medication

Regular visits to physician to check progress of therapy

Checking with physician before discontinuing medication; gradual dosage reduction may be needed

Caution if any kind of surgery, dental treatment, or emergency treatment is required

» Avoiding use of alcoholic beverages; not taking other CNS depressants unless prescribed by physician

» Possible drowsiness; caution when driving or doing other things requiring alertness

» Possible dizziness or lightheadedness; caution when getting up suddenly from a lying or sitting position

Caution if any laboratory tests required; possible interference with results of cyanocobalamin Co 57, metyrapone, or phentolamine tests.

Side/adverse effects

Signs of potential side effects, especially excitement or restlessness, allergic reaction, or megaloblastic anemia

General Dosing Information

Because primidone serum concentrations vary greatly among patients after oral administration, it is very important that the dosage be individualized. One of primidone's metabolites, phenobarbital, greatly influences its serum concentration, side effects, and interactions, as well as its therapeutic effect.

When primidone is to be discontinued, dosage should be reduced gradually. Abrupt withdrawal may precipitate status epilepticus.

When used with or to replace other anticonvulsant therapy, the dosage of primidone should be increased gradually while that of the other medication is maintained or decreased gradually in order to maintain seizure control. When therapy with primidone alone is the objective, the transition should not be completed in less than 2 weeks.

Many of the common side effects such as nausea, dizziness, and drowsiness diminish in frequency and intensity with continued use of the medication or reduction of dosage.

Diet/Nutrition

Patients on long-term anticonvulsant therapy have increased folate requirements. In addition, patients on long-term therapy may require vitamin D supplementation to prevent osteomalacia.

Oral Dosage Forms

Note: Bracketed uses in the *Dosage Forms* section refer to categories of use and/or indications that are not included in U.S. product labeling.

PRIMIDONE ORAL SUSPENSION USP

Usual adult and adolescent dose

Anticonvulsant—

Initial—

Oral, 100 or 125 mg once a day at bedtime for the first three days, the daily dose being increased to 100 or 125 mg two times a day for the fourth, fifth, and sixth days, and then increased to 100 or 125 mg three times a day for the seventh, eighth, and ninth days. On the tenth day a maintenance dosage of 250 mg three times a day may be established and then adjusted according to patient needs and tolerance but not to exceed 2 grams a day.

Note: Initial doses as low as 25 mg twice a day have been used in patients experiencing troublesome nausea and vomiting.

Maintenance—

Oral, 250 mg three or four times a day.

[Tremorlytic][1]—

Oral, initially 50 to 62.5 mg a day, the dosage being increased as needed and tolerated up to a maximum of 750 mg a day.

Usual pediatric dose

Anticonvulsant—

Children up to 8 years of age—

Initial—Oral, 50 mg at bedtime for the first three days, the daily dose being increased to 50 mg two times a day for the fourth, fifth, and sixth days and then increased to 100 mg two times a day for the seventh, eighth, and ninth days.

Maintenance—Oral, on the tenth day, 125 to 250 mg three times a day (or 10 to 25 mg per kg of body weight a day given in divided doses), the dosage being adjusted according to patient needs and tolerance.

Children 8 years of age and over—

See *Usual adult and adolescent dose.*

Strength(s) usually available

U.S.—

250 mg per 5 mL (Rx) [*Mysoline* (ammonia solution [diluted]; citric acid; D&C Yellow No. 10; FD&C Yellow No. 6; magnesium aluminum silicate; methylparaben; propylparaben; saccharin sodium; sodium alginate; sodium citrate; sodium hypochlorite solution; sorbic acid; sorbitan monolaurate; purified water; flavors)].

Canada—

Not commercially available.

Packaging and storage

Store below 40 °C (104 °F), preferably between 15 and 30 °C (59 and 86 °F), unless otherwise specified by manufacturer. Store in a tight, light-resistant container. Protect from freezing.

Auxiliary labeling

- Shake well.
- May cause drowsiness.
- Avoid alcoholic beverages.
- Do not freeze.

PRIMIDONE TABLETS USP

Usual adult and adolescent dose

See *Primidone Oral Suspension USP*.

Usual pediatric dose

See *Primidone Oral Suspension USP*.

Strength(s) usually available

U.S.—

50 mg (Rx) [*Mysoline* (lactose)].

250 mg (Rx) [*Myidone; Mysoline;* GENERIC].

Canada—

125 mg (Rx) [*Apo-Primidone; PMS Primidone; Sertan*].

250 mg (Rx) [*Apo-Primidone; Mysoline* (lactose); *PMS Primidone; Sertan;* GENERIC].

Packaging and storage

Store below 40 °C (104 °F), preferably between 15 and 30 °C (59 and 86 °F), unless otherwise specified by manufacturer. Store in a well-closed container.

Auxiliary labeling

- May cause drowsiness.
- Avoid alcoholic beverages.

PRIMIDONE CHEWABLE TABLETS

Usual adult and adolescent dose

See *Primidone Oral Suspension USP*.

Usual pediatric dose

See *Primidone Oral Suspension USP*.

Strength(s) usually available

U.S.—

Not commercially available.

Canada—

125 mg (Rx) [*Mysoline* (lactose)].

Packaging and storage
Store below 40 °C (104 °F), preferably between 15 and 30 °C (59 and 86 °F), in a well-closed container unless otherwise specified by manufacturer.

Auxiliary labeling
- Chew tablets before swallowing
- May cause drowsiness.
- Avoid alcoholic beverages.

[1]Not included in Canadian product labeling.

Revised: 08/16/1994

PROBENECID AND COLCHICINE Systemic

VA CLASSIFICATION (Primary): MS400

Commonly used brand name(s): *ColBenemid; Col-Probenecid; Proben-C.*

NOTE: The *Probenecid and Colchicine (Systemic)* monograph is maintained on the *USP DI* electronic data base. A copy of the most recent revision of the complete monograph can be accessed on the *USP DI* Updates Online website. See the front cover of book for details on accessing the site.

For information on the specific components of this combination, see the *USP DI* monographs for *Colchicine (Systemic)* and *Probenecid (Systemic)*.

The information that follows is selectively abstracted from the complete monograph and is provided to facilitate drug use review and patient counseling.

Note: For a listing of dosage forms and brand names by country availability, see *Dosage Forms* section(s).

Category
Antigout agent.

Indications

Accepted
Gouty arthritis, chronic (treatment)—Probenecid and colchicine combination is indicated for the treatment of chronic gouty arthritis in patients having frequent, recurrent acute attacks.

Probenecid is used to control hyperuricemia. Therapy with this uricosuric agent is recommended only for patients whose 24-hour renal excretion of urate is 800 mg (4.8 mmol) or lower (i.e., patients who are hyperuricemic as a result of underexcretion, rather than overproduction, of urate). The aim of probenecid therapy is to reduce the number of acute gout attacks. Probenecid therapy should not be initiated during an acute attack because it may produce fluctuations in urate concentration that may result in prolongation of the attack or initiation of a new attack. Even when probenecid therapy is started several weeks after an acute attack, the frequency of acute attacks may be increased during the early months of therapy. Therefore, prophylactic doses of the colchicine in this combination medication are usually administered for the first 3 to 6 months of probenecid therapy.

Unaccepted
Probenecid is not recommended in circumstances in which there is an especially high risk of adverse effects associated with crystallization and deposition of urate in renal tissues, such as formation of renal calculi and uric acid nephropathy. It therefore should not be used for treatment of gout in patients whose 24-hour urate excretion exceeds 800 mg (4.8 mmol) or who have extensive tophi. Allopurinol, which decreases the quantity of urate that reaches the kidneys in addition to decreasing the concentration of urate in the blood, is recommended in these circumstances.

Patient Consultation
As an aid to patient consultation, refer to *Advice for the Patient, Probenecid and Colchicine (Systemic).*

In providing consultation, consider emphasizing the following selected information (» = major clinical significance):

Before using this medication
» Conditions affecting use, especially:

Allergic reaction to probenecid or sensitivity to colchicine, history of

Pregnancy—Probenecid crosses the placenta; colchicine reported to be teratogenic in humans

Use in the elderly—Increased susceptibility to cumulative colchicine toxicity

Other medications, especially antibiotics, antivirals, bone marrow depressants or blood dyscrasia-causing medications, indomethacin, ketoprofen, antineoplastic agents, aspirin or other salicylates, including bismuth subsalicylate, heparin, methotrexate, nitrofurantoin, or zidovudine

Other medical problems, especially alcohol abuse, severe cardiac or gastrointestinal disorders; cancer being treated by cytolytic medication or radiation (x-ray) therapy; kidney stones or other kidney problems, especially if caused by uric acid, or history of; renal function impairment; hepatic function impairment; stomach ulcer or other stomach problems, and blood dyscrasias

Proper use of this medication
Taking with food or an antacid to minimize gastric irritation

Importance of not taking more medication than the amount prescribed

Several months of continuous therapy may be required for maximum effectiveness

» Medication does not relieve acute attacks of gout but rather helps to prevent them; need to continue taking probenecid and colchicine with medication prescribed for gout attacks

Importance of high fluid intake and compliance with therapy for alkalinization of urine, if prescribed

» Proper dosing

Missed dose: Taking as soon as possible; not taking if almost time for next dose; not doubling doses

» Proper storage

Precautions while using this medication
Regular visits to physician to check progress during therapy

Caution if any laboratory tests required; possible interference with test results

Diabetics: May cause false results with copper sulfate urine sugar tests, but not with glucose enzymatic urine sugar tests

» Aspirin or other salicylates may decrease uricosuric effects of probenecid; checking with physician regarding concurrent use, since effect is dependent on salicylate dose and duration of use

» Possibility that alcohol taken in large amounts may increase the risk of colchicine-induced gastrointestinal toxicity; also, may increase uric acid concentrations and thereby reduce effectiveness of medication

» For patients taking high doses (4 tablets a day): Discontinuing at once and notifying physician as soon as possible if symptoms of gastrointestinal toxicity occur

Side/adverse effects
Signs and symptoms of potential side effects, especially renal calculi, allergic dermatitis, anaphylaxis, anemia, aplastic anemia, hemolytic anemia, fever, hepatic necrosis, leukopenia, nephrotic syndrome, pain in back and/or ribs, renal colic, urate nephropathy, colchicine-induced gastrointestinal toxicity, and peripheral neuritis

Oral Dosage Forms

PROBENECID AND COLCHICINE TABLETS USP

Usual adult dose
Antigout agent—

Initial: Oral, 1 tablet a day for one week.

Maintenance: Oral, 1 tablet two times a day. In nongeriatric patients, if this dose does not control symptoms or if the 24-hour uric acid excretion is not above 700 mg, the daily dosage may be increased by 1 tablet every four weeks as tolerated (usually not above 4 tablets per day). If the increase in colchicine dosage is not desired or tolerated, administration of additional probenecid alone may be required.

Note: The initial dose may be eliminated, and treatment started with the usual maintenance dose, when patients previously controlled with other uricosuric therapy are transferred to probenecid.

When acute attacks of gout have not occurred for at least six months, and the serum uric acid concentrations remain within normal limits, the daily dose may be reduced by 1 tablet every six months until the lowest effective maintenance dose is reached. Alternatively, prophylactic use of colchicine may be discontinued and the patient treated with maintenance doses of probenecid alone.

Usual pediatric dose
Dosage has not been established.

Strength(s) usually available
U.S.—
500 mg of probenecid and 500 mcg (0.5 mg) of colchicine (Rx) [*ColBenemid; Col-Probenecid; Proben-C;* GENERIC].

Revised: 08/27/1994

PROCAINAMIDE Systemic

VA CLASSIFICATION (Primary): CV300

Commonly used brand name(s): *Procan SR; Promine; Pronestyl; Pronestyl-SR.*

Note: For a listing of dosage forms and brand names by country availability, see *Dosage Forms* section(s).

Category

Antiarrhythmic.

Indications

Note: Bracketed information in the *Indications* section refers to uses that are not included in U.S. product labeling.

Accepted

Arrhythmias, ventricular (treatment)—Procainamide is indicated in the treatment of life-threatening ventricular arrhythmias, such as sustained ventricular tachycardia. Parenteral procainamide also is indicated for treatment of ventricular extrasystoles and cardiac arrhythmias associated with anesthesia and surgery.

[Arrhythmias, supraventricular (treatment)]—Procainamide is used for the conversion and management of atrial fibrillation and paroxysmal atrial tachycardia.

Pharmacology/Pharmacokinetics

Physicochemical characteristics

Molecular weight—271.79.
pKa—9.23.

Mechanism of action/Effect

Direct cardiac effect—Decreases excitability, conduction velocity, automaticity, and membrane responsiveness with prolonged refractory period. No effect on contractility or cardiac output unless myocardial damage present. Larger doses may induce atrioventricular (AV) block. In the Vaughan Williams classification of antiarrhythmics, procainamide is considered to be a Class I antiarrhythmic.

Other actions/effects

Relatively weak anticholinergic action diminishes vagal transmission, resulting in increased heart rate, usually with higher dosages. Alpha-adrenergic blockade does not occur. Also causes peripheral vasodilation.

Absorption

Oral—Rapid; 75 to 95% complete but may vary.
Intramuscular—Rapid.
Intravenous—Immediate.

Protein binding

Low (15 to 20%).

Biotransformation

Hepatic; approximately 25% of dose is converted to the active metabolite *N*-acetylprocainamide (NAPA); up to 40% conversion occurs in patients who are rapid acetylators or those with renal function impairment.

Half-life

Procainamide—About 2.5 to 4.5 hours (11 to 20 hours in renal function impairment).
N-acetylprocainamide—About 6 hours.

Therapeutic serum concentration

Procainamide—4 to 10 mg per L; higher levels may be needed in some patients such as those with sustained ventricular tachycardia.

NAPA—10 to 30 mg per L.

Time to peak effect

Oral—60 to 90 minutes.
Intravenous—Immediately.
Intramuscular—15 to 60 minutes.

Elimination

Renal, 50 to 60% unchanged. The cardioactive metabolite, NAPA, has a slower excretion rate than the parent compound. In cases of renal function impairment or congestive heart failure, this metabolite tends to accumulate rapidly in the serum to toxic concentrations, while the serum concentration of procainamide appears to be within acceptable limits.

In dialysis—Procainamide and NAPA are removable by hemodialysis but not by peritoneal dialysis.

Precautions to Consider

Cross-sensitivity and/or related problems

Patients sensitive to procaine or other related agents may be sensitive to procainamide also.

Carcinogenicity/Mutagenicity

Long-term studies in animals have not been done.

Pregnancy/Reproduction

Pregnancy—Procainamide crosses the placenta. Adequate and well-controlled studies have not been done in humans. Some reports of procainamide use in pregnant women seem to indicate that although procainamide and *N*-acetylprocainamide (NAPA) appear in fetal serum, no adverse effects on the fetus or neonate have been noted. However, there is a potential risk of drug accumulation and maternal hypotension leading to uteroplacental insufficiency and ventricular arrhythmias.

FDA Pregnancy Category C.

Breast-feeding

Procainamide and NAPA are distributed into breast milk.

Pediatrics

Appropriate studies on the relationship of age to the effects of procainamide have not been performed in the pediatric population. Occasional use in pediatric patients has not demonstrated pediatrics-specific problems that would limit the usefulness of procainamide in these patients. However, dosage requirements to achieve and maintain effective therapeutic concentrations may be higher in some pediatric patients than in adults.

Geriatrics

Appropriate studies on the relationship of age to the effects of procainamide have not been performed in the geriatric population. However, elderly patients may be more prone to hypotension, especially with parenteral use or when very high doses are given. In addition, elderly patients are more likely to have age-related renal function impairment, which may require lower doses in patients receiving procainamide.

Dental

The leukopenic and thrombocytopenic effects of procainamide may result in an increased incidence of microbial infection, delayed healing, and gingival bleeding. If leukopenia or thrombocytopenia occurs, dental work should be deferred until blood counts have returned to normal, and patients should be instructed in proper oral hygiene, including caution in use of regular toothbrushes, dental floss, and toothpicks.

The secondary anticholinergic effects of procainamide may decrease or inhibit salivary flow, especially in middle-aged or elderly patients, thus contributing to the development of caries, periodontal disease, oral candidiasis, and discomfort.

Drug interactions and/or related problems

The following drug interactions and/or related problems have been selected on the basis of their potential clinical significance (possible mechanism in parentheses where appropriate)—not necessarily inclusive (» = major clinical significance):

Note: Combinations containing any of the following medications, depending on the amount present, may also interact with this medication.

» Antiarrhythmics, other
(concurrent use with procainamide may produce additive cardiac effects)

Anticholinergics, especially atropine or related compounds (see *Appendix II*), or
Antidyskinetics or
Antihistamines
(concurrent use with procainamide may intensify atropine-like side effects because of the secondary anticholinergic activities of procainamide; patients should be advised to report occurrence of gastrointestinal problems promptly since paralytic ileus may occur with concurrent therapy)

» Antihypertensives
(concurrent use with procainamide, especially intravenous procainamide, may produce additive hypotensive effects)

» Antimyasthenics
(neuromuscular blocking action and/or secondary anticholinergic activity of procainamide may antagonize the effect of antimyasthenics on skeletal muscle; dosage adjustments of antimyasthenics may be necessary to control symptoms of myasthenia gravis)

Bethanechol
(concurrent use with procainamide may antagonize the cholinergic effects of bethanechol)

Bone marrow depressants (see *Appendix II*)
(concurrent use of procainamide with these medications may increase the leukopenic and/or thrombocytopenic effects; if concurrent use is required, close observation for toxic effects should be considered)

Bretylium
(concurrent administration may counteract inotropic effect of bretylium and potentiate hypotension)

» Neuromuscular blocking agents
(effects of these medications may be prolonged or enhanced when they are used concurrently with procainamide; careful postoperative monitoring of the patient may be necessary following concurrent or sequential use, especially if there is a possibility of incomplete reversal of neuromuscular blockade)

» Pimozide
(concurrent use with procainamide may potentiate cardiac arrhythmias, which are seen on electrocardiogram [ECG] as prolongation of QT interval)

Laboratory value alterations

The following have been selected on the basis of their potential clinical significance (possible effect in parentheses where appropriate)—not necessarily inclusive (» = major clinical significance).

With diagnostic test results

Bentiromide
(administration of procainamide during a bentiromide test period will invalidate test results since procainamide is also metabolized to arylamines and will thus increase the percent of para-aminobenzoic acid [PABA] recovered; discontinuation of procainamide at least 3 days prior to the administration of bentiromide is recommended)

Edrophonium tests
(may be altered)

With physiology/laboratory test values

Alanine aminotransferase (ALT [SGPT]), serum and
Alkaline phosphatase, serum and
Aspartate aminotransferase (AST [SGOT]), serum and
Bilirubin, serum and
Lactate dehydrogenase (LDH), serum
(concentrations may be increased)

Antinuclear antibody (ANA) titers
(occur in 60 to 70% of patients after 1 to 2 months of procainamide therapy; may increase with continued therapy)

Direct antiglobulin (Coombs') tests
(may produce positive results)

ECG changes such as:
QRS widening, and less frequently
PR and QT prolongation and
Reduced voltage of QRS and T waves
(may occur with large doses)

Leukocyte counts, including neutrophils and
Platelet counts
(may rarely be decreased)

Medical considerations/Contraindications

The medical considerations/contraindications included have been selected on the basis of their potential clinical significance (reasons given in parentheses where appropriate)—not necessarily inclusive (» = major clinical significance).

Except under special circumstances, this medication should not be used when the following medical problems exist:

» Atrioventricular (AV) block, complete, and also 2nd and 3rd degree AV block unless controlled by electrical pacemaker
(risk of additive cardiac depression)

» Torsades de pointes
(procainamide may aggravate this arrhythmia)

Risk-benefit should be considered when the following medical problems exist:

» AV block or
» Bundle branch block or
» Digitalis intoxication, severe
(risk of additive cardiac depression and ventricular asystole or fibrillation)

Bronchial asthma
(possible hypersensitivity)

» Congestive heart failure or
Hepatic function impairment or
» Renal function impairment
(possible accumulation leading to toxicity; lower doses may be required in patients with congestive heart failure or renal function impairment)

» Lupus erythematosus, history of
(procainamide may precipitate active lupus)

» Myasthenia gravis
(procainamide may increase muscle weakness)

Sensitivity to procainamide

» Ventricular tachycardia during an occlusive coronary episode

Patient monitoring

The following may be especially important in patient monitoring (other tests may be warranted in some patients, depending on condition; » = major clinical significance):

Antinuclear antibody (ANA) titers
(recommended at periodic intervals during prolonged use of procainamide or if symptoms of a lupus-like reaction occur; procainamide should be withdrawn if a steady increase in ANA titer occurs)

Blood pressure determinations and
» Cardiac function monitoring, including ECG
(recommended at periodic intervals with oral therapy and concurrently with parenteral administration; procainamide should be withdrawn if an excessive blood pressure reduction or QRS widening occurs, and immediately if signs of impending heart block occur)

Complete blood cell counts (especially leukocyte counts)
(recommended every 2 weeks during the first 3 months of therapy, then at longer intervals throughout maintenance, especially in patients taking the extended-release dosage form or after cardiovascular surgery; procainamide should be withdrawn if leukocyte counts fall)

Plasma procainamide and *N*-acetylprocainamide (NAPA) concentrations
(recommended at periodic intervals to aid in dosage adjustment, especially in patients with congestive heart failure or hepatic or renal function impairment, and when switching from regular oral to extended-release dosage form; risk of toxicity may be increased when the summed concentration of procainamide and NAPA exceeds 25 to 30 mg/L)

Side/Adverse Effects

Note: Agranulocytosis, bone marrow depression, neutropenia, hypoplastic anemia, and thrombocytopenia have been reported with an incidence of about 0.5% in patients receiving procainamide. Fatalities have been reported, especially in cases of agranulocytosis (20 to 25% mortality in reported cases). Most cases have been noted in the first 12 weeks of therapy.

In the National Heart, Lung, and Blood Institute's Cardiac Arrhythmias Suppression Trial (CAST), treatment with encainide or flecainide was found to be associated with excessive mortality or increased nonfatal cardiac arrest rate, as compared with placebo, in patients with asymptomatic, non-life-threatening arrhythmias who had a recent myocardial infarction. The implications of these results for other patient populations or other antiarrhythmic agents are uncertain.

Tachycardia may occur at high plasma procainamide concentrations as a reflex sympathetic response to the hypotensive effect, due to the anticholinergic effect on the atrioventricular (AV) node, or in response to slowing of the atrial rate in treatment of atrial fibrillation. Tachycardia is especially hazardous in patients with myocardial damage, because of the risk of emboli. Adequate digitalization reduces, but does not abolish, the risk.

Intravenous administration may cause a transient but sometimes severe reduction in blood pressure, especially in conscious patients. Hypotension is less frequent with intramuscular administration and rare with oral use (except with excessive doses).

Ventricular asystole or fibrillation may occur, especially with too-rapid intravenous administration or excessive doses; death has occurred rarely.

The following side/adverse effects have been selected on the basis of their potential clinical significance (possible signs and symptoms in parentheses where appropriate)—not necessarily inclusive:

Those indicating need for medical attention

Incidence less frequent

Allergic reaction or systemic lupus erythematosus (SLE)–like syndrome (fever and chills; joint pain or swelling; pains with breathing; skin rash or itching)

Note: After extended maintenance therapy nearly 80% of patients treated show an increased titer of antinuclear antibodies (an early sign of developing SLE), often within 1 to 12 months of commencing therapy. Nearly 30% of these patients develop clinical symptoms that resemble SLE. This *SLE-like condition* is usually reversible with discontinuation of procainamide therapy.

Incidence rare

Central nervous system (CNS) effects (confusion; hallucinations; mental depression); ***Coombs' positive hemolytic anemia*** (unusual tiredness or weakness); ***leukopenia (neutropenia) and possible agranulocytosis, which may be fatal*** (fever, chills, or sore mouth, gums, or throat); ***thrombocytopenia*** (unusual bleeding or bruising)

Note: *Coombs' positive hemolytic anemia* may be related to the SLE-like syndrome.

Leukopenia may be more likely to occur with use of the extended-release dosage form, especially after cardiovascular surgery. Leukopenia usually occurs within the first 3 months of therapy, and counts recover within a few weeks after procainamide is withdrawn. Leukopenia also may occur in association with the SLE-like syndrome.

Thrombocytopenia may be related to the SLE-like syndrome.

Those indicating need for medical attention only if they continue or are bothersome

Incidence more frequent, especially with daily doses > 4 grams

Diarrhea; loss of appetite

Incidence less frequent

Dizziness or lightheadedness

Overdose

For more information on the management of overdose or unintentional ingestion, **contact a Poison Control Center** (see *Poison Control Center Listing*).

Clinical effects of overdose

The following effects have been selected on the basis of their potential clinical significance (possible signs and symptoms in parentheses where appropriate)—not necessarily inclusive:

Confusion; decrease in urination; dizziness, severe, or fainting; drowsiness; fast or irregular heartbeat; nausea and vomiting

Treatment of overdose

Treatment is primarily symptomatic and supportive. Gastric lavage, emesis, hemodialysis, pressor medication, and maintenance of airway are of possible benefit, according to the patient's condition.

Patient Consultation

As an aid to patient consultation, refer to *Advice for the Patient, Procainamide (Systemic).*

In providing consultation, consider emphasizing the following selected information (» = major clinical significance):

Before using this medication

» Conditions affecting use, especially:
- Sensitivity to procaine or other related agents
- Pregnancy—Procainamide crosses the placenta
- Breast-feeding—Procainamide and NAPA are distributed into breast milk
- Use in children—Higher doses may be needed to maintain adequate therapeutic concentrations in some patients
- Use in the elderly—May be more susceptible to hypotension
- Dental—May be more susceptible to microbial infection, delayed healing, and gingival bleeding because of risk of leukopenia and thrombocytopenia; may cause dryness of mouth
- Other medications, especially other antiarrhythmics, antihypertensives, antimyasthenics, neuromuscular blocking agents, and pimozide
- Other medical problems, especially atrioventricular block, torsades de pointes, severe digitalis intoxication, congestive heart failure, renal function impairment, lupus erythematosus, myasthenia gravis, or ventricular tachycardia during an occlusive coronary episode

Proper use of this medication

» Taking exactly as directed even if feeling well

Taking on empty stomach for faster absorption, or with food or milk to reduce stomach irritation

Proper administration of extended-release tablets: Swallowing tablets whole, without breaking, crushing, or chewing

» Importance of not missing doses and of taking at evenly spaced intervals

» Proper dosing

Missed dose: Taking as soon as possible if remembered within 2 hours (4 hours for extended-release tablets); not taking if remembered later; not doubling doses

» Proper storage

Precautions while using this medication

Regular visits to physician to check progress

» Checking with physician before discontinuing medication; gradual dosage reduction may be necessary to avoid worsening of condition

» Caution if any kind of surgery (including dental surgery) or emergency treatment is required

Carrying medical identification card or bracelet

» Possibility of dizziness with high dosage, especially in elderly; caution when driving or doing things requiring alertness

Caution if any laboratory tests required; possible interference with test results

Side/adverse effects

Signs of potential side effects, especially allergic reaction, SLE-like syndrome, CNS effects, Coombs' positive hemolytic anemia, leukopenia, and thrombocytopenia

Extended-release tablet matrix may be seen in stool and is to be expected

General Dosing Information

Dosage must be adjusted to meet the individual requirements of each patient, on the basis of clinical response.

Procainamide therapy should be withdrawn if signs or symptoms of systemic lupus erythematosus (SLE)–like syndrome, leukopenia, or hemolytic anemia occur.

For treatment of atrial fibrillation

Patients should be digitalized prior to administration of procainamide to reduce the risk of enhancing atrioventricular (AV) conduction, which may result in ventricular rate acceleration.

For oral dosage forms only

A period of 3 to 4 hours should elapse after the last intravenous dose before administration of the first oral dose.

For parenteral dosage forms only

Procainamide Hydrochloride Injection USP is always diluted before intravenous administration.

Intravenous administration should be limited to hospitals where monitoring facilities are available.

Intramuscular injection usually is used only when the oral or intravenous routes are not feasible.

Procainamide intravenous injection should be administered at a rate not exceeding 50 mg per minute.

Because hypotension may develop rapidly during intravenous administration, it is highly recommended that blood pressure be monitored continuously, with the patient in a supine position. Phenylephrine and norepinephrine injections should be available to counteract severe hypotension.

Diet/Nutrition

Oral procainamide should preferably be taken with a glass of water on an empty stomach (either 1 hour before or 2 hours after meals) for faster absorption; however, it may be taken with meals or immediately after meals to lessen gastrointestinal irritation.

Oral Dosage Forms

Note: Bracketed information in the *Indications* section refers to uses that are not included in U.S. product labeling.

PROCAINAMIDE HYDROCHLORIDE CAPSULES USP

Usual adult dose

[Atrial arrhythmias]—

Initial: Oral, 1.25 grams, followed in one to two hours by 750 mg if necessary; then 500 mg to 1 gram every two or three hours as needed and tolerated.

Maintenance: Oral, 500 mg to 1 gram every four to six hours, the dosage being adjusted as needed and tolerated.

Ventricular arrhythmias—

Oral, 50 mg per kg of body weight per day in eight divided doses (every three hours), the dosage being adjusted as needed and tolerated.

Note: Geriatric patients may be more sensitive to the hypotensive effects of the usual adult dose.

Geriatric patients or patients with renal, hepatic, or cardiac insufficiency may require lower doses or longer dosing intervals.

Usual adult prescribing limits

Maintenance—Up to 6 grams daily.

Usual pediatric dose

Antiarrhythmic—

Oral, 12.5 mg per kg of body weight or 375 mg per square meter of body surface four times a day.

Strength(s) usually available

U.S.—

250 mg (Rx) [*Promine; Pronestyl* (lactose); GENERIC].
375 mg (Rx) [*Promine; Pronestyl* (lactose); GENERIC].
500 mg (Rx) [*Promine; Pronestyl;* GENERIC].

Canada—

250 mg (Rx) [*Pronestyl*].
375 mg (Rx) [*Pronestyl*].
500 mg (Rx) [*Pronestyl;* GENERIC].

Packaging and storage

Store below 40 °C (104 °F), preferably between 15 and 30 °C (59 and 86 °F), unless otherwise specified by manufacturer. Store in a tight container.

Stability

Procainamide is hygroscopic.

Auxiliary labeling

- Keep container tightly closed.
- Do not take other medicines without your doctor's advice.

PROCAINAMIDE HYDROCHLORIDE TABLETS USP

Usual adult dose

See *Procainamide Hydrochloride Capsules USP.*

Usual pediatric dose

See *Procainamide Hydrochloride Capsules USP.*

Strength(s) usually available

U.S.—

250 mg (Rx) [*Pronestyl* (tartrazine); GENERIC].
375 mg (Rx) [*Pronestyl* (tartrazine)].
500 mg (Rx) [*Pronestyl* (tartrazine)].

Canada—

Not commercially available.

Packaging and storage

Store below 40 °C (104 °F), preferably between 15 and 30 °C (59 and 86 °F), unless otherwise specified by manufacturer. Store in a tight container.

Stability

Procainamide is hygroscopic.

Auxiliary labeling

- Keep container tightly closed.
- Do not take other medicines without your doctor's advice.

PROCAINAMIDE HYDROCHLORIDE EXTENDED-RELEASE TABLETS USP

Usual adult dose

[Atrial arrhythmias]—

Maintenance: Oral, 1 gram every six hours, the dosage being adjusted as needed and tolerated.

Ventricular arrhythmias—

Maintenance: Oral, 50 mg per kg of body weight per day in four divided doses (every six hours), the dosage being adjusted as needed and tolerated.

Note: The extended-release dosage form is intended for maintenance dosage, and not for initial dosage.

Geriatric patients may be more sensitive to the hypotensive effects of the usual adult dose.

Usual adult prescribing limits

Maintenance—Up to 6 grams daily.

Usual pediatric dose

Not generally used in children. See instead *Procainamide Hydrochloride Capsules USP.*

Strength(s) usually available

U.S.—

250 mg (Rx) [*Procan SR* (lactose; methylparaben; propylparaben); GENERIC].
500 mg (Rx) [*Procan SR* (scored; lactose; methylparaben; propylparaben); *Pronestyl-SR;* GENERIC].
750 mg (Rx) [*Procan SR;* GENERIC].
1 gram (Rx) [*Procan SR*].

Canada—

250 mg (Rx) [*Procan SR* (lactose; parabens)].
500 mg (Rx) [*Procan SR* (parabens); *Pronestyl-SR*].
750 mg (Rx) [*Procan SR* (scored)].
1 gram (Rx) [*Procan SR* (scored)].

Packaging and storage

Store below 30 °C (86 °F), unless otherwise specified by manufacturer. Store in a tight container.

Stability

Procainamide is hygroscopic.

Auxiliary labeling

- Keep container tightly closed.
- Do not take other medicines without your doctor's advice.
- Swallow tablets whole.

Note

Extended-release tablets utilize a wax matrix, which may be detected in the stool.

Parenteral Dosage Forms

PROCAINAMIDE HYDROCHLORIDE INJECTION USP

Usual adult dose

Antiarrhythmic—

Intramuscular—

50 mg per kg of body weight per day in divided doses given every three to six hours.

Intravenous—

Initial:

Intravenous (direct), 100 mg (diluted in an appropriate volume of 5% dextrose injection to facilitate control of dosage rate) administered slowly (not exceeding 50 mg per minute) and repeated every five minutes until arrhythmia is controlled or up to a maximum total dose of 1 gram, or

Intravenous infusion, 500 to 600 mg diluted and administered at a constant rate over a period of twenty-five to thirty minutes.

Maintenance:

Intravenous infusion, diluted and administered at a rate of 2 to 6 mg per minute to maintain control of arrhythmia.

Usual pediatric dose

Dosage has not been established.

Strength(s) usually available

U.S.—

100 mg per mL (Rx) [*Pronestyl* (benzyl alcohol; sodium bisulfite); GENERIC].
500 mg per mL (Rx) [*Pronestyl* (sodium bisulfite; methylparaben); GENERIC].

Canada—

100 mg per mL (Rx) [*Pronestyl* (benzyl alcohol; sodium bisulfite)].
500 mg per mL (Rx) [*Pronestyl* (sodium bisulfite; methylparaben)].

Packaging and storage

Store between 15 and 30 °C (59 and 86 °F), unless otherwise specified by manufacturer. Protect from freezing. Protect from light.

Preparation of dosage form

For administration by intravenous infusion, dilute 200 mg to l gram of Procainamide Hydrochloride Injection USP to a concentration of 2 or 4 mg per mL using a suitable volume of 5% dextrose injection.

Stability

A slight yellowing will not alter potency; however, do not use if markedly discolored (darker than light amber) or if a precipitate is present.

Revised: 08/04/1993

PROCAINE

—See *Anesthetics (Parenteral-Local)*

PROCARBAZINE Systemic

VA CLASSIFICATION (Primary): AN900
Commonly used brand name(s): *Matulane; Natulan.*

Note: For a listing of dosage forms and brand names by country availability, see *Dosage Forms* section(s).

Category

Antineoplastic.

Indications

Note: Bracketed information in the *Indications* section refers to uses that are not included in U.S. product labeling.

Accepted

Lymphomas, Hodgkin's (treatment) or
[Lymphomas, non-Hodgkin's (treatment)][1]—Procarbazine is indicated, in combination with other agents, for treatment of Hodgkin's disease (Stage III and IV) and some non-Hodgkin's lymphomas.

[Tumors, brain, primary (treatment)][1]—Procarbazine is indicated for treatment of primary brain tumors.

[Multiple myeloma (treatment)][1]—Procarbazine is indicated for treatment of multiple myeloma.

[1]Not included in Canadian product labeling.

Pharmacology/Pharmacokinetics

Physicochemical characteristics

Molecular weight—257.76.

Mechanism of action/Effect

Procarbazine is an alkylating agent. The exact mechanism of antineoplastic action is unknown but is thought to resemble that of the alkylating agents; procarbazine is cell cycle–specific for the S phase of cell division. Procarbazine is thought to inhibit DNA, RNA, and protein synthesis.

Other actions/effects

Procarbazine causes weak inhibition of monoamine oxidase (MAO). MAO inhibitors prevent the inactivation of tyramine by hepatic and gastrointestinal monoamine oxidase. Tyramine in the bloodstream releases norepinephrine from the sympathetic nerve terminals and produces a sudden increase in blood pressure.

Absorption

Rapidly and completely absorbed from the gastrointestinal tract.

Distribution

Crosses the blood-brain barrier.

Biotransformation

Hepatic.

Half-life

Approximately 10 minutes.

Elimination

Renal—70% (as metabolite).

Precautions to Consider

Carcinogenicity/Mutagenicity

Secondary malignancies are potential delayed effects of many antineoplastic agents, although it is not clear whether the effect is related to their mutagenic or immunosuppressive action. The effect of dose and duration of therapy is also unknown, although risk seems to increase with long-term use. Although information is limited, available data seem to indicate that the carcinogenic risk is greatest with the alkylating agents.

Procarbazine is a potent carcinogen in animals and, because it is an alkylating agent, is also likely to be carcinogenic in humans.

Pregnancy/Reproduction

Fertility—Gonadal suppression, resulting in amenorrhea or azoospermia, may occur in patients taking antineoplastic therapy, especially with the alkylating agents. In general, these effects appear to be related to dose and length of therapy and may be irreversible. Prediction of the degree of testicular or ovarian function impairment is complicated by the common use of combinations of several antineoplastics, which makes it difficult to assess the effects of individual agents. Procarbazine affects spermatogenesis in humans.

Pregnancy—Procarbazine is frequently teratogenic in animals and there have been reports of minor malformations or premature births when it is given later in pregnancy in humans.

First trimester: It is usually recommended that use of antineoplastics, especially combination chemotherapy, be avoided whenever possible, especially during the first trimester. Although information is limited because of the relatively few instances of antineoplastic administration during pregnancy, the mutagenic, teratogenic, and carcinogenic potential of these medications must be considered.

Other hazards to the fetus include adverse reactions seen in adults.

In general, use of a contraceptive is recommended during cytotoxic drug therapy.

FDA Pregnancy Category D.

Breast-feeding

Although very little information is available regarding distribution of antineoplastic agents into breast milk, breast-feeding is not recommended while procarbazine is being administered because of the risks to the infant (adverse effects, mutagenicity, carcinogenicity).

Pediatrics

Appropriate studies with procarbazine have not been performed in the pediatric population. However, pediatrics-specific problems that would limit the usefulness of this medication in children are not expected.

Geriatrics

Although appropriate studies with procarbazine have not been performed in the geriatric population, the potential for increased vascular accidents (especially in the event of sudden hypertensive episodes), increased sensitivity to hypotensive effects, and reduced metabolic capacity discourages the first-time use of MAO inhibitors in patients over 60 years of age. When an MAO inhibitor is prescribed for an elderly patient, the patient's history of depression, ability to comply with prescribing instructions, and any potential drug interactions must also be considered. In addition, elderly patients are more likely to have age-related renal function impairment, which may require a lower dosage or, in severe cases, avoidance of use of procarbazine.

Dental

The bone marrow depressant effects of procarbazine may result in an increased incidence of microbial infection, delayed healing, and gingival bleeding. Dental work, whenever possible, should be completed prior to initiation of therapy or deferred until blood counts have returned to normal. Patients should be instructed in proper oral hygiene during treatment, including caution in use of regular toothbrushes, dental floss, and toothpicks.

Procarbazine may also cause stomatitis that is associated with considerable discomfort.

The secondary anticholinergic effects of procarbazine may decrease or inhibit salivary flow, especially in middle-aged or elderly patients, thus contributing to the development of caries, periodontal disease, oral candidiasis, and discomfort.

Drug interactions and/or related problems

The following drug interactions and/or related problems have been selected on the basis of their potential clinical significance (possible mechanism in parentheses where appropriate)—not necessarily inclusive (» = major clinical significance):

Note: Combinations containing any of the following medications, depending on the amount present, may also interact with this medication.

Most drug interactions are due to procarbazine's monoamine oxidase–inhibiting activity.

» Alcohol
(concurrent use with procarbazine may result in a disulfiram-like reaction and additive central nervous system (CNS) depression and postural hypotension; also, possible tyramine content in alcoholic beverages, especially beer, wine, or ale, may induce hypertensive reactions)

» Anesthetics, local, with epinephrine or levonordefrin or
» Cocaine
(concurrent use with procarbazine may cause severe hypertension due to sympathomimetic effects)
(cocaine should not be administered during or within 14 days following administration of an MAO inhibitor)

» Anesthetics, spinal
(hypotensive effects may be potentiated when spinal anesthetics are used concurrently with procarbazine; discontinuation of procarbazine at least 10 days before elective surgery if spinal anesthesia is planned may be advisable)

» Anticholinergics or other medications with anticholinergic activity (see *Appendix II*) or
Antidyskinetic agents or
» Antihistamines
(concurrent use with procarbazine may intensify anticholinergic effects because of the secondary anticholinergic activities of MAO

inhibitors; also, MAO inhibitors may block detoxification of anticholinergics, thus potentiating their action; patients should be advised to report occurrence of gastrointestinal problems promptly since paralytic ileus may occur with concurrent therapy)

(concurrent use with MAO inhibitors may also prolong and intensify CNS depressant and anticholinergic effects of antihistamines; concurrent use is not recommended)

Anticoagulants, coumarin- and indandione-derivative
(concurrent use may increase anticoagulant activity; although the mechanism of action and clinical significance are unknown, caution is recommended)

Anticonvulsants
(concurrent use of anticonvulsants with procarbazine may lead to increased CNS depressant effects as well as a change in the pattern of epileptiform seizures; dosage adjustment of anticonvulsant may be necessary)

» Antidepressants, tricyclic
(in addition to increased anticholinergic effects, concurrent use with procarbazine may result in hyperpyretic crises, severe convulsions, and death; however, recent studies have shown that some tricyclic antidepressants can be used concurrently with MAO inhibitors with no adverse effects if both medications are initiated simultaneously at lower than usual doses and the doses raised gradually, or if the MAO inhibitor is gradually added to the tricyclic also at low doses; tricyclics should not be added to an established MAO inhibitor regimen; careful monitoring for side effects of either medication is necessary)

» Antidiabetic agents, sulfonylurea or
» Insulin
(procarbazine may enhance hypoglycemic effects; dosage reduction of hypoglycemic medication may be necessary during and after such combined therapy)

Antihypertensives or
Diuretics or
Hypotension-producing medications, other (see *Appendix II*)
(concurrent use with procarbazine may result in an enhanced hypotensive effect; dosage adjustment may be necessary)

(antihypertensives with CNS depressant effects, such as clonidine, guanabenz, methyldopa, or metyrosine, may increase CNS depression)

Beta-adrenergic blocking agents, including ophthalmic beta-blockers absorbed systemically
(possible significant hypertension may theoretically occur up to 14 days following discontinuation of procarbazine; however, sufficient clinical reports are lacking)

Blood dyscrasia-causing medications (see *Appendix II*)
(leukopenic and/or thrombocytopenic effects of procarbazine may be increased with concurrent or recent therapy if these medications cause the same effects; dosage adjustment of procarbazine, if necessary, should be based on blood counts)

» Bone marrow depressants, other (see *Appendix II*) or
Radiation therapy
(additive bone marrow depression may occur; dosage reduction may be required when two or more bone marrow depressants, including radiation, are used concurrently or consecutively)

Bromocriptine
(concurrent use may increase serum prolactin concentrations and interfere with effects of bromocriptine; dosage adjustment of bromocriptine may be necessary)

» Buspirone
(concurrent use with MAO inhibitors is not recommended because elevation of blood pressure may occur)

» Caffeine-containing preparations
(concurrent use of excessive amounts of caffeine, consumed in chocolate, coffee, cola, tea, or "stay awake" products, with procarbazine may produce dangerous cardiac arrhythmias or severe hypertension because of sympathomimetic effects of caffeine)

» Carbamazepine or
» Cyclobenzaprine or
» Maprotiline or
» Monoamine oxidase (MAO) inhibitors, other, including furazolidone and pargyline
(concurrent use with procarbazine is not recommended on an outpatient basis, as hyperpyretic crises, severe seizures, and death could result; prior to initiation of procarbazine therapy, 14 days should elapse after discontinuance of any of these medications)

» CNS depression-producing medications, other (see *Appendix II*)
(CNS depression and postural hypotension may be enhanced; concurrent use with antihistamines is not recommended)

» Dextromethorphan
(concurrent use with procarbazine may cause excitation, hypertension, and hyperpyrexia)

» Doxapram
(concurrent use may increase the pressor effects of either doxapram or procarbazine)

» Fluoxetine
(concurrent use may result in confusion, agitation, restlessness, and gastrointestinal symptoms, or possibly hyperpyretic episodes, severe convulsions, and hypertensive crises. Based on experience with tricyclic antidepressants, at least 14 days should elapse between discontinuation of an MAO inhibitor and initiation of fluoxetine. However, because of the long half-lives of fluoxetine and its active metabolite, at least 5 weeks [approximately 5 half-lives of norfluoxetine] should elapse between discontinuation of fluoxetine and initiation of therapy with an MAO inhibitor. Administration of an MAO inhibitor within 5 weeks of discontinuation of fluoxetine may increase the risk of serious events. While a causal relationship to fluoxetine has not been established, death has been reported following the initiation of an MAO inhibitor shortly after fluoxetine administration was stopped)

» Guanadrel or
» Guanethidine or
» Rauwolfia alkaloids
(administration to patients receiving procarbazine may result in sudden release of accumulated catecholamines and a hypertensive reaction; parenteral administration is not recommended during and for 1 week following procarbazine therapy)

(when an MAO inhibitor is added to existing therapy with a rauwolfia alkaloid, serious potentiation of CNS depressant effects may result; however, if a rauwolfia alkaloid is added to an MAO inhibitor regimen, CNS excitation and hypertension may result from release of excessive amounts of accumulated norepinephrine and serotonin)

Haloperidol or
Loxapine or
Molindone or
Phenothiazines or
Pimozide or
Thioxanthenes
(concurrent use may prolong and intensify the sedative, hypotensive, and anticholinergic effects of either these medications or procarbazine)

» Levodopa
(concurrent use with MAO inhibitors is not recommended, as the combination may result in sudden moderate to severe hypertensive crisis; a period of 2 to 4 weeks is recommended after withdrawal of MAO inhibitors before levodopa is administered)

» Meperidine and possibly other opioid (narcotic) analgesics
(concurrent use with procarbazine may produce immediate excitation, sweating, rigidity, and severe hypertension; in some patients, hypotension, severe respiratory depression, coma, convulsions, hyperpyrexia, vascular collapse, and death may occur; reactions may be due to accumulation of serotonin resulting from MAO inhibition; avoidance of meperidine use within 2 to 3 weeks following procarbazine is recommended; other opioid analgesics, such as morphine, are not likely to cause such severe reactions and may be used cautiously in reduced dosage in patients receiving MAO inhibitors; however, it is recommended that a small test dose [one quarter of the usual dose] or several small incremental test doses over a period of several hours should first be administered to permit observation of any adverse effects)

(caution is also recommended in the use of alfentanil, fentanyl, or sufentanil as an adjunct to anesthesia if the patient has received procarbazine within 14 days; although the risk of a significant interaction has been questioned, the use of a small test dose is advised to detect any possible interaction)

» Methyldopa
(concurrent use with procarbazine may cause hyperexcitability; also headache, severe hypertension, and hallucinations have been reported)

» Methylphenidate
(concurrent use with procarbazine may potentiate the CNS stimulant effects of methylphenidate, possibly resulting in a hypertensive crisis; should not be administered during or within 14 days following the administration of procarbazine)

Metrizamide
(concurrent use with procarbazine may lower the seizure threshold; procarbazine should be discontinued at least 48 hours before

myelography and should not be resumed for at least 24 hours after procedure)

Phenylephrine, nasal or ophthalmic
(if significant systemic absorption of nasal or ophthalmic phenylephrine occurs, concurrent use with procarbazine may potentiate pressor effects; these medications should not be administered during or within 14 days following the administration of procarbazine)

» Sympathomimetics
(concurrent use with procarbazine may prolong and intensify cardiac stimulant and vasopressor effects [including headache, cardiac arrhythmias, vomiting, sudden and severe hypertensive and hyperpyretic crises] of these medications because of release of catecholamines that accumulate in intraneuronal storage sites during MAO inhibitor therapy; these medications should not be administered during or within 14 days following the administration of procarbazine)

» Tryptophan
(concurrent use with MAO inhibitors may cause hyperreflexia, shivering, hyperventilation, hyperthermia, mania or hypomania, and disorientation or confusion; when tryptophan is added to an MAOI regimen, it should be started in low dosages and the dose titrated upwards gradually with close monitoring of mental status and blood pressure)

» Tyramine- or other high pressor amine-containing foods and beverages, such as aged cheese; beer; reduced-alcohol and alcohol-free beer and wine; red and white wines; sherry; liqueurs; yeast/protein extracts; fava or broad bean pods; smoked or pickled meats, poultry, or fish; fermented sausage (bologna, pepperoni, salami, summer sausage) or other fermented meat; and any over-ripe fruit
(concurrent use with procarbazine may cause sudden and severe hypertensive reactions; reactions are usually limited to a few hours and easily treated with phentolamine; severity depends on amount of tyramine ingested, rate of gastric emptying, and length of interval between dose of procarbazine and ingestion of tyramine; when procarbazine is discontinued, dietary restrictions must continue for at least 2 weeks; other tyramine- or high pressor amine-containing foods, such as yogurt, sour cream, cream cheese, cottage cheese, chocolate, and soy sauce, if eaten when fresh and in moderation, are considered unlikely to cause serious problems)

Vaccines, killed virus
(because normal defense mechanisms may be suppressed by procarbazine therapy, the patient's antibody response to the vaccine may be decreased. The interval between discontinuation of medications that cause immunosuppression and restoration of the patient's ability to respond to the vaccine depends on the intensity and type of immunosuppression-causing medication used, the underlying disease, and other factors; estimates vary from 3 months to 1 year)

» Vaccines, live virus
(because normal defense mechanisms may be suppressed by procarbazine therapy, concurrent use with a live virus vaccine may potentiate the replication of the vaccine virus, may increase the side/adverse effects of the vaccine virus, and/or may decrease the patient's antibody response to the vaccine; immunization of these patients should be undertaken only with extreme caution after careful review of the patient's hematologic status and only with the knowledge and consent of the physician managing the procarbazine therapy. The interval between discontinuation of medications that cause immunosuppression and restoration of the patient's ability to respond to the vaccine depends on the intensity and type of immunosuppression-causing medication used, the underlying disease, and other factors; estimates vary from 3 months to 1 year. Immunization with oral poliovirus vaccine should also be postponed in persons in close contact with the patient, especially family members)

Medical considerations/Contraindications

The medical considerations/contraindications included have been selected on the basis of their potential clinical significance (reasons given in parentheses where appropriate)—not necessarily inclusive (» = major clinical significance).

Except under special circumstances, this medication should not be used when the following medical problems exist:

» Alcoholism, active

» Congestive heart failure

» Hepatic function impairment, severe
(procarbazine may precipitate hepatic precoma in patients with cirrhosis, who are extremely sensitive to its effects)

» Pheochromocytoma
(pressor substances secreted by such tumors may alter blood pressure during therapy with MAO inhibitors)

» Renal function impairment, severe
(cumulative effects of procarbazine may occur because of reduced renal excretion)

Risk-benefit should be considered when the following medical problems exist:

» Bone marrow depression

» Cardiac arrhythmias

» Cardiovascular disease or coronary insufficiency
(ischemia may be aggravated as a result of reduced blood pressure)

Cerebrovascular disease
(cerebral ischemia may be aggravated as a result of reduced blood pressure)

» Chickenpox, existing or recent (including recent exposure) or
» Herpes zoster
(risk of severe generalized disease)

Diabetes mellitus
(procarbazine may alter insulin or oral hypoglycemic requirements)

Epilepsy
(pattern of epileptiform seizures may be changed)

» Headaches, severe or frequent
(headache as a first sign of hypertensive reaction during therapy may be masked)

» Hepatic function impairment
(procarbazine may precipitate hepatic precoma in patients with cirrhosis, who are extremely sensitive to its effects; lower dosage is recommended; use not recommended in severe function impairment)

Hyperthyroidism
(sensitivity to pressor amines may be increased)

» Infection

» Paranoid schizophrenia or other hyperexcitable personality states
(MAO inhibitors may cause excessive stimulation in schizophrenic patients; in manic-depressive states, may effect a swing from depressive to manic phase)

Parkinsonism
(may be aggravated)

» Renal function impairment
(cumulative effects may occur; lower dosage is recommended; use not recommended in severe function impairment)

Sensitivity to procarbazine

» Caution should be used also in patients who have had previous cytotoxic drug therapy or radiation therapy.

» In addition, caution should be used in patients who have undergone sympathectomy, who may be more sensitive to the hypotensive effects of MAO inhibitors.

Patient monitoring

The following may be especially important in patient monitoring (other tests may be warranted in some patients, depending on condition; » = major clinical significance):

» Alanine aminotransferase (ALT [SGPT]) values, serum and
» Aspartate aminotransferase (AST [SGOT]) values, serum and
» Bilirubin concentrations, serum and
» Lactate dehydrogenase (LDH) values, serum
(determinations recommended prior to initiation of therapy and at periodic intervals during therapy; frequency varies according to clinical state, agent, dose, and other agents being used concurrently)

Blood urea nitrogen (BUN) concentrations and
Creatinine concentrations, serum
(determinations recommended prior to initiation of therapy and at periodic intervals during therapy; frequency varies according to clinical state, agent, dose, and other agents being used concurrently)

» Bone marrow aspiration studies
(recommended prior to initiation of procarbazine therapy and at time of maximum hematologic response to ensure adequate bone marrow reserve)

» Hematocrit or hemoglobin and
» Platelet count and
» Total and, if appropriate, differential leukocyte count
(determinations recommended prior to initiation of therapy and at periodic intervals during therapy; frequency varies according to

clinical state, agent, dose, and other agents being used concurrently)

Side/Adverse Effects

Note: Many "side effects" of antineoplastic therapy are unavoidable and represent the medication's pharmacologic action. Some of these (for example, leukopenia and thrombocytopenia) are actually used as parameters to aid in individual dosage titration.

Except for hematologic, pulmonary, and gastrointestinal toxicity, adverse effects of procarbazine resemble those of the MAO inhibitors used in treating psychiatric disorders.

Toxicity is increased in patients with renal or hepatic function impairment or bone marrow depression.

The following side/adverse effects have been selected on the basis of their potential clinical significance (possible signs and symptoms in parentheses where appropriate)—not necessarily inclusive:

Those indicating need for medical attention

Incidence more frequent

Anemia; CNS stimulation, excessive (confusion; convulsions; hallucinations); ***immunosuppression, infection, or leukopenia*** (fever or chills; cough or hoarseness; lower back or side pain; painful or difficult urination)—usually asymptomatic; ***thrombocytopenia*** (unusual bleeding or bruising; black, tarry stools; blood in urine or stools; pinpoint red spots on skin)—usually asymptomatic; ***hemolytic anemia*** (continuing tiredness or weakness); ***missing menstrual periods; pneumonitis*** (cough; shortness of breath; thickening of bronchial secretions)

Note: With *leukopenia and thrombocytopenia*, the nadir of the platelet count occurs after about 4 weeks, followed by the leukocyte count, with recovery complete in about 6 weeks.

Missing menstrual periods occur with high doses.

Incidence less frequent

Gastrointestinal toxicity (diarrhea); ***hepatotoxicity*** (yellow eyes or skin); ***peripheral neuropathy*** (tingling or numbness of fingers or toes; unsteadiness or awkwardness); ***stomatitis*** (sores in mouth and on lips)

Incidence rare

Allergic reaction (skin rash, hives or itching; wheezing); ***hypertensive crisis*** (severe chest pain; enlarged pupils; fast or slow heartbeat; severe headache; increased sensitivity of eyes to light; increased sweating, possibly with fever or cold, clammy skin; stiff or sore neck); ***orthostatic hypotension*** (fainting)

Those indicating need for medical attention only if they continue or are bothersome

Incidence more frequent

CNS stimulation, excessive (drowsiness; muscle or joint pain; muscle twitching; nervousness; nightmares; trouble in sleeping); ***nausea and vomiting; unusual tiredness or weakness***

Incidence less frequent

Constipation; darkening of skin; difficulty in swallowing; dry mouth; feeling of warmth and redness in face; headache; loss of appetite; mental depression; orthostatic hypotension (dizziness or lightheadedness when getting up from a lying or sitting position)

Those not indicating need for medical attention

Incidence less frequent

Loss of hair

Overdose

For more information on the management of overdose or unintentional intestion, **contact a Poison Control Center** (see *Poison Control Center listing*).

Treatment of overdose

Note: Symptoms resulting from overdose may be absent or minimal for nearly 12 hours following ingestion, and develop slowly thereafter, reaching a maximum in 24 to 48 hours. Immediate hospitalization and close monitoring of patient are essential during this period.

Treatment may include the following:

Induction of vomiting or gastric lavage with protected airway followed by instillation of charcoal slurry in early overdose.

Treatment of signs and symptoms of CNS stimulation with diazepam, administered intravenously and slowly.

Treatment of hypotension and vascular collapse with intravenous fluids and a dilute pressor agent.

Support of respiration by management of the airway, and mechanical ventilation with the use of supplemental oxygen, as required.

Close monitoring of body temperature and vigorous treatment of hyperpyrexia with antipyretics and a cooling blanket. Maintenance of fluid and electrolyte balance is essential.

Reduction of symptoms of hypermetabolic state (coma, respiratory failure, hyperpyrexia, tachycardia, muscular rigidity, tremor, and hyperreflexia) with intravenous dantrolene sodium at 2.5 mg per kg of body weight (mg/kg) a day in divided doses, with careful monitoring for signs of hepatotoxicity and pleural or pericardial effusions.

Hemodialysis may be beneficial but is of unproven value.

Pathophysiologic effects of massive overdose may persist for several days; recovery from mild overdose may take 3 to 4 days.

Patient Consultation

As an aid to patient consultation, refer to *Advice for the Patient, Procarbazine (Systemic)*.

In providing consultation, consider emphasizing the following selected information (» = major clinical significance):

Before using this medication

» Conditions affecting use, especially:
- Sensitivity to procarbazine
- Pregnancy—Advisability of using contraception; telling physician immediately if pregnancy is suspected
- Breast-feeding—Not recommended because of risk of serious side effects
- Use in the elderly—Potential for increased vascular accidents, increased sensitivity to hypotensive effects; first-time use discouraged in patients over 60 years of age
- Other medications, especially alcohol, anticholinergics or other medications with anticholinergic activity, antihistamines, buspirone, caffeine-containing preparations, carbamazepine, CNS-depressants, cocaine, cyclobenzaprine, dextromethorphan, doxapram, fluoxetine, furazolidone, guanadrel, guanethidine, insulin, levodopa, local anesthetics with epinephrine or levonordefrin, maprotiline, meperidine and possibly other opioid analgesics, methyldopa, methylphenidate, other bone marrow depressants, other monoamine oxidase inhibitors, pargyline, previous cytotoxic drug or radiation therapy, rauwolfia alkaloids, spinal anesthetics, sulfyonylurea antidiabetic agents, sympathomimetics, tricyclic antidepressants, or tryptophan
- Other medical problems, especially active alcoholism, bone marrow depression, cardiac arrhythmias, chickenpox or recent exposure, congestive heart failure, coronary insufficiency, severe or frequent headaches, hepatic function impairment, herpes zoster, other infection, paranoid schizophrenia or other hyperexcitable personality states, pheochromocytoma, sympathectomy, or renal function impairment

Proper use of this medication

» Importance of not taking more or less medication than the amount prescribed

Caution in taking combination chemotherapy; taking each medication at the right time

» Frequency of nausea and vomiting; importance of continuing medication despite stomach upset

Checking with physician if vomiting occurs shortly after dose is taken

» Proper dosing

Missed dose: Taking as soon as remembered if within a few hours; not taking if several hours have passed or if almost time for next dose; not doubling doses

» Proper storage

Precautions while using this medication

» Importance of close monitoring by the physician

» Checking with hospital emergency room or physician if symptoms of hypertensive crisis develop

» Avoiding use of tyramine-containing foods, alcoholic beverages and large quantities of caffeine-containing beverages, over-the-counter cold and cough medicines, and other medication unless prescribed; having list of such for reference

» Obeying rules of caution during 14 days after discontinuing medication

» Caution in taking alcohol or other CNS depressants

» Caution if drowsiness occurs, especially when driving or doing things requiring alertness

» Avoiding immunizations unless approved by physician; other persons in patient's household should avoid immunizations with oral poliovirus vaccine; avoiding other persons who have taken oral poliovirus vaccine or wearing a protective mask that covers nose and mouth

Caution if bone marrow depression occurs:

» Avoiding exposure to persons with infections, especially during periods of low blood counts; checking with physician immediately if fever or chills, cough or hoarseness, lower back or side pain, or painful or difficult urination occurs

» Checking with physician immediately if unusual bleeding or bruising; black, tarry stools; blood in urine or stools; or pinpoint red spots on skin occur

Caution in use of regular toothbrush, dental floss, or toothpick; physician, dentist, or nurse may suggest alternatives; checking with physician before having dental work done

Not touching eyes or inside of nose unless hands washed immediately before

Using caution to avoid accidental cuts with use of sharp objects such as safety razor or fingernail or toenail cutters

Avoiding contact sports or other situations where bruising or injury could occur

Diabetics: Checking urine or blood sugar levels

» Caution if any kind of surgery (including dental surgery) or emergency treatment is required

Carrying medical identification card

Side/adverse effects

May cause adverse effects such as blood problems, loss of hair, hypertensive crisis, and cancer; importance of discussing possible effects with physician

Signs of potential side effects, especially anemia, excessive CNS stimulation, immunosuppression, infection, leukopenia, thrombocytopenia, hemolytic anemia, missing menstrual periods, pneumonitis, gastrointestinal toxicity, hepatotoxicity, peripheral neuropathy, stomatitis, allergic reaction, hypertensive crisis, and orthostatic hypotension

Physician or nurse can help in dealing with side effects

General Dosing Information

Patients receiving procarbazine should be under supervision of a physician experienced in cancer chemotherapy.

A variety of dosage schedules and regimens of procarbazine, alone or in combination with other antitumor agents, are used. The prescriber may consult medical literature as well as the manufacturer's literature in choosing a specific dosage.

Dosage must be adjusted to meet the individual requirements of each patient, based on clinical response and appearance or severity of toxicity.

Although dosages are based on the patient's actual weight, use of estimated lean body weight is recommended in obese patients or those with weight gain due to edema, ascites, or other abnormal fluid retention.

It is recommended that procarbazine therapy be discontinued promptly if any of the following occur:

Allergic reaction

Central nervous system signs or symptoms, such as paresthesias, neuropathies, or confusion

Diarrhea

Hemorrhage or bleeding tendencies

Leukopenia (< 4000 white blood cells per cubic millimeter)

Stomatitis

Thrombocytopenia (< 100,000 platelets per cubic millimeter)

Therapy may be resumed at a lower dosage when the clinical and laboratory examinations are satisfactory.

Because of the risk of enhanced bone marrow toxicity, an interval of at least 1 month (based on bone marrow studies) is recommended before starting procarbazine therapy after a patient has received radiation or chemotherapy with medications that depress bone marrow function.

After dosage is stopped, monoamine oxidase (MAO) inhibitor effects of this medication may persist for up to 2 weeks after withdrawal (time required for regeneration of enzyme). During this period, food and drug contraindications must be observed.

Special precautions are recommended in patients who develop thrombocytopenia as a result of administration of procarbazine. These may include extreme care in performing invasive procedures; regular inspection of intravenous sites, skin (including perirectal area), and mucous membrane surfaces for signs of bleeding or bruising; limiting frequency of venipuncture and avoiding intramuscular injections; testing urine, emesis, stool, and secretions for occult blood; care in use of regular toothbrushes, dental floss, toothpicks, safety razors, and fingernail and toenail cutters; avoiding constipation; and using caution to prevent falls and other injuries. Such patients should avoid alcohol and any aspirin intake because of the risk of gastrointestinal bleeding. Platelet transfusions may be required.

Patients who develop leukopenia should be observed carefully for signs of infection. Antibiotic support may be required. In neutropenic patients who develop fever, broad-spectrum antibiotic coverage should be initiated empirically, pending bacterial cultures and appropriate diagnostic tests.

Diet/Nutrition

Foods and beverages containing tyramine or other high pressor amines, such as aged cheese; beer; reduced-alcohol and alcohol-free beer and wine; red and white wines; sherry; liqueurs; yeast/protein extracts; fava or broad bean pods; smoked or pickled meats, poultry, or fish; fermented sausage (bologna, pepperoni, salami, summer sausage) or other fermented meat; and any overripe fruit, when used concurrently with MAO inhibitors, may cause sudden and severe hypertensive reactions. The reactions are usually limited to a few hours and are easily treated with phentolamine. The severity depends on the amount of tyramine ingested, rate of gastric emptying, and length of the interval between the dose of MAO inhibitor and ingestion of tyramine. When MAO inhibitors are discontinued, dietary restrictions must continue for at least 2 weeks. Other foods, such as yogurt, sour cream, cream cheese, cottage cheese, chocolate, and soy sauce, if eaten when fresh and in moderation, are considered unlikely to cause serious problems.

For treatment of hypertensive crisis

Recommended treatment includes:

- Discontinuing MAO inhibitor.
- Lowering blood pressure immediately with intravenous administration of 5 mg of phentolamine, with care being taken to inject slowly, to prevent excessive hypotensive effect.
- Reducing fever by external cooling.

Combination chemotherapy

Procarbazine may be used in combination with other agents in various regimens. As a result, incidence and/or severity of side effects may be altered and different dosages (usually reduced) may be used. For example, procarbazine is part of the following chemotherapeutic combinations (some commonly used acronyms are in parentheses):

—carmustine, cyclophosphamide, vinblastine, procarbazine, and prednisone (BCVPP).

—cyclophosphamide, doxorubicin, methotrexate, and procarbazine (CAMP).

—cyclophosphamide, vincristine, procarbazine, and prednisone (COPP).

—mechlorethamine, vincristine, procarbazine, and prednisone (MOPP).

For specific dosages and schedules, consult the literature. For information regarding each agent, consult the individual monographs.

Oral Dosage Forms

PROCARBAZINE HYDROCHLORIDE CAPSULES USP

Note: The doses and strength are expressed in terms of procarbazine base, not the hydrochloride salt.

Usual adult dose

Lymphomas, Hodgkin's—

Initial: Oral, 2 to 4 mg (base) per kg of body weight (to the nearest 50 mg) a day in single or divided doses for the first week, followed by 4 to 6 mg per kg of body weight a day until leukopenia, thrombocytopenia, or maximum response occurs.

Note: If hematologic toxicity occurs, the medication is withdrawn until the toxicity is resolved, then treatment may be resumed with 1 to 2 mg (base) per kg of body weight a day.

Maintenance: Oral, 1 to 2 mg (base) per kg of body weight a day.

Usual pediatric dose

Lymphomas, Hodgkin's—

Initial: Oral, 50 mg (base) per square meter of body surface area a day for the first week, followed by 100 mg per square meter of body surface area a day until leukopenia, thrombocytopenia, or maximum response occurs.

Note: If hematologic toxicity occurs, the medication is withdrawn until the toxicity is resolved, then treatment may be resumed with 50 mg (base) per square meter of body surface area a day.

Maintenance: Oral, 50 mg (base) per square meter of body surface area a day.

Note: This dosage schedule is a guideline only. Undue toxicity in the form of tremors, coma, and seizures has occurred; therefore, dosage must be individualized based on clinical response and appearance of toxicity.

Strength(s) usually available

U.S.—

50 mg (base) (Rx) [*Matulane*].

Canada—

50 mg (base) (Rx) [*Natulan*].

Packaging and storage
Store below 40 °C (104 °F), preferably between 15 and 30 °C (59 and 86 °F), unless otherwise specified by manufacturer. Store in a tight, light-resistant container.

Auxiliary labeling
- Avoid alcoholic beverages.
- May cause drowsiness.
- Avoid certain foods as directed.

Revised: 12/12/2002

PROCATEROL—See *Bronchodilators, Adrenergic (Inhalation-Local)*

PROCHLORPERAZINE—See *Phenothiazines (Systemic)*

PROCYCLIDINE—See *Antidyskinetics (Systemic)*

PROGESTERONE—See *Progestins (Systemic)*

PROGESTINS Systemic

Note: For information pertaining to the use of estrogens and progestins oral contraceptives, see *Estrogens and Progestins Oral Contraceptives (Systemic)* and for use of progesterone intrauterine device, see *Progesterone Intrauterine Device (IUD)*.

This monograph includes information on the following: 1) Hydroxyprogesterone†; 2) Levonorgestrel; 3) Medrogestone*; 4) Medroxyprogesterone; 5) Megestrol; 6) Norethindrone; 7) Norgestrel†; 8) Progesterone.

INN:
Hydroxyprogesterone caproate—Hydroxyprogesterone
Medroxyprogesterone acetate—Medroxyprogesterone
Megestrol acetate—Megestrol
Norethindrone—Norethisterone

BAN:
Hydroxyprogesterone caproate—Hydroxyprogesterone
Medroxyprogesterone acetate—Medroxyprogesterone
Megestrol acetate—Megestrol
Norethindrone—Norethisterone

VA CLASSIFICATION (Primary/Secondary):
Hydroxyprogesterone—HS103
Levonorgestrel—HS103/HS104
Medrogestone—HS103
Medroxyprogesterone—HS103/AN500; HS104
Megestrol—HS103/AN500
Norethindrone—HS103/HS104
Norgestrel—HS103/HS104
Progesterone—HS103

Commonly used brand name(s): *Alti-MPA*[4]; *Amen*[4]; *Apo-Megestrol*[5]; *Aygestin*[6]; *Colprone*[3]; *Crinone*[8]; *Curretab*[4]; *Cycrin*[4]; *Depo-Provera*[4]; *Depo-Provera Contraceptive Injection*[4]; *Gen-Medroxy*[4]; *Gesterol 50*[8]; *Gesterol LA 250*[1]; *Hy/Gestrone*[1]; *Hylutin*[1]; *Megace*[5]; *Megace OS*[5]; *Micronor*[6]; *NORPLANT System*[2]; *Nor-QD*[6]; *Norlutate*[6]; *Novo-Medrone*[4]; *Ovrette*[7]; *PMS-Progesterone*[8]; *Plan B*[2]; *Pro-Span*[1]; *Prochieve*[8]; *Prodrox*[1]; *Prometrium*[8]; *Provera*[4]; *Provera Pak*[4]; *depo-subQ provera 104*[4].

Another commonly used name for norethindrone is norethisterone.

Note: For a listing of dosage forms and brand names by country availability, see *Dosage Forms* section(s).

*Not commercially available in U.S.
†Not commercially available in Canada.

Category

Progestational agent—Hydroxyprogesterone; Medrogestone; Medroxyprogesterone (oral); Norethindrone; Norgestrel; Progesterone.
Antianoretic—Megestrol.
Anticachectic—Megestrol.
Antineoplastic—Medroxyprogesterone (parenteral); Megestrol.
Contraceptive (systemic)—Levonorgestrel; Medroxyprogesterone (parenteral); Norethindrone (base); Norgestrel.
Diagnostic aid (estrogen production)—Hydroxyprogesterone; Medroxyprogesterone (oral); Progesterone (parenteral).
Infertility therapy adjunct—Progesterone (vaginal).
Ovarian hormone therapy agent adjunct—Medroxyprogesterone (oral); Progesterone (oral)

Indications

Note: Bracketed information in the *Indications* section refers to uses that are not included in U.S. product labeling.

Accepted

Amenorrhea, secondary (treatment)
Dysfunctional uterine bleeding (treatment) or
Menses, induction of (treatment)—Hydroxyprogesterone, medrogestone, oral medroxyprogesterone, norethindrone acetate, and parenteral progesterone are indicated in the treatment of menstrual disorders, including secondary amenorrhea and dysfunctional uterine bleeding (DUB) caused by hormonal imbalance in the absence of organic pathology. Progesterone oral capsules[1] and progesterone vaginal gel are indicated in the treatment of secondary amenorrhea. The 8% strength of vaginal gel is used only if the patient fails to respond to treatment with the 4% progesterone vaginal gel. Hydroxyprogesterone is also indicated for the production of a secretory endometrium and desquamation. The uterus must be sufficiently primed with endogenous or exogenous estrogen for the progestins to produce a secretory-like endometrium and endometrial shedding after progestin use ends. Withdrawal bleeding usually occurs 3 to 7 days after discontinuation of the progestin for women with an intact uterus.

Anorexia (treatment)
Cachexia (treatment) or
Weight loss, significant (treatment)—Megestrol suspension is indicated in the treatment of anorexia, cachexia, unexplained significant weight loss (loss of 10% or more of base-line body weight) associated with acquired immunodeficiency syndrome (AIDS). [Megestrol tablets are indicated in the treatment of anorexia, cachexia, and unexplained significant weight loss associated with cancer].

Assisted reproductive technologies, in females or
[Corpus luteum insufficiency (treatment)][1]—Progesterone vaginal gel is indicated to replace the progesterone hormone in female patients whose infertility is due to partial or complete ovarian failure. Progesterone vaginal gel is indicated to supplement endogenous progesterone for luteal phase progesterone deficiency. Extemporaneously prepared [progesterone suppositories][1] have also been used for these indications.

Carcinoma, breast (treatment)—Megestrol and [oral and parenteral medroxyprogesterone] are indicated in the treatment of breast carcinoma; [medroxyprogesterone] is indicated for use in postmenopausal women only. It is used as adjunctive or palliative therapy in the treatment of advanced (inoperable, recurrent, or metastatic) hormonally dependent carcinoma.

Carcinoma, endometrial (treatment)—[Oral] or parenteral medroxyprogesterone, and megestrol are indicated for the treatment of endometrial carcinoma. It is used as adjunctive and/or palliative therapy in the treatment of advanced (recurrent or metastatic) hormonally dependent carcinoma.

Carcinoma, prostate (treatment)—[Megestrol] is indicated in the treatment of hormonally dependent and advanced prostate carcinoma as palliative therapy.

Carcinoma, renal (treatment)—Parenteral medroxyprogesterone is also indicated in the treatment of metastatic renal carcinoma as adjunctive and/or palliative therapy when used in the treatment of advanced (recurrent or metastatic) hormonally dependent carcinoma.

Contraception, emergency postcoital (prophylaxis)—Levonorgestrel, oral
Endometriosis (treatment)—Norethindrone acetate, [parenteral medroxyprogesterone], and [oral medroxyprogesterone][1] are indicated in the treatment of endometriosis.

Estrogen production, endogenous (diagnosis)—Hydroxyprogesterone, [oral medroxyprogesterone], and [parenteral progesterone] are indicated as a test for endogenous estrogen production and can be used to determine whether low levels of estrogen are present if withdrawal bleeding does not occur after a progestin challenge in menopausal women before estrogen-progestin ovarian hormone therapy is considered. However, determination that serum gonadotropins are elevated is the standard way to confirm menopause.

[Hot flashes][1]—Megesterol acetate and medroxyprogesterone acetate injection are indicated for the treatment of hot flashes.

[Hyperplasia, endometrial (treatment)][1] or Hyperplasia, endometrial, estrogen-induced (prophylaxis)—Megestrol and oral medroxyprogesterone have been used to treat endometrial hyperplasia without atypia, which is usually not a precursor of carcinoma. Complex atypical hyperplasia (previously called adenomatous hyperplasia) is usually best treated surgically, but in some high risk patients or when future pregnancy is desired, high continuous doses of progestins have been used.

For prevention, [oral medroxyprogesterone], [norethindrone][1], medrogestone, and [oral progesterone] can be used to oppose the effects of estrogen on the endometrium in menopausal women who take estrogens for ovarian hormone therapy (OHT), also called hormone replacement therapy (HRT) and estrogen replacement therapy (ERT). All menopausal patients receiving progestins do not have recognized endometrial shedding; there is frequently amenorrhea after several months of treatment with estrogen-progestin regimens. The optimal or recommended length for estrogen replacement after menopause has not been established. Studies have shown that administration of a progestin for a minimum of 10 to 14 days of an estrogen cycle in women with an intact uterus is required for major reduction of endometrial hyperplasia and endometrial carcinoma compared with an estrogen-only cycle. Other dosing regimens for estrogens and progestins, including low continuous daily dosing, are also used. Progestins without estrogens may be used for debilitating menopausal symptoms in patients who have breast cancer and are candidates for progestin therapy but cannot take estrogens.

Pain, endometriosis-associated (treatment)—Subcutaneous medroxyprogesterone is indicated for management of endometriosis-associated pain.

Pregnancy, prevention of—Levonorgestrel, parenteral medroxyprogesterone, norethindrone (base), and norgestrel are indicated for the prevention of pregnancy. Progestin-only oral contraceptives are also called minipills and progestin-only oral pills (POPs).

The following table presents the results of studies examining contraceptive failure rates calculated using the life-table method. The first column lists the contraceptive method used. The second column indicates the percentage of women experiencing an accidental pregnancy in the first year of use of a contraceptive method while using the method perfectly under clinical conditions. The range of failure rates in the clinical trials may be explained by interstudy variations in study design or patient population characteristics, such as motivation, fecundity, or socioeconomic factors (including education). The third column indicates contraceptive failure rates in the first year of contraceptive use under clinical conditions for typical couples who start using a method (not necessarily for the first time). Failure rates among adolescents may be higher due to poorer compliance than in other age groups.

Method used	Failure rate range (over 12 months) in clinical studies (%)	Typical first year failure rate (%)
None	78–94	85
Spermicides*	0.3–37	21
Periodic abstinence†	13–35	20
Withdrawal	7–22	19
Cervical cap with spermicide	6–27	18
Diaphragm with spermicide	2–23	18
Condom without spermicide	2–14	12
IUD		
Progesterone-releasing	1.9–2	2
Copper-T 200	3–3.6	
Copper-T 200Ag‡	0–1.2	
Copper-T 220C§	0.9–1.8	
Copper-T 380A	0.5–0.8	0.8
Copper-T 380S	0.9	
Oral contraceptive		3
Estrogen and progestin	0–6	
Progestin only	1–10	0.5
Progestin injection		
Medroxyprogesterone (90-day)	0–0.3	0.3
Levonorgestrel (subdermal)		
Six implants	0–0.09	0.09
Two rods	0–0.2	0.3
Sterilization		
Female#	0–8	0.4
Male	0–0.5	0.15

[Polycystic ovary syndrome (treatment)][1]—Medroxyprogesterone is used in the treatment of endometrial hyperplasia and its consequences in syndromes, such as polycystic ovary syndrome.

[Puberty, precocious (treatment)][1]—Parenteral medroxyprogesterone is accepted therapy for use in the treatment of precocious puberty but has been replaced by other treatment modalities.

Unaccepted

There is no evidence that progesterone is effective in the treatment of premenstrual syndrome.

Progestins are no longer recommended for use as pregnancy tests because of possible teratogenic effects with synthetic progestins; also, other tests available are quicker and easier to perform.

With the exception of progesterone in patients who are progesterone deficient, progestins have no proven value in the treatment of threatened abortion and are no longer recommended for such use.

Parenteral medroxyprogesterone for contraception is not indicated for use before menarche.

Unlike oral medroxyprogesterone, parenteral medroxyprogesterone is not recommended by the manufacturer for treatment of secondary amenorrhea or dysfunctional uterine bleeding.

Megestrol is not recommended for prophylactic use to avoid weight loss.

Levonorgestrel used for emergency postcoital contraception is not recommended for routine use as a contraceptive.

Levonorgestrel used for emergency postcoital contraception is not effective in terminating an existing pregnancy.

[1]Not included in Canadian product labeling.

Pharmacology/Pharmacokinetics

See *Table 1*, page 2443.

Physicochemical characteristics

Molecular weight—
- Hydroxyprogesterone caproate: 428.62.
- Levonorgestrel: 312.45.
- Medrogestone: 340.51.
- Medroxyprogesterone acetate: 386.53.
- Megestrol acetate: 384.52.
- Norethindrone: 298.43.
- Norethindrone acetate: 340.47.
- Norgestrel: 312.45.
- Progesterone: 314.47.

Mechanism of action/Effect

Progestins enter target cells by passive diffusion and bind to cytosolic (soluble) receptors that are loosely bound in the nucleus. The steroid receptor complex initiates transcription, resulting in an increase in protein synthesis.

Progestins are capable of affecting serum concentrations of other hormones, particularly estrogen. Estrogenic effects are modified by the progestins, either by reducing the availability or stability of the hormone receptor complex or by turning off specific hormone-responsive genes by direct interaction with the progestin receptor in the nucleus. In addition, estrogen priming is necessary to increase progestin effects by upregulating the number of progestin receptors and/or increasing progesterone production, causing a negative feedback mechanism that inhibits estrogen receptors.

Depending on the progestin and its dose, progestin may demonstrate varying degrees of progestational effects. Also, other hormonal effects, such as estrogenic-, anabolic-, androgenic-, or glucocorticoid-inducing or suppressing effects are demonstrated to different degrees and depend on the progestin type and dose. For example, an androgenic effect may be expressed by 19-nor derivatives of testosterone but not by other progestins. The androgenic effects of norethindrone are minor to moderate; norethindrone acetate is twice as potent as norethindrone. Norgestrel and levonorgestrel have androgenic effects if unopposed by estrogens. Rare cases of adrenal suppression have been reported in patients using megestrol. While the progestational effects dominate, the other effects can become important when choosing the appropriate progestin or monitoring side effects. Progestins are not used exclusively for other than their progestational effects, as the other effects are highly variable and unreliable.

Progestational agents—Progestins produce significant antiproliferative changes in the endometrium. As progestin levels fall after estrogen priming in the second half of the menstrual cycle, uterine bleeding may occur. Depending on the estrogen-progestin regimen, the progestin dose may be sufficient to cause amenorrhea.

Antianoretic or anticachectic—The mechanism that produces weight gain has not been fully elucidated; however, megestrol appears to have appetite-stimulant and metabolic effects that result in weight gain while causing minimal fluid retention. The underlying cause of wasting should be treated concurrently to optimize management of catabolism.

Antineoplastic—The mechanism has not been fully elucidated; however, several mechanisms may be involved that are dependent on the type and dose of progestin. In certain doses, progestins can produce a diminished response to endogenous hormones in tumor cells by decreasing the number of steroid hormone receptors (estrogen, progesterone, androgen, and glucocorticoid); the degree of variation of response is tissue- and progestin-dependent. The suppression of the growth of hormone-sensitive cells may be due to a direct cytotoxic effect or antiproliferative effects on cell cycle growth and an increased terminal cell differentiation. At higher doses, some progestins compete for the glucocorticoid receptor, resulting in suppressed adrenal production of estradiol and androstenedione. Still-higher progestin doses are able to completely suppress the hypothalamic-pituitary-adrenal axis (HPA axis), an effect that is important in the treatment of estrogen- or testosterone-sensitive tumors.

Contraceptive (systemic)—Inhibition of the secretion of gonadotropins from the anterior pituitary prevents ovulation and follicular maturation and is one of the contraceptive actions of levonorgestrel, parenteral medroxyprogesterone, norethindrone, and norgestrel. These effects do not occur with low-dose oral medroxyprogesterone, which is not used for contraception. In some patients using low-dose progestin-only contraceptives, particularly norethindrone (base) and levonorgestrel subdermal implants, ovulation is not suppressed consistently from cycle to cycle. The contraceptive effect of the progestin is achieved through other mechanisms that result in interference with fertilization and implantation in the luteal cycle, such as thickening of the cervical mucus and changes in the endometrium. In males, medroxyprogesterone suppresses the Leydig cell function.

Other actions/effects

Progestins increase body temperature, stimulate the respiratory center, and, in some cases, may provide pain relief. The mechanism by which progesterone and medroxyprogesterone mediate thermogenic effects is not clear. It has been suggested that progesterone influences neurotransmitters and neuropeptides in the brain, notably endogenous opioids, interleukin-1, and serotonin, that raise body temperature. Also, medroxyprogesterone may reduce hypercapnia in certain patients by stimulating the respiratory center. Pain relief from high-dose progestins may be due in part to an anti-inflammatory action.

Locally the progestins relax the uterine smooth muscle, sustain pregnancy, decrease the immune response, and, acting with estrogen, stimulate breast tissue growth.

Some progestins cause sodium and water retention. Progesterone doses of 50 to 100 mg may produce a moderate catabolic effect and transient increase in sodium chloride excretion. In addition, use of some progestins may result in dose-related adverse effects on carbohydrate and lipid metabolism.

Progestins influence bone density. When progestins have been used without estrogen, a positive effect has been shown in postmenopausal women and a possible negative effect in premenopausal women; the latter may depend on the degree to which a progestin can reduce ovarian estrogen production, a dose-dependent effect. When progestins have been used sequentially with continuously administered estrogen, a synergistic protective effect on bone density has been shown. Specifically, placebo-controlled studies of postmenopausal women showed that medroxyprogesterone decreased the rate of cortical bone loss but did not protect trabecular areas of the skeleton, such as the spine, equally from bone loss in all studies. A low-dose combination of continuously administered estrogen and sequentially administered progestin therapy showed protective effects against bone loss that were similar to those of higher doses of estrogen therapy alone. This effect may be due to an increase of progestin receptors caused by estrogen, to an antagonistic effect of progestin binding to glucocorticoid receptors, or to a stimulatory effect of progestin acting on progestin receptors within osteoblasts. Additional studies are needed to confirm and fully characterize these results.

Other health benefits of progestational hormone therapy may include less painful menstruation, less menstrual blood loss and anemia, fewer pelvic infections, and lower incidence of uterine cancers.

Absorption

Progestins—Well absorbed.

Levonorgestrel subdermal implants and parenteral medroxyprogesterone acetate—Well-absorbed during controlled release with wide intra- and intersubject variability. Initial release rate for a set of levonorgestrel subdermal implants is approximately 80 micrograms of levonorgestrel per 24 hours. This rate declines over the first 6 to 18 months to an approximately constant release rate of 30 micrograms of levonorgestrel per 24 hours over the remainder of the 5 years of use.

Progesterone—Micronized progesterone improves surface area contact and absorption compared to nonmicronized progesterone; both types have been used in extemporaneously prepared formulations.

Micronized progesterone, oral—Luteal phase concentrations of progesterone are maintained for approximately 9 to 12 hours after oral administration. Food significantly increases absorption as shown by increases in the area under the plasma concentration-time curve (AUC) and peak concentration, but the time to peak concentration is not affected.

Micronized progesterone, vaginal gel—Since the progesterone is soluble in both the water and oil phases, the vaginal gel (as an oil and water emulsion) provides a prolonged action and an absorption half-life of 25 to 50 hours.

Precautions to Consider

Carcinogenicity

The benefit of lowering the incidence of endometrial hyperplasia and endometrial cancer by adding progestin to an estrogen regimen in ovarian hormone therapy to counter estrogen's effect on the uterus is established.

Medroxyprogesterone—

Long-term studies in humans using parenteral medroxyprogesterone for contraception have found no increase in the overall risk of ovarian, liver, breast, or cervical cancer and have found a prolonged, protective effect of reducing the risk of endometrial cancer for at least 8 years. The possible protective effect may be lessened with concomitant use of estrogen; however, the lifetime risk for developing endometrial cancer is not increased in women with a uterus who take estrogen plus a progestin for 10 to 20 years. In the short-term, the initial risk of breast cancer with parenteral medroxyprogesterone exposure may be increased in the first 4 years after initial exposure in women under 35 years of age. The risk lessens with duration of use and results in no overall increase of risk for developing breast cancer.

Studies of monkeys administered doses of 3, 30, and 150 mg per kg (mg/kg) of body weight every 90 days for 10 years produced undifferentiated carcinoma of the uterus in a few monkeys dosed at 150 mg/kg. No uterine malignancies were reported in monkeys taking other doses or in the control monkeys; no uterine abnormalities were produced in similar studies of rats after 2 years. The relevance of these findings to humans is not known.

Tumorigenicity/Mutagenicity

Hydroxyprogesterone, levonorgestrel, medrogestone, norgestrel, norethindrone, and progesterone—

Studies have not been done.

Medroxyprogesterone—

Studies in humans have not been done.

Mammary nodules, some of which were malignant in the high-dose group, developed in a number of beagles given doses of 3 or 75 mg/kg of medroxyprogesterone every 90 days for 7 years. In studies of monkeys, doses of 3, 30, or 150 mg/kg of medroxyprogesterone given every 90 days for 10 years produced transient mammary nodules in the 3 and 30 mg/kg groups, with none reported in the 150 mg/kg group during the study; hyperplastic nodules had developed in 3 monkeys that had been administered 30 mg/kg of medroxyprogesterone; no breast abnormalities were produced in rats after 2 years. Caution is warranted in applying these results of animal studies of progestins to their use in humans because of the hormonal differences between species. Also, humans and beagles metabolize medroxyprogesterone differently, and beagles are particularly susceptible to this type of breast tumor and develop these tumors spontaneously without progestin use.

There was no mutagenic response in the Ames and micronucleus tests.

Megestrol—

Studies in humans have not been done.

Studies of female dogs given megestrol for up to 7 years showed an increased incidence of both benign and malignant tumors; 2-year studies of female rats demonstrated an increased incidence of pituitary tumors. These effects were not found in monkey studies.

Pregnancy/Reproduction

Fertility—Progestins cause a decrease in quantity and/or change the quality of cervical mucus and may interfere with sperm function, fertilization, and subsequently, the occurrence of pregnancy. This effect depends on the dose and type of the progestin. High-dose or long-term use of progestins may cause a delayed return to fertility.

Levonorgestrel subdermal implants—
After removal, 40% of those women wanting to conceive did so by 3 months; 76% conceived within 1 year, percentages are similar to normal pregnancy rates.

Medroxyprogesterone—
It has been reported that of the women who discontinued parenteral medroxyprogesterone to become pregnant, 68% conceived within 12 months, 83% conceived within 15 months, and 93% conceived within 18 months after discontinuation (range, 4 to 31 months; median 10 months). The return of fertility is a function of the uptake and metabolism of parenteral medroxyprogesterone; follicular activity has been reported to return 3 to 37 days after parenteral medroxyprogesterone is nondetectable in serum, whereas, luteal function is delayed by 14 to 102 days.
Animal studies with medroxyprogesterone have reported no impairment of fertility in first- or second-generation studies.

Megestrol—
Studies in humans have not been done.
Studies of rats given megestrol in doses of 0.05 to 12.5 mg per kg of body weight (mg/kg), which are lower than the human dose of 13.3 mg/kg, resulted in impaired reproductive capability of male offspring produced from megestrol-treated females; similar results were found in studies of dogs.

Progesterone—
Progesterone has been used successfully with assisted reproductive technologies to support embryo implantation and to maintain pregnancy if needed.

Pregnancy—Progestins, in general, should be withheld during pregnancy. Progestins cross the placenta. Although many studies fail to demonstrate an increase in teratogenicity when progestins are given in the first trimester, the possibility that genital abnormalities may appear in male and female fetuses exposed to progestins during that period has been suggested by some studies. The low number of abnormalities reported include an increased risk of hypospadias in male fetuses exposed to intrauterine progesterone and virilization of the female fetus' external genitalia when exposed to ethisterone and norethindrone. There is some controversy about the reliability of these reports. The significant concentration of endogenous natural progesterone produced during pregnancy is devoid of teratogenic effects.

Ectopic pregnancy is possible with contraception failure because some progestin-only contraceptives reduce ectopic pregnancy risk substantially, but prevent ectopic pregnancy less effectively than intrauterine pregnancy. For progestin-only oral contraceptives, the ectopic pregnancy rate reported is 4.1 per 100 pregnancies. The rate of ectopic pregnancy for a set of levonorgestrel subdermal implants is 1.3 per 1000 woman-years. This is lower than those for women not using any contraceptive method (2.7 to 3 ectopic pregnancies per 1000 woman-years). However, the risk may increase with longer duration of use of levonorgestrel subdermal implants and increased weight of the user; risk does not increase in women of normal weight.

Hydroxyprogesterone and progesterone—
Use is generally not recommended during pregnancy, unless prescribed in the treatment of female infertility due to progesterone deficiency. Hydroxyprogesterone and progesterone have been used to prevent habitual or threatened abortion within the first few months of pregnancy. There are no adequate and well-controlled studies in humans to document that such use is effective during the first 4 months of pregnancy in preventing miscarriage; use is generally limited to certain cases of hormonal imbalance. Progesterone has been used successfully with assisted reproductive technologies to support embryo implantation and maintain pregnancy. Progesterone may be used to treat corpus luteum deficiency in early pregnancy. Progesterone replacement or supplementation does not appear to be efficacious when a hormone imbalance does not exist. In addition, the progesterone's effects on the uterus may delay the spontaneous miscarriage of a defective ovum.
FDA Pregnancy Category D.

Levonorgestrel, norethindrone, and norgestrel—
Use is not recommended during pregnancy. Virilization of the female fetus has been reported with norethindrone in a few cases, but a causal relationship has not been conclusively proven.
FDA Pregnancy Category X.

Medroxyprogesterone—
Use is not recommended in pregnancy. Studies in humans have shown that medroxyprogesterone may decrease intrauterine growth. Polysyndactyly in the offspring of women who had used parenteral medroxyprogesterone during pregnancy was reported in a few case-reports; this effect has not been seen in major studies. Furthermore, there has been no evidence of problems associated with growth and development in children exposed *in utero* to medroxyprogesterone and followed to adolescence.
In studies of pregnant beagles given doses of 1, 10, and 30 mg/kg of body weight per day for 6 months, clitoral hypertrophy appeared in the female pups of the high-dose group; no abnormalities were reported in the male pups. No abnormalities were detected in the treated female pups' offspring. Caution is warranted in transferring this information to humans because beagle dogs metabolize medroxyprogesterone differently than do humans.
Medroxyprogesterone, parenteral—FDA Pregnancy Category X.
Note: An FDA pregnancy category has not been assigned for medroxyprogesterone tablets.

Megestrol—
Use is not recommended during pregnancy. Risk-benefit must be carefully considered.
Studies in pregnant rats given high doses of megestrol decreased fetal birth weight, produced fewer live births, and resulted in reversible feminization of some male fetuses.
Megestrol suspension—FDA Pregnancy Category X.
Megestrol tablets—FDA Pregnancy Category D.

Breast-feeding

Progestins are distributed into breast milk in variable amounts and, depending on the progestin and dose, may increase or decrease quantity or quality or have no effect on breast milk. The effect on the nursing infant has not been determined for many progestins.

No adverse effects on breast milk's quantity or quality have been seen with progestin-only contraceptives, or specifically, when norethindrone or medroxyprogesterone was used for contraception within 5 days postpartum or after the establishment of lactation. Progestin-only contraceptives are recommended in breast-feeding women when oral contraception is desired. The manufacturers and distributors of levonorgestrel subdermal implants and parenteral medroxyprogesterone for contraception recommend that their initial use for contraception begin at 6 weeks postpartum for exclusively breast-feeding mothers. Additionally, no adverse effects have been reported in a study of nursing infants exposed to parenteral medroxyprogesterone and followed through puberty or in another study of 80 nursing infants exposed to levonorgestrel subdermal implants 6 weeks after delivery and followed for 3 years.

Decrease in bone mass density can occur during lactation. Risk/benefit assessment should be considered for long-term use of parenteral medroxyprogesterone for contraception in women who breast-feed.

Progestins used in very high doses are not recommended for use by nursing mothers.

Pediatrics

No information is available on the relationship of age to the effects of progestins in pediatric patients. Safety and efficacy have not been established. Serious adverse effects have not been reported in small children who ingested large doses of oral contraceptives.

Adolescents

Safety and efficacy of progestin-only contraceptives are expected to be the same in postpubertal adolescents as they are in adults. However, special counseling for medication compliance and prevention of sexually transmitted diseases (STDs) is needed. Studies have shown that adolescents tend to have a higher failure rate with the use of any type of contraceptive that requires strict compliance, such as oral progestins for contraception, and its use is not generally recommended in this age group. Although parenteral medroxyprogesterone and levonorgestrel subdermal implants do not require daily compliance, readministration of their doses after 3 months (13 weeks) and after 5 years, respectively, is important. Furthermore, none of the progestin contraceptives protect against STDs, which are significant risk-factors for this age group.

Medroxyprogesterone injectable for contraception—
Injectable medroxyprogesterone for contraception is associated with significant bone mineral density (BMD) loss. This loss of BMD is of particular concern during adolescence, a critical period of bone accretion. It is unknown whether use by younger women will reduce peak bone mass and increase risk for osteoporotic fracture in later life. Evaluation of BMD should take into account patient age and skeletal maturity when considering long-term use in adolescents.

Geriatrics

No information is available on the relationship of age to the effects of progestins in geriatric patients.

Dental

Increased concentrations of progestins increase the normal oral flora growth rate, leading to an increase in inflammation of the gingival tissues and increased bleeding. A strictly enforced program of teeth cleaning by a professional, combined with plaque control by the patient, will minimize severity.

Drug interactions and/or related problems

The following drug interactions and/or related problems have been selected on the basis of their potential clinical significance (possible mechanism in parentheses where appropriate)—not necessarily inclusive (» = major clinical significance):

Note: Combinations containing any of the following medications, depending on the amount present, may also interact with this medication.

» Aminoglutethimide
(may significantly lower the serum concentrations of oral and parenteral medroxyprogesterone by an undetermined mechanism; it has been suggested that aminoglutethimide may decrease the intestinal absorption of oral medroxyprogesterone)

» Hepatic enzyme inducing medications, such as
Carbamazepine or
Phenobarbital or
Phenytoin or
Rifabutin or
Rifampin
(decreased efficacy of some progestins, including levonorgestrel subdermal implants, has been suggested to be caused by enhanced metabolism of the progestins by these drugs)
(phenytoin and rifampin increase the serum concentrations of sex hormone-binding globulin [SHBG]; this significantly decreases the serum concentration of free drug for some progestins, which is a special concern in patients using progestins for contraception)
(drug interaction data are not available for rifabutin, but because its structure is similar to that of rifampin, similar precautions with its use with progestins may be warranted. Megestrol has been shown not to affect the pharmacokinetics of rifabutin; whether rifabutin changes megestrol pharmacokinetics has not been studied)

Laboratory value alterations

The following have been selected on the basis of their potential clinical significance (possible effect in parentheses where appropriate)—not necessarily inclusive (» = major clinical significance).

With diagnostic test results
Biopsy
(pathologist should be notified of relevant specimens)

Glucose tolerance test
(varies with progestin and dose, glucose tolerance may be increased or decreased)

Metyrapone
(lower response than normally expected)

With laboratory test values
Apolipoprotein A and
High-density lipoproteins (HDL) and
Total cholesterol and
Triglycerides
(serum concentrations may be increased or decreased and may differ depending on type of progestin, dose, dosing, and duration of therapy. In general, all progestins will lower triglyceride and total cholesterol concentrations. Parenteral medroxyprogesterone, in low doses, produces no significant decrease in HDL cholesterol concentrations; oral doses may blunt an estrogen-induced increase of HDL. In contrast, 19-nor-testosterone–derived progestins significantly lower HDL cholesterol as well as total cholesterol)

Apolipoprotein B and
Low-density lipoproteins (LDL)
(serum concentrations may be increased and may differ depending on type of progestin, dose, dosing, and duration of therapy)
(LDL concentrations increased initially in some studies and then returned to normal or below normal baseline levels when progestins were given for a year. Additionally, serum estrogen concentrations seemed to influence the cyclicality and degree to which LDL concentration increased; progestins affected the values to a lesser extent when estrogen levels were normal)

Clotting factors II, VII, VIII, IX, and X and
Prothrombin
(serum concentrations may be increased although studies have not shown consistent results; no change in clotting factors has been reported with parenteral medroxyprogesterone for contraception)

Gonadotropin and
Sex hormone-binding globulin (SHBG)
(serum concentration may be decreased)

Liver function tests
(values may be increased; if abnormal with parenteral medroxyprogesterone use, liver tests may be repeated 4 to 6 months after its discontinuation)

T_3-uptake
(values may be decreased because of increase in thyroid-binding globulin [TBG]; free T_4 concentration is unaltered)

T_4, total
(unaffected by most progestins but concentrations are slightly decreased with levonorgestrel; free T_4 concentration is unaltered)

Medical considerations/Contraindications

The medical considerations/contraindications included have been selected on the basis of their potential clinical significance (reasons given in parentheses where appropriate)—not necessarily inclusive (» = major clinical significance).

Except under special circumstances, these medications should not be used when the following medical problems exist:

» Allergy to peanuts for oral or parenteral progesterone
» Breast malignancies or tumors, known or suspected
(may worsen conditions in some nonresponsive patients; however, some progestins are used for palliative treatment in select patients)
» Cerebral vascular disease or
» Thrombophlebitis or thromboembolic disease, active or past history of
(the large doses of progestins used to treat breast and prostate cancer have been associated with a slight risk of thrombogenic conditions; mechanism is unclear and may be due to underlying condition. Problems have not been associated with low doses used for contraception, including parenteral medroxyprogesterone, progestin-only oral contraceptives, and levonorgestrel subdermal implants)
» Hepatic disease, acute, including benign or malignant liver tumors
(metabolism of 19-nor derivatives of testosterone-type progestins may be impaired; also, progestins may worsen the condition)
Hypersensitivity to progestin prescribed or any of its components or any other progestin
» Pregnancy, known or suspected
(use of synthetic progestins during pregnancy may result in virilization of a female fetus and, in a small number of cases, increase the risk of hypospadias in a male fetus)
(use for pregnancy diagnosis is contraindicated)
» Urinary tract bleeding, undiagnosed or
» Uterine or genital bleeding, undiagnosed
(use of a progestin may delay diagnosis by masking underlying conditions, including cancer)

Risk-benefit should be considered when the following medical problems exist:

Asthma or
Cardiac insufficiency, significant or
Epilepsy or
Hypertension or
Migraine headaches or
Renal dysfunction, significant
(fluid retention may be caused by some progestins, especially in high doses, and may aggravate these conditions)

CNS disorders, such as depression or convulsions, history of
(progestins, such as levonorgestrel, medroxyprogesterone, or norethindrone, may make these conditions worse. Cases of convulsions have been reported with use of parenteral medroxyprogesterone; however, a clear association has not been established. In one small study of 14 women with uncontrolled seizures, medroxyprogesterone reduced their seizure frequency by 30%. However, use of many medications for seizure control reduce the contraceptive efficacy of many contraceptives)

Diabetes mellitus
(high doses of progestins may alter carbohydrate metabolism by an unknown mechanism, producing a mild decrease in glucose tolerance in some patients. New-onset diabetes mellitus and ex-

acerbation of preexisting diabetes mellitus have been reported in patients taking high or chronic doses of megestrol. Progestin-only oral contraceptives do not usually affect carbohydrate metabolism, but may occasionally affect lipid metabolism. No clinical significance on fasting blood glucose is seen in nondiabetics receiving low doses of oral progestins for contraception)

(levonorgestrel's effects on carbohydrate metabolism appear to be minimal for nondiabetics but are considered inconclusive for prediabetics and diabetics)

(parenteral medroxyprogesterone may decrease glucose tolerance for some patients by an undetermined mechanism; it has been used with caution for contraception in diabetics)

Hepatic disease or dysfunction, history of
(metabolism of progestins, specifically androgenic progestins, may be impaired and contribute to the hepatic condition)

Hyperlipidemia
(some progestins, specifically androgenic progestins, might increase LDL and lower HDL levels and aggravate problems in controlling hyperlipidemia)

» Osteoporosis risk factors such as
Anorexia nervosa or
Chronic alcohol and/or tobacco use or
Chronic use of drugs such as anticonvulsants or corticosteroids that can reduce bone mass
Metabolic bone disease or
Osteoporosis, strong family history of, or
» Other significant risk factors for low bone mineral density
(the overall effect on bone density for progestins has yet to be established and may depend on type of progestin, dose, and gender and age of patient. Specifically, parenteral medroxyprogesterone for contraception is associated with significant loss of bone mineral density [BMD] as bone metabolism accommodates to a lower estrogen level. The decrease in BMD appears to be at least partially reversible after parenteral medroxyprogesterone is discontinued. Bone loss is greater with increasing duration of use. Other birth control methods should be considered, especially for long-term use, in women and adolescents with osteoporosis risk factors because parenteral medroxyprogesterone can pose an additional risk in these patients. The greatest bone loss is evident in the early years of use, is usually reversible, and possibly reflects other factors, such as hypoestrogenism, when progestin is used alone. A prospective study has reported that the use of oral medroxyprogesterone alone for treatment of menopausal symptoms showed a protective effect against loss of bone; other studies, particularly those in which a progestin was combined with estrogen, have also shown a protective effect)

» Thromboembolic disorders, including cerebrovascular disease, pulmonary embolism, retinal thrombosis, history of or
Thrombophlebitis, history of
(the large doses of progestins used to treat breast and prostate cancer have been associated with a slight risk of thrombogenic conditions; mechanism is unclear and may be due to the underlying condition. Problems have also occurred with megestrol. Problems have not been associated with low doses used for contraception, including parenteral medroxyprogesterone, progestin-only oral contraceptives, or levonorgestrel subdermal implants for patients with a history of thromboembolic disorders or thrombophlebitis)

Patient monitoring

The following may be especially important in patient monitoring (other tests may be warranted in some patients, depending on condition; » = major clinical significance):

» Bone mineral density [BMD]
(should be evaluated if a woman needs to use parenteral medroxyprogesterone for endometriosis-associated pain management or contraception long term [longer than 2 years] and other birth control methods are inadequate; in adolescents, evaluation of BMD should take into account patient age and skeletal maturity)

Breast examinations
(should be performed routinely, especially with prolonged progestin use)

Papanicolaou (Pap) test and
Physical examination
(as determined by physician, with special attention being given to abdomen, breast and pelvic organs; pre- and post-inspection of site of insertion and removal of levonorgestrel subdermal implants with annual inspection of implantation site during use)

Side/Adverse Effects

The following side/adverse effects have been selected on the basis of their potential clinical significance (possible signs and symptoms in parentheses where appropriate)—not necessarily inclusive:

Those indicating need for medical attention

Incidence more frequent

Amenorrhea (stopping of menstrual periods); ***breakthrough menstrual bleeding or metromenorrhagia*** (medium to heavy uterine bleeding between regular monthly periods); ***hyperglycemia*** (dry mouth; frequent urination; loss of appetite; unusual thirst)—16% with high doses of megestrol; ***menorrhagia*** (increased amount of menstrual bleeding occurring at regular monthly periods); ***spotting*** (light uterine bleeding between regular monthly periods)—17% for levonorgestrel subdermal implants or oral progestins for contraception

Note: *For all progestins,* if *abnormal uterine bleeding* is persistent (longer than 10 days at a time) or recurring (heavier than normal menses occurring longer than 10 months after beginning therapy or more often than monthly), malignancy should be considered as a cause of the bleeding.

For progestins used for cycle control or as part of ovarian hormone therapy: Breakthrough uterine bleeding is not as prevalent as it is with progestin-only contraceptives; therefore, any unexpected uterine bleeding that persists for 3 to 6 months should be investigated.

For oral progestins for contraception: *Breakthrough menstrual bleeding* or *spotting* is common.

For parenteral medroxyprogesterone: Amenorrhea increases with duration of use (12 months—55% and 24 months—68%). *Breakthrough menstrual bleeding* occurs in 90% of users.

For levonorgestrel subdermal implants: After 1 year of use of levonorgestrel subdermal implants, total uterine blood loss decreases from baseline levels of 31 mL per month to 24 mL per month. *Amenorrhea* occurs in 9.4 to 15% of users of the subdermal implants and *breakthrough menstrual bleeding* occurs in 28% of users, persisting throughout treatment.

Incidence less frequent

Galactorrhea (unexpected or increased flow of breast milk); ***mental depression***; ***skin rash***

Incidence rare

Adrenal suppression or insufficiency or hypotension (dizziness; nausea or vomiting; unusual tiredness or weakness)—may occur during chronic megestrol treatment or on its withdrawal; ***Cushing's syndrome*** (backache; filling or rounding out of the face; irritability; menstrual irregularities; mental depression; unusual decrease in sexual desire or ability in men; unusual tiredness or weakness)—may occur during chronic megestrol treatment; ***thromboembolism or thrombus formation*** (headache or migraine; loss of or change in speech, coordination, or vision; pain or numbness in chest, arm, or leg; shortness of breath, unexplained)—severe and sudden, with high doses of progestins for noncontraceptive uses

Note: It is not clear if the *thromboembolism or thrombus formation* associated with use of progestins in high doses is due to the treatment or to the underlying condition that is being treated, such as cancer. Thrombophlebitis, pulmonary embolism, and heart failure have occurred with use of megestrol; fatalities occurred in some cases.

Incidence not determined—Observed during clinical practice for parenteral medroxyprogesterone for contraception; estimates of frequency can not be determined

Anaphylaxis/anaphylactoid reaction (cough; difficulty swallowing; dizziness; fast heartbeat; hives, itching, puffiness or swelling of the eyelids or around the eyes, face, lips or tongue; shortness of breath; skin rash; tightness in chest; unusual tiredness or weakness; wheezing); ***loss of bone mineral density; osteoporosis*** (pain in back, ribs, arms, or legs; decrease in height); ***osteoporotic fracture*** (pain or swelling in arms or legs without any injury)

Note: For parenteral medroxyprogesterone: If there is a sudden partial or complete loss of vision or if there is a sudden onset of proptosis, diplopia, or migraine, medication should not be readministered pending examination. If examination reveals papilledema or retinal vascular lesions, medication should not be readministered.

Those indicating need for medical attention only if they continue or are bothersome

Incidence more frequent

Abdominal pain or cramping; diarrhea—5% for oral levonorgestrel for postcoital contraception; ***dizziness; drowsiness***—for progesterone only; ***edema*** (bloating or swelling of ankles or feet); ***fatigue***—17% for oral levonorgestrel for postcoital contraception; ***headache, mild***—up to 24% with levonorgestrel subdermal implants; ***mood changes***—up to 16% for levonorgestrel subdermal implants; ***nausea***—23% for oral levonorgestrel for postcoital contraception; ***nervousness***; ***ovarian enlargement or ovarian cyst formation*** (abdominal pain)—10% for levonorgestrel subdermal implants; ***pain, redness, or skin irritation at the site of injection or implantation***—including local skin color change and residual lump; ***unusual tiredness or weakness; unusual or rapid weight gain; vomiting***—5% for oral levonorgestrel for postcoital contraception

Note: For parenteral medroxyprogesterone for contraception: Average *weight gain* is 2.5 to 7.5 kilograms (kg) after 1 to 6 years of use.

Ovarian enlargement or ovarian cyst formation occurring with levonorgestrel subdermal implants is almost always transient and rarely requires surgery.

For oral levonorgestrel for postcoital contraception: If vomiting occurs within one hour of taking a dose of levonorgestrel, the dose may have to be repeated.

Incidence less frequent

Acne; ***breast pain or tenderness; hot flashes; insomnia*** (trouble in sleeping); ***libido decrease*** (loss of sexual desire); ***loss or gain of body, facial, or scalp hair***, ***melasma*** (brown spots on exposed skin, which may persist after treatment stops); ***nausea***—subsides in 3 months for low dose progestins for contraception

Those indicating need for medical attention if they occur after medication is discontinued

Adrenal suppression or insufficiency or hypotension (dizziness; nausea or vomiting; unusual tiredness or weakness)—may occur on withdrawal of chronic megestrol treatment; ***delayed return of fertility in females*** (stopping of menstrual periods; unusual menstrual bleeding, continuing)

Note: Progestin-only oral contraceptives and progestins used for ovarian hormone therapy have not been shown to cause *adrenal suppression or insufficiency* or *delayed return of fertility.*

Patient Consultation

As an aid to patient consultation, refer to *Advice for the Patient, Progestins—For Noncontraceptive Use (Systemic)* or *Progestins—For Contraceptive Use (Systemic).*

In providing consultation, consider emphasizing the following selected information (» = major clinical significance):

Before using this medication

» Conditions affecting use, especially:

Allergy to peanuts (for oral or parenteral progesterone) or history of hypersensitivity to progestins or any component of the product prescribed

Carcinogenicity—Studies are ongoing and have not been done with all progestins. Use of progestins with estrogens in ovarian hormone therapy lowers the incidences of endometrial hyperplasia and endometrial cancer. Significantly, a prolonged (8-year) study in women using injectable medroxyprogesterone for contraception has found a protective effect against endometrial cancer. Long-term studies of parenteral medroxyprogesterone have found no increase in overall risk of breast, ovarian, liver, or cervical cancer. Women 35 years of age or younger may have an increased risk of breast cancer during the first four years following initial use

Pregnancy—With the exception of hydroxyprogesterone and progesterone, use is not recommended during pregnancy. When progestins are used in doses for contraception, ectopic pregnancy is possible, although rare. Alternative methods of contraception should be used by fertile and sexually active females when high dose progestins are used for noncontraceptive purposes, such as in treatment of cancer; physician should be told immediately if pregnancy is suspected

Breast-feeding—Progestins are distributed into breast milk in variable amounts; high doses may increase or decrease the quantity or quality of breast milk while low doses have no effect on breast milk and are recommended for use in breast-feeding women needing contraception; adverse effects in the nursing infant have not been reported

Decrease in bone mass density occurs during lactation; risk/benefit should be assessed in breast-feeding women who use parenteral medroxyprogesterone for contraception long-term

Use in adolescents—Adolescents tend to have a greater risk for sexually transmitted diseases (STDs) and have a higher failure rate for oral progestins for contraception because of compliance problems. Adolescents who are at increased risk for STDs or those failing to comply with strict dosing schedule for contraceptives (a strict 24-hour dose regimen for oral medications or replacement doses for contraceptive injection and implants) may be better served with another form of contraception

With parenteral medroxyprogesterone for contraception—Not known if use during adolescence and early adulthood, a critical time for bone accretion, will reduce peak bone mass and increase risk for osteoporotic fracture in later life; should take into account patient age and skeletal maturity in assessing bone mineral density in adolescence

Dental—May predispose patient to increased bleeding and inflammation of the gingival tissues; teeth cleaning and plaque control should minimize severity

Other medications, especially aminoglutethimide and hepatic enzyme inducers, such as carbamazepine, phenobarbital, phenytoin, rifabutin, or rifampin

Other medical problems, especially active thrombophlebitis or thromboembolic disease; acute hepatic disease, including benign or malignant tumors; cerebral vascular disease; history of thromboembolic disease; known or suspected breast malignancy or tumor; known or suspected pregnancy; undiagnosed genital, uterine, or urinary tract bleeding

Other medical problems for parenteral medroxyprogesterone for contraception or endometriosis-associated pain management observed during clinical practice, especially osteoporosis risk factors or other significant risk factors for low bone mineral density

Proper use of this medication

Reading patient directions

» Importance of not taking more or less medication than the amount prescribed

» Proper dosing

Missed dose for noncontraceptive uses of progestins (except for progesterone capsules): Taking as soon as possible; not taking if almost time for next dose; not doubling doses

Missed dose for progesterone capsules: If 200 mg at bedtime is missed, taking 100 mg in the morning, then going back to regular dose schedule. If 300 mg a day is missed, not taking the missed doses, then going back to regular dose schedule

Missed dose for medroxyprogesterone injection for contraceptive use: If next injection is delayed longer than 13 weeks, using a back-up method of contraception and checking with physician about continuing the medication

Missed dose for progestin-only oral contraceptives: If one or more tablets are missed or if dose is delayed by 3 hours or more, taking the missed dose as soon as remembered, continuing your regular dosing schedule, and using a backup method, such as condoms or spermicides, for the next 48 hours if planning to have sexual intercourse. A dose that is 3 hours late is considered a missed dose

» Proper storage

For contraception use

Caution that progestins do not protect against sexually transmitted diseases, including human immunodeficiency virus (HIV) infection or acquired immunodeficiency syndrome (AIDS)

For levonorgestrel subdermal implants

Insertion procedure by a health care professional takes 15 minutes under local anesthesia

» Caring for insertion site requires removing pressure dressing in 24 hours, leaving steristrips (sterile tape) on incisions for 3 days, keeping covered and dry, taking care not to bump site or to lift heavy objects for 24 hours, and expecting some swelling and bruising at site of insertion

» Full contraceptive protection begins within 24 hours when insertion is done within 7 days of the beginning of the menstrual period; otherwise, another birth control method must be used during the rest of the first menstrual cycle; protection ends immediately after removal

» Removal procedure may be done at any time by a health care professional. After 5 years of use the subdermal implants should be removed and, if desired, a new set of subdermal implants can be inserted at this time; the removal procedure takes 20 minutes or longer under local anesthesia; rarely, some difficult cases may require skin healing after an unsuccessful attempt

For levonorgestrel tablets

The medicine may be taken any time during the menstrual cycle

For medroxyprogesterone for contraception

» Importance of receiving an injection by a health care professional every 3 months

Stopping use by simply not receiving the injection

Full contraceptive protection begins immediately after initial injection without need for additional birth control methods if given within the first 5 days of a normal menstrual period, within the first 5 days postpartum if not breast-feeding, and, if exclusively breast-feeding, at the sixth postpartum week. Protection continues when an injection is given every 3 months

For oral progestins for contraception

» Compliance with therapy, taking medication at the same time each day at 24-hour intervals

When switching from estrogen and progestin oral contraceptives, the first dose of the progestin-only oral contraceptive should be taken the next day after the last active tablet of the oral estrogen and progestin oral contraceptive is administered. The placebo (inactive) tablets of the 28-day cycle can be discarded

(Also, when switching, full protection begins within 48 hours if the dose is taken on the first day of the menstrual period; if treatment is begun at other times, a back-up method should be used for 3 weeks as a conservative approach)

A chance of pregnancy is increased for each missed dose

For noncontraception use

Caution in taking combination therapy; taking each medication at the right time

Precautions while using this medication

» Regular visits to health care professional

» Caution when driving or doing things requiring alertness because the medication may cause dizziness; for progesterone capsules, dizziness or drowsiness may occur 1 to 4 hours after ingestion

Checking with doctor immediately if uterine bleeding (spotting or breakthrough menstrual bleeding) continues longer than 3 months or if menstruation is delayed by 45 days

» Contacting doctor immediately if pregnancy is suspected or a menstrual period is missed

If scheduled for laboratory tests, tell physician if taking progestins; certain blood tests may be affected

Possibility of dental problems, such as tenderness, swelling, or bleeding of gums; checking with dentist if there are questions about care of teeth or gums or if tenderness, swelling, or bleeding of gums occurs; patient should follow good cleaning procedures, such as regular brushing and flossing of teeth, massaging gums, and having dentist clean teeth regularly

For contraceptive use:

» Using a second method of birth control when taking medications that reduce effectiveness of progestins

If vomiting occurs for any reason shortly after taking the progestin-only oral contraceptive pill, do not take another dose, resume your normal dosing schedule and use an additional backup method for 48 hours

If vomiting occurs within 1 hour of taking either dose of the levonorgestrel tablets for emergency contraception, contact your physician to discuss whether the dose should be repeated

For noncontraceptive use:

» Advisability of using contraceptive methods while taking progestins for noncontraceptive uses if fertile and sexually active

For progesterone (vaginal) dosage form: Avoiding use of other vaginal products for 6 hours before and for 6 hours after administering progesterone vaginally to ensure its complete absorption

Side/adverse effects

Signs of potential side effects, especially amenorrhea; breakthrough menstrual bleeding or metromenorrhagia; hyperglycemia; menorrhagia; spotting; galactorrhea; mental depression; skin rash; adrenal suppression or insufficiency or hypotension (megestrol only); Cushing's syndrome (megestrol only), or thromboembolism or thrombus formation

Signs of potential side effects observed during clinical practice for parenteral medroxyprogesterone for contraception, especially anaphylaxis/anaphylactoid reaction, loss of bone mineral density, osteoporosis, or osteoporotic fracture

General Dosing Information

For all progestins

The cyclical administration of progestins is based on an assumed menstrual cycle of 28 days.

Onset of the female menopause may be masked by the use of progestins.

Follicular atresia may be delayed, allowing the growth and development of follicles that clinically may appear to be ovarian cysts, especially with levonorgestrel subdermal implants. In most cases, enlarged follicles disappear spontaneously, but, rarely, they may rupture, causing abdominal pain and requiring surgical intervention.

Discontinue medication pending eye examination if there is sudden partial or complete loss of vision or sudden onset of proptosis (exophthalmos or abnormal protrusion of the eyeball), diplopia (seeing double), or migraine. Also, discontinue medication if examination reveals papilledema or if thrombotic disorder occurs or is suspected.

The patient package insert is mandatory for progestational drugs to convey information regarding birth defects to premenopausal women unless childbearing is impossible. However, it is recommended that the patient package insert also be given to patients taking or using progestins for noncontraceptive purposes.

For contraception use

Although some progestin products protect against pregnancy, none protects against HIV infection or AIDS.

Another contraceptive method should be used and pregnancy should be ruled out before resuming use of hormonal contraceptives if two tablets or an injection is missed.

For levonorgestrel subdermal implants

Insertion (usually a 15-minute procedure using local anesthesia) should be performed within the first 7 days of a normal menstrual period or immediately postabortion. Insertion is not recommended by the manufacturer in the first 6-weeks postpartum for breast-feeding women.

All 6 implants are inserted subdermally in a fanlike pattern about 15 degrees apart (totaling 75 degrees) in the midportion of the upper arm (8 to 10 centimeters above the crease in the elbow).

Proper insertion technique for insertion or removal of subdermal implants reduces the incidence of hard-to-remove subdermal implants, expulsions, and improper placement of subdermal implants. Bruising and some scarring may occur with insertion or removal procedures. Insertion site complications at 1-year follow-up include 0.8% skin infection, 0.4% expulsion, and 4.7% local skin reaction; in approximately 41% of women with a skin infection, an expulsion of an implant resulted.

When an implant is expelled, a new subdermal implant may be inserted in the same incision, although any infection or unusual wound or incision site problems should heal before a new sterile subdermal implant is inserted. Other contraceptive methods should be used concurrently when fewer than 6 subdermal implants are in place. Also, if removal of all subdermal implants is not successful with the first attempt, the skin should be allowed to heal completely before a second attempt of removal.

Removal of the levonorgestrel implants (usually a 20-minute procedure) may occur on request at any time or at the end of the fifth year of use, and should be considered if prolonged immobilization is anticipated or if persistent infection develops at the implantation site. Used subdermal implants should be disposed of by using the Centers for Disease Control guidelines for biohazardous waste.

For oral levonorgestrel for postcoital contraception

The first dose (0.75 milligram) should be taken as soon as possible within 72 hours of intercourse. The second dose must be taken 12 hours later. Levonorgestrel may be taken at any time during the menstrual cycle.

Patients should be instructed to contact their health care if vomiting occurs within one hour of taking either dose of levonorgestrel to discuss whether the dose should be repeated

For oral progestins for contraception

When used as oral contraceptives, progestins are administered daily without interruption, regardless of menstrual cycle.

When switching a patient from estrogen and progestin oral contraceptives, a new progestin-only oral contraceptive is begun on the 22nd day; the inactive or placebo tablets of the 28-day cycle should be discarded. Full contraceptive protection begins within 48 hours if the first oral progestin dose is taken on Day 1 of the menstrual cycle. A back-up birth control method should be used for 3 weeks (a conservative approach) if the patient is started at any other time.

For parenteral medroxyprogesterone

The formulation of parenteral medroxyprogesterone for noncontraceptive use (400 mg/mL) should not be used for contraceptive uses, even if the proper dose (150 mg) is considered. Efficacy issues arose and resulted in discontinuation of a clinical trial conducted by the manufacturer using a lower volume dose than that used in the formulation of medroxyprogesterone for contraception. Dose adjustment is not necessary for body weight but it is reported that plasma concentration and duration decreased by a mean of 3.3 picograms/mL per kg increase of body weight because of its accumulation in fat cells; therefore, return to fertility may be especially prolonged in obese women.

Injecting into the deltoid muscle as opposed to the gluteal muscle is recommended by some clinicians to lessen absorption problems that may occur because of rubbing the injection site while sitting.

Although no studies exist addressing whether calcium and vitamin D may lessen bone mineral density loss in women using parenteral medroxyprogesterone for contraception, all patients should have adequate and calcium and vitamin D intake.

For noncontraceptive uses

For women who are using progestins for other reasons besides contraception, concurrent contraceptive methods should be used if fertile and sexually active.

Response rates are about 15 to 16% in patients using progestins for treating endometrial carcinoma with high-grade resistant tumors and may be significantly better with low-grade malignancy; response rate decreases for tumors of increasing grade and in those tumors negative for both estrogen and progesterone receptors; median survival is approximately 9 to 10 months.

Response rates are approximately 5% and of short duration in patients using progestins for treating renal carcinoma; routine receptor assay is not helpful in predicting appropriate patients.

Response rates of up to about 40% have been reported when high-dose oral medroxyprogesterone has been used to treat breast cancer.

Decisions to treat menopausal symptoms with hormones for a limited time (1 to 5 years) or to use hormones to prevent diseases in postmenopausal women for a longer period of time (10 to 20 years), or a lifetime, should be separate decisions. Counseling asymptomatic postmenopausal women about the benefits and risks of long-term estrogen and progestin ovarian hormone therapy to prevent disease and prolong life is complex. It is dependent on an individual's risk of breast cancer, osteoporosis, and coronary heart disease and whether a uterus is present (progestins are not needed when the uterus is absent). Adding a progestin to estrogen therapy may benefit postmenopausal women at risk for osteoporosis, slightly reduce estrogen's protective effect against coronary heart disease (women at more risk are provided the greatest benefit), and slightly increase the risk of breast cancer over that of non-users. Women should understand that the benefits and risks of preventive ovarian hormone therapy depend on their risk status.

For medroxyprogesterone

Reestablishment of menstrual cycle may be delayed (up to 18 months or longer) and is difficult to predict following the intramuscular administration of medroxyprogesterone. Because of the prolonged action and the resulting difficulty in predicting the time of withdrawal bleeding following injection, parenteral medroxyprogesterone is not recommended for treatment of secondary amenorrhea or dysfunctional uterine bleeding; oral medroxyprogesterone is the preferred mode of therapy.

For megestrol

The magnitude and rate of weight gain are highly dependent on megestrol dose and are significantly greater with higher doses. The greatest effect can be maintained at a lower dose of 400 mg a day in the second to fourth months when 800 mg a day is taken in the first month, although some studies have reported further benefit when the dose is not lowered.

Adrenal suppression may occur with normal dosing range; effects on HIV viral replication have not been determined.

For progesterone

For oral progesterone:

If only one dose of progesterone capsules is needed, it should be taken at bedtime to minimize the side effect of dizziness or drowsiness experienced by patients within 1 to 4 hours after taking 200 mg progesterone.

If a progesterone dose is taken in the morning, the patient should take it 2 hours after eating breakfast.

For vaginal progesterone:

Synthetic progestins are more potent than natural progesterone; i.e., 20 to 25 mg progesterone (intramuscular) has an effect equivalent to 100 mg progesterone (vaginal suppository) or 5 to 10 mg medroxyprogesterone (oral) or 50 mg medroxyprogesterone (intramuscular).

Use of other vaginal products should be avoided for at least 6 hours before or 6 hours after administering progesterone vaginally to ensure its complete absorption.

For treatment of adverse effects

For megesterol—

Reports of adrenal suppression or insufficiency have been reported in patients during treatment and at treatment discontinuation of high or chronic doses of megestrol, whereas Cushing's syndrome has been reported during treatment with high or chronic doses of megestrol. Recommended treatment of adrenal insufficiency consists of the following:

- Laboratory evaluation for adrenal insufficiency.
- Physiologic replacement doses of a rapid-acting glucocorticosteroid.

HYDROXYPROGESTERONE

Summary of Differences

Category:

Progestational agent; diagnostic aid.

Indications:

Amenorrhea, dysfunctional uterine bleeding, induction of menses, and test for endogenous estrogen production.

Pharmacology/pharmacokinetics:

More potent than progesterone with longer duration of action.

Synthetic 17-hydroxy derivative of progesterone with progestogenic, androgenic, and glucocorticoid effects.

Parenteral Dosage Forms

HYDROXYPROGESTERONE CAPROATE INJECTION USP

Usual adult and adolescent dose

Amenorrhea or

Dysfunctional uterine bleeding—

Intramuscular, 375 mg.

Estrogen production, endogenous, diagnosis or

Menses, induction of—

Intramuscular, 125 to 250 mg given on Day 10 of the menstrual cycle, repeated every seven days until suppression is no longer desired.

Note: Withdrawal bleeding usually occurs within three to seven days after discontinuing therapy.

Strength(s) usually available

U.S.—

125 mg per mL (Rx).

250 mg per mL (Rx) [*Gesterol LA 250; Hy/Gestrone; Hylutin; Prodrox; Pro-Span*].

Canada—

Not commercially available.

Packaging and storage

Store below 40 °C (104 °F), preferably between 15 and 30 °C (59 and 86 °F), unless otherwise specified by manufacturer. Protect from freezing.

Note

Castor or sesame oils are commonly used as the vehicle for intramuscular injection.

Include mandatory patient package insert (PPI) when dispensing to premenopausal patient unless reproduction is impossible.

LEVONORGESTREL

Summary of Differences

Category:

Contraceptive.

Indications:

Pregnancy prophylaxis; contraception, emergency postcoital (prophylaxis)

Pharmacology/pharmacokinetics:

19-nor derivative of testosterone; has progestational and androgenic effects.

Precautions:

Breast-feeding—Generally recommended for use 6 weeks postpartum in breast-feeding women but has been used 5 days postpartum after establishment of lactation.

Laboratory value alterations—Serum T_3 concentrations may be slightly elevated and T_4 concentrations may be decreased; total serum T_4 concentrations are unaffected.

Medical considerations/contraindications—Levonorgestrel subdermal implants have not caused thrombogenic disorders, but caution may be necessary with use in patients with a history of thrombosis. Caution is necessary in patients with a history of CNS disorders, such as depression or history of convulsions.

Side effects:

Breakthrough menstrual bleeding or spotting, reduced amount of menstrual bleeding, and amenorrhea are predominant side effects. These bleeding irregularities may persist but are less problematic with time. Other side effects include ovarian enlargement or cysts (usually reversible with continued use), acne, headaches, and mood changes.

Additional Dosing Information

See also *General Dosing Information*.

Special training for insertion, removal, and disposal of levonorgestrel subdermal implants includes knowledge and familiarity of procedures by physician and patient.

Oral Dosage Form

LEVONORGESTREL TABLETS

Usual adult and adolescent dose

Contraception, emergency postcoital (prophylaxis)—

The first dose of 0.75 milligram should be taken as soon as possible within 72 hours of intercourse. The second dose must be taken 12 hours later.

Strength(s) usually available

U.S.—

0.75 milligram (Rx) [*Plan B*].

Subdermal Dosage Form

LEVONORGESTREL IMPLANTS

Usual adult and adolescent dose

Pregnancy, prevention of—

Subdermally, one set of six implants surgically inserted every five years.

Strength(s) usually available

U.S.—

216 mg (Rx) [*NORPLANT System*].

Canada—

216 mg (Rx) [*NORPLANT System*].

Packaging and storage

Store below 40 °C (104 °F), preferably between 15 and 30 °C (59 and 86 °F), unless otherwise specified by manufacturer. Store away from excess heat or moisture.

Note

Include mandatory patient package insert (PPI) when dispensing progestins to premenopausal patient unless reproduction is impossible.

MEDROGESTONE

Summary of Differences

Category:

Progestational agent.

Indications:

Secondary amenorrhea, dysfunctional uterine bleeding, induction of menses, and, in conjunction with estrogens, for endometrial shedding in menopausal women.

Pharmacology/pharmacokinetics:

17-hydroxy derivative of progesterone; highly progestational, devoid of estrogenic, androgenic, glucocorticoid, or anti-androgenic effects.

Oral Dosage Forms

MEDROGESTONE TABLETS

Usual adult and adolescent dose

Amenorrhea, secondary or
Dysfunctional uterine bleeding or
Hyperplasia, endometrial, estrogen-induced, postmenopausal, prophylaxis or
Menses, induction of—

Oral, 5 to 10 mg a day on Days 15 through 25 of monthly cycle.

Note: Withdrawal bleeding usually occurs within three to seven days after discontinuing therapy.

An optimum secretory transformation of an endometrium that has been adequately primed with either endogenous or exogenous estrogens (Days 5 to 25 of the menstrual cycle) may be reestablished with three or more cycles.

Strength(s) usually available

U.S.—

Not commercially available.

Canada—

5 mg (Rx) [*Colprone* (scored)].

Packaging and storage

Store below 40 °C (104 °F), preferably between 15 and 30 °C (59 and 86 °F), unless otherwise specified by manufacturer. Store in a well-closed container.

MEDROXYPROGESTERONE

Summary of Differences

Category:

Oral medroxyprogesterone used as a progestational agent, antineoplastic agent, and diagnostic aid (test for endogenous estrogen production). Parenteral medroxyprogesterone used as adjunct in antineoplastic therapy and indicated as contraceptive agent in a special parenteral formulation.

Indications:

Oral and parenteral medroxyprogesterone indicated to treat breast carcinoma in postmenopausal women and endometrial hyperplasia in conditions such as polycystic ovary syndrome; however, only parenteral medroxyprogesterone is indicated for adjunct treatment of metastatic renal or endometrial carcinoma and endometriosis. Parenteral medroxyprogesterone is accepted therapy for precocious puberty, but has been replaced by other modalities. Unlike parenteral medroxyprogesterone, oral medroxyprogesterone is indicated for secondary amenorrhea, dysfunctional uterine bleeding, induction of menses, carcinoma, ovarian hormone therapy in menopause, and testing for endogenous estrogen production.

Unlike oral medroxyprogesterone, parenteral medroxyprogesterone is not recommended for treatment of secondary amenorrhea or dysfunctional uterine bleeding.

Pharmacology/pharmacokinetics:

17-hydroxy derivative of progesterone with progestogenic, androgenic, and glucocorticoid effects.

Precautions:

Fertility—Luteal function may be delayed after cessation of parenteral medroxyprogesterone treatment for contraception, especially in obese females of reproductive age.

Pregnancy—Use in pregnancy has produced problems in the fetus and is not recommended. Doses used for contraception have not appeared to produce problems for nursing infants after lactation is established.

Adolescents—Use of medroxyprogesterone contraceptive injection is associated with loss of bone mineral density. If is unknown if use of this drug during adolescence or early adulthood, a critical period of bone accretion, will reduce peak bone mass and increase risk for osteoporotic fracture in later life. When evaluating long-term use in adolescents, bone mineral density interpretation should take into account patient age and skeletal maturity.

Drug interactions—Use of aminoglutethimide may lower serum concentrations of medroxyprogesterone and interfere with intestinal absorption of oral dose.

Medical considerations/contraindications—Low dose parenteral medroxyprogesterone can be used with caution for contraception in women with diabetes mellitus. High doses (but not low doses) have rarely been associated with thromboembolic disorders or thrombophlebitis. Patients with risk factor(s) for osteoporosis and/or bone mineral density loss may be at greater risk when using parenteral medroxyprogesterone for contraception.

Side/adverse effects:

Bloating or swelling of face, ankles, or feet more likely with higher doses.

Additional Dosing Information

See also *General Dosing Information*.

Reestablishment of menstrual cycle can be delayed and difficult to predict following the parenteral dose. Also, only the 150 mg/mL formulation and a 150-mg dose should be used for contraception; a special dose adjustment for the obese patient is not needed; however, contraceptive efficacy in patients over 90 kg has not been evaluated.

Oral Dosage Forms

Note: Bracketed uses in the *Dosage Forms* section refer to categories of use or indications that are not included in U.S. product labeling.

MEDROXYPROGESTERONE ACETATE TABLETS USP

Usual adult or adolescent dose

Amenorrhea, secondary—
Oral, 5 to 10 mg a day for five to ten days, started any time during cycle.

Dysfunctional uterine bleeding—
Oral, 5 to 10 mg a day for five to ten days, commencing on the calculated Day 16 or Day 21 of the menstrual cycle.

Menses, induction of—
Oral, 10 mg daily for ten days starting on Day 16 of the menstrual cycle. If bleeding is controlled satisfactorily, two or more subsequent cycles of the treatment should be given.

[Hyperplasia, endometrial, estrogen-induced, postmenopausal, prophylaxis]—
There are several recommended dosing schedules
Oral, 5 to 10 mg medroxyprogesterone a day for ten or fourteen days beginning on Days 12 or 16 through Day 25, estrogen is taken on Day 1 through Day 25, and neither estrogen nor medroxyprogesterone is taken on the twenty-fifth day through the end of the month.
Oral, 5 to 10 mg medroxyprogesterone a day taken on the first ten to fourteen days along with continuous estrogen dosing.
Oral, 2.5 or 5 mg medroxyprogesterone a day taken continuously with continuous estrogen dosing.

Note: Other regimens may differ but also may be appropriate. Withdrawal bleeding usually occurs within three to seven days after discontinuing therapy.

[Carcinoma, breast, postmenopausal women]—
Oral, 400 mg a day in divided doses.

[Carcinoma, endometrial]—
Initial: Oral, 200 to 400 mg a day for two to three months.
Maintenance: Oral, 200 mg a day.

Note: Improvement may not be evident until eight to ten weeks following initiation of therapy for breast or endometrial carcinoma. However, treatment should be discontinued when there is rapid progression of the disease at any time during therapy.

[Endometriosis][1]—
Oral, 10 to 40 mg a day for six to nine months.

[Estrogen production, endogenous, diagnosis]—
Oral, 10 mg a day for five to ten days. Withdrawal bleeding will occur three to seven days following therapy if the uterus has been sufficiently primed with endogenous estrogen.

[Hyperplasia, endometrial, treatment][1]—
There are several recommended dosing schedules
Oral, 10 mg a day for three to six months.
Oral, 10 mg a day for twenty-one days each month for three months. Then the dose is reduced to 10 mg a day for ten to fourteen days a month.
Oral, 20 mg a day for thirty days every six months.

Note: Other regimens may differ but also may be appropriate.

Strength(s) usually available

U.S.—
2.5 mg (Rx) [*Cycrin* (scored); *Provera* (scored); GENERIC].
5 mg (Rx) [*Cycrin* (scored); *Provera* (scored); GENERIC].
10 mg (Rx) [*Amen* (scored); *Curretab* (scored); *Cycrin* (scored); *Provera* (scored); GENERIC].

Canada—
Note: Brand name *Provera Pak* contains 14 tablets in blister packaging.
2.5 mg (Rx) [*Alti-MPA; Gen-Medroxy* (scored); *Novo-Medrone* (scored); *Provera*].
5 mg (Rx) [*Alti-MPA; Gen-Medroxy* (scored); *Novo-Medrone* (scored); *Provera* (scored); *Provera Pak* (scored)].
10 mg (Rx) [*Alti-MPA; Gen-Medroxy* (scored); *Novo-Medrone* (scored); *Provera* (scored)].
100 mg (Rx) [*Provera* (scored)].

Packaging and storage

Store below 40 °C (104 °F), preferably between 15 and 30 °C (59 and 86 °F), unless otherwise specified by manufacturer.

Note

Include mandatory patient package insert (PPI) when dispensing progestins to premenopausal patient unless reproduction is impossible.

Parenteral Dosage Forms

Note: Bracketed uses in the *Dosage Forms* section refer to categories of use or indications that are not included in U.S. product labeling.

MEDROXYPROGESTERONE ACETATE INJECTABLE SUSPENSION INTRAMUSCULAR

Note: Formerly known as Sterile Medroxyprogesterone Acetate Suspension, USP.

Usual adult or adolescent dose

Carcinoma, endometrial or
Carcinoma, renal—
Initial: Intramuscular, 400 mg to 1 gram once a week until improvement and stabilization occur.
Maintenance: Intramuscular, 400 mg or more once a month.

[Carcinoma, breast]—
Initial: Intramuscular, 500 mg a day for twenty-eight days.
Maintenance: Intramuscular, 500 mg two times a week.

Note: Improvement may not be evident for eight to ten weeks of therapy for breast or endometrial carcinoma. However, treatment should be discontinued when there is rapid progression of the disease at any time during therapy.

[Endometriosis]—
There are several recommended dosing schedules
Intramuscular, 50 mg once a week for at least six months.
Intramuscular, 100 mg every two weeks for at least six months.
Intramuscular, 150 mg every 3 months for at least six months.

[Hot flashes][1]—
Intramuscular, 500 mg every two weeks.

Pregnancy, prevention of—
Intramuscular, 150 mg every three months.

Note: Dosage does not need to be adjusted for body weight in patients weighing less than 90 kg, but dosage has not been studied in patients weighing more than 90 kg. It is recommended that the first injection be given during the first five days after onset of a normal menstrual period; within five days postpartum if not breast-feeding, and if exclusively breast-feeding, at six weeks postpartum. A physician should determine that a patient is not pregnant if more than thirteen weeks will elapse between injections.

Strength(s) usually available

U.S.—
Note: Brand name *Depo-Provera Contraceptive Injection* is available in vials or as prefilled syringes.
150 mg per mL (Rx) [*Depo-Provera Contraceptive Injection*].
400 mg per mL (Rx) [*Depo-Provera*].

Canada—
50 mg per mL (Rx) [*Depo-Provera*].
150 mg per mL (Rx) [*Depo-Provera*].

Packaging and storage

Store below 40 °C (104 °F), preferably between 15 and 30 °C (59 and 86 °F), unless otherwise specified by manufacturer. Protect from freezing.

Preparation of dosage form

Should be shaken vigorously before administration.

Auxiliary labeling

- Shake well.

Note

Include mandatory patient package insert (PPI) when dispensing progestins to premenopausal patient unless reproduction is impossible.

MEDROXYPROGESTERONE ACETATE INJECTABLE SUSPENSION SUBCUTANEOUS

Usual adult or adolescent dose

Pain, endometriosis-associated (treatment) or
Pregnancy, prevention of—
Subcutaneous, 104 mg (in a 0.65 mL prefilled syringe) into the anterior thigh or abdomen every three months (12 to 14 weeks).
Dosage does not need to be adjusted for body weight. It is recommended that the first injection be given only during the first five

days after onset of a normal menstrual period in women who are sexually active and having regular menses and during or after the sixth postpartum week in women who are breast-feeding. For second and subsequent injections, dosing is every 12 to 14 weeks. If more than 14 weeks elapse between injections, pregnancy should be ruled out before the next injection.

If using for contraception and switching from another method—Subcutaneous medroxyprogesterone acetate should be given in a manner that ensures continuous contraceptive coverage. Patients switching from estrogen plus progestin contraceptives should have their first medroxyprogesterone injection within 7 days after the last day of using that method (7 days after taking the last active pill, removing the patch or ring). Contraceptive coverage will also be maintained if switching from intramuscular to subcutaneous medroxyprogesterone acetate, provided the next injection is given within the prescribed dosing period for the previous doseform.

Usual adult prescribing limits

Pain, endometriosis-associated (treatment)—
Treatment for longer than 2 years is not recommended due to impact of long-term medroxyprogesterone acetate on bone mineral density.

Strength(s) usually available

U.S.—
104 mg per 0.65 mL (160 mg per mL) (Rx) [*depo-subQ provera 104* (prefilled syringe; methylparaben 1.04 mg; propylparaben 0.098 mg; sodium chloride 5.2 mg; polyethylene glycol 18.688 mg; polysorbate 80 1.95 mg; monobasic sodium phosphate 0.451 mg; dibasic sodium phosphate 0.382 mg; methionine 0.975 mg; povidone 3.25 mg; water for injection; sodium hydroxide for pH adjustment if necessary; hydrochloric acid for pH adjustment if necessary)].

Packaging and storage

Store at 20 and 25 °C (68 and 77°F).

Preparation of dosage form

Should be shaken vigorously before administration.

Auxiliary labeling

- Shake well.

[1]Not included in Canadian product labeling.

MEGESTROL

Summary of Differences

Category:
Antianoretic, anticachectic, antineoplastic.

Indications:
Endometrial or breast carcinoma; anorexia, cachexia and significant weight loss, associated with cancer (tablets) and acquired immunodeficiency syndrome (AIDS) (suspension); and advanced prostate carcinoma. Not recommended for prophylactic avoidance of weight loss.

Pharmacology/pharmacokinetics:
17-hydroxy derivative of progesterone; progestogenic, glucocorticoid, and anti-estrogenic effects.

Precautions:
Fertility—Impaired fertility shown in male offspring of megestrol-treated females in studies in rats and dogs.
Pregnancy—Use is not recommended.

Additional Dosing Information

See also *General Dosing Information.*

Magnitude and rate of weight gain are dose-related; lower doses of 400 mg are recommended after the first month, although some results have shown weight gain continuing with 800 mg given continuously for 4 months.

Oral Dosage Forms

Note: Bracketed uses in the *Dosage Forms* section refer to categories of use or indications that are not included in U.S. product labeling.

MEGESTROL ACETATE SUSPENSION

Usual adult and adolescent dose

Anorexia or
Cachexia or
Weight-loss, significant—
For patients with AIDS: Oral, 800 mg a day the first month, then 400 or 800 mg a day for three more months.

Strength(s) usually available

U.S.—
40 mg per milliliter (mL) (Rx) [*Megace* (alcohol 0.06%; sucrose)].

Canada—
40 mg per milliliter (mL) (Rx) [*Megace OS* (alcohol 0.06%; sucrose)].

Packaging and storage

Store between 15 and 25 °C (59 and 77 °F). Protect from heat. Store in a well-closed container.

Auxiliary labeling

- Shake well.

Note

Include patient package insert (PPI) when dispensing.

MEGESTROL ACETATE TABLETS USP

Usual adult and adolescent dose

[Anorexia] or
[Cachexia] or
[Weight-loss, significant]—
For patients with cancer: Oral, 400 to 800 mg a day as a single daily dose.

Carcinoma, breast—
Oral, 160 mg a day as a single dose or in divided doses.

Carcinoma, endometrial—
Oral, 40 to 320 mg a day in divided doses.

[Carcinoma, prostate, advanced]—
Oral, 120 mg once a day with 0.1 mg diethylstilbesterol a day.

Note: At least two months of continuous treatment is considered an adequate period for determining the efficacy of megestrol.

[Hot flashes][1]—
Oral, 40 to 160 mg per day.

[Hyperplasia, endometrial, treatment][1]—
Oral, 20 to 40 mg a day for 14 days or longer every month.

Strength(s) usually available

U.S.—
20 mg (Rx) [*Megace* (scored); GENERIC].
40 mg (Rx) [*Megace* (scored); GENERIC].

Canada—
40 mg (Rx) [*Apo-Megestrol* (scored); *Megace* (scored)].
160 mg (Rx) [*Apo-Megestrol* (scored); *Megace*].

Packaging and storage

Store below 40 °C (104 °F), preferably between 15 and 30 °C (59 and 86 °F), unless otherwise specified by manufacturer. Store in a well-closed container.

Note

Include patient package insert (PPI) when dispensing.

[1]Not included in Canadian product labeling.

NORETHINDRONE

Summary of Differences

Category:
Indicated as a progestational agent (norethindrone base and acetate) and contraceptive agent (norethindrone base).

Indication:
Norethindrone acetate indicated for secondary amenorrhea, dysfunctional uterine bleeding, induction of menses, and endometriosis. Norethindrone base is indicated for contraception while the acetate form is not.

Oral Dosage Forms

NORETHINDRONE TABLETS USP

Usual adult and adolescent dose

Pregnancy, prevention of—
Oral, 350 mcg (0.35 mg) a day, starting on Day 1 of the menstrual cycle and continuing uninterrupted at the same time every day of the year, whether or not menstrual bleeding occurs.

Strength(s) usually available
U.S.—
350 mcg (0.35 mg) (Rx) [*Micronor; Nor-QD*].
Canada—
350 mcg (0.35 mg) (Rx) [*Micronor*].

Packaging and storage
Store below 40 °C (104 °F), preferably between 15 and 30 °C (59 and 86 °F), unless otherwise specified by manufacturer. Store in a well-closed container.

Note
Include mandatory patient package insert (PPI) when dispensing progestins to premenopausal patient unless reproduction is impossible.

NORETHINDRONE ACETATE TABLETS USP

Usual adult and adolescent dose
Amenorrhea, secondary or
Dysfunctional uterine bleeding—
Oral, 2.5 to 10 mg a day on Day 5 through Day 25 of the menstrual cycle or for five to ten days during the last half of menstrual cycle.

Note: Withdrawal bleeding occurs within three to seven days after progestin treatment ends.

Endometriosis—
Initial: Oral, 5 mg a day for two weeks, increasing by 2.5 mg a day at two-week intervals to reach a total dose of 15 mg a day.
Maintenance: Oral, 15 mg a day for six to nine months, unless temporarily discontinued because of breakthrough menstrual bleeding.

Strength(s) usually available
U.S.—
5 mg (Rx) [*Aygestin* (scored)].
Canada—
5 mg (Rx) [*Norlutate*].

Packaging and storage
Store below 40 °C (104 °F), preferably between 15 and 30 °C (59 and 86 °F), unless otherwise specified by manufacturer. Store in a well-closed container.

Note
Include mandatory patient package insert (PPI) when dispensing progestins to premenopausal patients unless reproduction is impossible.

NORGESTREL

Summary of Differences
Category:
Contraceptive agent.
Indication:
Pregnancy prophylaxis.
Pharmacology/pharmacokinetics:
19-nor derivative of testosterone; has progestogenic, estrogenic, androgenic, and anti-estrogenic effects.

Oral Dosage Forms

NORGESTREL TABLETS USP

Usual adult and adolescent dose
Pregnancy, prevention of—
Oral, 75 mcg (0.075 mg) a day, starting on Day 1 of menstrual cycle and continuing uninterrupted at the same time every day of the year whether or not menstrual bleeding occurs.

Strength(s) usually available
U.S.—
75 mcg (0.075 mg) (Rx) [*Ovrette*].
Canada—
Not commercially available.

Packaging and storage
Store below 40 °C (104 °F), preferably between 15 and 30 °C (59 and 86 °F), unless otherwise specified by manufacturer. Store in a well-closed container.

Note
Include mandatory patient package insert (PPI) when dispensing progestins to premenopausal patients unless reproduction is impossible.

PROGESTERONE

Summary of Differences
Category:
Progestational agent.
Indications:
Indicated for secondary amenorrhea and dysfunctional uterine bleeding but is also used for corpus luteum insufficiency.
Pharmacology/pharmacokinetics:
Natural hormone with progestational, androgenic, and anti-estrogenic effects.
Precautions:
Pregnancy—Although not proven effective, progesterone has been used during first few months of pregnancy to prevent habitual or threatened abortion due to hormonal imbalance but may also delay expulsion of a defective ovum.

Additional Dosing Information
See also *General Dosing Information.*

Twenty to 25 mg progesterone (intramuscular) produces an equivalent progestogenic effect compared to 100 mg progesterone (vaginal suppository).

Oral Dosage Forms

PROGESTERONE CAPSULES (Micronized)

Usual adult dose
Amenorrhea, secondary[1]—
Oral, 400 mg once a day in the evening for ten days.
[Hyperplasia, endometrial, estrogen-induced, postmenopausal, prophylaxis]—
Oral, 200 mg once a day at bedtime for fourteen days beginning Day 8 through Day 21 of a twenty-eight–day cycle or beginning Day 12 to Day 25 of a thirty-day cycle. A dose of 300 mg progesterone divided as 100 mg in the morning two hours after breakfast and 200 mg at bedtime may be required for patients taking doses of estrogen 1.25 mg or greater. The progestin dose should be adjusted until desired uterine response is achieved (regular withdrawal uterine bleeding or amenorrhea). In many treatment regimens, the last five to seven days of each month are often left free of hormone use.

Strength(s) usually available
U.S.—
100 mg (Rx) [*Prometrium* (glycerin; lecithin; peanut oil; titanium dioxide)].
Canada—
100 mg (Rx) [*Prometrium* (glycerin; lecithin; peanut oil; titanium dioxide)].

Packaging and storage
Store between 15 and 30 °C (59 and 86 °F), unless otherwise specified by manufacturer. Protect from light.

Auxiliary labeling
May cause dizziness or drowsiness.

Note
Include patient package insert (PPI) when dispensing progestins to premenopausal patients, unless reproduction is impossible.

Parenteral Dosage Forms
Note: Bracketed uses in the *Dosage Forms* section refer to categories of use or indications that are not included in U.S. product labeling.

PROGESTERONE INJECTION USP

Usual adult and adolescent dose
Amenorrhea, secondary—
Intramuscular, 5 to 10 mg a day for six to ten consecutive days or 100 to 150 mg injected intramuscularly as a single dose.

Note: If there has been sufficient ovarian activity to produce a proliferative endometrium or two weeks of prior estrogen therapy, withdrawal bleeding will occur forty-eight to seventy-two hours after the last injection. The patient should discontinue therapy if menstrual cycle occurs. This may be followed by spontaneous normal cycles. Progesterone should be discontinued if menses occurs during the series of injections.

Dysfunctional uterine bleeding—
Intramuscular, 5 to 10 mg a day for six consecutive days.

Note: Bleeding should cease within six days. When estrogen is being given, the administration of progesterone should begin after two weeks of estrogen therapy. Progesterone should be discontinued if menses occurs during the series of injections.

[Corpus luteum insufficiency][1]—
Intramuscular, 12.5 mg or more a day initiated within several days of ovulation. Treatment duration is usually two weeks, but it may be continued, if necessary, up to eleventh week of gestation.

[Estrogen production, endogenous, diagnosis][1]—
Intramuscular, 100 mg as a single dose.

Strength(s) usually available

U.S.—
50 mg per mL (Rx) [*Gesterol 50* (in sesame seed oil; benzyl alcohol 10%); GENERIC (in sesame seed or peanut oil)].

Canada—
50 mg per mL (Rx) [*PMS-Progesterone* (in sesame seed oil; benzyl alcohol 10%)].

Packaging and storage

Store below 40 °C (104 °F), preferably between 15 and 30 °C (59 and 86 °F), unless otherwise specified by manufacturer. Protect from freezing.

Auxiliary labeling

May cause dizziness or drowsiness.

Note

Include mandatory patient package insert (PPI) when dispensing progestins to premenopausal patients unless reproduction is impossible.

Vaginal Dosage Forms

PROGESTERONE GEL (Micronized)

Note: Bracketed uses in the *Dosage Forms* section refer to categories of use or indications that are not included in U.S. product labeling.

Usual adult and adolescent dose

Amenorrhea, secondary—
Vaginal, 45 mg (one applicatorful of 4% vaginal gel) once every other day for up to six doses. Dose may be increased to 90 mg (one applicatorful of 8% vaginal gel) once every other day for up to six doses.

Note: Increasing the dose to 90 mg by doubling the amount of the 4% vaginal gel used does not increase the amount of medication absorbed, and the 8% vaginal gel should be used instead.

Assisted reproductive technologies, in females or
[Corpus luteum insufficiency][1]—
For patients needing luteal phase support: Vaginal, 90 mg (one applicatorful of 8% vaginal gel) once a day for progesterone supplementation. For patients undergoing *in vitro* fertilization (IVF), treatment may begin within 24 hours of embryo transfer and continue through Day 30 post-transfer. If pregnancy occurs, treatment can be extended until placental autonomy is achieved, up to ten to twelve weeks.

For patients with partial or complete ovarian failure: Vaginal, 90 mg (one applicatorful of 8% vaginal gel) two times a day to receive full progesterone replacement doses while undergoing donor oocyte transfer procedure. If pregnancy occurs, treatment can be extended until placental autonomy is achieved, up to ten to twelve weeks.

Strength(s) usually available

U.S.—
Note: Available as single-use prefilled applicators. One applicatorful of 4% or 8% vaginal gel delivers 1.125 grams of gel.

4% (Rx) [*Crinone*].
8% (Rx) [*Crinone*].
4% (Rx) [*Prochieve* (glycerin; mineral oil; polycarbophil; carbomer 934P; hydrogenated palm oil glyceride; sorbic acid; sodium hydroxide; purified water)].
8% (Rx) [*Prochieve* (glycerin; mineral oil; polycarbophil; carbomer 934P; hydrogenated palm oil glyceride; sorbic acid; sodium hydroxide; purified water)].

Canada—
Not commercially available.

Packaging and storage

Store between 15 and 25 °C (59 and 77 °F), unless otherwise specified by manufacturer.

Auxiliary labeling

For vaginal use only.
May cause dizziness or drowsiness.

PROGESTERONE SUPPOSITORIES

Note: Because progesterone suppositories are not commercially available in the U.S. or Canada, the bracketed uses and the use of the superscript 1 in this *Dosage Forms* section reflect the lack of labeled (approved) indications for this product in these countries.

Usual adult and adolescent dose

[Assisted reproductive technologies, in females][1] or
[Corpus luteum insufficiency][1]—
Vaginal, 25 to 100 mg one to two times a day initiated within several days of ovulation. Treatment duration is usually continued if the patient is pregnant up to about the eleventh week of gestation.

Strength(s) usually available

U.S.—
Not commercially available. Compounding required for prescription.

Canada—
Not commercially available. Compounding required for prescription.

Packaging and storage

Store between 2 and 8 °C (36 and 46 °F), in a tight container.

Preparation of dosage form

A formulation that has been used for the extemporaneous compounding of progesterone suppositories is as follows:

- 710 mg (0.71 grams) progesterone powder
- 33.7 grams polyethylene glycol 400
- 22.3 grams polyethylene glycol 6000

Makes 28 suppositories, 25 mg progesterone per suppository.

Auxiliary labeling

- For vaginal use only.
- Refrigerate. Do not freeze.

[1]Not included in Canadian product labeling.

Selected Bibliography

Product Information: Depo-Provera® Contraceptive Injection, medroxyprogesterone acetate. Pharmacia & Upjohn, Kalamazoo, MI, (PI revised 11/2004) reviewed 11/2004.

General

American College of Physicians. Clinical Guideline. Guidelines for counseling postmenopausal women about preventive hormone therapy. Ann Intern Med 1992 Dec; 117(12): 1038-41.

Revised: 04/14/2005

Table 1. Pharmacokinetics

Drug	Protein* binding (%)	Biotransformation	Elimination half-life (hrs)	Time to peak concentration (hrs)	Peak serum concentration		Renal elimination (%)	Fecal elimination (%)
					ng/mL	Dose (mg)		
Natural:								
Progesterone†	Very high (90% or more)	Hepatic	Several minutes, after absorption				50–60	10
Oral, micronized				2–4	24.3	200		
IM				28	39.1	45		
IM				19.6	53.8	90		
Vaginal gel, micronized				55	13.2	45		
Vaginal gel, micronized				34.8	14.9	45		
Synthetic 17-hydroxy derivatives:								
Hydroxyprogesterone caproate	Very high (90% or more)	Hepatic						
Medroxyprogesterone acetate	Very high (90% or more)	Hepatic					15–22	45–80
Oral			30	Within 2–4	19–35	10		
IM		No first-pass hepatic effect	50 days	3 weeks	1–7	150‡		
Medrogestone			4	1				
Megestrol acetate	Very high (90% or more)	Hepatic	38 (13–104)				66	20
Oral				2–3	200	160		
Oral				2–3	753	600		
Synthetic 19-nor derivatives:								
Levonorgestrel subdermal implants	Very high§ (90% or more)	No first-pass hepatic effect	16 (8–30)	24	1.6, within first week	216**	45	32
3 months					0.4			
12 months					0.32			
60 months					0.26			
Norgestrel	Very high (90% or more)		20					
Norethindrone	Very high# (90% or more)	Hepatic first pass effect	8 (6–12)	2			50	20–40
Norethindrone acetate	Very high (90% or more)	Hepatic first pass effect	8					

*Sex hormone-binding globulin (SHBG) synthesis is stimulated by estrogens and inhibited by androgens; levels are twice as high in women as in men.

†Progesterone binds strongly to cortisol binding globulin (CBG) 17.7%, SHBG 0.6%, and weakly to albumin 79.3%. Absorption is the rate-limiting step for the elimination half-life.

‡Pertains to parenteral medroxyprogesterone for contraception injection formulation (150mg/mL) only given every 3 months.

§Levonorgestrel: Free, 1.1–1.7%; SHBG 92–62%; albumin 37.56%, but suppresses SHBG by 33%.

#Norethindrone: Free 3.5%; SHBG 35.5%; albumin 61%.

**216 mg is the loading dose for 6 levonorgestrel implants; a mean dose of 35 mcg levonorgestrel is released daily.

PROMAZINE—See *Phenothiazines (Systemic)*

PROMETHAZINE—See *Antihistamines, Phenothiazine-derivative (Systemic)*

PROPAFENONE Systemic

VA CLASSIFICATION (Primary): CV300

Commonly used brand name(s): *Rythmol; Rythmol SR*.

Note: For a listing of dosage forms and brand names by country availability, see *Dosage Forms* section(s).

Category

Antiarrhythmic.

Indications

Note: Bracketed information in the *Indications* section refers to uses that are not included in U.S. product labeling.

Accepted

Arrhythmias, ventricular (treatment)—Propafenone is indicated for suppression of documented life-threatening ventricular arrhythmias, such as sustained ventricular tachycardia.

Note: Propafenone is a class IC antiarrhythmic agent (Vaughan Williams classification) with some similarities in antiarrhythmic action to the class IC antiarrhythmic agents encainide and flecainide, and the class IA agent moricizine. In a multicenter, randomized, placebo-controlled trial called the Cardiac Arrhythmias Suppression Trial (CAST), patients with prior myocardial infarction received either encainide, flecainide, or moricizine during an open-label titration phase, and the same drug or a matching placebo for the remaining long-term phase of the trial. The objective of the trial was to determine if suppression of asymptomatic or mildly symptomatic ventricular arrhythmias would reduce the incidence of death due to arrhythmia.

After a mean follow-up of 10 months, the encainide and flecainide arms of the study were terminated due to an excessive mortality or nonfatal cardiac arrest rate (7.7%), compared with that seen in patients assigned to matching placebo (3%). The moricizine arm of the trial was continued in a second trial (CAST II), but this trial also was terminated early because of an increase in mortality in the moricizine-treated patients during the first 14-day period of the trial.

Scientists have speculated that the adverse results of the CAST trials may be attributed to proarrhythmic effects of the study drugs. Because these and previous studies with class I agents to suppress ventricular arrhythmias in patients after myocardial infarction did not result in a decrease in mortality, propafenone is generally not recommended for treating less severe ventricular arrhythmias.

Arrhythmias, supraventricular (treatment)—Propafenone is indicated in patients without structural heart disease to prolong the time to recurrence of paroxysmal atrial fibrillation or flutter and paroxysmal supraventricular tachycardia associated with disabling symptoms.

[Arrhythmias, supraventricular, other (treatment)][1]—Propafenone has been used for the treatment of supraventricular arrhythmias, such as intranodal and extranodal re-entrant tachycardias (e.g., Wolff-Parkinson-White Syndrome).

Unaccepted

Propafenone should not be used to control ventricular rate during atrial fibrillation.

Propafenone use in patients with permanent atrial fibrillation or in patients exclusively with atrial flutter or PSVT has not been evaluated.

---

[1]Not included in Canadian product labeling.

Pharmacology/Pharmacokinetics

Physicochemical characteristics

Molecular weight—377.91.
pKa—9.

Mechanism of action/Effect

Propafenone reduces the inward sodium current in Purkinje and myocardial cells. Consequently, it decreases excitability, conduction velocity, and automaticity in atrioventricular (AV) nodal, His-Purkinje, and intraventricular tissue, and causes a slight but significant prolongation of refractory periods in AV nodal tissue. The greatest effect is on the His-Purkinje system. Propafenone decreases the rate of rise of the action potential without markedly affecting its duration. Also, propafenone prolongs both antegrade and retrograde conduction velocity and the effective refractory periods of accessory pathways. As observed electrocardiographically, propafenone prolongs the PR interval and increases the duration of the QRS complex. These effects are dose-related. In the Vaughan Williams classification of antiarrhythmics, propafenone is considered to be a class IC agent.

Other actions/effects

Propafenone has a negative inotropic effect. It has approximately one fortieth of the beta-adrenergic blocking activity of propranolol, which may become clinically significant in some patients. Propafenone has weak calcium channel blocking properties and local anesthetic activity approximately equal to that of procaine.

Absorption

Rapid and nearly complete, with more than 90% of an oral dose absorbed. Systemic bioavailability ranges from 5 to 50%, reflecting significant first-pass metabolism. Such a wide range in systemic bioavailability is related to two factors. The presence of food increases bioavailability for extensive metabolizers (more than 90% of patients). In addition, bioavailability increases as dosage increases. Absolute bioavailability is 3.4% for a 150-mg tablet compared to 10.6% for a 300-mg tablet.

Distribution

Volume of distribution (Vol_D)—1.1 L/kg for central compartment; about 252 L total

Protein binding

Very high (97%); decreases to 88% in patients with severe hepatic dysfunction.

Biotransformation

Hepatic; significant first-pass effect. In over 90% of patients, rapidly and extensively metabolized to two active metabolites, 5-hydroxypropafenone and *N*-depropylpropafenone, which have antiarrhythmic activity comparable to propafenone but which are present in concentrations less than 20% of propafenone concentrations. In less than 10% of patients and in patients also receiving quinidine, more slowly metabolized (these patients also have a diminished ability to metabolize debrisoquin, encainide, metoprolol, and dextromethorphan); little, if any, 5-hydroxypropafenone is present in plasma.

Half-life

Elimination—
In extensive metabolizers (more than 90% of patients)—2 to 10 hours.
In poor metabolizers (less than 10% of patients)—10 to 32 hours.

Time to peak plasma concentration

1 to 3.5 hours; 3 to 8 hours for extended-release.

Time to steady-state plasma concentration

Multiple doses—4 to 5 days.

Steady-state plasma concentrations

Wide interindividual variability. In extensive metabolizers, pharmacokinetics are nonlinear; because of saturable first-pass metabolism, a 3-fold increase in dose may result in a 10-fold increase in steady-state plasma concentrations; however, in poor metabolizers, pharmacokinetics are linear.

Peak plasma concentration

In poor metabolizers, concentrations are 1.5 to 2 times those of extensive metabolizers at doses of 675 to 900 mg per day.

Elimination

Renal—38% as metabolites; less than 1% as unchanged drug.
Fecal—53% as metabolites.

Precautions to Consider

Carcinogenicity

Studies in rats and mice at oral doses of up to 270 mg per kg of body weight (mg/kg) per day and 360 mg/kg per day, respectively, revealed no evidence of carcinogenicity.

Mutagenicity

The mouse dominant lethal test, rat bone marrow chromosome analysis, Chinese hamster bone marrow and spermatogonia chromosome analysis, Chinese hamster micronucleus test, and Ames bacterial test were negative.

Pregnancy/Reproduction

Fertility—A reversible reduction in sperm count (within normal range) occurred after short-term administration in humans, but chronic administration did not have this effect.

Reversible impairment of spermatogenesis occurs in monkeys, dogs, and rabbits after high intravenous doses.

Pregnancy—Adequate and well-controlled studies in humans have not been done.

Studies in rats and rabbits at doses of up to 40 and 10 times the maximum recommended human dose, respectively, have not shown that propafenone causes teratogenicity in the fetus; however, a perinatal and postnatal study in rats at doses of 6 times the maximum recommended human dose or greater found a dose-related increase in maternal and neonatal mortality, decreased maternal and pup body weight gain, and reduced neonatal physiological development.

FDA Pregnancy Category C.

Breast-feeding

Propafenone and 5-hydroxypropafenone, a metabolite of propafenone, are distributed into breast milk at concentrations lower than those found in maternal plasma. Breast-feeding is not recommended during propafenone use because of the potential for adverse effects in the nursing infant.

Pediatrics

Safety and efficacy have not been established. However, limited use of propafenone in neonates, infants, and children seems to indicate that the incidence of side effects in pediatric patients is similar to that reported in adults. Proarrhythmic effects have been reported in the pediatric population, as in the adult population, including an incident of sudden death which may or may not have been related to propafenone. Therefore, propafenone should be used with caution in pediatric patients.

Geriatrics

Although appropriate studies on the relationship of age to the effects of propafenone have not been performed in the geriatric population, no geriatrics-specific problems have been documented to date. However, elderly patients are more likely to have age-related hepatic and renal function impairment, which may require dosage reduction in patients receiving propafenone.

Surgical

The central nervous system (CNS) side/adverse effects of propafenone may be increased when propafenone is used concurrently with local anesthetics during surgery, dental procedures, or pacemaker implantation.

Drug interactions and/or related problems

The following drug interactions and/or related problems have been selected on the basis of their potential clinical significance (possible mechanism in parentheses where appropriate)—not necessarily inclusive (» = major clinical significance):

» Amiodarone
(concomitant use can affect conduction and repolarization and is not recommended)

Beta-adrenergic blocking agents
(propafenone has weak beta-adrenergic blocking activity, which may be additive if it is used concurrently with a beta-adrenergic blocking agent; however, an increased incidence of side effects in patients receiving both medications concurrently was not reported in clinical trials; concurrent use of propranolol or metoprolol with propafenone results in significant increases in plasma concentrations and half-life of propranolol and metoprolol, without affecting plasma propafenone concentrations; this interaction may result from propafenone-induced inhibition of the hydroxylation pathways of these drugs; a dosage reduction of the beta-blocker may be necessary)

Cimetidine
(concurrent use of cimetidine produces a 20% [approximate] increase in plasma concentrations of propafenone; however, because of wide interindividual variability in plasma concentrations and, therefore, lack of direct correlation with clinical effect, effects of propafenone on electrocardiogram parameters are unchanged)

» Class Ia and III antiarrhythmic agents
(should be withheld for at least five half-lives prior to dosing with propafenone; concomitant use not recommended)

Cyclosporine
(concurrent use may increase cyclosporine plasma concentrations)

CYP1A2 inhibitors or
CYP2D6 inhibitors such as
Desipramine or
Paroxetine or
Ritonavir or
Sertraline or
CYP3A4 inhibitors such as
Erythromycin or
Grapefruit juice or
Ketoconazole or
Ritonavir or
Saquinavir
(can be expected to increase propafenone plasma levels; appropriate monitoring recommended with concomitant use)

CYP2D6 metabolizers such as
Desipramine or
Haloperidol or
Imipramine or
Venlafaxine
(concomitant use may increase plasma levels of these drugs)

» Digoxin
(concurrent use with propafenone results in an increase in serum digoxin concentrations ranging from 35 to 85%, which appears to be unrelated to digoxin renal clearance but which may be related to a decrease in volume of distribution and nonrenal clearance; careful monitoring of digoxin concentrations and dosage reduction of digoxin are recommended when propafenone is initiated; subsequent dosage adjustments should be based on plasma digoxin concentrations)

Desipramine
(concurrent use has resulted in increased serum desipramine concentrations, possibly due to competition for cytochrome P450 metabolic pathways)

» Drugs that prolong QT interval including:
Antiarrhythmics or
Bepridil or
Cisapride or
Macrolides, oral or
Phenothiazines or
Tricyclic antidepressants
(concomitant use has not been extensively studied and is not recommended)

Fluoxetine
(concomitant use increases propafenone AUC and C_{max})

Lidocaine
(may increase risk of CNS side effects)

Orlistat
(may limit the fraction of propafenone available for absorption; post-marketing reports show abrupt cessation of orlistat in patients stabilized on propafenone has resulted in severe adverse events including convulsions, atrioventricular block, and acute circulatory failure)

Quinidine
(small doses of quinidine completely inhibit hydroxylation of propafenone, effectively making patients poor metabolizers of propafenone; however, dosage adjustment of propafenone is usually not necessary)

Rifampin
(concurrent use may decrease propafenone plasma concentrations as a result of rifampin-induced increased metabolism of propafenone)

Theophylline
(concurrent use may increase theophylline plasma concentrations and possibly lead to theophylline toxicity)

» Warfarin
(concurrent use with propafenone results in a significant increase [approximately 40%] in mean steady-state warfarin plasma concentrations, with a corresponding increase in prothrombin time of approximately 25%; monitoring of prothrombin time and appropriate adjustment of warfarin dosage are recommended during concurrent use)

Laboratory value alterations

The following have been selected on the basis of their potential clinical significance (possible effect in parentheses where appropriate)—not necessarily inclusive (» = major clinical significance).

With physiology/laboratory test values
Antinuclear antibody (ANA) titers, positive
(may occur rarely; reversible after withdrawal and sometimes during continued propafenone treatment; usually not symptomatic, but one case of lupus erythematosus, which reversed on withdrawal, has been reported)

Medical considerations/Contraindications

The medical considerations/contraindications included have been selected on the basis of their potential clinical significance (reasons given in parentheses where appropriate)—not necessarily inclusive (» = major clinical significance).

Except under special circumstances, this medication should not be used when the following medical problems exist:

Asthma or
Bronchospasm, nonallergic (e.g., chronic bronchitis, emphysema)
(because of its beta-adrenergic blocking effect, propafenone may aggravate bronchospasm)

» Atrioventricular (AV), intraventricular, and sinoatrial conduction or impulse generation disorders (without an artificial pacemaker), such as
AV block or
Sick sinus syndrome or
» Sinus bradycardia
(propafenone slows AV conduction and decreases the automaticity of latent or subsidiary pacemakers [Purkinje fibers], worsening the existing condition; in patients with sick sinus syndrome, propafenone prolongs the sinus node recovery time)

» Cardiogenic shock or
» Hypotension, severe
(the beta-adrenergic blocking effects of propafenone may aggravate these conditions)

» Congestive heart failure, uncontrolled
(propafenone has a direct negative inotropic effect and a beta-adrenergic blocking effect, both of which may worsen this condition; these patients should be fully compensated before receiving propafenone)

» Electrolyte imbalance, clinically manifest
(electrolyte disturbances can potentiate the proarrhythmic effects of propafenone and, therefore, should be corrected prior to its administration)

» Hypersensitivity to propafenone

Risk-benefit should be considered when the following medical problems exist:

» Congestive heart failure
(the negative inotropic and beta-adrenergic blocking effects of propafenone may worsen or cause new congestive heart failure; caution should be used)

Hepatic function impairment
(severe liver function impairment increases the bioavailability of propafenone to approximately 70% [compared to a range of 3 to 40% in patients with normal liver function]; in patients with moderate to severe liver dysfunction, the mean half-life of propafenone was approximately 9 hours; dosage of propafenone should be reduced to approximately 20 to 30% of the usual dose, with careful monitoring)

Myasthenia gravis
(propafenone has been reported to exacerbate myasthenia gravis)

Pacemaker, permanent or
Pacing electrodes, temporary
(propafenone may increase endocardial pacing thresholds and may suppress ventricular escape rhythms; use is not recommended in patients with existing poor thresholds or nonprogrammable pacemakers unless suitable pacing rescue is available)

Renal function impairment
(because 18.5 to 38% of propafenone metabolites are eliminated in the urine, propafenone should be administered with caution in patients with renal function impairment)

Patient monitoring

The following may be especially important in patient monitoring (other tests may be warranted in some patients, depending on condition; » = major clinical significance):

» Electrocardiogram (ECG)
(recommended prior to initiation of therapy and at periodic intervals during therapy to help assess efficacy and detect possible proarrhythmic effects)

Side/Adverse Effects

Note: Adverse cardiac effects reported with propafenone administration include new or exacerbated ventricular arrhythmias (seen as an increase in frequency of premature ventricular contractions, or a worsening or new appearance of ventricular tachycardia or ventricular fibrillation) in about 4.7% of patients; new or exacerbated congestive heart failure in 1% or less of patients; first, second, or third degree atrioventricular (AV) block in 2.5%, 0.6%, and 0.2% of patients, respectively; sinus bradycardia in 1.5% of patients; and rarely, sinus pause or sinus arrest.

Incidence of cardiac and other effects is at least partially dose-related.

The following side/adverse effects have been selected on the basis of their potential clinical significance (possible signs and symptoms in parentheses where appropriate)—not necessarily inclusive:

Those indicating need for medical attention

Incidence less frequent

Angina (chest pain); ***atrial flutter or fibrillation; bradycardia*** (slow heartbeat); ***bundle branch block; congestive heart failure*** (shortness of breath, swelling of feet or lower legs, weight gain); ***first or second degree AV block; intraventricular conduction delay; ventricular arrhythmias, including*** *torsades de pointes* (fast or irregular heartbeat, dizziness, and/or fainting)

Note: Propafenone may induce new arrhythmias (proarrhythmia) and/or worsen an existing arrhythmia. *Ventricular arrhythmias,* such as *torsades de pointes,* are potentially fatal. In clinical trials, a worsening of ventricular tachycardia occurred in patients with a history of ventricular tachycardia or ventricular tachycardia and/or ventricular fibrillation, coronary artery disease, or myocardial infarction.

Incidence rare

Agranulocytosis (chills, fever, and weakness); ***hypotension*** (dizziness or lightheadedness); ***joint pain; trembling or shaking***

Those indicating need for medical attention only if they continue or are bothersome

Incidence more frequent

Dizziness; taste disturbance (change in taste; bitter or metallic taste)

Incidence less frequent

Blurred vision; constipation or diarrhea; dryness of mouth; headache; nausea and/or vomiting; skin rash; unusual tiredness or weakness

Overdose

For more information on the management of overdose or unintentional ingestion, **contact a Poison Control Center** (see *Poison Control Center Listing*).

Clinical effects of overdose

The following effects have been selected on the basis of their potential clinical significance (possible signs and symptoms in parentheses where appropriate)—not necessarily inclusive:

Acute and/or chronic

Bradycardia (slow heartbeat); ***hypotension*** (dizziness, lightheadedness, or fainting); ***intra-atrial and intraventricular conduction disturbances; seizures; somnolence*** (sleepiness); ***ventricular arrhythmias***

Treatment of overdose

Treatment is primarily supportive and symptomatic and may include: Defibrillation and infusion of dopamine and isoproterenol to control rhythm and blood pressure; intravenous diazepam for convulsions; mechanical respiratory assistance and external cardiac massage.

Supportive care—Patients in whom intentional overdose is confirmed or suspected should be referred for psychiatric consultation.

Patient Consultation

As an aid to patient consultation, refer to *Advice for the Patient, Propafenone (Systemic).*

In providing consultation, consider emphasizing the following selected information (» = major clinical significance):

Before using this medication

» Conditions affecting use, especially:
Hypersensitivity to propafenone
Pregnancy—Reduces fertility in monkeys, dogs, and rabbits; in rats, causes increased maternal and neonatal mortality, decreased maternal and infant weight gain, and reduced neonatal development
Breast-feeding—Caution should be exercised in administering to a nursing woman.
Use in the elderly—Greater sensitivity in some older individuals can not be ruled out.
Other medications, especially amiodarone, class Ia and III antiarrhythmic agents, digoxin, drugs that prolong QT interval, or warfarin
Other medical problems, especially asthma or nonallergic bronchospasm; atrioventricular (AV), intraventricular, and sinoatrial conduction or impulse generation disorders without an artificial pacemaker, such as AV block or sick sinus syndrome; cardiogenic shock; clinically manifest electrolyte imbalance; congestive heart failure; severe hypotension; or sinus bradycardia

Proper use of this medication

» Compliance with therapy; taking exactly as directed; not taking more or less medication than is prescribed
» Importance of not missing doses and taking at evenly spaced intervals
» Not drinking grapefruit juice or eating grapefruit
Taking with or without food
Missed dose: Taking as soon as possible if remembered within 4 hours; not taking if remembered later; not doubling doses
» Proper storage

Precautions while using this medication

Seeing the physician regularly to check progress of therapy
Telling your doctor about all medications you are taking, prescription and nonprescription
Carrying medical identification card or bracelet
» Caution if any kind of surgery (including dental surgery) or emergency treatment is required
Caution when driving or doing things requiring alertness because of possible dizziness

Side/adverse effects

Signs of potential side effects, especially angina, atrial flutter or fibrillation; bradycardia; bundle branch block; congestive heart failure; first or second degree atrioventricular (AV) block; intraventricular conduction delay; ventricular arrhythmias, including *torsades de pointes;* agranulocytosis; hypotension; joint pain; and trembling or shaking

General Dosing Information

Because of wide interindividual variability in plasma concentrations, careful titration of dosage is recommended. However, because steady-state concentrations are achieved after the same amount of time in both extensive and poor metabolizers, and because the difference in peak plasma concentrations decreases at high doses and the active 5-hydroxy metabolite is absent in poor metabolizers, the recommended dosage regimen is the same for both groups of patients.

Propafenone should not be used to control the ventricular rate during atrial fibrillation. Patients with atrial flutter when treated with propafenone have developed 1:1 conduction across the atrioventricular (AV) node, causing an increase in the ventricular rate. It is recommended that other agent(s) that increase the AV refractory period be used concurrently with propafenone, to avoid an increase in the ventricular rate.

Dosage increments should be made no more frequently than every 5 days.

It is recommended that treatment be initiated in the hospital because of the increased risk of proarrhythmic effects associated with propafenone administration.

In general, it is recommended that previous antiarrhythmic therapy be withdrawn 2 to 5 half-lives before initiation of propafenone therapy.

In patients with pacemakers, pacing threshold should be monitored and programmed at periodic intervals during propafenone therapy.

Diet/Nutrition

Propafenone may be taken with or without food.

Oral Dosage Forms

PROPAFENONE HYDROCHLORIDE EXTENDED-RELEASE CAPSULES

Usual adult dose

Antiarrhythmic—

Oral, initially 225 mg once every 12 hours. Dose must be individually titrated on the basis of response and tolerance and may be increased at a minimum of 5-day intervals up to 325 mg every twelve hours.

Note: Dosage reduction should be considered in patients with hepatic impairment or who have significant widening of the QRS complex or second or third degree AV block.

Usual adult prescribing limits

450 mg every 12 hours

Usual pediatric dose

Safety and efficacy have not been established.

Usual geriatric dose

See *Usual adult dose*

Strength(s) usually available

U.S.—

225 mg (Rx) [*Rythmol SR* (antifoam; gelatin; hypromellose; red iron oxide; magnesium stearate; shellac; sodium lauryl sulfate; sodium dodecyl sulfate; soy lecithin; titanium dioxide)].

325 mg (Rx) [*Rythmol SR* (antifoam; gelatin; hypromellose; red iron oxide; magnesium stearate; shellac; sodium lauryl sulfate; sodium dodecyl sulfate; soy lecithin; titanium dioxide)].

425 mg (Rx) [*Rythmol SR* (antifoam; gelatin; hypromellose; red iron oxide; magnesium stearate; shellac; sodium lauryl sulfate; sodium dodecyl sulfate; soy lecithin; titanium dioxide)].

Packaging and storage

Store at 25 °C excursions permitted between 15 and 30 °C (59 and 86 °F), in a tight container.

Auxiliary labeling

- Tell your doctor about all medications you are taking, prescription and nonprescription
- Swallow whole. Do not crush or chew.
- Grapefruit and grapefruit juice should not be taken with this medication

PROPAFENONE HYDROCHLORIDE TABLETS

Usual adult dose

Antiarrhythmic—Ventricular or

Antiarrhythmic—Supraventricular or

[Antiarrhythmic—Supraventricular, other][1]—

Oral, initially 150 mg every eight hours, increased, if necessary, after three to four days to 225 mg every eight hours (U.S. labeling) or 300 mg every twelve hours (Canadian labeling); may be further increased after an additional three to four days, if necessary, to 300 mg every eight hours.

Usual adult prescribing limits

900 mg per day.

Usual pediatric dose

Safety and efficacy have not been established.

Strength(s) usually available

U.S.—

150 mg (Rx) [*Rythmol* (scored)].

225 mg (Rx) [*Rythmol* (scored)].

300 mg (Rx) [*Rythmol* (scored)].

Canada—

150 mg (Rx) [*Rythmol*].

300 mg (Rx) [*Rythmol* (scored)].

Packaging and storage

Store between 15 and 30 °C (59 and 86 °F), in a tight, light-resistant container.

[1]Not included in Canadian product labeling.

Selected Bibliography

Echt DS, Liebson PR, Mitchell LB, et al. Mortality and morbidity in patients receiving encainide, flecainide, or placebo: the cardiac arrhythmia suppression trial. N Engl J Med 1991; 324: 781-8.

The Cardiac Arrhythmia Suppression Trial II Investigators. Effect of the antiarrhythmic agent moricizine on survival after myocardial infarction. N Engl J Med 1992 Jul 23; 327(4): 227-33.

Product Information: Rythmol SR, propafenone. Reliant Pharmaceutical, Liberty Corner, NJ, (PI revised) PI reviewed 12/2004.

Revised: 12/22/2004

PROPANTHELINE—See *Anticholinergics/Antispasmodics (Systemic)*

PROPARACAINE—See *Anesthetics (Ophthalmic)*

PROPOFOL Systemic

VA CLASSIFICATION (Primary/Secondary): CN203/CN206; CN309

Commonly used brand name(s): *Diprivan*.

Another commonly used name is disoprofol.

Note: For a listing of dosage forms and brand names by country availability, see *Dosage Forms* section(s).

Category

Anesthetic, general; anesthesia adjunct; sedative-hypnotic.

Indications

Accepted

Anesthesia, general or

Anesthesia, general, adjunct—Propofol is indicated for the induction of general anesthesia in adults and in pediatric patients greater than 3 years of age. It is also indicated for maintenance of anesthesia utilizing balanced techniques with other appropriate agents such as opioids and inhalation anesthetics in adults and pediatric patients greater than 2 months of age.

Sedation—Propofol is indicated for sedation in critically ill patients confined to intensive care units.

Propofol is indicated to produce sedation or amnesia as a supplement to local or regional anesthetics, and in diagnostic procedures, such as endoscopy (i.e., Monitored Anesthesia Care [MAC]).

Although cardiovascular, respiratory, and sedative effects must be carefully monitored, propofol provides good control of depth of sedation, and the rapid return of spontaneous ventilation following discontinuation of propofol infusion allows early extubation. Tachyphylaxis, delayed awakening, or cumulative effects have not been reported after prolonged administration of propofol as they have with prolonged infusion of thiopental, diazepam, or midazolam. In addition, propofol does not suppress adrenocortical function as does etomidate.

Unaccepted

Propofol is not indicated in pediatric patients for monitored anesthesia care (MAC) sedation or for sedation in intensive care.

Pharmacology/Pharmacokinetics

Physicochemical characteristics

Molecular weight—178.28.

pH—Propofol emulsion: 7 to 8.5.

Mechanism of action/Effect

Propofol is a short-acting hypnotic. Its mechanism of action has not been well-defined.

Other actions/effects

Hemodynamic effects—

Propofol's hemodynamic effects are generally more pronounced than those of other intravenous anesthetic agents. Arterial hypotension, with readings decreased by as much as 30% or more, has been reported, possibly due to inhibition of sympathetic vasoconstrictor nerve activity. Hypotensive effects are generally proportional to dose and rate of administration of propofol, and may be potentiated by opioid analgesics. Endotracheal intubation and surgical stimulation may increase arterial pressure; increases in heart rate and/or blood pressure to greater than baseline values, which occur frequently with other agents, are not as significant with propofol, possibly due to central sympatholytic and/or vagotonic effects. Propofol may also decrease systemic vascular resistance, myocardial blood flow, and oxygen consumption. The mechanism of these effects may involve direct vasodilation and negative inotropy. Effects such as decreased stroke volume and cardiac output have been demonstrated in some studies.

Respiratory effects—

Propofol is a respiratory depressant, frequently producing apnea that may persist for longer than 60 seconds, depending on factors such as premedication, rate of administration, dose administered, and presence of hyperventilation or hyperoxia. In addition, propofol may produce significant decreases in respiratory rate, minute volume, tidal volume, mean inspiratory flow rate, and functional residual capacity. These respiratory depressant effects may be the result of depression of the central inspiratory drive as opposed to a change in central timing. The ventilatory depressant effects of propofol may be counteracted by painful surgical stimulation.

Cerebral effects—

Propofol decreases cerebral blood flow, cerebral metabolic oxygen consumption, and intracranial pressure, and increases cerebrovascular resistance. It does not appear to affect cerebrovascular reactivity to changes in arterial carbon dioxide tension.

Other effects—

Preliminary findings suggest that in patients with normal intraocular pressure, propofol decreases intraocular pressure by as much as 30 to 50%. This decrease may be associated with a concomitant decrease in systemic vascular resistance.

Clinical studies have shown that propofol does not cause significant signs of histamine release or significant increases in plasma immunoglobulin or complement C_3 levels. Respiratory resistance after tracheal intubation is lower when propofol is used for induction of anesthesia than when thiopental or high-dose etomidate is used for induction of anesthesia.

Although propofol has the potential for affecting adrenal steroidogenesis, it does not appear to block cortisol and aldosterone secretion in response to surgical stress or adrenocorticotropic hormone (ACTH) in clinical practice. Although transient decreases in plasma cortisol concentrations have occurred, these reductions have not been sustained.

Propofol appears to have no analgesic activity. In addition, animal studies have demonstrated no significant effect on coagulation profiles.

Limited experience with propofol in susceptible patients and animal studies has not demonstrated a propensity to induce malignant hyperthermia.

Propofol has antiemetic properties. Anesthesia with propofol results in less nausea and vomiting than anesthesia with desflurane, enflurane, isoflurane, methohexital, nitrous oxide, or thiopental.

Distribution

Propofol is rapidly and extensively distributed in the body. It crosses the blood-brain barrier quickly, and its short duration of action is due to rapid redistribution from the CNS to other tissues, high metabolic clearance, and high lipophilicity.

Volumes of distribution—

Initial apparent (Vol_D): 13 to 76 liters (L).

Steady-state (Vol_{DSS}): 171 to 349 L.

Elimination (Vol_D): 209 to 1008 L.

Steady-state (Vol_{DSS}) in pediatric patients: 9.5 ± 3.71 liters per kg of body weight (L/kg).

Protein binding

Very high (95 to 99%).

Biotransformation

Hepatic; rapidly undergoes glucuronide conjugation to inactive metabolites. An unidentified route of extrahepatic metabolism may also exist, suggested by the fact that propofol clearance exceeds estimated hepatic blood flow.

Half-life

Distribution—

Two distribution phases:

Rapid—2 to 4 minutes.

Slower—30 to 64 minutes.

Elimination—

Terminal elimination half-life is 3 to 12 hours; prolonged administration of propofol may result in a longer duration.

Note: The long terminal elimination half-life of propofol does not reflect elimination, as more than 70% is eliminated during the first 2 phases. Some investigators believe that the second exponential phase half-life (30 to 64 minutes) best explains the properties of propofol in clinical practice.

Other—

Blood-brain equilibration half-life: 2.9 minutes.

Onset of action

Loss of consciousness occurs rapidly and smoothly, usually within 40 seconds (one arm-brain circulation time) from the start of intravenous injection of propofol. Loss of consciousness is dependent on the dose administered, the rate of administration, and the extent of premedication.

Plasma concentrations

Propofol concentrations of 1.5 to 6 mcg per mL (8.42 to 33.66 micromoles per liter [micromoles/L]) will maintain hypnosis, although needs vary with type of surgery and use of other anesthetic agents.

Duration of action

Mean duration following a single bolus dose of 2 to 2.5 mg per kg of body weight is 3 to 5 minutes.

Time to recovery

Recovery from anesthesia with propofol is rapid, with minimal psychomotor impairment. Emergence following induction (with 2 to 2.5 mg of propofol per kg) and maintenance (with 0.1 to 0.2 mg of propofol per kg per minute) for up to 2 hours occurs in most patients within 8 minutes. If an opioid has been used, recovery may take up to 19 minutes.

Recovery occurs faster than recovery following the use of etomidate, methohexital, midazolam, or thiopental. When anesthesia has included use of an opioid with propofol, recovery has occurred more quickly than with similar use of etomidate, midazolam, or thiopental.

Many investigators have noted clearheadedness in patients emerging from propofol anesthesia, and less residual impairment of performance than in patients who received methohexital has been reported.

Elimination

Renal; approximately 70% of a dose is excreted in the urine within 24 hours after administration, and 90% is excreted within 5 days. Clearance of propofol ranges from 1.6 to 3.4 liters per minute in healthy 70 kg patients. As the age of the patient increases, total body clearance of propofol may decrease. Clearance rates ranging from 1.4 to 2.2 liters per minute in patients 18 to 35 years of age have been reported, in contrast to clearance rates of 1 to 1.8 liters per minute in patients 65 to 80 years of age.

Note: Pharmacokinetic parameters of propofol appear to be unaffected by gender, obesity, chronic hepatic cirrhosis, and chronic renal failure.

Precautions to Consider

Carcinogenicity

Studies have not been done.

Mutagenicity

The Ames mutation test using *Salmonella* species, gene mutation/gene conversion using *Saccharomyces cerevisiae*, cytogenetic studies in Chinese hamsters, and a mouse micronucleus test have failed to demonstrate mutagenic potential by propofol.

Pregnancy/Reproduction

Fertility—Studies in rats given doses up to 6 times the human dose for varying lengths of time have shown no evidence of impaired fertility.

Pregnancy—Propofol crosses the placenta. Adequate and well-controlled studies in humans have not been done.

Studies in animals have shown propofol to cause increased maternal deaths in rats and rabbits and decreased pup survival during the lactating period when the dams received 6 times the recommended human dose.

FDA Pregnancy Category B.

Labor and delivery—A study was conducted in 74 patients comparing the use of propofol with that of thiamylal-isoflurane for induction and maintenance of anesthesia during cesarean section. The study did not show any problems in the mothers or in the neonates with the use of propofol. There was no difference between the neonates in the two groups in Apgar scores or the neurological and adaptive capacity scores (NACS). However, the manufacturer states that use of propofol is not recommended since data are insufficient to support its use in obstetrics, including cesarean section deliveries.

Breast-feeding

Propofol is distributed into breast milk. However, the effects of oral administration of small amounts of propofol are not known.

Pediatrics

Appropriate studies with propofol for sedation have not been performed in the pediatric population. There are case reports in the medical literature of pediatric patients developing metabolic acidosis after receiving propofol for sedation in the intensive care unit (ICU). Rarely, deaths have occurred. The role of propofol in these deaths is controversial. Other causes of metabolic acidosis could not be ruled out, and a causal relationship could not be established.

Note: Propofol is approved by the FDA for use in pediatric patients 3 years of age and older for induction of anesthesia and as a component of balanced anesthesia, and in pediatric patients 2 months of age and older for maintenance of anesthesia and as a component of balanced anesthesia.

Geriatrics

Dosage requirements are lower in geriatric patients than in younger adult patients, probably due to pharmacokinetic differences rather than pharmacodynamic differences in geriatric patients. Lower induction doses and a slower maintenance infusion rate should be used in geriatric patients, due to reduced total body clearance and volume of distribution in these patients.

Drug interactions and/or related problems

The following drug interactions and/or related problems have been selected on the basis of their potential clinical significance (possible mechanism in parentheses where appropriate)—not necessarily inclusive (» = major clinical significance):

Note: Combinations containing any of the following medications, depending on the amount present, may also interact with this medication.

» Alcohol or
» CNS depression-producing medications, other, including those commonly used for preanesthetic medication or induction or supplementation of anesthesia (see *Appendix II*)
(concurrent administration may increase the CNS-depressant, respiratory-depressant, or hypotensive effects of propofol, as well as decreasing anesthetic requirements and prolonging recovery from anesthesia; dosage adjustments may be required; propofol may also decrease the emetic effects of some opioid drugs)

Droperidol
(droperidol may compete with propofol for binding sites in the chemoreceptor trigger zone; concurrent use of propofol and droperidol to control nausea and vomiting is less effective than using propofol alone)

Fentanyl
(concomitant administration of fentanyl in pediatric patients may result in serious bradycardia)

Medical considerations/Contraindications

The medical considerations/contraindications included have been selected on the basis of their potential clinical significance (reasons given in parentheses where appropriate)—not necessarily inclusive (» = major clinical significance).

Except under special circumstances, this medication should not be used when the following medical problem exists:

» Hypersensitivity
(hypersensitivity to propofol or its components, including soybean oil, glycerol, egg lecithin, and disodium edetate)

Risk-benefit should be considered when the following medical problems exist:

Circulatory disorders or
Compromised cardiovascular function
(may be aggravated by cardiovascular-depressant and hypotensive effects)

Disorders of lipid metabolism, such as primary hyperlipoproteinemia, diabetic hyperlipemia, or pancreatitis
(may be aggravated by emulsion vehicle of propofol)

Increased intracranial pressure or
Impaired cerebral circulation
(substantial decreases in mean arterial pressure and cerebral perfusion may occur)

Caution is also recommended in geriatric, debilitated, and/or hypovolemic patients, because they may require lower induction and maintenance doses.

Side/Adverse Effects

Note: Postoperative infections and subsequent deaths have been reported following the use of propofol that was not administered using strict aseptic technique.

Rarely, a clinical syndrome including bronchospasm, erythema, and hypotension has occurred shortly after administration of propofol, and sequelae including anoxic brain damage and death have been reported; concurrent use of other agents makes a causal relationship unclear.

The following side/adverse effects have been selected on the basis of their potential clinical significance (possible signs and symptoms in parentheses where appropriate)—not necessarily inclusive:

Those indicating need for medical attention

Incidence more frequent

Apnea; bradycardia; hypotension

Incidence less frequent or rare

Hypertension; perioperative myoclonia, rarely including opisthotonus; pancreatitis (abdominal pain)—symptoms may not occur until after discharge from medical care following use of propofol

Those indicating need for medical attention only if they continue or are bothersome

Incidence more frequent

Involuntary muscle movements, temporary; nausea and/or vomiting; pain, burning, or stinging at injection site

Note: *Excitatory movements* reportedly occur more often than with thiopental but less often than with etomidate or methohexital.

Pain is usually mild and short-lived, and may be decreased by using the larger veins of the forearm or the antecubital fossa or a dedicated intravenous catheter. Pain may be decreased by prior intravenous injection of 10 to 20 mg of lidocaine. Post-injection thrombosis or phlebitis is rare.

Incidence less frequent or rare

Abdominal cramping; cough; dizziness; fever; flushing; headache; hiccups; tingling, numbness, or coldness at injection site

Overdose

For specific information on the management of a propofol overdose, see:
- *Atropine* in *Anticholinergics/Antispasmodics* monograph; and/or
- *Sympathomimetic Agents—Cardiovascular Use (Parenteral-Systemic)* monograph.

For more information on the management of overdose, **contact a Poison Control Center** (see *Poison Control Center Listing*).

Clinical effects of overdose

The following effects have been selected on the basis of their potential clinical significance (possible signs and symptoms in parentheses where appropriate)—not necessarily inclusive:

Acute

Cardiovascular depression; respiratory depression

Treatment of overdose

Specific treatment—
Discontinuation of propofol.
For respiratory depression: artificial ventilation with oxygen.
For cardiovascular depression: elevation of legs, increasing flow rate of intravenous fluids, and administration of pressor agents and/or anticholinergic agents.

Monitoring—
Patients should be continuously monitored for signs of significant hypotension and/or bradycardia.

Patient Consultation

As an aid to patient consultation, refer to *Advice for the Patient, Anesthetics, General (Systemic)*.

In providing consultation, consider emphasizing the following selected information (» = major clinical significance):

Before using this medication

» Conditions affecting use, especially:
Hyperensitivity to propofol or its components, including soybean oil, glycerol, egg lecithin, and disodium edetate
Pregnancy—Propofol crosses the placenta
Use of propofol is not recommended in labor and delivery because data are insufficient to support its use in obstetrics
Use in children—Propofol should not be used for sedation in pediatric intensive care unit patients or for monitored anesthesia care (MAC) sedation in pediatric patients because safety and efficacy have not been established

Use in the elderly—Lower induction and maintenance doses are recommended

Other medications, especially other CNS depressants

Proper use of this medication

» Proper dosing

Precautions after receiving this medication

Possibility of psychomotor impairment following use of anesthetics; for about 24 hours following anesthesia, using added caution in driving or performing other tasks requiring alertness and coordination

Avoiding use of alcohol or other CNS depressants within 24 hours following anesthesia except as directed by physician or dentist

Side/adverse effects

Signs of potential side effects, especially pancreatitis

General Dosing Information

Propofol should be administered only by individuals qualified in the use of general anesthetics. Appropriate resuscitative and endotracheal intubation equipment, oxygen, and medications for prevention and treatment of anesthetic emergencies must be immediately available. Airway patency must be maintained at all times.

Propofol emulsion is for intravenous administration only. Although clinical experience and animal studies have shown that inadvertent intra-arterial injection of propofol usually produces minimal tissue reaction, intra-arterial injection of propofol is not recommended.

To minimize the pain, burning, or stinging patients may experience at the site of injection of propofol, a larger vein of the forearm or the antecubital fossa may be used as the infusion site. Pretreatment of the injection site with one mL of 1% lidocaine may also decrease the incidence of this side effect.

Dosage of propofol must be individualized for each patient, with the dose titrated to achieve the desired clinical effect. Lower doses are usually required for elderly, debilitated, or higher risk surgical patients, or those with circulatory disorders. The dosage of intravenously administered propofol should be adjusted according to the type and amount of premedication used.

Rapid intravenous injection of propofol should not be used in elderly, debilitated, hypovolemic, or higher risk surgical patients. Rapid intravenous injection of propofol in these patients may result in cardiopulmonary depression including hypotension, apnea, airway obstruction and/or oxygen desaturation.

When propofol is administered by infusion, it is recommended that drop counters, syringe pumps, or volumetric pumps be utilized to control infusion rates.

When nitrous oxide, oxygen, and propofol are used for maintenance of general anesthesia, supplemental analgesic agents are generally required; neuromuscular blocking agents may also be required. Concurrent use of propofol with neuromuscular blocking agents does not significantly alter the onset, intensity, or duration of action of these agents.

Propofol injection contains 0.005% disodium edetate, but it is not an antimicrobially preserved product under USP standards. The vehicle is capable of supporting the rapid growth of microorganisms, and particulate or bacterial contamination may be difficult to detect because propofol injection is opaque. Rarely, failure to use strict aseptic technique has resulted in sepsis in patients to whom contaminated solution was administered. Therefore, strict aseptic technique must be maintained, and propofol injection should be administered promptly after opening. Unused portions of the injection, as well as reservoirs, intravenous lines, or solutions containing propofol injection, must be discarded at the end of the procedure or within 12 hours (6 hours if propofol was transferred from the original container).

Propofol should not be infused through filters with pore size smaller than 5 microns because infusion through a smaller filter may cause breakdown of the emulsion.

Parenteral Dosage Forms

PROPOFOL INJECTABLE EMULSION

Usual adult and adolescent dose

Dosage must be individualized and titrated to the desired clinical effect; however, as a general guideline—

Anesthesia, general (induction)—

Adults up to 55 years of age and/or American Society of Anesthesiologists (ASA) I or II patients:

Intravenous, 2 to 2.5 mg per kg of body weight (approximately 40 mg every ten seconds until onset of induction).

Cardiac patients:

Intravenous, 0.5 to 1.5 mg per kg of body weight (approximately 20 mg every ten seconds until onset of induction).

Elderly, debilitated, hypovolemic, and/or ASA III or IV patients:

Intravenous, 1 to 1.5 mg per kg of body weight (approximately 20 mg every ten seconds until onset of induction).

Neurosurgical patients:

Intravenous, 1 to 2 mg per kg of body weight (approximately 20 mg every ten seconds until onset of induction).

Note: Slow injection of the induction dose of propofol may result in longer induction times and a lower percentage of successful inductions, probably due to rapid redistribution from the CNS; however, slow injection of doses is preferable, in order to diminish some of the cardiovascular effects.

Rapid intravenous injection of propofol should not be used in elderly, debilitated, hypovolemic, or higher-risk surgical patients. Rapid intravenous injection of propofol in these patients may result in cardiopulmonary depression including hypotension, apnea, airway obstruction and/or oxygen desaturation.

Anesthesia, general, adjunct (maintenance)—

Adults up to 55 years of age and/or ASA I or II patients:

Intravenous infusion, 100 to 200 mcg (0.1 to 0.2 mg) per kg of body weight per minute (6 to 12 mg per kg of body weight per hour), with 60 to 70% nitrous oxide and oxygen.

Note: During the initial ten to fifteen minutes following induction, higher infusion rates of 150 to 200 mcg (0.15 to 0.2 mg) per kg of body weight per minute are generally required. Infusion rates should subsequently be decreased by 30 to 50% during the first half-hour of maintenance.

Infusion rates should always be titrated downward in the absence of light anesthesia to avoid administration of propofol at rates higher than clinically necessary. In general, rates of 50 to 100 mcg (0.05 to 0.1 mg) per kg of body weight per minute should be achieved during maintenance to optimize recovery times.

Intravenous intermittent injection, 20 to 50 mg increments, administered as needed. Alternatively, some clinicians recommend increments of 500 mcg (0.5 mg) per kg of body weight.

Adults receiving propofol for maintenance of general anesthesia for cardiac surgery:

Intravenous infusion, 50 to 150 mcg (0.05 to 0.15 mg) per kg of body weight per minute (3 to 9 mg per kg of body weight per hour). The use of an opioid as the primary anesthetic will result in a need for dosing of propofol at the lower end of this range, and the use of low-dose opioid as a secondary agent will result in a need for dosing of propofol at the higher end of this range.

Adults receiving propofol for maintenance of general anesthesia for neurosurgery:

Intravenous infusion, 100 to 200 mcg (0.1 to 0.2 mg) per kg of body weight per minute (6 to 12 mg per kg of body weight per hour).

Elderly, debilitated, hypovolemic, and/or ASA III or IV patients:

Intravenous infusion, 50 to 100 mcg (0.05 to 0.1 mg) per kg of body weight per minute (3 to 6 mg per kg of body weight per hour).

Sedation—

Intensive care:

Individualize dose by titrating to unconsciousness with minimal hypotension:

Initiation: Intravenous infusion, 5 mcg (0.005 mg) per kg of body weight per minute (0.3 mg per kg of body weight per hour) for at least 5 minutes.

Titrate: Intravenous infusion, increments of 5 to 10 mcg (0.005 to 0.010 mg) per kg of body weight per minute (0.3 to 0.6 mg per kg of body weight per hour) over 5 to 10 minutes.

Maintenance: Intravenous infusion, 5 to 50 mcg (0.005 to 0.050 mg) per kg of body weight per minute (0.3 to 3 mg per kg of body weight per hour). or higher may be required.

Daily reassessment of level of sedation and CNS function should be carried out during maintenance dosing of propofol to determine the minimum dose of propofol injectable emulsion required for sedation..

Note: The mean requirement for sedation in the intensive care unit is 27 mcg per kg of body weight per minute, but the requirements vary widely, from 2.8 to 130 mcg per kg of body weight per minute. Lower rates of administration may be sufficient for patients receiving benzodiazepines or opioid analgesics. Older patients (i.e., those 55 years of age and older) require less propofol for sedation than younger patients (i.e., those up to 55 years of age) (20 and 38 mcg per kg of body weight per minute, respectively). In all cases, the infusion should be initiated slowly and titrated to effect.

Monitored Anesthesia Care (MAC):

Initiation: Intravenous infusion, 100 to 150 mcg (0.1 to 0.15 mg) per kg of body weight per minute (6 to 9 mg per kg of body weight per hour) for three to five minutes; or slow intravenous injection over three to five minutes, 0.5 mg per kg of body weight.

Maintenance: Intravenous infusion, 25 to 50 mcg (0.025 to 0.05 mg) per kg of body weight per minute (1.5 to 3 mg per kg of body weight per hour).

Note: During the initial ten to fifteen minutes following induction, higher infusion rates of 25 to 75 mcg (0.025 to 0.075 mg) per kg of body weight per minute (1.5 to 4.5 mg per kg of body weight per hour) may be needed.

In titrating to clinical effect, two minutes should be allowed to observe effects after an adjustment in dose.

When propofol is used to provide MAC for elderly, debilitated, or ASA III or IV patients, the rate of administration and dose should be reduced to eighty percent of the usual adult dose.

Usual pediatric dose

Anesthesia, general (induction)—

Pediatric patients (ASA I or II) 3 years of age or older: Intravenous, 2.5 to 3.5 mg per kg of body weight.

Note: Propofol is approved for induction of anesthesia in pediatric patients 3 years of age and older. However, propofol has been used in pediatric patients younger than 3 years of age for induction of anesthesia. In one study, infants 1 to 6 months of age required 3 mg per kg of body weight for induction of anesthesia.

A lower dosage is recommended in pediatric patients classified as ASA III or IV.

Anesthesia, general, adjunct (maintenance)—

Pediatric patients (ASA I or II) 2 months of age to 16 years of age: Intravenous infusion, 125 to 300 mcg (0.125 to 0.3 mg) per kg of body weight per minute (7.5 to 18 mg per kg of body weight per hour), titrated to achieve the desired clinical effect.

Note: During the initial one-half hour following induction, higher infusion rates of 200 to 300 mcg (0.2 to 0.3 mg) per kg of body weight per minute (12 to 18 mg per kg of body weight per hour) may be needed. After one-half hour, the dose may be decreased to 125 to 150 mcg (0.125 to 0.15 mg) per kg of body weight per minute (7.5 to 9 mg per kg of body weight per hour) in most cases. Following the first half hour of maintenance, if clinical signs of light anesthesia are not present, the infusion rate should be decreased.

Children 5 years of age and younger may require larger weight-adjusted maintenance doses than older children.

Strength(s) usually available

U.S.—

10 mg per mL (Rx) [*Diprivan* (soybean oil 10% w/v; glycerol 2.25% w/v; purified egg phosphatide [lecithin] 1.2% w/v; disodium edetate 0.005%)].

Canada—

10 mg per mL (Rx) [*Diprivan* (soybean oil 10% w/v; glycerol 2.25% w/v; purified egg phosphatide [lecithin] 1.2% w/v; disodium edetate 0.005%)].

Packaging and storage

Store between 4 and 22 °C (40 and 72 °F). Refrigeration is not recommended. Protect from light.

Preparation of dosage form

Propofol is compatible with 5% dextrose in water, lactated Ringer's solution, lactated Ringer's and 5% dextrose in water, and combinations of 5% dextrose with 0.45% or 0.2% sodium chloride.

If propofol is diluted prior to administration, only 5% Dextrose Injection USP should be used as a diluent, and the final concentration should not be less than 2 mg per mL to preserve the emulsion base. The dilution is more stable in glass than in plastic.

Stability

Propofol injection contains 0.005% disodium edetate, but it is not an antimicrobially preserved product under USP standards. The vehicle is capable of supporting the rapid growth of microorganisms, and particulate or bacterial contamination may be difficult to detect because propofol injection is opaque. Therefore, strict aseptic technique must be maintained. Propofol injection should be administered promptly after opening. Unused portions of the injection, as well as reservoirs, IV lines, or solutions containing propofol injection, must be discarded at the end of the procedure or within 12 hours (6 hours if propofol was transferred from the original container).

Propofol should not be used if there is evidence of separation of the emulsion phases.

Incompatibilities

The manufacturer states that propofol emulsion should not be mixed with other therapeutic agents prior to administration. In addition, propofol should not be coadministered through the same IV catheter with blood or plasma; although the clinical significance is not known, *in vitro* studies have shown that the globular component of the emulsion vehicle has formed aggregates when in contact with human and animal blood, plasma, and serum.

Auxiliary labeling

- Shake well before use.
- Protect from light.

Selected Bibliography

Sebel P, Lowdon J. Propofol: a new intravenous anesthetic. Anesthesiology 1989; 71: 260-77.

White PF. Propofol: pharmacokinetics and pharmacodynamics. Seminars in Anesthesia 1988; 7 Suppl 1: 4-20.

Fulton B, Sorkin E. Propofol: an overview of its pharmacology and a review of its clinical efficacy in intensive care sedation. Drugs 1995; 50: 636-57.

Revised: 02/09/2006

PROPOXYPHENE—See *Opioid (Narcotic) Analgesics (Systemic)*

PROPRANOLOL—See *Beta-adrenergic Blocking Agents (Systemic)*

PROPYLTHIOURACIL—See *Antithyroid Agents (Systemic)*

PROTRIPTYLINE—See *Antidepressants, Tricyclic (Systemic)*

PSEUDOEPHEDRINE Systemic

VA CLASSIFICATION (Primary): RE200

Commonly used brand name(s): *Balminil Decongestant Syrup; Benylin Decongestant; Cenafed; Chlor-Trimeton Non-Drowsy Decongestant 4 Hour; Decofed; Dimetapp Decongestant; Dimetapp Decongestant Pediatric Drops; Drixoral N.D.; Drixoral Nasal Decongestant; Efidac/24; Eltor 120; Genaphed; Maxenal; Myfedrine; PediaCare Infants' Oral Decongestant Drops; Pseudo; Pseudo 60's; Robidrine; Sudafed; Sudafed 12 Hour; Sudafed Children's Nasal Decongestant Liquid Medication; Sudafed Decongestant; Sudafed Decongestant 12 Hour; Sudafed Decongestant Extra Strength; Triaminic AM Decongestant Formula; Triaminic Infant Oral Decongestant Drops.*

Note: For a listing of dosage forms and brand names by country availability, see *Dosage Forms* section(s).

Category

Decongestant, nasal (systemic).

Indications

Accepted

Congestion, nasal (treatment)
Congestion, sinus (treatment) or
Congestion, eustachian tube (treatment)—Pseudoephedrine is indicated for temporary relief of congestion associated with acute coryza, acute eustachian salpingitis, serous otitis media with eustachian tube congestion, vasomotor rhinitis, and aerotitis (barotitis) media. Pseudoephedrine also may be indicated as an adjunct to analgesics, antihistamines, antibiotics, antitussives, or expectorants for optimum results in allergic rhinitis, croup, acute and subacute sinusitis, acute otitis media, and acute tracheobronchitis.

Pharmacology/Pharmacokinetics

Physicochemical characteristics

Molecular weight—
Pseudoephedrine hydrochloride: 201.70.
Pseudoephedrine sulfate: 428.54.

Mechanism of action/Effect

Pseudoephedrine acts on alpha-adrenergic receptors in the mucosa of the respiratory tract, producing vasoconstriction. The medication shrinks swollen nasal mucous membranes; reduces tissue hyperemia, edema, and nasal congestion; and increases nasal airway patency. Also, drainage of sinus secretions may be increased and obstructed eustachian ostia may be opened.

Biotransformation

Pseudoephedrine is incompletely metabolized in the liver.

Onset of action

15 to 30 minutes.

Time to peak effect

Within 30 to 60 minutes.

Duration of action

Tablets, oral solution, and syrup—3 to 4 hours.
Extended-release capsules and tablets—8 to 12 hours.

Elimination

Renal. About 55 to 75% of a dose is excreted unchanged. The rate of excretion is accelerated in acidic urine.

Precautions to Consider

Cross-sensitivity and/or related problems

Patients sensitive to other sympathomimetics (for example, albuterol, amphetamines, ephedrine, epinephrine, isoproterenol, metaproterenol, norepinephrine, phenylephrine, phenylpropanolamine, terbutaline) may be sensitive to this medication also.

Pregnancy/Reproduction

Pregnancy—Studies in humans have not been done.
Studies in animals have not shown that pseudoephedrine causes teratogenic effects in the fetus. However, pseudoephedrine reduced average weight, length, and rate of skeletal ossification in the animal fetus.

FDA Pregnancy Category B.

Breast-feeding

Pseudoephedrine is distributed into breast milk; use by nursing mothers is not recommended, because of the higher than usual risk to infants, especially newborn and premature infants, of side effects from sympathomimetic amines.

Pediatrics

Pseudoephedrine should be used with caution in infants, especially newborn and premature infants, because of the higher than usual risk of side/adverse effects.

Geriatrics

No information is available on the relationship of age to the effects of pseudoephedrine in geriatric patients. However, elderly patients are more likely to have age-related prostatic hypertrophy, which may require adjustment of dosage in patients receiving pseudoephedrine.

Drug interactions and/or related problems

The following drug interactions and/or related problems have been selected on the basis of their potential clinical significance (possible mechanism in parentheses where appropriate)—not necessarily inclusive (» = major clinical significance):

Note: Combinations containing any of the following medications, depending on the amount present, may also interact with this medication.

Anesthetics, hydrocarbon inhalation, such as:
Chloroform
Cyclopropane
Enflurane
Halothane
Isoflurane
Methoxyflurane
Trichloroethylene
(administration of pseudoephedrine prior to or shortly after anesthesia with chloroform, cyclopropane, halothane, or trichloroethylene may increase the risk of severe ventricular arrhythmias, especially in patients with pre-existing heart disease, because these anesthetics greatly sensitize the myocardium to the effects of sympathomimetics)

(enflurane, isoflurane, or methoxyflurane may also cause some sensitization of the myocardium to the effects of sympathomimetics; caution is recommended in patients taking pseudoephedrine)

Antihypertensives or
Diuretics used as antihypertensives
(antihypertensive effects may be reduced when these medications are used concurrently with pseudoephedrine; the patient should be monitored carefully to confirm that the desired effect is being obtained)

» Beta-adrenergic blocking agents
(concurrent use with pseudoephedrine may inhibit the therapeutic effect of these medications; beta-blockade may result in unopposed alpha-adrenergic activity of pseudoephedrine, with a risk of hypertension and excessive bradycardia and possible heart block)

Central nervous system (CNS) stimulation-producing medications, other (see *Appendix II*)
(concurrent use with pseudoephedrine may result in additive CNS stimulation to excessive levels, which may cause unwanted effects such as nervousness, irritability, insomnia, or possibly convulsions or cardiac arrhythmias; close observation is recommended)

Citrates
(concurrent use may inhibit urinary excretion and prolong the duration of action of pseudoephedrine)

» Cocaine, mucosal-local
(in addition to increasing CNS stimulation, concurrent use with pseudoephedrine may increase the cardiovascular effects of either or both medications and the risk of adverse effects)

Digitalis glycosides
(concurrent use with pseudoephedrine may increase the risk of cardiac arrhythmias; caution and electrocardiographic monitoring are very important if concurrent use is necessary)

Levodopa
(concurrent use with pseudoephedrine may increase the possibility of cardiac arrhythmias; dosage reduction of the sympathomimetic is recommended)

» Monoamine oxidase (MAO) inhibitors, including furazolidone, procarbazine, and selegiline
(concurrent use may prolong and intensify the cardiac stimulant and vasopressor effects of pseudoephedrine because of release of catecholamines, which accumulate in intraneuronal storage sites during MAO inhibitor therapy, resulting in headache, cardiac arrhythmias, vomiting, or sudden and severe hypertensive and/or hyperpyretic crises; pseudoephedrine should not be administered during or within 14 days following administration of MAO inhibitors)

Nitrates
(concurrent use with pseudoephedrine may reduce the antianginal effects of these medications)

Rauwolfia alkaloids
(concurrent use may inhibit the action of pseudoephedrine by depleting catecholamine stores)

Sympathomimetics, other
(in addition to possibly increasing CNS stimulation, concurrent use may increase the cardiovascular effects of either the other sympathomimetics or pseudoephedrine and the potential for side effects)

Thyroid hormones
(concurrent use may increase the effects of either these medications or pseudoephedrine; thyroid hormones enhance risk of coronary insufficiency when sympathomimetic agents are administered to patients with coronary artery disease; dosage adjustment is recommended, although problem is reduced in euthyroid patients)

Medical considerations/Contraindications

The medical considerations/contraindications included have been selected on the basis of their potential clinical significance (reasons given in parentheses where appropriate)—not necessarily inclusive (» = major clinical significance).

Risk-benefit should be considered when the following medical problems exist:

Cardiovascular disease, including ischemic heart disease, or
» Coronary artery disease, severe or
Hypertension, mild to moderate or
» Hypertension, severe
(condition may be exacerbated due to drug-induced cardiovascular effects)

Diabetes mellitus
(may lead to increased blood glucose concentrations)

Glaucoma, predisposition to
(condition may be aggravated)

Hyperthyroidism
(symptoms may be exacerbated)

Prostatic hypertrophy
(urinary retention may be precipitated)

Sensitivity to pseudoephedrine or other sympathomimetics

Side/Adverse Effects

The following side/adverse effects have been selected on the basis of their potential clinical significance (possible signs and symptoms in parentheses where appropriate)—not necessarily inclusive:

Those indicating need for medical attention

Incidence rare—more frequent with high doses

Convulsions; hallucinations; irregular or slow heartbeat; shortness of breath or troubled breathing

Those indicating need for medical attention only if they continue or are bothersome

Incidence more frequent

Nervousness; restlessness; trouble in sleeping

Incidence less frequent

Difficult or painful urination; dizziness or lightheadedness; fast or pounding heartbeat; headache; increased sweating; nausea or vomiting; trembling; unusual paleness; weakness

Overdose

For more information on the management of overdose or unintentional ingestion, **contact a Poison Control Center** (see *Poison Control Center Listing*).

Clinical effects of overdose

The following effects have been selected on the basis of their potential clinical significance (possible signs and symptoms in parenthesis where appropriate)—not necessarily inclusive:

Acute and chronic effects

Convulsions; fast breathing; hallucinations; increase in blood pressure; irregular heartbeat, continuing; shortness of breath or troubled breathing, severe or continuing; slow or fast heartbeat, severe or continuing; unusual nervousness, restlessness, or excitement

Treatment of overdose

To decrease absorption—

Because pseudoephedrine is rapidly absorbed from the gut, emetics and gastric lavage should be instituted within 4 hours of overdosage in order to be effective. Charcoal is useful only if administered within 1 hour. However, if an extended-release preparation was taken, there will be more time for benefit from these measures.

To enhance elimination—

Forced diuresis will increase elimination of pseudoephedrine provided renal function is adequate; however, diuresis is not recommended for severe overdosage.

Specific treatment—

For delirium or convulsions, intravenous diazepam may be administered.

The cardiac state should be monitored and serum electrolytes measured. If there are signs of cardiac toxicity, intravenous propranolol may be indicated.

Hypokalemia may be treated, if necessary, with a slow infusion of a dilute potassium chloride solution; serum potassium concentration should be monitored during and for several hours after administration of potassium chloride.

Patient Consultation

As an aid to patient consultation, refer to *Advice for the Patient, Pseudoephedrine (Systemic)*.

In providing consultation, consider emphasizing the following selected information (» = major clinical significance):

Before using this medication

» Conditions affecting use, especially:

Sensitivity to pseudoephedrine or other sympathomimetics

Pregnancy—In animal studies, pseudoephedrine caused reduced average weight, length, and rate of skeletal ossification in animal fetus

Breast-feeding—Pseudoephedrine distributed into breast milk; use by nursing mothers not recommended because of higher than usual risk of side effects for infants, especially newborn and premature infants

Use in children—Caution should be used in infants, especially newborn and premature infants, because of higher than usual risk of side/adverse effects

Other medications, especially beta-adrenergic blocking agents, mucosal-local cocaine, or monoamine oxidase (MAO) inhibitors

Other medical problems, especially severe coronary artery disease or severe hypertension

Proper use of this medication

Proper administration of extended-release dosage forms

Swallowing capsules or tablets whole; if capsule too large to swallow, mixing contents with jam or jelly and swallowing without chewing

Not crushing or chewing capsules; not crushing, breaking, or chewing tablets

» Taking the medication a few hours before bedtime to minimize the possibility of insomnia

» Importance of not taking more medication than the amount recommended

» Proper dosing

Missed dose: Taking right away if remembered within an hour or so; not taking if remembered later; not doubling doses

» Proper storage

Precautions while using this medication

» Checking with physician if symptoms do not improve within 7 days or if fever is present

Side/adverse effects

Signs of potential side effects, especially convulsions, hallucinations, irregular or slow heartbeat, and shortness of breath or troubled breathing

General Dosing Information

To minimize the possibility of insomnia, the last dose of pseudoephedrine for each day should be administered a few hours before bedtime.

For patients who have difficulty in swallowing the extended-release capsule, the contents of the capsule may be mixed with jam or jelly and taken without chewing.

Oral Dosage Forms

PSEUDOEPHEDRINE HYDROCHLORIDE CAPSULES

Usual adult and adolescent dose

Decongestant, nasal—

Oral, 60 mg every four to six hours.

Usual adult prescribing limits

240 mg in twenty-four hours.

Usual pediatric dose

Decongestant, nasal—

Children up to 12 years of age: Use is not recommended.

Children 12 years of age and over: See *Usual adult and adolescent dose*.

Strength(s) usually available

U.S.—

30 mg (OTC) [*Dimetapp Decongestant*].

Canada—

60 mg (OTC) [*Benylin Decongestant*].

Packaging and storage

Store below 40 °C (104 °F), preferably between 15 and 30 °C (59 and 86 °F), in a well-closed container, unless otherwise specified by manufacturer.

PSEUDOEPHEDRINE HYDROCHLORIDE EXTENDED-RELEASE CAPSULES

Usual adult and adolescent dose

Decongestant, nasal—

Oral, 120 mg every twelve hours, or 240 mg every twenty-four hours.

Usual adult prescribing limits

240 mg in twenty-four hours.

Usual pediatric dose

Decongestant, nasal—

Children up to 12 years of age: Use is not recommended.

Children 12 years of age and over: See *Usual adult and adolescent dose.*

Strength(s) usually available

U.S.—

Not commercially available.

Canada—

120 mg (OTC) [GENERIC].

Packaging and storage

Store below 40 °C (104 °F), preferably between 15 and 30 °C (59 and 86 °F), in a tight container, unless otherwise specified by manufacturer. Protect from light.

Auxiliary labeling

- Swallow capsules whole.

PSEUDOEPHEDRINE HYDROCHLORIDE ORAL SOLUTION

Usual adult and adolescent dose

Decongestant, nasal—

See *Pseudoephedrine Hydrochloride Capsules.*

Usual adult prescribing limits

See *Pseudoephedrine Hydrochloride Capsules.*

Usual pediatric dose

Decongestant, nasal—

Oral, 4 mg per kg of body weight or 125 mg per square meter of body surface area per day, administered in four divided doses; or for

Children up to 2 years of age: Dosage must be individualized.

The manufacturer recommends the following dosing guidelines:

Children 4 to 12 months of age (5.4 to 7.7 kg)—

Oral, 7.5 mg every four to six hours not to exceed four doses (30 mg) in twenty-four hours.

Children 12 to 23 months of age (8.2 to 10.4 kg)—

Oral, 11.25 mg every four to six hours not to exceed four doses (45 mg) in twenty-four hours.

Children 2 to 6 years of age—

Oral, 15 mg every four to six hours, not to exceed 60 mg in twenty-four hours.

Children 6 to 12 years of age—

Oral, 30 mg every four to six hours, not to exceed 120 mg in twenty-four hours.

Children 12 years of age and over—

See *Pseudoephedrine Hydrochloride Capsules.*

Strength(s) usually available

U.S.—

7.5 mg per 0.8 mL (OTC) [*Dimetapp Decongestant Pediatric Drops; PediaCare Infants' Oral Decongestant Drops; Triaminic Infant Oral Decongestant Drops*].

15 mg per 5 mL (OTC) [*Sudafed Children's Nasal Decongestant Liquid Medication*].

30 mg per 5 mL (OTC) [*Decofed; Myfedrine*].

Canada—

Not commercially available.

Packaging and storage

Store below 40 °C (104 °F), preferably between 15 and 30 °C (59 and 86 °F), in a well-closed container, unless otherwise specified by manufacturer. Protect from freezing. Protect from light.

PSEUDOEPHEDRINE HYDROCHLORIDE SYRUP USP

Usual adult and adolescent dose

Decongestant, nasal—

See *Pseudoephedrine Hydrochloride Capsules.*

Usual adult prescribing limits

See *Pseudoephedrine Hydrochloride Capsules.*

Usual pediatric dose

Decongestant, nasal—

Children up to 12 years of age: See *Pseudoephedrine Hydrochloride Oral Solution.*

Children 12 years of age and over: See *Pseudoephedrine Hydrochloride Capsules.*

Strength(s) usually available

U.S.—

15 mg per 5 mL (OTC) [*Triaminic AM Decongestant Formula*].

30 mg per 5 mL (OTC) [*Cenafed;* GENERIC].

Canada—

30 mg per 5 mL (OTC) [*Balminil Decongestant Syrup* (alcohol); *Robidrine* (alcohol 1.4%); *Sudafed*].

Packaging and storage

Store below 40 °C (104 °F), preferably between 15 and 30 °C (59 and 86 °F), unless otherwise specified by manufacturer. Store in a tight, light-resistant container. Protect from freezing.

PSEUDOEPHEDRINE HYDROCHLORIDE TABLETS USP

Usual adult and adolescent dose

Decongestant, nasal—

See *Pseudoephedrine Hydrochloride Capsules.*

Usual adult prescribing limits

See *Pseudoephedrine Hydrochloride Capsules.*

Usual pediatric dose

Decongestant, nasal—

Children up to 12 years of age: See *Pseudoephedrine Hydrochloride Oral Solution.*

Children 12 years of age and over: See *Pseudoephedrine Hydrochloride Capsules.*

Strength(s) usually available

U.S.—

30 mg (OTC) [*Genaphed; Pseudo; Sudafed;* GENERIC].

60 mg (OTC) [*Cenafed; Pseudo 60's; Sudafed;* GENERIC].

Canada—

30 mg (OTC) [*Sudafed Decongestant*].

60 mg (OTC) [*Robidrine* (scored); *Sudafed Decongestant Extra Strength* (scored)].

Packaging and storage

Store below 40 °C (104 °F), preferably between 15 and 30 °C (59 and 86 °F), unless otherwise specified by manufacturer. Store in a tight container.

PSEUDOEPHEDRINE HYDROCHLORIDE EXTENDED-RELEASE TABLETS

Usual adult and adolescent dose

Decongestant, nasal—

See *Pseudoephedrine Hydrochloride Extended-Release Capsules.*

Usual adult prescribing limits

See *Pseudoephedrine Hydrochloride Extended-Release Capsules.*

Usual pediatric dose

Decongestant, nasal—

Children up to 12 years of age: Use is not recommended.

Children 12 years of age and over: See *Pseudoephedrine Hydrochloride Extended-Release Capsules.*

Strength(s) usually available

U.S.—

120 mg (OTC) [*Sudafed 12 Hour*].

240 mg (OTC) [*Efidac/24*].

Canada—

120 mg (OTC) [*Eltor 120; Maxenal; Sudafed Decongestant 12 Hour*].

Packaging and storage

Store below 40 °C (104 °F), preferably between 15 and 30 °C (59 and 86 °F), in a tight container, unless otherwise specified by manufacturer. Protect from light.

Auxiliary labeling

- Swallow tablets whole.

PSEUDOEPHEDRINE SULFATE TABLETS

Usual adult and adolescent dose

Decongestant, nasal—

See *Pseudoephedrine Hydrochloride Capsules.*

Usual adult prescribing limits

See *Pseudoephedrine Hydrochloride Capsules.*

Usual pediatric dose

Decongestant, nasal—

Children up to 12 years of age: See *Pseudoephedrine Hydrochloride Oral Solution.*

Children 12 years of age and over: See *Pseudoephedrine Hydrochloride Capsules.*

Strength(s) usually available

U.S.—

60 mg (OTC) [*Chlor-Trimeton Non-Drowsy Decongestant 4 Hour* (scored)].

Canada—

Not commercially available.

Packaging and storage

Store between 2 and 30 °C (36 and 86 °F), in a well-closed container, unless otherwise specified by manufacturer. Protect from light.

PSEUDOEPHEDRINE SULFATE EXTENDED-RELEASE TABLETS

Usual adult and adolescent dose

Decongestant, nasal—

See *Pseudoephedrine Hydrochloride Extended-Release Capsules.*

Usual adult prescribing limits

See *Pseudoephedrine Hydrochloride Extended-Release Capsules.*

Usual pediatric dose

Decongestant, nasal—

Children up to 12 years of age: Use is not recommended.

Children 12 years of age and over: See *Pseudoephedrine Hydrochloride Extended-Release Capsules.*

Strength(s) usually available

U.S.—

120 mg (OTC) [*Drixoral Nasal Decongestant*].

Canada—

120 mg (OTC) [*Drixoral N.D.*].

Packaging and storage

Store between 2 and 30 °C (36 and 86 °F), in a well-closed container, unless otherwise specified by manufacturer. Protect from light.

Auxiliary labeling

- Swallow tablets whole.

Revised: 12/14/1998

PSYLLIUM—See *Laxatives (Local)*

PSYLLIUM HYDROPHILIC MUCILLOID—See *Laxatives (Local)*

PYRAZINAMIDE Systemic

VA CLASSIFICATION (Primary): AM500

Commonly used brand name(s): *Tebrazid; pms-Pyrazinamide.*

Note: For a listing of dosage forms and brand names by country availability, see *Dosage Forms* section(s).

Category

Antibacterial (antimycobacterial).

Indications

General Considerations

Tuberculosis is a highly infectious life-threatening bacterial disease with 8 million new cases and 3 million deaths reported worldwide each year to the World Health Organization (WHO). The vast majority of these cases are in developing countries; however, tuberculosis also has emerged as an important public health problem in the U.S. in recent years after the decline in number of cases observed between 1950 and 1980.

The resurgence of tuberculosis in the U.S. has been complicated by an increase in the proportion of patients with strains resistant to antituberculosis medications. Outbreaks of multidrug-resistant tuberculosis have been documented in hospitals and prisons. Drug-resistant tuberculosis, particularly that caused by strains resistant to isoniazid and rifampin, is much harder to treat and often is fatal. Among acquired immunodeficiency syndrome (AIDS) patients infected with tuberculosis bacilli resistant to both rifampin and isoniazid, a case-fatality rate of 91% has been reported. Recent investigations of outbreaks of multidrug-resistant tuberculosis have found an extraordinarily high case-fatality rate, with the median time to mortality being reached between 4 and 16 weeks. In almost all instances, these outbreaks have involved patients with severe immunosuppression as a result of infection with the human immunodeficiency virus (HIV).

Acquired drug resistance develops during treatment for drug-sensitive tuberculosis with regimens that are poorly conceived or poorly complied with, allowing the emergence of naturally occurring drug-resistant mutations. Resistant organisms from affected patients may subsequently infect other people who have not been infected with *M. tuberculosis* previously, resulting in primary drug resistance.

Resistance to antituberculosis agents can develop not only in the strain that caused the initial disease, but also as a result of reinfection with a new strain of *M. tuberculosis* strain that is drug-resistant. Reinfection with a new multidrug-resistant *M. tuberculosis* can occur during therapy for the original infection or after completion of therapy. Most recent data suggest that outcomes can be improved if patients promptly begin therapy with two or more drugs that have *in vitro* activity against the multidrug-resistant isolate.

HIV infection is the strongest risk factor yet identified for the development of tuberculosis disease in persons infected with tuberculosis. In addition, persons with HIV infection are at an increased risk of tuberculosis resulting either from newly acquired disease or from reactivation of latent infections. Tuberculosis is a major clinical manifestation of immunodeficiency induced by HIV. In hospital-based retrospective studies, high rates of tuberculosis have been found among patients with AIDS. In communities where tuberculosis and HIV infection are common, the prevalence of HIV seropositivity among patients with tuberculosis is greatly increasing.

WHO has estimated that 5.6 million people worldwide and 80,000 people in the U.S. are infected with both HIV and tuberculosis. Persons dually infected with *M. tuberculosis* and HIV have a high risk of developing clinically active tuberculosis. One study of HIV-positive drug users with positive tuberculin skin test results found a rate of the development of active tuberculosis to be 8 cases per 100 person-years (8% yearly) as compared with the 10% lifetime risk (1 to 3% risk within the first year after skin test conversion) in the general population.

Persons who are known to be HIV-infected and who are contacts of patients with infectious tuberculosis should be carefully evaluated for evidence of tuberculosis. If there are no findings suggestive of current tuberculosis, preventive therapy with isoniazid should be given. Because HIV-infected contacts are not managed in the same way as those who are not HIV-infected, HIV testing is recommended if there are known or suspected risk factors for their acquiring HIV infection.

According to investigators at the National Institute of Allergy and Infectious Diseases (NIAID), levels of HIV in the bloodstream increase 5- to 160-fold in HIV-infected persons who develop active tuberculosis. Clinical and epidemiologic observations have demonstrated that HIV-infected individuals have an estimated 113-times higher risk and AIDS patients have a 170-times higher risk as compared with uninfected persons. Furthermore, the problem of drug resistance may worsen as the HIV epidemic spreads. Immunosuppressed patients with HIV infection who subsequently become infected with *M. tuberculosis* have an extraordinarily high risk of developing active tuberculosis within a short period of time.

In addition to the convincing evidence that HIV infection increases the risk and worsens the course of tuberculosis, there is increasing clinical evidence that coinfection with *M. tuberculosis* accelerates progression of disease caused by HIV infection. Understanding the interaction of these two pathogens is clinically important, given the high prevalence of patients coinfected with HIV and *M. tuberculosis* in both the U.S. and Africa; it is estimated that by the year 2000 about 500,000 deaths per year will occur in coinfected patients worldwide.

Persons with a positive tuberculin skin test and HIV infection, and persons with a positive tuberculin skin test and at risk of acquiring HIV infection with unknown HIV status should be considered for tuberculosis preventive therapy regardless of age. One study showed that isoniazid prophylaxis in HIV-infected, tuberculin-positive individuals not only decreased the incidence of tuberculosis disease, but also delayed the progression to AIDS and death.

Twelve months of preventive therapy is recommended for adults and children with HIV infection and other conditions associated with immunosuppression. Persons with HIV infection should receive at least 6 months of preventive therapy. The American Academy of Pediatrics recommends that children receive 9 months of therapy.

Tuberculosis control programs should ensure that drug susceptibility tests are performed on all initial isolates of *M. tuberculosis* and the results are reported promptly to the primary care provider and the local health department. Tuberculosis control programs should monitor local drug resistance rates to assess the effectiveness of local tuberculosis control efforts and to determine the appropriateness of the currently recommended initial tuberculosis treatment regimen for the area.

Relapse of rifampin-resistant tuberculosis has been reported in HIV-infected patients. Reinfection with new strains of *M. tuberculosis* has also been reported in these patients. Rifampin-resistant tuberculosis is a serious threat because responses to therapy are more difficult to achieve and require long courses of treatment. Therefore, careful follow-up of HIV-infected patients with treated tuberculosis is essential.

Multidrug-resistant tuberculosis also has been transmitted to persons without HIV infection in health care facilities. Together with the lack of effective agents for second-line treatment and methods of prophylaxis, the transmission of multidrug-resistant strains of *M. tuberculosis* may create a substantial reservoir of latently infected people and the potential for clinical multidrug-resistant tuberculosis for many years to come.

Several studies have documented a high prevalence of extrapulmonary disease in HIV-infected patients with clinical tuberculosis disease, particularly in conjunction with pulmonary manifestations. Cutaneous miliary tuberculosis, also known as *tuberculosis cutis miliaris disseminata*, was in the past a rare condition in adults, with only 24 cases reported in nearly a century. However, since the first reported case of cutaneous miliary tuberculosis in 1990 in a patient with AIDS, five additional cases have been reported in HIV-infected patients. Its appearance can be quite nondescript; therefore, a high level of suspicion must be maintained, particularly for patients with CD4+ cell counts of < 200 per cubic millimeter, in order to diagnose the condition and initiate therapy appropriately.

Accepted

Tuberculosis (treatment)—Pyrazinamide is indicated, in combination with other antimycobacterial drugs, in the treatment of tuberculosis. Pyrazinamide is effective only against mycobacteria.

Not all species or strains of a particular organism may be susceptible to pyrazinamide.

Unaccepted

Rifampin plus pyrazinamide generally should not be offered for treatment of latent tuberculosis infection [LTBI] for HIV-infected or HIV-negative persons, because of reports of an increased rate of hepatotoxicity with the rifampin-pyrazinamide regimen.

Pharmacology/Pharmacokinetics

Note: Preliminary data suggest that patients coinfected with the human immunodeficiency virus (HIV) and mycobacteria (*Mycobacterium tuberculosis* or *M. avium*) have altered pharmacokinetic profiles for antimycobacterial agents. In particular, malabsorption of these agents appears to occur frequently, and could seriously affect the efficacy of treatment.

Physicochemical characteristics

Molecular weight—123.11.

Mechanism of action/Effect

Unknown; pyrazinamide may be bacteriostatic or bactericidal, depending on its concentration and the susceptibility of the organism. It is active *in vitro* at an acidic pH of 5.6 or less, similar to that found in early, active tubercular inflammatory lesions.

Absorption

Rapidly and almost completely absorbed from the gastrointestinal tract.

Distribution

Wide, to most fluids and tissues, including liver, lungs, kidneys, and bile.

Pyrazinamide has excellent penetration into the cerebrospinal fluid (CSF), ranging from 87 to 105% of the corresponding serum concentration.

Vol_D—0.57 to 0.74 L per kg.

Protein binding

Pyrazinamide—Low (10 to 20%).
Pyrazinoic acid—Low (approximately 31%).

Biotransformation

Hepatic; hydrolyzed by a microsomal deamidase to pyrazinoic acid, an active metabolite, and then hydroxylated by xanthine oxidase to 5-hydroxypyrazinoic acid.

Half-life

Distribution—
- Approximately 1.6 hours.

Elimination—
- Pyrazinamide:
  - Normal renal function—Approximately 9.5 hours.
  - Chronic renal failure—Approximately 26 hours.
- Pyrazinoic acid:
  - Normal renal function—Approximately 12 hours.
  - Chronic renal failure—Approximately 22 hours.

Time to peak serum concentration

Pyrazinamide—1 to 2 hours.
Pyrazinoic acid—4 to 5 hours.

Peak serum concentration

Pyrazinamide—
- Approximately 19 mcg/mL after a single dose of 14 mg per kg of body weight (mg/kg).
- Approximately 39 mcg/mL after a single dose of 27 mg/kg.

Pyrazinoic acid—
- Approximately 3 mcg/mL after a single dose of 14 mg/kg.
- Approximately 4.5 mcg/mL after a single dose of 27 mg/kg.

Elimination

Renal; approximately 3% of unchanged pyrazinamide, 33% of pyrazinoic acid, and 36% of remaining identifiable metabolites excreted in urine within 72 hours.

In dialysis—A single 3- to 4-hour hemodialysis session reduced serum pyrazinamide concentrations by approximately 55% and pyrazinoic acid concentrations by 50 to 60%.

Precautions to Consider

Cross-sensitivity and/or related problems

Patients hypersensitive to ethionamide, isoniazid, niacin (nicotinic acid), or other chemically related medications may be hypersensitive to this medication also.

Carcinogenicity

Pyrazinamide was administered in the diets of rats and mice. The estimated daily dose was 2 grams per kg (grams/kg), or 40 times the maximum human dose, for the mouse, and 0.5 gram/kg, or 10 times the maximum human dose, for the rat. Pyrazinamide was not carcinogenic in rats or male mice. No conclusion was possible for female mice due to insufficient numbers of surviving control mice.

Mutagenicity

Pyrazinamide was not mutagenic in the Ames bacterial test, but it did induce chromosomal aberrations in human lymphocyte cell cultures.

Pregnancy/Reproduction

Note: Pregnant women with tuberculosis should be managed in concert with an expert in the management of tuberculosis. Women who have only pulmonary tuberculosis are not likely to infect the fetus until after delivery, and congenital tuberculosis is extremely rare. *In utero* infections with tubercle bacilli, however, can occur after maternal bacillemia occurs at different stages in the course of tuberculosis. Miliary tuberculosis can seed the placenta and thereby gain access to the fetal circulation. In women with tuberculous endometritis, transmission of infection to the fetus can result from fetal aspiration of bacilli at the time of delivery. A third mode of transmission is through ingestion of infected amniotic fluid *in utero*. If active disease is diagnosed during pregnancy, a 9-month regimen of isoniazid and rifampin, supplemented by an initial course of ethambutol if drug resistance is suspected, is recommended. Pyrazinamide usually is not given because of inadequate data regarding teratogenesis. Hence, a 9-month course of therapy is necessary for drug-susceptible disease. When isoniazid resistance is a possibility, isoniazid, ethambutol, and rifampin are recommended initially. One of these medications can be discontinued after 1 or 2 months, depending on results of susceptibility tests. If rifampin or isoniazid is discontinued, treatment is continued for a total of 18 months; if ethambutol is discontinued, treatment is continued for a total of 9 months. Prompt initiation of chemotherapy is mandatory to protect both the mother and fetus. If isoniazid or rifampin resistance is documented, an expert in the management of tuberculosis should be consulted.

Asymptomatic pregnant women with positive tuberculin skin tests and normal chest radiographs should receive preventive therapy with isoniazid for 9 months if they are HIV seropositive or have recently been in contact with an infectious person. For these individuals, preventive therapy should begin after the first trimester. In other circumstances in which none of these risk factors is present, although no harmful effects of isoniazid to the fetus have been observed, preventive therapy can be delayed until after delivery.

For all pregnant women receiving isoniazid, pyridoxine should be prescribed. Isoniazid, ethambutol, and rifampin appear to be relatively safe for the fetus. The benefit of ethambutol and rifampin for therapy of active disease in the mother outweighs the risk to the infant. Streptomycin and pyrazinamide should not be used unless they are essential to the control of the disease.

Pregnancy—Adequate and well-controlled studies in humans have not been done; the risk for teratogenicity has not been determined.

Animal reproduction studies have not been conducted with pyrazinamide.

FDA Pregnancy Category C.

Breast-feeding

Pyrazinamide is distributed into breast milk in small amounts.

Pediatrics

Note: If an infant is suspected of having congenital tuberculosis, a Mantoux tuberculin skin test, chest radiograph, lumbar puncture, and appropriate cultures should be performed promptly. Regardless of the skin test results, treatment of the infant should be initiated promptly with isoniazid, rifampin, pyrazinamide, and streptomycin or kanamycin. In addition, the mother should be evaluated for the presence of pulmonary or extrapulmonary (including uterine) tuberculosis. If the physical examination or chest radiograph support the diagnosis of tuberculosis, the patient should be treated with the same regimen as that used for tuberculous meningitis. The drug susceptibilities of the organism recovered from the mother and/or infant should be determined.

Possible isoniazid resistance should always be considered, particularly in children from population groups in which drug resistance is high, especially in foreign-born children from countries with a high prevalence of drug-resistant tuberculosis. For contacts who are likely to have been infected by an index case with isoniazid-resistant but rifampin-susceptible organisms, and in whom the consequences of the infection are likely to be severe (e.g., children up to 4 years of age), rifampin (10 mg per kg of body weight, maximum 600 mg, given daily in a single dose) should be given in addition to isoniazid (10 mg per kg, maximum 300 mg, given daily in a single dose) until susceptibility test results for the isolate from the index case are available. If the index case is known or proven to be excreting organisms resistant to isoniazid, then isoniazid should be discontinued and rifampin given for a total of 9 months. Isoniazid alone should be given if no proof of exposure to isoniazid-resistant organisms is found. Optimal therapy for children with tuberculosis infection caused by organisms resistant to isoniazid and rifampin is unknown. In deciding on therapy in this situation, consultation with an expert is advised.

Adjuvant treatment with corticosteroids in treating tuberculosis is controversial. Corticosteroids have been used for therapy in children with tuberculous meningitis to reduce vasculitis, inflammation, and, as a result, intracranial pressure. Data indicate that dexamethasone may lower mortality rates and lessen long-term neurologic impairment. The administration of corticosteroids should be considered in all children with tuberculous meningitis, and also may be considered in children with pleural and pericardial effusions (to hasten reabsorption of fluid), severe miliary disease (to mitigate alveolocapillary block), and endobronchial disease (to relieve obstruction and atelectasis). Corticosteroids should be given only when accompanied by appropriate antituberculosis therapy. Consultation with an expert in the treatment of tuberculosis should be obtained when corticosteroid therapy is considered.

Appropriate studies on the relationship of age to the effects of pyrazinamide have not been performed in the pediatric population. However, no pediatrics-specific problems have been documented to date.

Geriatrics

Appropriate studies on the relationship of age to the effects of pyrazinamide have not been performed in the geriatric population. However, no geriatrics-specific problems have been documented to date.

Drug interactions and/or related problems

The following drug interactions and/or related problems have been selected on the basis of their potential clinical significance (possible mechanism in parentheses where appropriate)—not necessarily inclusive (» = major clinical significance):

Note: Combinations containing any of the following medications, depending on the amount present, may also interact with this medication.

Allopurinol or
Colchicine or
Probenecid or
Sulfinpyrazone
(pyrazinamide may increase serum uric acid concentrations and decrease the efficacy of antigout therapy; dosage adjustments of these medications may be necessary to control hyperuricemia and gout when antigout medications are used concurrently with pyrazinamide)

Cyclosporine
(concurrent use with pyrazinamide may decrease the serum concentrations of cyclosporine, possibly leading to inadequate immunosuppression; cyclosporine serum concentrations should be monitored)

Laboratory value alterations

The following have been selected on the basis of their potential clinical significance (possible effect in parentheses where appropriate)—not necessarily inclusive (» = major clinical significance).

With diagnostic test results

Ketone determinations, urine
(may react with sodium nitroprusside tests, such as *Acetest* or *Chemstrip K;* both pyrazinamide and pyrazinoic acid produce an interfering pink-brown color reaction with nitroprusside)

With physiology/laboratory test values

Alanine aminotransferase (ALT [SGPT]) and
Aspartate aminotransferase (AST [SGOT])
(values may be increased)

Uric acid, serum
(concentration may be increased)

Medical considerations/Contraindications

The medical considerations/contraindications included have been selected on the basis of their potential clinical significance (reasons given in parentheses where appropriate)—not necessarily inclusive (» = major clinical significance).

Risk-benefit should be considered when the following medical problems exist:

Gout, history of
(pyrazinamide can increase serum uric acid concentrations and precipitate an acute attack of gout)

» Hepatic function impairment, severe
(pyrazinamide is metabolized in the liver and, in high doses, can be hepatotoxic)

» Hypersensitivity to pyrazinamide, ethionamide, isoniazid, niacin (nicotinic acid), or other chemically related medications

Patient monitoring

The following may be especially important in patient monitoring (other tests may be warranted in some patients, depending on condition; » = major clinical significance):

Hepatic function determinations
(AST [SGOT] and ALT [SGPT] determinations may be required prior to and every 2 to 4 weeks during treatment; however, elevated serum enzyme values may not be predictive of clinical hepatitis and values may return to normal despite continued treatment; patients with impaired hepatic function should not receive pyrazinamide unless it is crucial to therapy)

Uric acid concentrations, serum
(may be required during treatment since elevated serum uric acid concentrations frequently occur, possibly precipitating acute gout)

Side/Adverse Effects

The following side/adverse effects have been selected on the basis of their potential clinical significance (possible signs and symptoms in parentheses where appropriate)—not necessarily inclusive:

Those indicating need for medical attention

Incidence more frequent

Arthralgia (pain in the large and small joints)—related to hyperuricemia; usually mild and self-limiting

Incidence rare

Gouty arthritis (pain and swelling of joints, especially big toe, ankle, and knee; tense, hot skin over affected joints); ***hepatotoxicity*** (loss of appetite; unusual tiredness or weakness; yellow eyes or skin)—related to large doses, i.e., 40 to 50 mg per kg of body weight per day for prolonged periods of time

Those indicating need for medical attention only if they continue or are bothersome

Incidence rare

Itching; skin rash

Patient Consultation

As an aid to patient consultation, refer to *Advice for the Patient, Pyrazinamide (Systemic).*

In providing consultation, consider emphasizing the following selected information (» = major clinical significance):

Before using this medication

» Conditions affecting use, especially:
Hypersensitivity to pyrazinamide, ethionamide, isoniazid, niacin (nicotinic acid), or other chemically related medications
Breast-feeding—Pyrazinamide is distributed into breast milk
Other medical problems, especially severe hepatic function impairment

Proper use of this medication

» Compliance with full course of therapy, which may take months
» Proper dosing
Missed dose: Taking as soon as possible; not taking if almost time for next dose; not doubling doses
» Proper storage

Precautions while using this medication

» Regular visits to physician to check progress

Checking with physician if no improvement within 2 to 3 weeks

» Diabetics: May interfere with urine ketone determinations

Side/adverse effects

Signs of side effects, especially arthralgia, gouty arthritis, and hepatotoxicity

General Dosing Information

Since bacterial resistance may develop rapidly when pyrazinamide is administered alone in the treatment of tuberculosis, it only should be administered concurrently with other antitubercular medications.

The duration of treatment with an antituberculosis regimen is at least 6 months, and may be continued for 2 years. Uncomplicated pulmonary tuberculosis is often successfully treated within 6 to 12 months. Several different treatment regimens are currently recommended.

The duration of antituberculosis therapy is based on the patient's clinical and radiographic responses, smear and culture results, and susceptibility studies of *Mycobacterium tuberculosis* isolates from the patient or the suspect source case. With directly observed therapy (DOT), clinical evaluation is an integral component of each visit for administration of medication. Careful monitoring of the clinical and bacteriologic responses to therapy on a monthly basis in sputum-positive patients is important.

If therapy is interrupted, the treatment schedule should be extended to a later completion date. Although guidelines cannot be provided for every situation, the following factors need to be considered in establishing a new date for completion:
• The length of interruption;
• The time during therapy (early or late) in which interruption occurred; and
• The patient's clinical, radiographic, and bacteriologic status before, during, and after interruption. Consultation with an expert is advised.

Therapy should be administered based on the following guidelines, published by the American Thoracic Society (ATS) and by the Centers for Disease Control and Prevention (CDC), and endorsed by the American Academy of Pediatrics (AAP).
• A 6-month regimen consisting of isoniazid, rifampin, and pyrazinamide given for 2 months followed by isoniazid and rifampin for 4 months is the preferred treatment for patients infected with fully susceptible organisms who adhere to the treatment course.
• Ethambutol (or streptomycin in children too young to be monitored for visual acuity) should be included in the initial regimen until the results of drug susceptibility studies are available, and unless there is little possibility of drug resistance (i.e., there is less than 4% primary resistance to isoniazid in the community, and the patient has had no previous treatment with antituberculosis medications, is not from a country with a high prevalence of drug resistance, and has no known exposure to a drug-resistant case).
• Alternatively, a 9-month regimen of isoniazid and rifampin is acceptable for persons who cannot or should not take pyrazinamide. Ethambutol (or streptomycin in children too young to be monitored for visual acuity) should also be included until the results of drug susceptibility studies are available, unless there is little possibility of drug resistance. If isoniazid resistance is demonstrated, rifampin and ethambutol should be continued for a minimum of 12 months.
• Consideration should be given to treating all patients with DOT. DOT programs have been demonstrated to increase adherence in patients receiving antituberculosis chemotherapy in both rural and urban settings.
• Multidrug-resistant tuberculosis (i.e., resistance to at least isoniazid and rifampin) presents difficult treatment problems. Treatment must be individualized and based on susceptibility studies. In such cases, consultation with an expert in tuberculosis is recommended.
• Children should be managed in essentially the same ways as adults, but doses of the medications must be adjusted appropriately and specific important differences between the management of adults and children addressed. However, optimal therapy of tuberculosis in children with HIV infection has not been established. The Committee on Infectious Diseases of the AAP recommends that therapy always should include at least three drugs initially, and should be continued for a minimum period of 9 months. Isoniazid, rifampin, and pyrazinamide with or without ethambutol or an aminoglycoside should be given for at least the first 2 months. A fourth drug may be needed for disseminated disease and whenever drug-resistant disease is suspected.
• Extrapulmonary tuberculosis should be managed according to the principles and with the drug regimens outlined for pulmonary tuberculosis, except in children who have miliary tuberculosis, bone/joint tuberculosis, or tuberculous meningitis. These children should receive a minimum of 12 months of therapy.
• A 4-month regimen of isoniazid and rifampin is acceptable therapy for adults who have active tuberculosis and who are sputum smear– and culture–negative, if there is little possibility of drug resistance.

ATS, CDC, and AAP recommend preventive treatment of tuberculosis infection in the following patients:
• Preventive therapy with isoniazid given for 6 to 12 months is effective in decreasing the risk of future tuberculosis disease in adults and children with tuberculosis infection demonstrated by a positive tuberculin skin test reaction.
• Persons with a positive skin test and any of the following risk factors should be considered for preventive therapy regardless of age:
—Persons with HIV infection.
—Persons at risk for HIV infection with unknown HIV status.
—Close contacts of sputum-positive persons with newly diagnosed infectious tuberculosis.
—Newly infected persons (recent skin test convertors).
—Persons with medical conditions reported to increase the risk of tuberculosis (i.e., diabetes mellitus, corticosteroid therapy and other immunosuppressive therapy, intravenous drug users, hematologic and reticuloendothelial malignancies, end-stage renal disease, and clinical conditions associated with rapid weight loss or chronic malnutrition).
In some circumstances, persons with negative skin tests should be considered for preventive therapy. These include children who are close contacts of infectious tuberculosis cases and anergic HIV-infected adults at increased risk of tuberculosis, tuberculin-positive adults with abnormal chest radiographs showing fibrotic lesions probably representing old healed tuberculosis, adults with silicosis, and persons who are known to be HIV-infected and who are contacts of patients with infectious tuberculosis.
• In the absence of any of the above risk factors, persons up to 35 years of age with a positive skin test who are in the following high-incidence groups should be also considered for preventive therapy:
—Foreign-born persons from high-prevalence countries.
—Medically underserved low-income persons from high-prevalence populations (especially blacks, Hispanics, and Native Americans).
—Residents of facilities for long-term care (e.g., correctional institutions, nursing homes, and mental institutions).
• Twelve months of preventive therapy is recommended for adults and children with HIV infection and other conditions associated with immunosuppression. Persons without HIV infection should receive preventive therapy for at least 6 months.
• In persons younger than 35 years of age, routine monitoring for adverse effects of isoniazid should consist of a monthly symptom review. For persons 35 years of age and older, hepatic enzymes should be measured prior to starting isoniazid and monitored monthly throughout treatment, in addition to monthly symptom reviews.
• Persons who are presumed to be infected with isoniazid-resistant organisms should be treated with rifampin rather than with isoniazid.
• As with the treatment of active tuberculosis, the key to success of preventive treatment is patient adherence to the prescribed regimen. Although not evaluated in clinical studies, directly observed, twice-weekly preventive therapy may be appropriate for adults and children at risk, who cannot or will not reliably self-administer therapy.

Rifampin is an essential component of the currently recommended regimen for treating tuberculosis. This regimen is effective in treating HIV-infected patients with tuberculosis, and consists of isoniazid and rifampin for a minimum period of 6 months, plus pyrazinamide and either ethambutol or streptomycin for the first 2 months.

Because of the common association of tuberculosis with HIV infection, an increasing number of patients probably will be considered candidates for combined therapy with rifampin and protease inhibitors. Prompt initiation of appropriate pharmacologic therapy for patients with HIV infection who acquire tuberculosis is critical because tuberculosis may become rapidly fatal. The management of these patients is complex, requires an individualized approach, and should be undertaken only by or in consultation with an expert. In addition, all HIV-infected patients at risk for tuberculosis infection should be carefully evaluated and administered isoniazid preventive treatment if indicated, regardless of whether they are receiving protease inhibitor therapy.

For HIV-infected patients diagnosed with drug-susceptible tuberculosis and for whom protease inhibitor therapy is being considered but has not been initiated, the suggested management strategy is to complete tuberculosis treatment with a regimen containing rifampin before starting therapy with a protease inhibitor. The duration of antituberculosis regimen is at least 6 months, and therapy should be administered according to the guidelines developed by ATS and CDC, including the recommendation to carefully assess clinical and bacteriologic responses in patients coinfected with HIV and to prolong treatment if response is slow or suboptimal.

Health care or correctional institutions experiencing outbreaks of tuberculosis that are resistant to isoniazid and rifampin, or are resuming therapy for a patient with a prior history of antitubercular therapy, may need to begin five- or six-drug regimens as initial therapy. These regimens should include the four-drug regimen and at least three medications to which the suspected multidrug-resistant strain may be susceptible.

Most infants ≤ 12 months of age with tuberculosis are asymptomatic at the time of diagnosis, and the gastric aspirate cultures in these patients have a high yield for *M. tuberculosis*. When an infant is suspected of having tuberculosis, a thorough household investigation should be undertaken. A 6-month regimen of isoniazid and rifampin supplemented during the first 2 months by pyrazinamide has been found to be well-tolerated and effective in infants with pulmonary tuberculosis. Furthermore, twice-weekly DOT appears to be as effective as daily therapy, and is an essential alternative in patients for whom social issues prevent reliable daily therapy.

Physicians caring for children should be familiar with the clinical forms of the disease in infants to enable them to make an early diagnosis. Any child, especially one in a high-risk group or area, who has unexplained pneumonia, cervical adenitis, bone or joint infections, or aseptic meningitis should have a Mantoux tuberculin skin test performed, and a detailed epidemiologic history for tuberculosis should be obtained.

Management of a newborn infant whose mother, or other household contact, is suspected of having tuberculosis is based on individual considerations. If possible, separation of the mother, or contact, and infant should be minimized. The Committee on Infectious Diseases of the AAP offers the following recommendations in the management of the newborn infant whose mother, or any other household contact, has tuberculosis:

• *Mother, or any other household contact, with a positive tuberculin skin test reaction but no evidence of current disease:* Investigation of other members of the household or extended family to whom the infant may later be exposed is indicated. If no evidence of current disease is found in the mother or in members of the extended family, the infant should be tested with a Mantoux tuberculin skin test at 3 to 4 months of age. When the family members cannot be promptly tested, consideration should be given to administering isoniazid (10 mg per kg of body weight a day) to the infant until skin testing and other evaluation of the family members have excluded contact with a case of active tuberculosis. The infant does not need to be hospitalized during this time if adequate follow-up can be arranged, but adherence to medication administration should be closely monitored. The mother also should be considered for isoniazid therapy.

• *Mother with untreated (newly diagnosed) disease or disease that has been treated for 2 or more weeks and who is judged to be noncontagious at delivery:* Careful investigation of household members and extended family is mandatory. A chest radiograph and Mantoux tuberculin skin test should be performed on the infant at 3 to 4 months and at 6 months of age. Separation of the mother and infant is not necessary if adherence to treatment for the mother and infant is assured. The mother can breast-feed. The infant should receive isoniazid even if the tuberculin skin test and chest radiograph do not suggest clinical tuberculosis, since cell-mediated immunity of a degree sufficient to mount a significant reaction to tuberculin skin testing may develop as late as 6 months of age in an infant infected at birth. Isoniazid can be discontinued if the Mantoux skin test is negative at 3 to 4 months of age, the mother is adherent to treatment and has a satisfactory clinical response, and no other family members have infectious tuberculosis. The infant should be examined carefully at monthly intervals. If nonadherence is documented, the mother has an acid-fast bacillus (AFB)–positive sputum or smear, and supervision is impossible, the infant should be separated from the ill family member and Bacillus Calmette-Guérin (BCG) vaccine may be considered for the infant. However, the response to the vaccine in infants may be delayed and inadequate for prevention of tuberculosis.

• *Mother has current disease and is suspected of having been contagious at the time of delivery:* The mother and infant should be separated until the infant is receiving therapy or the mother is confirmed to be noncontagious. Otherwise, management is the same as when the disease is judged to be noncontagious to the infant at delivery.

• *Mother has hematogenously spread tuberculosis (e.g., meningitis, miliary disease, or bone involvement):* The infant should be evaluated for congenital tuberculosis. If clinical and radiographic findings do not support the diagnosis of congenital tuberculosis, the infant should be separated from the mother until she is judged to be noncontagious. The infant should be given isoniazid until 3 or 4 months of age, at which time the Mantoux skin test should be repeated. If the skin test is positive, isoniazid should be continued for a total of 12 months. If the skin test is negative and the chest radiograph is normal, isoniazid may be discontinued, depending on the status of the mother and whether there are other cases of infectious tuberculosis in the family. The infant should continue to be examined carefully at monthly intervals.

Patients with impaired renal function do not require a reduction in dose; however, patients on hemodialysis should receive the usual dose at the end of each dialysis session.

Oral Dosage Forms

PYRAZINAMIDE TABLETS USP

Usual adult and adolescent dose

Tuberculosis—

In combination with other antitubercular drugs: Oral, 15 to 30 mg per kg of body weight once a day; or 50 to 70 mg per kg of body weight two or three times a week, depending on the treatment regimen.

Note: The usual dose of pyrazinamide for persons infected with human immunodeficiency virus (HIV) is 20 to 30 mg per kg of body weight per day for the first two months of therapy.

Usual adult prescribing limits

A maximum of 2 grams when taken daily, 3 grams per dose for the three times a week regimen, 4 grams per dose for the two times a week regimen.

Usual pediatric dose

See *Usual adult and adolescent dose.*

Note: The usual maximum dose in children is 2 grams when taken daily, 3 grams per dose for the three times a week regimen, 4 grams per dose for the two times a week regimen.

Strength(s) usually available

U.S.—

500 mg (Rx) [GENERIC].

Canada—

500 mg (Rx) [*pms-Pyrazinamide; Tebrazid*].

Packaging and storage

Store below 40 °C (104 °F), preferably between 15 and 30 °C (59 and 86 °F), unless otherwise specified by the manufacturer. Store in a well-closed container.

Auxiliary labeling

• Continue medicine for full time of treatment.

Selected Bibliography

The American Thoracic Society (ATS). Ad Hoc Committee on the Scientific Assembly on Microbiology, Tuberculosis, and Pulmonary Infections. Treatment of tuberculosis and tuberculosis infection in adults and children. Clin Infect Dis 1995; 21: 9-27

Revised: 11/10/2003

PYRETHRINS AND PIPERONYL BUTOXIDE Topical

VA CLASSIFICATION (Primary): AP300

Commonly used brand name(s): *A-200 Gel Concentrate; A-200 Shampoo Concentrate; Barc; Blue; Licetrol; Pronto Lice Killing Shampoo Kit; Pyrinyl; R & C; Rid; Tisit; Tisit Blue; Tisit Shampoo; Triple X.*

Note: For a listing of dosage forms and brand names by country availability, see *Dosage Forms* section(s).

Category

Pediculicide.

Indications

Accepted

Pediculosis corporis (treatment)
Pediculosis capitis (treatment) or
Pediculosis pubis (treatment)—Pyrethrins and piperonyl butoxide combination is indicated for the treatment of pediculosis (lice) infestations caused by *Pediculus humanus* var. *corporis* (body louse), *P. humanus* var. *capitis* (head louse), and *Phthirus pubis* (pubic or crab louse).

Pharmacology/Pharmacokinetics

Physicochemical characteristics

Source—

Pyrethrins: Obtained from flowers of the pyrethrum plant, *Chrysanthemum cinerariaefolium,* which is related to the ragweed plant; esters formed by the combination of chrysanthenic and pyrethric acids and pyrethrolone, cinerolone, and jasmolone alcohols.

Piperonyl butoxide: A synthetic piperic acid derivative.

Mechanism of action/Effect

Pyrethrins—Are absorbed through the chitinous exoskeleton of arthropods and stimulate the nervous system, probably by competitively interfering with cationic conductances in the lipid layer of nerve cells, thereby blocking nerve impulse transmissions, which results in paralysis and death.

Piperonyl butoxide—Has little or no insecticidal activity but potentiates that of pyrethrins by inhibiting the hydrolytic enzymes responsible for metabolism of pyrethrins in arthropods, thereby increasing the insecticidal activity of pyrethrins by 2 to 12 times.

Absorption

Pyrethrins and piperonyl butoxide are poorly absorbed through intact skin when applied topically; if pyrethrins are absorbed, they are rapidly metabolized in mammals.

Precautions to Consider

Cross-sensitivity and/or related problems

Patients allergic to the ragweed or chrysanthemum plant may be allergic to the pyrethrins in this medication also.

Patients sensitive to kerosene may also be sensitive to the pyrethrins and piperonyl butoxide combination preparations that contain kerosene.

Pregnancy/Reproduction

Pregnancy—Problems in humans have not been documented; however, pyrethrins and piperonyl butoxide may be absorbed systemically in small amounts through intact skin.

Breast-feeding

Problems in humans have not been documented; however, pyrethrins and piperonyl butoxide may be absorbed systemically in small amounts through intact skin.

Pediatrics

Appropriate studies on the relationship of age to the effects of pyrethrins and piperonyl butoxide have not been performed in the pediatric population. However, no pediatrics-specific problems have been documented to date.

Geriatrics

Appropriate studies on the relationship of age to the effects of pyrethrins and piperonyl butoxide have not been performed in the geriatric population. However, no geriatrics-specific problems have been documented to date.

Medical considerations/Contraindications

The medical considerations/contraindications included have been selected on the basis of their potential clinical significance (reasons given in parentheses where appropriate)—not necessarily inclusive (» = major clinical significance).

Risk-benefit should be considered when the following medical problems exist:

Inflammation of skin, acute
(condition may be exacerbated)

Sensitivity to pyrethrins or piperonyl butoxide

Side/Adverse Effects

Note: Pyrethrins and piperonyl butoxide combination applied topically in recommended dosage appears to be relatively free of the risk of causing systemic toxicity.

When pyrethrins are injected or inhaled, they can cause nausea, vomiting, muscle paralysis, and even death; however, severe poisoning from pyrethrins is rare.

Piperonyl butoxide has been reported to cause nausea, vomiting, diarrhea, central nervous system (CNS) depression, and hemorrhagic enteritis when large amounts are ingested orally.

The following side/adverse effects have been selected on the basis of their potential clinical significance (possible signs and symptoms in parentheses where appropriate)—not necessarily inclusive:

Those indicating need for medical attention

Incidence less frequent or rare

Allergic reaction (skin rash; sudden attacks of sneezing; stuffy or runny nose; wheezing or difficulty in breathing); ***skin infection; skin irritation not present before therapy***

Patient Consultation

As an aid to patient consultation, refer to *Advice for the Patient, Pyrethrins and Piperonyl Butoxide (Topical).*

In providing consultation, consider emphasizing the following selected information (» = major clinical significance):

Before using this medication

» Conditions affecting use, especially:
  Allergy to ragweed or chrysanthemum plants or sensitivity to pyrethrins, piperonyl butoxide, or kerosene or other petroleum products

Proper use of this medication

» Importance of not using more medication than the amount recommended
» Importance of keeping away from mouth and not inhaling; harmful if swallowed or inhaled
» Applying in a well-ventilated room to minimize possibility of inhalation
» Avoiding contact with the eyes and mucous membranes, such as the inside of the nose, mouth, or vagina; flushing eyes thoroughly with water if medication accidentally gets in eyes
» Not using on eyelashes or eyebrows; checking with physician if they become infested

Proper administration

Reading patient directions carefully before using
Applying sufficient amount to thoroughly wet the dry hair and scalp or skin of affected areas
Allowing to remain on affected areas for exactly 10 minutes
Then
  For gel and solution dosage forms: Thoroughly washing affected areas with warm water and soap or regular shampoo
  For shampoo dosage form: Using small amount of water and working shampoo into the hair and scalp or skin until a lather forms
Rinsing thoroughly; drying with clean towel
Using nit removal comb to remove dead lice and eggs from hair
Washing hands immediately after using medication
Repeating treatment once in 7 to 10 days to kill any newly hatched lice

» Importance of all members of household being examined for infestation, and treated if infested
Importance of concurrent treatment of sexual partner in pediculosis pubis
» Proper dosing
» Proper storage

Precautions while using this medication

Using hygienic measures to control reinfestation or spread of infestation:

For head lice

Machine washing all clothing (including hats, scarves, and coats), bedding, towels, and washcloths in very hot water and drying them by using hot cycle of dryer for at least 20 minutes; for clothing or bedding not washable, dry-cleaning or sealing in a plastic bag for 2 weeks

Shampooing all wigs and hairpieces

Washing hairbrushes and combs in very hot soapy water (at least 130 °F) for 5 to 10 minutes; not sharing them with other people

Cleaning house or room by thoroughly vacuuming upholstered furniture, rugs, and floors

For body lice

Machine washing all clothing, bedding, towels, and washcloths in very hot water and drying them by using hot cycle of dryer for at least 20 minutes; for clothing or bedding not washable, dry-cleaning or sealing in a plastic bag for 2 weeks

Cleaning house or room by thoroughly vacuuming upholstered furniture, rugs, and floors

For pubic lice

Machine washing all clothing (especially underwear), bedding, towels, and washcloths in very hot water and drying them by using hot cycle of dryer for at least 20 minutes; for clothing or bedding not washable, dry-cleaning or sealing in a plastic bag for 2 weeks

Scrubbing toilet seats frequently

Side/adverse effects

Signs of potential side effects, especially allergic reaction, skin infection, or skin irritation not present before therapy

General Dosing Information

Following the initial treatment, a second treatment should be made in 7 to 10 days to kill any newly hatched lice.

When used in the treatment of pediculosis pubis (pubic or crab lice), the sexual partner should receive concurrent therapy, since the infestation may spread to persons in close contact.

For treatment of systemic toxicity

- For accidental ingestion—Primarily supportive treatment; induction of vomiting if patient is conscious; gastric lavage if patient is unconscious. Saline cathartics may be administered to minimize absorption of pyrethrins and piperonyl butoxide.
- For accidental inhalation—Artificial respiration, if necessary.

Topical Dosage Forms

PYRETHRINS AND PIPERONYL BUTOXIDE GEL

Usual adult and adolescent dose

Pediculicide—

Topical, to the hair and scalp or skin, for one application, repeated once in seven to ten days.

Usual adult prescribing limits

No more than two applications within twenty-four hours.

Usual pediatric dose

See *Usual adult and adolescent dose.*

Strength(s) usually available

U.S.—

0.18% pyrethrins, 2.2% piperonyl butoxide technical (equivalent to 1.76% [butylcarbityl] [6-propylpiperonyl] ether and 0.44% related compounds), and 4.80% petroleum distillate (OTC) [*Barc*].

0.3% pyrethrins, 3% piperonyl butoxide technical (equivalent to 2.4% [butylcarbityl] [6-propylpiperonyl] ether and 0.6% related compounds), and 1.2% petroleum distillate (OTC) [*Blue; Tisit Blue*].

0.33% pyrethrins, 4% piperonyl butoxide technical (equivalent to 3.2% [butylcarbityl] [6-propylpiperonyl] ether and 0.8% related compounds) (OTC) [*A-200 Gel Concentrate* (benzyl alcohol)].

Canada—

Not commercially available.

Packaging and storage

Store below 40 °C (104 °F), preferably between 15 and 30 °C (59 and 86 °F), in a well-closed container, unless otherwise specified by manufacturer. Protect from freezing.

Auxiliary labeling

- For external use only.
- Harmful if swallowed or inhaled.

Note

When dispensing, include patient instructions.

PYRETHRINS AND PIPERONYL BUTOXIDE SOLUTION SHAMPOO

Usual adult and adolescent dose

See *Pyrethrins and Piperonyl Butoxide Gel.*

Usual adult prescribing limits

See *Pyrethrins and Piperonyl Butoxide Gel.*

Usual pediatric dose

See *Usual adult and adolescent dose.*

Strength(s) usually available

U.S.—

0.3% pyrethrins, 3% piperonyl butoxide technical (equivalent to 2.4% [butylcarbityl] [6-propylpiperonyl] ether and 0.6% related compounds), and 1.2% petroleum distillate (OTC) [*R & C*].

0.3% pyrethrins, 3% piperonyl butoxide technical (equivalent to 2.4% [butylcarbityl] [6-propylpiperonyl] ether and 0.6% related compounds), 1.2% petroleum distillate, and 2.4% benzyl alcohol (OTC) [*Triple X*].

0.33% pyrethrins, 4% piperonyl butoxide technical (equivalent to 3.2% [butylcarbityl] [6-propylpiperonyl] ether and 0.8% related compounds) (OTC) [*A-200 Shampoo Concentrate* (benzyl alcohol); *Pronto Lice Killing Shampoo Kit*].

Canada—

0.3% pyrethrins, 3% piperonyl butoxide technical (equivalent to 2.4% [butylcarbityl] [6-propylpiperonyl] ether and 0.6% related compounds), and 1.2% petroleum distillate (OTC) [*R & C*].

Packaging and storage

Store below 40 °C (104 °F), preferably between 15 and 30 °C (59 and 86 °F), in a well-closed container, unless otherwise specified by manufacturer. Protect from freezing.

Auxiliary labeling

- For external use only.
- Harmful if swallowed or inhaled.

Note

When dispensing, include patient instructions.

PYRETHRINS AND PIPERONYL BUTOXIDE TOPICAL SOLUTION

Usual adult and adolescent dose

See *Pyrethrins and Piperonyl Butoxide Gel.*

Usual adult prescribing limits

See *Pyrethrins and Piperonyl Butoxide Gel.*

Usual pediatric dose

See *Usual adult and adolescent dose.*

Strength(s) usually available

U.S.—

0.18% pyrethrins, 2.2% piperonyl butoxide (equivalent to 1.76% [butylcarbityl] [6-propylpiperonyl] ether and 0.44% related compounds), and 5.52% petroleum distillate (OTC) [*Barc*].

0.2% pyrethrins, 2% piperonyl butoxide technical (equivalent to 1.6% [butylcarbityl] [6-propylpiperonyl] ether and 0.4% related compounds), and 0.8% deodorized kerosene or petroleum distillate (OTC) [*Licetrol; Pyrinyl*].

0.3% pyrethrins and 2% piperonyl butoxide technical (equivalent to 1.6% [butylcarbityl] [6-propylpiperonyl] ether and 0.4% related compounds) (OTC) [*Tisit*].

0.3% pyrethrins, 3% piperonyl butoxide technical (equivalent to 2.4% [butylcarbityl] [6-propylpiperonyl] ether and 0.6% related compounds), 1.2% petroleum distillate, and 2.4% benzyl alcohol (OTC) [*Rid; Tisit Shampoo*].

Canada—

Not commercially available.

Packaging and storage

Store below 40 °C (104 °F), preferably between 15 and 30 °C (59 and 86 °F), in a well-closed container, unless otherwise specified by manufacturer. Protect from freezing.

Auxiliary labeling

- For external use only.
- Harmful if swallowed or inhaled.

Note

When dispensing, include patient instructions.

Revised: 02/18/1994

PYRIDOSTIGMINE—See *Antimyasthenics (Systemic)*

QUAZEPAM—See *Benzodiazepines (Systemic)*

QUETIAPINE Systemic

VA CLASSIFICATION (Primary): CN709

Commonly used brand name(s): *Seroquel*.

Note: For a listing of dosage forms and brand names by country availability, see *Dosage Forms* section(s).

Category

Antipsychotic.

Indications

Accepted

Psychotic disorders (treatment)—Quetiapine is indicated for the treatment of the manifestations of psychotic disorders including schizophrenia. The effectiveness of quetiapine for more than 6 weeks has not been evaluated in controlled trials.

Unaccepted

Quetiapine is not approved for the treatment of behavioral symptoms in elderly patients with dementia.

Pharmacology/Pharmacokinetics

Physicochemical characteristics

Chemical Group—Dibenzothiazepine derivative.
Molecular weight—Quetiapine fumarate: 883.11.
Solubility—Quetiapine fumarate is moderately soluble in water.

Mechanism of action/Effect

The exact mechanism by which quetiapine exerts its antipsychotic effect is unknown. However, this effect may be mediated through antagonism of dopamine type 2 (D_2) and serotonin type 2 ($5\text{-}HT_2$) receptors.

Quetiapine is an antagonist at serotonin $5\text{-}HT_{1A}$ and $5\text{-}HT_2$, dopamine D_1 and D_2, histamine H_1, and adrenergic $alpha_1$ and $alpha_2$ receptors. Quetiapine has no significant affinity for cholinergic muscarinic or benzodiazepine receptors. Drowsiness and orthostatic hypotension associated with use of quetiapine may be explained by its antagonism of histamine H_1 and adrenergic $alpha_1$ receptors, respectively.

Other actions/effects

In clinical trials, quetiapine produced a dose-related decrease in total and free thyroxine (T_4) concentrations. This decrease was apparent early in treatment with quetiapine, and no further changes occurred during continued therapy. At the high end of the quetiapine therapeutic dosage range, total and free thyroxine concentrations were decreased by about 20%. About 0.4% (10/2386) of patients in clinical trials experienced increases in thyroid-stimulating hormone (TSH) concentrations and six of these patients required thyroid hormone replacement therapy.

Prolactin concentration increases, which were associated with an increased incidence of mammary gland neoplasia, were seen in rat studies with quetiapine. However, prolactin concentration increases were not demonstrated in human clinical trials.

Cataracts developed in the eyes of dogs during chronic quetiapine dosing. Also, changes in the lenses of the eyes have been observed in patients during long-term quetiapine therapy, although a causal relationship to quetiapine has not been established.

It is thought that quetiapine may have an anti-emetic effect, consistent with its antagonism of dopaminergic receptors.

Absorption

Rapidly and well absorbed. Food increases peak plasma concentration (C_{max}) and area under the plasma concentration-time curve (AUC) by 25% and 15%, respectively.

Distribution

Extensively distributed throughout the body, with an apparent volume of distribution (Vol_D) of 10 ± 4 L/kg.

Protein binding

High (83%) to plasma proteins; does not alter the binding of warfarin or diazepam to human serum albumin *in vitro* and quetiapine binding is not altered *in vitro* by warfarin or diazepam.

Biotransformation

Quetiapine is extensively metabolized in the liver. Less than 5% of an orally administered dose is excreted unchanged. The major metabolic pathways are sulfoxidation, which *in vitro* studies indicate is mediated by the cytochrome P450 3A4 (CYP3A4) isoenzyme, and oxidation. The major metabolites of quetiapine are inactive.

Half-life

Elimination—
Mean, about 6 to 7 hours.

Time to peak concentration

Peak plasma concentration is reached within 2 hours of dosing.

Pharmacokinetic parameters

The pharmacokinetics of quetiapine are linear within the clinical dose range of 50 to 600 mg/day, and are similar in both genders and in smokers and nonsmokers.

Elimination

Renal—
Approximately 73% of an orally administered dose is excreted renally.
Fecal—
Approximately 20% of an orally administered dose is excreted in the feces.

Precautions to Consider

Carcinogenicity/Tumorigenicity

Statistically significant increases in the incidence of thyroid gland follicular cell adenomas were seen in male mice receiving quetiapine at daily dosages that were equivalent to 1.5 and 4.5 times the maximum recommended human dose (MRHD) on a mg per square meter of body surface area (mg/m^2) basis and in male rats receiving three times the MRHD on a mg/m^2 basis, possibly as a result of chronic stimulation of the thyroid gland by thyroid-stimulating hormone (TSH). Although the results were not definitive, quetiapine toxicity studies in rats and mice showed changes in thyroxine concentrations, thyroxine clearance, and TSH concentrations that are consistent with the proposed mechanism of increased thyroxine clearance leading to increased TSH concentrations and increased thyroid gland stimulation.

Statistically significant increases in the incidence of mammary gland adenocarcinomas were seen in female rats receiving quetiapine at daily dosages that were equivalent to 0.3 to 3 times the MRHD on a mg/m^2 basis. In a 1-year quetiapine toxicity study, median serum prolactin concentrations were increased a maximum of 32-fold in male rats, and 13-fold in female rats. The mammary gland neoplasms seen in rodents after chronic administration of antipsychotic medications are considered to be prolactin-mediated.

The relevance of these findings to humans is unknown.

Mutagenicity

Quetiapine produced a reproducible increase in mutations in one of six strains in *in vitro* bacterial gene mutation assays in the presence of metabolic activation. An *in vitro* chromosomal aberration assay in cultured human lymphocytes and an *in vivo* micronucleus assay in rats found no evidence of clastogenic potential.

Pregnancy/Reproduction

Fertility—In male Sprague-Dawley rats, the interval to mate and the number of matings required to produce pregnancy increased at quetiapine doses equivalent to 0.6 and 1.8 times the MRHD on a mg/m^2 basis. These effects were still present 2 weeks after discontinuation of quetiapine in the rats that had received 1.8 times the MRHD. No effects on mating or fertility were seen in male rats receiving ≤ 0.3 times the MRHD on a mg/m^2 basis.

In female Sprague-Dawley rats, the interval to mate increased and the number of matings and the number of matings resulting in pregnancy decreased at a quetiapine dose equivalent to 0.6 times the MRHD on a mg/m^2 basis. Irregular estrus cycles increased at doses equivalent to 0.1 and 0.6 times the MRHD on a mg/m^2 basis. No effects on estrus, mating, or fertility were seen in female rats receiving ≤ 0.01 times the MRHD on a mg/m^2 basis.

Pregnancy—Adequate and well-controlled studies in humans have not been done.

Quetiapine showed no teratogenic potential in rats and rabbits dosed at 0.3 to 2.4 and 0.6 to 2.4 times the MRHD on a mg/m^2 basis, respectively, during the period of organogenesis. However, in rats, delays in skeletal ossification were seen in the fetuses at all doses. Also, reduced fetal body weight and reduced maternal weight gain and/or increased maternal deaths were seen at the highest dose used. In rabbits, reduced maternal weight gain and/or increased maternal deaths were seen at all doses, delays in skeletal ossification in the fetuses were seen at doses of 1.2 and 2.4 times the MRHD on a mg/m^2 basis, and reduced fetal body weight and an increased incidence of minor soft tissue anomaly in the fetuses were seen at the highest dose used. In a perinatal/postnatal study in rats receiving 0.01 to 0.24 times the MRHD on a mg/m² basis, no drug-related effects were observed. However, in a preliminary perinatal/postnatal study in rats receiving three times the MRHD on a mg/m² basis, increases in fetal and pup deaths and decreases in mean litter weight were found.

FDA Pregnancy Category C.

Labor and delivery—The effects of quetiapine on labor and delivery are unknown.

Breast-feeding

Quetiapine is distributed into the milk of animals. It is not known whether quetiapine is distributed into breast milk, but breast-feeding while taking quetiapine is not recommended.

Pediatrics

No information is available on the relationship of age to the effects of quetiapine in pediatric patients. Safety and efficacy have not been established.

Geriatrics

No geriatrics-specific problems that would limit the usefulness of quetiapine in the elderly were seen in studies that included subjects 65 years of age and older. However, the mean plasma clearance of quetiapine in elderly patients was 30 to 50% less than in younger patients. Reduced initial and target dosages, and slower dosage titration may be necessary in elderly patients.

According to an FDA Public Health Advisory, quetiapine is not approved for the treatment of behavioral symptoms in elderly patients with dementia. Clinical studies of quetiapine and other atypical antipsychotic drugs for treatment of behavioral symptoms in the elderly with dementia have shown a higher death rate associated with their use compared to patients receiving a placebo. Causes of death varied, but most seemed to be either heart-related (i.e., heart failure or sudden death) or from infections (i.e., pneumonia).

Drug interactions and/or related problems

The following drug interactions and/or related problems have been selected on the basis of their potential clinical significance (possible mechanism in parentheses where appropriate)—not necessarily inclusive (» = major clinical significance):

Note: Combinations containing any of the following medications, depending on the amount present, may also interact with this medication.

» Alcohol or
» Central nervous system (CNS) depression-producing medications, other (see *Appendix II*)
  (quetiapine has been shown to potentiate the cognitive and motor effects of alcohol)

Antihypertensive agents
  (hypotensive effects of these medications may be enhanced)

Cimetidine
  (oral clearance of quetiapine was decreased by 20% when coadministered with cimetidine 400 mg three times a day)

» Cytochrome P450 3A (CYP3A) isoenzyme inhibitors, such as:
  Clarithromycin
  Diltiazem
  Erythromycin
  Fluconazole
  Itraconazole
  Ketoconazole
  Nefazodone
  Verapamil
  (although there is no experience with the combination of quetiapine and a potent CYP3A enzyme inhibitor, caution is advised since quetiapine's major route of metabolism involves CYP3A4)

Dopamine agonists or
Levodopa
  (effects of these medications may be antagonized by quetiapine)

» Enzyme inducers, hepatic, cytochrome P450 (see *Appendix II*)
  (mean oral clearance of quetiapine was increased fivefold in patients receiving phenytoin; higher doses of quetiapine may be required during concomitant therapy with an enzyme-inducing medication; a decrease in quetiapine dosage may be required when enzyme-inducer therapy is discontinued)

Lorazepam
  (mean oral clearance of lorazepam was decreased by 20% when coadministered with quetiapine 250 mg three times a day)

Thioridazine
  (oral clearance of quetiapine was increased by 65% when coadministered with thioridazine 200 mg two times a day)

Laboratory value alterations

The following have been selected on the basis of their potential clinical significance (possible effect in parentheses where appropriate)—not necessarily inclusive (» = major clinical significance).

With physiology/laboratory test values
  Alanine aminotransferase (ALT [SGPT]) and
  Aspartate transaminase (AST [SGOT])
    (elevated values have been reported, usually during the first 2 months of quetiapine use; approximately 6% of patients in a sample of clinical trials experienced elevations of greater than three times the upper limit of normal; all patients were asymptomatic, and most elevations (80%) returned to baseline with continued use of quetiapine)

  Blood counts
    (Transient leukopenia, neutropenia, and eosinophilia have been reported during quetiapine therapy)

  Cholesterol, total and
  Triglycerides
    (increases from baseline of 11% and 17%, respectively, which were weakly related to body weight increases, were reported in patients in short-term, placebo-controlled trials)

  Gamma glutamyl transpepsidase (GGT)
    (elevated values have been reported; patients were asymptomatic, and values returned to baseline during continued quetiapine therapy)

  Thyroid function tests
    (a dose-related decrease in total and free thyroxine [T_4] concentrations, which averaged 20%, but was ≥50% in some cases, at the higher end of the therapeutic dose range, was seen in clinical trials; this decrease was apparent early in treatment with quetiapine, and no further changes occurred with continued therapy; about 0.4% [10/2386] of patients in clinical trials experienced increases in thyroid-stimulating hormone [TSH] concentrations and six of these patients required thyroid hormone replacement therapy)

Medical considerations/Contraindications

The medical considerations/contraindications included have been selected on the basis of their potential clinical significance (reasons given in parentheses where appropriate)—not necessarily inclusive (» = major clinical significance).

Except under special circumstances, this medication should not be used when the following medical problem exists:

» Hypersensitivity to quetiapine

Risk-benefit should be considered when the following medical problems exist:

Alzheimer's dementia
  (dysphagia associated with use of antipsychotic medications may increase risk of aspiration pneumonia)
  (possible increased risk of seizures because of lowered seizure threshold with Alzheimer's dementia)

» Breast cancer, or history of
  (although elevated prolactin concentrations have not been demonstrated in clinical trials of quetiapine, elevations have occurred with use of other antipsychotic medications and in animal studies of quetiapine; studies have found approximately one third of human breast cancers to be prolactin-dependent *in vitro*)

» Cardiovascular disease, including:
  Conduction abnormalities or
  Heart failure or
  Myocardial infarction or ischemia, or history of or
» Cerebrovascular disease or
» Conditions that would predispose to hypotension, including:
  Dehydration or
  Hypovolemia
  (orthostatic hypotension may be exacerbated or may exacerbate pre-existing cardiovascular or cerebrovascular conditions; if hypotension occurs during dosage titration, it is recommended that dosage be returned to the previous level)
  (dehydration may predispose patient to increased core body temperature, and antipsychotic medications may disrupt the body's ability to lower core body temperature, thus increasing the risk of heatstroke)

Drug abuse or dependence, history of
(patients should be observed closely for signs of misuse or abuse of quetiapine, as with any new CNS medication)

» Hepatic function impairment or
Renal function impairment, severe
(higher blood concentrations of quetiapine may occur; dosage adjustments may be necessary, especially in the initial dosing period)

Hypothyroidism
(decreases in total and free thyroxine (T_4) occurred during clinical trials of quetiapine)

Seizures, or history of
(seizures occurred rarely in premarketing studies of quetiapine; it is recommended that quetiapine be used with caution in patients with a history of seizures or a decreased seizure threshold)

Patient monitoring

The following may be especially important in patient monitoring (other tests may be warranted in some patients, depending on condition; » = major clinical significance):

Abnormal hepatic function
(transaminase values should be measured prior to quetiapine use in patients with known or suspected hepatic function impairment; periodic re-assessment should occur in these patients, as well as in patients who develop signs or symptoms suggestive of new onset liver disorders)

Careful supervision of patients with suicidal tendencies
(recommended in high-risk patients, since the possibility of suicide attempt is inherent in schizophrenia; prescribing the smallest quantity of medication necessary for good patient management is recommended to prevent overdosing)

» Ophthalmologic exams
(examination of the lens of the eye by methods adequate to detect cataract formation, such as slit lamp examination, is recommended at baseline and every 6 months during treatment with quetiapine; lens changes have been observed in patients during long-term quetiapine therapy and cataracts developed in dogs during chronic quetiapine dosing)

Side/Adverse Effects

Note: Disturbances of body temperature regulation have been associated with use of other antipsychotic agents. Caution is advised in administering quetiapine to patients who will be experiencing conditions that may contribute to an elevation in core body temperature, such as strenuous exercise, exposure to extreme heat, dehydration, or concomitant treatment with anticholinergic medications.

The neuroleptic malignant syndrome (NMS) has been associated with the use of antipsychotic agents. Two possible cases were reported during clinical trials with quetiapine. NMS is a potentially fatal symptom complex that may include: hyperpyrexia; muscle rigidity; altered mental status; and autonomic instability seen as irregular pulse or blood pressure, tachycardia, diaphoresis, and cardiac dysrhythmia. Elevated creatine kinase, myoglobinuria (rhabdomyolysis), and acute renal failure also may occur. Differential diagnosis should exclude serious medical illnesses, such as pneumonia or systemic infection, presenting in conjunction with extrapyramidal effects, as well as central anticholinergic toxicity, heatstroke, drug fever, and primary CNS pathology.

Tardive dyskinesia, a syndrome of potentially irreversible, involuntary, dyskinetic movements, has been reported in patients taking other antipsychotic medications. Tardive dyskinesia occurs more frequently in elderly patients, especially women, than in younger patients. The risk of developing the syndrome and of experiencing irreversible effects appears to increase with treatment duration and total cumulative dose, although it may develop at any time during antipsychotic therapy. There is no known treatment for tardive dyskinesia, although partial or complete remission may occur when the antipsychotic medication is withdrawn. Alternatively, the antipsychotic medication may suppress the signs of the syndrome, masking the underlying process. For these reasons, quetiapine should be used only in those patients with chronic illness that is responsive to antipsychotic medication, and for whom potentially less harmful treatments are unavailable or inappropriate. Also, the smallest effective dose of quetiapine should be used and the need for continuing treatment should be assessed periodically.

The following side/adverse effects have been selected on the basis of their potential clinical significance (possible signs and symptoms in parentheses where appropriate)—not necessarily inclusive:

Those indicating need for medical attention

Incidence less frequent

Dysarthria (trouble in speaking); ***dyspnea*** (trouble in breathing); ***extrapyramidal symptoms, parkinsonian*** (trouble in speaking or swallowing; loss of balance control; mask-like face; shuffling walk; slowed movements; stiffness of arms or legs; trembling and shaking of hands and fingers); ***flu-like symptoms*** (fever; chills; muscle aches); ***leukopenia*** (fever, chills, or sore throat); ***orthostatic hypotension*** (dizziness, lightheadedness, or fainting, especially when getting up from a lying or sitting position); ***peripheral edema*** (swelling of feet or lower legs); ***skin rash***

Incidence rare

Changes in lenses of eyes—usually asymptomatic; ***galactorrhea*** (unusual secretion of milk)—in females; ***hypothyroidism*** (loss of appetite; weight gain; dry, puffy skin; tiredness); ***hypotension*** (low blood pressure); ***menstrual changes; neuroleptic malignant syndrome (NMS)*** (difficult or unusually fast breathing; fast heartbeat or irregular pulse; high fever; high or low [irregular] blood pressure; increased sweating; loss of bladder control; severe muscle stiffness; seizures; unusually pale skin; unusual tiredness or weakness); ***seizures; tachycardia*** (fast, pounding, or irregular heartbeat; fainting)

Note: *Changes in the lenses of the eyes* have been observed in patients during long-term quetiapine therapy and cataracts have developed in dogs during chronic quetiapine dosing. Regular ophthalmologic examinations are recommended during quetiapine therapy.

Those indicating need for medical attention only if they continue or are bothersome

Incidence more frequent

Constipation; dizziness; drowsiness; dry mouth; dyspepsia (indigestion); ***increased weight***

Note: *Dyspepsia* and *increased weight* are dose-related. In pooled data from 3- to 6-week trials, 23% of patients receiving quetiapine and 6% of patients receiving placebo gained $\geq$ 7% of their baseline body weight.

Incidence less frequent

Abdominal pain; abnormal vision; anorexia (decrease in appetite); ***asthenia*** (decreased strength and energy); ***headache; hypertonia*** (increased muscle tone); ***increased sweating; palpitation*** (feeling of fast or irregular heartbeat); ***pharyngitis*** (sore throat); ***rhinitis*** (stuffy or runny nose)

Note: *Abdominal pain* is dose-related.

Overdose

For specific information on the agents used in the management of quetiapine overdose, see:

- *Antidyskinetics (Systemic)* monograph;
- *Charcoal, Activated (Oral-Local)* monograph;
- *Laxatives (Local)* monograph; and/or
- *Sympathomimetic Agents–Cardiovascular Use (Parenteral-Systemic)* monograph.

For more information on the management of overdose or unintentional ingestion, **contact a Poison Control Center** (see *Poison Control Center Listing*).

Clinical effects of overdose

Note: Effects of overdose may be similar to side effects experienced at therapeutic doses, but may be more severe or several effects may occur together.

The following effects have been selected on the basis of their potential clinical significance (possible signs and symptoms in parentheses where appropriate)—not necessarily inclusive:

Acute

Drowsiness; heart block (slow or irregular heartbeat); ***hypotension*** (low blood pressure); ***hypokalemia*** (weakness); ***tachycardia*** (fast heartbeat)

Note: First degree *heart block* and *hypokalemia* were seen in one patient after an estimated overdose of 9600 mg of quetiapine. Doses in excess of 10 grams have been taken; patients recovered without sequelae, and no fatalities were reported.

Treatment of overdose

Treatment is symptomatic and supportive.

To decrease absorption—Gastric lavage, following intubation in unconscious patients, and administration of charcoal with a laxative should be considered. Induction of emesis is not recommended due to risk of aspiration if patient is obtunded or experiencing seizures or dystonic reactions of the head and neck.

Specific treatment—Administering antiarrhythmic therapy, if needed. However, disopyramide, procainamide, and quinidine have the potential to add to the possible QT-interval–prolonging effects of quetiapine overdosage. Also, bretylium may add to the hypotensive effect of quetiapine, due to additive alpha-adrenergic receptor blockade. Hypotension may be treated with intravenous fluids and/or sympathomimetic agents. However, epinephrine and dopamine may exacerbate hypotension through beta-adrenergic stimulation in the presence of quetiapine-induced alpha-adrenergic receptor blockade. Anticholinergic (antidyskinetic) medication should be administered in the presence of severe extrapyramidal symptoms.

Monitoring—Continuous electrocardiographic (ECG) monitoring is recommended to detect possible arrhythmias.

Supportive care—Establish and maintain airway and ensure adequate oxygenation and ventilation. Patients in whom intentional overdose is confirmed or suspected should be referred for psychiatric consultation.

Patient Consultation

As an aid to patient consultation, refer to *Advice for the Patient, Quetiapine (Systemic)*.

In providing consultation, consider emphasizing the following selected information (» = major clinical significance):

Before using this medication

» Conditions affecting use, especially:
- Breast-feeding—Distributed into milk of animals; use in nursing mothers not recommended
- Use in the elderly—Not approved for the treatment of behavioral disorders in elderly patients with dementia; associated with a higher death rate
- Other medications, especially alcohol, CYP3A isoenzyme inhibitors, other CNS depression-producing medications, or hepatic enzyme inducers
- Other medical problems, especially breast cancer or history of breast cancer, cardiovascular disease, cerebrovascular disease, conditions that would predispose to hypotension, hepatic function impairment, hypersensitivity to quetiapine, or severe renal function impairment

Proper use of this medication

Compliance with therapy; not taking more or less medicine than prescribed

Taking with or without food, on a full or empty stomach, as directed by physician

» Importance of caregivers contacting doctor and not giving this medicine for treatment of behavioral problems in elderly patients with dementia

» Proper dosing

Missed dose: Taking as soon as remembered; skipping if almost time for next dose; not doubling doses.

» Proper storage

Precautions while using this medication

Possible drowsiness, especially during first 3 to 5 days of therapy; caution when driving, operating machinery, or doing other jobs that require alertness

Possible orthostatic hypotension; rising slowly from a sitting or lying position

Possible impairment of ability to regulate core body temperature; avoiding overheating and dehydration

Avoiding use of alcoholic beverages; not taking other CNS depressants unless prescribed by physician

Side/adverse effects

Signs of potential side effects, especially dysarthria, dyspnea, parkinsonian extrapyramidal symptoms, flu-like symptoms, galactorrhea, leukopenia, orthostatic hypotension, peripheral edema, skin rash, changes in lenses of eyes, hypothyroidism, hypotension, menstrual changes, neuroleptic malignant syndrome (NMS), seizures, and tachycardia,

General Dosing Information

Since the possibility of suicide is inherent in schizophrenia, patients should not have access to large quantities of quetiapine. To reduce the risk of overdose, the patient should be supplied with the smallest quantity of medication necessary for satisfactory patient management.

Diet/Nutrition

Quetiapine may be administered with or without food, on a full or empty stomach. Food marginally increases quetiapine absorption.

For treatment of adverse effects

Neuroleptic malignant syndrome (NMS)—Recommended treatment consists of the following:
- *Discontinuing quetiapine and other medications not essential to current therapy.*
- Providing intensive symptomatic treatment and medical monitoring.
- Treating any concomitant serious medical problems for which specific treatments are available.
- After recovery, giving careful consideration to the reintroduction of antipsychotic drug therapy in patients with severe psychosis requiring treatment, because of possible recurrence of NMS; closely monitoring patients in whom antipsychotic drug therapy is reintroduced after recovery from NMS.

Tardive dyskinesia—There is no known effective treatment. If signs and symptoms of tardive dyskinesia appear, discontinuation of quetiapine treatment should be considered if clinically feasible. To minimize the occurrence of tardive dyskinesia, chronic antipsychotic treatment should be in the smallest effective dose for the shortest duration necessary to produce a satisfactory clinical response.

Oral Dosage Form

Note: The available dosage form contains quetiapine fumarate, but dosage and strength are expressed in terms of the base.

QUETIAPINE TABLETS

Usual adult dose

Antipsychotic—

Oral, initially 25 mg (base) two times a day, with increases of 25 to 50 mg (base) two or three times a day to a target dosage range of 300 to 400 mg (base) a day, in divided doses given two or three times a day, by the fourth to seventh day. Further dosage adjustments may be made in increments or decrements of 25 to 50 mg (base) two times a day at intervals of two days. Some patients may require as little as 150 mg a day.

Note: A slower rate of dosage titration and a lower target dosage should be considered in geriatric patients and in patients with hepatic impairment, predisposition to hypotension, or other debilitation.

A dose-response study did not find dosages above 300 mg (base) a day to be more efficacious than a dosage of 300 mg (base) a day.

When reinstituting quetiapine therapy in a patient who has discontinued quetiapine for more than one week, the initial titration schedule should be followed. If discontinuation has been for less than one week, quetiapine may be reinstituted at the previous maintenance dosage.

Usual adult prescribing limits

800 mg (base) a day.

Usual pediatric dose

Antipsychotic—

Safety and efficacy have not been established.

Strength(s) usually available

U.S.—

25 mg (base) (Rx) [*Seroquel*].
100 mg (base) (Rx) [*Seroquel*].
200 mg (base) (Rx) [*Seroquel*].

Canada—

25 mg (base) (Rx) [*Seroquel* (film-coated; red ferric oxide)].
100 mg (base) (Rx) [*Seroquel* (film-coated)].
200 mg (base) (Rx) [*Seroquel* (film-coated)].

Packaging and storage

Store at temperatures between 15 and 30 °C (59 to 86 °F), unless otherwise specified by manufacturer.

Auxiliary labeling

- Avoid alcoholic beverages.
- May cause dizziness or drowsiness.

Revised: 08/22/2005
Developed: 12/19/1997

QUINAPRIL—See *Angiotensin-converting Enzyme (ACE) Inhibitors (Systemic)*

QUINETHAZONE—See *Diuretics, Thiazide (Systemic)*

QUINIDINE Systemic

VA CLASSIFICATION (Primary/Secondary): CV300/AP101

Commonly used brand name(s): *Apo-Quinidine; Biquin Durules; Cardioquin; Novoquinidin; Quin-Release; Quinaglute Dura-tabs; Quinate; Quinidex Extentabs.*

Note: For a listing of dosage forms and brand names by country availability, see *Dosage Forms* section(s).

Category

Antiarrhythmic; antimalarial.

Indications

Accepted

Ventricular arrhythmias (treatment)—Quinidine is indicated in the treatment of recurrent, documented, life-threatening ventricular arrhythmias, such as sustained ventricular tachycardia. Quinidine should not be used to treat ventricular arrhythmias of lesser severity, such as asymptomatic ventricular premature contractions.

Note: Quinidine is a class IA antiarrhythmic agent (Vaughan Williams classification) with some similarities in antiarrhythmic action to the class IC antiarrhythmic agents encainide and flecainide, and the class IA agent moricizine. In a multicenter, randomized, placebo-controlled trial called the Cardiac Arrhythmias Suppression Trial (CAST), patients with prior myocardial infarction received either encainide, flecainide, or moricizine during an open-label titration phase, and the same drug or a matching placebo for the remaining long-term phase of the trial. The objective of the trial was to determine whether suppression of asymptomatic or mildly symptomatic ventricular arrhythmias would reduce the rate of death due to arrhythmia.

After a mean follow-up of 10 months, the encainide and flecainide arms of the study were terminated due to an excessive mortality or nonfatal cardiac arrest rate (7.7%), compared with that seen in patients assigned to matching placebo (3%). The moricizine arm of the trial was continued in a second trial (CAST II), but this trial also was terminated early when an increase in mortality in the moricizine-treated patients occurred during the first 14-day period of the trial.

Scientists have speculated that the adverse results in the CAST trials may be attributed to proarrhythmic effects of the study drugs. Because these and previous studies with class I agents to suppress ventricular arrhythmias in patients after myocardial infarction have not resulted in a decrease in mortality, quinidine is generally not recommended for treating less severe ventricular arrhythmias.

Atrial fibrillation (treatment) or

Atrial flutter (treatment)—Quinidine is indicated in the treatment of symptomatic atrial fibrillation or flutter in patients whose symptoms are not controlled by measures to reduce the rate of ventricular response. When used in the treatment of atrial fibrillation or flutter, quinidine should be discontinued if sinus rhythm is not restored within a reasonable time.

Atrial fibrillation (prophylaxis) or

Atrial flutter (prophylaxis)—Chronic quinidine therapy is indicated for some patients at high risk for symptomatic atrial fibrillation or flutter, such as those who have had previous episodes that are so frequent and poorly tolerated as to outweigh the risks of prophylactic therapy with quinidine. Quinidine should be used only after alternative measures, such as use of other drugs to control the ventricular rate, have been found to be inadequate. In patients with histories of symptomatic episodes of atrial fibrillation or flutter, the goal of therapy should be to increase the average time between episodes.

Note: A meta-analysis of six clinical trials published between 1970 and 1984 found that patients treated with quinidine for the maintenance of sinus rhythm after cardioversion from chronic atrial fibrillation had a higher risk of mortality (2.9%) than patients in the control group (0.8%).

Malaria (treatment)[1]—Intravenous quinidine is indicated in the treatment of life-threatening *Plasmodium falciparum* malaria.

[1]Not included in Canadian product labeling.

Pharmacology/Pharmacokinetics

Physicochemical characteristics

Molecular weight—

Quinidine bisulfate: 494.56.
Quinidine gluconate: 520.58.
Quinidine sulfate: 782.96.
Quinidine polygalacturonate: 536.58.

Mechanism of action/Effect

Antiarrhythmic—Quinidine blocks open-state, inward-current sodium channels in cardiac tissues, causing a decrease in the rate and amplitude of phase 0 depolarization of the action potential. Because the sodium channels require a higher transmembrane potential (voltage) and longer time to recover from inactivation, the refractory period is prolonged. Outward-current potassium channels also are blocked, causing a prolongation of phase 3 repolarization. Quinidine also reduces the slope of phase 4 depolarization in Purkinje fibers, which results in decreased automaticity. Although quinidine directly affects the atrioventricular (AV) node, decreasing conduction, it also has a vagolytic effect (through an anticholinergic action), which can increase conduction through the AV node. On the electrocardiogram, quinidine widens the QRS complex and prolongs the QT interval. In the Vaughan Williams classification of antiarrhythmics, quinidine is considered to be a Class IA antiarrhythmic.

Antimalarial—Quinidine primarily kills the schizont parasite at the asexual intra-erythrocytic cycle stage of the *Plasmodium falciparum* malaria protozoan parasite. Quinidine also kills the gametocyte parasite stages of *Plasmodium malariae, Plasmodium vivax*, and *Plasmodium ovale.*

Other actions/effects

Quinidine acts as a vasodilator by blocking alpha-adrenergic receptors. It also has a negative inotropic effect. Quinidine inhibits the action of cytochrome P450 2D6 hepatic enzyme, which can interfere with the metabolism of certain medications. See *Drug interactions and/or related problems* section.

Absorption

Absolute bioavailability of quinidine is about 70% or greater, but interpatient bioavailability can vary due to first-pass hepatic metabolism. Food slows absorption, but does not affect the extent of absorption, of quinidine sulfate immediate-release tablets or quinidine polygalacturonate tablets. Food increases the rate and extent of absorption of quinidine gluconate extended-release tablets.

Distribution

Volume of distribution (Vol_D)—

Approximately 3 L/kg, but may be reduced in patients with congestive heart failure and increased in patients with cirrhosis.

Protein binding

High (approximately 70 to 90%).

Protein binding is mainly to alpha-1-acid glycoprotein and to albumin. Total serum concentrations of quinidine may be increased when alpha-1-acid glycoprotein concentrations are increased, such as in cases of trauma, surgery, cardiac arrest, and during acute myocardial infarction. Protein binding may be decreased in patients with liver disease, in neonates, and in infants younger than 18 months of age. Although total serum quinidine concentrations may be increased, the free fraction of the drug (the main determinant of the drug effect) may fall within a normal therapeutic range. In this instance, measuring the free fraction of serum quinidine concentrations (instead of total serum quinidine concentrations) may be helpful in guiding therapy.

Biotransformation

Hepatic—Quinidine undergoes oxidative metabolism in the liver by the P450 3A4 enzyme. Of several metabolites, the 3-hydroxyquinidine (3HQ) has approximately half of the antiarrhythmic activity of quinidine, can exceed quinidine serum concentrations, and has a larger volume of distribution than quinidine.

Half-life

Elimination—

Range, 4 to 17 hours; average, approximately 6 hours.

Time to peak concentration

Oral—

Quinidine bisulfate, extended-release: Approximately 4 hours.
Quinidine gluconate, extended-release: 3 to 5 hours.
Quinidine gluconate, immediate-release: 1 to 3 hours.
Quinidine polygalacturonate, immediate-release: Approximately 2 hours.
Quinidine sulfate, extended-release: Approximately 6 hours.
Quinidine sulfate, immediate-release: Approximately 2 hours.

Intramuscular—
Less than 2 hours.
Intravenous—
Immediate.

Therapeutic serum concentration

2 to 6 mcg per mL; however, this range refers to total serum quinidine concentrations (both the protein-bound and free fractions) and may not be an accurate predictor of the therapeutic or toxic effects of quinidine, especially in disease states in which protein binding of quinidine is altered (see *Protein binding* section). In such cases, measurement of the free fraction of quinidine might be helpful, although there is no established reference range for the unbound concentration. Therapy should be guided by individual patient response.

Elimination

Renal—Approximately 20% of quinidine is excreted unchanged in the urine when urine pH is below 7. Urinary excretion may decrease to as little as 5% in more alkaline urine. Renal elimination involves both glomerular filtration and active tubular secretion, moderated by pH-dependent tubular reabsorption.

In dialysis—
Quinidine is not adequately removed by dialysis.

Precautions to Consider

Cross-sensitivity and/or related problems

Patients sensitive to quinine or other cinchona alkaloids may be sensitive to quinidine. Quinidine should not be administered to patients who have experienced thrombocytopenic purpura with quinine.

Carcinogenicity/Mutagenicity

Adequate and well-controlled studies in humans have not been done.

Pregnancy/Reproduction

Fertility—Adequate and well-controlled studies in humans have not been done.

Pregnancy—Although adequate and well-controlled studies on the use of quinidine in pregnant women have not been done, quinidine has been used during pregnancy for the treatment of cardiac arrhythmias and is considered to be the class IA drug of choice in this patient population. Adverse effects that have occurred during pregnancy are mild uterine contractions, premature labor, and neonatal thrombocytopenia. At toxic doses, quinidine has been reported to cause spontaneous abortion and possible cranial nerve VIII injury; however, in general, adverse effects are uncommon.

FDA Pregnancy Category C.

Breast-feeding

Quinidine is distributed into breast milk and appears at concentrations slightly lower than maternal serum concentrations. A nursing infant's quinidine serum concentration will most likely be lower than that of the mother, although the lower level of protein binding of quinidine in a neonate may increase its risk for toxicity, even at low total serum concentrations; therefore, it is recommended that quinidine not be administered to nursing mothers.

Pediatrics

The pharmacokinetics and pharmacodynamics of quinidine have not been studied extensively in the pediatric population, and use of quinidine in the treatment of cardiac arrhythmias in children is largely empirical. Children may require a higher dose of quinidine than adults, possibly because children have a higher rate of clearance of quinidine, which may be related to a faster metabolism. Additionally, children may be more tolerant to the side effects of quinidine, experiencing fewer gastrointestinal side effects, such as vomiting, anorexia, and diarrhea.

In clinical trials for malaria, children received the same dose, on a mg per kg of body weight (mg/kg) basis, as adults, and quinidine was considered to be as safe and effective in children as in adults.

Geriatrics

Appropriate studies on the relationship of age to the effects of quinidine have not been performed in the geriatric population; however, it has been reported that quinidine's elimination half-life is increased and total clearance is decreased in healthy elderly volunteers when compared with younger individuals. Protein binding also may be slightly reduced in the elderly.

Surgical

Use of quinidine during surgery can prolong the blockade effects of nondepolarizing neuromuscular blocking agents.

Drug interactions and/or related problems

The following drug interactions and/or related problems have been selected on the basis of their potential clinical significance (possible mechanism in parentheses where appropriate)—not necessarily inclusive (» = major clinical significance):

Note: Combinations containing any of the following medications, depending on the amount present, may also interact with this medication.

Alkalizers, urinary, such as:
Carbonic anhydrase inhibitors
Diuretics, thiazide
Sodium bicarbonate
(concurrent use may reduce renal elimination of quinidine by increasing urinary pH, thereby enhancing renal reabsorption)

» Amiodarone
(concurrent use with quinidine may have additive effects on prolongation of the QT interval, increasing the risk of cardiac proarrhythmia, specifically *torsades de pointes* ventricular tachycardia. Additionally, concurrent use has been reported to increase serum quinidine concentrations, on average, by 32%; concurrent use of the two agents is not recommended except in unusual circumstances, in which case the dose of quinidine should be reduced by 30 to 50%)

Antacids
(concurrent use may decrease the bioavailability of quinidine and may decrease renal elimination by raising urine pH; it is recommended that quinidine and antacid administration be separated by at least 2 hours)

Anticholinergics (see *Appendix II*)
(concurrent use with quinidine may produce additive anticholinergic effects)

» Antidepressants, tricyclic, such as
Amitriptyline or
Clomipramine or
Desipramine or
Doxepin or
Imipramine or
Nortriptyline
(concurrent use with quinidine may have additive effects on prolongation of the QT interval, increasing the risk of cardiac proarrhythmia, specifically *torsades de pointes* ventricular tachycardia; additionally, quinidine inhibits the action of cytochrome P450 2D6 enzyme, which possibly can reduce the metabolism of amitriptyline, clomipramine, desipramine, imipramine, and nortriptyline)

Bretylium
(both bretylium and quinidine have alpha-adrenergic blocking activity, and concurrent use may have additive vasodilating [hypotensive] effects)

Cimetidine
(concurrent use with cimetidine has been reported to increase quinidine's elimination half-life and area under the plasma concentration-time curve [AUC] by 23% and 15%, respectively; the interaction may be a result of cimetidine-induced inhibition of cytochrome P450 3A4 enzyme metabolism of quinidine or competition for renal tubular secretion)

» Digitalis glycosides
(concurrent use with quinidine has resulted in increased plasma digoxin concentrations, possibly due to an initial displacement of digoxin from quinidine binding sites, and a reduction in the renal and nonrenal clearance and volume of distribution of digoxin; the extent of the interaction is proportional to plasma quinidine concentrations and, on average, concurrent use results in 100% increases in serum digoxin concentrations, although increases of over 300% have been reported; concurrent use of quinidine with digitoxin has resulted in increases in serum digitoxin concentrations of 30 to 67%, the smaller increases possibly resulting from impairment of extrarenal clearance of digitoxin by quinidine. Quinidine should not be administered during digitalis intoxication because the effects of the two medications, which slow AV conduction [by different mechanisms], are additive and can result in complete AV block)

» Erythromycin
(concurrent use with quinidine may have additive effects on QT interval prolongation, increasing the risk of cardiac proarrhythmia, specifically *torsades de pointes* ventricular tachycardia. Increases in quinidine serum concentrations as a result of a decrease in quinidine clearance have been reported with concurrent use of erythromycin; the mechanism of this interaction may be attributed either to competition for the same metabolic enzyme or to inhibition of cytochrome P450 3A4 enzyme metabolism of quinidine by metabolites of erythromycin)

» Haloperidol
(concurrent use with quinidine may have additive effects on QT interval prolongation, increasing the risk of cardiac proarrhythmia, specifically *torsades de pointes* ventricular tachycardia; additionally, because haloperidol undergoes partial or full metabolism by cytochrome P450 2D6 and/or cytochrome P450 3A4 enzymes, serum concentrations of haloperidol may be increased as a result of inhibition of and/or competition for these enzymes by quinidine)

Medications that induce metabolism by cytochrome P450 3A4 (and possibly other) hepatic enzymes, such as:
Phenobarbitol or
Phenytoin or
Rifampin
(concurrent use may increase the metabolism of quinidine)

Medications (or substances) that inhibit metabolism by cytochrome P450 3A4 (and possibly other) hepatic enzymes, such as:
Grapefruit juice or
Itraconazole or
Ketoconazole or
Ritonavir
(concurrent use may increase serum quinidine concentrations by inhibiting its metabolism; concurrent use with itraconazole has resulted in 58% and 59% increases in quinidine elimination half-life and peak plasma concentrations, respectively; grapefruit juice has been reported to have the potential to inhibit the *in vitro* metabolism of quinidine)

» Medications that prolong the QT interval, such as
Antiarrhythmic agents, other, such as
Disopyramide or
Ibutilide or
Sotalol or
Astemizole or
Bepridil or
Chloroquine or
Cisapride or
Clarithromycin or
Diphenhydramine or
Fludrocortisone or
Halofantrine or
Indapamide or
Maprotiline or
Pentamidine or
Pimozide or
Risperidone or
Sparfloxacin or
Tamoxifen or
Thiothixene or
Trimethoprim and sulfamethoxazole combination
(concurrent use with quinidine may have additive effects on prolongation of the QT interval, increasing the risk of cardiac proarrhythmia, specifically *torsades de pointes* ventricular tachycardia)

Medications that undergo full or partial hepatic metabolism by the cytochrome P450 3A4 enzyme, such as
Diltiazem or
Felodipine or
Nicardipine or
Nifedipine or
Nimodipine
(because quinidine also undergoes hepatic metabolism by the cytochrome P450 3A4 enzyme, competition for the same enzyme may, theoretically, affect the clearance of either or both drugs; increases in quinidine serum concentrations have been reported with concurrent use of diltiazem; inhibition of nifedipine metabolism has been reported with concurrent use of quinidine)

Medications that undergo full or partial metabolism by the cytochrome P450 2D6 enzyme, such as:
Codeine or
Dextromethorphan or
Encainide or
Flecainide or
Hydrocodone or
Propafenone
(quinidine inhibits the action of cytochrome P450 2D6 enzyme, possibly reducing the metabolism of these drugs. In the case of an active parent drug [e.g., flecainide, encainide, propafenone], plasma concentrations may be increased; in the case of an active metabolite, metabolic conversion may be inhibited [e.g., codeine, dextromethorphan, hydrocodone])

» Mefloquine
(mefloquine has been reported to have myocardial depressant effects [by a mechanism not fully defined], resulting in sinus bradycardia, first-degree atrioventricular [AV] block, and prolongation of the QTc interval; it is recommended that mefloquine not be administered concurrently with quinidine)

Neuromuscular blocking agents, such as:
Decamethonium or
d-Tubocurarine or
Pancuronium or
Succinylcholine
(quinidine can potentiate the blockade effects of these medications by blocking acetylcholine receptor channels and by suppressing the release of acetylcholine)

Quinine
(concurrent use with quinidine may increase the possibility of cinchonism)

» Phenothiazines, such as
Chlorpromazine or
Perphenazine or
Prochlorperazine or
Thioridazine
(concurrent use with quinidine may have additive effects on prolongation of the QT interval, increasing the risk of cardiac proarrhythmia, specifically *torsades de pointes* ventricular tachycardia; additionally, quinidine inhibits the action of cytochrome P450 2D6 enzyme, possibly reducing the metabolism of these drugs)

» Procainamide
(concurrent use may increase serum concentrations of procainamide, possibly by competing with quinidine for shared renal clearance pathways; in one patient, the addition of quinidine to procainamide therapy increased serum procainamide concentrations by 70%; additionally, concurrent use with quinidine may have additive effects on prolongation of the QT interval, increasing the risk of cardiac proarrhythmia, specifically *torsades de pointes* ventricular tachycardia)

Propranolol
(although some studies have reported increases in peak serum concentrations and decreases in the volume of distribution and total clearance of quinidine, in one study, concurrent use of propranolol and quinidine resulted in no significant change in quinidine half-life, peak serum concentration, or AUC)

Verapamil
(concurrent use may reduce hepatic clearance of quinidine and result in increased quinidine serum concentrations and half-life; additive hypotensive effects because of additive peripheral alpha-adrenergic receptor blockade also may occur)

Warfarin
(concurrent use may increase the anticoagulant effect of warfarin; a dosage adjustment of warfarin may be necessary)

Medical considerations/Contraindications

The medical considerations/contraindications included have been selected on the basis of their potential clinical significance (reasons given in parentheses where appropriate)—not necessarily inclusive (» = major clinical significance).

Except under special circumstances, this medication should not be used when the following medical problems exist:

» Atrioventricular (AV) block, complete or
» Pacemaker-dependent conduction disturbance, idioventricular or junctional, without an artificial pacemaker
(quinidine can cause further slowing of AV conduction and decrease the automaticity of latent or subsidiary pacemakers [i.e., Purkinje fibers])

» Hypersensitivity to quinidine

» Long-QT syndrome, pre-existing or
» QT interval prolongation occurring with quinidine or other QT interval–prolonging drugs, history of or
» *Torsades de pointes*, history of
(these conditions increase the risk for development of *torsades de pointes* with quinidine therapy; quinidine should not be administered to patients with pre-existing long-QT syndrome or a history of *torsades de pointes*)

» Myasthenia gravis or
» Other disease states adversely affected by an anticholinergic agent
(patients with myasthenia gravis may be at risk for increased paralysis with quinidine therapy; other disease states that are adversely affected by anticholinergic agents may be aggravated by the anticholinergic effects of quinidine)

» Thrombocytopenic purpura, quinidine or quinine-induced, history of (increased risk of recurrence with quinidine therapy)

Risk-benefit should be considered when the following medical problems exist:

» AV block, second-degree, without an artificial pacemaker or

» Intraventricular conduction defects, severe, without an artificial pacemaker or

» Sick sinus syndrome
(quinidine can cause further slowing of AV conduction, which can result in complete AV block in patients with pre-existing second degree AV block and/or severe intraventricular conduction defects, unless an artificial pacemaker is in place; quinidine can cause severe bradycardia and sinus node depression in patients with sick sinus syndrome)

» Bradycardia or

» Electrolyte disorders (resulting from dialysis, diarrhea, diuretic therapy or use of other medications, prolonged vomiting, etc.), such as

Hypocalcemia or

» Hypokalemia or

Hypomagnesemia
(these conditions increase the risk for development of *torsades de pointes* with quinidine therapy; electrolyte disturbances should be corrected prior to administration of quinidine)

Congestive heart failure
(the volume of distribution of quinidine may be reduced in patients with congestive heart failure, which can lead to an increased risk of quinidine toxicity; although quinidine has negative inotropic activity, this effect does not appear to predominate in patients with severe congestive heart failure; however, these patients may be especially sensitive to the hypotensive vasodilatory effects of quinidine)

Hepatic function impairment
(plasma protein binding of quinidine is decreased and volume of distribution of quinidine is increased in patients with hepatic function impairment; although clearance of quinidine is not affected, elimination half-life is prolonged [presumably due to the increased volume of distribution] in these patients, increasing the risk of toxicity)

Renal function impairment
(elimination of quinidine may be decreased in patients with renal function impairment)

Patient monitoring

The following may be especially important in patient monitoring (other tests may be warranted in some patients, depending on condition; » = major clinical significance):

» Blood pressure determinations
(blood pressure should be monitored continuously for 2 to 3 days while oral therapy is initiated and should be monitored continuously during intravenous therapy; quinidine therapy should be discontinued if significant hypotension occurs)

» Electrocardiogram (ECG) monitoring
(ECG should be monitored continuously [with frequent determinations of the QT interval] for 2 to 3 days during initiation of oral therapy and throughout intravenous administration of quinidine)

» Potassium concentrations, serum
(recommended for those patients at risk for developing hypokalemia, such as those concurrently taking diuretics)

Quinidine concentrations, serum
(monitoring of serum quinidine concentrations should begin 24 to 48 hours after initiation of quinidine, and sampling should be done 1 hour before the next dose; antiarrhythmic effects usually are seen with quinidine serum concentrations between 2 and 5 mcg per mL. However, this range refers to total serum quinidine concentrations [both the protein-bound and free fractions] and may not be an accurate predictor of the therapeutic or toxic effect of quinidine, especially in disease states in which protein binding of quinidine is altered [i.e., acute myocardial infarction, chronic renal failure, infection, and inflammatory arthritis]. In such cases, monitoring the free [or unbound] fraction of quinidine might be helpful [although there is no established reference range for the unbound concentration], but therapy should be guided by individual patient response; additionally, the QTc is a better predictor of quinidine-induced ventricular arrhythmias than serum quinidine concentrations)

Malaria patients:
Blood glucose determinations and
Hydration
(malaria can be complicated by dehydration, hypoglycemia, and hyperinsulinemia and quinidine has been reported to stimulate the release of insulin, aggravating malaria-induced hypoglycemia; therefore, it is recommended that hydration and blood glucose be monitored in malaria patients.)

Side/Adverse Effects

The following side/adverse effects have been selected on the basis of their potential clinical significance (possible signs and symptoms in parentheses where appropriate)—not necessarily inclusive:

Quinidine prolongs the electrocardiographic QT interval, which can be proarrhythmic. QT interval prolongation may induce *torsades de pointes*, a life-threatening ventricular tachycardia. Other electrocardiographic changes that may occur with quinidine (generally with overdosage) include P wave disappearance and QRS complex widening. Other ventricular arrhythmias that have occurred with quinidine therapy include frequent extrasystoles and ventricular tachycardia, fibrillation, and flutter.

When quinidine is used to treat atrial fibrillation or flutter, the change in the atrial rate may be preceded by a reduction in the degree of atrioventricular (AV) block, causing an increase in the rate of beats conducted to the ventricles. This may result in a paradoxical increase in the ventricular rate. This response may be minimized if partial AV block is achieved through prior digitalization or prior administration of verapamil, diltiazem, or a beta-adrenergic blocking agent.

Those indicating need for medical attention

Incidence less frequent

Cinchonism (confusion; blurred and/or double vision; delirium; disturbed color perception; dizziness or lightheadedness; headache; noises or ringing in the ear; visual intolerance of light); ***fever; hepatitis*** (primarily fever, but may include abdominal pain and/or yellow eyes or skin)—an incidence of 2.2% has been reported; ***hypotension*** (dizziness; lightheadedness); ***syncope*** (fainting)—episodes of syncope may be attributed to ventricular arrhythmias and may occur in 1 to 8% of quinidine-treated patients

Note: Symptoms of *cinchonism* usually are signs of quinidine intoxication, but symptoms have occurred after a single dose.

Quinidine-induced *hepatitis* usually occurs early during treatment (onset 3 to 44 days) and resolves once quinidine is discontinued. Although *fever* appears to be the distinguishing symptom of hepatitis, other symptoms may include a *bleeding tendency, gastrointestinal symptoms, rash*, and *thrombocytopenia*, suggesting a possible hypersensitivity reaction.

Hypotension is the result of quinidine-induced vasodilation and occurs more commonly after intravenous administration, especially with rapid infusion rates.

Incidence rare

Blood dyscrasias, such as hemolytic anemia (unusual tiredness; pale skin color); ***and thrombocytopenia*** (may be seen as nosebleeds or bleeding gums); ***skin rash; systemic lupus erythematosus–like condition*** (chest pain; fever; general discomfort; joint pain; joint swelling; muscle pain; skin rash)

Note: Quinidine therapy of a month or longer has been associated with a rare incidence of a condition resembling *systemic lupus erythematosus*. Clinical symptoms may include adenopathy, arthralgias, arthritis, fever, malaise, myalgias, pericarditis with or without effusions, pleuritis with or without effusions, and skin rash. Clinical symptoms usually resolve within days or weeks after discontinuation of quinidine, although the resolution of laboratory value changes, such as a positive ANA titer, may take weeks or months. Development of a positive ANA titer does not always lead to development of clinical symptoms; therefore, screening asymptomatic patients with serial ANA titers is not recommended.

Those indicating need for medical attention only if they continue or are bothersome

Incidence more frequent

Fatigue (unusual tiredness); ***gastrointestinal symptoms, including anorexia*** (loss of appetite); ***diarrhea; nausea; and vomiting; muscle weakness***

Note: As many as one third of patients experience *diarrhea, nausea*, and/or *vomiting*, which has resulted in discontinuation of quinidine therapy, although many patients may become tolerant to these effects. The occurrence of gastrointestinal adverse effects may be less frequent with administration of a sustained-release dosage form or if quinidine is administered with food.

Overdose

For specific information on the agents used in the management of quinidine overdose, see the following monographs:
- *Charcoal, Activated (Oral-Local);* and/or
- *Isoproterenol, Metaraminol,* and/or *Norepinephrine* in *Sympathomimetic Agents—Cardiovascular Use (Parenteral-Systemic);* and/or
- *Magnesium Sulfate (Systemic)*

For more information on the management of overdose or unintentional ingestion, **contact a Poison Control Center** (see *Poison Control Center Listing*).

Clinical effects of overdose

The following effects have been selected on the basis of their potential clinical significance (possible signs and symptoms in parentheses where appropriate)—not necessarily inclusive:

Acute and chronic

Abdominal pain; cardiac arrhythmias and conduction disturbances (dizziness, faint feeling or fainting, and/or palpitations); ***cinchonism*** (confusion; blurred and/or double vision; delirium; disturbed color perception; dizziness or lightheadedness; headache; noises or ringing in the ear; visual intolerance of light); ***coma*** (loss of consciousness); ***confusion; diarrhea; hypotension*** (dizziness, lightheadedness, or fainting); ***respiratory arrest*** (cessation of breathing); ***seizures; vomiting***

Note: *Cardiac arrhythmias* and *conduction disturbances* that have occurred with quinidine overdose include atrioventricular (AV) block, atrioventricular junctional or ventricular bradycardia, bundle branch block, depressed myocardial contractility, QRS complex widening, QT interval prolongation, sinus bradycardia, sinoatrial (SA) block, sinus tachycardia, *torsades de pointes*, ventricular fibrillation, ventricular tachycardia, and asystole.

Treatment of overdose

Treatment should be symptomatic and supportive and may include the following:

To decrease absorption—Although the use of gastric lavage decreased the elimination half-life of quinidine in one case report, the clinical benefit of gastric lavage has not been confirmed, and it should be used only if ingestion has occurred within 1 hour. Similarly, the use of activated charcoal should be considered only if ingestion has occurred within 1 hour.

To enhance elimination—Medications that delay the elimination of quinidine, such as urinary alkalizers (i.e., carbonic-anhydrase inhibitors, sodium bicarbonate, thiazide diuretics), should be withdrawn, if possible, to avoid prolonging the half-life of quinidine. However, attempting to facilitate quinidine elimination by acidifying the urine is not recommended and is considered hazardous.

Specific treatment:

For *torsades de pointes* ventricular tachycardia, quinidine should be withdrawn and cardioversion or overdrive pacing should be performed immediately. Further quinidine therapy should be guided by the length of the QT interval corrected for heart rate (QTc). To prevent the recurrence of *torsades de pointes*, sustained overdrive pacing or administration of isoproterenol may be used. If the postcardioversion QTc interval is prolonged, other factors that might contribute to QTc prolongation, such as hypokalemia, hypomagnesemia, and hypocalcemia, should be corrected. Intravenous magnesium sulfate also has been shown to be effective in the treatment of *torsades de pointes* in the absence of hypomagnesemia.

For hypotension due to quinidine-induced alpha-adrenergic receptor blockade (vasodilation) and not to an arrhythmia, treatment may involve Trendelenburg positioning and volume repletion (saline infusion). Other procedures may involve increasing peripheral vascular resistance by using vasopressors, such as norepinephrine or metaraminol.

Monitoring: The QTc interval is the best predictor of quinidine-induced ventricular arrhythmias, although serum quinidine concentrations can be monitored as well.

Supportive care: Patients in whom intentional overdose is confirmed or suspected should be referred for psychiatric consultation.

Patient Consultation

As an aid to patient consultation, refer to *Advice for the Patient, Quinidine (Systemic).*

In providing consultation, consider emphasizing the following selected information (» = major clinical significance):

Before using this medication

» Conditions affecting use, especially:
  Hypersensitivity to quinidine
  Pregnancy—Quinidine has caused mild uterine contractions, premature labor, and neonatal thrombocytopenia
  Breast-feeding—Quinidine is distributed into breast milk; it is not recommended in nursing mothers because of risk of toxicity in the neonate
  Other medications, especially amiodarone, digitalis glycosides, and medications that cause QT interval prolongation, such as amitriptyline, astemizole, bepridil, chloroquine, chlorpromazine, cisapride, clarithromycin, clomipramine, desipramine, diphenhydramine, disopyramide, doxepin, erythromycin, fludrocortisone, halofantrine, haloperidol, ibutilide, imipramine, indapamide, maprotiline, mefloquine, nortriptyline, pentamidine, perphenazine, pimozide, procainamide, prochlorperazine, resperidone, sotalol, sparfloxacin, tamoxifen, thioridazine, thiothixene, and trimethoprim and sulfamethoxazole combination
  Other medical problems, especially bradycardia; complete atrioventricular (AV) block; electrolyte disorders, such as hypocalcemia, hypokalemia, and hypomagnesemia; history of QTc interval lengthening occurring with quinidine or other drugs; history of quinidine- or quinine-induced thrombocytopenic purpura; history of *torsades de pointes;* idioventricular or junctional pacemaker-dependent conduction disturbance without an artificial pacemaker; myasthenia gravis or other disease state adversely affected by an anticholinergic agent; pre-existing long-QT syndrome; sick sinus syndrome; second degree AV block without an artificial pacemaker; or severe intraventricular conduction defects without an artificial pacemaker

Proper use of this medication

» Compliance with therapy; taking exactly as directed; not taking more or less medication than is prescribed
  Taking medication with food may lessen gastrointestinal irritation
  Proper administration of extended-release tablets:—Quinidine gluconate: Tablets may be broken in half, but should not be crushed or chewed
  Quinidine bisulfate and quinidine sulfate: Tablets should not be broken, crushed, or chewed. Patients taking quinidine bisulfate (*Biquin Durules*) may notice a leftover empty tablet shell in the stool
» Proper dosing
  Missed dose: Taking as soon as possible if remembered within 2 hours; if remembered later, not taking at all; not doubling doses
» Proper storage

Precautions while using this medication

Seeing the physician regularly to check progress of therapy
Checking with physician before discontinuing medication
Caution if any kind of surgery (including dental surgery) or emergency treatment is required
Possible dizziness or lightheadedness: Caution when getting up suddenly from a lying or sitting position
» Possible fainting: Caution when driving or doing things that may be dangerous if fainting occurs
» Checking with physician if fainting or other side/adverse effects occur
Carrying medical identification card

Side/adverse effects

Signs of potential side effects, especially signs of cinchonism, such as confusion, blurred and/or double vision, delirium, disturbed color perception, dizziness or lightheadedness, headache, noises or ringing in the ear, and visual intolerance of light; fever; hepatitis; hypotension; syncope; blood dyscrasias; skin rash; and systemic lupus erythematosus–like condition

General Dosing Information

The dosage of quinidine should be adjusted to meet the individual requirements of each patient on the basis of clinical response and may vary considerably depending upon the general condition and cardiovascular state of the patient.

Patients with symptomatic atrial fibrillation or flutter should be treated with quinidine only after control of the ventricular rate with agents such as digitalis or beta-adrenergic blocking agents has failed to provide satisfactory control of symptoms.

When used to convert atrial fibrillation or flutter to normal sinus rhythm, quinidine should be discontinued if sinus rhythm is not restored within a reasonable time.

For treatment of patients with life-threatening ventricular arrhythmias, quinidine therapy should be guided by the results of programmed electrical stimulation and/or Holter monitoring with exercise.

Quinidine therapy should be initiated in a hospital, and the patient should be monitored for 2 or 3 days. Dosage adjustments of quinidine in patients at risk for toxicity, such as those with structural heart disease, also should be performed in a hospital.

Oral Dosage Forms

QUINIDINE BISULFATE EXTENDED-RELEASE TABLETS

Note: 250 mg of quinidine bisulfate is equivalent to 200 mg of quinidine sulfate or 166 mg quinidine base.

Usual adult dose

Ventricular arrhythmias—

Oral, initially, a test dose of 200 mg of quinidine sulfate, administered in the morning to rule out hypersensitivity, followed by 500 mg quinidine bisulfate administered in the evening. Beginning the following day, 500 to 750 mg of quinidine bisulfate every twelve hours. The usual maintenance dose is 500 mg to 1.25 grams of quinidine bisulfate every morning and evening.

Atrial fibrillation or flutter, prior to scheduled conversion—

The above described regimen should be given, beginning two days before the scheduled cardioversion. The starting dose for maintenance after cardioversion is 750 mg of quinidine bisulfate every morning and evening.

Usual adult prescribing limits

2.5 grams of quinidine bisulfate daily.

Usual pediatric dose

Safety and efficacy have not been established.

Strength(s) usually available

U.S.—

Not commercially available.

Canada—

0.25 gram (equivalent to 0.2 gram of quinidine sulfate) (Rx) [*Biquin Durules*].

Packaging and storage

Store between 15 and 30 °C (59 and 86 °F), in a well-closed container, and protect from light.

Auxiliary labeling

- Do not take other medicines without advice from your doctor.
- Swallow tablets whole. Do not break or chew.

QUINIDINE GLUCONATE TABLETS

Note: 325 mg of quinidine gluconate is approximately equivalent to 202 mg of quinidine base.

Usual adult dose

Atrial fibrillation or flutter (treatment)—

Optimal dosing regimens for the conversion of atrial fibrillation or flutter to normal sinus rhythm have not been established. The following regimen has been used to treat atrial fibrillation: Oral, 325 mg of quinidine gluconate every two or three hours for five to eight doses, gradually increasing the dose daily until sinus rhythm is restored or toxic effects occur. Maintenance doses range from 325 mg to 488 mg of quinidine gluconate three or four times a day.

If at any point during administration of quinidine the QRS complex widens to 130% of its pretreatment duration; the QT interval corrected for heart rate (QTc) widens to 130% of its pretreatment duration and is then longer than 500 milliseconds (ms); P waves disappear; or the patient develops significant tachycardia, symptomatic bradycardia, or hypotension, then quinidine should be discontinued, and other means of conversion, such as direct-current cardioversion, should be considered.

Ventricular arrhythmias—

Dosing regimens for the treatment of ventricular arrhythmias have not been established.

Usual adult prescribing limits

6500 mg of quinidine gluconate daily.

Usual pediatric dose

[Atrial fibrillation or flutter or ventricular arrhythmias][1]—

Initial doses should be approximately 30 to 40 mg of quinidine gluconate per kg of body weight per day or 550 to 800 mg of quinidine gluconate per square meter of body surface area per day. Doses of up to 75 mg of quinidine gluconate per kg of body weight per day or 1500 mg of quinidine gluconate per square meter of body surface area per day may be necessary in some children.

Strength(s) usually available

U.S.—

Not commercially available.

Canada—

325 mg (Rx) [*Quinate*].

Packaging and storage

Store below 40 °C (104 °F), preferably between 15 and 30 °C (59 and 86 °F), in a well-closed container, unless otherwise specified by manufacturer. Protect from light.

Auxiliary labeling

- Do not take other medicines without advice from your doctor.

QUINIDINE GLUCONATE EXTENDED-RELEASE TABLETS

Note: 324 mg of quinidine gluconate is approximately equivalent to 202 mg of quinidine base.

Usual adult dose

Atrial fibrillation or flutter (treatment)—

An optimal quinidine dosing regimen for the conversion of atrial fibrillation or flutter to normal sinus rhythm has not been established. The following regimens have been used:

Oral, 648 mg of quinidine gluconate every eight hours. If conversion to normal sinus rhythm does not occur after three or four doses, the dose may be carefully increased.

Alternative regimen: Oral, 324 mg of quinidine gluconate every eight hours for two days; 648 mg of quinidine gluconate every twelve hours for two days, then 648 mg of quinidine gluconate every eight hours for up to four days. If a lower dose is the highest tolerated, it may be used during the last four-day dosing period.

If at any point during administration of quinidine the QRS complex widens to 130% of its pretreatment duration; the QT interval corrected for heart rate (QTc) widens to 130% of its pretreatment duration and is then longer than 500 milliseconds (ms); P waves disappear; or the patient develops significant tachycardia, symptomatic bradycardia, or hypotension, then quinidine should be discontinued, and other means of conversion, such as direct-current cardioversion, should be considered.

Atrial fibrillation or flutter (reduction of frequency of relapse)—

Oral, 324 mg of quinidine gluconate every eight or twelve hours. If the dose is well tolerated, quinidine serum concentrations are well within the therapeutic range, and the average time between arrhythmic episodes has not been satisfactorily prolonged, the dose may be carefully increased. If the QRS complex widens to 130% of its pretreatment duration; the QTc interval widens to 130% of its pretreatment duration and is then longer than 500 milliseconds (ms); P waves disappear; or the patient develops significant tachycardia, symptomatic bradycardia, or hypotension, the total daily dose should be reduced.

Ventricular arrhythmias—

Quinidine dosing regimens for the suppression of life-threatening ventricular arrhythmias have not been adequately studied. Regimens that have been used are similar to the regimen for the reduction of frequency of relapse of atrial fibrillation or flutter stated above.

Usual adult prescribing limits

1944 mg of quinidine gluconate daily.

Usual pediatric dose

[Atrial fibrillation or flutter or ventricular arrhythmias][1]—

Initial doses should be approximately 30 to 40 mg of quinidine gluconate per kg of body weight per day or 550 to 800 mg of quinidine gluconate per square meter of body surface area per day. Doses of up to 75 mg of quinidine gluconate per kg of body weight per day or 1500 mg of quinidine gluconate per square meter of body surface area per day may be necessary in some children.

Strength(s) usually available

U.S.—

324 mg (Rx) [*Quinaglute Dura-tabs; Quin-Release;* GENERIC].

Canada—

324 mg (Rx) [*Quinaglute Dura-tabs;* GENERIC].

Note: Quinaglute tablets may be broken in half for dosage titration but should not be crushed or chewed.

Packaging and storage

Store below 40 °C (104 °F), preferably between 15 and 30 °C (59 and 86 °F), in a well-closed container, unless otherwise specified by manufacturer. Protect from light.

Auxiliary labeling
- Swallow tablet whole. Do not crush or chew.
- Do not take other medicines without advice from your doctor.

QUINIDINE POLYGALACTURONATE TABLETS

Note: 275 mg of quinidine polygalacturonate is equivalent to 200 mg of quinidine sulfate or 166 mg of quinidine base.

Usual adult dose

Atrial fibrillation or flutter (treatment)—

An optimal quinidine dosing regimen for the conversion of atrial fibrillation or flutter to normal sinus rhythm has not been established. The following regimen has been used: Oral, 550 mg of quinidine polygalacturonate every six hours. If conversion to normal sinus rhythm has not occurred after four or five doses, the dose may be carefully increased. If at any time during administration of quinidine the QRS complex widens to 130% of its pretreatment duration; the QTc interval widens to 130% of its pretreatment duration and is then longer than 500 milliseconds (ms); P waves disappear; or the patient develops significant tachycardia, symptomatic bradycardia, or hypotension, then quinidine should be discontinued and other means of conversion, such as direct-current cardioversion, should be considered.

Atrial fibrillation or flutter (reduction of frequency of relapse)—

Oral, 275 mg of quinidine polygalacturonate every six to eight hours. If the dose is well tolerated, quinidine serum concentrations are well within the therapeutic range, and the time between episodes has not been satisfactorily prolonged, the dose may be carefully increased. If the QRS complex widens to 130% of its pretreatment duration; the QTc interval widens to 130% of its pretreatment duration and is then longer than 500 milliseconds (ms); P waves disappear; or the patient develops significant tachycardia, symptomatic bradycardia, or hypotension, the total daily dose should be reduced.

Ventricular arrhythmias—

Quinidine dosing regimens for the suppression of life-threatening ventricular arrhythmias have not been adequately studied. Regimens that have been used are similar to the regimen for the reduction of frequency of relapse of atrial fibrillation or flutter stated above. Where possible, therapy should be guided by the results of programmed electrical stimulation and/or Holter monitoring with exercise.

Usual pediatric dose

Atrial fibrillation or flutter or ventricular arrhythmias—

Safety and efficacy have not been established.

Strength(s) usually available

U.S.—

275 mg (equivalent to 200 mg of quinidine sulfate) (Rx) [*Cardioquin*].

Canada—

275 mg (equivalent to 200 mg of quinidine sulfate) (Rx) [*Cardioquin*].

Packaging and storage

Store below 40 °C (104 °F), preferably between 15 and 30 °C (59 and 86 °F), in a well-closed container, unless otherwise specified by manufacturer.

Auxiliary labeling

- Do not take other medicines without advice from your doctor.

QUINIDINE SULFATE TABLETS USP

Note: 200 mg of quinidine sulfate is equivalent to 166 mg of quinidine base.

Usual adult dose

Atrial fibrillation or flutter (treatment)—

An optimal quinidine dosing regimen for the treatment of atrial fibrillation or flutter has not been established. The following regimen has been used: Oral, 400 mg of quinidine sulfate every six hours. If conversion to normal sinus rhythm does not occur after four or five doses, the dose may be carefully increased. If at any point during administration the QRS complex widens to 130% of its pretreatment duration; the QTc interval widens to 130% of its pretreatment duration and is then longer than 500 milliseconds (ms); P waves disappear; or the patient develops significant tachycardia, symptomatic bradycardia, or hypotension, then quinidine should be discontinued, and other means of conversion, such as direct-current cardioversion, should be considered.

Atrial fibrillation or flutter (reduction of frequency of relapse)—

Oral, 200 mg of quinidine sulfate every six hours. If the dose is well tolerated, quinidine serum concentrations are well within the therapeutic range, and the time between episodes has not been satisfactorily prolonged, the dose may be carefully increased. If the QRS complex widens to 130% of its pretreatment duration; the QTc interval widens to 130% of its pretreatment duration and is then longer than 500 milliseconds (ms); P waves disappear; or the patient develops significant tachycardia, symptomatic bradycardia, or hypotension, the total daily dose should be reduced.

Ventricular arrhythmias—

Quinidine dosing regimens for the suppression of life-threatening ventricular arrhythmias have not been adequately studied. Regimens that have been used are similar to the regimen for the reduction of frequency of relapse of atrial fibrillation or flutter stated above.

Usual pediatric dose

[Atrial fibrillation or flutter or ventricular arrhythmias][1]—

Initial doses should be approximately 20 to 30 mg of quinidine sulfate per kg of body weight per day or 400 to 600 mg of quinidine sulfate per square meter of body surface area per day. Doses of up to 60 mg of quinidine sulfate per kg of body weight per day or 1100 mg of quinidine sulfate per square meter of body surface area per day may be necessary in some children.

Strength(s) usually available

U.S.—

200 mg (Rx) [GENERIC].

300 mg (Rx) [GENERIC].

Canada—

200 mg (Rx) [*Apo-Quinidine; Novoquinidin;* GENERIC].

Packaging and storage

Store below 40 °C (104 °F), preferably between 15 and 30 °C (59 and 86 °F), unless otherwise specified by manufacturer. Store in a well-closed, light-resistant container.

Auxiliary labeling

- Do not take other medicines without advice from your doctor.

QUINIDINE SULFATE EXTENDED-RELEASE TABLETS USP

Note: 300 mg of quinidine sulfate is equivalent to 249 mg of quinidine base.

Usual adult dose

Atrial fibrillation or flutter (treatment)—

An optimal quinidine dosing regimen for the treatment of atrial fibrillation or flutter has not been established. The following regimen has been used: Oral, 300 mg of quinidine sulfate every eight to twelve hours. If this regimen is well tolerated, if quinidine serum concentrations are still well within the therapeutic range, and if this regimen has not resulted in conversion, the dose may be cautiously increased. If at any point during administration the QRS complex widens to 130% of its pretreatment duration; the QTc interval widens to 130% of its pretreatment duration and is then longer than 500 milliseconds (ms); P waves disappear; or the patient develops significant tachycardia, symptomatic bradycardia, or hypotension, then quinidine should be discontinued, and other means of conversion, such as direct-current cardioversion, should be considered.

Atrial fibrillation or flutter (reduction of frequency of relapse)—

Oral, 300 mg of quinidine sulfate every eight to twelve hours. If the dose is well tolerated, quinidine serum concentrations are well within the therapeutic range, and the time between episodes has not been satisfactorily prolonged, the dose may be carefully increased. If the QRS complex widens to 130% of its pretreatment duration; the QTc interval widens to 130% of its pretreatment duration and is then longer than 500 milliseconds (ms); P waves disappear; or the patient develops significant tachycardia, symptomatic bradycardia, or hypotension, the total daily dose should be reduced.

Ventricular arrhythmias—

Quinidine dosing regimens for the suppression of life-threatening ventricular arrhythmias have not been adequately studied. Regimens that have been used are similar to the regimen for the reduction of frequency of relapse of atrial fibrillation or flutter stated above.

Usual pediatric dose

[Atrial fibrillation or flutter or ventricular arrhythmias][1]—

Initial doses should be approximately 20 to 30 mg of quinidine sulfate per kg of body weight per day or 400 to 600 mg of quinidine sulfate per square meter of body surface area per day. Doses of up to 60 mg of quinidine sulfate per kg of body weight per day or 1100 mg of quinidine sulfate per square meter of body surface area per day may be necessary in some children.

Strength(s) usually available

U.S.—

300 mg (Rx) [*Quinidex Extentabs*].

Canada—

300 mg (Rx) [*Quinidex Extentabs*].

Packaging and storage
Store between 15 and 30 °C (59 and 86 °F), unless otherwise specified by manufacturer. Store in a well-closed, light-resistant container.

Auxiliary labeling
- Swallow tablets whole. Do not break or chew.
- Do not take other medicines without advice from your doctor.

Parenteral Dosage Forms

QUINIDINE GLUCONATE INJECTION USP

Note: An overly rapid infusion rate of quinidine has been associated with nausea, vomiting, peripheral vascular collapse, and severe hypotension. If quinidine is to be administered intravenously, patients should be closely monitored with continuous electrocardiographic and blood pressure measurements. Use of quinidine injection by the intramuscular route is not recommended because absorption of quinidine from muscle is erratic and quinidine may cause local irritation and/or muscle necrosis.

800 mg of quinidine gluconate is equivalent to 500 mg of quinidine base.

Usual adult dose
Atrial fibrillation or flutter (treatment)—

Intravenous infusion, 800 mg of quinidine gluconate diluted with 5% Dextrose Injection USP to a total volume of 50 mL, administered slowly, under the control of a volumetric pump, at a rate no faster than 0.25 mg per kg of body weight per minute (no faster than 1 mL per kg per hour) with continuous electrocardiogram (ECG) and blood pressure monitoring. Most arrhythmias that will respond to intravenous quinidine will respond to a total dose of less than 5 mg per kg of body weight, but some patients may require as much as 10 mg per kg of body weight. If conversion to sinus rhythm has not been achieved after infusion of 10 mg per kg of body weight, the infusion should be discontinued and other means of conversion should be considered.

During the first few minutes of administration, the patient should be monitored closely for hypersensitivity or idiosyncratic reactions. The infusion should be discontinued as soon as sinus rhythm is restored. If at any point during administration the QRS complex widens to 130% of its pretreatment duration; the QTc interval widens to 130% of its pretreatment duration and is then longer than 500 milliseconds (ms); P waves disappear; or the patient develops significant tachycardia, symptomatic bradycardia, or hypotension, then quinidine should be discontinued.

Ventricular arrhythmias—

Quinidine dosing regimens for the suppression of life-threatening ventricular arrhythmias have not been adequately studied but are similar to the regimen for the treatment of symptomatic atrial fibrillation or flutter.

Malaria—

Note: Both the intermittent and the continuous regimens have been shown to be effective, with or without concurrent exchange transfusion; however, the continuous intravenous infusion may be associated with fewer side effects, possibly because high peak serum concentrations causing hypotension and cardiotoxicity can be avoided.

Malaria can be complicated by dehydration, hypoglycemia, and hyperinsulinemia. Quinidine has been reported to stimulate the release of insulin, aggravating malaria-induced hypoglycemia. It is recommended that hydration and blood glucose be monitored in malaria patients.

Intravenous infusion, intermittent—

Initially, 24 mg per kg of body weight of quinidine gluconate (15 mg per kg of body weight of quinidine base) in a volume of 250 mL of 0.9% sodium chloride or 5% dextrose infused over four hours. Starting eight hours after the beginning of the initial dose, 12 mg per kg of body weight of quinidine gluconate (7.5 mg per kg of body weight of quinidine base) infused over four hours every eight hours. This regimen should be continued for three to seven days (depending on the location in which the malaria was acquired, e.g., seven days in southeast Asia), except in patients able to swallow. For these patients, quinidine maintenance infusions may be discontinued and oral therapy used at approximately the same daily dose of quinidine, using 300-mg tablets of quinidine sulfate.

Intravenous infusion, continuous—

Initially, 10 mg per kg of body weight of quinidine gluconate (6.25 mg per kg of body weight of quinidine base) in approximately 5 mL per kg of 0.9% sodium chloride or 5% dextrose, infused over one to two hours. This dose is followed by a maintenance infusion of 20 mcg (0.02 mg) per kg of body weight of quinidine gluconate per minute (12.5 mcg per kg of body weight of quinidine base per minute). In patients able to swallow, the maintenance infusion may be discontinued and a daily amount of oral quinine sulfate, to provide approximately as much daily quinine base as the patient had been receiving of quinidine base, administered every eight hours. The intravenous quinidine or oral quinine therapy should be continued for three to seven days (depending on the location in which the infection was acquired, e.g., seven days in southeast Asia).

During or after completion of intravenous quinidine or oral quinine therapy, adult patients able to swallow should be administered tetracycline 250 mg four times a day for seven days, or sulfadoxine and pyrimethamine combination (*Fansidar*) as a single 1500 mg/75 mg dose. Patients unable to swallow should be administered intravenous doxycycline hyclate, 100 mg, two times a day for seven days. In clinical studies, most patients under this regimen also underwent exchange transfusion.

Note: The patient should undergo continuous ECG and blood pressure monitoring during intravenous quinidine administration. Quinidine infusion should be slowed if quinidine serum concentrations are greater than 6 mcg per mL, if the QT interval is greater than 0.6 second, or if the QRS complex widens to more than 25% beyond baseline.

Usual adult prescribing limits
0.25 mg per kg per minute.

Usual pediatric dose
Malaria—

In clinical studies for malaria, small children have been administered the adult dose of the continuous intravenous infusion without a dosage adjustment. See *Intravenous infusion, continuous*, above.

Strength(s) usually available
U.S.—

80 mg per mL (Rx) [GENERIC].

Canada—

80 mg per mL (Rx) [GENERIC].

Packaging and storage
Store between 15 and 30 °C (59 and 86 °F)

A solution diluted with 5% dextrose may be stored for up to 24 hours at room temperature or for up to 48 hours at 4 °C (39 °F).

Preparation of dosage form
It is recommended that the length of PVC tubing used to administer quinidine be minimized to avoid loss of the medicine. In one study, a length of 112 inches of tubing resulted in a 30% loss, whereas a length of 12 inches resulted in a loss of only 3%.

QUINIDINE SULFATE INJECTION

Usual adult dose
Atrial fibrillation or flutter (treatment)—

An initial test dose of 95 mg of quinidine sulfate given intramuscularly is recommended, followed by 190 to 380 mg of quinidine sulfate administered every two to four hours, up to a total dose of 3 grams of quinidine sulfate daily.

Usual adult prescribing limits
3 grams of quinidine sulfate daily.

Usual pediatric dose
Dosage has not been established.

Strength(s) usually available
U.S.—

Not commercially available.

Canada—

190 mg per mL (Rx) [GENERIC].

Packaging and storage
Store below 40 °C (104 °F), preferably between 15 and 30 °C (59 and 86 °F), unless otherwise specified by manufacturer. Protect from freezing. Protect from light.

---

[1]Not included in Canadian product labeling.

Revised: 05/26/1999

QUININE Systemic

VA CLASSIFICATION (Primary/Secondary): AP101/MS900

Note: For a listing of dosage forms and brand names by country availability, see *Dosage Forms* section(s).

Category

Antiprotozoal; antimyotonic.

Indications

Note: Bracketed information in the *Indications* section refers to uses that are not included in U.S. product labeling.

Accepted

Malaria (treatment)—Quinine is indicated in conjunction with doxycycline, clindamycin, or sulfadoxine/pyrimethamine combination in the treatment of uncomplicated chloroquine-resistant malaria caused by *Plasmodium falciparum* and [*Plasmodium vivax*] .

Note: The treatment of chloroquine-resistant malaria caused by *P. vivax* requires higher doses of quinine. Therefore, if quinine is considered for the treatment of chloroquine-resistant malaria caused by *P. vivax*, expert advice from an infectious or tropical disease specialist should be sought.

[Leg cramps (prophylaxis and treatment)]—Quinine is indicated in the prophylaxis and treatment of nocturnal recumbency leg muscle cramps, including those associated with arthritis, diabetes, varicose veins, thrombophlebitis, arteriosclerosis, and static foot deformities.

[Babesiosis (treatment)][1]—Quinine is used concurrently with clindamycin in the treatment of severe babesiosis caused by *Babesia microti*.

[1]Not included in Canadian product labeling.

Pharmacology/Pharmacokinetics

Physicochemical characteristics

Molecular weight—782.96.

Mechanism of action/Effect

Antiprotozoal—The precise mechanism of action of quinine in malaria has not been determined but may be based on its ability to concentrate in parasitic acid vesicles, causing an elevation of pH in intracellular organelles. This is thought to disrupt the intracellular transport of membrane components and macromolecules, and phospholipase activity. Quinine has a schizonticidal action. Its ability to concentrate in parasitized erythrocytes may account for its selective toxicity against the erythrocytic stages of the four malarial parasites, including *Plasmodium falciparum* strains resistant to chloroquine. The drug is also gametocidal against *Plasmodium vivax* and *Plasmodium malariae*.

Antimyotonic—Quinine increases the refractory period of skeletal muscle by direct action on the muscle fiber and the distribution of calcium within the muscle fiber, thereby diminishing the response to tetanic stimulation. It also decreases the excitability of the motor end-plate region, reducing the responses to repetitive nerve stimulation and to acetylcholine.

Absorption

Rapidly and almost completely absorbed. Bioavailability is approximately 80% in healthy subjects.

Distribution

Distribution of quinine may vary depending on the degree of illness; the volume of distribution is smaller in patients with cerebral malaria and increases with recovery. Children and pregnant women have a smaller volume of distribution than do nonpregnant female adults and male adults. Plasma and red blood cell (RBC) concentrations appear to be similar before infection; however, during a malaria attack, plasma concentrations are considerably higher than RBC concentrations. Quinine does not freely cross the blood-brain barrier; the cerebrospinal fluid to plasma ratio is approximately 7%. Quinine crosses the placenta and is distributed into breast milk; peak concentrations are reached in breast milk approximately 90 minutes after oral administration.

Vol_D—
- Adults:
  - Cerebral malaria—Approximately 1.2 liters per kg.
  - Uncomplicated malaria—Approximately 1.7 liters per kg.
- Children:
  - Uncomplicated malaria—Approximately 0.8 liter per kg.

Protein binding

Higher (> 90%) in patients with cerebral malaria, pregnant women, and children; approximately 85 to 90% in patients with uncomplicated malaria; and approximately 70% in healthy adults.

Biotransformation

Hepatic; > 80% metabolized by the liver. Metabolites have less activity than the parent drug.

Half-life

- Adults—
  - Cerebral malaria: Approximately 18 hours.
  - Uncomplicated malaria: Approximately 16 hours.
  - Healthy persons: Approximately 11 hours.
- Children—
  - Uncomplicated malaria: Approximately 12 hours.
- Acute overdose—
  - Approximately 26 hours.

Time to peak serum concentration

Acute malaria—Approximately 5.9 hours.

Convalescence—Approximately 3.2 hours.

Mean serum concentration

Approximately 7 mcg per mL, following chronic administration of total daily doses of 1 gram. Plasma concentrations are higher in patients with cerebral malaria due to reduced clearance and volume of distribution; concentrations decrease as patient recovers.

Elimination

Primarily renal, with about 20% excreted as unchanged drug. Excretion of quinine is increased in acidic urine.

Dialysis—Exchange transfusion, hemodialysis, peritoneal dialysis, and hemofiltration have little effect on plasma quinine concentrations.

Precautions to Consider

Cross-sensitivity and/or related problems

Patients hypersensitive to quinidine may be hypersensitive to this medication also.

Carcinogenicity

A study in rats given quinine sulfate in drinking water at a concentration of 0.1% for up to 20 months has not shown that quinine is carcinogenic.

Mutagenicity

Micronucleus tests in male and female mice given 2 intraperitoneal injections of quinine dihydrochloride 24 hours apart in doses of 0.5 millimole per kg of body weight have not shown that quinine is mutagenic. Direct *Salmonella typhimurium* tests were also negative. However, when mammalian liver homogenate was added, positive results were obtained.

Sister chromatid exchange (SCE) tests, micronucleus tests, and chromosome aberration tests in Chinese hamsters given quinine hydrochloride orally in doses of 100 mg per kg of body weight (mg/kg) have not shown that quinine is mutagenic.

Micronucleus tests and chromosome aberration tests in mice given quinine hydrochloride orally in doses of 100 mg/kg have not shown that quinine is mutagenic. However, the SCE test showed an increase in SCEs per cell. Tests were repeated in two inbred strains of mice, using oral doses of 55, 75, and 110 mg of quinine hydrochloride per kg of body weight. The effects were more pronounced in these mice and the increase in SCEs per cell demonstrated a linear dose relationship. One of the inbred strains of mice showed positive micronucleus test results. The chromosome aberration tests also showed an increase in chromatid breaks. In addition, the Ames test was negative for point mutation.

Pregnancy/Reproduction

Fertility—No information is available on the effect of quinine on fertility in animals or humans.

Pregnancy—Quinine crosses the placenta; one study found the cord plasma concentration to be approximately one third the concentration of quinine in maternal plasma. Quinine has been used to treat patients with *Plasmodium falciparum* malaria in the third trimester of pregnancy. However, the risk of quinine to the fetus must be balanced against the danger of *P. falciparum* malaria, which is potentially life-threatening, especially during pregnancy. Studies in humans have shown that quinine causes congenital malformations, especially when given in large doses (e.g., up to 30 grams for attempted abortion). These malformations include deafness related to auditory nerve hypoplasia, limb anomalies, visceral defects, and visual changes. In addition, quinine may have an oxytoxic action on the uterus and has been shown to cause abortion when taken in toxic amounts. Stillbirths have also been reported in mothers taking quinine during pregnancy.

Studies in rabbits and guinea pigs have shown that quinine is teratogenic. However, no teratogenic effects were seen in mice, rats, dogs, or monkeys.

FDA Pregnancy Category X.

Breast-feeding
Quinine is distributed into breast milk in small amounts. One study suggests that a breast-fed infant will receive approximately 1.5 to 3 mg per day of quinine base from maternal therapy. Problems in humans have not been documented.

Pediatrics
Appropriate studies on the relationship of age to the effects of quinine for use as an antimyotonic have not been performed in the pediatric population. Antimalarial studies performed to date have shown that children have a decreased elimination half-life and volume of distribution; however, pediatrics-specific problems that would limit the usefulness of quinine in children have not been documented.

Geriatrics
No information is available on the relationship of age to the effects of quinine in geriatric patients.

Drug interactions and/or related problems
The following drug interactions and/or related problems have been selected on the basis of their potential clinical significance (possible mechanism in parentheses where appropriate)—not necessarily inclusive (» = major clinical significance):

Note: Combinations containing any of the following medications, depending on the amount present, may also interact with this medication.

Antacids, aluminum-containing
(concurrent use of aluminum-containing antacids with quinine may decrease or delay the absorption of quinine)

Anticoagulants, coumarin- or indandione-derivative
(hypoprothrombinemic effects may be increased when these agents are used concurrently with quinine because of decreased hepatic synthesis of procoagulant factors; hypoprothrombinemia can be prevented by coadministration of vitamin K; dosage adjustments may be necessary during and after quinine therapy)

Antimyasthenics
(concurrent use of medications with neuromuscular blocking action may antagonize the effect of antimyasthenics on skeletal muscle; temporary dosage adjustments of antimyasthenics may be necessary to control symptoms of myasthenia gravis during and following concurrent use)

Cimetidine
(concurrent use of cimetidine with quinine may reduce the clearance of quinine)

Digitoxin or
Digoxin
(concurrent use of digoxin with quinine may result in increased digoxin serum concentrations and increased digoxin effect by decreasing the nonrenal clearance of digoxin; concurrent use of quinidine with digitoxin has been reported to result in increased digitoxin serum concentrations and increased digitoxin effect as well; because of the similarities of the digitalis glycosides and the similarities of quinine and quinidine, serum digoxin and digitoxin concentrations should be monitored periodically during concurrent therapy with quinine, and dosage adjustments made as indicated)

Hemolytics, other (see *Appendix II*) or
Neurotoxic medications, other (see *Appendix II*) or
Ototoxic medications, other, (see *Appendix II*)
(concurrent use of these medications with quinine may increase the potential for toxicity)

» Mefloquine
(concurrent use with quinine may result in an increased incidence of seizures and of electrocardiogram abnormalities, predisposing the patient to arrhythmias; it is recommended that mefloquine be administered at least 12 hours after the last dose of quinine)
(patients taking weekly mefloquine prophylaxis may be found to have mefloquine-resistant malaria that requires treatment with quinine; because mefloquine has a very long half-life [approximately 20 days], it will remain in the body long after the drug has been discontinued. Although there is insufficient information available, it is recommended that if quinine must be given, the patient be hospitalized, if possible, and monitored for QT prolongation and possible rhythm disturbances. Seizure activity also may be potentiated in these patients. In patients considered to be at high risk for a seizure, additional precautions and interventions may be indicated)

Neuromuscular blocking agents
(neuromuscular blockade may be potentiated when these agents are used concurrently with quinine)

Quinidine
(concurrent use with quinine may increase the possibility of QT prolongation or cinchonism)

Laboratory value alterations
The following have been selected on the basis of their potential clinical significance (possible effect in parentheses where appropriate)—not necessarily inclusive (» = major clinical significance).

With diagnostic test results
17-ketogenic steroid, urinary
(quinine may cause increased values for urinary 17-ketogenic steroids when the metyrapone or Zimmerman method is used)

Medical considerations/Contraindications
The medical considerations/contraindications included have been selected on the basis of their potential clinical significance (reasons given in parentheses where appropriate)—not necessarily inclusive (» = major clinical significance).

Risk-benefit should be considered when the following medical problems exist:

» Blackwater fever, history of
(interrupted or recurrent quinine therapy in patients with *Plasmodium falciparum* infections may predispose them to the complications of blackwater fever, including anemia and hemolysis with renal failure)

Cardiac arrhythmias, history of, or QT prolongation
(a prolonged QT interval has been noted in patients being treated for cerebral malaria, without correlation with plasma quinine concentration; patients with a history of cardiac arrhythmias or QT prolongation may be at risk for arrhythmias while taking quinine)

Glucose-6-phosphate dehydrogenase (G6PD) deficiency
(hemolysis or hemolytic anemia may occur in G6PD-deficient patients; however, quinine has been given safely in therapeutic doses to patients with G6PD deficiency)

» Hypersensitivity to quinine or quinidine

» Hypoglycemia
(quinine stimulates release of insulin from the pancreas; hypoglycemia may also be a complication of severe *P. falciparum* malaria, especially in children and during pregnancy)

» Myasthenia gravis
(quinine may exacerbate muscle weakness in myasthenia gravis due to its neuromuscular blocking effects)

» Purpura, thrombocytopenic, or history of
(quinine may cause thrombocytopenic purpura, especially in highly sensitive patients or in patients with a previous history of this reaction to quinine)

Side/Adverse Effects
The following side/adverse effects have been selected on the basis of their potential clinical significance (possible signs and symptoms in parentheses where appropriate)—not necessarily inclusive:

Those indicating need for medical attention
Incidence more frequent

Gastrointestinal disturbances (abdominal or stomach cramps or pain; diarrhea; nausea; vomiting)

Note: Symptoms of *gastrointestinal disturbances*, such as nausea and vomiting, may be related to central nervous system (CNS) effects of quinine.

Incidence less frequent

Blood dyscrasias such as agranulocytosis, leukopenia, and/or thrombocytopenia (black, tarry stools; blood in urine or stools; cough or hoarseness; fever or chills; lower back or side pain; painful or difficult urination; pinpoint red spots on skin; sore throat; unusual bleeding or bruising; unusual tiredness or weakness); ***hypoglycemia*** (anxiety; behavior change, similar to drunkenness; blurred vision; cold sweats; confusion; convulsions or coma; cool pale skin; difficulty in concentrating; drowsiness; excessive hunger; fast heartbeat; headache; nausea; nervousness; nightmares; restless sleep; shakiness; slurred speech; unusual tiredness or weakness)

Note: *Hypoglycemia*, which may be severe and recurrent, has been reported in some patients with severe malaria caused by *Plasmodium falciparum* who received quinine therapy, and there was some evidence that quinine-induced insulin secretion may have been one of several possible precipitating factors.

Incidence rare

Cinchonism (abdominal pain; blurred vision; change in color vision; diarrhea; headache; nausea; ringing or buzzing in ears; vomiting); ***hemolytic uremic syndrome*** (abdominal pain; bruising; fever or chills; increased sweating; muscle aches; nausea; vomiting); ***hypersensitivity reactions*** (abdominal pain; difficulty in breathing and/or swallowing; fever; hives; nausea; reddening of the skin, especially around ears; swelling of eyes, face, or inside of nose; unusual tiredness or weakness); ***hypoprothrombinemia*** (unusual bleeding or bruising); ***visual disturbances*** (blurred vision; disturbed color perception; double vision; night blindness)

Note: *Hemolytic uremic syndrome* (HUS) is a multi-system disorder that is characterized by hemolytic anemia, thrombocytopenia, disseminated intravascular coagulation (DIC), and acute renal failure. This reaction may occur within hours of a single ingestion of quinine. Several case reports have been published describing patients who have had an acute hypersensitivity reaction to quinine that resulted in adult HUS.

Hypoprothrombinemia may be reversed with vitamin K administration.

Those indicating need for medical attention if they occur or progress after medication is discontinued

Blurred vision or any other change in vision

Overdose

For specific information on the agents used in the management of quinine overdose, see:
- *Charcoal, Activated (Oral-Local)* monograph; and/or
- *Ipecac (Oral-Local)* monograph.

For more information on the management of overdose or unintentional ingestion, **contact a Poison Control Center** (see *Poison Control Center Listing*).

Clinical effects of overdose

The following effects have been selected on the basis of their potential clinical significance (possible signs and symptoms in parentheses where appropriate)—not necessarily inclusive:

Acute and chronic

Cardiovascular toxicity (blurred vision; chest pain; confusion; dizziness; fainting; lightheadedness; rapid or irregular heartbeat; unusual tiredness or weakness); ***central nervous system toxicity*** (coma; confusion; restlessness; seizures; shortness of breath or troubled breathing; sleepiness); ***cinchonism*** (abdominal pain; blurred vision; change in color vision; diarrhea; headache; nausea; ringing or buzzing in ears; vomiting); ***visual disturbances*** (blurred vision; complete blindness; double vision)—blindness usually is transitory, but rarely may be permanent

Treatment of overdose

Note: Treatment is mostly symptomatic with attention to maintaining blood pressure, renal function, and respiration, and treating arrhythmias.

Recommended treatment consists of the following:

To decrease absorption—

Using gastric lavage or inducing emesis with ipecac syrup to remove residual quinine from the stomach. Repeated dosing of activated charcoal every 4 hours may be beneficial in shortening the half-life of quinine in an overdose.

To enhance elimination—

Although excretion of quinine is increased in acidic urine, administration of forced acid diuresis has had little impact on quinine elimination by the kidney, which accounts for only 20% of the total body clearance. Peritoneal dialysis, hemodialysis, exchange transfusion, charcoal hemoperfusion, resin hemoperfusion, and plasmapheresis have not been found to be effective in the management of quinine overdose.

Specific treatment—

Stellate ganglionic block has not been shown to be of value in treating quinine-induced blindness and may cause an increase in complications. Caution should be used in administration of antiarrhythmics since quinine has class 1 antiarrhythmic properties that can be potentiated.

Supportive care—

Supportive measures such as maintaining an open airway, respiration, and circulation may be administered. Patients in whom intentional overdose is confirmed or suspected should be referred for psychiatric consultation.

Patient Consultation

As an aid to patient consultation, refer to *Advice for the Patient, Quinine (Systemic)*.

In providing consultation, consider emphasizing the following selected information (» = major clinical significance):

Before using this medication

» Conditions affecting use, especially:
- Hypersensitivity to quinine
- Pregnancy—Quinine has been found to be teratogenic; it has also caused stillbirths and abortions in pregnant women
- Breast-feeding—Quinine is distributed into breast milk
- Other medications, especially mefloquine
- Other medical problems, especially a history of blackwater fever, hypoglycemia, myasthenia gravis, and a history of thrombocytopenic purpura

Proper use of this medication

» Importance of not taking more medication than the amount recommended

» Taking medication with or after meals to minimize possible gastrointestinal irritation

» Compliance with full course of therapy in malaria

» Proper dosing

Missed dose: Taking as soon as possible; not taking if almost time for next dose; not doubling doses

» Proper storage

Precautions while using this medication

» Caution if blurred vision or change in color vision occurs

Side/adverse effects

Signs of side effects, especially gastrointestinal disturbances; blood dyscrasias such as agranulocytosis, leukopenia, and/or thrombocytopenia; hypoglycemia; cinchonism; hemolytic uremic syndrome; hypersensitivity reactions; hypoprothrombinemia; and visual disturbances

General Dosing Information

This medication should be taken with or after meals to minimize gastrointestinal irritation.

In the treatment of chloroquine-resistant *Plasmodium falciparum* malaria, quinine is given concurrently with tetracycline, clindamycin, or pyrimethamine in combination with sulfadiazine or sulfadoxine.

In the treatment of nocturnal recumbency leg cramps, quinine may be discontinued if leg cramps do not occur after several consecutive nights of therapy, to determine if continued therapy is needed.

Plasma concentrations above 10 mg per 100 mL may cause severe symptoms of cinchonism.

Bioequivalence information

Bioavailability of quinine is extensive and rapid in healthy subjects. Studies using various salts of quinine have indicated no marked difference in the rate and extent of absorption of quinine in the capsule and plain tablet dosage forms.

Oral Dosage Forms

Note: Bracketed uses in the *Dosage Forms* section refer to categories of use and/or indications that are not included in U.S. product labeling. The dosing and dosage forms available are expressed in terms of quinine sulfate (salt). Bioavailability studies have indicated no marked difference in the rate and extent of absorption of quinine in the capsule and plain tablet dosage forms.

QUININE SULFATE CAPSULES USP

Usual adult and adolescent dose

Malaria, *Plasmodium falciparum*, chloroquine-resistant (treatment)—

Oral, 600 to 650 mg every eight hours for at least three days in most areas of the world (seven days in Southeast Asia) with concurrent administration of 250 mg of tetracycline every six hours for seven days; or concurrent administration of 100 mg of doxycycline every twelve hours for seven days; or concurrent administration of 1.5 grams of sulfadoxine and 75 mg of pyrimethamine combination as a single dose; or concurrent administration of 900 mg of clindamycin three times a day for three days.

[Antimyotonic (treatment)]—

Nocturnal recumbency leg cramps: Oral, 200 to 300 mg at bedtime; if an additional dose of 200 to 300 mg is needed, it may be taken following the evening meal.

[Babesiosis (treatment)][1]—

Oral, 650 mg three or four times a day with concurrent intravenous administration of 300 to 600 mg clindamycin four times a day for seven to ten days.

Usual pediatric dose

Malaria, *Plasmodium falciparum*, chloroquine-resistant (treatment)—

Oral, 8.3 mg per kg of body weight every eight hours for at least three days in most areas of the world (seven days in Southeast Asia) with concurrent administration of 5 mg per kg of body weight of tetracycline every six hours for seven days in children older than 8 years of age; or concurrent administration of 6.7 to 13.3 mg per kg of body weight of clindamycin three times a day for three days; or concurrent administration of 1.25 mg per kg of body weight of pyrimethamine in combination with 25 mg per kg of body weight of sulfadoxine as a single dose.

[Antimyotonic (treatment)]—

Dosage has not been established.

[Babesiosis (treatment)][1]—

Dosage has not been established; however, based on one case report in an infant, the suggested dose is: Oral, 25 mg per kg of body weight per day with concurrent intravenous or intramuscular administration of 20 mg per kg of body weight per day of clindamycin for seven to ten days.

Strength(s) usually available

U.S.—

200 mg (Rx) [GENERIC].
300 mg (Rx) [GENERIC].
325 mg (Rx) [GENERIC].

Canada—

200 mg (Rx) [GENERIC].
300 mg (Rx) [GENERIC].

Packaging and storage

Store below 40 °C (104 °F), preferably between 15 and 30 °C (59 and 86 °F), unless otherwise specified by manufacturer. Store in a well-closed container.

Auxiliary labeling

- May cause vision problems.
- Continue medication for full time of treatment.

QUININE SULFATE TABLETS USP

Usual adult and adolescent dose

See *Quinine Sulfate Capsules USP*.

Usual pediatric dose

See *Quinine Sulfate Capsules USP*.

Strength(s) usually available

U.S.—

260 mg (Rx) [GENERIC].
325 mg (Rx) [GENERIC].

Canada—

Not commercially available.

Packaging and storage

Store below 40 °C (104 °F), preferably between 15 and 30 °C (59 and 86 °F), unless otherwise specified by manufacturer. Store in a well-closed container.

Auxiliary labeling

- May cause vision problems.
- Continue medication for full time of treatment.

Parenteral Dosage Forms

QUININE DIHYDROCHLORIDE INJECTION

Note: The dosing and strengths of the dosage form are expressed in terms of quinine dihydrochloride (salt).

Usual adult and adolescent dose

Malaria, *Plasmodium falciparum*, severe (treatment)—

Intravenous (if an infusion pump is available), 7 mg per kg of body weight over thirty minutes followed immediately by 10 mg per kg of body weight diluted in 10 mL per kg isotonic fluid over four hours; repeated every eight hours until oral treatment can be instituted.

or

Intravenous (if an infusion pump is not available), 20 mg per kg of body weight over four hours followed immediately by 10 mg per kg of body weight diluted in 10 mL per kg isotonic fluid over four hours; repeated every eight hours until oral treatment can be instituted.

Note: The two dosage regimens listed above are equally effective. Either regimen should be administered in conjunction with doxycycline, clindamycin, or sulfadoxine/pyrimethamine combination. Treatment should be switched to oral quinine sulfate when the patient can swallow, to complete a seven-day treatment course. If parenteral treatment is required for more than forty-eight hours, the maintenance dose of quinine should be reduced by one third to one half.

Usual pediatric dose

See *Usual adult and adolescent dose*.

Note: Quinine dihydrochloride injection is not commercially available in the U.S. or Canada. However, quinine dihydrochloride injection can be obtained in the U.S. from the Parasitic Diseases Drug Service of the Centers for Disease Control and Prevention (CDC), and in Canada from the Special Access Program, Health Canada.

Strength(s) usually available

U.S.—

Not commercially available.

Canada—

Not commercially available.

Packaging and storage

Store below 40 °C (104 °F), preferably between 15 and 30 °C (59 and 86 °F), unless otherwise specified by manufacturer. Protect from light.

---

[1]Not included in Canadian product labeling.

Revised: 05/24/1999

QUINUPRISTIN AND DALFOPRISTIN Systemic

VA CLASSIFICATION (Primary): AM900

Commonly used brand name(s): *Synercid*.

Note: For a listing of dosage forms and brand names by country availability, see *Dosage Forms* section(s).

Category

Antibacterial (systemic).

Indications

Note: Quinupristin and dalfopristin for injection is approved for marketing in the U.S. for the treatment of vancomycin-resistant *Enterococcus faecium* (VREF) bacteremia under FDA's accelerated approval process, using clearance of VREF from the blood stream as a surrogate end point. A well-controlled clinical study using traditional clinical end points is presently being conducted.

General Considerations

Quinupristin and dalfopristin are bacteriostatic against *Enterococcus faecium* and bactericidal against strains of methicillin-susceptible and methicillin-resistant staphylococci. They are **not active** against *Enterococcus faecalis*. Enterococcal species therefore must be differentiated to avoid misidentification of *Enterococcus faecalis* as *Enterococcus faecium*.

The mode of action of quinupristin and dalfopristin combination is different from that of other classes of antibacterial agent. When tested with the minimum inhibitory concentration method, there is **no** cross-resistance between the combination and β-lactams, aminoglycosides, glycopeptides, quinolones, macrolides, lincosamides or tetracyclines. Resistance to the combination is associated with the resistance to both quinupristin and dalfopristin.

Accepted

Septicemia, bacterial (treatment)—Quinupristin and dalfopristin for injection is indicated for the treatment of serious or life-threatening bacteremia caused by vancomycin-resistant *Enterococcus faecium*.

Skin and skin structure infections, complicated (treatment)—Quinupristin and dalfopristin for injection is indicated for the treatment of complicated skin and skin structure infection by *Staphylococcus aureus* (methicillin susceptible) or *Streptococcus pyogenes*.

Pharmacology/Pharmacokinetics

Physicochemical characteristics

Source—Quinupristin and dalfopristin combination, a streptogamin antibacterial agent for intravenous administration, is a sterile lyophilized formulation of two semisynthetic pristinamycin derivatives. Quinupristin is derived from pristinamycin I, while dalfopristin is derived from pristinamycin IIA. Quinupristin and dalfopristin are present in a ratio of 30 parts quinupristin to 70 parts of dalfopristin.

Chemical Group—Pristinamycin

Molecular weight—
- Quinupristin: 1022.24.
- Dalfopristin: 690.85.

Mechanism of action/Effect

Quinupristin and dalfopristin combination is bacteriostatic against *Enterococcus faecium* and bactericidal against strains of methicillin-susceptible and methicillin-resistant *staphylococci*. The site of action of quinupristin and dalfopristin combination is the bacterial ribosome. Dalfopristin inhibits the early phase of protein synthesis in the bacterial ribosome and quinupristin inhibits the late phase of protein synthesis. The combination of the two components acts synergistically and is more effective *in vitro* than each component alone. *In vitro* synergism of the major metabolites with the complimentary parent compound has been demonstrated.

Distribution

Distribution of unchanged quinupristin and dalfopristin in noninflamed blister fluid is approximately 19% and 11% of estimated plasma level, respectively. When combining with their major metabolites, the amount penetrated into the blister fluid is approximately 40% of plasma level.

Vol_D (steady–state)—

Quinupristin: 0.45 L/kg.

Dalfopristin: 0.24 L/kg.

Protein binding

Moderate

Biotransformation

Quinupristin and dalfopristin are biotransformed in the liver into several active metabolites. Quinupristin is converted into glutathione and cysteine conjugated metabolites, and dalfopristin is hydrolyzed into nonconjugated metabolite.

The *in vitro* transformation of the parent drugs is not dependent on cytochrome P450 or glutathione transferase enzyme. However, they are major inhibitors of cytochrome P450 3A4 isoenzyme.

Elimination

Quinupristin 0.85 hour
Dalfopristin 0.70 hour

Peak serum concentration

Quinupristin and metabolites: 3.2 mcg/mL at a dose of 7.5 mg/kg every 8 hours

Dalfopristin and metabolite: 7.96 mcg/mL at a dose of 7.5 mg/kg every 8 hours

In obese patients (body mass index ≥30): Quinupristin level increased by about 30% and dalfopristin level by about 40%

Elimination

Primary elimination is probably by biliary excretion

Fecal—Approximately 75 to 77% of dose of both parent drugs and their metabolites

Renal—Approximately 15% of quinupristin and 19% of dalfopristin dose

In dialysis—Not removed by peritoneal dialysis or hemodialysis

Precautions to Consider

Cross-sensitivity and/or related problems

Patients allergic to other streptogramins (e.g. pristinamycin or virginiamycin) may be allergic to quinupristin or dalfopristin also.

Carcinogenicity/Mutagenicity

Long-term carcinogenicity in animals has not been studied. Quinupristin and quinupristin-dalfopristin combination were negative in the bacterial reverse mutation assay, the Chinese hamster ovary cell HGPRT gene mutation assay, the unscheduled DNA synthesis assay in rat hepatocytes, the Chinese hamster ovary cell chromosome aberration assay, and the mouse micronucleus assay in bone marrow. Dalfopristin was associated with the production of structural chromosome aberrations in the Chinese hamster ovary cell chromosome aberration assay and was negative in the other four genetic toxicity tests.

Pregnancy/Reproduction

Fertility—There was no impairment of fertility observed in rats at doses up to 12 to 18 mg/kg (approximately 0.3 to 0.4 times the human dose based on body-surface area)

Pregnancy—Adequate and well-controlled studies in humans have not been done.

Reproductive studies in mice at doses up to 40 mg/kg per day (approximately half the human dose based on body-surface area), in rats at doses up to 120 mg/kg per day (approximately 2.5 times the human dose based on body-surface area), and in rabbits at doses up to 12 mg/kg per day (approximately half the human dose based on body-surface area) showed no evidence of teratogenic effects or impairment of fertility.

FDA Pregnancy Category B

Breast-feeding

It is not known whether quinupristin and dalfopristin are distributed into breast milk. However, problems in humans have not been documented.

Quinupristin and dalfopristin have been detected in the milk of lactating rats.

Pediatrics

Although quinupristin and dalfopristin have been used in a limited number of pediatric patients at a dose of 7.5 mg/kg every 8 or 12 hours, their safety and efficacy in patients younger than 16 years of age have not been established.

Geriatrics

Appropriate studies performed to date have not demonstrated geriatrics-specific problems that would limit the usefulness of quinupristin and dalfopristin in the elderly.

Drug interactions and/or related problems

The following drug interactions and/or related problems have been selected on the basis of their potential clinical significance (possible mechanism in parentheses where appropriate)—not necessarily inclusive (» = major clinical significance):

Note: Combinations containing any of the following medications, depending on the amount present, may also interact with this medication.

Note: *In vitro* drug interaction studies have demonstrated that quinupristin and dalfopristin combination significantly inhibits cytochrome P450 3A4 metabolism of some drugs primarily metabolized by the cytochrome P450 3A4 enzyme system. Therefore, concurrent administration of quinupristin and dalfopristin combination with drugs that are cytochrome P450 3A4 subtrates and possess a narrow therapeutic index requires caution and monitoring of these drugs. Concurrent medications metabolized by the cytochrome P450 3A4 enzyme system that may prolong the QTc interval should be avoided.

Quinupristin and dalfopristin combination does not significantly inhibit human cytochrome P450 1A2, 2A6, 2C9, 2C19, 2D6, or 2E1. Therefore, clinical interactions with drugs metabolized by these cytochrome P450 isoenzymes are not expected.

A drug interaction between quinupristin and dalfopristin combination and digoxin cannot be excluded but is unlikely to occur via CYP3A4 enzyme inhibition. Quinupristin and dalfopristin combination has shown *in vitro* activity against *Eubacterium lentium*. Digoxin is metabolized in part by bacteria in the gut and therefore, a drug interaction based on quinupristin and dalfopristin combination inhibition or digoxin's gut metabolism by *E. lentium* is possible.

Astemizole or
» Terfenadine
(concurrent use with quinupristin and dalfopristin may result in increased plasma concentrations of these antihistamines by inhibiting the cytochrome P450 3A4 metabolism of these agents, resulting in prolongation of their therapeutic effect and/or increased adverse reactions; plasma antihistamine concentrations should be monitored and dosage adjustment may be necessary)

Carbamazepine or
Disopyramide or
Lidocaine or
Quinidine
(concurrent use with quinupristin and dalfopristin may result in increased plasma concentrations of carbamazepine, disopyramide, lidocaine, or quinidine by inhibiting the cytochrome P450 3A4 metabolism of these agents, resulting in prolongation of their therapeutic effect and/or increased adverse reactions; plasma carbamazepine, disopyramide, lidocaine, and quinidine concentrations should be monitored and dosage adjustment may be necessary)

Cisapride
(concurrent use with quinupristin and dalfopristin may result in increased plasma concentrations of cisapride by inhibiting the cytochrome P450 3A4 metabolism of cisapride, resulting in prolongation of its effect and/or increased adverse reactions; plasma cisapride concentrations should be monitored and dosage adjustment may be necessary)

» Cyclosporine or
Tacrolimus
(concurrent use with quinupristin and dalfopristin may result in increased plasma concentrations of these immunosuppressives by inhibiting the cytochrome P450 3A4 metabolism of these agents, resulting in prolongation of their effect and/or increased adverse reactions; plasma concentrations of these immunosuppressive agents should be monitored and dosage adjustment may be necessary)

Delavirdine or
Indinavir or
Nevirapine or
Ritonavir
(concurrent use with quinupristin and dalfopristin may result in increased plasma concentrations of these non-nucleoside reverse transcriptase inhibitors [NNRTIs] and protease inhibitors by inhibiting the cytochrome P450 3A4 metabolism of these agents, resulting in prolongation of their therapeutic effect and/or increased adverse reactions; plasma NNRTI and protease inhibitor concentrations should be monitored and dosage adjustment may be necessary)

Diazepam or
» Midazolam
(concurrent use with quinupristin and dalfopristin may result in increased plasma concentrations of these benzodiazepines by inhibiting the cytochrome P450 3A4 metabolism of these agents, resulting in prolongation of their therapeutic effect and/or increased adverse reactions; plasma benzodiazepine concentrations should be monitored and dosage adjustment may be necessary)

Diltiazem or
» Nifedipine or
Verapamil
(concurrent use with quinupristin and dalfopristin may result in increased plasma concentrations of these calcium channel blocking agents by inhibiting the cytochrome P450 3A4 metabolism of these agents, resulting in prolongation of their therapeutic effect and/or increased adverse reactions; plasma calcium channel blocking agent concentrations should be monitored and dosage adjustment may be necessary)

Docetaxel or
Paclitaxel or
Vinblastine
(concurrent use with quinupristin and dalfopristin may result in increased plasma concentrations of these antineoplastic agents by inhibiting the cytochrome P450 3A4 metabolism of these agents, resulting in prolongation of their therapeutic effect and/or increased adverse reactions; plasma antineoplastic concentrations should be monitored and dosage adjustment may be necessary)

HMG-CoA reductase inhibitors, such as
Lovastatin
(concurrent use with quinupristin and dalfopristin may result in increased plasma concentrations of lovastatin by inhibiting the cytochrome P450 3A4 metabolism of lovastatin, resulting in prolongation of its effect and/or increased adverse reactions; plasma lovastatin concentrations should be monitored and dosage adjustment may be necessary)

Methylprednisolone
(concurrent use with quinupristin and dalfopristin may result in increased plasma concentrations of methylprednisolone by inhibiting the cytochrome P450 3A4 metabolism of methylprednisolone, resulting in prolongation of its effect and/or increased adverse reactions; plasma methylprednisolone concentrations should be monitored and dosage adjustment may be necessary)

Laboratory value alterations

The following have been selected on the basis of their potential clinical significance (possible effect in parentheses where appropriate)—not necessarily inclusive (» = major clinical significance).

With physiology/laboratory test values
Alanine aminotransferase (ALT [SGPT]) and
Alkaline phosphatase and
Aspartate aminotransferase (AST [SGOT]) and
Lactate dehydrogenase (LDH)
(values may be increased)

» Bilirubin, serum and
Blood urea nitrogen (BUN) and
Creatinine, serum and
Glucose, blood
(concentrations may be increased)

Hematocrit and
Hemoglobin
(concentrations may be decreased)

Platelet count
(may be increased or decreased)

Medical considerations/Contraindications

The medical considerations/contraindications included have been selected on the basis of their potential clinical significance (reasons given in parentheses where appropriate)—not necessarily inclusive (» = major clinical significance).

Risk-benefit should be considered when the following medical problems exist:

» Hypersensitivity to quinupristin, dalfopristin, or to other streptogramins

Hepatic function impairment
(plasma concentrations of quinupristin and dalfopristin may be significantly increased; however, the effect of dose reduction or increase in dosing interval on the pharmacokinetics of quinupristin and dalfopristin in patients with hepatic function impairment has not been studied; dosage adjustment may be necessary; however, there are no recommendations regarding the appropriate dose modification)

Patient monitoring

The following may be especially important in patient monitoring (other tests may be warranted in some patients, depending on condition; » = major clinical significance):

» Culture and sensitivity test

Liver function test

» Total and conjugated bilirubin

Side/Adverse Effects

Note: The safety of quinupristin and dalfopristin combination was evaluated in 1099 patients enrolled in five comparative clinical trials. In addition, four noncomparative clinical trials (3 prospective and 1 retrospective in design) were conducted in which 1199 patients received quinupristin and dalfopristin combination for infections due to gram-positive pathogens for which no other treatment option was available. In noncomparative trials, the patients were severely ill, and often with multiple clinical conditions, and may have been intolerant or failed other antibacterial therapies.

Approximately one-third of patients discontinued therapy in noncomparative trials due to adverse reactions. However, the discontinuation rate due to adverse reactions assessed by the investigator as possibly or probably related to quinupristin and dalfopristin combination therapy was approximately 5%.

The following side/adverse effects have been selected on the basis of their potential clinical significance (possible signs and symptoms in parentheses where appropriate)—not necessarily inclusive:

Those indicating need for medical attention

Incidence more frequent

Infusion site reaction (pain, redness, and/or swelling at the place of injection)

Incidence less frequent

Arthralgia (joint pain)—incidence 3.3%; ***myalgia*** (muscle pain)—incidence 3.1%; ***thrombophlebitis*** (pain at the injection site)—incidence 2.4%

Note: Episodes of *arthralgia* and *myalgia*, some severe, have been reported in patients treated with quinupristin and dalfopristin (systemic). In some patients improvement has been noted with a reduction in dose frequency to every 12 hours. In those patients available for follow-up, discontinuation of treatment has been followed by resolution of symptoms. The etiology of these myalgias and arthralgias is under investigation.

Incidence rare

Chest pain; palpitation (pounding or racing of the heart); ***hematuria*** (blood in urine); ***vaginitis*** (redness, burning sensation, or pain in vagina); ***pseudomembranous enterocolitis*** (abdominal or stomach cramps and pain, severe; abdominal tenderness; diarrhea, watery and severe, which may also be bloody; fever); ***maculopapular rash*** (skin rash with red patches); ***urticaria*** (hives)

Those indicating need for medical attention only if they continue or are bothersome

Incidence less frequent

Diarrhea—incidence 2.7%; ***headache; nausea; pain; pruritus*** (itching); ***rash; vomiting***

Incidence rare

Confusion; dizziness; hypertonia (unusual muscle tone); ***leg cramps; myasthenia*** (muscle weakness); ***paresthesia*** (numbness or tingling sensation); ***constipation; dyspepsia*** (stomach discomfort or bloating); ***oral moniliasis*** (oral yeast infection)

Overdose

For more information on the management of overdose or unintentional ingestion, **contact a poison control center** (see *Poison Control Center Listing*).

Note: In clinical trials, four patients received quinupristin and dalfopristin combination at doses three times the recommended dose. No adverse effect was considered possibly or probably related to quinupristin and dalfopristin combination overdosage. In animals given extremely high doses of quinupristin and dalfopristin combination dyspnea, emesis, tremors, and ataxia were observed. Therefore, patients who receive higher doses than the recommended dose should be carefully observed and given supportive treatment. Quinupristin and dalfopristin combination is not removed by peritoneal dialysis or hemodialysis.

Patient Consultation

As an aid to patient consultation, refer to *Advice for the Patient, Quinupristin and Dalfopristin (Systemic)*.

Consider advising the patient on the following (» = major clinical significance):

Before using this medication

» Conditions affecting use, especially:

Hypersensitivity to quinupristin, dalfopristin, or other streptogramins (e.g. pristinamycin or virginiamycin)

Breast-feeding—Quinupristin and dalfopristin are distributed into the milk of lactating rats; use with caution in mothers who are breast-feeding

Other medications, especially cyclosporine, midazolam, nifedipine, or terfenadine

Proper use of this medication

» Importance of receiving medication for full course of therapy and on regular schedule

» Proper dosing

Side/adverse effects

Signs of potential side effects, especially infusion site reaction, arthralgia, myalgia, thrombophlebitis, chest pain, palpitation, hematuria, vaginitis, pseudomembranous enterocolitis, maculopapular rash, or urticaria.

General Dosing Information

If quinupristin and dalfopristin combination is to be given concurrently with another medication, each medication should be given separately in accordance with the recommended dosage and route of administration for each drug. With intermittent infusion of quinupristin and dalfopristin combination and other agents through a common intravenous line, the line should be flushed before and after administration with 5% dextrose in water solution.

If moderate to severe venous irritation occurs following peripheral administration of quinupristin and dalfopristin combination diluted in 250 mL of dextrose 5% in water, consideration should be given to increasing the infusion volume to 500 or 750 mL, changing the infusion site, or infusing by a peripherally inserted central catheter. In clinical trials, concurrent administration of hydrocortisone or diphenhydramine did not appear to alleviate venous pain or inflammation.

Parenteral Dosage Forms

QUINUPRISTIN AND DALFOPRISTIN FOR INJECTION

Note: Dosage is expressed in terms of the combination of quinupristin and dalfopristin in a ratio of 30:70 (w/w). For example, a 500 milligram (mg) dose contains quinupristin 150 mg and dalfopristin 350 mg.

Usual adult dose

Bacterial septicemia—

Intravenous infusion, 7.5 mg per kg of body weight every 8 hours.

Note: The duration of treatment for vancomycin-resistant *Enterococcus faecium* infection should be determined based on the site and the severity of the infection.

Complicated skin and skin structure infection—

Intravenous infusion, 7.5 mg per kg of body weight every 12 hours for a minimum of 7 days.

Usual pediatric dose

Children up to 16 years of age—Safety and efficacy have not been established.

Usual geriatric dose

See *Usual adult dose*.

Size(s) usually available:

U.S.—

500 mg (quinupristin 150 mg and dalfopristin 350 mg) (Rx) [*Synercid*].

Canada—

Not commercially available.

Packaging and storage

Prior to reconstitution, store between 2 and 8 °C (36 and 46 °F).

Preparation of dosage form

Quinupristin and Dalfopristin for Injection is reconstituted for use by slowly adding 5 mL of 5% dextrose for injection or sterile water for injection to the single-dose vial to produce a solution containing 100 mg quinupristin and dalfopristin per mL. The vial should be gently swirled by manual rotation without shaking to ensure dissolution of contents while limiting foam formation. After the solution is allowed to sit for a few minutes until all the foam has disappeared, the resulting solution is clear.

Note: Quinupristin and Dalfopristin for Injection does not contain an antibacterial preservative. Therefore, it should be reconstituted under strict aseptic conditions. The reconstituted solution should be diluted within 30 minutes. The storage time of the diluted solution should be as short as possible to minimize the risk of microbial contamination.

Stability

Diluted solution is stable for 5 hours at room temperature or 54 hours if stored between 2 and 8 °C (36 and 46 °F). Do not freeze the solution.

Incompatibilities

Quinupristin and dalfopristin injection is not compatible with normal saline and should not be mixed with other drugs. However, it is compatible with aztreonam 20 mg/mL, ciprofloxacin 1 mg/mL, fluconazole 2 mg/mL, haloperidol 0.2 mg/mL, metoclopramide 5 mg/mL, and potassium chloride 40 mEq/L.

Developed: 12/20/1999

RABEPRAZOLE Systemic†

USA: Rabeprazole

INN: Rabeprazole

VA CLASSIFICATION (Primary): GA304

Commonly used brand name(s): *AcipHex*.

Note: For a listing of dosage forms and brand names by country availability, see *Dosage Forms* section(s).

†Not commercially available in Canada.

Category

Gastric acid pump inhibitor; antiulcer agent.

Indications

Accepted

Gastroesophageal reflux disease [GERD] (prophylaxis and treatment)—Rabeprazole is indicated for the short-term treatment 4-8 weeks for symptomatic relief and healing of erosive or ulcerative gastroesophageal reflex disease. Rabeprazole may be indicated for an additional 8 weeks of treatment for patients in whom healing has not occurred. Rabeprazole also is indicated to maintain healing of erosive or ulcerative gastroesophageal reflux disease.

Hypersecretory conditions, gastric (treatment)

Zollinger-Ellison syndrome (treatment)—Rabeprazole is indicated for the long-term treatment of pathological hypersecretory conditions, including Zollinger-Ellison syndrome.

Ulcer, duodenal (treatment)—Rabeprazole is indicated for short-term treatment (up to 4 weeks) in the healing and symptomatic relief of patients with active duodenal ulcers.

Ulcer, duodenal, *Helicobacter pylori*-associated (treatment adjunct)—Rabeprazole in combination with amoxicillin and clarithromycin as a three drug regimen, is indicated for the treatment of patients with *H. pylori* infection and duodenal ulcer disease (active or history within the past 5 years) to eradicate *H. pylori*. Eradication of *H. pylori* has been shown to reduce the risk of duodenal ulcer recurrence.

Pharmacology/Pharmacokinetics

Physicochemical characteristics

Chemical Group—Substituted benzimidazole

Molecular weight—381.43.

Mechanism of action/Effect

Rabeprazole is a selective and irreversible proton pump inhibitor. Rabeprazole suppresses gastric acid secretion by specific inhibition of the hydrogen-potassium adenosine triphosphatase (H^+, K^+-ATPase) enzyme system found at the secretory surface of parietal cells. It inhibits the final transport of hydrogen ions (via exchange with potassium ions) into the gastric lumen. Since the H^+, K^+-ATPase enzyme system is regarded as the acid (proton) pump of the gastric mucosa, rabeprazole is known as a gastric acid pump inhibitor. Rabeprazole does not have anticholinergic or histamine H_2-receptor antagonist properties.

Absorption

Since rabeprazole is acid-labile, it is administered as a delayed-release tablet so that it can pass through the stomach relatively intact. Once rabeprazole has left the stomach, absorption occurs within 1 hour of administration. The bioavailability is approximately 52%.

Distribution

Distributed in tissue, particularly gastric parietal cells.

Protein binding

Very high; approximately 96% bound to human plasma protein.

Biotransformation

Rabeprazole is extensively metabolized in the liver by the cytochrome P450 enzyme system to 2 main metabolites. These 2 metabolites do not have any significant antisecretory activity.

Elimination

Normal renal function: Approximately 1 to 2 hours

Hepatic function impairment: 2 to 6 hours

Onset of action

The anti-secretory effect of rabeprazole begins 1 hour following administration.

Time to peak concentration

Approximately 2 to 5 hours.

Peak serum concentration

The peak rabeprazole serum concentration is linear over an oral dosage range of 10 to 40 mg

Duration of action

More than 24 hours. The mean inhibitory effect of rabeprazole on 24-hour gastric acidity is 88% of maximal after the first dose.

Elimination

Renal—Approximately 90% of the rabeprazole dose is excreted in the urine as metabolites. These metabolites are mainly thioether carboxylic acid (TCA), the glucuronide of TCA, and mercapturic acid. No unchanged rabeprazole is detected in the urine.

Fecal—Approximately 10% as metabolites. No unchanged rabeprazole is detected in the feces.

In dialysis—Rabeprazole is highly protein bound and is not readily dialyzable.

Precautions to Consider

Carcinogenicity/Tumorigenicity

In a 1 to 2 year study of mice receiving a dose of rabeprazole resulting in 1.6 times the human exposure of the recommended doses, increase in tumor occurrence was demonstrated. Another study of 104 weeks in duration in which rabeprazole was administered at doses of up to 60 mg/kg/day in male rats and up to 120 mg/kg/day in female rats, enterochromaffin-like (ECL) cell hyperplasia was observed in both male and female rats. Only the female rats demonstrated ECL carcinoid tumors at all dosage levels (5, 15, 30, 60, and 120 mg/kg/day). The lowest dose tested in the female rats was 0.1 times the human exposure at the recommended rabeprazole dose for gastroesophageal reflux disease (GERD).

Mutagenicity

Some of the mutagenicity tests were positive, while other tests were negative for rabeprazole. The following tests were positive: the Ames test, the Chinese hamster ovary cell forward gene mutation test, and the mouse lymphoma cell forward gene test. The following tests were negative: the *in vitro* Chinese hamster lung cell chromosome aberration tests, the *in vivo* mouse micronucleus test, and the *in vivo* and *ex vivo* hepatocyte unscheduled DNA synthesis (UDS) tests.

Pregnancy/Reproduction

Fertility—Fertility studies in rats using a dose resulting in 10 times the human rabeprazole exposure at recommended doses demonstrated no effect on fertility.

Pregnancy—Adequate and well-controlled studies in human have not been done. Because animal reproduction studies are not always predictive of human response, this drug should be used during pregnancy only if clearly needed.

However, no teratogenic effects and impaired fertility were demonstrated at doses up to 13 and 8 times the human exposure at recommended dose for GERD in rats and rabbits, respectively.

FDA Pregnancy Category B

Breast-feeding

It is not known whether rabeprazole is distributed into human milk. However, in lactating rats, levels of rabeprazole were 2 to 7 times higher in milk than in blood. Administration of rabeprazole to rats in late gestation and during lactation at doses 195 times the human dose based on mg/m² resulted in decreases in body weight gain of the pups. A decision should be made whether to discontinue nursing or discontinue the drug, taking into account the importance of the drug to the mother.

Pediatrics

No information is available on the relationship of age to the effects of rabeprazole in pediatric patients. Safety and efficacy have not been established.

Geriatrics

No differences in safety and efficacy were observed in studies of patients over 65 and over 75 years old and younger patients. However, some geriatric patients may be more sensitive to rabeprazole.

Pharmacogenetics

Efficacy and adverse events were comparable between men and women.

Pharmacokinetic studies in healthy Japanese men using different formulations of rabeprazole showed approximately 50 to 60% increase in area under the plasma concentration-time curve (AUC) as compared to data from healthy men in the United States.

Drug interactions and/or related problems

The following drug interactions and/or related problems have been selected on the basis of their potential clinical significance (possible

mechanism in parentheses where appropriate)—not necessarily inclusive (» = major clinical significance):

Note: Rabeprazole increased gastric pH and has the potential to affect the bioavailability of any medication for which absorption is pH-dependent.

Combinations containing any of the following medications, depending on the amount present, may also interact with this medication.

Amoxicillin and
Clarithromycin
(combined administration consisting of rabeprazole, amoxicillin and clarithromycin may result in increased plasma levels of rabeprazole and 14–hydroxyclarithromycin)

» Cyclosporine
(concomitant use may inhibit cyclosporine metabolism and increase cyclosporine C_{max} significantly)

» Digoxin
(rabeprazole may increase gastrointestinal pH; concurrent use with rabeprazole resulted in increase of the serum peak concentration by 29% in normal subjects)

» Ketoconazole
(rabeprazole may increase gastrointestinal pH; concurrent use with rabeprazole resulted in 30% reduction of bioavailability)

» Warfarin
(reports of increased INR and prothrombin time with concomitant use which may lead to abnormal bleeding and even death)

Laboratory value alterations

The following have been selected on the basis of their potential clinical significance (possible effect in parentheses where appropriate)—not necessarily inclusive (» = major clinical significance).

With physiology/laboratory test values

Alanine aminotransferase (ALT), serum and
Aspartate aminotransferase (AST), serum
(values may be increased during therapy; incidence of an increase of 1.25 times baseline value was 0.2% as compared to 0.8% with placebo)

Gastrin, serum
(median fasting gastrin level increased in a dose-dependent manner in long-term therapy for up to 52 weeks; the median values were within the normal range)

Thyroid stimulating hormone (TSH)
(may be elevated according to worldwide post-marketing experience)

Medical considerations/Contraindications

The medical considerations/contraindications included have been selected on the basis of their potential clinical significance (reasons given in parentheses where appropriate)—not necessarily inclusive (» = major clinical significance).

Except under special circumstances, this medication should not be used when the following medical problem exists:

» Hypersensitivity to rabeprazole, substituted benzimidazoles or to any component of the formulation

Risk-benefit should be considered when the following medical problems exist:

Helicobacter pylori infection
(may develop mild or moderate inflammation in the gastric body or mild inflammation in the gastric antrum)

Hepatic impairment, mild to moderate
(may increase exposure and decrease elimination)

» Hepatic impairment, severe
(may increase exposure and decrease elimination; however, caution is recommended in patients with severe hepatic impairment)

Side/Adverse Effects

Note: Rabeprazole 10 or 20 mg/day for up to 1 year resulted in time- and dose-dependent increase in the incidence of enterochromaffin-like (ECL) cell hyperplasia. However, no patient developed carcinoid tumors or adenomatoid, dysplastic or neoplastic changes of ECL cells in the gastric mucosa.

The following side/adverse effects have been selected on the basis of their potential clinical significance (possible signs and symptoms in parentheses where appropriate)—not necessarily inclusive:

Those indicating need for medical attention

Incidence rare

Apnea (breathing interruptions); ***convulsions*** (seizures); ***hematologic abnormalities, specifically anemia*** (unusual tiredness or weakness); ***agranulocytosis*** (chills; fever; sore throat; unusual tiredness or weakness)—sometimes fatal; ***hemolytic anemia*** (continuing unusual tiredness or weakness); ***leukopenia or neutropenia*** (continuing ulcers or sores in mouth); ***pancytopenia or thrombocytopenia*** (unusual bleeding or bruising); ***hematuria*** (bloody urine); ***hepatitis*** (yellow eyes or skin)

Incidence unknown—Observed during clinical practice; estimates of frequency can not be determined

Anaphylaxis (cough; difficulty swallowing; dizziness; fast heartbeat; hives, itching, puffiness or swelling of the eyelids or around the eyes, face, lips or tongue; shortness of breath; skin rash; tightness in chest; unusual tiredness or weakness; wheezing); ***angioedema*** (large, hive-like swelling on face, eyelids, lips, tongue, throat, hands, legs, feet, sex organs); ***bullous and other drug eruptions of the skin*** (skin blisters); ***coma*** (change in consciousness; loss of consciousness); ***disorientation and delirium*** (confusion about identity, place, person, and time; unusual excitement, nervousness, or restlessness; hallucinations; holding false beliefs that cannot be changed by fact); ***erythema multiforme*** (blistering, peeling, loosening of skin; chills; cough; diarrhea; fever; itching; joint or muscle pain; red irritated eyes; sore throat; sores, ulcers, or white spots in mouth or on lips; unusual tiredness or weakness); ***hyperammonemia*** (increase in frequency of seizures; loss of appetite; continuing nausea or vomiting; swelling of face; tiredness and weakness; yellow eyes or skin); ***interstitial nephritis*** (bloody or cloudy urine; fever; skin rash; swelling of feet or lower legs; greatly decreased frequency of urination or amount of urine); ***interstitial pneumonia*** (cough; difficult breathing; fever; shortness of breath); ***jaundice*** (chills; clay-colored stools; dark urine; dizziness; fever; headache; itching; loss of appetite; nausea; abdominal or stomach pain; area rash; unpleasant breath odor; unusual tiredness or weakness; vomiting of blood; yellow eyes or skin); ***rhabdomyolysis*** (dark-colored urine; fever, muscle cramps or spasms; muscle pain or stiffness; unusual tiredness or weakness); ***Stevens-Johnson syndrome*** (blistering, peeling, loosening of skin; chills; cough; diarrhea; itching; joint or muscle pain; red irritated eyes; red skin lesions, often with a purple center; sore throat; sores, ulcers, or white spots in mouth or on lips; unusual tiredness or weakness); ***sudden death*** (no pulse; no blood pressure; no breathing); ***toxic epidermal necrolysis*** (blistering, peeling, loosening of skin; chills; cough; diarrhea; itching; joint or muscle pain; red irritated eyes; red skin lesions, often with a purple center; sore throat; sores, ulcers, or white spots in mouth or on lips; unusual tiredness or weakness)

Those indicating need for medical attention only if they continue or are bothersome

Incidence more frequent

Headache

Incidence less frequent or rare

Asthenia or; malaise (feeling weak); ***constipation; dizziness; dyspepsia*** (heartburn); ***flatulence*** (gas); ***nausea and vomiting; paresthesia*** (numbness, tingling, pain, or weakness in hands or feet); ***pruritus*** (itchy skin); ***somnolence*** (sleepiness); ***stomach pain***

Overdose

For more information on the management of overdose or unintentional ingestion, **contact a poison control center** (see *Poison Control Center Listing*).

Clinical effects of overdose

No large overdose with rabeprazole has been reported. There were no clinical signs or symptoms associated with the 7 reported overdoses of up to 80 mg.

Treatment of overdose

There is no specific antidote for rabeprazole. Treatment is essentially symptomatic and supportive. Rabeprazole is not appreciably removed by dialysis.

Patients in whom intentional overdose is confirmed or suspected should be referred for psychiatric consultation.

Patient Consultation

As an aid to patient consultation, refer to *Advice for the Patient, Rabeprazole (Systemic)*.

In providing consultation, consider advising the patient on the following (» = major clinical significance):

Before using this medication

» Conditions affecting use, especially:

Hypersensitivity to rabeprazole or substituted benzimidazoles products or to any component of the formulation.

Pregnancy—Should be used during pregnancy only if clearly needed

Breast-feeding—Distributed into milk of rats in animal studies; may cause potentially serious adverse effects in nursing infants.

Other medications, especially cyclosporine, digoxin, ketoconazole, or warfarin.

Proper use of this medication

» Swallowing tablet whole without crushing, breaking, chewing, or splitting

» Compliance with therapy

» Proper dosing

Missed dose: Taking as soon as possible; not taking if almost time for next dose; not doubling doses

» Proper storage

Precautions while using this medication

» Visits to physician to check progress if condition does not improve or worsen at predetermined time period

Side/adverse effects

Signs of potential side effects, especially apnea, convulsions, hematologic abnormalities, hematuria, or hepatitis.

Signs of potential side effects observed during clinical practice, especially anaphylaxis, angioedema, bullous and other drug eruptions of the skin, disorientation and delirium, erythema multiforme, hyperammonemia, interstitial nephritis, interstitial pneumonia, jaundice, rhabdomyolysis, Stevens-Johnson syndrome, sudden death, or toxic epidermal necrolysis

General Dosing Information

Rabeprazole delayed-released tablet should be swallowed whole, and not chewed, crushed, or split.

Symptomatic response to therapy does not preclude the presence of gastric malignancy.

Rabeprazole may be taken with antacid without affecting the plasma rabeprazole concentrations.

Diet/Nutrition

Rabeprazole, when used to treat duodenal ulcers, should be taken after the morning meal.

Rabeprazole, when used to treat *Helicobacter pylori*-associated duodenal ulcers as part of a three-drug regimen, should be taken with the morning and evening meals.

Oral Dosage Forms

RABEPRAZOLE DELAYED-RELEASE TABLETS

Usual adult dose

Gastroesophageal reflux disease (treatment)—

Oral, 20 mg once a day for 4 to 8 weeks. May be continued for an additional 8 weeks if necessary.

Gastroesophageal reflux disease (maintenance)—

Oral, 20 mg once a day.

Duodenal ulcers (treatment)—

Oral, 20 mg once a day after the morning meal for up to 4 weeks. A few patients may require additional therapy beyond the 4 weeks.

Duodenal ulcer, *Helicobacter pylori*-associated (treatment adjunct)—

Oral, 20 mg twice daily with amoxicillin 1000 mg twice daily and clarithromycin 500 mg twice daily as a three drug regimen for 7 days with the morning and evening meals.

Pathological hypersecretory conditions including Zollinger-Ellison Syndrome—

Oral, 60 mg once a day, the dosage may be adjusted as needed, and therapy continued for as long as clinically indicated. Dose up to 100 mg once a day or 60 mg twice a day for a period up to 1 year have been used.

Usual pediatric dose

Dosage has not been established.

Usual geriatric dose

See *Usual adult dose*

Strength(s) usually available

U.S.—

20 mg (Rx) [*AcipHex* (hydroxypropyl cellulose; magnesium oxide; talc; ferric oxide (yellow))].

Packaging and storage

Store at 25°C (77°F); excursion permitted to 15 and 30°C (59 and 86°F). Protect from moisture

Auxiliary labeling

Swallow whole. Do not crush or chew.

Revised: 07/13/2005
Developed: 12/02/1999

RABIES IMMUNE GLOBULIN Systemic

VA CLASSIFICATION (Primary): IM402

Commonly used brand name(s): *BayRab; Hyperab; Imogam; Imogam Rabies-HT*.

Other commonly used names are HRIG and RIG.

Note: For a listing of dosage forms and brand names by country availability, see *Dosage Forms* section(s).

Category

Immunizing agent (passive).

Indications

Accepted

Rabies (prophylaxis)—Rabies immune globulin is indicated for post-exposure immunization against rabies infection in persons who have not been previously immunized against rabies with rabies vaccine. Rabies immune globulin is used in conjunction with rabies vaccine.

Unaccepted

Post-exposure prophylaxis is not recommended for persons inadvertently exposed to modified live rabies virus (MLV) vaccines intended for animals. Although vaccine-induced rabies has occurred in animals administered these vaccines, there have been no reported rabies cases among humans resulting from exposure to needle sticks or sprays with licensed MLV vaccines.

Pharmacology/Pharmacokinetics

Physicochemical characteristics

Source—

Rabies immune globulin is an antirabies gamma globulin obtained from the plasma of hyperimmunized human donors. It is concentrated by cold ethanol fractionation. The rabies neutralizing antibody content is usually standardized to contain 150 International Units (IU) per mL.

The solvent/detergent treated immune globulin is isolated from solubilized Cohn Fraction II. The Fraction II solution is adjusted to a final concentration of 0.3% tri-*n*-butylphosphate; TNBP (solvent) and 0.2% sodium cholate (detergent). The solution is heated to 30°C and maintained at that temperature for not less than 6 hours. After the viral inactivation step, the reactants are removed by precipitation, filtration and finally ultrafiltration and diafiltration. BayRab is formulated as a 15% to 18% protein solution at a pH of 6.4 to 7.2. BayRab is then incubated in the final container for 21 to 28 days at 20 to 27°C.

A heat treated immune globulin undergoes a heat treatment process step (58 to 60°C for 10 hours) to inactivate viruses that has been added to further reduce any risk of blood-borne viral transmission. The inactivation and removal of model and laboratory strains of enveloped and non-enveloped viruses during the manufacturing and heat treatment process has been validated by spiking experiments. Removal and/or inactivation of the studied enveloped and non-enveloped model viruses was demonstrated at the precipitation II stage of manufacturing. In addition, inactivation was demonstrated during the 10 hour heat treatment process for the studied enveloped and non-enveloped viruses. Imogam Rabies-HT is formulated as a 10% to 18% protein solution at a pH of 6.8 ± 0.4 adjusted with sodium hydroxide or hydrochloric acid.

One Canadian product is standardized to contain 300 International Units (IU) per mL. The International Unit of potency is equivalent to the U.S. unit of potency.

Mechanism of action/Effect

Following intramuscular administration, rabies immune globulin provides immediate passive antibodies for a short period of time. This protects the patient until the patient can produce active antibodies from the rabies vaccine.

Protective effect

When the post-exposure prophylaxis regimen has included local wound treatment, passive immunization, and active immunization, 100% effectiveness has been shown. However, rabies has occasionally developed in persons when key elements of the rabies post-exposure prophylaxis regimen were omitted or incorrectly administered. This has occurred outside the United States in cases in which patients' wounds were not cleansed with soap and water or other antiviral agents, rabies vaccine was not administered in the deltoid area but rather in the gluteal area, and passive immunization was not administered around the wound site.

Time to protective effect

An adequate titer of passive antibody is present 24 hours after injection.

Duration of protective effect

Short; rabies immune globulin has a half-life of approximately 21 days.

Precautions to Consider

Cross-sensitivity and/or related problems

Patients sensitive to other human immune globulin products may be sensitive to rabies immune globulin (RIG) also.

Pregnancy/Reproduction

Pregnancy—Studies have not been done in humans. Because of the potential consequences of rabies virus infection, and because there is no indication that fetal abnormalities have been associated with use of RIG in pregnant women, pregnancy is not considered to be a contraindication to use.

Studies have not been done in animals.

FDA Pregnancy Category C.

Breast-feeding

Problems in humans have not been documented.

Pediatrics

Appropriate studies on the relationship of age to the effects of RIG have not been performed in the pediatric population. However, pediatrics-specific problems that would limit the usefulness of this medicine in children are not expected.

Geriatrics

No information is available on the relationship of age to the effects of RIG in geriatric patients.

Drug interactions and/or related problems

The following drug interactions and/or related problems have been selected on the basis of their potential clinical significance (possible mechanism in parentheses where appropriate)—not necessarily inclusive (» = major clinical significance):

Note: Combinations containing any of the following medications, depending on the amount present, may also interact with this medication.

Live virus vaccines
(antibodies contained in RIG may interfere with the body's immune response to certain live virus vaccines; live virus vaccines, such as measles, mumps, and rubella, should be administered at least 14 days prior to, or at least 3 months after, administration of RIG)

Medical considerations/Contraindications

The medical considerations/contraindications included have been selected on the basis of their potential clinical significance (reasons given in parentheses where appropriate)—not necessarily inclusive (» = major clinical significance).

Risk-benefit should be considered when the following medical problems exist:

» Immunoglobulin A (IgA) deficiencies, in patients who have known antibody to IgA
(small amounts of IgA may be present in RIG and may cause a severe allergic reaction in patients with antibody to IgA)

Sensitivity to RIG

Sensitivity to thimerosal
(some RIG available in the U.S. and Canada contain thimerosal)

Side/Adverse Effects

Note: Severe systemic adverse effects to rabies immune globulin (RIG) are rare.

Although not reported with RIG, anaphylaxis, angioneurotic edema, and nephrotic syndrome have been reported rarely with other immune globulin products.

If necessary, physicians should consult with the state public health department, the Centers for Disease Control (CDC), Canadian National Advisory Committee on Immunization (NACI), and/or the World Health Organization (WHO) regarding the management of serious adverse reactions.

There is no evidence that hepatitis B virus (HBV), human immunodeficiency virus (HIV), or other viruses have been transmitted by commercially available RIG in the U.S.

Since RIG is given in conjunction with rabies vaccine, adverse effects generally associated with rabies vaccine have also been temporally associated with RIG.

The following side/adverse effects have been selected on the basis of their potential clinical significance (possible signs and symptoms in parentheses where appropriate)—not necessarily inclusive:

Those indicating need for medical attention only if they continue or are bothersome

Incidence less frequent

Fever; pain, soreness, tenderness, or stiffness of the muscles at the place(s) of injection—may persist for several hours following injection

Patient Consultation

As an aid to patient consultation, refer to *Advice for the Patient, Rabies Immune Globulin (Systemic).*

In providing consultation, consider emphasizing the following selected information (» = major clinical significance):

Before using this medication

» Conditions affecting use, especially:
Sensitivity to rabies immune globulin, other human immune globulins, or thimerosal
Other medical problems, especially immunoglobulin A (IgA) deficiencies

Proper use of this medication

» Proper dosing

General Dosing Information

The recommended dose of rabies immune globulin (RIG) is 20 International Units (IU) per kg of body weight. Since RIG may partially suppress active production of rabies antibody, it is recommended that no more than the recommended dose be administered.

If anatomically feasible, up to one-half of the dose of RIG should be thoroughly infiltrated into the area(s) around the wound(s) and the rest should be administered intramuscularly in the gluteal area. Because of risk of injury to the sciatic nerve, the central region of the gluteal area should be avoided; only the upper, outer quadrant should be used.

Care should be taken to avoid injection of RIG into or near blood vessels or nerves.

RIG should **not** be administered intravenously because of the potential for serious reactions. Although systemic reactions are rare, epinephrine should be available for the treatment of acute anaphylactic reactions.

All post-exposure therapy should begin with immediate and thorough cleansing of all the patient's wounds with soap and water. Studies have shown that wound cleansing greatly reduces the likelihood of rabies.

Appropriate management of persons who may have been exposed to rabies depends on the assessment of the risk of infection. The incubation period for rabies infection varies with respect to the location and severity of the bite. The incubation period is usually 2 to 6 weeks, but can be longer. For bites to the face or extensive bites elsewhere on the body, the incubation period may be as short as 10 to 17 days. Decisions about management should be made promptly. Persons who have been bitten by animals suspected of being, or proven, rabid should begin therapy within 24 hours. If necessary, physicians should consult with the local or state public health department, the Centers for Disease Control (CDC), the Canadian National Advisory Committee on Immunization (NACI), and/or the World Health Organization (WHO) regarding the need for rabies prophylaxis.

The essential components of the rabies post-exposure prophylaxis regimen are local wound treatment, passive immunization with RIG (unless the patient has been previously immunized against rabies), and active immunization with rabies vaccine. Rabies has occasionally developed in persons when key elements of this regimen were omitted or incorrectly performed. In addition, tetanus prophylaxis and antibacterial medications may be administered as required. Both passive immunization with RIG (except for patients who have been previously immunized against rabies) and active immunization with rabies vaccine are required regardless of the interval between exposure and initiation of therapy. However, RIG should not be administered in the same syringe or into the same body site as the rabies vaccine.

Persons are considered to have been previously immunized against rabies (and as such should not receive RIG as part of the post-exposure therapy) if they have previously received complete regimens of pre- or post-exposure rabies prophylaxis with human diploid cell rabies vaccine (HDCV) or rabies vaccine adsorbed (RVA) or if they have been documented to have had an adequate antibody response to another rabies vaccine, such as duck embryo rabies vaccine. Regardless of the antibody titer that is present before post-exposure therapy occurs, an anamnestic antibody response should occur following the administration of the next dose of rabies vaccine.

RIG, when indicated, is administered only once, usually at the beginning of the post-exposure therapy regimen. RIG provides immediate passive antibodies until the patient can produce active antibodies from the rabies vaccine. If not given on the first day, RIG may be given any time up through the 7th day of the therapy regimen. Beyond the 7th day, RIG is not indicated, since an active antibody response to the rabies vaccine is presumed to have begun, and passive antibody may interfere with the body's active response.

If post-exposure prophylaxis is administered outside the U.S., additional prophylaxis may be desirable when the patient returns to the U.S. Physicians should contact the state public health department or the CDC for specific advice. This is important, since treatment regimens and products vary from country to country.

Parenteral Dosage Forms

RABIES IMMUNE GLOBULIN (HUMAN) (RIG) USP

Usual adult and adolescent dose

Immunizing agent (passive)—

Intramuscular: 20 International Units (IU) per kg of body weight. If anatomically feasible, up to one-half of the dose should be thoroughly infiltrated into the area(s) around the wound(s) and the rest should be administered intramuscularly in the gluteal area. Because of risk of injury to the sciatic nerve, the central region of the gluteal area should be avoided; only the upper, outer quadrant should be used.

Note: Rabies immune globulin (RIG) is used in conjunction with rabies vaccine and should be administered at the time of the first rabies vaccine dose or no later than the 7th day of rabies vaccine therapy.

Usual pediatric dose

See *Usual adult and adolescent dose.*

Strength(s) usually available

U.S.—

150 International Units (IU) per mL (Rx) [*BayRab* (preservative-free; glycine, 0.21 to 0.32 M); *Imogam* (thimerosal); *Imogam Rabies-HT* (preservative-free; glycine, 0.3M); *Hyperab* (thimerosal)].

Canada—

150 International Units (IU) per mL (Rx) [*Imogam* (thimerosal); *Hyperab* (thimerosal)].

300 International Units (IU) per mL (Rx) [GENERIC (may contain thimerosal)].

Note: The International Unit of potency is equivalent to the U.S. unit of potency.

Packaging and storage

Store between 2 and 8 °C (35 and 46 °F), unless otherwise specified by manufacturer. Do not freeze.

Stability

The solution should be discarded if it has been frozen.

The solution should not be used if it is discolored or contains particulate matter.

Rabies immune globulin (RIG) should not be heated. It may be warmed slightly by holding the vial in one's hands, but it should not be placed in warm water or an incubator.

Incompatibilities

RIG should not be administered in the same syringe or into the same body site as the rabies vaccine.

Auxiliary labeling

- Store in refrigerator.
- Do not freeze.
- Discard if vaccine has been frozen.

Selected Bibliography

Chabala S, Williams M, Amenta R, et al. Confirmed rabies exposure during pregnancy: treatment with human rabies immune globulin and human diploid cell vaccine. Am J Med 1991 Oct; 91: 423-4.

Centers for Disease Control and Prevention. Rabies prevention-United States, 1991: recommendations of the Immunization Practices Advisory Committee (ACIP). MMWR 1991 Mar 22; 40(RR-3): 1-19.

Frenia ML, Lafin SM, Barone JA. Features and treatment of rabies. Clin Pharm 1992 Jan; 11(1): 37-47.

Revised: 11/04/1999

RABIES VACCINE ADSORBED—See *Rabies Vaccine (Systemic)*

RABIES VACCINE, HUMAN DIPLOID CELL—See *Rabies Vaccine (Systemic)*

RALOXIFENE Systemic

VA CLASSIFICATION (Primary): HS900

Commonly used brand name(s): *Evista*.

Another commonly used name is keoxifene hydrochloride.

Note: For a listing of dosage forms and brand names by country availability, see *Dosage Forms* section(s).

Category

Estrogen receptor modulator, selective; osteoporosis prophylactic.

Indications

Accepted

Osteoporosis, postmenopausal (prophylaxis)—Raloxifene is indicated for the prevention of osteoporosis in postmenopausal women. The effects on risk of fracture are not known. Also, use of estrogens as ovarian hormone therapy (OHT) with raloxifene has not been studied and their concurrent use is not recommended. Safety and efficacy of raloxifene have not been studied in men. Supplemental calcium and/or vitamin D should be added to the diet if daily intake is inadequate.

Osteoporosis, postmenopausal (treatment)—Raloxifene is indicated for the treatment of osteoporosis in postmenopausal women. The effects on risk of fracture are not known. Also, use of estrogens as ovarian hormone therapy (OHT) with raloxifene has not been studied and their concurrent use is not recommended. Safety and efficacy of raloxifene have not been studied in men. Supplemental calcium and/or vitamin D should be added to the diet if daily intake is inadequate.

Unaccepted

Raloxifene is not effective in reducing the hot flashes or flushes of estrogen deficiency, such as those occurring during the menopause.

There is no indication for premenopausal use in women. Safety has not been established and its use is not recommended.

Pharmacology/Pharmacokinetics

Physicochemical characteristics

Note: Raloxifene shows high interindividual variability as seen by an approximate 30% coefficient of variation in most pharmacokinetic parameters.

Chemical Group—Nonsteroidal, benzothiophene derivative.

Molecular weight—Raloxifene hydrochloride: 510.06.

Mechanism of action/Effect

Selective estrogen receptor modulator—Estrogen receptors regulate gene expression by ligand-, tissue-, or gene-specific pathways or a combination of these. Raloxifene acts as a ligand for the estrogen receptor and, depending on the tissue's subtype of estrogen receptors or available cellular proteins, can cause an estrogenic agonist or antagonist reaction or may not cause any apparent change in a tissue's gene expression.

Osteoporosis prophylactic—Raloxifene has estrogen-like effects on bone and increases bone mineral density. It reduces resorption of bone and decreases overall bone turnover, as shown by radiocalcium kinetics studies and by bone turnover markers in the serum and urine. Postmenopausal females who took daily doses of 60 mg raloxifene and 400 to 600 mg of calcium showed a statistically significant increase in bone mineral density (BMD) in the hip, spine, and total body at 12 months that was maintained at 24 months as measured by dual-energy radiography (DXA) compared with women taking a placebo and similar calcium doses. The extent of bone density increase is less with use of raloxifene than with daily doses of 0.625 mg conjugated estrogens. The placebo/calcium females lost 1% of BMD over 24 months. The effects of raloxifene on the forearm have been inconsistent between studies. It is not established whether raloxifene's effect of increasing BMD results in a reduced number of skeletal fractures.

Other actions/effects

Raloxifene has estrogen-like effects for lowering serum total and low-density lipoprotein (LDL) cholesterol, but it does not affect serum concentrations of total high-density lipoprotein (HDL) cholesterol or triglycerides. Raloxifene has not been associated with other estrogen-like effects, such as endometrial proliferation, breast pain, or breast enlargement.

Absorption

Raloxifene is rapidly absorbed after oral administration. Absolute raloxifene bioavailability is 2%, approximately 60% of an oral dose is absorbed, and enterohepatic cycling occurs. Although not considered clinically significant, absorption may increase when raloxifene is given with a high-fat meal, as shown by a 28% increase in peak serum concentration (C_{max}) and a 16% increase in the area under the plasma concentration-time curve (AUC).

Distribution

For 30 to 150 mg single doses of raloxifene, the apparent volume of distribution (Vol_D) is 2348 L per kg (L/kg) and is not dose-dependent.

Protein binding

Raloxifene and its glucuronide conjugates are highly bound to plasma proteins albumin and alpha-1-acid glycoprotein, but not to sex hormone-binding globulin.

Biotransformation

First-pass metabolism to the glucuronide conjugate is extensive; 1% unconjugated raloxifene appears in the plasma as a result of interconversion between conjugated and unconjugated forms.

Half-life

Elimination—32.5 hours (range 15.8 to 86.6) with multiple dosing.

Elimination

Primarily fecal, 0.2% renal (unchanged) and 6% renal (glucuronide metabolite).

Precautions to Consider

Carcinogenicity/Tumorigenicity

Raloxifene did not increase the risk of endometrial or breast cancer in patients taking raloxifene for up to 58 months when compared with patients taking placebos.

In a 21-month study, there was an increased incidence of benign tumors of granulosal, thecal, or epithelial cell origin in female mice given raloxifene doses of 9 to 242 mg per kg of body weight (mg/kg) (corresponding to 0.3 to 34 times the systemic exposure of that achieved in postmenopausal women taking a 60-mg daily dose). Malignant tumors of granulosal/thecal origin occurred at the higher doses. There was an increased incidence of testicular interstitial cell tumors, prostatic adenomas, and adenocarcinomas in male mice given 41 mg/kg or 210 mg/kg of raloxifene (corresponding to 4.7 to 24 times the systemic exposure in humans); the higher dose showed incidence of prostatic leiomyoblastomas.

In a 2-year study, there was an increased incidence of benign granulosal or thecal cell ovarian tumors in nonovariectomized female rats of reproductive age given doses of 279 mg/kg of raloxifene (corresponding to approximately 400 times the systemic exposure of that achieved in humans).

The clinical relevance of the animal data to humans is not known.

Mutagenicity

Raloxifene was not found to be mutagenic in the following tests or assays: Ames test, unscheduled DNA synthesis assay in rat hepatocytes, mouse lymphoma assay for mammalian cell mutation, chromosomal aberration assay in Chinese hamster ovary cells, *in vivo* sister chromatid exchanges assay in Chinese hamsters, and *in vivo* micronucleus test in mice.

Pregnancy/Reproduction

Reproduction studies in rats given raloxifene are consistent with estrogen receptor activity.

Fertility—In rats given at least 5 mg/kg a day of raloxifene (corresponding to 0.8 times or more the human dose based on mg per squared meter [mg/m²] of body surface area), no pregnancies occurred. In male rats, 100 mg/kg of raloxifene a day for 2 weeks (corresponding to 16 times the human dose based on body surface area) did not affect sperm production or quality or reproductive performance. In female rats, 0.1 to 10 mg/kg a day of raloxifene (corresponding to 0.02 to 1.5 times the human dose based on body surface area) reversibly disrupted estrous cycles, inhibited ovulation, and delayed and disrupted embryo implantation, resulting in prolonged gestation and a small litter size.

Pregnancy—Raloxifene is not recommended during pregnancy.

Studies in animals have shown that raloxifene decreased neonatal survival, delayed and disrupted parturition, and caused fetal abortion, ventricular septal defects, hydrocephaly, wavy ribs, kidney cavitation, lymphoid compartment size reduction, growth reduction, and pituitary hormone content changes. Although no ovarian or vaginal pathology resulted, effects in adult offspring included uterine hypoplasia and reduced fertility.

FDA Pregnancy Category X.

Breast-feeding

It is not known whether raloxifene is distributed into breast milk. However, use of raloxifene during breast-feeding is not recommended.

Geriatrics

Appropriate studies performed to date have not demonstrated geriatrics-specific problems that would limit the usefulness of raloxifene in the elderly.

Surgical

Raloxifene should be discontinued for at least 72 hours prior to and during prolonged bed rest or immobilization, such as during postsurgical recovery, because of increased risk of venous thromboembolic events. The medication should be resumed only after the patient is fully ambulatory.

Drug interactions and/or related problems

The following drug interactions and/or related problems have been selected on the basis of their potential clinical significance (possible mechanism in parentheses where appropriate)—not necessarily inclusive (» = major clinical significance):

Note: Combinations containing any of the following medications, depending on the amount present, may also interact with this medication.

» Cholestyramine
(reduces the absorption and enterohepatic recycling of raloxifene by 60%; concomitant use is not recommended)

» Estrogens, systemic
(raloxifene is not recommended for use with estrogens)

Highly protein-bound drugs, such as:
Clofibrate
Diazepam
Diazoxide
Ibuprofen
Indomethacin
Lidocaine
Naproxen
(caution is recommended in using concurrently since raloxifene is highly bound to plasma proteins)

» Warfarin
(raloxifene alone does not affect the protein-binding of warfarin, but concurrent use has decreased the prothrombin time by 10% in single-dose studies; when given concurrently, prothrombin time should be monitored and the dose of warfarin may need an initial adjustment)

Laboratory value alterations

The following have been selected on the basis of their potential clinical significance (possible effect in parentheses where appropriate)—not necessarily inclusive (» = major clinical significance).

With physiology/laboratory test values
Albumin concentration, serum and
Calcium concentration, total, serum and
Phosphate concentration, serum and
Protein concentration, total, serum
(slightly decreased)

Cholesterol concentrations, total, serum and
Lipoproteins concentrations, low-density (LDL), serum
(compared with the patients' baselines, serum total cholesterol concentrations decreased 5% in 24-month data and 6.6% in a 6-month study; LDL decreased 8% in the 24-month data and 10.9% in a 6-month study)

Corticosteroid-binding globulin and
Sex steroid-binding globulin and
Thyroid-binding globulin
(may modestly increase serum protein–binding globulins without increasing the free fraction of corresponding hormones)

Fibrinogen concentration, serum and

Lipoprotein (a) concentration
(in a 6-month study, fibrinogen decreased by a median of 12.2% from patients' baselines and lipoprotein (a) decreased by a median of 4.1% from patients' baselines)

Lipoproteins concentrations, high-density-3 (HDL-3), serum
(serum HDL-3 concentrations decreased by a median of 2.5% compared with the patients' baselines in a 6-month study; no effect occurred for serum concentrations of triglycerides and serum total high-density lipoprotein [HDL] cholesterol)

Platelet count
(slightly decreased)

Triglycerides, serum
(values may increase with raloxifene treatment in some women with a history of marked hypertriglyceridemia (>5.6 mmol/L or >500 mg/dL) in response to treatment with oral estrogen plus progestin)

Medical considerations/Contraindications

The medical considerations/contraindications included have been selected on the basis of their potential clinical significance (reasons given in parentheses where appropriate)—not necessarily inclusive (» = major clinical significance).

Except under special circumstances, this medication should not be used when the following medical problem exists:

» Thromboembolic disorders, active or history of, including deep vein thrombosis, pulmonary embolism, and retinal vein thrombosis (may be exacerbated)

Risk-benefit should be considered when the following medical problems exist:

» Congestive heart failure or
» Neoplasia or
» Other conditions of increased thromboembolic risk
(underlying thromboembolic disorders may be exacerbated)

Hepatic function impairment
(may increase plasma concentrations of raloxifene. In patients with cirrhosis classified as Child-Pugh Class A, plasma concentrations of raloxifene were 2.5 times greater than expected, correlating with their total bilirubin concentrations; safety and efficacy in patients with severe hepatic function impairment have not been evaluated)

Sensitivity to raloxifene

Patient monitoring

The following may be especially important in patient monitoring (other tests may be warranted in some patients, depending on condition; » = major clinical significance):

Physical examination
(every year or more frequently as determined by physician, with special attention given to breast and pelvic organs)

Triglycerides, serum
(should be monitored during raloxifene treatment; limited clinical data suggests that some women with a history of marked hypertriglyceridemia (>5.6 mmol/L or >500 mg/dL) in response to treatment with oral estrogen plus progestin may develop increased levels of triglycerides when treated with raloxifene)

Side/Adverse Effects

The following side/adverse effects have been selected on the basis of their potential clinical significance (possible signs and symptoms in parentheses where appropriate)—not necessarily inclusive:

Those indicating need for medical attention

Incidence more frequent

Chest pain—4%; ***cystitis or urinary tract infection*** (bloody or cloudy urine; difficult, burning, or painful urination; frequent urge to urinate)—3.3 to 4%; ***endometrial disorder***—3.1%; ***fever***—3.1%; ***infection of the body as a whole; influenza-like syndrome; sinusitis; or pharyngitis*** (body aches or pain; congestion in throat; cough; dryness or soreness of throat; fever; loss of voice; runny nose)—7 to 15%; ***leg cramping***—5.9%; ***peripheral edema*** (swelling of hands, ankles, or feet)—3.3%; ***skin rash***—5.5%; ***vaginitis*** (vaginal itching)—4.3%

Incidence less frequent

Gastroenteritis (abdominal pain, severe; diarrhea; loss of appetite; nausea; weakness)—2.6%; ***laryngitis*** (cough; dryness or soreness of throat; hoarseness; trouble in swallowing)—2.2%; ***migraine headaches***—2.4%; ***pneumonia*** (aching body pains; congestion in lungs; difficulty in breathing; fever; sore throat)—2.6%

Incidence rare

Retinal vein occlusion (decreased vision or other changes in vision)—Observed during clinical practice; ***thromboembolism or thrombus formation*** (coughing blood; headache or migraine headache; loss of or change in speech, coordination, or vision; pain or numbness in chest, arm, or leg; shortness of breath, unexplained)

Those indicating need for medical attention only if they continue or are bothersome

Incidence less frequent

Arthralgia; arthritis; or myalgia (joint or muscle pain; swollen joints)—4 to 10.7%; ***gastrointestinal disturbances*** (nausea; passing of gas; upset stomach; vomiting); ***hot flashes*** (feelings of warmth; sudden sweating)—24.6%, especially common during the first 6 months of treatment; ***insomnia*** (trouble in sleeping)—5.5%; ***leukorrhea*** (increased white vaginal discharge)—3.3%; ***mental depression***—6.4%; ***sweating***—3.1%; ***weight gain, unexplained***—8.8%

Patient Consultation

As an aid to patient consultation, refer to *Advice for the Patient, Raloxifene (Systemic)*.

In providing consultation, consider emphasizing the following selected information (» = major clinical significance):

Before using this medication

» Conditions affecting use, especially:
Sensitivity to raloxifene or allergies to product's components
Pregnancy—Not recommended for use during pregnancy. Approved for use in postmenopausal women only. Raloxifene has been associated with fetal abnormalities in animals
Breast-feeding—Not recommended for use during breast-feeding
Surgical—Discontinue use 72 hours before surgery, until patient is fully mobilized
Other medications, especially cholestyramine; estrogens (systemic); or warfarin
Other medical problems, especially congestive heart failure, neoplasia, or other conditions of increased thromboembolic risk; or thromboembolic disorders, active or history of (deep vein thrombosis, pulmonary embolism, and retinal vein thrombosis)

Proper use of this medication

» Reading patient directions that come with medication carefully before using
» Not taking more or less of medication than your physician ordered
» Proper dosing
Missed dose: Skipping missed dose and resuming regular dosing schedule; not doubling dose
» Proper storage

Precautions while using this medication

» Regular visits to physician, keeping appointments even if feeling well

» Discussing continuing medication with physician before having surgery or periods of immobility, including the inactivity of long trips, because of potential increased risk of thromboembolism

» Stopping medication immediately and checking with physician if pregnancy is suspected; present use is for postmenopausal women only

» Reporting occurrences of vaginal bleeding, breast pain, or swelling of hands or feet

» Importance of weight-bearing exercise and calcium and vitamin D supplements for prevention of osteoporosis

Side/adverse effects

Signs of potential side effects, especially chest pain; cystitis or urinary tract infection; endometrial disorder; fever; infection of the body as a whole, influenza-like syndrome, sinusitis, or pharyngitis; leg cramping; peripheral edema; skin rash; vaginitis; gastroenteritis; laryngitis; migraine headaches; pneumonia; retinal vein occlusion; thromboembolism or thrombus formation

General Dosing Information

Because of increased risk of venous thromboembolic events, raloxifene should be discontinued for at least 72 hours prior to surgery and during prolonged bed rest or immobilization, such as in postsurgical recovery or during a long trip when mobility is not possible. To prevent thromboembolic events while taking raloxifene, the patient should understand the importance of mobility during a long trip. The medication may be resumed only after the patient is fully ambulatory.

If a pregnancy is possible and is suspected, patient should stop using the medication and contact physician immediately. Present use is for postmenopausal women only.

Since raloxifene does not act like an estrogen to stimulate the uterus or breast, patients should report any occurrences of vaginal bleeding, breast pain or enlargement, or swelling of hands or feet while on raloxifene.

Exercise can be recommended to all patients to prevent development of osteoporosis. Calcium supplementation should be considered as an additional preventive measure if patient's dietary intake is inadequate.

Diet/Nutrition
Raloxifene may be given without regard to meals.

Oral Dosage Forms

RALOXIFENE HYDROCHLORIDE TABLETS

Note: Formerly known as keoxifene hydrochloride.

Usual adult dose
Osteoporosis prophylactic—
Oral, 60 mg once a day, without regard to meals.
Osteoporosis treatment—
Oral, 60 mg once a day, without regard to meals.

Usual adult prescribing limits
Efficacy beyond 2 years for prevention of osteoporosis has not been determined.

Usual geriatric dose
See *Usual adult dose.*

Strength(s) usually available
U.S.—
60 mg (Rx) [*Evista* (anhydrous lactose; lactose monohydrate; polyethylene glycol; povidone; propylene glycol)].

Packaging and storage
Store between 15 and 30 °C (59 and 86 °F), preferably between 20 and 25 °C (68 and 77 °F), unless otherwise specified by manufacturer.

Caution
The previously available product *E-Vista*, the brand name for hydroxyzine hydrochloride, should not be confused with *Evista*, raloxifene hydrochloride. They are different products with completely different indications.

Note
Include patient information when dispensing.

Revised: 02/08/2002
Developed: 3/26/1998

RALTITREXED Systemic*

VA CLASSIFICATION (Primary): AN300

Commonly used brand name(s): *Tomudex*.

Note: For a listing of dosage forms and brand names by country availability, see *Dosage Forms* section(s).

*Not commercially available in U.S.

Category

Antineoplastic.

Indications

Accepted

Carcinoma, colorectal (treatment)—Raltitrexed is indicated in the treatment of advanced colorectal cancer.

Pharmacology/Pharmacokinetics

Physicochemical characteristics
Molecular weight—458.49.
pKa—The estimated pKa values of the two carboxylic acid groups are 4.5 and 5.7 at 25 °C.
Solubility—Solubility is susceptible to pH.

Mechanism of action/Effect
Raltitrexed is a quinazoline folate analogue that selectively inhibits thymidylate synthase (TS). Inhibition of TS leads to DNA fragmentation and cell death. Once transported into cells via a reduced folate carrier, raltitrexed is extensively polyglutamated, which enhances TS inhibitory potency and duration, which may increase the antitumor activity.

Distribution
Volume of distribution (Vol_D)—Steady state: 548 L.

Protein binding
Very high (93%).

Biotransformation
Raltitrexed is transported into cells via a reduced folate carrier and is then extensively polyglutamated by the enzyme folyl polyglutamate synthetase to polyglutamate forms.

Half-life
Half-life is triphasic.
Second phase—1.79 hours.
Terminal—198 hours.

Peak plasma concentration
Following intravenous administration at 3 mg/m^2—656 ng/mL.

The maximum concentrations of raltitrexed increased linearly with dose over the clinical dose range tested.

Elimination
Primarily excreted unchanged in the urine (approximately 50%).

Fecal excretion also occurs with approximately 15% of the dose being eliminated over a 10 day period.

In one study, approximately half of the radiolabeled raltitrexed was not recovered during the study period suggesting that a proportion (50%) of the dose is retained within tissues, perhaps as polyglutamates. Trace levels of radiolabeled raltitrexed were detected in red blood cells on Day 29.

Following intravenous administration at 3 mg/m^2:
- Renal clearance—25.1 mL/min.
- Total clearance—51.6 mL/min.

In patients with normal renal function, there was no clinically significant plasma accumulation of raltitrexed during repeat administration at three week intervals. In patients with mild to moderate renal impairment (creatinine clearance of 25 to 65 mL/min), plasma clearance was significantly reduced (approximately 50%).

In patients with mild (WHO grade 2) to moderate (WHO grade 3) hepatic impairment, plasma clearance was reduced by less than 25%.

Additional pharmacokinetic information
Pharmacokinetics are independent of age and gender.

Pharmacokinetics have not been evaluated in children.

Precautions to Consider

Carcinogenicity
The carcinogenic potential of raltitrexed has not been evaluated.

Mutagenicity
Raltitrexed was not mutagenic in the Ames test or in supplementary tests using *E. coli* or chinese hamster ovary cells. Raltitrexed caused increased levels of chromosome damage in an *in vitro* assay of human lymphocytes. An *in vivo* micronucleus study in the rat indicated that at cytotoxic dose levels, raltitrexed is capable of causing chromosome damage in the bone marrow.

Pregnancy/Reproduction
Fertility—In rats, raltitrexed can cause impairment of male fertility. Fertility returned to normal three months after dosing ceased.

Pregnancy—Raltitrexed is not recommended during pregnancy. Pregnancy should be excluded before treatment with raltitrexed is begun and should be avoided during treatment and for at least 6 months after discontinuation of treatment if either partner is receiving raltitrexed.

In pregnant rats, raltitrexed caused embryolethality and fetal abnormalities.

Breast-feeding
It is not known whether raltitrexed is distributed into breast milk. However, raltitrexed is not recommended in women who are breast-feeding.

Pediatrics
Raltitrexed is not recommended for use in children. Safety and efficacy have not been established.

Geriatrics
Elderly patients are more vulnerable to the toxic effects of raltitrexed, particularly gastrointestinal toxicity. Elderly patients are more likely to have age-related renal function impairment, which may require reduction of dosage in patients receiving raltitrexed.

Pharmacogenetics
Raltitrexed pharmacokinetics are independent of age and gender.

Dental
The bone marrow depressant effects of raltitrexed may result in an increased incidence of microbial infection, delayed healing, and gingival bleeding. Dental work, whenever possible, should be completed prior to initiation of therapy or deferred until blood counts have returned to normal. Patients should be instructed in proper oral hygiene during treatment, including caution in use of regular toothbrushes, dental floss, and toothpicks.

Drug interactions and/or related problems

The following drug interactions and/or related problems have been selected on the basis of their potential clinical significance (possible mechanism in parentheses where appropriate)—not necessarily inclusive (» = major clinical significance):

Blood dyscrasia-causing medications (see *Appendix II*)
(leukopenic and/or thrombocytopenic effects of raltitrexed may be increased with concurrent or recent therapy if these medications cause the same effects; dosage adjustment of raltitrexed, if necessary, should be based on blood counts)

» Bone marrow depressants, other (see *Appendix II*) or
Radiation therapy
(additive bone marrow depression may occur; dosage reduction may be required when two or more bone marrow depressants, including radiation, are used concurrently or consecutively)

» Folic acid or
» Leucovorin (folinic acid) or
» Vitamin preparations containing folic or folinic acid
(should not be given immediately prior to or during raltitrexed administration due to possible interference with the therapeutic effects of raltitrexed)

Immunosuppressants, other
(concurrent use with raltitrexed may increase the risk of infection and development of neoplasms)

Vaccines, killed virus
(because normal defense mechanisms may be suppressed by raltitrexed therapy, the patient's antibody response to the vaccine may be decreased. The interval between discontinuation of medications that cause immunosuppression and restoration of the patient's ability to respond to the vaccine depends on the intensity and type of immunosuppression-causing medication used, the underlying disease, and other factors; estimates vary from 3 months to 1 year)

» Vaccines, live virus
(because normal defense mechanisms may be suppressed by raltitrexed therapy, concurrent use with a live virus vaccine may potentiate the replication of the vaccine virus, may increase the side/adverse effects of the vaccine virus, and/or may decrease the patient's antibody response to the vaccine; immunization of these patients should be undertaken only with extreme caution after careful review of the patient's hematologic status and only with the knowledge and consent of the physician managing the raltitrexed therapy. The interval between discontinuation of medications that cause immunosuppression and restoration of the patient's ability to respond to the vaccine depends on the intensity and type of immunosuppression-causing medication used, the underlying disease, and other factors; estimates vary from 3 months to 1 year. Immunization with oral poliovirus vaccine should also be postponed in persons in close contact with the patient, especially family members)

Laboratory value alterations

The following have been selected on the basis of their potential clinical significance (possible effect in parentheses where appropriate)—not necessarily inclusive (» = major clinical significance).

With physiology/laboratory test values
Alanine aminotransferase (ALT [SGPT]), serum and
Alkaline phosphatase, serum and
Aspartate aminotransferase (AST [SGOT], serum
(values may be increased transiently)

Medical considerations/Contraindications

The medical considerations/contraindications included have been selected on the basis of their potential clinical significance (reasons given in parentheses where appropriate)—not necessarily inclusive (» = major clinical significance).

Except under special circumstances, this medication should not be used when the following medical problem exists:

» Hepatic function impairment, severe
» Renal function impairment, severe
» Sensitivity to raltitrexed

Risk-benefit should be considered when the following medical problems exist:

» Bone marrow depression
» Chickenpox, existing or recent (including recent exposure) or
» Herpes zoster
(risk of severe generalized disease)

Hepatic function impairment, mild to moderate
(elimination may be reduced)

» Infection

Renal function impairment, mild to moderate
(reduced elimination; lower dosage is recommended)

» Caution should be used also in patients who have had previous cytotoxic drug or radiation therapy

Patient monitoring

Alanine aminotransferase (ALT [SGPT]) values and
Alkaline phosphatase values and
Aspartate aminotransferase (AST [SGOT]) values and
Bilirubin concentrations, serum
(recommended prior to initiation of treatment and before each subsequent treatment)

» Blood counts, complete and
» Hematocrit or hemoglobin and
» Leukocyte count, total and, if appropriate, differential and
» Neutrophil count, absolute (ANC) and
» Platelet count
(recommended prior to initiation of treatment and before each subsequent treatment)

» Creatinine clearance and
» Creatinine, serum
(recommended prior to initiation of treatment and before each subsequent treatment)

Side/Adverse Effects

Note: Many "side effects" of antineoplastic therapy are unavoidable and represent the medication's pharmacologic action. Some of these (for example, leukopenia and thrombocytopenia) are actually used as parameters to aid in individual dosage titration.

Adverse effects associated with raltitrexed mainly include reversible effects on the gastrointestinal tract, hematopoietic system, and liver enzymes.

The following side/adverse effects have been selected on the basis of their potential clinical significance (possible signs and symptoms in parentheses where appropriate)—not necessarily inclusive:

Those indicating need for medical attention

Incidence more frequent

Anemia (pale skin; troubled breathing, exertional; unusual bleeding or bruising; unusual tiredness or weakness); ***leukopenia*** (black, tarry stools; chest pain; chills; cough; fever; painful or difficult urination; shortness of breath; sore throat; sores, ulcers, or white spots on lips or in mouth; swollen glands; unusual bleeding or bruising; unusual tiredness or weakness); ***diarrhea*** (increase in bowel movements; loose stools; soft stools)—can be severe

Note: *Anemia and leukopenia* are usually mild to moderate, reaching a nadir in the first or second week after treatment and recovering by the third week. Severe leukopenia of WHO grade 4 can occur and may be life-threatening or fatal, especially if associated with gastrointestinal toxicity.

Diarrhea is usually mild or moderate in intensity. However, severe diarrhea can occur, and may be associated with concurrent hematological suppression, especially leukopenia. Subsequent treatment may need to be discontinued or the dose reduced depending on the grade of toxicity.

Incidence less frequent

Arrhythmias (dizziness; fainting; fast, slow, or irregular heartbeat); ***congestive heart failure*** (chest pain; decreased urine output; dilated neck veins; extreme fatigue; irregular breathing; irregular heartbeat; shortness of breath; swelling of face, fingers, feet, or lower legs; tightness in chest; troubled breathing; weight gain; wheezing); ***thrombocytopenia*** (black, tarry stools; chest pain; chills; cough; fever; painful or difficult urination; shortness of breath; sore throat; sores, ulcers, or white spots on lips or in mouth; swollen glands; unusual bleeding or bruising; unusual tiredness or weakness)

Note: *Thrombocytopenia* is usually mild to moderate, reaching a nadir in the first or second week after treatment and recovering by the third week. Severe thrombocytopenia of WHO grade 4 can occur and may be life-threatening or fatal, especially if associated with gastrointestinal toxicity

Those indicating need for medical attention only if they continue or are bothersome

Incidence more frequent

Abdominal pain (stomach or abdomen pain); ***anorexia*** (loss of appetite; weight loss); ***constipation; nausea; stomatitis*** (swelling or inflammation of the mouth); ***vomiting; asthenia*** (lack or loss of strength); ***fever; flu syndrome*** (chills; cough; diarrhea; fever; general feeling of discomfort or illness; headache; joint pain; loss of appetite; muscle aches and pains; nausea; runny nose; shivering; sore throat; sweating; trouble sleeping; unusual tiredness or weakness; vomiting); ***rash***

Note: *Asthenia and fever* are usually mild to moderate and reversible. However, severe asthenia can occur and may be associated with malaise and a flu-like syndrome.

Nausea and vomiting are usually mild or moderate and responsive to antiemetics.

Incidence less frequent

Headache; peripheral edema (bloating or swelling of face, arms, hands, lower legs, or feet; rapid weight gain; tingling of hands or feet)

Those not indicating need for medical attention

Incidence more frequent

Alopecia (hair loss; thinning of hair)

Incidence less frequent

Taste disturbance (change in taste; bad unusual or unpleasant (after)taste); ***weight loss***

Those indicating need for medical attention only if they occur after medication is discontinued

Bone marrow depression (black, tarry stools; blood in urine or stools; cough or hoarseness; fever or chills; lower back or side pain; painful or difficult urination; pinpoint red spots on skin; unusual bleeding or bruising)

Overdose

For specific information on the agents used in the management of raltitrexed overdose, see: *Leucovorin (Systemic)*.

For more information on the management of overdose or unintentional ingestion, **contact a poison control center** (see *Poison Control Center Listing*).

Clinical effects of overdose

Expected manifestations of overdose are likely to be an exaggerated form of the adverse drug reactions anticipated with the administration of raltitrexed, particularly gastrointestinal and hematological toxicity.

Treatment of overdose

There is no clinically proven antidote to raltitrexed; however, consideration should be given to the administration of leucovorin. From clinical experience with other antifolates, leucovorin may be given at a dose of 25 mg/m^2 intravenously every 6 hours. Leucovorin should be administered as soon as possible following accidental raltitrexed overdosage. The efficacy of leucovorin in reducing raltitrexed toxicity may decrease as the time between raltitrexed administration and the initiation of leucovorin therapy increases.

Supportive care—Patients should be managed with appropriate supportive therapy, including intravenous hydration and bone marrow support. Patients in whom intentional overdose is confirmed or suspected should be referred for psychiatric consultation.

Patient Consultation

As an aid to patient consultation, refer to *Advice for the Patient, Raltitrexed (Systemic)*.

In providing consultation, consider emphasizing the following selected information (» = major clinical significance):

Before using this medication

» Conditions affecting use, especially:

Sensitivity to raltitrexed

Caused chromosome damage in an *in vitro* assay of human lymphocytes; caused chromosome damage in the bone marrow of rats, at cytotoxic dose levels

Pregnancy—Not recommended for use during pregnancy (while taking this medication and avoid pregnancy for at least 6 months after last dose)

Breast-feeding—Not recommended because of risk of serious side effects.

Use in children—Not recommended for use in children.

Other medications, especially folic acid, leucovorin (folinic acid), other bone marrow depressants, previous cytotoxic drug therapy or radiation therapy, or vitamin preparations containing folic or folinic acid

Other medical problems, especially bone marrow depression, chickenpox, herpes zoster, severe hepatic function impairment, infection, or severe renal function impairment

Proper use of this medication

Caution with combination therapy; taking each medication at the right time

Frequency of nausea and vomiting; importance of continuing medication despite stomach upset

» Proper dosing

Missed dose: Consult physician

Precautions while using this medication

» Importance of close monitoring by physician

» Raltitrexed may cause a general feeling of discomfort or illness and unusual tiredness or weakness following the infusion; this may impair the ability to drive or use machinery

» Avoiding immunizations unless approved by physician; other persons in patient's household should avoid immunizations with oral poliovirus vaccine; avoiding other persons who have taken oral poliovirus vaccine or wearing a protective mask that covers nose and mouth

Caution if bone marrow depression occurs:

» Avoiding exposure to persons with infections, especially during periods of low blood counts; checking with physician immediately if fever or chills, cough or hoarseness, lower back or side pain, or painful or difficult urination occurs

» Checking with physician immediately if unusual bleeding or bruising; black, tarry stools; blood in urine or stools; or pinpoint red spots on skin occur

Caution in use of regular toothbrush, dental floss, or toothpick; physician, dentist, or nurse may suggest alternatives; checking with physician before having dental work done

Not touching eyes or inside of nose unless hands are washed immediately before

Using caution to avoid accidental cuts with use of sharp objects such as safety razor or fingernail or toenail cutters

Avoiding contact sports or other situations where bruising or injury could occur

Side/adverse effects

Signs of potential side effects, especially anemia, leukopenia, diarrhea, arrhythmias, congestive heart failure, and thrombocytopenia

Physician or nurse can help in dealing with side effects

Possibility of hair loss; normal hair growth should resume after treatment has ended

General Dosing Information

Patients receiving raltitrexed should be under supervision of a physician experienced in cancer chemotherapy and in the management of related toxicities.

It is recommended that raltitrexed be administered as a single short, intravenous infusion in 0.9% sodium chloride or 5% dextrose (over a 15 minute period).

Prior to the initiation of treatment and before each subsequent treatment a full blood count (including a differential count and platelets), liver transaminases, serum bilirubin, and serum creatinine measurements should be performed. The total white cell count should be greater than 4000/mm^3, the neutrophil count greater than 2000/mm^3, and the platelet count greater than 100,000/mm^3 prior to treatment.

In the event of toxicity the next scheduled dose should be withheld until signs of toxic effects regress. Gastrointestinal and hematological toxicity should have resolved completely before subsequent treatment is permitted. Patients who develop signs of gastrointestinal toxicity should have their full blood counts monitored at least weekly for signs of hematological toxicity. Treatment in patients with elevated liver enzymes should be deferred until they show signs of reversibility to at least WHO grade 2.

Based on the worst grade of gastrointestinal and hematological toxicity observed on the previous treatment and provided that such toxicity has resolved completely, the following dose reductions are recommended for subsequent treatments:

- 25% dose reduction in patients with WHO grade 3 hematological toxicity (neutropenia or thrombocytopenia) or WHO grade 2 gastrointestinal toxicity (diarrhea or mucositis).
- 50% dose reduction in patients with WHO grade 4 hematological toxicity (neutropenia or thrombocytopenia) or WHO grade 3 gastrointestinal toxicity (diarrhea or mucositis).

Once a dose reduction has been made, all subsequent doses should be given at the reduced dose level.

Treatment should be discontinued in the event of any WHO grade 4 gastrointestinal toxicity (diarrhea or mucositis) or in the event of a WHO grade 3 gastrointestinal toxicity associated with WHO grade 4 hematological toxicity. Patients with mild to moderate renal impairment (creatinine clearance of 25 to 65 mL/min) will require a dosage adjustment. For patients with abnormal serum creatinine, before the first or any subsequent treatment, a creatinine clearance should be obtained.

Patients with mild (WHO grade 2) to moderate (WHO grade 3) hepatic impairment do not require a dosage adjustment. However, these patients should be monitored carefully.

Special precautions are recommended in patients who develop thrombocytopenia as a result of administration of raltitrexed. These may include extreme care in performing invasive procedures; regular inspection of intravenous sites, skin (including perirectal area), and mucous membrane surfaces for signs of bleeding or bruising; limiting frequency of venipuncture and avoiding intramuscular injections; testing urine, emesis, stool, and secretions for occult blood; care in use of regular toothbrushes, dental floss, toothpicks, safety razors, and fingernail and toenail cutters; avoiding constipation; and using caution to prevent falls and other injuries. Such patients should avoid alcohol and any aspirin intake because of the risk of gastrointestinal bleeding. Platelet transfusions may be required.

Patients who develop leukopenia should be observed carefully for signs of infection. Antibiotic support may be required. In neutropenic patients who develop fever, broad-spectrum antibiotic coverage should be initiated empirically, pending bacterial cultures and appropriate diagnostic tests.

Safety considerations for handling this medication

There is limited but increasing evidence and concern that personnel involved in preparation and administration of parenteral antineoplastics may be at some risk because of the potential mutagenicity, teratogenicity, and/or carcinogenicity of these agents, although the actual risk is unknown. USP advisory panels recommend cautious handling both in preparation and disposal of antineoplastic agents. Precautions that have been suggested include:

- Use of a biological containment cabinet during reconstitution and dilution of parenteral medications and wearing of disposable surgical gloves and masks.
- Use of proper technique to prevent contamination of the medication, work area, and operator during transfer between containers (including proper training of personnel in this technique).
- Cautious and proper disposal of needles, syringes, vials, ampuls, and unused medication.

A number of medical centers have developed detailed guidelines for handling of antineoplastic agents.

For treatment of adverse effects

WHO grade 4 gastrointestinal toxicity or WHO grade 3 gastrointestinal toxicity associated with WHO grade 4 hematological toxicity should be managed promptly with standard supportive care measures including intravenous hydration and bone marrow support.

To improve intestinal damage and recovery of neutrophil and platelet numbers, leucovorin (folinic acid) may be given at a dose of 25 mg/m^2 intravenously every 6 hours until the resolution of symptoms.

Parenteral Dosage Forms

RALTITREXED DISODIUM INJECTION

Usual adult and adolescent dose

Carcinoma, colorectal—

Intravenous, 3 mg per square meter of body surface area every 3 weeks.

Note: RENAL IMPAIRMENT: Adults with impaired renal function (creatinine clearance ≤ 65 mL/min) may require a change in dosing as follows:

Creatinine clearance	Dose as % of 3 mg/m²	Dosing interval
> 65 mL/min	Full dose	3–weekly
55 to 65 mL/min	75%	4–weekly
25 to 54 mL/min	% equivalent to mL/min*	4–weekly
< 25 mL/min	No therapy	Not applicable

*For example, if the creatinine clearance = 30 mL/min, 30% of the full dose should be given.

Note: HEPATIC IMPAIRMENT: Adults with mild (WHO grade 2) to moderate (WHO grade 3) hepatic impairment do not require a dosage adjustment. However, these patients should be monitored carefully.

Usual adult and adolescent prescribing limits

Dose escalation above 3 mg per square meter of body surface area is not recommended, since higher doses have been associated with an increased incidence of life-threatening or fatal toxicity.

Usual pediatric dose

Not recommended for use in children. Safety and efficacy have not been established.

Usual geriatric dose

See *Usual adult and adolescent dose*. See *Precautions* section.

Strength(s) usually available

U.S.—

Not commercially available.

Canada—

2 mg of raltitrexed disodium per single dose vial. (Rx) [*Tomudex* (sterile lyophilized powder; mannitol, dibasic sodium phosphate, sodium hydroxide)].

Packaging and storage

Store at 2 to 25 °C. Protect from light.

Preparation of dosage form

Each vial, containing 2 mg of raltitrexed, should be reconstituted with 4 mL of sterile water for injection to produce a 0.5 mg/mL solution. The appropriate dose of solution is diluted in 50 to 250 mL of either 0.9% sodium chloride or 5% dextrose solution.

Stability

The reconstituted solution is stable for 24 hours at 25 °C exposed to ambient light. The solution may be refrigerated (2 to 8 °C) for up to 24 hours. Reconstituted and diluted solutions do not need to be protected from light.

Incompatibilities

Raltitrexed should not be mixed with any other drug.

Caution

Raltitrexed should not be handled by pregnant women.

Developed: 08/08/2000

RAMELTEON Systemic†

VA CLASSIFICATION (Primary): CN309

Commonly used brand name(s): *Rozerem*.

Note: For a listing of dosage forms and brand names by country availability, see *Dosage Forms* section(s).

†Not commercially available in Canada.

Category

Sedative-hypnotic.

Indications

Accepted

Insomnia (treatment)—Rameltean is indicated for the treatment of insomnia characterized by difficulty with sleep onset.

Pharmacology/Pharmacokinetics

Physicochemical characteristics

Molecular weight—Ramelteon: 259.34.

Solubility—Freely soluble in organic solvents, such as methanol, ethanol, and dimethyl sulfoxide; soluble in 1-octanol and acetonitrile; and very slightly soluble in water and in aqueous buffers from pH 3 to 11.

Mechanism of action/Effect

Ramelteon is a melatonin receptor agonist with both high affinity for melatonin M_1 and M_2 receptors and selectivity over the M_3 receptor. The activity at the M_1 and M_2 receptors is believed to contribute to sleep-promoting properties as they are acted upon by endogenous melatonin.

Ramelteon has no appreciable affinity for the GABA receptor complex or for receptors that bind neuropeptides, cytokines, serotonin, dopamine, noradrenaline, acetylcholine and opiates. Ramelteon does not interfere with the activity of a number of selected enzymes in a standard panel.

Absorption

Rapidly absorbed following fasted oral administration. Absolute oral bioavailability is 1.8% due to extensive first-pass metabolism. When administered with a high fat meal, the $AUC_{0\text{-}inf}$ following a single 16 mg dose was 31% higher and the C_{max} was 22% lower than when given in a fasted state. Medium T_{max} was also delayed approximately 45 minutes when administered with food. Effects of food on the AUC values for M-II were similar.

AUC: In 24 hours elderly subjects, following a single 6 mg dose the mean $AUC_{0\text{-}inf}$ was 18.7 ng h per mL.

Distribution
Volume of distribution (Vol_D)—73.6 L, following intravenous administration, indicating substantial tissue distribution.

Protein binding
High (approximately 82%) in human serum; 70% to human serum albumin.

Biotransformation
Primarily oxidation to hydroxyl and carbonyl derivatives, with secondary glucuronide conjugates. These metabolites are formed rapidly and exhibit a monophasic decline and rapid elimination. Major metabolite M-II, is active and has one tenth and one fifth the binding affinity of the parent molecule for the human M_1 and M_2 receptors. M-II circulates at higher concentrations than the parent producing 20 -100 fold greater mean systemic exposure, compared with ramelteon. M-II has a weak affinity for the serotonin 5-HT_{2B} and no affinity to other receptors or enzymes. M-II does not interfere with the activity of a number of endogenous enzymes.

All other known metabolites of ramelteon are inactive.

Elimination
1 to 2.6 hours for ramelteon; 2 to 5 hours for M-II metabolite.

Time to peak concentration
0.75 hour (range, 0.5 to 1.5 hours).

Peak plasma concentration
In 24 elderly subjects, following a single 16 mg dose the mean C_{max} value was 11.6 ng/mL.

Elimination
Feces: 4%; < 0.1% unchanged drug

Urine: 84%; < 0.1% unchanged drug

Accumulation
Repeated daily administration does not result in significant accumulation.

Precautions to Consider

Carcinogenicity
Two-year carcinogenicity studies were done in B6C3F_1 mice given ramelteon at doses of 0, 30, 100, 300, or 1000 mg/kg/day by oral gavage. Male mice had a dose-related increase in the incidence of hepatic tumors at dose levels of 100 mg/kg/day and above including hepatic adenoma, carcinoma, and hepatoblastoma. Female mice developed a dose related increase in the incidence of hepatic adenomas at doses greater than or equal to 300 mg/kg/day, and hepatic carcinoma at doses of 1000 mg/kg/day. The no-effect level for hepatic tumors in male mice was 30 mg/kg/day, and 100 mg/kg/day in female mice.

Two-year carcinogenicity studies were done in Sprague-Dawley rats administered ramelteon at doses of 0, 15, 60, 250 or 1000 mg/kg/day by oral gavage. Male rats revealed a dose-related increase in the incidence of hepatic adenoma and benign Leydig cell tumors of the testis at doses of 250 mg/kg/day and higher and hepatic carcinoma at the 1000 mg/kg/day dose level. Female rats showed a dose-related increase in the incidence of hepatic adenoma at doses of 60 mg/kg/day or higher and hepatic carcinoma at 1000 mg/kg/day. The no-effect levels for hepatic tumors in male and female rats was 60 mg/kg/day and 15 mg/kg/day, respectively.

Hepatic tumors in rodents following chronic treatment with non-genotoxic compounds may be secondary to microsomal enzyme induction, a mechanism for tumor generation not thought to occur in humans. Leydig cell tumor development in rodents after treatment with non-genotoxic compounds has been linked to reductions in testosterone and increases in luteinizing hormone release. Rat Leydig cells are more sensitive to the stimulatory effects of luteinizing hormone than human Leydig cells.

The relevance of both rodent hepatic tumors and benign rat Leydig cell tumors following ramelteon treatment at excess levels of mean clinical plasma concentrations at the maximum recommended human dose (MRHD) to humans is not known.

Mutagenicity
Ramelteon showed no evidence of mutagenicity based on the *in vitro* bacterial reverse mutation assay (Ames) assay, *in vitro* mammalian cell gene mutation assay using the mouse lymphoma TK$^{+/-}$ cell line, *in vivo/in vitro* unscheduled DNA synthesis assay in rat hepatocytes, and in *in vivo* micronucleus assays in mouse and rat. Ramelteon was positive in the chromosomal aberration assay in Chinese hamster lung cells in the presence of S9 metabolic activation.

The M-II metabolite formed by the rat liver S9 fraction used in the *in vitro* genetic toxicity studies exceeded the concentration of ramelteon and, therefore, assessed the genotoxic potential of the M-II metabolite.

Pregnancy/Reproduction
Fertility—In rats given daily doses of 6 to 600 mg/kg/day of ramelteon, neither male nor female fertility was affected. However, female rats receiving ≥60 mg/kg/day (79 times the MRHD on a mg/m^2 basis) of ramelteon displayed irregular estrus cycles, reduction in the number of implants and reduction in the number of live embryos. A reduction in the number of corpora lutea occurred at the 600 mg/kg/day dose level. The no-effect dose for fertility was 20 mg/kg/day (26 times the MRHD on a mg/m^2 basis) in females and 600 mg/kg/day (786 times the MRHD on a mg/m^2 basis) in males.

Pregnancy—Adequate and well controlled studies in humans have not been done. Studies in animals have shown that ramelteon causes adverse effects in the fetus. Ramelteon should be used during pregnancy only if the potential benefit justifies the potential risk to the fetus.

Pregnant rats were given oral ramelteon at doses of 0, 10, 40, 150, or 600 mg/kg/day during gestation days 6-17. Maternal toxicity and fetal teratogenicity were observed at doses ≥150 mg/kg/day. Maternal toxicity was characterized by decreased body weight and, at 600 mg/kg/day, ataxia and decreased spontaneous movement. At doses ≥150 mg/kg/day, visceral malformations consisting of diaphragmatic hernia and minor anatomical variations of skeleton (irregular shaped scapula) were observed in the fetus, and at 600 mg/kg/day, reductions in fetal body weight and malformations including cysts on the external genitalia were also observed. The no effect level for teratogenicity was 40 mg/kg/day. Studies done in pregnant rabbits given oral ramelteon at doses of 0, 12, 60 or 300 mg/kg/day during gestation days 16-18, revealed maternal toxicity at the 300 mg/kg/day dose, and no evidence of fetal effects at any dose level.

Pre- and post-natal development studies were done in rats given oral ramelteon at doses of 0, 30, 100, or 300 mg/kg/day from day 6 of gestation through postnatal (lactation) day 21, when the offspring were weaned. Maternal toxicity was observed at the 100 mg/kg/day dose and higher and included reduced body weight gain and increased adrenal weight. Reduced body weight in the offspring was also observed at this dose. Offspring in the 300 mg/kg/day group demonstrated physical and developmental delays including eruption of the lower incisors, and acquisition of the righting reflex and an alteration of emotional response. Decrease in the viability of the offspring was noted in the 300 mg/kg/day group and was likely due to altered maternal behavior and function observed at this level. The no-effect level for pre- and post-natal development was 30 mg/kg/day (39 times higher than the MRHD on a mg/m^2 basis).

FDA Pregnancy Category C

Labor and delivery—Ramelteon has no established use in labor and delivery. The potential effects of ramelteon on the duration of labor and delivery for either mother or fetus, have not been studied.

Breast-feeding
Ramelteon is distributed into the milk of lactating rats. It is not known whether it is distributed into human milk. The use of ramelteon in nursing mothers is not recommended.

Pediatrics
Safety and effectiveness in pediatric patients have not been established.

Ramelteon has been associated with an effect on reproductive hormones in adults, including decreased testosterone levels and increased prolactin levels. It is not known what effect the use of ramelteon may have on the reproductive axis in developing humans.

Geriatrics
Appropriate studies performed to date have not demonstrated geriatrics-specific problems that would limit the usefulness or ramelteon in the elderly. However, pharmacokinetic studies suggest a higher total exposure (97%) in elderly subjects compared to younger adults.

Pharmacogenetics
There are no gender-related differences in the pharmacokinetics of ramelteon or its metabolites.

Drug interactions and/or related problems
The following drug interactions and/or related problems have been selected on the basis of their potential clinical significance (possible mechanism in parentheses where appropriate)—not necessarily inclusive (» = major clinical significance):

Note: Combinations containing any of the following medications, depending on the amount present, may also interact with this medication.

» Alcohol
(caution is advised with concomitant use of alcohol and ramelteon; additive effect on some measures of psychomotor performance)

» CYP inducers, strong such as
  Rifampin
  (efficacy of ramelteon may be reduced; concomitant administration resulted in approximately 80% decrease in total ramelteon exposure and metabolite M-II when administered with rifampin)

» CYP1A2 inhibitors, less potent
  (caution is advised with concomitant administration with ramelteon)

» CYP3A4 inhibitors, such as
  Ketoconazole
  (caution; ramelteon $AUC_{0\text{-}inf}$ increased 84%, and C_{max} increased 36% when administered with ketoconazole)

» Fluvoxamine (strong CYP1A2 inhibitor)
  (should not be used concomitantly; ramelteon $AUC_{0\text{-}inf}$ increased 190-fold, and C_{max} increased 70-fold)

Laboratory value alterations

The following have been selected on the basis of their potential clinical significance (possible effect in parentheses where appropriate)—not necessarily inclusive (» = major clinical significance).

Cortisol, blood
  (may be decreased)

Medical considerations/Contraindications

The medical considerations/contraindications included have been selected on the basis of their potential clinical significance (reasons given in parentheses where appropriate)—not necessarily inclusive (» = major clinical significance).

Except under special circumstances, this medication should not be used when the following medical problem exists:

» Hypersensitivity to ramelteon or to any component of its formulation

Risk-benefit should be considered when the following medical problems exist:

» Chronic obstructive pulmonary disease (COPD), severe

» Sleep apnea, severe
  (use is not recommended)

» Hepatic impairment, moderate and mild
  (caution; exposure to ramelteon increased 4-fold in patients with mild hepatic impairment following 7 days of dosing with 16 mg/day and increased more than 10-fold in patients with moderate hepatic impairment)

» Hepatic impairment, severe
  (use is not recommended, ramelteon has not been studied in patients with severe hepatic impairment [Child-Pugh Class C])

» Mental depression
  (condition may be intensified, resulting in suicidal ideation)

Patient monitoring

The following may be especially important in patient monitoring (other tests may be warranted in some patients, depending on condition; » = major clinical significance):

Prolactin levels
Testosterone levels
  (assessment should be considered in patients with unexplained amenorrhea, galactorrhea, decreased libido, or problems with fertility)

Side/Adverse Effects

The following side/adverse effects have been selected on the basis of their potential clinical significance (possible signs and symptoms in parentheses where appropriate)—not necessarily inclusive:

Those indicating need for medical attention only if they continue or are bothersome

Incidence more frequent

Dizziness; headache; somnolence (sleepiness or unusual drowsiness)

Incidence less frequent

Arthralgia (pain in joints; muscle pain or stiffness; difficulty in moving); ***blood cortisol decreased; depression*** (discouragement; feeling sad or empty; irritability; lack of appetite; loss of interest or pleasure; tiredness; trouble concentrating; trouble sleeping); ***diarrhea; dysgeusia*** (loss of taste; change in taste); ***fatigue; influenza*** (chills; cough; diarrhea; fever; general feeling of discomfort or illness; headache; joint pain; loss of appetite; muscle aches and pains; nausea; runny nose; shivering; sore throat; sweating; trouble sleeping; unusual tiredness or weakness; vomiting); ***insomnia exacerbated*** (sleeplessness; trouble sleeping; unable to sleep); ***myalgia*** (joint pain; swollen joints; muscle aching or cramping; muscle pains or stiffness; difficulty in moving); ***nausea; upper respiratory tract infection*** (ear congestion; nasal congestion; chills; cough; fever; sneezing, or sore throat; body aches or pain; headache; loss of voice; runny nose; unusual tiredness or weakness; difficulty in breathing)

Overdose

For more information on the management of overdose or unintentional ingestion, **contact a poison control center** (see *Poison Control Center Listing*).

Treatment of overdose

There is no known specific antidote to ramelteon. Treatment is generally symptomatic and supportive.

To decrease absorption—
  Performing gastric lavage immediately when appropriate.

To enhance elimination—
  Performing hemodialysis is NOT expected to enhance elimination of ramelteon.

Monitoring—
  Monitoring respiratory, pulse, blood pressure, and other appropriate vital signs.

Supportive care—
  Providing general symptomatic and supportive therapy as indicated, including administering intravenous fluids and maintaining adequate airway.
  Patients in whom intentional overdose is confirmed or suspected should be referred for psychiatric consultation.

Patient Consultation

As an aid to patient consultation, refer to *Advice for the Patient, Ramelteon (Systemic)*.

In providing consultation, consider emphasizing the following selected information (» = major clinical significance):

Before using this medication

» Conditions affecting use, especially:
  Hypersensitivity to ramelteon or to any component of its formulation
  Pregnancy—Adequate and well controlled studies in humans have not been done. Studies in animals have shown that ramelteon causes adverse effects in the fetus. Ramelteon should be used during pregnancy only if the potential benefit justifies the potential risk to the fetus.
  Breast-feeding—Ramelteon is distributed into the milk of lactating rats. It is not known whether it is distributed into human milk. The use of ramelteon in nursing mothers is not recommended.
  Use in children—Safety and effectiveness in pediatric patients have not been established.
  Other medications, especially alcohol, fluvoxamine, CYP1A2 inhibitors, CYP3A4 inhibitors such as ketoconazole, strong CYP inducers such as rifampin
  Other medical problems, especially chronic obstructive pulmonary disease (COPD), mental depression, hepatic impairment, or sleep apnea

Proper use of this medication

» Not taking ramelteon with or immediately after a high fat meal

» Taking medicine within 30 minutes prior to going to bed and confining activities to those necessary to prepare for bed

» Proper dosing
  Missed dose: Skipping missed dose; not doubling doses

» Proper storage

Precautions while using this medication

» Avoiding use of alcohol during therapy

» Avoiding hazardous activities such as operating a motor vehicle or heavy machinery after taking ramelteon

» Consulting your doctor if worsening of insomnia or any new behavioral signs or symptoms occur
  Consulting your doctor if you develop any unusual and strange thoughts or behavior while you are taking ramelteon.

» Telling your doctor if cessation of menses or galactorrhea (females), decreased libido, or problems with fertility occur

General Dosing Information

Because sleep disturbances may be the manifestation of a physical and/or psychiatric disorder, symptomatic treatment with ramelteon should be initiated only after careful evaluation of the patient.

Ramelteon should be taken within 30 minutes before going to bed.

After taking ramelteon, patients should confine their activities to those necessary to prepare for bed.

The failure of insomnia to remit after a reasonable period of treatment may indicate the presence of a primary psychiatric and/or medical illness that should be evaluated.

Ramelteon does not appear to produce physical dependence.

Diet/Nutrition
Patients should not take ramelteon with or immediately following a high fat meal.

Oral Forms

RAMELTEON TABLETS

Usual adult dose
Hypnotic—
Oral, one tablet (8 mg) at bedtime.

Usual pediatric dose
Safety and efficacy have not been established.

Usual geriatric dose
See *Usual adult dose.*

Strength(s) usually available
U.S.—
8 mg (Rx) [*Rozerem* (copovidone; hydroxypropyl cellulose; hypromellose; ink containing shellac and synthetic iron oxide black; lactose monohydrate; magnesium stearate; polyethylene glycol 8000; starch; titanium dioxide; yellow ferric oxide)].

Packaging and storage
Store at 25 °C (77 °F), excursions permitted to 15° to 30 °C (59° to 86 °F). Store in a tight container.

Auxiliary labeling
- May cause drowsiness.
- Avoid alcoholic beverages.

Developed: 09/14/2005

RAMIPRIL—See *Angiotensin-converting Enzyme (ACE) Inhibitors (Systemic)*

RANITIDINE—See *Histamine H_2-receptor Antagonists (Systemic)*

RASAGILINE Systemic†

VA CLASSIFICATION (Primary): CN500

Commonly used brand name(s): *Azilect.*

Note: For a listing of dosage forms and brand names by country availability, see *Dosage Forms* section(s).

†Not commercially available in Canada.

Category
Antidyskinetic (dopamine agonist).

Indications

Accepted
Parkinson's disease, idiopathic (treatment)—Rasagiline is indicated for the treatment of the signs and symptoms of idiopathic Parkinson's disease as initial monotherapy and as adjunct therapy to levodopa.

Pharmacology/Pharmacokinetics

Physicochemical characteristics
Molecular weight—Rasagiline mesylate—267.34.

Solubility—Freely soluble in water or ethanol; sparingly soluble in isopropanol.

Mechanism of action/Effect
Rasagiline irreversibly inhibits MAO type B (MAO-B), but adequate studies to establish whether rasagiline is selective for MAO-B in humans have not been conducted.

Rasagiline's mechanisms of action are unknown. One proposed mechanism is related to its MAO-B inhibitory activity, which causes increased extracellular dopamine levels in the striatum. The increased dopamine level and increased dopaminergic activity are likely to mediate rasagiline's beneficial effects seen in models of dopaminergic motor dysfunction.

Absorption
Absolute bioavailability—about 36%

A high fat meal decreased C_{max} and AUC by approximately 60% and 20%, respectively

Distribution
Volume of distribution (Vol_D)—87 L at steady-state

Protein binding
High, 88 to 94%

61 to 63% (mean extent of binding) to human albumin over concentration range of 1 to 100 ng per mL

Biotransformation
Almost complete in the liver prior to elimination through two main pathways: N-dealkylation and/or hydroxylation to yield 1-aminoindan (AI), 3-hydroxy-N-propargyl-1 aminoindan (3-OH-AI)

Rasagiline metabolism dependent on cytochrome P450 (CYP) system, with CYP1A2 being the major isoenzyme involved

Half-life
Mean steady-state—3 hours

Time to peak concentration
Approximately 1 hour

Elimination
Urine (primary)—62% of total dose over 7 days; less than 1% of rasagiline was eliminated as unchanged drug in the urine

Feces (secondary)—7% of total dose over 7 days

Total calculated recovery—84% over 38 days

Precautions to Consider

Cross-sensitivity and/or related problems

Carcinogenicity
In two year studies in CD-1 mice given oral doses of 1, 15 and 45 mg per kg of body weight per day, there was an increase in lung tumors (combined adenomas/carcinomas) at 15 and 45 mg per kg doses in males and females. Plasma exposures associated with the no-effect dose of 1 mg per kg were approximately 5 times those expected in humans at the maximum recommended dose (MRD).

In two year studies of Sprague-Dawley rates given oral doses of 0.3, 1 and 3 mg per kg (males) or 0.5, 2, 5, and 17 mg per kg (females), there was no increase in tumors at any dose. Plasma exposures at the highest dose were approximately 33 and 260 times, in male and female rats, respectively, the expected plasma exposures in humans at the MRD of 1 mg per day.

Carcinogenicity studies of rasagiline in combination with levodopa/carbidopa have not been done.

Mutagenicity
Rasagiline was clastogenic in *in vitro* chromosomal aberration assays in human lymphocytes in the presence of metabolic activation and was mutagenic and clastogenic in the *in vitro* mouse lymphoma tk assay in the absence and presence of metabolic activation. Rasagiline was negative in the *in vitro* bacterial reverse mutation Ames assay, the *in vivo* unscheduled DNA synthesis assay, and the *in vivo* micronucleus assay in CD-1 mice. Rasagiline was also negative in the *in vivo* micronucleus assay in CD-1 mice when administered in combination with levodopa/carbidopa.

Pregnancy/Reproduction
Fertility—Male and female rats treated with oral doses up to 3 mg per kg of body weight per day (approximately 30 times the expected plasma rasagiline AUC at the MRHD of 1 mg per day) prior to and throughout the mating period (males) or from prior to mating through day 17 of gestation (females) had no effect on mating performance or fertility.

The effect of rasagiline with levodopa/carbidopa on mating and fertility has not been studied.

Pregnancy—There are no adequate and well-controlled studied of rasagiline in pregnant women. Therefore, rasagiline should be used during pregnancy only if the potential benefit justifies the potential risk to the fetus.

Female rats treated with oral doses up to 3 mg per kg of body weight per day (approximately 30 times the expected plasma rasagiline AUC at the MRHD of 1 mg per day) showed no effect on embryo-fetal development.

In a study of pregnant rats doses with 0.1, 0.3, and 1 mg per kg of body weight per day of oral rasagiline from the beginning of organogenesis to day 20 post-partum, offspring survival was decreased and offspring body weight reduced at doses of 0.3 mg per kg per day and 1 mg per kg per day (10 and 16 times the expected plasma rasagiline AUC at the MRHD). Rasagiline's effect on physical and behavioral development was not adequately assessed in this study.

In another study in which pregnancy rats were dosed 0.1, 0.3, and 1 mg per kg of body weight per day of oral rasagiline alone and in combination with 20/20 mg per kg of body weight per day levodopa/carbidopa throughout organogenesis, there was an increased incidence of wavy ribs in fetuses from rats given 1 mg per kg per day rasagiline in combination with levodopa/carbidopa.

In a pregnant rabbit study in which doses of rasagiline alone (3 mg per kg) or in combination with levodopa/carbidopa (rasagiline: 0.1, 0.6, 1.2 mg per kg and levodopa/carbidopa 80/20 mg per kg per day) were given throughout the period of organogenesis, an increase in fetal death was noted at rasagiline doses of 0.6 and 1.2 mg per kg per day (approximately 7 and 13 times the MRHD). Levodopa/carbidopa alone increased cardiovascular abnormalities and the increase was greater with rasagiline at all doses combined with levodopa/carbidopa.

FDA Pregnancy Category C

Breast-feeding

It is not known whether rasagiline is distributed into breast milk. Because many drugs are distributed into human milk, caution should be exercised when rasagiline is administered to a nursing woman.

In rat studies, rasagiline was shown to inhibit prolactin secretion and may inhibit milk secretion in females.

Pediatrics

Appropriate studies have not been performed on the relationship of age to the effects of rasagiline in the pediatric population. Safety and efficacy have not been established in children less than 18 years of age.

Geriatrics

Appropriate studies performed to date have not demonstrated geriatrics-specific problems that would limit the usefulness of rasagiline in the elderly.

Surgical

Elective surgery requiring general anesthesia is **contraindicated** in patients taking rasagiline. Rasagiline should be discontinued at least 14 days prior to elective surgery. If surgery is necessary sooner, benzodiazepines, mivacurium, rapacuronium, fentanyl, morphine, and codeine may be used cautiously.

Drug interactions and/or related problems

The following drug interactions and/or related problems have been selected on the basis of their potential clinical significance (possible mechanism in parentheses where appropriate)—not necessarily inclusive (» = major clinical significance):

Note: Combinations containing any of the following medications, depending on the amount present, may also interact with this medication.

» Analgesic agents, including:
» Methadone or
» Propoxyphene or
» Tramadol
(**contraindicated** due to serious side effects with concomitant use)

Ciprofloxacin or
CYP1A2 inhibitors
(concomitant use may increase rasagiline concentrations up to 2-fold)

» Cocaine or
» Local anesthesia containing sympathomimetic vasoconstrictors
(**contraindicated** due to increased risk of serious adverse reactions)

» Cyclobenzaprine or
» Mirtazapine or
» St. John's Wort
(concomitant use **contraindicated**)

» Dextromethorphan
(**contraindicated** because of brief episodes of psychosis or bizarre behavior reported with MAO inhibitors and dextromethorphan)

» Fluoxetine
(prudent to avoid concomitant use due to reports of serious adverse events including behavioral and mental status changes progressing to agitation, delirium and coma; should allow a minimum of 5 weeks between discontinuation of rasagiline and initiation of fluoxetine treatment [may need to be longer if fluoxetine has been prescribed chronically and/or at higher doses] since fluoxetine and its metabolites have long half lives)

Levodopa or
Levodopa/carbidopa
(may be some rasagiline blood level increase in the presence of levodopa; effect is modest and adjustment of rasagiline dose not needed; use with levodopa may increase dyskinesia, postural hypotension, or hallucinations)

» MAO inhibitors including
» Selective MAO-B inhibitors
(**contraindicated** because of the increased risk of non-selective inhibition that may lead to a hypertensive crisis; a minimum of 14 days should elapse between discontinuation of rasagiline and initiation of MAO inhibitor treatment)

» Meperidine
(**contraindicated** due to serious reactions such as coma, severe hypertension or hypotension, severe respiratory depression, convulsions, malignant hyperpyrexia, excitation, peripheral vascular collapse and death with concomitant use; a minimum of 14 days should elapse between discontinuation of rasagiline and initiation of meperidine treatment)

» Selective serotonin reuptake inhibitors (SSRIs) or
» Serotonin-norepinephrine reuptake inhibitors (SNRIs) or
» Tricyclic antidepressants
(may cause serious adverse events including behavioral and mental status changes progressing to agitation, delirium and coma; prudent to avoid concomitant use; should allow a minimum of 14 days between discontinuation of rasagiline and initiation of treatment with an SSRI, SNRI, or tricyclic antidepressant)

» Sympathomimetic amines including:
» Amphetamines or
» Vasoconstrictor-containing cold and weight reducing products containing
Ephedrine or
Phenylephrine or
Phenylpropanolamine or
Pseudoephderine
(**contraindicated** due to severe hypertensive reactions that have followed concomitant use of sympathomimetics and non-selective MAO inhibitors)

Medical considerations/Contraindications

The medical considerations/contraindications included have been selected on the basis of their potential clinical significance (reasons given in parentheses where appropriate)—not necessarily inclusive (» = major clinical significance).

Except under special circumstances, this medication should not be used when the following medical problem exists:

» Hepatic impairment, moderate or severe
(may increase rasagiline plasma concentration by up to 7-fold)

» Pheochromocytoma

Risk-benefit should be considered when the following medical problems exist:

» Hepatic impairment, mild
(may increase rasagiline plasma concentration by up to 2-fold; dose adjustment to 0.5 mg per day needed)

Patient monitoring

The following may be especially important in patient monitoring (other tests may be warranted in some patients, depending on condition; » = major clinical significance):

» Melonomas
(increased risk of up to 2- to 4-fold higher for patients with Parkinson's disease; periodic skin examinations should be performed by dermatologists on a regular basis)

Side/Adverse Effects

The following side/adverse effects have been selected on the basis of their potential clinical significance (possible signs and symptoms in parentheses where appropriate)—not necessarily inclusive:

Those indicating need for medical attention

Incidence less frequent

Albuminuria (cloudy urine); ***allergic reaction*** (cough; difficulty swallowing; dizziness; fast heartbeat; hives, itching, puffiness or swelling of the eyelids or around the eyes, face, lips or tongue; shortness of breath; skin rash; tightness in chest; unusual tiredness or weakness; wheezing); ***angina pectoris*** (arm, back or jaw pain; chest pain or discomfort; chest tightness or heaviness; fast or irregular heartbeat; shortness of breath; sweating; nausea); ***chest pain; gastroenteritis*** (abdominal or stomach pain; diarrhea; loss of appetite; nausea; weakness); ***hallucinations*** (seeing, hearing, or feeling things that are not there); ***leukopenia*** (black, tarry stools; chest pain; chills; cough; fever; painful or difficult urination; shortness of breath; sore throat; sores, ulcers, or white spots on lips or in mouth; swollen glands; unusual bleeding or bruising; unusual tiredness or weakness); ***liver function tests abnormal*** (lab results that show problems with liver); ***postural hypotension*** (chills; cold sweats; confusion; dizziness, faintness, or lightheadedness when getting up from lying or sitting position); ***skin carcinoma*** (persistent non-healing sore; reddish patch or irritated area; shiny bump; pink growth; white, yellow or waxy scar-like area); ***syncope*** (fainting); ***vesiculobullous rash*** (redness, blistering, peeling, or loosening of the skin)

Those indicating need for medical attention only if they continue or are bothersome

Incidence more frequent

Arthralgia (pain in joints; muscle pain or stiffness; difficulty in moving); ***dyspepsia*** (acid or sour stomach; belching; heartburn; indigestion; stomach discomfort, upset, or pain); ***headache***

Incidence less frequent

Alopecia (hair loss; thinning of hair); ***anorexia*** (loss of appetite; weight loss); ***arthritis*** (pain, swelling, or redness in joints; muscle pain or stiffness; difficulty in moving); ***asthma*** (cough; difficulty breathing; noisy breathing; shortness of breath; tightness in chest; wheezing); ***conjunctivitis*** (redness, pain, swelling of eye, eyelid, or inner lining of eyelid; burning, dry or itching eyes; discharge; excessive tearing); ***depression*** (discouragement; feeling sad or empty; irritability; lack of appetite; loss of interest or pleasure; tiredness; trouble concentrating; trouble sleeping); ***ecchymosis*** (bruising; large, flat, blue or purplish patches in the skin); ***fall; fever; flu syndrome*** (chills; cough; diarrhea; fever; general feeling of discomfort or illness; headache; joint pain; loss of appetite; muscle aches and pains; nausea; runny nose; shivering; sore throat; sweating; trouble sleeping; unusual tiredness or weakness; vomiting); ***impotence*** (loss in sexual ability, desire, drive, or performance; decreased interest in sexual intercourse; inability to have or keep an erection); ***libido decreased*** (loss in sexual ability, desire, drive, or performance; decreased interest in sexual intercourse; inability to have or keep an erection); ***malaise*** (general feeling of discomfort or illness; unusual tiredness or weakness); ***neck pain; paresthesia*** (burning, crawling, itching, numbness, prickling, "pins and needles", or tingling feelings); ***rhinitis*** (stuffy nose; runny nose; sneezing); ***vertigo*** (dizziness or lightheadedness; feeling of constant movement of self or surroundings; sensation of spinning)

Overdose

For more information on the management of overdose or unintentional ingestion, **contact a poison control center** (see *Poison Control Center Listing*).

Clinical effects of overdose

The following effects have been selected on the basis of their potential clinical significance (possible signs and symptoms in parentheses where appropriate)—not necessarily inclusive:

Agitation (anxiety; nervousness; restlessness; irritability; dry mouth; shortness of breath; hyperventilation; trouble sleeping; irregular heartbeats; shaking); ***coma*** (change in consciousness; loss of consciousness); ***convulsions*** (seizures); ***cool, clammy skin; diaphoresis*** (increased sweating); ***dizziness; drowsiness*** (sleepiness); ***faintness*** (feeling like you will pass out); ***hallucinations*** (seeing, hearing, or feeling things that are not there); ***hyperactivity*** (restlessness; trouble sitting still); ***hyperpyrexia*** (fever); ***hypertension*** (blurred vision; dizziness; nervousness; headache; pounding in the ears; slow or fast heartbeat); ***hypotension*** (blurred vision; confusion; dizziness, faintness, or lightheadedness when getting up from a lying or sitting position suddenly; sweating; unusual tiredness or weakness); ***irritability; opisthotonus*** (severe spasm where the head and heels are bent backward and the body arched forward); ***precordial pain*** (pain in lower chest or upper abdomen); ***rapid and irregular pulse; respiratory depression and failure*** (pale or blue lips, fingernails, or skin; difficult or troubled breathing; irregular, fast or slow, or shallow breathing; shortness of breath); ***trismus*** (difficulty opening the mouth; lockjaw; muscle spasm, especially of neck and back); ***vascular collapse*** (chest pain or discomfort; cold, clammy, pale skin; confusion; dizziness; irregular heartbeats; shortness of breath; slow heart rate; weakness)

Treatment of overdose

Symptoms of overdose may not appear right away. Delays of up to 12 hours after ingestion may occur with the peak intensity of the syndrome not being reached for up to a day following the overdose. Death has resulted following MAOI overdose. Immediate hospitalization with close and continuous monitoring of patient is strongly recommended for a period of at least two days following the ingestion of rasagiline in overdose.

There is no known specific antidote to rasagiline. Treatment is generally symptomatic and supportive. These treatment options are offered based upon the assumption that rasagiline overdose may be modeled after non-selective MAO inhibitor poisoning. For more information on the management of MAO inhibitor overdose, see the *Antidepressants, Monoamine Oxidase (MAO) Inhibitor (Systemic)* monograph.

Specific treatment—
Intensive management of hypepyrexia may be required.
Maintenance of fluid and electrolyte balance is essential.

Monitoring—
Close monitoring of body temperature

Supportive care—
Respiration should be supported by appropriate measures, including management of the airway, use of supplemental oxygen, and mechanical ventilatory assistance.
Patients in whom intentional overdose is confirmed or suspected should be referred for psychiatric consultation.

Patient Consultation

In providing consultation, consider emphasizing the following selected information (» = major clinical significance):

Importance of diet

» Avoiding tyramine-containing foods, alcoholic beverages, and large quantities of caffeine-containing beverages, over-the-counter cold and cough medicines, and other medications, unless prescribed; having list of such for reference

Before using this medication

» Conditions affecting use, especially:
Hypersensitivity to rasagiline or any component of the product
Pregnancy—Risk-benefit considerations during pregnancy
Breast-feeding—Caution should be exercised
Use in children—Safety and efficacy not established in children less than 18 years of age
Surgical—Elective surgery requiring general anesthesia **contraindicated** in patients taking rasagiline; discontinuing rasagiline at least 14 days prior to elective surgery
Other **contraindicated** medications, especially analgesic agents (methadone, propoxyphene or tramadol), cocaine, cyclobenzaprine, dextromethorphan, local anesthesia containing sympathomimetic vasoconstrictors, MAO inhibitors (including selective MAO-B inhibitors), meperidine, mirtazapine, St. John's Wort, or sympathomimetic amines (amphetamines, vasoconstrictor-containing cold and weight reducing products [ephedrine, pheylephrine, phenylpropanolamine, pseudoephedrine])
Other medications, especially fluoxetine, selective serotonin reuptake inhibitors (SSRIs), serotonin-norepinephrine reuptake inhibitors (SNRIs), or tricyclic antidepressants
Other medical problems, especially moderate or severe hepatic impairment, pheochromocytoma, or mild hepatic impairment

Proper use of this medication

» Proper dosing
Missed dose: Not taking missed dose; taking at the usual time on the following day; not doubling doses
» Proper storage

Precautions while using this medication

» Telling doctor of all medicines currently being taken including prescription and nonprescription
» Importance of regular visits to a dermatologist for periodic skin examinations to check for melanoma
» *Seeking out immediate medical attention* for patients who experience symptoms of hypertensive crisis including severe headache, blurred vision, difficulty thinking, seizures, chest pain, unexplained nausea or vomiting, or stroke
Informing patient that there is possibility of increased dyskinesia and postural hypotension if taking rasagiline as adjunct to levodopa

Side/adverse effects

Signs of potential side effects, especially albuminuria, allergic reaction, angina pectoris, chest pain, gastroenteritis, hallucinations, leukopenia, liver function tests abnormal, postural hypotension, skin carcinoma, syncope, or vesiculobullous rash

General Dosing Information

Patients administered rasagiline as an adjunct to levodopa should be advised that there may be an increased risk of dyskinesia and postural hypotension.

Diet/Nutrition

Rasagiline can be administered with or without food.

Foods and beverages containing tyramine or other high pressor amines, such as aged cheese; fava or broad bean pods; yeast/protein extracts; smoked or pickled meats, poultry, or fish; fermented sausage (bologna, pepperoni, salami, summer sausage) or other fermented meat;

sauerkraut; beer; reduced-alcohol and alcohol-free beer and wine; red and white wines; sherry; and liqueurs, when used concurrently with rasagiline, may cause sudden and severe hypertensive reactions called "cheese reactions." Patients receiving rasagiline should be instructed about the tyramine content of foods and beverages and amine containing medications that should be avoided. When rasagiline is discontinued, it is also necessary to maintain this dietary tyramine restriction and avoidance of exogenous amines contained in medications for at least 2 weeks.

Oral Dosage Forms

RASAGILINE MESYLATE TABLETS

Usual adult dose

Parkinsonism—

Monotherapy: Oral, 1 mg once daily.

Adjunctive therapy with levodopa: Oral, 0.5 mg once daily. If clinical response is not achieved, dose may be increased to 1 mg once daily.

When rasagiline is used in combination with levodopa, a reduction of the levodopa dosage may be considered based upon individual response.

Concomitant use with ciprofloxacin and other CYP1A2 inhibitors: Oral, 0.5 mg daily.

Note: In patients with mild hepatic impairment, a dose of 0.5 mg daily should be administered.

In patients with moderate or severe hepatic impairment, rasagiline should NOT be administered.

Usual pediatric dose

Safety and efficacy have not been established in children less than 18 years of age.

Usual geriatric dose

See *Usual adult dose.*

Strength(s) usually available

U.S.—

0.5 mg rasagiline (Rx) [*Azilect* (mannitol; starch; pregelatinized starch; colloidal silicon dioxide; stearic acid; talc)].

1 mg rasagiline (Rx) [*Azilect* (mannitol; starch; pregelatinized starch; colloidal silicon dioxide; stearic acid; talc)].

Packaging and storage

Store between 25 °C (77 °F) with excursions permitted to 15 to 30 °C (59 to 86 °F).

Auxiliary labeling

• Tell doctor about all prescriptions you are taking: prescription and non-prescription.

Developed: 07/29/2006

RASBURICASE Systemic

VA CLASSIFICATION (Primary): AN700

Commonly used brand name(s): *Elitek; Fasturtec.*

Note: For a listing of dosage forms and brand names by country availability, see *Dosage Forms* section(s).

Category

Antineoplastic adjunct.

Indications

Accepted

Hyperuricemia, neoplasm-associated, pediatric (treatment)—Rasburicase is indicated for the initial management of plasma uric acid levels in pediatric patients with leukemia, lymphoma, and solid tumor malignancies who are receiving anti-cancer therapy expected to result in tumor lysis and subsequent elevation of plasma uric acid.

[Hyperuricemia, neoplasm-associated, adult (prophylaxis or treatment)]—Rasburicase is indicated for the prophylaxis and treatment of hyperuricemia in pediatric and adult cancer patients.

Pharmacology/Pharmacokinetics

Physicochemical characteristics

Source—Rasburicase is a recombinant urate-oxidase enzyme produced by a genetically modified *Saccharomyces cerevisiae* strain. The cDNA coding for rasburicase was cloned from a strain of *Aspergillus flavus.*

Chemical Group—Tetrameric protein

Molecular weight—34 kilodalton.

Mechanism of action/Effect

Uric acid is the final step in the catabolic pathway of purines. Rasburicase catalyzes oxidation of uric acid into an inactive and soluble metabolite (allantoin). Hydrogen peroxide is one of the major by-products of this conversion. Rasburicase is only active at the end of the purine catabolic pathway.

Distribution

Volume of distribution (Vol_D)—110 to 127 mL per kg in pediatric patients.

Half-life

Elimination—18 hours

Peak plasma concentration

Rasburicase pharmacokinetics were evaluated in two studies which included pediatric patients with lymphoid leukemia (B and T cells), non-Hodgkin's lymphoma (including Burkitt's lymphoma) or acute myelogenous leukemia. Rasburicase exposure, as measured by area under the curve ($AUC_{0\text{-}24\ hr}$) and peak plasma concentration (C_{max}), tended to increase linearly with doses over a limited dose range (0.15 to 0.20 mg per kg).

Precautions to Consider

Carcinogenicity

Long-term studies in animals to determine carcinogenic potential have not been performed.

Mutagenicity

Rasburicase was non-genotoxic in the Ames, unscheduled DNA synthesis, chromosome analysis, mouse lymphoma, and micronucleus tests.

Pregnancy/Reproduction

Fertility—Rasburicase did not affect reproductive performance or fertility in male or female rats at doses 8 fold higher than the human dose when corrected for body surface area.

Pregnancy—Studies in humans have not been done. Rasburicase should be given to a pregnant woman only if clearly needed.

Studies in animals have not been done.

FDA Pregnancy Category C

Breast-feeding

It is not known whether rasburicase is distributed into breast milk. Because many drugs are distributed in human milk, a decision should be made whether to discontinue nursing or discontinue therapy.

Pediatrics

Clinical studies have been performed in pediatric patients ranging in age from 1 month to 17 years of age. Pediatric patients less than 2 years of age had higher mean uric acid level and lower success rates of achieving maintenance uric acid concentration by 48 hours. This age group may be more prone to toxicity and adverse events such as vomiting, diarrhea, fever, and rash than those between the ages of 2 and 17.

Geriatrics

There is insufficient data to determine whether geriatric patients or adults in general respond differently from pediatric patients.

Pharmacogenetics

Patients of African or Mediterranean ancestry should be screened to rule out glucose 6 phosphate dehydrogenase (G6PD) deficiency, which could result in severe hemolysis.

Laboratory value alterations

The following have been selected on the basis of their potential clinical significance (possible effect in parentheses where appropriate)—not necessarily inclusive (» = major clinical significance).

With physiology/laboratory test values

Uric acid

(rasburicase will cause enzymatic degradation of uric acid within blood samples that are left at room temperature, resulting in low plasma uric acid assay readings; samples must be immediately placed into pre-chilled tubes containing heparin; samples may be stored for up to 4 hours in an ice water bath and must be analyzed within 4 hours of collection.)

Medical considerations/Contraindications

The medical considerations/contraindications included have been selected on the basis of their potential clinical significance (reasons

given in parentheses where appropriate)—not necessarily inclusive (» = major clinical significance).

Except under special circumstances, this medication should not be used when the following medical problem exists:

» Anaphylaxis, history of or
» Hemolytic reactions, history of or
» Hypersensitivity reactions, history of or
» Methemoglobinemia reactions, history of
(treatment with rasburicase should be discontinued permanently)
» Glucose-6-phosphate dehydrogenase (G6PD) deficiency
(may lead to severe hemolysis; if hemolysis develops, permanently discontinue treatment; individuals of African or Mediterranean ancestry should be screened before initiating therapy)

Risk-benefit should be considered when the following medical problems exist:

Tumor lysis syndrome, risk of
(intravenous hydration is required to manage plasma uric acid in patients at risk for tumor lysis syndrome)

Side/Adverse Effects

Rasburicase is immunogenic in healthy volunteers and can elicit antibodies that inhibit the activity of rasburicase *in vitro*.

Severe hypersensitivity reactions, including anaphylaxis, may occur. This can occur at any time during treatment including the first dose. Signs and symptoms of these reactions include bronchospasm, chest pain and tightness, dyspnea, hypoxia, hypotension, shock and/or urticaria. Rasburicase should be immediately and permanently discontinued in any patient developing evidence of a serious hypersensitivity reaction.

The following side/adverse effects have been selected on the basis of their potential clinical significance (possible signs and symptoms in parentheses where appropriate)—not necessarily inclusive:

Those indicating need for medical attention

Incidence more frequent

Mucositis (cracked lips; diarrhea; difficulty in swallowing; sores, ulcers, or white spots on lips, tongue, or inside mouth)—15%

Incidence less frequent

Arrhythmia (dizziness; fainting; fast, slow, or irregular heartbeat)—≤1%; ***cardiac arrest*** (stopping of heart; no blood pressure or pulse; unconsciousness)—≤1%; ***cardiac failure*** (chest pain or discomfort; dilated neck veins; extreme fatigue; irregular breathing; irregular heartbeat; shortness of breath; swelling of face, fingers, feet, or lower legs; weight gain; wheezing)—≤1%; ***cellulitis*** (itching, pain, redness, swelling, tenderness or warmth on skin)—≤1%; ***cerebrovascular disorder*** (blurred vision; headache, sudden and severe; inability to speak; seizures; slurred speech; temporary blindness; weakness in arm and/or leg on one side of the body, sudden and severe)—≤1%; ***chest pain***—≤1%; ***convulsions*** (seizures)—≤1%; ***cyanosis*** (bluish color of fingernails, lips, skin, palms, or nail beds)—≤1%; ***dehydration*** (confusion; decreased urination; dizziness; dry mouth; fainting; increase in heart rate; lightheadedness; rapid breathing; sunken eyes; thirst; unusual tiredness or weakness; wrinkled skin)—≤1%; ***hemorrhage*** (bleeding gums; coughing up blood; difficulty in breathing or swallowing; dizziness; headache; increased menstrual flow or vaginal bleeding; nosebleeds; paralysis; prolonged bleeding from cuts; red or dark brown urine; red or black, tarry stools; shortness of breath)—≤1%; ***ileus*** (abdominal pain; severe constipation; severe vomiting)—≤1%; ***infection*** (fever or chills; cough or hoarseness; lower back or side pain; painful or difficult urination)—≤1%; ***intestinal obstruction*** (abdominal pain; severe constipation; nausea; vomiting)—≤1%; ***myocardial infarction*** (chest pain or discomfort; pain or discomfort in arms, jaw, back or neck; shortness of breath; nausea; sweating, vomiting)—≤1%; ***neutropenia; neutropenia with fever*** (black, tarry stools; chills; cough; fever; lower back or side pain; painful or difficult urination; pale skin; shortness of breath; sore throat; ulcers, sores, or white spots in mouth; unusual bleeding or bruising; unusual tiredness or weakness)—2% and 4%, respectively; ***pancytopenia*** (high fever; chills; unexplained bleeding or bruising; bloody, black, or tarry stools; pale skin; unusual tiredness or weakness; cough; shortness of breath; sores, ulcers, or white spots on lips or in mouth; swollen glands)—≤1%; ***paresthesia*** (burning, crawling, itching, numbness, prickling, "pins and needles" or tingling feelings)—≤1%; ***pneumonia*** (chest pain; cough, fever or chills; sneezing; shortness of breath; sore throat; troubled breathing; tightness in chest; wheezing)—≤1%; ***pulmonary edema*** (chest pain; difficult, fast, noisy breathing, sometimes with wheezing; blue lips and fingernails; pale skin; increased sweating; coughing that sometimes produces a pink, frothy sputum; shortness of breath; swelling in legs and ankles)—≤1%; ***rash, severe***—1%; ***renal failure, acute*** (lower back/side pain; decreased frequency/amount of urine; bloody urine; increased thirst; loss of appetite; nausea; vomiting; unusual tiredness or weakness; swelling of face, fingers, lower legs; weight gain; troubled breathing; increased blood pressure)—≤1%; ***respiratory distress*** (shortness of breath; troubled breathing; tightness in chest or wheezing)—3%; ***retinal hemorrhage*** (decreased vision or other changes in vision)—≤1%; ***sepsis*** (chills; confusion; dizziness; lightheadedness; fainting; fast heartbeat; fever; rapid, shallow breathing)—3%; ***thrombophlebitis*** (changes in skin color; pain, tenderness, swelling of foot or leg)—≤1%; ***thrombosis*** (severe, headaches of sudden onset; sudden loss of coordination; pains in chest, groin, or legs, especially calves of legs; sudden onset of shortness of breath for no apparent reason; sudden onset of slurred speech; sudden vision changes)—≤1%

Incidence rare

Anaphylaxis (cough; difficulty swallowing; dizziness; fast heartbeat; hives; itching, puffiness or swelling of the eyelids or around the eyes, face, lips or tongue; shortness of breath; skin rash; tightness in chest; unusual tiredness or weakness; wheezing)—<1%; ***hemolysis*** (abdominal pain; back pain; dark urine; decreased urination; fever; tiredness; yellow eyes or skin)—<1%; ***methemoglobinemia*** (bluish-colored lips, fingernails, palms; dark urine; difficulty breathing; dizziness or lightheadedness; fatigue; fever; headache; pale skin; rapid heart rate; shortness of breath; sore throat; unusual bleeding or bruising; unusual tiredness or weakness)—<1%

Those indicating need for medical attention only if they continue or are bothersome

Incidence more frequent

Abdominal pain—20%; ***constipation*** (difficulty having a bowel movement)—20%; ***diarrhea***—20%; ***fever***—46%; ***headache***—26%; ***nausea***—27%; ***vomiting***—50%

Incidence less frequent

Hot flashes (feeling of warmth; redness of the face, neck, arms and occasionally, upper chest; sudden sweating)—≤1%; ***rigors*** (feeling unusually cold; shivering)—≤1%

Overdose

For more information on the management of overdose or unintentional ingestion, **contact a poison control center** (see *Poison Control Center Listing*).

Treatment of overdose

Specific treatment—
Overdose will lead to low or undetectable plasma uric acid concentration, which has no known clinical consequences.
See the package insert or *Rasburicase (Systemic)* for specific dosing guidelines for use of this product.
There is no specific antidote.

Supportive care—
Treatment should be primarily supportive and symptomatic.
Patients in whom intentional overdose is confirmed or suspected should be referred for psychiatric consultation.

Patient Consultation

As an aid to patient consultation, refer to *Advice for the Patient, Rasburicase (Systemic)*.

In providing consultation, consider emphasizing the following selected information (» = major clinical significance):

Before using this medication

» Conditions affecting use, especially:
Hypersensitivity to rasburicase or any of its excipients
Pregnancy—Should be used during pregnancy only if clearly needed
Breast-feeding—Risk-benefit considerations
Use in children—Increased frequency of toxicity and adverse effects such as vomiting, diarrhea, fever, and rash in pediatric patients less than two years of age compared to those between the ages of 2 and 17 due to higher mean uric acid levels.
Pharmacogenetics—Patients of African or Mediterranean ancestry are at higher risk for glucose-6-phosphate dehydrogenase (G6PD) deficiency which can cause severe hemolysis; screening recommended prior to starting rasburicase therapy
Other medical problems, especially history of anaphylaxis, history of hemolytic reactions, history of hypersensitivity, history of methemoglobinemia reactions, or G6PD deficiency

Proper use of this medication

» Not administering as a bolus infusion
» Adhering to the recommended treatment regimen of no more than a single course of treatment [once daily for 5 days]
Initiating chemotherapy 4 to 24 hours after the first dose of rasburicase

» Proper dosing
Proper storage

Precautions while using this medication

» Notifying physician immediately if signs and symptoms of allergic reaction occur

Side/adverse effects

Signs of potential side effects, especially acute renal failure, anaphylaxis, arrhythmia, cardiac arrest, cardiac failure, cellulitis, cerebrovascular disorder, chest pain, convulsions, cyanosis, hemolysis, hemorrhage, ileus, intestinal obstruction, mucositis, myocardial infarction, neutropenia, pancytopenia, paresthesia, pneumonia, pulmonary edema, acute renal failure, respiratory distress, retinal hemorrhage, severe rash, thrombophlebitis, and thrombosis.

General Dosing Information

The safety and efficacy of rasburicase have been established only for a single course of treatment (once daily for 5 days in United States and for up to 7 days in Canada). See *Parenteral Dosage Forms* for rasburicase dosing information.

Rasburicase should be administered via intravenous infusion over 30 minutes; *Do not administer as a bolus infusion.*

Rasburicase should be infused through a different line than that used for the infusion of other concomitant medications. If use of a separate line is not possible, the line should be flushed with at least 15 mL of saline solution prior to and after infusion with rasburicase.

For treatment of adverse effects

Rasburicase administration should be immediately and permanently discontinued in any patient developing clinical evidence of a serious anaphylactic, hypersensitivity reaction, hemolysis, or methemoglobinemia. Hemolysis patients should be appropriately monitored and transfusion support measures initiated. In patients developing methemoglobinemia, appropriate monitoring and support measures such as transfusion support and methylene-blue administration should be implemented.

Parenteral Dosage Forms

RASBURICASE FOR INJECTION

Usual adult dose

[Antiuricemic, adult (prophylaxis or treatment)]—

Intravenous infusion, 0.2 milligrams per kilogram of body weight administered over 30 minutes as a single daily dose for up to 7 days. Chemotherapy may be initiated as soon as 4 hours after the first dose of rasburicase.

Usual adult prescribing limits

See *Usual pediatric prescribing limits* below.

Usual pediatric dose

Antiuricemic, pediatric (treatment) or—

Intravenous infusion, 0.15 or 0.2 mg per kg of body weight administered over 30 minutes as a single daily dose for five days. Chemotherapy should be initiated 4 to 24 hours after the first dose of rasburicase

[Antiuricemic, pediatric (prophylaxis)]—

Intravenous infusion, 0.2 milligrams per kilogram of body weight administered over 30 minutes as a single daily dose for up to 7 days. Chemotherapy may be initiated as soon as 4 hours after the first dose of rasburicase.

Usual pediatric prescribing limits

Up to five days with daily doses of 0.15 or 0.2 mg per kg of body weight. Because the safety and effectiveness of other schedules have not been established, dosing beyond five days or administration of more than one course of rasburicase is not recommended. Safety and efficacy of rasburicase have been established only for a single course of treatment..

Usual geriatric dose

See *Usual pediatric dose.*

Usual geriatric prescribing limits

See *Usual pediatric prescribing limits.*

Strength(s) usually available

U.S.—

1.5 mg of rasburicase lyophilized powder per single-use vial with diluent in ampules (Rx) [*Elitek* (diluent ampule composed of 1 mL sterile Water for Injection, USP, and 1 mg Poloxamer 188; 10.6 mg mannitol; 15.9 mg l-alanine; between 12.6 and 14.3 mg of dibasic sodium phosphate)].

Canada—

1.5 mg of rasburicase lyophilized powder per single-use vial with diluent in ampule (Rx) [*Fasturtec* (diluent ampule composed of 1 mL sterile Water for Injection, USP, and 1 mg Poloxamer 188; 10.6 mg mannitol; 15.9 mg l-alanine; between 12.6 and 14.3 mg of dibasic sodium phosphate)].

Packaging and storage

Store the lyophilized drug and diluent for reconstitution between 2 and 8 °C (36 and 46 °F), in a tight container. Do not freeze. Protect from light.

The reconstituted or diluted solution can be stored between 2 and 8 °C (36 and 46 °F) up to 24 hours

Preparation of dosage form

The rasburicase lyophilized powder is reconstituted by adding 1 mL of the provided reconstitution solution (diluent) to each vial of rasburicase and mixing by swirling very gently. Do not shake or vortex. Do not administer the reconstituted solution without further dilution. The reconstituted solution must be further diluted in an infusion bag containing the appropriate volume of 0.9% sterile sodium chloride to achieve a final total volume of 50 mL. No filters should be used for the infusion. See the manufacturer's package insert for instructions.

Stability

After reconstitution, the solution may be stored up to 24 hours under refrigeration at 2 to 8°C (36 to 46°F). Rasburicase must be administered within 24 hours of reconstitution.

This product should be visually inspected for particulate matter and discoloration prior to administration. Samples containing visible particulates or samples that are discolored should not be used.

Incompatibilities

Rasburicase should be infused through a different line than that used for the infusion of other concomitant medications. If use of a separate line is not possible, the line should be flushed with at least 15 mL of saline solution prior to and after infusion with rasburicase.

Auxiliary labeling

- Dilute medication before use
- For single dose only. Discard unused drug.

Revised: 08/04/2005
Developed: 06/17/2003

RAUWOLFIA SERPENTINA—See *Rauwolfia Alkaloids (Systemic)*

REPAGLINIDE Systemic

VA CLASSIFICATION (Primary): HS509

Commonly used brand name(s): *Prandin.*

Note: For a listing of dosage forms and brand names by country availability, see *Dosage Forms* section(s).

Category

Antidiabetic agent.

Indications

Accepted

Diabetes, type 2 (treatment)—Repaglinide is indicated as adjunctive therapy to diet and exercise in the management of patients with type 2 diabetes (previously referred to as non-insulin-dependent diabetes mellitus [NIDDM]). It is also indicated in combination with metformin in patients whose hyperglycemia cannot be controlled by diet and exercise or by either metformin or repaglinide alone. In clinical trials, combination therapy with repaglinide and metformin demonstrated a synergistic improvement in glycosylated hemoglobin and fasting plasma glucose concentrations as compared with either medication alone. If adequate glycemic control is not achieved with combination therapy, repaglinide and metformin probably should be discontinued and insulin therapy instituted.

Pharmacology/Pharmacokinetics

Physicochemical characteristics

Class—Meglitinide.

Molecular weight—452.6.

Mechanism of action/Effect
Repaglinide lowers blood glucose concentrations by stimulating the release of insulin from functioning beta cells of pancreatic islet tissue. This is accomplished by a selective ion channel mechanism. Repaglinide inhibits adenosine triphosphate (ATP)-potassium channels on the beta cell membrane and potassium efflux. The resulting depolarization and calcium influx induces insulin secretion.

Absorption
Rapid and complete following oral administration.

Distribution
The mean absolute bioavailability is 56%. Volume of distribution at steady-state was 31 L following intravenous administration to healthy volunteers.

Protein binding
Very high (> 98%).

Biotransformation
Completely metabolized by oxidative biotransformation and direct conjugation with glucuronic acid. The major metabolites are an oxidized dicarboxylic acid (M2), the aromatic amine (M1), and the acyl glucuronide (M7), none of which contributes to the glucose-lowering effect. The cytochrome P450 3A4 isoenzyme has been shown to be involved in the *N*-dealkylation of repaglinide to M2 and the further oxidation to M1.

Half-life
Approximately 1 hour.

Time to peak concentration
Approximately 1 hour.

Peak plasma concentration
9.8, 18.3, 26, and 65.8 nanograms per mL following doses of 0.5, 1, 2, and 4 mg, respectively. The peak plasma concentration may be decreased by 20% when repaglinide is administered with food.

Elimination
Fecal (approximately 90%, 60% as M2 and < 2% as parent compound); renal (approximately 8%, 0.1% as parent compound). Total body clearance was 38 L per hour following intravenous administration to healthy volunteers.

In dialysis—

There is no evidence that repaglinide is dialyzable using hemodialysis.

Precautions to Consider

Carcinogenicity/Tumorigenicity
No evidence of carcinogenicity was found in mice or female rats administered repaglinide at doses up to and including 500 mg per kg of body weight (mg/kg) per day or 120 mg/kg per day, respectively, for 104 weeks. These doses represent approximately 125 or 60 times the clinical exposure on a mg per square meter of body surface area (mg/m^2) basis. However, in male rats there was an increased incidence of benign adenomas of the thyroid and liver at doses above 30 mg/kg per day for thyroid tumors and above 60 mg/kg per day for liver tumors. These doses represent 15 and 30 times, respectively, the clinical exposure on a mg/m^2 basis.

Mutagenicity
No evidence of mutagenicity was found in a series of *in vitro* and *in vivo* studies including the Ames test, *in vitro* forward cell mutation assay in V79 cells, *in vitro* chromosomal aberration assay in human lymphocytes, unscheduled and replicating DNA synthesis in rat liver, and *in vivo* mouse and rat micronucleus tests.

Pregnancy/Reproduction
Fertility—Repaglinide had no effect on the fertility of male and female rats administered doses of 300 mg/kg per day and up to 80 mg/kg per day, respectively. These doses represent greater than 40 times the clinical exposure on a mg/m^2 basis.

Pregnancy—Studies have not been done in humans.

It is recommended that insulin be used during pregnancy for maintenance of blood glucose concentrations as close to normal as possible. Abnormal maternal blood glucose concentrations have been associated with a higher incidence of congenital anomalies.

No evidence of teratogenicity was found in rats or rabbits administered 40 or 0.8 times, respectively, the clinical exposure on a mg/m^2 basis throughout pregnancy. However, rat pups developed skeletal deformities during the postnatal period when the dams were exposed to doses 15 times the clinical exposure on a mg/m^2 basis on days 17 to 22 of gestation.

FDA Pregnancy Category C.

Breast-feeding
It is not known whether repaglinide is distributed into breast milk. However, it is distributed into the milk of lactating rats and has been shown to lower glucose concentrations in the pups. In addition, some pups developed skeletal abnormalities, including shortening, thickening, and bending of the humerus during the postnatal period. Consideration should be given to discontinuing breast-feeding or discontinuing repaglinide and instituting insulin if blood glucose cannot be controlled by diet alone.

Pediatrics
Appropriate studies on the relationship of age to the effects of repaglinide have not been performed in the pediatric population. Safety and efficacy have not been established.

Geriatrics
Studies performed in approximately 415 patients 65 years of age or older have not demonstrated geriatrics-specific problems that would limit the usefulness of repaglinide in the elderly. However, hypoglycemia may be difficult to recognize in elderly patients.

Pharmacogenetics
In a 1-year study in the U.S., the glucose-lowering effect was comparable in black and white patients with type 2 diabetes. In a dose-response study in the U.S., there was no difference in the area under the plasma concentration-time curve (AUC) between Hispanic and white patients.

Drug interactions and/or related problems
The following drug interactions and/or related problems have been selected on the basis of their potential clinical significance (possible mechanism in parentheses where appropriate)—not necessarily inclusive (» = major clinical significance):

Note: Combinations containing any of the following medications, depending on the amount present, may also interact with this medication.

» Beta-adrenergic blocking agents or
Chloramphenicol or
Highly protein-bound medications, such as:
- Anticoagulants, coumarin-derivative
- Anti-inflammatory drugs, nonsteroidal (NSAIDs)
- Probenecid
- Salicylates or

Monoamine oxidase (MAO) inhibitors or
Sulfonamides

(these medications enhance the hypoglycemic effect of repaglinide; patients should be observed closely for symptoms of hypoglycemia or loss of glycemic control when repaglinide is added to or withdrawn from a regimen containing these medications)

(beta-adrenergic blocking agents may blunt some of the symptoms of hypoglycemia, making detection of this condition more difficult)

Erythromycin or
Ketoconazole or
Miconazole

(these medications may inhibit repaglinide metabolism; however, it is not known whether this effect on metabolism results in an increase in the plasma concentration of repaglinide)

Hyperglycemia-causing medications, such as:
- Calcium channel blocking agents
- Corticosteroids
- Diuretics, especially thiazide diuretics
- Estrogens
- Isoniazid
- Niacin
- Oral contraceptives
- Phenothiazines
- Phenytoin
- Sympathomimetic agents
- Thyroid hormones

(these medications may cause loss of glycemic control; patients should be observed closely for symptoms of hypoglycemia or loss of glycemic control when repaglinide is added to or withdrawn from a regimen containing these medications)

Other drugs metabolized by cytochrome P450 CYP3A4, such as:
- Barbiturates
- Carbamazepine
- Rifampin
- Troglitazone

(these medications may increase repaglinide metabolism; however, it is not known if this effect results in a decrease in the plasma concentration of repaglinide)

Laboratory value alterations

The following have been selected on the basis of their potential clinical significance (possible effect in parentheses where appropriate)—not necessarily inclusive (» = major clinical significance).

With physiology/laboratory test values

Electrocardiogram (ECG)
(rarely, may be abnormal)

Liver enzymes
(rarely, may be elevated)

Medical considerations/Contraindications

The medical considerations/contraindications included have been selected on the basis of their potential clinical significance (reasons given in parentheses where appropriate)—not necessarily inclusive (» = major clinical significance).

Except under special circumstances, this medication should not be used when the following medical problems exist:

» Diabetes, type 1 or
» Diabetic ketoacidosis, with or without coma
(these conditions should be treated with insulin)

Risk-benefit should be considered when the following medical problems exist:

Adrenal insufficiency or
Debilitated physical condition or
Hepatic function impairment or
Malnutrition or
Pituitary insufficiency
(these conditions may cause increased sensitivity to the glucose-lowering effect of repaglinide; caution is recommended)

» Hepatic function impairment
(AUC and peak plasma concentration [C_{max}] may be increased in patients with moderate or severe impairment; caution and longer intervals between dosage adjustments are recommended)

Infection or
Surgery or
Trauma or
Unusual stress
(these conditions may cause loss of glycemic control; temporary insulin therapy may be necessary)

» Renal function impairment
(AUC and C_{max} may be increased; adjustments to the initial dosage usually are not necessary, but subsequent increases in dosage should be made carefully in patients with renal function impairment or renal failure requiring hemodialysis)

Sensitivity to repaglinide

Patient monitoring

The following may be especially important in patient monitoring (other tests may be warranted in some patients, depending on condition; » = major clinical significance):

» Blood glucose determinations
(recommended periodically to determine the minimum effective dose of repaglinide, to confirm that blood glucose concentration is maintained within acceptable targets, and to detect inadequate lowering of glucose concentration after initial administration [primary failure] or loss of adequate glucose-lowering response after an initial period of efficacy [secondary failure])

» Glycosylated hemoglobin (hemoglobin A_{1c} [HbA_{1c}]) determinations
(recommended every 3 months to assess long-term glycemic control)

Side/Adverse Effects

Note: It has been suggested, based on a study conducted by the University Group Diabetes Program (UGDP), that certain sulfonylurea antidiabetic agents increase cardiovascular mortality in diabetic patients, a population that already has a greater risk of cardiovascular disease and mortality when blood glucose is not controlled. Despite questions regarding the interpretation of the results and the adequacy of the experimental design, the findings of the UGDP study provide an adequate basis for caution, especially for certain high-risk patients with coronary artery disease, congestive heart failure, or angina pectoris. Given the similarities in the mechanisms of action of sulfonylureas and repaglinide, the patient should be informed of the potential risks and advantages of repaglinide and of alternative modes of therapy.

The following side/adverse effects have been selected on the basis of their potential clinical significance (possible signs and symptoms in parentheses where appropriate)—not necessarily inclusive:

Those indicating need for medical attention

Incidence more frequent

Bronchitis (cough; fever; pain in the chest; shortness of breath); ***hypoglycemia*** (anxiety; behavior change similar to drunkenness; blurred vision; cold sweats; coma; confusion; cool pale skin; difficulty in concentrating; drowsiness; excessive hunger; fast heartbeat; headache; nausea; nervousness; nightmares; restless sleep; seizures; shakiness; slurred speech; unusual tiredness or weakness)—incidence 16% in clinical trials; ***sinusitis*** (headache; runny nose; sinus congestion with pain); ***upper respiratory infection*** (cough; fever; runny or stuffy nose; sneezing; sore throat)

Note: The incidence of *hypoglycemia* is greater in patients who have not previously been treated with oral antidiabetic agents and in patients whose hemoglobin A_{1c} is less than 8%.

Incidence less frequent

Allergic reaction (fever with or without chills; headache; nausea with or without vomiting; runny nose; shortness of breath, tightness in chest, trouble in breathing, or wheezing; skin rash, itching, or hives; tearing of eyes); ***angina; chest pain; tooth disorder; urinary tract infection*** (bloody or cloudy urine; burning, painful, or difficult urination; frequent urge to urinate)

Incidence rare

Cardiovascular effects including arrhythmias; hypertension; and myocardial infarction; leukopenia (cough or hoarseness; fever or chills; lower back or side pain; painful or difficult urination)—usually asymptomatic; ***thrombocytopenia*** (black, tarry stools; blood in urine or stools; pinpoint red spots on skin; unusual bleeding or bruising)—usually asymptomatic

Those indicating need for medical attention only if they continue or are bothersome

Incidence more frequent

Arthralgia (joint pain); ***back pain; diarrhea; headache; nausea; rhinitis*** (stuffy nose)

Incidence less frequent

Constipation; indigestion; paresthesias (sensation of burning, numbness, tightness, tingling, warmth, or heat); ***vomiting***

Overdose

For more information on the management of overdose or unintentional ingestion, **contact a Poison Control Center** (see *Poison Control Center Listing*).

Clinical effects of overdose

The following effects have been selected on the basis of their potential clinical significance (possible signs and symptoms in parentheses where appropriate)—not necessarily inclusive:

Hypoglycemia (anxiety; behavior change similar to drunkenness; blurred vision; cold sweats; coma; confusion; cool pale skin; difficulty in concentrating; drowsiness; excessive hunger; fast heartbeat; headache; nausea; nervousness; nightmares; restless sleep; seizures; shakiness; slurred speech; unusual tiredness or weakness)

Treatment of overdose

Specific treatment—

Mild hypoglycemia without neurologic symptoms or loss of consciousness should be treated with immediate ingestion of glucose and adjustments to medication dosage and/or meal patterns.

Severe hypoglycemia including coma, seizures, or other neurologic impairment requires immediate emergency medical assistance. The patient should immediately be given an intravenous injection of a 50% glucose solution followed by a continuous infusion of a 10% glucose solution to maintain a blood glucose concentration above 100 mg per dL.

Monitoring—

The patient should be monitored for at least 24 to 48 hours.

Patient Consultation

As an aid to patient consultation, refer to *Advice for the Patient, Repaglinide (Systemic)*.

In providing consultation, consider emphasizing the following selected information (» = major clinical significance):

Before using this medication

» Conditions affecting use, especially:
Sensitivity to repaglinide

Pregnancy—Use of insulin is recommended during pregnancy for maintenance of blood glucose concentrations as close to normal as possible
Breast-feeding—Breast-feeding should be discontinued, or repaglinide should be discontinued and insulin given, if blood glucose cannot be controlled by diet alone
Use in the elderly—Hypoglycemia may be difficult to recognize
Other medications, especially beta-adrenergic blocking agents
Other medical problems, especially diabetic ketoacidosis, hepatic function impairment, renal function impairment, or type 1 diabetes

Proper use of this medication

» Adhering to recommended regimens for diet, exercise, and glucose monitoring
» Taking medication 15 to 30 minutes before each meal
» Proper dosing
Missed dose: Skipping a dose if a meal is skipped; adding a dose if an extra meal is eaten
» Proper storage

Precautions while using this medication

» Regular visits to physician to check progress
» *Carefully following special instructions of health care team:*
Discussing use of alcohol
Not taking other medications unless discussed with physician
Getting counseling for family members to help the patient with diabetes; also, special counseling for pregnancy planning and contraception
Making travel plans that include readiness for diabetic emergencies and eating meals at the usual times, even with changing time zones
» Preparing for and understanding what to do in case of diabetic emergency; carrying medical history and current medication list and wearing medical identification
» Recognizing what brings on symptoms of hypoglycemia, such as using other antidiabetic medication; delaying or missing a meal; exercising more than usual; drinking significant amounts of alcohol; or illness, including vomiting or diarrhea
» Recognizing symptoms of hypoglycemia: anxiety; behavior change similar to drunkenness; blurred vision; cold sweats; confusion; cool, pale skin; difficulty in concentrating; drowsiness; excessive hunger; fast heartbeat; headache; nausea; nervousness; nightmares; restless sleep; shakiness; slurred speech; and unusual tiredness or weakness
» Knowing what to do if symptoms of hypoglycemia occur, such as eating glucose tablets or gel, corn syrup, honey, or sugar cubes; drinking fruit juice, nondiet soft drink, or sugar dissolved in water; or getting emergency medical assistance if symptoms are severe
» Recognizing what brings on symptoms of hyperglycemia, such as not taking enough antidiabetic medication, skipping a dose of antidiabetic medication, overeating or not following meal plan, having a fever or infection, or exercising less than usual
» Recognizing symptoms of hyperglycemia and ketoacidosis: blurred vision; drowsiness; dry mouth; flushed, dry skin; fruit-like breath odor; increased urination (frequency and volume); ketones in urine; loss of appetite; stomachache, nausea, or vomiting; tiredness; troubled breathing (rapid and deep); unconsciousness; and unusual thirst
» Knowing what to do if symptoms of hyperglycemia occur, such as checking blood glucose and contacting a member of the health care team

Side/adverse effects

Signs of potential side effects, especially bronchitis, hypoglycemia, sinusitis, upper respiratory infection, allergic reaction, angina, chest pain, tooth disorder, urinary tract infection, cardiovascular effects, leukopenia, and thrombocytopenia

General Dosing Information

Diet/Nutrition

Repaglinide may be taken 15 to 30 minutes before a meal.
Taking repaglinide with meals decreases the risk of hypoglycemia.

Oral Dosage Forms

REPAGLINIDE TABLETS

Usual adult dose

Antidiabetic agent—
For patients not previously treated with a blood glucose–lowering medication or whose hemoglobin A_{1c} (HbA_{1c}) is less than 8%: Oral, initially 0.5 mg fifteen to thirty minutes before each meal. The dose may be adjusted up to 4 mg as determined by blood glucose response (usually assessed by fasting concentration).
For patients previously treated with a blood glucose–lowering medication and whose HbA_{1c} is greater than or equal to 8%: Oral, initially 1 or 2 mg fifteen to thirty minutes before each meal. The dose may be adjusted up to 4 mg as determined by blood glucose response (usually assessed by fasting concentration).

Note: For both patients not previously treated and those previously treated with blood glucose–lowering medications, at least one week should elapse to assess response after each dose adjustment. However, in patients with hepatic function impairment, the interval between dose adjustments should be increased.
When repaglinide is taken in combination with metformin, the dosing guidelines are the same as for repaglinide monotherapy.
When used to replace therapy with other oral antidiabetic agents, repaglinide may be started on the day after the final dose of previous therapy is given. The patient should be monitored for possible overlapping hypoglycemic effects. Monitoring for up to one week or longer may be required when the patient is transferred from longer half-life agents, such as chlorpropamide.

Usual adult prescribing limits

16 mg per day.

Usual pediatric dose

Safety and efficacy have not been established.

Strength(s) usually available

U.S.—
0.5 mg (Rx) [*Prandin* (calcium hydrogen phosphate [anhydrous]; microcrystalline cellulose; maize starch; polacrilin potassium; povidone; glycerol 85%; magnesium stearate; meglumine; poloxamer)].
1 mg (Rx) [*Prandin* (calcium hydrogen phosphate [anhydrous]; microcrystalline cellulose; maize starch; polacrilin potassium; povidone; glycerol 85%; magnesium stearate; meglumine; poloxamer; iron oxide [yellow])].
2 mg (Rx) [*Prandin* (calcium hydrogen phosphate [anhydrous]; microcrystalline cellulose; maize starch; polacrilin potassium; povidone; glycerol 85%; magnesium stearate; meglumine; poloxamer; iron oxide [red])].

Packaging and storage

Store below 25 °C (77 °F), in a tight container. Protect from moisture.

Developed: 08/03/1998

RESERPINE—See *Rauwolfia Alkaloids (Systemic)*

RESPIRATORY SYNCYTIAL VIRUS IMMUNE GLOBULIN INTRAVENOUS Systemic

VA CLASSIFICATION (Primary): IM402
Commonly used brand name(s): *RespiGam*.
Another commonly used name is RSV-IGIV.

Note: For a listing of dosage forms and brand names by country availability, see *Dosage Forms* section(s).

Category

Immunizing agent (passive).

Indications

General Considerations

Respiratory syncytial virus (RSV), a negative-strand enveloped ribonucleic acid (RNA) virus of the paramyxovirus family, is considered to be a major cause of morbidity and mortality in the developing world. In the U.S., RSV causes an estimated 90,000 hospitalizations and 4500 deaths each year from lower respiratory tract infection in both infants and young children.

RSV strains are classified into groups A and B on the basis of the antigenic structure of the G protein. Among hospitalized infants, group A RSV infection results in greater disease severity than does group B infection. Unlike influenza, infection with RSV does not elicit long-term immunity, since RSV contains a single segment of RNA that does not facilitate major antigenic evolution. The mechanism by which group A RSV may cause more severe illness is unknown, but could result from functional differences in the viral genome or protein.

RSV activity in the U.S. is monitored by the National Respiratory and Enteric Virus Surveillance System (NREVSS), a voluntary, laboratory-based system. Outbreaks occur annually throughout the U.S. Onset of disease activity usually occurs in November and continues through April or early May, with peak activity occurring from late January through mid-February.

During the RSV season, health care providers should consider the role of RSV as a cause of acute respiratory disease in both children and adults. RSV is a common, but preventable, cause of nosocomially acquired infection; the risk for nosocomial transmission increases during community outbreaks. Nosocomial outbreaks or transmission of RSV can be controlled with strict attention to contact-isolation procedures.

Individuals at greatest risk for RSV-associated complications include preterm infants, children less than 6 months of age with chronic lung disease (especially those with bronchopulmonary dysplasia [BPD]) or congenital heart disease (CHD), immunocompromised individuals, and geriatric patients.

RSV causes acute respiratory illness in patients of any age. However, in infants and young children, it is the most important cause of bronchiolitis and pneumonia. Most severe manifestations of infection with RSV (e.g., bronchiolitis and pneumonia) occur in infants 2 to 6 months of age. During the first few weeks of life, particularly in preterm infants, respiratory signs can be minimal. Lethargy, irritability, and poor feeding, sometimes accompanied by apneic episodes, may be the major signs. RSV infection in older children and adults usually manifests as an upper respiratory tract illness, occasionally with bronchitis. Exacerbation of asthma or other chronic lung conditions is also common.

Nearly all children are infected by 2 years of age, and 1 to 2% of those infected require hospitalization. Among those admitted to the hospital with no apparent risk factors for severe disease, 4 to 15% are admitted to the intensive care unit (ICU), 1 to 5% require assisted ventilation, and $<$ 1% die. In contrast, among children with underlying heart and lung disease, prematurity (i.e., gestation $\leq$ 32 weeks), and young age (i.e., $\leq$ 6 weeks), the corresponding figures for ICU, ventilation, and mortality range from 10 to 40%, 8 to 27%, and up to 10%, respectively.

Although traditionally recognized as the most common cause of lower respiratory tract disease in young children, RSV also has been shown to be a cause of serious illness in elderly adults. RSV is a predictable cause of disease each winter in older persons living in the community, in nursing homes, or attending senior day care programs. Similar to influenza, a well-recognized pathogen in the elderly, peaks of RSV activity in the community are associated with excess rates of mortality in persons over 65 years of age.

Immunity to RSV is incomplete and reinfection throughout life is common. However, although reinfection with RSV occurs throughout life, analysis of immune mechanisms following natural infection suggests that both humoral and mucosal antibodies may contribute to at least partial protection. Illness severity in infants has been related to the level of serum antibody to RSV, and passively administered high-titer RSV immunoglobulin has been demonstrated to protect infants who are at greater risk of acquiring the most severe disease.

Respiratory syncytial virus immune globulin intravenous (RSV-IGIV) has demonstrated efficacy only in the prophylaxis of children at high risk for RSV-related lower respiratory tract infection. One clinical trial has demonstrated that RSV-IGIV treatment is safe, but not efficacious, in the treatment of children with BPD, CHD, or premature gestation who are hospitalized with RSV-related lower respiratory tract infection.

Accepted

Respiratory syncytial virus infection (prophylaxis)—Respiratory syncytial virus immune globulin intravenous (RSV-IGIV) is indicated for the prevention of serious lower respiratory tract infection caused by RSV in children younger than 24 months of age with bronchopulmonary dysplasia (BPD) or a history of premature birth (gestation $\leq$ 32 weeks).

Pharmacology/Pharmacokinetics

Physicochemical characteristics

Source—Respiratory syncytial virus immune globulin intravenous (RSV-IGIV) is a sterile solution of immune globulin G (IgG) purified from pooled adult human plasma selected for high titers of neutralizing antibody against respiratory syncytial virus (RSV). The product is purified using Cohn-Oncley cold ethanol fractionation and a solvent detergent partitioning method to inactivate blood-borne pathogens.

Mechanism of action/Effect

RSV-IGIV contains a high concentration of neutralizing and protective antibodies directed against RSV. *In vitro* tests demonstrated that RSV-IGIV can neutralize clinical isolates of RSV.

Protective effect

Studies in otherwise healthy children have shown that the frequency of primary and recurrent RSV infection is inversely correlated to the titer of RSV-neutralizing antibodies measured before the onset of the RSV season.

A randomized, double-blind, placebo-controlled, clinical trial was conducted at 54 centers in the U.S. (the PREVENT trial) during the 1994 to 1995 RSV season. This study included 510 children with bronchopulmonary dysplasia and/or a history of prematurity. These children were randomized to receive either 750 mg per kg of body weight (mg/kg) RSV-IGIV or placebo (1% albumin). In the study's comparison of treated patients with control patients, the incidence of RSV hospitalization was reduced by 41%, total days of RSV hospitalization were reduced by 53%, total RSV hospital days with increased supplemental oxygen requirements were reduced by 60%, and total RSV hospital days with a moderate or severe lower respiratory tract infection were reduced by 54%. The total days of hospitalization for respiratory illness per 100 randomized children were compared between placebo patients and RSV-IGIV patients. There were 317 days per 100 control children and 170 days per 100 treated children.

Time to protective efficacy

One month after the second, third, and fourth monthly infusion of respiratory syncytial virus immune globulin intravenous 750 mg/kg, titers were 1:477 $\pm$ 85, 1:490 $\pm$ 61, and 1:429 $\pm$ 23, respectively. Experts expect that protection against RSV infection is obtained with titers of 1:200 to 1:400.

Duration of effect

Studies of adult volunteers have shown that immunity to RSV frequently lasts only a few months. By the next annual RSV epidemic, most of the population is susceptible to reinfection by the same strain of virus.

Half-life

22 to 28 days.

Precautions to Consider

Cross-sensitivity and/or related problems

Respiratory syncytial virus immune globulin intravenous (RSV-IGIV) should be given with caution to patients with a history of prior systemic allergic reactions following the administration of human immunoglobulin preparations.

Pregnancy/Reproduction

Pregnancy—Studies have not been done in humans.

Studies have not been done in animals.

FDA Pregnancy Category C.

Breast-feeding

It is not known whether RSV-IGIV is distributed into breast milk. However, problems in humans have not been documented.

Pediatrics

Infants with underlying pulmonary disease may be sensitive to extra fluid volume. Infusion of RSV-IGIV, particularly in children with bronchopulmonary dysplasia (BPD), may precipitate symptoms of fluid overload. Therefore, RSV-IGIV should be administered with caution to infants with underlying pulmonary disease. Vital signs should be monitored to help indicate fluid overload, and, if indicated, a loop diuretic should be administered.

The safety and efficacy of RSV-IGIV in children with congenital heart disease (CHD) has not been established. In one study, although equivalent proportions of children in RSV-IGIV and control groups had adverse events, a large number of RSV-IGIV recipients had severe or life-threatening adverse reactions. These reactions were most frequently observed in infants with CHD with right to left shunts who underwent cardiac surgery before treatment with RSV-IGIV.

Geriatrics

No information is available on the relationship of age to the effects of RSV-IGIV in geriatric patients.

Drug interactions and/or related problems

The following drug interactions and/or related problems have been selected on the basis of their potential clinical significance (possible mechanism in parentheses where appropriate)—not necessarily inclusive (» = major clinical significance):

Note: Combinations containing any of the following medications, depending on the amount present, may also interact with this medication.

Live virus vaccines
(concurrent administration of RSV-IGIV with measles, mumps, rubella, or varicella live virus vaccines may interfere with the patient's immune response to these vaccines; immunization with measles, mumps, rubella, or varicella live virus vaccines should be deferred for 9 months after the last dose of RSV-IGIV; in addition, limited information available from infants who received RSV-IGIV concurrently with one or more doses of their primary immunization series indicates that antibody responses to diphtheria and tetanus toxoids, and pertussis vaccine, and *Haemophilus* b vaccine may be decreased; however, no changes are required to the primary immunization schedule for these agents)

Medical considerations/Contraindications

The medical considerations/contraindications included have been selected on the basis of their potential clinical significance (reasons given in parentheses where appropriate)—not necessarily inclusive (» = major clinical significance).

Except under special circumstances, this medication should not be used when the following medical problems exist:

» Allergic reaction to human immunoglobulins

» Immunoglobulin A (IgA) deficiencies, selective, in patients who are known to have antibodies to IgA
(small amounts of IgA may be present in RSV-IGIV and may cause a severe allergic reaction in patients with antibodies to IgA)

Risk-benefit should be considered when the following medical problem exists:

Sensitivity to RSV-IGIV

Patient monitoring

The following may be especially important in patient monitoring (other tests may be warranted in some patients, depending on condition; » = major clinical significance):

Vital signs
(infants with underlying pulmonary disease who may be sensitive to extra fluid volume may be at risk of developing hypotension, anaphylaxis, or a severe allergic reaction, which may lead to shock; the patient's vital signs should be monitored continuously, and the patient should be observed carefully throughout the infusion)

Side/Adverse Effects

Note: Severe reactions, such as anaphylaxis or angioneuropathy, have been reported in association with intravenous immunoglobulins, even in patients not known to be sensitive to human immunoglobulins or blood products. In one clinical trial, serious allergic reactions were noted in two patients who received respiratory syncytial virus immune globulin intravenous (RSV-IGIV). These reactions were manifested as an acute episode of cyanosis, mottling, and fever in one patient, and as respiratory distress in the other.

Rare occurrences of aseptic meningitis syndrome (AMS) have been reported in association with immune globulin intravenous (IGIV) treatment. AMS usually begins within several hours to 2 days following IGIV treatment and is characterized by symptoms and signs that include severe headache, drowsiness, fever, photophobia, painful eye movements, muscle rigidity, and nausea and vomiting. Cerebrospinal fluid studies generally demonstrate pleocytosis, predominantly granulocytic, and elevated protein levels. Patients exhibiting such symptoms and signs should be thoroughly evaluated to rule out other causes of meningitis. AMS may occur more frequently in association with high-dose (2 grams per kg of body weight) IGIV treatment. Discontinuation of IGIV treatment has resulted in remission of AMS within several days without sequelae.

Except for hypersensitivity reactions, adverse reactions to IGIV are related to the rate of infusion, and may be relieved by decreasing the rate or temporarily stopping infusion. Loop diuretics should be available for the management of patients who are at risk of fluid overload.

The following side/adverse effects have been selected on the basis of their potential clinical significance (possible signs and symptoms in parentheses where appropriate)—not necessarily inclusive:

Those indicating need for medical attention

Incidence rare

Anaphylactic reaction (difficulty in breathing and swallowing; hives; itching, especially of feet and hands; reddening of skin, especially around ears; swelling of eyes, face, or inside of nose; unusual tiredness or weakness, sudden and severe); ***fever of 39.2 °C (102.6 °F) or more; respiratory distress; tachycardia*** (increased heart rate); ***vomiting***

Patient Consultation

As an aid to patient consultation, refer to *Advice for the Patient, Respiratory Syncytial Virus Immune Globulin Intravenous (Systemic)*.

In providing consultation, consider emphasizing the following selected information (» = major clinical significance):

Before using this medication

» Conditions affecting use, especially:
Sensitivity to respiratory syncytial virus immune globulin intravenous (RSV-IGIV)
Use in children—Using with caution in children with bronchopulmonary dysplasia; safety and efficacy of RSV-IGIV in children with congenital heart disease have not been established
Other medical problems, especially history of allergic reactions to human immunoglobulins, or selective IgA deficiencies

Proper use of this medication

» Proper dosing

Side/adverse effects

Signs of potential side effects, especially, anaphylactic reaction, fever of 39.2 °C (102.6 °F), respiratory distress, tachycardia, and vomiting

General Dosing Information

Although systemic reactions to human immunoglobulin preparations are rare, serious allergic reactions were reported following respiratory syncytial virus immune globulin intravenous (RSV-IGIV) administration. Therefore, appropriate precautions should be taken prior to RSV-IGIV infusion to prevent allergic or other unwanted reactions. These precautions should include review of the patient's history regarding possible sensitivity and the ready availability of epinephrine 1:1000 and other appropriate agents used to control immediate allergic reactions.

RSV-IGIV has been approved for use in infants and children younger than 24 months with bronchopulmonary dysplasia (BPD) or a history of premature birth (≤ 32 weeks of gestation). In addition to BPD and prematurity, other factors may influence the decision about the use of RSV-IGIV prophylaxis. These include conditions that predispose to respiratory complications (e.g., neurologic disease in very-low-birth-weight infants), the number of young siblings, child care center attendance, exposure to cigarette smoke in the home, anticipated cardiac surgery, ease of intravenous access, medication- and infusion-related costs, practicality and tolerability of monthly infusions, and the distance to and availability of hospital care for severe respiratory illness. For many infants qualifying for the approved indications, the risk of rehospitalization for serious respiratory illness will be low, and the cost of logistic difficulties associated with RSV-IGIV use may outweigh potential benefits. The effectiveness of RSV-IGIV for children who receive an incomplete single infusion or less than the recommended total monthly infusions has not been assessed.

The Committee on Infectious Diseases and the Committee on Fetus and Newborn of the American Academy of Pediatrics (AAP) offer the following recommendations on the use of RSV-IGIV in infants and children:

- RSV-IGIV prophylaxis should be considered for infants and children younger than 2 years of age with BPD who currently are receiving or have received oxygen therapy within the 6 months before the anticipated respiratory syncytial virus (RSV) season. Patients with BPD with more severe underlying lung disease may benefit clinically from prophylaxis for two RSV seasons, whereas those with less severe underlying disease may benefit only for the first season. Decisions regarding individual patients may need additional input from neonatologists, intensive care specialists, or pulmonologists.
- Infants born at 32 weeks or less of gestation without BPD also may benefit from RSV-IGIV prophylaxis. In these infants, major risk factors to consider are gestational age and chronologic age at the start of the RSV season. Infants born at 28 weeks of gestation or less may benefit from prophylaxis up to 12 months of age. Infants born at 29 to 32 weeks of gestation may benefit from prophylaxis up to 6 months of age. Decisions regarding each patient should be individualized. Practitioners may wish to use RSV rehospitalization data from their own region to assist in the decision-making process.
- RSV-IGIV is not approved for patients with congenital heart disease (CHD). Available data indicate that RSV-IGIV should not be used in patients who have cyanotic CHD. However, patients with BPD and/or prematurity who meet the criteria in recommendations mentioned above and who also have asymptomatic acyanotic CHD (e.g., patent ductus arteriosus or ventricular septal defect) may benefit from prophylaxis.
- RSV-IGIV use, either prophylactically or therapeutically, has not been evaluated in randomized trials in immunocompromised pediatric patients. Although specific recommendations for all immunocompro-

mised patients cannot be made, children with severe immunodeficiencies (e.g., severe combined immunodeficiency or severe acquired immunodeficiency syndrome [AIDS]) may benefit from RSV-IGIV. If these infants and children are receiving immune globulin intravenous (IGIV) monthly, providers may consider substituting RSV-IGIV during the RSV season.

• RSV is known to be transmitted in the hospital setting and to cause serious disease in high-risk infants. In high-risk hospitalized infants, the major means to prevent RSV disease is strict observance of infection control practices, including the use of rapid means to identify RSV-infected infants. If an RSV outbreak is documented in a high-risk unit (e.g., pediatric intensive care unit), primary emphasis should be placed on proper infection control practices. The need for, and efficacy of, RSV-IGIV prophylaxis in these situations have not been documented.

• RSV-IGIV prophylaxis should be initiated before the onset of the RSV season and terminated at the end of the RSV season. In most areas of the U.S., the usual time for the beginning of RSV outbreaks is October to December and termination is March to May, but regional differences occur. The onset of RSV occurs earlier in the southern states than in the northern states. Practitioners should check with health departments and/or diagnostic virology laboratories in their geographic areas to determine the optimal schedule.

• In infants and children receiving RSV-IGIV prophylaxis (750 mg per kg of body weight [mg/kg] dose), immunization with measles, mumps, and rubella virus vaccine live and varicella live virus vaccine should be deferred for 9 months after the last dose. There are no data on the use of RSV-IGIV and the response to hepatitis B vaccine, but there is no reason to anticipate any interference because RSV-IGIV does not contain antibodies to hepatitis B surface antigen. RSV-IGIV use should not alter the primary immunization schedule for diphtheria and tetanus toxoids, whole-cell or acellular pertussis vaccine, *Haemophilus* b vaccine, and poliovirus vaccines (inactivated poliovirus vaccine [IPV] or oral poliovirus vaccine [OPV]).

• A critical aspect of RSV prevention in high-risk infants is education of parents and other care givers about the importance of reducing exposure to, and transmission of, RSV. Preventive measures include limiting, where feasible, exposure to cigarette smoke and contagious settings (e.g., child care centers) and emphasis on hand washing in all settings, including the home, especially during periods when contacts of high-risk children have respiratory infections.

For treatment of adverse effects

Recommended treatment consists of the following:

• For mild hypersensitivity reaction—Administering antihistamines, and, if necessary, corticosteroids.

• For severe hypersensitivity or anaphylactic reaction—Administering epinephrine. Antihistamines or corticosteroids also may be administered as required.

Parenteral Dosage Forms

RESPIRATORY SYNCYTIAL VIRUS IMMUNE GLOBULIN INTRAVENOUS INJECTION

Usual adult and adolescent dose

Use is not recommended.

Usual pediatric dose

Respiratory syncytial virus infection (prophylaxis)—

Children younger than 2 years of age: Intravenous infusion, the maximum recommended total dosage is 750 mg per kg of body weight administered as a single monthly infusion beginning in September or October and continuing for a total of five doses.

Note: Respiratory syncytial virus immune globulin intravenous should be administered intravenously at a rate of 1.5 mL per kg of body weight per hour for 15 minutes. If not contraindicated by the patient's clinical condition, the rate can be increased to 3 mL per kg of body weight per hour for 15 minutes, and finally to a maximum rate of 6 mL per kg of body weight per hour. The maximum recommended rate of infusion should not be exceeded. The patient should be monitored closely during and after each rate change. A slower rate of infusion may be indicated in children who are volume sensitive, such as those with bronchopulmonary dysplasia (BPD) or prematurity.

Children 2 years of age and older: Use is not recommended.

Strength(s) usually available

U.S.—

Each 50-mL vial contains 2500 mg ± 500 mg immunoglobulin, primarily IgG and trace amounts of IgA and IgM (Rx) [*RespiGam*].

Canada—

Each 50-mL vial contains 2500 mg ± 500 mg immunoglobulin, primarily IgG and trace amounts of IgA and IgM (Rx) [*RespiGam*].

Packaging and storage

Store between 2 and 8 °C (36 and 46 °F), unless otherwise specified by the manufacturer. Protect from freezing.

Stability

A solution that has been frozen should be discarded.

Auxiliary labeling

• Do not freeze.

Selected Bibliography

American Academy of Pediatrics. Recommendations of the Committee on Infectious Diseases and the Committee on Fetus and Newborn: respiratory syncytial virus immune globulin intravenous—indications for use. Pediatrics 1997; 99(4): 645-50.

Connor E, Top F, Kramer A, et al. The PREVENT Study Group. Reduction of respiratory syncytial virus hospitalization among premature infants and infants with bronchopulmonary dysplasia using respiratory syncytial virus immune globulin prophylaxis. Pediatrics 1997; 99(1): 93-9.

Revised: 07/29/1998

RIBAVIRIN—See *Ribavirin and Interferon Alfa-2b, Recombinant (Systemic)*

RIBAVIRIN Systemic

VA CLASSIFICATION (Primary): AM890

Commonly used brand name(s): *Copegus; Rebetol; Virazole.*

Another commonly used name is tribavirin.

Note: For a listing of dosage forms and brand names by country availability, see *Dosage Forms* section(s).

Category

Antiviral (systemic)

Note: Ribavirin is a broad-spectrum antiviral active *in vitro* against a wide variety of DNA and RNA viruses.

Indications

Note: Bracketed information in the *Indications* section refers to uses that are not included in U.S. product labeling.

Accepted

Chronic hepatitis C (treatment)—Ribavirin capsules and ribavirin oral solution (Rebetol®) are indicated in combination with interferon alfa–2b, recombinant injection (Intron A®) for the treatment of chronic hepatitis C in patients 3 years of age and older with compensated liver disease previously untreated with alpha interferons or in patients 18 years of age and older who have relapsed following alpha interferon therapy.

Ribavirin capsules (Rebetol®) are indicated in combination with peginterferon alfa-2b, recombinant injection (Peg-Intron®) for the treatment of chronic hepatitis C in patients with compensated liver disease who have not been previously treated with interferon alpha and are at least 18 years of age.

Ribavirin tablets (Copegus®) are indicated in combination with peginterferon alfa-2a (Pegasys®) for the treatment of adults with chronic hepatitis C virus infection who have compensated liver disease and have not previously been treated with interferon alpha. Patients in whom efficacy was demonstrated included patients with compensated liver disease and histological evidence of cirrhosis (Child-Pugh class A) and patients with HIV disease that is clinically stable (e.g., antiretroviral therapy not required or receiving stable antiretroviral therapy).

Note: Ribavirin monotherapy is not effective for the treatment of chronic hepatitis C virus infection and should not be used alone for this indication.

Respiratory syncytial virus (RSV) infection, lower respiratory tract (treatment)—Ribavirin inhalation solution is for the treatment of severe lower respiratory tract infections (including bronchiolitis and pneumonia) caused by respiratory syncytial virus (RSV) in hospitalized infants and young children who are at high risk for severe or complicated RSV infection; this category includes premature infants and infants with structural or physiologic cardiopulmonary disorders, bronchopulmonary dysplasia, immunodeficiency, or imminent respiratory failure. Ribavirin is indicated in the treatment of RSV infections in infants requiring mechanical ventilator assistance.

[Influenza A (treatment)][1] or

[Influenza B (treatment)][1]—Ribavirin inhalation solution is used as a secondary agent in the treatment of influenza A and B in young adults when treatment is started early (e.g., within 24 hours of initial symptoms) in the course of the disease.

[Lassa fever (prophylaxis and treatment)][1] or

[Viral hemorrhagic fever (prophylaxis and treatment)][1]—Oral and intravenous ribavirin are used in the treatment of Lassa fever and as postexposure prophylaxis in contacts at high risk. It may be similarly effective with other viral hemorrhagic fevers, including hemorrhagic fever with renal syndrome, Crimean-Congo hemorrhagic fever, and Rift Valley fever.

Unaccepted

Ribavirin is not indicated in children with mild RSV lower respiratory tract involvement who require a shorter hospitalization than that required for completion of a full course of ribavirin treatment (i.e., 3 to 7 days).

The safety and efficacy of ribavirin capsules or oral solution with interferons other than Intron A® (interferon alfa-2b, recombinant) or Peg-Intron® (peginterferon alfa-2b, recombinant) products has not been established.The safety and efficacy of ribavirin tablets (Copegus®) have only been established when used together with Pegasys™, pegylated interferon alfa-2a, recombinant.

The safety and efficacy of ribavirin/interferon alfa–2a therapy and ribavirin/peginterferon alfa–2b therapy for the treatment of adenovirus, RSV, parainfluenza, or influenza infections have not been established.

The safety and efficacy of oral ribavirin/interferon alfa–2a therapy has not been established in liver or other organ transplant patients, patients with decompensated liver disease due to hepatitis C infection, or patients who are non-responders to interferon therapy, or patients coinfected with HBV and HIV.

---

[1]Not included in Canadian product labeling.

Pharmacology/Pharmacokinetics

Physicochemical characteristics

Molecular weight—244.21.

Mechanism of action/Effect

Virustatic; mechanism not completely understood, but does not alter viral attachment, penetration, or uncoating and does not induce cellular production of interferon; however, reversal of its antiviral action by guanosine and xanthosine suggests that ribavirin may act as a competitive inhibitor of cellular enzymes that act on these metabolites. Ribavirin is rapidly transported into cells and acts within virus-infected cells. Ribavirin is readily phosphorylated intracellularly by adenosine kinase to ribavirin mono-, di-, and triphosphate metabolites. Ribavirin triphosphate (RTP) is a potent competitive inhibitor of inosine monophosphate (IMP) dehydrogenase, influenza virus RNA polymerase, and messenger RNA (mRNA) guanylyltransferase, the latter resulting in inhibition of the capping of mRNA. These diverse effects result in a marked reduction of intracellular guanosine triphosphate (GTP) pools and inhibition of viral RNA and protein synthesis. Ultimately, viral replication and spreading to other cells are prevented or greatly inhibited.

The mechanism of inhibition of hepatitis C virus (HCV) RNA by combination therapy with interferon products has not been established.

Other actions/effects

May have immunologic effects; decreases in neutralizing antibody responses to respiratory syncytial virus (RSV) infection have been reported in ribavirin-treated patients. The clinical significance of this effect is unknown. Ribavirin has also been shown to significantly reduce viral shedding in RSV-infected patients.

Absorption

Inhalation—A small amount is systemically absorbed following inhalation.

Oral—Rapidly absorbed from the gastrointestinal tract following oral administration; bioavailability is approximately 64%.

Bioavailability of a single oral dose was increased by 70% when coadministered with a high-fat meal.

Distribution

Distributed to plasma, respiratory tract secretions, and erythrocytes (RBCs). Large amounts of ribavirin triphosphate are sequestered in RBCs, reaching a plateau in approximately 4 days and remaining sequestered for weeks after administration. Significant concentrations (greater than 67%) may be found in the cerebrospinal fluid after prolonged administration.

Vol_D Inhalation/Parenteral = Approximately 647 to 802 liters.

Vol_D Oral = 2825 liters

Protein binding

No significant plasma protein binding.

Biotransformation

Hepatic (probable); phosphorylated intracellularly to mono-, di-, and triphosphate metabolites, the latter being active; metabolized also to 1,2,4-triazole carboxamide metabolite; secondary metabolic pathway involves amide hydrolysis to tricarboxylic acid, deribosylation, and breakdown of the triazole ring.Ribavirin is not a substrate of CYP450 enzymes.

Half-life

Distribution—
- Intravenous:
  - Approximately 0.2 hours.

Elimination—
- Inhalation: 9.5 hours.
- Intravenous and oral (single dose): 0.5 to 2 hours.
- In erythrocytes: 40 days.

Terminal—
- Intravenous and oral:
  - Single dose—27 to 36 hours.
  - Single oral dose tablet—120 to 170 hours
  - Steady state—Approximately 151 hours.
- Mean:
  - multiple oral dosing, capsule—298 hours

Time to peak plasma concentration

Intravenous—End of infusion.

Oral—1 to 2 hours.

Oral, pediatric—1.9 hours

Time to steady state concentration—
- Oral Dosing—4 weeks

Therapeutic plasma concentration

Therapeutically effective concentrations depend primarily on the duration of exposure and patient minute volume. Concentrations in respiratory tract secretions are much higher than corresponding plasma concentrations.

Mean peak plasma concentration

Inhalation—
- Mean plasma concentration is 0.76 micromolar (range 0.44 to 1.55 micromolar) in pediatric patients receiving ribavirin aerosol by face mask 2.5 hours per day for 3 days.
- Mean plasma concentration is 6.8 micromolar (range 1.5 to 4.3 micromolar) in pediatric patients receiving ribavirin aerosol by face mask or mist tent 20 hours per day for 5 days.

Intravenous—
- Approximately 43 micromoles per liter after a single 600 mg dose.
- Approximately 72 micromoles per liter after a single 1200 mg dose.

Oral—
- Approximately 5 micromoles per liter at the end of the first week of administration of 200 mg every 8 hours.
- Approximately 11 micromoles per liter at the end of the first week of administration of 400 mg every 8 hours.
- Oral, capsule: 3680 ng per mL for multiple dose (600 mg twice daily)
- Oral, tablet: 2748 ng per mL following 1200 mg per day with food for 12 weeks
- Oral, solution: 2200 ng per mL following 600 mg twice daily for 4 weeks
- Oral, pediatric: 3275 ng/mL for 15 mg/kg/day as 2 divided doses.

Elimination

Inhalation—
- Renal: Approximately 30 to 55% excreted as the 1,2,4-triazole carboxamide metabolite in urine within 72 to 80 hours.
- Fecal: Approximately 15% excreted in feces within 72 hours.

Intravenous—
- Approximately 19% excreted unchanged in 24 hours; approximately 24% excreted unchanged in 48 hours.

Oral—
- Approximately 7% excreted unchanged in 24 hours; approximately 10% excreted unchanged in 48 hours.
- Approximately 61% renal; 12% fecal; 17% unchanged in 336 hours
- Apparent clearance, single oral dose: 26 L per hour

In dialysis—
- Significant amounts of ribavirin are not removed by hemodialysis.

Precautions to Consider

Carcinogenicity/Tumorigenicity

Ribavirin did not cause an increase in any tumor type when administered for 6 months in the transgenic p53 deficient mouse model at doses up to 300 mg/kg (estimated human equivalent of 25 mg/kg based on body surface area adjustment for a 60 kg adult); approximately 1.9 times the maximum recommended human daily dose). Ribavirin was noncarcinogenic when administered for 2 years to rats at doses up to 40 mg/kg (estimated human equivalent of 5.71 mg/kg based on body surface area adjustment for a 60 kg adult). However, this dose was less than the maximum tolerated dose, and therefore the study was not adequate to fully characterize the carcinogenic potential of ribavirin.

Mutagenicity

Studies have shown that ribavirin is mutagenic to mammalian cells (L5178Y) in culture. However, microbial mutagenicity assays and dominant lethal assays in mice have not shown that ribavirin is mutagenic. Ribavirin demonstrated increased incidences of mutation and cell transformation in multiple genotoxic assays. Ribavirin was active in the Balb/3T3 *in vitro* cell transformation assay. Mutagenic activity was observed in the mouse lymphoma assay, and at doses of 20–200 mg/kg (estimated human equivalent of 1.67 to 16.7 mg/kg based on body surface area adjustment for a 60 kg adult), 0.1 - 1 times the maximum recommended human 24 hour dose of ribavirin) in a mouse micronucleus assay. A dominant lethal assay in rats was negative, indicating that if mutations occurred in rats they were not transmitted through male gametes.

Pregnancy/Reproduction

Fertility—Although the effects of lower doses have not been studied, studies have shown that ribavirin causes testicular lesions (tubular atrophy) in adult rats given oral doses as low as 16 mg/kg daily. Ribavirin demonstrated significant embryocidal and teratogenic effects at doses well below the recommended human dose in all animal species in which adequate studies have been conducted. Fertile women and partners of fertile women should not receive ribavirin unless appropriate contraception methods are being used. Ribavirin should be used with caution in fertile men. In studies in mice to evaluate the time course and reversibility of ribavirin-induced testicular degeneration at doses of 15 to 150 mg/kg/day (estimated human equivalent of 1.25—12.5 mg/kg/day, based on body surface area adjustment for a 60 kg adult); 0.1–0.8 times the maximum human 24–hour dose of ribavirin) administered for 3 or 6 months, abnormalities in sperm occurred. Upon cessation of treatment, essentially total recovery from ribavirin-induced testicular toxicity was apparent within 1 or 2 spermatogenesis cycles.

Pregnancy—Ribavirin is contraindicated during pregnancy. Studies in humans have not been done. In some cases healthcare workers and visitors who spend time at the patient's bedside may become environmentally exposed to ribavirin. Female healthcare workers and visitors who are pregnant, or may become pregnant, should be advised of the potential risks of exposure. Extreme care must be taken to avoid pregnancy in female patients and female partners of male patients. Therapy should not be started until a report of a negative pregnancy test has been obtained immediately prior to planned initiation of therapy. The patient should be instructed to use at least two forms of effective contraception during treatment and for 6 months after discontinuation of treatment. Male patients and their female partners must practice effective contraception (two reliable forms) during treatment and for at least 6 months following treatment. If pregnancy occurs in a patient or a partner of a patient during treatment or during the 6 months after treatment cessation, physicians should report such cases by calling 1–800–593–2214,

Ribavirin crosses the placenta and studies in other animals have shown that it is teratogenic and/or embryocidal in all species tested at doses as low as one-twentieth the recommended human dose. Malformations of the skull, palate, eye, jaw, skeleton, and gastrointestinal tract have been observed in animal studies, and survival of fetuses and offspring was reduced. The incidence and severity of teratogenic effects increased with the escalation of the drug dose. Survival of fetuses and offspring was reduced. Studies in rabbits given daily oral doses as low as 1 mg/kg have shown that ribavirin is embryocidal.

FDA Pregnancy Category X.

Breast-feeding

It is not known whether ribavirin is excreted in human breast milk. However, ribavirin is excreted in the breast milk of animals and has been shown to be toxic to lactating animals and their offspring. Ribavirin aerosol is not indicated in the treatment of nursing mothers since respiratory syncytial virus (RSV) infection is self-limited in this population. Because of the potential for serious adverse reactions from the drug in nursing infants, a decision should be made whether to discontinue nursing or whether to delay or discontinue therapy with ribavirin.

Pediatrics

Ribavirin inhalation solution is indicated in the treatment of RSV infection only in children.

Tablet forms: Safety and effectiveness have not been established in pediatric patients.

Capsule forms: Safety and efficacy has not been established in those less than 5 years of age

Oral Solution: Safety and efficacy has not been established in those less than 3 years of age.

Suicidal ideation or attempts occurred more frequently, primarily in adolescents, as compared to adult patients during treatment and off- therapy follow-up. As in adult patients, pediatric patients experienced other psychiatric adverse events (e.g., depression, emotional lability, somnolence), anemia, and neutropenia. During a 48–week course of therapy there was a decrease in the rate of weight gain (mean percentile assignment decrease of 13%). A general reversal of these trends was noted during the 24 week post-treatment period.

Evidence of disease progression, such as hepatic inflammation and fibrosis, as well as prognostic factors for response, HCV genotype and viral load, should be considered when deciding to treat a pediatric patient. The benefits of treatment should be weighed against the safety findings observed for pediatric patients in clinical trials.

Geriatrics

Ribavirin inhalation solution is not indicated for use in geriatric patients.

Appropriate studies on the effects of ribavirin have not been performed in the geriatric population. Dose selection should be done with caution as ribavirin is known to be excreted by the kidney, and the risk of toxic reactions to this drug may be greater in patients with impaired renal function. Dose selection should start at the lower end of the dosing range, reflecting the greater frequency of decreased hepatic and/or cardiac function, and of concomitant disease or other drug therapy.

Drug interactions and/or related problems

The following drug interactions and/or related problems have been selected on the basis of their potential clinical significance (possible mechanism in parentheses where appropriate)—not necessarily inclusive (» = major clinical significance):

For further information pertaining to the combination of Ribavirin and Interferon Alfa 2–b see the Medication Advisory Screening section of *Ribavirin and Interferon Alfa 2–b (Systemic)*

Note: Combinations containing any of the following medications, depending on the amount present, may also interact with this medication.

» Didanosine
(coadministration with oral ribavirin is not recommended; cases of fatal hepatic failure, peripheral neuropathy, pancreatitis, and symptomatic hyperlactemia/lactic acidosis have been reported in clinical trials)

» Lamivudine or
» Stavudine or
» Zidovudine
(ribavirin may antagonize the *in vitro* antiviral activity of lamivudine, stavudine and zidovudine against HIV; concomitant use of ribavirin with any of these drugs should be avoided)

Laboratory value alterations

The following have been selected on the basis of their potential clinical significance (possible effect in parentheses where appropriate)—not necessarily inclusive (» = major clinical significance).

With diagnostic test results
Bilirubin and
Uric acid
(increases in both were noted in clinical trials; most were moderate and reversed within 4 weeks of discontinuation of treatment; occurs most frequently in patients with a previous diagnosis of Gilbert's syndrome; this has not been associated with hepatic dysfunction or clinical morbidity.)

» Hemoglobin
(hemoglobin decreases begin at week 1 with stabilization by week 4; values should return to pretreatment levels within 4 to 8 weeks of cessation of therapy)

Medical considerations/Contraindications

The medical considerations/contraindications included have been selected on the basis of their potential clinical significance (reasons given in parentheses where appropriate)—not necessarily inclusive (» = major clinical significance).

Except under special circumstances, this medication should not be used when the following medical problem exists:

Anemia, severe
(may cause anemia and result in worsening of cardiac disease that has led to fatal and non-fatal myocardial infarctions)

» Autoimmune hepatitis
(use of ribavirin and interferon alfa-2b therapy is contraindicated in these patients; using these medications can make the condition worse.)

» Cardiac disease, history of
(patients with a history of significant stable or unstable cardiac disease should not use ribavirin oral dosage forms; fatal and non-fatal myocardial infarctions have been reported and cardiac disease may be worsened by drug-induced anemia)

» Creatinine clearance, abnormal
(ribavirin should not be used in patients whose creatinine clearance is less than 50 mL/min)

» Hemoglobinopathies, such as
» Sickle-cell anemia or
» Thalassemia major
(Use is contraindicated in these patients)

» Hepatic decompensation (Child Pugh class B and C) in cirrhotic chronic hepatitis C monoinfected patients or in cirrhotic chronic hepatitis C patients coinfected with HIV
(use of ribavirin and peginterferon alfa 2–b therapy is contraindicated in these patients who have this condition before starting treatment or those who develop it during treatment)

Hypersensitivity to ribavirin or any of its components

Risk-benefit should be considered when the following medical problems exist:

» Cardiac disease, underlying
(patients should be assessed for underlying cardiac disease before initiation of therapy; if there is any deterioration of cardiac status therapy should be suspended or discontinued)

» Mental depression, history of
(should be used with caution in patients with a history of depression; significant adverse events can include severe depression and suicidal ideation; occurred more frequently in adolescent patients)

» Pancreatitis
(therapy should be suspended in patients with signs and symptoms of pancreatitis and discontinued for patients with confirmed pancreatitis)

Patient monitoring

The following may be especially important in patient monitoring (other tests may be warranted in some patients, depending on condition; » = major clinical significance):

Complete blood counts with differential white blood counts and
Platelet counts
(should be obtained before initiating treatment and periodically thereafter)

» Electrocardiograms
(patients with pre-existing cardiac disease should have electrocardiograms administered before treatment, and should be appropriately monitored during therapy)

» Hematocrit or
» Hemoglobin
(Inhalation and Parenteral dosage forms: hematocrit should be monitored periodically since intravenous and oral ribavirin may cause anemia)
(Capsule and Tablet dosage forms: values should be obtained pretreatment and at week 2 and week 4 of therapy, or more frequently if clinically indicated; patients should then be followed as clinically appropriated; anemia associated with ribavirin usually occurs within 1 to 2 weeks of initiation of therapy with the maximum effect on hemoglobin occurring during the first 8 weeks)

Liver function tests and
TSH
(should be done before initiating treatment and periodically thereafter)

» Pregnancy testing
(testing should occur monthly during therapy and for six months after therapy has stopped)

Pulmonary infiltrates or pulmonary symptoms including dyspnea, pulmonary infiltrates, pneumonitis and pneumonia; sarcoidosis and sarcoidosis exacerbations have been reported; closely monitor patient for signs and symptoms; if appropriate therapy may need to be discontinued
Pulmonary function impairment

Pulmonary pressure
(for aerosolized ribavirin for inhalation monitor pulmonary pressure every 2 to 4 hours)

Renal function
(renal function should be monitored in geriatric patients and dose adjustments should be done accordingly)

» Respiratory status and
Fluid status
(sudden deterioration of respiratory function has been associated with aerosolized ribavirin in infants; respiratory function should be carefully monitored; patients with severe lower respiratory tract infection due to respiratory syncytial virus (RSV) need optimum monitoring and attention to respiratory and fluid status)

Side/Adverse Effects

Note: The primary toxicity of ribavirin is hemolytic anemia. The anemia associated with ribavirin therapy may result in worsening of cardiac disease that has lead to fatal and non-fatal myocardial infarctions. Patients with a history of significant or unstable cardiac disease should not be treated with ribavirin.

The most common life-threatening or fatal events induced or aggravated by peginterferon alfa-2b and ribavirin were depression, suicide, relapse of drug abuse/overdose and bacterial infections including sepsis, osteomyelitis, endocarditis, pyelonephritis and pneumonia. The most commonly reported adverse reactions were psychiatric reactions including depression, irritability, anxiety, and flu-like symptoms such as fatigue, pyrexia, myalgia, headache and rigors.

For further information pertaining to the combination of Ribavirin and Interferon Alfa-2b see *Ribavirin and Interferon Alfa-2b (Systemic)*

The following side/adverse effects have been selected on the basis of their potential clinical significance (possible signs and symptoms in parentheses where appropriate)—not necessarily inclusive:

Those indicating need for medical attention

Incidence more frequent

Anemia (pale skin; troubled breathing with exertion; unusual bleeding or bruising; unusual tiredness or weakness); ***chest pain; dyspnea*** (shortness of breath; difficult or labored breathing; tightness in chest; wheezing); ***lymphopenia*** (fever or chills; cough or hoarseness; lower back or side pain; painful or difficult urination); ***neutropenia*** (black, tarry, stools; chills; cough; fever; lower back or side pain; painful or difficult urination; pale skin; shortness of breath; sore throat; ulcers, sores, or white spots in mouth; unusual bleeding or bruising; unusual tiredness or weakness); ***thrombocytopenia*** (black, tarry stools; bleeding gums; blood in urine or stools; pinpoint red spots on skin; unusual bleeding or bruising)

Those indicating need for medical attention only if they continue or are bothersome

Incidence more frequent—Oral dosage forms

Asthenia (lack or loss of strength); ***depression*** (discouragement; feeling sad or empty; irritability; lack of appetite; loss of interest or pleasure; tiredness; trouble concentrating; trouble sleeping); ***dizziness; dyspepsia*** (acid or sour stomach; belching; heartburn; indigestion; stomach discomfort, upset, or pain); ***irritability; pruritus*** (itching skin); ***rigors*** (feeling unusually cold; shivering)

Incidence less frequent—Oral dosage forms

CNS effects (fatigue; headache; insomnia)—usually with higher doses; ***emotional lability*** (crying; depersonalization; dysphoria; euphoria; mental depression; paranoia; quick to react or overreact emotionally; rapidly changing moods); ***fever; gastrointestinal effects*** (anorexia; nausea); ***myalgia*** (joint pain; swollen joints; muscle aching or cramping; muscle pains or stiffness; difficulty in moving); ***nervousness; rash; sinusitis*** (pain or tenderness around eyes and cheekbones; fever; stuffy or runny nose; headache; cough; shortness of breath or troubled breathing; tightness of chest or wheezing); ***taste perversion*** (change in taste); ***vomiting***

Incidence rare—inhalation only

In patients

Skin irritation due to prolonged drug contact; skin rash

In healthcare worker

Headache; itching, redness, or swelling of eye

Patient Consultation

As an aid to patient consultation, refer to *Advice for the Patient, Ribavirin (Systemic).*

In providing consultation, consider emphasizing the following selected information (» = major clinical significance):

Before using this medication

» Conditions affecting use, especially:
Hypersensitivity to ribavirin, interferon alfa-2a, or peginterferon alfa-2a or any of its components

Pregnancy—Ribavirin is contraindicated during pregnancy, can cause birth defects and/or death of the exposed fetus; female healthcare workers and visitors who are pregnant or may become pregnant may become environmentally exposed to ribavirin (inhalation form) and should be advised of the potential risks of exposure; effective contraception necessary during therapy and for 6 months after discontinuation of therapy; importance of avoiding pregnancy in female patients and female partners of male patients

FDA Pregnancy Category X

Breast-feeding—Decision must be made whether to discontinue nursing or discontinue treatment based on the potential for adverse reactions; not recommended for use in nursing women

Use in the elderly—Elderly patients are more likely to have age related problems that may be more severe; caution should be used

Other medications, especially didanosine, lamivudine, stavudine, or zidovudine

Other medical problems, especially anemia, autoimmune hepatitis, cardiac disease, hemoglobinopathies, hepatic decompensation (before or during treatment), history of mental depression, pancreatitis, renal impairment, sickle-cell anemia, thalassemia major

Proper use of this medication

» Reading accompanying patient information before using this medication

» For women of reproductive potential—Negative pregnancy test is needed before beginning treatment and monthly during treatment to ensure that the patient is not pregnant. Women of reproductive age are required to use two forms of contraception during treatment and continuing for 6 months after medication is discontinued

Take with food

» Importance of receiving medication for full course of therapy and on regular or continuous schedule

» Proper dosing

» Proper storage

Precautions while using this medication

» Caution while driving or operating machinery until you are familiar with this drug's effects

» Stopping medication immediately and checking with physician if pregnancy is suspected, since ribavirin can cause birth defects and/or possible fetal death

Side/adverse effects

Signs of potential side effects, especially anemia, chest pain, depression, dyspnea, infection, lymphopenia, neutropenia, suicidal ideation, or thrombocytopenia

General Dosing Information

Inhalation/Parenteral Dosage Forms

Use of ribavirin inhalation solution in infants requiring mechanical ventilation should be undertaken only by health care workers familiar with this mode of administration and the specific ventilator being used. The dose for infants requiring mechanical ventilation is the same as for those who do not. Precipitation of ribavirin within the ventilator apparatus, including endotracheal tubes, may cause obstruction, resulting in increased positive end expiratory pressure and increased positive inspiratory pressure. Accumulation of fluid in the tubing ("rain out") has also been observed. To try to avoid this, instructions must be followed carefully. Either a pressure or volume cycle ventilator may be used in conjunction with the SPAG-2. Patients should have their endotracheal tubes suctioned every 1 to 2 hours, and their pulmonary pressures monitored frequently (every 2 to 4 hours). For both pressure and volume ventilators, heated wire connective tubing and bacteria filters in series in the expiratory limb of the system must be used to minimize the risk of ribavirin precipitation in the system and the subsequent risk of ventilator dysfunction. Bacteria filters must be changed frequently, i.e., every 4 hours. Water column pressure release valves should be used in the ventilator circuit for pressure cycled ventilators, and may be utilized with volume cycled ventilators. Refer to the SPAG-2 manual for detailed instructions.

Sudden deterioration of respiratory function has been associated with initiation of aerosolized ribavirin use in infants, respiratory function should be carefully monitored during treatment. If initiation of aerosolized ribavirin treatment appears to produce sudden deterioration of respiratory function, treatment should be stopped and reinstituted only with extreme caution, continuous monitoring and consideration of concomitant administration of bronchodilators.

Ribavirin aerosolization, using a small particle aerosol generator, produces particles of 1.2 to 1.6 microns (mass mean diameter) in size. Ribavirin inhalation solution has been administered by this method at the rate of 12.5 liters per minute via an infant oxygen hood or mask, tent, or tubing of a respirator. Using a ribavirin concentration of 20 mg per mL, this method delivers approximately 1.8 mg per kg of body weight (mg/kg) per hour in infants and children up to 6 years of age.

Although ribavirin treatment may be initiated before the results of diagnostic tests are received, treatment should not be continued without laboratory confirmation of respiratory syncytial virus (RSV) infection.

Ribavirin inhalation solution treatment is generally effective when initiated within the first 3 days of RSV pneumonia. Early treatment may be necessary to achieve efficacy and to avoid further damage to the patient's lungs.

Healthcare workers who are pregnant should consider avoiding direct care of patients who are receiving aerosolized ribavirin. If close patient contact cannot be avoided, precautions to limit exposure should be taken. These include administration of ribavirin in negative pressure rooms; adequate room ventilation (at least six air exchanges per hour); the use of ribavirin aerosol scavenging devices; turning off the SPAG-2 device for 5 to 10 minutes prior to prolonged patient contact; and wearing appropriately filtered respirator masks. Surgical masks do not provide adequate filtration of ribavirin particles.

RSV infection should be documented by a rapid diagnostic method such as demonstration of viral antigen in respiratory tract secretions by immunofluorescence or ELISA before or during the first 24 hours of treatment. Treatment may be initiated while awaiting rapid diagnostic test results. Treatment should not be continued without documentation of RSV infection. Non-culture antigen detection techniques my have false positive or false negative results. Assessment of the clinical situation, the time of year, and other parameters may warrant reevaluation of the laboratory diagnosis.

Oral dosage forms

Treatment with ribavirin and peginterferon alfa-2a should be administered under the guidance of a qualified physician and may lead to moderate to severe adverse experiences requiring dose reduction, temporary dose cessation or discontinuation of therapy.

The entrance criteria used for clinical studies of ribavirin and peginterferon alfa-2b may be considered as a guideline for acceptable baseline values for initiation of treatment.

- Platelet Count ≥ 90,000 cells/mm^3
- Absolute neutrophil count (ANC) ≥ 1500 cells/mm^3
- TSH and T_4 within normal limits or adequately controlled thyroid function
- ECG

There are significant adverse events caused by ribavirin and interferon alfa-2b or by ribavirin and peginterferon alfa-2b therapy, including severe depression and suicidal ideation, hemolytic anemia, suppression of bone marrow function, autoimmune and infectious disorders, pulmonary dysfunction, pancreatitis, and diabetes. The package inserts for these medicines should be reviewed in their entirety prior to initiation of combination treatment for additional safety information.

Inhalation Dosage Forms

RIBAVIRIN FOR INHALATION SOLUTION USP

Usual adult and adolescent dose

Respiratory syncytial virus (RSV) infection, lower respiratory tract—
Dosage has not been established.

Usual pediatric dose

Respiratory syncytial virus (RSV) infection, lower respiratory tract—
Oral inhalation, via a Viratek Small Particle Aerosol Generator (SPAG) Model SPAG-2 utilizing a 20-mg-per-mL ribavirin concentration in the reservoir, over a twelve- to eighteen-hour period per day for at least three to a maximum of seven days. The average aerosol concentration over a 12–hour period would be 190 micrograms per liter of air.

Note: Various ribavirin dosage regimens have been utilized in RSV pneumonia and other infections, including virtually continuous aerosolization for three to six days and aerosolization over a four-hour period three times a day for three days.

Note: Administration by a face mask or oxygen tent may be necessary if a hood cannot be employed. The volume and condensation area are larger in a tent and this may alter the delivery dynamics of the drug.

Strength(s) usually available

U.S.—
6 grams (Rx) [*Virazole*].

Canada—
6 grams (Rx) [*Virazole*].

Packaging and storage

Prior to reconstitution, store between 15 and 25 °C (59 and 78 °F), in a dry place.

Reconstituted solutions may be stored under sterile conditions at room temperature 20 to 30°C (68 to 86°F) for 24 hours.

Preparation of dosage form

To prepare initial dilution for oral inhalation, using sterile technique, add a minimum of 75 mL of sterile USP water for injection or inhalation, (no preservatives, antimicrobial agents, or other substances added) in the original 100-milliliter vial. Shake well. Transfer the resulting solution to a clean, sterilized 500 mL SPAG-2 reservoir. Further dilute the solution to a final volume of 300 mL with sterile USP water for injection or inhalation to provide a final concentration of 20 mg per mL.

Prior to administration, visually inspect the final solution for particulate matter and discoloration.

When the solution level in the SPAG-2 reservoir is low, discard the remaining solution before adding freshly reconstituted solution to the reservoir.

Stability

The stability of ribavirin for inhalation solution (lyophilized powder) is unaffected by temperature, light, and moisture.

After reconstitution, solutions retain their potency at room temperature (20 to 30 °C [68 to 86 °F]) for 24 hours.

Solutions which have been placed in the SPAG-2 unit should be discarded at least every 24 hours.

Ribavirin solutions are colorless.

Incompatibilities

Ribavirin for inhalation solution should not be administered concurrently with other medications administered by aerosolization.

Oral Dosage Forms

RIBAVIRIN CAPSULES

Usual adult and adolescent dose

Chronic hepatitis C virus infection (treatment)—

Body Weight	Ribavirin Capsules
≤ 75 kg	2 x 200 mg capsules AM 3 x 200 mg capsules PM daily p.o.
> 75 kg	3 x 200 mg capsules AM 3 x 200 mg capsules PM daily p.o.

Ribavirin oral and Interferon alfa-2b injection combination therapy—

Oral, dose depends on body weight, may be administered without regard to food, but should be administered in a consistent manner with respect to food intake.

Duration of treatment for patients previously untreated with interferon is 24 to 48 weeks. The duration of treatment should be individualized to the patient depending on baseline disease characteristics, response to therapy, and tolerability of the regimen. After 24 weeks the virological response should be assessed and discontinuation considered for patients who have not achieved an HCV RNA below the limit of detection of the assay by 24 weeks. In patients who relapse following interferon therapy, the recommended duration of treatment is 24 weeks.

Dosing modifications:

If severe adverse reactions or laboratory abnormalities develop during combination ribavirin and interferon alfa–2b the dose should be modified, or discontinued if appropriate until the adverse reactions abate. If intolerance persists after dose adjustment therapy should be discontinued.

- Cardiovascular disease, stable: Permanent dose reduction to 600 mg per day is required if the hemoglobin decreases by ≥ 2 g/dL during any 4 week period. In addition, if the hemoglobin remains <12 g/dL after 4 weeks on a reduced dose therapy should be discontinued.
- Hematological: In patients with hemoglobin levels below 10 g/dL the ribavirin dose should be reduced to 600 mg/day (1 x 200–mg capsule AM, 2 x 200 mg capsules PM). A patient whose hemoglobin falls below 8.5 g/dL should be permanently discontinued from ribavirin therapy.

Ribavirin oral and peginterferon alfa-2b injection combination therapy—

Oral, 800 mg a day in two divided doses: two capsules (400 mg) in the morning with food and two capsules (400 mg) in the evening with food.

Usual pediatric dose

Children less than 5 years of age: Safety and efficacy have not been established in pediatric patients

Children 5 years of age and older:

Body Weight	Ribavirin Capsules	Interferon alfa–2b
25–36 kg	1 x 200 mg capsules AM 1 x 200 mg capsules PM daily p.o.	3 million IU per m² 3 times weekly s.c.
37–49 kg	1 x 200 mg capsules AM 2x 200 mg capsules PM daily p.o.	3 million IU per m² 3 times weekly s.c.
50–61 kg	2 x 200 mg capsules AM 2 x 200 mg capsules PM daily p.o.	3 million IU per m² 3 times weekly s.c.
> 61 kg	See Usual Adult Dose	See Usual Adult Dose

Usual geriatric dose

Caution should be exercised in the use of ribavirin and dosing should begin at the low end of the dosing range due to the possible greater severity of adverse reactions and systemic effects in this population.

Strength(s) usually available

U.S.—

200 mg [*Rebetol* (microcrystalline cellulose; lactose monohydrate; croscarmellose sodium; magnesium stearate)].

Canada—

Not commercially available.

Packaging and storage

Store at 25 °C (77°F), excursions permitted to 15 to 30°C (59 to 86°F).

RIBAVIRIN FOR ORAL SOLUTION

Note: Ribavirin for Inhalation Solution USP is the dosage form being used because an oral solution is not commercially available for this indication.

Usual adult and adolescent dose

[Lassa fever (prophylaxis)][1]—

Oral, 500 mg every six hours for seven to ten days.

Usual pediatric dose

Children 10 years of age and older—See *Usual adult and adolescent dose.*

Children 6 to 9 years of age—Oral, 400 mg every six hours for seven to ten days.

Children less than 6 years of age—Dosage has not been established.

Strength(s) usually available

U.S.—

Dosage form not commercially available. Compounding required for prescription.

Canada—

Dosage form not commercially available. Compounding required for prescription.

Packaging and storage

Prior to reconstitution, store between 15 and 25 °C (59 and 78 °F), in a dry place.

Preparation of dosage form

To prepare initial dilution for oral solution, add a measured quantity of sterile water for injection (without antimicrobial agents or other added substances) or sterile water for inhalation, sufficient for dissolution, to each 6-gram vial. Add dissolved solution to 0.9% sodium chloride or 5% dextrose in water.

Stability

The stability of ribavirin for inhalation solution (lyophilized powder) is unaffected by temperature, light, and moisture.

After reconstitution, solutions retain their potency at room temperature (20 to 30 °C [68 to 86 °F]) for 24 hours.

Ribavirin solutions are colorless.

RIBAVIRIN ORAL SOLUTION

Usual adult and adolescent dose

Note: Oral solution is not commonly used in adult patients

Usual pediatric dose

Chronic hepatitis C virus infection (treatment)—

Children less than 3 years of age: Safety and efficacy have not been established

Children 3 years of age and older: Oral, 15 mg/kg per day in divided doses (AM and PM), may be administered without regard to food but should be administered in a consistent manner with respect to food intake.

Genotype	Duration
Genotype 1	48 weeks
Genotype 2/ 3	24 weeks

Note: After 24 weeks of treatment the virologic response should be assessed. Discontinuation should be considered in any patient who has not achieved an HCV RNA below the limit of detection of the assay by this time.

Note: For children weighing ≥ 25 kg, either the oral solution or the 200–mg capsule can be administered. See recommended dosing table below

Body Weight (kg)	Ribavirin Capsules	Interferon alfa-2b Injection
25 to 36	1x 200 mg capsule AM 1 x 200 mg capsule PM daily p.o.	3 million IU/m² 3 times weekly s.c.
37 to 49	1 x 200 mg capsule AM 2 x 200 mg capsules PM daily p.o.	3 million IU/m² 3 times weekly s.c.
50 to 61	2 x 200 mg capsule AM 2 x 200 mg capsules PM daily p.o.	3 million IU/m² 3 times weekly s.c.
> 61 kg	Refer to adult dosing table	Refer to adult dosing table

Dosing modifications—

The peginterferon alfa-2a/ribavirin dose should be modified or discontinued if severe adverse reactions or laboratory abnormalities develop until the adverse reactions abate, if appropriate. If intolerance persists after dose adjustment, combination therapy should be discontinued. Ribavirin should be administered with caution to patients with pre-existing cardiac disease. Patients should be assessed before commencement of therapy and should be appropriately monitored during therapy. If there is any deterioration of cardiac status, therapy should be stopped.

Laboratory Values	Reduce Only Ribavirin dose to 7.5 mg/kg/day if:	Discontinue Ribavirin if:
Hemoglobin in patients with no cardiac disease	< 10 g/dL	<8.5 g/dL
Hemoglobin in patients with history of stable cardiac disease	≥ 2 g/dL decrease in hemoglobin during any 4 week period of treatment	< 12 g/dL despite 4 weeks at reduced dose

Dose Modification and Discontinuation for Anemia—

Usual geriatric dose

Oral solution is not commonly used in adult patients

Strength(s) usually available

U.S.—

40 mg/mL [*Rebetol* (sodium citrate; citric acid; sodium benzoate; glycerin; sucrose; sorbitol; propylene glycol; water)].

Canada—

Dosage form not commercially available.

Packaging and storage

Store between 2 and 8°C (36 and 46°F) or at 25°C (77°F); excursions permitted to 15 to 30°C (59 to 86°F).

RIBAVIRIN TABLETS

Usual adult and adolescent dose

Chronic hepatitis C virus monoinfection (treatment)—

Genotype	Peginterferon Alfa-2a Dose	Ribavirin Dose	Duration
Genotype 1, 4	180 mcg	<75 kg =1000 mg ≥75 kg =1200 mg	48 weeks 48 weeks
Genotype 2, 3	180 mcg	800 mg	24 weeks

Ribavirin oral and peginterferon alfa-2a combination injection therapy—

Oral, 800 mg to 1200 mg in two divided doses, taken with food. The dose should be individualized according to baseline disease characteristics, response to therapy, and tolerability of regimen. Duration of treatment for patients previously untreated with interferon is 24 to 48 weeks.

Once ribavirin has been withheld due to either a laboratory abnormality or clinical manifestation, and attempt may be made to restart ribavirin at 600 mg daily and further increase the dose to 800 mg daily depending on the physicians judgment. It is not recommended that ribavirin be increased to its original assigned dose (1000 to 1200 mg).

Note: Genotypes non-1 showed no increased response to treatment beyond 24 weeks.

Data on genotypes 5 and 6 are insufficient for dosing recommendations.

Chronic hepatitis C with HIV coinfection (treatment)—

Ribavirin oral and peginterferon alfa-2a combination injection therapy—

Oral, 800 mg ribavirin daily and 180 mcg peginterferon alfa-2a subcutaneously once weekly for a total of 48 weeks, regardless of phenotype.

Laboratory Values	Reduce Only Ribavirin dose to 600 mg/day if:	Discontinue Ribavirin if:
Hemoglobin in patients with no cardiac disease	< 10 g/dL	<8.5 g/dL
Hemoglobin in patients with history of stable cardiac disease	≥ 2 g/dL decrease in hemoglobin during any 4 week period of treatment	< 12 g/dL despite 4 weeks at reduced dose

Dosing modifications—

The peginterferon alfa-2a/ribavirin dose should be modified or discontinued if severe adverse reactions or laboratory abnormalities develop until the adverse reactions abate, if appropriate. If intolerance persists after dose adjustment, combination therapy should be discontinued. Ribavirin should be administered with caution to patients with pre-existing cardiac disease. Patients should be assessed before commencement of therapy and should be appropriately monitored during therapy. If there is any deterioration of cardiac status, therapy should be stopped.

Note: Ribavirin should not be used in patients with creatinine clearance less than 50 mL per minute.

Usual pediatric dose

Safety and efficacy have not been established in patients less than 18 years of age.

Usual geriatric dose

Caution should be exercised in the use of ribavirin and dosing should begin at the low end of the dosing range due to the possible greater severity of adverse reactions and systemic effects in this population. See *Usual adult and adolescent dose*.

Strength(s) usually available

U.S.—

200 mg [*Copegus* (pregelatinized starch; microcrystalline cellulose; sodium starch glycolate; corn starch; magnesium stearate)].

Canada—

Not commercially available

Packaging and storage

Store at 25°C (77°F); excursions permitted between 15 and 30°C (59 and 86°F). Keep bottle tightly closed.

Parenteral Dosage Forms

Note: Bracketed uses in the *Dosage Forms* section refer to categories of use and/or indications that are not included in U.S. product labeling.

RIBAVIRIN FOR INJECTION

Note: Ribavirin for Inhalation Solution USP is the dosage form being used because a parenteral solution is not commercially available.

Usual adult and adolescent dose

[Lassa fever (treatment)][1]—

Intravenous infusion, 30 mg per kg of body weight loading dose, then 16 mg per kg of body weight every six hours for four days, then 8 mg per kg of body weight every eight hours for six more days. Infuse over 15 to 20 minutes.

Usual pediatric dose

Dosage has not been established.

Strength(s) usually available

U.S.—

Dosage form not commercially available. Compounding required for prescription.

Canada—

Dosage form not commercially available. Compounding required for prescription.

Packaging and storage
Prior to reconstitution, store between 15 and 25 °C (59 and 78 °F), in a dry place.

Preparation of dosage form
To prepare initial dilution for parenteral use, add a measured quantity of sterile water for injection (without antimicrobial agents or other added substances) or sterile water for inhalation, sufficient for dissolution, to each 6-gram vial. Add to 0.9% sodium chloride or 5% dextrose in water and infuse over 15 to 20 minutes.

Stability
The stability of ribavirin for inhalation solution (lyophilized powder) is unaffected by temperature, light, and moisture.
After reconstitution, solutions retain their potency at room temperature (20 to 30 °C [68 to 86 °F]) for 24 hours.
Ribavirin solutions are colorless.

[1]Not included in Canadian product labeling.

Selected Bibliography

McCormick JB, et al. Lassa fever-effective therapy with ribavirin. New Engl J Med 1986; 314(1): 20-6.
Frankel LR, Wilson CW, Demers RR, et al. A technique for the administration of ribavirin to mechanically ventilated infants with severe respiratory syncytial virus infection. Crit Care Med 1987; 15: 1051-4.
Outwater KM, Meissner HC, Peterson MB. Ribavirin administration to infants receiving mechanical ventilation. Am J Dis Child 1988; 142: 512-5.
Demers RR, Parker J, Frankel LR, et al. Administration of ribavirin to neonatal and pediatric patients during mechanical ventilation. Respir Care 1986; 31: 1188-96.

Revised: 11/14/2005

RIBAVIRIN AND INTERFERON ALFA-2B, RECOMBINANT Systemic

VA CLASSIFICATION (Primary): AM810

Commonly used brand name(s): *Intron A; Rebetol; Rebetron (in combination with Intron A); Rebetron (in combination with Rebetol).*

NOTE: The *Ribavirin and Interferon, Alfa-2b (Systemic)* monograph is maintained on the *USP DI* electronic data base. A copy of the most recent revision of the complete monograph can be accessed on the *USP DI* Updates Online website. See the front cover of book for details on accessing the site.

For information on the specific components of this combination, see the *USP DI* monographs for *Ribavirin (Systemic),* and *Interferons, Alfa (Systemic).*

The information that follows is selectively abstracted from the complete monograph and is provided to facilitate drug use review and patient counseling.

Note: For a listing of dosage forms and brand names by country availability, see *Dosage Forms* sections(s).

Category
Antiviral.

Indications

Accepted
Hepatitis C, chronic, active (treatment)—Ribavirin and recombinant interferon alfa-2b combination is indicated for the treatment of chronic hepatitis C in patients with compensated liver disease previously untreated with alpha interferon or who have relapsed following alpha interferon therapy.

Patient Consultation
As an aid to patient consultation, refer to *Advice for the Patient, Ribavirin and Interferon Alfa-2b, Recombinant (Systemic).*

Consider advising the patient on the following (» = major clinical significance):

Before using this medication
» Conditions affecting use, especially:
Sensitivity to ribavirin or alpha interferons
Pregnancy—Ribavirin is contraindicated during pregnancy
Breast-feeding—Consider risk-benefit before initiating combination ribavirin and recombinant interferon alfa-2b or continuing to breast-feed while on combination therapy
Use in adolescents—Safety and efficacy have not been established in pediatric patients younger than 18 years of age
Other medical conditions especially, severe anemia, autoimmune hepatitis, cardiac disease, hemoglobinopathies, pancreatitis, and psychiatric illness

Proper use of this medication
» Using as directed by physician and reading patient package insert carefully with regard to:
—Preparation of the injection
—Use of disposable syringes
—Proper administration technique
—Stability of the injection
Administration at bedtime to minimize inconvenience of fatigue
Patients should be well hydrated, especially during the initial stages of treatment
» Proper dosing
Missed dose: Skipping missed dose and going back to regular schedule; not doubling doses; checking with physician.
» Proper storage

Precautions while using this medication
» Importance of close monitoring by physician.
» Counseling women of childbearing potential on the importance of using two reliable forms of effective contraception
» Caution in taking alcohol or other central nervous system depressants during therapy
» Caution when driving or doing anything else requiring alertness because of possible fatigue and dizziness
» Importance of contacting physician if depression or suicidal tendencies occur
» Frequency of fever, headache, and flu-like symptoms; possible need for analgesics/antipyretics before and after a dose is given

Caution if bone marrow depression occurs:
» Avoiding exposure to persons with bacterial infections, especially during periods of low blood counts; checking with physician immediately if fever or chills, cough or hoarseness, lower back or side pain, or painful or difficult urination occur
» Checking with physician immediately if unusual bleeding or bruising; black, tarry stools; blood in urine or stools; or pinpoint red spots on skin occur
Caution in use of regular toothbrush, dental floss, or toothpick; physician, dentist, or nurse may suggest alternatives; checking with physician before having dental work done
Not touching eyes or inside of nose unless hands washed immediately before
Using caution to avoid accidental cuts with use of sharp objects such as safety razor or fingernail or toenail cutters
Avoiding contact sports or other situations where bruising injury could occur

Follow Up
Emphasize the importance of follow-up with physician for the required laboratory tests

Side/adverse effects
» Signs of potential serious side adverse effects such as chest pain, depression, dyspnea, anemia, thyroid function abnormalities, and suicidal behavior and severe psychiatric adverse effects

Oral and Parenteral Dosage Forms

RIBAVIRIN and INTERFERON ALFA-2B, RECOMBINANT, CAPSULES and INJECTION

Usual adult dose
Hepatitis C, chronic (treatment)—
Table 1 shows recommended dosing for both oral ribavirin and subcutaneous interferon alfa-2b, recombinant. The recommended duration of treatment for patients previously untreated with interferon is twenty-four to forty-eight weeks. For patients who relapse following interferon therapy, the recommended duration is twenty-four weeks.

Table 1. Recommended dosing

Body weight*	Ribavirin capsules ORAL†	interferon alfa-2b, recombinant injection SUBCUTANEOUSLY††
≤ 75 kg	400 mg every morning 600 mg every evening	3 million IU 3 times a week
> 75 kg	600 mg every morning 600 mg every evening	3 million IU 3 times a week

*kg=kilograms †mg=milligrams ††IU=International Units.

Note: Ribavirin may be administered without regard to food.

Table 2 shows the guidelines for dose modifications for both ribavirin and interferon based on hematological (hemoglobin, white blood cell count, neutrophil count and platelet count) abnormalities.

Table 2. Guidelines for Dose Modifications

	Dose Reduction* Ribavirin 600 mg** daily interferon alfa-2b, recombinant 1.5 million IU*** three times weekly	Permanent Discontinuation of Treatment ribavirin and interferon alfa-2b, recombinant
Hemoglobin†	<10g/dL (ribavirin) Cardiac History patients only: ≥2g/dL decrease during any 4–week period during treatment (ribavirin and interferon alfa-2b), recombinant	<8.5g/dL Cardiac History patients only: <12g/dL after 4 weeks of dose reduction
White blood cell count††	$<1.5\times10^9$/L (interferon alfa-2b, recombinant)	$<1.0\times10^9$/L
Neutrophil count††	$<0.75\times10^9$/L (interferon alfa-2b, recombinant)	$<0.5\times10^9$/L
Platelet††	$<50\times10^9$/L (interferon alfa-2b, recombinant)	$<25\times10^9$/L

*Study medication to be dose reduced is shown in parenthesis.
**mg=milligrams
**IU=International Units
†g/dL=grams/deciliter
††L=liters

Usual pediatric dose

Safety and effectiveness in patients younger than 18 years of age have not been established.

Strength(s) usually available

U.S.—

Ribavirin:

200 milligrams (Rx) [*Rebetol* (Croscarmellose sodium; lactose monohydrate; magnesium stearate; microcrystalline cellulose); *Rebetron (in combination with Intron A)*].

Interferon alfa-2b, recombinant:

3 million International Units (IU) per 0.5 mL (Rx) [*Intron A* (Albumin (human) free; m-cresol; polysorbate 80); *Rebetron (in combination with Rebetol)*].

18 million IU multidose vial (22.8 million IU per 3.8 milliliters (mL [3 million IU per 0.5 mL]) (Rx) [*Intron A* (Albumin (human) free; m-cresol; polysorbate 80); *Rebetron (in combination with Rebetol)*].

18 million IU multidose pen (22.5 million IU per 1.5 mL [3 million IU per 0.2 mL]) (Rx) [*Intron A* (Albumin (human) free; m-cresol; polysorbate 80); *Rebetron (in combination with Rebetol)*].

Canada—

Ribavirin:

200 milligrams (Rx) [*Rebetol* (Croscarmellose sodium; lactose monohydrate; magnesium stearate; microcrystalline cellulose); *Rebetron (in combination with Intron A)*].

Interferon alfa-2b:

3 million International Units (IU) per 0.5 mL (Rx) [*Intron A* (Albumin (human) free; m-cresol; polysorbate 80); *Rebetron (in combination with Rebetol)*].

Revised: 05/16/2001
Developed: 10/1/1999

RICE SYRUP SOLIDS AND ELECTROLYTES—See *Carbohydrates and Electrolytes (Systemic)*

RIFABUTIN Systemic

VA CLASSIFICATION (Primary): AM900

Commonly used brand name(s): *Mycobutin*.

Note: For a listing of dosage forms and brand names by country availability, see *Dosage Forms* section(s).

Category

Antibacterial (antimycobacterial).

Indications

Note: Bracketed information in the *Indications* section refers to uses that are not included in U.S. product labeling.

Accepted

Mycobacterium avium complex (MAC) disease (prophylaxis)—Rifabutin is indicated for the prevention of disseminated MAC disease in patients with advanced human immunodeficiency virus (HIV) infection (CD4+ cell count ≤ 200/mm^3 with an acquired immunodeficiency syndrome [AIDS]–defining diagnosis, or CD4+ cell count ≤ 100/mm^3 without an AIDS–defining diagnosis).

[Tuberculosis (in HIV-infected patients on antiretroviral therapy) (treatment)][1]—Rifabutin is indicated for the treatment of HIV-infected patients with tuberculosis who are undergoing antiretroviral therapy (see *General Dosing Information*).

Unaccepted

Rifabutin must not be administered as single drug therapy for *Mycobacterium avium* complex (MAC) disease prophylaxis in patients with active tuberculosis, due to the possibility of the development of resistance.

There is no evidence that rifabutin is effective prophylaxis against *Mycobacterium tuberculosis*. Patients requiring prophylaxis against both *M. tuberculosis* and *M. avium* complex may be given isoniazid and rifabutin concurrently.

[1]Not included in Canadian product labeling.

Pharmacology/Pharmacokinetics

Physicochemical characteristics

Source—Rifabutin is a spiro-piperidyl-rifamycin derived from rifamycin-S. It is structurally related to and shares many of the properties of rifampin.

Molecular weight—847.02.

Mechanism of action/Effect

The antimicrobial activity of rifabutin is produced by inhibition of DNA-dependent RNA polymerase and subsequent initiation of transcription. This results in inhibition of protein synthesis. Rifabutin has a broad spectrum of antimicrobial activity. This includes activity against mycobacteria (atypical mycobacteria, including the *Mycobacterium avium* complex [MAC], *Mycobacterium leprae*, and *Mycobacterium tuberculosis*), a variety of gram-positive and gram-negative bacteria, *Chlamydia trachomatis*, and *Toxoplasma gondii*.

Absorption

Readily absorbed from the gastrointestinal tract. High-fat meals slow the rate, but not the extent, of absorption. In a multiple-dose study, the mean absolute bioavailability assessed in human immunodeficiency virus (HIV)-positive patients was 20% on day 1 and 12% on day 28.

Distribution

Highly lipophilic; widely distributed with extensive intracellular tissue uptake. Rifabutin crosses the blood-brain barrier; cerebrospinal fluid (CSF) concentrations are approximately 50% of the corresponding serum concentration.

Vol_D = 9.3 ± 1.5 liters per kg.

Protein binding

High 85%.

Biotransformation

Hepatic; 5 metabolites have been identified.

Half-life

Mean terminal—45 hours (range, 16 to 69 hours).

Time to peak concentration

2 to 4 hours.

Peak serum concentration
375 nanograms per mL after a single oral dose of 300 mg in healthy volunteers.

Elimination
30% fecal; 5% unchanged in the urine; 5% unchanged in the bile; 53% in urine as metabolites.
In dialysis—Hemodialysis is not expected to enhance elimination.

Precautions to Consider

Cross-sensitivity and/or related problems
Patients sensitive to other rifamycins (e.g., rifampin and rifapentine) may also be sensitive to rifabutin.

Carcinogenicity
Long-term carcinogenicity studies found that rifabutin was not carcinogenic in mice at doses of up to 180 mg per kg of body weight (mg/kg) per day, or approximately 36 times the recommended human daily dose. Rifabutin was not carcinogenic in rats at doses of up to 60 mg/kg per day, or 12 times the recommended human dose.

Mutagenicity
Rifabutin was not mutagenic in the Ames test using both rifabutin-susceptible and rifabutin-resistant strains or in *Schizosaccharomyces pombe P_1* and was not genotoxic in V-79 Chinese hamster cells, human lymphocytes *in vitro* , or mouse bone marrow cells *in vivo*.

Pregnancy/Reproduction
Fertility—Fertility was impaired in male rats given 160 mg/kg of rifabutin, or 32 times the recommended human daily dose.

Pregnancy—Adequate and well-controlled studies have not been done in humans.
No teratogenicity was seen in rats and rabbits given rifabutin at doses of up to 200 mg/kg (40 times the recommended human daily dose). There was a decrease in fetal viability in rats given 200 mg/kg per day. At 40 mg/kg per day, rifabutin caused an increase in fetal skeletal variants in rats. In rabbits, rifabutin was maternotoxic and there was an increase in fetal skeletal anomalies at 80 mg/kg per day.
FDA Pregnancy Category B.

Breast-feeding
It is not known whether rifabutin is distributed into human breast milk.

Pediatrics
The safety and efficacy of rifabutin in the prophylaxis of *Mycobacterium avium* complex (MAC) in children have not been established. Limited data are available about the use of rifabutin in children; it was used, along with 2 other antimycobacterials, to treat MAC in 22 HIV-positive children. The mean doses used were 18.5 mg/kg in infants 1 year of age, 8.6 mg/kg in children 2 to 10 years of age, and 4 mg/kg in adolescents 14 to 16 years of age. Side effects seen in children were similar to those seen in adults. Some pediatric patients receiving rifabutin as part of a multiple drug regimen have exhibited tiny, almost transparent, asymptomatic, peripheral and central corneal deposits which do not impair vision.

Geriatrics
Rifabutin administered as a single dose has been evaluated in 24 healthy, elderly (71 to 80 years of age) volunteers. The pharmacokinetic profile of rifabutin is not modified significantly by age, although the interindividual variability in this age group was higher slightly when compared with younger (25 to 37 years of age) volunteers.

Dental
The leukopenic and thrombocytopenic effects of rifabutin may result in an increased incidence of certain microbial infections, delayed healing, and gingival bleeding. If leukopenia or thrombocytopenia occurs, dental work should be deferred until blood counts have returned to normal. Patients should be instructed in proper oral hygiene, including caution in use of regular toothbrushes, dental floss, and toothpicks.

Drug interactions and/or related problems
The following drug interactions and/or related problems have been selected on the basis of their potential clinical significance (possible mechanism in parentheses where appropriate)—not necessarily inclusive (» = major clinical significance):

Note: Rifabutin has hepatic cytochrome P450–inducing properties. The structurally related rifampin is known to reduce the activity of many drugs due to its hepatic enzyme-inducing properties. Rifabutin appears to be a less potent enzyme inducer of the hepatic cytochrome P450 system than rifampin. However, because of the structural similarity of rifabutin and rifampin, rifabutin is expected to have some effects on these drugs as well.

Combinations containing any of the following medications, depending on the amount present, may also interact with this medication.

Aminophylline or
Oxtriphylline or
(rifabutin may increase the metabolism of aminophylline and oxtriphylline by induction of hepatic microsomal enzymes, resulting in increased clearance of these medications)

» Amprenavir or
» Indinavir or
» Nelfinavir or
» Ritonavir or
» Saquinavir
(rifabutin accelerates the metabolism of human immunodeficiency virus (HIV)-protease inhibitors, such as amprenavir, indinavir, nelfinavir, ritonavir, and saquinavir through induction of hepatic P450 cytochrome oxidases, resulting in subtherapeutic levels of protease inhibitors; in addition, protease inhibitors retard the metabolism of rifabutin, resulting in increased serum levels of rifabutin; dosage adjustments may be required when rifabutin is administered with an HIV-protease inhibitor; *See General Dosing Information*)

Antidiabetic agents, oral
(concurrent use with rifabutin may enhance the metabolism of sulfonylureas by induction of hepatic microsomal enzymes, resulting in lower serum sulfonylurea concentrations; dosage adjustments may be required)

Azole antifungals
(concurrent use with rifabutin may increase the metabolism of azole antifungals, lowering their plasma concentrations; depending on the clinical situation, the dose of an azole antifungal may need to be increased)

Barbiturates or
Beta-adrenergic blocking agents, systemic
(concurrent use with rifabutin may enhance the metabolism of these agents by induction of hepatic microsomal enzymes, resulting in lower serum concentrations; dosage adjustment may be required)

Chloramphenicol
(concurrent use with rifabutin may enhance the metabolism of chloramphenicol by induction of hepatic microsomal enzymes, resulting in significantly lower serum chloramphenicol concentrations; dosage adjustment may be required)

Clofibrate
(concurrent use with rifabutin may enhance the metabolism of clofibrate by induction of hepatic microsomal enzymes, resulting in significantly lower serum clofibrate concentrations; dosage adjustment may be required)

» Contraceptives, estrogen-containing oral
(concurrent use with rifabutin may decrease the effectiveness of estrogen-containing oral contraceptives because of stimulation of estrogen metabolism or reduction in enterohepatic circulation of estrogens, resulting in menstrual irregularities, intermenstrual bleeding, and unplanned pregnancies; patients should be advised to change to nonhormonal methods of birth control)

Corticosteroids, glucocorticoid and mineralocorticoid
(concurrent use with rifabutin may enhance the metabolism of corticosteroids by induction of hepatic microsomal enzymes, resulting in a considerable decrease in corticosteroid plasma concentrations; dosage adjustment may be required)

Cyclosporine
(rifabutin may enhance the metabolism of cyclosporine by induction of hepatic microsomal enzymes and intestinal cytochrome P450 enzymes; dosage adjustment may be required)

CYP3A enzyme substrates:
Clarithromycin or
Itraconazole or
Saquinavir
(rifabutin may reduce the plasma concentrations of these medicines; this effect may reduce the efficacy of these medications.)

(the area under the plasma concentration-time curve [AUC] of clarithromycin may decrease by 50%; the AUC of rifabutin may increase by 75%)

CYP3A enzyme inhibitors:
Clarithromycin or
Fluconazole
(drugs that inhibit CYP3A enzymes may significantly increase the plasma concentrations of rifabutin and may increase the risk of adverse reactions.)

Dapsone
(concurrent use with rifabutin may decrease the effect of dapsone because of increased metabolism resulting from stimulation of hepatic microsomal activity; dapsone concentrations may be decreased)

Diazepam
(concurrent use with rifabutin may enhance the metabolism of diazepam, resulting in decreased plasma concentrations; dosage adjustment may be required)

Digitalis glycosides
(concurrent use with rifabutin may enhance the metabolism of digoxin or digitoxin by induction of hepatic microsomal enzymes, resulting in significantly lower serum digoxin and digitoxin concentrations; dosage adjustments may be required)

» Delavirdine or
» Efavirenz or
» Nevirapine
(rifabutin accelerates the metabolism of nonnucleoside reverse transcriptase inhibitors (NNRTIs), such as delavirdine, efavirenz, and nevirapine through induction of hepatic P450 cytochrome oxidases, resulting in subtherapeutic levels of NNRTIs; in addition NNRTIs retard the metabolism of rifabutin, resulting in increased serum levels of rifabutin; a dosage adjustment may be required when rifabutin is administered with an NNRTI*See General Dosing Information*)
(given the expected drug interactions that would result in markedly decreased serum levels of delavirdine, and given the overlapping toxicities, the coadministration of rifabutin with delavirdine is contraindicated)

Fluconazole
(pharmacokinetic studies with fluconazole and rifabutin show that fluconazole appears to increase the serum concentration of rifabutin; however, this is not thought to have clinical significance and rifabutin dosing does not need to be modified in patients receiving fluconazole; in addition, the pharmacokinetics of fluconazole are unchanged)

Methadone
(concurrent administration with rifabutin has no significant effect on the pharmacokinetics of methadone; however, a few patients may require methadone dosage modification if symptoms of narcotic withdrawal occur)

Quinidine or
Verapamil, oral
(concurrent use with rifabutin may enhance the metabolism of these agents by induction of hepatic microsomal enzymes, resulting in lower serum concentrations; dosage adjustment may be required)

Sulfamethoxazole-trimethoprim
(the AUC of sulfamethoxazole and trimethoprim may be decreased by 15–20%)

Trimethoprim
(the AUC of trimethoprim may be decreased by 14%; the peak concentration of trimethoprim may decrease by 6%)

» Zidovudine
(steady-state plasma concentrations and the area under the plasma concentration-time curve [AUC] of zidovudine were decreased after repeated rifabutin dosing in healthy volunteers and HIV-positive patients in phase I trials; the mean decreases in peak plasma concentration and AUC were 48% and 32%, respectively. However, a population pharmacokinetic analysis of zidovudine concentration versus time data from two phase III studies showed a nonsignificant trend for rifabutin to increase the apparent clearance of zidovudine. *In vitro* studies have demonstrated that rifabutin does not affect the inhibition of HIV by zidovudine)

Laboratory value alterations

The following have been selected on the basis of their potential clinical significance (possible effect in parentheses where appropriate)—not necessarily inclusive (» = major clinical significance).

With diagnostic test results
Tuberculin, purified protein derivative (PPD)
(patients are likely to have a nonreactive PPD test despite active tuberculous disease)

Urinalyses based on spectrometry or color reaction
(rifabutin may interfere with urinalyses that are based on spectrometry or color reaction due to rifabutin's reddish-orange to reddish-brown discoloration of urine)

With physiology/laboratory test values
Alanine aminotransferase (ALT [SGPT]) and
Alkaline phosphatase and
Aspartate aminotransferase (AST [SGOT])
(values may be increased)

Medical considerations/Contraindications

The medical considerations/contraindications included have been selected on the basis of their potential clinical significance (reasons given in parentheses where appropriate)—not necessarily inclusive (» = major clinical significance).

Except under special circumstances, this medication should not be used when the following medical problem exists:
» Hypersensitivity to rifabutin, rifampin, or rifapentine

Risk-benefit should be considered when the following medical problems exist:
» Renal insufficiency, severe (creatinine clearance below 30 mL per min)
(may increase AUC by up to 71%; a reduced dose is recommended)

Renal insufficiency, mild to moderate (creatinine clearance between 30 and 61 mL per min)
(may increase AUC by up to 41%)

Patient monitoring

The following may be especially important in patient monitoring (other tests may be warranted in some patients, depending on condition; » = major clinical significance):

Platelet count

» Tuberculosis
(patients who develop complaints consistent with active tuberculosis while on prophylaxis with rifabutin should be evaluated immediately and a proper combination regimen for tuberculosis be initiated to prevent the development of resistance.)

White blood cell count
(recommended periodically since rifabutin may cause neutropenia and, rarely, thrombocytopenia)

Side/Adverse Effects

The following side/adverse effects have been selected on the basis of their potential clinical significance (possible signs and symptoms in parentheses where appropriate)—not necessarily inclusive:

Those indicating need for medical attention

Incidence more frequent
Allergic reaction (skin itching and/or rash); ***gastrointestinal intolerance*** (anorexia [loss of appetite]; diarrhea; dyspepsia [heartburn, indigestion and/or sour stomach]; nausea; vomiting); ***neutropenia*** (fever; sore throat)

Incidence less frequent
Asthenia (loss of strength or energy); ***myalgia*** (muscle pain)

Incidence rare
Arthralgia (joint pain); ***dysgeusia*** (change in taste); ***leukopenia or neutropenia*** (black, tarry, stools; chills; cough; fever; lower back or side pain; painful or difficult urination; pale skin; shortness of breath; sore throat; ulcers, sores, or white spots in mouth; unusual bleeding or bruising; unusual tiredness or weakness); ***myositis*** (muscle inflammation or pain; unusual tiredness or weakness); ***pseudojaundice*** (yellow skin); ***thrombocytopenia*** (bruising or purple spots on skin); ***uveitis*** (eye pain; loss of vision)

Note: *Uveitis* usually is associated with doses larger than 1050 mg per day.

Those indicating need for medical attention only if they continue or are bothersome

Incidence more frequent
Abdominal pain; chest pain; eructation (belching; bloated, full feeling; excess air or gas in stomach); ***fever; flatulence; rash; taste perversion***

Incidence less frequent
Headache; insomnia (trouble in sleeping)

Note: Some pediatric patients may exhibit tiny, almost transparent, asymptomatic, peripheral and central corneal deposits which do not impair vision.

Those not indicating need for medical attention
Incidence more frequent
Reddish–orange to reddish–brown discoloration of urine, feces, saliva, skin, sputum, sweat, and tears
Note: Tears discolored by rifabutin may also permanently discolor soft contact lenses.

Overdose

For specific information on the agent used in the management of rifabutin overdose, see:
• *Charcoal, Activated (Oral-Local)* monograph;

For more information on the management of overdose or unintentional ingestion, **contact a Poison Control Center** (see *Poison Control Center Listing*).

No information is available on accidental overdosage in humans. However, uveitis has been reported with doses larger than 1050 mg per day.

Clinical effects of overdose

The following effects have been selected on the basis of their potential clinical significance (possible signs and symptoms in parentheses where appropriate)—not necessarily inclusive:

Acute and chronic
Uveitis (eye pain; loss of vision)
Note: In clinical trials, *uveitis* was reversible when administration of rifabutin was discontinued and topical therapy with corticosteroids was initiated.

Treatment of overdose

Since there is no specific antidote, treatment of rifabutin should be symptomatic and supportive.

To decrease absorption—
While there is no experience in the treatment of overdose with rifabutin, clinical experience with other rifamycins suggests that gastric lavage to empty the stomach (within a few hours of overdose), followed by instillation of activated charcoal slurry into the stomach, may help absorb any remaining rifabutin from the gastrointestinal tract.

Note: Forced diuresis and hemodialysis are of no benefit in the treatment of rifabutin overdose.

Supportive care—
Supportive measures such as securing and maintaining a patent airway, administering oxygen, and instituting assisted or controlled respiration may be required. Patients in whom intentional overdose is confirmed or suspected should be referred for psychiatric consultation.

Patient Consultation

As an aid to patient consultation, refer to *Advice for the Patient, Rifabutin (Systemic)*.

In providing consultation, consider emphasizing the following selected information (» = major clinical significance):

Before using this medication

» Conditions affecting use, especially:
Hypersensitivity to rifabutin, rifampin, or rifapentine
Other medications, especially amprenavir, delavirdine, efavirenz, estrogen-containing contraceptives, indinavir, nelfinavir, nevirapine, ritonavir, saquinavir, or zidovudine
Other medical conditions such as severe renal insufficiency.

Proper use of this medication

Taking on an empty stomach, or with food if gastrointestinal irritation occurs
» Compliance with full course of therapy, which may take months
» Proper dosing, especially reduced dosing in severe renal insufficiency
Missed dose: Taking as soon as possible; not taking if almost time for next dose; not doubling doses
» Proper storage

Precautions while using this medication

» Regular visits to physician to check progress
Caution in use of regular toothbrush, dental floss, or toothpick; physician, dentist, or nurse may suggest alternatives; checking with physician before having dental work done
» Medication causes tears to turn reddish-orange to reddish-brown and may also permanently discolor soft contact lenses; avoiding the use of soft contact lenses during treatment
Monitoring patient for signs of active tuberculosis

Side/adverse effects

Signs of potential side effects, especially allergic reaction, gastrointestinal intolerance, leukopenia, neutropenia, asthenia, arthralgia, dysgeusia, myalgia, myositis, pseudojaundice, thrombocytopenia, and uveitis
Reddish-orange to reddish-brown discoloration of urine, stools, saliva, skin, sputum, sweat, and tears may be alarming to patient, although medically insignificant
Tears discolored by rifabutin may also permanently discolor soft contact lenses.

General Dosing Information

Rifabutin is absorbed more rapidly if taken on an empty stomach. However, if gastrointestinal irritation occurs, administering rifabutin at doses of 150 mg two times a day with food may help to reduce stomach upset.

Contents of rifabutin capsules may be mixed with applesauce for patients who are unable to swallow the capsules.

Human immunodeficiency virus (HIV) infection confers the greatest known risk for the development of tuberculosis, both for the reactivation of latent infection and for progressive primary disease. Moreover, once active tuberculosis develops in HIV-infected persons, mortality is high, despite good clinical and microbiological response to antituberculosis therapy.

Rifampin is an essential component of the currently recommended regimen for treating tuberculosis. Because of the common association of tuberculosis with HIV infection, an increasing number of patients probably will be considered candidates for combined therapy with rifampin and antiretroviral agents. The management of these patients is complex, requires an individualized approach, and should be undertaken only by or in consultation with an expert. In addition, all HIV-infected patients at risk for tuberculosis infection should be carefully evaluated and administered isoniazid preventive treatment if indicated, regardless of whether they are receiving protease inhibitor therapy.

Antiretroviral agents such as protease inhibitors and nonnucleoside reverse transcriptase inhibitors (NNRTIs) have substantive interactions with the rifamycins (rifampin, rifabutin, and rifapentine) used to treat mycobacterial infections commonly observed in HIV-infected patients. Rifamycins accelerate the metabolism of these agents through induction of hepatic cytochrome P450 oxidases, resulting in subtherapeutic levels of these antiretroviral agents. In addition, protease inhibitors and NNRTIs retard the metabolism of rifamycins, resulting in increased serum levels of rifamycins and the likelihood of increased drug toxicity. Rifabutin is a less potent P450 inducer than rifampin and thus can be used with dosage adjustments concurrently with certain NNRTIs or with certain protease inhibitors.

Nucleoside reverse transcriptase inhibitors (NRTIs) (e.g., zidovudine, didanosine, zalcitabine, stavudine, lamivudine, abacavir) are not metabolized by cytochrome P450 isoenzymes. Concurrent use of NRTIs and rifamycins is not contraindicated and does not require dose adjustments.

The Centers for Disease Control and Prevention (CDC) provides the following recommendations for the treatment of tuberculosis in HIV-infected patients who also are receiving antiretroviral treatment with either HIV-protease inhibitors or NNRTIs:
• The initial phase of a 6-month tuberculosis regimen consists of isoniazid, rifabutin, pyrazinamide, and ethambutol.
• Isoniazid, rifabutin, pyrazinamide, and ethambutol should be administered daily for 8 weeks, or
• Isoniazid, rifabutin, pyrazinamide, and ethambutol should be administered daily for at least the first 2 weeks, followed by twice-a-week dosing for 6 weeks, to complete the 2-month induction phase.
• The second phase of treatment consists of isoniazid and rifabutin administered daily or twice a week for 4 months.
• The minimum duration of short-course rifabutin-containing tuberculosis treatment regimens is 6 months. To complete these regimens, doses should be administered as follows:
—At least 180 doses, i.e., one dose per day for 6 months; or
—14 induction doses, i.e., one dose per day for 2 weeks followed by 12 induction doses, i.e., two doses per week for 6 weeks plus 36 continuation doses, i.e., two doses per week for 18 weeks.
• The final decision on the duration of therapy should consider the patient's response to treatment. For patients with delayed response to treatment, the duration of rifabutin-based regimens should be prolonged from 6 months to 9 months or to 4 months after culture conversion is documented.
• Recommendations for coadministering different antiretroviral drugs with the antimycobacterial drug rifabutin-United States, 2000:

Antiretroviral	Use in combination with rifabutin	Comments
Saquinavir* Hard- or soft-gel capsules	Hard-gel capsules: Possibly[1], if antiretroviral regimen also includes ritonavir Soft-gel capsules: Probably[2]	Coadministration of saquinavir soft-gel capsules with usual-dose rifabutin (300 mg daily or two or three times per week) is a possibility (patients receiving saquinavir soft-gel capsules and two NRTIs, the usual dose of rifabutin should not be decreased). The combination of saquinair soft- or hard-gel capsules and ritonavir, coadministered with reduced dose rifabutin (150 mg two or three times per week) is a possibility. Pharmacokinetic data and clinical experience for these combinations are limited.
Ritonavir	Probably	If the combination of ritonavir and rifabutin is used (with or without saquinavir), then a substantially reduced-dose rifabutin regimen (150 mg two or three times per week) is recommended.
Indinavir	Yes	There is limited, but favorable, clinical experience with coadministration of indinavir with a reduced daily dose of rifabutin (150 mg) or with the usual dose of rifabutin (300 mg two or three times per week). (Usual recommended dose of indinavir is 800 mg every 8 hours. Some experts recommend increasing the indinavir dose to 1000 mg every 8 hours if used in combination with rifabutin)
Nelfinavir	Yes	There is limited, but favorable, clinical experience with coadministration of nelfinavir with a reduced daily dose of rifabutin (150 mg) or with the usual dose of rifabutin (300 mg two or three times per week). (Usual recommended dose of nelfinavir is 750 mg three times per day or 1250 mg twice daily. Some experts recommend increasing the nelfinavir dose to 1000 mg if the three-times-per-day dosing is used and nelfinavir is used in combination with rifabutin).
Amprenavir	Yes	Coadministration of amprenavir with a reduced daily dose of rifabutin (150 mg) or with the usual dose of rifabutin (300 mg two or three times per week) is a possibility, but there is no published clinical experience.
Nevirapine	Yes	Coadministration of nevirapine with usual-dose rifabutin (300 mg daily or two or three times per week) is a possibility based on pharmacokinetic study data. However, there is no published clinical experience for this combination.
Delavirdine	No	Coadministration is contraindicated because rifabutin markedly decreases concentrations of delavirdine.
Efavirenz	Probably	Coadministration of efavirenz with increased-dose rifabutin (450 mg or 600 mg daily, or 600 mg two or three times per week) is a possibility, though there is no published clinical experience.

*Usual recommended doses are 400 mg two times per day for each of these protease inhibitors and 400 mg of ritonavir.

[1]Despite limited data and clinical experience, the use of this combination is potentially successful.

[2]Based on available data and clinical experience, the successful use of this combination is likely.

- For patients undergoing therapy with complex combinations of protease inhibitors or NNRTIs, the use of antituberculosis regimens containing no rifamycins can be considered.
- Isoniazid does not interact with either the protease inhibitors or NNRTIs, and the use of a 9–month regimen of isoniazid is recommended as the preferred option for treatment for latent Mycobacterium tuberculosis infection (LTBI). However, 2–month regimens of a rifamycin and pyrazinamide also are recommended for LTBI therapy. If these regimen options are chosen for HIV-infected patients with LTBI, the drug-drug interactions and dose adjustment for antiretroviral drugs and rifamycins apply.

Oral Dosage Forms

RIFABUTIN CAPSULES

Usual adult and adolescent dose

Mycobacterium avium complex (MAC) disease (prophylaxis)—

Oral, 300 mg once a day, or 150 mg two times a day.

[Tuberculosis (in HIV-infected patients on antiretroviral therapy), (treatment)][1]—

See General Dosing Information.

Note: The recommended daily dose of rifabutin is 300 mg administered with or without food. However, for those patients who experience nausea, vomiting, or other gastrointestinal upsets, it may be useful to split the rifabutin dose in half, i.e., one 150 mg capsule twice a day administered with food.

Note: Patients with severe renal impairment (creatinine clearance less than 30 mL per min) should have their dose reduced by 50%.

Usual pediatric dose

Dosage has not been established; however, MAC prophylaxis should follow recommendations similar to those for adults and adolescents. Limited data are available about the use of rifabutin in children; it has been used in the treatment of MAC in HIV-positive children. The mean doses used were 18.5 mg per kg of body weight in infants 1 year of age, 8.6 mg per kg of body weight in children 2 to 10 years of age, and 4 mg per kg of body weight in adolescents 14 to 16 years of age. Side effects seen in children were similar to those seen in adults.

Strength(s) usually available

U.S.—

150 mg (Rx) [*Mycobutin*].

Canada—

150 mg (Rx) [*Mycobutin*].

Packaging and storage

Store between 15 and 30 °C (59 and 86 °F). Store in a tightly closed container.

Auxiliary labeling

- Continue medicine for full time of treatment.
- May discolor body fluids.

[1]Not included in Canadian product labeling.

Revised: 11/22/2002

RIFAMPIN Systemic

INN: Rifampicin

VA CLASSIFICATION (Primary/Secondary): AM500/AM900

Commonly used brand name(s): *Rifadin; Rifadin IV; Rimactane; Rofact.*

Note: For a listing of dosage forms and brand names by country availability, see *Dosage Forms* section(s).

Category

Antibacterial (antimycobacterial; antileprosy agent).

Indications

Note: Bracketed information in the *Indications* section refers to uses that are not included in U.S. product labeling.

General Considerations

Tuberculosis is a highly infectious life-threatening bacterial disease with 8 million new cases and 3 million deaths reported worldwide each year to the World Health Organization (WHO). The vast majority of these cases are in developing countries; however, tuberculosis also has emerged as an important public health problem in the U.S. in recent years after the decline in number of cases observed between 1950 and 1980.

The resurgence of tuberculosis in the U.S. has been complicated by an increase in the proportion of patients with strains resistant to antituberculosis medications. Outbreaks of multidrug-resistant tuberculosis have been documented in hospitals and prisons. Drug-resistant tuberculosis, particularly that caused by strains resistant to isoniazid and rifampin, is much harder to treat and often is fatal. Among acquired immunodeficiency syndrome (AIDS) patients infected with tuberculosis bacilli resistant to both rifampin and isoniazid, a case-fatality rate of 91% has been reported. Recent investigations of outbreaks of multidrug-resistant tuberculosis have found an extraordinarily high case-fatality rate, with the median time to mortality being reached between 4 and 16 weeks. In almost all instances, these outbreaks have involved patients with severe immunosuppression by infection with the human immunodeficiency virus (HIV).

Acquired drug resistance develops during treatment for drug-sensitive tuberculosis with regimens that are poorly conceived or poorly complied with, allowing the emergence of naturally occurring drug-resistant mutations. Resistant organisms from affected patients may subsequently infect other people who have not been infected with *M. tuberculosis* previously, resulting in primary drug resistance.

Resistance to antituberculosis agents can develop not only in the strain that caused the initial disease, but also as a result of reinfection with a new strain of *M. tuberculosis* that is drug-resistant. Reinfection with a new multidrug-resistant *M. tuberculosis* strain can occur during therapy for the original infection or after completion of therapy. Most recent data suggest that outcomes can be improved if patients promptly begin therapy with two or more drugs that have *in vitro* activity against the multidrug-resistant isolate.

HIV infection is the strongest risk factor yet identified for the development of active tuberculosis disease in persons infected with tuberculosis. In addition, persons with HIV infection are at an increased risk of tuberculosis resulting either from newly acquired disease or from reactivation of latent infections. Tuberculosis is a major clinical manifestation of immunodeficiency induced by HIV. In hospital-based retrospective studies, high rates of tuberculosis have been found among patients with AIDS. In communities where tuberculosis and HIV infection are common, the prevalence of HIV seropositivity among patients with tuberculosis is greatly increasing.

WHO has estimated that 5.6 million people worldwide and 80,000 people in the U.S. are infected with both HIV and tuberculosis. Persons dually infected with *M. tuberculosis* and HIV have a high risk of developing clinically active tuberculosis. One study of HIV-positive drug users with positive tuberculin skin test results found a rate of the development of active tuberculosis to be 8 cases per 100 person-years (8% yearly) as compared with the 10% lifetime risk (1 to 3% risk within the first year after skin test conversion) in the general population.

Persons who are known to be HIV-infected and who are contacts of patients with infectious tuberculosis should be carefully evaluated for evidence of tuberculosis. If there are no findings suggestive of current tuberculosis, preventive therapy with isoniazid should be given. Because HIV-infected contacts are not managed in the same way as those who are not HIV-infected, HIV testing is recommended if there are known or suspected risk factors for their acquiring HIV infection.

According to investigators at the National Institute of Allergy and Infectious Diseases (NIAID), levels of HIV in the bloodstream increase 5- to 160-fold in HIV-infected persons who develop active tuberculosis. Clinical and epidemiologic observations have demonstrated that HIV-infected individuals have an estimated 113-times higher risk and AIDS patients have a 170-times higher risk compared with uninfected persons. Furthermore, the problem of drug resistance may worsen as the HIV epidemic spreads. Immunosuppressed patients with HIV infection who subsequently become infected with *M. tuberculosis* have an extraordinarily high risk of developing active tuberculosis within a short period of time.

In addition to the convincing evidence that HIV infection increases the risk and worsens the course of tuberculosis, there is increasing clinical evidence that coinfection with *M. tuberculosis* accelerates progression of disease caused by HIV infection. Understanding the interaction of these two pathogens is clinically important, given the high prevalence of patients coinfected with HIV and *M. tuberculosis* in both the U.S. and Africa; it is estimated that by the year 2000 about 500,000 deaths per year will occur in coinfected patients worldwide.

Persons with a positive tuberculin skin test and HIV infection, and persons with a positive tuberculin skin test and at risk of acquiring HIV infection with unknown HIV status should be considered for tuberculosis preventive therapy regardless of age. One study showed that isoniazid prophylaxis in HIV-infected, tuberculin-positive individuals not only decreased the incidence of tuberculosis disease, but also delayed the progression to AIDS and death.

Twelve months of preventive therapy is recommended for adults and children with HIV infection and other conditions associated with immunosuppression. Persons with HIV infection should receive at least 6 months of preventive therapy. The American Academy of Pediatrics recommends that children receive 9 months of therapy.

Tuberculosis control programs should ensure that drug susceptibility tests are performed on all initial isolates of *M. tuberculosis* and the results are reported promptly to the primary care provider and the local health department. Tuberculosis control programs should monitor local drug resistance rates to assess the effectiveness of local tuberculosis control efforts and to determine the appropriateness of the currently recommended initial tuberculosis treatment regimen for the area.

Relapse of rifampin-resistant tuberculosis has been reported in HIV-infected patients. Reinfection with new strains of *M. tuberculosis* has also been reported in these patients. Rifampin-resistant tuberculosis is a serious threat because responses to therapy are more difficult to achieve and require long courses of treatment. Therefore, careful follow-up of HIV-infected patients with treated tuberculosis is essential.

Multidrug-resistant tuberculosis also has been transmitted to persons without HIV infection in health care facilities. Together with the lack of effective agents for second-line treatment and methods of prophylaxis, the transmission of multidrug-resistant strains of *M. tuberculosis* may create a substantial reservoir of latently infected people and the potential for clinical multidrug-resistant tuberculosis for many years to come.

Several studies have documented a high prevalence of extrapulmonary disease in HIV-infected patients with clinical tuberculosis disease, particularly in conjunction with pulmonary manifestations. Cutaneous miliary tuberculosis, also known as *tuberculosis cutis miliaris disseminata*, was in the past a rare condition in adults, with only 24 cases reported in nearly a century. However, since the first reported case of cutaneous miliary tuberculosis in 1990 in a patient with AIDS, five additional cases have been reported in HIV-infected patients. Its appearance can be quite nondescript; therefore, a high level of suspicion must be maintained, particularly for patients with CD4+ cell counts of < 200 per cubic millimeter, in order to diagnose the condition and initiate therapy appropriately.

Accepted

Tuberculosis (treatment)—Rifampin is indicated in combination with other antituberculosis medications in the treatment of all forms of tuberculosis, including tuberculous meningitis.

Meningococcal infections (prophylaxis)—Rifampin is indicated in the treatment of close contacts of patients with proved or suspected infection caused by *Neisseria meningitidis.* These contacts include other household members, children in nurseries, persons in day care centers, and closed populations, such as military recruits. Health care providers who have intimate exposure (e.g., mouth-to-mouth resuscitation) with index cases also should receive prophylactic therapy.

[*Haemophilus influenzae* type b infection (prophylaxis)][1]—Rifampin is used in the treatment of close contacts of patients with proved or suspected infections caused by *H. influenzae* type b if at least one of the contacts is 4 years of age or younger. A close contact is defined as one who has spent 4 or more hours per day for 5 of the 7 most recent days with the index case.

[Leprosy (treatment)][1]—Rifampin is used in combination with other agents in the treatment of leprosy (Hansen's disease).

[Mycobacterial infections, atypical (treatment)][1]—Rifampin is used in combination with other agents in the treatment of certain atypical (nontuberculous) mycobacterial infections, such as those caused by *Mycobacterium avium* complex (MAC).

[Rifampin, administered concurrently with other antistaphylococcal agents, also may be used in the treatment of serious infections caused by *Staphylococcus* species (including methicillin-resistant and multidrug-resistant strains)][1].

Unaccepted

Rifampin is not indicated as a sole agent in the treatment of meningococcal infections because of the possibility of the rapid emergence of resistant organisms.

Rifampin plus pyrazinamide generally should not be offered for treatment of latent tuberculosis infection [LTBI] for HIV-infected or HIV-negative persons, because of reports of an increased rate of hepatotoxicity with the rifampin-pyrazinamide regimen.

---

[1]Not included in Canadian product labeling.

Pharmacology/Pharmacokinetics

Note: Preliminary data suggest that patients coinfected with human immunodeficiency virus (HIV) and mycobacteria (*Mycobacterium tuberculosis* or *M. avium*) have altered pharmacokinetic profiles for antimycobacterial drugs. In particular, malabsorption of these agents appears to occur frequently, and could seriously affect the efficacy of treatment.

Physicochemical characteristics

Molecular weight—822.96.

Mechanism of action/Effect

Rifampin, a semisynthetic broad-spectrum bactericidal antibiotic, inhibits bacterial RNA synthesis by binding strongly to the beta subunit of DNA-dependent RNA polymerase, preventing attachment of the enzyme to DNA, and thus blocking initiation of RNA transcription.

Absorption

Well absorbed from the gastrointestinal tract.

Distribution

Diffuses well to most body tissues and fluids, including the cerebrospinal fluid (CSF), where concentrations are increased if the meninges are inflamed; concentrations in the liver, gallbladder, bile, and urine are higher than those found in the blood; therapeutic concentrations are achieved in the saliva, reaching 20% of serum concentrations; crosses the placenta, with fetal serum concentrations at birth found to be approximately 33% of the maternal serum concentration; penetrates into aqueous humor; and is distributed into breast milk. Being lipid-soluble, rifampin may reach and kill susceptible intracellular, as well as extracellular, bacteria including *Mycobacteria* species.

Vol_D—1.6 L per kg.

Protein binding

High to very high (89%).

Biotransformation

Hepatic; rapidly deacetylated by auto-induced microsomal oxidative enzymes to active metabolite (25-*O*-desacetylrifampin). Other identified metabolites include rifampin quinone, desacetyl rifampin quinone, and 3-formylrifampin.

Half-life

Absorption half-life—
Approximately 0.6 hour.

Elimination half-life—
Initially, 3 to 5 hours; with repeated administration, half-life decreases to 2 to 3 hours.

Time to peak concentration

1.5 to 4 hours after oral administration; peak concentration may be decreased and delayed following administration with food.

Peak plasma concentration

Oral—
Adults: 7 to 9 mcg/mL after a dose of 600 mg.
Children (6 to 58 months old): Approximately 11 mcg/mL after a dose of 10 mg per kg of body weight (mg/kg) mixed in applesauce or simple syrup.

Intravenous—
Adults: Approximately 17.5 mcg/mL after a 30 minute infusion of 600 mg.
Children (3 months to 12 years old): Approximately 26 mcg/mL after a 30 minute infusion of 300 mg per square meter.

Elimination

Biliary/fecal; enterohepatic recirculation of rifampin, but not of its deacetylated active metabolite; 60 to 65% of dose appears in feces.

Renal; 6 to 15% excreted as unchanged drug, and 15% excreted as active metabolite in urine; 7% excreted as inactive 3-formyl derivative.

Rifampin does not accumulate in patients with impaired renal function; its rate of excretion is increased during the first 6 to 10 days of therapy, probably because of auto-induction of hepatic microsomal oxidative enzymes; after high doses, excretion may be slower because of saturation of its biliary excretory mechanism.

In dialysis—
Rifampin is not removed from the blood by either hemodialysis or peritoneal dialysis.

Precautions to Consider

Tumorigenicity

Studies in female mice of a strain known to be particularly susceptible to the spontaneous development of hepatomas have shown that rifampin, given in doses of 2 to 10 times the maximum human dose for 1 year, causes a significant increase in the development of hepatomas. However, studies in male mice of the same strain, in other strains of male or female mice, or in rats have not shown that rifampin is tumorigenic.

Pregnancy/Reproduction

Note: Tuberculosis in pregnancy should be managed in concert with an expert in the management of tuberculosis. Women who have only pulmonary tuberculosis are not likely to infect the fetus until after delivery, and congenital tuberculosis is extremely rare. *In utero* infections with tubercle bacilli, however, can occur after maternal bacillemia occurs at different stages in the course of tuberculosis. Miliary tuberculosis can seed the placenta and thereby gain access to the fetal circulation. In women with tuberculous endometritis, transmission of infection to the fetus can result from fetal aspiration of bacilli at the time of delivery. A third mode of transmission is through ingestion of infected amniotic fluid *in utero*.

If active disease is diagnosed during pregnancy, a 9-month regimen of isoniazid and rifampin, supplemented by an initial course of ethambutol if drug resistance is suspected, is recommended. Pyrazinamide usually is not given because of inadequate data regarding teratogenesis. Hence, a 9-month course of therapy is necessary for drug-susceptible disease. When isoniazid resistance is a possibility, isoniazid, ethambutol, and rifampin are recommended initially. One of these medications can be discontinued after 1 or 2 months, depending on results of susceptibility tests. If rifampin or isoniazid is discontinued, treatment is continued for a total of 18 months; if ethambutol is discontinued, treatment is continued for a total of 9 months. Prompt initiation of chemotherapy is mandatory to protect both the mother and fetus. If isoniazid or rifampin resistance is documented, an expert in the management of tuberculosis should be consulted.

Asymptomatic pregnant women with positive tuberculin skin tests and normal chest radiographs should receive preventive therapy with isoniazid for 9 months if they are HIV seropositive or have recently been in contact with an infectious person. For these individuals, preventive therapy should begin after the first trimester. In other circumstances in which none of these risk factors is present, although no harmful effects of isoniazid to the fetus have been observed, preventive therapy can be delayed until after delivery.

For all pregnant women receiving isoniazid, pyridoxine should be prescribed. Isoniazid, ethambutol, and rifampin appear to be relatively safe for the fetus. The benefit of ethambutol and rifampin for therapy of active disease in the mother outweighs the risk to the infant. Streptomycin and pyrazinamide should not be used unless they are essential to the control of the disease.

Pregnancy—Rifampin crosses the placenta. It has rarely caused postnatal hemorrhages in the mother and infant when administered during the last few weeks of pregnancy; vitamin K may be indicated. Neonates should be carefully observed for evidence of adverse effects.

Imperfect osteogenesis and embryotoxicity were reported in rabbits given up to 20 times the usual daily human dose. Studies in rodents have shown that rifampin given in doses of 150 to 250 mg per kg of body weight (mg/kg) daily causes congenital malformations, primarily cleft palate and spina bifida.

FDA Pregnancy Category C.

Breast-feeding

Rifampin is distributed into breast milk. Problems in humans have not been documented.

Pediatrics

Note: If an infant is suspected of having congenital tuberculosis, a Mantoux tuberculin skin test, chest radiograph, lumbar puncture, and appropriate cultures should be performed promptly. Regardless of the skin test results, treatment of the infant should be initiated promptly with isoniazid, rifampin, pyrazinamide, and streptomycin or kanamycin. In addition, the mother should be evaluated for the presence of pulmonary or extrapulmonary (including uterine) tuberculosis. If the physical examination or chest radiograph support the diagnosis of tuberculosis, the patient should be treated with the same regimen as that used for tuberculous meningitis. The drug susceptibilities of the organism recovered from the mother and/or infant should be determined.

Possible isoniazid resistance should always be considered, particularly in children from population groups in which drug resistance is high, especially in foreign-born children from countries with a high prevalence of drug-resistant tuberculosis. For contacts who are likely to have been infected by an index case with isoniazid-resistant but rifampin-susceptible organisms, and in whom the consequences of the infection are likely to be severe (e.g., children up to 4 years of age), rifampin (10 mg per kg of body weight, maximum 600 mg, given daily in a single dose) should be given in addition to isoniazid (10 mg per kg, maximum 300 mg, given daily in a single dose) until susceptibility test results for the isolate from the index case are available. If the index case is known or proven to be excreting organisms resistant to isoniazid, then isoniazid should be discontinued and rifampin given for a total of 9 months. Isoniazid alone should be given if no proof of exposure to isoniazid-resistant organisms is found. Optimal therapy for children with tuberculosis infection caused by organisms resistant to isoniazid and rifampin is unknown. In deciding on therapy in this situation, consultation with an expert is advised.

Adjuvant treatment with corticosteroids in treating tuberculosis is controversial. Corticosteroids have been used for therapy in children with tuberculous meningitis to reduce vasculitis, inflammation, and, as a result, intracranial pressure. Data indicate that dexamethasone may lower mortality rates and lessen long-term neurologic impairment. The administration of corticosteroids should be considered in all children with tuberculous meningitis, and also may be considered in children with pleural and pericardial effusions (to hasten reabsorption of fluid), severe miliary disease (to mitigate alveolocapillary block), and endobronchial disease (to relieve obstruction and atelectasis). Corticosteroids should be given only when accompanied by appropriate antituberculosis therapy. Consultation with an expert in the treatment of tuberculosis should be obtained when corticosteroid therapy is considered.

Appropriate studies performed to date have not demonstrated pediatrics-specific problems that would limit the usefulness of rifampin in children.

Geriatrics

Appropriate studies on the relationship of age to the effects of rifampin have not been performed in the geriatric population. However, no geriatrics-specific problems have been documented to date.

Dental

The leukopenic and thrombocytopenic effects of rifampin may result in an increased incidence of certain microbial infections, delayed healing, and gingival bleeding. If leukopenia or thrombocytopenia occurs, dental work should be deferred until blood counts have returned to normal. Patients should be instructed in proper oral hygiene, including caution in use of regular toothbrushes, dental floss, and toothpicks.

Rifampin may cause a hypersensitivity reaction of sore mouth or tongue.

Drug interactions and/or related problems

The following drug interactions and/or related problems have been selected on the basis of their potential clinical significance (possible mechanism in parentheses where appropriate)—not necessarily inclusive (» = major clinical significance):

Note: Combinations containing any of the following medications, depending on the amount present, may also interact with this medication.

» Alcohol
(concurrent daily consumption of alcohol may increase the risk of rifampin-induced hepatotoxicity and increased metabolism of rifampin; dosage adjustments of rifampin may be necessary, and patients should be monitored closely for signs of hepatotoxicity)

» Aminophylline or
» Oxtriphylline or
» Theophylline
(rifampin may increase metabolism of theophylline, oxtriphylline, and aminophylline by induction of hepatic microsomal enzymes, resulting in increased theophylline clearance)

» Amprenavir or
» Indinavir or
» Nelfinavir or
» Ritonavir or
» Saquinavir
(rifampin accelerates the metabolism of protease inhibitors, such as amprenavir, indinavir, nelfinavir, ritonavir, and saquinavir through induction of hepatic P450 cytochrome oxidases, resulting in subtherapeutic levels of the protease inhibitors; in addition, protease inhibitors retard the metabolism of rifampin, resulting in increased serum levels of rifampin and the likelihood of increased toxicity; concurrent use of HIV protease inhibitors with rifampin is only recommended under specific circumstances *See General Dosing Information*)

Anesthetics, hydrocarbon inhalation, except isoflurane
(chronic use of hepatic enzyme-inducing agents prior to anesthesia, except isoflurane, may increase anesthetic metabolism, leading to increased risk of hepatotoxicity)

» Anticoagulants, coumarin- or indandione-derivative
(concurrent use with rifampin may enhance the metabolism of these anticoagulants by induction of hepatic microsomal enzymes, resulting in a considerable decrease in the activity and effectiveness of the anticoagulants; prothrombin time determinations may be required as frequently as once a day; dosage adjustments of anticoagulants may be required before and after rifampin therapy)

» Antidiabetic agents, oral
(concurrent use with rifampin may enhance the metabolism of tolbutamide, chlorpropamide, and glyburide by induction of hepatic microsomal enzymes, resulting in lower serum sulfonylurea concentrations; although not documented, other oral antidiabetic agents may also interact with rifampin; dosage adjustment may be required)

» Azole antifungals
(concurrent use may increase the metabolism of the azole antifungals, lowering their plasma concentrations; depending on the clinical situation, the dose of an azole antifungal may need to be increased during concurrent use with rifampin)

Barbiturates
(concurrent use with rifampin may enhance the metabolism of hexobarbital by induction of hepatic microsomal enzymes, resulting in lower serum concentrations; there are conflicting data on rifampin's effect on phenobarbital; dosage adjustment may be required)

Beta-adrenergic blocking agents, systemic
(concurrent use of metoprolol or propranolol with rifampin has resulted in reduced plasma concentrations of these two beta-adrenergic blocking agents due to enhanced metabolism of hepatic microsomal enzymes by rifampin; although not documented, other beta-adrenergic blocking agents may also interact with rifampin)

Bone marrow depressants (see *Appendix II*)
(concurrent use of bone marrow depressants with rifampin may increase the leukopenic and/or thrombocytopenic effects; if concurrent use is required, close observation for myelotoxic effects should be considered)

» Chloramphenicol
(concurrent use with rifampin may enhance the metabolism of chloramphenicol by induction of hepatic microsomal enzymes, resulting in significantly lower serum chloramphenicol concentrations; dosage adjustment may be necessary)

Clofazimine
(concurrent use with rifampin has resulted in reduced absorption of rifampin, delaying its time to peak concentration, and increasing its half-life)

Clofibrate
(concurrent use with rifampin may enhance the metabolism of clofibrate by induction of hepatic microsomal enzymes, resulting in significantly lower serum clofibrate concentrations)

» Contraceptives, estrogen-containing, oral
(concurrent use with rifampin may decrease the effectiveness of estrogen-containing oral contraceptives because of stimulation of estrogen metabolism or reduction in enterohepatic circulation of estrogens, resulting in menstrual irregularities, intermenstrual bleeding, and unplanned pregnancies; patients should be advised

to use an additional method of contraception throughout the whole cycle while taking rifampin and estrogen-containing oral contraceptives concurrently)

» Corticosteroids, glucocorticoid and mineralocorticoid
(concurrent use with rifampin may enhance the metabolism of corticosteroids by induction of hepatic microsomal enzymes, resulting in a considerable decrease in corticosteroid plasma concentrations; dosage adjustment may be required; rifampin has also counteracted endogenous cortisol and produced acute adrenal insufficiency in patients with Addison's disease)

Cyclosporine
(rifampin may enhance metabolism of cyclosporine by induction of hepatic microsomal enzymes and intestinal cytochrome P450 enzymes; dosage adjustment may be required)

Dapsone
(concurrent use with rifampin may decrease the effect of dapsone because of increased metabolism resulting from stimulation of hepatic microsomal enzyme activity; dapsone concentrations may be decreased by half; dapsone dosage adjustments are not required during concurrent therapy with rifampin for leprosy)

» Delavirdine or
» Efavirenz or
» Nevirapine
(rifampin accelerates the metabolism of nonnucleoside reverse transcriptase inhibitors (NNRTIs), such as delavirdine, efavirenz, and nevirapine through induction of hepatic P450 cytochrome oxidases, resulting in subtherapeutic levels of NNRTIs; in addition NNRTIs retard the metabolism of rifampin, resulting in increased serum levels of rifampin and the likelihood of increased toxicity; concurrent use of NNRTIs with rifampin is only recommended under specific circumstances *See General Dosing Information*)

Diazepam
(concurrent use with rifampin may enhance the elimination of diazepam, resulting in decreased plasma concentrations; whether this effect applies to other benzodiazepines has not been determined; dosage adjustment may be necessary)

» Digitalis glycosides
(concurrent use with rifampin may enhance the metabolism of digoxin or digitoxin by induction of hepatic microsomal enzymes, resulting in significantly lower serum digoxin or digitoxin concentrations; dosage adjustment may be necessary)

» Disopyramide or
» Mexiletine or
Propafenone or
» Quinidine or
» Tocainide
(concurrent use with rifampin may enhance the metabolism of these antiarrhythmics by induction of hepatic microsomal enzymes, resulting in significantly lower serum antiarrhythmic concentrations; serum antiarrhythmic concentrations should be monitored and dosage adjustment may be necessary)

» Estramustine or
» Estrogens
(concurrent use of estramustine or estrogens with rifampin may result in significantly reduced estrogenic effect because of stimulation of estrogen metabolism or reduction in enterohepatic circulation of estrogens)

» Hepatotoxic medications, other (see *Appendix II*)
(concurrent use of rifampin and other hepatotoxic medications may increase the potential for hepatotoxicity; patients should be monitored closely for signs of hepatotoxicity)

» Isoniazid
(concurrent use of isoniazid with rifampin may increase the risk of hepatotoxicity, especially in patients with pre-existing hepatic function impairment and/or in fast acetylators of isoniazid; patients should be monitored closely for signs of hepatotoxicity during the first 3 months of therapy)

» Methadone
(concurrent use with rifampin may decrease the effects of methadone because of stimulation of hepatic microsomal enzyme activity and/or impaired absorption, resulting in symptoms of methadone withdrawal if the patient is dependent on methadone; dosage adjustments may be necessary during and after rifampin therapy)

» Phenytoin
(concurrent use with rifampin may stimulate the hepatic metabolism of phenytoin, increasing its elimination and thus counteracting its anticonvulsant effects; careful monitoring of serum hydantoin concentrations and dosage adjustments may be necessary before and after rifampin therapy)

Probenecid
(may compete with rifampin for hepatic uptake when used concurrently, resulting in increased and more prolonged rifampin serum concentrations and/or toxicity; however, the effect on rifampin serum concentrations is inconsistent, and concurrent use of probenecid to increase rifampin serum concentrations is not recommended)

Trimethoprim
(concurrent use with rifampin may significantly increase the elimination and shorten the elimination half-life of trimethoprim)

» Verapamil, oral
(rifampin has been found to accelerate the metabolism of oral verapamil, resulting in a significant decrease in serum verapamil concentration and reversing its cardiovascular effects; concurrent use of intravenous verapamil with rifampin was found to have only minor effects on verapamil's clearance and no significant effect on cardiovascular effects)

Laboratory value alterations

The following have been selected on the basis of their potential clinical significance (possible effect in parentheses where appropriate)—not necessarily inclusive (» = major clinical significance).

With diagnostic test results

Coombs' (antiglobulin) tests, direct
(may become positive rarely during rifampin therapy)

Dexamethasone suppression test
(rifampin may prevent the inhibitory action of a standard dexamethasone dose administered for the overnight suppression test, rendering the test abnormal; it is recommended that rifampin therapy be discontinued 15 days before the dexamethasone suppression test is administered)

Folate determinations, serum and
Vitamin B_{12} determinations, serum
(therapeutic concentrations of rifampin may interfere with standard microbiological assays for serum folate and vitamin B_{12}; alternative methods must be considered when determining serum folate and vitamin B_{12} concentrations in patients taking rifampin)

Sulfobromophthalein (BSP) uptake and excretion
(hepatic uptake and excretion of BSP in liver function tests may be delayed by rifampin, resulting in BSP retention; the BSP test should be performed prior to the daily dose of rifampin to avoid false-positive test results)

Urinalyses based on spectrometry or color reaction
(rifampin may interfere with urinalyses that are based on spectrometry or color reaction due to rifampin's reddish-orange to reddish-brown discoloration of urine)

With physiology/laboratory test values

Alanine aminotransferase (ALT [SGPT]) and
Alkaline phosphatase and
Aspartate aminotransferase (AST [SGOT])
(values may be increased)

Bilirubin, serum and
Blood urea nitrogen (BUN) and
Uric acid, serum
(concentrations may be increased)

Medical considerations/Contraindications

The medical considerations/contraindications included have been selected on the basis of their potential clinical significance (reasons given in parentheses where appropriate)—not necessarily inclusive (» = major clinical significance).

Risk-benefit should be considered when the following medical problems exist:

» Alcoholism, active or in remission or
» Hepatic function impairment
(rifampin is metabolized in the liver and may also be hepatotoxic)

Hypersensitivity to rifampin

Patient monitoring

The following may be especially important in patient monitoring (other tests may be warranted in some patients, depending on condition; » = major clinical significance):

» Hepatic function determinations
(ALT [SGPT], AST [SGOT], alkaline phosphatase, and serum bilirubin determinations may be indicated prior to and monthly or more frequently during treatment; however, elevated serum enzyme values may not be predictive of clinical hepatitis and may return to normal despite continued treatment)

Side/Adverse Effects

Note: Intermittent use of rifampin may increase the chance of a patient developing the "flu-like" syndrome, as well as acute hemolysis or renal failure. These reactions are thought to be immunologically mediated and intermittent use should be limited to those conditions, such as leprosy, in which its safety and efficacy have been established.

The following side/adverse effects have been selected on the basis of their potential clinical significance (possible signs and symptoms in parentheses where appropriate)—not necessarily inclusive:

Those indicating need for medical attention

Incidence less frequent

"Flu-like" syndrome (chills; difficult breathing; dizziness; fever; headache; muscle and bone pain; shivering); ***hypersensitivity*** (itching; redness; skin rash)

Incidence rare

Blood dyscrasias (sore throat; unusual bleeding or bruising); ***hepatitis*** (yellow eyes or skin); ***hepatitis prodromal symptoms*** (loss of appetite; nausea or vomiting; unusual tiredness or weakness); ***interstitial nephritis*** (bloody or cloudy urine, greatly decreased frequency of urination or amount of urine)

Those indicating need for medical attention only if they continue or are bothersome

Incidence more frequent

Gastrointestinal disturbances (diarrhea; stomach cramps)

Incidence less frequent

Fungal overgrowth (sore mouth or tongue)

Those not indicating need for medical attention

Incidence more frequent

Reddish-orange to reddish-brown discoloration of urine, feces, saliva, sputum, sweat, and tears

Note: Tears discolored by rifampin may also discolor soft contact lenses.

Overdose

The information below applies to the clinical effects and treatment of rifampin overdose.

Clinical effects of overdose

The following effects have been selected on the basis of their potential clinical significance (possible signs and symptoms in parentheses where appropriate)—not necessarily inclusive:

Acute and chronic effects

Mental obtundation (mental changes); ***periorbital or facial edema*** (swelling around the eyes or the whole face); ***pruritus, generalized*** (itching over the whole body); ***Redman syndrome*** (red-orange discoloration of skin, mucous membranes, and sclera)

Note: Fatalities are more likely to occur if there is underlying hepatic disease, frequent use or abuse of alcohol, or concurrent intake of other hepatotoxic medications.

Treatment of overdose

To decrease absorption—

Evacuating stomach contents using ipecac syrup or gastric lavage.

Administering an activated charcoal slurry to help adsorb residual rifampin in the gastrointestinal tract.

Supportive care—

Supportive therapy.

Patient Consultation

As an aid to patient consultation, refer to *Advice for the Patient, Rifampin (Systemic)*.

In providing consultation, consider emphasizing the following selected information (» = major clinical significance):

Before using this medication

» Conditions affecting use, especially:

Hypersensitivity to rifampin

Pregnancy—Rifampin crosses the placenta and has rarely caused postnatal hemorrhages in the mother and infant when administered during the last few weeks of pregnancy

Breast-feeding—Rifampin is distributed into breast milk

Dental—Patients who develop blood dyscrasias may be at increased risk of microbial infections, delayed healing, and gingival bleeding

Other medications, especially aminophylline, azole antifungals, corticosteroids, coumarin- or indandione-derivative anticoagulants, oral antidiabetic agents, chloramphenicol, estrogen-containing oral contraceptives, digitalis glycosides, disopyramide, estramustine, estrogens, hepatotoxic medications, HIV protease inhibitors such as amprenavir, indinavir, nelfinavir, ritonavir, and saquinavir, isoniazid, methadone, mexiletine, non-nucleoside reverse transcriptase inhibitors (NNRTIs) such as delavirdine, efavirenz, and nevirapine, oxtriphylline, phenytoin, quinidine, tocainide, theophylline, or oral verapamil

Other medical problems, especially alcoholism, active or in remission, or impairment of hepatic function

Proper use of this medication

Taking with a full glass (240 mL) of water on an empty stomach, 1 hour before or 2 hours after a meal, or with food if gastrointestinal irritation occurs

Proper administration technique for patients unable to swallow capsules

» Compliance with full course of therapy, which may take months or years to complete

» Proper dosing

Missed dose: Taking as soon as possible; not taking if almost time for next dose; not doubling doses; intermittent dosing may result in more frequent and/or severe side effects

» Proper storage

Precautions while using this medication

» Regular visits to physician to check progress

Checking with physician if no improvement within 2 to 3 weeks

» Using an alternative method of contraception if taking estrogen-containing oral contraceptives concurrently

» Avoiding alcoholic beverages concurrently with this medication

» Need to report prodromal signs of hepatotoxicity to physician

» Medication causes urine, feces, saliva, sputum, sweat, and tears to turn reddish-orange to reddish-brown and may also permanently discolor soft contact lenses; avoiding the wearing of soft contact lenses

Using caution in use of regular toothbrushes, dental floss, and toothpicks; deferring dental work until blood counts have returned to normal; checking with physician or dentist concerning proper oral hygiene

Possible interference with laboratory values

Side/adverse effects

Reddish-orange to reddish-brown discoloration of urine, stools, saliva, sputum, sweat, and tears may be alarming to patient, although medically insignificant; however, tears discolored by rifampin may also discolor soft contact lenses

Signs of potential side effects, especially "flu-like" syndrome, hypersensitivity, blood dyscrasias, hepatitis, hepatitis prodromal symptoms, and interstitial nephritis

General Dosing Information

Rifampin preferably should be taken with a full glass (240 mL) of water on an empty stomach (either 1 hour before or 2 hours after a meal) to obtain optimum absorption. However, it may be taken with food if gastrointestinal irritation occurs.

Contents of rifampin capsules may be mixed with applesauce or jelly for patients who are unable to swallow the capsules.

Since bacterial resistance may develop rapidly when rifampin is administered alone in the treatment of tuberculosis, it should be administered only concurrently with other antituberculosis medications.

The duration of treatment with an antituberculosis regimen is at least 6 months and may be continued for to 2 years. Uncomplicated pulmonary tuberculosis is often successfully treated within 6 to 12 months. Several different treatment regimens are currently recommended.

The duration of antituberculosis therapy is based on the patient's clinical and radiographic responses, smear and culture results, and susceptibility studies of *Mycobacterium tuberculosis* isolates from the patient or the suspect source case. With directly observed therapy (DOT), clinical evaluation is an integral component of each visit for administration of medication. Careful monitoring of the clinical and bacteriologic responses to therapy on a monthly basis in sputum-positive patients is important.

If therapy is interrupted, the treatment schedule should be extended to a later completion date. Although guidelines cannot be provided for every situation, the following factors need to be considered in establishing a new date for completion:

- The length of interruption;

- The time during therapy (early or late) in which interruption occurred; and
- The patient's clinical, radiographic, and bacteriologic status before, during, and after interruption. Consultation with an expert is advised.

Therapy should be administered based on the following guidelines, published by the American Thoracic Society (ATS) and by the Centers for Disease Control and Prevention (CDC), and endorsed by the American Academy of Pediatrics (AAP).

- A 6-month regimen consisting of isoniazid, rifampin, and pyrazinamide given for 2 months followed by isoniazid and rifampin for 4 months is the preferred treatment for patients infected with fully susceptible organisms who adhere to the treatment course.
- Ethambutol (or streptomycin in children too young to be monitored for visual acuity) should be included in the initial regimen until the results of drug susceptibility studies are available, and unless there is little possibility of drug resistance (i.e., there is less than 4% primary resistance to isoniazid in the community, and the patient has had no previous treatment with antituberculosis medications, is not from a country with a high prevalence of drug resistance, and has no known exposure to a drug-resistant case).
- Alternatively, a 9-month regimen of isoniazid and rifampin is acceptable for persons who cannot or should not take pyrazinamide. Ethambutol (or streptomycin in children too young to be monitored for visual acuity) should also be included until the results of drug susceptibility studies are available, unless there is little possibility of drug resistance. If isoniazid resistance is demonstrated, rifampin and ethambutol should be continued for a minimum of 12 months.
- Consideration should be given to treating all patients with DOT. DOT programs have been demonstrated to increase adherence in patients receiving antituberculosis chemotherapy in both rural and urban settings.
- Multidrug-resistant tuberculosis (i.e., resistance to at least isoniazid and rifampin) presents difficult treatment problems. Treatment must be individualized and based on susceptibility studies. In such cases, consultation with an expert in tuberculosis is recommended.
- Children should be managed in essentially the same ways as adults, but doses of the medications must be adjusted appropriately and specific important differences between the management of adults and children addressed. However, optimal therapy of tuberculosis in children with HIV infection has not been established. The Committee on Infectious Diseases of the AAP recommends that therapy always should include at least three drugs initially, and should be continued for a minimum period of 9 months. Isoniazid, rifampin, and pyrazinamide with or without ethambutol or an aminoglycoside should be given for at least the first 2 months. A fourth drug may be needed for disseminated disease and whenever drug-resistant disease is suspected.
- Extrapulmonary tuberculosis should be managed according to the principles and with the drug regimens outlined for pulmonary tuberculosis, except in children who have miliary tuberculosis, bone/joint tuberculosis, or tuberculous meningitis. These children should receive a minimum of 12 months of therapy.
- A 4-month regimen of isoniazid and rifampin is acceptable therapy for adults who have active tuberculosis and who are sputum smear– and culture–negative, if there is little possibility of drug resistance.

ATS, CDC, and AAP recommend preventive treatment of tuberculosis infection in the following patients:

- Preventive therapy with isoniazid given for 6 to 12 months is effective in decreasing the risk of future tuberculosis disease in adults and children with tuberculosis infection demonstrated by a positive tuberculin skin test reaction.
- Persons with a positive skin test and any of the following risk factors should be considered for preventive therapy regardless of age:
  - —Persons with HIV infection.
  - —Persons at risk for HIV infection with unknown HIV status.
  - —Close contacts of sputum-positive persons with newly diagnosed infectious tuberculosis.
  - —Newly infected persons (recent skin test convertors).
  - —Persons with medical conditions reported to increase the risk of tuberculosis (i.e., diabetes mellitus, corticosteroid therapy and other immunosuppressive therapy, intravenous drug users, hematologic and reticuloendothelial malignancies, end-stage renal disease, and clinical conditions associated with rapid weight loss or chronic malnutrition).

  In some circumstances, persons with negative skin tests should be considered for preventive therapy. These include children who are close contacts of infectious tuberculosis cases and anergic HIV-infected adults at increased risk of tuberculosis, tuberculin-positive adults with abnormal chest radiographs showing fibrotic lesions probably representing old healed tuberculosis, adults with silicosis, and persons who are known to be HIV-infected and who are contacts of patients with infectious tuberculosis.
- In the absence of any of the above risk factors, persons up to 35 years of age with a positive skin test who are in the following high-incidence groups should be also considered for preventive therapy:
  - —Foreign-born persons from high-prevalence countries.
  - —Medically underserved low-income persons from high-prevalence populations (especially blacks, Hispanics, and Native Americans).
  - —Residents of facilities for long-term care (e.g., correctional institutions, nursing homes, and mental institutions).
- Twelve months of preventive therapy is recommended for adults and children with HIV infection and other conditions associated with immunosuppression. Persons without HIV infection should receive preventive therapy for at least 6 months.
- In persons younger than 35 years of age, routine monitoring for adverse effects of isoniazid should consist of a monthly symptom review. For persons 35 years of age and older, hepatic enzymes should be measured prior to starting isoniazid and monitored monthly throughout treatment, in addition to monthly symptom reviews.
- Persons who are presumed to be infected with isoniazid-resistant organisms should be treated with rifampin rather than with isoniazid.
- As with the treatment of active tuberculosis, the key to success of preventive treatment is patient adherence to the prescribed regimen. Although not evaluated in clinical studies, directly observed, twice-weekly preventive therapy may be appropriate for adults and children at risk, who cannot or will not reliably self-administer therapy.

Antiretroviral agents such as protease inhibitors and nonnucleoside reverse transcriptase inhibitors (NNRTIs) have substantive interactions with the rifamycins (rifampin, rifabutin, and rifapentine) used to treat mycobacterial infections commonly observed in HIV-infected patients. Rifamycins accelerate the metabolism of these agents through induction of hepatic cytochrome P450 oxidases, resulting in subtherapeutic levels of these antiretroviral agents. In addition, protease inhibitors and NNRTIs retard the metabolism of rifamycins, resulting in increased serum levels of rifamycins and the likelihood of increased drug toxicity. Nucleoside reverse transcriptase inhibitors (NRTIs) (e.g., zidovudine, didanosine, zalcitabine, stavudine, lamivudine, abacavir) are not metabolized by cytochrome P450 isoenzymes. Concurrent use of NRTIs and rifamycins is not contraindicated and does not require dose adjustments.

Rifampin is an essential component of the currently recommended regimen for treating tuberculosis. This regimen is effective in treating HIV-infected patients with tuberculosis, and consists of isoniazid and rifampin for a minimum period of 6 months, plus pyrazinamide and either ethambutol or streptomycin for the first 2 months. Therefore, information concerning the pharmacokinetic interactions between antiretroviral agents (i.e., protease inhibitors, NNRTIs) and rifampin is important for health care workers involved in tuberculosis control and the care of patients coinfected with tuberculosis and HIV, because clinicians may decrease or restrict the use of rifampin in the treatment of patients who are candidates for therapy with both antiretrovirals and rifampin. Because of the common association of tuberculosis with HIV infection, an increasing number of patients probably will be considered candidates for combined therapy with rifampin and antiretrovirals. Prompt initiation of appropriate pharmacologic therapy for patients with HIV infection who acquire tuberculosis is critical because tuberculosis may become rapidly fatal. The management of these patients is complex, requires an individualized approach, and should be undertaken only by, or in consultation with, a physician with experience in the care of patients with these two diseases. In addition, all HIV-infected patients at risk for tuberculosis infection should be carefully evaluated and administered isoniazid preventive treatment if indicated, regardless of whether they are receiving protease inhibitor therapy.

Use of rifampin to treat active tuberculosis (TB) has been contraindicated for patients who take any of the protease inhibitors or nonnucleoside reverse transcriptase inhibitors (NNRTIs); however, according to the Centers for Disease Control and Prevention (CDC), rifampin can be used for the treatment of active TB in three situations:

- In patients whose antiretroviral regimen includes the NNRTI efavirenz and two nucleoside reverse transcriptase inhibitors (NRTIs)
- In patients whose antiretroviral regimen includes the protease inhibitor ritonavir and one or more NRTIs
- In patients whose antiretroviral regimen includes the combination of two protease inhibitors (ritonavir and either saquinavir hard-gel capsule or saquinavir soft-gel capsule)

Recommendations for coadministering different antiretroviral drugs with the antimycobacterial drug rifampin-United States, 2000:

Antiretroviral	Use in combination with rifampin	Comments
Saquinavir* Hard- or soft-gel capsules	Possibly, if antiretroviral regimen also includes ritonavir	The combination of saquinavir and ritonavir, coadministered with usual-dose rifampin (600 mg daily or two or three times per week) is a possibility. Coadministration of saquinavir hard- or soft-gel capsules is not recommended because rifampin markedly decreases concentrations of saquinavir.
Ritonavir	Probably	Coadministration of ritonavir with usual-dose rifampin (600 mg daily or two or three times per week) is a possibility, though pharmacokinetic data and clinical experience are limited.
Indinavir	No	Coadministration is not recommended because rifampin markedly decreases concentrations of indinavir.
Nelfinavir	No	Coadministration is not recommended because rifampin markedly decreases concentrations of nelfinavir.
Amprenavir	No	Coadministration is not recommended because rifampin markedly decreases concentrations of amprenavir.
Nevirapine	Possibly	Data are insufficient to assess whether dose adjustments are necessary when rifampin is coadministered with nevirapine. The combination should only be used if clearly indicated and with careful monitoring.
Delavirdine	No	Coadministration is contraindicated because rifampin markedly decreases concentrations of delavirdine.
Efavirenz	Probably	Coadministration of efavirenz with usual-dose rifampin (600 mg daily or two or three times per week) is a possibility, though there is no published clinical experience. (Usual recommended dose of efavirenz is 600 mg daily. Some experts recommend increasing the efavirenz dose to 800 mg daily if used in combination with rifampin)

*Usual recommended doses are 400 mg two times per day for each of these protease inhibitors and 400 mg of ritonavir.

For patients undergoing therapy with complex combinations of protease inhibitors or NNRTIs, the use of antituberculosis regimens containing no rifamycins can be considered.

Isoniazid does not interact with either the protease inhibitors or NNRTIs, and the use of a 9–month regimen of isoniazid is recommended as the preferred option for treatment for latent Mycobacterium tuberculosis infection (LTBI). However, 2–month regimens of a rifamycin and pyrazinamide also are recommended for LTBI therapy. If these regimen options are chosen for HIV-infected patients with LTBI, the drug-drug interactions and dose adjustment for antiretroviral drugs and rifamycins apply

For HIV-infected patients diagnosed with drug-susceptible tuberculosis and for whom protease inhibitor therapy is being considered but has not been initiated, one suggested management strategy is to complete tuberculosis treatment with a regimen containing rifampin before starting therapy with a protease inhibitor. The duration of antituberculosis regimen is at least 6 months, and therapy should be administered according to the guidelines developed by ATS and CDC, including the recommendation to carefully assess clinical and bacteriologic responses in patients coinfected with HIV and to prolong treatment if response is slow or suboptimal.

Three other options for managing HIV-infected patients with tuberculosis who are undergoing protease inhibitor therapy when tuberculosis is diagnosed have been provided by the Centers for Disease Control and Prevention (CDC). Option I is discontinuation of therapy with the protease inhibitor while a tuberculosis treatment regimen that includes rifampin is followed. However, because that interruption in the administration of the prescribed protease inhibitor can induce HIV resistance to the protease inhibitor and possibly to other medications within the protease inhibitor class, and because discontinuation of the protease inhibitor therapy may be detrimental to the patient's clinical status, some clinicians may be reluctant to discontinue protease inhibitor therapy for the duration of tuberculosis treatment. In such cases, option II and option III may be considered. Because the risks and benefits of all of these options are unknown, clinicians should make management decisions on a case-by-case basis to provide optimal patient care.

- Option I. This option involves discontinuing therapy with the protease inhibitor and completing a short (minimum 6 months) course of tuberculosis treatment with a regimen containing rifampin. The antituberculosis regimen should be administered according to the guidelines developed by ATS and CDC, and the duration of therapy should be prolonged in patients with slow or suboptimal responses. Protease inhibitor therapy may be resumed when treatment with rifampin is discontinued. Antiretroviral agents other than protease inhibitors may be used concurrently with rifampin. Although the risks associated with complete discontinuation of protease inhibitor therapy during tuberculosis treatment are unclear, they may be serious; however, the risks and complications associated with tuberculosis treatment regimens that do not include rifampin are known. Potential consequences include prolonged duration of therapy to at least 18 to 24 months, increased likelihood of treatment failure and mortality, slower conversion of sputum culture to negative with patients remaining infectious for longer periods of time, and the adverse effect of tuberculous disease on the progression of HIV infection. Therefore, antituberculosis treatment regimens without rifampin are not recommended for the treatment of rifampin-susceptible tuberculosis.
- Option II. To minimize the interruption of protease inhibitor therapy, one option is to use a four-drug tuberculosis treatment regimen that includes rifampin (i.e., daily isoniazid, pyrazinamide, rifampin, and ethambutol or streptomycin) for a minimum of 2 months, and until bacteriologic response is achieved (i.e., sputum conversion to culture-negative status) and the results from the susceptibility testing are available. After bacteriologic response and drug susceptibility have been documented (usually 3 months), treatment may be modified to a 16-month continuation-phase regimen consisting of isoniazid (15 mg per kg of body weight) and ethambutol (50 mg per kg of body weight) two times per week. This regimen allows the reintroduction of protease inhibitor therapy. Some experts recommend adding a third agent, such as streptomycin, during this continuation phase if the infecting organism is not resistant to the agent. Option II cannot be recommended for patients with proven isoniazid-resistant tuberculosis.
- Option III. Another management option is to continue protease inhibitor therapy with indinavir (800 mg every 8 hours) and administer a four-drug, 9-month tuberculosis treatment regimen containing daily rifabutin (150 mg a day) instead of rifampin. When this option is used for tuberculosis management, clinicians should conduct careful monitoring, possibly including measurement of serum concentrations of rifabutin. This alternative tuberculosis therapy is recommended based on the pharmacokinetic characteristics of rifabutin and limited data from clinical trials. Rifabutin is a rifamycin derivative with comparable antituberculosis activity *in vitro* , but with less hepatic cytochrome P450 enzyme-inducing effect than rifampin. An international multicenter study indicated that a 6-month regimen containing rifabutin at a daily dose of either 150 or 300 mg is as effective in treating tuberculosis as a similar regimen containing rifampin. In a small clinical trial, a rifabutin-containing regimen was effective in treating tuberculosis in patients coinfected with HIV. In addition, limited data from pharmacokinetic studies suggest that the combination of rifabutin 150 mg a day and indinavir resulted in acceptable levels of both agents. Option III cannot be recommended for patients undergoing therapy with ritonavir or saquinavir. For these patients, the decision to change the prescribed protease inhibitor to indinavir and to prescribe rifabutin for tuberculosis therapy should be made in consultation with an expert in the use of protease inhibitors to manage HIV infection.

Neither option II nor option III has been studied in large clinical trials of HIV-infected patients or patients undergoing protease inhibitor therapy during tuberculosis treatment. For these reasons, if either of these options is selected for managing patients with tuberculosis, CDC recommends the following interim guidelines until additional data are available and formal guidelines are issued:

- On initiation of therapy, frequent bacteriologic evaluations should be performed to document sputum conversion to culture-negative status, and after culture conversion, to detect any possible treatment failures.

• The duration of therapy should be extended to at least 18 months for option II or 9 months for option III.
• Only indinavir should be used with option III.
• Monitoring for drug toxicity should be performed carefully.
• DOT should be used throughout treatment.
• During the first 2 years after completion of therapy, periodic evaluation should be performed (including an assessment of bacteriologic status at 6 months), and patients should be instructed to report symptoms indicating relapse of tuberculous disease promptly.

HIV-infected patients diagnosed with drug-resistant tuberculosis or diagnosed clinically with tuberculosis but without culture and susceptibility test results should be evaluated on a case-by-case basis and managed in consultation with a tuberculosis expert.

Most infants ≤ 12 months of age with tuberculosis are asymptomatic at the time of diagnosis, and the gastric aspirate cultures in these patients have a high yield for *M. tuberculosis.* When an infant is suspected of having tuberculosis, a thorough household investigation should be undertaken. A 6-month regimen of isoniazid and rifampin supplemented during the first 2 months by pyrazinamide has been found to be well-tolerated and effective in infants with pulmonary tuberculosis. Furthermore, twice-weekly DOT appears to be as effective as daily therapy, and is an essential alternative in patients for whom social issues prevent reliable daily therapy.

Physicians caring for children should be familiar with the clinical forms of the disease in infants to enable them to make an early diagnosis. Any child, especially one in a high-risk group or area, who has unexplained pneumonia, cervical adenitis, bone or joint infections, or aseptic meningitis should have a Mantoux tuberculin skin test performed, and a detailed epidemiologic history for tuberculosis should be obtained.

Management of a newborn infant whose mother, or other household contact, is suspected of having tuberculosis is based on individual considerations. If possible, separation of the mother, or contact, and infant should be minimized. The Committee on Infectious Diseases of the AAP offers the following recommendations in the management of the newborn infant whose mother, or any other household contact, has tuberculosis:

• *Mother, or any other household contact, with a positive tuberculin skin test reaction but no evidence of current disease:* Investigation of other members of the household or extended family to whom the infant may later be exposed is indicated. If no evidence of current disease is found in the mother or in members of the extended family, the infant should be tested with a Mantoux tuberculin skin test at 3 to 4 months of age. When the family members cannot be promptly tested, consideration should be given to administering isoniazid (10 mg per kg of body weight a day) to the infant until skin testing and other evaluation of the family members have excluded contact with a case of active tuberculosis. The infant does not need to be hospitalized during this time if adequate follow-up can be arranged, but adherence to medication administration should be closely monitored. The mother also should be considered for isoniazid therapy.

• *Mother with untreated (newly diagnosed) disease or disease that has been treated for 2 or more weeks and who is judged to be noncontagious at delivery:* Careful investigation of household members and extended family is mandatory. A chest radiograph and Mantoux tuberculin skin test should be performed on the infant at 3 to 4 months and at 6 months of age. Separation of the mother and infant is not necessary if adherence to treatment for the mother and infant is assured. The mother can breast-feed. The infant should receive isoniazid even if the tuberculin skin test and chest radiograph do not suggest clinical tuberculosis, since cell-mediated immunity of a degree sufficient to mount a significant reaction to tuberculin skin testing may develop as late as 6 months of age in an infant infected at birth. Isoniazid can be discontinued if the Mantoux skin test is negative at 3 to 4 months of age, the mother is adherent to treatment and has a satisfactory clinical response, and no other family members have infectious tuberculosis. The infant should be examined carefully at monthly intervals. If nonadherence is documented, the mother has an acid-fast bacillus (AFB)–positive sputum or smear, and supervision is impossible, the infant should be separated from the ill family member and Bacillus Calmette-Guérin (BCG) vaccine may be considered for the infant. However, the response to the vaccine in infants may be delayed and inadequate for prevention of tuberculosis.

• *Mother has current disease and is suspected of having been contagious at the time of delivery:* The mother and infant should be separated until the infant is receiving therapy or the mother is confirmed to be noncontagious. Otherwise, management is the same as when the disease is judged to be noncontagious to the infant at delivery.

• *Mother has hematogenously spread tuberculosis (e.g., meningitis, miliary disease, or bone involvement):* The infant should be evaluated for congenital tuberculosis. If clinical and radiographic findings do not support the diagnosis of congenital tuberculosis, the infant should be separated from the mother until she is judged to be noncontagious. The infant should be given isoniazid until 3 or 4 months of age, at which time the Mantoux skin test should be repeated. If the skin test is positive, isoniazid should be continued for a total of 12 months. If the skin test is negative and the chest radiograph is normal, isoniazid may be discontinued, depending on the status of the mother and whether there are other cases of infectious tuberculosis in the family. The infant should continue to be examined carefully at monthly intervals.

Health care or correctional institutions experiencing outbreaks of tuberculosis that are resistant to isoniazid and rifampin, or that are resuming therapy for a patient with a prior history of antitubercular therapy, may need to begin five- or six-drug regimens as initial therapy. These regimens should include the four-drug regimen and at least three medications to which the suspected multi-drug-resistant strain may be susceptible.

Side effects may be more frequent and/or severe with intermittent administration (600 mg once or twice weekly).

Patients with severe hepatic function impairment usually require a 50% reduction in dose of rifampin.

Patients with renal function impairment do not require a reduction in dose. In addition, rifampin plasma concentrations are not significantly altered in patients with decreased glomerular filtration rates (GFR) or in anuric patients.

Oral Dosage Forms

Note: Bracketed uses in the *Dosage Forms* section refer to categories of use and/or indications that are not included in U.S. product labeling.

RIFAMPIN CAPSULES USP

Usual adult and adolescent dose

Tuberculosis—
In combination with other antituberculosis medications: Oral, 600 mg once a day for the entire treatment period; or 10 mg per kg of body weight, up to 600 mg, two or three times a week, depending on the treatment regimen.

Meningococcal infection (prophylaxis)—
Oral, 600 mg once a day for four days.

[*Haemophilus influenzae* infection (prophylaxis)][1]—
Oral, 600 mg once a day for four days.

[Leprosy][1]—
In combination with other antileprosy agents:
For multibacillary leprosy—Oral, 600 mg once a month for a minimum of two years or until smear is negative, whichever is longer.
For paucibacillary leprosy—Oral, 600 mg once a month for a minimum of six months.

Note: Debilitated patients—Oral, 10 mg per kg of body weight once a day.

Usual adult prescribing limits

600 mg daily.

Usual pediatric dose

Infants up to 1 month of age—
Tuberculosis: In combination with other antituberculosis medications—Oral, 10 to 20 mg per kg of body weight once a day; or 10 to 20 mg per kg of body weight, two or three times a week, depending on the treatment regimen.

Meningococcal infection (prophylaxis)—
Oral, 5 mg per kg of body weight every twelve hours for two days.

[*Haemophilus influenzae* infection (prophylaxis)][1]—
Oral, 10 mg per kg of body weight once a day for four days.

Children 1 month of age and over—
Tuberculosis: In combination with other antituberculosis medications—Oral, 10 to 20 mg per kg of body weight, up to 600 mg, once a day; or 10 to 20 mg per kg of body weight, up to 600 mg, two or three times a week, depending on the treatment regimen.
Meningococcal infection (prophylaxis): Oral, 10 mg per kg of body weight every twelve hours for two days.

[*Haemophilus influenzae* infection (prophylaxis)][1]—
Oral, 20 mg per kg of body weight once a day for four days.

Note: The maximum daily dose should not exceed 600 mg.

Usual geriatric dose

Tuberculosis—
Oral, 10 mg per kg of body weight once a day.

Strength(s) usually available

U.S.—
150 mg (Rx) [*Rifadin*].
300 mg (Rx) [*Rifadin; Rimactane;* GENERIC].

Canada—
150 mg (Rx) [*Rifadin; Rimactane; Rofact*].
300 mg (Rx) [*Rifadin; Rimactane; Rofact*].

Packaging and storage

Store below 40 °C (104 °F). Store in a tight, light-resistant container.

Auxiliary labeling

- Continue medicine for full time of treatment.
- Avoid alcoholic beverages.
- May discolor body fluids.

Note

Contents of the capsules may also be mixed with applesauce or jelly.

RIFAMPIN ORAL SUSPENSION USP

Usual adult and adolescent dose

See *Rifampin Capsules USP*.

Usual adult prescribing limits

600 mg daily.

Usual pediatric dose

See *Rifampin Capsules USP*.

Note: The maximum daily dose should not exceed 600 mg.

Usual geriatric dose

See *Rifampin Capsules USP*.

Strength(s) usually available

U.S.—
Not commercially available. Compounding required for prescription.

Canada—
Not commercially available. Compounding required for prescription.

Packaging and storage

Preserve in a tight, light-resistant glass or plastic prescription bottle, with a child-resistant closure. Store at controlled room temperature.

Preparation of dosage form

Rifampin oral suspension is compounded as follows:
Rifampin—1.2 grams
Syrup, a sufficient quantity to make—120 mL

Transfer 1.2 grams of rifampin, or the contents of rifampin capsules, into a mortar. If necessary, gently crush the capsule contents with a pestle to produce a fine powder. Add about 2 mL of syrup to the mortar, and triturate until a smooth paste is formed. Add about 10 mL of syrup, and triturate to form a suspension. Continue to add syrup, until about 80 mL has been added. Transfer this suspension to a 120-mL precalibrated light-resistant glass or plastic prescription bottle. Rinse the mortar and pestle with successive small portions of syrup, and add the rinses to the bottle. Shake vigorously. If necessary, add citric acid or sodium citrate to adjust to a pH of 5. Add a suitable flavor if desired. Add sufficient syrup to make the product measure 120 mL, and shake vigorously.

Stability

Rifampin suspension compounded for oral use should be discarded 30 days after the day on which it was compounded.

Auxiliary labeling

- Continue medicine for full time of treatment.
- Avoid alcoholic beverages.
- May discolor body fluids.
- Shake well before using.

Parenteral Dosage Forms

Note: Bracketed uses in the *Dosage Forms* section refer to categories of use and/or indications that are not included in U.S. product labeling.

RIFAMPIN FOR INJECTION USP

Usual adult and adolescent dose

Tuberculosis—
In combination with other antituberculosis medications: Intravenous, 600 mg once a day for the entire treatment period; or 10 mg per kg of body weight, up to 600 mg, two or three times a week, depending on the treatment regimen.

Meningococcal infection (prophylaxis)—Intravenous, 600 mg two times a day for two days.

[Leprosy]—In combination with other antileprosy agents: Intravenous, 600 mg once a month for a minimum of two years or until smear is negative, whichever is longer.

Note: Debilitated patients—Intravenous, 10 mg per kg of body weight once a day.

Usual adult prescribing limits

600 mg daily.

Usual pediatric dose

Infants up to 1 month of age—
Tuberculosis: In combination with other antituberculosis medications—Intravenous, 10 to 20 mg per kg of body weight once a day; or 10 to 20 mg per kg of body weight two or three times a week, depending on the treatment regimen.
Meningococcal infection (prophylaxis): Intravenous, 5 mg per kg of body weight every twelve hours for two days.

Children 1 month of age and over—
Tuberculosis: In combination with other antituberculosis medications—Intravenous, 10 to 20 mg per kg of body weight, up to 600 mg, once a day; or 10 to 20 mg per kg of body weight, up to 600 mg, two or three times a week, depending on the treatment regimen.
Meningococcal infection (prophylaxis): Intravenous, 10 mg per kg of body weight every twelve hours for two days.

Note: The maximum daily dose should not exceed 600 mg.

Usual geriatric dose

Tuberculosis: Intravenous, 10 mg per kg of body weight once a day.

Strength(s) usually available

U.S.—
600 mg (Rx) [*Rifadin IV*].

Canada—
Not commercially available.

Packaging and storage

Store below 40 °C (104 °F). Store in a tight, light-resistant container.

Preparation of dosage form

To prepare for initial dilution for intravenous use, 10 mL of sterile water for injection should be added to each 600-mg vial. Vial should be gently swirled to completely dissolve the rifampin.

For intermittent infusion, the calculated amount of reconstituted rifampin to be administered should be added to 500 mL of normal saline or 5% dextrose in water and infused over 3 hours. In some cases, the calculated amount of rifampin may be added to 100 mL of normal saline or 5% dextrose in water and infused over 30 minutes.

Stability

5% dextrose in water is the recommended infusion medium. Sterile saline may be used; however, this slightly reduces the stability of rifampin. Other solutions are not recommended.

After reconstitution, the solution of 60 mg per mL is stable at room temperature for 24 hours. After dilution in 100 or 500 mL, solutions prepared with normal saline are also stable at room temperature for 24 hours, while those prepared with 5% dextrose in water are stable at room temperature for 4 hours. Other infusion media are not recommended.

[1]Not included in Canadian product labeling.

Selected Bibliography

The American Thoracic Society (ATS). Ad Hoc Committee on the Scientific Assembly on Microbiology, Tuberculosis, and Pulmonary Infections. Treatment of tuberculosis and tuberculosis infection in adults and children. Clin Infect Dis 1995; 21: 9-27

Revised: 11/10/2003

RIFAMPIN AND ISONIAZID Systemic

INN: Rifampin—Rifampicin
VA CLASSIFICATION (Primary): AM500
Commonly used brand name(s): *Rifamate*.

NOTE: The *Rifampin and Isoniazid (Systemic)* monograph is maintained on the *USP DI* electronic data base. A copy of the most recent revision of the complete monograph can be accessed on the *USP DI* Updates Online website. See the front cover of book for details on accessing the site.

For information on the specific components of this combination, see the *USP DI* monographs for *Isoniazid (Systemic)* and *Rifampin (Systemic)*.

The information that follows is selectively abstracted from the complete monograph and is provided to facilitate drug use review and patient counseling.

Note: For a listing of dosage forms and brand names by country availability, see *Dosage Forms* section(s).

Category

Antibacterial (antimycobacterial).

Indications

General Considerations

Tuberculosis is a highly infectious life-threatening bacterial disease with 8 million new cases and 3 million deaths reported worldwide each year to the World Health Organization (WHO). The vast majority of these cases are in developing countries; however, tuberculosis also has emerged as an important public health problem in the U.S. in recent years after the decline in number of cases observed between 1950 and 1980.

The resurgence of tuberculosis in the U.S. has been complicated by an increase in the proportion of patients with strains resistant to antituberculosis medications. Outbreaks of multidrug-resistant tuberculosis have been documented in hospitals and prisons. Drug-resistant tuberculosis, particularly that caused by strains resistant to isoniazid and rifampin, is much harder to treat and often is fatal. Among acquired immunodeficiency syndrome (AIDS) patients infected with tuberculosis bacilli resistant to both rifampin and isoniazid, a case-fatality rate of 91% has been reported. Recent investigations of outbreaks of multidrug-resistant tuberculosis have found an extraordinarily high case-fatality rate, with the median time to mortality being reached between 4 and 16 weeks. In almost all instances, these outbreaks have involved patients with severe immunosuppression by infection with the human immunodeficiency virus (HIV).

Acquired drug resistance develops during treatment for drug-sensitive tuberculosis with regimens that are poorly conceived or poorly complied with, allowing the emergence of naturally occurring drug-resistant mutations. Resistant organisms from affected patients may subsequently infect other people who have not been infected with *M. tuberculosis* previously, resulting in primary drug resistance.

Resistance to antituberculosis agents can develop not only in the strain that caused the initial disease, but also as a result of reinfection with a new strain of *M. tuberculosis* that is drug-resistant. Reinfection with a new multidrug-resistant *M. tuberculosis* strain can occur during therapy for the original infection or after completion of therapy. Most recent data suggest that outcomes can be improved if patients promptly begin therapy with two or more drugs that have *in vitro* activity against the multidrug-resistant isolate.

HIV infection is the strongest risk factor yet identified for the development of active tuberculosis disease in persons infected with tuberculosis. In addition, persons with HIV infection are at an increased risk of tuberculosis resulting either from newly acquired disease or from reactivation of latent infections. Tuberculosis is a major clinical manifestation of immunodeficiency induced by HIV. In hospital-based retrospective studies, high rates of tuberculosis have been found among patients with AIDS. In communities where tuberculosis and HIV infection are common, the prevalence of HIV seropositivity among patients with tuberculosis is greatly increasing.

WHO has estimated that 5.6 million people worldwide and 80,000 people in the U.S. are infected with both HIV and tuberculosis. Persons dually infected with *M. tuberculosis* and HIV have a high risk of developing clinically active tuberculosis. One study of HIV-positive drug users with positive tuberculin skin test results found a rate of the development of active tuberculosis to be 8 cases per 100 person-years (8% yearly) as compared with the 10% lifetime risk (1 to 3% risk within the first year after skin test conversion) in the general population.

Persons who are known to be HIV-infected and who are contacts of patients with infectious tuberculosis should be carefully evaluated for evidence of tuberculosis. If there are no findings suggestive of current tuberculosis, preventive therapy with isoniazid should be given. Because HIV-infected contacts are not managed in the same way as those who are not HIV-infected, HIV testing is recommended if there are known or suspected risk factors for their acquiring HIV infection.

According to investigators at the National Institute of Allergy and Infectious Diseases (NIAID), levels of HIV in the bloodstream increase 5- to 160-fold in HIV-infected persons who develop active tuberculosis. Clinical and epidemiologic observations have demonstrated that HIV-infected individuals have an estimated 113-times higher risk and AIDS patients have a 170-times higher risk as compared with uninfected persons. Furthermore, the problem of drug resistance may worsen as the HIV epidemic spreads. Immunosuppressed patients with HIV infection who subsequently become infected with *M. tuberculosis* have an extraordinarily high risk of developing active tuberculosis within a short period of time.

In addition to the convincing evidence that HIV infection increases the risk and worsens the course of tuberculosis, there is increasing clinical evidence that coinfection with *M. tuberculosis* accelerates progression of disease caused by HIV infection. Understanding the interaction of these two pathogens is clinically important, given the high prevalence of patients coinfected with HIV and *M. tuberculosis* in both the U.S. and Africa; it is estimated that by the year 2000 about 500,000 deaths per year will occur in coinfected patients worldwide.

Persons with a positive tuberculin skin test and HIV infection, and persons with a positive tuberculin skin test and at risk of acquiring HIV infection with unknown HIV status should be considered for tuberculosis preventive therapy regardless of age. One study showed that isoniazid prophylaxis in HIV-infected, tuberculin-positive individuals not only decreased the incidence of tuberculosis disease, but also delayed the progression to AIDS and death.

Twelve months of preventive therapy is recommended for adults and children with HIV infection and other conditions associated with immunosuppression. Persons with HIV infection should receive at least 6 months of preventive therapy. The American Academy of Pediatrics recommends that children receive 9 months of therapy.

Tuberculosis control programs should ensure that drug susceptibility tests are performed on all initial isolates of *M. tuberculosis* and the results are reported promptly to the primary care provider and the local health department. Tuberculosis control programs should monitor local drug resistance rates to assess the effectiveness of local tuberculosis control efforts and to determine the appropriateness of the currently recommended initial tuberculosis treatment regimen for the area.

Relapse of rifampin-resistant tuberculosis has been reported in HIV-infected patients. Reinfection with new strains of *M. tuberculosis* has also been reported in these patients. Rifampin-resistant tuberculosis is a serious threat because responses to therapy are more difficult to achieve and require long courses of treatment. Therefore, careful follow-up of HIV-infected patients with treated tuberculosis is essential.

Multidrug-resistant tuberculosis also has been transmitted to persons without HIV infection in health care facilities. Together with the lack of effective agents for second-line treatment and methods of prophylaxis, the transmission of multidrug-resistant strains of *M. tuberculosis* may create a substantial reservoir of latently infected people and the potential for clinical multidrug-resistant tuberculosis for many years to come.

Several studies have documented a high prevalence of extrapulmonary disease in HIV-infected patients with clinical tuberculosis disease, particularly in conjunction with pulmonary manifestations. Cutaneous miliary tuberculosis, also known as *tuberculosis cutis miliaris disseminata*, was in the past a rare condition in adults, with only 24 cases reported in nearly a century. However, since the first reported case of cutaneous miliary tuberculosis in 1990 in a patient with AIDS, five additional cases have been reported in HIV-infected patients. Its appearance can be quite nondescript; therefore, a high level of suspicion must be maintained, particularly for patients with CD4+ cell counts of < 200 per cubic millimeter, in order to diagnose the condition and initiate therapy appropriately.

Accepted

Tuberculosis (treatment)—Rifampin and isoniazid combination is indicated in the treatment of pulmonary tuberculosis when the patient has been titrated on the individual components and the efficacy of the combination has been established.

Unaccepted

Rifampin and isoniazid combination is not indicated for initial treatment or prophylaxis of pulmonary tuberculosis, for meningococcal infections, or in the treatment of asymptomatic meningococcal carriers to eliminate *Neisseria meningitidis* from the nasopharynx.

Patient Consultation

As an aid to patient consultation, refer to *Advice for the Patient, Rifampin and Isoniazid (Systemic)*.

In providing consultation, consider emphasizing the following selected information (» = major clinical significance):

Before using this medication

» Conditions affecting use, especially:
- Hypersensitivity to rifampin, isoniazid, ethionamide, pyrazinamide, niacin (nicotinic acid), or other chemically related medications
- Pregnancy—Isoniazid and rifampin cross the placenta. It is recommended that isoniazid and rifampin be used to treat pregnant women with tuberculosis; however, rifampin has rarely caused postnatal hemorrhage in the mother and infant when administered during the last few weeks of pregnancy
- Breast-feeding—Isoniazid and rifampin are distributed into breast milk
- Use in children—Use of the fixed-dose combination is not recommended in pediatric patients
- Use in the elderly—Patients over the age of 50 have the highest incidence of hepatitis

Dental—Patients who develop blood dyscrasias may be at increased risk of microbial infections, delayed healing, and gingival bleeding

Other medicines, especially daily alcohol use, alfentanil, aminophylline, coumarin- or indandione-derivative anticoagulants, oral antidiabetic agents, azole antifungals, carbamazepine, chloramphenicol, corticosteroids, digitalis glycosides, disopyramide, disulfiram, estramustine, estrogens, ketoconazole, other hepatotoxic medications, methadone, mexiletine, oral estrogen-containing contraceptives, oxtriphylline, phenytoin, quinidine, theophylline, tocainide, or verapamil

Other medical problems, especially alcoholism, active or in remission, or hepatic function impairment

Proper use of this medication

Taking this medication with food or antacids, but not within 1 hour of aluminum-containing antacids, if gastrointestinal irritation occurs

» Compliance with full course of therapy, which may take months or years

» Taking pyridoxine concurrently to prevent or minimize symptoms of peripheral neuritis

» Proper dosing

Missed dose: Taking as soon as possible; not taking if almost time for next dose; not doubling doses; intermittent dosing may result in more frequent and/or severe side effects

» Proper storage

Precautions while using this medication

» Regular visits to physician to check progress, as well as ophthalmologic examinations if signs of optic neuritis occur

Checking with physician if no improvement within 2 to 3 weeks

» Using an alternate method of contraception if taking estrogen-containing oral contraceptives concurrently

» Avoiding alcoholic beverages concurrently with this medication

Checking with physician if vascular reactions occur following concurrent ingestion of cheese or fish with isoniazid-containing medications

» Medication causes urine, feces, saliva, sputum, sweat, and tears to turn reddish-orange to reddish-brown and may also permanently discolor soft contact lenses; avoiding the wearing of soft contact lenses

» Need to report to physician promptly prodromal signs of hepatitis or peripheral neuritis

Caution in use of regular toothbrushes, dental floss, and toothpicks; deferring dental work until blood counts have returned to normal; checking with physician or dentist concerning proper oral hygiene

Possible interference with diagnostic tests

Side/adverse effects

Signs of potential side effects, especially blood dyscrasias, hepatitis, hepatitis prodromal symptoms, hypersensitivity, neurotoxicity, optic neuritis, peripheral neuritis, "flu-like" syndrome, and interstitial nephritis

Hepatitis may be more likely to occur in patients over 50 years of age

Reddish-orange to reddish-brown discoloration of urine, stools, saliva, sputum, sweat, and tears may be alarming to patient, although medically insignificant; however, tears discolored by rifampin may also discolor soft contact lenses

Oral Dosage Forms

RIFAMPIN AND ISONIAZID CAPSULES USP

Usual adult and adolescent dose

Tuberculosis—

Oral, 600 mg of rifampin and 300 mg of isoniazid once a day for the entire treatment period.

Usual pediatric dose

Use of the fixed-dose combination is not recommended in pediatric patients.

Note: See individual components for dosage recommendations.

Strength(s) usually available

U.S.—

300 mg of rifampin and 150 mg of isoniazid (Rx) [*Rifamate*].

Canada—

Not commercially available.

Auxiliary labeling

- Continue medicine for full time of treatment.
- Avoid alcoholic beverages.
- May discolor body fluids.

Revised: 08/29/1997

RIFAMPIN, ISONIAZID, AND PYRAZINAMIDE Systemic

VA CLASSIFICATION (Primary): AM500

Commonly used brand name(s): *Rifater*.

NOTE: The *Rifampin, Isoniazid, and Pyrazinamide (Systemic)* monograph is maintained on the *USP DI* electronic data base. A copy of the most recent revision of the complete monograph can be accessed on the *USP DI* Updates Online website. See the front cover of book for details on accessing the site.

For information on the specific components of this combination, see the *USP DI* monographs for *Isoniazid (Systemic)*, *Pyrazinamide (Systemic)*, and *Rifampin (Systemic)*.

The information that follows is selectively abstracted from the complete monograph and is provided to facilitate drug use review and patient counseling.

Note: For a listing of dosage forms and brand names by country availability, see *Dosage Forms* section(s).

Category

Antibacterial (antimycobacterial).

Indications

General Considerations

Tuberculosis is a highly infectious life-threatening bacterial disease with 8 million new cases and 3 million deaths reported worldwide each year to the World Health Organization (WHO). The vast majority of these cases are in developing countries; however, tuberculosis also has emerged as an important public health problem in the U.S. in recent years after the decline in number of cases observed between 1950 and 1980.

The resurgence of tuberculosis in the U.S. has been complicated by an increase in the proportion of patients with strains resistant to antituberculosis medications. Outbreaks of multidrug-resistant tuberculosis have been documented in hospitals and prisons. Drug-resistant tuberculosis, particularly that caused by strains resistant to isoniazid and rifampin, is much harder to treat and often is fatal. Among acquired immunodeficiency syndrome (AIDS) patients infected with tuberculosis bacilli resistant to both rifampin and isoniazid, a case-fatality rate of 91% has been reported. Recent investigations of outbreaks of multidrug-resistant tuberculosis have found an extraordinarily high case-fatality rate, with the median time to mortality being reached between 4 and 16 weeks. In almost all instances, these outbreaks have involved patients with severe immunosuppression by infection with the human immunodeficiency virus (HIV).

Acquired drug resistance develops during treatment for drug-sensitive tuberculosis with regimens that are poorly conceived or poorly complied with, allowing the emergence of naturally occurring drug-resistant mutations. Resistant organisms from affected patients may subsequently infect other people who have not been infected with *Mycobacterium tuberculosis* previously, resulting in primary drug resistance.

Resistance to antituberculosis agents can develop not only in the strain that caused the initial disease, but also as a result of reinfection with a new strain of *M. tuberculosis* that is drug-resistant. Reinfection with a new multidrug-resistant *M. tuberculosis* strain can occur during therapy for the original infection or after completion of therapy. Most recent data suggest that outcomes can be improved if patients promptly begin therapy with two or more drugs that have *in vitro* activity against the multidrug-resistant isolate.

HIV infection is the strongest risk factor yet identified for the development of active tuberculosis disease in persons infected with tuberculosis. In addition, persons with HIV infection are at an increased risk of tuberculosis resulting either from newly acquired disease or from reactivation of latent infections. Tuberculosis is a major clinical manifestation of immunodeficiency induced by HIV. In hospital-based retrospective studies, high rates of tuberculosis have been found among patients with AIDS. In communities where tuberculosis and HIV infection are common, the prevalence of HIV seropositivity among patients with tuberculosis is greatly increasing.

WHO has estimated that 5.6 million people worldwide and 80,000 people in the U.S. are infected with both HIV and tuberculosis. Persons dually infected with *M. tuberculosis* and HIV have a high risk of developing clinically active tuberculosis. One study of HIV-positive drug users with positive tuberculin skin test results found a rate of the development of active tuberculosis to be 8 cases per 100 person-years (8% yearly) as compared with the 10% lifetime risk (1 to 3% risk within the first year after skin test conversion) in the general population.

Persons who are known to be HIV-infected and who are contacts of patients with infectious tuberculosis should be carefully evaluated for evidence of tuberculosis. If there are no findings suggestive of current tuberculosis, preventive therapy with isoniazid should be given. Because HIV-infected contacts are not managed in the same way as those who are not HIV-infected, HIV testing is recommended if there are known or suspected risk factors for their acquiring HIV infection.

According to investigators at the National Institute of Allergy and Infectious Diseases (NIAID), levels of HIV in the bloodstream increase 5- to 160-fold in HIV-infected persons who develop active tuberculosis. Clinical and epidemiologic observations have demonstrated that HIV-infected individuals have an estimated 113-times higher risk and AIDS patients have a 170-times higher risk compared with uninfected persons. Furthermore, the problem of drug resistance may worsen as the HIV epidemic spreads. Immunosuppressed patients with HIV infection who subsequently become infected with *M. tuberculosis* have an extraordinarily high risk of developing active tuberculosis within a short period of time.

In addition to the convincing evidence that HIV infection increases the risk and worsens the course of tuberculosis, there is increasing clinical evidence that coinfection with *M. tuberculosis* accelerates progression of disease caused by HIV infection. Understanding the interaction of these two pathogens is clinically important, given the high prevalence of patients coinfected with HIV and *M. tuberculosis* in both the U.S. and Africa; it is estimated that by the year 2000 about 500,000 deaths per year will occur in coinfected patients worldwide.

Persons with a positive tuberculin skin test and HIV infection, and persons with a positive tuberculin skin test and at risk of acquiring HIV infection with unknown HIV status should be considered for tuberculosis preventive therapy regardless of age. One study showed that isoniazid prophylaxis in HIV-infected, tuberculin-positive individuals not only decreased the incidence of tuberculosis disease, but also delayed the progression to AIDS and death.

Twelve months of preventive therapy is recommended for adults and children with HIV infection and other conditions associated with immunosuppression. Persons with HIV infection should receive at least 6 months of preventive therapy. The American Academy of Pediatrics recommends that children receive 9 months of therapy.

Tuberculosis control programs should ensure that drug susceptibility tests are performed on all initial isolates of *M. tuberculosis* and that the results are reported promptly to the primary care provider and the local health department. Tuberculosis control programs should monitor local drug resistance rates to assess the effectiveness of local tuberculosis control efforts and to determine the appropriateness of the currently recommended initial tuberculosis treatment regimen for the area.

Relapse of rifampin-resistant tuberculosis has been reported in HIV-infected patients. Reinfection with new strains of *M. tuberculosis* has also been reported in these patients. Rifampin-resistant tuberculosis is a serious threat because responses to therapy are more difficult to achieve and require long courses of treatment. Therefore, careful follow-up of HIV-infected patients with treated tuberculosis is essential.

Multidrug-resistant tuberculosis also has been transmitted to persons without HIV infection in health care facilities. Together with the lack of effective agents for second-line treatment and methods of prophylaxis, the transmission of multidrug-resistant strains of *M. tuberculosis* may create a substantial reservoir of latently infected people and the potential for clinical multidrug-resistant tuberculosis for many years to come.

Several studies have documented a high prevalence of extrapulmonary disease in HIV-infected patients with clinical tuberculosis disease, particularly in conjunction with pulmonary manifestations. Cutaneous miliary tuberculosis, also known as *tuberculosis cutis miliaris disseminata*, was in the past a rare condition in adults, with only 24 cases reported in nearly a century. However, since the first reported case of cutaneous miliary tuberculosis in 1990 in a patient with AIDS, five additional cases have been reported in HIV-infected patients. Its appearance can be quite nondescript; therefore, a high level of suspicion must be maintained, particularly for patients with CD4+ cell counts of < 200 per cubic millimeter, in order to diagnose the condition and initiate therapy appropriately.

Accepted

Tuberculosis (treatment)—Rifampin, isoniazid, and pyrazinamide combination is indicated in the initial phase of the short-course treatment of all forms of tuberculosis. During this phase, usually lasting 2 months, rifampin, isoniazid, and pyrazinamide combination should be administered on a daily, continuous basis. Additional medications are indicated if multidrug-resistant tuberculosis is suspected.

Patient Consultation

As an aid to patient consultation, refer to *Advice for the Patient, Rifampin, Isoniazid, and Pyrazinamide (Systemic)*.

In providing consultation, consider emphasizing the following selected information (» = major clinical significance):

Before using this medication

» Conditions affecting use, especially:
- Hypersensitivity to rifampin, isoniazid, pyrazinamide, ethionamide, niacin (nicotinic acid), rifabutin, or other chemically related medications
- Pregnancy—Isoniazid and rifampin cross the placenta
- Breast-feeding—Isoniazid, pyrazinamide, and rifampin are distributed into breast milk
- Use in children—Use of the fixed-dose combination is not recommended in pediatric patients up to 15 years of age
- Use in the elderly—Patients 50 years of age and older have the highest incidence of hepatitis with use of isoniazid
- Other medications, especially daily alcohol consumption, alfentanil, aminophylline, coumarin- or indandione-derivative anticoagulants, oral antidiabetic agents, azole antifungals, carbamazepine, chloramphenicol, oral estrogen-containing contraceptives, corticosteroids, digitalis glycosides, disopyramide, disulfiram, estramustine, estrogens, other hepatotoxic medications, HIV protease inhibitors, ketoconazole, methadone, mexiletine, oxtriphylline, phenytoin, quinidine, theophylline, tocainide, or oral verapamil
- Other medical problems, especially alcoholism, active or in remission, or hepatic function impairment

Proper use of this medication

Taking this medication with food or antacids, but not within 1 hour of aluminum-containing antacids, if gastrointestinal irritation occurs

» Compliance with full course of therapy, which may take months or years

» Taking pyridoxine concurrently to prevent or minimize symptoms of peripheral neuritis

» Proper dosing

Missed dose: Taking as soon as possible; not taking if almost time for next dose; not doubling doses; intermittent dosing may result in more frequent and/or severe side effects

» Proper storage

Precautions while using this medication

» Regular visits to physician to check progress, as well as ophthalmologic examinations if signs of optic neuritis occur

Checking with physician if no improvement within 2 to 3 weeks

» Using an alternate method of contraception if taking estrogen-containing oral contraceptives concurrently

» Avoiding alcoholic beverages while taking this medication

» Checking with physician if vascular reactions occur following concurrent ingestion of cheese or fish with isoniazid-containing medication

» Medication causes urine, feces, saliva, sputum, sweat, and tears to turn reddish-orange to reddish-brown and may also permanently discolor soft contact lenses; avoiding the wearing of soft contact lenses

» Need to report to physician promptly prodromal signs of hepatitis or peripheral neuritis

Using caution in use of regular toothbrushes, dental floss, and toothpicks; deferring dental work until blood counts have returned to normal; checking with physician or dentist concerning proper oral hygiene

Possible interference with diagnostic tests

» Diabetics: May interfere with urine ketone determinations

Side/adverse effects

Hepatitis caused by isoniazid is more likely to occur in patients 50 years of age and older

Reddish-orange to reddish-brown discoloration of urine, stools, saliva, sputum, sweat, and tears may be alarming to patient, although medically insignificant; however, tears discolored by rifampin may also discolor soft contact lenses

Signs of potential side effects, especially arthralgia, hepatitis, hepatitis prodromal symptoms, peripheral neuritis, "flu-like" syndrome, hypersensitivity, blood dyscrasias, interstitial nephritis, neurotoxicity, and optic neuritis

Oral Dosage Forms

RIFAMPIN, ISONIAZID AND PYRAZINAMIDE TABLETS

Note: *Rifater* contains rifampin 120 mg, isoniazid 50 mg, and pyrazinamide 300 mg. However, the World Health Organization (WHO) recommends the fixed-dose combination of rifampin 150 mg, isoniazid 75 mg, and pyrazinamide 400 mg for the daily administration in the initial phase of tuberculosis treatment. The WHO also recommends the fixed-dose combination of rifampin 150 mg, isoniazid 150 mg, and pyrazinamide 500 mg for intermittent (3 times weekly) administration during the continuation phase of tuberculosis treatment. Neither of these WHO-recommended fixed-dose combinations are commercially available in the U.S.

Usual adult dose

Tuberculosis—

Patients weighing 44 kg or less: Oral, 4 tablets once a day.

Patients weighing between 45 and 54 kg: Oral, 5 tablets once a day.

Patients weighing 55 kg or more: Oral, 6 tablets once a day.

Usual pediatric dose

Tuberculosis—

Children and adolescents up to 15 years of age: Use of the fixed-dose combination is not recommended.

Adolescents 15 years of age and older: See *Usual adult dose*.

Note: See individual components for dosage recommendations.

Strength(s) usually available

U.S.—

120 mg rifampin, 50 mg isoniazid, and 300 mg pyrazinamide (Rx) [*Rifater*].

Canada—

Not commercially available.

Auxiliary labeling

- Continue taking the medicine for full time of treatment.
- Avoid alcoholic beverages.
- May discolor body fluids.

Revised: 09/17/1998

RIFAXIMIN Oral-Local†

VA CLASSIFICATION (Primary/Secondary): GA208/AM900

Commonly used brand name(s): *Xifaxan*.

Note: For a listing of dosage forms and brand names by country availability, see *Dosage Forms* section(s).

†Not commercially available in Canada.

Category

Antidiarrheal; antibacterial (non-systemic).

Indications

Accepted

Diarrhea (treatment)—Rifaximin is indicated for the treatment of patients ≥ 12 years of age with travelers' diarrhea caused by noninvasive strains of *Escherichia coli*.

Unaccepted

Rifaximin should not be used if diarrhea is accompanied by fever, blood in the stool or diarrhea due to pathogens other than *Escherichia coli*.

Pharmacology/Pharmacokinetics

Physicochemical characteristics

Source—Rifaximin is a semi-synthetic, non-systemic antibiotic.

Molecular weight—Rifaximin: 785.9.

Mechanism of action/Effect

Rifaximin inhibits bacterial RNA synthesis by binding to the beta-subunit of bacterial DNA-dependent RNA polymerase.

Absorption

Poorly absorbed from the gastrointestinal tract.

Distribution

80 to 90% in the gut, less than 0.2% in the liver and kidney and less than 0.01% in other tissues after oral administration.

Biotransformation

Rifaximin did not inhibit hepatic cytochrome P450 isoenzymes: 1A2, 2A6, 2B6, 2C9, 2C19, 2D6, 2E1 and 3A4. However, it did induce cytochrome P450 3A4 in an *in vitro* hepatocyte induction model.

Peak plasma concentration:

- 0.81 to 3.4 ng/mL (range) on Day 1 after 3 consecutive doses.
- 0.68 to 2.26 ng/mL (range) on Day 3 after 9 consecutive doses.

Elimination

Fecal—almost exclusively and completely as unchanged drug.

Renal—0.32% of dose.

Precautions to Consider

Carcinogenicity

Carcinogenicity studies with rifaximin have not been done.

Mutagenicity

Rifaximin was not genotoxic in the bacterial reverse mutation assay, chromosomal aberration assay, rat bone marrow micronucleus assay, and the CHO/HGPRT mutation assay.

Pregnancy/Reproduction

Fertility—Reproduction studies in rats have shown that rifaximin administered in doses up to 300 milligrams per kilogram (approximately 5 times the clinical dose, adjusted for body surface area) does not effect fertility.

Pregnancy—Adequate and well controlled studies in pregnant women have not been done. Studies in animals have shown that rifaximin causes adverse effects in the fetus. Rifaximin should be used during pregnancy only if the potential benefit outweighs the potential risk to the fetus.

Rifaximin was teratogenic in rats at doses (approximately 2.5 to 5 times the clinical dose, adjusted for body surface area), and in rabbits at doses (approximately 2 to 33 times the clinical dose, adjusted for body surface area). The effects included cleft palate, agnatha, jaw shortening, hemorrhage, eye partially open, small eyes, brachygnathia, incomplete ossification, and increased thoracolumbar vertebrae.

FDA Pregnancy Category C

Breast-feeding

It is not known if rifaximin is distributed into breast milk. Because many drug are distributed in human milk and because of the potential for adverse reactions in nursing infants, a decision should be made whether to discontinue nursing or to discontinue treatment with rifaximin.

Pediatrics

The safety and effectiveness of rifaximin in pediatric patients under 12 years of age have not been established.

Geriatrics

No information is available on the relationship of age to the effects of rifaximin in geriatric patients.

Pharmacogenetics

The effects of gender on the pharmacokinetics of rifaximin have not been studied.

Medical considerations/Contraindications

The medical considerations/contraindications included have been selected on the basis of their potential clinical significance (reasons given in parentheses where appropriate)—not necessarily inclusive (» = major clinical significance).

Except under special circumstances, this medication should not be used when the following medical problem exists:

» Hypersensitivity to rifaximin, any of the rifamycin antimicrobial agents, or any of the components in the tablet.

Patient monitoring

The following may be especially important in patient monitoring (other tests may be warranted in some patients, depending on condition; » = major clinical significance):

» Pseudomembranous colitis
(monitor patient for development of diarrhea subsequent to rifaximin therapy)

Side/Adverse Effects

The following side/adverse effects have been selected on the basis of their potential clinical significance (possible signs and symptoms in parentheses where appropriate)—not necessarily inclusive:

Those indicating need for medical attention

Incidence not determined—Observed during clinical practice; estimates of frequency cannot be determined

Hypersensitivity reactions including; allergic dermatitis (skin rash, hives, itching, or redness); ***angioneurotic edema*** (large, hive-like swelling on face, eyelids, lips, tongue, throat, hands, legs, feet, sex organs); ***pruritus*** (itching skin); ***rash; urticaria*** (hives or welts; itching; redness of skin; skin rash)

Those indicating need for medical attention only if they continue or are bothersome

Incidence more frequent

Headache

Incidence less frequent

Constipation (difficulty having a bowel movement (stool)); ***vomiting***

Overdose

For more information on the management of overdose or unintentional ingestion, **contact a poison control center** (see *Poison Control Center Listing*).

Treatment of overdose

There is no known specific antidote to rifaximin. Treatment is generally symptomatic and supportive.

Supportive care—

Patients in whom intentional overdose is confirmed or suspected should be referred for psychiatric consultation.

Patient Consultation

As an aid to patient consultation, refer to *Advice for the Patient, Rifaximin (Oral-Local)*.

In providing consultation, consider emphasizing the following selected information (» = major clinical significance):

Before using this medication

» Conditions affecting use, especially:

Hypersensitivity to rifaximin, any of the rifamycin antimicrobial agents, or any of the components in the tablet.

Pregnancy—Not recommended for use during pregnancy

Breast-feeding—It is not known if rifaximin is distributed in human milk. Because many drugs are distributed in human milk, and because of the potential for adverse reactions in nursing infants, a decision should be made whether to discontinue nursing or to discontinue treatment with rifaximin.

Use in children—Safety and effectiveness of rifaximin in pediatric patients under 12 years of age have not been established.

Other medical problems, especially pseudomembranous colitis.

Proper use of this medication

» Not using if diarrhea is accompanied by fever or blood in the stool; contacting physician.

» Proper dosing

Missed dose: Taking as soon as possible; not taking if almost time for next scheduled dose; not doubling doses.

» Proper storage

Precautions while using this medication

» Consulting physician if diarrhea is not controlled within 48 hours and/or fever develops.

Side/adverse effects

Signs of potential side effects, especially hypersensitivity reactions including allergic dermatitis, angioneurotic edema, pruritus, rash or urticaria.

General Dosing Information

No adjustment in dose is required in patients with hepatic impairment.

Rifaximin tablets may be taken with or without food.

The use of antibiotics may promote the overgrowth of nonsusceptible organisms. Should superinfection occur during therapy, appropriate measures should be taken.

Rifaximin is not effective in patients with diarrhea complicated by fever and/or blood in the stool or pathogens other than *Escherichia coli*.

Rifaximin should not be used in patients where *Campylobacter jejuni*, *Shigella spp.*, or *Salmonella spp.* is suspected to be the causative agent.

In patients where diarrhea symptoms get worse or persist more than 24 to 48 hours, rifaximin should be discontinued and alternative antibiotic therapy should be considered.

For treatment of adverse effects

Pseudomembranous colitis—Mild cases usually respond to drug discontinuation alone. In moderate to severe cases, consideration should be given to management with fluids and electrolytes, protein supplementation, and treatment with an antibacterial drug clinically effective against *Clostridium difficile*.

Oral Dosage Forms

RIFAXIMIN TABLETS

Usual adult and adolescent dose

Diarrhea—

Oral, 200 mg tablet taken three times a day for 3 days.

Usual pediatric dose

Safety and efficacy in pediatric patients below 12 years of age have not been established.

Usual geriatric dose

See *Usual adult and adolescent dose.*

Strength(s) usually available

U.S.—

200 mg (Rx) [*Xifaxan* (colloidal silicon dioxide; disodium edetate; glycerol palmitostearate; hypromellose; microcrystalline cellulose; propylene glycol; red iron oxide; sodium starch glycolate; talc; titanium dioxide)].

Canada—

Not commercially available.

Packaging and storage

Store between 20 and 25°C (68 and 77°F), in a tight container; excursions permitted between 15 and 30°C (59 and 86°F).

Auxiliary labeling

- This medication can be taken with of without food.

Developed: 08/31/2004

RIMANTADINE Systemic†

VA CLASSIFICATION (Primary): AM890

Commonly used brand name(s): *Flumadine*.

Note: For a listing of dosage forms and brand names by country availability, see *Dosage Forms* section(s).

†Not commercially available in Canada.

Category

Antiviral (systemic).

Indications

Accepted

Influenza A (prophylaxis and treatment)—Rimantadine is indicated for the prophylaxis of respiratory tract infections caused by influenza A virus in adults and children, and the treatment of respiratory tract infections caused by influenza A virus in adults.

Influenza A virus strains that are resistant to amantadine or rimantadine are cross-resistant to the other medication.

Although rimantadine is structurally similar to amantadine, differing only in the 10-carbon ring side chain, rimantadine, unlike amantadine, is not effective in the control of Parkinson's disease.

Pharmacology/Pharmacokinetics

Physicochemical characteristics

Molecular weight—215.77.

Mechanism of action/Effect

Rimantadine is thought to exert its inhibitory effect early in the viral replicative cycle, possibly by blocking or greatly reducing the uncoating of viral RNA within host cells. Genetic studies suggest that a single amino acid change on the transmembrane portion of the M2 protein can completely eliminate influenza A virus' susceptibility to rimantadine.

Absorption

Well absorbed; tablets and syrup are absorbed equally well after oral administration.

Distribution

Vol_D—

Adults: 17 to 25 L/kg.

Children: Mean of 289 L.

Concentrations in the nasal mucus average 50% higher than those in plasma.

Protein binding
Moderate (approximately 40%).

Biotransformation
Extensively metabolized in the liver; glucuronidation and hydroxylation are the major metabolic pathways.

Half-life
Young adults (22 to 44 years old)—25 to 30 hours.
Older adults (71 to 79 years old) and patients with chronic liver disease—Approximately 32 hours.
Children (4 to 8 years old)—13 to 38 hours.

Time to peak concentration
1 to 4 hours.

Peak serum concentration
Steady state—
100 mg once a day: Approximately 181 nanograms per mL.
100 mg twice a day: Approximately 416 nanograms per mL.
Rimantadine concentrations in elderly nursing home patients were found to be nearly 3 times those of younger adults.

Elimination
Renal; > 90% recovered in the urine within 72 hours, mostly as metabolites. Less than 25% excreted in urine as unchanged drug.
In dialysis—Hemodialysis has a negligible effect on the clearance of rimantadine.

Precautions to Consider

Cross-sensitivity and/or related problems
Patients who are hypersensitive to amantadine may also be hypersensitive to rimantadine.

Carcinogenicity
Carcinogenicity studies in animals have not been performed.

Mutagenicity
No mutagenic effects were seen when rimantadine was evaluated in several standard mutagenicity assays.

Pregnancy/Reproduction
Fertility—A study in male and female rats given doses of up to 60 mg per kg of body weight (mg/kg) per day (3 times the maximum human dose based on body surface area comparisons) showed no impairment of fertility.

Pregnancy—Adequate and well-controlled studies in humans have not been done.
Rimantadine crosses the placenta in mice. It has been shown to be embryotoxic in rats when given at a dose of 200 mg/kg per day (11 times the maximum human dose based on body surface area comparisons), and has caused fetal resorption. Maternal toxicity included ataxia, tremors, seizures, and significantly reduced weight gain. Rimantadine was not embryotoxic when given to rabbits in doses of up to 50 mg/kg per day (5 times the maximum human dose based on body surface area comparisons). However, there was evidence of a change in the ratio of fetuses with 12 ribs to fetuses with 13 ribs; normally the ratio is 50:50 in a litter, but the ratio was 80:20 after rimantadine treatment.

FDA Pregnancy Category C.

Breast-feeding
It is not known whether rimantadine is distributed into breast milk. However, it is distributed into the milk of rats. Rimantadine concentrations in the milk of rats were twice those found in serum 2 to 3 hours after administration.

Pediatrics
Appropriate studies on the relationship of age to the effects of rimantadine have not been performed in neonates and infants up to one year of age. However, use of rimantadine in children older than I year of age has not been shown to cause any pediatrics-specific problems that would limit its usefulness in children.

Geriatrics
Elderly patients, particularly those in chronic care facilities, are more likely than younger adults or children to experience adverse effects associated with rimantadine, primarily central nervous system (CNS) and gastrointestinal side effects.

Drug interactions and/or related problems
The following drug interactions and/or related problems have been selected on the basis of their potential clinical significance (possible mechanism in parentheses where appropriate)—not necessarily inclusive (» = major clinical significance):

Note: Combinations containing any of the following medications, depending on the amount present, may also interact with this medication.

Acetaminophen or
Aspirin
(concurrent use of acetaminophen or aspirin with rimantadine reduces the peak serum concentration of rimantadine by approximately 11%; the clinical significance is thought to be minimal at this time)

Cimetidine
(concurrent use of a single dose of rimantadine with cimetidine reduces rimantadine clearance by 18% in healthy adults; the clinical significance is thought to be minimal at this time)

Medical considerations/Contraindications
The medical considerations/contraindications included have been selected on the basis of their potential clinical significance (reasons given in parentheses where appropriate)—not necessarily inclusive (» = major clinical significance).

Risk-benefit should be considered when the following medical problems exist:
» Epilepsy, history of, or other seizure disorders
(amantadine increases the risk of seizures; seizures have also been reported with rimantadine in 2 patients with a history of seizures who had previously been withdrawn from their anticonvulsants)

» Hepatic function impairment
(a single-dose study done in patients with severe liver dysfunction showed a reduction in rimantadine clearance by 50% compared to healthy subjects)

Hypersensitivity to amantadine or rimantadine
» Renal function impairment, severe
(a single-dose study done in patients with end-stage renal failure showed a reduction in rimantadine clearance by 40%, and an increase in elimination half-life by 60%, compared to healthy subjects; a dosage reduction is recommended in patients with a creatinine clearance of ≤ 10 mL/min [0.17 mL/second])

Side/Adverse Effects

Note: Rimantadine has fewer CNS side effects than does amantadine. Elderly patients have a higher incidence of side effects, primarily CNS and gastrointestinal side effects, than do younger patients at conventional doses.

The following side/adverse effects have been selected on the basis of their potential clinical significance (possible signs and symptoms in parentheses where appropriate)—not necessarily inclusive:

Those indicating need for medical attention only if they continue or are bothersome
Incidence less frequent
CNS effects (difficulty in concentrating; difficulty in sleeping; dizziness; headache; nervousness; unusual tiredness); ***gastrointestinal disturbances*** (dryness of mouth; loss of appetite; nausea; stomach pain; vomiting)

Patient Consultation

As an aid to patient consultation, refer to *Advice for the Patient, Rimantadine (Systemic)*.
In providing consultation, consider emphasizing the following selected information (» = major clinical significance):

Before using this medication
» Conditions affecting use, especially:
Hypersensitivity to amantadine or rimantadine
Pregnancy—High doses were embryotoxic and maternotoxic in rats
Other medical problems, especially epilepsy or a history of seizures, liver function impairment and renal function impairment

Proper use of this medication
» Receiving a flu shot if recommended by your doctor
» Taking before exposure or as soon as possible after exposure
» Compliance with full course of therapy
» Importance of not missing doses and taking at evenly spaced times
Proper administration technique for oral liquid
» Proper dosing
Missed dose: Taking as soon as possible; not taking if almost time for next dose; not doubling doses
» Proper storage

Precautions while using this medication
Caution if dizziness occurs
Checking with physician if no improvement within a few days

General Dosing Information

Chemoprophylactic administration should be started in anticipation of contact with, or as soon as possible after exposure to, persons having influenza A virus infections. Administration should be continued for at least 10 days following exposure. During an influenza epidemic, rimantadine should be given daily, usually for 6 to 8 weeks in most communities or until active immunity can be expected from administration of inactivated influenza A virus vaccine. Rimantadine has been reported to be effective for post-exposure prophylaxis of household contacts, but appeared to be less effective when used prophylactically in members of households in which index cases were being treated concurrently for influenza A. Failure was apparently due to transmission of drug-resistant strains of the virus.

If administered concurrently with inactivated influenza A virus vaccine until protective antibodies develop, rimantadine should be continued chemoprophylactically for 2 to 3 weeks after the vaccine has been administered. However, since the vaccine is only 70 to 80% effective, continued administration of rimantadine may be beneficial in elderly or high-risk patients. If the vaccine is unavailable or contraindicated, rimantadine should be administered for up to 90 days in cases of possible repeated or unknown exposure.

Treatment of influenza A virus infection with rimantadine should be started within 24 to 48 hours after the onset of symptoms and should be continued for 5 to 7 days. Optimal duration of therapy has not been established.

Oral Dosage Forms

RIMANTADINE HYDROCHLORIDE SYRUP

Usual adult and adolescent dose

Antiviral—

Prophylaxis: Oral, 100 mg two times a day.

Treatment: Oral, 100 mg two times a day for approximately five to seven days from the inital onset of symptoms.

Note: In adults with impaired renal function (creatinine clearance ≤ 10 mL/minute [0.17 mL/second]) or severe hepatic dysfunction, and in elderly nursing home patients, a dose of 100 mg once a day is recommended.

Although the manufacturer recommends twice-a-day dosing, once-a-day dosing has been well-tolerated and as effective because of the long elimination half-life of rimantadine.

Usual pediatric dose

Antiviral—Prophylaxis:—

Children up to 10 years of age: Oral, 5 mg per kg of body weight once a day. Maximum daily dose should not exceed 150 mg.

Children 10 years of age and over: See *Usual adult and adolescent dose*.

Strength(s) usually available

U.S.—

100 mg per 5 mL (Rx) [*Flumadine* (methylparaben; propylparaben; sodium saccharin)].

Canada—

Not commercially available.

Packaging and storage

Store below 40 °C (104 °F), preferably between 15 and 30 °C (59 and 86 °F), unless otherwise specified by manufacturer.

Auxiliary labeling

- Continue medicine for full time of treatment.

RIMANTADINE HYDROCHLORIDE TABLETS

Usual adult and adolescent dose

See *Rimantadine Hydrochloride Syrup.*

Usual pediatric dose

See *Rimantadine Hydrochloride Syrup.*

Strength(s) usually available

U.S.—

100 mg (Rx) [*Flumadine*].

Canada—

Not commercially available.

Packaging and storage

Store below 40 °C (104 °F), preferably between 15 and 30 °C (59 and 86 °F), unless otherwise specified by manufacturer.

Auxiliary labeling

- Continue medicine for full time of treatment.

Developed: 03/29/1994

RISEDRONATE Systemic

VA CLASSIFICATION (Primary): HS303

Commonly used brand name(s): *Actonel.*

Note: For a listing of dosage forms and brand names by country availability, see *Dosage Forms* section(s).

Category

Bone resorption inhibitor.

Indications

Accepted

Osteoporosis, glucocorticoid-induced (prophylaxis and treatment)[1]—Risedronate is indicated for the prevention and treatment of glucocorticoid-induced osteoporosis in men and women who are either initiating or continuing systemic glucocorticoid treatment for chronic diseases.

Osteoporosis, postmenopausal (prophylaxis)—Risedronate is indicated for the prevention of osteoporosis in postmenopausal women. It may be considered in postmenopausal women who are at risk of developing osteoporosis and for whom the desired clinical outcome is to maintain bone mass and to reduce the risk of fracture.

Osteoporosis, postmenopausal (treatment)—Risedronate is indicated for the treatment of postmenopausal osteoporosis in women. It increases the bone mineral density and reduces the incidence of vertebral fractures and a composite endpoint of nonvertebral osteoporosis fractures.

Paget's disease of bone (treatment)—Risedronate is indicated for the treatment of Paget's disease of bone (osteitis deformans) in patients with alkaline phosphatase concentrations that are at least two times the upper limit of normal, those who are symptomatic, or those at risk for future complications from the disease. Signs and symptoms of Paget's disease may include bone pain, deformity, and/or fractures; increased concentrations of *N*-telopeptide of type I collagen, serum alkaline phosphatase, and/or urinary hydroxyproline; neurologic disorders associated with skull lesions and spinal deformities; and elevated cardiac output and other vascular disorders associated with increased vascularity of bones.

Acceptance not established

Safety and efficacy have been demonstrated in clinical studies in men receiving risedronate both for Paget's disease and for treatment and prevention of glucocorticoid-induced osteoporosis. However, the safety and effectiveness in men for osteoporosis due to other causes have not been established.

[1]Not included in Canadian product labeling.

Pharmacology/Pharmacokinetics

Physicochemical characteristics

Chemical Group—A pyridinyl bisphosphonate.

Molecular weight—

Anhydrous: 305.1.

Hemi-pentahydrate: 350.13.

Solubility—Soluble in water and in aqueous solutions, and essentially insoluble in common organic solvents.

Mechanism of action/Effect

Risedronate binds to bone hydroxyapatite and, at the cellular level, inhibits osteoclasts. Although the osteoclasts adhere normally to the bone surface, they show evidence of reduced active resorption (e.g., lack of ruffled border). Evidence from studies in rats and dogs indicates that risedronate treatment reduces bone turnover (activation frequency, i.e., the number of sites at which bone is remodeled) and bone resorption at remodeling sites.

Absorption

Rapid and independent of dose, occurring throughout the upper gastrointestinal tract. Mean oral bioavailability is 0.63% and is decreased when administered with food. Administration either 0.5 hour before breakfast or 2 hours after dinner reduces the extent of absorption by 55% compared to the fasting state (no food or drink for 10 hours before or 4 hours after administration). Administration 1 hour before breakfast reduces the extent of absorption by 30% compared with the fasting state.

Distribution

Studies in rats and dogs with intravenously administered single doses of radiolabeled risedronate showed that approximately 60% of the dose was distributed to bone.

The mean steady-state volume of distribution is 6.3 liters per kg of body weight in humans.

Protein binding

Plasma—Low (about 24%).

Biotransformation

There is no evidence that risedronate is metabolized in humans or animals.

Half-life

Initial—
Approximately 1.5 hours.
Terminal exponential—
480 hours (which may represent the dissociation of risedronate from the surface of bone).

Time to peak concentration

1 hour.

Time to peak effect

3 months in one study.

Duration of action

At least 16 months in one study.

Elimination

Fecal, unabsorbed drug (unchanged).

Renal, unchanged, approximately 50% of the absorbed dose within 24 hours, 85% over 28 days. Mean renal clearance is 105 mL per minute (mL/min) and mean total clearance is 122 mL/min, the difference primarily reflecting nonrenal clearance or clearance due to adsorption to bone.

Note: Renal clearance is not concentration-dependent and there is a linear relationship between renal clearance and creatinine clearance.

Precautions to Consider

Carcinogenicity

No significant drug-induced tumor findings were observed in male or female rats in a 104-week carcinogenicity study when rats were administered daily oral doses up to 24 mg per kg of body weight per day (approximately 7.7 times the maximum recommended human daily dose of 30 mg based on surface area) or in male or female mice in an 80-week carcinogenicity study when mice were administered daily oral doses up to 32 mg per kg of body weight per day (approximately 6.4 times the maximum recommended human daily dose of 30 mg based on surface area).

Mutagenicity

Risedronate was not found to be mutagenic in a number of assays, including *in vitro* bacterial mutagenesis in *Salmonella* and *Escherichia coli* (Ames assay), mammalian cell mutagenesis in CHO/HGPRT assay, unscheduled DNA synthesis in rat hepatocytes, and an assessment of chromosomal aberrations *in vivo* in rat bone marrow. Positive results were obtained in a chromosomal aberration assay in CHO cells at highly cytotoxic concentrations (> 675 mcg per mL, survival of 6% to 7%); however, when the assay was repeated at doses exhibiting appropriate cell survival (29%), there was no evidence of chromosomal damage.

Pregnancy/Reproduction

Fertility—Studies in female rats at oral doses of 16 mg per kg of body weight (mg/kg) per day (approximately five times the human 30-mg dose on a mg per square meter of body surface area [mg/m^2] basis) found inhibition of ovulation. At doses of 7 and 16 mg/kg per day (two and five times the human 30-mg dose on a mg/m^2 basis), decreased implantation was noted. Studies in male rats at doses of 40 mg/kg per day (13 times the human 30-mg dose on a mg/m^2 basis) found testicular and epididymal atrophy and inflammation. Studies in male dogs at a dose of 8 mg/kg per day (approximately eight times the human 30-mg dose on a mg/m^2 basis) found moderate to severe spermatid maturation block after 13 weeks. Studies in male rats at doses of 16 mg/kg per day (five times the human 30-mg dose on a mg/m^2 basis) found testicular atrophy after 13 weeks. Findings tended to show an increased severity with increased dose and exposure time.

Pregnancy—Adequate and well-controlled studies in humans have not been done. Risedronate should be used during pregnancy only if the potential benefit justifies the potential risk to the mother and fetus.

Bisphosphonates are incorporated into the bone matrix, from which they are gradually released over periods of weeks to years. The amount of bisphosphonate incorporation into adult bone, and hence, the amount available for release back into the systemic circulation, is directly related to the dose and duration of bisphosphonate use. There are no data on fetal risk in humans. However, there is a theoretical risk of fetal harm, predominantly skeletal, if a woman becomes pregnant after completing a course of bisphosphonate therapy. The impact of variables such as time between cessation of bisphosphonate therapy to conception, the particular bisphosphonate used, and the route of administration (intravenous versus oral) on this risk has not been studied.

Studies in rats at doses of 16 and 80 mg/kg per day (5 and 27 times the human 30-mg dose on a mg/m^2 basis) during gestation found decreased survival of neonates. Body weight was increased in neonates from dams treated with 7.1 and 16 mg/kg (two and five times the human 30-mg dose on a mg/m^2 basis), but decreased in neonates from dams treated with 80 mg/kg (27 times the human 30-mg dose based on a mg/m^2 basis). In rats treated during gestation, the number of fetuses exhibiting incomplete ossification of sternebrae or skull was statistically significantly decreased at 3.2 mg/kg per day, but increased at 7.1 mg/kg per day (one and two times the human 30-mg dose on a mg/m^2 basis). Statistically significant decreases in the number of fetuses exhibiting unossified fetal sternebrae occurred at these same doses. In rats treated with 16 and 80 mg/kg per day (5 and 27 times the human 30-mg dose on a mg/m^2 basis), both incomplete ossification and the number of unossified sternebrae were increased. When female rats were treated with 3.2 and 7.1 mg/kg per day (one and two times the human 30-mg dose on a mg/m^2 basis), a low incidence of cleft palate was observed in fetuses. Studies in rabbits at doses of up to 10 mg/kg per day during gestation (seven times the human 30-mg dose on a mg/m^2 basis) found no significant fetal ossification effects. However, in rabbits treated with 10 mg/kg per day, 1 of 14 litters was aborted and 1 of 14 litters was delivered prematurely.

Like other bisphosphonates, risedronate in doses as low as 3.2 mg/kg per day (equal to the human 30-mg dose on a mg/m^2 basis) during mating and gestation has resulted in periparturient hypocalcemia and mortality in pregnant rats allowed to deliver.

FDA Pregnancy Category C.

Breast-feeding

It is not known whether risedronate passes into human breast milk. However, a small degree of lacteal transfer has been detected in lactating rats for a 24-hour period post dosing. A decision should be made whether to discontinue nursing or to discontinue the drug, taking into account the importance of the drug to the mother, because of the potential for serious adverse reactions in nursing infants from bisphosphonates.

Pediatrics

Studies on the relationship of age to the effects of risedronate in pediatric patients (younger than 18 years of age) have not been done. Safety and efficacy have not been established.

Geriatrics

Studies indicate that bioavailability and disposition of risedronate are similar in patients older than 60 years of age to those in younger adults. No dosage adjustment is necessary.

Dental

Patients undergoing dental procedures and receiving risedronate treatment may be at increased risk for osteonecrosis, primarily of the jaw. Most cases of osteonecrosis have been in cancer patients undergoing dental procedures such as tooth extraction.

Drug interactions and/or related problems

The following drug interactions and/or related problems have been selected on the basis of their potential clinical significance (possible mechanism in parentheses where appropriate)—not necessarily inclusive (» = major clinical significance):

Note: Combinations containing any of the following medications, depending on the amount present, may also interact with this medication.

» Antacids containing calcium or
» Calcium-containing preparations
(simultaneous use may interfere with the absorption of risedronate)

Anti-inflammatory agents, nonsteroidal or
Aspirin
(concurrent use may result in increased gastrointestinal irritation)

Laboratory value alterations

The following have been selected on the basis of their potential clinical significance (possible effect in parentheses where appropriate)—not necessarily inclusive (» = major clinical significance).

With diagnostic test results
Bone imaging
(bisphosphonates are known to interfere with the use of bone imaging agents)

With physiology/laboratory test values
Calcium and
Phosphorus
(small, asymptomatic decreases in serum concentrations have occurred in some patients)
Liver function tests
(abnormal values are rare [incidence less than 0.1%])

Medical considerations/Contraindications

The medical considerations/contraindications included have been selected on the basis of their potential clinical significance (reasons given in parentheses where appropriate)—not necessarily inclusive (» = major clinical significance).

Except under special circumstances, this medication should not be used when the following medical problems exist:

» Hypersensitivity to risedronate or any component of the product

» Hypocalcemia
(disturbances of bone and mineral metabolism, especially hypocalcemia, should be effectively treated before starting risedronate therapy)

» Inability to stand or sit upright for at least 30 minutes
(patient must take risedronate in an upright position and not lie down for 30 minutes after taking this medicine to facilitate delivery to the stomach and reduce the potential for esophageal irritation)

Risk-benefit should be considered when the following medical problems exist:

Gastrointestinal disorders, upper
(bisphosphonates may cause upper gastrointestinal disorders such as dysphagia, esophagitis, esophageal ulcer, and gastric ulcer; caution is recommended with use of risedronate in these conditions)

» Renal function impairment, severe
(renal clearance is significantly decreased [by about 70%] in patients with creatinine clearance of approximately 30 mL per minute [mL/min]; use is not recommended in patients with creatinine clearance less than 30 mL/min; no dosage adjustment is necessary when creatinine clearance is 30 mL/min or higher)

Patient monitoring

The following may be especially important in patient monitoring (other tests may be warranted in some patients, depending on condition; » = major clinical significance):

» Alkaline phosphatase, serum values
(determinations recommended to confirm effectiveness of risedronate therapy)

Side/Adverse Effects

The following side/adverse effects have been selected on the basis of their potential clinical significance (possible signs and symptoms in parentheses where appropriate)—not necessarily inclusive:

Those indicating need for medical attention

Incidence more frequent (incidence 11.5%)
Abdominal or stomach pain; skin rash

Note: *Abdominal or stomach pain* may be associated with dysphagia, esophagitis, esophageal ulcers, or gastric ulcer.

Incidence less frequent (incidence 3 to 5%)
Belching; bone pain; colitis (abdominal or stomach pain, severe; cramping)

Note: *Belching* may be a symptom of esophagitis.

Incidence rare
Iritis, acute (red, sore eyes); ***neoplasm*** (tumor)

Those indicating need for medical attention only if they continue or are bothersome

Incidence more frequent (incidence 18 to 33%)
Arthralgia (joint pain); ***back pain; diarrhea; headache; infection*** (fever or chills; cough or hoarseness; lower back or side pain; painful or difficult urination)

Incidence less frequent (incidence 3 to 10%)
Amblyopia (blurred vision or a change in vision); ***asthenia*** (weakness); ***bronchitis*** (cough); ***chest pain; constipation; dizziness; dry eyes; dyspepsia*** (acid or sour stomach; belching; heartburn; indigestion; stomach discomfort, upset, or pain); ***flu-like syndrome*** (fever; general feeling of discomfort or illness); ***hypertension*** (blurred vision; dizziness; nervousness; headache; pounding in the ears; slow or fast heartbeat); ***joint disorder*** (difficulty in moving; muscle pain or stiffness; pain, swelling, or redness in joints); ***leg cramps; myasthenia*** (weakness); ***nausea; pain; peripheral edema*** (swelling of feet or lower legs); ***pharyngitis*** (body aches or pain; congestion; cough; dryness or soreness of throat; fever; hoarseness; runny nose; tender, swollen glands in neck; trouble in swallowing; voice changes); ***sinusitis*** (headache); ***tinnitus*** (ringing in the ears); ***urinary tract infection*** (bladder pain; bloody or cloudy urine; difficult, burning, or painful urination; frequent urge to urinate; lower back or side pain)

Incidence rare (incidence less than 3%)
Anemia (pale skin; troubled breathing with exertion; unusual bleeding or bruising; unusual tiredness or weakness); ***anxiety*** (fear; nervousness); ***bursitis*** (pain and inflammation at the joints); ***duodenitis*** (abdominal discomfort); ***gastrointestinal disorder*** (diarrhea; loss of appetite; nausea or vomiting; stomach pain, fullness, or discomfort; indigestion; passing of gas); ***glossitis*** (redness, swelling, or soreness of tongue); ***pneumonia*** (chest pain; cough; fever or chills; sneezing; shortness of breath; sore throat; troubled breathing; tightness in chest; wheezing); ***pruritus*** (itching skin); ***syncope*** (fainting); ***vomiting***

Incidence not determined—Observed during clinical practice; estimates of frequency can not be determined
Hypersensitivity and skin reactions including; angioedema (large, hive-like swelling on face, eyelids, lips, tongue, throat, hands, legs, feet, sex organs); ***bullous skin reactions*** (skin blisters); ***or rash, generalized; muscle pain***

Overdose

For more specific information on the agents used in the management of risedronate overdose, see:
- *Calcium Supplements (Systemic)* monograph.

For more information on the management of overdose or unintentional ingestion, **contact a Poison Control Center** (see *Poison Control Center Listing*).

Clinical effects of overdose

Although overdose with risedronate has not been reported, decreases in serum calcium (including signs and symptoms of hypocalcemia) would be expected to occur with substantial overdose in some patients.

Treatment of overdose

To decrease absorption—Gastric lavage may remove unabsorbed drug. Administration of milk or antacids to chelate risedronate may be helpful.

Specific treatment—Standard procedures for treatment of hypocalcemia, including administration of intravenous calcium, would be expected to restore physiologic amounts of ionized calcium and to relieve signs and symptoms of hypocalcemia.

Patient Consultation

As an aid to patient consultation, refer to *Advice for the Patient, Risedronate (Systemic)*.

In providing consultation, consider emphasizing the following selected information (» = major clinical significance):

Before using this medication

» Conditions affecting use, especially:
Hypersensitivity to risedronate or any component of the product
Pregnancy—Studies in animals showed decreased weight gain, incomplete fetal ossification, and decreased survival of the fetus
Breast-feeding—Distributed into milk in lactating rats; risk-benefit should be considered
Dental—Patients undergoing dental procedures and receiving risedronate may be at increased risk for osteonecrosis of the jaw.
Other medications, especially calcium-containing antacids or other calcium-containing preparations
Other medical problems, especially hypocalcemia, inability to stand or sit upright for at least 30 minutes, and severe renal function impairment

Proper use of this medication

» Taking with 6 to 8 ounces of plain water on empty stomach, at least 30 minutes before first food, beverage, or medication of the day

» Not lying down for at least 30 minutes after taking risedronate

Importance of taking risedronate according to the dosing instructions as clinical benefits may be compromised by failure to do so

Possible need for calcium and vitamin D supplementation

Importance of weight-bearing exercise and modification of excessive cigarette smoking and/or alcohol consumption

Importance of reading the Patient Information before starting therapy and reading again each time the prescription is renewed

» Proper dosing

Missed dose: For daily dosing—Not taking later in the day; continuing usual schedule the next morning

For weekly dosing—Taking one tablet on the morning after they remember and returning to taking one tablet once a week, as originally scheduled on their chosen day. Not doubling doses.

» Proper storage

Precautions while using this medication
Importance of close monitoring by physician
» Importance of telling all of their health care providers an accurate medication history, including risedronate.
Importance of telling your doctor about new medical problems, especially problems with teeth or jaws and severe bone, joint, and/or muscle pain.

Side/adverse effects
Signs of potential side effects, especially abdominal or stomach pain, skin rash, belching, bone pain, colitis, acute iritis, or neoplasm

General Dosing Information
To facilitate delivery of risedronate to the stomach and reduce esophageal irritation, patients should not lie down for at least 30 minutes after taking risedronate.

Patients should not chew or suck on the tablet because of a potential for oropharyngeal irritation.

Hypocalcemia and other disturbances of bone and mineral metabolism should be treated effectively before risedronate therapy is initiated.

Patients should be instructed that if they develop symptoms of esophageal disease such as difficulty or pain upon swallowing, retrosternal pain, or severe persistent or worsening heartburn, they should consult their physician before continuing risedronate.

Weight-bearing exercise should be considered along with the modification of certain behavioral factors, such as excessive cigarette smoking, and/or alcohol consumption, if these factors exist.

Diet/Nutrition
Risedronate should be taken with 6 to 8 ounces of plain water. Absorption of risedronate is best when it is taken in the morning, at least 30 minutes before the first food, beverage, or medication of the day. Waiting longer than 30 minutes will improve the absorption of risedronate.

A well-balanced diet with adequate intake of calcium and vitamin D should be maintained. Calcium and vitamin D supplements may be prescribed if necessary.

Calcium supplements and any medications containing calcium, aluminum, and/or magnesium may interfere with the absorption of risedronate and should be taken at a different time of the day.

Treatment of musculoskeletal pain
For severe and occasionally incapacitating bone, joint, and/or muscle pain in patients taking bisphosphonates, most patients experienced relief of symptoms by stopping the medication. In some patients, rechallenge with the same drug or another bisphosphonate may result in recurrence of symptoms.

Oral Dosage Forms

RISEDRONATE SODIUM TABLETS

Usual adult dose
Glucocorticoid-induced osteoporosis (prophylaxis)[1]
Glucocorticoid-induced osteoporosis (treatment),[1]—
Oral, 5 mg daily at least thirty minutes before the first food or drink of the day other than water.

Paget's disease of bone (treatment)—
Oral, 30 mg once a day for two months. Re-treatment may be considered, after a posttreatment observation period of at least two months, if relapse occurs, or if treatment fails to normalize serum alkaline phosphatase values. For retreatment, the dose and duration of therapy are the same as for initial treatment.

Postmenopausal osteoporosis (prophylaxis), and
Postmenopausal osteoporosis (treatment)—
Oral, 5 mg daily or 35 mg once a week at least thirty minutes before the first food or drink of the day other than water.

Usual pediatric dose
Safety and efficacy in children younger than 18 years of age have not been established.

Strength(s) usually available
U.S.—
5 mg (Rx) [*Actonel* (lactose monohydrate; crospovidone; ferric oxide yellow; hydroxypropyl cellulose; hydroxypropyl methylcellulose; magnesium stearate; microcrystalline cellulose; polyethylene glycol; silicon dioxide; titanium dioxide)].
30 mg (Rx) [*Actonel* (lactose monohydrate; crospovidone; hydroxypropyl cellulose; hydroxypropyl methylcellulose; magnesium stearate; microcrystalline cellulose; polyethylene glycol; silicon dioxide; titanium dioxide)].
35 mg (Rx) [*Actonel* (ferric oxide, red; ferric oxide, yellow; hydroxypropyl cellulose; hydroxypropyl methylcellulose; magnesium stearate; microcrystalline cellulose; polyethylene glycol; silicon dioxide; titanium dioxide)].

Canada—
5 mg (Rx) [*Actonel*].
30 mg (Rx) [*Actonel*].
35 mg (Rx) [*Actonel*].

Packaging and storage
Store between 20 and 25 °C (68 and 77 °F).

Auxiliary labeling
- Take on an empty stomach.
- Take with 8 ounces of water at least 30 minutes prior to first food/beverage/drug of day. Do not lie down for 30 minutes.
- You should take this medication exactly as prescribed. Do not skip or discontinue unless directed.
- Please read patient information leaflet enclosed

[1]Not included in Canadian product labeling.

Revised: 10/25/2005
Developed: 08/12/1998

RISPERIDONE Systemic

VA CLASSIFICATION (Primary): CN709

Commonly used brand name(s): *Risperdal; Risperdal M-Tab.*

Note: For a listing of dosage forms and brand names by country availability, see *Dosage Forms* section(s).

Category
Antipsychotic

Note: Risperidone is considered by some experts to be an atypical antipsychotic. Universal acceptance of the exact parameters that define an antipsychotic as an atypical agent has not been established. Differences in binding affinities and activity at various receptor sites may explain the differing profiles of the newer antipsychotics.

Indications

Accepted
Psychotic disorders (treatment)—Risperidone is used to treat the manifestations of psychotic disorders. It appears to produce a significant improvement in both the positive and negative symptoms of schizophrenia.

Unaccepted
Risperidone is not approved for the treatment of behavioral symptoms in elderly patients with dementia.

Pharmacology/Pharmacokinetics

Physicochemical characteristics
Chemical Group—A benzisoxazole derivative.
Molecular weight—410.49.
pKa_1—8.24.
pKa_2—3.11.

Mechanism of action/Effect
The mechanism by which risperidone exerts its antipsychotic effect is unknown. Risperidone is a selective monoaminergic antagonist with a strong affinity for serotonin type 2 ($5\text{-}HT_2$) receptors and a slightly weaker affinity for dopamine type 2 (D_2) receptors. The antipsychotic activity of risperidone may be mediated through antagonism at a combination of these receptor sites, particularly through blockade of cortical serotonin receptors and limbic dopamine systems.

Risperidone also has moderate affinity for the $alpha_1$-adrenergic, $alpha_2$-adrenergic, and H_1-histaminergic receptors. The affinity of risperidone for the serotonin $5\text{-}HT_{1A}$, $5\text{-}HT_{1C}$, and $5\text{-}HT_{1D}$ receptors is low to moderate, while its affinity for dopamine D_1 receptors and the haloperidol-sensitive sigma site is weak.

Risperidone has negligible affinity for cholinergic-muscarinic, beta-adrenergic, and serotonin $5\text{-}HT_{1B}$ and $5\text{-}HT_3$ receptors.

Other actions/effects
Cardiovascular effects reflect the vascular alpha-adrenergic antagonistic activity of risperidone, as evidenced by such dose-related effects as hypotension and reflex tachycardia. The potential for proarrhythmic effects exists, due to risperidone's ability to prolong the QT interval in some patients.

Risperidone changes sleep architecture by promoting deep slow-wave sleep, thereby improving sleep patterns. This effect is most likely due to risperidone's blockade of serotonin receptors.

Substantial and sustained elevations in serum prolactin levels are induced by risperidone. It appears that tolerance to hyperprolactinemia does not occur, but the condition is reversible upon withdrawal of risperidone. Increases in prolactin concentrations are likely due to risperidone's blockade of dopamine receptors.

Preliminary reports suggest that risperidone may suppress pre-existing dyskinesias and may exhibit a low propensity for inducing extrapyramidal symptoms or tardive dyskinesia. However, some clinicians believe that risperidone is likely to cause tardive movement disorders because of its relatively potent blockade of D_2 receptors. Additional data from long-term studies are needed to resolve these issues.

Risperidone exerts an antiemetic effect in animals that may also occur in humans, potentially masking signs and symptoms of other medical problems.

Disturbances of body temperature regulation have been reported with the use of other antipsychotics; both hypothermia and hyperthermia have been reported with the use of risperidone.

Absorption

Rapid and extensive. Food does not significantly affect the extent of absorption; therefore, risperidone may be given without respect to meals.

The relative bioavailability of risperidone from a tablet is 94% when compared with a solution. The absolute oral bioavailability of risperidone is 70%; the absolute bioavailability of the active moiety (risperidone plus 9-hydroxy-risperidone) approaches 100%, irrespective of the route of administration or the metabolic phenotype status of the patient.

Distribution

Rapid and extensive. The volume of distribution (Vol_D) at steady state is about 1.1 L per kg. In animals, risperidone and 9-hydroxy-risperidone are distributed into milk, reaching concentrations comparable to plasma concentrations.

Protein binding

Risperidone—Very high (90%).

9-hydroxy-risperidone—High (77%).

Note: In plasma, risperidone is predominantly bound to albumin and alpha$_1$-acid glycoprotein (AGP). Although the pharmacokinetics of risperidone in patients with hepatic function impairment are similar to those in healthy young controls, the mean free fraction of risperidone in plasma is increased by about 35% due to decreased concentrations of albumin and AGP.

Biotransformation

Risperidone is extensively metabolized in the liver by the cytochrome P450 2D6 (CYP2D6) isoenzyme. The main metabolic pathway, hydroxylation, yields the major active metabolite 9-hydroxy-risperidone. The pharmacologic activity, potency, and safety of this metabolite are comparable to those of its parent compound.

Half-life

Elimination—

Overall mean elimination half-life of the active moiety (risperidone plus 9-hydroxy-risperidone) ranges from 20 to 24 hours.

In patients with renal function impairment, increased elimination half-lives have been reported. Dosage reductions for patients with renal function impairment are recommended.

Time to peak concentration

Mean peak risperidone plasma concentrations occur within 1 to 2 hours following oral administration.

Time to steady-state plasma concentrations

Steady-state concentrations of the active moiety (risperidone plus 9-hydroxy-risperidone) are achieved within 5 to 6 days.

Peak plasma concentration

In one study in healthy volunteers, peak plasma concentrations of the active moiety (risperidone plus 9-hydroxy-risperidone) ranging from 9 to 16 nanograms/mL were reported following oral administration of 1 mg of risperidone. However, no correlation between plasma concentrations and therapeutic effect has been definitively established.

Plasma concentrations

Although interindividual plasma concentrations vary considerably, plasma concentrations of risperidone, 9-hydroxy-risperidone, and the active moiety (risperidone plus 9-hydroxy-risperidone) are dose-proportional and linear over the therapeutic dosing range.

Elimination

Renal—

In patients with normal renal function: Approximately 70% of administered oral dose.

In patients with moderate to severe renal function impairment: Renal clearance of the active moiety (risperidone plus 9-hydroxy-risperidone) may be decreased by 60 to 80%.

Fecal—

Approximately 15% of administered oral dose.

Precautions to Consider

Carcinogenicity/Tumorigenicity

Significant increases in the incidence of mammary gland adenocarcinomas and pituitary adenomas occurred in female Swiss albino mice that received risperidone for 18 months at doses of 2.4 and 9.4 times, respectively, the maximum recommended human dose (MRHD) on a mg per kg of body weight (mg/kg) basis (0.2 and 0.75 times, respectively, the MRHD on a mg per square meter of body surface area [mg/m^2] basis). In Wistar rats that received risperidone for 25 months, males dosed at 9.4 times the MRHD on a mg/kg basis (1.5 times the MHRD on a mg/m^2 basis) exhibited increased incidences of endocrine pancreas adenomas and mammary gland neoplasms; also, mammary gland adenocarcinomas were reported in males dosed at 37.5 times the MRHD on a mg/kg basis (6 times the MRHD on a mg/m^2 basis) and in females dosed at 2.4 times the MRHD on a mg/kg basis (0.4 times the MRHD on a mg/m^2 basis).

Risperidone, like other agents that antagonize dopamine D_2 receptors, elevates prolactin concentrations; the elevation persists during chronic administration. Tissue culture experiments indicate that approximately one-third of human breast cancers are prolactin-dependent *in vitro*, a factor of potential importance if use of this medication is contemplated in a patient with a previously detected breast cancer. Although disturbances such as galactorrhea, amenorrhea, gynecomastia, and impotence have been reported, the clinical significance of elevated serum prolactin concentrations is unknown for most patients. An increase in pituitary gland, mammary gland, and pancreatic islet cell hyperplasia and/or neoplasia has been found in rodents after chronic administration of medications (including risperidone) that increase prolactin release. However, neither clinical studies nor epidemiologic studies conducted to date have shown an association between chronic administration of these medications and tumorigenesis in humans; the available evidence is considered too limited to be conclusive at this time.

Mutagenicity

Risperidone demonstrated no mutagenic potential in the following tests: Ames reverse mutation test, mouse lymphoma assay, *in vitro* rat hepatocyte DNA-repair assay, *in vivo* micronucleus test in mice, the sex-linked recessive lethal test in *Drosophila*, and the chromosomal aberration test in human lymphocytes or Chinese hamster cells.

Pregnancy/Reproduction

Fertility—In three reproductive studies, risperidone was shown to impair mating but not fertility in Wistar rats that received 0.1 to 3 times the MRHD on a mg/m^2 basis; this effect apparently occurred only in female rats. In a study in beagle dogs, sperm motility and concentration were decreased at risperidone doses of 0.6 to 10 times the MRHD on a mg/m^2 basis. Dose-related decreases in serum testosterone were also noted. Serum testosterone and sperm parameters partially recovered but remained decreased after discontinuation of risperidone.

Pregnancy—Adequate and well-controlled studies in humans have not been done.

Agenesis of the corpus callosum in an infant exposed to risperidone *in utero* has been reported. However, a causal relationship to risperidone therapy has not been established.

In three teratogenicity studies conducted in rats and rabbits that received 0.4 to 6 times the MRHD of risperidone on a mg/m^2 basis, the incidence of malformations was not increased as compared with controls. In three reproductive studies in rats, there was an increase in pup deaths during the first 4 days of lactation at doses of 0.1 to 3 times the MRHD on a mg/m^2 basis; it is not known whether these deaths were due to a direct effect on the fetuses or pups, or to effects on the dams. In another study in rats receiving risperidone doses of 1.5 times the MRHD on a mg/m^2 basis, there was an increase in the number of stillborn pups.

Risperidone should be used during pregnancy only if the potential benefit justifies potential risk to the fetus.

FDA Pregnancy Category C

Labor and delivery—The effect of risperidone on labor and delivery is not known.

Breast-feeding

Risperidone and 9-hydroxy-risperidone are distributed into human breast milk. Women receiving risperidone should not breast feed.

Pediatrics
No information is available on the relationship of age to the effects of risperidone in pediatric patients. Safety and efficacy in children up to 18 years of age have not been established.

Geriatrics
There is limited experience in the use of risperidone in the elderly. In healthy elderly patients, decreases in renal clearance and increases in the elimination half-life of the active moiety (risperidone plus 9-hydroxy-risperidone) have been reported. Also, geriatric patients generally have decreased renal function, decreased hepatic function, decreased cardiac function, increased occurrence of dementia, and an increased tendency to postural hypotension. Therefore, reduced risperidone doses are recommended.

According to an FDA Public Health Advisory, risperidone is not approved for the treatment of behavioral symptoms in elderly patients with dementia. Clinical studies of risperidone and other atypical antipsychotic drugs for treatment of behavioral symptoms in the elderly with dementia have shown a higher death rate associated with their use compared to patients receiving a placebo. Causes of death varied, but most seemed to be either heart-related (i.e., heart failure or sudden death) or from infections (i.e., pneumonia).

The use of risperidone in elderly patients with dementia may be associated with an increased incidence of reports of cerebrovascular adverse events such as stroke and transient ischemic attacks, including fatalities. Risperidone should be used with caution, after less toxic alternatives have been considered and/or found ineffective. Recommended doses should not be exceeded, and the patient should be carefully monitored during therapy for signs and symptoms of potential cerebrovascular adverse events such as sudden weakness or numbness in the face, arms or legs, and speech or vision problems, so that diagnosis can be made and treatment options considered, including discontinuation of risperidone.

Pharmacogenetics
Hydroxylation of risperidone via the cytochrome P450 2D6 (CYP2D6) isoenzyme is subject to genetic polymorphism. About 6 to 8% of Caucasians and a low percentage of Asians have little or no CYP2D6 activity and are considered poor metabolizers. Patients taking risperidone who have normal CYP2D6 activity (considered extensive metabolizers) have lower plasma concentrations of risperidone and higher concentrations of 9-hydroxy-risperidone than do patients who are poor metabolizers. Although blood levels of risperidone and 9-hydroxy-risperidone can differ by up to sevenfold, there is no difference in the area under the plasma concentration-time curve (AUC) for the combination, and clinical data do not indicate that the ratio affects either therapeutics or incidence of adverse effects. Overall, the pharmacokinetic parameters of the active moiety (risperidone plus 9-hydroxy-risperidone) are similar in all metabolizers. Therefore, the metabolic phenotype status of patients is not considered to have clinically significant effects on risperidone therapy.

Drug interactions and/or related problems
The following drug interactions and/or related problems have been selected on the basis of their potential clinical significance (possible mechanism in parentheses where appropriate)—not necessarily inclusive (» = major clinical significance):

Note: Medications that inhibit the cytochrome P450 2D6 (CYP2D6) isoenzyme potentially could inhibit the metabolism of risperidone. However, since only the relative amounts of risperidone and 9-hydroxy-risperidone and not the total concentration of active moiety (risperidone plus 9-hydroxy-risperidone) would be affected, no marked changes in activity should occur. *In vitro*, medications metabolized by other P450 isoenzymes (including CYP1A1, CYP1A2, CYP2C9, MP, and CYP3A4) are only weak inhibitors of risperidone metabolism.

Similarly, risperidone potentially could interfere with the metabolism of other medications metabolized via CYP2D6; however, risperidone is bound relatively weakly to the enzyme, so these effects seem unlikely to be clinically significant.

In vitro studies have shown no significant interactions caused by other highly protein-bound agents displacing or being displaced by risperidone.

Combinations containing any of the following medications, depending on the amount present, may also interact with this medication.

» Alcohol or
» Central nervous system (CNS) depression-producing medications, other (see *Appendix II*)
(additive CNS depressant effects may occur)

» Bromocriptine or
» Levodopa or
» Pergolide
(risperidone may antagonize the effects of levodopa and dopamine agonists)

» Carbamazepine
(chronic administration of carbamazepine may increase the clearance of risperidone)

Cimetidine or
Ranitidine
(increased bioavailability of risperidone, but only marginally increased plasma concentration of the active antipsychotic fraction)

» Clozapine
(chronic administration of clozapine may decrease the clearance of risperidone)

» Fluoxetine or
» Paroxetine
(may increase the plasma concentration of the antipsychotic fraction by raising the concentration of risperidone; when either concomitant fluoxetine or paroxetine is initiated or discontinued, physician should re-evaluate risperidone dosing)

» Hypotension-producing medications, other (see *Appendix II*)
(potential hypotensive effects of these medications can enhance hypotensive effects of risperidone)

» Medications that prolong the QT interval (see *Appendix II*)
(concomitant use of other drugs that prolong the QT interval have been associated with the occurrence of *torsades de pointes*, a life-threatening arrhythmia.)

Valproate
(after concomitant administration of risperidone, there was a 20% increase in valproate peak plasma concentration [C_{max}])

Laboratory value alterations
The following have been selected on the basis of their potential clinical significance (possible effect in parentheses where appropriate)—not necessarily inclusive (» = major clinical significance).

With physiology/laboratory test values

Blood glucose
(patients with a diagnosis of or risk factors for diabetes mellitus should undergo fasting blood glucose testing at the beginning of treatment and periodically during treatment)

Electrocardiogram
(prolongation of the QT interval has occurred in some patients)

Prolactin concentrations, serum
(sustained elevations occur during therapy with risperidone)

Medical considerations/Contraindications
The medical considerations/contraindications included have been selected on the basis of their potential clinical significance (reasons given in parentheses where appropriate)—not necessarily inclusive (» = major clinical significance).

Except under special circumstances, this medication should not be used when the following medical problem exists:

» Hypersensitivity to risperidone or any components of the product

Risk-benefit should be considered when the following medical problems exist:

Aspiration pneumonia, risk of
(antipsychotic drug use has been associated with esophageal dysmotility and aspiration; may be especially dangerous in patients with advanced Alzheimer's dementia)

Brain tumor or
Intestinal obstruction or
Medication overdose or
Reye's syndrome
(risperidone's antiemetic effect may mask signs and symptoms of these conditions)

» Breast cancer
(prolactin-dependent cancer may be exacerbated)

» Cardiovascular disease, including heart failure, conduction abnormalities, or history of myocardial infarction or ischemia or
» Cerebrovascular disease
(condition may be exacerbated by risperidone-induced hypotension)

» Dehydration or
» Hypovolemia
(these conditions may increase likelihood or severity of risperidone-induced hypotension)

» Dementia
(may increase occurrence of cerebrovascular adverse events (CVAE) such as stroke and transient ischemic attacks including

fatalities; patients and/or caregivers should be instructed to report signs of CVAEs such as weakness, numbness, and problems with speech or vision)

» Diabetes mellitus or
» Risk factors for diabetes mellitus such as
Obesity or
Family history of diabetes
(epidemiological studies suggest an increased risk of treatment-emergent hyperglycemia-related adverse events including keto-acidosis, hyperosmolar coma, or death in patients treated with the atypical antipsychotics including risperidone; patients should be monitored carefully)

Drug abuse or dependence, history of
(although no evidence of drug-seeking behavior was seen in clinical trials, patients with a history of drug abuse should be observed closely for any signs of misuse of risperidone, as with any new CNS medication)

» Hepatic function impairment, severe
(metabolism and protein binding of risperidone may be decreased; reduced dosage is recommended)

» Parkinson's disease
(may be exacerbated)

Phenylketonuria (PKU)
(*Risperdal M-Tab* brand of risperidone oral disintegrating tablets contains aspartame, which is metabolized to phenylalanine)

» Renal function impairment, severe
(excretion of the active moieties of risperidone may be decreased; reduced dosage is recommended)

» Risk factors for *torsades de pointes*, including bradycardia, electrolyte imbalance, or concomitant intake of other medications that prolong the QT interval
(risk of *torsades de pointes* may be increased)

» Seizures, history of
(seizure threshold may be lowered)

Patient monitoring

The following may be especially important in patient monitoring (other tests may be warranted in some patients, depending on condition; » = major clinical significance):

Abnormal-movement determinations
(recommended at periodic intervals to detect extrapyramidal symptoms)

Careful observation for early signs of tardive dyskinesia
(recommended at periodic intervals; since there is no known effective treatment if the syndrome develops, risperidone should be discontinued, if clinically feasible, at the earliest signs, usually fine, worm-like movements of the tongue, to stop further development)

Hyperglycemia
(patients should be monitored for symptoms of hyperglycemia including polydipsia, polyuria, polyphagia, and weakness; patients developing these symptoms should undergo fasting blood glucose testing)

Suicide attempts
(potential is inherent in schizophrenia; close supervision of high risk patients should accompany therapy)

Side/Adverse Effects

The following side/adverse effects have been selected on the basis of their potential clinical significance (possible signs and symptoms in parentheses where appropriate)—not necessarily inclusive:

Post-marketing studies in elderly patients with dementia suggest that the use of risperidone in dementia patients may be associated with an increased incidence of cerebrovascular adverse events such as stroke and transient ischemic attacks.

Those indicating need for medical attention

Incidence more frequent

Akathisia (restlessness or need to keep moving); ***anxiety or nervousness; changes in vision, including disturbances of accommodation and blurred vision; sexual dysfunction or decreased libido*** (decreased sexual performance or desire); ***dizziness; dysmenorrhea or menorrhagia*** (menstrual changes); ***extrapyramidal effects, dystonic*** (muscle spasms of face, neck and back; tic-like or twitching movements; twisting movements of body; inability to move eyes; weakness of arms and legs); ***extrapyramidal effects, parkinsonian*** (difficulty in speaking or swallowing; loss of balance control; mask-like face; shuffling walk; stiffness of arms or legs; trembling and shaking of hands and fingers); ***insomnia*** (trouble in sleeping); ***micturition disturbances or polyuria*** (problems in urination or increase in amount of urine); ***mood or mental changes, including aggressive behavior, agitation, difficulty in concentration, and memory problems; skin rash or itching***

Note: *Extrapyramidal symptoms* are dose-related; *sexual dysfunction* and *decreased libido*, or *vision changes* may be dose-related.

Menorrhagia may be associated with increased prolactin concentrations.

Incidence less frequent

Amenorrhea (menstrual changes); ***back pain; cardiovascular effects, including orthostatic hypotension*** (dizziness or lightheadedness)—especially when getting up from a lying or sitting position; ***orthostatic dizziness; hypotension; palpitation*** (fast or irregular heartbeat); ***chest pain, and reflex tachycardia or tachycardia*** (fast heartbeat); ***cerebrovascular adverse events, including stroke, transient ischemic attacks*** (sudden weakness or numbness in the face, arms or legs; speech or vision problems)—disease state may be a contributing factor; ***dyspnea*** (trouble in breathing); ***galactorrhea*** (unusual secretion of milk)

Note: *Amenorrhea* and *galactorrhea* are associated with increased prolactin concentrations. *Orthostatic dizziness, palpitation,* and *tachycardia* may be dose-related.

Incidence rare

Anorexia (loss of appetite); ***hyperthermia*** (dizziness; fast, shallow breathing; fast, weak heartbeat; headache; muscle cramps; pale, clammy skin; thirst); ***or hypothermia*** (confusion; drowsiness; poor coordination; shivering); ***mania or hypomania*** (talking, feeling, and acting with excitement and activity that cannot be controlled); ***neuroleptic malignant syndrome (NMS)*** (difficult or unusually fast breathing; fast heartbeat or irregular pulse; high fever; high or low [irregular] blood pressure; increased sweating; loss of bladder control; severe muscle stiffness; seizures; unusually pale skin; unusual tiredness or weakness); ***polydipsia*** (extreme thirst); ***priapism*** (prolonged, painful, inappropriate erection of the penis); ***seizures*** (convulsions); ***tardive dyskinesia*** (lip smacking or puckering; puffing of cheeks; rapid or worm-like movements of tongue; uncontrolled chewing movements; uncontrolled movements of arms and legs); ***tardive dystonia*** (increased blinking or spasms of eyelid; unusual facial expressions or body positions; uncontrolled twisting movements of neck, trunk, arms, or legs); ***thrombocytopenic purpura*** (unusual bleeding or bruising)

Incidence not determined—Observed during clinical practice, estimates of frequency cannot be determined

Anaphylactic reaction (cough; difficulty swallowing; dizziness; fast heartbeat; hives; itching; puffiness or swelling of the eyelids or around the eyes, face, lips or tongue; shortness of breath; skin rash; tightness in chest; unusual tiredness or weakness; wheezing); ***angioedema*** (large, hive-like swelling on face, eyelids, lips, tongue, throat, hands, legs, feet, sex organs); ***apnea*** (bluish lips or skin; not breathing); ***atrial fibrillation*** (fast or irregular heartbeat; dizziness; fainting); ***diabetes mellitus, aggravation of; diabetic ketoacidosis*** (blurred vision; confusion; dry mouth; fatigue; flushed, dry skin; fruit-like breath odor; increased hunger; increased thirst; increased urination; loss of consciousness; nausea; stomachache; sweating; troubled breathing; unexplained weight loss; vomiting); ***hyperglycemia*** (abdominal pain; blurred vision; dry mouth; fatigue; flushed, dry skin; fruit-like breath odor; increased hunger; increased thirst; increased urination; nausea; sweating; troubled breathing; unexplained weight loss; vomiting); ***intestinal obstruction*** (abdominal pain; severe constipation; nausea; vomiting); ***jaundice*** (chills; clay-colored stools; dark urine; dizziness; fever; headache; itching; loss of appetite; nausea; abdominal or stomach pain; area rash; unpleasant breath odor; unusual tiredness or weakness; vomiting of blood; yellow eyes or skin); ***pancreatitis*** (bloating; chills; constipation; darkened urine; fast heartbeat; fever; indigestion; loss of appetite; nausea; pains in stomach, side, or abdomen, possibly radiating to the back; vomiting; yellow eyes or skin); ***Parkinson's disease, aggravation of; pulmonary embolism*** (anxiety; chest pain; cough; fainting; fast heartbeat; sudden shortness of breath or troubled breathing; dizziness or lightheadedness)

Note: Adverse events reported since market introduction were temporally (but not causally) related to risperidone therapy.

There have been rare reports of sudden death and/or cardiopulmonary arrest in patients receiving risperidone. It is important to note that sudden and unexpected death may occur in psychotic patients whether they remain untreated or whether they are treated with other antipsychotic drugs.

Those indicating need for medical attention only if they continue or are bothersome

Incidence more frequent

Asthenia, fatigue, or lassitude (unusual tiredness or weakness); ***constipation; cough; decreased salivation or dryness of mouth; diarrhea; drowsiness; dyspepsia*** (heartburn); ***headache; increased dream activity; increased duration of sleep; nausea; pharyngitis*** (sore throat); ***rhinitis*** (stuffy or runny nose); ***somnolence*** (sleepiness or unusual drowsiness); ***weight gain***

Note: *Asthenia, lassitude, or fatigue, drowsiness, increased duration of sleep,* and *weight gain* may be dose-related. *Rhinitis* is most likely due to alpha-adrenoceptor–mediated nasal congestion.

Incidence less frequent

Abdominal pain; arthralgia (joint pain); ***back pain; dry skin; increased pigmentation*** (darkening of skin color); ***increased salivation*** (increased watering of mouth); ***increased sweating; photosensitivity*** (increased sensitivity of the skin to sun); ***seborrhea*** (dandruff; oily skin); ***sinusitis*** (pain or tenderness around eyes and cheekbones; fever; stuffy or runny nose; headache; cough; shortness of breath or troubled breathing; tightness of chest or wheezing); ***toothache; upper respiratory infection*** (ear congestion; nasal congestion; chills; cough; fever; sneezing; sore throat; body aches or pain; headache; loss of voice; runny nose; unusual tiredness or weakness; difficulty in breathing); ***vomiting; weight loss***

Note: *Increased pigmentation* may be dose-related.

Incidence rare

Hyperkinesia (increase in body movements)

Those indicating the need for medical attention if they occur after the medication is discontinued

Withdrawal emergent dyskinesia (lip smacking or puckering; puffing of cheeks; rapid or worm-like movements of tongue; uncontrolled chewing movements; uncontrolled movements of arms and legs)

Overdose

For specific information on the agents used in the management of risperidone overdose, see *Charcoal, Activated (Oral-Local)* monograph.

For more information on the management of overdose or unintentional ingestion, **contact a Poison Control Center** (see *Poison Control Center Listing*).

Clinical effects of overdose

The following effects have been selected on the basis of their potential clinical significance (possible signs and symptoms in parentheses where appropriate)—not necessarily inclusive:

Acute and chronic effects

Drowsiness; extrapyramidal symptoms; electrocardiogram (ECG) abnormalities, especially prolonged QT interval; electrolyte disturbances; hypotension; seizures; tachycardia

Treatment of overdose

There is no specific antidote for risperidone. Treatment is essentially symptomatic and supportive.

To decrease absorption—

Gastric lavage should be considered. Activated charcoal may be administered with a laxative. The risk of aspiration with induced emesis is increased if the patient is obtunded, seizing, or experiencing dystonic movements of the head and neck.

Specific treatment—

For treatment of severe extrapyramidal symptoms: Administration of anticholinergic agents may be indicated.

For treatment of arrhythmias caused by risperidone toxicity: Selection of an appropriate antiarrhythmic agent—Use of disopyramide, procainamide, or quinidine may add to risperidone toxicity by prolonging the QT interval. Also, the alpha-adrenergic blocking properties of bretylium may add to risperidone's effects, producing problematic hypotension.

For treatment of hypotension or circulatory collapse: Selection of an appropriate sympathomimetic—Beta-adrenergic stimulation properties of epinephrine or dopamine may worsen the hypotension induced by risperidone's alpha-adrenergic blockade.

Monitoring—

Cardiovascular monitoring should be initiated immediately to detect arrhythmias. Serum electrolytes should also be monitored.

Supportive care—

Supportive measures such as establishing intravenous lines, hydration, correction of electrolyte imbalance, oxygenation, and support of ventilatory function are essential for maintaining the vital functions of the patient. Patients in whom intentional overdose is confirmed or suspected should be referred for psychiatric consultation.

Patient Consultation

As an aid to patient consultation, refer to *Advice for the Patient, Risperidone (Systemic)*.

In providing consultation, consider emphasizing the following selected information (» = major clinical significance):

Before using this medication

» Conditions affecting use, especially:

Hypersensitivity to risperidone or any component of the product

Note: Phenylketonurics—Oral disintegrating tablets may contain aspartame.

Pregnancy—Agenesis of the corpus callosum reported in one infant, but causal relationship not established. Risk/benefit should be considered.

Breast-feeding—Risperidone is distributed in human breast milk. Women receiving risperidone should not breast feed.

Use in the elderly—Older patients may be at increased risk for adverse effects; reduced dosage recommended

Use of risperidone in elderly patients with dementia may be at increase risk for cerebrovascular adverse events such as stroke and transient ischemic attacks; Not approved for the treatment of behavioral disorders in elderly patients with dementia; associated with a higher death rate.

Other medications, especially alcohol, bromocriptine, carbamazepine, clozapine, CNS depressants, fluoxetine, hypotension-producing medications, levodopa, medications that prolong the QT interval, paroxetine, or pergolide

Other medical problems, especially breast cancer, cardiovascular disease, cerebrovascular disease, dehydration, dementia, diabetes mellitus or risk factors for diabetes mellitus, hepatic function impairment, history of seizures, hypovolemia, Parkinson's disease, renal function impairment, or risk factors for *torsades de pointes*

Proper use of this medication

» Compliance with therapy; not taking more or less medicine than prescribed

» Importance of caregivers contacting doctor and not giving this medicine for treatment of behavioral problems in elderly patients with dementia

» Proper dosing

Stirring measured dose of oral solution into water, coffee, orange juice, or low-fat milk prior to use; not mixing with cola or tea

Missed dose: Taking as soon as possible; if almost time for next dose, skipping missed dose; not doubling doses

» Proper storage

Precautions while using this medication

» Regular visits to physician to check progress of therapy

» Checking with physician before discontinuing medication; gradual dosage reduction may be needed

» Avoiding use of alcoholic beverages; not taking other CNS depressants unless prescribed by physician

» Caution if any kind of surgery, dental treatment, or emergency treatment is required; telling physician or dentist in charge about treatment with risperidone because of possible drug interactions or adverse effects

» Possible blurred vision, dizziness, or drowsiness; caution when driving or doing jobs requiring alertness or clear vision

» Possible dizziness or lightheadedness; caution when getting up suddenly from a lying or sitting position

» Possible skin photosensitivity; avoiding unprotected exposure to sun; wearing protective clothing; using a sun block product that includes protection against both UVA-caused photosensitivity reactions and UVB-caused sunburn reactions; avoiding use of sunlamp, tanning bed, or tanning booth

Possible heatstroke or hypothermia; caution during exercise, hot baths, or exposure to extreme temperatures

Side/adverse effects

Signs of potential side effects, especially akathisia; anxiety or nervousness; changes in vision; sexual dysfunction or decreased libido; dizziness; dysmenorrhea or menorrhagia; extrapyramidal effects; insomnia; micturition disturbances or polyuria; mood or mental changes; skin rash or itching; amenorrhea; back pain; cardiovascular effects; cerebrovascular adverse events; dyspnea; galactorrhea; seborrhea; anorexia; hyperthermia or hypothermia; mania or hypomania; neuroleptic malignant syndrome; polydipsia; priapism; seizures; tardive dyskinesia; tardive dystonia; or thrombocytopenic purpura

Signs of potential side effects observed during clinical practice, especially anaphylactic reaction; angioedema; apnea; atrial fibrillation; diabetes mellitus aggravation; hyperglycemia; intestinal obstruction; jaundice; pancreatitis; Parkinson's disease aggravation; or pulmonary embolism

General Dosing Information

Risperidone dosage must be individualized by cautious titration from the lower dosage range, to avoid orthostatic hypotension. The need for risperidone should be reassessed periodically, and the patient maintained at the lowest possible dosage level. The physician who elect to use risperidone for extended periods should periodically re-evaluate the long term usefulness of the drug for the individual patient.

Since the possibility of suicide is inherent in schizophrenia, patients should not have access to large quantities of this medication. To reduce the risk of overdose, some clinicians recommend that the patient be supplied with the smallest quantity of medication necessary for satisfactory patient management.

There is a significant curvilinear dose-response relationship over the range of 1 to 16 mg of risperidone a day. This represents an "optimal dose" curve; maximum activity of risperidone occurs at doses of 4 to 8 mg a day. In trials using two-times-a-day dosing, daily doses greater than 6 mg of risperidone were not proven to be more efficacious than lower risperidone doses and were associated with increased adverse effects. In a trial using once-a-day dosing, the 8-mg dose was generally more effective than the 4-mg dose.

Oral disintegrating tablets may contain aspartame, which is metabolized to phenylalanine. This substance must be used with caution in patients with phenylketonuria.

Diet/Nutrition

Risperidone may be given without regard to food.

Bioequivalence information

The oral solution and 1-mg tablet forms of risperidone are bioequivalent.

The orally disintegrating tablets and the tablet forms of risperidone are bioequivalent.

Directions for use of Orally Disintegrating Tablets

Tablet Accessing—

Do not open blister until ready to administer. For single tablet removal, separate one of the four blister units by tearing apart at the perforations. Bend the corner where indicated. Peel back foil to expose tablet. ***Do not*** push the tablet through the foil because this could damage the tablet.

Tablet Administration—

Using dry hands, remove the tablet from the blister unit and immediately place the entire orally disintegrating tablet on the tongue. The tablet should be consumed immediately, as the tablet cannot be stored once removed from the blister unit. The orally disintegrating tablets disintegrate in the mouth within seconds and can be swallowed subsequently with or without liquid. Patients should not attempt to split or chew the tablet.

For treatment of adverse effects

Neuroleptic malignant syndrome (NMS)—Treatment is essentially symptomatic and supportive and may include the following:

- *Discontinuing risperidone immediately.*
- Hyperthermia—Administering antipyretics (aspirin or acetaminophen); using cooling blanket.
- Dehydration—Restoring fluids and electrolytes.
- Cardiovascular instability—Monitoring blood pressure and cardiac rhythm closely; use of sodium nitroprusside may allow vasodilation with subsequent heat loss from the skin in patients with less dominant muscle rigidity.
- Hypoxia—Administering oxygen; considering airway insertion and assisted ventilation.
- Muscle rigidity—Administering dantrolene sodium (100 to 300 mg per day in divided doses, or 1.25 to 1.5 mg per kg of body weight, intravenously) for muscle relaxation; or amantadine (100 mg two times a day) or bromocriptine (5 mg three times a day) to restore central balance of dopamine and acetylcholine at the receptor site.
- If neuroleptics must be continued because of severe psychosis, initial treatment may consist of:
  —At least 5 days of neuroleptic abstinence before rechallenge.
  —Use of a neuroleptic of a different class from the one causing NMS.
  —Use of a low dose.
  —Using the neuroleptic only for controlling the psychosis.

Tardive dyskinesia or tardive dystonia—No known effective treatment. Dosage of risperidone should be lowered or medication discontinued, if clinically feasible, at earliest signs of tardive dyskinesia or tardive dystonia to prevent possible irreversible effects.

Oral Dosage Forms

RISPERIDONE ORAL SOLUTION

Note: The oral solution and 1-mg tablet forms of risperidone are bioequivalent.

Usual adult dose

Antipsychotic—

Oral, 1 mg on the first day; the dose may be increased to 2 mg on the second day, and further increased to 3 mg on the third day. Risperidone may be administered on either a once a day or twice a day schedule. However, although this regimen was employed in early trials of risperidone, many patients reportedly have been unable to tolerate such rapid titration. Slower titration may be necessary in many patients. Further dosage adjustments should be made as needed and tolerated in increments or decrements of 1 to 2 mg a day at intervals of no less than one week, thus enabling steady-state plasma concentrations to be reached before further dosage changes are instituted. Total daily doses of up to 8 mg may be administered in a single dose or in two divided doses.

Note: Dosing regimens for risperidone are somewhat controversial. Some clinicians advocate an initial dosing schedule of 0.5 to 1 mg two times a day, with the dosage being increased as needed and tolerated at intervals of three to five days, until a total daily dose of 4 to 8 mg is reached; that dosage level usually is maintained for one to two weeks prior to any further changes in dose.

Efficacy in schizophrenia was demonstrated in a dose range of 4 to 16 mg per day in short-term clinical trials supporting the effectiveness of risperidone, however, maximal effect was seen in a range of 4 to 8 mg per day. Doses above 6 mg per day for BID dosing were not demonstrated to be more efficacious than lower doses, were associated with more extrapyramidal symptoms and other adverse effects, and are not generally recommended. In a single study supporting QD dosing, the efficacy results were generally stronger for 8 mg than for 4 mg.

Maintenance Therapy—While there is no body of evidence available to answer the question of how long the patient should remain on risperidone therapy, the effectiveness of 2 mg per day to 8 mg per day at delaying relapse was demonstrated in a controlled trial in patients who had been clinically stable for at least 4 weeks and then were followed for a period of 1 to 2 years. In this trial, risperidone was administered on a once daily schedule, at 1 mg once daily initially, with increases to 2 mg once daily on day 2, and to a target dose of 4 mg once daily on day 3.

Debilitated patients, as well as those who have severe hepatic or renal function impairment, and those who are predisposed to hypotension or for whom hypotension would pose a risk, should receive reduced doses, following the regimen described in the *Usual geriatric dose* section.

If risperidone treatment is to be reinitiated in a patient who previously was receiving risperidone therapy, the initial titration schedule should be followed.

When switching from other antipsychotics to risperidone, immediate discontinuation of the previous treatment may be acceptable for some patients, while more gradual discontinuation may be most appropriate for other patients. In all cases, the period of overlapping antipsychotic administration should be minimized. When switching patients from depot antipsychotics, risperidone may be instituted in place of the next scheduled depot injection, if medically appropriate. The need for continuing administration of medication to control extrapyramidal symptoms should be re-evaluated periodically.

Usual adult prescribing limits

16 mg per day.

Note: In adults with severe hepatic function impairment, the usual prescribing limit is 4 mg per day.

Usual pediatric dose

Safety and efficacy in children younger than 18 years of age have not been established.

Usual geriatric dose

Antipsychotic—

Oral, initially 0.5 mg two times a day. The dose may be increased as needed and tolerated in increments of 0.5 mg two times a day.

Increases to dosages above 1.5 mg two times a day generally should occur at intervals of at least one week. It is recommended that titration to the target dosage be accomplished on a two-times-a-day regimen. Once-a-day dosing may be instituted after at least two to three days at the target dosage.

Note: There is potential for accumulation of risperidone in the elderly In Canada, the dosing schedule in elderly patients is oral, 0.25 mg two times daily, adjusted slowly to a maximum daily dose of 3 mg.

Usual geriatric prescribing limits
3 mg per day

Strength(s) usually available
U.S.—
1 mg per mL (Rx) [*Risperdal* (benzoic acid; purified water; sodium hydroxide; tartaric acid)].
Canada—
1 mg per mL (Rx) [*Risperdal*].

Packaging and storage
Store at controlled room temperature, between 15 and 25 °C (59 and 77 °F), unless otherwise specified by manufacturer. Protect from light and freezing.

Preparation of dosage form
Measure the dose with the pipette provided and thoroughly stir the dose into about 100 mL (3 to 4 ounces) of a compatible beverage. Compatible beverages include water, coffee, orange juice, and low-fat milk.

Incompatibilities
Risperidone oral solution is not compatible with cola or tea.

Auxiliary labeling
- Avoid alcoholic beverages.
- Dilute dose before taking.
- May cause drowsiness.
- Keep out of the reach of children
- Protect from light and freezing.

Note
When dispensing, include the manufacturer-provided calibrated dispensing pipette.

RISPERIDONE ORALLY DISINTEGRATING TABLETS

Note: The orally disintegrating tablets and the tablet forms of risperidone are bioequivalent.

Usual adult dose
See *Risperidone Oral Solution*.

Usual adult prescribing limits
See *Risperidone Oral Solution*.

Usual pediatric dose
See *Risperidone Oral Solution*.

Usual geriatric dose
See *Risperidone Oral Solution*.

Usual geriatric prescribing limits
See *Risperidone Oral Solution*.

Strength(s) usually available
U.S.—
0.5 mg (Rx) [*Risperdal M-Tab* (Amberlite™ resin; gelatin; mannitol; glycine; simethicone; carbomer; sodium hydroxide; aspartame; red ferric oxide; peppermint oil)].
1 mg (Rx) [*Risperdal M-Tab* (Amberlite™ resin; gelatin; mannitol; glycine; simethicone; carbomer; sodium hydroxide; aspartame; red ferric oxide; peppermint oil)].
2 mg (Rx) [*Risperdal M-Tab* (Amberlite™ resin; gelatin; mannitol; glycine; simethicone; carbomer; sodium hydroxide; aspartame; red ferric oxide; peppermint oil; xanthan gum)].
3 mg (Rx) [*Risperdal M-Tab* (Amberlite™ resin; gelatin; mannitol; glycine; simethicone; carbomer; sodium hydroxide; aspartame; red ferric oxide; peppermint oil; xanthan gum)].
4 mg (Rx) [*Risperdal M-Tab* (Amberlite™ resin; gelatin; mannitol; glycine; simethicone; carbomer; sodium hydroxide; aspartame; red ferric oxide; peppermint oil; xanthan gum)].
Canada—
Not commercially available

Packaging and storage
Store at controlled room temperature, between 15 and 25 °C (59 and 77 °F).

Auxiliary labeling
- Avoid alcoholic beverages.
- May cause drowsiness.
- Keep out of the reach of children
- May be swallowed with or without liquid
- Use dry hands when handling tablets

Caution
Risperdal M-Tab brand of oral disintegrating tablets contains aspartame, which is metabolized to phenylalanine and must be used with caution in patients with phenylketonuria.

RISPERIDONE TABLETS

Note: The oral solution and 1-mg tablet forms of risperidone are bioequivalent.

Usual adult dose
See *Risperidone Oral Solution*.

Usual adult prescribing limits
See *Risperidone Oral Solution*.

Usual pediatric dose
See *Risperidone Oral Solution*.

Usual geriatric dose
See *Risperidone Oral Solution*.

Usual geriatric prescribing limits
See *Risperidone Oral Solution*.

Strength(s) usually available
U.S.—
0.25 mg (Rx) [*Risperdal* (scored; colloidal silicon dioxide; corn starch; hydroxypropyl methylcellulose; lactose; magnesium stearate; microcrystalline cellulose; propylene glycol; sodium lauryl sulfate; talc; titanium dioxide; yellow iron oxide)].
0.5 mg (Rx) [*Risperdal* (scored; colloidal silicon dioxide; corn starch; hydroxypropyl methylcellulose; lactose; magnesium stearate; microcrystalline cellulose; propylene glycol; red iron oxide; sodium lauryl sulfate; talc; titanium dioxide)].
1 mg (Rx) [*Risperdal* (scored; colloidal silicon dioxide; corn starch; hydroxypropyl methylcellulose; lactose; magnesium stearate; microcrystalline cellulose; propylene glycol; sodium lauryl sulfate)].
2 mg (Rx) [*Risperdal* (colloidal silicon dioxide; corn starch; FD&C Yellow No. 6 Aluminum Lake; hydroxypropyl methylcellulose; lactose; magnesium stearate; microcrystalline cellulose; propylene glycol; sodium lauryl sulfate; talc; titanium dioxide)].
3 mg (Rx) [*Risperdal* (colloidal silicon dioxide; corn starch; D&C Yellow No. 10; hydroxypropyl methylcellulose; lactose; magnesium stearate; microcrystalline cellulose; propylene glycol; sodium lauryl sulfate; talc; titanium dioxide)].
4 mg (Rx) [*Risperdal* (colloidal silicon dioxide; corn starch; D&C Yellow No. 10; FD&C Blue No. 2 Aluminum Lake; hydroxypropyl methylcellulose; lactose; magnesium stearate; microcrystalline cellulose; propylene glycol; sodium lauryl sulfate; talc; titanium dioxide)].
Canada—
0.25 mg (Rx) [*Risperdal* (scored; lactose)].
0.5 mg (Rx) [*Risperdal* (lactose)].
1 mg (Rx) [*Risperdal* (scored; lactose)].
2 mg (Rx) [*Risperdal* (lactose)].
3 mg (Rx) [*Risperdal* (lactose)].
4 mg (Rx) [*Risperdal* (lactose)].

Packaging and storage
Store at controlled room temperature, between 15 and 25 °C (59 and 77 °F), unless otherwise specified by manufacturer. Protect from light and moisture.

Auxiliary labeling
- Avoid alcoholic beverages.
- May cause drowsiness.
- Keep out of the reach of children
- Protect from light and moisture.

Selected Bibliography

Product Information: Risperdal®, risperidone. Janssen Pharmaceutica Products, L.P., Titusville, NJ (PI Revised 11/2002) PI reviewed 12/2002.

Health Canada: Updated Safety Information for Risperdal® (Risperidone) and Cerebrovascular Adverse Events in Placebo-controlled Dementia Trials. Janssen-Ortho Inc., Drug Safety and Surveillance, Toronto, Canada. 10/11/2002.

Risperdal® product monograph (Janssen-Ortho). In: Repchinsky C (editor). CPS Compendium of pharmaceuticals and specialties. Toronto: Canadian Pharmacists Association, 2002: 1486-1490 (PI Revised 2002) PI reviewed 10/2002.

Revised: 05/04/2005
Developed: 09/12/1995

RITONAVIR Systemic

VA CLASSIFICATION (Primary): AM830

Commonly used brand name(s): *Norvir; Norvir SEC.*

Note: For a listing of dosage forms and brand names by country availability, see *Dosage Forms* section(s).

Category

Antiviral (systemic).

Indications

General Considerations

Cross-resistance between ritonavir (a protease inhibitor) and reverse transcriptase inhibitors is thought to be unlikely because each affects a different part of human immunodeficiency virus (HIV) replication.

Varying degrees of cross-resistance among protease inhibitors have been observed. Continued administration of ritonavir therapy following loss of viral suppression may increase the likelihood of cross-resistance to other protease inhibitors.

Accepted

Human immunodeficiency virus (HIV) infection (treatment)—Ritonavir is indicated in combination with other antiretroviral agents for the treatment of HIV infection.

Pharmacology/Pharmacokinetics

Physicochemical characteristics

Molecular weight—720.95.

Mechanism of action/Effect

Ritonavir is a protease inhibitor. It inhibits both human immunodeficiency virus proteases (HIV-1 and HIV-2), which leaves these enzymes incapable of processing the gag-pol polyprotein precursor. This leads to the production of noninfectious immature HIV particles.

Absorption

In one study, when ritonavir oral solution was administered with food, the peak plasma concentration was decreased by 23% and the extent of absorption was decreased by 7% as compared with administration under fasting conditions. However, administration of the oral solution with chocolate milk, *Advera®*, or *Ensure®* did not significantly affect the extent and rate of absorption. When administered with food, 600 mg of ritonavir capsules and oral solution yielded comparable areas under the plasma concentration-time curve in two studies. The extent of absorption of ritonavir from the capsules was 15% higher when administered with a meal than under fasting conditions.

In children less than 2 years of age, the area under the ritonavir plasma concentration-time (AUC) curve and trough concentrations following twice-daily administration of 350 or 450 mg per m^2 were approximately 16% and 60% lower, respectively, compared with adults receiving 600 mg twice daily.

In children less than 2 years of age, higher ritonavir exposures were not evident in those given 450 mg per m^2 twice daily with those given 350 mg per m^2 twice daily.

Protein binding

Very high (98 to 99%).

Biotransformation

Hepatic; five metabolites have been identified in the urine and feces. Isopropylthiazole oxidation metabolite (M-2) is the major metabolite and has antiviral activity similar to that of ritonavir; however, plasma concentrations of M-2 are low. The cytochrome P450 enzymes CYP3A and CYP2D6 are primarily involved in ritonavir metabolism.

Half-life

3 to 5 hours.

Time to peak concentration

Two hours after administration of 600 mg of oral solution under fasting conditions.

Four hours after administration of 600 mg of oral solution with food.

Peak serum concentration

Approximately 11 micrograms per mL after administration of 600 mg every 12 hours.

In children less than 2 years of age, ritonavir trough concentrations following twice-daily administration of 350 or 450 mg per m^2 were somewhat lower compared with adults receiving 600 mg twice daily. However, ritonavir concentrations were comparable.

Elimination

Fecal; approximately 86% of the dose was excreted in the feces, with approximately 34% excreted as unchanged drug.

Renal; approximately 11% of the administered dose was excreted into the urine, with approximately 4% excreted as unchanged drug.

There was a 1.5 to 1.7 times faster steady-state oral clearance ($CL/F/m^2$) in pediatric patients compared with adult patients across dose groups.

Precautions to Consider

Carcinogenicity

Carcinogenicity studies in mice and rats have been done. In male mice, at levels of 50, 100 or 200 mg/kg/day, there was a dose dependent increase in the incidence of both adenomas and combined adenomas and carcinomas in the liver. Based on AUC measurements, the exposure at the high dose was approximately 0.3–fold for male that of the exposure in humans with the recommended therapeutic dose (600 mg BID). There were no carcinogenic effects seen in females at the dosages tested. The exposure at the high dose was approximately 0.6–fold for the females that of the exposure in humans.

In rats dosed at levels of 7,15, or 30 mg/kg/day there were no carcinogenic effects. In this study, the exposure at the high dose was approximately 6% that of the exposure in humans with the recommended therapeutic dose. Based on the exposures achieved in animal studies, the significance of the observed effects is not known.

Mutagenicity

Ritonavir was not found to be mutagenic in a series of *in vitro* and *in vivo* assays, including bacterial reverse mutation (Ames test) using *Salmonella typhimurium* and *Escherichia coli*, mouse lymphoma, mouse micronucleus, and human lymphocyte chromosome aberration assays.

Pregnancy/Reproduction

Fertility—There was no effect on the fertility of rats receiving ritonavir exposures approximately 40% (male) and 60% (female) of those achieved with the recommended human therapeutic dose. Use of higher doses was not feasible due to hepatic toxicity.

Pregnancy—Adequate and well-controlled studies have not been done in humans. Because animal reproduction studies are not always predictive of human response, this drug should be used during pregnancy only if clearly needed.

When ritonavir was administered to pregnant rats and rabbits, no treatment-related malformations were observed. Early resorptions, decreased fetal body weight, ossification delays, and developmental variations occurred in rats at a maternally toxic dosage, equivalent to approximately 30% of the recommended therapeutic dose. There was a slight increase in cryptorchidism in rats exposed to approximately 22% of the recommended therapeutic dose. Resorptions, decreased litter size, and decreased fetal weights also occurred in rabbits administered a maternally toxic dosage equivalent to 1.8 times the recommended therapeutic dose on a mg per square meter of body surface area basis.

An Antiretroviral Pregnancy Registry has been established to monitor the maternal and fetal outcomes of pregnant women exposed to ritonavir. Physicians are encouraged by the manufacturer to register patients by calling (800) 258-4263.

FDA Pregnancy Category B.

Breast-feeding

It is not known whether ritonavir is distributed into breast milk. However, the U.S. Public Health Service Centers for Disease Control and Prevention advises HIV-infected women not to breast-feed, to avoid postnatal transmission of HIV to an uninfected child.

Pediatrics

The antiviral activity and adverse event profile seen during clinical trials and through postmarketing experience in HIV-infected patients less than 1 month to 21 years of age receiving ritonavir was similar to that of adults.

Geriatrics

No information is available on the relationship of age to the effects of ritonavir in geriatric patients. Pharmacokinetic studies have not been done in older patients. Dose selection should be done with caution. Elderly patients are more likely to have age related problems such as hepatic, renal, or cardiac function, and concomitant diseases or other drug therapy.

Drug interactions and/or related problems

The following drug interactions and/or related problems have been selected on the basis of their potential clinical significance (possible mechanism in parentheses where appropriate)—not necessarily inclusive (» = major clinical significance):

Note: Combinations containing any of the following medications, depending on the amount present, may also interact with this medication.

Ritonavir clearance may be increased by the use of other medications that increase the activity of the cytochrome P450 enzyme CYP3A, resulting in decreased ritonavir plasma concentrations. Also, ritonavir may produce a large increase in the plasma concentration of certain highly metabolized medications due to ritonavir's high affinity for several cytochrome P450 enzyme isoforms. The affinity for the isoforms is in the following rank order: CYP3A > CYP2D6 > CYP2C9, CYP2C19 > CYP2A6, CYP1A2, CYP2E1.

Medications that are contraindicated or should not be co-administered with ritonavir

» Alfuzosin or
» Amiodarone or
» Astemizole or
» Bepridil or
» Cisapride or
» Dihydroergotamine or
» Ergonovine or
» Ergotamine or
» Flecainide or
» Lovastatin or
» Methylergonovine or
» Midazolam or
» Pimozide or
» Propafenone or
» Quinidine or
» Simvastatin or
» St. John's Wort (Hypericum perforatum) or
» Terfenadine or
» Triazolam
(these medications should not be co-administered with ritonavir due to the expected magnitude of interaction and potential for serious adverse events)

Note: Post marketing reports indicate that coadministration of ritonavir with ergotamine or dihydroergotamine has been associated with acute ergot toxicity characterized by peripheral vasospasm and ischemia of the extremities.

Established drug interactions—alteration in dose or regimen is recommended

» Clarithromycin
(concomitant use with ritonavir may result in increased clarithromycin concentrations; dosage reduction of clarithromycin is recommended for patients with renal impairment)

» Desipramine
(concomitant use with ritonavir may result in increased desipramine concentrations; monitor concentration of desipramine and dosage reduction of desipramine is recommended)

» Didanosine
(concomitant use of ritonavir may result in decreased didanosine concentrations due to formulation incompatibility; dosing of didanosine and ritonavir should be separated by 2.5 hours)

» Disulfiram
(concomitant use of ritonavir may result in a disulfiram reaction due to ethanol in formulation of soft gelatin capsules and oral solution)

» Ethinyl estradiol-containing oral contraceptives
(concomitant use of ritonavir may result in decreased ethinyl estradiol concentrations; dosage increase of ethinyl estradiol or use of alternate contraceptive measures should be considered)

» Fluticasone, inhaled or nasal
(coadministration not recommended unless potential benefit outweighs risk; concomitants use increases fluticasone propionate plasma concentrations resulting in significantly reduced serum cortisol concentrations; Cushing's syndrome and adrenal suppression have been reported)

» Indinavir
(concurrent use of **reduced doses** of both indinavir and ritonavir may result in increased indinavir C_{min} concentration)

» Ketoconazole
(concomitant use of ritonavir may result in increased ketoconazole concentrations; ketoconazole doses > 200 mg per day are not recommended)

» Meperidine
(concomitant use of ritonavir may result in increased risk of CNS stimulation [e.g., seizures] due to increased concentrations of meperidine metabolite, normeperidine)

» Methadone
(concurrent use of ritonavir may result in decreased methadone concentrations; dosage increase of methadone may be considered)

» Metronidazole
(concomitant use of ritonavir may produce a disulfiram-like reaction due to ethanol in formulation of soft gelatin capsules and oral solution)

» Rifabutin
(concomitant use of ritonavir may result in increased rifabutin and rifabutin metabolite concentrations; dosage and/or regimen reduction is recommended; concomitant use of ritonavir and rifabutin is contraindicated in Canada)

» Rifampin
(concomitant use of ritonavir may result in decreased ritonavir concentrations and loss of virologic response; alternate antimycobacterial is recommended)

» Saquinavir
(concurrent use of **reduced doses** of both saquinavir and ritonavir may result in increased saquinavir concentrations)

» Sildenafil
(concurrent use of ritonavir may result in increased sildenafil concentrations; sildenafil should not exceed a maximum single dose of 25 mg in a 48-hour period in patients receiving concomitant ritonavir therapy)

» Theophylline
(concurrent use of ritonavir may result in decreased theophylline concentrations; consider therapeutic monitoring and increased dosage of theophylline)

Predicted drug interactions—use with caution and consider dose decrease of co-administered drug

Atorvastatin or
Bupropion or
Carbamazepine or
Cerivastatin or
Clonazepam or
Clorazepate or
Cyclosporine or
Dexamethasone or
Diazepam or
Diltiazem or
Disopyramide or
Dronabinol or
Estazolam or
Ethosuximide or
Flurazepam or
Itraconazole or
Lidocaine or
Methamphetamine or
Metoprolol or
Mexiletine or
Nefazodone or
Nifedipine or
Perphenazine or
Prednisone or
Propoxyphene or
Risperidone or
Quinine or
Selective serotonin reuptake inhibitors (SSRI) or
Sirolimus (rapamycin) or
Tacrolimus or
Thioridazine or
Timolol or
Tramadol or
Trazodone or
Tricyclic antidepressants or
Verapamil or
Zolpidem
(use with caution—consider careful monitoring of therapy and dosage **reduction** of co-administered drug)

Predicted drug interactions—use with caution and consider dose increase of co-administered drug

Atovaquone or
Divalproex or

Lamotrigine or
Phenytoin or
Warfarin
(use with caution—consider careful monitoring of therapy and dose **increase** of co-administered drug)

Laboratory value alterations

The following have been selected on the basis of their potential clinical significance (possible effect in parentheses where appropriate)—not necessarily inclusive (» = major clinical significance).

With physiology/laboratory test values
Alanine aminotransferase (ALT [SGPT]), serum and
Aspartate aminotransferase (AST [SGOT]), serum and
Cholesterol and
Creatine kinase (CK) and
Gamma-glutamyltransferase (GGT)
(values may be increased)

Glucose, plasma and
Triglycerides, serum and
Uric acid, serum
(concentrations may be increased)

Hematocrit and
Hemoglobin and
Neutrophils and
RBC and
WBC
(values may be decreased)

Medical considerations/Contraindications

The medical considerations/contraindications included have been selected on the basis of their potential clinical significance (reasons given in parentheses where appropriate)—not necessarily inclusive (» = major clinical significance).

Except under special circumstances, this medication should not be used when the following medical problem exists:
» Hypersensitivity to ritonavir or any of its components

Risk-benefit should be considered when the following medical problems exist:
Diabetes mellitus or
Hyperglycemia
(new onset diabetes mellitus, exacerbation of pre-existing diabetes mellitus, and hyperglycemia have been reported during postmarketing surveillance in HIV-infected patients receiving protease inhibitor therapy; a causal relationship has not been established)

Hemophilia
(increased bleeding, including spontaneous skin hematomas and hemarthrosis, has been reported in patients with hemophilia types A and B who are receiving protease inhibitor therapy; a causal relationship has not been established)

Hepatic function impairment
(because ritonavir is primarily metabolized by the liver, it should be used with caution in patients with pre-existing liver diseases, liver enzyme abnormalities, or hepatitis)

Patient monitoring

The following may be especially important in patient monitoring (other tests may be warranted in some patients, depending on condition; » = major clinical significance):

Alanine aminotransferase (ALT [SGPT]), serum and
Aspartate aminotransferase (AST [SGOT]), serum and
(recommended to closely monitor patients with hepatic impairments; especially during the first three months of treatment)

Alanine aminotransferase (ALT [SGPT]), serum and
Aspartate aminotransferase (AST [SGOT]), serum and
Cholesterol and
Creatine kinase (CK) and
Gamma-glutamyltransferase (GGT) and
Triglycerides, serum and
Uric acid, serum
(appropriate laboratory testing should be performed prior to initiating ritonavir therapy and at periodic intervals or if any clinical signs or symptoms occur during therapy)

Blood glucose determinations
(recommended to monitor closely patient's plasma glucose concentrations; development of hyperglycemia or diabetes may be associated with the use of protease inhibitors)

Cholesterol and
Triglycerides, serum
(should be monitored prior to initiation of therapy, and at periodic intervals during therapy)

Side/Adverse Effects

The following side/adverse effects have been selected on the basis of their potential clinical significance (possible signs and symptoms in parentheses where appropriate)—not necessarily inclusive:

The redistribution or accumulation of body fat, including central obesity, dorsocervical fat enlargement (buffalo hump), peripheral wasting, breast enlargement, and "cushingoid appearance" have been reported in patients on protease inhibitor therapy. A causal relationship between these events and use of protease inhibitors has not been confirmed.

Pancreatitis has been observed in patients receiving ritonavir therapy, including those who developed hypertriglyceridemia. In some cases fatalities have been observed. Patients with advanced HIV disease may be at increased risk of elevated triglycerides and pancreatitis. Pancreatitis should be considered if clinical symptoms (nausea, vomiting, abdominal pain) or abnormalities in lab values (such as increased serum lipase or amylase values) suggestive of pancreatitis should occur. Patients who exhibit these signs or symptoms should be evaluated and ritonavir therapy should be discontinued if a diagnosis of pancreatitis is made.

Cardiac and neurologic events have been reported when ritonavir has been co-administered with disopyramide, mexiletine, nefazodone, fluoxetine, and beta blockers. The possibility of drug interaction can not be excluded.

Reports of allergic reactions have included angioedema, bronchospasm, mild skin eruptions, and urticaria. There are rare reports of anaphylaxis and Stevens-Johnson syndrome.

Orthostatic hypotension, renal insufficiency, and syncope have been reported without known dehydration.

Those indicating need for medical attention

Incidence less frequent

Syncope (fainting); ***vasodilation*** (feeling of warmth or heat; flushing or redness of skin, especially on face and neck; headache; feeling faint, dizzy, or light-headedness; sweating)

Incidence rare

Diabetes or hyperglycemia (dry or itchy skin; fatigue; hunger, increased; thirst, increased; unexplained weight loss; urination, increased); ***ketoacidosis*** (confusion; dehydration; mouth odor, fruity; nausea; vomiting; weight loss)

Incidence not determined—Observed during clinical practice; estimates of frequency can not be determined

Dehydration (confusion; decreased urination; dizziness; dry mouth; fainting; increase in heart rate; lightheadedness; rapid breathing; sunken eyes; thirst; unusual tiredness or weakness; wrinkled skin)—usually associated with gastrointestinal symptoms; ***seizures*** (convulsions; muscle spasm or jerking of all extremities; sudden loss of consciousness; loss of bladder control)

Note: There have been post-marketing reports of dehydration sometimes resulting in hypotension, syncope, or renal insufficiency.

Those indicating need for medical attention only if they continue or are bothersome

Incidence more frequent

Abdominal pain; anorexia (loss of appetite, weight loss); ***asthenia*** (generalized weakness); ***diarrhea; dizziness; dyspepsia*** (acid or sour stomach, belching, heartburn, indigestion, stomach discomfort, upset, or pain); ***fever; headache; insomnia*** (sleeplessness, trouble sleeping, unable to sleep); ***nausea; paresthesia*** (burning, crawling, itching, numbness, prickling, pins and needles, or tingling feelings)—circumoral or peripheral; ***somnolence*** (sleepiness or unusual drowsiness); ***taste perversion*** (change in sense of taste); ***vomiting***

Incidence less frequent

Abnormal thinking (confusion, delusions, dementia); ***anxiety*** (fear, nervousness); ***arthralgia*** (pain in joints, muscle pain or stiffness, difficulty in moving); ***confusion*** (mood or mental changes); ***constipation; depression*** (discouragement, feeling sad or empty, irritability, lack of appetite, loss of interest or pleasure, tiredness, trouble concentrating, trouble sleeping); ***flatulence*** (bloated full feeling, excess air or gas in stomach or intestines, passing gas); ***local throat irritation; malaise*** (general feeling of discomfort or illness, unusual tiredness or weakness); ***myalgia*** (joint pain; swollen joints; muscle aching or cramping; muscle pains or stiffness; difficulty in moving); ***nocturia*** (waking to urinate at night, increased urge to urinate during the night); ***pain, unspecified; pharyngitis*** (body aches or pain, congestion, cough, dryness or soreness of throat, fever, hoarseness, runny nose, tender, swollen glands in neck, trouble in swallowing voice changes); ***rash; sweating; throat irritation; weight loss***

Overdose

Information on ritonavir overdose in humans is limited. There is one report of a patient who took 1500 mg a day of ritonavir for two days. The patient experienced paresthesias, which resolved after the dose was decreased. One case of renal failure with eosinophilia has also been reported with ritonavir overdose. The approximate lethal dose was found to be more than 20 times the recommended human dose in rats and 10 times the recommended human dose in mice.

Ritonavir oral solution contains 43% alcohol by volume. Accidental ingestion of the product by a young child could result in a significant alcohol-related toxicity and could approach the potential lethal dose of alcohol.

For more information on the management of overdose or unintentional ingestion, **contact a Poison Control Center** (see *Poison Control Center Listing*).

Treatment of overdose

To decrease absorption—Induction of emesis or performing gastric lavage.

To enhance elimination—Administration of activated charcoal. Since ritonavir is extensively metabolized by the liver and highly protein bound, dialysis is unlikely to be beneficial in significant removal of the drug.

Monitoring—Monitoring of vital signs and observation of the clinical status of the patient.

Supportive care—Patients in whom intentional overdose is known or suspected should be referred for psychiatric consultation.

Patient Consultation

As an aid to patient consultation, refer to *Advice for the Patient, Ritonavir (Systemic).*

In providing consultation, consider emphasizing the following selected information (» = major clinical significance):

Before using this medication

» Conditions affecting use, especially:
- Hypersensitivity to ritonavir or any of its components
- Pregnancy—Should be used during pregnancy only if clearly needed
- Breast-feeding—The U.S. Public Health Service Centers for Disease Control and Prevention advises HIV-infected women not to breast-feed, to avoid postnatal transmission of HIV to an uninfected child.
- Use in children—Safety and effectiveness have not been established in infants one month of age or less.
- Other medications, especially alfuzosin, amiodarone, astemizole, bepridil, cisapride, clarithromycin, desipramine, didanosine, dihydroergotamine, disulfiram, ergonovine, ergotamine, ethinyl estradiol-containing oral contraceptives, flecainide, fluticasone (inhaled or nasal), indinavir, ketoconazole, lovastatin, meperidine, methadone, methylergonovine, metronidazole, midazolam, pimozide, propafenone, quinidine, rifabutin, rifampin, saquinavir, sildenafil, simvastatin, St. John's Wort (hypericum perforatum), terfenadine, theophylline, or triazolam

Proper use of this medication

» Importance of taking ritonavir with food

» For oral solution formulation:
- Importance of shaking the bottle well before using.
- Importance of using a calibrated oral syringe to accurately measure each dose.

» Importance of not taking more medication than prescribed; importance of not discontinuing ritonavir without checking with physician

» Compliance with full course of therapy

» Importance of not missing doses and of taking at evenly spaced times

Not sharing medication with others

» Proper dosing

Missed dose: Taking as soon as possible; not taking if almost time for next dose; not doubling doses

» Proper storage

Soft gelatin capsule formulation—store in refrigerator

Oral solution formulation—store at room temperature

Precautions while using this medication

» Because ritonavir may interact with other medications, not taking any other medications (prescription or nonprescription) without first checking with physician

» Regular visits to physician for blood tests and monitoring of blood glucose concentrations

» Using an additional method of contraception if taking estrogen-containing oral contraceptives concurrently

Side/adverse effects

Signs of potential side effects, especially redistribution or accumulation of body fat, pancreatitis, cardiac and neurologic events, allergic reactions, orthostatic hypotension, renal insufficiency, syncope, vasodilation, diabetes or hyperglycemia, or ketoacidosis

Signs of potential side effects observed during clinical practice, especially dehydration or seizures

General Dosing Information

If an adult or adolescent patient experiences nausea or other adverse events upon initiation of 600 mg two times a day, the following dose escalation may be beneficial: 300 mg two times a day, then increasing the dose by 100 mg two times a day up to 600 mg two times a day.

If a pediatric patient cannot tolerate a dose of 400 mg per square meter of body surface area two times a day due to adverse events, the highest tolerated dose should be used for maintenance therapy in combination with other antiretroviral agents.

Patients who are initiating both ritonavir and nucleoside analogs may improve gastrointestinal tolerance by initiating ritonavir alone and then adding the nucleoside analog within 2 weeks.

The taste of ritonavir oral solution may be improved by mixing with chocolate milk, *Ensure*®, or *Advera*® within one hour of dosing. The effects of antacids on the absorption of ritonavir have not been studied.

Diet/Nutrition

It is recommended that ritonavir be taken with meals, if possible.

Oral Dosage Forms

RITONAVIR CAPSULES

Usual adult and adolescent dose

Antiviral—

Recommended dosage—

Oral, 600 mg two times a day with food. Ritonavir should be started at no less than 300 mg twice daily and increased at 2 to 3 day intervals by 100 mg twice daily.

Concomitant therapy—

Rifabutin: Oral, dose reduction of rifabutin by at least three-quarters of the usual dose of 300 mg/day; further reduction may be necessary

Saquinavir: Oral, ritonavir dose has not been determined; saquinavir should be reduced to 400 mg twice daily. The combination regimen was better tolerated in patients who received ritonavir 400 mg twice daily.

Sildenafil: Oral, maximum sildenafil dose 25 mg in 48 hours

Note: Renally impaired patients with concomitant clarithromycin administration: CL_{CR} 30 to 60 mL/min clarithromycin dose should be reduced by 50%; $CL_{CR} < 30$ mL/min clarithromycin dose should be reduced by 75%.

Usual pediatric dose

This dosage form usually is not used in children. See *Ritonavir Oral Solution.*

Strength(s) usually available

U.S.—

100 mg (Rx) [*Norvir* (ethanol; butylated hydroxytoluene; gelatin; iron oxide; oleic acid; polyoxyl 35 castor oil; titanium dioxide)].

Canada—

100 mg (Rx) [*Norvir SEC* (ethanol; butylated hydroxytoluene; fractionated coconut oil; gelatin; glycerin; iron oxide; lecithin; oleic acid; polyoxyl 35 castor oil; purified water; sorbitol; titanium dioxide)].

Packaging and storage

Store in the refrigerator between 2 and 8 °C (36 and 46 °F) until dispensed. Protect from light.

Storage after dispensing to patient: refrigeration is recommended, but is not required if used within 30 days and stored below 25 °C (77 °F). Avoid exposure to excessive heat.

Auxiliary labeling

- Take with food.
- Continue medicine for full time of treatment.
- Refrigerate.
- Do not take other medications without physician's advice.

RITONAVIR ORAL SOLUTION

Usual adult and adolescent dose

This dosage form usually is not used in adults or adolescents. See *Ritonavir Capsules.*

Usual pediatric dose

Infants greater than one month of age: Oral, 350 to 400 mg per square meter [mg/m^2] of body surface area and should not exceed 600 mg twice daily.

Starting dose: Oral, 250 mg/m^2 of body surface area two times a day, increasing by 50 mg/m^2 of body surface area two times a day in two- to three-day intervals, up to a total dosage of 400 mg/m^2 of body surface area two times a day, according to the following table:

Body Surface Area (m^2)	250 mg/m^2 (given two times a day)	300 mg/m^2 (given two times a day)	350 mg/m^2 (given two times a day)	400 mg/m^2 (given two times a day)
0.2	0.6 mL (50 mg)	0.75 mL (60 mg)	0.9 mL (70 mg)	1 mL (80 mg)
0.25	0.8 mL (62.5 mg)	0.9 mL (75 mg)	1.1 mL (87.5 mg)	1.25 mL (100 mg)
0.5	1.6 mL (125 mg)	1.9 mL (150 mg)	2.2 mL (175 mg)	2.5 mL (200 mg)
1	3.1 mL (250 mg)	3.75 mL (300 mg)	4.4 mL (350 mg)	5 mL (400 mg)
1.25	3.9 mL (312.5 mg)	4.7 mL (375 mg)	5.5 mL (437.5 mg)	6.25 mL (500 mg)
1.5	4.7 mL (375 mg)	5.6 mL (450 mg)	6.6 mL (525 mg)	7.5 mL (600 mg)

Note: Body surface area (m^2) = the square root of [(Height [cm] X Weight [kg])/3600]

Usual pediatric prescribing limits

1200 mg per day.

Strength(s) usually available

U.S.—

80 mg per mL (Rx) [*Norvir* (ethanol; saccharin sodium; FD&C Yellow No. 6)].

Canada—

80 mg per mL (Rx) [*Norvir* (ethanol; anhydrous citric acid; creamy carmel flavoring; FD&C Yellow No. 6; peppermint oil; polyoxyl 35 castor oil; propylene glycol; saccharin sodium water)].

Packaging and storage

Store at room temperature between 20 and 25 °C (68 and 77 °F); it should not be refrigerated. The oral solution should be stored in the original container. Keep cap tightly closed. Avoid exposure to excessive heat. Use by product expiration date.

Auxiliary labeling

- Shake well.
- Take with food.
- Continue medicine for full time of treatment.
- Do not take other medications without physician's advice.

Revised: 11/03/2005
Developed: 01/27/1997

RITUXIMAB Systemic

VA CLASSIFICATION (Primary): AN900

Commonly used brand name(s): *Rituxan*.

Note: For a listing of dosage forms and brand names by country availability, see *Dosage Forms* section(s).

Category

Monoclonal antibody; antineoplastic.

Indications

Note: Bracketed information in the *Indications* section refers to uses that are not included in U.S. product labeling.

Accepted

Lymphomas, non-Hodgkin's (treatment)—Rituximab is indicated for the treatment of patients with relapsed or refractory low-grade or follicular CD20-positive, B-cell non-Hodgkin's lymphoma. Rituximab is also indicated for use in first-line treatment, as a single agent, in combination with the CHOP regimen, anthracycline-based chemotherapy regimens, or [other agents][1] active in this disease. For responders and patients with stable disease, [re-induction treatment][1] with rituximab, is also appropriate.

Rituximab is also indicated in [relapsed or refractory diffuse aggressive non-Hodgkin's lymphoma, as a single agent, in combination with the CHOP regimen, or in combination with other agents active in this disease.][1] [Use as a single agent, for first-line treatment, is appropriate only in selected elderly patients with diffuse aggressive non-Hodgkin's lymphoma.][1]

Lymphomas, non-Hodgkin's, (in combination for first-line treatment)—Rituximab is indicated for the first-line treatment of diffuse large B-cell, CD20-positive, non-Hodgkin's lymphoma in combination with CHOP or other anthracycline-based chemotherapy regimens.

[Chronic lymphocytic leukemia, in combination for first line treatment][1]—Rituximab has demonstrated activity in combination with fludarabine and with fludarabine and cyclophosphamide in the first line treatment of chronic lymphocytic leukemia. Overall response rates of 87% to 95% have been reported during concurrent first line treatment. In a trial of sequential versus concurrent rituximab, the concurrent treatment protocol yielded a 90% overall response rate while the sequential protocol yielded a 77% overall response rate. Complete response rates varied per trial from 23% to 70%. Infections and hematologic toxicities were the most commonly reported adverse effects.

[Leukemia, chronic lymphocytic (treatment)][1]—Rituximab is indicated for the treatment of relapsed/refractory chronic lymphocytic leukemia (CLL).

[Waldenstrom's macroglobulinemia (treatment)][1]—Rituximab is indicated for the treatment of relapsed/refractory Waldenstrom's macroglobulinemia.

[Thrombocytopenic purpura, immune or idiopathic (treatment)][1]—Rituximab is indicated for the treatment of immune or idiopathic thrombocytopenic purpura.

Acceptance not established

Autoimmune hemolytic anemia, in adult and pediatric patients—Rituximab is a promising agent in the treatment of autoimmune hemolytic anemia (AIHA) in adult and pediatric patients. Small, open-label, single-arm, published clinical trials have resulted in responses to rituximab in adult patients with either previously untreated or refractory, idiopathic or secondary, cold agglutinin AIHA or AIHA of chronic lymphocytic leukemia and in refractory AIHA with various associated features in pediatric patients. Additional small, open-label, single-arm, unpublished clinical trials have resulted in responses in adult patients with warm agglutinin AIHA. An unpublished summary of case reports in adult patients with a variety of types of AIHA reported a response rate of 72% in a total of 92 patients. Rituximab was well-tolerated with transient, mild to moderate infusion reactions, rare cases of reversible hematologic toxicity and infection.

[1]Not included in Canadian product labeling.

Pharmacology/Pharmacokinetics

Physicochemical characteristics

Source—Synthetic (genetically engineered) chimeric murine/human monoclonal antibody, an IgG1-kappa immunoglobulin containing murine light- and heavy-chain variable region sequences and human constant region sequences. It is composed of two heavy chains of 451 amino acids and two light chains of 213 amino acids (based on cDNA analysis). The chimeric anti-CD20 antibody is produced by mammalian cell (Chinese hamster ovary) suspension culture in a nutrient medium containing gentamicin (although gentamicin does not appear in the final product). Purification procedure includes affinity and ion exchange chromatography, as well as specific viral inactivation and removal procedures.

Molecular weight—145 kilodaltons.

pH—6.5.

Binding affinity—For CD20 antigen: Approximately 8 nanomolar.

Mechanism of action/Effect

Rituximab, a murine/human monoclonal antibody, binds to the antigen CD20 (human B-lymphocyte–restricted differentiation antigen, Bp35). This antigen is a hydrophobic transmembrane protein, with a molecular weight of approximately 35,000 daltons, that is located on pre-B and mature B lymphocytes. It is also expressed on more than 90% of B-cell non-Hodgkin's lymphomas but not expressed on hematopoietic stem cells, pro-B cells, normal plasma cells, or other normal tissues. CD20 regulates an early step or steps in the activation process for cell cycle initiation and differentiation and may also function as a calcium ion channel. It is not shed from the cell surface and does not internalize upon antibody binding. No free CD20 antigen is found in the circulation.

The mechanism of antineoplastic action may involve mediation of B cell lysis (seen *in vitro*) by means of binding of the Fab domain of rituximab to the CD20 antigen on B lymphocytes and by recruitment of immune effector functions by the Fc domain. Cell lysis may be the result of complement-dependent cytotoxicity (CDC) and antibody-dependent cellular cytotoxicity (ADCC). In addition, the antibody has been shown to induce apoptosis in the DHL-4 human B-cell lymphoma line.

Rituximab binds to lymphoid cells in the thymus, the white pulp of the spleen, and a majority of B lymphocytes in peripheral blood and lymph nodes. However, there appears to be little or no binding to non-lymphoid tissues.

Half-life

Intravenous infusion (for four doses)—

After the first dose: Mean, 59.8 hours (range, 11.1 to 104.6 hours).

After the fourth dose: Mean, 174 hours (range, 26 to 442 hours).

Note: The wide range may be related to variable tumor burden among patients, as well as the changes that were seen in CD20-positive (normal and malignant) B-cell populations with repeated administration.

No difference has been found in the rate of elimination of rituximab, as measured by serum half-life, in responders versus nonresponders.

Rituximab has been found to be detectable in serum for 3 to 6 months after completion of treatment.

Onset of action

Depletion of circulating B cells (measured as CD19-positive cells)—Within the first three doses.

Depletion of tissue-based B cells (measured in lymph node biopsies)—Fourteen days after a single dose.

Note: Rituximab treatment results in depletion of both circulating and tissue-based B cells.

Peak serum concentration

Inversely correlated with baseline values for the number of circulating CD20-positive B cells and measures of disease burden.

Note: Trough serum concentrations also are inversely correlated with baseline values for the number of circulating CD20-positive B cells and measures of disease burden.

Median steady-state serum concentrations have been found to be higher in responders than in nonresponders.

Serum concentrations have been found to be higher in patients with International Working Formulation (IWF) subtypes B, C, and D as compared to those with subtype A.

Duration of action

Depletion of circulating B cells (measured as CD19-positive cells)—Up to 6 to 9 months after treatment, with median B-cell levels returning to normal by 12 months following completion of treatment.

Note: Sustained and statistically significant reductions in IgG and IgM serum concentrations occurred from the fifth through the eleventh month after administration, but only 14% of patients experienced reductions in IgG and/or IgM serum concentrations to values below the normal range.

Precautions to Consider

Cross-sensitivity and/or related problems

Patients sensitive to murine proteins may also be sensitive to rituximab.

Carcinogenicity

Long-term studies in animals have not been done.

Mutagenicity

Long-term studies in animals have not been done.

Pregnancy/Reproduction

Fertility—Studies in animals have not been done.

Pregnancy—Studies in humans have not been done.

Studies in animals have not been done.

Immunoglobulin G (IgG) is known to cross the placenta and therefore could cause fetal B cell depletion.

It is recommended that women of childbearing potential use effective contraception during treatment and for up to 12 months following treatment with rituximab. Risk-benefit should be considered before use of rituximab during pregnancy.

FDA Pregnancy Category C.

Breast-feeding

It is not known whether rituximab is distributed into human breast milk. However, human IgG is distributed into human milk, although the potential for absorption and consequent immunosuppression in the infant is unknown. It is recommended that women treated with rituximab not breast-feed until circulating drug levels are no longer detectable.

Pediatrics

Safety and efficacy have not been established.

Geriatrics

Appropriate studies performed to date have not demonstrated geriatrics-specific problems that would limit the usefulness of rituximab in the elderly. Adverse reactions, including incidence, severity and type of adverse reaction were similar between older and younger patients.

Pharmacogenetics

In the reported cases of severe infusion reactions, female gender was one factor more frequently associated with fatal outcomes.

Drug interactions and/or related problems

The following drug interactions and/or related problems have been selected on the basis of their potential clinical significance (possible mechanism in parentheses where appropriate)—not necessarily inclusive (» = major clinical significance):

Antihypertensive medications
(withholding of antihypertensive medications for 12 hours prior to rituximab administration should be considered because rituximab may cause hypotension)

Chemotherapy
(majority of reported hepatitis B virus [HBV] reactivation with fulminant hepatitis, hepatic failure, and death were in patients receiving rituximab in combination with chemotherapy)

» Cisplatin
(renal toxicity was seen with concurrent administration in clinical trials; cisplatin and rituximab combination is not an approved treatment regimen; extreme caution should be exercised and patients should be monitored closely for renal failure)

Vaccines, killed virus or
Vaccines, live virus
(rituximab theoretically may inhibit the generation of an anamnestic or humoral response to any vaccine)

Laboratory value alterations

The following have been selected on the basis of their potential clinical significance (possible effect in parentheses where appropriate)—not necessarily inclusive (» = major clinical significance).

With physiology/laboratory test values

B-cell counts and
Immunoglobulin concentrations
(may be decreased; B cell depletion is associated with a decrease in serum immunoglobulin concentrations in a minority of patients; however, incidence of infection does not appear to be increased)

Blood pressure
(may be increased or decreased)

Creatinine, serum
(may increase with rituximab treatment; discontinuation should be considered with rising concentrations)

Glucose, serum
(increases in concentrations [hyperglycemia] have been reported infrequently)

Hemoglobin concentrations and
Hematocrit
(may be decreased)

Lactate dehydrogenase (LDH), serum
(increases in values have been reported infrequently)

Neutrophil counts and
Platelet counts
(may be decreased)

Medical considerations/Contraindications

The medical considerations/contraindications included have been selected on the basis of their potential clinical significance (reasons given in parentheses where appropriate)—not necessarily inclusive (» = major clinical significance).

Except under special circumstances, this medication should not be used when the following medical problems exist:

» Anaphylaxis to murine proteins, rituximab, or any component of this product or

» IgE-mediated hypersensitivity to murine proteins, rituximab, or any component of this product
(severe hypersensitivity reactions could occur in these patients)

Risk-benefit should be considered when the following medical problems exist:

Cardiacconditions (history of), including
Angina

Arrhythmias
Pulmonary conditions (history of)
(recurrences in patients with pre-existing cardiac and pulmonary conditions and those with prior clinically significant cardiopulmonary adverse events have been reported during rituximab therapy; monitoring throughout the infusion and immediately post-infusion is recommended)

» Hepatitis B virus [HBV], high risk of or carriers
(reported HBV reactivation with fulminant hepatitis, hepatic failure and death in some patients with hematologic malignancies treated with rituximab)

» High numbers of circulating malignant cells (>25,000 per mm³) or
» High tumor burden or
» Renal dysfunction
(patients with these conditions are at higher risk for severe infusion reactions, tumor lysis syndrome [TLS], or renal toxicity; prophylaxis for TLS should be considered; close monitoring for severe infusion reactions recommended during first and all subsequent infusions)

Patient monitoring

The following may be especially important in patient monitoring (other tests may be warranted in some patients, depending on condition; » = major clinical significance):

» Blood counts, complete and
Platelet counts
(recommended at periodic intervals during therapy, more frequently in patients who develop cytopenias)

» Creatinine, serum
(may be increased; discontinuation of rituximab should be considered in patients with rising serum creatinine or oliguria)

Electrocardiogram (ECG)
(continuous monitoring recommended during administration of rituximab and during the immediate post-infusion period in patients with pre-existing cardiac conditions, including angina and arrhythmias; for patients who develop clinically significant arrhythmias during rituximab administration, continuous monitoring is recommended during subsequent administrations)

» Hepatitis B virus [HBV] clinical and laboratory signs
(high risk patients should be screened before initiation of rituximab; carriers of hepatitis B should be closely monitored for clinical and laboratory signs of active HBV infection and for signs of hepatitis during and for up to several months following rituximab therapy)

Side/Adverse Effects

Note: Severe and life-threatening (grades 3 and 4) reactions have occurred in approximately 57% of patients. These included (in some cases, only in one patient) abdominal pain, anemia, angioedema, anxiety, arthralgia, arrhythmia, asthenia, asthma, back pain, bronchiolitis obliterans, bronchospasm, chills, coagulation disorder, diarrhea, dizziness, dyspnea, fever, headache, hyperglycemia, hypertension, hypotension, hypoxia, increased cough, infection, leukopenia, lymphopenia, myalgia, nausea, neutropenia, night sweats, pain, pruritus, rhinitis, skin rash, thrombocytopenia, urticaria, and vomiting.

Human antichimeric antibody [HACA] was detected in 4 out of 356 patients; 3 had an objective clinical response. Development of HACA is associated with allergic or hypersensitivity reactions in patients treated with murine or chimeric monoclonal antibodies.

In most cases, incidence of side/adverse effects is the same for one course or several courses of treatment. However, side/adverse effects seen more frequently in re-treated subjects have included anemia, anorexia, asthenia, dizziness, flushing, leukopenia, mental depression, night sweats, peripheral edema, pruritus, respiratory symptoms, tachycardia, throat irritation, and thrombocytopenia.

The incidence of any side/adverse effect in patients with bulky disease versus those with lesions less than 10 centimeters in diameter was similar. However, incidence of specific side/adverse effects (abdominal pain, anemia, dyspnea, hypotension, and neutropenia) was higher in patients with lesions greater than 10 centimeters in diameter.

Rituximab induced B cell depletion in 70 to 80% of patients, with an associated decrease in serum immunoglobulins in a minority of patients. The lymphopenia lasted a median of 14 days. Infectious events included bacterial, viral, fungal, and unknown infections. Serious infectious events (Grade 3 or 4), including sepsis, occurred in 2% of patients.

Rare reports of prolonged pancytopenia and bone marrow hypoplasia have been received in postmarketing data.

Grade 3 or 4 cardiac-related events include hypotension. Rare, fatal cardiac failure with symptomatic onset weeks after rituximab administration also has been reported.

Pulmonary events such as increased cough, rhinitis, bronchospasm, dyspnea, and sinusitis have been reported. Acute bronchospasms, acute pneumonitis (1 to 4 weeks post-infusion), and bronchiolitis obliterans have been reported in temporal association with rituximab infusion as a single agent. The safety of resuming or continuing administration of rituximab in patients with pneumonitis or bronchiolitis obliterans is unknown.

The following side/adverse effects have been selected on the basis of their potential clinical significance (possible signs and symptoms in parentheses where appropriate)—not necessarily inclusive:

Those indicating need for medical attention

Incidence more frequent

Anemia (pale skin, troubled breathing with exertion, unusual bleeding or bruising, unusual tiredness or weakness); ***hyperglycemia*** (abdominal pain, blurred vision, dry mouth, fatigue, flushed, dry skin, fruit-like breath odor, increased hunger, increased thirst, increased urination, nausea, sweating, troubled breathing, unexplained weight); ***hypertension*** (blurred vision, dizziness, nervousness, headache, pounding in the ears, slow or fast heartbeat)—symptomatic or asymptomatic; ***infection*** (fever or chills, cough or hoarseness lower back or side pain, painful or difficult urination); ***infusion-related reaction; including angioedema*** (feeling of swelling of tongue or throat); ***bronchospasm or dyspnea*** (shortness of breath); ***fatigue*** (unusual tiredness); ***fever and chills; flushing of face; headache; hypotension*** (dizziness); ***nausea; pruritus*** (itching); ***rhinitis*** (runny nose); ***urticaria*** (skin rash); ***and vomiting; leukopenia*** (black, tarry stools, chest pain, chills, cough, fever, painful or difficult urination, shortness of breath, sore throat, sores, ulcers, or white spots on lips or in mouth, swollen glands, unusual bleeding or bruising, unusual tiredness or weakness); ***lymphopenia*** (fever or chills, cough or hoarseness, lower back or side pain, painful or difficult urination); ***neutropenia*** (black, tarry, stools, chills, cough, fever, lower back or side pain, painful or difficult urination, pale skin, shortness of breath, sore throat, ulcers, sores, or white spots in mouth, unusual bleeding or bruising, unusual tiredness or weakness); ***peripheral edema*** (bloating or swelling of face, arms, hands, lower legs, or feet, rapid weight gain, tingling of hands or feet, unusual weight gain or loss); ***sinusitis*** (pain or tenderness around eyes and cheekbones, fever, stuffy or runny nose, headache, cough, shortness of breath or troubled breathing, tightness of chest or wheezing); ***thrombocytopenia*** (black, tarry stools; bleeding gums; blood in urine or stools; pinpoint red spots on skin; unusual bleeding or bruising)

Note: *Fever and chills* occur in a majority of patients during the first rituximab infusion. *Infusion-related reactions* usually occur within 30 minutes to 2 hours of the beginning of the first infusion and can be resolved by slowing or interrupting the infusion and administering supportive care (diphenhydramine, acetaminophen, intravenous saline, and vasopressors). Patients also may be premedicated with diphenhydramine prior to starting the infusion. The incidence of these reactions is decreased with subsequent infusions.

Mild to moderate *hypotension* may require interruption of the infusion, with or without administration of intravenous saline (sodium chloride).

Severe infusion reactions have been reported and have been associated with fatal outcomes. These severe reactions typically occurred during the first infusion with time to onset of 30 to 120 minutes. Signs and symptoms of severe infusion reactions may include hypotension, angioedema, hypoxia, or bronchospasm. The most severe manifestations include pulmonary infiltrates, acute respiratory distress syndrome, myocardial infarction, ventricular fibrillation, and cardiogenic shock. Factors more frequently associated with fatal outcomes include female gender, pulmonary infiltrates, and chronic lymphocytic leukemia or mantle cell lymphoma. Interruption of treatment may be needed and supportive care measures should be started as deemed medically needed. Treatment may be resumed at a 50% reduced rate when symptoms have completely resolved.

Isolated cases of a severe *infusion-related reaction* requiring administration of epinephrine have been reported with use of rituximab for indications other than the labeled indication.

Approximately 25% of patients who experienced *bronchospasm* have required treatment with bronchodilators.

Incidence less frequent

Arthritis (pain, swelling, or redness in joints, muscle pain or stiffness, difficulty in moving); **conjunctivitis** (red, itchy lining of eye); **depression** (discouragement, feeling sad or empty, irritability, lack of appetite, loss of interest or pleasure, tiredness, trouble concentrating, trouble sleeping); **mucocutaneous reactions, severe; including paraneoplastic pemphigus** (blisters in the mouth; blisters on the trunk, scalp, or other areas; itching); **Stevens-Johnson syndrome** (blistering, peeling, loosening of skin; chills; cough; diarrhea; itching; joint or muscle pain; red irritated eyes; red skin lesions, often with a purple center; sore throat; sores, ulcers, or white spots in mouth or on lips; unusual tiredness or weakness); **lichenoid dermatitis; vesiculobullous dermatitis; and toxic epidermal necrolysis** (blistering, peeling, loosening of skin; chills; cough; diarrhea; itching; joint or muscle pain; red irritated eyes; red skin lesions, often with a purple center; sore throat; sores, ulcers, or white spots in mouth or on lips; unusual tiredness or weakness); **neuritis** (numbness or tingling of hands, feet, or face); **neuropathy** (burning, tingling, numbness or pain in the hands, arms, feet, or legs, sensation of pins and needles stabbing pain); **paresthesia** (burning, crawling, itching, numbness, prickling, "pins and needles", or tingling feelings); **tumor lysis syndrome; resulting in acute renal failure** (lower back or side pain; decreased frequency or amount of urine; bloody urine; increased thirst; loss of appetite; nausea; vomiting; unusual tiredness or weakness; swelling of face, fingers, lower legs; weight gain; troubled breathing; increased blood pressure)

Note: Mucocutaneous reactions, some with fatal outcome, have been reported with the onset of the reaction varying from 1 to 13 weeks following rituximab exposure. Patients experiencing a severe mucocutaneous reaction should not receive any further infusions and seek prompt medical evaluation. Skin biopsy may help to distinguish among different mucocutaneous reactions and guide subsequent treatment. The safety of readministration of rituximab to patients with any of these mucocutaneous reactions has not been determined.

Note: Tumor lysis syndrome [TLS] (a rapid reduction in tumor volume followed by acute renal failure, hyperkalemia, hypocalcemia, hyperuricemia, or hyperphosphatasemia) has been reported within 12 to 24 hours after the first infusion; risks appear to be greater in patients with high numbers of circulating malignant cells or high tumor burden. Rare instances of fatal outcome have been reported in the setting of TLS following treatment with rituximab. Prophylaxis for TLS should be considered for patients at high risk. Correction of electrolyte abnormalities, monitoring of renal function and fluid balance, and administration of supportive care, including dialysis, should be initiated as indicated. Following complete resolution of the complications of TLS, rituximab has been tolerated when readministered in conjunction with prophylactic therapy for TLS in a limited number of cases.

Note: During the treatment period, and for up to 30 days following the last dose, severe *anemia*, *neutropenia*, or *thrombocytopenia* has been reported in 1%, 1.9%, and 1.3% of patients, respectively.

Incidence rare

Angina (chest pain); **cardiac arrhythmias, including ventricular tachycardia, supraventricular tachycardia, trigeminy, and irregular pulse** (irregular heartbeat)

Note: Bradycardia also has been reported.

Incidence not determined—Observed during clinical practice; estimates of frequency can not be determined

Abdominal pain (stomach pain); **bowel obstruction and perforation** (abdominal or stomach cramps or pain; black, tarry stools; diarrhea; fever; severe vomiting, sometimes with blood); **herpes simplex virus** (burning or stinging of skin; painful cold sores or blisters on lips, nose, eyes, or genitals); **hyperviscosity syndrome in Waldenstrom's macroglobulinemia** (fatigue; rash; nosebleeds; weight loss; vision changes); **increased fatal infections in HIV-associated lymphoma** (fever or chills; cough or hoarseness; lower back or side pain; painful or difficult urination); **lupus-like syndrome** (fever or chills; general feeling of discomfort, illness, or weakness); **optic neuritis** (blindness; blue-yellow color blindness; blurred vision; decreased vision; eye pain); **pleuritis** (chest pain; chills and fever; dry cough; troubled breathing); **polyarticular arthritis** (pain in many joints; swelling, stiffness redness, or warmth around many joints); **serum sickness** (feeling of discomfort; fever; inflammation of joints; itching; muscle aches; rash; swollen lymph glands); **systemic vasculitis** (severe abdominal pain); **uveitis** (eye pain, tearing; sensitivity of eye to light; redness of eye, or blurred vision or other change in vision); **vasculitis with rash** (redness, soreness or itching skin; fever; sores, welting or blisters); **viral infections** (chills; cough or hoarseness; fever; cold flu-like symptoms)—new, reactivated or exacerbated; occurring up to 1 year after discontinuation of rituximab

Note: Abdominal pain, bowel obstruction and perforation, in some cases leading to death, were observed in patients receiving rituximab in combination with chemotherapy for diffuse large B-cell lymphoma (DLBCL). In post-marketing reports, the mean time to onset of symptoms was 6 days in patients with documented gastrointestinal perforation. Complaints of abdominal pain, especially early in the course of treatment, should prompt a thorough diagnostic evaluation and appropriate treatment.

The viral infections listed above have been identified in clinical studies or postmarketing reports as either new, reactivated, or exacerbated. The majority of these patients received rituximab in combination with chemotherapy or as part of a hematopoietic stem cell transplant. In some cases, the viral infections occurred up to one year following rituximab discontinuation and have resulted in death.

Those indicating need for medical attention only if they continue or are bothersome

Incidence more frequent

Anxiety (fear, nervousness); **arthralgia** (pain in joints, muscle pain or stiffness, difficulty in moving); **asthenia** (lack or loss of strength); **back pain; diarrhea; dizziness; increased cough; myalgia** (joint pain, swollen joints, muscle aching or cramping, muscle pains or stiffness, difficulty in moving); **night sweats; pain; rash; throat irritation**

Incidence less frequent—1 to 5%

Agitation; anorexia (loss of appetite); **back pain; change in taste; diarrhea; dyspepsia** (heartburn); **hyperkinesia** (increase in body movements); **hypertonia** (excessive muscle tone, muscle tension or tightness, muscle stiffness); **hypesthesia or paresthesia** (numbness or tingling of hands or feet); **injection site pain; insomnia** (trouble in sleeping); **lacrimation disorder** (dry eyes); **loss of appetite; malaise** (general feeling of discomfort or illness); **nervousness; somnolence** (sleepiness or unusual drowsiness); **vertigo** (dizziness or lightheadedness; feeling of constant movement of self or surroundings, sensation of spinning); **weight decrease**

Those indicating the need for medical attention if they occur after medication is discontinued

Anemia (unusual tiredness or weakness)—usually asymptomatic; **neutropenia** (fever or chills; cough or hoarseness; lower back or side pain; painful or difficult urination)—usually asymptomatic; **thrombocytopenia** (unusual bleeding or bruising; black, tarry stools; blood in urine or stools; pinpoint red spots on skin)

Note: During the treatment period, and for up to 30 days following the last dose, severe *anemia*, *neutropenia*, or *thrombocytopenia* has been reported in 1%, 1.9%, and 1.3% of patients, respectively.

Patient Consultation

As an aid to patient consultation, refer to *Advice for the Patient, Rituximab (Systemic)*.

In providing consultation, consider emphasizing the following selected information (» = major clinical significance):

Before using this medication

» Conditions affecting use, especially:

Known anaphylaxis or IgE-mediated hypersensitivity to murine proteins, rituximab, or any component of this product

Pregnancy—Use of contraception recommended in women of childbearing potential; risk-benefit should be considered during pregnancy

Breast-feeding—Not recommended as long as rituximab is detectable in the blood because of the risk of absorption and consequent immunosuppression in the infant

Pharmacogenetics—Women more frequently associated with fatal outcomes in patients with severe infusion reactions caused by rituximab

Other medications, especially cisplatin

Other medical problems, especially hepatitis B virus (high risk of or carriers), high numbers of circulating malignant cells, high tumor burden, or renal dysfunction

Proper use of this medication

» Proper dosing

Precautions while using this medication

Importance of monitoring patients who are at high risk or carriers of hepatitis B virus [HBV]

Evaluating complaints of abdominal pain, especially those early in the course of treatment, due to possibility of bowel obstruction or perforation

Side/adverse effects

Signs of potential side effects, especially anemia, hyperglycemia, hypertension, infection, infusion-related reaction (angioedema, bronchospasm or dyspnea, fatigue, fever and chills, flushing of face, headache, hypotension, nausea, pruritus, rhinitis, urticaria, vomiting), leukopenia, lymphopenia, neutropenia, peripheral edema, sinusitis, thrombocytopenia, arthritis, conjunctivitis, depression, neuritis, neuropathy, paresthesia, tumor lysis syndrome (resulting in acute renal failure), angina, and cardiac arrhythmias (ventricular tachycardia, supraventricular tachycardia, trigeminy, and irregular pulse).

Signs of potential side effects observed during clinical practice, especially abdominal pain, bowel obstruction and perforation, herpes simplex virus, hyperviscosity syndrome in Waldenstrom's macroglobulinemia, increased fatal infections in HIV-associated lymphoma, lupus-like syndrome, optic neuritis, pleuritis, polyarticular arthritis, serum sickness, systemic vasculitis, uveitis, vasculitis with rash or viral infections (new, reactivated or exacerbated)

Asymptomatic side effects, including anemia, hypertension, and neutropenia.

General Dosing Information

Rituximab is recommended for administration by intravenous infusion only. Rapid intravenous (push or bolus) administration is not recommended.

It is recommended that medications for hypersensitivity reactions (e.g., epinephrine, antihistamines, corticosteroids) be available for each administration of rituximab.

Premedication with acetaminophen and diphenhydramine may attenuate the hypersensitivity reaction and should be considered before each dose of rituximab.

If a severe infusion-related hypersensitivity (non-IgE-mediated) reaction occurs, it is recommended that the infusion be discontinued. Hypotension, bronchospasm, and angioedema have occurred in association with rituximab infusion. The infusion may be resumed at a 50% reduction in rate (e.g., from 100 mg/hr to 50 mg/hr) when symptoms have completely resolved. Treatment of symptoms with diphenhydramine and acetaminophen is recommended, along with bronchodilators or intravenous sodium chloride if indicated. In most cases, the occurrence of non-life-threatening reactions has not prevented completion of the full course of therapy.

If a serious or life-threatening cardiac arrhythmia occurs, it is recommended that the infusion be discontinued. Cardiac monitoring during and following subsequent infusions is recommended in patients who develop clinically significant arrhythmias.

In patients who develop viral hepatitis, rituximab and any concomitant chemotherapy should be discontinued and appropriate treatment including antiviral therapy initiated. There are insufficient data regarding the safety of resuming rituximab therapy in patients who develop hepatitis subsequent to hepatitis B virus [HBV] reactivation.

Parenteral Dosage Forms

Note: Bracketed uses in the *Dosage Forms* section refer to categories of use and/or indications that are not included in U.S. product labeling.

RITUXIMAB CONCENTRATE FOR INJECTION

Usual adult dose

Lymphomas, non-Hodgkin's (treatment)—

Single therapy—Intravenous infusion, initial therapy is given at 375 mg per square meter of body surface area once weekly for four or eight doses. Retreatment therapy is given at 375 mg per square meter of body surface area once weekly for four doses (on days 1, 8, 15, and 22). Currently there are limited data concerning more than 2 courses..

For responders and patients with stable low-grade or follicular CD20-positive, B-cell non-Hodgkin's lymphoma, dosing with rituximab may continue [beyond the initial four or eight doses, as re-induction treatment][1]. The dosing interval for [re-induction treatment][1] is at the discretion of the treating physician.

Note: An initial intravenous infusion rate of 50 mg per hour (mg/hr) is recommended. If hypersensitivity or other infusion-related events do not occur, the infusion rate may be increased in 50 mg/hr increments every thirty minutes up to a maximum rate of 400 mg/hr. For subsequent infusions, an initial rate of 100 mg/hr may be used, increased in 100 mg/hr increments at thirty-minute intervals up to a maximum rate of 400 mg/hr.

Note: In the [first-line treatment of low-grade non-Hodgkin's lymphoma][1], [first-line treatment of diffuse aggressive non-Hodgkin's lymphoma][1], and treatment of [relapsed or refractory diffuse aggressive non-Hodgkin's lymphoma][1], several doses and regimens using rituximab are showing activity. Therefore, no individual dose/regimen is listed here. Consult the medical literature and/or experts in the field of oncology for information on dosage.

Concomitant therapy with ibritumomab tiuxetan—Intravenous infusion, 250 mg per square meter of body surface area infused within four hours prior to the administration of Indium-111 [In-111] ibritumomab tiuxetan and within four hours of Yttrium-90 [Y-90] ibritumomab tiuxetan. Administration of In-111-ibritumomab tiuxetan with rituximab should precede rituximab and Y-90 ibritumomab tiuxetan by 7 to 9 days.

Note: Rituximab is a required component of the ibritumomab tiuxetan therapeutic regimen. See the manufacturer's package insert for ibritumomab tiuxetan for full prescribing information regarding this therapeutic regimen.

Lymphomas, non-Hodgkin's, (adjuvant, first-line treatment)—

Intravenous infusion, 375 mg per m^2 given on Day 1 of each cycle of chemotherapy for up to 8 infusions.

[Leukemia, chronic lymphocytic][1] or
[Waldenstrom's macroglobulinemia][1]—

Because several doses and regimens using rituximab are working well, no individual dose/regimen is listed here. Consult the medical literature and/or experts in the field of oncology for information on dosage.

[Thrombocytopenic purpura, immune or idiopathic (treatment)][1]—

Intravenous infusion, 375 mg per square meter of body surface area once a week for four weeks..

Usual pediatric dose

Safety and efficacy have not been established.

Strength(s) usually available

U.S.—

10 mg per mL (Rx) [*Rituxan* (sodium chloride; sodium citrate dihydrate; polysorbate 80)].

Packaging and storage

Store vials between 2 and 8 °C (36 and 46 °F) for 24 hours. Protect from direct sunlight.

Preparation of dosage form

Rituximab concentrate for injection is prepared for administration by intravenous infusion by withdrawing the necessary amount of drug and diluting it, in an infusion bag, to a final concentration of 1 to 4 mg per mL (mg/mL) with 0.9% sodium chloride injection or 5% dextrose injection. The bag is then gently inverted to mix the solution.

Stability

Contains no preservative; any unused portion of a vial should be discarded. Rituximab solutions prepared for intravenous infusion are stable for 24 hours at 2 to 8 °C (36 to 46 °F). Incompatibilities between rituximab and polyvinyl chloride or polyethylene infusion bags have not been observed.

Auxiliary labeling

- Do not freeze
- Do not shake

[1]Not included in Canadian product labeling.

Revised: 06/13/2006
Developed: 03/23/1998

RIVASTIGMINE Systemic

VA CLASSIFICATION (Primary): CN900

Commonly used brand name(s): *Exelon*.

Some other commonly used names are:
ENA 713;
SDZ ENA 713;
SDZ-212713

Note: For a listing of dosage forms and brand names by country availability, see *Dosage Forms* section(s).

Category
Dementia symptoms treatment adjunct.

Indications
Accepted
Dementia, Alzheimer's type, mild to moderate (treatment)—Rivastigmine is indicated for the symptomatic treatment of mild to moderate dementia of the Alzheimer's type.

Pharmacology/Pharmacokinetics
Physicochemical characteristics
Molecular weight—Rivastigmine tartrate 400.4.
Solubility—Very soluble in water; soluble in ethanol and acetonitrile; slightly soluble in octanol; very slightly soluble in ethyl acetate.

Mechanism of action/Effect
While many neuronal systems are affected in Alzheimer's disease, the decline in central cholinergic activity is one of the most pronounced neurotransmitter deficits. This defecit occurs early in the disease process and correlates with decreased scores on dementia ratings scales. Rivastigmine's primary effect is the reversible inhibition of cholinesterase. This inhibition is thought to increase the level of acetylcholine available in the central nervous system. Increased levels of acetylcholine have been found in the cerebrospinal fluid of patients receiving rivastigmine.

There is no evidence that rivastigmine alters the underlying dementing process, and its effect may lessen as the disease progresses.

Other actions/effects
Because of its cholinomimetic action, rivastigmine may have vagotonic effects on the heart, including bradycardia, and may increase the activity of the gastrointestinal and urinary tracts.

Absorption
Rivastigmine is rapidly absorbed. The absolute bioavailability is about 40%. Rivastigmine shows linear pharmacokinetics with doses up to 3 milligrams twice daily but is non-linear at higher doses. There is a 3–fold increase in area under the curve when the dose is doubled from 3 to 6 milligrams twice daily. Food delays absorption.

Distribution
Mean volume of distribution (Vol_D) is 1.8 to 2.7 L/kg. Rivastigmine penetrates the blood—brain barrier.

Protein binding
Moderate (40%)

Biotransformation
Rivastigmine is is rapidly metabolized, primarily via cholinesterase-mediated hydrolysis. The cytochrome 450 isozymes are minimally involved.

Half-life
Elimination—1.5 hours.

Time to peak concentration
1 hour

Duration of action
Anticholinesterase activity is present in CSF for 10 hours

Elimination
Mostly as metabolites via the urine. After a radiolabeled dose was administered, 97% and 0.4% were recovered in the urine and feces, respectively, over 120 hours. The sulfate conjugate of the decarbamylated metabolite represents 40% of the dose in the urine.

Precautions to Consider
Cross-sensitivity and/or related problems
Patients hypersensitive to other carbamate derivatives may be hypersensitive to rivastigmine.

Carcinogenicity/Tumorgenicity/mutagenicity
Rivastigmine was not carcinogenic in rats and mice at dose of 1.1 mg-base/kg/day and 1.6 mg-base/kg/day, respectively. These doses are 0.9 and 0.7 times the maximum recommended human daily dose, respectively.

Pregnancy/Reproduction
Fertility—Studies showed no effect on fertility or reproductive performance in rats at dose levels up to 1.1 mg-base/kg/day. This dose is 0.9 times the maximum recommended human daily dose.

Pregnancy—Studies have not been done in humans. Studies conducted in pregnant rats and rabbits at doses approximately 2 to 4 times, respectively, the maximum recommended human dose on a mg/m^2) basis showed no evidence of teratogenic potential.

FDA Pregnancy Category B

Breast-feeding
Problems in humans have not been documented. It is not known whether rivastigmine is distributed into breast milk. However, use of rivastigmine is not recommended in nursing mothers.

Pediatrics
No information is available on the relationship of age to the effects of rivastigmine in the pediatric population. Safety and efficacy have not been established.

Geriatrics
Clinical trials of rivastigmine have included Alzheimer's disease patients with a mean age of 73 years of age; information available on the effects of rivastigmine is based upon this population. Elderly patients are more likely to have age-related prostate problems, which may require caution in patients receiving rivastigmine, especially if urinary tract obstruction is present.

Surgical
Because rivastigmine is a cholinesterase inhibitor, it may be likely to prolong or exaggerate succinylcholine-type muscle relaxation during anesthesia.

Drug interactions and/or related problems
The following drug interactions and/or related problems have been selected on the basis of their potential clinical significance (possible mechanism in parentheses where appropriate)—not necessarily inclusive (» = major clinical significance):

Combinations containing any of the following medications, depending on the amount present, may also interact with this medication.

Anticholinergics (See *Appendix II)*
(concurrent use may decrease the effects of either these medications or rivastigmine)

Cholinomimetics (e.g., bethanecol) and cholinesterase inhibitors (e.g., neostigmine)
(concurrent use may increase the effects of these medications or rivastigmine and increase the potential for toxicity)

» Neuromuscular blocking agents metabolized by plasma cholinesterase (e.g., succinylcholine, mivacurium)
(rivastigmine inhibits cholinesterase and may prolong or exaggerate muscle relaxation)

» Nonsteroidal anti-inflammatory drugs (NSAIDs)
(rivastigmine may increase gastric acid secretion, which may contribute to gastrointestinal irritation; patient should be monitored for occult gastrointestinal bleeding)

Medical considerations/Contraindications
The medical considerations/contraindications included have been selected on the basis of their potential clinical significance (reasons given in parentheses where appropriate)—not necessarily inclusive (» = major clinical significance).

Except under special circumstances, this medication should not be used when the following medical problem exists:

» Known hypersensitivity to rivastigmine or other carbamate derivatives

Risk-benefit should be considered when the following medical problems exist:

» Asthma, bronchial, active or latent
(asthma attack may be precipitated)

» Cardiovascular conditions, such as:
Bradycardia or
Sick sinus syndrome
(vagotonic effect on heart may exacerbate pre-existing conditions)

» Epilepsy or history of seizures or

» Metabolic disorders, unstable
(seizures may occur)

» Gastrointestinal obstruction or

» Urinary tract obstruction (increased activity of gastrointestinal tract or urinary bladder may be harmful)
(increased activity of gastrointestinal tract or urinary bladder may be harmful)

Note: Because of their pharmacological action, cholinesterase inhibitors may be expected to increase gastric acid secretion due to increased cholinergic activity. Therefore, patients should be monitored closely for symptoms of active or occult gastrointestinal bleeding, especially those at increased risk for developing ulcers (e.g., those with a history of ulcer or those receiving concurrent nonsteroidal antiinflammatory drugs [NSAIDs]).

» Peptic ulcer, active or history of
(increased gastric acid secretion may exacerbate or reactivate condition)

Patient monitoring

The following may be especially important in patient monitoring (other tests may be warranted in some patients, depending on condition; » = major clinical significance):

» Cognitive function
(periodic objective assessment of cognitive status is recommended to determine effectiveness of rivastigmine treatment)

» Gastrointestinal effects
(post-marketing experience indicates that rivastigmine patients have a very high incidence of nausea and vomiting with the possibility of anorexia and weight loss)

Side/Adverse Effects

The following side/adverse effects have been selected on the basis of their potential clinical significance (possible signs and symptoms in parentheses where appropriate)—not necessarily inclusive:

Those indicating need for medical attention

Incidence more frequent
Anorexia (loss of appetite); ***asthenia*** (loss of strength); ***diarrhea; dyspepsia*** (indigestion); ***nausea; vomiting; weight loss***

Note: Rivastigmine use is associated with significant gastrointestinal adverse reactions, including *nausea and vomiting, anorexia, and weight loss.* One post-marketing report detailed a specific incident in which a patient suffered severe vomiting with esophageal rupture following inappropriate restart of treatment with a 4.5-mg dose after 8 weeks of treatment interruption. In controlled clinical trials, more patients treated with rivastigmine developed gastrointestinal adverse reactions compared to the placebo-treated patients. Rates of gastrointestinal toxicity were higher in women than men.

Incidence less frequent
Hypertension (high blood pressure); ***syncope*** (fainting)

Incidence rare
Aggression; seizures (convulsions); ***tremors*** (trembling and shaking of hands and fingers); ***urinary obstruction*** (trouble in urinating)

Those indicating need for medical attention only if they continue or are bothersome

Incidence more frequent
Abdominal or stomach pain or cramping; confusion; constipation; mental depression; dizziness; fatigue; flatulence (bloated full feeling); ***hallucinations*** (seeing, hearing, or feeling things that are not there); ***headache; insomnia*** (trouble in sleeping)

Incidence less frequent
Malaise (general feeling of discomfort or illness); ***rhinitis*** (runny nose); ***sweating increased***

Overdose

For specific information on the agents used in the management of rivastigmine overdose, see:
• *Atropine* in *Anticholinergics/Antispasmodics (Systemic)* monograph.

For more information on the management of overdose or unintentional ingestion, **contact a poison control center** (see *Poison Control Center Listing*).

Clinical effects of overdose

The following effects have been selected on the basis of their potential clinical significance (possible signs and symptoms in parentheses where appropriate)—not necessarily inclusive:

Bradycardia (slow heart beat); ***hypotension*** (low blood pressure; dizziness; fainting); ***increased salivation*** (drooling; watering of mouth); ***increased sweating; respiratory depression*** (slow or troubled breathing)—increasing muscle weakness may affect respiratory muscles, resulting in death; ***seizures*** (convulsions); ***severe nausea and vomiting***

Note: The clinical effects mentioned above are symptoms of cholinergic crisis.

Treatment of overdose

Specific treatment—
Tertiary anticholinergics, such as atropine, may be used as an antidote for rivastigmine overdosage. Intravenous (IV) atropine sulfate titrated to effect is recommended: an initial dose of 1 to 2 mg IV with subsequent dosing based upon clinical response. Atypical responses in blood pressure and heart rate have been reported with other cholinomimetics when co-administered with quaternary anticholinergics such as glycopyrrolate.
In overdose associated with by severe nausea and vomiting, the use of antiemetics should be considered.
Note: Hemodialysis, peritoneal dialysis, and hemofiltration are not clinically useful in rivastigmine overdose, due to the short half-life of this agent.

Supportive care—
General supportive measures should be utilized.
Patients in whom intentional overdose is confirmed or suspected should be referred for psychiatric consultation.

Patient Consultation

As an aid to patient consultation, refer to *Advice for the Patient, Rivastigmine (Systemic).*

In providing consultation, consider emphasizing the following selected information (» = major clinical significance):

Before using this medication

» Conditions affecting use, especially:
Hypersensitivity to rivastigmine or other carbamate derivatives
Surgical—Rivastigmine is a cholinesterase inhibitor and may prolong or exaggerate succinylcholine-type muscle relaxation during anesthesia.
Other medications, especially neuromuscular blocking agents metabolized by plasma cholinesterase or nonsteroidal anti-inflammatory drugs (NSAIDs)
Other medical problems, especially asthma, cardiovascular conditions (such as bradycardia, hypotension, or sick sinus syndrome), epilepsy or history of seizures, gastrointestinal or urinary tract obstruction, peptic ulcer, and unstable metabolic disorders

Proper use of this medication

» Not taking more medication than the amount prescribed because of increased risk of adverse effects
Taking rivastigmine with food
Taking doses at regular intervals for maximum efficacy
» Proper dosing
Missed dose: Taking as soon as possible if remembered within an hour or so; not taking if remembered later; not doubling doses
» Proper storage

Precautions while using this medication

» Importance of complying with monitoring schedule and keeping appointments with physician and/or laboratory

Informing physician when new symptoms arise or when previously noted symptoms increase in severity

» Caution if any kind of surgery or emergency treatment is required; informing physician or dentist in charge that rivastigmine is being taken

» Caution if dizziness, clumsiness, or unsteadiness occurs

» Suspected overdose: Getting emergency help at once

Side/adverse effects

Signs of potential side effects, especially aggression, anorexia, asthenia, seizures, diarrhea, dyspepsia, hallucinations, hypertension, nausea, syncope, tremors, urinary obstruction, vomiting, and weight loss

General Dosing Information

Rivastigmine should only be prescribed by (or following consultation with) clinicians who are experienced in the diagnosis and management of Alzheimer's Disease.

Rivastigmine should be taken with food, preferably in the morning and the evening at regular intervals.

Dosage must be gradually titrated according to patient tolerance. Dosage increases should be made after a minimum of two weeks of treatment.

The patient should be carefully observed for side effects following initiation of therapy and following every dosage increase.

Dosage of rivastigmine in patients who smoke or use tobacco products may need to be adjusted, since nicotine increases the clearance of rivastigmine in these patients.

For treatment of adverse effects

Post-marketing experience indicates that rivastigmine causes a very high incidence of gastrointestinal problems. If nausea, vomiting, abdominal pain, or loss of appetite cause intolerance during treatment, the patient should discontinue treatment for several doses and then restart at the same or next lower dose level.

If rivastigmine therapy is interrupted for more than several days, treatment should be restarted at the lowest dose to reduce the possibility of serious gastrointestinal toxicity.

Oral Dosage Forms

Note: The available dosage form contains rivastigmine tartrate, but dosage and strength are expressed in terms of rivastigmine base.

RIVASTIGMINE CAPSULES

Usual adult dose

Alzheimer's dementia—

Oral, initially 1.5 mg twice daily in the morning and evening. After at least 2 weeks of treatment if the patient is tolerating treatment well, the dose may be increased to 3 mg twice daily. Additional increases to 4.5 mg twice daily and 6 mg twice daily should be attempted after a minimum of 2 weeks at the previous dose.

Note: If adverse effects (especially gastrointestinal) cause intolerance during treatment, patient should discontinue treatment for several doses and then restart at the same or next lower dose level. If treatment is interrupted for longer than several days, begin treatment again with the lowest daily dose and then titrate to a higher dose.

Usual adult prescribing limits

12 mg daily.

Usual pediatric dose

Safety and efficacy have not been established.

Usual geriatric dose

See *Usual adult dose*.

Usual geriatric prescribing limits

See *Usual adult prescribing limits*.

Strength(s) usually available

U.S.—

1.5 mg (base) (Rx) [*Exelon* (hydroxypropyl methylcellulose; magnesium stearate; microcrystalline cellulose; silicon dioxide; gelatin; titanium dioxide; red and/or yellow iron oxides)].

3 mg (base) (Rx) [*Exelon* (hydroxypropyl methylcellulose; magnesium stearate; microcrystalline cellulose; silicon dioxide; gelatin; titanium dioxide; red and/or yellow iron oxides)].

4.5 mg (base) (Rx) [*Exelon* (hydroxypropyl methylcellulose; magnesium stearate; microcrystalline cellulose; silicon dioxide; gelatin; titanium dioxide; red and/or yellow iron oxides)].

6 mg (base) (Rx) [*Exelon* (hydroxypropyl methylcellulose; magnesium stearate; microcrystalline cellulose; silicon dioxide; gelatin; titanium dioxide; red and/or yellow iron oxides)].

Canada—

1.5 mg (base) (Rx) [*Exelon* (hydroxypropyl methylcellulose; magnesium stearate; microcrystalline cellulose; silicon dioxide; gelatin; titanium dioxide; red and/or yellow iron oxides)].

3 mg (base) (Rx) [*Exelon* (hydroxypropyl methylcellulose; magnesium stearate; microcrystalline cellulose; silicon dioxide; gelatin; titanium dioxide; red and/or yellow iron oxides)].

4.5 mg (base) (Rx) [*Exelon* (hydroxypropyl methylcellulose; magnesium stearate; microcrystalline cellulose; silicon dioxide; gelatin; titanium dioxide; red and/or yellow iron oxides)].

6 mg (base) (Rx) [*Exelon* (hydroxypropyl methylcellulose; magnesium stearate; microcrystalline cellulose; silicon dioxide; gelatin; titanium dioxide; red and/or yellow iron oxides)].

Packaging and storage

Store below 25 °C (77 °F),

Auxiliary labeling

- May cause dizziness
- Take exactly as directed

Revised: 03/05/2001
Developed: 08/07/2000

RIZATRIPTAN Systemic†

VA CLASSIFICATION (Primary): CN105

Note: For a listing of dosage forms and brand names by country availability, see *Dosage Forms* section(s).

†Not commercially available in Canada.

Category

Antimigraine.

Indications

General Considerations

Rizatriptan should be prescribed only for patients who have an established clear diagnosis of migraine.

Accepted

Headache, migraine (treatment)—Rizatriptan is indicated to relieve (abort) acute migraine headaches (with or without aura).

Unaccepted

Rizatriptan is not recommended for treatment of basilar artery migraine or hemiplegic migraine.

Rizatriptan is not recommended for treatment of cluster headaches. Efficacy and safety of rizatriptan in this condition have not been established.

Pharmacology/Pharmacokinetics

Physicochemical characteristics

Molecular weight—Rizatriptan benzoate: 269.4.

Mechanism of action/Effect

Rizatriptan's mechanism of action has not been established. It is thought that agonist activity at the 5-hydroxytryptamine $(5\text{-HT})_{1B}$ and 5-HT_{1D} receptor subtypes provides relief of headaches. Rizatriptan is a highly selective agonist at these receptor subtypes; it has no significant activity at 5-HT_2 or 5-HT_3 receptor subtypes or at adrenergic, dopaminergic, histamine, muscarinic, or benzodiazepine receptors. It has been proposed that constriction of cerebral vessels resulting from $5\text{-HT}_{1B/1D}$ receptor stimulation reduces the pulsation that may be responsible for the pain of migraine headaches. It has also been proposed that rizatriptan may relieve migraine headaches by decreasing the release of pro-inflammatory neuropeptides.

Absorption

Oral—Rapid; bioavailability is 45%. Food has no effect on the bioavailability of rizatriptan. However, administering rizatriptan with food will delay by 1 hour the time to reach peak plasma concentration. The rate of absorption is not affected by the presence of a migraine attack.

Protein binding

Low (14%).

Biotransformation

Rizatriptan is metabolized by monoamine oxidase A isoenzyme (MAO-A) to an inactive indole acetic acid metabolite. In addition, several other inactive metabolites are formed. An active metabolite, *N*-monodesmethyl-rizatriptan, with pharmacological activity similar to that of the parent compound has been identified in small concentrations (14%) in the plasma.

Half-life

Approximately 2 to 3 hours.

Elimination

Renal; following administration of a radiolabeled rizatriptan dose, approximately 82% and 12% of the dose was excreted in the urine and feces, respectively, within 120 hours. Approximately 14% of rizatriptan was excreted in the urine as unchanged and 51% as an indole acetic acid metabolite.

Precautions to Consider

Carcinogenicity/Tumorigenicity

Lifetime carcinogenic studies were done in a 100-week study in mice and a 106-week study in rats receiving doses of rizatriptan of 125 mg per kg of body weight (mg/kg) per day by oral gavage. However, the exposure data were not obtained in these studies. A 5-week study in mice and a 21-week study in rats exposed to the highest dose level of rizatriptan (reflects the area under the plasma concentration-time curve [AUC] exposure of 150 and 240 times the maximum recommended human dose [MRHD], respectively) reported no evidence of tumorigenicity.

Mutagenicity

Rizatriptan demonstrated no mutagenic or clastogenic effects in the microbial mutagenesis (Ames) assay or in the *in vitro* studies, including mammalian cell mutagenic assay in V-79 Chinese hamster lung cells, alkaline elution assay in rat hepatocytes, chromosomal aberration assay in Chinese hamster ovary cells, or in the *in vivo* chromosomal aberration assay in mouse bone marrow.

Pregnancy/Reproduction

Fertility—A fertility study in female rats receiving oral doses of rizatriptan of up to 100 mg/kg per day (approximately 225 times the AUC in humans receiving the MRHD) found changes in estrus cyclicity and delays in time to mating. The no-effect dose was 10 mg/kg per day (approximately 15 times the human exposure at the MRHD). Also, a reproductive study in male rats receiving 250 mg/kg per day (approximately 550 times the human exposure at the MRHD) found no impairment of fertility or reproductive performance.

Pregnancy—Adequate and well-controlled trials have not been done in pregnant women.

A reproductive study in female rats receiving doses of rizatriptan of up to 10 and 100 mg/kg per day prior to and during mating and throughout gestation and lactation (AUC approximately 15 and 225 times the MRHD, respectively) found reduced birth weights and pre- and post-weaning weight gain in the offspring of the rats. Although there was no apparent maternal toxicity, developmental effects on offspring growth occurred. The developmental no-effect dose of rizatriptan was 2 mg/kg per day (maternal exposure approximately 1.5 times the MRHD). Since high doses were not evaluated in this reproduction study, the full spectrum of developmental toxicity is unknown. A rat dose-finding study reported an increase in pup mortality at maternally toxic doses (250 mg/kg per day or greater).

No teratogenic effects were observed in embryofetal developmental studies in pregnant rats and rabbits receiving rizatriptan doses of 100 mg/kg per day and 50 mg/kg per day during organogenesis, respectively. Maternal exposures at the highest doses, approximately 225 and 115 times the human exposure at the MRHD in rats and rabbits, respectively, resulted in decreased fetal weight and maternal weight gain. In both rats and rabbits, the developmental no-effect dose was 10 mg/kg per day (maternal exposure approximately 15 times the MRHD).

Rizatriptan crosses the placenta in rats and rabbits.

FDA Pregnancy Category C.

Breast-feeding

It is not known whether rizatriptan is distributed into human breast milk. However, rizatriptan is distributed into the milk of rats at a concentration at least fives times greater than the maternal plasma level.

Pediatrics

No information is available on the relationship of age to the effects of rizatriptan in patients up to 18 years of age. Safety and efficacy have not been established.

Geriatrics

Pharmacokinetic studies performed to date have not demonstrated geriatrics-specific problems that would limit the use of rizatriptan in geriatric patients. In patients older than 65 years of age, there was no difference in efficacy or overall side effects compared with younger adults.

Drug interactions and/or related problems

The following drug interactions and/or related problems have been selected on the basis of their potential clinical significance (possible mechanism in parentheses where appropriate)—not necessarily inclusive (» = major clinical significance):

Note: Combinations containing any of the following medications, depending on the amount present, may also interact with this medication.

» Dihydroergotamine or
» Ergotamine or
» Methysergide or
» Other 5-hydroxytryptamine (5HT) agonists such as:
Naratriptan or
Sumatriptan or
Zolmitriptan
(a delay of 24 hours between administration of dihydroergotamine, ergotamine, methysergide, or other $5HT_1$ agonists and rizatriptan is recommended because of the possibility of additive and/or prolonged vasoconstriction)

Serotonergics (see Appendix II), such as:
Fluoxetine
Fluvoxamine
Paroxetine
Sertraline
(concurrent use may result in weakness, hyperreflexia, and incoordination; monitoring is recommended; a pharmacokinetic study evaluating rizatriptan 10 mg and paroxetine observed no clinical interactions)

» Monoamine oxidase (MAO) inhibitors, including furazolidone, procarbazine, and selegiline
(concurrent use may increase systemic exposure of rizatriptan; rizatriptan should not be taken concurrently with or within 14 days following administration of an MAO inhibitor)

Propranolol
(propranolol has been reported to increase the plasma concentration of rizatriptan by 70%; if given concurrently, a 5-mg dose of rizatriptan is recommended and a maximum of three doses in a 24-hour period)

Laboratory value alterations

The following have been selected on the basis of their potential clinical significance (possible effect in parentheses where appropriate)—not necessarily inclusive (» = major clinical significance).

With physiology/laboratory test values
Blood pressure
(may be increased; in healthy volunteers, blood pressure elevations of approximately 2 to 3 mm Hg were observed)

Medical considerations/Contraindications

The medical considerations/contraindications included have been selected on the basis of their potential clinical significance (reasons given in parentheses where appropriate)—not necessarily inclusive (» = major clinical significance).

Except under special circumstances, this medication should not be used when the following medical problems exist:

» Coronary artery disease, especially:
Angina pectoris or
Myocardial infarction, history of or
Myocardial ischemia, silent, documented or
Prinzmetal's angina or
» Other conditions in which coronary vasoconstriction would be detrimental
(rizatriptan may cause coronary vasospasms)

» Hypertension, uncontrolled
(may be exacerbated)

Risk-benefit should be considered when the following medical problems exist:

» Coronary artery disease, predisposition to
(rizatriptan may cause serious coronary adverse effects; patients in whom coronary artery disease is a possibility on the basis of age or the presence of other risk factors, such as diabetes, hypercholesterolemia, obesity, a strong family history of coronary artery disease, or tobacco smoking, should be evaluated for the presence of cardiovascular disease before rizatriptan is prescribed; even after a satisfactory evaluation, the advisability of administering the patient's first dose under medical supervision should be considered)

» Hepatic function impairment, moderate or
» Renal function impairment, severe
(studies have shown decreased rizatriptan clearance in patients with moderate hepatic or severe renal disease; caution is recommended)

Sensitivity to rizatriptan or aspartame

Patient monitoring

The following may be especially important in patient monitoring (other tests may be warranted in some patients, depending on condition; » = major clinical significance):

Electrocardiogram (ECG)
(monitoring is recommended for long-term intermittent users of rizatriptan who have risk factors for coronary artery disease)

Side/Adverse Effects

The following side/adverse effects have been selected on the basis of their potential clinical significance (possible signs and symptoms in parentheses where appropriate)—not necessarily inclusive:

Those indicating need for medical attention

Incidence more frequent

Chest pain, severe; dyspnea (shortness of breath); ***heaviness, tightness, or pressure in chest and/or neck; palpitations*** (pounding heartbeat); ***paresthesias*** (sensation of burning, warmth, heat, numbness, tightness, or tingling)

Incidence less frequent

Arrhythmia (irregular heartbeat); ***bradycardia*** (slow heartbeat); ***tachycardia*** (increased heartbeat)

Those indicating need for medical attention only if they continue or are bothersome

Incidence more frequent

Asthenia (unusual tiredness or muscle weakness); ***dizziness; dry mouth; fatigue*** (unusual tiredness); ***hot flashes; nausea and/or vomiting; somnolence*** (sleepiness)

Incidence less frequent

Arthralgia (joint pain); ***central nervous system (CNS) effects; including agitation; anxiety; confusion; depression; irritability; eye problems; including blurred vision; dry eyes; eye irritation; chills; constipation; diarrhea; dyspepsia*** (heartburn); ***dysphagia*** (difficulty swallowing); ***euphoria*** (unusual feeling of well-being); ***flatulence*** (gas); ***heat sensitivity; hypertension*** (dizziness; headache, severe or continuing; increased blood pressure); ***increased sweating; increased thirst; insomnia*** (inability to sleep); ***muscle or joint stiffness, tightness, or rigidity; muscle pain or spasms; polyuria*** (sudden, large increase in frequency and quantity of urine); ***pruritus*** (itching of the skin); ***tinnitus*** (ringing or buzzing in ears); ***tremor*** (trembling or shaking of hands or feet); ***vertigo*** (feeling of constant movement of self or surroundings); ***warm and/or cold sensations***

Overdose

For specific information on the agents used in the management of rizatriptan overdose, see:

- *Charcoal, Activated (Oral-Local)* monograph.

For more information on the management of overdose or unintentional ingestion, **contact a Poison Control Center** (see *Poison Control Center Listing*).

Clinical effects of overdose

The following effects have been selected on the basis of their potential clinical significance (possible signs and symptoms in parentheses where appropriate)—not necessarily inclusive:

Acute and/or chronic

Bradycardia (slow heartbeat); ***dizziness; hypertension*** (dizziness; headache, severe or continuing; increased blood pressure); ***somnolence*** (sleepiness); ***syncope*** (fainting); ***vomiting***

Treatment of overdose

To decrease absorption—Gastric lavage with activated charcoal may be employed.

Monitoring—Patients should be monitored for at least 12 hours after an overdose.

To enhance elimination—The effectiveness of hemodialysis is unknown.

Supportive care—General supportive measures should be instituted. Patients in whom intentional overdose is confirmed or suspected should be referred for psychiatric consultation.

Patient Consultation

As an aid to patient consultation, refer to *Advice for the Patient, Rizatriptan (Systemic)*.

In providing consultation, consider emphasizing the following selected information (» = major clinical significance):

Before using this medication

» Conditions affecting use, especially:

Sensitivity to rizatriptan or aspartame

Pregnancy—Rizatriptan crosses the placenta in animals

Breast-feeding—Studies found that rizatriptan was distributed into the milk of lactating rats

Other medications, especially dihydroergotamine, ergotamine, methysergide, monamine oxidase inhibitors, or other 5-hydroxytryptamine agonists

Other medical problems, especially coronary artery disease, predisposition to coronary artery disease, or other conditions that may be adversely affected by coronary artery constriction; hepatic function impairment (moderate); renal function impairment (severe); or hypertension

Proper use of this medication

» Proper administration:

Orally disintegrating tablet—

Remove tablet from blister pack just prior to dosing

Place tablet on tongue; avoid eating, drinking, smoking, or using tobacco while tablet is dissolving

» Not administering if atypical headache symptoms are present; checking with physician instead

Administering after onset of headache pain

Additional benefit may be obtained if the patient lies down in a quiet, dark room after administering medication

» Not taking additional doses if first dose does not provide substantial relief; taking alternate medication as previously advised by physician, then checking with physician as soon as possible

» Taking additional doses, if needed, for return of migraine headache after initial relief was obtained, provided that prescribed limits (quantity used and frequency of administration) are not exceeded

» Compliance with prophylactic therapy, if prescribed

» Proper dosing

» Proper storage

Precautions while using this medication

Avoiding alcohol, which aggravates headaches

» Caution when driving or doing anything else requiring alertness because of possible drowsiness, dizziness, lightheadedness, impairment of physical or mental abilities

Side/adverse effects

Signs of potential side effects, especially chest pain; dyspnea; heaviness, tightness, or pressure in chest and/or neck; palpitations; paresthesias; arrhythmia; bradycardia; and tachycardia

General Dosing Information

The phenylalanine (component of aspartame) in the rizatriptan orally disintegrating tablet should be considered when administering to phenylketonuric patients.

Oral Dosage Forms

Note: The dosing and strengths of the dosage forms available are expressed in terms of rizatriptan base (not the benzoate salt).

RIZATRIPTAN BENZOATE TABLETS

Usual adult dose

Antimigraine agent—

Oral, 5 or 10 mg (base) as a single dose. If necessary, additional doses may be taken at intervals of at least two hours.

Usual adult prescribing limits

30 mg in twenty-four hours.

Usual pediatric dose

Safety and efficacy have not been established in children up to 18 years of age.

Usual geriatric dose

See *Usual adult dose*.

Strength(s) usually available

U.S.—

5 mg (base) (Rx) [*Maxalt* (lactose monohydrate; microcrystalline cellulose; pregelatinized starch; ferric acid (red); magnesium stearate)].

10 mg (base) (Rx) [*Maxalt* (lactose monohydrate; microcrystalline cellulose; pregelatinized starch; ferric acid (red); magnesium stearate)].

Packaging and storage

Store at room temperature, preferably between 15 and 30 °C (59 and 86 °F).

RIZATRIPTAN BENZOATE ORALLY DISINTEGRATING TABLETS

Usual adult dose

Antimigraine agent—

Oral, 5 or 10 mg (base) as a single dose. If necessary, additional doses may be taken at intervals of at least two hours.

Usual adult prescribing limits

30 mg in twenty-four hours.

Usual pediatric dose

Safety and efficacy have not been established in children up to 18 years of age.

Usual geriatric dose

See *Usual adult dose*.

Strength(s) usually available

U.S.—

5 mg (base) (Rx) [*Maxalt-MLT* (orally disintegrating; gelatin; mannitol; glycine; aspartame (1.05 mg); peppermint flavor)].

10 mg (base) (Rx) [*Maxalt-MLT* (orally disintegrating; gelatin; mannitol; glycine; aspartame (2.1 mg); peppermint flavor)].

Packaging and storage

Store at room temperature, preferably between 15 and 30 °C (59 and 86 °F).

Developed: 11/11/1998

ROPINIROLE Systemic

VA CLASSIFICATION (Primary): CN500

Commonly used brand name(s): *Requip*.

Note: For a listing of dosage forms and brand names by country availability, see *Dosage Forms* section(s).

Category

Antidyskinetic (dopamine agonist).

Indications

Accepted

Parkinson's disease, idiopathic (treatment)—Ropinirole is used to treat the symptoms of idiopathic Parkinson's disease. Its efficacy has been demonstrated in patients with early Parkinson's disease, as well as in patients with advanced disease receiving concomitant levodopa therapy.

Restless legs syndrome (treatment)—Ropinirole is indicated for the treatment of moderate-to-severe primary Restless Legs Syndrome (RLS).

Note: Key diagnostic criteria for RLS are: an urge to move the legs usually accompanied or caused by uncomfortable and unpleasant leg sensations; symptoms begin or worsen during periods of rest or inactivity such as lying or sitting; symptoms are partially or totally relieved by movement such as walking or stretching at least as long as the activity continues; and symptoms are worse or occur only in the evening or night. Difficulty falling asleep may frequently be associated with moderate-to-severe RLS.

Pharmacology/Pharmacokinetics

Physicochemical characteristics

Molecular weight—

Ropinirole: 260.38.

Ropinirole hydrochloride: 296.84.

Mechanism of action/Effect

Ropinirole is a non-ergoline dopamine agonist with a high relative *in vitro* specificity and full intrinsic activity at the D_2 and D_3 dopamine receptor subtypes; it binds with higher affinity to D_3 than to D_2 or D_4 receptor subtypes. The relevance of this binding specificity in Parkinson's disease is not known.

Ropinirole's mechanism of action in the treatment of Parkinson's disease is not precisely known, but is believed to be due to the stimulation of post-synaptic dopamine D_2–type receptors within the caudate-putamen in the brain. This conclusion is supported by studies in various animal models of Parkinson's disease that show that ropinirole improves motor function. In particular, ropinirole attenuates the motor deficits induced by lesioning the ascending striatonigral dopaminergic pathway with the neurotoxin 1-methyl-4-phenyl-1,2,3,6-tetrahydropyridine (MPTP) in primates.

The precise mechanism of action of ropinirole as a treatment cor restless legs syndrome is unknown. Although the pathology of restless legs syndrome is largely unknown, neuropharmacological evidence suggests primary dopaminergic system involvement. Positron emission tomographic studies suggest that a mild striatal presynaptic dopaminergic dysfunction may be involved in the pathogenesis of restless legs syndrome.

Other actions/effects

Ropinirole has moderate *in vitro* affinity for opioid receptors. Ropinirole and its metabolites have negligible *in vitro* affinity for dopamine D_1, 5-HT_1, 5-HT_2, benzodiazepine, GABA, muscarinic, $alpha_1$, $alpha_2$, and beta adrenoreceptors.

Absorption

Ropinirole is rapidly and fully absorbed. Absolute bioavailability is 55%, indicating a first pass effect. Relative bioavailability from a tablet compared with an oral solution is 85%. Food does not affect the extent of absorption.

Distribution

Ropinirole is widely distributed throughout the body, with an apparent volume of distribution (Vol_D) of 7.5 L per kg. Studies in rats have shown that ropinirole and/or its metabolites cross the placenta and are distributed into breast milk.

Protein binding

Up to 40%. Ropinirole has a blood-to-plasma ratio of 1:1.

Biotransformation

Hepatic. Ropinirole is extensively metabolized to inactive metabolites via *N*-despropylation and hydroxylation pathways. *In vitro* studies indicate that the major cytochrome P450 isoenzyme involved in the metabolism of ropinirole is CYP1A2.

Half-life

Elimination—Approximately 6 hours.

Time to peak concentration

Median time to peak concentration (T_{max}) is approximately 1.5 hours. T_{max} is increased by 2.5 hours when ropinirole is taken with a meal.

Peak serum concentration

Approximate dose-normalized mean peak serum concentration (C_{max}) is 2 nanograms per mL per mg ([nanograms/mL]/mg). The C_{max} of ropinirole is decreased by an average of 25% when the medication is taken with a meal.

Time to steady-state concentration

Steady-state concentrations are expected to be achieved within 2 days of dosing. Single dosing predicts that accumulation will occur with multiple dosing. Ropinirole displays linear kinetics over the therapeutic dosing range of 1 to 8 mg three times a day.

Elimination

Renal. Over 88% of a radiolabeled dose is recovered in urine; less than 10% of an administered dose is excreted as unchanged drug.

In dialysis—

Although the effect of hemodialysis on ropinirole removal is not known, removal is unlikely because of the relatively high apparent volume of distribution of the medication.

Precautions to Consider

Carcinogenicity/Tumorigenicity

Patients with Parkinson's disease have a higher risk of developing melanoma than the general population according to some epidemiologic studies. Ropinirole has not been associated with an increased risk of melanoma specifically, its role as a risk factor has not been systematically studied. Patients using ropinirole should undergo periodic dermatologic screening.

Two-year carcinogenicity studies were conducted in Charles River CD-1 mice at doses of 5, 15, and 50 mg per kg of body weight (mg/kg) per day and in Sprague-Dawley rats at doses of 1.5, 15, and 50 mg/kg per day (top doses equivalent to 10 times and 20 times, respectively, the maximum recommended human dose [MRHD] of 24 mg per day on a mg per square meter of body surface area [mg/m^2] basis). In the male rat, there was a significant increase in testicular Leydig cell adenomas at all doses tested, i.e., $\geq$ 1.5 mg/kg (0.6 times the MRHD on a mg/m^2 basis). This finding is of questionable significance because the endocrine mechanisms believed to be involved in the production of Leydig cell hyperplasia and adenomas in rats are not relevant to humans. In the female mouse, there was an increase in benign uterine endometrial polyps at a dose of 50 mg/kg per day (10 times the MRHD on a mg/m^2 basis).

Mutagenicity

Ropinirole was not mutagenic or clastogenic in the *in vitro* Ames test, the *in vitro* chromosome aberration test in human lymphocytes, the *in vitro* mouse lymphoma (L1578Y cells) assay, and the *in vivo* mouse micronucleus test.

Pregnancy/Reproduction

Fertility—When administered to female rats prior to and during mating and throughout pregnancy, ropinirole caused disruption of implantation at doses of 20 mg/kg per day (8 times the MRHD on a mg/m^2 basis) or greater. This effect is thought to be due to the prolactin-lowering effect of ropinirole. In humans, chorionic gonadotropin, not prolactin, is essential for implantation. In rat studies, low doses of ropinirole (5 mg/kg) given during the prolactin-dependent phase of early pregnancy (gestation days 0 to 8) did not affect female fertility at dosages of up to 100 mg/kg per day (40 times the MRHD on a mg/m^2 basis). No effect on male fertility was observed in rats at dosages of up to 125 mg/kg per day (50 times the MRHD on a mg/m^2 basis).

Pregnancy—Adequate and well-controlled studies have not been done in humans. Ropinirole should be used during pregnancy only if the potential benefit outweighs the potential risk to the fetus.

In animal reproduction studies, ropinirole has been shown to have adverse effects on embryo-fetal development, including teratogenic effects. Ropinirole given to pregnant rats during organogenesis (20 mg/kg on gestation days 6 and 7, followed by 20, 60, 90, 120, or 150 mg/kg on gestation days 8 through 15) resulted in decreased fetal body weight at 60 mg/kg per day, increased fetal death at 90 mg/kg per day, and digital malformations at 150 mg/kg per day (24, 36, and 60 times the maximum recommended clinical dose on a mg/m^2 basis, respectively). The combined administration of ropinirole (10 mg/kg per day [8 times the MRHD on a mg/m^2 basis]) and levodopa (250 mg/kg per day) to pregnant rabbits during organogenesis produced a greater incidence and severity of fetal malformations (primarily digit defects) than were seen in the offspring of rabbits treated with levodopa alone. No indication of an effect on development of the conceptus was observed in rabbits when a maternally toxic dose of ropinirole was administered alone (20 mg/kg per day [16 times the MRHD on a mg/m^2 basis]). In a perinatal-postnatal study in rats, 10 mg/kg per day (4 times the MRHD on a mg/m^2 basis) of ropinirole impaired growth and development of nursing offspring and altered neurological development of female offspring.

FDA Pregnancy Category C.

Breast-feeding

Studies in rats have shown that ropinirole and/or its metabolites are distributed into breast milk. Dopamine agonist activity is a possibility in the nursing infant. Because many drugs are distributed in human milk and because of the potential for serious adverse reactions in nursing infants from ropinirole, a decision should be made whether to discontinue nursing or to discontinue the drug, taking into account the importance of the drug to the mother.

Pediatrics

Appropriate studies on the relationship of age to the effects of ropinirole have not been performed in the pediatric population. Safety and efficacy have not been established.

Geriatrics

Ropinirole clearance is reduced by 30% in patients older than 65 years of age as compared with that in younger patients. Dosage adjustments are not necessary because dose titration is based on individual clinical response.

The incidence of hallucinations appears to be greater in the elderly.

Pharmacogenetics

The influence of race on the pharmacokinetics of ropinirole has not been evaluated.

Drug interactions and/or related problems

The following drug interactions and/or related problems have been selected on the basis of their potential clinical significance (possible mechanism in parentheses where appropriate)—not necessarily inclusive (» = major clinical significance):

Note: Since *in vitro* metabolism studies have shown that CYP1A2 is the major enzyme responsible for the metabolism of ropinirole, substrates or inhibitors of this enzyme, when coadministered with ropinirole, have the potential to alter its clearance. Therefore, if a potent inhibitor of CYP1A2 is initiated or discontinued during ropinirole therapy, dosage adjustments may be necessary.

Combinations containing any of the following medications, depending on the amount present, may also interact with this medication.

» Alcohol or
» CNS depressants such as
  Antidepressants or
  Antipsychotics or
  Benzodiazepines
  (caution should be used with concomitant use due to possible additive sedative effects)

» Carbidopa and levodopa combination and
» Levodopa
  (administration of 2 mg of ropinirole three times a day increased the mean steady-state concentration of levodopa by 20%; however, the area under the plasma concentration-time curve [AUC] was unaffected; when ropinirole is administered concomitantly, the dose of levodopa may be gradually reduced as needed and tolerated)
  (ropinirole may potentiate the dopaminergic side effects of levodopa and may cause or exacerbate preexisting dyskinesia; reducing the dosage of levodopa may ameliorate this effect)

» Ciprofloxacin
  (coadministration of ciprofloxacin with ropinirole increased the AUC of ropinirole by 84% on average, and the peak plasma concentration by 60% through inhibition of the metabolism of ropinirole via the hepatic isoenzyme CYP1A2)

Dopamine antagonists, including:
  Butyrophenones
  Metoclopramide
  Phenothiazines
  Thioxanthenes
  (since ropinirole is a dopamine agonist, its actions may be diminished by dopamine antagonists)

Estrogens
  (population pharmacokinetic analysis revealed that estrogens [mainly ethinyl estradiol, with an intake of 0.6 to 3 mg over a 4-month to 23-year period] reduced the oral clearance of ropinirole by 36% in 16 patients; with careful clinical titration, dosage adjustments of ropinirole may not be needed unless estrogen therapy is initiated or discontinued during ropinirole treatment)

Tobacco, smoking
  (increased clearance of ropinirole is expected, since smoking induces the CYP1A2 isoenzyme)

Laboratory value alterations

The following have been selected on the basis of their potential clinical significance (possible effect in parentheses where appropriate)—not necessarily inclusive (» = major clinical significance).

With physiology/laboratory test values
  Alkaline phosphatase
  (values may be increased)
  Prolactin concentrations
  (prolactin secretion in healthy male volunteers is suppressed by ropinirole at doses as low as 0.2 mg)

Medical considerations/Contraindications

The medical considerations/contraindications included have been selected on the basis of their potential clinical significance (reasons given in parentheses where appropriate)—not necessarily inclusive (» = major clinical significance).

Except under special circumstances, this medication should not be used when the following medical problem exists:

» Hypersensitivity to ropinirole or any components of the product

Risk-benefit should be considered when the following medical problems exist:

Fibrotic complications from ergot-derived dopaminergic agents, history of
  (condition may recur)

» Hallucinations
  (condition may be exacerbated)

Hepatic function impairment
  (the pharmacokinetics of ropinirole have not been studied in patients with impaired hepatic function; however, these patients may have higher plasma concentrations and lower clearance than do patients with normal hepatic function; doses should be titrated with caution in this patient population)

» Hypotension or
» Orthostatic hypotension
  (condition may be exacerbated; Parkinson's patients may require careful monitoring, especially during dose escalation and should be informed of risk)

Renal impairment, severe
  (use of ropinirole in patients with this condition has not been studied)

Retinal degeneration, or retinal problems
  (studies in albino rats have shown retinal degeneration; the potential significance of this effect in humans has not been established; however, disruption of disk shedding [a mechanism universally present in vertebrates] may be involved)

Restless leg syndrome with augmentation and rebound
  (ropinirole may make these symptoms worse; patients with augmentation and rebound have not been evaluated in controlled clinical trials)

» Sleep disorders or
Somnolence, history of
(many increase the chance of falling asleep without warning during activities of daily living, including driving)

Patient monitoring

The following may be especially important in patient monitoring (other tests may be warranted in some patients, depending on condition; » = major clinical significance):

Dermatologic screening
(periodic dermatologic screening for melanoma is recommended in patients with Parkinson's disease)

Monitoring for symptoms of orthostatic hypotension
(particularly important during dose escalation)

Side/Adverse Effects

Note: Dopamine agonists appear to impair the systemic regulation of blood pressure, with resulting orthostatic hypotension, especially during dose escalation. In addition, patients with Parkinson's disease appear to have an impaired capacity to respond to an orthostatic challenge.

Retinal degeneration was observed in albino rats that received ropinirole in the premarketing carcinogenicity study. This effect was not noted in albino mice, pigmented rats, or monkeys. The potential significance for humans has not been established; however, this effect cannot be disregarded because it may involve disruption of disk shedding, a mechanism that is universally present in vertebrates.

A symptom complex (characterized by elevated temperature, muscular rigidity, altered consciousness, and autonomic instability) that resembles neuroleptic malignant syndrome and has no other obvious etiology has been reported in association with rapid dose reduction, withdrawal of, or changes in antiparkinsonian therapy. This effect was not observed during premarketing trials of ropinirole, but potentially could occur with the use of this dopaminergic agent.

Fibrotic complications, including retroperitoneal fibrosis, pulmonary infiltrates, pleural effusion, and pleural thickening, have been reported in some patients treated with ergot-derived dopaminergic agents. These complications may resolve upon discontinuation of the medication, but complete resolution does not always occur. Although these effects are believed to be associated with the ergoline structure of these compounds, it is not known if non–ergot-derived dopamine agonists such as ropinirole may produce similar adverse effects.

The following side/adverse effects have been selected on the basis of their potential clinical significance (possible signs and symptoms in parentheses where appropriate)—not necessarily inclusive:

Those indicating need for medical attention

Incidence more frequent

Asthenia (unusual tiredness or weakness); ***confusion; dependent edema*** (swelling of legs); ***dizziness; dyskinesia*** (twisting, twitching, or other unusual body movements)—may be dose-related; ***falling; hallucinations*** (seeing, hearing, or feeling things that are not there)—may be dose-related; ***nausea; orthostatic hypotension*** (dizziness, lightheadedness, or fainting, especially when standing up); ***somnolence*** (drowsiness); ***syncope*** (fainting); ***viral infection; worsening of parkinsonism***

Note: In placebo-controlled premarketing trials conducted in patients with early Parkinson's disease, *hallucinations* were observed in 5.2% of patients receiving ropinirole, as compared with 1.4% of patients receiving placebo. Among those patients with advanced Parkinson's disease who were concomitantly receiving levodopa, 10.1% of patients receiving ropinirole experienced hallucinations, as compared with 4.2% of patients receiving placebo. The incidence of hallucinations appears to be higher in elderly patients.

Syncope, sometimes associated with bradycardia, was observed in placebo-controlled trials in patients receiving ropinirole alone or in combination with levodopa. In patients with early Parkinson's disease who were receiving ropinirole, 11.5% experienced syncope, as compared with 1.4% of patients who were receiving placebo. In patients with advanced Parkinson's disease, 2.9% of those receiving ropinirole plus levodopa reported syncope, as compared with 1.7% of those receiving placebo plus levodopa.

Incidence less frequent

Abdominal pain; amnesia (loss of memory); ***bronchitis*** (cough; shortness of breath; tightness in chest; wheezing); ***cardiac arrhythmias*** (irregular or pounding heartbeat); ***chest pain; difficulty in concentrating; diplopia, xeropthalmia, or other eye or vision problems; dyspnea*** (troubled breathing); ***hematuria*** (blood in urine); ***hypertension; hypotension; mental depression; pain; pain in arms or legs; paresthesia*** (tingling, numbness, or prickly feelings); ***pharyngitis*** (sore throat); ***tachycardia*** (fast heartbeat); ***urinary tract infection*** (burning, pain, or difficulty in urinating); ***vomiting***

Incidence rare

Anxiety or nervousness; chills; dysphagia (trouble in swallowing); ***fever; joint pain; muscle cramps, pain, or spasms; sinus infection*** (fever; headache; nasal congestion); ***tinnitus*** (buzzing or ringing in ears); ***upper respiratory infection*** (cough; fever; runny nose; sneezing); ***urinary incontinence*** (loss of bladder control)

Those indicating need for medical attention only if they continue or are bothersome

Incidence less frequent

Abnormal dreams; anorexia (loss of appetite); ***constipation; diarrhea; dryness of mouth; flushing; headache; heartburn or gas; hot flashes; impotence*** (decrease in sexual desire or performance); ***increased sweating; malaise*** (general feeling of discomfort or illness); ***tremor; weight loss; yawning***

Overdose

For information on the management of ropinirole overdose or unintentional ingestion, **contact a Poison Control Center** (see *Poison Control Center Listing*).

Clinical effects of overdose

Symptoms of ropinirole overdose will most likely be related to its dopaminergic activity.

The following effects have been selected on the basis of their potential clinical significance (possible signs and symptoms in parentheses where appropriate)—not necessarily inclusive:

Agitation; chest pain; confusion; fatigue; grogginess; increased coughing; increased dyskinesia, including mild oro-facial dyskinesia; nausea; orthostatic hypotension; sedation; syncope; vasovagal syncope; vomiting

Treatment of overdose

To decrease absorption—Gastric lavage may be indicated.

Supportive care—General supportive measures are recommended. Vital signs should be maintained. Patients in whom intentional overdose is confirmed or suspected should be referred for psychiatric consultation.

Patient Consultation

As an aid to patient consultation, refer to *Advice for the Patient, Ropinirole (Systemic)*.

In providing consultation, consider emphasizing the following selected information (» = major clinical significance):

Before using this medication

» Conditions affecting use, especially:
Hypersensitivity to ropinirole or any component of the product
Patients with Parkinson's disease may be at increased risk of developing melanoma.
Pregnancy—Animal studies have shown adverse effects on embryo-fetal development, including teratogenicity; risk/benefit considerations
Breast-feeding—Potential for serious adverse effects in nursing infant
Use in the elderly—Age-related reductions in renal function may require dosage adjustments; also, increased risk of occurrence of hallucinations
Other medications, especially alcohol, ciprofloxacin, CNS depressants, carbidopa and/or levodopa
Other medical problems, especially hallucinations, hypotension, orthostatic hypotension, or sleep disorders

Proper use of this medication

» Reading Patient Information leaflet before starting therapy and each time prescription is refilled.
» Compliance with therapy; not taking more or less medication than prescribed
» Proper dosing
Missed dose: Taking dose as soon as possible; not taking if almost time for next dose; not doubling doses
» Proper storage

Precautions while using this medication

» Regular visits to physician to check progress of therapy

» Checking with physician before discontinuing medication; gradual dosage reduction may be needed

» Possible drowsiness, dizziness, lightheadedness, vision problems, weakness, or muscular incoordination; caution when driving or doing jobs requiring alertness, clear vision, and coordination

» Possible falling asleep without warning during daily living activities, including driving which have resulted in accidents.

» Caution when getting up suddenly from lying or sitting position

» Possible occurrence of hallucinations

» If taking ropinirole for Parkinson's disease, regular visits to physician to check skin for melanoma.

Side/adverse effects

Signs of potential side effects, especially asthenia; confusion; dependent edema; dizziness; dyskinesia; falling; hallucinations; nausea; orthostatic hypotension; somnolence; syncope; viral infection; worsening of parkinsonism; abdominal pain; amnesia; bronchitis; cardiac arrhythmias; chest pain; difficulty in concentrating; diplopia, xeropthalmia, or other eye or vision problems; dyspnea; hematuria; hypertension; hypotension; mental depression; pain; pain in arms or legs; paresthesia; pharyngitis; tachycardia; urinary tract infection; vomiting; anxiety or nervousness; chills; dysphagia; fever; joint pain; muscle cramps, pain, or spasms; sinus infection; tinnitus; upper respiratory infection; and urinary incontinence

General Dosing Information

Ropinirole doses should be titrated slowly in all patients. Dosage goal should be to achieve maximum therapeutic effect balanced against the principal side effects of nausea, dizziness, somnolence, and dyskinesia.

When ropinirole is used in combination with levodopa, the required dosage of levodopa may be reduced. In clinical trials, the levodopa dose was reduced on average by 31% from baseline.

For Parkinson's disease: It is recommended that ropinirole be discontinued gradually over a 7-day period. The frequency of administration should be reduced to two times a day for 4 days, then to once a day for the remaining 3 days before complete withdrawal of ropinirole.

For restless leg syndrome (RLS): Ropinirole can be discontinued without a taper.

If significant interruption in therapy with ropinirole has occurred, retitration of therapy may be warranted.

Diet/Nutrition

Ropinirole may be taken with or without food. Taking this medication with food possibly may reduce the occurrence of nausea.

Oral Dosage Forms

ROPINIROLE HYDROCHLORIDE TABLETS

Note: In clinical studies, dosage was initiated at subtherapeutic levels and gradually titrated to therapeutic response.

Usual adult dose

Parkinson's disease, idiopathic—

Oral, initially 0.25 mg three times a day. Based on patient response, dosage should be increased at weekly intervals. A suggested schedule for titration follows:

Ascending Dosage Schedule of Ropinirole

Week	Dosage	Total Daily Dose
1	0.25 mg three times a day	0.75 mg
2	0.5 mg three times a day	1.5 mg
3	0.75 mg three times a day	2.25 mg
4	1 mg three times a day	3 mg

Restless legs syndrome (RLS) (treatment)—

Oral, initially 0.25 mg once daily, 1 to 3 hours before bedtime. Patients should be titrated based on clinical response and tolerability to achieve efficacy according to the following schedule:

Dose Titration Schedule for RLS

Day/Week	Dosage to be taken once daily, 1 to 3 hours before bedtime
Days 1 and 2	0.25 mg
Days 3-7	0.5 mg
Week 2	1 mg
Week 3	1.5 mg
Week 4	2 mg
Week 5	2.5 mg
Week 6	3 mg
Week 7	4 mg

Usual adult prescribing limits

Parkinson's disease idiopathic—

24 mg a day.

Restless legs syndrome (treatment)—

4 mg per day.

Usual pediatric dose

Safety and efficacy have not been established.

Strength(s) usually available

U.S.—

0.25 mg (Rx) [*Requip* (croscarmellose sodium; hydrous lactose; magnesium stearate; microcrystalline cellulose; carmine; FD&C Blue No. 2 aluminum lake; FD&C Yellow No. 6 aluminum lake; hypromellose; iron oxides; polyethylene glycol; polysorbate 80; titanium dioxide)].

0.5 mg (Rx) [*Requip* (croscarmellose sodium; hydrous lactose; magnesium stearate; microcrystalline cellulose; carmine; FD&C Blue No. 2 aluminum lake; FD&C Yellow No. 6 aluminum lake; hypromellose; iron oxides; polyethylene glycol; polysorbate 80; titanium dioxide)].

1 mg (Rx) [*Requip* (croscarmellose sodium; hydrous lactose; magnesium stearate; microcrystalline cellulose; carmine; FD&C Blue No. 2 aluminum lake; FD&C Yellow No. 6 aluminum lake; hypromellose; iron oxides; polyethylene glycol; polysorbate 80; titanium dioxide)].

2 mg (Rx) [*Requip* (croscarmellose sodium; hydrous lactose; magnesium stearate; microcrystalline cellulose; carmine; FD&C Blue No. 2 aluminum lake; FD&C Yellow No. 6 aluminum lake; hypromellose; iron oxides; polyethylene glycol; polysorbate 80; titanium dioxide)].

3 mg (Rx) [*Requip* (croscarmellose sodium; hydrous lactose; magnesium stearate; microcrystalline cellulose; carmine; FD&C Blue No. 2 aluminum lake; FD&C Yellow No. 6 aluminum lake; hypromellose; iron oxides; polyethylene glycol; polysorbate 80; titanium dioxide)].

4 mg (Rx) [*Requip* (croscarmellose sodium; hydrous lactose; magnesium stearate; microcrystalline cellulose; carmine; FD&C Blue No. 2 aluminum lake; FD&C Yellow No. 6 aluminum lake; hypromellose; iron oxides; polyethylene glycol; polysorbate 80; titanium dioxide)].

5 mg (Rx) [*Requip* (croscarmellose sodium; hydrous lactose; magnesium stearate; microcrystalline cellulose; Aluminum Lake; FD&C Blue No. 2; hypromellose; iron oxides; polyethylene glycol; polysorbate 80; talc; titanium dioxide)].

Canada—

0.25 mg (Rx) [*Requip* (sucrose-, tartrazine-, azo dyes-free)].

1 mg (Rx) [*Requip* (sucrose-, tartrazine-, azo dyes-free)].

2 mg (Rx) [*Requip* (sucrose-, tartrazine-, azo dyes-free)].

5 mg (Rx) [*Requip* (sucrose-, tartrazine-, azo dyes-free)].

Packaging and storage

Store at controlled room temperature between 20 and 25 °C (68 and 77 °F). Protect from light.

Stability

Protect from moisture. Close container tightly after each use.

Auxiliary labeling

• This drug alone or with alcohol may cause drowsiness. Use care when driving or operating machinery.
• May cause dizziness or drowsiness

Revised: 11/20/2005
Developed: 11/17/1997

ROSIGLITAZONE Systemic

VA CLASSIFICATION (Primary): HS505

Commonly used brand name(s): *Avandia.*

Note: For a listing of dosage forms and brand names by country availability, see *Dosage Forms* section(s).

Category

Antidiabetic agent.

Indications

Accepted

Diabetes, type 2 (treatment)—Rosiglitazone is indicated as monotherapy as an adjunctive therapy to diet and exercise in the management of patients with type 2 diabetes mellitus (previously referred to as non-insulin-dependent diabetes mellitus [NIDDM]). Rosiglitazone is also indicated for use in combination with a sulfonylurea, metformin, or insulin when diet, exercise, and either rosiglitazone alone, a sulfonylurea alone, metformin alone or insulin alone do not result in adequate glycemic control in patients with type 2 diabetes. Rosiglitazone is also indicated for use in combination with a sulfonylurea plus metformin when diet, exercise, and both agents do not result in adequate glycemia control.

Note: In Canada, rosiglitazone is not currently indicated for combination use with insulin.

Pharmacology/Pharmacokinetics

Physicochemical characteristics

Chemical Group—Thiazolidinedione

Molecular weight—473.52 (357.44 free base).

pKa—6.8 and 6.1.

Solubility—Readily soluble in ethanol and buffered aqueous solution with pH of 2.3.

Mechanism of action/Effect

Rosiglitazone is a thiazolidinedione antidiabetic agent that is effective only in the presence of insulin. Its primary action is to decrease insulin resistance at peripheral sites and in the liver. This results in increased insulin-dependent glucose disposal and decreased hepatic glucose output. These effects are accomplished by selective binding at the peroxisome proliferator-activated receptor-gamma (PPAR-gamma) which is found in adipose tissue, skeletal muscle, and the liver. Activation of these receptors modulates transcription of several insulin responsive genes that control glucose and lipid metabolism.

Absorption

Absolute bioavailability: 99%

Rapid. Food decreases the maximum concentration (approximately 28%) and delays the time to achieve the maximum concentration (approximately 1.75 hours); however, these changes are not likely to be clinically significant.

Distribution

The mean oral apparent volume of distribution is 17.6 liters.

The mean intravenous apparent volume of distribution at steady state in healthy subjects is approximately 14.1 liters.

Studies have shown that both oral clearance and oral steady state volume of distribution increase with increases in body weight.

Protein binding

Very high (>99.8%); primarily to serum albumin

Biotransformation

Rosiglitazone is extensively metabolized in the liver to inactive metabolites via N-demethylation, hydroxylation, and conjugation with sulfate and glucuronic acid.

In vitro data have shown that Cytochrome (CYP) P450 isoenzyme 2C8 (CYP2C8) and to a minor extent CYP2C9 are involved in the hepatic metabolism of rosiglitazone.

Half-life

Elimination—3 to 4 hours

Peak plasma concentration

Maximum plasma concentration (C_{max}) and the area under the curve ($AUC_{0\text{-}inf}$) of rosiglitazone increase in a dose-proportional manner.

Time to peak concentration

1 hour

Elimination

Fecal—23%

Renal—64%

Precautions to Consider

Carcinogenicity

In rats, a significant increase in benign adipose tissue tumors (lipomas) was found at doses ≥ 0.3 mg per kg of body weight (mg/kg) per day for 104 weeks. These doses represented area under the plasma concentration-time curve (AUC) values 2 times that of the maximum recommended human daily dose. In mice, rosiglitazone was not carcinogenic; however, the incidence of adipose hyperplasia increased at doses ≥ 1.5 mg/kg/day (approximately 2 times the human AUC at the maximum recommended human daily dose).

Mutagenicity

No evidence of mutagenicity or clastogenicity was found in the *in-vitro* bacterial assays for gene mutation, the *in-vitro* chromosome aberration test in human lymphocytes, the *in-vivo,* mouse micronucleus test, and the *in-vivo/in-vitro* rat UDS assay. When metabolic activation was used in the *in-vitro* mouse lymphoma assay, an increase (about 2-fold) in mutation was observed

Pregnancy/Reproduction

Fertility—Rosiglitazone therapy may cause resumption of ovulation in premenopausal anovulatory patients with insulin resistance

No evidence of impaired fertility or reproductive capability was found in male rats given up to 40 mg/kg per day of rosiglitazone (corresponding to 116 times the human exposure based on AUC at maximum recommended human daily dose). However, in female rats, fertility was decreased at a dose of 40 mg per kg per day and estrous cyclicity was altered at 2 mg per kg per day, but these effects were not noted at doses less than 0.2 mg/kg per day. These effects were attributed to altered plasma levels of progesterone and estradiol. In monkeys administered 0.6 and 4.6 mg/kg/day of rosiglitazone, the follicular phase rise in serum estradiol was decreased with reduction in the luteinizing hormone surge and luteal phase progesterone levels. Amenorrhea was also observed

Pregnancy—Studies have not been done in humans

It is recommended that insulin alone be used during pregnancy for maintenance of blood glucose concentrations that are as close to normal as possible. Abnormal maternal blood glucose concentrations have been associated with a higher incidence of congenital anomalies and increased neonatal morbidity and mortality

No evidence of teratogenicity was found in rats and rabbits given up to 3 mg/kg and 100 mg/kg, respectively (corresponding to 20 and 75 times the human AUC at the maximum recommended human daily dose, respectively). In rats and rabbits, rosiglitazone treatment during mid-late gestation was associated with fetal death and growth retardation. Administration of rosiglitazone to rats during gestation through lactation reduced litter size, neonatal viability, and postnatal growth. However, postnatal growth retardation was reversible after puberty.

FDA Pregnancy Category C

Labor and delivery—In humans, the effect of rosiglitazone on labor and delivery is not known

Breast-feeding

It is not known whether rosiglitazone is distributed into human breast milk. However, it is distributed into the milk of lactating rats. Rosiglitazone is not recommended for use by nursing mothers

Pediatrics

Appropriate studies on the relationship of age to the effects of rosiglitazone have not been performed in the pediatric population. Safety and efficacy have not been established

Geriatrics

In pharmacokinetic studies, 331 patients were 65 years of age or older. These studies demonstrated no geriatrics-specific problems that would limit the usefulness of rosiglitazone in the elderly

Race

The pharmacokinetics of rosiglitazone and its metabolites are similar among various ethnic groups

Drug interactions and/or related problems

The following drug interactions and/or related problems have been selected on the basis of their potential clinical significance (possible mechanism in parentheses where appropriate)—not necessarily inclusive (» = major clinical significance):

» CYP2C8 inducers such as
  Rifampin
    (concomitant use may increase rosiglitazone metabolism; changes in diabetes treatment may be needed based on clinical response)

» CYP2C8 inhibitors such as
  Gemfibrozil
    (concomitant use may decrease rosiglitazone metabolism; decrease in rosiglitazone dose may be needed when gemfibrozil is

introduced due to the potential for dose-related adverse events with rosiglitazone)

Hypoglycemic agents, especially insulin secreting agents such as:
Insulin or
Sulfonylurea
(may be at risk for hypoglycemia; reduction in the dose of the concomitant agent may be needed)
(thiazolidinediones in combination with insulin may increase the risk of cardiovascular adverse events)

Laboratory value alterations

The following have been selected on the basis of their potential clinical significance (possible effect in parentheses where appropriate)—not necessarily inclusive (» = major clinical significance).

With physiology/laboratory test values

Alanine aminotransferase (ALT [SGPT]) and
Aspartate aminotransferase (AST [SGOT])
(during controlled clinical trials, reversible elevations greater than three times the upper limit of normal were observed in 0.2% of rosiglitazone-treated patients versus 0.2% of placebo-treated patients and 0.5% of active comparator-treated patients; however, ALT elevations were not clearly related to rosiglitazone)

Cholesterol, total and
High-density lipoproteins (HDL) and
Low-density lipoproteins (LDL)
(increases in total cholesterol (C), LDL-C, and HDL-C were observed during clinical trials)

Hematocrit and
Hemoglobin concentration
(decreased by ≤ 3.3% and ≤ 1 gram/dL, respectively, in patients treated with rosiglitazone, alone and in combination with other hypoglycemic agents. Decreases have been attributed to dilutional effects caused by increased plasma volume.)

Triglycerides
(effect was variable and generally not different than placebo or glyburide controls)

Medical considerations/Contraindications

The medical considerations/contraindications included have been selected on the basis of their potential clinical significance (reasons given in parentheses where appropriate)—not necessarily inclusive (» = major clinical significance).

Except under special circumstances, this medication should not be used when the following medical problems exist:

» Diabetes mellitus, type I
» Diabetic ketoacidosis
(rosiglitazone lowers plasma glucose concentrations only in the presence of insulin)

» Hepatic function impairment
(rosiglitazone should NOT be started in patients with clinical evidence of active liver disease or in patients with an alanine aminotransferase greater than 2.5 times the upper limit of normal)

Hypersensitivity to rosiglitazone

» Jaundice
(discontinue therapy if jaundice is observed)

Risk-benefit should be considered when the following medical problem exists:

» Congestive heart failure or
Cardiac effects, other
(can cause fluid retention; may exacerbate or lead to heart failure; not recommended in patients with NYHA class 3 and 4 cardiac states)
(increased risk of cardiovascular events in patients with congestive heart failure (CHF) New York Heart Association (NYHA) Class 1 and 2 who take rosiglitazone)

» Diabetic macular edema
(post-marketing reports of exacerbation with rosiglitazone)

» Edema
(due to the possibility of an increase in median plasma volume, rosiglitazone should be used with caution in patients with edema)

Patient monitoring

The following may be especially important in patient monitoring (other tests may be warranted in some patients, depending on condition; » = major clinical significance):

» Cardiac function
(rosiglitazone alone or in combination therapy with other antidiabetic agents can cause fluid retention which may exacerbate or lead to heart failure patients should be observed for signs and symptoms of heart failure; rosiglitazone therapy should be discontinued if any deterioration in cardiac status occurs)

» Eye examinations
(important in patients with diabetes to have regular exams with ophthalmologist; visual symptoms should be reported and patient promptly referred to an ophthalmologist regardless of underlying medications or other physical findings due to post-marketing reports of macular edema)

» Glucose concentrations, fasting blood
(monitor regularly to assess therapeutic efficacy)

» Glycosylated hemoglobin
(monitor regularly to assess long-term glycemic control)

» Transaminase values
(monitor before starting treatment, every 2 months for the first year, and periodically thereafter; if symptoms of hepatic dysfunction develop, serum transaminases should be obtained, the cause of the elevation should be determined, treatment following mild elevations should be met with caution and more frequent enzyme monitoring, if ALT levels ever exceed 3 times the upper limit of normal, levels should be rechecked as soon as possible, therapy should be discontinued if levels remain at 3 times the upper limit)
(if symptoms suggesting hepatic dysfunction, which include unexplained nausea, vomiting, abdominal pain, fatigue, anorexia, and/or dark urine, liver enzymes should be checked)

» Weight
(patients who experience unusually rapid increases in weight and increases in excess of that generally observed in clinical trials [approximately 3 to 6 kilograms over 26 weeks] should be assessed for fluid accumulation and volume-related events such as excessive edema and congestive heart failure)

Side/Adverse Effects

Note: Rosiglitazone does not stimulate insulin secretion and, administered alone, is not expected to cause hypoglycemia

In a clinical trial that included healthy volunteers, treatment with rosiglitazone 8 mg once daily for 8 weeks resulted in a statistically significant increase in median plasma volume of 1.8 mL/kg compared to placebo. Patients with New York Heart Association class III and IV cardiac status were not studied during the clinical trials. Use of rosiglitazone is not recommended in patients with New York Heart Association Class III or IV cardiac status unless the expected benefit is believed to outweigh the potential risk. Rosiglitazone, alone or in combination with other antidiabetic agents, can cause fluid retention, which may exacerbate or lead to heart failure.

In post-marketing experience with rosiglitazone, reports of hepatic enzyme elevations of three or more times the upper limit of normal have been received. Very rarely, these reports have involved hepatic failure with and without fatal outcome, although causality has not been established.

The following side/adverse effects have been selected on the basis of their potential clinical significance (possible signs and symptoms in parentheses where appropriate)—not necessarily inclusive:

Those indicating need for medical attention

Incidence less frequent

Edema, severe (decrease in amount of urine; noisy, rattling breathing; shortness of breath; swelling of fingers, hands, feet, or lower legs; troubled breathing at rest; weight gain)—may be dose related; ***hyperglycemia*** (abdominal pain; blurred vision; dry mouth; fatigue; flushed, dry skin; fruit-like breath odor; increased hunger; increased thirst; increased urination; nausea; sweating; troubled breathing; unexplained weight loss; vomiting); ***ischemic heart disease*** (chest pain or discomfort; irregular heartbeat; nausea or vomiting; pain in the shoulders, arms, jaw or neck; sweating)

Incidence rare

Congestive heart failure (edema; shortness of breath; weight gain, rapid or unusual); ***hepatic failure*** (abdominal or stomach pain; dark urine; loss of appetite; nausea; unusual tiredness or weakness; vomiting); ***hypoglycemia*** (anxiety; blurred vision; chills; cold sweats; coma; confusion; cool pale skin; depression; dizziness; fast heartbeat; headache; increased hunger; nausea; nervousness; nightmares; seizures; shakiness; slurred speech; unusual tiredness or weakness)

Incidence not determined—Observed during clinical practice; estimates of frequency can not be determined

Angioedema (large, hive-like swelling on face, eyelids, lips, tongue, throat, hands, legs, feet, sex organs); ***decreased visual acuity*** (decreased vision); ***diabetic macular edema*** (blurred vision or other change in vision); ***urticaria*** (hives or welts, itching, redness of skin, skin rash)

Those indicating need for medical attention only if they continue or are bothersome

Incidence more frequent

Headache—incidence 5.9%; ***injury; upper respiratory infection*** (fever, runny or stuffy nose)

Incidence less frequent

Anemia (dizziness, light-headedness)—incidence 1.9%; ***back pain; diarrhea; edema, mild*** (swelling of hands, ankles, feet, or lower legs); ***fatigue*** (unusual tiredness or weakness); ***sinusitis*** (pain or tenderness around eyes and cheekbones; fever; stuffy or runny nose; headache; cough; shortness of breath or troubled breathing; tightness of chest or wheezing); ***weight gain***

Patient Consultation

As an aid to patient consultation, refer to *Advice for the Patient, Rosiglitazone (Systemic).*

Consider advising the patient on the following (» = major clinical significance):

Before using this medication

» Conditions affecting use, especially:
- Hypersensitivity to rosiglitazone
- Pregnancy—Use of insulin alone is recommended during pregnancy for maintenance of blood glucose concentrations as close to normal as possible
- Breast-feeding—Not recommended for use by nursing mothers
- Other medications, especially CYP2C8 inducers or CYP2C8 inhibitors
- Other medical problems, especially congestive heart failure, diabetic ketoacidosis, diabetic macular edema, edema, hepatic function impairment, or type 1 diabetes

Proper use of this medication

» Importance of adherence to recommended regimens for diet, exercise, and glucose monitoring

May take with or without food

» Proper dosing

Missed dose: Taking as soon as possible if remembered the same day; if dose is missed on one day, not doubling dose the following day

» Proper storage

Precautions while using this medication

» Reporting symptoms, such as abdominal pain, anorexia, dark urine, fatigue, jaundice, nausea, or vomiting, that are suggestive of hepatic dysfunction to physician immediately

» Telling your doctor right away if you are rapidly gaining weight and/or have excessive swelling of hands, wrist, ankles, or feet.

» Telling your doctor right away if you develop shortness of breath or other symptoms of heart failure.

» Rosiglitazone may increase the chance of a premenopausal women with type 2 diabetes getting pregnant. Reliable birth control is recommended. Talk to your health care professional about choices, risks, and benefits.

» Regular visits to physician to check progress and monitor liver function

» *Carefully following special instructions of health care team:*

Discussing use of alcohol

Not taking other medications unless discussed with physician

Getting counseling for family members to help the patient with diabetes; also, special counseling for pregnancy planning and contraception

Making travel plans that include readiness for diabetic emergencies and eating meals at the usual times, even with changing time zones

» Preparing for and understanding what to do in case of diabetic emergency; carrying medical history and current medication list and wearing medical identification

» Recognizing what brings on symptoms of hypoglycemia, such as using other antidiabetic medication; delaying or missing a meal; exercising more than usual; drinking significant amounts of alcohol; or illness, including vomiting or diarrhea

» Recognizing symptoms of hypoglycemia: anxiety; behavior change similar to drunkenness; blurred vision; cold sweats; confusion; cool, pale skin; difficulty in concentrating; drowsiness; excessive hunger; fast heartbeat; headache; nausea; nervousness; nightmares; restless sleep; shakiness; slurred speech; or unusual tiredness or weakness

» Knowing what to do if symptoms of hypoglycemia occur, such as eating glucose tablets or gel, corn syrup, honey, or sugar cubes; drinking fruit juice, non-diet soft drink, or sugar dissolved in water; or injecting glucagon if symptoms are severe

» Recognizing what brings on symptoms of hyperglycemia, such as not taking enough or skipping a dose of antidiabetic medication, overeating or not following meal plan, having a fever or infection, or exercising less than usual

» Recognizing symptoms of hyperglycemia and ketoacidosis: blurred vision; drowsiness; dry mouth; flushed, dry skin; fruit-like breath odor; increased urination (frequency and volume); ketones in urine; loss of appetite; stomachache, nausea, or vomiting; tiredness; troubled breathing (rapid and deep); unconsciousness; and unusual thirst

» Knowing what to do if symptoms of hyperglycemia occur, such as checking blood glucose and contacting a member of the health care team

Patients with diabetes—
- Having regular eye exams by an ophthalmologist
- Reporting any kind of visual symptom and obtaining a referral to an ophthalmologist, regardless of underlying medications or other physical findings

Side/adverse effects

Signs of potential side effects, especially congestive heart failure, hepatic failure, hyperglycemia, hypoglycemia, ischemic heart disease, or severe edema

Signs of potential side effects observed during clinical practice, especially angioedema; decreased visual ascuity; diabetic macular edema; hepatitis and hepatic enzyme elevations to three or more times the upper limit of normal; pleural effusions, unusually rapid increases in weight, or urticaria.

General Dosing Information

Therapy with rosiglitazone may result in ovulation in some premenopausal anovulatory women. As a result, these patients may be at an increased risk for pregnancy while taking rosiglitazone. So, adequate contraception in premenopausal women should be recommended.

Diet/Nutrition

Rosiglitazone may be taken with or without food.

Diet control should be included in the management of type 2 diabetes with rosiglitazone therapy. Caloric restriction, weight loss, and exercise are essential for the proper treatment because they help improve insulin sensitivity.

Oral Dosage Forms

ROSIGLITAZONE MALEATE TABLETS

Usual adult dose

Antidiabetic agent—

As monotherapy—

Oral, initially 4 milligrams per day administered once daily or divided and administered twice daily without regard to meals. If the patient has an inadequate response to rosiglitazone after 8 to 12 weeks, as determined by reduction in FPG, the dose may be increased to 8 mg per day administered once daily or divided and administered twice daily.

In patients with renal impairment, no dosage adjustment is necessary.

In combination with metformin—

Oral, initially 4 milligrams per day administered once daily or divided and administered twice daily without regard to meals. It is unlikely that the dose of metformin will require adjustment due to hypoglycemia during combination therapy with rosiglitazone.

In combination with a sulfonylurea—

Oral, 4 milligrams per day administered once daily or divided and administered twice daily without regard to meals. If patients report hypoglycemia, the dose of the sulfonylurea should be decreased. Doses of rosiglitazone greater than 4 mg daily in combination with a sulfonylurea have not been studied in adequate and well-controlled clinical trials. However, in Canada, the dose may be increased to 8 mg per day after 8 to 12 weeks if the patient had an inadequate response to the lower dose.

In combination with insulin—

Oral, 4 milligrams per day. Adjustments should be individualized based on glucose-lowering response. Doses greater than 4 mg daily in combination with insulin are not currently indicated. It is recommended that the insulin dose be decreased by 10% to 25% if the patient reports hypoglycemia or if FPG concentrations decrease to less than 100 mg per dL.

Note: Canadian manufacturer states that rosiglitazone is not currently indicated for combination use with insulin.

In combination with sulfonylurea plus metformin—
Oral, 4 milligrams per day administered once daily or divided and administered twice daily without regard to meals. If patients report hypoglycemia, the dose of the sulfonylurea should be decreased.

Usual adult prescribing limits
8 milligrams per day as monotherapy and in combination with metformin, sulfonylurea, or sulfonylurea plus metformin; doses greater than 4 mg per day in combination with insulin are not currently indicated.

Usual pediatric dose
Safety and efficacy have not been established.

Usual geriatric dose
See *Usual adult dose.*

Strength(s) usually available
U.S.—
2 mg (base) (Rx) [*Avandia* (hypromellose 2910; lactose monohydrate; magnesium stearate; microcrystalline cellulose; polyethylene glycol 3000; sodium starch glycolate; titanium dioxide; triacetin; synthetic red and/or yellow iron oxides; talc)].
4 mg (base) (Rx) [*Avandia* (hypromellose 2910; lactose monohydrate; magnesium stearate; microcrystalline cellulose; polyethylene glycol 3000; sodium starch glycolate; titanium dioxide; triacetin; synthetic red and/or yellow iron oxides; talc)].
8 mg (base) (Rx) [*Avandia* (hypromellose 2910; lactose monohydrate; magnesium stearate; microcrystalline cellulose; polyethylene glycol 3000; sodium starch glycolate; titanium dioxide; triacetin; synthetic red and/or yellow iron oxides; talc)].

Canada—
2 mg (base) (Rx) [*Avandia* (hydroxypropyl methylcellulose; lactose monohydrate; magnesium stearate; microcrystalline cellulose; polyethylene glycol 3000; sodium starch glycolate; titanium dioxide; triacetin; synthetic red and/or yellow iron oxides; talc)].
4 mg (base) (Rx) [*Avandia*].
8 mg (base) (Rx) [*Avandia*].

Packaging and storage
Store at 25 °C (77 °F) with excursions 15 °C to 30 °C (59 °F to 86 °F). Protect from light.

Revised: 07/29/2006
Developed: 01/20/2000

ROSIGLITAZONE AND METFORMIN Systemic

VA CLASSIFICATION (Primary): HS509

Commonly used brand name(s): *Avandamet.*

Note: For a listing of dosage forms and brand names by country availability, see *Dosage Forms* section(s).

Category

Antidiabetic agent.

Indications

Accepted

Diabetes, type 2 (treatment)—The combination of rosiglitazone and metformin is indicated as an adjunctive therapy to diet and exercise to improve glycemic control in patients with type 2 diabetes mellitus. The combination of rosiglitazone and metformin also is indicated when diet, exercise, and initial treatment with rosiglitazone or metformin do not result in adequate glycemic control in patients with type 2 diabetes.

Acceptance not established

The safety and efficacy of rosiglitazone and metformin as initial pharmacologic therapy for patients with type 2 diabetes mellitus after a trial of caloric restriction, weight loss, and exercise has not been established.

Unaccepted

Rosiglitazone and metformin combination therapy is not indicated for use in combination with insulin.

Rosiglitazone and metformin should not be used in patients with type 1 diabetes. Due to its mechanism of action, rosiglitazone is active only in the presence of endogenous insulin.

Pharmacology/Pharmacokinetics

Physicochemical characteristics

Chemical Group—
Metformin—Biguanide
Rosiglitazone—Thiazolidinedione

Molecular weight—
Metformin: 165.63.
Rosiglitazone: 473.52 (357.44 free base).

pKa—
Metformin: 12.4.
Rosiglitazone: 6.8 and 6.1.

Solubility—
Metformin hydrochloride—soluble in water and 95% ethanol; practically insoluble in acetone, ether and chloroform.
Rosiglitazone maleate—readily soluble in ethanol and a buffered aqueous solution with pH of 2.3; solubility decreases with increasing pH in the physiological range.

pH—
Metformin: 6.68 (1% aqueous solution of metformin hydrochloride)
Rosiglitazone: 3.3 (saturated solution of rosiglitazone maleate in water) and 3.4 (in 0.9% saline)

Mechanism of action/Effect

Metformin hydrochloride is an antihyperglycemic agent, which improves glucose tolerance in patients with type 2 diabetes, lowering both basal and postprandial plasma glucose. Metformin decreases hepatic glucose production, decreases intestinal absorption of glucose and increases peripheral glucose uptake and utilization. Unlike sulfonylureas, metformin does not produce hypoglycemia in either patients with type 2 diabetes or normal subjects (except in special circumstances, refer to *Side/Adverse Effects, Rosiglitazone and Metformin*) and does not cause hyperinsulinemia. With metformin therapy, insulin secretion remains unchanged while fasting insulin levels and day-long plasma insulin response may actually decrease.

Rosiglitazone, a thiazolidinedione class of antidiabetic agents, improves glycemic control by improving insulin sensitivity while reducing circulating insulin levels. Rosiglitazone is a highly selective and potent agonist for the for the peroxisome proliferator-activated receptor-gamma (PPARγ). PPAR receptors are found in key target tissues for insulin action such as adipose tissue, skeletal muscle and liver. Activation of PPARγ nuclear receptors regulates the transcription of insulin-responsive genes involved in the control of glucose production, transport, and utilization. PPARγ-responsive genes also participate in the regulation of fatty acid metabolism.

Absorption

Metformin—absolute bioavailability is 50% to 60% under fasting conditions
Rosiglitazone—absolute bioavailability is 99%

Distribution

Metformin: apparent volume of distribution is 654 ± 358 liters; partitions into erythrocytes
Rosiglitazone: mean oral volume of distribution is approximately 17.6 liters

Protein binding

Metformin—negligibly bound to plasma proteins
Rosiglitazone—very high (99.8%); bound to plasma protein, primarily albumin.

Biotransformation

Metformin is not metabolized.
Rosiglitazone is extensively metabolized. The major routes of metabolism are N-demethylation and hydroxylation, followed by conjugation with sulfate and glucuronic acid. All the circulating metabolites are considerably less potent than parent and, therefore, are not expected to contribute to the insulin-sensitizing activity of rosiglitazone. In vitro data demonstrate that rosiglitazone is predominantly metabolized by cytochrome P450 (CYP) isoenzyme 2C8, with CYP2C9 contributing as the minor pathway.

Elimination

Metformin—6.2 hours (plasma); 17.6 hours (blood). In patients with decreased renal function the plasma and blood half-life is prolonged.
Rosiglitazone elimination half-life is 3 to 4 hours, independent of dose; plasma half-life of [^{14}C] related material ranged from 103 to 158 hours. In patients with hepatic impairment the elimination half-life for rosiglitazone was about 2 hours longer.

Onset of action

Rosiglitazone and metformin combination therapy can begin to take effect 1 to 2 weeks after initiation; the full effect of glycemic improvement may take 2 to 3 months

Time to peak concentration

Rosiglitazone—approximately 1 hour after dosing

Time to steady state plasma concentration—

Metformin—steady state is reached within 24 to 48 hours

Note: Although not clinically significant, administration with food delays time to peak concentration for both components (1.5 hours for rosiglitazone and 0.5 hours for metformin, respectively).

Peak serum concentration

Peak plasma concentration:—

Rosiglitazone—maximum plasma concentration and the area under the curve increase in a dose-proportional manner over a therapeutic dose range.

Note: Unbound oral clearance of rosiglitazone was significantly lower in patients with moderate to severe hepatic impairment (Child-Pugh Class B/C), as a result, unbound C_{max} and $AUC_{0\text{-}inf}$ were increased 2- and 3-fold, respectively.

Steady state plasma concentration—

Metformin—less than 1 microgram per milliliter; maximum plasma levels did not exceed 5 micrograms per milliliter, even at maximum doses. Administration with food decreases peak plasma concentrations by 15% for metformin.

Elimination

Renal—

Metformin—approximately 90% of the absorbed drug is eliminated within the first 24 hours; renal clearance is approximately 3.5 times greater than creatinine clearance which indicates that tubular secretion is the major route of metformin elimination. In patients with impaired renal function, the renal clearance is decreased in proportion to the decrease in creatine clearance.

Rosiglitazone—approximately 64% of the dose was eliminated in urine following oral or intravenous administration of [^{14}C] rosiglitazone

In dialysis—Hemodialysis with clearance of up to 170 mL per minute may be useful for removal of accumulated metformin.

Fecal—

Metformin—intravenous studies demonstrate no biliary elimination

Rosiglitazone—approximately 23% of [^{14}C] rosiglitazone dose is eliminated in the feces following oral or intravenous administration.

Precautions to Consider

Carcinogenicity

Metformin: Long term carcinogenicity studies in rats and in mice for 104 weeks and 91 weeks, respectively, at three times the recommended human daily dose showed no evidence of carcinogenicity in either male or female mice.

Rosiglitazone: In mice, rosiglitazone was not carcinogenic.

Tumorigenicity

Metformin: A study in male rats showed no evidence of tumorigenicity; however, female rats given three times the recommended human daily dose on a mg per kg of body weight (mg/kg) basis, or 900 mg a day, had an increased incidence of benign stromal uterine polyps.

Rosiglitazone: In rats, a significant increase in benign adipose tissue tumors (lipomas) was found at doses ≥ 0.3 mg per kg of body weight (mg/kg) per day for 104 weeks. These doses represented area under the plasma concentration-time curve (AUC) values 2 times that of the maximum recommended human daily dose. In mice, the incidence of adipose hyperplasia increased at doses ≥ 1.5 mg per kg of body weight per day (approximately 2 times the human AUC at the maximum recommended human daily dose).

Mutagenicity

Metformin: Not found to be mutagenic in the Ames test, gene mutation test (mouse lymphoma cells), chromosome aberration test (human lymphocytes), or *in vivo* micronucleus test.

Rosiglitazone: No evidence of mutagenicity or clastogenicity was found in the *in vitro* bacterial assays for gene mutation, the *in vitro* chromosome aberration test in human lymphocytes, the *in vivo* mouse micronucleus test, and the *in vivo/in vitro* rat UDS assay. When metabolic activation was used in the *in vitro* mouse lymphoma assay, an increase (about 2–fold) in mutation was observed.

Pregnancy/Reproduction

Fertility—Metformin: Problems in humans have not been documented. No evidence of impairment of fertility was found in male or female rats given three times the recommended human daily dose of metformin.

Rosiglitazone:

Rosiglitazone therapy may cause resumption of ovulation in premenopausal anovulatory patients with insulin resistance. In premenopausal women, adequate contraception should be recommended.

No evidence of impaired fertility or reproductive capability was found in male rats given up to 40 mg per kg of body weight per day of rosiglitazone (corresponding to 116 times the human exposure based on AUC at maximum recommended human daily dose). However, in female rats, fertility was decreased at a dose of 40 mg per kg per day and estrous cyclicity was altered at 2 mg per kg per day, but these effects were not noted at doses less than 0.2 mg per kg per day. These effects were attributed to altered plasma levels of progesterone and estradiol. In monkeys administered 0.6 and 4.6 mg per kg per day of rosiglitazone, the follicular phase rise in serum estradiol was decreased with reduction in the luteinizing hormone surge and luteal phase progesterone levels. Amenorrhea was also observed.

Pregnancy—Rosiglitazone and metformin should not be used in pregnant women unless the potential benefit justifies the potential risk to the fetus.

It is recommended that insulin alone be used during pregnancy for maintenance of blood glucose concentrations that are as close to normal as possible. Abnormal maternal blood glucose concentrations have been associated with a higher incidence of congenital anomalies and increased neonatal morbidity and mortality.

Metformin: Adequate and well-controlled studies in humans have not been done. Metformin was not teratogenic in rats and rabbits at doses up to 600 mg per kg of body weight per day. This represents an exposure of about two and six times the maximum recommended human daily dose of the 2000 mg based on body surface area comparisons for rats and rabbits, respectively. Determination of fetal concentrations demonstrated a partial placental barrier to metformin.

Rosiglitazone: Adequate and well-controlled studies in humans have not been done. No evidence of teratogenicity was found in rats and rabbits given up to 3 and 100 mg per kg of body weight, respectively (corresponding to 20 and 75 times the human AUC at the maximum recommended human daily dose, respectively). In rats and rabbits, rosiglitazone treatment during mid-late gestation was associated with fetal death and growth retardation. Administration of rosiglitazone to rats during gestation through lactation reduced litter size, neonatal viability, and postnatal growth. However, postnatal growth retardation was reversible after puberty.

FDA Pregnancy Category C

Labor and delivery—The effect of rosiglitazone and metformin on labor and delivery is unknown.

Breast-feeding

It is not known whether rosiglitazone and metformin combination is distributed into human breast milk. In studies performed with the individual components both rosiglitazone-related material and metformin were detectable in the milk of lactating rats. Because many drugs pass into human breast milk it is recommended that nursing mothers not take rosiglitazone and metformin combination. If rosiglitazone and metformin combination is discontinued, and if diet alone is inadequate for controlling blood glucose, insulin therapy should be considered.

Pediatrics

Appropriate studies on the relationship of age to the effects of rosiglitazone and metformin have not been performed in the pediatric population. Safety and efficacy have not been established.

Geriatrics

Appropriate studies on the relationship of age to the effects of rosiglitazone and metformin have not been performed in the geriatric population. Metformin is known to be substantially excreted by the kidney and because the risk of serious adverse reactions to the drug is greater in patients with impaired renal function, rosiglitazone and metformin combination should only be used in patients with normal renal function. Elderly patients are more likely to have age-related problems such as decreased renal function and should be used with caution as age increases. Dose selection should be done with caution and it should be based on careful and regular monitoring of renal function. Generally, geriatric patients should not be titrated to the maximum dose.

Pharmacogenetics

Efficacy was demonstrated with no gender differences in glycemic response in studies of rosiglitazone and metformin given as a combined formulation.

Surgical

Treatment with rosiglitazone and metformin combination should be discontinued until patient's oral intake has been reestablished to presurgical levels and renal function is normal.

Drug interactions and/or related problems

The following drug interactions and/or related problems have been selected on the basis of their potential clinical significance (possible mechanism in parentheses where appropriate)—not necessarily inclusive (» = major clinical significance):

Note: Combinations containing any of the following medications, depending on the amount present, may also interact with this medication.

» Alcohol intake, acute or chronic
(alcohol is known to potentiate the effect of metformin on lactate metabolism; patients should be warned against excessive alcohol intake, acute or chronic)

» Beta-adrenergic blocking agents
(hypoglycemia may be difficult to recognize in patients taking a beta-adrenergic blocking agent)

» Cimetidine or
Cationic medications excreted by renal tubular transport, such as:
Amiloride or
Digoxin or
Morphine or
Procainamide or
Quinidine or
Quinine or
Ranitidine or
Triamterene or
Trimethoprim or
Vancomycin
(potential for interaction because of competition for common renal tubular transport systems; careful patient monitoring and dose adjustment of either drug is recommended)
(cimetidine inhibits the renal tubular secretion of metformin; increases peak plasma concentrations and whole blood concentrations of metformin by 60%; 40% increase in plasma and whole blood metformin AUC; clinical significance is not known, but dosage reduction of metformin should be considered if cimetidine is administered concomitantly)

» CYP2C8 inducers such as
Rifampin
(concomitant use may increase rosiglitazone metabolism; changes in diabetes treatment may be needed based on clinical response)

» CYP2C8 inhibitors such as
Gemfibrozil
(concomitant use may decrease rosiglitazone metabolism; decrease in rosiglitazone dose may be needed when gemfibrozil is introduced due to the potential for dose-related adverse events with rosiglitazone)

» Furosemide
(in one study, furosemide increased the AUC of metformin by 15% in normal healthy volunteers; renal clearance was not affected and clinical significance is not known, but dosage reduction of metformin potentially may be needed)

Hyperglycemia-causing medications, such as:
Calcium channel blocking drugs or
Contraceptives, estrogen-containing, oral or
Corticosteroids or
Diuretics, thiazide or
Estrogens or
Isoniazid or
Niacin or
Phenothiazines, especially chlorpromazine or
Phenytoin or
Sympathomimetic agents or
Thyroid hormones
(these medications may contribute to hyperglycemia; patients should be closely observed to maintain adequate glycemic control)

Hypoglycemia-causing medications, such as:
Insulin or
Sulfonylureas
(hypoglycemia does not occur in patients receiving metformin alone under usual circumstances, but could occur during concomitant use with hypoglycemic agents)
(thiazolidinediones in combination with insulin may increase the risk of cardiovascular adverse events)

Nifedipine
(coadministration of nifedipine increased plasma metformin C_{max} and AUC by 20% and 9% respectively; amount excreted in urine increased; metformin absorption appears to be enhanced by nifedipine)

Laboratory value alterations

The following have been selected on the basis of their potential clinical significance (possible effect in parentheses where appropriate)—not necessarily inclusive (» = major clinical significance).

With physiology/laboratory test values

Alanine aminotransferase (ALT [SGPT]) and
Aspartate aminotransferase (AST [SGOT])
(During controlled clinical trials, reversible elevations greater than three times the upper limit of normal were observed in 0.2% of rosiglitazone-treated patients versus 0.2% of placebo-treated patients and 0.5% of active comparator-treated patients; however, ALT elevations were not clearly related to rosiglitazone)

Hematocrit and
Hemoglobin concentrations and
Red blood cell indices and
White blood cell counts
(Decreases occurred in a dose related fashion in patients treated with rosiglitazone)

Lipids, serum
(Changes in serum lipids have been observed in patients treated with rosiglitazone)

Medical considerations/Contraindications

The medical considerations/contraindications included have been selected on the basis of their potential clinical significance (reasons given in parentheses where appropriate)—not necessarily inclusive (» = major clinical significance).

Except under special circumstances, this medication should not be used when the following medical problem exists:

Conditions associated with hypoxemia, such as:
» Cardiovascular collapse (shock) or
» Dehydration or
» Myocardial infarction, acute or
» Sepsis
(these conditions have been associated with lactic acidosis; may also cause prerenal azotemia; if these conditions occur rosiglitazone and metformin combination therapy should be promptly discontinued.)

» Diabetic ketoacidosis, with or without coma or
» Lactic acidosis, history of or
» Metabolic acidosis, acute or chronic
(Rosiglitazone and metformin is contraindicated in patients with these conditions; diabetic ketoacidosis should be treated with insulin)

» Diagnostic radiologic studies using intravascular iodinated contrast media such as:
Angiography or
Cholangiography, intravenous or
Computed tomography (CT) scan or
Urogram, intravenous
(intravascular contrast studies with iodinated contrast materials can lead to acute alteration of renal function and have been associated with lactic acidosis in patients receiving metformin; rosiglitazone and metformin should be temporarily discontinued at the time of or prior to the procedure and withheld 48 hours after the procedure; therapy should be reinstituted only after renal function has been reevaluated and found to be normal)

» Heart failure, congestive
(rosiglitazone and metformin combination therapy is contraindicated in patients with congestive heart failure requiring pharmacological management, in particular those with unstable or acute congestive heart failure who are at risk for hypoperfusion and hypoxemia, are at increased risk for lactic acidosis)
(caution should be used since rosiglitazone use can cause fluid retention, which can exacerbate or lead to congestive heart failure)
(increased risk of cardiovascular events in patients with congestive heart failure (CHF) New York Heart Association (NYHA) Class 1 and 2 who take rosiglitazone)

» Hepatic function, impaired
(impaired hepatic function has been associated with some cases of lactic acidosis; decreased hepatic function may significantly limit the ability to clear lactate; patients with clinical or laboratory evidence of hepatic disease generally should avoid using rosiglitazone and metformin)

» Hypersensitivity to rosiglitazone maleate, metformin hydrochloride, or any of its components

» Renal dysfunction
(rosiglitazone and metformin combination therapy is contraindicated in patients with renal disease or renal failure [serum creatinine ≥ 1.5 mg per dL in males, ≥ 1.4 mg per dL in females, or abnormal creatinine clearance] the risk of lactic acidosis increases with the degree of renal dysfunction and the patient's age)

» Surgical procedures
(use of rosiglitazone and metformin combination therapy should be temporarily suspended for any surgical procedure [except for minor procedures not associated with the restricted intake of food and fluids] and should not be restarted until the patients oral intake has resumed and renal function has been evaluated as normal.)

» Type 1 diabetes
(rosiglitazone is only active in the presence of endogenous insulin and the combination of rosiglitazone and metformin should not be used in patients with type 1 diabetes)

Risk-benefit should be considered when the following medical problems exist:

» Diabetic macular edema
(post-marketing reports of exacerbation with rosiglitazone)

Edema
(should be used with caution in patients with edema; rosiglitazone can cause fluid retention, which can exacerbate or lead to congestive heart failure; patients with ongoing edema are more likely to have adverse events associated with edema if started on combination therapy with insulin and rosiglitazone)

» Hypoglycemia-causing conditions, such as:
Adrenal insufficiency, not optimally controlled or
Alcohol intoxication or
Caloric intake, deficient or
Elderly patients or
Debilitated physical condition or
Malnourished physical condition or
Pituitary insufficiency, not optimally controlled
(These conditions, which inherently predispose patients to the risk of developing hypoglycemia, increase the patient's risk of developing severe hypoglycemia during treatment; may be difficult to recognize in the elderly and in patients taking beta-adrenergic blocking drugs)

» Jaundice
(Rosiglitazone and metformin should not be used in patients who experienced jaundice while taking troglitazone; safety and efficacy have not been established in patients who experienced liver abnormalities, jaundice, or hepatic dysfunction while taking troglitazone)

» Stress, such as
Fever or
Infection or
Surgery or
Trauma
(when a patient stabilized on any diabetic regimen is exposed to stress, a temporary loss of glycemic control may occur; it may be necessary to withhold rosiglitazone and metformin and temporarily administer insulin; treatment may be restarted after the acute episode is resolved)

Patient monitoring

The following may be especially important in patient monitoring (other tests may be warranted in some patients, depending on condition; » = major clinical significance):

Anion gap and
Electrolyte concentrations, serum and
Glucose, blood and
Ketone, urine and
Lactic acid, blood and
Lactic acid/pyruvate ratio and
Metformin concentration, plasma and
pH, blood
(any patient with type 2 diabetes previously well controlled who develops laboratory abnormalities or clinical illness [especially vague and poor defined illness] should be promptly evaluated for evidence of ketoacidosis or lactic acidosis; if acidosis of either form occurs rosiglitazone and metformin should be stopped immediately and appropriate measures initiated)

» Cardiac function
(rosiglitazone can cause fluid retention which may exacerbate or lead to heart failure; in combination with insulin, thiazolidinediones may also increase the risk of other cardiovascular adverse events; patients should be monitored for signs and symptoms of heart failure; rosiglitazone therapy should be discontinued if any deterioration in cardiac status occurs)

» Eye examinations
(important in patients with diabetes to have regular exams with ophthalmologist; visual symptoms should be reported and patient promptly referred to an ophthalmologist regardless of underlying medications or other physical findings due to post-marketing reports of macular edema)

Folic acid and
» Hematocrit and
» Hemoglobin concentrations and
» Red blood cell indices and
Vitamin B_{12} concentrations, serum
(initial and periodic monitoring of hematologic parameters [hematocrit, hemoglobin, and red blood cell indices] on an annual basis is advised in all patients; any abnormalities should be investigated and managed; certain individuals appear to be predisposed to developing subnormal vitamin B_{12} levels and routine serum measurements should be done at one- to three-year intervals in patients on long-term treatment with rosiglitazone and metformin)

» Glucose concentration, in blood, fasting and
» Glycosylated hemoglobin (HbA_{1c} measurements)
(should be routinely performed to monitor therapeutic response)

» Hepatic function determinations
(recommended prior to initiation of therapy, every 2 months for the first 12 months, and periodically thereafter; patients with mildly elevated enzymes [ALT levels ≤ 2.5 times upper limit of normal] at baseline or during therapy with rosiglitazone and metformin should proceed with caution and include more frequent liver enzyme monitoring; if ALT levels increase to >3 times the upper limit of normal, levels should be rechecked as soon as possible; if levels remain >3 times the upper limit of normal, therapy should be discontinued)
(liver enzymes should be checked if the patient develops symptoms suggesting hepatic dysfunction such as unexplained nausea, vomiting, abdominal pain, fatigue, anorexia, and/or dark urine; if jaundice is observed drug therapy should be discontinued)
(if the presence of hepatic disease or hepatic dysfunction of sufficient magnitude is confirmed and is of sufficient magnitude to predispose to lactic acidosis, drug therapy should be discontinued)

» Renal function
(prior to initiation of therapy and annually thereafter, renal function should be assessed and verified as normal; in patients in whom development of renal dysfunction is anticipated [e.g., in older adults] it should be assessed more frequently and the drug should be discontinued if evidence of renal impairment is present)

» Weight
(patients who experience unusually rapid increases in weight and increases in excess of that generally observed in clinical trials should be assessed for fluid accumulation and volume-related events such as excessive edema and congestive heart failure)

Side/Adverse Effects

Lactic acidosis is a rare, but serious, metabolic complication that can occur due to metformin accumulation during treatment with rosiglitazone and metformin combination therapy and when it occurs, is fatal in approximately 50% of cases. Reported cases have occurred primarily in diabetic patients with significant renal insufficiency, including both intrinsic renal disease and renal hypoperfusion. Patients with congestive heart failure requiring pharmacologic management, in particular those with unstable or acute congestive heart failure who are at risk of hypoperfusion and hypoxemia, are at an increased risk of lactic acidosis. The risk of lactic acidosis increases with the degree of renal dysfunction and the patient's age. Symptoms of lactic acidosis include malaise, myalgias, respiratory distress, increasing somnolence and nonspecific abdominal distress. Hypothermia, hypotension and resistant bradyarrhythmias may occur in more severe lactic acidosis.

Hypoglycemia does not occur in patients receiving metformin alone under usual circumstances of use. Hypoglycemia could occur when caloric intake is deficient, when strenuous exercise is not compensated by caloric supplementation, or during concomitant use with hypoglycemic agents (such as insulin or sulfonylureas) or ethanol. Older adults, debilitated or malnourished patients, and those with adrenal or pituitary insufficiency or alcohol intoxication are particularly susceptible to hypoglycemic effects. Hypoglycemia may be difficult to recognize in people who are taking beta-adrenergic blocking drugs or in older adults.

The following side/adverse effects have been selected on the basis of their potential clinical significance (possible signs and symptoms in parentheses where appropriate)—not necessarily inclusive:

Those indicating need for medical attention

Incidence more frequent

Anemia (pale skin; troubled breathing with exertion; unusual bleeding or bruising; unusual tiredness or weakness)

Note: In studies of metformin in combination therapy, pretreatment concentrations of hemoglobin and hematocrit were lower and may have contributed to the higher reporting rate of anemia (7.1% vs 2.2% or less).

Incidence less frequent

Cardiac failure (chest pain or discomfort; dilated neck veins; extreme fatigue; irregular breathing; irregular heartbeat; shortness of breath; swelling of face, fingers, feet, or lower legs; weight gain; wheezing); ***edema*** (swelling)—rosiglitazone with maximum dose of metformin; ***hypoglycemia*** (anxiety; blurred vision; chills; cold sweats; coma; confusion; cool pale skin; depression; dizziness; fast heartbeat; headache; increased hunger; nausea; nervousness; nightmares; seizures; shakiness; slurred speech; unusual tiredness or weakness)

Incidence rare

Lactic acidosis (abdominal discomfort; decreased appetite; diarrhea; fast, shallow breathing; general feeling of discomfort; muscle pain or cramping; nausea; shortness of breath; sleepiness; unusual tiredness or weakness)

Incidence not determined—Observed during clinical practice; estimates of frequency can not be determined

Angioedema (large, hive-like swelling on face, eyelids, lips, tongue, throat, hands, legs, feet, sex organs); ***congestive heart failure*** (chest pain; decreased urine output; dilated neck veins; extreme fatigue; irregular breathing; irregular heartbeat; shortness of breath; swelling of face, fingers, feet, or lower legs; tightness in chest; troubled breathing; weight gain; wheezing); ***decreased visual acuity*** (decreased vision); ***diabetic macular edema*** (blurred vision or other change in vision); ***hepatic effects, including*** (dark urine; loss of appetite; nausea; stomach pain; unusual tiredness or weakness; vomiting; weight loss); ***hepatitis; hepatic enzymes, increased***—ALT > 3 times upper limit of normal; ***jaundice; pleural effusions*** (chest pain; shortness of breath); ***pulmonary edema*** (chest pain; difficult, fast, noisy breathing, sometimes with wheezing; blue lips and fingernails; pale skin; increased sweating; coughing that sometimes produces a pink frothy sputum; shortness of breath; swelling in legs and ankles); ***urticaria*** (hives or welts; itching; redness of skin; skin rash); ***weight gain, excessive***

Those indicating need for medical attention only if they continue or are bothersome

Incidence more frequent

Diarrhea; fatigue (unusual tiredness or weakness); ***headache; injury; sinusitis*** (pain or tenderness around eyes and cheekbones; fever; stuffy or runny nose; headache; cough; shortness of breath or troubled breathing; tightness of chest or wheezing); ***upper respiratory tract infection*** (ear congestion; nasal congestion; chills; cough, fever, sneezing, or sore throat; body aches or pain; headache; loss of voice; runny nose; unusual tiredness or weakness; difficulty in breathing)

Incidence less frequent

Arthralgia (pain in joints; muscle pain or stiffness; difficulty in moving); ***back pain; viral infection*** (chills; cough or hoarseness; fever; cold flu-like symptoms)

Overdose

For more information on the management of overdose or unintentional ingestion, **contact a poison control center** (see *Poison Control Center Listing*).

Metformin: Hypoglycemia has not been seen with ingestion of up to 85 grams, although lactic acidosis has occurred in such circumstances. Metformin is dialyzable with a clearance of up to 170 mL per minute under good hemodynamic conditions. Hemodialysis may be useful for removal of accumulated metformin from patients in whom a metformin overdosage is suspected.

Rosiglitazone: Limited data are available with regard to overdosage in humans. In clinical studies in volunteers, rosiglitazone has been administered at single oral doses of up to 20 mg and was well-tolerated. In the event of an overdose, appropriate supportive treatment should be initiated as dictated by the patients clinical status.

Patient Consultation

As an aid to patient consultation, refer to *Advice for the Patient, Rosiglitazone and Metformin (Systemic)*.

In providing consultation, consider emphasizing the following selected information (» = major clinical significance):

Before using this medication

» Conditions affecting use, especially:

Hypersensitivity to rosiglitazone or metformin

Pregnancy—Use not recommended; diet or diet plus insulin monotherapy is recommended to prevent maternal and fetal problems; importance of controlling and monitoring blood glucose during pregnancy; alerting physician if planning to become pregnant

FDA Pregnancy Category C

Breast-feeding—Use not recommended; it is not known whether rosiglitazone or metformin passes into human breast milk, however rosiglitazone and metformin have been detected in milk from lactating rats.

Use in children—Safety and efficacy not established in children.

Use in the elderly—Elderly patients should not be titrated to the maximum dose. Elderly patients may be more susceptible to serious adverse reactions due to decreased renal function. Rosiglitazone and metformin should not be used in patients 80 years of age or older unless measurement of creatinine clearance demonstrates that renal function is not reduced.

Surgical—Treatment should be temporarily suspended for any surgical procedure (except minor procedures); should not be restarted until oral intake has been reestablished to pre-surgical levels and renal function is normal.

Other medications, especially alcohol, amiloride, beta-adrenergic blocking agent, cimetidine, CYP2C8 inducers, CYP2C8 inhibitors, digoxin, furosemide, morphine, procainamide, quinidine, quinine, ranitidine, triamterene, trimethoprim, vancomycin, or any other cationic medication excreted by renal transport

Other medical problems, especially cardiovascular collapse (shock), congestive heart failure, dehydration, acute myocardial infarction, sepsis, diagnostic radiologic studies using intravascular iodinated contrast media, impaired hepatic function, metabolic acidosis, diabetic ketoacidosis, history of lactic acidosis, renal dysfunction, surgical procedures, type 1 diabetes, diabetic macular edema, fever, hypoglycemia-causing conditions, infection, jaundice, or trauma

Proper use of this medication

» Proper dosing

Missed dose: Taking as soon as possible; not taking if almost time for next scheduled dose; not doubling doses

» Importance of adherence to recommended regimens for diet, exercise, and glucose monitoring

Should take with food to reduce gastrointestinal side effects

You may begin to see an effect on blood glucose control in 1 to 2 weeks after starting rosiglitazone and metformin combination therapy or following a dosage adjustment; full effect of glycemic improvement may take 2 to 3 months after starting therapy or following a dosage adjustment

» Proper storage

Precautions while using this medication

» Reporting symptoms, such as abdominal pain, anorexia, dark urine, fatigue, jaundice, nausea, or vomiting, that are suggestive of hepatic dysfunction to physician immediately

» Regular visits to physician to check progress and monitor kidney and liver function

» *Carefully following special instructions of health care team:*

Discussing use of alcohol

Not taking other medications unless discussed with physician

Getting counseling for family members to help the patient with diabetes; also, special counseling for pregnancy planning and contraception

Making travel plans that include readiness for diabetic emergencies and eating meals at the usual times, even with changing time zones

» Preparing for and understanding what to do in case of diabetic emergency; carrying medical history and current medication list and wearing medical identification

» Recognizing what brings on symptoms of hypoglycemia, such as using other antidiabetic medication; delaying or missing a meal; exercising more than usual; drinking significant amounts of alcohol; or illness, including vomiting or diarrhea

» Recognizing symptoms of hypoglycemia: anxiety; behavior change similar to drunkenness; blurred vision; cold sweats; confusion; cool, pale skin; difficulty in concentrating; drowsiness; excessive hunger; fast heartbeat; headache; nausea; nervousness; nightmares; restless sleep; shakiness; slurred speech; or unusual tiredness or weakness

» Knowing what to do if symptoms of hypoglycemia occur, such as eating glucose tablets or gel, corn syrup, honey, or sugar cubes; drinking fruit juice, nondiet soft drink, or sugar dissolved in water; or injecting glucagon if symptoms are severe

» Recognizing what brings on symptoms of hyperglycemia, such as not taking enough or skipping a dose of antidiabetic medication, overeating or not following meal plan, having a fever or infection, or exercising less than usual

» Recognizing symptoms of hyperglycemia and ketoacidosis: blurred vision; drowsiness; dry mouth; flushed, dry skin; fruit-like breath odor; increased urination (frequency and volume); ketones in urine; loss of appetite; stomachache, nausea, or vomiting; tiredness; troubled breathing (rapid and deep); unconsciousness; and unusual thirst

» Knowing what to do if symptoms of hyperglycemia occur, such as checking blood glucose and contacting a member of the health care team

» Informing physician of metformin therapy when medical examinations that require administration of contrast media are scheduled or when surgery is scheduled; metformin should be discontinued before surgery or appropriate medical tests and may be reinstated 48 hours postprocedure if renal function is normal

» Recognizing symptoms of lactic acidosis, such as diarrhea, fast and shallow breathing, severe muscle pain or cramping, unusual sleepiness, and unusual tiredness and weakness

» Knowing what to do if symptoms of lactic acidosis occur, such as checking blood glucose and getting immediate emergency medical help; checking with physician if vomiting occurs

» Recognizing symptoms of heart failure, such as chest pain or discomfort; dilated neck veins; extreme fatigue; irregular breathing; irregular heartbeat; shortness of breath; swelling of face, fingers, feet, or lower legs; weight gain; wheezing

» Knowing what to do if symptoms of heart failure occur, such as immediately contacting a member of the health care team.

» Patients with diabetes—
- Having regular eye exams by an ophthalmologist
- Reporting any kind of visual symptom and obtaining a referral to an ophthalmologist, regardless of underlying medications or other physical findings

Side/adverse effects

Signs of potential side effects, especially anemia, cardiac failure, edema, hypoglycemia, or, lactic acidosis

Signs of potential side effects observed during clinical practice, especially angioedema, congestive heart failure, decreased visual ascuity, diabetic macular edema, hepatic effects, pleural effusions, pulmonary edema, urticaria, or excessive weight gain

General Dosing Information

For oral dosing forms:

Management of type 2 diabetes mellitus should include diet control. Caloric restriction, weight loss, and exercise are essential for proper treatment of the diabetic patient because they help improve insulin sensitivity. This is important not only in the primary treatment of type 2 diabetes, but also in maintaining the efficacy of drug therapy. Prior to initiation or escalation of oral antidiabetic therapy in patients with type 2 diabetes mellitus, secondary causes of poor oral glycemic control, e.g., infection, should be investigated and treated.

The safety and efficacy of using rosiglitazone and metformin in patients previously treated with other oral hypoglycemic agents and switched to rosiglitazone and metformin have not been established. Any change in therapy of type 2 diabetes should be undertaken with care and appropriate monitoring as changes in glycemic control can occur.

The use of rosiglitazone in combination therapy with insulin is not indicated and therefore the combination of rosiglitazone and metformin is not indicated for use in combination with insulin.

Therapy with rosiglitazone may result in ovulation in some premenopausal anovulatory women. As a result, these patients may be at an increased risk for pregnancy while taking rosiglitazone and metformin combination. Adequate contraception in premenopausal women is recommended.

Once a patient is stabilized on any dose level of rosiglitazone and metformin, gastrointestinal symptoms, which are common during initiation of therapy, are unlikely to be drug related. Later occurrence of gastrointestinal symptoms could be due to lactic acidosis or other serious disease.

Levels of fasting venous plasma lactate above the upper limit of normal but less than 5 mmol/L in patients taking rosiglitazone and metformin do not necessarily indicate impending lactic acidosis and may be explainable by other mechanisms, such as poorly controlled diabetes or obesity, vigorous physical activity or technical problems in sampling handling.

Bioequivalence information

The tablet formulation containing 4 mg rosiglitazone and 500 mg metformin was bioequivalent to one tablet containing 4 mg of rosiglitazone coadministered with one tablet containing 500 mg metformin under fasted conditions.

Oral Dosage Forms

ROSIGLITAZONE MALEATE AND METFORMIN HYDROCHLORIDE TABLETS

Usual adult dose

The selection of dose of rosiglitazone plus metformin should be based on the patient's current doses of rosiglitazone and/or metformin.

The following recommendations regarding the use of rosiglitazone plus metformin in patients inadequately controlled on rosiglitazone and metformin monotherapies are based on clinical practice experience with rosiglitazone and metformin combination therapy.
- The dosage of antidiabetic therapy with rosiglitazone and metformin should be individualized on the basis of effectiveness and tolerability while not exceeding the maximum recommended daily dose.
- Rosiglitazone plus metformin should be given in divided doses with meals, with gradual dose escalation. This reduces GI side effects (largely due to metformin) and permits determination of the maximum effective dose for the individual patient.
- Sufficient time should be given to assess adequacy of therapeutic response. Fasting plasma glucose (FPG) should be used to determine the therapeutic response. After an increase in metformin dosage, dose titration is recommended if patients are not adequately controlled in 1 to 2 weeks. After an increase in rosiglitazone dosage, dose titration is recommended if patients are not adequately controlled after 8 to 12 weeks.

Type 2 diabetes—

For drug naive patients (initial therapy)—

Oral, 2 mg rosiglitazone/500 mg metformin once or twice daily. The dose may be increased in increments of 2 mg/500 mg per day to a maximum of 8 mg/2000 mg per day given in divided doses if patients are not adequately controlled after 4 weeks.

Note: For patients with HbA1c> 11% or FPG>270 mg per dL—Starting dose of 2 mg rosiglitazone/500 mg metformin twice daily may be considered.

For patients inadequately controlled on metformin therapy—

Oral, 4 mg rosiglitazone (total daily dose) plus the dose of metformin already being taken (see table titled *Rosiglitazone and Metformin Starting Dose*).

For patients inadequately controlled on rosiglitazone therapy—

Oral, 1000 mg metformin (total daily dose) plus the dose of rosiglitazone already being taken (see table titled *Rosiglitazone and Metformin Starting Dose*).

PRIOR THERAPY Total Daily Dose	Tablet Strength	Number of Tablets
Metformin HCL 1000 mg/day	2 mg/500 mg	1 tablet twice a day
2000 mg/day	2 mg/1000 mg	1 tablet twice a day
Rosiglitazone 4 mg/day	2 mg/500 mg	1 tablet twice a day
8 mg/day	4 mg/500 mg	1 tablet twice a day

Note: In Canada, patients on 2000 mg per day of metformin should receive 2 tablets of tablet strength 1 mg rosiglitazone with 500 mg metformin twice daily.

For patients on doses of metformin between 1000 mg and 2000 mg/day, initiation of rosiglitazone and metformin requires individualization of therapy. In Canada, for patients on 1500 mg, 1750 mg, or 2500 mg of metformin, initiation of rosiglitazone and metformin requires individualization of therapy.

Rosiglitazone and Metformin Starting Dose—

Switching from combination therapy of rosiglitazone plus metformin as separate tablets—

Oral, the usual starting dose of rosiglitazone plus metformin is the dose of rosiglitazone plus metformin already being taken.

If additional glycemic control is needed—
Oral, the daily dose of rosiglitazone plus metformin may be increased by increments of 4 mg rosiglitazone and/or 500 mg metformin, up to the maximum recommended daily dose.

Note: Therapy should not be initiated in the following patients:
- Increased serum transaminase levels—ALT > 2.5 times the upper limit of normal at start of therapy.
- Clinical evidence of active liver disease

Usual adult prescribing limits
Maximum recommended daily dose: 8 mg of rosiglitazone and 2000 mg of metformin

Usual pediatric dose
Safety and efficacy have not been established.

Usual geriatric dose
See *Usual adult dose.*

Dose selection for elderly patients should be done with caution due to the greater frequency of geriatric specific problems. Initial and maintenance dosing should be conservative due to the potential for decreased renal function. Geriatric patients should not be titrated to the maximum dose.

Note: Renal function monitoring is necessary to aid in the prevention of metformin associated lactic acidosis.

Strength(s) usually available
U.S.

1 mg rosiglitazone maleate and 500 mg metformin hydrochloride (Rx) [*Avandamet* (hypromellose 2910; lactose monohydrate; magnesium stearate; microcrystalline cellulose; polyethylene glycol 400; povidone 29–32; sodium starch glycolate; titanium dioxide; red and/or yellow iron oxides)].

2 mg rosiglitazone maleate and 500 mg metformin hydrochloride (Rx) [*Avandamet* (hypromellose 2910; lactose monohydrate; magnesium stearate; microcrystalline cellulose; polyethylene glycol 400; povidone 29–32; sodium starch glycolate; titanium dioxide; red and/or yellow iron oxides)].

2 mg rosiglitazone maleate and 1000 mg metformin hydrochloride (Rx) [*Avandamet* (hypromellose 2910; lactose monohydrate; magnesium stearate; microcrystalline cellulose; polyethylene glycol 400; povidone 29–32; sodium starch glycolate; titanium dioxide; red and/or yellow iron oxides)].

4 mg rosiglitazone maleate and 500 mg metformin hydrochloride (Rx) [*Avandamet* (hypromellose 2910; lactose monohydrate; magnesium stearate; microcrystalline cellulose; polyethylene glycol 400; povidone 29–32; sodium starch glycolate; titanium dioxide; red and/or yellow iron oxides)].

4 mg rosiglitazone maleate and 1000 mg metformin hydrochloride (Rx) [*Avandamet* (hypromellose 2910; lactose monohydrate; magnesium stearate; microcrystalline cellulose; polyethylene glycol 400; povidone 29–32; sodium starch glycolate; titanium dioxide; red and/or yellow iron oxides)].

Canada—

1 mg rosiglitazone maleate and 500 mg metformin hydrochloride (Rx) [*Avandamet* (hydroxypropyl methylcellulose; lactose monohydrate; magnesium stearate; microcrystalline cellulose; polyethylene glycol 400; povidone 29–32; sodium starch glycolate; titanium dioxide; red and/or yellow iron oxides)].

2 mg rosiglitazone maleate and 500 mg metformin hydrochloride (Rx) [*Avandamet* (hydroxypropyl methylcellulose; lactose monohydrate; magnesium stearate; microcrystalline cellulose; polyethylene glycol 400; povidone 29–32; sodium starch glycolate; titanium dioxide; red and/or yellow iron oxides)].

4 mg rosiglitazone maleate and 500 mg metformin hydrochloride (Rx) [*Avandamet* (hydroxypropyl methylcellulose; lactose monohydrate; magnesium stearate; microcrystalline cellulose; polyethylene glycol 400; povidone 29–32; sodium starch glycolate; titanium dioxide; red and/or yellow iron oxides)].

Packaging and storage
Store at 25 °C (77 °F); excursions permitted to 15 to 30 °C (59 to 86 °F). Keep in a tight, light resistant container.

Auxiliary labeling
- Avoid alcohol while taking this medication
- Take with food
- *For control of diabetes. Do not stop unless directed by physician.*

Revised: 07/29/2006
Developed: 11/20/2003

ROSUVASTATIN Systemic

VA CLASSIFICATION (Primary): CV351

Commonly used brand name(s): *Crestor.*

Note: For a listing of dosage forms and brand names by country availability, see *Dosage Forms* section(s).

Category
Antihyperlipidemic; HMG-CoA reductase inhibitor.

Indications
Accepted
Hyperlipidemia (treatment)—Rosuvastatin is indicated as an adjunct to diet to reduce elevated total cholesterol (total-C), low-density lipoprotein cholesterol (LDL-C), apolipoprotein B (Apo B), non-high-density lipoprotein cholesterol (HDL-C), and triglyceride (TG) concentrations and to increase high-density lipoprotein cholesterol (HDL-C) in patients with primary hypercholesterolemia (heterozygous familial and nonfamilial) and mixed dyslipidemia (Fredrickson Types IIa and IIb).

Rosuvastatin is indicated as an adjunct to diet for the treatment of patients with elevated serum triglyceride levels (Fredrickson Type IV).

Rosuvastatin is also indicated to reduce LDL-C, total-C, and Apo B in patients with homozygous familial hypercholesterolemia as an adjunct to other lipid-lowering treatments, such as low-density lipoprotein apheresis, or if such treatments are unavailable.

For additional information on initial therapeutic guidelines related to the treatment of hyperlipidemia, see *Appendix III.*

Acceptance not established
Rosuvastatin has not been studied in Fredrickson Type I, III, and V dyslipidemias.

Pharmacology/Pharmacokinetics
Physicochemical characteristics
Molecular weight—Rosuvastatin calcium—1001.14.

Solubility—
Sparingly soluble in water and methanol.
Slightly soluble in ethanol.

Partition coefficient—Octanol/water at pH of 7—0.13

Mechanism of action/Effect
Rosuvastatin is a selective and competitive inhibitor of HMG-CoA reductase, the rate-limiting enzyme that converts 3-hydroxy-3-methylglutaryl coenzyme A to mevalonate, a precursor of cholesterol. Rosuvastatin produces its lipid-modifying effects in two ways. First, it increases the number of hepatic LDL receptors on the cell-surface to enhance uptake and catabolism of LDL. Second, rosuvastatin inhibits hepatic synthesis of VLDL, which reduces the total number of VLDL and LDL particles. Rosuvastatin reduces total cholesterol, LDL-C, Apo B, and nonHDL-C in patients with homozygous and heterozygous familial hypercholesterolemia, nonfamilial forms of hypercholesterolemia, and mixed dyslipidemia. Rosuvastatin also reduces TG and produces increases in HDL-C. Rosuvastatin reduces total-C, LDL-C, VLDL-cholesterol, Apo B, nonHDL-C and TG, and increases HDL-C in patients with isolated hypertriglyceridemia.

Absorption
Bioavailability: 20%; food decreased rate of drug absorption

Distribution
Volume of distribution (Vol_D) at steady state—134 L

Protein binding
High (88%), primarily bound to albumin

Biotransformation
Rosuvastatin is metabolized by cytochrome P450 2C9. Approximately 10% of radiolabeled dose is recovered as metabolite. The major metabolite is N-desmethyl rosuvastatin, which has approximately one-sixth to one-half the HMG-CoA reductase inhibitory activity of rosuvastatin.

Half-life
Elimination: 19 hours

Time to peak concentration
3 to 5 hours

Elimination
Fecal: 90%

In hemodialysis, rosuvastatin clearance is not significantly enhanced.

Pharmacogenetics
Pharmacokinetic differences in different race populations have been observed. Japanese subjects residing in Japan and Chinese subjects residing in Singapore had a 2-fold elevation in median exposure (AUC) when compared with Caucasians residing in North America and Europe.

Precautions to Consider

Carcinogenicity
In a 104-week carcinogenicity study in rats at dose levels of 2, 20, 60, or 80 mg per kg per day by oral gavage, the incidence of uterine stromal polyps was significantly increased in females at 80 mg per kg per day at systemic exposure 20 times the human exposure at 40 mg per day based on AUC. In a 107-week carcinogenicity study in mice given 10, 60, or 200 mg per kg per day by oral gavage, an increased incidence of hepatocellular adenoma/carcinoma was observed at 200 mg per kg per day at systemic exposures 20 times human exposure at 40 mg per day based on AUC.

Mutagenicity
Rosuvastatin was not mutagenic or clastogenic with or without metabolic activation in the Ames test with *Salmonella typhimurium* and *Escherichia coli*, the mouse lymphoma assay, and the chromosomal aberration assay in Chinese hamster lung cells. Rosuvastatin was negative in the *in vivo* mouse micronucleus test.

Pregnancy/Reproduction
Fertility—No changes in fertility were observed in studies in rats given doses of up to 50 mg/kg (10 times the human exposure) of rosuvastatin. Spermatidic giant cells were observed in dogs and monkeys exposed to 20 and 10 times the human exposure, respectively. Similar findings have been reported with other HMG-CoA reductase inhibitors.

Pregnancy—Rosuvastatin is **contraindicated** during pregnancy. If rosuvastatin is administered to a woman with reproductive potential, she should be apprised of the potential hazard to the fetus.

Rosuvastatin crosses the placenta. It is believed that HMG-CoA reductase inhibitors may decrease biologically active substances derived from cholesterol and may cause fetal harm.

Decreased fetal body weight, delayed ossification, and a decrease in survival rate have been seen in the pups of female rats given rosuvastatin 2 to 50 mg per kg per day. Decreased fetal viability and maternal mortality was observed when pregnant rabbits were given rosuvastatin 0.3, 1, and 3 mg per kg per day.

FDA Pregnancy Category X

Breast-feeding
It is not known whether rosuvastatin is distributed in breast milk. Because of the potential for serious side effects in nursing infants from rosuvastatin, a decision should be made to discontinue nursing or discontinue the administration of the drug.

Pediatrics
Safety and efficacy have not been established. Appropriate studies have not been performed on the relationship of age to the effects of rosuvastatin in the pediatric population in children up to 8 years of age. Studies performed to date have not demonstrated pediatrics-specific problems that would limit the usefulness of rosuvastatin in children 8 years of age and older.

Geriatrics
Geriatrics-specific problems have not been established.

Pharmacogenetics
A 2-fold elevation in median exposure (AUC) was found in Japanese subjects residing in Japan and in Chinese subjects residing in Singapore when compared with Caucasians residing in North America and Europe.

Surgical
Rosuvastatin therapy should be temporarily withheld or discontinued in any patient having a risk factor, such as major surgery, predisposing to the development of renal failure secondary to rhabdomyolysis.

Drug interactions and/or related problems
The following drug interactions and/or related problems have been selected on the basis of their potential clinical significance (possible mechanism in parentheses where appropriate)—not necessarily inclusive (» = major clinical significance):

Note: Combinations containing any of the following medications, depending on the amount present, may also interact with this medication.

» Aluminium and magnesium hydroxide combination antacids
 (concurrent administration of aluminum and magnesium hydroxide combination antacids and rosuvastatin may result in decreased concentrations of rosuvastatin; administer the antacid at least 2 hours after rosuvastatin administration)

» Cyclosporine or
» Gemfibrozil
 (may lead to significant increases in rosuvastatin C_{max} and AUC and increase the risk of myopathy; dosage reduction of rosuvastatin is recommended)

» Fibrates or
» Niacin or
» Other lipid-lowering therapies
 (risk of myopathy may be increased; risk benefit of combination therapy for further alterations in lipid levels should be carefully weighed)

Medications that may decrease the concentrations or activity of endogenous steroid hormones, such as:
 Cimetidine or
 Ketoconazole or
 Spironolactone
 (concomitant use with rosuvastatin may decrease the levels or activity of endogenous steroid hormones)

Oral contraceptives
 (concurrent use of ethinyl estradiol and norgestrel oral contraceptives may result in increased plasma concentration of ethinyl estradiol and norgestrel)

» Warfarin
 (coadministration of rosuvastatin to patients on stable warfarin therapy resulted in clinically significant rises in the International Normalized Ratio [INR]; monitor INR before starting rosuvastatin and frequently during early therapy to ensure that no significant alteration of INR occurs)

Laboratory value alterations
The following have been selected on the basis of their potential clinical significance (possible effect in parentheses where appropriate)—not necessarily inclusive (» = major clinical significance).

With physiology/laboratory test values
 Alkaline phosphatase, serum or
 Bilirubin, serum or
» Creatinine phosphokinase (CPK), serum or
 Glucose, blood or
 Glutamyl transpeptidase or
» Transaminases, serum
 (values may be elevated and usually transient)

Protein, urine
 (dipstick-positive proteinuria and microscopic hematuria were observed among rosuvastatin-treated patients, especially those receiving 40 mg therapy; proteinuria was transient and not associated with worsening renal function)

Thyroid function
 (abnormalities may occur)

Medical considerations/Contraindications
The medical considerations/contraindications included have been selected on the basis of their potential clinical significance (reasons given in parentheses where appropriate)—not necessarily inclusive (» = major clinical significance).

Except under special circumstances, this medication should not be used when the following medical problem exists:

» Hypersensitivity to rosuvastatin or any of its components

» Liver disease, active or
» Transaminases, serum, unexplained, persistent elevation of
 (rosuvastatin is contraindicated in patients with active liver disease or with unexplained persistent elevations of serum transaminases.)

Risk-benefit should be considered when the following medical problems exist:

» Alcoholism or
» Hepatic disease, history of
 (use with caution; rosuvastatin concentrations may increase and increase the risk of adverse effects)

Chinese or Japanese ancestry
 (2-fold elevation in median exposure in Japanese and Chinese subjects residing in Japan and Singapore, respectively; increased risk of myopathy during treatment with rosuvastatin may occur in these patients)

» Myopathy or
 Predisposing factors for myopathy, such as:
 Age, advanced or
 Hypothyroidism, inadequately treated or

Renal impairment
(use with caution; rosuvastatin therapy should be temporarily withheld in any patient with an acute, serious condition suggestive of myopathy or predisposing to the development of renal failure secondary to rhabdomyolysis)

Proteinuria, unexplained, persistent
(a dose reduction should be considered when this condition is present in those using the 40 mg therapy)

» Renal impairment, severe, not on hemodialysis
(may increase rosuvastatin plasma concentrations; rosuvastatin should be used with caution in these patients because they may be predisposed to myopathy; dosage reduction of rosuvastatin is recommended)

» Serious conditions suggestive of myopathy, such as:
Electrolyte disorders, severe or
Endocrine disorders, severe or
Hypotension or
Metabolic disorders, severe or
Seizures, uncontrolled or
Sepsis or
Surgery, major or
Trauma
(rosuvastatin therapy should be temporarily withheld in any patient with an acute, serious condition suggestive of myopathy or predisposing to the development of renal failure secondary to rhabdomyolysis)

Patient monitoring
The following may be especially important in patient monitoring (other tests may be warranted in some patients, depending on condition; » = major clinical significance):

» International Normalized Ratio (INR)
(measurements should be taken prior to the initiation of and throughout therapy in patients taking coumarin anticoagulants and rosuvastatin concomitantly)

» Lipid profile
(total-C, LDL-C, HDL-C, and TG measurements should be recorded prior to initiating therapy; after initiation and/or dosage adjustments, lipid levels should be analyzed within 2 to 4 weeks and dosage adjusted accordingly)

» Liver function tests
(recommended before and at 12 weeks following both the initiation of therapy and any elevation of dose, and semiannually thereafter; reduction in dose or withdrawal from therapy is recommended if an increase in ALT or AST of more than 3 times the upper limit of normal [ULN] persist)

Side/Adverse Effects
The following side/adverse effects have been selected on the basis of their potential clinical significance (possible signs and symptoms in parentheses where appropriate)—not necessarily inclusive:

Rosuvastatin therapy should also be temporarily withheld in any patient with an acute, serious condition suggestive of myopathy or predisposing to the development of renal failure secondary to rhabdomyolysis including sepsis, hypotension, dehydration, major surgery, trauma, severe metabolic, endocrine, and electrolyte disorders, or uncontrolled seizures.

Those indicating need for medical attention
Incidence rare

Myopathy (muscular pain, tenderness, wasting or weakness); ***rhabdomyolysis*** (dark-colored urine; fever; muscle cramps or spasms; muscle pain or stiffness; unusual tiredness or weakness)

Incidence not determined—Observed during clinical practice; estimates of frequency can not be determined

Jaundice (chills; clay-colored stools; dark urine; dizziness; fever; headache; itching; loss of appetite; nausea; abdominal or stomach pain; area rash; unpleasant breath odor; unusual tiredness or weakness; vomiting of blood; yellow eyes or skin)

Those indicating need for medical attention only if they continue or are bothersome
Incidence more frequent

Headache; pharyngitis (body aches or pain; congestion; cough; dryness or soreness of throat; fever; hoarseness; runny nose; tender, swollen glands in neck; trouble in swallowing; voice changes)

Incidence less frequent

Abdominal pain (stomach pain); ***accidental injury; anemia*** (pale skin; troubled breathing with exertion; unusual bleeding or bruising; unusual tiredness or weakness); ***angina pectoris*** (arm, back or jaw pain; chest pain or discomfort; chest tightness or heaviness; fast or irregular heartbeat; shortness of breath; sweating; nausea); ***anxiety*** (fear; nervousness); ***arthralgia*** (joint pain); ***arthritis*** (pain, swelling, or redness in joints; muscle pain or stiffness; difficulty in moving); ***asthenia*** (lack or loss of strength); ***asthma*** (cough; difficulty breathing; noisy breathing; shortness of breath; tightness in chest; wheezing); ***back pain; bronchitis*** (cough producing mucus; difficulty breathing; shortness of breath; tightness in chest; wheezing); ***chest pain; constipation*** (difficulty having a bowel movement (stool)); ***cough increased; depression*** (discouragement; feeling sad or empty; irritability; lack of appetite; loss of interest or pleasure; tiredness; trouble concentrating; trouble sleeping); ***diabetes mellitus*** (blurred vision; dry mouth; fatigue; flushed, dry skin; fruit-like breath odor; increased hunger; increased thirst; increased urination; loss of consciousness; nausea; stomach ache; sweating; troubled breathing; unexplained weight loss; vomiting); ***diarrhea; dizziness; dyspepsia*** (acid or sour stomach; belching; heartburn; indigestion; stomach discomfort, upset or pain); ***dyspnea*** (shortness of breath; difficult or labored breathing; tightness in chest; wheezing); ***ecchymosis*** (bruising; large, flat, blue or purplish patches in the skin); ***edema, peripheral*** (swelling of hands, ankles, feet, or lower legs); ***flatulence*** (bloated; full feeling; excess air or gas in stomach or intestines; passing gas); ***flu syndrome*** (chills; cough; diarrhea; fever; general feeling of discomfort or illness; headache; joint pain; loss of appetite; muscle aches and pains; nausea; runny nose; shivering; sore throat; sweating; trouble sleeping; unusual tiredness or weakness; vomiting); ***gastritis*** (burning feeling in chest or stomach; tenderness in stomach area; stomach upset; indigestion); ***gastroenteritis*** (abdominal or stomach pain; diarrhea; loss of appetite; nausea; weakness); ***hypertension*** (blurred vision; dizziness; nervousness; headache; pounding in the ears; slow or fast heartbeat); ***hypertonia*** (excessive muscle tone; muscle tension or tightness; muscle stiffness); ***infection*** (fever or chills; cough or hoarseness; lower back or side pain; painful or difficult urination); ***insomnia*** (sleeplessness; trouble sleeping; unable to sleep); ***myalgia*** (muscle pain); ***nausea; neck pain; neuralgia*** (nerve pain); ***pain; palpitation*** (fast, irregular, pounding, or racing heartbeat or pulse); ***paresthesia*** (burning, crawling, itching, numbness, prickling, "pins and needles", or tingling feelings); ***pathological fracture*** (pain or swelling in arms or legs without any injury); ***pelvic pain; periodontal abscess*** (accumulation of pus, swollen, red, tender area of infection of the gum); ***pneumonia*** (chest pain; cough; fever or chills; sneezing; shortness of breath; sore throat; troubled breathing; tightness in chest; wheezing); ***pruritus*** (itching skin); ***rash; rhinitis*** (stuffy nose; runny nose; sneezing); ***sinusitis*** (pain or tenderness around eyes and cheekbones; fever; stuffy or runny nose; headache; cough; shortness of breath); ***urinary tract infection*** (bladder pain; bloody or cloudy urine; difficult, burning, or painful urination; frequent urge to urinate; lower back or side pain); ***vasodilation*** (feeling of warmth or heat; flushing or redness of skin especially on face and neck; headache; feeling faint; dizzy, or lightheadedness; sweating); ***vertigo*** (dizziness or lightheadedness; feeling of constant movement of self or surroundings; sensation of spinning); ***vomiting***

Overdose
For more information on the management of overdose or unintentional ingestion, **contact a poison control center** (see *Poison Control Center Listing*).

Treatment of overdose
To enhance elimination—
Hemodialysis does not significantly enhance the clearance of rosuvastatin.

Specific treatment—
There is no specific treatment for overdose of rosuvastatin.

Supportive care—
Treatment should be symptomatic and supportive.
Patients in whom intentional overdose is confirmed or suspected should be referred for psychiatric consultation.

Patient Consultation
As an aid to patient consultation, refer to *Advice for the Patient, Rosuvastatin (Systemic)*

In providing consultation, consider emphasizing the following selected information (» = major clinical significance):

Before using this medication
» Conditions affecting use, especially:
Hypersensitivity to rosuvastatin or any component of the product
Carcinogenicity—An increased incidence of carcinomas was seen in animal studies using rosuvastatin

Pregnancy—Rosuvastatin crosses the placenta and is **contraindicated** during pregnancy. Risk-benefit must be carefully considered.

Breast-feeding—It is not known whether rosuvastatin is distributed in breast milk. Because of the potential for serious side effects in nursing infants from rosuvastatin, a decision should be made to discontinue nursing or discontinue the administration of the drug.

Use in children—Safety and efficacy have not been established.

Surgical—Increased risk of development of renal failure secondary to rhabdomyolysis with major surgery.

Other medications, especially aluminum and magnesium hydroxide combination antacids, cyclosporine, fibrates, gemfibrozil, niacin, other lipid-lowering therapies, and warfarin.

Other medical problems, especially liver disease, unexplained, persistent elevations of transaminases, alcoholism, myopathy, renal impairment, severe electrolyte disorders, severe endocrine disorders, hypotension, severe metabolic disorders, uncontrolled seizures, sepsis, major surgery, or trauma.

Proper use of this medication

» Proper dosing

Compliance with therapy; taking medication at the same time each day to maintain the antihyperlipidemic effect

Compliance with prescribed diet during treatment

» If you take an aluminum and magnesium hydroxide combination antacid, the antacid should be taken at least 2 hours after you take your rosuvastatin.

Missed dose: Taking as soon as possible; not taking if almost time for next scheduled dose; not doubling doses

» Proper storage

Precautions while using this medication

» Regular visits to physician to check progress and monitor for side effects.

» Checking with your doctor right away if you have unexplained muscle pain, tenderness, or weakness, especially if you also have fever or unusual tiredness.

Side/adverse effects

Signs of potential side effects, especially myopathy or rhabdomyolysis

Signs of potential side effects observed during clinical practice, especially jaundice

General Dosing Information

For oral dosing forms:

Before instituting therapy with rosuvastatin, an attempt should be made to control hypercholesterolemia with appropriate diet and exercise, weight reduction in obese patients, and treatment of underlying medical problems.

As with other HMG-CoA reductase inhibitors, reports of rhabdomyolysis with acute renal failure secondary to myoglobinuria with rosuvastatin are rare, but higher at the highest marketed dose (40 mg). *Consequently, the 40 mg dose of rosuvastatin is reserved only for those patients who have not achieved their LDL-C goal utilizing the 20 mg dose of rosuvastatin once daily.*

Patients should be placed on a standard cholesterol-lowering diet before receiving rosuvastatin and should continue on this diet during treatment.

Rosuvastatin can be administered as a single dose at any time of day, with or without food.

Oral Dosage Forms

Note: Bracketed information in the *Indications* section refers to uses that are not included in U.S. product labeling.

ROSUVASTATIN CALCIUM TABLETS

Note: Before instituting therapy with rosuvastatin, an attempt should be made to control hypercholesterolemia with appropriate diet and exercise, weight reduction in obese patients, and treatment of underlying medical problems.

Usual adult dose

Antihyperlipidemic—

Heterozygous familial and nonfamilial hypercholesterolemia and mixed dyslipidemia (Fredrickson Types IIa and IIb)—

Oral, initially 10 mg once a day. The dosage range is 5 to 40 mg once a day, to be administered at any time of the day, with or without food. After initiation or titration of atorvastatin, lipid concentrations should be measured within 2 to 4 weeks and the dosage adjusted accordingly.

Homozygous familial hypercholesterolemia—

Oral, recommended starting dose of 20 mg once daily

Note: Rosuvastatin should be used in these patients as an adjunct to other lipid-lowering treatments, such as LDL apheresis, or if such treatments are unavailable. Response to therapy should be estimated from pre apheresis LDL-C levels

Concomitant Therapy—

Cyclosporine: Oral dose reduction of rosuvastatin to 5 mg once daily.

Gemfibrozil: Oral dose reduction of rosuvastatin to 10 mg once daily.

Note: Renal insufficiency: Dosage adjustment in patients with mild to moderate renal insufficiency is not necessary. Rosuvastatin should be started at 5 mg once daily and not to exceed 10 mg once daily in patients with severe renal impairment ($CL_{cr} <$ 30 mL per min per 1.73 m^2) not on hemodialysis.

Asian patients: Initiation of rosuvastatin therapy with 5 mg once daily should be considered. The potential for increased systemic exposures relative to Caucasians is relevant when considering escalation of dose in cases where hypercholesterolemia is not adequately controlled at doses of 5, 10, or 20 mg once daily.

Initiation of therapy with 5 mg once daily should also be considered in patients requiring less aggressive LDL-C reductions, who have predisposing factors for myopathy.

The goal of therapy is to lower LDL-C. The National Cholesterol Education Program (NCEP) recommends that LDL-C concentrations be used to initiate and assess treatment response. Only if LDL-C concentrations are not available should total-C be used to monitor therapy.

Usual adult prescribing limits

Up to 40 mg daily

Usual geriatric dose

See *Usual adult dose*.

Usual geriatric prescribing limits

See *Usual adult prescribing limits*.

Strength(s) usually available

U.S.—

5 mg tablets of rosuvastatin (Rx) [*Crestor* (crospovidone NF; hypromellose NF; lactose monohydrate NF; magnesium stearate NF; microcrystalline cellulose NF; red ferric oxide NF; titanium dioxide USP; triacetin NF; tribasic calcium phosphate NF; yellow ferric oxide NF)].

10 mg tablets of rosuvastatin (Rx) [*Crestor* (crospovidone NF; hypromellose NF; lactose monohydrate NF; magnesium stearate NF; microcrystalline cellulose NF; red ferric oxide NF; titanium dioxide USP; triacetin NF; tribasic calcium phosphate NF; yellow ferric oxide NF)].

20 mg tablets of rosuvastatin (Rx) [*Crestor* (crospovidone NF; hypromellose NF; lactose monohydrate NF; magnesium stearate NF; microcrystalline cellulose NF; red ferric oxide NF; titanium dioxide USP; triacetin NF; tribasic calcium phosphate NF; yellow ferric oxide NF)].

40 mg tablets of rosuvastatin (Rx) [*Crestor* (crospovidone NF; hypromellose NF; lactose monohydrate NF; magnesium stearate NF; microcrystalline cellulose NF; red ferric oxide NF; titanium dioxide USP; triacetin NF; tribasic calcium phosphate NF; yellow ferric oxide NF)].

Canada—

10 mg tablets of rosuvastatin (Rx) [*Crestor* (calcium phosphate; crospovidone; glycerol triacetate; hydroxypropyl methylcellulose; lactose monohydrate; microcrystalline cellulose; magnesium stearate; ferric oxide red; titanium dioxide)].

20 mg tablets of rosuvastatin (Rx) [*Crestor* (calcium phosphate; crospovidone; glycerol triacetate; hydroxypropyl methylcellulose; lactose monohydrate; microcrystalline cellulose; magnesium stearate; ferric oxide red; titanium dioxide)].

40 mg tablets of rosuvastatin (Rx) [*Crestor* (calcium phosphate; crospovidone; glycerol triacetate; hydroxypropyl methylcellulose; lactose monohydrate; microcrystalline cellulose; magnesium stearate; ferric oxide red; titanium dioxide)].

Packaging and storage

Store between 20 and 25 °C (68 and 77 °F), in a tight container. Protect from moisture.

In Canada, store between 15 and 30 °C (59 and 86 °F)

Revised: 03/10/2005
Developed: 02/04/2004

SALICYLATES Systemic

This monograph includes information on the following: 1) Aspirin‡; 2) Aspirin, Buffered‡; 3) Choline Salicylate†; 4) Choline and Magnesium Salicylates; 5) Magnesium Salicylate; 6) Salsalate; 7) Sodium Salicylate.

VA CLASSIFICATION (Primary/Secondary):

Aspirin
- Tablets—CN103/CN104; CN850; MS101; BL117
- Chewable Tablets—CN103/CN104; CN850; MS101; BL117
- Chewing Gum Tablets—CN103
- Delayed-release Tablets—CN103/CN104; CN850; MS101; BL117
- Extended-release Tablets—CN103/CN104; CN850; MS101
- Suppositories—CN103/CN104; CN850; MS101

Aspirin and Caffeine—CN103/CN104; CN850; MS101
Aspirin, Buffered—CN103/CN104; CN850; MS101; BL117
Aspirin and Caffeine, Buffered—CN103/CN104; CN850; MS101; BL117
Choline Salicylate—CN103/CN104; CN850; MS101
Choline and Magnesium Salicylates—CN103/CN104; CN850; MS101
Magnesium Salicylate—CN103/CN104; CN850; MS101
Salsalate—MS101/CN103; CN104; CN850
Sodium Salicylate—CN103/CN104; CN850; MS101

Note: For information on a buffered aspirin product that is used for its antacid as well as its analgesic and antithrombotic effects, see *Aspirin, Sodium Bicarbonate, and Citric Acid (Systemic).*

Commonly used brand name(s): *Aspirin, Coated*[1]; *217*[1]; *217 Strong*[1]; *Acuprin 81*[1]; *Amigesic*[6]; *Anacin*[1]; *Anacin Caplets*[1]; *Anacin Extra Strength*[1]; *Anacin Maximum Strength*[1]; *Anacin Tablets*[1]; *Anaflex 750*[6]; *Antidol*[1]; *Apo-ASA*[1]; *Apo-ASEN*[1]; *Arco Pain Tablet*[1]; *Arthrisin*[1]; *Arthritis Pain Ascriptin*[2]; *Arthritis Pain Formula*[2]; *Arthritis Strength Bufferin*[2]; *Arthropan*[3]; *Artria S.R*[1]; *Aspergum*[1]; *Aspir-Low*[1]; *Aspirin Caplets*[1]; *Aspirin Children's Tablets*[1]; *Aspirin, Coated*[1]; *Aspirin Plus Stomach Guard Extra Strength*[2]; *Aspirin Plus Stomach Guard Regular Strength*[2]; *Aspirin Regimen Bayer Adult Low Dose*[1]; *Aspirin Regimen Bayer Regular Strength Caplets*[1]; *Aspirin Tablets*[1]; *Aspirtab*[1]; *Aspirtab-Max*[1]; *Astone*[1]; *Astrin*[1]; *Backache Caplets*[5]; *Bayer Children's Aspirin*[1]; *Bayer Select Maximum Strength Backache Pain Relief Formula*[5]; *Bufferin Caplets*[2]; *Bufferin Extra Strength Caplets*[2]; *Bufferin Tablets*[2]; *Buffex*[2]; *Buffinol*[2]; *Buffinol Extra*[2]; *C2*[1]; *C2 Buffered*[2]; *CMT*[4]; *Calmine*[1]; *Cama Arthritis Pain Reliever*[2]; *Cope*[2]; *Coryphen*[1]; *Disalcid*[6]; *Doan's Backache Pills*[5]; *Doan's Regular Strength Tablets*[5]; *Dodd's Extra Strength*[7]; *Dodd's Pills*[7]; *Dolomine*[1]; *Easprin*[1]; *Ecotrin Caplets*[1]; *Ecotrin Tablets*[1]; *Empirin*[1]; *Entrophen 10 Super Strength Caplets*[1]; *Entrophen 15 Maximum Strength Tablets*[1]; *Entrophen Caplets*[1]; *Entrophen Extra Strength*[1]; *Entrophen Tablets*[1]; *Extended-release Bayer 8-Hour*[1]; *Extra Strength Bayer Arthritis Pain Formula Caplets*[1]; *Extra Strength Bayer Aspirin Caplets*[1]; *Extra Strength Bayer Aspirin Tablets*[1]; *Extra Strength Bayer Plus Caplets*[2]; *Gensan*[1]; *Genuine Bayer Aspirin Caplets*[1]; *Genuine Bayer Aspirin Tablets*[1]; *Gin Pain Pills*[7]; *Halfprin*[1]; *Headache Tablet*[1]; *Healthprin Adult Low Strength*[1]; *Healthprin Full Strength*[1]; *Healthprin Half-Dose*[1]; *Herbopyrine*[1]; *Instantine*[1]; *Kalmex*[1]; *Magan*[5]; *Magnaprin*[2]; *Marthritic*[6]; *Maximum Strength Arthritis Foundation Safety Coated Aspirin*[1]; *Maximum Strength Ascriptin*[2]; *Maximum Strength Doan's Analgesic Caplets*[5]; *Mobidin*[5]; *Mono-Gesic*[6]; *Nervine*[1]; *Norwich Aspirin*[1]; *Novasen*[1]; *Novasen Sp.C*[1]; *P-A-C Revised Formula*[1]; *PMS-ASA*[1]; *Pain Aid*[1]; *Regular Strength Ascriptin*[2]; *Salflex*[6]; *Salsitab*[6]; *Sero-Gesic*[5]; *Sloprin*[1]; *St. Joseph Adult Chewable Aspirin*[1]; *Tri-Buffered ASA*[2]; *Tricosal*[4]; *Trilisate*[4]; *ZORprin*[1].

Other commonly used names are Acetylsalicylic Acid [Aspirin‡] ASA [Aspirin‡] Choline Magnesium Trisalicylate [Choline and Magnesium Salicylates] Salicylsalicylic Acid [Salsalate]

Note: For a listing of dosage forms and brand names by country availability, see *Dosage Forms* section(s).

†Not commercially available in Canada.
‡*Aspirin* is a brand name in Canada; acetylsalicylic acid is the generic name. ASA, a commonly used designation for aspirin (or acetylsalicylic acid) in both the U.S. and Canada, is the term used in Canadian product labeling.

Category

Note: All of the salicylates have analgesic, anti-inflammatory, and antipyretic actions; however, clinical uses among specific agents or dosage formulations may vary because of actual pharmacokinetic differences, lack of specific testing, and/or lack of clinical-use data.

Analgesic—Aspirin; Aspirin, Buffered; Choline Salicylate; Choline and Magnesium Salicylates; Magnesium Salicylate; [Salsalate]; Sodium Salicylate.

Anti-inflammatory (nonsteroidal)—Aspirin; Aspirin, Buffered; Choline Salicylate; Choline and Magnesium Salicylates; Magnesium Salicylate; [Salsalate]; Sodium Salicylate.

Antipyretic—Aspirin; Aspirin, Buffered; Choline Salicylate; Choline and Magnesium Salicylates; [Magnesium Salicylate]; [Salsalate]; Sodium Salicylate.

Antirheumatic (nonsteroidal anti-inflammatory)—Aspirin; Aspirin, Buffered; Choline Salicylate; Choline and Magnesium Salicylates; Magnesium Salicylate; Salsalate; Sodium Salicylate.

Platelet aggregation inhibitor—Aspirin Tablets; Aspirin Tablets (Chewable); Aspirin Delayed-release Tablets; Aspirin, Buffered.

Antithrombotic—Aspirin Tablets; Aspirin Tablets (Chewable); Aspirin Delayed-release Tablets; Aspirin, Buffered.

Myocardial infarction prophylactic—Aspirin Tablets; Aspirin Tablets (Chewable); Aspirin Delayed-release Tablets; Aspirin, Buffered.

Myocardial reinfarction prophylactic—Aspirin Tablets; Aspirin Tablets (Chewable); Aspirin Delayed-release Tablets; Aspirin, Buffered

Indications

Note: Bracketed information in the *Indications* section refers to uses that are not included in U.S. product labeling.

Accepted

Pain (treatment) or
Fever (treatment)—Salicylates are indicated to relieve mild to moderate pain such as headache, toothache, and menstrual cramps and to reduce fever. These medications provide only symptomatic relief; additional therapy to treat the cause of the pain or fever should be instituted when necessary. However, the presence of an illness that may predispose toward Reye's syndrome (i.e., an acute febrile illness, especially influenza or varicella) should be ruled out before salicylate therapy is initiated in a pediatric or adolescent patient.

Salicylates are recommended for relief of mild to moderate bone pain caused by metastatic neoplastic disease. However, careful patient selection is necessary, especially in patients receiving chemotherapy, because of the platelet aggregation-inhibiting effect of aspirin and because salicylates may cause hypoprothrombinemia or gastrointestinal or renal toxicity.

Delayed-release formulations containing aspirin or sodium salicylate may not be as useful as immediate-release formulations for single-dose administration for analgesia or antipyresis because the delayed absorption prolongs the onset of action.

Note: The FDA has proposed that caffeine (present as an analgesic adjuvant in some aspirin products) be classified as a Category III ingredient (i.e., lacking documentation of efficacy) in OTC analgesic/antipyretic medications.

Inflammation, nonrheumatic (treatment)—Salicylates are indicated to relieve myalgia, musculoskeletal pain, and other symptoms of nonrheumatic inflammatory conditions such as athletic injuries, bursitis, capsulitis, tendinitis, and nonspecific acute tenosynovitis.

Arthritis, rheumatoid (treatment)
Arthritis, juvenile (treatment) or
Osteoarthritis (treatment)—Salicylates are indicated for the symptomatic relief of acute and chronic rheumatoid arthritis, juvenile arthritis, osteoarthritis, and related rheumatic diseases. Aspirin is usually the first agent to be used and may be the drug of choice in patients able to tolerate prolonged therapy with high doses. These agents do not affect the progressive course of rheumatoid arthritis.

Concurrent treatment with a glucocorticoid or a disease-modifying antirheumatic agent may be needed, depending on the condition being treated and patient response.

[Salicylates are also used to reduce arthritic complications associated with systemic lupus erythematosus.]

Rheumatic fever (treatment)—Salicylates are indicated to reduce fever and inflammation in rheumatic fever. However, they do not prevent cardiac or other complications associated with this condition. Sodium salicylate should be avoided in rheumatic fever if congestive cardiac complications are present because of its sodium content. Also, large doses of any salicylate should be avoided in rheumatic fever if severe carditis is present because of possible adverse cardiovascular effects.

Platelet aggregation (prophylaxis)—Aspirin (tablets, chewable tablets, delayed-release capsules or tablets, and buffered formulations) is indicated as a platelet aggregation inhibitor in the following:
Ischemic attacks, transient, in males (prophylaxis)
Thromboembolism, cerebral (prophylaxis) or

[Thromboembolism, cerebral, recurrence (prophylaxis)][1]—Aspirin is indicated in the treatment of men who have had transient brain ischemia due to fibrin platelet emboli to reduce the recurrence of transient ischemic attacks (TIAs) and the risk of stroke and death.

[Aspirin is also used in the treatment of women with transient brain ischemia due to fibrin platelet emboli. However, its efficacy in preventing stroke and death in female patients has not been established.][1]

[Aspirin is also indicated in the treatment of patients with documented, unexplained TIAs associated with mitral valve prolapse. However, if TIAs continue to occur after an adequate trial of aspirin therapy, aspirin should be discontinued and an oral anticoagulant administered instead.][1]

[Aspirin is also indicated to prevent initial or recurrent cerebrovascular embolism, TIAs, and stroke following carotid endarterectomy.]

[Aspirin is indicated in the treatment of patients who have had a completed thrombotic stroke, to prevent a recurrence.][1]

Myocardial infarction (prophylaxis) or
Myocardial reinfarction (prophylaxis)—Aspirin is indicated to prevent myocardial infarction in patients with unstable angina pectoris and to prevent recurrence of myocardial infarction in patients with a history of myocardial infarction.

In one study, aspirin significantly reduced the rate of reocclusion, reinfarction, stroke, and death when a single dose was administered within a few hours after the onset of symptoms of acute myocardial infarction and daily thereafter. The benefit of early treatment with aspirin was additive to that of streptokinase. Therefore, it is recommended that aspirin therapy be initiated as soon as possible after the onset of symptoms, even if the patient is receiving thrombolytic therapy.

[One study has shown that aspirin may also prevent myocardial infarction in individuals 50 years of age and older who have no history of unstable angina pectoris or myocardial infarction. However, the incidence of hemorrhagic stroke (but not the total number of hemorrhagic plus thrombotic strokes) was slightly increased in subjects receiving aspirin. Also, the incidence of myocardial infarction, although higher in the placebo group than in the aspirin group, was low in both groups. Therefore, aspirin's benefit in apparently healthy individuals has not been established. However, aspirin may be indicated for prevention of an initial myocardial infarction in selected patients, especially those who may be at risk because of the presence of chronic stable coronary artery disease (as shown by exertional or episodic angina pectoris, abnormal coronary arteriogram, or positive stress test) and/or other risk factors.][1]

[Thromboembolism (prophylaxis)]—Aspirin is used in low doses to decrease the risk of thromboembolism following orthopedic (hip) surgery (especially total hip replacement) and in patients with arteriovenous shunts.

Platelet aggregation inhibitors, although not as consistently effective as an anticoagulant or an anticoagulant plus dipyridamole, may provide some protection against the development of thromboembolic complications in patients with mechanical prosthetic heart valves. Therefore, administration of aspirin, alone or in combination with dipyridamole, may be considered if anticoagulant therapy is contraindicated for these patients. Patients with bioprosthetic cardiac valves who are in normal sinus rhythm generally do not require prolonged antithrombotic therapy, but long-term aspirin administration may be considered on an individual basis.[1]

Aspirin is also indicated, alone[1] or in combination with dipyridamole, to reduce the risk of thrombosis and/or reocclusion of saphenous vein aortocoronary bypass grafts following coronary bypass surgery.

Aspirin is also indicated, alone or in combination with dipyridamole, to reduce the risk of thrombosis and/or reocclusion of prosthetic or saphenous vein femoral popliteal bypass grafts.[1]

Because the patient may be at risk for thromboembolic complications, including myocardial infarction and stroke, long-term aspirin therapy may also be indicated for maintaining patency following coronary or peripheral vascular angioplasty and for treating patients with peripheral vascular insufficiency caused by arteriosclerosis.[1]

Prolonged antithrombotic therapy is generally not needed to maintain vessel patency following vascular reconstruction procedures in high-flow, low-resistance arteries larger than 6 mm in diameter. However, long-term aspirin therapy may be indicated, because patients requiring such procedures may be at risk for other thrombotic complications.[1]

[Kawasaki disease (treatment)][1]—Aspirin is indicated for its anti-inflammatory, antipyretic, and antithrombotic effects in the treatment of Kawasaki disease (Kawasaki syndrome, mucocutaneous lymph node syndrome) in children. It reduces fever, relieves inflammation (e.g., lymphadenitis, mucositis, conjunctivitis, serositis), and may reduce the occurrence of cardiovascular complications. However, the combination of high-dose intravenous gamma globulin and aspirin has been shown to be more effective than aspirin alone in reducing the formation of coronary artery abnormalities.

[1]Not included in Canadian product labeling.

Pharmacology/Pharmacokinetics

Physicochemical characteristics

Note: Aspirin is an acetylated salicylate; the other salicylates are nonacetylated.

Molecular weight—
- Aspirin: 180.16.
- Choline salicylate: 241.29.
- Magnesium salicylate: 370.60 (tetrahydrate); 298.53 (anhydrous).
- Salsalate: 258.23.
- Sodium salicylate: 160.11.

pKa—
- Aspirin: 3.5.

Note: The other salicylates are also acidic.

Mechanism of action/Effect

The analgesic, antipyretic, and anti-inflammatory effects of aspirin are due to actions by both the acetyl and the salicylate portions of the intact molecule as well as by the active salicylate metabolite. The actions of other salicylates are due only to the salicylate portion of the molecule. Aspirin directly inhibits the activity of the enzyme cyclo-oxygenase to decrease the formation of precursors of prostaglandins and thromboxanes from arachidonic acid. Salicylate may competitively inhibit prostaglandin formation. Although many of the therapeutic and adverse effects of these medications may result from inhibition of prostaglandin synthesis (and consequent reduction of prostaglandin activity) in various tissues, other actions may also contribute significantly to the therapeutic effects.

Analgesic—

Salicylates: Produce analgesia through a peripheral action by blocking pain impulse generation and via a central action, possibly in the hypothalamus. The peripheral action may predominate and probably involves inhibition of the synthesis of prostaglandins, and possibly inhibition of the synthesis and/or actions of other substances, which sensitize pain receptors to mechanical or chemical stimulation.

Caffeine: A mild central nervous system (CNS) stimulant. Caffeine-induced constriction of cerebral blood vessels, which leads to a decrease in cerebral blood flow and in the oxygen tension of the brain, may contribute to relief of some types of headache. It has been suggested that the addition of caffeine to aspirin may provide a more rapid onset of action and/or enhanced pain relief with lower doses of analgesic. However, the FDA has determined that studies performed to date have not demonstrated that caffeine is an effective analgesic adjuvant or that it does not interfere with aspirin's efficacy as an antipyretic.

Anti-inflammatory (nonsteroidal)—

Exact mechanisms have not been determined. Salicylates may act peripherally in inflamed tissue, probably by inhibiting the synthesis of prostaglandins and possibly by inhibiting the synthesis and/or actions of other mediators of the inflammatory response. Inhibition of leukocyte migration, inhibition of the release and/or actions of lysosomal enzymes, and actions on other cellular and immunological processes in mesenchymal and connective tissues may be involved.

Antipyretic—

May produce antipyresis by acting centrally on the hypothalamic heat-regulating center to produce peripheral vasodilation resulting in increased cutaneous blood flow, sweating, and heat loss. The central action may involve inhibition of prostaglandin synthesis in the hypothalamus; however, there is some evidence that fevers caused by endogenous pyrogens that do not act via a prostaglandin mechanism may also respond to salicylate therapy.

Antirheumatic (nonsteroidal anti-inflammatory)—

Act via analgesic and anti-inflammatory mechanisms; the therapeutic effects are not due to pituitary-adrenal stimulation.

Platelet aggregation inhibitor—

The platelet aggregation-inhibiting effect of aspirin specifically involves the compound's ability to act as an acetyl donor to the platelet membrane; the nonacetylated salicylates have no clinically significant effect on platelet aggregation. Aspirin affects platelet function by inhibiting the enzyme prostaglandin cyclooxygenase in platelets, thereby preventing the formation of the aggregating agent thromboxane A_2. This action is irreversible; the effects persist for the life of the platelets exposed. Aspirin may also inhibit formation of the platelet aggregation inhibitor prostacyclin (prostaglandin I_2) in blood vessels; however, this action is reversible. These actions may be dose-dependent. Although there is some evidence that doses lower than 100 mg per day may not inhibit prostacyclin synthesis, optimum dosage that will suppress thromboxane A_2 formation without suppressing prostacyclin generation has not been determined.

Other actions/effects

It is proposed that the gastrointestinal toxicity of salicylates, especially aspirin, may be caused primarily by reduction of the activity of prostaglandins (which exert a protective effect on the gastrointestinal mucosa) because upper gastrointestinal toxicity has been reported following rectal or parenteral administration of nonsteroidal anti-inflammatory drugs. However, when administered orally, these acidic medications (unless administered in an enteric-coated formulation) probably also exert a direct irritant or erosive effect on the mucosa.

Absorption

Salicylates—

Absorption is generally rapid and complete following oral administration but may vary according to specific salicylate used, dosage form, and other factors such as tablet dissolution rate and gastric or intraluminal pH.

Food decreases the rate, but not the extent, of absorption.

Absorption from enteric-coated formulations is generally delayed.

Absorption of aspirin from the chewing gum tablet is incomplete as compared with absorption from the oral tablet.

Following rectal administration of aspirin, absorption is delayed and incomplete as compared with absorption following oral administration of equal doses.

Absorption of aspirin is impaired during the early febrile stage of Kawasaki disease, then increases toward normal in the convalescent stage.

Caffeine—

Well absorbed from the gastrointestinal tract.

Distribution

In breast milk—

Aspirin: Peak salicylate concentrations of 173 to 483 mcg per mL have been measured 5 to 8 hours after maternal ingestion of a single 650-mg dose.

Sodium salicylate: A total of 3 to 4 mg of salicylate is excreted following maternal ingestion of a single dose of 20 mg per kg of body weight (mg/kg).

Protein binding

Salicylate—High (to albumin); decreases as plasma salicylate concentration increases, with reduced plasma albumin concentration or renal dysfunction, and during pregnancy.

Caffeine—Low.

Biotransformation

Salicylate compounds are largely hydrolyzed in the gastrointestinal tract, liver, and blood to salicylate, which is further metabolized primarily in the liver.

Caffeine—Hepatic.

Half-life

Aspirin—

15 to 20 minutes (for intact molecule); rapidly hydrolyzed to salicylate.

In breast milk (as salicylate)—3.8 to 12.5 hours (average 7.1 hours) following a single 650-mg dose of aspirin.

Salicylate—

Dependent on dose and on urinary pH; about 2 to 3 hours with low or single doses and 20 hours or longer with very high doses; with repeated dosing using antirheumatic doses, may range from 5 to 18 hours.

Caffeine—

3 to 4 hours.

Time to peak plasma concentration

Generally 1 to 2 hours with single doses; may be more rapid with liquid dosage forms; may be delayed with salsalate (as compared with aspirin) or with delayed-release tablet or capsule formulations.

Time to steady-state plasma concentration

Increases as daily dosage and plasma concentrations are increased; with large (antirheumatic) doses of aspirin, may require up to 7 days.

Therapeutic plasma concentration

Salicylate—

Analgesic and antipyretic: 25 to 50 mcg per mL (2.5 to 5 mg per 100 mL); these concentrations are generally reached with single analgesic/antipyretic doses.

Anti-inflammatory/antirheumatic: 150 to 300 mcg per mL (15 to 30 mg per 100 mL). Steady-state plasma concentrations within this range are usually reached with therapeutic antirheumatic doses. However, because of interindividual differences in salicylate kinetics, wide variations in steady-state plasma concentrations may be produced in different patients by the same dose. Also, with large or repeated doses, major metabolic pathways become saturated; small changes in dosage may result in large changes in plasma concentration.

Time to peak effect

Antirheumatic—May require 2 to 3 weeks or more of continuous therapy.

Elimination

Aspirin and salicylate salts—

Renal; primarily as free salicylic acid and conjugated metabolites.

Salsalate—

About 13% of a dose excreted as conjugated salsalate; small amounts also excreted unchanged. The remainder of the dose is excreted as free or conjugated salicylate.

Note: Total salicylate excretion does not increase proportionately with dose, but excretion of unmetabolized salicylic acid is increased with higher doses; also, there are large interindividual differences in elimination kinetics. In addition, the rate of excretion of total salicylate and the quantity of free salicylic acid eliminated are increased in alkaline urine and decreased in acidic urine.

In dialysis—Salicylate—

Hemodialysis—Clearances of 35 to 100 mL per minute have been reported.

Peritoneal dialysis—Removed more slowly than with hemodialysis; clearances of 45 to 90 mL per hour have been reported in infants.

Caffeine—Renal; primarily as metabolites. About 1 to 2% of a dose is excreted unchanged.

Precautions to Consider

Cross-sensitivity and/or related problems

Patients sensitive to one salicylate, including methyl salicylate (oil of wintergreen), or to other nonsteroidal anti-inflammatory drugs (NSAIDs) may be sensitive to other salicylates also.

Patients sensitive to aspirin may not necessarily be sensitive to nonacetylated salicylates.

Patients sensitive to tartrazine dye may be sensitive to aspirin also, and vice versa.

Cross-sensitivity between aspirin and other NSAIDs that results in bronchospastic or cutaneous reactions may be eliminated if the patient undergoes a desensitization procedure (See *General Dosing Information*).

Patients sensitive to other xanthines (aminophylline, dyphylline, oxtriphylline, theobromine, theophylline) may be sensitive to caffeine also.

Pregnancy/Reproduction

Fertility—Salicylates have caused increased numbers of fetal resorptions in animal studies.

Pregnancy—

First trimester—

For salicylates—Salicylates readily cross the placenta. Although it has been reported that salicylate use during pregnancy may increase the risk of birth defects in humans, controlled studies using aspirin have not shown proof of teratogenicity. Studies in humans with other salicylates have not been done. Studies in animals have shown that salicylates cause birth defects including fissure of the spine and skull; facial clefts; eye defects; and malformations of the CNS, viscera, and skeleton (especially the vertebrae and ribs). (Aspirin extended-release tablets: FDA Pregnancy Category D; Magnesium salicylate and salsalate: FDA Pregnancy Category C.)

For caffeine—Caffeine crosses the placenta and achieves blood and tissue concentrations similar to maternal concentrations. Studies in humans have not shown that caffeine causes birth defects. However, studies in animals have shown that caffeine causes skeletal abnormalities in the digits and phalanges (when given in doses equivalent to the caffeine content of 12 to 24 cups of coffee daily throughout pregnancy or when given in very large single doses, i.e., 50 to 100 mg per kg of body weight [mg/kg]) and retarded skeletal development (when given in lower doses).

Third trimester—
Chronic, high-dose salicylate therapy may result in prolonged gestation, increased risk of postmaturity syndrome (fetal damage or death due to decreased placental function if pregnancy is greatly prolonged), and increased risk of maternal antenatal hemorrhage. Also, ingestion of salicylates, especially aspirin, during the last 2 weeks of pregnancy may increase the risk of fetal or neonatal hemorrhage. The possibility that regular use late in pregnancy may result in constriction or premature closure of the fetal ductus arteriosus, possibly leading to persistent pulmonary hypertension and heart failure in the neonate, must also be considered. Overuse or abuse of aspirin late in pregnancy has been reported to increase the risk of stillbirth or neonatal death, possibly because of antenatal hemorrhage or premature ductus arteriosus closure, and to decrease birthweight; however, studies using therapeutic doses of aspirin have not shown these adverse effects. Pregnant women should be advised not to take aspirin during the last trimester of pregnancy unless such therapy is prescribed and monitored by a physician.

Labor and delivery—Chronic, high-dose salicylate therapy late in pregnancy may result in prolonged labor, complicated deliveries, and increased risk of maternal or fetal hemorrhage.

Breast-feeding

For salicylates—
Problems in humans with usual analgesic doses have not been documented. However, salicylate is distributed into breast milk; with chronic, high-dose use, intake by the infant may be high enough to cause adverse effects.

In one study, peak salicylate concentrations of 173 to 483 mcg per mL were measured in breast milk 5 to 8 hours after maternal ingestion of a single dose of 650 mg of aspirin. The half-life in breast milk was 3.8 to 12.5 hours (average 7.1 hours).

Following maternal ingestion of 20 mg/kg of sodium salicylate, a total of 3 to 4 mg of salicylate is distributed into breast milk.

For caffeine—
Caffeine is distributed into breast milk in very small amounts; at recommended dosages, concentration in the infant is considered to be insignificant.

Pediatrics

For salicylates—
Aspirin use may be associated with the development of Reye's syndrome in children and teenagers with acute febrile illnesses, especially influenza and varicella. It is recommended that salicylate therapy not be initiated in febrile pediatric or adolescent patients until after the presence of such an illness has been ruled out. Also, it is recommended that chronic salicylate therapy in these patients be discontinued if a fever occurs, and not resumed until it has been determined that an illness that may predispose to Reye's syndrome is not present or has run its course. Other forms of salicylate toxicity may also be more prevalent in pediatric patients, especially children who have a fever or are dehydrated.

Especially careful monitoring of the serum salicylate concentration is recommended in pediatric patients with Kawasaki disease. Absorption of aspirin is impaired during the early febrile stage of the disease; therapeutic anti-inflammatory plasma salicylate concentrations may be extremely difficult to achieve. Also, as the febrile stage passes, absorption is improved; salicylate toxicity may occur if dosage is not readjusted.

For caffeine—
Pediatric patients are especially susceptible to overdose of caffeine and its adverse CNS effects.

Geriatrics

Geriatric patients may be more susceptible to the toxic effects of salicylates, possibly because of decreased renal function. Lower doses than those usually recommended for adults, especially for long-term use or for use of long-acting salicylates (such as choline and magnesium salicylates and salsalate), may be required.

Drug interactions and/or related problems

The following drug interactions and/or related problems have been selected on the basis of their potential clinical significance (possible mechanism in parentheses where appropriate)—not necessarily inclusive (» = major clinical significance):

Note: Combinations containing any of the following medications, depending on the amount present, may also interact with this medication.

In addition to the interactions listed below, the possibility should be considered that additive or multiple effects leading to impaired blood clotting and/or increased risk of bleeding may occur if a salicylate, especially aspirin, is used concurrently with any medication having a significant potential for causing hypoprothrombinemia, thrombocytopenia, or gastrointestinal ulceration or hemorrhage.

For all salicylates

Acetaminophen
(prolonged concurrent use of acetaminophen with a salicylate is not recommended because chronic, high-dose administration of the combined analgesics [1.35 grams daily, or cumulative ingestion of 1 kg annually, for 3 years or longer] significantly increases the risk of analgesic nephropathy, renal papillary necrosis, end-stage renal disease, and cancer of the kidney or urinary bladder; also, it is recommended that for short-term use the combined dose of acetaminophen plus a salicylate not exceed that recommended for acetaminophen or a salicylate given individually)

Acidifiers, urinary, such as:
Ammonium chloride
Ascorbic acid (Vitamin C)
Potassium or sodium phosphates
(acidification of the urine by these medications decreases salicylate excretion, leading to increased salicylate plasma concentrations; initiation of therapy with these medications in patients stabilized on a salicylate may lead to toxic salicylate concentrations)

(aspirin may increase urinary excretion of ascorbic acid; clinical significance is unclear, but some clinicians recommend ascorbic acid supplementation in patients receiving prolonged high-dose aspirin therapy)

Alcohol or
» Nonsteroidal anti-inflammatory drugs (NSAIDs), other
(concurrent use of these medications with a salicylate may increase the risk of gastrointestinal side effects, including ulceration and gastrointestinal blood loss; also, concurrent use of a salicylate with an NSAID may increase the risk of severe gastrointestinal side effects without providing additional symptomatic relief and is therefore not recommended)

(aspirin may decrease the bioavailability of many NSAIDs, including diflunisal, fenoprofen, indomethacin, meclofenamate, piroxicam [to 80% of the usual plasma concentration], and the active sulfide metabolite of sulindac; aspirin has also been shown to decrease the protein binding and increase the plasma clearance of ketoprofen, and to decrease the formation and excretion of ketoprofen conjugates)

(concurrent use of other NSAIDs with aspirin may also increase the risk of bleeding at sites other than the gastrointestinal tract because of additive inhibition of platelet aggregation)

» Alkalizers, urinary, such as:
Carbonic anhydrase inhibitors
Citrates
Sodium bicarbonate or
Antacids, chronic high-dose use, especially calcium- and/or magnesium-containing
(alkalinization of the urine by these medications increases salicylate excretion, leading to decreased salicylate plasma concentrations, reduced effectiveness, and shortened duration of action; also, withdrawal of a urinary alkalizer from a patient stabilized on a salicylate may increase the plasma salicylate concentration to a toxic level; however, the antacids present in buffered aspirin formulations may not be present in sufficient quantity to alkalinize the urine)

(metabolic acidosis induced by carbonic anhydrase inhibitors may increase penetration of salicylate into the brain and increase the risk of salicylate toxicity in patients taking large [antirheumatic] doses of salicylate; if acetazolamide is used to produce forced alkaline diuresis in the treatment of salicylate poisoning, the increased risk of severe metabolic acidosis and increased salicylate toxicity must be considered and an alkaline intravenous solution given concurrently)

» Anticoagulants, coumarin- or indandione-derivative or
» Heparin or
» Thrombolytic agents, such as:
Alteplase
Anistreplase
Streptokinase
Urokinase
(salicylates may displace a coumarin- or indandione-derivative anticoagulant from its protein-binding sites, and, in high doses, may cause hypoprothrombinemia, leading to increased anticoagulation and risk of bleeding)

(the potential occurrence of gastrointestinal ulceration or hemorrhage during salicylate, especially aspirin, therapy may cause increased risk to patients receiving anticoagulant or thrombolytic therapy)

(because aspirin-induced inhibition of platelet function may lead to prolonged bleeding time and increased risk of hemorrhage, concurrent use of aspirin with an anticoagulant or a thrombolytic agent is recommended only within a carefully monitored antithrombotic regimen; although a recent study has shown that initiation of therapy with 160 mg of aspirin a day concurrently with short-term [1-hour] intravenous infusion of streptokinase in patients with acute coronary arterial occlusion significantly decreases the risk of reocclusion, reinfarction, stroke, and death without increasing the risk of adverse effects [as compared with streptokinase alone], other studies using higher doses of aspirin and/or more prolonged administration of a thrombolytic agent have demonstrated an increased risk of bleeding)

Anticonvulsants, hydantoin
(salicylates may decrease hydantoin metabolism, leading to increases in hydantoin plasma concentrations, efficacy, and/or toxicity; adjustment of hydantoin dosage may be required when chronic salicylate therapy is initiated or discontinued)

» Antidiabetic agents, oral or
Insulin
(effects of these medications may be increased by large doses of salicylates; dosage adjustments may be necessary; potentiation of oral antidiabetic agents may be caused partially by displacement from serum proteins; glipizide and glyburide, because of their nonionic binding characteristics, may not be affected as much as the other oral agents; however, caution in concurrent use is recommended)

Antiemetics, including antihistamines and phenothiazines
(antiemetics may mask the symptoms of salicylate-induced ototoxicity, such as dizziness, vertigo, and tinnitus)

Bismuth subsalicylate
(ingestion of large repeated doses as for traveler's diarrhea may produce substantial plasma salicylate concentrations; concurrent use with large doses of analgesic salicylates may increase the risk of salicylate toxicity)

» Cefamandole or
» Cefoperazone or
» Cefotetan or
» Plicamycin or
» Valproic acid
(these medications may cause hypoprothrombinemia; in addition, plicamycin or valproic acid may inhibit platelet aggregation; concurrent use with aspirin may increase the risk of bleeding because of additive interferences with blood clotting)

(hypoprothrombinemia induced by large doses of salicylates, and the potential occurrence of gastrointestinal ulceration or hemorrhage during salicylate, especially aspirin, therapy, may increase the risk of bleeding complications in patients receiving these medications)

(concurrent use of aspirin with valproic acid has also been reported to increase the plasma concentration of valproic acid and induce valproic acid toxicity)

Corticosteroids or
Corticotropin (ACTH), chronic therapeutic use of
(corticosteroids or corticotropin may increase salicylate excretion, resulting in lower plasma concentrations and increased salicylate dosage requirements; salicylism may result when corticosteroids or corticotropin dosage is subsequently decreased or discontinued, especially in patients receiving large [antirheumatic] doses of salicylate; also, the risk of gastrointestinal side effects, including ulceration and gastrointestinal blood loss, may be increased; however, concurrent use in the treatment of arthritis may provide additive therapeutic benefit and permit reduction of corticosteroid or corticotropin dosage)

(because corticosteroids and corticotropin may cause sodium and fluid retention, caution in concurrent use with large doses of sodium salicylate is recommended)

Furosemide
(in addition to increasing the risk of ototoxicity, concurrent use of furosemide with high doses of salicylate may lead to salicylate toxicity because of competition for renal excretory sites)

Laxatives, cellulose-containing
(concurrent use may reduce the salicylate effect because of physical binding or other absorptive hindrance; medications should be administered 2 hours apart)

» Methotrexate
(salicylates may displace methotrexate from its binding sites and decrease its renal clearance, leading to toxic methotrexate plasma concentrations; if they are used concurrently, methotrexate dosage should be decreased, the patient observed for signs of toxicity, and/or methotrexate plasma concentration monitored; also, it is recommended that salicylate therapy be discontinued 24 to 48 hours prior to administration of a high-dose methotrexate infusion, and not resumed until the plasma methotrexate concentration has decreased to a nontoxic level [usually at least 12 hours postinfusion])

Ototoxic medications, other (See *Appendix II*), especially
» Vancomycin
(concurrent or sequential administration of these medications with a salicylate should be avoided because the potential for ototoxicity may be increased; hearing loss may occur and may progress to deafness even after discontinuation of the medication; these effects may be reversible, but usually are permanent)

» Platelet aggregation inhibitors (See *Appendix II*)
(concurrent use with aspirin is not recommended, except in a monitored antithrombotic regimen, because the risk of bleeding may be increased)

(the potential occurrence of gastrointestinal ulceration or hemorrhage during salicylate therapy, and the hypoprothrombinemic effect of large doses of salicylate, may cause increased risk to patients receiving a platelet aggregation inhibitor)

» Probenecid or
» Sulfinpyrazone
(concurrent use of a salicylate is not recommended when these medications are used to treat hyperuricemia or gout, because the uricosuric effect of these medications may be decreased by doses of salicylates that produce serum salicylate concentrations above 5 mg per 100 mL; also, these medications may inhibit the uricosuric effect achieved when serum salicylate concentrations are above 10 to 15 mg per 100 mL)

(probenecid may decrease renal clearance and increase plasma concentrations and toxicity of salicylates)

(sulfinpyrazone may decrease salicylate excretion and/or displace salicylate from its protein binding sites, possibly leading to increased salicylate concentrations and toxicity)

(although low doses of sulfinpyrazone and aspirin have been used concurrently to provide additive inhibition of platelet aggregation, the efficacy of the combination has not been established and the increased risk of bleeding must be considered; also, concurrent use of sulfinpyrazone with aspirin may increase the risk of gastrointestinal ulceration or hemorrhage)

Salicylic acid or other salicylates, topical
(concurrent use with systemic salicylates may increase the risk of salicylate toxicity if significant quantities are absorbed)

Vitamin K
(requirements for this vitamin may be increased in patients receiving high doses of salicylate)

Zidovudine
(in theory, aspirin may competitively inhibit the hepatic glucuronidation and decrease the clearance of zidovudine, leading to potentiation of zidovudine toxicity; the possibility must be considered that aspirin toxicity may also be increased)

For buffered aspirin formulations, choline and magnesium salicylates, and magnesium salicylate (in addition to those interactions listed above as applying to all salicylates)

» Ciprofloxacin or
» Enoxacin or
» Itraconazole or
» Ketoconazole or
» Lomefloxacin or
» Norfloxacin or
» Ofloxacin or
» Tetracyclines, oral
(antacids present in buffered aspirin formulations, and the magnesium in choline and magnesium salicylates or magnesium salicylate, interfere with absorption of these medications; if used concurrently, the interacting salicylate should be taken at least 6 hours before or 2 hours after ciprofloxacin or lomefloxacin, 8 hours before or 2 hours after enoxacin, 2 hours after itraconazole, 3 hours before or after ketoconazole, 2 hours before or after norfloxacin or ofloxacin, and 3 to 4 hours before or after a tetracycline)

For enteric-coated formulations (in addition to those interactions listed above as applying to all salicylates)

Antacids or

Histamine H_2-receptor antagonists

(concurrent administration of these medications, which increase intragastric pH, with an enteric-coated medication may cause premature dissolution, and loss of the protective effect, of the enteric coating)

For formulations containing caffeine (in addition to those interactions listed above as applying to all salicylates)

CNS stimulation-producing medications, other (See *Appendix II*)

(concurrent use with caffeine may result in excessive CNS stimulation, which may cause unwanted effects such as nervousness, irritability, insomnia, or possibly convulsions or cardiac arrhythmias; close observation is recommended)

Lithium

(caffeine increases urinary excretion of lithium, thereby possibly reducing its therapeutic effect)

Monoamine oxidase (MAO) inhibitors, including furazolidone, pargyline, and procarbazine

(concurrent use of large amounts of caffeine with MAO inhibitors may produce dangerous cardiac arrhythmias or severe hypertension because of the sympathomimetic side effects of caffeine)

Laboratory value alterations

The following have been selected on the basis of their potential clinical significance (possible effect in parentheses where appropriate)—not necessarily inclusive (» = major clinical significance).

With diagnostic test results

For all salicylates

Copper sulfate urine sugar tests

(false-positive test results may occur with chronic use of salicylates in doses equivalent in salicylate content to 2.4 grams or more of aspirin a day, i.e., 3.2 grams of choline salicylate, 2.4 grams of choline and magnesium salicylates, 2 grams of magnesium salicylate, 1.8 grams of salsalate, or 2.4 grams of sodium salicylate a day)

Gerhardt test for urine aceto-acetic acid

(interference may occur because reaction with ferric chloride produces a reddish color that persists after boiling)

Glucose enzymatic urine sugar tests

(false-negative test results may occur with chronic use of salicylates in doses equivalent in salicylate content to 2.4 grams or more of aspirin a day, i.e., 3.2 grams of choline salicylate, 2.4 grams of choline and magnesium salicylates, 2 grams of magnesium salicylate, 1.8 grams of salsalate, or 2.4 grams of sodium salicylate a day)

Renal function test using phenolsulfonphthalein (PSP)

(salicylate may competitively inhibit renal tubular secretion of PSP, thereby decreasing urinary PSP concentration and invalidating test results)

Serum uric acid determinations

(falsely increased values may occur with colorimetric assay methods when plasma salicylate concentrations exceed 13 mg per 100 mL; the uricase assay method is not affected)

Thyroid imaging, radionuclide

(chronic salicylate administration may depress thyroid function; salicylate therapy should be discontinued at least 1 week prior to administration of the radiopharmaceutical; however, a rebound effect may occur following discontinuation of salicylate therapy, resulting in a period of 3 to 10 days of increased thyroidal uptake)

Urine vanillylmandelic acid (VMA) determinations

(values may be falsely increased or decreased, depending on method used)

For aspirin only (in addition to those interferences listed above for all salicylates)

Protirelin-induced thyroid-stimulating hormone (TSH) release determinations

(TSH response to protirelin may be decreased by 2 to 3.6 grams of aspirin daily; peak TSH concentrations occur at the same time after administration, but are reduced)

Urine 5-hydroxyindoleacetic acid (5-HIAA) determinations

(aspirin may alter results when fluorescent method is used)

For caffeine-containing formulations (in addition to the diagnostic interferences listed above)

Myocardial perfusion imaging, radionuclide, when adenosine or dipyridamole is used as an adjunct to the radiopharmaceutical

(caffeine may reverse the effects of adenosine or dipyridamole on myocardial blood flow, thereby interfering with test results; patients should be advised to avoid caffeine for at least 8 to 12 hours prior to the test)

With physiology/laboratory test values

For all salicylates

Liver function tests, including:

Serum alanine aminotransferase (ALT [SGPT]) and

Serum alkaline phosphatase and

Serum aspartate aminotransferase (AST [SGOT])

(abnormalities may occur, especially in patients with juvenile rheumatoid arthritis, systemic lupus erythematosus, or pre-existing history of liver disease, or when plasma salicylate concentrations exceed 25 mg per 100 mL; liver function test values may return to normal despite continued use or when dosage is decreased; however, if severe abnormalities occur, or if there is evidence of active liver disease, the medication should be discontinued and used with caution in the future)

Prothrombin time

(may be prolonged with large doses of salicylates, especially if plasma concentrations exceed 30 mg per 100 mL)

Serum cholesterol concentrations

(may be decreased by chronic use of salicylates in doses equivalent in salicylate content to 5 grams or more of aspirin per day, i.e., 6.7 grams of choline salicylate, 5 grams of choline and magnesium salicylates, 4.1 grams of magnesium salicylate, 3.8 grams of salsalate, or 5 grams of sodium salicylate a day)

Serum potassium concentrations

(may be decreased because of increased potassium excretion caused by direct effect on renal tubules)

Serum thyroxine (T_4) concentrations and

Serum triiodothyronine (T_3) concentrations

(may be decreased when determined by radioimmunoassay—with large doses of salicylates)

Serum uric acid concentrations

(may be increased or decreased, depending on salicylate dosage; plasma salicylate concentrations below 10 to 15 mg per 100 mL increase serum uric acid concentrations and higher plasma salicylate concentrations decrease uric acid concentrations)

T_3 resin uptake

(may be increased with large doses of salicylates)

For aspirin only (in addition to the interferences listed above)

Bleeding time

(may be prolonged by aspirin for 4 to 7 days because of suppressed platelet aggregation; as little as 40 mg of aspirin affects platelet function for at least 96 hours following administration; however, clinical bleeding problems have not been reported with small doses [150 mg or less])

Medical considerations/Contraindications

The medical considerations/contraindications included have been selected on the basis of their potential clinical significance (reasons given in parentheses where appropriate)—not necessarily inclusive (» = major clinical significance).

Except under special circumstances, this medication should not be used when the following medical problems exist:

For all salicylates

» Bleeding ulcers or

» Hemorrhagic states, other active

(may be exacerbated, especially by aspirin)

» Hemophilia or other bleeding problems, including coagulation or platelet function disorders

(increased risk of hemorrhage, especially with aspirin)

For aspirin only (in addition to the contraindications listed above for all salicylates)

» Angioedema, anaphylaxis, or other severe sensitivity reaction induced by aspirin or other NSAIDs, history of or

» Nasal polyps associated with asthma, induced or exacerbated by aspirin

(high risk of severe sensitivity reaction to aspirin)

» Thrombocytopenia

(increased risk of bleeding because aspirin inhibits platelet aggregation)

For choline and magnesium salicylates and for magnesium salicylate only (in addition to the contraindications listed above for all salicylates)

» Renal insufficiency, chronic advanced

(risk of hypermagnesemic toxicity)

Risk-benefit should be considered when the following medical problems exist:

For all salicylates

Anemia
(may be exacerbated by gastrointestinal blood loss during salicylate, especially aspirin, therapy; also, salicylate-induced peripheral vasodilation may lead to pseudoanemia)

Conditions predisposing to fluid retention, such as:
Compromised cardiac function or
Hypertension
(in patients with carditis, high doses of salicylates may precipitate congestive heart failure or pulmonary edema)
(patients with congestive heart disease may be more susceptible to adverse renal effects)
(sodium content of sodium salicylate may be detrimental to these patients when large doses are administered chronically)

» Gastritis, erosive or
» Peptic ulcer
(may be exacerbated because of ulcerogenic effects, especially with aspirin; risk of gastrointestinal bleeding is increased)

Gout
(salicylates may increase serum uric acid concentrations and may interfere with efficacy of uricosuric agents)

Hepatic function impairment
(salicylates metabolized hepatically; also, patients with decompensated hepatic cirrhosis may be more susceptible to adverse renal effects)
(in severe hepatic impairment, inhibition of platelet function by aspirin may increase the risk of hemorrhage)

Hypoprothrombinemia or
Vitamin K deficiency
(increased risk of bleeding because of antiplatelet action of aspirin and the hypoprothrombinemic effect of high doses of salicylates)

Renal function impairment
(salicylate elimination may be reduced; also, the risk of renal adverse effects may be increased)
(choline and magnesium salicylates or magnesium salicylate should be used with caution in patients with mild or moderate renal impairment because of the risk of hypermagnesemic toxicity; however, as stated above, these medications should *not* be used if chronic advanced renal insufficiency is present)

Sensitivity reaction, mild, to aspirin or other NSAIDs, history of
(risk of sensitivity reaction, especially with aspirin)

Symptoms of nasal polyps associated with bronchospasm, or angioedema, anaphylaxis, or other severe allergic reactions induced by aspirin or other NSAIDs
(although cross-sensitivity leading to severe reactions occurs very rarely with the nonacetylated salicylates, caution is recommended; however, as indicated above, aspirin should *not* be used)

Thyrotoxicosis
(may be exacerbated by large doses)

For aspirin only (in addition to those listed above for all salicylates)

» Asthma
(increased risk of bronchospastic sensitivity reaction)

Glucose-6-phosphate dehydrogenase (G6PD) deficiency
(rarely, aspirin has caused hemolytic anemia in these patients)

For formulations containing caffeine

Cardiac disease, severe
(high doses of caffeine may increase risk of tachycardia or extrasystoles, which may lead to heart failure)

Sensitivity to caffeine, history of
(risk of allergic reaction)

Patient monitoring

The following may be especially important in patient monitoring (other tests may be warranted in some patients, depending on condition; » = major clinical significance):

For all salicylates

Hematocrit determinations
(may be required at periodic intervals during prolonged high-dose therapy because of the possibility of gastrointestinal blood loss, especially with aspirin)

Hepatic function determinations
(may be required prior to initiation of antirheumatic therapy and if symptoms of hepatotoxicity occur during therapy; salicylate-induced hepatotoxicity may be especially likely to occur in patients, especially children, with rheumatic fever, systemic lupus erythematosus, juvenile arthritis, or pre-existing hepatic disease)

Serum salicylate concentrations
(monitoring required at periodic intervals during prolonged high-dose therapy as a guide to dosage, safety, and efficacy, especially in children; because aspirin absorption in children with Kawasaki disease is erratic and varies at different stages of the disease, monitoring of plasma salicylate concentration in these patients is critical)

For choline and magnesium salicylates and magnesium salicylate only (in addition to those listed above for all salicylates)

Serum magnesium concentration
(monitoring recommended during therapy with large doses in patients with renal insufficiency because of the possibility of hypermagnesemic toxicity)

Side/Adverse Effects

In July 2005, the Food and Drug Administration (FDA) asked all manufacturers of NSAIDs, including salsalate, to revise the labeling for their products to include a boxed warning, highlighting the potential for increased risk of cardiovascular (CV) events including stroke and the well described, serious potential life-threatening gastrointestinal (GI) bleeding associated with their use.

Note: Salicylates may decrease renal function, especially when serum salicylate concentrations reach 250 mcg per mL (25 mg per 100 mL). However, the risk of complications due to this action appears minimal in patients with normal renal function.

Aspirin-induced bronchospasm is most likely to occur in patients with the triad of asthma, allergies, and nasal polyps induced by aspirin. Nonacetylated salicylates may rarely cause bronchospastic reactions in susceptible people when very large doses are given.

Angioedema or urticaria may be more likely to occur in patients with a history of recurrent idiopathic angioedema or urticaria.

Gastrointestinal side effects are more likely to occur with aspirin than with other salicylates; also, they may be more likely to occur with chronic, high-dose administration than with occasional use. Use of enteric-coated formulations may reduce the potential for gastrointestinal side effects.

Adverse effects are more likely to occur at serum salicylate concentrations of 300 mcg per mL (30 mg per 100 mL) or above; however, they may also occur at lower serum concentrations, especially in patients 60 years of age or older. Serum concentrations at which adverse or toxic effects have been reported during chronic therapy include:

Salicylate Concentration (mcg per mL/ mg per 100 mL)	Effect
195–210/19.5–21	Mild toxicity (tinnitus, decreased hearing)
250/25	Hepatotoxicity (abnormal liver function tests)
250/25	Decreased renal function
300/30	Decreased prothrombin time
310/31	Deafness
350/35	Hyperventilation
> 400/40	Metabolic acidosis, other signs of severe toxicity

The following side/adverse effects have been selected on the basis of their potential clinical significance (possible signs and symptoms in parentheses where appropriate)—not necessarily inclusive:

Those indicating need for medical attention

Incidence less frequent or rare

Anaphylactoid reaction (bluish discoloration or flushing or redness of skin; coughing; difficulty in swallowing; dizziness or feeling faint, severe; skin rash, hives [may include giant urticaria], and/or itching; stuffy nose; swelling of eyelids, face, or lips; tightness in chest, troubled breathing, and/or wheezing, especially in asthmatic patients); ***anemia*** (unusual tiredness or weakness)—for aspirin or buffered aspirin only; may occur secondary to gastrointestinal microbleeding; ***anemia, hemolytic*** (troubled breathing, exertional; unusual tiredness or weakness)—reported with aspirin only, almost always in patients with glucose-6-phosphate (G6PD) deficiency; ***bronchospastic allergic reaction*** (shortness of breath, troubled breathing, tightness in chest, and/or wheezing); ***dermatitis, allergic*** (skin rash, hives, or itching); ***gastrointestinal ulceration, possibly with bleeding*** (bloody or black, tarry stools; stomach pain, severe; vomiting of blood or material that looks like coffee grounds)

Incidence unknown

Rectal irritation—for aspirin suppository dosage form

Those indicating need for medical attention only if they continue or are bothersome

Incidence more frequent with aspirin; less frequent with enteric-coated or buffered formulations and with other salicylates

Gastrointestinal irritation (mild stomach pain; heartburn or indigestion; nausea with or without vomiting)

Incidence less frequent

For caffeine-containing formulations

CNS stimulation (trouble in sleeping, nervousness, or jitters)

Overdose

For specific information on the agents used in the management of salicylate overdose, see:

- Vitamin K_1—Phytonadione in *Vitamin K (Systemic)* monograph.

For more information on the management of overdose or unintentional ingestion, **contact a Poison Control Center** (see *Poison Control Center Listing*).

Clinical effects of overdose

The following effects have been selected on the basis of their potential clinical significance (possible signs and symptoms in parentheses where appropriate)—not necessarily inclusive:

Acute and chronic

Mild overdose

Salicylism (Continuing ringing or buzzing in ears or hearing loss; confusion; severe or continuing diarrhea, stomach pain, and or headache; dizziness or lightheadedness; severe drowsiness; fast or deep breathing; continuing nausea and/or vomiting; uncontrollable flapping movements of the hands, especially in elderly patients; increased thirst; vision problems)—tinnitus and/or headache may be the earliest symptoms of salicylism

Severe overdose

Bloody urine; convulsions; hallucinations; severe nervousness, excitement, or confusion; shortness of breath or troubled breathing; unexplained fever

Note: In young children, the only signs of an overdose may be changes in behavior, severe drowsiness or tiredness, and/or fast or deep breathing.

Laboratory findings in overdose may indicate encephalographic abnormalities, alterations in acid-base balance (especially respiratory alkalosis and metabolic acidosis), hyperglycemia or hypoglycemia (especially in children), ketonuria, hyponatremia, hypokalemia, and proteinuria.

Treatment of overdose

To decrease absorption—Emptying the stomach via induction of emesis (taking care to guard against aspiration) or gastric lavage.

Administering activated charcoal.

To enhance elimination—Inducing forced alkaline diuresis to increase salicylate excretion. However, bicarbonate should not be administered orally for this purpose because salicylate absorption may be increased. Also, if acetazolamide is used, the increased risk of severe metabolic acidosis and salicylate toxicity (caused by increased penetration of salicylate into the brain because of metabolic acidosis) must be considered. Some emergency care practitioners recommend that acetazolamide not be used at all in the treatment of salicylate overdose. Others state that acetazolamide may be used, provided that precautions are taken to prevent systemic metabolic acidosis, such as concurrent administration of an alkaline intravenous solution, e.g., one that contains sodium bicarbonate or sodium lactate.

Institution of exchange transfusion, hemodialysis, peritoneal dialysis, or hemoperfusion as needed in severe overdose.

Specific treatment—Administering blood or vitamin K_1 if necessary to treat hemorrhaging.

Monitoring—Monitoring for pulmonary edema and convulsions and instituting appropriate therapy if required.

Monitoring serum salicylate concentration until it is apparent that the concentration is decreasing to the nontoxic range. When a large single dose of an immediate-release formulation has been ingested, salicylate concentrations of 500 mcg per mL (50 mg per 100 mL; 3.62 mmol/L) 2 hours after ingestion indicate serious toxicity; salicylate concentrations above 800 mcg per mL (80 mg per 100 mL; 5.79 mmol/L) 2 hours after ingestion indicate possible fatality. In addition, prolonged monitoring may be necessary in massive overdosage because absorption may be delayed; if a determination performed prior to 6 hours after ingestion fails to show a toxic salicylate concentration, the determination should be repeated. Although the following values are not reliable for predicting the severity of toxicity after chronic or repeated ingestions, or after ingestion of a large single dose of a delayed-release (enteric-coated) or extended-release formulation, salicylate concentrations considered indicative of varying degrees of toxicity are as follows:

Time After Ingestion	Salicylate Concentration		
	mcg/mL	mg/100 mL	mmol/L
Mild toxicity			
6 hr	450–650	45–65	3.26–4.71
12 hr	350–550	35–55	2.53–3.98
Moderate toxicity			
6 hr	650–900	65–90	4.71–6.52
12 hr	550–750	55–75	3.98–5.43
Severe toxicity			
6 hr	> 900	> 90	> 6.52
12 hr	> 750	> 75	> 5.43

Supportive care—Monitoring and supporting vital functions. Correcting hyperthermia; fluid, electrolyte, and acid-base imbalances; ketosis; and plasma glucose concentration as needed. Patients in whom intentional overdose is known or suspected should be referrred for psychiatric consultation.

Patient Consultation

As an aid to patient consultation, refer to *Advice for the Patient, Salicylates (Systemic)*.

In providing consultation, consider emphasizing the following selected information (» = major clinical significance):

Before using this medication

» Conditions affecting use, especially:

Sensitivity to any of the salicylates, including methyl salicylate, or nonsteroidal anti-inflammatory drugs (NSAIDs), history of

Pregnancy—Salicylates and caffeine (present in some formulations) cross the placenta; high-dose chronic use or abuse of aspirin in the third trimester may be hazardous to the mother as well as the fetus and/or neonate, causing heart problems in fetus or neonate and/or bleeding in mother, fetus, or neonate; high-dose chronic use or abuse of any salicylate late in pregnancy may also prolong and complicate labor and delivery; not taking aspirin during the third trimester unless prescribed by physician

Breast-feeding—Salicylates and caffeine (present in some formulations) are excreted in breast milk

Use in children and adolescents—Checking with physician before giving to children or teenagers with symptoms of acute febrile illness, especially influenza or varicella, because of the risk of Reye's syndrome; determining ahead of time what physician wants done if a child receiving chronic therapy develops fever or other symptoms of acute illness that may predispose to Reye's syndrome; also, increased susceptibility to salicylate toxicity in children, especially with fever and dehydration

Use in the elderly—Increased susceptibility to salicylate toxicity

Other medications, especially anticoagulants, antidiabetic agents (oral), those cephalosporins that may cause hypoprothrombinemia, plicamycin, valproic acid, methotrexate, NSAIDs, platelet aggregation inhibitors, probenecid, sulfinpyrazone, urinary alkalizers, and vancomycin; also, for buffered aspirin, choline and magnesium salicylates, and magnesium salicylate: fluoroquinolone antibiotics, itraconazole, ketoconazole, and oral tetracyclines

Other medical problems, especially coagulation or platelet function disorders, gastrointestinal problems such as ulceration or erosive gastritis (especially a bleeding ulcer), thyrotoxicosis, and (for choline and magnesium salicylates and for magnesium salicylate) chronic advanced renal insufficiency

Diet—Sodium content of sodium salicylate must be considered for patients on a sodium-restricted diet, especially with chronic use of antirheumatic doses

Proper use of this medication

» Taking nonenteric-coated oral dosage forms after meals or with food to minimize stomach irritation

» Taking all tablet or capsule dosage forms with a full glass of water and not lying down for 15 to 30 minutes after taking

» Not taking aspirin or buffered aspirin if it has a strong vinegar-like odor

Not chewing aspirin or buffered aspirin dosage forms within 7 days after tonsillectomy, tooth extraction, or other oral surgery

Not placing aspirin or buffered aspirin tablet directly on tooth or gum surface, to prevent tissue damage

Proper administration of

Aspirin

Chewable tablets—May be chewed, dissolved in liquid, crushed, or swallowed whole

Delayed-release tablets—Must be swallowed whole

Extended-release tablets—May be broken or crumbled (but not ground up) if necessary, unless specified by manufacturer to be swallowed whole; see manufacturer's prescribing information

Suppository—Proper administration technique

Choline and magnesium salicylates oral solution

Liquid may be mixed with fruit juice just prior to taking, if desired

Sodium salicylate delayed-release tablets

Tablets must be swallowed whole

Importance of not taking more medication than prescribed by physician or dentist or recommended on package label

Unless otherwise directed by physician, children not taking more often than 5 times daily

Compliance with therapy (for arthritis); may take 2 to 3 weeks or longer for maximum effectiveness

» Proper dosing

Missed dose: If on scheduled dosing regimen—taking as soon as possible; not taking if almost time for next dose; not doubling doses

» Proper storage

Precautions while using this medication

» Possibility of overdose if other medications containing aspirin or other salicylates (possibly including topical products) are used

» Regular visits to physician to check progress if long-term or high-dose therapy is prescribed

» Importance of immediately reporting to physician symptoms of edema, gastrointestinal bleeding or ulceration, cardiovascular events, unusual weight gain, or skin rash

Checking with physician if:

Taking for pain or fever, and pain persists for longer than 10 days for adults or 5 days for children, fever persists for longer than 3 days, condition becomes worse, new symptoms occur, or redness or swelling is present

Taking for sore throat, and sore throat is severe, persists for longer than 2 days, or occurs together with or is followed by fever, headache, rash, nausea, or vomiting

Symptoms of ringing or buzzing in ears or headache occur during long-term therapy

Patients taking aspirin as a platelet aggregation inhibitor:

» Taking only the amount of aspirin prescribed; checking with prescribing physician about proper medication to use for relief of pain, fever, or arthritis

» Not discontinuing treatment for any reason without first consulting prescribing physician

» Not taking acetaminophen, ibuprofen, or other NSAIDs concurrently with salicylates for longer than a few days, unless specifically prescribed by physician or dentist, especially if using salicylates on a long-term and/or high-dose basis

Diabetics:

Possibility of false urine sugar test results with prolonged use (per day) of—

8 or more 325-mg (5-grain), 4 or more 500-mg or 650-mg (10-grain), 3 or more 800-mg or 975-mg (15-grain) doses of aspirin

8 or more 325-mg (5-grain) or 4 or more 500-mg or 650-mg (10-grain) doses of buffered aspirin or sodium salicylate

4 or more 870-mg doses of choline salicylate

5 or more 500-mg, 4 or more 750-mg, or 2 or more 1000-mg, doses of choline and magnesium salicylates

7 or more regular strength, or 4 or more extra-strength, tablets of magnesium salicylate

4 or more 500-mg, or 3 or more 750-mg, doses of salsalate

Checking with physician, nurse, or pharmacist if unsure of daily dose being taken, if changes in urine sugar test results occur, or if any other questions, especially if diabetes not well-controlled

Caution if any kind of surgery is required; not taking aspirin for 5 days prior to surgery unless otherwise directed by physician or dentist because of risk of bleeding

Checking with health care professional before using buffered aspirin, choline and magnesium salicylates, or magnesium salicylate concurrently with a fluoroquinolone antibiotic, itraconazole, ketoconazole, or an oral tetracycline; these salicylate formulations may interfere with absorption of the anti-infective agent

Not taking a cellulose-containing laxative within 2 hours of a salicylate

Alcohol consumption may increase probability of stomach problems (for oral dosage forms only)

Checking with physician if rectal irritation occurs with aspirin suppositories

Caution if any laboratory tests required; possible interference with some test results by salicylates; possible interference with dipyridamole-assisted myocardial imaging by formulations containing caffeine

» Suspected overdose: Getting emergency help immediately

Side/adverse effects

Signs of potential side effects, especially allergic reactions, anemia, and gastrointestinal toxicity and, with aspirin suppositories, rectal irritation

General Dosing Information

A reduction in initial dosage is recommended for geriatric patients, especially those receiving long-acting salicylates (e.g., choline and magnesium salicylates, salsalate) or prolonged therapy. These patients may be more susceptible to salicylate toxicity, especially if accumulation occurs because of impaired renal function. If the reduced dosage is not effective, dosage may gradually be increased as tolerated.

For treatment of arthritis, dosage is usually increased gradually until symptoms are relieved, therapeutic plasma concentrations are achieved, or signs of toxicity, such as tinnitus or headache, occur. If these signs should appear, dosage should be reduced. However, tinnitus is not a reliable index of maximum salicylate tolerance, especially in very young or geriatric patients or those with impaired hearing.

For treatment of arthritis, dosage adjustments should not be made more frequently than once weekly, unless a reduction in dosage is required because of side effects, because up to 7 days may be required to achieve steady-state plasma concentrations.

The risk of Reye's syndrome must be considered when salicylates are administered to children and teenagers. It is recommended that salicylates be withheld from pediatric and adolescent patients with a fever or other symptoms of an illness that may predispose to Reye's syndrome until it has been determined that such an illness is not present or has run its course.

Dosage should be reduced if fever or illness causes fluid depletion, especially in children.

In general, it is recommended that aspirin therapy be discontinued 5 days before surgery to prevent possible occurrence of bleeding problems.

Patients who experience bronchospastic or cutaneous allergic reactions to aspirin may be desensitized to these effects by administration of initially small and gradually increasing doses of aspirin. *Desensitization must be carried out only by clinicians who are familiar with the technique, and only in a facility having trained personnel, medications, and equipment immediately available for treating any adverse reaction to the medication (especially anaphylaxis or severe bronchospasm).* This procedure also desensitizes the patient to other nonsteroidal anti-inflammatory drugs (NSAIDs). However, unless aspirin or another NSAID is then administered on a daily basis, sensitivity to these medications redevelops within a few days.

For oral dosage forms only

These medications (except enteric-coated formulations) should be administered after meals or with food to lessen gastric irritation.

It is recommended that tablet and capsule dosage forms of these medications always be administered with a full glass (240 mL) of water and that the patient remain in an upright position for 15 to 30 minutes after administration. These measures may reduce the risk of the medication becoming lodged in the esophagus, which has been reported to cause prolonged esophageal irritation and difficulty in swallowing in some patients receiving NSAIDs.

It is recommended that aspirin or buffered aspirin products not be chewed before swallowing for at least 7 days following tonsillectomy or oral surgery because of possible injury to oral tissues from prolonged contact with aspirin.

Aspirin or buffered aspirin tablets should not be placed directly on a tooth or gum surface because of possible injury to tissues.

Concurrent use of an antacid and/or a histamine (H_2)-receptor antagonist (cimetidine, famotidine, or ranitidine) may protect against salicylate-induced gastric irritation or ulceration. However, the fact that chronic, high-dose antacid use may alkalinize the urine and increase salicylate excretion must be considered. Also, because these medications may cause premature dissolution, and loss of the protective effect, of enteric coatings, they will not provide additive protection against gastric irritation when administered concurrently with enteric-coated dosage forms.

ASPIRIN

Summary of Differences

Category/indications:

Aspirin (tablets, chewable tablets, and delayed-release tablets) also indicated as a platelet aggregation inhibitor.

Pharmacology/pharmacokinetics:

Aspirin irreversibly inhibits platelet aggregation.

Precautions:

Cross-sensitivity and/or related problems—

Risk of cross-sensitivity with other nonsteroidal anti-inflammatory drugs (NSAIDs) significantly greater than with other salicylates.

Drug interactions and/or related problems—

May increase ascorbic acid requirement (prolonged high-dose use).

Theoretically, may decrease zidovudine clearance.

Higher risk of bleeding (compared with other salicylates) when used concurrently with other medications that may inhibit blood clotting or cause gastrointestinal ulceration or bleeding.

Laboratory value alterations—

Interferes with urine 5-hydroxyindoleacetic acid determinations.

Interferes with protirelin-induced thyroid-stimulating hormone release determinations.

Prolongs bleeding time.

Medical considerations/contraindications—

Should not be used in patients with a history of severe sensitivity reactions to aspirin, other NSAIDs, nasal polyps and asthma, or thrombocytopenia

Should be used with caution in patients with asthma or glucose-6-phosphate dehydrogenase (G6PD) deficiency.

Side/adverse effects:

More ulcerogenic than other salicylates.

Rarely, causes hemolytic anemia (in patients with G6PD deficiency).

Suppository dosage form may cause rectal bleeding.

Additional Dosing Information

See also *General Dosing Information.*

Salicylate toxicity requiring treatment generally occurs with doses of 200 mg per kg of body weight (mg/kg), especially in children.

The general doses for aspirin products other than aspirin chewing gum tablets are based on the FDA's dosing recommendations for aspirin. The dosage unit of 80 mg (1.23 grains) is used for pediatric doses; the dosage unit of 325 mg (5 grains) is used for adult doses. The conversion factor of 1 grain equal to 65 mg is used. Strengths of specific products may vary, depending on the manufacturer.

The extended-release tablet, the suppository, and the chewing gum tablet dosage forms may give incomplete or unreliable absorption.

Chewable aspirin tablets may be chewed, dissolved in liquid, or swallowed whole.

The delayed-release tablets must be swallowed whole.

Some extended-release tablets may be broken or crumbled but must not be ground up before swallowing. Others must be swallowed whole. Consult manufacturers" prescribing information for individual products.

Oral Dosage Forms

Note: Bracketed uses in the *Dosage Forms* section refer to categories of use and/or indications that are not included in U.S. product labeling.

ASPIRIN TABLETS USP

Usual adult and adolescent dose

Analgesic/antipyretic—

Oral, 325 to 500 mg every three hours, 325 to 650 mg every four hours, or 650 mg to 1000 mg every six hours as needed, while symptoms persist.

Note: For patient self-medication, it is recommended that the total daily dose not exceed 4 grams, and that a physician be consulted if pain is not relieved within ten days, fever within three days, or sore throat within two days.

Antirheumatic (nonsteroidal anti-inflammatory)—

Oral, 3.6 to 5.4 grams a day in divided doses.

Note: In acute rheumatic fever, up to 7.8 grams a day in divided doses may be given.

Platelet aggregation inhibitor—

Oral, 80 to 325 mg a day, with the following exceptions

Ischemic attacks, transient, in males or

[Thromboembolism, cerebral, recurrence][1]—

Oral, 1 gram a day. Dosage may be reduced to 325 mg a day if the patient is unable to tolerate the higher dose.

[Ischemic attacks, transient, occurring in association with mitral valve prolapse][1]—

Oral, 325 mg to 1 gram a day.

[Prevention of thrombosis or occlusion of coronary bypass graft]—

Oral, 325 mg seven hours postoperatively (via a nasogastric tube), then 325 mg three times daily, concurrently with 75 mg of dipyridamole. Dipyridamole may be discontinued one week postoperatively, but aspirin should be continued indefinitely.

Platelet aggregation inhibitor therapy is most effective when it is initiated two days prior to scheduled surgery. However, preoperative administration of aspirin has been shown to increase perisurgical bleeding and is not recommended. Therapy is therefore initiated with dipyridamole (recommended dosage 100 mg four times a day for two days prior to surgery and 100 mg one hour postoperatively [via a nasogastric tube]). Dipyridamole therapy is continued postoperatively (recommended dosage 75 mg seven hours postoperatively, via a nasogastric tube, then 75 mg three times a day, concurrently with aspirin) for at least one week.

Note: Although the doses recommended above for use of aspirin as a platelet aggregation inhibitor have been found effective in clinical studies, optimum dosage has not been established. For indications other than prevention of transient ischemic attacks or recurrence of cerebral thromboembolism, lower doses are often used. A few studies have shown that 160 mg of aspirin every twenty-four hours, or 325 mg every forty-eight hours, may effectively inhibit platelet aggregation while minimizing the risk of aspirin-induced side effects. Other studies have shown that single doses of 40 to 80 mg also inhibit platelet aggregation.

Usual pediatric dose

Analgesic/antipyretic—

Oral, 1.5 grams per square meter of body surface a day in four to six divided doses; or for

Children up to 2 years of age: Dosage must be individualized by physician.

Children 2 to 4 years of age: Oral, 160 mg every four hours as needed, while symptoms persist.

Children 4 to 6 years of age: Oral, 240 mg every four hours as needed, while symptoms persist.

Children 6 to 9 years of age: Oral, 320 to 325 mg every four hours as needed, while symptoms persist.

Children 9 to 11 years of age: Oral, 320 to 400 mg every four hours as needed, while symptoms persist.

Children 11 to 12 years of age: Oral, 320 to 480 mg every four hours as needed, while symptoms persist.

Note: It is recommended that children up to 12 years of age receive no more than five doses in each twenty-four-hour period, unless otherwise directed by a physician, and that a physician be consulted if pain is not relieved within five days, fever within three days, or sore throat within two days.

Antirheumatic (nonsteroidal anti-inflammatory)—

Oral, 80 to 100 mg per kg of body weight a day in divided doses.

Note: If an adequate response is not achieved within one or two weeks, dosage adjustment should be based on measurement of plasma salicylate concentration. Up to 130 mg per kg of body weight per day may be required in some patients.

[Kawasaki disease][1]—

During the early febrile stage: Oral, 80 to 120 mg (average 100 mg) per kg of body weight a day in four divided doses for fourteen days or until inflammation has subsided. However, absorption may be impaired or erratic during this stage of the illness, and considerably higher doses may be required. It is recommended that dosage be adjusted to achieve and maintain a plasma salicylate concentration of 20 to 30 mg per 100 mL.

During the convalescent stage: Oral, 3 to 5 mg per kg of body weight a day as a single dose. If no coronary artery abnormalities occur, treatment is usually continued for a minimum of eight weeks. If coronary artery abnormalities occur, it is recommended that treatment be continued for at least one year, even if the abnormalities regress, and longer if abnormalities persist.

Strength(s) usually available

U.S.—

81 mg (OTC) [*Aspir-Low; Healthprin Adult Low Strength* (scored); GENERIC].

162.5 mg (OTC) [*Healthprin Half-Dose* (scored)].

325 mg (OTC) [*Aspirtab; Empirin; Genuine Bayer Aspirin Caplets; Genuine Bayer Aspirin Tablets; Healthprin Full Strength* (scored); *Norwich Aspirin;* GENERIC].
500 mg (OTC) [*Aspirtab-Max; Extra Strength Bayer Aspirin Caplets; Extra Strength Bayer Aspirin Tablets; Norwich Aspirin;* GENERIC].
650 mg (OTC) [GENERIC].

Canada—
300 mg of ASA (OTC) [*Headache Tablet*].
325 mg of ASA (OTC) [*Apo-ASA; Aspirin Caplets; Aspirin Tablets; PMS-ASA;* GENERIC].
500 mg of ASA (OTC) [*Aspirin Caplets; Aspirin Tablets*].

Note: Strengths of specific products labeled in grains may vary, depending on the manufacturer.

Packaging and storage

Store below 40 °C (104 °F), preferably between 15 and 30 °C (59 and 86 °F), unless otherwise specified by manufacturer. Store in a tight container.

Auxiliary labeling

- Take with food and a full glass of water.

ASPIRIN TABLETS (CHEWABLE) USP

Usual adult and adolescent dose

See *Aspirin Tablets USP.*

Usual pediatric dose

See *Aspirin Tablets USP.*

Strength(s) usually available

U.S.—
81 mg (OTC) [*Bayer Children's Aspirin; St. Joseph Adult Chewable Aspirin;* GENERIC].

Canada—
80 mg of ASA (OTC) [*Aspirin Children's Tablets*].

Packaging and storage

Store below 40 °C (104 °F), preferably between 15 and 30 °C (59 and 86 °F), unless otherwise specified by manufacturer. Store in a tight container.

Auxiliary labeling

- May be chewed.
- Take with food and a full glass of water.

ASPIRIN CHEWING GUM TABLETS

Usual adult and adolescent dose

Analgesic—
Oral, 454 to 650 mg. May be repeated every four hours as needed.

Note: For patient self-medication, it is recommended that a physician be consulted if pain is not relieved within ten days or sore throat within two days.

Usual pediatric dose

Analgesic—
Children up to 3 years of age: Dosage must be individualized by physician.
Children 3 to 6 years of age: Oral, 227 mg. May be repeated up to three times a day.
Children 6 to 12 years of age: Oral, 227 to 454 mg. May be repeated up to four times a day.

Note: It is recommended that children up to 12 years of age receive no more than five doses in each twenty-four-hour period, unless otherwise directed by a physician, and that a physician be consulted if pain is not relieved within five days or sore throat within two days.

Strength(s) usually available

U.S.—
227 mg (OTC) [*Aspergum*].

Canada—
325 mg of ASA (OTC) [*Aspergum*].

Packaging and storage

Store below 40 °C (104 °F), preferably between 15 and 30 °C (59 and 86 °F), unless otherwise specified by manufacturer.

Auxiliary labeling

- To be chewed.
- Take with food.
- Drink a full glass of water after chewing.

ASPIRIN DELAYED-RELEASE TABLETS USP

Usual adult and adolescent dose

See *Aspirin Tablets USP.*

Usual pediatric dose

See *Aspirin Tablets USP.*

Strength(s) usually available

U.S.—
81 mg (OTC) [*Acuprin 81; Aspirin Regimen Bayer Adult Low Dose; Ecotrin Caplets; Ecotrin Tablets; Halfprin;* GENERIC].
162 mg (OTC) [*Halfprin*].
325 mg (OTC) [*Aspirin Regimen Bayer Regular Strength Caplets; Ecotrin Caplets; Ecotrin Tablets; Norwich Aspirin;* GENERIC].
500 mg (OTC) [*Ecotrin Caplets; Ecotrin Tablets; Extra Strength Bayer Arthritis Pain Formula Caplets; Maximum Strength Arthritis Foundation Safety Coated Aspirin; Norwich Aspirin;* GENERIC].
650 mg (OTC) [GENERIC].
975 mg (Rx) [*Easprin;* GENERIC].

Canada—
325 mg of ASA (OTC) [*Apo-ASEN; Aspirin, Coated; Astrin; Coryphen; Entrophen Caplets; Entrophen Tablets; Novasen; Novasen Sp.C;* GENERIC].
500 mg of ASA (OTC) [*Aspirin, Coated; Entrophen Extra Strength*].
650 mg of ASA (OTC) [*Apo-ASEN; Coryphen; Entrophen 10 Super Strength Caplets; Novasen; Novasen Sp.C;* GENERIC].
975 mg of ASA (OTC) [*Entrophen 15 Maximum Strength Tablets;* GENERIC].

Packaging and storage

Store below 40 °C (104 °F), preferably between 15 and 30 °C (59 and 86 °F), unless otherwise specified by manufacturer. Store in a tight container.

Auxiliary labeling

- Swallow tablets whole.
- Take with a full glass of water.

ASPIRIN EXTENDED-RELEASE TABLETS USP

Usual adult and adolescent dose

Analgesic—
Oral, 650 mg to 1.3 grams as 650-mg tablets every eight hours, or 1.6 grams as 800-mg tablets twice a day.

Note: The extended-release tablets have not been recommended by FDA for use as a platelet aggregation inhibitor.
For treatment of arthritis, the recommended analgesic dose may be administered initially, then adjusted according to patient requirements and response.

Usual pediatric dose

Pediatric strength not available.

Strength(s) usually available

U.S.—
650 mg (OTC) [*Extended-release Bayer 8-Hour* (scored)].
800 mg (Rx) [*Sloprin; ZORprin;* GENERIC].
975 mg (Rx) [GENERIC].

Canada—
325 mg of ASA (OTC) [*Arthrisin*].
650 mg of ASA (OTC) [*Arthrisin; Artria S.R*].

Packaging and storage

Store below 40 °C (104 °F), preferably between 15 and 30 °C (59 and 86 °F), unless otherwise specified by manufacturer. Store in a tight container.

Auxiliary labeling

- Take with food and a full glass of water.
- Swallow tablets whole (if specified by manufacturer).

ASPIRIN AND CAFFEINE CAPSULES

Usual adult and adolescent dose

See *Aspirin Tablets USP.* Dosage is based only on the aspirin component.

Usual pediatric dose

Analgesic/Antipyretic—
Children up to 6 years of age: Product of suitable strength not available.
Children 6 years of age and older: Oral, 325 mg every four hours as needed, while symptoms persist.

Note: It is recommended that children up to 12 years of age receive no more than five doses in each twenty-four-hour period, unless otherwise directed by a physician, and that a physician be consulted if pain is not relieved within five days, fever within three days, or sore throat within two days.

Antirheumatic (nonsteroidal anti-inflammatory)—
Oral, 80 to 100 mg per kg of body weight a day in divided doses.

Note: If an adequate response is not achieved within one or two weeks, dosage adjustment should be based on measurement of plasma salicylate concentration. Up to 130 mg per kg of body weight per day may be required in some patients.

Strength(s) usually available
U.S.—
Not commercially available.
Canada—
325 mg of ASA and 55 mg of caffeine (OTC) [*Astone*].

Packaging and storage
Store below 40 °C (104 °F), preferably between 15 and 30 °C (59 and 86 °F), in a well-closed container, unless otherwise specified by manufacturer.

Auxiliary labeling
- Take with food and a full glass of water.

ASPIRIN AND CAFFEINE TABLETS

Usual adult and adolescent dose
See *Aspirin Tablets USP*. Dosage is based only on the aspirin component.

Usual pediatric dose
Analgesic/Antipyretic—
Children up to 9 years of age: Product of suitable strength not available.
Children 9 years of age and older: Oral, 325 to 400 mg every four hours as needed, while symptoms persist.
Note: It is recommended that children up to 12 years of age receive no more than five doses in each twenty-four-hour period, unless otherwise directed by a physician, and that a physician be consulted if pain is not relieved within five days, fever within three days, or sore throat within two days.

Antirheumatic (nonsteroidal anti-inflammatory)—
Oral, 80 to 100 mg per kg of body weight a day in divided doses.
Note: If an adequate response is not achieved within one or two weeks, dosage adjustment should be based on measurement of plasma salicylate concentration. Up to 130 mg per kg of body weight per day may be required in some patients.

Strength(s) usually available
U.S.—
400 mg of aspirin and 32 mg of caffeine (OTC) [*Anacin Caplets; Anacin Tablets; Gensan; P-A-C Revised Formula*].
500 mg of aspirin and 32 mg of caffeine (OTC) [*Anacin Maximum Strength*].
Canada—
325 mg of ASA and 4 mg of caffeine [*Kalmex*].
325 mg of ASA and 15 mg of caffeine (OTC) [*C2* (double-scored)].
325 mg of ASA and 30 mg of caffeine citrate equivalent to 15 mg of caffeine base (OTC) [*Herbopyrine; 217* (scored)].
325 mg of ASA and 30 mg of caffeine (OTC) [*Nervine*].
325 mg of ASA and 32 mg of caffeine (OTC) [*Anacin*].
325 mg of ASA and 32.4 mg of caffeine (OTC) [*Antidol*].
325 mg of ASA and 33 mg of caffeine (OTC) [*Calmine; Dolomine*].
325 mg of ASA and 65 mg of caffeine (OTC) [*Instantine*].
375 mg of ASA and 30 mg of caffeine citrate equivalent to 15 mg of caffeine base [*Arco Pain Tablet*].
500 mg of ASA and 30 mg of caffeine citrate equivalent to 15 mg of caffeine base (OTC) [*217 Strong*].
500 mg of ASA and 32 mg of caffeine (OTC) [*Anacin Extra Strength; Pain Aid*].

Packaging and storage
Store below 40 °C (104 °F), preferably between 15 and 30 °C (59 and 86 °F), in a well-closed container, unless otherwise specified by manufacturer.

Auxiliary labeling
- Take with food and a full glass of water.

Rectal Dosage Forms

Note: Bracketed uses in the *Dosage Forms* section refer to categories of use and/or indications that are not included in U.S. product labeling.

ASPIRIN SUPPOSITORIES USP

Usual adult and adolescent dose
Analgesic/antipyretic—
Rectal, 325 to 650 mg every four hours as needed, while symptoms persist.
Note: For patient self-medication, it is recommended that the total daily dose not exceed 4 grams, and that a physician be consulted if pain is not relieved within ten days, fever within three days, or sore throat within two days.

Antirheumatic (nonsteroidal anti-inflammatory)—
Rectal, 3.6 to 5.4 grams a day in divided doses.
Note: In acute rheumatic fever, up to 7.8 grams a day in divided doses may be given.

Platelet aggregation inhibitor—
The suppositories have not been recommended by FDA for use as a platelet aggregation inhibitor.

Usual pediatric dose
Analgesic/antipyretic—
Rectal, 1.5 grams per square meter of body surface a day in four to six divided doses; or for
Children up to 2 years of age—Dosage must be individualized by physician.
Children 2 to 4 years of age—Rectal, 160 mg every four hours as needed, while symptoms persist.
Children 4 to 6 years of age—Rectal, 240 mg every four hours as needed, while symptoms persist.
Children 6 to 9 years of age—Rectal, 325 mg every four hours as needed, while symptoms persist.
Children 9 to 11 years of age—Rectal, 325 to 400 mg every four hours as needed, while symptoms persist.
Children 11 to 12 years of age—Rectal, 325 to 480 mg every four hours as needed, while symptoms persist.
Note: Do not exceed 2.5 grams per square meter of body surface per day. It is recommended that children up to 12 years of age receive no more than five doses in each twenty-four-hour period, unless otherwise directed by a physician, and that a physician be consulted if pain is not relieved within five days, fever within three days, or sore throat within two days.

Antirheumatic (nonsteroidal anti-inflammatory)—
Rectal, 80 to 100 mg per kg of body weight a day in divided doses.
Note: If an adequate response is not achieved within one or two weeks, dosage adjustment should be based on measurement of plasma salicylate concentration. Up to 130 mg per kg of body weight per day may be required in some patients.

[Kawasaki disease][1]—
During the early febrile stage: Rectal, 80 to 120 mg (average 100 mg) per kg of body weight a day in four divided doses for fourteen days or until inflammation has subsided. However, absorption may be impaired or erratic during this stage of the illness, and considerably higher doses may be required. It is recommended that dosage be adjusted to achieve and maintain a plasma salicylate concentration of 20 to 30 mg per 100 mL.
During the convalescent stage: Rectal, 3 to 5 mg per kg of body weight a day as a single dose. If no coronary artery abnormalities occur, treatment is usually continued for a minimum of eight weeks. If coronary artery abnormalities occur, it is recommended that treatment be continued for at least one year, even if the abnormalities regress, and longer if abnormalities persist.

Strength(s) usually available
U.S.—
60 mg (OTC) [GENERIC].
120 mg (OTC) [GENERIC].
125 mg (OTC) [GENERIC].
200 mg (OTC) [GENERIC].
300 mg (OTC) [GENERIC].
325 mg (OTC) [GENERIC].
600 mg (OTC) [GENERIC].
650 mg (OTC) [GENERIC].
1.2 grams (OTC) [GENERIC].
Canada—
150 mg of ASA (OTC) [*PMS-ASA;* GENERIC].
650 mg of ASA (OTC) [*PMS-ASA;* GENERIC].
Note: The strengths of the specific products may not conform to the recommended pediatric doses. Also, the strengths of some products labeled in grains may vary, depending on the manufacturer.

Packaging and storage
Store between 8 and 15 °C (46 and 59 °F), unless otherwise specified by manufacturer. Store in a well-closed container, in a cool place.

Auxiliary labeling
- Store in a cool place. May be refrigerated.
- For rectal use only.

[1]Not included in Canadian product labeling.

ASPIRIN, BUFFERED

Summary of Differences

Category/indications:
Aspirin, buffered, also indicated as a platelet aggregation inhibitor.

Pharmacology/pharmacokinetics:
Aspirin irreversibly inhibits platelet aggregation.

Precautions:
Cross-sensitivity and/or related problems—
Risk of cross-sensitivity with other nonsteroidal anti-inflammatory drugs (NSAIDs) significantly greater with aspirin than with other salicylates.

Drug interactions and/or related problems—
Aspirin may increase ascorbic acid requirement (prolonged high-dose use).
Theoretically, aspirin may decrease zidovudine clearance.
Higher risk of bleeding (compared with other salicylates) when aspirin is used concurrently with other medications that may inhibit blood clotting or cause gastrointestinal ulceration or bleeding.
Antacids present as buffering agents may decrease absorption of fluoroquinolone antibiotics, itraconazole, ketoconazole, and oral tetracyclines.

Laboratory value alterations—
Aspirin interferes with urine 5-hydroxyindoleacetic acid determinations.
Aspirin interferes with protirelin-induced thyroid stimulating hormone release determinations.
Aspirin prolongs bleeding time.

Medical considerations/contraindications—
Aspirin should not be used in patients with a history of severe sensitivity reactions to aspirin, other NSAIDs, nasal polyps and asthma, or thrombocytopenia.
Aspirin should be used with caution in patients with asthma or glucose-6-phosphate dehydrogenase (G6PD) deficiency.

Side/adverse effects:
Aspirin is more ulcerogenic than other salicylates.
Rarely, aspirin causes hemolytic anemia (in patients with G6PD deficiency).

Additional Dosing Information

See also *General Dosing Information.*

The doses for buffered aspirin formulations are based on the FDA's dosing recommendations for aspirin. The dosage unit of 325 mg (5 grains) is used. The conversion factor of 1 grain equal to 65 mg is used. Strengths of specific products may vary, depending on the manufacturer.

The amount and type of buffering may vary among products.

Oral Dosage Forms

Note: Bracketed uses in the *Dosage Forms* section refer to categories of use and/or indications that are not included in U.S. product labeling.

ASPIRIN, ALUMINA, AND MAGNESIA TABLETS USP

Usual adult and adolescent dose

Analgesic/antipyretic—
Oral, 500 mg every three or four hours or 1000 mg every six hours as needed, while symptoms persist.
Note: For patient self-medication, it is recommended that the total daily dose not exceed 4 grams, and that a physician be consulted if pain is not relieved within ten days, fever within three days, or sore throat within two days.

Antirheumatic (nonsteroidal anti-inflammatory)—
Oral, 3.6 to 5.4 grams a day in divided doses.
Note: In acute rheumatic fever, up to 7.8 grams a day in divided doses may be given.

Platelet aggregation inhibitor—
Oral, 325 mg a day, with the following exceptions:
Ischemic attacks, transient, in males or—
[Thromboembolism, cerebral, recurrence][1]—
Oral, 1 gram a day. Dosage may be reduced to 325 mg a day if the patient is unable to tolerate the higher dose.
[Ischemic attacks, transient, occurring in association with mitral valve prolapse][1]—
Oral, 325 mg to 1 gram a day.
[Prevention of thrombosis or occlusion of coronary bypass graft]—
Oral, 325 mg seven hours postoperatively (via a nasogastric tube), then 325 mg three times daily, concurrently with 75 mg of dipyridamole. Dipyridamole may be discontinued one week postoperatively, but aspirin should be continued indefinitely.
Platelet aggregation inhibitor therapy is most effective when it is initiated two days prior to scheduled surgery. However, preoperative administration of aspirin has been shown to increase perisurgical bleeding and is not recommended. Therapy is therefore initiated with dipyridamole (recommended dosage 100 mg four times a day for two days prior to surgery and 100 mg one hour postoperatively [via a nasogastric tube]). Dipyridamole therapy is continued postoperatively (recommended dosage 75 mg seven hours postoperatively, via a nasogastric tube, then 75 mg three times a day, concurrently with aspirin) for at least one week.

Note: Although the doses recommended above for use of aspirin as a platelet aggregation inhibitor have been found effective in clinical studies, optimum dosage has not been established. For indications other than prevention of transient ischemic attacks or recurrence of cerebral thromboembolism, lower doses are often used. A few studies have shown that 160 mg of aspirin every twenty-four hours, or 325 mg every forty-eight hours, may effectively inhibit platelet aggregation while minimizing the risk of aspirin-induced side effects.
For most antithrombotic indications, lower doses than can be achieved with the aspirin, alumina, and magnesia formulation are used. However, this formulation may be used when 500-mg or 1-gram doses are appropriate.

Usual pediatric dose

Analgesic/antipyretic—
Product of suitable strength not available.

Antirheumatic (nonsteroidal anti-inflammatory)—
Oral, 80 to 100 mg per kg of body weight a day in divided doses.
Note: If an adequate response is not achieved within one or two weeks, dosage adjustment should be based on measurement of plasma salicylate concentration. Up to 130 mg per kg of body weight per day may be required in some patients.

[Kawasaki disease][1]—
During the early febrile stage: Oral, 80 to 120 mg (average 100 mg) per kg of body weight a day in four divided doses for fourteen days or until inflammation has subsided. However, absorption may be impaired or erratic during this stage of the illness, and considerably higher doses may be required. It is recommended that dosage be adjusted to achieve and maintain a plasma salicylate concentration of 20 to 30 mg per 100 mL.
During the convalescent stage: Oral, 3 to 5 mg per kg of body weight a day as a single dose. If no coronary artery abnormalities occur, treatment is usually continued for a minimum of eight weeks. If coronary artery abnormalities occur, it is recommended that treatment be continued for at least one year, even if the abnormalities regress, and longer if abnormalities persist.

Strength(s) usually available

U.S.—
500 mg of aspirin, with 27 mg of aluminum hydroxide and 100 mg of magnesium hydroxide (OTC) [*Arthritis Pain Formula*].

Canada—
Not commercially available.

Packaging and storage

Store below 40 °C (104 °F), preferably between 15 and 30 °C (59 and 86 °F), unless otherwise specified by manufacturer. Store in a tight container.

Auxiliary labeling

- Take with food and a full glass of water.

ASPIRIN, ALUMINA, AND MAGNESIUM OXIDE TABLETS USP

Usual adult and adolescent dose

Analgesic/antipyretic or
Antirheumatic (nonsteroidal anti-inflammatory)—
See *Aspirin, Alumina, and Magnesia Tablets USP.* Dosage is based only on the aspirin component.

Platelet aggregation inhibitor—
See *Aspirin, Alumina, and Magnesia Tablets USP.* Dosage is based only on the aspirin component. For most antithrombotic indications, lower doses than can be achieved with the aspirin, alumina, and magnesium oxide formulation are used. However, this formulation may be used when 500-mg or 1-gram doses are appropriate.

Usual pediatric dose

See *Aspirin, Alumina, and Magnesia Tablets USP.* Dosage is based only on the aspirin component.

Strength(s) usually available

U.S.—

500 mg of aspirin, with dried aluminum hydroxide gel equivalent to 125 mg of aluminum hydroxide and 150 mg of magnesium oxide (OTC) [*Cama Arthritis Pain Reliever*].

Canada—

Not commercially available.

Packaging and storage

Store below 40 °C (104 °F), preferably between 15 and 30 °C (59 and 86 °F), unless otherwise specified by manufacturer. Store in a tight container.

Auxiliary labeling

• Take with food and a full glass of water.

BUFFERED ASPIRIN TABLETS USP

Usual adult and adolescent dose

Analgesic/antipyretic—

Oral, 325 to 500 mg every three hours, 325 to 650 mg every four hours, or 650 mg to 1000 mg every six hours as needed, while symptoms persist.

Note: For patient self-medication, it is recommended that the total daily dose not exceed 4 grams, and that a physician be consulted if pain is not relieved within ten days, fever within three days, or sore throat within two days.

Platelet aggregation inhibitor—

See *Aspirin, Alumina, and Magnesia Tablets USP*.

Usual pediatric dose

Analgesic/antipyretic—

Oral, 1.5 grams of aspirin per square meter of body surface a day in four to six divided doses; or for

Children up to 2 years of age: Dosage must be individualized by physician.

Children 2 to 4 years of age: Oral, ½ of a 325-mg tablet every four hours as needed, while symptoms persist.

Children 4 to 6 years of age: Oral, ¾ of a 325-mg tablet every four hours as needed, while symptoms persist.

Children 6 to 9 years of age: Oral, 1 tablet (325 mg) every four hours as needed, while symptoms persist.

Children 9 to 11 years of age: Oral, 1 to 1¼ tablets (325 mg each) every four hours as needed, while symptoms persist.

Children 11 to 12 years of age: Oral, 1 to 1½ tablets (325 mg each) every four hours as needed, while symptoms persist.

Note: It is recommended that children up to 12 years of age receive no more than five doses in each twenty-four-hour period, unless otherwise directed by a physician, and that a physician be consulted if pain is not relieved within five days, fever within three days, or sore throat within two days.

Antirheumatic (nonsteroidal anti-inflammatory)—

Oral, 80 to 100 mg of aspirin per kg of body weight a day in divided doses.

Note: If an adequate response is not achieved within one or two weeks, dosage adjustment should be based on measurement of plasma salicylate concentration. Up to 130 mg per kg of body weight of aspirin per day may be required in some patients.

[Kawasaki disease][1]—

During the early febrile stage: Oral, 80 to 120 mg (average 100 mg) per kg of body weight a day in four divided doses for fourteen days or until inflammation has subsided. However, absorption may be impaired or erratic during this stage of the illness, and considerably higher doses may be required. It is recommended that dosage be adjusted to achieve and maintain a plasma salicylate concentration of 20 to 30 mg per 100 mL.

During the convalescent stage: Oral, 3 to 5 mg per kg of body weight a day as a single dose. If no coronary artery abnormalities occur, treatment is usually continued for a minimum of eight weeks. If coronary artery abnormalities occur, it is recommended that treatment be continued for at least one year, even if the abnormalities regress, and longer if abnormalities persist.

Strength(s) usually available

U.S.—

325 mg of aspirin (OTC) [*Arthritis Pain Ascriptin; Bufferin Caplets; Bufferin Tablets; Buffex; Buffinol; Magnaprin; Regular Strength Ascriptin;* GENERIC].

500 mg of aspirin (OTC) [*Arthritis Strength Bufferin; Buffinol Extra; Extra Strength Bayer Plus Caplets; Maximum Strength Ascriptin*].

Canada—

325 mg of ASA (OTC) [*Aspirin Plus Stomach Guard Regular Strength; Bufferin Caplets; Tri-Buffered ASA;* GENERIC].

500 mg of ASA (OTC) [*Aspirin Plus Stomach Guard Extra Strength; Bufferin Extra Strength Caplets;* GENERIC].

Note: See individual product label for buffering agent(s).

The strengths of the specific products may not conform to the recommended pediatric doses.

Packaging and storage

Store below 40 °C (104 °F), preferably between 15 and 30 °C (59 and 86 °F), unless otherwise specified by manufacturer. Store in a tight container.

Auxiliary labeling

• Take with food and a full glass of water.

BUFFERED ASPIRIN AND CAFFEINE TABLETS

Usual adult and adolescent dose

See *Buffered Aspirin Tablets USP*. Dosage is based only on the aspirin component.

Usual pediatric dose

Analgesic/antipyretic—

Oral, 1.5 grams of aspirin per square meter of body surface a day in four to six divided doses; or for

Children up to 2 years of age: Dosage must be individualized by physician.

Children 2 to 4 years of age: Oral, ½ of a 325-mg tablet every four hours as needed, while symptoms persist.

Children 4 to 6 years of age: Oral, ¾ of a 325-mg tablet every four hours as needed, while symptoms persist.

Children 6 to 9 years of age: Oral, 1 tablet (325 mg) every four hours as needed, while symptoms persist.

Children 9 to 11 years of age: Oral, 1 to 1¼ tablets (325 mg each) every four hours as needed, while symptoms persist.

Children 11 to 12 years of age: Oral, 1 to 1½ tablets (325 mg each) or 1 tablet (421 mg) every four hours as needed, while symptoms persist.

Note: It is recommended that children up to 12 years of age receive no more than five doses in each twenty-four-hour period, unless otherwise directed by a physician, and that a physician be consulted if pain is not relieved within five days, fever within three days, or sore throat within two days.

Antirheumatic (nonsteroidal anti-inflammatory)—

Oral, 80 to 100 mg of aspirin per kg of body weight a day in divided doses.

Note: If an adequate response is not achieved within one or two weeks, dosage adjustment should be based on measurement of plasma salicylate concentration. Up to 130 mg per kg of body weight of aspirin per day may be required in some patients.

Strength(s) usually available

U.S.—

421 mg of aspirin and 32 mg of caffeine (OTC) [*Cope*].

Canada—

325 mg of ASA and 15 mg of caffeine (OTC) [*C2 Buffered* (scored)].

Note: See individual product label for buffering agent(s).

The strengths of the specific products may not conform to the recommended pediatric doses.

Packaging and storage

Store below 40 °C (104 °F), preferably between 15 and 30 °C (59 and 86 °F), unless otherwise specified by manufacturer. Store in a tight container.

Auxiliary labeling

• Take with food and a full glass of water.

---

[1]Not included in Canadian product labeling.

CHOLINE SALICYLATE

Summary of Differences

Pharmacology/pharmacokinetics:

Choline salicylate does not have a clinically significant effect on platelet aggregation.

Precautions:

Cross-sensitivity and/or related problems—Lower risk than with aspirin of cross-sensitivity to nonsteroidal anti-inflammatory drugs (NSAIDs).

Drug interactions and/or related problems—Lower risk of bleeding (compared with aspirin) when used concurrently with other medications that may inhibit blood clotting or cause gastrointestinal ulceration or bleeding.

Medical considerations/contraindications—May be used in patients with a history of severe sensitivity reactions to aspirin or other NSAIDs, although caution is advised.

Side/adverse effects:

Less ulcerogenic than aspirin.

Additional Dosing Information

See also *General Dosing Information.*

The nonarthritic doses are based on the FDA's dosing recommendations for aspirin.

A 435-mg dose of choline salicylate is equivalent in salicylate content to 325 mg of aspirin.

Oral Dosage Forms

CHOLINE SALICYLATE ORAL SOLUTION

Usual adult and adolescent dose

Analgesic/antipyretic—

Oral, 435 to 669 mg (equivalent in salicylate content to 325 to 500 mg of aspirin) every three hours, 435 to 870 mg (equivalent in salicylate content to 325 to 650 mg of aspirin) every four hours, or 870 to 1338 mg (equivalent in salicylate content to 650 to 1000 mg of aspirin) every six hours as needed, while symptoms persist.

Note: For patient self-medication, it is recommended that the total daily dose not exceed 5352 mg, and that a physician be consulted if pain is not relieved within ten days, fever within three days, or sore throat within two days.

Antirheumatic (nonsteroidal anti-inflammatory)—

Oral, 4.8 to 7.2 grams (equivalent in salicylate content to 3.6 to 5.4 grams of aspirin) a day in divided doses.

Usual pediatric dose

Analgesic/antipyretic—

Oral, 2 grams (equivalent in salicylate content to 1.5 grams of aspirin) per square meter of body surface a day in four to six divided doses; or for

Children up to 2 years of age: Dosage must be individualized by physician.

Children 2 to 4 years of age: Oral, 217.5 mg (equivalent in salicylate content to 162.5 mg of aspirin) every four hours as needed, while symptoms persist.

Children 4 to 6 years of age: Oral, 326.5 mg (equivalent in salicylate content to 243.8 mg of aspirin) every four hours as needed, while symptoms persist.

Children 6 to 9 years of age: Oral, 435 mg (equivalent in salicylate content to 325 mg of aspirin) every four hours as needed, while symptoms persist.

Children 9 to 11 years of age: Oral, 435 to 543.8 mg (equivalent in salicylate content to 325 to 406.3 mg of aspirin) every four hours as needed, while symptoms persist.

Children 11 to 12 years of age: Oral, 435 to 652.5 mg (equivalent in salicylate content to 325 to 487.5 mg of aspirin) every four hours as needed, while symptoms persist.

Note: It is recommended that children up to 12 years of age receive no more than five doses in each twenty-four-hour period, unless otherwise directed by a physician, and that a physician be consulted if pain is not relieved within five days, fever within three days, or sore throat within two days.

Antirheumatic (nonsteroidal anti-inflammatory)—

Oral, 107 to 133 mg (equivalent in salicylate content to 80 to 100 mg of aspirin) per kg of body weight a day in divided doses.

Note: If an adequate response is not achieved within one or two weeks, dosage adjustment should be based on measurement of plasma salicylate concentration. Up to 174 mg (equivalent in salicylate content to 130 mg of aspirin) per kg of body weight per day may be required in some patients.

Strength(s) usually available

U.S.—

870 mg (equivalent in salicylate content to 650 mg of aspirin) per 5 mL (OTC) [*Arthropan*].

Canada—

Not commercially available.

Packaging and storage

Store below 40 °C (104 °F), preferably between 15 and 30 °C (59 and 86 °F), in a well-closed container, unless otherwise specified by manufacturer. Protect from freezing.

Auxiliary labeling

• Take with food or a full glass of water.

CHOLINE AND MAGNESIUM SALICYLATES

Summary of Differences

Pharmacology/pharmacokinetics:

This medication does not have a clinically significant effect on platelet aggregation.

Precautions:

Cross-sensitivity and/or related problems—

Lower risk than with aspirin of cross-sensitivity to nonsteroidal anti-inflammatory drugs (NSAIDs).

Drug interactions and/or related problems—

Lower risk of bleeding (compared with aspirin) when used concurrently with other medications that may inhibit blood clotting or cause gastrointestinal ulceration or bleeding.

Magnesium may decrease absorption of fluoroquinolone antibiotics, itraconazole, ketoconazole, and oral tetracyclines.

Medical considerations/contraindications—

Should not be used in patients with chronic advanced renal impairment because of risk of hypermagnesemic toxicity.

May be used in patients with a history of severe sensitivity reactions to aspirin or other NSAIDs, although caution is advised.

Patient monitoring—

Monitoring of serum magnesium concentration recommended if large doses administered to patients with renal insufficiency.

Side/adverse effects:

Less ulcerogenic than aspirin.

Additional Dosing Information

See also *General Dosing Information.*

Choline and magnesium salicylates oral solution may be mixed with fruit juices just prior to administration.

Oral Dosage Forms

CHOLINE AND MAGNESIUM SALICYLATES ORAL SOLUTION

Usual adult and adolescent dose

Analgesic or

Antipyretic—

Oral, 2 to 3 grams of salicylate a day in two or three divided doses.

Anti-inflammatory (nonsteroidal) or

Antirheumatic—

Oral, 3 grams of salicylate a day in a single dose at bedtime, or in two or three divided doses, initially. Dosage must then be adjusted according to the requirements and response of the individual patient.

Usual pediatric dose

Analgesic

Antipyretic or

Anti-inflammatory (nonsteroidal)—

Children weighing up to 37 kg: Oral, 50 mg of salicylate per kg of body weight per day in two divided doses.

Children weighing more than 37 kg: Oral, 2.2 grams of salicylate a day in two divided doses.

Strength(s) usually available

U.S.—

500 mg of salicylate (contains 293 mg of choline salicylate and 362 mg of magnesium salicylate) per 5 mL. (Rx) [*Trilisate*].

Note: Each 5-mL dose of this medication is equivalent in salicylate content to 650 mg of aspirin.

Canada—

Not commercially available.

Packaging and storage

Store below 40 °C (104 °F), preferably between 15 and 30 °C (59 and 86 °F), unless otherwise specified by manufacturer. Protect from freezing.

Auxiliary labeling

• Take with food or a full glass of water.

CHOLINE AND MAGNESIUM SALICYLATES TABLETS

Usual adult and adolescent dose

See *Choline and Magnesium Salicylates Oral Solution.*

Usual pediatric dose
See *Choline and Magnesium Salicylates Oral Solution.*

Strength(s) usually available
U.S.—
500 mg of salicylate (contains 293 mg of choline salicylate and 362 mg of magnesium salicylate) (Rx) [*CMT; Tricosal; Trilisate* (scored); GENERIC].
750 mg of salicylate (contains 440 mg of choline salicylate and 544 mg of magnesium salicylate) (Rx) [*CMT; Tricosal; Trilisate* (scored); GENERIC].
1000 mg of salicylate (contains 587 mg of choline salicylate and 725 mg of magnesium salicylate) (Rx) [*CMT; Tricosal; Trilisate* (scored); GENERIC].
Canada—
500 mg of salicylate (contains 293 mg of choline salicylate and 362 mg of magnesium salicylate) (Rx) [*Trilisate* (scored)].

Note: Each 500-mg tablet is equivalent in salicylate content to 650 mg of aspirin. Each 750-mg tablet is equivalent in salicylate content to 975 mg of aspirin. Each 1000-mg tablet is equivalent in salicylate content to 1.3 grams of aspirin.

Packaging and storage
Store below 40 °C (104 °F), preferably between 15 and 30 °C (59 and 86 °F), in a well-closed container, unless otherwise specified by manufacturer.

Auxiliary labeling
- Take with food and a full glass of water.

MAGNESIUM SALICYLATE

Summary of Differences

Pharmacology/pharmacokinetics:
Magnesium salicylate does not have a clinically significant effect on platelet aggregation.
Precautions:
Cross-sensitivity and/or related problems—
Lower risk than with aspirin of cross-sensitivity to nonsteroidal anti-inflammatory drugs (NSAIDs).
Drug interactions and/or related problems—
Lower risk of bleeding (compared with aspirin) when used concurrently with other medications that may inhibit blood clotting or cause gastrointestinal ulceration or bleeding.
Magnesium may decrease absorption of fluoroquinolone antibiotics, itraconazole, ketoconazole, and oral tetracyclines.
Medical considerations/contraindications—
Should not be used in patients with chronic advanced renal impairment.
May be used in patients with a history of severe sensitivity reactions to aspirin or other NSAIDs, although caution is advised.
Patient monitoring—
Monitoring of serum magnesium concentration recommended if large doses are administered to patients with renal insufficiency.
Side/adverse effects:
Less ulcerogenic than aspirin.

Additional Dosing Information

See also *General Dosing Information.*

A 545-mg dose of magnesium salicylate is equivalent in salicylate content to 650 mg of aspirin.

Oral Dosage Forms

MAGNESIUM SALICYLATE TABLETS USP

Usual adult and adolescent dose
Analgesic/antipyretic
Antirheumatic (nonsteroidal anti-inflammatory)—
Oral, 2 regular-strength tablets (containing the equivalent of 303.7 mg of anhydrous magnesium salicylate per tablet) every four hours as needed, up to a maximum of 12 tablets a day, or
Oral, 2 extra-strength tablets (containing the equivalent of 467 mg of anhydrous magnesium salicylate, or more, per tablet) every six hours as needed, up to a maximum of 8 tablets a day.

Note: For patient self-medication, it is recommended that a physician be consulted if pain is not relieved within ten days, fever within three days, or sore throat within two days.

Usual pediatric dose
Dosage has not been established.

Strength(s) usually available
U.S.—
377 mg of magnesium salicylate tetrahydrate equivalent to 303.7 mg of anhydrous magnesium salicylate (OTC) [*Doan's Regular Strength Tablets*].
545 mg (Rx) [*Magan*].
580 mg of magnesium salicylate tetrahydrate equivalent to 467 mg of anhydrous magnesium salicylate (OTC) [*Backache Caplets; Bayer Select Maximum Strength Backache Pain Relief Formula; Maximum Strength Doan's Analgesic Caplets*].
600 mg (Rx) [*Mobidin* (scored)].
Canada—
325 mg (OTC) [*Doan's Backache Pills*].
650 mg (OTC) [*Sero-Gesic*].

Packaging and storage
Store below 40 °C (104 °F), preferably between 15 and 30 °C (59 and 86 °F), unless otherwise specified by manufacturer. Store in a tight container.

Auxiliary labeling
- Take with food and a full glass of water.

SALSALATE

Summary of Differences

Pharmacology/pharmacokinetics:
Salsalate does not have a clinically significant effect on platelet aggregation.
Precautions:
Cross-sensitivity and/or related problems—Lower risk than with aspirin of cross-sensitivity to nonsteroidal anti-inflammatory drugs (NSAIDs).
Drug interactions and/or related problems—Lower risk of bleeding (compared with aspirin) when used concurrently with other medications that may inhibit blood clotting or cause gastrointestinal ulceration or bleeding.
Medical considerations/contraindications—May be used in patients with a history of severe sensitivity reactions to aspirin or other NSAIDs, although caution is advised.
Side/adverse effects:
Less ulcerogenic than aspirin.

Additional Dosing Information

Bioequivalence information
Bioavailability or bioequivalence problems among different brands of Salsalate Tablets USP have not been documented.

Oral Dosage Forms

SALSALATE CAPSULES USP

Usual adult and adolescent dose
Antirheumatic—
Oral, 1 gram three times a day initially. Dosage may then be titrated according to patient response.

Usual pediatric dose
Dosage has not been established.

Strength(s) usually available
U.S.—
500 mg (Rx) [*Disalcid;* GENERIC].
750 mg (Rx) [GENERIC].
Canada—
Not commercially available.

Packaging and storage
Store between 15 and 30 °C (59 and 86 °F), in a light-resistant container, unless otherwise specified by manufacturer. Store in a tight container.

Auxiliary labeling
- Take with food and a full glass of water.

SALSALATE TABLETS USP

Note: Bioavailability or bioequivalence problems among different brands of Salsalate Tablets USP have not been documented.

Usual adult and adolescent dose
Analgesic/antipyretic or
Antirheumatic—
Oral, 500 mg to 1 gram two or three times a day initially. Dosage may then be titrated according to patient response.

Usual pediatric dose
Dosage has not been established.

Strength(s) usually available
U.S.—
500 mg (Rx) [*Amigesic; Disalcid* (scored); *Mono-Gesic; Salflex; Salsitab;* GENERIC].
750 mg (Rx) [*Amigesic* (scored); *Anaflex 750; Disalcid* (scored); *Marthritic; Mono-Gesic* (scored); *Salflex* (scored); *Salsitab* (scored); GENERIC].
Canada—
500 mg (Rx) [*Disalcid* (scored)].
750 mg (Rx) [*Disalcid* (scored)].

Packaging and storage
Store between 15 and 30 °C (59 and 86 °F), in a light-resistant container, unless otherwise specified by manufacturer. Store in a tight container.

Auxiliary labeling
- Take with food and a full glass of water.

SODIUM SALICYLATE

Summary of Differences

Pharmacology/pharmacokinetics:
Sodium salicylate does not have a clinically significant effect on platelet aggregation.
Precautions:
Cross-sensitivity and/or related problems—
Lower risk than with aspirin of cross-sensitivity to nonsteroidal anti-inflammatory drugs (NSAIDs).
Drug interactions and/or related problems—
Caution required when large doses administered concurrently with sodium-retaining medications.
Lower risk of bleeding (compared with aspirin) when used concurrently with other medications that may inhibit blood clotting or cause gastrointestinal ulceration or bleeding.
Medical considerations/contraindications—
Caution required in hypertensive patients or those on a sodium-restricted diet because of sodium content.
May be used in patients with a history of severe sensitivity reactions to aspirin or other NSAIDs, although caution is advised.
Side/adverse effects:
Less ulcerogenic than aspirin.

Additional Dosing Information

See also *General Dosing Information.*

The nonarthritic doses are based on the FDA's dosing recommendations for sodium salicylate. The dosage unit of 325 mg (5 grains) is used for adult doses. The conversion factor of 65 mg equal to 1 grain is used. Strengths of specific products may vary, depending on the manufacturer.

The uncoated tablet form of sodium salicylate should be administered with food or a full glass (240 mL) of water to lessen gastric irritation.

Each 325-mg tablet of sodium salicylate contains 2 mEq (46 mg) of sodium.

Oral Dosage Forms

SODIUM SALICYLATE TABLETS USP

Usual adult and adolescent dose
Analgesic/antipyretic—
Oral, 325 to 650 mg every four hours as needed, while symptoms persist.
Note: For patient self-medication, it is recommended that the total daily dose not exceed 4 grams, and that a physician be consulted if pain is not relieved within ten days, fever within three days, or sore throat within two days.
Antirheumatic (nonsteroidal anti-inflammatory)—
Oral, 3.6 to 5.4 grams a day in divided doses.

Usual pediatric dose
Analgesic/antipyretic—
Oral, 1.5 grams per square meter of body surface a day in four to six divided doses; or for
Children up to 6 years of age: Product of suitable strength not available.
Children 6 years of age and older: Oral, 325 mg every four hours as needed, while symptoms persist.
Note: It is recommended that children up to 12 years of age receive no more than five doses in each twenty-four-hour period, unless otherwise directed by a physician, and that a physician be consulted if pain is not relieved within five days, fever within three days, or sore throat within two days.
Antirheumatic (nonsteroidal anti-inflammatory)—
Oral, 80 to 100 mg per kg of body weight a day in divided doses.
Note: If an adequate response is not achieved within one or two weeks, dosage adjustment should be based on measurement of plasma salicylate concentration. Up to 130 mg per kg of body weight per day may be required in some patients.

Strength(s) usually available
U.S.—
Not commercially available.
Canada—
325 mg (OTC) [*Dodd's Pills; Gin Pain Pills*].
500 mg [*Dodd's Extra Strength*].
Note: The strengths of the specific products may not conform to the recommended pediatric dose. Also, the strengths of individual products labeled in grains may vary, depending on the manufacturer.

Packaging and storage
Store below 40 °C (104 °F), preferably between 15 and 30 °C (59 and 86 °F), unless otherwise specified by manufacturer. Store in a well-closed container.

Auxiliary labeling
- Take with food and a full glass of water.

SODIUM SALICYLATE DELAYED-RELEASE TABLETS

Usual adult and adolescent dose
See *Sodium Salicylate Tablets USP.*

Usual pediatric dose
See *Sodium Salicylate Tablets USP.*

Strength(s) usually available
U.S.—
325 mg (OTC) [GENERIC].
650 mg (OTC) [GENERIC].
Canada—
Not commercially available.
Note: Strengths of individual products labeled in grains may vary, depending on the manufacturer.

Packaging and storage
Store between 15 and 30 °C (59 and 86 °F), in a well-closed container, unless otherwise specified by manufacturer.

Auxiliary labeling
- Swallow tablets whole.
- Take with a full glass of water.

Revised: 08/04/2005

SALMETEROL—See *Bronchodilators, Adrenergic (Inhalation-Local)*

SALSALATE—See *Salicylates (Systemic)*

SAQUINAVIR Systemic

VA CLASSIFICATION (Primary): AM830

Commonly used brand name(s): *Fortovase; Invirase.*

Another commonly used name is SQV

Note: For a listing of dosage forms and brand names by country availability, see *Dosage Forms* section(s).

Category

Antiviral (systemic).

Indications

General Considerations

Saquinavir is a human immunodeficiency virus (HIV) protease inhibitor. Cross-resistance between saquinavir (following prolonged [24 to 127 weeks] treatment with saquinavir mesylate capsules) and other HIV protease inhibitors, such as indinavir, nelfinavir, and ritonavir, has been observed in clinical isolates. However, cross-resistance between saquinavir and reverse transcriptase inhibitors is thought to be unlikely because they affect different parts of HIV replication.

The key mutations conferring viral resistance to saquinavir are at codons L90M and G48V. In clinical isolates from patients treated with either saquinavir mesylate capsules or saquinavir soft gelatin capsules, the L90M mutation predominated. Although the mutations in HIV protease characterizing resistance to saquinavir differ from those seen in patients treated with indinavir, nelfinavir, or ritonavir, additional mutations may occur during long-term treatment. The mutations may lead to resistance to other protease inhibitors.

Accepted

Human immunodeficiency virus (HIV) infection (treatment)—Saquinavir, in combination with other antiretroviral agents, is indicated in the treatment of HIV infection.

Note: Saquinavir mesylate is indicated in combination with ritonavir and other antiretroviral agents for the treatment of HIV infection.

Invirase must be combined with ritonavir (and other antiretrovirals).

Fortovase may be used with or without ritonavir (and other antiretrovirals).

Pharmacology/Pharmacokinetics

Note: Two capsule formulations of saquinavir currently are available: saquinavir mesylate capsules (*Invirase*) and saquinavir soft gelatin capsules (*Fortovase*). Unless otherwise indicated, the information provided in this monograph refers to both capsule formulations of saquinavir. Saquinavir is the active ingredient in both products.

Physicochemical characteristics

Molecular weight—
Saquinavir base: 670.86.
Saquinavir mesylate: 766.96.

Mechanism of action/Effect

Saquinavir inhibits the activity of human immunodeficiency virus (HIV) protease. HIV protease cleaves viral polyprotein precursors in HIV-infected cells to generate functional proteins that are essential for maturation of the virus. Inhibition of HIV protease results in the production of immature, noninfectious virus particles.

Absorption

Saquinavir mesylate capsules (*Invirase*)—

Absolute bioavailability averaged 4% (range, 1 to 9%) in healthy volunteers who received a single 600-mg dose following a high-fat meal; low bioavailability was thought to be due to incomplete absorption and extensive first-pass metabolism. The area under the plasma concentration-time curve (AUC) and peak plasma concentration (C_{max}) values were 2.5 times higher in HIV-infected patients following multiple dosing than after a single dose. HIV-infected patients had AUC and C_{max} values that were approximately twice those of healthy volunteers when both groups were administered the same treatment regimen.

Administration of saquinavir with a high-fat meal increased the AUC and C_{max} to approximately twice the concentrations seen following administration with a low-calorie, lower-fat meal. The effect of food persisted for up to 2 hours.

Saquinavir soft gelatin capsules (*Fortovase*)—

The bioavailability of the soft gelatin capsule formulation was estimated to be 331% of that of the original saquinavir mesylate capsule formulation. In healthy volunteers receiving single doses of saquinavir soft gelatin capsules (300 to 1200 mg), or in HIV-infected patients receiving multiple doses (400 to 1200 mg three times a day), a greater than dose-proportional increase in the plasma concentration of saquinavir was observed.

Distribution

In two patients, distribution into the cerebrospinal fluid was minimal when compared with concentrations from corresponding plasma samples.

Vol_D—Approximately 700 liters (mean) at steady state.

Protein binding

Very high (98%).

Biotransformation

Hepatic; over 90% of saquinavir is metabolized by the cytochrome P450 isoenzyme CYP3A4. Saquinavir is thought to undergo extensive first-pass metabolism and is rapidly metabolized to a variety of inactive mono- and di-hydroxylated compounds.

Elimination

Fecal—Approximately 88% of orally administered saquinavir is eliminated fecally as unchanged saquinavir and metabolites within 5 days of dosing.

Renal—Approximately 1% of orally administered saquinavir is eliminated unchanged in the urine within 5 days of dosing.

Precautions to Consider

Carcinogenicity

Carcinogenicity studies found no carcinogenic activity in rats and mice administered saquinavir for approximately 2 years. Because of limited bioavailability of saquinavir in animals, the respective plasm exposures (AUC values) were approximately 29% using rat and 65% using mouse of those obtained in humans at the recommended clinical dose boosted with ritonavir.

Mutagenicity

Mutagenicity and genotoxicity studies, with and without metabolic activation where appropriate, have not shown saquinavir to be mutagenic *in vitro* in the Ames test or the Chinese hamster lung V79/HPRT test. Saquinavir does not induce chromosomal damage *in vivo* in the mouse micronucleus assay or *in vitro* in human peripheral blood lymphocytes, and does not induce primary DNA damage *in vitro* in the unscheduled DNA synthesis test.

Pregnancy/Reproduction

Fertility—Fertility and reproduction were not affected in rats given saquinavir at plasma exposures (area under the plasma concentration-time curve [AUC] values) of up to five times those achieved in humans at the recommended dose for saquinavir mesylate capsules (or approximately 50% of AUC values achieved in humans at the recommended dose for saquinavir soft gelatin capsules). Because of limited bioavailability of saquinavir in animals, the maximal plasma exposures achieved in rats were approximately 26% of those obtained in humans at the recommended clinical dose boosted with ritonavir.

Pregnancy—Adequate and well-controlled studies have not been done in humans.

Embryotoxicity and teratogenicity were not seen in rats given saquinavir at plasma exposures (AUC values) of up to five times those achieved in humans at the recommended dose for saquinavir mesylate capsules (1800 mg per day) (or approximately 50% of AUC values achieved in humans at the recommended dose for saquinavir soft gelatin capsules), or in rabbits at plasma exposures of four times those achieved at the recommended clinical dose for saquinavir mesylate capsules (or approximately 40% of AUC values achieved in humans at the recommended dose for saquinavir soft gelatin capsules). Studies in rats administered saquinavir from late pregnancy through lactation at plasma concentrations (AUC values) of up to five times those achieved in humans at the recommended dose for saquinavir mesylate capsules (or approximately 50% of AUC values achieved in humans at the recommended dose for saquinavir soft gelatin capsules) showed that saquinavir had no effect on survival, growth, and development of offspring to the time of weaning. Saquinavir should be used during pregnancy only if potential benefit justified potential risk to the fetus.

To monitor maternal-fetal outcomes of pregnant women exposed to antiretroviral medications, including saquinavir, an Antiretroviral Pregnancy Registry has been established. Physicians are encouraged to register patients by calling 1-800-258-4263.

FDA Pregnancy Category B.

Breast-feeding

It is not known whether saquinavir is distributed into breast milk. The U.S. Public Health Services Centers for Disease Control and Prevention advises human immunodeficiency virus (HIV)-infected women not to breast-feed, to avoid potential postnatal transmission of HIV to a child who may not be infected.

Pediatrics

No information is available on the relationship of age to the effects of saquinavir in pediatric patients. Safety, efficacy, and pharmacokinetics of saquinavir in HIV-infected children up to 16 years of age have not been established.

Geriatrics

No information is available on the relationship of age to the effects of saquinavir in geriatric patients. Safety, efficacy, and pharmacokinetics of saquinavir have not been studied in HIV-infected patients older than 65 years of age. However, caution should be taken when dosing saquinavir in elderly patients due to the greater frequency of decreased hepatic, renal, or cardiac function, and of concomitant disease or other drug therapy.

Drug interactions and/or related problems

The following drug interactions and/or related problems have been selected on the basis of their potential clinical significance (possible mechanism in parentheses where appropriate)—not necessarily inclusive (» = major clinical significance):

Note: Combinations containing any of the following medications, depending on the amount present, may also interact with this medication.

» Antiarrhythmics such as
» Amiodarone or
» Bepridil or
» Flecainide or
» Propafenone
» Quinidine
(concomitant use with saquinavir **contraindicated**)

» Astemizole or
» Cisapride or
» Ergot derivatives or
» Midazolam or
» Pimozide or
» Terfenadine or
» Triazolam
(concurrent use of saquinavir with terfenadine has resulted in an increase in the plasma concentrations of terfenadine; competition for the cytochrome P450 enzyme CYP3A by saquinavir may also inhibit the metabolism of astemizole, cisapride, ergot derivatives, midazolam, pimozide, or triazolam; due to the potential for serious and/or life-threatening cardiac arrhythmias or prolonged sedation, concurrent use of any of these medications with saquinavir mesylate capsules or saquinavir soft gelatin capsules is **contraindicated**)

Atorvastatin or
Cerivastatin or
Lovastatin or
Simvastatin
(concurrent use of saquinavir with lovastatin or simvastatin not recommended; saquinavir mesylate and HMG CoA reductase inhibitors compete for CYP3A4 pathway for metabolism and may result in increased HMG CoA reductase inhibitors concentration, rarely leads to myopathy including rhabdomyolysis)

(concurrent use of saquinavir and atorvastatin at lowest possible dose may be considered; careful monitoring advised)

Benzodiazepines including
Alprazolam or
Clorazepate or
Diazepam or
Flurazepam
(may increase benzodiazepine concentration; clinical significance unknown; however, benzodiazepine dose decrease may be needed)

» Calcium channel blocking agents or
Dapsone or
(concurrent administration of saquinavir mesylate capsules with these medications, which are substrates of the CYP3A4 isoenzyme of the cytochrome P450 enzyme system, may result in elevated plasma concentrations of these medications; patients should be monitored for toxicities associated with these medications)

» Carbamazepine or
» Dexamethasone or
» Phenobarbital or
» Phenytoin or
» Other medications that are metabolic inducers of the cytochrome P450 enzyme system (see *Appendix II*)
(; carbamazepine, dexamethasone, phenobarbital, phenytoin, or other medications that induce CYP3A4 may reduce saquinavir plasma concentrations; use of alternative medications should be considered if patients are taking either formulation of saquinavir)

Clarithromycin
(concurrent use of saquinavir soft gelatin capsules with clarithromycin has resulted in a 177% increase in the AUC for saquinavir, a 45% increase in the AUC for clarithromycin, and a 24% decrease in the AUC for the active metabolite 14-hydroxyclarithromycin; consider dosage adjustment of clarithromycin in patients with renal impairment)

Cyclosporines or
Sirolimus or
Tacrolimus
(concentration of these drugs may increase when coadministered with saquinavir; therapeutic concentration monitoring recommended)

» Delavirdine or
(concurrent use of delavirdine and saquinavir mesylate has resulted in a fivefold increase in the AUC for saquinavir mesylate capsules; in one small, preliminary study, hepatic enzyme activities were elevated in 15% of subjects during the first several weeks of dual therapy with delavirdine and saquinavir mesylate capsules; hepatic function should be monitored if these medications are administered concurrently)

» Efavirenz
(concurrent use reduces concentrations of both saquinavir and efavirenz)

» Ethinyl estradiol-containing oral contraceptives
(concomitant use with saquinavir/ritonavir may result in decreased ethinyl estradiol concentrations; use of additional or alternate contraceptive measures should be considered)

» Garlic capsules
(should not be used while taking saquinavir as sole protease inhibitor due to the risk of decreased saquinavir plasma concentrations)

Indinavir or
Nelfinavir or
» Ritonavir
(concurrent administration of saquinavir mesylate capsules or saquinavir soft gelatin capsules with indinavir has resulted in a 364% increase in the AUC for saquinavir; concurrent administration of saquinavir mesylate capsules or saquinavir soft gelatin capsules with nelfinavir has resulted in a 392% increase in the AUC for saquinavir and an 18% increase in the AUC for nelfinavir; there are currently no safety and efficacy data from the use of these combinations)

(in HIV-infected patients, concurrent administration of saquinavir mesylate capsules [400 or 600 mg two times a day] with ritonavir [400 or 600 mg two times a day] has resulted in AUC values for saquinavir that were at least 17-fold greater than historical AUC values in patients receiving saquinavir 600 mg three times a day without ritonavir; when used in combination therapy for up to 24 weeks, doses greater than 400 mg two times a day of either ritonavir or saquinavir mesylate capsules were associated with an increase in adverse events; plasma exposures achieved with saquinavir mesylate capsules [400 mg two times a day] and ritonavir [400 mg two times a day] are similar to those achieved with saquinavir soft gelatin capsules [400 mg two times a day] and ritonavir [400 mg two times a day])

Itraconazole or
Ketoconazole
(concurrent use of ketoconazole with saquinavir mesylate capsules has resulted in steady-state AUC and C_{max} values for saquinavir that were three times those seen with saquinavir alone; no dosage adjustment is necessary when these two medications are administered together; the pharmacokinetics of ketoconazole are unaffected)

(concurrent use with saquinavir soft gelatin capsules increases the saquinavir plasma AUC by 130%)

(similar increase in saquinavir plasma concentrations could occur with itraconazole)

Lidocaine
(may increase lidocaine concentration; caution warranted and therapeutic concentration monitoring when lidocaine is given with saquinavir)

Lopinavir/ritonavir
(concomitant use increases saquinavir concentration; effect on lopinavir not well established)

» Methadone
(may decrease methadone concentration; concomitant use with saquinavir/ritonavir may require increase in methadone dose)

» Nevirapine
(concurrent use of nevirapine and saquinavir mesylate has resulted in a 24% decrease in saquinavir plasma AUC)

Other drugs metabolized by CYP3A4 such as
Alfentanyl or
Disopyramide or
Fentanyl or
Quinine
(caution should be used; these drugs may have elevated plasma concentrations when coadministered with saquinavir)

» Phosphodiesterase type 5 inhibitors including
» Sildenafil or
» Tadalafil or
» Vardenafil
(sildenafil, tadalafil, and vardenafil concentrations may be increased with concomitant use; caution should be used with increased adverse event monitoring and dose adjustments when coadministered with saquinavir)

» Rifabutin
(saquinavir concentration decreases and rifabutin concentration increases with concomitant use)

» Rifampin
(concomitant use contraindicated)

St. John's wort (*hypericum perforatum*)
(concomitant use not recommended; coadministration of protease inhibitors expected to substantially decrease protease-inhibitor concentration which may result in lower levels of saquinavir and lead to loss of virologic response and possible resistance to saquinavir or to the class of protease inhibitors)

Tricyclic antidepressants such as
Amitriptyline or
Imipramine
(may increase tricyclic antidepressant concentration; therapeutic concentration monitoring recommended for these drugs when coadministered with saquinavir/ritonavir)

Warfarin
(may effect warfarin concentrations; recommended international normalized ratio [INR] monitoring)

Zalcitabine or
Zidovudine
(concurrent administration of saquinavir with zalcitabine and zidovudine as triple therapy resulted in no change in absorption, metabolism, or elimination for any of these medications)

Laboratory value alterations

The following have been selected on the basis of their potential clinical significance (possible effect in parentheses where appropriate)—not necessarily inclusive (» = major clinical significance):

With physiology/laboratory test values
Alanine aminotransferase (ALT [SGPT]), serum or
Amylase, serum or
Aspartate aminotransferase (AST [SGOT]), serum or
Creatine kinase (CK) or
Gamma-glutamyltransferase or
Lactase dehydrogenase (LDH), serum
(values may be increased)

Bilirubin or
Calcium or
Potassium or
Sodium
(concentrations may be increased; calcium, potassium, and sodium concentrations may also be decreased)

Cholesterol and/or
Triglyceride
(may be elevated)

Glucose, plasma
(concentrations may be decreased or increased)

Neutrophils or
Platelets or
White blood cells
(may be decreased)

Thyroid-stimulating hormone (TSH)
(may be increased)

Medical considerations/Contraindications

The medical considerations/contraindications included have been selected on the basis of their potential clinical significance (reasons given in parentheses where appropriate)—not necessarily inclusive (» = major clinical significance).

Except under special circumstances, this medication should not be used when the following medical problem exists:

» Hepatic function impairment severe
(saquinavir is **contraindicated** in patients with this condition)

» Hypersensitivity to saquinavir or any of the components contained in the product formulation

Risk-benefit should be considered when the following medical problems exist:

Alcoholism, chronic or
Cirrhosis or
Hepatitis B or
Hepatitis C or
Other liver abnormalities
(reports of worsening liver disease in patients with these underlying conditions)

Diabetes mellitus or
Hyperglycemia
(new onset diabetes mellitus, exacerbation of pre-existing diabetes mellitus, and hyperglycemia have been reported during postmarketing surveillance in HIV-infected patients receiving protease inhibitor therapy; a causal relationship has not been established)

Hemophilia
(increased bleeding, including spontaneous skin hematomas and hemarthrosis, has been reported in patients with hemophilia types A and B who are receiving protease inhibitor therapy; a causal relationship has not been established)

Hepatic function impairment
(saquinavir is metabolized primarily by the liver; in patients with underlying hepatitis B or C, cirrhosis, or other hepatic abnormalities, there have been reports of exacerbation of chronic hepatic dysfunction, including portal hypertension, with saquinavir therapy; although a causal relationship has not been established, caution should be used when administering saquinavir to patients with hepatic function impairment)

Lactose intolerance
(saquinavir mesylate contains lactose; although this quantity should not induce intolerance symptoms, caution is advised)

Renal impairment, severe
(caution should be exercised as saquinavir use in patients with this condition have not been studied)

Patient monitoring

The following may be especially important in patient monitoring (other tests may be warranted in some patients, depending on condition; » = major clinical significance):

» Blood glucose determinations
(close monitoring of patient's plasma glucose concentrations is recommended; development of hyperglycemia or diabetes may be associated with the use of protease inhibitors)

Cholesterol and
Triglyceride
(levels should be monitored prior to initiating saquinavir therapy and at periodic intervals while on such therapy)

Clinical chemistry tests and
CD_4 counts and
Viral load
(should be performed prior to initiating saquinavir therapy and at appropriate intervals thereafter)

Side/Adverse Effects

Note: Saquinavir is indicated in combination with other antiretroviral agents. Saquinavir was not found to alter the pattern, frequency, or severity of toxicities associated with nucleoside analog reverse transcriptase inhibitors. Most side effects were considered to be mild. However, ketoacidosis has been reported in rare cases for patients receiving protease inhibitor therapy.

If saquinavir is being taken in combination with ritonavir, see *Ritonavir (Systemic)* for additional side and adverse effects.

If a serious or severe toxicity occurs during treatment with saquinavir, saquinavir therapy should be interrupted until the cause of the event is identified or the toxicity resolves. At that time, resumption of treatment with full-dose saquinavir may be considered.

The redistribution or accumulation of body fat, including central obesity, dorsocervical fat enlargement (buffalo hump), facial wasting, peripheral wasting, breast enlargement, and "cushingoid appearance" have been reported in patients on protease inhibitor therapy. A causal relationship between these events and use of protease inhibitors has not been confirmed.

The following side/adverse effects have been selected on the basis of their potential clinical significance (possible signs and symptoms in parentheses where appropriate)—not necessarily inclusive:

Those indicating need for medical attention

Chest pain

Incidence rare

Diabetes or hyperglycemia (dry or itchy skin; fatigue; hunger, increased; thirst, increased; unexplained weight loss; urination, increased); ***ketoacidosis*** (confusion; dehydration; mouth odor, fruity; nausea; vomiting; weight loss); ***paresthesia*** (burning or prickling sensation); ***skin rash***

Those indicating need for medical attention only if they continue or are bothersome

Incidence less frequent

Anxiety (fear, nervousness); ***appetite decreased; asthenia*** (weakness); ***constipation*** (difficulty having a bowel movement (stool)); ***depression*** (discouragement; feeling sad or empty; irritability; lack of appetite; loss of interest or pleasure; tiredness; trouble concentrating; trouble sleeping); ***dyspepsia*** (acid or sour stomach; belching; heartburn; indigestion; stomach discomfort, upset, or pain); ***eczema*** (skin rash encrusted, scaly and oozing); ***fatigue*** (unusual tiredness or weakness); ***flatulence*** (bloated full feeling; excess air or gas in stomach or intestines; passing gas); ***gastrointestinal disturbances*** (abdominal pain; diarrhea; mouth ulcers; nausea); ***insomnia*** (sleeplessness; trouble sleeping; unable to sleep); ***libido disorder*** (loss in sexual ability, desire, drive, or performance; decreased interest in sexual intercourse; inability to have or keep an erection); ***taste alteration*** (change in taste); ***verruca*** (skin wart); ***vomiting***

Incidence rare

Headache

Overdose

For more information on the management of overdose or unintentional ingestion, **contact a Poison Control Center** (see *Poison Control Center Listing*).

Clinical effects of overdose

No acute toxicities were seen in one patient who ingested a single dose of 8 grams of saquinavir mesylate capsules; emesis was induced within 2 to 4 hours after ingestion. No serious toxicities were reported in patients taking 7200 mg per day for 25 weeks in a phase II study.

Treatment of overdose

To decrease absorption—Patients may benefit from treatment with activated charcoal.

Monitoring—Patient's vital signs should be monitored.

Supportive care—Supportive therapy. Patients in whom intentional overdose is confirmed or suspected should be referred for psychiatric consultation.

Patient Consultation

As an aid to patient consultation, refer to *Advice for the Patient, Saquinavir (Systemic)*.

In providing consultation, consider emphasizing the following selected information (» = major clinical significance):

Before taking this medication

» Conditions affecting use, especially:

Hypersensitivity to saquinavir

Pregnancy—Risk benefit should be considered

Breast-feeding—It is recommended that HIV-infected mothers do not breast-feed to avoid potential postnatal transmission of HIV to an uninfected infant

Use in children—Saquinavir has not been studied in children up to 16 years of age

Use in the elderly—Caution due to greater frequency of decreased hepatic, renal or cardiac function, and of concomitant disease or other drug therapy in the elderly

Other medications, especially antiarrhythmics, astemizole, calcium channel blocking agents, carbamazepine, cisapride, delavirdine, dexamethasone, efavirenz, ergot derivatives, ethinyl estradiol-containing oral contraceptives, garlic capsules, methadone, midazolam, pimozide, nevirapine, phenobarbital, phenytoin, phosphodiesterase type 5 inhibitors (sildenafil, tadalafil, vardenafil), quinidine, rifabutin, rifampin, ritonavir, terfenadine, triazolam, or other medications that are metabolic inducers of the cytochrome P450 enzyme system

Other medical problems, especially severe hepatic function impairment

Proper use of this medication

» Importance of taking saquinavir within 2 hours after a meal

» Importance of not taking more medication than prescribed; importance of not discontinuing saquinavir or other antiretroviral agents without checking with physician

» Importance of not switching from one brandname of saquinavir to another brandname. They may not contain the same amount of medicine.

» Using *Invirase* only if it is being combined with ritonavir

» Compliance with full course of therapy

» Importance of not missing doses and of taking at evenly spaced times

Not sharing medication with others

Discussing alternative treatment regimens with patients on *Fortovase* due to its discontinuation by February 15, 2006

» Proper dosing

Missed dose: Taking as soon as possible; not taking if almost time for next dose; not doubling doses

» Proper storage

Precautions while using this medication

» Because saquinavir may interact with other medications, not taking any other medications (prescription or nonprescription) without first consulting your physician

» Regular visits to physician for blood tests and monitoring of blood glucose concentrations

» Using an additional method of contraception if taking estrogen-containing oral contraceptives concurrently

» Being aware that saquinavir therapy does not reduce the risk of transmitting HIV to others through sexual contact or contamination through blood

Side/adverse effects

Signs of potential side effects, especially chest pain, diabetes or hyperglycemia, ketoacidosis, paresthesia, and skin rash

General Dosing Information

Saquinavir should be taken with a meal or within 2 hours after a meal.

Bioequivalence information

Invirase (saquinavir mesylate) capsules and *Fortovase* (saquinavir) soft gelatin capsules **are not bioequivalent and cannot be used interchangeably** when used as the sole protease inhibitor. Only *Fortovase* should be used for the initiation of therapy that includes saquinavir as a sole protease inhibitor since *Fortovase* soft gelatin capsules provide greater bioavailability and efficacy than *Invirase* capsules.

Saquinavir mesylate (*Invirase*) may be used only if combined with ritonavir to inhibit the metabolism of saquinavir and provide plasma saquinavir levels at least equal to those achieved with saquinavir (*Fortovase*).

Oral Dosage Forms

Note: The dosing and strength of the dosage forms available are expressed in terms of saquinavir base.

SAQUINAVIR SOFT GELATIN CAPSULES

Usual adult dose

Human immunodeficiency virus (HIV) infection—

Oral, 1200 mg three times a day with a meal or within two hours of eating a meal, in combination with other appropriate antiretroviral agents.

With ritonavir—Oral, 1000 mg twice per day (5 x 200-mg capsules) in combination with ritonavir 100 mg twice per day taken at the same time within two hours of eating a meal

Dosing adjustments

—Clarithromycin dose in patients with renal impairment taking saquinavir concomitantly—

- CL_{CR} 30 to 60 ml/min: reduce by 50%
- CL_{CR} less than 30 ml/min: decrease by 75%

PDE5 inhibitor doses in patients taking saquinavir concomitantly—

- Sildenafil: reduced to 25 mg every 48 hours
- Tadalafil: reduced to no more than 10 mg every 72 hours
- Vardenafil: reduced to no more than 2.5 mg every 72 hours

Usual pediatric dose

Children up to 16 years of age—Safety and efficacy have not been established.

Strength(s) usually available

U.S.—

Note: Roche Laboratories will be discontinuing *Fortovase* from the market by February 15, 2006 due to the declining clinical demand for the product. Prescribing health care providers are encouraged to discuss appropriate alternative treatment regimens with their patients currently receiving *Fortovase*.

200 mg (Rx) [*Fortovase*].

Canada—

200 mg (Rx) [*Fortovase*].

Packaging and storage

Store in a refrigerator between 2 and 8 °C (36 and 46 °F) in a tight container.

Stability

Capsules stored in the refrigerator remain stable until the expiration date printed on the label. Capsules that are brought to room temperature (25 °C [77 °F]) are stable for up to 3 months.

Auxiliary labeling

- Refrigerate.
- Continue for full time of treatment.
- Take with food.
- Do not take other medications without physician's advice.

SAQUINAVIR MESYLATE CAPSULES

Usual adult dose

Human immunodeficiency virus (HIV) infection—

Oral, 1000 mg (5 x 200-mg capsule) twice per day within two hours of eating a meal, in combination with ritonavir 100 mg twice per day at the same time.

Note: *Invirase* doses less than 1000 mg with 100 mg ritonavir twice daily are not recommended since lower doses have not shown antiviral activity. For recipients of combination therapy with saquinavir and ritonavir, dose adjustments may be necessary. These adjustments should be based on the known toxicity profile of the individual agent and the pharmacokinetic interaction between saquinavir and the coadministered drug. Physicians should refer to the complete product information for these drugs for comprehensive dose adjustment recommendations and drug-associated adverse reactions of nucleoside analogues.

Dosing adjustments—

Clarithromycin dose in patients with renal impairment taking saquinavir concomitantly—

- CL_{CR} 30 to 60 ml/min: reduce by 50%
- CL_{CR} less than 30 ml/min: decrease by 75%

PDE5 inhibitor doses in patients taking saquinavir concomitantly—

- Sildenafil: reduced to 25 mg every 48 hours
- Tadalafil: reduced to no more than 10 mg every 72 hours
- Vardenafil: reduced to no more than 2.5 mg every 72 hours

Usual pediatric dose

Children up to 16 years of age—Safety and efficacy have not been established.

Strength(s) usually available

U.S.—

200 mg (base) (Rx) [*Invirase* (lactose)].

Canada—

200 mg (base) (Rx) [*Invirase* (lactose)].

Packaging and storage

Store between 15 and 30 °C (59 and 86 °F) in a tight container.

Auxiliary labeling

- Continue for full time of treatment.
- Take with food.
- Do not take other medications without physician's advice.

SAQUINAVIR MESYLATE TABLETS

Usual adult dose

Human immunodeficiency virus (HIV) infection—

Oral, 1000 mg (2 x 500-mg tablets) twice per day within two hours of eating a meal, in combination with ritonavir 100 mg twice per day at the same time.

Note: *Invirase* doses less than 1000 mg with 100 mg ritonavir twice daily are not recommended since lower doses have not shown antiviral activity. For recipients of combination therapy with saquinavir and ritonavir, dose adjustments may be necessary. These adjustments should be based on the known toxicity profile of the individual agent and the pharmacokinetic interaction between saquinavir and the coadministered drug. Physicians should refer to the complete product information for these drugs for comprehensive dose adjustment recommendations and drug-associated adverse reactions of nucleoside analogues.

Dosing adjustments—

Clarithromycin dose in patients with renal impairment taking saquinavir concomitantly—

- CL_{CR} 30 to 60 ml/min: reduce by 50%
- CL_{CR} less than 30 ml/min: decrease by 75%

PDE5 inhibitor doses in patients taking saquinavir concomitantly—

- Sildenafil: reduced to 25 mg every 48 hours
- Tadalafil: reduced to no more than 10 mg every 72 hours
- Vardenafil: reduced to no more than 2.5 mg every 72 hours

Usual pediatric dose

Children up to 16 years of age—Safety and efficacy have not been established.

Strength(s) usually available

U.S.—

500 mg (base) (Rx) [*Invirase* (film-coated; lactose; microcrystalline cellulose; povidone K30; croscarmellose sodium; magnesium stearate; hypromellose; titanium dioxide; talc; iron oxide yellow; iron oxide red; triacetin)].

Packaging and storage

Store at 25 °C (77 °F) 15 to 30 °C (59 and 86 °F) in a tight container.

Auxiliary labeling

- Continue for full time of treatment.
- Take with food.
- Do not take other medications without physician's advice.

Revised: 11/15/2005
Developed: 01/27/1997

SARGRAMOSTIM—See *Colony Stimulating Factors (Systemic)*

SCOPOLAMINE—See *Anticholinergics/Antispasmodics (Systemic), Scopolamine (Ophthalmic)*

SECOBARBITAL—See *Barbiturates (Systemic)*

SELEGILINE Systemic

VA CLASSIFICATION (Primary): CN500

Commonly used brand name(s): *Apo-Selegiline; Carbex; Eldepryl; Gen-Selegiline; Novo-Selegiline; Nu-Selegiline; SD Deprenyl; Selegiline-5.*

Other commonly used names are deprenil and deprenyl.

Note: For a listing of dosage forms and brand names by country availability, see *Dosage Forms* section(s).

Category

Antidyskinetic.

Indications

Note: Bracketed information in the *Indications* section refers to uses that are not included in U.S. product labeling.

Accepted

Parkinsonism (treatment adjunct)—Selegiline is indicated for use with levodopa or levodopa and carbidopa combination in the treatment of idiopathic Parkinson's disease (paralysis agitans).

[Some studies have suggested that the initial use of selegiline may delay the need for addition of levodopa to the treatment regimen; in addition, these studies have shown that selegiline alone or in combination with levodopa may slow the progression of Parkinson's disease, possibly by preventing selective destruction of dopaminergic neurons in the substantia nigra. One retrospective study showed selegiline to possibly prolong the life span of patients with idiopathic Parkinson's disease.]

[The addition of selegiline to levodopa in patients experiencing fluctuating responses ("wearing off" effect or "on-off" phenomenon) may be of moderate benefit. However, the initial response to selegiline may not be sustained, with the degree of improvement declining over 6 months to 4 years. Selegiline is ineffective in advanced disease with extreme fluctuations. Motor control fluctuations may be due to factors other than the central pharmacokinetics of dopamine; hence prolongation of dopamine effects may fail in some cases to improve this problem.]

Note: Preliminary studies have demonstrated that selegiline may be useful as an antidepressant, usually when given in doses greater than those used for its antidyskinetic effect. However, there are *insufficient data* to definitively establish effectiveness of selegiline and criteria for its use in mental depression.

Pharmacology/Pharmacokinetics

Physicochemical characteristics

Molecular weight—223.75.

Mechanism of action/Effect

The action of selegiline is thought to be related to its irreversible inhibition of monoamine oxidase type B (MAO B), the major form of the enzyme in the human brain. MAO B, which is involved in the oxidative deamination of dopamine in the brain, is inhibited when selegiline binds covalently and stoichiometrically to the isoalloxazine flavin adenine dinucleotide (FAD) at its active center. Administration of 10 mg of selegiline a day produces almost complete inhibition of MAO B in the brain. Selegiline becomes a nonselective inhibitor of all monoamine oxidase (MAO) at higher doses, possibly at 20 to 40 mg a day. At these doses, tyramine-mediated hypertensive reactions from MAO A blockade ("cheese reactions") may occur.

Selegiline (or its metabolites) may also act through other mechanisms to increase dopaminergic activity, including interfering with dopamine reuptake at the synapse.

Absorption

Rapidly absorbed from the gastrointestinal tract.

Distribution

Crosses the blood-brain barrier.

Biotransformation

Rapidly and completely metabolized to *N*-desmethyldeprenyl, l-methamphetamine, and l-amphetamine.

Half-life

The mean half-lives of the 3 active metabolites that were found in serum and urine following a single dose of selegiline are as follows—
N-desmethyldeprenyl: 2 hours.
l-amphetamine: 17.7 hours.
l-methamphetamine: 20.5 hours.

Elimination—
Selegiline: 39 (range, 16 to 69) hours.

Time to peak plasma concentration

0.5 to 2 hours.

Duration of action

Duration of clinical action depends on the regeneration time of MAO B.

Elimination

Renal; slow. 45% of a 10 mg dose appears in the urine as metabolites (*N*-desmethyldeprenyl, l-amphetamine, and l-methamphetamine) within 48 hours of ingestion.

Precautions to Consider

Carcinogenicity

Long-term animal studies have revealed no evidence of carcinogenic effects.

Pregnancy/Reproduction

Pregnancy—Studies in humans have not been done.

Studies in animals have not shown that selegiline causes adverse effects on the fetus. Reproduction studies in rats and rabbits given approximately 250 and 350 times the comparable human dose, respectively, have revealed no evidence of teratogenic effects.

FDA Pregnancy Category C.

Breast-feeding

It is not known whether selegiline is excreted in breast milk.

Pediatrics

No published pediatrics-specific information is available. Safety and efficacy have not been established.

Geriatrics

No geriatrics-related problems have been documented in studies done to date that included elderly patients.

Dental

Selegiline may decrease or inhibit salivary flow, thus contributing to the development of caries, periodontal disease, oral candidiasis, and discomfort.

Drug interactions and/or related problems

The following drug interactions and/or related problems have been selected on the basis of their potential clinical significance (possible mechanism in parentheses where appropriate)—not necessarily inclusive (» = major clinical significance):

Note: Combinations containing any of the following medications, depending on the amount present, may also interact with this medication.

For all doses of selegiline

» Antidepressants, tricyclic
(asystole, diaphoresis, hypertension, syncope, changes in behavior and mental status, impaired consciousness, hyperpyrexia, seizures, muscular rigidity, and tremors have occurred with concurrent use of selegiline and tricyclic antidepressants. Concurrent use is not recommended; at least 14 days should elapse between discontinuation of selegiline and initiation of a tricyclic antidepressant)

» Fluoxetine or
» Fluvoxamine or
» Nefazodone or
» Paroxetine or
» Sertraline or
» Venlafaxine
(a reaction resembling the serotonin syndrome has been reported rarely following concurrent use of selegiline with selective serotonin re-uptake inhibitors (SSRIs). [The serotonin syndrome may occur as the result of combining a serotonergic agent with an MAO inhibitor. The syndrome may be manifest by mental status changes (confusion, hypomania), restlessness, myoclonus, hyperreflexia, diaphoresis, shivering, tremor, diarrhea, incoordination, and/or fever. If recognized early, the syndrome usually resolves quickly upon withdrawal of the offending agents.] Concurrent use of selegiline with SSRIs is not recommended because of the potential for autonomic instability, muscular rigidity, severe agitation, or delirium. At least 14 days should elapse between discontinuation of an MAO inhibitor and initiation of an SSRI. However, because of the long half-lives of fluoxetine and its active metabolite, at least 5 weeks [approximately 5 half-lives] should elapse between discontinuation of fluoxetine and initiation of therapy with an MAO inhibitor. Also, based on the half-life of venlafaxine, at least 7 days should elapse between discontinuation of venlafaxine and initiation of therapy with an MAO inhibitor.)

Levodopa
(although selegiline is used in conjunction with levodopa, it may enhance levodopa-induced dyskinesias, nausea, orthostatic hypotension, confusion, and hallucinations; reduction of levodopa dosage may be necessary within 2 to 3 days after the initiation of selegiline therapy)

» Meperidine, and possibly other opioid (narcotic) analgesics
(at least one interaction of meperidine with selegiline has been reported; concurrent use of meperidine with nonselective monoamine oxidase inhibitors [MAOIs] may produce immediate excitation, sweating, rigidity, and severe hypertension; in some patients, hypotension, severe respiratory depression, coma, convulsions, hyperpyrexia, vascular collapse, and death may occur; avoidance of meperidine use within 2 to 3 weeks following MAO inhibition is recommended; other opioid analgesics such as morphine are not likely to cause such severe reactions and may be used cautiously in reduced dosage in patients receiving MAOIs; however, it is recommended that a small test dose [one quarter of the usual dose] or several small incremental test doses over a period of several hours should first be administered to permit observation of any adverse effects; caution is also recommended in the use of alfentanil, fentanyl, or sufentanil as an adjunct to anesthesia if the patient has received an MAOI within 14 days; because the risk of a significant interaction has been questioned, the use of a small test dose is advised to detect any possible interaction)

For doses of 20 mg or more of selegiline per day

» Tyramine- or other high pressor amine-containing foods and beverages, such as aged cheese; fava or broad bean pods; yeast/protein extracts; smoked or pickled meats, poultry, or fish; fermented sausage (bologna, pepperoni, salami, summer sausage) or other fermented meat; sauerkraut; any overripe fruit; beer; reduced-alcohol and alcohol-free beer and wine; red and white wines; sherry; and liqueurs
(concurrent use with MAOIs, including selegiline in doses of 20 mg a day or greater, may cause sudden and severe hypertensive re-

actions; reactions are usually limited to a few hours and are easily treated with rapidly acting hypotensive agents [such as labetalol, nifedipine, or, if necessary in severe cases refractory to other agents, phentolamine]; severity of reaction depends on amount of tyramine ingested, rate of gastric emptying, and length of interval between dose of MAOI and ingestion of tyramine; when MAOIs are discontinued, dietary restrictions must continue for at least 2 weeks; other tyramine- or high pressor amine-containing foods, such as yogurt, sour cream, cream cheese, cottage cheese, chocolate, and soy sauce, if eaten when fresh and in moderation, are considered unlikely to cause serious problems)

Medical considerations/Contraindications

The medical considerations/contraindications included have been selected on the basis of their potential clinical significance (reasons given in parentheses where appropriate)—not necessarily inclusive (» = major clinical significance).

Risk-benefit should be considered when the following medical problems exist:

Dementia, profound or
Psychosis, severe or
Tardive dyskinesia or
Tremor, excessive
(condition may be exacerbated)

» Peptic ulcer disease, history of
(activation of pre-existing ulcers may occur, probably due to stimulation of the H_2 receptors in the stomach or inhibition of MAO-mediated gastric histamine catabolism)

Sensitivity to selegiline

Side/Adverse Effects

Note: Selegiline enhances the dose-related side effects of levodopa, but few side effects are attributable to selegiline itself. When selegiline is used as an adjunct to levodopa or levodopa and carbidopa combination, adverse effects can usually be ameliorated by reducing the dose of levodopa or levodopa and carbidopa.

In addition, selegiline may cause elevation of liver enzymes.

The following side/adverse effects have been selected on the basis of their potential clinical significance (possible signs and symptoms in parentheses where appropriate)—not necessarily inclusive:

Those indicating need for medical attention

Incidence more frequent

Dyskinesias (increase in unusual movements of body); ***mood or other mental changes***

Incidence less frequent or rare

Angina pectoris, new or increased (chest pain); ***arrhythmias*** (irregular heartbeat); ***asthma*** (wheezing, difficulty in breathing, or tightness in chest); ***bradycardia, sinus*** (slow heartbeat); ***edema, peripheral*** (swelling of feet or lower legs); ***motor/coordination/extrapyramidal effects*** (difficulty in speaking; loss of balance control; uncontrolled movements, especially of face, neck, and back; restlessness or desire to keep moving; twisting movements of body); ***gastrointestinal bleeding*** (bloody or black, tarry stools; severe stomach pain; vomiting of blood or material that looks like coffee grounds); ***hallucinations; headache, severe; hypertension, severe; orthostatic hypotension*** (dizziness or lightheadedness, especially when getting up from a lying or sitting position); ***prostatic hypertrophy*** (difficult or frequent urination); ***tardive dyskinesia*** (lip smacking or puckering; puffing of cheeks; rapid or worm-like movements of tongue; uncontrolled chewing movements; uncontrolled movements of arms and legs)

Symptoms of hypertensive crisis

Chest pain, severe; enlarged pupils; fast or slow heartbeat; headache, severe; increased sensitivity of eyes to light; increased sweating, possibly with fever or cold, clammy skin; nausea or vomiting, severe; stiff or sore neck

Those indicating need for medical attention only if they continue or are bothersome

Incidence more frequent

Abdominal or stomach pain; dizziness or feeling faint; dryness of mouth; insomnia (trouble in sleeping); ***nausea or vomiting***

Incidence less frequent or rare

Anxiety, nervousness, or restlessness; apraxia, increased (inability to move); ***blepharospasm*** (sudden closing of eyelids); ***blurred or double vision; body ache or back or leg pain; bradykinesia, increased*** (slowed movements); ***chills; constipation or diarrhea; diaphoresis*** (increased sweating); ***drowsiness; headache; heartburn; hypertension or hypotension*** (high or low blood pressure); ***impaired memory***—more frequent with doses greater than 10 mg a day; ***slow or difficult urination; frequent urge to urinate; irritability, temporary; loss of appetite or weight loss; muscle cramps or numbness of fingers or toes; palpitations or tachycardia*** (pounding or fast heartbeat); ***paresthesias, circumoral*** (burning of lips or mouth); ***or burning of throat; photosensitivity*** (increased sensitivity of skin and eyes to sunlight); ***skin rash; tinnitus*** (ringing or buzzing in ears); ***taste changes; unusual feeling of well-being; unusual tiredness or weakness***

With doses greater than 10 mg a day

Bruxism (clenching, gnashing, or grinding teeth); ***muscle twitches or myoclonic jerks*** (sudden jerky movements of body)

Note: *Bruxism* and *myoclonic jerks* may be considered to be adverse effects only if not previously present and beginning shortly after the start of therapy with selegiline.

Overdose

For specific information in the agents used in the management of selegiline overdose, see:

- *Charcoal, Activated (Oral-Local)* monograph.

For more information on the management of overdose of unintentional ingestion, **contact a Poison Control Center** (see *Poison Control Center Listing*).

Clinical effects of overdose

No specific information is available regarding overdoses with selegiline. Since overdose is likely to cause significant inhibition of both MAO type A and type B, symptoms of overdose may resemble those of nonselective MAO inhibitors.

Symptoms of MAOI overdose

Agitation or irritability; chest pain; convulsions; cool, clammy skin; diaphoresis (increased sweating); ***dizziness, severe, or fainting; fast or irregular pulse, continuing; high or low blood pressure; hyperpyrexia*** (high fever); ***opisthotonus*** (severe spasm where the head and heels are bent backward and the body arched forward); ***respiratory depression*** (troubled breathing); ***trismus*** (difficulty opening the mouth; lockjaw)

Note: Symptoms resulting from overdose may be absent or minimal for nearly 12 hours after ingestion, and develop slowly thereafter, reaching a maximum in 24 to 48 hours. Death has resulted. Immediate hospitalization and close monitoring of patient is essential during this period.

Treatment of overdose

Treatment may include the following:

To decrease absorption—
Induction of emesis or gastric lavage with protected airway followed by instillation of charcoal slurry in early overdose.

Specific treatment—
Treatment of signs and symptoms of central nervous system (CNS) stimulation with diazepam, administered intravenously and slowly. Phenothiazine derivatives should be avoided.
Treatment of hypotension and vascular collapse with intravenous fluids and, if necessary, a dilute pressor agent. Adrenergic agents may produce a markedly increased pressor response.
Vigorous treatment of hyperpyrexia with antipyretics and a cooling blanket.

Monitoring—
Close monitoring of body temperature.

Supportive care—
Maintenance of fluid and electrolyte balance.
Support of respiration by management of the airway, and mechanical ventilation with the use of supplemental oxygen, as required.
Patients in whom intentional overdose is confirmed or suspected should be referred for psychiatric consultation.

Patient Consultation

As an aid to patient consultation, refer to *Advice for the Patient, Selegiline (Systemic).*

In providing consultation, consider emphasizing the following selected information (» = major clinical significance):

Before using this medication

» Conditions affecting use, especially:
Sensitivity to selegiline
Other medications, especially fluoxetine, fluvoxamine, meperidine and possibly other narcotic (opioid) analgesics, nefazodone, paroxetine, sertraline, tricyclic antidepressants, or venlafaxine
Other medical problems, especially a history of peptic ulcer disease

Proper use of this medication

» Importance of not taking more medication than the amount prescribed; to do so may increase the risk of side effects

Missed dose: Taking as soon as possible; not taking in the late afternoon or evening; not taking if almost time for next dose; not doubling doses.

» Proper storage

Precautions while using this medication

» If taking 20 mg or more of selegiline a day, avoiding tyramine-containing foods, alcoholic beverages, and large quantities of caffeine-containing beverages, over-the-counter cold and cough medicines, and other medications, unless prescribed

» Checking with hospital emergency room or physician if symptoms of hypertensive crisis develop

» Possibility of orthostatic hypotension; caution when getting up suddenly from a lying or sitting position

Possible dryness of mouth; using sugarless candy or gum, ice, or saliva substitute for relief; checking with physician or dentist if dryness of mouth continues for more than 2 weeks

Side/adverse effects

Signs of potential side effects, especially dyskinesias, mood or mental changes, angina pectoris, arrhythmias, asthma, bradycardia, peripheral edema, extrapyramidal effects, hallucinations, severe headache, severe hypertension, gastrointestinal bleeding, orthostatic hypotension, prostatic hypertrophy, and tardive dyskinesia

General Dosing Information

Selegiline should not be used in the treatment of Parkinson's disease at doses exceeding 10 mg a day because of the risks associated with nonselective inhibition of monoamine oxidase (MAO). A tyramine-mediated hypertensive reaction has been reported when selegiline was administered at a dose of 20 mg a day. In addition, selegiline in doses greater than 10 mg a day has not demonstrated increased effectiveness in the treatment of Parkinson's disease.

When selegiline is used as an adjunct to levodopa or levodopa and carbidopa combination, adverse effects such as involuntary movements or hallucinations may result, and doses of levodopa may need to be reduced. If necessary, doses of levodopa should be reduced after 2 to 3 days by 10 to 30%, and possibly by as much as 50% with continued therapy.

Because selegiline may produce insomnia, it should not be administered in the late afternoon or evening.

Diet/Nutrition

Selegiline should be administered with breakfast and lunch to minimize possible nausea and insomnia.

When monoamine oxidase inhibitors, including selegiline at doses of 20 mg a day or greater, are used concurrently with foods and beverages containing tyramine or other high pressor amines, sudden and severe hypertensive reactions may result. These reactions are usually limited to a few hours and are easily treated with rapidly acting hypotensive agents (such as labetalol, nifedipine, or, if necessary in severe cases refractory to other agents, phentolamine). The severity of the reaction depends on the amount of tyramine ingested, the rate of gastric emptying, and the length of the interval between the dose of MAO inhibitor and ingestion of tyramine. When MAO inhibitors are discontinued, dietary restrictions must continue for at least 2 weeks. Foods and beverages containing tyramine or other high pressor amines include aged cheese; fava or broad bean pods; yeast/protein extracts; smoked or pickled meats, poultry, or fish; fermented sausage (bologna, pepperoni, salami, summer sausage) or other fermented meat; sauerkraut; any overripe fruit; beer; reduced-alcohol and alcohol-free beer and wine; red and white wines; sherry; and liqueurs. Other foods, such as yogurt, sour cream, cream cheese, cottage cheese, chocolate, and soy sauce, if eaten when fresh and in moderation, are considered unlikely to cause serious problems.

Oral Dosage Forms

SELEGILINE HYDROCHLORIDE CAPSULES

Usual adult dose

Parkinsonism—

Oral, 5 mg two times a day, at breakfast and lunch.

Note: In some cases, some clinicians recommend that the total daily dose be divided (2.5 mg four times a day) to decrease the side effects induced by concomitant administration of levodopa.

Usual pediatric dose

Safety and efficacy have not been established.

Usual geriatric dose

See *Usual adult dose.*

Strength(s) usually available

U.S.—

5 mg (Rx) [*Eldepryl*].

Canada—

Not commercially available.

Packaging and storage

Store below 40 °C (104 °F), preferably between 15 and 30 °C (59 and 86 °F), in a well-closed container, unless otherwise specified by manufacturer.

Auxiliary labeling

- Avoid alcoholic beverages.

SELEGILINE HYDROCHLORIDE TABLETS USP

Usual adult dose

See *Selegiline Hydrochloride Capsules.*

Usual pediatric dose

See *Selegiline Hydrochloride Capsules.*

Usual geriatric dose

See *Selegiline Hydrochloride Capsules.*

Strength(s) usually available

U.S.—

5 mg (Rx) [*Carbex*; GENERIC].

Canada—

5 mg (Rx) [*Apo-Selegiline; Eldepryl; Gen-Selegiline; Novo-Selegiline; Nu-Selegiline; SD Deprenyl; Selegiline-5*].

Packaging and storage

Store below 40 °C (104 °F), preferably between 15 and 30 °C (59 and 86 °F), in a well-closed container, unless otherwise specified by manufacturer.

Auxiliary labeling

- Avoid alcoholic beverages.

Selected Bibliography

Yahr MD. R-(—)-Deprenyl and parkinsonism. J Neural Transm 1987; 25(Suppl): 5-12.

Golbe LI. Deprenyl as symptomatic therapy in Parkinson's disease. Clin Neuropharmacol 1988 Oct; 11(5): 387-400.

Revised: 01/21/1998

SELENIOUS ACID—See *Selenium Supplements (Systemic)*

SELENIUM—See *Selenium Supplements (Systemic)*

SENNA—See *Laxatives (Local)*

SENNOSIDES—See *Laxatives (Local)*

SERTACONAZOLE Topical†

VA CLASSIFICATION (Primary): DE102

Commonly used brand name(s): *Ertaczo.*

Note: For a listing of dosage forms and brand names by country availability, see *Dosage Forms* section(s).

†Not commercially available in Canada.

Category

Antifungal (topical).

Indications

Accepted

Interdigital tinea pedis (treatment)—Sertaconazole is indicated for the topical treatment of interdigital tinea pedis, caused by *Trichophyton rubrum, Trichophyton mentagrophytes,* and *Epidermophyton floccosum* in immunocompetent patients 12 years of age and older.

Pharmacology/Pharmacokinetics

Physicochemical characteristics
Chemical Group—Imidazole antifungal
Molecular weight—500.8.
Solubility—Practically insoluble in water; soluble in methanol; sparingly soluble in alcohol and in methylene chloride.

Mechanism of action/Effect
While the exact mechanism of action of this class of antifungals is not known, it is believed that they act primarily by inhibiting the cytochrome P450-dependent synthesis of ergosterol. Ergosterol is a key component of the cell membrane of fungi, and lack of this component leads to fungal cell injury primarily by leakage of key constituents in the cytoplasm from the cell.

Pharmacokinetics
In a multiple dose pharmacokinetic study that included 5 male patients with interdigital tinea pedis (range of diseased area, 42 – 140 cm^2; mean 93 cm^2), sertaconazole was topically applied every 12 hours for a total of 13 doses to the diseased skin (0.5 grams sertaconazole nitrate per 100 cm). Sertaconazole concentrations in plasma measured by serial blood sampling for 72 hours after the thirteenth dose were below the limit of quantitation (2.5 ng/mL) of the analytical method used.

Precautions to Consider

Cross-sensitivity and/or related problems
Physicians should exercise caution when prescribing sertaconazole cream to patients known to be sensitive to imidazole antifungals, since cross-reactivity may occur.

Carcinogenicity/Tumorigenicity
Long-term studies to evaluate the carcinogenic potential of sertaconazole have not been conducted. No clastogenic potential was observed in a mouse micronucleus test. Sertaconazole was considered negative for sister chromatid exchange (SCE) in the *in vivo* mouse bone marrow SCE assay. There was no evidence that sertaconazole induced unscheduled DNA synthesis in rat primary hepatocyte cultures.

Pregnancy/Reproduction
Fertility—Sertaconazole exhibited no toxicity or adverse effects on reproductive performance or fertility of male or female rats given up to 60 mg/kg/day orally by gastric intubation (16 times the maximum recommended human dose based on a body surface area comparison).

Pregnancy—There are no adequate and well-controlled studies that have been conducted on topically applied sertaconazole in pregnant women. Because animal reproduction studies are not always predictive of human response sertaconazole should be used during pregnancy only if clearly needed.

Oral reproduction studies in rats and rabbits did not produce any evidence of maternal toxicity, embryotoxicity or teratogenicity of sertaconazole at an oral dose of 160 mg/kg/day (40 times (rats) and 80 times (rabbits) the maximum recommended human dose on a body surface area comparison). In an oral peri-postnatal study in rats, a reduction in live birth indices and an increase in the number of still-born pups was seen at 80 and 160 mg/kg/day.

FDA Pregnancy Category C.

Breast-feeding
It is not known if sertaconazole is excreted in human milk. Because many drugs are excreted in human milk, caution should be exercised when prescribing sertaconazole to a nursing woman.

Pediatrics
Appropriate studies on the relationship of age (under 12 years) to the effects of sertaconazole have not been performed in the pediatric population. Pediatrics-specific problems that would limit the usefulness of this medication in children are not expected. The efficacy and safety of sertaconazole have not been established in pediatric patients below the age of 12 years.

Geriatrics
Appropriate studies on the relationship of age to the effects of sertaconazole have not been performed in the geriatric population. Studies of sertaconazole did not include sufficient numbers of subjects aged 65 and over to determine whether they respond differently than younger subjects. However, no geriatrics-specific problems have been reported to date.

Medical considerations/Contraindications
The medical considerations/contraindications included have been selected on the basis of their potential clinical significance (reasons given in parentheses where appropriate)—not necessarily inclusive (» = major clinical significance).

Except under special circumstances, this medication should not be used when the following medical problem exists:

» Sertaconazole is contraindicated in patients who have a known or suspected sensitivity to sertaconazole or any of its components or to other imidazoles.

Patient monitoring
The following may be especially important in patient monitoring (other tests may be warranted in some patients, depending on condition; » = major clinical significance):

» Skin irritation or
Skin sensitivity
(if irritation or sensitivity develops with the use of sertaconazole cream treatment should be discontinued and appropriate therapy instituted)

Side/Adverse Effects
The following side/adverse effects have been selected on the basis of their potential clinical significance (possible signs and symptoms in parentheses where appropriate)—not necessarily inclusive:

Those indicating need for medical attention only if they continue or are bothersome
Incidence unknown—Observed during clinical trials and non-US postmarketing

Application site reaction (burning, itching, redness, skin rash, swelling, or soreness at site); ***burning skin; contact dermatitis*** (blistering, burning, crusting, dryness or flaking of skin; itching, scaling, severe redness, soreness or swelling of skin); ***desquamation*** (peeling of skin); ***dry skin; erythema*** (flushing, redness of skin; unusually warm skin); ***hyperpigmentation*** (darkening of skin); ***pruritus*** (itching skin); ***skin tenderness; vesiculation*** (blistering, peeling, or loosening of the skin)

Overdose
For more information on the management of overdose or unintentional ingestion, **contact a poison control center** (see *Poison Control Center Listing*).

Overdosage with sertaconazole has not been reported to date. Sertaconazole is intended for topical dermatologic use only.

Patient Consultation
As an aid to patient consultation, refer to *Advice for the Patient, Sertaconazole (Topical).*

In providing consultation, consider emphasizing the following selected information (» = major clinical significance):

Before using this medication
» Conditions affecting use, especially:
Hypersensitivity to sertaconazole or any of its components or to other imidazoles

Proper use of this medication
Proper administration technique
Compliance with full course of therapy
Sertaconazole is for external use only
Not applying occlusive dressing over this medication unless directed to do so by physician
» Proper dosing
Missed dose: Applying as soon as possible; not applying if almost time for next dose
Avoiding contact with eyes, nose, mouth and other mucus membranes
Washing hands after applying medicine
» Proper storage

Precautions while using this medication
» Checking with physician if no improvement within 2 weeks or if condition worsens
Importance of checking with physician if application area shows signs of irritation, redness, itching, burning, blistering, swelling or oozing

General Dosing Information
For topical dosing forms:

Sufficient sertaconazole cream should be applied to cover both the affected areas between the toes and immediately surrounding healthy skin of patients with interdigital tinea pedis. If a patient shows no clinical improvement 2 weeks after the treatment period, the diagnosis should be reviewed.

Diagnosis of the disease should be confirmed either by direct microscopic examination of infected superficial epidermal tissue in a solution of potassium hydroxide or by culture on an appropriate medium.

Sertaconazole is intended for topical dermatologic use only. It is not for oral, ophthalmic, or intravaginal use.

Topical Dosage Forms

SERTACONAZOLE CREAM

Usual adult dose

Tinea pedis—

Topical, applied twice daily for 4 weeks.

Usual pediatric dose

For pediatric patients over the age of 12: See *Usual adult dose.*

Usual geriatric dose

See *Usual adult dose.*

Strength(s) usually available

U.S.—

2% (Rx) [*Ertaczo* (17.5 mg of sertaconazole in a white cream base; ethylene glycol; polyethylene glycol; palmitostearate; glyceryl isostearate; light mineral oil; methylparaben; polyoxyethylened saturated glycerides; glycolized saturated glycerides; sorbic acid; purified water)].

Canada—

Not commercially available

Packaging and storage

Store at 25°C (77°F); excursions permitted to 15-30°C (59-86°F).

Auxiliary labeling

- For external use only
- Not for oral use
- Apply to clean, dry area of skin
- Continue medicine for full time of treatment

Developed: 03/01/2004

SERTRALINE Systemic

VA CLASSIFICATION (Primary/Secondary): CN603/CN900

Commonly used brand name(s): *Zoloft*.

Note: For a listing of dosage forms and brand names by country availability, see *Dosage Forms* section(s).

Category

Antianxiety agent; antidepressant; antiobsessional agent; antipanic agent; posttraumatic stress disorder therapy agent; premenstrual dysphoric disorder (PMDD) therapy agent.

Indications

Accepted

Depressive disorder, major (treatment)—Sertraline is indicated for the treatment of major depressive disorder. Treatment of acute depressive episodes typically requires 6 to 12 months of antidepressant therapy. Patients with recurrent or chronic depression may require long-term treatment. Sertraline showed effective maintenance of antidepressant response for up to 52 weeks of treatment in a placebo-controlled trial.

Obsessive-compulsive disorder (treatment)—Sertraline is indicated for the treatment of obsessions and compulsions in adults and children[1] 6 years of age and older with obsessive-compulsive disorder.

Panic disorder (treatment)—Sertraline is indicated for the treatment of panic disorder with or without agoraphobia.

Posttraumatic stress disorder (treatment)[1]—Sertraline is indicated for the treatment of posttraumatic stress disorder (PTSD) in adults. In placebo-controlled trials for up to 28 weeks, sertraline was shown to be effective in sustaining symptom improvement and preventing relapse of PTSD.

Premenstrual dysphoric disorder (treatment)[1]—Sertraline is indicated for the treatment of premenstrual dysphoric disorder (PMDD).

Social anxiety disorder (treatment)[1]—Sertraline is indicated for the treatment of social anxiety disorder, also known as social phobia.

[Premature ejaculation (treatment)][1]—Sertraline is indicated for the treatment of premature ejaculation.

[1]Not included in Canadian product labeling.

Pharmacology/Pharmacokinetics

Physicochemical characteristics

Chemical Group—Naphthylamine derivative. Chemically unrelated to tricyclic or tetracyclic antidepressants.

Molecular weight—Sertraline hydrochloride: 342.7.

Solubility—Sertraline hydrochloride is slightly soluble in water and sparingly soluble in ethyl alcohol.

Mechanism of action/Effect

Sertraline is a potent and selective inhibitor of neuronal uptake of serotonin (5-hydroxytryptamine [5-HT]). It has only weak effects on neuronal uptake of norepinephrine and dopamine. Chronic administration of sertraline in animals has resulted in down-regulation of postsynaptic beta-adrenergic receptors. Sertraline's inhibition of serotonin reuptake enhances serotonergic transmission, which results in subsequent inhibition of adrenergic activity in the locus ceruleus. Specifically, sertraline depresses the firing of the raphe serotonin neurons; this, in turn, increases the activity of the locus ceruleus, with consequent desensitization of the postsynaptic beta-receptors and presynaptic $alpha_2$-receptors.

Sertraline lacks affinity for adrenergic ($alpha_1$, $alpha_2$, or beta) receptors, muscarinic-cholinergic receptors, gamma aminobutyric acid (GABA) receptors, dopaminergic receptors, histaminergic receptors, serotonergic ($5\text{-}HT_{1A}$, $5\text{-}HT_{1B}$, $5\text{-}HT_2$) receptors, and benzodiazepine receptors. Sertraline does not inhibit monoamine oxidase.

Other actions/effects

Sertraline inhibits the isoenzyme cytochrome P450 2D6 (CYP2D6). When used in low clinical doses, sertraline probably inhibits CYP2D6 less than other selective serotonin reuptake inhibitors.

Sertraline blocks the uptake of serotonin into human platelets as well as into neurons. There have been rare reports of altered platelet function and of abnormal bleeding or purpura in patients taking sertraline.

Sertraline has anorectic effects.

Absorption

Slow but consistent. Bioavailability and absorption rate are increased if sertraline is taken with food.

Distribution

Both sertraline and its metabolites are extensively distributed into tissues. In animal studies, the volume of distribution (Vol_D) exceeded 20 liters/kilogram (L/kg).

Protein binding

Very high (98%). However, at concentrations up to and greater than those achieved during therapeutic dosing of sertraline, neither sertraline nor its major metabolite, *N*-desmethylsertraline, altered plasma protein binding of warfarin or propranolol *in vitro* .

Biotransformation

Undergoes extensive first-pass metabolism in the liver. The primary initial pathway is *N*-demethylation to form *N*-desmethylsertraline, which is substantially less active than the parent compound, exhibiting only about 1/8 of its activity. Animal testing has shown that *N*-desmethylsertraline does not contribute appreciably to the pharmacologic activity or toxicity of the parent compound. Both sertraline and *N*-desmethylsertraline undergo oxidative deamination and subsequent reduction, hydroxylation, and glucuronide conjugation.

Half-life

Elimination—

Sertraline: 24 to 26 hours.

N-desmethylsertraline: 62 to 104 hours.

Onset of action

Antidepressant and antipanic effects—2 to 4 weeks.

Antiobsessional effects may take longer to achieve.

Time to peak concentration

Time to reach mean peak plasma concentration (T_{max}) following administration of 50 to 200 mg of sertraline once daily for 14 days ranged from 4.5 to 8.4 hours. When sertraline was administered with food, T_{max} fell from 8 hours to 5.5 hours post-dosing.

Time to steady-state concentration

After once-daily dosing of sertraline in adult subjects, steady-state plasma concentrations were reached in about 7 days. Based on a 14-day kinetics study, steady state should be reached after 2 to 3 weeks in older patients.

Peak plasma concentration

Mean peak plasma concentration (C_{max}) and area under the plasma concentration-time curve (AUC) after a single dose of sertraline were proportional to dose over the range of 50 to 200 mg, demonstrating linear pharmacokinetics. When sertraline was administered with food, C_{max} increased by 25% and AUC increased slightly.

Elimination

Renal—

In two healthy male subjects, about 40 to 45% of an administered radioactive dose was recovered in the urine within 9 days, with less than 0.2% recovered unchanged.

Fecal—

In two healthy male subjects, about 40 to 45% of an administered radioactive dose was recovered in feces within 9 days, including 12 to 14% unchanged sertraline.

In dialysis—

Due to large volume of distribution, dialysis is not believed to be effective.

Precautions to Consider

Carcinogenicity

In lifetime carcinogenicity studies, there was a dose-related increase in the incidence of liver adenomas in male CD-1 mice receiving sertraline at doses of 10 to 40 mg per kg of body weight (mg/kg) per day (less than and equal to the maximum recommended human dose [MRHD] on a mg per square meter of body surface area [mg/m^2] basis). However, liver adenomas have a variable rate of spontaneous occurrence in the CD-1 mouse, and the significance of this finding to use in humans is unknown. No increase in liver adenomas was seen in Long-Evans rats or in female CD-1 mice receiving doses of up to 40 mg/kg. No increase in the incidence of hepatocellular carcinomas was seen in the studies. Female rats receiving 40 mg/kg (two times the MRHD on a mg/m^2 basis) had an increase in follicular adenomas of the thyroid, unaccompanied by thyroid hyperplasia. Rats receiving 10 to 40 mg/kg (0.5 to 2 times the MRHD on a mg/m^2 basis) showed an increase in uterine adenocarcinomas compared with placebo controls, but this effect was not clearly drug-related.

Mutagenicity

Sertraline had no genotoxic effects, with or without metabolic activation, based on the bacterial mutation assay, mouse lymphoma mutation assay, or tests for cytogenic aberrations *in vivo* in mouse bone marrow and *in vitro* in human lymphocytes.

Pregnancy/Reproduction

Fertility—A decrease in fertility was seen in one of two studies in rats that received 80 mg/kg of sertraline per day (four times the MRHD on a mg/m^2 basis).

Pregnancy—There are no adequate and well-controlled studies in pregnant women. Sertraline should be used during pregnancy only if the potential benefit justifies the potential risk to the fetus.

In neonates whose mothers had been treated with sertraline during pregnancy and in an infant whose mother discontinued sertraline treatment during breast feeding, there have been isolated reports in the neonates of reactions such as difficulty breathing, hypertonia, hyperreflexia, jitteriness, restlessness, and tremors.

A prospective study compared birth outcomes of 267 pregnancies that were exposed to the selective serotonin reuptake inhibitors (SSRIs) sertraline (50 mg/day, range 25 to 250 mg/day), paroxetine (30 mg/day, range 10 to 60 mg/day), or fluvoxamine (50 mg/day, range 25 to 200 mg/day) with those of 267 pregnancies that were exposed to medications or medical treatments that are known to be nonteratogenic. Sertraline was taken at some time during 147 of the SSRI-exposed pregnancies. Based on interviews with the mothers 6 to 9 months after the births, no differences in the infants' gestational ages or mean birth weights, or in the rates of major malformations, spontaneous or elective abortions, or stillbirths were found between the two groups. Also, no differences were found between infants exposed to SSRIs during the first trimester only and infants exposed to SSRIs throughout gestation. The behavioral effects of *in utero* sertraline exposure were not examined.

No teratogenic effects were demonstrated in studies in rats and rabbits receiving approximately four times the MRHD on a mg/m^2 basis. However, delayed ossification occurred in fetuses of rats and rabbits given sertraline dosages of 10 mg/kg per day (one half the MRHD on a mg/m^2 basis) and 40 mg/kg per day (four times the MRHD on a mg/m^2 basis), respectively, during the period of organogenesis. Also, an increase in pup stillbirths and pup deaths during the first 4 days of life and a decrease in pup weights were seen in rats when dams were given a sertraline dose of 20 mg/kg per day (equal to the MRHD on a mg/m^2 basis) through the last one third of gestation and through lactation. There was no effect on pup mortality at doses $\leq$ 10 mg/kg per day (one half the MRHD on a mg/m^2 basis). The decrease in pup survival was due to *in utero* exposure to sertraline. The clinical significance of these effects is unknown.

FDA Pregnancy Category C.

Labor and delivery—The effect of sertraline on labor and delivery is not known.

Breast-feeding

Sertraline is distributed into breast milk. Very low levels of sertraline and/or *N*-desmethylsertraline (< 2 nanograms/mL) were detected in the plasma of breast-fed infants of mothers who were receiving sertraline. However, no adverse effects in the infants were seen during the short-term (< 2 years) follow-up. Because sertraline is distributed into human breast milk, caution should be used when sertraline is administered to a nursing woman.

In an infant whose mother discontinued sertraline treatment during breast feeding and in neonates whose mothers had been treated with sertraline during pregnancy, there have been isolated reports in the neonates of reactions such as difficulty breathing, hypertonia, hyperreflexia, jitteriness, restlessness, and tremors.

Pediatrics

The efficacy of sertraline in pediatric patients with major depressive disorder, panic disorder, posttraumatic stress disorder [PTSD], premenstrual dysphoric disorder [PMDD], or social anxiety disorder has not been established.

Sertraline has been tested in children 6 to 17 years of age with obsessive compulsive disorder and, in effective doses, has not been shown to cause different side effects or problems than it does in adults. However, the effects of long-term use of sertraline on the growth, development, and maturation of children and adolescents are unknown. Because of the anorectic effect of sertraline, body weight and growth should be monitored in children receiving long-term treatment.

Antidepressants increase the risk of suicidal thinking and behavior (suicidality) in children and adolescents with major depressive disorder (MDD) and other psychiatric disorders. Anyone considering the use of sertraline or any other antidepressant in a child or adolescent must balance this risk with the clinical need.

Pooled analyses of short-term placebo controlled trials of nine antidepressant drugs in children and adolescents with MDD, obsessive compulsive disorder, or other psychiatric disorders have revealed a greater risk of adverse events representing suicidality during the first few months of treatment in those receiving antidepressants.

Geriatrics

No geriatrics-specific problems have been documented in studies done to date that included elderly patients. However, in one study, clearance of sertraline in 16 elderly patients was about 40% lower than clearance in a group of younger subjects, indicating that steady-state will take 2 to 3 weeks to achieve in elderly patients. A reduced initial dosage is recommended in elderly patients. Greater sensitivity of some older individuals taking sertraline cannot be ruled out.

Drug interactions and/or related problems

The following drug interactions and/or related problems have been selected on the basis of their potential clinical significance (possible mechanism in parentheses where appropriate)—not necessarily inclusive (» = major clinical significance):

Note: Sertraline inhibits cytochrome P450 2D6 (CYP2D6) and a potential exists for clinically significant interactions with medications that are metabolized by this isoenzyme, particularly medications having a narrow therapeutic index, such as tricyclic antidepressants and the type 1C antiarrhythmics propafenone and flecainide. A lower dosage of these medications may be needed when they are used concomitantly with sertraline, and an increase in dosage may be necessary after discontinuation of sertraline following concomitant use.

In vivo interaction studies indicate that sertraline's extent of inhibition of P450 3A4 activity is not likely to be of clinical significance. Sertraline did not increase plasma concentrations of cisapride, carbamazepine, or terfenadine in these studies.

Combinations containing any of the following medications, depending on the amount present, may also interact with this medication.

Alcohol
(although sertraline has not been shown to alter alcohol metabolism and does not appear to potentiate cognitive and psychomotor effects of alcohol in normal subjects, concomitant use is not recommended)

» Antidepressants, tricyclic (TCAs) or
» Type 1C antiarrhythmics, such as:
» Flecainide or
» Propafenone or
Other drugs metabolized by P450 2D6 and have a narrow therapeutic index

(concomitant use of a drug metabolized by P450 2D6 and sertraline has the potential for clinically important 2D6 inhibition and may require reducing the dose of the other drug; when sertraline is withdrawn from co-therapy the dose of the other drug may need to be increased)

» Astemizole or
(because sertraline inhibits cytochrome P450 enzymes and may increase plasma concentrations of these medications, thereby increasing the risk of cardiac arrhythmias, concurrent use is not recommended)

Cimetidine
(AUC, C_{max}, and mean half-life of sertraline were increased by 50%, 24%, and 26%, respectively, compared with placebo values, when a single dose of 100 mg of sertraline was administered on the second day of administration of 800 mg per day of cimetidine)

Cisapride
(concurrent use of cisapride and sertraline may induce the metabolism of cisapride; cisapride AUC and C_{max} were reduced by about 35%)

CNS active drugs such as
Diazepam
(after 21 days of dosing with sertraline or placebo, clearance of diazepam following a single intravenous dose was decreased from baseline by 32% in subjects administered sertraline and by 19% in subjects administered placebo; however, the clinical significance of this interaction is unknown)

CNS active drugs, especially antidepressants, antiobsessional, antipanic, or agents used to treat posttraumatic stress disorder or premenstrual dysphoric disorder
(caution is advised if concomitant administration of sertraline and other CNS active drugs is required)
(caution is advised when switching from other CNS active drugs or from one selective serotonin reuptake inhibitor to another; the duration of an appropriate washout period may not be established)

» Disulfiram
(sertraline **oral concentrate** contains 12% alcohol; concomitant use with disulfiram is **contraindicated**)

Electroconvulsive therapy
(combined use of electroconvulsive therapy [ECT] and sertraline has not been established)

» Highly protein-bound medications, especially:
Digitoxin
Warfarin
(caution in concurrent use with sertraline is recommended because of possible displacement of either medication from protein-binding sites, leading to increased plasma concentrations of the free [unbound] medications and increased risk of adverse effects)
(after single oral doses of warfarin in six healthy males, the prothrombin time was increased and the protein binding of warfarin was decreased compared with both baseline and the placebo group values after 21 days of sertraline dosing that was escalated from 50 mg per day to 200 mg per day; changes were small but statistically significant; prothrombin time should be carefully monitored when sertraline therapy is initiated or stopped in patients taking warfarin)

Lithium
(although a placebo-controlled clinical trial in normal volunteers demonstrated no alteration in steady-state lithium levels or renal clearance of lithium, close monitoring of lithium concentrations is recommended; also, concurrent use may lead to an increased incidence of serotonin-associated side effects)

» Moclobemide
(because of the potentially fatal effects of concomitant use of sertraline and nonselective, irreversible monoamine oxidase [MAO] inhibitors, and the increased risk of development of the serotonin syndrome with concomitant use of sertraline and the selective, reversible MAO-A inhibitor moclobemide, concurrent use is not recommended; allowing a washout period of 3 to 7 days is advised between discontinuing moclobemide and initiating sertraline therapy, and allowing a washout period of 2 weeks is advised between discontinuing sertraline and initiating moclobemide therapy)

» Monoamine oxidase (MAO) inhibitors, including furazolidone, procarbazine, and selegiline
(concurrent use of MAO inhibitors with sertraline may result in hyperpyretic episodes, severe convulsions, hypertensive crises, or the serotonin syndrome; fatalities have occurred; concomitant use of MAO inhibitors with sertraline is **contraindicated**; a wash-out period of at least 14 days should elapse between discontinuation of either medication [the MAO inhibitor or sertraline] and initiation of the other.)

» Pimozide
(controlled study co-administration of a 2 mg pimozide as a single dose and 200 mg sertraline given once daily was associated with a mean increase in pimozide AUC and C_{max} of about 40%; due to the narrow therapeutic index of pimozide and due to the interaction noted at a low dose of pimozide, concomitant administration of sertraline and pimozide is **contraindicated**)

» Serotonergics or other medications or substances with serotonergic activity (see *Appendix II*)
(increased risk of developing the serotonin syndrome, a rare but potentially fatal hyperserotonergic state; symptoms typically occur shortly [hours to days] after the addition of a serotonergic agent to a regimen that includes other serotonin-enhancing drugs, such as sertraline, or an increase in dosage of a serotonergic agent; symptoms include agitation, diaphoresis, diarrhea, fever, hyperreflexia, incoordination, mental status changes [confusion, hypomania], myoclonus, shivering, or tremor; the syndrome usually resolves shortly after the discontinuation of the serotonergic agents)

» St. John's wort
(concomitant use of sertraline and St. John's wort may result in an increase in undesirable effects)

Sumatriptan
(rare post-marketing reports of patients with weakness, hyperreflexia, and incoordination following the use of a selective serotonin reuptake inhibitor [SSRI] and sumatriptan; if concomitant use is clinically warranted, appropriate patient observation is advised)

Tolbutamide
(in a placebo-controlled study in 25 healthy male volunteers, clearance of tolbutamide following a single intravenous dose was decreased by 16% from baseline after 22 days of sertraline dosing that was escalated from 50 mg per day to 200 mg per day; blood glucose should be monitored, and the dosage of tolbutamide reduced if hypoglycemia occurs)

Laboratory value alterations

The following have been selected on the basis of their potential clinical significance (possible effect in parentheses where appropriate)—not necessarily inclusive (» = major clinical significance):

With physiology/laboratory test values
Alanine aminotransferase (ALT [SGPT]) or
Aspartate aminotransferase (AST [SGOT])
(values increased to ≥ 3 times the upper limit of normal have been reported infrequently; increases usually occur within 1 to 9 weeks of initiation of therapy, with values generally normalizing after sertraline is discontinued)

Bilirubin
(increase observed during postmarketing evaluation of sertraline)

Total cholesterol or
Triglycerides
(mean increases of 3% and 5%, respectively, have been reported)

Uric acid, serum
(mean decreases of approximately 7% have been reported)

Medical considerations/Contraindications

The medical considerations/contraindications included have been selected on the basis of their potential clinical significance (reasons given in parentheses where appropriate)—not necessarily inclusive (» = major clinical significance).

Except under special circumstances, this medication should not be used when the following medical problem exists:

» Hypersensitivity to latex (**oral concentrate only**)
(use of oral concentrate is contraindicated in patients with latex hypersensitivity; dropper dispenser for sertraline oral concentrate contains natural dry rubber)

» Hypersensitivity to sertraline or any of its components
(use is contraindicated in these patients)

Risk-benefit should be considered when the following medical problems exist:

Dehydration or
Hyponatremia
(conditions may be exacerbated; more prevalent in elderly individuals, some patients were taking diuretics)

Diseases or conditions affecting hemodynamic responses, such as:
Heart disease, unstable or
Myocardial infarction, recent history of
(caution is advisable in these patients)

» Hepatic function impairment
(in a single-dose study, mean elimination half-life of sertraline was prolonged from 22 hours in healthy subjects to 52 hours in patients with mild, stable cirrhosis; peak concentrations and AUC were increased 1.7 and 4.4 times, respectively, in patients with hepatic impairment; decreased dosage or less frequent dosing is recommended)

Mania, history of
(activation of mania or hypomania was reported in approximately 0.4% of patients during premarketing testing of sertraline, and occurs most frequently in patients with bipolar disorder)

Neurological impairment, including developmental delay
(risk of seizures may be increased)

Platelet function, altered or abnormal
(altered platelet function, abnormal platelet function laboratory results, abnormal bleeding or purpura have been reported rarely in patients taking sertraline; use with caution and monitor for signs of abnormal bleeding or purpura)

Renal function impairment
(results of an open-label study showed no difference between pharmacokinetic parameters of sertraline in patients with renal impairment ranging from mild to severe [but not requiring regular hemodialysis] and those of a matched healthy group with no renal impairment; however, since clinical experience with long-term sertraline treatment in patients with renal impairment is lacking, caution is recommended)

Seizure disorders
(seizures occurred in approximately 0.2% of subjects in clinical trials of sertraline for obsessive-compulsive disorder, with most cases occurring in patients with a pre-existing seizure disorder or a family history of seizure disorder; as with other antidepressants, sertraline should be introduced with care)

Weight loss
(although the weight loss associated with sertraline use is usually about one to two pounds [0.4 to 0.9 kg], there have been rare reports of significant weight loss; significant weight loss may be undesirable in some patients)

Patient monitoring

The following may be especially important in patient monitoring (other tests may be warranted in some patients, depending on condition; » = major clinical significance):

Careful evaluation and supervision of patients with a history of drug abuse
(patients should be followed closely observing them for signs of sertraline misuse or abuse)

Careful supervision of depressed patients including those with:
Abnormal behaviors (i.e., agitation, panic attacks, hostility) or
Clinical worsening of their depression or
Suicidal ideation and behavior (suicidality)
(recommended especially during early treatment phase before peak effectiveness of sertraline is achieved or at the time of increases or decreases in dose; prescribing the smallest number of tablets necessary for good patient management is recommended to decrease the risk of overdose; consideration should be given to changing the therapeutic regimen, including possibly discontinuing the medicine, in patients whose depression is persistently worse or whose emergent suicidality or other symptoms are severe, abrupt in onset, or were not part of the patient's presenting symptoms)

Glucose, blood
(Careful monitoring of blood glucose is recommended in patients treated with sertraline and oral hypoglycemic medications or insulin.)

Prothombin time
(should be carefully monitored when sertraline therapy is initiated or stopped in patients on warfarin therapy)

Side/Adverse Effects

Note: Side effects may be dose-related and time-related. Severity of side effects appears to lessen with decreased doses or after administration for longer than 2 weeks.

The following side/adverse effects have been selected on the basis of their potential clinical significance (possible signs and symptoms in parentheses where appropriate)—not necessarily inclusive:

Those indicating need for medical attention

Incidence more frequent

Sexual dysfunction (decreased sexual desire or ability); ***ejaculation failure; ejaculation failure*** (failure to discharge semen (in men))

Note: *Sexual dysfunction* may include decreased libido, impotence, delayed ejaculation, or anorgasmia. Delayed ejaculation is the most commonly seen form of sexual dysfunction associated with sertraline use.

Incidence less frequent or rare

Abnormal bleeding (red or purple spots on skin; nose bleeds); ***aggressive reaction***—in pediatric patients; ***akathisia*** (inability to sit still; restlessness); ***breast tenderness or enlargement; or galactorrhea*** (unusual secretion of milk)—in females; ***extrapyramidal effects, dystonic*** (unusual or sudden body or facial movements or postures); ***fever; hyperkinesia*** (increase in body movements)—in pediatric patients; ***hyponatremia*** (confusion; drowsiness; dryness of mouth; increased thirst; lack of energy; seizures); ***mania or hypomania*** (fast talking and excited feelings or actions that are out of control)—may be more frequent in patients with bipolar disorder; ***palpitation*** (fast or irregular heartbeat); ***seizure*** (convulsions; muscle spasm or jerking of all extremities; sudden loss of consciousness; loss of bladder control); ***serotonin syndrome*** (diarrhea; fever; increased sweating; mood or behavior changes; overactive reflexes; racing heartbeat; restlessness; shivering or shaking); ***skin rash, hives, or itching; urinary incontinence*** (loss of bladder control)—in pediatric patients

Note: *Hyponatremia* is probably the result of the syndrome of inappropriate antidiuretic hormone secretion (SIADH). Most cases have been in elderly patients or in volume-depleted patients, such as patients taking diuretics.

The *serotonin syndrome* is most likely to occur shortly (within hours to days) after an increase in sertraline dosage or the addition of another serotonergic agent to the patient's regimen. The syndrome may include cardiac arrhythmias, coma, disseminated intravascular coagulation, hypertension or hypotension, renal failure, respiratory failure, seizures, or severe hyperthermia.

Incidence not determined—Observed during clinical practice, estimates of frequency cannot be determined

Acute renal failure (agitation, coma, confusion, decreased urine output, depression, dizziness, headache, hostility, irritability, lethargy, muscle twitching, nausea, rapid weight gain, seizures, stupor, swelling of face, ankles, or hands, unusual tiredness or weakness); ***agranulocytosis*** (cough or hoarseness, fever with or without chills, general feeling of tiredness or weakness, lower back or side pain, painful or difficult urination, sore throat, sores, ulcers, or white spots on lips or in mouth, unusual bleeding or bruising); ***anaphylactoid reaction*** (cough, difficulty swallowing, dizziness, fast heartbeat, hives, itching, puffiness or swelling of the eyelids or around the eyes, face, lips or tongue, shortness of breath, skin rash, tightness in chest, unusual tiredness or weakness, wheezing); ***angioedema*** (large, hive-like swelling on face, eyelids, lips, tongue, throat, hands, legs, feet, sex organs); ***aplastic anemia*** (chest pain, chills, cough, fever, headache, shortness of breath, sores, ulcers, or white spots on lips or in mouth, swollen or painful glands, tightness in chest, unusual bleeding or bruising, unusual tiredness or weakness, wheezing); ***atrial arrhythmias*** (dizziness, fainting, fast, slow, or irregular heartbeat); ***atrioventricular [AV] block*** (chest pain, dizziness, fainting, pounding, slow heartbeat, troubled breathing, unusual tiredness or weakness); ***blindness; bradycardia*** (chest pain or discomfort, lightheadedness, dizziness or fainting, shortness of breath, slow or irregular heartbeat, unusual tiredness); ***cataract*** (blindness, blurred vision, decreased vision); ***extrapyramidal symptoms*** (difficulty in speaking, drooling, loss of balance control, muscle trembling, jerking, or stiffness, restlessness, shuffling walk, stiffness of limbs, twisting movements of body, uncontrolled movements, especially of face, neck, and back); ***hepatitis*** (dark urine, general tiredness and weakness, light-colored stools, nausea and vomiting, upper right abdominal pain, yellow eyes and skin); ***hepatomegaly*** (right upper abdominal pain and fullness.); ***hypothyroidism*** (constipation; depressed mood; dry skin and hair; feeling cold; hair loss; hoarseness or husky voice; muscle cramps and stiffness; slowed heartbeat; weight gain; unusual tiredness or weakness); ***increased coagulation times; jaundice*** (chills, clay-colored stools, dark urine, dizziness, fever, headache, itching, loss of appetite, nausea, abdominal or stomach pain, rash, unpleasant breath odor, unusual tiredness or weakness, vomiting of blood, yellow eyes or skin); ***leukopenia*** (black, tarry stools, chest pain, chills, cough, fever, painful or difficult urination, shortness of breath, sore throat, sores, ulcers, or white spots on lips or in mouth, swollen glands, unusual bleeding or bruising, unusual tiredness or weakness); ***liver failure*** (headache, stomach pain, continuing vomiting, dark-colored urine, general feeling of tiredness or weakness, light-colored stools, yellow eyes or skin); ***lupus-like syndrome*** (fever or chills, general feeling of discomfort, illness, or weakness); ***neuroleptic malignant syndrome-like events*** (convulsions, difficulty in breathing, fast heartbeat, high fever, high or low blood pressure, increased sweating, loss of bladder control, severe muscle stiffness, unusually pale skin, tiredness); ***oculogyric crisis*** (fixed position of eye); ***optic neuritis*** (blindness, blue-yellow color blindness, blurred vision, decreased vision, eye pain); ***pancreatitis*** (bloating, chills, constipation, darkened urine, fast heartbeat, fever, indigestion, loss of appetite, nausea, pains in stomach, side, or abdomen, possibly radiating to the back, vomiting, yellow eyes or skin); ***pancytopenia*** (high fever; chills; unexplained bleeding or bruising; bloody, black, or tarry stools; pale skin; unusual tiredness or weakness; cough; shortness of breath; sores, ulcers, or white spots on lips or in mouth; swollen glands); ***psychosis*** (feeling that others can hear your thoughts, feeling that others are watching you or controlling your behavior, feeling, seeing, or hearing things that are not there, severe mood or mental changes, unusual behavior); ***pulmonary hypertension*** (shortness of breath); ***QT-interval prolongation; Steven-Johnson syndrome*** (blistering, peeling, loosening of skin, chills, cough, diarrhea, itching, joint or muscle pain, red irritated eyes, red skin lesions, often with a purple center, sore throat, sores, ulcers, or white spots in mouth or on lips, unusual tiredness or weakness); ***serum sickness*** (feeling of discomfort, fever, inflammation of joints, itching, muscle aches, rash, swollen lymph glands); ***thrombocytopenia*** (black, tarry stools; bleeding gums; blood in urine or stools; pinpoint red spots on skin; unusual bleeding or bruising); ***vasculitis*** (redness, soreness or itching skin; fever; sores, welting or blisters); ***ventricular tachycardia*** (fainting; fast, pounding, or irregular heartbeat or pulse; palpitations)—including torsade de pointes-type arrhythmias

Those indicating need for medical attention only if they continue or are bothersome

Incidence more frequent

Dizziness; drowsiness; fatigue (unusual tiredness or weakness); ***gastrointestinal effects; including anorexia*** (decrease in appetite); ***diarrhea or loose stools; dryness of mouth; dyspepsia*** (acid or sour stomach; belching; heartburn; indigestion; stomach discomfort upset or pain); ***nausea; stomach or abdominal cramps, gas, or pain; or weight loss; headache; increased sweating; insomnia*** (trouble in sleeping); ***somnolence*** (sleepiness or unusual drowsiness); ***tiredness or weakness; tremor*** (trembling or shaking)

Note: *Weight loss* in patients in controlled trials was usually about one to two pounds [0.4 to 0.9 kg]. Significant weight loss was reported rarely.

Incidence less frequent

Anxiety, agitation, or nervousness; changes in vision, including blurred vision; constipation; flushing or redness of skin, with feeling of warmth or heat; increased appetite; paresthesias (burning, crawling, itching, numbness, prickling, "pins and needles", or tingling feelings); ***sinusitis*** (pain or tenderness around eyes and cheekbones; fever; stuffy or runny nose; headache; cough; shortness of breath or troubled breathing; tightness of chest; wheezing)—in pediatric patients; ***urinary tract infection*** (bladder pain; bloody or cloudy urine; difficult, burning, or painful urination; frequent urge to urinate; lower back or side pain)—in older adults; ***vomiting; yawning***

Incidence not determined—Observed during clinical practice, estimates of frequency cannot be determined

Hyperglycemia (abdominal pain, blurred vision, dry mouth, fatigue, flushed, dry skin, fruit-like breath odor, increased hunger, increased thirst, increased urination, nausea, sweating, troubled breathing, unexplained weight loss. vomiting); ***hyperprolactinemia*** (swelling of breasts or unusual milk production); ***photosensitivity*** (increased sensitivity of skin to sunlight, itching, redness or other discoloration of skin, severe sunburn, skin rash)

Those indicating the need for medical attention if they occur after medication is discontinued or dose is reduced

Abnormal dreams; agitation; anxiety; dizziness; gait instability (trouble in walking); ***headache; increased sweating; insomnia*** (trouble in sleeping); ***nausea; sensory disturbances, including; electric shock sensations; paresthesias*** (burning, crawling, itching, numbness, prickling, "pins and needles", or tingling feelings); ***tremor*** (trembling or shaking); ***unusual tiredness; vertigo*** (feeling of constant movement of self or surroundings); ***vomiting***

Note: Discontinuation symptoms are usually mild, and are often mistaken for influenza.

Overdose

For specific information on the agents used in the management of sertraline overdose, see *Charcoal, Activated (Oral-Local)* monograph.

For more information on the management of overdose or unintentional ingestion, **contact a Poison Control Center** (see *Poison Control Center Listing*).

Clinical effects of overdose

Note: Sertraline has a wide margin of safety in overdose. However, deaths have occurred in overdoses involving sertraline in combination with other drugs and/or alcohol.

Symptoms of overdose resemble the side/adverse effects occurring with therapeutic doses, but may be more intense or several symptoms may occur together.

The following effects have been selected on the basis of their potential clinical significance (possible signs and symptoms in parentheses where appropriate)—not necessarily inclusive:

Acute

Agitation; anxiety; bradycardia (chest pain or discomfort, lightheadedness, dizziness or fainting, shortness of breath, slow or irregular heartbeat, unusual tiredness); ***bundle branch block*** (chest pain or discomfort, fainting, shortness of breath, slow or irregular heartbeat, sweating); ***coma*** (change in consciousness, loss of consciousness); ***convulsions; delirium*** (unusual excitement, nervousness, or restlessness. hallucinations, confusion as to time, place, or person holding false beliefs that cannot be changed by fact); ***dizziness; drowsiness; electrocardiogram (ECG) changes; hallucinations*** (seeing, hearing, or feeling things that are not there); ***hypertension*** (blurred vision, dizziness, nervousness, headache, pounding in the ears, slow or fast heartbeat); ***hypotension*** (blurred vision, confusion, dizziness, faintness, or lightheadedness when getting up from a lying or sitting position suddenly, sweating, unusual tiredness or weakness); ***manic reaction*** (actions that are out of control, irritability, nervousness, talking, feeling, and acting with excitement); ***mydriasis*** (unusually large pupils); ***nausea; pancreatitis*** (bloating, chills, constipation, darkened urine, fast heartbeat, fever, indigestion, loss of appetite, nausea, pains in stomach, side, or abdomen, possibly radiating to the back, vomiting, yellow eyes or skin); ***QT-interval prolongation; serotonin syndrome*** (agitation, confusion, diarrhea, fever, overactive reflexes, poor coordination, restlessness, shivering, sweating, talking or acting with excitement you cannot control, trembling or shaking, twitching); ***somnolence*** (sleepiness or unusual drowsiness); ***stupor*** (decreased awareness or responsiveness; severe sleepiness); ***syncope*** (fainting); ***tachycardia*** (unusually fast heartbeat); ***tremor*** (trembling or shaking of hands or feet, shakiness in legs, arms, hands, feet); ***vomiting***

Note: Some patients may develop the serotonin syndrome, a potentially fatal symptom complex, in response to acute overdose with sertraline. The serotonin syndrome may be manifested by mental status changes, restlessness, myoclonus, hyperreflexia, diaphoresis, shivering, tremor, diarrhea, incoordination, and/or fever.

Treatment of overdose

There is no specific antidote for sertraline. Treatment is essentially symptomatic and supportive.

To decrease absorption—Administering activated charcoal, which may be used with sorbitol, may be as effective as or more effective than emesis or gastric lavage.

Monitoring—Monitoring cardiac function and vital signs.

Supportive care—Establishing and maintaining airway. Patients in whom intentional overdose is confirmed or suspected should be referred for psychiatric consultation.

Note: Dialysis, forced diuresis, hemoperfusion, and exchange transfusions are unlikely to be of benefit due to sertraline's large volume of distribution and high degree of protein binding.

Patient Consultation

As an aid to patient consultation, refer to *Advice for the Patient, Sertraline (Systemic)*.

In providing consultation, consider emphasizing the following selected information (» = major clinical significance):

Before using this medication

» Conditions affecting use, especially:

Pregnancy—No difference in birth outcome was found between 267 SSRI-exposed pregnancies (147 to sertraline) and 267 pregnancies exposed to known nonteratogenic medications or procedures; behavioral effects were not studied; risk benefit should be determined before administering sertraline to a pregnant woman

Use in children—Difficulty breathing, hypertonia, hyperreflexia, jitteriness, restlessness, and tremors may occur in neonates exposed to sertraline *in utero*.

FDA Pregnancy Category C

Breast-feeding—Distributed into breast milk; the long-term effects on nursing infants are unknown; caution should be used when administering sertraline to a nursing woman

Difficulty breathing, hypertonia, hyperreflexia, jitteriness, restlessness, and tremors may occur in infants exposed to sertraline in breast milk.

Use in children—The efficacy of sertraline in pediatric patients with major depressive disorder, panic disorder, posttraumatic stress disorder [PTSD], premenstrual dysphoric disorder [PMDD], or social anxiety disorder has not been established.

Body weight and growth should be monitored during long-term treatment because of anorectic effect

Because of Food and Drug Administration [FDA] reports of the occurrence of suicidality in clinical trials for various antidepressant drugs in pediatric patients with major depressive disorder [MDD], sertraline must be used with caution in treating pediatric patients for MDD.

Use in the elderly—Clearance is reduced; reduced initial dosage is recommended

Contraindicated medications—Disulfiram (oral concentrate only); MAO inhibitors; pimozide

Other medications, especially astemizole, digitoxin, flecainide, moclobemide, propafenone, warfarin and serotonergics or other medications or substances with serotonergic activity, St. John's wort, or tricyclic antidepressants

Other medical problems, especially hypersensitivity to sertraline or any of its components, hypersensitivity to latex (oral concentrate only) or hepatic dysfunction

Proper use of this medication

» Compliance with therapy; not taking more or less medicine than prescribed

Taking with or without food, as directed by physician

» Four weeks or more of therapy may be required before antidepressant or antipanic effects are achieved; antiobsessional effects may take longer to achieve

» Proper dosing

Missed dose: Discussing with physician what to do about any missed doses since some patients take sertraline in the morning and other patients take sertraline in the evening

» Proper storage

Precautions while using this medication

Regular visits to physician to check progress of therapy

» Not taking sertraline with or within 14 days of taking an MAO inhibitor; not taking an MAO inhibitor within 14 days of taking sertraline

» Importance of patient or caregiver notifying physician immediately if any signs of abnormal behavior, worsening depression or suicidality occur

Avoiding use of alcoholic beverages

» Possible drowsiness, impairment of judgment, thinking, or motor skills; caution when driving or doing jobs requiring alertness or coordination until effects of medication are known

» Checking with physician before discontinuing sertraline; dosage tapering may be required

Side/adverse effects

Signs of potential side effects, especially sexual dysfunction; abnormal bleeding; aggressive reaction (in children); akathisia; breast tenderness or enlargement, or galactorrhea (in females); extrapyramidal effects, dystonic; fever; hyperkinesia; hyponatremia; mania or hypomania; palpitation; seizure; serotonin syndrome; skin rash, hives, or itching; urinary incontinence (in children)

Signs of potential side effects following discontinuation or dose reduction of sertraline, especially abnormal dreams, agitation, anxiety, dizziness, gait instability, headache, increased sweating, insomnia, nausea, sensory disturbances such as paresthesias and electric shock sensations, tremor, unusual tiredness, vertigo or vomiting

Signs of potential side effects observed during clinical practice, especially acute renal failure, agranulocytosis, anaphylactoid reaction, angioedema, aplastic anemia, atrial arrhythmias, atrioventricular [AV] block, blindness, bradycardia, cataract, extrapyramidal symptoms, hepatitis, hepatomegaly, hypothyroidism, increased coagulation times, jaundice, leukopenia, liver failure, lupus-like syndrome, neuroleptic malignant syndrome-like events, oculogyric crisis, optic neuritis, pancreatitis, pancytopenia, psychosis, pulmonary hypertension, QT-interval prolongation, Steven-Johnson syndrome, serum sickness, thrombocytopenia, vasculitis, or ventricular tachycardia

General Dosing Information

Potentially suicidal patients, particularly those who may use alcohol excessively, should not have access to large quantities of this medication since they may continue to exhibit suicidal tendencies until significant improvement occurs. Some clinicians recommend that the patient be supplied with the least amount of medication necessary for satisfactory patient management.

Activation of hypomania or mania has been reported in patients treated with sertraline. Risk is greatest in patients with a history of bipolar disorder.

Sertraline should be administered once daily, either in the morning or evening.

Physicians who prescribe sertraline for extended periods should periodically reevaluate the long-term usefulness of the drug for the individual patient.

When discontinued, sertraline should be withdrawn gradually to help avoid the occurrence of discontinuation symptoms, including abnormal dreams, agitation, anxiety, dizziness, gait instability, headache, increased sweating, insomnia, nausea, sensory disturbances such as paresthesias and electric shock sensations, tremor, unusual tiredness, vertigo, or vomiting. Discontinuation symptoms are usually mild and are often mistaken for influenza.

Diet/Nutrition

Sertraline may be taken with or without food. Some clinicians advise their patients to take this medication with food to lessen gastrointestinal side effects.

For treatment of adverse effects

Serotonin syndrome—The serotonin syndrome usually resolves shortly after discontinuation of serotonergic medications. Treatment is essentially symptomatic and supportive. However, the nonspecific serotonergic receptor antagonists cyproheptadine and methysergide have been reported to be of some use in shortening the duration of the serotonin syndrome.

Oral Dosage Forms

Note: The dosing and strengths of the dosage forms available are expressed in terms of sertraline base.

SERTRALINE HYDROCHLORIDE CAPSULES

Usual adult dose

Depression or
Obsessive-compulsive disorder—

Oral, initially 50 mg (base) a day as a single morning or evening dose. The dosage may be increased after several weeks in increments of 50 mg, with increases made at intervals of at least one week, as needed and tolerated.

Note: Some clinicians recommend an initial dosage of 25 mg a day for one to two days.

Panic disorder
Posttraumatic stress disorder[1]
Social anxiety disorder[1]—

Oral, initially 25 mg (base) a day, as a single morning or evening dose. After one week, the dosage should be increased to 50 mg (base) a day, as a single dose. Further dosage increases may be made in increments of 50 mg, at intervals of at least one week, as needed and tolerated.

Premenstrual dysphoric disorder [PMDD][1]—

Oral, 50 mg per day, either daily throughout the menstrual cycle or limited to the luteal phase of the menstrual cycle, depending on physician assessment; dose may be increased at 50 mg increments per menstrual cycle.

[Premature ejaculation][1]—

Oral, initially 25 mg (base) a day as a single morning or evening dose. The dose may be increased to 50 mg a day.

Note: Patients with hepatic function impairment should receive a lower dosage or less frequent dosing than patients with normal hepatic function.

Usual adult prescribing limits

For major depressive disorder, obsessive-compulsive disorder, panic disorder, posttraumatic stress disorder, or social anxiety disorder—200 mg (base) a day.

For PMDD—150 mg per day when dosing daily throughout the menstrual cycle; 100 mg per day when dosing during the luteal phase of the menstrual cycle

Usual pediatric dose

Depression or
Panic disorder

Posttraumatic stress disorder
Premenstrual dysphoric disorder or
Social anxiety disorder—
Safety and efficacy have not been established.
Obsessive-compulsive disorder[1]—
Children 6 to 12 years of age: Oral, initially 25 mg (base) a day as a single morning or evening dose. Dosage may be increased at intervals of at least one week, as needed and tolerated.
Children 13 to 17 years of age: Oral, initially 50 mg (base) a day as a single morning or evening dose. Dosage may be increased at intervals of at least one week, as needed and tolerated.

Note: To avoid excessive dosing when the dosage is being increased, consideration should be given to the generally lower body weights of children as compared with adult body weights.

Usual pediatric prescribing limits
See *Usual adult prescribing limits.*

Usual geriatric dose
Depression or
Obsessive-compulsive disorder
Panic disorder
Posttraumatic stress disorder[1] or
Social anxiety disorder[1]—
Oral, initially 25 mg (base) a day, as a single morning or evening dose; dosage may be increased gradually as needed and tolerated.

Usual geriatric prescribing limits
See *Usual adult prescribing limits.*

Strength(s) usually available
U.S.—
Not commercially available.
Canada—
Note: Capsule is hard gelatin shell.
25 mg (base) (Rx) [*Zoloft* (anhydrous lactose; corn starch; magnesium stearate; sodium lauryl sulfate); GENERIC].
50 mg (base) (Rx) [*Zoloft* (anhydrous lactose; corn starch; magnesium stearate; sodium lauryl sulfate); GENERIC].
100 mg (base) (Rx) [*Zoloft* (anhydrous lactose; corn starch; magnesium stearate; sodium lauryl sulfate); GENERIC].

Packaging and storage
Store between 15 and 30 °C (59 and 86 °F), unless otherwise specified by manufacturer.

Auxiliary labeling
- May cause dizziness or drowsiness.
- Avoid alcoholic beverages.

SERTRALINE HYDROCHLORIDE ORAL CONCENTRATE

Usual adult dose
See *Sertraline Hydrochloride Capsules.*

Usual adult prescribing limits
See *Sertraline Hydrochloride Capsules.*

Usual pediatric dose
See *Sertraline Hydrochloride Capsules.*

Usual pediatric prescribing limits
See *Sertraline Hydrochloride Capsules.*

Strength(s) usually available
U.S.—
20 mg (base) per mL (Rx) [*Zoloft* (alcohol 12%; butylated hydroxytoluene; glycerin; menthol)].
Canada—
Not commercially available

Packaging and storage
Store between 15 and 30 °C (59 and 86 °F), unless otherwise specified by manufacturer.

Preparation of dosage form
Mix the required amount of sertraline oral concentrate with 4 ounces of water, ginger ale, lemon/lime soda, lemonade or orange juice only. Solution should be ingested immediately after mixing.
A slight haze may appear after mixing.

Auxiliary labeling
- May cause dizziness or drowsiness.
- Avoid alcoholic beverages.
- Dilute medication before use.

SERTRALINE HYDROCHLORIDE TABLETS

Usual adult dose
See *Sertraline Hydrochloride Capsules.*

Usual adult prescribing limits
See *Sertraline Hydrochloride Capsules.*

Usual pediatric dose
See *Sertraline Hydrochloride Capsules.*

Usual pediatric prescribing limits
See *Sertraline Hydrochloride Capsules.*

Usual geriatric dose
Depression or
Obsessive-compulsive disorder or
Panic disorder—
Oral, initially 12.5 to 25 mg (base) a day, as a single morning or evening dose; dosage may be increased gradually as needed and tolerated.
Posttraumatic stress disorder[1] or
Social anxiety disorder[1]—
Oral, initially 50 mg (base) a day, as a single morning or evening dose; dosage may be increased gradually as needed and tolerated.

Usual geriatric prescribing limits
See *Sertraline Hydrochloride Capsules.*

Strength(s) usually available
U.S.—
25 mg (base) (Rx) [*Zoloft* (scored; dibasic calcium phosphate dihydrate; D&C Yellow #10 aluminum lake; FD&C Blue #2 aluminum lake; FD&C Red #40 aluminum lake; hydroxypropyl cellulose; hypromellose; magnesium stearate; microcrystalline cellulose; polyethylene glycol; polysorbate 80; sodium starch glycolate; titanium dioxide)].
50 mg (base) (Rx) [*Zoloft* (scored; dibasic calcium phosphate dihydrate; FD&C Blue #2 aluminum lake; hydroxypropyl cellulose; hypromellose; magnesium stearate; microcrystalline cellulose; polyethylene glycol; polysorbate 80; sodium starch glycolate; titanium dioxide)].
100 mg (base) (Rx) [*Zoloft* (scored; dibasic calcium phosphate dihydrate; hydroxypropyl cellulose; hypromellose; magnesium stearate; microcrystalline cellulose; polyethylene glycol; polysorbate 80; sodium starch glycolate; synthetic yellow iron oxide; titanium dioxide)].
Canada—
Not commercially available.

Packaging and storage
Store at 25 °C (77 °F), excursions permitted between between 15 and 30 °C (59 and 86 °F), unless otherwise specified by manufacturer.

Auxiliary labeling
- May cause dizziness or drowsiness.
- Avoid alcoholic beverages.

[1]Not included in Canadian product labeling.

Revised: 02/01/2005

SIBUTRAMINE Systemic†

VA CLASSIFICATION (Primary): GA751
Note: Controlled substance classification
U.S.: Schedule IV
Commonly used brand name(s): *Meridia*.
Note: For a listing of dosage forms and brand names by country availability, see *Dosage Forms* section(s).

†Not commercially available in Canada.

Category
Appetite suppressant.

Indications
General Considerations
Cardiac valve dysfunction and primary pulmonary hypertension have been associated with the use of centrally acting appetite suppressants. Sibutramine does not promote the release of serotonin (5-hydroxytryptamine, 5-HT) from nerve terminals as do the appetite suppressants that were associated with these adverse events most commonly. A comparison of echocardiograms performed on patients after 0.5 to 16 months (mean 7.6 months) of treatment with 15 mg per

day of sibutramine (132 patients) or placebo (77 patients) showed no difference in the incidence of valvular heart disease between the two groups. A second study in 25 patients comparing echocardiograms administered at baseline with those administered after 3 months of treatment with 5 to 30 mg per day of sibutramine detected no cases of valvular heart disease.

In two 12-month studies of sibutramine in obese subjects, maximum weight loss was achieved by 6 months and statistically significant weight loss was maintained over 12 months. Among patients receiving 15 mg per day of sibutramine in clinical weight-loss trials, more than 50% lost ≥ 5% of their baseline body weight and about 25% lost ≥ 10% of their baseline body weight. However, some weight was regained after discontinuation of sibutramine.

Accepted

Obesity, exogenous (treatment)—Sibutramine is indicated for the management of obesity, including weight loss and maintenance of weight loss, in patients on a reduced-calorie diet. Sibutramine should be used only in obese patients with an initial body mass index ≥ 30 kg of body weight per square meter of height (kg/m^2) or with an initial body mass index ≥ 27 kg/m^2 in the presence of other risk factors, such as hypertension, diabetes, or dyslipidemia. Safety and efficacy of sibutramine use for more than 1 year have not been evaluated in controlled trials.

Pharmacology/Pharmacokinetics

Physicochemical characteristics

Chemical Group—Cyclobutanemethanamine.

Molecular weight—Sibutramine hydrochloride monohydrate: 334.33.

Solubility—In water at pH 5.2: 2.9 mg/mL.

Partition coefficient—Octanol:water at pH 5: 30.9.

Mechanism of action/Effect

Sibutramine is a serotonin (5-hydroxytryptamine, 5-HT) and norepinephrine (NE) reuptake inhibitor (SNRI). *In vitro* testing found sibutramine to be much less potent than its primary and secondary amine metabolites in inhibiting monoamine reuptake. Therefore, the pharmacological actions of sibutramine are thought to be due predominantly to its active metabolites. The metabolites of sibutramine inhibit 5-HT and NE reuptake with potencies comparable to those of fluoxetine and desipramine, respectively. Combined NE and 5-HT reuptake inhibition is thought to promote a sense of satiety, leading to a decrease in energy intake, and, possibly, to increase resting metabolic rate. Randomized, placebo-controlled, double-blind studies in obese and in nonobese subjects have shown significant reductions in self-rated premeal hunger and in energy intake with sibutramine use, even in the absence of an imposed reduced-calorie diet. One study found no difference in the decrease in resting energy expenditure associated with weight loss between subjects receiving sibutramine and subjects receiving placebo, in spite of significantly greater weight loss in the sibutramine group. In another study, basal metabolic rate, as measured by indirect calorimetry, increased more in sibutramine-treated patients than in patients receiving placebo; however, this finding has not been consistent.

The degree of weight loss occurring with sibutramine use is dose-related. Also, the subcutaneous to visceral fat ratio was found to be significantly increased from baseline in sibutramine-treated patients, possibly indicating a preferential reduction in visceral fat.

Studies in rodents indicate that sibutramine administration leads to rapid down-regulation of alpha$_2$-adrenergic receptors, with a greater effect on postsynaptic than on presynaptic receptors, and down-regulation of beta$_1$-adrenergic receptors. Sibutramine's metabolites inhibit the reuptake of dopamine *in vivo*, but much less potently than they inhibit the reuptake of NE and 5-HT. Neither sibutramine nor its active metabolites, at clinically relevant concentrations, cause the release of monoamines or inhibit monoamine oxidase. Also, all active moieties have low affinity for serotonin (5-HT$_1$, 5-HT$_{1A}$, 5-HT$_{1B}$, 5-HT$_{2A}$, 5-HT$_{2C}$), norepinephrine (beta$_1$, beta$_2$, beta$_3$, alpha$_1$, alpha$_2$), dopamine (D$_1$, D$_2$), benzodiazepine, and glutamate (NMDA) receptors, and they show no evidence of anticholinergic or antihistaminergic actions.

Other actions/effects

Inhibits 5-HT uptake by platelets as well as by neurons, which may affect platelet functioning.

Absorption

Rapidly absorbed following oral administration; undergoes extensive first-pass metabolism in the liver to form mono- and di-desmethyl active metabolites (M1, a secondary amine, and M2, a primary amine, respectively). Absolute bioavailability is unknown, but mass balance studies indicate that at least 77% of a single oral dose is absorbed.

Food increases the time to peak plasma concentration and decreases the peak plasma concentrations of the desmethyl metabolites by about 3 hours and 30%, respectively, but does not affect the area under the plasma concentration-time curves (AUCs) of the desmethyl metabolites.

Distribution

Rapidly and extensively distributed into tissues.

Protein binding

Sibutramine—Very high (97%); to human plasma proteins.

M1 and M2—Very high (94%); to human plasma proteins.

Although protein binding is very high, interactions with other highly protein-bound medications are not anticipated because of the low therapeutic concentrations and basic characteristics of sibutramine and its active metabolites.

Biotransformation

Hepatic. Sibutramine is metabolized principally by the cytochrome P450 3A4 (CYP3A4) isoenzyme to two active desmethyl metabolites, monodesmethylsibutramine (M1, a secondary amine) and di-desmethylsibutramine (M2, a primary amine), which are hydroxylated and conjugated to inactive metabolites. Mild to moderate hepatic impairment does not significantly alter the pharmacokinetics of sibutramine or its active metabolites.

Half-life

Elimination—
- Sibutramine: 1.1 hours.
- M1: 14 hours.
- M2: 16 hours.

Time to peak plasma concentration

Sibutramine—1.2 hours.

M1 and M2—3 to 4 hours.

Time to steady-state plasma concentration

Steady-state plasma concentrations of M1 and M2 are reached within 4 days with once-a-day dosing.

Peak plasma concentration

In 18 obese subjects, after each received a single 15-mg dose of sibutramine, the mean peak plasma concentrations of M1 and M2 were 4 nanograms/mL (range 3.2 to 4.8 nanograms/mL) and 6.4 nanograms/mL (range 5.6 to 7.2 nanograms/mL), respectively.

Steady-state plasma concentration

Steady-state plasma concentrations of M1 and M2 are linearly related to sibutramine dosage and are approximately twofold higher than single-dose plasma concentrations.

Elimination

Primarily renal, as inactive metabolites. Renal function impairment did not significantly affect maximum plasma concentrations, half-life, or AUC of sibutramine or its active metabolites in 18 nonobese patients.

Precautions to Consider

Carcinogenicity/tumorigenicity

Two-year studies in rats and mice given sibutramine in daily doses that resulted in combined area under the plasma concentration-time curves (AUCs) of the two active metabolites that were 0.5 to 21 times those seen in patients taking the maximum recommended human dose (MRHD) showed an increased incidence of benign tumors of the testicular interstitial cells in male rats. These tumors are commonly seen in rats, and the clinical significance of this finding is unknown. No evidence of carcinogenicity was seen in mice or in female rats.

Mutagenicity

The two active metabolites of sibutramine had equivocal bacterial mutagenic activity in the Ames test. However, neither sibutramine nor its active metabolites showed evidence of mutagenicity in a number of other appropriate tests.

Pregnancy/Reproduction

Fertility—Studies in rats showed no evidence of impairment of fertility with sibutramine administration.

Pregnancy—Adequate and well-controlled studies in humans have not been done.

No evidence of teratogenicity was seen in studies in which pregnant rats were given daily doses of sibutramine that produced an AUC of the active metabolites that was approximately 43 times that produced in humans receiving the MRHD. However, maternal toxicity and impaired nest-building behavior, which led to decreased pup survival, were seen. Maternal toxicity and increased incidences of broad short snout, short rounded pinnae, short tail, and short thickened long bones in the limbs of offspring were seen when pregnant Dutch Belted rabbits were given daily doses of sibutramine that produced an AUC of the active metabolites greater than five times that produced in humans receiving the MRHD. Using comparable doses, two studies in New Zealand White rabbits yielded conflicting results. One study found an increased incidence and the other a decreased incidence of cardiovascular anomalies in the offspring of rabbits given sibutramine compared with the offspring of control rabbits.

FDA Pregnancy Category C.

Breast-feeding

It is not known whether sibutramine or its metabolites are distributed into breast milk.

Pediatrics

Appropriate studies on the relationship of age to the effects of sibutramine have not been performed in the pediatric population. Safety and efficacy in children up to 16 years of age have not been established.

Geriatrics

Appropriate studies on the relationship of age to the effects of sibutramine have not been performed in the geriatric population. However, no geriatrics-specific problems have been documented to date and plasma concentrations of sibutramine's active metabolites were similar in subjects 61 to 77 years of age and subjects 19 to 30 years of age after a single 15-mg dose.

Pharmacogenetics

Although pharmacokinetic data indicate that mean maximum plasma concentrations and AUCs are slightly higher in females than in males, this difference is not likely to be clinically significant, and no dosage adjustments based on gender are recommended.

Dental

Use of sibutramine may decrease or inhibit salivary flow, thus contributing to the development of dental caries, periodontal disease, oral candidiasis, and discomfort.

Drug interactions and/or related problems

The following drug interactions and/or related problems have been selected on the basis of their potential clinical significance (possible mechanism in parentheses where appropriate)—not necessarily inclusive (» = major clinical significance):

Note: In a 52-day, single-blind, placebo controlled study of 11 healthy female volunteers, 28 days of treatment with 15 mg per day of sibutramine did not interfere with the efficacy of combined steroid oral contraceptives.

Combinations containing any of the following medications, depending on the amount present, may also interact with this medication.

Alcohol
(a single-dose study found no clinically significant psychomotor effects with concomitant use; however, use of excess alcohol with sibutramine is not recommended)

» Appetite suppressants, other
(sibutramine has not been studied and should not be used in combination with other centrally acting appetite suppressants)

Medications that inhibit cytochrome P450 3A4 (CYP3A4), such as:
Cimetidine or
Erythromycin or
Ketoconazole
(CYP3A4 is involved in sibutramine metabolism and the potential exists for a decrease in sibutramine clearance; in small clinical drug interaction studies, the effects of erythromycin and ketoconazole on sibutramine clearance were small to moderate, and the effects of cimetidine on sibutramine clearance were very small)

Medications that may increase blood pressure and/or heart rate, other, such as:
Ephedrine or
Phenylpropanolamine or
Pseudoephedrine or
Cough, cold, and allergy products that contain such agents
(sibutramine may increase blood pressure and/or heart rate; concurrent use has not been evaluated)

» Moclobemide
(because of the potentially fatal consequences of combining nonselective, irreversible monoamine oxidase inhibitors with sibutramine, and the increased risk of developing the serotonin syndrome with combined use of sibutramine and the reversible monoamine oxidase–A inhibitor moclobemide, concurrent use is not recommended and a wash-out period of 3 to 7 days is advised between the use of one medication [sibutramine or moclobemide] and the use of the other)

» Monoamine oxidase (MAO) inhibitors, including furazolidone, procarbazine, and selegiline
(there have been reports of serious, sometimes fatal, reactions in patients taking MAO inhibitors in combination with other serotonergic agents; concurrent use is **contraindicated** and at least 2 weeks should elapse between discontinuing one medication [MAO inhibitor or sibutramine] and beginning the other)

» Serotonergics or medications or substances with serotonergic activity (see *Appendix II*)
(increased risk of development of the serotonin syndrome, a rare but potentially fatal hyperserotonergic state that may occur in patients receiving serotonergic medications, usually in combination; symptoms typically occur shortly [hours to days] after the addition of a serotonergic agent to a regimen that includes serotonin-enhancing drugs or an increase in dosage of a serotonergic agent; symptoms include agitation, diaphoresis, diarrhea, fever, hyperreflexia, incoordination, mental status changes [confusion, hypomania], myoclonus, shivering, or tremor; cardiac arrhythmias, coma, disseminated intravascular coagulation, hypertension or hypotension, renal failure, respiratory failure, seizures, and severe hyperthermia also have been reported; the syndrome usually resolves shortly after discontinuation of serotonergic medications; treatment is essentially symptomatic and supportive)

Laboratory value alterations

The following have been selected on the basis of their potential clinical significance (possible effect in parentheses where appropriate)—not necessarily inclusive (» = major clinical significance).

With physiology/laboratory test values

» Blood pressure and
» Heart rate
(mean increases of 1 to 3 mm Hg in systolic and diastolic blood pressure and four to five beats per minute in heart rate occurred during clinical trials of sibutramine. However, some patients experienced substantial increases in blood pressure, leading to discontinuation of sibutramine in 0.4% of patients. Tachycardia also led to discontinuation of sibutramine in 0.4% of patients. Placebo discontinuation rates for hypertension and tachycardia were 0.4% and 0.1%, respectively. If a sustained increase in blood pressure or heart rate occurs, a reduction in sibutramine dosage or discontinuation of sibutramine therapy should be considered)

(in an 8-week, parallel-group, double-blind study of 20 obese hypertensive patients [10 sibutramine, 10 placebo recipients], during which diet was monitored to minimize weight loss, 24-hour ambulatory blood pressure and heart rate monitoring showed statistically significant increases over baseline values in the sibutramine group compared with the placebo group. Overall, diastolic blood pressure changed from baseline by a decrease of 8 mm Hg in the placebo group and by an increase of 2.2 mm Hg in the sibutramine group during week 4 of the study, and by a decrease of 7.7 mm Hg in the placebo group and by an increase of 3.7 mm Hg in the sibutramine group during week 8 of the study. The magnitude of the diastolic blood pressure increases in the sibutramine group was greatest during the nocturnal hours. Overall, mean arterial pressure was increased from baseline in the sibutramine group and was decreased from baseline in the placebo group; however, the difference between the two groups in mean arterial pressure was not statistically significant. Heart rate increased in both groups, with overall increases of 3.5 and 15.1 beats per minute in the placebo and sibutramine groups, respectively)

(in a 12-week, parallel-group, double-blind study of 113 obese hypertensive patients [54 sibutramine, 59 placebo recipients], during which patients were to follow dietary advice directed toward weight loss, diastolic and systolic blood pressures decreased in both groups. Although the weight loss in the sibutramine group was significantly greater than that in the placebo group, the decrease in blood pressure was greater, though not significantly so, in the placebo group. Heart rate changes from baseline were significantly different between placebo [decreases of 4.3 and 5.8 beats per minute supine and standing, respectively] and sibutramine [increase of 2.4 and decrease of 0.6 beats per minute supine and standing, respectively] groups)

Lipids, serum and
Uric acid, serum
(weight loss induced by sibutramine has been accompanied by increases in serum high-density lipoprotein cholesterol concentrations and by decreases in serum triglyceride, total cholesterol, low-density lipoprotein cholesterol, and uric acid concentrations)

Liver function tests
(increases in serum concentrations of aspartate aminotransferase [AST (SGOT)], alanine aminotransferase [ALT (SGPT)], gamma-glutamyltransferase [GGT], lactate dehydrogenase [LDH], alkaline phosphate, and bilirubin were reported in 1.6% of sibutramine-treated obese patients and 0.8% of placebo-control patients in clinical trials; clinically significant elevations were rare; abnormal

values were sporadic, did not show a clear dose-response relationship, and often diminished with continued treatment)

Medical considerations/Contraindications

The medical considerations/contraindications included have been selected on the basis of their potential clinical significance (reasons given in parentheses where appropriate)—not necessarily inclusive (» = major clinical significance).

Except under special circumstances, this medication should not be used when the following medical problems exist:

» Anorexia nervosa or
» Hypertension, uncontrolled or poorly controlled
(may be exacerbated)

Risk-benefit should be considered when the following medical problems exist:

» Cardiac arrhythmia, or history of or
» Congestive heart failure, or history of or
» Coronary artery disease, or history of or
» Stroke, or history of
(sibutramine is not recommended for use in these patients, because of its association with increases in blood pressure and heart rate)

Drug abuse or dependence, history of
(although the abuse potential of sibutramine was found to be very low in rat and human studies, clinical use data are limited and patients should be observed carefully for signs of misuse of sibutramine, such as increasing dosage and drug-seeking behavior)

Gallstones, or history of
(weight loss may precipitate or exacerbate gallstone formation)

Glaucoma, narrow angle
(sibutramine can cause mydriasis and should be used with caution in patients with narrow angle glaucoma)

» Hepatic function impairment, severe or
» Renal function impairment, severe
(pharmacokinetic studies indicate that no dosage adjustment is needed in patients with mild to moderate hepatic function impairment, and a study in 18 nonobese patients with renal function impairment found insignificant changes in the pharmacokinetics of sibutramine's active moieties; however, sibutramine has not been studied in patients with severe hepatic or renal function impairment and use is not recommended in these patients)

» Hypertension, well-controlled or
» Hypertension, history of
(may be exacerbated; sibutramine should be used with caution in these patients and should not be used in patients with uncontrolled or poorly controlled hypertension)

Neurological impairment, including developmental delay or
Seizures, history of
(increased risk of seizures occurring; seizures were reported in < 0.1% of patients in premarketing studies of sibutramine)

Sensitivity to sibutramine

Patient monitoring

The following may be especially important in patient monitoring (other tests may be warranted in some patients, depending on condition; » = major clinical significance):

» Blood pressure and
» Heart rate
(recommended in all patients before starting therapy with sibutramine and at regular intervals during treatment; tachycardia or hypertension, when seen in patients during clinical trials, usually developed during the first 8 weeks of sibutramine treatment; if sustained elevations occur, a decrease in sibutramine dosage or discontinuation of sibutramine therapy should be considered)

Side/Adverse Effects

The following side/adverse effects have been selected on the basis of their potential clinical significance (possible signs and symptoms in parentheses where appropriate)—not necessarily inclusive:

Those indicating need for medical attention

Incidence less frequent

Dysmenorrhea (painful menstruation); ***edema*** (swelling of body or of feet and ankles); ***hypertension*** (increased blood pressure); ***influenza-like symptoms*** (chills; achiness); ***mental depression; palpitation or tachycardia*** (fast or irregular heartbeat)

Incidence rare

Abnormal bleeding (bruising or red spots or patches on skin; excessive bleeding following injury); ***acute interstitial nephritis*** (swelling of body or of feet and ankles; unusual weight gain); ***emotional lability*** (rapidly changing moods); ***migraine*** (severe headache); ***seizures; skin rash***

Note: *Abnormal bleeding* may be related to inhibition of serotonin uptake into platelets caused by sibutramine and its metabolites.

A single case of biopsy-confirmed *acute interstitial nephritis* was reported during premarketing studies. The patient fully recovered after discontinuing sibutramine and receiving dialysis and oral corticosteroids.

Seizures were reported in < 0.1% of patients in premarketing studies of sibutramine. Some of these patients had predisposing factors, including prior history of epilepsy or brain tumor. If seizures develop, sibutramine should be discontinued.

Those indicating need for medical attention only if they continue or are bothersome

Incidence more frequent

Central nervous system (CNS) stimulation; including anxiety; insomnia (trouble in sleeping); ***irritability or unusual impatience; or nervousness; constipation; dizziness; dryness of mouth; headache; rhinitis*** (stuffy or runny nose)

Incidence less frequent

Abdominal pain; back pain; diarrhea; drowsiness; dyspepsia (indigestion); ***increased appetite; increased sweating; increased thirst; nausea; paresthesia*** (burning, itching, prickling, or tingling of skin); ***taste perversion*** (change in sense of taste); ***vasodilation*** (unusual warmth or flushing of skin)

Overdose

For specific information on the agents used in the management of sibutramine overdose, see *Beta-adrenergic Blocking Agents (Systemic)* monograph.

For more information on the management of overdose or unintentional ingestion, **contact a Poison Control Center** (see *Poison Control Center Listing*).

Clinical effects of overdose

Note: Experience with sibutramine overdose is very limited. In reported cases, few adverse effects and no apparent sequelae occurred. Increased heart rate (120 beats per minute) was reported in a 45-year-old male who ingested 400 mg of sibutramine.

Treatment of overdose

Treatment of sibutramine overdose is symptomatic and supportive.

Specific treatment—Beta-adrenergic blocking agents may be used cautiously to control elevated blood pressure or tachycardia.

Monitoring—Cardiac and vital signs should be monitored.

Supportive care—Establish and maintain patent airway. Patients in whom intentional overdose is confirmed or suspected should be referred for psychiatric consultation.

Note: Forced diuresis and hemodialysis are of unknown benefit in the treatment of sibutramine overdose.

Patient Consultation

As an aid to patient consultation, refer to *Advice for the Patient, Sibutramine (Systemic)*.

In providing consultation, consider emphasizing the following selected information (» = major clinical significance):

Before using this medication

» Conditions affecting use, especially:
Dental—Decreased salivary flow may contribute to caries, periodontal disease, oral candidiasis, and discomfort
Contraindicated medications—Monoamine oxidase (MAO) inhibitors
Other medications, especially other appetite suppressants, serotonergics, or medications or substances with serotonergic activity
Other medical problems, especially anorexia nervosa; cardiac arrhythmia, or history of; congestive heart failure, or history of; coronary artery disease, or history of; hepatic or renal function impairment, severe; hypertension, or history of; or stroke, or history of

Proper use of this medication

» Taking as directed; not increasing dose, not taking more frequently, and not taking for a longer time than directed by physician, because of potential cardiovascular adverse effects
Following reduced-calorie diet, as directed by physician
Taking with or without food, on a full or empty stomach, as directed by physician

» Proper dosing

Missed dose: Taking as soon as possible if remembered within 2 to 3 hours; not taking if remembered later; returning to regular dosing schedule; not doubling doses

» Proper storage

Precautions while using this medication

» Importance of regular visits to physician to check progress of therapy and monitor blood pressure and heart rate

» Not increasing dosage if effect diminishes; checking with physician

» Not taking an MAO inhibitor within 2 weeks of taking sibutramine; not taking sibutramine within 2 weeks of taking an MAO inhibitor

Limiting alcohol consumption

» Notifying physician as soon as possible if skin rash, hives, or other allergic reaction occurs

» Possible dizziness, drowsiness, or impaired judgment; caution in driving or doing other things that require alertness and sound judgment until effects are known

Possible dryness of mouth; using sugarless candy or gum, ice, or saliva substitute for relief; checking with physician or dentist if dry mouth continues for more than 2 weeks

Side/adverse effects

Signs of potential side effects, especially dysmenorrhea, edema, hypertension, influenza-like symptoms, mental depression, palpitation or tachycardia, abnormal bleeding, acute interstitial nephritis, emotional lability, migraine, seizures, and skin rash

General Dosing Information

Sibutramine should not be prescribed until organic causes for obesity, such as untreated hypothyroidism, have been ruled out.

In sibutramine obesity trials of 6 months or longer, the patients who lost at least 1.8 kg (4 pounds) of body weight during the first 4 weeks of treatment were much more likely than the patients who lost less than this to subsequently lose at least 5% of their initial body weight at a given dose. If a patient does not lose at least 1.8 kg (4 pounds) in the first 4 weeks of sibutramine treatment, therapy should be re-evaluated and sibutramine dosage should be increased, or sibutramine use should be discontinued.

The abuse potential of sibutramine was found to be very low in rat and human studies designed to assess potential for abuse as a psychostimulant and in rat studies designed to assess potential for abuse as an hallucinogen.

Diet/Nutrition

Sibutramine may be taken with or without food.

A reduced-calorie diet must be followed during sibutramine therapy in order to achieve significant weight loss.

Oral Dosage Form

SIBUTRAMINE HYDROCHLORIDE MONOHYDRATE CAPSULES

Usual adult dose

Obesity, exogenous—

Oral, initially 10 mg once a day, usually in the morning. If weight loss is inadequate (< 1.8 kg [4 pounds]) after four weeks of therapy, dosage may be increased to 15 mg once a day, taking into consideration effects on heart rate and blood pressure.

Note: Patients who do not tolerate the 10-mg dose may benefit from a 5-mg dose.

Usual adult prescribing limits

15 mg per day.

Usual pediatric dose

Safety and efficacy in children up to 16 years of age have not been established.

Usual geriatric dose

See *Usual adult dose*.

Note: Dosing in elderly patients should be approached cautiously because of the high incidence of concomitant disease states and medication use in this population.

Strength(s) usually available

U.S.—

5 mg (Rx) [*Meridia* (colloidal silicon dioxide; D&C Yellow No. 10; FD&C Blue No. 2; gelatin; lactose monohydrate; microcrystalline cellulose; magnesium stearate; titanium dioxide)].

10 mg (Rx) [*Meridia* (colloidal silicon dioxide; FD&C Blue No. 2; gelatin; lactose monohydrate; microcrystalline cellulose; magnesium stearate; titanium dioxide)].

15 mg (Rx) [*Meridia* (colloidal silicon dioxide; D&C Yellow No. 10; gelatin; lactose monohydrate; microcrystalline cellulose; magnesium stearate; titanium dioxide)].

Canada—

Not commercially available.

Packaging and storage

Store at 25 °C (77 °F), with excursions between 15 and 30 °C (59 and 86 °F) permitted, in a tight, light-resistant container, unless otherwise specified by manufacturer. Protect from heat and moisture.

Auxiliary labeling

- May cause dizziness or drowsiness

Note

Sibutramine is a controlled substance in the U.S.

Developed: 04/26/1999

SILDENAFIL Systemic

VA CLASSIFICATION (Primary/Secondary): GU900/CV900

Note: For a listing of dosage forms and brand names by country availability, see *Dosage Forms* section(s).

Category

Impotence therapy agent (systemic); antihypertensive (pulmonary).

Indications

General Considerations

Erectile dysfunction that is medication-induced or caused by endocrine problems, such as hypogonadism or hypothyroidism or hyperthyroidism, should be evaluated and appropriately treated before sildenafil treatment is considered.

Cardiac risk associated with sexual activity should be individually assessed prior to initiating any treatment for erectile dysfunction.

Accepted

Erectile dysfunction (treatment)—Sildenafil is indicated for the treatment of erectile dysfunction.

Sildenafil has been evaluated in 3000 patients (19 to 87 years of age) in 21 studies of up to 6 months. Compared with patients taking a placebo, patients taking sildenafil demonstrated statistically significant improvement in treatment of erectile dysfunction of organic, psychogenic, or mixed etiologies (mean onset of 5 years). Sildenafil was effective in a broad range of patients, including those with a history of coronary artery disease, hypertension, other cardiac disease, peripheral vascular disease, diabetes mellitus, depression, coronary artery bypass graft (CABG), radical prostatectomy, transurethral resection of the prostate (TURP), and spinal cord injury. Sildenafil was also effective in patients taking antidepressant, antipsychotic, antihypertensive, or diuretic medications.

Pulmonary arterial hypertension (treatment)—Sildenafil is indicated for the treatment of pulmonary arterial hypertension (WHO Group I) to improve exercise ability.

Pharmacology/Pharmacokinetics

Note: The pharmacokinetics of sildenafil are dose-proportional over the recommended dosage range (25 mg to 100 mg).

Physicochemical characteristics

Molecular weight—666.7.

Mechanism of action/Effect

Impotence therapy agent—Sildenafil is a selective inhibitor of phosphodiesterase type 5 (PDE5), an enzyme responsible for degrading cyclic guanosine monophosphate (cGMP) in the corpus cavernosum. By diminishing the effect of PDE5, sildenafil facilitates the effect of nitric oxide during sexual stimulation: cGMP levels increase, smooth muscle relaxes, and blood flows into the corpus cavernosum, producing an erection. Without sexual stimulation, sildenafil has no effect on erections.

Pulmonary antihypertensive agent—Sildenafil is an inhibitor of cGMP specific phosphodiesterase type-5 (PDE5) in the smooth muscle of the pulmonary vasulature, where PDE5 is responsible for degradation of cGMP. Sildenafil, therefore, increases cGMP within pulmonary vascular smooth muscle cells resulting in relaxation. In patients with pulmonary hypertension, this can lead to vasodilation of the pulmonary vascular bed and, to a lesser degree, vasodilatation in the systemic circulation.

In vitro studies show that sildenafil's potency for action on phosphodiesterases differs. Sildenafil's action is greater for PDE5 than for the following phosphodiesterases: PDE1 (> 80 times); PDE2 and PDE4 (> 1000 times); PDE3 (about 4000 times), and PDE6 (about 10 times). PDE3 controls cardiac contractility and PDE6, an enzyme found in the retina, may be involved in color vision abnormalities reported for the higher dose of sildenafil. The active metabolite of sildenafil has approximately 50% potency for PDE5, and contributes approximately 20% of sildenafil's effect.

Other actions/effects

Pulmonary antihypertensive agent—In addition to vascular smooth muscle and the corpus cavernosum, PDE5 is also found in other tissues including vascular and visceral smooth muscle and in platelets. The inhibition of PDE5 in these tissues by sildenafil may be the basis for the enhanced platelet anti-aggregatory activity of nitric oxide observed in vitro, and the mild peripheral arterial-venous dilatation in vivo.

Absorption

Rapidly absorbed; absolute bioavailability is approximately 40%. A high-fat meal reduces absorption as shown by reducing the maximum plasma concentration (C_{max}) by 29% and delaying time to peak concentration (T_{max}) by 60 minutes.

Distribution

The mean steady state volume of distribution (Vol_{ss}) is 105 liters. Less than 0.001% of sildenafil remained in the semen of healthy volunteers at 90 minutes.

Protein binding

Very high (96% bound to plasma proteins); independent of total plasma concentration.

Biotransformation

Hepatic metabolism, via cytochrome P450 (CYP) 3A4 (major route) and CYP2C9 (minor route). Sildenafil is converted by *N*-desmethylation to an active metabolite with properties similar to those of the parent, sildenafil. Parent and active metabolite are metabolized further.

Half-life

4 hours (terminal half-life for parent and major metabolite).

Onset of action

Within 0.5 hour after administration.

Time to peak concentration

30 to 120 minutes under fasting conditions; attainment of peak concentration level is delayed by 60 minutes when given with a high-fat meal.

Peak serum concentration

Sildenafil—Approximately 440 nanograms per mL; major metabolite has 40% of the serum concentration of sildenafil.

Duration of action

Up to 4 hours, but with less response than that seen at 2 hours.

Elimination

Feces (80% of the administered dose as metabolites); urine (13% of the administered dose as metabolites).

Precautions to Consider

Carcinogenicity

In 24-month animal studies, sildenafil was not found to be carcinogenic in male rats given 29 times the maximum recommended human dose (MRHD) or in female rats given 42 times the MRHD of a 100-mg dose. In 18- to 21-month studies, sildenafil was not carcinogenic in mice given 10 mg per kg of body weight (mg/kg) a day, corresponding to 0.6 times the MRHD (based on a mg per square meter of body surface area).

Mutagenicity

Sildenafil was not found to be mutagenic in an *in vivo* mouse micronucleus assay or an *in vitro* human lymphocytes assay and bacterial or Chinese hamster ovary cell assays.

Pregnancy/Reproduction

Fertility—Single doses of 100 mg sildenafil given to males did not impair sperm motility or morphology.

In animal studies, sildenafil did not impair fertility in rats given sildenafil in doses of 60 mg/kg a day for 36 days in females and for 102 days in males, corresponding to an area under the plasma concentration-time curve (AUC) that was greater than 25 times that produced in humans.

Pregnancy—Adequate and well-controlled studies in humans have not been done. Sildenafil is not indicated for use in females for erectile dysfunction.

In animal studies, sildenafil was not teratogenic, embryotoxic, or fetotoxic in rats and rabbits given up to 200 mg/kg a day during organogenesis, corresponding to 20 to 40 times the MRHD as calculated per body surface area of a 50-kg person.

FDA Pregnancy Category B.

Breast-feeding

Problems in humans have not been documented; sildenafil is not indicated for use in females for erectile dysfunction. Caution should be used when sildenafil is administered to nursing women for pulmonary arterial hypertension.

Pediatrics

Safety and effectiveness of sildenafil in pediatric pulmonary hypertension patients have not been established.

Geriatrics

Healthy volunteers 65 years of age and over cleared sildenafil less effectively from the plasma than did healthy younger volunteers 18 to 45 years of age as shown by a 40% increase of AUC in older adults. Using an initial lower dose of 25 mg is recommended for patients 65 years of age and over. In general, dose selection for an elderly patient should be cautious, reflecting the greater frequency of decreased hepatic, renal, or cardiac function, and of concomitant disease or other drug therapy.

Drug interactions and/or related problems

The following drug interactions and/or related problems have been selected on the basis of their potential clinical significance (possible mechanism in parentheses where appropriate)—not necessarily inclusive (» = major clinical significance):

Note: Combinations containing any of the following medications, depending on the amount present, may also interact with this medication.

The safety and efficacy of combining sildenafil treatment with other impotence therapy agents have not been studied.

» Alpha-blockers
(administration of sildenafil to a patient taking alpha-blocker therapy may lead to symptomatic hypotension in some patients; sildenafil doses above 25 mg should not be taken within 4 hours of taking an alpha-blocker)

Antihypertensive medications
(concurrent use may potentiate the hypotensive effect of these medications; a mean additional reduction in supine blood pressure, 8 mm Hg systolic and 7 mm Hg diastolic, was observed in a study when sildenafil was given concurrently with amlodipine in either 5-mg or 10-mg strengths)

» Bosentan
(efficacy of sildenafil as pulmonary antihypertensive has not been evaluated in patients currently on bosentan therapy; coadministration increases AUC and C_{max} of bosentan and dosage adjustments may be necessary)

» Enzyme inhibitors, hepatic, cytochrome P450 (CYP) 3A4 including:
Cimetidine
Erythromycin
Itraconazole
Ketoconazole
Mibefradil
Saquinavir
(an increase in sildenafil plasma concentrations is likely to occur with CYP3A4 inhibitors because they reduce the metabolism and clearance of sildenafil; using a lower dose of 25 mg is recommended for patients taking these medications. Plasma concentrations of sildenafil increased 56% when a 50-mg dose of sildenafil was administered with cimetidine 800 mg; AUC of sildenafil increased 182% when a single 100-mg dose of sildenafil was administered after steady-state concentrations of erythromycin were achieved at 5 days; similar reactions are expected with stronger CYP3A4 inhibitors, such as ketoconazole, itraconazole, and mibefradil; coadministration of saquinavir (1200 mg 3 times a day at steady state) and sildenafil 100 mg, or ritonavir (500 mg twice a day at steady state) and sildenafil 100 mg resulted in a 140% and 300% increase in sildenafil C_{max} and a 210% and 1000% increase in sildenafil AUC, respectively)

Enzyme inducers, hepatic, cytochrome P450 (CYP) 3A4, including rifampin
(a decrease in sildenafil plasma concentrations is likely to occur with CYP3A4 inducers because they increase the metabolism and clearance of sildenafil)

» Erectile dysfunction treatments
(safety and efficacy of combinations of sildenafil with other treatments for erectile dysfunction have not been studied; use of such combinations is not recommended)

» Nitrates, including nitroglycerin
(sildenafil potentiates the hypotensive effect of nitrates; concomitant use is contraindicated)

Note: It has not been determined when patients may safely receive nitrates, if they are considered necessary, after having taken sildenafil. Although plasma concentrations of sildenafil (100 mg) at 24 hours postdose (approximately 2 nanograms per mL) are much lower than at peak concentration (approximately 440 nanograms per mL), it is not known if nitrates may be administered safely at that point. Also, these plasma concentration data are taken from healthy volunteers. Hepatic or renal impairment, concurrent administration of a CYP 3A4 inhibitor, or an age > 65 years may result in an increase in the plasma concentration of sildenafil to three to eight times that seen in healthy volunteers.

» Ritonavir
(concomitant administration substantially increases sildenafil serum concentrations and is not recommended)

Vitamin K antagonists
(concomitant use in pulmonary arterial hypertensive patients resulted in a greater incidence of reports of bleeding [primarily epistaxis] compared with placebo)

Medical considerations/Contraindications

The medical considerations/contraindications included have been selected on the basis of their potential clinical significance (reasons given in parentheses where appropriate)—not necessarily inclusive (» = major clinical significance).

Except under special circumstances, this medication should not be used when the following medical problem exists:

» Hypersensitivity to sildenafil or any component of the product

Risk-benefit should be considered when the following medical problems exist:

Abnormalities of the penis, such as:
Anatomical deformity
Angulation of the penis
Cavernosal fibrosis
Hypospadia, severe
Peyronie's disease
(patients who have an anatomical deformity, angulation of the penis, cavernosal fibrosis, or Peyronie's disease are at increased risk of developing problems when using impotence therapy agents, including sildenafil)

Age >50 years or
Coronary artery disease
Diabetes or
Hyperlipidemia or
Hypertension or
Smoking
(NAION has been reported rarely postmarketing in temporal association with the use of PDE5 inhibitors with most of these patients having one of these underlying anatomic or vascular risk factors for development of NAION; it is not possible to determine whether these events are related directly to the use of PDE5 inhibitors, to the patient's underlying vascular risk factors or anatomical defects, to a combination of these factors or other factors)

Bleeding disorders, including peptic ulcer, active or
Coagulation defects, severe
(risk of bleeding may be increased since sildenafil may inhibit platelet aggregation as shown in *in vitro* studies; further study is needed. Safety information is not available for use of sildenafil in these patients)

Autonomic dysfunction or
Coronary artery disease causing unstable angina or
Fluid depletion or
Hypertension resulting in a blood pressure > 170/100 mm Hg or
Hypotension resulting in a blood pressure < 90/50 mm Hg or
Left ventricular outflow obstruction, severe, or
Life-threatening arrhythmia, history of (within the previous 6 months) or
Myocardial infarction, history of (within the previous 6 months) or
Stroke, history of (within the previous 6 months)
(it is recommended that sildenafil be prescribed with caution in these patients since controlled clinical data regarding safety and efficacy are not yet available; also, cardiac risk associated with sexual activity should be assessed individually prior to initiation of any treatment for erectile dysfunction)
(consideration as to whether these patients could be adversely affected by the vasodilatory effects of sildenafil, such as the transient decreases in supine blood pressure [mean maximum decrease 8.4/5.5 mm Hg], is recommended)

Cardiovascular disease, other
(serious, life-threatening cardiovascular events with a temporal relationship to dosing with sildenafil have been described in postmarketing reports; these have included myocardial infarction, hypertension, ventricular arrhythmia, cerebrovascular hemorrhage, sudden cardiac death, and transient ischemic attacks. Cardiac risk associated with sexual activity should be assessed individually prior to initiation of any treatment for erectile dysfunction; consideration as to whether these patients could be adversely affected by the vasodilatory effects of sildenafil, such as the transient decreases in supine blood pressure [mean maximum decrease 8.4/5.5 mm Hg], is recommended)

Cardiac failure
(patients with stable cardiac disease experienced a mean decrease of 7% in cardiac output after receiving a total dose of sildenafil 40 mg intravenously over 4 infusions)

» Cirrhosis or
» Hepatic function impairment, severe
(sildenafil clearance was reduced in volunteers with hepatic cirrhosis [Child-Pugh A and B], resulting in an increase of AUC by 84% and of C_{max} by 47% when compared with data of age-matched volunteers who had no hepatic impairment; using a lower initial dose of 25 mg of sildenafil is recommended for these patients)

Leukemia or
Myeloma, multiple or
Polycythemia or
Priapism, history of or
Sickle cell disease or
Thrombocythemia
(patients with these predisposing conditions have an increased risk of priapism)

NAION in one eye, previous
(may increase risk of NAION recurring; these patients could be adversely affected by use of vasodilators such as PDE5 inhibitors)

» Pulmonary veno-occlusive disease (PVOD)
(administration of sildenafil to these patients not recommended; no clinical data on administration of sildenafil to patients with PVOD and pulmonary vasodilators may significantly worsen the cardiovascular status of patients with PVOD)

» Renal function impairment, severe
(creatinine clearance of less than 30 mL/min [severe renal insufficiency] significantly reduced sildenafil clearance, approximately doubling AUC and C_{max} compared with those of age-matched volunteers who had no renal impairment; using a lower initial dose of 25 mg of sildenafil is recommended for these patients. Creatinine clearance of 30 to 80 mL/min [mild to moderate renal insufficiency] did not alter pharmacokinetics of 50 mg sildenafil as a single dose)

Retinitis pigmentosa
(a minority of patients with this condition also experience genetic disorders of retinal phosphodiesterases; due to a lack of data on safety and efficacy, it is recommended that sildenafil be prescribed with caution in these patients)

Side/Adverse Effects

Note: Serious cardiovascular events, including myocardial infarction, sudden cardiac death, ventricular arrhythmia, cerebrovascular hemorrhage, transient ischemic attack (TIA), and hypertension, have occurred with use of sildenafil; these effects had not been reported prior to its approval by the Food and Drug Administration (FDA). Most, but not all, of the patients who experienced these events had pre-existing cardiovascular risk factors. Many of these events occurred during or shortly following sexual activity; however, a few occurred shortly after the use of sildenafil in the absence of sexual activity. It is unknown at present whether these events are related directly to sildenafil, to sexual activity, to underlying cardiovascular disease, to a combination of these factors, or to other factors. See also the *Medical considerations/Contraindications* section.

Sildenafil produces a transient decrease in blood pressure through vasodilation. Single oral doses of 100 mg of sildenafil have produced a decrease in the supine blood pressure (mean maximum decrease of 8.4/5.5 mm Hg). This hypotensive effect was most prominent at 1 to 2 hours after the dose was administered. Since similar results were observed with the 25-mg and 50-mg doses of sildenafil, this effect does not appear to be related to either the dose or plasma concentration.

The following side/adverse effects have been selected on the basis of their potential clinical significance (possible signs and symptoms in parentheses where appropriate)—not necessarily inclusive:

Those indicating need for medical attention

Incidence less frequent—2 to 3%

Abnormal vision, including blurred vision; color change perception (seeing shades of colors differently than before); ***or sensitivity to light***—may be mild and transient; ***dizziness; urinary tract infection or cystitis*** (bladder pain; cloudy or bloody urine; increased frequency of urination; pain on urination)

Note: In fixed-dose studies, *abnormal vision* was more common at the 100-mg dose (incidence of 11%) than at lower doses.

Incidence rare

Hematuria (blood in urine); ***ophthalmic effects, such as diplopia*** (double vision); ***increased intraocular pressure; paramacular edema*** (blurred vision or other changes in vision); ***redness, burning or swelling of the eye; retinal vascular disease or bleeding*** (changes in vision; bleeding of eye); ***vision loss, temporary; or vitreous detachment or traction*** (decrease in vision or other changes in vision); ***prolonged erection; priapism*** (prolonged, painful, inappropriate erection of penis); ***seizures***

Note: The following side/adverse effects reported in clinical trials or following the approval of sildenafil have not been established as being caused by sildenafil.

Allergic reaction (skin rash; hives; itching of skin); ***anemia or asthenia*** (unusual tiredness or weakness); ***arthrosis; arthritis; gout or hyperuricemia; synovitis or tenosynovitis; tendon rupture*** (bone pain; lower back or side pain; painful, swollen joints); ***breast enlargement; cardiovascular effects, such as angina pectoris*** (chest pain); ***AV block*** (fainting; trouble in breathing; unusual weakness); ***cardiac arrest or sudden cardiac death*** (heart failure); ***cerebral thrombosis*** (confusion; numbness of hands); ***cerebrovascular hemorrhage*** (headache, severe or continuing; seizures; sudden weakness; vision changes, such as blurred vision or temporary blindness); ***hypertension*** (dizziness, severe; headache, continuing); ***hypotension, including orthostatic hypotension*** (dizziness or lightheadedness, especially when getting up from a lying or sitting position; low blood pressure); ***intracerebral or subarachnoid hemorrhage*** (confusion; headache, sudden, severe, and continuing; nausea and vomiting); ***migraine headache; myocardial ischemia, myocardial infarction or transient ischemic attack*** (chest pain; fainting; fast heartbeat; increased sweating; nausea, continuing or severe; nervousness; shortness of breath; weakness); ***palpitation*** (pounding heartbeat); ***pulmonary hemorrhage*** (coughing up blood; shortness of breath); ***syncope*** (fainting); ***tachycardia*** (fast heartbeat); ***and ventricular arrhythmia*** (irregular heartbeat); ***chills; deafness; edema*** (swelling of face, hands, feet, or lower legs); ***hyperglycemia*** (faintness; nausea; paleness of skin; sweating); ***or hypoglycemia reaction*** (anxiety; behavior change similar to drunkenness; blurred vision; cold sweats; confusion; cool, pale skin; difficulty in concentrating; drowsiness; excessive hunger; fast heartbeat; headache; nausea; nervousness; nightmares; restless sleep; shakiness; slurred speech; unusual tiredness or weakness)—especially for patients with diabetes mellitus; ***hypernatremia*** (confusion; convulsions; decrease in amount of urine or in frequency of urination; dizziness; fast heartbeat; headache; increased thirst; swelling of feet or lower legs; twitching of muscles; unusual tiredness or weakness); ***leukopenia*** (sore throat and fever or chills); ***myasthenia*** (weakness of muscles); ***ophthalmic effects, such as cataracts; conjunctivitis*** (feeling of something in the eye; redness, itching, or tearing of eyes); ***dry eyes; eye hemorrhage*** (eye pain); ***and mydriasis*** (increase in size of pupil); ***shock*** (fainting); ***skin effects, such as contact dermatitis; pruritus; or urticaria*** (hives; itching; redness of skin); ***exfoliative dermatitis*** (dryness, redness, scaling, or peeling of the skin); ***herpes simplex*** (groups of skin lesions with swelling; unusual feeling of burning or stinging of skin); ***and skin ulcers***

Incidence not determined—Observed during clinical practice; estimates of frequency can not be determined

Non-arteritic anterior ischemic optic neuropathy (NAION) (blindness; blurred vision; decreased vision)

Those indicating need for medical attention only if they continue or are bothersome

Incidence more frequent

Diarrhea; dyspepsia (stomach discomfort following meals)—7%; ***dyspnea*** (shortness of breath; difficult or labored breathing; tightness in chest; wheezing); ***epistaxis*** (bloody nose); ***erythema*** (flushing, redness of skin; unusually warm skin); ***flushing***—10%; ***headache***—16%; ***insomnia*** (trouble in sleeping); ***myalgia*** (aches or pains in muscles); ***nasal congestion***—4%; ***pyrexia*** (fever)

Note: In fixed-dose studies, *dyspepsia* was more common at the 100-mg dose (incidence of 17%) than at lower doses.

Incidence less frequent

Gastritis (burning feeling in chest or stomach; tenderness in stomach area; stomach upset; indigestion); ***paresthesia*** (burning, crawling, itching, numbness, prickling, "pins and needles", or tingling feelings); ***rhinitis*** (stuffy nose; runny nose; sneezing); ***sinusitis*** (pain or tenderness around eyes and cheekbones; fever; stuffy or runny nose; headache; cough; shortness of breath or troubled breathing; tightness of chest or wheezing)

Incidence rare

Anxiety

Note: The following side/adverse effects reported in clinical trials of sildenafil have not been established as being caused by sildenafil.

Abdominal pain; central nervous system (CNS) symptoms, such as abnormal dreams; ataxia (clumsiness or unsteadiness); ***decreased reflexes*** (lack of coordination); ***hypertonia*** (tense muscles); ***hypesthesia*** (increased skin sensitivity); ***mental depression; neuralgia; neuropathy; or tremor*** (aches, pains, or weakness of muscles; numbness or tingling of hands, legs, or feet; trembling and shaking; unusual feeling of burning or stinging of skin); ***somnolence*** (sleepiness); ***and vertigo*** (sensation of motion, usually whirling, either of one's self or of one's surroundings); ***ear pain; gastrointestinal effects, such as colitis*** (severe diarrhea or stomach cramps); ***dry mouth, esophagitis, and stomatitis*** (difficulty in swallowing; redness or irritation of the tongue; sores in mouth and on lips); ***gastroenteritis*** (abdominal pain; diarrhea, severe; nausea); ***gingivitis*** (redness, soreness, swelling, or bleeding of gums); ***rectal bleeding; and vomiting; increased amount of saliva; increased sweating or thirst; respiratory effects, such as asthma; bronchitis; laryngitis; pharyngitis; and sinusitis*** (cough; shortness of breath or troubled breathing; tightness of chest or wheezing); ***tinnitus*** (ringing or buzzing in ears); ***urogenital effects, such as abnormal ejaculation or anorgasmia*** (failure to experience a sexual orgasm; sexual problems in men, continuing); ***nocturia*** (waking to urinate at night); ***urinary frequency, and urinary incontinence*** (loss of bladder control)

Overdose

For more information on the management of overdose or unintentional ingestion, **contact a poison control center** (see *Poison Control Center Listing*).

Clinical effects of overdose

In studies with healthy volunteers taking single doses of up to 800 mg, adverse events were similar to those seen at lower doses but incidence rates were increased.

Treatment of overdose

To enhance elimination—Renal dialysis is not expected to accelerate clearance of sildenafil; sildenafil is highly bound to plasma proteins and is not eliminated in the urine.

Supportive care—Supportive treatment should be adopted as required. Patients in whom intentional overdose is confirmed or suspected should be referred for psychiatric consultation.

Patient Consultation

As an aid to patient consultation, refer to *Advice for the Patient, Sildenafil (Systemic)*.

In providing consultation, consider emphasizing the following selected information (» = major clinical significance):

Before using this medication

» Conditions affecting use, especially:

Hypersensitivity to sildenafil or any component of the product

Breast-feeding—For pulmonary arterial hypertension: Caution should be used

Use in children—Safety and effectiveness in pediatric pulmonary hypertension not established

Use in the elderly—For erectile dysfunction: Patients 65 years of age and older should be started at 25 mg of sildenafil because of their slower metabolism and clearance and should be monitored more often for side/adverse effects.

For pulmonary arterial hypertension: Dose selection should be cautious.

Other medications, especially alpha-blockers, bosentan, enzyme inhibitors, hepatic, cytochrome P450 3A4, including cimetidine, erythromycin, itraconazole, ketoconazole, mibefradil, ritonavir, and saquinavir; erectile dysfunction treatments, or nitrates, including nitroglycerin

Other medical problems, especially cirrhosis or severe hepatic function impairment, pulmonary veno-occlusive disease (PVOD), or renal function impairment

Proper use of this medication

» Reading patient package insert

Knowing that medication begins to work within 30 minutes after taking it and effect continues for up to 4 hours, lessening after 2 hours for erectile dysfunction

» Proper dosing

» Proper storage

Precautions while using this medication

» Concurrent use of other impotence therapy agents is not presently recommended

» Complying with therapy dose recommendations; importance of not exceeding prescribed dosage and frequency of use

Sildenafil does not protect against sexually transmitted diseases; counseling patient on proper protection

» Checking with physician immediately if a prolonged erection, 4 or more hours in duration, occurs

Importance of physician knowing patient's cardiac risk factors and pre-existing cardiovascular disease states

Advising patient to seek medical attention if sudden loss of vision in one or both eyes occurs

Side/adverse effects

Signs of potential side effects, especially abnormal vision, including blurred vision, color change perception, and sensitivity to light; dizziness; urinary tract infection or cystitis; hematuria; ophthalmic effects, such as diplopia, increased intraocular pressure, paramacular edema, redness, burning, or swelling of the eye, retinal vascular disease or bleeding, temporary vision loss, or vitreous detachment or traction; prolonged erection; priapism; seizures

Signs of potential side effects (although not proven to be caused by sildenafil, but reported in clinical trials or in postmarketing experience), especially allergic reaction; anemia or asthenia; arthrosis, arthritis, gout or hyperuricemia, synovitis (including tenosynovitis), tendon rupture; breast enlargement; cardiovascular effects, such as angina pectoris, AV block, cardiac arrest or sudden cardiac death, cerebral thrombosis, cerebrovascular hemorrhage, hypertension, hypotension (including orthostatic hypotension), intracerebral or subarachnoid hemorrhage, migraine headache, myocardial ischemia, myocardial infarction or transient ischemic attack palpitation, pulmonary hemorrhage, syncope, tachycardia, and ventricular arrhythmia; chills; deafness; edema; hyperglycemia or hypoglycemia—especially for patients with diabetes mellitus; hypernatremia; leukopenia; myasthenia; ophthalmic effects, such as cataracts, conjunctivitis, dry eyes, eye hemorrhage, mydriasis; shock; or skin effects, such as contact dermatitis, pruritus, urticaria, exfoliative dermatitis, herpes simplex, and skin ulcer

Signs of potential side effects observed during clinical practice, especially non-arteritic anterior ischemic optic neuropathy (NAION)

General Dosing Information

For treatment of untreated erectile dysfunction—Sildenafil improved frequency, firmness, and maintenance of erections; frequency of orgasm; frequency and level of desire; frequency, satisfaction, and enjoyment of intercourse; and overall relationship satisfaction.

For treatment of erectile dysfunction due to a radical prostatectomy—Across all trials, sildenafil improved the erections of 43% of patients compared with improvement in 15% of the patients taking a placebo.

For treatment of erectile dysfunction due to complications of diabetes mellitus—Sildenafil improved frequency of successful penetration during sexual activity and maintenance of erections after penetration, compared to patients taking a placebo. Fifty-seven percent of patients taking sildenafil reported improved erections compared with 10% of patients taking a placebo.

For treatment of erectile dysfunction due to a spinal cord injury—Sildenafil improved frequency of successful penetration during sexual activity and maintenance of erections after penetration. Eighty-three percent of patients taking sildenafil reported improved erections compared with 12% of patients taking a placebo.

For treatment of erectile dysfunction due to psychogenic etiology—Sildenafil improved frequency of successful penetration during sexual activity and maintenance of erections after penetration. Eighty-four percent of patients taking sildenafil reported improved erections compared with 26% of patients taking a placebo.

For treatment of pulmonary arterial hypertension—Dosages lower than 20 mg three times per day were not tested and efficacy is not known.

Diet/Nutrition

Sildenafil can be taken with or without food.

Treatment of prolonged erection or priapism

A prolonged erection should be treated if it persists longer than 4 hours; priapism should be treated immediately. If priapism is not treated promptly, penile tissue damage and/or permanent loss of potency may result. Procedures for detumescence are listed below:

- Aspirate 40 to 60 mL of blood from either left or right corpora using vacutainer and holder for drawing blood. Apply ice for 20 minutes post aspiration if erection remains.
- If the above procedure is unsuccessful, put patient in supine position. Dilute phenylephrine 10 mg into 20 mL sterile water for injection. Using an insulin syringe, inject 0.1 to 0.2 mL (50 to 100 mcg) into the corpora every 2 to 5 minutes until detumescence occurs.
- Patients may develop transient bradycardia and hypertension due to phenylephrine injections. Monitor patient's blood pressure and pulse every 10 minutes. Patients with cardia arrhythmia and diabetes may be at higher risk. Do not give phenylephrine to patients on MAO inhibitors. Phenylephrine is usually effective in the majority of patients if used within 12 hours of erection.
- If the above measures fail to detumesce the patient, consult a urologist as soon as possible.

Oral Dosage Forms

SILDENAFIL CITRATE TABLETS

Usual adult dose

Erectile dysfunction—

Oral, 50 mg (base) one hour (range, one half to four hours) before sexual intercourse once a day if needed. As tolerated, subsequent doses may be increased to 100 mg or decreased to 25 mg once a day.

Note: For patients with hepatic impairment, severe renal impairment (creatinine clearance less than 30 mL per min), or patients concomitantly using a CYP3A4 inhibitor (ketoconazole, itraconazole, erythromycin, and saquinavir), a starting dose of 25 mg should be considered due to increased plasma levels of sildenafil associated with these conditions.

Pulmonary arterial hypertension (treatment)—

Oral 20 mg (base) three times a day approximately 4 to 6 hours apart, with or without food.

Note: For pulmonary arterial hypertension treatment: No dose adjustments are required for patients with renal impairment (including severe renal impairment, creatinine clearance less than 30 mL per min) or for patients with hepatic impairment (Child Pugh class A and B).

Usual adult prescribing limits

For erectile dysfunction—100 mg once a day.

For pulmonary arterial hypertension—20 mg three times per day.

Usual geriatric dose

Erectile dysfunction—

Oral, 25 mg (base) one hour (range, one half to four hours) before sexual intercourse once a day if needed. As tolerated, subsequent doses may be increased.

Pulmonary arterial hypertension (treatment)—

See *Usual adult dose*.

Strength(s) usually available

U.S.—

20 mg (base) (Rx) [*Revatio* (white film-coated; microcrystalline cellulose; anhydrous dibasic calcium phosphate; croscarmellose sodium; magnesium stearate; hypromellose; titanium dioxide; lactose monohydrate; triacetin)].

25 mg (base) (Rx) [*Viagra* (film-coated; croscarmellose sodium; lactose; magnesium stearate)].

50 mg (base) (Rx) [*Viagra* (film-coated; croscarmellose sodium; lactose; magnesium stearate)].

100 mg (base) (Rx) [*Viagra* (film-coated; croscarmellose sodium; lactose; magnesium stearate)].

Canada—

25 mg (base) (Rx) [*Viagra* (FD&C Blue #2 aluminum lake; lactose)].

50 mg (base) (Rx) [*Viagra* (FD&C Blue #2 aluminum lake; lactose)].

100 mg (base) (Rx) [*Viagra* (FD&C Blue #2 aluminum lake; lactose)].

Packaging and storage

Store below 40 °C (104 °F), preferably between 15 and 30 °C (59 and 86 °F).

Note
Include patient information insert (PPI) when dispensing.

Revised: 08/11/2005
Developed: 05/28/1998

SILVER SULFADIAZINE Topical

VA CLASSIFICATION (Primary/Secondary): DE101/DE102

Commonly used brand name(s): *Flamazine; SSD; SSD AF; Silvadene; Thermazene.*

Note: For a listing of dosage forms and brand names by country availability, see *Dosage Forms* section(s).

Category

Antibacterial (topical); antifungal (topical).

Note: Silver sulfadiazine is a broad-spectrum antibacterial agent having an antibacterial spectrum similar to that of mafenide.

Indications

Note: Bracketed information in the *Indications* section refers to uses that are not included in U.S. product labeling.

Accepted

Burn wound infections (prophylaxis and treatment)—Silver sulfadiazine is indicated [as a primary agent] in the topical prophylaxis and treatment of burn wound infections caused by *Acinetobacter calcoaceticus, Candida albicans (Monilia albicans), Citrobacter* species, *Clostridium perfringens, Corynebacterium diphtheriae, Enterobacter* species (including *E. cloacae*), enterococci, *Escherichia coli, Klebsiella* species, *Mima-Herellea* species, *Morganella morganii (Proteus morganii), P. mirabilis, P. vulgaris, Providencia rettgeri (Proteus rettgeri), Pseudomonas aeruginosa, Serratia* species, *Staphylococcus aureus, S. epidermidis Xanthomonas (Pseudomonas) maltophilia*, and beta-hemolytic streptococci in patients with second- and third-degree burns.

[Skin infections, bacterial, minor (treatment)] or
[Ulcer, dermal (treatment)]—Silver sulfadiazine is used in the topical treatment of minor bacterial skin infections such as those involving skin grafts, incisions and other clean lesions, abrasions, minor cuts and wounds; and dermal ulcer such as leg ulcer.

Not all species or strains of a particular organism may be susceptible to silver sulfadiazine.

Pharmacology/Pharmacokinetics

Physicochemical characteristics

Molecular weight—357.13.

Other characteristics—
Sulfonamides have certain chemical similarities to some goitrogens, diuretics (acetazolamide and thiazides), and oral antidiabetic agents.

Mechanism of action/Effect

Bactericidal for many gram-positive and gram-negative organisms. Mechanism of action differs from that of silver nitrate or sodium sulfadiazine. Acts only on the cell membrane and cell wall.

Other actions/effects

Also active against yeasts and *Candida albicans (M. albicans).*

Absorption

Varies, depending on the percentage of body surface area to which silver sulfadiazine is applied and extent of tissue damage.

Peak serum concentration

Serum sulfadiazine concentrations may approach therapeutic concentrations (up to 8 to 12 mg per 100 mL) when used in burns over extensive areas of the body.

Precautions to Consider

Cross-sensitivity and/or related problems

Patients sensitive to other sulfonamides, furosemide, thiazide diuretics, sulfonylureas, or carbonic anhydrase inhibitors may be sensitive to this medication also.

Carcinogenicity

Long-term dermal toxicity studies in rats (24 months) and mice (18 months), using 3 to 10% silver sulfadiazine, have shown no evidence of carcinogenicity.

Pregnancy/Reproduction

Pregnancy—Adequate and well-controlled studies in humans have not been done. However, absorbed sulfonamides may displace bilirubin from protein-binding sites in the fetal plasma, thus increasing the possibility of kernicterus in the neonate.

Studies in rabbits, treated with 3 to 10% silver sulfadiazine cream, have not shown that silver sulfadiazine causes adverse effects on the fetus.

FDA Pregnancy Category B.

Breast-feeding

It is not known whether silver sulfadiazine, applied topically, is distributed into breast milk. However, silver sulfadiazine may be absorbed systemically in variable amounts following topical application. Caution is recommended in nursing women since systemically administered sulfonamides are distributed into breast milk and may cause kernicterus in nursing infants. Also, sulfonamides may cause hemolytic anemia in glucose-6-phosphate dehydrogenase (G6PD)–deficient infants.

Pediatrics

Use is not recommended in premature or newborn infants up to 2 months of age since sulfonamides may cause kernicterus in these neonates. Appropriate studies on the relationship of age to the effects of silver sulfadiazine have not been performed in the pediatric population. However, pediatrics-specific problems that would limit the usefulness of this medication in older infants and children are not expected.

Geriatrics

No information is available on the relationship of age to the effects of silver sulfadiazine in geriatric patients.

Drug interactions and/or related problems

The following drug interactions and/or related problems have been selected on the basis of their potential clinical significance (possible mechanism in parentheses where appropriate)—not necessarily inclusive (» = major clinical significance):

Note: Combinations containing any of the following medications, depending on the amount present, may also interact with this medication.

» Cimetidine
(concurrent use with cimetidine may increase the incidence of leukopenia)

» Collagenase or
» Papain or
» Sutilains
(concurrent use of proteolytic enzymes with silver sulfadiazine is not recommended since heavy metal salts may inactivate the enzymes)

Medical considerations/Contraindications

The medical considerations/contraindications included have been selected on the basis of their potential clinical significance (reasons given in parentheses where appropriate)—not necessarily inclusive (» = major clinical significance).

Risk-benefit should be considered when the following medical problems exist:

Blood dyscrasias
(sulfonamides may cause blood dyscrasias)

Glucose-6-phosphate dehydrogenase (G6PD) deficiency
(sulfonamides may cause hemolytic anemia in G6PD-deficient patients)

Hepatic function impairment
(sulfonamides are metabolized in the liver and may cause hepatitis; if hepatic function impairment occurs, discontinuation of therapy should be considered)

Porphyria
(sulfonamides may precipitate an acute attack of porphyria)

Renal function impairment
(if renal function impairment with decreased elimination occurs, discontinuation of therapy should be considered)

Sensitivity to silver sulfadiazine

Patient monitoring

The following may be especially important in patient monitoring (other tests may be warranted in some patients, depending on condition; » = major clinical significance):

» Complete blood counts (CBCs)
(may be required prior to and weekly during treatment to detect blood dyscrasias in patients with extensive burns; therapy should

be discontinued if a significant decrease in the count of any formed blood elements occurs)

Serum sulfadiazine concentrations

(may be required periodically during treatment in patients with extensive burns since serum sulfadiazine concentrations may approach adult therapeutic concentrations)

Urinalyses

(may be required prior to and periodically during treatment to detect crystalluria and/or urinary calculi formation in patients on long-term or high-dose therapy and in patients with impaired renal function)

Side/Adverse Effects

Note: Hyperosmolality, due to the propylene glycol–containing vehicle, has been reported very rarely in infants during therapy with silver sulfadiazine cream.

If significant absorption occurs, side/adverse effects (e.g., Stevens-Johnson syndrome, Lyell's syndrome, blood dyscrasias, crystalluria) usually seen with systemic sulfonamides may occur with silver sulfadiazine therapy, although few have been reported.

If allergic reactions or hepatic or renal function impairment with decreased elimination occurs, discontinuation of therapy with silver sulfadiazine should be considered.

The following side/adverse effects have been selected on the basis of their potential clinical significance (possible signs and symptoms in parentheses where appropriate)—not necessarily inclusive:

Those indicating need for medical attention

Incidence rare

Erythema multiforme (blistering, peeling, loosening of skin; red skin lesions, often with a purple center); ***fungal proliferation in and below the eschar*** (intense itching of burn wounds); ***increased sensitivity of skin to sunlight***—especially in patients with burns on large areas; ***interstitial nephritis*** (bloody or cloudy urine, greatly decreased frequency of urination or amount of urine); ***leukopenia*** (chills; cough; decreased neutrophil count; fever; painful or difficult urination; shortness of breath; sore throat; sores, ulcers, or white spots on lips or in mouth; swollen glands; unusual bleeding or bruising; unusual tiredness or weakness)—transient and may recover without discontinuation of treatment; ***skin necrosis*** (blue-green to black skin discoloration; pain, redness, or sloughing of skin)

Those indicating need for medical attention only if they continue or are bothersome

Incidence more frequent

Burning feeling on treated area(s)

Incidence less frequent or rare

Brownish-gray skin discoloration; itching or skin rash

Patient Consultation

As an aid to patient consultation, refer to *Advice for the Patient, Silver Sulfadiazine (Topical)*

In providing consultation, consider emphasizing the following selected information (» = major clinical significance):

Before using this medication

» Conditions affecting use, especially:

Sensitivity to other sulfonamides, furosemide, thiazide diuretics, sulfonylureas, or carbonic anhydrase inhibitors

Pregnancy—Absorbed sulfonamides may increase the possibility of kernicterus in the neonate

Breast-feeding—May cause kernicterus in nursing infants; may cause hemolytic anemia in G6PD-deficient infants

Use in children—Not recommended in premature or newborn infants up to 2 months of age; may cause kernicterus

Other medications, especially cimetidine and proteolytic enzymes such as collagenase, papain, or sutilains

Proper use of this medication

To use

Before applying, cleansing affected area(s); removing necrotic or burned skin and other debris

Wearing a sterile glove to apply the medication; applying a thin layer (approximately 1.5 mm) to affected area(s); keeping affected area(s) covered with the medication at all times

Reapplying silver sulfadiazine that has been removed by patient activity or washed off by bathing, showering, or use of a whirlpool bath

After applying, covering treated area(s) with a dressing or leaving treated area(s) uncovered as desired

» Compliance with full course of therapy; continuing medication until burn has healed or is ready for skin grafting

» Proper dosing

Missed dose: Applying as soon as possible; not applying if almost time for next dose

» Proper storage

Precautions while using this medication

Regular visits to physician to check progress

Checking with physician if no improvement within a few days or weeks (for more serious burns or burns over more extensive areas)

May rarely stain skin brownish gray

Side/adverse effects

Signs of potential side effects, especially erythema multiforme, fungal proliferation in and below the eschar, increased sensitivity of skin to sunlight, interstitial nephritis, leukopenia, and skin necrosis

General Dosing Information

Before application, burn wounds should be cleansed and debrided following control of shock and pain. A sterile glove should be worn to apply the medication. A thin layer (approximately 1.5 mm) of silver sulfadiazine should then be applied to the affected area(s). The burn area(s) should be kept covered with silver sulfadiazine at all times. When necessary, silver sulfadiazine should be reapplied to any area(s) from which it has been removed by patient activity or washed off by bathing, showering, or use of a whirlpool bath.

Dressings, although not required, may be applied if necessary.

Treatment with silver sulfadiazine should be continued until satisfactory healing has occurred or until the burn site is ready for skin grafting. Therapy should not be discontinued while the possibility of infection exists, unless significant toxicity occurs.

Burn patients should be bathed daily, if feasible, to aid in debridement of the burned area(s). Whirlpool baths are particularly helpful, although burn patients may be bathed in bed or in a shower. Following this, silver sulfadiazine should be reapplied.

Topical Dosage Forms

Note: Bracketed information in the *Indications* section refers to uses that are not included in U.S. product labeling.

SILVER SULFADIAZINE CREAM USP

Usual adult and adolescent dose

Burn wound infections or
[Skin infections, bacterial, minor] or
[Ulcer, dermal]—

Topical, to the affected area(s), one or two times a day, applied in a thin layer approximately 1.5 mm thick.

Note: In some other countries, silver sulfadiazine is customarily applied less frequently (e.g., three times a week), in a 3- to 5-mm layer. However, USP medical experts prefer application one or two times a day in a 1.5-mm layer.

Usual pediatric dose

Burn wound infections or
[Skin infections, bacterial, minor] or
[Ulcer, dermal]—

Premature and newborn infants up to 2 months of age—Use is not recommended, since sulfonamides may cause kernicterus in these neonates.

Infants and children 2 months of age and over—See *Usual adult and adolescent dose*.

Strength(s) usually available

U.S.—

1% (Rx) [*Silvadene* (propylene glycol; methylparaben 0.3%; white petrolatum); *SSD* (cetyl alcohol; propylene glycol; methylparaben 0.3%); *SSD AF* (propylene glycol; methylparaben 0.3%); *Thermazene* (propylene glycol; methylparaben 0.3%)].

Canada—

1% (Rx) [*Flamazine*].

Packaging and storage

Store between 15 and 30 °C (59 and 86 °F), in a well-closed container, unless otherwise specified by manufacturer. Protect from freezing.

Auxiliary labeling

- For external use only.
- May discolor skin.
- Continue medicine for full time of treatment.

Additional information
Silver sulfadiazine cream is available in a water-miscible base containing silver sulfadiazine in micronized form.

Revised: 03/17/2000

SIMETHICONE Oral-Local

VA CLASSIFICATION (Primary/Secondary): GA900/DX900

Commonly used brand name(s): *Baby's Own Infant Drops; Degas; Extra Strength Maalox Anti-Gas; Extra Strength Maalox GRF Gas Relief Formula; Flatulex; Gas Relief; Gas-X; Gas-X Extra Strength; Genasyme; Maalox Anti-Gas; Maalox GRF Gas Relief Formula; Maximum Strength Gas Relief; Maximum Strength Mylanta Gas Relief; Maximum Strength Phazyme; My Baby Gas Relief Drops; Mylanta Gas; Mylanta Gas Relief; Mylicon Drops; Ovol; Ovol-160; Ovol-40; Ovol-80; Phazyme; Phazyme Drops; Phazyme-125; Phazyme-95.*

Note: For a listing of dosage forms and brand names by country availability, see *Dosage Forms* section(s).

Category
Antiflatulent; diagnostic aid (gastroscopy; radiography of the bowel).

Indications
Note: Bracketed information in the *Indications* section refers to uses that are not included in U.S. product labeling.

Accepted
Gas, gastrointestinal (treatment)—Simethicone's clinical use is based on its antifoam properties demonstrated *in vitro*. It is indicated in the treatment of functional conditions in which the retention of gas may be a problem.

[Gastroscopy adjunct][1] and
[Radiography, bowel, adjunct][1]—Simethicone is used as an antifoaming agent during gastroscopy to enhance visualization and prior to radiography of the bowel to reduce gas shadows.

Unaccepted
The clinical effectiveness of simethicone in such conditions as aerophagia, functional dyspepsia, peptic ulcer, spastic or irritable colon, or diverticulitis, beyond that of placebo, has not been established.

Simethicone is not recommended for use in infant colic.

[1]Not included in Canadian product labeling.

Pharmacology/Pharmacokinetics

Mechanism of action/Effect
Acts *in vitro* to lower the surface tension of gas bubbles. Its relevance to action *in vivo* is not clearly established.

Elimination
Fecal, as unchanged drug.

Precautions to Consider

Pregnancy/Reproduction
Pregnancy—Problems in humans have not been documented.

Breast-feeding
Problems in humans have not been documented.

Pediatrics
Appropriate studies performed to date have not demonstrated pediatrics-specific problems that would limit the usefulness of simethicone in children.

Geriatrics
No information is available on the relationship of age to the effects of simethicone in geriatric patients.

Medical considerations/Contraindications
The medical considerations/contraindications included have been selected on the basis of their potential clinical significance (reasons given in parentheses where appropriate)—not necessarily inclusive (» = major clinical significance).

Risk-benefit should be considered when the following medical problem exists:
Sensitivity to simethicone

Patient Consultation
As an aid to patient consultation, refer to *Advice for the Patient, Simethicone (Oral).*

In providing consultation, consider emphasizing the following selected information (» = major clinical significance):

Before using this medication
» Conditions affecting use, especially:
Sensitivity to simethicone
Importance of proper diet and exercise to prevent gas problem

Proper use of this medication
Following physician's or manufacturer's instructions
» Taking after meals and at bedtime for best results
For chewable tablet dosage form
Chewing tablets thoroughly for faster and more complete results
For oral suspension dosage form
Proper use of dropper bottle or measuring spoon
» Proper dosing
Missed dose: If on regular dosing schedule—Taking as soon as possible; not taking if almost time for next dose; not doubling doses
» Proper storage

General Dosing Information
Dosage or frequency of administration may be doubled with the advice of a physician.

Pediatric dosage should be based on the severity of the condition and the surface area of the patient rather than on body weight.

Oral Dosage Forms
Note: Bracketed uses in the *Dosage Forms* section refer to categories of uses and/or indications that are not included in the U.S. product labeling.

SIMETHICONE CAPSULES USP

Usual adult and adolescent dose
Antiflatulent—
Oral, 95 or 125 mg four times a day, after meals and at bedtime, or as needed.

Note: For OTC use, it is recommended that no more than 500 mg be taken in each twenty-four-hour period.

Usual pediatric dose
Dosage must be individualized by physician.

Usual geriatric dose
See *Usual adult and adolescent dose.*

Strength(s) usually available
U.S.—
125 mg (OTC) [*Gas-X Extra Strength; Maximum Strength Phazyme*].
Canada—
95 mg (OTC) [*Phazyme-95*].
125 mg (OTC) [*Phazyme-125*].

Packaging and storage
Store between 15 and 30 °C (59 and 86 °F), unless otherwise specified by manufacturer. Store in a well-closed container.

SIMETHICONE ORAL SUSPENSION USP

Usual adult and adolescent dose
Antiflatulent—
Oral, 40 to 95 mg four times a day, after meals and at bedtime, or as needed.
[Diagnostic aid (gastroscopy; radiography of the bowel)][1]—
Oral, 67 mg in 2.5 mL of water, as a single dose.

Note: For OTC use, it is recommended that no more than 500 mg be taken in each twenty-four-hour period.

Usual pediatric dose
Dosage must be individualized by physician.

Usual geriatric dose
See *Usual adult and adolescent dose.*

Strength(s) usually available
U.S.—
40 mg per 0.6 mL (OTC) [*Flatulex; Gas Relief; My Baby Gas Relief Drops; Mylicon Drops; Phazyme;* GENERIC].
Canada—
40 mg per 0.6 mL (OTC) [*Baby's Own Infant Drops; Phazyme Drops*].
40 mg per mL (OTC) [*Ovol*].
95 mg per 1.425 mL (OTC) [*Phazyme-95*].

Packaging and storage
Store below 40 °C (104 °F), preferably between 15 and 30 °C (59 and 86 °F), unless otherwise specified by manufacturer. Store in a tight, light-resistant container. Protect from freezing.

Auxiliary labeling
- Shake well.

Note
Dispense in dropper bottle or with measuring spoon.

SIMETHICONE TABLETS USP

Usual adult and adolescent dose
Antiflatulent—

Oral, 60 to 95 mg four times a day, after meals and at bedtime, or as needed.

Note: For OTC use, it is recommended that no more than 500 mg be taken in each twenty-four-hour period.

Usual pediatric dose
Dosage must be individualized by physician.

Usual geriatric dose
See *Usual adult and adolescent dose*.

Strength(s) usually available
U.S.—

60 mg (OTC) [*Phazyme* (sugar-coated)].
80 mg (OTC) [*Flatulex; Genasyme* (scored); GENERIC].
95 mg (OTC) [*Phazyme-95*].

Canada—

Not commercially available.

Packaging and storage
Store below 40 °C (104 °F), preferably between 15 and 30 °C (59 and 86 °F), unless otherwise specified by manufacturer. Store in a well-closed container.

SIMETHICONE TABLETS (CHEWABLE) USP

Usual adult and adolescent dose
Antiflatulent—

Oral, 40 to 125 mg four times a day, after meals and at bedtime, or as needed; or, 150 mg three times a day, after meals, or as needed.

Note: For OTC use, it is recommended that no more than 500 mg be taken in each twenty-four-hour period.

Usual pediatric dose
Dosage must be individualized by physician.

Usual geriatric dose
See *Usual adult and adolescent dose*.

Strength(s) usually available
U.S.—

40 mg (OTC) [*Mylanta Gas*].
80 mg (OTC) [*Degas; Gas Relief; Gas-X* (scored); *Maalox Anti-Gas; Mylanta Gas Relief;* GENERIC].
125 mg (OTC) [*Maximum Strength Gas Relief; Maximum Strength Mylanta Gas Relief; Maximum Strength Phazyme*].
150 mg (OTC) [*Extra Strength Maalox Anti-Gas*].

Canada—

40 mg (OTC) [*Ovol-40* (scored)].
80 mg (OTC) [*Maalox GRF Gas Relief Formula; Ovol-80* (scored)].
150 mg (OTC) [*Extra Strength Maalox GRF Gas Relief Formula*].
160 mg (OTC) [*Ovol-160*].

Packaging and storage
Store below 40 °C (104 °F), preferably between 15 and 30 °C (59 and 86 °F), unless otherwise specified by manufacturer. Store in a well-closed container.

Auxiliary labeling
- Chew tablets well before swallowing.

[1]Not included in Canadian product labeling.

Revised: 08/14/1998

SIMVASTATIN—See *HMG-CoA Reductase Inhibitors (Systemic)*

SIROLIMUS Systemic

VA CLASSIFICATION (Primary): IM403

Commonly used brand name(s): *Rapamune*.

Another commonly used name is
Rapamycin

Note: For a listing of dosage forms and brand names by country availability, see *Dosage Forms* section(s).

Category
Immunosuppressant.

Indications

Accepted
Transplant rejection, kidney (prophylaxis)—Sirolimus is indicated for the prevention of rejection of transplanted kidney allografts. It is recommended that sirolimus be used initially in a regimen with cyclosporine and corticosteroids.

Acceptance not established
Safety and efficacy of conversion from calcineurin inhibitors to sirolimus in maintenance renal transplant population has not been established. In an ongoing study in maintenance renal transplant patients, enrollment was stopped in the subset of patients with a baseline glomerular filtration rate of less than 40 mL per minute. There was a higher rate of serious adverse events including pneumonia, acute rejections, graft loss and death in this sirolimus treatment arm.

Unaccepted
The safety and efficacy of sirolimus as immunosuppressive therapy have not been established in liver or lung transplant patients. Therefore, such use is not recommended.

Pharmacology/Pharmacokinetics

Physicochemical characteristics
Source—*Streptomyces hygroscopicus*.
Chemical Group—Macrocyclic lactone
Molecular weight—914.2.
Solubility—Freely soluble in acetone, acetonitrile, benzyl alcohol, and chloroform; insoluble in water.

Mechanism of action/Effect
Immunosuppressant, systemic—Sirolimus inhibits cytokine (Interleukin (IL)–2, IL-4, and IL-15)—stimulated T lymphocyte activation and proliferation; it also inhibits antibody production. This may occur through formation of an immunosuppressive complex with FK Binding Protein-12 (FKBP-12). Although the sirolimus-(FKBP-12) complex is inactive against calcineurin activity, the complex binds to and inhibits activation of a key regulatory kinase, mammalian Target of Rapamycin (mTOR). This is believed to suppress cytokine-driven T-cell proliferation, inhibiting cell cycle progression from the G_1 to S phase.

Absorption
Rapid, from the gastrointestinal tract. Bioavailability is approximately 14%. Rate of absorption is decreased in the presence of a high-fat diet. The rate and extent of absorption is reduced in black patients.

Distribution
The volume of distribution (Vol D) of sirolimus is 12 ± 8 liters per kg of body weight; extensive uptake by formed blood elements is found (95% concentrated in red blood cells).

Protein binding
Very high (approximately 92%), primarily to serum albumin, α_1-acid glycoprotein, and lipoproteins.

Biotransformation
Hepatic, extensive, by cytochrome P450 3A enzymes in the intestinal wall and liver and undergoes counter-transport from enterocytes of the small intestine into the gut lumen by the P-glycoprotein (P-gp) drug efflux pump. Sirolimus is recycled between enterocytes and the gut lumen to allow continued metabolism by CYP3A4. Therefore, absorption and subsequent elimination of systemically absorbed sirolimus may be influenced by drugs that affect these proteins including CYP3A4 and P-gp inhibitors and inducers. Major metabolites include hydroxysirolimus, demethylsirolimus, and hydroxydemethylsirolimus.

Elimination
57 to 63 hours. May be significantly increased (up to 72 hours) in males. However, no adjustment in dosage is required.

Time to peak concentration
1 to 3 hours, after oral administration. A mean time-to-peak concentration of 2 hours after multiple oral doses in renal transplant patients.

Peak blood concentration
12.2 ± 6.2 and 37.4 ± 21 nanograms per mL (ng/mL) in renal transplant patients administered 2 mg and 5 mg, respectively, of sirolimus in combination with cyclosporine and corticosteroids.

Whole blood trough concentration
As measured by immunoassay—9 ng/mL in patients who received 2 mg of sirolimus per day; 17 ng/mL in patients who received 5 mg of sirolimus per day. Results from other assays may differ from those found with immunoassay.

Duration of action
The immunosuppressant effect of sirolimus lasted up to 6 months after discontinuation of therapy in some animal studies.

Elimination
Only a minor amount (2.2%) is eliminated in urine; the majority of metabolites (91%) are recovered from the feces.

Precautions to Consider

Carcinogenicity/Tumorigenicity
Malignant lymphoma was statistically increased at dosages of 6 to 25 mg per kg of body weight (approximately 16 to 135 times the clinical dose based on body surface area) per day given for 86 weeks to female mice. There was a statistically significant increased incidence of testicular adenoma in rats given 0.2 mg per kg of body weight (approximately 0.4 to 1 times the clinical dose based on body surface area) per day for 104 weeks.

Mutagenicity
Mutagenicity was not observed in the *in vitro* bacterial reverse mutation assay, the Chinese hamster ovary cell chromosomal aberration assay, the mouse lymphoma cell forward mutation assay, nor with *in vivo* mouse micronucleus testing.

Pregnancy/Reproduction
Fertility—Adequate and well-controlled studies have not been conducted in humans. Sirolimus was not observed to affect fertility in female and male rats at doses of approximately 1 to 3 times (0.5 mg per kg of body weight) and 4 to 11 times (2 mg per kg of body weight) the clinical doses adjusted for body surface area, respectively. Reductions in testicular weights and/or histological lesions were observed in rats following dosages of 0.65 mg per kg of body weight (approximately 1 to 3 times the clinical dose based on body surface area) and above and in monkeys following dosages of 0.1 mg per kg of body weight (approximately 0.4 to 1 times the clinical dose based on body surface area) and above. Sperm counts were reduced following the administration of sirolimus at dosages of 6 mg per kg of body weight (approximately 12 to 32 times the clinical dose based on body surface area) for 13 weeks, but resolved 3 months after discontinuation of sirolimus in male rats.

Pregnancy—Adequate and well-controlled studies in humans have not been done.

Sirolimus should be used during pregnancy only if the potential benefit outweighs the potential risk to the embryo/fetus. Effective contraception must be initiated before sirolimus therapy, during sirolimus therapy, and for 12 weeks after sirolimus therapy has been stopped.

Sirolimus was associated with embryo and fetal toxicity in rats; there was no teratogenicity observed. Increased mortality and reduced fetal weights (with associated delays in skeletal ossification) occurred at dosages of 0.1 mg per kg of body weight and above (approximately 0.2 to 0.5 times the clinical doses adjusted for body surface area). Embryo and fetal mortality increased in rats on combination sirolimus and cyclosporine compared to sirolimus alone. No effects on rabbit development at the maternally toxic dose of 0.05 mg per kg of body weight (approximately 0.3 to 0.8 times the clinical dose based on body surface area) were observed.

FDA Pregnancy Category C.

Breast-feeding
It is not known whether sirolimus is distributed in human breast milk. However, trace amounts of sirolimus is distributed in the milk of lactating rats. Because similar drugs are known to be distributed in human milk, and because of the risk for adverse reactions in nursing infants, a decision should be made whether to discontinue nursing or to discontinue the drug, taking into account the importance of the drug to the mother.

Pediatrics
Appropriate studies have not been performed on the relationship of age to the effects of sirolimus in the pediatric population in children up to 13 years of age. Safety and efficacy have not been established in children less than 13 years of age.

Adolescents
Safety and efficacy of sirolimus have been established in children 13 years of age and older judged to be at low to moderate immunologic risk and use of sirolimus tablets and oral solution is supported in this group.

Safety and efficacy information in pediatric and adolescent children less than 18 years of age judged to be at high immunologic risk, defined as a history of one or more acute rejection episodes and/or the presence of chronic allograft nephropathy, does not support the use of sirolimus tablets and oral solution in combination with calcineurin inhibitors and corticosteroids in this group. Use is not supported due to the increased risk of lipid abnormalities and deterioration of renal function associated with these immunosuppressive regimens, without increased benefit with respect to acute rejection, graft survival, or patient survival.

Geriatrics
No information is available on the relationship of age to the effects of sirolimus in geriatric patients. Preliminary data pertaining to sirolimus trough concentrations infer that it is unnecessary to adjust doses based upon age in the geriatric renal transplant patient.

Pharmacogenetics
When comparing the safety profile of sirolimus oral solution versus tablets, it was found that tremor occurred more frequently in the tablet group, particularly in black patients. Hispanic patients in the tablet group experienced hyperglycemia more frequently than those in the oral solution group.

Dental
The immunosuppressant effects of sirolimus may result in an increased incidence of microbial infection and delayed healing. Dental work, whenever possible, should be completed prior to initiation of therapy and undertaken with caution during therapy. Patients should be instructed in proper oral hygiene during treatment, including caution in use of regular toothbrushes, dental floss, and toothpicks.

Drug interactions and/or related problems
The following drug interactions and/or related problems have been selected on the basis of their potential clinical significance (possible mechanism in parentheses where appropriate)—not necessarily inclusive (» = major clinical significance):

» Antibiotics such as
 » Rifabutin or
 » Rifapentine
» Anticonvulsants such as
 » Carbamazepine or
 » Phenobarbital or
 » Phenytoin
 (these drugs decrease sirolimus concentrations due to CYP3A4 and P-glycoprotein [P-gp] induction; co-administration of sirolimus with strong CYP3A4 and/or P-gp inducers is not recommended; alternative therapeutic agents with less potential for induction should be considered.)

Antifungal agents such as
 Clotrimazole or
 Fluconazole or
 » Itraconazole or
 » Voriconazole
Bromocriptine
Calcium channel blockers such as
 Nicardipine
 » Verapamil
Cimetidine
Danazol
Gastrointestinal prokinetic agents such as
 Cisapride or
 Metoclopramide or
Macrolide antibiotics such as
 » Clarithromycin or
 » Erythromycin or
 » Telithromycin or
 Troleanodomycin
Protease inhibitors, human immunodeficiency virus including
 Indinavir or
 Ritonavir
 (sirolimus is a known CYP3A4 isoenzyme and P-gp substrate; inhibition of the CYP3A4 enzyme-mediated metabolism of sirolimus, can result in elevations in sirolimus blood concentrations and toxicity; concomitant use of strong inhibitors of CYP3A4 and/or P-gp including clarithromycin, erythromycin, itraconazole, telithromycin,

and voriconazole and sirolimus is not recommended; co-administration of sirolimus and verapamil significantly affected bioavailability of both; sirolimus concentrations should be monitored and a dose adjustment may be necessary when administered with verapamil)

» Calcineurin inhibitors
(concomitant use may increase the risk of calcineurin inhibitor-induced hemolytic uremic syndrome/thrombotic thrombocytopenic purpura/thrombotic microangiopathy [HUS/TTP/TMA])

» Cyclosporine
(coadministration in renal transplantation patients increases the susceptibility to infection and possible developments of lymphomas and malignancy, especially of the skin; patients should be monitored with adequate laboratory and supportive medical resources)

(sirolimus is a known CYP3A4 and P-glycoprotein substrate. Impairment of the CYP3A4 enzyme-mediated metabolism of sirolimus, may lead to elevations in sirolimus blood concentrations and toxicity.The drug interactions between sirolimus and cyclosporine have been observed clinically in either patients or healthy human subjects.)

(coadministration in liver transplant patients has resulted in excess mortality, graft loss and hepatic artery thrombosis [HAT], most cases of HAT occurred within 30 days post-transplantation)

(because of the effect of cyclosporine capsules [modified], it is recommended that sirolimus should be taken 4 hours after administration of cyclosporine oral solution [modified] and/or cyclosporine capsules [modified])

» Diltiazem or
» Ketoconazole
(sirolimus is a known CYP3A4 and P-glycoprotein substrate; impairment of the CYP3A4 enzyme-mediated metabolism of sirolimus, may lead to elevations in sirolimus blood concentrations and toxicity; if diltiazem is administered, sirolimus concentrations should be monitored and a dose adjustment may be necessary; co-administration of sirolimus oral solution or tablets and ketoconazole is not recommended)

» Grapefruit juice
(reduces CYP3A4-mediated drug metabolism and potentially enhances P-gp mediated drug counter-transport from enterocytes of the small intestine; must not be taken with or used to dilute sirolimus)

HMG-CoA reductase inhibitors
(monitoring for rhabdomyolysis and other adverse effects as described in the respective labeling is recommended when these medications are administered concurrently with sirolimus and cyclosporine)

Nephrotoxic medications (see *Appendix II*), such as:
Aminoglycosides or
Amphotericin B
(may cause additive or synergistic impairment of renal function)

Other drugs that affect P-gp
(sirolimus is a substrate for the multidrug efflux pump, P-gp, in the small intestine; absorption of sirolimus may be influenced)

» Rifampin
(significant increases in sirolimus clearance occurs when administered with rifampin due to CYP3A4 induction by rifampin; an alternative antibacterial agent with less enzyme induction potential should be considered; co-administration of sirolimus oral solution or tablets and rifampin is not recommended)

» St. John's wort
(because St. John's wort [*hypericum perforatum*] induces the activity of CYP3A4 and P-glycoprotein and sirolimus is a substrate of both, concurrent use of St. John's wort with sirolimus may result in decreased sirolimus concentrations)

» Tacrolimus
(may cause excess mortality, graft loss and hepatic artery thrombosis [HAT] in liver transplant patients, most cases of HAT occurred within 30 days post-transplantation)

Vaccines, killed virus
(immune response to vaccines may be decreased)

» Vaccines, live virus
(avoid the use of live vaccines such as measles, mumps, rubella, oral polio, BCG, yellow fever, varicella, and TY21a typhoid)

Laboratory value alterations

The following have been selected on the basis of their potential clinical significance (possible effect in parentheses where appropriate)—not necessarily inclusive (» = major clinical significance):

With physiology/laboratory test values

Albumin in urine or
Sugar in urine
(values may be increased indicating abnormal amounts of albumin or sugar in the urine; called albuminuria and glycosuria, respectively)

Alkaline phosphatase or
ALT/SGPT or
AST/SGOT or
Blood urea nitrogen [BUN] or
Creatine phosphokinase or
Lactic dehydrogenase
(may be increased)

Blood glucose or
Calcium
(values may be increased or decreased)

Cholesterol and
Triglycerides
(values may be increased; in clinical trials, 42 to 52% of patients required treatment with lipid-lowering medications)

Creatinine, serum
(values may be increased; may indicate nephrotoxicity)

Glomerular filtration rate and
Hematocrit value and
Hemoglobin concentration
(may be decreased)

Leukocytes (neutrophils [WBC])
(blood counts may be increased or decreased)

Magnesium or
Sodium
(may be decreased)

Platelets
(blood counts may be decreased)

Medical considerations/Contraindications

The medical considerations/contraindications included have been selected on the basis of their potential clinical significance (reasons given in parentheses where appropriate)—not necessarily inclusive (» = major clinical significance).

Except under special circumstances, this medication should not be used when the following medical problems exist:

» Hypersensitivity to sirolimus or its derivatives

» Liver transplantation
(sirolimus not recommended for immunosuppressive therapy in liver transplants. Use in liver transplantation has resulted in excess mortality, graft loss and hepatic artery thrombosis.)

» Lung transplantation
(sirolimus use not recommended as immunosuppressive therapy; cases of bronchial anastomotic dehiscence, most fatal, reported in lung transplant patients when sirolimus was used as part of an immunosuppressive regimen)

» Malignancy, current
(sirolimus use is associated with an increased susceptibility to lymphoma)

Risk-benefit should be considered when the following medical problems exist:

» Chickenpox, existing or recent (including recent exposure) or
» Herpes zoster
(risk of severe generalized disease)

» Hepatic impairment
(prolonged half-life from 79 ± 12 hours to 113 ± 41 hours occurs in patients with impaired hepatic function. Dosage adjustment is necessary in patients with mild to moderate hepatic impairment.)

Hyperlipidemia
(risk/benefit should be carefully considered before initiating therapy because renal transplant patients are at increased risk of developing clinically significant hyperlipidemia)

» Infection
(immunosuppression may exacerbate infections)

Patient monitoring

The following may be especially important in patient monitoring (other tests may be warranted in some patients, depending on condition; » = major clinical significance):

Blood urea nitrogen (BUN) and
» Creatinine, serum
(recommended during administration of maintenance immunosuppression regimens; dosage adjustment may be necessary in patients with increased serum creatinine concentrations)

Cholesterol, serum and
Triglycerides, serum
(diet and exercise modifications and/or lipid-lowering agents may be required if cholesterol or triglyceride concentrations increase.)

Complete blood counts (CBCs)
(monitoring of CBC recommended to detect sirolimus-induced blood dyscrasias; changes in the neutrophil count may also indicate infection)

» Infection
(increased susceptibility to infection may result from immunosuppression; oversuppression of the immune system can also increase susceptibility to infection including opportunistic infections, fatal infections, and sepsis)

» Sirolimus concentration, whole blood, trough
(recommended in patients likely to have altered drug metabolism, in patients ≥ 13 years of age who weigh less than 40 kilograms, in patients with hepatic impairment, during concurrent administration of potent cytochrome CYP3A4 inducers and inhibitors, and/or if cyclosporine dosing is markedly reduced or discontinued; should be monitored at least 3 to 4 days after loading dose(s))

Side/Adverse Effects

The following side/adverse effects have been selected on the basis of their potential clinical significance (possible signs and symptoms in parentheses where appropriate)—not necessarily inclusive:

Those indicating need for medical attention

Incidence more frequent

Abnormal liver function tests (lab results that show problems with liver); ***abscess*** (accumulation of pus; swollen, red, tender area of infection; fever); ***acidosis*** (drowsiness, fatigue, headache, nausea, troubled breathing, vomiting); ***anemia*** (unusual bleeding or bruising; unusual tiredness or weakness; trouble breathing on exertion); ***asthma*** (cough; difficulty breathing; noisy breathing; shortness of breath; tightness in chest; wheezing); ***atelectasis*** (coughing; difficult breathing; fever; rapid heartbeat); ***atrial fibrillation*** (irregular heartbeat); ***bone necrosis*** (pain in bones); ***bronchitis*** (cough producing mucus; difficulty breathing; shortness of breath; tightness in chest; wheezing); ***cataracts*** (blindness; blurred vision; decreased vision); ***cellulitis*** (itching, pain, redness, swelling, tenderness, warmth on skin); ***chest pain; congestive heart failure*** (chest pain; decreased urine output; dilated neck veins; extreme fatigue; irregular breathing; irregular heartbeat; shortness of breath; swelling of face, fingers, feet, or lower legs; tightness in chest; troubled breathing; weight gain; wheezing); ***conjunctivitis*** (redness, pain, swelling of eye, eyelid, or inner lining of eyelid; burning, dry or itching eyes; discharge; excessive tearing); ***Cushing's syndrome*** (backache; blurred vision; loss of sexual desire or ability; facial hair growth in females; fractures; full or round face, neck, or trunk; increased thirst or urination; irritability; menstrual irregularities; muscle wasting; unusual tiredness or weakness); ***deafness; diabetes mellitus*** (blurred vision; dry mouth; fatigue; flushed, dry skin; fruit-like breath odor; increased hunger; increased thirst; increased urination; loss of consciousness; nausea; stomachache; sweating; troubled breathing; unexplained weight loss; vomiting); ***dyspnea*** (shortness of breath); ***dysuria*** (difficult or painful urination; burning while urinating); ***ecchymosis*** (bruising; large, flat, blue or purplish patches in the skin); ***hematuria*** (blood in urine); ***hemorrhage*** (bleeding gums; coughing up blood; difficulty in breathing or swallowing; dizziness; headache; increased menstrual flow or vaginal bleeding; nosebleeds; paralysis; prolonged bleeding from cuts; red or dark brown urine; red or black, tarry stools; shortness of breath); ***hernia*** (abdominal pain; lump in abdomen); ***herpes simplex infection*** (burning or stinging of skin; painful cold sores or blisters on lips, nose, eyes, or genitals); ***herpes zoster infection*** (painful blisters on trunk of body); ***hydronephrosis*** (swelling of face, hands, legs, and feet; cloudy urine); ***hypercholesteremia; hyperkalemia*** (abdominal pain; confusion; irregular or slow heartbeat; nausea or vomiting; numbness or tingling around lips, hands, or feet; shortness of breath or trouble breathing; unusual tiredness or weakness; weakness or heaviness of legs; unexplained anxiety); ***hyperlipidemia; hypertension; hypervolemia*** (blurred vision; cough; dizziness; fast or slow heartbeat; headache; rapid breathing; shortness of breath; swelling of lower legs or arms; weight gain); ***hypokalemia*** (convulsions; decreased urine output; fast or irregular heartbeat; increased thirst; loss of appetite; mood changes; muscle pain or cramps; nausea or vomiting; numbness or tingling in hands, feet, or lips; shortness of breath; unusual tiredness or weakness); ***hypophosphatemia*** (bone pain; convulsions; loss of appetite; muscle weakness; difficulty breathing; unusual tiredness or weakness); ***hypoxia*** (confusion; dizziness; fast heartbeat; shortness of breath; weakness); ***ileus*** (abdominal pain; severe constipation; severe vomiting); ***kidney tubular necrosis*** (bloody or cloudy urine; difficult or painful urination; sudden decrease in amount of urine); ***leukocytosis*** (chills; cough; eye pain; fever; general feeling of illness; headache; sore throat; unusual tiredness); ***leukopenia*** (black, tarry stools; chest pain; chills; cough; fever; painful or difficult urination; shortness of breath; sore throat; sores, ulcers, or white spots on lips or in mouth; swollen glands; unusual bleeding or bruising; unusual tiredness or weakness); ***lung edema*** (chest pain; difficult, fast, noisy breathing, sometimes with wheezing; blue lips and fingernails; pale skin; increased sweating; coughing that sometimes produces a pink frothy sputum; shortness of breath; swelling in legs and ankles); ***lymphadenopathy*** (swollen, painful, or tender lymph glands in neck, armpit, or groin); ***lymphoma*** (black, tarry stools; general feeling of illness; swollen glands; weight loss, unusual; yellow skin and eyes); ***neuropathy*** (burning, tingling, numbness or pain in the hands, arms, feet, or legs; sensation of pins and needles; stabbing pain); ***oral moniliasis*** (sore mouth or tongue; white patches in mouth and/or on tongue); ***otitis media*** (earache; redness or swelling in ear); ***palpitation*** (fast, irregular, pounding, or racing heartbeat or pulse); ***peritonitis*** (abdominal or stomach pain; chills; fever; nausea or vomiting); ***peripheral edema*** (swelling of hands, ankles, feet, or lower legs); ***peripheral vascular disorder*** (cold hands and feet); ***pleural effusion*** (chest pain; shortness of breath); ***pneumonia*** (chest pain; cough; fever or chills; sneezing; shortness of breath; sore throat; troubled breathing; tightness in chest; wheezing); ***polycythemia*** (abdominal pain; bleeding from gums or nose; dizziness; eye pain; headache; ringing in the ears; tiredness; weakness); ***postural hypotension*** (chills; cold sweats; confusion; dizziness, faintness, or lightheadedness when getting up from lying or sitting position); ***pyelonephritis*** (chills; fever; frequent or painful urination; headache; stomach pain); ***pyuria*** (pus in the urine); ***rash; sepsis*** (chills; confusion; dizziness; lightheadedness; fainting; fast heartbeat; fever; rapid, shallow breathing); ***syncope*** (fainting); ***tachycardia*** (fast, pounding, or irregular heartbeat or pulse); ***tetany*** (abdominal cramps; confusion; convulsions; difficulty in breathing; irregular heartbeats; mood or mental changes; muscle cramps in hands, arms, feet, legs, or face; numbness and tingling around the mouth, fingertips, or feet; shortness of breath; tremor); ***thrombocytopenia*** (unusual bleeding or bruising); ***thrombophlebitis*** (changes in skin color; pain, tenderness, swelling of foot or leg); ***thrombosis*** (tenderness, pain, swelling, warmth, skin discoloration, and prominent superficial veins over affected area); ***thrombotic thrombocytopenic purpura (hemolytic-uremic syndrome)*** (change in mental status; dark or bloody urine; difficulty speaking; fever; pale color of skin; pinpoint red spots on skin; seizures; weakness; yellow eyes or skin); ***toxic nephropathy*** (bloody or cloudy urine; difficult or painful urination; sudden decrease in amount of urine); ***upper respiratory infection*** (ear congestion; nasal congestion; chills; cough; fever; sneezing; sore throat, body aches or pain; headache; loss of voice; runny nose; unusual tiredness or weakness; difficulty in breathing); ***urinary tract infection*** (bloody or cloudy urine; difficult, burning, or painful urination; frequent urge to urinate; lower back or side pain); ***vasodilation*** (feeling of warmth or heat; flushing or redness of skin, especially on face and neck; headache; feeling faint, dizzy, or lightheadedness; sweating); ***venous thromboembolism*** (pain in chest, groin, or legs, especially the calves; difficulty breathing; severe, sudden headache; slurred speech; sudden, unexplained shortness of breath; sudden loss of coordination; sudden, severe weakness or numbness in arm or leg; vision changes)

Incidence less frequent

Epstein-Barr virus infections (black, tarry stools; chest pain; chills; cough; difficult urination; fever; muscle pain; pale skin; shortness of breath; skin rash; sore throat; trouble breathing; tightness in chest; unusual bleeding or bruising; unusual tiredness or weakness; wheezing); ***hypotension*** (blurred vision; confusion; dizziness; faintness, or lightheadedness when getting up from a lying or sitting position suddenly; sweating; unusual tiredness or weakness); ***lymphocele***—occurred more frequently in a dose-related fashion; appropriate operative measures should be considered to minimize this complication; ***melanoma*** (new mole; change in size, shape or color of existing mole; mole that leaks fluid or bleeds); ***mycobacterial infections*** (fever or chills; cough or hoarseness; lower back or side pain; painful or difficult urination); ***pancreatitis*** (bloating; chills; constipation; darkened urine; fast heartbeat; fever; indigestion; loss of appetite; nausea; pains in stomach, side, or abdomen, possibly radiating to the back; vomiting; yellow eyes or skin); ***skin ulcer*** (sores on skin)

Note: To minimize the occurrence of *lymphocele*, appropriate postoperative measures should be employed.

Incidence rare

Capillary leak syndrome (fever; low blood pressure; swelling of legs and feet; weight gain)

Incidence not determined—Observed during clinical practice; estimates of frequency can not be determined

Abnormal healing—fascial dehiscence and anastomotic disruption, including wound, vascular, airway, ureteral, biliary following transplant surgery; ***anaphylactic reaction*** (cough; difficulty swallowing; dizziness; fast heartbeat; hives; itching; puffiness or swelling of the eyelids or around the eyes, face, lips or tongue; shortness of breath; skin rash; tightness in chest; unusual tiredness or weakness; wheezing); ***angioedema*** (large, hive-like swelling on face, eyelids, lips, tongue, throat, hands, legs, feet, sex organs); ***hepatic necrosis*** (abdominal or stomach pain; black, tarry stools; chills; light-colored stools; dark urine; dizziness; fever; headache; itching; loss of appetite; nausea; rash; unpleasant breath odor; unusual tiredness or weakness; vomiting of blood; yellow eyes or skin); ***hepatotoxicity*** (abdominal pain or tenderness; clay colored stools; dark urine; decreased appetite; fever; headache; itching; loss of appetite; nausea and vomiting; skin rash; swelling of feet or lower legs; unusual tiredness or weakness; yellow eyes or skin); ***hypersensitivity vasculitis*** (chills; fever; sore throat; muscle aches, pains, or weakness; shortness of breath; troubled breathing; tightness in chest; wheezing); ***interstitial lung disease*** (cough; difficult breathing; fever; shortness of breath); ***lymphedema*** (swelling of arms or legs; yellow nails lacking a cuticle; nails loose or detached); ***neutropenia*** (black, tarry, stools; chills; cough; fever; lower back or side pain; painful or difficult urination; pale skin; shortness of breath; sore throat; ulcers, sores, or white spots in mouth; unusual bleeding or bruising; unusual tiredness or weakness); ***pancytopenia*** (high fever; chills; unexplained bleeding or bruising; bloody, black, or tarry stools; pale skin; unusual tiredness or weakness; cough; shortness of breath; sores, ulcers, or white spots on lips or in mouth; swollen glands); ***pneumonitis*** (chest pain; chills; cough; fever; general feeling of discomfort or illness; shortness of breath; thickening of bronchial secretions; troubled breathing); ***pulmonary fibrosis*** (fever; cough; shortness of breath)

Those indicating need for medical attention only if they continue or are bothersome

Incidence more frequent

Abdomen enlarged; abdominal pain; abnormal vision (changes in vision); ***acne; anorexia*** (loss of appetite, weight loss); ***anxiety*** (fear, nervousness); ***arthralgia*** (difficulty in moving; muscle pain or stiffness; pain); ***arthrosis*** (degenerative disease of the joint); ***ascites*** (stomach pain and bloating); ***asthenia*** (loss of energy or weakness); ***back pain; bladder pain*** (lower abdominal pain); ***chills; confusion*** (mood or mental changes); ***constipation; cough increased; dehydration*** (confusion, decreased urination, dizziness, dry mouth, fainting, increase in heart rate, lightheadedness, rapid breathing, sunken eyes, thirst, unusual tiredness or weakness, wrinkled skin); ***depression*** (discouragement, feeling sad or empty, irritability, lack of appetite, loss of interest or pleasure, tiredness, trouble concentrating, trouble sleeping); ***diarrhea; dizziness; dysphagia*** (difficulty swallowing); ***ear pain; emotional lability*** (crying; depersonalization; dysphoria; euphoria; mental depression; paranoia; quick to react or overreact emotionally; rapidly changing moods); ***eructation*** (belching, bloated full feeling, excess air or gas in stomach); ***esophagitis*** (difficulty in swallowing, pain or burning in throat, chest pain, heartburn, vomiting, sores, ulcers, or white spots on lips or tongue or inside the mouth); ***fever; flatulence*** (bloated full feeling; excess air or gas in stomach or intestines; passing gas); ***flu syndrome*** (chills; cough; diarrhea; fever; general feeling of discomfort or illness; headache; joint pain; loss of appetite; muscle aches and pains; nausea; runny nose; shivering; sore throat; sweating; trouble sleeping; unusual tiredness or weakness; vomiting); ***fungal dermatitis*** (blistering, crusting, irritation, itching, or reddening of skin; cracked, dry, scaly skin; swelling); ***gastritis or gastroenteritis*** (abdominal or stomach pain; burning feeling in chest or stomach; tenderness in stomach area; stomach upset; indigestion; diarrhea; loss of appetite; nausea; weakness); ***generalized edema*** (swelling); ***gingivitis*** (bleeding gums; irritation in mouth; redness and swelling of gums; mouth ulcers); ***gum hyperplasia*** (bleeding, tender, or enlarged gums); ***headache; hirsutism*** (increased hair growth, especially on the face); ***hypertonia*** (excessive muscle tone, muscle tension or tightness; muscle stiffness); ***hypesthesia*** (burning, crawling, itching, numbness, prickling, "pins and needles", or tingling feelings); ***hypotonia*** (unusual weak feeling; loss of strength or energy; muscle pain or weakness); ***impotence*** (loss in sexual ability, desire, drive, or performance; decreased interest in sexual intercourse; inability to have or keep an erection); ***insomnia*** (trouble in sleeping); ***kidney pain; leg cramps; malaise*** (general feeling of discomfort or illness, unusual tiredness or weakness); ***mouth ulceration; myalgia*** (joint pain; swollen joints; muscle aching or cramping; muscle pains or stiffness; difficulty in moving); ***nausea; nocturia*** (waking to urinate at night; increased urge to urinate during the night); ***oliguria*** (decrease in amount of urine); ***osteoporosis*** (pain in back, ribs, arms, or legs; decrease in height); ***paresthesia*** (burning, crawling, itching, numbness, prickling, "pins and needles", or tingling feelings); ***pelvic pain; pruritus*** (itching skin); ***rhinitis*** (stuffy nose; runny nose; sneezing); ***scrotal edema*** (swelling of the scrotum); ***sinusitis*** (pain or tenderness around eyes and cheekbones; fever; stuffy or runny nose; headache; cough; shortness of breath or troubled breathing; tightness of chest or wheezing); ***skin hypertrophy*** (thickening of the skin); ***somnolence*** (sleepiness or unusual drowsiness); ***stomatitis*** (swelling or inflammation of the mouth); ***sweating; testis disorder; tinnitus*** (continuing ringing or buzzing or other unexplained noise in ears, hearing loss); ***tremor*** (shaking or trembling); ***urinary frequency; urinary incontinence*** (loss of bladder control); ***urinary retention*** (decrease in urine volume; decrease in frequency of urination; difficulty in passing urine [dribbling]; painful urination); ***vomiting; weight gain, unusual; weight loss***

Incidence less frequent

Epistaxis (nosebleed); ***facial edema*** (swelling of the face)

Overdose

For more information on the management of overdose or unintentional ingestion, **contact a poison control center** (see *Poison Control Center Listing*).

Clinical effects of overdose

There was minimal experience with overdose of sirolimus during clinical trials. In mice and rats, the acute oral lethal dose was greater than 800 mg per kg of body weight.

In general, the adverse effects of overdose of sirolimus are consistent with those listed in the Side/Adverse Effects section. For more information, see *Side/Adverse Effects* of this monograph or consult the manufacturer's package insert.

The following effects have been selected on the basis of their potential clinical significance (possible signs and symptoms in parentheses where appropriate)—not necessarily inclusive:

Atrial fibrillation (irregular heartbeat)—transient; occurred in one patient accidentally ingesting 150 mg in clinical trials

Treatment of overdose

Supportive care—

Treatment of overdose of sirolimus is generally symptomatic and supportive. Patients in whom intentional overdose is confirmed or suspected should be referred for psychiatric consultation.

To enhance elimination—

Due to the high erythrocyte binding and low aqueous solubility of sirolimus, dialysis is unlikely to offer any significant clinical benefit in the management of sirolimus overdose.

Patient Consultation

As an aid to patient consultation, refer to *Advice for the Patient, Sirolimus (Systemic)*.

Consider advising the patient on the following (» = major clinical significance):

Before using this medication

» Conditions affecting use, especially:

Hypersensitivity to sirolimus or its derivatives

Pregnancy—Effective contraception is recommended prior to, during and 12 weeks after sirolimus therapy. Increased embryo/fetal mortality has occurred in animal studies.

Breast-feeding—It is unknown if sirolimus is distributed into human breast milk. Breast feeding is not recommended during sirolimus therapy, due to risk of side effects in infants.

Use in adolescents—Safety/efficacy established in patients ≥13 years of age at low to moderate immunologic risk; safety/efficacy NOT established in patients ≥13 years of age at high immunologic risk

Dental—Dental work should be completed prior to initiation of therapy whenever possible.

Other medications, especially calcineurin inhibitors, carbamazepine, clarithromycin, cyclosporine, diltiazem, erythromycin, itraconazole, ketoconazole, phenobarbital, phenytoin, rifabutin, rifampin, rifapentine, St. John's wort, telithromycin, tacrolimus, live vaccines, verapamil, or voriconazole

Other medical problems, especially chickenpox, current malignancy, hepatic impairment, herpes zoster infection, liver transplantation, lung transplantation, or other infection

Proper use of this medication

» Reading patient package insert carefully

» Taking medication only as directed by physician

Establishing the routine of taking medication at the same time each day

Taking medication consistently in relation to the timing of the intake of food to help increase compliance and maintain steady blood concentrations

» Checking with physician before discontinuing or changing medication; possible need for lifelong therapy

» Importance of checking with physician before discontinuing cyclosporine after 4 months of combination therapy of sirolimus and cyclosporine; physician must assess risk-benefit of continuing cyclosporine

Taking sirolimus 4 hours after cyclosporine modified oral solution (*Neoral*) or cyclosporine modified capsules (*Neoral*)

Mixing oral solution of sirolimus with at least 2 ounces (¼ cup, 60 mL) of water or orange juice in a glass or plastic container, stirring well and drinking immediately, then rinsing the glass with at least 4 ounces (½ cup, 120 mL) of additional liquid, stirring well, and drinking that liquid also to make sure that all of the medication is taken

» Proper dosing

Missed dose: Taking as soon as possible if remembered within 12 hours; not taking if almost time for next dose; not doubling doses

» Proper storage

Precautions while using this medication

» Importance of close monitoring by physician

Maintaining good dental hygiene and seeing dentist regularly for teeth cleaning

» Not eating raw oysters or other shellfish; making sure they are fully cooked before eating

» Continuing recommended vaccination schedule (except for live vaccines)

Avoiding people with colds or other infections

» Not drinking grapefruit juice or eating grapefruit

» Limiting exposure to sunlight and UV light by wearing protective clothing and using a sunscreen with a high protection factor because of the increased risk for skin cancer

Side/adverse effects

Signs of potential side effects, especially abnormal liver function tests, abscess, acidosis, anemia, asthma, atelectasis, atrial fibrillation, bone necrosis, bronchitis, cataracts, cellulitis, chest pain, congestive heart failure, conjunctivitis, Cushing's syndrome, deafness, diabetes mellitus, dyspnea, dysuria, ecchymosis, hematuria, hemorrhage, hernia, herpes simplex infection, herpes zoster infection, hydronephrosis, hypercholesteremia, hyperkalemia, hyperlipidemia, hypertension, hypervolemia, hypokalemia, hypophosphatemia, hypoxia, ileus, kidney tubular necrosis, leukocytosis, leukopenia, lung edema, lymphadenopathy, lymphoma, neuropathy, oral moniliasis, otitis media, palpitation, peritonitis, peripheral edema, peripheral vascular disorder, pleural effusion, pneumonia, polycythemia, postural hypotension, pyelonephritis, pyuria, rash, sepsis, syncope, tachycardia, tetany, thrombocytopenia, thrombotic thrombocytopenic purpura (hemolytic-uremic syndrome), thrombophlebitis, thrombosis, toxic nephropathy, upper respiratory infection, urinary tract infection, vasodilation, venous thromboembolism, Epstein-Barr virus infections, hemolytic-uremic syndrome, hypotension, lymphocele, melanoma, mycobacterial infections, pancreatitis, skin ulcer, and capillary leak syndrome

Signs of potential side effects observed during clinical practice, especially abnormal healing following transplant surgery, anaphylactic reaction, angioedema, hepatic necrosis, hepatotoxicity, hypersensitivity vasculitis, interstitial lung disease, lymphedema, neutropenia, pancytopenia, pneumonitis, and pulmonary fibrosis

General Dosing Information

Only physicians experienced in immunosuppressive therapy and management of organ transplant patients should use sirolimus. Patients receiving sirolimus should be managed in facilities equipped and staffed with adequate laboratory and supportive medical resources. The physician responsible for maintenance therapy should have complete information requisite for the follow-up of the patient.

Sirolimus is indicated for use in conjunction with cyclosporine and corticosteroids. Because of the effect of cyclosporine capsules (modified), it is recommended that sirolimus be taken 4 hours after cyclosporine solution (modified) and/or cyclosporine capsules (modified).

Oral sirolimus is to be administered once daily. It is recommended that the initial dose be administered as soon as possible after transplantation.

Because sirolimus is extensively metabolized by the liver, it is recommended that the maintenance dose be reduced by approximately one third in patients with impaired hepatic function. However, adjustment of the loading dose is not necessary.

Although a daily maintenance dose of 5 mg, with a loading dose of 15 mg was shown to be safe and effective in clinical trials, no efficacy advantage over the 2-mg dose could be established for renal transplant patients. Patients receiving 2 mg of sirolimus oral solution per day demonstrated an overall better safety profile than those receiving a 5-mg per day dose.

Frequent sirolimus dose adjustments based on non-steady-state sirolimus concentrations can lead to overdosing or underdosing because sirolimus has a long half-life. Once sirolimus maintenance dose is adjusted, patients should be retained on the new maintenance dose at least 7 to 14 days before further dosage adjustment with concentration monitoring.

In clinical trials, sirolimus has been administered concurrently with corticosteroids and with the following formulations of cyclosporine:

- Cyclosporine injection (Sandimmune® Injection)
- Cyclosporine oral solution (Sandimmune® Oral Solution)
- Cyclosporine capsules (Sandimmune® Soft Gelatin Capsules)
- Cyclosporine capsules [MODIFIED] (Neoral® Soft Gelatin Capsules)
- Cyclosporine oral solution [MODIFIED] (Neoral® Oral Solution)

Safety and efficacy of sirolimus use in combination with other immunosuppressive agents has not been determined.

Safety and efficacy of cyclosporine withdrawal in high-risk patients have not been adequately studied and it is, therefore, not recommended. This includes patients with Banff grade III acute rejection or vascular rejection prior to cyclosporine withdrawal, those who are dialysis-dependent or with serum creatinine >4.5 mg per dL, black patients, retransplants, multi-organ transplants, and patients with high panel of reactive antibodies.

Safety and efficacy of conversion from calcineurin inhibitors to sirolimus in maintenance renal transplant population have not been established. In an ongoing study in maintenance renal transplant patients, enrollment was stopped in the subset of patients with a baseline glomerular filtration rate of less than 40 mL per minute. There was a higher rate of serious adverse events including pneumonia, acute rejections, graft loss and death in this sirolimus treatment arm.

In patients with low to moderate immunologic risk, continuation of combination therapy with cyclosporine beyond 4 months following transplantation should only be considered when the benefits outweigh the risks of this combination for the individual patients.

At 2 to 4 months following transplantation, cyclosporine should be progressively discontinued over 4 to 8 weeks and sirolimus dose adjusted accordingly to obtain whole blood trough concentrations within the range of 12 to 24 ng per mL. Careful attention should also be paid to clinical signs/symptoms, tissue biopsy, and laboratory parameters when adjusting sirolimus dose. Cyclosporine inhibits the metabolism and transport of sirolimus. Consequently, sirolimus concentrations will decrease when cyclosporine is discontinued unless the sirolimus dose is increased. Sirolimus dose will need to be approximately 4-fold higher to account for both the absence of the pharmacokinetic interaction and the augmented immunosuppressive requirement in the absence of cyclosporine.

Antimicrobial prophylaxis against *Pneumocystis carinii* pneumonia is recommended for 1 year following transplantation.

Antiviral prophylaxis against cytomegalovirus (CMV) is recommended for 3 months following transplantation, especially in patients at increased risk for developing CMV disease.

Diet/Nutrition

It is recommended that sirolimus be taken consistently either with or without food, in order to minimize variability of absorption.

Grapefruit juice significantly reduces the CYP3A4–mediated metabolism of sirolimus, and should not be taken with the drug nor used for dilution. Conversely, the rate of absorption of sirolimus is decreased in the presence of a high-fat diet.

Bioequivalence information
Two milligrams (mg) of sirolimus oral solution has been demonstrated to be clinically equivalent to a 2-mg sirolimus oral tablet making them interchangeable on a mg to mg basis. However, it is not known if higher doses of sirolimus oral solution are clinically equivalent to higher doses of tablets on a mg to mg basis.

Cyclosporine oral solution USP (*Sandimmune*) is not bioequivalent to cyclosporine modified capsules (*Neoral*) and, therefore, these dosage forms cannot be used interchangeably.

Safety considerations for handling this medication
Special precautions for handling sirolimus are unnecessary. However, wash thoroughly with soap and water, if direct contact with the skin or mucous membranes occurs; rinse eyes with plain water.

Oral Dosage Forms

SIROLIMUS ORAL SOLUTION

Usual adult and adolescent dose
Transplant rejection, kidney (prophylaxis)—

Oral, loading dose of 6 mg and a maintenance dose of 2 mg once daily. Loading dose for *de novo* transplant recipients is 3 times the maintenance dose. For adolescents above the age of 13 years weighing less than 40 kg, the dose should be adjusted based upon body surface area, to 1 mg per square meter per day, following a 3 mg per square meter loading dose. In most patients, dose adjustments can be based on simple proportion:

• New sirolimus dose = current dose x (target concentration / current concentration)

A loading dose should be considered in addition to a new maintenance dose when it is necessary to considerably increase sirolimus trough concentrations:

• Sirolimus loading dose = 3 x (new maintenance dose − current maintenance dose

Once sirolimus maintenance dose is adjusted, patients should be retained on the new maintenance dose at least for 7 to 14 days before further dosage adjustment with concentration monitoring.

Note: Reduce the dose by approximately one third in patients with hepatic impairment; an adjustment in the loading dose is unnecessary. Dosage does not need to be adjusted for patients with renal impairment

Usual adult prescribing limits
Not to exceed 40 mg once daily. If an estimated daily dose exceeds 40 mg due to the addition of a loading dose, the loading dose should be administered over 2 days.

Usual pediatric dose
Transplant rejection, kidney (prophylaxis)—

Children up to 13 years of age—Safety and efficacy have not been established.

Children 13 years of age or older—See *Usual adult and adolescent dose.*

Usual geriatric dose
See *Usual adult and adolescent dose*

Strength(s) usually available
U.S.—

1 mg per 1 mL (Rx) [*Rapamune* (Phosal 50 PG® (phosphatidylcholine, propylene glycol, mono- and di-glycerides, ethanol 1.5%—2.5%, soy fatty acids, and ascorbyl palmitate) and polysorbate 80, NF)].

Canada—

1 mg per 1 mL (Rx) [*Rapamune* (ascorbyl palmitate; ethanol; phosphatidylcholine; propylene glycol; soybean oil fatty acids; sunflower mono and diglycerides; polysorbate 80)].

Packaging and storage
Store between 2 and 8° (C) (36 and 46° F). Brief periods of storage (not more than 15 days) at room temperatures up to 25° C (77° F) are tolerated. The solution should be protected from light.

Sirolimus oral solution may be stored in the syringe for up to 24 hours at room temperature up to 25 °C (77 °F) or refrigerated at temperatures between 2 and 8 °C (36 and 46 °F).

Preparation of dosage form
Oral sirolimus should be diluted in a glass or plastic container with at least 2 fluid ounces (¼ cup, 60 mL) of water or orange juice. The drug should not be diluted in grapefruit juice or any other liquid. See the manufacturer's package insert for instructions.

Stability
Stable for up to 24 months in protected, unopened bottles. The solution should be used within one month after bottle opening. The solution should be used immediately after dilution. The syringe should be discarded after one use.

Note: When dispensing, include the calibrated oral dose syringes provided by the manufacturer.

Auxiliary labeling
• For oral use only.
• Refrigerate- Do not freeze.
• Dilute medication before use.
• Grapefruit and grapefruit juice should not be taken with this medicine.
• Limit exposure to sunlight and UV light by wearing protective clothing and using a sunscreen with a high protection factor because of the increased risk for skin cancer.

Additional information
Sirolimus oral solution in bottles may develop a slight haze when refrigerated. If such a haze occurs, allow the product to stand at room temperature and shake gently until the haze disappears. The presence of this haze does not affect the quality of the product.

SIROLIMUS TABLETS

Usual adult and adolescent dose
Transplant rejection, kidney (prophylaxis)—

Oral, loading dose of 6 mg and a maintenance dose of 2 mg once daily. Loading dose for *de novo* transplant recipients is 3 times the maintenance dose. For adolescents above the age of 13 years weighing less than 40 kg, the dose should be adjusted based upon body surface area, to 1 mg per square meter per day, following a 3 mg per square meter loading dose. In most patients, dose adjustments can be based on simple proportion:

• New sirolimus dose = current dose x (target concentration / current concentration)

A loading dose should be considered in addition to a new maintenance dose when it is necessary to considerably increase sirolimus trough concentrations:

• Sirolimus loading dose = 3 x (new maintenance dose − current maintenance dose

Once sirolimus maintenance dose is adjusted, patients should be retained on the new maintenance dose at least for 7 to 14 days before further dosage adjustment with concentration monitoring.

Note: Reduce the maintenance dose by approximately one third in patients with hepatic impairment; an adjustment in the loading dose is unnecessary. Dosage does not need to be adjusted for patients with renal impairment.

Usual adult prescribing limits
Not to exceed 40 mg once daily. If an estimated daily dose exceeds 40 mg due to the addition of a loading dose, the loading dose should be administered over 2 days.

Usual pediatric dose
Transplant rejection, kidney (prophylaxis)—

Children up to 13 years of age—Safety and efficacy have not been established.

Children 13 years of age or older—See *Usual adult and adolescent dose.*

Usual geriatric dose
See *Usual adult and adolescent dose.*

Strength(s) usually available
U.S.—

1 mg (Rx) [*Rapamune* (sucrose; lactose; polyethylene glycol 8000; calcium sulfate; microcrystalline cellulose; pharmaceutical glaze; talc; titanium dioxide; magnesium stearate; povidone; poloxamer 188; polyethylene glycol 20,000; glycerol monooleate; carnauba wax; and other ingredients)].

2 mg [*Rapamune* (sucrose; lactose; polyethylene glycol 8000; calcium sulfate; microcrystalline cellulose; pharmaceutical glaze; talc; titanium dioxide; magnesium stearate; povidone; poloxamer 188; polyethylene glycol 20,000; glycerol monooleate; carnauba wax; iron oxide yellow 10; iron oxide brown 70; and other ingredients)].

Packaging and storage
Store between 20 and 25°C (68 and 77°F).

Auxiliary labeling
• Protect from light.
• Grapefruit and grapefruit juice should not be taken with this medicine.

• Limit exposure to sunlight and UV light by wearing protective clothing and using a sunscreen with a high protection factor because of the increased risk for skin cancer.

Revised: 04/19/2006
Developed: 04/06/2000

SKELETAL MUSCLE RELAXANTS Systemic

This monograph includes information on the following: 1) Carisoprodol; 2) Chlorphenesin†; 3) Chlorzoxazone†; 4) Metaxalone†; 5) Methocarbamol; 6) Orphenadrine.

VA CLASSIFICATION (Primary):
Carisoprodol—MS200
Chlorphenesin—MS200
Chlorzoxazone—MS200
Metaxalone—MS200
Methocarbamol—MS200
Orphenadrine Citrate—MS200
Orphenadrine Hydrochloride—AU305

Commonly used brand name(s): *Antiflex*[6]; *Banflex*[6]; *Carbacot*[5]; *Disipal*[6]; *EZE-DS*[3]; *Flexoject*[6]; *Maolate*[2]; *Mio-Rel*[6]; *Myolin*[6]; *Myotrol*[6]; *Norflex*[6]; *Orfro*[6]; *Orphenate*[6]; *Paraflex*[3]; *Parafon Forte DSC*[3]; *Relaxazone*[3]; *Remular*[3]; *Remular-S*[3]; *Robaxin*[5]; *Robaxin-750*[5]; *Skelaxin*[4]; *Soma*[1]; *Strifon Forte DSC*[3]; *Vanadom*[1].

Note: For a listing of dosage forms and brand names by country availability, see *Dosage Forms* section(s).

†Not commercially available in Canada.

Category

Skeletal muscle relaxant—Carisoprodol; Chlorphenesin; Chlorzoxazone; Metaxalone; Methocarbamol; Orphenadrine Citrate.

Parkinsonism therapy adjunct—Orphenadrine Hydrochloride.

Indications

Accepted

Spasm, skeletal muscle (treatment)—Skeletal muscle relaxants are indicated as adjuncts to other measures, such as rest and physical therapy, for the relief of muscle spasm associated with acute, painful musculoskeletal conditions.

Parkinsonism (treatment adjunct)—Orphenadrine hydrochloride is indicated (but is rarely used) as an adjunct to physical therapy and other medications in the treatment of postencephalic, arteriosclerotic, or idiopathic parkinsonism. It produces symptomatic relief of tremor. The medication may be used concurrently with reduced dosages of more potent medications in treating patients who cannot tolerate effective doses of the other medications.

Unaccepted

Methocarbamol is also FDA-approved for control of the neuromuscular manifestations of tetanus. However, it has largely been replaced in the treatment of tetanus by diazepam, or, in severe cases, a neuromuscular blocking agent such as pancuronium. Such therapy is used as an adjunct to other measures, such as debridement, tetanus antitoxin, penicillin, tracheotomy, fluid and electrolyte replacement, and supportive treatment.

Pharmacology/Pharmacokinetics

See *Table 1*, page 2630.
See *Table 2*, page 2631.

Physicochemical characteristics

Molecular weight—
Carisoprodol: 260.34.
Chlorphenesin carbamate: 245.66.
Chlorzoxazone: 169.57.
Metaxalone: 221.26.
Methocarbamol: 241.25.
Orphenadrine citrate: 461.51.
Orphenadrine hydrochloride: 305.85.

Mechanism of action/Effect

Skeletal muscle relaxant—Precise mechanism of action has not been determined. These agents act in the central nervous system (CNS) rather than directly on skeletal muscle. Several of these medications have been shown to depress polysynaptic reflexes preferentially. The muscle relaxant effects of most of these agents may be related to their CNS depressant (sedative) effects. Carisoprodol blocks interneuronal activity in the descending reticular formation and in the spinal cord. Chlorzoxazone acts primarily at the spinal cord level and at subcortical areas of the brain. Orphenadrine has analgesic activity, which may contribute to its skeletal muscle relaxant properties.

Parkinsonism therapy adjunct—Orphenadrine has mild anticholinergic actions, which produce its beneficial effect in parkinsonism.

Other actions/effects

Orphenadrine also has anticholinergic properties.

Precautions to Consider

Cross-sensitivity and/or related problems

Patients sensitive to other carbamate derivatives (for example, carbromal, meprobamate, mebutamate, or tybamate) may be sensitive to carisoprodol also.

Carcinogenicity

Methocarbamol—
Long-term studies to evaluate the carcinogenic potential of methocarbamol have not been performed.

Mutagenicity

Methocarbamol—
No studies have been conducted to assess the effect of methocarbamol on mutagenesis.

Pregnancy/Reproduction

Fertility—
Methocarbamol—
No studies have been conducted to assess the effect of methocarbamol on its potential to impair fertility.

Pregnancy—
Carisoprodol, chlorzoxazone—
Problems in humans have not been documented.
Chlorphenesin—
Studies have not been done in either animals or humans.
Metaxalone—
Although studies in humans have not been done, studies in rats have not shown that metaxalone causes adverse effects in the fetus.
Methocarbamol—
Although studies in humans have not been done, there have been rare reports of fetal and congenital abnormalities following in utero exposure to methocarbamol. Methocarbamol should not be used in women who are or may become pregnant and particularly during early pregnancy unless in the judgment of the physician the potential benefits outweigh the possible risk to the fetus.

Methocarbamol—FDA Pregnancy Category C
Orphenadrine—
Problems in humans have not been documented.
Studies in animals have not been done.

Orphenadrine citrate—FDA Pregnancy Category C.

Breast-feeding

Carisoprodol—
Carisoprodol is distributed into breast milk in concentrations that may reach 2 to 4 times the maternal plasma concentrations; use by nursing mothers may cause sedation and gastrointestinal upset in the infant.
Chlorphenesin, chlorzoxazone, metaxalone, methocarbamol, and orphenadrine—
It is not known whether these medications are distributed into breast milk. However, problems in humans have not been documented.
Methocarbamol—
It is not known if methocarbamol is distributed into breast milk. However, methocarbamol and/or its metabolites are distributed in the milk of dogs. Because many drugs are distributed in human milk, caution should be exercised when methocarbamol is administered to a nursing women.

Pediatrics

Carisoprodol—
Although appropriate studies with carisoprodol have not been performed in the pediatric population, the medication has been used in children. Pediatrics-specific problems that would limit the use of carisoprodol in these patients have not been documented.

Chlorphenesin, metaxalone, methocarbamol, and orphenadrine—
No information is available on the relationship of age to the effects of these medications in pediatric patients. Safety and efficacy have not been established.

Chlorzoxazone—
This medication has been used in children. Pediatrics-specific problems that would limit use of chlorzoxazone in these patients have not been documented.

Methocarbamol—
Safety and effectiveness of methocarbamol injection in pediatric patients have not been established except in tetanus.

Geriatrics

No information is available on the relationship of age to the effects of skeletal muscle relaxants in geriatric patients. However, elderly males are more likely to have age-related prostatic hypertrophy and may therefore be adversely affected by orphenadrine's anticholinergic activity. Also, elderly patients are more likely to have age-related renal function impairment, which may require that parenteral methocarbamol not be used at all and that other skeletal muscle relaxants be used with caution.

Methocarbamol—
The mean elimination half-life of methocarbamol in elderly healthy volunteers was slightly prolonged and the fraction of bound methocarbamol was slightly decreased compared to younger healthy volunteers.

Dental

Orphenadrine—
The peripheral anticholinergic effects of orphenadrine may decrease or inhibit salivary flow, thus contributing to the development of caries, periodontal disease, oral candidiasis, and discomfort.

Drug interactions and/or related problems

The following drug interactions and/or related problems have been selected on the basis of their potential clinical significance (possible mechanism in parentheses where appropriate)—not necessarily inclusive (» = major clinical significance):

Note: Combinations containing any of the following medications, depending on the amount present, may also interact with this medication.

For all skeletal muscle relaxants
» Alcohol or
» CNS depression-producing medications, other (See *Appendix II*)
(concurrent use with a skeletal muscle relaxant may result in additive CNS depressant effects; caution is recommended and dosage of one or both agents should be reduced)

For orphenadrine (in addition to the interaction listed above)
Anticholinergics or other medications with anticholinergic action (See *Appendix II*)
(anticholinergic effects may be intensified when these medications are used concurrently with orphenadrine because of orphenadrine's secondary anticholinergic activity)

Laboratory value alterations

The following have been selected on the basis of their potential clinical significance (possible effect in parentheses where appropriate)—not necessarily inclusive (» = major clinical significance):

With diagnostic test results
For metaxalone
Copper sulfate urine sugar tests
(false-positive test results may occur, possibly because of the presence of an unknown reducing substance; results of tests using glucose oxidase are not affected)

For methocarbamol
5-Hydroxyindoleacetic acid (5-HIAA), in urine, determinations
(values may be falsely increased when the nitrosonaphthol reagent is used)
Vanillylmandelic acid (VMA), in urine, determinations
(values may be falsely increased when the Gitlow screening method is used; no error occurs when the quantitative procedure of Sunderman is used)

With physiology/laboratory test values
For metaxalone
Cephalin flocculation tests
(elevations may occur without concurrent changes in other liver function tests)

Medical considerations/Contraindications

The medical considerations/contraindications included have been selected on the basis of their potential clinical significance (reasons given in parentheses where appropriate)—not necessarily inclusive (» = major clinical significance).

See *Table 3*, page 2631.

Patient monitoring

The following may be especially important in patient monitoring (other tests may be warranted in some patients, depending on condition; » = major clinical significance):

For metaxalone
Liver function tests
(recommended periodically during prolonged metaxalone therapy, especially if the patient has pre-existing hepatic function impairment or disease)

For methocarbamol
Renal function determinations
(recommended if parenteral therapy lasts 3 days or more because the polyethylene glycol 300 vehicle may be nephrotoxic)

For orphenadrine
Blood count and
Liver function tests and
Renal function tests
(recommended during prolonged therapy since the safety of continuous long-term use has not been established)

Side/Adverse Effects

See *Table 4*, page 2632.

Note: Rarely, an idiosyncratic reaction to carisoprodol may occur within minutes or hours following the first dose of the medication. Reported symptoms include agitation, ataxia, confusion, disorientation, dizziness, euphoria, extreme weakness, speech disturbances, temporary loss of vision or other vision disturbances, and transient quadriplegia. Symptoms usually subside within several hours, but in some cases, supportive and symptomatic therapy, including hospitalization, may be necessary.

Psychological dependence and abuse have occurred very rarely with carisoprodol. Signs of abstinence have not been reported with clinical usage; however, in one study abrupt withdrawal of 100 mg per kg of body weight (mg/kg) per day of carisoprodol (5 times the recommended daily dose) produced withdrawal symptoms including abdominal cramps, insomnia, chills, headache, and nausea.

Overdose

For more information on the management of overdose or unintentional ingestion, **contact a Poison Control Center** (see *Poison Control Center Listing*).

Treatment of overdose

Carisoprodol

To decrease absorption—Emptying the stomach via induction of emesis or gastric lavage.

Specific treatment—Administering respiratory assistance, CNS stimulants, and pressor agents cautiously, if necessary.

To enhance elimination—Removing carisoprodol from the body via induction of diuresis, osmotic (mannitol) diuresis, peritoneal dialysis, or hemodialysis.

Monitoring—Monitoring urinary output.

Taking care to prevent overhydration.

Monitoring the patient for relapse due to incomplete gastric emptying and delayed absorption, and administering additional treatment as required.

Supportive care—Administering supportive treatment of observed symptoms.

Chlorphenesin—

To decrease absorption—Emptying the stomach via institution of saline catharsis or gastric lavage.

Supportive care—Administering supportive therapy of observed symptoms.

Chlorzoxazone—

To decrease absorption—Emptying the stomach via induction of emesis or gastric lavage.

Specific treatment—Administering oxygen and artificial respiration for respiratory depression and plasma volume expanders or vasopressors for hypotension.

Supportive care—Administering supportive treatment of observed symptoms.

Note: Cholinergic medications and analeptic medications are of no value in chlorzoxazone overdose and should not be used.

Metaxalone—

Experience with overdose causing major toxicity is extremely limited.

To decrease absorption—Emptying the stomach via induction of emesis or gastric lavage.

Supportive care—Administering supportive treatment of observed symptoms.

Methocarbamol—

To decrease absorption—Emptying the stomach via induction of emesis or gastric lavage (if administered orally).

To enhance elimination—The usefulness of forced diuresis or hemodialysis in treating overdose has not been determined.

Supportive care—Administering supportive treatment of observed symptoms.

Orphenadrine—

To decrease absorption—Emptying the stomach via induction of emesis or gastric lavage (if administered orally).

To enhance elimination—Maintaining a high-volume urinary output.

Institution of hemodialysis or peritoneal dialysis may be of some benefit if the serum concentration exceeds 4 mcg per mL.

Supportive care—Administering intravenous fluids and circulatory support as required. Administering supportive treatment of observed symptoms.

Note: Patients in whom intentional overdose is known or suspected should be referred for psychiatric consultation.

Patient Consultation

See *Table 5*, page 2633.

CARISOPRODOL

Summary of Differences

Pharmacology/pharmacokinetics:

Physicochemical characteristics—Molecular weight: 260.34.

Biotransformation—Hepatic; one metabolite is meprobamate.

Half-life—8 hours.

Onset of action—0.5 hour.

Time to peak concentration—4 hours (350-mg single dose).

Peak serum concentration—4–7 mcg per mL.

Duration of action—4–6 hours.

Elimination—Renal, <1% as unchanged carisoprodol. Carisoprodol is dialyzable.

Precautions:

Cross-sensitivity and/or related problems—May occur with other carbamate derivatives.

Breast-feeding—Distributed into breast milk in significant quantities; may cause sedation and gastrointestinal upset in the nursing infant.

Medical considerations/contraindications—

Should not be used in patients with known or suspected acute intermittent porphyria.

Caution also recommended in patients with a history of drug abuse or dependence.

Side/adverse effects:

Idiosyncratic reactions may occur shortly after first dose.

Psychological dependence and abuse reported very rarely.

Also may cause orthostatic hypotension, fast heartbeat, mental depression, clumsiness or unsteadiness, fever (allergic), stinging or burning of eyes, angioedema, bronchospastic allergic reaction, blurred vision, and flushing.

Oral Dosage Forms

CARISOPRODOL TABLETS USP

Usual adult and adolescent dose

Skeletal muscle relaxant—

Oral, 350 mg four times a day.

Usual pediatric dose

Skeletal muscle relaxant—

Children up to 5 years of age: Dosage has not been established.

Children 5 to 12 years of age: Oral, 6.25 mg per kg of body weight four times a day.

Strength(s) usually available

U.S.—

350 mg (Rx) [*Soma; Vanadom;* GENERIC].

Canada—

350 mg (Rx) [*Soma*].

Packaging and storage

Store below 40 °C (104 °F), preferably between 15 and 30 °C (59 and 86 °F), unless otherwise specified by manufacturer. Store in a well-closed container.

Auxiliary labeling

- May cause drowsiness.
- Avoid alcoholic beverages.

CHLORPHENESIN

Summary of Differences

Pharmacology/pharmacokinetics:

Physicochemical characteristics—Molecular weight: 245.66.

Absorption—Rapid; complete.

Biotransformation—Hepatic; at least partially metabolized.

Half-life—2.3–5 hours.

Time to peak concentration—1–3 hours.

Peak serum concentration—3.8–17 mcg per mL (800-mg single dose).

Elimination—Renal; 85% of a dose excreted within 24 hours as the glucuronide metabolite.

Side/adverse effects:

Gastrointestinal bleeding reported, but causal relationship not established.

Also may cause fever (allergic), agranulocytosis, leukopenia, or thrombocytopenia.

Additional Dosing Information

The safety of administering chlorphenesin for longer than 8 weeks has not been established.

Oral Dosage Forms

CHLORPHENESIN CARBAMATE TABLETS

Usual adult and adolescent dose

Skeletal muscle relaxant—

Oral, 800 mg three times a day initially; may be decreased to 400 mg four times a day or less, as required to maintain the desired response.

Usual pediatric dose

Safety and efficacy have not been established.

Strength(s) usually available

U.S.—

400 mg (Rx) [*Maolate*].

Canada—

Not commercially available.

Packaging and storage

Store below 40 °C (104 °F), preferably between 15 and 30 °C (59 and 86 °F), in a well-closed container, unless otherwise specified by manufacturer.

Auxiliary labeling

- May cause drowsiness.
- Avoid alcoholic beverages.

CHLORZOXAZONE

Summary of Differences

Pharmacology/pharmacokinetics:

Physicochemical characteristics—Molecular weight: 169.57.

Absorption—Rapid; complete.

Biotransformation—Hepatic.

Half-life—1.1 hours.

Onset of action—Within 1 hour.

Time to peak concentration—1–2 hours.
Peak serum concentration—10–30 mcg per mL (750-mg single dose).
Duration of action—3–4 hours.
Elimination—Renal; <1% as unchanged chlorzoxazone.

Precautions:
Medical considerations/contraindications: Also should be used with caution in patients with allergies (or history of).

Side/adverse effects:
Also may cause agranulocytosis, gastrointestinal bleeding, angioedema, anemia, diarrhea, heartburn, and constipation.
Hepatotoxicity reported, but causal association not established.

Additional Dosing Information

Discontinuation of chlorzoxazone therapy is recommended if symptoms of hepatotoxicity or sensitivity (e.g., skin rash, hives, or itching) occur.

Oral Dosage Forms

CHLORZOXAZONE TABLETS USP

Usual adult and adolescent dose

Skeletal muscle relaxant—
Oral, 250 to 750 mg three or four times a day; usually 500 mg three or four times a day initially and increased or decreased as determined by patient response.

Usual pediatric dose

Skeletal muscle relaxant—
Oral, 20 mg per kg of body weight or 600 mg per square meter of body surface, in three or four divided doses; or 125 to 500 mg three or four times a day, according to the child's age and weight.

Strength(s) usually available

U.S.—
250 mg (Rx) [*Paraflex; Remular-S;* GENERIC].
500 mg (Rx) [*EZE-DS; Parafon Forte DSC* (scored); *Relaxazone; Remular; Strifon Forte DSC;* GENERIC].

Canada—
Not commercially available.

Packaging and storage

Store between 15 and 30 °C (59 and 86 °F), unless otherwise specified by manufacturer. Store in a tight container.

Preparation of dosage form

Single dose—Tablets may be crushed and mixed with food or liquid for ease of administration.

Auxiliary labeling

- May cause drowsiness.
- Avoid alcoholic beverages.

METAXALONE

Summary of Differences

Pharmacology/pharmacokinetics:
Physicochemical characteristics—Molecular weight 221.26.
Biotransformation—Hepatic.
Half-life—2–3 hours
Onset of action—1 hour.
Time to peak concentration—2 hours (800-mg single dose).
Peak serum concentration—295 mcg per mL (800-mg single dose).
Elimination—Renal.

Precautions:
Laboratory value alterations—
May interfere with copper sulfate urine sugar test results.
May cause liver function test abnormalities.
Medical considerations/contraindications—Also should not be used in patients with hemolytic anemia or a history of hemolytic anemia, especially if drug-induced.
Patient monitoring—Liver function tests recommended during prolonged therapy.

Side/adverse effects:
Also may cause hemolytic anemia and hepatotoxicity.

Additional Dosing Information

Discontinuation of metaxalone therapy is recommended if signs of hepatotoxicity occur.

Oral Dosage Forms

METAXALONE TABLETS

Usual adult and adolescent dose

Skeletal muscle relaxant—
Oral, 800 mg three or four times a day.

Usual pediatric dose

Safety and efficacy have not been established.

Strength(s) usually available

U.S.—
400 mg (Rx) [*Skelaxin* (scored)].

Canada—
Not commercially available.

Packaging and storage

Store below 40 °C (104 °F), preferably between 15 and 30 °C (59 and 86 °F), in a well-closed container, unless otherwise specified by manufacturer.

Auxiliary labeling

- May cause drowsiness.
- Avoid alcoholic beverages.

METHOCARBAMOL

Summary of Differences

Pharmacology/pharmacokinetics:
Physicochemical characteristics—Molecular weight: 241.25.
Absorption—Rapid.
Biotransformation—Probably hepatic.
Half-life (elimination)—0.9–2.2 hours.
Onset of action—
Oral: Within 0.5 hour.
Intravenous: Immediate.
Time to peak concentration—
Oral: 2 hours (2-gram single dose).
Intravenous: Almost immediate.
Peak serum concentration—
Oral: 16 mcg per mL (2-gram single dose).
Intravenous: 19 mcg per mL (1-gram single dose).
Elimination—
Renal and fecal.

Precautions:
Laboratory value alterations—Urinary 5-Hydroxyindoleacetic acid (5-HIAA) values may be falsely increased (with nitrosonaphthol reagent).
Urinary vanillylmandelic acid (VMA) values may be falsely increased (with the Gitlow screening method).
Medical considerations/contraindications—
Methocarbamol may inhibit the effect of pyridostigmine bromide. Use with caution in patients with myasthenia gravis receiving anticholinesterase agents.
Parenteral dosage form should not be used in patients with renal function impairment or disease because the polyethylene glycol 300 vehicle is nephrotoxic.
Parenteral dosage form also should be used with caution in patients with epilepsy.
Patient monitoring—Renal function determinations recommended if parenteral therapy lasts 3 days or more.

Side/adverse effects:
Parenteral dosage form also reported to cause convulsions, fainting, slow heartbeat, muscle weakness, nystagmus, and facial flushing, especially when given too rapidly.
Parenteral dosage form may also cause pain or peeling of skin at injection site and thrombophlebitis.
Also may cause fever (allergic), conjunctivitis and nasal congestion, and leukopenia.
May be more likely than other muscle relaxants to cause blurred or double vision.

Additional Dosing Information

For parenteral dosage forms only

The injection may be given intravenously or intramuscularly. Subcutaneous administration is not recommended.

The parenteral dosage form vial stopper contains dry natural rubber that may cause hypersensitivity reactions in persons with known or possible latex sensitivity.

The polyethylene glycol 300 vehicle in the parenteral dosage form may be nephrotoxic.

The medication may be administered intravenously undiluted at a rate not to exceed 3 mL (300 mg) per minute. It may also be given as an intravenous infusion in sodium chloride injection or 5% dextrose injection.

The patient should lie down during and for at least 10 to 15 minutes following intravenous administration.

Extravasation should be avoided, since the injection is hypertonic and may cause thrombophlebitis.

The manufacturer's labeling should be consulted for special directions for use in tetanus.

Not more than 5 mL (500 mg) should be given intramuscularly into each gluteal region at one time. The injections may be repeated at 8-hour intervals, if necessary.

Oral Dosage Forms

METHOCARBAMOL TABLETS USP

Usual adult and adolescent dose

Skeletal muscle relaxant—

Initial: Oral, 1.5 grams four times a day for the first forty-eight to seventy-two hours of therapy. For severe conditions, 8 grams a day may be administered initially.

Maintenance: Oral, 750 mg every four hours; 1 gram four times a day; or 1.5 grams three times a day.

Note: If used as adjunctive therapy in the treatment of tetanus—Via nasogastric tube, up to 24 grams a day depending on patient response.

Usual pediatric dose

Safety and efficacy have not been established.

Strength(s) usually available

U.S.—

500 mg (Rx) [*Carbacot; Robaxin;* GENERIC].
750 mg (Rx) [*Carbacot; Robaxin-750;* GENERIC].

Canada—

500 mg (OTC) [*Robaxin* (scored)].
750 mg (OTC) [*Robaxin-750* (scored)].

Packaging and storage

Store below 40 °C (104 °F), preferably between 15 and 30 °C (59 and 86 °F), unless otherwise specified by manufacturer. Store in a tight container.

Preparation of dosage form

For administration via nasogastric tube—Crush tablets and suspend in water or saline solution.

Auxiliary labeling

- May cause drowsiness.
- Avoid alcoholic beverages.

Parenteral Dosage Forms

METHOCARBAMOL INJECTION USP

Usual adult and adolescent dose

Skeletal muscle relaxant—

Intramuscular or intravenous, 1 to 3 grams a day for three days. Following a drug-free interval of forty-eight hours, the course may be repeated if necessary.

Note: If used as adjunctive therapy in the treatment of tetanus—Intravenous, 1 or 2 grams by direct intravenous injection. An additional 1 or 2 grams may be administered by intravenous infusion, so that a total initial dose of up to 3 grams is administered. This regimen should be repeated every six hours until therapy via a nasogastric tube can be instituted.

Usual adult prescribing limits

Total adult dosage should not exceed 3 grams per day. Also, the medication should not be administered for more than three consecutive days except in the treatment of tetanus.

Usual pediatric dose

Skeletal muscle relaxant—

Safety and efficacy in children up to 12 years of age have not been established for conditions other than tetanus.

Note: If used as adjunctive therapy in the treatment of tetanus—Intravenous, 15 mg per kg of body weight or 500 mg per square meter of body surface area every six hours if required. The maintenance dose may be given by injection into tubing or by IV infusion with an appropriate quantity of fluid.

Usual pediatric prescribing limits

The total dose should not exceed 1.8 grams per square meter of body surface are for 3 consecutive days.

Strength(s) usually available

U.S.—

100 mg per mL (1 gram per 10-mL single-dose vial) (Rx) [*Robaxin;* GENERIC].

Canada—

100 mg per mL (1 gram per 10-mL single-dose vial) [GENERIC].

Packaging and storage

Store at 20 to 25 °C (68 to 77 °F), excursions permitted to 15 to 30 °C (59 to 86 °F).

Preparation of dosage form

For intravenous infusion—Dilute with sodium chloride injection or 5% dextrose injection; 10 mL (1 gram) of medication should be diluted to not more than 250 mL of infusion. After dilution, the injection should not be refrigerated.

ORPHENADRINE

Summary of Differences

Category:
Hydrochloride salt indicated to relieve tremor in parkinsonism.

Pharmacology/pharmacokinetics—
Physicochemical characteristics—Molecular weight—
Orphenadrine citrate—461.51.
Orphenadrine hydrochloride—305.85.

Mechanism of action (parkinsonism therapy adjunct)—
Has anticholinergic activity.

Protein binding—
Low.

Biotransformation—
Hepatic.

Half-life—
14 hours (parent compound; half-life of metabolites may range from 2 to 25 hours).

Onset of action—
Orphenadrine citrate:
Oral (extended-release tablets)—Within 1 hour.
Intramuscular—5 minutes.
Intravenous—Immediate.
Orphenadrine hydrochloride:
Oral—Within 1 hour.

Time to peak concentration—
Orphenadrine citrate:
Oral (extended-release tablets)—6–8 hours (100-mg single dose).
Intramuscular—0.5 hour (60-mg single dose).
Intravenous—Immediate.
Orphenadrine hydrochloride:
Oral—3 hours (50-mg single dose).

Peak serum concentration—
Orphenadrine citrate:
Oral (extended-release tablets)—60–120 nanograms per mL (100-mg single dose).
Orphenadrine hydrochloride: Oral—110–210 nanograms per mL (100-mg single dose).

Elimination—
Renal and fecal.

Precautions:
Dental—May cause dryness of mouth.
Medical considerations/contraindications—
Also should not be used in patients with medical conditions in which anticholinergic actions are detrimental.
Also should be used with caution in patients with cardiac disease or arrhythmias, especially tachycardia.
Patient monitoring—Blood count and hepatic and renal function tests recommended during prolonged therapy.

Side/adverse effects:
Also may cause side effects typical of anticholinergics and aplastic anemia.
Also may cause hallucinations, syncope, confusion (especially in the elderly), and blurred or double vision; anticholinergic as well as CNS actions may contribute to these effects.

Additional Dosing Information

The safety of continuous long-term administration of orphenadrine has not been established.

Oral Dosage Forms

ORPHENADRINE CITRATE EXTENDED-RELEASE TABLETS

Usual adult and adolescent dose

Skeletal muscle relaxant—

Oral, 100 mg two times a day, in the morning and evening.

Usual pediatric dose

Safety and efficacy have not been established.

Strength(s) usually available

U.S.—

100 mg (Rx) [*Norflex;* GENERIC].

Canada—

100 mg (OTC) [*Norflex*].

Packaging and storage

Store below 40 °C (104 °F), preferably between 15 and 30 °C (59 and 86 °F), in a tight, light-resistant container, unless otherwise specified by manufacturer.

Auxiliary labeling

- May cause drowsiness.
- Avoid alcoholic beverages.

ORPHENADRINE HYDROCHLORIDE TABLETS

Usual adult and adolescent dose

Skeletal muscle relaxant and Parkinsonism therapy adjunct—

Oral, 50 mg three times a day.

Note: Smaller doses may suffice if other antiparkinson medications are being administered concurrently.

Usual adult prescribing limits

Up to 250 mg a day.

Usual pediatric dose

Dosage has not been established.

Strength(s) usually available

U.S.—

Not commercially available.

Canada—

50 mg (OTC) [*Disipal*].

Packaging and storage

Store below 40 °C (104 °F), preferably between 15 and 30 °C (59 and 86 °F), in a tight container, unless otherwise specified by manufacturer.

Auxiliary labeling

- May cause drowsiness.
- Avoid alcoholic beverages.

Parenteral Dosage Forms

ORPHENADRINE CITRATE INJECTION USP

Usual adult and adolescent dose

Skeletal muscle relaxant—

Intramuscular or intravenous, 60 mg every twelve hours as needed.

Usual pediatric dose

Safety and efficacy have not been established.

Strength(s) usually available

U.S.—

30 mg per mL (Rx) [*Antiflex; Banflex; Flexoject; Mio-Rel; Myolin; Myotrol; Norflex; Orfro; Orphenate;* GENERIC].

Canada—

30 mg per mL (OTC) [*Norflex* (sodium bisulfite)].

Packaging and storage

Store below 40 °C (104 °F), preferably between 15 and 30 °C (59 and 86 °F), unless otherwise specified by manufacturer. Protect from light. Protect from freezing.

Selected Bibliography

Elenbaas JK. Central acting oral skeletal muscle relaxants. Am J Hosp Pharm 1980; 37: 1313-23.

Waldman HJ. Centrally acting skeletal muscle relaxants and associated drugs. J Pain Symptom Manage 1994; 9: 434-41.

Revised: 11/02/2004

Table 1. Pharmacology/Pharmacokinetics

Drug	Absorption	Protein Binding (%)	Biotransformation	Half-life (hr)	Elimination Primary (% Excreted Unchanged)/ Secondary
Carisoprodol			Hepatic*	8	Renal (<1)†
Chlorphenesin	Rapid; complete		Hepatic‡	2.3–5	Renal§
Chlorzoxazone	Rapid; complete		Hepatic	1.1	Renal (<1)
Metaxalone			Hepatic	2–3	Renal
Methocarbamol	Rapid		Probably hepatic	0.9–2.2	Renal/fecal
Orphenadrine		Low	Hepatic	14#	Renal/fecal

*One of the metabolites is meprobamate.

†Distributed into breast milk; concentration may reach 2 to 4 times the maternal plasma concentration. Also, may be removed from the circulation via hemodialysis and peritoneal dialysis.

‡At least partially metabolized.

§85% of a dose excreted within 24 hours as the glucuronide metabolite.

#For the parent compound; half-life of metabolites may range from 2 to 25 hours.

Table 2. Pharmacology/Pharmacokinetics

Drug	Onset of Action	Time to Peak Concentration (hr) (single dose)	Peak Serum Concentration (single dose)	Duration of Action (hr)
Carisoprodol	0.5 hr	4 (350 mg)	4–7 mcg/mL	4–6
Chlorphenesin		1–3	3.8–17 mcg/mL (800 mg)	
Chlorzoxazone	Within 1 hr	1–2	10–30 mcg/mL (750 mg)	3–4
Metaxalone	1 hr	2 (800 mg)	295 mcg/mL (800 mg)	
Methocarbamol				
Oral	Within 0.5 hr	2 (2 grams)	16 mcg/mL (2 grams)	
IV (300 mg/min)	Immediate	Almost immediate	19 mcg/mL (1 gram)	
Orphenadrine citrate*				
Oral (extended-release tablets)	Within 1 hr	6 to 8 (100 mg)	60–120 nanograms/mL (100 mg)	12
IM	5 min	0.5 (60 mg)		
IV	Immediate	Immediate		
Orphenadrine hydrochloride†	Within 1 hr	3 (50 mg)	110–210 nanograms/mL (100 mg)	8

*Relief of muscle spasm.
†In parkinsonism.

Table 3. Medical considerations/Contraindications

The medical considerations/contraindications included have been selected on the basis of their potential clinical significance (reasons given in parentheses where appropriate)—not necessarily inclusive (» = major clinical significance).

Legend:
I=Carisoprodol
II=Chlorphenesin
III=Chlorzoxazone
IV=Metaxalone
V =Methocarbamol
VI=Orphenadrine

	I	II	III	IV	V	VI
Except under special circumstances, these medications should not be used when the following medical problems exist:						
» Achalasia or						✓
» Bladder neck obstruction or						✓
» Glaucoma, or predisposition to, or						✓
» Myasthenia gravis or						✓
» Peptic ulcer, stenosing, or						✓
» Prostatic hypertrophy or						✓
» Pyloric or duodenal obstruction (anticholinergic actions detrimental in these conditions)						✓
» Hemolytic anemia, or history of, especially if drug-induced (may be induced by metaxalone)				✓		
» Porphyria, acute intermittent, known or suspected	✓					
» Renal function impairment or disease (for parenteral dosage form only—polyethylene glycol 300 vehicle is nephrotoxic and may cause increased urea retention and acidosis in these patients)					✓	
Risk-benefit should be considered when the following medical problems exist:						
Allergic reaction to the medication considered for use, history of	✓	✓	✓	✓	✓	✓
Allergies or history of			✓			
Cardiac disease or arrhythmias or tachycardia (orphenadrine may cause tachycardia)						✓ ✓
CNS depression (may be exacerbated)	✓	✓	✓	✓	✓	✓
Drug abuse or dependence, history of (psychological dependence and abuse reported rarely)	✓					
Epilepsy (for parenteral dosage form only—may increase risk of seizures)					✓	
Hepatic function impairment (metabolized in liver)	✓	✓			✓	✓
» Hepatic function impairment or disease (metabolized in liver; also, potentially hepatotoxic)			✓	✓		
Renal function impairment (excreted via kidneys)	✓	✓	✓	✓	✓	✓
» Renal function impairment, severe (excreted via kidneys)				✓		

Table 4. Side/Adverse Effects*

The following side/adverse effects have been selected on the basis of their potential clinical significance (possible signs and symptoms in parentheses where appropriate)—not necessarily inclusive:

Legend: I=Carisoprodol; II=Chlorphenesin; III=Chlorzoxazone; IV=Metaxalone; V=Methocarbamol; VI=Orphenadrine

	I	II	III	IV	V	VI
Medical attention needed						
Anticholinergic effects, specifically:						
Decreased urination	—	—	—	—	—	L
Increased intraocular pressure (eye pain)	—	—	—	—	—	L
Cardiovascular effects, specifically:						
Fast heartbeat—with orphenadrine, anticholinergic activity may contribute to this effect	L	U	U	U	U	L
Pounding heartbeat	U	U	U	U	U	L
Slow heartbeat—with parenteral dosage form only	—	—	—	—	L‡	U
Thrombophlebitis (local pain, tenderness, heat, redness, swelling at site of affected vein)—with parenteral administration only	—	—	—	—	R	U
Central nervous system effects, specifically:						
Convulsions	U	U	U	U	R‡	U
Fainting—with carisoprodol, may also be caused by orthostatic hypotension	L	U	U	U	R‡	L
Hallucinations—orphenadrine's anticholinergic activity may contribute to this effect	U	U	U	U	U	R
Mental depression	L	U	U	U	U	U
Gastrointestinal bleeding (bloody or black, tarry stools; vomiting of blood or material that looks like coffee grounds)	U	R†	R	U	U	U
Hematologic effects, specifically:						
Agranulocytosis (fever with or without chills; sores, ulcers, or white spots on lips or in mouth; sore throat)	U	R	R	U	U	U
Anemia (unusual tiredness or weakness)	U	U	R	U	U	U
Anemia, aplastic [pancytopenia] (shortness of breath, troubled breathing, tightness in chest, and/or wheezing; sores, ulcers, or white spots on lips or in mouth; swollen and/or painful glands; unusual bleeding or bruising; unusual tiredness or weakness)	R†	U	U	U	U	R
Anemia, hemolytic (troubled breathing, exertional; unusual tiredness or weakness)	U	U	U	R	U	U
Leukopenia (usually asymptomatic; rarely, fever or chills, cough or hoarseness, lower back or side pain, painful or difficult urination)	R†	R	U	R	R	U
Thrombocytopenia (usually asymptomatic; rarely, unusual bleeding or bruising; black, tarry stools; blood in urine or stools; pinpoint red spots on skin)	U	R	U	U	U	U
Hepatotoxicity (yellow eyes or skin)	U	U	R†	R	R	U
Hypersensitivity reactions, specifically:						
Anaphylactic or anaphylactoid reaction (changes in facial skin color; skin rash, hives, and/or itching; fast or irregular breathing; puffiness or swelling of the eyelids or around the eyes; shortness of breath, troubled breathing, tightness in chest, and/or wheezing)—with carisoprodol, anaphylactic shock with sudden, severe decrease in blood pressure and collapse has also occurred	R	R	R	R	R	U
Angioedema (hive-like swellings, large, on face, eyelids, mouth, lips, and/or tongue)	L	U	R	U	R	U
Bronchospastic allergic reaction (shortness of breath, troubled breathing, tightness in chest, and/or wheezing)	L	U	U	U	U	U
Conjunctivitis and nasal congestion (stuffy nose and red or bloodshot eyes)	U	U	U	U	L	U
Dermatitis, allergic (skin rash, hives, itching, and/or redness)—with carisoprodol, fixed drug eruptions with cross-sensitivity to meprobamate have also been reported; with chlorzoxazone, petechial rashes and ecchymoses have also been reported	L	R	R	R	L	U
Eosinophilia	R	U	U	U	U	U
Erythema multiforme (fever with or without chills; muscle cramps or pain; skin rash; sores, ulcers, or white spots on lips or in mouth)	R	U	U	U	U	U
Fever, allergic	L	R	U	U	L	U
Stinging or burning of eyes	L	U	U	U	U	U
Medical attention needed only if continuing or bothersome						
Anticholinergic effects (dryness of mouth [more frequent], confusion, difficult urination, constipation, unusually large pupils, blurred or double vision, weakness)	—	—	—	—	—	L
Central nervous system effects, specifically:						
Blurred or double vision or any change in vision—with orphenadrine, anticholinergic activity may also contribute to this effect	R	U	U	U	M	L
Clumsiness or unsteadiness	R	U	U	U	U	U
Confusion—with orphenadrine, anticholinergic activity may also contribute to this effect, especially in elderly patients	U	L	U	U	R	L
Dizziness or lightheadedness—with carisoprodol, orthostatic hypotension may also contribute to this effect	L	L	M	M	M	L
Drowsiness	M	L	M	M	M	L

Table 4. Side/Adverse Effects* *(continued)*

The following side/adverse effects have been selected on the basis of their potential clinical significance (possible signs and symptoms in parentheses where appropriate)—not necessarily inclusive:

Legend: I=Carisoprodol; II=Chlorphenesin; III=Chlorzoxazone; IV=Metaxalone; V=Methocarbamol; VI=Orphenadrine

	I	II	III	IV	V	VI
Headache	L	R	L	M	L	L
Muscle weakness	U	R	U	U	L‡	R
Nystagmus (uncontrolled movements of eyes)	U	U	U	U	L‡	U
Stimulation, paradoxical (excitement, nervousness, restlessness, irritability, trouble in sleeping)	L	R	L	M	U	L
Trembling	L	U	U	U	U	L
Flushing or redness of face	L	U	U	U	L‡	U
Gastrointestinal irritation, specifically: Abdominal or stomach cramps or pain	L	R	L	M	U	L
Constipation—with orphenadrine, anticholinergic activity may contribute to this effect	U	U	L	U	U	L
Diarrhea	U	U	L	U	U	U
Heartburn	U	U	L	U	R	U
Hiccups	L	U	U	U	U	U
Nausea or vomiting	L	R	L	M	L	L
Pain or peeling at place of injection	—	—	—	—	L‡	U

*Differences in frequency of occurrence may reflect either lack of clinical-use data or actual pharmacologic distinctions among agents (although their pharmacologic similarity suggests that side effects occurring with one may occur with the others, except for those caused by anticholinergic activity, which is specific for orphenadrine). M = more frequent; L = less frequent; R = rare; U = unknown.

†A causal association has not been established.

‡Usually reported with too-rapid intravenous administration.

Table 5. Patient Consultation

As an aid to patient consultation, refer to *Advice for the Patient, Skeletal Muscle Relaxants (Systemic)* or *Orphenadrine (Systemic)*.

In providing consultation, consider emphasizing the following selected information (» = major clinical significance):

Legend: I=Carisoprodol; II=Chlorphenesin; III=Chlorzoxazone; IV=Metaxalone; V=Methocarbamol; VI=Orphenadrine

	I	II	III	IV	V	VI
Before using this medication						
» Conditions affecting use, especially:						
Sensitivity to the muscle relaxant considered for use, history of, and, for carisoprodol, sensitivity to other carbamate derivatives	✓	✓	✓	✓	✓	✓
Breast-feeding—Carisoprodol distributed into breast milk and may cause sedation and gastrointestinal upset in the infant; problems in nursing infants have not been reported with other skeletal muscle relaxants	✓					
Other medications, especially other CNS depression-producing medications	✓	✓	✓	✓	✓	✓
Other medical problems, especially:						
Acute intermittent porphyria (known or suspected)	✓					
Conditions that may be adversely affected by anticholinergic activity						✓
Hemolytic anemia, or history of				✓		
Hepatic function impairment or disease	✓	✓	✓	✓	✓	✓
Renal function impairment or disease	✓	✓	✓	✓	✓	✓
Proper use of this medication						
Tablets may be crushed and mixed with food or liquid for ease of administration			✓	✓	✓	
» Proper dosing	✓	✓	✓	✓	✓	✓
Missed dose: Taking if remembered within an hour or so; not taking if remembered later; not doubling doses	✓	✓	✓	✓	✓	✓
» Proper storage	✓	✓	✓	✓	✓	✓
Precautions while using this medication						
Regular visits to physician to check progress during prolonged therapy	✓	✓	✓	✓	✓	✓
» Avoiding use of alcohol or other CNS depressants during therapy unless prescribed or otherwise approved by physician	✓	✓	✓	✓	✓	✓
» Caution if any of the following occur:						
Blurred vision or other vision problems	✓				✓	✓
Clumsiness or unsteadiness	✓				✓	
Dizziness or lightheadedness	✓	✓	✓	✓	✓	✓
Drowsiness	✓	✓	✓	✓	✓	✓
Faintness	✓				✓	✓
Muscle weakness						✓
Possible dryness of mouth; using sugarless gum or candy, ice, or saliva substitute for relief; checking with dentist if dry mouth continues for more than 2 weeks						✓
Diabetics: May cause false-positive urine sugar tests				✓		

Table 5. Patient Consultation *(continued)*

As an aid to patient consultation, refer to *Advice for the Patient, Skeletal Muscle Relaxants (Systemic)* or *Orphenadrine (Systemic)*.

In providing consultation, consider emphasizing the following selected information (» = major clinical significance):

Legend: I=Carisoprodol, II=Chlorphenesin, III=Chlorzoxazone, IV=Metaxalone, V=Methocarbamol, VI=Orphenadrine

	I	II	III	IV	V	VI
Side/adverse effects						
Signs and symptoms of potential side effects, especially:						
Allergic reactions	✓	✓	✓	✓	✓	✓
Anticholinergic effects						✓
Blood dyscrasias		✓	✓	✓	✓	✓
Convulsions					✓*	
Fainting	✓				✓*	✓
Fast heartbeat	✓					✓
Gastrointestinal bleeding			✓			
Hallucinations						✓
Hepatotoxicity				✓	✓	
Mental depression	✓					
Pounding heartbeat						✓
Slow heartbeat					✓*	
Medication may color urine orange or reddish purple			✓			
Medication may color urine black, brown, or green, especially if allowed to stand					✓	

*For parenteral administration only.

SODIUM ASCORBATE—See *Ascorbic Acid (Systemic)*

SODIUM CHLORIDE Ophthalmic†

VA CLASSIFICATION (Primary): OP900

Commonly used brand name(s): *Muro 128*.

Note: For a listing of dosage forms and brand names by country availability, see *Dosage Forms* section(s).

†Not commercially available in Canada.

Category

Antiedemic (cornea).

Indications

Note: Bracketed information in the *Indications* section refers to uses that are not included in U.S. product labeling.

Accepted

Edema, corneal (treatment)—Sodium chloride 5% ophthalmic solutions is for the temporary relief of corneal edema.

Pharmacology/Pharmacokinetics

Mechanism of action/Effect

A sterile ophthalmic solution used to draw water out of the cornea of the eye.

Precautions to Consider

Pregnancy/Reproduction

Pregnancy—No information is available regarding the use of sodium chloride 5% ophthalmic solution in pregnant women.

FDA Pregnancy Category—none provided

Breast-feeding

No information is available regarding the use of sodium chloride 5% ophthalmic solution in lactating women or distribution into breast milk.

Pediatrics

No information is available regarding the use of sodium chloride 5% ophthalmic solution in pediatric patients.

Geriatrics

No information is available regarding the use of sodium chloride 5% ophthalmic solution in geriatric patients.

Medical considerations/Contraindications

The medical considerations/contraindications included have been selected on the basis of their potential clinical significance (reasons given in parentheses where appropriate)—not necessarily inclusive (» = major clinical significance).

Except under special circumstances, this medication should not be used when the following medical problem exists:

» Hypersensitivity to any of the inactive ingredients

Side/Adverse Effects

The following side/adverse effects have been selected on the basis of their potential clinical significance (possible signs and symptoms in parentheses where appropriate)—not necessarily inclusive:

Those indicating need for medical attention only if they continue or are bothersome

Incidence more frequent

Burning eyes, temporary; eye irritation, temporary

Overdose

For more information on the management of overdose or unintentional ingestion, **contact a poison control center** (see *Poison Control Center Listing*).

Treatment of overdose

Supportive care—

Treatment is symptomatic and supportive.

Patients in whom intentional overdose is confirmed or suspected should be referred for psychiatric consultation.

Patient Consultation

As an aid to patient consultation, refer to *Advice for the Patient, Sodium Chloride (Ophthalmic)*.

In providing consultation, consider emphasizing the following selected information (» = major clinical significance):

Before using this medication

» Conditions affecting use, especially:

Other medical problems, especially prior allergic reaction to any ingredients

Proper use of this medication

» Proper dosing

Missed dose: Using as soon as possible; not using if almost time for next scheduled dose; using next dose at regularly scheduled time; not doubling doses

» Proper storage

Precautions while using this medication

» Use only under the advice and supervision of a doctor.

» Consult your doctor if you have eye pain, changes in vision, continued redness or irritation of the eye, or if the condition worsens or persists.

» Importance of not contaminating the product. Do not touch the tip of the container to the eye or any surface.

» Do not use if the solution changes color or becomes cloudy.

Replace cap after use.

General Dosing Information

Use of product should be under the advice and supervision of a doctor.

Avoid contamination of the product. Do not touch the tip of the container to any surface.

Do not use if the solution changes color or becomes cloudy.

Ophthalmic Dosage Forms

Note: Bracketed information in the *Indications* section refers to uses that are not included in U.S. product labeling.

SODIUM CHLORIDE OPHTHALMIC SOLUTION

Usual adult dose

Antiedemic, corneal—

Topical to the conjunctiva, 1 or 2 drops in the affected eye(s) every 3 or 4 hours, or as directed by a doctor.

Strength(s) usually available

U.S.—

5% (Rx) [*Muro 128* (sterile; boric acid; hydroxypropyl methylcellulose 2910; propylene glycol; sodium borate; purified water; sodium hydroxide and/or hydrochloric acid may be added to adjust pH; methylparaben; propylparaben)].

Packaging and storage

Store between 15 and 30 °C (59 and 86 °F), in a tight container. Store upright and immediately replace cap after use.

Auxiliary labeling

- For the eye.
- Do not touch or contaminate the tip of the container.
- Keep in the original container. Close container tightly after use.
- Keep out of reach of children.

Developed: 02/16/2005

SODIUM CITRATE AND CITRIC ACID—See *Citrates (Systemic)*

SODIUM FERRIC GLUCONATE—See *Iron Supplements (Systemic)*

SODIUM FLUORIDE Systemic

VA CLASSIFICATION (Primary): TN407

Commonly used brand name(s): *Flozenges; Fluor-A-Day; Fluoritab; Fluoritabs; Fluorodex; Fluorosol; Flura; Flura-Drops; Flura-Loz; Karidium; Luride; Luride Lozi-Tabs; Luride-SF Lozi-Tabs; PDF; Pedi-Dent; Pediaflor; Pharmaflur; Pharmaflur 1.1; Pharmaflur df; Phos-Flur; Solu-Flur.*

Note: For a listing of dosage forms and brand names by country availability, see *Dosage Forms* section(s).

Category

Dental caries prophylactic; nutritional supplement (mineral).

Indications

Accepted

Dental caries (prophylaxis)—Sodium fluoride is indicated as a dietary supplement for prevention of dental caries in children in those areas where the level of naturally occurring fluoride in the drinking water is inadequate. In optimally fluoridated communities, sodium fluoride supplementation may be necessary in infants that are totally breast-fed or receive ready-to-use formulas or in children consuming nonfluoridated bottled water rather than tap water. Sodium fluoride supplementation may also be indicated in those situations where home water filtration systems remove fluoride. This usually occurs with reverse osmosis or distillation units, but not with carbon charcoal filters.

Evidence that oral systemic fluoride supplements reduce dental caries in adults is lacking.

Note: Sodium fluoride has been used to treat osteoporosis and otospongiosis in adults; however, its use is controversial and further studies are needed. The doses used in osteoporosis and otospongiosis have potential for toxicity, including skeletal fluorosis, osteomalacia, widening of unmineralized osteoid seams, and upper gastrointestinal ulceration.

Pharmacology/Pharmacokinetics

Physicochemical characteristics

Molecular weight—41.99.

Mechanism of action/Effect

Fluoride ion becomes incorporated into and stabilizes the apatite crystal of bone and teeth. Fluoride acts primarily to promote remineralization of decalcified enamel and may interfere with growth and development of dental plaque bacteria. Deposition of fluoride ion in the enamel surface of teeth increases resistance to acid and to development of caries.

Absorption

Fluorides in solution or in the form of rapidly soluble salts are readily and almost completely absorbed from the gastrointestinal tract.

Storage

In bone and developing teeth.

Time to peak serum concentration

30 to 60 minutes.

Elimination

Primarily renal (approximately 50%), with small amounts in feces and sweat.

Precautions to Consider

Carcinogenicity

Fluoride in the concentrations shown to be effective against tooth decay has not been shown to cause cancer in individuals who receive fluoride over prolonged periods.

Pregnancy/Reproduction

Problems in humans have not been documented with intake of normal daily recommended amounts. Fluoride readily crosses the placenta.

There is conflicting evidence as to whether administration of fluoride supplements to women during pregnancy will help prevent caries in the child.

Breast-feeding

Problems in humans have not been documented with intake of normal daily recommended amounts. Trace amounts of fluoride are distributed into breast milk, although the concentration is not high enough to provide benefits to the infant.

Pediatrics

Problems in pediatrics have not been documented with intake of normal daily recommended amounts. Chronic overdose may cause fluorosis of the teeth (if given during the period of tooth-enamel formation) and osseous changes.

Geriatrics

Problems in geriatrics have not been documented with intake of normal daily recommended amounts. Elderly patients are more likely to have age-related renal failure, which may require caution if patients are receiving large doses for osteoporosis or otospongiosis. The elderly are also more likely to develop stress fractures, gastrointestinal ulceration, and arthralgia from large doses of sodium fluoride.

Dental

Excessive doses of sodium fluoride may result in fluorosis of teeth if taken during tooth formation years.

Drug interactions and/or related problems

The following drug interactions and/or related problems have been selected on the basis of their potential clinical significance (possible mechanism in parentheses where appropriate)—not necessarily inclusive (» = major clinical significance):

Note: Combinations containing any of the following, depending on the amount present, may also interact with this medication.

Aluminum hydroxide
(may decrease absorption and increase fecal excretion of fluoride; aluminium hydroxide–containing medications should be taken 2 hours before or after sodium fluoride)

Calcium supplements
(concurrent use with sodium fluoride may cause the calcium ions to complex with fluoride and inhibit absorption of both fluoride and calcium; if sodium fluoride is used with calcium supplements to treat osteoporosis, a 1- to 2-hour interval should elapse between doses of the two)

Laboratory value alterations

The following have been selected on the basis of their potential clinical significance (possible effect in parentheses where appropriate)—not necessarily inclusive (» = major clinical significance).

With diagnostic test results

Alkaline phosphatase concentrations, serum
(results may be elevated)

Aspartate aminotransferase (AST [SGOT]) concentrations, serum
(may be falsely increased)

Medical considerations/Contraindications

The medical considerations/contraindications included have been selected on the basis of their potential clinical significance (reasons given in parentheses where appropriate)—not necessarily inclusive (» = major clinical significance).

Except under special circumstances, this medication should not be used when the following medical conditions exist:

Arthralgia or
Gastrointestinal ulceration
(conditions may be exacerbated, especially with high doses)

Renal insufficiency, severe
(condition may be exacerbated; may lead to higher blood levels of fluoride due to a decrease in excretion of fluoride; dosage reduction may be necessary)

Risk-benefit should be considered when the following medical problems exist:

High dental fluorosis, or prevalence in other members of the immediate community

Patient monitoring

The following may be especially important in patient monitoring (other tests may be warranted in some patients, depending on condition; » = major clinical significance):

Dental examination
(recommended once or twice a year in most patients, and more frequently in those highly prone to developing caries)

Side/Adverse Effects

The following side/adverse effects have been selected on the basis of their potential clinical significance (possible signs and symptoms in parentheses where appropriate)—not necessarily inclusive:

Those indicating need for medical attention

Incidence rare

Ulceration of oral mucous membranes (sores in mouth and on lips)

Overdose

For specific information on the agents used in the management of fluoride overdose, see

- *Calcium Supplements (Systemic)* monograph.

For more information on the management of overdose or unintentional ingestion **contact a Poison Control Center** (see *Poison Control Center Listing*).

Clinical effects of overdose

Note: Stomach upset may occur with ingestion of 5 to 20 mg of sodium fluoride. The lethal dose is not known, but has been estimated as 5 to 10 grams of sodium fluoride in untreated adults and 5 mg of fluoride ion per kilogram of body weight in children.

Severe acute fluoride overdose can cause hypocalcemia and tetany and bone pain, especially in the feet and ankles, of uncertain cause; electrolyte disturbances and cardiac arrhythmias have been reported, progressing to cardiac failure or respiratory arrest in some cases.

Osseous changes, including skeletal fluorosis, osteomalacia, and osteosclerosis, may also result from excessive, chronic doses.

The following effects have been selected on the basis of their potential clinical significance (possible signs and symptoms in parentheses where appropriate)—not necessarily inclusive:

Chronic effects (fluorosis and osteosclerosis)

Pain and aching of bones, stiffness, or white, brown, or black discoloration of teeth—occur only during periods of tooth development in children

Acute effects

Black, tarry stools; bloody vomit; diarrhea; drowsiness; faintness; increased watering of mouth; nausea or vomiting; shallow breathing; stomach cramps or pain; tremors; unusual excitement; watery eyes; weakness

Treatment of overdose

For treatment of acute overdoseSpecific treatment—

Administration of intravenous dextrose.

Gastric lavage with calcium chloride or calcium hydroxide solution to precipitate fluoride.

Intravenous calcium gluconate if hypocalcemia occurs.

Monitoring—

Monitor respiration, blood pressure, and ECG.

Supportive care—

Maintenance of high urine output.

Patients in whom intentional overdose is confirmed or suspected should be referred for psychiatric consultation.

Patient Consultation

As an aid to patient consultation, refer to *Advice for the Patient, Sodium Fluoride (Systemic)*.

In providing consultation, consider emphasizing the following selected information (» = major clinical significance):

Importance of diet

Importance of proper nutrition; fluoride may be needed because of inadequate dietary intake

Dietary sources of fluoride; effects of processing

Recommended daily intake for fluoride

Remembering not to take more than recommended

Before using this medication

» Conditions affecting use, especially:

Pregnancy—Fluoride crosses the placenta

Breast-feeding—Trace amount distributed into breast milk

Use in children—Chronic overdose may cause dental fluorosis and osseous changes

Use in the elderly—High doses used for osteoporosis or otospongiosis not recommended in elderly patients with arthralgia, gastrointestinal ulceration, or renal insufficiency

Dental—Excessive doses taken during tooth formation years may result in tooth fluorosis

Proper use of this medication

» Importance of not using more medication than the amount prescribed

» Proper dosing

Missed dose: Taking as soon as possible; not taking if almost time for next dose; not doubling doses

For individuals taking the chewable tablet dosage form

Chewing or crushing tablets before swallowing

Advisability of taking at bedtime after brushing teeth; not eating or drinking for at least 15 minutes after taking

For individuals taking the oral solution dosage form

Proper use of the dropper bottle

» Avoiding use of glass with fluoride-containing solutions since fluoride etches glass

May be dropped directly into the mouth or mixed with cereal, fruit juice, or other food (except calcium-containing foods or beverages)

» Proper storage

Precautions while using this medication

Checking with health care professional as soon as possible after moving to another geographic area to see if continued treatment at the same dosage is necessary, since fluoride levels of community drinking water vary; also checking if changing infant feeding habits, drinking water, or filtration

Not taking calcium supplements or aluminum hydroxide-containing products and sodium fluoride at the same time; use should be separated by 2 hours

» Informing health care professional if teeth show signs of mottling

Side/adverse effects

Signs of potential side effects especially oral mucous membrane ulceration

General Dosing Information

Optimal benefit of fluorides must be established on an individual basis, taking into consideration the fluoride content of the water supply when determining the dose. Some studies have found that systemic fluoride ingestion from toothpaste use in young children is significant.

The amount of fluoride from all sources should be taken into account when determining the therapeutic dose. For example, infant formulas made with fluoridated water provide a significant amount. Also, some schools in communities without water fluoridation have added up to 4.5 times the optimal fluoride level to the school's water supply to ensure that children receive adequate fluoride.

Use of fluoride supplements is generally not recommended when community drinking water contains more than 0.6 parts per million (ppm) of fluoride.

A fluoride level of approximately 1 ppm (0.6 to 1.2 ppm) in water is generally considered optimal for development of decay-resistant teeth without causing fluorosis, the actual value depending on the annual mean maximum daily temperature of the geographic area.

2.2 mg of sodium fluoride is equivalent to 1 mg of fluoride ion.

Since therapy with oral, systemic fluoride supplements is most effective on unerupted teeth, it is recommended that children receive oral fluoride supplementation until the age of 13 (or when the second molars have erupted) to provide maximum benefit to both deciduous and permanent teeth. Subsequent periodic topical application of fluoride for life may be advisable to prolong the cariostatic benefits, since beneficial effects, particularly in caries-prone individuals, appear to be lost a year or two after topical use is discontinued.

The recommended dose should not be exceeded, since prolonged overdosage may cause dental fluorosis in children and osseous changes in children and adults.

Mottling of tooth enamel (dental fluorosis) occurs with excessive ingestion of fluoride (e.g., continual use of drinking water containing greater than 2 ppm of fluoride) during the period of tooth development in children.

Stiffness (skeletal fluorosis) occurs with chronic ingestion of water containing 4 to 14 ppm of fluoride.

Generalized effects (renal damage, albuminuria, goiter) occur only after chronic ingestion of large amounts of fluoride over 10 to 20 years.

It is recommended that fluoride preparations (especially the chewable tablets) taken on a once-a-day basis be taken at bedtime after the teeth have been thoroughly brushed (to also provide some topical benefit from the fluoride).

Sodium fluoride (25 to 60 mg a day) may stabilize the progression of hearing loss in some patients with otospongiosis.

Diet/Nutrition

Nausea (although rare with doses of fluoride taken for dental caries) may be reduced by taking sodium fluoride with or just after meals, provided that the foods do not contain calcium, since calcium may interfere with fluoride absorption.

The oral solution may be administered undiluted or mixed with cereal, fluids, or other food. However, absorption of sodium fluoride may be reduced when taken with calcium-rich foods or beverages.

Recommended dietary intakes for fluoride are defined differently worldwide.

For U.S.—

The Recommended Dietary Allowances (RDAs) for vitamins and minerals are determined by the Food and Nutrition Board of the National Research Council and are intended to provide adequate nutrition in most healthy persons under usual environmental stresses. In addition, a different designation may be used by the FDA for food and dietary supplement labeling purposes, as with Daily Value (DV). DVs replace the previous labeling terminology United States Recommended Daily Allowances (USRDAs).

For Canada—

Recommended Nutrient Intakes (RNIs) for vitamins, minerals, and protein are determined by Health and Welfare Canada and provide recommended amounts of a specific nutrient while minimizing the risk of chronic diseases.

There is no RDA or RNI established for fluoride. Daily recommended intakes for fluoride are generally defined as follows:

Infants and children:

Birth to 3 years: 0.1 to 1.5 mg.

4 to 6 years: 1 to 2.5 mg.

7 to 10 years: 1.5 to 2.5 mg.

Adolescents and adults:

1.5 to 4 mg.

Sources of fluoride other than fluoridated drinking water include fish that are consumed with their bones and tea. Cooking foods in fluorinated water can increase their fluoride content as can cooking with Teflon- (a fluoride-containing polymer) coated utensils and pans. However, cooking foods in utensils and pans with an aluminum surface can decrease their fluoride content.

Oral Dosage Forms

SODIUM FLUORIDE LOZENGES

Usual pediatric dose

Dental caries prophylactic or

Nutritional supplement—

Dosage of fluoride recommended by the American Dental Association, the American Academy of Pediatrics, and the American Academy of Pediatric Dentistry for communities where the level of fluoride in drinking water is 0.6 ppm or less

Water Fluoride (ppm)	Age (yr)	Dose of Fluoride Ion (mg per day)
<0.3	Birth to 0.5	0
	0.5 to 3	0.25
	3 to 6	0.5
	6 to 16	1
0.3–0.6	Birth to 3	0
	3 to 6	0.25
	6 to 16	0.5
>0.6	Birth to 16	0

Note: In Canada a different dosing schedule may be used. The Canadian Dental Association recommendations differ from that of the American Dental Association.

Strength(s) usually available

U.S.—

2.2 mg (1 mg of fluoride ion) (Rx) [*Flura-Loz*].

Canada—

1.1 mg (OTC) [*Flozenges*].

2.2 mg (OTC) [*Flozenges*].

Packaging and storage

Store below 40 °C (104 °F), preferably between 15 and 30 °C (59 and 86 °F), unless otherwise specified by manufacturer. Store in a tight container.

SODIUM FLUORIDE ORAL SOLUTION USP

Usual pediatric dose

See *Sodium Fluoride Lozenges*.

Strength(s) usually available

U.S.—

0.275 mg (0.125 mg of fluoride ion) per drop (Rx) [*Karidium; Luride*; GENERIC].

0.44 mg (0.2 mg of fluoride ion) per mL (Rx) [*Phos-Flur*].

0.55 mg (0.25 mg of fluoride ion) per drop (Rx) [*Fluoritab; Flura-Drops*].

1.1 mg (0.5 mg of fluoride ion) per mL (Rx) [*Pediaflor* (alcohol less than 0.5%)].

Canada—

2 mg (0.905 mg of fluoride ion) per mL (OTC) [*PDF*].

2.2 mg (1 mg of fluoride ion) per 4 drops (Rx) [*Solu-Flur*].

2.21 mg (1 mg of fluoride ion) per 8 drops (0.5 mL) (OTC) [*Karidium*].

5.56 mg (1 mg of fluoride ion) per mL (OTC) [*Fluor-A-Day*].

6.9 mg (3.12 mg of fluoride ion) per mL (OTC) [*Fluorosol; Pedi-Dent*; GENERIC].

Packaging and storage

Store below 40 °C (104 °F), preferably between 15 and 30 °C (59 and 86 °F), unless otherwise specified by manufacturer. Store in a tight, plastic container. Protect from freezing.

Auxiliary labeling

- Keep out of reach of children.

Note

To reduce the risk associated with accidental ingestion and overdosage, it is recommended that no more than 264 mg of sodium fluoride be dispensed at one time. The American Dental Association Council on Dental Therapeutics considers a limit of 300 mg acceptable when sodium fluoride is dispensed to children in prepackaged containers.

Since size of drop dispensed and strength vary among commercial preparations, always dispense the same brand for refills on a prescription.

SODIUM FLUORIDE TABLETS USP

Usual pediatric dose

See *Sodium Fluoride Lozenges*.

Strength(s) usually available

U.S.—

1.1 mg (0.5 mg of fluoride ion) (Rx) [GENERIC].

2.2 mg (1 mg of fluoride ion) (Rx) [*Flura; Karidium*; GENERIC].

Canada—

2.2 mg (1 mg fluoride ion) (OTC) [*Fluorosol; Karidium*; GENERIC].

Packaging and storage

Store below 40 °C (104 °F), preferably between 15 and 30 °C (59 and 86 °F), unless otherwise specified by manufacturer. Store in a tight container.

Auxiliary labeling

- Keep out of reach of children.

Note

To reduce the risk associated with accidental ingestion and overdosage, it is recommended that no more than 264 mg of sodium fluoride be dispensed at one time. The American Dental Association Council on Dental Therapeutics considers a limit of 300 mg acceptable when sodium fluoride is dispensed to children in prepackaged containers.

SODIUM FLUORIDE CHEWABLE TABLETS USP

Usual pediatric dose

See *Sodium Fluoride Lozenges*.

Strength(s) usually available

U.S.—

0.55 mg (0.25 mg of fluoride ion) (Rx) [*Luride Lozi-Tabs*].

1.1 mg (0.5 mg of fluoride ion) (Rx) [*Fluoritab* (scored); *Fluorodex; Luride Lozi-Tabs; Pharmaflur 1.1;* GENERIC].

2.2 mg (1 mg of fluoride ion) (Rx) [*Fluoritab; Fluorodex; Karidium; Luride Lozi-Tabs; Luride-SF Lozi-Tabs; Pharmaflur; Pharmaflur df;* GENERIC].

Canada—

2.2 mg (1 mg of fluoride ion) (OTC) [*Fluor-A-Day; Fluoritabs; Pedi-Dent; Solu-Flur;* GENERIC].

Packaging and storage

Store below 40 °C (104 °F), preferably between 15 and 30 °C (59 and 86 °F), unless otherwise specified by manufacturer. Store in a tight container.

Auxiliary labeling

- Keep out of reach of children.

Note

To reduce the risk associated with accidental ingestion and overdosage, it is recommended that no more than 264 mg of sodium fluoride be dispensed at one time. The American Dental Association Council on Dental Therapeutics considers a limit of 300 mg acceptable when sodium fluoride is dispensed to children in prepackaged containers.

Revised: 08/07/1995

SODIUM OXYBATE Systemic†

VA CLASSIFICATION (Primary): CN900

Note: Controlled substance classification

U.S.: Schedule III

Commonly used brand name(s): *Xyrem*.

Another commonly used name is GHB

Note: For a listing of dosage forms and brand names by country availability, see *Dosage Forms* section(s).

†Not commercially available in Canada.

Category

Anticataplectic.

Indications

Accepted

Cataplexy (treatment)—Sodium oxybate is indicated for the treatment of cataplexy in patients with narcolepsy.

Pharmacology/Pharmacokinetics

Physicochemical characteristics

Molecular weight—126.09 grams/mole.

Mechanism of action/Effect

Sodium oxybate is a central nervous system depressant with anti-cataplectic activity in patients with narcolepsy. The precise mechanism by which sodium oxybate produces an effect on cataplexy is unknown.

Absorption

Sodium oxybate is a hydrophilic compound that is rapidly but incompletely absorbed after oral administration with bioavailability approximately 25%.

Administration of sodium oxybate immediately after a high fat meal results in delayed and decreased absorption.

In a clinical study performed in 16 cirrhotic patients, AUC values were double with apparent oral clearance reduced from 9.1 in healthy adults to between 4.1 (patients without ascites) and 4.5 mL per min per kg (patients with ascites).

Distribution

Volume of distribution (Vol_D)—averaging 190 to 384 milliliters per kilogram.

Protein binding

Very low (less than 1%), binding to plasma proteins at concentrations ranging from 3 to 300 micrograms per milliliter.

Half-life

Elimination—0.5 to 1 hour.

In a clinical study performed in 16 cirrhotic patients, the elimination half-life was significantly longer (mean of 59 and 32 versus 22 minutes in healthy patients).

Time to peak concentration

Following oral administration—T_{max} ranges from 0.5 to 1.25 hours; plasma levels increase more than proportionally with increasing dose.

Note: Administration of sodium oxybate after a high fat meal results in delayed absorption; time to peak concentration (T_{max}) increased from 0.75 hours to 2.0 hours.

Peak plasma concentration:

Concentrations of 78 and 142 micrograms per milliliter—(First peak and second peak, respectively) following administration of a 9 gram daily dose divided into two equivalent doses given four hours apart; plasma levels increase more than proportionally with increasing dose.

Note: Administration of sodium oxybate after a high fat meal results in delayed absorption; peak plasma level (C_{max}) decreased by a mean of 58%; area under the curve, (AUC) decreased by 37%.

Elimination

Sodium oxybate is almost entirely eliminated by biotransformation to carbon dioxide, which is then eliminated by expiration. Less than 5% of unchanged drug appears in urine within 6 to 8 hours after dosing. Fecal elimination is negligible.

Precautions to Consider

Carcinogenicity and Mutagenicity

Studies in mice and rats found no evidence of carcinogenicity or mutagenicity (negative Ames microbial mutagen test, *in vitro* chromosomal aberration assay, and *in vivo* rat micronucleus assay).

Pregnancy/Reproduction

Fertility—Studies in rats found no impairment of fertility at doses equal to the maximum recommended human daily dose on a mg per m² basis.

Pregnancy—Adequate and well controlled studies in humans have not been done. Studies in rats have shown that sodium oxybate may decrease pup weight gain and no effects were seen on other developmental parameters.

FDA Pregnancy Category B

Labor and delivery—Sodium oxybate has not been studied in labor or delivery. In obstetric anesthesia using an injectable formulation, newborns had stable cardiovascular and respiratory measure, but were very sleepy causing a slight decrease in Apgar scores. There was a fall in the rate of uterine contractions 20 minutes after injection. Placental transfer is rapid, but umbilical vein levels were no more than 25% of the maternal concentrations. No levels were detected in the infant's blood 30 minutes after delivery.

Breast-feeding

It is not known whether sodium oxybate is distributed into human breast milk. However, caution should be exercised.

Pediatrics

Safety and efficacy have not been established in those under 16 years of age.

Geriatrics

There is limited information available on the relationship of age to the effects of sodium oxybate in geriatric patients. However, elderly patients should be monitored closely for impaired motor and/or cognitive function.

Drug interactions and/or related problems

The following drug interactions and/or related problems have been selected on the basis of their potential clinical significance (possible mechanism in parentheses where appropriate)—not necessarily inclusive (» = major clinical significance):

Note: Combinations containing any of the following medications, depending on the amount present, may also interact with this medication.

» Central Nervous System (CNS) depressants (see *Appendix II-Drug induced effects*) especially:

» Alcohol or

» Sedative hypnotics
(strong warning against concomitant therapy which may result in potentiation of the CNS-depressant effects especially respiratory depression)

Medical considerations/Contraindications

The medical considerations/contraindications included have been selected on the basis of their potential clinical significance (reasons given in parentheses where appropriate)—not necessarily inclusive (» = major clinical significance).

Except under special circumstances, this medication should not be used when the following medical problem exists:

» Succinic semialdehyde dehydrogenase deficiency
(contraindicated in patients with this rare inborn metabolism deficiency)

Risk-benefit should be considered when the following medical problems exist:

» Depression, history of, or
» Suicide, attempted
(close monitoring is recommended)
» Drug abuse or dependence, history of
(should evaluate carefully for history of drug dependence and follow such patients closely for signs of dependence)

Heart failure, history of, or
Hypertension or
Renal function impairment
(daily sodium intake from sodium oxybate ranges from 0.5g (for a 3g sodium oxybate dose) to 1.6g (for a 9g sodium oxybate dose))

» Hepatic dysfunction
(may increase both AUC values and elimination half-life, may reduce oral clearance; reduce the starting dose by one-half and monitor dose increments)
» Respiratory function, compromised including:
» Hypopnea or
» Sleep apnea
(may lead to impaired respiratory drive; life threatening respiratory depression has been reported following overdose)

Patient monitoring

The following may be especially important in patient monitoring (other tests may be warranted in some patients, depending on condition; » = major clinical significance):

» Geriatric patients
(monitor for signs of impaired motor and/or cognitive function.)
» Neuropsychiatric symptoms, including:
» Confusion or
» Depressive symptoms
(patients with a previous history of a depressive illness and/or suicide attempt should be monitored carefully; monitor patient for signs of confusion and evaluate for appropriate intervention)
» Sleepwalking
(monitor patient for confused behavior occurring at night associated with wandering to avoid self injury; fully evaluate and take appropriate intervention measures.)
» Symptoms of abuse, dependence and tolerance
(illicit misuse and abuse have been reported; patients should be monitored for signs of abuse, dependence, or tolerance such as increase in size or frequency of dosing, drug-seeking behavior, and/or feigned cataplexy)

Side/Adverse Effects

Sodium oxybate is GHB, a known drug of abuse. GHB abuse has been associated with some important central nervous system adverse events including seizures, respiratory depression and profound decreases in level of consciousness, with instances of coma and death. Signs of use and misuse include increase in size or frequency of dosing and drug seeking behavior.

The following side/adverse effects have been selected on the basis of their potential clinical significance (possible signs and symptoms in parentheses where appropriate)—not necessarily inclusive:

Those indicating need for medical attention

Incidence more frequent

Amblyopia (blurred vision; change in vision; impaired vision); ***amnesia*** (loss of memory; problems with memory); ***asthenia*** (lack or loss of strength); ***confusion; depression*** (discouragement; feeling sad or empty; irritability; lack of appetite; loss of interest or pleasure; tiredness; trouble concentrating; trouble sleeping); ***hypesthesia*** (burning, crawling, itching, numbness, prickling, "pins and needles" or tingling feelings); ***hypertension*** (blurred vision; dizziness; nervousness; headache; pounding in the ears; slow or fast heartbeat); ***myasthenia*** (loss of strength or energy; muscle pain or weakness); ***sleepwalking; urinary incontinence*** (loss of bladder control)

Those indicating need for medical attention only if they continue or are bothersome

Incidence more frequent

Abdominal pain; abnormal thinking; anxiety (fear; nervousness); ***back pain; dreams, abnormal; diarrhea; dizziness; dysmenorrhea*** (pain; cramps; heavy bleeding); ***dyspepsia*** (acid or sour stomach; belching; heartburn; indigestion; stomach discomfort, upset, or pain); ***flu syndrome*** (chills; cough; diarrhea; fever; general feeling of discomfort or illness; headache; joint pain; loss of appetite; muscle aches and pains; nausea; runny nose; shivering; sore throat; sweating; trouble sleeping; unusual tiredness or weakness; vomiting); ***headache; infection*** (fever or chills; cough or hoarseness; lower back or side pain; painful or difficult urination); ***nausea; nervousness; pain; pharyngitis*** (body aches or pain; congestion; cough; dryness or soreness of throat; fever; hoarseness; runny nose; tender, swollen glands in neck; trouble in swallowing; voice changes); ***rhinitis*** (stuffy nose; runny nose; sneezing); ***sinusitis*** (pain or tenderness around eyes and cheekbones; fever; stuffy or runny nose; headache; cough; shortness of breath or troubled breathing; tightness of chest or wheezing); ***sleep disorder; somnolence*** (sleepiness or unusual drowsiness); ***sweating; viral infection*** (chills; cough or hoarseness; fever; cold flu-like symptoms); ***vomiting***

Incidence less frequent

Insomnia (sleeplessness; trouble sleeping; unable to sleep)

Those indicating need for medical attention only if they occur after medication is discontinued

Incidence unknown—Occurring during abrupt discontinuation; estimates of frequency not determined

Abstinence syndrome including; insomnia (sleeplessness; trouble sleeping; unable to sleep); ***restlessness; anxiety*** (fear; nervousness); ***psychosis*** (feeling that others can hear your thoughts; feeling that others are watching you or controlling your behavior; feeling, seeing, or hearing things that are not there; severe mood or mental changes; unusual behavior); ***lethargy*** (unusual drowsiness; dullness; tiredness; weakness or feeling of sluggishness); ***nausea; tremor*** (trembling or shaking of hands or feet; shakiness in legs, arms, hands, feet); ***sweating; muscle cramps; tachycardia*** (fast, pounding, or irregular heartbeat or pulse)

Note: Symptoms of abstinence syndrome generally abated in 3 to 14 days.

Overdose

For more information on the management of overdose or unintentional ingestion, **contact a poison control center** (see *Poison Control Center Listing*).

Clinical effects of overdose

The following effects have been selected on the basis of their potential clinical significance (possible signs and symptoms in parentheses where appropriate)—not necessarily inclusive:

Apnea (bluish lips or skin, not breathing); ***ataxia*** (shakiness and unsteady walk; trembling, or other problems with muscle control or coordination); ***bradycardia*** (chest pain or discomfort; lightheadedness, dizziness or fainting; shortness of breath; slow or irregular heartbeat; unusual tiredness); ***Cheyne Stokes respiration*** (alternating periods of shallow and deep breathing); ***coma; confusional, agitated combative state; consciousness, depressed; diaphoresis*** (increased sweating); ***headache; hypothermia*** (clumsiness; confusion; drowsiness; low body temperature; muscle aches or weakness; shivering; sleepiness; weak or feeble pulse); ***hypotonia, muscular*** (unusual weak feeling loss of strength or energy muscle pain or weakness); ***incontinence*** (inability to hold bowel movement and/or urine); ***psychomotor skills, impaired*** (generalized slowing of mental and physical activity); ***seizures, tonic-clonic and myoclonus*** (convulsions); ***vision, blurred; vomiting***

Treatment of overdose

To decrease absorption—
Gastric decontamination may be considered if co-ingestants are suspected.

To enhance elimination—
Hemodialysis is not warranted, due to the rapid metabolism of sodium oxybate.

Specific treatment—
Appropriate posture, left lateral recumbent position, and protection of the airway by intubation may be warranted due to emesis even when obtunded.

Rapid sequence induction, *without* the use of a sedative, should be considered due to the possibility of combativeness during intubation, even in unconscious patients.

Overdose induced bradycardia has been responsive to intravenous administration of atropine.

Monitoring—

Vital signs and consciousness should be closely monitored.

Supportive care—

Patients in whom intentional overdose is confirmed or suspected should be referred for psychiatric consultation.

Patient Consultation

As an aid to patient consultation, refer to *Advice for the Patient, Sodium Oxybate (Systemic)*.

In providing consultation, consider emphasizing the following selected information (» = major clinical significance):

Before using this medication

» Conditions affecting use, especially:

Use in the elderly—Elderly patients should be monitored closely for impaired motor and/or cognitive function.

Other medications, especially central nervous system depressants including alcohol or sedative hypnotics

Other medical problems, especially succinic semialdehyde dehydrogenase deficiency, apnea, hypopnea, history of depression, attempted suicide, history of drug abuse or dependence, hepatic dysfunction, or compromised respiratory function

Proper use of this medication

Monitoring patient for signs of abuse, dependence or tolerance, impaired motor or cognitive function especially in the elderly, neuropsychiatric symptoms, such as confusion or depression, and sleepwalking,

Importance of taking first dose at bedtime and second dose 2.5 to 4 hours later;

Taking several hours after eating well and adhering to a consistent schedule with the medication and meals

Proper administration technique for oral liquid

Diluting each dose with two ounces of water before taking

» Proper dosing, especially decreased dosing in hepatic insufficiency.

Proper storage

Precautions while using this medication

» Avoiding the use of alcohol or other CNS depressants while taking this medication

» Not engaging in hazardous occupations or activities requiring complete mental alertness or motor coordination, such as operating machinery, driving a motor vehicle or flying an airplane for at least six hours after ingesting sodium oxybate; using extreme care when engaging in any hazardous occupations or activities the following day until the carry over effects of the medication are known

» Frequent visits to the physician during the course of treatment to evaluate adverse reactions to the medication

Side/adverse effects

Signs of potential side effects, especially amblyopia, amnesia, asthenia, confusion, depression, hypesthesia, hypertension, myasthenia, sleepwalking or urinary incontinence

General Dosing Information

The first dose of sodium oxybate should be taken at bedtime while in bed and the second taken 2.5 to 4 hours later while sitting in bed. Patients will probably need to set an alarm to awaken for the second dose. The second dose must be prepared prior to ingesting the first dose, and should be placed in close proximity to the patient's bed. After ingesting each dose patients should then lie down and remain in bed.

Care should be taken to prevent access to this medication by children and pets. Each bottle has a child resistant cap and two dosing cups with child resistant caps.

Diet/Nutrition

Because food significantly reduces the bioavailability of sodium oxybate, it should be taken several hours after eating well. Patients should try to minimize variability in the timing of dosing in relation to meals.

Safety considerations for handling this medication

It is safe to dispose of sodium oxybate oral solution down the sanitary sewer.

For treatment of adverse effects

If a patient experiences urinary or fecal incontinence during sodium oxybate therapy, investigations to rule out underlying etiologies such as worsening sleep apnea or nocturnal seizures should be considered.

Episodes of sleepwalking, which refers to confused behavior occurring at night and at times, associated with wandering, should be fully evaluated and appropriate interventions considered.

The emergence of thought disorders, behavior abnormalities, and/or depression requires careful and immediate evaluation.

Patients being treated with sodium oxybate who become confused should be evaluated fully, and appropriate intervention should be considered on an individual basis.

Oral Dosage Forms

Note: Sodium oxybate is available only through restricted distribution, the Xyrem Success Program, by calling 1–866–XYREM88 (1-866-997-3688) and following the appropriate prescribing procedures.

SODIUM OXYBATE ORAL SOLUTION

Usual adult dose

Cataplexy treatment—

Oral, 4.5 grams per day divided into two equal doses of 2.25 grams. Dosage can be increased in increments of 1.5 grams per day (0.75 grams per dose) with two weeks recommended between dosage increases up to 9 grams per day. The first dose should be taken at bedtime and the second dose taken 2.5 to 4 hours later.

Note: For hepatic insufficient patients, the starting dose should be decreased by one-half to 1.125 grams per dose and dose increments should titrated to effect while closely monitoring potential adverse events.

Usual adult prescribing limits

9 grams per day. Sodium oxybate is effective at doses of 6 to 9 grams per day. The efficacy and safety of sodium oxybate at doses higher than 9 grams per day have not been investigated, and doses greater than 9 grams per day ordinarily should not be administered.

Usual pediatric dose

Safety and efficacy in patients under 16 years of age have not been established.

Usual geriatric dose

See *Usual adult dose.*

Note: Elderly patients should be monitored closely for impaired motor and/or cognitive function when taking sodium oxybate.

Usual geriatric prescribing limits

See *Usual adult prescribing limits.*

Strength(s) usually available

U.S.—

500 mg per mL (Rx) [*Xyrem* (purified water, USP; malic acid to adjust pH)].

Canada—

Not commercially available.

Packaging and storage

Store at 25 °C (77 °F), USP controlled room temperature, excursions permitted up to 15 to 30 °C (59 to 86 °F).

Preparation of dosage form

Prior to administration, each dose of sodium oxybate must be diluted with two ounces (60 mL, ¼ cup, or 4 tablespoons) of water.

Stability

Following dilution, sodium oxybate solution should be consumed within 24 hours to minimize bacterial growth and contamination.

Auxiliary labeling

• Caution: Federal law prohibits the transfer of this drug to any person other than the patient for whom it was prescribed.

• Avoid alcoholic beverages.

• May cause slowed motor coordination or lack of mental alertness due to the CNS depressant effects. Be careful while engaging in hazardous occupations or activities such as operating machinery, driving a motor vehicle, or flying an airplane. Use caution until you become familiar with its effects.

• Please read the enclosed medication guide.

Note

Controlled substance—Federal and state regulations apply.

Revised: 04/11/2003

SODIUM PHOSPHATE—See *Laxatives (Local)*

SODIUM PHOSPHATES—See *Laxatives (Local), Phosphates (Systemic)*

SODIUM SALICYLATE—See *Salicylates (Systemic)*

SODIUM TETRADECYL SULFATE Systemic†

VA CLASSIFICATION (Primary): CV600

Commonly used brand name(s): *Sotradecol*.

Note: For a listing of dosage forms and brand names by country availability, see *Dosage Forms* section(s).

†Not commercially available in Canada.

Category

Sclerosing agent.

Indications

Accepted

Varicose veins, small uncomplicated (treatment)—Sodium tetradecyl sulfate is indicated in the treatment of small uncomplicated varicose veins of the lower extremities that show simple dilation with competent valves. The benefit-to-risk ratio should be considered in selected patients who are great surgical risks.

Pharmacology/Pharmacokinetics

Physicochemical characteristics

Molecular weight—Sodium tetradecyl sulfate: 316.44.

Mechanism of action/Effect

Sodium tetradecyl sulfate is a sclerosing agent. Injection into a vein causes intima inflammation and thrombus formation, usually occluding the injected vein. The subsequent formation of fibrous tissue results in partial or complete vein obliteration that may or may not be permanent.

Precautions to Consider

Carcinogenicity

No long term carcinogenicity studies in animals have been performed.

Mutagenicity

Sodium tetradecyl sulfate was not found to be mutagenic when tested in the L5178YTK +/- mouse lymphoma assay.

Pregnancy/Reproduction

Fertility—Animal reproduction studies have not been done with sodium tetradecyl sulfate.

Pregnancy—Studies have not been done in humans.
Studies have not been done in animals.
Sodium tetradecyl sulfate should be given to a pregnant woman only if clearly needed and the benefits outweigh the risks.

FDA Pregnancy Category C

Breast-feeding

It is not known whether sodium tetradecyl sulfate is distributed in human milk. Because many drugs are distributed in human milk, caution should be exercised when sodium tetradecyl sulfate is administered to a nursing woman.

Pediatrics

Safety and effectiveness in pediatric patients have not been established.

Drug interactions and/or related problems

The following drug interactions and/or related problems have been selected on the basis of their potential clinical significance (possible mechanism in parentheses where appropriate)—not necessarily inclusive (» = major clinical significance):

Note: Combinations containing any of the following medications, depending on the amount present, may also interact with this medication.

» Antiovulatory drugs
(well-controlled studies have not been done; physician judgement and evaluation prior to initiating therapy)

Medical considerations/Contraindications

The medical considerations/contraindications included have been selected on the basis of their potential clinical significance (reasons given in parentheses where appropriate)—not necessarily inclusive (» = major clinical significance).

Except under special circumstances, this medication should not be used when the following medical problem exists:

» Hypersensitivity to sodium tetradecyl sulfate

» Allergic conditions or
» Bedridden patients or
» Cellulitis, acute or
» Deep vein incompetence or
» Huge superficial veins with wide open communications to deeper veins or
» Infections, acute or
» Migrans, phlebitis or
» Respiratory diseases, acute or
» Skin diseases, acute or
» Thrombophlebitis, acute superficial or
» Valvular vein incompetence or
» Varicosities caused by abdominal and pelvic tumors (unless the tumor has been removed)
(use is contraindicated)

» Systemic diseases, uncontrolled such as
» Asthma or
» Blood dyscrasias or
» Diabetes or
» Hyperthyroidism, toxic or
» Neoplasm or
» Sepsis or
» Tuberculosis
(use is contraindicated)

Risk-benefit should be considered when the following medical problems exist:

» Arterial diseases such as
Peripheral arteriosclerosis, marked or
Thromboangiitis obliterans (Buerger's Disease)
(extreme caution must be exercised)

Side/Adverse Effects

The following side/adverse effects have been selected on the basis of their potential clinical significance (possible signs and symptoms in parentheses where appropriate)—not necessarily inclusive:

Those indicating need for medical attention

Incidence not determined

Allergic reactions including (burning; itching; nausea; redness; skin rash; vomiting); ***anaphylactic shock*** (cough; difficulty swallowing; dizziness; fast heartbeat; hives; itching; puffiness or swelling of the eyelids or around the eyes, face, lips or tongue; shortness of breath; skin rash; tightness in chest; unusual tiredness or weakness; wheezing); ***asthma*** (cough; difficulty breathing; noisy breathing; shortness of breath; tightness in chest; wheezing); ***hayfever; hives*** (raised red swellings on the skin, lips, tongue, or in the throat); ***deep vein thrombosis*** (pain, redness, or swelling in arm or leg); ***pulmonary embolism*** (anxiety; chest pain; cough; fainting; fast heartbeat; sudden shortness of breath or troubled breathing; dizziness or lightheadedness)

Those indicating need for medical attention only if they continue or are bothersome

Incidence not determined

Extravasation (pale skin at site of injection; pain or redness at site of injection); ***headache; nausea; necrosis*** (peeling or sloughing of skin); ***pain, local; permanent discoloration of sclerosed vein segment; urticaria, local*** (hives or welts; itching; redness of skin; skin rash); ***ulceration at site of injection; vomiting***

Overdose

For more information on the management of overdose or unintentional ingestion, **contact a poison control center** (see *Poison Control Center Listing*).

The intravenous LD_{50} of sodium tetradecyl sulfate in mice was 90 +/- 5 mg/kg. In rats the intravenous LD_{50} is estimated to be between 72 mg/kg and 108 mg/kg.

Purified sodium tetradecyl sulfate had an LD_{50} of 2 g/kg when administered orally by stomach tube as a 25% aqueous solution to rats. However, no appreciable toxicity was seen in rats given 0.15 g/kg in drinking water for 30 days.

Patient Consultation

As an aid to patient consultation, refer to *Advice for the Patient, Sodium Tetradecyl Sulfate (Systemic)*.

In providing consultation, consider emphasizing the following selected information (» = major clinical significance):

Before using this medication

» Conditions affecting use, especially:

Hypersensitivity to sodium tetradecyl sulfate

Pregnancy—Not recommended for use during pregnancy; should be given to a pregnant woman only if clearly needed and the benefits outweigh the risks.

Breast-feeding—Caution should be exercised when administering to a nursing woman.

Use in children—Safety and effectiveness not established

Other medications, especially antiovulatory drugs

Other medical problems, especially acute cellulitis, acute infections, acute respiratory diseases, acute skin diseases, acute superficial thrombophlebitis, allergic conditions, arterial diseases such as marked peripheral arteriosclerosis, or thromboangiitis obliterans (Buerger's disease); bedridden patients, deep vein incompetence, huge superficial veins with wide open communications to deeper veins, migrans, phlebitis, systemic diseases, uncontrolled such as asthma, blood dyscrasias, diabetes, toxic hyperthyroidism, neoplasm, sepsis, or tuberculosis; valvular vein incompetence, or varicosities caused by abdominal and pelvic tumors (unless the tumor has been removed)

Proper use of this medication

» The importance of a preinjection evaluation for valvular competency

» The importance of slow injections with a small amount (preferably 1 mL maximum) for each injection, and a maximum single treatment of 10 mL

» Proper dosing

» Proper storage

Precautions while using this medication

» The occurrence of embolism up to 4 weeks following injection of sodium tetradecyl sulfate

» The possible development of deep vein thrombosis

Side/adverse effects

Signs of potential side effects, especially allergic reactions including anaphylactic shock, asthma, deep vein thrombosis, hayfever, hives, or pulmonary embolism

General Dosing Information

Sodium tetradecyl sulfate injections should only be administered by a physician familiar with venous anatomy and the diagnosis and treatment of conditions affecting the venous system and familiar with proper injection technique.

A thorough preinjection evaluation for valvular competency should be performed due to the danger of thrombosis extension into the deep venous system.

Extreme care in intravenous needle placement and the minimal effective volume should be used at each injection site.

As a precaution against anaphylactic shock, it is recommended that 0.5 mL of sodium tetradecyl sulfate be injected into a varicosity, followed by several hours of patient observation before the administration of a second or larger dose.

Deep venous patency must be determined by angiography or noninvasive testing such as duplex ultrasound; and, venous sclerotherapy should not be done if significant valvular or deep venous incompetence exist.

Post-treatment follow-up of sufficient duration should be done to assess for the development of deep vein thrombosis.

For treatment of adverse effects

Emergency resuscitation equipment should be readily available including treatment for anaphylactic shock; allergic reactions including fatal anaphylaxis have been reported.

Adequate post-treatment compression should be used to decrease the incidence of deep vein thrombosis.

Parenteral Dosage Forms

SODIUM TETRADECYL SULFATE INJECTION

Usual adult dose

Sclerosing agent—

Intravenous, 0.5 mL to 2 mL (preferably 1 mL max) for each injection. The strength of solution required depends on the size and degree of varicosity; the 1% solution will be found most useful with the 3% solution preferred for larger varicosities.

Usual adult prescribing limits

Up to 1 mL maximum for each injection and 10 mL per single treatment.

Usual pediatric dose

Safety and effectiveness in pediatric patients have not been established.

Usual geriatric dose

See *Usual adult dose*.

Usual geriatric prescribing limits

See *Usual adult prescribing limits*.

Strength(s) usually available

U.S.—

1% (salt) (Rx) [*Sotradecol* (benzyl alcohol; dibasic sodium phosphate anhydrous; water for injection; sodium phosphate monobasic; sodium hydroxide)].

3% (salt) (RX) [*Sotradecol* (benzyl alcohol; dibasic sodium phosphate anhydrous; water for injection; sodium phosphate monobasic; sodium hydroxide)].

Packaging and storage

Store between 20 and 25 °C (68 and 77 °F).

Preparation of dosage form

Inspect visually for particulate matter and discoloration prior to administration. Do not use if precipitated or discolored.

Incompatibilities

Heparin should not be used in the same syringe as sodium tetradecyl sulfate because the two are incompatible.

Developed: 03/08/2006

SOLIFENACIN Systemic†

VA CLASSIFICATION (Primary): GU201

Commonly used brand name(s): *VESIcare*.

Note: For a listing of dosage forms and brand names by country availability, see *Dosage Forms* section(s).

†Not commercially available in Canada.

Category

Antispasmodic (urinary).

Indications

Accepted

Bladder hyperactivity (treatment)—Solifenacin is indicated for the treatment of overactive bladder with symptoms of urinary incontinence, urgency, or urinary frequency.

Pharmacology/Pharmacokinetics

Physicochemical characteristics

Molecular weight—Solifenacin succinate: 480.55.

Solubility—Solifenacin succinate is freely soluble at room temperature in water, glacial acetic acid, dimethyl sulfoxide, and methanol.

Mechanism of action/Effect

Solifenacin is an antispasmodic, antimuscarinic agent. It is an antagonist on the effects of muscarinic receptors in cholinergically mediated functions, including contractions of the urinary bladder smooth muscle and stimulation of salivary secretion.

Absorption

Following oral administration the absolute bioavailability in healthy volunteers is approximately 90%, and plasma concentrations are proportional to the administered dose. Food has no effect on the pharmacokinetics of solifenacin.

Distribution

Highly distributed to non-CNS tissue.

Volume of distribution (Vol_D)—Steady state: 600 L.

Protein binding
Very high (98%) to plasma protein; principally alpha$_1$-acid glycoprotein.

Biotransformation
Extensively metabolized in the liver. Primary metabolic route through N-oxidation of the quinuclidin ring and 4R-hydroxylation of tetrahydroisoquinoline ring to active metabolite 4R-hydroxy solifenacin, and three inactive metabolites.

Half-life
Elimination—45 to 68 hours following chronic dosing.

Time to peak concentration
3 to 8 hours following oral administration.

Steady state
32.3 to 62.9 ng/mL for the 5 and 10 mg dose, respectively.

Elimination
Urine: 69.2%; less then 15% intact solifenacin; major metabolites N-oxide of solifenacin, 4R-hydroxy solifenacin, and 4R-hydroxy-N-oxide of solifenacin.

Fecal: 22.5%, major metabolite 4R-hydroxy solifenacin.

Precautions to Consider

Carcinogenicity
Carcinogenicity studies with solifenacin succinate were done in mice and rats. No increase in tumors was found in a 104-week study in male and female mice given doses up to 200 mg/kg/day (5 and 9 times the human exposure at the maximum recommended human dose [MRHD]), and in male and female rats given doses up to 20 and 15 mg/kg/day, respectively (<1 times exposure at the MRHD) for 104 weeks.

Mutagenicity
Solifenacin succinate was negative for mutagenicity in the *in vitro* Salmonella typhimurium or Escherichia coli test, or the chromosomal aberration test in human peripheral blood lymphocytes with or without metabolic activation, or the *in vivo* micronucleus test in rats.

Pregnancy/Reproduction
Fertility—Fertility studies done in mice given doses 250 mg/kg/day (13 times exposure at the MRHD) of solifenacin succinate or male rats given 50 mg/kg/day (<1 times exposure at the MRHD) or female rats given 100 mg/kg/day (1.7 times exposure at the MRHD) had no effect on reproductive function, fertility or early embryonic development of the fetus.

Pregnancy—Adequate and well controlled studies in humans have not been done. Studies in animals have shown that solifenacin succinate can cause adverse effects in the fetus. Because animal reproduction studies are not alway predictive of human response, solifenacin should be used during pregnancy only if the potential benefit justifies the potential risk to the fetus.

Studies done in pregnant mice given solifenacin succinate at doses of 30 mg/kg/day (1.2 times exposure at the MRHD) produced no embryotoxic or teratogenic effects. However, pregnant mice given doses of 100 mg/kg day and greater (3.6 times exposure at the MRHD) resulted in reduced fetal body weights, and pregnant mice given 250 mg/kg (7.9 times exposure at the MRHD) resulted in increased incidence of cleft palate. In utero and lactational exposures to maternal doses of 100 mg/kg and greater (3.6 times exposure at the MRHD) resulted in reduced peripartum and postnatal survival, reductions in body weight gain and delayed physical development (eye opening and vaginal patency). Increase in the percentage of male offspring was also observed in litters exposed to doses of 250 mg/kg/day (7.9 times exposure at the MRHD). No embryotoxic effects were observed in rats given up to 50 mg/kg day (<1 times the MRHD) or in rabbits given up to 50 mg/kg day (1.8 times exposure at the MRHD).

FDA Pregnancy Category C

Labor and delivery—The effect of solifenacin on labor and delivery in humans has not been studied.

Labor and delivery—Studies in mice given 30 mg/kg day (1.2 times the MRHD) revealed no effects on delivery; however, mice administered 100 mg/kg/day (3.6 times the MRHD) of solifenacin succinate revealed increased peripartum pup mortality.

Breast-feeding
It is not known whether solifenacin is distributed into human breast milk. Because many drugs are distributed into human milk, solifenacin should not be administered to nursing women. A decision should be made whether to discontinue nursing or to discontinue solifenacin.

Pups of female mice treated with solifenacin succinate at doses of 100 mg/kg/day (3.6 times exposure at the MRHD) or greater revealed reduced body weights, postpartum pup mortality or delays in the onset of reflex and physical development during the lactation period.

Pediatrics
Safety and effectiveness of solifenacin in pediatric patients have not been established.

Geriatrics
Appropriate studies performed to date have not demonstrated geriatrics-specific problems that would limit the usefulness of solifenacin in the elderly.

Drug interactions and/or related problems
The following drug interactions and/or related problems have been selected on the basis of their potential clinical significance (possible mechanism in parentheses where appropriate)—not necessarily inclusive (» = major clinical significance):

Note: Combinations containing any of the following medications, depending on the amount present, may also interact with this medication.

» CYP3A4 inhibitors such as
» Ketoconazole
(may increase solifenacin C_{max} and AUC; reduced dose of solifenacin is recommended)

Medications that prolong the QT interval
(care should be taken due to the potential for QT prolongation)

Laboratory value alterations
The following have been selected on the basis of their potential clinical significance (possible effect in parentheses where appropriate)—not necessarily inclusive (» = major clinical significance).

With diagnostic test results

Cardiac Electrophysiology or
ECG
(may be prolonged in patients with a known history of QT prolongation or patients taking medication known to prolong the QT interval)

Medical considerations/Contraindications
The medical considerations/contraindications included have been selected on the basis of their potential clinical significance (reasons given in parentheses where appropriate)—not necessarily inclusive (» = major clinical significance).

Except under special circumstances, this medication should not be used when the following medical problem exists:

» Hypersensitivity to solifenacin or any components of the product
» Gastric rentention or
» Narrow-angle glaucoma, uncontrolled or
» Urinary rentention
(use is contraindicated in patients with these conditions)

Risk-benefit should be considered when the following medical problems exist:

» Bladder outflow obstruction
(caution; risk of urinary retention)

Gastrointestinal obstructive disorders or
Decreased gastrointestinal motility
(administer with caution in patients with these conditions)

» Hepatic function impairment, moderate
(administer with caution in patients with reduced hepatic function [Child-Pugh B])

» Hepatic function impairment, severe
(use is not recommended in patients with severe hepatic impairment [Child-Pugh C])

Narrow-angle glaucoma, controlled
(use with caution in patients being treated for narrow-angle glaucoma)

QT prolongation, congenital or acquired
(should use with caution; solifenacin may make this condition worse)

» Renal function impairment, severe
(dose modification is recommended)

Side/Adverse Effects
The following side/adverse effects have been selected on the basis of their potential clinical significance (possible signs and symptoms in parentheses where appropriate)—not necessarily inclusive:

Those indicating need for medical attention only if they continue or are bothersome
Incidence more frequent

Constipation (difficulty having a bowel movement (stool)); ***dry mouth***

Incidence less frequent

Blurred vision; cough; depression (discouragement; feeling sad or empty; irritability; lack of appetite; loss of interest or pleasure; tiredness; trouble concentrating; trouble sleeping); ***dizziness; dry eyes; dyspepsia*** (acid or sour stomach; belching; heartburn; indigestion; stomach discomfort upset or pain); ***edema lower limb*** (swelling of the legs); ***fatigue*** (unusual tiredness or weakness); ***hypertension*** (blurred vision; dizziness; nervousness; headache pounding in the ears; slow or fast heartbeat); ***influenza*** (chills; cough; diarrhea; fever; general feeling of discomfort or illness; headache; joint pain; loss of appetite; muscle aches and pains; nausea; runny nose; shivering; sore throat; sweating; trouble sleeping; unusual tiredness or weakness; vomiting); ***nausea; pharyngitis*** (body aches or pain; congestion; cough; dryness or soreness of throat; fever; hoarseness; runny nose; tender, swollen glands in neck; trouble in swallowing; voice changes); ***upper abdominal pain*** (upper stomach pain); ***urinary retention*** (decrease in urine volume decrease in frequency of urination difficulty in passing urine [dribbling] painful urination); ***urinary tract infection*** (bladder pain; bloody or cloudy urine; difficult, burning, or painful urination; frequent urge to urinate; lower back or side pain); ***vomiting***

Overdose

For more information on the management of overdose or unintentional ingestion, **contact a poison control center** (see *Poison Control Center Listing*).

Clinical effects of overdose

The following effects have been selected on the basis of their potential clinical significance (possible signs and symptoms in parentheses where appropriate)—not necessarily inclusive:

Acute

Anticholinergic effects, severe (blurred vision; dizziness; drowsiness; confusion; delirium or hallucinations; nausea; vomiting; constipation; difficult urination; eye pain; dry eyes, mouth, nose, or throat; flushing or redness of face; troubled breathing; fast heartbeat)

Chronic

Anticholinergic effects, intolerable (fixed and dilated pupils; blurred vision; failure of heel-to-toe exam; tremors; dry skin)

Treatment of overdose

Treatment is essentially symptomatic and supportive.

To decrease absorption—

Emptying the stomach with gastric lavage.

Supportive care—

Patients in whom intentional overdose is confirmed or suspected should be referred for psychiatric consultation.

Patient Consultation

As an aid to patient consultation, refer to *Advice for the Patient, Solifenacin (Systemic)*.

In providing consultation, consider emphasizing the following selected information (» = major clinical significance):

Before using this medication

» Conditions affecting use, especially:

Hypersensitivity to solifenacin or any of its ingredients

Pregnancy—Adequate and well controlled studies in humans have not been done. Studies in animals have shown that solifenacin succinate can cause adverse effects in the fetus. Because animal reproduction studies are not alway predictive of human response, solifenacin should be used during pregnancy only if the potential benefit justifies the potential risk to the fetus.

Breast-feeding—It is not known whether solifenacin is distributed into breast milk. Because many drugs are distributed into breast milk, solifenacin should not be administered to nursing women. A decision should be made whether to discontinue nursing or to discontinue solifenacin.

Use in children—Safety and effectiveness of solifenacin in pediatric patients have not been established.

Other medications, especially CYP3A4 inhibitors such as ketoconazole.

Other medical problems, especially bladder outflow obstruction, gastric retention, hepatic function impairment (moderate or severe), narrow-angle glaucoma (uncontrolled), QT prolongation, congenital or acquired, renal function impairment, or urinary retention

Proper use of this medication

Taking solifenacin with liquids and swallowing the tablet whole.

» Proper dosing

Missed dose: If you miss a dose of this medicine, skip the missed dose and go back to your regular dosing schedule. Do not double doses.

Proper storage

Precautions while using this medication

» Caution during exercise or hot weather, overheating may result in heat exhaustion

» Caution if vision problems occur; caution while driving or doing dangerous activities

» Constipation; call your doctor if you get severe stomach pain or become constipated for 3 or more days.

Possible dryness of mouth; checking with physician or dentist if dry mouth continues

General Dosing Information

It is important to take the tablet with liquids and swallow it whole.

Solifenacin can be taken with or without food.

Oral Dosage Forms

SOLIFENACIN SUCCINATE TABLETS

Usual adult dose

Urologic disorders, symptoms of—

Oral, one tablet (5 mg) once daily. If well tolerated the dose may be increased to 10 mg once daily.

Note: For patients with severe renal impairment (CL_{cr} <30 mL per min), a dose greater than 5 mg is not recommended.

For patients with moderate hepatic impairment (Child-Pugh B), a dose greater than 5 mg is not recommended. In patients with severe hepatic impairment (Child-Pugh C), solifenacin is not recommended.

For patients receiving therapeutic doses of ketoconazole or other CYP3A4 inhibitors, doses of solifenacin should not exceed the 5 mg daily dose.

Usual adult prescribing limits

Up to 10 mg daily.

Usual pediatric dose

Safety and efficacy have not been established.

Usual geriatric dose

See *Usual adult dose.*

Usual geriatric prescribing limits

See *Usual adult prescribing limits.*

Strength(s) usually available

U.S.—

5 mg (Rx) [*VESIcare* (lactose monohydrate; corn starch; hypromellose 2910; magnesium stearate; talc; polyethylene glycol 8000; titanium dioxide with yellow ferric oxide)].

10 mg [*VESIcare* (lactose monohydrate; corn starch; hypromellose 2910; magnesium stearate; talc; polyethylene glycol 8000; titanium dioxide with red ferric oxide)].

Packaging and storage

Store between at 25 °C (77 °F), excursions permitted from 15 °C to 30 °C (59 to 86 °F).

Auxiliary labeling

- May cause drowsiness. Be careful while driving or operating machinery. Use caution until you become familiar with its effects.
- May cause blurred vision.
- Dry mouth may occur when taking this medicine.

Developed: 01/18/2005

SOMATREM—See *Growth Hormone (Systemic)*

SOMATROPIN, RECOMBINANT—See *Growth Hormone (Systemic)*

SORAFENIB Systemic†

VA CLASSIFICATION (Primary): AN900

Commonly used brand name(s): *Nexavar.*

Note: For a listing of dosage forms and brand names by country availability, see *Dosage Forms* section(s).

†Not commercially available in Canada.

Category

Antineoplastic.

Indications

Accepted

Carcinoma, advanced renal (treatment)—Sorafenib is indicated for the treatment of patients with advanced renal cell carcinoma.

Pharmacology/Pharmacokinetics

Physicochemical characteristics

Molecular weight—Sorafenib: 637 g/mole.

Solubility—Practically insoluble in aqueous media and slightly soluble in ethanol and soluble in PEG 400.

Mechanism of action/Effect

Sorafenib is a multikinase inhibitor that decreases tumor cell proliferation *in vitro*. Sorafenib has been shown to interact with multiple intracellular (CRAF, BRAF, and mutant BRAF) and cell surface kinases (KIT, FLT-3, VEGFR-2, VEGFR-3 and PDGFR-β). Many of these kinases are thought to be involved in angiogenesis.

Absorption

Bioavailability is 38 to 49% following oral administration in the fasted state or when given with a moderate-fat meal. Bioavailability is reduced by 29% when given with a high fat meal.

Protein binding

Very high, 99.5% to human plasma proteins.

Biotransformation

Primarily in the liver by CYP3A4 and glucuronidation mediated by UGT1A9 to eight metabolites, five of which have been detected in plasma. Main metabolite pyridine N-oxide comprises of 9-16% of circulating analytes while sorafenib accounts for 70-85% of the circulating analytes in plasma at steady state.

Half-life

Elimination—Approximately 25 to 48 hours

Time to peak plasma concentration

Approximately 3 hours

Elimination

Fecal: 77% of the administered oral dose of 100 mg; 51% unchanged drug

Urine: 19% of the administered oral dose of 100 mg, as glucuronidated metabolites

Precautions to Consider

Carcinogenicity

Carcinogenicity studies with sorafenib have not been conducted.

Mutagenicity

Sorafenib was clastogenic in an *in vitro* mammalian cell assay with metabolic activation. Sorafenib was negative for mutagenicity in the Ames bacterial cell assay and was not clastogenic in an *in vivo* mouse micronucleus assay.

One intermediate, in the manufacturing process, which is also present in the final drug substance was positive for mutagenicity in an *in vitro* bacterial cell assay (Ames test) when tested independently.

Pregnancy/Reproduction

Fertility—Studies in animals to evaluate the effects of sorafenib on fertility have not been conducted. Results from repeat-dose toxicity studies suggest a potential for sorafenib to impair reproductive performance and fertility. Adverse effects including testicular atrophy or degeneration, degeneration of epididymis, prostate, and seminal vesicles, central necrosis of the corpora lutea and arrest of follicular development were observed in male or female rats given daily oral doses ≥30 mg/m². Dogs given sorafenib showed tubular degeneration in the testes at doses of 600 mg/m²/day and oligospermia at doses of 1200 mg/m²/day.

Pregnancy—Sorafenib crosses the placenta and has been shown to cause adverse effects. Risk-benefit must be carefully considered when this medication is required in life threatening situations or in serious diseases for which other medications cannot be used or are ineffective.

Studies in rats and rabbits given doses below the recommended human dose have shown sorafenib to be teratogenic and to induce embryofetal toxicity (i.e., increased post-implantation loss, resorptions, skeletal retardations, and retarded fetal weight). Adverse intrauterine development effects were seen at doses ≥1.2 mg/m²/day in rats and 3.6 mg/m²/day in rabbits. A no observed adverse effect level was not defined for either species.

FDA Pregnancy Category D.

Breast-feeding

It is not known whether sorafenib is distributed into breast milk. However, sorafenib is distributed into the milk of lactating rats. Because many drugs are distributed in human milk and because the effects of sorafenib on infants have not been studied, women should be advised against breast-feeding while receiving sorafenib.

Pediatrics

Safety and effectiveness in pediatric patients have not been established.

Geriatrics

Appropriate studies performed to date have not demonstrated geriatrics-specific problems that would limit the usefulness of sorafenib in the elderly. However, greater sensitivity of some older individuals cannot be ruled out.

Pharmacogenetics

Japanese patients showed a 45% lower systemic exposure compared with Caucasian patients. Clinical significance is unknown.

Surgical

Temporary interruption of sorafenib therapy is recommended in patients undergoing major surgical procedures.

Drug interactions and/or related problems

The following drug interactions and/or related problems have been selected on the basis of their potential clinical significance (possible mechanism in parentheses where appropriate)—not necessarily inclusive (» = major clinical significance):

Note: Combinations containing any of the following medications, depending on the amount present, may also interact with this medication.

CYP2B6 substrate or
CYP2C8 substrate
(caution as systemic exposure may increase when co-administered with sorafenib)

CYP3A4 inducers such as
Carbamazepine or
Dexamethasone or
Phenobarbital or
Phenytoin or
Rifampin or
St. John's wort
(may increase metabolism of sorafenib and decrease its concentration)

» Doxorubicin
(caution should be used; concomitant administration with sorafenib increased doxorubicin AUC 21%)

» UGT1A1 substrates such as
Irinotecan
(caution should be used; increased irinotecan AUC 26-42% and active metabolite SN-38 AUC 67-120%)

UGT1A9 substrates
(systemic exposure of substrates may increase)

Warfarin
(infrequent bleeding events or elevations in the International Normalized Ratio (INR) have been reported; patients should be monitored regularly for changes in prothrombin time, INR, or clinical bleeding)

Laboratory value alterations

The following have been selected on the basis of their potential clinical significance (possible effect in parentheses where appropriate)—not necessarily inclusive (» = major clinical significance).

With diagnostic test results

Alkaline phosphatase values, serum
Transaminases
(transient increases may occur)

Bilirubin
(may be increased)

Amylase or
Lipase
(elevated levels very common and many were transient)

Medical considerations/Contraindications

The medical considerations/contraindications included have been selected on the basis of their potential clinical significance (reasons given in parentheses where appropriate)—not necessarily inclusive (» = major clinical significance).

Except under special circumstances, this medication should not be used when the following medical problem exists:

» Hypersensitivity to sorafenib or to any of its components

Risk-benefit should be considered when the following medical problems exist:

Hepatic function impairment
(sorafenib has not been studied in Child-Pugh C hepatic impairment; systemic exposure and safety comparable in Child-Pugh A and Child-Pugh B hepatic impairment)

Renal function impairment, severe
(caution should be used; sorafenib has not been studied in patient with severe renal impairment [CrCl <30 ml/min] or undergoing dialysis)

Patient monitoring

The following may be especially important in patient monitoring (other tests may be warranted in some patients, depending on condition; » = major clinical significance):

Blood pressure
(should be monitored weekly during first 6 weeks of sorafenib therapy; thereafter, should be monitored and treated if required, in accordance with standard medical practice)

Side/Adverse Effects

The following side/adverse effects have been selected on the basis of their potential clinical significance (possible signs and symptoms in parentheses where appropriate)—not necessarily inclusive:

Those indicating need for medical attention

Incidence more frequent

Hemorrhage (bleeding gums; coughing up blood; difficulty in breathing or swallowing; dizziness; headache; increased menstrual flow or vaginal bleeding; nosebleeds; paralysis; prolonged bleeding from cuts; red or dark brown urine; red or black, tarry stools; shortness of breath); ***hypertension*** (blurred vision; dizziness; nervousness; headache; pounding in the ears; slow or fast heartbeat)

Reported during clinical trials

Anemia (pale skin, troubled breathing with exertion, unusual bleeding or bruising, unusual tiredness or weakness); ***hypersensitivity reactions*** (difficulty in breathing and/or swallowing; fever; hives; nausea; reddening of the skin, especially around ears; swelling of eyes, face, or inside of nose; unusual tiredness or weakness); ***hypertensive crisis*** (severe chest pain; enlarged pupils; fast or slow heartbeat; severe headache; increased sensitivity of eyes to light; increased sweating, possibly with fever or cold; clammy skin; stiff or sore neck); ***hyponatremia*** (coma; confusion; convulsions; decreased urine output; dizziness; fast or irregular heartbeat; headache; increased thirst; muscle pain or cramps; nausea or vomiting; shortness of breath; swelling of face, ankles, or hands; unusual tiredness or weakness); ***hypophosphatemia*** (bone pain; convulsions; loss of appetite; trouble breathing; unusual tiredness or weakness); ***hypothyroidism*** (constipation; depressed mood; dry skin and hair; feeling cold; hair loss; hoarseness or husky voice; muscle cramps and stiffness; slowed heartbeat; weight gain; unusual tiredness or weakness); ***increased bilirubin*** (chills; clay-colored stools; dark urine; dizziness; fever; headache; itching; loss of appetite; nausea; abdominal or stomach pain; area rash; unpleasant breath odor; unusual tiredness or weakness; vomiting of blood; yellow eyes or skin); ***leukopenia*** (black, tarry stools; chest pain; chills; cough; fever; painful or difficult urination; shortness of breath; sore throat; sores, ulcers, or white spots on lips or in mouth; swollen glands; unusual bleeding or bruising; unusual tiredness or weakness); ***lymphopenia*** (fever or chills; cough or hoarseness; lower back or side pain; painful or difficult urination); ***myalgia*** (joint pain; swollen joints; muscle aching or cramping; muscle pains or stiffness; difficulty in moving); ***myocardial infarction*** (chest pain or discomfort; pain or discomfort in arms, jaw, back or neck; shortness of breath; nausea; sweating; vomiting); ***myocardial ischemia*** (chest pain or discomfort; nausea; pain or discomfort in arms, jaw, back or neck; shortness of breath; sweating; vomiting); ***neutropenia*** (black, tarry, stools; chills; cough; fever; lower back or side pain; painful or difficult urination; pale skin; shortness of breath; sore throat; ulcers, sores, or white spots in mouth; unusual bleeding or bruising; unusual tiredness or weakness); ***pancreatitis*** (bloating; chills; constipation; darkened urine; fast heartbeat; fever; indigestion; loss of appetite; nausea; pains in stomach, side, or abdomen, possibly radiating to the back; vomiting; yellow eyes or skin); ***thrombocytopenia*** (black, tarry stools; bleeding gums; blood in urine or stools; pinpoint red spots on skin; unusual bleeding or bruising); ***tinnitus*** (continuing ringing or buzzing or other unexplained noise in ears; hearing loss)

Those indicating need for medical attention only if they continue or are bothersome

Incidence more frequent

Abdominal pain (stomach pain); ***alopecia*** (hair loss; thinning of hair); ***anorexia*** (loss of appetite; weight loss); ***constipation*** (difficulty having a bowel movement (stool)); ***cough; diarrhea; dry skin; dyspnea*** (shortness of breath; difficult or labored breathing; tightness in chest; wheezing); ***headache; fatigue*** (unusual tiredness or weakness); ***hand-foot skin reaction*** (blistering, peeling, redness, and/or swelling of palms of hands or bottoms of feet; numbness, pain, tingling, or unusual sensations in palms of hands or bottoms of feet); ***joint pain; nausea; neuropathy-sensory*** (burning, tingling, numbness or pain in the hands, arms, feet, or legs; sensation of pins and needles; stabbing pain); ***pruritus*** (itching skin); ***rash; vomiting; weight loss***

Reported during clinical trials

Arthralgia (pain in joints; muscle pain or stiffness; difficulty in moving); ***asthenia*** (lack or loss of strength); ***bone pain; decreased appetite; dehydration*** (confusion; decreased urination; dizziness; dry mouth; fainting; increase in heart rate; lightheadedness; rapid breathing; sunken eye; thirst; unusual tiredness or weakness; wrinkled skin); ***depression*** (discouragement; feeling sad or empty; irritability; lack of appetite; loss of interest or pleasure; tiredness; trouble concentrating; trouble sleeping); ***dyspepsia*** (acid or sour stomach; belching; heartburn; indigestion; stomach discomfort upset or pain); ***dysphagia*** (loss of ability to use or understand speech or language); ***eczema*** (skin rash encrusted, scaly and oozing); ***erectile dysfunction*** (loss in sexual ability, desire, drive, or performance; decreased interest in sexual intercourse; inability to have or keep an erection); ***erythema*** (flushing, redness of skin; unusually warm skin); ***erythema multiforme*** (blistering, peeling, loosening of skin; chills; cough; diarrhea; fever; itching; joint or muscle pain; red irritated eyes; sore throat; sores, ulcers, or white spots in mouth or on lips; unusual tiredness or weakness); ***exfoliative dermatitis*** (cracks in the skin; loss of heat from the body; red, swollen skin, scaly skin); ***acne; flushing*** (feeling of warmth, redness of the face, neck, arms and occasionally, upper chest); ***folliculitis*** (burning, itching, and pain in hairy areas; pus at root of hair); ***gastritis*** (burning feeling in chest or stomach; tenderness in stomach area; stomach upset; indigestion); ***gastrointestinal reflux*** (bloating; diarrhea; gas; heartburn; indigestion; loss of appetite; nausea; stomach pain; vomiting); ***gynecomastia*** (swelling of the breasts or breast soreness in both females and males); ***hoarseness*** (rough, scratchy sound to voice); ***infection*** (fever or chills; cough or hoarseness; lower back or side pain; painful or difficult urination); ***influenza-like illness*** (chills; cough; diarrhea; fever; general feeling of discomfort or illness; headache; joint pain; loss of appetite; muscle aches and pains; nausea; runny nose; shivering; sore throat; sweating; trouble sleeping; unusual tiredness or weakness; vomiting); ***mouth pain; mucositis*** (cracked lips; diarrhea; difficulty in swallowing; sores, ulcers, or white spots on lips, tongue, or inside mouth); ***muscle pain; pyrexia*** (fever); ***rhinorrhea*** (runny nose); ***stomatitis*** (swelling or inflammation of the mouth)

Overdose

For more information on the management of overdose or unintentional ingestion, **contact a poison control center** (see *Poison Control Center Listing*).

Clinical effects of overdose

The following effects have been selected on the basis of their potential clinical significance (possible signs and symptoms in parentheses where appropriate)—not necessarily inclusive:

Diarrhea; dermatologic events (flushing; impaired wound healing; increased sweating; suppressed reaction to skin tests; thin, fragile skin)

Treatment of overdose

There is no known specific antidote to sorafenib. Treatment is generally symptomatic and supportive.

Supportive care—

In cases of suspected overdose, sorafenib should be withheld and supportive care instituted.

Patients in whom intentional overdose is confirmed or suspected should be referred for psychiatric consultation.

Patient Consultation

As an aid to patient consultation, refer to *Advice for the Patient, Sorafenib (Systemic).*

In providing consultation, consider emphasizing the following selected information (» = major clinical significance):

Before using this medication

» Conditions affecting use, especially:

Hypersensitivity to sorafenib or to any of its ingredients.

Pregnancy—Use not recommended; advisability of using contraception; telling physician immediately if pregnancy is suspected.

Breast-feeding—Not recommended.

Use in children—Safety and effectiveness in pediatric patients not established
Use in the elderly—May have greater sensitivity
Other medications, especially doxorubicin or UGT1A1 metabolizers such as irinotecan

Proper use of this medication

» The importance of reading the patient information leaflet before taking sorafenib and each time prescription is refilled.
» Taking exactly as prescribed.
» Swallowing the tablet whole with water.
» Taking on an empty stomach (at least 1 hour before or 2 hours after a meal).
» The importance of using effective birth control during sorafenib treatment and for at least 2 weeks after stopping treatment for both male and female patients.
» Proper dosing
Missed dose: Taking as soon as possible; not taking if almost time for next scheduled dose; not doubling doses
» Proper storage

Precautions while using this medication

» Regular visits to physician to check your blood pressure.
» Checking with physician if any redness, pain, swelling or blisters on the palms of hands or soles of feet.
» Checking with physician if any episodes of chest pain or other symptoms of cardiac ischemia and/or infarction.
» Promptly reporting any episodes of bleeding.

Side/adverse effects

Signs of potential side effects, especially anemia, hemorrhage, hypertension, hypersensitivity reactions, hypertensive crisis, hyponatremia, hypophosphatemia, hypothyroidism, increased bilirubin, leukopenia, lymphopenia, myalgia, myocardial infarction, myocardial ischemia, neutropenia, pancreatitis, thrombocytopenia, tinnitus

General Dosing Information

Sorafenib treatment should continue until the patient is no longer clinically benefiting or until unacceptable toxicity occurs.

For treatment of adverse effects

Management of dermatologic toxicities may include topical therapies for symptomatic relief, temporary interruption and/or dose modification, or in severe or persistent cases, discontinuation of sorafenib therapy.

In cases of severe or persistent hypertension, temporary or permanent discontinuation of sorafenib should be considered.

If any bleeding event necessitates medical intervention, permanent discontinuation of sorafenib should be considered.

For patients who develop cardiac ischemia and/or infarction, temporary or permanent discontinuation should be considered.

Oral Dosage Forms

SORAFENIB TABLETS

Usual adult dose

Carcinoma, renal—
Oral, 400 mg (2 x 200 mg tablets) taken twice daily, without food (at least 1 hour before or 2 hours after a meal).

Note: For Skin Toxicity Grade 1: Any occurrence—continue sorafenib treatment and consider topical therapy for symptomatic relief.

For Skin Toxicity Grade 2:
- 1st occurrence—Continue sorafenib treatment and consider topical therapy for symptomatic relief.
- No improvement within 7 days or 2nd or 3rd occurrence—Interrupt sorafenib treatment until toxicity resolves to grade 0-1; when resuming treatment decrease dose by one dose level (400 mg daily or 400 mg every other day).
- 4th occurrence—Discontinue sorafenib treatment.

For Skin Toxicity Grade 3:
- 1st or 2nd occurrence—Interrupt sorafenib treatment until toxicity resolves to grade 0-1; when resuming treatment decrease dose by one dose level (400 mg daily or 400 mg every other day).
- 3rd occurrence—Discontinue sorafenib treatment.

Usual pediatric dose

Safety and efficacy have not been established.

Usual geriatric dose

See *Usual adult dose*.

Strength(s) usually available

U.S.—
200 mg (Rx) [*Nexavar* (croscarmellose sodium; microcrystalline cellulose; hypromellose; sodium lauryl sulphate; magnesium stearate; polyethylene glycol; titanium dioxide; ferric oxide red)].

Packaging and storage

Store at 25 °C (77 °F), excursions permitted to 15 to 30 °C (59 to 86 °F). Store in a dry place.

Developed: 12/30/2005

SOTALOL—See *Beta-adrenergic Blocking Agents (Systemic)*

SPARFLOXACIN—See *Fluoroquinolones (Systemic)*

SPIRONOLACTONE—See *Diuretics, Potassium-sparing (Systemic)*

SPIRONOLACTONE AND HYDROCHLOROTHIAZIDE—See *Diuretics, Potassium-sparing and Hydrochlorothiazide (Systemic)*

STANOZOLOL—See *Anabolic Steroids (Systemic)*

STAVUDINE Systemic

VA CLASSIFICATION (Primary): AM890

Commonly used brand name(s): *Zerit; Zerit XR*.

Another commonly used name is d4T.

Note: For a listing of dosage forms and brand names by country availability, see *Dosage Forms* section(s).

Category

Antiviral (systemic).

Indications

Accepted

Human immunodeficiency virus (HIV) infection (treatment)—Stavudine in combination with other antiretroviral agents is indicated for the treatment of HIV–1 infection. Additionally, stavudine is indicated for the treatment of patients with HIV infection who have received prolonged previous treatment with zidovudine.

The duration of clinical benefit from antiretroviral therapy may be limited. If disease progression occurs during stavudine treatment, an alternative antiretroviral therapy is recommended.

Pharmacology/Pharmacokinetics

Physicochemical characteristics

Molecular weight—224.22.

Mechanism of action/Effect

Stavudine, a nucleoside analog of thymidine, is rapidly phosphorylated by cellular enzymes to its active moiety, stavudine triphosphate. Stavudine triphosphate inhibits human immunodeficiency virus (HIV) replication by competing with the natural substrate, deoxythymidine triphosphate, and by inhibiting viral DNA synthesis by acting as a terminator of chain elongation. In addition, stavudine triphosphate inhibits cellular DNA polymerases beta and gamma, and markedly reduces the synthesis of mitochondrial DNA.

A concentration of stavudine ranging from 0.009 to 4 micromolesis required to inhibit HIV replication by 50% *in vitro* . The *in vitro* potency of stavudine against HIV is similar to that of zidovudine.

Absorption

Stavudine is rapidly absorbed with an oral bioavailability of 68.2 to 104.6% in adults, and 44.2 to 108.6% in children (ages 5 weeks to 15 years).

Peak plasma concentrations (C_{max}) and area under the plasma concentration-time curve (AUC) increased in proportion to dose.

Stavudine may be taken with food or on an empty stomach. Administration with food results in a decrease in C_{max} of approximately 45%; however, the systemic availability, as measured by the AUC, remains unchanged.

Distribution

Crosses the blood-brain barrier and distributes into the cerebrospinal fluid (CSF); the mean CSF to plasma concentration ratio was59% (range, 24 to 94%) when measured in 8 children. Binding of stavudine to serum proteins was negligible over the concentration range of 0.01 to 11.4 micrograms/mL. Also, stavudine distributes equally between red blood cells and plasma.

Vol_D—
- Adults: 0.8 to 1.1 L per kg (L/kg)
- Children: Approximately 0.73 L/kg (following 1 hour IV infusion).

Protein binding

Negligible.

Biotransformation

Phosphorylated intracellularly to stavudine triphosphate, the active substrate for HIV-reverse transcriptase.

Half-life

Normal renal function—
- Adults: 0.8 to 1.5 hours (intravenous); 1.14 to 1.74 hours (oral).
- Children (5 weeks to 15 years): 0.83 to 1.39 hours (intravenous); 0.7 to 1.22 hours (oral).
- Neonates (14 to 28 days): 1.3 to 1.88 hours (oral).
- Neonates (day of birth): 3.26 to 7.28 hours (oral).

Renal function impairment (creatinine clearance >50 mL/min)—
- Approximately 1.3 to 2.1 hours

Renal function impairment (creatinine clearance 26 to 50 mL/min)—
- Approximately 1 to 6 hours

Renal function impairment (creatinine clearance 9 to 25 mL/min)—
- Approximately 3.7 to 5.5 hours.

Renal function impairment (hemodialysis patients)—
- Approximately 4.0 to 6.8 hours

Intracellular half-life of stavudine triphosphate—
- Approximately 3.5 hours.

Time to peak concentration

0.5 to 1.5 hour.

Peak serum concentration

Approximately 1.4 micrograms/mL (6.2 micromoles/L) after a single oral dose of 70 mg.

Elimination

Adults
- Renal—16 to 62% recovered in urine
- Total body clearance—6.0 to 10.6 mL/min/kg (following 1 hour IV infusion)
- Apparent oral clearance—5.4 to 10.6 mL/min/kg (following single oral dose)

Children (ages 5 weeks to 15 years)
- Renal—18 to 50% recovered in urine
- Total body clearance—5.99 to 13.51 mL/min/kg (following single oral dose)
- Apparent oral clearance—9.46 to 18.04 mL/min/kg (following single oral dose)

Neonates (ages 14 to 28 days)
- Apparent oral clearance—5.59 to 17.45 mL/min/kg (following single oral dose)

Neonates (day of birth)
- Apparent oral clearance—2.28 to 7.88 mL/min/kg (following single oral dose)

Those with renal impairment

Creatinine clearance >50 mL/min
- Apparent oral clearance—278 to 392 mL/min
- Renal clearance—102 to 232 mL/min

Creatinine clearance 26 to 50 mL/min
- Apparent oral clearance—152 to 230 mL/min
- Renal clearance—55 to 91 mL/min

Creatinine clearance 9 to 25 mL/min
- Apparent oral clearance—91 to 141 mL/min
- Renal clearance—14 to 20 mL/min

Creatinine clearance for hemodialysis patients (determined while patients were off dialysis)
- Apparent oral clearance—88 to 122 mL/min

Approximately 50% of an administered dose undergoes nonrenal elimination. Although the exact metabolic fate is unknown, stavudine may be cleaved to thymine, and the subsequent degradation and/or utilization of thymine may account for the unrecovered stavudine.

In dialysis—
- Hemodialysis clearance of stavudine was 120 ± 18 mL per minute (mean ± standard deviation) in a study of 12 patients.
- Stavudine dose recovered in the dialysate, timed to occur between 2 to 6 hours post-dose, was 31 ± 5 % (mean ± standard deviation).
- It is not know whether stavudine is removed by peritoneal dialysis.

Precautions to Consider

Carcinogenicity

From 2-year studies in mice and rats, stavudine was not carcinogenic at doses equivalent to 39 and 168 times the recommended human clinical exposures (AUC), respectively.

Mutagenicity

No evidence of mutagenicity was found in the Ames test, *Escherichia coli* reverse mutation assay, or the CHO/HGPRT mammalian cell forward gene mutation assay, with and without metabolic activation. Positive results were produced in the *in vitro* human lymphocyte clastogenesis and mouse fibroblast assays, and in the *in vivo* mouse micronucleus test. In the *in vitro* assays, stavudine produced an increased frequency of chromosome aberrations in human lymphocytes at concentrations of 25 to 250 micrograms per mL (mcg/mL), without metabolic activation, and increased the frequency of transformed foci in mouse fibroblast cells at concentrations of 25 to 2500 mcg/mL, with and without metabolic activation. In the *in vivo* micronucleus assay, stavudine was clastogenic in bone marrow cells of mice following administration of oral doses of 600 to 2000 mg per kg of body weight (mg/kg) per day for 3 days.

Pregnancy/Reproduction

Fertility—No evidence of impaired fertility was seen in rats given stavudine at doses that resulted in peak serum concentrations that were up to 216 times those observed in humans who received a clinical dosage of 1 mg/kg per day.

Pregnancy—*An Antiretroviral Pregnancy Registry has been established to monitor the outcomes of pregnant women exposed to stavudine. Physicians are encouraged by the manufacturer to register patients by calling (800) 258-4263.*

Fatal lactic acidosis has been reported in pregnant women who received the combination of didanosine and stavudine with other antiretroviral agents. It is unclear if pregnancy augments the risk of lactic acidosis/hepatic steatosis syndrome reported in non-pregnant individuals receiving nucleoside analogues. The combination of didanosine and stavudine should be used with caution during pregnancy and is recommended only if the potential benefit clearly outweighs the potential risk.

Adequate and well-controlled studies have not been done in humans. It is not known whether stavudine crosses the placenta in humans. Also, it is not known whether stavudine reduces perinatal transmission of HIV infection, as does zidovudine. Stavudine should be used during pregnancy only if clearly needed.

Stavudine crosses the placenta in rats. Reproduction studies done in rats and rabbits exposed to levels of stavudine up to 399 and 183 times, respectively, those seen at a clinical dosage in humans of 1 mg/kg per day, based on peak serum concentrations, revealed no evidence of teratogenicity. The incidence of common skeletal variation, unossified or incomplete ossification of sternebra, in fetuses was increased in rats at 399 times the human exposure, but not at 216 times the human exposure. A slight postimplantation loss was seen at 216 times the human exposure, but no effect was seen at approximately 135 times the human exposure. An increase in rat neonatal mortality occurred at 399 times the human exposure, while survival was unaffected at approximately 135 times the human exposure. The concentration of stavudine in rat fetal tissue was approximately one-half the concentration of that in maternal plasma.

FDA Pregnancy Category C.

Breast-feeding

It is not known whether stavudine is distributed into human breast milk. However, it has been found to pass readily into the milk of lactating rats. Mothers should not breast-feed if they are taking stavudine.

There have been case reports of HIV being transmitted from an infected mother to her nursing infant through breast milk. Therefore, breast-feeding is not recommended in HIV-infected mothers, to avoid potential postnatal transmission of HIV to the nursing infant.

Pediatrics

Various pharmacokinetic studies have been done in children between birth and 15 years of age. The pharmacokinetic and side effect profiles of stavudine in children and neonates were similar to those in adults.

Safety and efficacy of stavudine extended-release capsules have not been established in pediatric patients.

Geriatrics

Although appropriate studies on the relationship of age to the effects of stavudine have not been performed in the geriatric population, geriatrics-specific problems are not expected to limit the usefulness of stavudine in the elderly. However, elderly patients are more likely to have age-related renal function impairment which may require the monitoring of renal function and a possible reduction in dose.

Elderly patients should be closely monitored for signs and symptoms of peripheral neuropathy due to higher than expected incidence of peripheral neuropathy or peripheral neuropathic symptoms in elderly patients in the monotherapy Expanded Access Program for patients with advanced HIV infection.

Drug interactions and/or related problems

The following drug interactions and/or related problems have been selected on the basis of their potential clinical significance (possible mechanism in parentheses where appropriate)—not necessarily inclusive (» = major clinical significance):

Note: Combinations containing any of the following medications, depending on the amount present, may also interact with this medication.

Medications that may cause peripheral neuropathy, such as:
» Chloramphenicol or
» Cisplatin or
» Dapsone or
» Didanosine or
» Ethambutol or
» Ethionamide or
» Hydralazine or
» Isoniazid or
» Lithium or
» Metronidazole or
» Nitrofurantoin or
» Phenytoin or
» Vincristine or
» Zalcitabine
(since stavudine has been shown to cause peripheral neuropathy, other medications associated with the development of neuropathy should be avoided during stavudine therapy or, if concurrent use is necessary, used with caution)

» Didanosine or
» Hydroxyurea
(these medications in combination with stavudine may increase the risk of potentially fatal hepatotoxicity or pancreatitis; patients receiving concomitant therapy should be closely monitored for signs of liver toxicity)
(reported fatal lactic acidosis in pregnant women who received combination of stavudine and didanosine with other antiretroviral agents; combination of stavudine and didanosine should be used with caution during pregnancy and is recommended only if potential benefit clearly outweighs potential risk)

Doxorubicin or
Ribavirin
(phosphorylation of stavudine inhibited at relevant concentrations by doxorubicin and ribavirin as indicated by *in vitro* data)

» Zidovudine (AZT)
(*in vitro* studies detected an antagonistic antiviral effect between stavudine and zidovudine at a molar ratio of 20 to 1, respectively; concurrent use is not recommended until *in vivo* studies demonstrate that these medications are not antagonistic in their anti-HIV activity; zidovudine may competitively inhibit the intracellular phosphorylation of stavudine and so these two medications in combination should be avoided)

Laboratory value alterations

The following have been selected on the basis of their potential clinical significance (possible effect in parentheses where appropriate)—not necessarily inclusive (» = major clinical significance).

With physiology/laboratory test values
» Alanine aminotransferase (ALT [SGPT]) and
Alkaline phosphatase and
» Aspartate aminotransferase (AST [SGOT])
Gamma-glutamyl transferase (GGT)
(serum values have increased to greater than 5 times the upper normal limit, but returned to baseline when therapy was discontinued)

Amylase
Bilirubin
Mean corpuscular volume (MCV)
(may be increased)

Medical considerations/Contraindications

The medical considerations/contraindications included have been selected on the basis of their potential clinical significance (reasons given in parentheses where appropriate)—not necessarily inclusive (» = major clinical significance).

Except under special circumstances, this medication should not be used when the following medical problem exists:
» Hypersensitivity to stavudine or any components of the product

Risk-benefit should be considered when the following medical problems exist:
Alcoholism, active or a history of, or
Hepatic function impairment
(stavudine may exacerbate hepatic dysfunction in patients with pre-existing liver disease or a history of alcohol abuse)

» Hepatic disease or
» Risk factors for hepatic disease including:
» Female gender or
» Obesity or
» Prolonged nucleoside exposure
(lactic acidosis and severe hepatomegaly with steatosis have been reported in patients with the use of nucleoside analogues alone or in combination; fatal cases have been reported; female gender [majority of cases have been in women], obesity and prolonged nucleoside exposure may be risk factors; treatment should be suspended in patients with evidence of lactic acidosis or pronounced hepatotoxicity which may include hepatomegaly and steatosis even in the absence of marked transaminase elevations)

» Peripheral neuropathy
(stavudine may cause peripheral neuropathy; if symptoms of peripheral neuropathy develop, stavudine therapy should be interrupted; if symptoms resolve completely, reinstatement of therapy at a lower dose may be considered)

» Renal function impairment
(patients with renal function impairment may be at increased risk of toxicity due to decreased clearance of stavudine; patients with a creatinine clearance of < 50 mL/min [0.83 mL/sec] may require a reduction in dose)

Patient monitoring

The following may be especially important in patient monitoring (other tests may be warranted in some patients, depending on condition; » = major clinical significance):

» Alanine aminotransferase (ALT [SGPT]) and
Alkaline phosphatase and
» Aspartate aminotransferase (AST [SGOT])
(serum values may be increased to greater than 5 times the upper normal limit)

Amylase, serum and
Lipase, serum
(values may be increased)

» Signs and symptoms of hyperlactatemia/lactic acidosis syndrome
(generalized fatigue, digestive symptoms [nausea, vomiting, abdominal pain, and unexplained weight loss]; respiratory symptoms [tachypnea and dyspnea]; or neurologic symptoms [motor weakness] might be indicative of the development of these conditions; if lactic acidosis is suspected, stavudine should be immediately suspended; if lactic acidosis is confirmed, permanent discontinuation of stavudine should be considered)

Side/Adverse Effects

Note: Lactic acidosis and severe hepatomegaly with steatosis, including fatal cases, have been reported with the use of nucleoside analogues alone or in combination, including stavudine and other antiretroviral agents. Symptoms may include generalized fatigue, nausea, vomiting, abdominal pain, and sudden unexplained weight loss, tachypnea, dyspnea, or motor weakness. Patients should be informed of the importance of early recognition of symptoms of lactic acidosis.Fatal lactic acidosis has been reported in pregnant women who received the combination of didanosine and stavudine with other antiretroviral agents. The combination of didanosine and stavudine should be used with caution during pregnancy and is recommended only if the potential benefit clearly outweighs the potential risk.

Note: Fatal and nonfatal pancreatitis have occurred during therapy when stavudine was part of a combination regimen that included didanosine, with or without hydroxyurea, regardless of the degree of immunosuppression.

The following side/adverse effects have been selected on the basis of their potential clinical significance (possible signs and symptoms in parentheses where appropriate)—not necessarily inclusive:

Those indicating need for medical attention

Incidence more frequent

Peripheral neuropathy (tingling, burning, numbness, or pain in the hands or feet)

Note: Stavudine has been associated with *peripheral sensory neuropathy* which is dose related and can be severe. It occurs more frequently in patients being treated with neurotoxic drug therapy, including didanosine, in patients with advanced HIV infection, or in patients who have previously experienced peripheral neuropathy. *Peripheral sensory neuropathy* may also be seen with severe HIV disease. Therefore, differentiation between this side effect of stavudine and the complications of HIV disease may be difficult. *Peripheral neuropathy* occurred in 19 to 24% of adult patients with advanced HIV infection who were treated with stavudine, compared with 13% of adult patients with less advanced HIV infection who were treated with stavudine. It may resolve if stavudine therapy is stopped promptly. Symptoms may become worse temporarily after discontinuation of therapy. If symptoms resolve completely, resumption of treatment at a lower dose may be considered.

Incidence less frequent

Arthralgia (joint pain); ***hypersensitivity or allergic reaction*** (cough; difficulty swallowing; dizziness; fast heartbeat; hives; itching; puffiness or swelling of the eyelids or around the eyes, face, lips or tongue; shortness of breath; skin rash; tightness in chest; unusual tiredness or weakness; wheezing); ***myalgia*** (muscle pain)

Incidence rare

Anemia (unusual tiredness or weakness); ***pancreatitis*** (nausea, vomiting, severe abdominal pain)

Note: *Pancreatitis* was reported in 1% of patients enrolled in clinical trials.

Incidence not determined—Observed during clinical practice, estimates of frequency can not be determined

Hepatic steatosis (dark urine; light-colored stools; nausea and vomiting; upper right abdominal pain; yellow eyes and skin); ***hepatitis*** (dark urine; general tiredness and weakness; light-colored stools; nausea and vomiting; upper right abdominal pain; yellow eyes and skin); ***lactic acidosis*** (abdominal pain; dyspnea; generalized fatigue; motor weakness; nausea; sudden unexplained weight loss; tachypnea; vomiting); ***leukopenia*** (black, tarry stools; chest pain; chills; cough; fever; painful or difficult urination; shortness of breath; sore throat; sores, ulcers, or white spots on lips or in mouth; swollen glands; unusual bleeding or bruising; unusual tiredness or weakness); ***liver failure*** (headache; stomach pain; continuing vomiting; dark-colored urine; general feeling of tiredness or weakness; light-colored stools; yellow eyes or skin); ***severe motor weakness*** (shakiness and unsteady walk; unsteadiness. trembling, or other problems with muscle control or coordination); ***thrombocytopenia*** (black, tarry stools; bleeding gums; blood in urine or stools; pinpoint red spots on skin; unusual bleeding or bruising)

Note: In rare cases, *severe motor weakness* has been reported in patients receiving combination antiretroviral therapy including stavudine. Although most cases occurred in the setting of lactic acidosis, it may mimic the clinical presentation of Guillain-Barre syndrome including respiratory failure and symptoms may continue or worsen following discontinuation of therapy.

Those indicating need for medical attention only if they continue or are bothersome

Incidence more frequent

Anorexia (loss of appetite; weight loss); ***chills and fever; rash***

Incidence less frequent

Asthenia (lack of strength or energy; weakness); ***gastrointestinal disturbances*** (abdominal pain; diarrhea; loss of appetite; nausea or vomiting); ***headache; insomnia*** (difficulty in sleeping)

Incidence not determined—Observed during clinical practice, estimates of frequency can not be determined

Fat redistribution (breast enlargement; buffalo hump; central obesity; facial wasting; peripheral wasting)

Overdose

For more information on the management of overdose or unintentional ingestion, **contact a poison control center** (see *Poison Control Center Listing*).

Clinical effects of overdose

The following effects have been selected on the basis of their potential clinical significance (possible signs and symptoms in parentheses where appropriate)—not necessarily inclusive:

Acute

Adults treated with 12 to 24 times the recommended daily dose of stavudine showed no acute toxicity.

Chronic

Hepatotoxicity (dark or amber urine; loss of appetite; pale stools; stomach pain; unusual tiredness or weakness; yellow eyes or skin); ***peripheral neuropathy*** (tingling, burning, numbness, or pain in the hands or feet)

Treatment of overdose

To enhance elimination—

Stavudine can be removed by hemodialysis; the mean hemodialysis clearance of stavudine is 120 mL/min (±18 mL/min SD). Peritoneal dialysis has not been studied for stavudine.

Supportive care—

Patients in whom intentional overdose is confirmed or suspected should be referred for psychiatric consultation.

Patient Consultation

As an aid to patient consultation, refer to *Advice for the Patient, Stavudine (Systemic)*.

In providing consultation, consider emphasizing the following selected information (» = major clinical significance):

Before using this medication

» Conditions affecting use, especially:

Hypersensitivity to stavudine or any of its components

Pregnancy—Stavudine should be used during pregnancy only if the potential benefit clearly outweighs the potential risk. In addition, fatal lactic acidosis has been reported in pregnant women who received the combination of stavudine and didanosine with other antiretroviral agents.

Breast-feeding—Breast-feeding is not recommended, because of potential postnatal transmission of HIV to the nursing infant and because of the potential for serious adverse reactions in nursing infants.

Use in children—The pharmacokinetic and side effect profiles of stavudine in children and neonates were similar to those in adults; safety/efficacy of stavudine extended-release capsules not established

Use in the elderly—Elderly patients should be closely monitored for signs and symptoms of peripheral neuropathy.

Other medications, especially didanosine, hydroxyurea, zidovudine (AZT) or those associated with hepatotoxicity, pancreatitis, and peripheral neuropathy

Other medical problems, especially alcoholism, hepatic disease, hepatic function impairment, pancreatitis (or history of pancreatitis), peripheral neuropathy, renal function impairment, and risk factors for hepatic disease (female gender, obesity, prolonged nucleoside exposure)

Proper use of this medication

» Importance of not taking more medication than prescribed; importance of not discontinuing medication without checking with physician

» Compliance with full course of therapy

» Importance of not missing doses and of taking at evenly spaced times

Not sharing medication with others

» Proper dosing

Missed dose: Taking as soon as possible; not taking if almost time for next dose; not doubling doses

» Proper storage

Precautions while using this medication

» Regular visits to physician for blood tests

» Importance of not taking other medications including prescription, nonprescription, vitamin supplements, and herbal preparations concurrently without checking with physician

» Taking steps to avoid spreading HIV infection

Importance of telling doctor if signs or symptoms of hyperlactatemia/lactic acidosis, peripheral neuropathy, or pancreatitis occur

Side/adverse effects

Signs of potential side effects, especially peripheral neuropathy, arthralgia, hypersensitivity or allergic reaction, myalgia, anemia, pancreatitis, hepatic steatosis, hepatitis, lactic acidosis, liver failure, severe motor weakness, and thrombocytopenia.

General Dosing Information

Patients with symptoms of peripheral neuropathy or clinically significant elevations in serum concentrations of hepatic transaminases should discontinue taking stavudine. If symptoms or serum enzyme elevations resolve completely, stavudine may be reintroduced at 50% of the regular dose. However, if peripheral neuropathy recurs after resuming stavudine treatment, permanent discontinuation should be considered.

Since urinary excretion is a major route of elimination for stavudine in pediatric patients, the clearance of stavudine may be altered in children with renal impairment. Although insufficient data exists to recommend a dose adjustment for pediatric patients, a reduction in the dose and/or an increase in the interval between doses should be considered.

Diet/Nutrition
Stavudine may be taken with or without food.

Oral Dosage Forms

STAVUDINE CAPSULES

Usual adult and adolescent dose
Human immunodeficiency virus (HIV) infection—

Adults and adolescents 60 kg of body weight or greater: Oral, 40 mg every twelve hours.

Adults and adolescents less than 60 kg of body weight: Oral, 30 mg every twelve hours.

Note: Patients with renal function impairment may require a reduction in dose as follows:

Creatinine clearance (mL/min)/(mL/sec)	Recommended dose based on patient's body weight	
	≥ 60 kg	< 60 kg
> 50/0.83	See *Usual adult and adolescent dose*	See *Usual adult and adolescent dose*
26-50/0.43-0.83	20 mg every 12 hours	15 mg every 12 hours
10-25/0.17-0.42	20 mg every 24 hours	15 mg every 24 hours

Data are insufficient to recommend a dose for patients with creatinine clearance < 10 mL per minute (0.17 mL per second).

Recommended dose for hemodialysis patients is 20 mg every 24 hours (patients weighing 60 kg or more) *or* 15 mg every 24 hours (patients weighing less than 60 kg), administered after hemodialysis completion and at the same time of day on non-dialysis days.

Usual pediatric dose
This dosage form is usually not used for children. See *Stavudine for Oral Solution.*

Strength(s) usually available
U.S.—

15 mg (Rx) [*Zerit* (lactose)].
20 mg (Rx) [*Zerit* (lactose)].
30 mg (Rx) [*Zerit* (lactose)].
40 mg (Rx) [*Zerit* (lactose)].

Canada—

15 mg (Rx) [*Zerit* (lactose)].
20 mg (Rx) [*Zerit* (lactose)].
30 mg (Rx) [*Zerit* (lactose)].
40 mg (Rx) [*Zerit* (lactose)].

Packaging and storage
Store at controlled room temperature, preferably between 15 and 30 °C (59 and 86 °F), in a tight container.

Auxiliary labeling
- Continue medicine for full time of treatment.

STAVUDINE EXTENDED-RELEASE CAPSULES

Usual adult and adolescent dose
Human immunodeficiency virus (HIV) infection—

Adults and adolescents 60 kg of body weight or greater: Oral, 100 mg once daily.

Adults and adolescents less than 60 kg of body weight: Oral, 75 mg once daily.

Note: Patients with renal function impairment may require a reduction in dose of extended-release stavudine capsules as follows:

Creatinine clearance (mL/min)	Recommended dose based on patient's body weight	
	≥ 60 kg	< 60 kg
> 50	100 mg once daily	75 mg once daily
26-50	50 mg once daily	37.5 mg once daily
10-25	50 mg every 48 hours	37.5 mg every 48 hours
Hemodialysis patients	50 mg every 48 hours	37.5 mg every 48 hours

Hemodialysis patients: The recommended dose is 50 mg every 48 hours (≥60 kg) or 37.5 mg every 48 hours (less than 60 kg), administered after the completion of hemodialysis and at the same time of day on nondialysis days.

If peripheral neuropathy symptoms develop during treatment and are resolved satisfactorily after temporary withdrawal, extended-release stavudine may be resumed at 50% or the recommended dosage (i.e., 50 mg once daily for patients ≥60 kg and 37.5 mg once daily for patients less than 60 kg). If peripheral neuropathy recurs, permanent discontinuation should be considered.

Usual pediatric dose
This dosage form has not been studied in pediatric patients. See *Stavudine Capsules* or *Stavudine for Oral Solution.*

Strength(s) usually available
U.S.—

37.5 mg (Rx) [*Zerit XR* (contain extended-release beads; distilled acetylated monoglycerides; ethylcellulose aqueous dispersion; hypromellose; lactose monohydrate; magnesium stearate; microcrystalline cellulose; talc; gelatin; iron oxide colorant; silicon dioxide; sodium lauryl sulfate; titanium dioxide)].

50 mg (Rx) [*Zerit XR* (contain extended-release beads; distilled acetylated monoglycerides; ethylcellulose aqueous dispersion; hypromellose; lactose monohydrate; magnesium stearate; microcrystalline cellulose; talc; gelatin; iron oxide colorant; silicon dioxide; sodium lauryl sulfate; titanium dioxide)].

75 mg (Rx) [*Zerit XR* (contain extended-release beads; distilled acetylated monoglycerides; ethylcellulose aqueous dispersion; hypromellose; lactose monohydrate; magnesium stearate; microcrystalline cellulose; talc; gelatin; iron oxide colorant; silicon dioxide; sodium lauryl sulfate; titanium dioxide)].

100 mg (Rx) [*Zerit XR* (contain extended-release beads; distilled acetylated monoglycerides; ethylcellulose aqueous dispersion; hypromellose; lactose monohydrate; magnesium stearate; microcrystalline cellulose; talc; gelatin; iron oxide colorant; silicon dioxide; sodium lauryl sulfate; titanium dioxide)].

Packaging and storage
Store at 25 °C (77 °F), excursions permitted between 15 and 30 °C (59 and 86 °F), in a tight container.

Auxiliary labeling
- Swallow whole. Do not crush or chew.
- Ask your doctor or pharmacist before using nonprescription drugs.
- You should take this medication exactly as prescribed. Do not skip or discontinue unless directed.

Additional information
For patients who have difficulty swallowing intact capsules, the capsule can be carefully opened and the contents mixed with 2 tablespoons of yogurt or applesauce. Patients should be cautioned not to chew or crush the beads while swallowing.

STAVUDINE FOR ORAL SOLUTION

Usual adult and adolescent dose
See *Stavudine Capsules.*

Usual pediatric dose
Human immunodeficiency virus (HIV) infection—

Infants and children 30 kg of body weight or greater: Oral, 30 mg every twelve hours.

Infants and children at least 14 days and less than 30 kg of body weight: Oral, 1 mg per kg of body weight every twelve hours.

Infants from birth to 13 days: Oral, 0.5 mg per kg of body weight every 12 hours.

Strength(s) usually available
U.S.—

1 mg per mL (when reconstituted according to manufacturer's instructions) (available in 200-mL bottles) (Rx) [*Zerit* (antifoaming and flavoring agents; methylparaben; propylparaben; sucrose)].

Canada—

Not commercially available.

Packaging and storage
Prior to reconstitution, store at controlled room temperature, preferably between 15 and 30 °C (59 and 86 °F), in a tight container. Protect from excessive moisture.

After reconstitution, store in a refrigerator (2 to 8 °C [36 to 46 °F]).

Preparation of dosage form
To prepare stavudine for oral solution, add 202 mL of purified water to each bottle and shake vigorously to dissolve. This will provide 200 mL of dispensable solution. The solution may appear slightly hazy.

Stability
Reconstituted solutions are stable for up to 30 days when refrigerated.

Auxiliary labeling
- Shake prior to use.
- Continue medicine for full time of treatment.

Additional information
When dispensing, use original container with measuring cup provided.

Revised: 05/04/2005
Developed: 11/28/1994

STREPTOKINASE—See *Thrombolytic Agents (Systemic)*

STREPTOMYCIN—See *Aminoglycosides (Systemic)*

SUCCINYLCHOLINE CHLORIDE—See *Neuromuscular Blocking Agents (Systemic)*

SUCRALFATE Oral-Local

VA CLASSIFICATION (Primary): GA302

Commonly used brand name(s): *Apo-sucralfate; Carafate; Sulcrate; Sulcrate Suspension Plus.*

Note: For a listing of dosage forms and brand names by country availability, see *Dosage Forms* section(s).

Category
Antiulcer agent; gastric mucosa protectant.

Indications
Note: Bracketed information in the *Indications* section refers to uses that are not included in U.S. product labeling.

Accepted
Ulcer, duodenal (treatment)—Sucralfate is indicated in the short-term (up to 8 weeks) treatment of duodenal ulcer.

Ulcer, duodenal (prophylaxis)—Sucralfate is used in the prevention of duodenal ulcer recurrence.

[Ulcer, gastric (treatment)]—Sucralfate is used for the short-term treatment of benign gastric ulcer.

[Arthritis, rheumatoid (treatment adjunct)][1]—Sucralfate is used for the relief of gastrointestinal symptoms associated with the use of nonsteroidal anti-inflammatory drugs in the treatment of rheumatoid arthritis.

[Stress-related mucosal damage (prophylaxis and treatment)]—Sucralfate is used to prevent and treat gastrointestinal, stress-induced ulceration and bleeding, especially in intensive care patients.

[Reflux, gastroesophageal (treatment)]—Sucralfate is used in the treatment of gastroesophageal reflux disease.

[1]Not included in Canadian product labeling.

Pharmacology/Pharmacokinetics

Physicochemical characteristics
Sucralfate is an aluminum salt of a sulfated disaccharide.

Mechanism of action/Effect
Exact mechanism of action is not known; however, sucralfate is thought to form an ulcer-adherent complex with proteinaceous exudate, such as albumin and fibrinogen, at the ulcer site, protecting it against further acid attack. To a lesser extent, sucralfate forms a viscous, adhesive barrier on the surface of intact mucosa of the stomach and duodenum. Sucralfate also inhibits pepsin activity and has been found to bind bile salts *in vitro.* Recent information suggests that sucralfate may increase the production of prostaglandin E_2 and gastric mucus.

Absorption
Up to 5% of the disaccharide component and less than 0.02% of aluminum is absorbed from the gastrointestinal tract following an oral sucralfate dose.

Elimination
Mostly fecal; small amounts of sulfate disaccharide are eliminated in the urine.

Precautions to Consider

Pregnancy/Reproduction
Pregnancy—Studies in humans have not been done.

Studies in animals have not shown that sucralfate causes adverse effects on the fetus.

FDA Pregnancy Category B.

Breast-feeding
Problems in humans have not been documented.

Pediatrics
Appropriate studies to date have not demonstrated pediatrics-specific problems that would limit the usefulness of sucralfate in children.

Geriatrics
Although adequate and well-controlled studies on the relationship of age to the effects of sucralfate have not been performed in the geriatric population, no geriatrics-specific problems have been documented to date.

Drug interactions and/or related problems
The following drug interactions and/or related problems have been selected on the basis of their potential clinical significance (possible mechanism in parentheses where appropriate)—not necessarily inclusive (» = major clinical significance):

Note: Combinations containing any of the following medications, depending on the amount present, may also interact with this medication.

Aluminum-containing medications, such as:
Antacids
Antidiarrheals
Aspirin, buffered with aluminum
Vaginal douches
(concurrent use with sucralfate in patients with renal failure may cause aluminum toxicity)

Antacids
(concurrent use with antacids in the treatment of duodenal ulcer may be indicated for the relief of pain; however, simultaneous administration is not recommended since antacids may interfere with binding of sucralfate to the mucosa; patient should be advised not to take antacids within ½ hour before or after sucralfate)

Cimetidine or
Ranitidine
(concurrent use with sucralfate may decrease the absorption of cimetidine or ranitidine; patients should be advised to take cimetidine or ranitidine 2 hours before sucralfate)

» Ciprofloxacin or
» Norfloxacin or
» Ofloxacin
(concurrent use with sucralfate may decrease the absorption of ciprofloxacin, norfloxacin, or ofloxacin by chelation, resulting in lower serum and urine concentrations of these 3 medicines; patients should be advised to take ciprofloxacin, norfloxacin, or ofloxacin 2 to 3 hours before sucralfate)

» Digoxin or
» Theophylline
(concurrent use with sucralfate may decrease the absorption of digoxin or theophylline; patients should be advised not to take sucralfate within 2 hours of digoxin or theophylline)

» Phenytoin
(concurrent use with sucralfate may decrease the absorption of phenytoin enough to reduce the steady-state blood concentrations of phenytoin with a resultant loss of seizure control; patients should be advised not to take sucralfate within 2 hours of phenytoin)

Tetracyclines, oral
(absorption may be decreased when oral tetracyclines are used concurrently with sucralfate, since sucralfate is an aluminum salt and may form nonabsorbable complexes with tetracycline; patients should be advised not to take sucralfate within 2 hours of tetracyclines)

Medical considerations/Contraindications
The medical considerations/contraindications included have been selected on the basis of their potential clinical significance (reasons given in parentheses where appropriate)—not necessarily inclusive (» = major clinical significance).

Risk-benefits should be considered when the following medical problems exist:
Dysphagia or

Gastrointestinal tract obstruction disease
(patients with these conditions may be at risk of bezoar formation because of the protein-binding properties of sucralfate)

Renal failure
(absorption of the aluminum in sucralfate in patients with renal failure may cause aluminum toxicity, especially with long-term use)

Sensitivity to sucralfate

Patient monitoring

The following may be especially important in patient monitoring (other tests may be warranted in some patients, depending on condition; » = major clinical significance):

Serum aluminum concentrations
(determinations may be increased in patients with renal failure)

Side/Adverse Effects

Note: Occurrence of drowsiness progressing to seizures in patients with renal failure may indicate aluminum toxicity.

The following side/adverse effects have been selected on the basis of their potential clinical significance (possible signs and symptoms in parentheses where appropriate)—not necessarily inclusive:

Those indicating need for medical attention only if they continue or are bothersome

Incidence more frequent
Constipation

Incidence less frequent or rare
Backache; diarrhea; dizziness or lightheadedness; drowsiness; dryness of mouth; indigestion; nausea; skin rash, hives, or itching; stomach cramps or pain

Patient Consultation

As an aid to patient consultation, refer to *Advice for the Patient, Sucralfate (Oral)*.

In providing consultation, consider emphasizing the following selected information (» = major clinical significance):

Before using this medication

» Conditions affecting use, especially:
Sensitivity to sucralfate
Other medications, especially ciprofloxacin, digoxin, norfloxacin, ofloxacin, phenytoin, and theophylline

Proper use of this medication

Taking on empty stomach 1 hour before meals and at bedtime
Compliance with full course of therapy and keeping appointments for check-ups
» Proper dosing
Missed dose: Taking as soon as possible; not taking if almost time for next dose; not doubling doses
» Proper storage

Precautions while using this medication

» Not taking antacids within ½ hour before or after sucralfate

Side/adverse effects

Signs of potential side effects, especially aluminum toxicity

General Dosing Information

Sucralfate should be taken with water on an empty stomach, 1 hour before each meal and at bedtime, for maximum effectiveness.

Short-term treatment with sucralfate may result in complete healing of the ulcer but it may not alter the posthealing frequency or severity of duodenal ulceration.

If required, antacids may be administered ½ hour before or after sucralfate for the relief of pain.

Even though the symptoms of duodenal ulcers may subside, unless healing has been documented by x-ray or endoscopic examination, therapy should continue for at least 4 to 8 weeks.

Use of sucralfate in a nasogastric feeding tube has resulted in bezoar formation with other medications or enteral feedings, due to the protein-binding properties of sucralfate.

Oral Dosage Forms

Note: Bracketed uses in the *Dosage Forms* section refer to categories of use and/or indications that are not included in U.S. product labeling.

SUCRALFATE ORAL SUSPENSION

Usual adult and adolescent dose

Duodenal ulcer (treatment)—
Oral, 1 gram four times a day one hour before each meal and at bedtime; or 2 grams two times a day on waking and at bedtime on an empty stomach.

[Gastroesophageal reflux]—
Oral, 1 gram four times a day one hour before each meal and at bedtime.

[Stress-related mucosal damage (prophylaxis)]—
Oral, 1 gram four to six times a day.

Note: Duration of treatment for prophylaxis of stress ulceration must be individually determined and should be continued for as long as risk factors are present; usually, treatment does not continue longer than fourteen days.

Usual pediatric dose

Duodenal ulcer (treatment)—
Dosage has not been established.

[Gastroesophageal reflux]—
Oral, 500 mg to 1 gram four times a day one hour before each meal and at bedtime.

Strength(s) usually available

U.S.—
500 mg per 5 mL (Rx) [*Carafate*].

Canada—
500 mg per 5 mL (Rx) [*Sulcrate*].
1 gram per 5 mL (Rx) [*Sulcrate Suspension Plus* (caramel-flavored)].

Packaging and storage

Store below 40 °C (104 °F), preferably between 15 and 30 °C (59 and 86 °F), in a tight container, unless otherwise specified by manufacturer. Protect from freezing.

Auxiliary labeling

- Shake well.

SUCRALFATE TABLETS USP

Usual adult and adolescent dose

Duodenal ulcer (treatment)—
Oral, 1 gram four times a day one hour before each meal and at bedtime.

Duodenal ulcer (prophylaxis)—
Oral, 1 gram two times a day on an empty stomach.

[Gastric ulcer (treatment)] or—
Oral, 1 gram four times a day one hour before each meal and at bedtime.

[Gastroesophageal reflux]—
Oral, 1 gram four times a day one hour before each meal and at bedtime.

Usual pediatric dose

Duodenal ulcer (treatment)—
Dosage has not been established.

[Gastroesophageal reflux]—
Oral, 500 mg four times a day one hour before each meal and at bedtime.

Strength(s) usually available

U.S.—
1 gram (Rx) [*Carafate;* GENERIC].

Canada—
1 gram (Rx) [*Apo-sucralfate; Sulcrate*].

Packaging and storage

Store below 40 °C (104 °F), preferably between 15 and 30 °C (59 and 86 °F), in a tight container, unless otherwise specified by manufacturer.

Auxiliary labeling

- Continue medicine for full time of treatment.

Revised: 03/24/1998

SUFENTANIL—See *Fentanyl Derivatives (Systemic)*

SULFACETAMIDE—See *Sulfonamides (Ophthalmic)*

SULFADIAZINE—See *Sulfonamides (Systemic)*

SULFAMETHIZOLE—See *Sulfonamides (Systemic)*

SULFAMETHOXAZOLE—See *Sulfonamides (Systemic)*

SULFANILAMIDE—See *Sulfonamides (Vaginal)*

SULFASALAZINE Systemic

INN: none; BAN: Sulphasalazine.

JAN: Salazosulfapyridine.

VA CLASSIFICATION (Primary/Secondary): GA400/MS109

Commonly used brand name(s): *Alti-Sulfasalazine; Alti-Sulfasalazine (Enteric-Coated); Azulfidine; Azulfidine EN-Tabs; PMS-Sulfasalazine; PMS-Sulfasalazine E.C.; S.A.S. Enteric-500; S.A.S.-500; Salazopyrin; Salazopyrin EN-Tabs.*

Another commonly used name is salicylazosulfapyridine.

Note: For a listing of dosage forms and brand names by country availability, see *Dosage Forms* section(s).

Category

Bowel disease (inflammatory) suppressant; antirheumatic (disease-modifying).

Indications

Note: Bracketed information in the *Indications* section refers to uses that are not included in U.S. product labeling.

Accepted

Bowel disease, inflammatory (prophylaxis and treatment)—Sulfasalazine is indicated to treat and to maintain remission of inflammatory bowel disease (e.g., ulcerative colitis or Crohn's disease affecting the colon). It is indicated in the treatment of mild to moderate ulcerative colitis and as adjunctive treatment of severe ulcerative colitis.

Arthritis, rheumatoid (treatment)—Sulfasalazine is indicated for the treatment of rheumatoid arthritis in patients who have responded inadequately to, or who are intolerant of, analgesics or other nonsteroidal anti-inflammatory drugs (NSAIDs).

Arthritis, juvenile rheumatoid; poly-articular course (treatment)[1]—Sulfasalazine delayed release tablets are indicated for the treatment of pediatric patients who have responded inadequately to salicylates or other non-steroidal anti-inflammatory drugs.

[Ankylosing spondylitis (treatment)][1]—Sulfasalazine is used in the treatment of ankylosing spondylitis.

[1]Not included in Canadian product labeling.

Pharmacology/Pharmacokinetics

Physicochemical characteristics

Molecular weight—398.39.

Mechanism of action/Effect

Bowel disease (inflammatory) suppressant—Uncertain; may be related to sulfasalazine's immunosuppressant effects, which have been observed in animals, its affinity for connective tissue, and/or its relatively high concentrations in serous fluids, the liver, and intestinal wall. Sulfasalazine is considered a vehicle for carrying its principal metabolites to the colon. Unabsorbed sulfasalazine is cleaved in the colon by intestinal bacteria to form sulfapyridine and mesalamine (5-aminosalicylic acid; 5-ASA), both of which may act locally within the gut. Mesalamine, which is different from aminosalicylates used to treat tuberculosis, is thought to be the major active moiety. Mucosal production of arachidonic acid metabolites, both through the cyclooxygenase and the lipoxygenase pathways, is increased in patients with inflammatory bowel disease. Mesalamine appears to diminish inflammation by inhibiting cyclooxygenase and lipoxygenase, thereby decreasing the production of prostaglandins, and leukotrienes and hydroxyeicosatetraenoic acids (HETEs), respectively. It is also believed that mesalamine acts as a scavenger of oxygen-derived free radicals, which are produced in greater numbers in patients with inflammatory bowel disease.

Antirheumatic (disease-modifying)—Uncertain; sulfapyridine moiety may suppress the activity of natural killer cells and impair lymphocyte transformation.

Absorption

Sulfasalazine—Poorly absorbed; approximately 20% of ingested sulfasalazine dose reaches the systemic circulation. The remaining ingested dose is split by colonic bacteria into its components, sulfapyridine and mesalamine.

Sulfapyridine—Most of the sulfapyridine metabolized from sulfasalazine (60–80%) is absorbed in the colon following oral administration.

Mesalamine (5-ASA)—Approximately 25% of the mesalamine metabolized from sulfasalazine is absorbed in the colon following oral administration.

Distribution

Distributed to serum, connective tissue, serous fluids, liver, and intestinal wall. The apparent volume of distribution (Vol_D) of sulfasalazine in 8 healthy volunteers was 64 L. The Vol_D of sulfapyridine was found to be 0.4 to 1.2 L per kg.

Protein binding

Sulfasalazine—Very high (Approximately 99%).

Sulfapyridine—Moderate (Approximately 50%).

Mesalamine (5-ASA)—Moderate (Approximately 43%).

Biotransformation

Sulfasalazine (unabsorbed)—Cleaved in the colon by intestinal bacteria to form sulfapyridine and mesalamine.

Sulfapyridine (absorbed)—Acetylated and hydroxylated in the liver, followed by conjugation with glucuronic acid.

Mesalamine (5-ASA) (absorbed)—Acetylated in the intestinal mucosal wall and the liver.

Half-life

Sulfasalazine—5 to 10 hours.

Sulfapyridine—6 to 14 hours, depending on acetylator status.

Mesalamine (5-ASA)—0.6 to 1.4 hours.

Time to peak serum concentration

Sulfasalazine oral suspension—
- Sulfasalazine: Approximately 1.5 to 6 hours.
- Sulfapyridine: Approximately 9 to 24 hours.

Sulfasalazine tablets—
- Sulfasalazine: Approximately 1.5 to 6 hours.
- Sulfapyridine: Approximately 6 to 24 hours.

Sulfasalazine enteric-coated tablets—
- Sulfasalazine: Approximately 3 to 12 hours.
- Sulfapyridine: Approximately 12 to 24 hours.

Mean peak serum concentration

Sulfasalazine oral suspension—
- Sulfasalazine: Approximately 20 mcg per mL 3 hours following a single oral 2-gram dose.
- Sulfapyridine: Approximately 19 mcg per mL 12 hours following a single oral 2-gram dose.
- Mesalamine (5-ASA): Approximately 4 mcg per mL following a single oral 2-gram dose.

Sulfasalazine tablets—
- Sulfasalazine: Approximately 14 mcg per mL 3 hours following a single oral 2-gram dose.
- Sulfapyridine: Approximately 21 mcg per mL 12 hours following a single oral 2-gram dose.
- Mesalamine (5-ASA): Approximately 4 mcg per mL following a single oral 2-gram dose.

Sulfasalazine enteric-coated tablets—
- Sulfasalazine: Approximately 6 mcg per mL 6 hours following a single oral 2-gram dose.
- Sulfapyridine: Approximately 13 mcg per mL 12 hours following a single oral 2-gram dose.
- Mesalamine (5-ASA): Approximately 4 mcg per mL following a single oral 2-gram dose.

Elimination

Fecal—Trace amounts of sulfasalazine, approximately 5% of sulfapyridine, and approximately 67% of mesalamine are found in feces.

Renal—Approximately 75 to 91% of sulfasalazine and sulfapyridine metabolites excreted in urine within 3 days, depending on the dosage form used. Mesalamine is excreted in urine mostly in acetylated form.

Precautions to Consider

Cross-sensitivity and/or related problems

Patients allergic to one sulfonamide may be allergic to other sulfonamides also.

Patients allergic to salicylates, furosemide, thiazide diuretics, sulfonylureas, or carbonic anhydrase inhibitors may be allergic to this medication also.

Carcinogenicity/Tumorigenicity

Long-term studies in humans have not been done to evaluate the carcinogenic potential of sulfasalazine. However, long-term administration of sulfonamides to rats has been shown to result in thyroid malignancies. In addition, rats appear to be especially susceptible to the goitrogenic effects of sulfonamides.

Two year oral carcinogenicity studies were done in male and female rats and mice. An increase in the incidence of urinary bladder transitional cell papillomas was seen in male rats, and transitional cell papilloma of the kidney was observed in a small percentage of female rats (4%). The increased occurrence of neoplasms in the rats was also associated with an increase in renal calculi formulation and hyperplasia of the transitional cell epithelium.

There was an increase in the incidence of hepatocellular adenoma or carcinoma in both male and female mice in all of the doses that were tested.

Mutagenicity

Sulfasalazine did not show mutagenicity in the bacterial reverse mutation assay (Ames test) or in the L51784 mouse lymphoma cell assay at the HGPRT gene. Equivocal mutagenic response was seen in the micronucleus assay of mouse and rat bone marrow and mouse peripheral RBC and in the sister chromatid exchange, chromosomal aberration and the micronucleus assays in lymphocytes obtained from humans.

Pregnancy/Reproduction

Fertility—Studies in rats and rabbits given doses of up to 6 times the human dose have not shown that sulfasalazine impairs female fertility. However, these studies have shown that sulfasalazine does impair male fertility. In addition, oligospermia and infertility, reported to be reversible upon discontinuation of sulfasalazine, have been reported in men.

Pregnancy—Sulfasalazine and sulfapyridine cross the placenta. Adequate and well-controlled studies in humans have not been done. However, a national survey of 186 women with inflammatory bowel disease (IBD) who took sulfasalazine, alone or concurrently with corticosteroids, showed an incidence of adverse effects in the fetus comparable to that in 245 untreated IBD pregnancies. Another study of 1445 pregnancies in which sulfonamides, including sulfasalazine, were taken did not show that sulfasalazine causes fetal malformations.

Appropriate studies have not been performed on the effect of sulfasalazine on growth, development, and functional maturation of children whose mothers received sulfasalazine during pregnancy.

Studies in rats and rabbits given doses of up to 6 times the human dose have not shown that sulfasalazine causes adverse effects in the fetus.

FDA Pregnancy Category B.

Breast-feeding

Uncleaved sulfasalazine is distributed into breast milk in small amounts. Sulfapyridine is distributed into breast milk in concentrations that are 30 to 60% of those in the maternal serum. Although sulfonamides may displace bilirubin from protein-binding sites in the fetal plasma, hyperbilirubinemia has occurred rarely.

Sulfonamides may cause hemolytic anemia in glucose-6-phosphate dehydrogenase (G6PD)–deficient neonates.

Pediatrics

Use is contraindicated in infants and children up to 2 years of age because sulfonamides may cause kernicterus.

Geriatrics

Appropriate studies performed to date have not demonstrated geriatrics-specific problems that would limit the usefulness of sulfasalazine in the elderly.

Pharmacogenetics

Mean serum concentrations of sulfapyridine and its metabolites may be significantly increased in patients who are slow acetylators. Eskimo, Oriental, and American Indian populations have the lowest prevalence of slow acetylators, while Egyptian, Israeli, Scandinavian, other Caucasian, and black populations have the highest prevalence of slow acetylators.

Dental

The leukopenic and thrombocytopenic effects of sulfasalazine may result in an increased incidence of certain microbial infections, delayed healing, and gingival bleeding. If leukopenia or thrombocytopenia occurs, dental work should be deferred until blood counts have returned to normal. Patients should be instructed in proper oral hygiene, including caution in use of regular toothbrushes, dental floss, and toothpicks.

Drug interactions and/or related problems

The following drug interactions and/or related problems have been selected on the basis of their potential clinical significance (possible mechanism in parentheses where appropriate)—not necessarily inclusive (» = major clinical significance):

Note: Combinations containing any of the following medications, depending on the amount present, may also interact with this medication.

» Anticoagulants, coumarin- or indandione-derivative or
» Anticonvulsants, hydantoin or
» Antidiabetic agents, oral
(may be displaced from protein binding sites and/or metabolism may be inhibited by sulfonamides, resulting in increased or prolonged effects and/or toxicity; dosage adjustments may be necessary during and after sulfonamide therapy)

Bone marrow depressants (see *Appendix II*)
(concurrent use of sulfasalazine with bone marrow depressants may increase the leukopenic and/or thrombocytopenic effects; if concurrent use is required, close observation for myelotoxic effects should be considered)

Digitalis glycosides or
Folic acid
(sulfasalazine may inhibit absorption and lower the serum concentrations of these medications; folic acid requirements may be increased in patients receiving sulfasalazine; patients taking digitalis glycosides should be monitored closely for evidence of altered digitalis effect)

» Hemolytics, other (see *Appendix II*)
(concurrent use with sulfasalazine may increase the potential for toxic side effects)

» Hepatotoxic medications, other (see *Appendix II*)
(concurrent use with sulfonamides may result in an increased incidence of hepatotoxicity; patients, especially those on prolonged administration or those with a history of liver disease, should be carefully monitored)

» Methotrexate or
Phenylbutazone or
Sulfinpyrazone
(the effects of these medications may be potentiated during concurrent use with sulfonamides because of displacement from plasma protein binding sites; phenylbutazone and sulfinpyrazone have also been reported to potentiate the effects of sulfonamides)

Laboratory value alterations

The following have been selected on the basis of their potential clinical significance (possible effect in parentheses where appropriate)—not necessarily inclusive (» = major clinical significance).

With diagnostic test results
Bentiromide
(administration of sulfonamides during a bentiromide test period will invalidate test results because sulfonamides are also metabolized to arylamines and will thus increase the percent of *p*-aminobenzoic acid (PABA) recovered; discontinuation of sulfonamides at least 3 days prior to the administration of bentiromide is recommended)

Medical considerations/Contraindications

The medical considerations/contraindications included have been selected on the basis of their potential clinical significance (reasons given in parentheses where appropriate)—not necessarily inclusive (» = major clinical significance).

Except under special circumstances, this medication should not be used when the following medical problem exists:

» Intestinal obstruction or
» Urinary obstruction
» Previous allergic reaction to sulfasalazine, sulfonamides, salicylates, furosemide, thiazide diuretics, sulfonylureas, or carbonic anhydrase inhibitors

Risk-benefit should be considered when the following medical problems exist:

» Allergy, severe or
» Asthma, bronchial
(risk of hypersensitivity reaction to sulfasalazine may be increased with use of sulfasalazine)

» Blood dyscrasias
(sulfasalazine may cause agranulocytosis, aplastic anemia, or other blood dyscrasias)

» Glucose-6-phosphate dehydrogenase (G6PD) deficiency
(sulfasalazine may cause hemolytic anemia in G6PD-deficient patients)

» Hepatic function impairment
(sulfonamides are metabolized in the liver and may cause hepatitis)

» Porphyria
(sulfonamides may precipitate an acute attack of porphyria)

» Renal function impairment
(the metabolite, sulfapyridine, is excreted primarily through the kidneys)

Patient monitoring

The following may be especially important in patient monitoring (other tests may be warranted in some patients, depending on condition; » = major clinical significance):

» Complete blood counts (CBCs)
(recommended prior to, and every 2 to 3 weeks for the first 2 to 3 months of treatment, then every 3 to 6 months during treatment to detect blood dyscrasias in patients on prolonged therapy; therapy should be discontinued if a significant decrease in the count of any formed blood elements occurs)

» Liver function tests
(recommended prior to, and every 2 weeks for the first 3 months of treatment, then monthly during the second 3 months of treatment, and thereafter once every 3 months and as clinically indicated during treatment to detect hepatotoxicity)

Proctoscopy and Sigmoidoscopy
(may be required periodically during treatment to determine patient response and dosage adjustments)

Sulfapyridine concentrations, serum
(determinations may be useful since concentrations greater than 50 mcg/mL appear to be associated with an increased incidence of adverse reactions)

Urinalyses
(may be required prior to and periodically during treatment)

Side/Adverse Effects

Note: Deaths have been reported from hypersensitivity reactions, agranulocytosis, aplastic anemia, other blood dyscrasias, renal and hepatic damage, irreversible neuromuscular and central nervous system (CNS) changes, and fibrosing alveolitis in patients taking sulfasalazine. If toxic or hypersensitivity reactions occur, sulfasalazine should be discontinued immediately.

Oligospermia and infertility, reported to be reversible upon discontinuation of sulfasalazine, have been reported in males taking this medication.

Daily doses of 4 grams or more and total sulfapyridine serum concentrations > 50 mcg per mL may be associated with an increased incidence of side/adverse effects.

The following side/adverse effects have been selected on the basis of their potential clinical significance (possible signs and symptoms in parentheses where appropriate)—not necessarily inclusive:

Those indicating need for medical attention

Incidence more frequent

Headache, continuing; hypersensitivity reaction (aching of joints; fever; itching; skin rash); ***photosensitivity*** (increased sensitivity of skin to sunlight); ***serum sickness-like syndrome*** (fever; headache; nausea; rash; vomiting)—seen in pediatric patients being treated for juvenile rheumatoid arthritis

Incidence less frequent or rare

Blood dyscrasias, including agranulocytosis or neutropenia (fever and sore throat); ***aplastic anemia*** (fever, chills, or sore throat; unusual bleeding or bruising; unusual tiredness or weakness); ***Heinz body or hemolytic anemia*** (back, leg, or stomach pains; loss of appetite; pale skin; unusual tiredness or weakness; fever); ***leukopenia*** (fever, chills, or sore throat); ***or thrombocytopenia*** (unusual bleeding or bruising); ***cyanosis*** (bluish fingernails, lips, or skin); ***exacerbation of ulcerative colitis*** (bloody diarrhea; fever; rash); ***hepatitis*** (yellow eyes or skin); ***interstitial pneumonitis*** (cough; difficult breathing; fever); ***Stevens-Johnson syndrome*** (aching of joints and muscles; redness, blistering, peeling, or loosening of skin; unusual tiredness or weakness); ***systemic lupus erythematosus (SLE)–like syndrome*** (blisters on skin; chest pain; general feeling of discomfort or illness; skin rash, hives, and/or itching); ***toxic epidermal necrolysis*** (difficulty in swallowing; redness, blistering, peeling, or loosening of skin)

Those indicating need for medical attention only if they continue or are bothersome

Incidence more frequent

Gastrointestinal disturbances (abdominal or stomach pain or upset; diarrhea; loss of appetite; nausea or vomiting)

Those not indicating need for medical attention

Incidence more frequent

Orange-yellow discoloration of urine or skin

Overdose

For specific information on the agents used in the management of sulfasalazine overdose, see *Ipecac (Oral-Local)* monograph.

For more information on the management of overdose or unintentional ingestion, **contact a Poison Control Center** (see *Poison Control Center Listing*).

The severity of sulfasalazine toxicity is directly related to the total serum sulfapyridine concentration. Daily doses of 4 grams or more and total sulfapyridine serum concentrations > 50 mcg per mL may be associated with an increased incidence of side/adverse effects.

Clinical effects of overdose

The following effects have been selected on the basis of their potential clinical significance (possible signs and symptoms in parentheses where appropriate)—not necessarily inclusive:

Anuria, crystalluria, or hematuria (blood in urine; lack of urination; lower back pain; pain or burning while urinating); ***drowsiness; gastrointestinal disturbances*** (abdominal or stomach pain or upset; diarrhea; loss of appetite; nausea or vomiting); ***seizures***

Treatment of overdose

To decrease absorption—the stomach may be emptied by inducing emesis with ipecac syrup (taking care to guard against aspiration) or by gastric lavage.

To enhance elimination—The urine may be alkalinized and, if kidney function is normal, fluids forced. If anuria is present, fluids and salt should be restricted. Catheterization of the ureters may be indicated when there is complete renal blockage by crystals. The low molecular weight of sulfasalazine and its metabolites may facilitate removal by dialysis.

Monitoring—Serum sulfapyridine concentrations may be monitored so that the progress of recovery can be followed.

Supportive care—Patients in whom intentional overdose is confirmed or suspected should be referred for psychiatric consultation.

Patient Consultation

As an aid to patient consultation, refer to *Advice for the Patient, Sulfasalazine (Systemic)*.

In providing consultation, consider emphasizing the following selected information (» = major clinical significance):

Before using this medication

» Conditions affecting use, especially:
Allergies to sulfasalazine, sulfonamides, salicylates, furosemide, thiazide diuretics, sulfonylureas, carbonic anhydrase inhibitors
Pregnancy—Sulfasalazine and sulfapyridine cross the placenta
Breast-feeding—Sulfasalazine and sulfapyridine are distributed into breast milk
Use in children—Use is contraindicated in infants and children up to 2 years of age because sulfonamides may cause kernicterus
Other medications, especially coumarin- or indandione-derivative anticoagulants, hemolytics, hepatotoxic medications, hydantoin anticonvulsants, methotrexate, and oral antidiabetic agents
Other medical problems, especially intestinal obstruction, urinary obstruction, severe allergies, bronchial asthma, blood dyscrasias, G6PD deficiency, hepatic function impairment, porphyria, and renal function impairment

Proper use of this medication

» Not giving to infants up to 2 years of age; sulfasalazine may cause kernicterus
Taking after meals or with food to lessen gastrointestinal irritation
» Maintaining adequate fluid intake
Proper administration technique for enteric-coated tablets
» Compliance with full course of therapy
» Proper dosing
Missed dose: Taking as soon as possible; not taking if almost time for next dose; not doubling doses
» Proper storage

Precautions while using this medication

» Regular visits to physician to check blood counts in patients on long-term therapy
Checking with physician if no improvement within 1 or 2 months

Using caution in use of regular toothbrushes, dental floss, and toothpicks; deferring dental work until blood counts have returned to normal; checking with physician or dentist concerning proper oral hygiene

» Possible photosensitivity reactions

» Caution if dizziness occurs

Possible interference with bentiromide diagnostic test for pancreatic function

Side/adverse effects

Signs of potential side effects, especially headache (continuing), hypersensitivity reaction, photosensitivity, blood dyscrasias, cyanosis, exacerbation of ulcerative colitis, hepatitis, interstitial pneumonitis, Stevens-Johnson syndrome, systemic lupus erythematosus (SLE)–like syndrome, and toxic epidermal necrolysis

Orange-yellow discoloration of alkaline urine or skin may be alarming to patient although medically insignificant

General Dosing Information

Fluid intake should be sufficient to maintain urine output of at least 1200 to 1500 mL per day in adults.

Sulfasalazine should preferably be taken immediately after meals or with food. Also, when sulfasalazine is being taken for inflammatory bowel disease, the total daily dose may be spread evenly over a 24-hour period. In some patients it may be necessary to initiate therapy with smaller doses (e.g., 1 to 2 grams daily) to lessen gastrointestinal irritation.

When endoscopic examination confirms satisfactory improvement, dosage may be reduced to maintenance level. If diarrhea recurs, dosage should be increased to previously effective level.

Patients with impaired renal function may require a reduction in dose.

Adverse reactions tend to increase with total daily doses of 4 grams or more or with serum concentrations greater than the equivalent of 50 mcg of sulfapyridine per mL.

Patients experiencing mild hypersensitivity reactions may be "desensitized" to allow continued treatment with sulfasalazine. Desensitization involves withdrawal of the medication followed by reinstitution, beginning with a lower dose and increasing it slowly over at least 23 days. Desensitization should not be attempted in patients with a history of agranulocytosis. Some medical experts believe that with the availability of mesalamine preparations, desensitization may no longer be indicated.

Diet/Nutrition

Folic acid requirements may be increased in patients on sulfasalazine therapy, because sulfasalazine inhibits the absorption of folic acid.

For treatment of adverse effects

Recommended treatment consists of the following:

- Discontinuing the drug immediately if agranulocytosis or hypersensitivity reactions occur.
- Controlling hypersensitivity reactions with antihistamines and/or corticosteroids.

Oral Dosage Forms

SULFASALAZINE TABLETS USP

Usual adult and adolescent dose

Bowel disease (inflammatory) suppressant—

Initial: Oral, 1 gram every six to eight hours. An initial dose of 500 mg every six to twelve hours may be recommended to lessen gastrointestinal side effects.

Maintenance: Oral, 500 mg every six hours, adjusted according to patient response and tolerance.

Antirheumatic (disease-modifying)—

Oral, 500 mg to 1 gram daily for the first week, with the daily dose being increased by 500 mg each week, up to a maintenance dose of 2 grams daily. The dose may be administered two times a day. If no response is seen after two months, the dose may be increased to 3 grams daily.

Usual adult prescribing limits

Total daily doses of greater than 4 grams may increase the risk of side effects and toxicity.

Usual pediatric dose

Bowel disease (inflammatory) suppressant—

Infants and children up to 2 years of age—

Use is contraindicated because sulfonamides may cause kernicterus.

Children 2 years of age and older—

Initial—Oral, 6.7 to 10 mg per kg of body weight every four hours; 10 to 15 mg per kg of body weight every six hours; or 13.3 to 20 mg per kg of body weight every eight hours.

Maintenance—Oral, 7.5 mg per kg of body weight every six hours.

Antirheumatic (disease-modifying)—

Safety and efficacy have not been established.

Usual geriatric dose

See *Usual adult and adolescent dose.*

Strength(s) usually available

U.S.—

500 mg (Rx) [*Azulfidine;* GENERIC].

Canada—

500 mg (Rx) [*Alti-Sulfasalazine* (scored); *PMS-Sulfasalazine* (scored); *Salazopyrin* (scored); *S.A.S.-500* (scored); GENERIC].

Packaging and storage

Store below 40 °C (104 °F), preferably between 15 and 30 °C (59 and 86 °F), unless otherwise specified by manufacturer. Store in a well-closed container.

Auxiliary labeling

- Take with a full glass of water.
- Avoid use of sunlamp and unprotected exposure to sun.
- Continue medicine for full time of treatment.
- May discolor urine.

SULFASALAZINE DELAYED-RELEASE TABLETS USP

Usual adult and adolescent dose

See *Sulfasalazine Tablets USP.*

Usual adult prescribing limits

See *Sulfasalazine Tablets USP.*

Usual pediatric dose

Bowel disease (inflammatory) suppressant—

Infants and children up to 2 years of age—

Safety and efficacy have not been established.

Children 6 years of age and older—

See *Sulfasalazine Tablets USP*

Antirheumatoid (treatment)[1]—

Infants and children up to 2 years of age—

Safety and efficacy have not been established.

Children 6 years of age and older—

Oral, 30 to 50 mg per kg of body weight a day divided into two equal doses. To lessen gastrointestinal side effects, lower doses (a quarter to a third of the planned maintenance dose) may be recommended and increased every week until reaching the maintenance dose at one month.

Note: Desensitization-like regimens may be used in some patients who may be sensitive to treatment with sulfasalazine. If the symptoms of sensitivity recur, sulfasalazine should be discontinued. Desensitization should not be attempted in patients with a history of agranulocytosis or an anaphylactoid reaction while receiving sulfasalazine previously.

Usual pediatric prescribing limits

Maximum dose is typically 2 grams per day.

Usual geriatric dose

See *Sulfasalazine Tablets USP.*

Strength(s) usually available

U.S.—

500 mg (Rx) [*Azulfidine EN-Tabs* (cellulose acetate phthalate); GENERIC].

Canada—

500 mg (Rx) [*Alti-Sulfasalazine (Enteric-Coated); PMS-Sulfasalazine E.C.; Salazopyrin EN-Tabs; S.A.S. Enteric-500;* GENERIC].

Packaging and storage

Store below 40 °C (104 °F), preferably between 15 and 30 °C (59 and 86 °F), unless otherwise specified by manufacturer. Store in a well-closed container.

Auxiliary labeling

- Take with a full glass of water.
- Take after meals.
- Avoid use of sunlamp and unprotected exposure to sun.
- Continue medicine for full time of treatment.
- May discolor urine.
- Swallow tablets whole.

Note

Dissolution of enteric-coated tablets is much more variable and unreliable than that of nonenteric-coated tablets.

Rectal Dosage Forms

SULFASALAZINE RECTAL SUSPENSION

Usual adult and adolescent dose

Bowel disease (inflammatory) suppressant—
Rectal, 3 grams each night at bedtime.

Usual pediatric dose

Bowel disease (inflammatory) suppression—
Infants and children up to 2 years of age: Use is contraindicated because sulfonamides cause kernicterus.
Children 2 years of age and older: Dosage has not been established.

Usual geriatric dose

See *Usual adult and adolescent dose.*

Strength(s) usually available

U.S.—
Not commercially available.

Canada—
3 grams per 100-mL unit (Rx) [*Salazopyrin*].

Packaging and storage

Store below 40 °C (104 °F), preferably between 15 and 30 °C (59 and 86 °F), unless otherwise specified by manufacturer.

Auxiliary labeling

- For rectal use.
- Shake well.
- Continue medicine for full time of treatment.

[1]Not included in Canadian product labeling.

Selected Bibliography

Allgayer H. Sulfasalazine and 5-ASA compounds. Gastrointest Pharmacol 1992; 21: 643-57.

Revised: 06/01/2001

SULFISOXAZOLE—See *Sulfonamides (Ophthalmic), Sulfonamides (Systemic)*

SULFONAMIDES Ophthalmic

This monograph includes information on the following: 1) Sulfacetamide; 2) Sulfisoxazole.

INN: Sulfisoxazole—Sulfafurazole

BAN:
Sulfacetamide—Sulphacetamide
Sulfisoxazole—Sulphafurazole

VA CLASSIFICATION (Primary): OP201

Commonly used brand name(s): *Ak-Sulf[1]; Bleph-10[1]; Cetamide[1]; Gantrisin[2]; I-Sulfacet[1]; Isopto-Cetamide[1]; Ocu-Sul-10[1]; Ocu-Sul-15[1]; Ocu-Sul-30[1]; Ocusulf-10[1]; Ophthacet[1]; Sodium Sulamyd[1]; Steri-Units Sulfacetamide[1]; Sulf-10[1]; Sulfair[1]; Sulfair 10[1]; Sulfair 15[1]; Sulfair Forte[1]; Sulfamide[1]; Sulfex[1]; Sulten-10[1].*

Note: For a listing of dosage forms and brand names by country availability, see *Dosage Forms* section(s).

Category

Antibacterial (ophthalmic).

Indications

Note: Bracketed information in the *Indications* section refers to uses that are not included in U.S. product labeling.

Accepted

Conjunctivitis, bacterial (treatment) or
Ocular infections, other (treatment)—Ophthalmic sulfonamides are indicated in the treatment of conjunctivitis and other superficial ocular infections caused by susceptible organisms.

Trachoma (treatment) or
Chlamydial infections, other (treatment)—Ophthalmic sulfonamides are indicated concurrently with systemic sulfonamides in the treatment of trachoma and other chlamydial infections.

[Blepharitis, bacterial (treatment)]—Ophthalmic sulfonamides are used in the treatment of bacterial blepharitis.

[Blepharoconjunctivitis (treatment)]—Ophthalmic sulfonamides are used in the treatment of blepharoconjunctivitis.

[Keratitis, bacterial (treatment)]—Ophthalmic sulfonamides are used in the treatment of bacterial keratitis.

[Keratoconjunctivitis, bacterial (treatment)]—Ophthalmic sulfonamides are used in the treatment of bacterial keratoconjunctivitis.

Note: Not all species or strains of a particular organism may be susceptible to a specific sulfonamide.

Pharmacology/Pharmacokinetics

Physicochemical characteristics

Molecular weight—
Sulfacetamide sodium: 254.24.
Sulfisoxazole diolamine: 372.44.

Mechanism of action/Effect

Sulfonamides are broad-spectrum, bacteriostatic anti-infectives. They are structural analogs of aminobenzoic acid (PABA) and competitively inhibit a bacterial enzyme, dihydropteroate synthetase, that is responsible for incorporation of PABA into dihydrofolic acid. This blocks the synthesis of dihydrofolic acid and decreases the amount of metabolically active tetrahydrofolic acid, a cofactor for the synthesis of purines, thymidine, and DNA.

Susceptible bacteria are those that must synthesize folic acid. The action of sulfonamides is antagonized by PABA and its derivatives (e.g., procaine and tetracaine) and by the presence of pus or tissue breakdown products, which provide the necessary components for bacterial growth.

Absorption

Following topical application of sulfacetamide (30% solution) to the eye, small amounts may be absorbed into the cornea.

Precautions to Consider

Cross-sensitivity and/or related problems

Patients sensitive to one sulfonamide may be sensitive to other sulfonamides also.

Patients sensitive to furosemide, thiazide diuretics, sulfonylureas, or carbonic anhydrase inhibitors may be sensitive to sulfonamides also.

Pregnancy/Reproduction

Problems in humans have not been documented.

Breast-feeding

Problems in humans have not been documented.

Pediatrics

Appropriate studies on the relationship of age to the effects of sulfonamides have not been performed in the pediatric population.

Geriatrics

Appropriate studies on the relationship of age to the effects of sulfonamides have not been performed in the geriatric population. However, no geriatrics-specific problems have been documented to date.

Drug interactions and/or related problems

The following drug interactions and/or related problems have been selected on the basis of their potential clinical significance (possible mechanism in parentheses where appropriate)—not necessarily inclusive (» = major clinical significance):

Note: Combinations containing any of the following medications, depending on the amount present, may also interact with this medication.

» Silver preparations, such as silver nitrate, mild silver protein (topical sulfonamides are incompatible with silver salts; concurrent use is not recommended)

Medical considerations/Contraindications

The medical considerations/contraindications included have been selected on the basis of their potential clinical significance (reasons given in parentheses where appropriate)—not necessarily inclusive (» = major clinical significance).

Risk-benefit should be considered when the following medical problem exists:
Sensitivity to sulfonamides

Side/Adverse Effects

The following side/adverse effects have been selected on the basis of their potential clinical significance (possible signs and symptoms in parentheses where appropriate)—not necessarily inclusive:

Those indicating need for medical attention

Incidence more frequent

Hypersensitivity (itching, redness, swelling, or other sign of irritation not present before therapy)

Patient Consultation

As an aid to patient consultation, refer to *Advice for the Patient, Sulfonamides (Ophthalmic).*

In providing consultation, consider emphasizing the following selected information (» = major clinical significance):

Before using this medication

» Conditions affecting use, especially:

Sensitivity to sulfonamides, furosemide, thiazide diuretics, sulfonylureas, or carbonic anhydrase inhibitors

Other medications, especially silver preparations, such as silver nitrate or mild silver protein

Proper use of this medication

Proper administration technique for ophthalmic solution and ophthalmic ointment

» Compliance with full course of therapy

» Proper dosing

Missed dose: Applying as soon as possible; not applying if almost time for next dose

» Proper storage

Precautions while using this medication

Blurred vision after application of ophthalmic ointments

Possibility of stinging or burning after application

Checking with physician if no improvement within a few days

Side/adverse effects

Signs of potential side effects, especially hypersensitivity

General Dosing Information

At night the ophthalmic ointment may be used as an adjunct to the ophthalmic solution to provide prolonged contact with the medication.

Although some manufacturers recommend a dose of 2 drops of an ophthalmic solution at appropriate intervals, the conjunctival sac will usually hold only 1 drop.

SULFACETAMIDE

Ophthalmic Dosage Forms

SULFACETAMIDE SODIUM OPHTHALMIC OINTMENT USP

Usual adult and adolescent dose

Ophthalmic antibacterial—

Topical, to the conjunctiva, a thin strip (approximately 1.25 to 2.5 cm) of ointment four times a day and at bedtime.

Usual pediatric dose

Dosage has not been established.

Strength(s) usually available

U.S.—

10% (Rx) [*Ak-Sulf; Bleph-10; Cetamide; Ocu-Sul-10; Sodium Sulamyd; Sulfair 10;* GENERIC].

Canada—

10% (Rx) [*Cetamide; Sodium Sulamyd*].

Packaging and storage

Store below 40 °C (104 °F), preferably between 15 and 30 °C (59 and 86 °F), unless otherwise specified by manufacturer. Protect from freezing.

Auxiliary labeling

- For the eye.
- Continue medicine for full time of treatment.

SULFACETAMIDE SODIUM OPHTHALMIC SOLUTION USP

Usual adult and adolescent dose

Ophthalmic antibacterial—

Topical, to the conjunctiva, 1 drop every one to three hours during the day and less frequently during the night.

Usual pediatric dose

Dosage has not been established.

Strength(s) usually available

U.S.—

10% (Rx) [*Ak-Sulf; Bleph-10; I-Sulfacet; Ocu-Sul-10; Ocusulf-10; Ophthacet; Sodium Sulamyd; Sulf-10; Sulfair; Sulfair 10; Sulfamide; Sulten-10;* GENERIC].

15% (Rx) [*Isopto-Cetamide; I-Sulfacet; Ocu-Sul-15; Steri-Units Sulfacetamide; Sulfair; Sulfair 15;* GENERIC].

30% (Rx) [*I-Sulfacet; Ocu-Sul-30; Sodium Sulamyd; Sulfair; Sulfair Forte;* GENERIC].

Canada—

10% (Rx) [*Ak-Sulf; Bleph-10; Isopto-Cetamide; Sodium Sulamyd; Sulfex*].

30% (Rx) [*Sodium Sulamyd*].

Packaging and storage

Store between 8 and 15 °C (46 and 59 °F). Store in a tight, light-resistant container.

Stability

Sulfonamide solutions become dark brown with time. When this occurs, solutions should be discarded.

Auxiliary labeling

- For the eye.
- Keep in a cool place.
- Continue medicine for full time of treatment.
- Discard if dark brown.

Note

Dispense in original unopened container.

SULFISOXAZOLE

Ophthalmic Dosage Forms

Note: The dosing and strengths of the dosage forms available are expressed in terms of sulfisoxazole base.

SULFISOXAZOLE DIOLAMINE OPHTHALMIC OINTMENT USP

Usual adult and adolescent dose

Ophthalmic antibacterial—

Topical, to the conjunctiva, a thin strip (approximately 1.25 to 2.5 cm) of ointment one to three times a day and at bedtime.

Usual pediatric dose

See *Usual adult and adolescent dose*.

Strength(s) usually available

U.S.—

4% (base) (each gram of ophthalmic ointment contains 55.6 mg of sulfisoxazole diolamine, equivalent to approximately 40 mg of sulfisoxazole) (Rx) [*Gantrisin* (phenylmercuric nitrate 1:50,000)].

Packaging and storage

Store below 40 °C (104 °F), preferably between 15 and 30 °C (59 and 86 °F), unless otherwise specified by manufacturer. Protect from freezing.

Auxiliary labeling

- For the eye.
- Continue medicine for full time of treatment.

SULFISOXAZOLE DIOLAMINE OPHTHALMIC SOLUTION USP

Usual adult and adolescent dose

Ophthalmic antibacterial—

Topical, to the conjunctiva, 1 drop three or more times a day.

Usual pediatric dose

Ophthalmic antibacterial—

Infants up to 2 months of age: Use is not recommended.

Infants and children over 2 months of age: See *Usual adult and adolescent dose*.

Strength(s) usually available

U.S.—

4% (base) (each mL of ophthalmic solution contains 55.6 mg of sulfisoxazole diolamine, equivalent to approximately 40 mg of sulfisoxazole) (Rx) [*Gantrisin* (phenylmercuric nitrate 1:100,000)].

Packaging and storage

Store below 40 °C (104 °F), preferably between 15 and 30 °C (59 and 86 °F), unless otherwise specified by manufacturer. Store in a tight, light-resistant container. Protect from freezing.

Auxiliary labeling
- For the eye.
- Continue medicine for full time of treatment.

Note
Dispense in original unopened container.

Revised: 07/01/1993

SULFONAMIDES Systemic

This monograph includes information on the following: 1) Sulfadiazine; 2) Sulfamethizole†; 3) Sulfamethoxazole; 4) Sulfisoxazole.

INN: Sulfisoxazole—Sulfafurazole

BAN:
Sulfadiazine—Sulphadiazine
Sulfamethizole—Sulphamethizole
Sulfamethoxazole—Sulphamethoxazole
Sulfisoxazole—Sulphafurazole

JAN:
Sulfamethoxazole—Acetylsulfamethoxazole
Sulfamethoxazole—Sulfamethoxazole sodium

VA CLASSIFICATION (Primary): AM650

Commonly used brand name(s): *Apo-Sulfamethoxazole*[3]; *Apo-Sulfisoxazole*[4]; *Gantanol*[3]; *Gantrisin*[4]; *Novo-Soxazole*[4]; *Sulfizole*[4]; *Thiosulfil Forte*[2]; *Urobak*[3].

Note: For a listing of dosage forms and brand names by country availability, see *Dosage Forms* section(s).

†Not commercially available in Canada.

Category

Antibacterial (urinary)—Sulfamethizole.
Antibacterial (systemic)—Sulfadiazine; Sulfamethoxazole; Sulfisoxazole.
Antiprotozoal—Sulfadiazine; Sulfamethoxazole; Sulfisoxazole

Indications

Note: Bracketed information in the *Indications* section refers to uses that are not included in U.S. product labeling.

General Considerations

Sulfonamides are active *in vitro* against a broad spectrum of gram-positive and gram-negative bacteria. They also have activity *in vitro* against *Actinomyces, Chlamydia trachomatis, Nocardia asteroides, Plasmodium falciparum*, and *Toxoplasma gondii*. Susceptibility of an organism to sulfonamides is variable; many bacteria have become resistant to sulfonamides, with resistance occurring in more than 20% of community and nosocomial bacterial isolates. Resistance has developed in strains of staphylococci, *Neisseria gonorrhoeae, N. meningitidis*, Enterbacteriaceae, and *Pseudomonas* species.

Accepted

Chancroid (treatment)—Sulfonamides are indicated in the treatment of chancroid caused by *Haemophilus ducreyi*. However, other agents, such as erythromycin and ceftriaxone, are considered to be first line agents.

Chlamydial infections, endocervical and urethral (treatment)[1]—Sulfonamides are indicated in the treatment of endocervical and urethral infections caused by *Chlamydia trachomatis*. However, other agents, such as doxycycline and azithromycin, are considered to be first line agents.

Conjunctivitis, inclusion (treatment)—Sulfonamides are indicated in the treatment of neonatal inclusion conjunctivitis caused by *Chlamydia trachomatis*. However, other agents, such as erythromycin, are considered to be first line agents.

Malaria (treatment)—Sulfonamides are indicated as adjunctive therapy in the treatment of chloroquine-resistant *Plasmodium falciparum*.

Meningitis (prophylaxis)[1]—Sulfonamides are indicated in the prophylaxis of meningitis caused by susceptible strains of *Neisseria meningitidis*. However, other agents, such as rifampin, are considered to be first line agents.

Nocardiosis (treatment)—Sulfonamides are indicated in the treatment of nocardiosis caused by *Nocardia asteroides*.

Otitis media (treatment)[1]—Sulfonamides are indicated in combination with other antibacterials in the treatment of otitis media caused by susceptible strains of *H. influenzae*, streptococci, and pneumococci.

Rheumatic fever (prophylaxis)[1]—Sulfadiazine, [sulfamethoxazole], and [sulfisoxazole] are indicated in the prophylaxis of rheumatic fever associated with group A beta-hemolytic streptococcal infections. However, other agents, such as penicillin, are considered to be first line agents.

Toxoplasmosis (treatment)[1]—Sulfonamides are indicated in combination with pyrimethamine in the treatment of toxoplasmosis caused by *Toxoplasma gondii*.

Trachoma (treatment)—Sulfonamides are indicated in the treatment of ocular trachoma caused by *Chlamydia trachomatis*. However, other agents, such as doxycycline and azithromycin, are considered to be first line agents.

Urinary tract infections, bacterial (treatment)—Sulfonamides are indicated in the treatment of acute, uncomplicated urinary tract infections caused by susceptible bacteria. Because sulfamethizole produces low plasma levels and is rapidly eliminated, it is recommended only for use in urinary tract infections, not systemic infections. Sulfadiazine is not recommended for the treatment of urinary tract infections because of its relatively lower urine solubility and the increased chance of crystalluria; other, more soluble agents, such as sulfisoxazole, are generally preferred.

[Lymphogranuloma venereum (treatment)][1]—Sulfonamides are used in the treatment of lymphogranuloma venereum caused by *Chlamydia* species. However, other agents, such as doxycycline and erythromycin, are considered to be first line agents.

[Paracoccidioidomycosis (treatment)][1]—Sulfadiazine is used in the treatment of paracoccidioidomycosis caused *Paracoccidioides brasiliensis*.

Not all species or strains of a particular organism may be susceptible to a specific sulfonamide.

Unaccepted

Sulfonamides should not be used in the treatment of Group A beta-hemolytic streptococcal tonsillopharyngitis since they may not eradicate streptococci and therefore may not prevent sequelae such as rheumatic fever.

Sulfonamides are also not effective in treating rickettsial, viral, tuberculous, actinomycotic, fungal, or mycoplasmal infections. They are also not effective in the treatment of shigellosis.

[1]Not included in Canadian product labeling.

Pharmacology/Pharmacokinetics

Physicochemical characteristics

Molecular weight—
Sulfadiazine: 250.28.
Sulfamethizole: 270.34.
Sulfamethoxazole: 253.28.
Sulfisoxazole: 267.31.
Sulfisoxazole acetyl: 309.35.

Mechanism of action/Effect

Sulfonamides are broad-spectrum, bacteriostatic anti-infectives. They are structural analogs of para-aminobenzoic acid (PABA) and competitively inhibit a bacterial enzyme, dihydropteroate synthetase, that is responsible for incorporation of PABA into dihydrofolic acid, the immediate precursor of folic acid. This blocks the synthesis of dihydrofolic acid and decreases the amount of metabolically active tetrahydrofolic acid, a cofactor for the synthesis of purines, thymidine, and DNA.

Susceptible bacteria are those that must synthesize folic acid. Mammalian cells require preformed folic acid and cannot synthesize it. The action of sulfonamides is antagonized by PABA and its derivatives (e.g., procaine and tetracaine) and by the presence of pus or tissue breakdown products, which provide the necessary components for bacterial growth.

Absorption

All sulfonamides are rapidly and well absorbed (70–100%).

Distribution

Widely distributed throughout body tissues and fluids, including pleural, peritoneal, synovial, and ocular fluids, as well as the vagina and middle ear. Sulfadiazine is distributed throughout total body water, while sulfisoxazole is distributed primarily to extracellular fluid (ECF). Sulfadiazine, sulfamethoxazole, and sulfisoxazole penetrate into the cerebrospinal fluid (CSF); sulfadiazine reaches 32 to 65%, sulfamethoxazole reaches 14 to 30%, and sulfisoxazole reaches 30 to 50% of corresponding blood concentrations. Sulfonamides may be detected in the urine in approximately 30 minutes. They readily cross the placenta and are distributed into breast milk, also.

Urine solubility—
Sulfadiazine: Less soluble in urine; increased risk of crystalluria.
Sulfamethizole: Highly soluble in urine.
Sulfamethoxazole: Acetylated metabolite less soluble in urine; increased risk of crystalluria.
Sulfisoxazole: Highly soluble in urine.

Vol_D—
Sulfamethoxazole: Approximately 0.15 L per kg of body weight (L/kg).
Sulfisoxazole: Approximately 0.21 L/kg.

Protein binding

Variable; acetylated metabolites are more highly protein bound than the free drug. Sulfonamides compete with bilirubin for binding to albumin. Kernicterus may develop in premature infants or neonates. Binding is decreased in patients with severely impaired renal function. Only free, unbound drug has antibacterial activity.
Sulfadiazine—38 to 48%.
Sulfamethizole—Approximately 90%.
Sulfamethoxazole—60 to 70%.
Sulfisoxazole—85 to 90%.

Biotransformation

Hepatic; primarily by acetylation to inactive metabolites, which retain the toxicity of the parent compound. Some hepatic glucuronide conjugation may occur. Metabolism is increased with renal function impairment and decreased with hepatic failure.

Half-life

Sulfadiazine—
Normal renal function: Approximately 10 hours.
Renal failure: Approximately 34 hours.

Sulfamethizole—
Normal renal function: Approximately 1.5 hours.

Sulfamethoxazole—
Normal renal function: 6 to 12 hours.
Renal failure: 20 to 50 hours.

Sulfisoxazole—
Normal renal function: 3 to 7 hours.
Renal failure: 6 to 12 hours.

Time to peak concentration

Sulfadiazine—3 to 6 hours.
Sulfamethoxazole—2 to 4 hours.
Sulfisoxazole—2 to 4 hours.

Peak serum concentration

Free unbound sulfonamide—
Sulfadiazine: Single 2-gram dose—Approximately 30 to 60 mcg/mL.
Sulfamethoxazole: Single 2-gram dose—Approximately 80 to 100 mcg/mL.
Sulfisoxazole: Single 2-gram dose—40 to 50 mcg/mL.

Duration of action

Sulfadiazine—Short-acting sulfonamide.
Sulfamethizole—Short-acting sulfonamide.
Sulfamethoxazole—Intermediate-acting sulfonamide.
Sulfisoxazole—Short-acting sulfonamide.

Elimination

Renal, by glomerular filtration, with some tubular secretion and reabsorption of both active medication and metabolites. Excretion is increased in alkaline urine; small amounts are excreted in the feces, bile, and other body secretions.

Percent of medication unchanged in the urine—
Sulfadiazine: 60 to 85% in 48 to 72 hours.
Sulfamethizole: Approximately 95%.
Sulfamethoxazole: 20 to 40%.
Sulfisoxazole: Approximately 52% in 48 hours.
Sulfisoxazole acetyl: Approximately 58% in 72 hours.

In dialysis—
Peritoneal dialysis is not effective and hemodialysis is only moderately effective in removing sulfonamides.

Precautions to Consider

Cross-sensitivity and/or related problems

Patients allergic to one sulfonamide may be allergic to other sulfonamides also.
Patients allergic to furosemide, thiazide diuretics, sulfonylureas, or carbonic anhydrase inhibitors may be allergic to sulfonamides also.

Carcinogenicity

Sulfamethoxazole—
Long-term studies to evaluate the carcinogenic potential of sulfamethoxazole have not been done.

Sulfisoxazole—
Studies in mice given daily oral doses of up to 18 times the highest recommended human daily dose for 103 weeks, and rats given 4 times the highest recommended human daily dose have not shown that sulfisoxazole is carcinogenic in either male or female mice or rats.

Mutagenicity

Sulfamethizole—
No long-term mutagenicity studies have been done in animals or humans.

Sulfamethoxazole—
Bacterial mutagenicity studies with sulfamethoxazole have not been done. Studies in human leukocytes cultured *in vitro* with sulfamethoxazole using concentrations that exceeded therapeutic serum concentrations have not shown that sulfamethoxazole causes chromosomal damage.

Sulfisoxazole—
Bacterial mutagenicity studies with sulfisoxazole have not been done. However, sulfisoxazole has not been shown to be mutagenic when tested in *Escherichia coli* Sd-4-73 strains in the absence of a metabolic activating system.

Pregnancy/Reproduction

Fertility—
Sulfamethizole—
No long-term fertility studies have been done in animals or humans.

Sulfamethoxazole—
Studies in rats, given oral doses of 350 mg of sulfamethoxazole per kg of body weight daily, have not shown that it causes any adverse effects on fertility or general reproductive performance.

Sulfisoxazole—
Studies in rats given daily doses of 7 times the highest recommended daily dose have not shown that sulfisoxazole causes adverse effects on mating behavior, conception rate, or fertility index (percent of animals pregnant).

Pregnancy—
Sulfadiazine—
FDA Pregnancy Category C.

Sulfamethizole—
FDA Pregnancy Category C.

Sulfamethoxazole—
Sulfamethoxazole crosses the placenta. Large, adequate, and well-controlled studies in humans have not been done.
Studies in rats given oral doses of 533 mg of sulfamethoxazole per kg of body weight have shown that it causes teratogenic effects (primarily cleft palates). However, doses of 512 mg of sulfamethoxazole per kg of body weight did not cause cleft palates in rats.
Studies in rabbits given doses of 150 to 350 mg of sulfamethoxazole per kg of body weight daily have shown that sulfamethoxazole causes increased maternal mortality but has no adverse effects on the fetus.
FDA Pregnancy Category C.

Sulfisoxazole—
Sulfisoxazole crosses the placenta and enters the fetal circulation. Adequate and well-controlled studies in humans have not been done.
Studies in rats and rabbits given daily doses of 7 times the highest recommended human daily dose have not shown that sulfisoxazole is teratogenic. However, in studies in rats and mice given doses of 9 times the highest recommended human daily dose, sulfisoxazole caused cleft palates in both mice and rats and skeletal defects in rats.
FDA Pregnancy Category C.

Labor and delivery—Sulfonamides are not recommended at term since sulfonamides may cause kernicterus in the newborn.

Breast-feeding

Sulfonamides are distributed into breast milk. Use is not recommended in nursing women since sulfonamides may cause kernicterus in nursing infants. Also, sulfonamides may cause hemolytic anemia in glucose-6-phosphate dehydrogenase (G6PD)–deficient infants.

Pediatrics

Except as concurrent adjunctive therapy with pyrimethamine in the treatment of congenital toxoplasmosis, use of sulfonamides is contraindicated in infants up to 2 months of age. Sulfonamides compete for bilirubin binding sites on plasma albumin, increasing the risk of kernicterus in the newborn. Also, because the acetyltransferase system is not fully developed in the newborn, increased blood concentrations of the free sulfonamide can further increase the risk of kernicterus.

Geriatrics

Elderly patients may be at increased risk of severe side/adverse effects. Severe skin reactions, generalized bone marrow depression, and decreased platelet count (with or without purpura) are the most frequently reported severe side/adverse effects in the elderly. An increased incidence of thrombocytopenia with purpura has been reported in elderly patients who are receiving diuretics, primarily thiazides, concurrently with sulfamethoxazole. The potential for these problems should also be considered for elderly patients taking other sulfonamide medications.

Pharmacogenetics

Sulfonamides are metabolized primarily by acetylation. Patients can be divided into 2 groups, slow and fast acetylators. Slow acetylators have a higher incidence of severe sulfonamide reactions, although a slow acetylator phenotype is not thought to be the sole reason for sulfonamide toxicity. The incidence of the slow acetylator phenotype is approximately 50% in North American blacks and whites. Approximately 30% of the Hispanic population and 10% of the Asian population are slow acetylators. Also, acquired immunodeficiency syndrome (AIDS) patients with acute illness, but not AIDS patients who are stable or human immunodeficiency virus (HIV)-infected patients without AIDS, have an increased incidence of slow acetylation.

Dental

The leukopenic and thrombocytopenic effects of sulfonamides may result in an increased incidence of certain microbial infections, delayed healing, and gingival bleeding. If leukopenia or thrombocytopenia occurs, dental work should be deferred until blood counts have returned to normal. Patients should be instructed in proper oral hygiene, including caution in use of regular toothbrushes, dental floss, and toothpicks.

Drug interactions and/or related problems

The following drug interactions and/or related problems have been selected on the basis of their potential clinical significance (possible mechanism in parentheses where appropriate)—not necessarily inclusive (» = major clinical significance):

Note: Combinations containing any of the following medications, depending on the amount present, may also interact with this medication.

» Anticoagulants, coumarin- or indandione-derivative or
» Anticonvulsants, hydantoin or
» Antidiabetic agents, oral
(these medications may be displaced from protein binding sites and/or their metabolism may be inhibited by some sulfonamides, resulting in increased or prolonged effects and/or toxicity; dosage adjustments may be necessary during and after sulfonamide therapy)

Bone marrow depressants (See *Appendix II*)
(concurrent use of bone marrow depressants with sulfonamides may increase the leukopenic and/or thrombocytopenic effects; if concurrent use is required, close observation for myelotoxic effects should be considered)

Contraceptives, estrogen-containing, oral
(concurrent long-term use of sulfonamides may result in increased incidence of breakthrough bleeding and pregnancy)

Cyclosporine
(concurrent use with sulfonamides may increase the metabolism of cyclosporine, resulting in decreased plasma concentrations and potential transplant rejection, and additive nephrotoxicity; plasma cyclosporine concentrations and renal function should be monitored)

» Hemolytics, other (See *Appendix II*)
(concurrent use with sulfonamides may increase the potential for toxic side effects)

» Hepatotoxic medications, other (See *Appendix II*)
(concurrent use with sulfonamides may result in an increased incidence of hepatotoxicity; patients, especially those on prolonged administration or those with a history of liver disease, should be carefully monitored)

» Methenamine
(in acid urine, methenamine breaks down into formaldehyde, which may form an insoluble precipitate with certain sulfonamides, especially those that are less soluble in urine, and may also increase the danger of crystalluria; concurrent use is not recommended)

» Methotrexate or
Phenylbutazone or
Sulfinpyrazone
(the effects of methotrexate may be potentiated during concurrent use with sulfonamides because of displacement from plasma protein binding sites; phenylbutazone and sulfinpyrazone may displace sulfonamides from plasma protein binding sites, increasing sulfonamide concentrations)

Penicillins
(since bacteriostatic drugs may interfere with the bactericidal effect of penicillins in the treatment of meningitis or in other situations where a rapid bactericidal effect is necessary, it is best to avoid concurrent therapy)

Laboratory value alterations

The following have been selected on the basis of their potential clinical significance (possible effect in parentheses where appropriate)—not necessarily inclusive (» = major clinical significance).

With diagnostic test results

Benedict's test
(sulfonamides may produce a false-positive Benedict's test for urine glucose)

Jaffé alkaline picrate reaction assay
(sulfamethoxazole may interfere with the Jaffé alkaline picrate reaction assay for creatinine, resulting in overestimations of approximately 10% in the normal values for creatinine)

Sulfosalicylic acid test
(sulfonamides may produce a false-positive sulfosalicylic acid test for urine protein)

Urine urobilinogen test strip (e.g., Urobilistix)
(sulfonamides may interfere with the urine urobilinogen [Urobilistix] test for urinary urobilinogen)

With physiology/laboratory test values

Alanine aminotransferase (ALT [SGPT]), serum and
Aspartate aminotransferase (AST [SGOT]), serum and
Bilirubin, serum
(values may be increased)

Blood urea nitrogen (BUN) and
Creatinine, serum
(concentrations may be increased)

Medical considerations/Contraindications

The medical considerations/contraindications included have been selected on the basis of their potential clinical significance (reasons given in parentheses where appropriate)—not necessarily inclusive (» = major clinical significance).

Except under special circumstances, this medication should not be used when the following medical problems exist:

Allergy to sulfonamides, furosemide, thiazide diuretics, sulfonylureas, or carbonic anhydrase inhibitors

Risk-benefit should be considered when the following medical problems exist:

» Blood dyscrasias or
» Megaloblastic anemia due to folate deficiency
(sulfonamides may cause blood dyscrasias)

» Glucose-6-phosphate dehydrogenase (G6PD) deficiency
(hemolysis may occur)

» Hepatic function impairment
(sulfonamides are metabolized in the liver; delayed metabolism may increase the risk of toxicity; also, sulfonamides may cause fulminant hepatic necrosis)

» Porphyria
(sulfonamides may precipitate an acute attack of porphyria)

» Renal function impairment
(sulfonamides are renally excreted; delayed elimination may increase the risk of toxicity; also, sulfonamides may cause tubular necrosis or interstitial nephritis)

Patient monitoring

The following may be especially important in patient monitoring (other tests may be warranted in some patients, depending on condition; » = major clinical significance):

Complete blood counts (CBCs)
(may be required prior to and monthly during treatment to detect blood dyscrasias in patients on prolonged therapy; therapy should be discontinued if a significant decrease in the count of any formed blood elements occurs)

Urinalyses
(may be required prior to and periodically during treatment to detect crystalluria and/or urinary calculi formation in patients on long-term or high-dose therapy and in patients with impaired renal function)

Side/Adverse Effects

Note: Fatalities have occurred, although rarely, due to severe reactions such as Stevens-Johnson syndrome, toxic epidermal necrolysis, fulminant hepatic necrosis, agranulocytosis, aplastic anemia, and other blood dyscrasias. Therapy should be discontinued at the first appearance of skin rash or any serious side/adverse effects.

Patients with acquired immunodeficiency syndrome (AIDS) may have a greater incidence of side/adverse effects, especially rash, fever, and leukopenia, than do non-AIDS patients.

The multiorgan toxicity of sulfonamides is thought to be the result of the way sulfonamides are metabolized in certain patients. It is probably due to the inability of the body to detoxify reactive metabolites. Sulfonamides are metabolized primarily by acetylation. Patients can be divided into slow and fast acetylators. Slow acetylation of sulfonamides makes more of the medication available for metabolism by the oxidative pathways of the cytochrome P-450 system. These pathways produce reactive toxic metabolites, such as hydroxylamine and nitroso compounds. The metabolites are normally detoxified by scavengers, such as glutathione. However, some populations, such as human immunodeficiency virus (HIV)-infected patients, have low concentrations of glutathione and these metabolites accumulate, producing toxicity. Patients who are slow acetylators have a higher incidence of sulfonamide hypersensitivity reactions, although severe toxicity has also been seen in fast acetylators. Acetylation status alone cannot fully explain sulfonamide toxicity since approximately 50% of North American blacks and whites are slow acetylators and severe reactions occur in less than 1% of patients treated with sulfonamides. However, decreased acetylation may increase the amount of sulfonamide metabolized to toxic metabolites.

Crytalluria is more likely to occur with a less soluble sulfonamide, such as sulfadiazine. It occurs most often with the administration of high doses, and can be minimized by maintaining a high urine flow and alkalinizing the urine.

The following side/adverse effects have been selected on the basis of their potential clinical significance (possible signs and symptoms in parentheses where appropriate)—not necessarily inclusive:

Those indicating need for medical attention

Incidence more frequent

Hypersensitivity (fever; itching; skin rash); ***photosensitivity*** (increased sensitivity of skin to sunlight)

Incidence less frequent

Blood dyscrasias (fever and sore throat; pale skin; unusual bleeding or bruising; unusual tiredness or weakness); ***hepatitis*** (yellow eyes or skin); ***Lyell's syndrome*** (difficulty in swallowing; redness, blistering, peeling, or loosening of skin); ***Stevens-Johnson syndrome*** (aching joints and muscles; redness, blistering, peeling, or loosening of skin; unusual tiredness or weakness)

Incidence rare

Central nervous system toxicity (confusion; disorientation; euphoria; hallucination; mental depression); *Clostridium difficile* ***colitis*** (severe abdominal or stomach cramps and pain; abdominal tenderness; watery and severe diarrhea, which may also be bloody; fever); ***crystalluria or hematuria*** (blood in urine; lower back pain; pain or burning while urinating); ***goiter or thyroid function disturbance*** (swelling of front part of neck); ***interstitial nephritis or tubular necrosis*** (greatly increased or decreased frequency of urination or amount of urine; increased thirst; loss of appetite; nausea; vomiting)

Note: *C. difficile colitis* may occur up to several weeks after discontinuation of these medications.

Those indicating need for medical attention only if they continue or are bothersome

Incidence more frequent

Central nervous system effects (dizziness; headache; lethargy); ***gastrointestinal disturbances*** (diarrhea; loss of appetite; nausea or vomiting)

Patient Consultation

As an aid to patient consultation, refer to *Advice for the Patient, Sulfonamides (Systemic).*

In providing consultation, consider emphasizing the following selected information (» = major clinical significance):

Before using this medication

» Conditions affecting use, especially:

Allergy to sulfonamides, furosemide, thiazide diuretics, sulfonylureas, carbonic anhydrase inhibitors

Pregnancy—Sulfonamides cross the placenta; not recommended at term since sulfonamides may cause kernicterus in newborn

Breast-feeding—Sulfonamides are distributed into breast milk; may cause kernicterus in nursing infants

Use in children—Sulfonamides are contraindicated in infants up to 2 months of age since sulfonamides may cause kernicterus in neonates

Use in the elderly—Elderly patients may be at increased risk of severe side/adverse effects

Other medications, especially coumarin- or indandione-derivative anticoagulants, hydantoin anticonvulsants, oral antidiabetic agents, other hemolytics, other hepatotoxic medications, methenamine, or methotrexate

Other medical problems, especially blood dyscrasias, G6PD deficiency, hepatic function impairment, megaloblastic anemia, porphyria, and renal function impairment

Proper use of this medication

» Not giving to infants under 2 months of age

» Maintaining adequate fluid intake

Proper administration technique for oral liquids

» Compliance with full course of therapy

» Importance of not missing doses and taking at evenly spaced times

» Proper dosing

Missed dose: Taking as soon as possible; not taking if almost time for next dose; not doubling doses

» Proper storage

Precautions while using this medication

» Regular visits to physician to check blood counts

Checking with physician if no improvement within a few days

Using caution in use of regular toothbrushes, dental floss, and toothpicks; deferring dental work until blood counts have returned to normal; checking with physician or dentist concerning proper oral hygiene

» Possible photosensitivity reactions

» Caution if dizziness occurs

Side/adverse effects

Severe skin problems and blood problems may be more likely to occur in the elderly who are taking sulfamethoxazole, especially if taking diuretics concurrently

Signs of potential side effects, especially hypersensitivity, photosensitivity, blood dyscrasias, hepatitis, Lyell's syndrome, Stevens-Johnson syndrome, central nervous system toxicity, *C. difficile* colitis, crystalluria or hematuria, goiter or thyroid function disturbance, and interstitial nephritis or tubular necrosis

General Dosing Information

Fluid intake should be sufficient to maintain urine output of at least 1200 mL per day in adults.

SULFADIAZINE

Summary of Differences

Indications: Because of its relatively low urine solubility and the increased chance of crystalluria, sulfadiazine is not recommended for the treatment of urinary tract infections. Sulfadiazine is used for the prophylaxis of rheumatic fever and, in combination with pyrimethamine, for the treatment of toxoplasmosis and malaria caused by chloroquine-resistant *P. falciparum*.

Additional Dosing Information

Fluid intake should be sufficient to maintain urine output of at least 1200 mL per day in adults.

Patients with impaired renal function may require a reduction in dose.

Oral Dosage Forms

SULFADIAZINE TABLETS USP

Usual adult and adolescent dose

Antibacterial (systemic) or
Antiprotozoal—

Oral, 2 to 4 grams initially, then 1 gram every four to six hours.

Meningitis (prophylaxis)—

Oral, 1 gram every twelve hours for two days.

Rheumatic fever (prophylaxis)—

Oral, 1 gram once a day.

Toxoplasmosis—
AIDS patients: Oral, 1 to 2 grams of sulfadiazine every 6 hours with 50 to 100 mg of pyrimethamine per day and 10 to 25 mg of leucovorin per day.
Pregnant women: Oral, 1 gram of sulfadiazine every 6 hours with 25 mg of pyrimethamine per day after week 16 of the pregnancy. With this regimen, 5 to 15 mg of leucovorin per day is administered.

Usual pediatric dose

Antibacterial (systemic) or
Antiprotozoal—
Infants up to 2 months of age: Use is not recommended.
Infants 2 months of age and over: Oral, 75 mg per kg of body weight initially, then 37.5 mg per kg of body weight every six hours or 25 mg per kg of body weight every four hours.
Toxoplasmosis: Oral, 50 mg of sulfadiazine per kg of body weight two times a day, administered concurrently with 2 mg of pyrimethamine per kg of body weight per day for two days, then 1 mg of pyrimethamine per kg of body weight per day for two to six months, then of 1 mg pyrimethamine per kg of body weight per day three times per week. With this regimen, 5 mg of leucovorin is administered three times a week. The three medications should be given for a total of twelve months.

Note: The maximum dose for children should not exceed 6 grams daily.

Strength(s) usually available

U.S.—
500 mg (Rx) [GENERIC].
Canada—
500 mg (Rx) [GENERIC].

Packaging and storage

Store below 30 °C (86 °F), unless otherwise specified by manufacturer. Store in a tight container. Protect from light.

Auxiliary labeling

- Take with a full glass of water.
- Avoid too much sun or use of sunlamp.
- May cause dizziness.
- Continue medicine for full time of treatment.

SULFAMETHIZOLE

Summary of Differences

Indications: Sulfamethizole is recommended for use only in the treatment of urinary tract infections, not systemic infections.

Additional Dosing Information

Fluid intake should be sufficient to maintain urine output of at least 1200 mL per day in adults.

Patients with impaired renal function may require a reduction in dose.

Oral Dosage Forms

SULFAMETHIZOLE TABLETS USP

Usual adult and adolescent dose

Antibacterial—
Oral, 500 mg to 1 gram every six to eight hours.

Usual pediatric dose

Antibacterial—
Infants up to 2 months of age: Use is not recommended.
Infants 2 months of age and over: Oral, 7.5 to 11.25 mg per kg of body weight every six hours.

Strength(s) usually available

U.S.—
500 mg (Rx) [*Thiosulfil Forte*].
Canada—
Not commercially available.

Packaging and storage

Store below 30 °C (86 °F), unless otherwise specified by manufacturer. Store in a tight container.

Auxiliary labeling

- Take with a full glass of water.
- Avoid too much sun or use of sunlamp.
- May cause dizziness.
- Continue medicine for full time of treatment.

SULFAMETHOXAZOLE

Additional Dosing Information

Fluid intake should be sufficient to maintain urine output of at least 1200 mL per day in adults.

Although sulfamethoxazole has a greater tendency to cause crystalluria than sulfisoxazole because of slower absorption and excretion, alkalinization of the urine is usually unnecessary.

Therapy should be continued for at least 7 to 10 days in urinary tract infections.

Patients with impaired renal function may require a reduction in dose.

Oral Dosage Forms

SULFAMETHOXAZOLE TABLETS USP

Usual adult and adolescent dose

Antibacterial (systemic) or
Antiprotozoal—
Mild to moderate infections: Oral, 2 grams initially, then 1 gram every eight to twelve hours.
Severe infections: Oral, 4 grams initially, then 2 grams every eight to twelve hours.

Usual pediatric dose

Antibacterial (systemic) or
Antiprotozoal—
Infants up to 2 months of age: Except as concurrent adjunctive therapy with pyrimethamine in the treatment of congenital toxoplasmosis, use is contraindicated since sulfonamides may cause kernicterus in neonates.
Infants and children 2 months of age and over: Oral, 50 to 60 mg per kg of body weight (maximum—2 grams) initially, then 25 to 30 mg per kg of body weight every twelve hours.

Note: The maximum dose for children should not exceed 75 mg per kg of body weight per day.

Strength(s) usually available

U.S.—
500 mg (Rx) [*Gantanol; Urobak*].
Canada—
500 mg (Rx) [*Apo-Sulfamethoxazole* (scored); GENERIC].

Packaging and storage

Store below 40 °C (104 °F), preferably between 15 and 30 °C (59 and 86 °F), unless otherwise specified by manufacturer. Store in a well-closed, light-resistant container.

Auxiliary labeling

- Take with a full glass of water.
- May cause dizziness.
- Avoid too much sun or use of sunlamp.
- Continue medicine for full time of treatment.

SULFISOXAZOLE

Additional Dosing Information

Fluid intake should be sufficient to maintain urine output of at least 1200 mL per day in adults.

Because of its relatively high solubility even in acid urine, the risk of crystalluria with sulfisoxazole is low and alkalinization of the urine is usually unnecessary.

Therapy should be continued for at least 7 to 10 days in urinary tract infections.

Patients with impaired renal function may require a reduction in dose.

Oral Dosage Forms

SULFISOXAZOLE TABLETS USP

Usual adult and adolescent dose

Antibacterial (systemic) or
Antiprotozoal—
Oral, 2 to 4 grams initially, then 750 mg to 1.5 grams every four hours; or 1 to 2 grams every six hours.

Usual adult prescribing limits

Up to 8 grams daily.

Usual pediatric dose
Antibacterial (systemic) or
Antiprotozoal—
Infants up to 2 months of age: Except as concurrent adjunctive therapy with pyrimethamine in the treatment of congenital toxoplasmosis, use is contraindicated since sulfonamides may cause kernicterus in neonates.
Infants and children 2 months of age and over: Oral, 75 mg per kg of body weight or 2 grams per square meter of body surface initially, then 25 mg per kg of body weight or 667 mg per square meter of body surface every four hours; or 37.5 mg per kg of body weight or 1 gram per square meter of body surface every six hours.

Note: The maximum dose for children should not exceed 6 grams daily.

Strength(s) usually available
U.S.—
500 mg (Rx) [*Gantrisin* (scored); GENERIC].
Canada—
500 mg (Rx) [*Apo-Sulfisoxazole; Novo-Soxazole; Sulfizole*].

Packaging and storage
Store below 40 °C (104 °F), preferably between 15 and 30 °C (59 and 86 °F), unless otherwise specified by manufacturer. Store in a well-closed, light-resistant container.

Auxiliary labeling
- Take with a full glass of water.
- May cause dizziness.
- Avoid too much sun or use of sunlamp.
- Continue medicine for full time of treatment.

SULFISOXAZOLE ACETYL ORAL SUSPENSION USP

Usual adult and adolescent dose
See *Sulfisoxazole Tablets USP*.

Usual adult prescribing limits
See *Sulfisoxazole Tablets USP*.

Usual pediatric dose
See *Sulfisoxazole Tablets USP*.

Strength(s) usually available
U.S.—
500 mg per 5 mL (Rx) [*Gantrisin* (alcohol 0.3%; parabens; sucrose); GENERIC].
Canada—
Not commercially available.

Packaging and storage
Store below 40 °C (104 °F), preferably between 15 and 30 °C (59 and 86 °F), unless otherwise specified by manufacturer. Store in a tight, light-resistant container. Protect from freezing.

Auxiliary labeling
- Shake well.
- Take with a full glass of water.
- May cause dizziness.
- Avoid too much sun or use of sunlamp.
- Continue medicine for full time of treatment.

Note
When dispensing, include a calibrated liquid-measuring device.

SULFISOXAZOLE ACETYL ORAL SYRUP

Usual adult and adolescent dose
See *Sulfisoxazole Tablets USP*.

Usual adult prescribing limits
See *Sulfisoxazole Tablets USP*.

Usual pediatric dose
See *Sulfisoxazole Tablets USP*.

Strength(s) usually available
U.S.—
500 mg per 5 mL (Rx) [*Gantrisin*].
Canada—
Not commercially available.

Packaging and storage
Store below 40 °C (104 °F), preferably between 15 and 30 °C (59 and 86 °F), unless otherwise specified by manufacturer. Store in a tight, light-resistant container. Protect from freezing.

Auxiliary labeling
- Take with a full glass of water.
- May cause dizziness.
- Avoid too much sun or use of sunlamp.
- Continue medicine for full time of treatment.

Note
When dispensing, include a calibrated liquid-measuring device.

Revised: 08/25/1995

SULFONAMIDES AND TRIMETHOPRIM Systemic

This monograph includes information on the following: 1) Sulfadiazine and Trimethoprim; 2) Sulfamethoxazole and Trimethoprim.

BAN:
Sulfadiazine—Sulphadiazine
Sulfamethoxazole—Sulphamethoxazole

JAN:
Sulfamethoxazole—Acetylsulfamethoxazole
Sulfamethoxazole—Sulfamethoxazole sodium

VA CLASSIFICATION (Primary): AM650

Commonly used brand name(s): *Apo-Sulfatrim*[2]; *Apo-Sulfatrim DS*[2]; *Bactrim*[2]; *Bactrim DS*[2]; *Bactrim I.V.*[2]; *Bactrim Pediatric*[2]; *Cofatrim Forte*[2]; *Coptin*[1]; *Coptin 1*[1]; *Cotrim*[2]; *Cotrim DS*[2]; *Cotrim Pediatric*[2]; *Novo-Trimel*[2]; *Novo-Trimel D.S.*[2]; *Nu-Cotrimox*[2]; *Nu-Cotrimox DS*[2]; *Roubac*[2]; *Septra*[2]; *Septra DS*[2]; *Septra Grape Suspension*[2]; *Septra I.V.*[2]; *Septra Suspension*[2]; *Sulfatrim*[2]; *Sulfatrim Pediatric*[2]; *Sulfatrim S/S*[2]; *Sulfatrim Suspension*[2]; *Sulfatrim-DS*[2].

Other commonly used names are:
Cotrimazine Sulfadiazine and Trimethoprim
Cotrimoxazole Sulfamethoxazole and Trimethoprim
SMZ-TMP Sulfamethoxazole and Trimethoprim

NOTE: The *Sulfonamides and Trimethoprim (Systemic)* monograph is maintained on the *USP DI* electronic data base. A copy of the most recent revision of the complete monograph can be accessed on the *USP DI* Updates Online website. See the front cover of book for details on accessing the site.

For information on the specific components of this combination, see the *USP DI* monographs for *Sulfonamides (Systemic)* and *Trimethoprim (Systemic)*.

The information that follows is selectively abstracted from the complete monograph and is provided to facilitate drug use review and patient counseling.

Note: For a listing of dosage forms and brand names by country availability, see *Dosage Forms* section(s).

Category

Antibacterial (systemic)—Sulfadiazine and Trimethoprim; Sulfamethoxazole and Trimethoprim.
Antiprotozoal—Sulfamethoxazole and Trimethoprim

Indications

Note: Bracketed information in the *Indications* section refers to uses that are not included in U.S. product labeling.

General Considerations
Sulfonamides, such as sulfadiazine and sulfamethoxazole, used together with trimethoprim, produce synergistic antibacterial activity. Sulfadiazine and sulfamethoxazole have equal antibacterial properties, covering the same spectrum of activity. These sulfonamides, in combination with trimethoprim, are active *in vitro* against many gram-positive and gram-negative aerobic organisms. They have minimal activity against anaerobic bacteria. Susceptible gram-positive organisms include many *Staphylococcus aureus*, including some methicillin-resistant strains, *S. saprophyticus*, some group A beta-hemolytic streptococci, *Streptococcus agalactiae*, and most but not all strains of *S. pneumoniae*. Gram-negative organisms that are susceptible include *Escherichia coli*, many *Klebsiella* species, *Citrobacter diversus* and *C. freundii*, *Enterobacter* species, *Salmonella* species, *Shigella* species, *Haemophilus influenzae*, including some ampicillin-resistant strains, *H. ducreyi*, *Morganella morganii*, *Proteus vulgaris* and *P. mirabilis*, and some *Serratia* species. Sulfonamide and trimethoprim combinations also have activity against *Acinetobacter* species, *Pneumocystis carinii*, *Providencia rettgeri*, *P. stuarti*, *Aeromonas*, *Brucella*, and *Yersinia* species. They are also usually active against *Neisseria meningitidis*, *Branhamella (Moraxella) catarrhalis*, and some, but not all, *N. gonorrhoeae*. *Pseudomonas aeruginosa* is usually resistant, but *P. cepacia* and *P. maltophilia* may be sensitive.

The major difference between sulfadiazine and sulfamethoxazole exists in their respective pharmacokinetics. The primary distinction is that sulfadiazine is metabolized to a much lesser extent than is sulfamethoxazole. This allows for a higher urinary concentration of unchanged sulfadiazine, as well as an increased risk of crystalluria when it is administered in high doses; the antibacterial urinary concentration of sulfadiazine is maintained over a 24-hour interval, allowing for once-a-day dosing in adults. Also, sulfadiazine achieves higher concentrations in the bile and cerebrospinal fluid.

Accepted

Bronchitis (treatment)—Oral sulfamethoxazole and trimethoprim combination is indicated in adults in the treatment of acute exacerbations of chronic bronchitis caused by susceptible organisms.

Enterocolitis, *Shigella* species (treatment)—Oral and parenteral sulfamethoxazole and trimethoprim combinations are indicated in the treatment of enterocolitis caused by susceptible strains of *Shigella flexneri* and *S. sonnei*.

Otitis media, acute (treatment)—Oral sulfamethoxazole and trimethoprim combination is indicated in the treatment of acute otitis media caused by susceptible organisms in children.

Pneumonia, *Pneumocystis carinii* (prophylaxis)[1]—Oral sulfamethoxazole and trimethoprim combination is indicated in the prophylaxis of *Pneumocystis carinii* pneumonia (PCP) in patients who are immunocompromised and considered to be at increased risk of developing PCP, including patients with acquired immunodeficiency syndrome (AIDS). It is considered to be the treatment of choice for this indication. Sulfamethoxazole and trimethoprim combination is indicated in both secondary prophylaxis (patients who have already had at least one episode of PCP), and primary prophylaxis (HIV-infected adults with a CD4 lymphocyte count less than or equal to 200 cells per cubic millimeter and/or less than 20% of total lymphocytes; all children born to HIV-infected mothers, beginning at 4 to 6 weeks of age, and subsequent prophylaxis given as determined on the basis of age-specific CD4 lymphocyte count) of PCP.

Pneumonia, *Pneumocystis carinii* (treatment)—Oral and parenteral sulfamethoxazole and trimethoprim combinations are indicated as primary agents in the treatment of *Pneumocystis carinii* pneumonia (PCP) in immunocompromised patients, including patients with acquired immunodeficiency syndrome (AIDS). Pentamidine is considered an alternative agent for PCP.

Traveler's diarrhea (treatment)—Oral sulfamethoxazole and trimethoprim combination is indicated in the treatment of traveler's diarrhea caused by susceptible strains of enterotoxigenic *Escherichia coli* and *Shigella* species.

Urinary tract infections, bacterial (treatment)—Sulfadiazine and trimethoprim combination and oral and parenteral sulfamethoxazole and trimethoprim combinations are indicated in the treatment of urinary tract infections caused by susceptible organisms.

[Biliary tract infections (treatment)]—Sulfamethoxazole and trimethoprim combination is used in the treatment of biliary tract infections caused by susceptible organisms.

[Bone and joint infections (treatment)]—Sulfamethoxazole and trimethoprim combination is used in the treatment of bone and joint infections caused by susceptible organisms.

[Chancroid (treatment)][1]—Sulfamethoxazole and trimethoprim combination is used as an alternative agent in the treatment of chancroid.

[Chlamydial infections (treatment)][1]—Sulfamethoxazole and trimethoprim combination is used as an alternative agent in the treatment of chlamydial infections.

[Cyclospora infections (treatment)][1]—Sulfamethoxazole and trimethoprim combination is used in the treatment of diarrhea caused by *Cyclospora cayetanensis*, but may not completely eradicate the organism.

[Endocarditis, bacterial (treatment)][1]—Sulfamethoxazole and trimethoprim combination is used as an alternative agent in the treatment of bacterial endocarditis caused by susceptible organisms.

[Gonorrhea, endocervical and urethral, uncomplicated (treatment)]—Sulfamethoxazole and trimethoprim combination is used as an alternative agent in the treatment of gonorrhea caused by susceptible organisms.

[Granuloma inguinale (treatment)][1]—Sulfamethoxazole and trimethoprim combination is used as an alternative agent in the treatment of granuloma inguinale.

[HIV-related infections in Africa (prophylaxis)][1]—Sulfamethoxazole and trimethoprim combination is used in the prophylaxis of HIV-related infections in Africa.

Given the large number of patients with HIV-related infections throughout Africa and the high mortality they experience, sulfamethoxazole and trimethoprim combination prophylaxis if widely applicable and implemented could significantly affect care and survival (i.e., could significantly lower morbidity and mortality) among HIV-infected patients in Africa.

[Isosporiasis (prophylaxis and treatment)][1]—Sulfamethoxazole and trimethoprim combination is used in the prophylaxis and treatment of isosporiasis caused by *Isospora belli*.

[Lymphogranuloma venereum (treatment)][1]—Sulfamethoxazole and trimethoprim combination is used in the treatment of lymphogranuloma venereum.

[Meningitis (treatment)]—Sulfamethoxazole and trimethoprim combination is used as an alternative agent in the treatment of meningitis caused by susceptible organisms.

[Nocardiosis (treatment)]—Sulfamethoxazole and trimethoprim combination is used in the treatment of nocardiosis.

[Paracoccidioidomycosis (treatment)][1]—Sulfamethoxazole and trimethoprim combination is used in the treatment of paracoccidioidomycosis.

[Paratyphoid fever (treatment)] or
[Typhoid fever (treatment)]—Sulfamethoxazole and trimethoprim combination is used as an alternative agent in the treatment of paratyphoid and typhoid fevers caused by susceptible strains.

[Septicemia, bacterial (treatment)]—Sulfamethoxazole and trimethoprim combination is used as an alternative agent in the treatment of bacterial septicemia caused by susceptible organisms.

[Sinusitis (treatment)][1]—Sulfamethoxazole and trimethoprim combination is used in the treatment of sinusitis caused by susceptible organisms.

[Skin and soft tissue infections (treatment)]—Sulfamethoxazole and trimethoprim combination is used in the treatment of skin and soft tissue infections, including burn wound infections caused by susceptible organisms.

[Toxoplasmosis (prophylaxis)][1]—Sulfamethoxazole and trimethoprim combination is used in the primary prophylaxis of toxoplasmosis in patients with AIDS.

[Urinary tract infections, bacterial (prophylaxis)][1]—Sulfamethoxazole and trimethoprim combination is used in the prophylaxis of bacterial urinary tract infections.

[Whipple's disease (treatment)][1]—Sulfamethoxazole and trimethoprim combination is used in the treatment of Whipple's disease.

Not all strains of a particular organism may be susceptible to sulfonamide and trimethoprim combinations.

Unaccepted

Sulfamethoxazole and trimethoprim combination is not indicated for prophylaxis or prolonged therapy in otitis media. Sulfamethoxazole and trimethoprim combination is not effective in the treatment of syphilis and *Ureaplasm urealyticum*.

Sulfamethoxazole and trimethoprim combination should not be used in the treatment of group A beta-hemolytic streptococcal tonsillopharyngitis since it may not eradicate streptococci and therefore may not prevent sequelae such as rheumatic fever.

---

[1]Not included in Canadian product labeling.

Patient Consultation

As an aid to patient consultation, refer to *Advice for the Patient, Sulfonamides and Trimethoprim (Systemic)*.

In providing consultation, consider emphasizing the following selected information (» = major clinical significance):

Before using this medication

» Conditions affecting use, especially:

Allergy to sulfonamides, furosemide, thiazide diuretics, sulfonylureas, carbonic anhydrase inhibitors, sulfites, or trimethoprim

Pregnancy—Sulfonamides and trimethoprim cross the placenta; trimethoprim may interfere with folic acid metabolism; use is not recommended at term since sulfonamides may cause jaundice, hemolytic anemia, and kernicterus in neonates

Breast-feeding—Sulfonamides and trimethoprim are distributed into breast milk; sulfonamides may cause kernicterus in nursing infants; trimethoprim may interfere with folic acid metabolism

Use in children—Sulfadiazine and trimethoprim combination is contraindicated in infants up to 3 months of age and sulfamethoxazole and trimethoprim combination is contraindicated in infants up to 2 months of age for most indications since sulfonamides may cause kernicterus in neonates; however, sulfamethoxazole and trimethoprim combination is indicated in all infants born to human immunodeficiency virus (HIV)-infected mothers, starting at 4 to 6 weeks

Use in the elderly—Elderly patients, especially those also taking diuretics, may be at increased risk of severe side/adverse effects

Other medications, especially coumarin- or indandione-derivative anticoagulants, hydantoin anticonvulsants, oral antidiabetic agents, other hemolytics, other hepatotoxic medications, methenamine, or methotrexate

Other medical problems, especially blood dyscrasias, G6PD deficiency, hepatic function impairment, megaloblastic anemia due to folic acid deficiency, porphyria, and renal function impairment

Proper use of this medication

» Not giving sulfadiazine and trimethoprim combination to infants under 3 months of age, or sulfamethoxazole and trimethoprim combination to infants under 2 months of age, except under special circumstances

» Maintaining adequate fluid intake

Proper administration technique for oral liquids

» Compliance with full course of therapy

» Importance of not missing doses and taking at evenly spaced times

» Proper dosing

Missed dose: Taking as soon as possible; not taking if almost time for next dose; not doubling doses

» Proper storage

Precautions while using this medication

» Regular visits to physician to check blood counts

Checking with physician if no improvement within a few days

Caution in use of regular toothbrushes, dental floss, and toothpicks; deferring dental work until blood counts have returned to normal; checking with physician or dentist concerning proper oral hygiene

» Possible skin photosensitivity

» Caution if dizziness occurs

Side/adverse effects

Severe skin problems and blood problems may be more likely to occur in elderly patients who are taking sulfamethoxazole and trimethoprim combination, especially if diuretics are being taken concurrently.

Signs of potential side effects, especially hypersensitivity, photosensitivity, blood dyscrasias, cholestatic hepatitis, pancreatitis, Stevens-Johnson syndrome, toxic epidermal necrolysis, aseptic meningitis, central nervous system toxicity, *Clostridium difficile* colitis, crystalluria, hematuria, goiter, thyroid function disturbance, interstitial nephritis, tubular necrosis, methemoglobinemia, rhabdomyolysis and thrombophlebitis

SULFADIAZINE AND TRIMETHOPRIM

Summary of Differences

Indications: Sulfadiazine and trimethoprim combination is recommended for use only in the treatment of urinary tract infections.

Pharmacology/pharmacokinetics: Compared to sulfamethoxazole, sulfadiazine achieves higher concentrations in the bile and cerebrospinal fluid, is metabolized to a lesser extent, and a higher percentage of active medication is eliminated in the urine.

Additional Dosing Information

The usual length of therapy when treating an uncomplicated lower urinary tract infection with sulfadiazine and trimethoprim combination is three to five days in women and seven to ten days in men. Therapy should be continued for fourteen days or more in upper urinary tract infections.

Oral Dosage Forms

SULFADIAZINE AND TRIMETHOPRIM ORAL SUSPENSION

Usual adult and adolescent dose

Antibacterial—

Oral, 820 mg of sulfadiazine and 180 mg of trimethoprim once a day.

Usual pediatric dose

Antibacterial—

Infants up to 3 months of age: Use is not recommended.

Children 3 months to 12 years of age: Oral, 7 mg of sulfadiazine and 1.5 mg of trimethoprim per kg of body weight every twelve hours.

Children over 12 years of age: See *Usual adult and adolescent dose*.

Strength(s) usually available

U.S.—

Not commercially available.

Canada—

205 mg of sulfadiazine and 45 mg of trimethoprim per 5 mL (Rx) [*Coptin*].

Auxiliary labeling

- Shake well.
- Take with a full glass of water.
- May cause dizziness.
- Avoid too much sun or use of sunlamp.
- Continue medicine for full time of treatment.

SULFADIAZINE AND TRIMETHOPRIM TABLETS

Usual adult and adolescent dose

See *Sulfadiazine and Trimethoprim Oral Suspension*.

Usual pediatric dose

See *Sulfadiazine and Trimethoprim Oral Suspension*.

Strength(s) usually available

U.S.—

Not commercially available.

Canada—

410 mg of sulfadiazine and 90 mg of trimethoprim (Rx) [*Coptin*].

820 mg of sulfadiazine and 180 mg of trimethoprim (Rx) [*Coptin 1*].

Auxiliary labeling

- Take with a full glass of water.
- May cause dizziness.
- Avoid too much sun or use of sunlamp.
- Continue medicine for full time of treatment.

SULFAMETHOXAZOLE AND TRIMETHOPRIM

Summary of Differences

Pharmacology/pharmacokinetics: Sulfamethoxazole is more soluble in urine than is sulfadiazine.

Additional Dosing Information

Therapy should be continued for at least ten to fourteen days in acute exacerbations of chronic bronchitis; as single-dose therapy or for three to five days in urinary tract infections; for five to seven days in shigellosis; for ten days in acute otitis media in children; for five days in travelers diarrhea; and for fourteen to twenty-one days in *Pneumocystis carinii* pneumonia. Sulfamethoxazole and trimethoprim combination may also be given for one or two days or as single-dose therapy for lower urinary tract infections. Therapy should be continued for fourteen days or more in upper urinary tract infections.

Oral Dosage Forms

Note: Bracketed uses in the *Dosage Forms* section refer to categories of use and/or indications that are not included in U.S. product labeling.

SULFAMETHOXAZOLE AND TRIMETHOPRIM ORAL SUSPENSION USP

Usual adult and adolescent dose

Antibacterial (systemic)—

Oral, 800 mg of sulfamethoxazole and 160 mg of trimethoprim every twelve hours.

Antiprotozoal—

Pneumocystis carinii pneumonia—

Treatment:

Oral, 18.75 to 25 mg of sulfamethoxazole and 3.75 to 5 mg of trimethoprim per kg of body weight every six hours for fourteen to twenty-one days.

Prophylaxis[1]:

Oral, 800 mg of sulfamethoxazole and 160 mg of trimethoprim once a day.

Acceptable alternative dosing schedules include—

Oral, 800 mg of sulfamethoxazole and 160 mg of trimethoprim three times a week (e.g., Monday, Wednesday, Friday).

Oral, 400 mg of sulfamethoxazole and 80 mg of trimethoprim once a day.

[Toxoplasmosis (prophylaxis)][1]—

Oral, 800 mg of sulfamethoxazole and 160 mg of trimethoprim once a day.

Acceptable alternative dosing schedules include:

Oral, 800 mg of sulfamethoxazole and 160 mg of trimethoprim three times a week (e.g., Monday, Wednesday, Friday).

Oral, 400 mg of sulfamethoxazole and 80 mg of trimethoprim once a day.

[HIV-related infection in Africa (prophylaxis)][1]—

Oral, 800 mg of sulfamethoxazole and 160 mg of trimethoprim once a day.

Usual pediatric dose

Antibacterial (systemic)—

Infants up to 2 months of age—

Use is not recommended since sulfonamides may cause kernicterus in neonates.

Infants 2 months of age and over—

Infants and children up to 40 kg of body weight—Oral, 20 to 30 mg of sulfamethoxazole and 4to 6 mg of trimethoprim per kg of body weight every twelve hours.

Children 40 kg of body weight and over—See *Usual adult and adolescent dose.*

Antiprotozoal—

Pneumocystis carinii pneumonia (PCP)—

Treatment:

Oral, 18.75 to 25 mg of sulfamethoxazole and 3.75 to 5 mg of trimethoprim per kg of body weight every six hours for fourteen to twenty-one days.

Prophylaxis[1]:

Children 4 weeks of age and over—

Oral, 375 mg of sulfamethoxazole per square meter and 75 mg of trimethoprim per square meter of body surface two times a day, three times a week on consecutive days (e.g., Monday, Tuesday, Wednesday).

Acceptable alternative dosing schedules include—

Oral, 750 mg of sulfamethoxazole per square meter and 150 mg of trimethoprim per square meter of body surface as a single daily dose three times a week on consecutive days (e.g., Monday, Tuesday, Wednesday).

Oral, 375 mg of sulfamethoxazole per square meter and 75 mg of trimethoprim per square meter of body surface two times a day seven days a week.

Oral, 375 mg of sulfamethoxazole per square meter and 75 mg of trimethoprim per square meter of body surface two times a day, three times a week on alternate days (e.g., Monday, Wednesday, Friday).

Note: PCP prophylaxis is recommended for all infants born to HIV-infected mothers starting at 4 weeks of age, regardless of their CD4 lymphocyte counts. However, if the infant is receiving zidovudine during the first 6 weeks of life for the prevention of perinatal HIV transmission, sulfamethoxazole and trimethoprim combination prophylaxis should be delayed until zidovudine is discontinued at 6 weeks of age, to reduce the chance of anemia that may occur if these two medications are given concurrently.

[Toxoplasmosis (prophylaxis)][1]—

Oral, 375 mg of sulfamethoxazole per square meter and 75 mg of trimethoprim per square meter of body surface two times a day, three times a week on consecutive days (e.g., Monday, Tuesday, Wednesday).

Acceptable alternative dosing schedules include:

Oral, 750 mg of sulfamethoxazole per square meter and 150 mg of trimethoprim per square meter of body surface as a single daily dose three times a week on consecutive days (e.g., Monday, Tuesday, Wednesday).

Oral, 375 mg of sulfamethoxazole per square meter and 75 mg of trimethoprim per square meter of body surface two times a day seven days a week.

Oral, 375 mg of sulfamethoxazole per square meter and 75 mg of trimethoprim per square meter of body surface two times a day, three times a week on alternate days (e.g., Monday, Wednesday, Friday).

[HIV-related infection in Africa (prophylaxis)][1]—

Studies have not been performed in children.

Strength(s) usually available

U.S.—

200 mg of sulfamethoxazole and 40 mg of trimethoprim per 5 mL (Rx) [*Bactrim Pediatric* (edetate disodium; glycerin; microcrystalline cellulose; polysorbate 80; saccharin; simethicone; sorbitol; FD&C Yellow No. 6; FD&C Red No. 40; flavors); *Cotrim Pediatric; Septra Suspension* (sodium benzoate 0.1%; carboxymethylcellulose sodium; citric acid; FD&C Red No. 40; FD&C Yellow No. 6; flavor; glycerin; microcrystalline cellulose; polysorbate 80; saccharin; sorbitol); *Septra Grape Suspension* (sodium benzoate 0.1%; carboxymethylcellulose sodium; citric acid; FD&C Red No. 40; FD&C Blue No. 1; flavor; glycerin; microcrystalline cellulose; polysorbate 80; saccharin; sorbitol); *Sulfatrim Pediatric; Sulfatrim Suspension*].

Canada—

200 mg of sulfamethoxazole and 40 mg of trimethoprim per 5 mL (Rx) [*Apo-Sulfatrim; Bactrim; Novo-Trimel; Nu-Cotrimox; Septra*].

Auxiliary labeling

- Shake well.
- Take with a full glass of water.
- May cause dizziness.
- Avoid too much sun or use of sunlamp.
- Continue medicine for full time of treatment.

SULFAMETHOXAZOLE AND TRIMETHOPRIM TABLETS USP

Usual adult and adolescent dose

See *Sulfamethoxazole and Trimethoprim Oral Suspension USP.*

Usual adult prescribing limits

See *Sulfamethoxazole and Trimethoprim Oral Suspension USP.*

Usual pediatric dose

See *Sulfamethoxazole and Trimethoprim Oral Suspension USP.*

Strength(s) usually available

U.S.—

400 mg of sulfamethoxazole and 80 mg of trimethoprim (Rx) [*Bactrim* (magnesium stearate; pregelatinized starch; sodium starch glycolate; FD&C Blue No. 1 lake; FD&C Yellow No. 6 lake; FD&C Yellow No. 10 lake); *Cotrim; Septra* (docusate sodium 0.4 mg; FD&C Red No. 40; magnesium stearate; povidone; sodium starch glycolate); *Sulfatrim; Sulfatrim S/S*].

800 mg of sulfamethoxazole and 160 mg of trimethoprim (Rx) [*Bactrim DS* (magnesium stearate; pregelatinized starch; sodium starch glycolate); *Cofatrim Forte; Cotrim DS; Septra DS* (docusate sodium 0.8 mg; FD&C Red No. 40; magnesium stearate; povidone; sodium starch glycolate); *Sulfatrim-DS*].

Canada—

100 mg of sulfamethoxazole and 20 mg of trimethoprim (Rx) [*Apo-Sulfatrim*].

400 mg of sulfamethoxazole and 80 mg of trimethoprim (Rx) [*Apo-Sulfatrim* (scored); *Bactrim; Novo-Trimel* (scored); *Nu-Cotrimox; Septra*].

800 mg of sulfamethoxazole and 160 mg of trimethoprim (Rx) [*Apo-Sulfatrim DS; Bactrim DS* (scored); *Novo-Trimel D.S.* (scored); *Nu-Cotrimox DS; Roubac; Septra DS*].

Auxiliary labeling

- Take with a full glass of water.
- May cause dizziness.
- Avoid too much sun or use of sunlamp.
- Continue medicine for full time of treatment.

Parenteral Dosage Forms

SULFAMETHOXAZOLE AND TRIMETHOPRIM FOR INJECTION CONCENTRATE USP

Usual adult and adolescent dose

Antibacterial (systemic)—

Intravenous infusion, 10 to 12.5 mg of sulfamethoxazole and 2 to 2.5 mg of trimethoprim per kg of body weight every six hours; 13.3 to 16.7 mg of sulfamethoxazole and 2.7 to 3.3 mg of trimethoprim per kg of body weight every eight hours; or 20 to 25 mg of sulfamethoxazole and 4 to 5 mg of trimethoprim per kg of body weight every twelve hours.

Antiprotozoal—

Pneumocystis carinii pneumonia: Intravenous infusion, 18.75 to 25 mg of sulfamethoxazole and 3.75 to 5 mg of trimethoprim per kg of body weight every six hours; or 25 to 33.3 mg of sulfamethoxazole and 5.0 to 6.7 mg of trimethoprim per kg of body weight every eight hours for fourteen days.

Usual pediatric dose

Infants up to 2 months of age—Use is not recommended since sulfonamides may cause kernicterus in neonates.

Infants 2 months of age and over—See *Usual adult and adolescent dose.*

Strength(s) usually available

U.S.—

400 mg of sulfamethoxazole and 80 mg of trimethoprim per 5 mL (Rx) [*Bactrim I.V.* (diethanolamine 0.3%; sodium hydroxide); *Septra I.V.* (diethanolamine 0.3%; sodium hydroxide)].

Canada—

400 mg of sulfamethoxazole and 80 mg of trimethoprim per 5 mL (Rx) [*Septra*].

Preparation of dosage form

The contents of each vial (5 mL) must be diluted. Each 5 mL of solution should be added to 75 to 125 mL of 5% dextrose injection prior to administration by intravenous infusion. The resulting solution should be administered by intravenous infusion over a 60- to 90-minute period.

Caution: Use of products containing benzyl alcohol is not recommended for use in neonates. A fatal toxic syndrome consisting of metabolic acidosis, CNS depression, respiratory problems, renal failure, hypotension, and possibly seizures and intracranial hemorrhages has been associated with this use.

[1]Not included in Canadian product labeling.

Revised: 08/08/2000

SULINDAC—See *Anti-inflammatory Drugs, Nonsteroidal (Systemic)*

SUMATRIPTAN Systemic

VA CLASSIFICATION (Primary): CN105

Commonly used brand name(s): *Imitrex*.

Note: For a listing of dosage forms and brand names by country availability, see *Dosage Forms* section(s).

Category

Antimigraine agent.

Indications

General Considerations

Sumatriptan should not be prescribed for a patient who has not previously been diagnosed as a migraineur, or administered to a migraineur with atypical symptoms, until it has been determined that the patient's headache is not occurring secondary to an evolving potentially serious neurological condition (e.g., cerebrovascular accident or subarachnoid hemorrhage).

Accepted

Headache, migraine (treatment)—Sumatriptan is indicated to relieve (abort) acute migraine headaches (with or without aura) in patients who do not obtain sufficient relief with analgesics, such as acetaminophen, aspirin, or nonsteroidal anti-inflammatory drugs (NSAIDs). Sumatriptan also relieves the nausea, vomiting, photophobia, and phonophobia that frequently occur in association with migraine headaches.

When incapacitating migraines occur more frequently than twice a month, prophylactic treatment is recommended to reduce the severity and duration, as well as the number, of headaches. Sumatriptan is not used for this purpose. Beta-adrenergic blocking agents, calcium channel blocking agents, tricyclic antidepressants, monoamine oxidase inhibitors, methysergide, pizotyline (pizotifen [not commercially available in the U.S.]), and sometimes cyproheptadine (especially in children) are used for prophylaxis. Other measures that may reduce the need for medication in migraineurs include identification and avoidance of headache precipitants and relaxation and/or biofeedback techniques.

Headache, cluster (treatment)—Sumatriptan injection is indicated for the relief of acute cluster headache episodes. Cluster headaches may occur daily, often more than once a day, for several months (a cluster period), followed by a headache-free interval.

Unaccepted

Sumatriptan is not recommended for long-term migraine prophylaxis.

Sumatriptan is not recommended for treatment of basilar artery migraine or hemiplegic migraine. Efficacy and safety in these conditions have not been established.

Pharmacology/Pharmacokinetics

Physicochemical characteristics

Source—Synthetic. Sumatriptan is structurally related to serotonin (5-hydroxytryptamine, 5-HT).

Molecular weight—Sumatriptan succinate: 413.5

pKa—

Sumatriptan succinate—

pKa_1 (succinic acid)—4.21 and 5.67

pKa_2 (tertiary amine group)—9.63pKa_3 (sulfonamide group)—> 12

Solubility—Sumatriptan succinate: Readily soluble in water and in 0.9% sodium chloride solution.

Mechanism of action/Effect

Although sumatriptan's mechanism of action has not been established, suppression of migraine headaches may result from sumatriptan-induced decreases in the firing of serotonergic (5-hydroxytryptaminergic, 5-HT) neurons. Specifically, it is thought that agonist activity at the 5-HT_{1D} receptor subtype provides relief of acute headache. Sumatriptan is a highly selective agonist at this receptor subtype; it has no significant activity at other 5-HT receptor subtypes or at adrenergic, dopaminergic, muscarinic, or benzodiazepine receptors.

It has been proposed that constriction of cerebral blood vessels resulting from 5-HT_{1D} receptor stimulation reduces the pulsation that may be responsible for the pain of vascular headaches. Studies in humans have shown that blood flow velocity in the middle cerebral arteries is significantly reduced during a migraine on the side of the headache, that relief of the headache by sumatriptan is accompanied by return of the blood flow velocity in these vessels to normal, and that sumatriptan treatment does not induce other changes in cerebral hemispheric blood flow. However, other studies have not consistently shown a significant correlation between dilatation of cerebral blood vessels and pain or other symptoms of migraine headaches, or between medication-induced vasoconstriction and relief of these headaches.

It has also been proposed that neurogenic inflammation in areas innervated by the trigeminal nerve may contribute to the development of migraine headaches. Although the cause of the inflammation has not been established, there is some evidence that serotonergic mechanisms may be involved. Sumatriptan may also relieve migraines by decreasing release of neuropeptides and other mediators of inflammation and by reducing extravasation of plasma proteins. A study in humans has demonstrated that concentrations of calcitonin gene-related peptide, a substance that increases vascular permeability and promotes plasma protein extravasation, are elevated during a migraine and return to normal as the headache is relieved by sumatriptan.

Absorption

Nasal—Rapid; bioavailability is low (approximately 17%), primarily because of presystemic hepatic metabolism and incomplete absorption.

Oral—Rapid; bioavailability is low (approximately 15% of a dose), primarily because of presystemic hepatic metabolism and, to a lesser extent, because of incomplete absorption. The rate and extent of absorption are not affected to a clinically significant extent by administration with food or by the gastric stasis that may accompany migraine headaches.

Subcutaneous—Rapid; bioavailability is approximately 97% of that achieved with an intravenous injection.

Distribution

Sumatriptan is rapidly and extensively distributed to tissues but passage across the blood-brain barrier is limited.

Protein binding

In plasma—Low (14 to 21%)

Biotransformation

Hepatic and extensive; approximately 80% of a dose is metabolized. The major metabolite is an inactive indole acetic acid derivative.

In vitro studies with human hepatic microsomes indicate that sumatriptan is metabolized by monoamine oxidase (MAO), primarily the A isoenzyme (MAO-A).

Half-life

Distribution—

Subcutaneous administration: Approximately 15 minutes

Elimination—

Subcutaneous or oral administration: Approximately 2.5 hours. One study reported a terminal half-life of approximately 7 hours that became apparent about 12 hours after administration of multiple oral doses, but did not contribute substantially to the overall disposition of the medication.

Nasal administration: Approximately 2 hours.

Onset of action

Nasal—

Within 15 minutes

Oral—

Within 30 minutes

Subcutaneous—

Relief of headache pain: Within 10 minutes

Relief of migraine-associated nausea, vomiting, photophobia, phonophobia: Within 20 minutes

Time to peak serum concentration

Nasal (single 5-mg, 10-mg, or 20-mg dose): Between 1 and 1.5 hours

Oral (single 100-mg dose): Approximately 2 hours (range, 0.5 to 5 hours). The wide interindividual variability found in pharmacokinetic studies may be related to the appearance of multiple peaks in the concentration over time. Approximately 80% of the maximum value is achieved within 45 minutes.

Subcutaneous (single 6-mg dose): Approximately 12 minutes (range, 5 to 20 minutes).

Peak serum concentration

Nasal (5-mg and 20-mg dose): Approximately 5 nanograms per mL (0.012 micromoles/L) and 16 nanograms/mL (0.039 micromoles/L), respectively.

Oral (single 100-mg dose): Approximately 54 nanograms per mL (0.13 micromoles/L) (range, 26.7 to 137 nanograms per mL [0.06 to 0.33 micromoles/L]).

Subcutaneous (single 6-mg dose): Approximately 72 to 74 nanograms per mL; (0.17 to 0.18 micromoles/L) (range, 54.9 to 108.4 nanograms per mL [0.13 to 0.26 micromoles/L]).

Time to peak effect

Relief of headache (i.e., moderate or severe pain being reduced to mild or no pain)—

Oral (single 100-mg dose): Within 2 hours in 50 to 75%, and within 4 hours in an additional 15 to 25%, of patients.

Subcutaneous (single 6-mg dose): Within 1 hour in 70%, and within 2 hours in an additional 12%, of patients.

Relief of associated symptoms (nausea, vomiting, photophobia, phonophobia)—

Oral (single 100-mg dose): Within 2 hours.

Subcutaneous (single 6-mg dose): Within 1 hour in 68%, and within 2 hours in an additional 13%, of patients.

Duration of action

Return of migraine headache occurs within 24 to 48 hours in approximately 40% of patients who initially obtain a beneficial response to sumatriptan, i.e., after moderate or severe headache pain has been reduced to mild or no pain. Whether this represents development of a new migraine or breakthrough of a prolonged migraine after the effects of sumatriptan have worn off has not been established.

Elimination

Renal, via active renal tubular secretion, following hepatic metabolism. Approximately 80% of a dose is eliminated as metabolites. After nasal administration, approximately 3% of the dose is eliminated as unchanged sumatriptan and 35% as the indole acetic acid metabolite. After oral administration, approximately 57% of a dose is eliminated in the urine (3% of the dose as unchanged sumatriptan, 35% as the indole acetic acid metabolite, and 8% as the glucuronide conjugate of the indole acetic acid metabolite) and another 38% of the dose is eliminated in the feces (9% as unchanged sumatriptan and 11% as the indole acetic acid metabolite). After subcutaneous administration, approximately 22% of a dose is eliminated in the urine as unchanged sumatriptan and another 38% as the indole acetic acid metabolite. Only 0.6% and 3.3% of a dose are eliminated in the feces as unchanged sumatriptan and the indole acetic acid metabolite, respectively.

The effects of renal function impairment on clearance of sumatriptan have not been studied. Approximately 80% of the total clearance is via hepatic biotransformation; therefore, hepatic function impairment may produce clinically significant elevations in the bioavailability of orally administered sumatriptan. However, the elevation in the bioavailability of intranasal sumatriptan is not clinically significant.

Precautions to Consider

Tumorigenicity

No evidence of tumorigenicity was found in a 104-week study in rats given sumatriptan by oral gavage in quantities sufficient to achieve peak concentrations up to > 100 times higher than are achieved in humans with a 6-mg subcutaneous dose. Also, although no evidence of tumorigenicity was found in a 78-week study in mice given sumatriptan continuously in drinking water, this study did not use the maximum tolerated dose and is therefore considered inadequate for evaluating potential tumorigenicity in the mouse.

Mutagenicity

No evidence of mutagenicity was found in a variety of *in vitro* and *in vivo* studies.

Pregnancy/Reproduction

Fertility—A treatment-related decrease in fertility was observed secondary to a decrease in mating in male and female rats treated with 50 and 500 mg per kg of body weight per day dosed daily with oral sumatriptan prior to and throughout the mating period.

Fertility studies were not conducted in which sumatriptan was administered by the intranasal route.

No adverse effects on fertility were found in reproduction studies in rats given up to 60 mg per kg of body weight (mg/kg) per day subcutaneously or up to 500 mg/kg per day orally.

Pregnancy—*A Pregnancy Registry has been established to monitor the outcomes of pregnant women exposed to sumatriptan. Physicians are encouraged by the manufacturer to register patients by calling (800) 336-2176.*

Adequate and well-controlled studies have not been done in pregnant women. Studies in rats receiving daily subcutaneous injections of sumatriptan prior to and during pregnancy showed no evidence of teratogenicity or embryolethality. Also, embryolethality did not occur in studies in rats receiving sumatriptan intravenously throughout organogenesis in doses producing plasma concentrations > 50 times higher than those produced by the recommended human subcutaneous dose. However, maternal toxicity and embryotoxicity occurred in rats given oral doses of 1000 mg/kg per day, but not those given 500 mg/kg per day, during organogenesis. Also, term fetuses from Dutch Stride rabbits treated during organogenesis with oral sumatriptan exhibited an increased incidence of cervicothoracic vascular defects and minor skeletal abnormalities. The functional significance of these abnormalities is not known. In other studies, daily administration of sumatriptan to pregnant rabbits throughout the period of organogenesis using oral doses of 100 mg/kg per day or intravenous doses sufficient to produce peak concentrations > 3 times those produced in humans after a 6-mg subcutaneous dose resulted in maternal toxicity and/or embryolethality.

FDA Pregnancy Category C.

Breast-feeding

Sumatriptan is distributed into human breast milk. However, problems in humans have not been documented.

Pediatrics

Appropriate studies on the relationship of age to the effects of sumatriptan have not been done in patients up to 18 years of age. Safety and efficacy have not been established.

Adolescents

Controlled clinical trials have not established the efficacy of oral or intranasal sumatriptan compared to placebo in the treatment of migraine in adolescent patients aged 12 to 17 years. In these clinical trials, adverse events observed were similar in nature to those reported in clinical trials in adults. Serious adverse events have occurred in the pediatric population after use of subcutaneous, oral and/or intranasal sumatriptan during postmarketing experience. The events reported were similar in nature to those reported rarely in adults, including stroke, visual loss, and death.

Geriatrics

The use of sumatriptan in the elderly patient is not recommended. The elderly patient is more likely to have decreased hepatic function, is at higher risk for CAD, and blood pressure increases may be more pronounced.

No unusual adverse, age-related phenomena occurred in patients older than 60 years of age who participated in clinical trials. However, most published studies report excluding patients older than 65 years of age. Studies in a limited number of healthy subjects 65 to 86 years of age found no differences in pharmacokinetic parameters between these older individuals and younger subjects.

Drug interactions and/or related problems

The following drug interactions and/or related problems have been selected on the basis of their potential clinical significance (possible mechanism in parentheses where appropriate)—not necessarily inclusive (» = major clinical significance):

Note: Combinations containing any of the following medications, depending on the amount present, may also interact with this medication.

Antidepressants, selective 5-hydroxytryptamine uptake inhibitor or

Lithium or

» Monoamine oxidase (MAO) inhibitors, including furazolidone, procarbazine, and selegiline

(concurrent use of any of these agents with sumatriptan may lead to a potentially dangerous hyperserotonergic state or other adverse effects; sumatriptan should be used with caution in patients receiving these medications)

(sumatriptan is metabolized by the MAO-A isoenzyme; pretreatment of human subjects with an MAO-A inhibitor has been shown to decrease sumatriptan clearance, resulting in substantial increases in the area under the sumatriptan plasma concentration-time curve and the sumatriptan half-life. MAOIs that inhibit the MAO-A isoenzyme include furazolidone, isocarboxazid, moclobemide, phenelzine, toloxatone, and tranylcypromine. MAOIs that inhibit only the MAO-B isoenzyme, such as selegiline, did not produce these effects)

Oral and intranasal sumatriptan should not be used during or within 14 days following administration of an MAO inhibitor; concurrent use of sumatriptan injection with MAO inhibitors is not generally recommended; however, concurrent use would require a dosage adjustment of sumatriptan injection

Dihydroergotamine or

Ergotamine or

Methysergide
(a delay of 24 hours between administration of dihydroergotamine, ergotamine, or methysergide and sumatriptan is recommended because of the possibility of additive and/or prolonged vasoconstriction)

Selective serotonin reuptake inhibitors, such as:
Fluoxetine
Fluvoxamine
Paroxetine
Sertraline
(concurrent use may result in weakness, hyperreflexia, and incoordination; careful monitoring is recommended)

Laboratory value alterations

The following have been selected on the basis of their potential clinical significance (possible effect in parentheses where appropriate)—not necessarily inclusive (» = major clinical significance):

With physiology/laboratory test values
Blood pressure and
Peripheral vascular resistance
(may be increased, although increases are generally mild and transient; in clinical studies, clinically significant blood pressure elevations [increase in systolic pressure by 20 mm Hg or to 180 mm Hg; increase in diastolic pressure by 15 mm Hg or to 105 mm Hg] occurred in fewer than 1% of the patients; blood pressure changes after oral administration are smaller and occur more slowly than after subcutaneous administration)

Medical considerations/Contraindications

The medical considerations/contraindications included have been selected on the basis of their potential clinical significance (reasons given in parentheses where appropriate)—not necessarily inclusive (» = major clinical significance).

Except under special circumstances, this medication should not be used when the following medical problems exist:

» Coronary artery disease, especially:
Angina pectoris or
Myocardial infarction, history of or
Myocardial ischemia, silent documented or
Prinzmetal's angina or
» Other conditions in which coronary vasoconstriction would be detrimental
(although sumatriptan has only a slight vasoconstrictive effect on coronary arteries, sumatriptan-induced myocardial ischemia has been documented, primarily in patients with a history of coronary artery disease or susceptibility to coronary artery vasospasm)
» Hypertension, uncontrolled
(may be exacerbated)

Risk-benefit should be considered when the following medical problems exist:

Cardiac arrhythmias, especially:
» Tachycardia or
» Cerebrovascular accident, history of
(sumatriptan may cause cerebral hemorrhage, subarachnoid hemorrhage, or stroke; caution should be used when administering in patients at risk for cerebrovascular events)
» Coronary artery disease, predisposition to
(sumatriptan has rarely caused serious coronary adverse effects; patients in whom coronary artery disease is a possibility on the basis of age or the presence of other risk factors, such as diabetes, hypercholesterolemia, obesity, a strong family history of coronary artery disease, or tobacco smoking should be evaluated for the presence of cardiovascular disease before sumatriptan is prescribed; even after a satisfactory evaluation, the advisability of administering the patient's first dose under medical supervision should be considered)
» Hepatic function impairment or
Renal function impairment
(caution is recommended because clearance of sumatriptan may be impaired; because about 80% of the total clearance is via hepatic biotransformation, hepatic function impairment should be more likely than renal function impairment to produce clinically significant increases in sumatriptan concentration; dosage adjustment is recommended in patients with hepatic impairment)
Hypertension, controlled
(elevations of systolic and diastolic blood pressure may occur, especially after subcutaneous administration, although these effects are generally mild and transient in hypertensive patients whose blood pressure is adequately controlled by medication; in clinical studies, patients with controlled hypertension experienced mean peak increases of 6 mm Hg, which usually started within 30 minutes after subcutaneous administration and persisted for less than an hour)
» Sensitivity to sumatriptan

Side/Adverse Effects

Note: Most of the adverse effects reported with sumatriptan are mild and transient (lasting less than 1 hour after subcutaneous injection and 2 hours or less after oral administration) and resolve without treatment. Although several deaths have been reported after administration of sumatriptan, a direct causal relationship could not be established in most cases. Most of the fatalities occurred 3 hours or more after administration and probably were spontaneous events or were caused by underlying disease. Some of the deaths were attributed to strokes, cerebral hemorrhages, or other cerebrovascular events. However, migraineurs are known to be at increased risk of cerebrovascular accidents or transient ischemic attacks; in many of these cases a cerebrovascular event, rather than a migraine, may have been causing the symptoms that led to sumatriptan administration.

Some of the adverse events reported after administration of sumatriptan (e.g., nausea, vomiting, malaise, fatigue, dizziness, vertigo, weakness, drowsiness, sedation) often occur during and/or following a migraine headache; whether sumatriptan contributes to their occurrence has not been established.

Although a causal relationship to sumatriptan has not been established, the following adverse events have also been reported in open, uncontrolled studies (incidences < 1%) and/or postmarketing: cardiac arrhythmias (atrial fibrillation, ventricular fibrillation, ventricular tachycardia, sinus arrhythmia), other transient changes in the electrocardiogram (ST segment elevations, other ST or T-wave changes, prolongation of PR or QTc intervals, nonsustained ventricular premature beats, isolated junctional ectopic beats, atrial ectopic beats, delayed activation of the right ventricle), hypotension, bradycardia, syncope, Prinzmetal's angina, vasodilatation, Raynaud's disease, acute renal failure, seizures, cerebrovascular accident, dysphagia, subarachnoid hemorrhage, polydipsia, dehydration, gastrointestinal reflux, dyspnea, erythema, pruritus, skin rashes, peptic ulceration, gallstones, swelling of extremities, transient hemiplegia, hysteria, globus hystericus, intoxication, mental depression, myoclonia, monoplegia or diplegia, dystonia, dysuria, urinary frequency, renal calculus, photosensitivity, and exacerbation of sunburn.

Note: Sumatriptan causes corneal opacities and defects in the corneal epithelium in dogs; this raises the possibility that these changes may occur in humans. There is not systematic evaluation for these effects in clinical trials, and no specific recommendations for monitoring are being offered, but health care professionals should be aware of the possibility of changes.

The following side/adverse effects have been selected on the basis of their potential clinical significance (possible signs and symptoms in parentheses where appropriate)—not necessarily inclusive:

Those indicating need for medical attention

Incidence less frequent (1 to 3%) with subcutaneous administration; less frequent or rare (< 1%) with oral or nasal administration

Chest pain, severe; difficulty in swallowing; heaviness, tightness, or pressure in chest and/or neck

Note: Although *chest pain* and *heaviness, tightness, or pressure in the chest and neck* are suggestive of angina pectoris, monitoring of the electrocardiogram (ECG) during such symptoms in clinical studies failed to detect evidence of myocardial ischemia. Conversely, ECG monitoring detected new T-wave abnormalities in a small number of patients, most of whom had abnormal pretreatment ECGs, who were not experiencing relevant symptoms. However, sumatriptan-induced coronary artery vasospasm resulting in symptomatic myocardial ischemia and myocardial infarction have been documented in a few patients, primarily patients with a history of coronary artery disease or susceptibility to coronary artery vasospasm. Several fatalities associated with such complications have been reported following administration of sumatriptan, but in most cases a causal relationship has not been established.

Incidence rare

Anaphylactic or anaphylactoid reaction (changes in facial skin color; skin rash, hives, and/or itching; fast or irregular breathing; puffiness or swelling of the eyelids or around the eyes, face, or lips; shortness of breath, troubled breathing, tightness in chest, and/or wheezing); ***dermatitis, allergic*** (skin rash, hives, and/or itching); ***seizures***

Those indicating need for medical attention only if they continue or are bothersome

Incidence more frequent

Injection site reaction (burning, pain, or redness); ***irritation in the nose*** (burning; discharge; pain; or soreness)—occurs with nasal spray only; ***nausea or vomiting; taste perversion*** (change in sense of taste)—occurs with nasal spray only

Note: *Nausea* and *vomiting* often occur in conjunction with migraine headaches; they are not necessarily caused by (and may actually be relieved by) sumatriptan. However, these effects occurred more frequently after oral than after subcutaneous administration of sumatriptan in clinical trials, possibly because of the unpleasant taste of the dispersible tablet used in the studies.

Incidence up to 13.5% with subcutaneous administration; less frequent (1 to 3%) or rare (< 1%) with nasal or oral administration

Atypical sensations (sensation of burning, warmth, heat, numbness, tightness, or tingling; feeling cold; "strange" feeling); ***discomfort in jaw, mouth, throat, tongue, nasal cavity, or sinuses; dizziness; drowsiness; flushing; lightheadedness; muscle aches, cramps, or stiffness; weakness***

Note: *Flushing* and sensations of *burning, warmth,* or *heat* generally disappear within 10 to 30 minutes after administration of a subcutaneous dose.

Incidence less frequent (1 to 3%) with subcutaneous administration; less frequent or rare (< 1%) with oral and nasal administration

Anxiety; general feeling of illness or tiredness; vision changes

Overdose

For specific information on the agents used in the management of sumatriptan overdose, see:

- *Nitroglycerin* in *Nitrates (Systemic).*

For more information on the management of overdose or unintentional ingestion **contact a Poison Control Center** (see *Poison Control Center Listing*).

Clinical effects of overdose

Overdose has not been reported in humans. Signs and symptoms that might be anticipated, based on animal studies, include ataxia, convulsions, cyanosis, erythema of extremities, inactivity, injection site reactions (desquamation, hair loss, scab formation), mydriasis, paralysis, reduced respiratory rate, and tremor.

Treatment of overdose

Although there is no experience with overdose of sumatriptan, treatment may involve:

To decrease absorption—Emptying the stomach by induction of emesis or performing gastric lavage (if ingested orally).

Monitoring—For continuing chest pain or other symptoms consistent with angina pectoris: Monitoring the electrocardiogram for evidence of ischemia and administering appropriate treatment (e.g., nitroglycerin or other coronary artery vasodilators) as needed. Some patients may require further evaluation to determine whether previously undiagnosed coronary artery disease is present. See the package insert or *Nitroglycerin* in *Nitrates (Systemic)* for specific dosing guidelines for use of this product.

Monitoring of patients who have received an overdose of sumatriptan nasal spray should continue for at least 10 hours or while signs or symptoms persist.

Supportive care—Monitoring the patient and instituting supportive treatment as needed. Patients in whom intentional overdose is confirmed or suspected should be referred for psychiatric consultation.

Patient Consultation

As an aid to patient consultation, refer to *Advice for the Patient, Sumatriptan (Systemic).*

In providing consultation, consider emphasizing the following selected information (» = major clinical significance):

Before using this medication

» Conditions affecting use, especially:

Hypersensitivity to sumatriptan or any of its components

Pregnancy—There are no adequate studies in pregnant women. However, sumatriptan crosses the placenta in rats and rabbits and can harm the fetus.

Breast-feeding—Sumatriptan is distributed to human breast milk.

Use in children—Safety and efficacy of sumatriptan have not been established in patients under 18 years of age.

Use in the elderly—Use in elderly patients is not recommended.

Other medications, especially monoamine oxidase inhibitors

Other medical problems, especially cerebrovascular accident (history of); coronary artery disease, predisposition to coronary artery disease, or other conditions that may be adversely affected by coronary artery constriction; hepatic function impairment; hypertension (uncontrolled); and tachycardia

Proper use of this medication

» Not administering if atypical headache symptoms are present; checking with physician instead

Administering after onset of headache pain

Additional benefit may be obtained if the patient lies down in a quiet, dark room after administering medication

» Not using additional doses if a first dose does not provide substantial relief; additional sumatriptan is not likely to be effective in these circumstances; taking alternate medication as previously advised by physician, then checking with physician as soon as possible

» Taking additional doses, if needed, for return of migraine after initial relief was obtained, provided that prescribed limits (quantity used and frequency of administration) are not exceeded

» Compliance with prophylactic therapy, if prescribed

Proper administration of

Tablets

Swallowing whole; not breaking, crushing or chewing before taking; taking with full glass of water

Injection

Reading patient instructions provided with medication

Proper injection technique

Discarding used cartridge as directed in patient instructions, using container provided; not discarding autoinjector unit because refill cartridges are available

Nasal

Reading patient instructions provided with medication

» Proper dosing

» Proper storage

Precautions while using this medication

Checking with physician if usual dose fails to relieve three consecutive headaches, or frequency and/or severity of headaches increases

Avoiding alcohol, which aggravates headache

» Caution if drowsiness or dizziness occurs

Side/adverse effects

Contacting physician immediately if severe chest pain or signs and symptoms of anaphylactoid reaction occur

Contacting physician at once if mild pain or tightness in chest or throat occurs and persists for more than 1 hour; even if symptoms are of shorter duration, not using medication again without first consulting physician

Signs and symptoms of other potential side effects, including dysphagia, palpitation, and skin rash or eruptions

General Dosing Information

Clinical studies have not shown a correlation between the duration of a migraine prior to administration of sumatriptan and its ability to abort an acute attack. Because a recent study has shown that administration of sumatriptan during a preheadache aura may neither prevent nor significantly delay the onset of the headache, it is recommended that sumatriptan not be administered prior to the appearance of headache pain.

Lying down and relaxing in a quiet, darkened room after administering a dose of antimigraine medication may contribute to relief of migraines.

Additional doses of sumatriptan should not be administered to patients who do not obtain substantial relief (reduction of initially moderate or severe headache pain to mild or no pain) within 1 or 2 hours after the initial dose. Several clinical trials have failed to demonstrate that a second dose benefits these patients. It is recommended that an analgesic be used as "rescue" medication in the event of an unsatisfactory response to sumatriptan; use of dihydroergotamine, ergotamine, or methysergide is not recommended because of the possibility of additive or prolonged vasoconstriction. Also, the prescriber should be contacted as soon as possible if sumatriptan is ineffective because of the possibility that the patient's symptoms are being caused by a cerebrovascular event. However, patients who do not respond to sumatriptan during one migraine attack may obtain a satisfactory response during subsequent attacks.

Return of migraine headache occurs within 24 to 48 hours in about 40% of patients who initially obtain a beneficial response to sumatriptan. Whether this represents development of a new migraine or breakthrough of a prolonged migraine after the effects of sumatriptan have worn off has not been established. Recurrences following an initial beneficial response may be treated with additional sumatriptan.

Tolerance to the effects of sumatriptan did not occur when the medication was used intermittently to relieve acute migraines for longer than 6 months.

The possibility that overuse of sumatriptan by migraineurs may lead to dependence on the medication and to the development of withdrawal (rebound) or chronic, intractable headaches (as has been documented with too-frequent use of ergotamine and/or analgesics by these patients) has not been evaluated. Some headache specialists recommend that, until more definitive information about the risk of cumulative toxicity and/or dependence is available, courses of sumatriptan treatment should not be administered more often than every five to seven days.

For oral dosage form only

Sumatriptan tablets are to be swallowed whole (i.e., with the film coating intact) because the unpleasant taste of the contents may cause taste disturbances and/or an increased risk of nausea and vomiting.

For parenteral dosage form only

Sumatriptan is not to be given intravenously. Clinical trials have shown that intravenous administration is associated with a higher incidence of adverse effects than subcutaneous administration. Specifically, the risk of coronary artery vasospasm and angina may be increased. Long-term users with risk factors of coronary artery disease should receive periodic cardiovascular evaluations.

Oral Dosage Forms

Note: Sumatriptan tablets contain sumatriptan succinate. However, dosage and strength are expressed in terms of sumatriptan base.

SUMATRIPTAN TABLETS

Usual adult dose

Antimigraine agent—

Oral, 25, 50 or 100 mg (base) as a single dose. If necessary, additional doses up to 100 mg may be taken at intervals of at least two hours, up to a maximum of 200 mg a day. Individuals vary in response to doses of sumatriptan. The choice of dose should be made on an individual basis.

For relief of migraine headache that returns after an initial treatment with sumatriptan tablets: the dose may be repeated after two hours, up to a maximum of 200 mg once a day

For relief of migraine headache that returns after an initial treatment with sumatriptan injection, additional single oral doses of up to 100 mg a day may be given at intervals of at least two hours between tablet doses, up to a maximum of 200 mg a day.

The maximum single dose for patients with hepatic impairment should not exceed 50 mg.

Note: There is evidence that an initial doses of 50 mg and 100 mg provides substantially greater relief than a dose of 25 mg. There is also evidence that doses of 100 mg do not provide a greater effect than 50 mg.

Usual adult prescribing limits

Antimigraine agent—

Oral, not more than 200-mg (base) in twenty-four hours.

Usual pediatric dose

Safety and efficacy in patients up to 18 years of age have not been established.

Strength(s) usually available

U.S.—

25 mg (base [as the succinate salt]) (Rx) [*Imitrex* (lactose)].
50 mg (base [as the succinate salt]) (Rx) [*Imitrex* (lactose)].
100 mg (base [as the succinate salt]) (Rx) [*Imitrex* (lactose)].

Canada—

50 mg (base [as the succinate salt]) (Rx) [*Imitrex* (lactose)].
100 mg (base [as the succinate salt]) (Rx) [*Imitrex* (lactose)].

Packaging and storage

Store between 2 and 30 °C (36 and 86 °F), unless otherwise specified by manufacturer.

Auxiliary labeling

- Swallow tablets whole.
- Take with a full glass of water.

Nasal Dosage Forms

SUMATRIPTAN NASAL SOLUTION

Usual adult dose

Antimigraine agent—

Intranasal, 5 mg, 10 mg or 20 mg into **one** nostril were effective for the acute treatment of migraine in adults.

Additional doses should not be administered for the same migraine attack. However, a dose may be administered for subsequent attacks provided a minimum of two hours has elapsed since the last dose.

Usual adult prescribing limits

Antimigraine agent—

Nasal, not more than 40 mg in twenty-four hours.

The safety of treating an average of more than 4 headaches in a 30-day period has not been established.

Usual pediatric dose

Safety and efficacy in patients up to 18 years of age have not been established.

Strength(s) usually available

U.S.—

5 mg (base [as the hemisulphate salt]) (Rx) [*Imitrex* (monobasic potassium phosphate; anhydrous dibasic sodium phosphate; sulfuric acid; sodium hydroxide; purified water)].
20 mg (base [as the hemisulphate salt]) (Rx) [*Imitrex* (monobasic potassium phosphate; anhydrous dibasic sodium phosphate; sulfuric acid; sodium hydroxide; purified water)].

Canada—

5 mg (base [as the hemisulphate salt]) (Rx) [*Imitrex* (monobasic potassium phosphate; anhydrous dibasic sodium phosphate; sulfuric acid; sodium hydroxide; purified water)].
20 mg (base [as the hemisulphate salt]) (Rx) [*Imitrex* (monobasic potassium phosphate; anhydrous dibasic sodium phosphate; sulfuric acid; sodium hydroxide; purified water)].

Packaging and storage

Store between 2 and 30 °C (36 and 86 °F), protected from light and from freezing, unless otherwise specified by manufacturer.

Parenteral Dosage Forms

Note: Sumatriptan injection contains sumatriptan succinate. However, dosage and strength are expressed in terms of sumatriptan base.

SUMATRIPTAN INJECTION

Usual adult dose

Antimigraine agent—

Subcutaneous, injected into the outer thigh or the outer upper arm, 6 mg (base). If a beneficial response to this dose is not obtained within one or two hours, an additional 6-mg dose may be administered, at least one hour after the first dose, if headache pain returns or increases in severity. Controlled clinical trials have not shown that there is a clear benefit associated with the administration of a second 6–mg dose in patients who failed to respond to the first injection.

Note: Lower doses may be administered if the patient does not tolerate the usual dose. The auto-injector should not be used for this purpose; doses should be withdrawn from the single-dose vial, using a separate syringe.

One study compared the effects of 6-mg and 8-mg subcutaneous doses of sumatriptan (base) in migraineurs. The 8-mg dose was not significantly more effective than the 6-mg dose; therefore, doses higher than 6 mg are not recommended.

Usual adult prescribing limits

Antimigraine agent—

Single subcutaneous doses should not exceed 6 mg (base), and should be separated by at least one hour. No more than two 6-mg doses should be administered within twenty-four hours.

Note: Some clinicians recommend administering no more than two 6-mg doses within forty-eight hours.

Usual pediatric dose

Safety and efficacy in patients up to 18 years of age have not been established.

Strength(s) usually available

U.S.—

6 mg (base [as the succinate salt]) per 0.5 mL (Rx) [*Imitrex* (sodium chloride 3.5 mg per 0.5 mL)].

Canada—

6 mg (base [as the succinate salt]) per 0.5 mL (Rx) [*Imitrex*].

Packaging and storage

Store between 2 and 30 °C (36 and 86 °F), protected from light and from freezing, unless otherwise specified by manufacturer.

Selected Bibliography

Cady RK, Wendt JK, Kirchner JR, et al. Treatment of acute migraine with subcutaneous sumatriptan. JAMA 1991; 265: 2831-5.

Subcutaneous Sumatriptan International Study Group. Treatment of migraine attacks with sumatriptan. N Engl J Med 1991; 325: 316-21.

Brown EG, Endersby CA, Smith RM, et al. The safety and tolerability of sumatriptan: an overview. Eur Neurol 1991; 31: 339-44.

Revised: 12/06/2004
Developed: 03/25/1998

SUPROFEN—See *Anti-inflammatory Drugs, Nonsteroidal (Ophthalmic)*

TACROLIMUS Systemic

JAN: Tacrolimus Hydrate.

VA CLASSIFICATION (Primary): IM403

Commonly used brand name(s): *Prograf*.

Another commonly used name is FK 506.

Note: For a listing of dosage forms and brand names by country availability, see *Dosage Forms* section(s).

Category

Immunosuppressant.

Indications

Note: Bracketed information in the *Indications* section refers to uses that are not included in U.S. product labeling.

Accepted

Transplant rejection, solid organ (prophylaxis)—Tacrolimus is useful for the prevention of rejection of transplanted *heart*[1], kidney[1], liver, *[lung]*[1], *[pancreas]*[1], and *[small bowel]*[1] allografts.

In heart transplant recipients, it is recommended that tacrolimus be used in conjunction with azathioprine or mycophenolate mofetil (MMF).

[Transplant rejection, solid organ (treatment)]—Tacrolimus is useful for the treatment of rejection of transplanted *heart*[1], *kidney*[1], *liver*, *lung*[1], *pancreas*[1], and small bowel[1] allografts.

[Graft-versus-host disease (prophylaxis)][1] or

[Graft-versus-host disease (treatment)][1]—Tacrolimus is useful for the prevention and treatment of graft-versus-host disease in patients receiving bone marrow transplants.

[Uveitis, severe, refractory (treatment)][1]—Tacrolimus is useful for the treatment of severe, refractory uveitis.

Acceptance not established

Tacrolimus has been studied for the treatment of *atopic dermatitis*, *nephrotic syndrome*, *pediatric autoimmune enteropathy*, *primary sclerosing cholangitis*, *psoriasis*, *psoriatic arthritis*, and *pyoderma gangrenosum*. More data are needed to assess the place in therapy of tacrolimus for these indications.

There have been additional reports of the use of tacrolimus for other conditions, including:

- *alopecia universalis*;
- *autoimmune chronic active hepatitis*;
- *inflammatory bowel disease*;
- *multiple sclerosis*;
- *primary biliary cirrhosis*; and
- *scleroderma*.

The use of tacrolimus for these conditions cannot be assessed at this time.

Safety and efficacy of the use of tacrolimus with sirolimus have not been established.

---

[1]Not included in Canadian product labeling.

Pharmacology/Pharmacokinetics

Physicochemical characteristics

Source—Tacrolimus is a macrolide immunosuppressant produced by *Streptomyces tsukubaensis*.

Molecular weight—822.05.

Solubility—Freely soluble in ethanol; very soluble in chloroform and methanol; practically insoluble in water.

Mechanism of action/Effect

Tacrolimus inhibits T-lymphocyte activation. This may occur through formation of a complex with FK 506-binding proteins (FKBPs). The complex inhibits calcineurin phosphatase. This is believed to inhibit interleukin-2 (IL-2) gene expression in T-helper lymphocytes.

Tacrolimus also binds to the steroid receptor–associated heat-shock protein 56. This ultimately results in inhibition of transcription of proinflammatory cytokines such as granulocyte–macrophage colony-stimulating factor (GM-CSF), interleukin-1 (IL-1), interleukin-3 (IL-3), interleukin-4 (IL-4), interleukin-5 (IL-5), interleukin-6 (IL-6), interleukin-8 (IL-8), and tumor necrosis factor alpha (TNF alpha).

Absorption

Rapid, variable, and incomplete from the gastrointestinal tract; the mean bioavailability of the oral dosage form is 27%, range 5 to 65%; rate of absorption is decreased in the presence of food, but the extent of absorption may or may not be affected, depending on the type of food ingested.

Pediatric patients may have decreased bioavailability as compared to adult patients.

Distribution

The volume of distribution (Vol_D) when based on plasma obtained from blood samples at 37 °C (98.6 °F) is 5 to 65 L per kg of body weight (L/kg). The Vol_D based on plasma concentration is much higher than the Vol_D based on whole blood concentrations, the difference reflecting the binding of tacrolimus to the red blood cells. The mean Vol_D for patients with liver allografts when measured in whole blood is 0.9 L/kg.

Protein binding

High to very high (75 to 99%), primarily to albumin and alpha$_1$-acid glycoprotein.

Biotransformation

Hepatic, extensive, primarily by the cytochrome P450 3A enzymes.

Half-life

Distribution—

0.9 hour.

Elimination—

Biphasic, variable: Terminal—11.3 hours (range, 3.5 to 40.5 hours).

Time to peak concentration

0.5 to 4 hours after oral administration.

Note: The rate of absorption is reduced when tacrolimus is given with food.

Peak serum concentration

Plasma or blood—Whole blood concentrations may be 12 to 67 times the plasma concentrations.

Elimination

Tacrolimus is eliminated by metabolism. Less than 1% of the dose is eliminated unchanged in urine.

Pediatric patients may have increased clearance as compared with adult patients.

In dialysis—

Tacrolimus is not removed by dialysis.

Precautions to Consider

Cross-sensitivity and/or related problems

Patients allergic to castor oil derivatives may be allergic to the injectable dosage form of tacrolimus also, since the injection contains a polyoxyl 60 hydrogenated castor oil vehicle.

Carcinogenicity

Tacrolimus is associated with an increased risk of malignancy, especially lymphomas and skin malignancies. The increased risk is attributed to the intensity and duration of immunosuppression. The incidence of lymphomas is comparable to that observed with cyclosporine-based immunosuppressive regimens.

Tumorigenicity

Studies in mice and rats did not show a relationship between the dose of tacrolimus and the incidence of tumors.

Mutagenicity

Mutagenicity was not observed in bacterial or Chinese hamster cell *in vitro* testing, or *in vivo* tests performed in mice or rat hepatocytes.

Pregnancy/Reproduction

Fertility—Adequate and well-controlled studies have not been done in humans.

Pregnancy—Tacrolimus crosses the placenta. Pregnancy in patients treated with tacrolimus is possible, with low incidences of hypertension and pre-eclampsia. The use of tacrolimus during pregnancy is associated with premature birth, and hyperkalemia and reversible renal function impairment in neonates. One case of intrauterine growth retardation has been reported. In one series, 27 pregnancies in 21 liver transplant recipients managed with tacrolimus did not result in the loss of any allografts. Prenatal growth and postnatal infant growth for postpartum age were normal. Two of the 27 infants died after being delivered at 23 and 24 weeks gestation. The unsuccessful pregnancies were conceived a few weeks and 11.7 months following the liver transplantations.

Studies in rats showed that tacrolimus use during organogenesis was associated with an increase in late fetal resorptions and a decrease in the number of live births.

FDA Pregnancy Category C.

Breast-feeding

Tacrolimus is distributed into breast milk. Breast-feeding should be avoided during tacrolimus therapy.

Pediatrics

Pediatric patients require higher doses of tacrolimus per kg of body weight to maintain trough concentrations similar to those of adult patients. Pediatric patients may have decreased bioavailability and increased clearance as compared with adult patients.

Post-transplant lymphoproliferative disorder (PTLD) may be more common in pediatric patients than in adult patients, especially in pediatric patients up to 3 years of age.

Geriatrics

No information is available on the relationship of age to the effects of tacrolimus in geriatric patients. Tacrolimus has been used in geriatric patients undergoing transplantation; however, information has not been published on the age-related effects of tacrolimus in these patients. Elderly patients are more likely to have age-related renal function impairment, which may require adjustment of dosage.

Dental

The immunosuppressive effects of tacrolimus may result in an increased incidence of certain microbial infections and delayed healing. Dental work, whenever possible, should be completed prior to initiation of therapy and undertaken with caution during therapy. Patients should be instructed in proper oral hygiene.

Drug interactions and/or related problems

The following drug interactions and/or related problems have been selected on the basis of their potential clinical significance (possible mechanism in parentheses where appropriate)—not necessarily inclusive (» = major clinical significance):

Note: Combinations containing any of the following medications, depending on the amount present, may also interact with this medication.

The drug interactions between tacrolimus and clarithromycin, clotrimazole, danazol, erythromycin, fluconazole, hyperkalemia-causing medications, nephrotoxic medications, and rifampin have been observed clinically in patients. The drug interactions between tacrolimus and aluminum hydroxide gel, bromocriptine, cimetidine, cyclosporine, dexamethasone, diltiazem, ethinyl estradiol, itraconazole, ketoconazole, magnesium oxide, nifedipine, omeprazole, sodium bicarbonate, and verapamil have been demonstrated *in vitro* or in experimental animal models.

The extent of induction or inhibition of cytochrome P450 enzymes may depend on the dose of the inducer or inhibitor.

Aluminum hydroxide gel
(absorbs tacrolimus; may lead to reduced blood concentrations of tacrolimus)

Note: No interaction between fluconazole and tacrolimus was noted in one study in which the medications were administered intravenously to patients receiving bone marrow transplantation. The mechanism of this interaction may be inhibition of metabolism of tacrolimus in the gut, leading to increased absorption. This interaction may not occur to the same extent when tacrolimus is given intravenously as when it is given orally.

Bromocriptine or
Cimetidine or
Cisapride or
Chloramphenicol or
Cimetidine or
Clarithromycin or
Clotrimazole or
» Danazol or
Diltiazem or
Ethinyl estradiol or
» Erythromycin or
» Fluconazole or
» Itraconazole or
» Ketoconazole or
» Lansoprazole or
Magnesium-aluminum-hydroxide or
Methylprednisolone or
Metoclopramide or
Nefazodone or
Nicardipine or
Nifedipine or
Omeprazole or
Protease inhibitors or
Troleandomycin or
Verapamil or
Voriconazole
(may inhibit the metabolism of tacrolimus, leading to increased tacrolimus blood concentrations and toxicity; some agents inhibiting the metabolism of tacrolimus [e.g., azole antifungal agents and calcium channel blocking agents] may be used therapeutically so that lower doses of tacrolimus can be used)
(lansoprazole may potentially inhibit tacrolimus metabolism and substantially increase tacrolimus whole blood concentrations, especially in transplant patients who are intermediate or poor CYP2C19 metabolizers compared with those who are efficient CYP2C19 metabolizers)

Carbamazepine or
Caspofungin or
Phenobarbital or
Phenytoin or
Rifabutin or
Sirolimus or
St. John's Wort
(may increase tacrolimus drug concentrations)

» Cyclosporine
(increased immunosuppression; tacrolimus may increase the bioavailability of cyclosporine, or may inhibit the metabolism of cyclosporine, leading to increased cyclosporine blood concentrations and toxicity; increased risk of nephrotoxicity with concurrent use)
(patients switched from cyclosporine to tacrolimus should receive the first dose of tacrolimus no sooner than 24 hours after the last cyclosporine dose)

Dexamethasone or
» Rifampin
(may induce cytochrome P450 3A enzymes, leading to increased metabolism of tacrolimus and lower blood concentrations)

Drugs metabolized by CYP3A such as
» Nelfinavir or
Ritonavir
(coadministration of nelfinavir and tacrolimus increased tacrolimus blood concentrations significantly and required a tacrolimus dose reduction of 16-fold on average to maintain mean trough tacrolimus blood concentrations; appropriate dosage adjustments are essential when nelfinavir is used concomitantly)

» Grapefruit juice
(affects CYP3A-mediated metabolism of tacrolimus and should be avoided)

Hyperkalemia-causing medications (see *Appendix II*), especially:
» Diuretics, potassium-sparing
(concurrent use with tacrolimus may result in hyperkalemia)

Magnesium oxide or
Sodium bicarbonate
(tacrolimus is degraded by an alkaline environment, resulting in decreased bioavailability of tacrolimus; the same interaction may occur with other antacids; a single-dose study examining the effect of magnesium oxide did not show decreased bioavailability)

Muromonab-CD3
(increased incidence of post-transplant lymphoproliferative disorder [PTLD] with concurrent use)

Nephrotoxic medications (see *Appendix II*), such as:
Aminoglycosides or
Amphotericin B or
Anti-inflammatory drugs, nonsteroidal or
Ganciclovir or
Vancomycin
(may be additive or synergistic impairment of renal function)

Vaccines, killed virus
(immune response to vaccines may be decreased)

» Vaccines, live virus
(the immunosuppressive effect of tacrolimus may potentiate the replication of the vaccine virus, may increase the side/adverse effect of the vaccine, and/or may decrease the immune response to the vaccine)

Laboratory value alterations

The following have been selected on the basis of their potential clinical significance (possible effect in parentheses where appropriate)—not necessarily inclusive (» = major clinical significance).

With physiology/laboratory test values
Alanine aminotransferase (ALT [SGPT]) and

Alkaline phosphatase and
Amylase
Aspartate aminotransferase (AST [SGOT])
(values may be increased; may indicate hepatotoxicity)

Bilirubin, serum
(concentrations may be increased; may indicate hepatotoxicity)

Blood urea nitrogen (BUN) and
» Creatinine, serum
(concentrations may be increased; may indicate nephrotoxicity)

Calcium and
» Magnesium, serum
(concentrations may be decreased)

Cholesterol, serum
(values may be increased)

» Glucose, blood and
Triglycerides, serum
(concentrations may be increased)

Glucose, urine
(glucosuria has been observed during clinical practice)

Hematocrit value and
Hemoglobin concentration
(may be decreased)

Leukocytes (neutrophils [WBC])
(blood counts may be increased or decreased)

Platelets
(blood counts may be decreased)

Phosphate and
» Potassium
(serum concentrations may be increased)

Medical considerations/Contraindications

The medical considerations/contraindications included have been selected on the basis of their potential clinical significance (reasons given in parentheses where appropriate)—not necessarily inclusive (» = major clinical significance).

Except under special circumstances, this medication should not be used when the following medical problems exist:

» Allergy to polyoxyl 60 hydrogenated castor oil
(patients with an allergy to castor oil derivatives may be allergic to tacrolimus injection also, since tacrolimus injection has a castor oil vehicle; intravenous administration of castor oil derivatives has been associated with anaphylactic reactions; the use of tacrolimus injection in patients with an allergy to castor oil derivatives is contraindicated)

» Allergy to tacrolimus, history of

» Malignancy, current
(Tacrolimus use is associated with an increased susceptibility to malignancies)

Risk-benefit should be considered when the following medical problems exist:

» Chickenpox, existing or recent (including recent exposure) or
» Herpes zoster
(risk of severe generalized disease)

Diabetes mellitus
(risk of loss of glucose control)

Hepatic function impairment or
Hepatitis B or C infection, chronic or
» Renal function impairment
(dosage reduction may be required; patients with post-transplant hepatic function impairment may have an increased risk of renal toxicity when taking tacrolimus)

Hyperkalemia
(tacrolimus may exacerbate hyperkalemia)

» Infection
(immunosuppression may exacerbate infections)

Neurologic function impairment
(dosage reduction may be required)

Patient monitoring

The following may be especially important in patient monitoring (other tests may be warranted in some patients, depending on condition; » = major clinical significance):

Note: Monitoring intervals may need to be altered based on the condition of the patient.

Alanine aminotransferase (ALT [SGPT]) and
Alkaline phosphatase and
Aspartate aminotransferase (AST [SGOT]) and
Bilirubin, serum
(recommended periodically to monitor hepatic function; more frequent monitoring required in the early post-transplant period)

Blood urea nitrogen (BUN) and
» Creatinine, serum
(recommended to monitor for nephrotoxicity; nephrotoxicity occurs most often in the early post-transplant period, especially if intravenous tacrolimus is administered)

» Blood pressure measurements
(frequent measurements recommended)

Calcium and
» Magnesium and
Phosphate and
» Potassium
(frequent monitoring recommended in the early post-transplant period; periodic monitoring recommended thereafter)

Cholesterol, serum and
Triglycerides, serum
(periodic monitoring recommended)

Complete blood counts (CBCs)
(monitoring of CBC recommended to detect tacrolimus-induced blood dyscrasias; changes in the neutrophil count may also indicate infection)

» Echocardiographic evaluation
(consider if patient develops renal failure or clinical manifestations of ventricular dysfunction while receiving tacrolimus therapy; dosage reduction or discontinuation of tacrolimus should be considered if myocardial hypertrophy is diagnosed)

» Glucose, blood
(frequent monitoring recommended in the early post-transplant period; periodic monitoring recommended thereafter)

» Tacrolimus concentrations, whole blood, trough
(target blood concentrations vary depending on the indication and the transplant center protocol; trough whole blood concentrations of 10 to 20 mcg per mL [mcg/mL] [12.2 to 24.4 micromoles per L (micromoles/L)] are used by some centers in the first month following transplantation; for the subsequent 2 months, lower blood concentrations [i.e., 5 to 15 mcg/mL (6.1 to 18.3 micromoles/L)] are often recommended; after 3 months some centers lower the target blood concentrations to 5 to 10 mcg/mL [6.1 to 12.2 micromoles/L]; higher concentrations are used in intestinal transplantation)
(target blood concentrations vary for pediatric patients, depending on indication and transplant center; for liver transplantation, a consortium of transplant centers recommends trough concentrations of 12 to 15 mcg/L [14.6 to 18.3 micromoles/L] in the first month following transplantation, 10 to 12 mcg/L [12.2 to 14.6 micromoles/L] for the subsequent 2 months, and 5 to 10 mcg/L [6.1 to 12.2 micromoles/L] thereafter; for renal transplantation, one transplant center recommends trough blood concentrations of 20 to 25 mcg/L [24.4 to 30.5 micromoles/L] in the first 2 weeks following transplantation, 15 to 20 mcg/mL [18.3 to 24.4 micromoles/L] for the second 2 weeks following transplantation, 10 to 15 mcg/L [12.2 to 18.3 micromoles/L] for the following 3 months, and 5 to 9 mcg/L [6.1 to 11 micromoles/L] thereafter)
(trough blood concentrations should be measured frequently in the early post-transplant period; tacrolimus blood concentrations often are measured daily until good graft function and good renal function are achieved, and then every other day during the early post-transplant hospitalization; concentrations should be measured after adjustment in the tacrolimus dose, and after the addition or removal of medications that may alter tacrolimus absorption or clearance)
(high tacrolimus blood concentrations are correlated with toxicity; low tacrolimus blood concentrations are not as well-correlated with episodes of rejection; tacrolimus blood concentrations should always be considered in conjunction with the patients' clinical condition when assessing the adequacy of the tacrolimus dose)

Side/Adverse Effects

Note: Hyperglycemia, nephrotoxicity, and neurotoxicity are the most significant adverse effects resulting from the use of tacrolimus. Other adverse effects (e.g., infection, post-transplant lymphoproliferative disorder [PTLD]) result from the degree of immunosuppression, *not specifically from the use of tacrolimus.*

The following side/adverse effects have been selected on the basis of their potential clinical significance (possible signs and symptoms in parentheses where appropriate)—not necessarily inclusive:

Those indicating need for medical attention

Incidence more frequent

Asthenia (loss of energy or weakness); ***blood dyscrasias including red cell aplasia*** (fever and sore throat; pale skin; unusual bleeding or bruising; unusual tiredness or weakness); ***gastrointestinal disturbance, including abdominal pain; diarrhea; loss of appetite; nausea; vomiting; hyperglycemia*** (frequent urination); ***hyperkalemia*** (abdominal pain; nausea or vomiting; weakness); ***hypomagnesemia*** (muscle trembling or twitching); ***infection*** (fever or chills); ***nephrotoxicity; neurotoxicity, including abnormal dreams; agitation; anxiety; confusion; depression; dizziness; hallucinations*** (seeing or hearing things that are not there); ***headache; insomnia*** (trouble in sleeping); ***nervousness; seizures; tremor*** (trembling and shaking of hands); ***paresthesia*** (tingling); ***peripheral edema*** (swelling of ankles, feet, or lower legs); ***pleural effusion*** (shortness of breath); ***pruritus*** (itching); ***skin rash***

Incidence less frequent

Cardiovascular effects, including cardiomyopathy (shortness of breath); ***chest pain; hyperlipidemia; hypertension; hyperesthesia*** (increased sensitivity to pain); ***muscle cramps; neuropathy*** (numbness or pain in legs); ***osteoporosis; sweating; tinnitus*** (ringing in ears); ***visual disturbance*** (blurred vision)

Incidence rare

Anaphylaxis (flushing of face or neck; shortness of breath; wheezing)—with parenteral use; ***hepatotoxicity*** (flu-like symptoms); ***myocardial hypertrophy, spontaneous*** (enlarged heart); ***PTLD*** (fever; general feeling of discomfort and illness; weight loss)

Note: PTLD may be more common in pediatric patients than in adult patients, especially in pediatric patients up to 3 years of age.

Incidence not determined and indicating the need for medical attention—Observed during clinical practice; estimates of frequency cannot be determined

Cardiac arrhythmia (chest pain or discomfort; dizziness; fainting; fast, slow, or irregular heartbeat; lightheadedness; pounding or rapid pulse); ***gastroenteritis*** (abdominal or stomach pain; diarrhea; loss of appetite; nausea; weakness); ***glycosuria*** (sugar in the urine); ***hearing loss; hemolytic-uremic syndrome*** (black, tarry, stools; stomach pain; blood in urine; fever increased or decreased; urination; pinpoint red spots on skin; swelling of face, fingers, feet, or lower legs; unusual bleeding or bruising; unusual tiredness or weakness; yellow eyes or skin); ***leukoencephalopathy*** (back pain; blurred vision; confusion; convulsions; dizziness; drowsiness; fever; headache; unusual tiredness or weakness); ***pancreatitis*** (bloating; chills; constipation; darkened urine; fast heartbeat; fever; indigestion; loss of appetite; nausea; pains in stomach, side, or abdomen, possibly radiating to the back; vomiting; yellow eyes or skin); ***QT prolongation*** (irregular heartbeat; recurrent fainting); ***renal failure, acute*** (Lower back/side pain; decreased frequency /amount of urine; bloody urine; increased thirst; loss of appetite; nausea; vomiting; unusual tiredness or weakness; swelling of face, fingers, lower legs; weight gain; troubled breathing; increased blood pressure); ***Stevens Johnson syndrome*** (blistering; peeling; loosening of skin; chills; cough; diarrhea; itching; joint or muscle pain; red irritated eyes; red skin lesions, often with a purple center; sore throat; sores; ulcers, or white spots in mouth or on lips; unusual tiredness or weakness); ***stomach ulcer*** (abdominal or stomach pain; cramping or burning; black, tarry stools; constipation; diarrhea; vomiting of blood or material that looks like coffee grounds; nausea; heartburn; indigestion); ***Toursade de Pointes*** (chest pain or discomfort; irregular or slow heart rate; fainting; shortness of breath)

Overdose

For more information on the management of overdose or unintentional ingestion, **contact a Poison Control Center** (see *Poison Control Center Listing*).

Clinical effects of overdose

Early clinical trials used doses of tacrolimus that were later determined to be overdoses. The patients experienced the same side effects as patients receiving lower doses, but the incidence of these effects was greater in patients receiving higher doses of tacrolimus. The patients receiving the overdoses of tacrolimus experienced more new-onset diabetes, nephrotoxicity, and neurotoxicity as compared to patients receiving lower doses.

There is limited literature on the effects of massive overdoses of tacrolimus in humans. Overdoses of up to 7 mg per kg of body weight (mg/kg) have been reported. Most patients did not develop symptoms associated with the overdose.

In toxicity studies in rats, mortalities first occurred at intravenous doses 16 times the recommended human dose.

Treatment of overdose

Treatment is symptomatic and supportive. Clearance of tacrolimus cannot be enhanced by dialysis because tacrolimus is extensively bound to erythrocytes and plasma proteins.

Patients in whom intentional overdose is confirmed or suspected should be referred for psychiatric consultation.

Patient Consultation

As an aid to patient consultation, refer to Advice for the Patient, Tacrolimus (Systemic).

In providing consultation, consider emphasizing the following selected information (» = major clinical significance):

Before using this medication

» Conditions affecting use, especially:

Allergy to tacrolimus or castor oil derivatives

Carcinogenicity—Use of tacrolimus is associated with an increased incidence of malignancy

Pregnancy—Tacrolimus crosses the placenta; transplant patients should not conceive shortly after transplantation or while being treated for transplant-related complications

Breast-feeding—Tacrolimus is distributed into breast milk; breast-feeding should be avoided

Dental—Dental work should be completed prior to initiation of therapy whenever possible

Other medications, especially cyclosporine, danazol, erythromycin, fluconazole, itraconazole, ketoconazole, lansoprazole, nelfinavir, potassium-sparing diuretics, or rifampin

Other medical problems, especially allergy to polyoxyl 60 hydrogenated castor oil, chickenpox, current malignancy, herpes zoster infection, or renal function impairment

Proper use of this medication

» Importance of not using more or less medication than the amount prescribed

Getting into the habit of taking at the same time each day and in a consistent relationship to the type and timing of the intake of food to help increase compliance and maintain steady blood concentrations

» Not drinking grapefruit juice or eating grapefruit

» Checking with physician before discontinuing or changing medication; possible need for lifelong therapy

» Proper dosing

Missed dose: Taking as soon as possible if remembered within 12 hours; not taking if almost time for next dose; not doubling doses

» Proper storage

Precautions while using this medication

» Importance of close monitoring by physician

Maintaining good dental hygiene and seeing dentist frequently for teeth cleaning

Use of sunscreen with high protection and by wearing protective clothing to protect skin from exposure to sun light

» Not eating raw oysters or other shellfish; making sure they are fully cooked before eating

» Continuing recommended vaccination schedule (except for live vaccines)

» Avoiding exposure to chickenpox, measles, mumps, and rubella; if exposed, seeing physician for prophylactic therapy

Not traveling to another country without making sure a supply of tacrolimus will be available

Side/adverse effects

Signs of potential side effects, especially asthenia, blood dyscrasias, abdominal pain, diarrhea, loss of appetite, nausea, vomiting, hyperglycemia, hyperkalemia, hypomagnesemia, infection, nephrotoxicity, abnormal dreams, agitation, anxiety, confusion, depression, dizziness, hallucinations, headache, insomnia, nervousness, seizures, tremor, paresthesia, peripheral edema, pleural effusion, pruritus, skin rash, cardiomyopathy, chest pain, hyperlipidemia, hypertension, hyperesthesia, muscle cramps, neuropathy, osteoporosis, sweating, tinnitus, visual disturbance, anaphylaxis, hepatotoxicity, and post-transplant lymphoproliferative disorder

General Dosing Information

Dosage regimens for tacrolimus vary among transplant centers. Dosage of tacrolimus should be adjusted based on the clinical response of each patient. Whole blood trough concentrations can be used as a guide to appropriate dosing. High whole blood trough concentrations are associated with an increase in toxicity.

Tacrolimus usually is used in conjunction with other immunosuppressants (e.g., corticosteroids and azathioprine). Corticosteroids typically are tapered following transplantation to target doses of prednisone for adult patients of 2.5 to 5 mg per day six months after transplantation. In some cases, it may be possible to wean the patient from other immunosuppressants and maintain the patient on tacrolimus monotherapy.

When converting from cyclosporine to tacrolimus, it is recommended that cyclosporine be discontinued 24 hours before initiating tacrolimus therapy. In some transplant centers, cyclosporine whole blood concentrations are measured, and tacrolimus therapy started if cyclosporine concentrations are less than 100 micrograms per liter (mcg/L).

Patients receiving lower-quality hepatic allografts or with poor early hepatic graft function should receive lower doses of tacrolimus initially. Liver transplant patients with poor hepatic graft function have increased risk for developing renal function impairment.

Antiviral prophylaxis, i.e., with acyclovir, ganciclovir, and immune globulins, may be advisable for some patients receiving tacrolimus, especially cytomegalovirus (CMV) prophylaxis in patients who have not been exposed to CMV prior to transplantation who receive a CMV-positive graft.

Vaccination schedules should be continued, except for live vaccines. Vaccinations against hepatitis A and B are recommended. Inactivated poliovirus vaccine should be used instead of oral poliovirus vaccine for both the patient and for people living in the same household as the patient. Vaccines given to immunosuppressed patients may not result in a protective antibody response. Protective antibody concentrations should be checked after the vaccine has been administered.

If a patient is exposed to measles, mumps, rubella, or varicella for the first time while receiving tacrolimus, the patient should receive prophylactic therapy with immune globulin, i.e., pooled human immune globulin or varicella immune globulin.

For parenteral dosage forms only

Because parenteral tacrolimus is associated with the development of more adverse effects, including anaphylaxis and renal function impairment, than is oral tacrolimus, parenteral tacrolimus should be used only in patients unable to take tacrolimus orally. When receiving parenteral tacrolimus, patients should be monitored closely for anaphylaxis, especially during the first 30 minutes of the infusion. Patients receiving tacrolimus parenterally should be switched to oral tacrolimus as soon as it can be tolerated.

Diet/Nutrition

The rate of absorption of oral tacrolimus is decreased in the presence of food, but the extent of absorption may or may not be affected, depending on the type of food ingested. Tacrolimus should be given consistently with relation to food.

Bioavailability of tacrolimus may be increased by ingestion of grapefruit or grapefruit juice, resulting in toxic blood concentrations of tacrolimus.

Raw oysters or other shellfish may contain bacteria that can cause serious illness, and possibly death. Even eating oysters from "clean" water or good restaurants does not guarantee that the oysters do not contain the bacteria. Symptoms of this infection include sudden chills, fever, nausea, vomiting, blood poisoning, and sometimes death. Eating raw shellfish is not a problem for most healthy people; however, patients with the following conditions may be at greater risk: cancer, immune disorders, immunosuppression following organ transplantation, long-term corticosteroid use (as for asthma, arthritis, or prevention of graft rejection in organ transplantation), liver disease (including viral hepatitis), excessive alcohol intake (two to three drinks or more per day), diabetes, stomach problems (including previous stomach surgery and low stomach acid), and hemochromatosis.

For treatment of adverse effects

Recommended treatment consists of the following:

- Many adverse effects (e.g., cardiomyopathy, gastrointestinal toxicity, hyperglycemia, hyperkalemia, hypomagnesemia, nephrotoxicity, neurotoxicity, pruritus, rash) may respond to a reduction in dose. If adverse effects do not respond to a reduction in dose, it may be advisable to convert the patient to a cyclosporine-based immunosuppressant regimen.

Oral Dosage Forms

Note: Bracketed uses in the Dosage Forms section refer to categories of use and/or indications that are not included in U.S. product labeling.

TACROLIMUS CAPSULES

Usual adult and adolescent dose

Transplant rejection, heart (prophylaxis)[1]—

Oral, 0.075 mg per kg of body weight per day, in two divided doses every 12 hours, initially. The dose should be based on typical whole blood trough concentrations of 10 to 20 ng per mL (month 1 through 3) and 5 to 15 ng per mL (month ≥ 4). Oral therapy should be given 8 to 12 hours after discontinuation of intravenous infusion.

Transplant rejection, liver (prophylaxis) or
[Transplant rejection, solid organ, other (prophylaxis)][1] or
[Transplant rejection, liver (treatment)] or
[Transplant rejection, solid organ, other (treatment)][1]—

Oral, 0.1 to 0.15 mg per kg of body weight per day, in two divided doses, initially. The dose should be adjusted based on trough blood concentrations.

Transplant rejection, kidney (prophylaxis)[1] or—

Oral, 0.2mg per kg per day in 2 divided doses

[Graft-versus-host disease (prophylaxis)][1]—

Oral, 0.12 mg per kg of body weight per day in two divided doses, starting when the patient can tolerate oral medications. The dose should be adjusted based on trough blood concentrations.

[Graft-versus-host disease (treatment)][1]—

Oral, 0.3 mg per kg of body weight per day in two divided doses, starting when the patient can tolerate oral medications. The dose should be adjusted based on trough blood concentrations.

Tacrolimus is used as part of a regimen to treat graft-versus-host disease. Other agents used to treat graft-versus-host disease may include methotrexate and/or corticosteroids.

[Uveitis, severe, refractory (treatment)][1]—

Oral, 0.1 to 0.15 mg per kg of body weight per day in two divided doses.

Usual pediatric dose

Transplant rejection, liver (prophylaxis) or
Transplant rejection, kidney (prophylaxis)[1] or
[Transplant rejection, solid organ, other (prophylaxis)][1] or
[Transplant rejection, liver (treatment)] or
[Transplant rejection, solid organ, other (treatment)][1]—

Oral, 0.15 to 0.2 mg per kg of body weight per day, in two divided doses, initially. The dose should be adjusted based on trough blood concentrations.

[Graft-versus-host disease (prophylaxis)][1]—

See *Usual adult and adolescent dose*. Pediatric patients may require higher doses to attain therapeutic blood trough concentrations.

[Graft-versus-host disease (treatment)][1]—

See *Usual adult and adolescent dose*. Pediatric patients may require higher doses to attain therapeutic blood trough concentrations.

Usual geriatric dose

See *Usual adult and adolescent dose*.

Strength(s) usually available

U.S.—

0.5 mg (Rx) [*Prograf* (anhydrous; croscarmellose sodium; gelatin; hydroxypropyl methylcellulose; lactose; magnesium stearate; titanium dioxide)].

1 mg (Rx) [*Prograf* (anhydrous; croscarmellose sodium; gelatin; hydroxypropyl methylcellulose; lactose; magnesium stearate; titanium dioxide)].

5 mg (Rx) [*Prograf* (anhydrous; croscarmellose sodium; ferric oxide; gelatin; hydroxypropyl methylcellulose; lactose; magnesium stearate; titanium dioxide)].

Canada—

1 mg (Rx) [*Prograf* (anhydrous; croscarmellose sodium; gelatin; hydroxypropyl methylcellulose; lactose; magnesium stearate; titanium dioxide)].

5 mg (Rx) [*Prograf* (anhydrous; croscarmellose sodium; ferric oxide; gelatin; hydroxypropyl methylcellulose; lactose; magnesium stearate; titanium dioxide)].

Packaging and storage

Store between 15 and 30 °C (59 and 86 °F).

Note: Tacrolimus suspension has been extemporaneously compounded by mixing the contents of 5-mg capsules with equal amounts of Ora-Plus®, a suspending vehicle for oral extemporaneous preparations, and Simple Syrup NF, to a final concentration of 0.5 mg per mL (mg/mL). The extemporaneously prepared tacrolimus suspension was found to be stable for at least 56 days in glass and plastic amber bottles stored between 24 and 26 °C (75.2 and 78.8 °F). Bioavailability testing has not been performed using the extemporaneously compounded suspension.

Parenteral Dosage Forms

Note: Bracketed uses in the Dosage Forms section refer to categories of use and/or indications that are not included in U.S. product labeling.

TACROLIMUS FOR INJECTION

Note: Tacrolimus injection is intended for intravenous infusion only.

Parenteral tacrolimus should be used only in patients unable to take tacrolimus orally. Patients receiving tacrolimus parenterally should be switched to oral tacrolimus as soon as it can be tolerated.

Usual adult and adolescent dose

Transplant rejection, heart (prophylaxis), in patients unable to take oral medications—

Begin treatment no sooner than 6 hours after transplantation. Continuous intravenous infusion, as follows:

Time after transplantation	Caucasian patients Dose (mg/kg of body weight)	Caucasian patients Trough concentrations (ng/mL)	Black patients Dose (mg/kg of body weight)	Black patients Trough concentrations (ng/mL)
Day 7	0.18	12	0.23	10.9
Month 1	0.17	12.8	0.26	12.9
Month 6	0.14	11.8	0.24	11.5
Month 12	0.13	10.1	0.19	11

Transplant rejection, liver (prophylaxis), in patients unable to take oral medications or

Transplant rejection, kidney (prophylaxis), in patients unable to take oral medications[1] or

[Transplant rejection, solid organ, other (prophylaxis), in patients unable to take oral medications][1] or

[Transplant rejection, liver (treatment), in patients unable to take oral medications] or

[Transplant rejection, solid organ, other (treatment), in patients unable to take oral medications][1]—

Continuous intravenous infusion, 0.01 to 0.05 mg per kg of body weight per day, beginning no sooner than six hours after transplantation. The dose should be adjusted based on trough blood concentrations.

[Graft-versus-host disease (prophylaxis)][1]—

Intravenous infusion, 0.04 mg per kg of body weight per day as a continuous infusion started the day prior to bone marrow transplantation. The dose should be adjusted based on trough blood concentrations.

[Graft-versus-host disease (treatment)][1]—

Intravenous infusion, 0.1 mg per kg of body weight per day in two divided doses administered over four hours for each infusion. The dose should be adjusted based on trough blood concentrations.

Usual pediatric dose

Transplant rejection, liver (prophylaxis), in patients unable to take oral medications or

Transplant rejection, kidney (prophylaxis), in patients unable to take oral medications[1] or

[Transplant rejection, solid organ, other (prophylaxis), in patients unable to take oral medications][1] or

[Transplant rejection, liver (treatment), in patients unable to take oral medications] or

[Transplant rejection, solid organ, other (treatment), in patients unable to take oral medications][1]—

See *Usual adult and adolescent dose.*

[Graft-versus-host disease (prophylaxis)][1]—

See *Usual adult and adolescent dose.* Pediatric patients may require higher doses to attain therapeutic blood trough concentrations.

[Graft-versus-host disease (treatment)][1]—

Intravenous infusion, 0.1 mg per kg of body weight per day as a continuous infusion.

Usual geriatric dose

See *Usual adult and adolescent dose.*

Strength(s) usually available

U.S.—

5 mg per mL (Rx) [*Prograf* (anhydrous; alcohol 80% v/v; polyoxyl 60 hydrogenated castor oil 200 mg per mL)].

Canada—

5 mg per mL (Rx) [*Prograf* (anhydrous; alcohol 80% v/v; polyoxyl 60 hydrogenated castor oil 200 mg per mL)].

Packaging and storage

Store between 5 and 25 °C (41 and 77 °F).

Preparation of dosage form

Tacrolimus should be diluted with 5% dextrose injection or 0.9% sodium chloride injection to a concentration between 0.004 and 0.02 mg per mL (mg/mL).

Stability

Diluted tacrolimus for injection should be used within 24 hours. The prepared solution should be inspected for particulate matter and clarity before administration to the patient, and should be discarded if particulate matter is present.

Incompatibilities

Tacrolimus for injection should not be stored in polyvinyl chloride (PVC) containers because the solution may be absorbed by PVC containers, and leaching of phthalates in the PVC container may occur.

[1]Not included in Canadian product labeling.

Selected Bibliography

The US Multicenter FK506 Liver Study Group. A comparison of tacrolimus (FK 506) and cyclosporine for immunosuppression in liver transplantation. N Engl J Med 1994; 331: 1110-5.

Venkataramanan R, Swaminathan A, Prasad T, et al. Clinical pharmacokinetics of tacrolimus. Clin Pharmacokinet 1995; 404-30.

Peters D, Fitton A, Plosker G. Tacrolimus. A review of its pharmacology and therapeutic potential in hepatic and renal transplantation. Drugs 1993; 46: 746-94

Starzl T, Todo S, Fung J, et al. FK 506 for liver, kidney, and pancreas transplantation. Lancet 1989; 2: 1000-4.

Revised: 05/02/2006
Developed: 08/14/1997

TACROLIMUS Topical

VA CLASSIFICATION (Primary): DE900

Commonly used brand name(s): *Protopic.*

Note: For a listing of dosage forms and brand names by country availability, see *Dosage Forms* section(s).

Category

Immunomodulator (topical).

Indications

Accepted

Dermatitis, atopic, moderate to severe, second-line (treatment)—Tacrolimus ointment, both 0.03% and 0.1% for adults, and only 0.03% for children aged 2 to 15 years, is indicated as *second-line therapy* for the short-term and non-continuous chronic treatment of moderate to severe atopic dermatitis in non-immunocompromised adults and children who have failed to respond adequately to other topical prescription treatments for atopic dermatitis, or when those treatments are not advisable.

Unaccepted

Studied have not evaluated the safety and efficacy of tacrolimus in the treatment of clinically infected atopic dermatitis.

Tacrolimus ointment is not indicated for children younger than 2 years of age.

Long-term safety of topical calcineurin inhibitors, including tacrolimus, has not been established.

The safety of tacrolimus ointment under occlusion, which may promote systemic exposure, has not been evaluated.

Pharmacology/Pharmacokinetics

Physicochemical characteristics

Molecular weight—822.05.

Mechanism of action/Effect

The exact mechanism of action of tacrolimus in atopic dermatitis is not known.Tacrolimus inhibits T-lymphocyte activation by first binding to an intracellular protein FKBP-12, by forming a complex with FKBP-12, calcium, calmodulin, and calcineurin, inhibiting the phosphatase activity of calcineurin. This is believed to prevent the formation of lymphokines (IL-2, gamma interferon).

Tacrolimus also inhibits the transcription of genes which encode IL-3, IL-4, IL-5, GM-CSF, and TNF-α, inhibits the release of pre-formed mediators from skin mast cells and basophils, and downregulates Fc (epsilon) RI expression on Langerhans cells.

Absorption
Absolute bioavailability is unknown. Using historial intravenous data for comparison, bioavailability is less than 0.5%.

Peak blood concentration:
Blood—Range from undetectable to 20 ng per mL in adult patients and below 1.6 ng per mL in pediatric patients.

Precautions to Consider

Carcinogenicity / Tumorigenicity
Application of tacrolimus ointment with concurrent UV exposure, in a 52-week photocarcinogenicity study (40 weeks of treatment followed by 12 weeks of observation) has been shown to decrease the median time to onset of skin tumor formation in hairless mice. Lymphomas were noted in the mouse dermal carcinogenicity study at a daily dose of 3.5 mg per kg (26 times the maximum recommended human dose [MRHD]) but none were noted with a daily dose of 1.1 mg per kg (10 times the MRHD). A 104 week dermal carcinogenicity study in which mice were given 1.1 to 118 mg per kg per day of tacrolimus ointment showed a significant elevation in the incidence of pleomorphic lymphoma in high dose male and female animals and in the incidence of undifferentiated lymphoma in high dose females. Carcinogenicity studies conducted with topical application of tacrolimus in mice demonstrated a dose-dependent development of lymphoma. The systemic administration of tacrolimus in kidney and liver transplant patients has been associated with development of lymphoma and skin malignancies.However, the incidence of skin tumor formation was minimal and not associated with the topical application of tacrolimus, under ambient lighting.

The systemic form of tacrolimus is known to cause both skin cancers and lymphoma in humans by suppressing the body's normal immune defenses against cancer. The cancer risk increases with higher doses and longer treatment courses of oral tacrolimus.

Mutagenicity
No evidence of genotoxicity was seen in bacterial or mammalian *in vitro* assays of mutagenicity, or *in vivo* clastogenicity assays performed in mice. Unscheduled DNA synthesis was not seen in rodent hepatocytes.

Pregnancy/Reproduction
Fertility—There are no adequate and well controlled studies on the effects of topical tacrolimus on fertility. However, studies in which tacrolimus was administered orally showed no reduction in fertility in male or female rats. Oral administration at 1.0 mg/kg (0.12 times the MRHD) in rats was associated with embryolethality and adverse effects on female reproduction, indicated by a higher rate of pre-implantation loss and increased numbers of undelivered and nonviable pups. Doses of 3.2 mg/kg (0.43 times the MRHD), was associated with maternal and paternal toxicity and reproductive toxicity including marked effects on estrous cycles, parturition, pup viability, and pup malformations.

Pregnancy—Tacrolimus crosses the placenta. There are no adequate and well-controlled studies of topically administered tacrolimus in pregnant women. Use of systemic tacrolimus during pregnancy has been associated with neonatal hyperkalemia and renal dysfunction. Studies in animals have shown that orally administered tacrolimus causes adverse effects on the fetus. Tacrolimus ointment should be used during pregnancy only if the potential benefit to the mother justifies a potential risk to the fetus.

FDA Pregnancy Category C.

Breast-feeding
Systemic absorption of topical tacrolimus is minimal, although potential adverse effects on nursing infants exist. Tacrolimus is distributed in human breast milk following oral administration. A decision on the use of topical tacrolimus by nursing mothers should consider the benefit to the mother as well as the potential for adverse effects on the infant.

Pediatrics
Only the lower concentration tacrolimus ointment 0.03% is recommended for use by pediatric patients 2 to 15 years of age.

Appropriate studies have not been performed on the relationship of age to the effects of tacrolimus in children up to 2 years of age. Tacrolimus ointment is not indicated for children less than 2 years of age. The effect of tacrolimus on the developing immune system in infants and children is not known.

Tacrolimus is sometimes absorbed through the skin, though usually at very low amounts. Occasionally, children who have been treated with topical tacrolimus have had measurable blood level of the drug, in the range of patients treated with oral tacrolimus.

Geriatrics
Appropriate studies performed to date have not demonstrated geriatrics-specific problems that would limit the usefulness of tacrolimus ointment in the elderly.

Drug interactions and/or related problems
The following drug interactions and/or related problems have been selected on the basis of their potential clinical significance (possible mechanism in parentheses where appropriate)—not necessarily inclusive (» = major clinical significance):

Note: Minimal systemic absorption of topically applied tacrolimus should preclude the potential for significant interactions with other oral medications.

CYP3A4 hepatic enzyme inhibitors, such as:
Calcium channel blockers or
Cimetidine
Erythromycin
Fluconazole
Itraconazole
Ketoconazole
(patients with widespread and/or erythrodermic disease should use caution; systemic absorption of topical tacrolimus is minimal, but drug interactions with these systemic drugs known to interact with systemic tacrolimus cannot be ruled out; may inhibit metabolism of tacrolimus, leading to increased tacrolimus blood concentrations and toxicity)

Medical considerations/Contraindications
The medical considerations/contraindications included have been selected on the basis of their potential clinical significance (reasons given in parentheses where appropriate)—not necessarily inclusive (» = major clinical significance).

Except under special circumstances, this medication should not be used when the following medical problem exists:

» Hypersensitivity to tacrolimus or any other component of the preparation

» Immunocompromised patients
(should not be used in these patients)

» Infections, active cutaneous viral, or
» Infected atopic dermatitis
(tacrolimus should not be applied topically to areas of active cutaneous viral infections or to clinically infected atopic dermatitis; before commencing treatment with tacrolimus, infections at treatment sites should be cleared)

» Netherton's syndrome
(potential for increased systemic absorption)

» Pre-malignant skin conditions or
» Malignant skin conditions
(tacrolimus use should be avoided; some malignant skin conditions, such as cutaneous T-cell lymphoma (CTCL), may mimic atopic dermatitis)

Risk-benefit should be considered when the following medical problems exist:

Eczema herpeticum (Kaposi's varicelliform eruption) or
Herpes simplex virus infection or
Varicella zoster virus infection
(increased risk may be associated with these conditions)

Erythroderma, generalized
(safety and efficacy has not been established)

Lymphoma
(increased risk for developing lymphoma in transplant patients receiving systemic immunosuppressant regimens, such as systemic tacrolimus; consider discontinuation of topical tacrolimus if lymphadenopathy without a clear etiology develops or in the presence of acute infectious mononucleosis)

» Renal impairment, predisposition to
(rare post-marketing reports of acute renal failure in patients treated with tacrolimus; caution should be exercised)

Patient monitoring
The following may be especially important in patient monitoring (other tests may be warranted in some patients, depending on condition; » = major clinical significance):

Reevaluation at 6 weeks
(if no improvement in signs and symptoms of atopic dermatitis within 6 weeks, patients should be reexamined by healthcare provider for diagnosis confirmation)

Side/Adverse Effects

Between December 2000 and 2004, the FDA had received 19 cases of postmarketing reports linking topical tacrolimus with cancer-related adverse events. Three cases occurred in children up to 16 years of age, and 16 cases occurred in adults. Two deaths in adults were reported related to complications of the cancers, and 8 hospitalizations were reported, including 2 in pediatric patients.

The 19 postmarketing cases included 9 lymphomas, 10 cutaneous tumors, of which 7 occurred at the site of tacrolimus application, as well as cases of squamous cell carcinoma, cutaneous sarcoma, malignant melanoma and other tumor types. Median time was 150 days after initiation of tacrolimus treatment until diagnosis, with a 21 to 790 day range. Six cases also reported lymphadenopathy. Two cases reported pre-existing malignancy. Three additional cases were confounded by other possible risk factors, including environmental exposure, or pre-existing conditions that may have been pre-malignant.

The potential for systemic immunosuppression is unknown and the role of topical tacrolimus in the development of the cancer-related events in the individual postmarketing cases is also uncertain.

The following side/adverse effects have been selected on the basis of their potential clinical significance (possible signs and symptoms in parentheses where appropriate)—not necessarily inclusive:

Those indicating need for medical attention

Incidence not determined—Observed during clinical practice; estimates of frequency can not be determined

Acute renal failure (agitation; coma; confusion; decreased urine output; depression; dizziness; headache; hostility; irritability; lethargy; muscle twitching; nausea; rapid weight gain; seizures; stupor; swelling of face, ankles, or hands; unusual tiredness or weakness); ***basal cell carcinoma*** (sore that will not heal; growth or bump on skin); ***bullous impetigo*** (red rash with watery, yellow-colored, or pus filled blisters; thick yellow to honey-colored crusts); ***lymphomas*** (swollen glands; weight loss; general feeling of illness; black, tarry stools; yellow skin and eyes); ***malignant melanoma*** (new mole; change in size, shape or color of existing mole; mole that leaks fluid or bleeds); ***osteomyelitis*** (increase in bone pain); ***renal impairment*** (lower back/side pain; decreased frequency/amount of urine; bloody urine; increased thirst; loss of appetite; nausea; vomiting; unusual tiredness or weakness; swelling of face, fingers, lower legs; weight gain; troubled breathing; increased blood pressure); ***rosacea*** (spider-like blood vessels on the face; burning or stinging sensation of face; redness of face); ***seizures*** (convulsions, muscle spasm or jerking of all extremities; sudden loss of consciousness; loss of bladder control); ***septicemia*** (fever; chills; looks very ill); ***squamous cell carcinoma*** (small, red skin lesion, growth, or bump unusually on face, ears, neck, hands, or arms)

Those indicating need for medical attention only if they continue or are bothersome

Incidence more frequent

Alcohol intolerance (skin flushing in areas of ointment application); ***fever***—in pediatric patients; ***flu like symptoms*** (cough; fever; headache; loss of appetite; general aches and pains; sneezing; weakness); ***headache; pruritis*** (itching skin)—in pediatric patients; ***skin burning***

Incidence less frequent

Allergic reaction (itching, pain, redness, or swelling of eye or eyelid; watering of eyes; troubled breathing or wheezing; severe skin rash or hives; flushing; headache; fever; chills; runny nose; increased sensitivity to sunlight; joint pain; swollen glands); ***acne; back pain; cyst; dyspepsia*** (acid or sour stomach; belching; heartburn; indigestion; stomach discomfort upset or pain); ***folliculitis*** (burning, itching, or pain in hairy areas; pus at root of hair); ***hyperesthesia*** (increased skin sensitivity); ***myalgia*** (muscle aches or pain); ***rash; skin tingling; sinusitis*** (pain or tenderness around eyes and cheekbones; fever; stuffy or runny nose; headache; cough; shortness of breath; troubled breathing; tightness of chest; wheezing); ***vesiculobullous rash*** (skin blisters)—in pediatric patients

Note: Other side effects have occurred, but have not been reasonably associated with the use of topical tacrolimus.

Overdose

For specific information on the clinical effects of systemic tacrolimus overdose, see the *Tacrolimus (Systemic)* monograph.

For more information on the management of overdose or unintentional ingestion, **contact a poison control center** (see *Poison Control Center Listing*).

Treatment of overdose

Treatment is symptomatic and supportive. Clearance of tacrolimus cannot be enhanced by dialysis because tacrolimus is extensively bound to erythrocytes and plasma proteins.

If oral ingestion occurs, medical advice should be sought. Oral ingestion may lead to adverse effects associated with systemic administration of tacrolimus.

Patients in whom intentional overdose is confirmed or suspected should be referred for psychiatric consultation.

Patient Consultation

As an aid to patient consultation, refer to *Advice for the Patient, Tacrolimus (Topical).*

In providing consultation, consider emphasizing the following selected information (» = major clinical significance):

Before using this medication

» Conditions affecting use, especially:
- Hypersensitivity to tacrolimus or any component of the preparation
- Pregnancy—Crosses the placenta; systemic tacrolimus associated with neonatal hyperkalemia and renal dysfunction; risk/benefit considerations
- Breast-feeding—Distributed in human breast milk following oral administration; risk/benefit considerations
- Use in children—Tacrolimus ointment not indicated for children less than 2 years of age; only lower concentration (0.03%) ointment recommended for pediatric use in patients 2 to 15 years; occasionally, children treated with tacrolimus have had measurable blood levels of the drug
- Other medical problems, especially active cutaneous viral infections, infected atopic dermatitis, immunocompromised patients, Netherton's syndrome, pre-malignant skin conditions, malignant skin conditions, or predisposition to renal impairment

Proper use of this medication

Using minimum amount of tacrolimus needed to control patient's symptoms

Using for short periods of time, not continuously and not using beyond one year of non-continuous use

Seeing healthcare provider for diagnosis confirmation if no improvement in signs and symptoms within 6 weeks

Clearing clinical infections at treatment sites before initiating topical tacrolimus treatment

Using on dry skin

Washing hands after application if hands are not an area for treatment

» Proper dosing, especially no occlusive dressings

Missed dose: Using as soon as possible; not using if almost time for next scheduled dose; not doubling doses

» Proper storage

Precautions while using this medication

» Importance of close monitoring by a physician

Reporting any adverse reactions to physician

Not using tacrolimus ointment for any disorder other than that for which it was prescribed

» Minimizing or avoiding exposure to natural or artificial sunlight (tanning beds or UVA/B treatment)

Side/adverse effects

Between December 2000 and 2004, 19 postmarketing reports linking topical tacrolimus with cancer-related adverse events have been reported to the FDA with two deaths related to complications of the cancers, and 8 hospitalizations, including 2 in pediatric patients.

Signs of potential side effects observed during clinical practice, especially acute renal failure, basal cell carcinoma, bullous impetigo, lymphomas, malignant melanoma, osteomyelitis, renal impairment, rosacea, seizures, septicemia, or squamous cell carcinoma.

General Dosing Information

Skin should be completely dry prior to application

The minimum amount of tacrolimus needed to control the patient's symptoms should be used.

Showering, bathing, or swimming directly after application may wash off the ointment.

Tacrolimus ointments should not be used with occlusive dressings.

Tacrolimus ointments are not for oral use.

Tacrolimus should be used for short period of time, not continuously. The long term safety of topical tacrolimus is unknown.

If signs and symptoms (e.g., itch, rash, and redness) do not improve within 6 weeks, patients should be re-examined by their healthcare provider to confirm the diagnosis of atopic dermatitis.

The safety of tacrolimus ointment has not been established beyond one year of non-continuous use.

Topical Dosage Forms

TACROLIMUS OINTMENT

Usual adult dose

Atopic dermatitis—

Topical, as 0.03% or 0.1% ointment, the minimum amount should be rubbed in gently and completely to the affected areas of the skin twice daily. Stop using when signs and symptoms of atopic dermatitis resolve.

Usual pediatric dose

Atopic dermatitis—

Children 2 to 15 years of age—Topical, as 0.03% ointment only, the minimum amount should be rubbed in gently and completely to the affected areas of the skin twice daily. Stop using when signs and symptoms of atopic dermatitis resolve.

Children less than 2 years of age—Safety and efficacy have not been established.

Usual geriatric dose

See *Usual adult dose.*

Strength(s) usually available

U.S.—

0.03% (Rx) [*Protopic* (mineral oil; paraffin; propylene carbonate; white petrolatum; white wax)].

0.1% (Rx) [*Protopic* (mineral oil; paraffin; propylene carbonate; white petrolatum; white wax)].

Packaging and storage

Store at 25 °C (77 °F), excursions permitted from 15 to 30°C (59 to 86°F).

Auxiliary labeling

- Avoid extended exposure to sunlight or tanning beds while taking this drug
- External use only
- Use sparingly and rub well into affected area

Revised: 03/27/2006
Developed: 05/24/2001

TADALAFIL Systemic

VA CLASSIFICATION (Primary): GU900

Note: For a listing of dosage forms and brand names by country availability, see *Dosage Forms* section(s).

Category

Impotence therapy agent (systemic).

Indications

Accepted

Erectile dysfunction (treatment)—Tadalafil is indicated for the treatment of erectile dysfunction

Pharmacology/Pharmacokinetics

Physicochemical characteristics

Molecular weight—389.41.

Solubility—Insoluble in water; slightly soluble in ethanol.

Mechanism of action/Effect

Penile erection during sexual stimulation is caused by increased penile blood flow resulting from the relaxation of penile arteries and corpus cavernosum smooth muscle. This response is mediated by the release of nitric oxide (NO) from nerve terminals and endothelial cells, which stimulates the synthesis of cyclic guanosine monophosphate (GMP) in smooth muscle cells. Cyclic GMP causes smooth muscle relaxation and increased blood flow into the corpus cavernosum. The inhibition of phosphodiesterase type 5 (PDE5) enhances erectile function by increasing the amount of cyclic GMP. Tadalafil inhibits PDE5. Because sexual stimulation is required to initiate the local release of nitric oxide, the inhibition of PDE5 by tadalafil has no effect in the absence of sexual stimulation.

Studies *in vitro* have demonstrated that tadalafil is a selective inhibitor of PDE5. PDE5 is found in corpus cavernosum smooth muscle, vascular and visceral smooth muscle, skeletal muscle, platelets, kidney, lung, cerebellum, and pancreas.

In vitro studies have shown that the effect of tadalafil is more potent on PDE5 than on other phosphodiesterases. These studies have shown that tadalafil is >10,000-fold more potent for PDE5 than for PDE1, PDE2, PDE4, and PDE7 enzymes, which are found in the heart, brain, blood vessels, liver, leukocytes, skeletal muscle, and other organs. Tadalafil is >10,000-fold more potent for PDE5 than for PDE3, an enzyme found in the heart and blood vessels. Additionally, tadalafil is 700-fold more potent for PDE5 than for PDE6, which is found in the retina and is responsible for phototransduction. Tadalafil is >9000-fold more potent for PDE5 than for PDE8, PDE9, PDE10 and 14-fold more potent for PDE5 than for PDE11A1, an enzyme found in human skeletal muscle. Tadalafil inhibits human recombinant PDE11A1 activity at concentrations within the therapeutic range. The physiological role and clinical consequence of PDE11 inhibition in humans have not been defined.

Absorption

T_{max}: 30 minutes to 6 hours (median 2 hours)

Absolute bioavailability has not been determined; rate and extent of absorption are not influenced by food

Distribution

Vol_D: 63 L; indicating distribution into tissues

Less than 0.0005% of administered dose was found in the semen of healthy subjects

Protein binding

94%

Biotransformation

Hepatic metabolism, mainly by CYP3A4

Tadalafil is predominantly metabolized by CYP3A4 to a catechol metabolite. The catechol metabolite undergoes extensive methylation and glucuronidation to form the methylcatechol and methylcatechol glucuronide conjugate, respectively. The major circulating metabolite is the methylcatechol glucuronide. Methylcatechol concentrations are less than 10% of glucuronide concentrations. *In vitro* data suggests that metabolites are not expected to be pharmacologically active at observed metabolite concentrations.

Half-life

Terminal: 17.5 hours

Steady State Plasma Concentrations

5 days with once daily dosing

Elimination

Mean oral clearance: 2.5 L per hour

Fecal: 61%

Urine: 36%

Pharmacokinetics in special populations

Geriatric: Healthy male subjects (65 years of age and older) had a lower oral clearance of tadalafil, resulting in 25% higher exposure (AUC) with no effect on C_{max} relative to that observed in healthy subjects 19 to 45 years of age; no dose adjustment is warranted based on age alone

Hepatic Impairment: In clinical pharmacology studies, tadalafil exposure (AUC) in subjects with mild or moderate hepatic impairment (Child-Pugh Class A or B) was comparable to that in healthy subjects when a dose of 10 mg was administered; there are no available data for doses higher than 10 mg of tadalafil in patients with hepatic impairment; insufficient data are available for subjects with severe hepatic impairment (Child-Pugh Class C); use in patients with severe impairment is not recommended.

Renal Insufficiency: In clinical pharmacology studies using single dose tadalafil (5 to 10 mg), tadalafil exposure (AUC) doubled in subjects with mild (creatinine clearance 51 to 80 mL per min) or moderate (creatinine clearance 31 to 50 mL per min) renal insufficiency. In subjects with end-stage renal disease on hemodialysis, there was a two-fold increase in C_{max} and 2.7–to 4.1–fold increase in AUC following single dose administration of 10 or 20 mg of tadalafil. Exposure to methylcatechol (unconjugated plus glucuronide) was 2–to 4–fold higher in subjects with renal impairment, compared to those with normal renal function. Hemodialysis (performed between 24 and 30 hours post dose) contributed negligibly to tadalafil or metabolite elimination. Dose reductions are needed in patients with moderate or severe renal insufficiency.

Diabetes mellitus: In male patients with diabetes mellitus receiving a 10 mg tadalafil dose, exposure (AUC) was reduced approximately 19% and C_{max} was 5% lower than observed in healthy subjects. No dose adjustment is warranted.

Precautions to Consider

Carcinogenicity

Tadalafil was not carcinogenic to rats or mice when administered daily for up to two years at doses up to 400 mg per kg per day. Systemic drug exposures, as measured by AUC of unbound tadalafil, were approximately 10-fold for mice, and 14- and 26-fold for male and female rats, respectively, above the exposures in human males given the Maximum Recommended Human Dose (MRHD) of 20 mg.

Mutagenicity

Tadalafil was not mutagenic in the *in vitro* bacterial Ames assay or the forward mutation test in mouse lymphoma cells. Tadalafil was not clastogenic in the *in vitro* chromosomal aberration test in human lymphocytes or the *in vivo* rat micronucleus assays.

Pregnancy/Reproduction

Fertility—There were no effects on fertility, reproductive performance or reproductive organ morphology in male or female rats given oral doses of tadalafil up to 400 mg per kg per day, a dose producing AUCs for unbound tadalafil of 14-fold for males or 26-fold for females above the exposures observed in human males given the MRHD of 20 mg. In beagle dogs given tadalafil daily for 3 to 12 months, there was treatment-related non-reversible degeneration and atrophy of the seminiferous tubular epithelium in the testes in 20 to 100% of the dogs that resulted in decreased spermatogenesis in 40 to 75% of the dogs at doses of ≥ 10 mg per kg per day. Systemic exposure (based on AUC) at no-observed-adverse-effect-level (NOAEL) (10 mg per kg per day) for unbound tadalafil was similar to that expected in humans at the MRHD of 20 mg.

There were no treatment-related testicular findings in rats or mice treated with doses up to 400 mg per kg per day for 2 years.

In men, there were no clinically relevant effects on sperm concentration, motility, or morphology in placebo-controlled studies of daily doses of tadalafil 10 mg (N=204) or 20 mg (N=217) for 6 months. In addition, tadalafil had no effect on serum levels of testosterone, luteinizing hormone, or follicle stimulating hormone in males.

Pregnancy—Adequate and well-controlled studies in women have not been done. Tadalafil is not indicated for use in females.

Tadalafil and/or its metabolites cross the placenta, resulting in fetal exposure in rats.

There was no evidence of teratogenicity, fetotoxicity, or embryotoxicity in rat or mouse fetuses that received up to 1000 mg per kg per day during the major organ development. Plasma exposure at this dose is approximately 11-fold greater than the AUC values for unbound tadalafil in humans given he MRHD of 20 mg. In a rat prenatal and postnatal development study at doses of 60, 200, and 1000 mg per kg, there was a reduction in postnatal survival of pups. The no-observed-effect-level (NOEL) for maternal toxicity was 200 mg per kg per day and for developmental toxicity was 30 mg per kg per day, which gives approximately 16- and 10- fold exposure multiples, respectively, of the human AUC for the MRHD dose of 20 mg.

FDA Pregnancy Category B

Breast-feeding

It is not known whether tadalafil is distributed into human breast milk. However, tadalafil and/or its major metabolites were secreted into the milk of lactating rats at concentrations approximately 2.4-fold greater than found in the plasma. Following a single-oral dose of 10 mg per kg, approximately 0.1% of the total radioactive dose was distributed into the milk within 3 hours. Tadalafil is not indicated for use in females and the use of tadalafil in nursing mothers is not recommended.

Pediatrics

No information is available on the relationship of age to the effects of tadalafil in the pediatric population. Tadalafil is not indicated for use in pediatric patients.

Geriatrics

Approximately 25% of patients in the primary efficacy and safety studies of tadalafil were greater than 65 years of age. No overall differences were observed between older and younger patients. No dose adjustment is warranted based on age alone. However, greater sensitivity to medications in some older individuals should be considered.

Drug interactions and/or related problems

The following drug interactions and/or related problems have been selected on the basis of their potential clinical significance (possible mechanism in parentheses where appropriate)—not necessarily inclusive (» = major clinical significance):

Note: Combinations containing any of the following medications, depending on the amount present, may also interact with this medication.

» Potent CYP3A4 inhibitors, such as
» Protease inhibitors, including
» Ritonavir or
» Saquinavir or
» Ketoconazole

(tadalafil is a substrate of and predominantly metabolized by CYP3A4; studies have shown that drugs that are potent inhibitors of CYP3A4 can increase tadalafil exposure; the dose of tadalafil should be limited to 10 mg not more than once every 24 hours)

(ketoconazole [400 mg daily] increased tadalafil 20 mg single dose AUC by 312% and C_{max} by 22%; ketoconazole [200 mg daily] increased tadalafil 10 mg single dose AUC by 107% and C_{max} by 15%)

(ritonavir [200 mg twice daily] increased tadalafil 20 mg single dose exposure (AUC) by 124% with no change in C_{max}; although specific interactions have not been studied, other HIV protease inhibitors would likely increase tadalafil exposure.)

» Cytochrome P450 3A4 (CYP3A4) inhibitors, others, such as
» Erythromycin or
» Grapefruit juice or
» Itraconazole

(although specific interactions have not been studied these may likely increase tadalafil exposure)

» Erectile dysfunction treatments

(the safety and efficacy of combinations of tadalafil and other medications for the treatment of erectile dysfunctions have not been studied; use of combinations is not recommended)

» Nitrates

(administration of tadalafil to patients who are using any form of organic nitrates, either regularly and/or intermittently, is **contraindicated;** in clinical pharmacology studies tadalafil was shown to potentiate the hypotensive effects of nitrates; this is thought to result from the combined effects of nitrates and tadalafil on the nitric oxide/cGMP pathway)

(a significant interaction between tadalafil and nitroglycerin was observed to last up to 48 hours; at least 48 hours should elapse after the last dose of tadalafil before nitrate administration is considered)

CYP3A4 inducers, such as
Carbamazepine or
Phenytoin or
Phenobarbital or
Rifampin

(studies have shown that drugs that induce CYP3A4 can decrease tadalafil exposure)

(rifampin [600 mg daily] reduced tadalafil 10 mg single dose exposure [AUC] by 88% and C_{max} by 46%; although specific interactions have not been studied, other CYP3A4 inducers would likely decrease tadalafil exposure; no dose adjustment is warranted)

Antacids

(simultaneous administration of an antacid [magnesium hydroxide/aluminum hydroxide] and tadalafil reduced the apparent rate of absorption of tadalafil without altering the exposure [AUC] to tadalafil)

» Alcohol

(tadalafil did not affect alcohol plasma concentrations and alcohol did not affect tadalafil plasma concentrations)

(both alcohol and tadalafil act as mild vasodilators; when mild vasodilators are taken in combination, blood-pressure lowering effects of each individual compound may be increased; substantial consumption of alcohol [e.g., 5 units or greater] in combination with tadalafil can increase the potential for orthostatic signs and symptoms, including increase in heart rate, decrease in standing blood pressure, dizziness, and headache)

» Alpha-adrenergic blockers

(doxazosin [8 mg daily] and tadalafil [20 mg daily] administered to healthy subjects resulted in potentially clinically significant augmentation of the blood-pressure-lowering effect of doxazosin)

(tamsulosin 0.4 mg [a selective alpha-adrenergic blocker] showed no significant decreases in blood pressure of subjects receiving 10 or 20 mg of tadalafil)

(caution is advised with concomitant use due to the additive lowering effect on blood pressure which may lead to symptomatic hypotension [i.e., fainting]; consideration should be given to insuring patient is stable on one drug prior to instituting the other at lowest possible dose)

Antihypertensive agents, other, such as
Amlodipine or
Metoprolol or
Bendrofluazide or
Enalapril

(small reactions in blood pressure were observed when tadalafil was taken with these medications; systolic blood pressure was reduced by 3 to 6 mm Hg and diastolic blood pressure was reduced by 1 to 4 mm Hg)

Angiotensin II receptor blockers
(blood pressure was reduced by 8/4 mm Hg in systolic/diastolic blood pressure when tadalafil was taken with angiotensin II receptor blockers)

Laboratory value alterations

The following have been selected on the basis of their potential clinical significance (possible effect in parentheses where appropriate)—not necessarily inclusive (» = major clinical significance).

With physiology/laboratory test values

Abnormal liver function tests
(abnormal liver function tests were observed in less than 2% of patients in clinical trials)

Gamma glutamyl transpeptidase (GGTP)
(increased GGTP values were observed in less than 2% of patients in clinical trials)

Medical considerations/Contraindications

The medical considerations/contraindications included have been selected on the basis of their potential clinical significance (reasons given in parentheses where appropriate)—not necessarily inclusive (» = major clinical significance).

Except under special circumstances, this medication should not be used when the following medical problem exists:

» Angina occurring during sexual intercourse or
» Heart failure (New York Heart Association Class 2 or greater), within last 6 months, or
» Hereditary degenerative retinal disorders, including retinitis pigmentosa, or
» Hypotension (< 90/50 mm Hg) or
» Myocardial infarction, within 90 days, or
» Stroke, within last 6 months, or
» Uncontrolled arrhythmias or
» Uncontrolled hypertension (>170/100 mm Hg) or
» Unstable angina
(groups of patients with these conditions were not included in clinical safety and efficacy trials; use is not recommended in these groups until further information is available)

» Degenerative retinal disorders, known hereditary, including Retinitis pigmentosa
(patients with this condition not included in clinical trials; use in these patients is not recommended)

» Hepatic impairment, severe (Child-Pugh Class C)
(tadalafil should not be used in patients with severe hepatic impairment)

» Hypersensitivity to tadalafil or any component of the tablet

» Renal insufficiency, severe or end-stage
(dose should be adjusted; should be used with caution)

Risk-benefit should be considered when the following medical problems exist:

Age >50 years or
Coronary artery disease or
Diabetes or
Hyperlipidemia or
Hypertension or
Low cup to disc ratio ("crowded disc") or
Smoking
(NAION has been reported rarely postmarketing in temporal association with the use of PDE5 inhibitors with most of these patients having one of these underlying anatomic or vascular risk factors for development of NAION; it is not possible to determine whether these events are related directly to the use of PDE5 inhibitors, to the patient's underlying vascular risk factors or anatomical defects, to a combination of these factors or other factors)

» Cardiovascular status, current and underlying
(cardiovascular status of patients should be considered since there is a degree of risk associated with sexual activity; treatments for erectile dysfunction, including tadalafil, should not be used in men for whom sexual activity is inadvisable as a result of their underlying cardiac status)
(as with other PDE5 inhibitors, tadalafil has mild vasodilatory properties that may result in transient decreases in blood pressure; patients with underlying cardiovascular disease could be adversely affected by such vasodilatory effects; careful consideration should be given to patients with this condition)

Left ventricular outflow obstruction, such as
Aortic stenosis or
Idiopathic hypertrophic subaortic stenosis
(these conditions may cause patients to be sensitive to the action of vasodilators, including PDE5 inhibitors)

Leukemia or
Multiple myeloma or
Sickle cell anemia
(tadalafil should be used with caution in patients with these conditions that may predispose them to priapism)

Anatomical deformation of the penis, such as
Angulation or
Cavernosal fibrosis or
Peyronie's disease
(tadalafil should be used with caution in patients with these conditions that may predispose them to priapism or painful erections)

Hepatic impairment, mild to moderate
(dose should not exceed 10 mg; use with caution)

NAION in one eye, previous
(may increase risk of NAION recurring; these patients could be adversely affected by use of vasodilators such as PDE5 inhibitors)

Renal insufficiency, moderate or severe
(dose should be adjusted; use with caution)

Bleeding disorders or
Active peptic ulceration, significant
(use should be based upon careful risk-benefit assessment and should be used with caution; tadalafil has not been studied in patients with bleeding disorders or significant peptic ulceration)

Side/Adverse Effects

The following side/adverse effects have been selected on the basis of their potential clinical significance (possible signs and symptoms in parentheses where appropriate)—not necessarily inclusive:

There have been rare reports of prolonged erections (longer than 4 hours) and priapism (painful erections greater than 6 hours in duration) for this class of compounds, including tadalafil. Priapism, if not treated promptly, can result in irreversible damage to erectile tissue. Patients who have an erection lasting longer than 4 hours, whether painful or not, should be instructed to seek emergency medical attention.

Those indicating need for medical attention

Incidence less frequent (less than 2%)

Angina pectoris (arm, back or jaw pain; chest pain or discomfort; chest tightness or heaviness; fast or irregular heartbeat; shortness of breath; sweating; nausea); ***chest pain; dyspnea*** (shortness of breath; difficult or labored breathing; tightness in chest; wheezing); ***hypertension*** (blurred vision; dizziness; nervousness; headache; pounding in the ears; slow or fast heartbeat); ***hypotension*** (blurred vision; confusion; dizziness, faintness, or lightheadedness when getting up from a lying or sitting position suddenly; sweating; unusual tiredness or weakness); ***myocardial infarction*** (chest pain or discomfort; pain or discomfort in arms, jaw, back or neck; shortness of breath; nausea; sweating; vomiting); ***palpitations*** (irregular heartbeat); ***postural hypotension*** (chills; cold sweats; confusion; dizziness, faintness, or lightheadedness when getting up from lying or sitting position); ***syncope*** (fainting); ***tachycardia*** (fast, pounding, or irregular heartbeat or pulse)

Incidence rare

Priapism (painful or prolonged erection of the penis)

Incidence not determined—Observed during clinical practice; estimates of frequency can not be determined

Exfoliative dermatitis (cracks in the skin; loss of heat from the body; red, swollen skin; scaly skin); ***hypersensitivity reactions*** (abdominal or stomach pain; diarrhea; fever; joint or muscle pain; nausea; numbness or tingling of face, hands, or feet; redness and soreness of eyes; skin rash; shortness of breath; sores in mouth; swelling of feet or lower legs; vomiting); ***non-arteritic anterior ischemic optic neuropathy (NAION)*** (blindness; blurred vision; decreased vision); ***retinal vein occlusion*** (blurred vision; change in vision); ***Stevens-Johnson syndrome*** (blistering, peeling, loosening of skin; chills; cough; diarrhea; itching; joint or muscle pain; red irritated eyes; red skin lesions, often with a purple center; sore throat; sores, ulcers, or white spots in mouth or on lips; unusual tiredness or weakness); ***stroke*** (confusion; difficulty in speaking; slow speech; inability to speak; inability to move arms, legs, or facial muscles; double vision; headache); ***sudden cardiac death; urticaria*** (hives or welts; itching; redness of skin; skin rash); ***visual field defect*** (blurred vision; decrease or change in vision)

Those indicating need for medical attention only if they continue or are bothersome

Incidence more frequent

Back pain; dyspepsia (acid or sour stomach; belching; heartburn; indigestion; stomach discomfort, upset, or pain); ***headache***

Incidence less frequent

Arthralgia (muscle or joint pain); ***asthenia*** (lack or loss of strength); ***blurred vision; conjunctivitis*** (redness, pain, swelling of eye, eyelid, or inner lining of eyelid; burning; dry or itching eyes; discharge excessive; tearing); ***diarrhea; dizziness; dry mouth; dysphagia*** (difficulty swallowing); ***epistaxis*** (bloody nose); ***erection increased; esophagitis*** (difficulty in swallowing; pain or burning in throat; chest pain; heartburn; vomiting; sores, ulcers, or white spots on lips or tongue or inside the mouth); ***eye pain; face edema*** (swelling or puffiness of eye or face); ***fatigue*** (unusual tiredness or weakness); ***flushing*** (feeling of warmth redness of the face, neck, arms and occasionally, upper chest); ***gastritis*** (burning feeling in chest or stomach; tenderness in stomach area; stomach upset; indigestion); ***gastroesophageal reflux*** (heartburn; vomiting); ***hypesthesia*** (reduced sensitivity to touch); ***insomnia*** (sleeplessness; trouble sleeping; unable to sleep); ***lacrimation increased*** (watering of eyes); ***loose stools; myalgia*** (joint pain; swollen joints; muscle aching or cramping; muscle pains or stiffness; difficulty in moving); ***nasal congestion; nausea; neck pain; pain; pain in limbs; paresthesia*** (burning, crawling, itching, numbness, prickling, “pins and needles”, or tingling feelings); ***pharyngitis*** (body aches or pain; congestion; cough; dryness or soreness of throat; fever; hoarseness; runny nose; tender, swollen glands in neck; trouble in swallowing; voice changes); ***pruritis*** (itching skin); ***rash; somnolence*** (sleepiness or unusual drowsiness); ***spontaneous penile erection; sweating; swelling of eyelids; upper abdominal pain; vertigo*** (dizziness or lightheadedness; feeling of constant movement of self or surroundings; sensation of spinning); ***vomiting***

Incidence rare

Changes in color vision

Overdose

For more information on the management of overdose or unintentional ingestion, **contact a poison control center** (see *Poison Control Center Listing*).

Treatment of overdose

Single doses up to 500 mg have been given to healthy subjects, and multiple daily doses up to 100 mg have been given to patients. Adverse events were similar to those seen at lower doses. In cases of overdose, standard supportive measures should be adopted as required. Hemodialysis contributes negligibly to tadalafil elimination.

Supportive care—Patients in whom intentional overdose is confirmed or suspected should be referred for psychiatric consultation.

Patient Consultation

As an aid to patient consultation, refer to *Advice for the Patient, Tadalafil (Systemic)*.

In providing consultation, consider emphasizing the following selected information (» = major clinical significance):

Before using this medication

» Conditions affecting use, especially:
- Hypersensitivity to tadalafil or any component of the tablet
- Other medications, especially alcohol, alpha adrenergic blockers (other than 0.4 mg tamsulosin once daily), erectile dysfunction treatments, erythromycin, grapefruit juice, itraconazole, ketoconazole, nitrates, ritonavir
- Other medical problems, especially bleeding disorders, cardiovascular conditions, known hereditary degenerative retinal disorders (including retinitis pigmentosa), peptic ulceration, hepatic impairment, renal insufficiency

Proper use of this medication

» Proper dosing; importance of taking exactly as prescribed

Proper storage

Patients should read patient leaflet before starting therapy and each time the prescription is renewed or refilled

Precautions while using this medication

» Concurrent use of other impotence therapy agents is not recommended

Importance of seeking emergency medical attention if a prolonged erection, more than 4 hours, occurs

Tadalafil does not protect against sexually transmitted diseases; counsel patient on proper protection

Importance of physician knowing patient’s cardiac risk factors and preexisting cardiovascular disease states

Advising patient to seek medical attention if sudden loss of vision in one or both eyes occurs

Concurrent use of substantial amounts of alcohol can increase the potential for orthostatic signs and symptoms

Importance of patients understanding the effects of using tadalafil in combination with other medicines

Importance of seeking immediate medical attention if anginal chest pain occurs after taking tadalafil; importance of knowing that 48 hours should elapse after the last dose of tadalafil before nitroglycerin is administered

Side/adverse effects

Signs of potential side effects, especially angina pectoris, chest pain, dyspnea, hypertension, hypotension, myocardial infarction, palpitations, postural hypertension, priapism, syncope, tachycardia

Signs of potential side effects observed during clinical practice, especially exfoliative dermatitis, hypersensitivity reactions, non-arteritic anterior ischemic optic neuropathy (NAION), retinal vein occlusion, Stevens-Johnson syndrome, stroke, sudden cardiac death, urticaria, or visual field defect

General Dosing Information

For oral dosing forms:

Evaluation of erectile dysfunction should include an appropriate medical assessment to identify potential underlying causes, as well as treatment options.

Onset of action of tadalafil generally occurs within 30 minutes. Tadalafil was shown to improve erectile function compared to placebo up to 36 hours following dosing. Therefore, when advising patients on optimal use of tadalafil, timing should be taken into consideration.

Physicians should discuss with patients the contraindication of tadalafil with regular and/or intermittent use of organic nitrates. Patients should be counseled that concomitant use of tadalafil with nitrates could cause blood pressure to suddenly drop to an unsafe level, resulting in dizziness, syncope, or even heart attack or stroke.

Physicians should discuss with patients the contraindication of tadalafil use with alpha-adrenergic antagonists other than tamsulosin 0.4 mg taken once daily. Patients should be counseled that concomitant use of tadalafil with alpha blockers (other than tamsulosin 0.4 mg taken once daily) may cause symptomatic hypotension in some patients.

Diet/Nutrition

Tadalafil may be taken without regard to food.

Treatment of adverse effects

Patients who have an erection lasting longer than 4 hours, whether painful or not, should seek emergency medical attention. Priapism, if not treated promptly, can lead to irreversible damage to the erectile tissue.

Physicians should discuss with patients the appropriate action in the event that they experience anginal chest pain requiring nitroglycerin following intake of tadalafil. When nitrate administration is deemed medically necessary for a life-threatening situation in a patient who has taken tadalafil, at least 48 hours should have elapsed after the last dose of tadalafil before nitrate administration is considered. In such circumstances, nitrates should still only be administered under close medical supervision with appropriate hemodynamic monitoring. Therefore, patients who experience anginal chest pain after taking tadalafil should seek immediate medical attention.

Oral Dosage Forms

TADALAFIL TABLETS

Usual adult dose

Erectile dysfunction—

Oral, 10 mg taken prior to sexual activity, no more than once a day. If necessary, the dose may be increased up to 20 mg once a day or decreased to 5 mg once a day, based on individual efficacy and tolerability.

Renal Insufficiency

Creatinine Clearance (mL/min)	Tadalafil Dose
Mild (51 to 80 mL/min)	No dose adjustment needed
Moderate (31 to 50 mL/min)	Starting dose: 5 mg taken not more than once a day Maximum Dose: 10 mg taken not more than once in 48 hours
Severe (>30 mL/min), on hemodialysis	Maximum Dose: 5 mg

Hepatic Impairment

Hepatic Impairment (Child-Pugh)	Tadalafil Dose
Mild (Child-Pugh Class A)	Dose not to exceed 10 mg per day
Moderate (Child-Pugh Class B)	Dose not to exceed 10 mg per day
Severe (Child-Pugh Class C)	Use is not recommended

Concomitant Medications

Concomitant Medications	Tadalafil Dose
Ketoconazole, Ritonavir or other potent CYP3A4 inhibitors	Maximum dose is 10 mg, not to exceed once every 72 hours

Usual adult prescribing limits

The maximum recommended dosing frequency is once per day in most patients.

Usual geriatric dose

See *Usual adult dose*.

Usual geriatric prescribing limits

See *Usual adult prescribing limits*.

Strength(s) usually available

U.S.—

5 mg (Rx) [*Cialis* (croscarmellose sodium; hydroxypropyl cellulose; hypromellose; iron oxide; lactose monohydrate; magnesium stearate; microcrystalline cellulose; sodium laurel sulfate; talc; titanium dioxide; triacetin)].

10 mg (Rx) [*Cialis* (croscarmellose sodium; hydroxypropyl cellulose; hypromellose; iron oxide; lactose monohydrate; magnesium stearate; microcrystalline cellulose; sodium laurel sulfate; talc; titanium dioxide; triacetin)].

20 mg (Rx) [*Cialis* (croscarmellose sodium; hydroxypropyl cellulose; hypromellose; iron oxide; lactose monohydrate; magnesium stearate; microcrystalline cellulose; sodium laurel sulfate; talc; titanium dioxide; triacetin)].

Canada—

10 mg (Rx) [*Cialis* (croscarmellose sodium; hydroxypropylcellulose; hydroxypropylmethylcellulose; iron oxide; lactose monohydrate; magnesium stearate; microcrystalline cellulose; sodium laurel sulfate; talc; titanium dioxide; triacetin)].

20 mg (Rx) [*Cialis* (croscarmellose sodium; hydroxypropylcellulose; hydroxypropylmethylcellulose; iron oxide; lactose monohydrate; magnesium stearate; microcrystalline cellulose; sodium laurel sulfate; talc; titanium dioxide; triacetin)].

Packaging and storage

Store at 25°C (77 °F), excursions permitted to 15 to 30°C (59 to 86 °F)

Auxiliary labeling

- Keep out of the reach of children

Revised: 08/09/2005
Developed: 01/22/2004

TAMOXIFEN Systemic

VA CLASSIFICATION (Primary): AN500

Commonly used brand name(s): *Apo-Tamox; Gen-Tamoxifen; Nolvadex; Nolvadex-D; Novo-Tamoxifen; PMS-Tamoxifen; Tamofen; Tamone.*

Note: For a listing of dosage forms and brand names by country availability, see *Dosage Forms* section(s).

Category

Antineoplastic.

Indications

Note: Bracketed information in the *Indications* section refers to uses that are not included in U.S. product labeling.

Accepted

Carcinoma, breast (treatment)—Node-negative: Tamoxifen is indicated for adjuvant treatment of axillary node-negative breast cancer in women following total mastectomy or segmental mastectomy, axillary dissection, and breast irradiation. Data are insufficient to predict which women are most likely to benefit and to determine if tamoxifen provides any benefit in women with tumors of less than 1 cm.

Node-positive: Tamoxifen is indicated for adjuvant treatment of axillary node-positive breast cancer in postmenopausal women following total mastectomy or segmental mastectomy, axillary dissection, and breast irradiation. In some tamoxifen adjuvant studies, most of the benefit to date has been in the subgroup with four or more positive axillary nodes.

Note: The estrogen and progesterone receptor values may help to predict whether adjuvant tamoxifen therapy is likely to be beneficial in node-negative or node-positive breast cancer.

Advanced disease: Tamoxifen is indicated in the treatment of metastatic breast cancer in men and women.

The labeling states that tamoxifen is effective in premenopausal women as an alternative to oophorectomy or ovarian irradiation. Available evidence indicates that women whose tumors are estrogen receptor–positive are more likely to benefit from tamoxifen therapy.

Data from clinical trials support five years of adjuvant tamoxifen therapy for patients with breast cancer.Carcinoma, breast (prophylaxis)[1]

Tamoxifen is indicated to reduce the risk of developing breast cancer in women who have been determined to be at high risk for developing this cancer. A woman is considered to be at high risk if she is at least 35 years of age and has a 5-year predicted risk of developing breast cancer greater than or equal to 1.67% (based on the Gail Model Risk Assessment Tool).

Risk factors that predict a 5-year risk of ≥ 1.67%:

- *Age ≥ 35 years and any of the following combinations of factors:*
  —One first-degree relative with a history of breast cancer, two or more benign biopsies, and a history of a breast biopsy that has shown atypical hyperplasia; or
  —At least two first-degree relatives with a history of breast cancer, and a personal history of at least one benign breast biopsy; or
  —Lobular carcinoma in situ (LCIS)
- *Age ≥ 40 years and any of the following combinations of factors:*
  —One first-degree relative with a history of breast cancer, two or more benign biopsies, age at first live birth was ≥ 25 years of age, and age at menarche was ≤ 11 years of age; or
  —At least two first-degree relatives with a history of breast cancer and age at first live birth was ≤ 19 years of age; or
  —One first-degree relative with a history of breast cancer and a personal history of benign breast biopsy that has shown atypical hyperplasia
- *Age ≥ 45 years and any of the following combinations of factors:*
  —At least two first-degree relatives with a history of breast cancer and age at first live birth was ≤ 24 years of age; or
  —One first-degree relative with a history of breast cancer, a personal history of benign breast biopsy, age at first live birth was ≥ 20 years of age, and age at menarche was ≤ 11 years of age
- *Age ≥ 50 years and any of the following combinations of factors:*
  —At least two first-degree relatives with a history of breast cancer; or
  —History of one benign breast biopsy showing atypical hyperplasia, age at first live birth was ≥ 30 years of age, and age at menarche was ≤ 11 years of age; or
  —History of at least two breast biopsies with a history of atypical hyperplasia and age at first live birth was ≥ 30 years of age
- *Age ≥ 55 years and any of the following combinations of factors:*
  —One first-degree relative with a history of breast cancer, a personal history of benign breast biopsy, and age at menarche was ≤ 11 years of age; or
  —History of at least two breast biopsies with a history of atypical hyperplasia and age at first live birth was ≥ 20 years of age
- *Age ≥ 60 years:*
  —5 year predicted risk of breast cancer ≥ 1.67 %, as calculated by the Gail Model

Note: Women whose risk factors are not described in the above examples should have their absolute breast cancer risk estimated using the Gail Model. The Gail Model Risk Assessment Tool is available for health care professionals by calling 1-800-544-2007.

The effect of tamoxifen on breast cancer incidence in women with inherited mutations (BRCA1, BRCA2) has not been adequately studied.

The decision regarding therapy with tamoxifen for the reduction in breast cancer incidence should be based upon an individual assessment of benefits and risks of tamoxifen therapy. Tamoxifen treatment in the NSABP P-1 trial lowered the risk of developing breast cancer during the follow-up period of the trial, however it did not eliminate breast cancer risk.

Carcinoma, breast, ductal, in situ (prophylaxis)[1]—Tamoxifen is indicated to reduce the risk of invasive breast cancer in women with ductal carcinoma in situ (DCIS) who have undergone breast surgery and radiation treatment.

[Melanoma, malignant (treatment)][1]—Tamoxifen is indicated, in combination with other agents, in the treatment of malignant melanoma.

[Carcinoma, endometrial (treatment)][1]—Tamoxifen, in combination with other agents, is considered reasonable medical therapy at some point in the management of endometrial carcinoma (Evidence rating: IA).

[1]Not included in Canadian product labeling.

Pharmacology/Pharmacokinetics

Note: Pharmacokinetic studies have been done in women only.

Physicochemical characteristics

Molecular weight—563.62.
pKa—8.85.

Mechanism of action/Effect

Tamoxifen is a nonsteroidal agent with potent antiestrogenic properties. The antiestrogen effects may be related to tamoxifen's ability to compete with estrogen for binding sites in target tissues such as breast.

Tamoxifen competes with estradiol for estrogen receptor protein in cytosols derived from human breast adenocarcinomas.

Tamoxifen has been shown to inhibit the induction of rat mammary carcinoma induced by dimethylbenzanthracene (DMBA) and causes the regression of already established DMBA-induced tumors. Tamoxifen appears to exert its antitumor effects by binding the estrogen receptors in this rat model.

Other actions/effects

Tamoxifen may induce ovulation in anovulatory women, stimulating release of gonadotropin-releasing hormone from the hypothalamus, which in turn stimulates release of pituitary gonadotropins. In oligospermic males, tamoxifen increases serum concentrations of luteinizing hormone (LH), follicle-stimulating hormone (FSH), testosterone, and estrogen.

Biotransformation

Hepatic. Tamoxifen is extensively metabolized after oral administration. N-desmethyl tamoxifen is the major metabolite found in plasma. N-desmethyl tamoxifen activity is similar to tamoxifen. 4-Hydroxytamoxifen and a side chain primary alcohol derivative of tamoxifen have been identified as minor metabolites in plasma. Tamoxifen is a substrate of cytochrome P450 CYP3A, CYP2C9 and CYP2D6, and an inhibitor of P-glycoprotein.

Half-life

Distribution—7 to 14 hours; secondary peaks at 4 or more days may be due to enterohepatic circulation.

Elimination—Terminal: 5 to 7 days following a single oral dose of 20 milligrams of tamoxifen and approximately 14 days following chronic administration of 20 milligrams of tamoxifen per day given for three months

Onset of action

An objective response usually occurs within 4 to 10 weeks of therapy, but may take several months in patients with bone metastases.

Time to peak concentration

Approximately 5 hours following a single oral dose of 20 milligrams of tamoxifen.

Time to steady state concentration

Steady state—approximately 4 weeks for steady state concentrations of tamoxifen and approximately 8 weeks for steady state concentrations of N-desmethyl tamoxifen

Peak plasma concentration:

Tamoxifen

Single oral dose—approximately 40 nanograms per milliliter (range: 35 to 45 nanograms per milliliter)

Chronic administration—approximately of 120 nanograms per milliliter (range: 67 to 183 nanograms per milliliter)

N-desmethyl tamoxifen

Single oral dose—approximately 15 nanograms per milliliter (range: 10 to 20 nanograms per milliliter)

Chronic administration—approximately 336 nanograms per milliliter (range: 148 to 706 nanograms per milliliter)

Duration of action

Estrogen antagonism may persist for several weeks following a single dose.

Elimination

Primary route—Biliary/fecal, mostly as polar conjugates. Studies in women receiving 20 milligrams of ^{14}C tamoxifen have shown that approximately 65% of the administered dose was eliminated from the body over a 2 week period. Unchanged drug and unconjugated metabolites account for less than 30% of the fecal radioactivity.

Secondary route—Renal (only small amounts).

Precautions to Consider

Note: Unless otherwise noted, information in this section is based on reports on women treated with tamoxifen.

Carcinogenicity

An increased incidence of endometrial cancer has been associated with tamoxifen treatment in humans. A large randomized study in Sweden found a significantly increased incidence of uterine cancer in women who took tamoxifen as compared with those who received placebo. Estimated incidence rates per 1,000 women per year for endometrial adenocarcinoma was 2.2 for tamoxifen treated women compared with 0.71 for women receiving placebo and for uterine sarcoma was 0.17 for tamoxifen treated women compared with 0 for women receiving placebo. Similar increased incidence in endometrial adenocarcinoma and uterine sarcoma were observed among women receiving tamoxifen in five other NSABP clinical trials. Some uterine malignancies were fatal.

Liver cancer has been reported in a small number of tamoxifen-treated patients. Hepatic carcinogenicity of tamoxifen in rats is well established. Studies in rats at doses of 5, 20, and 35 mg per kg of body weight (mg/kg) per day for up to 2 years found an increased incidence of hepatocellular carcinoma at all doses; the incidence was highest at doses of 20 or 35 mg/kg per day. In a 13-month study of endocrine changes in immature and mature mice, granulosa cell ovarian tumors and interstitial cell testicular tumors were found in tamoxifen-treated mice but not in controls.

Mutagenicity

No genotoxic potential was found in a conventional battery of *in vivo* and *in vitro* tests with prokaryotic and eukaryotic test systems with drug-metabolizing systems present. However, increased levels of DNA adducts have been found in the livers of rats exposed to tamoxifen. Tamoxifen also has been found to increase levels of micronucleus formation *in vitro* in human lymphoblastoid cell line (MCL-5).

Pregnancy/Reproduction

Fertility—Tamoxifen may induce ovulation in women.

Tamoxifen affects reproductive function in rats at doses somewhat higher than the human dose.

Pregnancy—Tamoxifen may cause fetal harm when administered to a pregnant woman. Women should be advised not to become pregnant while taking tamoxifen or within 2 months of discontinuing tamoxifen.

Although adequate and well-controlled studies have not been done in humans, spontaneous abortions, birth defects, fetal deaths, and vaginal bleeding have been reported. Because of tamoxifen's estrogenic effect, the possibility of a diethylstilbestrol (DES)-like syndrome in females whose mothers took tamoxifen during pregnancy should be kept in mind. In rodent models of fetal reproductive tract development, at doses of 0.3 to 2.4 times the maximum recommended human dose (MRHD), tamoxifen caused changes in both sexes that are similar to those caused by estradiol, ethynylestradiol, and DES; some of these changes, especially vaginal adenosis, are similar to those found in young women who were exposed *in utero* to DES and who have a 1 in 1000 risk of developing clear-cell adenocarcinoma of the vagina or cervix. Duration of follow-up of the few women exposed to tamoxifen *in utero* to date has not been long enough to confirm or disprove this risk with its use in humans.

In general, use of a barrier or nonhormonal contraceptive is recommended during (and for about 2 months after) tamoxifen therapy in sexually active women.

At dose levels at or below the human dose, reversible nonteratogenic developmental skeletal changes occurred in rats, and a lower incidence of embryo implantation and higher incidence of fetal death or retarded *in utero* growth occurred in rats and rabbits, as well as impaired learning behavior in some rat pups.

For reducing the risk of breast cancer in high-risk women—

Tamoxifen should not be used to reduce the risk of breast cancer in women who are pregnant or who plan on becoming pregnant. For women of child-bearing age, it is recommended that tamoxifen therapy be initiated during menstruation or if there are menstrual irregularities, it is recommended that a negative beta-human chorionic gonadotropin (*B*-HCG) test be obtained immediately prior to initiation of treatment with tamoxifen.

FDA Pregnancy Category D

Breast-feeding

It is not known whether tamoxifen is distributed into breast milk. Although very little information is available regarding distribution of antineoplastic agents into breast milk, breast-feeding is not recommended during chemotherapy because of the risks to the infant (adverse effects, mutagenicity, carcinogenicity).

Geriatrics

Appropriate studies on the relationship of age to the effects of tamoxifen have not been performed in the geriatric population. However, this medication is commonly used in elderly patients and geriatrics-specific problems that would limit the usefulness of this medication in the elderly have not been reported and are not expected.

Drug interactions and/or related problems

The following drug interactions and/or related problems have been selected on the basis of their potential clinical significance (possible mechanism in parentheses where appropriate)—not necessarily inclusive (» = major clinical significance):

Note: Because tamoxifen and its metabolites are potent inhibitors of cytochrome P450 mixed function oxidases, there is a potential for interaction with medications that require mixed function oxidases for activation.

Combinations containing any of the following medications, depending on the amount present, may also interact with this medication.

Aminoglutethimide
(concomitant use may decrease plasma concentrations of tamoxifen and N-desmethyl tamoxifen)

» Anticoagulants, coumarin-derivative
(concomitant use may result in significant increase in anticoagulant effect; use is contraindicated in women for reducing the risk of breast cancer in high-risk women and women with ductal carcinoma in situ [DCIS])

Bromocriptine
(concomitant use may increase serum levels of tamoxifen and N-desmethyl tamoxifen)

» Cytotoxic agents
(concomitant use may result in increased risk of thromboembolic events)

Estrogens
(may interfere with tamoxifen's therapeutic effect)

Letrozole
(concomitant use may reduce plasma concentrations of letrozole)

Medroxyprogesterone
(concomitant use may result in decreased plasma concentrations of N-desmethyl tamoxifen)

Phenobarbital or
Rifampin
(concomitant use may decrease plasma concentrations of tamoxifen)

Laboratory value alterations

The following have been selected on the basis of their potential clinical significance (possible effect in parentheses where appropriate)—not necessarily inclusive (» = major clinical significance).

With physiology/laboratory test values

Calcium concentrations, serum
(may be increased infrequently, usually in patients with bone metastases; the effect appears to be transient; if effect is serious, discontinue tamoxifen)

Cholesterol and
Triglycerides
(increases in serum concentrations have been seen infrequently)

Hepatic enzymes
(serum values may be increased; rarely, more severe abnormalities, including fatty liver, cholestasis, and hepatitis, have occurred; fatalities have been reported)

Karyopyknotic index on vaginal smears
(variations have been seen infrequently in postmenopausal women treated with tamoxifen)

Papanicolaou (Pap) test
(various degrees of estrogen effect have been seen infrequently in postmenopausal women treated with tamoxifen)

Thyroxine (T_4)
(increases in serum concentrations have been reported in a few patients, possibly as a result of increases in thyroid-binding globulin; however, clinical hyperthyroidism has not been reported)

Medical considerations/Contraindications

The medical considerations/contraindications included have been selected on the basis of their potential clinical significance (reasons given in parentheses where appropriate)—not necessarily inclusive (» = major clinical significance).

Except under special circumstances, this medication should not be used when the following medical problem exists:

When used for reducing the risk of breast cancer in high-risk women or in women with DCIS

» Stroke, history of or
» Thromboembolic events, history of or
» Uterine malignancies, history of
(Stroke, thromboembolic events (including pulmonary emboli and deep venous thrombosis), and uterine malignancies have occurred in women treated with tamoxifen)

Risk-benefit should be considered when the following medical problems exist:

Cataracts or vision disturbances
(visual disturbances, including corneal changes, cataracts, color vision perception changes, retinal vein thrombosis, and retinopathy, have been reported in patients receiving tamoxifen)

Hyperlipidemia
(increased serum lipid concentrations have been reported infrequently)

» Hypersensitivity to tamoxifen

Leukopenia
(leukopenia has been reported occasionally in patients receiving tamoxifen)

Thrombocytopenia
(thrombocytopenia has been reported occasionally in patients receiving tamoxifen, although platelet counts recovered even with continued therapy; hemorrhagic events may rarely occur)

Patient monitoring

The following may be especially important in patient monitoring (other tests may be warranted in some patients, depending on condition; » = major clinical significance):

» Calcium concentrations, serum
(recommended at periodic intervals in patients with bone metastases during initial period of therapy)

Cholesterol concentrations, serum and
Triglyceride concentrations, serum
(may be recommended at periodic intervals in patients with preexisting hyperlipidemias)

Complete blood count
(may be appropriate at periodic intervals, although leukopenia and thrombocytopenia have not been definitely attributed to tamoxifen)

» Gynecologic examinations
(recommended at regular intervals in women taking tamoxifen to detect possible endometrial cancers)

Hepatic function tests
(recommended at periodic intervals during therapy)

Ophthalmologic examinations
(recommended prior to initiation of therapy and at periodic intervals during therapy)

Prothrombin time
(when coadministered with coumarin-type anticoagulants, careful monitoring of the patients prothrombin time is recommended)

When used for reducing the risk of breast cancer in high-risk women:

» Breast examinations and
» Mammograms
(recommended prior to initiation of therapy and at periodic intervals during therapy)

Side/Adverse Effects

Note: Side/adverse effects usually are relatively mild.

Although information is limited, the side effect profile in men seems to be similar to that in women.

A transient, sometimes severe, increase in bone or tumor pain may occur shortly after initiation of therapy but usually subsides with continued tamoxifen treatment. Analgesics may be required during this time.

Tamoxifen induces ovulation, which puts women at risk for becoming pregnant.

Ovarian cysts have been reported in a small number of premenopausal women treated with tamoxifen for advanced breast carcinoma.

An increased incidence of uterine malignancies has been reported in association with tamoxifen treatment. Most uterine malignancies seen are classified as adenocarcinoma of the endometrium. Rare uterine sarcomas, including malignant mixed mullerian tumors, have also been reported. Uterine sarcoma has been reported to occur more frequently among long-term users (≥2 years) of tamoxifen than nonusers. Some of the uterine malignancies (endometrial carcinoma or uterine sarcoma) have been fatal.

There is evidence of an increased incidence of thromboembolic events, including deep vein thrombosis, stroke, and pulmonary embolism during tamoxifen treatment. Coadministration of tamoxifen with chemotherapy may increase the risk for thromboembolic effects. Some thromboembolic events were fatal.

The following side/adverse effects have been selected on the basis of their potential clinical significance (possible signs and symptoms in parentheses where appropriate)—not necessarily inclusive:

Those indicating need for medical attention

Incidence less frequent or rare

In both females and males

Confusion; erythema multiforme, bullous pemphigoid, or Stevens-Johnson syndrome (blistering, peeling, or loosening of skin and mucous membranes); ***hepatotoxicity*** (yellow eyes or skin)—usually asymptomatic; ***ocular toxicity, including retinopathy, keratopathy, cataracts, and optic neuritis*** (blurred vision)—may be asymptomatic initially; ***pulmonary embolism*** (anxiety; chest pain; cough; fainting; fast heartbeat; sudden shortness of breath or troubled breathing; dizziness or lightheadedness); ***thrombosis*** (pain or swelling in legs); ***weakness or sleepiness***

Note: *Hepatotoxicity* usually consists of elevated hepatic enzyme values. However, more serious liver abnormalities, including fatty liver, cholestasis, and hepatitis, have occurred; fatalities have been reported.

Ocular toxicity previously was thought to occur only after high (240 to 320 mg per day), prolonged (17 months or more) tamoxifen dosage. However, there are reports of retinopathy or keratopathy occurring at lower doses (10 to 40 mg per day) and after only a few weeks of tamoxifen therapy, although they are still most commonly associated with several months' therapy. Ocular toxicity may or may not be reversible following withdrawal of tamoxifen. A number of reports included recommendations for baseline and periodic ocular examinations during tamoxifen therapy to detect subclinical toxicity and permit withdrawal of tamoxifen at early stages of toxicity.

In females only

Allergy (dizziness; fast heartbeat; shortness of breath; skin rash or itching over the entire body; sweating; weakness; wheezing); ***deep vein thrombosis*** (pain, redness, or swelling in arm or leg); ***endometrial hyperplasia, endometrial polyps, or endometrial carcinoma*** (change in vaginal discharge; pain or feeling of pressure in pelvis; vaginal bleeding); ***infection or sepsis*** (chills; confusion; cough or hoarseness; dizziness; fainting; fast heartbeat; fever; lightheadedness; lower back or side pain; painful or difficult urination; rapid shallow breathing)

Incidence not determined—Observed during clinical practice; estimates of frequency can not be determined

Angioedema (large, hive-like swelling on face, eyelids, lips, tongue, throat, hands, legs, feet, sex organs); ***bullous pemphigoid*** (large, hard skin blisters); ***erythema multiforme*** (blistering, peeling, loosening of skin; chills; cough; diarrhea; fever; itching; joint or muscle pain; red irritated eyes; sore throat; sores, ulcers, or white spots in mouth or on lips; unusual tiredness or weakness); ***interstitial pneumonitis*** (cough; difficult breathing; fever; shortness of breath); ***pancreatitis*** (bloating; chills; constipation; darkened urine; fast heartbeat; fever; indigestion; loss of appetite; nausea; pain in stomach, side, or abdomen, possibly radiating to the back; vomiting; yellow eyes or skin); ***Stevens-Johnson syndrome*** (blistering, peeling, loosening of skin; chills; cough; diarrhea; itching; joint or muscle pain; red irritated eyes; red skin lesions, often with a purple center; sore throat; sores, ulcers, or white spots in mouth or on lips; unusual tiredness or weakness)

Those indicating need for medical attention only if they continue or are bothersome

Incidence more frequent

In females only

Altered menses; menstrual disorder (menstrual changes); ***amenorrhea*** (absent, missed, or irregular menstrual periods; stopping of menstrual bleeding); ***bone pain; fluid retention*** (decrease in amount of urine; noisy, rattling breathing; shortness of breath; swelling of fingers, hands, feet, or lower legs; troubled breathing at rest; weight gain); ***hot flashes*** (feeling of warmth redness of the face, neck, arms and occasionally, upper chest; sudden sweating)—(≥ 10%); ***nausea; oligomenorrhea*** (absent, missed or irregular menstrual periods; stopping of menstrual bleeding); ***skin changes; vaginal bleed; vaginal discharge*** (white or brownish vaginal discharge); ***weight gain***—(≥ 10%); ***weight loss***—(≥ 5%)

Note: *Weight gain* is an effect of estrogen.

Incidence less frequent

In both females and males

Headache; nausea and/or vomiting, mild; skin rash or dryness; transient local disease flare (bone pain)

Note: Incidence of *nausea and/or vomiting* is higher with higher doses.

Transient local disease flare may also consist of hypercalcemia and/or spinal cord compression, as well as a sudden increase in the size of pre-existing lesions in patients with soft tissue disease, sometimes associated with marked erythema within and surrounding the lesions and/or the development of new lesions. Bone pain or other disease flare usually occurs shortly after initiation of therapy and subsides within 1 to 2 weeks.

In females only

Abdominal cramps; anorexia (loss of appetite; weight loss); ***changes in menstrual period; constipation; itching in genital area; cough; depression*** (discouragement; feeling sad or empty; irritability; lack of appetite; loss of interest or pleasure; tiredness; trouble concentrating; trouble sleeping); ***edema*** (swelling); ***fatigue*** (unusual tiredness or weakness); ***musculoskeletal pain*** (muscle or bone pain); ***pain; ovarian cyst*** (bloating; stomach or pelvic discomfort, aching, or heaviness); ***thrombocytopenia*** (black, tarry stools; bleeding gums; blood in urine or stools; pinpoint red spots on skin; unusual bleeding or bruising)

In males only

Impotence or decrease in sexual interest (loss in sexual ability, desire, drive, or performance; decreased interest in sexual intercourse; inability to have or keep an erection)

Incidence rare

In females only

Superficial phlebitis (bluish color changes in skin color; pain, tenderness, swelling of foot or leg)

Those not indicating need for medical attention

Incidence less frequent or rare

Hair thinning or partial hair loss

Overdose

For more information on the management of overdose or unintentional ingestion, **contact a Poison Control Center** (see *Poison Control Center Listing*).

Clinical effects of overdose

Acute tamoxifen overdose has not been reported. However, acute neurotoxicity, including tremors, hyperflexia, unsteady gait, and dizziness, has been reported following administration of very high doses of tamoxifen (> 400 mg per square meter of body surface area [mg/m^2], followed by maintenance doses of 150 mg/m^2 twice a day). Prolonged QT intervals have been reported in patients who were given doses of tamoxifen greater than 250 mg/m^2 (loading dose), followed by maintenance doses of 80 mg/m^2 twice a day.

Treatment of overdose

Neurotoxic symptoms begin 3 to 5 days after the initiation of high-dose tamoxifen therapy and resolve within 2 to 5 days after withdrawal of tamoxifen.

There is no specific treatment for overdose of tamoxifen. Patients should be treated symptomatically.

Patient Consultation

As an aid to patient consultation, refer to *Advice for the Patient, Tamoxifen (Systemic).*

In providing consultation, consider emphasizing the following selected information (» = major clinical significance):

Before using this medication

» Conditions affecting use, especially:

Hypersensitivity to tamoxifen

Carcinogenicity—An increased incidence of uterine malignancies has been reported. The benefits of tamoxifen outweigh the risks in women already diagnosed with breast cancer. In women considering tamoxifen to reduce their risk of developing breast cancer, your healthcare professional should discuss with you the potential benefits and potential risks of tamoxifen therapy.

Pregnancy—Use not recommended because of risk of miscarriage, death of the fetus, birth defects, and vaginal bleeding;

advisability of using nonhormonal contraception during (and for about 2 months following) therapy; telling physician immediately if pregnancy is suspected

FDA Pregnancy Category D

Breast-feeding—Not recommended because of risk of serious side effects

Other medications, especially courmarin-derivative anticoagulants and cytotoxic agents

Other medical problems, especially history of stroke, thromboembolic events or uterine malignancies

Proper use of this medication

» Importance of not taking more or less medication than the amount prescribed

» Swallow tablets whole with a drink of water. Can be taken with or without food.

» Frequency of nausea and vomiting; importance of continuing medication despite stomach upset

Checking with physician if vomiting occurs shortly after dose is taken

» Proper dosing

Missed dose: Not taking at all; not doubling doses

» Proper storage

Precautions while using this medication

» Importance of close monitoring by the physician

» Contact your healthcare professional if you notice any of the following:

- New breast lumps
- Vaginal bleeding
- Changes in your menstrual cycle
- Changes in your vaginal discharge
- Pelvic pain or pressure
- Swelling or tenderness in your calf
- Unexplained breathlessness (shortness of breath)
- Sudden chest pain
- Coughing up blood
- Changes in your vision

If you seek medical attention for any reason, make sure you tell your healthcare professional that you take tamoxifen or have previously take tamoxifen.

For women: May increase fertility; advisability of using nonhormonal contraception during therapy; telling physician immediately if pregnancy is suspected

Side/adverse effects

Signs of potential side effects, especially confusion, erythema multiforme, bullous pemphigoid, Stevens-Johnson syndrome, hepatotoxicity, retinopathy, keratopathy, cataracts, optic neuritis, pulmonary embolus, thrombosis, weakness or sleepiness

For women: Signs of additional potential side effects, especially deep vein thrombosis, endometrial hyperplasia, endometrial polyps, endometrial carcinoma, infection or sepsis

Mild hair loss may occur in some women.

General Dosing Information

Patients receiving tamoxifen should be under the supervision of a physician experienced in cancer chemotherapy.

If side effects are severe, dosage may sometimes be reduced without loss of control of the disease.

If severe hypercalcemia occurs, tamoxifen should be discontinued.

Ophthalmologic examination is recommended if visual disturbances occur, and withdrawal of tamoxifen should be considered if retinopathy or keratopathy is detected.

Current data from clinical trials supports 5 years of adjuvant tamoxifen therapy for patients with breast cancer. And, there is no data to support the use of tamoxifen other than for 5 years.

Bioequivalence information

In a crossover study, a 10-milligram tablet of Nolvadex® given twice daily was found to be bioequivalent to a 20-milligram tablet of Nolvadex® given once daily.

Oral Dosage Forms

Note: Bracketed uses in the *Dosage Forms* section refer to categories of use and/or indications that are not included in U.S. product labeling.

TAMOXIFEN CITRATE TABLETS USP

Note: The dosing and strengths available are expressed in terms of tamoxifen base.

Usual adult dose

Breast carcinoma—

Node-negative or node-positive: In women—Oral, 10 mg (base) two times a day (in the morning and evening).

Metastatic: In men and women—Oral, 20 to 40 mg (base) daily. Dosages greater than 20 mg (base) per day should be given in divided doses in the morning and evening.

Note: Data from clinical trials support 5 years of adjuvant tamoxifen therapy for patients with breast cancer.

Breast carcinoma (prophylaxis)[1]—

Oral, 20 mg (base) daily for five years.

[Melanoma, malignant][1] or

[Carcinoma, endometrial][1]—

Consult medical literature and manufacturer's literature for specific dosages.

Ductal carcinoma in situ (prophylaxis)[1]—

Oral, 20 mg (base) daily for 5 years.

Strength(s) usually available

U.S.—

10 mg (base) (Rx) [*Nolvadex* (carboxymethylcellulose calcium; magnesium stearate; mannitol; starch); GENERIC].

20 mg (base) (Rx) [*Nolvadex* (carboxymethylcellulose calcium; magnesium stearate; mannitol; starch); GENERIC].

Canada—

10 mg (base) (Rx) [*Apo-Tamox; Gen-Tamoxifen; Nolvadex; Novo-Tamoxifen; PMS-Tamoxifen; Tamofen; Tamone;* GENERIC].

20 mg (base) (Rx) [*Apo-Tamox; Gen-Tamoxifen; Nolvadex-D; Novo-Tamoxifen; PMS-Tamoxifen; Tamofen; Tamone;* GENERIC].

Packaging and storage

Store between 20 and 25 °C (68 and 77 °F), unless otherwise specified by manufacturer. Store in a well-closed, light-resistant container.

[1]Not included in Canadian product labeling.

Revised: 09/12/2003

TAMSULOSIN Systemic

VA CLASSIFICATION (Primary): GU700

Commonly used brand name(s): *Flomax*.

Note: For a listing of dosage forms and brand names by country availability, see *Dosage Forms* section(s).

Category

Benign prostatic hyperplasia therapy agent.

Indications

Accepted

Benign prostatic hyperplasia (treatment)—Tamsulosin is indicated in the treatment of symptomatic benign prostatic hyperplasia (BPH). It has been shown to improve urinary flow and the symptoms of BPH.

Unaccepted

Tamsulosin is not intended for use as an antihypertensive agent.

Pharmacology/Pharmacokinetics

Physicochemical characteristics

Molecular weight—444.98.

Mechanism of action/Effect

Tamsulosin is an alpha$_1$-adrenergic blocking agent exhibiting selectivity for alpha$_1$ receptors in the human prostate. Relaxation of smooth muscle in the bladder neck and prostate produced by alpha$_1$-adrenergic blockade results in improvement in urine flow rate and a reduction in symptoms of BPH.

Absorption

Absorption is $>$ 90% following oral administration of a 0.4-mg dose under fasting conditions. Bioavailability is increased by 30% and peak concentration is increased by 40 to 70% when tamsulosin is taken in the fasting state compared to the nonfasting state.

Distribution

Animal studies have found that tamsulosin is widely distributed to most tissues, including aorta, brown fat, gallbladder, heart, kidney, liver, and prostate; it is minimally distributed into the brain, spinal cord, and testes.

Protein binding
Very high (94 to 99%) to plasma proteins, primarily to alpha-1 glycoprotein; binding is linear over a wide concentration range (20 to 600 nanograms per mL).

Biotransformation
Tamsulosin is extensively metabolized by cytochrome P450 enzymes in the liver, with < 10% of the dose excreted in the urine unchanged. The metabolites undergo extensive conjugation to glucuronide or sulfate prior to renal excretion.

Half-life
Healthy individuals (fasting state)—9 to 13 hours.
Target population—14 to 15 hours.
Elimination—
5 to 7 hours in plasma following intravenous or oral administration of an immediate-release formulation of tamsulosin.

Time to peak concentration
4 to 5 hours under fasting conditions and 6 to 7 hours when administered with food.

Peak serum concentration
Peak plasma concentrations achieved with a 0.4-mg once-daily dose are 10.1 ± 4.8 nanograms per mL after a light breakfast and 17.1 ± 17.1 nanograms per mL in the fasting state; peak plasma concentrations after administration of a 0.8-mg dose are 29.8 ± 10.3 nanograms per mL after a light breakfast, 29.1 ± 11 nanograms per mL after a high-fat breakfast, and 41.6 ± 15.6 nanograms per mL in the fasting state.

Elimination
After administration of a radiolabeled dose of tamsulosin, 76% of the dose is recovered in the urine and 21% is recovered in the feces over 168 hours.
In dialysis—
Tamsulosin is unlikely to be removed because of its high protein binding (94 to 99%).

Precautions to Consider

Carcinogenicity
Male rats given doses of up to 43 mg per kg of body weight (mg/kg) a day and female rats given doses of 52 mg/kg a day had no increase in tumor incidence, with the exception of a modest increase in the frequency of mammary gland fibroadenomas in female rats receiving doses ≥ 5.4 mg/kg. There were no significant tumor findings in male mice receiving doses of up to 127 mg/kg a day. However, female mice treated for 2 years had statistically significant increases in the incidence of mammary gland fibroadenomas and adenocarcinomas with the highest doses given (45 and 158 mg/kg a day). The highest dose concentrations of tamsulosin evaluated in the rat and mice carcinogenicity studies produced systemic exposures (area under the plasma concentration-time curve [AUC]) in rats and mice eight times the exposures in men receiving 0.8 mg of tamsulosin a day. The increased incidences of mammary gland neoplasms in female rats and mice were considered secondary to tamsulosin-induced hyperprolactinemia. It is not known if tamsulosin elevates prolactin secretion in humans.

Mutagenicity
Tamsulosin was found nonmutagenic *in vitro* in the Ames reverse mutation test, the mouse lymphoma thymidine kinase assay, the unscheduled DNA repair synthesis assay, and the chromosomal aberration assays in Chinese hamster ovary cells or human lymphocytes. There were no mutagenic effects in the *in vivo* sister chromatid exchange and mouse micronucleus assay.

Pregnancy/Reproduction
Fertility—Studies in rats receiving tamsulosin in single or multiple daily doses of 300 mg/kg a day (AUC exposure in rats approximately 50 times the maximum human exposure using the maximum therapeutic dose) found a significant reduction in fertility in males. This reduction is thought to be due to an effect of the compound on the vaginal plug formation in female rats, possibly due to changes of semen content or impairment of ejaculation. These effects were reversible, showing improvement by 3 days after a single dose and by 4 weeks after multiple dosing; the effects were completely reversed 9 weeks after discontinuation of multiple dosing. Multiple doses of 10 and 100 mg/kg a day (1/5 and 16 times the anticipated human AUC exposure, respectively) produced no significant effects on fertility in male rats. Studies in female rats found a significant reduction in fertility after single or multiple dosing using 300 mg/kg a day of the R-isomer or a racemic mixture of tamsulosin, respectively. In female rats, the reductions in fertility after single doses of tamsulosin were considered to be associated with impairments in fertilization. Multiple dosing with 10 or 100 mg/kg a day of the racemic mixture of tamsulosin did not significantly alter fertility in female rats.

Pregnancy—Tamsulosin is not indicated for use in women.
Administration of tamsulosin to pregnant female rats at doses of up to 300 mg/kg a day (approximately 50 times the human therapeutic AUC exposure) and to pregnant rabbits at doses of up to 50 mg/kg a day produced no evidence of fetal harm.

FDA Pregnancy Category B.

Breast-feeding
Tamsulosin is not indicated for use in women.

Pediatrics
Tamsulosin is not indicated for use in children.

Geriatrics
Appropriate studies performed to date have not demonstrated geriatrics-specific problems that would limit the usefulness of tamsulosin in the elderly. However, greater sensitivity of some elderly patients cannot be ruled out. Studies indicate that the pharmacokinetic disposition of tamsulosin may be slightly prolonged in geriatric males resulting in a 40% overall higher exposure (AUC) in patients 55 to 75 years of age compared to those 20 to 32 years of age.

Drug interactions and/or related problems
The following drug interactions and/or related problems have been selected on the basis of their potential clinical significance (possible mechanism in parentheses where appropriate)—not necessarily inclusive (» = major clinical significance):

Note: Combinations containing any of the following medications, depending on the amount present, may also interact with this medication.

Tamsulosin is extensively metabolized by cytochrome P450 enzymes in the liver. Potential interactions with other cytochrome P450–metabolized compounds have not been determined.

» Alpha$_1$-adrenergic blocking agents, other, such as doxazosin, phentolamine, prazosin, and terazosin
(concurrent administration may produce an additive effect)

Cimetidine
(concurrent administration resulted in a 26% decrease in the clearance of tamsulosin and a 44% increase in tamsulosin AUC; tamsulosin should be used with caution in combination with cimetidine, particularly at daily doses higher than 0.4 mg)

» Warfarin
(caution should be exercised with concurrent administration because of inconclusive results from *in vitro* and *in vivo* studies)

Medical considerations/Contraindications
The medical considerations/contraindications included have been selected on the basis of their potential clinical significance (reasons given in parentheses where appropriate)—not necessarily inclusive (» = major clinical significance).

Except under special circumstances, this medication should not be used when the following medical problems exists:
» Hypersensitivity to tamsulosin or any component of the product

Risk-benefit should be considered when the following medical problem exists:
Cataract surgery
(Inoperative Floppy Iris Syndrome [IFIS] observed during cataract surgery in some patients treated with alpha-1 blockers; most patients taking alpha-1 blocker when IFIS occurred, but some had been stopped prior to surgery [2 to 14 days] a few had been stopped a longer period [5 weeks to 9 months]; ophthalmologists should be prepared for possible surgical technique modifications; benefit of stopping alpha-1 blocker therapy prior to cataract surgery not established)

Sulfa allergy
(allergic reaction to tamsulosin rarely reported in these patients; caution warranted when administering tamsulosin if patient reports serious or life threatening sulfa allergy)

Side/Adverse Effects

The following side/adverse effects have been selected on the basis of their potential clinical significance (possible signs and symptoms in parentheses where appropriate)—not necessarily inclusive:

Those indicating need for medical attention only if they continue or are bothersome
Incidence more frequent—(5 to 21%, except as indicated)
Abnormal ejaculation; asthenia (unusual weakness); ***back pain; diarrhea***—incidence 4.3% with 0.8-mg dose; ***dizziness; headache; rhinitis*** (stuffy or runny nose)

Note: Incidence of *abnormal ejaculation* is 8.4% with the 0.4-mg dose and 18% with the 0.8-mg dose.

Incidence less frequent—(< 5%)

Chest pain; decreased libido; drowsiness; insomnia (difficulty in sleeping); ***nausea; orthostatic hypotension*** (dizziness, fainting, or lightheadedness, especially when getting up from a lying or sitting position)

Incidence not determined—Observed during clinical practice; estimates of frequency cannot be determined

Priapism (painful or prolonged erection of the penis)

Overdose

For more information on the management of overdose or unintentional ingestion, **contact a Poison Control Center** (see *Poison Control Center Listing*).

Clinical effects of overdose

The following effects have been selected on the basis of their potential clinical significance (possible signs and symptoms in parentheses where appropriate)—not necessarily inclusive:

Treatment of overdose

Specific treatment—Intravenous fluids and vasopressors should be administered if needed.

Monitoring—Renal function should be monitored.

Supportive care—Cardiovascular system must be maintained; to restore blood pressure and normalize the heart rate, patient should be kept in the supine position. Patients in whom intentional overdose is confirmed or suspected should be referred for psychiatric consultation.

Patient Consultation

As an aid to patient consultation, refer to *Advice for the Patient, Tamsulosin (Systemic)*.

In providing consultation, consider emphasizing the following selected information (» = major clinical significance):

Before using this medication

» Conditions affecting use, especially:

Hypersensitivity to tamsulosin or any component

Use in the elderly—May have greater sensitivity; studies show 40% higher AUC in men 55 to 75 years of age compared with those 20 to 32 years of age

Other medications, especially alpha$_1$-adrenergic blocking agents or warfarin

Proper use of this medication

Taking at the same time each day to help increase compliance

Not crushing, chewing, or opening capsules, unless otherwise directed by a physician

» Proper dosing

Missed dose: Taking as soon as possible; not taking if almost time for next dose; not doubling doses

» Proper storage

Precautions while using this medication

Regular visits to physician to check progress

» Caution when getting up suddenly from a lying or sitting position

» Possible dizziness; caution when driving or doing things requiring alertness

» Calling doctor or seeking emergency treatment immediately if prolonged erection occurs

Side/adverse effects

Signs of potential side effects, especially abnormal ejaculation, decreased libido, or orthostatic hypotension

Signs of potential side effects observed during clinical practice, especially priapism

General Dosing Information

Diet/Nutrition

Tamsulosin should be taken once a day one-half hour after the same meal each day.

Oral Dosage Forms

TAMSULOSIN HYDROCHLORIDE CAPSULES

Usual adult dose

Benign prostatic hyperplasia—

Oral, 0.4 mg once a day, approximately one-half hour after the same meal each day. If there is no response after two to four weeks, the dose may be increased to 0.8 mg once a day.

Note: If tamsulosin administration is discontinued or interrupted for several days at either dose, therapy should be restarted with the 0.4-mg dose.

Usual geriatric dose

See *Usual adult dose*.

Strength(s) usually available

U.S.—

0.4 mg (Rx) [*Flomax*].

Packaging and storage

Store at 20 to 25 °C (68 to 77 °F).

Auxiliary labeling

- Do not crush, chew, or open capsules.

Revised: 05/02/2006
Developed: 03/02/1998

TEGASEROD Systemic

VA CLASSIFICATION (Primary): GA900

Commonly used brand name(s): *Zelnorm*.

Note: For a listing of dosage forms and brand names by country availability, see *Dosage Forms* section(s).

Category

Serotonin agonist.

Indications

Accepted

Bowel syndrome, irritable (treatment)—Tegaserod is indicated for the short-term treatment of women with irritable bowel syndrome (IBS) whose primary bowel symptom is constipation.

Constipation, idiopathic, chronic (treatment)—Tegaserod is indicated for the treatment of women less than 65 years of age with chronic idiopathic constipation.

Pharmacology/Pharmacokinetics

Physicochemical characteristics

Molecular weight—Tegaserod maleate—417.47.

Solubility—Tegaserod maleate—Slightly soluble in ethanol and very slightly soluble in water.

Mechanism of action/Effect

Tegaserod is a serotonin type-4 (5-HT4) receptor partial agonist. Tegaserod binds with high affinity at human 5-HT4 receptors present on caudate membranes; whereas it has no appreciable affinity for 5-HT3 receptors or dopamine D2 receptors. It has moderate affinity for 5-HT1 receptors. Tegaserod, by acting as an agonist at neuronal 5-HT4 receptors, triggers the release of further neurotransmitters such as calcitonin gene-related peptide from sensory neurons. The activation of 5-HT4 receptors in the gastrointestinal tract stimulates the peristaltic reflex and intestinal secretion, as well as inhibits visceral sensitivity. *In vivo* studies have demonstrated that tegaserod enhanced basal motor activity and normalized impaired motility throughout the gastrointestinal tract.

Absorption

Rapidly absorbed after oral administration. Absolute bioavailability is approximately 10% when administered to fasting subjects; bioavailability reduced 40% to 65% when administered with food.

Distribution

Volume of distribution (Vol_D)—Steady state: 368 ± 223 liters; pronounced distribution into tissues following intravenous dosing.

Protein binding

Very high—98% bound to plasma proteins, predominately alpha-1-acid glycoprotein.

Biotransformation

Tegaserod is metabolized mainly via two pathways. The first is a presystemic acid catalyzed hydrolysis in the stomach followed by oxidation and conjugation which produces the main metabolite of tegaserod, 5-methoxyindole-3-carboxylic acid glucuronide. The main metabolite has negligible affinity for 5-HT4 receptors *in vitro*. Systemic exposure to tegaserod was not altered at neutral gastric pH values. The second metabolic pathway of tegaserod is direct glucuronidation which leads to generation of three isomeric N-glucuronides.

Half-life

Terminal—approximately 11 ± 5 hours following intravenous dosing.

Time to peak concentration

Approximately 1 hour; prolonged 1 to 2 hours when administered after a meal; decreased to 0.7 hours when taken 30 minutes prior to a meal.

AUC

Renal impairment—The area under the curve (AUC) of the main pharmacologically inactive metabolite of tegaserod, 5-methoxy-indole-3-carboxylic acid glucuronide, increased 10-fold in patients with severe renal impairment.

Hepatic impairment—Mean AUC was 31 to 43% higher in patients with mild to moderate hepatic impairment compared to patients with normal hepatic function.

Peak plasma concentration:

Approximately 20% to 40% reduction in maximum plasma concentration (C_{max}) when administered with food; similar reduction occurs when administered to patients within 30 minutes prior to a meal or 2.5 hours after a meal.

Renal Impairment—Peak plasma concentration (C_{max}) of the main pharmacologically inactive metabolite of tegaserod, 5-methoxy-indole-3-carboxylic acid glucuronide, increased 2-fold in patients with severe renal impairment.

Hepatic Impairment—C_{max} was 16 to 18% higher in patients with mild to moderate hepatic impairment compared to patients with normal hepatic function.

Elimination

Fecal—approximately 67% of the orally administered dose is eliminated unchanged.

Renal—approximately 33% of orally administered dose eliminated primarily as the main metabolite.

Plasma clearance of tegaserod is approximately 77 ± 15 liters per hour.

In hemodialysis—No change in the pharmacokinetics of tegaserod was observed in subjects with severe renal impairment requiring hemodialysis (creatinine clearance ≤ 15 mL per minute per 1.73 square meters of body surface area.

Precautions to Consider

Carcinogenicity

Tegaserod was not carcinogenic in rats given up to 180 mg per kg per day (93 to 111 times the maximum recommended human dose [MRHD]). Mucosal hyperplasia and adenocarcinoma of the small intestine were seen when mice were given 600 mg per kg per day (83 to 110 times the MRHD). However, no evidence of carcinogenicity was found when mice were given 200 mg per kg per day (24 to 35 times the MRHD).

Mutagenicity

Tegaserod was not genotoxic in the *in vitro* Chinese hamster lung fibroblast cell chromosomal aberration test, the *in vitro* Chinese hamster lung fibroblast cell forward mutation test, the *in vitro* rat hepatocyte unscheduled DNA synthesis test or the *in vivo* mouse micronucleus test. The results of Ames test for mutagenicity were ambiguous.

Pregnancy/Reproduction

Fertility—No effect on fertility or reproductive performance was seen when either male or female rats were given tegaserod (57 and 42 times the MRHD, respectively).

Pregnancy—Adequate and well controlled studies in humans have not been done.

Studies in rats and rabbits have not shown that tegaserod causes adverse effects in the fetus. Because animal reproduction studies are not always predictive of human response, this drug should be used during pregnancy only if clearly needed.

FDA Pregnancy Category B

Breast-feeding

It is not known whether tegaserod is distributed into human breast milk. However, tegaserod and its metabolites are distributed in the milk of lactating rats with a high milk to plasma ratio. A decision should be made whether to discontinue the drug or discontinue nursing, taking into account the importance of the drug to the mother.

Pediatrics

Safety and efficacy have not been established in pediatric patients below the age of 18.

Geriatrics

IBS with constipation—Appropriate studies performed to date have not demonstrated geriatrics-specific problems that would limit the usefulness of tegaserod in the elderly.

Chronic idiopathic constipation—Efficacy in patients 65 years of age or greater showed no significant difference between drug and placebo responses. Patients 65 years of age or greater who received tegaserod experienced a higher incidence of diarrhea and discontinuation due to diarrhea than patients younger than 65 years of age. Tegaserod is not indicated for patients with chronic idiopathic constipation who are 65 years of age or older.

Pharmacogenetics

The safety and effectiveness of tegaserod in men has not been established.

Drug interactions and/or related problems

The following drug interactions and/or related problems have been selected on the basis of their potential clinical significance (possible mechanism in parentheses where appropriate)—not necessarily inclusive (» = major clinical significance):

In vitro data with tegaserod indicated no inhibition of the cytochrome P450 isoenzymes CYP2C8, CYP2C9, CYP2C19, CYP2E1, and CYP3A4. Inhibition of CYP1A2 and CYP2D6 could not be excluded. No clinically relevant drug-drug interactions have been observed with dextromethorphan, digoxin, oral contraceptives, theophylline, and warfarin.

Laboratory value alterations

The following have been selected on the basis of their potential clinical significance (possible effect in parentheses where appropriate)—not necessarily inclusive (» = major clinical significance).

With physiology/laboratory test values

Alanine aminotransferase (ALT [SGPT]) or
Aspartase aminotransferase (AST [SGOT])
(values may be increased)

Bilirubin, serum
(concentrations may be increased)

Medical considerations/Contraindications

The medical considerations/contraindications included have been selected on the basis of their potential clinical significance (reasons given in parentheses where appropriate)—not necessarily inclusive (» = major clinical significance).

Except under special circumstances, this medication should not be used when the following medical problem exists:

» Abdominal pain, new or sudden worsening of
(discontinue therapy immediately)

» Adhesions, abdominal or
» Bowel obstruction, history of or
» Gallbladder disease, symptomatic or
» Hepatic impairment, moderate or severe or
» Hypersensitivity to tegaserod or any of its excipients or
» Renal impairment, severe or
» Sphincter of Oddi dysfunction, suspected
(use is contraindicated)

» Diarrhea
(serious consequences of diarrhea, including hypovolemia, hypotension, and syncope have been reported with use of tegaserod; in some cases; hospitalization was required for rehydration; tegaserod use should be discontinued immediately in patients who develop hypotension or syncope; use should not be initiated in patients currently experiencing or frequently experiencing diarrhea)

Patient monitoring

The following may be especially important in patient monitoring (other tests may be warranted in some patients, depending on condition; » = major clinical significance):

» Ischemic colitis
(monitor for symptoms of ischemic colitis, such as rectal bleeding, bloody diarrhea or new or worsening abdominal pain; tegaserod should be discontinued immediately in patients developing these symptoms and patient should be evaluated promptly with appropriate diagnostic testing performed; treatment should not be resumed in patients who develop findings consistent with ischemic colitis)

Side/Adverse Effects

The following side/adverse effects have been selected on the basis of their potential clinical significance (possible signs and symptoms in parentheses where appropriate)—not necessarily inclusive:

Patients who experience severe diarrhea or new or worsening abdominal pain (not typical of their IBS symptoms) during therapy with tegaserod should contact their healthcare professional.

An increase in abdominal surgeries was observed in tegaserod-treated patients (0.3%) when compared to placebo-treated patients (0.2%).

There was a numerical imbalance in cholecystectomies in the tegaserod-treated group. A causal relationship between abdominal surgeries and tegaserod has not been established.

Those indicating need for medical attention

Incidence more frequent

Abdominal pain (stomach pain); ***diarrhea***

Incidence less frequent

Dizziness; facial edema (swelling or puffiness of face); ***flushing*** (feeling of warmth; redness of the face, neck, arms and occasionally, upper chest); ***pruritus*** (itching skin)

Incidence not determined—Observed during clinical practice; estimates of frequency cannot be determined

Bile duct stone (severe stomach pain with nausea and vomiting); ***cholecystitis*** (indigestion; stomach pain; severe nausea; vomiting)—with elevated transaminases; ***gangrenous bowel*** (bloody diarrhea; new or worsening abdominal pain; rectal bleeding); ***ischemic colitis*** (abdominal pain and tenderness; bloody stools; rectal bleeding); ***mesenteric ischemia*** (abdominal pain, usually after eating a meal; constipation; diarrhea; nausea; vomiting); ***rectal bleeding*** (black, tarry stools; blood in stools); ***sphincter of Oddi spasm*** (severe stomach pain with nausea and vomiting); ***syncope*** (fainting)

Those indicating need for medical attention only if they continue or are bothersome

Incidence more frequent

Flatulence (bloated, full feeling; excess air or gas in stomach or intestines; passing gas); ***headache; nausea***

Incidence less frequent or rare

Arthropathy (disease or abnormality of the joint); ***back pain; leg pain; migraine*** (headache, severe and throbbing)

Overdose

For more information on the management of overdose or unintentional ingestion, **contact a poison control center** (see *Poison Control Center Listing*).

Clinical effects of overdose

The following effects have been selected on the basis of their potential clinical significance not necessarily inclusive.

Abdominal pain (stomach pain); ***diarrhea; flatulence*** (bloated full feeling; excess air or gas in stomach or intestines; passing gas); ***headache; hypotension, orthostatic*** (chills; cold sweats; confusion; dizziness, faintness, or lightheadedness when getting up from lying or sitting position); ***nausea; vomiting***

Note: These symptoms were reported following single oral doses of 120 mg tegaserod or 90 to 180 mg tegaserod per day for several days.

Treatment of overdose

To enhance elimination—

It is unlikely that tegaserod could be removed by dialysis due to high protein binding and large distribution volume of tegaserod.

Specific treatment—

There is no known specific antidote to tegaserod.

Treatment should be symptomatic and supportive.

Supportive care—

Patients in whom intentional overdose is confirmed or suspected should be referred for psychiatric consultation.

Patient Consultation

As an aid to patient consultation, refer to *Advice for the Patient, Tegaserod (Systemic)*.

In providing consultation, consider emphasizing the following selected information (» = major clinical significance):

Before using this medication

» Conditions affecting use, especially:

Hypersensitivity to tegaserod or any of its excipients

Pregnancy—Because animal reproduction studies are not always predictive of human response, this drug should be used during pregnancy only if clearly needed.

FDA Pregnancy Category B

Breast-feeding—Decision should be made whether to discontinue nursing or discontinue tegaserod, taking into account the importance of the drug to the mother

Use in children—Safety and efficacy have not been established in pediatric patients below the age of 18.

Use in the elderly—No geriatric-specific differences in safety were found in patients being treated for IBS with constipation.

Tegaserod is not indicated for patients with chronic idiopathic constipation who are 65 years of age or older.

Pharmacogenetics—The safety and effectiveness of tegaserod in men have not been established.

Other medical problems, especially abdominal adhesions, new or sudden worsening abdominal pain, history of bowel obstructions, diarrhea, symptomatic gallbladder disease, severe or moderate hepatic impairment, severe renal impairment, or suspected Sphincter of Oddi dysfunction

Proper use of this medication

» Proper dosing especially taking on empty stomach before eating a meal.

Missed dose: If you miss a dose of this medicine, skip the missed dose and go back to your regular dosing schedule. Do not double doses.

» Proper storage

Precautions while using this medication

Checking with your physician or pharmacist if you are taking or plan to take any prescription or over-the-counter medicines while taking tegaserod

» Tell your doctor immediately if you become pregnant or are planning to become pregnant.

» Patients should consult their doctor if they experience severe diarrhea, or if the diarrhea is accompanied by severe cramping, abdominal pain, or dizziness. Patients should also consult their physician if they experience new or worsening abdominal pain.

» Do not take this medication if you have diarrhea now or have diarrhea often.

May cause dizziness.

Side/adverse effects

Signs of potential side effects, especially abdominal pain, diarrhea, dizziness, facial edema, flushing, or pruritus

Signs of potential side effects observed during clinical practice, especially bile duct stone, cholecystitis, gangrenous bowel, ischemic colitis, mesenteric ischemia, rectal bleeding, sphincter of Oddi spasm, or syncope

General Dosing Information

The efficacy of tegaserod beyond 12 weeks has not been studied.

Diet/Nutrition

Medication should be taken on an empty stomach shortly before eating a meal.

Take with a glass of water.

Bioequivalence information

Each 1.385 mg of tegaserod as the maleate is equivalent to 1 mg tegaserod.

Oral Dosage Forms

TEGASEROD MALEATE TABLETS

Note: The safety and effectiveness of tegaserod in men have not been established.

Usual adult dose

Chronic idiopathic constipation (treatment)—

Oral, 6 mg twice daily before meals. Physicians and patients should periodically assess the need for continued therapy.

Irritable bowel syndrome (treatment)—

Oral, 6 mg (base) twice daily before meals for 4 to 6 weeks

For those patients who respond to therapy in 4 to 6 weeks, an additional 4 to 6 week course can be considered.

Usual adult prescribing limits

Note: The efficacy of tegaserod for treatment of IBS with constipation or chronic idiopathic constipation has not been studied beyond 12 weeks.

Canadian manufacturer states that maximum duration of treatment is 12 weeks for treatment of irritable bowel syndrome and treatment should be discontinued if there has been no response after 4 weeks.

Usual pediatric dose

Safety and efficacy have not been established in pediatric patients below the age of 18.

Usual geriatric dose

Chronic idiopathic constipation (treatment)—

The effectiveness of tegaserod in patients 65 years of age or older with chronic idiopathic constipation has not been established.

Irritable bowel syndrome (treatment)—

See *Usual adult dose*.

Usual geriatric prescribing limits

Irritable bowel syndrome (treatment)—

See *Usual adult prescribing limits.*

Strength(s) usually available

U.S.—

2 mg (base) (Rx) [*Zelnorm* (crospovidone; glyceryl monostearate; hydroxypropyl methylcellulose; lactose monohydrate; poloxamer 188; polyethylene glycol 4000)].

6 mg (base) (Rx) [*Zelnorm* (crospovidone; glyceryl monostearate; hydroxypropyl methylcellulose; lactose monohydrate; poloxamer 188; polyethylene glycol 4000)].

Canada—

6 mg (base) (Rx) [*Zelnorm* (crospovidone; glyceryl monostearate; hydroxypropyl methylcellulose; lactose monohydrate; poloxamer 188; polyethylene glycol 4000)].

Packaging and storage

Store at 25 °C (77 °F), excursions permitted to 15 to 30 °C (59 and 86 °F). Protect from moisture.

Auxiliary labeling

- Take 30 minutes before a meal
- May cause dizziness
- Ask your doctor or pharmacist before taking any prescription or nonprescription medications
- Do not give this medication to other people, even if they have the same symptoms that you have.

Revised: 09/24/2004
Developed: 06/05/2003

TELITHROMYCIN Systemic

USA:

VA CLASSIFICATION (Primary): AM900

Commonly used brand name(s): *Ketek*.

Note: For a listing of dosage forms and brand names by country availability, see *Dosage Forms* section(s).

Category

Antibacterial (systemic).

Indications

Note: Bracketed information in the *Indications* section refers to uses that are not included in U.S. product labeling.

General Considerations

To reduce the development of drug resistant bacteria and maintain antibacterial effectiveness telithromycin should be used only to treat infections that are proven or are strongly suspected to be caused by susceptible bacteria.

Accepted

Bronchitis, chronic (treatment)—Telithromycin is indicated in the treatment of acute bacterial exacerbation of chronic bronchitis due to *Streptococcus pneumoniae*, *Haemophilus influenzae*, or *Moraxella catarrhalis*.

[Pharyngitis (treatment)] or
[Tonsillitis (treatment)]—Telithromycin is indicated for the treatment of group A-β Hemolytic Streptococcus as an alternative when β-lactam antibiotics are not appropriate.

Pneumonia, community-acquired (treatment)—Telithromycin is indicated in the treatment of community-acquired pneumonia due to *Streptococcus pneumoniae* (including multi-drug resistant isolates [MDRSP]), *Haemophilus influenzae*, *Chlamydophila pneumoniae*, *Mycoplasma pneumoniae*, or *Moraxella catarrhalis*[1].

Sinusitis, acute bacterial (treatment)[1]—Telithromycin is indicated in the treatment of acute bacterial sinusitis due to *Streptococcus pneumoniae*, *Haemophilus influenzae*, *Moraxella catarrhalis*, or *Staphylococcus aureus*

[1]Not included in Canadian product labeling.

Pharmacology/Pharmacokinetics

Physicochemical characteristics

Source—Telithromycin is a semisynthetic antibacterial..

Chemical Group—Telithromycin belonging to the group ketolide differs chemically from the macrolide group by lack of α-L-cladinose at position 3 of the erythronolide A ring, resulting in a 3-keto function.

Molecular weight—Telithromycin: 812.03.

pKa—Pyridinium ring: 2.4; imidazole ring: 5.1; dimethylamine function: 8.7.

Solubility—Freely soluble in dichloromethane, ethanol, methanol, acetonitrile and acetone; very slightly soluble in water.

Partition coefficient—c = 3.05 mg/0.1 mL of octanol at 25°C.

Mechanism of action/Effect

Antibacterial—Telithromycin inhibits bacterial protein synthesis by blocking translation of the bacterial 23S ribosomal RNA and also by inhibiting the assembly of new bacterial ribosomes. Telithromycin blocks protein synthesis by binding to two sites on the 50S ribosomal subunit: domain II and V of the 23S rRNA. The greater affinity in binding strength can be attributed to the C11–C12 carbamate side chain.

Absorption

Rapidly absorbed, absolute bioavailability is 57% in both young and elderly patients. The rate and extent of absorption are unaffected by food.

The AUC following an single dose is 8.25 mcg h/mL and 12.5 mcg h/mL following multiple dosing.

Distribution

Volume of distribution (Vol_D)—2.9 L/kg following an intervenous infusion.

Widely distributed throughout the body.

Telithromycin is distributed into breast milk of rats.

Protein binding

Moderate-High (60 to 70%)

Protein binding is not modified in elderly patients or patients with hepatic impairment.

Biotransformation

Hepatic; 37% of the dose is metabolized by the liver

Metabolism accounts for approximately 70% of the dose. The main metabolite represented 12.6% of the AUC while three other metabolites quantified represented 3% or less of the AUC of telithromycin.

Half-life

Elimination—10 hours following oral dosing.

Time to peak concentration

About 1 hour.

Time to steady state concentration:

2 to 3 days for 800 mg once daily.

Peak plasma concentration

1.9 mcg/mL following a single 800 mg dose.

2.27 mcg/mL following multiple doses (7 days), 800 mg dose once daily.

Time to peak effect

About 1 hour.

Elimination

Biliary/fecal—7% unchanged.

Renal—13% unchanged.

Precautions to Consider

Carcinogenicity

Long term studies in animals have not been performed with telithromycin to determine potential carcinogenicity.

Mutagenicity

Telithromycin showed no evidence of genotoxicity in gene mutation in bacterial cells, gene mutation in mammalian cells, chromosome aberration in human lymphocytes, and the micronucleus test in mice.

Pregnancy/Reproduction

Fertility—Moderate reductions in fertility were observed in male and female animals treated with telithromycin at doses 1.8–3.6 times the human daily dose. No evidence of impaired fertility was observed in rats at doses approximately 0.61 times the daily human dose.

Pregnancy—Adequate and well controlled studies in humans have not been done. Since there are no adequate and well controlled studies in pregnant women telithromycin should be used during pregnancy only if the potential benefit justifies the potential risk to the fetus.

Studies in rats and rabbits given doses higher than 900 mg/m^2 and 240 mg/m^2 have shown that telithromycin may delay fetal maturation. Reproduction studies in rats and rabbits with effect on pre-post natal development found no evidence of adverse effects to the fetus at doses approximately 1.8 and 0.49 times the daily human dose.

FDA Pregnancy Category C

Breast-feeding
Telithromycin is distributed into the breast milk of rats. Telithromycin may also be distributed in human milk. Because many drugs are distributed in human milk, caution should be exercised when telithromycin is administered to a nursing mother.

Pediatrics
No information is available on the relationship of age to the effects of telithromycin in pediatric patients below 18 years of age. Safety and efficacy have not been established.

Geriatrics
Appropriate studies performed to date have not demonstrated geriatrics-specific problems that would limit the usefulness of telithromycin in the elderly. However, greater sensitivity of some older individuals cannot be ruled out. No dosage adjustment is required based on age alone.

Pharmacogenetics
Studies done to compare the difference between males and females showed no significant differences.

Drug interactions and/or related problems
The following drug interactions and/or related problems have been selected on the basis of their potential clinical significance (possible mechanism in parentheses where appropriate)—not necessarily inclusive (» = major clinical significance):

Note: Combinations containing any of the following medications, depending on the amount present, may also interact with this medication.

» Amiodarone or
» Dofetilide or
» Procainamide or
» Quinidine
(use is not recommended in patients taking Class IA or Class III antiarrhythmic agents; potential to prolong the QTc interval of the electrocardiogram resulting in increased risk for ventricular arrhythmias including torsades de pointes)

» Atorvastatin or
» Lovastatin or
» Simvastatin
(concomitant use is not recommended; if telithromycin is prescribed, therapy should be suspended during the course of treatment)

» Carbamazepine
(decreases efficacy of telithromycin and increases carbamazepine exposure)

» Cyclosporine or
» Hexobarbital or
» Phenytoin or
» Sirolimus or
» Tacrolimus
(elevated serum levels of these drugs may be observed, resulting in increases or prolongation of the therapeutic and/or adverse effects of the concomitant drug)

» Cisapride
(use with telithromycin is contraindicated; significant increases in QTc have been reported)

» Digoxin
(concurrent administration with telithromycin has been shown to increase serum digoxin concentrations; monitoring of digoxin serum concentrations or side effect should be considered in patients receiving digoxin and telithromycin concurrently)

» Dihydroergotamine or
» Ergotamine
(use is not recommended; acute ergot toxicity characterized by severe peripheral vasospasm and dysesthesia have been reported with ergot alkaloid derivatives co-administration with telithromycin)

Itraconazole or
Ketoconazole or
Ritonavir
(may increase telithromycin plasma concentrations)

» Metoprolol
(may increase metoprolol plasma concentrations; co-administration of telithromycin and metoprolol in patients with heart failure should be considered with caution)

» Midazolam
(may increase midazolam AUC; patients should be monitored and dosage adjustments of midazolam should be considered if necessary)

» Other benzodiazepines such as
Triazolam
(caution; when telithromycin is administered with other benzodiazepines which are metabolized by CYP 3A4 and undergo a high first-pass effect, serum levels of the other benzodiazepines may increase)

Phenobarbital or
Phenytoin or
St. John's wort
(may result in subtherapeutic levels of telithromycin and loss of effect)

» Pimozide
(use is **contraindicated;** risk of increased pimozide levels)

» Rifampin
(concomitant treatment should be avoided)

» Sotalol
(in addition to the interaction, may decrease C_{max} and AUC due to decreased absorption)

» Theophylline
(co-administration with telithromycin may worsen gastrointestinal side effects such as nausea and vomiting; theophylline and telithromycin should be taken a least 1 hour apart.)

Laboratory value alterations
The following have been selected on the basis of their potential clinical significance (possible effect in parentheses where appropriate)—not necessarily inclusive (» = major clinical significance).

With physiology/laboratory test values
Alanine aminotransferase (ALT [SGPT]) or
Alkaline phosphatase or
Aspartase aminotransferase (AST [SGOT]) or
Bilirubin, serum or
Eosinophil count or
Liver function test, abnormal or
Platelet count
(transient rise in values has been reported)

Medical considerations/Contraindications
The medical considerations/contraindications included have been selected on the basis of their potential clinical significance (reasons given in parentheses where appropriate)—not necessarily inclusive (» = major clinical significance).

Except under special circumstances, this medication should not be used when the following medical problem exists:
» Hepatitis, previous history of or
» Jaundice, previous history of
(should NOT be used if these conditions were associated with telithromycin or any macrolide antibiotic use in the past)
» Hypersensitivity to telithromycin and/or any components of telithromycin tablet, or any macrolide antibiotic

Risk-benefit should be considered when the following medical problems exist:
» Congenital prolongation of the QTc interval or
» Proarrhythmic conditions, ongoing such as
» Bradycardia or
» Hypokalemia, uncorrected or
» Hypomagnesemia
(telithromycin is not recommended; potential to prolong the QTc interval of the electrocardiogram resulting in an increased risk for ventricular arrhythmias including torsades de pointes.)

» Myasthenia gravis
(use is not recommended in patients with myasthenia gravis unless no other therapeutic alternatives are available; telithromycin may exacerbate this condition; patients must be advised that if they experience exacerbations of their symptoms they should discontinue telithromycin treatment and seek medical attention.)

» Renal function impairment (severe)
(patients with severe renal impairment are prone to conditions that may impair their metabolic clearance)

Patient monitoring
The following may be especially important in patient monitoring (other tests may be warranted in some patients, depending on condition; » = major clinical significance):

Liver function tests
(monitor for signs and symptoms of hepatitis including elevated bilirubin transaminase levels)

» Pseudomembranous colitis
(monitor patient for development of diarrhea subsequent to telithromycin therapy)

Side/Adverse Effects

The following side/adverse effects have been selected on the basis of their potential clinical significance (possible signs and symptoms in parentheses where appropriate)—not necessarily inclusive:

Those indicating need for medical attention

Incidence more frequent

Erythema multiforme (blistering, peeling, loosening of skin; chills; cough; diarrhea; fever; itching; joint or muscle pain; red irritated eyes; sore throat; sores, ulcers, or white spots in mouth or on lips; unusual tiredness or weakness); ***hepatitis (with or without jaundice)*** (dark urine; general tiredness and weakness; light-colored stools; nausea and vomiting; upper right abdominal pain; yellow eyes and skin)

Incidence rare

Allergic reaction, severe (cough; difficulty swallowing; dizziness; fast heartbeat; hives, itching, puffiness or swelling of the eyelids or around the eyes, face, lips or tongue; shortness of breath; skin rash; tightness in chest; unusual tiredness or weakness; wheezing); ***anaphylaxis*** (cough; difficulty swallowing; dizziness; fast heartbeat; hives, itching, puffiness or swelling of the eyelids or around the eyes, face, lips or tongue; shortness of breath; skin rash; tightness in chest; unusual tiredness or weakness; wheezing); ***angioedema*** (large, hive-like swelling on face, eyelids, lips, tongue, throat, hands, legs, feet, sex organs); ***antibiotic associated colitis*** (stomach cramps, tenderness, or pain; watery or bloody diarrhea; fever); ***arrhythmias, atrial*** (dizziness; fainting; fast, slow, or irregular heartbeat); ***blood bilirubin, elevated; bradycardia*** (chest pain or discomfort; lightheadedness; dizziness or fainting; shortness of breath; slow or irregular heartbeat; unusual tiredness); ***eosinophilia*** (increased eosinophil count); ***hyperkalemia*** (abdominal pain; confusion; irregular heartbeat; nausea or vomiting; nervousness; numbness or tingling in hands, feet, or lips; shortness of breath; difficult breathing; weakness or heaviness of legs); ***hypokalemia*** (convulsions; decreased urine; dry mouth; irregular heartbeat; increased thirst; loss of appetite; mood changes; muscle pain or cramps; nausea or vomiting; numbness or tingling in hands, feet, or lips; shortness of breath; unusual tiredness or weakness); ***hypotension*** (blurred vision; confusion; dizziness; faintness, or lightheadedness when getting up from a lying or sitting position suddenly; sweating; unusual tiredness or weakness); ***increased blood alkaline phosphatase; myasthenia gravis, exacerbation*** (difficulty in breathing, chewing, swallowing, or talking; double vision; drooping eyelids; muscle weakness; severe tiredness)

Incidence unknown—Observed during clinical practice; estimates of frequency cannot be determined

Fulminant hepatitis (abdominal or stomach pain; chills; clay-colored stools; dark urine; diarrhea; dizziness; fever; headache; itching; loss of appetite; nausea; rash; unpleasant breath odor; unusual tiredness or weakness; vomiting of blood; yellow eyes or skin); ***hepatic failure*** (headache; stomach pain; continuing vomiting; dark-colored urine; general feeling of tiredness or weakness; light-colored stools; yellow eyes or skin); ***hepatic necrosis*** (abdominal or stomach pain; black, tarry stools; chills; light-colored stools; dark urine; dizziness; fever; headache; itching; loss of appetite; nausea; rash; unpleasant breath odor; unusual tiredness or weakness; vomiting of blood; yellow eyes or skin); ***hepatoxicity*** (abdominal pain or tenderness; clay colored stools; dark urine; decreased appetite; fever; headache; itching; loss of appetite; nausea and vomiting; skin rash; swelling of feet or lower legs; unusual tiredness or weakness; yellow eyes or skin)

Those indicating need for medical attention only if they continue or are bothersome

Incidence more frequent

Diarrhea; nausea

Incidence less frequent or rare

Abdominal distention (swelling of abdominal or stomach area; full or bloated feeling or pressure in the stomach); ***abdominal pain*** (stomach pain); ***abnormal dream; abnormal liver function test results*** (lab results that show problems with liver); ***ageusia*** (loss of sense of taste); ***anorexia*** (loss of appetite; weight loss); ***anxiety*** (fear; nervousness); ***asthenia*** (lack or loss of strength); ***blurred vision; constipation*** (difficulty having a bowel movement (stool)); ***difficulty focusing eyes; diplopia*** (double vision; seeing double); ***dizziness; disturbed attention; dry lips; dry mouth; dry skin; dyspepsia*** (acid or sour stomach; belching; heartburn; indigestion; stomach discomfort, upset or pain); ***dysgeusia*** (loss of taste; change in taste); ***eczema*** (skin rash encrusted, scaly and oozing); ***esophagitis*** (difficulty in swallowing; pain or burning in throat; chest pain; heartburn; vomiting; sores, ulcers, or white spots on lips or tongue or inside the mouth); ***eructation*** (belching; bloated full feeling; excess air or gas in stomach); ***facial edema*** (swelling or puffiness of face); ***fatigue*** (unusual tiredness or weakness); ***flatulence*** (bloated full feeling; excess air or gas in stomach or intestines; passing gas); ***flushing*** (feeling of warmth, redness of the face, neck, arms and occasionally, upper chest); ***fungal vaginosis*** (change in the color, amount or odor of vaginal discharge); ***gastritis*** (burning feeling in chest or stomach; tenderness in stomach area; stomach upset; indigestion); ***gastroenteritis*** (abdominal or stomach pain; diarrhea; loss of appetite; nausea; weakness); ***gastrointestinal upset*** (diarrhea; loss of appetite; nausea; vomiting; stomach cramps or pain); ***glossitis*** (redness, swelling, or soreness of tongue); ***headache; increased platelet count; increased sweating; insomnia*** (sleeplessness; trouble sleeping; unable to sleep); ***loose stools; muscle cramps; nervousness; oral candidiasis*** (sore mouth or tongue; white patches in mouth and/or on tongue); ***palpitation*** (fast, irregular, pounding, or racing heartbeat or pulse); ***paresthesias*** (burning, crawling, itching, numbness, prickling, "pins and needles", or tingling feelings); ***parosmia*** (change in sense of smell); ***polyuria*** (frequent urination; increased volume of pale, dilute urine); ***pruritus*** (itching skin); ***rash; somnolence*** (sleepiness or unusual drowsiness); ***stomatitis*** (swelling or inflammation of the mouth); ***tooth discoloration; tremor*** (trembling or shaking of hands or feet; shakiness in legs, arms, hands, feet); ***upper abdominal pain*** (upper stomach pain); ***urine discoloration; urticaria*** (hives or welts; itching, redness of skin; skin rash); ***vaginal candidiasis*** (itching of the vagina or outside genitals pain during sexual intercourse; thick, white curd-like vaginal discharge without odor or with mild odor); ***vaginal irritation*** (vaginal burning or itching); ***vaginitis*** (itching of the vagina or genital area; pain during sexual intercourse; thick, white vaginal discharge with no odor or with a mild odor); ***vasculitis*** (redness, soreness or itching skin; fever; sores, welting or blisters); ***vertigo*** (dizziness or lightheadedness; feeling of constant movement of self or surroundings; sensation of spinning); ***vomiting; watery stools***

Overdose

For more information on the management of overdose or unintentional ingestion, **contact a poison control center** (see *Poison Control Center Listing*).

Treatment of overdose

To decrease absorption—

Emptying stomach with gastric lavage.

The effectiveness of hemodialysis is unknown.

Monitoring—

Carefully monitor for cardiovascular function (e.g., ECG).

Supportive care—

Treatment should be symptomatic and supportive.

Adequate hydration should be maintained.

Patients in whom intentional overdose is confirmed or suspected should be referred for psychiatric consultation.

Patient Consultation

As an aid to patient consultation, refer to *Advice for the Patient, Telithromycin (Systemic)*.

In providing consultation, consider emphasizing the following selected information (» = major clinical significance):

Before using this medication

» Conditions affecting use, especially:

Hypersensitivity to telithromycin or other macrolides

Pregnancy—Since there are no adequate and well controlled studies in pregnant women telithromycin should be used during pregnancy only if the potential benefit justifies the potential risk to the fetus.

Breast-feeding—Because many drugs are distributed in human milk, caution should be exercised when telithromycin is administered to a nursing mother.

Use in children—Safety and efficacy have not been established in pediatric patients below the age of 18 years

Use in the elderly—Elderly patients may have a greater sensitivity to telithromycin.

Other contraindicated medications, especially cisapride and pimozide

Other medications, especially amiodarone, atorvastatin, carbamazepine, cyclosporine, digoxin, dihydroergotamine, dofetilide, ergotamine, hexobarbital, lovastatin, metoprolol, midazolam, other benzodiazepines such as triazolam; phenytoin, procainamide, quinidine, rifampin, simvastatin, sirolimus, sotalol, tacrolimus, or theophylline

Other medical problems, especially hepatitis or jaundice (history of, associated with use of telithromycin), congenital prolongation of the QT_C interval, myasthenia gravis, proarrhythmic conditions such as bradycardia, hypokalemia, and hypomagnesemia, or renal impairment (severe).

Proper use of this medication

» Compliance with full course of therapy

» Proper dosing

Missed dose: Taking as soon as possible; not taking if almost time for next scheduled dose; not doubling doses

» Proper storage

Precautions while using this medication

» *Not taking telithromycin if there is a history of hepatitis and/or jaundice with previous use of telithromycin or other macrolides*

» *Discontinuing telithromycin and immediately seeking medical evaluation* if signs or symptoms of hepatitis such as fatigue, malaise, anorexia, nausea, jaundice, bilirubinuria, acholic stools, liver tenderness, or hepatomegaly occur

» Report any fainting while taking this medication

» Report any severe diarrhea during or following treatment with telithromycin

» Not taking with cisapride or pimozide

Checking with physician if no improvement within a few days

» May cause visual disturbances. Be careful while driving or operating machinery until you become familiar with the effects of telithromycin.

Side/adverse effects

Signs of potential side effects, especially allergic reaction (severe), anaphylaxis, angioedema, antibiotic associated colitis, arrhythmias, atrial, blood bilirubin, elevated, bradycardia, eosinophilia, erythema multiforme, hepatitis (with or without jaundice), hyperkalemia, hypokalemia, hypotension, increased blood alkaline phosphatase, increased eosinophil count, or myasthenia gravis exacerbation

Signs of potential side effects observed during clinical practice, especially fulminant hepatitis, hepatic failure, hepatic necrosis, or hepatoxicity

General Dosing Information

No adjustment in dose is required in patients with hepatic impairment.

Telithromycin tablets may be taken with or without food.

Treatment of side and adverse effects

Pseudomembranous colitis—mild cases usually respond to drug discontinuation alone. In moderate to severe cases, consideration should be given to management with fluids and electrolytes, protein supplementation, and treatment with an antibacterial drug clinically effective against *Clostridium difficile*, which is one primary cause of antibiotic associated colitis. Other causes of colitis should also be considered.

Oral Dosage Forms

Note: Bracketed information in the *Indications* section refers to uses that are not included in U.S. product labeling.

TELITHROMYCIN TABLETS

Usual adult dose

Bronchitis, chronic, bacterial exacerbation due to *Streptococcus pneumoniae* or *Moraxella catarrhalis*—

Oral, 800 mg (two tablets of 400 mg) once daily for 5 days.

[Pharyngitis/Tonsillitis due to group A-β Hemolytic Streptococcus as an alternative when β-lactam antibiotics are not appropriate.]—

Oral, 800 mg (two tablets of 400 mg) once daily for 5 days.

Pneumonia, community-acquired due to *Streptococcus pneumoniae* (including multi-drug resistant isolates [MDRSP]), *Haemophilus influenzae, Chlamydia pneumoniae, Mycoplasma pneumoniae*, or *Moraxella catarrhalis*[1]—

Oral, 800 mg (two tablets of 400 mg) once daily for 7 to 10 days.

Sinusitis, acute bacterial due to *Streptococcus pneumoniae, Haemophilus influenzae, Moraxella catarrhalis*, or *Staphylococcus aureus*[1]—

Oral, 800 mg (two tablets of 400 mg) once daily for 5 days.

Note: In patients with hepatic impairment, telithromycin may be administered without dosage adjustment.

In the US, patients with severe renal impairment (CL_{CR} less than 30 mL per minute), including patients who need dialysis, the dose should be reduced to 600 mg once daily. In patients undergoing hemodialysis, telithromycin should be given after the dialysis session on dialysis days.

In the US, patients with severe renal impairment (CL_{CR} less than 30 mL per minute) and coexisting hepatic impairment, the dose should be reduced to 400 mg once daily.

In the presence of severe renal impairment (creatinine clearance < 30 mL/min), the recommended dose in Canada should be reduced to 400 mg once daily and for hemodialysis patients, on dialysis days, 800 mg should be given after each dialysis session.

Usual pediatric dose

Safety and efficacy in pediatric patients below 18 years of age have not been established.

Usual geriatric dose

See *Usual adult dose.*

Strength(s) usually available

U.S.—

400 mg (Rx) [*Ketek* (cornstarch; croscarmellose sodium; hypromellose; lactose monohydrate; magnesium stearate; microcrystalline cellulose; polyethylene glycol; povidone; red ferric oxide; talc; titanium dioxide; yellow ferric oxide)].

Canada—

400 mg (Rx) [*Ketek* (cornstarch; croscarmellose sodium; lactose monohydrate; magnesium stearate; microcrystalline cellulose; polyethylene glycol; povidone; red ferric oxide; talc; titanium dioxide; yellow ferric oxide)].

Packaging and storage

Store at 25 °C (77 °F); excursions permitted to 15 to 30°C (59 to 86 °F).

Auxiliary labeling

- Continue medicine for full time of treatment.
- May cause blurred vision.
- This medication can be taken with of without food.

[1]Not included in Canadian product labeling.

Revised: 07/29/2006
Developed: 06/22/2004

TELMISARTAN Systemic

VA CLASSIFICATION (Primary/Secondary): CV805/CV409

Commonly used brand name(s): *Micardis.*

Note: For a listing of dosage forms and brand names by country availability, see *Dosage Forms* section(s).

Category

Antihypertensive.

Indications

Accepted

Hypertension (treatment)—Telmisartan is indicated for the treatment of hypertensionwhen diuretic or beta-adrenergic blocker therapy has failed, or is contraindicated, or in the event that side effects of these agents are too severe. It may be used alone or in combination with other antihypertensive medications.

For additional information on initial therapeutic guidelines related to the treatment of hypertension, see *Appendix III.*

Pharmacology/Pharmacokinetics

Physicochemical characteristics

Molecular weight—Telmisartan: 514.63.

Mechanism of action/Effect

Telmisartan is a nonpeptide angiotensin II antagonist that selectively blocks the binding of angiotensin II to the AT_1 receptors in vascular smooth muscle and the adrenal gland. In the renin-angiotensin system, angiotensin I is converted by angiotensin-converting enzyme (ACE) to form angiotensin II. Angiotensin II stimulates the adrenal cortex to synthesize and secrete aldosterone, which decreases the excretion of sodium and increases the excretion of potassium. Angiotensin II also acts as a vasoconstrictor in vascular smooth muscle. By blocking the binding of angiotensin II to the AT_1 receptors, telmisartan causes vasodilation and decreases the effects of aldosterone. The negative feedback regulation of angiotensin II on renin secretion also is inhibited, resulting in a rise in plasma renin concentrations and a consequent rise in angiotensin II plasma concentrations; however, these effects do not counteract the blood pressure-lowering effect that occurs.

Other actions/effects

Telmisartan may have an inhibitory effect on cytochrome P450 2C19 isozyme and may affect the metabolism of medications that are metabolized by this enzyme.

Absorption

Absolute bioavailability of telmisartan increases (with greater than proportional increments) with increasing doses. Food slightly decreases the bioavailability of telmisartan; a decrease of about 6% is seen when the 40-mg dose is administered with food.

Distribution

Vol_D—Approximately 500 liters (L).

Protein binding

Very high (> 99.5%), mainly to albumin and alpha$_1$-acid glycoprotein. Protein binding is constant, not affected by changes in dose.

Biotransformation

Elimination of telmisartan is primarily as unchanged drug. Telmisartan undergoes conjugation to form an inactive acylglucuronide metabolite, the only metabolite identified in human plasma and urine.

Half-life

Elimination—
Approximately 24 hours.

Time to peak concentration

0.5 to 1 hour.

Elimination

Elimination of telmisartan is primarily as unchanged drug.
After intravenous or oral administration—
Renal—Less than 1%.
Fecal (biliary)—Greater than 97%.
In dialysis—
Telmisartan is not removable by hemodialysis.

Precautions to Consider

Carcinogenicity

No evidence of carcinogenicity was found when telmisartan was given to mice or rats for up to 2 years in doses of up to 1000 and 100 mg per kg of body weight (mg/kg) per day, respectively. These doses represent approximately 59 and 13 times, respectively, the maximum recommended human daily dose (MRHDD) of 80 mg and provide an average systemic exposure to telmisartan of more than 100 and 25 times, respectively, the systemic exposure in humans.

Mutagenicity

Telmisartan was not found to be mutagenic in the Ames bacterial mutagenicity test with *Salmonella* and *Escherichia coli*, a gene mutation test with Chinese hamster V79 cells, a cytogenetic test with human lymphocytes, and a mouse micronucleus test.

Pregnancy/Reproduction

Fertility—Reproductive performance was not affected in male and female rats given telmisartan at doses of 100 mg/kg per day, resulting in an average systemic exposure (as determined by the area under the plasma concentration-time curve [AUC] on day 6 of pregnancy) of approximately 50 times the average systemic exposure in humans at the MRHDD of 80 mg per day. This dose represents about 13 times the MRHDD of telmisartan on a milligram per square meter of body surface area (mg/m^2) basis.

Pregnancy—Medications that act directly on the renin-angiotensin system can cause fetal and neonatal morbidity and mortality when administered to pregnant women during the second and third trimesters. Telmisartan should be discontinued as soon as possible when pregnancy is detected, unless no alternative therapy can be used. In the latter instance, serial ultrasound examinations should be performed to assess the intra-amniotic environment. If oligohydramnios is observed, telmisartan should be discontinued unless it is considered life-saving for the mother. Perinatal diagnostic tests, such as contraction-stress testing (CST), a nonstress test (NST), or biophysical profiling (BPP) may be appropriate during the applicable week of pregnancy. However, oligohydramnios may not appear until after the fetus has sustained irreversible damage.

Fetal exposure to drugs that act directly on the renin-angiotensin system during the second and third trimesters can cause hypotension, reversible or irreversible renal failure, anuria, neonatal skull hypoplasia, and death in the fetus or neonate. Maternal oligohydramnios, which may result from decreased fetal renal function, has been reported and is associated with fetal limb contractures, craniofacial deformation, and hypoplastic lung development. Other adverse effects that have been reported are prematurity, intrauterine growth retardation, and patent ductus arteriosus, although it is not clear how these effects are related to drug exposure. When limited to the first trimester, exposure to this medication does not appear to be associated with these adverse effects.

Infants exposed in utero to angiotensin II receptor antagonists should be observed closely for hypotension, oliguria, and hyperkalemia. Oliguria should be treated with support of blood pressure and renal perfusion. Dialysis or exchange transfusion may be necessary to reverse hypotension and/or substitute for disordered renal function.

No teratogenic effects were observed in pregnant rats given oral doses of telmisartan of up to 50 mg/kg per day or in pregnant rabbits given oral doses of up to 45 mg/kg per day. Maternal toxicity in rabbits (as determined by reduced body weight gain and food consumption), at a dose of 45 mg/kg of body weight per day, resulted in embryolethality. This dose represents about 6.4 times the MRHDD of 80 mg on a mg/m^2 basis. Maternal toxicity in rats (as determined by a reduction in body weight gain and food consumption) given telmisartan in doses of 15 mg/kg per day during late gestation and lactation produced adverse effects in neonates, including reduced viability, low birth weight, delayed maturation, and decreased weight gain. This dose represents about 1.9 times the MRHDD on a mg/m^2 basis. Telmisartan has been shown to be present in rat fetuses during late gestation and in the milk of rats. The no-observed-effect doses for developmental toxicity in rats and rabbits, 5 and 15 mg/kg per day, respectively, are about 0.64 and 3.7 times, on a mg/m^2 basis, the MRHDD of telmisartan (80 mg per day).

FDA Pregnancy Category C (first trimester).

FDA Pregnancy Category D (second and third trimesters).

Breast-feeding

It is not known whether telmisartan is distributed into human breast milk. However, telmisartan is distributed into the milk of lactating rats. Because of the potential for adverse effects in the nursing infant, it is recommended that telmisartan not be administered to mothers who are breast-feeding.

Pediatrics

No information is available on the relationship of age to the effects of telmisartan in pediatric patients. Safety and efficacy have not been established.

Geriatrics

Use of telmisartan in patients 65 years of age and older (18.6% of patient in clinical trials) has not demonstrated geriatrics-specific problems that would limit the usefulness of telmisartan in the elderly. The pharmacokinetics of telmisartan have not been shown to differ between individuals younger or older than 65 years of age.

Pharmacogenetics

Females generally have twofold to threefold higher plasma concentrations of telmisartan than do males; however, no significant increases in blood pressure response or in the incidence of orthostatic hypotension have been found in women and no dosage adjustment is necessary.

Black patients have a somewhat smaller response to the blood pressure-lowering effects of telmisartan.

Drug interactions and/or related problems

The following drug interactions and/or related problems have been selected on the basis of their potential clinical significance (possible mechanism in parentheses where appropriate)—not necessarily inclusive (» = major clinical significance):

Note: Safety and efficacy of concurrent use of telmisartan with other angiotensin-converting enzyme inhibitors or beta-adrenergic blocking agents have not been established.

Note: Combinations containing any of the following medications, depending on the amount present, may also interact with this medication.

Digoxin
(concurrent use with telmisartan has resulted in median increases in digoxin peak plasma concentrations of 49% and in trough concentrations of 20%; digoxin plasma concentrations should be monitored when initiating, adjusting, and discontinuing telmisartan)

Diuretics
(concurrent use with telmisartan may have additive hypotensive effects)

Warfarin
(concurrent use with telmisartan for a period of 10 days has resulted in a slight decrease in the mean warfarin trough plasma concentration; however, this did not result in a change in international normalized ratio [INR])

Laboratory value alterations

The following have been selected on the basis of their potential clinical significance (possible effect in parentheses where appropriate)—not necessarily inclusive (» = major clinical significance).

With physiology/laboratory test values
Blood urea nitrogen (BUN) and
Creatinine, serum
(increases in serum creatinine of 0.5 mg per dL or greater occurred in 0.4% of patients treated with telmisartan; one patient discontinued treatment with telmisartan due to increases in serum creatinine and blood urea nitrogen)

Cholesterol
(marked increases in serum cholesterol were reported in 6 patients (0.4%) treated with telmisartan; two of these patients were followed over time and their cholesterol levels returned to baseline values)

Hemoglobin
(in clinical studies, small decreases in hemoglobin values of > 2 grams per dL occurred in 0.8% of patients treated with telmisartan; no patients discontinued telmisartan due to anemia)

Liver function tests
(in clinical studies, elevations of liver enzymes and/or serum bilirubin occurred infrequently in telmisartan-treated patients; no patients discontinued telmisartan due to abnormal hepatic function)

Serum uric acid
(clinically significant hyperuricemia (>10 mEq/L) was observed in 2.3% of telmisartan patients, primarily in those receiving in combination with hydrochlorothiazide)

Medical considerations/Contraindications

The medical considerations/contraindications included have been selected on the basis of their potential clinical significance (reasons given in parentheses where appropriate)—not necessarily inclusive (» = major clinical significance).

Except under special circumstances, this medication should not be used when the following medical problem exists:

» Hypersensitivity to telmisartan or to any component of this product

Risk-benefit should be considered when the following medical problems exist:

» Congestive heart failure, severe
(therapy with angiotensin receptor–antagonists in these patients, who may be especially susceptible to changes in the renin-angiotensin-aldosterone system, has been associated with oliguria, azotemia, acute renal failure, and/or death)

Dehydration
(sodium or volume depletion, due to excessive perspiration, vomiting, diarrhea, prolonged diuretic therapy, dialysis, or dietary salt restriction)
(patients with reduced salt or fluid volume may have an increased risk of symptomatic hypotension)

Hepatic function impairment
(because telmisartan is eliminated primarily by the biliary route, patients with hepatic function impairment or biliary obstructive disorders may have increased plasma concentrations due to reduced elimination of telmisartan; the absolute bioavailability of telmisartan in patients with hepatic function impairment is close to 100%)

Renal artery stenosis, unilateral or bilateral or
Renal function impairment
(increases in serum creatinine or blood urea nitrogen [BUN] have occurred in patients with unilateral or bilateral renal artery stenosis and treated with angiotensin-converting enzyme [ACE] inhibitors; similar increases also may occur in patients treated with telmisartan. Changes in renal function as a result of therapy with angiotensin receptor–antagonists in patients susceptible to changes in the renin-angiotensin-aldosterone system [such as patients with severe congestive heart failure] have been associated with oliguria, progressive azotemia, acute renal failure, and/or death)
(patients on dialysis may develop orthostatic hypotension; their blood pressure should be closely monitored)

» Valvular stenosis
(There is a theoretical risk of decreased coronary perfusion for patients with aortic stenosis, because they do not develop as much afterload reduction.)

Patient monitoring

The following may be especially important in patient monitoring (other tests may be warranted in some patients, depending on condition; » = major clinical significance):

» Blood pressure measurements
(periodic monitoring is necessary for titration of dose according to the patient's response; importance of monitoring patients' blood pressure if they are on dialysis)

Side/Adverse Effects

The following side/adverse effects have been selected on the basis of their potential clinical significance (possible signs and symptoms in parentheses where appropriate)—not necessarily inclusive:

Those indicating need for medical attention

Incidence rare

Angioedema (large hives); ***changes in vision; hypotension or syncope*** (dizziness, lightheadedness, or fainting)—usually seen in volume- or salt-depleted patients, such as those treated with diuretics, especially upon standing; ***tachycardia*** (fast heartbeat)

Incidence not determined—Observed during clinical practice; estimates of frequency can not be determined

Aggravated hypertension (blurred vision; dizziness; nervousness; headache; pounding in the ears; slow or fast heartbeat); ***angioneurotic edema*** (large, hive-like swelling on face, eyelids, lips, tongue, throat, hands, legs, feet, sex organs); ***atrial fibrillation*** (fast or irregular heartbeat; dizziness; fainting); ***chest pain; congestive heart failure*** (chest pain; decreased urine output; dilated neck veins; extreme fatigue; irregular breathing; irregular heartbeat; shortness of breath; swelling of face, fingers, feet, or lower legs; tightness in chest; troubled breathing; weight gain; wheezing); ***erythema*** (flushing; redness of skin; unusually warm skin); ***hyperkalemia*** (abdominal pain; confusion; irregular heartbeat; nausea or vomiting; nervousness; numbness or tingling in hands, feet, or lips; shortness of breath; difficult breathing; weakness or heaviness of legs); ***hypersensitivity*** (fast heartbeat; fever; hives; itching; irritation; hoarseness; joint pain, stiffness, or swelling; rash; redness of skin; shortness of breath; swelling of eyelids, face, lips, hands, or feet; tightness in chest; troubled breathing or swallowing; wheezing); ***increased blood pressure*** (headache; dizziness; weakness, numbness or tingling in arms or legs; trouble thinking, speaking or walking); ***myocardial infarction*** (chest pain or discomfort; pain or discomfort in arms, jaw, back or neck; shortness of breath; nausea; sweating; vomiting); ***rhabdomyolysis*** (dark-colored urine; fever; muscle cramps or spasms; muscle pain or stiffness; unusual tiredness or weakness); ***urticaria*** (hives or welts; itching; redness of skin; skin rash)

Those indicating need for medical attention only if they continue or are bothersome

Incidence less frequent

Abdominal pain; acid reflux or dyspepsia (heartburn); ***appetite changes; back pain; diarrhea; dizziness; dry mouth; edema in extremities*** (swelling in hands, lower legs, and feet); ***fatigue*** (general tiredness or weakness); ***flatulence*** (bloating or gas); ***increased sweating; muscle pain or spasm; nausea; nervousness; pharyngitis*** (sore throat); ***sinusitis*** (headache; stuffy nose); ***skin rash; urinary tract infection*** (painful urination or changes in urinary frequency); ***upper respiratory tract infection*** (coughing; ear congestion or pain; fever; head congestion; nasal congestion; runny nose; sneezing; sore throat)

Incidence not determined—Observed during clinical practice; estimates of frequency can not be determined

Asthenia (lack or loss of strength); ***coughing; dyspepsia*** (acid or sour stomach; belching; heartburn; indigestion; stomach discomfort, upset, or pain); ***edema*** (swelling); ***erectile dysfunction*** (loss in sexual ability, desire, drive, or performance; decreased interest in sexual intercourse; inability to have or keep an erection); ***facial edema*** (swelling or puffiness of face); ***headache; muscle cramps (including leg cramps); myalgia*** (joint pain; swollen joints; muscle aching or cramping; muscle pains or stiffness; difficulty in moving); ***weakness***

Overdose

For more information on the management of overdose or unintentional ingestion, **contact a Poison Control Center** (see *Poison Control Center Listing*).

Clinical effects of overdose

The following effects have been selected on the basis of their potential clinical significance (possible signs and symptoms in parentheses where appropriate)—not necessarily inclusive:

Acute and/or chronic

Bradycardia (slow heartbeat)—as a result of parasympathetic (vagal) stimulation; ***dizziness; hypotension*** (dizziness, lightheadedness, or fainting); ***tachycardia*** (fast heartbeat)

Treatment of overdose

Treatment should be symptomatic and supportive.

Telmisartan is not removed by hemodialysis.

Supportive care—Patients in whom intentional overdose is confirmed or suspected should be referred for psychiatric consultation.

Patient Consultation

As an aid to patient consultation, refer to *Advice for the Patient, Telmisartan (Systemic)*.

In providing consultation, consider emphasizing the following selected information (» = major clinical significance):

Before using this medication

» Conditions affecting use, especially:

Hypersensitivity to telmisartan or to any component of the product

Pregnancy—Fetal and neonatal hypotension, skull hypoplasia, renal failure, and death have been reported; telmisartan should be discontinued as soon as possible when pregnancy is detected

Breast-feeding—Telmisartan is distributed into the milk of lactating rats; not recommended in mothers who are breast-feeding

Pharmacogenetics—Plasma concentrations of telmisartan may be higher in women; black patients may have a somewhat smaller therapeutic response

Other medical problems, especially severe congestive heart failure and valvular stenosis

Proper use of this medication

» Compliance with therapy; taking medication at the same time each day to maintain the antihypertensive effect

Protecting tablets from moisture and keeping in blister pack until immediately before use

» Proper dosing

Missed dose: Taking as soon as possible; not taking if almost time for next scheduled dose; not doubling doses

» Proper storage

Precautions while using this medication

Visiting the physician regularly to check progress

Notifying physician immediately if pregnancy is suspected

Not taking other medications without consulting the physician

Caution when driving, using machines, or doing other things that may be dangerous if dizziness or light-headedness occurs from hypotension

To prevent dehydration and hypotension, checking with physician if severe nausea, vomiting, or diarrhea occurs and continues

Caution when exercising or during exposure to hot weather, because of the risk of dehydration and hypotension due to reduced fluid volume

Side/adverse effects

Signs of potential side effects, especially angioedema, changes in vision, hypotension or syncope, and tachycardia

Signs of potential side effect observed during clinical practice, especially aggravated hypertension, angioneurotic edema, atrial fibrillation, chest pain, congestive heart failure, erythema, hyperkalemia, hypersensitivity, increased blood pressure, myocardial infarction, rhabdomyolysis, and urticaria

General Dosing Information

Dosage must be adjusted, on the basis of clinical response, to meet the individual requirements of each patient.

Telmisartan may be administered with other antihypertensive agents.

Diet/Nutrition

Telmisartan may be taken with or without food.

For treatment of adverse effects

Recommended treatment consists of the following:

- Treatment of symptomatic hypotension involves placing the patient in a supine position and, if needed, administering normal saline intravenously.

Oral Dosage Forms

TELMISARTAN TABLETS

Usual adult dose

Antihypertensive—

Oral, initially 40 mg once a day. Telmisartan may be administered in total daily doses ranging from 20 to 80 mg. The antihypertensive effect is considerable within two weeks of therapy, and maximal antihypertensive effect usually is attained within four weeks of therapy. If blood pressure is not controlled by telmisartan alone at a dose of 80 mg, a diuretic may be added

Note: Patients with volume depletion (e.g., from diuretic treatment), on dialysis, with biliary obstructive disorders, or with hepatic function impairment should be closely monitored during initiation of therapy

No dosage adjustment is necessary in patients with renal impairment, including those on hemodialysis.

Usual adult prescribing limits

80 mg per day.

Usual pediatric dose

Safety and efficacy have not been established.

Usual geriatric dose

See *Usual adult dose*.

Strength(s) usually available

U.S.—

20 mg (Rx) [*Micardis* (sodium hydroxide; meglumine; povidone; sorbitol; magnesium stearate)].

40 mg (Rx) [*Micardis* (magnesium stearate; meglumine; povidone; sodium hydroxide; sorbitol)].

80 mg (Rx) [*Micardis* (magnesium stearate; meglumine; povidone; sodium hydroxide; sorbitol)].

Canada—

40 mg (Rx) [*Micardis* (sodium hydroxide; meglumine; povidone; sorbitol; magnesium stearate)].

80 mg (Rx) [*Micardis* (sodium hydroxide; meglumine; povidone; sorbitol; magnesium stearate)].

Packaging and storage

Store at 25 °C (77 °F). Fluctuations between 15 and 30 °C (59 and 86 °F) are acceptable. Telmisartan is hygroscopic and requires protection from moisture; therefore, the tablets should not be removed from the blister packaging until immediately before administration.

Auxiliary labeling

- Do not take other medicines without your doctor's advice.

Revised: 10/03/2005
Developed: 01/04/1999

TELMISARTAN AND HYDROCHLOROTHIAZIDE Systemic

VA CLASSIFICATION (Primary): CV408

Commonly used brand name(s): *Micardis HCT; Micardis Plus.*

NOTE: The *Telmisartan and Hydrochlorothiazide (Systemic)* monograph is maintained on the *USP DI* electronic data base. A copy of the most recent revision of the complete monograph can be accessed on the *USP DI* Updates Online website. See the front cover of book for details on accessing the site.

For information on the specific components of this combination, see the *USP DI* monographs for *Telmisartan (Systemic)*, and *Diuretics, Thiazide (Systemic)*.

The information that follows is selectively abstracted from the complete monograph and is provided to facilitate drug use review and patient counseling.

Note: For a listing of dosage forms and brand names by country availability, see *Dosage Forms* section(s).

Category

Antihypertensive.

Indications

Note: Bracketed information in the *Indications* section refers to uses that are not included in U.S. product labeling.

Accepted

Hypertension (treatment)—Telmisartan and hydrochlorothiazide combination is indicated for the treatment of mild to moderate hypertension in patients that have failed to achieve the desired antihypertensive effect through monotherapy. The fixed dose combination is not indicated as initial therapy and is reserved for patients in whom treatment with [diuretic or beta-adrenergic blocking agent] monotherapy was ineffective or was associated with unacceptable adverse effects.

For additional information on initial therapeutic guidelines related to the treatment of hypertension, see *Appendix III.*

Patient Consultation

As an aid to patient consultation, refer to *Advice for the Patient, Telmisartan and Hydrochlorothiazide (Systemic)*.

In providing consultation, consider emphasizing the following selected information (» = major clinical significance):

Before using this medication

» Conditions affecting use, especially:

Hypersensitivity to telmisartan and hydrochlorothiazide or any of its components

Hypersensitivity to any other sulfonamide-derived drugs

Pregnancy—When used during the second and third trimesters, drugs that act directly on the renin-angiotensin system can cause injury and even death to the developing fetus. When pregnancy is detected, telmisartan and hydrochlorothiazide should be discontinued as soon as possible.

Thiazides cross the placental barrier and appear in core blood. There is a risk of fetal or neonatal jaundice, thrombocytopenia, other adverse effects seen in adults.

Breast-feeding—It is not known whether telmisartan is distributed in human breast milk. However, telmisartan is distributed into the milk of rats. Because of the potential for adverse effects on the nursing infant, a decision should be made whether to discontinue nursing or discontinue the drug, taking into account the importance of the drug to the mother. Hydrochlorothiazide is distributed in breast milk.

Other medications, especially alcohol, barbiturates, diuretics, lithium, and narcotics

Other medical problems, especially anuria, severe congestive heart failure, systemic lupus erythematosus, renal function impairment and hepatic insufficiency

Proper use of this medication

» Compliance with therapy; taking medication at the same time each day to maintain the antihypertensive effect

Possible need for control of weight and diet, especially sodium intake; risks associated with sodium depletion; not taking potassium supplements or salt substitutes containing potassium unless approved by physician.

» Importance of taking medication even if feeling well; possible life-long therapy; checking with physician before discontinuing medication.

Medication may be taken with or without food.

» Proper dosing

Missed dose: Taking as soon as possible; not taking if almost time for next scheduled dose; not doubling doses

Proper storage

Precautions while using this medication

Visiting the physician regularly to check progress

» Notifying physician immediately if pregnancy is suspected

Not taking other medications without consulting the physician

Caution when driving, using machines, or doing other things that may be dangerous if dizziness, light-headedness or drowsiness occur while taking telmisartan and hydrochlorothiazide

To prevent dehydration and hypotension, checking with physician if severe nausea, vomiting, or diarrhea occurs and continues

» Caution should be taken when standing from a lying or sitting position.

Caution when exercising or during exposure to hot weather, because of the risk of dehydration and hypotension due to reduced fluid volume

Diabetics: May increase blood sugar levels

Side/adverse effects

Signs of potential side effects, especially angioedema, hypokalemia, tachycardia, urinary tract infection.

Oral dosage forms

TELMISARTAN AND HYDROCHLOROTHIAZIDE TABLETS

Usual adult dose

Antihypertensive—

Oral, initially one tablet containing 40 mg of telmisartan and 12.5 mg of hydrochlorothiazide once daily.

Note: The fixed dose combination is not indicated for initial therapy.

Usual adult prescribing limits

160 mg of telmisartan and 25 mg of hydrochlorothiazide once daily.

Usual pediatric dose

Antihypertensive—

Safety and efficacy have not been established.

Usual geriatric dose

See *Usual adult dose*.

Usual geriatric prescribing limits

See *Usual adult prescribing limits*.

Strength(s) usually available

U.S.—

40 mg of telmisartan and 12.5 mg of hydrochlorothiazide (Rx) [*Micardis HCT* (iron oxide red; lactose monohydrate; magnesium stearate; maize starch; meglumine; microcrystalline cellulose; povidone; sodium hydroxide; sodium starch glycolate; sorbitol)].

80 mg of telmisartan and 12.5 mg of hydrochlorothiazide (Rx) [*Micardis HCT* (iron oxide red; lactose monohydrate; magnesium stearate; maize starch; meglumine; microcrystalline cellulose; povidone; sodium hydroxide; sodium starch glycolate; sorbitol)].

Canada—

80 mg of telmisartan and 12.5 mg of hydrochlorothiazide (Rx) [*Micardis Plus* (iron oxide red; lactose monohydrate; magnesium stearate; maize starch; meglumine; microcrystalline cellulose; povidone; sodium hydroxide; sodium starch glycolate; sorbitol)].

Auxiliary labeling

May be administered with or without food.

Revised: 06/13/2002
Developed: 02/21/2002

TEMAZEPAM—See *Benzodiazepines (Systemic)*

TEMOZOLOMIDE Systemic

VA CLASSIFICATION (Primary): AN100

Commonly used brand name(s): *Temodal; Temodar.*

Note: For a listing of dosage forms and brand names by country availability, see *Dosage Forms* section(s).

Category

Antineoplastic.

Indications

Note: Bracketed information in the *Indications* section refers to uses that are not included in U.S. product labeling.

Accepted

Anaplastic astrocytoma of brain, refractory (treatment)—Temozolomide is indicated for treatment of adult patients with refractory anaplastic astrocytoma, i.e. patients who have experienced disease progression on an existing drug regimen containing a nitrosourea and procarbazine.

Glioblastoma multiforme of brain, newly diagnosed (treatment)—Temozolomide is indicated for the treatment of adult patients with newly diagnosed glioblastoma multiforme concomitantly with radiotherapy and then as maintenance treatment.

[Melanoma, metastatic (treatment)][1]—Temozolomide is indicated, as a single agent, for the treatment of metastatic melanoma, including metastases to the brain.

Acceptance not established

Use of temozolomide for the treatment of brain metastases of other solid tumors has not been established, due to insufficient data supporting safety and efficacy, low response rate as a single agent, substantial side effects, and an undefined role in combination therapy.

[1]Not included in Canadian product labeling.

Pharmacology/Pharmacokinetics

Physicochemical characteristics

Chemical Group—Imidazotetrazine derivative.

Molecular weight—194.15.

Temozolomide is a prodrug, which hydrolyzes to 5-(3-methyltriazen-1-yl)imidazole-4-carboxamide (MTIC) at neutral and alkaline pH values. MTIC is the active form of the drug.

Mechanism of action/Effect

Temozolomide is rapidly converted to the active form, MTIC. MTIC alkylates DNA at the O^6 and N^7 positions of guanine, and thus is cytotoxic.

Absorption

Rapid and complete absorption of temozolomide occurs in the gastrointestinal tract. Food reduces the rate and extent of absorption.

Distribution
Mean apparent volume of distribution (Vol_D)—0.4 L per kg of body weight (L/kg).

Protein binding
Low (15%).

Biotransformation
Temozolomide is non-enzymatically hydrolyzed to MTIC and temozolomide acid metabolite at physiologic pH. MTIC undergoes further hydrolysis to 5-amino-imidazole-4-carboxamide (AIC), which is an intermediate in purine and nucleic acid synthesis and to methylhydrazine, which is thought to be the active alkylating species. Cytochrome P450 enzymes constitute only a minor metabolic pathway in the metabolism of MTIC and temozolomide.

Half-life
Elimination—

Approximately 1.8 hours.

Time to peak plasma concentration
1 hour; doubles (to 2.25 hours) when administered after a high fat meal.

Peak plasma concentration
Decreased by 32% when administered after a high fat meal.

Elimination
Renal—Over 7 days, 37.7% of a temozolomide dose is recovered; 5.6% as unchanged temozolomide, 12% as AIC, 2.3% as temozolomide acid metabolite, and 17% as unidentified polar metabolite(s).

Fecal—Over 7 days, 0.8% of a temozolomide dose.

Precautions to Consider

Cross-sensitivity and/or related problems
Patients allergic to dacarbazine may be allergic to temozolomide; both drugs are metabolized to MTIC.

Carcinogenicity/Tumorigenicity
Patients treated with temozolomide may experience myelosuppression. Very rare cases of myelodysplastic syndrome and secondary malignancies, including myeloid leukemia have also been observed.

Male and female rats treated with 200 mg per square meter of body surface area (mg/m^2) of temozolomide (equivalent to the maximum recommended daily human dose) for 5 consecutive days out of every 28-day cycle for 3 cycles developed mammary carcinomas. Rats given 25, 50, or 125 mg/m^2 (equivalent to one eighth to one half of the maximum daily recommended human dose) for 6 cycles developed mammary carcinomas and malignant tumors in various organs and glands including the eyes, heart, prostate, salivary glands, seminal vesicles, and uterus. Adenomas of the lung, pituitary, skin, and thyroid were observed at the highest dose.

Mutagenicity
Temozolomide was mutagenic *in vitro* in the Ames assay and clastogenic in human peripheral blood lymphocyte assays.

Pregnancy/Reproduction
Fertility—Temozolomide can have genotoxic effects. Effective contraception should also be used by male patients taking temozolomide and they should not father a child for up to 6 months after treatment. In addition, males are advised to seek advice on cryoconservation of sperm prior to treatment because of the possibility of irreversible infertility due to therapy with temozolomide. Testicular toxicity has been demonstrated in rats and dogs given doses equivalent to one fourth and five eighths, respectively, of the maximum recommended human dose on a body surface area basis.

Pregnancy—Adequate and well-controlled studies have not been performed in humans. Due to potential hazard to the fetus, women of childbearing potential should be advised against becoming pregnant while taking temozolomideand in the 6 months after the treatment ends. Risk-benefit must be carefully considered when this medication is required in life-threatening situations or in serious diseases for which other medications cannot be used or are ineffective.

Administration of temozolomide for 5 consecutive days at doses of 75 mg/m^2 per day to rats and 150 mg/m^2 per day to rabbits (three eighths and three fourths of the maximum recommended human dose, respectively) resulted in malformations of the external organs, skeleton, and soft tissues in both species. Doses of 150 mg/m^2 per day administered to rats and rabbits resulted in an increased incidence of fetal resorptions.

FDA Pregnancy Category D.

Breast-feeding
It is not known whether temozolomide is distributed into human breast milk. Because many drugs are distributed into breast milk and because of the potential harm to an infant, nursing should be discontinued prior to temozolomide administration.

Pediatrics
Appropriate studies on the relationship of age to the effects of temozolomide have not been performed in children up to 3 years of age. Clearance and half-life values in pediatric patients 3 to 17 years of age are similar to those found in adult patients. Safety and efficacy have not been established.

Geriatrics
Studies performed to date have not demonstrated geriatrics-specific problems that would limit the usefulness of temozolomide in the elderly. However, elderly patients 70 years of age or older demonstrated a higher incidence of Grade 4 neutropenia and thrombocytopenia in the first cycle of therapy than did younger patients. Caution should be used when treating elderly patients.

Pharmacogenetics
Women have a lower clearance (approximately 5%) and higher incidences of Grade 4 neutropenia and thrombocytopenia in the first cycle of therapy than men.

Pharmacokinetic differences between different races have not been studied.

Dental
The bone marrow depressant effects of temozolomide may result in an increased incidence of microbial infection, delayed healing, and gingival bleeding. Dental work, whenever possible, should be completed prior to initiation of therapy or deferred until blood counts have returned to normal. Patients should be instructed in proper oral hygiene during treatment, including caution in use of regular toothbrushes, dental floss, and toothpicks.

Drug interactions and/or related problems
The following drug interactions and/or related problems have been selected on the basis of their potential clinical significance (possible mechanism in parentheses where appropriate)—not necessarily inclusive (» = major clinical significance):

Note: Combinations containing any of the following medications, depending on the amount present, may also interact with this medication.

» Blood dyscrasia-causing medications (see *Appendix II*)
(leukopenic and/or thrombocytopenic effects of temozolomide may be increased with concurrent or recent therapy if these medications cause the same effects; dosage adjustment of the bone marrow depressant, if necessary, should be based on blood counts)

» Bone marrow depressants, other (see *Appendix II*)
(additive bone marrow depression may occur; dosage reduction may be required when two or more bone marrow depressants are used concurrently or consecutively)

Vaccines, killed virus
(because normal defense mechanisms may be suppressed by temozolomide therapy, the patient's antibody response to the vaccine may be decreased. The interval between discontinuation of medications that cause immunosuppression and restoration of the patient's ability to respond to the vaccine depends on the intensity and type of immunosuppression-causing medication used, the underlying disease, and other factors; estimates vary from 3 months to 1 year)

» Vaccines, live virus
(because normal defense mechanisms may be suppressed by temozolomide therapy, concurrent use with a live virus vaccine may potentiate the replication of the vaccine virus, may increase the side/adverse effects of the vaccine virus, and/or may decrease the patient's antibody response to the vaccine; immunization of these patients should be undertaken only with extreme caution after careful review of the patient's hematologic status and only with the knowledge and consent of the physician managing the temozolomide therapy. The interval between discontinuation of medications that cause immunosuppression and restoration of the patient's ability to respond to the vaccine depends on the intensity and type of immunosuppression-causing medication used, the underlying disease, and other factors; estimates vary from 3 months to 1 year. Immunization with oral poliovirus vaccine should be postponed in persons in close contact with the patient, especially family members)

Valproic acid
(concurrent use decreases the clearance of temozolomide by 5%)

Medical considerations/Contraindications
The medical considerations/contraindications included have been selected on the basis of their potential clinical significance (reasons

given in parentheses where appropriate)—not necessarily inclusive (» = major clinical significance).

Except under special circumstances, this medication should not be used when the following medical problem exists:

» Hypersensitivity to temozolomide or any of its components or dacarbazine (DTIC)
(both drugs are metabolized to MTIC)

Risk-benefit should be considered when the following medical problems exist:

» Bone marrow depression (especially severe), existing
(patients treated with temozolomide may experience myelosuppression; geriatric patients and women have been shown to have higher risk of developing myelosuppression as shown in clinical trials; very rare cases of myelodysplastic syndrome and secondary malignancies, including myeloid leukemia, also observed)

» Chickenpox, existing or recent (including recent exposure) or
» Herpes zoster
(risk of severe generalized disease)

Hepatic function impairment, severe
(caution should be exercised)

» Infection

Renal function impairment, severe
(caution should be exercised; temozolomide has not been studied in patients with creatinine clearances less than 36 mL per minute per square meter of body surface area or in patients on dialysis)

» Caution should be used also in patients who have had previous cytotoxic drug therapy or radiation therapy.

Patient monitoring

» Absolute neutrophil count (ANC) and
» Complete blood count
(recommended prior to treatment and at periodic intervals during treatment; complete blood count should be performed 21 days after the first dose or within 48 hours of that day and at weekly intervals until recovery if the ANC falls below 1.5×10^9 cells/L and the platelet count falls below 100×10^9 cells/L; complete blood counts should be obtained weekly during concomitant temozolomide and radiotherapy treatment)

Side/Adverse Effects

Note: Many "side effects" of antineoplastic therapy are unavoidable and represent the medication's pharmacologic action. Some of these (for example, leukopenia and thrombocytopenia) actually are used as parameters to aid in individual dosage titration.

Very rare cases of myelodysplastic syndrome and secondary malignancies, including myeloid leukemia, have also been observed.

The following side/adverse effects have been selected on the basis of their potential clinical significance (possible signs and symptoms in parentheses where appropriate)—not necessarily inclusive:

Those indicating need for medical attention

Incidence less frequent or rare—occurring in up to 30% of patients

Amnesia; fever; hemiparesis or paresis (muscle weakness or paralysis on one or both sides of the body); ***infection; leukopenia or neutropenia*** (cough or hoarseness; fever or chills; lower back or side pain; painful or difficult urination)—usually asymptomatic; ***peripheral edema*** (swelling of feet or lower legs); ***seizures; thrombocytopenia*** (black, tarry stools; blood in urine or stools; pinpoint red spots on skin; unusual bleeding or bruising)—usually asymptomatic

Note: With *neutropenia*, the nadir of the neutrophil count occurs 28 (range 1–44) days after administration, returning to normal within 14 days of the nadir; cumulative myelosuppression has not been reported.

With *thrombocytopenia*, the nadir of the platelet count occurs 26 (range 21–40) days after administration, returning to normal within 14 days of the nadir; cumulative myelosuppression has not been reported.

Incidence not determined and indicating the need for medical attention—Observed during clinical practice; estimates of frequency cannot be determined

Anaphylaxis (cough; difficulty swallowing; dizziness; fast heartbeat; hives; itching; puffiness or swelling of the eyelids or around the eyes, face, lips or tongue; shortness of breath; skin rash; tightness in chest; unusual tiredness or weakness; wheezing); ***erythema multiforme*** (blistering, peeling, loosening of skin; chills; cough; diarrhea; fever; itching; joint or muscle pain; red irritated eyes; sore throat; sores, ulcers or white spots in mouth or on lips; unusual tiredness or weakness); ***opportunistic infections including: pneumocystis carinii pneumonia (PCP)*** (chest pain, cough, fever or chills, sneezing, shortness of breath, sore throat, troubled breathing, tightness in chest, wheezing)

Those indicating need for medical attention only if they continue or are bothersome

Incidence more frequent—occurring in more than 30% of patients

Constipation; headache; nausea and vomiting—may require antiemetic prophylaxis; ***unusual tiredness or weakness***

Incidence less frequent or rare—occurring in up to 30% of patients

Abdominal pain; anorexia (loss of appetite); ***anxiety; back pain; blurred or double vision; breast pain***—in females; ***confusion; cough; diarrhea; dizziness; drowsiness; dysphasia*** (difficulty in speaking); ***insomnia*** (trouble in sleeping); ***loss of muscle coordination; mental depression; muscle pain; paresthesia*** (burning or prickling sensation on the skin); ***pharyngitis*** (sore throat); ***sinusitis*** (runny or stuffy nose); ***skin rash or itching; urinary incontinence or increased urge to urinate; weight gain, unusual***

Overdose

For more information on the management of overdose or unintentional ingestion, **contact a poison control center** (see *Poison Control Center Listing*).

Up to 1000 milligrams per square meter of body surface area (mg/m²) or over 6.6 times the initial dose of 150 mg/m² has been taken as a single dose, resulting in expected effects of neutropenia and thrombocytopenia.

Clinical effects of overdose

The following effects have been selected on the basis of their potential clinical significance (possible signs and symptoms in parentheses where appropriate)—not necessarily inclusive:

Neutropenia (cough or hoarseness; fever or chills; lower back or side pain; painful or difficult urination); ***thrombocytopenia*** (black, tarry stools; blood in urine or stools; pinpoint red spots on skin; unusual bleeding or bruising)

Treatment of overdose

Monitoring—Hematologic evaluation including absolute neutrophil counts, and complete blood counts.

Supportive care—Antibiotic therapy, blood transfusions, colony-stimulating factors, intensive care, and platelet transfusions as necessary. Patients in whom intentional overdose is confirmed or suspected should be referred for psychiatric consultation.

Patient Consultation

As an aid to patient consultation, refer to *Advice for the Patient, Temozolomide (Systemic)*.

In providing consultation, consider emphasizing the following selected information (» = major clinical significance):

Before using this medication

» Conditions affecting use, especially:

Hypersensitivity to temozolomide or any component of the product or dacarbazine

Pregnancy—Use not recommended because of mutagenic, teratogenic, and carcinogenic potential; advisability of using contraception; telling physician immediately if pregnancy is suspected; waiting for 6 months after treatment before conception; consider possibility of sterility for males after treatment

Breast-feeding—Not recommended because of risk of serious side effects

Other medications, especially other blood dyscrasia-causing medications, other bone marrow depressants, or previous cytotoxic drug or radiation therapy

Other medical problems, especially chickenpox, existing blood marrow depression, herpes zoster, or infection

Proper use of this medication

» Importance of taking medication exactly as directed
» Probability of nausea and vomiting; importance of continuing medication despite stomach upset; taking the medication on an empty stomach or at bedtime to reduce nausea and vomiting

Taking medication at the same time each day in relation to meals

» Swallowing capsules whole with a full glass of water without chewing, crushing, or breaking open; avoiding contact with capsule contents if accidentally opened
» Proper dosing

Missed dose: Not doubling doses; checking with physician for instructions

» Proper storage

Precautions while using this medication

» Importance of close monitoring by the physician

» Importance of prophylaxis against pneumocystis carinii pneumonia (PCP) for all patients receiving concomitant temzolomide and radiotherapy for the 42 day regimen

» Avoiding immunizations unless approved by physician; other persons in patient's household should avoid immunizations with oral poliovirus vaccine; avoiding persons who have taken oral poliovirus vaccine or wearing a protective mask that covers nose and mouth

Caution if bone marrow depression occurs:

» Avoiding exposure to persons with infections, especially during periods of low blood counts; checking with physician immediately if fever or chills, cough or hoarseness, lower back or side pain, or painful or difficult urination occurs

» Checking with physician immediately if unusual bleeding or bruising; black, tarry stools; blood in urine or stools; or pinpoint red spots on skin occur

Caution in use of regular toothbrush, dental floss, or toothpick; physician, dentist, or nurse may suggest alternatives; checking with physician before having dental work done

Not touching eyes or inside of nose unless hands are washed immediately before

Using caution to avoid accidental cuts with use of sharp objects such as safety razor or fingernail or toenail cutters

Avoiding contact sports or other situations where bruising or injury could occur

Side/adverse effects

Signs of potential side effects, especially amnesia, fever, hemiparesis or paresis, infection, leukopenia or neutropenia, peripheral edema, seizures, and thrombocytopenia; importance of discussing possible effects with physician

Signs of potential side effects observed during clinical practice, especially anaphylaxis, erythema multiforme, opportunistic infections (including *pneumocystis carinii* pneumonia [PCP])

(Very rare cases of myelodysplastic syndrome and secondary malignancies, including myeloid leukemia, also observed)

Physician or nurse can help in dealing with side effects

General Dosing Information

Patients receiving temozolomide should be under supervision of a physician experienced in cancer chemotherapy.

A variety of dosage schedules and regimens of temozolomide are used. The prescriber may consult the medical literature as well as the manufacturer's literature in choosing a specific dosage.

Dosage must be adjusted to meet the individual requirements of each patient, on the basis of clinical response and degree of bone marrow depression.

Although in clinical trials temozolomide therapy was continued for up to 2 years, the optimum duration of therapy is not known. Therapy may be continued until disease progression occurs.

If marked neutropenia or thrombocytopenia occurs, temozolomide treatment should be postponed until neutrophil and platelet counts return to satisfactory levels.

Special precautions are recommended in patients who develop thrombocytopenia as a result of administration of temozolomide. These may include extra care in performing invasive procedures, regular inspection of intravenous sites, skin (including perirectal area), and mucous membrane surfaces for signs of bleeding or bruising; limiting frequency of venipuncture and avoiding intramuscular injections; testing urine, emesis, stool, and secretions for occult blood; care in use of regular toothbrushes, dental floss, toothpicks, safety razors, and fingernail and toenail cutters; avoiding constipation; and using caution to prevent falls and other injuries. Such patients should avoid alcohol and aspirin intake because of the risk of gastrointestinal bleeding. Platelet transfusion may be required.

Pneumocystis carinii pneumonia (PCP) prophylaxis is required during the concomitant administration of temozolomide and radiotherapy and should be continued in patients who develop lymphocytopenia until recovery from lymphocytopenia (common toxicity criteria grade ≤ 1). There may be a higher occurrence of PCP when temozolomide is administered during a longer dosing regimen. However, all patients receiving temozolomide, particularly patients receiving steroids should be observed closely for the development of PCP regardless of the regimen.

Patients who develop leukopenia should be observed carefully for signs of infection. Antibiotic support may be required. In neutropenic patients who develop fever, broad-spectrum antibiotic coverage should be initiated empirically, pending bacterial cultures and appropriate diagnostic tests.

Diet/Nutrition

Temozolomide may be taken with or without food. However, because food affects the rate and extent of temozolomide absorption, consistency of administration with respect to food is recommended.

Nausea and vomiting may be reduced by taking temozolomide on an empty stomach.

Safety considerations for handling this medication

Great care should be taken to avoid contact with or inhalation of capsule contents if capsules are accidentally damaged or opened, since temozolomide has been shown to cause the rapid appearance of malignant tumors in rats.

A number of medical centers have developed detailed guidelines for handling of antineoplastic agents; procedures for appropriate handling and disposal of temozolomide should be considered.

Oral Dosage Forms

Note: Bracketed information in the *Dosage Forms* section refer to categories of use and/or indications that are not included in U.S. product labeling.

TEMOZOLOMIDE CAPSULES

Usual adult dose

Note: Dosage of temozolomide capsules must be adjusted according to nadir neutrophil and platelet counts in the previous cycle and the neutrophil and platelet counts at the time of initiating the next cycle. For dosage calculations based on body surface area or suggested capsule combinations on a daily dose, see the manufacturer's package insert.

Anaplastic astrocytoma of brain, refractory (treatment)[1]—

Oral, initially, 150 mg per square meter of body surface area (mg/m^2) once daily for five consecutive days per 28-day treatment cycle. Dose may be increased to 200 mg/m^2 once daily for five consecutive days per 28-day treatment cycle if the nadir and Day 29, Day 1 of next cycle absolute neutrophil counts are ≥ 1.5 x 10^9 cells per L (1500 cells per microliter) and the nadir and Day 29, Day 1 of next cycle platelet counts are ≥ 100 x 10^9 cells per L (100,000 cells per microliter).

Note: If at any time during therapy the absolute neutrophil count falls below 1 x 10^9 cells per L (1000 cells per microliter) or the platelet count falls below 50 x 10^9 cells per L (50,000 cells per microliter), the dose for the next cycle should be decreased by 50 mg per square meter of body surface area but not to a dose less than 100 mg per square meter of body surface area, which is the lowest recommended dose.

Glioblastoma multiforme of brain, newly diagnosed (treatment)—

Concomitant Radiotherapy Phase: Oral, 75 mg per m^2 daily for 42 days concomitant with focal radiotherapy (60 Gy administered in 30 fractions) followed by maintenance temozolomide for 6 cycles. Focal radiotherapy includes the tumor bed or resection site with a 2 to 3 centimeter margin. No dose reductions are recommended during the concomitant phase; however, dose interruptions or discontinuation may occur based on toxicity. Temozolomide dose should be continued throughout the 42 day concomitant period up to 49 days if all the following conditions are met:

- absolute neutrophil count≥1.5 x 10^9 per L
- platelet count≥100 x 10^9 per L
- common toxicity criteria (CTC) non-hematological toxicity ≤ grade 1 (except for alopecia, nausea, and vomiting)

Temozolomide dosing should be interrupted or discontinued during concomitant phase according to the hematological and non-hematological toxicity criteria in the following table: *Table 1*

Toxicity	TMZ Interruption	TMZ Discontinuation
Absolute Neutrophil Count	≥0.5 and <1.5 x 10(9) per L	<0.5 x 10(9) per L
Platelet Count	≥10 and <100 x 10(9) per L	<10 x 10(9) per L
CTC Non-hematological Toxicity (except for alopecia, nausea, vomiting)	CTC Grade 2	CTC Grade 3 or 4

TMZ = temozolomide; CTC = Common Toxicity Criteria. Four weeks after completing the temozolomide plus radiotherapy phase, temozolomide is administered for an additional 6 cycles of maintenance treatment.

Maintenance Phase Cycle 1: Oral, 150 mg per m^2 once daily for 5 days followed by 23 days without treatment

Maintenance Phase Cycles 2 through 6: Oral, 200 mg per m² once daily if all the following conditions are met:

- absolute neutrophil count≥1.5 x 10^9 per L
- platelet count≥100 x 10^9 per L
- CTC non-hematological toxicity ≤ grade 2 (except for alopecia, nausea, and vomiting)

The dose remains at 200 mg per m² for the first 5 days of each subsequent cycle except if toxicity occurs. If dose was not escalated at Cycle 2, escalation should NOT be done in subsequent cycles. Dose should be reduced to 100 mg per m² once daily for prior toxicity. Dose reductions during the next cycle should be based on the lowest blood counts and worst non-hematologic toxicity during the previous cycle. Dose reductions or discontinuations during the maintenance phase should be applied according to the following table: *Table 2*

Toxicity	Reduce TMZ by 1 Dose Level	Discontinue TMZ
Absolute Neutrophil Count	<1.0 x 10(9) per L	See note below
Platelet Count	<50 x 10(9) per L	See note below
CTC Non-hematological Toxicity (except for alopecia, nausea, vomiting)	CTC Grade 3	CTC Grade 4

Note: Dose level -1=100 mg/m²/day (reduction for prior toxicity); Dose level 0= 150 mg/m²/day (dose during Cycle 1); Dose level 1= 200 mg/m²/day (dose during Cycle 2 to 6 in absence of toxicity); TMZ is to be discontinued if dose reduction to <100 mg per m² is required or if the same Grade 3 non-hematological toxicity (except for alopecia, nausea, vomiting) recurs after dose reduction.

[Melanoma, metastatic][1]—

As single-agent therapy, patients have benefited from oral doses of 150 to 200 mg/m² on Days 1 to 5 of a 28-day treatment cycle.

Usual geriatric dose

Anaplastic astrocytoma of brain, refractory (treatment) and Glioblastoma multiforme of brain, newly diagnosed (treatment) and [Glioblastoma multiforme, anaplastic, refractory]—

See *Usual adult dose*.

Note: Patients over 70 years of age may experience a higher rate of Grade 4 neutropenia and Grade 4 thrombocytopenia in the first cycle of therapy than younger patients.

Strength(s) usually available

U.S.—

5 mg (Rx) [*Temodar* (lactose anhydrous; colloidal silicon dioxide; gelatin; iron oxides; sodium starch glycolate; stearic acid; tartaric acid; titanium dioxide)].

20 mg (Rx) [*Temodar* (lactose anhydrous; colloidal silicon dioxide; gelatin; iron oxides; sodium starch glycolate; stearic acid; tartaric acid; titanium dioxide)].

100 mg (Rx) [*Temodar* (lactose anhydrous; colloidal silicon dioxide; gelatin; iron oxides; sodium starch glycolate; stearic acid; tartaric acid; titanium dioxide)].

250 mg (Rx) [*Temodar* (lactose anhydrous; colloidal silicon dioxide; gelatin; iron oxides; sodium starch glycolate; stearic acid; tartaric acid; titanium dioxide)].

Canada—

5 mg (Rx) [*Temodal* (lactose anhydrous; colloidal silicon dioxide; gelatin; iron oxides; sodium lauryl sulfate; sodium starch glycolate; stearic acid; tartaric acid; titanium dioxide)].

20 mg (Rx) [*Temodal* (lactose anhydrous; colloidal silicon dioxide; gelatin; iron oxides; sodium lauryl sulfate; sodium starch glycolate; stearic acid; tartaric acid; titanium dioxide)].

100 mg (Rx) [*Temodal* (lactose anhydrous; colloidal silicon dioxide; gelatin; iron oxides; sodium lauryl sulfate; sodium starch glycolate; stearic acid; tartaric acid; titanium dioxide)].

250 mg (Rx) [*Temodal* (lactose anhydrous; colloidal silicon dioxide; gelatin; iron oxides; sodium lauryl sulfate; sodium starch glycolate; stearic acid; tartaric acid; titanium dioxide)].

Packaging and storage

Store at controlled room temperature between 15 and 30 °C (59 and 86 °F).

Auxiliary labeling

- Swallow capsules whole with a full glass of water without breaking, chewing, or crushing.
- Take at the same time each day in relation to meals.

[1]Not included in Canadian product labeling.

Revised: 04/12/2005
Developed: 11/29/1999

TENOFOVIR Systemic†

VA CLASSIFICATION (Primary): AM840

Commonly used brand name(s): *Viread*.

Note: For a listing of dosage forms and brand names by country availability, see *Dosage Forms* section(s).

†Not commercially available in Canada.

Category

Antiviral (systemic).

Indications

Note: Bracketed information in the *Indications* section refers to uses that are not included in U.S. product labeling.

Accepted

Human immunodeficiency virus (HIV) infection (treatment)—Tenofovir is indicated, in combination with other antiretroviral agents, for treatment of HIV-1 infection.

Note: This indication is based on analyses of plasma HIV-1 RNA levels and CD4 cell counts in a controlled study of tenofovir of 24 weeks duration and in a controlled, dose ranging study of tenofovir of 48 weeks duration. Both studies were conducted in treatment experienced adults with evidence of HIV-1 viral replication despite ongoing antiretroviral therapy. Studies in antiretroviral naive patients are ongoing; consequently, the risk-benefit ratio for this population has yet to be determined.

There have been no studies to demonstrate the effect of tenofovir on the clinical progression of HIV.

[Hepatitis B virus (HBV) infection, chronic, in patients co-infected with HIV (treatment)][1]—Tenofovir is indicated, in combination with other antiretroviral agents, for the treatment of chronic hepatitis B virus infection in patients who are also infected with HIV. Tenofovir has been shown to be effective in reducing the viral load in patients with and without lamivudine-resistant HBV.

Note: When tenofovir is discontinued in patients who are co-infected with HBV and HIV, severe acute exacerbations of hepatitis B have been reported.

[1]Not included in Canadian product labeling.

Pharmacology/Pharmacokinetics

Physicochemical characteristics

Molecular weight—635.52.

pH—6.5

Partition coefficient—
1.25 at 25°C

Mechanism of action/Effect

Tenofovir disoproxil fumarate is an acyclic nucleoside phosphonate diester analog of adenosine monophosphate. Tenofovir disoproxil fumarate requires initial diester hydrolysis for conversion to tenofovir and subsequent phosphorylations by cellular enzymes to form tenofovir diphosphate. Tenofovir diphosphate inhibits the activity of HIV reverse transcriptase by competing with the natural substrate deoxyadenosine 5'-triphosphate and, after incorporation into DNA, by DNA chain termination. Tenofovir diphosphate is a weak inhibitor of mammalian DNA polymerases α, β, and mitochondrial DNA polymerase γ.

Absorption

Oral bioavailability of tenofovir in fasted patients is approximately 25%. Following a single oral dose of 300 mg, the area under the plasma concentration-time curve (AUC) is 2287 ± 685 nanogram*hours per mL.

Note: Administration of food (high fat meal containing 40 to 50% fat) increases the oral bioavailability, with an increase in the AUC of approximately 40%.

Distribution

Volume of distribution (Vol_D) at steady-state—1.3 ± 0.6 L per kg and 1.2 ± 0.4 L per kg, following intravenous administration of tenofovir at doses of 1 and 3 mg per kg of body weight, respectively.

Protein binding

Very low (Less than 0.7% to human plasma proteins; less than 7.2% to serum proteins).

Half-life

approximately 17 hours

Time to peak concentration
1 ± 0.4 hours following a 300-mg oral dose given in a fasted state.

Note: Administration of food (high fat meal containing 40 to 50% fat) delays the time to peak serum concentration by approximately 1 hour.

Peak serum concentration
296 ± 90 nanograms per mL.

Note: Administration of food (high fat meal containing 40 to 50% fat) increased the C_{max} by 14%.

Elimination
Renal—Following intravenous administration, approximately 70-80% of tenofovir is eliminated unchanged in the urine within 72 hours; following multiple oral doses of tenofovir 300 mg once a day (under fed conditions), 32 ± 10% of the administered dose is recovered in urine over 24 hours.

Tenofovir is eliminated by a combination of glomerular filtration and active tubular secretion. There may be competition for elimination with other compounds that are also renally eliminated.

In hemodialysis: Tenofovir is efficiently removed by hemodialysis with an extraction coefficient of approximately 54%. One four-hour hemodialysis session removed approximately 10% of a single 300-mg dose of tenofovir.

Precautions to Consider

Carcinogenicity
Liver adenomas were increased in female mice at exposures 16 times that in humans. The long-term carcinogenicity study was negative in rats at exposures up to 5 times that observed in humans at the therapeutic dose.

Mutagenicity
Tenofovir was mutagenic in the *in vitro* mouse lymphoma assay and negative in an *in vitro* bacterial mutagenicity test (Ames test). In an *in vivo* mouse micronucleus assay, tenofovir was negative at doses up to 2000 mg per kg of body weight (mg/kg) when administered to male mice.

Pregnancy/Reproduction
Fertility—There were no effects on fertility, mating performance or early embryonic development when tenofovir was administered at doses of 600 mg/kg per day to male rats for 28 days prior to mating and to female rats for 15 days prior to mating through day seven of gestation. There was, however, an alteration of the estrous cycle in female rats. A dose of 600 mg/kg per day is equivalent to 10 times the human dose based on surface area comparisons.

Pregnancy—Adequate and well-controlled studies have not been done in humans.

Studies have been done in rats and rabbits with administered doses up to 14 and 19 times, respectively, the human dose based on body surface area. There was no evidence of impaired fertility or harm to the fetus due to tenofovir.

FDA Pregnancy Category B.

Note: Physicians are encouraged to register patients in the Antiretroviral Pregnancy Registry, a registry set up to monitor maternal-fetal outcomes of exposure to tenofovir during pregnancy, by calling 800-258-4263.

Breast-feeding
It is not known whether tenofovir is distributed into human breast milk. However, it is distributed into the milk in lactating rats. In addition, the Centers for Disease Control and Prevention recommends that HIV-infected mothers refrain from breast-feeding their infants to avoid risking postnatal transmission of HIV. Breast-feeding is not recommended during therapy with tenofovir.

Pediatrics
No information is available on the relationship of age to the effects of tenofovir in the pediatric population. Safety and efficacy have not been established.

Geriatrics
Although appropriate studies on the relationship of age to the effects of tenofovir have not been performed specifically in the geriatric population, no geriatrics-specific problems have been documented to date. However, elderly patients are more likely to have age-related renal function impairment, which may require caution in patients receiving tenofovir.

Drug interactions and/or related problems
The following drug interactions and/or related problems have been selected on the basis of their potential clinical significance (possible mechanism in parentheses where appropriate)—not necessarily inclusive (» = major clinical significance):

Note: Combinations containing any of the following medications, depending on the amount present, may also interact with this medication.

» Atazanavir
(concurrent use of atazanavir and tenofovir may result in increased concentrations of tenofovir and decreases in the AUC and C_{min} of atazanavir; monitor patients for tenofovir-associated adverse events and administer atazanavir with ritonavir; discontinue tenofovir in patients who develop tenofovir-associated adverse events)

» Didanosine
(concurrent use of didanosine and tenofovir should be undertaken with caution; monitor patients closely for didanosine-associated adverse events; discontinue didanosine in patients who develop didanosine-associated adverse events)

Indinavir
(concurrent administration of 800 mg of indinavir three times a day for 7 days resulted in an average 14% increase in peak plasma concentration of tenofovir, and an average 11% decrease in the peak plasma concentration of indinavir)

Lamivudine
(concurrent administration of 150 mg of lamivudine twice daily for 7 days resulted in an average 24% decrease in the peak plasma concentration of lamivudine)

» Lopinavir and ritonavir combination
(concurrent administration of tenofovir with 400 mg of lopinavir and 100 mg of ritonavir twice daily for 14 days resulted in a 32% increase in AUC and a 51% increase in C_{min} of tenofovir)

Renally eliminated drugs, such as:
Acyclovir
Adefovir dipivoxil
Cidofovir
Ganciclovir
Valacyclovir
Valganciclovir
(concurrent administration of tenofovir with drugs that are primarily renally eliminated may increase serum concentrations of either tenofovir or the concurrently administered drug due to competition for this elimination pathway; drugs that decrease renal function also may increase serum concentrations of tenofovir)

Laboratory value alterations
The following have been selected on the basis of their potential clinical significance (possible effect in parentheses where appropriate)—not necessarily inclusive (» = major clinical significance).

With physiology/laboratory test results
Alanine aminotransferase (ALT [SGPT]) and
Aspartate aminotransferase (AST [SGOT])
(values may be increased)

Amino acids, urine
(may be increased)

Creatinine, serum
(may be increased)

Glucose, urine
(concentration may be increased)

Neutrophil count
(may be decreased)

Phosphate, serum
(may be decreased)

Phosphate, urine
(may be increased)

Protein, urine
(may be increased)

Medical considerations/Contraindications
The medical considerations/contraindications included have been selected on the basis of their potential clinical significance (reasons given in parentheses where appropriate)—not necessarily inclusive (» = major clinical significance).

Except under special circumstances, this medication should not be used when the following medical problem exists:
» Hypersensitivity to tenofovir

Risk-benefit should be considered when the following medical problems exist:
» Hepatic disease or

» Hepatic disease, risk factors for
(lactic acidosis and severe hepatomegaly with steatosis may occur in patients with liver disease or a predisposition toward liver dysfunction; fatal cases have been reported; treatment should be stopped in patients with evidence of lactic acidosis or hepatomegaly. Obesity and prolonged nucleoside exposure may be risk factors, however cases have been reported in patients with no known risk factors)

» Hepatitis B Virus infection
(the safety and efficacy of tenofovir have not been established in patients co-infected with HBV and HIV; severe acute exacerbations of hepatitis B have been reported when tenofovir is discontinued)

» Renal impairment
(tenofovir should not be administered to patients with renal insufficiency [creatinine clearance < 60 mL per minute] until data becomes available describing the disposition of tenofovir in these patients)

Patient monitoring
The following may be especially important in patient monitoring (other tests may be warranted in some patients, depending on condition; » = major clinical significance):

» Hepatic function
(should be monitored closely with both clinical and laboratory follow-up for at least several months in patients who discontinue tenofovir and are co-infected with HIV and HBV)

» Hepatitis B Virus
(all patients with HIV should be tested for the presence of chronic hepatitis B virus (HBV) before initiating antiretroviral therapy; tenofovir is not indicated for the treatment of chronic HBV infection and the safety and efficacy of tenofovir have not been established in patients co-infected with HBV and HIV)

Serum creatinine and
Serum phosphorous
(monitoring of signs of renal dysfunction should be considered in patients at risk or with a history of renal dysfunction)

Side/Adverse Effects
Lactic acidosis and severe hepatomegaly with steatosis, including fatal cases, have been reported with the use of nucleoside analogs alone or in combination with other antiretrovirals.

Although a causal relationship has not been established, accumulation and redistribution of body fat, including breast enlargement, central obesity, cushingoid appearance, dorsocervical fat enlargement (buffalo hump), facial wasting, and peripheral wasting, have been seen in patients receiving antiretroviral therapy. The mechanism and long-term consequences of these effects are not known.

It is not known if long-term (more than 1 year) use of tenofovir causes bone abnormalities. It is recommended that appropriate consultation be obtained if bone abnormalities are suspected.

The following side/adverse effects have been selected on the basis of their potential clinical significance (possible signs and symptoms in parentheses where appropriate)—not necessarily inclusive:

Those indicating need for medical attention
Incidence rare

Hepatotoxicity, including lactic acidosis (abdominal discomfort; decreased appetite; diarrhea; fast, shallow breathing; general feeling of discomfort; muscle pain or cramping; nausea; shortness of breath; sleepiness; unusual tiredness or weakness)

Note: *Hepatotoxicity*, consisting of *lactic acidosis* and severe hepatomegaly with steatosis, has been reported with nucleoside therapy (including tenofovir), alone or in combination. Fatalities have occurred. The majority of cases have occurred in women. Possible risk factors include obesity and prolonged nucleoside exposure, as well as other risk factors for liver disease, although cases have occurred in the absence of any known risk factors. Treatment with tenofovir should be discontinued if clinical or laboratory findings suggestive of lactic acidosis or pronounced hepatotoxicity (possibly including hepatomegaly and steatosis, with or without marked transaminase elevations) occur.

Incidence is not determined—Observed during clinical practice; estimates of frequency can not be determined

Allergic reaction (cough; difficulty swallowing; dizziness; fast heartbeat; hives; itching; puffiness or swelling of the eyelids or around the eyes, face, lips or tongue; shortness of breath; skin rash; tightness in chest; unusual tiredness or weakness; wheezing); ***dyspnea*** (shortness of breath; difficult or labored breathing; tightness in chest; wheezing); ***fanconi syndrome; hypophosphatemia*** (bone pain; convulsions; loss of appetite; trouble breathing; unusual tiredness or weakness); ***pancreatitis*** (bloating; chills; constipation; darkened urine; fast heartbeat; fever; indigestion; loss of appetite; nausea; pains in stomach, side, or abdomen, possibly radiating to the back; vomiting; yellow eyes or skin); ***proximal tubulopathy; renal failure or insufficiency*** (lower back or side pain; decreased frequency or amount of urine; bloody urine; increased thirst; loss of appetite; nausea; vomiting; unusual tiredness or weakness; swelling of face, fingers, lower legs; weight gain; troubled breathing; increased blood pressure); ***renal failure, acute*** (agitation; coma; confusion; decreased urine output; depression; dizziness; headache; hostility; irritability; lethargy; muscle twitching; nausea; rapid weight gain; seizures; stupor; swelling of face, ankles, or hands; unusual tiredness or weakness); ***tubular necrosis, acute*** (bloody or cloudy urine; difficult or painful urination; sudden decrease in amount of urine)

Those indicating need for medical attention only if they continue or are bothersome
Incidence more frequent

Asthenia (lack or loss of strength); ***diarrhea; nausea or vomiting***

Incidence less frequent

Abdominal pain; anorexia (loss of appetite; weight loss); ***flatulence*** (passing of gas)

Overdose
For more information on the management of overdose or unintentional ingestion, **contact a poison control center** (see *Poison Control Center Listing*).

Clinical effects of overdose
In one study, 600 mg of tenofovir disoproxil fumarate was administered to 8 patients orally for 28 days. No severe adverse reactions were reported. The effects of higher doses are not known.

Treatment of overdose
To enhance elimination—
It is not known whether peritoneal dialysis or hemodialysis increases the rate of elimination of tenofovir. However, given its pharmacokinetics, it would be expected that tenofovir would be removed by these techniques. It is unknown whether extracorporeal removal would change the clinical course or outcome after overdose.

Monitoring—
Monitor for evidence of toxicity.

Supportive care—
Treatment should be symptomatic and supportive.
Patients in whom intentional overdose is confirmed or suspected should be referred for psychiatric consultation.

Patient Consultation
As an aid to patient consultation, refer to *Advice for the Patient, Tenofovir (Systemic)*.

In providing consultation, consider emphasizing the following selected information (» = major clinical significance):

Before using this medication
» Conditions affecting use, especially:
Hypersensitivity to tenofovir
Breast-feeding—Not recommended because of the potential for postnatal transmission of HIV
Other medications, especially atazanavir, didanosine, or lopinavir and ritonavir combination therapy
Other medical problems, especially hepatic disease (or risk factors for), hepatitis B virus infection, or renal impairment

Proper use of this medication
» Compliance with therapy; importance of not discontinuing medication without checking with physician
» May be taken with or without food
» Importance of keeping amount of medication in blood constant
» Proper dosing
Missed dose: Taking as soon as possible; not taking if almost time for next scheduled dose; not doubling doses
» Proper storage

Precautions while using this medication
» Regular visits to physician to check progress
» Consulting physician immediately if symptoms of hepatotoxicity or lactic acidosis occur

Side/adverse effects
Signs of potential side effects, especially acute renal failure; acute tubular necrosis; allergic reaction; dyspnea; Fanconi syndrome; hepatotoxicity, including lactic acidosis; hypophosphatemia; pancreatitis; proximal tubulopathy; or renal failure or insufficiency

General Dosing Information

It is recommended that tenofovir therapy be withdrawn if clinical or laboratory findings suggestive of lactic acidosis or pronounced hepatotoxicity (possibly including hepatomegaly and steatosis, with or without marked transaminase elevations) occur.

The use of tenofovir should be considered for treating adult patients with HIV strains that are expected to be susceptible to tenofovir as assessed by laboratory testing or treatment history.

Diet/Nutrition

Tenofovir may be taken with or without food.

Oral Dosage Forms

Note: Bracketed uses in the *Dosage Forms* section refer to categories of use and/or indications that are not included in U.S. product labeling.

TENOFOVIR DISOPROXIL FUMARATE TABLETS

Usual adult dose

Human immunodeficiency virus (HIV) infection (treatment)—
Oral, 300 mg once a day.

Note: The dosing interval of tenofovir should be adjusted in patients with baseline creatinine clearance < 50 mL per minute.
- Creatinine clearance = 50 mL per min: oral, 300 mg every 24 hours
- Creatinine clearance 30 to 49 mL per min: oral, 300 mg every 48 hours
- Creatinine clearance 10 to 29 mL per min: oral, 300 mg twice a week
- Hemodialysis patients: oral, 300 mg every 7 days or after a total of approximately 12 hours of dialysis

[Hepatitis B virus (HBV) infection, chronic, in patients co-infected with HIV (treatment)][1]—
Oral, 300 mg once a day with a meal.

Usual pediatric dose

Safety and efficacy have not been established.

Usual geriatric dose

See *Usual Adult Dose.*

Note: Dose selection for elderly patients should be cautious because of the possibility of age-related renal function impairment.

Strength(s) usually available

U.S.—
300 mg (equivalent to 245 mg of tenofovir disoproxil) (Rx) [*Viread* (croscarmellose sodium; lactose monohydrate; magnesium stearate; microcrystalline cellulose; pregelatinized starch)].

Canada—
Not commercially available.

Packaging and storage

Store at 25 °C (77 °F), excursions permitted to 15 to 30 °C (59 to 86 °F).

Auxiliary labeling

- You should take this medicine exactly as prescribed. Do not skip or discontinue unless directed.

[1]Not included in Canadian product labeling.

Revised: 07/26/2004
Developed: 12/03/2001

TENOXICAM—See *Anti-inflammatory Drugs, Nonsteroidal (Systemic)*

TERAZOSIN Systemic

VA CLASSIFICATION (Primary/Secondary): CV150/CV409; GU900

Commonly used brand name(s): *Hytrin*.

Note: For a listing of dosage forms and brand names by country availability, see *Dosage Forms* section(s).

Category

Antihypertensive; benign prostatic hyperplasia therapy agent.

Indications

Accepted

Hypertension (treatment)—Terazosin is indicated in the treatment of hypertension.

For additional information on initial therapeutic guidelines related to the treatment of hypertension, see *Appendix III.*

Benign prostatic hyperplasia[1]—Terazosin is indicated in the treatment of symptomatic benign prostatic hyperplasia (BPH). It has been shown to improve urinary flow and symptoms of BPH. However, the long-term effects of terazosin on the incidence of surgery, acute urinary obstruction, or other complications of BPH have not yet been determined.

[1]Not included in Canadian product labeling.

Pharmacology/Pharmacokinetics

Physicochemical characteristics

Molecular weight—459.93.
pKa—7.04.

Mechanism of action/Effect

Terazosin has a peripheral post-synaptic alpha$_1$-adrenergic blocking action, which is thought to account primarily for its effects.

Hypertension—
Terazosin produces vasodilation and reduces peripheral resistance but generally has little effect on cardiac output. Antihypertensive effect with chronic dosing is usually not accompanied by reflex tachycardia. There is little or no effect on renal blood flow or glomerular filtration rate.

Benign prostatic hyperplasia—
Relaxation of smooth muscle in the bladder neck, prostate, and prostate capsule produced by alpha$_1$-adrenergic blockade results in a reduction in urethral resistance and pressure, bladder outlet resistance, and urinary symptoms.

Other actions/effects

Terazosin may affect serum lipids. The most consistent changes observed are a decrease in levels of serum total cholesterol and low density lipoprotein (LDL) cholesterol plus very low density lipoprotein (VLDL) cholesterol fraction. However, the implications of these changes are unclear.

Absorption

Rapid and nearly complete; not affected by food; minimal first-pass metabolism; bioavailability approximately 90%.

Protein binding

Very high (90 to 94%).

Biotransformation

Hepatic; four metabolites have been identified, one of which (the piperazine derivative of terazosin) has antihypertensive activity.

Half-life

Approximately 12 hours; does not appear to be significantly influenced by renal insufficiency.

Onset of action

Single dose—15 minutes.

Time to peak plasma concentration

Approximately 1 hour.

Time to peak effect

Single dose—2 to 3 hours.

Multiple doses—Up to 6 to 8 weeks.

Duration of action

Single dose—24 hours.

Elimination

Fecal (biliary)—40%.
Fecal (unchanged)—20%.
Renal—40% (10% unchanged).

Precautions to Consider

Carcinogenicity

Studies in rats for two years at doses of 250 mg per kg of body weight (mg/kg) per day (695 times the maximum recommended human dose [MRHD]) found an increase in benign adrenal medullary tumors in male, but not in female, rats. Studies in mice for two years at a maximum tolerated dose of 32 mg/kg per day found no oncogenic effect.

Mutagenicity

Both *in vivo* and *in vitro* tests (Ames test, *in vivo* cytogenetics, dominant lethal test in mice, *in vivo* Chinese hamster chromosome aberration test, V_{79} forward mutation assay) found no evidence of mutagenicity.

Pregnancy/Reproduction

Fertility—Testicular atrophy occurred in rats given 40 and 250 mg/kg per day for 1 to 2 years, but not in those given 8 mg/kg per day. Testicular atrophy also occurred in dogs given 300 mg/kg per day (more than 800 times the MRHD) for 3 months, but not in those given 20 mg/kg per day for 1 year.

Pregnancy—Adequate and well-controlled studies in humans have not been done.

Studies in rats given oral doses of 480 mg/kg per day (approximately 1330 times the MRHD) found an increased incidence of fetal resorptions. In offspring of rabbits given 165 times the MRHD, there were increased fetal resorptions, decreased fetal weight, and an increased number of supernumerary ribs. No teratogenicity occurred in either rats or rabbits in these studies.

In peri- and postnatal development studies with rats given 120 mg/kg per day (approximately 300 times the MRHD), postpartum death of pups was increased.

FDA Pregnancy Category C.

Breast-feeding

It is not known whether terazosin is distributed into breast milk. However, problems in humans have not been documented.

Pediatrics

Appropriate studies on the relationship of age to the effects of terazosin have not been performed in the pediatric population. Safety and efficacy have not been established.

Geriatrics

Although appropriate studies on the relationship of age to the effects of terazosin have not been performed in the geriatric population, clinical trials have included patients over 65 years of age and have not demonstrated geriatrics-specific problems that would limit the usefulness of terazosin in the elderly. However, the elderly may be more sensitive to the hypotensive effects of terazosin.

Drug interactions and/or related problems

The following drug interactions and/or related problems have been selected on the basis of their potential clinical significance (possible mechanism in parentheses where appropriate)—not necessarily inclusive (» = major clinical significance):

Note: Combinations containing any of the following medications, depending on the amount present, may also interact with this medication.

Anti-inflammatory drugs, nonsteroidal (NSAIDs), especially indomethacin
(indomethacin, and probably other NSAIDs, may antagonize the antihypertensive effect of terazosin by inhibiting renal prostaglandin synthesis and/or by causing sodium and fluid retention; the patient should be carefully monitored to confirm that the desired effect is being obtained)

Hypotension-producing medications, other (See *Appendix II*)
(antihypertensive effects may be potentiated when these medications are used concurrently with terazosin; although some antihypertensive and/or diuretic combinations are frequently used to therapeutic advantage, when used concurrently dosage adjustments are necessary)

Sympathomimetics
(antihypertensive effects of terazosin may be reduced when it is used concurrently with these agents; the patient should be carefully monitored to confirm that the desired effect is being obtained)

(concurrent use of terazosin antagonizes the peripheral vasoconstriction produced by high doses of dopamine)

(concurrent use of terazosin may decrease the pressor response to ephedrine)

(concurrent use of terazosin may block the alpha-adrenergic effects of epinephrine, possibly resulting in severe hypotension and tachycardia)

(concurrent use of terazosin usually decreases, but does not reverse or completely block, the pressor effect of metaraminol)

(prior administration of terazosin may decrease the pressor effect and shorten the duration of action of methoxamine and phenylephrine)

Laboratory value alterations

The following have been selected on the basis of their potential clinical significance (possible effect in parentheses where appropriate)—not necessarily inclusive (» = major clinical significance).

With physiology/laboratory test values

Albumin and
Total protein
(serum concentrations may be decreased)

Hemoglobin and hematocrit and
White blood cells
(serum concentrations may be decreased)

Medical considerations/Contraindications

The medical considerations/contraindications included have been selected on the basis of their potential clinical significance (reasons given in parentheses where appropriate)—not necessarily inclusive (» = major clinical significance).

Risk-benefit should be considered when the following medical problems exist:

Angina or
Cardiac disease, severe
(may induce angina or aggravate pre-existing angina)

Hepatic function impairment
(although studies in patients with impaired hepatic function have not been done, terazosin undergoes hepatic metabolism, and, therefore, increased sensitivity or prolonged terazosin effect may occur)

Renal function impairment
(approximately 40% of terazosin dose is eliminated by the kidneys as parent drug or metabolites; therefore, prolonged hypotensive effects may occur)

Sensitivity to terazosin

Patient monitoring

The following may be especially important in patient monitoring (other tests may be warranted in some patients, depending on condition; » = major clinical significance):

» Blood pressure measurements
(recommended at periodic intervals in patients being treated for hypertension; selected patients may be trained to perform blood pressure measurements at home and report the results at regular physician visits)

Side/Adverse Effects

Note: A "first-dose orthostatic hypotensive reaction" sometimes occurs, most frequently 30 minutes to 2 hours after the initial dose of terazosin, and may be severe. Syncope or other postural symptoms, such as dizziness, may occur. Subsequent occurrence with dosage increases is also possible. Incidence appears to be dose-related; thus, it is important that therapy be initiated with a 1-mg dose given at bedtime. Patients who are volume-depleted or sodium-restricted may be more sensitive to the orthostatic hypotensive effects of terazosin, and the effect may be exaggerated after exercise.

The following side/adverse effects have been selected on the basis of their potential clinical significance (possible signs and symptoms in parentheses where appropriate)—not necessarily inclusive:

Those indicating need for medical attention

Incidence more frequent

Dizziness

Incidence less frequent

Angina (chest pain); ***dyspnea*** (shortness of breath); ***edema, peripheral*** (swelling of feet or lower legs); ***orthostatic hypotension*** (dizziness or lightheadedness, when getting up from a lying or sitting position; sudden fainting); ***palpitations*** (pounding heartbeat); ***tachycardia*** (fast or irregular heartbeat)

Note: Rarely, weight gain (usually 1 kg [2 lb] or less) may occur with *peripheral edema.*

Those indicating need for medical attention only if they continue or are bothersome

Incidence more frequent

Asthenia (unusual tiredness or weakness); ***headache***

Incidence less frequent

Back or joint pain; blurred vision; nasal congestion (stuffy nose); ***nausea or vomiting; somnolence*** (drowsiness)

Overdose

For more information on the management of overdose or unintentional ingestion, **contact a Poison Control Center** (see *Poison Control Center Listing*).

Treatment of overdose

Recommended treatment for terazosin overdose includes: Treatment of circulatory failure, either by placing the patient in the supine position and elevating the legs or by using additional measures if shock is present, is most important; volume expanders may be used to treat shock, followed, if necessary, by administration of a vasopressor; symptomatic, supportive treatment and monitoring of fluid and electrolyte status.

Patient Consultation

As an aid to patient consultation, refer to *Advice for the Patient, Terazosin (Systemic)*.

In providing consultation, consider emphasizing the following selected information (» = major clinical significance):

Before using this medication

» Conditions affecting use, especially:
- Sensitivity to quinazolines
- Use in the elderly—Increased sensitivity to hypotensive effects
- Other medical problems, especially angina, severe cardiac disease, hepatic function impairment, or renal function impairment

Proper use of this medication

- Compliance with therapy; taking medication at the same time each day to maintain the therapeutic effect
- » Proper dosing
- Missed dose: Taking as soon as possible the same day; not taking if not remembered until next day; not doubling doses
- » Proper storage

For use as an antihypertensive
- Possible need for control of weight and diet, especially sodium intake
- » Patient may not experience symptoms of hypertension; importance of taking medication even if feeling well
- » Does not cure, but helps control hypertension; possible need for lifelong therapy; serious consequences of untreated hypertension

For use in benign prostatic hyperplasia (BPH)
- Relieves symptoms of BPH but does not change the size of the prostate; may not prevent the need for surgery in the future
- May require 2 to 6 weeks of therapy before patient experiences improvement of symptoms

Precautions while using this medication

- Making regular visits to physician to check progress
- » Caution if dizziness, lightheadedness, or sudden fainting occurs, especially after initial dose; taking first dose at bedtime
- » Caution when getting up suddenly from a lying or sitting position
- » Caution in using alcohol, while standing for long periods or exercising, and during hot weather because of enhanced orthostatic hypotensive effects
- » Possibility of drowsiness
- » Caution when driving or doing anything else requiring alertness because of possible drowsiness, dizziness, or lightheadedness
- » Not taking other medication, especially nonprescription sympathomimetics, unless discussed with physician

Side/adverse effects

Signs of potential side effects, especially angina, dizziness, dyspnea, orthostatic hypotension, palpitations, peripheral edema, and tachycardia

General Dosing Information

In order to minimize the "first-dose orthostatic hypotensive reaction," an initial dose of 1 mg is recommended, with gradual increments as needed. Administration of the initial dose at bedtime is recommended, as well as for the initial dose at each increment.

For use as an antihypertensive

Dosage of terazosin should be adjusted to meet the individual requirements of each patient, on the basis of blood pressure response.

Terazosin may be used alone or in combination with a thiazide diuretic or beta-adrenergic blocker, both of which reduce the tendency for sodium and water retention, although they also produce additive hypotension. If combination therapy is indicated, individual titration is required to ensure the lowest possible therapeutic dose of each drug.

When a diuretic or other antihypertensive agent is added to terazosin therapy, the dose of terazosin should be reduced, followed by titration of dosage of the combination. When terazosin is added to existing diuretic or antihypertensive therapy, the dose of the other agent should be reduced and terazosin started at a dose of 1 mg once a day.

For use in benign prostatic hyperplasia

Prior to initiation of terazosin therapy, the presence of prostate carcinoma should be ruled out, since prostate carcinoma can present with symptoms similar to those associated with BPH.

Oral Dosage Forms

TERAZOSIN HYDROCHLORIDE CAPSULES

Note: The dosing and strengths of the dosage forms available are expressed in terms of terazosin base (not the hydrochloride salt).

Usual adult dose

Antihypertensive—
- Initial: Oral, 1 mg (base) once a day, at bedtime.
- Maintenance: Oral, adjusted gradually to meet individual requirements, usually 1 to 5 mg (base) once a day.

Note: If the antihypertensive effect is not maintained for a full 24 hours, twice daily dosing may be more effective.

Geriatric patients may be more sensitive to the effects of the usual adult dose.

Benign prostatic hyperplasia[1]—
- Initial: Oral, 1 mg (base), at bedtime.
- Maintenance: Oral, adjusted gradually up to 5 to 10 mg (base) once a day. Doses of 10 mg once a day are generally required for an adequate response.

Usual adult prescribing limits

Daily doses higher than 20 mg (base) usually do not have increased efficacy.

Usual pediatric dose

Safety and efficacy have not been established.

Strength(s) usually available

U.S.—
- 1 mg (base) (Rx) [*Hytrin*].
- 2 mg (base) (Rx) [*Hytrin*].
- 5 mg (base) (Rx) [*Hytrin*].
- 10 mg (base) (Rx) [*Hytrin*].

Canada—
- 1 mg (base) (Rx) [*Hytrin*].
- 2 mg (base) (Rx) [*Hytrin*].
- 5 mg (base) (Rx) [*Hytrin*].
- 10 mg (base) (Rx) [*Hytrin*].

Packaging and storage

Store below 40 °C (104 °F), preferably between 15 and 30 °C (59 and 86 °F), unless otherwise specified by manufacturer.

Auxiliary labeling
- Do not take other medicines without your doctor's advice.
- May cause dizziness.

Note

Check refill frequency to determine compliance in hypertensive patients.

[1]Not included in Canadian product labeling.

Selected Bibliography

The fifth report of the Joint National Committee on Detection, Evaluation, and Treatment of High Blood Pressure (JNC V). Arch Intern Med 1993; 153(2): 154-83.

Revised: 08/19/1998

TERBINAFINE Systemic

VA CLASSIFICATION (Primary): AM700

Commonly used brand name(s): *Lamisil*.

Note: For a listing of dosage forms and brand names by country availability, see *Dosage Forms* section(s).

Category

Antifungal (systemic).

Indications

Note: Bracketed information in the *Indications* section refers to uses that are not included in U.S. product labeling.

General Considerations
Terbinafine has *in vitro* activity against yeasts and a wide range of dermatophyte, filamentous, dimorphic, and dematiaceous fungi. It is fungicidal against dermatophytes, such as *Trichophyton* species, *Microsporum* species, and *Epidermophyton floccosum*, as well as against *Aspergillus* species, *Scopulariopsis brevicaulis, Blastomyces dermatitidis, Cryptococcus neoformans, Sporothrix schenckii, Histoplasma capsulatum, Candida parapsilosis*, and *Pityrosporum* yeasts. Terbinafine has also been shown to be active *in vitro* against the protozoal organisms *Trypanosoma cruzi* and *Leishmania mexicana mexicana*. However, clinical efficacy has not been demonstrated in the treatment of infections caused by *B. dermatitidis, H. capsulatum, S. schenckii, C. neoformans, T. cruzi*, and *L. mexicana mexicana*. Also, terbinafine is only fungistatic against *Candida albicans*. Clinical studies have found terbinafine to be only moderately effective against skin infections caused by *Candida* species, with a mycological cure of only 65% after 2 to 4 weeks of treatment.

Accepted
Onychomycosis (treatment)—Terbinafine is indicated in the treatment of onychomycosis (fungal infection of the nails) caused by dermatophyte fungi.

[Tinea capitis (treatment)][1]—Limited data suggest that terbinafine may be used in the treatment of tinea capitis (ringworm of the scalp).

[Tinea corporis (treatment)]—Terbinafine is indicated in the treatment of tinea corporis (ringworm of the body).

[Tinea cruris (treatment)]—Terbinafine is indicated in the treatment of tinea cruris (ringworm of the groin; jock itch).

[Tinea pedis (treatment)]—Terbinafine is indicated in the treatment of interdigital or plantar tinea pedis (ringworm of the foot; athlete's foot).

Unaccepted
Terbinafine is not effective in the treatment of pityriasis versicolor because concentrations of oral terbinafine reached in the stratum corneum are not high enough to treat this condition adequately.

---

[1]Not included in Canadian product labeling.

Pharmacology/Pharmacokinetics

Physicochemical characteristics
Chemical Group—Allylamine class.

Molecular weight—Terbinafine hydrochloride: 327.9.

Mechanism of action/Effect
Terbinafine interferes with fungal ergosterol biosynthesis by inhibiting squalene epoxidase in the fungal cell membrane. This leads to a deficiency of ergosterol and an intracellular accumulation of squalene, thus disrupting fungal membrane function and cell wall synthesis, and resulting in fungal cell death.

Other actions/effects
Unlike azole antifungal agents, terbinafine does not inhibit cytochrome P450 activity and is only weakly bound to hepatic cytochrome P450, resulting in a low propensity for interference with cytochrome P450 enzymes involved in drug metabolism and synthesis of steroid hormones and prostaglandins. Terbinafine also has no effect on 14 alpha-demethylation.

Terbinafine's mechanism of action against protozoal organisms is thought to involve inhibition of sterol synthesis.

Absorption
Readily absorbed from gastrointestinal tract. Bioavailability is 70 to 80% and is not affected by the presence of food.

Distribution
Terbinafine is lipophilic and extensively distributed. It rapidly diffuses from the vascular system, passes through the dermis and epidermis, and concentrates in the lipophilic stratum corneum. It is also distributed via the sebum to hair follicles and sebum-rich skin, resulting in high concentrations in hair follicles, hair, sebum-rich skin, and the nail plate within the first few weeks of therapy. It is also highly distributed to adipose tissue. After 12 days of treatment, concentrations in the stratum corneum exceed those in plasma by a factor of 75 and concentrations in the epidermis and dermis exceed those in plasma by a factor of 25. Blood cells contain approximately 8% of administered terbinafine. Terbinafine is not detected in sweat.

Vol_D at steady state is approximately 948 L.

Protein binding
Very high (> 99%), with binding evenly distributed among all plasma fractions.

Biotransformation
Terbinafine undergoes first pass metabolism. It is extensively metabolized in the liver by N-demethylation of the central nitrogen atom, alkyl side-chain oxidation (alkyl oxidation), and arene oxide formation followed by hydrolysis to the corresponding dihydrodiol. Metabolism involves only a small fraction (< 5%) of total hepatic cytochrome P450 capacity. Fifteen metabolites have been identified, but none are active.

Half-life
Absorption—
- Approximately 0.8 hour.

Distribution—
- Approximately 4.6 hours.

Elimination—
- Plasma: 11 to 17 hours.
- Sebum: 3 to 5 days.
- Stratum corneum: 3 to 5 days.

Terminal—
- Sebum: 18 days.
- Plasma: 22 days, due to accumulation in adipose tissue and gradual release after discontinuation of treatment.
- Stratum corneum: 22 days.
- Hair and nails: 24 days.
- Dermis and epidermis: 28 days.

Time to peak concentration
Plasma—Approximately 2 hours. Steady state is reached in 10 to 14 days.

Stratum corneum—Maximum concentrations in the stratum corneum were found on Day 12 of treatment. However, terbinafine was detected in lower levels of the stratum corneum 24 hours after a single oral dose, and fungicidal concentrations were found across the whole of the stratum corneum within 7 days.

Nails—Detected in distal nail clippings as early as 3 weeks after the beginning of therapy. Fungicidal levels in nails were maintained for several weeks after discontinuation of therapy.

Peak serum concentration
Serum—0.8 to 1.5 mg per L (2.4 to 4.6 micromoles per L).

Nails—250 to 550 nanograms per mg, detected in toenails 3 to 18 weeks after starting therapy, with no progressive increase thereafter during the 48 weeks of therapy.

Elimination
Renal—Approximately 80% of an administered dose is excreted in the urine as metabolites.

Fecal—Approximately 20% is eliminated in feces.

Precautions to Consider

Carcinogenicity
An increase in liver tumors was observed in male rats at the highest dose level (69 mg per kg of body weight [mg/kg] per day) during a 123-week carcinogenicity study. Other changes included increased enzyme activity, peroxisome proliferation, and altered triglyceride metabolism. These changes were not seen in mice or monkeys.

Mutagenicity
In vitro and *in vivo* mutagenicity testing of terbinafine revealed no specific mutagenic or genotoxic properties. *In vitro* tests of cell transformation to malignancy were negative.

Pregnancy/Reproduction
Fertility—Fertility studies in animals suggest no adverse effects.

Pregnancy—Adequate and well-controlled studies in humans have not been done.

Fetal toxicity studies in animals suggest no adverse effects.

FDA Pregnancy Category B.

Breast-feeding
Terbinafine is distributed into breast milk. In 2 women, totals of 0.2 and 0.7 mg of terbinafine were detected in the breast milk after a single oral 500-mg dose in the ablactation period.

Pediatrics
No information is available on the relationship of age to the effects of terbinafine in pediatric patients. Safety and efficacy have not been established. However, terbinafine has been used to treat tinea capitis in a small number of children 3 to 16 years of age and was generally well tolerated.

Geriatrics
No information is available on the relationship of age to the effects of terbinafine in geriatric patients. However, elderly patients are more likely to have age-related renal function impairment, which may require an adjustment of dosage in patients receiving terbinafine.

Drug interactions and/or related problems
The following drug interactions and/or related problems have been selected on the basis of their potential clinical significance (possible

mechanism in parentheses where appropriate)—not necessarily inclusive (» = major clinical significance):

Note: Combinations containing any of the following medications, depending on the amount present, may also interact with this medication.

» Alcohol or
» Hepatotoxic medications, other (see *Appendix II*)
(severe hepatitis has been reported rarely with terbinafine; concurrent use of other hepatotoxic medications may increase the risk of hepatotoxicity)

Caffeine
(terbinafine was found to decrease the clearance of caffeine by 20%)

Cyclosporine
(Terbinafine increases the clearance of cyclosporine by 15%)

» Enzyme inducers, hepatic, cytochrome P450 (see *Appendix II*)
(because terbinafine is hepatically metabolized, medications, such as rifampin, that induce the cytochrome P450 system may increase the clearance of terbinafine)

» Enzyme inhibitors, hepatic, cytochrome P450
(because terbinafine is hepatically metabolized, medications, such as cimetidine, that inhibit the cytochrome P450 system may decrease the clearance of terbinafine)

Laboratory value alterations

The following have been selected on the basis of their potential clinical significance (possible effect in parentheses where appropriate)—not necessarily inclusive (» = major clinical significance).

With physiology/laboratory test values
Absolute lymphocyte counts (ALC)
(values may be transiently decreased.)

Alanine aminotransferase (ALT [SGPT]) and
Aspartate aminotransferase (AST [SGOT])
(values may rarely be transiently increased)

Complete blood count (CBC)
(isolated cases of severe neutropenia have been reported. if neutrophil count is less than or equal to 1,000 cells/mm^3 then terbinafine should be discontinued and supportive management started.)

Medical considerations/Contraindications

The medical considerations/contraindications included have been selected on the basis of their potential clinical significance (reasons given in parentheses where appropriate)—not necessarily inclusive (» = major clinical significance).

Risk-benefit should be considered when the following medical problems exist:

» Alcoholism, active or in remission or
» Hepatic function impairment or
Liver disease, chronic or acitve
(rare cases of liver failure, some leading to death or liver transplant have occurred; hepatoxicity has occured in patients with and without pre-existing liver disease; pretreatment serum transaminase tests (ALT and AST) are advised before starting treatment.)

» Hypersensitivity to terbinafine

» Renal function impairment
(the clearance of terbinafine was decreased by approximately 50% in patients with renal impairment [creatinine clearance ≤ 50 mL per min (0.83 mL per sec)]; the use of terbinafine is not recommended)

Patient monitoring

The following may be especially important in patient monitoring (other tests may be warranted in some patients, depending on condition; » = major clinical significance):

Clinical assessment
(a follow-up clinical assessment is recommended after terbinafine therapy has ended, to determine whether relapse has occurred; the timing of this assessment depends on the condition being treated; for tinea corporis, tinea cruris, and tinea pedis, it is recommended that the assessment be performed at 6 to 8 weeks following cessation of treatment, for onychomycosis of the fingernails, it is recommended that the assessment be at 4 to 6 months, and for onychomycosis of the toenails, it is recommended that the assessment be at 6 to 9 months following cessation of treatment)

Hepatic function determinations
(liver function tests (ALT and AST) are recommended before therapy, and periodically during terbinafine treatment, in all patients, especially in those with hepatic function impairment, alcoholic patients, or patients taking hepatotoxic medications concurrently)

Side/Adverse Effects

Note: Loss of taste has been reported rarely during terbinafine treatment, with the onset occurring 5 to 8 weeks after the start of therapy. This effect is reversible upon discontinuation of terbinafine, but recovery may take 2 to 6 weeks. There also has been one case of tongue discoloration associated with terbinafine.

The following side/adverse effects have been selected on the basis of their potential clinical significance (possible signs and symptoms in parentheses where appropriate)—not necessarily inclusive:

Those indicating need for medical attention

Incidence less frequent
Hypersensitivity (skin rash or itching)

Incidence rare
Hepatitis or hepatic failure (dark urine; fatigue; loss of appetite; pale stools; yellow eyes or skin); ***neutropenia*** (fever, chills, or sore throat); ***pancytopenia*** (fever, chills, or sore throat; pale skin; unusual bleeding or bruising; unusual tiredness or weakness); ***Stevens-Johnson syndrome*** (aching joints and muscles; redness, blistering, peeling, or loosening of skin; unusual tiredness or weakness); ***toxic epidermal necrolysis*** (difficulty in swallowing; redness, blistering, peeling, or loosening of skin)

Those indicating need for medical attention only if they continue or are bothersome

Incidence more frequent
Gastrointestinal disturbances (diarrhea; loss of appetite; nausea and vomiting; stomach pain, mild)

Incidence less frequent
Change of taste or loss of taste

Patient Consultation

As an aid to patient consultation, refer to *Advice for the Patient, Terbinafine (Systemic)*.

In providing consultation, consider emphasizing the following selected information (» = major clinical significance):

Before using this medication

» Conditions affecting use, especially:
Hypersensitivity to terbinafine
Breast-feeding—Terbinafine is distributed into breast milk
Other medications, especially alcohol, cytochrome P450 enzyme inducers and inhibitors, and other hepatotoxic medications
Other medical problems, especially alcoholism, hepatic function impairment, and renal function impairment

Proper use of this medication

May be taken with or without food
» Compliance with full course of therapy
» Importance of not missing doses and taking at evenly spaced times
» Proper dosing
Missed dose: Taking as soon as possible; not taking if almost time for next dose; not doubling doses
» Proper storage

Precautions while using this medication

Regular visits to physician to check progress during therapy

Checking with physician if no improvement within a few weeks (or months for onychomycosis)

Caution in drinking alcoholic beverages during terbinafine therapy

Reporting any signs of hepatic failure to physician immediately

Side/adverse effects

Signs of potential side effects, especially hypersensitivity, hepatitis, neutropenia, pancytopenia, Stevens-Johnson syndrome, and toxic epidermal necrolysis

General Dosing Information

Terbinafine may be taken with or without food.

To prevent relapse, therapy should be continued until the infecting organism is completely eradicated as determined by clinical or laboratory examination. Representative treatment periods are: onychomycosis, 6 weeks to 3 months; tinea corporis and tinea cruris, 2 to 4 weeks; and tinea pedis, 2 to 6 weeks.

Hepatotoxicity may occur in patients with and without preexisting liver disease and patients should be warned to report any symptoms immediately (persistent nausea, anorexia, fatigue, vomiting, right upper abdominal pain or jaundice, dark urine or pale stools). Terbinafine should be temporarily discontinued and the patient's liver function should be immediately evaluated.

Terbinafine is not recommended in patients with impaired renal function (creatinine clearance ≤ 50 mL per min [0.83 mL per sec]).

Oral Dosage Forms

Note: Bracketed uses in the Dosage Forms section refer to categories of use and/or indications that are not included in U.S. product labeling.

TERBINAFINE HYDROCHLORIDE TABLETS

Note: The dosing and strengths available are expressed in terms of terbinafine base.

Usual adult and adolescent dose

Antifungal—

Onychomycosis: Oral, 250 mg (base) once a day, for six weeks (for fingernail infections) to twelve weeks (for toenail infections). Some toenail infections may require longer therapy, depending on the extent of the infection.

[Tinea capitis][1]: Oral, 250 mg (base) once a day, for four to six weeks.

[Tinea corporis]: Oral, 250 mg (base) once a day, for two to four weeks.

[Tinea cruris]: Oral, 250 mg (base) once a day, for two to four weeks.

[Tinea pedis (interdigital or plantar)]: Oral, 250 mg (base) once a day, for two to six weeks.

Usual pediatric dose

Dosage has not been established. However, in one study the following doses were used in the treatment of tinea capitis in children 3 to 16 years of age—

Children 12.5 to 18.5 kg of body weight: Oral, 62.5 mg (base) once a day.

Children 18.5 to 25 kg of body weight: Oral, 125 mg (base) once a day.

Children more than 25 kg of body weight: Oral, 250 mg (base) once a day.

Strength(s) usually available

U.S.—

250 mg (base) (Rx) [*Lamisil*].

Canada—

250 mg (base) (Rx) [*Lamisil*].

Packaging and storage

Store below 40 °C (104 °F), preferably between 15 and 30 °C (59 and 86 °F), unless otherwise specified by manufacturer.

Auxiliary labeling

- Continue medicine for full time of treatment.

[1]Not included in Canadian product labeling.

Selected Bibliography

Balfour JA, Faulds D. Terbinafine. A review of its pharmacodynamic and pharmacokinetic properties, and therapeutic potential in superficial mycoses. Drugs 1992; 43(2): 259-84.

Revised: 06/27/2001

TERBINAFINE Topical

VA CLASSIFICATION (Primary): DE102

Commonly used brand name(s): *Lamisil.*

Note: For a listing of dosage forms and brand names by country availability, see *Dosage Forms* section(s).

Category

Antifungal (topical).

Indications

Note: Bracketed information in the *Indications* section refers to uses that are not included in U.S. product labeling.

Accepted

Tinea corporis (treatment)

Tinea cruris (treatment)

Tinea pedis, interdigital (treatment) or

Tinea pedis, plantar (treatment)—Terbinafine is indicated as a primary agent in the topical treatment of tinea corporis (ringworm of the body), tinea cruris (ringworm of the groin; jock itch), interdigital tinea pedis (ringworm of the foot; athlete's foot) caused by *Trichophyton rubrum, Trichophyton mentagrophytes,* or *Epidermophyton floccosum (Acrothesium floccosum),* and plantar tinea pedis (moccasin-type) caused by *T. mentagrophytes* or *T. rubrum.*

Tinea versicolor (treatment)—Terbinafine [cream] and solution are indicated for the topical treatment of tinea versicolor due to *Malassezia furfur (Pityrosporum orbiculare).*

[Candidiasis, cutaneous (treatment)]—Terbinafine cream is indicated for the topical treatment of yeast infections of the skin, principally those caused by the genus *Candida*, e.g., *Candida albicans.*

Pharmacology/Pharmacokinetics

Physicochemical characteristics

Source—A synthetic allylamine derivative.

Molecular weight—Terbinafine hydrochloride: 327.9.

Mechanism of action/Effect

May be fungicidal; inhibits squalene epoxidase (a key enzyme in sterol biosynthesis in fungi), which results in a deficiency in ergosterol and a corresponding increase in squalene within the fungal cell, causing fungal cell death. Also fungistatic; interferes with membrane synthesis and growth.

Absorption

Limited systemic absorption may occur; less than 5% of the topically applied terbinafine cream is absorbed.

Distribution

Terbinafine rapidly diffuses through the dermis and concentrates in the lipophilic stratum corneum.

Protein binding

Approximately 99% is bound to plasma proteins.

Half-life

Elimination—

The elimination half-life of topically absorbed terbinafine is approximately 21 hours.

Onset of action

Terbinafine cream has a rapid onset of action.

Elimination

Approximately 75% of topically absorbed terbinafine is eliminated in the urine, mostly as inactive metabolites.

Precautions to Consider

Cross-sensitivity and/or related problems

Patients sensitive to the oral form of terbinafine may be sensitive to the topical form also.

Carcinogenicity/Tumorigenicity

A 2-year carcinogenicity study in mice showed a 4% incidence of splenic hemangiosarcomas and a 6% incidence of leiomyosarcoma-like tumors of the seminal vesicles in males administered terbinafine orally in doses of 156 mg per kg of body weight (mg/kg) per day. A carcinogenicity study in rats showed a 6% incidence of liver tumors, which were associated with peroxisomal proliferation, increased enzyme activity, altered triglyceride metabolism, and skin lipomas in males administered terbinafine orally in doses of 69 mg/kg per day.

Mutagenicity

In vitro and *in vivo* genotoxicity tests, including Ames test, mutagenicity evaluation in Chinese hamster ovarian cells, chromosome aberration test, sister chromatid exchanges, and mouse micronucleus test, revealed no evidence of mutagenic or clastogenic potential of terbinafine.

Pregnancy/Reproduction

Fertility—Reproductive studies in rats administered terbinafine orally in doses of up to 300 mg/kg per day did not show any adverse effects on fertility. In addition, terbinafine in doses of 150 mg per day administered intravaginally to pregnant rabbits did not increase the incidence of abortions or premature deliveries and did not affect fetal parameters.

Pregnancy—Adequate and well-controlled studies in humans have not been done.

Terbinafine was not teratogenic when it was administered orally at doses of up to 300 mg/kg per day during organogenesis in rats and rabbits, administered subcutaneously at doses of up to 100 mg/kg per day in rats, or administered percutaneously at doses of up to 150 mg/kg per day in rabbits.

FDA Pregnancy Category B.

Breast-feeding

Terbinafine is distributed into breast milk after oral administration. However, it is not known whether terbinafine is distributed into breast milk after topical administration. Breast-feeding women should avoid applying topical terbinafine to the breasts.

Terbinafine was administered orally in single 500-mg doses to two breast-feeding women. The total amounts of terbinafine recovered in the breast milk during the following 72-hour period were 0.65 mg and 0.15 mg. These amounts corresponded to 0.13% and 0.03% of the administered dose, respectively.

Pediatrics

No information is available on the relationship of age to the effects of terbinafine in pediatric patients. Safety and efficacy have not been established in infants and children up to 12 years of age.

Geriatrics

No information is available on the relationship of age to the effects of terbinafine in geriatric patients.

Medical considerations/Contraindications

The medical considerations/contraindications included have been selected on the basis of their potential clinical significance (reasons given in parentheses where appropriate)—not necessarily inclusive (» = major clinical significance).

Risk-benefit should be considered when the following medical problem exists:

Onychomycosis

(patients with onychomycosis are less likely to have a favorable response to terbinafine therapy for plantar tinea pedis)

Side/Adverse Effects

The following side/adverse effects have been selected on the basis of their potential clinical significance (possible signs and symptoms in parentheses where appropriate)—not necessarily inclusive:

Those indicating need for medical attention

Incidence rare

Dryness, redness, itching, burning, peeling, rash, stinging, tingling, or other signs of skin irritation that were not present before use of this medicine

Overdose

For more information on the management of overdose or unintentional ingestion, **contact a Poison Control Center** (see *Poison Control Center Listing*).

Treatment of overdose

Acute overdosage with topical application of terbinafine hydrochloride is unlikely due to the limited absorption of the topically applied drug and would not be expected to lead to a life-threatening situation.

Patient Consultation

As an aid to patient consultation, refer to *Advice for the Patient, Terbinafine (Topical)*.

In providing consultation, consider emphasizing the following selected information (» = major clinical significance):

Before using this medication

» Conditions affecting use, especially:

Sensitivity to terbinafine

Proper use of this medication

If using cream, applying sufficient medication to cover affected and surrounding areas, and rubbing in gently

If using solution, applying sufficient medication to wet thoroughly the affected and surrounding areas, and letting it dry

» Avoiding contact with the eyes, nose, mouth, and other mucous membranes; the solution may be especially irritating to the eyes

Not applying the solution to the face

» Not applying occlusive dressing over this medication unless directed to do so by physician

» Proper dosing

» Compliance with full course of therapy; fungal infections may require prolonged therapy

Missed dose: Applying as soon as possible; not applying if almost time for next dose

» Proper storage

Precautions while using this medication

Discontinuing therapy and checking with physician if irritation or possible sensitization occurs while using the medication

Checking with physician if no improvement occurs after 1 week of treatment

» *Using hygienic measures to help cure infection and prevent reinfection:*

For tinea corporis

Carefully drying the body after bathing

Avoiding excess heat and humidity if possible; keeping moisture from accumulating on affected areas of the body

Wearing well-ventilated, loose-fitting clothing

Using a bland, absorbent powder once or twice daily; using the powder after the cream or solution has been applied and has disappeared into the skin

For tinea cruris

Avoiding underwear that is tight-fitting or made from synthetic materials; wearing loose-fitting cotton underwear instead

Using a bland, absorbent powder on the skin; using the powder between administration times for terbinafine

For tinea pedis

Carefully drying feet, especially between toes, after bathing

Avoiding socks made from wool or synthetic materials; wearing clean, cotton socks and changing them daily or more often if feet perspire excessively

Wearing sandals or well-ventilated shoes

Using a bland, absorbent powder between toes, on feet, and in socks and shoes liberally once or twice daily; using the powder between administration times for terbinafine

Side/adverse effects

Signs of potential side effects, especially, dryness, redness, itching, burning, peeling, rash, stinging, tingling, or other signs of skin irritation that were not present before use of this medicine

General Dosing Information

For cream dosage form

Improvement is gradual. In many patients treated with shorter durations of therapy (1-2 weeks), improvement may continue during the 2 to 6 weeks after completion of therapy. Patients should not be considered therapeutic failures until after the 2-to-6-week observation period. The patient's diagnosis should be reviewed if a successful outcome is not achieved by the end of the 6-week posttherapy period.

A gauze strip may be placed over the cream if intertriginous infections are present.

For solution dosage form

Relief of signs and symptoms usually begins within the 1-week treatment period. Continued improvement may occur over a period of 2 to 7 weeks after therapy has been completed.

Topical Dosage Forms

Note: Bracketed uses in the *Dosage Forms* section refer to categories of use and/or indications that are not included in U.S. product labeling.

TERBINAFINE HYDROCHLORIDE CREAM

Usual adult and adolescent dose

Tinea corporis or
Tinea cruris—

Topical, to the skin and surrounding areas, one or two times a day. Treatment should be continued for at least one week *and* until there is significant improvement in the clinical signs and symptoms of the disease. Treatment should not be continued beyond four weeks.

Tinea pedis, interdigital—

Topical, to the skin and surrounding areas, two times a day. Treatment should be continued for at least one week *and* until there is significant improvement in the clinical signs and symptoms of the disease. Treatment should not be continued beyond four weeks.

Tinea pedis, plantar—

Topical, to the skin and surrounding areas, two times a day. Treatment should be continued for two weeks. Treatment may be affected by the presence of onychomycosis. Patients with a toenail infection may be less likely to respond favorably to terbinafine therapy.

[Tinea versicolor]—

Topical, to the skin and surrounding areas, one or two times a day for two weeks.

[Cutaneous candidiasis]—

Topical, to the skin and surrounding areas, one or two times a day for one or two weeks.

Usual pediatric dose

Tinea corporis or
Tinea cruris or
Tinea pedis—

Infants and children younger than 12 years of age: Safety and efficacy have not been established.

Children 12 years of age and older: See *Usual adult and adolescent dose*.

[Tinea versicolor] or

[Cutaneous candidiasis]—
Safety and efficacy have not been established for these indications.

Strength(s) usually available
U.S.—
1% (Rx) [*Lamisil* (benzyl alcohol; cetyl alcohol; cetyl palmitate; isopropyl myristate; polysorbate 60; purified water; sodium hydroxide; sorbitan monostearate; stearyl alcohol)].

Canada—
1% (Rx) [*Lamisil* (benzyl alcohol; cetyl alcohol; cetyl palmitate; isopropyl myristate; polysorbate 60; purified water; sodium hydroxide; sorbitan monostearate; stearyl alcohol)].

Packaging and storage
Store between 5 and 30 °C (41 and 86 °F), unless otherwise specified by manufacturer.

Auxiliary labeling
- For external use only.
- Continue medicine for full time of treatment.

TERBINAFINE HYDROCHLORIDE SOLUTION

Usual adult and adolescent dose
Tinea corporis or
Tinea cruris—
Topical, to the skin and surrounding areas, once a day for one week. Treatment should be continued for at least one week *even though* symptoms of the disease may have improved.

Tinea pedis or
Tinea versicolor—
Topical, to the skin and surrounding areas, two times a day for one week. Treatment should be continued for at least one week *even though* symptoms of the disease may have improved.

Usual pediatric dose
Tinea corporis or
Tinea cruris or
Tinea pedis or
Tinea versicolor—
Safety and efficacy have not been established for these indications.

Strength(s) usually available
U.S.—
1% pump spray (Rx) [*Lamisil* (cetomacrogol 1000; ethanol 28.7%; propylene glycol; purified water)].

Canada—
Not commercially available.

Packaging and storage
Store between 5 and 25 °C (41 and 77 °F), unless otherwise specified by the manufacturer. Do not refrigerate.

Auxiliary labeling
- For external use only.
- Do not refrigerate.
- Continue using medicine for full time of treatment.

Selected Bibliography
Berman B, Ellis C, Leydon J, et al. Efficacy of a 1-week twice-daily regimen of terbinafine 1% cream in the treatment of interdigital tinea pedis. J Am Acad Dermatol 1992 Jun; 26(6): 956-60.

Revised: 03/04/1999

TERBUTALINE—See *Bronchodilators, Adrenergic (Inhalation-Local), Bronchodilators, Adrenergic (Systemic)*

TERCONAZOLE—See *Antifungals, Azole (Vaginal)*

TERFENADINE—See *Antihistamines (Systemic)*

TESTOSTERONE—See *Androgens (Systemic)*

TESTOSTERONE Systemic†

VA CLASSIFICATION (Primary): HS101

Note: Controlled substance classification
U.S.: Schedule III

Commonly used brand name(s): *Striant.*

Note: For a listing of dosage forms and brand names by country availability, see *Dosage Forms* section(s).

†Not commercially available in Canada.

Category
Androgen.

Indications

Accepted
Androgen deficiency, due to primary or secondary hypogonadism (treatment)—Androgens are primarily indicated in males as replacement therapy when congenital or acquired endogenous androgen absence or deficiency is associated with primary or secondary hypogonadism. Primary hypogonadism includes conditions such as: testicular failure due to cryptorchidism, bilateral torsion, orchitis, or vanishing testis syndrome; orchidectomy, Klinefelter's syndrome, chemotherapy, or toxic damage from alcohol or heavy metals. Hypogonadotropic hypogonadism (secondary hypogonadism) conditions include idiopathic gonadotropin or LHRH deficiency, or pituitary-hypothalamic injury as a result of tumors, trauma, or radiation and are the most common forms of hypogonadism seen in older adults

[Female-to-male transsexualism in patients with gender identity disorder]—Administration of testosterone was effective in producing male characteristics in female-to-male transsexual patients with gender identity disorder in open-label, time-series clinical trials. Significant improvements have been reported in body weight, body mass index, suppression of menses, and many secondary sex characteristics. Long-term effects of testosterone in these patients have not been extensively studied but one trial reports detrimental effects on cholesterol and triglyceride levels. The Harry Benjamin International Gender Dysphoria Association recommends the use of testosterone as a standard of care in appropriate individuals.

Pharmacology/Pharmacokinetics

Physicochemical characteristics
Molecular weight—Testosterone: 288.42.

Mechanism of action/Effect
Buccal testosterone delivers physiologic amounts of testosterone to the systemic circulation producing concentrations in hypogonadal males that are equivalent to the physiologic levels seen in healthy young men (300−1050 ng/dL). During exogenous administration of androgens, endogenous testosterone release may be inhibited through feedback inhibition of pituitary luteinizing hormone. With large doses of exogenous testosterone spermatogenesis may also be suppressed through feedback inhibition of pituitary follicle-stimulation hormone.

Absorption
When applied to the buccal mucosa testosterone is slowly released allowing absorption through gum and check surfaces that are in contact with the buccal system. Since venous drainage from the mouth is to the superior vena cava, trans-buccal delivery of testosterone circumvents hepatic metabolism.

Distribution
The distribution of bioactive and nonbioactive androgen is determined by the amount sex hormone binding globulin in the serum and the total testosterone level.

Protein binding
Moderate (approximately 40% to sex hormone-binding globulin); 2% remains free and the rest is bound to albumin and other proteins. However, the albumin-bound testosterone easily dissociates and is presumed to be bioactive, while the portion bound to the sex hormone-binding globulin is not considered biologically active.

Biotransformation
Testosterone is metabolized to 17-keto steroids through two different pathways. The major active metabolites are estradiol and dihydrotestosterone (DHT).

Half-life
Variable, 10 to 100 minutes.

Time to peak concentration
Within 10 to 12 hours.

Peak serum concentration
Within the normal physiologic range.

Elimination
Renal—about 90% excreted in urine as glucuronic and sulfuric acid conjugates of testosterone and its metabolites.
Fecal—about 6% unconjugated form.

Precautions to Consider

Carcinogenicity/Tumorigenicity/Mutagenicity
Studies done in rats and mice given testosterone by subcutaneous injection have suggested that in some strains of female mice there were increases in susceptibility to hepatoma. Testosterone is also known to increase the number of tumors and decrease the degree of chemically induced carcinomas of the liver in rats.
In patients receiving long-term therapy with high doses of androgens there were rare cases of hepatocellular carcinoma. Withdrawal of the drug did not lead to regression of the tumors in all cases.
Patients receiving testosterone for one year showed no cancer related to the drug. However, safety of patients beyond one year of therapy has not been established.
Studies done in rats and mice given testosterone by implantation showed that the implant induced cervical-uterine tumors, which in some cases metastasized.

Pregnancy/Reproduction
Pregnancy—Testosterone is not indicated for women and must not be used in women.
FDA Pregnancy Category X

Breast-feeding
Testosterone is not indicated for women and must not be used in women.

Pediatrics
Safety and effectiveness in pediatric male patients below 18 years of age have not been established.

Geriatrics
Appropriate studies performed to date have not demonstrated geriatrics-specific problems that would limit the usefulness of testosterone in the elderly. However geriatric patients treated with androgens may be at increased risk for development of prostatic hyperplasia and prostatic carcinoma. Geriatric patients with risk factors associated with prostate cancer should be evaluated for the presence of prostate cancer prior to initiation of testosterone replacement therapy.

Pharmacogenetics
Studies comparing the pharmacokinetics of testosterone in different racial groups or patients with compromised renal or hepatic function have not been done.

Drug interactions and/or related problems
The following drug interactions and/or related problems have been selected on the basis of their potential clinical significance (possible mechanism in parentheses where appropriate)—not necessarily inclusive (» = major clinical significance):

Note: Combinations containing any of the following medications, depending on the amount present, may also interact with this medication.

ACTH or
Corticosteroids
(caution, may enhance edema formation particularly in patients with cardiac or hepatic disease.)

» Insulin
(in diabetic patients, androgens may decrease blood glucose requiring insulin adjustments.)

Oxyphenbutazone
(concurrent use may result in elevated serum levels of oxyphenbutazone.)

Laboratory value alterations
The following have been selected on the basis of their potential clinical significance (possible effect in parentheses where appropriate)—not necessarily inclusive (» = major clinical significance).

With physiology/laboratory test values
Hematocrit or
Lipids (serum) or
Liver function test
(may increase)

Thyroxine-binding globulin
(may be decreased, resulting in decreased total T_4 serum concentrations and increased resin uptake of T_3 and T_4; free thyroid hormone levels remain unchanged, showing no clinical evidence of thyroid impairment.)

Medical considerations/Contraindications
The medical considerations/contraindications included have been selected on the basis of their potential clinical significance (reasons given in parentheses where appropriate)—not necessarily inclusive (» = major clinical significance).

Except under special circumstances, this medication should not be used when the following medical problem exists:

» Breast cancer in males or
» Prostate cancer, known
(use is contraindicated)

» Hypersensitivity to testosterone USP (that is chemically synthesized from soy) or any of its ingredients.

Risk-benefit should be considered when the following medical problems exist:

» Cardiac function impairment or
» Hepatic function impairment or
» Renal function impairment
(may cause fluid retention resulting in edema with or without congestive heart failure; in addition to discontinuation of testosterone, diuretics may be required.)

Diabetes mellitus
(blood glucose may decrease and insulin adjustments may be required)

Sleep apnea
(treatment with testosterone esters may potentiate sleep apnea especially those with risk factors such as obesity or chronic lung disease)

Patient monitoring
The following may be especially important in patient monitoring (other tests may be warranted in some patients, depending on condition; » = major clinical significance):

Cholesterol and
High density lipoproteins (HDL) and
Hepatic function determinations and
Prostate-specific antigen
(should be checked periodically)

Hematocrit determinations and
Hemoglobin
(should be checked periodically to detect polycythemia in patients on long-term androgen therapy.)

Prostate cancer surveillance
(should be consistent with current practices for eugonadal men)

Testosterone, total, serum
(maximum serum concentrations may be determined 4 to 12 weeks after initiating treatment with testosterone; in the rare circumstance where concentrations are in excess, therapy with testosterone should be discontinued and an alternative treatment considered.)

Side/Adverse Effects
The following side/adverse effects have been selected on the basis of their potential clinical significance (possible signs and symptoms in parentheses where appropriate)—not necessarily inclusive:

Those indicating need for medical attention only if they continue or are bothersome
Incidence more frequent

Gum or mouth irritation

Incidence less frequent

Abdominal cramp (stomach cramps); ***abnormal renal function; acne*** (blemishes on the skin, pimples); ***anxiety*** (fear; nervousness); ***asthma*** (cough; difficulty breathing; noisy breathing; shortness of breath; tightness in chest; wheezing); ***breast enlargement; breast pain; buccal inflammation; depression*** (discouragement; feeling sad or empty; irritability; lack of appetite; loss of interest or pleasure; tiredness; trouble concentrating; trouble sleeping); ***dry mouth; emotional lability*** (crying; depersonalization; dysphoria; euphoria; mental depression; paranoia; quick to react or overreact emotionally; rapidly changing moods); ***fatigue*** (unusual tiredness or weakness); ***gastrointestinal disorder*** (diarrhea; loss of appetite; nausea or vomiting; stomach pain, fullness, or discomfort; indigestion; passing of gas); ***gingivitis*** (bleeding gums; irritation in mouth; redness and swelling of gums; mouth ulcers); ***gum blister; gum edema*** (swelling of gums); ***gum pain; gum tenderness; headache; hypertension*** (blurred vision; dizziness; nervousness; headache; pounding in the ears; slow or fast heartbeat); ***infection*** (fever or chills; cough or hoarseness;

lower back or side pain; painful or difficult urination); ***liver function test abnormal; micturition disturbances*** (trouble in holding or releasing urine; painful urination); ***nausea; nose edema*** (swelling of the nose); ***pruritus*** (itching skin); ***stinging of lips; stomatitis*** (swelling or inflammation of the mouth); ***taste bitter; taste perversion*** (change in taste; bad unusual or unpleasant (after)taste); ***toothache***

Overdose

For more information on the management of overdose or unintentional ingestion, **contact a poison control center** (see *Poison Control Center Listing*).

Clinical effects of overdose

The following effects have been selected on the basis of their potential clinical significance (possible signs and symptoms in parentheses where appropriate)—not necessarily inclusive:

For testosterone enanthate

Cerebrovascular accident (blurred vision; headache; sudden and severe inability to speak; seizures; slurred speech; temporary blindness; weakness in arm and/or leg on one side of the body, sudden and severe)

Note: One report has described acute overdosage with testosterone enanthate. Testosterone concentrations of up to 11,400 ng/dL were implicated in a cerebrovascular accident.

Treatment of overdose

Supportive care—

Treatment should be symptomatic and supportive.

Patients in whom intentional overdose is confirmed or suspected should be referred for psychiatric consultation.

Patient Consultation

As an aid to patient consultation, refer to *Advice for the Patient, Testosterone (Systemic)*.

In providing consultation, consider emphasizing the following selected information (» = major clinical significance):

Before using this medication

» Conditions affecting use, especially:

Hypersensitivity to testosterone or any of its ingredients.

Hepatocellular carcinoma is associated with long-term therapy, with high doses of androgens

Fertility—Studies in animals given testosterone by implantation showed that the implant induced cervical-uterine tumors, which in some cases metastasized.

Pregnancy—Not recommended for use during pregnancy. Testosterone is not indicated for women.

Breast-feeding—Not recommended. Testosterone is not indicated for women.

Use in children—Safety and effectiveness in pediatric male patients below the age of 18 have not been established.

Use in the elderly—Elderly patients may have an increased risk of prostatic hyperplasia or prostatic carcinoma.

Dental—May increase possibility of moderate gingivitis, gum abnormalities, or mild gum edema

Other medications, especially insulin or oxyphenbutazone

Other medical problems, especially breast cancer in males, cardiac function impairment, hepatic function impairment, prostate cancer, or renal function impairment

Proper use of this medication

» Importance of reading the directions carefully before using the buccal system

» Proper administration technique

» Proper dosing

Missed dose: If the buccal system fails to properly adhere to the gum or should fall off during the 12–hour dosing interval, the old one should be removed and a new buccal system applied. If the old one falls out within 4 hours prior to the next dose, a new system should be applied and it may remain in place until the time of the next regularly scheduled dosing; not doubling doses.

» Proper storage

Precautions while using this medication

» Regular visits to physician to check progress during therapy

» Reporting too frequent or persistent erections of the penis

» Reporting nausea, vomiting, changes in skin color or swelling of the ankles

» Reporting breathing disturbances, including those associated with sleep

» Regularly inspecting the gum region where the buccal system is applied and reporting any abnormalities to a healthcare professional.

» Diabetics: May decrease blood glucose and therefore insulin requirements

General Dosing Information

For buccal dosing forms:

The dosing schedule for testosterone is one buccal application twice daily (morning and evening) to the gum region.

Testosterone should be positioned just above the incisor tooth on either side of the mouth, alternating sides with each application.

The buccal application should be placed rounded side against the gum, held in place with a finger over the lip against the product for 30 seconds to ensure adhesion.

If the buccal system fails to properly adhere to the gum or should fall off during the 12–hour dosing interval, the old one should be removed and a new buccal system applied. If the old one falls out within 4 hours prior to the next dose, a new system should be applied and it may remain in place until the time of the next regularly scheduled dosing.

Patients should take care to avoid dislodging the buccal system, and check regularly to see if it is in place especially after brushing, eating and drinking.

To remove the buccal system gently slide it downwards from the gum toward the tooth, careful to avoid scratching the gum.

It is recommended that patients frequently inspect their own gum region where the buccal system is applied and promptly report any abnormal findings to their physician.

Damaged blister packs should not be used.

Buccal Dosage Forms

TESTOSTERONE BUCCAL SYSTEM USP

Usual adult dose

Androgen deficiency, due to primary or secondary hypogonadism—

Buccal, one buccal system (30 mg) applied to the gum region twice daily, morning and evening (about 12 hours apart)

Usual pediatric dose

Safety and effectiveness in pediatric male patients below the age of 18 years have not been established.

Usual geriatric dose

See *Usual adult dose.*

Strength(s) usually available

U.S.—

30 mg of testosterone per buccal application (Rx) [*Striant* (anhydrous lactose NF; carbomer 934P; hypomellose USP; magnesium stearate NF; lactose monohydrate NF; polycarbophil USP; colloidal silicon dioxide NF; starch NF; talc USP)].

Canada—

Not commercially available

Packaging and storage

Store between 20 and 25 °C (68 and 77 °F), in a tight container. Protect from heat and moisture.

Testosterone is supplied in transparent blister packages. Each package contains 6 blister packs, with 10 buccal systems per blister pack, and 30 mg testosterone per buccal system.

Auxiliary labeling

- Do not chew or swallow
- Dispose of properly. Discard away from children and pets.

Note

Controlled substance in the U.S.

Revised: 07/19/2006
Developed: 05/17/2004

TETANUS AND DIPHTHERIA TOXOIDS (TD)—See *Diphtheria and Tetanus Toxoids (Systemic)*

TETANUS IMMUNE GLOBULIN Systemic

VA CLASSIFICATION (Primary): IM402

Note: This monograph is specific to the sterile solution of tetanus immune globulin prepared from large pools of plasma obtained from individuals immunized with tetanus toxoid.

Commonly used brand name(s): *BayTet*.

Another commonly used name is TIG.

Note: For a listing of dosage forms and brand names by country availability, see *Dosage Forms* section(s).

Category

Immunizing agent (passive).

Indications

General Considerations

Tetanus (lockjaw) is a neurologic disease charcterized by severe muscular spasms. It is caused by the neurotoxin produced by the anaerobic bacterium *Clostridium tetani* in a contaminated wound. Onset is gradual, occurring over 1 to 7 days, and progresses to severe generalized muscle spasms (severe enough to cause spinal fractures), which frequently are aggravated by any external stimulus. Severe spasms persist for 1 week or more and subside in a period of weeks in those who recover. Neonatal tetanus, a common cause of neonatal mortality in developing countries but rare in the U.S., is caused by contamination of the umbilical stump. Local tetanus is manifested by local muscle spasms in areas contiguous to a wound infected with *Clostridium tetani*.

Wound cleaning, debridement when indicated, and proper immunization are important in the prevention and management of tetanus. The need for tetanus toxoid (active immunization), with or without tetanus immune globulin (passive immunization), depends on both the condition of the wound and the patient's vaccination history.

Determining whether the wound is clean or dirty is extremely important in categorizing patients. A wound is considered to be dirty if it is more than 6 hours old, if there is debris in the wound, if the wound is penetrating or deep, if the instrument that caused the wound is contaminated, if the wound is infected, if the wound is caused by a deep partial- or full-thickness burn, or if it is a crush injury.

A thorough attempt must be made to determine whether a patient has completed primary vaccination. Patients with unknown or uncertain previous vaccination histories should be considered to have had no previous tetanus toxoid doses. Patients who have not completed a primary series may require tetanus toxoid and passive immunization with tetanus immune globulin at the time of wound cleaning and debridement.

Tetanus immune globulin provides protection for a longer time than does antitoxin of animal origin, and causes fewer adverse reactions. Therefore, if passive immunization is needed, tetanus immune globulin is the product of choice.

A recent U.S. serologic survey of tetanus immunity indicated that in the majority of the population, tetanus immunity decreases with time after the recipient's most recent vaccination. If a contraindication to using tetanus toxoid–containing preparations exists for a person who has not completed a primary series of tetanus toxoid immunizations and that person has a wound that is neither clean nor minor, only passive immunization should be given, using tetanus immune globulin.

In the U.S., tetanus is primarily a disease of older adults. Of the 99 tetanus patients with complete information reported to the Centers for Disease Control and Prevention (CDC) during 1987 and 1988, 68% were 50 years of age or older. The age distribution of recent cases and the results of serosurveys indicate that many U.S. adults are not protected against tetanus.

Accepted

Clostridium tetani infection (prophylaxis)—Tetanus immune globulin is indicated for prophylaxis against *C. tetani* infection, and the severe complications that arise from the toxins produced by *C. tetani*, following injury in patients whose immune status against tetanus is uncertain or incomplete.

Pharmacology/Pharmacokinetics

Physicochemical characteristics

Source—Tetanus immune globulin is a sterile solution of tetanus hyperimmune immunoglobulin, primarily immunoglobulin G (IgG), containing 15 to 18% protein, of which not less than 90% is gamma globulin. Tetanus immune globulin is prepared from large pools of plasma obtained from individuals immunized with tetanus toxoid. Tetanus immune globulin is stabilized with 0.21 to 0.32 molar glycine and contains no preservative. Tetanus immune globulin is standardized against the U.S. standard antitoxin and the U.S. control tetanus toxin and contains not less than 250 tetanus antitoxin units per vial.

pH—Adjusted to between 6.4 and 7.2 with sodium carbonate or acetic acid.

Mechanism of action/Effect

Following intramuscular injection, tetanus immune globulin provides immunity to those individuals who have low or no immunity to the toxin produced by the tetanus organism, *Clostridium tetani*. The antibodies act to neutralize the free form of the powerful exotoxin, tetanospasmin, produced by this bacterium.

Protective effect

Therapeutic passive immunization with tetanus immune globulin decreases fatalities in humans. While the therapeutic dose of tetanus immune globulin does not prevent the effects of toxin already bound to the nerve tissue, it should be given promptly because it may modify the course of toxin that has not yet been bound and later may cause symptoms.

Time to protective effect

Peak blood concentrations of immunoglobulin G (IgG) are obtained approximately 2 days after intramuscular injection.

Duration of protective effect

Short; the half-life of IgG in the circulation of individuals with normal IgG concentrations is approximately 23 days.

Precautions to Consider

Pregnancy/Reproduction

Pregnancy—Studies have not been done in humans. However, there is no evidence to suspect that tetanus immune globulin causes problems in pregnant women.

Studies have not been done in animals.

FDA Pregnancy Category C.

Breast-feeding

It is not known whether tetanus immune globulin is distributed into breast milk. However, problems in humans have not been documented.

Pediatrics

Appropriate studies on the relationship of age to the effects of tetanus immune globulin have not been performed in the pediatric population. However, pediatrics-specific problems that would limit the usefulness of tetanus immune globulin in children are not expected.

Geriatrics

No information is available on the relationship of age to the effects of tetanus immune globulin in geriatric patients. However, there is no evidence that increasing age enhances the risk or diminishes the efficacy of tetanus immune globulin, or that its effects differ from those in younger persons.

Drug interactions and/or related problems

The following drug interactions and/or related problems have been selected on the basis of their potential clinical significance (possible mechanism in parentheses where appropriate)—not necessarily inclusive (» = major clinical significance):

Note: Combinations containing any of the following medications, depending on the amount present, may also interact with this medication.

Live virus vaccines
(antibodies in immunoglobulin preparations may interfere with the response to live virus vaccines such as measles, oral poliovirus, and rubella; use of live virus vaccines should be deferred until approximately 3 months after tetanus immune globulin administration; the effect of immune globulin preparations on the response to mumps and varicella vaccines is unknown, but commercial immune globulin preparations contain antibodies to these viruses)

Medical considerations/Contraindications

The medical considerations/contraindications included have been selected on the basis of their potential clinical significance (reasons given in parentheses where appropriate)—not necessarily inclusive (» = major clinical significance).

Risk-benefit should be considered when the following medical problem exists:

Sensitivity to tetanus immune globulin

Side/Adverse Effects

Note: Sensitization to repeated injections of human immunoglobulin preparations is extremely rare, even though slight soreness at the site of injection and slight temperature elevation may be noted at times.

In the course of routine injections of large numbers of persons with immunoglobulin preparations, there have been a few isolated occurrences of angioneuropathic edema, nephrotic syndrome, and anaphylactic shock after injection.

The following side/adverse effects have been selected on the basis of their potential clinical significance (possible signs and symptoms in parentheses where appropriate)—not necessarily inclusive:

Those indicating need for medical attention

Incidence rare

Anaphylactic reaction (difficulty in breathing or swallowing; hives; itching, especially of soles or palms; reddening of skin, especially around ears; swelling of eyes, face, or inside of nose; unusual tiredness or weakness, sudden and severe)

Patient Consultation

As an aid to patient consultation, refer to *Advice for the Patient, Tetanus Immune Globulin (Systemic).*

In providing consultation, consider emphasizing the following selected information (» = major clinical significance):

Before receiving this medication

» Conditions affecting use, especially:

Sensitivity to tetanus immune globulin

Proper use of this medication

» Proper dosing

Side/adverse effects

Signs of potential side effects, especially anaphylactic reaction

General Dosing Information

Skin tests for allergy should not be performed prior to administration of tetanus immune globulin. The intradermal injection of concentrated immunoglobulin G (IgG) solution often causes localized inflammation due to tissue irritation, which can be misinterpreted as a positive allergic reaction. True allergic responses to human IgG are rare.

Although systemic reactions to human immunoglobulin preparations are rare, appropriate precautions should be taken prior to tetanus immune globulin injection to prevent allergic or other unwanted reactions. These should include review of the patient's history regarding possible sensitivity and the ready availability of epinephrine 1:1000 and other appropriate agents used to control immediate allergic reactions.

Tetanus immune globulin is administered intramuscularly. The preferred sites for intramuscular injections are the anterolateral aspect of the upper thigh and the deltoid muscle of the upper arm. It should not be injected intravenously. Intravenous injection of immune globulin intended for intramuscular use can, on occasion, cause a rapid fall in blood pressure. Therefore, injections should only be made intramuscularly; care should be taken to draw back on the plunger of the syringe before injection in order to be certain that the needle is not in a blood vessel.

It is important to convey immediate passive protection against tetanus, and at the same time begin formation of tetanus antibodies in the injured individual in order to preclude future need for antitoxin. Passive immunization with tetanus immune globulin may be undertaken simultaneously with active immunization using tetanus toxoid in those persons who must receive an immediate injection of tetanus immune globulin and in whom it is desirable to begin or continue (for those patients who have had only one dose of tetanus toxoid) the process of active immunization.

Since tetanus is actually a local infection, proper initial wound care is of paramount importance. The use of tetanus immune globulin is an adjunct to treatment of the wound. However, in approximately 10% of recent tetanus cases, no wound or other break in the skin or mucous membranes could be implicated. Current recommendations for wound management of patients definitely known to have completed a full tetanus toxoid series indicate only a booster dose of tetanus toxoid if more than 5 to 10 years have elapsed since the last dose of toxoid.

Tetanus immune globulin does not interfere with the immune response to tetanus toxoid. However, the two injections should not be given in the same syringe or injected at the same site, since neutralization of the toxoid may occur.

The optimum therapeutic dose for the treatment of tetanus infection has not been established. However, the Committee on Infectious Diseases of the American Academy of Pediatrics (AAP) recommends a single dose of 3000 to 6000 units of tetanus immune globulin for the treatment of tetanus infection.

Antibodies in immune globulin preparations may interfere with the response to live virus vaccines such as oral poliovirus, and rubella. Therefore, use of live virus vaccines should be deferred until approximately 3 months after tetanus immune globulin administration. The concurrent administration of tetanus immune globulin should not interfere with the immune response to oral typhoid vaccine.

Recent evidence suggests high doses of immune globulin can inhibit the immune response to measles vaccine for more than 3 months after administration. Administration of immune globulin can also inhibit the response to rubella vaccine. The effect of immune globulin preparations on the response to mumps and varicella vaccines is unknown, but commercial immune globulin preparations contain antibodies to these viruses.

Blood-containing products, such as immune globulins, can diminish the immune response to measles, mumps, and rubella virus vaccine live or its individual component vaccines. Therefore, after an immune globulin preparation is received, these vaccines should not be administered before the recommended interval. However, the postpartum vaccination of rubella-susceptible women with rubella virus vaccine live or measles, mumps, and rubella virus vaccine live should not be delayed because immune globulin was received during the last trimester of pregnancy or at delivery. These women should be vaccinated immediately after delivery and, if possible, tested at least 3 months later to ensure immunity to rubella and, if necessary, to measles.

If administration of an immune globulin preparation becomes necessary because of imminent exposure to disease, measles, mumps, and rubella virus vaccine live or its individual component vaccines can be administered simultaneously with the immune globulin preparation, although vaccine-induced immunity could be compromised. The vaccine should be administered at an injection site remote from that chosen for the immune globulin inoculation. Unless serologic testing indicates that specific antibodies have been produced, vaccination should be repeated after the recommended interval.

If administration of an immune globulin preparation becomes necessary after measles, mumps, and rubella virus vaccine live or its individual component vaccines have been administered, interference can occur. Usually, vaccine virus replication and stimulation of immunity will occur 1 to 2 weeks after vaccination. Thus, if the interval between administration of any of these vaccines and subsequent administration of an immune globulin preparation is less than 14 days, vaccination should be repeated after the recommended interval, unless serologic testing indicates that antibodies were produced.

Immune globulin preparations interact less with inactivated vaccines and toxoids than with live virus vaccines. Therefore, administration of inactivated vaccines and toxoids either simultaneously with, or at any interval before or after, receipt of immune globulins should not substantially impair the development of a protective antibody response. The vaccine or toxoid and the immune globulin preparation should be administered at different injection sites using the standard recommended dose of vaccine. Increasing the vaccine dose or number of vaccinations for inactivated vaccines or toxoids is not indicated or recommended.

Immunocompromised persons, including those infected with human immunodeficiency virus (HIV), should receive tetanus immune globulin for the same indications and in the same doses as immunocompetent persons.

For emergency tetanus prophylaxis of wounds

• If uncertain of number or less than three primary doses of tetanus toxoid have been administered: For clean, minor wounds, tetanus and diphtheria toxoids should be administered as soon as possible. For children younger than 7 years of age, diphtheria and tetanus toxoids adsorbed (for pediatric use), diphtheria and tetanus toxoids and pertussis vaccine adsorbed (DTP), or a combination DTP and poliovirus vaccine should be given as part of the routine childhood immunization. For all other wounds, tetanus immune globulin also should be administered.

• If three or more doses of tetanus toxoid have been administered alone or in combination with other vaccines such as DTP: For clean, minor wounds, if more than 10 years have passed since the last dose of tetanus toxoid, tetanus and diphtheria toxoids should be administered as soon as possible. For other, more severe tetanus-prone wounds, if more than 5 years have passed since the last dose of tetanus toxoid, tetanus and diphtheria toxoids should be administered as soon as possible. Generally, tetanus immune globulin is not required in either case.

For treatment of adverse effects

Recommended treatment consists of the following:

- For mild hypersensitivity reaction—Administering antihistamines, and, if necessary, corticosteroids.
- For severe hypersensitivity or anaphylactic reaction—Administering epinephrine. Antihistamines or corticosteroids also may be administered as required.

Parenteral Dosage Forms

TETANUS IMMUNE GLOBULIN INJECTIONUSP

Usual adult and adolescent dose

Immunizing agent (passive)—

Deep intramuscular injection, 250 units.

Note: In cases of severe or highly contaminated wounds, or when treatment is delayed for more than twenty-four hours, a dose of 500 units may be required. If the threat of tetanus infection persists, repeat doses of tetanus immune globulin can be given at four-week intervals.

Usual pediatric dose

Immunizing agent (passive)—

See *Usual adult and adolescent dose.*

Note: The pediatric dose is the same as for adults. Alternatively, in children younger than 7 years of age, tetanus immune globulin can be given in doses of 4 units per kilogram of body weight.

Strength(s) usually available

U.S.—

Not less than 250 units in each prefilled disposable syringe (Rx) [*BayTet*].

Canada—

Not less than 250 units in each prefilled disposable syringe (Rx) [GENERIC].

Packaging and storage

Store between 2 and 8 °C (36 and 46 °F), unless otherwise specified by manufacturer.

Stability

Tetanus immune globulin should not be used if exposed to freezing temperatures.

Incompatibilities

Do not administer in the same syringe or at the same body site as tetanus toxoid.

Auxiliary labeling

- Do not freeze.

Developed: 06/27/1997

TETRACAINE—See *Anesthetics (Ophthalmic), Anesthetics (Parenteral-Local), Anesthetics (Topical)*

TETRACAINE AND MENTHOL—See *Anesthetics (Topical)*

TETRACYCLINE—See *Tetracycline Periodontal Fibers (Mucosal-Local), Tetracyclines (Ophthalmic), Tetracyclines (Systemic), Tetracyclines (Topical)*

TETRACYCLINES Ophthalmic*†

This monograph includes information on the following: 1) Chlortetracycline†; 2) Tetracycline†.

VA CLASSIFICATION (Primary): OP201

Commonly used brand name(s):.

Note: For a listing of dosage forms and brand names by country availability, see *Dosage Forms* section(s).

*Not commercially available in U.S.

†Not commercially available in Canada.

Category

Antibacterial (ophthalmic).

Indications

Note: Because chlortetracycline and tetracycline are not commercially available in the U.S. or Canada, the bracketed information and the use of the superscript 1 in this monograph reflect the lack of labeled (approved) indications for this medication in these countries.

Accepted

[Ocular infections (treatment)][1]—Ophthalmic chlortetracycline is indicated in the treatment of superficial ocular infections caused by *Staphylococcus aureus, Streptococcus epidemicus (Streptococcus pyogenes), Neisseria gonorrhoeae, Streptococcus pneumoniae (Diplococcus pneumoniae), Haemophilus influenzae, Haemophilus ducreyi, Klebsiella pneumoniae, Francisella tularensis (Pasteurella tularensis), Yersinia pestis (Pasteurella pestis), Escherichia coli, Bacillus anthracis,* and *Lymphogranuloma venereum.*

Ophthalmic tetracycline is indicated in the treatment of superficial ocular infections caused by *Staphylococcus aureus*, streptococci including *Streptococcus epidemicus (Streptococcus pyogenes)* and *Streptococcus pneumoniae (Diplococcus pneumoniae), Neisseria gonorrhoeae*, and *Escherichia coli.*

[Ophthalmia neonatorum (prophylaxis)][1]—Ophthalmic chlortetracycline and tetracycline are indicated in the prophylaxis of ophthalmia neonatorum caused by *N. gonorrhoeae* and *Chlamydia trachomatis.*

[Trachoma (treatment)][1]—Ophthalmic chlortetracycline and tetracycline are indicated in the treatment of trachoma caused by *Chlamydia trachomatis*. They should be used concurrently with oral tetracyclines.

[Blepharitis, bacterial (treatment)][1]
[Blepharoconjunctivitis (treatment)][1]
[Conjunctivitis, bacterial (treatment)][1]
[Keratitis, bacterial (treatment)][1]
[Keratoconjunctivitis, bacterial (treatment)] or[1]
[Meibomianitis (treatment)][1]—Ophthalmic chlortetracycline and tetracycline are used in the treatment of bacterial blepharitis, blepharoconjunctivitis, bacterial conjunctivitis, bacterial keratitis, bacterial keratoconjunctivitis, and meibomianitis.

[Chlamydial infections (treatment)] or[1]
[Rosacea, ocular (treatment)][1]—Ophthalmic tetracycline is used in the treatment of chlamydial infections and ocular rosacea.

Note: Not all species or strains of a particular organism may be susceptible to a specific tetracycline.

Unaccepted

Tetracycline is not effective against *Haemophilus influenzae, Klebsiella* species, *Enterobacter (Aerobacter)* species, *Pseudomonas aeruginosa*, or *Serratia marcescens.*

[1]Not included in Canadian product labeling.

Pharmacology/Pharmacokinetics

Physicochemical characteristics

Molecular weight—

Chlortetracycline hydrochloride: 515.35.
Tetracycline hydrochloride: 480.9.

Mechanism of action/Effect

Tetracyclines are broad-spectrum bacteriostatic agents and act by inhibiting protein synthesis by blocking the binding of aminoacyl tRNA (transfer RNA) to the mRNA (messenger RNA) ribosome complex. Reversible binding occurs primarily at the 30 S ribosomal subunit of susceptible organisms. Bacterial cell wall synthesis is not inhibited.

Precautions to Consider

Cross-sensitivity and/or related problems

Patients sensitive to one tetracycline, tetracycline combination, or tetracycline derivative may be sensitive to other tetracyclines also.

Pregnancy/Reproduction

Pregnancy—Problems in humans have not been documented.

Breast-feeding

Problems in humans have not been documented.

Pediatrics

Appropriate studies on the relationship of age to the effects of ophthalmic tetracyclines have not been performed in the pediatric population. However, no pediatrics-specific problems have been documented to date.

Geriatrics
Appropriate studies on the relationship of age to the effects of tetracyclines have not been performed in the geriatric population. However, no geriatrics-specific problems have been documented to date.

Medical considerations/Contraindications
The medical considerations/contraindications included have been selected on the basis of their potential clinical significance (reasons given in parentheses where appropriate)—not necessarily inclusive (» = major clinical significance).

Risk-benefit should be considered when the following medical problem exists:
Sensitivity to tetracyclines

Patient Consultation

As an aid to patient consultation, refer to *Advice for the Patient, Tetracyclines (Ophthalmic)*.

In providing consultation, consider emphasizing the following selected information (» = major clinical significance):

Before using this medication
» Conditions affecting use, especially:
Sensitivity to tetracycline, chlortetracycline, or any related antibiotic, such as demeclocycline, doxycycline, methacycline, minocycline, or oxytetracycline

Proper use of this medication
Proper administration technique for ophthalmic ointment
» Compliance with full course of therapy
» Proper dosing
Missed dose: Applying as soon as possible; not applying if almost time for next dose
» Proper storage

Precautions while using this medication
Blurred vision after application of ophthalmic ointments

Checking with physician if no improvement within a few days

General Dosing Information

Blurred vision after application of ophthalmic ointments is to be expected.

Therapy should be continued for 1 to 2 months or longer in acute and chronic trachoma. Severe infections may also require concurrent oral therapy for trachoma.

In term infants born to mothers with clinically apparent gonorrhea, a single intramuscular or intravenous dose of 50,000 Units of penicillin G potassium is administered concurrently with ophthalmic tetracycline. In low-birth-weight infants, the dose is 20,000 Units.

CHLORTETRACYCLINE

Ophthalmic Dosage Forms

Note: Because chlortetracycline is not commercially available in the U.S. or Canada, the bracketed uses and the use of the superscript 1 in this monograph reflect the lack of labeled (approved) indications for this medication in these countries.

CHLORTETRACYCLINE HYDROCHLORIDE OPHTHALMIC OINTMENT USP

Usual adult and adolescent dose
[Ocular infections][1]—
Topical, to the conjunctiva, a thin strip (approximately 1 cm) of ointment every two to four hours or more frequently.

Usual pediatric dose
See *Usual adult and adolescent dose.*

Strength(s) usually available
U.S.—
Not commercially available.
Canada—
Not commercially available.

Packaging and storage
Store below 40 °C (104 °F), preferably between 15 and 30 °C (59 and 86 °F), unless otherwise specified by manufacturer. Store in a collapsible ophthalmic ointment tube. Protect from freezing.

Auxiliary labeling
• For the eye.
• Continue medicine for full time of treatment.

[1]Not included in Canadian product labeling.

TETRACYCLINE

Ophthalmic Dosage Forms

Note: Because tetracycline is not commercially available in the U.S. or Canada, the bracketed uses and the use of the superscript 1 in this monograph reflect the lack of labeled (approved) indications for this medication in these countries.

TETRACYCLINE HYDROCHLORIDE OPHTHALMIC OINTMENT USP

Usual adult and adolescent dose
[Ocular infections][1]—
Topical, to the conjunctiva, a thin strip (approximately 1 cm) of ointment every two to four hours or more frequently.
[Ophthalmia neonatorum][1]—
Topical, to the conjunctiva, a thin strip (approximately 1 cm) of ointment as a single dose.

Usual pediatric dose
See *Usual adult and adolescent dose.*

Strength(s) usually available
U.S.—
Not commercially available.
Canada—
Not commercially available.

Packaging and storage
Store below 40 °C (104 °F), preferably between 15 and 30 °C (59 and 86 °F), unless otherwise specified by manufacturer. Store in a collapsible ophthalmic ointment tube. Protect from freezing.

Auxiliary labeling
• For the eye.
• Continue medicine for full time of treatment.

[1]Not included in Canadian product labeling.

Revised: 06/15/1999

TETRACYCLINES Systemic

This monograph includes information on the following: 1) Demeclocycline; 2) Doxycycline; 3) Minocycline; 4) Oxytetracycline†; 5) Tetracycline.

VA CLASSIFICATION (Primary/Secondary):
Demeclocycline—AM250/AP109; CV709
Doxycycline—AM250/AP101; AP109; DE751
Minocycline—AM250/AP109; DE751; MS109
Oxytetracycline—AM250/AP109
Tetracycline—AM250/AP101; AP109; DE751; IP100

Commonly used brand name(s): *Achromycin V[5]; Alti-Doxycycline[2]; Alti-Minocycline[3]; Apo-Doxy[2]; Apo-Doxy-Tabs[2]; Apo-Minocycline[3]; Apo-Tetra[5]; Declomycin[1]; Doryx[2]; Doxycin[2]; Doxytec[2]; Dynacin[3]; Gen-Minocycline[3]; Minocin[3]; Monodox[2]; Novo-Doxylin[2]; Novo-Minocycline[3]; Novo-Tetra[5]; Nu-Doxycycline[2]; Nu-Tetra[5]; Terramycin[4]; Vibra-Tabs[2]; Vibra-Tabs C-Pak[2]; Vibramycin[2].*

Note: For a listing of dosage forms and brand names by country availability, see *Dosage Forms* section(s).

†Not commercially available in Canada.

Category

Antibacterial; antiprotozoal—Demeclocycline; Doxycycline; Minocycline; Oxytetracycline; Tetracycline.
Antiacne agent—Doxycycline; Minocycline (oral); Tetracycline.
Antimalarial; intrapleural sclerosing agent—Doxycycline; Tetracycline.
Antirheumatic—Minocycline (oral).
Diuretic (syndrome of inappropriate antidiuretic hormone)—Demeclocycline

Indications

Note: Bracketed information in the *Indications* section refers to uses that are not included in U.S. product labeling.

Accepted
Acne vulgaris (treatment adjunct)[1]—Doxycycline, minocycline, and tetracycline are indicated as adjunctive treatments for acne. Doxycycline and minocycline are generally no more effective in the initial treatment of acne, are more likely to cause photosensitivity reaction, and are

more expensive than tetracycline; however, doxycycline and minocycline may be taken less frequently per day than tetracycline. Oral minocycline may be more effective in severe or resistant acne, and it may be effective in acne unresponsive to tetracycline or where poor absorption of tetracycline is suspected.

Actinomycosis (treatment)—Systemic tetracyclines are indicated in the treatment of actinomycosis caused by *Actinomyces* species in patients who cannot take penicillins.

Amebiasis, intestinal (treatment adjunct)—Systemic tetracyclines are indicated as treatment adjuncts for acute intestinal amebiasis.

Anthrax (treatment)—Systemic tetracyclines are indicated in the treatment of anthrax caused by *Bacillus anthracis* in patients who cannot take penicillins.

Bartonellosis (treatment)[1]—Systemic tetracyclines are indicated for the treatment of bartonellosis caused by *Bartonella bacilliformis.*

Brucellosis (treatment)—Systemic tetracyclines, in conjunction with streptomycin, are indicated in the treatment of brucellosis caused by *Brucella* species.

Chancroid (treatment)—Systemic tetracyclines are indicated in the treatment of chancroid caused by *Haemophilus ducreyi.*

Cholera (treatment)—Oral doxycycline, oral minocycline, and tetracycline are indicated in the treatment of cholera caused by *Vibrio cholerae (Vibrio comma).*

Conjunctivitis, inclusion (treatment)—Oral tetracyclines are indicated in the treatment of inclusion conjunctivitis caused by *Chlamydia trachomatis.*

Genitourinary tract infections (treatment)—Systemic tetracyclines are indicated in the treatment of genitourinary tract infections as follows:

	Infectious agent		
Infection	*Chlamydia trachomatis*	*Neisseria gonorrhoeae*	*Ureaplasma urealyticum*
Endocervical infections	Doxycycline Tetracycline	Demeclocycline Doxycycline Minocycline Tetracycline	
Epididymoorchitis	Doxycycline	Demeclocycline Doxycycline	
Rectal infections	Doxycycline Tetracycline		
Urethral infections	Doxycycline Minocycline Tetracycline	Demeclocycline Doxycycline Minocycline Tetracycline	Doxycycline Minocycline

Gingivostomatitis, necrotizing ulcerative (treatment)—Systemic tetracyclines are indicated in the treatment of necrotizing ulcerative gingivostomatitis (Vincent's infection) caused by *Fusobacterium fusiforme* in patients who cannot take penicillins.

Gonorrhea (treatment)—Systemic tetracyclines are indicated for the treatment of uncomplicated gonorrhea caused by *Neisseria gonorrhoeae* in patients who cannot take penicillins.

Granuloma inguinale (treatment)—Systemic tetracyclines are indicated in the treatment of granuloma inguinale caused by *Calymmatobacterium granulomatis.*

Listeriosis (treatment)—Systemic tetracyclines are indicated in the treatment of listeriosis caused by *Listeria monocytogenes* in patients who cannot take penicillins.

Lymphogranuloma venereum (treatment)—Systemic tetracyclines are indicated in the treatment of lymphogranuloma venereum caused by *Chlamydia* species.

Malaria (prophylaxis)[1]—Systemic doxycycline is indicated in the prophylaxis of malaria due to *Plasmodium falciparum* in travelers going to areas with chloroquine-resistant strains. Doxycycline is also often used for chloroquine-sensitive strains in patients who cannot take chloroquine.

Meningococcal carriers (treatment)[1]—Oral minocycline is indicated in the treatment of asymptomatic meningococcal carriers to eliminate *Neisseria meningitidis* from the nasopharynx.

Mycobacterial infections, atypical (treatment)[1]—Oral minocycline is indicated in the treatment of infections caused by *Mycobacterium marinum.*

Treatment of infections caused by *Mycobacterium avium intracellulare, Mycobacterium fortuitum, Mycobacterium haemophilum, Mycobacterium kansasii,* or *Mycobacterium vaccae* with tetracyclines, in combination with other anti-infective agents, has been reported. However, controlled clinical studies need to be done before tetracyclines can be recommended for use in the treatment of these atypical mycobacterial infections.

Plague (treatment)—Systemic tetracyclines are indicated in the treatment of plague caused by *Yersinia (Pasteurella) pestis.*

Pneumonia, mycoplasmal (treatment)—Systemic tetracyclines are indicated in the treatment of pneumonia and other respiratory tract infections caused by *Mycoplasma pneumoniae.*

Psittacosis (treatment)—Systemic tetracyclines are indicated in the treatment of psittacosis (ornithosis) caused by *Chlamydia psittaci.*

Q fever (treatment)
Rickettsial pox (treatment)
Rocky Mountain spotted fever (treatment) or
Typhus infections (treatment)—Systemic tetracyclines are indicated in the treatment of Q fever, rickettsial pox, Rocky Mountain spotted fever (including tick fevers), and typhus infections caused by Rickettsiae.

Relapsing fever (treatment)—Systemic tetracyclines are indicated in the treatment of relapsing fever caused by *Borrelia recurrentis.*

Respiratory tract infections (treatment)—Systemic tetracyclines are indicated in the treatment of respiratory tract infections caused by susceptible strains of *Haemophilus influenzae* and *Klebsiella* species. Doxycycline and minocycline are also indicated for the treatment of upper respiratory tract infections caused by susceptible strains of *Streptococcus pneumoniae.*

[Demeclocycline is indicated in the treatment of primary atypical pneumonia.]

Tetracyclines are not recommended as the first choice of treatment for acute throat infections or any staphylococcal infection.

Skin and soft tissue infections (treatment)—Systemic tetracyclines are indicated in the treatment of skin and soft tissue infections, including burn wound infections, caused by susceptible *Staphylococcus aureus* strains. However, some USP medical experts do not recommend the use of tetracyclines for infections caused by *S. aureus.*

[Systemic tetracyclines are also indicated in the treatment of abscess, furunculosis, impetigo, and pyoderma caused by susceptible *Escherichia coli, Proteus* species, *S. aureus, Staphylococcus epidermidis,* or *Streptococcus pyogenes* strains.]

Syphilis (treatment)—Oral tetracyclines are indicated in the treatment of syphilis caused by *Treponema pallidum.*

Trachoma (treatment)—Systemic tetracyclines are indicated in the treatment of trachoma caused by *C. trachomatis,* although the infectious agent is not always eliminated as judged by immunofluorescence.

Tularemia (treatment)—Systemic tetracyclines are indicated in the treatment of tularemia caused by *Francisella (Pasteurella) tularensis.*

Urinary tract infections, bacterial (treatment)—Systemic tetracyclines are indicated in the treatment of urinary tract infections caused by *Klebsiella* species.

[Systemic tetracyclines also are indicated in the treatment of urinary tract infections caused by susceptible *E. coli, Enterobacter aerogenes,* and *Proteus* species].

Yaws (treatment)—Systemic tetracyclines are indicated in the treatment of yaws caused by *Treponema pertenue* in patients who cannot take penicillins.

[Amebiasis, extraintestinal (treatment)]—Tetracycline, an intraluminal amebicide, is indicated concurrently or sequentially with metronidazole in the treatment of extraintestinal amebiasis caused by *Entamoeba histolytica.*

[Arthritis, gonococcal (treatment)][1]—Systemic tetracyclines are indicated in the treatment of gonococcal arthritis caused by susceptible strains of *Neisseria gonorrhoeae* in patients who cannot take more appropriate medications.

[Arthritis, rheumatoid (treatment)][1]—Oral minocycline is indicated in the treatment of early (< 2 years), mild rheumatoid arthritis.

[Chlamydial infections (treatment)][1]—Systemic tetracycline is indicated in the treatment of chlamydial infections (Evidence rating: III).

[Enterocolitis, *Shigella* species (prophylaxis and treatment)][1]—Doxycycline is indicated in the prophylaxis and treatment of enterocolitis (shigellosis) caused by susceptible *Shigella* species.

[Gallbladder infections (treatment)]—Minocycline is indicated in the treatment of gallbladder infections caused by *E. coli.*

[Leprosy (treatment)][1]—Minocycline, in combination with other anti-infective agents, is indicated as an alternative agent (alone or in combination with other appropriate agents) in the treatment of lepromatous leprosy caused by *Mycobacterium leprae.*

[Lyme disease (treatment)][1]—Doxycycline and tetracycline are indicated in the treatment of early Lyme disease caused by *Borrelia burgdorferi*.

[Malaria (treatment)][1]—Oral doxycycline and tetracycline, in combination with antimalarial agents such as quinine, are indicated in the treatment of malaria caused by *Plasmodium falciparum*.

[Malignant effusions, pleural (treatment)][1]—Doxycycline is indicated as a sclerosing agent in the treatment of malignant pleural effusions by instillation into the pleural cavity.

[Nocardiosis (treatment)][1]—Doxycycline and minocycline are indicated as alternative agents in the treatment of nocardiosis in patients who cannot take sulfa medications.

[Pneumothorax (prophylaxis)][1]—Tetracycline is indicated as an alternative intrapleural sclerosing agent for the prophylaxis of recurrent, spontaneous pneumothorax. Some clinicians are using doxycycline because parenteral tetracycline is no longer commercially available. Chemical pleurodesis should often be accompanied by bullectomy.

[Rosacea, ocular (treatment)][1]—Oral doxycycline and tetracycline are indicated in the treatment of ocular rosacea.

[Syndrome of inappropriate antidiuretic hormone (SIADH) (treatment)][1]—Demeclocycline is indicated in the treatment of syndrome of inappropriate (excess) antidiuretic hormone (SIADH).

[Travelers' diarrhea (treatment)]—Doxycycline can be used in the treatment of travelers' diarrhea caused by susceptible strains of enterotoxigenic *Escherichia coli*, *Salmonella* species, and *Shigella* species in high-risk patients in whom diarrhea and dehydration may result in serious consequences because of chronic underlying health problems. However, doxycycline is generally not used as a first choice of therapy for this indication.

Tetracyclines are indicated in the treatment of infections due to *N. gonorrhoeae* in patients who cannot take penicillins. Tetracyclines are also indicated in the treatment of infections due to *Campylobacter (Vibrio) fetus* or *Clostridium* species.

Demeclocycline, doxycycline, and tetracycline are indicated in the treatment of infections due to *Bacteroides* species.

Not all species or strains of a particular organism may be susceptible to a specific tetracycline.

Acceptance not established

Tetracycline is reported to have been used in the treatment of *bacterial septicemia* in a limited number of patients. However, controlled clinical studies need to be done to establish the role of tetracycline for this indication.

Unaccepted

Oral minocycline is not indicated in the treatment of meningococcal infections.

Use of doxycycline for prophylaxis of *travelers' diarrhea* is considered obsolete and, therefore, is no longer recommended. Tetracycline resistance is extensive in most areas of the world, and more effective medications are currently available.

[1]Not included in Canadian product labeling.

Pharmacology/Pharmacokinetics

Physicochemical characteristics

Molecular weight—
- Demeclocycline hydrochloride: 501.32.
- Doxycycline: 462.46.
- Doxycycline hyclate: 1025.89.
- Minocycline hydrochloride: 493.95.
- Oxytetracycline: 496.47.
- Oxytetracycline hydrochloride: 496.9.
- Tetracycline: 444.44.
- Tetracycline hydrochloride: 480.9.

Mechanism of action/Effect

Antibacterial (systemic); antiprotozoal—Tetracyclines are broad-spectrum bacteriostatic agents that act by inhibiting protein synthesis by blocking the binding of aminoacyl-tRNA (transfer RNA) to the mRNA (messenger RNA)-ribosome complex. Reversible binding occurs primarily at the 30 S ribosomal subunit of susceptible organisms. Bacterial cell wall synthesis is not inhibited.

Diuretic (syndrome of inappropriate antidiuretic hormone [SIADH])—In the treatment of SIADH, demeclocycline acts by inhibiting ADH-induced water reabsorption in the distal portion of the convoluted tubules and collecting ducts of the kidneys, thereby causing water diuresis.

Absorption

Drug	Absorbed orally (%)	Effect of food on absorption
Demeclocycline	66	Decreased
Doxycycline	90–100	Insignificant
Minocycline	90–100	Insignificant
Oxytetracycline	58	Decreased
Tetracycline	75–77	Decreased

Distribution

Doxycycline—Achieves therapeutic concentrations in the eye; prostatic concentrations are approximately 60% of serum concentrations.

Minocycline—Achieves high concentrations in saliva, sputum, and tears.

All tetracyclines—Readily distributed to most body fluids, including bile, sinus secretions, and synovial, pleural, ascitic, and gingival crevicular fluids. Cerebrospinal fluid (CSF) concentrations vary and may achieve 10 to 25% of plasma concentrations following parenteral administration. Concentrations in gingival crevicular fluid may be three to seven times the serum concentrations. Tetracyclines tend to localize in bone, liver, spleen, tumors, and teeth; tetracyclines also cross the placenta and distribute into breast milk.

Biotransformation

Doxycycline and minocycline are partially inactivated by hepatic metabolism.

Half-life

Drug	Half-life Normal (hr)	Half-life Anuric (hr)
Demeclocycline	10–17	40–60
Doxycycline	12–22	12–22
Minocycline	11–23	11–23
Oxytetracycline	6–10	47–66
Tetracycline	6–11	57–108

Onset of action

SIADH (demeclocycline)—24 to 48 hours.

Time to peak concentration

Tetracycline—2 to 3 days may be necessary to achieve therapeutic concentrations of tetracycline.

Other tetracyclines—2 to 4 hours (oral).

Elimination

Renal; unchanged, via glomerular filtration.

Fecal; unchanged, via biliary secretion, gastrointestinal secretion, or poor absorption.

Dialysis—Tetracyclines are slowly removed by hemodialysis; however, doxycycline is not removed by hemodialysis. Peritoneal dialysis does not effectively remove tetracyclines.

Note: Gastrointestinal secretion is an important route of excretion when doxycycline is administered to patients with renal function impairment or azotemia.

Drug	Volume of distribution* (L/kg)	Excretion routes† (primary/secondary [% excreted unchanged])	Protein binding
Demeclocycline	1.79	Renal/biliary (42)	High (91%)
Doxycycline	0.7	Biliary/renal (35)	High (93%)
Minocycline	0.14–0.7	Biliary/renal (5–10)	Moderate (76%)
Oxytetracycline	0.9–1.9	Renal/biliary (70)	Low (35%)
Tetracycline	1.3–1.6	Renal/biliary (60)	Moderate (65%)

*Diffuses readily into most body tissues, fluids, and/or cavities.

†Biliary route involves concentration by the liver and excretion via the bile into the intestine from which partial reabsorption occurs.

Precautions to Consider

Cross-sensitivity and/or related problems

Patients hypersensitive to one tetracycline may be hypersensitive to other tetracyclines also.

Patients hypersensitive to lidocaine, procaine, or other "caine-type" local anesthetics may also be hypersensitive to the lidocaine component of oxytetracycline injection.

Pregnancy/Reproduction

Pregnancy—Tetracyclines cross the placenta; use is not recommended during the last half of pregnancy since tetracyclines may cause permanent discoloration of teeth, enamel hypoplasia, and inhibition of skeletal growth in the fetus. In addition, fatty infiltration of the liver may occur in pregnant women, especially with high intravenous doses.

FDA Pregnancy Category D.

Breast-feeding

Tetracyclines are distributed into breast milk; although tetracyclines may form nonabsorbable complexes with breast-milk calcium, use is not recommended because of the possibility of their causing permanent staining of teeth, enamel hypoplasia, inhibition of linear skeletal growth, photosensitivity reactions, and oral and vaginal thrush in infants. In addition, vestibular disturbances may occur with minocycline.

Pediatrics

In infants and children 8 years of age and younger, tetracyclines may cause permanent staining of teeth, enamel hypoplasia, and a decrease in linear skeletal growth rate. Therefore, use is not recommended in patients in these age groups unless other antibacterials are unlikely to be effective or are contraindicated.

Bulging fontanels have been reported in young infants who received full therapeutic doses of tetracyclines. This side effect disappeared rapidly upon discontinuation of the medication.

Geriatrics

No information is available on the relationship of age to the effects of tetracyclines in geriatric patients.

Dental

Use of systemic tetracyclines during pregnancy or in infants and children 8 years of age and younger may cause permanent discoloration of teeth and enamel hypoplasia. Therefore, use is not recommended in patients in these age groups unless other antibacterials are unlikely to be effective or are contraindicated. Vital bleaching or aesthetic restoration may be required if staining is objectionable.

Systemic tetracyclines also may contribute to the development of oral candidiasis.

Drug interactions and/or related problems

The following drug interactions and/or related problems have been selected on the basis of their potential clinical significance (possible mechanism in parentheses where appropriate)—not necessarily inclusive (» = major clinical significance):

Note: Combinations containing any of the following medications, depending on the amount present, may also interact with this medication.

» Antacids or
» Calcium supplements such as calcium carbonate or
» Choline and magnesium salicylates or
» Iron supplements or
» Magnesium salicylate or
» Magnesium-containing laxatives or
Sodium bicarbonate
(concurrent use may result in formation of nonabsorbable complexes; also, concurrent use with antacids or sodium bicarbonate may result in decreased absorption of oral tetracyclines because of increased intragastric pH; patients should be advised not to take these medications within 1 to 3 hours of oral tetracyclines)

Barbiturates or
Carbamazepine or
Phenytoin
(concurrent use with doxycycline may result in decreased doxycycline serum concentrations due to induction of microsomal enzyme activity; adjustment of doxycycline dosage or substitution of another tetracycline may be necessary)

» Cholestyramine or
» Colestipol
(concurrent use with cholestyramine or colestipol may result in binding of oral tetracyclines, thus impairing their absorption; an interval of several hours between administration of cholestyramine or colestipol and oral tetracyclines is recommended)

» Contraceptives, estrogen-containing, oral
(concurrent long-term use with tetracyclines may result in reduced contraceptive reliability and increased incidence of breakthrough bleeding)

Digoxin
(although no cases of clinical toxicity have been reported, concurrent use of oral antibiotics may increase serum digoxin concentrations in some individuals; in these individuals, alteration of the gut flora by antibiotics may diminish digoxin conversion to inactive metabolites, resulting in increased serum digoxin concentrations; although limited data are available, this interaction has been reported with oral use of erythromycins, neomycin, and tetracyclines)

Methoxyflurane
(concurrent use with tetracyclines may increase the potential for nephrotoxicity)

» Penicillins
(since bacteriostatic drugs may interfere with the bactericidal effect of penicillins in the treatment of meningitis or in other situations where a rapid bactericidal effect is necessary, concurrent therapy is not recommended)

Vitamin A
(concurrent use with tetracycline has been reported to cause benign intracranial hypertension)

Laboratory value alterations

The following have been selected on the basis of their potential clinical significance (possible effect in parentheses where appropriate)—not necessarily inclusive (» = major clinical significance).

With diagnostic test results
Catecholamine determinations, urine
(may produce false elevations of urinary catecholamines because of interfering fluorescence)

With physiology/laboratory test values
Alanine aminotransferase (ALT [SGPT]) and
Alkaline phosphatase and
Amylase and
Aspartate aminotransferase (AST [SGOT])
(serum values may be increased)

Bilirubin
(serum concentrations may be increased)

Blood urea nitrogen (BUN)
(antianabolic effect of tetracyclines [except doxycycline] may increase BUN concentrations; in patients with significantly impaired renal function, increased serum concentrations of tetracyclines may lead to azotemia, hyperphosphatemia, and acidosis)

Medical considerations/Contraindications

The medical considerations/contraindications included have been selected on the basis of their potential clinical significance (reasons given in parentheses where appropriate)—not necessarily inclusive (» = major clinical significance).

Risk-benefit should be considered when the following medical problems exist:

Asthma
(doxycycline calcium oral suspension contains sodium metabisulfite, and oxytetracycline contains sodium formaldehyde sulfoxylate, each of which may form a potential sulfiting agent upon oxidation; sulfite sensitivity may be seen more frequently in asthmatic patients and may cause allergic-type reactions, including anaphylactic symptoms and life-threatening or less-severe asthmatic episodes, in certain susceptible individuals)

» Diabetes insipidus, nephrogenic
(demeclocycline induces a reversible nephrogenic diabetes insipidus)

Hepatic function impairment
(doxycycline and minocycline are partially metabolized in the liver; hepatic function impairment may prolong the elimination half-life)

Hypersensitivity to tetracyclines, or “caine-type” local anesthetics (e.g., lidocaine)

» Renal function impairment
(the half-life of tetracyclines, except doxycycline or minocycline, is prolonged in patients with renal function impairment)

Side/Adverse Effects

Note: Tetracycline-induced hepatotoxicity is usually seen as a fatty degeneration of the liver. It is more likely to occur in pregnant women, in patients receiving high-dose intravenous therapy, and in patients with renal function impairment. However, hepatotoxicity also has occurred in patients without these predisposing conditions. Tetracycline-induced pancreatitis also has been described in association with hepatotoxicity, and without associated liver disease.

The following side/adverse effects have been selected on the basis of their potential clinical significance (possible signs and symptoms in parentheses where appropriate)—not necessarily inclusive:

Those indicating need for medical attention

Incidence more frequent
Staining of infants' or children's teeth; photosensitivity (increased sensitivity of skin to sunlight)

Incidence less frequent

Nephrogenic diabetes insipidus (greatly increased frequency of urination or amount of urine; increased thirst; unusual tiredness or weakness)—with demeclocycline; ***pigmentation of skin and mucous membranes***—primarily with minocycline

Incidence rare

Benign intracranial hypertension (anorexia; bulging fontanel in infants; headache; papilledema; visual changes; vomiting); ***hepatotoxicity*** (abdominal pain; nausea and vomiting; yellowing skin); ***pancreatitis*** (abdominal pain; nausea and vomiting)

Those indicating need for medical attention only if they continue or are bothersome

Incidence more frequent

CNS toxicity (dizziness; lightheadedness; unsteadiness)—primarily with minocycline; ***gastrointestinal disturbances*** (cramps or burning of the stomach; diarrhea; nausea or vomiting)

Incidence less frequent

Fungal overgrowth (itching of the rectal or genital areas; sore mouth or tongue); ***hypertrophy of the papilla*** (darkened or discolored tongue)

Patient Consultation

As an aid to patient consultation, refer to *Advice for the Patient, Tetracyclines (Systemic)*.

In providing consultation, consider emphasizing the following selected information (» = major clinical significance):

Before using this medication

» Conditions affecting use, especially:

Sensitivity to tetracyclines or to "caine-type" local anesthetics

Pregnancy—Tetracyclines cross the placenta; use is not recommended during the last half of pregnancy since tetracyclines may cause permanent staining of teeth, enamel hypoplasia, and inhibition of skeletal growth in the fetus; also, fatty infiltration of the liver may occur in pregnant women, especially with high intravenous doses

Breast-feeding—Tetracyclines are distributed into breast milk; although tetracyclines may form nonabsorbable complexes with breast-milk calcium, use is not recommended because of the possibility of their causing permanent staining of teeth, enamel hypoplasia, inhibition of linear skeletal growth, photosensitivity reactions, and oral and vaginal thrush in infants

Use in children—In infants and children 8 years of age and younger, tetracyclines may cause permanent discoloration of teeth, enamel hypoplasia, and a decrease in linear skeletal growth rate

Other medications, especially antacids, calcium supplements, cholestyramine, choline and magnesium salicylates, colestipol, estrogen-containing oral contraceptives, iron supplements, magnesium salicylate, magnesium-containing laxatives, or penicillins

Other medical problems, especially nephrogenic diabetes insipidus or renal function impairment

Proper use of this medication

» Not giving to children 8 years of age and younger

Taking with at least a full glass of water while in an upright position, to avoid esophageal ulceration and to decrease gastrointestinal irritation

» Avoiding concurrent use of milk or other dairy products when taking oral demeclocycline, oxytetracycline, and tetracycline; if gastrointestinal irritation occurs, these medicines may be taken with food

Oral doxycycline and minocycline may be taken with food or milk if gastric irritation occurs

» Discarding outdated or decomposed tetracyclines (decomposed products may be toxic)

» Compliance with full course of therapy

» Importance of not missing doses and taking at evenly spaced times

» Proper dosing

Missed dose: Taking as soon as possible; not taking if almost time for next dose; not doubling doses

» Proper storage

Precautions while using this medication

Checking with physician if no improvement of symptoms within a few days (or a few weeks or months for acne patients)

» Concurrent administration of any of the tetracyclines and antacids is not recommended. If concurrent use cannot be avoided, tetracyclines should be taken at least 1 to 3 hours before antacids. Because staggered administration may not be completely reliable, physicians should monitor for continued antibiotic efficacy.

» Concurrent administration of any of the tetracyclines and iron is not recommended. If both medications must be used concurrently, iron salts should be taken not less than three hours before or two hours after the tetracycline dose.

» Use of an alternate or additional method of contraception if concurrently taking estrogen-containing oral contraceptives

Caution if surgery with general anesthesia is required

» Possible photosensitivity reactions

» Caution if dizziness, lightheadedness, or unsteadiness occurs

Side/adverse effects

Signs of potential side effects such as discoloration of infant's or children's teeth, photosensitivity, nephrogenic diabetes insipidus (with demeclocycline), pigmentation of skin and mucous membranes (with minocycline), benign intracranial hypertension, hepatotoxicity, and pancreatitis

General Dosing Information

Use of tetracyclines (except doxycycline and minocycline) in patients with impaired renal function is not recommended.

For oral dosage forms only

All tetracyclines should be taken with a full glass (240 mL) of water to avoid esophageal ulceration and to decrease gastrointestinal irritation.

In addition, most tetracyclines (except doxycycline and minocycline) should preferably be taken on an empty stomach (either 1 hour before or 2 hours after meals) to obtain optimum serum concentrations.

DEMECLOCYCLINE

Summary of Differences

Indications:

Also used as a diuretic (syndrome of inappropriate antidiuretic hormone [SIADH]).

Pharmacology/pharmacokinetics:

Different mechanism of action in SIADH.

Precautions:

Medical considerations/contraindications—Caution needed in nephrogenic diabetes insipidus.

Side/adverse effects:

May cause greatly increased frequency of urination or amount of urine, increased thirst, or unusual tiredness or weakness (nephrogenic diabetes insipidus).

Oral Dosage Forms

Note: Bracketed uses in the *Dosage Forms* section refer to categories of use and/or indications that are not included in U.S. product labeling.

The dosing and strengths of the dosage forms available are expressed in terms of demeclocycline hydrochloride.

DEMECLOCYCLINE HYDROCHLORIDE TABLETS USP

Usual adult and adolescent dose

Gonorrhea[1]—

Oral, 600 mg initially, then 300 mg every twelve hours for four days for a total dose of 3 grams.

[Syndrome of inappropriate antidiuretic hormone (SIADH)][1]—

Oral, 3.25 to 3.75 mg per kg of body weight every six hours.

For all other infections—

Oral, 150 mg every six hours; or 300 mg every twelve hours.

Usual adult prescribing limits

1.2 grams per day for SIADH.

Usual pediatric dose

For all infections—

Children older than 8 years of age: Oral, 1.65 to 3.3 mg per kg of body weight every six hours; or 3.3 to 6.6 mg per kg of body weight every twelve hours.

Note: Infants and children 8 years of age and younger—All tetracyclines form a stable calcium complex in any bone-forming tissue. As a result, tetracyclines may cause permanent yellow-gray-brown staining of the teeth, as well as enamel hypoplasia. Also, a decrease in linear skeletal growth rate may occur in premature infants. Therefore, use of tetracyclines is not recommended in patients in these age groups unless other medications are unlikely to be effective or are contraindicated.

Strength(s) usually available

U.S.—

150 mg (Rx) [*Declomycin* (sorbitol)].

300 mg (Rx) [*Declomycin* (sorbitol)].

Canada—

150 mg (Rx) [*Declomycin*].

300 mg (Rx) [*Declomycin*].

Packaging and storage
Store below 40 °C (104 °F), preferably between 15 and 30 °C (59 and 86 °F), unless otherwise specified by manufacturer. Store in a tight, light-resistant container.

Auxiliary labeling
- Continue medicine for full time of treatment.
- Do not take within 1 to 3 hours of other medicines, milk, or other dairy products.
- Avoid too much sun or use of sunlamp.
- Keep container tightly closed in a dry place.

[1]Not included in Canadian product labeling.

DOXYCYCLINE

Summary of Differences
Precautions:

Drug interactions and/or related problems—

Interacts with barbiturates, carbamazepine, and phenytoin.

No interaction with methoxyflurane.

Laboratory value alterations—

No increase in BUN concentrations.

Medical considerations/contraindications—

Caution not needed in renal impairment.

Increased sensitivity of asthmatic patients to sodium metabisulfite in doxycycline calcium oral suspension.

General dosing information:

No dosage reduction in renal impairment.

May be taken with food, milk, or carbonated beverages.

Additional Dosing Information
Even though approximately 40% of a dose of doxycycline may be eliminated through the kidneys in patients with normal renal function, patients with impaired renal function do not generally require a reduction in dose since doxycycline alternatively may be eliminated through the liver, biliary tract, and gastrointestinal tract and does not have the antianabolic effect of other tetracyclines.

For oral dosage forms only:
- Doxycycline may be taken with food or milk if gastrointestinal irritation occurs.

Oral Dosage Forms
Note: Bracketed uses in the *Dosage Forms* section refer to categories of use and/or indications that are not included in U.S. product labeling.

The dosing and strengths of the dosage forms available are expressed in terms of doxycycline base.

DOXYCYCLINE CAPSULES USP

Usual adult and adolescent dose
Endocervical, rectal, or urethral infection, uncomplicated, caused by *Chlamydia trachomatis*—

Oral, 100 mg (base) two times a day for seven days.

Epididymo-orchitis caused by *C. trachomatis* or *Neisseria gonorrhoeae* or Nongonococcal urethritis caused by *C. trachomatis* or *Ureaplasma urealyticum*—

Oral, 100 mg (base) two times a day for at least ten days.

Gonococcal infections, uncomplicated (except anorectal infections in men)—

Oral, 100 mg (base) every twelve hours for seven days; or 300 mg initially, then 300 mg one hour later.

[Lyme disease][1]—

Oral, 100 mg (base) two times a day.

Malaria prophylaxis[1]—

Oral, 100 mg (base) once a day. Prophylaxis should begin one to two days before travel to the malarious area and be continued daily during travel and for four weeks after the traveler leaves the malarious area.

Syphilis (early), for penicillin-allergic patients—

Oral, 100 mg (base) two times a day for two weeks.

Syphilis (of > 1 year's duration), for penicillin-allergic patients—

Oral, 100 mg (base) two times a day for four weeks.

For all other infections—

Mild to moderate: Oral, 100 mg (base) every twelve hours on the first day, and 100 mg once a day or 50 mg two times a day thereafter.

Severe: Oral, 100 mg (base) every twelve hours.

Usual adult prescribing limits
600 mg (base) per day for five days in acute gonococcal infections; 300 mg per day for all other infections.

Usual pediatric dose
[Lyme disease][1]—

Children older than 8 years of age: Oral, 1 to 2 mg (base) per kg of body weight two times a day.

Malaria (prophylaxis)[1]—

Children older than 8 years of age: Oral, 2 mg (base) per kg of body weight, up to 100 mg, once a day. Prophylaxis should begin one or two days before travel to the malarious area and be continued daily during travel and for four weeks after the traveler leaves the malarious area.

For all other infections—

Children older than 8 years of age and weighing more than 45 kg: See *Usual adult and adolescent dose.*

Children older than 8 years of age and weighing 45 kg or less: Oral, 2.2 mg (base) per kg of body weight two times a day on the first day; then either 2.2 to 4.4 mg per kg of body weight once a day or 1.1 to 2.2 mg per kg of body weight two times a day.

Note: Infants and children 8 years of age and younger—All tetracyclines form a stable calcium complex in any bone-forming tissue. As a result, tetracyclines may cause permanent yellow-gray-brown staining of the teeth, as well as enamel hypoplasia. Also, a decrease in linear skeletal growth rate may occur in premature infants. Therefore, use of tetracyclines is not recommended in patients in these age groups unless other medications are unlikely to be effective or are contraindicated.

Strength(s) usually available
U.S.—

50 mg (base) [*Monodox*].

100 mg (base) [*Monodox*].

Canada—

Not commercially available.

Packaging and storage
Store below 40 °C (104 °F), preferably between 15 and 30 °C (59 and 86 °F), unless otherwise specified by manufacturer. Store in a tight, light-resistant container.

Auxiliary labeling
- Continue medicine for full time of treatment.
- Do not take within 1 to 3 hours of other medicines.
- Avoid too much sun or use of sunlamp.
- Keep container tightly closed in a dry place.

DOXYCYCLINE FOR ORAL SUSPENSION USP

Usual adult and adolescent dose
See *Doxycycline Capsules USP*.

Usual adult prescribing limits
See *Doxycycline Capsules USP*.

Usual pediatric dose
See *Doxycycline Capsules USP*.

Strength(s) usually available
U.S.—

25 mg (base) per 5 mL, when reconstituted according to manufacturer's instructions (Rx) [*Vibramycin* (methylparaben; propylparaben; sucrose)].

Canada—

Not commercially available.

Packaging and storage
Prior to reconstitution, store below 40 °C (104 °F), preferably between 15 and 30 °C (59 and 86 °F), unless otherwise specified by manufacturer. Store in a tight, light-resistant container.

Stability
After reconstitution, suspensions retain their potency for 14 days at room temperature.

Auxiliary labeling
- Shake well.
- Continue medicine for full time of treatment.
- Do not take within 1 to 3 hours of other medicines.
- Avoid too much sun or use of sunlamp.
- Beyond-use date.

Note
When dispensing, include a calibrated liquid-measuring device.

DOXYCYCLINE CALCIUM ORAL SUSPENSION USP

Usual adult and adolescent dose
See *Doxycycline Capsules USP*.

Usual adult prescribing limits
See *Doxycycline Capsules USP*.

Usual pediatric dose
See *Doxycycline Capsules USP*.

Strength(s) usually available
U.S.—
50 mg (base) per 5 mL (Rx) [*Vibramycin* (butylparaben; propylparaben; sodium metabisulfate; sorbitol solution)].
Canada—
Not commercially available.

Packaging and storage
Store below 40 °C (104 °F), preferably between 15 and 30 °C (59 and 86 °F), unless otherwise specified by manufacturer. Store in a tight, light-resistant container. Protect from freezing.

Auxiliary labeling
- Shake well.
- Continue medicine for full time of treatment.
- Do not take within 1 to 3 hours of other medicines.
- Avoid too much sun or use of sunlamp.

Note
When dispensing, include a calibrated liquid-measuring device.

DOXYCYCLINE HYCLATE CAPSULES USP

Usual adult and adolescent dose
See *Doxycycline Capsules USP*.

Usual adult prescribing limits
See *Doxycycline Capsules USP*.

Usual pediatric dose
See *Doxycycline Capsules USP*.

Strength(s) usually available
U.S.—
50 mg (base) (Rx) [*Vibramycin;* GENERIC].
100 mg (base) (Rx) [*Vibramycin;* GENERIC].
Canada—
100 mg (base) (Rx) [*Alti-Doxycycline; Apo-Doxy; Doxycin; Doxytec* (lactose); *Novo-Doxylin; Nu-Doxycycline; Vibramycin*].

Packaging and storage
Store below 40 °C (104 °F), preferably between 15 and 30 °C (59 and 86 °F), unless otherwise specified by manufacturer. Store in a tight, light-resistant container.

Auxiliary labeling
- Continue medicine for full time of treatment.
- Do not take within 1 to 3 hours of other medicines.
- Avoid too much sun or use of sunlamp.
- Keep container tightly closed in a dry place.

DOXYCYCLINE HYCLATE DELAYED-RELEASE CAPSULES USP

Usual adult and adolescent dose
See *Doxycycline Capsules USP*.

Usual adult prescribing limits
See *Doxycycline Capsules USP*.

Usual pediatric dose
See *Doxycycline Capsules USP*.

Strength(s) usually available
U.S.—
100 mg (base) (Rx) [*Doryx* (lactose)].
Canada—
Not commercially available.

Packaging and storage
Store below 40 °C (104 °F), preferably between 15 and 30 °C (59 and 86 °F), unless otherwise specified by manufacturer. Store in a tight, light-resistant container.

Auxiliary labeling
- Continue medicine for full time of treatment.
- Do not take within 1 to 3 hours of other medicines.
- Avoid too much sun or use of sunlamp.
- Keep container tightly closed in a dry place.
- Swallow capsules whole.

Note
Doxycycline Delayed-release Capsules USP contain enteric-coated pellets.

DOXYCYCLINE HYCLATE TABLETS USP

Usual adult and adolescent dose
See *Doxycycline Capsules USP*.

Usual adult prescribing limits
See *Doxycycline Capsules USP*.

Usual pediatric dose
See *Doxycycline Capsules USP*.

Strength(s) usually available
U.S.—
100 mg (base) (Rx) [*Vibra-Tabs;* GENERIC].
Canada—
100 mg (base) (Rx) [*Alti-Doxycycline; Apo-Doxy-Tabs; Doxycin; Novo-Doxylin; Nu-Doxycycline; Vibra-Tabs; Vibra-Tabs C-Pak*].

Packaging and storage
Store below 40 °C (104 °F), preferably between 15 and 30 °C (59 and 86 °F), unless otherwise specified by manufacturer. Store in a tight, light-resistant container.

Auxiliary labeling
- Continue medicine for full time of treatment.
- Do not take within 1 to 3 hours of other medicines.
- Avoid too much sun or use of sunlamp.
- Keep container tightly closed in a dry place.

Parenteral Dosage Forms

Note: The dosing and strengths of the dosage forms available are expressed in terms of doxycycline base.

DOXYCYCLINE HYCLATE FOR INJECTION USP

Usual adult and adolescent dose
Syphilis (primary and secondary)—
Intravenous infusion, 150 mg (base) every twelve hours for at least ten days.
For all other infections—
Intravenous infusion, 200 mg (base) once a day or 100 mg every twelve hours for the first day, then 100 to 200 mg once a day; or 50 to 100 mg every twelve hours.

Usual adult prescribing limits
300 mg (base) daily.

Usual pediatric dose
For all infections—
Children older than 8 years of age and weighing more than 45 kg: See *Usual adult and adolescent dose.*
Children older than 8 years of age and weighing 45 kg or less: Intravenous infusion, 4.4 mg (base) per kg of body weight once a day; or 2.2 mg per kg of body weight every twelve hours for the first day, then 2.2 to 4.4 mg per kg of body weight once a day or 1.1 to 2.2 mg per kg of body weight every twelve hours.

Note: Infants and children 8 years of age and younger—All tetracyclines form a stable calcium complex in any bone-forming tissue. As a result, tetracyclines may cause permanent yellow-gray-brown staining of the teeth, as well as enamel hypoplasia. Also, a decrease in linear skeletal growth rate may occur in premature infants. Therefore, use of tetracyclines is not recommended in patients in these age groups unless other medications are unlikely to be effective or are contraindicated.

Strength(s) usually available
U.S.—
100 mg (base) (Rx) [*Vibramycin*].
200 mg (base) (Rx) [*Vibramycin*].
Canada—
Not commercially available.

Packaging and storage
Prior to reconstitution, store below 40 °C (104 °F), preferably between 15 and 30 °C (59 and 86 °F), unless otherwise specified by manufacturer. Protect from light.

Preparation of dosage form
To prepare initial dilution for intravenous use, add 10 mL of sterile water for injection or other suitable diluents (see manufacturer's package insert) to each 100-mg vial or 20 mL of diluent to each 200-mg vial. The resulting solution containing the equivalent of 100 to 200 mg of doxycycline may be further diluted in 100 to 1000 mL or in 200 to 2000 mL of suitable diluent, respectively.

Stability
After reconstitution, intravenous infusions of doxycycline hyclate retain their potency for 12 hours at room temperature or for 72 hours if refrigerated at concentrations of 100 mcg (0.1 mg) to 1 mg per mL in suitable fluids (see manufacturer's package insert). Intravenous infusions of doxycycline hyclate retain their potency for 6 hours at room temperature at concentrations of 100 mcg (0.1 mg) to 1 mg per mL in lactated Ringer's injection or 5% dextrose and lactated Ringer's injec-

tion. Infusions must be protected from direct sunlight during administration.

If frozen immediately after reconstitution with sterile water for injection, solutions at concentrations of 10 mg per mL retain their potency up to 8 weeks at −20 °C (−4 °F). Once thawed, solutions should not be refrozen.

Additional information

Concentrations less than 100 mcg (0.1 mg) per mL or greater than 1 mg per mL are not recommended.

Infusions may be administered over a 1- to 4-hour period. Avoid rapid administration.

Do not administer intramuscularly or subcutaneously.

[1]Not included in Canadian product labeling.

MINOCYCLINE

Summary of Differences

Precautions:
- Laboratory value alterations—No increase in BUN concentrations.
- Medical considerations/contraindications—Caution not needed in renal impairment.

Side/adverse effects:
- May cause dizziness, light-headedness, or unsteadiness (central nervous system [CNS] toxicity); and pigmentation of skin and mucous membranes.

General dosing information:
- No dosage reduction in renal impairment.
- May be taken with food or milk.

Additional Dosing Information

For oral dosage forms only:

- Minocycline may be taken with food or milk if gastrointestinal irritation occurs.

Oral Dosage Forms

Note: Bracketed uses in the *Dosage Forms* section refer to categories of use and/or indications that are not included in U.S. product labeling.

The dosing and strengths of the dosage forms available are expressed in terms of minocycline base.

MINOCYCLINE HYDROCHLORIDE CAPSULES USP

Usual adult and adolescent dose

Gonococcal infections, uncomplicated—
- Urethral (in men): Oral, 100 mg (base) every twelve hours for five days.
- Infections other than urethral or anorectal (in men): Oral, 200 mg (base) initially, then 100 mg every twelve hours for at least four days.

Infections, urethral, caused by *Chlamydia trachomatis* or *Ureaplasma urealyticum*[1]—
- Oral, 100 mg (base) every twelve hours for at least seven days.

Meningococcal carriers[1]—
- Oral, 100 mg (base) every twelve hours for five days.

Mycobacterium marinum infections[1]—
- Oral, 100 mg (base) every twelve hours for six to eight weeks.

[Rheumatoid arthritis][1]—
- Oral, 100 mg (base) two times a day.

Syphilis—
- Oral, 200 mg (base) initially, then 100 mg every twelve hours for ten to fifteen days; or 100 to 200 mg initially, then 50 mg every six hours for ten to fifteen days.

For all other infections—
- Oral, 200 mg (base) initially, then 100 mg every twelve hours; or 100 to 200 mg initially, then 50 mg every six hours.

Usual adult prescribing limits

350 mg (base) the first day; then 200 mg a day.

Usual pediatric dose

For all infections—
- Children older than 8 years of age: Oral, 4 mg (base) per kg of body weight initially, then 2 mg per kg of body weight every twelve hours.

Note: Infants and children 8 years of age and younger—All tetracyclines form a stable calcium complex in any bone-forming tissue. As a result, tetracyclines may cause permanent yellow-gray-brown staining of the teeth, as well as enamel hypoplasia. Also, a decrease in linear skeletal growth rate may occur in premature infants. Therefore, use of tetracyclines is not recommended in patients in these age groups unless other medications are unlikely to be effective or are contraindicated.

Strength(s) usually available

U.S.—
- 50 mg (base) (Rx) [*Dynacin; Minocin;* GENERIC].
- 100 mg (base) (Rx) [*Dynacin; Minocin;* GENERIC].

Canada—
- 50 mg (base) (Rx) [*Alti-Minocycline; Apo-Minocycline; Gen-Minocycline; Minocin; Novo-Minocycline*].
- 100 mg (base) (Rx) [*Alti-Minocycline; Apo-Minocycline; Gen-Minocycline; Minocin; Novo-Minocycline*].

Packaging and storage

Store below 40 °C (104 °F), preferably between 15 and 30 °C (59 and 86 °F), unless otherwise specified by manufacturer. Store in a tight, light-resistant container.

Auxiliary labeling

- Continue medicine for full time of treatment.
- Do not take within 1 to 3 hours of other medicines.
- Avoid too much sun or use of sunlamp.
- Keep container tightly closed in a dry place.
- May cause dizziness.

MINOCYCLINE HYDROCHLORIDE ORAL SUSPENSION USP

Usual adult and adolescent dose

See *Minocycline Hydrochloride Capsules USP*.

Usual adult prescribing limits

See *Minocycline Hydrochloride Capsules USP*.

Usual pediatric dose

See *Minocycline Hydrochloride Capsules USP*.

Strength(s) usually available

U.S.—
- 50 mg (base) (Rx) [*Minocin* (alcohol 5% v/v; butylparaben 0.06%; propylparaben 0.1%)].

Canada—
- Not commercially available.

Packaging and storage

Store below 40 °C (104 °F), preferably between 15 and 30 °C (59 and 86 °F), unless otherwise specified by manufacturer. Store in a tight, light-resistant container. Protect from freezing.

Auxiliary labeling

- Shake well.
- Continue medicine for full time of treatment.
- Do not take within 1 to 3 hours of other medicines.
- Avoid too much sun or use of sunlamp.
- May cause dizziness.

Note

When dispensing, include a calibrated liquid-measuring device.

Parenteral Dosage Forms

Note: The dosing and strengths of the dosage forms available are expressed in terms of minocycline base.

MINOCYCLINE FOR INJECTION USP

Usual adult and adolescent dose

Intravenous infusion, 200 mg (base) initially, then 100 mg every twelve hours.

Usual adult prescribing limits

400 mg (base) daily.

Usual pediatric dose

For all infections—
- Children older than 8 years of age: Intravenous infusion, 4 mg (base) per kg of body weight initially, then 2 mg per kg of body weight every twelve hours.

Note: Infants and children 8 years of age and younger—All tetracyclines form a stable calcium complex in any bone-forming tissue. As a result, tetracyclines may cause permanent yellow-gray-brown staining of the teeth, as well as enamel hypoplasia. Also, a decrease in linear skeletal growth rate may occur in premature infants. Therefore, use of tetracyclines is not recommended in patients in these age groups unless other medications are unlikely to be effective or are contraindicated.

Strength(s) usually available

U.S.—
- 100 mg (base) (Rx) [*Minocin*].

Canada—
Not commercially available.

Packaging and storage
Prior to reconstitution, store below 40 °C (104 °F), preferably between 15 and 30 °C (59 and 86 °F), unless otherwise specified by manufacturer. Protect from light.

Preparation of dosage form
To prepare initial dilution for intravenous use, add 5 to 10 mL of sterile water for injection to each 100-mg vial.

The resulting solution may be further diluted in 500 to 1000 mL of 0.9% sodium chloride injection, dextrose injection, dextrose and sodium chloride injection, Ringer's injection, or lactated Ringer's injection, but not in other calcium-containing solutions since a precipitate may form. Administration should be started immediately, but avoid rapid administration.

Stability
After reconstitution, solutions retain their potency for 24 hours at room temperature.

---

[1]Not included in Canadian product labeling.

OXYTETRACYCLINE

Additional Dosing Information
For parenteral dosage forms only:
- Serum concentrations should not exceed 15 mcg per mL, especially in pregnant or postpartum patients with pyelonephritis.

Oral Dosage Forms
Note: The dosing and strengths of the dosage forms available are expressed in terms of oxytetracycline base.

OXYTETRACYCLINE HYDROCHLORIDE CAPSULES USP

Usual adult and adolescent dose
Brucellosis—
Oral, 500 mg (base) every six hours for three weeks, given concurrently with 1 gram of streptomycin intramuscularly every twelve hours for the first week and once a day for the second week.

Gonorrhea, uncomplicated—
Oral, 1.5 grams (base) initially, then 500 mg every six hours for a total dose of 9 grams.

Syphilis—
Oral, 500 mg to 1 gram (base) every six hours for ten to fifteen days for a total dose of 30 to 40 grams.

For all other infections—
Oral, 250 to 500 mg (base) every six hours.

Usual adult prescribing limits
4 grams (base) daily.

Usual pediatric dose
For all infections—
Children older than 8 years of age: Oral, 6.25 to 12.5 mg (base) per kg of body weight every six hours.

Note: Infants and children 8 years of age and younger—All tetracyclines form a stable calcium complex in any bone-forming tissue. As a result, tetracyclines may cause permanent yellow-gray-brown staining of the teeth, as well as enamel hypoplasia. Also, a decrease in linear skeletal growth rate may occur in premature infants. Therefore, use of tetracyclines is not recommended in patients in these age groups unless other medications are unlikely to be effective or are contraindicated.

Strength(s) usually available
U.S.—
250 mg (base) (Rx) [*Terramycin;* GENERIC].

Canada—
Not commercially available.

Packaging and storage
Store below 40 °C (104 °F), preferably between 15 and 30 °C (59 and 86 °F), unless otherwise specified by manufacturer. Store in a tight, light-resistant container.

Auxiliary labeling
- Continue medicine for full time of treatment.
- Do not take within 1 to 3 hours of other medicines, milk, or other dairy products.
- Avoid too much sun or use of sunlamp.
- Keep container tightly closed in a dry place.

Parenteral Dosage Forms

OXYTETRACYCLINE INJECTION USP

Usual adult and adolescent dose
For all infections—
Intramuscular, 100 mg every eight hours; 150 mg every twelve hours; or 250 mg once a day.

Usual adult prescribing limits
500 mg daily.

Usual pediatric dose
For all infections—
Children older than 8 years of age: Intramuscular, 5 to 8.3 mg per kg of body weight every eight hours; or 7.5 to 12.5 mg per kg of body weight every twelve hours. Maximum daily dose should not exceed 250 mg.

Note: Infants and children 8 years of age and younger—All tetracyclines form a stable calcium complex in any bone-forming tissue. As a result, tetracyclines may cause permanent yellow-gray-brown staining of the teeth, as well as enamel hypoplasia. Also, a decrease in linear skeletal growth rate may occur in premature infants. Therefore, use of tetracyclines is not recommended in patients in these age groups unless other medications are unlikely to be effective or are contraindicated.

Usual pediatric prescribing limits
250 mg per day.

Strength(s) usually available
U.S.—
Note: Injection contains 2% of lidocaine.

50 mg per mL (Rx) [*Terramycin*].
100 mg per 2 mL (Rx) [*Terramycin*].
250 mg per 2 mL (Rx) [*Terramycin*].

Canada—
Not commercially available.

Packaging and storage
Store below 40 °C (104 °F), preferably between 15 and 30 °C (59 and 86 °F), unless otherwise specified by manufacturer. Protect from light. Protect from freezing.

Additional information
Cross-sensitivity with other "caine-type" local anesthetics may also occur.

For deep intramuscular use only. Do not administer intravenously.

May cause intense pain and local irritation at the site of intramuscular injections.

Since intramuscular administration of oxytetracycline produces lower serum concentrations than oral administration in recommended doses, patients should be changed to an oral dosage form as soon as feasible.

TETRACYCLINE

Oral Dosage Forms
Note: Bracketed uses in the *Dosage Forms* section refer to categories of use and/or indications that are not included in U.S. product labeling.

The dosing and strengths of the dosage forms available are expressed in terms of tetracycline hydrochloride.

TETRACYCLINE ORAL SUSPENSION USP

Usual adult and adolescent dose
Antiacne agent—
Oral, 500 mg to 2 grams per day in divided doses initially, as adjunctive therapy, in moderate to severe cases. When improvement is noted (usually after three weeks), dosage should be reduced gradually to a maintenance dose of 125 mg to 1 gram per day. Adequate remission of lesions may also be possible with alternate-day or intermittent therapy.

Brucellosis—
Oral, 500 mg four times a day for three weeks, in combination with intramuscular streptomycin 1 gram two times a day for the first week and 1 gram once a day for the second week.

Gonorrhea—
Oral, 1.5 grams initially, then 500 mg every six hours for four days, for a total dose of 9 grams.

[Lyme disease][1]—
Oral, 250 to 500 mg four times a day.

Syphilis—
Oral, 30 to 40 grams over a period of ten to fifteen days.

Uncomplicated endocervical, rectal, or urethral infections caused by *Chlamydia trachomatis*—
Oral, 500 mg four times a day for at least seven days.

For all other infections—
Oral, 250 to 500 mg every six hours; or 500 mg to 1 gram every twelve hours.

Usual adult prescribing limits

4 grams daily.

Usual pediatric dose

[Lyme disease][1]—
Children older than 8 years of age: Oral, 6.25 to 12.5 mg per kg of body weight four times a day.

For all other infections—
Children older than 8 years of age: Oral, 6.25 to 12.5 mg per kg of body weight every six hours; or 12.5 to 25 mg per kg of body weight every twelve hours.

Note: Infants and children 8 years of age and younger—All tetracyclines form a stable calcium complex in any bone-forming tissue. As a result, tetracyclines may cause permanent yellow-gray-brown staining of the teeth, as well as enamel hypoplasia. Also, a decrease in linear skeletal growth rate may occur in premature infants. Therefore, use of tetracyclines is not recommended in patients in these age groups unless other medications are unlikely to be effective or are contraindicated.

Strength(s) usually available

U.S.—
Not commercially available.

Canada—
125 mg per 5 mL (Rx) [*Novo-Tetra*].

Packaging and storage

Store below 40 °C (104 °F), preferably between 15 and 30 °C (59 and 86 °F), unless otherwise specified by manufacturer. Store in a tight, light-resistant container. Protect from freezing.

Auxiliary labeling

- Shake well.
- Continue medicine for full time of treatment.
- Do not take within 1 to 3 hours of other medicines, milk, or other dairy products.
- Avoid too much sun or use of sunlamp.

Note

When dispensing, include a calibrated liquid-measuring device.

TETRACYCLINE HYDROCHLORIDE CAPSULES USP

Usual adult and adolescent dose

See *Tetracycline Oral Suspension USP*.

Usual adult prescribing limits

See *Tetracycline Oral Suspension USP*.

Usual pediatric dose

See *Tetracycline Oral Suspension USP*.

Strength(s) usually available

U.S.—
250 mg (Rx) [*Achromycin V;* GENERIC].
500 mg (Rx) [*Achromycin V;* GENERIC].

Canada—
250 mg (Rx) [*Apo-Tetra; Novo-Tetra; Nu-Tetra*].

Packaging and storage

Store below 40 °C (104 °F), preferably between 15 and 30 °C (59 and 86 °F), unless otherwise specified by manufacturer. Store in a tight, light-resistant container.

Auxiliary labeling

- Continue medicine for full time of treatment.
- Do not take within 1 to 3 hours of other medicines, milk or other dairy products.
- Avoid too much sun or use of sunlamp.
- Keep container tightly closed in a dry place.

[1]Not included in Canadian product labeling.

Revised: 05/14/2001

THALIDOMIDE Systemic†

VA CLASSIFICATION (Primary/Secondary): IM900/MS102
Commonly used brand name(s): *THALOMID*.

Note: For a listing of dosage forms and brand names by country availability, see *Dosage Forms* section(s).

†Not commercially available in Canada.

Category

Immunomodulator; anti-inflammatory; antiangiogenesis agent.

Indications

Note: Bracketed information in the *Indications* section refers to uses that are not included in U.S. product labeling.

General Considerations

Thalidomide was first synthesized in 1954. It produced marked sedation in laboratory animals. Dose-escalation studies in rodents failed to show lethality even when thalidomide was given in excess of 10 grams per kilogram of body weight, suggesting that thalidomide was a safe drug. Although the studies were limited in scope, thalidomide was tested in over 1000 adults and children: it was well tolerated, had minimal addictive potential, and appeared to be an effective alternative to barbiturates. Thus, thalidomide was marketed in Europe in the late 1950's as a sedative/hypnotic (thalidomide was not approved for sale in the U.S.). However, in the early 1960's it became evident that the incidences of a relatively rare birth defect, phocomelia, and of other severe malformations of internal organs were increasing. These specific birth defects soon reached epidemic proportions (more than 10,000 children with birth defects were reported), and retrospective epidemiological research firmly established the causative agent to be thalidomide taken early in the course of pregnancy. Because of its established teratogenicity, thalidomide was withdrawn from the market worldwide.

Due to the attention given to thalidomide's dramatic, previously unknown side effects, lines of research into thalidomide's other properties were abandoned. Research into the anti-inflammatory properties that had been suggested by animal and human studies, including follow-up of surgical patients, was not pursued. Ironically, it was the sedative properties of thalidomide that resulted in its eventual acceptance as an immunomodulatory agent. In 1964, a patient with severe erythema nodosum leprosum (ENL), or type II leprosy reaction, was given thalidomide for sedation (the patient's pain had been so severe that he could not sleep). The patient's ENL lesions had regressed after a few doses of thalidomide, and this response was reversed when treatment was stopped temporarily. Thus, investigation into thalidomide's immunologic activities began, and in 1998 the Food and Drug Administration (FDA) approved the use of thalidomide for the treatment and suppression of ENL.

Due to thalidomide's toxicity, and in an effort to make the chance of fetal exposure to thalidomide as negligible as possible, thalidomide has been approved for marketing in the U.S. only under a special restricted distribution program approved by the FDA. This program is called the System for Thalidomide Education and Prescribing Safety (STEPS®). Registration is available to all health care providers who agree to comply with the STEPS® program. Under this restricted distribution program, only prescribers and pharmacists registered with the program are allowed to prescribe and dispense thalidomide. In addition, patients must be advised of, agree to, and comply with the requirements of the STEPS® program to receive the product.

Any suspected fetal exposure to thalidomide must be reported immediately to the FDA via the MedWATCH number at 1-800-FDA-1088 and also to Celgene Corporation (1-888-423-5436).The patient should be referred to an obstetrician/gynecologist experienced in reproductive toxicity for further evaluation and counseling.

Accepted

Note: **FOR WOMEN WITH CHILDBEARING POTENTIAL, SEE THE PREGNANCY/REPRODUCTION SECTION OF *PRECAUTIONS TO CONSIDER* FOR RESTRICTIONS ON THE USE OF THALIDOMIDE.**

Erythema nodosum leprosum (ENL) (treatment)[1]—Thalidomide is indicated for the treatment of the cutaneous manifestations of moderate to severe ENL. Thalidomide is not indicated as monotherapy for such ENL treatment in the presence of moderate to severe neuritis.

Erythema nodosum leprosum (ENL), recurrent (suppression)[1]—Thalidomide is indicated as maintenance therapy for prevention and suppression of the cutaneous manifestations of ENL recurrence.

Multiple myeloma, newly diagnosed (treatment)—Thalidomide in combination with dexamethasone is indicated for the treatment of patients with newly diagnosed multiple myeloma.

[Behcet's syndrome (treatment)][1]—Thalidomide is indicated for the treatment of the mucocutaneous lesions associated with Behcet's syndrome (*Evidence rating: I*).

[Human immunodeficiency virus (HIV)–associated wasting syndrome (treatment)][1]—Thalidomide is indicated for the treatment of HIV-associated wasting syndrome (*Evidence rating: I*).

[Stomatitis, aphthous (treatment)][1] or

[Stomatitis, aphthous, immunodeficiency-associated (treatment)][1]—Thalidomide is indicated in the treatment of aphthous stomatitis in immunocompetent and HIV-infected patients who do not respond to colchicine, dapsone, or corticosteroid treatment (*Evidence rating: I*). An infectious cause of the lesion should be excluded before thalidomide therapy is considered.

[Multiple myeloma (treatment)][1]—Thalidomide is indicated in the treatment of advanced, refractory multiple myeloma.

[Ulcer, esophageal, aphthous, human immunodeficiency virus (HIV)-associated (treatment)][1]—Thalidomide is indicated in the treatment of esophageal aphthous ulcers in HIV-infected patients.

Acceptance not established

The use of thalidomide for the treatment of the cutaneous lesions associated with *lupus erythematosus* refractory to other therapies has been studied (*Evidence rating: III*). Although thalidomide appeared to be effective in the small number of patients reported thus far, comparative clinical studies need to be done to determine the role of thalidomide in this indication.

Thalidomide also has been used in the treatment of chronic *graft-versus-host disease* (GVHD) (*Evidence rating: III*). There is currently not enough medical literature or clinical experience to recommend the use of thalidomide for this indication.

Use of thalidomide for the treatment of Kaposi's sarcoma has not been established.

Use of thalidomide for the treatment of prostate carcinoma has not been established, due to safety concerns (venous thrombosis) and insufficient data regarding efficacy. Use should be reserved for desperate clinical situations.

Use of thalidomide for the treatment of renal cell carcinoma has not been established. Toxicity exceeds what is acceptable for the occasional stable response. Safety and efficacy data is needed using lower doses (less toxic), in combination with other agents. Use should be reserved for desperate clinical situations.

Use of thalidomide for the treatment of first-line or relapsed/refractory melanoma is not established, due to insufficient data supporting efficacy.

Use of thalidomide for the treatment of myelodysplastic syndromes has not been established, due to insufficient data supporting safety and efficacy.

Unaccepted

Thalidomide is not indicated as monotherapy for erythema nodosum leprosum treatment in the presence of moderate to severe neuritis.

---

[1]Not included in Canadian product labeling.

Pharmacology/Pharmacokinetics

Physicochemical characteristics

Chemical class—
Glutamic acid derivative; chemically related to glutethimide and chlorthalidone.

Molecular weight—258.23.

Mechanism of action/Effect

Thalidomide is a racemic mixture of two optical isomers in equal amounts. The R-configuration and the S-configuration are more toxic individually than the racemic mixture; the dose at which 50% of animals would be killed (lethal dose $[LD]_{50}$) could not be established in mice for racemic thalidomide, whereas LD_{50} values for the R and S configurations are reported to be 0.4 to 0.7 grams per kilogram of body weight (grams/kg) and 0.5 to 1.5 grams/kg, respectively. However, it should be noted that chirally pure thalidomide converts to the racemic mixture when administered. Early studies suggested that the R-configuration is responsible for the sleep-inducing effects of thalidomide, while the S-configuration confers its teratogenicity. More recent studies suggest that the S-configuration may be selectively responsible for all of the sedative, teratogenic, and immunomodulatory properties of thalidomide. It is not clear whether the configuration of the thalidomide molecule determines its neurotoxicity.

The mechanism(s) responsible for the clinical activity of thalidomide are as yet unknown. Although thalidomide was first recognized as a sedating agent, little information is available to ascertain a potential mechanism underlying this effect, and thalidomide is no longer used for this purpose. The teratogenic effects of thalidomide currently are explained by three leading hypotheses: disruption of neural crest development; inhibition of angiogenesis; and down-regulation of adhesion receptors on early limb-bud cells and on cells of the heart in embryos. It has been well established that thalidomide has no antibacterial or antimycotic activity. Thus, the clinical usefulness of thalidomide appears to reside in its anti-inflammatory and/or immunomodulatory properties.

Although the underlying mechanisms of these activities have not yet been defined, detailed pharmacological analyses indicate that the clinical effects result from the thalidomide molecule itself and not from any of its metabolites. Results from *in vitro* and *in vivo* studies demonstrate that thalidomide inhibits the production of tumor necrosis factor–alpha (TNF-alpha) in monocytes, ostensibly by accelerating the degradation of TNF-alpha ribonucleic acid (RNA) transcripts. Other studies suggest that thalidomide may induce the down-regulation of integrin receptors and other surface adhesion proteins, reduce IgM production. alter CD4/CD8 T-cell ratios, and/or inhibit angiogenesis. However, lymphocyte proliferation does not appear to be affected by thalidomide.

Thalidomide has been used successfully to treat various inflammatory conditions characterized by tissue infiltration with polymorphonuclear leukocytes (PMNLs), e.g., erythema nodosum leprosum (ENL) and recurrent mucocutaneous aphthous ulceration. Therapeutic benefit has been attributed to depression of PMNL chemotaxis and, possibly, PMNL phagocytosis. However, thalidomide has been reported also to be effective in other inflammatory processes with predominantly mononuclear cell accumulation, including discoid lupus erythematosus. Thalidomide was found to reduce both monocyte phagocytosis and chemiluminescence, indicating that thalidomide may decrease tissue inflammation and injury by suppressing production of oxygen-derived free radicals and other mediators involved in inflammatory responses.

Erythema nodosum leprosum (ENL)—Thalidomide has been found to reduce circulating TNF-alpha in patients with ENL; this action may be related to thalidomide's ability to reduce the local and systemic symptoms of ENL, and reduce the number of neutrophils and CD4 T-cells in the ENL lesions.

Human immunodeficiency virus (HIV) infection—Thalidomide may suppress viral replication, decrease viral burden, and enhance patient well-being by reducing TNF-alpha–induced fever, malaise, muscle weakness, and cachexia in the immunodepressed host. *In vitro* studies suggest that thalidomide selectively inhibits TNF-alpha production by monocytes. Additionally, *in vitro* experiments in primary macrophages suggest that thalidomide works through the nuclear factor kappa-B (NF-kappa-B) pathway to inhibit HIV-1 viral replication. However, *in vitro* inhibition of HIV-1 by thalidomide cannot be reproduced consistently, and this inhibition has not been shown *in vivo* or in HIV-infected patients. Contrarily, there is some *in vivo* evidence that HIV RNA levels are increased in HIV-infected patients treated with thalidomide (compared with HIV-infected patients treated with placebo).

Graft-versus-host disease (GVHD)—Thalidomide has been found to bind less avidly to helper T-lymphocytes than to suppressor and cytotoxic T-lymphocytes. This binding pattern suppresses the activity of helper T-lymphocytes while allowing the development of the cytotoxic and suppressor T-lymphocytes; these latter cells play a critical role in keeping GVHD in check and in promoting transplant tolerance.

Other actions/effects

Results from human and animal studies suggest that thalidomide also has an effect on the endocrine system. Hyperthyroid states improved in some patients who were receiving thalidomide. Iodine uptake by the thyroid gland was decreased slightly, and myxedema was seen occasionally. An increase in the urinary secretion of 17-hydroxycorticosteroids associated with hypoglycemia also has been reported.

Absorption

Half-life—Approximately 1.7 hours

Distribution

Approximately 121 liters in healthy subjects and 78 liters in HIV-infected patients.

In animal studies, high concentrations of thalidomide were found in the gastrointestinal tract, liver, and kidney; and lower concentrations were found in the muscle, brain, and adipose tissue. Thalidomide crosses the placenta. In a pharmacokinetic study of thalidomide in HIV-seropositive adult male subjects receiving thalidomide 100 mg/day, thalidomide was detectable in the semen.

Patients with Hansen's disease may have an increased bioavailability of thalidomide compared with healthy subjects.

Protein binding

Highly bound to plasma proteins (55% and 66% for the (+)R and (−)S enantiomers, respectively).

Biotransformation
Studies on thalidomide metabolism in humans have not been done. In animals, nonenzymatic hydrolytic cleavage appears to be the main pathway of degradation, producing seven major and at least five minor hydrolysis products. Thalidomide may be metabolized hepatically by enzymes of the cytochrome P450 enzyme system. Thalidomide does not appear to induce or inhibit its own metabolism. However, it may interfere with enzyme induction caused by other compounds.

The end product of metabolism, phthalic acid, is excreted as a glycine conjugate.

Half-life
Elimination—

In healthy subjects, following a single dose of:

50 mg—5.52 hours

200 mg—5.53 hours

400 mg—7.29 hours

In HIV-positive patients, following a single dose of:

100 mg—6.5 ± 3.4 hours

300 mg—5.7 ± 0.6 hours

In patients with Hansen's disease, following a single dose of:

400 mg—6.86 hours

Time to peak concentration
In healthy subjects, following a single dose of—

50 mg: 2.9 hours

200 mg: 3.5 to 4.4 hours

400 mg: 4.3 hours

Taking thalidomide with a high-fat meal increases the time to peak concentration to 6 hours

In HIV-positive patients, following a single dose of—

100 mg: 3.4 ± 1.8 hours

300 mg: 3.4 ± 1.5 hours

In patients with Hansen's disease, following a single dose of—

400 mg: 5.7 hours

Peak plasma concentration
In healthy subjects, following a single dose of—

50 mg: 0.62 microgram per milliliter (mcg/mL)

200 mg: 1.15 to 1.76 mcg/mL

400 mg: 2.82 mcg/mL

In HIV-positive patients, following a single dose of—

100 mg: 1.17 ± 0.21 mcg/mL

300 mg: 3.47 ± 1.14 mcg/mL

In patients with Hansen's disease, following a single dose of—

400 mg: 3.44 mcg/mL

Taking thalidomide with a high-fat meal does not significantly alter peak plasma concentration values (< 10% change).

Elimination
Thalidomide has a renal clearance of 1.15 mL per minute; less than 0.7% of the total dose is excreted unchanged.

Thalidomide appears to be well tolerated in patients with severe liver and kidney disease.

Precautions to Consider

Mutagenicity
Thalidomide was not mutagenic in *Salmonella typhimurium* or *Escherichia coli* gene mutation assays, in L5178YTK $^{+/-}$ mouse lymphoma cell assays, or in AS52/XPRT mammalian cell forward gene mutation assays, with or without metabolic activation. It was not clastogenic in chromosomal aberration assays using Chinese hamster ovary cells, human lymphocytes, grasshopper neuroblasts (although some unusual chromosome morphology was observed), or *Drosophila melanogaster* somatic cells; in human lymphocyte micronucleus assays; or in bone marrow micronucleus assays using male and female mice and female rabbits.

Note: The unusual chromosome morphologies observed in the grasshopper cytogenetic studies indicate a potential for thalidomide to interact with chromosomal proteins. However, this potential was not evident in the human lymphocyte micronucleus assays, and thalidomide was apparently not reactive to the proteins of mouse skin, as it gave negative results in a mouse local lymph node assay for skin sensitizing agents.

Pregnancy/Reproduction
Fertility—Studies on the effects of thalidomide on fertility in humans or in animals have not been performed. In a pharmacokinetic study, thalidomide was detected in the semen of HIV-seropositive adult males given 100 mg per day.

Pregnancy—**Thalidomide is teratogenic in humans**. The window of embryopathy is small (thought to be from day 21 to day 56 after conception); however, during that time, one dose, producing a serum concentration of as little as 0.9 mcg per mL, can cause birth defects. Malformations include amelia and phocomelia; polydactyly; syndactyly; facial capillary hemangiomas; hydrocephalus; intestinal, cardiovascular, and renal anomalies; and eye, ear, and cranial nerve defects. Other malformations include facial and oculomotor paresthesias; other ocular defects; anal stenoses; vaginal and uterine defects; and heart malformations, which are generally fatal. Mortality at or shortly after birth has been reported at about 40%.

Thalidomide is contraindicated in women of childbearing potential, unless all of the following criteria have been met (women who have undergone hysterectomy or 24 consecutive months of menopause are not considered to have childbearing potential):

- Patient is reliable in understanding and carrying out instructions.
- Patient understands that even a single dose (1 capsule) taken by a pregnant woman can cause severe birth defects.
- Patient is capable of complying with the mandatory contraceptive measures, pregnancy testing, patient registration, and patient survey as described by the STEPS® program.
- Patient has received both oral and written warnings of the risk of possible contraception failure; and of the need to continuously abstain from heterosexual sexual contact, or to use simultaneously two reliable forms of contraception, for at least 1 month before thalidomide therapy, during therapy, and for 1 month following discontinuation of therapy. The two reliable forms of contraception include at least one highly effective method (e.g., intrauterine device [IUD], hormonal contraception, tubal ligation, partner's vasectomy) and one additional effective method (e.g., latex condom, diaphragm, cervical cap). If hormonal or IUD contraception is medically contraindicated, two other effective or highly effective methods may be used.
- Patient acknowledges, in writing, her understanding of these warnings and of the need for using two reliable methods of contraception for 1 month before starting thalidomide therapy, during therapy, and for 1 month following discontinuation of therapy.
- Pregnancy has been definitely excluded through a negative pregnancy test with a sensitivity of at least 50 mIU per mL and appropriate history and physical examination. The pregnancy test should be performed within the 24 hours before beginning thalidomide therapy, weekly during the first month of therapy, and monthly thereafter in women with regular menstrual cycles or every 2 weeks in women with irregular menstrual cycles.
- If the patient is between 12 and 18 years of age, her parent or legal guardian must have read this material and agreed to ensure compliance with the above.

Thalidomide is contraindicated in sexually mature males, unless all of the following criteria have been met:

- Patient can reliably understand and carry out instructions.
- Patient is capable of complying with the mandatory contraceptive measures that are appropriate for men, the patient registration, and the patient survey as described by the STEPS® program.
- Patient has received both oral and written warnings of the hazards of taking thalidomide and exposing a fetus to this medicine.
- Patient has received both oral and written warnings of the risk of possible contraception failure and of the presence of thalidomide in semen. Patient has been instructed that he must always use barrier contraception (latex condom) during any sexual contact with women of childbearing potential, even if he has undergone successful vasectomy.
- Patient acknowledges, in writing, his understanding of these warnings and of the need for using barrier contraception (latex condom) during any sexual contact with women of childbearing potential, even if he has undergone successful vasectomy, when having sexual intercourse with women with childbearing potential.
- If the patient is between 12 and 18 years of age, his parent or legal guardian must have read this material and agreed to ensure compliance with the above.

FDA Pregnancy Category X.

Breast-feeding
It is not known whether thalidomide is distributed into breast milk. Thalidomide was given to nursing mothers in the late 1950's. Although the mothers awakened easily to nurse their babies, no information was provided about the effects thalidomide had on the nursing infants. Because of the potential for serious adverse reactions from thalidomide in nursing infants, a decision should be made whether to discontinue nursing or to discontinue taking thalidomide, taking into account the importance of the medication to the mother.

Pediatrics
Appropriate studies have not been performed on the relationship of age to the effects of thalidomide in children up to 12 years of age. Safety and efficacy have not been established.

Geriatrics

Appropriate studies performed to date have not demonstrated geriatrics-specific problems that would limit the usefulness of thalidomide in the elderly. However, greater sensitivity of some older individuals cannot be ruled out.

Drug interactions and/or related problems

The following drug interactions and/or related problems have been selected on the basis of their potential clinical significance (possible mechanism in parentheses where appropriate)—not necessarily inclusive (» = major clinical significance):

Note: The pharmacokinetic profiles of the hormonal contraceptive agents norethindrone (1 mg) and ethinyl estradiol (75 grams) are not changed significantly when coadministered with thalidomide (200 mg per day, to steady-state levels).

Combinations containing any of the following medications, depending on the amount present, may also interact with this medication.

» Alcohol or
» Barbiturates or
» Chlorpromazine or
» CNS depression-producing medications, other (see *Appendix II*) or
» Reserpine
(because thalidomide is a strong sedative, concurrent use may increase the CNS depressant effects of these medications; caution is recommended; the dosage of thalidomide or the other CNS depressant may need to be reduced)

» Chloramphenicol or
» Cisplatin or
» Dapsone or
» Didanosine or
» Ethambutol or
» Ethionamide or
» Hydralazine or
» Isoniazid or
» Lithium or
» Metronidazole or
» Nitrofurantoin or
» Nitrous oxide or
» Phenytoin or
» Stavudine or
» Vincristine or
» Zalcitabine or
» Other medications associated with peripheral neuropathy
(since thalidomide has been shown to cause peripheral neuropathy, which may be irreversible, other medications associated with the development of neuropathy should be used with caution during thalidomide therapy; if concurrent use is necessary, the patient should be monitored closely)

» Carbamazepine or
» Griseofulvin or
» Human immunodeficiency virus (HIV)–protease inhibitors or
» Rifabutin or
» Rifampin
(use of these medications with hormonal contraceptive agents may reduce the effectiveness of the contraception; women requiring treatment with one or more of these medications must abstain from heterosexual sexual intercourse or use two *other* effective or highly effective methods of contraception)

Medical considerations/Contraindications

The medical considerations/contraindications included have been selected on the basis of their potential clinical significance (reasons given in parentheses where appropriate)—not necessarily inclusive (» = major clinical significance).

Except under special circumstances, this medication should not be used when the following medical problems exist:

» Hypersensitivity to thalidomide—more common in HIV-infected patients

» Neutropenia
(decreased white blood cell counts, including neutropenia, have been reported in association with the clinical use of thalidomide; thalidomide treatment should not be initiated with an absolute neutrophil count [ANC] of < 750 per cubic millimeter)

» Peripheral neuropathy
(thalidomide may cause peripheral neuropathy, which may be irreversible; because nerve damage can occur before the patient has any symptoms, thalidomide should not be used in any patient with pre-existing neuropathy or encephalopathy; neuropathy secondary to thalidomide is uncommon in leprosy patients, possibly because high doses are used only for 1 or 2 weeks)

Risk-benefit should be considered when the following medical problems exist:

» Epilepsy or
» Other factors that predispose to seizures
(seizures, including grand mal seizures, have been reported during post-approval use in clinical practice. Most patients had disorders that may have predisposed them to seizure activity, and it is not currently known whether thalidomide has any epileptogenic influence. Patients with a history of seizures or with other risk factors for the development of seizures should be monitored closely for clinical changes that could precipitate acute seizure activity.)

Patient monitoring

The following may be especially important in patient monitoring (other tests may be warranted in some patients, depending on condition; » = major clinical significance):

» Clinical neurological examinations and
» Nerve conduction studies
(thalidomide may cause peripheral neuropathy, which may be irreversible; although peripheral neuropathy generally occurs over a period of months following long-term use of thalidomide, reports following relatively short-term use also exist; patients should be examined at monthly intervals for the first 3 months of thalidomide therapy for detection of early signs of neuropathy, including numbness, tingling, or pain in the hands and feet; patients should be evaluated periodically thereafter during treatment, and counseled, questioned, and evaluated regularly for signs or symptoms of peripheral neuropathy; electrophysiological testing, consisting of measurement of sensory nerve action potential [SNAP] amplitudes at baseline and every 6 months thereafter, may be considered; the variability in SNAP amplitudes may be limited by having the same examiner perform the baseline and follow-up tests, and by measuring several SNAPs on each occasion; if symptoms of medication-induced neuropathy develop, thalidomide should be *discontinued immediately* to limit further damage; treatment with thalidomide should be reinitiated only if the neuropathy returns to baseline status)

» HIV-viral load
(plasma HIV ribonucleic acid [RNA] levels were found to increase in HIV-positive patients treated with thalidomide compared with HIV-positive patients treated with placebo; it is recommended that HIV-viral load be measured in HIV-positive patients after the first and third months of thalidomide treatment and every 3 months thereafter)

Side/Adverse Effects

Note: Thalidomide may cause **peripheral neuropathy**, characterized by axonal degeneration without demyelination, affecting mainly sensory fibers in the lower limbs. Neuropathy is manifested initially by paresthesia of the feet, then the hands, followed by burning sensations in the extremities and by muscle cramps. Distribution is generally in a stocking-glove pattern.

Thalidomide does not cause major motor disability, although distal weakness in the feet and depression of the ankle deep tendon reflexes do occur late in the course of the neuropathy; on discontinuation, motor signs revert more readily and completely than sensory symptoms. Patients with mild, new onset, or progressive symptoms of peripheral neuropathy should discontinue thalidomide treatment. Thalidomide-induced neuropathy progresses gradually, over a period of weeks to months; neuropathy generally is reversible if thalidomide treatment is stopped in the early stages of neuropathy. However, symptoms may occur some time after thalidomide treatment has been stopped. Although some researchers have suggested a relationship between the total dose given and the neuropathy, others found no statistically significant correlation between the severity of this effect and total dose. However, the risk of developing polyneuropathy may be 10% or higher in chronically treated patients who do not have Hansen's disease. Results from one clinical study have suggested that smoking may have a protective effect against the development of peripheral neuropathy.

Electrophysiological abnormalities detected before the onset of subjective symptoms have been reported. The most prominent electrophysiological alteration was a decreased sensory nerve action potential (SNAP) amplitude, but decreased sensory and motor conduction velocities, as well as alterations in latencies, were also observed. The number of patients found to have developed neuropathy was consistently higher if electrophysiological tests, rather than clinical symptoms alone, were used for diagnosis. The reduced or absent sensitivity in the extremities was frequently irreversible or was only partially reversible over a long period. The incidence of peripheral neuropathy has ranged widely, from 0.5 to 50%. In human immunodeficiency virus (HIV)-infected patients, the incidence reportedly varies from 15 to 50%. Patients with preexisting neuropathies may be more sensitive to the development of thalidomide-induced neuropathy. However, neuropathy may also be seen in HIV disease itself. The side effects of thalidomide appear to be more severe and more poorly tolerated in HIV-infected patients.

Detecting thalidomide-induced neuropathy in erythema nodosum leprosum (ENL) patients may be difficult because of the similarity of clinical symptoms and changes in electrophysiological measurements that result from the underlying ENL disease. The incidence of peripheral neuropathy due to thalidomide appears to be low in patients being treated for ENL; this may be because peripheral nerves are consistently affected in lepromatous leprosy and thalidomide improves the neuritis of ENL by reducing inflammation. Gradual dose escalation may be efficacious in avoiding adverse reactions.

Serious dermatologic reactions including Stevens-Johnson syndrome and toxic epidermal necrolysis, which may be fatal, have been reported.

Seizures, including grand mal convulsions, have been reported during post-approval use of thalidomide in clinical practice. Because these events are reported voluntarily from a population of unknown size, estimates of frequency cannot be made. Most patients had disorders that may have predisposed them to seizure activity, and it is not currently known whether thalidomide has any epileptogenic influence. During therapy with thalidomide, patients with a history of seizures or with other risk factors for the development of seizures should be monitored closely for clinical changes that could precipitate acute seizure activity.

The following side/adverse effects have been selected on the basis of their potential clinical significance (possible signs and symptoms in parentheses where appropriate)—not necessarily inclusive:

Those indicating need for medical attention

Incidence more frequent

Deep vein thrombosis (pain, redness, or swelling in arm or leg); ***peripheral neuropathy*** (tingling, burning, numbness, or pain in the hands, arms, feet, or legs; muscle weakness); ***pulmonary embolus*** (anxiety; chest pain; cough; fainting; fast heartbeat; sudden shortness of breath or troubled breathing; dizziness or lightheadedness)

Note: If symptoms of thalidomide-induced neuropathy develop, thalidomide should be *discontinued immediately* to limit further damage. Usually, treatment with thalidomide should be reinitiated only if the neuropathy returns to baseline status.

Patients should undergo a baseline neurological exam before beginning thalidomide treatment.

Incidence rare

Fever; irregular heartbeat; low blood pressure; neutropenia (fever, chills, or sore throat); ***renal failure*** (blood in urine; decreased urination); ***skin rash***—seen more frequently in HIV-infected patients; may be moderate to severe

Those indicating need for medical attention only if they continue or are bothersome

Incidence more frequent

Dizziness; drowsiness; gastrointestinal intolerance (constipation; diarrhea; nausea; stomach pain)

Incidence less frequent

Dryness of mouth; dry skin; headache; increased appetite; mood alterations; swelling in the legs

Incidence not determined and indicating the need for medical attention—Reported during use of thalidomide; estimates of frequency cannot be determined

Seizures, including grand mal convulsions (muscle jerking of extremities; loss of consciousness; vision changes; atypical headache); ***Stevens-Johnson syndrome*** (peeling or loosening of skin; itching; red skin lesions, often with a purple center; sores, ulcers, or white spots in mouth or on lips); ***toxic epidermal necrolysis*** (blistering of skin; red irritated eyes; chills; red lesions with a purple center; unusual tiredness)

Overdose

For more information on the management of overdose or unintentional ingestion, **contact a Poison Control Center** (see *Poison Control Center Listing*).

Clinical effects of overdose

The toxicity of thalidomide is so low that a dose at which 50% of animals would be killed (LD_{50}) could not be established. Patients who have attempted suicide or have accidentally overdosed have survived without detectable sequelae. Overdoses of up to 14 grams of thalidomide taken with alcohol have resulted only in somnolence. No respiratory or circulatory problems have been reported.

Treatment of overdose

Supportive care—Patients in whom intentional overdose is confirmed or suspected should be referred for psychiatric consultation.

Patient Consultation

As an aid to patient consultation, refer to *Advice for the Patient, Thalidomide (Systemic).*

In providing consultation, consider emphasizing the following selected information (» = major clinical significance):

Before using this medication

» Conditions affecting use, especially:

Hypersensitivity to thalidomide

Pregnancy—Thalidomide is **contraindicated** during pregnancy; it is a known teratogen to the human fetus; women with childbearing potential should have a pregnancy test within 24 hours before starting thalidomide treatment, weekly during the first month of treatment, and every 2 to 4 weeks thereafter; two effective methods of contraception should be used simultaneously for at least 1 month before starting thalidomide treatment, during treatment, and for at least 1 month following discontinuation of treatment

Other medications, especially alcohol, barbiturates, carbamazepine, chloramphenicol, chlorpromazine, cisplatin, dapsone, didanosine, ethambutol, ethionamide, griseofulvin, HIV–protease inhibitors, hydralazine, isoniazid, lithium, metronidazole, nitrofurantoin, nitrous oxide, phenytoin, reserpine, rifabutin, rifampin, stavudine, vincristine, zalcitabine, other CNS depressants, and other medications associated with peripheral neuropathy

Other medical problems, especially neutropenia, epilepsy or other factors that predispose to seizures and peripheral neuropathy

Proper use of this medication

» Importance of not taking more medication than prescribed; not discontinuing medication without checking with physician

» Not sharing this medicine with others

» Importance of concomitant prophylactic anticoagulation or aspirin treatment to benefit certain patients with multiple myeloma

» Proper dosing

Missed dose: Taking as soon as possible; not taking if almost time for next dose; not doubling doses

» Proper storage

Precautions while using this medication

» Avoiding the use of alcoholic beverages and other medicines that cause drowsiness

» Having a pregnancy test done within 24 hours before starting thalidomide treatment, weekly during the first month of treatment, and every 2 to 4 weeks thereafter in women with childbearing potential

» Abstaining from heterosexual sexual contact unless using two effective methods of contraception simultaneously for at least 1 month before starting thalidomide, during treatment, and for at least 1 month following discontinuation of treatment, for women with childbearing potential

» For men, always using a condom during sexual contact with women of childbearing potential while taking thalidomide and for 4 weeks after discontinuing it

» Discontinuing thalidomide and calling physician immediately if mild, new onset, or progressive symptoms of peripheral neuropathy occur

» *Seeking out immediate medical care* if symptoms of thromboembolism such as shortness of breath, chest pain, or arm or leg swelling occur

Side/adverse effects

Signs of potential side effects, especially deep venous thrombosis, peripheral neuropathy, pulmonary embolus, fever, irregular heartbeat, low blood pressure, neutropenia, renal failure, seizures, Stevens-Johnson syndrome, skin rash and toxic epidermal necrolysis

General Dosing Information

Because of the toxicity and in an effort to make the enhance of fetal exposure to thalidomide as negligible as possible, thalidomide is approved for marketing only under a special restricted distribution program approved by the FDA. This program is called "System for Thalidomide Education and Prescribing Safety (STEPS®)." **Thalidomide must only be administered in compliance with all of the terms outlined in the STEPS® program and may only be prescribed and dispensed by prescribers and pharmacists registered with the program.**

Thalidomide should be taken with water, at least 1 hour after the evening meal, preferably at bedtime to minimize the impact of its sedative effect, which occurs in nearly all patients when therapy is started. Many patients rapidly adjust to this effect and are able to resume their normal daily activities.

The use of thalidomide for multiple myeloma results in an increased risk of venous thrombolic events. Preliminary data indicates that patients who are appropriate candidates may benefit from concomitant prophylactic anticoagulation or aspirin treatment.

Patients with newly diagnosed multiple myeloma who develop constipation, oversedation, or peripheral neuropathy may benefit from the discontinuation of thalidomide or continuing at a lower dose. When the side effects subside, thalidomide may be started at a lower dose or at the previous dose based on clinical judgment.

Dosing of thalidomide for erythema nodosum leprosum (ENL) generally should continue until signs and symptoms of active reaction have subsided, usually a period of at least 2 weeks. Patients may then be tapered off thalidomide in 50-mg decrements every 2 to 4 weeks. However, ENL recurrence is very common, often necessitating prolonged (up to several years) suppressive therapy.

Some patients (26% from one clinical study) receiving thalidomide for recurrent aphthous stomatitis have been able to discontinue thalidomide treatment after approximately 27 months of therapy, and a further 43% of patients remained in remission with continued low doses of thalidomide.

Because thalidomide is present in the semen, males receiving thalidomide must always use a latex condom during any sexual contact with women of childbearing potential. Males also must continue to use condoms during sexual contact for at least 4 weeks after discontinuing use of thalidomide.

Oral Dosage Forms

Note: Bracketed uses in the *Dosage Forms* section refer to categories of use and/or indications that are not included in U.S. product labeling.

THALIDOMIDE CAPSULES USP

Usual adult and adolescent dose

Erythema nodosum leprosum (ENL)[1]—

Cutaneous ENL, treatment: Oral, 100 to 300 mg once a day with water, taken at bedtime or at least one hour after the evening meal. Patients weighing less than 50 kilograms should be started at the low end of the dosing range.

Severe cutaneous ENL, treatment: Oral, up to 400 mg once a day at bedtime or in divided doses with water, at least one hour after meals.

Note: In patients with moderate to severe neuritis associated with a severe ENL reaction, corticosteroids may be started concomitantly with thalidomide. Corticosteroid use can be tapered and discontinued when the neuritis has ameliorated.

Recurrent ENL, suppression: Patients who have a documented history of requiring prolonged maintenance treatment to prevent the recurrence of cutaneous ENL or who flare during tapering should be maintained on the minimum dose necessary to control the reaction. Tapering the dosage of thalidomide should be attempted every three to six months, in decrements of 50 mg every two to four weeks.

Newly diagnosed multiple myeloma—

Oral, 200 mg once daily with water in combination dexamethasone in 28-day treatment cycles.

Dexamethasone dose—Oral, 40 mg once daily on days 1 through 4, 9 through 12, and 17 through 20, every 28 days.

[Behcet's syndrome][1]—

Oral, 100 to 300 mg a day with water, at bedtime or at least one hour after meals.

[Human immunodeficiency virus (HIV)–associated wasting syndrome][1]—

Oral, 100 or 200 mg once a day with water, at bedtime or at least one hour after the evening meal; or 100 mg two times a day with water, at least one hour after meals. Up to 300 mg per day may be required in some patients.

[Stomatitis, aphthous][1]—

Oral, 50 to 200 mg once a day with water, at bedtime or at least one hour after the evening meal, for four weeks. A maintenance dose of 50 mg four times a day may be required for some patients.

[Multiple myeloma][1]—

Because several doses using thalidomide are showing activity, no individual dose is listed here. Consult the medical literature and/or experts in the field of oncology for information on dosage

[Ulcer, esophageal, aphthous, human immunodeficiency virus (HIV)-associated][1]—

Oral, 200 mg once a day at bedtime with water.

Usual pediatric dose

Safety and efficacy not established in children below 12 years of age.

Strength(s) usually available

U.S.—

50 mg (Rx) [*THALOMID* (anhydrous lactose)].

Canada—

Not commercially available.

Note: In the U.S., thalidomide has orphan drug status for the treatment and maintenance of reactional lepromatous leprosy (Sponsor: Pediatric Pharmaceuticals, Westfield, NJ); for the treatment and prevention of graft-versus-host disease (GVHD) in patients receiving bone marrow transplantation (Sponsors: Andrulis Research Corporation, Bethesda, MD, and Pediatric Pharmaceuticals, Westfield, NJ); for the treatment of the clinical manifestations of mycobacterial infection caused by *Mycobacterium tuberculosis* and nontuberculous mycobacteria (Sponsor: Celgene Corporation, Warren, NJ); for the treatment and prevention of recurrent aphthous ulcers in severely, terminally immunocompromised patients (Sponsors: Celgene Corporation, Warren, NJ, and Andrulis Research Corporation, Bethesda, MD); and for the treatment of human immunodeficiency virus (HIV)–associated wasting syndrome (Sponsor: Celgene Corporation, Warren, NJ).

Canada revoked the total ban on thalidomide in 1984; thalidomide is now available on a limited basis, upon specific authorization, for emergency purposes only.

Packaging and storage

Store between 15 and 30 °C (59 and 86 °F). Protect from light.

Preparation of dosage form

For patients who cannot swallow oral solids—Thalidomide capsules may be opened and the powder mixed with a semi-solid food such as applesauce, gelatin, ice cream, or pudding. The food should then be eaten immediately. Because thalidomide is not very water-soluble, it may not mix well with beverages. Extemporaneous compounding of thalidomide solutions or suspensions also is not recommended.

Auxiliary labeling

- Take with water.
- May cause drowsiness.
- Continue medicine for full time of treatment.

Caution

Direct contact with the powder content of thalidomide capsules should be avoided.

Note: Before dispensing thalidomide, the pharmacist must activate the authorization number on every prescription by calling the Celgene customer care center at 1-888-4-CELGENE (1-888-423-5436) and obtain a confirmation number. Pharmacist must also write the confirmation number on the prescription and accept a prescription only if it has been issued within the previous 7 days (telephone prescriptions are not permitted); dispense no more than a 4-week (28-day) supply, with no automatic refills; dispense blister packs intact (capsules cannot be repackaged); dispense subsequent prescriptions only if fewer than 7 days of therapy remain on the previous prescription, and educate all staff pharmacists about the dispensing procedure for thalidomide.

[1]Not included in Canadian product labeling.

Revised: 07/21/2006

THEOPHYLLINE—See *Bronchodilators, Theophylline (Systemic)*

THIOPENTAL—See *Anesthetics, Barbiturate (Systemic)*

THIOPROPERAZINE—See *Phenothiazines (Systemic)*

THIORIDAZINE—See *Phenothiazines (Systemic)*

THIOTHIXENE—See *Thioxanthenes (Systemic)*

THROMBOLYTIC AGENTS
Systemic

This monograph includes information on the following: 1) Alteplase, Recombinant; 2) Anistreplase; 3) Streptokinase; 4) Urokinase.

VA CLASSIFICATION (Primary): BL115

Commonly used brand name(s): *Abbokinase*[4]; *Abbokinase Open-Cath*[4]; *Activase*[1]; *Activase rt-PA*[1]; *Cathflo Activase*[1]; *Eminase*[2]; *Streptase*[3].

Other commonly used names for [Anistreplase] are anisoylated plasminogen-streptokinase activator complex and APSAC.

Other commonly used names for [Alteplase, Recombinant], are tissue-type plasminogen activator (recombinant), t-PA, and rt-PA.

Note: For a listing of dosage forms and brand names by country availability, see *Dosage Forms* section(s).

Category

Thrombolytic.

Indications

Note: Bracketed information in the *Indications* section refers to uses that are not included in U.S. product labeling.

General Considerations

The selection of thrombolytic therapy must be evaluated individually for each patient based on confirmation of thrombotic disease and assessment of patient condition and history. Some of the indications for thrombolytic therapy are identical to those for heparin or coumarin- or indanedione-derivative anticoagulants. However, the goals of thrombolytic therapy and anticoagulant therapy are different. Thrombolytic agents are used primarily to lyse obstructive thrombi and restore blood flow in a recently occluded blood vessel, whereas anticoagulants are used primarily to prevent thrombus formation and extension of existing thrombi. The potential benefit of thrombolytic therapy must be weighed against the risk of bleeding because the risk of hemorrhage may be greater with thrombolytic agents than with heparin or coumarin- or indanedione-derivative anticoagulants.

Accepted

Thrombosis, coronary arterial, acute (treatment)—Alteplase, anistreplase, streptokinase, and urokinase are indicated to lyse acute coronary arterial thrombi associated with evolving transmural myocardial infarction. Alteplase and anistreplase are indicated for use via intravenous infusion; streptokinase is indicated for use via intravenous and intracoronary infusion; and urokinase is indicated for use only via intracoronary infusion. Various studies with intracoronary arterial injection have reported recanalization rates of 72 to 96%. In patients who received urokinase by intracoronary infusion within 6 hours following the onset of symptoms of a transmural myocardial infarction, 60% of the occluded coronary vessels were opened. However, it has not been established that the administration of urokinase during an evolving transmural myocardial infarction results in a preservation of myocardial tissue or a reduction in mortality. Additionally, intracoronary arterial administration requires prior identification of the site of the thrombus by coronary angiography. Intravenous infusion does not require coronary angiography and is the preferred route of administration because therapy can be instituted more rapidly and can be initiated in locations that lack facilities for cardiac catheterization.

Thrombolytic therapy, via intravenous or intracoronary routes of administration, may relieve chest pain, reduce the incidence of congestive heart failure, improve left ventricular function, limit cardiac damage (i.e., infarct size), and decrease the risk of early death if coronary arterial blood flow is restored before irreversible cardiac damage occurs. The reperfusion rate is dependent on the interval between the onset of symptoms and the initiation of therapy. Higher reperfusion rates are achieved when thrombolytic therapy is started within 4 hours after symptoms of ischemia first appear. However, reductions in mortality can be achieved if thrombolytic therapy is started up to 24 to 36 hours after the onset of symptoms.

Thrombolytic therapy is not a substitute for other measures that may be required to treat acute myocardial infarction or prevent reinfarction. Restoration of coronary arterial blood flow via thrombolysis does not correct underlying conditions that may promote thrombus formation. Recurrent ischemia, with or without reocclusion or overt reinfarction, may occur following initially successful thrombolysis. The risk of reocclusion may depend on the extent of residual stenosis in the affected vessel. Following successful thrombolytic therapy, long-term anticoagulation, platelet aggregation inhibitor therapy, percutaneous transluminal coronary angioplasty (PTCA), or coronary artery bypass graft (CABG) surgery may be required to provide long-lasting protection against reocclusion. However, initial thrombolytic therapy may permit a revascularization procedure to be performed on a delayed or elective, rather than on an emergency, basis.

Stroke, acute ischemic (treatment)—Alteplase[1] is indicated for the management of acute ischemic stroke in adults; it is used to improve neurologic recovery and reduce the incidence of disability. However, the safety and efficacy of alteplase therapy in patients with minor neurologic deficit, or with rapidly improving symptoms prior to the initiation of treatment, have not been evaluated.

Thromboembolism, pulmonary, acute (treatment)—Alteplase[1], streptokinase, and urokinase are indicated, and may be the therapy of choice in selected patients, for the lysis of acute, massive pulmonary emboli producing obstruction or significant filling defects involving two or more lobar pulmonary arteries or an equivalent degree of obstruction in other pulmonary vessels. These agents are also indicated for lysing pulmonary emboli accompanied by unstable hemodynamics, i.e., failure to maintain blood pressure without supportive measures. Heparin is recommended for the treatment of subacute or small emboli; however, some clinicians recommend thrombolytic therapy for comparatively small emboli in patients with limited cardiopulmonary reserve caused by significant cardiac or pulmonary disease. Prior to administration of a thrombolytic agent, the diagnosis should be confirmed by objective means such as pulmonary angiography via an upper extremity vein (preferred) or ventilation-perfusion lung scanning.

Thrombosis, deep venous (treatment)—Streptokinase and [urokinase][1] are indicated for the lysis of acute, extensive, deep venous thrombi in the popliteal or more proximal vessels. Thrombolytic therapy may be the treatment of choice for deep venous thrombosis in selected patients. [These agents are also used for the lysis of acute, extensive thrombi in the axillary subclavian veins and vena cavae in selected patients.] However, anticoagulants are recommended for treatment of calf-vein thrombi. Prior to administration of a thrombolytic agent, the diagnosis should be confirmed, preferably by ascending venography or by Doppler ultrasound.

Thromboembolism, arterial, acute (treatment) and
Thrombosis, arterial, acute (treatment)—Streptokinase and [urokinase] are indicated for use via intravenous infusion for the lysis of acute arterial thrombi or emboli. [These agents are also administered locally (via a catheter positioned adjacent to or inserted into the substance of the thrombus as shown by arteriogram) to lyse arterial thrombi or emboli.] Studies have shown that thrombolytic therapy alone may be ineffective for treating chronic arterial occlusion. Angioplasty or distal bypass may be required following initial thrombolytic therapy in order to salvage the affected limb.

Streptokinase has been used in the treatment (lysis) of arterial occlusions in pediatric patients from younger than 1 month of age up to 16 years of age; however, the evidence of clinical benefits and risks in these patients is based solely on anecdotal reports. Adverse events associated with the use of streptokinase in the pediatric population are similar in nature to those associated with its use in adults, including bleeding at catheter sites.[1]

Cannula, arteriovenous, clearance—Streptokinase and [urokinase][1] are indicated to clear totally or partially occluded arteriovenous cannulae, as an alternative to surgical revision, when acceptable flow cannot be achieved by conventional mechanical measures.

Catheter, intravenous, clearance—Alteplase and urokinase are indicated to restore patency to intravenous catheters, including central venous catheters, obstructed by clotted blood or fibrin deposits.

[Peripheral arterial occlusive disease (treatment)][1]—Alteplase is indicated via intra-arterial infusion for the treatment of peripheral arterial occlusive disease. However, because of the risks associated with this use, treatment should be limited to patients who are poor surgical candidates.

[Thrombolytic agents are also used to treat renal artery thrombosis, retinal blood vessel occlusions, hemolytic uremic syndrome, and impending renal cortical necrosis. However, controlled studies are required to establish the safety and effectiveness of such therapy in these conditions.][1]

Unaccepted

Thrombolytic agents should *not* be used to treat superficial thrombophlebitis.

Alteplase has not been sufficiently studied, and is currently not recommended, for treatment of deep venous thrombosis or arterial thrombosis not associated with evolving acute myocardial infarction or for clearing occluded arteriovenous cannulae or obstructed intravenous catheters.

Alteplase and streptokinase are not recommended for treatment of arterial emboli originating in the left side of the heart (e.g., mitral stenosis accompanied by atrial fibrillation) because of the risk of cerebral embolism.

Streptokinase is *not* indicated for restoration of patency of intravenous catheters.

---

[1]Not included in Canadian product labeling.

Pharmacology/Pharmacokinetics

Physicochemical characteristics

Source—

Alteplase: Glycoprotein enzyme (serine protease) containing 527 amino acids; produced by recombinant DNA technology utilizing the complementary DNA (cDNA) for natural human tissue-type plasminogen activator obtained from a human melanoma cell line.

Anistreplase: P-anisoylated derivative of a fibrinolytic enzyme (protein) complex consisting of human plasma-derived lys-plasminogen and bacterially derived streptokinase.

Streptokinase: Co-enzyme (protein) obtained from cultures of group C, beta-hemolytic streptococci.

Urokinase: Enzyme (protein) obtained from cultures of primary human neonatal kidney cells.

Molecular weight—

Alteplase: About 68,000 daltons.

Anistreplase: About 131,000 daltons.

Streptokinase: About 46,000 daltons.

Urokinase: About 33,000 daltons.

Mechanism of action/Effect

Thrombolytic agents activate the endogenous fibrinolytic system by cleaving the arginine$_{560}$–valine$_{561}$ bond in plasminogen to produce plasmin, an enzyme that degrades fibrin clots, fibrinogen, and other plasma proteins, including the procoagulant factors V and VIII. Alteplase and urokinase cleave the peptide bond directly. Anistreplase and streptokinase act indirectly; they combine with plasminogen to form streptokinase-plasminogen complexes that are converted to streptokinase-plasmin complexes. These activator complexes, rather than streptokinase itself, convert residual plasminogen to plasmin. These complexes are inactivated, in part, by antistreptococcal antibodies.

Conversion of plasminogen to plasmin occurs within the thrombus or embolus as well as on its surface and in circulating blood. Thrombolytic agents lyse fibrin deposits wherever they exist and can be reached by the plasmin generated; therefore, thrombolytic agents also promote lysis of fibrin deposits responsible for hemostasis.

Alteplase is more clot-selective than the other thrombolytic agents, binding more readily to the fibrin-plasminogen complex within a clot than to circulating (free) plasminogen. However, limited systemic fibrinolysis does occur with usual therapeutic doses.

Other actions/effects

Fibrinogenolysis and fibrinolysis induced by thrombolytic agents increase the concentration of fibrinogen-degradation and fibrin-degradation products (FDP/fdp) in the blood. The FDP/fdp exert an anticoagulant effect, probably by impairing fibrin polymerization and possibly by decreasing thrombin generation and/or interfering with platelet function. Alteplase usually reduces the circulating fibrinogen concentration and increases FDP/fdp concentrations to a lesser extent than does streptokinase, but to about the same extent that urokinase does. However, studies have not shown a significantly lower incidence of bleeding with alteplase than has been reported with the other thrombolytic agents, probably because factors other than the concentrations of fibrinogen and/or FDP/fdp also significantly influence the risk of bleeding (see *Side/Adverse Effects*). Specifically, the risk of bleeding complications associated with thrombolytic therapy may be more dependent on the presence of vascular injury than on the extent of systemic fibrinolysis induced by a specific agent.

Anistreplase has potent proteolytic activity in the systemic circulation. In addition to decreasing plasma concentrations of fibrinogen, the medication lowers plasma concentrations of plasminogen, procoagulant factors V and VIII, and the fibrinolysis inhibitor alpha-2-antiplasmin.

Anistreplase, streptokinase, and urokinase have also been reported to decrease plasma viscosity and erythrocyte aggregation, probably as a result of reduced fibrinogen concentration.

Streptokinase and the streptokinase component of anistreplase are antigenic and induce the formation of antibodies. Elevation of the anti-streptokinase antibody titer usually occurs about 5 to 7 days following administration, reaches a peak after 2 to 3 weeks, and may persist for 1 year or longer. The antibodies may cause resistance to subsequent streptokinase or anistreplase therapy, and possibly an increased risk of anaphylaxis or other severe allergic reactions.

Biotransformation

Alteplase—Hepatic; rapid.

Streptokinase—Hepatic; no metabolites identified.

Urokinase—Hepatic; rapid.

Half-life

Alteplase—

Distribution: Less than 5 minutes.

Elimination: Approximately 35 minutes.

Anistreplase—

The half-life of anistreplase's fibrinolytic activity is 70 to 120 minutes (average about 90 minutes). The deacylation half-life of the complex is about 105 to 120 minutes. The plasma clearance and duration of fibrinolytic activity of the medication are probably controlled primarily by its deacylation rate.

Streptokinase—

Following intravenous administration of 1.5 million International Units (IU) over a 1-hour period: the half-life of the activator complexes (streptokinase-plasminogen and/or streptokinase-plasmin) is 23 minutes.

Urokinase—

Up to 20 minutes. The half-life may be prolonged in patients with hepatic function impairment.

Time to peak effect

Reperfusion of the myocardium generally occurs 20 minutes to 2 hours (average 45 minutes) following initiation of intravenous therapy.

Duration of action

Thrombolysis may continue for approximately 4 hours following administration of alteplase, streptokinase, or urokinase; the hyperfibrinolytic effect disappears within a few hours following discontinuation of administration. Following administration of anistreplase, thrombolysis may continue for approximately 6 hours, and a systemic hyperfibrinolytic state, as demonstrated by euglobulin clot lysis time determinations, may persist for more than 2 days. For all thrombolytic agents, the prothrombin time may rarely be prolonged for 12 to 24 hours following cessation of therapy because of the decreased plasma concentration of fibrinogen, decreased plasma concentration of factor V and possibly other coagulant factors, and/or the anticoagulant effects of FDP/fdp. However, prolonged, high FDP/fdp concentrations may potentiate bleeding for a longer period of time, especially after administration of non–clot-selective thrombolytic agents.

Elimination

Alteplase—Renal; approximately 80% of a dose is excreted in the urine, as metabolites, within 18 hours.

Urokinase—Small quantities are eliminated via the renal and biliary routes.

Precautions to Consider

Cross-sensitivity and/or related problems

Patients allergic to streptokinase will be allergic to anistreplase also, and vice versa.

Carcinogenicity

Alteplase, anistreplase, and *urokinase*—Long-term studies to determine whether alteplase, anistreplase, and urokinase have carcinogenic potential have not been done.

Mutagenicity

Alteplase—No mutagenicity was demonstrated in the Ames test or in chromosomal aberration assays in human lymphocytes.

Anistreplase—No mutagenicity was demonstrated in chromosomal aberration assays in human lymphocytes.

Pregnancy/Reproduction

Fertility—*Alteplase*: Studies have not been done in animals.

Anistreplase: Studies have not been done in humans.

Studies have not been done in animals.

Urokinase: Studies in mice and rats have not shown that urokinase causes impaired fertility.

Pregnancy—It has been suggested that administration of a thrombolytic agent during the first 18 weeks of pregnancy may increase the risk of premature separation of the placenta because fetal attachments to the uterus during this time are composed primarily of fibrin. However, this problem has not been reported following administration of streptokinase or urokinase to patients during the first 2 trimesters of pregnancy.

Alteplase and anistreplase—

Studies have not been done in humans.

Studies have not been done in animals.

FDA Pregnancy Category C.

Streptokinase—

Streptokinase apparently crosses the human placenta minimally if at all. However, antibodies to streptokinase do cross the placenta. Studies in pregnant women (treated mostly during the second and third trimesters) have not shown evidence of abnormalities or induction of fibrinolysis in the fetus.

Studies have not been done in animals.

FDA Pregnancy Category C.

Urokinase—

Adequate and well-controlled studies have not been done in humans.

Studies in mice and rats have not shown that urokinase causes fetal harm when administered in doses up to 1000 times the human dose. Because animal reproduction studies are not always predictive of human response, this drug should be used during pregnancy only if clearly needed.

FDA Pregnancy Category B.

Postpartum—

Thrombolytic agents should be administered with great caution during the first 10 days postpartum because of the increased risk of hemorrhage.

Breast-feeding

It is not known whether thrombolytic agents are distributed into breast milk. However, problems in humans have not been documented. Because many drugs are distributed in human milk, caution should be exercised when a thrombolytic agent is administered to a nursing woman.

Pediatrics

Safety and efficacy have not been established.

Although controlled clinical studies have not been conducted to determine the safety and efficacy of using streptokinase in pediatric patients, a significant number of anecdotal reports exist supporting the use of streptokinase in children, particularly for the treatment of arterial occlusions. In patients from younger than 1 month of age up to 16 years of age, the use of streptokinase for the treatment of acute arterial occlusions resulted in bleeding complications in as many as 50% of catheter sites in some studies. Occasionally, bleeding has required blood transfusion. Careful monitoring of the patient is therefore recommended.

Geriatrics

Geriatric patients generally have a poorer prognosis than younger adults following an acute myocardial infarction. Also, they may be more likely than younger adults to have pre-existing conditions that tend to increase the risk of intracranial bleeding or other hemorrhagic complications. Because the risks of thrombolytic therapy, as well as its potential benefits, are increased in older patients, careful patient selection and monitoring are recommended.

Drug interactions and/or related problems

The following drug interactions and/or related problems have been selected on the basis of their potential clinical significance (possible mechanism in parentheses where appropriate)—not necessarily inclusive (» = major clinical significance):

Note: Combinations containing any of the following medications, depending on the amount present, also may interact with this medication.

In addition to the interactions listed below, the possibility should be considered that multiple effects leading to further impairment of blood clotting and/or increased risk of hemorrhage may occur if a thrombolytic agent is administered to a patient receiving any medication having a significant potential for causing hypoprothrombinemia, thrombocytopenia, or gastrointestinal ulceration or hemorrhage.

» Anticoagulants, coumarin- or indanedione-derivative or

» Enoxaparin or

» Heparin

(concurrent use with antithrombotic or thrombolytic agents increases the risk of hemorrhage; however, heparin is often administered concurrently with intravenous thrombolytic therapy for the treatment of acute coronary arterial occlusion or with low doses of thrombolytic agents given intra-arterially; in one clinical study, no increased risk of hemorrhage was shown with concurrent use of heparin during intracoronary administration of urokinase; also, thrombolytic therapy may be administered following initial anticoagulant therapy)

(anticoagulants are recommended to prevent additional thrombus formation following thrombolytic therapy for most indications; however, following intravenous thrombolytic therapy for acute coronary arterial occlusion, the need for anticoagulant administration should be determined on an individual basis; if an anticoagulant is administered under these circumstances, careful monitoring of the patient is recommended because studies have shown that heparin, when administered after intravenous streptokinase for this indication, increases the risk of hemorrhage)

(although an initial dose of heparin is recommended prior to intracoronary use of urokinase, anticoagulants including heparin should not be given concurrently with large doses of intravenous urokinase, when used to treat pulmonary embolism, because of an increased risk of hemorrhage; if heparin has been given, it should be discontinued and the aPTT should be less than twice the normal control value before thrombolytic therapy is started)

(after infusing urokinase, anticoagulation treatment is recommended to prevent recurrent thrombosis; do not begin anticoagulation until the aPTT has decreased to less than twice the normal control value; if heparin is used, do not administer a loading dose of heparin; treatment should be followed by oral anticoagulants)

» Antifibrinolytic agents, such as:

Aminocaproic acid

Aprotinin

Tranexamic acid

(the actions of antifibrinolytic agents and of thrombolytic agents are mutually antagonistic; although antifibrinolytic agents may be effective in treating severe hemorrhage caused by thrombolytic agents, controlled studies to verify their efficacy and safety have not been done)

Antihypertensive agents or

Other hypotension-producing medications

(the risk of severe hypotension may be increased, especially when streptokinase is administered rapidly for treatment of coronary arterial occlusion)

» Cefamandole or

» Cefoperazone or

» Cefotetan or

» Plicamycin or

» Valproic acid

(these medications may cause hypoprothrombinemia; in addition, plicamycin or valproic acid may inhibit platelet aggregation; concurrent use with a thrombolytic agent may increase the risk of severe hemorrhage and is not recommended)

Corticosteroids, glucocorticoids or

Corticotropin, chronic therapeutic use or

Ethacrynic acid or

Salicylates, nonacetylated

(gastrointestinal ulceration or hemorrhage may occur during therapy with these medications and cause increased risk of severe hemorrhage in patients receiving thrombolytic therapy)

» Nonsteroidal anti-inflammatory drugs (NSAIDs), especially:

Indomethacin

Phenylbutazone or

» Platelet aggregation inhibitors (see *Appendix II*), especially:

Aspirin

Dipyridamole or

GP IIb and IIa inhibitors or

Sulfinpyrazone or

Ticlopidine

(concurrent use of a platelet aggregation inhibitor and a thrombolytic agent may increase the risk of bleeding and is generally not recommended [except when aspirin therapy for acute myocardial infarction is initiated concurrently with thrombolytic therapy])

(initiation of aspirin therapy [160 mg per day] before or during intravenous administration of alteplase, anistreplase, or streptokinase for treatment of acute coronary arterial occlusion may reduce significantly the risk of reocclusion, reinfarction, stroke, and death without increasing the risk of adverse effects [as compared to the thrombolytic agent or aspirin alone]; however, larger doses of aspirin have been shown to increase the risk of bleeding in patients receiving thrombolytic agents for other indications; the possibility of hemorrhage should be considered and the patient carefully monitored) (the potential occurrence of gastrointestinal ulceration and/or hemorrhage during therapy with NSAIDs [including analgesic or antirheumatic doses of aspirin] or sulfinpyrazone also may cause increased risk to patients receiving thrombolytic therapy)

Thiotepa
(urokinase may increase the efficacy of thiotepa in the treatment of bladder cancer by acting as a plasminogen activator and increasing the amount of thiotepa in tumor tissue)

Thrombolytic agents, other
(administration of urokinase prior to, during, or after other thrombolytic agents may increase the risk of serious bleeding)

Laboratory value alterations

The following have been selected on the basis of their potential clinical significance (possible effect in parentheses where appropriate)—not necessarily inclusive (» = major clinical significance).

With diagnostic test results

Coagulation tests and
Tests for systemic fibrinolysis
(the fibrinolytic activity of thrombolytic agents persists *in vitro;* unless the patient is extremely resistant to thrombolytic therapy, degradation of fibrinogen in blood samples will lead to unreliable test results [when specific measurements of fibrinogen, rather than a general indication that fibrinolysis is occurring, are required]; the addition of a fibrinolysis inhibitor, e.g., aprotinin [150 to 200 Kallikrein Inhibitor Units per mL of blood], or aminocaproic acid may reduce this effect)

With physiology/laboratory test values

Activated partial thromboplastin time (APTT) and
Prothrombin time (PT) and
Thrombin time (TT)
(values will be increased unless the patient is extremely resistant to thrombolytic therapy)

$Alpha_2$-antiplasmin activity and
Factor V activity and
Factor VIII activity and
Fibrinogen activity and
Plasminogen activity
(will be decreased unless the patient is extremely resistant to thrombolytic therapy; significant recovery of fibrinogen activity may occur within 18 to 36 hours after discontinuation of thrombolytic therapy, but return of fibrinogen activity to pretreatment values may require up to 48 hours after discontinuation of thrombolytic therapy; recovery of plasminogen activity also may require more than 30 hours)

Blood pressure
(may be decreased, especially when a thrombolytic agent is administered rapidly for treatment of acute coronary arterial occlusion; a decrease in blood pressure [not secondary to anaphylaxis or bleeding], which may be severe, has also been reported in about 10% of anistreplase-treated patients)

Fibrinogen-degradation and fibrin-degradation products (FDP/fdp) concentrations
(will be increased unless the patient is extremely resistant to thrombolytic therapy; return to pretreatment values may require up to 48 hours after discontinuation of thrombolytic therapy)

Hematocrit values and
Hemoglobin concentrations
(moderate reduction not related to clinical bleeding has been reported in 20% of patients receiving thrombolytic therapy)

Medical considerations/Contraindications

The medical considerations/contraindications included have been selected on the basis of their potential clinical significance (reasons given in parentheses where appropriate)—not necessarily inclusive (» = major clinical significance).

Except under special circumstances, this medication should not be used when the following medical problems exist:

For all thrombolytic agents

» Aneurysm, dissecting and/or intracranial, confirmed or suspected or
» Arteriovenous malformation or
» Bleeding, active or
» Brain tumor, primary, or neoplasm metastatic to the central nervous system (CNS) from other primary sites or
» Cerebrovascular accident, or history of or
» Neurosurgery, intracranial or intraspinal, within past 2 months or
» Surgery, thoracic, recent or
» Trauma to the CNS, recent
(increased risk of uncontrollable hemorrhage)
» Hypertension, severe, uncontrolled, i.e., ≥ 200 mm Hg systolic and/or ≥ 120 mm Hg diastolic
(increased risk of cerebral hemorrhage)

For alteplase used to treat acute ischemic stroke (in addition to medical problems listed above)

» Bleeding diathesis, such as
Heparin therapy within 48 hours preceding the onset of stroke along with an elevated APTT at presentation
Oral anticoagulant therapy with a PT > 15 seconds
Platelet count < 100,000 per mm^3 or
» Hemorrhage, intracranial, evidence of on pretreatment evaluation, or history of or
» Hemorrhage, subarachnoid, suspected or
» Hypertension, severe, uncontrolled, i.e., > 185 mm Hg systolic or > 110 mm Hg diastolic or
» Seizure at the onset of stroke or
» Stroke, recent
(increased risk of bleeding, which could result in significant disability or death)

For anistreplase, streptokinase, and urokinase (in addition to medical problems listed above)

» Anaphylaxis or other severe allergic reaction to anistreplase, streptokinase, or urokinase, history of
(increased risk of anaphylaxis)

For urokinase (in addition to medical problems listed above)

» Bleeding diatheses, known
(increased risk of bleeding)

Risk-benefit should be considered when the following medical problems exist:

For all thrombolytic agents

Allergic reaction, mild, to the thrombolytic agent considered for use, history of
Any condition in which the risk of bleeding or hemorrhage is present or would be difficult to control because of its location, such as:
Cardiopulmonary resuscitation with possibility of internal injury, recent
Cerebrovascular disease
» Childbirth within past 10 days
» Coagulation defects, uncontrolled, or other hemostatic defects, including those secondary to severe hepatic or renal disease
» Endocarditis, bacterial, subacute
» Gastrointestinal bleeding, severe, within past 10 days
Gastrointestinal lesion or ulcer, active or history of
Genitourinary bleeding within past 10 days
Hemorrhagic retinopathy, diabetic, or other hemorrhagic ophthalmic conditions
Hepatic function impairment, severe
Hypertension, moderate, not optimally controlled, i.e., 180 to 200 mm Hg systolic and/or 110 to 120 mm Hg diastolic
Invasive procedure, such as lumbar puncture, paracentesis, or thoracentesis, recent
Knitted dacron graft
» Neurosurgical procedure more than 2 months previously
» Organ biopsy within past 10 days
Pregnancy
» Puncture of noncompressible blood vessel within past 10 days
» Surgery, major, other than neurosurgery or thoracic surgery, within past 10 days
Trauma, minor, recent, other than to the CNS
» Trauma, severe, recent, other than to the CNS
Tuberculosis, active, with cavitation of recent onset
Infection at or near site of thrombus, obstructed intravenous catheter, or occluded arteriovenous cannula
(risk of spreading the infection into and via the circulation)
» Mitral stenosis with atrial fibrillation or other indications of probable left heart thrombus
(risk of new embolic phenomena including those to cerebral vessels)
Pericarditis, acute
(risk of hemopericardium, which may lead to cardiac tamponade)

For alteplase used to treat acute ischemic stroke (in addition to medical problems listed above)

» Infarct signs, major, on cranial computed tomographic scan, e.g., substantial edema, mass effect, or midline shift or
» Neurologic deficit, severe, i.e., National Institutes of Health Stroke Scale score > 22 at presentation
(increased risk of intracranial hemorrhage)

For anistreplase and streptokinase (in addition to medical problems listed above)

» Anistreplase or streptokinase therapy within past 5 days to 1 year or
» Streptococcal infection, recent
(antistreptococcal antibodies are likely to be present in the circulation; these antibodies may cause a temporary resistance to the therapeutic effects of anistreplase or streptokinase and/or an in-

creased risk of severe allergic reactions to the medication; although resistance may be overcome by increasing the dosage, use of an alternate thrombolytic agent [alteplase or urokinase] is advisable if thrombolytic therapy is needed within 1 year after anistreplase or streptokinase therapy or streptococcal infection)

Patient monitoring

The following may be especially important in patient monitoring (other tests may be warranted in some patients, depending on condition; » = major clinical significance):

Note: Initiation of therapy for acute coronary arterial occlusion must **not** be delayed until the results of the tests recommended below are available. However, blood may be drawn prior to initiation of therapy so that appropriate tests can be performed to determine the hemostatic status of the patient, especially if a potential bleeding problem exists or is suspected, and/or to establish baseline values.

Prior to initiation of therapy

» Coagulation tests, such as:
Activated partial thromboplastin time (APTT)
Fibrin/fibrinogen degradation product (FDP/fdp) titer
Fibrinogen concentration
Prothrombin time (PT)
Thrombin time (TT) and

» Hematocrit values and

» Hemoglobin concentrations and

» Platelet count
(recommended prior to initiation of therapy to determine the hemostatic status of the patient and/or to establish baseline values so that the presence of fibrinolysis can be confirmed during therapy; heparin therapy should be discontinued before thrombolytic therapy is instituted unless the heparin is being given in conjunction with urokinase for intracoronary administration; also the APTT or TT should be less than 2 times the control value before thrombolytic therapy is instituted)

» Electrocardiogram (ECG)
(recommended when acute coronary arterial thrombosis is suspected, to confirm diagnosis and to aid in selecting patients in whom thrombolytic therapy is likely to be most beneficial)

During and/or following therapy

Coagulation tests, such as APTT, PT, or TT and/or

Tests of fibrinolytic activity, such as fibrinogen concentration, FDP/fdp titer, reptilase clotting time, and/or whole blood euglobulin lysis time
(recommended 3 to 4 hours following initiation of intravenous therapy for indications other than acute coronary arterial thrombosis; these tests may be repeated every 12 hours for the duration of therapy, if necessary, to determine that a fibrinolytic state exists; however, such tests do not reliably predict either efficacy of medication or risk of bleeding and are not currently recommended for determining maintenance dosage; a TT value equal to or greater than 1.5 times the control value in seconds, or a decrease of fibrinogen concentration to 50% or less of the control value [with alteplase or anistreplase, a reduction to 75% of the control value may be sufficient], indicates that fibrinolysis is occurring)

Note: Confirmation of fibrinolysis does **not** require that all of the tests listed above be used for each patient. The selection of a particular test for monitoring thrombolytic therapy depends upon physician preference and available laboratory facilities.

Because heparin also prolongs APTT, PT, and TT, the results of these determinations may be misleading if heparin has been or is being administered; tests that more directly measure fibrinolytic activity may be more reliable.

Computed tomography and/or

Impedance plethysmography and/or

Quantitative Doppler effect determination and/or

Visualization of affected vessel via angiography or venography
(may be useful in assessing restoration of blood flow; also, may aid in determining optimum duration of therapy; however, repeated venograms are not recommended)

Coronary angiography and/or

Myocardial scanning, radionuclide
(may be useful for monitoring effectiveness of therapy for coronary arterial thrombosis in evolving transmural myocardial infarction; coronary angiography and myocardial scanning also may be useful for assessing the patency of the coronary vasculature and for determining whether further treatment to prevent reocclusion is needed; however, coronary angiography increases the risk of adverse effects, including severe bleeding, when performed within several days after thrombolytic therapy; it is recommended that the procedure be performed only when necessary [as determined by signs and symptoms of persistent ischemia], preferably after a delay of 7 to 10 days following thrombolytic therapy)

Creatine kinase activity or other cardiac enzyme determination
(may be useful for monitoring effectiveness of therapy for acute coronary arterial thrombosis)

» Electrocardiogram (ECG)
(monitoring during and following administration for treatment of acute coronary arterial thrombosis is recommended to detect reperfusion atrial or ventricular arrhythmias; also, may be useful as a means of determining effectiveness of treatment because reversal of some abnormalities may occur with recanalization)

Hematocrit values
(monitoring recommended to detect possible blood loss during and following thrombolytic therapy)

» Mental status and

» Neurologic status
(monitoring recommended because altered sensorium or neurologic changes may be indicative of intracranial bleeding)

Stool tests for occult blood loss and

Urine tests for hematuria
(recommended periodically during therapy)

» Vital signs, such as blood pressure, pulse, respiratory rate, and temperature
(continuous monitoring recommended during therapy for acute coronary arterial occlusion to detect adverse effects such as bradycardia, hypotension, and allergic reactions; a reduction in the infusion rate is usually sufficient to correct hypotension)
(monitoring recommended at least every 4 hours during therapy for other indications; however, a lower extremity should **not** be used for blood pressure determinations when there is a risk of dislodging deep vein thrombi that may be present)

Side/Adverse Effects

Note: Rarely, thrombolysis causes clot fragmentation with migration of the fragments resulting in additional embolic complications. Patients should be monitored for new embolic phenomena.

Bleeding, the most common side effect encountered during thrombolytic therapy, occurs most frequently at invaded sites (e.g., sites of arterial punctures, venous cutdowns, recent surgery) because thrombolytic agents promote lysis of the fibrin deposits that are needed to maintain hemostasis at these sites. The risk of bleeding at invaded sites is not reduced by administration of a relatively clot-selective agent such as alteplase. Studies comparing alteplase with streptokinase have shown a similar incidence of internal bleeding with both agents. However, most patients in these studies also received heparin or other potentially hemorrhagic medications concurrently with and/or immediately following the thrombolytic agent. Therefore, the frequency of hemorrhage attributable solely to the thrombolytic agent has not been determined. In some patients, bleeding may be severe enough to result in anemia or shock.

Chest pain or cardiac arrhythmias may occur during or following thrombolytic therapy for acute coronary arterial thrombosis. These are not direct effects of the medication. Chest pain may indicate treatment failure or reocclusion. Cardiac arrhythmias may be associated with the myocardial infarction itself, or may be induced by sudden reperfusion. Specific arrhythmias that have been reported include sinus bradycardia, accelerated idioventricular rhythm, ventricular premature depolarizations, ventricular tachycardia, second- and third-degree atrioventricular block, atrial fibrillation, and (especially in patients with coronary instrumentation) ventricular fibrillation. Hypotension may occur in association with reperfusion bradyarrhythmias.

Nausea and vomiting have also been reported during thrombolytic therapy. However, a causal relationship to the medication has not been established because these symptoms occur frequently during acute myocardial infarction.

The lys-plasminogen used in manufacturing anistreplase is obtained from human plasma. To reduce the risk of the patient's contracting viral infections that may be transmitted via human blood-derived products, the material is tested for viral antigens or particles and heat-treated to inactivate viral particles. Hepatitis has not been reported to date.

Urokinase is made from human neonatal kidney cells grown in tissue culture. Products made from human source material may contain infectious agents, such as viruses, that can cause disease. The risk that urokinase will transmit an infectious agent has been reduced by screening donors for prior exposure to certain viruses, by testing donors for the presence of certain current virus infections, by testing for certain viruses during manufacturing, and by inactivating and/or removing certain viruses during manufacturing. Despite these measures, urokinase may carry a risk of transmitting infectious agents including those that cause the Creutzfeldt-Jakob disease [CJD] or other diseases. Therefore, the risk of transmission of infectious agents cannot be totally eliminated. All infections that may have been transmitted by urokinase should be reported by the healthcare professional to the manufacturer.

The following effects have been selected on the basis of their potential clinical significance (possible signs and symptoms in parentheses where appropriate)—not necessarily inclusive:

Those indicating need for medical attention

Incidence more frequent

Bleeding or oozing from cuts, invaded or disturbed sites, wounds, or gums; decreased blood pressure, not secondary to bleeding or to streptokinase-induced anaphylaxis—may be severe, especially when a thrombolytic agent is given rapidly and/or when other medications having hypotensive actions, such as vasodilators or morphine, are used concurrently

Incidence more frequent with anistreplase and streptokinase; less frequent with urokinase

Fever

Note: Elevations of body temperature by about 1.5 °F occur in up to 33%, and body temperature as high as 104 °F has been reported in about 3.5%, of patients receiving streptokinase. Approximately 2 to 3% of patients receiving urokinase develop a febrile reaction to the medication. *Fever* has also been reported with alteplase, but a causal relationship has not been established.

Incidence less frequent or rare

Allergic reaction (flushing or redness of skin; mild headache; mild muscle pain; nausea; skin rash, hives, or itching; troubled breathing or wheezing)—less frequent with streptokinase and rare with alteplase or urokinase; ***bleeding into subcutaneous tissues*** (bruising); ***cholesterol embolism/embolization may include: acute renal failure*** (agitation, coma, confusion, decreased urine output, depression, dizziness, headache, hostility, irritability, lethargy, muscle twitching, nausea, rapid weight gain, seizures, stupor, swelling of face, ankles, or hands, unusual tiredness or weakness); ***bowel infarction; cerebral or spinal cord infarction*** (blurred vision; confusion; numbness or tingling in face, arms, legs; severe headache; trouble speaking or walking); ***gangrenous digits; hypertension*** (blurred vision, dizziness, nervousness, headache, pounding in the ears, slow or fast heartbeat); ***livedo reticularis*** (purplish red, net-like, blotchy spots on skin); ***myocardial infarction*** (chest pain or discomfort, pain or discomfort in arms, jaw, back or neck, shortness of breath, nausea, sweating, vomiting); ***pancreatitis*** (bloating, chills, constipation, darkened urine, fast heartbeat, fever, indigestion, loss of appetite, nausea, pains in stomach, side, or abdomen, possibly radiating to the back, vomiting, yellow eyes or skin); ***"purple toe" syndrome*** (blue or purple toes, pain in toes); ***retinal artery occlusion; rhabdomyolysis*** (dark-colored urine, fever, muscle cramps or spasms, muscle pain or stiffness, unusual tiredness or weakness)—with alteplase, anistreplase, streptokinase, and urokinase; ***internal bleeding*** (abdominal pain or swelling; back pain or backaches; bloody urine; bloody or black, tarry stools; constipation caused by hemorrhage-induced paralytic ileus or intestinal obstruction; coughing up blood; dizziness; headaches, sudden, severe, and/or continuing; joint pain, stiffness, or swelling; muscle pain or stiffness, severe or continuing; nosebleeds; unexpected or unusually heavy bleeding from vagina; vomiting of blood or material that looks like coffee grounds); ***stroke, hemorrhagic or thromboembolic*** (confusion; double vision; impairment of speech; weakness in arms or legs)—more frequent with alteplase

Note: Individual symptoms of *internal bleeding* depend on the site of bleeding and have not necessarily been reported with all of the thrombolytic agents; internal bleeding has been reported following intracoronary arterial administration as well as following intravenous administration; with alteplase, the incidences of gastrointestinal, genitourinary, and retroperitoneal bleeding are 5%, 4%, and < 1%, respectively; the incidence of intracranial hemorrhage (ICH) in patients with acute myocardial infarction treated with alteplase is 0.4% with total doses of 100 mg or 1 to 1.4 mg per kg of body weight (mg/kg) and 1.3% with a total dose of 150 mg; the incidence of ICH in patients treated with alteplase for acute ischemic stroke was found to be 15.4% in trials.

Incidence rare—for anistreplase, streptokinase, and urokinase

Allergic reaction, severe, or anaphylaxis (changes in facial skin color; fast or irregular breathing; large, hive-like swellings on eyelids, face, mouth, lips, or tongue; puffiness or swelling of the eyelids or around the eyes; shortness of breath, troubled breathing, tightness in chest, and/or wheezing; skin rash, hives, and/or itching)—also may include anaphylactic shock with sudden, severe decrease in blood pressure

Note: An *anaphylactic reaction* has been reported in a patient following a second course of streptokinase given 1 month after the first course for clearance of an occluded arteriovenous shunt. Therefore, the probability of systemic absorption of streptokinase following use for this purpose must be considered.

Incidence not determined—Observed during clinical practice for urokinase, estimates of frequency cannot be determined

Allergic-type reactions such as bronchospasm (cough, difficulty breathing, noisy breathing, shortness of breath, tightness in chest, wheezing); ***orolingual edema*** (swelling of the tongue and mouth); ***urticaria*** (hives or welts, itching, redness of skin, skin rash); ***skin rash; pruritus*** (itching skin); ***infusion reaction may include: acidosis*** (drowsiness, fatigue, headache, nausea, troubled breathing, vomiting); ***back pain; chills/rigors*** (feeling unusually cold, shivering); ***cyanosis*** (bluish color of fingernails, lips, skin, palms, or nail beds); ***dyspnea*** (shortness of breath, difficult or labored breathing, tightness in chest, wheezing); ***fever; hypertension*** (blurred vision, dizziness, nervousness, headache, pounding in the ears, slow or fast heartbeat); ***hypotension*** (blurred vision, confusion, dizziness, faintness or lightheadedness when getting up from a lying or sitting position suddenly, sweating, unusual tiredness or weakness); ***hypoxia*** (confusion, dizziness, fast heartbeat, shortness of breath, weakness); ***nausea; tachycardia*** (fast, pounding, or irregular heartbeat or pulse); ***vomiting***

Those indicating need for medical attention only if they continue or are bothersome

Incidence rare

Skin lesions—with streptokinase

Patient Consultation

As an aid to patient consultation, refer to *Advice for the Patient, Thrombolytic Agents (Systemic).*

In providing consultation, consider emphasizing the following selected information (» = major clinical significance):

Before receiving this medication

» Conditions affecting use, especially:

Allergic reaction to the thrombolytic agent considered for use, history of, especially a severe allergic reaction to anistreplase, streptokinase, or urokinase

Pregnancy—Thrombolytic agents should be used during pregnancy only if clearly needed.

Breast-feeding—Because many drugs are distributed in human milk, caution should be exercised when a thrombolytic agent is administered to a nursing woman.

Use in the elderly—May have conditions which increase the risk of hemorrhage

Other medications, especially anticoagulants, antifibrinolytic agents, enoxaparin, heparin, hypoprothrombinemia-inducing cephalosporins, nonsteroidal anti-inflammatory drugs, platelet aggregation inhibitors, plicamycin, and valproic acid

Other medical problems for all thrombolytic agents, especially conditions leading to an increased risk of uncontrollable or cerebral hemorrhage. Other medical problems for anistreplase and streptokinase, especially prior treatment with either agent (within the past 12 months). Other medical problems for anistreplase, streptokinase, and urokinase, especially history of anaphylaxis or severe allergic reaction to any of these agents. Other medical problems for alteplase and urokinase, especially bleeding diatheses.

Proper use of this medication

» Proper dosing

Precautions after receiving this medication

» Importance of compliance with strict bed rest or other measures to minimize bleeding

Side/adverse effects

Signs of potential side effects, especially bleeding or oozing from cuts, invaded or disturbed sites, wounds, or gums; decreased blood pressure, not secondary to bleeding or streptokinase-induced anaphylaxis; fever; allergic reaction; bleeding into subcutaneous tissues; cholesterol embolism/embolization; internal bleeding; hemorrhagic or thromboembolic stroke; and severe allergic reaction or anaphylaxis

(Signs of potential side effects observed during clinical practice for urokinase, especially allergic-type reactions or infusion reactions)

General Dosing Information

The activity and doses of alteplase are expressed in milligrams, the activity and doses of anistreplase are expressed in units, and the activity and doses of streptokinase and urokinase are expressed in International Units (IU). However, in some countries, individual products may be labeled in other units. Different tests and standards are used to determine activity of each thrombolytic agent.

Thrombolytic therapy for indications other than acute coronary arterial thrombosis and catheter clearance should be performed only in a hospital with the facilities and trained personnel necessary for performance of the recommended diagnostic and monitoring techniques.

Thrombolytic therapy should be instituted as soon as possible following the onset of clinical symptoms because resistance to lysis increases with the age of the thrombus. For coronary arterial thrombosis or occlusion in evolving transmural myocardial infarction, rapid initiation of treatment is critical. However, patients receiving treatment within 6 to 12 hours following the onset of symptoms also may benefit from thrombolytic therapy. In patients who experience intermittent symptoms resulting from alternating coronary artery occlusion and spontaneous recanalization, thrombolytic therapy may limit the extent of myocardial damage even if given late. In addition, late thrombolytic therapy may limit myocardial damage by providing collateral flow in the event of subsequent coronary artery occlusion. For other indications, treatment should preferably be started within:

- Pulmonary embolism—5 to 7 days.
- Deep venous thrombosis—3 to 4 days, although treatment started later may be somewhat successful.
- Arterial thrombosis or thromboembolism (noncoronary)—3 days, although treatment started later may be successful.

Factors that may affect the success of thrombolytic therapy include the age, size, and location of the thrombus, and the extent of pretreatment perfusion, with most failures occurring when no blood is flowing past the thrombus (grade 0 flow as defined in the Thrombolysis in Myocardial Infarction [TIMI] trials). Factors that decrease the efficiency or activation potential of the fibrinolytic system include extremes in body temperature, elevated concentration of endogenous inhibitors, the presence of abnormal proteins or dysfunctional components of the fibrinolytic system, and the presence of high titers of antistreptokinase antibodies.

Prior to initiation of intravenous thrombolytic therapy for indications other than acute coronary arterial thrombosis, heparin (if being given) should be discontinued and the patient's thrombin time (TT) or activated partial thromboplastin time (APTT) should be less than twice the control value.

Thrombolytic agents should be administered via a constant infusion pump. A separate intravenous line, which should be established prior to initiation of thrombolytic therapy to reduce the need for venipuncture during treatment, should be used for administration of other medications, if required.

To minimize the risk of bleeding during thrombolytic therapy, the patient should be kept on strict bed rest and pressure dressings applied to recently invaded sites. *Nonessential handling or moving of the patient, invasive procedures (biopsy, etc.), and intramuscular injections must be avoided. Only essential procedures or diagnostic tests should be performed.* Cutdowns should be performed only if unavoidable. Venipunctures should be performed as carefully and infrequently as possible, preferably only in arm vessels, using a 23-gauge (or smaller) needle. If an arterial puncture is necessary, an upper extremity distal vessel should be used. Manual pressure should be applied for 30 minutes after the arterial puncture, followed by application of a pressure dressing. The puncture site should be checked frequently for signs of bleeding. Profuse bleeding may persist for a prolonged period of time.

Therapy should be discontinued immediately if bleeding not controllable by local pressure occurs. Some clinicians recommend that thrombolytic therapy be discontinued permanently if such bleeding occurs. However, other clinicians suggest that reinstitution of therapy using one half the original maintenance dose may be considered if the results of blood coagulation tests performed shortly after the bleeding episode show values higher than the normal therapeutic range. These clinicians further suggest that therapy not be reinstituted until the results of blood coagulation tests have returned to within the normal therapeutic range, and, if bleeding recurs, that therapy be discontinued permanently.

Anticoagulation with heparin (preferably by continuous intravenous infusion) followed, if necessary, by a coumarin or indanedione derivative is recommended following thrombolytic therapy for deep venous thrombosis or pulmonary embolism to prevent further thrombus formation. It is usually recommended that heparin be administered only after the patient's TT or APTT returns to less than twice the normal control value. This usually occurs within 2 to 4 hours after cessation of thrombolytic therapy. However, heparin therapy may be instituted earlier, depending on clinical circumstances. A loading dose of heparin is generally not recommended, but may be required in some circumstances, especially if the TT or APTT has fallen to substantially less than twice the control value. Administration of a coumarin- or indanedione-derivative anticoagulant, if necessary, should be started at least 5 days prior to discontinuation of heparin.

Angioplasty, coronary bypass surgery, or another revascularization procedure may be necessary to provide long-lasting protection against reocclusion, especially if extensive stenosis (> 80%) persists in the affected artery. Performance of these procedures within several days after thrombolytic therapy increases the risk of adverse effects, including hemorrhage, and should therefore be delayed if possible. If such a procedure cannot be postponed, replacement of fibrinogen to 50% of normal activity by administration of cryoprecipitate may reduce the risk of bleeding complications. If systemic fibrinolysis induced by the thrombolytic agent has not yet ceased, administration of an antifibrinolytic agent (e.g., aminocaproic acid, tranexamic acid) will be necessary to prevent immediate lysis of the infused fibrinogen, but the risks of administering an antifibrinolytic agent to a patient undergoing a revascularization procedure must be carefully considered.

For treatment of acute coronary arterial thrombosis

A suitable antiarrhythmic agent may be administered prior to or concurrently with the thrombolytic agent to prevent reperfusion arrhythmias.

It has been shown that aspirin, administered in conjunction with streptokinase for treatment of coronary arterial thrombosis, significantly decreases the occurrence of reocclusion, reinfarction, stroke, and death, as compared to aspirin or streptokinase administered alone. Although the benefit of aspirin administered with alteplase or anistreplase has not been studied, it is widely held that the combination of aspirin and any thrombolytic agent is likely to have benefit similar to that of aspirin and streptokinase. It is therefore recommended that at least 160 mg of aspirin be administered as soon as possible after myocardial infarction is suspected. It is also recommended that the aspirin be chewed so that it reaches the bloodstream rapidly.

Heparin (in dosage sufficient to prolong the APTT to 1.5 to 2 times the control value) has been administered in conjunction with thrombolytic therapy for acute coronary arterial occlusion. However, recent studies have found that the addition of heparin to a regimen of aspirin and thrombolysis does not significantly improve survival, but does increase the risk of major bleeding and cerebral hemorrhage. In addition, there are little data to show that heparin contributes to sustained coronary artery patency when administered with aspirin and streptokinase or with aspirin and anistreplase. When administered with aspirin and alteplase, intravenous heparin seems to improve coronary artery patency slightly, but the benefit must be weighed against the risk of hemorrhage associated with the use of intravenous heparin.

For arteriovenous cannula occlusion clearance

First, the cannula should be cleared by careful syringe technique, using heparinized saline solution. If this procedure is unsuccessful, a thrombolytic agent may be used after the effects of prior anticoagulation have been allowed to diminish. After the thrombolytic agent has been instilled in the cannula, the affected cannula limb(s) should be clamped for 2 hours and the patient closely observed for possible adverse effects. After treatment, the contents of the affected cannula limb(s) should be aspirated, and the cannula flushed with saline solution and reconnected.

For intravenous catheter obstruction clearance

The manufacturer's product information for urokinase should be consulted for a complete description of the recommended procedure.

Streptokinase is not indicated for restoration of patency of intravenous catheters. Under postmarketing surveillance, an increased number of serious adverse events have been reported. Most have involved the use of high doses of streptokinase in small volumes (250,000 IU in 2 mL). Uses of lower doses of streptokinase in infusions over several hours, generally into partially occluded catheters, or local instillation into the catheter lumen and subsequent aspiration, have been described in the medical literature.

Excessive pressure should be avoided when instilling a thrombolytic agent into the catheter in order to avoid rupture of the catheter or expulsion of the clot into the circulation.

To prevent air from entering an open central venous catheter, the patient should be instructed to exhale and hold his or her breath any time the catheter is not connected to intravenous tubing or to a syringe.

Intravenous catheters may be obstructed by substances not responsive to thrombolysis (i.e., substances other than clotted blood or fibrin). The possibility that such a precipitate may be forced into the circulation must be considered.

For treatment of adverse effects

Recommended treatment includes

- For minor bleeding—Applying local measures, such as pressure at the site of bleeding. Although efficacy has not been proved, topical application of an antifibrinolytic agent such as aminocaproic acid may help to stop stubborn minor bleeding. Thrombolytic therapy need not be discontinued unless such measures are unsuccessful and it is determined that the risk to the patient outweighs the benefit of continuing treatment.
- For uncontrollable or internal bleeding—Discontinuing thrombolytic therapy. If necessary, replacement of lost blood and reversal of the bleeding tendency can be accomplished by administration of fresh whole blood, packed red blood cells, cryoprecipitate or fresh frozen plasma, platelets, and/or desmopressin. Plasma volume expanders may be administered; however, dextran should **not** be used, because of its platelet aggregation-inhibiting activity. Heparin, if being given, should be discontinued and consideration given to administration of the heparin antagonist protamine. Also, an antifibrinolytic agent, such as aminocaproic acid (5 grams initially or over a period of 1 hour, followed by 1 gram per hour for approximately 4 to 8 hours or until the desired response has been obtained), or tranexamic acid may be administered intravenously (preferably by continuous infusion) or orally. However, the efficacy of aminocaproic acid or other antifibrinolytic agents in the treatment of thrombolytic agent-induced hemorrhage has not been documented by controlled studies in humans. Also, the risk of reocclusion or other thrombotic complications must be considered.
- For bradycardia—If necessary, atropine may be administered.
- For reperfusion arrhythmias—Administering a suitable antiarrhythmic agent, such as lidocaine or procainamide. Electrical cardioversion may be needed for ventricular tachycardia or fibrillation.
- For mild hypersensitivity reaction—Administering antihistamines and, if necessary, glucocorticoids.
- For severe hypersensitivity or anaphylactic reaction—Discontinuing thrombolytic therapy and administering epinephrine. Antihistamines and/or glucocorticoids also may be administered as required.
- For sudden hypotension—If sudden hypotension occurs during rapid, high-dose administration, reducing the infusion rate. If sudden hypotension occurs in other circumstances or does not respond to a reduction in the infusion rate, placing the patient in the Trendelenburg position and/or administering volume expanders (other than dextrans), atropine, and/or a vasopressor, e.g., dopamine, as clinical circumstances permit.
- For fever—Administering acetaminophen if treatment is required. Administration of multiple antipyretic doses of aspirin is not recommended.

ALTEPLASE, RECOMBINANT

Summary of Differences

Indications:

Indicated in the treatment of acute coronary arterial thrombosis, acute ischemic stroke, acute pulmonary thromboembolism, and in the clearance of central intravenous catheters.

Pharmacology/pharmacokinetics:

Mechanism of action/effect—

Acts directly to convert plasminogen to plasmin.

May be more clot-selective than anistreplase, streptokinase, or urokinase.

Half-life—

Biphasic; about 4 minutes for distribution phase and 35 minutes for elimination phase.

Side/adverse effects:

Incidence of stroke and cerebral hemorrhage greater than with other thrombolytic agents. Incidence and severity of allergic reactions lower than with anistreplase or streptokinase.

Additional Dosing Information

Alteplase is not antigenic (as are anistreplase and streptokinase) and does not promote antibody formation. Therefore, a second course of alteplase therapy can be administered, if reocclusion occurs, without resistance having developed to the effects of alteplase and without risk of precipitating an anaphylactic reaction. In one study, a second course of alteplase therapy was shown to be effective, without producing significant bleeding complications, in patients exhibiting signs and symptoms of reocclusion following initial thrombolytic therapy for treatment of acute myocardial infarction. However, it must still be considered that a second course of therapy, if initiated before systemic effects of the first dose have subsided, may increase the risk of severe hemorrhage.

A large multi-center study has shown that alteplase, administered in an accelerated or front-loaded dosing regimen within 6 hours of the onset of symptoms of myocardial infarction, may achieve earlier and more complete patency of the infarct-affected artery than does streptokinase in combination with intravenous or subcutaneous heparin, or a combination of alteplase, streptokinase, and intravenous heparin. Twenty-four-hour and 30-day mortality was also lower with the accelerated or front-loaded alteplase regimen than with these combinations.

For treatment of acute ischemic stroke

The treatment of acute ischemic stroke with alteplase should be limited to facilities that can provide appropriate evaluation and management of intracranial hemorrhage.

Treatment should be initiated only within 3 hours after the onset of stroke symptoms, and after exclusion of intracranial hemorrhage by a cranial computed tomographic scan or other diagnostic imaging method sensitive to the presence of hemorrhage.

In patients who have not recently been treated with oral anticoagulants or heparin, alteplase may be given prior to the availability of coagulation study results. However, treatment should be stopped if either a pretreatment prothrombin time > 15 seconds or an elevated APTT is identified.

Blood pressure should be monitored frequently and controlled with appropriate medication during and following alteplase administration.

The safety and efficacy of concomitant administration of heparin and aspirin during the first 24 hours after symptom onset have not been investigated.

Parenteral Dosage Forms

ALTEPLASE, RECOMBINANT, FOR INJECTION

Usual adult dose

Intravenous catheter clearance—

After the intravenous tubing has been disconnected and catheter occlusion confirmed, the catheter should be filled with a solution containing 1 mg per mL of alteplase. The solution should be administered as follows:

Initial Dose

For patients weighing 30 kg or more—Intravenous, 2 mg in 2 mL.

For patients weighing at least 10 kg and less than 30 kg—Intravenous, 110% of internal lumen volume of the catheter, not to exceed 2 mg in 2 mL.

Second dose

If catheter function is not restored at 120 minutes after dose 1, a second dose may be administered.

Note: There is no efficacy or safety information on dosing in excess of 2 mg per dose for this indication. Studies have not been performed with administration of total doses greater than 4 mg (two 2 mg doses).

Thrombosis, coronary arterial, acute—

Standard regimen—

For patients weighing less than 65 kg—Intravenous, 1.25 mg per kg of body weight administered over a period of three hours, as follows:

First hour—60% of the total dose. Initially, 6 to 10% of the total dose is given by direct intravenous injection within the first one or two minutes. The next 50 to 54% of the total dose is given via intravenous infusion during the remainder of the hour.

Second hour—20% of the total dose, via intravenous infusion.

Third hour—20% of the total dose, via intravenous infusion.

For patients weighing 65 kg or more—Intravenous, 100 mg, administered over a period of three hours, as follows:

First hour—60 mg. Initially, 6 to 10 mg is given by direct intravenous injection within the first one or two minutes. The next 50 to 54 mg is given via intravenous infusion during the remainder of the hour.

Second hour—20 mg, via intravenous infusion.

Third hour—20 mg, via intravenous infusion.

Accelerated regimen—

For patients weighing less than 67 kg—Intravenous, initially 15 mg followed by an infusion of 0.75 mg per kg of body weight, up to 50 mg, administered over a period of thirty minutes. The infusion should continue for an additional sixty minutes at a dose of 0.5 mg per kg of body weight, up to 35 mg.

For patients weighing 67 kg or more—Intravenous, initially 15 mg by direct intravenous injection, followed by 50 mg infused over the next thirty minutes, and then 35 mg infused over the next sixty minutes.

Note: It is recommended that intravenous heparin be administered in conjunction with accelerated-dose alteplase at an initial dose of 5000 USP Heparin Units, followed by 1000 USP Heparin Units per hour (1200 USP Heparin Units per hour for patients weighing more than 80 kg), with the dose adjusted to raise the activated partial thromboplastin time to between sixty and eighty-five seconds.

Stroke, acute ischemic[1]—

Intravenous, 0.9 mg per kg of body weight (up to a maximum of 90 mg) infused over sixty minutes, with 10% of the total dose administered by direct intravenous injection over the first minute.

Thromboembolism, pulmonary, acute[1]—

Intravenous infusion, 100 mg, administered over a period of two hours.

Note: It is recommended that heparin be used in conjunction with alteplase for treatment of acute pulmonary embolism. Heparin should be administered only if the patient's activated partial thromboplastin time or thrombin time value is no higher than twice the control value, near the end of or immediately following the alteplase infusion.

[Peripheral arterial occlusive disease][1]—

Intra-arterial, 0.05 to 0.1 mg per kg of body weight per hour (weight-based dosing) or 0.5 to 5 mg per hour (non–weight-based dosing) not to exceed 40 mg or twenty-four hours.

Usual pediatric dose
Safety and efficacy have not been established.

Strength(s) usually available
U.S.—

50 mg (Rx) [*Activase* (vials contain a vacuum; l-arginine 1.7 grams; phosphoric acid 0.5 gram; polysorbate 80 $\leq$ 4 mg)].

100 mg (Rx) [*Activase* (vials do *not* contain a vacuum; l-arginine 3.5 grams; phosphoric acid 1 gram; polysorbate 80 $\leq$ 11 mg)].

2.2 mg vial [*Cathflo Activase* (vials contain 2.2 mg which includes a 10% overfill supplying a 2 mg dose; 77 mg of L-arginine, 0.2 mg polysorbate 80, phosphoric acid)].

Canada—

50 mg (Rx) [*Activase rt-PA* (vials contain a vacuum; l-arginine; phosphoric acid; polysorbate 80)].

100 mg (Rx) [*Activase rt-PA* (vials do *not* contain a vacuum; l-arginine; phosphoric acid; polysorbate 80)].

Packaging and storage
Store between 2 and 30 °C (36 and 86 °F), unless otherwise specified by manufacturer. Protect from excessive exposure to light.

Store Cathflo Activase between 2 and 8°C (36 and 46°F). May be used within 8 hours of reconstitution when stored between 2 and 30 °C (36 and 86 °F). Protect from excessive exposure to light.

Preparation of dosage form
Alteplase should be reconstituted using Sterile Water for Injection, USP (diluent may or may not be provided). Bacteriostatic water for injection must not be used. A large-bore (18-gauge) needle or the transfer device (for use with the 100-mg vials) should be used to direct the stream of diluent directly into the lyophilized material.

If a vacuum is not present in the 50-mg vial, it should not be used.

When reconstituting the 100-mg vials using the transfer device, the vial of sterile water for injection, with the transfer device inserted, is held upright while the vial of alteplase is held upside down and pushed down onto the piercing pin of the transfer device. The vials are then inverted to allow the sterile water for injection to flow into the alteplase vial. The resulting colorless to pale yellow, transparent solution will contain 1 mg of alteplase per mL. This solution may be used without further dilution or it may be diluted to a concentration of 0.5 mg per mL using an equal volume of 0.9% sodium chloride injection or 5% dextrose injection. Other infusion solutions or preservative-containing solutions should not be used when further diluting the reconstituted solution. The solution may be mixed with gentle swirling and/or slow inversion; excessive agitation should be avoided. Slight foaming may occur during reconstitution; however, large bubbles dissipate when the solution is left undisturbed for a few minutes.

When reconstituting alteplase 2 mg for intracatheter installation, aseptically withdraw 2.2 ml of sterile water for injection USP and inject into the cathflow activase vial directing the diluent stream into the powder. Let the vial stand undisturbed until all large bubbles have dissipated. Do not shake. Mix by swirling until the contents are completely dissolved. Complete dissolution results in a pale yellow transparent solution containing 1 mg per ml and should occur within 3 minutes.

Stability
The reconstituted solution should be used within 8 hours when stored between 2 and 30 °C (36 and 86 °F). It should be discarded if not used within this time. However, because alteplase for injection contains no preservatives, it should not be reconstituted until immediately prior to use. Any unused solution must be discarded.

Incompatibilities
Do not add any other medication to the container of alteplase solution or administer other medications through the same intravenous line.

[1]Not included in Canadian product labeling.

ANISTREPLASE

Summary of Differences
Indications:

Indicated in the treatment of acute coronary arterial thrombosis.

Pharmacology/pharmacokinetics:

Mechanism of action/effect—Acts indirectly to promote conversion of plasminogen to plasmin.

Other actions/effects—Antigenic; promotes antibody formation.

Half-life—70 to 120 minutes (average about 90 minutes). The deacylation half-life of the complex is about 105 to 120 minutes.

Precautions:

Medical considerations/contraindications—Caution is required in patients who have had a severe hypersensitivity reaction to prior anistreplase or streptokinase therapy or a prior course of anistreplase or streptokinase therapy within the past 12 months.

Side/adverse effects:

Incidence of mild hypersensitivity and febrile reactions greater than with alteplase or urokinase.

May cause severe hypersensitivity reactions including anaphylaxis.

Additional Dosing Information
It is recommended that equipment and medications (such as epinephrine, glucocorticoids, and antihistamines) for treating anaphylaxis be immediately available whenever anistreplase is administered. Some investigators have administered a glucocorticoid (e.g., 100 mg of hydrocortisone or methylprednisolone, intravenously) and/or an antihistamine (e.g., 50 mg of diphenhydramine, intravenously) prior to anistreplase administration, to decrease the risk of severe hypersensitivity and febrile reactions. However, the prophylactic efficacy of these medications has not been established.

Resistance to anistreplase therapy may occur because of the presence of high titers of antibodies following a prior course of anistreplase or streptokinase therapy. A significant titer of these antibodies generally occurs 5 to 7 days following administration of anistreplase or streptokinase and may persist for 1 year (up to 4 years in some patients). Alteplase or urokinase may be administered if thrombolytic therapy is indicated during this time. A recent streptococcal infection also may result in high titers of antibodies and resistance to anistreplase.

Parenteral Dosage Forms

ANISTREPLASE FOR INJECTION

Usual adult dose
Thrombosis, coronary arterial, acute—

Intravenous, 30 units, administered over two to five minutes.

Usual pediatric dose
Safety and efficacy have not been established.

Strength(s) usually available
U.S.—

30 Units per single-dose vial (Rx) [*Eminase* (human albumin 30 mg; dimethylsulfoxide < 3 mg; epsilon-aminocaproic acid 1.3 mg; glycerol < 2 mg; l-lysine 46 mg; mannitol 100 mg; p-amidinophenyl-p'-anisate 150 mcg; sodium hydroxide < 0.2 mg)].

Canada—

30 Units per single-dose vial (Rx) [*Eminase* (human albumin 30 mg; dimethylsulfoxide < 3 mg; epsilon-aminocaproic acid 1.3 mg; glycerol < 2 mg; l-lysine 46 mg; mannitol 100 mg; p-amidinophenyl-p'-anisate 150 mcg; sodium hydroxide < 0.2 mg)].

Packaging and storage
Store between 2 and 8 °C (36 and 46 °F), unless otherwise specified by manufacturer.

Preparation of dosage form
Five mL of sterile water for injection should be slowly added to the vial containing anistreplase for injection; the stream of water should be

directed against the side of the vial. The vial should then be gently rolled (not shaken), to mix the powder with the liquid. Other measures to minimize foaming should also be used.

Stability

The reconstituted solution is to be administered within 30 minutes after reconstitution.

The medication contains no preservative. Each vial is intended to provide a single dose only; any unused solution should be discarded.

Incompatibilities

Do not add any other medication to the container of anistreplase solution or administer other medications through the same intravenous line.

STREPTOKINASE

Summary of Differences

Indications:
Indicated in the treatment of acute coronary arterial thrombosis, acute pulmonary thromboembolism, deep venous thrombosis, and acute arterial thromboembolism and thrombosis. Also indicated to clear totally or partially occluded arteriovenous cannulae.
Not indicated for restoration of patency of intravenous catheters.

Pharmacology/pharmacokinetics:
Mechanism of action/effect—Acts indirectly to promote conversion of plasminogen to plasmin.
Other actions/effects—Antigenic; promotes antibody formation.
Half-life—Following rapid, high-dose administration: 23 minutes (as active activator complex activity).

Precautions:
Medical considerations/contraindications—Caution required in patients who have had a severe hypersensitivity reaction to prior streptokinase therapy or a prior course of streptokinase therapy within the past 12 months.

Side/adverse effects:
Incidence of mild hypersensitivity and febrile reactions greater than with urokinase or alteplase.
May cause severe hypersensitivity reactions including anaphylaxis or, rarely, skin lesions.

Additional Dosing Information

It is recommended that equipment and medications (such as epinephrine, glucocorticoids, and antihistamines) for treating anaphylaxis be immediately available whenever streptokinase is administered. Some investigators have administered a glucocorticoid (e.g., 100 mg of hydrocortisone or methylprednisolone, intravenously) and/or an antihistamine (e.g., 50 mg of diphenhydramine, intravenously) prior to streptokinase administration, to decrease the risk of severe hypersensitivity and febrile reactions. However, the prophylactic efficacy of these medications has not been established.

Resistance to streptokinase therapy may occur because of the presence of high titers of antibodies to streptokinase following a prior course of streptokinase or anistreplase therapy. A significant titer of these antibodies generally occurs 5 to 7 days following administration of anistreplase or streptokinase and may persist for 1 year (up to 4 years in some patients). Alteplase or urokinase may be administered if thrombolytic therapy is indicated during this time. A recent streptococcal infection also may result in high titers of antibodies and resistance to streptokinase.

For intravenous administration of streptokinase (for indications other than acute coronary arterial thrombosis), a loading dose of 250,000 International Units (IU) is recommended to overcome mild resistance caused by exposure (without recent active infection) to streptococci. Since this loading dose successfully overcomes resistance in 85 to 90% of patients, many clinicians state that a previously recommended resistance test is now considered unnecessary. However, if a thrombin time (TT) determination or other test of fibrinolysis performed after 4 hours of therapy indicates minimal or no fibrinolytic activity, and no clinical improvement is apparent, the possibility of excessive resistance to streptokinase should be considered. Streptokinase should be discontinued and an alternate thrombolytic agent (alteplase or urokinase, but not anistreplase) administered instead.

A previously recommended regimen of variable maintenance dosage with frequent laboratory monitoring has not been shown to increase the efficacy or safety of streptokinase therapy. Therefore, this regimen is not currently recommended and has been replaced by a fixed maintenance dosage schedule.

The dosage and duration of intravenous therapy vary with the condition being treated. For the individual patient, tests to determine restoration of blood flow, such as angiography or venography of the affected blood vessel, computed tomography, impedance plethysmography, or quantitative Doppler effect, may be useful in determining the optimum duration of administration.

Parenteral Dosage Forms

STREPTOKINASE FOR INJECTION

Usual adult dose

Thrombosis, coronary arterial, acute—
Intravenous, 1,500,000 IU, administered within one hour.
Intra-arterial (via a coronary artery catheter placed via the Judkins or Sones technique), 20,000 IU initially, followed by 2000 IU per minute for one hour.

Note: Recanalization may occur in less than one hour; however, treatment should be continued following recanalization, to ensure complete lysis of all thrombotic material.

Thromboembolism, pulmonary, acute—
Intravenous, 250,000 IU as an initial loading dose over thirty minutes, followed by 100,000 IU per hour as a continuous infusion for twenty-four hours (seventy-two hours if concurrent deep venous thrombosis)

Thrombosis, deep venous—
Intravenous, 250,000 IU as an initial loading dose over thirty minutes, followed by 100,000 IU per hour as a continuous infusion for seventy-two hours

Thromboembolism or thrombosis, arterial, acute—
Intravenous, 250,000 IU as an initial loading dose over thirty minutes, followed by 100,000 IU per hour as a continuous infusion for twenty-four to seventy-two hours

Cannula, arteriovenous, clearance—
100,000 to 250,000 IU, instilled slowly into each occluded cannula limb.

Usual pediatric dose

Thromboembolism or thrombosis, arterial, acute—
Intravenous, 1000 IU (up to 3000 IU) per kg of body weight initially over five to thirty minutes, followed by 1000 IU (up to 1500 IU) per kg of body weight per hour for twelve to twenty-four hours.

Note: Controlled clinical studies have not been conducted to determine the safety and efficacy of using streptokinase in pediatric patients. The evidence of clinical benefits and risks is based solely on anecdotal reports in patients from younger than 1 month of age up to 16 years of age.

Strength(s) usually available

U.S.—
250,000 IU (Rx) [*Streptase* (albumin human 100 mg; cross-linked gelatin polypeptides 25 mg; sodium hydroxide; sodium l-glutamate 25 mg)].
750,000 IU (Rx) [*Streptase* (albumin human 100 mg; cross-linked gelatin polypeptides 25 mg; sodium hydroxide; sodium l-glutamate 25 mg)].
1,500,000 IU (Rx) [*Streptase* (albumin human 100 mg; cross-linked gelatin polypeptides 25 mg; sodium hydroxide; sodium l-glutamate 25 mg)].

Canada—
250,000 IU (Rx) [*Streptase* (albumin human 100 mg; cross-linked gelatin polypeptides 25 mg; sodium hydroxide; sodium l-glutamate 25 mg)].
750,000 IU (Rx) [*Streptase* (albumin human 100 mg; cross-linked gelatin polypeptides 25 mg; sodium hydroxide; sodium l-glutamate 25 mg)].
1,500,000 IU (Rx) [*Streptase* (albumin human 100 mg; cross-linked gelatin polypeptides 25 mg; sodium hydroxide; sodium l-glutamate 25 mg)].

Packaging and storage

Store between 15 and 30 °C (59 and 86 °F), unless otherwise specified by manufacturer.

Preparation of dosage form

For intracoronary artery or intravenous administration—Manufacturer's prescribing information should be consulted for recommendations for reconstituting and further diluting the individual product.

For arteriovenous cannula obstruction clearance—Two mL of sodium chloride injection or 5% dextrose injection should be added to each 250,000-IU vial of streptokinase.

Stability

Streptokinase for injection should be reconstituted immediately prior to use.

If not administered shortly following reconstitution, the solution should be stored at 2 to 8 °C (36 to 46 °F). If not used within 8 hours after reconstitution, the solution should be discarded.

One manufacturer states that slight flocculation (described as thin translucent fibers) may occur after reconstitution. Shaking the solution during reconstitution may increase flocculation or cause foaming and should be avoided. The solution may be administered if slight flocculation is present but should be discarded if flocculation is extensive.

Incompatibilities

Do not add any other medication to the container of streptokinase solution or administer other medications through the same intravenous line.

UROKINASE

Summary of Differences

Indications:
- Indicated for the lysis of acute massive pulmonary emboli and pulmonary emboli accompanied by unstable hemodynamics.

Pharmacology/pharmacokinetics:
- Mechanism of action/effect—Acts directly to convert plasminogen to plasmin.
- Half-life—Up to 20 minutes; may be prolonged in patients with hepatic function impairment.

Side/adverse effects:
- Incidence of allergic or febrile reactions lower than with anistreplase or streptokinase.
- May cause anaphylaxis and other infusion reactions and cholesterol embolization

Additional Dosing Information

The dosage and duration of urokinase therapy may vary with the condition being treated. For the individual patient, tests to determine restoration of blood flow, such as angiography or venography of the affected blood vessel, computed tomography, impedance plethysmography, or quantitative Doppler effect, may be useful in determining the optimum duration of administration.

For lysis of coronary artery thrombi

Prior to intracoronary arterial administration of urokinase, it is recommended that 2500 to 10,000 USP Heparin Units be administered via direct intravenous injection. Prior heparin administration should be considered when calculating heparin dosage.

Parenteral Dosage Forms

UROKINASE FOR INJECTION

Usual adult dose

Pulmonary emboli lysis—
- Intravenous, 4400 IU per kg of body weight initially over a ten-minute period, followed by 4400 IU per kg of body weight per hour for approximately twelve hours.

Note: Manufacturer's product information should be consulted for recommendations concerning the rate of infusion, based on recommended dilution volume of the product.

Heparin should be discontinued during the intravenous administration of urokinase.

Usual pediatric dose

Safety and efficacy have not been established.

Strength(s) usually available

U.S.—
- 250,000 IU (Rx) [*Abbokinase* (preservative-free; albumin human 250 mg; mannitol 25 mg; sodium chloride 50 mg)].

Canada—
- 5000 IU (Rx) [*Abbokinase Open-Cath* (gelatin; mannitol; monobasic sodium phosphate anhydrous; sodium chloride)].
- 250,000 IU (Rx) [*Abbokinase* (albumin human 250 mg; mannitol 25 mg; sodium chloride 50 mg)].

Note: The 250,000-IU size is intended for intravenous and intracoronary infusion only. After initial reconstitution, the solution prepared from one 250,000-IU size contains approximately 50,000 IU of urokinase per mL; however, further dilution is required prior to use.

The 5000-IU size is intended for intravenous catheter clearance only. Premeasured diluent is included. After reconstitution, the solution prepared from the 5000-IU size contains 5000 IU of urokinase per mL.

Packaging and storage

Store between 2 and 8 °C (36 and 46 °F), unless otherwise specified by manufacturer. Store *Abbokinase Open-Cath* below 25 °C (77 °F). Protect from freezing.

Preparation of dosage form

For the 250,000-IU size only—Five mL of sterile water for injection *without preservatives* should be added to each 250,000-IU vial. Bacteriostatic water for injection should not be used. The vial should be rolled and tilted (not shaken) to facilitate reconstitution.

For intravenous administration—Manufacturer's prescribing information should be consulted for recommendations for further diluting the product. Intravenous urokinase should be administered by a constant infusion pump capable of delivering a total volume of 195 mL.

For intracoronary arterial administration—The contents of the three reconstituted 250,000-IU vials should be added to 500 mL of 5% dextrose injection to make a solution containing approximately 1500 IU per mL.

For intravenous catheter clearance (for the 5000-IU size only)—Manufacturer's prescribing information should be consulted for instructions for reconstituting product in vials containing premeasured diluent.

Stability

Because urokinase for injection contains no preservatives, it should not be reconstituted until immediately prior to use. Also, any unused solution must be discarded.

Translucent filaments may form in the solution during reconstitution but do not affect the potency of the product. Shaking the vial should be avoided. If necessary, the solution may be filtered through a 0.45-micron or smaller cellulose membrane filter.

After reconstitution, urokinase should be visually inspected for discoloration and particulate matter. The solution should be pale and straw-colored; highly colored solutions should not be used.

Incompatibilities

Do not add any other medication to the container of urokinase solution or administer other medications through the same intravenous line.

Selected Bibliography

Anderson HV, Willerson JT. Thrombolysis in acute myocardial infarction. N Engl J Med 1993; 329: 703-9.

Revised: 12/17/2003

THYROGLOBULIN—See *Thyroid Hormones (Systemic)*

THYROID—See *Thyroid Hormones (Systemic)*

THYROID HORMONES Systemic

This monograph includes information on the following: 1) Levothyroxine; 2) Liothyronine; 3) Liotrix†; 4) Thyroglobulin†; 5) Thyroid.

VA CLASSIFICATION (Primary/Secondary):
- Levothyroxine—HS851/AN500; DX900
- Liothyronine—HS851/AN500; DX900
- Liotrix—HS851/AN500
- Thyroglobulin—HS851/AN500
- Thyroid—HS851/AN500

Commonly used brand name(s): *Armour Thyroid*[5]; *Cytomel*[2]; *Eltroxin*[1]; *Levo-T*[1]; *Levothroid*[1]; *Levoxyl*[1]; *PMS-Levothyroxine Sodium*[1]; *Synthroid*[1]; *Thyrar*[5]; *Thyroid Strong*[5]; *Triostat®*[2]; *Westhroid*[5].

Another commonly used name for Levothyroxine is L-Thyroxine.

Note: For a listing of dosage forms and brand names by country availability, see *Dosage Forms* section(s).

---

*Not commercially available in U.S.

†Not commercially available in Canada.

Category

Thyroid hormone—Levothyroxine; Liothyronine; Liotrix; Thyroglobulin; Thyroid.

Antineoplastic—Levothyroxine; Liothyronine; Liotrix; Thyroglobulin; Thyroid.

Diagnostic aid (thyroid function)—Levothyroxine; Liothyronine

Indications

Accepted

Hypothyroidism (diagnosis and treatment)—Thyroid hormones are indicated as replacement therapy in the treatment of thyroid hormone deficiency (hypothyroidism) of any etiology (except transient hypothyroidism during the recovery phase of subacute thyroiditis), as well as for simple (nonendemic) goiter and chronic lymphocytic (Hashimoto's) thyroiditis[1].

In general, levothyroxine is the preferred thyroid hormone for use in the treatment of hypothyroidism because of the absence of variability and the ease of monitoring of plasma concentrations; it is the drug of choice in the treatment of congenital hypothyroidism. Liothyronine is recommended by some clinicians because of its short half-life and readily reversible effects for initial therapy in myxedema and myxedema coma, as well as for hypothyroid patients who also have heart disease, although there are significant risks associated with the latter use. Liothyronine may also be preferred during preparation for radioisotope scanning procedures or when gastrointestinal absorption processes are impaired. Disadvantages of thyroid extract and thyroglobulin tablets are their variable potencies and the fact that triiodothyronine (T_3) and thyroxine (T_4) concentrations fluctuate and cannot be used to regulate dosage. Liotrix is no longer considered advantageous because of the natural conversion of T_4 to T_3 in the tissues.

Goiter (prophylaxis[1] and treatment)—Thyroid hormones are indicated to suppress the growth of some adenomatous goiters, and to prevent the goitrogenic effects of other medications such as lithium, aminosalicylic acid, and some sulfonamide compounds.

Carcinoma, thyroid (prophylaxis and treatment)[1]—Thyroid hormones are indicated in the treatment of thyrotropin-dependent thyroid gland carcinoma. Some clinicians believe that prophylactic administration of thyroid hormones after neck irradiation will prevent development of thyroid gland carcinoma.

Thyroid function studies—Levothyroxine[1] and liothyronine are indicated as diagnostic aids (for example, the T_3 suppression test), although this use has generally been replaced by other tests.

Unaccepted

Use of thyroid hormones to treat vague symptoms such as dry skin, fatigue, constipation, abnormalities of reproductive function, growth retardation, or obesity without laboratory confirmation of contributing hypothyroidism is inappropriate and may cause hyperthyroidism in euthyroid individuals.

---

[1]Not included in Canadian product labeling.

Pharmacology/Pharmacokinetics

Physicochemical characteristics

Source—
- Natural products include thyroglobulin and thyroid.
- Synthetic products include levothyroxine, liothyronine, and liotrix.

Composition—
- Levothyroxine: T_4 (thyroxine), with approximately 30% being converted to T_3 in peripheral tissues.
- Liothyronine: T_3 (triiodothyronine).
- Liotrix, thyroglobulin, and thyroid: T_3 and T_4.

Molecular weight—
- Levothyroxine sodium: 798.86 (anhydrous).
- Liothyronine sodium: 672.96.

Equivalent strength (approximate), based on clinical response—
- Levothyroxine: 100 mcg (0.1 mg) or less.
- Liothyronine: 25 mcg (0.025 mg).
- Liotrix—
  - Levothyroxine and liothyronine: 60 mcg (0.06 mg) and 15 mcg (0.015 mg), or 50 mcg (0.05 mg) and 12.5 mcg (0.0125 mg), respectively.

Thyroglobulin: 60 mg.
Thyroid USP: 60 mg.

Note: Because of the difficulty in measuring actual hormonal content of thyroglobulin and Thyroid USP, the measurable amounts of levothyroxine and liothyronine in these preparations may be less than the clinical equivalent. However, for purposes of dosage adjustment, the above equivalent strengths are appropriate.

Mechanism of action/Effect

The action of thyroid hormones is not completely understood, but they have both catabolic (calorigenic) and anabolic effects and are therefore involved in normal metabolism, growth, and development, especially the development of the central nervous system (CNS) of infants. A feedback system involving the hypothalamus, anterior pituitary, and thyroid normally regulates circulating thyroid hormone concentrations.

Absorption

Oral—
- Levothyroxine: Incomplete and variable, especially when taken with food; average 50 to 75%.
- Liothyronine: Approximately 95%.

Note: Absorption may be reduced in patients with congestive heart failure, malabsorption syndromes, or diarrhea.

Protein binding

Very high (more than 99%), but not firmly bound.

Biotransformation

As for endogenous thyroid hormone; levothyroxine (approximately 30%) is deiodinated in peripheral tissues; small amounts are metabolized in the liver and excreted in bile.

Half-life

Levothyroxine—
- Euthyroid: 6 to 7 days.
- Hypothyroid: 9 to 10 days.
- Hyperthyroid: 3 to 4 days.

Liothyronine—
- Euthyroid: 1 day.
- Hypothyroid: 1.4 days.
- Hyperthyroid: 0.6 day.

Note: Because thyroid and thyroglobulin contain varying amounts of thyroxine and triiodothyronine, their half-lives will vary but will be somewhere between that for T_4 and T_3.

Time to peak therapeutic effect

With chronic stable oral dosing—
- Levothyroxine, thyroglobulin, thyroid: 3 to 4 weeks.
- Liothyronine: 48 to 72 hours.

Duration of therapeutic action

After withdrawal of chronic therapy—
- Levothyroxine, thyroglobulin, thyroid: 1 to 3 weeks.
- Liothyronine: Up to 72 hours.

Precautions to Consider

Note: The following precautions apply to patients with *abnormal thyroid status* (hypothyroidism or, in some cases, hyperthyroidism). Patients in stable euthyroid condition as a result of continuing thyroid hormone therapy may be expected to respond in the same way as individuals with normal thyroid function and, therefore, the following precautions (except for *Patient monitoring*) do not usually apply in those circumstances.

Carcinogenicity/Mutagenicity

Studies have not been done in animals. A reported association with breast cancer has not been confirmed and does not justify withholding thyroid hormone treatment.

Pregnancy/Reproduction

Pregnancy—Thyroid hormones cross the placenta, but only to a limited extent. However, clinical experience in humans has not shown that appropriate use of thyroid hormones causes adverse effects in the fetus. Monitoring of maternal dose is important as maternal dose requirements may change during pregnancy. Intra-amniotic levothyroxine has been used to treat fetal hypothyroidism.

FDA Pregnancy Category A.

Breast-feeding

Problems in humans have not been documented with appropriate use of thyroid hormones in women who are breast-feeding. Minimal amounts of exogenous thyroid hormones are distributed into breast milk.

Pediatrics

Studies performed to date have not demonstrated pediatrics-specific problems that would limit the usefulness of thyroid hormones in children. However, caution is necessary in interpreting results of thyroid function tests in neonates, because serum T_4 concentrations are transiently elevated and serum T_3 concentrations are transiently low, and the infant pituitary is relatively insensitive to the negative feedback effect of thyroid hormones.

Geriatrics

The elderly may be more sensitive to the effects of thyroid hormones. Thyroid hormone replacement requirements are about 25% lower in some patients over the age of 60 years than in younger adults; therefore, individualization of dose is recommended.

Drug interactions and/or related problems

The following drug interactions and/or related problems have been selected on the basis of their potential clinical significance (possible mechanism in parentheses where appropriate)—not necessarily inclusive (» = major clinical significance):

Note: Combinations containing any of the following medications, depending on the amount present, may also interact with this medication.

In most cases, relative need for thyroid hormone dosage adjustment will depend on the thyroid state of the patient and the dosages of all medications involved. Dosage adjustment should be based on results of thyroid function tests and clinical status.

» Anticoagulants, coumarin- or indandione-derivative
(the effects of the oral anticoagulant may be altered, depending on the thyroid status of the patient; an increase in dosage of thyroid hormone may necessitate a decrease in oral anticoagulant dosage; adjustment of oral anticoagulant dosage on the basis of prothrombin time is recommended)

Antidepressants, tricyclic
(concurrent use with thyroid hormones may increase the therapeutic and toxic effects of both drugs, possibly due to increased receptor sensitivity to catecholamines; toxic effects include cardiac arrhythmias and CNS stimulation; also the onset of action of tricyclics may be accelerated)

Antidiabetic agents, sulfonylurea or
Insulin
(thyroid hormones may increase insulin or antidiabetic agent requirements; careful monitoring of diabetic control is recommended, especially when thyroid therapy is started, changed, or discontinued)

Beta-adrenergic blocking agents
(may decrease peripheral conversion of T_4 [thyroxine] to T_3 [triiodothyronine])

» Cholestyramine or
» Colestipol
(concurrent use may decrease the effects of thyroid hormones by binding and delaying or preventing absorption; an interval of 4 to 5 hours between administration of the two medications and regular monitoring of thyroid function tests are recommended)

Corticosteroids, glucocorticoid with mineralocorticoid activity or
Corticosteroids, mineralocorticoid or
Corticotropin (ACTH)
(changes in the thyroid status of the patient that may occur as a result of administration, changes in dosage, or discontinuation of thyroid hormones may necessitate adjustment of corticosteroid dosage because metabolic clearance of corticosteroids is decreased in hypothyroid patients and increased in hyperthyroid patients)

Digitalis glycosides
(hypothyroid patients may have an increased risk for digitalis toxicity; thyroid hormone replacement therapy increases the metabolic rate, which may necessitate an increase in the digitalis dose)

Estrogens
(increase serum thyroxine-binding globulin; in patients with a nonfunctioning thyroid gland, thyroid hormone requirements may be increased)

Hepatic enzyme inducers (See *Appendix II*)
(increase hepatic degradation of levothyroxine, which may result in increased requirements; dosage adjustment may be necessary)

(phenytoin also reduces serum protein binding of levothyroxine, and reduces total and free serum T_4 by 15 to 25%; despite this, most patients remain euthyroid and dosage of thyroid hormone does not need to be adjusted)

Ketamine
(concurrent use may produce marked hypertension and tachycardia; cautious administration to patients receiving thyroid hormone therapy is recommended)

Maprotiline
(concurrent use with thyroid hormones may enhance the possibility of cardiac arrhythmias; dosage adjustment may be necessary)

Sodium iodide I 123 or
Sodium iodide I 131 or
Sodium pertechnetate Tc 99m
(thyroid hormones may decrease the normal thyroidal uptake of I 123, I 131, or pertechnetate ion)

Somatrem or
Somatropin
(concurrent excessive use of thyroid hormones with somatrem or somatropin may accelerate epiphyseal closure. However, untreated hypothyroidism may interfere with growth response to somatrem or somatropin; prior and/or concurrent thyroid hormone replacement is recommended)

» Sympathomimetics
(concurrent use may increase the effects of these medications or thyroid hormone; thyroid hormones enhance risk of coronary insufficiency when sympathomimetic agents are administered to patients with coronary artery disease)

Medical considerations/Contraindications

The medical considerations/contraindications included have been selected on the basis of their potential clinical significance (reasons given in parentheses where appropriate)—not necessarily inclusive (» = major clinical significance).

Risk-benefit should be considered when the following medical problems exist:

» Adrenocortical insufficiency
(must be corrected while thyroid replacement therapy is being given, to prevent precipitation of acute adrenocortical insufficiency)

» Cardiovascular disease, including angina pectoris, arteriosclerosis, coronary artery disease, hypertension, myocardial infarction
(because of the risks associated with overly rapid thyroid hormone replacement and increased metabolic demands; mobilization of myxedema fluid may produce pitting edema 1 to 3 or more weeks after a change in dosage)

Diabetes mellitus
(possible reduced glucose tolerance and increased insulin or oral antidiabetic agent requirements)

» Hyperthyroidism, history of
(residual autonomous thyroid function may be present after therapy for hyperthyroidism, necessitating lower than typical doses)

Malabsorption states, such as celiac disease
(absorption, especially of levothyroxine, is reduced; dosage adjustment may be necessary)

» Pituitary insufficiency
(associated adrenocortical insufficiency must be corrected before thyroid replacement therapy is initiated, to prevent precipitation of acute adrenocortical insufficiency)

Sensitivity to thyroid hormone

» Thyrotoxicosis being treated with antithyroid medication

» Caution is required also in patients with long-standing hypothyroidism or myxedema, who may be more sensitive to effects of thyroid hormones.

Patient monitoring

The following may be especially important in patient monitoring (other tests may be warranted in some patients, depending on condition; » = major clinical significance):

Note: In patients receiving levothyroxine, liotrix, or thyroid extract for primary hypothyroidism, serum free T_4 index (total serum T_4 and T_3 resin uptake) or serum free T_4 together with a serum thyroid-stimulating hormone (TSH) are the most useful tests for monitoring replacement therapy. Serum TSH measurements are not useful in hypothyroidism secondary to pituitary insufficiency. In the rare patient receiving liothyronine replacement, serum T_4 concentrations will remain low and normalization of serum TSH indicates that treatment is adequate. Overdosage with liothyronine can best be recognized by clinical symptoms of hyperthyroidism and/or by a decrease in serum TSH to subnormal levels.

Many medications affect the results of thyroid function tests and may produce false results.

Caution is necessary in interpreting results of thyroid function tests in neonates, because serum T_4 concentrations are transiently elevated and serum T_3 concentrations are transiently low, and the infant pituitary is relatively insensitive to the negative feedback effect of thyroid hormones.

The following have been found to be the most useful in general and may be especially important in patient monitoring (other tests may be warranted in some patients, depending on condition; » = major clinical significance):

» Free T_4 (thyroxine) index determinations or
Free (unbound) T_4 determinations
(recommended at periodic intervals in most patients)

Measurement of bone age and
» Measurement of growth and

» Measurement of psychomotor development
(recommended at periodic intervals in children with congenital hypothyroidism)

» Observation for signs of ischemia or tachyarrhythmias
(recommended in hypothyroid patients with cardiovascular disease to aid in adjustment of dosage and to prevent overdosage or overly rapid increase in dosage)

» TSH (thyroid-stimulating hormone) determinations and
» T_3 (triiodothyronine) or T_4 resin uptake determinations and
» Total serum T_4 determinations, by radioimmunoassay and
» Total serum T_3 determinations, by radioimmunoassay
(which thyroid function tests are most useful for a particular patient depends on the agent, condition being treated, other agents used concomitantly, and existing conditions that are capable of altering test results by altering serum thyroxine-binding globulin [TBG] concentrations)

Side/Adverse Effects

Note: Side/adverse effects are dose-related and the dose at which they occur varies with each patient; incidence may be reduced by slowly increasing the initial dose to the minimum effective dose.

Side/adverse effects may occur more rapidly with liothyronine than with levothyroxine or thyroid because of its rapid onset of action.

In infants, excessive doses may result in craniosynostosis.

Partial loss of hair may occur in children during the first few months of treatment; normal hair growth usually returns, even with continued treatment.

The following side/adverse effects have been selected on the basis of their potential clinical significance (possible signs and symptoms in parentheses where appropriate)—not necessarily inclusive:

Those indicating need for medical attention

Incidence less frequent or rare

Allergic reaction (skin rash or hives); ***hyperthyroidism or overdosage*** (changes in appetite; changes in menstrual periods; chest pain; diarrhea; fast or irregular heartbeat; fever; hand tremors; headache; irritability; leg cramps; nervousness; sensitivity to heat; shortness of breath; sweating; trouble in sleeping; vomiting; weight loss); ***pseudotumor cerebri, in children*** (severe headache)

Those indicating need for medical attention only if they continue or are bothersome

Hypothyroidism or underdosage (changes in menstrual periods; clumsiness; coldness; constipation; dry, puffy skin; headache; listlessness; muscle aches; sleepiness; tiredness; weakness; weight gain)

Overdose

For specific information on the agents used in the management of thyroid hormones overdose, see:
- *Beta-adrenergic Blocking Agents (Systemic)* monograph;
- *Charcoal, Activated (Oral-Local)* monograph;
- *Hydrocortisone* in *Corticosteroids—Glucocorticoid Effects (Systemic)* monograph; and/or
- *Digitalis Glycosides (Systemic)* monograph.

For more information on the management of overdose or unintentional ingestion, **contact a Poison Control Center** (see *Poison Control Center Listing*).

Clinical effects of overdose

The following effects have been selected on the basis of their potential clinical significance (possible signs and symptoms in parentheses when appropriate)—not necessarily inclusive:

Changes in appetite; changes in menstrual periods; chest pain; diarrhea; fast or irregular heartbeat; fever; hand tremors; headache; irritability; leg cramps; nervousness; sensitivity to heat; shortness of breath; sweating; thyroid storm–like effects (confusion; fever; jaundice, mild; mood swings; muscle wasting; psychosis; restlessness, extreme; weakness, marked)—following massive overdose; ***trouble in sleeping; vomiting; weight loss***

Treatment of overdose

If symptoms of hyperthyroidism occur, it is recommended that thyroid hormone therapy be withdrawn for 2 to 6 days (1 to 2 days for liothyronine), then resumed at a lower dose.

To decrease absorption—
Acute massive overdose is treated by reducing gastrointestinal absorption, if possible, by means of vomiting, followed by emptying of the stomach and/or use of a charcoal instillation, which may be useful up to 3 to 4 hours after oral ingestion of toxic doses of thyroid hormones.

Specific treatment—
Cardiac glycosides if congestive heart failure develops.
Beta-adrenergic blocking agents such as propranolol for treatment of increased sympathetic activity.
Intravenous hydrocortisone to partially inhibit conversion of T_4 to T_3.

Supportive care—
Administration of oxygen. Implementation of measures to control fever, hypoglycemia, or fluid loss. Patients in whom intentional overdose is confirmed or suspected should be referred for psychiatric consultation.

Patient Consultation

As an aid to patient consultation, refer to *Advice for the Patient, Thyroid Hormones (Systemic)*.

In providing consultation, consider emphasizing the following selected information (» = major clinical significance):

Before using this medication

» Conditions affecting use, especially:
Allergy to thyroid hormones
Pregnancy—Crosses the placenta to a limited extent and has not caused problems in the fetus with appropriate doses; regular monitoring is necessary as maternal dose requirements may change during pregnancy
Breast-feeding—Small amounts are distributed into breast milk
Use in the elderly—Sensitivity to thyroid effects is greater in the elderly than in younger age groups and dose adjustment may be necessary
Other medications, especially cholestyramine, colestipol, coumarin- or indandione-derivative anticoagulants, or sympathomimetics
Other medical problems, especially adrenocortical insufficiency, cardiovascular disease, history of hyperthyroidism, pituitary insufficiency, thyroid sensitivity with long-standing hypothyroidism or myxedema, or thyrotoxicosis

Proper use of this medication

» Importance of not taking more or less medication than the amount prescribed; taking medication at the same time every day for consistent effect

» Possible need for lifelong therapy; checking with physician before discontinuing medication

» Proper dosing
Missed dose: Taking as soon as possible; not taking if almost time for next dose and not doubling doses; notifying physician if two or more doses in a row are missed

» Proper storage

Precautions while using this medication

» Importance of close monitoring by the physician
Caution with angina or coronary artery disease; heavy exercise or exertion may precipitate angina

» Caution if any kind of surgery (including dental surgery) or emergency treatment is required

Avoiding other medications unless prescribed by physician because of possible interference with effects of thyroid hormone

Side/adverse effects

Signs of potential side effects, especially allergic reaction, hyperthyroidism, and pseudotumor cerebri

General Dosing Information

Dosage must be adjusted to meet the individual requirements of each patient, on the basis of clinical response and results of thyroid function tests.

Levothyroxine is the preferred form of thyroid replacement therapy.

Patients who are more than mildly hypothyroid initially should be treated with less than a full replacement dose, with doses then being increased gradually over a period of weeks. Otherwise, nervousness and rapid heart rate may occur.

Thyroid hormone replacement therapy for congenital hypothyroidism should be initiated as soon as possible after birth to minimize impaired mental and physical development. Treatment after about 3 months of age may reverse many of the physical effects but not all of the mental effects of hypothyroidism. Treatment should be continued for life, unless transient hypothyroidism is suspected, in which case therapy may be withdrawn for 2 to 8 weeks after 3 years of age; if thyroid-stimulating hormone (TSH) and thyroxine (T_4) concentrations remain normal throughout the withdrawal period, treatment is no longer necessary.

Suppression of TSH to normal levels must not be used as the sole criterion of adequacy of dose in congenital hypothyroidism, since TSH concentrations may remain elevated despite adequate or even excessive doses of thyroid hormone. Maintenance of appropriate T_4 concentrations for age is a more accurate guideline during infancy and childhood.

In general, thyroid hormone therapy is begun at a low dose, which is increased gradually to obtain a euthyroid state, followed by the dose required to maintain the response. However, this is not necessary in neonates, in whom rapid replacement is important, and who may be started at the full replacement dose. Adverse effects such as hyperactivity in the older child may be lessened by utilizing a starting dose of one-fourth the full replacement dose, and increasing the dose by one-fourth weekly until the full replacement dose is reached.

Rapid replacement of thyroid hormone is associated with less risk in younger adults than in older ones.

In hypothyroid patients with adrenocortical insufficiency or panhypopituitarism, replacement therapy with thyroid hormones must be preceded by adequate amounts of corticosteroids to prevent precipitation of acute adrenocortical insufficiency by the increase in metabolism. Supplemental corticosteroids may also be necessary for patients with prolonged or severe hypothyroidism, including myxedema.

In hypothyroid patients with myxedema or cardiovascular disease, the initial dosage of thyroid hormones should be very small and must be increased very gradually to prevent precipitation of angina, coronary occlusion, or stroke. If cardiovascular reactions occur, a reduction in thyroid hormone dosage may be required. Although some clinicians prefer to use liothyronine in these patients because its effects disappear more rapidly after withdrawal, regulation of dosage is more difficult and its rapid onset of action may also produce adverse cardiac effects as a result of abrupt changes in metabolic demands.

If, after prolonged therapy (2 to 6 months), no response occurs with physiologic doses or a response occurs only with large doses of thyroid hormone, it is recommended that the diagnosis be reevaluated.

For treatment of myxedema coma

It has been recommended that corticosteroids be administered initially in the emergency treatment of all patients with myxedema coma. Patients with pituitary myxedema should receive adrenocortical hormone replacement therapy prior to or when beginning therapy with liothyronine. Similarly, patients with primary myxedema should receive adrenocortical hormone replacement therapy to prevent acute adrenocortical insufficiency and shock, which may occur following a rapid return to normal body metabolism from a hypothyroid state.

Artificial rewarming is contraindicated in conjunction with administration of liothyronine in patients with myxedema coma. The external heat causes peripheral vasodilation that further decreases circulation to vital organs and increases shock if it is present. If heat loss is prevented by keeping the patient in a warm room covered with blankets, administration of liothyronine usually restores normal body temperature within 24 to 48 hours.

LEVOTHYROXINE

Summary of Differences

Indications: Usual drug of choice. Advantage over thyroid and thyroglobulin is a predictable effect because of standard hormonal content.

Pharmacology/pharmacokinetics: Absorption after oral administration is incomplete and variable, especially when taken with food.

Precautions: Medical problems/contraindications—Absorption may be significantly reduced in patients with malabsorption states.

Oral Dosage Forms

LEVOTHYROXINE SODIUM TABLETS USP

Usual adult dose

Mild hypothyroidism—

Initial: Oral, 50 mcg (0.05 mg) as a single daily dose, with increments of 25 to 50 mcg (0.025 to 0.05 mg) at two- to three-week intervals until the desired result is obtained.

Maintenance: Oral, 75 to 125 mcg (0.075 to 0.125 mg) per day (or 1.5 mcg per kg of body weight per day) as a single daily dose. A higher maintenance dose (up to 200 mcg per day) may be necessary in some patients (e.g., those with malabsorption).

Severe hypothyroidism—

Initial: Oral, 12.5 to 25 mcg (0.0125 to 0.025 mg) as a single daily dose, with increments of 25 mcg (0.025 mg) at two- to three-week intervals until the desired result is obtained.

Maintenance: Oral, 75 to 125 mcg (0.075 to 0.125 mg) per day (or 1.5 mcg per kg of body weight per day) as a single daily dose. A higher maintenance dose (up to 200 mcg per day) may be necessary in some patients (e.g., those with malabsorption).

Note: In the elderly and in patients with long-standing hypothyroidism, myxedematous infiltration, or cardiovascular dysfunction, the initial dose is usually 12.5 to 25 mcg (0.0125 to 0.025 mg) a day, and dosage is incremented at three- to four-week intervals. In the elderly, the maintenance dose is usually about 75 mcg (0.075 mg) per day.

Usual adult prescribing limits

Failure to respond to a daily dose of 150 mcg (0.15 mg) or more may indicate erroneous diagnosis of hypothyroidism, malabsorption, or poor compliance.

Usual pediatric dose

Children less than 6 months of age—Oral, 5 to 6 mcg (0.005 to 0.006 mg) per kg of body weight per day or 25 to 50 mcg (0.025 to 0.05 mg) per day as a single daily dose.

Children 6 to 12 months of age—Oral, 5 to 6 mcg (0.005 to 0.006 mg) per kg of body weight per day or 50 to 75 mcg (0.05 to 0.075 mg) per day as a single daily dose.

Children 1 to 5 years of age—Oral, 3 to 5 mcg (0.003 to 0.005 mg) per kg of body weight per day or 75 to 100 mcg (0.075 to 0.1 mg) per day as a single daily dose.

Children 6 to 10 years of age—Oral, 4 to 5 mcg (0.004 to 0.005 mg) per kg of body weight per day or 100 to 150 mcg (0.1 to 0.15 mg) per day as a single daily dose.

Children over 10 years of age—Oral, 2 to 3 mcg (0.002 to 0.003 mg) per kg of body weight per day as a single daily dose until the adult dose is reached (usually 150 mcg [0.15 mg] per day) up to 200 mcg (0.2 mg) per day.

Note: Premature infants weighing less than 2000 grams, or infants at risk for cardiac failure receive a starting dose of 25 mcg (0.025 mg) a day which may be increased to 50 mcg (0.05 mg) a day in four to six weeks.

Usual geriatric dose

See *Usual adult dose.*

Strength(s) usually available

U.S.—

25 mcg (0.025 mg) (Rx) [*Levo-T* (scored); *Levothroid; Levoxyl; Synthroid* (scored); GENERIC].

50 mcg (0.05 mg) (Rx) [*Levo-T* (scored); *Levothroid; Levoxyl; Synthroid* (scored); GENERIC].

75 mcg (0.075 mg) (Rx) [*Levo-T* (scored); *Levothroid; Levoxyl; Synthroid* (scored); GENERIC].

88 mcg (0.088 mg) (Rx) [*Levothroid; Levoxyl; Synthroid* (scored)].

100 mcg (0.1 mg) (Rx) [*Levo-T* (scored); *Levothroid; Levoxyl; Synthroid* (scored); GENERIC].

112 mcg (0.112 mg) (Rx) [*Levothroid; Levoxyl; Synthroid* (scored)].

125 mcg (0.125 mg) (Rx) [*Levo-T* (scored); *Levothroid; Levoxyl; Synthroid* (scored); GENERIC].

137 mcg (0.137 mg) (Rx) [*Levothroid; Levoxyl*].

150 mcg (0.15 mg) (Rx) [*Levo-T* (scored); *Levothroid; Levoxyl; Synthroid* (scored); GENERIC].

175 mcg (0.175 mg) (Rx) [*Levothroid; Levoxyl; Synthroid* (scored)].

200 mcg (0.2 mg) (Rx) [*Levo-T* (scored); *Levothroid; Levoxyl; Synthroid* (scored); GENERIC].

300 mcg (0.3 mg) (Rx) [*Levo-T* (scored); *Levothroid; Levoxyl; Synthroid* (scored); GENERIC].

Canada—

25 mcg (0.025 mg) (Rx) [*PMS-Levothyroxine Sodium* (scored); *Synthroid* (scored)].

50 mcg (0.05 mg) (Rx) [*Eltroxin; PMS-Levothyroxine Sodium* (scored); *Synthroid* (scored)].

75 mcg (0.075 mg) (Rx) [*PMS-Levothyroxine Sodium* (scored); *Synthroid* (scored)].

88 mcg (0.088 mg) (Rx) [*Synthroid* (scored)].

100 mcg (0.1 mg) (Rx) [*Eltroxin; PMS-Levothyroxine Sodium* (scored); *Synthroid* (scored)].

112 mcg (0.112 mg) (Rx) [*Synthroid* (scored)].

125 mcg (0.125 mg) (Rx) [*PMS-Levothyroxine Sodium* (scored); *Synthroid* (scored)].

150 mcg (0.15 mg) (Rx) [*Eltroxin; PMS-Levothyroxine Sodium* (scored); *Synthroid* (scored)].

175 mcg (0.175 mg) (Rx) [*Synthroid* (scored)].

200 mcg (0.2 mg) (Rx) [*Eltroxin; PMS-Levothyroxine Sodium* (scored); *Synthroid* (scored)].

300 mcg (0.3 mg) (Rx) [*Eltroxin; PMS-Levothyroxine Sodium* (scored); *Synthroid* (scored)].

Packaging and storage

Store below 40 °C (104 °F), preferably between 15 and 30 °C (59 and 86 °F), unless otherwise specified by manufacturer. Store in a tight, light-resistant container.

Auxiliary labeling
- Take on empty stomach.
- Do not take other medicines without your doctor's advice.

Note
Caution is recommended when changing products because of the potential difference in actual levothyroxine content between brands.

Parenteral Dosage Forms

LEVOTHYROXINE SODIUM INJECTION

Usual adult dose
Hypothyroidism—
Intravenous or intramuscular, 50 to 100 mcg (0.05 to 0.1 mg) as a single daily dose.
Myxedema coma or stupor—
Initial: Intravenous, 200 to 500 mcg (0.2 to 0.5 mg), even in the elderly; an additional 100 to 300 mcg (0.1 to 0.3 mg) may be given on the second day if improvement has not occurred, followed by continuous daily administration of smaller doses, until the patient can tolerate oral administration.
Note: Smaller doses may be required in patients with concomitant cardiovascular disease.

Usual pediatric dose
Hypothyroidism—
Intravenous or intramuscular, daily dose equal to 75% of the usual oral pediatric dose.

Usual geriatric dose
See *Usual adult dose*.

Strength(s) usually available
U.S.—
Not commercially available.
Canada—
Not commercially available.

Packaging and storage
Store below 40 °C (104 °F), preferably between 15 and 30 °C (59 and 86 °F), unless otherwise specified by manufacturer.

LEVOTHYROXINE SODIUM FOR INJECTION

Usual adult dose
See *Levothyroxine Sodium Injection*.

Usual pediatric dose
See *Levothyroxine Sodium Injection*.

Usual geriatric dose
See *Levothyroxine Sodium Injection*.

Strength(s) usually available
U.S.—
200 mcg (0.2 mg) (Rx) [*Levothroid; Synthroid;* GENERIC].
500 mcg (0.5 mg) (Rx) [*Levothroid; Synthroid;* GENERIC].
Canada—
500 mcg (0.5 mg) (Rx) [*Synthroid*].

Packaging and storage
Store below 40 °C (104 °F), preferably between 15 and 30 °C (59 and 86 °F), unless otherwise specified by manufacturer. Protect from light.

Preparation of dosage form
Levothyroxine sodium for injection may be reconstituted for parenteral use by adding 0.5, 2, or 5 mL of Sodium Chloride Injection USP (without preservative) to the 50-, 200-, or 500-mcg vial, respectively, and shaking to dissolve, producing a solution containing 100 mcg (0.1 mg) per mL.

Stability
Solution should be freshly reconstituted immediately prior to each dose. Any unused portion should be discarded.

LIOTHYRONINE

Summary of Differences
Indications:
Advantage over thyroid and thyroglobulin is a predictable effect because of standard hormonal content. May be preferred over levothyroxine when a rapid effect or rapidly reversible effect is desired, or when gastrointestinal absorption processes or peripheral conversion of T_4 (thyroxine) to T_3 (triiodothyronine) is impaired; however, regulation of dosage is more difficult and rapid onset of action may also produce adverse cardiac effects as a result of abrupt changes in metabolic demands.
Pharmacology/pharmacokinetics:
Maximal effects with continued use occur within 48 to 72 hours and persist for up to 72 hours after withdrawal.
Side/adverse effects:
May occur more rapidly with liothyronine than with levothyroxine or thyroid.
General dosing information:
Rapid action and abrupt increase in metabolic demands may produce adverse cardiac effects.
If symptoms of hyperthyroidism occur, withdrawal for 2 to 3 days is recommended before resumption at a lower dose.

Additional Dosing Information
See also *General Dosing Information*.

When a patient is transferred to liothyronine from other thyroid therapy, the other therapy is discontinued and liothyronine is initiated at a low dosage, increased gradually on the basis of patient response. Keep in mind that the effects of liothyronine occur rapidly, while the effects of other thyroid hormones may persist for several weeks.

Liothyronine may be given in divided daily doses to minimize fluctuations in T_3 concentrations.

Oral Dosage Forms

LIOTHYRONINE SODIUM TABLETS USP

Usual adult dose
Mild hypothyroidism—
Initial: Oral, 25 mcg (0.025 mg) a day, with increments of 12.5 or 25 mcg (0.0125 or 0.025 mg) every one or two weeks until the desired result is obtained.
Maintenance: Oral, 25 to 50 mcg (0.025 to 0.05 mg) a day.
Myxedema—
Initial: Oral, 2.5 to 5 mcg (0.0025 to 0.005 mg) a day, with increments of 5 to 10 mcg (0.005 to 0.01 mg) every one or two weeks. When 25 mcg (0.025 mg) a day is reached, increments may sometimes be by 12.5 to 25 mcg (0.0125 to 0.025 mg) every one or two weeks.
Maintenance: Oral, 25 to 50 mcg (0.025 to 0.05 mg) a day.
Simple (nontoxic) goiter—
Initial: Oral, 5 mcg (0.005 mg) a day, with increments of 5 to 10 mcg (0.005 to 0.01 mg) every one or two weeks. When 25 mcg (0.025 mg) a day is reached, increments may be by 12.5 or 25 mcg (0.0125 or 0.025 mg) every week.
Maintenance: Oral, 50 to 100 mcg (0.05 to 0.1 mg) a day.
Note: In patients with cardiovascular disease, the initial dose is 5 mcg (0.005 mg) a day, with increments of no more than 5 mcg every two weeks. In the elderly also, the initial dose is 5 mcg a day, with increments of no more than 5 mcg at the recommended intervals.

Usual pediatric dose
Cretinism—
USP Advisory Panels do not recommend use for cretinism in children because of significant question about T_3 crossing the blood-brain barrier.

Usual geriatric dose
See *Usual adult dose*.

Strength(s) usually available
U.S.—
5 mcg (0.005 mg) (Rx) [*Cytomel*].
25 mcg (0.025 mg) (Rx) [*Cytomel* (scored); GENERIC].
50 mcg (0.05 mg) (Rx) [*Cytomel* (scored)].
Canada—
5 mcg (0.005 mg) (base) (Rx) [*Cytomel*].
25 mcg (0.025 mg) (base) (Rx) [*Cytomel* (scored)].

Packaging and storage
Store below 40 °C (104 °F), preferably between 15 and 30 °C (59 and 86 °F), unless otherwise specified by manufacturer. Store in a tight container.

Auxiliary labeling
- Do not take other medicines without your doctor's advice.

Parenteral Dosage Forms

LIOTHYRONINE SODIUM INJECTION

Usual adult dose
Myxedema coma/precoma—
Initial: Intravenous, 25 to 50 mcg every four to twelve hours. Subsequent doses should be determined on the basis of continuous monitoring of the patient's clinical condition and response to the previous injection.

In patients with confirmed or suspected cardiovascular disease, an initial dose of 10 to 20 mcg is suggested.

Note: Oral therapy should be resumed as soon as clinically possible. When switching a patient to liothyronine sodium tablets, liothyronine sodium injection should be discontinued, and oral therapy should be initiated at a low dosage and increased gradually based on the patient's response. When switching a patient to levothyroxine sodium tablets, liothyronine sodium injection should be gradually discontinued because there is a delay in the onset of action of levothyroxine.

Usual adult prescribing limits
Clinical experience with total daily doses greater than 100 mcg per day is limited.

Usual pediatric dose
Safety and efficacy have not been established.

Strength(s) usually available
U.S.—
10 mcg per mL (Rx) [*Triostat*® (alcohol 6.8% by volume; anhydrous citric acid 0.175 mg; ammonia 2.19 mg [as ammonium hydroxide])].

Canada—
Not commercially available.

Packaging and storage
Store between 2 and 8 °C (35 and 46 °F), unless otherwise specified by manufacturer.

LIOTRIX

Summary of Differences

Indications: Advantage over thyroid and thyroglobulin is a predictable effect because of standard hormonal content; provision of a product containing T_3 (triiodothyronine) no longer considered an advantage because of natural conversion of T_4 (thyroxine) to T_3 in the tissues.

Oral Dosage Forms

LIOTRIX TABLETS USP

Usual adult and adolescent dose
Hypothyroidism without myxedema—
Initial: Oral, 50 mcg (0.05 mg) of levothyroxine and 12.5 mcg (0.0125 mg) of liothyronine a day, with increments of a like amount at monthly intervals until the desired result is obtained.
Maintenance: Oral, 50 to 100 mcg (0.05 to 0.1 mg) of levothyroxine and 12.5 to 25 mcg (0.0125 to 0.025 mg) of liothyronine a day.

Myxedema or hypothyroidism with cardiovascular disease—
Initial: Oral, 12.5 mcg (0.0125 mg) of levothyroxine and 3.1 mcg (0.0031 mg) of liothyronine a day, with increments of a like amount at two- to three-week intervals until the desired result is obtained.
Maintenance: Oral, 50 to 100 mcg (0.05 to 0.1 mg) of levothyroxine and 12.5 to 25 mcg (0.0125 to 0.025 mg) of liothyronine a day.

Note: In the elderly, the initial dose is one-fourth to one-half the usual adult dose, doubled at six- to eight-week intervals until the desired result is obtained.

Usual pediatric dose
Cretinism or severe hypothyroidism—
See *Usual adult and adolescent dose* for myxedema.

Hypothyroidism—
See *Usual adult and adolescent dose* for hypothyroidism without myxedema.

Note: Increments in dosage are made at two-week intervals in children.

Dosage should always be based on results of thyroid function tests.

Usual geriatric dose
See *Usual adult and adolescent dose.*

Strength(s) usually available
U.S.—

Levothyroxine sodium (mcg)	Liothyronine sodium (mcg)	Brand name
12.5	3.1	*Thyrolar* (Rx)
25	6.25	*Thyrolar* (Rx)
50	12.5	*Thyrolar* (Rx)
100	25	*Thyrolar* (Rx)
150	37.5	*Thyrolar* (Rx)

Canada—
Not commercially available.

Packaging and storage
Store below 40 °C (104 °F), preferably between 15 and 30 °C (59 and 86 °F), unless otherwise specified by manufacturer. Store in a tight container.

Auxiliary labeling
- Do not take other medicines without your doctor's advice.

Note
Be very careful always to dispense the same brand of liotrix that a patient has received previously.

THYROGLOBULIN

Summary of Differences

Indications: Disadvantages include variable hormonal content of commercial preparations and fluctuation of T_3 (triiodothyronine) and T_4 (thyroxine) concentrations produced.

Oral Dosage Forms

THYROGLOBULIN TABLETS USP

Usual adult and adolescent dose
Hypothyroidism without myxedema—
Initial: Oral, 32 mg a day, with increments every one or two weeks until the desired result is obtained.
Maintenance: Oral, 65 to 160 mg a day.

Myxedema or hypothyroidism with cardiovascular disease—
Initial: Oral, 16 to 32 mg a day, with increments of a like amount every two weeks until the desired result is obtained.
Maintenance: 65 to 160 mg a day.

Usual pediatric dose
Cretinism or severe hypothyroidism—
See *Usual adult and adolescent dose* for myxedema.

Hypothyroidism—
See *Usual adult and adolescent dose* for hypothyroidism without myxedema.

Note: Dosage should always be based on results of thyroid function tests.

Levothyroxine is considered the drug of choice in the treatment of congenital hypothyroidism.

Strength(s) usually available
U.S.—
Not commercially available.

Canada—
Not commercially available.

Packaging and storage
Store below 40 °C (104 °F), preferably between 15 and 30 °C (59 and 86 °F), unless otherwise specified by manufacturer. Store in a tight container.

Auxiliary labeling
- Do not take other medicines without your doctor's advice.

THYROID

Summary of Differences

Indications: Disadvantages include variable hormonal content of commercial preparations and fluctuation of T_3 (triiodothyronine) and T_4 (thyroxine) concentrations produced.

Oral Dosage Forms

THYROID TABLETS USP

Usual adult and adolescent dose
Hypothyroidism without myxedema—
Initial: Oral, 60 mg a day, with increments of 30 mg at monthly intervals until the desired result is obtained.
Maintenance: Oral, 60 to 120 mg a day.

Myxedema or hypothyroidism with cardiovascular disease—
Initial: Oral, 15 mg a day, increased to 30 mg a day after two weeks, and to 60 mg a day after a further two weeks. Careful clinical assessment is recommended after one month and two months of treatment at 60 mg a day. If necessary, dosage may then be in-

creased to 120 mg a day. If necessary, further increases of 30 or 60 mg may be made.

Maintenance: Oral, 60 to 120 mg a day.

Note: An initial dose of 7.5 to 15 mg a day is recommended in the elderly; this dose may be doubled every six to eight weeks until the desired result is obtained.

Usual pediatric dose

Cretinism or severe hypothyroidism—

See *Usual adult and adolescent dose* for myxedema.

Hypothyroidism—

See *Usual adult and adolescent dose* for hypothyroidism without myxedema.

Note: Dosage should always be based on results of thyroid function tests.

Levothyroxine is considered the drug of choice in the treatment of congenital hypothyroidism.

Usual geriatric dose

See *Usual adult and adolescent dose*.

Strength(s) usually available

U.S.—

Regular:

15 mg (Rx) [*Armour Thyroid;* GENERIC].

30 mg (Rx) [*Armour Thyroid; Westhroid;* GENERIC].

60 mg (Rx) [*Armour Thyroid; Westhroid;* GENERIC].

90 mg (Rx) [*Armour Thyroid*].

120 mg (Rx) [*Armour Thyroid; Westhroid;* GENERIC].

180 mg (Rx) [*Armour Thyroid; Westhroid;* GENERIC].

240 mg (Rx) [*Armour Thyroid; Westhroid*].

300 mg (Rx) [*Armour Thyroid; Westhroid;* GENERIC].

Bovine:

30 mg (Rx) [*Thyrar*].

60 mg (Rx) [*Thyrar*].

120 mg (Rx) [*Thyrar*].

Strong (contains iodine 0.3%):

30 mg (Rx) [*Thyroid Strong*].

60 mg (Rx) [*Thyroid Strong*].

120 mg (Rx) [*Thyroid Strong*].

180 mg (Rx) [*Thyroid Strong*].

Canada—

Regular:

30 mg (Rx) [GENERIC].

60 mg (Rx) [GENERIC].

125 mg (Rx) [GENERIC].

Note: Administration of strengths above 120 mg may result in thyrotoxic symptoms.

Packaging and storage

Store below 40 °C (104 °F), preferably between 15 and 30 °C (59 and 86 °F), unless otherwise specified by manufacturer. Store in a tight container.

Auxiliary labeling

- Do not take other medicines without your doctor's advice.

Revised: 06/21/2000

TIAGABINE Systemic

VA CLASSIFICATION (Primary): CN400

Commonly used brand name(s): *Gabitril*.

Note: For a listing of dosage forms and brand names by country availability, see *Dosage Forms* section(s).

Category

Anticonvulsant.

Indications

Accepted

Epilepsy (treatment adjunct)—Tiagabine is indicated as an adjunct to other anticonvulsant medications in the treatment of partial seizures in adults and children 12 years of age and older.

Pharmacology/Pharmacokinetics

Physicochemical characteristics

Molecular weight—Tiagabine hydrochloride: 412.

Mechanism of action/Effect

The precise mechanism of tiagabine's antiseizure effects is unknown. *In vitro* experiments have documented tiagabine's ability to enhance the activity of gamma-aminobutyric acid (GABA), the major inhibitory neurotransmitter in the central nervous system (CNS). These experiments have shown that tiagabine binds to recognition sites associated with the GABA uptake carrier. It is thought that this binding enables tiagabine to block GABA uptake into presynaptic neurons, permitting more GABA to be available for receptor binding on the surfaces of post-synaptic cells. Inhibition of GABA uptake has been shown for synaptosomes, neuronal cell cultures, and glial cell cultures.

In vitro binding studies have shown that tiagabine does not significantly inhibit the uptake of dopamine, norepinephrine, serotonin, glutamate, or choline, and shows little or no binding to dopamine D_1 and D_2; muscarinic; serotonin $5HT_{1A}$, $5HT_2$, and $5HT_3$; beta$_1$- and beta$_2$-adrenergic; alpha$_1$- and alpha$_2$-adrenergic; histamine H_2 and H_3; adenosine A_1 and A_2; opiate mu and K_1; *N*-methyl-*D*-aspartate (NMDA) glutamate; and $GABA_A$ receptors. Tiagabine also lacks significant affinity for sodium or calcium channels. At concentrations 20 to 400 times those inhibiting the uptake of GABA, tiagabine binds to histamine H_1, serotonin $5HT_{1B}$, benzodiazepine, and chloride channel receptors.

Absorption

Tiagabine is rapidly and nearly completely absorbed (> 95%), with an absolute bioavailability of about 90%. Food slows the rate but not the extent of absorption.

Protein binding

Very high (96%), mainly to serum albumin and alpha-1–acid glycoprotein.

Biotransformation

Hepatic; not fully elucidated. At least two metabolic pathways have been identified: thiophene ring oxidation, leading to an inactive metabolite, and glucuronidation. Tiagabine is most likely metabolized primarily by the 3A isoform subfamily of hepatic cytochrome P450 (CYP3A); contributions to the metabolism of tiagabine from isoenzymes CYP1A2, CYP2D6, or CYP2C19 have not been excluded.

In patients with moderate hepatic impairment (Child-Pugh Class B), clearance of unbound tiagabine was reduced by about 60%. Patients with impaired liver function may require lower initial and maintenance doses of tiagabine and/or longer dosing intervals than patients with normal hepatic function.

Half-life

Elimination—

Normal volunteers: 7 to 9 hours.

Epileptic patients taking hepatic enzyme-inducing drugs: 4 to 7 hours.

Note: In clinical trials, most patients were induced.

Time to peak concentration

Approximately 45 minutes following an oral dose administered in the fasting state. The presence of food (i.e., a high fat meal) may prolong the time to reach maximum concentration to 2.5 hours.

Other pharmacokinetic parameters

A diurnal effect was observed on the pharmacokinetics of tiagabine. Mean steady-state minimum plasma concentration (C_{min}) values were 40% lower in the evening than in the morning. The area under the plasma concentration-time curve (AUC) values at steady-state were 15% lower following the evening dose as compared to the AUC values following the morning dose.

Elimination

Approximately 2% of an oral dose of tiagabine is excreted unchanged. Of the remaining dose, 25% and 63% are excreted into the urine and feces, respectively, primarily as metabolites.

Precautions to Consider

Carcinogenicity/Tumorigenicity

A carcinogenicity study in rats receiving 200 mg of tiagabine per kg of body weight (mg/kg) a day (36 to 100 times the maximum recommended human dosage [MRHD] of 56 mg a day) for 2 years resulted in small but statistically significant increases in the incidences of hepatocellular adenomas in female rats and Leydig cell tumors of the testis in male rats. The significance of these findings relative to the use of tiagabine in humans is not known. The no effect dosage for induction of tumors in this study was 100 mg/kg a day (17 to 50 times the MRHD). No statistically significant increases in tumor formation were noted in mice at dosages of up to 250 mg/kg a day (20 times the MRHD on a mg per square meter of body surface area [mg/m^2] basis).

Mutagenicity

Tiagabine produced an increase in structural chromosome aberration frequency in human lymphocytes *in vitro* in the absence of metabolic activation; no increase in chromosomal aberration frequencies was demonstrated in this assay in the presence of metabolic activation. No evidence of genetic toxicity was found in the *in vitro* bacterial gene mutation assays, the *in vitro* HGPRT forward mutation assay in Chinese hamster lung cells, the *in vivo* mouse micronucleus test, or an unscheduled DNA synthesis assay.

Pregnancy/Reproduction

Fertility—Studies in male and female rats receiving tiagabine prior to and during mating, gestation, and lactation have shown no impairment of fertility at doses of up to 100 mg/kg a day (approximately 16 times the MRHD on a mg/m² basis). Lowered maternal weight gain and decreased viability and growth in the rat pups did occur at this dose.

Pregnancy—Adequate and well-controlled studies in humans have not been done.

Tiagabine has been shown to have adverse effects on embryo-fetal development, including teratogenic effects, when administered to pregnant rats and rabbits at doses greater than the human therapeutic dose.

An increased incidence of malformed fetuses (various craniofacial, appendicular, and visceral defects) and decreased fetal weights were observed following oral administration of 100 mg/kg a day to pregnant rats during the period of organogenesis. This dose is approximately 16 times the MRHD on a mg/m² basis. Maternal toxicity (transient weight loss and reduced maternal weight gain during gestation) was associated with this dose, but there was no evidence to suggest that the teratogenic effects were secondary to the maternal effects. No adverse maternal or embryo-fetal effects were seen at a dose of 20 mg/kg a day (3 times the MRHD on a mg/m² basis).

Decreased maternal weight gain, increased resorption of embryos, and increased incidence of fetal variations, but not malformations, were observed when pregnant rabbits were administered 25 mg of tiagabine per kg a day (8 times the MRHD on a mg/m² basis) during organogenesis. The no effect level for maternal and embryo-fetal toxicity in rabbits was 5 mg/kg a day (equivalent to the MRHD on a mg/m² basis).

Decreased maternal weight gain during gestation, an increase in stillbirths, and decreased postnatal offspring viability and growth were observed in female rats that received tiagabine 100 mg/kg a day during late gestation and throughout parturition and lactation.

FDA Pregnancy Category C.

Breast-feeding

It is not known whether tiagabine and/or its metabolites are distributed into human milk or what effects it may have on the nursing infant. Animal studies have shown that tiagabine and/or its metabolites appear in the milk of rats. Risk-benefit must be considered.

Pediatrics

Adequate and well-controlled studies have not been conducted in children up to 12 years of age. However, pharmacokinetic studies in a small number of children 3 to 10 years of age showed that apparent clearance (per unit of body surface area) and volume of distribution (per kg) of tiagabine were similar to those in adults when both groups were receiving enzyme-inducing anticonvulsants (e.g., carbamazepine or phenytoin). In children taking a non–enzyme-inducing anticonvulsant (e.g., valproate), the clearance of tiagabine based upon body weight and body surface area was 2- and 1.5-fold higher, respectively, than in uninduced adults with epilepsy. Safety and efficacy in children up to 12 years of age have not been established.

Geriatrics

The pharmacokinetic profile of tiagabine in healthy elderly adults was similar to that in healthy young adults. However, only a small number of patients over 65 years of age were exposed to tiagabine during clinical evaluation; therefore, safety and efficacy in this age group have not been established.

Pharmacogenetics

Population pharmacokinetic analyses indicated that tiagabine clearance values were not significantly different in white, black, or Hispanic patients with epilepsy.

Drug interactions and/or related problems

The following drug interactions and/or related problems have been selected on the basis of their potential clinical significance (possible mechanism in parentheses where appropriate)—not necessarily inclusive (» = major clinical significance):

Note: Administration of hepatic enzyme-inducing medications will increase the clearance of tiagabine.

Combinations containing any of the following medications, depending on the amount present, may also interact with this medication.

Alcohol or
Central nervous system (CNS) depression-producing medications, other (see *Appendix II*)
(increased CNS depression may occur)

» Carbamazepine
(tiagabine clearance is increased by 60% in patients taking carbamazepine)

» Phenobarbital
(tiagabine clearance is increased by 60% in patients taking phenobarbital)

» Phenytoin
(tiagabine clearance is increased by 60% in patients taking phenytoin)

» Primidone
(tiagabine clearance is increased by 60% in patients taking primidone)

Valproic acid
(tiagabine causes a slight decrease [about 10%] in steady-state valproate concentrations; *in vitro* studies have shown that valproate decreased the protein binding of tiagabine from 96.3 to 94.8%, resulting in an increase of approximately 40% in the free tiagabine concentration; clinical relevance of this finding is unknown)

Medical considerations/Contraindications

The medical considerations/contraindications included have been selected on the basis of their potential clinical significance (reasons given in parentheses where appropriate)—not necessarily inclusive (» = major clinical significance).

Risk-benefit should be considered when the following medical problems exist:

Electroencephalogram (EEG) abnormalities
(patients with a history of spike and wave discharges on EEG have been reported to have exacerbations of EEG abnormalities associated with cognitive/neuropsychiatric events; these clinical events may, in some cases, be a manifestation of underlying seizure activity; dosage adjustments may be required)

Hepatic function impairment
(dosage reductions or longer dosing intervals may be required)

Sensitivity to tiagabine

Status epilepticus, history of
(condition may be precipitated)

Patient monitoring

The following may be especially important in patient monitoring (other tests may be warranted in some patients, depending on condition; » = major clinical significance):

Therapeutic monitoring of plasma concentrations
(a therapeutic range for tiagabine plasma concentrations has not been established; in controlled trials, trough plasma concentrations observed in patients randomized to tiagabine doses that were statistically significantly more effective than placebo ranged from < 1 nanogram/mL to 234 nanograms/mL; because of the potential for interactions between tiagabine and drugs that induce or inhibit hepatic metabolizing enzymes, obtaining tiagabine plasma concentrations before and after changes are made in the patient's medication regimen may be useful)

Side/Adverse Effects

Note: In studies in dogs receiving a single dose of radiolabeled tiagabine, residual binding in the retina and uvea after 3 weeks was apparent. Binding to melanin is likely. The ability of available tests to detect potentially adverse consequences of the binding of tiagabine to melanin-containing tissue is unknown, and no systematic monitoring for relevant ophthalmologic changes during the clinical development of tiagabine was conducted. However, long-term (up to 1 year) toxicological studies of tiagabine in dogs showed no treatment-related ophthalmoscopic changes, and macro- and microscopic examinations of the eye were unremarkable. Although there are no specific recommendations for periodic ophthalmologic monitoring, the possibility of long-term ophthalmologic effects exists.

The following side/adverse effects have been selected on the basis of their potential clinical significance (possible signs and symptoms in parentheses where appropriate)—not necessarily inclusive:

Those indicating need for medical attention

Incidence more frequent

Difficulty in concentrating or paying attention—may be dose-related; ***ecchymosis*** (blue or purple spots on skin)

Incidence less frequent

Ataxia (clumsiness or unsteadiness); ***confusion; mental depression; paresthesias*** (burning, numbness, or tingling sensations); ***pruritus*** (itching); ***speech and/or language problems***

Incidence rare

Abnormal gait (walking in unusual manner); ***agitation; emotional lability*** (quick to react or overreact emotionally); ***generalized weakness; hostility; memory problems; nystagmus*** (uncontrolled back-and-forth and/or rolling eye movements); ***rash; urinary tract infection*** (bloody or cloudy urine; burning, pain, or difficulty in urinating; frequent urge to urinate)

Note: Moderately severe to incapacitating *generalized weakness* has been reported in about 1% of patients with epilepsy following administration of tiagabine. Weakness resolved in all cases following a reduction in dose or discontinuation of tiagabine.

Four patients treated with tiagabine during premarketing clinical testing developed serious *rashes;* two cases were described as maculopapular, one case was described as vesiculobullous, and one case was diagnosed as Stevens-Johnson syndrome. A causal relationship to tiagabine has not been established. However, drug-associated rash can, if extensive and serious, cause irreversible morbidity, even death.

Those indicating need for medical attention only if they continue or are bothersome

Incidence more frequent

Asthenia (unusual tiredness or weakness)—may be dose-related; ***diarrhea; dizziness; influenza-like syndrome*** (chills; fever; headache; muscle aches or pain); ***nervousness; pharyngitis*** (sore throat); ***somnolence*** (drowsiness); ***tremor***—may be dose-related; ***vomiting***

Incidence less frequent

Abdominal pain; amblyopia (impaired vision); ***cough, increased; increased appetite; insomnia*** (trouble in sleeping); ***mouth ulcers; muscle weakness; myalgia*** (muscle ache or pain); ***nausea; pain (unspecified); vasodilation*** (flushing)

Overdose

For information on the management of overdose or unintentional ingestion of tiagabine, **contact a Poison Control Center** (see *Poison Control Center Listing*).

Clinical effects of overdose

The following effects have been selected on the basis of their potential clinical significance (possible signs and symptoms in parentheses where appropriate)—not necessarily inclusive:

Acute

Agitation, severe; ataxia, severe (clumsiness or unsteadiness); ***confusion, severe; hostility; impaired consciousness*** (coma); ***lethargy*** (sluggishness); ***mental depression; myoclonus*** (severe muscle twitching or jerking); ***precipitation of a tonic-clonic seizure*** (increase in seizures); ***somnolence, severe*** (drowsiness); ***speech problems, severe; weakness***

Treatment of overdose

There is no specific antidote for overdose with tiagabine.

To decrease absorption—Elimination of unabsorbed drug by inducing emesis or by gastric lavage, if indicated; usual precautions to maintain the airway should be taken.

To enhance elimination—Since tiagabine is primarily metabolized by the liver and highly protein-bound, dialysis is not likely to be beneficial.

Monitoring—Monitoring of vital signs.

Supportive care—General supportive care, including observation of clinical status. Patients in whom intentional overdose is confirmed or suspected should be referred for psychiatric consultation.

Patient Consultation

As an aid to patient consultation, refer to *Advice for the Patient, Tiagabine (Systemic)*.

In providing consultation, consider emphasizing the following selected information (» = major clinical significance):

Before using this medication

» Conditions affecting use, especially:
  Sensitivity to tiagabine
  Pregnancy—Teratogenicity and maternal toxicity have been demonstrated in animal studies
  Other medications, especially carbamazepine, phenobarbital, phenytoin, or primidone

Proper use of this medication

Compliance with therapy; not taking more or less medicine than prescribed

Taking with food

» Proper dosing
  Missed dose: Taking as soon as possible; if almost time for next dose, skipping missed dose and returning to regular dosing schedule; not doubling doses

» Proper storage

Precautions while using this medication

» Possible dizziness, drowsiness, impairment of thinking or motor skills; caution when driving or doing jobs requiring alertness or coordination

Discussing alcohol use or use of other CNS depressants with physician

» Not discontinuing tiagabine abruptly; consulting physician about gradually reducing dosage

Side/adverse effects

Signs of potential side effects, especially difficulty in concentrating or paying attention, ecchymosis, ataxia, confusion, mental depression, paresthesias, pruritus, speech and/or language problems, abnormal gait, agitation, emotional lability, generalized weakness, hostility, memory problems, nystagmus, rash, and urinary tract infection

General Dosing Information

Anticonvulsants should not be abruptly discontinued because of the possibility of increasing seizure frequency. Unless safety concerns require a more rapid withdrawal, tiagabine should be withdrawn gradually.

Diet/Nutrition

Tiagabine should be taken with food.

Oral Dosage Forms

TIAGABINE HYDROCHLORIDE TABLETS

Note: Clinical trials of adjunctive use of tiagabine were conducted in patients taking enzyme-inducing anticonvulsants (e.g., barbiturates, carbamazepine, phenytoin). Patients taking only non–enzyme-inducing anticonvulsants (e.g., gabapentin, lamotrigine, valproate) may require a lower dose or slower titration of tiagabine. Patients taking a combination of inducing and non-inducing anticonvulsants should be considered to be induced.

Usual adult dose

Anticonvulsant—

Oral, initially 4 mg once a day. The total daily dose may be increased by 4 to 8 mg at weekly intervals until clinical response is achieved or a dose of 56 mg a day is reached. The total daily dose should be given in divided doses two to four times a day.

Note: Dosage modification of concomitant anticonvulsants is not necessary, unless clinically indicated.

A typical dosing titration regimen for patients taking enzyme-inducing anticonvulsants follows:

Week	Initiation and titration schedule	Total daily dose
1	Initiate at 4 mg once a day	4 mg/day
2	Increase total daily dose by 4 mg	8 mg/day (in two divided doses)
3	Increase total daily dose by 4 mg	12 mg/day (in three divided doses)
4	Increase total daily dose by 4 mg	16 mg/day (in two to four divided doses)
5	Increase total daily dose by 4 to 8 mg	20 to 24 mg/day (in two to four divided doses)
6	Increase total daily dose by 4 to 8 mg	24 to 32 mg/day (in two to four divided doses)
Usual adult maintenance dose	32 to 56 mg/day in two to four divided doses	

Note: Dosage reduction may be necessary in patients with liver disease due to reduced clearance of tiagabine.

Usual adult prescribing limits

56 mg a day.

Note: Doses above 56 mg a day have not been evaluated in adequate and well-controlled studies.

Usual pediatric dose

Anticonvulsant—

Children 12 to 18 years of age: Oral, initially 4 mg once a day. The total daily dose may be increased by 4 mg at the beginning of the second week of therapy. Thereafter, the total daily dose may be further increased by 4 to 8 mg at weekly intervals until clinical response is achieved or a dose of 32 mg a day is reached. The total daily dose should be given in divided doses two to four times a day.

Note: Dosage modification of concomitant anticonvulsants is not necessary, unless clinically indicated.

Children up to 12 years of age: Safety and efficacy have not been established.

Usual adolescent prescribing limits

32 mg a day.

Note: Doses above 32 mg a day have been tolerated in a small number of adolescent patients for a relatively short time.

Usual geriatric dose

See *Usual adult dose.*

Strength(s) usually available

U.S.—

4 mg (Rx) [*Gabitril* (film-sealed; ascorbic acid; colloidal silicon dioxide; crospovidone; hydrogenated vegetable oil wax; hydroxypropyl cellulose; hydroxypropyl methylcellulose; lactose; magnesium stearate; microcrystalline cellulose; pregelatinized starch; stearic acid; titanium dioxide; D&C Yellow No. 10)].

12 mg (Rx) [*Gabitril* (film-sealed; ascorbic acid; colloidal silicon dioxide; crospovidone; hydrogenated vegetable oil wax; hydroxypropyl cellulose; hydroxypropyl methylcellulose; lactose; magnesium stearate; microcrystalline cellulose; pregelatinized starch; stearic acid; titanium dioxide; D&C Yellow No. 10; FD&C Blue No. 1)].

16 mg (Rx) [*Gabitril* (film-sealed; ascorbic acid; colloidal silicon dioxide; crospovidone; hydrogenated vegetable oil wax; hydroxypropyl cellulose; hydroxypropyl methylcellulose; lactose; magnesium stearate; microcrystalline cellulose; pregelatinized starch; stearic acid; titanium dioxide; D&C Blue No. 2)].

20 mg (Rx) [*Gabitril* (film-sealed; ascorbic acid; colloidal silicon dioxide; crospovidone; hydrogenated vegetable oil wax; hydroxypropyl cellulose; hydroxypropyl methylcellulose; lactose; magnesium stearate; microcrystalline cellulose; pregelatinized starch; stearic acid; titanium dioxide; D&C Red No. 30)].

Packaging and storage

Store between 20 and 25 °C (68 and 77 °F). Protect from light and moisture.

Auxiliary labeling

- Take with food.
- May cause drowsiness.
- May cause dizziness.

Revised: 09/07/2001

TIAPROFENIC ACID—See *Anti-inflammatory Drugs, Nonsteroidal (Systemic)*

TICARCILLIN—See *Penicillins (Systemic)*

TICLOPIDINE Systemic

VA CLASSIFICATION (Primary): BL117

Commonly used brand name(s): *Ticlid.*

Note: For a listing of dosage forms and brand names by country availability, see *Dosage Forms* section(s).

Category

Antithrombotic; platelet aggregation inhibitor.

Indications

Accepted

Stroke, thromboembolic, initial or recurrent (prophylaxis)—Ticlopidine is indicated to reduce the risk of a recurrent thromboembolic stroke in patients who have had a completed thrombotic stroke. It is also indicated to reduce the risk of an initial completed thromboembolic stroke in patients who have experienced stroke precursors, such as transient ischemic attack, transient monocular blindness (amarurosis fugax), reversible ischemic neurological deficit (RIND), or minor stroke. In one study in patients who had experienced an ischemic stroke, ticlopidine produced slight but significant neurologic improvement.

Although ticlopidine was somewhat more effective than aspirin in preventing initial strokes in patients with stroke precursors in a major study, it caused significantly more adverse effects than aspirin. Also, ticlopidine may cause neutropenia, agranulocytosis, aplastic anemia and thrombotic thrombocytopenic purpura (TTP). It is therefore recommended that ticlopidine therapy be reserved for patients unable to take aspirin for stroke prophylaxis and patients who develop strokes despite aspirin therapy, and only when close hematologic monitoring is possible.

Thrombosis, subacute coronary artery stent-related (prophylaxis)[1]—Ticlopidine is indicated as an adjunctive therapy with aspirin to reduce the incidence of subacute stent thrombosis in patients undergoing successful coronary stent implantation.

---

[1]Not included in Canadian product labeling.

Pharmacology/Pharmacokinetics

Physicochemical characteristics

Chemical Group—Thienopyridine derivative.

Molecular weight—300.25.

Mechanism of action/Effect

Ticlopidine is an inhibitor of platelet aggregation; doses of 250, 375, and 500 mg a day inhibit platelet aggregation by 20 to 50%, 30 to 60%, and 50 to 70%, respectively. Doses higher than 500 mg per day do not produce a significant additional increase in the extent of inhibition.

The mechanism by which ticlopidine inhibits platelet aggregation has not been fully characterized. Ticlopidine inhibits adenosine diphosphate (ADP)-induced binding of fibrinogen to the platelet membrane at a specific receptor site (the glycoprotein IIb-IIIa complex). Release of platelet granule constituents, platelet-platelet interactions, and platelet adhesion to the endothelium and to atheromatous plaque are inhibited. Ticlopidine has no significant inhibitory effect on other endogenous substances known to promote platelet aggregation; it does not interfere with the synthesis or activity of cyclo-oxygenase, phosphodiesterase, or platelet cyclic adenosine monophosphate (cAMP), or with adenosine uptake. Also, ticlopidine does not alter mobilization or influx of calcium ions.

There is a lag time of several days for ticlopidine to exert its maximum effect on platelet function, probably by acting on platelet membranes during megakaryocytopoietic development rather than on circulating platelets. Ticlopidine-induced inhibition of platelet aggregation persists for the life of the platelet.

Ticlopidine prolongs the template bleeding time, but has no effect in usual assays of coagulation or fibrinolysis.

Ticlopidine also reduces fibrinogen concentrations and blood viscosity, and increases the filterability rates of both whole blood and red cells, which may contribute to the beneficial effects in patients with vascular disease.

Absorption

Rapid; 80% or more of a dose is absorbed. Absorption is increased when the medication is taken after a meal.

Protein binding

Very high (98%), primarily to serum albumin and lipoproteins, and, to a lesser extent (15% or less), to alpha-1-acid glycoprotein. Protein binding of metabolites is about 40 to 50%.

Biotransformation

Hepatic; extensive. At least 20 metabolites have been identified. It has been proposed that 1 or more active metabolites may account for ticlopidine's activity, because ticlopidine itself is an extremely weak platelet aggregation inhibitor *in vitro* at the concentrations achieved *in vivo*. However, no active metabolite has been identified.

Biotransformation of ticlopidine may be saturable; plasma concentrations achieved after a single dose increase disproportionately to the dose. Also, steady-state plasma concentrations are approximately twice as high as those achieved after administration of a single dose. In addition, the percentage of unmetabolized ticlopidine present in the circulation is 5% after a single dose and 15% at steady-state.

Half-life

Elimination—

Single 250-mg dose: About 7.9 hours in subjects 20 to 43 years of age; about 12.6 hours in subjects 65 to 76 years of age.

Repeated dosing with 250 mg twice a day: About 4 days in subjects 20 to 43 years of age; about 5 days in subjects 65 to 76 years of age.

Onset of action

Repeated dosing with 250 mg twice a day—Inhibition of platelet aggregation is detectable within 2 days; clinically significant inhibition (more than 50%) occurs within 4 days.

Time to peak concentration

Single 250-mg dose—About 2 hours.

Peak concentration

Single 250-mg dose—0.4 to 0.6 mcg per mL (mcg/mL) (1.33 to 1.99 micromoles/L); subject to substantial inter- and intrasubject variation. Values obtained when the medication is taken with meals are about 20% higher than those obtained when the medication is taken on an empty stomach. Values obtained when the medication is taken following an aluminum- and magnesium-containing antacid are about 18% lower than those obtained when the medication is not taken after an antacid.

Plasma concentrations may be increased slightly in patients with hepatic function impairment (advanced cirrhosis) and significantly increased in patients with renal function impairment. The area under the curve is increased by about 28% in patients with mild renal function impairment (creatinine clearances of 50 to 80 mL per minute) and by about 60% in patients with moderate renal function impairment (creatinine clearances of 20 to 50 mL per minute).

Time to steady-state concentration

Repeated administration of 250 mg twice a day—14 to 21 days.

Steady-state concentration

Repeated administration of 250 mg twice a day—About 1 to 2 mcg/mL (3.33 to 6.66 micromoles/L); may be increased in elderly patients. The area under the curve in elderly subjects receiving 250 mg twice a day for 21 days is 2 to 3 times as high as in younger subjects.

Time to peak effect

Repeated dosing with 250 mg twice a day: Maximal inhibition of platelet aggregation (60 to 70%) is achieved in 8 to 11 days.

Duration of action

After discontinuation of treatment, recovery of platelet function occurs as exposed platelets are replaced. In the majority of patients, bleeding time and other platelet function tests return to pretreatment levels within 1 to 2 weeks.

Elimination

Renal (about 60% of a dose) and biliary/fecal (about 23% of a dose). Unchanged ticlopidine accounts for trace amounts of the quantity eliminated in the urine and about 33% of the quantity eliminated in the feces.

The plasma clearance rate after administration of 250 mg twice a day for 21 days is about 1.52 L per minute in young subjects (average age 29 years) and about 0.56 L per minute in elderly subjects (average age 70 years). The plasma clearance rate is decreased by about 37% in patients with mild renal function impairment (creatinine clearances 50 to 80 mL per minute) and by about 52% in patients with moderate renal function impairment (creatinine clearances 20 to 50 mL per minute).

Precautions to Consider

Carcinogenicity/Tumorigenicity

No evidence of carcinogenicity or tumorigenicity was found in a 2-year study in rats receiving oral doses of up to 100 mg per kg of body weight (mg/kg) per day (610 mg per square meter of body surface area [mg/m^2] per day). These doses are equivalent to up to 14 times the human clinical dose on a mg/kg basis and 2 times the clinical dose on a mg/m^2 basis (based on a human weighing 70 kg and having a body surface area of 1.73 m^2). Also, no evidence of tumorigenicity or carcinogenicity was found in a 78-week study in mice receiving oral doses of up to 275 mg/kg per day (1180 mg/m^2 per day). These doses are equivalent to up to 40 times the clinical dose on a mg/kg basis and 4 times the clinical dose on a mg/m^2 basis.

Mutagenicity

No evidence of mutagenic activity was found in the Ames test, rat hepatocyte DNA-repair assay, Chinese hamster fibroblast chromosomal aberration test (all *in vitro*) or in the mouse spermatozoid morphology test, Chinese hamster micronucleus test, and Chinese hamster bone marrow cell sister chromatid exchange test (all *in vivo*).

Pregnancy/Reproduction

Fertility—Ticlopidine had no effect on fertility in male or female rats in doses of up to 400 mg/kg per day.

Pregnancy—Adequate and well-controlled studies have not been performed in pregnant women.

No evidence of teratogenicity was found in studies in mice receiving up to 200 mg/kg per day, rats receiving up to 400 mg/kg per day, or rabbits receiving up to 200 mg/kg per day. However, maternal toxicity (decreased food intake and weight gain) and fetotoxicity occurred in mice receiving 200 mg/kg per day, rats receiving 400 mg/kg per day, and rabbits receiving 100 mg/kg per day.

FDA Pregnancy Category B.

Breast-feeding

It is not known whether ticlopidine is distributed into human breast milk. However, problems in humans have not been documented.

Pediatrics

No information is available on the relationship of age to the effects of ticlopidine in pediatric patients. Safety and efficacy have not been established.

Geriatrics

Appropriate studies performed to date have not demonstrated geriatrics-specific problems that would limit the usefulness of ticlopidine in the elderly. In major clinical trials, approximately 45% of the patients were 65 years of age or older; 12% were more than 75 years of age. Although clearance of ticlopidine is lower in elderly patients than in younger adults, and plasma concentrations are higher than in younger adults, elderly individuals in these studies did not receive lower doses. No overall differences in efficacy or safety were observed.

Dental

Because of the risk of increased blood loss, it is recommended that ticlopidine be discontinued 10 to 14 days prior to dental surgery.

Ticlopidine may cause neutropenia and aplastic anemia, which may result in an increased incidence of microbial infection, delayed healing, and gingival bleeding. If severe neutropenia occurs, dental work should be deferred until blood counts have returned to normal. Also, patients should be instructed in proper oral hygiene, including caution in use of regular toothbrushes, dental floss, and toothpicks.

Surgical

Because of the risk of increased surgical blood loss, it is recommended that ticlopidine be discontinued 10 to 14 days prior to elective surgery. In emergency situations, transfusion of fresh platelets may improve hemostasis. It is recommended that therapy with ticlopidine be discontinued and that thrombotic thrombocytopenic purpura (TTP) and aplastic anemia be ruled out if a patient develops thrombocytopenia while taking ticlopidine. Platelet transfusions should, if possible, be avoided in patients with TTP as they may accelerate the thrombosis associated with TTP. Although intravenous administration of 20 mg of methylprednisolone to ticlopidine-treated patients has been shown to return the bleeding time to normal within 2 hours, the effect of such treatment on perisurgical hemostasis has not been established.

Drug interactions and/or related problems

The following drug interactions and/or related problems have been selected on the basis of their potential clinical significance (possible mechanism in parentheses where appropriate)—not necessarily inclusive (» = major clinical significance):

Note: Combinations containing any of the following medications, depending on the amount present, may also interact with this medication.

In addition to the interactions listed below, the possibility should be considered that additive or multiple effects leading to an increased risk of bleeding may occur if ticlopidine is administered concurrently with any other medication or herbal product that has significant platelet aggregation-inhibiting activity or a significant potential for causing hypoprothrombinemia, thrombocytopenia, or gastrointestinal ulceration or hemorrhage.

Antacids, aluminum- and magnesium-containing
(plasma concentrations of ticlopidine are decreased by about 18% when it is administered after an aluminum- and magnesium-containing antacid; information about the effects of single-ingredient antacids on ticlopidine concentrations is not available, but the possibility of a similar effect should be considered; it is recommended that ticlopidine and an antacid be administered at least 1 to 2 hours apart)

» Anticoagulants, coumarin- or indandione-derivative or
» Heparin or
» Low molecular weight heparin or
» Thrombolytic agents, such as:
Alteplase
Anistreplase
Streptokinase

Urokinase
(the possibility of additive effects on blood clotting mechanisms leading to an increased risk of bleeding cannot be discounted; particularly careful clinical monitoring of the patient is recommended if concurrent use is necessary)
(in one study, concurrent administration of warfarin and ticlopidine was associated with an increased risk of medication-induced hepatitis)

» Aspirin or
» Nonsteroidal anti-inflammatory drugs (NSAIDs) or
» Platelet aggregation inhibitors, other (see *Appendix II*)
(concurrent use of ticlopidine with these agents may increase the risk of bleeding because of additive inhibition of platelet aggregation; also, the potential for aspirin- or NSAID-induced gastrointestinal ulceration or hemorrhage exists)
(in one study, the risk of bleeding was higher, and bleeding episodes occurred earlier, in patients receiving combined therapy with low doses of aspirin and ticlopidine [81 mg and 100 mg per day, respectively] than in patients receiving larger doses of either agent alone; studies have also shown that the combination of medications prolongs bleeding time to a greater extent than either agent alone; these effects are probably due to potentiation by ticlopidine of aspirin-mediated inhibition of platelet aggregation, since studies have shown that inhibition of collagen-induced platelet aggregation [an effect of aspirin], but not of adenosine diphosphate [ADP]–induced platelet aggregation [an effect of ticlopidine] is increased in the presence of both agents)

Cimetidine
(chronic administration of cimetidine may reduce the clearance of a single dose of ticlopidine by 50%.)

» Phenytoin
(several cases of elevated phenytoin plasma concentrations with associated somnolence and lethargy have been reported following ticlopidine administration)

» Xanthines, such as:
Aminophylline
Oxtriphylline
Theophylline
(theophylline elimination half-life may be increased by about 40%, and total plasma clearance of theophylline decreased by about 35%, when a xanthine is administered to a patient receiving ticlopidine)

Laboratory value alterations

The following have been selected on the basis of their potential clinical significance (possible effect in parentheses where appropriate)—not necessarily inclusive (» = major clinical significance).

With physiology/laboratory test values

Alkaline phosphatase and
Bilirubin and
Transaminases
(values may be elevated; in clinical studies, the incidence of elevations to more than twice the upper limit of normal was 7.6% for alkaline phosphatase and 3.1% for aspartate aminotransferase [AST (SGOT)]; increases generally occurred within 1 to 4 months after initiation of therapy; although no progressive increases were reported, treatment was discontinued in most patients)

» Bleeding time
(prolongation to 2 to 5 times the pretreatment value is expected during ticlopidine treatment, although maximal effects on bleeding time may be delayed for some time after platelet aggregation tests indicate maximal inhibition; ticlopidine-induced prolongation of bleeding time may be reduced in patients receiving chronic glucocorticoid treatment, although ticlopidine's effect on ADP-induced platelet aggregation is not altered; also, prolongation of bleeding time may be reversed by a single intravenous dose of 20 mg of methylprednisolone)

Cholesterol, total and
Triglycerides
(serum concentrations may be elevated; in clinical studies, total serum cholesterol was increased by 8 to 10% after about 1 month of ticlopidine treatment, but further increases did not occur thereafter; also, the ratios of lipoprotein subfractions were not altered)

» Neutrophil count and
Platelet count
(may be decreased; in clinical trials, the overall incidence of neutropenia [absolute neutrophil count (ANC) $<$ 1200 neutrophils/mm^3] was 2.4%, and that of severe neutropenia [ANC $<$ 450 neutrophils/mm^3] about 0.8%; neutropenia generally occurs between 3 and 12 weeks after initiation of treatment, is associated with inhibition of granulocyte cell line maturation, and is generally reversed within a few weeks after discontinuation of treatment)
(thrombocytopenia may occur in conjunction with, or independently of, neutropenia, generally between 3 and 12 weeks after initiation of treatment; in clinical trials, the incidence of thrombocytopenia was 0.4%; recovery generally occurs after discontinuation)

Medical considerations/Contraindications

The medical considerations/contraindications included have been selected on the basis of their potential clinical significance (reasons given in parentheses where appropriate)—not necessarily inclusive (» = major clinical significance).

Except under special circumstances, this medication should not be used when the following medical problems exist:

» Bleeding or
» Hemophilia or other coagulation defects or hemostatic disorders
(risk of severe bleeding)

» Hematopoietic disorders such as:
Neutropenia
Thrombocytopenia
(may be exacerbated)

» Hepatic function impairment, severe
(increased risk of bleeding because severe hepatic function impairment may result in decreased synthesis of clotting factor precursors)

» Thrombotic thrombocytopenic purpura, history of
(risk of recurrence)

Risk-benefit should be considered when the following medical problems exist:

» Any condition in which there is a significant risk of bleeding, such as:
Gastrointestinal ulceration
Surgery
Trauma

» Renal function impairment, severe
(clearance of ticlopidine decreases, and concentrations increase, with increasing degrees of renal function impairment; although ticlopidine is well tolerated by patients with mild or moderate degrees of renal function impairment, caution and close monitoring are recommended in patients with severe renal disease because experience in such patients is limited; a reduction in dosage may be needed, but studies with reduced doses of ticlopidine have not been done)

Sensitivity to ticlopidine

Patient monitoring

The following may be especially important in patient monitoring (other tests may be warranted in some patients, depending on condition; » = major clinical significance):

Bleeding time and
Platelet count
(determinations may be needed to assess the risk of bleeding complications when procedures that have a significant risk of bleeding, such as surgery or dental work, are needed during or shortly following ticlopidine therapy)

» Complete blood count and
» Platelet count and
» Red blood cell morphology (peripheral smear) and
» White blood cell differentials
(because of the risk of severe hematological adverse reactions, these checks must be performed every 2 weeks, starting at baseline before treatment is begun, for the first 3 months of treatment; more frequent monitoring may be needed for patients with clinical signs suggesting hematological adverse reactions, whose absolute neutrophil counts are declining or are 30% below the baseline count, or who have decreases in hematocrit or platelet count since severe hematological adverse reactions may develop rapidly [over a few days]. The incidence of thrombotic thrombocytopenic purpura (TTP) peaks after about 3 to 4 weeks of therapy and neutropenia peaks at approximately 4 to 6 weeks, with both declining thereafter. Treatment should be discontinued if clinical evaluation and repeat laboratory testing confirm the presence of neutropenia or thrombocytopenia [neutrophil count reduced to 1200 per cubic millimeter or lower; platelet count reduced to 80,000 per cubic millimeter or lower]. Any acute, unexplained reduction in hemoglobin or platelet count should prompt further investigation for a diagnosis of TTP, and the appearance of schistocytes (fragmented red blood cells) on the peripheral smear should be treated as presumptive evidence of TTP. If treatment is discontinued for any reason within

the first 3 months, continued monitoring for at least another 2 weeks following discontinuation is recommended because of ticlopidine's long plasma half-life. Because the risk of these complications decreases substantially after the first 3 months of therapy [although cases have been reported after several months or even years of treatment], further testing is needed only if signs and symptoms suggestive of severe neutropenia or thrombocytopenia occur)

Side/Adverse Effects

Note: Most of the side/adverse effects reported with ticlopidine, including *aplastic anemia, neutropenia or agranulocytosis, thrombotic thrombocytopenic purpura, thrombocytopenia, gastrointestinal disturbances*, and *skin rash*, appear within the first 3 months of treatment, although some may occur or recur several months later. Rarely, *aplastic anemia, neutropenia, thrombocytopenia, or thrombotic thrombocytopenic purpura* has occurred after years of treatment. Fatalities associated with *severe neutropenia, agranulocytosis, pancytopenia, aplastic anemia, immune thrombocytopenia*, or *thrombotic thrombocytopenic purpura* have been reported.

Ticlopidine-induced *gastrointestinal disturbances* may occur in up to 40% of the patients receiving the medication. They are generally mild and usually disappear within 1 or 2 weeks without discontinuation of treatment; however, about 13% of the patients withdrew from clinical studies because of them. In some cases of severe or bloody diarrhea, colitis was later diagnosed.

In addition to the side/adverse effects listed below, rare cases of the following have been reported in postmarketing surveillance programs: *pancytopenia, hemolytic anemia with reticulocytosis, allergic pneumonitis, systemic lupus erythematosus, peripheral neuropathy, vasculitis, serum sickness, arthropathy, nephrotic syndrome, myositis, hyponatremia, immune thrombocytopenia, eosinophilia, bone marrow depression, aplastic anemia, hepatocellular jaundice, hepatic necrosis, peptic ulcer, renal failure, sepsis, and angioedema.* A causal relationship has not always been established.

The following side/adverse effects have been selected on the basis of their potential clinical significance (possible signs and symptoms in parentheses where appropriate)—not necessarily inclusive:

Those indicating need for medical attention

Incidence more frequent

Skin rash—incidence 5.1%

Note: Usually disappears within several days after treatment is discontinued, and may not recur upon reinstitution of treatment. However, there have been rare reports of severe rashes including Stevens-Johnson syndrome, erythema multiforme, and exfoliative dermatitis.

Incidence less frequent

Bleeding complications (abdominal pain [severe] or swelling; back pain; blood in eyes; blood in urine; bloody or black, tarry stools; bruising or purple areas on skin; coughing up blood; decreased alertness; dizziness; headache, severe or continuing; joint pain or swelling; nosebleeds; paralysis or problems with coordination; stammering or other difficulty in speaking; unusually heavy bleeding or oozing from cuts or wounds; unusually heavy or unexpected menstrual bleeding; vomiting of blood or material that looks like coffee grounds)—depending on the site of bleeding; in clinical studies the incidence of intracerebral bleeding was 0.5% and that of epistaxis was 0.5 to 1%; ***itching of skin***—incidence 1.3%; ***neutropenia, including agranulocytosis*** (fever, chills, sore throat, other signs of infection; ulcers, sores, or white spots in mouth)—incidence 2.4% overall, 0.8% severe [absolute neutrophil count (ANC) < 450 neutrophils/mm^3]; ***purpura*** (red or purple spots on skin, varying in size from pinpoint to large bruises)—incidence 2.2%

Incidence rare

Aplastic anemia (ulcers; unusual tiredness); ***hepatitis or cholestatic jaundice*** (yellow eyes or skin); ***hives***—incidence 0.5 to 1%; ***ringing or buzzing in ears***—incidence 0.5 to 1%; ***skin rash, severe, including erythema multiforme*** (fever; malaise; red skin lesions, often with a purple center); ***or Stevens-Johnson syndrome*** (blistering, peeling, or loosening of skin and mucous membranes; fever; malaise); ***or exfoliative dermatitis*** (fever; malaise; red, thickened, or scaly skin); ***thrombocytopenia*** (unusual bleeding or bruising; black, tarry stools; blood in urine or stools; pinpoint red spots on skin)—usually asymptomatic; incidence 0.4%; ***thrombotic thrombocytopenic purpura*** (change in mental status; dark or bloody urine; difficulty speaking; fever; pale color of skin; pinpoint red spots on skin; seizures; weakness; yellow eyes or skin)

Note: Bulla formation involving the eyes or other organ systems may occur with *Stevens-Johnson syndrome*.

Aplastic anemia and thrombocytopenia may occur independently of, or in conjunction with, neutropenia.

Clinical symptoms of *thrombotic thrombocytopenic purpura (TTP)* may precede laboratory findings by hours or days. With prompt treatment (often including plasmapheresis), 70 to 80% of patients will survive with minimal or no sequelae.

If TTP develops, ticlopidine should be discontinued. Ticlopidine should not be used to treat TTP because of its possible causative association with the syndrome. Platelet transfusions should, if possible, be avoided in patients with TTP as they may accelerate the thrombosis associated with TTP.

Those indicating need for medical attention only if they continue or are bothersome

Incidence more frequent

Abdominal pain—incidence 3.7%; ***diarrhea***—incidence 12.5%; ***indigestion***—incidence 7%; ***nausea***—incidence 7%

Incidence less frequent

Bloating or gas—incidence 1.5%; ***dizziness***—incidence 1.1%; ***vomiting***—incidence 1.9%

Overdose

Only one case of overdose has been reported, in which a single 6000-mg dose was ingested by a 38-year-old male. The patient's bleeding time was prolonged and the alanine aminotransferase (ALT [SGPT]) value was increased. There were no other abnormalities or symptoms, and the patient recovered without treatment.

For more information on the management of overdose or unintentional ingestion, **contact a Poison Control Center** (see *Poison Control Center Listing*).

Patient Consultation

As an aid to patient consultation, refer to *Advice for the Patient, Ticlopidine (Systemic)*.

In providing consultation, consider emphasizing the following selected information (» = major clinical significance):

Before using this medication

» Conditions affecting use, especially:

Sensitivity to ticlopidine

Dental—Risk of increased blood loss during dental procedures

Other medications, especially anticoagulants, aspirin, heparin, low molecular weight heparin, nonsteroidal anti-inflammatory drugs (NSAIDs), other platelet aggregation inhibitors, phenytoin, thrombolytic agents, or xanthines, including theophylline

Other medical problems, especially bleeding (active), medical problems in which there is a significant risk of bleeding, hematopoietic disorders, history of thrombotic thrombocytopenic purpura, severe hepatic function impairment, and severe renal function impairment

Surgical—Risk of increased blood loss during surgical procedures

Proper use of this medication

Taking medication with food to increase absorption and to reduce the risk of gastrointestinal irritation

Compliance with prescribed treatment regimen

» Proper dosing

Missed dose: Taking as soon as possible; not taking if almost time for next dose; not doubling doses

» Proper storage

Precautions while using this medication

» Importance of regular blood tests to detect potential adverse effects during the first 3 months of treatment

» Need to inform all health care providers of use of medication; medication should be discontinued 10 to 14 days prior to elective procedures with a risk of bleeding

» Because of risk of bleeding, obtaining physician's opinion before participating in activities with substantial risk of injury and contacting physician immediately if injury occurs

» Notifying physician immediately if signs and symptoms of bleeding, infection, thrombotic thrombocytopenic purpura, or thrombocytopenia occur

Possibility that risk of bleeding may continue for 1 to 2 weeks after treatment is discontinued

Side/adverse effects

Signs of potential side effects, especially skin rash, bleeding complications, itching of skin, neutropenia, agranulocytosis, purpura, aplastic anemia, hepatitis or cholestatic jaundice, hives, ringing or buzzing in the ears, erythema multiforme, Stevens-Johnson syndrome, exfoliative dermatitis, thrombocytopenia, and thrombotic thrombocytopenic purpura

General Dosing Information

Ticlopidine should be taken with meals to achieve maximum absorption and reduce the risk of gastrointestinal side effects.

It is recommended that ticlopidine therapy be discontinued temporarily if an injury that results in a substantial risk of bleeding occurs.

It is recommended that ticlopidine therapy be discontinued 10 to 14 days prior to elective surgery, including dental extraction, because of the risk of increased blood loss.

Diet/Nutrition

Absorption of ticlopidine is increased when the medication is taken after a meal.

For treatment of adverse effects

Recommended treatment consists of the following:

- In general—Monitoring the patient and instituting supportive measures as needed.
- For bleeding complications—Although administration of methylprednisolone (20 mg, intravenously) returns the bleeding time to normal in ticlopidine-treated patients, clinical experience indicating that such treatment improves hemostasis is lacking. Platelet transfusions may be helpful, although they are usually not indicated for thrombotic thrombocytopenic purpura occuring in patients taking ticlopidine. In addition, other measures to control bleeding in specific areas must be employed as needed.

Oral Dosage Forms

TICLOPIDINE HYDROCHLORIDE TABLETS

Usual adult dose

Antithrombotic—
Oral, 250 mg twice a day, taken with food.

Antithrombotic adjunct, coronary artery stenting[1]—
Oral, 500 mg immediately before the procedure followed by 250 mg twice daily together with food and antiplatelet doses of aspirin for up to 30 days following successful stent implantation.

Usual pediatric and adolescent dose

Safety and efficacy in patients up to 18 years of age have not been established.

Usual geriatric dose

See *Usual adult dose.*

Strength(s) usually available

U.S.—
250 mg (Rx) [*Ticlid* (citric acid; magnesium stearate; microcrystalline cellulose; povidone; starch; stearic acid)].

Canada—
250 mg (Rx) [*Ticlid* (citric acid; magnesium stearate; microcrystalline cellulose; povidone; corn starch; stearic acid)].

Packaging and storage

Store below 40 °C (104 °F), preferably between 15 and 30 °C (59 and 86 °F), unless otherwise specified by manufacturer.

Auxiliary labeling

- Take with food.

[1]Not included in Canadian product labeling.

Selected Bibliography

Gent M, Blakely JA, Easton JD, et al. The Canadian American ticlopidine study (CATS) in thromboembolic stroke. Lancet 1989; 333: 1215-20.

Hass WK, Easton D, Adams HP Jr, et al. A randomized trial comparing ticlopidine hydrochloride with aspirin for the prevention of stroke in high-risk patients. N Engl J Med 1989; 321: 501-7.

Revised: 12/14/2001

TIMOLOL—See *Beta-adrenergic Blocking Agents (Ophthalmic), Beta-adrenergic Blocking Agents (Systemic)*

TINIDAZOLE Systemic†

VA CLASSIFICATION (Primary): AM900

Commonly used brand name(s): *Tindamax.*

Note: For a listing of dosage forms and brand names by country availability, see *Dosage Forms* section(s).

†Not commercially available in Canada.

Category

Antiprotozoal.

Indications

Accepted

Amebiasis, extraintestinal (treatment)—Oral tinidazole is indicated in the treatment of amebic liver abscess caused by *Entamoeba histolytica* in both adults and pediatric patients older that three years of age.

Amebiasis, intestinal (treatment)—Oral tinidazole is indicated in the treatment of intestinal amebiasis caused by *Entamoeba histolytica* in both adults and pediatric patients older that three years of age.

Giardiasis (treatment)—Oral tinidazole is indicated for the treatment of giardiasis caused by *Giardia duodenalis (also termed Giardia lamblia)* in both adults and pediatric patients older that three years of age.

Trichomoniasis (treatment)—Oral tinidazole is indicated for the treatment of trichomoniasis, in males and females, caused by *Trichomonas vaginalis.*

Unaccepted

Tinidazole is not indicated for the treatment of asymptomatic cyst passage.

Pharmacology/Pharmacokinetics

Mechanism of action/Effect

Antiprotozoal—The nitro group of tinidazole is reduced by cell extracts of *Trichomonas.* As a result of this reduction a free nitro radical is generated which may be responsible for the antiprotozoal activity. The mechanism by which tinidazole exhibits activity against *Giardia and Entamoeba* species is not known.

Tinidazole demonstrates activity both *in vitro* and clinical infections against *Trichomonas vaginalis, Giardia duodenalis (also termed Giardia lamblia),* and *Entamoeba histolytica.*

Tinidazole does not appear to have activity against most strains of vaginal lactobacilli.

Absorption

Under fasted conditions tinidazole is rapidly and completely absorbed. Administration with food resulted in a delay in T_{max} of approximately 2 hours and a decline in C_{max} of approximately 10% and an AUC of 901.6 ± 126.5 mcg hr/mL

Distribution

Tinidazole is distributed into virtually all tissues and body fluids. Tinidazole also crosses the blood-brain barrier, placental barrier and is distributed into breast milk.

Volume of distribution (Vol_D)—About 50 L.

Biotransformation

Significantly biotransformed by CYP3A4 and partly metabolized by oxidation, hydroxylation and conjugation prior to excretion. Tinidazole is the major drug-related constituent in plasma with a small amount of the metabolite, 2-hydroxymethyl tinidazole.

Half-life

Elimination—13.2 (±1.4) hours.
Plasma—approximately 12 to 14 hours.

Time to peak concentration

1.6 (±0.7) hours.

Time to steady state

Steady state conditions are reached in 2.5 to 3 days of multi-day dosing.

Peak plasma concentration

47.7 (±7.5) mcg/mL.

Elimination

Renal—20 to 25% as unchanged drug.
Fecal—12%.
In hemodialysis—43% eliminated during 6-hour hemodialysis session.

Precautions to Consider

Carcinogenicity

Carcinogenicity studies with tinidazole in rats, mice, or hamsters have not been reported. However metronidazole, a chemically-related nitroimidazole, has been reported to be carcinogenic in mice and rats but not hamsters.

Mutagenicity

Tinidazole was found to be mutagenic in the TA 100, *S. typhimurium* tester strain both with and without the metabolic activation system and was not mutagenic in the TA 98 strain. However mutagenicity results were mixed both positive and negative in the TA 1535, 1537, and 1538 strains. Tinidazole was also positive in a tester strain of *Klebsiella pneumonia* and positive for *in vivo* genotoxicity in the mouse micronucleus assay. Tinidazole was negative for mutagenicity in a mammalian cell culture system with Chinese hamster lung V79 cells and negative for genotoxicity in the Chinese hamster ovary sister chromatid exchange assay.

Pregnancy/Reproduction

Fertility—Sixty-day fertility study done in male rats given doses (600 mg/kg/day) of tinidazole, resulted in reduced fertility and produced testicular histopathology. Spermatogenic effects resulted from dose levels of 300 and 600 mg/kg/day, while the no observed adverse effects dose level was 100 mg/kg/day (approximately 0.5-fold the highest human therapeutic dose based upon body surface area conversions). These effects are characteristic of agents in the 5-nitroimidazole class.

Pregnancy—Tinidazole crosses the placenta, and enters fetal circulation. Therefore, it should not be administered to pregnant women during the first trimester. Adequate and well-controlled studies in humans have not been done.

Studies in rats have shown that tinidazole may have mutagenic potential. Because animal studies are not always predictive of human response the potential benefits must be weighed against the possible risks to both the mother and the fetus.

FDA Pregnancy Category C

Breast-feeding

Tinidazole is distributed into breast milk at concentrations similar to those in serum. Because tinidazole can be detected in breast milk for up to 72 hours after administration, interruption of breast-feeding during tinidazole therapy and for three days following the last dose is recommended.

Pediatrics

Other than for use in the treatment of giardiasis and amebiasis in pediatric patients older that three years of age, safety and effectiveness of tinidazole in pediatric patients have not been established.

Geriatrics

No information is available on the relationship of age to the effects of tinidazole in geriatric patients. However, elderly patients are more likely to have age-related renal function impairment, decreased hepatic or cardiac function and concomitant disease or other drug therapy which may require caution in dosing selection.

Drug interactions and/or related problems

The following drug interactions and/or related problems have been selected on the basis of their potential clinical significance (possible mechanism in parentheses where appropriate)—not necessarily inclusive (» = major clinical significance):

Note: Drug interaction studies with tinidazole have not been done. However the following drug interactions were reported for metronidazole, a chemically-related nitroimidazole.

» Alcohol, ethyl or
» Ethanol-containing preparations or
» Propylene glycol
(it is recommended that these substances not be used concurrently with tinidazole, or for 3 days following tinidazole therapy; abdominal cramps, nausea, vomiting, headache, or flushing may occur)

» Anticoagulants, coumarin
(effects may be enhanced when these agents are used concurrently with tinidazole resulting in prolongation of prothrombin time; dosage of oral anticoagulants may need to be adjusted during tinidazole therapy and up to 8 days after discontinuation)

Cholestyramine
(cholestyramine may decrease oral bioavailability; separate dosing of cholestyramine and tinidazole is recommended)

Cyclosporine or
Tacrolimus
(tinidazole may increase levels of these drugs; monitor for signs of calcineurin-inhibitor associated toxicities)

Cytochrome P450 inducers such as
Fosphenytoin or
Phenobarbital or
Phenytoin or
Rifampin
(may increase elimination and decrease plasma concentration of tinidazole)

Cytochrome P450 inhibitors such as
Cimetidine or
Ketoconazole
(may prolong half-life and decrease plasma clearance of tinidazole resulting in increased plasma levels)

» Disulfiram
(it is recommended that tinidazole not be used concurrently with, or for 2 weeks following, disulfiram in alcoholic patients; such use may result in confusion and psychotic reactions because of combined toxicity)

Fluorouracil
(tinidazole may decrease the clearance of fluorouracil resulting in increased side effects; if co-administration cannot be avoided monitor for fluorouracil-associated toxicities.)

» Lithium
(lithium concentrations may increase when tinidazole therapy is introduced; serum lithium and serum creatinine levels should be monitored several days after beginning tinidazole in order to detect possible lithium intoxication)

Oxytetracycline
(may antagonize the therapeutic effect of tinidazole)

Phenytoin, intravenous or
Fosphenytoin, intravenous
(concomitant administration with tinidazole increases half life and decreases clearance of phenytoin)

Laboratory value alterations

The following have been selected on the basis of their potential clinical significance (possible effect in parentheses where appropriate)—not necessarily inclusive (» = major clinical significance).

With physiology/laboratory test values
Alanine aminotransferase (ALT [SGPT]), serum and
Aspartate aminotransferase (AST [SGOT]), serum and
Hexokinase glucose and
Lactate dehydrogenase (LDH) and
Triglycerides
(potential interference is due to the similarity of absorbance peaks of NADH and tinidazole; interference has been shown to involve enzymatic coupling of the assay to oxidation-reduction of nicotinamide-adenine dinucleotide)

Medical considerations/Contraindications

The medical considerations/contraindications included have been selected on the basis of their potential clinical significance (reasons given in parentheses where appropriate)—not necessarily inclusive (» = major clinical significance).

Except under special circumstances, this medication should not be used when the following medical problem exists:

» Hypersensitivity to tinidazole, any component of the tablet or other nitroimidazole derivatives

Risk-benefit should be considered when the following medical problems exist:

» Blood dyscrasia, history of
(administer with caution)

» Central nervous system (CNS) diseases
(administer with caution; convulsive seizures and peripheral neuropathy have been reported; appearance of abnormal neurologic signs demand prompt discontinuation of tinidazole therapy)

» Hepatic function impairment, severe
(caution; metabolized in the liver; hepatic dysfunction may lead to decreased plasma clearance and accumulation of tinidazole)

» Known or previously unrecognized candidiasis
(tinidazole may present more prominent symptoms requiring treatment with an antifungal agent)

Patient monitoring

The following may be especially important in patient monitoring (other tests may be warranted in some patients, depending on condition; » = major clinical significance):

Leukocyte counts, total and differential
(recommended if retreatment is necessary)

Side/Adverse Effects

The following side/adverse effects have been selected on the basis of their potential clinical significance (possible signs and symptoms in parentheses where appropriate)—not necessarily inclusive:

Those indicating need for medical attention

Incidence rare

Bronchospasm (cough; difficulty breathing; noisy breathing; shortness of breath; tightness in chest; wheezing); ***coma*** (change in consciousness, loss of consciousness); ***dyspnea*** (shortness of breath; difficult or labored breathing; tightness in chest; wheezing)

Incidence unknown

Angioedema (large, hive-like swelling on face, eyelids, lips, tongue, throat, hands, legs, feet, sex organs); ***convulsions*** (seizures); ***hepatic abnormalities including; increased transaminase levels; hypersensitivity*** (difficulty in breathing and/or swallowing; fever; hives; nausea; reddening of the skin, especially around ears; swelling of eyes, face, or inside of nose; unusual tiredness or weakness); ***leukopenia*** (black, tarry stools; chest pain; chills; cough; fever; painful or difficult urination; shortness of breath; sore throat; sores, ulcers, or white spots on lips or in mouth; swollen glands; unusual bleeding or bruising; unusual tiredness or weakness); ***neutropenia*** (black, tarry, stools; chills; cough; fever; lower back or side pain; painful or difficult urination; pale skin; shortness of breath; sore throat; ulcers, sores, or white spots in mouth; unusual bleeding or bruising; unusual tiredness or weakness); ***palpitation*** (fast, irregular, pounding, or racing heartbeat or pulse); ***peripheral neuropathy*** (burning, numbness, tingling, or painful sensations; weakness in arms, hands, legs, or feet, unsteadiness or awkwardness); ***thrombocytopenia*** (black, tarry stools; bleeding gums; blood in urine or stools; pinpoint red spots on skin; unusual bleeding or bruising)

Those indicating need for medical attention only if they continue or are bothersome

Incidence more frequent

Bitter taste; metallic taste

Incidence less frequent

Anorexia (loss of appetite, weight loss); ***constipation*** (difficulty having a bowel movement (stool)); ***cramps; dizziness; dyspepsia*** (acid or sour stomach; belching; heartburn; indigestion; stomach discomfort upset or pain); ***epigastric pain*** (pain or discomfort in chest, upper stomach, or throat; heartburn); ***fatigue*** (unusual tiredness or weakness); ***headache; malaise*** (general feeling of discomfort or illness; unusual tiredness or weakness); ***nausea; vomiting; weakness***

Incidence rare

Confusion (mood or mental changes); ***depression; furry tongue*** (coating on tongue; white patches on tongue); ***pharyngitis*** (body aches or pain; congestion; cough; dryness or soreness of throat; fever; hoarseness; runny nose; tender, swollen glands in neck; trouble in swallowing; voice changes)

Incidence unknown

Arthralgia (pain in joints; muscle pain or stiffness; difficulty in moving); ***arthritis*** (pain; swelling, or redness in joints; muscle pain or stiffness; difficulty in moving); ***ataxia*** (shakiness and unsteady walk; unsteadiness; trembling, or other problems with muscle control or coordination); ***candida overgrowth; candidiasis, oral*** (white patches in the mouth or throat or on the tongue,); ***darkened urine; diarrhea; drowsiness*** (sleepiness); ***giddiness; insomnia*** (sleeplessness; trouble sleeping; unable to sleep); ***myalgia*** (joint pain; swollen joints; muscle aching or cramping; muscle pains or stiffness; difficulty in moving); ***paresthesias*** (burning, crawling, itching, numbness, prickling, "pins and needles," or tingling feelings); ***stomatitis*** (swelling or inflammation of the mouth); ***tongue discoloration; vaginal discharge, increased*** (white or brownish vaginal discharge); ***vertigo*** (dizziness or lightheadedness; feeling of constant movement of self or surroundings; sensation of spinning)

Overdose

For more information on the management of overdose or unintentional ingestion, **contact a poison control center** (see *Poison Control Center Listing*).

Clinical effects of overdose

There have been no reported overdoses with tinidazole in humans.

Treatment of overdose

There is no known specific antidote to tinidazole. Treatment is generally symptomatic and supportive, possibly including:

To decrease absorption—
Emptying stomach with gastric lavage.

To enhance elimination—
Hemodialysis may be considered; 43% of the amount present in the body is eliminated during a 6-hour hemodialysis session.

Supportive care—
Patients in whom intentional overdose is confirmed or suspected should be referred for psychiatric consultation.

Patient Consultation

As an aid to patient consultation, refer to *Advice for the Patient, Tinidazole (Systemic)*.

In providing consultation, consider emphasizing the following selected information (» = major clinical significance):

Before using this medication

» Conditions affecting use, especially:

Hypersensitivity to tinidazole, any component of the tablet, or other nitroimidazole derivatives.

Pregnancy—Tinidazole crosses the placenta; use is not recommended during the first trimester of pregnancy

Breast-feeding—Tinidazole is distributed into breast milk; tinidazole is not recommended during breast-feeding

Other than for use in the treatment of giardiasis and amebiasis in pediatric patients older that three years of age, safety and effectiveness of tinidazole in pediatric patients have not been established

Other medications, especially alcohol, coumarin anticoagulants, disulfiram, or lithium

Other medical problems, especially active organic disease of the CNS, a history of blood dyscrasias, known or previously unrecognized candidiasis, or severe hepatic function impairment

Proper use of this medication

Taking with meals or a snack to minimize gastrointestinal irritation

» Compliance with full course of therapy

» Importance of not missing doses and taking at evenly spaced times

» Proper dosing

Missed dose: Taking as soon as possible; not taking if almost time for next scheduled dose; not doubling doses

» Proper storage

Precautions while using this medication

Follow-up visit to physician after treatment for giardiasis to ensure that infection has been eradicated.

Checking with physician if no improvement within a few days.

» Avoiding use of alcoholic beverages or other alcohol-containing preparations while taking and for at least 3 days after discontinuing this medication

Prevention of reinfection in trichomoniasis; possible need for concurrent treatment of sexual partner and the use of a condom

Side/adverse effects

Signs of potential side effects, especially angioedema, bronchospasm, coma, convulsions, dyspnea, hypersensitivity, leukopenia, neutropenia, palpitation, peripheral neuropathy, or thrombocytopenia

General Dosing Information

For oral dosing forms:

For children and patients unable to swallow tablets, tinidazole may be crushed in artifical cherry syrup to be taken with food.

Caution should be used when administering tinidazole to patients with severely impaired hepatic function.

When tinidazole is used in the treatment of trichomoniasis, sexual partners should receive concurrent therapy in order to prevent reinfection.

Parenteral Dosage Forms

Note: Bracketed information in the *Indications* section refers to uses that are not included in U.S. product labeling.

TINIDAZOLE TABLETS

Usual adult dose

Antiprotozoal—

Amebiasis: Oral, 2 grams per day for 3 days taken with food.

Amebic liver abscess: Oral, 2 grams per day for 3 to 5 days taken with food.

Giardiasis: Oral, a single 2-gram dose taken with food.

Trichomoniasis: Oral, a single 2-gram dose taken with food.

Note: If tinidazole is administered on a day when dialysis is performed, it is recommended that an additional dose of tinidazole equivalent to one half of the recommended dose be administered after the end of hemodialysis.

Usual pediatric dose
Antiprotozoal—
Amebiasis: Oral, 50 mg/kg/day (up to 2 grams) for 3 days taken with food.
Amebic liver abscess: Oral, 50 mg/kg/day (up to 2 grams) for 3 to 5 days taken with food.
Giardiasis: Oral, a single 50 mg/kg (up to 2 grams) dose taken with food.

Usual pediatric prescribing limits
Antiprotozoal—
Up to 2 grams daily.

Usual geriatric dose
See *Usual adult dose*.

Strength(s) usually available
U.S.—
250 mg (Rx) [*Tindamax* (scored; croscarmellose sodium; FD&C Red 40 lake; FD&C Yellow 6 lake; hypromellose; magnesium stearate; microcrystalline cellulose; polydextrose; polyethylene glycol; pregelatinized corn starch; titanium dioxide; triacetin)].
500 mg [*Tindamax* (scored; croscarmellose sodium; FD&C Red 40 lake; FD&C Yellow 6 lake; hypromellose; magnesium stearate; microcrystalline cellulose; polydextrose; polyethylene glycol; pregelatinized cornstarch; titanium dioxide; triacetin)].

Canada—
Not commercially available.

Packaging and storage
Store at controlled room temperature 20-25° C (68-77 °F). Protect form light.

Auxiliary labeling
- Take with food.
- Avoid alcoholic beverages.

Developed: 08/24/2004

TINZAPARIN Systemic

VA CLASSIFICATION (Primary): BL111

Commonly used brand name(s): *Innohep*.

Note: For a listing of dosage forms and brand names by country availability, see *Dosage Forms* section(s).

Category

Anticoagulant; antithrombotic

Note: Tinzaparin is one of a group of substances known as low molecular weight heparins (LMWHs).

Indications

Note: Bracketed information in the *Indications* section refers to uses that are not included in U.S. product labeling.

Accepted

[Thromboembolism, (prophylaxis)]—Tinzaparin is indicated for the prevention of postoperative venous thromboembolism in patients undergoing orthopedic surgery and in patients undergoing general surgery who are at high risk of developing postoperative venous thromboembolism.

Thromboembolism, pulmonary (treatment adjunct); and[1]
Thrombosis, deep venous (treatment adjunct)[1]—Tinzaparin is indicated for the treatment of acute symptomatic deep vein thrombosis with or without pulmonary embolism when administered in conjunction with warfarin sodium.

[Thromboembolism, pulmonary (treatment); and]
[Thrombosis, deep venous (treatment)]—Tinzaparin is indicated for the treatment of deep vein thrombosis and pulmonary embolism

[Thrombosis of the extracorporeal system during hemodialysis (prophylaxis)]—Tinzaparin is indicated for the prevention of clotting in indwelling intravenous lines for hemodialysis and extracorporeal circulation in patients without high bleeding risk

[1]Not included in Canadian product labeling.

Pharmacology/Pharmacokinetics

Physicochemical characteristics
Source—Tinzaparin is obtained by enzymatic depolymerization of unfractionated heparin from porcine intestinal mucosa using heparinase from *Flavobacterium heparinum*.
Molecular weight—Averages between 5500 and 7500 daltons.
pH—5.0 to 7.5

Mechanism of action/Effect
Tinzaparin's antithrombotic properties are achieved by enhancing the inhibition of coagulation factor Xa and thrombin (factor IIa) by binding to the plasma protease inhibitor, antithrombin III (ATIII). However, other mechanisms may also be involved since tinzaparin potentiates the inhibition of several activated coagulation factors.
Tinzaparin has high anti-Xa activity, but a relatively low inhibitory effect on factor IIa activity compared to unfractionated heparin. The ratio of anti-Xa to anti-IIa activity for tinzaparin is 2 ± 0.5, whereas it is 1 for unfractionated heparin. The higher ratio of anti-Xa to anti-IIa has the potential of providing equivalent antithrombotic effect with reduced hemorrhagic complications.
Bleeding time is usually unaffected by tinzaparin. Activated partial thromboplastin time (aPTT) occasionally may be prolonged by therapeutic doses of tinzaparin. Prothrombin time (PT) may be slightly prolonged with tinzaparin, but usually remains within the normal range. However, neither aPTT nor PT can be used for therapeutic monitoring of tinzaparin.

Other actions/effects
Tinzaparin does not have intrinsic fibrinolytic activity; therefore it does not lyse existing clots. Tinzaparin induces release of tissue factor pathway inhibitor, which may contribute to the antithrombotic effect.

Absorption
Based on anti-Xa activity, absolute bioavailability is 86.7% following subcutaneous injection. Based on anti-IIa activity, bioavailability following subcutaneous injection is 67%.

Distribution
Volume of distribution (Vol_D)—3.1 L to 5.0 L.

Vol_D of anti-Xa activity is 4 L.

Vol_D of anti-IIa activity is 10.9 L.

Tinzaparin does not appear to cross the placenta.

Biotransformation
Low molecular weight heparins are partially metabolized by desulphation and depolymerization.

Half-life
Absorption—
- Anti-Xa activity—200 minutes.
- Anti-IIa activity—257 minutes.

Elimination—approximately 3 to 4 hours following subcutaneous injection, based on anti-Xa activity.
- Anti-Xa activity—82 minutes
- Anti-IIa activity—71 minutes

The elimination half-life of anti-Xa activity for low molecular weight heparins (including tinzaparin) is prolonged in patients with impaired renal function relative to people with normal function.

Onset of action
Plasma levels of anti-Xa activity increase in the first 2 to 3 hours following subcutaneous injection.

Time to peak concentration
Peak plasma anti-Xa activity occurs approximately 4 to 6 hours following subcutaneous injection.

Peak plasma concentration:
Plasma anti-Xa activity can be measured as an indication of serum tinzaparin levels; however, clinical trials have not demonstrated a linear correlation between anti-Xa activity and antithrombotic effect.

Following single subcutaneous doses of 4500 International Units (IU) (approximately 64.3 IU/kg) and 175 IU/kg, peak concentrations of plasma anti-Xa activity were 0.25 and 0.87 IU/mL, respectively.

Dose (anti-Xa IU)	Peak Plasma Anti-Xa Activity (Units/mL)	Peak Plasma Anti-IIa Activity (Units/mL)
2500	0.12	0.02
5000	0.28	0.03
10000	0.54	0.08

Time to peak effect

Peak plasma anti-Xa activity occurs approximately 4 to 6 hours following subcutaneous injection.

Duration of action

Detectable anti-Xa activity persists for 24 hours after subcutaneous injection.

Elimination

The primary route of elimination is renal.

Hepatic elimination is not involved.

Clearance following intravenous administration of 4500 IU tinzaparin is approximately 1.7 L/hr.

Neither age nor gender significantly alter tinzaparin clearance based on anti-Xa activity; however, weight is an important factor for the prediction of tinzaparin clearance.

In patients receiving tinzaparin (175 IU/kg), clearance based on anti-Xa activity was related to creatinine clearance (calculated by Cockroft Gault equation). In patients with moderate (30 to 50 mL/min) and severe renal impairment (<30 mL/min), tinzaparin clearance was reduced. Patients with severe renal impairment exhibited a 24% reduction in tinzaparin clearance.

Precautions to Consider

Cross-sensitivity and/or related problems

Patients with known hypersensitivity to heparin, low molecular weight (LMW) heparins, sulfites, benzyl alcohol, or to pork products may be sensitive to tinzaparin also.

Carcinogenicity

No long-term animal studies have been performed with tinzaparin to determine its carcinogenic potential.

Mutagenicity

Tinzaparin was not mutagenic in the *in vitro* Ames test, the *in vitro* chinese hamster ovary cell forward gene mutation test, the *in vitro* human lymphocyte chromosomal aberration test, and the *in vivo* mouse micronucleus test.

Pregnancy/Reproduction

Fertility—In rats, subcutaneous doses up to 1800 International Units per kg of body weight per day (IU/kg/day) (about 2 times the maximum recommended human dose based on body surface area) was found to have no effect on fertility and reproductive performance.

Pregnancy—Tinzaparin does not appear to cross the placenta.

Adequate and well-controlled studies in humans have not been done.

There have been cases of cleft palate, optic nerve hypoplasia, pulmonary hypoplasia, muscular hypotonia, trisomy 21 (Down's) syndrome, and cutis aplasia of the scalp reported in infants of women who received tinzaparin during pregnancy. However, a cause and effect relationship has not been established. In addition, there have been reports of fetal death/miscarriage in pregnant women receiving tinzaparin who had high risk pregnancies and/or a prior history of spontaneous abortion. Approximately 6% of pregnancies were complicated by fetal distress.

Approximately 10% of pregnant women receiving tinzaparin experienced significant vaginal bleeding. A cause and effect relationship has not been established.

Studies in pregnant rats and rabbits given subcutaneous doses of tinzaparin up to 1800 IU/kg/day (about 2 times the maximum recommended human dose based on body surface area) and 1900 IU/kg/day (about 4 times the maximum recommended human dose based on body surface area), respectively, showed no evidence of embryotoxic or teratogenic effects.

Tinzaparin should not be used to prevent thromboembolism in pregnant women with prosthetic heart valves. Safety, effectiveness or dosage in pregnant women with prosthetic heart valves can not be determined.

FDA Pregnancy Category B.

Note: The multi-dose vial contains 10 mg of benzyl alcohol per mL, which is not recommended for use during pregnancy since benzyl alcohol may cross the placenta.

Breast-feeding

It is not known whether tinzaparin is distributed into breast milk.Breast-feeding is not recommended for women receiving tinzaparin.

In lactating rats, very low levels of tinzaparin were found in breast milk following subcutaneous administration.

Pediatrics

No information is available on the relationship of age to the effects of tinzaparin in pediatric patients. Safety and efficacy have not been established.

Note: The multi-dose vial contains 10 mg of benzyl alcohol per mL, which is not recommended for use in neonates. Cases of "Gasping Syndrome" have occurred in premature infants when large amounts of benzyl alcohol have been administered (99-404 mg/kg/day).

Geriatrics

Appropriate studies performed to date have not demonstrated geriatrics-specific problems that would limit the usefulness of tinzaparin in the elderly.

No increased bleeding tendency has been observed in the clinical studies with tinzaparin in elderly patients with normal kidney and liver function. However, since renal function is known to decline with age, elderly patients may show reduced elimination of tinzaparin.

Drug interactions and/or related problems

The following drug interactions and/or related problems have been selected on the basis of their potential clinical significance (possible mechanism in parentheses where appropriate)—not necessarily inclusive (» = major clinical significance):

Note: Spinal or epidural hematomas have occurred with concurrent use of LMWHs and spinal/epidural anesthesia, resulting in long-term or permanent paralysis. There may be an increased risk with the use of post-operative epidural catheters or with the concomitant use of NSAIDs, platelet aggregation inhibitors, or other drugs affecting coagulation.

Anticoagulants, coumarin- or indandione-derivative, or
Platelet aggregation inhibitors (see *Appendix II*) such as:
» Anti-inflammatory drugs, nonsteroidal (NSAIDs), including ketorolac, ticlopidine, and clopidogrel
» Aspirin
Dextran
Dipyridamole
Sulfinpyrazone
(increased risk of bleeding must be considered)

Thrombolytic agents, such as:
Alteplase (rt-PA)
Anistreplase (APSAC)
Streptokinase
Urokinase
(concurrent or sequential use may increase the risk of bleeding)

Laboratory value alterations

The following have been selected on the basis of their potential clinical significance (possible effect in parentheses where appropriate)—not necessarily inclusive (» = major clinical significance).

With physiology/laboratory test values

Alanine aminotransferase (ALT [SGPT]) and
Aspartate aminotransferase (AST [SGOT])

(asymptomatic reversible increases in serum values may occur during tinzaparin therapy; the usefulness of these enzymes in the differential diagnosis of myocardial infarction, pulmonary embolism, or liver disease may, therefore, be decreased; similar increases in transaminase levels have also been observed in patients and healthy volunteers treated with heparin and other low molecular weight heparins)

(levels greater than 3 times the upper limit of normal of the laboratory reference range have been reported in up to 8.8% and 13% for AST and ALT, respectively; elevated levels are rarely associated with increases in bilirubin)

(transaminase increases are dose-dependent and have been observed at doses as low as 50 IU/kg/day; no consistent irreversible liver damage has been observed; transaminase increases occurred after more than 3 days of treatment in clinical studies; normalization of transaminase levels can be expected within 2 to 4 weeks of the last dose of tinzaparin)

Medical considerations/Contraindications

The medical considerations/contraindications included have been selected on the basis of their potential clinical significance (reasons given in parentheses where appropriate)—not necessarily inclusive (» = major clinical significance).

Except under special circumstances, this medication should not be used when the following medical problem exists:

» Cerebrovascular accidents, hemorrhagic or acute cerebral insults (increased risk of bleeding)

» Bleeding, major, active (may be exacerbated)

» Hypertension, severe, uncontrolled (increased risk of cerebral hemorrhage)

» Patients with prosthetic heart valves (cases of thrombosis among patients treated with low molecular weight heparin; safety not established with tinzaparin)

Sensitivity to tinzaparin, low molecular weight (LMW) heparins, heparin, sulfites, benzyl alcohol, or pork products

» Thrombocytopenia associated with positive *in vitro* tests for antiplatelet antibody in the presence of tinzaparin or

» Thrombocytopenia, tinzaparin- or heparin-induced, with disseminated thrombosis, history of or (risk of recurrence; may result in complications of organ infarction with secondary organ dysfunction or limb ischemia and in some cases death)

Risk-benefit should be considered when the following medical problems exist:

Any medical procedure or condition in which the risk of bleeding or hemorrhage is present, such as: (risk of epidural or spinal hematoma, which can result in long-term or permanent paralysis; this risk is increased with the use of indwelling epidural catheters or by the concomitant use of medications that affect hemostasis, such as nonsteroidal anti-inflammatory drugs, platelet inhibitors, or other anticoagulants; the risk also may be increased by traumatic or repeated epidural or spinal puncture; see *General Dosing Information* for guidelines regarding the use of regional anesthesia in patients receiving perioperative tinzaparin)

» Abortion, threatened
» Anesthesia, epidural or spinal
» Bleeding disorders, congenital or acquired (e.g., hemophilia)
» Endocarditis, bacterial, acute or subacute
» Hepatic function impairment, severe
» Platelet defects
» Renal function impairment, severe
» Retinopathy, diabetic, hypertensive or hemorrhagic
» Surgery, brain, ophthalmic, otic, or spinal, recent
» Ulcers, other lesions, or recent bleeding of the gastrointestinal tract, active

Patient monitoring

The following may be especially important in patient monitoring (other tests may be warranted in some patients, depending on condition; » = major clinical significance):

Note: Routine anticoagulation tests such as prothrombin time (PT), activated partial thromboplastin time (aPTT), and thrombin clotting time (TT) are relatively insensitive measures of tinzaparin's anticoagulant activity and, therefore, are unsuitable for monitoring. However, prolongation of aPTT can be used as a criteria of overdose. Dose increases aimed at prolonging aPTT to the same extent as with unfractionated heparin could cause overdose and bleeding.

Alanine aminotransferase (ALT [SGPT]) and
Aspartate aminotransferase (AST [SGOT])
(asymptomatic reversible increases in serum values may occur during tinzaparin therapy)

» Anti-factor Xa activity
(plasma anti-Xa activity can be measured as an indication of serum tinzaparin levels; however, clinical trials have not demonstrated a linear correlation between anti-Xa activity and antithrombotic effect; patients receiving tinzaparin are at risk for major bleeding complications when plasma anti-Xa levels approach 2.0 IU/mL)

Blood counts, complete (CBC), including:
Hematocrit
Hemoglobin
(recommended periodically during therapy; an unexplained fall in hematocrit or hemoglobin may indicate a hemorrhagic event; some cases of hemorrhage have been reported to result in death or permanent disability)

Blood pressure measurement
(recommended periodically during therapy; an unexplained drop in blood pressure may signal occult bleeding; some cases of hemorrhage have been reported to result in death or permanent disability)

» Neurologic status
(monitor for signs and symptoms of neurological impairment such as paresthesias, leg weakness, sensory loss, motor deficit, or bowel/bladder dysfunction, which may indicate a potential epidural or spinal hematoma)

» Platelet aggregation test
(recommended prior to the initiation of therapy in patients who have congenital, or a history of drug-induced, thrombocytopenia or platelet defects; if the result is negative, tinzaparin therapy may be instituted, with daily monitoring of the platelet count; however, if the result is positive, tinzaparin should not be given)

» Platelet count
(recommended prior to the initiation of therapy, then twice weekly for the duration of therapy to detect occult bleeding or any degree of thrombocytopenia)

Stool tests for occult blood
(recommended periodically during therapy)

Side/Adverse Effects

The following side/adverse effects have been selected on the basis of their potential clinical significance (possible signs and symptoms in parentheses where appropriate)—not necessarily inclusive:

Those indicating need for medical attention

Incidence more frequent

Hematoma at injection site (deep, dark purple bruise, pain, or swelling at place of injection)

Incidence less frequent

Anemia (pale skin; troubled breathing, exertional; unusual bleeding or bruising; unusual tiredness or weakness); ***thrombocytopenia*** (black, tarry stools; chest pain; chills; cough; fever; painful or difficult urination; shortness of breath; sore throat; sores, ulcers, or white spots on lips or in mouth; swollen glands; unusual bleeding or bruising; unusual tiredness or weakness); ***angina pectoris*** (chest pain; chest tightness; fast or irregular heartbeat; shortness of breath); ***hypertension*** (blurred vision; dizziness; severe or continuing dull nervousness; headache; pounding in the ears; slow or fast heartbeat); ***hypotension*** (blurred vision; confusion; dizziness, faintness, or lightheadedness when getting up from a lying or sitting position suddenly; sweating; unusual tiredness or weakness); ***tachycardia*** (fainting; fast, pounding, or irregular heartbeat or pulse; palpitations); ***hematuria*** (blood in urine; lower back pain; pain or burning while urinating); ***hemorrhage*** (bleeding gums; coughing up blood; difficulty in breathing or swallowing; dizziness; headache; increased menstrual flow or vaginal bleeding; nosebleeds; paralysis; prolonged bleeding from cuts; red or dark brown urine; red or black, tarry stools; shortness of breath; unexplained pain, swelling, or discomfort, especially in the chest, abdomen, joints, or muscles; unusual bruising; vomiting of blood or coffee ground-like material; weakness); ***pulmonary embolism*** (chest pain; cough; fainting; fast heartbeat; sudden shortness of breath or troubled breathing; dizziness or lightheadedness); ***skin rash; urinary tract infection*** (bladder pain; bloody or cloudy urine; difficult, burning, or painful urination; frequent urge to urinate; lower back or side pain)

Note: In addition to the symptoms listed for *hemorrhage*, the possibility of hemorrhage should be considered in evaluating the condition of any anticoagulated patient with complaints which do not indicate an obvious diagnosis.

Incidence rare

Allergic reaction (fever; skin rash, hives, or itching); ***anaphylactoid reaction*** (cough; difficulty swallowing; dizziness; fast heartbeat; hives; itching; puffiness or swelling of the eyelids or around the eyes, face, lips or tongue; shortness of breath; skin rash; tightness in chest; unusual tiredness or weakness; wheezing); ***epidural or spinal hematoma*** (back pain; bowel/bladder dysfunction; leg weakness; numbness; paralysis; paresthesias)—back pain is not a typical presentation but some patients may experience this symptom; ***skin necrosis*** (blue-green to black skin discoloration; pain, redness, or sloughing of skin at place of injection)

Incidence not determined—Observed during clinical practice, estimates of frequency can not be determined

Abscess (accumulation of pus; swollen, red, tender area of infection; fever); ***acute febrile reaction*** (chills or sudden fever; fatigue; headache; malaise; muscle cramps; excessive thirst; weakness); ***agranulocytosis*** (cough or hoarseness; fever with or without chills; general feeling of tiredness or weakness; lower back or side pain; painful or difficult urination; sore throat; sores, ulcers, or white spots on lips or in mouth; unusual bleeding or bruising); ***allergic purpura*** (raised red swellings on the skin, the buttocks, legs or ankles; large, flat, blue or purplish patches in the skin; painful knees and ankles; fever; stomach pain; bloody or black, tarry stools; blood in urine); ***angioedema*** (large, hive-like swelling on face, eyelids, lips, tongue, throat, hands, legs, feet, sex organs); ***cholestatic hepatitis*** (abdominal or stomach pain; chills; clay-colored stools; dark urine; diarrhea; dizziness; fever; headache; itching; loss of appetite; nausea; rash; unpleasant breath odor; unusual tiredness or weakness; vomiting of blood; yellow eyes or skin); ***epidermal necrolysis*** (redness, tenderness, itching, burning, or peeling of skin; red or irritated eyes; sore throat; fever; chills); ***hemoptysis*** (coughing or spitting up blood); ***increased hepatic enzymes*** (dark urine; light-colored stools; loss of appetite; nausea and vomiting; unusual tiredness; yellow eyes or skin; fever with or without chills; stomach pain); ***ischemic necrosis or necrosis*** (break in the skin, especially associated with blue-black discoloration, swelling, or drainage of fluid); ***hematoma*** (collection of blood under the skin; dark, purple bruise; pain, redness, or swelling); ***ocular hemorrhage*** (red or bloodshot eye; change in vision; seeing floating spots before the eyes); ***pancytopenia*** (high fever; chills; unexplained bleeding or bruising; bloody, black, or tarry stools; pale skin; unusual tiredness or weakness; cough; shortness of breath; sores, ulcers, or white spots on lips or in mouth; swollen glands); ***peripheral ischemia*** (itching of skin; numbness and tingling of face, fingers, or toes; pain in arms legs, or lower back, especially pain in calves and/or heels upon exertion; pale, bluish-colored, or cold hands or feet; weak or absent pulses in legs); ***rectal bleeding*** (black, tarry stools; blood in stools); ***Steven-Johnson syndrome*** (redness, tenderness, burning, blistering or peeling of skin (usually on the backs of arms and the fronts of legs, mouth, eyes or hands and feet); fever; chills; headache; unusual tiredness or weakness); ***thrombocythemia*** (pain, warmth, or burning in fingers, toes and legs; headache; dizziness; problems with vision or hearing)

Those indicating need for medical attention only if they continue or are bothersome

Incidence less frequent

Back pain; headache; confusion; constipation; dizziness; insomnia (trouble in sleeping); ***nausea and vomiting; pain at injection site***

Incidence rare

Priapism (prolonged, painful, inappropriate erection of the penis)

Incidence not determined—Observed during clinical practice, estimates of frequency can not be determined

Urticaria (hives or welts; itching; redness of skin; skin rash)

Overdose

For specific information on the agents used in the management of tinzaparin overdose, see the *Protamine (Systemic)* monograph.

For more information on the management of overdose or unintentional ingestion, **contact a poison control center** (see *Poison Control Center Listing*).

Clinical effects of overdose

The following effects have been selected on the basis of their potential clinical significance (possible signs and symptoms in parentheses where appropriate)—not necessarily inclusive:

Acute

Bleeding complications or hemorrhage (bleeding gums; coughing up blood; difficulty in breathing or swallowing; dizziness; headache; increased menstrual flow or vaginal bleeding; nosebleeds; paralysis; prolonged bleeding from cuts; red or dark brown urine; red or black, tarry stools; shortness of breath; unexplained pain, swelling, or discomfort, especially in the chest, abdomen, joints, or muscles; unusual bruising; vomiting of blood or coffee ground-like material; weakness)

Treatment of overdose

Specific treatment—

Most patients who have bleeding complications while receiving tinzaparin can be controlled by discontinuing tinzaparin, applying pressure to the site, if possible, and replacing volume and hemostatic blood elements (e.g., red blood cells, fresh frozen plasma, platelets) as required.

Administration of protamine, a heparin antagonist, may be required. One mg of protamine sulfate (1% solution) per 100 anti-factor Xa International Units (IU) of tinzaparin is given as a slow intravenous injection. If the activated partial thromboplastin time (aPTT) measured 2 to 4 hours after the first injection remains prolonged, a second injection of 0.5 mg protamine sulfate per 100 anti-factor Xa IU of tinzaparin may be administered. However, the aPTT may remain more prolonged with tinzaparin than with conventional heparin, despite the additional dosing of protamine. Protamine only partially neutralizes tinzaparin anti-Xa activity (approximately 60%).

Protamine sulfate should be administered with great care to avoid an overdose. Severe hypotensive and anaphylactoid reactions, possibly fatal, may occur with protamine sulfate. In order to avoid these reactions the rate of administration of protamine should not exceed 20 mg/minute. Protamine should be administered only when resuscitation techniques and treatment of anaphylactic shock are readily available..

See the package insert or *Protamine (Systemic)* for specific dosing guidelines for use of this product.

Monitoring—

Monitor platelet count and other coagulation parameters.

Patient Consultation

As an aid to patient consultation, refer to *Advice for the Patient, Tinzaparin (Systemic)*.

In providing consultation, consider emphasizing the following selected information (» = major clinical significance):

Before using this medication

» Conditions affecting use, especially:

Sensitivity to tinzaparin, low molecular weight (LMW) heparins, heparin, sulfites, benzyl alcohol, or to pork products

Pregnancy—Multi-dose vials contain benzyl alcohol, which is not recommended for use during pregnancy since benzyl alcohol may cross the placenta

Not for use in pregnant women with prosthetic heart valves

Breast-feeding—Unknown if distributed into human breast milk; use is not recommended

Use in children—Multi-dose vials contain benzyl alcohol, which is not recommended for use in neonates

Other medications, especially platelet aggregation inhibitors, such as aspirin and nonsteroidal anti-inflammatory drugs including ketorolac,

Other medical problems, especially abortion, threatened; anesthesia, epidural or spinal; cerebrovascular accidents, hemorrhagic or acute cerebral insults; bleeding, major, active; bleeding disorders; endocarditis, bacterial, acute or subacute; hepatic function impairment; hypertension, severe, uncontrolled; patients with prosthetic heart valves; platelet defects; renal function impairment; retinopathy, diabetic, hypertensive or hemorrhagic; surgery, recent; thrombocytopenia; and ulcers, other lesions, or recent bleeding of the gastrointestinal tract

Proper use of this medication

» Proper injection technique

» Safe handling and disposal of syringe

» Proper dosing

Missed dose: Discuss with physician

» Proper storage

Precautions while using this medication

» Need to inform all physicians and dentists that this medicine is being used

» Notifying physician immediately if signs and symptoms of bleeding or epidural/spinal hematoma occur

Side/adverse effects

Signs of potential side effects, especially hematoma at injection site, anemia, thrombocytopenia, angina pectoris, hypertension, hypotension, tachycardia, hematuria, hemorrhage, pulmonary embolism, skin rash, urinary tract infection, allergic reaction, anaphylactoid reaction, epidural or spinal hematoma, skin necrosis, abscess, acute febrile reaction, agranulocytosis, allergic purpura, angioedema, cholestatic hepatitis, epidermal necrolysis, increased hepatic enzymes, ischemic necrosis or necrosis, hematoma, ocular hemorrhage, pancytopenia, peripheral ischemia, rectal bleeding, Steven-Johnson syndrome, thrombocythemia

General Dosing Information

Tinzaparin cannot be used interchangeably (unit for unit) with unfractionated heparin or other low molecular weight heparins.

Tinzaparin should not be mixed with other injections or infusions. Due to the risk of hematoma, intramuscular injection of other medications should be avoided during anticoagulant treatment with tinzaparin.

All patients should be evaluated for bleeding disorders prior to administration of tinzaparin.

Tinzaparin is administered by deep subcutaneous injection. It must not be administered by intramuscular or intravenous injection.

Injection technique: Proper subcutaneous administration is necessary to prevent pain and bruising at the site of injection. The patient should be sitting or lying down during the injection. Administration should be alternated between the left and right anterolateral and left and right posterolateral abdominal wall. Alternatively, tinzaparin can be injected into the side of the thigh, provided care is taken not to inject into muscle tissue. The site should be varied daily. The entire length of the needle should be inserted into a skin fold held between the thumb and forefinger; the skin fold should be held throughout the injection. To minimize bruising, do not rub the injection site after completion of the injection.

For treatment of adverse effects

If bleeding complications or hemorrhage occurs during tinzaparin therapy, tinzaparin should be discontinued. In most cases bleeding complications can be controlled by applying pressure to the site, if possible, and replacing volume and hemostatic blood elements as required. However, in some cases administration of protamine may be required. One mg of protamine sulfate (1% solution) per 100 anti-factor Xa International Units (IU) of tinzaparin is given as a slow intravenous injection. If the activated partial thromboplastin time (aPTT) measured 2 to 4 hours after the first injection remains prolonged, a second injection of 0.5 mg protamine sulfate per 100 anti-factor Xa IU of tinzaparin may be administered.

Parenteral Dosage Forms

Note: Bracketed uses in the *Dosage Forms* section refer to categories of use and/or indications that are not included in U.S. product labeling.

TINZAPARIN SODIUM INJECTION

Usual adult dose

[Thromboembolism (prophylaxis)]—

For prevention of postoperative venous thromboembolism in orthopedic surgery

• Hip Surgery—Subcutaneous, 50 anti-Xa International Units (IU) per kg of body weight 2 hours prior to surgery followed by 50 anti-Xa IU per kg of body weight once daily for 7 to 10 days or 75 anti-Xa IU per kg of body weight given postoperatively once daily for 7 to 10 days.

• Knee Surgery—Subcutaneous, 75 anti-Xa International Units (IU) per kg of body weight given postoperatively once daily for 7 to 10 days.

For prevention of postoperative venous thromboembolism in general surgery

Subcutaneous, 3500 anti-Xa International Units (IU) 2 hours prior to surgery followed by 3500 anti-Xa IU once daily for 7 to 10 days.

Thromboembolism, pulmonary (treatment adjunct); and[1]
Thrombosis, deep venous (treatment adjunct)[1]—

Subcutaneous, 175 anti-Xa International Units (IU) per kg of body weight once daily for at least 6 days and until the patient is adequately anticoagulated with warfarin (INR at least 2.0 for two consecutive days). Warfarin therapy is usually initiated within 1 to 3 days of tinzaparin initiation.

Note: To calculate the volume (mL) of an tinzaparin 175 anti-Xa IU per kg subcutaneous dose for treatment of deep vein thrombosis the following equation may be used:

Patient weight (kg) $\times$ 0.00875 mL/kg = volume to be administered (mL) subcutaneously.

[Thromboembolism, pulmonary (treatment) and]
[Thrombosis, deep venous (treatment)]—

Subcutaneous, 175 anti-Xa International Units (IU) per kg of body weight once daily at the same time every day.

Note: Treatment with vitamin K antagonists is usually initiated immediately. Treatment with tinzaparin should be continued until a therapeutic oral anticoagulant effect has been achieved (INR 2.0 to 3.0), usually within 5 days. The average duration of tinzaparin therapy is 7 days.

[Thrombosis of the extracorporeal system during hemodialysis (prophylaxis)]—

Chronic renal failure patients with a low risk of bleeding—

Dialysis lasting up to four hours—Intravenous or as a single injection into the arterial dialyser, 4500 International Units (IU), at the start of dialysis. Optimization of dosage is required for each individual patient. Dosage adjustments should consider the outcome of the previous dialysis session and should be made by increasing or decreasing the dose in steps of 500 IU until an adequate dose is obtained.

Dialysis lasting longer than 4 hours—A larger starting dose may be given. Doses in subsequent dialysis sessions should be adjusted as required.

Chronic renal failure patients with a risk of bleeding—

Dialysis sessions may be carried out using halved doses. An additional smaller dose may be given during dialysis for sessions lasting longer than 4 hours. The dose in subsequent dialysis sessions should be adjusted as required to achieve plasma levels within the range of 0.2 to 0.4 IU anti-Xa/mL. No anticoagulant should be added to the dialyser circuit when using this regimen.

Usual adult prescribing limits

The maximum daily dose has not been clearly established; however, maximum daily doses ranging from 18,000 to 21,000 have been cited by the manufacturer.

Usual pediatric dose

Safety and efficacy have not been established.

Usual geriatric dose

See *Usual adult dose*.

Usual geriatric prescribing limits

See *Usual adult prescribing limits*.

Strength(s) usually available

U.S.—

20,000 anti–Xa IU per mL (Rx) [*Innohep* (in 2 mL multiple-dose vials; 3.1 mg/mL sodium metabisulfite; 10 mg/mL benzyl alcohol; and sodium hydroxide)].

Canada—

3500 anti-Xa IU per 0.35 mL (Rx) [*Innohep* (in single pre-filled unit-dose syringes; 1.75 mg sodium acetate; sodium hydroxide; water for injection)].

4500 anti-Xa IU per 0.45 mL (Rx) [*Innohep* (in single pre-filled unit-dose syringes; 2.25 mg sodium acetate; sodium hydroxide; water for injection)].

10,000 anti-Xa IU per 0.5 mL (Rx) [*Innohep* (in single unit-dose graduated syringes; 0.92 mg sodium metabisulphite; sodium hydroxide; water for injection)].

14,000 anti-Xa IU per 0.7 mL (Rx) [*Innohep* (in single unit-dose graduated syringes; 1.27 mg sodium metabisulphite; sodium hydroxide; water for injection)].

18,000 anti-Xa IU per 0.9 mL (Rx) [*Innohep* (in single unit-dose graduated syringes; 1.65 mg sodium metabisulphite; sodium hydroxide; water for injection)].

10,000 anti-Xa IU per mL (Rx) [*Innohep* (in 1 mL multiple-dose vials; 1.8 mg sodium metabisulphite; 10 mg benzyl alcohol; sodium hydroxide; water for injection)].

20,000 anti-Xa IU per mL (Rx) [*Innohep* (in 1 mL multiple-dose vials; 3.1 mg sodium metabisulphite; 10 mg benzyl alcohol; sodium hydroxide; water for injection)].

Packaging and storage

Store between 15°C and 25 °C (59°F and 77 °F). Protect from light.

Stability

Because the unit-dose syringes contain no preservative, each syringe should be used to administer a single dose only.

Auxiliary labeling

• Keep out of the reach of children.

Additional information

The multiple-dose vials contain benzyl alcohol, which is not recommended for use in neonates. A fatal syndrome consisting of metabolic acidosis, central nervous system depression, respiratory problems, renal failure, hypotension, and possibly seizures and intracranial hemorrhage has been associated with the administration of benzyl alcohol to neonates.

Because benzyl alcohol may cross the placenta, tinzaparin preserved with benzyl alcohol should be used with caution in pregnant women.

---

[1]Not included in Canadian product labeling.

Revised: 12/12/2002
Developed: 08/11/2000

TIOCONAZOLE—See *Antifungals, Azole (Vaginal)*

TIOCONAZOLE Topical*

VA CLASSIFICATION (Primary): DE102

Commonly used brand name(s): *Trosyd AF; Trosyd J.*

Note: For a listing of dosage forms and brand names by country availability, see *Dosage Forms* section(s).

*Not commercially available in U.S.

Category

Antifungal (topical).

Indications

Accepted

Candidiasis, cutaneous (treatment)—Tioconazole is indicated in the topical treatment of cutaneous candidiasis caused by *Candida albicans.*

Tinea corporis (treatment) or
Tinea cruris (treatment) or
Tinea pedis (treatment)—Tioconazole is indicated in the topical treatment of tinea corporis (ringworm of the body), tinea cruris (ringworm of the groin; jock itch), and tinea pedis (ringworm of the foot; athlete's foot) caused by *Trichophyton rubrum, Trichophyton mentagrophytes,* or *Epidermophyton floccosum.*

Tinea versicolor (treatment)—Tioconazole is indicated in the topical treatment of tinea versicolor (pityriasis versicolor; "sun fungus") caused by *Malassezia furfur (Pityrosporon orbiculare).*

Pharmacology/Pharmacokinetics

Physicochemical characteristics

Chemical Group—Imidazole class of antifungals.

Molecular weight—387.7.

Solubility—Virtually insoluble in water; moderately soluble in chloroform, methanol, ethanol, and ethyl acetate.

Mechanism of action/Effect

Fungistatic; may be fungicidal, depending on concentration; inhibits biosynthesis of ergosterol or other sterols by blocking C-14 demethylation, damaging the fungal cell wall membrane and altering its permeability; as a result, loss of essential intracellular elements may occur.

Absorption

Tioconazole was not detectable in plasma after patients made repeated applications of tioconazole 2% cream to single or multiple superficial fungal infection sites on the skin through 28 days of treatment (detection limit 100 micrograms/liter [mcg/L]). Plasma concentrations of less than 10 mcg/L occurred after tioconazole 2% cream at a nominal dose of 40 mg per day was applied to the skin of the abdomen of normal subjects for 14 days.

Biotransformation

Orally administered tioconazole is extensively metabolized; the major metabolites are glucuronide conjugates.

Time to peak concentration

5.2 and 8 hours, following vaginal application of a single 300–mg ovule or a single dose of 6.5% ointment, respectively.

1 to 3 hours, following oral administration of single doses of 250 mg to 1 g or multiple doses of up to 3.5 g over 4 days.

Peak serum concentration

24.7 mcg/L and 18 mcg/L, following vaginal application of a single 300–mg ovule or a single dose of 6.5% ointment, respectively.

Elimination

Fecal—Primary route of excretion, following oral administration.

Renal—No unchanged drug; metabolites only, following oral administration.

Precautions to Consider

Cross-sensitivity and/or related problems

Patients sensitive to other forms of tioconazole or other imidazole antifungal agents may be sensitive to this medication also.

Carcinogenicity

Studies to evaluate the long-term carcinogenic potential of tioconazole have not been done.

Mutagenicity

No mutagenic or cytogenic effects of tioconazole were observed in animal studies.

Pregnancy/Reproduction

Fertility—Spermatogenic arrest occurred in 2 out of 5 male rabbits after 30 daily applications of tioconazole 2% cream 1 milliliter/kilogram (mL/kg) per day to shaven but not abraded skin.

Pregnancy—Adequate and well controlled studies of topical tioconazole in humans have not been done. In limited uncontrolled clinical use, tioconazole vaginal ointment and suppositories, applied as a single dose to approximately 20 patients during various stages of pregnancy, did not appear to interfere with the normal progress of the pregnancy or delivery.

Local and systemic administration in rats produced adverse effects related to parturition and/or fetal development. An increased incidence of stillbirths (range 37% to 100%) was observed on post-mating days 24 or 25 in rats given oral doses up to 150 milligrams/kilogram (mg/kg) per day or subcutaneous doses up to 20 mg/kg/day throughout gestation or during the last third of gestation.

Breast-feeding

It not known whether tioconazole applied topically is distributed into human breast milk. However, problems in humans have not been documented.

Pediatrics

Appropriate studies on the relationship of age to the effects of topical tioconazole have not been performed in the pediatric population. Limited clinical experiences have not demonstrated pediatrics-specific problems that would limit the usefulness of topical tioconazole in children. Use of topical tioconazole in children less than 2 years of age should be under the direction of a physician; use in children under 12 years of age should be supervised by an adult.

Geriatrics

Appropriate studies on the relationship of age to the effects of topical tioconazole have not been performed in the geriatric population. However, no geriatric-specific problems have been documented to date.

Medical considerations/Contraindications

The medical considerations/contraindications included have been selected on the basis of their potential clinical significance (reasons given in parentheses where appropriate)—not necessarily inclusive (» = major clinical significance).

Risk-benefit should be considered when the following medical problems exist:

Sensitivity to topical tioconazole

Side/Adverse Effects

Note: In human studies, tioconazole applied topically showed no evidence of sensitization, skin irritation, or local or systemic side effects.

No evidence of photo-irritation was seen when tioconazole 2% cream was applied to the upper back of healthy volunteers for 72 hours (under occlusion), with subsequent exposure of the treated area to sunlight or longwave ultraviolet light.

The following side/adverse effects have been selected on the basis of their potential clinical significance (possible signs and symptoms in parentheses where appropriate)—not necessarily inclusive:

Those indicating need for medical attention

Less common

Burning, itching, redness, skin rash, swelling, or other signs of skin irritation not present before therapy

Overdose

For more information on the management of overdose or unintentional ingestion, **contact a poison control center** (see *Poison Control Center Listing*).

Patient Consultation

As an aid to patient consultation, refer to *Advice for the Patient, Tioconazole (Topical).*

In providing consultation, consider emphasizing the following selected information (» = major clinical significance):

Before using this medication

» Conditions affecting use, especially:

Sensitivity to topical tioconazole or other imidazole derivatives such as miconazole or econazole

Proper use of this medication

Applying sufficient medication to cover affected and surrounding areas, and rubbing in gently

» Avoiding contact with the eyes

» Not applying occlusive dressing over this medication unless directed to do so by physician

» Compliance with full course of therapy; fungal infections may require prolonged therapy
» Proper dosing
Missed dose: Applying as soon as possible; not applying if almost time for next dose
Proper storage

Precautions while using this medication
Checking with physician if condition becomes worse or if it does not improve within: 2 weeks for tinea cruris; 2 to 4 weeks for cutaneous candidiasis or tinea corporis; 1 to 4 weeks for tinea versicolor; 6 weeks for tinea pedis
» Using hygienic measures to help cure infection or to help prevent re-infection
For tinea cruris:
Avoiding underwear that is tight-fitting or made from synthetic materials; wearing loose-fitting cotton underwear instead
Using a bland, absorbent powder or an antifungal powder on the skin; not using cream and powder concurrently
For tinea pedis:
Carefully drying feet, especially between toes, after bathing
Avoiding socks made from wool or synthetic materials; wearing clean, cotton socks and changing them daily or more often if feet perspire excessively
Wearing well-ventilated shoes or sandals
Using a bland, absorbent powder or an antifungal powder between toes, on feet, and in socks and shoes liberally once or twice daily; not using cream and powder concurrently

Side/adverse effects
Signs of potential side effects, especially burning, itching, redness, rash, swelling, or other signs of irritation not present before therapy

General Dosing Information

To reduce the possibility of recurrence, *Candida* infections and tinea corporis should be treated for 2 to 4 weeks, tinea cruris should be treated for up to 2 weeks, tinea pedis should be treated for up to 6 weeks, and tinea versicolor should be treated for 1 to 4 weeks.

Topical Dosage Forms

TIOCONAZOLE CREAM USP

Usual Adult and adolescent dose
Candidiasis, cutaneous or
Tinea corporis—
Topical, to the skin two times a day, morning and evening, for 2 to 4 weeks.
Tinea cruris—
Topical, to the skin two times a day, morning and evening, for up to 14 days.
Tinea pedis—
Topical, to the skin two times a day, morning and evening, for up to 6 weeks.
Tinea versicolor—
Topical, to the skin two times a day, morning and evening, for 7 to 28 days.

Note: For infection in intertriginous areas, tioconazole cream should be applied sparingly and smoothed in well to avoid macerating effects.

Usual pediatric dose
For children 2 to 12 years of age—
See *Usual adult and adolescent dose.*
For children up to 2 years of age—
Dosage has not been established.

Note: Tioconazole use in children under 2 years of age should be under the direction of a physician; use in children under 12 years of age should be supervised by an adult.

Strength(s) usually available
U.S.—
Not commercially available.
Canada—
1% w/w (Rx) [*Trosyd AF* (10 mg of tioconazole per gram of vanishing cream base; benzyl alcohol; ethoxylated cetostearyl alcohol; mineral oil; white petrolatum; propylene glycol; stearic acid; stearyl alcohol; purified water); *Trosyd J* (10 mg of tioconazole per gram of vanishing cream base; benzyl alcohol; ethoxylated cetostearyl alcohol; mineral oil; white petrolatum; propylene glycol; stearic acid; stearyl alcohol; purified water)].

Packaging and storage
Store between 15 and 30 °C (59 and 86 °F). Avoid freezing.

Auxiliary labeling
• For external use only.
• Continue medicine for full time of treatment.

Developed: 06/12/2000

TIOTROPIUM Inhalation-Local

VA CLASSIFICATION (Primary): RE150

Commonly used brand name(s): *Spiriva; Spiriva HandiHaler.*

Note: For a listing of dosage forms and brand names by country availability, see *Dosage Forms* section(s).

Category

Bronchodilator.

Indications

Accepted
Bronchitis, chronic (treatment) or
Emphysema, pulmonary (treatment) or
Pulmonary disease, chronic obstructive, other (treatment)—Tiotropium is indicated for the long term, once daily, maintenance treatment of bronchospasm associated with chronic obstructive pulmonary disease (COPD), including chronic bronchitis and emphysema.

Unaccepted
Tiotropium is not indicated for the initial treatment of acute episodes of bronchospasm.

Pharmacology/Pharmacokinetics

Note: Tiotropium is administered by dry powder inhalation. In common with other inhaled drugs, the majority of the delivered dose is deposited in the gastrointestinal tract and, to a lesser extent, in the lung, the intended organ. Many of the pharmacokinetic data described below were obtained with higher doses than recommended for therapy.

Physicochemical characteristics
Molecular weight—490.4 (tiotropium bromide monohydrate).
Solubility—Sparingly soluble in water; soluble in methanol.

Mechanism of action/Effect
Tiotropium is a long-acting, anitmuscarinicantimuscarinic agent, which is often referred to as an anticholinergic. It has similar affinity to the subtypes of muscarinic receptors, M_1 to M_5. In the airways, it exhibits pharmacological effects through inhibition of M_3-receptors at the smooth muscle leading to bronchodilation. The competitive and reversible nature of antagonism was shown with human and animal origin receptors and isolated organ preparations. In pre-clinical *in vitro* as well as *in vivo* studies prevention of methacholine-induced bronchoconstriction effects were dose-dependent and lasted longer than 24 hours. The bronchodilation following inhalation of tiotropium is predominantly a site-specific effect.

Absorption
Absolute bioavailability: 19.5%
It is suggested from the chemical structure of the compound that tiotropium is poorly absorbed from the intestinal tract; food is not expected to influence absorption; oral solutions have an absolute bioavailability of 2 to 3%

Distribution
Vol_D: 33 L per kg; studies in rats have shown that tiotropium does not readily cross the blood-brain barrier

Protein binding
72% bound to plasma proteins

Biotransformation
Extent of biotransformation appears to be small
A fraction of administered dose is metabolized by cytochrome P450–dependent oxidation and subsequent glutathione conjugation to a variety of Phase II metabolites. This enzymatic pathway can be inhibited by CYP450D and 3A4 inhibitors, such as quinidine, ketoconazole, and gestodene. Thus, CYP450D 2D6 and 3A4 are involved in the metabolic pathway that is responsible for the elimination of a small part of the administered dose.

Half-life
Terminal elimination: 5 to 6 days following inhalation

Time to peak concentration
Inhalation-5 minutes

Peak plasma concentration:
Steady-state peak plasma concentrations were 17 to 19 pg per mL; local concentrations in the lung are not known

Time to peak effect
Steady state was reached after 2 to 3 weeks with no accumulation thereafter.

Elimination
Urinary: 14%; remainder being mainly non-absorbed drug in the gut which is eliminated via the feces.

Precautions to Consider

Carcinogenicity/Tumorigenicity/Mutagenicity
No evidence of tumorigenicity was observed in a 104- week inhalation study in rats at tiotropium doses up to 0.059 mg per kg per day, in an 83- week inhalation study in female mice at doses up to 0.145 mg per kg per day, and in a 101- week inhalation study in male mice at doses up to 0.002 mg per kg per day. These doses correspond to 25, 35, and 0.5 times the Recommended Human Daily Dose (RHDD) on a mg per m^2 basis, respectively. These dose multiples may be overestimated due to difficulties in measuring deposited doses in animal inhalation studies.
Tiotropium bromide demonstrated no evidence of mutagenicity or clastogenicity in the following assays: the bacterial gene mutation assay, the V79 Chinese hamster cell mutagenesis assay, the chromosomal aberration assays in human lymphocytes *in vitro* and mouse micronucleus formation *in vivo*, and the unscheduled DNA synthesis in primary rat hepatocyte *in vitro* assay.

Pregnancy/Reproduction
Fertility—In rats, decreases in the number of corpora lutea and the percentage of implants were noted at inhalation tiotropium doses of 0.078 mg per kg per day or greater (approximately 35 times the RHDD on a mg per m^2 basis. No such effects were observed at 0.009 mg per kg per day (approximately 4 times the RHDD on a mg per m^2 basis). The fertility index, however, was not affected at inhalation doses up to 1.689 mg per kg per day (approximately 760 times the RHDD on a mg per m^2 basis). These dose multiples may be overestimated due to difficulties in measuring deposited doses in animal inhalation studies.
Pregnancy—There are no adequate and well controlled studies in pregnant women. Tiotropium should only be used during pregnancy if the potential benefit justifies the potential risk to the fetus.
No evidence of structural alterations was observed in rats and rabbits at inhalational tiotropium doses of up to 1.471 and 0.007 mg per kg per day, respectively. These doses correspond to approximately 660 and 6 times the recommended human daily dose (RHDD) on a mg per m^2 basis. However, in rats, fetal resorption, litter loss, decreases in number of live pups at birth and the mean pup weights, and a delay in the pup sexual maturation was observed at inhalational tiotropium doses of ≥ 0.078 mg per kg (approximately 35 times the RHDD on a mg per m^2 basis). In rabbits, an increase in post-implantation loss was observed at an inhalation dose of 0.4 mg per kg per day (approximately 360 times the RHDD on a mg per m^2 basis). Such effects were not observed at inhalation doses of 0.009 and up to 0.088 mg per kg per day in rats and rabbits, respectively. These dose multiples may be overestimated due to difficulties in measuring deposited doses in animal inhalation studies.
FDA Pregnancy Category C

Breast-feeding
It is not known whether tiotropium is distributed into breast milk. However, it is distributed into the milk of lactating rats. Caution should be exercised in administering tiotropium to nursing women.

Pediatrics
Appropriate studies on the relationship of age to the effects of tiotropium have not been performed in the pediatric population. Safety and efficacy in pediatric patients have not been established.
Tiotropium is used for the maintenance treatment of bronchospasm associated with chronic obstructive pulmonary disease, including chronic bronchitis and emphysema. This disease does not normally occur in children.

Geriatrics
Appropriate studies performed to date have not demonstrated geriatrics-specific problems that would limit the usefulness of tiotropium in the elderly. There was no overall difference in effectiveness observed and no adjustment of dosage in geriatric patients is warranted.

Drug interactions and/or related problems
The following drug interactions and/or related problems have been selected on the basis of their potential clinical significance (possible mechanism in parentheses where appropriate)—not necessarily inclusive (» = major clinical significance):

Note: Combinations containing any of the following medications, depending on the amount present, may also interact with this medication.

» Anticholinergic containing drugs, such as
Ipratropium
(co-administration has not been studied and is not recommended)

Medical considerations/Contraindications
The medical considerations/contraindications included have been selected on the basis of their potential clinical significance (reasons given in parentheses where appropriate)—not necessarily inclusive (» = major clinical significance).

Except under special circumstances, this medication should not be used when the following medical problem exists:
» Hypersensitivity to atropine or its derivatives, including tiotropium or ipratropium, or to any component of the product, including inhaled lactose

Risk-benefit should be considered when the following medical problems exist:
» Bladder-neck obstruction or
» Narrow angle glaucoma or
» Prostatic hyperplasia or
(as an anticholinergic drug, tiotropium may potentially worsen symptoms and signs of these conditions; should be used with caution)

Patient monitoring
The following may be especially important in patient monitoring (other tests may be warranted in some patients, depending on condition; » = major clinical significance):

Hypersensitivity reactions
(immediate hypersensitivity reactions, including angioedema, may occur after administration; therapy should be stopped at once and alternative treatments considered)

Paradoxical bronchospasm
(inhaled medications may cause paradoxical bronchospasm; treatment should be stopped immediately and other treatments considered)

» Renal impairment, moderate to severe
(as a predominantly renally excreted drug, patients with moderate to severe renal impairment (creatinine clearance of ≤ 50 mL per min) should be monitored closely)

Narrow-angle glaucoma
(eye pain or discomfort, blurred vision, visual halos or colored images in association with red eyes from conjunctival congestion and corneal edema may be signs of acute narrow-angle glaucoma; patients should be informed to contact a physician immediately; miotic eye drops alone are not considered effective treatment.)

Side/Adverse Effects

The following side/adverse effects have been selected on the basis of their potential clinical significance (possible signs and symptoms in parentheses where appropriate)—not necessarily inclusive:

Those indicating need for medical attention
Incidence more frequent
Angina pectoris (arm, back or jaw pain; chest pain or discomfort; chest tightness or heaviness; fast or irregular heartbeat; shortness of breath; sweating; nausea)—including aggravated angina pectoris

Incidence less frequent
Allergic reaction (cough; difficulty swallowing; dizziness; fast heartbeat; hives; itching; puffiness or swelling of the eyelids or around the eyes, face, lips or tongue; shortness of breath; skin rash; tightness in chest; unusual tiredness or weakness; wheezing); ***herpes zoster*** (painful blisters on trunk of body)

Incidence rare
Angioedema (large, hive-like swelling on face, eyelids, lips, tongue, throat, hands, legs, feet, sex organs); ***atrial fibrillation*** (fast or irregular heartbeat, dizziness, fainting); ***supraventricular tachycardia*** (fainting; fast, pounding, or irregular heartbeat or pulse; palpitations)

Those indicating need for medical attention only if they continue or are bothersome
Incidence more frequent
Chest pain; dry mouth; dyspepsia (acid or sour stomach; belching; heartburn; indigestion; stomach discomfort, upset or pain); ***pharyn-***

gitis (body aches or pain; congestion; cough; dryness or soreness of throat; fever; hoarseness; runny nose; tender, swollen glands in neck; trouble in swallowing; voice changes); ***rhinitis*** (stuffy nose; runny nose; sneezing); ***sinusitis*** (pain or tenderness around eyes and cheekbones; fever; stuffy or runny nose; headache; cough; shortness of breath or troubled breathing; tightness of chest or wheezing); ***upper respiratory tract infection*** (ear congestion; nasal congestion; chills; cough, fever, sneezing, or sore throat; body aches or pain; headache; loss of voice; runny nose; unusual tiredness or weakness; difficulty in breathing); ***urinary tract infection*** (bladder pain; bloody or cloudy urine; difficult, burning, or painful urination; frequent urge to urinate; lower back or side pain)

Incidence less frequent

Abdominal pain; constipation (difficulty having a bowel movement (stool)); ***depression*** (discouragement; feeling sad or empty; irritability; lack of appetite; loss of interest or pleasure; tiredness; trouble concentrating; trouble sleeping); ***dysphonia*** (hoarseness; sore throat; voice changes); ***edema*** (swelling); ***epistaxis*** (bloody nose); ***gastroesophageal reflux*** (heartburn; vomiting); ***hypercholesterolemia*** (large amount of cholesterol in the blood); ***hyperglycemia*** (abdominal pain; blurred vision; dry mouth; fatigue; flushed, dry skin; fruit-like breath odor; increased hunger; increased thirst; increased urination; nausea; sweating; troubled breathing; unexplained weight loss; vomiting); ***infection*** (fever or chills; cough or hoarseness; lower back or side pain; painful or difficult urination); ***laryngitis*** (cough; dryness or soreness of throat; hoarseness; trouble in swallowing; voice changes); ***leg pain; moniliasis*** (sore mouth or tongue; white patches in mouth and/or on tongue); ***myalgia*** (muscle pain); ***paresthesia*** (burning, crawling, itching, numbness, prickling, "pins and needles", or tingling feelings); ***skeletal pain; stomatitis*** (swelling or inflammation of the mouth; canker sores; sores, ulcers, or white spots on lips or tongue or inside the mouth)—including ulcerative stomatitis; ***rash; vomiting***

Incidence rare

Urinary retention (painful or difficult urination)

Incidence not determined—Observed during clinical practice

palpitations (irregular heartbeat); ***pruritus*** (itching skin); ***urticaria*** (hives or welts; itching; redness of skin; skin rash)

Overdose

For more information on the management of overdose or unintentional ingestion, **contact a poison control center** (see *Poison Control Center Listing*).

High doses of tiotropium may lead to anticholinergic signs and symptoms. However, there were no systemic anticholinergic adverse effects following a single inhaled dose of up to 282 mcg tiotropium in healthy volunteers. In a study of 12 healthy volunteers, bilateral conjunctivitis and dry mouth were seen following repeated once-daily inhalation of 141 mcg of tiotropium.

Acute intoxication by inadvertent oral ingestion of tiotropium is unlikely since it is not well absorbed systematically.

A case of overdose has been reported from post-marketing experience. A female patient was reported to have inhaled 30 capsules over a 2.5 day period, and developed altered mental status, tremors, abdominal pain, and severe constipation. The patient was hospitalized, tiotropium was discontinued, and the constipation was treated with an enema. The patient recovered and was discharged on the same day.

Treatment of overdose

Supportive care—

Patients in whom intentional overdose is confirmed or suspected should be referred for psychiatric consultation.

Patient Consultation

As an aid to patient consultation, refer to *Advice for the Patient, Tiotropium (Inhalation-Local)*.

In providing consultation, consider emphasizing the following selected information (» = major clinical significance):

Before using this medication

» Conditions affecting use, especially:

Hypersensitivity to atropine or its derivatives, including ipratropium or tiotropium, or to any component of the product, including inhaled lactose

Pregnancy—Not recommended for use during pregnancy

Breast-feeding—Not recommended for use during breast feeding

Other medications, especially anticholinergic containing drugs

Other medical problems, especially bladder-neck obstruction, narrow angle glaucoma, prostatic hyperplasia

Proper use of this medication

» Proper dosing and handling of medicine

» Do not swallow capsules; Use only with Handihaler® inhalation device

Importance of not using more medication than the amount prescribed

Importance of using medication as a once-daily maintenance bronchodilator and not as a rescue medication

» Reading patient instructions carefully before using

» Knowing correct administration technique and proper handling of inhaler device

Missed dose: Taking as soon as possible; not taking if almost time for next scheduled dose; not doubling doses

» Proper storage

Capsules should be stored in sealed blisters and only removed immediately before use. Capsules that are inadvertently exposed to air (i.e., not intended for immediate use) should be discarded

Precautions while using this medication

» Regular visits to physician to check progress

» Understanding symptoms and signs of acute narrow-angle glaucoma

Keep powder out of eyes

Side/adverse effects

Signs of potential side effects, especially angina pectoris, allergic reaction, herpes zoster, angioedema, atrial fibrillation, supraventricular tachycardia

General Dosing Information

For inhalation dosing forms:

Tiotropium is intended as a once-daily maintenance treatment for COPD and is not indicated for the initial treatment of acute episodes of bronchospasm, i.e., rescue therapy.

It is important for patients to understand how to correctly administer tiotropium capsules using the HandiHaler inhalation device. Tiotropium capsules should only be administered via the HandiHaler device and the HandiHaler device should not be used for administering any other medications.

After using the first capsule, the 2 remaining capsules should be used over the next 2 consecutive days. Capsules should always be stored in the blister and only removed immediately before use. The foil lidding should only be peeled back as far as the *STOP* line printed on the blister foil to prevent exposure of more than one capsule. The drug should be used immediately after the packaging over an individual capsule is opened.

For administration of tiotropium, a capsule is placed in the center chamber of the HandiHaler device. The capsule is pierced by pressing and releasing the button on the side of the inhalational device. The tiotropium formulation is dispersed into the air stream when the patient inhales through the mouthpiece.

The HandiHaler device is gray colored with a green button. It is imprinted with Spiriva HandiHaler (tiotropium bromide inhalation powder), the Boehringer Ingelheim company logo, and the Pfizer company logo. It is also imprinted to indicate that tiotropium capsules should not be stored in the HandiHaler device and that the HandiHaler device is only to be used with tiotropium (Spiriva) capsules.

Care must be taken to not allow powder to enter into the eyes as this may cause blurring of vision and pupil dilation.

Treatment of adverse events

Eye pain or discomfort, blurred vision, visual halos or colored images in association with red eyes from conjunctival congestion and corneal edema may be signs of acute narrow-angle glaucoma. Patients should be informed to contact a physician immediately if any of these side effects occur. Miotic eye drops alone are not considered effective treatment.

Inhalation Dosage Forms

TIOTROPIUM BROMIDE MONOHYDRATE FOR INHALATION CAPSULES

Usual adult dose

Bronchitis (treatment)

Emphysema (treatment) or

Pulmonary disease, chronic obstructive, other (treatment)—

Oral inhalation, 18 mcg (1 capsule) once a day.

Patients with moderate to severe renal impairment should be monitored closely.

Usual geriatric dose

See *Usual adult dose*.

Strength(s) usually available

U.S.—

18 mcg base (Rx) [*Spiriva HandiHaler* (lactose monohydrate)].

Canada—
18 mcg (Rx) [*Spiriva* (lactose monohydrate)].

Packaging and storage
Store at 25 °C (77 °F), excursions permitted to 15 - 30 °C (59 - 86 °F); protect from light and moisture

Auxiliary labeling
- For oral inhalation only
- Keep out of reach of children
- Store away from heat and direct sunlight
- Do not swallow

Note
Include patient instructions when dispensing.

Demonstrate inhalation technique to patient when dispensing.

Developed: 04/08/2004

TIROFIBAN Systemic

VA CLASSIFICATION (Primary): BL117

Commonly used brand name(s): *Aggrastat.*

Note: For a listing of dosage forms and brand names by country availability, see *Dosage Forms* section(s).

Category
Platelet aggregation inhibitor.

Indications

Accepted
Thrombosis, acute coronary syndrome–related (prophylaxis)—Tirofiban is indicated, in combination with heparin, for the prevention of acute cardiac ischemic complications in patients with acute coronary syndrome (unstable angina or non–Q-wave myocardial infarction). These patients are at high risk for myocardial infarction and sudden death due to progression of total coronary artery occlusion, whether managed medically or with percutaneous coronary intervention (PCI).

Note: Acute coronary syndrome is defined as prolonged (≥ 10 minutes) or repetitive symptoms of cardiac ischemia occurring at rest or with minimal exertion, associated with either ST-T wave changes on electrocardiogram or elevated cardiac enzymes. This definition includes unstable angina and non–Q-wave myocardial infarction but excludes myocardial infarction that is associated with Q waves or nontransient ST-segment elevation.

Tirofiban has been studied in settings that included the use of aspirin and heparin.

Pharmacology/Pharmacokinetics

Physicochemical characteristics
Molecular weight—495.08.

pH—Tirofiban hydrochloride injection or premixed injection: 5.5 to 6.5.

Mechanism of action/Effect
Tirofiban inhibits platelet aggregation by reversibly binding to the platelet receptor glycoprotein (GP) IIb/IIIa of human platelets, thus preventing the binding of fibrinogen. Inhibition of platelet aggregation occurs in a dose- and concentration-dependent manner.

Distribution
The steady-state volume of distribution ranges from 22 to 42 liters.

Protein binding
Not highly bound to plasma proteins; protein binding is concentration-independent over the range of 0.01 to 25 mcg per mL. Unbound fraction in human plasma is 35%.

Biotransformation
Metabolism appears to be limited.

Half-life
Elimination—
Approximately 2 hours.

Time to peak effect
> 90% platelet inhibition by the end of the 30-minute intravenous infusion.

Elimination
Renal, 65% (largely unchanged).

Fecal, 25% (largely unchanged).

In dialysis—
Removable by hemodialysis.

Note: Plasma clearance in healthy subjects has been found to be 213 to 314 mL per minute (mL/min), with renal clearance accounting for 39 to 69% of plasma clearance. In patients with coronary artery disease, plasma clearance ranges from 152 to 267 mL/min, with renal clearance accounting for 39% of plasma clearance.

Precautions to Consider

Carcinogenicity
No studies have been done.

Mutagenicity
Tirofiban was not found to be mutagenic *in vitro* in the microbial mutagenesis and V-79 mammalian cell mutagenesis assays, alkaline elution assays, or chromosomal aberrations assays, or *in vivo* in the bone marrow cells of male mice after administration of intravenous doses of up to 5 mg per kg of body weight (mg/kg) (about three times the maximum recommended daily human dose [MRHD] when compared on a body surface area basis).

Pregnancy/Reproduction
Fertility—Fertility and reproductive performance were not affected in studies with male and female rats given intravenous doses of up to 5 mg/kg per day (about five times the MRHD when compared on a body surface area basis).

Pregnancy—Adequate and well-controlled studies in humans have not been done.

Tirofiban crosses the placenta in pregnant rats and rabbits. Studies in rats and rabbits at intravenous doses of up to 5 mg/kg per day (about five and 13 times the MRHD, respectively, when compared on a body surface area basis) found no adverse effects on the fetus.

Risk-benefit should be considered before use of tirofiban during pregnancy.

FDA Pregnancy Category B.

Breast-feeding
It is not known whether tirofiban is distributed into breast milk. However, it is distributed in significant concentrations into the milk in lactating rats. Risk-benefit should be considered before breast-feeding during treatment with tirofiban.

Mothers may resume nursing 24 hours after cessation of treatment with tirofiban.

Pediatrics
Safety and efficacy of tirofiban in children younger than 18 years of age have not been established.

Geriatrics
In clinical studies including elderly patients (42.8% were 65 years of age or older and 11.7% were 75 years of age and older), no apparent differences in efficacy were observed between elderly patients and younger adults.

An increased frequency of bleeding complications was observed in elderly patients in clinical trials, although the incremental risk of bleeding in patients treated with tirofiban in combination with heparin compared to the risk in patients treated with heparin alone was similar, regardless of age. The incidence of non-bleeding side effects was also increased in elderly patients.

Plasma clearance is approximately 19 to 26% lower in patients older than 65 years of age with coronary artery disease than it is in younger adults.

No dosage adjustment is recommended for the elderly population; however, elderly patients are more likely to have age-related renal function impairment, which may require adjustment of dosage in patients receiving tirofiban.

Drug interactions and/or related problems
The following drug interactions and/or related problems have been selected on the basis of their potential clinical significance (possible mechanism in parentheses where appropriate)—not necessarily inclusive (» = major clinical significance):

Note: Combinations containing any of the following medications, depending on the amount present, may also interact with this medication.

» Anticoagulants, coumarin- or indandione-derivative or

» Other medications that affect hemostasis
(caution is recommended because of the increased risk of bleeding; tirofiban has been studied in settings that included the use of aspirin and heparin)

» Platelet aggregation inhibitors, other (especially inhibitors of platelet receptor GP IIb/IIIa)
(concurrent use is not recommended)

Medical considerations/Contraindications

The medical considerations/contraindications included have been selected on the basis of their potential clinical significance (reasons given in parentheses where appropriate)—not necessarily inclusive (» = major clinical significance).

Except under special circumstances, this medication should not be used when the following medical problems exist:

» Aneurysm, history of or
» Angina or
» Aortic dissection, suggested by history, symptoms, or findings or
» Arteriovenous malformation, history of or
» Bleeding, internal, active or
» Bleeding diathesis within the last year or
» Cerebrovascular accident (CVA) within the past 30 days or
» Hemorrhage, intracranial, history of or
» Hemorrhagic stroke, history of or
» Hypertension, severe, i.e., > 180 mm Hg systolic and/or > 110 mm Hg diastolic or
» Liver disease or
» Neoplasm, intracranial, history of or
» Pericarditis, acute or
» Platelet disorder or
» Surgery, major, recent (within 30 days) or
» Trauma, physical, severe (within 30 days)
(increased risk of bleeding with tirofiban)
» Hypersensitivity to tirofiban
» Thrombocytopenia, history of
(risk of recurrence)

Risk-benefit should be considered when the following medical problems exist:

» Cerebrovascular disease, history of (within 1 year)
(caution is recommended)
» Renal function impairment, severe or
(plasma clearance of tirofiban is significantly decreased [> 50%] in patients with creatinine clearance < 30 mL per minute; it is recommended that dosage be reduced by half in these patients)
» Retinopathy, hemorrhagic
(caution is recommended)
» Thrombocytopenia (< 150,000 per mm ^{3})
(caution is recommended)

Patient monitoring

The following may be especially important in patient monitoring (other tests may be warranted in some patients, depending on condition; » = major clinical significance):

» Activated clotting time (ACT)
(it is recommended that the ACT be checked before removal of the arterial sheath; the sheath should not be removed unless the ACT is less than 180 seconds)
» Activated partial thromboplastin time (aPTT)
(should be monitored 6 hours after the start of the heparin infusion to monitor unfractionated heparin)
(it is recommended that the aPTT be maintained at approximately two times the control value)
(it is recommended that the aPTT be checked before removal of the arterial sheath; the sheath should not be removed unless the aPTT is less than 45 seconds)
» Hematocrit and
» Hemoglobin and
» Platelet count
(recommended prior to initiation of tirofiban therapy, within 6 hours following the loading infusion, and at least daily during therapy, or more frequently if there is a significant decrease in counts; if the platelet count falls to < 90,000 per mm ^{3}, additional platelet counts should be performed to exclude pseudothrombocytopenia)

Side/Adverse Effects

The following side/adverse effects have been selected on the basis of their potential clinical significance (possible signs and symptoms in parentheses where appropriate)—not necessarily inclusive:

Those indicating need for medical attention

Incidence more frequent
Bleeding

Note: *Bleeding* is the most common complication of tirofiban therapy. Intracranial, gastrointestinal, genitourinary, and retroperitoneal bleeding are rare.
Most *major bleeding* occurs at the arterial access site for cardiac catheterization.

Incidence less frequent
Coronary artery dissection; vasovagal reflex

Incidence rare
Thrombocytopenia

Those indicating need for medical attention only if they continue or are bothersome

Incidence less frequent
Blood in feces; blood in urine; bradycardia; dizziness; edema; fever; headache; leg pain; nausea; pelvic pain; sweating

Overdose

Clinical effects of overdose

The following effects have been selected on the basis of their potential clinical significance (possible signs and symptoms in parentheses where appropriate)—not necessarily inclusive:

Acute
Bleeding (bleeding from gums; bleeding at the site of cardiac catheterization)

Note: Inadvertent overdose has occurred in doses up to five times and two times the recommended dose for bolus administration and loading infusion, respectively. Inadvertent overdosage has occurred in doses up to 9.8 times the 0.15 mcg per kg of body weight per minute maintenance infusion rate. The most frequently reported effect was *bleeding*, which was usually minor.

Treatment of overdose

Following assessment of the patient's clinical condition, treatment consists of cessation or adjustment of the tirofiban infusion as appropriate.

Tirofiban can be removed by hemodialysis.

General Dosing Information

Tirofiban intravenous solution should not be removed directly from the bag with a syringe.

Plastic containers should not be used in series connections, since such use can result in air embolism by drawing air from the first container if it is empty of solution.

Because of the risk of bleeding, arterial and venous punctures, intramuscular injections, and the use of urinary catheters, nasotracheal intubation, and nasogastric tubes should be minimized. Noncompressible sites, such as subclavian or jugular veins, should be avoided when obtaining intravenous access.

If bleeding occurs and cannot be controlled with pressure, it is recommended that the infusion of tirofiban and heparin be discontinued.

It is recommended that tirofiban intravenous infusion be continued through angiography and for 12 to 24 hours after angioplasty or atherectomy.

It is recommended that tirofiban and heparin therapy be discontinued, and appropriate monitoring and therapy initiated, if a confirmed platelet count decrease to less than 90,000 per mm ^{3} occurs and pseudothrombocytopenia has been ruled out.

Care of femoral artery access site in patients undergoing percutaneous coronary intervention (PCI)

Because tirofiban therapy is associated with increased bleeding rates, particularly at the site of arterial access for femoral sheath placement, care should be taken when attempting vascular access that only the anterior wall of the femoral artery is punctured. Prior to pulling the sheath, it is recommended that heparin be discontinued for 3 to 4 hours and an activated clotting time (ACT) of less than 180 seconds or an activated partial thromboplastin time (aPTT) of less than 45 seconds be documented. Care should also be taken to obtain proper hemostasis after removal of the sheaths using standard compressive techniques, followed by close observation. While the vascular sheath is in place, maintenance of patients on complete bed rest with the head of the bed elevated 30° and the affected limb restrained in a straight position is recommended. Sheath hemostasis should be achieved at least 4 hours before hospital discharge.

Parenteral Dosage Forms

Note: Tirofiban hydrochloride injection contains tirofiban hydrochloride monohydrate. Strength and dosage are expressed in terms of tirofiban.

TIROFIBAN HYDROCHLORIDE INJECTION

Usual adult dose

Note: For a dosing chart providing infusion rates in mL per hour by patient weight, see the *Aggrastat* package insert.

Acute coronary syndrome—
Initial—
Intravenous infusion, 0.4 micrograms per kg of body weight per minute for thirty minutes, immediately followed by—

Maintenance—
Intravenous infusion, 0.1 micrograms per kg of body weight per minute.

Note: In clinical studies, patients also received aspirin, unless it was contraindicated, and heparin.

It is recommended that the infusion rate be reduced by half in patients with severe renal function impairment (creatinine clearance less than 30 mL per minute).

Usual pediatric dose
Safety and efficacy have not been established in children younger than 18 years of age.

Strength(s) usually available
U.S.—
50 mcg (0.05 mg) per mL (25 mg per 500-mL container) (Rx) [*Aggrastat* (premixed solution **for intravenous infusion**)].
250 mcg (0.25 mg) per mL (12.5 mg per 50-mL vial) (Rx) [*Aggrastat* (concentrated solution **for dilution**)].
Canada—
50 mcg (0.05 mg) per mL (25 mg per 500-mL container) (Rx) [*Aggrastat* (premixed solution **for intravenous infusion**)].

Packaging and storage
Store between 15 and 30°C (59 and 86°F), preferably at 25 °C (77 °F). Protect from light during storage. Protect from freezing.An environment of 2–8°C is recommended during in-use storage.

Preparation of dosage form
- For tirofiban injection (250 mcg [0.25 mg] per mL, 50-mL vial):

This concentrated solution must be diluted prior to administration by intravenous infusion.

The solution is diluted for administration by first withdrawing and discarding 100 mL from a 500-mL bag of 0.9% sodium chloride injection or 5% dextrose injection, and then replacing this volume with 100 mL (2 vials) of tirofiban injection (total of 25 mg of tirofiban) and mixing well, to produce a solution containing 50 mcg (0.05 mg) of tirofiban per mL. Alternatively, a volume of 50 mL can be withdrawn from a 250-mL bag of 0.9% sodium chloride injection or 5% dextrose injection and replaced with 50 mL (1 vial) of concentrated tirofiban injection (total of 12.5 mg of tirofiban) and mixing well, to produce a solution containing 50 mcg (0.05 mg) of tirofiban per mL.

Note: The Canadian manufacturer recommends discarding 50 mL from a 250-mL bag of .9% sodium chloride injection or 5% dextrose injection. Replace with 50 mL of tirofiban injection.

- For tirofiban injection premixed (50 mcg [0.05 mg] per mL, 500-mL container):

This premixed solution may be administered undiluted by intravenous infusion.

The plastic container is prepared by tearing off the dust cover and checking for leaks by squeezing the inner bag firmly. If any leaks are found, sterility cannot be guaranteed and the bag should be discarded. The plastic bag may appear somewhat opaque at first because of moisture absorption during sterilization, but should clear gradually. The container is then suspended by its eyelet support, the plastic protector is removed from the outlet port, and a conventional administration set is attached.

Stability
It is recommended that any unused solution be discarded 24 hours following the start of the infusion.

Incompatibilities
Tirofiban may be administered in the same intravenous line as heparin.
Tirofiban should not be administered in the same intravenous line as any other medications.

Auxiliary labeling
When dispensed, the 50-mL vial should carry a label indicating that it "MUST BE DILUTED BEFORE USE." When dispensed, the 500-mL container should carry a label indicating that it is "FOR CONTINUOUS INTRAVENOUS INFUSION."

Caution
It is very important to distinguish between the 50-mL vial that must be diluted before administration and the 500-mL container that contains premixed infusion solution. The 50-mL vial must first be diluted to the same strength as the premixed solution.

Revised: 03/13/2001

TITANIUM DIOXIDE—See *Sunscreen Agents (Topical)*

TIXOCORTOL—See *Corticosteroids (Rectal)*

TIZANIDINE Systemic†

VA CLASSIFICATION (Primary): MS900
Commonly used brand name(s): *Zanaflex*.

Note: For a listing of dosage forms and brand names by country availability, see *Dosage Forms* section(s).

†Not commercially available in Canada.

Category
Antispastic.

Indications

Accepted
Spasticity (treatment)—Tizanidine is indicated in the acute and intermittent management of increased muscle tone associated with spasticity related to multiple sclerosis and spinal cord injury. It is especially useful in relieving muscle spasms and clonus. Studies comparing the efficacy of tizanidine with that of other current treatment agents, such as baclofen and diazepam, found tizanidine to be as effective as the other agents in reducing spasticity. In addition, clinical studies have demonstrated that tizanidine reduces muscle tone without causing excessive muscle weakness.

Acceptance not established
Preliminary studies and case reports suggest that tizanidine may be used as an alternative treatment in patients with *chronic tension headaches and cluster headaches* who are resistant to other types of drug therapy. However, data are insufficient to establish safety and efficacy of tizanidine for these indications.

A preliminary study suggests tizanidine may be used as an alternative to clonidine as an *adjunct in anesthesia*. Results of a small study in healthy volunteers have shown that the effects of a single 12-mg dose of tizanidine were comparable to those of a 150-mcg dose of oral clonidine. However, data are currently insufficient to establish safety and efficacy for this indication.

Pharmacology/Pharmacokinetics

Physicochemical characteristics
Chemical Group—Imidazoline.
Molecular weight—290.18.

Mechanism of action/Effect
Tizanidine is an alpha-adrenergic agonist. It acts by increasing presynaptic inhibition of motor neurons at the alpha$_2$-adrenergic receptor sites, possibly by reducing the release of excitatory amino acids and inhibiting facilitory caeruleospinal pathways, resulting in a reduction in spasticity. Some studies suggest a possible postsynaptic action at the excitatory amino acid receptors. In addition, tizanidine may have some activity at the imidazoline receptors. A study in animals found that tizanidine acts mainly on the polysynaptic pathways, thereby reducing facilitation of spinal motor neurons. Tizanidine may also have minor effects on monosynaptic reflexes, which are associated with the facilitory effect of the caeruleospinal pathways. The exact mechanism of action of tizanidine is unknown.

Other actions/effects
Tizanidine produces antihypertensive effects, possibly by binding to the imidazoline receptors. Pharmacologic studies done in animals found tizanidine to have one fiftieth to one tenth of the potency of clonidine, an alpha$_2$-adrenergic agonist, in lowering blood pressure. These antihypertensive effects are mild and transitory in relation to its activity as a muscle relaxant.

Tizanidine also has antinociceptive effects. However, these effects may be mediated through an alpha$_2$-adrenergic receptor mechanism rather than a narcotic or endorphin mechanism. The antinociceptive action has been confirmed at doses lower than those producing a muscle relaxant action.

In addition, various studies have shown that tizanidine has anticonvulsant, hypothermic, gastrointestinal, and sympatholytic effects.

Absorption

Well-absorbed following oral administration. Due to extensive metabolism, bioavailability is low (approximately 40%).

Fed state, *tablet*: increases extent of absorption by about 30%

Fed state, *capsule*: increases extent of absorption by about 10%

Note: The amount absorbed from the capsule is about 80% that of the tablet when administered with food.

Under fasting conditions, administration of capsule contents on applesauce compared with the intact capsule results in a 15 to 20% increase in AUC.

Distribution

Tizanidine is widely distributed. The apparent volume of distribution (Vol_D) following intravenous administration is approximately 2.4 L per kg of body weight (L/kg).

Protein binding

Low (30%).

Biotransformation

Hepatic; 95% metabolized to inactive metabolites.

Half-life

Tizanidine—Approximately 2.5 hours.

Metabolites—Approximately 20 to 40 hours.

Approximately 2 hours (following oral administration of tizanidine tablet or capsule [in the fasted state])

Time to peak concentration

Approximately 1.5 hours.

Note: Following single doses of up to 8 mg, a linear relationship is observed among the dose, plasma concentration, and antispastic action.

Fasted state, tablet or capsule: 1 hour

Fed state, two 4-mg *tablets*: 1 hour 25 minutes

Fed state, two 4-mg *capsules*: 3 hours

Note: Tizanidine tablets and capsules are bioequivalent under fasted conditions but not under fed conditions.

Under fasting conditions, administration of capsule contents on applesauce compared with the intact capsule results in a 15 minute decrease in the time to peak concentration.

Peak plasma concentration

Fed state, two 4-mg *tablets*: C_{max} increased by approximately 30%

Fed state, two 4-mg *capsules*: C_{max} decreased by 20%

Note: Mean C_{max} for capsule is approximately two-thirds that for tablets when administered with food

Under fasting conditions, administration of capsule contents on applesauce compared with the intact capsule results in a 15 to 20% increase in C_{max}.

Elimination

Renal—Approximately 60%.

Fecal—Approximately 20%.

Precautions to Consider

Carcinogenicity

No evidence of carcinogenicity was found in rats and mice given tizanidine at doses of up to 16 mg per kg of body weight (mg/kg) (2 times the maximum recommended human dose [MRHD] on a mg per square meter of body surface area [mg/m²] basis) for 78 weeks and doses of up to 9 mg/kg (2.5 times the MRHD on a mg/m² basis) for 104 weeks, respectively.

Mutagenicity

Tizanidine demonstrated no mutagenic or clastogenic potential in *in vitro* studies, including the bacterial Ames test, the mammalian gene mutation test, and chromosomal aberration test in Chinese hamster cells. In addition, there was no evidence of mutagenic potential in *in vivo* studies in mice, including the bone marrow micronucleus test, dominant lethal mutagenicity test, and unscheduled DNA synthesis test; or in *in vivo* Chinese hamster studies, including the bone marrow micronucleus test and cytogenicity test.

Pregnancy/Reproduction

Fertility—Studies in male and female rats given doses of 10 mg/kg (approximately 2.7 times the MRHD) and 3 mg/kg (approximately equal to the MRHD on a mg/m² basis), respectively, found no evidence of impairment of fertility. However, another study in male and female rats receiving 30 mg/kg (8 times the MRHD on a mg/m² basis) and 10 mg/kg (2.7 times the MRHD on a mg/m² basis), respectively, revealed reduced fertility. Abnormal maternal behavior, marked sedation, weight loss, and ataxia were also observed with doses used in the latter study.

Pregnancy—Adequate and well-controlled studies have not been done in humans. Tizanidine should be given to pregnant women only if clearly needed.

Reproduction studies in rats and rabbits given doses of 3 mg/kg (equal to the MRHD) and 30 mg/kg (16 times the MRHD on a mg/m² basis), respectively, found no evidence of teratogenicity. However, a study in rats given doses equal to and up to eight times the MRHD on a mg/m² basis found an increase in gestation period. In addition, prenatal and postnatal pup loss increased and developmental retardation occurred. Another study in rabbits given doses of 1 mg/kg or greater (equal to or greater than 0.5 times the MRHD on a mg/m² basis) reported an increase in postimplantation loss.

FDA Pregnancy Category C.

Labor and delivery—The effect of tizanidine on labor and delivery is unknown.

Breast-feeding

It is not known whether tizanidine is distributed into breast milk. Since tizanidine is lipid soluble, it may pass into the breast milk. However, problems in humans have not been documented.

Pediatrics

Appropriate studies on the relationship of age to the effects of tizanidine have not been performed in the pediatric population. Safety and efficacy have not been established.

Geriatrics

Tizanidine clearance is decreased fourfold in geriatric patients. In addition, geriatric patients are more likely to have age-related renal function impairment, which may require dosage adjustment.

Dental

Prolonged use of tizanidine may decrease or inhibit salivary flow, thus contributing to the development of caries, periodontal disease, oral candidiasis, and discomfort.

Drug interactions and/or related problems

The following drug interactions and/or related problems have been selected on the basis of their potential clinical significance (possible mechanism in parentheses where appropriate)—not necessarily inclusive (» = major clinical significance):

Note: Combinations containing any of the following medications, depending on the amount present, may also interact with this medication.

Acetaminophen
(in clinical trials, concurrent use of acetaminophen and tizanidine resulted in a delay in the time to peak effect of tizanidine by 16 minutes; the delay was not reported to be clinically significant)

Alcohol or
CNS depression-producing medications, other (see *Appendix II*)
(concurrent use with tizanidine may enhance the central nervous system [CNS] depressant effects)

CYP1A2 inhibitors such as
Antiarrhythmics including
Amidarone or
Mexiletine or
Propafenone or
Cimetidine or
Fluoroquinolones including Ciprofloxacin or
Norfloxacin or
Ticlopidine
(caution is recommended with concomitant use)

» Fluvoxamine
(concomitant use is **contraindicated;** significant alterations of tizanidine AUC and half-life, increased oral bioavailability and decreased plasma clearance observed with concomitant fluvoxamine administration; post-marketing reports of bradycardia, dizziness, significant hypotension, and somnolence with concomitant use)

» Hypotension-producing medications, other (see *Appendix II*)
(concurrent use may potentiate antihypertensive effects; caution is recommended; concurrent use with other alpha$_2$-adrenergic agonists is not recommended)

» Oral contraceptives
(concurrent use may reduce the clearance of tizanidine by approximately 50%; caution and dosage adjustments are recommended)

» Phenytoin
(in one study, a patient receiving 6 mg of phenytoin per day experienced an increase in the trough serum concentration of phenytoin from a baseline of approximately 75 micromoles per liter to 100 micromoles per liter, after one week of concurrent use with tizanidine; careful monitoring of serum hydantoin concentrations and dosage adjustments may be necessary)

Rofecoxib
(may potentiate adverse effects of tizanidine; eight post-marketing case reports of potential drug interaction identified mostly involving the nervous system and cardiovascular system; adverse events resolved after discontinuation of tizanidine and/or rofecoxib)

Laboratory value alterations

The following have been selected on the basis of their potential clinical significance (possible effect in parentheses where appropriate)—not necessarily inclusive (» = major clinical significance).

With physiology/laboratory test values

Alanine aminotransferase (ALT [SGPT]) and
Alkaline phosphatase and
Aspartate aminotransferase (AST [SGOT])
(in controlled clinical studies, the values have been increased up to three times the upper limit of normal)

Medical considerations/Contraindications

The medical considerations/contraindications included have been selected on the basis of their potential clinical significance (reasons given in parentheses where appropriate)—not necessarily inclusive (» = major clinical significance).

Except under special circumstances, this medication should not be used when the following medical problem exists:

» Hypersensitivity to tizanidine or any of its ingredients

Risk-benefit should be considered when the following medical problems exist:

» Hepatic function impairment or
» Renal function impairment
(studies have shown increased plasma concentrations of tizanidine in patients with hepatic or renal function impairment; a study evaluating six patients between 42 and 82 years of age receiving a single 4-mg dose of tizanidine reported an increase in mean maximum plasma concentration, mean elimination half-life, and mean area under the plasma concentration-time curve compared with those patients without renal impairment; adjustment of tizanidine dosage may be necessary)

Patient monitoring

The following may be especially important in patient monitoring (other tests may be warranted in some patients, depending on condition; » = major clinical significance):

Hepatic function determinations
(recommended during the first 6 months of treatment and periodically thereafter)

Hypotension
(chance of significant hypotension may possibly be minimized by titration of the dose and by focusing attention on signs and symptoms of hypotension prior to dose advancement)

Side/Adverse Effects

Note: A study comparing tizanidine (single dose of 3 or 6 mg) with diazepam (10 mg) reported no evidence of psychological dependence associated with tizanidine.

Tizanidine use has been associated with hallucinations. In two controlled clinical studies, hallucinations or delusions have been reported in 5 of 170 patients (3%) with the 5 cases occurring within the first 6 weeks. Most of the patients were aware that the events were unreal. One patient developed psychoses in association with the hallucinations. One patient continued to have problems for at least 2 weeks following discontinuation of tizanidine.

The following side/adverse effects have been selected on the basis of their potential clinical significance (possible signs and symptoms in parentheses where appropriate)—not necessarily inclusive:

Those indicating need for medical attention

Incidence more frequent

Bradycardia (chest pain or discomfort; lightheadedness; dizziness or fainting; shortness of breath; slow or irregular heartbeat; unusual tiredness); ***CNS effects, including nervousness; and paresthesias*** (tingling, burning, or prickling sensations); ***fever; hepatotoxicity*** (loss of appetite; nausea and/or vomiting; yellow eyes or skin); ***infection*** (fever or chills; cough or hoarseness; lower back or side pain; painful or difficult urination); ***skin ulcers*** (sores on the skin); ***urinary tract infections*** (pain or burning while urinating)

Incidence less frequent

Arrhythmias (irregular heartbeat); ***blood dyscrasias, including anemia*** (unusual tiredness or weakness); ***leukocytosis; or leukopenia*** (chills, fever, or sore throat); ***gastrointestinal hemorrhage*** (black, tarry stools; bloody vomit); ***hypothyroidism*** (coldness; dry, puffy skin; unusual tiredness; weight gain); ***liver injury*** (pruritus; dark urine; persistent anorexia; yellow eyes or skin; influenza (flu)-like symptoms; right upper quadrant tenderness); ***mood or mental changes, including delusions; or visual hallucinations*** (seeing things that are not there); ***renal calculi*** (kidney stones); ***seizures; syncope*** (fainting); ***upper respiratory tract infections*** (cough, fever, or sore throat); ***visual disturbances, including amblyopia*** (blurred vision); ***eye pain; or visual field defects*** (blurred vision)

Incidence not determined—observed during clinical practice; estimates of frequency can not be determined

Liver failure (headache; stomach pain; continuing vomiting; dark-colored urine; general feeling of tiredness or weakness; light-colored stools; yellow eyes or skin)

Those indicating need for medical attention only if they continue or are bothersome

Incidence more frequent

Anxiety; asthenia (unusual tiredness and/or weakness)—dose-related; ***back pain; constipation; depression; dizziness***—dose-related; ***drowsiness***—dose-related; ***dry mouth***—dose-related; ***dyskinesia*** (uncontrolled movements of the body); ***dyspepsia*** (heartburn); ***hypotension*** (dizziness or lightheadedness, especially when getting up from a lying or sitting position); ***gastrointestinal effects*** (diarrhea; stomach pain; vomiting); ***increased muscle spasms or tone***—dose-related; ***increased sweating; myasthenia*** (muscle weakness); ***pharyngitis*** (pain or burning in throat); ***rhinitis*** (runny nose); ***skin rash; somnolence*** (sleepiness)—dose-related; ***speech disorder*** (difficulty in speaking)

Incidence less frequent

Alopecia (loss of hair); ***arthritis*** (joint or muscle pain or stiffness); ***cellulitis*** (swollen area that feels warm and tender); ***dry skin; dysphagia*** (difficulty swallowing); ***edema*** (swelling of feet or lower legs); ***flu syndrome*** (chills; cough; diarrhea; fever; general feeling of discomfort or illness; headache; joint pain; loss of appetite; muscle aches and pains; nausea; runny nose; shivering; sore throat; sweating; trouble sleeping; unusual tiredness or weakness; vomiting); ***migraine headache; mood or mental changes, including agitation; euphoria*** (unusual feeling of well-being); ***or depersonalization; neck pain; tremor*** (trembling or shaking); ***urinary frequency*** (increased need to urinate; passing urine more often); ***weight loss***

Overdose

For specific information on the agents used in the management of tizanidine overdose, see:

- *Furosemide* in *Diuretics, Loop (Systemic)* monograph; and/or
- *Mannitol (Systemic)* monograph.

For more information on the management of overdose or unintentional ingestion, **contact a Poison Control Center** (see *Poison Control Center Listing*).

Clinical effects of overdose

A safety surveillance database search revealed a total of 18 cases of tizanidine overdose. Of the 14 intentional overdoses, 5 have resulted in fatality. Other CNS depressants were involved in at least three of these cases. One fatality was secondary to pneumonia and sepsis, which were sequelae of the ingestion. In general, symptoms resolve within one to three days following discontinuation of tizanidine and administration of appropriate therapy.

The following effects have been selected on the basis of their potential clinical significance (possible signs and symptoms in parentheses where appropriate)—not necessarily inclusive:

Acute and chronic

Bradycardia (chest pain or discomfort; lightheadedness, dizziness or fainting; shortness of breath; slow or irregular heartbeat; unusual tiredness); ***coma*** (change in consciousness; loss of consciousness); ***hypotension*** (blurred vision; confusion, dizziness, faintness, or lightheadedness when getting up from a lying or sitting position suddenly; sweating; unusual tiredness or weakness); ***respiratory depression or failure*** (pale or blue lips, fingernails, or skin; difficult or troubled breathing; irregular, fast or slow, or shallow breathing; shortness of breath); ***somnolence*** (sleepiness or unusual drowsiness); ***stupor*** (decreased awareness or responsiveness; severe sleepiness)

Treatment of overdose

Monitoring—Cardiovascular and respiratory systems

To enhance elimination—Gastric lavage and forced diuresis with furosemide and mannitol.

Supportive care—May include maintaining an open airway and breathing, maintaining proper fluid and electrolyte balance, correcting hypotension, and controlling seizures. Patients in whom intentional overdose is confirmed or suspected should be referred for psychiatric consultation.

Due to the similar mechanism of action, symptoms and management of tizanidine overdose are similar to those following clonidine overdose. For specific information on the management of clonidine overdose, see *Clonidine (Systemic)*.

Patient Consultation

As an aid to patient consultation, refer to *Advice for the Patient, Tizanidine (Systemic)*.

In providing consultation, consider emphasizing the following selected information (» = major clinical significance):

Before using this medication

» Conditions affecting use, especially:
- Hypersensitivity to tizanidine or any of its ingredients
- Pregnancy—Should be given to pregnant women only if clearly needed
- Breast-feeding—May be distributed into breast milk
- Use in the elderly—Clearance may be reduced. Also, elderly people are more likely to have age-related renal function impairment, which may require dosage adjustment
- Other medications, especially fluvoxamine, hypotension-producing medications, oral contraceptives, or phenytoin
- Other medical problems, especially hepatic or renal function impairment

Proper use of this medication

Not taking more medication than the amount prescribed to minimize possibility of side effects

» Advising patient that changes in absorption of tablets versus capsules as well as intact capsules versus capsules sprinkled over applesauce occur when administering with food; potential for changes in efficacy and adverse effects

» Proper dosing

Missed dose: Taking if remembered within an hour; not taking if not remembered until later; not doubling doses

» Proper storage

Precautions while using this medication

Regular visits to physician to check progress during therapy

» Checking with physician before discontinuing medication; gradual dosage adjustment may be necessary; rebound hypertension and tachycardia may occur with sudden discontinuation

» Avoiding use of alcohol or other CNS depressants during therapy unless approved by physician

» Caution when driving or doing anything else requiring alertness because of possible drowsiness, dizziness, lightheadedness, impairment of physical or mental abilities, false sense of well-being, or visual disturbances

Possible dryness of mouth; using sugarless gum or candy, ice, or saliva substitute for relief; checking with physician or dentist if dry mouth continues for more than 2 weeks

» Caution when getting up suddenly from a lying or sitting position

» Using this medicine with caution where spasticity is utilized to sustain posture and balance in locomotion or whenever spasticity is utilized to obtain increased function

Side/adverse effects

Signs of potential side effects, especially bradycardia, CNS effects, fever, hepatotoxicity, infection, skin ulcer, urinary tract infections, arrhythmias, blood dyscrasias, gastrointestinal hemorrhage, hypothyroidism, liver injury, mood or mental changes, renal calculi, seizures, syncope, upper respiratory tract infections, and visual disturbances

Signs of potential side effects observed during clinical practice, especially liver failure

Oral Dosage Forms

TIZANIDINE HYDROCHLORIDE CAPSULES

Note: Dose and strength of tizanidine hydrochloride capsules are expressed in terms of the base.

Usual adult dose

Antispastic—

See *Tizanidine Hydrochloride Tablets*.

Usual pediatric dose

Safety and efficacy have not been established.

Usual geriatric dose

See *Tizanidine Hydrochloride Tablets*.

Strength(s) usually available

U.S.—

- 2 mg (base) (Rx) [*Zanaflex* (hydroxypropyl methyl cellulose; silicon dioxide; sugar spheres; titanium dioxide; gelatin; colorants)].
- 4 mg (base) (Rx) [*Zanaflex* (hydroxypropyl methyl cellulose; silicon dioxide; sugar spheres; titanium dioxide; gelatin; colorants)].
- 6 mg (base) (Rx) [*Zanaflex* (hydroxypropyl methyl cellulose; silicon dioxide; sugar spheres; titanium dioxide; gelatin; colorants)].

Canada—

Not commercially available.

Packaging and storage

Store at 25 °C (77 °F); excursions permitted to 15 to 30 °C (59 to 86 °F).

Auxiliary labeling

- May cause drowsiness.
- Avoid alcoholic beverages.

Additional information

Tizanidine tablets and capsules are bioequivalent to each other under fasted conditions, but not under fed conditions.

Administration of the capsule contents sprinkled on apple sauce is NOT bioequivalent to administration of an intact capsule under fasting conditions. Administration of the capsule contents on applesauce results in a 15 to 20% increase in C_{max} and AUC of tizanidine compared to administration of an intact capsule while fasting, and a 15 minute decrease in the median lag time and time to peak concentration.

TIZANIDINE HYDROCHLORIDE TABLETS

Note: Dose and strength of tizanidine hydrochloride tablets are expressed in terms of the base.

Usual adult dose

Antispastic—

Oral, 8 mg every six to eight hours as needed.

Note: Due to the dose-related nature of the side effects and the various responses to doses among patients, the dose may be started at 4 mg and gradually titrated to optimum effect in 2- to 4-mg increments on an individual basis over a two- to four-week period.

Usual adult prescribing limits

36 mg per day.

Usual pediatric dose

Safety and efficacy have not been established.

Usual geriatric dose

See *Usual adult dose.*

Note: Dosage adjustment may be required.

Strength(s) usually available

U.S.—

- 2 mg (base) (Rx) [*Zanaflex* (silicon dioxide colloidal; stearic acid; microcrystalline cellulose; anhydrous lactose)].
- 4 mg (base) (Rx) [*Zanaflex* (silicon dioxide colloidal; stearic acid; microcrystalline cellulose; anhydrous lactose)].

Canada—

Not commercially available.

Packaging and storage

Store below 40 °C (104 °F), preferably between 15 and 30 °C (59 and 86 °F), unless otherwise specified by the manufacturer.

Auxiliary labeling

- May cause drowsiness.
- Avoid alcoholic beverages.

Additional information

Tizanidine tablets and capsules are bioequivalent to each other under fasted conditions, but not under fed conditions.

Selected Bibliography

Lataste X, Emre M, Davis C, et al. Comparative profile of tizanidine in the management of spasticity. Neurology 1994; 44 Suppl 9: S53-S59.

Wagstaff AJ, Bryson HM. Tizanidine: a review of its pharmacology, clinical efficacy and tolerability in the management of spasticity associated with cerebral and spinal disorders. Drugs 1997; 53(3): 435-52.

Revised: 06/09/2005

TOBRAMYCIN—See *Aminoglycosides (Systemic), Tobramycin (Ophthalmic)*

TOBRAMYCIN Ophthalmic

VA CLASSIFICATION (Primary): OP201

Commonly used brand name(s): *AKTob; Tobrex.*

Note: For a listing of dosage forms and brand names by country availability, see *Dosage Forms* section(s).

Category

Antibacterial (ophthalmic).

Indications

Note: Bracketed information in the *Indications* section refers to uses that are not included in U.S. product labeling.

Accepted

Ocular infections (treatment)—Ophthalmic tobramycin is indicated in the treatment of external ocular infections caused by susceptible organisms.

[Blepharitis, bacterial (treatment)]
[Blepharoconjunctivitis (treatment)]
[Conjunctivitis, bacterial (treatment)]
[Dacryocystitis (treatment)]
[Keratitis, bacterial (treatment)]
[Keratoconjunctivitis (treatment)] or
[Meibomianitis (treatment)]—Ophthalmic tobramycin is used as a primary agent in the treatment of bacterial blepharitis, blepharoconjunctivitis, bacterial conjunctivitis, dacryocystitis, bacterial keratitis, keratoconjunctivitis, and meibomianitis caused by coagulase-negative and coagulase-positive staphylococci, *Pseudomonas aeruginosa*, indole-positive and indole-negative *Proteus* species, *Escherichia coli, Klebsiella pneumoniae, Haemophilus influenzae, Haemophilus aegyptius, Enterobacter aerogenes, Moraxella lacunata* (Morax-Axenfeld bacillus), and *Neisseria* species, including *N. gonorrhoeae.*

[Keratitis, exposure (treatment)] or
[Keratitis, neuroparalytic (treatment)]—Ophthalmic tobramycin is used in the treatment of exposure keratitis and neuroparalytic keratitis when a secondary bacterial infection is present.

Note: Not all species or strains of a particular organism may be susceptible to tobramycin.

Unaccepted

Tobramycin is not effective against most strains of group D streptococci.

Pharmacology/Pharmacokinetics

Physicochemical characteristics

Chemical Group—Aminoglycoside.
Molecular weight—467.52.

Mechanism of action/Effect

Actively transported across the bacterial cell membrane, tobramycin binds to a specific receptor protein on the 30 S subunit of bacterial ribosomes and interferes with an initiation complex between messenger RNA (mRNA) and the 30 S subunit, thus inhibiting protein synthesis. The mRNA base sequence may be misread, thus producing nonfunctional proteins.

Note: Aminoglycosides are bactericidal, while most other antibiotics that interfere with protein synthesis are bacteriostatic.

Absorption

May be absorbed in minute quantities following topical application to the eye.

Precautions to Consider

Cross-sensitivity and/or related problems

Patients sensitive to other aminoglycosides may be sensitive to this medication also.

Pregnancy/Reproduction

Fertility—Adequate and well-controlled studies in humans have not been done.

Studies in three types of animals, given tobramycin at doses of up to 33 times the usual human systemic dose, have not shown that tobramycin causes impaired fertility.

Pregnancy—Adequate and well-controlled studies in humans have not been done.

Studies in three types of animals, given tobramycin at doses of up to 33 times the usual human systemic dose, have not shown that tobramycin causes adverse effects on the fetus.

FDA Pregnancy Category B.

Breast-feeding

Ophthalmic aminoglycosides may be absorbed, especially if tissue damage is present. However, ophthalmic tobramycin is unlikely to be distributed into breast milk in significant amounts since the ophthalmic dose is small. In addition, aminoglycosides are poorly absorbed from the gastrointestinal tract. Therefore, it is unlikely that the nursing infant would absorb significant amounts of tobramycin or that it would cause serious problems in the nursing infant.

Pediatrics

Studies performed to date have not demonstrated pediatrics-specific problems that would limit the usefulness of ophthalmic tobramycin in children.

Geriatrics

No information is available on the relationship of age to the effects of ophthalmic tobramycin in geriatric patients.

Drug interactions and/or related problems

If topical ophthalmic tobramycin is administered while the patient is on a systemic aminoglycoside antibiotic, the patient's total serum aminoglycoside concentration should be monitored.

Medical considerations/Contraindications

The medical considerations/contraindications included have been selected on the basis of their potential clinical significance (reasons given in parentheses where appropriate)—not necessarily inclusive (» = major clinical significance).

Risk-benefit should be considered when the following medical problem exists:

Sensitivity to tobramycin

Side/Adverse Effects

Note: Ophthalmic tobramycin should be discontinued if hypersensitivity reactions occur.

Prolonged use of anti-infective agents including tobramycin may result in the overgrowth of nonsusceptible organisms, including fungi.

The following side/adverse effects have been selected on the basis of their potential clinical significance (possible signs and symptoms in parentheses where appropriate)—not necessarily inclusive:

Those indicating need for medical attention

Incidence less frequent

Hypersensitivity (itching, redness, swelling, or other sign of eye or eyelid irritation not present before therapy)

Those indicating need for medical attention only if they continue or are bothersome

Incidence less frequent

Burning or stinging of the eyes

Those not indicating need for medical attention

For ophthalmic ointment dosage form only

Blurred vision

Overdose

For more information on the management of overdose or unintentional ingestion, **contact a Poison Control Center** (see *Poison Control Center Listing*).

Clinical effects of overdose

The following effects have been selected on the basis of their potential clinical significance (possible signs and symptoms in parentheses where appropriate)-not necessarily inclusive:

Acute and chronic

Increased watering of the eyes; itching, redness, or swelling of the eyes or eyelids; punctate keratitis (painful irritation of the clear front part of the eye)

Patient Consultation

As an aid to patient consultation, refer to *Advice for the Patient, Tobramycin (Ophthalmic)*.

In providing consultation, consider emphasizing the following selected information (» = major clinical significance):

Before using this medication

» Conditions affecting use, especially:
   Sensitivity to tobramycin or other aminoglycosides

Proper use of this medication

Proper administration technique for ophthalmic solution and ointment
» Compliance with full course of therapy
» Proper dosing
Missed dose: Applying as soon as possible; not applying if almost time for next dose
» Proper storage

Precautions while using this medication

Checking with physician if no improvement of symptoms occurs within a few days

Side/adverse effects

Ophthalmic ointments may cause blurred vision for a few minutes after application
Signs of potential side effects, especially hypersensitivity or punctate keratitis

General Dosing Information

Tobramycin ophthalmic solution is not for injection into the eye.

Although some manufacturers recommend doses of 2 drops of ophthalmic solutions at appropriate intervals, the conjunctival sac usually holds less than 1 drop.

When instilling two different ophthalmic solutions, wait at least 5 minutes between instillations to avoid a "wash-out" effect.

At night the ophthalmic ointment may be used as an adjunct to the ophthalmic solution to provide prolonged contact of the medicine with the infection.

If hypersensitivity develops, therapy with ophthalmic tobramycin should be discontinued.

For treatment of adverse effects

Recommended treatment consists of the following:

- For superinfection—Treatment with ophthalmic tobramycin should be discontinued and appropriate alternative therapy started.

Ophthalmic Dosage Forms

TOBRAMYCIN OPHTHALMIC OINTMENT USP

Usual adult and adolescent dose

Mild to moderate infections—
   Topical, to the conjunctiva, a thin strip (approximately 1.25 cm) of ointment every eight to twelve hours.

Severe infections—
   Topical, to the conjunctiva, a thin strip (approximately 1.25 cm) of ointment every three to four hours. Treatment should be continued until improvement occurs; then the frequency of administration should be reduced.

Usual pediatric dose

Mild to moderate infections—
   See *Usual adult and adolescent dose*.

Severe infections—
   See *Usual adult and adolescent dose*.

Strength(s) usually available

U.S.—
   0.3% (Rx) [*Tobrex* (chlorobutanol 0.5%; mineral oil; white petrolatum)].

Canada—
   0.3% (Rx) [*Tobrex* (chlorobutanol 0.5%; mineral oil; petrolatum base)].

Packaging and storage

Store between 8 and 27 °C (46 and 80 °F). Protect from freezing.

Auxiliary labeling

- For the eye.
- Continue medicine for full time of treatment.

TOBRAMYCIN OPHTHALMIC SOLUTION USP

Usual adult and adolescent dose

Mild to moderate infections—
   Topical, to the conjunctiva, 1 drop every four hours.

Severe infections—
   Topical, to the conjunctiva, 1 drop every hour. Treatment should be continued until improvement occurs; then the frequency of administration should be reduced.

Usual pediatric dose

Mild to moderate infections—
   See *Usual adult and adolescent dose*.

Severe infections—
   See *Usual adult and adolescent dose*.

Strength(s) usually available

U.S.—
   0.3% (Rx) [*AKTob* (boric acid; sodium sulfate; sodium chloride; tyloxapol; sodium hydroxide; sulfuric acid); *Tobrex* (benzalkonium chloride 0.01%; boric acid; sodium sulfate; sodium chloride; tyloxapol; sodium hydroxide; sulfuric acid); GENERIC].

Canada—
   0.3% (Rx) [*Tobrex* (benzalkonium chloride 0.01%; boric acid; sodium chloride; sodium hydroxide; sulfuric acid; sodium sulfate; tyloxapol)].

Packaging and storage

Store between 8 and 27 °C (46 and 80 °F). Protect from freezing.

Auxiliary labeling

- For the eye.
- Continue medicine for full time of treatment.

Revised: 03/15/1999

TOBRAMYCIN AND DEXAMETHASONE Ophthalmic†

VA CLASSIFICATION (Primary/Secondary): OP301/OP201

Commonly used brand name(s): *Tobradex*.

Note: For a listing of dosage forms and brand names by country availability, see *Dosage Forms* section(s).

†Not commercially available in Canada.

Category

Corticosteroid (ophthalmic); anti-inflammatory (steroidal), ophthalmic; antibacterial (ophthalmic).

Indications

General Considerations

Tobramycin is active against staphylococci, including *Staphylococcus aureus* and *Staphylococcus epidermidis* (coagulase-positive and coagulase-negative), including penicillin-resistant strains. It is also active against streptococci, including some of the Group A beta-hemolytic species, some nonhemolytic species, and some *Streptococcus pneumoniae*. In addition, it is active against *Pseudomonas aeruginosa*, *Escherichia coli*, *Klebsiella pneumoniae*, *Enterobacter aerogenes*, *Proteus mirabilis*, *Morganella morganii*, most *Proteus vulgaris* strains, *Haemophilus influenzae*, and *Haemophilus aegyptius*, *Moraxella lacunata*, *Acinetobacter calcoaceticus*, and some *Neisseria* species.

In some cases, according to bacterial susceptibility studies, microorganisms resistant to gentamicin will also be resistant to tobramycin.

Accepted

Inflammation, ocular (treatment) and
Ocular infections, superficial (treatment)—Tobramycin and dexamethasone in combination are indicated by topical administration for treatment of steroid-responsive inflammatory ocular conditions for which a corticosteroid is indicated and where superficial bacterial ocular infection or a risk of bacterial ocular infection exists.

Ocular corticosteroids are indicated in inflammatory conditions of the palpebral and bulbar conjunctiva, cornea, and anterior segment of the globe. Use is accepted even in certain infective conjunctivitides when necessary to reduce edema and inflammation. Use is also indicated in chronic anterior uveitis and corneal injury from chemical, radiation, or thermal burns, or penetration of foreign bodies. Addition of an antibacterial is indicated when the risk of superficial ocular infection is high or when potentially dangerous numbers of bacteria are expected to be present in the eye.

Unaccepted

The combination of tobramycin and dexamethasone is not indicated for treatment of epithelial herpes simplex keratitis (dendritis keratitis); for vaccinia, varicella, and many other viral diseases of the cornea and conjunctiva; for mycobacterial infection of the eye; or for fungal disease of ocular structures.

Pharmacology/Pharmacokinetics

Mechanism of action/Effect

Corticosteroids suppress the inflammatory response to a variety of agents and, as a result, probably delay or slow healing. Dexamethasone is a potent corticosteroid.

Tobramycin has antibacterial activity against susceptible organisms. Antibacterial activity provides protection against infection when the body's defense mechanisms are inhibited by corticosteroids.

Absorption

No data on the extent of systemic absorption after ophthalmic application are available. However, in general, some systemic absorption occurs with ocularly applied medications. If the entire ophthalmic dose of the medication were absorbed systemically, which is highly unlikely, the daily dose of dexamethasone would exceed the normal physiologic replacement dose.

Precautions to Consider

Cross-sensitivity and/or related problems

Patients sensitive to other aminoglycosides may also be sensitive to tobramycin.

Carcinogenicity

Studies have not been done.

Mutagenicity

Studies have not been done.

Pregnancy/Reproduction

Pregnancy—Adequate and well-controlled studies in humans have not been done.

Corticosteroids are teratogenic in animals. Studies in two groups of rabbits with ocular administration of 0.1% dexamethasone found a 15.6% and 32.3% incidence of fetal anomalies. Chronic dexamethasone therapy in rats has been associated with fetal growth retardation and increased mortality rates.

Reproduction studies with tobramycin in rats and rabbits at parenteral doses of up to 100 mg per kg of body weight (mg/kg) per day revealed no evidence of harm to the fetus.

Risk-benefit should be considered before use of ophthalmic tobramycin and dexamethasone during pregnancy.

FDA Pregnancy Category C.

Breast-feeding

It is not known whether ophthalmic administration of corticosteroids results in enough systemic absorption to produce detectable quantities in breast milk. Systemically administered corticosteroids are distributed into human breast milk and may suppress growth, interfere with endogenous corticosteroid production, or cause other untoward effects in the infant. Risk-benefit should be considered before use of ophthalmic tobramycin and dexamethasone during breast-feeding.

Pediatrics

Safety and efficacy have not been established.

Geriatrics

No information is available on the relationship of age to the effects of ophthalmic tobramycin and dexamethasone in geriatric patients.

Drug interactions and/or related problems

The following drug interactions and/or related problems have been selected on the basis of their potential clinical significance (possible mechanism in parentheses where appropriate)—not necessarily inclusive (» = major clinical significance):

Note: Combinations containing any of the following medications, depending on the amount present, may also interact with this medication.

Aminoglycoside antibiotics, systemic
(monitoring of total serum concentration is recommended during concurrent use with ophthalmic tobramycin)

Medical considerations/Contraindications

The medical considerations/contraindications included have been selected on the basis of their potential clinical significance (reasons given in parentheses where appropriate)—not necessarily inclusive (» = major clinical significance).

Except under special circumstances, this medication should not be used when the following medical problems exist:

» Fungal disease, ocular or
» Herpes simplex keratitis, epithelial (dendritis keratitis) or
» Mycobacterial infection, ocular or
» Viral infection of the cornea and conjunctiva, including vaccinia and varicella
(corticosteroids reduce resistance to bacterial, fungal, and viral infections; application may exacerbate existing infections and encourage the development of new or secondary infections)
(in acute purulent conditions of the eye, corticosteroids may mask infection or exacerbate existing infection)

Risk-benefit should be considered when the following medical problems exist:

Diseases causing thinning of the cornea or sclera
(use of ophthalmic dexamethasone may result in perforation)
» Glaucoma
(prolonged use of corticosteroids may increase intraocular pressure)
» Infections of the cornea or conjunctiva, other
(risk of exacerbation or development of secondary infections with ophthalmic corticosteroid use)
(in acute purulent conditions of the eye, corticosteroids may mask infection or exacerbate existing infection)
» Sensitivity to dexamethasone or tobramycin

Patient monitoring

The following may be especially important in patient monitoring (other tests may be warranted in some patients, depending on condition; » = major clinical significance):

Intraocular pressure
(determinations recommended at periodic intervals during prolonged therapy to detect possible glaucoma; may be difficult in children and uncooperative patients)

Ophthalmic examinations, such as slit lamp biomicroscopy or fluorescein staining
(recommended at periodic intervals)

Side/Adverse Effects

Note: Exact incidence figures for side/adverse effects are not available.

Secondary infections may occur because corticosteroids suppress the host response and may occur even with combinations of corticosteroids and antimicrobials. With prolonged use of corticosteroids, overgrowth of nonsusceptible organisms, including bacteria and fungi, may occur. Fungal infections of the cornea are particularly likely to occur and should be considered when any persistent corneal ulceration occurs in patients treated with corticosteroids.

The following side/adverse effects have been selected on the basis of their potential clinical significance (possible signs and symptoms in parentheses where appropriate)—not necessarily inclusive:

Those indicating need for medical attention

Incidence less frequent

Sensitivity or localized ocular toxicity (itching and swelling of eyelid; redness of eye)—incidence less than 4%

Note: *Sensitivity or local ocular toxicity* is related to the tobramycin component.

Incidence rare

Cataract, posterior subcapsular (blurred vision)—with prolonged use; ***delayed wound healing; increased intraocular pressure with possible development of glaucoma and possible optic nerve damage*** (may be asymptomatic; gradual blurring or loss of vision; eye pain)—with prolonged use

Note: *Delayed wound healing* is related to the corticosteroid (dexamethasone) component.

Prolonged use of corticosteroids may lead to *posterior subcapsular cataract* formation and *glaucoma*, with possible damage to the optic nerve and defects in visual acuity and fields of vision.

Overdose

For more information on the management of overdose or unintentional ingestion, **contact a Poison Control Center** (see *Poison Control Center Listing*).

Clinical effects of overdose

Signs and symptoms of ophthalmic overdose (i.e., punctate keratitis, erythema, increased lacrimation, edema, and itching of eyelid) may be similar to the side/adverse effects seen in some patients.

Patient Consultation

As an aid to patient consultation, refer to *Advice for the Patient, Tobramycin and Dexamethasone (Ophthalmic)*.

In providing consultation, consider emphasizing the following selected information (» = major clinical significance):

Before using this medication

» Conditions affecting use, especially:
Sensitivity to dexamethasone, tobramycin, or other aminoglycosides
Pregnancy—Teratogenic in animals
Breast-feeding—Discussing with physician before breast-feeding; systemically administered corticosteroids are distributed into human breast milk and may suppress growth, interfere with endogenous corticosteroid production, or cause other untoward effects in the infant
Other medical problems, especially fungal disease, ocular; glaucoma; herpes simplex keratitis, epithelial (dendritis keratitis); infections of the cornea or conjunctiva, other; mycobacterial infection, ocular; and viral infection of the cornea and conjunctiva, including vaccinia and varicella

Proper use of this medication

Shaking suspension vigorously before applying
Proper administration technique
Preventing contamination: Not touching applicator tip to any surface and keeping container tightly closed
» Proper dosing
Missed dose: Using as soon as possible; not using if almost time for next dose
» Proper storage

Precautions while using this medication

Need for ophthalmologic examinations during long-term therapy (more than a few weeks)

Side/adverse effects

Signs of potential side effects, especially sensitivity or localized ocular toxicity, posterior subcapsular cataract, delayed wound healing, and increased intraocular pressure

General Dosing Information

It is recommended that appropriate therapy be initiated if secondary infection occurs.

It is recommended that treatment with ophthalmic tobramycin and dexamethasone be withdrawn if a sensitivity reaction occurs.

Ophthalmic Dosage Forms

TOBRAMYCIN AND DEXAMETHASONE OPHTHALMIC OINTMENT

Usual adult dose

Ophthalmic disorders (treatment)—
Topical, to the conjunctiva, a thin strip (approximately one-half inch) up to three or four times a day.

Usual pediatric dose

Ophthalmic disorders (treatment)—
Safety and efficacy have not been established.

Strength(s) usually available

U.S.—
Tobramycin 3 mg per gram (0.3%) and dexamethasone 1 mg per gram (0.1%) (Rx) [*Tobradex* (chlorobutanol 0.5%; mineral oil; white petrolatum)].

Packaging and storage

Store between 8 and 27 °C (46 and 80 °F), unless otherwise specified by manufacturer.

Auxiliary labeling

- For the eye.

Note

It is recommended that no more than 8 grams of medication be prescribed initially and no refills be authorized without further evaluation of the condition.

TOBRAMYCIN AND DEXAMETHASONE OPHTHALMIC SUSPENSION

Usual adult dose

Ophthalmic disorders (treatment)—
Topical, to the conjunctiva, 1 or 2 drops every four to six hours. The dose may be increased, during the initial twenty-four to forty-eight hours of treatment, to 1 or 2 drops every two hours.

Note: The frequency of dosing should be decreased gradually as clinical signs improve. Treatment should not be discontinued prematurely.

Usual pediatric dose

Ophthalmic disorders (treatment)—
Safety and efficacy have not been established.

Strength(s) usually available

U.S.—
Tobramycin 3 mg per mL (0.3%) and dexamethasone 1 mg per mL (0.1%) (Rx) [*Tobradex* (benzalkonium chloride 0.01%; tyloxapol; edetate disodium; sodium chloride; hydroxyethyl cellulose; sodium sulfate; sulfuric acid and/or sodium hydroxide; purified water)].

Packaging and storage

Store between 8 and 27 °C (46 and 80 °F), unless otherwise specified by manufacturer.

Auxiliary labeling

- For the eye.
- Store bottle upright.

Note

It is recommended that no more than 20 mL of medication be prescribed initially and no refills be authorized without further evaluation of the condition.

Developed: 05/17/1999

TOLAZAMIDE—See *Antidiabetic Agents, Sulfonylurea (Systemic)*

TOLBUTAMIDE—See *Antidiabetic Agents, Sulfonylurea (Systemic)*

TOLMETIN—See *Anti-inflammatory Drugs, Nonsteroidal (Systemic)*

TOLTERODINE Systemic

VA CLASSIFICATION (Primary): AU305

Commonly used brand name(s): *Detrol; Detrol LA.*

Note: For a listing of dosage forms and brand names by country availability, see *Dosage Forms* section(s).

Category

Antispasmodic (urinary bladder).

Indications

Accepted

Bladder hyperactivity (treatment)—Tolterodine is indicated for the treatment of overactive bladder with symptoms of urinary frequency, urgency, or urge incontinence.

Pharmacology/Pharmacokinetics

Physicochemical characteristics

Molecular weight—325.5.

Mechanism of action/Effect

Both tolterodine and its active metabolite, 5-hydroxymethyl, exhibit similar antimuscarinic activity. In human studies, the effects of administration of a single, 5-mg dose were a decrease in detrusor pressure and an increase in residual urine, reflecting an incomplete emptying of the bladder.

Absorption

Rapid, at least 77% of a 5-mg radiolabeled oral dose was absorbed. It was found that food intake increased the bioavailability of tolterodine by an average of 53%, but did not affect the 5-hydroxymethyl metabolite concentrations in extensive metabolizers. There appeared to be no safety concerns related to this increased bioavailability and a dosage adjustment was not needed.

Distribution

Vol_D—113 ± 26.7 L following a 1.28 mg intravenous dose.

Protein binding

Very high (approximately 96.3%); to plasma proteins, primarily alpha acid glycoprotein. The 5-hydroxymethyl metabolite is approximately 64% protein bound.

Biotransformation

Tolterodine is transformed in the liver to 5-hydroxymethyl, its major pharmacologically active metabolite.

Half-life

Apparent—
1.9 to 3.7 hours.

Time to peak concentration

1 to 2 hours.

Elimination

Following administration of a 5-mg oral, radioactive dose of tolterodine in healthy males, 77% was recovered in the urine and 17% was recovered in the feces. Less than 1% (< 2.5% in poor metabolizers) of the dose was recovered as intact tolterodine and 5 to 14% (< 1% in poor metabolizers) was recovered as the active 5-hydroxymethyl metabolite.

Precautions to Consider

Carcinogenicity

Carcinogenicity studies with tolterodine in mice given 30 mg per kg of body weight (mg/kg) a day, female rats given 20 mg/kg a day, and male rats given 30 mg/kg a day (representing a 9- to 14-fold higher dose than the maximum tolerated dose in humans) found no increase in tumors.

Mutagenicity

Tolterodine was found nonmutagenic in the Ames test (using four strains of *Salmonella typhimurium* and two strains of *Escherichia coli*), a gene mutation assay in L5178Y mouse lymphoma cells, and chromosomal aberration tests in human lymphocytes. It was also negative in the bone marrow micronucleus test in the mouse.

Pregnancy/Reproduction

Fertility—In female mice treated with 20 mg/kg a day for 2 weeks before mating (a systemic exposure 15-fold higher in animals than in humans based on the area under the plasma concentration-time curve [AUC] of about 500 mcg • hour per L), no effects on fertility or on reproductive performance were observed. A dose of 30 mg/kg a day did not induce any adverse effects on fertility in male mice.

Pregnancy—Studies in humans have not been done. Tolterodine should be used during pregnancy only if the potential benefit for the mother justifies the potential risk for the fetus.

No anomalies or malformations were observed in mice given oral doses of 20 mg/kg a day (approximately 14 times the human exposure). Tolterodine was found to cause embryolethality, a reduced fetal weight, and an increased incidence of fetal abnormalities (cleft palate, digital abnormalities, intra-abdominal hemorrhage, and various skeletal abnormalities, primarily reduced ossification) in mice given doses of 30 to 40 mg/kg a day (approximately 20- to 25-fold higher than the human dose based on AUC). No embryotoxicity or teratogenicity was noted in rabbits treated with subcutaneous tolterodine doses of 0.8 mg/kg a day (threefold higher than the human dose based on AUC of 100 mcg • hour per L).

FDA Pregnancy Category C.

Breast-feeding

It is not known whether tolterodine is distributed into human breast milk; therefore its use should be discontinued during nursing. Tolterodine is distributed into the milk of mice. Offspring of female mice treated with 20 mg/kg a day of tolterodine during lactation had a slightly reduced body weight gain, but they regained the weight during the maturation phase.

Pediatrics

No information is available on the relationship of age to the effects of tolterodine in pediatric patients. Safety and efficacy have not been established.

Geriatrics

Appropriate studies performed to date have not demonstrated geriatrics-specific problems that would limit the usefulness of tolterodine in the elderly.

Pharmacogenetics

A subset of the population (approximately 7%) is devoid of cytochrome P450 2D6, the enzyme responsible for the formation of the 5-hydroxymethyl metabolite of tolterodine; the identified pathway of metabolism for these individuals is dealkylation via cytochrome P450 3A4 to *N*-dealkylated tolterodine. These individuals are referred to as poor metabolizers, while the remainder of the population is referred to as extensive metabolizers. Tolterodine is metabolized at a slower rate in poor metabolizers, resulting in significantly higher serum concentrations of tolterodine and negligible serum concentrations of the 5-hydroxymethyl metabolite. Because of differences in the protein binding characteristics of tolterodine and the 5-hydroxymethyl metabolite, the sum of unbound serum concentrations of tolterodine and the 5-hydroxymethyl metabolite is similar in extensive and poor metabolizers at steady state. Since tolterodine and the 5-hydroxymethyl metabolite have similar antimuscarinic effects, the net activity of tolterodine is expected to be similar in extensive and poor metabolizers.

Drug interactions and/or related problems

The following drug interactions and/or related problems have been selected on the basis of their potential clinical significance (possible mechanism in parentheses where appropriate)—not necessarily inclusive (» = major clinical significance):

Clarithromycin or
Cyclosporine or
Erythromycin or
Itraconazole or
Ketoconazole or
Miconazole or
Vinblastine
(oral use of these medications may inhibit cytochrome P450 3A4, which could lead to increased tolterodine concentrations in certain subpopulations; if given concurrently, the dose for tolterodine should not be higher than 1 mg two times a day, and for patients taking the extended release capsules, the dose for tolterodine should not be higher than 2 mg once daily)

Fluoxetine
(fluoxetine, a selective serotonin reuptake inhibitor and cytochrome P450 2D6 inhibitor, significantly inhibits the metabolism of tolterodine in extensive metabolizers; however, no dosage adjustment is necessary)

Medical considerations/Contraindications

The medical considerations/contraindications included have been selected on the basis of their potential clinical significance (reasons given in parentheses where appropriate)—not necessarily inclusive (» = major clinical significance).

Except under special circumstances, this medication should not be used when the following medical problems exist:

» Gastric retention or
» Glaucoma, narrow angle, uncontrolled or
» Urinary retention
(tolterodine may aggravate these conditions)

» Hypersensitivity to tolterodine tartrate

Risk-benefit should be considered when the following medical problems exist:

» Bladder outflow obstruction, clinically significant
(should be used with caution because of risk of urinary retention)

» Gastrointestinal obstructive disease such as aspyloric stenosis
(should be used with caution because of risk of gastric retention)

Glaucoma, narrow-angle, controlled
(caution should be used)

» Hepatic function impairment, severe
(patients with severe hepatic function impairment should not receive doses higher than 1 mg of tolterodine two times a day, and for patients taking the extended release capsules, the dose for tolterodine should not be higher than 2 mg once daily)

» Renal function impairment, severe
(patients taking extended release capsules, the dose of tolterodine should not be higher than 2 mg once daily)

Side/Adverse Effects

The following side/adverse effects have been selected on the basis of their potential clinical significance (possible signs and symptoms in parentheses where appropriate)—not necessarily inclusive:

Those indicating need for medical attention

Incidence more frequent

Abnormal vision, including problems with accommodation (difficulty adjusting to distances)—incidence 4.7%; ***urinary tract infection*** (difficult, burning, or painful urination; frequent urge to urinate; bloody or cloudy urine)—incidence 5.5%

Those indicating need for medical attention only if they continue or are bothersome

Incidence more frequent

Chest pain—incidence 3.4%; ***dizziness***—incidence 8.6%; ***dry mouth***—incidence 39.5%; ***fatigue***—incidence 6.8%; ***gastrointestinal symptoms, specifically abdominal pain***—incidence 7.6%; ***constipation***—incidence 6.5%; ***diarrhea***—incidence 4%; ***dyspepsia*** (upset stomach)—incidence 5.9%; ***nausea***—incidence 4.2%; ***headache***—incidence 11%; ***influenza-like symptoms*** (joint pain)—incidence 4.4%; ***somnolence*** (drowsiness)—incidence 3%; ***xerophthalmia*** (dry eyes)—incidence 3.8%

Incidence less frequent

Dysuria (difficult urination)—incidence 2.5%; ***hypertension*** (dizziness)—incidence 1.5%

Those not indicating need for medical attention

Incidence less frequent

Flatulence (stomach gas)—incidence 1.3%

Overdose

For more information on the management of overdose or unintentional ingestion, **contact a Poison Control Center** (see *Poison Control Center Listing*).

Treatment of overdose

Tolterodine overdose has the potential to result in severe central anticholinergic effects and should be treated accordingly.

Monitoring—Monitoring of electrocardiogram (ECG) is recommended because QT interval changes were observed in animal studies, but not in humans at doses of up to 4 mg two times a day.

Supportive care—Patients in whom intentional overdose is confirmed or suspected should be referred for psychiatric consultation.

Patient Consultation

As an aid to patient consultation, refer to *Advice for the Patient, Tolterodine (Systemic)*.

In providing consultation, consider emphasizing the following selected information (» = major clinical significance):

Before using this medication

» Conditions affecting use, especially:

Pregnancy—Risk benefit considerations due to increased embryo death, reduced fetal weight, and increased incidence of fetal abnormalities with high doses of tolterodine in animal studies

Breast-feeding—Should not be administered during nursing because not known if it is distributed in human milk

Use in children—Efficacy not demonstrated

Pharmacogenetics—Although overall effect thought to be negligible, 7% of population devoid of cytochrome P450 2D6, enzyme responsible for 5-hydroxymethyl metabolite formation

Other medical problems, especially bladder outflow obstruction; gastric retention; gastrointestinal obstructive disorders; glaucoma, narrow angle (uncontrolled); hepatic function impairment (severe); hypersensitivity to tolterodine tartrate; renal function impairment (severe); or urinary retention

Proper use of this medication

Importance of not taking more medication than the amount prescribed

» Taking extended release capsules with liquids and swallowing capsules whole

» Proper dosing

Missed dose: Using as soon as possible; not using if almost time for next dose; not doubling doses

» Proper storage

Precautions while using this medication

» Caution if vision problems occur

» Possible dizziness or drowsiness; caution when driving or doing things requiring alertness

Possible dryness of mouth; using sugarless candy or gum, ice, or saliva substitute for relief; checking with physician or dentist if dry mouth continues for more than 2 weeks

Side/adverse effects

Signs of potential side effects, especially abnormal vision (including accommodation problems) or urinary tract infection

Oral Dosage Forms

TOLTERODINE TARTRATE TABLETS

Usual adult and adolescent dose

Urologic disorders, symptoms of—

Oral, 2 mg two times a day; the dose may be lowered to 1 mg two times a day based on individual response and tolerance.

Note: For patients with significantly reduced hepatic function or those who are currently taking drugs that inhibit cytochrome P450 3A4, a dose no greater than of 1 mg two times a day is recommended.

Usual pediatric dose

Safety and efficacy have not been established.

Strength(s) usually available

U.S.—

1 mg (Rx) [*Detrol*].

2 mg (Rx) [*Detrol*].

Packaging and storage

Store below 40 °C (104 °F), preferably between 15 and 30 °C (59 and 86 °F), unless otherwise specified by manufacturer.

Auxiliary labeling

- May cause vision problems.
- May cause drowsiness.

TOLTERODINE TARTRATE EXTENDED-RELEASE CAPSULES

Usual adult and adolescent dose

Urologic disorders, symptoms of—

Oral, 4 mg once a day; the dose may be lowered to 2 mg once a day based on individual response and tolerance.

Note: For patients with significantly reduced hepatic or renal function or those who are currently taking drugs that inhibit cytochrome P450 3A4, a dose no greater than 2 mg once a day is recommended.

Usual pediatric dose

Safety and efficacy have not been established.

Strength(s) usually available

U.S.—

2 mg (Rx) [*Detrol LA*].

4 mg (Rx) [*Detrol LA*].

Packaging and storage

Store at 25°C (77°F); excursions permitted to 15–30°C (59–86°F). Store in a light-resistant container.

Auxiliary labeling

- Take with liquids
- Swallow whole
- May cause vision problems.
- May cause drowsiness.

Revised: 07/20/2006

TOPIRAMATE Systemic

VA CLASSIFICATION (Primary): CN400

Commonly used brand name(s): *Topamax*.

Note: For a listing of dosage forms and brand names by country availability, see *Dosage Forms* section(s).

Category

Anticonvulsant; migraine headache prophylactic.

Indications

Note: Bracketed information in the Indications section refers to uses that are not included in U.S. product labeling.

Accepted

Epilepsy (treatment)—Topiramate is indicated as initial monotherapy in patients 10 years of age and older with partial onset or primary generalized tonic-clonic seizures.

Epilepsy (treatment adjunct)—Topiramate is indicated for use in the adjunctive treatment of partial onset seizures in adults and pediatric patients ages 2 to 16 years. Topiramate is also indicated for use in the treatment of primary generalized tonic-clonic seizures in adults and in pediatric patients ages 2 to 16 years.

Epilepsy, Lennox-Gastaut syndrome (treatment adjunct)[1]—Topiramate is indicated for use in the treatment of seizures associated with Lennox-Gastaut syndrome in patients 2 years of age and older.

Headache, migraine (prophylaxis)—Topiramate is indicated for adults for the prophylaxis of migraine headache.

Unaccepted

The usefulness of topiramate in the acute treatment of migraine headache has not been studied.

---

[1]Not included in Canadian product labeling.

Pharmacology/Pharmacokinetics

Physicochemical characteristics

Chemical Group—Sulfamate-substituted monosaccharide.
Molecular weight—339.36.

Mechanism of action/Effect

The precise mechanism of action is unknown. Electrophysiological and biochemical studies on cultured neurons demonstrated that topiramate blocks the action potentials elicited repetitively by a sustained depolarization of the neurons in a time-dependent manner; this effect suggests a state-dependent sodium channel blocking action. Also, topiramate increases the frequency at which gamma-aminobutyric acid (GABA) activates $GABA_A$ receptors, thereby enhancing GABA-induced influx of chloride ions into neurons. Thus, it appears that topiramate exerts its effects by potentiation of the activity of the inhibitory neurotransmitter, GABA. In addition, topiramate antagonizes the ability of kainate to activate the kainate/AMPA (alpha-amino-3-hydroxy-5-methylisoxazole-4-propionic acid; non-NMDA) subtype of excitatory amino acid (glutamate) receptor, but has no apparent effect on the activity of N-methyl-D-aspartate (NMDA) at the NMDA receptor subtype. These effects of topiramate are concentration-dependent within the range of 1 to 200 micromoles.

Other actions/effects

Topiramate also inhibits some isoenzymes of carbonic anhydrase (CA-II and CA-IV). This pharmacologic effect is generally weak and may not be a major contributing factor to the antiepileptic activity of topiramate.

Absorption

Rapid. The relative bioavailability of the tablet dosage form is about 80% as compared with that from a solution. Food does not affect the bioavailability of topiramate.

Protein binding

Low (13 to 17% over the concentration range of 1 to 250 mcg per mL).

Biotransformation

Topiramate is not extensively metabolized. Six metabolites (formed by hydroxylation, hydrolysis, and glucuronidation) have been identified in humans, with none constituting more than 5% of an administered dose.

Half-life

Elimination—

21 hours (mean) following single or multiple dosing.

Time to peak concentration

Approximately 2 hours following administration of a 400-mg oral dose.

Time to steady state concentration

In patients with normal renal function, steady state is reached in about 4 days.

Note: The pharmacokinetics of topiramate are linear, with dose-proportional increases in the plasma concentration over the range of 200 to 800 mg a day.

Elimination

Renal; approximately 70% of an administered dose is eliminated unchanged. Evidence from rat studies has shown that renal tubular reabsorption of topiramate occurs.

With impaired renal function—

Topiramate clearance was reduced by 42% in patients with moderate renal function impairment (creatinine clearance of 30 to 69 mL per minute per 1.73 square meters of body surface area), and by 54% in patients with severe renal impairment (creatinine clearance less than 30 mL per minute per 1.73 square meters of body surface area,) as compared with the clearance in subjects with normal renal function. Topiramate is presumed to undergo significant tubular reabsorption, but it is not certain if changes in clearance can be generalized to all cases of renal impairment. Some forms of renal disease may affect glomerular filtration rate and tubular reabsorption differently, resulting in a topiramate clearance rate not predicted by creatinine clearance. In general, one half of the usual dose is recommended in patients with moderate or severe renal impairment.

With impaired hepatic function—

The clearance of topiramate may be decreased in patients with impaired hepatic function; the mechanism of this effect is not well understood.

In hemodialysis—

120 mL per minute with blood flow through the dialyzer at 400 mL per minute (using a high efficiency, counterflow, single pass–dialysate hemodialysis procedure). This high clearance, as compared with 20 to 30 mL per minute total clearance of the oral dose in healthy adults, removes a clinically significant amount of topiramate from the patient over the hemodialysis treatment period; dosage adjustments may be necessary.

Precautions to Consider

Carcinogenicity

An increase in urinary bladder tumors was observed in mice given topiramate (20, 75, and 300 mg per kg of body weight [mg/kg]) in the diet for 21 months. The statistically significant increased incidence of bladder tumors in male and female mice receiving 300 mg/kg was due primarily to the increased occurrence of a smooth muscle tumor considered histomorphologically unique to mice. Plasma exposures in mice receiving 300 mg/kg were approximately 0.5 to 1 time the steady-state exposures measured in patients receiving topiramate monotherapy at the recommended human dose of 400 mg, and 1.5 to 2 times the steady-state topiramate exposures in patients receiving 400 mg topiramate plus phenytoin. The relevance of this finding to human carcinogenic risk is uncertain. No evidence of carcinogenicity was seen in rats following oral administration of topiramate for 2 years at doses of up to 120 mg/kg (approximately three times the recommended human dose on a mg per square meter of body surface area [mg/m^2] basis).

Mutagenicity

Topiramate did not demonstrate genotoxic potential when tested in a battery of *in vitro* and *in vivo* assays. Topiramate was not mutagenic in the Ames test or the *in vitro* mouse lymphoma assay; it did not increase unscheduled DNA synthesis in rat hepatocytes *in vitro;* and it did not increase chromosomal aberrations in human lymphocytes *in vitro* or in rat bone marrow *in vivo*.

Pregnancy/Reproduction

Fertility—No adverse effects on male or female fertility were observed in rats receiving up to 2.5 times the recommended human dose on a mg per square meter of body surface area (mg/m^2) basis.

Pregnancy—Studies have not been done in humans. Post-marketing cases of hypospadias in male infants exposed in utero to topiramate, with or without other convulsants, have been reported; however, a causal relationship has not been established. Topiramate should be used during pregnancy only if the potential benefit outweighs the potential risk to the fetus.

Topiramate has demonstrated selective developmental toxicity, including teratogenicity, in animal studies.

Incidence of fetal malformations (primarily craniofacial defects) was increased in pregnant mice that received oral topiramate doses of 20, 100, or 500 mg/kg during the period of organogenesis. Fetal body weights and skeletal ossification were reduced at doses of 500 mg/kg; decreased maternal body weight gain also occurred at this dose. In studies in rats, the frequency of limb malformations (ectrodactyly, micromelia, and amelia) was increased among the offspring of dams treated with 400 mg of topiramate per kg or greater during the organogenesis period of pregnancy. Clinical signs of maternal toxicity were seen at doses of 400 mg/kg and above, and maternal body weight gain was reduced during treatment with doses of 100 mg/kg or greater. Embryotoxicity (reduced fetal body weights, increased incidence of structural variations) was observed at doses as low as 20 mg/kg.

In studies in rabbits receiving topiramate, embryo/fetal mortality was increased at doses of 35 mg/kg and greater, and teratogenic effects (primarily rib and vertebral malformations) were observed at doses of 120 mg/kg. Evidence of maternal toxicity (decreased body weight gain, clinical signs, and/or mortality) was seen at doses of 35 mg/kg and greater.

Offspring of female rats treated with topiramate during the latter part of gestation and throughout lactation exhibited decreased viability and delayed physical development at doses of 200 mg/kg, and reductions in pre- and/or postweaning body weight gain at doses of 2 mg/kg and greater. Maternal toxicity (decreased body weight gain, other clinical signs) was evident at doses of 100 mg/kg or greater.

In a rat embryo/fetal development study with a postnatal component, pups of dams receiving topiramate exhibited delayed physical development at doses of 400 mg/kg and persistent reductions in body weight gain at doses of 30 mg/kg and higher.

FDA Pregnancy Category C.

Labor and delivery—The effect of topiramate on labor and delivery in humans is unknown. In studies in rats in which dams were allowed to deliver pups naturally, no drug-related effects on gestation length or parturition were observed at doses of up to 200 mg/kg per day.

Breast-feeding

It is not known if topiramate is distributed into breast milk; however, it is distributed into the milk of lactating rats. Since many drugs are distributed in human milk, and because the potential for serious adverse reactions in nursing infants to topiramate is unknown, potential benefit to the mother should be weighed against potential risk to the infant when considering recommendations regarding nursing.

Pediatrics

Safety and efficacy of topiramate in pediatric patients below 2 years of age have not been established for the adjunctive therapy treatment of partial onset seizures, primary generalized tonic-clonic seizures, or seizures associated with Lennox-Gastaut.

Safety and efficacy in patients below the age of 10 years have not been established for the monotherapy treatment of epilepsy.

Safety and efficacy in pediatric patients have not been established for the prophylaxis treatment of migraine headache.

Pharmacokinetic profiles obtained after 1 week at topiramate doses of 1, 3, and 9 mg per kg of body weight per day in patients aged 4 to 17 years receiving one or two other antiepileptic medications showed that clearance was independent of dose. Pediatric patients have a 50% higher clearance and shorter elimination half-life than adults. The plasma concentration for the same milligram/kilogram dose may be lower in pediatric patients compared to adults.

Geriatrics

In clinical trials, 3% of patients were over 60 years of age. No age-related differences in the efficacy of topiramate were observed, and no pharmacokinetic differences related to age alone were found. However, elderly patients are more likely to have age-related renal function impairment, which may require topiramate dosage reductions.

Pharmacogenetics

The clearance of topiramate was not affected by race or gender.

Drug interactions and/or related problems

The following drug interactions and/or related problems have been selected on the basis of their potential clinical significance (possible mechanism in parentheses where appropriate)—not necessarily inclusive (» = major clinical significance):

Note: Combinations containing any of the following medications, depending on the amount present, may also interact with this medication.

Alcohol or
Central nervous system (CNS) depression-producing medications, other (see *Appendix II*)
(CNS depression may be enhanced)

Amitriptyline
(12% increase in amitriptyline AUC and C_{max} with concomitant use; some patients may experience a large increase in amitriptyline concentration in the presence of topiramate; amitriptyline dose adjustments should be made according to patient's clinical response and not on basis of plasma levels)

» Anticholinergics or (see *Appendix II*)
» Carbonic anhydrase inhibitors such as
Acetazolamide or
Dichlorphenamide
(these drugs predispose patients to heat-related disorders; caution should be used when administered concurrently with topiramate)
(carbonic anhydrase inhibitors may create a physiological environment that increases risk of renal stone formation; concomitant use should be avoided)

» Carbamazepine
(mean carbamazepine area under the plasma concentration-time curve [AUC] was unchanged or changed by less than 10%, whereas the AUC of topiramate was decreased by 40% when these two medications were given concurrently during controlled clinical studies)

» Contraceptives, estrogen-containing, oral
(efficacy of oral contraceptives may be compromised when used concurrently with topiramate; patients should be instructed to report any change in their bleeding patterns)

Digoxin
(in a single-dose study, serum digoxin area under the plasma concentration-time curve [AUC] was decreased by 12% with concomitant topiramate administration; clinical relevance has not been established)

Hydrochlorothiazide
(concomitant use of hydrochlorothiazide and topiramate may increase peak concentration and AUC of topiramate, dosage reduction of topiramate may be required)

Lithium
(lithium AUC and C_{max} decreased by 20% with multiple dosing of topiramate)

Metformin
(concomitant use of metformin and topiramate may increase the peak concentration and AUC of metformin, routine monitoring for adequate control of diabetic disease state is recommended when topiramate is added or withdrawn in patients on metformin)

» Phenytoin
(mean phenytoin area under the plasma concentration-time curve [AUC] was unchanged, changed by less than 10%, or increased by 25%, whereas the AUC of topiramate was decreased by 48% when these two medications were given concurrently during controlled clinical studies; increases in phenytoin plasma concentrations generally occurred in patients receiving phenytoin doses two times a day)

Risperidone
(25% decrease in exposure to risperidone with concomitant use; patients receiving risperidone and topiramate concomitantly should be closely monitored for clinical response)

» Valproic acid
(mean valproic acid area under the plasma concentration-time curve [AUC] was decreased by 11%, whereas the AUC of topiramate was decreased by 14% when these two medications were given concurrently during controlled clinical studies)
(concomitant administration has been associated with hyperammonemia with or without encephalopathy in patients who have tolerated either drug alone; although not studied, an interaction of topiramate and valproic acid may exacerbate existing metabolism defects or unmask deficiencies in susceptible persons)

Medical considerations/Contraindications

The medical considerations/contraindications included have been selected on the basis of their potential clinical significance (reasons given in parentheses where appropriate)—not necessarily inclusive (» = major clinical significance).

Except under special circumstances, this medication should not be used when the following medical problem exists:

» Hypersensitivity to topiramate or any component of this product

Risk-benefit should be considered when the following medical problems exist:

» Diarrhea or
» Ketogenic diet or
» Renal disease or
» Respiratory disorder, severe, or
» Status epilepticus or
» Surgery
(these conditions all predispose to metabolic acidosis; may be additive to the bicarbonate lowering effects of topiramate)

Hepatic function impairment or
» Renal function impairment including hemodialysis
(clearance of topiramate and its metabolites may be decreased; dosage adjustments may be necessary)

Renal calculi, predisposition to
(increased risk of occurrence of renal calculi)

Patient monitoring

The following may be especially important in patient monitoring (other tests may be warranted in some patients, depending on condition; » = major clinical significance):

» Bicarbonate, serum
(baseline and periodic measurements during topiramate treatment recommended; consideration should be given to reducing dose or discontinuing topiramate [using dose tapering]; if decision is made to continue topiramate treatment with persistent acidosis, alkali treatment should be considered)

» Body temperature elevation and/or

» Decreased sweating
(monitor closely in patients, especially pediatric patients or patients exposed to warm or hot weather; could indicate oligohidrosis or hyperthermia)

» Tonometry
(Monitoring for elevated levels of intraocular pressure as signs of ocular syndrome characterized by acute myopia and secondary angle glaucoma is recommended at initiation of therapy and at periodic intervals during treatment; symptoms typically occur within the first month of therapy.)

Side/Adverse Effects

Note: Since topiramate is indicated for use as adjunctive therapy, the side/adverse effects reported in this section occurred in clinical trials in which patients were receiving additional antiepileptic medication.

The following side/adverse effects have been selected on the basis of their potential clinical significance (possible signs and symptoms in parentheses where appropriate)—not necessarily inclusive:

Those indicating need for medical attention

Incidence more frequent

Asthenia (unusual tiredness or weakness); ***ataxia*** (clumsiness or unsteadiness); ***confusion; difficulty with concentration or attention; diplopia or other vision problems*** (double vision or other vision problems); ***dizziness; dysmenorrhea or other menstrual changes*** (menstrual pain or other changes); ***fatigue; memory problems; myopia, acute and secondary angle closure glaucoma*** (blurred vision; eye pain; eye redness; increased eye pressure; rapidly decreasing vision)—typically occur within the first month after starting treatment; ***nervousness; nystagmus*** (uncontrolled back-and-forth and/or rolling eye movements); ***paresthesia*** (burning, prickling, or tingling sensations); ***psychomotor retardation*** (generalized slowing of mental and physical activity); ***somnolence*** (drowsiness); ***speech or language problems***—particularly word-finding difficulties

Note: *Fatigue* and *somnolence* are usually mild to moderate and appear early in therapy. The incidence of *fatigue* appears to increase at doses greater than 400 mg of topiramate a day. *Confusion, difficulty with concentration or attention, nervousness,* and *speech or language problems* appear to be dose-related.

Incidence less frequent

Abdominal pain; anorexia (loss of appetite); ***chills; gingivitis*** (red, irritated, or bleeding gums); ***hypoesthesia*** (lessening of sensations or perception); ***leukopenia*** (fever; chills; sore throat); ***mood or mental changes, including aggression, agitation, apathy, irritability, and mental depression; pharyngitis*** (sore throat); ***weight loss***

Note: *Anorexia, mood or mental changes,* and *weight loss* appear to be dose-related.

Incidence rare

Anemia (pale skin; unusual tiredness or weakness); ***conjunctivitis*** (red or irritated eyes); ***dyspnea*** (troubled breathing); ***edema*** (swelling); ***epistaxis*** (nosebleeds); ***eye pain; hematuria*** (blood in urine); ***impotence or decreased libido*** (decrease in sexual performance or desire); ***pruritus*** (itching); ***renal calculi*** (flank pain; difficult or painful urination); ***skin rash; tinnitus*** (ringing or buzzing in ears; hearing loss); ***urinary problems, including dysuria*** (pain on urination); ***urinary frequency*** (frequent urination); ***and incontinence*** (loss of bladder control)

Note: *Renal calculi* occurred in about 1.5% of the patients exposed to topiramate during its development, an incidence which is about two to four times that expected in the general population. Incidence of stone formation was higher in males, as is usual for the general population. As a weak carbonic anhydrase inhibitor, topiramate may promote stone formation by reducing urinary citrate excretion and by increasing urinary pH. Concomitant use with other carbonic anhydrase inhibitors may increase the risk of stone formation and should be avoided. Hydration is recommended to reduce new stone formation; increased fluid intake increases urinary output, thus lowering the concentration of substances involved in stone formation.

Incidence not determined—Observed during clinical practice; estimates of frequency cannot be determined

Erythema multiforme (blistering, peeling, loosening of skin; chills; cough; diarrhea; fever; itching; joint or muscle pain; red irritated eyes; sore throat; sores, ulcers, or white spots in mouth or on lips; unusual tiredness or weakness); ***hepatic failure*** (abdominal or stomach pain; clay-colored stools; fatigue; fever); ***hepatitis*** (pain or tenderness in upper abdomen; yellow eyes or skin; fever); ***pancreatitis*** (bloating; constipation; loss of appetite; pains in stomach); ***pemphigus*** (blisters in the mouth; blisters on the trunk, scalp, or other areas; itching); ***renal tubular acidosis*** (fatigue; confusion; increased rate of breathing; muscle pain); ***Stevens-Johnson syndrome or toxic epidermal necrolysis*** (blistering, peeling, loosening of skin; chills; cough; diarrhea; itching; joint or muscle pain; red irritated eyes; red skin lesions, often with a purple center; sore throat; sores, ulcers, or white spots in mouth or on lips; unusual tiredness or weakness)

Those indicating need for medical attention only if they continue or are bothersome

Incidence more frequent

Breast pain in females; nausea; tremor—appears to be dose-related

Incidence less frequent

Back pain; chest pain; constipation; dyspepsia (heartburn); ***hot flushes; increased sweating; leg pain***

Those not indicating need for medical attention

Incidence less frequent

Taste perversion (change in sense of taste)

Overdose

For more information on the management of overdose or unintentional ingestion, **contact a Poison Control Center** (see *Poison Control Center Listing*).

Treatment of overdose

To decrease absorption—If ingestion is recent, the stomach should be emptied immediately by lavage or by induction of emesis. Since activated charcoal has not been shown to adsorb topiramate *in vitro* , its use in overdosage is not recommended.

To enhance elimination—Hemodialysis is an effective means of removing topiramate from the body.

Supportive care—Treatment should be appropriately supportive. Patients in whom intentional overdose is confirmed or suspected should be referred for psychiatric consultation.

Patient Consultation

As an aid to patient consultation, refer to *Advice for the Patient, Topiramate (Systemic).*

In providing consultation, consider emphasizing the following selected information (» = major clinical significance)

Before using this medication

» Conditions affecting use, especially:
Hypersensitivity to topiramate or any component of the product
Pregnancy—In animal studies, topiramate has demonstrated selective developmental toxicity, including teratogenicity
Use in children—Topiramate is not approved for migraine headache prevention in pediatric patients. Oligohidrosis, sometimes resulting in heat stroke and hospitalization, and hyperthermia have been reported in pediatric patients after receiving topiramate for seizure treatment.
Other medications, especially anticholinergics, carbamazepine, carbonic anhydrase inhibitors, oral estrogen-containing contraceptives, phenytoin, or valproic acid
Other medical problems, especially diarrhea, hemodialysis, hepatic function impairment, history of renal calculi, ketogenic diet, renal disease, renal function impairment, severe respiratory disorder, status epilepticus, or surgery

Proper use of this medication

» Compliance with therapy; taking every day exactly as directed
Not breaking tablets, due to the bitter taste
Swallowing the sprinkle capsule formulation whole, or opening and sprinkling contents on soft food

» Proper dosing
Missed dose: Taking as soon as possible; not taking if almost time for next dose; not doubling doses

» Proper storage

Precautions while using this medication

» Importance of regular visits to physician to check progress of therapy

» Caution when driving, using machines, or doing other jobs requiring alertness

» Discussing alcohol use or use of other CNS depressants with physician

» Using alternative contraceptive method or additional means of birth control with oral estrogen-containing contraceptives

» Caution during exercise or hot weather; overheating may result in heat stroke

» Importance of telling your doctor if you have blurred vision or eye pain

» Checking with physician immediately if a child taking topiramate is not sweating as usual

» Importance of contacting doctor immediately if symptoms of metabolic acidosis including hyperventilation, fatigue, anorexia, cardiac arrhythmias or stupor occur

» Importance of adequate fluid intake during therapy to help prevent kidney stone formation

» Not discontinuing topiramate abruptly; checking with physician about gradually reducing dosage before stopping completely

Side/adverse effects

Signs of potential side effects, especially acute myopia and secondary angle closure glaucoma asthenia, ataxia, confusion, difficulty with concentration or attention, diplopia or other vision problems, dizziness, dysmenorrhea or other menstrual changes, fatigue, memory problems, acute myopia and secondary angle closure glaucoma, nervousness, nystagmus, paresthesia, psychomotor retardation, somnolence, speech or language problems, abdominal pain, anorexia, chills, gingivitis, hypoesthesia, leukopenia, mood or mental changes, pharyngitis, weight loss, anemia, conjunctivitis, dyspnea, edema, epistaxis, eye pain, hematuria, impotence or decreased libido, pruritus, renal calculi, skin rash, tinnitus, and urinary problems

Signs of potential side effects observed during clinical practice, especially erythema multiforme, hepatic failure, hepatitis, pancreatitis, pemphigus, renal tubular acidosis, Stevens-Johnson syndrome or toxic epidermal necrolysis

Taste perversion may be of concern to the patient, but usually does not require medical attention

General Dosing Information

In the controlled trials, there was no correlation between trough plasma concentrations of topiramate and clinical efficacy; thus, monitoring of topiramate plasma concentrations to optimize therapy is not necessary.

Dosage adjustments may be required when topiramate is added to or withdrawn from antiepileptic dosing regimens. Similarly, when other agents are added to or withdrawn from a regimen that includes topiramate, dosage adjustments may be necessary (see *Drug Interactions* section).

Antiepileptic medications, including topiramate, should be withdrawn gradually to minimize the potential of increased seizure frequency.

Patients, particularly those with predisposing factors, should be instructed to maintain an adequate fluid intake in order to minimize the risk of renal stone formation.

Because of the bitter taste, tablets should not be broken.

Diet/Nutrition

Topiramate may be taken without regard to meals.

The capsules may be swallowed whole, or opened and the contents sprinkled on a small amount (teaspoon) of soft food (such as applesauce, custard, ice cream, oatmeal, pudding, or yogurt) and swallowed, not chewed, immediately after preparation.

Bioequivalence information

The sprinkle capsule formulation is bioequivalent to the immediate-release tablet.

Oral Dosage Forms

TOPIRAMATE TABLETS

Usual adult dose

Epilepsy (treatment)—

Oral, recommended total daily dose of 400 mg per day administered in two divided doses. The dose should be achieved by titrating according to the following schedule

	Morning Dose	Evening Dose
Week 1	25 mg	25 mg
Week 2	50 mg	50 mg
Week 3	75 mg	75 mg
Week 4	100 mg	100 mg
Week 5	150 mg	150 mg
Week 6	200 mg	200 mg

Epilepsy (treatment adjunct)—

Oral, 400 mg a day, administered in two divided doses. Dosage should be initiated at 25 to 50 mg a day for the first week, and increased at weekly intervals by 25 to 50 mg a day until an effective dose is reached. Titrating in increments of 25 mg per week may delay time to reach an effective dose.

Note: A daily dose of 200 mg has inconsistent effects and is less effective than 400 mg a day. Doses above 400 mg a day have not been shown to improve responses.

Migraine headache (prophylaxis)[1]—

Oral, recommended total daily dose of 100 mg per day administered in two divided doses. Recommended titration rate to 100 mg per day of topiramate is as follows:

	Morning Dose	Evening Dose
Week 1	None	25 mg
Week 2	25 mg	25 mg
Week 3	25 mg	50 mg
Week 4	50 mg	50 mg

If required, longer intervals between dose adjustments can be used. Dose and titration should be guided by clinical outcome.

Note: In patients with renal function impairment, one half of the usual adult dose is recommended. These patients will require a longer time to reach steady-state plasma concentrations at each dose. Similarly, patients with hepatic function impairment may have increased topiramate plasma concentrations, and dosage adjustments may be needed.

In patients undergoing hemodialysis, topiramate is cleared by hemodialysis at a rate four to six times greater than in a normal individual. Prolonged periods of dialysis may decrease topiramate concentrations below levels required to maintain seizure control. To avoid rapid decreases in topiramate plasma concentrations during hemodialysis, a supplemental topiramate dose may be required. The duration of dialysis, the clearance rate of the dialysis system employed, and the effective renal clearance of topiramate in the dialysis patient, should be considered when making dosage adjustments.

Usual adult prescribing limits

Epilepsy: 1600 mg per day

Usual pediatric dose

Safety and efficacy below the age of 2 have not been established.

Anticonvulsant—

Oral, 5 to 9 milligrams/kilogram (mg/kg) per day administered in two divided doses. Dosage should be initiated at 25 mg nightly for the first week, and increased at 1 or 2 week intervals by 1 to 3 mg/kg per day administered in two divided doses until an effective dose is reached.

Migraine headache (prophylaxis)[1]—

Safety and efficacy have not been established.

Usual geriatric dose

See *Usual adult dose.*

Strength(s) usually available

U.S.—

25 mg (Rx) [*Topamax* (coated tablets; lactose monohydrate; pregelatinized starch; microcrystalline cellulose; sodium starch glycolate; magnesium stearate; purified water; carnauba wax; hypromellose; titanium dioxide; polyethylene glycol; polysorbate 80)].

50 mg (Rx) [*Topamax* (coated tablets; lactose monohydrate; pregelatinized starch; microcrystalline cellulose; sodium starch glycolate; magnesium stearate; purified water; carnauba wax; hypromellose; titanium dioxide; polyethylene glycol; polysorbate 80)].

100 mg (Rx) [*Topamax* (coated tablets; lactose monohydrate; pregelatinized starch; microcrystalline cellulose; sodium starch glycolate; magnesium stearate; purified water; carnauba wax; hypromellose; titanium dioxide; polyethylene glycol; synthetic iron oxide; polysorbate 80)].

200 mg (Rx) [*Topamax* (coated tablets; lactose monohydrate; pregelatinized starch; microcrystalline cellulose; sodium starch glycolate; magnesium stearate; purified water; carnauba wax; hypromellose; titanium dioxide; polyethylene glycol; synthetic iron oxide; polysorbate 80)].

Canada—

25 mg (Rx) [*Topamax* (coated tablets; lactose monohydrate; pregelatinized starch; microcrystalline cellulose; sodium starch glycolate; magnesium stearate; purified water; carnauba wax; hydroxypropyl methylcellulose; titanium dioxide; polyethylene glycol; polysorbate 80; and may contain synthetic iron oxide)].

100 mg (Rx) [*Topamax* (coated tablets; lactose monohydrate; pregelatinized starch; microcrystalline cellulose; sodium starch glycolate; magnesium stearate; purified water; carnauba wax; hydroxypropyl methylcellulose; titanium dioxide; polyethylene glycol; synthetic iron oxide; polysorbate 80)].

200 mg (Rx) [*Topamax* (coated tablets; lactose monohydrate; pregelatinized starch; microcrystalline cellulose; sodium starch glycolate; magnesium stearate; purified water; carnauba wax; hydroxy-

propyl methylcellulose; titanium dioxide; polyethylene glycol; synthetic iron oxide; polysorbate 80)].

Packaging and storage

Store tablets in tightly closed containers between 15 and 30 °C (59 and 86 °F). Protect from moisture.

Auxiliary labeling

- May cause drowsiness.
- Avoid alcoholic beverages.
- Do not break tablets.

TOPIRAMATE CAPSULES

Usual adult dose

See *Topiramate Tablets.*

Usual pediatric dose

See *Topiramate Tablets.*

Usual geriatric dose

See *Topiramate Tablets.*

Strength(s) usually available

U.S.—

15 mg (Rx) [*Topamax* (Sprinkle capsules; sucrose and starch sugar spheres; povidone; cellulose acetate; gelatin; silicone dioxide; sodium lauryl sulfate; titanium dioxide; black pharmaceutical ink)].

25 mg (Rx) [*Topamax* (Sprinkle capsules; sucrose and starch sugar spheres; povidone; cellulose acetate; gelatin; silicone dioxide; sodium lauryl sulfate; titanium dioxide; black pharmaceutical ink)].

Canada—

15 mg (Rx) [*Topamax* (Sprinkle capsules; sucrose and starch sugar spheres; povidone; cellulose acetate; gelatin; silicone dioxide; sodium lauryl sulfate; titanium dioxide; black pharmaceutical ink)].

25 mg (Rx) [*Topamax* (Sprinkle capsules; sucrose and starch sugar spheres; povidone; cellulose acetate; gelatin; silicone dioxide; sodium lauryl sulfate; titanium dioxide; black pharmaceutical ink)].

Packaging and storage

Store sprinkle capsules at or below 25 °C (77 °F). Protect from moisture.

Auxiliary labeling

- May cause drowsiness.
- Avoid alcoholic beverages.
- Sprinkle capsule contents on a small amount of food or swallow whole

[1]Not included in Canadian product labeling.

Revised: 10/17/2005

TOPOTECAN Systemic

VA CLASSIFICATION (Primary): AN900

Commonly used brand name(s): *Hycamtin.*

Note: For a listing of dosage forms and brand names by country availability, see *Dosage Forms* section(s).

Category

Antineoplastic.

Indications

Note: Bracketed information in the *Indications* section refers to uses that are not included in U.S. product labeling.

Accepted

Carcinoma, ovarian (treatment)—Topotecan is indicated for the treatment of metastatic ovarian carcinoma after failure of first-line or subsequent chemotherapy.

Carcinoma, lung, small cell (SCLC) (treatment)—Topotecan is indicated for the treatment of SCLC in patients who have responded to chemotherapy with other agents and who have relapsed more than 2 or 3 months after completion of chemotherapy.

[Carcinoma, lung, non-small cell (NSCLC) (treatment)][1]—Topotecan is indicated for the treatment of NSCLC (Evidence rating: IIIA). Topotecan is not recommended as first-line therapy, but may be considered for use at a later point in the management of patients with this disease.

[Myelodysplastic syndrome (treatment)][1]—Topotecan is indicated, alone or as part of a combination regimen containing cytarabine and/or amifostine, for the treatment of myelodysplastic syndromes (MDS). There was not a clear consensus by the USP medical experts, regarding combination use with amifostine. Some of the experts are hesitant about the use of amifostine and suggest reserving amifostine combination regimens for salvage treatment. Individual case factors (e.g., International Prognostic Scoring System [IPSS] risk group, patient characteristics, etc.) be considered when choosing an appropriate treatment (Evidence rating: II/IIID). Preliminary evidence indicates that topotecan may correct genetic abnormalities and prolong survival in patients with these diseases, for whom treatment options are limited.

[Chronic myelomonocytic leukemia (CMML) (treatment)][1]—Topotecan is indicated, alone or in combination with cytarabine for the treatment of CMML(Evidence rating: IIID). Preliminary evidence indicates that topotecan may correct genetic abnormalities and prolong survival in patients with this disease, for whom treatment options are limited.

Acceptance not established

Use of topotecan for the first-line treatment of small cell lung carcinoma has not been established.

Use of topotecan for the treatment of acute leukemias, including lymphocytic, lymphoblastic, and myeloid forms, has not been established.

Use of topotecan for the treatment of cervical carcinoma has not been established, due to insufficient data supporting efficacy.

Use of topotecan for the treatment of endometrial carcinoma has not been established, due to insufficient data supporting efficacy and safety.

[1]Not included in Canadian product labeling.

Pharmacology/Pharmacokinetics

Physicochemical characteristics

Source—Semisynthetic analog of camptothecin, a plant alkaloid obtained from the *Camptotheca acuminata* tree.

Molecular weight—457.92.

pH—After reconstitution, topotecan injection has a pH of 2.5 to 3.5.

Solubility—Soluble in water.

Mechanism of action/Effect

Topotecan inhibits the action of topoisomerase I, an enzyme essential for cell growth and proliferation. Topoisomerase I produces single strand breaks in DNA, thereby relieving torsional strain and allowing DNA replication to proceed, then repairs the strand. Topotecan binds to the topoisomerase I–DNA complex and prevents religation of the DNA strand, resulting in double strand DNA breakage and cell death.

Distribution

Topotecan is evenly distributed between plasma and blood cells. Significant quantities of topotecan are distributed into cerebrospinal fluid.

Volume of distribution—130 liters; decreased by approximately 25% in patients with moderate renal function impairment (creatinine clearance 20 to 39 mL per minute [mL/min]).

Protein binding

Moderate (35%).

Biotransformation

Topotecan undergoes reversible, pH-dependent hydrolysis of the active lactone moiety, forming an open-ring hydroxyacid, which is inactive. Whereas only the lactone form is present at pH $\leq$ 4, the hydroxyacid form predominates at physiologic pH.

Relatively small quantities of topotecan are metabolized via hepatic microsomal enzymes to an *N*-demethylated derivative. Neither the lactone nor the hydroxyacid form of topotecan is metabolized to a significant extent.

Half-life

Terminal—

Normal renal and hepatic function: Approximately 2 to 3 hours.

Moderate renal function impairment (creatinine clearance 20 to 39 mL/min): Approximately 5 hours.

Hepatic function impairment: May be increased slightly.

Onset of action

Tumor responses were observed at a median of 9 to 12 weeks (range, approximately 3 to 24 weeks) in clinical trials.

Serum concentration

Total exposure (as indicated by the area under the concentration-time curve [AUC]) is approximately proportional to the administered dose.

Elimination

Renal; approximately 30% of a dose. Some topotecan is also eliminated via the biliary route.

Plasma clearance—

Normal renal and hepatic function: Approximately 1030 mL/min; approximately 24% higher in males than in females because of differences in body size. Studies in female patients have not shown significant age-related differences in clearance.

Renal function impairment:

Mild (creatinine clearance 40 to 60 mL/min)—Decreased by approximately 33%.

Moderate (creatinine clearance 20 to 39 mL/min)—Decreased by approximately 66%.

Hepatic function impairment (serum bilirubin 1.7 to 15 mg per deciliter): Decreased by approximately 33%.

Precautions to Consider

Carcinogenicity

Secondary malignancies are potential delayed effects of many antineoplastic agents, although it is not clear whether the effect is related to their mutagenic or immunosuppressive action. The effect of dose and duration of therapy is also unknown, although risk seems to increase with long-term use. There is some evidence linking therapy with topoisomerase I inhibitors such as topotecan to the development of acute leukemias associated with specific chromosomal translocations.

Long-term animal studies to evaluate the carcinogenic potential of topotecan have not been done. However, topotecan is genotoxic to mammalian cells and is a probable carcinogen.

Mutagenicity

In vitro studies have shown that topotecan, with or without metabolic activation, is mutagenic to L5178Y mouse lymphoma cells and clastogenic to cultured human lymphocytes. In an *in vivo* study, clastogenicity was also demonstrated in mouse bone marrow cells. However, topotecan did not cause mutations in bacterial cells.

Pregnancy/Reproduction

Fertility—Administration of 0.23 mg of topotecan per kg of body weight (mg/kg) per day to rats (equivalent to the recommended human dose on a mg per square meter of body surface area [mg/m^2] basis) from day 14 prior to conception through day 6 of gestation caused fetal resorptions and pre-implant losses.

Pregnancy—Studies in humans have not been done.

It is usually recommended that use of antineoplastics, especially combination chemotherapy, be avoided whenever possible, especially during the first trimester. Although information is limited because of the relatively few instances of antineoplastic therapy during pregnancy, the mutagenic, teratogenic, and carcinogenic potential of these medications must be considered.

Other potential hazards to the fetus include adverse reactions seen in adults.

In general, use of a contraceptive is recommended during therapy with cytotoxic medications.

Administration to rabbits of 0.1 mg/kg of topotecan per day (equivalent to the recommended human dose on a mg/m^2 basis) on days 6 through 20 of gestation resulted in maternal and fetal toxicity (diminished fetal body weight and embryolethality). Also, administration to rats of 0.23 mg/kg per day (equivalent to the recommended human dose on a mg/m^2 basis) from 14 days prior to conception through day 6 of gestation caused microphthalmia and mild maternal toxicity, and administration to rats of 0.1 mg/kg per day (approximately one half the recommended human dose on a mg/m^2 basis) from days 6 through 17 of gestation caused increases in post-implantation mortality and malformations of the eye (microphthalmia, anophthalmia, rosette formation of the retina, coloboma of the retina, ectopic orbit), brain (dilated lateral and third ventricles), skull, and vertebrae.

FDA Pregnancy Category D.

Breast-feeding

Although very little information is available regarding distribution of antineoplastic agents into breast milk, breast-feeding is not recommended while topotecan is being administered because of the risks to the infant (adverse effects, mutagenicity, carcinogenicity). It is not known whether topotecan is distributed into breast milk.

Pediatrics

Topotecan has been studied in a limited number of pediatric patients. One dose-finding study has shown that severe topotecan-induced myelotoxicity may occur at lower doses in children than in adults. Safety and efficacy have not been established.

Geriatrics

Clinical trials with topotecan have included patients 65 years of age and older. No geriatrics-specific problems have been documented to date. Pharmacokinetic studies have not been performed specifically in elderly individuals, but studies in female patients did not identify age as a significant factor in topotecan clearance. Dosage adjustment on the basis of advanced age is not necessary. However, elderly patients are more likely to have age-related renal function impairment, which may require dosage adjustment in patients receiving topotecan.

Dental

The bone marrow depressant effects of topotecan may result in an increased incidence of microbial infection, delayed healing, and gingival bleeding. Dental work, whenever possible, should be completed prior to initiation of therapy or deferred until blood counts have returned to normal. Patients should be instructed in proper oral hygiene during treatment, including caution in use of regular toothbrushes, dental floss, and toothpicks.

Topotecan may cause stomatitis, which is usually mild. In clinical trials, stomatitis occurred in 24% of the patients. The incidences of grade 3 and grade 4 stomatitis were 2% and < 1%, respectively.

Drug interactions and/or related problems

The following drug interactions and/or related problems have been selected on the basis of their potential clinical significance (possible mechanism in parentheses where appropriate)—not necessarily inclusive (» = major clinical significance):

Note: Combinations containing any of the following medications, depending on the amount present, may also interact with this medication.

Blood dyscrasia-causing medications (see *Appendix II*)
(leukopenic and/or thrombocytopenic effects of topotecan may be increased with concurrent or recent therapy if these medications cause the same effects; dosage adjustment of topotecan, if necessary, should be based on blood counts)

» Bone marrow depressants, other (see *Appendix II*) or
» Radiation therapy
(additive bone marrow depression may occur; dosage reduction may be required when two or more bone marrow depressants, including radiation, are used concurrently or consecutively)
(in a dose-finding study, concurrent use of topotecan and cisplatin caused unexpectedly severe myelosuppression and grade 3 or 4 nonhematologic effects, such as diarrhea, nausea, vomiting, and lethargy, without providing increased benefit over established regimens. A safe and effective regimen utilizing topotecan and cisplatin has not been established)

Filgrastim (rG-CSF)
(filgrastim may be used to decrease the incidence and shorten the duration of severe topotecan-induced neutropenia; however, filgrastim treatment must be started no sooner than 24 hours after the last dose of topotecan in a cycle because concurrent use of the two medications may actually prolong the duration of topotecan-induced neutropenia)

» Immunosuppressants, other, such as:
Azathioprine
Chlorambucil
Corticosteroids, glucocorticoid
Cyclophosphamide
Cyclosporine
Mercaptopurine
Muromonab CD-3
Tacrolimus
(concurrent use with topotecan may increase the risk of infection)

Probenecid
(in a study in mice, probenecid decreased renal clearance of topotecan by 50% and significantly increased systemic exposure to the medication, as demonstrated by an increase in the area under the topotecan concentration-time curve [AUC]; the possibility of a similar effect in humans leading to a higher risk of severe topotecan-induced myelotoxicity should be considered)

Vaccines, killed virus
(because normal defense mechanisms may be suppressed by topotecan therapy, the patient's antibody response to the vaccine may be decreased. The interval between discontinuation of medications that cause immunosuppression and restoration of the patient's ability to respond to the vaccine depends on the intensity and type of immunosuppression-causing medication used, the underlying disease, and other factors; estimates vary from 3 months to 1 year)

» Vaccines, live virus
(because normal defense mechanisms may be suppressed by topotecan therapy, concurrent use with a live virus vaccine may potentiate the replication of the vaccine virus, may increase the side/adverse effects of the vaccine virus, and/or may decrease the patient's antibody response to the vaccine; immunization of these patients should be undertaken only with extreme caution after careful review of the patient's hematologic status and only with the knowledge and consent of the physician managing the topotecan therapy. The interval between discontinuation of medications that cause immunosuppression and restoration of the patient's ability to respond to the vaccine depends on the intensity and type of

immunosuppression-causing medication used, the underlying disease, and other factors; estimates vary from 3 months to 1 year. In addition, immunization with oral poliovirus vaccine should be postponed in persons in close contact with the patient, especially family members)

Laboratory value alterations

The following have been selected on the basis of their potential clinical significance (possible effect in parentheses where appropriate)—not necessarily inclusive (» = major clinical significance).

With physiology/laboratory test values

Alanine aminotransferase (ALT [SGPT]) and
Alkaline phosphatase and
Aspartate aminotransferase (AST [SGOT]) and
Bilirubin concentration, serum
(values may be increased; in clinical trials, transient grade 1 increases in aminotransferase values, and grade 3 or 4 elevations of aminotransferase values, and grade 3 or 4 increases in bilirubin concentration occurred in 5%, < 1%, and < 3%, respectively, of the patients)

» Hematocrit/hemoglobin values and
» Leukocyte, especially neutrophil, count and
» Platelet count
(may be decreased; hematocrit or hemoglobin values, neutrophil count, and platelet count usually reach their nadirs at medians of 15, 11, and 15 days, respectively, after a treatment. The median durations of grade 3 or 4 anemia, neutropenia, and thrombocytopenia are generally 7, 7, and 5 days, respectively)

Medical considerations/Contraindications

The medical considerations/contraindications included have been selected on the basis of their potential clinical significance (reasons given in parentheses where appropriate)—not necessarily inclusive (» = major clinical significance).

Except under special circumstances, this medication should not be used when the following medical problems exist:

» Bone marrow depression, pre-existing or treatment-related
(topotecan therapy should not be initiated if baseline neutrophil and platelet counts are lower than 1500 cells per cubic millimeter [cells/mm^3] and 100,000 cells/mm^3, respectively. Also, if severe topotecan-induced anemia, neutropenia, or thrombocytopenia occurs during treatment, subsequent courses of therapy should be delayed until the hemoglobin concentration recovers to 9 grams per deciliter [with transfusion, if necessary], neutrophil counts recover to > 1000 cells/mm^3, and platelet counts recover to > 100,000 cells/mm^3)

» Renal function impairment, severe (creatinine clearance less than 20 mL per minute)
(topotecan elimination will be greatly decreased, resulting in increased and prolonged plasma concentrations and half-life and an increased risk of toxicity; use in patients with severe renal function impairment is not recommended because a suitable dose for these patients has not been established)

Risk-benefit should be considered when the following medical problems exist:

» Chickenpox, existing or recent (including recent exposure) or
» Herpes zoster
(risk of severe, generalized disease)

» Hypersensitivity to topotecan

» Infection, pre-existing
(recovery may be impaired)

» Renal function impairment, moderate (creatinine clearance 20 to 39 mL per minute)
(topotecan elimination will be decreased by approximately 66%, resulting in increased and prolonged plasma concentrations and half-life and an increased risk of toxicity; a 50% reduction in dose is recommended for patients with moderate renal function impairment)

» Caution should also be used in patients who have had previous cytotoxic drug therapy or radiation therapy

Patient monitoring

The following may be especially important in patient monitoring (other tests may be warranted in some patients, depending on condition; » = major clinical significance):

» Hematocrit or hemoglobin and
» Leukocyte count, total and differential and
» Platelet count
(determinations recommended prior to initiation of therapy and at frequent intervals during therapy; topotecan therapy should not be initiated if baseline neutrophil and platelet counts are lower than 1500 cells/mm^3 and 100,000 cells/mm^3, respectively. Also, if severe topotecan-induced anemia, neutropenia, or thrombocytopenia occurs during treatment, subsequent courses of therapy should be delayed until the hemoglobin concentration recovers to 9 grams per deciliter [with transfusion, if necessary], neutrophil counts recover to > 1000 cells/mm^3, and platelet counts recover to > 100,000 cells/mm^3. A reduction in dose or administration of a colony stimulating factor [e.g., filgrastim] is recommended for subsequent courses of therapy if severe neutropenia occurs)

Side/Adverse Effects

The following side/adverse effects have been selected on the basis of their potential clinical significance (possible signs and symptoms in parentheses where appropriate)—not necessarily inclusive:

Those indicating need for medical attention

Incidence more frequent

Anemia (unusual tiredness or weakness); ***dyspnea*** (shortness of breath or troubled breathing); ***fever***—not necessarily associated with neutropenia; ***leukopenia or neutropenia, with or without infection (febrile neutropenia)*** (fever or chills; cough or hoarseness; lower back or side pain; painful or difficult urination)—usually asymptomatic; ***thrombocytopenia*** (unusual bleeding or bruising; black, tarry stools; blood in urine or stools; pinpoint red spots on skin)—usually asymptomatic

Note: *Anemia* may be severe; red blood cell transfusions were required by 56% of patients in clinical trials. The red blood cell nadir occurred at a median of 15 days, and the median duration of grade 3 or 4 anemia was 7 days.

Neutropenia, the dose-limiting toxicity associated with topotecan therapy, is dose-related and not cumulative. In clinical trials, neutrophil counts of <1500 cells per cubic millimeter (cells/mm^3) and < 500 cells/mm^3 occurred in 98% and 81%, respectively, of the patients, and febrile neutropenia (grade 4 neutropenia with fever and/or infection) occurred in 26%. The neutrophil nadir occurred at a median of 11 days. Severe neutropenia occurred primarily during the first course of therapy (filgrastim was not used until after the first cycle) and lasted for a median of 7 days.

In clinical trials, platelet count nadirs occurred at a median of 15 days, and *thrombocytopenia* lasted for a median of 5 days. Platelet transfusions were required by 13% of patients. There have been rare reports (postmarketing) of severe bleeding associated with topotecan-induced thrombocytopenia.

Incidence rare

Allergic reactions, including anaphylactoid reactions (changes in facial skin color; skin rash, hives, and/or itching; fast or irregular breathing; puffiness or swelling of the eyelids or around the eyes; shortness of breath, troubled breathing, tightness in chest, and/or wheezing); ***angioedema*** (large, hive-like swellings on face, eyelids, mouth, lips, and/or tongue); ***and dermatitis, severe*** (skin rash and/or itching, severe)

Those indicating need for medical attention only if they continue or are bothersome

Incidence more frequent

Abdominal pain; anorexia (loss of appetite); ***constipation; diarrhea; fatigue; headache; nausea or vomiting; neurological effects, including asthenia*** (muscle weakness); ***or paresthesia*** (burning or tingling in hands or feet); ***stomatitis*** (sores, ulcers, or white spots on lips or tongue or inside the mouth)

Incidence unknown

Bruising or redness at place of injection—if extravasation occurs

Those not indicating need for medical attention

Incidence more frequent

Alopecia (loss of hair)

Overdose

For more information on the management of overdose or unintentional ingestion, **contact a Poison Control Center** (see *Poison Control Center Listing*).

Clinical effects of overdose

The following effects have been selected on the basis of their potential clinical significance (possible signs and symptoms in parentheses where appropriate)—not necessarily inclusive:

Acute and chronic

Bone marrow suppression, including anemia (unusual tiredness or weakness); ***leukopenia or neutropenia, including febrile neutropenia*** (fever with or without chills; cough or hoarseness; lower back or side pain; painful or difficult urination); ***and/or thrombocytopenia*** (black, tarry stools; blood in urine or stools; pinpoint red spots on skin; unusual bleeding or bruising)

Treatment of overdose

It is recommended that the patient be hospitalized for close monitoring of vital functions and treatment of observed effects. Severe bone marrow depression may require transfusion of required blood components. Febrile neutropenia should be treated empirically with broad-spectrum antibiotics, pending bacterial cultures and appropriate diagnostic tests.

Patient Consultation

As an aid to patient consultation, refer to *Advice for the Patient, Topotecan (Systemic).*

In providing consultation, consider emphasizing the following selected information (» = major clinical significance):

Before using this medication

» Conditions affecting use, especially:

Hypersensitivity to topotecan

Pregnancy—Use is not recommended because of embryotoxic, fetotoxic, and carcinogenic potential; advisability of using contraception; informing physician immediately if pregnancy is suspected

Breast-feeding—Not recommended because of potential serious adverse effects

Other medications, especially other bone marrow depressants and immunosuppressants, and radiation therapy

Other medical problems, especially chickenpox, herpes zoster, pre-existing infection, and renal function impairment

Proper use of this medication

Frequency of nausea and vomiting; importance of continuing treatment despite stomach upset

» Proper dosing

Precautions while using this medication

» Importance of close monitoring by the physician

» Avoiding immunizations unless approved by physician; other persons in patient's household should avoid immunizations with oral poliovirus vaccine; avoiding other persons who have taken oral poliovirus vaccine or wearing a protective mask that covers nose and mouth

Caution if bone marrow depression occurs:

» Avoiding exposure to persons with infections, especially during periods of low blood counts; checking with physician immediately if fever with or without chills, cough or hoarseness, lower back or side pain, or painful or difficult urination occurs

» Checking with physician immediately if unusual bleeding or bruising; black, tarry stools; blood in urine or stools; or pinpoint red spots on skin occur

Caution in use of regular toothbrush, dental floss, or toothpick; physician, dentist, or nurse may suggest alternatives; checking with physician before having dental work done

Not touching eyes or inside of nose unless hands washed immediately before

Using caution to avoid accidental cuts when using sharp objects such as safety razor or fingernail or toenail cutters

Avoiding contact sports or other situations where bruising or injury could occur

Side/adverse effects

May cause adverse effects such as blood problems; importance of discussing possible effects with physician

Signs of potential side effects, especially anemia, dyspnea, fever, febrile neutropenia, thrombocytopenia, and allergic reactions

Some side effects may be asymptomatic, including anemia, leukopenia or neutropenia, and thrombocytopenia

Physician or nurse can help in dealing with side effects

Possibility of hair loss; regrowth should return after treatment has ended

General Dosing Information

Topotecan should be administered only under the supervision of a physician experienced in cancer chemotherapy. Adequate facilities and medications for diagnosis and treatment of complications should be readily available.

Topotecan is to be administered only by intravenous infusion.

A reduction in subsequent doses is recommended for patients who develop severe neutropenia (neutrophil count < 500 cells per cubic millimeter) that persists for 7 days or more. Alternatively, a colony stimulating factor (e.g., filgrastim) may be administered during subsequent cycles, starting at least 24 hours after the last dose of topotecan (i.e, on day 6 of the cycle).

Patients who develop leukopenia should be observed carefully for signs and symptoms of infection. Antibiotic support may be required. In neutropenic patients who develop fever, broad-spectrum antibiotic coverage should be initiated empirically, pending bacterial cultures and appropriate diagnostic tests.

Special precautions are recommended for patients who develop thrombocytopenia as a result of topotecan therapy. These may include extreme care in performing invasive procedures; regular inspection of intravenous access sites, skin (including perirectal area), and mucous membrane surfaces for signs of bleeding or bruising; testing urine, emesis, stool, and secretions for occult blood; care in use of regular toothbrushes, dental floss, toothpicks, safety razors, and fingernail and toenail cutters; avoiding constipation; and using caution to prevent falls and other injuries. Such patients should avoid alcohol and aspirin intake because of the risk of gastrointestinal bleeding. Platelet transfusions may be required.

Safety considerations for handling this medication

There is limited but increasing evidence and concern that personnel involved in preparation and administration of parenteral antineoplastics may be at some risk because of the potential mutagenicity, teratogenicity, and/or carcinogenicity of these agents, although the actual risk is unknown. USP advisory panels recommend cautious handling both in preparation and disposal of antineoplastic agents. Precautions that have been suggested include:

- Use of a biological containment cabinet during reconstitution and dilution of parenteral medications and wearing of disposable surgical gloves and masks.
- Use of proper technique to prevent contamination of the medication, work area, and operator during transfer between containers (including proper training of personnel in this technique).
- Cautious and proper disposal of needles, syringes, vials, ampuls, and unused medication.

A number of medical centers have developed detailed guidelines for handling of antineoplastic agents.

If topotecan comes into contact with the skin, the skin should be washed immediately and thoroughly with soap and water. If the medication comes into contact with a mucous membrane, the area should be immediately and thoroughly flushed with water.

Parenteral Dosage Forms

Note: Topotecan for injection contains topotecan hydrochloride. However, dosing and strengths are expressed in terms of topotecan base.

Bracketed information in the *Dosage Forms* section refers to uses that are not included in U.S. product labeling.

TOPOTECAN FOR INJECTION

Usual adult dose

Carcinoma, ovarian or

[Carcinoma, lung, non-small cell][1]—

Intravenous infusion (over thirty minutes), 1.5 mg (base) per square meter of body surface area per day for five consecutive days, repeated every twenty-one days.

Carcinoma, lung, small cell—

Intravenous infusion (over thirty minutes), 1.25 to 2 (usually 1.5) mg per square meter of body surface area per day for five consecutive days, repeated every twenty-one days.

[Myelodysplastic syndrome][1]—

Intravenous infusion, 2 mg per square meter of body surface area per day as a twenty-four-hour continuous intravenous infusion for five consecutive days every three to four weeks until remission, then once a month. Consult medical literature and/or experts in the field of hematology/oncology for specific information on dosage in combination regimens.

[Chronic myelomonocytic leukemia][1]—

Intravenous infusion, 2 mg per square meter of body surface area per day as a twenty-four-hour continuous intravenous infusion for five consecutive days every three to four weeks until remission, then once a month.

Note: For patients with moderate renal function impairment (creatinine clearance 20 to 39 mL per minute), a reduction in dose to 0.75 mg (base) per square meter of body surface area is recommended. Adjustment of topotecan dosage is generally not required for patients with mild renal function impairment (creatinine clearance 40 to 60 mL per minute) or patients with hepatic function impairment (serum bilirubin concentration between 1.5 and 10 mg per deciliter).

If severe neutropenia occurs and persists for more than seven days, dosage for subsequent cycles should be reduced by 0.25 mg (base) per square meter of body surface area or therapy with a colony stimulating factor initiated no sooner than twenty-four hours after the last dose of topotecan.

Topotecan treatment should be continued for a minimum of four cycles. In clinical studies, the median time to response was nine to twelve weeks. Responses may be missed if therapy is discontinued prematurely.

Usual pediatric dose
Safety and efficacy have not been established.

Usual geriatric dose
See *Usual adult dose.*

Strength(s) usually available
U.S.—
4 mg (base) (Rx) [*Hycamtin* (mannitol 48 mg; tartaric acid 20 mg; hydrochloric acid and/or sodium hydroxide if needed to adjust pH)].

Canada—
4 mg (base) (Rx) [*Hycamtin* (mannitol 48 mg; tartaric acid 20 mg; hydrochloric acid and/or sodium hydroxide if needed to adjust pH)].

Packaging and storage
Store between 20 and 25 °C (68 and 77 °F), protected from light, unless otherwise specified by manufacturer.

Preparation of dosage form
Topotecan for injection is reconstituted for intravenous use by adding 4 mL of sterile water for injection to the vial. The resulting yellow to yellow-green solution will contain 1 mg per mL. An appropriate volume of the injection should be further diluted with 5% dextrose injection or 0.9% sodium chloride injection. Final concentrations and volumes of 20 to 200 mcg per mL in 50 to 100 mL of diluent have been recommended.

Stability
Although topotecan for injection is stable after reconstitution, it contains no antimicrobial agent and preferably should be used immediately. However, the reconstituted injection may be stored in a refrigerator for up to 24 hours, if necessary. After further dilution for intravenous infusion, the product is stable for up to 24 hours when stored between 20 and 25 °C (68 and 77 °F).

---

[1]Not included in Canadian product labeling.

Selected Bibliography

ten Bokkel Huinink W, Carmichael J, et al. Efficacy and safety of topotecan in the treatment of advanced ovarian carcinoma. Semin Oncol 1997; 24 Suppl 5: S5-19–S5-25.

ten Bokkel Huinink W, Gore M, Carmichael J, et al. Topotecan versus paclitaxel for the treatment of recurrent epithelial ovarian cancer. J Clin Oncol 1997; 15: 2183-93.

Revised: 02/25/2004

TOREMIFENE Systemic

VA CLASSIFICATION (Primary): AN500

Commonly used brand name(s): *Fareston.*

Note: For a listing of dosage forms and brand names by country availability, see *Dosage Forms* section(s).

Category
Antineoplastic.

Indications

Accepted
Carcinoma, breast (treatment)—Toremifene is indicated for treatment of metastatic breast cancer in postmenopausal women with estrogen-receptor–positive or unknown tumors.

Pharmacology/Pharmacokinetics

Physicochemical characteristics
Chemical Group—Nonsteroidal triphenylethylene derivative.
Molecular weight—Toremifene citrate: 598.1.
pKa—8.
Solubility—Water solubility at 37 °C is 0.63 mg per mL (mg/mL) and solubility in hydrochloric acid at 37 °C is 0.38 mg/mL.

Mechanism of action/Effect
Toremifene binds to estrogen receptors. Its effects are mainly antiestrogenic (as indicated by a decrease in the estradiol-induced vaginal cornification index in some postmenopausal women), but it also has some estrogenic effects (as indicated by a decrease in serum gonadotropin [follicle-stimulating hormone (FSH) and luteinizing hormone (LH)] concentrations). The antitumor effect in breast cancer is thought to be related primarily to its antiestrogenic effects (i.e., competition with estrogen for binding sites in the cancer), thereby blocking the growth-stimulating effects of estrogen in the tumor.

Absorption
Well absorbed; not affected by food.

Distribution
Apparent volume of distribution is 580 liters.

Protein binding
Very high (more than 99.5%), mainly to albumin.

Biotransformation
Hepatic, extensive, mainly by cytochrome CYP3A4 to *N*-demethyltoremifene, which has antiestrogenic effects but weak *in vivo* antitumor activity.

Half-life
Distribution—
Mean, about 4 hours.
Elimination—
Toremifene: About 5 days.
N-demethyltoremifene: 6 days.
Deaminohydroxy toremifene: 4 days.
Note: Enterohepatic recirculation contributes to the slow elimination of toremifene.

Note: Mean total clearance of toremifene is approximately 5 liters per hour.

Time to peak concentration
Plasma—Within 3 hours.

Note: Time to steady-state concentrations is about 4 to 6 weeks. Serum concentrations of *N*-demethyltoremifene, the main metabolite, are two to four times higher than those of toremifene at steady state.
Pharmacokinetics are linear after single oral doses of 10 to 680 mg; with multiple doses, dose proportionality occurs for doses of 10 to 400 mg.

Elimination
Fecal, as metabolites.
Renal, about 10% within 1 week.

Precautions to Consider

Carcinogenicity
Studies in rats at doses of 0.12 to 12 mg per kg of body weight per day (mg/kg per day) (about.01 to 1.5 times the daily maximum recommended human dose [MRHD] on a mg per square meter of body surface area [mg/m^2] basis) for up to 2 years did not find evidence of carcinogenicity. Studies in mice given doses of 1 to 30 mg/kg per day (about.07 to 2 times the daily MRHD on a mg/m^2 basis) for up to 2 years showed increased incidence of ovarian and testicular tumors, and an increased incidence of osteoma and osteosarcoma; the significance is uncertain because toremifene is predominantly estrogenic, rather than antiestrogenic, in mice.

Some patients treated with toremifene have developed endometrial cancer, but because of other factors present (short duration of treatment, prior antiestrogen therapy, premalignant conditions) a direct causal relationship has not been established.

Mutagenicity
Toremifene has not been found to be mutagenic in *in vitro* tests (Ames and *Escherichia coli* bacterial tests). It is clastogenic *in vitro* (chromosomal aberrations and micronuclei formation in human lymphoblastoid MCL-5 cells) and *in vivo* (chromosomal aberrations in rat hepatocytes). Use of ^{32}P post-labeling in liver DNA from rats given toremifene produced no detectable adduct formation compared with tamoxifen at similar doses. In addition, in a study in cultured human

lymphocytes, adducting activity of toremifene (detected using ^{32}P post-labeling) was approximately one sixth that of tamoxifen at approximately equipotent concentrations. In a study in salmon sperm, adducting activity of toremifene (detected using ^{32}P post-labeling) was one sixth and one fourth that observed with tamoxifen at equivalent concentrations following activation by rat and human microsomal systems, respectively. However, toremifene exposure is fourfold that of tamoxifen based on human area under the plasma concentration-time curve (AUC) in serum at recommended clinical doses.

Pregnancy/Reproduction

Fertility—Studies in male and female rats at doses of 25 and 0.14 mg per kg of body weight per day (mg/kg per day) (about 3.5 times and.02 the daily MRHD on a mg/m² basis) or higher, respectively, found impairment of fertility and conception. At these doses, atrophy of seminal vesicles and prostate were seen in males and sperm counts, fertility indices, and conception rates were reduced. In females, fertility and reproductive indices were reduced markedly with increased pre- and postimplantation loss. Reproductive indices were also depressed in offspring of treated rats. Studies in dogs showed that doses of 3 mg/kg per day (about 1.5 times the daily MRHD on a mg/m² basis) or higher for 16 weeks produced ovarian atrophy. Studies in monkeys for 52 weeks at doses of 1 mg/kg per day (about one fourth of the daily MRHD on a mg/m² basis) or higher found cystic ovaries and reduction in endometrial stromal cellularity.

Pregnancy—Studies in humans have not been done.

Studies in rats at doses of 1 mg/kg per day (about one fourth of the daily MRHD on a mg/m² basis) or higher given during the period of organogenesis found toremifene to be embryotoxic and fetotoxic, as indicated by intrauterine mortality, increased resorption, reduced fetal weight, and fetal anomalies (including malformation of limbs, incomplete ossification, misshapen bones, ribs/spine anomalies, hydroureter, hydronephrosis, testicular displacement, and subcutaneous edema). Fetal anomalies may be the result of maternal toxicity. Toremifene crosses the placenta and accumulates in the rodent fetus.

In rodent models of fetal reproductive tract development, toremifene inhibits uterine development in female pups in a manner similar to that of diethylstilbestrol and tamoxifen, although the clinical relevance of these effects is unknown.

Studies in rabbits at doses of 1.25 mg/kg per day and 2.5 mg/kg per day (about one third and two thirds of the daily MRHD on a mg/m² basis) found embryotoxicity and fetotoxicity, respectively. Fetal anomalies included incomplete ossification and anencephaly.

Women who are or may become pregnant should be advised of the potential risks to the fetus or the risk for loss of the pregnancy.

FDA Pregnancy Category D.

Breast-feeding

It is not known whether toremifene is distributed into breast milk. However, it is distributed into the milk of lactating rats.

Geriatrics

The median ages in controlled clinical trials of toremifene ranged from 60 to 66 years; no age-related differences in efficacy or safety were noted.

Drug interactions and/or related problems

The following drug interactions and/or related problems have been selected on the basis of their potential clinical significance (possible mechanism in parentheses where appropriate)—not necessarily inclusive (» = major clinical significance):

Note: Combinations containing any of the following medications, depending on the amount present, may also interact with this medication.

» Anticoagulants, coumarin-derivative
 (concurrent use may result in an increased prothrombin time)

» Cytochrome P450 3A4 enzyme inducers, such as:
 Carbamazepine
 Phenobarbital
 Phenytoin
 (may increase the rate of metabolism of toremifene, leading to lower steady-state serum concentrations)

Cytochrome P450 CYP3A4-6 inhibitors, such as:
 Erythromycin and similar macrolides
 Ketoconazole and similar antimycotics
 (theoretically may inhibit metabolism of toremifene; this interaction has not been studied)

Medications that decrease renal excretion of calcium, such as
 Diuretics, thiazide
 (risk of hypercalcemia may be increased)

Laboratory value alterations

The following have been selected on the basis of their potential clinical significance (possible effect in parentheses where appropriate)—not necessarily inclusive (» = major clinical significance).

With physiology/laboratory test values
 Alkaline phosphatase values, serum, and
 Aspartate aminotransferase (AST [SGOT]) values, serum, and
 Bilirubin concentrations, serum
 (may be increased; dose-related)
 Calcium
 (serum concentrations may be increased infrequently, usually in patients with bone metastases)

Medical considerations/Contraindications

The medical considerations/contraindications included have been selected on the basis of their potential clinical significance (reasons given in parentheses where appropriate)—not necessarily inclusive (» = major clinical significance).

Except under special circumstances, this medication should not be used when the following medical problem exists:

» Thromboembolic disease, history of
 (use of toremifene is generally not recommended)

Risk-benefit should be considered when the following medical problems exist:

Bone metastases
 (close monitoring for hypercalcemia is recommended during the first weeks of toremifene therapy)

» Endometrial hyperplasia, pre-existing
 (long-term use is not recommended)

Leukopenia or
Thrombocytopenia
 (since leukopenia and thrombocytopenia have been reported rarely during treatment with toremifene, monitoring of leukocyte and platelet counts is recommended)

Sensitivity to toremifene

Patient monitoring

The following may be especially important in patient monitoring (other tests may be warranted in some patients, depending on condition; » = major clinical significance):

» Calcium concentrations, serum
 (recommended at periodic intervals during treatment)

Complete blood count
 (recommended at periodic intervals during treatment)

Hepatic function tests
 (recommended at periodic intervals during treatment)

Side/Adverse Effects

Note: Side/adverse effects are mostly related to the antiestrogenic hormonal effects of toremifene and usually occur at the beginning of treatment.

Some patients have developed endometrial cancer, but because of other factors present (short duration of treatment, prior antiestrogen therapy, premalignant conditions) a direct causal relationship with toremifene therapy has not been established.

Leukopenia and thrombocytopenia have been reported but have not been attributed definitely to toremifene.

The following side/adverse effects have been selected on the basis of their potential clinical significance (possible signs and symptoms in parentheses where appropriate)—not necessarily inclusive:

Those indicating need for medical attention

Incidence more frequent

Hepatotoxicity—usually asymptomatic

Note: *Hepatotoxicity* usually consists of elevated hepatic enzyme and bilirubin levels. However, jaundice has been seen rarely.

Incidence less frequent

Endometrial hyperplasia (change in vaginal discharge; pain or feeling of pressure in pelvis; vaginal bleeding); ***hypercalcemia*** (confusion; increased urination; loss of appetite; unusual tiredness); ***ocular toxicity, including abnormal visual fields, cataracts, corneal keratopathy, glaucoma*** (blurred vision; changes in vision)—may be asymptomatic initially

Note: *Endometrial hyperplasia* of the uterus has also been seen in monkeys following doses of 1 mg per kg of body weight (mg/kg) (about one fourth of the daily maximum recommended human dose [MRHD] on a mg per square meter of body surface area [mg/m^2] basis) or higher for 52 weeks, and in dogs following doses of 3 mg/kg (about 1.4 times the daily MRHD on a mg/m^2 basis) or higher for 16 weeks.

Hypercalcemia may occur in some patients, usually those with bone metastases, during the first weeks of treatment.

Incidence rare

Cardiac failure (swelling of feet or lower legs); ***myocardial infarction*** (chest pain); ***pulmonary embolus*** (shortness of breath); ***thrombophlebitis or thrombosis*** (pain or swelling in legs)

Those indicating need for medical attention only if they continue or are bothersome

Incidence more frequent

Hot flashes (sudden sweating and feelings of warmth); ***nausea***

Note: *Nausea* is dose-related.

Incidence less frequent

Dizziness; dry eyes; tumor flare (bone pain); ***vomiting***

Note: *"Tumor flair,"* a transient increase in bone or tumor pain (characterized by diffuse musculoskeletal pain and erythema with increased size of tumor lesions) may occur during the first few weeks after initiation of therapy. It is often accompanied by hypercalcemia. This temporary "tumor flair" subsequently regresses and does not imply treatment failure or tumor progression.

Overdose

For more information on the management of overdose or unintentional ingestion, **contact a Poison Control Center** (see *Poison Control Center Listing*).

Clinical effects of overdose

The following effects have been selected on the basis of their potential clinical significance (possible signs and symptoms in parentheses where appropriate)—not necessarily inclusive:

Acute and/or chronic

Dizziness; headache; nausea and/or vomiting

Note: The symptoms listed above have been reported with administration of a daily dose of 680 mg for 5 days; they appeared in two of five healthy subjects during the third day of treatment and disappeared within 2 days after withdrawal of the medication. In a study in postmenopausal breast cancer patients, a dose of 400 mg per square meter of body surface area per day caused similar symptoms, as well as reversible hallucinations and ataxia in one patient.

Theoretical symptoms of toremifene overdose include antiestrogenic effects such as hot flashes, estrogenic effects such as vaginal bleeding, or nervous system disorders such as vertigo, dizziness, ataxia, or nausea.

Treatment of overdose

Treatment is symptomatic.

There is no specific antidote.

Patient Consultation

As an aid to patient consultation, refer to *Advice for the Patient, Toremifene (Systemic)*.

In providing consultation, consider emphasizing the following selected information (» = major clinical significance):

Before using this medication

» Conditions affecting use, especially:
- Sensitivity to toremifene
- Pregnancy—Risk of miscarriage, death of the fetus, and birth defects; telling physician immediately if pregnancy is suspected
- Other medications, especially anticoagulants (coumarin-derivative), carbamazepine, phenobarbital, or phenytoin
- Other medical problems, especially endometrial hyperplasia or history of thromboembolic disease

Proper use of this medication

» Proper dosing

» Proper storage

Side/adverse effects

Possible increased risk of endometrial carcinoma

Signs of potential side effects, especially endometrial hyperplasia, hypercalcemia, ocular toxicity, cardiac failure, myocardial infarction, pulmonary embolus, and thrombophlebitis or thrombosis

Asymptomatic side effects including hepatotoxicity and ocular toxicity

General Dosing Information

If hypercalcemia occurs, appropriate measures should be taken. If it is severe, toremifene should be discontinued.

Oral Dosage Forms

TOREMIFENE CITRATE TABLETS

Note: The dosing and strengths available are expressed in terms of toremifene base (not the salt).

Usual adult dose

Breast carcinoma—

Oral, 60 mg (base) once a day.

Usual geriatric dose

See *Usual adult dose*.

Strength(s) usually available

U.S.—

60 mg (base) (Rx) [*Fareston* (lactose)].

Packaging and storage

Store at 25 °C (77 °F). Protect from light.

Developed: 03/23/1998

TORSEMIDE Systemic†

INN: Torasemide; BAN: Torasemide

VA CLASSIFICATION (Primary/Secondary): CV702/CV409

Commonly used brand name(s): *Demadex*.

Note: For a listing of dosage forms and brand names by country availability, see *Dosage Forms* section(s).

†Not commercially available in Canada.

Category

Diuretic; antihypertensive.

Indications

Accepted

Edema (treatment)—Torsemide is indicated in treatment of edema associated with congestive heart failure, renal disease, and hepatic disease (cirrhosis).

Hypertension (treatment)—Torsemide is indicated, alone or in combination with other antihypertensive agents, in the treatment of hypertension.

For additional information on initial therapeutic guidelines related to the treatment of hypertension, see *Appendix III*.

Pharmacology/Pharmacokinetics

Physicochemical characteristics

Molecular weight—348.43.

pKa—7.1.

Mechanism of action/Effect

Diuretic—Torsemide is a loop diuretic. It inhibits reabsorption of sodium and chloride in the luminal membrane of the ascending limb of the loop of Henle by interfering with the chloride binding site of the 1Na+, 1K+, 2Cl− cotransport system. This increases the rate of delivery of tubular fluid and electrolytes to the distal sites of hydrogen and potassium ion secretion, while plasma volume contraction increases aldosterone production. The increased delivery and high aldosterone levels promote sodium reabsorption at the distal tubules, thus increasing the loss of potassium and hydrogen ions. Torsemide's effects in other portions of the nephron have not been demonstrated.

Antihypertensive—Diuretics lower blood pressure initially by reducing plasma and extracellular fluid volume; cardiac output also decreases. Eventually, cardiac output returns to normal with an accompanying decrease in peripheral resistance.

Absorption

Rapidly absorbed following oral administration; not affected by food. Bioavailability is approximately 80%.

Distribution

Volume of distribution (Vol_D)—0.14 to 0.19 L per kg.

Protein binding

Very high (97 to greater than 99%).

Biotransformation
Metabolized via the hepatic cytochrome P-450 system to 5 metabolites. The major metabolite, M5, is pharmacologically inactive. There are 2 minor metabolites, M1, possessing one-tenth the activity of torsemide, and M3, equal in activity to torsemide. Overall, torsemide appears to account for 80% of the total diuretic activity, while metabolites M1 and M3 account for 9% and 11%, respectively.

Half-life
Elimination—2.2 to 3.8 hours; not affected by moderate renal failure. However, metabolite M1 may accumulate in renal failure.

Onset of action
Diuretic—
Oral: Within 1 hour.
Intravenous: Within 10 minutes.

Time to peak concentration
Oral—1 to 2 hours.

Time to peak effect
Diuretic—
Oral: 1 to 2 hours.
Intravenous: Within 1 hour.

Duration of action
Diuretic—6 to 8 hours.

Elimination
Renal; 24% as parent compound.
In dialysis—Torsemide is not significantly removed by hemodialysis.

Precautions to Consider

Cross-sensitivity and/or related problems
Patients sensitive to bumetanide, furosemide, or sulfonamides (including thiazide diuretics) may be sensitive to torsemide also.

Carcinogenicity/Tumorigenicity
Lifetime administration of torsemide to rats and mice at doses up to 9 and 32 mg per kg of body weight (mg/kg) per day, respectively, did not increase overall tumor incidence. These doses are equivalent to 27 and 96 times, respectively, a human dose of 20 mg on a body weight basis. However, renal tubular injury, interstitial inflammation, and a statistically significant increase in renal adenomas and carcinomas were observed in the high-dose female group of rats.

Mutagenicity
No mutagenic activity was seen in a variety of *in vitro* and *in vivo* tests.

Pregnancy/Reproduction
Fertility—No adverse effect on fertility was seen in male or female rats given doses up to 25 mg/kg per day (equivalent to 75 times a human dose of 20 mg on a body weight basis).

Pregnancy—Adequate and well-controlled studies have not been done in humans. Routine use of diuretics during normal pregnancy is not recommended because use may expose the mother and fetus to unnecessary hazard. However, diuretics may be continued during pregnancy if they were used to treat hypertension that existed prior to gestation. Diuretics do not prevent development of toxemia of pregnancy, and there is no satisfactory evidence that they are useful in the treatment of toxemia. Diuretics are indicated only in the treatment of edema due to pathologic causes or as a short course of treatment in patients with severe hypervolemia.

No fetotoxicity or teratogenicity was observed in rats and rabbits given doses up to 15 and 5 times, respectively, a human dose of 20 mg on a mg/kg basis. However, administration of doses 4 and 5 times larger in rats and rabbits, respectively, resulted in decreased average body weight, increased fetal resorption, and delayed fetal ossification.

FDA Pregnancy Category B.

Breast-feeding
It is not known whether torsemide is distributed into breast milk.

Pediatrics
No information is available on the relationship of age to the effects of torsemide in pediatric patients. Safety and efficacy have not been established.

Geriatrics
Studies that included patients over 65 years of age have not demonstrated geriatrics-specific problems that would limit the usefulness of torsemide in the elderly.

Drug interactions and/or related problems
The following drug interactions and/or related problems have been selected on the basis of their potential clinical significance (possible mechanism in parentheses where appropriate)—not necessarily inclusive (» = major clinical significance):

Note: Combinations containing any of the following medications, depending on the amount present, may also interact with this medication.

Alcohol or
Hypotension-producing medications, other (see *Appendix II*)
(hypotensive and/or diuretic effects may be potentiated when these medications are used concurrently with torsemide; although some antihypertensive and/or diuretic combinations are frequently used for therapeutic advantage, dosage adjustments may be necessary during concurrent use)

» Amphotericin B, parenteral
(concurrent and/or sequential administration with torsemide should be avoided since the potential for nephrotoxicity may be increased, especially in the presence of renal function impairment; in addition, concurrent use with torsemide may intensify electrolyte imbalance, particularly hypokalemia; frequent electrolyte determinations are recommended and potassium supplementation may be required)

Angiotensin-converting enzyme (ACE) inhibitors
(sudden and severe hypotension may occur within the first 1 to 5 hours after the initial dose of an ACE inhibitor, particularly in patients who are sodium- and volume-depleted as a result of diuretic therapy. Withdrawal of the diuretic or increase of salt intake approximately 1 week before start of captopril therapy or 2 to 3 days before start of benazepril, enalapril, fosinopril, lisinopril, quinapril, or ramipril therapy, or initiation of ACE inhibitor therapy at lower doses, will minimize the reaction; this reaction does not usually recur with subsequent doses, although caution in increasing doses is recommended; diuretics may be reinstituted as necessary)
(risk of renal failure may be increased in patients who are sodium- and volume-depleted as a result of diuretic therapy)
(ACE inhibitors may reduce the secondary aldosteronism and hypokalemia caused by diuretics)

Antiarrhythmic agents
(concurrent use with torsemide may lead to an increased risk of arrhythmias associated with hypokalemia)

» Anticoagulants, coumarin- or indandione-derivative, or
Heparin or
Streptokinase or
Urokinase
(anticoagulant effects may be decreased when these medications are used concurrently with torsemide, as a result of reduction of plasma volume leading to concentration of procoagulant factors in the blood; in addition, diuretic-induced improvement of hepatic congestion may lead to improved hepatic function, resulting in increased procoagulant factor synthesis; dosage adjustments may be necessary)

Antidiabetic agents, oral, or
Insulin
(torsemide may rarely raise blood glucose concentrations or interfere with the hypoglycemic effects of these agents; for non-insulin-dependent diabetics, dosage adjustment of hypoglycemic medications may be necessary)

Anti-inflammatory drugs, nonsteroidal (NSAIDs), especially indomethacin
(indomethacin, and possibly other NSAIDs, may reduce the natriuretic action of torsemide; NSAIDs may also reduce the antihypertensive effect or the increase in urine volume caused by torsemide, possibly by inhibiting renal prostaglandin synthesis and/or by causing sodium and fluid retention)
(in addition, concurrent use of NSAIDs with a diuretic may increase the risk of renal failure secondary to a decrease in renal blood flow caused by inhibition of renal prostaglandin synthesis)

Digitalis glycosides
(concurrent use with torsemide may enhance the possibility of digitalis toxicity associated with hypokalemia and hypomagnesemia)

» Hypokalemia-causing medications, other (see *Appendix II*)
(risk of severe hypokalemia due to other hypokalemia-causing medications may be increased; monitoring of serum potassium concentrations and cardiac function and potassium supplementation may be required)

» Lithium
(concurrent use with torsemide may promote lithium toxicity because of reduced renal clearance; concurrent use is not recommended unless patient can be closely monitored)

» Nephrotoxic medications, other, (see *Appendix II*) or
Ototoxic medications, other (see *Appendix II*)
(concurrent and/or sequential administration with torsemide is not recommended since the potential for ototoxicity and nephrotoxicity

may be increased, especially in the presence of renal function impairment)

Neuromuscular blocking agents, nondepolarizing
(torsemide may induce hypokalemia, which may enhance the blockade of nondepolarizing neuromuscular blocking agents; serum potassium determinations may be necessary prior to administration of nondepolarizing neuromuscular blocking agents; careful postoperative monitoring of the patient may be necessary following concurrent or sequential use, especially if there is a possibility of incomplete reversal of neuromuscular blockade)

Probenecid
(concurrent use with torsemide may decrease the diuretic activity of torsemide because probenecid reduces secretion of torsemide into the proximal tubule)

» Salicylates, high-dose
(concurrent use with torsemide may increase the risk of salicylate toxicity because torsemide and salicylates compete for secretion by the renal tubules)

Sympathomimetics
(concurrent use may reduce the antihypertensive effects of torsemide; the patient should be carefully monitored to confirm that the desired effect is being obtained)

Laboratory value alterations

The following have been selected on the basis of their potential clinical significance (possible effect in parentheses where appropriate)—not necessarily inclusive (» = major clinical significance).

With physiology/laboratory test values

Blood urea nitrogen (BUN) and
Uric acid, serum
(concentrations may be increased)

Calcium and
Magnesium and
Potassium
(serum concentrations may be decreased)

Glucose
(blood glucose concentrations may be increased; hyperglycemia has been reported rarely)

Medical considerations/Contraindications

The medical considerations/contraindications included have been selected on the basis of their potential clinical significance (reasons given in parentheses where appropriate)—not necessarily inclusive (» = major clinical significance).

Risk-benefit should be considered when the following medical problems exist:

» Anuria
(may impair effectiveness of torsemide; possible reduced clearance may increase risk of ototoxicity)

Diabetes mellitus
(torsemide may increase serum glucose concentrations)

Gout, history of or
Hyperuricemia
(torsemide may increase serum uric acid concentrations)

Hearing function impairment
(condition may be exacerbated if ototoxic effects occur)

Hepatic function impairment with cirrhosis and ascites
(sudden alterations in fluid and electrolyte balance may precipitate hepatic coma; hospitalization during initiation of torsemide therapy is recommended)

Myocardial infarction, acute
(excessive diuresis should be avoided because of the danger of precipitating shock)

Sensitivity to torsemide, other loop diuretics, or sulfonylureas

Caution is recommended in patients who are at increased risk if hypokalemia occurs, including those taking concurrent digitalis and those with cardiovascular disease, because of the risk of arrhythmias.

Patient monitoring

The following may be especially important in patient monitoring (other tests may be warranted in some patients, depending on condition; » = major clinical significance):

Blood pressure measurements
(recommended at periodic intervals in patients being treated for hypertension; selected patients may be taught to monitor their blood pressure at home and report the results at regular physician visits)

Blood urea nitrogen (BUN) and
Glucose, serum and
Hepatic function and
Renal function and
Uric acid, serum
(determinations recommended at periodic intervals)

» Electrolytes, serum, especially potassium
(determinations recommended at periodic intervals)

Hearing examinations
(recommended at periodic intervals in patients receiving prolonged high-dose intravenous therapy)

For use as a diuretic (in addition to the above)

Weight measurements
(recommended prior to initiation of therapy and at periodic intervals during therapy to monitor fluid loss)

Side/Adverse Effects

The following side/adverse effects have been selected on the basis of their potential clinical significance (possible signs and symptoms in parentheses where appropriate)—not necessarily inclusive:

Those indicating need for medical attention

Incidence less frequent

Electrolyte imbalance such as hyponatremia, hypochloremic alkalosis, and hypokalemia (dryness of mouth; fast or irregular heartbeat; increased thirst; mood or mental changes; muscle pain or cramps; nausea or vomiting; unusual tiredness or weakness)

Incidence rare

Allergic reaction (skin rash); ***gastrointestinal hemorrhage*** (black, tarry stools); ***hypotension, orthostatic*** (dizziness when getting up from a sitting or lying position); ***ototoxicity*** (ringing or buzzing in the ears or any loss of hearing)

Note: *Ototoxicity* may be more likely to occur with rapid intravenous administration or with use of very high doses.

Those indicating need for medical attention only if they continue or are bothersome

Incidence more frequent

Constipation; dizziness; gastrointestinal disturbance (stomach upset); ***headache***

Overdose

For more information on the management of overdose or unintentional ingestion, **contact a Poison Control Center** (see *Poison Control Center Listing*).

Treatment of overdose

Fluid and electrolyte replacement.

Symptomatic and supportive care.

Patient Consultation

As an aid to patient consultation, refer to *Advice for the Patient, Torsemide (Systemic)*.

In providing consultation, consider emphasizing the following selected information (» = major clinical significance):

Before using this medication

» Conditions affecting use, especially:
Sensitivity to loop diuretics or sulfonamides
Pregnancy—Not recommended for routine use
Other medications, especially amphotericin B, anticoagulants, hypokalemia-causing medications, lithium, other nephrotoxic medications, or high-dose salicylates
Other medical problems, especially anuria

Proper use of this medication

Diuretic effects of the medication and timing of doses to minimize inconvenience of diuresis

Compliance with therapy; taking medication at the same time(s) each day to maintain the therapeutic effect

» Proper dosing

Missed dose: Taking as soon as possible; not taking if almost time for next dose; not doubling doses

» Proper storage

For use as an antihypertensive

Possible need for control of weight and diet, especially sodium intake

» Patient may not experience symptoms of hypertension; importance of taking medication even if feeling well

» Does not cure, but controls hypertension; possible need for lifelong therapy; serious consequences of untreated hypertension

Precautions while using this medication

Making regular visits to physician to check progress

» Possibility of hypokalemia; possible need for additional potassium in diet; not changing diet without first checking with physician

To prevent dehydration, notifying physician if severe nausea, vomiting, or diarrhea occurs and continues

Caution if any kind of surgery (including dental surgery) is required

» Caution when getting up suddenly from a lying or sitting position

» Caution in using alcohol, while standing for long periods or exercising, and during hot weather because of enhanced orthostatic hypotensive effects

Diabetics: May increase blood sugar levels

For use as an antihypertensive:

» Not taking other medications, especially nonprescription sympathomimetics, unless discussed with physician

Side/adverse effects

Signs of potential side effects, especially electrolyte imbalance, allergic reaction, gastrointestinal hemorrhage, orthostatic hypotension, and ototoxicity

General Dosing Information

Dosage must be adjusted to meet the individual requirements of each patient, on the basis of clinical response. The lowest effective dosage should be utilized to minimize potential fluid and electrolyte imbalance.

Concurrent administration of potassium supplements or potassium-sparing diuretics may be indicated in patients considered to be at higher risk for developing hypokalemia.

When torsemide is added to an antihypertensive regimen, the dose of other antihypertensive agents may have to be reduced to prevent an excessive drop in blood pressure.

For parenteral dosage forms only

Intravenous injections should be administered slowly, over a period of 2 minutes.

Diet/Nutrition

Torsemide may be taken at any time in relation to a meal.

Bioequivalence information

Because of the high bioavailability of torsemide tablets, oral and intravenous doses of torsemide are equivalent.

Oral Dosage Forms

TORSEMIDE TABLETS

Usual adult dose

Diuretic—

Congestive heart failure—

Oral, 10 or 20 mg once a day, the dosage being increased as needed, up to 200 mg, for desired therapeutic effect.

Hepatic cirrhosis—

Oral, 5 or 10 mg once a day, administered with an aldosterone antagonist or a potassium-sparing diuretic.

Renal failure, chronic—

Oral, 20 mg once a day, the dosage being increased by doubling as needed until adequate diuretic response is achieved.

Antihypertensive—

Oral, 5 mg once a day for four to six weeks, the dosage being increased thereafter to 10 mg once a day if blood pressure response is not adequate.

Usual adult prescribing limits

Congestive heart failure—Single dose: 200 mg.
Hepatic cirrhosis—Single dose: 40 mg.
Renal failure, chronic—Single dose: 200 mg.

Usual pediatric dose

Safety and efficacy have not been established.

Usual geriatric dose

See *Usual adult dose.*

Strength(s) usually available

U.S.—

5 mg (Rx) [*Demadex*].
10 mg (Rx) [*Demadex*].
20 mg (Rx) [*Demadex*].
100 mg (Rx) [*Demadex*].

Canada—

Not commercially available.

Packaging and storage

Store below 40 °C (104 °F), preferably between 15 and 30 °C (59 and 86 °F). Protect from freezing.

Auxiliary labeling

- Do not take other medicines without your doctor's advice.

Parenteral Dosage Forms

TORSEMIDE INJECTION

Usual adult dose

Diuretic—

Congestive heart failure—

Intravenous, 10 or 20 mg once a day, the dosage being increased as needed, up to 200 mg, for desired therapeutic effect.

Hepatic cirrhosis—

Intravenous, 5 or 10 mg once a day, administered with an aldosterone antagonist or a potassium-sparing diuretic.

Renal failure, chronic—

Intravenous, 20 mg once a day, the dosage being increased by doubling as needed until adequate diuretic response is achieved.

Usual adult prescribing limits

See *Torsemide Tablets.*

Usual pediatric dose

Safety and efficacy have not been established.

Usual geriatric dose

See *Usual adult dose.*

Strength(s) usually available

U.S.—

10 mg per mL (Rx) [*Demadex*].

Canada—

Not commercially available.

Packaging and storage

Store below 40 °C (104 °F), preferably between 15 and 30 °C (59 and 86 °F). Protect from freezing.

Stability

Do not use if solution is discolored.

Selected Bibliography

Friedel HA, Buckley MM. Torasemide. A review of its pharmacological properties and therapeutic potential. Drugs 1991; 41(1): 81-103.

The fifth report of the Joint National Committee on Detection, Evaluation, and Treatment of High Blood Pressure (JNC V). Arch Intern Med 1993; 153(2): 154-83.

Revised: 08/19/1998

TOSITUMOMAB AND IODINE I 131 TOSITUMOMAB Systemic

VA CLASSIFICATION (Primary): AN900

Commonly used brand name(s): *Bexxar.*

Note: For a listing of dosage forms and brand names by country availability, see *Dosage Forms* section(s).

Category

Antineoplastic (radioactive); Monoclonal antibody.

Indications

Accepted

Lymphomas, non-Hodgkin's (treatment)—Tositumomab and iodine I-131 tositumomab is indicated for the treatment of patients with CD20 antigen expressing relapsed or refractory, low grade, follicular, or transformed non-Hodgkin's lymphoma, including patients with Rituximab-refractory non-Hodgkin's lymphoma. Determination of the effectiveness of this regimen is based on overall response rates in patients whose disease is refractory to chemotherapy alone or to chemotherapy and rituximab. The effects of this regimen on survival are not known.

Unaccepted

The tositumomab and iodine I-131 tositumomab regimen is not indicated for the initial treatment of patients with CD20 positive non-Hodgkin's lymphoma.

Physical Properties

Nuclear Data

Radionuclide (half-life)	Mode of decay	Principal photons (keV)
Iodine 131 (8.04 days)	Beta	Beta (191.6), Gamma (364.5)

Pharmacology/Pharmacokinetics

Physicochemical characteristics

Source—
Tositumomab—Tositumomab is a murine IgG_{2a} lambda monoclonal antibody directed against the CD20 antigen, which is found on the surface of normal and malignant B lymphocytes. Tositumomab is produced in an antibiotic-free culture of mammalian cells and is composed of two murine gamma 2a heavy chains of 451 amino acids each and two lambda light chains of 220 amino acids each.
Iodine I 131 tositumomab—This radio-iodated derivative of tositumomab has been covalently linked to Iodine-131. Unbound radioiodine and other reactants have been removed by chromatographic purification steps.

Molecular weight—Tositumomab—150 kD.

pH—
Tositumomab—7.2
Iodine I 131 tositumomab—7.0

Mechanism of action/Effect

Tositumomab binds specifically to the CD20 antigen. This antigen is expressed on pre-B lymphocytes, mature B lymphocytes and B-cell non-Hodgkin's lymphomas. Possible mechanisms of action for the tositumomab and iodine I 131 tositumomab therapeutic regimen include induction of apoptosis, complement-dependent cytotoxicity, and antibody-dependent cellular cytotoxicity mediated by the antibody. Additionally, cell death is associated with ionizing radiation from the radioisotope.

Half-life

Approximately 67 hours

Radiation dosimetry

Estimated radiation absorbed doses		
From Organ ROIs	**Iodine I131 tositumomab (mGy/MBq)** Median	**Range**
Thyroid	2.71	1.4–6.2
Kidneys	1.96	1.5–2.5
Upper large intestinal wall	1.34	0.8–1.7
Lower large intestinal wall	1.3	0.8–1.6
Heart wall	1.25	0.5–1.8
Spleen	1.14	0.7–5.4
Testes	0.83	0.3–1.3
Liver	0.82	0.6–1.3
Lungs	0.79	0.5–1.1
Red marrow	0.65	0.5–1.1
Stomach wall	0.4	0.2–0.8
From Whole Body ROIs		
Urine bladder wall	0.64	0.6–0.9
Bone surfaces	0.41	0.4–0.6
Pancreas	0.31	0.2–0.4
Gall bladder wall	0.29	0.2–0.3
Adrenals	0.28	0.2–0.3
Ovaries	0.25	0.2–0.3
Small intestine	0.23	0.2–0.3
Thymus	0.22	0.1–0.3
Uterus	0.2	0.2–0.2
Muscle	0.18	0.1–0.2
Breasts	0.16	0.1–0.2
Skin	0.13	0.1–0.2
Brain	0.13	0.1–0.2
Total body	0.24	0.2–0.3

Elimination

Renal—Approximately 67% of Iodine-131 dose is excreted in the urine over 5 days.

Precautions to Consider

Carcinogenicity/Mutagenicity

No long-term studies have been performed to establish the carcinogenic or mutagenic potential of the tositumomab and Iodine I 131 Tositumomab therapeutic regimen. However, radiation is a potential carcinogen and mutagen. Administration of this therapeutic regimen results in delivery of a significant radiation dose to the testes. The radiation dose to the ovaries has not been established. There have been no studies to evaluate whether administration of this regimen causes mutagenic alterations to germ cells. Myelodysplastic syndrome (MDS) and/or acute leukemia were reported by some patients (10% in clinical trials, 3% in expanded access programs). The median time to development of MDS/leukemia was 31 months following treatment

Non-hematological malignancies have also been reported. Approximately 50% of these were non-melanomatous skin cancers.

Pregnancy/Reproduction

Fertility—No long-term animal studies have been performed to determine the effects on fertility in males or females. There have been no studies to evaluate whether the administration of the tositumomab and iodine I 131 tositumomab therapeutic regimen causes hypogonadism, premature menopause, or azospermia. There is a potential risk that this regimen may cause toxic effects on male and female gonads.

Pregnancy—The tositumomab and iodine I 131 tositumomab therapeutic regimen is contraindicated during pregnancy. Effective contraceptive methods should be used during treatment and for 12 months following administration. Studies have shown that this regimen may cause harm to the fetal thyroid gland and severe, possibly irreversible hypothyroidism in neonates. If the patient becomes pregnant while being treated with this regimen, the patient should be apprised of the potential hazard to the fetus

FDA Pregnancy Category X

Breast-feeding

Both radioiodine and immunoglobulins are distributed in breast milk. Although very little information is available regarding distribution of antineoplastic agents into breast milk, breast-feeding is not recommended during chemotherapy because of the potential risks to the infant. Therefore, formula feedings should be substituted for breast feedings before starting treatment.

Pediatrics

No information is available on the relationship of age to the effects of the tositumomab and iodine I 131 tositumomab therapeutic regimen in the pediatric population. Safety and efficacy have not been established.

Geriatrics

Although appropriate studies on the relationship of age to the effects of the tositumomab iodine I 131 tositumomab therapeutic regimen have not been performed in the geriatric population, geriatrics-specific problems are not expected to limit its usefulness in the elderly. However, some elderly patients may lower response rate and a shorter duration of the response.

Drug interactions and/or related problems

The following drug interactions and/or related problems have been selected on the basis of their potential clinical significance (possible mechanism in parentheses where appropriate)—not necessarily inclusive (» = major clinical significance):

Note: Combinations containing any of the following medications, depending on the amount present, may also interact with this medication.

» Anticoagulants
(tositumomab and iodine I 131 tositumomab therapeutic regimen results in severe and prolonged cytopenias in most patients; the potential benefits of medications which interfere with coagulation should be weighed against the potential increased risks of bleeding and hemorrhage in these patients.)

» Bone marrow depressants (see *Appendix II*)
(tositumomab and iodine I 131 tositumomab therapeutic regimen results in severe and prolonged cytopenias in most patients; the tositumomab and iodine I 131 tositumomab should not be administered to patients with impaired bone marrow reserves.)

» Platelet function, interferes with (see *Appendix II*)
(tositumomab and iodine I 131 tositumomab therapeutic regimen results in severe and prolonged cytopenias in most patients; the potential benefits of medications which interfere with platelet function should be weighed against the potential increased risks of bleeding and hemorrhage in these patients.)

Vaccines
(safety of immunization with live viral vaccines following the tositumomab and iodine I 131 tositumomab therapeutic regimen has not been studied.)
(the ability of patients who received the tositumomab and iodine I 131 tositumomab therapeutic regimen to generate a primary or anamnestic humoral response to any vaccine has not be studied.)

Laboratory value alterations

The following have been selected on the basis of their potential clinical significance (possible effect in parentheses where appropriate)—not necessarily inclusive (» = major clinical significance).

With physiology/laboratory test values
Hemoglobin concentrations, or
Hematocrit
(may be decreased)

Human anti-murine antibodies (HAMA)
(may be increased; may affect the accuracy of the results of *in vitro* and *in vivo* diagnostic tests that rely on murine antibody technology)

» Neutrophil counts, or
» Platelet counts
(severe and prolonged decreases can be expected)

Medical considerations/Contraindications

The medical considerations/contraindications included have been selected on the basis of their potential clinical significance (reasons given in parentheses where appropriate)—not necessarily inclusive (» = major clinical significance).

Except under special circumstances, this medication should not be used when the following medical problem exists:

Bone marrow reserve, impaired

Lymphoma marrow involvement, high
(therapeutic regimen should not be administered to patients with >25% lymphoma marrow involvement, a platelet count ≤ 100,000 cells per mm^3, or neutrophil count ≤ 1,500 cells per mm^3)

» Hypersensitivity to the tositumomab, iodine I 131 tositumomab, or any of its components or

» Hypersensitivity to murine proteins
(serious hypersensitivity reactions including some with fatal outcomes have been reported; patients who experience hypersensitivity reactions should have infusions discontinued and receive medical attention)

Risk-benefit should be considered when the following medical problems exist:

Renal function impairment
(may decrease the rate of excretion of the radiolabeled iodine and increase patient exposure to the radioactive component)

Patient monitoring

The following may be especially important in patient monitoring (other tests may be warranted in some patients, depending on condition; » = major clinical significance):

» Complete blood count
(should be obtained prior to treatment and weekly thereafter for at least 10 to 12 weeks or until severe cytopenias have completely resolved)

Creatinine, serum
(levels should be measured immediately prior to administration)

» Pregnancy status
(should be assessed in women of child bearing potential)

Thyroid stimulating hormone
(levels should be determined prior to treatment; evaluations for signs and symptoms of hypothyroidism as well as screenings for biochemical evidence should be done annually)

Side/Adverse Effects

Note: The majority of patients who received the tositumomab and iodine I 131 tositumomab therapeutic regimen experienced severe thrombocytopenia and neutropenia. This regimen should not be administered to patients with >25% lymphoma marrow involvement and/or impaired bone marrow reserve.

Hypersensitivity reactions—Intravenous administration of proteins to patients may cause anaphylactic and other hypersensitivity reactions.

Human anti-mouse antibodies (HAMA) should be screened for in patients with prior exposure to murine proteins. Patients with evidence of HAMA may be at increased risk of allergic or serious hypersensitivity reactions during the administration of this therapeutic regimen.

Infectious events—45% of the patients experienced one or more adverse events possibly related to infection. The majority were viral or other minor infections. Serious infections that required hospitalization were experienced by 9% of the patients.

Note: Many side effects of antineoplastic therapy are unavoidable and represent the medication's pharmacologic action.

The following side/adverse effects have been selected on the basis of their potential clinical significance (possible signs and symptoms in parentheses where appropriate)—not necessarily inclusive:

Those indicating need for medical attention

Incidence more frequent

Allergic reaction (cough; difficulty swallowing; dizziness; fast heartbeat; hives; itching; puffiness or swelling of the eyelids or around the eyes, face, lips or tongue; shortness of breath; skin rash; tightness in chest; unusual tiredness or weakness; wheezing); ***anemia*** (pale skin; troubled breathing with exertion; unusual bleeding or bruising; unusual tiredness or weakness); ***angioedema*** (large, hive-like swelling on face, eyelids, lips, tongue, throat, hands, legs, feet, sex organs); ***hemorrhage while thrombocytopenic*** (bleeding gums; coughing up blood; difficulty in breathing or swallowing; dizziness; headache; increased menstrual flow or vaginal bleeding; nosebleeds; paralysis; prolonged bleeding from cuts; red or dark brown urine; red or black, tarry stools; shortness of breath)—resulting in deaths; ***hypothyroidism*** (constipation; depressed mood; dry skin and hair; feeling cold; hair loss; hoarseness or husky voice; muscle cramps and stiffness; slowed heartbeat; weight gain; unusual tiredness or weakness); ***infection*** (fever or chills; cough or hoarseness; lower back or side pain; painful or difficult urination); ***leukemia, secondary*** (bone pain); ***myelodysplasia*** (chest pain; chills; cough or hoarseness; fever; lower back or side pain; painful or difficult urination; shortness of breath; sores, ulcers, or white spots on lips or in mouth; swollen glands; unusual bleeding or bruising; unusual tiredness or weakness); ***neutropenia*** (chills; cough; fever; sore throat; sores, ulcers, or white spots on lips or in mouth; swollen glands); ***pneumonia*** (chest pain; cough; fever or chills; sneezing; shortness of breath; sore throat; troubled breathing; tightness in chest; wheezing); ***thrombocytopenia*** (black, tarry stools; bleeding gums; blood in urine or stools; pinpoint red spots on skin; unusual bleeding or bruising)

Incidence unknown

Bronchospasm (cough; difficulty breathing; noisy breathing; shortness of breath; tightness in chest; wheezing)

Those indicating need for medical attention only if they continue or are bothersome

Incidence more frequent

Abdominal pain; anorexia; arthralgia (pain in joints; muscle pain or stiffness; difficulty in moving); ***asthenia*** (lack or loss of strength); ***chest pain; chills***—seek medical attention if associated with signs or symptoms of infection; ***dehydration; diarrhea; constipation*** (difficulty having a bowel movement (stool)); ***cough; dizziness; dyspepsia*** (acid or sour stomach; belching; heartburn; indigestion; stomach discomfort, upset or pain); ***dyspnea*** (difficult or labored breathing; shortness of breath; tightness in chest; wheezing); ***edema, peripheral*** (swelling of hands, ankles, feet, or lower legs); ***fever***—seek medical attention if associated with signs or symptoms of infection; ***gastrointestinal symptoms*** (abdominal pain or stomach pain; diarrhea or increased bowel movements; loose or liquid stools; nausea or feeling of upset stomach or feeling like you may vomit; vomiting); ***headache, mild*** (pain in one or more areas of the head.)—seek medical attention if severe; ***hypotension*** (blurred vision; confusion; dizziness; faintness or lightheadedness when getting up from a lying or sitting position; sudden sweating; unusual tiredness or weakness); ***myalgia*** (joint pain; swollen joints; muscle aching or cramping; muscle pains or stiffness; difficulty in moving); ***nausea; neck pain; pain; pain, back; pharyngitis*** (body aches or pain; congestion; cough; dryness or soreness of throat; fever; hoarseness; runny nose; tender, swollen glands in neck; trouble in swallowing; voice changes); ***pleural effusion*** (chest pain; shortness of breath); ***pruritus*** (itching skin); ***rash; rhinitis*** (stuffy nose; runny nose; sneezing); ***somnolence*** (sleepiness or unusual drowsiness); ***sweating; vasodilation*** (feeling of warmth or heat; flushing or redness of skin, especially on face and neck; headache; feeling faint, dizzy, or light-headedness; sweating); ***vomiting; weight loss***

Overdose

For more information on the management of overdose or unintentional ingestion, **contact a poison control center** (see *Poison Control Center Listing*).

Clinical effects of overdose

Two of 3 patients given total body doses of 85 cGy of iodine I 131 tositumomab developed grade 4 toxicity of 5 weeks duration. One patient developed grade 3 hematologic toxicity of 18 days duration following a total body dose of 88 cGy.

Treatment of overdose

Specific treatment—
See the package insert or *Tositumomab and Iodine I 131 Tositumomab (Systemic)* for specific dosing guidelines for use of this product.

Monitoring—
Careful monitoring for and management of cytopenias and radiation related toxicity.

Supportive care—
The effectiveness of hematopoietic stem cell transplantation as a supportive care measure for marrow injury has not been studied.

Patient Consultation

As an aid to patient consultation, refer to *Tositumomab and Iodine I 131 (Systemic)*.

In providing consultation, consider emphasizing the following selected information (» = major clinical significance):

Before using this medication

» Conditions affecting use, especially:

Carcinogenicity/Mutagenicity—Radiation is a potential carcinogen and mutagen. Myelodysplastic syndrome (MDS) and/or acute leukemia were reported by some patients.

Pregnancy—Not recommended for use during pregnancy. Effective contraceptive methods should be used during treatment and for 12 months following administration.

Breast-feeding—Not recommended during tositumomab and iodine I 131 tositumomab therapy.

Use in children—Safety and efficacy have not been established

Use in the elderly—Geriatrics-specific problems are not expected to limit its usefulness in the elderly.

Other medications, especially anticoagulants, bone marrow depressants, vaccines, platelet function altering medications, or thyroid blocking agents.

Other medical problems, especially impaired bone marrow reserve, previous allergic reactions, or previous hypersensitivity reactions

Precautions while using this medication

» Avoiding immunizations unless approved by physician

» Caution if bone marrow depression occurs:

Avoiding exposure to persons with bacterial infections, especially during periods of low blood counts; checking with physician immediately if fever or chills, cough or hoarseness, lower back or side pain, or painful or difficult urination occur

Checking with physician immediately if unusual bleeding or bruising; black, tarry stools; blood in urine or stools; or pinpoint red spots on skin occur

Caution in use of regular toothbrush, dental floss, or toothpick; physician, dentist, or nurse may suggest alternatives; checking with physician before having dental work done

Not touching eyes or inside of nose unless hands washed immediately before

Using caution to avoid accidental cuts with use of sharp objects such as safety razor or fingernail or toenail cutters

Avoiding contact sports or other situations where bruising or injury could occur

Patients should be advised that they will have radioactive material in their bodies for several days following the therapeutic regimen. After discharge, patients should be given oral and written instructions for minimizing exposure of others.

Side/adverse effects

Signs of potential side effects, especially anemia, angioedema, bronchospasm, hemorrhage, infection, neutropenia, thrombocytopenia, allergic reaction, apnea, gastrointestinal hemorrhage, severe infection, hematoma, cerebral hemorrhage, tachycardia

General Dosing Information

For parenteral dosing forms:

Any institutional radiation safety practices or applicable federal guidelines should be followed closely in order to minimize the exposure of medical personnel and other patients.

The tositumomab and iodine I 131 tositumomab therapeutic regimen should be administered only by physicians and other health care professionals qualified by training in the safe use and handling of radionuclides. This regimen should be administered only by physicians who are in the process of being or have been certified by Corxia Corporation in dose calculation and administration of this regimen.

The dosimetric dose of iodine I 131 tositumomab should be given only to patients who have received at least three doses of saturated solution potassium iodide, three doses of Lugol's solution, or one dose of potassium iodide.

For treatment of adverse effects

Medications for the treatment of severe hypersensitivity reactions, including epinephrine, antihistamines, and corticosteroids should be available for immediate use.

Hematologic supportive care measures may be necessary following a therapeutic dose.

Acetaminophen 650 mg orally and diphenhydramine 50 mg orally were administered to all patients in the clinical trials as a pretreatment for infusional toxicity. However the value of the premedication is preventing infusion-related toxicity was not evaluated.

Parenteral Dosage Forms

TOSITUMOMAB AND IODINE I 131 TOSITUMOMAB INJECTION

Usual adult dose

Lymphomas, non-Hodgkin's (treatment)—

Tositumomab and Iodine I 131 tositumomab therapeutic regimen is administered in two steps, a dosimetric step and a therapeutic step:

- Dosimetric step—Intravenous infusion, tositumomab 450 mg over 1 hour preceding an intravenous dose of iodine I 131 tositumomab over 20 minutes
- Wait 7 to 14 days. Assess biodistribution. If biodistribution is not acceptable, do not proceed.
- Therapeutic step—Intravenous infusion, tositumomab 450 mg over 1 hour preceding an intravenous dose of iodine I 131 tositumomab; dose of iodine I 131 must be calculated, see full product information for details.

Note: Reduce the rate of infusion 50% for mild to moderate infusion toxicity; interrupt the infusion for severe infusional toxicity; infusion may be resumed at 50% the normal rate after resolution of severe infusion toxicity

Patients with mild thrombocytopenia—The dose of iodine I 131 tositumomab (in Step 2) should be reduced to that which will delivers 65 cGy total body irradiation and 35 mg tositumomab for patients with a baseline platelet count between 100,000 and 149,000 cells per cubic millimeter and that which delivers 75 cGy total body irradiation and 35 mg tositumomab for patients with a baseline platelet count greater than 150,000 cells per cubic millimeter.

Thyroid-blocking medications should be initiated at least 24 hours before receiving the dosimetric dose and continued until 14 days after the therapeutic dose.

Usual pediatric dose

Safety and efficacy have not been established.

Usual geriatric dose

See *Usual adult dose*.

Usual geriatric prescribing limits

See *Usual adult prescribing limits*.

Strength(s) usually available

U.S.—

Note: The components are shipped from separate sites. When ordering, ensure that the components are scheduled to arrive on the same day.

14 mg per mL tositumomab in maltose, sodium chloride, phosphate and water (Rx) [*Bexxar* (Dosimetric kit contains 4 vials—Two single use 225 mg vials, 1 single-use 35 mg vial of tositumomab, and one single-use vial of iodine I 131 (containing not less than 20 mL of iodine I 131 tositumomab at 0.1 mg per mL and 0.61 mCi per mL, respectively; Therapeutic kit contains 4 or 5 vials—Two single use 225 mg vials, 1 single-use 35 mg vial of tositumomab, and one or two single-use vials of iodine I 131 (containing not less than 20 mL of iodine I 131 tositumomab at nominal protein and activity concentrations of 1.1 mg per mL and 5.6 mCi per mL, respectively)].

Packaging and storage

Tositumomab—Store refrigerated at 2° to 8°C (36° to 46°F) prior to dilution. Protect from strong light. Do not shake. Do not freeze. Diluted solutions are stable for up to 24 hours when stored at 2° to 8°C (36° to 46°F) and for up to 8 hours at room temperature. Do not freeze diluted solutions.

Iodine I 131 tositumomab—Store frozen in lead pot at −20°C or below. Thawed doses are stable for up to 8 hours at 2° to 8°C (36° to 46°F) or at room temperature. Diluted doses should be stored at 2° to 8°C (36° to 46°F). Do not freeze diluted doses.

Preparation of dosage form

Read all directions thoroughly and assemble all materials before starting the radiolabeling procedure.

See the manufacturer's package insert for instructions.

The patient dose should be measured by a suitable radioactivity calibration system immediately prior to administration. The dose calibrator must be operated in accordance with the manufacturer's specifications and quality control for the measurement of In-131.

Proper aseptic technique and precautions for handling radioactive materials should be employed. Waterproof gloves should be utilized in the preparation and administration of the product. Appropriate shielding should be used during preparation and administration of the product.

Discard needles, syringes, and vials in accordance with local, state, and federal regulations governing radioactive and biohazardous waste.

Caution
Radioactive material

Developed: 04/25/2005

TRAMADOL Systemic†

VA CLASSIFICATION (Primary): CN103

Commonly used brand name(s): *Ultram; Ultram ER*.

Note: For a listing of dosage forms and brand names by country availability, see *Dosage Forms* section(s).

†Not commercially available in Canada.

Category

Analgesic.

Indications

Accepted

Pain (treatment)—Tramadol is indicated for the management of moderate to moderately severe pain. It has been used to treat pain following orthopedic and gynecological procedures, including cesarean section.

Pain, chronic (treatment)—Extended-release tramadol is indicated for the management of moderate to moderately severe chronic pain in adults who require around-the-clock treatment of their pain for an extended period of time.

Acceptance not established

Tramadol has been used for long-term treatment of *chronic pain* such as low back pain, neuropathic pain, orthopedic and joint conditions, and cancer pain. Tramadol may be a therapeutic option for patients who are intolerant to or inappropriate candidates for nonsteroidal anti-inflammatory drugs (NSAIDs); however, more studies evaluating safety and efficacy need to be established for long-term use.

Tramadol has been evaluated and has shown promise as an adjunct to NSAIDs for patients experiencing inadequate relief from *dental pain* with NSAIDs alone. Although tramadol would not be effective in patients needing only anti-inflammatory treatment, it would be effective in enhancing the suppression of pain. A small study found a single dose of tramadol given concomitantly with a single dose of ibuprofen enhanced suppression of dental pain caused by inflammation. However, additional studies need to be done to evaluate the use of tramadol and NSAIDs concomitantly as a therapeutic combination to enhance analgesic efficacy.

Pharmacology/Pharmacokinetics

Physicochemical characteristics

Source—Synthetic.

Molecular weight—299.84.

pKa—9.41.

Mechanism of action/Effect

Tramadol is a centrally-acting synthetic opioidanalgesic. The mechanism of action of tramadol is not completely understood, but it may bind to mu-opioid receptors and inhibit the reuptake of norepinephrine (NE) and serotonin. The ability of tramadol to inhibit the neuronal uptake of monoamines in the same concentration range at which it binds to mu-opioid receptors differentiates it from typical opioids. Tramadol consists of (+) and (−) enantiomers that appear to interact synergistically to produce antinociception. The (+) enantiomer is fivefold more potent in 5-hydroxytryptamine (5-HT) uptake and has a greater affinity for mu receptor binding than for NE uptake. The (−) enantiomer is five- to tenfold more potent in NE uptake inhibition and has less affinity for mu receptor binding than for 5-HT uptake. Electrophysiological studies show that tramadol, like morphine, depresses motor and sensory responses of the spinal nociceptive system by a spinal and a supraspinal action. Some opioid activity is derived from low-affinity binding of the parent compound and higher-affinity binding of the mono-*O*-desmethyltramadol (M1) metabolite to the opioid receptors. The analgesic potency of M1 is about six times greater than that of tramadol in animal models and 200 times more potent in mu-opioid receptor binding.

Note: It has been estimated that the analgesic potency of tramadol is one-tenth that of morphine.

Other actions/effects

Tramadol suppresses the cough reflex by binding to the mu-opioid receptor binding sites. Due to the high affinity binding of the M1 metabolite to the mu receptor, the metabolite has been found to have more cough suppressant activity than the parent compound.

Unlike morphine, tramadol has not been shown to cause histamine release.

Absorption

Oral—Rapid and almost complete. Mean absolute bioavailability of a 100-mg dose is approximately 75%. The rate or extent of absorption is not significantly affected by administration with food.

Distribution

The volume of distribution is 2.6 and 2.9 liters per kilogram of body weight (L/kg) in males and females, respectively, following a 100-mg intravenous dose. Tramadol crosses the blood-brain barrier in rats and possibly in humans. In women given tramadol during labor, the mean ratio of tramadol concentration in the umbilical veins compared to maternal veins was 0.83.

Protein binding

Low (20%). Independent of concentration up to 10 micrograms per mL (mcg/mL); saturation of binding occurs only at concentrations outside of the clinically relevant range.

Biotransformation

Hepatic. Extensively metabolized via *N*- and *O*-demethylation and glucuronidation or sulfation. The production of the active metabolite mono-*O*-desmethyltramadol (M1) is dependent on the CYP2D6 isoenzyme of cytochrome P450. The inactive metabolites are formed by *N*-demethylation.

Half-life

Terminal—

Individuals with normal renal function:

Tramadol—Approximately 6.3 hours (increased to 7 hours with multiple dosing [not clinically significant] and in individuals over 75 years of age [clinically significant]); approximately 7.9 hours for 200-mg extended-release tablet.

M1 metabolite—Approximately 7.4 hours; approximately 8.8 hours for 200-mg extended-release tablet.

Onset of action

Dose-dependent; generally within 1 hour.

Time to peak concentration

Plasma—

Following a single 100-mg dose:

Tramadol—2 hours.

M1 metabolite—3 hours.

Following an extended-release 200-mg tablet:

Tramadol—12 hours.

M1 metabolite—15 hours.

Time to steady state concentration

Plasma—

After administration of 100 mg four times a day:

About 2 days.

Peak serum concentration

Plasma—

Following a single 100-mg dose:

Tramadol—308 nanograms per mL ±78 nanograms/mL.

M1 metabolite—55 nanograms/mL ± 20 nanograms/mL.

Time to peak effect

Tramadol—2 hours.

M1 metabolite—3 hours.

Elimination

Renal—

30% unchanged; 60% as metabolites. Clearance rate is slightly higher in females than in males.

In dialysis—

7% of an administered dose is removed by hemodialysis.

Precautions to Consider

Carcinogenicity

No carcinogenicity was observed in mice given oral doses up to 150 mg per kg of body weight per day (approximately 2-fold the maximum daily human dose based on body surface conversion) for 26 weeks and in rats given oral doses up to 75 mg per kg of body weight per day for males and 100 mg per kg per day for females for two years. However, the excessive decrease in body weight gain observed in the rat study might reduced their sensitivity to any carcinogenic effect of the drug.

Tumorigenicity
Evidence of a statistically significant increase in two common murine tumors (pulmonary and hepatic) was observed in mice receiving oral doses up to 30 mg per kg of body weight (mg/kg) for approximately 2 years. However, no tumors were observed in a rat carcinogenicity study.

Mutagenicity
No evidence of mutagenicity was found in the Ames test, CHO/HPRT mammalian cell assay, mouse lymphoma assay, dominant lethal mutation test in mice, chromosome aberration test in Chinese hamsters, or bone marrow micronucleus tests in mice and Chinese hamsters. Weakly mutagenic results occurred in the presence of metabolic activation in the mouse lymphoma assay and micronucleus test in rats.

Pregnancy/Reproduction
Fertility—No impairment of fertility was observed at oral dose levels up to 50 mg/kg in male rats and 75 mg/kg in female rats.

Pregnancy—Tramadol has been shown to cross the placenta. Well-controlled studies in humans have not been done. Tramadol should be used during pregnancy only if the potential benefit justifies the potential risk to the fetus.

Studies have shown tramadol to be embryotoxic and fetotoxic in mice, rats, and rabbits at maternally toxic doses (3 to 15 times the maximum human dose or higher); however, it was found not to be teratogenic at these levels. Studies done in progeny of mice, rats, and rabbits given tramadol by various routes (up to 140 mg/kg for mice, 80 mg/kg for rats, or 300 mg/kg for rabbits) found no drug-related teratogenic effects. Transient delays in the developmental and behavioral parameters during the delivery of pups from rat dams were observed. At maternally toxic levels, fetal toxicity and embryotoxicity primarily included decreased fetal weights, skeletal ossification, and increased supernumerary ribs. A study in rabbits reported embryo and fetal lethality caused by extreme maternal toxicity at doses of 300 mg/kg. In peri- and postnatal studies in rats, decreased weights were observed in the progeny of dams that received oral (gavage) doses of 50 mg/kg or greater. At doses of 80 mg/kg (6 to 10 times the maximum human dose), pup survival was decreased early in lactation. The progeny of dams receiving 8, 10, 20, 25, or 40 mg/kg showed no signs of toxicity. Evidence of severe maternal toxicity was observed at higher doses; however, maternal toxicity was found at all dose levels.

Tramadol caused a decrease in neonatal body weight and survival in rats given an oral dose of 80 mg per kg of body weight during late gestation throughout lactation period. Neonatal seizures, neonatal withdrawal syndrome, fetal death and still birth have been noted in post-market reports.

FDA Pregnancy Category C.

Labor and delivery—Tramadol is not recommended for use in pregnant women prior to or during labor unless the potential benefits outweigh the risks, because safe use in pregnancy has not been established. Long-term use of tramadol during pregnancy may lead to physical dependence and postpartum withdrawal symptoms in the newborn.

Breast-feeding
Following a single intravenous 100-mg dose of tramadol, the cumulative distribution in breast milk within 16 hours postdose was 100 micrograms (mcg) of tramadol (0.1% of the maternal dose) and 27 mcg of M1. Use of oral tramadol is not recommended for obstetrical preoperative medication or postdelivery analgesia in nursing mothers because of lack of studies on its safety in infants and newborns.

Pediatrics
Tramadol tablets—No information is available on the relationship of age to the effects of tramadol in patients under 16 years of age. Safety and efficacy have not been established.

Tramadol extended-release tablets—Safety and efficacy in children under 18 years of age have not been established. The use of extended-release tramadol in the pediatric population is not recommended.

Geriatrics
Studies have shown that, in subjects over the age of 75 years, serum concentrations are slightly elevated and the elimination half-life is slightly prolonged. In addition, elderly patients are more likely to have age-related renal function impairment that may require dosage adjustment. Dose selection should be cautious, especially in those older than 75 years of age.

Drug interactions and/or related problems
The following drug interactions and/or related problems have been selected on the basis of their potential clinical significance (possible mechanism in parentheses where appropriate)—not necessarily inclusive (» = major clinical significance):

» Alcohol or
» Anesthetic agents or
» Central nervous system (CNS) depression-producing medications, other (see *Appendix II*), such as:
  Antidepressants, tricyclics
  Opioid analgesics
  Phenothiazines
  Sedative hypnotics
  Selective serotonin re-uptake inhibitors (SSRI antidepressants or anorectics)
  Tranquilizers
    (caution is recommended because concurrent use may potentiate the CNS and respiratory depressant effects; tricyclic antidepressants, SSRIs, and other opioids may increase the risk of seizures; SSRIs increase risk of serotonin syndrome; dosage reduction is recommended)

» Carbamazepine
  (causes a significant increase in tramadol metabolism, presumably through metabolic enzyme induction; may have a significantly reduced analgesic effect of tramadol; because carbamazepine increases tramadol metabolism and because of increased seizure risk associated with tramadol, concomitant use not recommended)

CYP2D6 inhibitors such as
  Amitriptyline or
  Fluoxetine or
  Paroxetine
    (concomitant administration could result in some inhibition of the metabolism of tramadol)

CYP3A4 inducers such as
  Rifampin or
  St. John's Wort

CYP3A4 inhibitors such as
  Erythromycin or
  Ketoconazole
    (concomitant use may affect the metabolism of tramadol leading to altered tramadol exposure)

Digoxin or
Warfarin
  (rare post-marketing reports of digoxin toxicity and alteration of warfarin effect, including elevation of prothrombin times with concomitant use)

» Monoamine oxidase (MAO) inhibitors, including furazolidone and procarbazine or
» Neuroleptics or
» Other drugs that reduce seizure threshold
  (tramadol inhibits the uptake of norepinephrine and serotonin; serotonin is believed to be the biogenic amine responsible for the toxic interactions; concurrent use may decrease seizure threshold; caution is recommended)

Quinidine
  (concurrent use may increase concentrations of tramadol and decrease concentration of the M1 metabolite by competitively inhibiting the CYP2D6 isoenzyme; clinical consequences of these findings are unknown)

Propafenone
  (concurrent use may increase concentrations of tramadol and decrease concentration of the M1 metabolite by inhibiting the CYP2D6 isoenzyme)

Medical considerations/Contraindications
The medical considerations/contraindications included have been selected on the basis of their potential clinical significance (reasons given in parentheses where appropriate)—not necessarily inclusive (» = major clinical significance).

Note: Tramadol does not affect the bile duct sphincter, which indicates that it is less likely than opioids to cause urinary retention, constipation, or worsening of pancreatic or biliary disorders.

Except under special circumstances, this medication should not be used when the following medical problems exist:

» Acute intoxication with alcohol, hypnotics, centrally-acting analgesics, opioids, or psychotropic drugs
  (risk of respiratory depression and may worsen central nervous system depression)

» Addiction prone or
» Suicidal
  (tramadol should not be prescribed)

» Drug abuse or dependence, current or history of, including alcoholism
  (patient predisposition to drug abuse)

» Hypersensitivity to tramadol or any other component of the product or
» Hypersensitivity to opioids

Risk-benefit should be considered when the following medical problems exist:

Acute abdominal conditions
  (diagnosis may be obscured)

Epilepsy or
History of seizures or
Recognized risk for seizure such as
Alcohol and drug withdrawal
CNS infections
Head trauma
Metabolic disorders
(risk of convulsions may increase in these patients)

» Hepatic function impairment
(metabolism of tramadol and M1 is reduced in patients with advanced cirrhosis of the liver; dosage reduction is recommended; delay in achievement of steady state may result from the prolonged half-life in this condition)

Increased intracranial pressure or
Head trauma
(tramadol causes pupillary changes [miosis] that may obscure the existence, extent, or course of intracranial pathology; clinicians should consider the possibility of a drug effect when evaluating mental status)

» Renal function impairment
(decreased rate and extent of excretion of tramadol and its active metabolite M1; dosage reduction is recommended in patients with creatinine clearance of less than 30 mL per minute [mL/min]; delay in achievement of steady-state may result from the prolonged half-life in this condition)

» Respiratory depression, risk of
(tramadol may decrease respiratory drive and increase airway resistance in patients with this condition; although there is absence of significant respiratory depression following epidural and intravenous use, caution is still recommended with administration of oral tramadol in patients at risk for respiratory depression; may also occur with concurrent administration of anesthetic medication or alcohol)

Side/Adverse Effects

Note: Tramadol can produce drug dependence of the mu-opioid type and may potentially be abused. Tolerance development, drug-seeking behavior and craving have been associated with the use of tramadol. The active metabolite of tramadol may be responsible for some delay in onset of activity and some extension of the duration of mu-opioid activity. Delayed mu-opioid activity is believed to reduce drug abuse liability. One case has been reported in which a patient developed tolerance to and dependence on oral tramadol (increase in daily dose by 500% over 6 years, from 50 to 300 mg per day). However, in a 3-week study no tolerance developed to oral tramadol. A few studies found no or very little development of tolerance with parenteral administration of tramadol.

The following side/adverse effects have been selected on the basis of their potential clinical significance (possible signs and symptoms in parentheses where appropriate)—not necessarily inclusive:

Those indicating need for medical attention

Incidence less frequent or rare

Abnormal gait (change in walking and balance); ***allergic reaction*** (severe redness, swelling, and itching of the skin); ***amnesia*** (loss of memory); ***appendicitis*** (stomach or lower abdominal pain; severe cramping; bloating; nausea; vomiting; fever); ***blood pressure increased; chest pain; cholecystitis*** (indigestion; stomach pain; severe nausea; vomiting); ***cholelithiasis*** (abdominal fullness; gaseous abdominal pain; recurrent fever; yellow eyes or skin); ***cognitive dysfunction*** (trouble performing routine tasks); ***drug withdrawal syndrome*** (abdominal pain; seizures; nervousness; shaking; nausea; vomiting; sweats); ***dyspnea*** (shortness of breath); ***hallucinations*** (seeing, hearing, or feeling things that are not there); ***heart rate increased; hematuria*** (blood in urine); ***hypoaesthesia*** (abnormal or decreased touch sensation); ***myocardial infarction*** (chest pain or discomfort; pain or discomfort in arms, jaw, back or neck; shortness of breath; nausea; sweating; vomiting); ***orthostatic hypotension*** (dizziness or lightheadedness when getting up from a lying or sitting position); ***palpitations*** (irregular heartbeat); ***pancreatitis*** (bloating; chills; constipation; darkened urine; fast heartbeat; fever; indigestion; loss of appetite; nausea; pains in stomach, side, or abdomen, possibly radiating to the back; vomiting; yellow eyes or skin); ***paresthesia*** (numbness, tingling, pain, or weakness in hands or feet); ***peripheral ischemia*** (itching of skin; numbness and tingling of face, fingers, or toes; pain in arms, legs, or lower back, especially pain in calves and/or heels upon exertion; pale, bluish-colored, or cold hands or feet; weak or absent pulses in legs); ***seizures; syncope*** (fainting); ***tachycardia*** (fast heartbeat); ***tremor*** (trembling and shaking of hands or feet); ***urinary frequency*** (frequent urge to urinate); ***urinary retention*** (difficult urination); ***urticaria*** (redness, swelling, and itching of the skin); ***vesicles*** (blisters under the skin); ***visual disturbances*** (blurred vision)

Those indicating need for medical attention only if they continue or are bothersome

Incidence more frequent

Abdominal or stomach pain; anorexia (loss of appetite); ***asthenia*** (loss of strength or weakness); ***central nervous system (CNS) stimulation*** (agitation; anxiety; nervousness; spasticity; unusual feeling of excitement); ***constipation; depression*** (discouragement; feeling sad or empty; irritability; lack of appetite; loss of interest or pleasure; tiredness; trouble concentrating; trouble sleeping); ***diarrhea; dizziness or vertigo; drowsiness; dry mouth; dyspepsia*** (heartburn); ***flushing*** (feeling of warmth; redness of the face, neck, arms and occasionally, upper chest); ***headache; influenza-like illness*** (chills; cough; diarrhea; fever; general feeling of discomfort or illness; headache; joint pain; loss of appetite; muscle aches and pains; nausea; runny nose; shivering; sore throat; sweating; trouble sleeping; unusual tiredness or weakness; vomiting); ***nasal congestion*** (stuffy nose); ***nausea; pruritus*** (itching of the skin); ***restlessness; rhinorrhea*** (runny nose); ***rigors*** (feeling unusually cold; shivering); ***skin rash; somnolence*** (sleepiness or unusual drowsiness); ***sweating; vomiting; weakness***

Note: Tramadol may produce opioid-like effects, including *constipation, dizziness, drowsiness, nausea, pruritus,* and *sweating,* but causes less respiratory depression than morphine.

Less frequent or rare

Abnormal dreams; appetite decreased; arthralgia (pain in joints; muscle pain or stiffness; difficulty in moving); ***back pain; bronchitis*** (cough producing mucus; difficulty breathing; shortness of breath; tightness in chest; wheezing); ***cellulitis*** (itching, pain, redness, swelling, tenderness, warmth on skin); ***confusion; contusion*** (pain; swelling; skin discoloration); ***clamminess; cough; difficulty in micturition*** (trouble in holding or releasing urine; painful urination); ***dysuria*** (difficult or painful urination; burning while urinating); ***ear infection*** (change in hearing; earache or pain in ear; ear drainage; fever); ***edema lower limb*** (swelling of legs and feet); ***dermatitis*** (blistering, crusting, irritation, itching, or reddening of skin; cracked, dry, scaly skin; swelling); ***disturbance in attention; euphoric mood*** (false or unusual sense of well-being); ***fall; feeling hot; feeling jittery; flatulence*** (excessive gas); ***gastroenteritis viral*** (abdominal or stomach pain; diarrhea; loss of appetite; nausea; weakness); ***influenza*** (chills; cough; diarrhea; fever; general feeling of discomfort or illness; headache; joint pain; loss of appetite; muscle aches and pains; nausea; runny nose; shivering; sore throat; sweating; trouble sleeping; unusual tiredness or weakness; vomiting); ***irritability; joint sprain; joint stiffness; joint swelling; libido decreased*** (loss in sexual ability, desire, drive, or performance; decreased interest in sexual intercourse; inability to have or keep an erection); ***malaise*** (general feeling of bodily discomfort); ***menopausal symptoms*** (hot flashes); ***migraine*** (headache, severe and throbbing); ***muscle cramps, spasms or twitching; muscle injury; myalgia*** (joint pain; swollen joints; muscle aching or cramping; muscle pains or stiffness; difficulty in moving); ***nasopharyngitis*** (stuffy or runny nose; muscle aches; unusual tiredness or weakness; fever; sore throat; headache); ***neck pain; night sweats; osteoarthritis aggravated*** (difficulty in moving; muscle pain or stiffness; pain, swelling, or redness in joints); ***pain; pain in limb; peripheral swelling*** (swelling of hands, ankles, feet, or lower legs); ***piloerection*** (goosebumps); ***pneumonia*** (chest pain; cough; fever or chills; sneezing; shortness of breath; sore throat; troubled breathing; tightness in chest; wheezing); ***pyrexia*** (fever); ***sedation*** (drowsiness; sleepiness; relaxed and calm); ***shivering; sleep disorder*** (trouble in sleeping); ***sinus congestion*** (stuffy nose; headache); ***sinusitus*** (pain or tenderness around eyes and cheekbones; fever; stuffy or runny nose; headache; cough; shortness of breath or troubled breathing; tightness of chest or wheezing); ***sneezing; sore throat; upper respiratory tract infection*** (ear congestion; nasal congestion; chills; cough, fever, sneezing, or sore throat; body aches or pain; headache; loss of voice; runny nose; unusual tiredness or weakness; difficulty in breathing); ***urinary tract infection*** (bladder pain; bloody or cloudy urine; difficult, burning, or painful urination; frequent urge to urinate; lower back or side pain); ***vasodilation*** (flushing or redness of the skin); ***viral infection*** (chills; cough or hoarseness; fever; cold flu-like symptoms); ***weight increased or decreased; yawning***

Those indicating possible withdrawal and the need for medical attention if they occur after medication is discontinued

Anxiety; body aches; diarrhea; fast heartbeat; fever, runny nose, or sneezing; gooseflesh; hypertension (high blood pressure); ***increased sweating; increased yawning; loss of appetite; nausea or vomiting; nervousness, restlessness, or irritability; shivering***

or trembling; stomach cramps; trouble in sleeping; unusually large pupils; weakness

Note: The *signs and symptoms of withdrawal* listed above are characteristics of the abstinence syndrome produced by abrupt discontinuation of a mu-receptor agonist. Tramadol does have some activity involving the mu-receptor; therefore, abrupt discontinuation may include some of these signs and symptoms. However, these effects may be milder compared with opiate agonists. Tapering the dose of tramadol may prevent some of the signs and symptoms of withdrawal from occurring. Minimal withdrawal signs have been observed in naloxone-precipitation studies.

Overdose

For specific information on the agents used in the management of tramadol overdose, see:

- *Diazepam* in *Benzodiazepines (Systemic)* monograph; and/or
- *Naloxone (Systemic)* monograph.

For more information on the management of overdose or unintentional ingestion, **contact a Poison Control Center** (see *Poison Control Center Listing*).

Clinical effects of overdose

The following effects have been selected on the basis of their potential clinical significance (possible signs and symptoms in parentheses where appropriate)—not necessarily inclusive:

Acute and chronic effects

Bradycardia (chest pain or discomfort; lightheadedness; dizziness or fainting; shortness of breath; slow or irregular heartbeat; unusual tiredness); ***cold, clammy skin; coma*** (change in consciousness; loss of consciousness); ***confusion; convulsions; death; dizziness, severe; drowsiness, severe; nervousness or restlessness, severe; pinpoint pupils of eyes; skeletal muscle flaccidity*** (no muscle tone); ***slow heartbeat; seizures; slow or troubled breathing; stupor*** (decreased awareness or responsiveness; severe sleepiness); ***weakness, severe***

Note: Studies have found the administration of intravenous tramadol may produce respiratory depression. However, morphine causes more clinically significant respiratory depression than tramadol. Clinical studies evaluating oral doses have not reported any clinically relevant respiratory depressant effects.

Deaths due to tramadol overdose have been reported with abuse and misuse by ingesting, inhaling, or injecting crushed tablets. Case report reviews have indicated that fatal overdose risk is increased when tramadol is abused concomitantly with alcohol or other CNS depressants, including other opioids.

Treatment of overdose

To decrease absorption—

Gastric lavage may be performed.

Specific treatment—

Administration of the opioid antagonist naloxone, which will reverse some, but not all, symptoms caused by overdosage with tramadol. Administer naloxone with caution because it may precipitate seizures. See the package insert or *Naloxone (Systemic)* for specific dosing guidelines for use of this product.

For treatment of convulsions caused by tramadol toxicity: Diazepam has been effective in treating convulsions. See the package insert or *Diazepam* in *Benzodiazepines (Systemic)* for specific dosing guidelines for use of this product.

Cardiac arrest or arrhythmias may require cardiac massage or defibrillation.

Supportive care—

Supportive measures such as establishing intravenous lines, hydration, correction of electrolyte imbalance, oxygenation, and support of ventilatory function are essential for maintaining the vital functions of the patient. Patients in whom intentional overdose is confirmed or suspected should be referred for psychiatric consultation.

Note: Hemodialysis is not recommended in overdose, since it removes less than 7% of the administered dose in a 4-hour dialysis period.

Patient Consultation

As an aid to patient consultation, refer to *Advice for the Patient, Tramadol (Systemic)*.

In providing consultation, consider emphasizing the following selected information (» = major clinical significance):

Before using this medication

» Conditions affecting use, especially:

Hypersensitivity to tramadol or any component of the product or opioids

Pregnancy—Crosses the placenta; safe use in pregnancy has not been established; should be used during pregnancy only if potential benefit justifies potential risk to fetus

Breast-feeding—Distributed into breast milk; use is not recommended

Use in children—Tablets: safety/efficacy not established in children under 16 years of age; extended-release tablets: safety/efficacy not established in children under 18 years of age

Other medications, especially alcohol, anesthetic agents, CNS depression-producing medications, carbamazepine, MAOIs, neuroleptics, or other drugs that reduce seizure threshold

Other medical problems, especially acute intoxication with alcohol, hypnotics, centrally-acting analgesics, opioids, or psychotropic drugs; addiction prone or suicidal individuals; current drug abuse or dependence; hepatic function impairment; renal function impairment; or risk of respiratory depression

Proper use of this medication

» Not increasing dose if medication is less effective after a few weeks; checking with physician first

» Importance of not taking more medication than the amount prescribed because of danger of overdose

» Proper dosing

Missed dose (if on scheduled dosing): Taking as soon as possible; not taking if almost time for next dose; not doubling doses

» Proper storage

Precautions while using this medication

» Avoiding use of alcoholic beverages or other CNS depressants during therapy unless prescribed or otherwise approved by physician

» Caution if dizziness, drowsiness, or lightheadedness occurs

» Caution when getting up from a lying or sitting position

Lying down if nausea or vomiting, or dizziness or lightheadedness occurs

Informing physician or dentist of use of medication if any kind of surgery (including dental surgery) or emergency treatment is required

» Suspected overdose: Getting emergency help at once

Side/adverse effects

Signs of potential side effects, especially abnormal gait, allergic reaction, amnesia, appendicitis, blood pressure increased, chest pain, cholecystitis, cholelithiasis, cognitive dysfunction, drug withdrawal syndrome, dyspnea, hallucinations, heart rate increased, hematuria, hypoaesthesia, myocardial infarction, orthostatic hypotension, palpitations, pancreatitis, paresthesia, peripheral ischemia, seizures, syncope, tachycardia, tremor, urinary frequency, urinary retention, urticaria, vesicles, and visual disturbances

Oral Dosage Forms

TRAMADOL HYDROCHLORIDE EXTENDED-RELEASE TABLETS

Usual adult dose

Analgesic for chronic pain—Oral, 100 mg once daily and titrated up as necessary by 100-mg increments every five days to relief of pain and depending upon tolerability.

Note: Extended-release tramadol should not used in patients with impaired renal function (creatinine clearance less than 30 mL/minute [mL/min]).

Extended-release tramadol should not used in patients with impaired hepatic function (Child-Pugh Class C).

Usual adult prescribing limits

Not to exceed 300 mg per day.

Usual pediatric dose

Children up to 18 years of age—Safety and efficacy have not been established.

Usual geriatric dose

See *Usual adult and adolescent dose* with consideration that dose selection in patients over 65 years of age should be cautious, usually starting at the low end of the dosing range. Even greater caution should be used in patients over 75 years due to the greater frequency of adverse events in this population.

Strength(s) usually available

U.S.—

100 mg (Rx) [*Ultram ER* (ethylcellulose; dibutyl sebacate; polyvinyl pyrrolidone; sodium stearyl fumarate; colloidal silicon dioxide; polyvinyl alcohol)].

200 mg (Rx) [*Ultram ER* (ethylcellulose; dibutyl sebacate; polyvinyl pyrrolidone; sodium stearyl fumarate; colloidal silicon dioxide; polyvinyl alcohol)].

300 mg (Rx) [*Ultram ER* (ethylcellulose; dibutyl sebacate; polyvinyl pyrrolidone; sodium stearyl fumarate; colloidal silicon dioxide; polyvinyl alcohol)].

Canada—

Not commercially available.

Packaging and storage

Store at 25 °C (77 °F); excursions permitted between 15 and 30 °C (59 and 86 °F), in a tight container.

Auxiliary labeling

- May cause drowsiness.
- Avoid alcoholic beverages.

Note: Tramadol is not a controlled substance in the U.S.

TRAMADOL HYDROCHLORIDE TABLETS

Usual adult and adolescent dose

Analgesic—Oral, 25 to 100 mg every four to six hours as needed.

Note: In patients with moderate to moderately severe chronic pain not requiring rapid onset of analgesic effect, the tolerability of tramadol can be improved by initiating therapy with the following titration regimen: tramadol should be started at 25 mg once daily in the morning and titrated in 25 mg increments as separate doses every 3 days to reach 100 mg daily (25 mg four times a day). Thereafter, the total dose may be increased by 50 mg as tolerated every 3 days to reach 200 mg daily (50 mg four times a day). After titration, tramadol 50 to 100 mg can be administered as needed for pain relief every four to six hours.

In patients needing rapid onset of analgesic effect, the higher 50 to 100 mg initial dose may be warranted if the benefits outweigh the risk of discontinuation due to adverse events associated with higher initial doses.

Patients with impaired renal function (creatinine clearance less than 30 mL/minute [mL/min]) should receive 50 to 100 mg every twelve hours.

The recommended dose in patients with cirrhosis is 50 mgevery twelve hours.

Patients on hemodialysis can receive their usual dose on the day of dialysis.

Usual adult prescribing limits

Oral, 400 mg per day (200 mg per day in patients with creatinine clearance of less than 30 mL/min).

Usual pediatric dose

Children up to 16 years of age—Safety and efficacy have not been established.

Children 16 years of age and over—See *Usual adult and adolescent dose.*

Usual geriatric dose

See *Usual adult and adolescent dose* with consideration that dose selection in patients over 65 years of age should be cautious, usually starting at the low end of the dosing range.

Usual geriatric prescribing limits

In patients over 75 years of age, the limit is 300 mg per day in divided doses.

Strength(s) usually available

U.S.—

50 mg (Rx) [*Ultram* (lactose)].

Canada—

Not commercially available.

Packaging and storage

Store between 15 and 30 °C (59 and 86 °F), in a tight container.

Auxiliary labeling

- May cause drowsiness.
- Avoid alcoholic beverages.

Note: Tramadol is not a controlled substance in the U.S.

Selected Bibliography

Levien TL, Baker DE. Reviews of tramadol and tretinoin. Hosp Pharm 1996; 31(1): 54-67.

Preston KL, Jasinski DR, Testa M. Abuse potential and pharmacological comparison of tramadol and morphine. Drug and Alcohol Depend 1991; 27: 7-17.

Sunshine A, Olson N, Zighelboim I, et al. Analgesic oral efficacy of tramadol hydrochloride in postoperative pain. Clin Pharmacol Ther 1992; 51: 740-6.

Revised: 03/09/2006

TRAMADOL AND ACETAMINOPHEN Systemic

VA CLASSIFICATION (Primary): CN101

Commonly used brand name(s): *Ultracet.*

NOTE: The *Tramadol and Acetaminophen (Systemic)* monograph is maintained on the *USP DI* electronic data base. A copy of the most recent revision of the complete monograph can be accessed on the *USP DI* Updates Online website. See the front cover of book for details on accessing the site.

For information on the specific components of this combination, see the *USP DI* monographs for *Tramadol (Systemic),* and *Acetaminophen (Systemic).*

The information that follows is selectively abstracted from the complete monograph and is provided to facilitate drug use review and patient counseling.

Note: For a listing of dosage forms and brand names by country availability, see *Dosage Forms* section(s).

Category

Analgesic.

Indications

Accepted

Acute pain (treatment)—Tramadol and acetaminophen combination is indicated for short-term (five days or less) management of acute pain.

Patient Consultation

As an aid to patient consultation, refer to *Advice for the Patient, Tramadol and Acetaminophen (Systemic).*

In providing consultation, consider emphasizing the following selected information (» = major clinical significance):

Before using this medication

» Conditions affecting use, especially:

Hypersensitivity to tramadol, opioids or acetaminophen

Pregnancy—Tramadol crosses the placenta; not recommended for use during pregnancy

Breast-feeding—Tramadol is distributed into breast milk; use is not recommended

Other medications, especially alcohol, antidepressants (TCA and SSRI), carbamazepine, CNS depressants or anesthetic agents, MAO inhibitors, neuroleptics, other acetaminophen-containing products, other opioid analgesics or oral anticoagulants

Other medical problems, especially acute intoxication with alcohol, hypnotics, centrally-acting analgesics, opioids, or psychotropic drugs; alcohol or drug withdrawal; central nervous system infection; drug abuse or dependence; epilepsy; head trauma; hepatic function impairment; metabolic disorders; physical dependence on opioids; renal function impairment; or risk of respiratory depression

Proper use of this medication

» Importance of not taking more medication than the amount prescribed because of danger of overdose

» Proper dosing

» Proper storage

Precautions while using this medication

» Avoiding use of alcoholic beverages or other CNS depressants during therapy unless prescribed or otherwise approved by physician

» Caution if dizziness, drowsiness, or lightheadedness occurs

» Caution when getting up from a lying or sitting position

Lying down if nausea or vomiting, or dizziness or lightheadedness occurs

Informing physician or dentist of use of medication if any kind of surgery (including dental surgery) or emergency treatment is required

» Possible dryness of mouth; using sugarless candy or gum, ice, or saliva substitute for relief of dry mouth; checking with physician or dentist if dry mouth continues for more than 2 weeks

» Importance of not stopping medication abruptly without consulting physician

Side/adverse effects

Signs of potential side effects, especially allergic reaction, anaphylactoid reactions, chest pain, and seizures

Oral Dosage Forms

TRAMADOL HYDROCHLORIDE AND ACETAMINOPHEN TABLETS

Usual adult and adolescent dose

Analgesic—

Oral, two tablets (75 mg tramadol, 650 mg acetaminophen) every four to six hours as needed for up to five days.

Note: Patients with impaired renal function (creatinine clearance less than 30 mL/minute), the dosing interval should be increased not to exceed 2 tablets every twelve hours.

Usual adult prescribing limits

Oral, 8 tablets per day (4 tablets per day in patients with creatinine clearance of less than 30 mL/min for up to five days.)

Usual pediatric dose

Children up to 16 years of age—Safety and efficacy have not been established.

Usual geriatric dose

See *Usual adult and adolescent dose.*

Note: In elderly patients, dose selection should be cautious, reflecting the greater frequency of decreased hepatic, renal, cardiac function, concomitant disease and multiple drug therapy.

Strength(s) usually available

U.S.—

37.5 mg tramadol and 325 mg acetaminophen (Rx) [*Ultracet* (powdered cellulose; pregelatinized starch; sodium starch glycolate; starch; purified water; magnesium stearate; OPADRY light yellow; carnauba wax)].

Canada—

Not commercially available.

Auxiliary labeling

- May cause drowsiness.
- Avoid alcoholic beverages.

Revised: 05/06/2002

TRANDOLAPRIL—See *Angiotensin-converting Enzyme (ACE) Inhibitors (Systemic)*

TRANDOLAPRIL AND VERAPAMIL Systemic

VA CLASSIFICATION (Primary): CV401

Commonly used brand name(s): *Tarka*.

NOTE: The *Trandolapril and Verapamil (Systemic)* monograph is maintained on the *USP DI* electronic data base. A copy of the most recent revision of the complete monograph can be accessed on the *USP DI* Updates Online website. See the front cover of book for details on accessing the site.

For information on the specific components of this combination, see the *USP DI* monographs for *Trandolapril (Systemic)*, and *Calcium Channel Blocking Agents (Systemic)*.

The information that follows is selectively abstracted from the complete monograph and is provided to facilitate drug use review and patient counseling.

Note: For a listing of dosage forms and brand names by country availability, see *Dosage Forms* section(s).

Category

Antihypertensive.

Indications

Accepted

Hypertension (treatment)—The combination of trandolapril and verapamil is indicated for the treatment of hypertension. However, it is not indicated for initial treatment of hypertension.

For additional information on initial therapeutic guidelines related to the treatment of hypertension, see *Appendix III*.

Patient Consultation

As an aid to patient consultation, refer to *Advice for the Patient, Trandolapril and Verapamil (Systemic)*.

In providing consultation, consider emphasizing the following selected information (» = major clinical significance):

Before using this medication

» Conditions affecting use, especially:

Hypersensitivity to trandolapril, other angiotensin-converting enzyme (ACE) inhibitors, or verapamil

Pregnancy—ACE inhibitor-associated fetal and neonatal hypotension, skull hypoplasia, renal failure, and death reported in humans

Breast-feeding—Verapamil is distributed into breast milk; use of the combination product is not recommended in nursing mothers

Use in the elderly—Bioavailability and AUC of trandolapril and verapamil are increased; increased elimination half-life of verapamil; elderly patients may experience greater sensitivity to drug effects

Surgical—Anesthesia with hypotension-producing agents may cause excessive hypotension; prolonged recovery from neuromuscular blockade

Other medications, especially beta-adrenergic blocking agents, digitalis glycosides, disopyramide, diuretics, potassium-containing salt substitutes, potassium-sparing diuretics, or potassium supplements

Other medical problems, especially accessory bypass tract accompanied by atrial flutter or fibrillation, cardiogenic shock, congestive heart failure, hepatic function impairment, history of ACE inhibitor-associated angioedema, hypertrophic cardiomyopathy (HCM), hypotension (systolic pressure less than 90 mm Hg), renal function impairment, second- or third-degree atrioventricular (AV) block (except in patients with a functioning artificial ventricular pacemaker), severe left ventricular dysfunction, sick sinus syndrome (except in patients with a functioning artificial ventricular pacemaker), and ventricular dysfunction with concurrent beta-adrenergic blocking agent use

Proper use of this medication

» Compliance with therapy; taking medication at the same time each day to maintain the therapeutic effect

Swallowing tablets whole without crushing or chewing

Taking with food

» Proper dosing

Missed dose: Taking as soon as possible; not taking if almost time for next scheduled dose; not doubling doses

» Proper storage

Precautions while using this medication

Regular visits to the physician to check progress

Notifying physician immediately if pregnancy is suspected

Not taking other medications, especially potassium supplements or salt substitutes that contain potassium, unless discussed with physician

Caution when driving or doing other things requiring alertness because of possible dizziness, lightheadedness, and syncope due to symptomatic hypotension

Reporting any signs of infection (fever, sore throat, chills) to physician because of risk of neutropenia

Reporting any signs of facial or extremity swelling and difficulty in swallowing or breathing because of risk of angioedema

To prevent dehydration and hypotension, checking with physician if severe nausea, vomiting, or diarrhea occurs and continues

Caution when exercising or during hot weather because of the risk of dehydration and hypotension due to reduced fluid volume

Caution if any kind of surgery (including dental surgery) or emergency treatment is required

Side/adverse effects

Signs of potential side effects, especially angioedema, bradycardia, bronchitis, chest pain, dyspnea, edema, hepatotoxicity, hyperkalemia, hypotension, neutropenia or agranulocytosis

Oral Dosage Forms

TRANDOLAPRIL AND VERAPAMIL HYDROCHLORIDE EXTENDED-RELEASE TABLETS

Usual adult dose

Antihypertensive—

Oral, 1 or 2 tablets a day, as determined by individual titration with the component agents.

Usual adult prescribing limits

4 mg trandolapril and 240 mg verapamil hydrochloride.

Usual pediatric dose
Safety and efficacy have not been established in patients below 18 years of age.

Strength(s) usually available
U.S.—

1 mg trandolapril in immediate-release form and 240 mg verapamil hydrochloride in extended-release form (Rx) [*Tarka*].

2 mg trandolapril in immediate-release form and 180 mg verapamil hydrochloride in extended-release form (Rx) [*Tarka*].

2 mg trandolapril in immediate-release form and 240 mg verapamil hydrochloride in extended-release form (Rx) [*Tarka*].

4 mg trandolapril in immediate-release form and 240 mg verapamil hydrochloride in extended-release form (Rx) [*Tarka*].

Auxiliary labeling
- Do not take other medicines without your doctor's advice.
- Take with food.

Developed: 08/10/1998

TRANEXAMIC ACID Systemic

VA CLASSIFICATION (Primary/Secondary): BL116/IM900

Commonly used brand name(s): *Cyklokapron.*

NOTE: The *Tranexamic Acid (Systemic)* monograph is maintained on the *USP DI* electronic data base. A copy of the most recent revision of the complete monograph can be accessed on the *USP DI* Updates Online website. See the front cover of book for details on accessing the site.

The information that follows is selectively abstracted from the complete monograph and is provided to facilitate drug use review and patient counseling.

Note: For a listing of dosage forms and brand names by country availability, see *Dosage Forms* section(s).

Category
Antifibrinolytic; antihemorrhagic.

Indications
Note: Bracketed information in the *Indications* section refers to uses that are not included in U.S. product labeling.

Accepted
Hemorrhage, following dental and oral surgery, in patients with hemophilia (prophylaxis and treatment)

[Hemorrhage, oral, in patients with hemophilia (treatment)[1]]

[Hemorrhage, postsurgical (treatment)] or

[Hemorrhage, hyperfibrinolysis-induced (treatment)]—Tranexamic acid is indicated for the management of hemophilic patients (those having Factor VIII or Factor IX deficiency) who have [oral mucosal bleeding[1]], or are undergoing tooth extraction [or other oral surgical procedures[1]]. The medication prevents or decreases hemorrhaging in these patients and reduces the need for administration of clotting factors, particularly when desmopressin is also used.

[Tranexamic acid is indicated for the treatment of severe localized bleeding secondary to hyperfibrinolysis, including epistaxis, hyphema, or hypermenorrhea (menorrhagia) and hemorrhage following certain surgical procedures, such as conization of the cervix.]

[Antifibrinolytic agents are used to treat severe hemorrhaging caused by thrombolytic agents such as alteplase (tissue-type plasminogen activator, recombinant), anistreplase (anisoylated plasminogen-streptokinase activator complex), streptokinase, or urokinase.][1] However, controlled studies to demonstrate their efficacy have not been done in humans.

[Bleeding responsive to antifibrinolytic therapy also may occur following heart surgery (with or without cardiac bypass procedures) and portacaval shunt, prostatectomy, nephrectomy, or bladder surgery, and in association with hematologic disorders (such as aplastic anemia), abruptio placentae, hepatic cirrhosis, neoplastic disease, and polycystic or neoplastic diseases of the genitourinary system.][1]

[Angioedema, hereditary (treatment)]—Tranexamic acid is indicated for the treatment of hereditary angioedema. It is used to reduce the frequency and severity of acute attacks in patients with this disorder.

Note: Antifibrinolytic agents are ineffective in bleeding caused by loss of vascular integrity; a definite clinical diagnosis or confirmation of hyperfibrinolysis (hyperplasminemia) via laboratory studies is required before tranexamic acid is used to treat hemorrhage. However, some conditions and laboratory findings suggestive of hyperfibrinolysis are also present in disseminated intravascular coagulation; differentiation between the two conditions is essential because antifibrinolytic agents may promote thrombus formation in patients with disseminated intravascular coagulation and must *not* be used unless heparin is administered concurrently. The following criteria may be useful in differential diagnosis:

Test	Primary Hyperfibrinolysis Results	Disseminated Intravascular Coagulation Results
Platelet count*	Normal	Decreased
Protamine para-coagulation test	Negative	Positive
Euglobulin clotlysis time	Decreased	Normal

*Following extracorporeal circulation (during cardiovascular surgery), decreased platelet count may not be useful for differentiating between primary hyperfibrinolysis and disseminated intravascular coagulation; the other criteria may be more useful in differential diagnosis in these patients.

[1]Not included in Canadian product labeling.

Patient Consultation
As an aid to patient consultation, refer to *Advice for the Patient, Antifibrinolytic Agents (Systemic).*

In providing consultation, consider emphasizing the following selected information (» = major clinical significance):

Before using this medication
» Conditions affecting use, especially:

Sensitivity to tranexamic acid, history of

Pregnancy—Tranexamic acid crosses the placenta, but has not been reported to cause problems when given to pregnant women

Breast-feeding—Tranexamic acid is distributed into breast milk

Other medical problems, especially defective color vision, hematuria of upper urinary tract origin, predisposition to or history of thrombosis, renal function impairment, and subarachnoid hemorrhage

Proper use of this medication
» Importance of not using more or less medication than the amount prescribed

» Proper dosing

Missed dose: Taking as soon as possible, then returning to regular dosing schedule; not doubling doses

» Proper storage

Precautions while using this medication
Possible need for regular ophthalmologic examinations during long-term therapy

Side/adverse effects
Signs of potential side effects, especially blurred vision or other changes in vision, hypotension, and thrombosis or thromboembolism.

Oral Dosage Forms
Note: Bracketed uses in the *Dosage Forms* section refers to categories of use and/or indications that are not included in U.S. product labeling.

TRANEXAMIC ACID TABLETS

Usual adult and adolescent dose
Prevention and treatment of [oral hemorrhage[1]], including hemorrhage following dental surgery, in hemophilic patients—

Presurgical: Oral, 25 mg per kg of body weight every six to eight hours, beginning one day before the dental procedure. However, intravenous administration of the medication immediately prior to surgery may be preferred. When tranexamic acid is used, a single factor VIII infusion of 40 International Units per kg of body weight, or coagulation factor IX infusion of 60 International Units per kg of body weight prior to surgery is often enough for normal hemostasis.

Note: Because of an increased risk of thrombotic complications when tranexamic acid and Factor IX or anti-inhibitor coagulant complex are administered concurrently, some hematologists recommend that tranexamic acid not be administered within eight hours of these clotting factor concentrates.

Postsurgical: Oral, 25 mg per kg of body weight every six to eight hours for two to eight days after surgery. In addition to systemic tranexamic acid, an oral rinse may be used topically (see *Tranexamic Acid Oral Solution*).

[Hemorrhage, postsurgical–conization of the cervix]—
Oral, 1 to 1.5 grams every eight to twelve hours for twelve days after surgery.

[Hemorrhage, postsurgical–prostatectomy][1] or
[Bladder surgery][1]—
Oral, 1 gram three to four times a day starting on the fourth day after surgery (the medication having been administered intravenously for the first three days postoperatively). Therapy should be continued until macroscopic hematuria is no longer present.

[Hemorrhage, hyperfibrinolysis-induced–epistaxis]—
Oral, 1 to 1.5 grams three or four times a day for 10 days.

[Hemorrhage, hyperfibrinolysis-induced–hypermenorrhea]—
Oral, 1 to 1.5 grams three or four times a day for three or four days, starting after copious bleeding has begun.

[Hemorrhage, hyperfibrinolysis-induced–hyphema]—
Oral, 1 to 1.5 grams three or four times a day for seven days.

[Angioedema, hereditary]—
Oral, 1 to 1.5 grams two or three times a day. Some patients can sense the onset of attacks and may be treated intermittently, with therapy being started at the first sign of an attack and continued for several days. Other patients should be treated on a continuing basis.

Note: Because of the risk of tranexamic acid accumulation, the following dosage regimens are recommended for patients with moderate to severe renal function impairment:

Serum Creatinine (micromoles/L)	Dose
120–250 (1.36–2.83 mg/dL)	15 mg/kg two times a day
250–500 (2.83–5.66 mg/dL)	15 mg/kg a day
>500 (>5.66 mg/dL)	15 mg/kg every 48 hours or 7.5 mg/kg every 24 hours

Usual pediatric dose

Prevention and treatment of [oral hemorrhage[1]], including hemorrhage following dental surgery, in hemophilic patients—
See *Usual adult and adolescent dose.*

Strength(s) usually available

U.S.—
500 mg (Rx) [*Cyklokapron* (microcrystalline cellulose; talc; magnesium stearate; silicon dioxide; povidone)].

Canada—
500 mg (Rx) [*Cyklokapron*].

TRANEXAMIC ACID ORAL SOLUTION

Usual adult and adolescent dose

Prevention and treatment of [oral hemorrhage[1]], including hemorrhage following dental surgery, in hemophilic patients—
Postsurgical: Topically, as an oral rinse, 10 mL of a 5% solution for two minutes four times a day for five to seven days after surgery, in addition to systemic tranexamic acid (see *Tranexamic Acid Tablets*).

Usual pediatric dose

Prevention and treatment of [oral hemorrhage[1]], including hemorrhage following dental surgery, in hemophilic patients—
See *Usual adult and adolescent dose.*

Strength(s) usually available

U.S.—
Dosage form not commercially available in the U.S. Compounding required for prescriptions.

Canada—
Dosage form not commercially available in Canada. Compounding required for prescriptions.

Preparation of dosage form

A 5% oral rinse is prepared by diluting 5 mL of 10% tranexamic acid injection with 5 mL of sterile water.

Parenteral Dosage Forms

Note: Bracketed uses in the *Dosage Forms* section refers to categories of use and/or indications that are not included in U.S. product labeling.

TRANEXAMIC ACID INJECTION

Usual adult and adolescent dose

Prevention and treatment of [oral hemorrhage[1]], including hemorrhage following dental surgery, in hemophilic patients—
Presurgical: Intravenous, 10 mg per kg of body weight, administered immediately prior to surgery. When tranexamic acid is used, a single factor VIII infusion of 40 International Units per kg of body weight, or coagulation factor IX infusion of 60 International Units per kg of body weight prior to surgery is often enough for normal hemostasis.

Note: Because of an increased risk of thrombotic complications when tranexamic acid and Factor IX or anti-inhibitor coagulant complex are administered concurrently, some hematologists recommend that tranexamic acid not be administered within eight hours of these clotting factor concentrates.

Postsurgical (for patients unable to take medication orally): Intravenous, 10 mg per kg of body weight every six to eight hours for seven to ten days.

[Hemorrhage, postsurgical]—
Following prostatectomy or bladder surgery: Intravenous, 1 gram, administered during surgery initially, then every eight hours for three days. Therapy is then continued, using orally administered tranexamic acid, until macroscopic hematuria is no longer present.

Note: Tranexamic acid injection may also be used as an irrigation following bladder surgery. One gram of tranexamic acid in one liter of 0.9% sodium chloride irrigation is instilled into the bladder at a rate of 1 mL per minute once a day for two to five days following surgery.

[Hemorrhage, hyperfibrinolysis-induced]—
Intravenous, 15 mg per kg of body weight or 1 gram every six to eight hours. Therapy should be continued until there is evidence of cessation of bleeding or laboratory determinations of fibrinolysis indicate that treatment is no longer needed.

Note: For other specific indications listed under *Tranexamic Acid Tablets*, patients unable to take medication orally may receive intravenous administration of 10 mg per kg of body weight of tranexamic acid according to the dosing schedule recommended for that indication.

For relief of severe epistaxis, tranexamic acid injection has also been applied topically to the nasal mucosa, as a spray or by packing the nasal cavity with a gauze strip that has been soaked in the solution.

Because of the risk of tranexamic acid accumulation, the following dosage regimens are recommended for patients with moderate to severe renal function impairment:

Serum Creatinine (micromoles/L)	Dose
120–250 (1.36–2.83 mg/dL)	10 mg/kg two times a day
250–500 (2.83–5.66 mg/dL)	10 mg/kg a day
>500 (>5.66 mg/dL)	10 mg/kg every 48 hours or 5 mg/kg every 24 hours

Usual pediatric dose

Prevention and treatment of [oral hemorrhage[1]], including hemorrhage following dental surgery, in hemophilic patients—
See *Usual adult and adolescent dose.*

Strength(s) usually available

U.S.—
100 mg per mL (in 10-mL ampuls) (Rx) [*Cyklokapron*].

Canada—
100 mg per mL (in 5- and 10-mL ampuls) (Rx) [*Cyklokapron*].

Preparation of dosage form

Tranexamic acid injection may be mixed with intravenous infusion solutions, including solutions containing electrolytes, carbohydrates, amino acids, or dextran.

Heparin may be added to the tranexamic acid injection, if necessary.

[1]Not included in Canadian product labeling.

Revised: 10/01/2004

TRANYLCYPROMINE—See *Antidepressants, Monoamine Oxidase (MAO) Inhibitor (Systemic)*

TRASTUZUMAB Systemic

VA CLASSIFICATION (Primary): AN900

Commonly used brand name(s): *Herceptin.*

Note: For a listing of dosage forms and brand names by country availability, see *Dosage Forms* section(s).

Category

Monoclonal antibody; antineoplastic.

Indications

General Considerations

Patient eligibility was determined by immunohistochemical assessment of tumor tissue for human epidermal growth factor receptor 2 [HER2] protein overexpression using the Clinical Trial Assay (CTA). Patients with 2+ or 3+ HER2 protein overexpression were eligible for treatment with trastuzumab. The results from both clinical trials suggest that patients with the highest level (3+) of HER2 protein overexpression may benefit most from treatment with trastuzumab.

Accepted

Carcinoma, breast (treatment)—Trastuzumab is indicated as a single agent for the treatment of metastatic breast cancer in patients whose tumors overexpress the HER2 protein and who have received at least one chemotherapy regimen previously. Trastuzumab also is indicated, in combination with paclitaxel, for treatment of metastatic breast cancer in patients whose tumors overexpress the HER2 protein and who have not previously received chemotherapy for metastatic disease.

[Breast cancer, adjuvant][1]—Trastuzumab has demonstrated activity as an adjuvant agent in combination with doxorubicin, cyclophosphamide, and paclitaxel for the treatment of HER-2 positive breast cancer. Interim results of two large pivotal trials have been presented in oral presentation/abstract format. Statistically significant improvement in overall survival was reported in one trial thus far. Decreases in disease recurrence were reported in both trials. The incidence of cardiotoxicity was higher for the trastuzumab-treated patients in both trials. Duration of treatment in all trials was no more than two years, thus safety and efficacy data exist for only 1 to 2 years of treatment.

[1]Not included in Canadian product labeling.

Pharmacology/Pharmacokinetics

Physicochemical characteristics

Source—Recombinant DNA-derived humanized monoclonal antibody derived from a mammalian cell (Chinese Hamster Ovary) suspension culture in a nutrient medium containing gentamicin (although gentamicin does not appear in the final product).

Molecular weight—148 kilodaltons.

pH—Approximately 6 (after reconstitution).

Binding affinity—High for the extracellular domain of the human epidermal growth factor receptor 2 [HER2] protein.

Mechanism of action/Effect

Trastuzumab, a recombinant DNA-derived humanized monoclonal antibody, binds to the extracellular domain of the HER2 protein, which is overexpressed in 25 to 30% of primary breast cancers. By binding to the HER2 protein, trastuzumab inhibits the growth of tumor cells and mediates antibody-dependent cellular cytotoxicity (ADCC) in cancer cells that overexpress the HER2 protein.

Distribution

Volume of distribution—Approximately 44 mL per kg of body weight (approximates serum volume).

Half-life

Dose-related—1.7 and 12 days for doses of 10 and 500 mg once a week, respectively.

5.8 days (range 1 to 32) for a loading dose of 4 mg per kg of body weight (mg/kg) followed by a maintenance dose of 2 mg/kg once a week.

Peak serum concentration

At steady state—123 micrograms per mL for a loading dose of 4 mg per kg of body weight (mg/kg) followed by a maintenance dose of 2 mg/kg once a week.

377 micrograms per mL for a dose of 500 mg once a week.

Trough serum concentration

At steady state—79 micrograms per mL for a loading dose of 4 mg per kg of body weight (mg/kg) followed by a maintenance dose of 2 mg/kg once a week.

In combination with paclitaxel—The average trough serum concentration is approximately 1.5-fold greater than the trough serum concentration associated with trastuzumab used in combination with an anthracycline and cyclophosphamide.

Time to peak effect

At a loading dose of 4 mg per kg of body weight (mg/kg) followed by a maintenance dose of 2 mg/kg once a week, steady-state serum concentrations are reached between 16 and 32 weeks.

Elimination

In combination with paclitaxel—Clearance of trastuzumab was decreased twofold in primate studies.

Precautions to Consider

Cross-sensitivity and/or related problems

Patients sensitive to Chinese hamster ovary cell proteins or components of the product formulation may also be sensitive to trastuzumab.

Carcinogenicity

Studies have not been done to evaluate the carcinogenic potential of trastuzumab.

Mutagenicity

Trastuzumab, at concentrations of up to 5000 micrograms per mL (mcg/mL), was not mutagenic in Ames tests, using six test strains of bacteria, with and without metabolic activation. Mutagenicity was also not detected in an *in vitro* test of human peripheral blood lymphocytes treated with concentrations of up to 5000 mcg/mL trastuzumab, with and without metabolic activation. An *in vivo* micronucleus assay detected no evidence of chromosomal damage to mouse bone marrow cells following bolus doses of 118 mg per kg of body weight.

Pregnancy/Reproduction

Fertility—Studies in monkeys at doses of up to 25 times the weekly human maintenance dose found no effect on fertility.

Pregnancy—Trastuzumab crosses the placenta in monkeys during early (days 20 to 50) and late (days 120 to 150) gestation. Adequate and well-controlled studies in humans have not been done. Because animal studies are not always predictive of human response, trastuzumab should be used during pregnancy only if the potential benefit to the mother justifies the potential risk to the fetus.

Studies in monkeys at doses of up to 25 times the weekly human maintenance dose found no harmful effects in the fetus. However, many embryonic tissues, including neural and cardiac tissues, express high amounts of HER2 protein and animal studies have shown that early embryo death occurs in mutant mice that lack HER2 protein.

In postmarketing studies, oligohydramnios has been reported in women who received trastuzumab either as a single agent or in combination with chemotherapy during pregnancy. However, due to the limited number of reported cases, the high background rate of occurrences of oligohydramnios, the lack of clear temporal relationships between drug use and clinical findings, and the lack of supportive findings in animal studies, an association has not been established.

FDA Pregnancy Category B.

Breast-feeding

It is not known if trastuzumab is distributed into breast milk. Human immunoglobulin G (IgG) is distributed into human milk, although the potential for absorption and consequent immunosuppression in the infant is unknown. Trastuzumab is distributed into the milk of lactating monkeys given 25 times the weekly human maintenance dose; however, the presence of trastuzumab in infant monkey serum did not adversely affect development or growth during the first 3 months after birth.

It is recommended that women treated with trastuzumab not breast-feed during therapy and for 6 months after the last dose of trastuzumab.

Pediatrics

No information is available on the relationship of age to the effects of trastuzumab in pediatric patients. Safety and efficacy have not been established.

Geriatrics

Appropriate studies performed to date have not demonstrated geriatrics-specific problems that would limit the usefulness of trastuzumab in the elderly. However, elderly patients are more likely to have age-related cardiac dysfunction, which may require caution in patients receiving trastuzumab.

Drug interactions and/or related problems

The following drug interactions and/or related problems have been selected on the basis of their potential clinical significance (possible mechanism in parentheses where appropriate)—not necessarily inclusive (» = major clinical significance):

Note: Combinations containing any of the following medications, depending on the amount present, may also interact with this medication.

» Cyclophosphamide or
» Doxorubicin or
» Epirubicin
(concurrent use increases risk of developing cardiac dysfunction)

Paclitaxel
(concurrent use may increase serum levels and effects of trastuzumab)

Medical considerations/Contraindications

The medical considerations/contraindications included have been selected on the basis of their potential clinical significance (reasons given in parentheses where appropriate)—not necessarily inclusive (» = major clinical significance).

Risk-benefit should be considered when the following medical problems exist:

» Cardiac disease, pre-existing or

» Prior cardiotoxic therapy (e.g., anthracycline or radiation therapy to chest)
(may decrease ability to tolerate trastuzumab; however, data not adequate to evaluate correlation between trastuzumab-induced cardiotoxicity and these factors)

» Cardiac dysfunction, pre-existing
(increased risk of developing cardiomyopathy [ventricular dysfunction and congestive heart failure]; extreme caution is recommended for patients with pre-existing cardiac dysfunction)

» Hypersensitivity to trastuzumab, Chinese hamster ovary cell proteins, or to any component of this product (including benzyl alcohol)
(should be used with caution)

» Pre-existing pulmonary compromise
(increased risk of serious events including hypersensitivity reactions, infusion reactions, and pulmonary events, including adult respiratory distress syndrome and death; extreme caution is recommended for patients with pulmonary compromise secondary to intrinsic lung disease and/or malignant pulmonary involvement)

Patient monitoring

The following may be especially important in patient monitoring (other tests may be warranted in some patients, depending on condition; » = major clinical significance):

Baseline cardiac assessment, including history and physical
(recommended prior to initiation of therapy)

Delayed severe reactions
(patients should be informed and monitored for the possibility of hypersensitivity, infusion, and pulmonary reactions which may occur 24 hours or more after the infusion)

Echocardiogram or
Electrocardiogram (ECG) studies or
Multigated angiogram scan (MUGA)
(recommended prior to initiation of therapy and frequently during therapy)

Side/Adverse Effects

Note: The side/adverse effects and frequencies reported below occur when trastuzumab is administered as a single agent. These effects may occur at a higher rate of frequency when trastuzumab is administered in combination with chemotherapy.

The following side/adverse effects have been selected on the basis of their potential clinical significance (possible signs and symptoms in parentheses where appropriate)—not necessarily inclusive:

Those indicating need for medical attention

Incidence more frequent (≥ 20%)

Infusion reaction (dizziness; fever or chills; headache; nausea or vomiting; shortness of breath; skin rash; weakness)—usually mild to moderate in severity, however, some reactions have resulted in fatal outcomes

Note: An *infusion reaction* may occur during the first dose, but infrequently occurs with subsequent doses. Severe reactions may be delayed for 24 hours or more after infusion.

Incidence less frequent (5 to 19%)

Cardiotoxicity, usually in the form of congestive heart failure (fast or irregular heartbeat; increased cough; shortness of breath; swelling of feet and lower legs)

Note: Signs and symptoms of cardiac dysfunctions, such as dyspnea, increased cough, paroxysmal nocturnal d yspnea, peripheral edema, S_3 gallop, or reduced ejection fraction, have been observed in patients treated with trastuzumab. Severe *congestive heart failure*, including cardiac failure, mural thrombosis leading to stroke, and death, has been reported.

Incidence rare (< 5%)

Anaphylaxis/allergic reaction (chills; hives; fever; shortness of breath; tightness in chest; trouble in breathing; wheezing; skin rash)—may result in fatal outcome; ***angioedema*** (large, hive-like swelling on face, eyelids, lips, tongue, throat, hands, legs, feet, sex organs); ***urticaria*** (hives or welts; itching; redness of skin; skin rash); ***adult respiratory distress syndrome*** (shortness of breath; tightness in chest; troubled breathing; wheezing); ***bronchospasm*** (cough; difficulty breathing; noisy breathing; shortness of breath; tightness in chest; wheezing); ***anemia*** (unusual tiredness or weakness); ***dyspnea*** (shortness of breath; difficult or labored breathing; tightness in chest; wheezing); ***hypotension*** (blurred vision; confusion; dizziness, faintness, or light-headedness when getting up from a lying or sitting position; sudden sweating; unusual tiredness or weakness); ***leukopenia*** (fever or chills; cough or hoarseness; lower back or side pain; painful or difficult urination)—usually asymptomatic; ***noncardiogenic pulmonary edema*** (chest pain; difficult, fast, noisy breathing, sometimes with wheezing; blue lips and fingernails; pale skin; increased sweating; coughing; shortness of breath); ***pleural effusions*** (chest pain; shortness of breath); ***pulmonary infiltrates*** (cough; chest pain; unusual tiredness or weakness); ***pulmonary insufficiency and hypoxia requiring supplemental oxygen or ventilatory support; wheezing*** (difficulty in breathing or troubled breathing)

Note: *Anemia* and *leukopenia* occur less frequently (14%) and more frequently (24%), respectively, in patients receiving trastuzumab and chemotherapy. Symptoms were mild to moderate in severity, with < 1% Grade III toxicity and no Grade IV toxicity reported.

Allergic reactions usually occur during the first dose but may be delayed for 24 hours or more after the infusion. Patients should be informed of the possibility of delayed severe reactions.

Pulmonary events may be fatal, however, most patients with fatal reactions had significant pre-existing pulmonary compromise secondary to intrinsic lung disease and/or malignant pulmonary involvement. These patients should be treated with extreme caution. Severe reactions may be delayed for 24 hours or more after infusion. Patients should be informed of the possibility of delayed reaction.

Incidence not determined—Observed during clinical practice; estimates of frequency can not be determined

Febrile neutropenia (black, tarry stools; chills; cough; fever; lower back or side pain; painful or difficult urination; pale skin; shortness of breath; sore throat; ulcers, sores, or white spots in mouth; unusual bleeding or bruising; unusual tiredness or weakness)—trastuzumab and myelosuppressive chemotherapy

Those indicating need for medical attention only if they continue or are bothersome

Incidence more frequent (≥ 20%)

Asthenia (unusual weakness); ***diarrhea***—usually mild to moderate in severity; ***infection*** (fever or chills; cough or hoarseness)—usually mild with little clinical significance; ***nausea; pain; vomiting***

Note: Incidence of *diarrhea* and *infection* is more frequent in patients receiving trastuzumab in combination with chemotherapy.

Incidence less frequent (5 to 19%)

Insomnia (trouble in sleeping); ***loss of appetite; paresthesia*** (numbness or tingling of hands or feet); ***rhinitis*** (runny nose); ***skin rash***

Patient Consultation

As an aid to patient consultation, refer to *Advice for the Patient, Trastuzumab (Systemic).*

In providing consultation, consider emphasizing the following selected information (» = major clinical significance):

Before using this medication

» Conditions affecting use, especially:
Hypersensitivity to trastuzumab, Chinese hamster ovary cell proteins, or other components of the product formulation
Pregnancy—Trastuzumab crosses the placenta in monkeys; risk/benefit considerations
Breast-feeding—Use is not recommended (while taking this medication and for 6 months after the last dose)
Other medications, especially cyclophosphamide, doxorubicin, or epirubicin
Other medical problems, especially pre-existingcardiac disease, prior cardiotoxic therapy (anthracycline or radiation therapy to chest, pre-existing cardiac dysfunction, and pre-existing pulmonary compromise

Proper use of this medication

» Proper dosing

» Discarding bacteriostatic water for injection if patient has a known hypersensitivity to benzyl alcohol and reconstituting with sterile water for injection instead

Precautions while using this medication

» Importance of regular monitoring by physician. Serious adverse events may occur during infusion or 24 hours or more after infusion.

» Importance of seeking immediate medical attention if signs of cardiac dysfunction occur

Side/adverse effects

Signs of potential side effects, especially infusion reactions (including some with fatal outcomes), cardiotoxicity, allergic reactions (including fatal anaphylaxis), angioedema, urticaria, adult respiratory distress syndrome, bronchospasm, anemia, dyspnea, hypotension, leukopenia, noncardiogenic pulmonary edema, pleural effusions, pulmonary infiltrates, pulmonary insufficiency and hypoxia requiring supplemental oxygen or ventilatory support, and wheezing

Signs of potential side effects observed during clinical practice, especially febrile neutropenia

General Dosing Information

Trastuzumab is recommended for administration by intravenous infusion only. Rapid intravenous (push or bolus) administration is not recommended.

Trastuzumab is recommended for use only in patients whose tumors overexpress the HER2 protein.

If clinically significant congestive heart failure occurs, it is recommended that discontinuation of trastuzumab therapy be seriously considered.

Discontinuation of trastuzumab should be strongly considered for patients who develop anaphylaxis, angioedema, or acute respiratory distress syndrome.

Infusion-related reactions can occur with the first dose, but usually do not reappear with subsequent doses. It is recommended that patients be observed for symptoms of an infusion-related reaction, which can be treated with acetaminophen, diphenhydramine, and meperidine, with or without reducing the rate of the infusion. If the initial infusion is well-tolerated, subsequent doses may be administered over 30 minutes.

Parenteral Dosage Forms

TRASTUZUMAB FOR INJECTION

Usual adult dose

Carcinoma, breast—

Loading dose: Intravenous infusion (over ninety minutes), 4 mg per kg of body weight.

Maintenance: Intravenous infusion (over thirty minutes), 2 mg per kg of body weight administered every seven days.

Usual adult prescribing limits

Single doses greater than 500 mg have not been tested in clinical trials.

Usual pediatric dose

Safety and efficacy have not been established.

Strength(s) usually available

U.S.—

440 mg (Rx) [*Herceptin* (L-histidine HCL; L-histidine; alpha,alpha-trehalose dihydrate; polysorbate 20)].

Canada—

440 mg (Rx) [*Herceptin*].

Packaging and storage

Store between 2 and 8 °C (36 and 46 °F).

Preparation of dosage form

Trastuzumab is reconstituted for intravenous use by adding to the vial, using asceptic technique, 20 mL of bacteriostatic water for injection (with benzyl alcohol), provided by the manufacturer. This produces a multidose solution containing 21 mg of trastuzumab per mL. Sterile water for injection should be used for initial dilution if the patient is hypersensitive to benzyl alcohol.

Trastuzumab for injection is prepared for intravenous infusion by withdrawing the necessary amount of drug and diluting it, in an infusion bag, with 250 mL 0.9% sodium chloride injection. The bag should be inverted gently to mix the solution, producing a colorless to pale yellow transparent solution. The prepared solution should be inspected visually for particulate matter and discoloration prior to administration.

Stability

After reconstitution, solutions stored in bacteriostatic water for injection at a concentration of 21 mg per mL retain their potency for 28 days if refrigerated at 2 to 8 °C (36 to 46 °F). Solutions stored in sterile water for injection should be used immediately.

Infusion solutions prepared in 0.9% sodium chloride injection are stable for up to 24 hours prior to use if refrigerated at 2 to 8 °C (36 to 46 °F) and for 24 hours at room temperature (between 15 and 30 °C [59 and 86 °F]). However, because diluted trastuzumab effectively contains no preservative, the manufacturer recommends that diluted solutions be stored in a refrigerator at 2 to 8 °C (36 to 46 °F).

Incompatibilities

Trastuzumab should not be mixed or diluted in any dextrose solution or with any other drugs. Incompatibilities between trastuzumab and polyvinyl chloride or polyethylene infusion bags have not been observed.

Caution

For patients with a known hypersensitivity to benzyl alcohol (the preservative in Bacteriostatic Water for Injection), reconstitute trastuzumab with Sterile Water for Injection.

Revised: 09/19/2005

TRAVOPROST Ophthalmic†

VA CLASSIFICATION (Primary): OP116

Commonly used brand name(s): *Travatan*.

Note: For a listing of dosage forms and brand names by country availability, see *Dosage Forms* section(s).

†Not commercially available in Canada.

Category

Antiglaucoma agent (ophthalmic); antihypertensive, ocular.

Indications

Accepted

Glaucoma, open-angle (treatment) or

Hypertension, ocular (treatment)—Travoprost is indicated for the treatment of elevated intraocular pressure (IOP) in patients with ocular hypertension or open-angle glaucoma who are intolerant of similar medications or not responsive (failed to achieve target IOP determined after multiple measurements over time) to another intraocular pressure lowering medication.

Acceptance not established

Ophthalmic travoprost has not been studied in patients with angle-closure, inflammatory, or neovascular glaucoma.

Pharmacology/Pharmacokinetics

Physicochemical characteristics

Chemical Group—Prostaglandin $F_{2-alpha}$ analog (synthetic)

Molecular weight—500.56.

Solubility—Very soluble in acetonitrile, chloroform, methanol, and octanol, and insoluble in water.

pH—6.0.

Mechanism of action/Effect

Antiglaucoma agent—Travoprost (free acid), a selective FP prostanoid receptor agonist, is thought to lower intraocular pressure (IOP) by increasing the uveoscleral outflow; however, the exact mechanism of action is unknown.

Absorption

Travoprost is systemically absorbed when administered to the eye.

Biotransformation

Travoprost, an isopropyl ester prodrug, is hydrolyzed by esterases in the cornea to its biologically active free acid. After absorption, systemic travoprost free acid is metabolized to inactive metabolites via oxidation, beta-oxidation, and reduction of the carboxylic acid chain.

Onset of action

Reduction of IOP starts after approximately two hours after ophthalmic administration

Time to peak concentration

Peak plasma concentrations of travoprost free acid were reached within 30 minutes after ophthalmic administration.

Peak plasma concentration:

Peak plasma concentration of travoprost free acid was approximately 25 picograms per mL within 30 minutes after ophthalmic administration.

Time to peak effect

12 hours after ophthalmic administration.

Elimination

Rapid elimination and is undetectable within one hour following ophthalmic dosing.

Precautions to Consider

Carcinogenicity
Studies have not been performed.

Tumorigenicity
Studies have not been performed.

Mutagenicity
Travoprost was not mutagenic in the Ames test, mouse micronucleus test, and the rat chromosome aberration assay. In the presence of rat S-9 activation enzymes, a slight increase in the mutant frequency was observed in one of two mouse lymphoma assays.

Pregnancy/Reproduction
Fertility—Travoprost did not affect mating or fertility indices in male or female rats at subcutaneous doses up to 10 mcg per kg per day (mcg/kg/day). When given at doses of 10 mcg/kg/day or more, or approximately 250 times the maximum recommended human ocular dose (MRHOD), the mean number of corpora lutea was reduced, and the postimplantation losses were increased.

Pregnancy—Adequate and well-controlled studies in humans have not been done. Travoprost may interfere with the maintenance of pregnancy and should not be used by women during pregnancy or by women attempting to get pregnant.

Travoprost was teratogenic in rats, at an intravenous doses from 3 to 10 mcg/kg/day (250 times the MRHOD), as shown by increases in skeletal malformation incidence and other malformations, such as fused sternebrae, domed head, and hydrocephaly. At intravenous doses of more than 3 mcg/kg/day (75 times the MRHOD) in rats or subcutaneous doses of more than 0.3 mcg/kg/day (7.5 times the MRHOD) in mice, travoprost increased postimplantation losses and decreased fetal viability.

For the offspring of female rats that were subcutaneously dosed at more than 0.12 mcg/kg/day (3 times MRHOD) with travoprost from day 7 of pregnancy to lactation day 21, postnatal mortality incidence increased and the neonatal body weight gain decreased. Neonatal development was also affected and was demonstrated by delayed eye opening, pinna detachment and preputial separation, and decreased motor activity.

FDA Pregnancy Category C

Breast-feeding
It not known whether travoprost is distributed into human breast milk. A study in lactating rats demonstrated that radiolabeled travoprost and/or its metabolites were distributed in breast milk. It is recommended that caution should be exercised when given to a nursing woman.

Pediatrics
Appropriate studies have not been performed on the relationship of age to the effects of travoprost in the pediatric population. Safety and efficacy have not been established.

Geriatrics
Appropriate studies on the relationship of age to the effects of travoprost have not been performed in the geriatric population. However, no geriatrics-specific problems have been documented to date.

Medical considerations/Contraindications
The medical considerations/contraindications included have been selected on the basis of their potential clinical significance (reasons given in parentheses where appropriate)—not necessarily inclusive (» = major clinical significance).

Except under special circumstances, this medication should not be used when the following medical problem exists:

» Hypersensitivity to travoprost or benzalkonium chloride

Pregnancy

Risk-benefit should be considered when the following medical problems exist:

» Aphakia or

» Macular edema or

» Pseudophakia

(macular edema, including cystoid macular edema, has been reported during treatment with prostaglandin $F_{2\alpha}$ analogs; aphakic patients, pseudophakic patients with a torn posterior lens capsule, or patients with risk factors for macular edema have mainly been affected)

Hepatic function impairment or

Renal function impairment

(although studies with travoprost have not been done in patients with hepatic or renal function impairment, use with caution in these patients)

Iritis or

Uveitis

(travoprost should be used with caution in patients with active intraocular inflammation [iritis/uveitis])

Patient monitoring
The following may be especially important in patient monitoring (other tests may be warranted in some patients, depending on condition; » = major clinical significance):

Ophthalmic examinations

(patients should be examined regularly and, depending on the clinical situation, treatment may be stopped if increased brown pigmentation of iris occurs)

Side/Adverse Effects

Note: Changes in pigmented tissues may occur with use of travoprost. Travoprost may gradually change eye color by increasing the number of melanosomes (pigment granules) in the melanocytes, thereby increasing the amount of brown pigment in the iris. The mechanism of this increased pigmentation is probably not associated with proliferation of the melanocytes, but rather with stimulation of melanin production within the melanocytes of the iris stroma. The long-term effects on the melanocytes, the consequences of potential injury to the melanocytes, and the possibility of deposition of pigment granules to other areas of the eye are not known. The change in iris color occurs slowly and may not be noticeable for several months to years. In addition, travoprost has been reported to cause increased pigmentation of the periorbital tissue (eyelid). Also, travoprost may gradually change eyelashes. The changes to the lashes include increased length, thickness, pigmentation, and the number of lashes. Patients should be advised of all the effects listed above and informed that if only one eye is treated with the medication, only one eye will be affected (heterochromia between the eyes). The changes in pigmentation and eyelash growth may be permanent.

Macular edema, including cystoid macular edema, has been reported during treatment with travoprost, mainly in patients with aphakia, in patients with pseudophakia who have a torn posterior lens capsule, or in patients with known risk factors for macular edema. It is recommended that travoprost be used with caution in these patients.

The following side/adverse effects have been selected on the basis of their potential clinical significance (possible signs and symptoms in parentheses where appropriate)—not necessarily inclusive:

Those indicating need for medical attention
Incidence less frequent

Abnormal vision (change in vision); ***angina pectoris*** (chest pain; chest tightness; fast or irregular heartbeat; shortness of breath); ***anxiety; arthritis*** (pain, swelling, or redness in joints; muscle pain or stiffness; difficulty in moving); ***back pain; blepharitis*** (redness, swelling, and/or itching of eyelid); ***blurred vision; bradycardia*** (slow or irregular heartbeat [less than 50 beats per minute]); ***bronchitis*** (cough producing mucus; difficulty breathing; shortness of breath; tightness in chest; wheezing); ***cataract*** (blindness; blurred vision; decreased vision); ***cold syndrome*** (runny nose; sore throat); ***conjunctivitis*** (redness, pain, swelling of eye, eyelid, or inner lining of eyelid; burning, dry or itching eyes; discharge; excessive tearing); ***depression*** (mood or mental changes); ***dyspepsia*** (acid or sour stomach; belching; heartburn; indigestion; stomach discomfort, upset or pain); ***gastrointestinal disorder*** (diarrhea; loss of appetite; nausea and vomiting; stomach cramps or pain); ***headache; hypercholesterolemia*** (high cholesterol); ***keratitis*** (irritation or inflammation of eye); ***hypertension*** (high blood pressure); ***hypotension*** (low blood pressure); ***infection*** (fever or chills); ***iris discoloration*** (eye color changes); ***prostate disorder*** (pelvic pain); ***sinusitis*** (pain or tenderness around eyes and cheekbones; fever; stuffy or runny nose; headache; cough; shortness of breath or troubled breathing; tightness of chest or wheezing); ***subconjunctival hemorrhage*** (decreased vision or any change in vision); ***urinary incontinence*** (loss of bladder control); ***urinary tract infection*** (blood in urine; lower back pain; pain or burning while urinating)

Those indicating need for medical attention only if they continue or are bothersome
Incidence more frequent

Decreased visual acuity (decreased vision); ***eye discomfort; eye pain; eye pruritus*** (itching eye); ***foreign body sensation*** (feeling of having something in the eye); ***ocular hyperemia*** (redness of eye)—reported in 35 to 50% of patients

Incidence less frequent

Dry eye; lid margin crusting (crusting in corner of eye); ***photophobia*** (increased sensitivity of eyes to sunlight); ***tearing***

Overdose

For more information on the management of overdose or unintentional ingestion, **contact a poison control center** (see *Poison Control Center Listing*).

Treatment of overdose

Supportive care—
No information is available on overdosage in humans. Treatment is generally symptomatic.
Patients in whom intentional overdose is confirmed or suspected should be referred for psychiatric consultation.

Patient Consultation

As an aid to patient consultation, refer to *Advice for the Patient, Travoprost (Ophthalmic)*

In providing consultation, consider emphasizing the following selected information (» = major clinical significance):

Before using this medication

» Conditions affecting use, especially:
Hypersensitivity to travoprost or benzalkonium chloride
Pregnancy—Not recommended for use during pregnancy
Breast-feeding—Caution should be exercised when travoprost is administered to nursing women, since it is not known whether travoprost or its metabolites are distributed into breast milk
Other medical problems, especially aphakia; macular edema, including cystoid macular edema, risk factors for; and pseudophakia

Proper use of this medication

» Using medication only as directed; not using more of it or using it more often than directed; to do so may increase absorption and the chance of side effects

Removing contact lenses prior to administration of travoprost; reinserting lenses, if desired, at least 15 minutes after administration

» Proper administration technique; preventing contamination of medication in bottle; not touching applicator tip to any surface; keeping container tightly closed

Waiting at least 5 minutes between applications of two different ophthalmic preparations to prevent second medication from "washing out" the first one

» Proper dosing

Missed dose: Applying as soon as possible; not applying if almost time for next scheduled dose; not doubling doses

» Proper storage

Precautions while using this medication

Regular visits to physician to check progress during therapy

» Checking with physician if signs of ocular allergic reaction occur

» Checking with physician about possible need for a fresh bottle of medication to use in case of surgery, injury, or infection

» Possibility of iris of eye becoming more brown in color; change in color of iris is usually noticeable within several months to years while using medication; in addition, possibility of the darkening of eyelid skin color; also, possibility of increased length, thickness, pigmentation, and the number of lashes; iris, eyelid, and lash pigmentation and other lash changes may be permanent even if medication is stopped; the color and lash changes will occur only to the eye being treated; if only one eye is treated, there is a possibility of having differently colored eyes and differently appearing eyelashes

Possibility of medication causing eyes to become more sensitive to light than they are normally; wearing sunglasses and avoiding too much exposure to bright light may help lessen discomfort

» Temporary blurring of vision may occur following administration; caution in driving or operating machinery

Side/adverse effects

Signs of potential side effects, especially abnormal vision, angina pectoris, anxiety, arthritis, back pain, blepharitis, blurred vision, bradycardia, bronchitis, cataract, cold syndrome, conjunctivitis, chest pain, depression, dyspepsia, gastrointestinal disorder, headache, hypercholesterolemia, keratitis, hypertension, hypotension, infection, iris discoloration, prostate disorder, sinusitis, subconjunctival hemorrhage, urinary incontinence, or urinary tract infection

General Dosing Information

Travoprost may be used alone or in combination with other antiglaucoma agents. If more than one topical ophthalmic medication is being used by the patient, administration of medications should be at least 5 minutes apart.

Travoprost contains benzalkonium chloride, which may be absorbed by contact lenses. Contact lenses should be removed before administration of travoprost and can be reinserted 15 minutes after instillation of medication.

Since prostaglandins are biologically active and may be absorbed through the skin, women who are pregnant or attempting to become pregnant should exercise appropriate precautions to avoid direct exposure to the contents of the dispenser bottle. In case of accidental contact with travoprost, thoroughly cleanse the area with soap and water immediately.

Once-daily dosing of travoprost should not be exceeded. More frequent administration may decrease the intraocular pressure-lowering effect of the medication.

Ophthalmic Dosage Forms

TRAVOPROST OPHTHALMIC SOLUTION

Usual adult dose

Glaucoma, open-angle (treatment)
Hypertension, ocular (treatment)—
Topical, to the conjunctiva, 1 drop in the affected eye(s) once a day in the evening.

Usual adult prescribing limits

No more than one dose per day.

Usual pediatric dose

Safety and efficacy have not been established.

Usual geriatric dose

See *Usual adult dose*.

Strength(s) usually available

U.S.—
0.004% (40 micrograms per mL) (Rx) [*Travatan* (benzalkonium chloride, 0.015%; polyoxyl 40 hydrogenated castor oil; boric acid; castor oil; edetate disodium; mannitol; tromethamine; sodium hydroxide (and/or hydrochloric acid [to adjust pH]); purified water)].

Canada—
Not commercially available.

Packaging and storage

Store between 2 and 25 °C (36 and 77 °F).

Stability

Discard container within 6 weeks of removing it from the sealed pouch.

Auxiliary labeling

• For the eye.

Developed: 07/23/2001

TRAZODONE Systemic

VA CLASSIFICATION (Primary/Secondary): CN609/CN103

Commonly used brand name(s): *Desyrel*.

Note: For a listing of dosage forms and brand names by country availability, see *Dosage Forms* section(s).

Category

Antidepressant; antineuralgic.

Indications

Note: Bracketed information in the *Indications* section refers to uses that are not included in U.S. product labeling.

Accepted

Depression, mental (treatment)—Trazodone is indicated in the treatment of major depressive episodes with or without prominent anxiety.

[Pain, neurogenic (treatment)][1]—Trazodone has been used to treat painful diabetic neuropathy and other types of chronic pain.

[1]Not included in Canadian product labeling.

Pharmacology/Pharmacokinetics

Physicochemical characteristics

Molecular weight—408.33.

Other characteristics—
Trazodone is *not* chemically related to tricyclic, tetracyclic, or other known antidepressants.

Mechanism of action/Effect
Not completely established in humans. Animal studies indicate that trazodone selectively inhibits serotonin re-uptake in the brain, causes beta-receptor subsensitivity, and induces significant changes in serotonin-receptor binding with only a slight effect on alpha-adrenergic receptors. Also, trazodone potentiates the behavioral changes in animals induced by 5-hydroxytryptophan, a serotonin precursor.

Absorption
Well absorbed. When trazodone is taken with or shortly after ingestion of food, there may be an increase in the amount of drug absorbed, a decrease in maximum concentration, and a lengthening of time to reach peak concentration.

Protein binding
Very high (89 to 95%).

Biotransformation
Hepatic; extensive, by hydroxylation.

Half-life
Biphasic. More rapid, 3 to 6 hours; slower, 5 to 9 hours.

Onset of therapeutic action
In clinical trials, significant therapeutic results occurred after 2 weeks of therapy in 75% of the patients responsive to the medication, with some patients showing definite improvement after 1 week of therapy; 25% of the responding patients required 2 to 4 weeks of therapy before noticeable improvement occurred.

Time to peak concentration
Fasting, l hour; with food, 2 hours.

Elimination
Biliary—
20%
Renal—
75%, mostly as inactive metabolites.

Precautions to Consider

Carcinogenicity
No evidence of carcinogenicity was observed in rats receiving up to 300 mg per kg of body weight (mg/kg) a day for 18 months.

Pregnancy/Reproduction
Pregnancy—Studies in humans have not been done.

Studies in animals have shown that trazodone causes congenital anomalies and increased fetal resorptions when given in doses up to 50 times those used in humans.

FDA Pregnancy Category C.

Breast-feeding
Problems in humans have not been documented; however, trazodone and its metabolites have been shown to be present in human milk and in the milk of lactating test animals.

Pediatrics
Safety and effectiveness have not been established in children below the age of 18 years.

Antidepressants increase the risk of suicidal thinking and behavior (suicidality) in children and adolescents with major depressive disorder (MDD) and other psychiatric disorders. Anyone considering the use of trazodone or any other antidepressant in a child or adolescent must balance this risk with the clinical need.

Pooled analyses of short-term placebo controlled trials of nine antidepressant drugs in children and adolescents with MDD, obsessive compulsive disorder, or other psychiatric disorders have revealed a greater risk of adverse events representing suicidality during the first few months of treatment in those receiving antidepressants.

Geriatrics
Elderly patients are more likely than younger adults to experience the sedative or hypotensive effects of trazodone; therefore, initial doses as low as half the recommended adult dose should be used in elderly patients, with adjustments made as needed and tolerated.

Dental
Peripheral anticholinergic effects, although they occur much less frequently with trazodone than with tricyclic antidepressants, may decrease or inhibit salivary flow, especially in middle-aged or elderly patients, thus contributing to the development of caries, periodontal disease, oral candidiasis, and discomfort.

Drug interactions and/or related problems
The following drug interactions and/or related problems have been selected on the basis of their potential clinical significance (possible mechanism in parentheses where appropriate)—not necessarily inclusive (» = major clinical significance):

Note: Combinations containing any of the following medications, depending on the amount present, may also interact with this medication.

» Alcohol or
» Central nervous system (CNS) depression-producing medications, other (See *Appendix II*)
(concurrent use with trazodone may result in potentiation of CNS depressant effects)

Anticholinergics or other medications with anticholinergic activity (See *Appendix II*) or
Antidyskinetics or
Antihistamines
(concurrent use with trazodone may intensify anticholinergic effects because of secondary anticholinergic activities of trazodone)
(also, concurrent use of trazodone with antihistamines may potentiate the CNS depressant effects of either medication)

Antidepressants, tricyclic or
Haloperidol or
Loxapine or
Maprotiline or
Molindone or
Phenothiazines or
Pimozide or
Thioxanthenes
(concurrent use may prolong and intensify the sedative and anticholinergic effects of either these medications or trazodone)

» Antihypertensives
(concurrent use with trazodone may increase the likelihood of hypotension; dosage reduction of the antihypertensive medication may be necessary; also, antihypertensives with CNS depressant effects, such as clonidine, guanabenz, methyldopa, metyrosine, and rauwolfia alkaloids, may potentiate CNS depression when used concurrently with trazodone)

Digoxin
(concurrent use with trazodone may increase serum concentration of digoxin and may result in digoxin toxicity)

Phenytoin and possibly other hydantoin anticonvulsants
(increased plasma phenytoin concentrations have been reported when phenytoin was used concurrently with trazodone; caution and close monitoring are suggested)

Laboratory value alterations
The following have been selected on the basis of their potential clinical significance (possible effect in parentheses where appropriate)—not necessarily inclusive (» = major clinical significance).

With physiology/laboratory test values
Leukocyte counts and
Neutrophil counts
(may occasionally be reduced, although not enough to be clinically significant)

Medical considerations/Contraindications
The medical considerations/contraindications included have been selected on the basis of their potential clinical significance (reasons given in parentheses where appropriate)—not necessarily inclusive (» = major clinical significance).

Except under special circumstances, this medication should not be used when the following medical problem exists:

» Myocardial infarction, during the acute recovery period

Risk-benefit should be considered when the following medical problems exist:

Alcoholism, active
(possible excessive CNS depression)

» Cardiac disease, especially arrhythmias
(ventricular arrhythmias, premature ventricular contractions, and ventricular tachycardia may be potentiated)

» Hepatic function impairment
(possible serum trazodone accumulation resulting in potentiation of side effects)

» Renal function impairment
(may result in prolonged trazodone effects)

Sensitivity to trazodone

Patient monitoring

The following may be especially important in patient monitoring (other tests may be warranted in some patients, depending on condition; » = major clinical significance):

Cardiac function
(monitoring is recommended, especially for patients with pre-existing cardiac disease; reports indicate that trazodone may initiate arrhythmias, including isolated premature ventricular contractions [PVC], ventricular couplets, and short episodes of ventricular tachycardia, in such patients)

Careful supervision of depressed patients including those with:
Abnormal behaviors (i.e., agitation, panic attacks, hostility) or
Clinical worsening of their depression or
Suicidal ideation and behavior (suicidality)
(recommended especially during early treatment phase before peak effectiveness of trazodone is achieved or at the time of increases or decreases in dose; prescribing the smallest number of tablets necessary for good patient management is recommended to decrease the risk of overdose; consideration should be given to changing the therapeutic regimen, including possibly discontinuing the medicine, in patients whose depression is persistently worse or whose emergent suicidality or other symptoms are severe, abrupt in onset, or were not part of the patient's presenting symptoms)

Leukocyte and neutrophil counts
(recommended particularly during extended treatment or if symptoms of systemic infection such as fever and sore throat develop; trazodone should be discontinued if patient's leukocyte or absolute neutrophil counts fall below normal)

Side/Adverse Effects

The following side/adverse effects have been selected on the basis of their potential clinical significance (possible signs and symptoms in parentheses where appropriate)—not necessarily inclusive:

Those indicating need for medical attention

Incidence less frequent
CNS effects (confusion; muscle tremors); ***hypotension*** (fainting)

Incidence rare
Allergic reaction (skin rash); ***fast or slow heartbeat; priapism*** (prolonged, painful, inappropriate penile erection); ***unusual excitement***

Note: When *abnormal erectile activity* occurs, the patient should be advised to discontinue medication immediately and consult with physician.

Those indicating need for medical attention only if they continue or are bothersome

Incidence more frequent
Dizziness or lightheadedness; drowsiness; dryness of mouth, usually mild; headache; nausea and vomiting; unpleasant taste

Incidence less frequent or rare
Blurred vision; constipation; diarrhea; muscle aches or pains; unusual tiredness or weakness

Overdose

For specific information on the agents used in the management of trazodone overdose, see:
- *Charcoal, Activated (Oral-Local)* monograph.

For more information on the management of overdose or unintentional ingestion, **contact a Poison Control Center** (see *Poison Control Center Listing*).

Clinical effects of overdose

The following effects have been selected on the basis of their potential clinical significance (possible signs and symptoms in parentheses were appropriate)—not necessarily inclusive:

Drowsiness; loss of muscle coordination; nausea and vomiting

Treatment of overdose

There is no specific antidote for trazodone. Treatment may include:

To decrease absorption—
Emptying stomach by gastric lavage.
Administering activated charcoal slurry followed by a stimulant cathartic.

To enhance elimination—
Forced diuresis may be helpful.

Supportive care—
Maintaining respiratory and cardiac function.
Providing symptomatic and supportive treatment in the event of hypotension or excessive sedation.

Patients in whom intentional overdose is known or suspected should be referred for psychiatric consultation.

Patient Consultation

As an aid to patient consultation, refer to *Advice for the Patient, Trazodone (Systemic)*.

In providing consultation, consider emphasizing the following selected information (» = major clinical significance):

Before using this medication

» Conditions affecting use, especially:
Sensitivity to trazodone
Pregnancy—Animal studies have shown congenital anomalies and increased fetal resorptions with large doses
Breast-feeding—Excreted in breast milk
Use in the elderly—Elderly are more prone to develop sedative and hypotensive effects
Dental—Dry mouth may result in caries, periodontal disease, oral candidiasis, and discomfort
Other medications, especially alcohol or other CNS depression-producing medications, or antihypertensives
Other medical problems, especially myocardial infarction, arrhythmias or other cardiac disease, hepatic function impairment, or renal function impairment

Proper use of this medication

Taking with or soon after a meal or light snack to minimize stomach upset and dizziness or lightheadedness
» Compliance with therapy
» May require up to 4 weeks to produce significant therapeutic results, although 75% of responding patients benefit within 2 weeks
» Proper dosing
Missed dose: Taking as soon as possible; not taking if within 4 hours of next scheduled dose; not doubling doses
» Proper storage

Precautions while using this medication

Regular visits to physician to check progress during therapy
» Checking with physician before discontinuing medication; gradual dosage reduction may be needed
» Caution if any kind of surgery, dental treatment, or emergency treatment is required
» Avoiding use of alcohol or other CNS depressants during therapy
» Possible drowsiness; caution when driving or doing other things requiring alertness
» Possible dizziness; caution when getting up suddenly from a lying or sitting position
Possible dryness of mouth; using sugarless gum or candy, ice, or saliva substitute for relief; checking with physician or dentist if dry mouth continues for more than 2 weeks

Side/adverse effects

Sedative and hypotensive side effects more likely to occur in the elderly
Priapism may occur; discontinuing medication and checking with physician immediately
Signs of potential side effects, especially CNS effects, fast or slow heartbeat, hypotension, priapism, unusual excitement, or allergic reaction

General Dosing Information

Dosage of trazodone must be individualized for each patient by titration.

Potentially suicidal patients should not have access to large quantities of this medication since depressed patients, particularly those who may use alcohol excessively, may continue to exhibit suicidal tendencies until significant improvement occurs. Some clinicians recommend that the patient be supplied with the least amount of medication necessary for satisfactory patient management.

Daily dosage should be divided into at least two doses, because of trazodone's short elimination half-life. Trazodone should not be given as a single daily dose.

When side effects such as excessive drowsiness or dizziness might be bothersome or dangerous during waking hours, a larger portion (about two-thirds) of the total daily dose may be given at bedtime, with the balance being administered in the morning or during the day in divided doses.

To avoid a possible increase in side effects or aggravation of the patient's condition, any change or discontinuation of dosage should be accomplished gradually.

Diet/Nutrition
Each dose is best taken with or shortly after a meal or light snack. Food reduces the incidence and severity of side effects such as nausea or dizziness, by slowing trazodone's rate of absorption, decreasing the maximum concentration, and lengthening the time to maximum concentration.

For treatment of priapism
Treatment may include
- In patients with mild or no ischemia (as differentiated by intracorporeal blood gas and pressure monitoring)—Irrigation of the corpora with metaraminol, epinephrine or norepinephrine.
- In patients with severe ischemia—Stagnant blood should be evacuated and a shunt procedure performed to allow metabolic replenishment of tissue.

Oral Dosage Forms

TRAZODONE HYDROCHLORIDE TABLETS USP
Note: The dosing and strengths of the dosage forms available are expressed in terms of trazodone hydrochloride.

Usual adult and adolescent dose
Antidepressant—
Oral, initially 150 mg a day in divided doses, the dosage being increased by 50 mg per day at three- or four-day intervals, as needed and tolerated.

Usual adult prescribing limits
Outpatients—
Up to 400 mg a day.
Inpatients—
Up to 600 mg a day.

Usual pediatric dose
Antidepressant—
Children up to 6 years of age: Dosage has not been established.
Children 6 to 18 years of age: Oral, initially 1.5 to 2 mg per kg of body weight a day in divided doses, the dosage being increased gradually at three- or four-day intervals as needed and tolerated up to a maximum of 6 mg per kg of body weight a day.

Usual geriatric dose
Antidepressant—
Oral, initially 75 mg a day in divided doses, the dosage being increased gradually at three- or four-day intervals, as needed and tolerated.

Strength(s) usually available
U.S.—
50 mg (Rx) [*Desyrel* (scored); GENERIC].
100 mg (Rx) [*Desyrel* (scored); GENERIC].
150 mg (Rx) [*Desyrel* (scored); GENERIC].
300 mg (Rx) [*Desyrel* (scored); GENERIC].
Canada—
50 mg (Rx) [*Desyrel* (scored; cornstarch; dibasic calcium phosphate; FD&C yellow No. 6 (aluminum lake); lactose; magnesium stearate; microcrystalline cellulose; povidone; sodium starch glycolate)].
100 mg (Rx) [*Desyrel* (scored; cornstarch; dibasic calcium phosphate; lactose; magnesium stearate; microcrystalline cellulose; povidone; sodium starch glycolate)].
150 mg (Rx) [*Desyrel* (scored; FD&C yellow No. 6 (aluminum lake); magnesium stearate; microcrystalline cellulose; pregelatinized starch; stearic acid)].

Packaging and storage
Store below 40 °C (104 °F), preferably between 15 and 30 °C (59 and 86 °F), in a tight, light-resistant container, unless otherwise specified by manufacturer.

Auxiliary labeling
- May cause drowsiness.
- Avoid alcoholic beverages.
- Take with or immediately after food.

Additional information
The 150-mg tablet may be broken to yield doses of 50, 75, or 100 mg.
The 300-mg tablet may be broken to yield three 100-mg doses, two 150-mg doses, or one 200-mg dose.

Revised: 01/05/2005

TREPROSTINIL Systemic†

VA CLASSIFICATION (Primary): CV402
Commonly used brand name(s): *Remodulin*.
Note: For a listing of dosage forms and brand names by country availability, see *Dosage Forms* section(s).

†Not commercially available in Canada.

Category
Antihypertensive (pulmonary); Vasodilator.

Indications

Accepted
Hypertension, pulmonary arterial (treatment)—Treprostinil is indicated as a continuous subcutaneous infusion or intravenous infusion (for those not able to tolerate a subcutaneous infusion) for the treatment of pulmonary arterial hypertension (PAH) in patients with NYHA Class II-IV symptoms to diminish symptoms associated with exercise.

Treprostinil is indicated to diminish the rate of clinical deterioration in patient requiring transition from Flolan® (epoprostenol sodium); the risk and benefits of each drug should be carefully considered prior to transition.

Pharmacology/Pharmacokinetics

Physicochemical characteristics
Molecular weight—412.49.

Mechanism of action/Effect
The major pharmacological actions of treprostinil are direct vasodilation of pulmonary and systemic arterial vascular beds and inhibition of platelet aggregation. Studies in animals have demonstrated vasodilatory effects such as, reduction in right and left ventricular afterload and increased cardiac output and stroke volume. Other studies have shown that treprostinil causes a dose-related negative inotropic and lusitropic effect. There were no major effects on cardiac conduction.

Absorption
Treprostinil absorption is relatively rapid and complete after subcutaneous infusion, with an absolute bioavailability approximately 100%.

In patients with mild (n=4) or moderate (n=5) hepatic insufficiency and portopulmonary hypertension following a subcutaneous dose of 10 ng per kg of body weight per min for 150 mins the $AUC_{0-\infty}$ was increased 3-fold and 5-fold respectively.

Distribution
Volume of distribution (Vol_D) approximately 14 L per 70 kg ideal body weight

Protein binding
Human plasma protein binding is approximately 91% in *in vitro* concentrations ranging from 330 to 10,000 mcg per L

Biotransformation
Treprostinil is metabolized by the liver however, the precise enzymes are unknown. Five metabolites have been described (HU1 through HU5) however, the biological activity and metabolic fate of these are unknown. The chemical structure of HU1 is unknown. The metabolite HU5 is the glucuronide conjugate of treprostinil. The other metabolites are formed by oxidation of the 3-hydroxyoctyl side chain (HU2) and subsequent additional oxidation (HU3) or dehydration (HU4). Study results of *in vitro* human hepatic cytochrome P450 demonstrates that treprostinil does not inhibit CYP-1A2, 2C9, 2C19, 2D6, 2E1, or 3A. Whether treprostinil induces these enzymes has not been studied.

Half-life
Approximately 2 to 4 hours

Time to peak concentration
Steady state concentration—approximately 10 hours

Peak serum concentration
In patients with mild (n=4) or moderate (n=5) hepatic insufficiency and portopulmonary hypertension following a subcutaneous dose of 10 ng per kg of body weight per min for 150 mins the C_{max} was increased 2-fold and 4-fold respectively.

Concentrations in patients treated with an average dose of 9.3 ng per kg of body weight per min were approximately 2 mcg per L.

Trepostinil's linear pharmacokinetics can be described by a two compartment model resulting in plasma concentrations of 0.03 to 8 mcg per L with a dosage range of 1.25 to 22.5 ng per kg of body weight per min.

Elimination
Renal—approximately 79%; dose eliminated as 4% unchanged drug and 64% identified metabolites.

Fecal—approximately 13%
Systemic clearance—approximately 30 liters per hour for a 70 kg ideal body weight patient.
Hepatic insufficiency—reduced clearance by up to 80% compared to healthy adults.

Precautions to Consider

Carcinogenesis and Mutagenesis

Long-term studies to evaluate the carcinogenic potential of treprostinil have not been done. *In vitro* and *in vivo* mutagenicity studies did not demonstrate any mutagenic or clastogenic effects of treprostinil.

Pregnancy/Reproduction

Fertility—In animal studies no evidence of impaired fertility was found in male or female rats given continuous subcutaneous infusion rates of up to 450 ng per kg of body weight per min [about 59 times the recommended starting human rate of infusion (1.25 ng per kg of body weight per min) and about 8 times the average rate (9.3 ng per kg of body weight per min) achieved in clinical trials, on a ng per m² body surface area basis]. In this study, males were dosed from 10 weeks prior to mating and through the 2-week mating period. Females were dosed from 2 weeks prior to mating until gestational day six.

Pregnancy—Adequate and well-controlled studies in humans have not been done. The use of treprostinil during pregnancy is only recommended if clearly needed.

In animal studies continuous subcutaneous infusion of treprostinil in pregnant rats during organogenesis and late gestational development, at rates as high as 900 ng per kg of body weight per min (about 117 times the starting human rate of infusion, on a ng per m² body surface area basis and about 16 times the average rate achieved in clinical trials) resulted in no evidence of harm to fetus. In rats, continuous subcutaneous infusion of treprostinil from implantation to the end of lactation, at rates of up to 450 ng per kg of body weight per min, did not affect the growth and development of offspring.

In pregnant rabbits, effects of continuous subcutaneous infusion of treprostinil during organogenesis were limited to an increased incidence of fetal skeletal variations (bilateral full rib or right rudimentary rib on lumbar 1) associated with maternal toxicity (reduction in body weight and food consumption) at an infusions rate of 150 ng per kg of body weight per min (about 41 times the starting human rate of infusion, on a ng per m² body surface area basis, and 5 times the average rate used in clinical trials).

FDA Pregnancy Category B

Breast-feeding

It is not known whether treprostinil is distributed into human breast milk or absorbed systemically after ingestion.

Pediatrics

No information is available on the relationship of age to the effects of treprostinil in the pediatric population ≤ 16 years of age. Safety and efficacy have not been established

Geriatrics

No information is available on the relationship of age to the effects of treprostinil in geriatric patients. Treprostinil was not studied in a sufficient number of patients 65 years of age and older to determine whether the elderly respond differently than younger patients.

Drug interactions and/or related problems

The following drug interactions and/or related problems have been selected on the basis of their potential clinical significance (possible mechanism in parentheses where appropriate)—not necessarily inclusive (» = major clinical significance):

Note: Combinations containing any of the following medications, depending on the amount present, may also interact with this medication.

» Anticoagulants
(treprostinil inhibits platelet aggregation, therefore, there is an increased risk of bleeding among patients maintained on anticoagulants)

» Antihypertensive agents, or
» Diuretics, or
» Vasodilators
(reduction in blood pressure caused by treprostinil may be exacerbated by medications that alter blood pressure)

Bosentan or
Epoprostenol
(treprostinil has not been studied in conjunction with either of these drugs)

Medical considerations/Contraindications

The medical considerations/contraindications included have been selected on the basis of their potential clinical significance (reasons given in parentheses where appropriate)—not necessarily inclusive (» = major clinical significance).

Except under special circumstances, this medication should not be used when the following medical problem exists:

» Hypersensitivity to treprostinil or to structurally related compounds

Risk-benefit should be considered when the following medical problems exist:

Hepatic insufficiency, or
Portopulmonary hypertension with hepatic insufficiency
(Use in patients with portopulmonary hypertension, and mild (n=4) or moderate (n=5) hepatic insufficiency had a C_{max} that was increased 2-fold and 4-fold, respectively, and $AUC_{0-\infty}$ was increased 3-fold and 5-fold, when given treprostinil at a subcutaneous dose of 10 ng per kg of body weight per min for 150 minutes. Clearance in patients with hepatic insufficiency was reduced by up to 80% compared to healthy patients. Dose reduction is recommended.

Note: Treprostinil has not been studied in patients with severe hepatic insufficiency.)

Renal impairment
(use with caution; metabolites of treprostinil are excreted in the urine)

Side/Adverse Effects

The following side/adverse effects have been selected on the basis of their potential clinical significance (possible signs and symptoms in parentheses where appropriate)—not necessarily inclusive:

Those indicating need for medical attention

Incidence more frequent

Edema (swelling); ***infusion site reaction- including erythema, induration or rash*** (accumulation of blood at site of injection; dry, red, hot, or irritated skin; hardening of site of injection); ***vasodilation*** (feeling of warmth or heat; flushing or redness of skin, especially on face and neck; feeling faint, dizzy, or light-headedness)

Incidence less frequent

Hypotension (blurred vision; confusion; dizziness, faintness, or lightheadedness when getting up from a lying or sitting position; sudden sweating; confusion; unusual tiredness or weakness)

Those indicating need for medical attention only if they continue or are bothersome

Incidence more frequent

Diarrhea; dizziness; headache; infusion site pain; jaw pain; nausea; pruritus (itching skin); ***rash***

Overdose

For more information on the management of overdose or unintentional ingestion, **contact a poison control center** (see *Poison Control Center Listing*).

Clinical effects of overdose

In clinical trials, fourteen patients received some level of overdose; in only two cases the excess delivery produced an event of substantial hemodynamic concern (hypotension, near-syncope).

The following effects have been selected on the basis of their potential clinical significance (possible signs and symptoms in parentheses where appropriate)—not necessarily inclusive:

Diarrhea; flushing (feeling of warmth; redness of the face, neck, arms and occasionally, upper chest); ***headache; hypotension*** (blurred vision; confusion; dizziness, faintness, or lightheadedness when getting up from a lying or sitting position; sudden sweating; unusual tiredness or weakness); ***nausea; vomiting***

Treatment of overdose

There is no known antidote to treprostinil. Treatment is generally symptomatic and supportive. Most events were self-limiting and resolved with reduction or withholding of treprostinil.

Supportive care—Patients in whom intentional overdose is confirmed or suspected should be referred for psychiatric consultation.

Patient Consultation

As an aid to patient consultation, refer to *Advice for the Patient, Treprostinil (Systemic)*.

In providing consultation, consider emphasizing the following selected information (» = major clinical significance):

Before using this medication

» Conditions affecting use, especially:
Hypersensitivity to treprostinil or to structurally related compounds
Other medications, especially anticoagulants, antihypertensive agents, diuretics, and vasodilators

Proper use of this medication

Informing patient that subsequent disease management may require the initiation of an alternative intravenous postacyclin therapy, Flolan® (epoprostenol sodium)

» Proper dosing

Missed dose: Treprostinil is administered by continuous subcutaneous or intravenous infusion and should not be stopped abruptly.

» Proper storage

Precautions while using this medication

May cause dizziness.

» Treprostinil for subcutaneous infusion is given without further dilution.

» Treprostinil for intravenous infusion is given diluted.

Side/adverse effects

Signs of potential side effects, especially edema, hypotension, infusion site reactions including erythema, induration or rash and vasodilation.

General Dosing Information

Treprostinil is administered by continuous subcutaneous infusion via a self-inserted subcutaneous catheter, using an infusion pump designed for subcutaneous delivery or by continuous intravenous infusion through a surgically placed indwelling central venous catheter, using an infusion pump designed for intravenous delivery.

For subcutaneous infusion, treprostinil is delivered without further dilution.

For intravenous infusion, treprostinil must be diluted with either 0.9% sodium chloride injection or sterile water for injection.

Continuous subcutaneous or intravenous infusion with treprostinil must be performed in a setting with adequate personnel and equipment for monitoring and emergency care. Treprostinil should be used only by clinicians experienced in the diagnosis and treatment of pulmonary arterial hypertension (PAH)

Since treprostinil may be used for prolonged periods, possibly years, careful consideration should be given to the patient's ability to accept and care for a catheter and to use an infusion pump. Aseptic technique must be used in preparation and administration of treprostinil in order to reduce the risk of infection.

The goal of chronic dosage adjustments is to establish a dose at which PAH symptoms are improved, while minimizing excessive pharmacological effects of treprostinil. In order to avoid symptoms associated with the use of treprostinil, therapy should not be withdrawn abruptly or the infusion rate suddenly reduced. Abrupt withdrawal or sudden large reductions in dosage of treprostinil may result in worsening of PAH symptoms and should be avoided

To avoid potential interruptions in drug delivery, the patient must have immediate access to a backup infusion pump and subcutaneous infusion sets.

The drug dose rate must be individualized according to the patient's body weight and according to the desired rapidity and extent of pharmacodynamic effect. For specific information on treprostinil infusion delivery rates refer to the manufacturer's product information.

Dose should be increased for lack of improvement in, or worsening of, symptoms and it should be decreased for excessive pharmacological effects or for unacceptable infusion site symptoms.

The infusion pump minimum and maximum flow rates and reservoir capacity should be compatible with the concentration of the treprostinil solution used. The infusion pump should also have the following features:

- Small, lightweight, and portable
- Adjustable infusion rates to 0.002 mL per hr
- Alarm capability for detecting occlusion/no delivery, end of infusion, low battery, programming error and motor malfunctions
- Accuracy to at least ± 6% of the programmed rate
- Positive pressure driven
- Polyvinyl chloride, polypropylene, or glass reservoir

Prior to administration, parenteral drugs should be inspected visually for particulate matter and discoloration. If particulate matter or discoloration is noted, treprostinil should not be administered.

Parenteral Dosage Forms

TREPROSTINIL SODIUM INJECTION

Usual adult dose

Pulmonary arterial hypertension—

Initiation: Subcutaneous or intravenous injection, 1.25 ng per kg of body weight per min. Depending on clinical response, the infusion rate should be reduced to 0.625 ng per kg of body weight per min if the initial dose cannot be tolerated. If the preferred subcutaneous route is not tolerated because of severe site pain or reaction, treprostinil can be administered by a central intravenous line.

Note: Patients with mild or moderate hepatic insufficiency, the initial dose of treprostinil should be decreased to 0.625 ng per kg of ideal body weight per min and should be increased cautiously

Maintenance: Subcutaneous or intravenous injection increased in increments of no more than 1.25 ng per kg of body weight per min per week for the first four weeks and then no more than 2.5 ng per kg of body weight per min per week for the remaining duration of infusion, depending on clinical response.

Note: Sudden large reductions in dosage or abrupt withdrawal of treprostinil may result in worsening of PAH symptoms and should be avoided.

For subcutaneous Infusion Rate, treprostinil is delivered without further dilution.

For intravenous infusion, treprostinil must be diluted with either 0.9% sodium chloride injection or sterile water for injection.

Treprostinil Subcutaneous Infusion Rate (in mL per hour):

- Infusion rate formula for treprostinil 1 mg per mL is calculated using the following formula: Patient weight (kg) x dose (ng/kg/min) x 0.00006
- Infusion rate formula for treprostinil 2.5 mg per mL is calculated using the following formula: Patient weight (kg) x dose (ng/kg/min) x 0.000024
- Infusion rate formula for treprostinil 5 mg per mL is calculated using the following formula: Patient weight (kg) x dose (ng/kg/min) x 0.000012
- Infusion rate formula for treprostinil 10 mg per mL is calculated using the following formula: Patient weight (kg) x dose (ng/kg/min) x 0.000006
- *Diluted Intravenous Treprostinil Concentration (in mg per mL)* is calculated using the following formula: [Dose (ng/kg/min) x Patient weight (kg) x 0.00006]/[Intravenous Infusion rate (mL/hr)]
- *Amount of Treprostinil Injection (mL)* is calculated using the following formula: [Diluted Intravenous Treprostinil Concentration (mg/mL)/ treprostinil vial strength (mg/mL)] x [total volume of diluted treprostinil solution in reservoir (mL)]
- To achieve the desired total volume in the reservoir (usually 50 or 100 mL), sufficient volume of diluent (sterile water for injection or 0.9% sodium chloride injection) should be added to the reservoir with the amount of treprostinil injection.

In patients requiring transition from Flolan® (epoprostenol)Transition from epoprostenol to treprostinil is accomplished by initiating the infusion of treprostinil and increasing it, while simultaneously reducing the dose of intravenous epoprostenol. The transition to treprostinil should take place in a hospital with constant observation of response (e.g., walk distance and signs and symptoms of disease progression). During the transition, treprostinil is initiated at a recommended dose of 10% of the current epoprostenol dose, and then escalated as the epoprostenol dose is decreased.

Patients are individually titrated to a dose that allows transition from epoprostenol therapy to treprostinil while balancing prostacylin-limiting adverse events. Increases in the patient's symptoms of PAH should be first treated with increases in the dose of treprostinil. Side effects normally associated with prostacyclin and prostacyclin analogs are to be first treated by decreasing the dose of epoprostenol.

Recommended Transition Dose Changes

Step	Epoprostenol dose	Treprostinil dose
1	Unchanged	10% starting epoprostenol dose
2	80% starting epoprostenol dose	30% starting epoprostenol dose
3	60% starting epoprostenol dose	50% starting epoprostenol dose
4	40% starting epoprostenol dose	70% starting epoprostenol dose
5	20% starting epoprostenol dose	90% starting epoprostenol dose
6	5% starting epoprostenol dose	110% starting epoprostenol dose
7	0	110% starting epoprostenol dose + additional 5 to 10% increments as needed

Usual adult prescribing limits

There is little experience with administered doses greater than 40 ng/kg/min

Usual pediatric dose

Safety and efficacy have not been established. Dose selection should be cautious.

Usual geriatric dose

Dose selection should be cautious due to the greater frequency of geriatric-specific problems.

Strength(s) usually available

U.S.—

1 mg/mL (base) (Rx) [*Remodulin* (Each mL contains 5.3 mg sodium chloride; 3.0 mg metacresol; 6.3 mg sodium citrate; water for injection; sodium hydroxide and hydrochloric acid to adjust pH between 6.0 and 7.2)].

2.5 mg/mL (base) (Rx) [*Remodulin* (Each mL contains 5.3 mg sodium chloride; 3.0 mg metacresol; 6.3 mg sodium citrate; water for injection; sodium hydroxide and hydrochloric acid to adjust pH between 6.0 and 7.2)].

5 mg/mL (base) (Rx) [*Remodulin* (Each mL contains 5.3 mg sodium chloride; 3.0 mg metacresol; 6.3 mg sodium citrate; water for injection; sodium hydroxide and hydrochloric acid to adjust pH between 6.0 and 7.2)].

10 mg/mL (base) (Rx) [*Remodulin* (Each mL contains 4.0 mg sodium chloride; 3.0 mg metacresol; 6.3 mg sodium citrate; water for injection; sodium hydroxide and hydrochloric acid to adjust pH between 6.0 and 7.2)].

Packaging and storage

Unopened vials stored at 15-25°C (59 to 77°F) are stable until the date indicated.

Store at 25°C (77°F), with excursions permitted to 15-30°C (59 to 86°F).

Stability

During use, a single reservoir syringe of undiluted treprostinil can be administered up to 72 hours at 37°C.

During use, diluted treprostinil solution can be administered up to 48 hours at 37 °C when diluted in sterile water for injection or 0.9% sodium chloride injection at concentration as low as 0.004 mg per mL.

Single vials of treprostinil should be used for no more than 30 days after the initial introduction into the vial.

Auxiliary labeling

- May cause dizziness

Revised: 04/26/2006
Developed: 09/19/2002

TRETINOIN Systemic

VA CLASSIFICATION (Primary): AN900

Commonly used brand name(s): *Vesanoid*.

Note: For a listing of dosage forms and brand names by country availability, see *Dosage Forms* section(s).

Category

Antineoplastic.

Indications

Accepted

Leukemia, acute promyelocytic (treatment)—Tretinoin is indicated for induction of remission in patients with acute promyelocytic leukemia (APL) (French-American-British [FAB] subtype M3, including the M3 variant, of acute myelocytic leukemia). Responses to tretinoin have not been observed in patients who lack the genetic marker characteristic of APL, i.e., the t(15;17) translocation that produces the PML/RAR *alpha* gene; other treatment should be considered for patients in whom a diagnosis of APL cannot be confirmed by detection of t(15;17) translocation or PML/RAR *alpha* fusion. Tretinoin should be used only for patients who are refractory to, or who have relapsed from, anthracycline-based chemotherapy, or for whom anthracycline-based chemotherapy is contraindicated.

Note: After induction therapy with tretinoin has been completed, the patient should receive appropriate remission consolidation and/or maintenance therapy with other agent(s).

Pharmacology/Pharmacokinetics

Physicochemical characteristics

Chemical Group—Tretinoin (all- *trans* retinoic acid) is a retinoid chemically related to retinol (Vitamin A).

Molecular weight—300.44.

Mechanism of action/Effect

The precise mechanism of action has not been established. Tretinoin is not a cytolytic agent. It induces cytodifferentiation and decreases proliferation of acute promyelocytic leukemia cells. In patients who achieve complete remission, tretinoin therapy results in an initial maturation of the primitive promyelocytes derived from the leukemic clone, followed by a repopulation of the bone marrow and peripheral blood with normal, polyclonal hematopoietic cells.

Absorption

Tretinoin is well absorbed after oral administration. Whether coadministration with food affects tretinoin absorption has not been established. However, administration with food has been shown to enhance absorption of other retinoids.

Protein binding

Very high (> 95%), primarily to albumin.

Biotransformation

Hepatic, via oxidative metabolism by cytochrome *P*-450 (CYP) enzymes. Tretinoin probably induces its own metabolism; after 1 week of continuous therapy, the plasma concentration and the area under the tretinoin concentration-time curve (AUC) are substantially lower than on the first day of treatment.

Half-life

Elimination—0.5 to 2 hours.

Time to peak plasma concentration:

1 to 2 hours after an oral dose.

Peak plasma concentration:

Following a single oral dose of 45 mg per square meter of body surface area (mg/m^2)—347 ± 266 nanograms/mL.

Note: In a study in seven patients, plasma concentrations determined after 1 week of treatment with 45 mg/m^2 per day were approximately one-third of those measured on Day 1 of treatment.

Time to peak effect

Median time to complete remission in clinical trials was 40 to 50 days (range, 2 to 120 days).

Elimination

Renal and fecal; in studies using radiolabeled tretinoin, approximately 63% of the radioactivity was recovered in the urine within 72 hours and 31% in the feces within 6 days.

Precautions to Consider

Cross-sensitivity and/or related problems

Patients sensitive to other retinoids may be sensitive to tretinoin also.

Carcinogenicity/Tumorigenicity

Long-term studies in animals have not been done. In short-term studies in mice receiving 30 mg per kg of body weight (mg/kg) per day (approximately twice the human dose on a mg per square meter of body surface area [mg/m^2] basis), tretinoin increased the rate of diethylnitrosamine-induced hepatic adenomas and carcinomas.

Mutagenicity

No evidence of mutagenicity was found in the Ames and Chinese hamster V79 cell HGPRT tests. Tretinoin produced a twofold increase in sister chromatid exchange in human diploid fibroblasts. However, no clastogenic or aneuploidogenic effect was demonstrated in other chromosome aberration assays, including an *in vitro* assay in human peripheral lymphocytes and an *in vivo* mouse micronucleus test.

Pregnancy/Reproduction

Fertility—Tretinoin caused increased fetal resorptions in all animal species studied (mice, rats, hamsters, rabbits, and pigtail monkeys), but caused no other adverse effects on fertility or on reproductive performance in rats given up to 5 mg/kg per day (approximately two-thirds the human dose on a mg/m^2 basis). Testicular degeneration and increased numbers of immature spermatozoa were observed in a 6-week study in dogs receiving 10 mg/kg per day (approximately 4 times the human dose on a mg/m^2 basis).

Pregnancy—Adequate and well-controlled studies with tretinoin have not been done in humans, but other retinoids have caused spontaneous abortions and major fetal abnormalities. Reported defects, some of which were fatal, include abnormalities of the central nervous system (CNS), musculoskeletal system, external ear, thymus, eye, and great vessels; facial dysmorphia; cleft palate; parathyroid hormone deficiency; and cases of below-average intelligence (intelligence quotient lower than 85) with or without apparent CNS abnormalities. **There is a high risk of a severely deformed infant being born to a woman receiving tretinoin during pregnancy.**

Administration of tretinoin to a female patient requires that the following criteria be met:

- Two reliable forms of contraception should be used simultaneously during, and for 1 month after discontinuation of, tretinoin therapy. Contraception should be used even after menopause, unless a hysterectomy has been performed.
- Pregnancy testing using a highly sensitive test should be performed within 1 week before treatment is started. If possible, treatment should be delayed until the test results are available. If treatment cannot be delayed, the patient should be placed on two forms of contraception.
- The patient must receive full information and warnings about the risk to the fetus if she becomes pregnant, the possibility of contraception failure, and the need to use two forms of contraception simultaneously during and following treatment. Proof that the patient understands and acknowledges the need for using two methods of contraception simultaneously should be obtained.
- Pregnancy testing and contraception counseling should be repeated on a monthly basis during treatment.

Pregnancy—If a patient becomes pregnant during tretinoin therapy, the physician and patient should discuss the advisability of continuing or terminating the pregnancy.

Tretinoin demonstrated teratogenic and embryotoxic effects and caused a decrease in the number of live fetuses in all animal species studied (mice, rats, hamsters, rabbits, and pigtail monkeys). Gross external, soft tissue, and skeletal abnormalities occurred with doses higher than 0.7 mg/kg per day in mice, 2 mg/kg per day in rats, and 7 mg/kg per day in hamsters, and with a dose of 10 mg/kg per day (the only dose studied) in pigtail monkeys. These doses are approximately equivalent to one-twentieth, one-fourth, one-half, and four times the human dose on a mg/m^2 basis, respectively.

FDA Pregnancy Category D.

Breast-feeding

It is not known whether tretinoin is distributed into breast milk. However, because of the risk of serious adverse effects in nursing infants, it is recommended that breast-feeding be discontinued prior to initiation of tretinoin therapy.

Pediatrics

Patients younger than 1 year of age: Safety and efficacy have not been established.

Patients 1 year of age and older: Clinical data in pediatric patients is limited. Fifteen patients 1 to 16 years of age received tretinoin in clinical trials. Complete remission was achieved in 10 patients (67%). However, particular caution is recommended when tretinoin is administered to children because the risk of retinoid-induced severe headache and pseudotumor cerebri is higher in this age group than in adults. Also, studies have shown that the maximal tolerated dose is lower in children than in adults (60 mg/m^2 per day versus 195 mg/m^2 per day, respectively). A reduction in dose may be considered if serious and/or intolerable toxicity occurs during treatment. However, the efficacy and safety of tretinoin in doses lower than 45 mg/m^2 per day have not been evaluated in pediatric patients.

Drug interactions and/or related problems

The following drug interactions and/or related problems have been selected on the basis of their potential clinical significance (possible mechanism in parentheses where appropriate)—not necessarily inclusive (» = major clinical significance):

Note: Combinations containing any of the following medications, depending on the amount present, may also interact with this medication.

» Agents that cause pseudotumor cerebri/intracranial hypertension including:

» Tetracyclines
(may increase the risk of this condition)

» Antifibrinolytic agents including:

» Aminocaproic Acid or

» Aprotinin or

» Tranexemic Acid
(may lead to serious, potentially fatal, thrombotic complications when taken concomitantly with tretinoin)

» Enzyme inducers, hepatic (see *Appendix II*)
(inducers of hepatic cytochrome *P*-450 [CYP] enzymes, such as glucocorticoids, pentobarbital, phenobarbital, and rifampin, may alter the pharmacokinetics of tretinoin; however, whether concurrent use of a hepatic CYP enzyme inducer alters the safety or efficacy of tretinoin has not been established)

» Enzyme inhibitors, hepatic (see *Appendix II*), especially

» Ketoconazole
(administration of 400 to 1000 mg of ketoconazole 1 hour prior to administration of tretinoin on the 29th day of tretinoin therapy resulted in a 72% increase in the mean area under the tretinoin concentration-time curve [AUC]; other medications that generally inhibit hepatic CYP enzymes, such as cimetidine, cyclosporine, diltiazem, erythromycin, and verapamil, may also alter the pharmacokinetics of tretinoin. However, whether concurrent use of a hepatic CYP enzyme inhibitor alters the safety or efficacy of tretinoin has not been established.)

» Vitamin A
(tretinoin, like all other retinoids, should not be used concomitantly with vitamin A; symptoms of hypervitaminosis may be aggravated)

Laboratory value alterations

The following have been selected on the basis of their potential clinical significance (possible effect in parentheses where appropriate)—not necessarily inclusive (» = major clinical significance).

With physiology/laboratory test values

Calcium, serum
(concentrations may be elevated; may lead to hypercalcemia)

» Cholesterol, serum, and

» Triglycerides, serum
(concentrations were increased in up to 60% of tretinoin-treated patients in clinical trials, but usually returned to pretreatment values after discontinuation of therapy; although the risks of temporary elevations of cholesterol and triglyceride concentrations have not been established, venous thrombosis and myocardial infarction have been reported in patients considered to be at low risk of developing these conditions)

Hepatic function tests
(elevated hepatic function test results occurred in 50 to 60% of tretinoin-treated patients in clinical trials, but values generally returned to normal during or following completion of therapy)

» Leukocyte count
(a rapidly evolving increase in leukocyte count may occur during treatment, especially in patients with pre-existing leukocytosis)

White blood cell count
(elevated levels of white blood cells have been recorded; may lead to basophilia)

Medical considerations/Contraindications

The medical considerations/contraindications included have been selected on the basis of their potential clinical significance (reasons given in parentheses where appropriate)—not necessarily inclusive (» = major clinical significance).

Risk-benefit should be considered when the following medical problems exist:

» Leukemia, promyelotic (APL)
(may be at higher risk in general and may experience severe adverse reactions to trentinoin; administer only to patients with APL under strict supervision of a physician who is experienced in the management of patients with acute leukemia and in a facility with laboratory and supportive services sufficient to monitor drug tolerance and protect and maintain a patient compromised by drug toxicity)

» Leukocytosis, pre-existing (leukocyte count > 5 x 10^9/L)
(high risk of further rapid increase in leukocyte count during therapy, which increases the risk of life-threatening complications, especially the retinoic acid–acute promyelocytic leukemia [RA-APL] syndrome; institution of concurrent full-dose chemotherapy, including an anthracycline if not contraindicated, on Day 1 or Day 2 of tretinoin treatment may decrease the risk of the RA-APL syndrome and should be considered for patients with pre-existing leukocytosis)

» Sensitivity to tretinoin or other retinoids

Sensitivity to parabens

Patient monitoring

The following may be especially important in patient monitoring (other tests may be warranted in some patients, depending on condition; » = major clinical significance):

Cholesterol concentrations and
Triglyceride concentrations
(should be monitored frequently during therapy)

Coagulation profile
(monitor frequently)

Hematopoietic profile, especially

» White blood cell (WBC) count
(should be monitored frequently during therapy; rapidly evolving leukocytosis occurs in approximately 40% of patients during tretinoin treatment, which increases the risk of life-threatening complications, especially the RA-APL syndrome. If the WBC count reaches ≥ 6 x 10^9/L by Day 5, ≥ 10 x 10^9/L by Day 10, or ≥ 15 x 10^9/L by Day 28 of tretinoin therapy, immediate institution of full-dose chemotherapy, including an anthracycline if not contraindicated, may decrease the risk of the RA-APL syndrome and should be considered.)

» Hepatic function
(should be monitored frequently during therapy; although abnormalities detected in clinical trials usually resolved during or after treatment, approximately 3% of the patients developed hepatitis. Temporary withdrawal of tretinoin should be considered if hepatic function test values are elevated to more than five times the upper limit of normal.)

Side/Adverse Effects

Note: Almost all patients will experience tretinoin-related adverse effects during treatment, especially fatigue, fever, headache, and weakness. These effects are seldom permanent and generally do not require interruption of therapy.

In addition to the adverse effects listed below, adverse events that are common in patients with acute promyelocytic leukemia were reported in clinical trials, including hemorrhage (incidence 60%), infections (incidence 58%), gastrointestinal bleeding (incidence 34%), disseminated intravascular coagulation (incidence 26%), pneumonia (incidence 14%), cerebral hemorrhage (incidence 9%), hepatosplenomegaly (incidence 9%), and lymph disorders (incidence 6%).

The following side/adverse effects have been selected on the basis of their potential clinical significance (possible signs and symptoms in parentheses where appropriate)—not necessarily inclusive:

Those indicating need for medical attention

Incidence more frequent (10% or higher)

Abdominal distention (swelling of abdomen); ***cardiac arrhythmias*** (irregular heartbeat); ***dyspnea*** (shortness of breath difficult or labored breathing tightness in chest wheezing); ***earache or feeling of fullness in the ear; edema*** (swelling of face, fingers, hands, feet, or lower legs); ***fever; gastrointestinal hemorrhage*** (black, tarry stools; bloody stools; vomiting of blood or material that looks like coffee grounds); ***hypertension*** (increase in blood pressure); ***hypotension*** (decrease in blood pressure); ***mental depression; phlebitis*** (pain and swelling in foot or leg); ***rales; renal insufficiency*** (decreased urination; swelling of face, fingers, hands, feet, or lower legs); ***retinoic acid–acute promyelocytic leukemia (RA-APL) syndrome*** (bone pain; discomfort or pain in chest; fever; shortness of breath, troubled breathing, tightness in chest, or wheezing; weight gain); ***retinoid toxicity, including mucositis*** (crusting, redness, pain, or sores in mouth or nose; cracked lips); ***ocular disorders and visual disturbances*** (any change in vision); ***respiratory tract disorders*** (coughing, sneezing, sore throat, stuffy or runny nose); ***and skin rash***

Note: The *RA-APL syndrome* occurs in approximately 25% of tretinoin-treated patients and is characterized, in addition to the symptoms listed above, by radiographic pulmonary infiltrates and pleural and/or pericardial effusions. This syndrome has resulted in impaired myocardial contractility, episodic hypotension, progressive hypoxemia requiring respiratory assistance, and fatalities due to multiorgan failure. This complication usually occurs during the first month of treatment; a few cases have appeared following the first dose of tretinoin. Although the RA-APL syndrome may occur without concomitant leukocytosis, the risk may be increased if rapidly evolving leukocytosis occurs during treatment.

Incidence less frequent (3 to 9%)

Acidosis (drowsiness; fatigue; headache; nausea; troubled breathing; vomiting); ***bone inflammation; bronchial asthma*** (shortness of breath, troubled breathing, tightness in chest, or wheezing); ***cardiac arrest*** (stopping of heart; no blood pressure or pulse; unconsciousness); ***cardiac failure*** (chest pain; shortness of breath or troubled breathing); ***cardiomyopathy, secondary*** (chest discomfort or pain; difficulty breathing; dizziness; faintness; fast irregular or pounding heartbeat; shortness of breath; swelling of feet or lower legs; troubled breathing; unusual tiredness or weakness); ***cellulitis*** (swollen area that feels warm and tender); ***cerebellar edema*** (confusion; headache; nausea; vomiting); ***CNS depression*** (confusion; difficulty sleeping; disorientation; dizziness; drowsiness; coma; hallucination; headache; lethargy; lightheadedness; mood or other mental changes; trouble breathing; unusual tiredness or weakness); ***coma*** (loss of consciousness); ***convulsions; dementia*** (mood, mental, or personality changes); ***difficult or painful urination; encephalopathy*** (agitation; back pain; blurred vision; coma; confusion; dizziness; drowsiness; fever; hallucinations; headache; irritability; mood or mental changes; seizures; stiff neck; unusual tiredness or weakness; vomiting); ***enlarged heart; erythema nodosum*** (fever; pain in ankles or knees; painful, red lumps under the skin, mostly on the legs); ***flank pain*** (pain in lower back or side); ***fluid imbalance; gastrointestinal tract ulcer*** (cramping or pain in stomach, severe; heartburn, indigestion, or nausea, severe and continuing); ***hallucinations; hearing loss***—may rarely be irreversible; ***heart murmur*** (irregular heartbeat); ***hemiplegia*** (inability to move legs or arms; paralysis of one side of the body); ***hepatitis or other hepatic disorder*** (yellow eyes or skin); ***hypotaxia*** (confusion; dizziness; fast heartbeat; shortness of breath; weakness); ***intracranial hypertension*** (decrease in vision; double vision; headache; severe nausea; blurred vision; change in ability to see colors, especially blue or yellow; vomiting); ***ischemia*** (chest pain or discomfort; irregular heartbeat; nausea or vomiting; pain in the shoulders, arms, jaw or neck; sweating); ***laryngeal edema*** (shortness of breath or troubled breathing); ***myocardial infarction*** (feeling of heaviness in chest; pain in back, chest, or left arm; shortness of breath or troubled breathing); ***myocarditis*** (chest pain or discomfort; fever and chills; fast heartbeat; trouble breathing); ***myositis*** (muscle pain unusual tiredness or weakness); ***neurologic reaction*** (confusion; fever; headache; seizures; excessive sleepiness; unusual irritability; vomiting); ***pancreatitis*** (bloating; chills; constipation; darkened urine; fast heartbeat; fever; indigestion; loss of appetite; nausea; pains in stomach, side, or abdomen, possibly radiating to the back; vomiting; yellow eyes or skin); ***pericarditis; prostate enlarged*** (painful or difficult urination); ***pseudotumor cerebri*** (headache, severe; nausea and vomiting; papilledema; vision problems)—especially in children; ***pulmonary disease*** (shortness of breath); ***pulmonary edema*** (chest pain; difficult, fast, noisy breathing, sometimes with wheezing; blue lips and fingernails; pale skin; increased sweating; coughing that sometimes produces a pink frothy sputum; shortness of breath; swelling in legs and ankles); ***renal failure, acute*** (decreased urination; swelling of face, hands, fingers, feet, or lower legs); ***renal tubular necrosis; somnolence*** (drowsiness, very severe and continuing); ***stroke*** (difficulty in speaking, slow speech, or inability to speak; inability to move arms, legs, or facial muscles); ***Sweet's syndrome*** (fever sores on skin); ***thrombosis, venous or arterial*** (tenderness; pain; swelling; warmth; skin discoloration; and prominent superficial veins over affected area)

Those indicating need for medical attention only if they continue or are bothersome

Incidence more frequent

Alopecia (hair loss; thinning of hair); ***Anxiety; confusion; constipation; diarrhea; dizziness; dyspepsia*** (acid or sour stomach; belching; heartburn; indigestion; stomach discomfort, upset, or pain); ***flushing; general feeling of discomfort or illness; indigestion; injection site reaction*** (bleeding; blistering; burning; coldness; discoloration of skin; feeling of pressure; hives; infection; inflammation; itching; lumps; numbness; pain; rash; redness; scarring; soreness; stinging; swelling; tenderness; tingling; ulceration; or warmth at site); ***insomnia*** (trouble sleeping); ***loss of appetite; malaise*** (general feeling of discomfort or illness; unusual tiredness or weakness); ***muscle pain; myalgia*** (joint pain; swollen joints; muscle aching or cramping; muscle pains or stiffness; difficulty in moving); ***pallor*** (paleness of skin); ***paresthesia*** (burning, crawling, or tingling feeling in the skin); ***pruritus*** (itching skin); ***retinoid effects*** (dryness of skin, mouth, or nose; hair loss; headache; itching of skin; nausea and vomiting); ***shivering; sweating, increased; weight loss***

Incidence less frequent

Agitation (anxiety and restlessness); ***agnosia; aphasia*** (problems with speech or speaking); ***ascites*** (stomach pain and bloating); ***clumsiness or unsteadiness when walking; dysarthia*** (trouble in speaking; slurred speech; changes in patterns and rhythms of speech); ***dysuria*** (difficult or painful urination; burning while urinating); ***forgetfulness; frequent urination; hypothermia*** (clumsiness; confusion; drowsiness; low body temperature; muscle aches; muscle weakness; shivering; sleepiness; tiredness; weak or feeble pulse; weight gain); ***organomegaly; trembling, sometimes with a flapping movement; ulceration of the genitals*** (sores on genitals); ***vasculitis*** (redness, soreness or itching skin; fever; sores, welting or blisters); ***weakness in legs***

Overdose

For information on the management of overdose or unintentional ingestion, **contact a Poison Control Center** (see *Poison Control Center listing*).

There is no experience with acute overdose of tretinoin in humans. Overdose of other retinoids has caused symptoms such as abdominal pain, ataxia, cheilosis, dizziness, facial flushing, and transient headache. These symptoms resolved without apparent residual effects.

Patient Consultation

As an aid to patient consultation, refer to *Advice for the Patient, Tretinoin (Systemic)*.

In providing consultation, consider emphasizing the following selected information (» = major clinical significance):

Before taking this medication

» Conditions affecting use, especially:
Sensitivity to tretinoin or other retinoids
Pregnancy—High risk of fetal abnormalities if taken during pregnancy; need to use two effective methods of birth control simultaneously during and for 1 month following therapy
Breast-feeding—Discontinuing breast-feeding prior to treatment because of the risk of adverse effects in nursing infants
Use in children—Higher risk of severe headache and pseudotumor cerebri during treatment
Other medications, especially aminocaproic acid, aprotinin, tetracycline, tranexemic acid, hepatic enzyme inducers or inhibitors, or vitamin A

Proper use of this medication

» Compliance with therapy; not taking more medication than the amount prescribed
» Proper dosing
Missed dose: Taking as soon as possible; checking with physician if not remembered until almost time for next dose
» Proper storage

Precautions while using this medication

» Importance of regular visits to physician during therapy
» Continuing to take medication despite occurrence of expected side effects, such as fever, headache, tiredness, and weakness
» Notifying physician immediately if symptoms of retinoic acid–acute promyelocytic (RA-APL) syndrome or pseudotumor cerebri occur

Side/adverse effects

Notifying physician immediately if fever or symptoms of acidosis, bone inflammation, RA-APL syndrome, bronchial asthma, cardiac failure, cerebellar edema, CNS depression, convulsions, dyspnea, encephalopathy, enlarged heart, erythema nodosum, GI hemorrhage, heart murmur, hemiplegia, hypotaxia, ischemia, laryngeal edema, myocardial infarction, myocarditis, myositis, pancreatitis, pericarditis, prostate enlarged, pseudotumor cerebri, pulmonary disease, pulmonary edema, rales, stroke, Sweet's syndrome, or thrombosis, venous or arterial, occur

Signs of other potential side effects, especially abdominal distention, cardiac arrhythmias, earache or feeling of fullness in the ear, edema, hypertension, hypotension, mental depression, phlebitis, renal insufficiency, retinoid toxicity, cellulitis, dementia, difficult or painful urination, flank pain, gastrointestinal tract ulcer, hallucinations, hearing loss, hepatitis or other hepatic disorder, and somnolence

General Dosing Information

Tretinoin is to be used only under the supervision of a physician experienced in the management of patients with acute leukemia. Use of this medication also requires the availability of laboratory and supportive services capable of monitoring drug tolerance and treating a patient compromised by drug toxicity, including respiratory impairment.

After remission has been achieved with tretinoin, the patient should receive a standard consolidation and/or maintenance chemotherapy regimen for acute promyelocytic leukemia, unless otherwise contraindicated.

For treatment of adverse effects

For the retinoic acid–acute promyelocytic leukemia syndrome: High-dose corticosteroid treatment may reduce morbidity and mortality. It is recommended that such therapy (e.g., 10 mg of dexamethasone intravenously every 12 hours for 3 days or until symptoms abate) be initiated at the first signs and symptoms suggestive of this complication. Discontinuation of tretinoin therapy is usually not necessary.

Oral Dosage Forms

TRETINOIN CAPSULES

Usual adult and adolescent dose

Leukemia, acute promyelocytic—
Oral, 45 mg per square meter of body surface area per day, administered in two evenly divided doses. Treatment should be continued for thirty days after complete remission has been achieved or for a maximum of ninety days, whichever occurs first.

Usual pediatric dose

Leukemia, acute promyelocytic—
See *Usual adult and adolescent dose.* A decrease in the dose may be considered for patients who experience serious or intolerable toxicity. However, the efficacy and safety of lower doses have not been established.

Strength(s) usually available

U.S.—
10 mg (Rx) [*Vesanoid* (beeswax; butylated hydroxyanisole; edetate disodium; hydrogenated soybean oil flakes; hydrogenated vegetable oils and soybean oil; glycerin; yellow iron oxide; red iron oxide; titanium dioxide; methylparaben; propylparaben)].

Packaging and storage

Store between 15 and 30 °C (59 and 86 °F).

Revised: 10/21/2004

TRETINOIN Topical

VA CLASSIFICATION (Primary/Secondary):
Oil-in-water cream—DE752/DE500
Water-in-oil cream—DE900
Gel—DE752/DE500
Solution—DE752/DE500

Commonly used brand name(s): *Avita; Renova; Retin-A; Retin-A MICRO; Retisol-A; Stieva-A; Stieva-A Forte; Vitamin A Acid; Vitinoin.*

Some other commonly used names are:
Some commonly used names are retinoic acid, all- *trans*-retinoic acid, and vitamin A acid.

Note: For a listing of dosage forms and brand names by country availability, see *Dosage Forms* section(s).

Category

Antiacne agent (topical)—Cream (oil-in-water); Gel; Solution; Keratolytic (topical)—Cream (oil-in-water); Gel; Solution; Hypopigmenting agent (topical)—Cream (water-in-oil); Photoaging mitigative agent (topical)—Cream (water-in-oil).

Indications

Note: Bracketed information in the *Indications* section refers to uses that are not included in U.S. product labeling.

Accepted

Acne vulgaris (treatment)—Tretinoin cream (oil-in-water formulation), gel, and topical solution are indicated in the topical treatment of acne vulgaris. Although use of tretinoin alone is effective in the topical treatment of mild acne vulgaris (Grades I to III), the therapeutic effect may be increased when tretinoin is used in combination with topical antibiotics or benzoyl peroxide when acne consists predominately of comedones, papules, and pustules. Tretinoin may be used with systemic antibiotics for treatment of all grades of acne, including severe (Grade IV) acne conglobata; however, tretinoin is not effective when used alone for severe acne conglobata. The water-in-oil formulation of the cream is not indicated for treatment of acne vulgaris.

Hyperpigmentation, mottled, facial, due to photoaging (treatment adjunct) or
Skin roughness, facial, due to photoaging (treatment adjunct) or
Wrinkling, fine facial, due to photoaging (treatment adjunct)—The water-in-oil formulation of tretinoin cream is indicated as palliative or adjunctive treatment to skin care and sun avoidance programs to lessen the roughness of facial skin, reduce hyperpigmentation, and decrease the number and severity of fine facial wrinkles caused by photoaging. Although studies to prevent photoaging were conducted with the water-in-oil formulation, there is no reason to expect other formulations to be inactive. Patients who have been compliant but unsuccessful when using skin care and sun avoidance programs alone may benefit by adding tretinoin to the regimen. Skin care and sun avoidance programs include use of sunscreens, protective clothing, and moisturizing lotions or creams. Tretinoin improves the histological process of photoaging but cannot completely repair sun-damaged skin or eliminate all wrinkles.

There are insufficient data to show tretinoin to be safe and effective for daily use longer than 48 weeks when used as a photoaging mitigative agent. Although the clinical significance is not known, some patients using the water-in-oil formulation of tretinoin cream 0.05% for longer than 48 weeks have experienced adverse effects, such as increased dermal elastosis and atypical changes in melanocytes and keratinocytes. Safety and efficacy have not been established for patients 50 years of age and older, for patients with a history of skin cancer, or for patients who have moderately to heavily pigmented skin.

[Keratosis follicularis (treatment)][1] or

[Verruca plana (treatment)][1]—Tretinoin as an oil-in-water cream, a gel, or a solution is used to treat disorders of keratinization, such as keratosis follicularis (Darier's disease, Darier-White disease), and verruca plana (flat warts).

Acceptance not established

The safety and efficacy of topical tretinoin for the treatment or prevention of *actinic keratoses* or *skin neoplasms* have not been established.

Unaccepted

Tretinoin is not indicated for and does not reduce coarse or deep wrinkling, skin yellowing, telangiectasia, skin laxity, melanocytic atypia, or dermal elastosis.

---

[1]Not included in Canadian product labeling.

Pharmacology/Pharmacokinetics

Physicochemical characteristics

Molecular weight—300.44.

Chemical names—

Retinoic acid or all-*trans*-retinoic acid.

Description—

Aqueous gel formulation: Tretinoin is adsorbed on an acrylate copolymer, rendering the active ingredient water-soluble. May be referred to as a microsphere or microsponge system by the manufacturer.

Mechanism of action/Effect

The exact mechanism of tretinoin, a hormone and vitamin A analog, is not known. One possible explanation is altered gene expression causing changes in protein synthesis. Tretinoin diffuses across cell membranes and complexes with specific cytoplasmic receptors, which can then enter the cell's nucleus and bind to DNA. Depending on the tissue, either a transcription process begins—messenger RNA (mRNA) increases and results in subsequent protein synthesis—or transrepression occurs. Transrepression results when the hormone-receptor complex (i.e., cytoplasmic tretinoin receptor) cannot activate the gene transcription factors or the hormone-response element. When gene expression is suppressed, protein synthesis cannot occur. Transrepression is thought to contribute to the photoaging mitigative and hypopigmenting effects.

Antiacne agent or keratolytic agent—

By stimulating the transcription process, tretinoin increases epidermal cell mitosis and epidermal cell turnover. The increased permeability of the skin causes water loss and weakens the horny cell layer, making it less cohesive and easier to peel. This action facilitates the removal of existing comedones and may inhibit the formation of new comedones. It has been proposed that increased turnover in the follicular epithelium prevents formation of keratinous plugs. Tretinoin has also been reported to suppress keratin synthesis.

Photoaging mitigative agent—

Pretreatment of the skin with tretinoin inhibits a sun-induced effect of stimulating the gene transcription factor, AP-I. This transrepression effect stops the sun-induced production of the metalloproteinase enzymes, which responsively remove cells that potentially may be harmed by ultraviolet light from the skin's matrix. Tretinoin does not appreciably absorb ultraviolet light, cannot be regarded as a sunscreen, and will not protect the skin from redness. In addition, tretinoin is thought to increase the growth and differentiation of various epithelial cells, increase the glycosaminoglycan-like substance in the compacted stratum corneum, increase the number of anchoring fibrils, and improve epidermal dysplastic changes. Some studies showed no appreciable change in collagen or elastin tissue content in human skin; other studies did show an increase in collagen content.

Whether tretinoin reverses, partially reverses, or only helps to mitigate the damage associated with ultraviolet light exposure is still considered controversial. This is partly because attentive skin care measures (sunscreens, protective clothing, moisturizers, mild soaps, and sun avoidance programs) used in the protocol of these studies also contributed to the overall efficacy against photoaging; even the placebo cream contributed positive effects. The long-term effects of suppressing the removal of potentially harmed DNA by the metalloproteinase enzymes within human skin are not known.

In a placebo-controlled study in which the water-in-oil formulation of 0.05% tretinoin cream was applied for 24 weeks, patients averaged a 27.1% reduction in fine wrinkling, 37% decrease in mottled hyperpigmentation, and 29.3% decrease in roughness of skin. Total improvement of severity was considered mild and averaged only 1 to 2 units based on a scale of 0 to 9 units.

Hypopigmenting agent—

Tretinoin inhibits melanogenesis. Lightening occurs because tretinoin reduces the melanin content in the epidermis, compacts the stratum corneum, and thickens the epidermis; it is not a result of a change of number or size of melanocytes. Tretinoin may improve but not clearly resolve hyperpigmented skin.

Other actions/effects

Tretinoin has shown some activity for increased wound healing, hair growth, and some antitumor effects that still need to be established. These actions may be due to increased rates of epidermal cell turnover, angiogenesis, protein synthesis, and increased cell differentiation.

Absorption

Systemic absorption—Up to 8% of the administered dose of the nonaqueous formulations may be absorbed systemically with repeated application for 10 days; only 1.41% of the administered dose was absorbed with the aqueous formulations. Absorption may be increased when medication is applied to large surface areas, or for long periods of time in chronic extensive dermatoses.

Duration of action

Although gradual, most patients will show some improvement in skin condition within the first 6 to 7 weeks for the treatment of acne and within 24 weeks for the treatment of photoaging.

Elimination

Renal—4.45% of applied dose.

Biliary—1.58% of applied dose.

Precautions to Consider

Cross-sensitivity and/or related problems

Patients sensitive to acitretin, etretinate, isotretinoin, or other vitamin A derivatives may be sensitive to tretinoin also, since it is a vitamin A derivative.

Carcinogenicity/Tumorigenicity

A lifetime study in CD-1 mice receiving a topical tretinoin dose of 100 and 200 times the average recommended human dose resulted in a few skin tumors in female mice and liver tumors in male mice. These tumors occurred at a rate similar to that of the untreated mice. The clinical significance of this study as related to humans is not known.

In animal (hairless albino mice) studies, tretinoin has been shown to increase the rate of cutaneous tumor formation induced by ultraviolet radiation. However, the results have not been consistently reproduced in mouse skin *in vivo* or yeast cells *in vitro* and the significance of these studies as related to humans is unknown.

Dermal carcinogenicity studies for tretinoin aqueous gel, including the copolymer component, have not been done.

Mutagenicity

The micronucleus assay in mice and the Ames assay are negative for tretinoin.

The Ames assay for the copolymer used in the tretinoin aqueous gel is negative. The copolymer's components, when individually evaluated, were not mutagenic in one study. Other studies show the copolymer to be potentially mutagenic and teratogenic if given long-term at doses several times greater than the recommended human dose. The copolymer is not considered a significant risk to humans when used topically at recommended doses, since the tretinoin aqueous gel contains less than 25 parts per million of the copolymer.

Pregnancy/Reproduction

Pregnancy—Adequate and well-controlled studies in humans have not been done. Although not clearly associated, 30 cases of congenital malformations have been reported for topical tretinoin during 2 decades of clinical use. Five cases showed a rare defect of incomplete midline development of the forebrain, called holoprosencephaly. It is recommended that topical tretinoin not be used during pregnancy.

Rat, mouse, and rabbit studies have not shown tretinoin to be toxic or teratogenic when subchronic topical doses were used. Topical tretinoin has been shown to be fetotoxic in rabbits given 100 times the usual topical human dose. Teratogenicity studies in Wistar rabbits given 200 times the usual topical human dose showed evidence of a shortened or kinked tail. Doses 80 times the usual human topical dose resulted in domed head and hydrocephaly in the offspring of New Zealand white rabbits. Furthermore, topical tretinoin has caused delayed ossification in a number of bones in the offspring of rats and rabbits given 100 to 320 times the usual topical human dose, respectively. However, the delayed ossification is usually corrected after weaning.

FDA Pregnancy Category C.

Breast-feeding

It is not known whether tretinoin is distributed into breast milk. Risk-benefit should be considered.

Pediatrics

Appropriate studies on the relationship of age to the effects of tretinoin have not been performed in the pediatric population. However, no pediatrics-specific problems have been documented to date in children 12 years of age and older.

Safety and efficacy have not been established for children up to 12 years of age for all uses of tretinoin or for children 12 years of age and older for treatment of photoaging. Problems due to photoaging are unlikely to occur in children or adolescents.

Geriatrics

Appropriate studies on the relationship of age to the effects of tretinoin have not been performed in the geriatric population. However, no geriatrics-specific problems have been documented to date. Significant acne vulgaris is not likely to occur in this age group. Safety and efficacy have not been established for tretinoin's use in treatment of photoaging for adults 50 years of age and older.

Drug interactions and/or related problems

The following drug interactions and/or related problems have been selected on the basis of their potential clinical significance (possible mechanism in parentheses where appropriate)—not necessarily inclusive (» = major clinical significance):

Note: Combinations containing any of the following medications, depending on the amount present, may also interact with this medication.

Acne products, topical, or topical products containing a peeling agent, such as
- Antibiotics, topical, such as
- Clindamycin, topical
- Erythromycin, topical
- Benzoyl peroxide
- Resorcinol
- Salicylic acid
- Sulfur or

Alcohol-containing products, topical, such as
- After-shave lotions
- Astringents
- Cosmetics or soaps with a strong drying effect
- Shaving creams or lotions or

Hair products, skin-irritating, such as hair permanents or hair removal products or

Products containing lime or spices, topical or

Soaps or cleansers, abrasive

(concurrent use with tretinoin may cause a cumulative irritant or drying effect, especially with the application of peeling, desquamating, or abrasive agents, resulting in excessive irritation of the skin. If irritation results, the strength or dose of tretinoin may need to be reduced or temporarily discontinued until the skin is less sensitive.)

(use of benzoyl peroxide or topical antibiotics with tretinoin on the same area of the skin at the same time is not recommended. A physical incompatibility between the medications or a change in pH may reduce tretinoin's efficacy if used simultaneously. When used together for clinical effect, it is recommended that these medications be used at different times of the day, such as morning and night, to minimize possible skin irritation. If irritation results, tretinoin's strength or dose may need to be reduced or temporarily discontinued until the skin is less sensitive.)

Minoxidil, topical

(tretinoin increases the rate and extent of systemic absorption of topical minoxidil and may enhance hair growth according to preliminary studies; however, increased skin irritation may occur. Use of these medications together is not recommended.)

Photosensitizing medications, such as
- Fluoroquinolones
- Phenothiazines
- Sulfonamides
- Thiazide diuretics

(concurrent use with these medications may increase risk of photosensitivity, partly due to tretinoin's ability to induce dryness, peeling, and scaling that is especially prominent during the first several months of use; if skin becomes sunburned or irritated, the strength or dose of tretinoin may need to be reduced or temporarily discontinued until the skin is less sensitive.)

Retinoids, such as
- » Acitretin
- » Etretinate
- Isotretinoin
- » Tretinoin, oral

(retinoids are not used together due to their cumulative mucocutaneous drying or irritative effects. Rarely, isotretinoin has been used together with topical tretinoin to treat acne; however, the strength or dose of one of the retinoids may need to be reduced or one or both retinoids temporarily discontinued if skin irritation results.)

Medical considerations/Contraindications

The medical considerations/contraindications included have been selected on the basis of their potential clinical significance (reasons given in parentheses where appropriate)—not necessarily inclusive (» = major clinical significance).

Risk-benefit should be considered when the following medical problems exist:

Dermatitis, seborrheic or

» Eczema

(tretinoin may cause severe irritation)

Sensitivity to tretinoin

» Sunburn

(irritation may be increased; tretinoin should be discontinued until the skin is less sensitive)

Patient monitoring

The following may be especially important in patient monitoring (other tests may be warranted in some patients, depending on condition; » = major clinical significance):

Monitoring for side/adverse effects and efficacy during prolonged therapy

(recommended for patients receiving tretinoin for prolonged periods, especially for treatment of photoaging, since long-term safety has not been established beyond 48 weeks)

Side/Adverse Effects

The following side/adverse effects have been selected on the basis of their potential clinical significance (possible signs and symptoms in parentheses where appropriate)—not necessarily inclusive:

Those indicating need for medical attention

Incidence more frequent

Burning or stinging sensation of skin, severe; erythema, severe (redness of skin, severe); ***hypopigmentation of treated skin*** (lightening of treated skin)—may correspond with therapeutic use; ***scaling of skin, severe*** (severe peeling of skin); ***unusually dry skin, severe***

Note: If the retinoid reaction (*erythema, stinging, or burning sensation of skin,* and *scaling of skin*) is severe, tretinoin should be discontinued for 1 to 3 days until the symptoms subside.

Not only does *hypopigmentation* occur in hyperpigmented skin but lightening of normal pigmented skin also may be statistically significant although clinically minimal. This may be a greater concern for patients with constitutionally dark complexions.

Incidence rare

Hyperpigmentation of treated skin (darkening of treated skin)

Those indicating need for medical attention only if they continue or are bothersome

Incidence more frequent

Burning sensation, stinging, or tingling of skin, mild—transient upon application; ***erythema, mild*** (redness of skin; unusually warm skin, mild); ***scaling of skin, mild*** (chapping and slight peeling of skin); ***unusually dry skin, mild***

Note: A mild to moderate retinoid reaction (*erythema, mild burning sensation, stinging, or tingling of skin,* and *mild scaling*) occurs within the first few weeks in more than 70 to 90% of patients using therapeutic doses. This reaction peaks within 2 weeks for the 0.05% cream and at 2 months for the 0.1% cream; symptoms may occur less often and be less severe for weaker strengths. *Unusually dry skin* and *mild scaling of skin* are more persistent, peaking at 12 to 16 weeks for the 0.05% cream.

Patient Consultation

As an aid to patient consultation, refer to *Advice for the Patient, Tretinoin (Topical).*

In providing consultation, consider emphasizing the following selected information (» = major clinical significance):

Before using this medication

» Conditions affecting use, especially:

Sensitivity to etretinate, isotretinoin, tretinoin, or vitamin A derivatives

Pregnancy—Not recommended during pregnancy; although not clearly associated, rare cases of fetal problems have occurred with topical use of tretinoin

Breast-feeding—Consulting with physician before breast-feeding.

Other medications, especially acitretin, etretinate, and oral tretinoin

Other medical problems, especially eczema and sunburn

Proper use of this medication

» Importance of not using more medication than the amount prescribed

» Not applying medication to windburned or sunburned skin or on open wounds

» Avoiding contact with the eyes, mouth, and nose

Reading patient directions carefully before use

Proper administration technique

Before applying—Washing skin with mild or nonallergenic soap or cleanser and warm water; gently patting dry; avoid harsh scrubbing of face with washcloth or sponge

» Waiting 20 to 30 minutes for complete drying of skin; applying to wet skin can cause skin irritation

For cream or gel dosage form

Applying very sparingly to affected areas and rubbing in gently but well; a pea-sized amount is sufficient to cover the face

For solution dosage form

Using fingertips, gauze pad, or cotton swab and applying very sparingly to affected areas

Not oversaturating gauze pad or cotton swab to prevent medication from running into areas not intended for treatment

Washing hands afterwards to remove any lingering medication

» Proper dosing

Missed dose: Applying next dose at regularly scheduled time; not doubling doses

» Proper storage

Precautions while using this medication

Possibility that skin will become irritated or that acne may appear to worsen during the first 3 weeks of therapy; checking with health care professional at any time that skin irritation becomes severe or if acne does not improve within 8 to 12 weeks

Not washing the areas of the skin treated with tretinoin for at least 1 hour after application

» Avoiding use of any topical product on the same area within 1 hour before or after application of tretinoin to avoid physical incompatibilities or excessive skin irritation; applying tretinoin at bedtime helps to avoid this when other topical products are used during the day

» Either checking with health care professional before using or avoiding use of other topical acne or skin products containing a peeling agent (benzoyl peroxide, resorcinol, salicylic acid, or sulfur), irritating hair products (permanents or hair removal products), sunsensitizing skin products (could contain limes or spices), alcohol-containing skin products, or drying or abrasive skin products (some cosmetics or soaps or skin cleansers); sometimes benzoyl peroxide is used with tretinoin for acne treatment but is applied at different times of the day to lessen skin irritation

» Minimizing exposure of treated areas to sunlight, wind, and cold temperatures to avoid sunburn, dryness, or irritation, especially during the first 6 months of treatment with tretinoin. Also, avoiding use of artificial sunlight or sunlamp

Using sunscreen preparations (minimum sun protection factor [SPF] of 15) or wearing protective clothing over treated areas when sunlight exposure cannot be avoided

» Checking with doctor at any time skin becomes too dry or irritated; choosing proper skin product to reduce skin dryness or irritation

For patients using tretinoin to treat acne:

Using light water-based skin products, especially regular use of moisturizers, to help reduce skin irritation or dryness

For patients using tretinoin to treat photoaging, hyperpigmentation, or fine wrinkling:

» Complying continually with sun avoidance measures

» Using oil-based skin products, especially regular use of moisturizers, to help reduce any skin irritation or dryness resulting from weather or tretinoin

Side/adverse effects

The side/adverse effects of tretinoin are reversible upon discontinuation of therapy; however, hyperpigmentation or hypopigmentation may persist for months

Signs of potential side effects, especially burning or stinging sensation of skin (severe); erythema (severe); hypopigmentation of treated skin—may correspond with therapeutic effect; scaling of skin (severe); unusually dry skin (mild or severe); hyperpigmentation of treated skin

General Dosing Information

Since tretinoin potentially can cause severe irritation and peeling, therapy may be initiated or maintained on an alternate-day or, occasionally, every-third-day regimen, preferably with the less irritating and low-concentration cream or gel dosage form. If tolerated, the more potent liquid or higher-concentration cream or gel preparation may then be used. Alcohol-containing gels and solutions are considered more potent because of the dryness produced from the volatility of their vehicles, an effect appropriate for hot, wet climates and summer months.

If severe irritation occurs, tretinoin should not be applied until the skin is healed or less irritated. Tretinoin should not be applied to mucous membranes; contact near the eyes, lips, or nose should be avoided.

Patients should be counseled on the importance of protecting the skin from the sun, wind, cold temperatures, and excessive dryness by using sunscreens of at least SPF 15, moisturizers, and protective clothing. Artificial sunlight, such as sunlamps, should be avoided.

Any topical products, medications, or agents should not be applied simultaneously but should be delayed at least 1 hour after the application of tretinoin. Topical acne products, such as antibiotics or benzoyl peroxide, are used therapeutically with tretinoin to treat acne but can increase the risk of skin irritation.

The areas to be treated should be cleansed thoroughly before the medication is applied. Using the fingertips when washing the skin helps clean the skin and remove resulting scales and peeling of skin; harsh scrubbing of skin with sponges or cloths should be avoided. Tretinoin should be applied to dry skin (20 to 30 minutes should be allowed after washing) to reduce possible skin irritation that worsens or occurs more often if tretinoin is applied any earlier to nondry skin. Treated areas of skin should not be washed for at least 1 hour after applying tretinoin. When considering dosage adjustments, a pea-sized amount (0.4 inch or 1 centimeter) is enough to cover the entire face.

For the treatment of acne

Within the first few weeks, acne can worsen because of exacerbation of deep, previously unseen lesions. Therapeutic results may be noticeable after 2 to 3 weeks of therapy, but more so after 6 weeks, with optimal results achieved after 3 months of therapy for most patients.

For the treatment of photoaging, hyperpigmentation, or fine wrinkling

In a dose-response study of water-in-oil tretinoin cream, the 0.01% strength was marginally effective, the 0.001% strength showed no difference from the vehicle, and the 0.05% strength provided the best clinical response. Improvement persists for at least 2 months post-therapy, followed by partial and gradual regression.

For the treatment of keratosis follicularis

Irritation caused by tretinoin may be minimized by use of adequate, yet threshold, concentrations of tretinoin or by concurrent use of topical steroids.

For treatment of verruca plana

In the treatment of flat warts, therapy is initiated with a weak concentration of tretinoin. If there is no response, the concentration of the tretinoin preparation and/or frequency of application should be increased.

Topical Dosage Forms

Note: Bracketed information in the *Dosage Forms* section refers to categories of use and/or indications that are not included in U.S. product labeling.

TRETINOIN CREAM (Oil-in-water) USP

Usual adult and adolescent dose

Acne vulgaris—

Initial: Topical, to the skin of affected areas, once a day at bedtime. After the first seven to ten days of use, dose may be increased to two times a day if excessive drying of skin has not occurred.

Maintenance: Topical, to the skin of affected areas, once a day at bedtime or less often as needed.

[Keratosis follicularis][1] or

[Verruca plana][1]—

Topical, to the skin of affected areas, one or two times a day.

Strength(s) usually available

U.S.—

0.025% (Rx) [*Retin-A* (stearyl alcohol); *Avita* (stearyl alcohol)].
0.05% (Rx) [*Retin-A* (stearyl alcohol)].
0.1% (Rx) [*Retin-A* (stearyl alcohol)].

Canada—

Note: *Retisol-A* contains sunscreens with a sun protection factor (SPF) of 15.

0.01% (Rx) [*Retin-A; Retisol-A; Stieva-A* (cetyl alcohol; edetate disodium; methylparaben; propylparaben; stearyl alcohol); *Vitamin A Acid*].
0.025% (Rx) [*Retin-A; Retisol-A* (light mineral oil; Parsol MCX 7.5%; Parsol 1789 2%; sodium hydroxide; stearyl alcohol); *Stieva-A* (cetyl alcohol; edetate disodium; methylparaben; propylparaben; stearyl alcohol); *Vitamin A Acid; Vitinoin*].
0.05% (Rx) [*Retin-A; Retisol-A* (light mineral oil; Parsol MCX 7.5%; Parsol 1789 2%; sodium hydroxide; stearyl alcohol); *Stieva-A* (cetyl alcohol; edetate disodium; methylparaben; propylparaben; stearyl alcohol); *Vitamin A Acid; Vitinoin*].
0.1% (Rx) [*Retin-A; Retisol-A* (light mineral oil; Parsol MCX 7.5%; Parsol 1789 2%; sodium hydroxide; stearyl alcohol); *Stieva-A Forte* (cetyl alcohol; edetate disodium; methylparaben; propylparaben; stearyl alcohol; titanium dioxide); *Vitamin A Acid; Vitinoin*].

Packaging and storage

Store between 15 and 27 °C (59 and 81 °F), unless otherwise specified by manufacturer. Store in a tight, light-resistant container. Protect from freezing.

Incompatibilities

Tretinoin and benzoyl peroxide should not be extemporaneously combined, since there is a physical incompatibility between the two medications.

Auxiliary labeling

- For external use only.
- Avoid prolonged or excessive exposure to direct and/or artificial sunlight while using this medication.

Note

Include patient instructions when dispensing.

TRETINOIN CREAM (Water-in-oil) USP

Usual adult and adolescent dose

Hyperpigmentation, mottled, facial, due to photoaging (treatment adjunct) or
Skin roughness, facial, due to photoaging (treatment adjunct) or
Wrinkling, fine facial, due to photoaging (treatment adjunct)—

Adults up to 50 years of age: Topical, to the skin of the face, a thin film once a day, usually at bedtime.

Adults 50 years of age and older: Safety and efficacy have not been established.

Note: Dosing is individualized to minimize irritation while maintaining efficacy. Alternate-day dosing, a smaller volume, or a weaker strength can be used initially or when skin becomes too irritated. If irritation becomes severe, tretinoin should be discontinued until irritation substantially lessens or heals.

Safety and efficacy have not been established for daily use for more than forty-eight weeks. Some clinicians recommend only two or three applications per week following use for eight to twelve months to maintain effects.

Usual geriatric dose

Hyperpigmentation, mottled, facial, due to photoaging (treatment adjunct) or
Skin roughness, facial, due to photoaging (treatment adjunct) or
Wrinkling, fine facial, due to photoaging (treatment adjunct)—

Adults 50 years of age and older: Safety and efficacy have not been established.

Strength(s) usually available

U.S.—

0.05% (Rx) [*Renova* (edetate disodium; light mineral oil; methylparaben; purified water; sorbital solution; stearyl alcohol)].

Canada—

0.05% (Rx) [*Renova* (edetate disodium; light mineral oil; methylparaben; purified water; sorbital solution; stearyl alcohol)].

Packaging and storage

Store between 15 and 27 °C (59 and 81 °F), unless otherwise specified by manufacturer. Store in a tight, light-resistant container. Protect from freezing.

Incompatibilities

Tretinoin and benzoyl peroxide should not be extemporaneously combined, since there is a physical incompatibility between the two medications.

Insoluble in water, mineral oil, and glycerin.

Auxiliary labeling

- For external use only.
- Avoid prolonged or excessive exposure to direct and/or artificial sunlight while using this medication.

Note

Include patient instructions when dispensing.
For facial use only.

TRETINOIN GEL USP

Usual adult and adolescent dose

Acne vulgaris or
[Keratosis follicularis][1] or
[Verruca plana][1]—

See *Tretinoin Cream USP (Oil-in-water)*.

Strength(s) usually available

U.S.—

0.01% (alcohol-based) (Rx) [*Retin-A* (butyl alcohol 90% w/w)].
0.025% (alcohol-based) (Rx) [*Retin-A* (butyl alcohol 90% w/w); *Avita* (ethanol 83% w/w)].
0.1% (aqueous-based) (Rx) [*Retin-A MICRO* (benzyl alcohol; butylated hydroxytoluene; carbomer 934P; cyclomethicone and dimethicone copolyol; disodium EDTA; glycerin; PPG-20 methyl glucose ether distearate; propylene glycol; purified water; sorbic acid)].

Canada—

Note: *Vitinoin* gel contains moisturizers.

0.01% (alcohol-based) (Rx) [*Retin-A; Stieva-A* (alcohol); *Vitamin A Acid* (methylparaben; propylparaben)].
0.025% (alcohol-based) (Rx) [*Retin-A; Stieva-A* (alcohol); *Vitamin A Acid* (methylparaben; propylparaben); *Vitinoin*].
0.05% (alcohol-based) (Rx) [*Stieva-A* (alcohol); *Vitamin A Acid* (methylparaben; propylparaben)].

Packaging and storage

Store between 15 and 25 °C (59 and 77 °F) unless otherwise specified by manufacturer. Store in a tight container. Protect from light.

Incompatibilities

Tretinoin and benzoyl peroxide should not be extemporaneously combined, since there is a physical incompatibility between the two medications.

Auxiliary labeling

- For external use only.
- Avoid prolonged or excessive exposure to direct and/or artificial sunlight while using this medication.

Note

Include patient instructions when dispensing.
Protect from heat and flame.

TRETINOIN TOPICAL SOLUTION USP

Usual adult and adolescent dose

Acne vulgaris or
[Keratosis follicularis][1] or
[Verruca plana][1]—

See *Tretinoin Cream USP (Oil-in-water)*.

Strength(s) usually available

U.S.—

0.05% (Rx) [*Retin-A* (alcohol 55% w/w)].

Canada—

0.025% (Rx) [*Stieva-A*].
0.05% (Rx) [*Stieva-A*].

Packaging and storage

Store between 15 and 30 °C (59 and 86 °F), unless otherwise specified by manufacturer. Store in a tight, light-resistant container.

Incompatibilities

Tretinoin and benzoyl peroxide should not be extemporaneously combined, since there is a physical incompatibility between the two medications.

Auxiliary labeling

- For external use only.
- Keep container tightly closed.
- Avoid prolonged or excessive exposure to direct and/or artificial sunlight while using this medication.

Note

Include patient instructions when dispensing.

[1]Not included in Canadian product labeling.

Selected Bibliography

Fisher GJ, Datta SC, Talwar HS, et al. Molecular basis of sun-induced premature skin aging and retinoid antagonism. Nature 1996 Jan 25; 379: 335-9.

Olsen EA, Katz I, Levine N, et al. Tretinoin moisturizers cream: a new therapy for photodamaged skin. J Am Acad Dermatol 1992 Feb; 26(2Pt1): 283-4.

Muller SA, Belcher RW, Esterly NB. Keratinizing dermatoses. Arch Dermatol 1977 Aug; 113(8): 1052-4.

Revised: 04/24/1998

TRIAMCINOLONE—See *Corticosteroids—Glucocorticoid Effects (Systemic), Corticosteroids (Inhalation-Local), Corticosteroids (Nasal), Corticosteroids (Topical)*

TRIAMTERENE—See *Diuretics, Potassium-sparing (Systemic)*

TRIAMTERENE AND HYDROCHLOROTHIAZIDE—See *Diuretics, Potassium-sparing and Hydrochlorothiazide (Systemic)*

TRIAZOLAM—See *Benzodiazepines (Systemic)*

TRICHLORMETHIAZIDE—See *Diuretics, Thiazide (Systemic)*

TRICITRATES—See *Citrates (Systemic)*

TRIFLUOPERAZINE—See *Phenothiazines (Systemic)*

TRIFLUPROMAZINE—See *Phenothiazines (Systemic)*

TRIFLURIDINE Ophthalmic

VA CLASSIFICATION (Primary): OP203

Commonly used brand name(s): *Viroptic.*

Another commonly used name is trifluorothymidine.

Note: For a listing of dosage forms and brand names by country availability, see *Dosage Forms* section(s).

Category

Antiviral (ophthalmic).

Indications

Accepted

Keratitis, herpes simplex virus (treatment) or

Keratoconjunctivitis, herpes simplex virus (treatment)—Trifluridine is indicated in the treatment of keratoconjunctivitis and recurrent epithelial keratitis caused by herpes simplex virus (HSV), types 1 and 2. Trifluridine may be useful in patients who do not respond to idoxuridine or vidarabine or when ocular toxicity or hypersensitivity to idoxuridine occurs.

Unaccepted

Trifluridine is not indicated in the prophylaxis of HSV keratoconjunctivitis or epithelial keratitis.

Trifluridine is not effective against bacterial, fungal, or chlamydial infections of the cornea or in nonviral trophic lesions.

Pharmacology/Pharmacokinetics

Physicochemical characteristics

Molecular weight—296.20.

pH—5.5 to 6

Mechanism of action/Effect

Trifluridine, also called trifluorothymidine, closely resembles thymidine. It inhibits thymidylic phosphorylase and specific DNA polymerases, which are necessary for the incorporation of thymidine into viral DNA. Trifluridine is incorporated in place of thymidine into viral DNA, resulting in faulty DNA and the inability to reproduce or to infect or destroy tissue. Trifluridine also is incorporated into mammalian DNA.

Absorption

Systemic absorption of trifluridine from the eye is negligible.

Distribution

Intraocular penetration occurs after topical administration of trifluridine. Decreased corneal integrity or stromal or uveal infections may increase trifluridine's penetration into the aqueous humor.

Half-life

Approximately 12 to 18 minutes.

Precautions to Consider

Carcinogenicity

Lifetime carcinogenicity bioassays have been performed in rats and mice given daily subcutaneous doses of trifluridine. Rats given doses of 1.5, 7.5, or 15 mg per kg of body weight (mg/kg) per day had increased incidences of adenocarcinomas of the intestinal tract and mammary glands, hemangiosarcomas of the spleen and liver, carcinosarcomas of the prostate gland, and granulosa-thecal cell tumors of the ovary. Mice given doses of 10 mg/kg per day (but not those given 1 or 5 mg/kg per day) had significantly increased incidences of adenocarcinomas of the intestinal tract and uterus. These mice also had a significantly higher incidence of testicular atrophy than vehicle control mice.

Mutagenicity

Studies in various standard *in vitro* test systems have shown that trifluridine exerts mutagenic, DNA-damaging, and cell-transforming effects and that it is clastogenic in *Vicia faba* cells. Chromosomal aberrations in bone marrow cells were induced in female, but not male, rats given daily 700 mg/kg subcutaneous injections for five days. Thus the possibility exists that unknown mutagenic agents may cause genetic damage in humans.

Pregnancy/Reproduction

Pregnancy—Adequate and well-controlled studies in humans have not been done.

Subcutaneous doses of trifluridine equal to up to 5 mg/kg daily (23 times the estimated human exposure) given to rats and rabbits were not teratogenic. However, at doses of 2.5 and 5 mg/kg daily in rats and 2.5 mg/kg daily in rabbits, fetal toxicity (delayed skeletal ossification) occurred. Doses of 2.5 and 5 mg/kg daily in rabbits caused increased fetal death or resorption. One mg/kg daily (equivalent to 5 times the estimated human exposure) was a no-effect level for rats and rabbits. No teratogenic or fetotoxic effects were noted after topical 1% trifluridine application to the eyes of pregnant rabbits on the sixth through 18th days of pregnancy. Trifluridine injected directly into the yolk sac of chicken eggs has been shown to be teratogenic.

FDA Pregnancy Category C.

Breast-feeding

Trifluridine is unlikely to be distributed into breast milk following ophthalmic administration, since the total daily dose is small (5 mg or less), and since trifluridine is diluted in body fluids and has an extremely short half-life (approximately 12 minutes).

Pediatrics

Appropriate studies on the relationship of age to the effects of trifluridine have not been performed in the pediatric population in children up to 6 years of age. However, no pediatrics-specific problems have been documented to date.

Geriatrics

Appropriate studies on the relationship of age to the effects of trifluridine have not been performed in the geriatric population. However, no geriatrics-specific problems have been documented to date.

Medical considerations/Contraindications

The medical considerations/contraindications included have been selected on the basis of their potential clinical significance (reasons

given in parentheses where appropriate)—not necessarily inclusive (» = major clinical significance).

Risk-benefit should be considered when the following medical problem exists:
Sensitivity to trifluridine

Patient monitoring
The following may be especially important in patient monitoring (other tests may be warranted in some patients, depending on condition; » = major clinical significance):
Ophthalmologic, including slit-lamp, examinations
(may be required periodically during therapy)

Side/Adverse Effects

The following side/adverse effects have been selected on the basis of their potential clinical significance (possible signs and symptoms in parentheses where appropriate)—not necessarily inclusive:

Those indicating need for medical attention
Incidence rare
Epithelial keratopathy; superficial punctate keratopathy (blurred vision or other change in vision); ***hyperemia*** (redness of eye); ***hypersensitivity*** (itching, redness, swelling, or other sign of irritation not present before therapy); ***increased intraocular pressure; keratitis sicca*** (dryness of eye); ***stromal edema*** (irritation of eye)

Those indicating need for medical attention only if they continue or are bothersome
Incidence more frequent
Burning or stinging

Patient Consultation

As an aid to patient consultation, refer to *Advice for the Patient, Trifluridine (Ophthalmic)*.

In providing consultation, consider emphasizing the following selected information (» = major clinical significance):

Before using this medication
» Conditions affecting use, especially:
Sensitivity to trifluridine

Proper use of this medication
Proper administration technique for ophthalmic solution
Washing hands before and after administration
» Not using more frequently or for longer than ordered by physician
» Compliance with full course of therapy
» Proper dosing
Missed dose: Applying as soon as possible; not applying if almost time for next dose
» Proper storage

Precautions while using this medication
Importance of keeping appointments with physician; checking with physician if symptoms become worse

Side/adverse effects
Signs of potential side effects, especially epithelial keratopathy, superficial punctate keratopathy, hyperemia, hypersensitivity, increased intraocular pressure, keratitis sicca, or stromal edema

General Dosing Information

Trifluridine may be administered concurrently with cycloplegics, mydriatics, antibiotics, sulfonamides, vasoconstrictors, miotics, adrenergics, and corticosteroids. Corticosteroids can accelerate the spread of viral infections and are usually contraindicated in superficial herpes simplex virus keratitis. However, steroids may be used concurrently with trifluridine in the treatment of herpes simplex stromal infections. Trifluridine should be continued for a few days after the steroid has been discontinued.

Treatment should not be continued for more than a total of 21 days, because of potential ocular toxicity, or for more than 7 days after healing is complete. If there are no signs of improvement after 7 days of therapy, or if complete re-epithelialization has not occurred after 14 days of therapy, other forms of therapy should be considered.

Herpetic keratitis may recur if trifluridine is discontinued before microscopic staining with fluorescein has cleared.

Ophthalmic Dosage Forms

TRIFLURIDINE OPHTHALMIC SOLUTION

Usual adult and adolescent dose
HSV keratitis and keratoconjunctivitis—
Topical, to the conjunctiva, 1 drop every two hours while awake. Treatment should be continued until re-epithelialization of the cornea is complete Dose may then be reduced to 1 drop every four hours while awake (minimum of 5 drops daily) for an additional seven days.

Usual adult prescribing limits
Up to 9 drops daily.
If there are no signs of improvement after 7 days of therapy, or if complete re-epithelialization has not occurred after 14 days of therapy, other forms of therapy should be considered.

Usual pediatric dose
For children 6 years of age and older, see *Usual adult and adolescent dose.*
For children up to 6 years of age, safety and efficacy have not been established.

Strength(s) usually available
U.S.—
1% (Rx) [*Viroptic* (thimerosal 0.001%)].
Canada—
1% (Rx) [*Viroptic* (benzalkonium chloride)].

Packaging and storage
Store between 2 and 8 °C (36 and 46 °F), unless otherwise specified by manufacturer.

Auxiliary labeling
- Refrigerate.
- For the eye.
- Continue medicine for full time of treatment.
- Do not use more often or longer than ordered.

Note
Dispense in original unopened container.

Revised: 03/29/2000

TRIHEXYPHENIDYL—See *Antidyskinetics (Systemic)*

TRIKATES—See *Potassium Supplements (Systemic)*

TRIMEPRAZINE—See *Antihistamines, Phenothiazine-derivative (Systemic)*

TRIMETHADIONE—See *Anticonvulsants, Dione (Systemic)*

TRIMETHOBENZAMIDE Systemic†

INN: Trimethobenzamide

VA CLASSIFICATION (Primary): GA609

Commonly used brand name(s): *Benzacot; Stemetic; Tebamide; Tigan; Tribenzagan; Trimazide.*

Note: For a listing of dosage forms and brand names by country availability, see *Dosage Forms* section(s).

†Not commercially available in Canada.

Category

Antiemetic.

Indications

Accepted
Nausea and vomiting (prophylaxis and treatment)—Trimethobenzamide is indicated for the control of nausea and vomiting.

Pharmacology/Pharmacokinetics

Physicochemical characteristics
Molecular weight—424.92.

Mechanism of action/Effect
Thought to inhibit the medullary chemoreceptor trigger zone.

Biotransformation
Hepatic.

Elimination
Renal; biliary.

Precautions to Consider

Cross-sensitivity and/or related problems
The suppository dosage form contains 2% of benzocaine. Patients sensitive to benzocaine or similar local anesthetics should not use the suppository dosage form of trimethobenzamide.

Pregnancy/Reproduction
Pregnancy—Adequate and well-controlled studies in humans have not been done.

Reproduction studies in animals have not shown that trimethobenzamide causes teratogenic effects in the fetus; however, it has been shown to cause increased embryonic resorptions and stillbirths.

Breast-feeding
It is not known if trimethobenzamide is distributed into breast milk.

Pediatrics
Trimethobenzamide is not recommended for treatment of uncomplicated vomiting in children. Caution is required because of the suspicion that centrally acting antiemetics, when used in the presence of viral illnesses, may contribute to the development of Reye's syndrome.

Geriatrics
No information is available on the relationship of age to the effects of trimethobenzamide in geriatric patients.

Drug interactions and/or related problems
The following drug interactions and/or related problems have been selected on the basis of their potential clinical significance (possible mechanism in parentheses where appropriate)—not necessarily inclusive (» = major clinical significance):

Note: Combinations containing any of the following medications, depending on the amount present, may also interact with this medication.

Apomorphine
(prior administration of trimethobenzamide may decrease the emetic response to apomorphine; also, concurrent use may potentiate the central nervous system [CNS] effects of either apomorphine or trimethobenzamide)

» CNS depression-producing medications (see *Appendix II*)
(concurrent use may potentiate the effects of either these medications or trimethobenzamide; in addition, use of trimethobenzamide as well as other antiemetic agents in patients who have recently received other medications with CNS effects, such as phenothiazines, barbiturates, or the belladonna alkaloids, has resulted in opisthotonos, convulsions, coma, and extrapyramidal symptoms)

Ototoxic medications (see *Appendix II*)
(concurrent use with trimethobenzamide may mask the symptoms of ototoxicity, such as tinnitus, dizziness, and vertigo)

Medical considerations/Contraindications
The medical considerations/contraindications included have been selected on the basis of their potential clinical significance (reasons given in parentheses where appropriate)—not necessarily inclusive (» = major clinical significance).

Risk-benefit should be considered when the following medical problems exist:

Dehydration or
Electrolyte imbalance or
Encephalitis or
Fever, high or
Gastroenteritis
(CNS reactions such as opisthotonos, convulsions, coma, and extrapyramidal symptoms have been reported after administration of trimethobenzamide, especially in children and in elderly or debilitated patients, or in those who have recently received other medications with CNS effects)

Sensitivity to trimethobenzamide

Note: Antiemetic action of trimethobenzamide may impede diagnosis of such conditions as appendicitis and obscure signs of toxicity from overdosage of other medications.

Side/Adverse Effects
The following side/adverse effects have been selected on the basis of their potential clinical significance (possible signs and symptoms in parentheses where appropriate)—not necessarily inclusive:

Those indicating need for medical attention
Incidence rare

Allergic reactions (skin rash); ***blood dyscrasias*** (sore throat or fever; unusual tiredness); ***convulsions; hepatic function impairment*** (yellow eyes or skin); ***mental depression; opisthotonos*** (body spasm with head and heels bent backward and body bowed forward); ***Parkinson-like syndrome*** (shakiness or tremors); ***Reye's syndrome*** (convulsions; severe or continuing vomiting)

Those indicating need for medical attention only if they continue or are bothersome
Incidence more frequent

Drowsiness

Incidence less frequent

Blurred vision; diarrhea; dizziness; headache; muscle cramps

Patient Consultation
As an aid to patient consultation, refer to Advice for the Patient, Trimethobenzamide (Systemic).

In providing consultation, consider emphasizing the following selected information (» = major clinical significance):

Before using this medication
» Conditions affecting use, especially:
Sensitivity to trimethobenzamide or to benzocaine (for suppository form)
Pregnancy—Animal studies have shown increased fetal resorptions and stillbirths
Use in children—Trimethobenzamide is not recommended for treatment of uncomplicated vomiting, due to the possible contribution of centrally acting antiemetics to the development of Reye's syndrome
Other medications, especially CNS depression-producing medications
Other medical problems, especially dehydration, electrolyte imbalance, encephalitis, high fever, or gastroenteritis

Proper use of this medication
Not giving to children unless prescribed; giving medication only as directed
Taking medication only as directed
Proper administration of this medication (for suppository dosage form only)
» Proper dosing
Missed dose: Taking as soon as possible; not taking if almost time for next dose; not doubling doses
» Proper storage

Precautions while using this medication
» Avoiding use of alcohol or other CNS depression-producing medications
» Possible dizziness, lightheadedness, or drowsiness; caution when driving or doing anything else requiring alertness
May mask ototoxic effects of large doses of salicylates

Side/adverse effects
Signs of potential side effects, especially allergic reactions, blood dyscrasias, convulsions, hepatic function impairment, mental depression, opisthotonos, Parkinson-like syndrome, and Reye's syndrome

General Dosing Information

For parenteral dosage form only
Intravenous injection is not recommended.

Intramuscular administration should be made by deep injection into the upper outer quadrant of the gluteal area in order to minimize irritation at the site of injection.

Oral Dosage Forms

TRIMETHOBENZAMIDE HYDROCHLORIDE CAPSULES USP

Usual adult and adolescent dose
Antiemetic—
Oral, 250 mg three or four times a day as needed.

Usual pediatric dose

Antiemetic—

Oral, 15 mg per kg of body weight a day as needed, divided into three or four doses; or for

Children weighing 15 to 45 kg: Oral, 100 to 200 mg three or four times a day, as needed.

Strength(s) usually available

U.S.—

100 mg (Rx) [*Tigan*].

250 mg (Rx) [*Tigan;* GENERIC].

Canada—

Not commercially available.

Packaging and storage

Store between 15 and 30 °C (59 and 86 °F), unless otherwise specified by manufacturer. Store in a well-closed container.

Auxiliary labeling

- May cause drowsiness.
- Avoid alcoholic beverages.

Parenteral Dosage Forms

TRIMETHOBENZAMIDE HYDROCHLORIDE INJECTION USP

Usual adult and adolescent dose

Antiemetic—

Intramuscular, 200 mg three or four times a day as needed.

Usual pediatric dose

Use is not recommended.

Strength(s) usually available

U.S.—

100 mg per mL (Rx) [*Benzacot; Stemetic; Tigan* (parabens [methyl and propyl] 0.2%—in 2-mL ampuls; phenol 0.45%—in 20-mL vials; phenol 0.45%, disodium edetate 0.2 mg—in 2-mL syringes); *Tribenzagan;* GENERIC].

Canada—

Not commercially available.

Packaging and storage

Store between 15 and 30 °C (59 and 86 °F), unless otherwise specified by manufacturer. Protect from freezing.

Rectal Dosage Forms

TRIMETHOBENZAMIDE HYDROCHLORIDE SUPPOSITORIES

Usual adult and adolescent dose

Antiemetic—

Rectal, 200 mg three or four times a day as needed.

Usual pediatric dose

Antiemetic—

Rectal, 15 mg per kg of body weight a day as needed, divided into three or four doses; or for

Children weighing less than 15 kg: Rectal, 100 mg three or four times a day as needed.

Children weighing 15 to 45 kg: Rectal, 100 to 200 mg three or four times a day as needed.

Note: Premature and full-term neonates—Use is not recommended.

Strength(s) usually available

U.S.—

100 mg (Rx) [*Tigan* (2% benzocaine); GENERIC].

200 mg (Rx) [*Tebamide; Tigan* (2% benzocaine); *Trimazide;* GENERIC].

Canada—

Not commercially available.

Packaging and storage

Store between 15 and 30 °C (59 and 86 °F), unless otherwise specified by manufacturer.

Auxiliary labeling

- May cause drowsiness.
- Avoid alcoholic beverages.

Revised: 01/29/1999

TRIMETHOPRIM Systemic

VA CLASSIFICATION (Primary): AM900

Commonly used brand name(s): *Proloprim; Trimpex.*

Note: For a listing of dosage forms and brand names by country availability, see *Dosage Forms* section(s).

Category

Antibacterial (systemic).

Indications

Note: Bracketed information in the *Indications* section refers to uses that are not included in U.S. product labeling.

Accepted

Urinary tract infections, bacterial (treatment)—Trimethoprim is indicated in the treatment of initial, uncomplicated urinary tract infections caused by susceptible strains of *Escherichia coli*, *Proteus mirabilis*, *Klebsiella pneumoniae*, *Enterobacter* species, and coagulase-negative *Staphylococcus* species, including *S. saprophyticus*.

[Urinary tract infections, bacterial (prophylaxis)][1]—Trimethoprim is used in the prophylaxis of bacterial urinary tract infections.

[Pneumonia, *Pneumocystis carinii* (treatment)][1]—Trimethoprim is used in combination with dapsone in the treatment of mild to moderate pneumonia caused by *Pneumocystis carinii* (PCP).

Not all species or strains of a particular organism may be susceptible to trimethoprim.

Unaccepted

Trimethoprim is not effective against *Pseudomonas aeruginosa*, *Bacteroides* species, or *Lactobacillus* species.

[1]Not included in Canadian product labeling.

Pharmacology/Pharmacokinetics

Physicochemical characteristics

Molecular weight—290.32.

Mechanism of action/Effect

Bacteriostatic lipophilic weak base structurally related to pyrimethamine, binds to and reversibly inhibits the bacterial enzyme dihydrofolate reductase, selectively blocking conversion of dihydrofolic acid to its functional form, tetrahydrofolic acid. This depletes folate, an essential cofactor in the biosynthesis of nucleic acids, resulting in interference with bacterial nucleic acid and protein production. Bacterial dihydrofolate reductase is approximately 50,000 to 60,000 times more tightly bound by trimethoprim than by the corresponding mammalian enzyme.

Exerts its effect at a step in the folate biosynthesis immediately subsequent to the one in which sulfonamides exert their effect. When administered concurrently with sulfonamides, synergism occurs and is attributed to inhibition of tetrahydrofolate production at two sequential steps in its biosynthesis.

Absorption

Rapidly and almost completely (90 to 100%) absorbed from the gastrointestinal tract.

Distribution

Rapidly and widely distributed to various tissues and fluids, including kidneys, liver, spleen, bronchial secretions, saliva, and seminal fluid. Trimethoprim has also been demonstrated in bile; aqueous humor; bone marrow and spongy, but not compact, bone.

Concentrations of trimethoprim in the urine are significantly higher than serum concentrations of trimethoprim.

Trimethoprim is distributed into vaginal secretions at approximately 1.6 times the serum concentration. Sufficient trimethoprim is excreted in the feces to markedly reduce or eliminate the organisms present in the fecal flora that are susceptible to trimethoprim.

Cerebrospinal fluid (CSF) concentrations—

30 to 50% of serum concentrations.

Prostatic tissue and fluid—

2 to 3 times the serum concentration.

Crosses the placenta and is distributed into breast milk.

Vol_D—

Adults:

1.3 to 1.8 liters per kg.

Children:

Newborns—Approximately 2.7 liters per kg.

Age 1 to 10 years old—Approximately 1 liter per kg.

Protein binding
Moderate (approximately 45%).

Biotransformation
Hepatic; 10 to 20% metabolized to inactive metabolites by O-demethylation, ring N-oxidation, and alpha-hydroxylation; metabolites may be free or conjugated.

Half-life
Adults—
Normal renal function: 8 to 10 hours.
Anuric patients: 20 to 50 hours.

Children—
Newborns: Approximately 19 hours.
Age 1 to 10 years: 3 to 5.5 hours.

Time to peak concentration
Time to mean peak serum concentration—
1 to 4 hours; steady-state concentrations are achieved within 2 to 3 days of daily administration.

Peak serum concentration
Mean peak serum concentration—
Approximately 1 mcg per mL, following a single 100-mg dose. A single 200-mg dose results in serum concentrations approximately twice as high.

Mean minimum steady-state concentration—
Approximately 1.1 mcg per mL.

Elimination
Renal, 50 to 60% excreted within 24 hours, primarily by glomerular filtration and tubular secretion; of this amount, 80 to 90% excreted unchanged and remainder excreted as inactive metabolites. Excretion increased in acid urine and decreased in alkaline urine.

Small amounts excreted in the feces (approximately 4%) and bile.

In dialysis—Moderate amount of trimethoprim is removed from the blood by hemodialysis. Peritoneal dialysis is not effective in removing trimethoprim from the blood.

Precautions to Consider

Carcinogenicity
Long-term studies in animals to evaluate the carcinogenic potential of trimethoprim have not been done.

Mutagenicity
Trimethoprim has not been shown to be mutagenic in the Ames assay. No chromosomal damage was seen in human leukocytes that were cultured *in vitro* with trimethoprim, using concentrations that exceeded serum concentrations following normal doses of trimethoprim.

Pregnancy/Reproduction
Fertility—Trimethoprim has not been shown to cause adverse effects on fertility or reproductive performance in rats given oral doses as high as 70 mg per kg of body weight (mg/kg) daily in males and 14 mg/kg daily in females.

Pregnancy—Trimethoprim crosses the placenta. Adequate and well-controlled studies in humans have not been done. Trimethoprim may interfere with folic acid metabolism. However, a retrospective study of 186 pregnancies, in which mothers received trimethoprim plus sulfamethoxazole or placebo, has shown a lower incidence of congenital malformations (3.3% versus 4.5%) in the trimethoprim-treated group. There were no abnormalities in the 10 children whose mothers received trimethoprim during the first trimester. Also, another study found no congenital abnormalities in 35 children whose mothers received trimethoprim plus sulfamethoxazole at the time of conception or shortly thereafter.

Studies in rats given oral doses of 70 mg/kg daily during the third trimester and throughout parturition have not shown that trimethoprim causes adverse effects on gestation or pup growth and survival. However, studies in rats given doses of 40 times the human dose have shown that trimethoprim is teratogenic. Studies in rabbits given doses of 6 times the human dose have shown an increase in fetal loss (dead, resorbed, and malformed fetuses).

FDA Pregnancy Category C.

Breast-feeding
Trimethoprim is distributed into breast milk in concentrations equal to or greater than those in the maternal serum and may interfere with folic acid metabolism in nursing infants. However, no significant problems in humans have been documented.

Pediatrics
Safety has not been established in infants less than 2 months of age. Appropriate studies on the relationship of age to the effects of trimethoprim have not been performed in children up to 12 years of age. However, in studies performed in children over 12 years of age, no pediatrics-specific problems have been documented to date.

Geriatrics
An increased incidence of thrombocytopenia with purpura has been reported in elderly patients who are receiving diuretics, primarily thiazides, concurrently with trimethoprim.

Dental
The leukopenic and thrombocytopenic effects of trimethoprim may result in an increased incidence of certain microbial infections, delayed healing, and gingival bleeding. If leukopenia or thrombocytopenia occurs, dental work should be deferred until blood counts have returned to normal. Patients should be instructed in proper oral hygiene, including caution in use of regular toothbrushes, dental floss, and toothpicks.

Drug interactions and/or related problems
The following drug interactions and/or related problems have been selected on the basis of their potential clinical significance (possible mechanism in parentheses where appropriate)—not necessarily inclusive (» = major clinical significance):

Note: Combinations containing any of the following medications, depending on the amount present, may also interact with this medication.

Bone marrow depressants (see *Appendix II*)
(concurrent use of bone marrow depressants with trimethoprim may increase the leukopenic and/or thrombocytopenic effects; if concurrent use is required, close observation for myelotoxic effects should be considered)

Cyclosporine
(concurrent use of cyclosporine with trimethoprim may increase the incidence of nephrotoxicity)

Dapsone
(concurrent use with trimethoprim will usually increase the plasma concentrations of both dapsone and trimethoprim, possibly due to an inhibition in dapsone metabolism, and/or competition for renal secretion between the 2 medications; increased serum dapsone concentrations may increase the number and severity of side effects, especially methemoglobinemia)

» Folate antagonists, other (see *Appendix II*)
(concurrent use with trimethoprim or use of trimethoprim between courses of other folic acid antagonists, such as methotrexate or pyrimethamine, is not recommended because of the possibility of an increased incidence of megaloblastic anemia)

Phenytoin
(trimethoprim may inhibit the hepatic metabolism of phenytoin, increasing the half-life of phenytoin by up to 50% and decreasing its clearance by 30%)

Procainamide
(concurrent use with trimethoprim may increase the plasma concentration of both procainamide and its metabolite NAPA by decreasing their renal clearance)

Rifampin
(concurrent use may significantly increase the elimination and shorten the elimination half-life of trimethoprim)

Warfarin
(trimethoprim may potentiate the anticoagulant activity of warfarin by inhibiting its metabolism)

Laboratory value alterations
The following have been selected on the basis of their potential clinical significance (possible effect in parentheses where appropriate)—not necessarily inclusive (» = major clinical significance).

With diagnostic test results
Creatinine determinations
(trimethoprim may interfere with the Jaffé alkaline picrate assay for creatinine, resulting in creatinine values that are approximately 10% higher than actual values)

Serum methotrexate assays
(trimethoprim may interfere with serum methotrexate assays if measured by the competitive binding protein technique [CBPA] using a bacterial dihydrofolate reductase as the binding protein; no interference occurs if methotrexate is measured by radioimmunoassay [RIA])

With physiology/laboratory test values
Alanine aminotransferase (ALT [SGPT]), serum and
Aspartate aminotransferase (AST [SGOT]), serum and
Bilirubin, serum and
Blood urea nitrogen (BUN) and
Creatinine, serum
(concentrations may be increased)

Medical considerations/Contraindications

The medical considerations/contraindications included have been selected on the basis of their potential clinical significance (reasons given in parentheses where appropriate)—not necessarily inclusive (» = major clinical significance).

Risk-benefit should be considered when the following medical problems exist:

Hypersensitivity to trimethoprim

» Megaloblastic anemia due to folic acid deficiency
(trimethoprim may worsen megaloblastic anemia caused by folic acid deficiency)

» Renal function impairment
(trimethoprim is primarily renally excreted)

Hepatic function impairment
(10 to 20% of trimethoprim is metabolized by the liver; delayed metabolism may increase the risk of toxicity)

Patient monitoring

The following may be especially important in patient monitoring (other tests may be warranted in some patients, depending on condition; » = major clinical significance):

Complete blood counts (CBCs)
(may be required in patients on long-term treatment or those predisposed to folate deficiency if signs of blood dyscrasias occur during treatment; trimethoprim should be discontinued if there is a significant reduction in the count of any formed blood elements)

Side/Adverse Effects

The following side/adverse effects have been selected on the basis of their potential clinical significance (possible signs and symptoms in parentheses where appropriate)—not necessarily inclusive:

Those indicating need for medical attention

Incidence less frequent

Skin rash; pruritus (itching)

Incidence rare

Anaphylaxis (shortness of breath; swelling of face; changes in facial skin color); ***aseptic meningitis*** (headache; neck stiffness; malaise; nausea); ***blood dyscrasias, such as leukopenia or neutropenia*** (chills, fever, or sore throat); ***megaloblastic anemia*** (unusual tiredness or weakness); ***and thrombocytopenia*** (rarely, unusual bleeding or bruising; black, tarry stools; blood in urine or stools; pinpoint red spots on skin); ***methemoglobinemia*** (bluish fingernails, lips, or skin; difficult breathing; pale skin; sore throat and fever; unusual bleeding or bruising; unusual tiredness or weakness); ***glossitis*** (redness, swelling, or soreness of tongue); ***phototoxicity*** (blisters; itching; rash; redness of skin; sensation of skin burning; swelling); ***severe skin reactions, such as erythema multiforme*** (fever; general feeling of discomfort or illness; red skin lesions, often with a purple center); ***exfoliative dermatitis*** (fever; general feeling of discomfort or illness; red, thickened, or scaly skin); ***Stevens-Johnson syndrome*** (joint or muscle pain; blistering, peeling, or loosening of skin and mucous membranes; fever; general feeling of discomfort or illness); ***and toxic epidermal necrolysis [Lyell's syndrome]*** (redness, tenderness, itching, burning, or peeling of skin; sore throat; fever with or without chills)

Those indicating need for medical attention only if they continue or are bothersome

Incidence less frequent

Gastrointestinal disturbances (diarrhea; loss of appetite; nausea or vomiting; stomach cramps or pain); ***headache***

Overdose

For specific information on the agents used in the management of trimethoprim overdose, see:

- *Leucovorin (Systemic)* monograph.

For more information on the management of overdose or unintentional ingestion, **contact a Poison Control Center** (see *Poison Control Center Listing*).

Clinical effects of overdose

Acute

Note: Signs of acute overdose may occur following the ingestion of one gram or more of trimethoprim.

Bone marrow depression (chills, fever, or sore throat; unusual tiredness or weakness; rarely, unusual bleeding or bruising; black, tarry stools; blood in urine or stools; pinpoint red spots on skin); ***confusion; dizziness; headache; mental depression; nausea or vomiting***

Chronic

Signs of bone marrow depression, such as leukopenia (chills, fever, or sore throat); ***megaloblastic anemia*** (unusual tiredness or weakness); ***or thrombocytopenia*** (rarely, unusual bleeding or bruising; black, tarry stools; blood in urine or stools; pinpoint red spots on skin)

Treatment of overdose

Recommended treatment consists of the following:

To decrease absorption—Administering gastric lavage and general supportive measures.

Specific treatment—

Acidifying the urine to promote renal excretion of trimethoprim.

Using hemodialysis to remove a moderate amount of trimethoprim from the blood, although peritoneal dialysis is not effective.

Discontinuing trimethoprim and administering leucovorin, 3 to 6 mg intramuscularly per day for 5 to 7 days or as necessary, to restore normal hematopoiesis if signs of bone marrow depression occur.

Supportive care—Patients in whom intentional overdose is known or suspected should be referred for psychiatric consultation.

Patient Consultation

As an aid to patient consultation, refer to *Advice for the Patient, Trimethoprim (Systemic)*.

In providing consultation, consider emphasizing the following selected information (» = major clinical significance):

Before using this medication

» Conditions affecting use, especially:
  Hypersensitivity to trimethoprim
  Pregnancy—Trimethoprim crosses the placenta; may interfere with folic acid metabolism in the fetus
  Breast-feeding—Trimethoprim is distributed into breast milk; may interfere with folic acid metabolism in the newborn
  Other medications, especially folic acid antagonists
  Other medical problems, especially megaloblastic anemia due to folic acid deficiency and renal function impairment

Proper use of this medication

» Not giving this medication to infants or children under twelve years of age unless directed by physician

Taking on an empty stomach or, if gastrointestinal irritation occurs, with food

» Compliance with full course of therapy

» Importance of not missing doses and taking at evenly spaced times

» Proper dosing

Missed dose: Taking as soon as possible; not taking if almost time for next dose; not doubling doses

» Proper storage

Precautions while using this medication

Importance of regular visits to physician to check progress if on prolonged therapy

Checking with physician if no improvement within a few days

Importance of taking folic acid concurrently if anemia occurs

Using caution in use of regular toothbrushes, dental floss, and toothpicks; deferring dental work until blood counts have returned to normal; checking with physician or dentist concerning proper oral hygiene

» Possible skin photosensitivity; checking with physician if severe reaction from sun occurs

Side/adverse effects

Signs of potential side effects, especially skin rash; pruritus; anaphylaxis; aseptic meningitis; blood dyscrasias, such as leukopenia or neutropenia, megaloblastic anemia, and thrombocytopenia; methemoglobinemia; glossitis; phototoxicity; and severe skin reactions, such as erythema multiforme, exfoliative dermatitis, Stevens-Johnson syndrome, and toxic epidermal necrolysis (Lyell's syndrome)

General Dosing Information

Trimethoprim may be taken on an empty stomach or, if gastrointestinal irritation occurs, it may be taken with food.

If trimethoprim causes folic acid deficiency, folates may be administered concurrently without interfering with the antibacterial activity of trimethoprim since bacteria are unable to utilize preformed folates. If signs of bone marrow depression occur, trimethoprim should be discontinued. Leucovorin (folinic acid) 3 to 6 mg may be given intramuscularly once a day for 3 days or as required to restore normal hematopoiesis. In chronic overdose of trimethoprim, leucovorin may be given in high doses and/or for an extended period of time.

Oral Dosage Forms

Note: Bracketed uses in the *Dosage Forms* section refer to categories of use and/or indications that are not included in U.S. product labeling.

TRIMETHOPRIM TABLETS USP

Usual adult and adolescent dose

Antibacterial—

Treatment of urinary tract infections: Oral, 100 mg every twelve hours for ten days; or 200 mg once a day for ten days.

[Pneumonia, *Pneumocystis carinii* (treatment)][1]: Oral, 20 mg per kg of body weight per day of trimethoprim in combination with 100 mg of dapsone once a day for 21 days.

[Prophylaxis of urinary tract infections][1]: Oral, 100 mg once a day.

Note: Adults with impaired renal function may require a reduction in dose as follows:

Creatinine Clearance (mL/min)/(mL/sec)	Dose
> 30/0.5	See *Usual adult and adolescent dose*
15–30/0.25–0.5	50 mg every twelve hours
< 15/<0.25	Use is not recommended

Usual adult prescribing limits

Doses greater than 600 mg are often used when treating *Pneumocystis carinii* pneumonia.

Usual pediatric dose

Antibacterial—

Infants and children up to 12 years of age: Dosage has not been established; however, a dose of 3 mg per kg of body weight two times a day has been effectively used in children.

Children 12 years of age and over: See *Usual adult and adolescent dose.*

Note: Safety and efficacy have not been established in infants up to 2 months of age. Efficacy has not been established in children up to 12 years of age.

Strength(s) usually available

U.S.—

100 mg (Rx) [*Proloprim; Trimpex;* GENERIC].

200 mg (Rx) [*Proloprim;* GENERIC].

Canada—

100 mg (Rx) [*Proloprim* (scored)].

200 mg (Rx) [*Proloprim* (scored)].

Packaging and storage

Store below 40 °C (104 °F), preferably between 15 and 30 °C (59 and 86 °F), unless otherwise specified by manufacturer. Store in a tight, light-resistant container.

Auxiliary labeling

- Continue medicine for full time of treatment.

[1]Not included in Canadian product labeling.

Revised: 06/14/1999

TRIMIPRAMINE—See *Antidepressants, Tricyclic (Systemic)*

TRIPLE SULFA—See *Sulfonamides (Vaginal)*

TRIPTORELIN Systemic

VA CLASSIFICATION (Primary): AN500

Commonly used brand name(s): *Trelstar Depot.*

Note: For a listing of dosage forms and brand names by country availability, see *Dosage Forms* section(s).

Category

Antineoplastic.

Indications

Accepted

Carcinoma, prostate (treatment)—Triptorelin is indicated for the palliative treatment of advanced prostatic carcinoma.

Pharmacology/Pharmacokinetics

Physicochemical characteristics

Molecular weight—

Triptorelin: 1311. 45.

Triptorelin pamoate: 1699.9.

Mechanism of action/Effect

Triptorelin is a synthetic luteinizing hormone releasing hormone (LHRH) analog. Like naturally occurring LHRH that is produced by the hypothalamus, initial or intermittent administration of triptorelin stimulates release of gonadotropins, luteinizing hormone (LH) and follicle-stimulating hormone (FSH), from the anterior pituitary. Long-term, sustained use of triptorelin is associated with an early phase of increased LH and FSH levels, followed by their suppression.

In males, the release of LH and FSH results in a transient increase in testosterone concentrations. However, monthly administration of triptorelin in the treatment of prostatic carcinoma suppresses secretion of LH and FSH, with a resultant fall in testosterone concentrations and a pharmacologic castration within 4 weeks following initial administration.

Other actions/effects

A transient surge in circulating estradiol also occurs following initiation of triptorelin therapy, but chronic and continuous administration results in a marked reduction of ovarian steroidogenesis.

Distribution

Following intravenous administration of 0.5 mg of triptorelin, the apparent volume of distribution was 30–33 L in healthy male volunteers.

Protein binding

There is no evidence that triptorelin, at clinically relevant concentrations, binds to plasma proteins.

Biotransformation

The mechanism by which triptorelin is metabolized is unknown. Hepatic microsomal enzymes (specifically, the P-450 system) is unlikely to be involved, but the activity of other drug-metabolizing enzymes in unknown; no metabolites of triptorelin have been identified. Pharmacokinetic data suggest that C-terminal fragments produced by tissue degradation are either completely degraded in the tissues, rapidly degraded in the plasma, or are cleared by the kidneys.

Half-life

Following intravenous administration of 0.5 mg of triptorelin peptide—

Males with normal renal function (average creatinine clearance 150 mL per minute [mL/min]): 2.81 hours.

Males with moderate renal function impairment (average creatinine clearance 40 mL/min): 6.56 hours.

Males with severe renal function impairment (average creatinine clearance 9 mL/min): 7.65 hours.

Males with liver function impairment (average creatinine clearance 90 mL/min): 7.58 hours.

Although half-life is increased in patients with liver or renal function impairment, it is unknown whether dosage adjustment is required.

Onset of action

Transient increases in testosterone occurs within the first 4 days of therapy. A decline in testosterone concentrations to castration levels occurs within 4 weeks.

Time to peak concentration

1 hour (range, 1 to 3 hours).

Peak plasma concentration:

Mean, 28.43 nanograms per mL following intramuscular administration of 3.75 mg of triptorelin pamoate to healthy male volunteers

Duration of action

Suppression of testosterone concentrations to castration levels persists for the duration of therapy. Plasma concentrations decreased to 0.84 nanograms/mL at 4 weeks in healthy males that received 3.75 mg of triptorelin pamoate intramuscularly; at 8 weeks following administration, testosterone plasma concentrations had returned to near baseline levels.

Elimination

Following intravenous administration of 0.5 mg of triptorelin peptide—

Hepatic: unknown amount.

Renal: 42% as intact peptide; increases to 62% in patients with liver disease and decreased creatinine clearance.

Precautions to Consider

Cross-sensitivity and/or related problems

Patients with a known hypersensitivity to other LHRH agonists or to LHRH may be sensitive to triptorelin.

Carcinogenicity

The incidence of benign and malignant pituitary tumors and histiosarcomas, as well as mortality, increased with dose in rats given 0.3, 2 and 8 times the recommended human therapeutic dose (based on body surface area) over 13-19 months. No oncogenic effect was noted in mice given approximately 8 times the human therapeutic dose (based on body surface area) every 28 days for 18 months.

Mutagenicity

No evidence of mutagenicity has been demonstrated with triptorelin in the Ames test, chromosomal aberration test in Chinese hamster ovary (CHO) cells or an *in vivo* mouse micronucleus test.

Pregnancy/Reproduction

Fertility—No adverse effects on fertility or general reproductive performance were noted in female rats given doses of 0.2, 2 and 16 times the recommended human therapeutic doses (based on body surface area), or 20 mcg per kg daily. Additionally, no adverse effects were noted in the F_1 generation offspring. No studies have been conducted to assess the effect of triptorelin on male fertility.

Pregnancy—

Studies have not been done in humans.

Maternal toxicity and embryotoxicity were exhibited in rats receiving doses of 0.2, 0.8, and 8 times the recommended human doses (based on body surface area); no fetotoxicity or teratogenicity was demonstrated.

FDA Pregnancy Category X.

Breast-feeding

It is not known whether triptorelin is distributed into breast milk. Breast-feeding is not recommended due to the potential for serious unwanted effects in the nursing infant.

Pediatrics

Appropriate studies have not been performed on the relationship of age to the effects of triptorelin in the pediatric population. Safety and efficacy have not been established.

Geriatrics

Appropriate studies on the relationship of age to the effects of triptorelin have not been performed in the geriatric population. However, clinical trials were conducted mainly in men with a mean age of 71 years, and geriatrics-specific problems that would limit the usefulness of this medication in the elderly are not expected.

Pharmacogenetics

In clinical trials, no differences in the response to triptorelin were demonstrated between racial groups defined as caucasian or black.

Drug interactions and/or related problems

Note: No drug-drug interaction studies have been conducted with triptorelin. However, hyperprolactinemic drugs should not be used concomitantly with triptorelin, since hyperprolactinemia reduces the number of pituitary gonadotrophin releasing hormone (GnRH) receptors.

Laboratory value alterations

The following have been selected on the basis of their potential clinical significance (possible effect in parentheses where appropriate)—not necessarily inclusive (» = major clinical significance).

With diagnostic test results

Tests of pituitary-gonadal function
(chronic triptorelin therapy suppresses the pituitary-gonadal axis)

Medical considerations/Contraindications

The medical considerations/contraindications included have been selected on the basis of their potential clinical significance (reasons given in parentheses where appropriate)—not necessarily inclusive (» = major clinical significance).

Except under special circumstances, this medication should not be used when the following medical problem exists:

» Hypersensitivity to triptorelin, other LHRH agonists or LHRH
(anaphylactic shock and angioedema have been reported; therapy should be immediately discontinued)

Risk-benefit should be considered when the following medical problems exist:

» Urinary tract obstruction or

» Vertebral lesions, metastatic
(initial, transient increases in serum testosterone levels may cause worsening of existing symptoms; close observation is warranted)

Patient monitoring

The following may be especially important in patient monitoring (other tests may be warranted in some patients, depending on condition; » = major clinical significance):

» Prostate-specific antigen (PSA) and

» Testosterone concentrations, serum

Side/Adverse Effects

The following side/adverse effects have been selected on the basis of their potential clinical significance (possible signs and symptoms in parentheses where appropriate)—not necessarily inclusive:

Those indicating need for medical attention

Note: Transient increases in testosterone levels following initial treatment may cause worsening of disease signs and symptoms including bone pain, neuropathy, hematuria, and urethral or bladder outlet obstruction. These levels generally return to normal by the end of the second week of treatment.

Cases of spinal cord compression, which may contribute to paralysis with or without fatal complications, have been reported. If spinal cord compression or renal impairment occurs, standard treatment of these complications should be initiated. In extreme cases, immediate orchiectomy may need to be considered.

Instances of angioedema and anaphylactic shock have been reported in post-marketing surveillance.

Incidence less frequent

Anemia (pale skin; troubled breathing, exertional; unusual bleeding or bruising; unusual tiredness or weakness); ***hypertension*** (high blood pressure); ***urinary retention*** (decrease in urine volume; decrease in frequency of urination; difficulty in passing urine [dribbling]; painful urination); ***urinary tract infection*** (bladder pain; bloody or cloudy urine; difficult, burning, or painful urination; frequent urge to urinate; lower back or side pain)

Those indicating need for medical attention only if they continue or are bothersome

Incidence more frequent

Headache; hot flushes (feeling of warmth redness of the face, neck, arms and occasionally, upper chest; sudden sweating)—occurs in > 50% of patients; ***impotence*** (loss in sexual ability, desire, drive, or performance; decreased interest in sexual intercourse; inability to have or keep an erection); ***skeletal pain***

Note: *Hot flushes* and *impotence* are expected pharmacologic responses to testosterone suppression therapy.

Incidence less frequent

Diarrhea; dizziness; emotional lability (crying; mental depression; paranoia; quick to react or overreact emotionally; rapidly changing moods); ***fatigue*** (unusual tiredness or weakness); ***injection site pain; insomnia*** (trouble sleeping or getting to sleep); ***leg pain; pruritus*** (itching); ***vomiting***

Patient Consultation

As an aid to patient consultation, refer to *Advice for the Patient, Triptorelin (Systemic).*

In providing consultation, consider emphasizing the following selected information (» = major clinical significance):

Before using this medication

» Conditions affecting use, especially:
Sensitivity to triptorelin, other LHRH products or LHRH
Pregnancy—Embryotoxicity and maternal toxicity reported; FDA Category X
Breast-feeding—Not recommended for use in nursing mothers due to potential for serious adverse effects in infant
Other medical problems, especially urinary tract obstruction or metastatic vertebral lesions

Proper use of this medication

» Proper dosing
Missed dose: Taking as soon as possible then returning to normal dosing schedule

» Proper storage

Precautions while using this medication

» Regular visits to physician to check progress

Side/adverse effects

Signs of potential side effects, especially anemia, hypertension, urinary retention or urinary tract infection

General Dosing Information

Patients receiving triptorelin should be under supervision of a physician experienced in prostate cancer therapy.

Treatment of Adverse Effects

If spinal cord compression or renal impairment develops, standard treatment of these complications should be implemented. In extreme cases, an immediate surgical orchiectomy should be considered.

Parenteral Dosage Forms

Note: Triptorelin injection contains triptorelin pamoate. However, the dosage and strength of the injection are expressed in terms of triptorelin base (not the pamoate salt).

TRIPTORELIN FOR INJECTION

Usual adult dose

Prostate carcinoma—

Intramuscular, 3.75 mg once per month.

Usual pediatric dose

Safety and efficacy have not been established.

Usual geriatric dose

See *Usual adult dose*.

Strength(s) usually available

U.S.—

Note: The commercially available product contains lyophilized microgranules of triptorelin pamoate incorporated in a biodegradable copolymer of lactic and glycolic acids.

3.75 mg (Rx) [*Trelstar Depot* (poly-*d, l*-lactide-co-glycolide (170 mg); mannitol USP (85 mg); carboxymethylcellulose sodium USP (30 mg); polysorbate 80 NF (2 mg))].

Packaging and storage

Store at 25 °C (77 °F), excursions permitted to 15–30 °C (59–86 °F)

Preparation of dosage form

Triptorelin for injection is reconstituted by adding 2 mL of sterile water for injection, USP. The vial should be shaken well to disperse the microgranules and form a milky suspension.

Stability

Reconstituted triptorelin suspension should be discarded if not used immediately after preparation.

Developed: 11/10/2000

TROLAMINE SALICYLATE—See *Sunscreen Agents (Topical)*

TROSPIUM Systemic†

VA CLASSIFICATION (Primary): AU305

Commonly used brand name(s): *Sanctura*.

Note: For a listing of dosage forms and brand names by country availability, see *Dosage Forms* section(s).

†Not commercially available in Canada.

Category

Antispasmodic (urinary bladder).

Indications

Accepted

Bladder hyperactivity (treatment)—Trospium is indicated for the treatment of overactive bladder with symptoms of urinary incontinence, urgency, or urinary frequency.

Pharmacology/Pharmacokinetics

Physicochemical characteristics

Molecular weight—Trospium chloride: 427.97.

Solubility—Trospium's solubility in water is approximately 1 gram per 2 milliliters.

Mechanism of action/Effect

Trospium is an antispasmodic, antimuscarinic agent. It antagonizes the effect of acetylcholine on muscarinic receptors in cholinergically innervated organs and its parasympatholytic action reduces the tonus of smooth muscle in the bladder.

Studies found that trospium increases maximum cystometric bladder capacity and volume at first detrusor contraction.

Absorption

Less than 10% absorbed following oral administration. Food (high fat meal) reduces absorption, with AUC and C_{max} values 70 to 80% lower than those obtained during a fasting state.

Mean absolute bioavailability of a 20 mg dose is 9.6% (4 to 16.1% range)

$AUC_{0-\infty}$, single dose, 20 mg: 36.4 ± 21.8ng/mL hr

Distribution

Volume of distribution (Vol_D)—following a 20 mg oral dose: 395 (± 140) liters

Plasma to whole blood ratio: 1.6 to 1

Protein binding

High (50-85%)

Biotransformation

The metabolic pathway of trospium has not been fully defined. The major metabolic pathway hypothesized is ester hydrolysis with subsequent conjugation of benzylic acid to form azoniaspironortropanol with glucuronic acid. Of the 10% of the dose absorbed, metabolites account for approximately 40% of the excreted dose following oral administration. Cytochrome P450 is not expected to contribute significantly to elimination of trospium.

Half-life

Plasma—approximately 20 hours.

Time to peak concentration

5 to 6 hours post-dose.

Peak plasma concentration single dose:

3.5 ± 4 ng/mL

Elimination

Fecal: 85%; Renal 5.8%, 60% in urine was unchanged drug.

Mean renal clearance: 29.07 L/hr; suggests that active tubular secretion is a major route of elimination

Precautions to Consider

Carcinogenicity

Carcinogenicity studies with trospium chloride were done in mice and rats. No evidence of a carcinogenic effect was found in a 78-week study in mice or a 104-week study in rats given doses of 2, 20, and 200 milligrams per kilogram per day (mg/kg/day). The 200 mg/kg/day dose represents approximately 25 and 60 times the human dose based on body surface area.

Mutagenicity

Trospium was negative for mutagenicity in the (Ames test) detection of gene mutations in bacteria and mammalian cells, and in the *in vivo* rat micronucleus test.

Pregnancy/Reproduction

Fertility—Fertility studies in rats given doses up to 200 mg/kg/day (approximately 10 times the expected clinical exposure via AUC) showed no evidence of impaired fertility.

Pregnancy—Adequate and well controlled studies in humans have not been done. Studies in animals have shown that trospium causes adverse effects in the fetus. Trospium should be used during pregnancy only if the potential benefit justifies the potential risk to the fetus.

Studies done in rats given doses approximately 10 times the expected clinical exposure have been shown to cause maternal toxicity and a decrease in fetal survival. The no effect levels were approximately 5 to 6 times the expected clinical exposure in rabbits. No malformations or developmental delays were observed.

FDA Pregnancy Category C

Breast-feeding

It is not known whether trospium is distributed into breast milk. However, trospium is distributed into the milk of lactating rats. Because many drugs are distributed in human milk, caution should be exercised when trospium is administered to a nursing woman. Trospium should be used during lactation only when the potential benefit justifies the potential risk to the newborn.

Pediatrics

Safety and effectiveness in pediatric patients have not been established.

Geriatrics

Appropriate studies performed to date have not demonstrated geriatric-specific problems that would limit the usefulness of trospium in the elderly. However elderly patients are more likely to have enhanced sensitivity to anticholinergic agents. Therefore, based on tolerability the dose frequency of trospium may be reduced in patients 75 years of age and older.

Pharmacogenetics

Studies comparing the pharmacokinetics in gender had conflicting results. When trospium was given as a single 40 mg dose to elderly patients, exposure was 45% lower in females compared to males. However, when a 20 mg dose was given to elderly patients for 4 days, AUC and C_{max} were 26% and 68% higher in females without hormone replacement therapy than in males.

Drug interactions and/or related problems

The following drug interactions and/or related problems have been selected on the basis of their potential clinical significance (possible mechanism in parentheses where appropriate)—not necessarily inclusive (» = major clinical significance):

Note: Combinations containing any of the following medications, depending on the amount present, may also interact with this medication.

Digoxin or
Metformin or
Morphine or
Pancuronium or
Procainamide or
Tenofovir or
Vancomycin
(may increase the serum concentration of trospium and/or the coadministered drug due to competition for active tubular secretion pathway; careful monitoring is recommended)

Other anticholinergic agents
(concurrent administration may increase the frequency and/or severity of adverse effects, and may potentially alter the absorption of some concomitantly administered drugs due to anticholinergic effects on gastrointestinal motility)

Laboratory value alterations

The following have been selected on the basis of their potential clinical significance (possible effect in parentheses where appropriate)—not necessarily inclusive (» = major clinical significance).

Studies on interactions between trospium and laboratory tests have not been done.

Medical considerations/Contraindications

The medical considerations/contraindications included have been selected on the basis of their potential clinical significance (reasons given in parentheses where appropriate)—not necessarily inclusive (» = major clinical significance).

Except under special circumstances, this medication should not be used when the following medical problem exists:

» Gastric retention or
» Narrow-angle glaucoma, uncontrolled or
» Urinary retention
(use is contraindicated in patients with these conditions)

Hypersensitivity to trospium or any of its ingredients

Risk-benefit should be considered when the following medical problems exist:

» Hepatic function impairment, moderate or severe
(administer with caution)

» Intestional atony or
» Myasthenia gravis or
» Ulcerative colitis
(caution; may decrease gastrointestinal motility)

Narrow-angle glaucoma, controlled
(administer only if the potential benefits outweigh the risks, and in that circumstance only with careful monitoring)

» Renal function impairment, severe
(dose modification is recommended)

Urinary retention, risk of
(administer with caution)

Side/Adverse Effects

The following side/adverse effects have been selected on the basis of their potential clinical significance (possible signs and symptoms in parentheses where appropriate)—not necessarily inclusive:

Those indicating need for medical attention

Incidence not determined—Observed during clinical practice; estimates of frequency cannot be determined

Abnormal vision (changes in vision); ***anaphylactic reaction*** (cough; difficulty swallowing; dizziness; fast heartbeat; hives; itching; puffiness or swelling of the eyelids or around the eyes, face, lips or tongue; shortness of breath; skin rash; tightness in chest; unusual tiredness or weakness; wheezing); ***delirium*** (unusual excitement, nervousness, or restlessness; hallucinations; confusion as to time, place, or person; holding false beliefs that cannot be changed by fact); ***hallucinations*** (seeing, hearing, or feeling things that are not there); ***hypertensive crisis*** (severe chest pain; enlarged pupils; fast or slow heartbeat; severe headache; increased sensitivity of eyes to light; increased sweating, possibly with fever or cold; clammy skin; stiff or sore neck); ***rhabdomyolysis*** (dark-colored urine; fever; muscle cramps or spasms; muscle pain or stiffness; unusual tiredness or weakness); ***Stevens-Johnson syndrome*** (blistering, peeling, loosening of skin; chills; cough; diarrhea; itching; joint or muscle pain; red irritated eyes; red skin lesions, often with a purple center; sore throat; sores, ulcers, or white spots in mouth or on lips; unusual tiredness or weakness)

Those indicating need for medical attention only if they continue or are bothersome

Incidence more frequent

Constipation (difficulty having a bowel movement (stool)); ***dry mouth***

Incidence less frequent

Constipation, aggravated (unable to have a bowel movement); ***dry eyes; dyspepsia*** (acid or sour stomach; belching; heartburn; indigestion; stomach discomfort upset or pain); ***fatigue*** (unusual tiredness or weakness); ***flatulence*** (bloated full feeling; excess air or gas in stomach or intestines; passing gas); ***headache; upper abdominal pain*** (upper stomach pain); ***urinary retention*** (trouble in urinating)

Incidence unknown

Abdominal distension (swelling of abdominal or stomach area; full or bloated feeling or pressure in the stomach); ***dysgeusia*** (loss of taste; change in taste); ***dry throat; dry skin; tachycardia*** (fast, pounding, or irregular heartbeat or pulse); ***vision blurred; vomiting***

Incidence not determined—Observed during clinical practice; estimates of frequency cannot be determined

Chest pain; gastritis (burning feeling in chest or stomach; tenderness in stomach area; stomach upset; indigestion); ***palpitations*** (fast, irregular, pounding, or racing heartbeat or pulse); ***supraventricular tachycardia*** (fainting; fast, pounding, or irregular heartbeat or pulse; palpitations); ***syncope*** (fainting)

Overdose

For more information on the management of overdose or unintentional ingestion, **contact a poison control center** (see *Poison Control Center Listing*).

Clinical effects of overdose

The following effects have been selected on the basis of their potential clinical significance (possible signs and symptoms in parentheses where appropriate)—not necessarily inclusive:

Anticholinergic effects, severe (blurred vision; dizziness; drowsiness; confusion, delirium, or hallucinations; nausea; vomiting; constipation; difficult urination; eye pain; dry eyes, mouth, nose, or throat; flushing or redness of face; troubled breathing; fast heartbeat); ***mydriasis*** (bigger, dilated, or enlarged pupils [black part of eye]; increased sensitivity of eyes to light); ***tachycardia*** (fast, pounding, or irregular heartbeat or pulse)

Treatment of overdose

Treatment should be symptomatic and supportive.

To enhance elimination—
Administering medicinal charcoal

Monitoring—
Monitoring for cardiovascular function (ECG)

Supportive care—
Patients in whom intentional overdose is confirmed or suspected should be referred for psychiatric consultation.

Patient Consultation

As an aid to patient consultation, refer to *Advice for the Patient, Trospium (Systemic)*.

In providing consultation, consider emphasizing the following selected information (» = major clinical significance):

Before using this medication

» Conditions affecting use, especially:

Hypersensitivity to trospium or any of its ingredients

Pregnancy—Adequate and well controlled studies in humans have not been done. Studies in rats found maternal toxicity and a decrease in fetal survival when trospium was given at doses 10 times the expected clinical exposure. Trospium should be used during pregnancy only if the potential benefit justifies the potential risk to the fetus.

Breast-feeding—Trospium is distributed into the milk of lactating rats. Because many drugs are distributed in human milk, caution should be exercised when trospium is administered to a nursing woman.

Use in the elderly—Elderly patients are more likely to have increased sensitivity to anticholinergic effects

Other medical problems, especially gastric retention, hepatic function impairment (moderate or severe), intestional atony, myasthenia gravis, narrow-angle glaucoma (uncontrolled), renal function impairment, ulcerative colitis, or urinary retention

Proper use of this medication

Take 1 hour before meals or take on an empty stomach.

» Proper dosing

Take next dose 1 hour before next meal; not taking if almost time for next scheduled dose; not doubling doses

Proper storage

Precautions while using this medication

» Caution during exercise or hot weather, overheating may result in heat stroke

» Caution if vision problems occur

» Possible dizziness; caution when driving or doing things requiring alertness

» Avoid use of alcohol; may increase risk of drowsiness

Possible dryness of mouth; checking with physician or dentist if dry mouth continues

Side/adverse effects

Signs of potential side effects, especially abnormal vision, anaphylactic reaction, delirium, hallucinations, hypertensive crisis, rhabdomyolysis, or Stevens-Johnson syndrome

General Dosing Information

For oral dosing forms:

Trospium should be taken at least one hour before meals or taken on an empty stomach.

Oral Dosage Forms

TROSPIUM CHLORIDE TABLETS

Usual adult dose

Urologic disorders, symptoms of—

Oral, one tablet (20 mg) twice daily

Note: For patients with severe renal impairment (CL_{cr},30 mL per min), the recommended dose is 20 mg once daily at bedtime

Usual pediatric dose

Safety and efficacy have not been established

Usual geriatric dose

For geriatric patients < 75 years of age, see *Usual adult dose*.

For geriatric patients ≥ 75 years of age, dose may be titrated down to 20 mg once daily based upon tolerability

Strength(s) usually available

U.S.—

20 mg (Rx) [*Sanctura* (calcium carbonate; carboxymethylcellulose sodium; carnauba wax; colloidal silicon dioxide; croscarmellose sodium; ferric oxide; lactose monohydrate; magnesium stearate; microcrystalline cellulose; polyethylene glycol 8000; povidone; stearic acid; sucrose; talc; titanium dioxide; wheat starch; white wax)].

Canada—

Not commercially available.

Packaging and storage

Store between 20 and 25°C (68 and 77°F).

Auxiliary labeling

• This drug alone or with alcohol may cause drowsiness. Use care when driving or operating machinery.

• Dry mouth may occur when taking this medicine

Developed: 09/02/2004

TUBERCULIN, PURIFIED PROTEIN DERIVATIVE Parenteral-Local

VA CLASSIFICATION (Primary): DX300

Commonly used brand name(s): *Aplisol; Aplitest; Tuberculin PPD TINE TEST; Tubersol.*

Note: For a listing of dosage forms and brand names by country availability, see *Dosage Forms* section(s).

Category

Diagnostic aid (tuberculosis).

Indications

Accepted

Tuberculosis (diagnosis)—Tuberculin, purified protein derivative (PPD) is indicated as a diagnostic aid in the detection of *Mycobacterium tuberculosis* infection. It is also indicated when BCG vaccination or isoniazid prophylaxis is being considered.

Pharmacology/Pharmacokinetics

Physicochemical characteristics

Tuberculin PPD is a sterile isotonic solution of tuberculin. It is obtained from a human strain of *Mycobacterium tuberculosis* grown on a protein-free synthetic medium and buffered with potassium and sodium phosphates

Mechanism of action/Effect

Intradermally injected tuberculin PPD causes a delayed (cellular) hypersensitivity reaction in individuals sensitized by mycobacterial infection. Following infection with mycobacteria, sensitization of T-cells occurs primarily in the regional lymph nodes. Natural infection with *M. tuberculosis* usually initiates a cell-mediated immune response against mycobacterial antigens. T-cells proliferate in response to the infection and give rise to T-cells specifically sensitized to mycobacterial antigens. After several weeks, these T-lymphocytes enter the bloodstream and circulate for a long period of time. Subsequent restimulation of these T-lymphocytes with intradermal injection of tuberculin PPD evokes a local reaction mediated by these cells.

Onset of action

5 to 6 hours after intradermal injection of tuberculin PPD. The reaction reaches its peak more than 24 (usually 48 to 72) hours after administration.

Precautions to Consider

Pregnancy/Reproduction

Fertility—Studies on effects of tuberculin PPD on fertility have not been done.

Pregnancy—Studies have not been done in humans. It is not known whether tuberculin PPD can cause harm to the fetus when administered to a pregnant woman. However, during pregnancy known positive reactors may demonstrate a negative response to the PPD tine test.

Studies have not been done in animals.

FDA Pregnancy Category C.

Breast-feeding

It is not known whether tuberculin PPD is distributed into breast milk. However, problems in humans have not been documented.

Pediatrics

Appropriate studies on the relationship of age to the effects of tuberculin PPD have not been performed in the pediatric population. However, no pediatrics-specific problems have been documented to date.

Geriatrics

In geriatric patients, reactions may develop slowly and may not peak until after 72 hours.

Drug interactions and/or related problems

The following drug interactions and/or related problems have been selected on the basis of their potential clinical significance (possible mechanism in parentheses where appropriate)—not necessarily inclusive (» = major clinical significance):

Note: Combinations containing any of the following medications, depending on the amount present, may also interact with this medication.

Bacillus Calmette-Guérin (BCG) vaccine

(individuals previously given BCG vaccine will usually show a positive reaction to tuberculin test administered within 6 to 12 weeks after BCG vaccination; a few years after BCG vaccination, reaction to tuberculin tests may be either positive or negative; a positive reaction to tuberculin PPD years after BCG vaccination suggests tuberculous infection)

Corticosteroids or

Immunosuppressive agents
(reactivity to the tuberculin test may be suppressed or enhanced in patients receiving these medications)

Vaccines, killed or live virus
(the reaction to tuberculin PPD may be suppressed if the test is given within 4 to 6 weeks following immunization with killed or live virus vaccines)

Diagnostic interference

The following drug interactions and/or related problems have been selected on the basis of their potential clinical significance (possible mechanism in parentheses where appropriate)—not necessarily inclusive (» = major clinical significance):

With Results of *this* test

Due to medical problems or conditions
Acquired immunodeficiency syndrome (AIDS) or
Anergy or
Atopic dermatitis or sun-damaged skin or
Human immunodeficiency virus (HIV) infection or
Illness that affects the lymphoid system (Hodgkin's disease, lymphoma, chronic lymphocytic leukemia) or
Pregnancy or
Stress, severe
(may cause false-negative test results)

Medical considerations/Contraindications

The medical considerations/contraindications included have been selected on the basis of their potential clinical significance (reasons given in parentheses where appropriate)—not necessarily inclusive (» = major clinical significance).

Except under special circumstances, this medication should not be used when the following medical problem exists:

» Known positive tuberculin reaction
(in highly sensitive persons the reaction at the test site can be severe, resulting in vesiculation, ulceration, or necrosis)

Side/Adverse Effects

The following side/adverse effects have been selected on the basis of their potential clinical significance (possible signs and symptoms in parentheses where appropriate)—not necessarily inclusive:

Those indicating need for medical attention

Incidence rare

Allergic reactions (skin rash or itching); ***necrosis, ulceration, or vesiculation at the site of injection*** (redness, blistering, peeling, or loosening of the skin)

Those indicating need for medical attention only if they continue or are bothersome

Incidence less frequent

Erythematous reaction (redness at the site of injection); ***granuloma*** (sores at and around the site of injection); ***pain; pruritus*** (itching)

Note: Discomfort and transient bleeding may be observed at the PPD tine puncture site.

Patient Consultation

As an aid to patient consultation, refer to *Advice for the Patient, Tuberculin, Purified Protein Derivative (PPD) Injection.*

In providing consultation, consider emphasizing the following selected information (» = major clinical significance):

Before using this medication

» Conditions affecting use, especially:
Sensitivity to tuberculin PPD
Other medical problems, especially known positive tuberculin reaction

Side/adverse effects

» Signs of potential side effects, especially allergic reactions and necrosis, ulceration, or vesiculation at the site of injection

General Dosing Information

Anergy to tuberculin among asymptomatic HIV-positive persons is common, making interpretation of tuberculin tests difficult. Therefore, the Centers for Disease Control (CDC) has produced guidelines for assessing delayed-type hypersensitivity in these patients. Concurrent administration of at least 2 other skin test antigens is recommended. The CDC suggests choosing from among mumps skin test antigen, candida antigen, and tetanus toxoid. The test antigens are given concurrently with the tuberculin skin test and the response is measured 48 to 72 hours later. Any amount of induration is considered evidence of delayed-type hypersensitivity; failure to elicit a response is considered evidence of anergy. HIV-positive persons and others at risk of anergy are considered to have a significant reaction to a standard Mantoux test if the induration reaction measures 5 mm or more in diameter, regardless of the reaction to the other antigens. It is very important to perform anergy testing in a population at increased risk of tuberculosis.

Booster effect—The ability of persons who have TB infection to react to tuberculin may gradually wane. For example, if tested with tuberculin, adults who were infected during their childhood may have a negative reaction. However, the tuberculin could boost the hypersensitivity, and the size of the reaction could be larger on a subsequent test. This boosted reaction may be misinterpreted as a tuberculin test conversion from a newly acquired infection. Misinterpretation of a boosted reaction as a new infection could result in unnecessary investigations of laboratory and patient records in an attempt to identify the source of infection and in unnecessary prescription of preventive therapy for health care workers. Although this booster effect can occur among persons in any age group, the likelihood of the effect increases with the age of the person being tested.

Two-step testing—When tuberculin testing of an adult is to be repeated periodically, 2-step testing can be used to reduce the likelihood that a boosted reaction will be misinterpreted as a new infection. Two-step testing should be performed on all newly employed health care workers who have an initial negative tuberculin test at the time of employment and have not had a documented negative tuberculin test result during the 12 months preceding the initial test. A second test should be performed 1 to 3 weeks after the first test. If the second test result is positive, this is most likely a boosted reaction, and the patient should be classified as previously infected. If the second test result is negative, the patient is classified as uninfected, and a positive reaction to a subsequent test is likely to represent a new infection with *M. tuberculosis.*

It is recommended that children at high risk for tuberculosis be given tuberculin skin tests annually by the Mantoux method. Children considered at high risk include those from areas with a high prevalence of the disease; those from households with 1 or more cases of tuberculosis; black, Hispanic, Asian, native American, and native Alaskan children, and others who are socioeconomically deprived; children from Asia, Africa, the Middle East, Latin America, or the Caribbean and children of parents who have immigrated from these areas; and children with medical risk factors for tuberculosis.

It is recommended that individuals with signs and/or symptoms suggestive of current tuberculous disease be given tuberculin skin test routinely by the Mantoux method. These individuals include persons who are recent contacts of known cases of clinical tuberculosis or are suspected of having tuberculosis; persons with abnormal chest radiographs compatible with past tuberculosis; persons with medical conditions that increase the risk of tuberculosis; HIV-infected individuals; immigrants from Asia, Africa, Latin America, and Oceania; inner-city and skid row populations.

Tuberculin PPD is administered by intradermal injection (the Mantoux method) or by using a disposable multiple-puncture device. These 2 commonly used test methods are briefly described below.

The Mantoux test method: The test is performed by intradermally injecting exactly 0.1 mL of diluted tuberculin PPD. The result is read 48 to 72 hours later and only induration is considered in interpreting the test. Induration is a hard, raised area with clearly defined margins at, and around, the injection site. Erythema may develop at the injection site but has no diagnostic value. The test is performed as follows:

- The site of the test is usually the flexor surface of the forearm, about 4 inches below the elbow. Other skin sites may be used, but the flexor surface of the forearm is preferred. The site of the test should be free of lesions and away from the veins.
- The skin at the injection site is cleansed with 70% alcohol or another suitable antiseptic agent and allowed to dry.
- The test material is administered with a tuberculin syringe (0.5 or 1.0 mL) fitted with a short (one-half-inch) 26- or 27- gauge needle.
- The syringe and needle should be a sterile, disposable, single-use type or should have been sterilized by autoclaving, boiling, or the use of dry heat. A separate sterile unit should be used for each person tested.
- The diaphragm of the vial-stopper should be wiped with 70% alcohol.
- The needle is inserted through the stopper diaphragm of the inverted vial. Exactly 0.1 mL is added to the syringe, with care being taken to exclude air bubbles and to keep the lumen of the needle filled.
- The point of the needle is inserted into the most superficial layers of the skin with the needle bevel pointed upward. As the tuberculin solution is injected, a pale bleb 6 to 10 mm in size will rise over the point of the needle. This is quickly absorbed, and no dressing is re-

quired. In the event that the injection is delivered subcutaneously (in this case no bleb will form) or if a significant part of the dose leaks from the injection site, the test should be repeated immediately at another site at least 5 cm (2 inches) removed from the first site.
• The test site should be examined by trained personnel 48 to 72 hours after the injection. The examination should be performed in good light with the arm slightly flexed at the elbow. The reaction should be measured and recorded in millimeters. Any induration reaction that measures 5 mm or more in diameter is considered positive in persons who have had recent close contact with tuberculosis; persons who have chest radiographs consistent with tuberculosis (including stable lesions consistent with "inactive" tuberculosis); immunosuppressed persons (including HIV-infected persons and patients on immunosuppressive therapy); and persons with cancer (including leukemia or lymphoma), Hodgkin's disease, or end-stage renal disease. Induration of 10 mm or more is considered a positive reaction in foreign-born persons; substance abusers (alcoholics and intravenous drug users); residents and employees of correctional institutions and nursing homes; hospital employees; persons over age 70; low-income populations, including the homeless; and persons with medical conditions including diabetes mellitus, post gastrectomy, silicosis, prolonged corticosteroid therapy, and 10% or more below ideal body weight. Induration of 15 mm or more is considered a positive reaction in all other persons (general population with no known tuberculosis risk factors).

The multiple-puncture (Tine) test method: Each test unit provides for the intradermal administration of 1 test-dose of tuberculin PPD. The test is performed as follows:
• The preferred site of the test is the flexor surface of the forearm about 4 inches below the elbow. Other suitable skin sites, such as the dorsal surface of the forearm, may be used. Areas without adequate subcutaneous tissue, such as skin over a tendon, as well as hairy areas, should be avoided.
• The skin at the test site should be cleaned with 70% alcohol or another suitable antiseptic agent such as acetone, ether, or soap and water and allowed to dry thoroughly.
• To expose the 4 impregnated tines, remove the protective cap while holding the plastic handle.
• The patient's forearm should be grasped firmly to stretch the skin taut at the test site and to prevent any jerking motion of the arm that could cause scratching with the tines.
• The test unit should be applied firmly without twisting to the test area for approximately 1 second. Sufficient pressure should be exerted to ensure that all 4 tines have penetrated the skin.
• Used units should be disposed of carefully to avoid accidents. Do not reuse.
• The test site should be examined by trained personnel 48 to 72 hours after application of the test. The examination should be performed in good light with the arm slightly flexed at the elbow. The presence of vesiculation indicates a positive reaction to the test. The test reaction is negative if both induration and vesiculation are absent. Induration reactions less than 2 mm in diameter may be considered negative. However, unless vesiculation is present, individuals with any size induration reaction should be retested using a standard Mantoux test.
• The dose of tuberculin PPD introduced into the skin with currently available multiple-puncture devices cannot be precisely controlled. Therefore, this test should not be used for the periodic surveillance of individuals likely to be exposed to clinical tuberculosis or for the evaluation of individuals who are suspected of having tuberculosis or are contacts of persons with clinical tuberculosis.

The Heaf test method: The test is performed using the Heaf multiple-puncture apparatus. The result is read 3 to 10 days later and only induration is considered in interpreting the test.
• The site of the test is usually the volar surface of the left forearm. The skin at the test site is cleansed with alcohol or another suitable antiseptic agent and allowed to dry. The undiluted tuberculin is transferred using a syringe needle or loop and smoothed over a circular area of about 1 cm in diameter.
• The needle points of the apparatus are placed on the forearm to give a puncture of 1 mm (for children under 2 years of age) or 2 mm (for older children and adults).
• With the apparatus held at a right angle to the skin, the end plate is placed firmly and evenly in the center of the film of tuberculin and the handle pressed to release the needles. No dressing need be applied. It is very important that the apparatus be properly sterilized after each application or that a disposable end plate be used.
• A positive result should be recorded only when there is palpable induration around at least 4 puncture points. The induration is best felt by passing the finger lightly over the punctures. If no resistance is felt, a negative result should be recorded.
• Four grades of positive response are recognized:

Grade 1—At least 4 small indurated papules.
Grade 2—An indurated ring formed by confluent papules.
Grade 3—A solid induration 5 to 10 mm wide.
Grade 4—Induration over 10 mm wide.

For treatment of adverse effects
Recommended treatment consists of the following:
• If strongly positive reactions, including vesiculation, ulceration, or necrosis, occur, cold packs or topical steroid preparations may be used for symptomatic relief of the associated pain, pruritus, and discomfort.

Parenteral Dosage Forms

TUBERCULIN (Purified Protein Derivative [PPD] Injection) USP

Usual adult and adolescent dose
Tuberculosis (diagnosis)—
Intradermal, 5 U.S. units (tuberculin units [TU]).

Note: The 1-TU-per-test-dose preparation is used for individuals suspected of being highly sensitized, since larger initial doses may result in severe skin reactions. The preparation containing 250 TU per test dose should be used exclusively for the testing of individuals who fail to react to a previous injection of 5 TU; under no circumstances is it to be used for the initial injection.

Usual pediatric dose
See *Usual adult and adolescent dose.*

Strength(s) usually available
U.S.—
1 U.S. unit (TU) per test dose (0.1 mL) (Rx) [*Tubersol*].
5 U.S. units (TU) per test dose (0.1 mL) (Rx) [*Aplisol; Tubersol*].
250 U.S. units (TU) per test dose (0.1 mL) (Rx) [*Tubersol*].
Canada—
1 U.S. unit (TU) per test dose (0.1 mL) (Rx) [*Tubersol*].
5 U.S. units (TU) per test dose (0.1 mL) (Rx) [*Tubersol*].
250 U.S. units (TU) per test dose (0.1 mL) (Rx) [*Tubersol*].

Packaging and storage
Store between 2 and 8 °C (36 and 46 °F). Protect from light.

Additional information
Vials of tuberculin PPD that have been opened should be discarded after 1 month of use, since oxidation and degradation may have reduced the potency.

TUBERCULIN (Purified Protein Derivative [PPD] Multiple-Puncture Device) USP

Usual adult and adolescent dose
Tuberculosis (diagnosis)—
Intradermal, equivalent to or more potent than 5 U.S. units (tuberculin units [TU]).

Usual pediatric dose
See *Usual adult and adolescent dose.*

Strength(s) usually available
U.S.—
Equivalent to or more potent than 5 U.S. units in individually capped test units (Rx) [*Aplitest; Tuberculin PPD TINE TEST*].
Canada—
Not commercially available.

Packaging and storage
Store below 30 °C (86 °F). Do not refrigerate.

Selected Bibliography

Menzies R, Vissandjee B, Rocher I, Germain YS. The booster effect in two-step tuberculin testing among young adults in Montreal. Ann Intern Med 1994; 120(3): 190-8.

Developed: 08/01/1995

TUBOCURARINE—See *Neuromuscular Blocking Agents (Systemic)*

TYROPANOATE—See *Cholecystographic Agents, Oral (Systemic)*

UNOPROSTONE Ophthalmic

VA CLASSIFICATION (Primary): OP119

Commonly used brand name(s): *Rescula*.

Note: For a listing of dosage forms and brand names by country availability, see *Dosage Forms* section(s).

Category

Antiglaucoma agent (ophthalmic); antihypertensive, ocular.

Indications

Accepted

Glaucoma, open-angle (treatment) or

Hypertension, ocular (treatment)—Unoprostone is indicated in the treatment of elevated intraocular pressure in patients with ocular hypertension or open-angle glaucoma who are intolerant of or unresponsive to other agents.

Pharmacology/Pharmacokinetics

Physicochemical characteristics

Molecular weight—424.62.

pH—5.0–6.5

Mechanism of action/Effect

Unoprostone decreases elevated intraocular pressure by increasing the outflow of aqueous humor, however the exact mechanism is unknown.

Absorption

Unoprostone is absorbed via the cornea and conjunctival epithelium. There is little systemic absorption of unoprostone.

Biotransformation

Unoprostone is hydrolyzed to unoprostone free acid via esterase activity in the cornea and conjunctival epithelium.

Half-life

Elimination—

14 minutes

Elimination

Predominately renal

Precautions to Consider

Carcinogenicity

Unoprostone administered to male and female rats in doses of approximately 580 and 240 fold the recommended human dose, respectively, was not found to be carcinogenic over a two-year period.

Mutagenicity

Unoprostone isopropyl and unoprostone free acid were not mutagenic in an Ames assay, nor were they clastogenic in a chromosome aberration assay in Chinese-hamster fibroblasts. Unoprostone isopropyl was not genotoxic in a mouse lymphoma mutation assay or clastogenic in an *in vivo* chromosomal aberration test in mouse bone marrow.

Pregnancy/Reproduction

Fertility—Unoprostone did not impair fertility of male or female rats when given in doses up to 10,000 fold the recommended human dose.

Pregnancy—Adequate and well-controlled studies have not been performed in humans.

Studies in rats showed an increase in miscarriages and a decrease in the live birth index when unoprostone was administered subcutaneously during organogenesis. Increases in miscarriages and resorptions and decrease in the number of live births were noted in rabbits given unoprostone subcutaneously during organogenesis.

FDA Pregnancy Category C

Breast-feeding

It is not known whether unoprostone is distributed into human breast milk. However, intravenous administration of unoprostone to rats has resulted in measurable breast milk concentrations. It is not known whether topical ocular administration will result in distribution into breast milk.

Pediatrics

Appropriate studies on the relationship of age to the effects of unoprostone have not been performed in the pediatric population. Safety and efficacy have not been established.

Geriatrics

Appropriate studies performed to date have not demonstrated geriatrics-specific problems that would limit the usefulness of unoprostone in the elderly.

Medical considerations/Contraindications

The medical considerations/contraindications included have been selected on the basis of their potential clinical significance (reasons given in parentheses where appropriate)—not necessarily inclusive (» = major clinical significance).

Except under special circumstances, this medication should not be used when the following medical problem exists:

» Hypersensitivity to unoprostone isopropyl or benzalkonium chloride

Risk-benefit should be considered when the following medical problems exist:

Intraocular inflammation, active
(caution is recommended)

Patient monitoring

The following may be especially important in patient monitoring (other tests may be warranted in some patients, depending on condition; » = major clinical significance):

» Pigmentation changes
(unoprostone may gradually and permanently affect eye pigmentation, increasing the amount of brown pigment in the iris; the long term consequences of this effect are unknown)

Side/Adverse Effects

The following side/adverse effects have been selected on the basis of their potential clinical significance (possible signs and symptoms in parentheses where appropriate)—not necessarily inclusive:

Those indicating need for medical attention

Incidence less frequent

Cataracts (blurred vision or eye pain); ***corneal lesion*** (eye irritation or redness); ***ocular hemorrhage*** (blood in whites of the eye)

Incidence rare

Acute elevated intraocular pressure (eye pain or blurred vision); ***color blindness; corneal deposits*** (blurred vision); ***corneal edema*** (blurred vision; decreased vision); ***optic atrophy*** (blindness; blurred vision; decreased vision; eye pain); ***retinal hemorrhage*** (decreased vision or other changes in vision)

Those indicating need for medical attention only if they continue or are bothersome

Incidence more frequent

Abnormal vision; burning or stinging of eyes; diplopia (double vision); ***dry eyes; flu-like syndrome*** (chills; cough; diarrhea; fever; general feeling of discomfort or illness; headache; joint pain; loss of appetite; muscle aches and pains; nausea; runny nose; shivering; sore throat; sweating; trouble sleeping; unusual tiredness or weakness; vomiting); ***itching of eyes; lacrimation disorder*** (abnormal tearing of eyes)

Incidence less frequent or rare

Blepharitis or conjunctivitis (redness, pain, swelling of eye, eyelid, or inner lining of eyelid; burning, dry or itching eyes; discharge; excessive tearing); ***discharge from eye; eye pain; keratitis*** (irritation or inflammation of eye); ***iritis*** (sensitivity to light; tearing; throbbing pain)

Those not indicating need for medical attention

Incidence more frequent

Foreign body sensation (feeling of having something in the eye); ***increased or decreased length of eyelashes***

Incidence less frequent or rare

Hyperpigmentation of iris or eyelid; increased number of eyelashes; photophobia (difficulty seeing at night; increased sensitivity of eyes to sunlight)

Note: *Hyperpigmentation of the iris* occurs slowly and may not be noticeable for months to several years. This color change may be permanent.

Overdose

For more information on the management of overdose or unintentional ingestion, **contact a poison control center** (see *Poison Control Center Listing*).

Treatment of overdose

There is no specific information regarding overdose with unoprostone. Treatment should be symptomatic and supportive.

Patients in whom intentional overdose is confirmed or suspected should be referred for psychiatric consultation.

Patient Consultation

As an aid to patient consultation, refer to *Advice for the Patient, Unoprostone (Ophthalmic)*.

In providing consultation, consider emphasizing the following selected information (» = major clinical significance):

Before using this medication

» Conditions affecting use, especially:
Hypersensitivity to unoprostone isopropyl or benzalkonium chloride

Proper use of this medication

Proper administration technique for ophthalmic solution
Preventing contamination: Not touching applicator tip to any surface; keeping container tightly closed
» Importance of not using more medication than the amount prescribed
» Importance of removing contact lenses prior to administration of medication
Waiting 5 minutes between the use of 2 different ophthalmic preparations
» Proper dosing
Missed dose: Using as soon as possible; not using if almost time for next scheduled dose; not doubling doses
Proper storage

Precautions while using this medication

» Regular visits to physician to check eye pressure during therapy
Checking with physician immediately if having ocular surgery, if trauma to the eye occurs, or an eye infection develops to determine if the present multidose container should continue to be used
» Caution when driving or using machinery because of possible blurred vision
Possible sensitivity of eyes to sunlight or bright light; wearing sunglasses and avoiding exposure to bright light

Side/adverse effects

Signs of potential side effects, especially cataracts, corneal lesion, ocular hemorrhage, acute elevated intraocular pressure, color blindness, corneal deposits, corneal edema, optic atrophy, and retinal hemorrhage
(Hyperpigmentation of the iris or eyelid may occur; change in color of iris may not be noticeable for months to several years and may be permanent)

General Dosing Information

Because the preservative, benzalkonium chloride, may be absorbed by contact lenses, it is recommended that they be removed prior to administration of unoprostone. The lenses may be reinserted 15 minutes after administration of the medication.

Unoprostone may be used concurrently with other medications instilled in the eye to lower intraocular pressure. However, the medications should be administered at least 5 minutes apart.

Patients should be cautioned that permanent alterations in iris color are possible. These changes may be very gradual and occur over a period of several months to years

Ophthalmic Dosage Forms

UNOPROSTONE ISOPROPYL OPHTHALMIC SOLUTION

Usual adult dose

Open-angle glaucoma or
Ocular hypertension—
Topical to the conjunctiva, 1 drop in the affected eye(s) two times a day.

Usual pediatric dose

Safety and efficacy have not been established.

Usual geriatric dose

See *Usual adult dose.*

Strength(s) usually available

U.S.—
1.5 mg per 1 mL (Rx) [*Rescula* (benzalkonium chloride 0.015%; Edetate disodium; mannitol; polysorbate 80; sodium hydroxide or hydrochloric acid; water for injection)].

Packaging and storage

Store between 2 and 25 °C (36 and 77 °F)

Auxiliary labeling

• For the eye.

Developed: 10/10/2000

UROKINASE—See *Thrombolytic Agents (Systemic)*

URSODIOL Systemic

INN: Ursodeoxycholic acid
BAN: Ursodeoxycholic acid
JAN: Ursodesoxycholic acid
VA CLASSIFICATION (Primary): GA900

Commonly used brand name(s): *Actigall; URSO; URSO 250; Ursofalk.*

Another commonly used name is UDCA.

Note: For a listing of dosage forms and brand names by country availability, see *Dosage Forms* section(s).

Category

Anticholelithic.

Indications

Note: Bracketed information in the *Indications* section refers to uses that are not included in U.S. product labeling.

Accepted

Gallstone disease (treatment)—Ursodiol is indicated for patients with radiolucent, noncalcified gallbladder stones < 20 mm in greatest diameter in whom elective cholecystectomy would be undertaken except for the presence of increased surgical risk due to systemic disease, advanced age, idiosyncratic reaction to general anesthesia, or for patients who refuse surgery. Safety of use of ursodiol beyond 24 months is not established.

Ursodiol therapy is more likely to be effective if the stones are small (≤ 20 mm) and of the floatable type.

Body weight and dietary factors may influence gallstone formation and/or dissolution rate.

Gallstone formation (prophylaxis)[1]—Ursodiol is indicated for the prevention of gallstone formation in obese patients experiencing rapid weight loss.

Cirrhosis, biliary (treatment)—Ursodiol is indicated for the treatment of patients with primary biliary cirrhosis [PBC].

[Atresia, biliary (treatment)][1]
[Cholangitis, sclerosing (treatment)][1]
[Cirrhosis, alcoholic (treatment)][1]
[Hepatic disease, cholestatic (treatment)]
[Hepatic disease, cystic fibrosis–associated (treatment)][1] and
[Hepatitis, chronic (treatment)][1]—Ursodiol is used for the treatment of some chronic liver diseases, primary sclerosing cholangitis, cystic fibrosis–associated liver disease, biliary atresia, chronic hepatitis, and alcoholic cirrhosis.

[Transplant rejection, liver (prophylaxis)][1]—Ursodiol is used as adjuvant therapy following orthotopic liver transplantation to prevent early graft rejection.

Unaccepted

Ursodiol is *not* indicated when there are calcified cholesterol stones, radiopaque stones (calcium-containing), or radiolucent bile pigment stones; when the gallbladder is not functioning; or when surgery for gallstones is clearly indicated.

[1]Not included in Canadian product labeling.

Pharmacology/Pharmacokinetics

Physicochemical characteristics

Molecular weight—392.58.

Mechanism of action/Effect

Anticholelithic—Although the exact mechanism of ursodiol's anticholelithic action is not completely understood, it is known that when administered orally ursodiol is concentrated in bile and decreases biliary cholesterol saturation by suppressing hepatic synthesis and secretion of cholesterol, and by inhibiting its intestinal absorption. The reduced cholesterol saturation permits the gradual solubilization of cholesterol from gallstones, resulting in their eventual dissolution.

Other actions/effects

Ursodiol increases bile flow. In chronic cholestatic liver disease, ursodiol appears to reduce the detergent properties of the bile salts, thus reducing their cytotoxicity. Also, ursodiol may protect liver cells from the damaging activity of toxic bile acids (e.g., lithocholate, deoxycholate, and chenodeoxycholate), which increase in concentration in patients with chronic liver disease.

Absorption

Absorbed from the small bowel (about 90% of dose).

Protein binding
High.

Biotransformation
Hepatic (first-pass hepatic clearance). Exogenous ursodiol is metabolized in the liver to its taurine and glycine conjugates. The resulting conjugates are secreted into bile.

Time to peak concentration
1 to 3 hours.

Elimination
Primarily fecal; very small amounts are excreted into urine. Small amount of unabsorbed ursodiol passes into the colon where it undergoes bacterial degradation (7-dehydroxylation); the resulting lithocholic acid is partly absorbed from the colon but is sulfated in the liver and rapidly eliminated in the feces as the sulfolithocholyl glycine or sulfolithocholyl taurine conjugate.

Precautions to Consider

Cross-sensitivity and/or related problems
Patients sensitive to other bile acid products may be sensitive to ursodiol also.

Carcinogenicity/Tumorigenicity
Studies in rats with intrarectal instillation of lithocholic acid and other metabolites of ursodiol and chenodiol did not show evidence of tumorigenicity, except when these substances were administered in conjunction with a carcinogenic agent. Epidemiologic studies suggest that bile acids might be involved in the pathogenesis of human colon cancer in patients who have undergone a cholecystectomy; however, conclusive evidence is lacking.

Pregnancy/Reproduction
Fertility—Studies in rats and rabbits given ursodiol doses of 20- to 100-fold the human dose in rats and 5-fold the human dose in rabbits revealed no evidence of impaired fertility. Studies using 100- to 200-fold the human dose in rats have shown some reduction in fertility and litter size.

Pregnancy—Adequate and well-controlled studies have not been done in humans. However, 4 women were inadvertently exposed to therapeutic doses of ursodiol in the first trimester of pregnancy during clinical trials which led to no evidence of effects on the fetus or newborn baby.

Studies in rats at doses 20 to 100 times the human dose, and in rabbits at doses 5 times the human dose, have not shown that ursodiol causes adverse effects in the fetus. Although it seems unlikely, the possibility that ursodiol can cause fetal harm cannot be ruled out. Therefore, ursodiol is not recommended for use during pregnancy.

FDA Pregnancy Category B.

Breast-feeding
It is not known whether ursodiol is distributed into breast milk. Because many drugs are excreted in human milk, caution should be exercised when ursodiol is administered to a nursing mother.

Pediatrics
Appropriate studies on the relationship of age to the effects of ursodiol when used as an anticholelithic have not been performed in the pediatric population. However, studies performed to date in children and infants with cholestatic liver disease and biliary atresia have not demonstrated pediatrics-specific problems that would limit the usefulness of ursodiol in children.

Geriatrics
Clinical studies have not demonstrated age related differences in safety and efficacy. However, dose selection for elderly patients should be cautious reflecting the greater sensitivity and small differences in efficacy of some elderly patients.

Drug interactions and/or related problems
The following drug interactions and/or related problems have been selected on the basis of their potential clinical significance (possible mechanism in parentheses where appropriate)—not necessarily inclusive (» = major clinical significance):

Note: Combinations containing any of the following medications, depending on the amount present, may also interact with this medication.

Antacids, aluminum-containing or
Cholestyramine or
Colestipol
(concurrent use may result in binding of ursodiol, thus decreasing its absorption)

Antihyperlipidemics, especially clofibrate or
Estrogens or
Neomycin or
Oral contraceptives or
Progestins
(concurrent use of these medications with ursodiol may decrease ursodiol's ability to dissolve cholesterol gallstones, since these medications increase hepatic cholesterol secretion and encourage cholesterol gallstone formation)

Laboratory value alterations
The following have been selected on the basis of their potential clinical significance (possible effect in parentheses where appropriate)—not necessarily inclusive (» = major clinical significance).

With physiology/laboratory test values

Creatinine, serum
(may be elevated during ursodiol treatment)

Transaminase (mainly serum alanine aminotransferase [ALT (SGPT)])
(although this effect has not been clearly demonstrated, serum concentrations of liver enzymes may be increased due to the inability of some patients to form sulfate conjugates of lithocholic acid; however, these concentrations may be decreased in patients with primary biliary cirrhosis, with other cholestatic conditions, and with chronic active hepatitis)

Medical considerations/Contraindications
The medical considerations/contraindications included have been selected on the basis of their potential clinical significance (reasons given in parentheses where appropriate)—not necessarily inclusive (» = major clinical significance).

Except under special circumstances, this medication should not be used when the following medical problem exists:

» Allergy to bile acids or ursodiol
(ursodiol use contraindicated)

» Gallstone complications, such as:
Biliary-gastrointestinal fistula
Biliary obstruction
Cholangitis
Cholecystitis
Pancreatitis
(patients with these conditions are not candidates for ursodiol therapy; medical treatment with ursodiol would be too lengthy; surgery may be indicated)

Risk-benefit should be considered when the following medical problems exist:

Deficiency in sulfation, congenital or acquired
(may predispose patient to lithocholate-induced liver damage)

Hepatic function impairment, chronic
(bile acid metabolism may be further impaired; however, in some studies ursodiol had a normalizing effect on previously abnormal liver test findings. Data suggest a possible therapeutic role for ursodiol in chronic cholestatic liver disease, in which cholestasis [impaired bile formation or flow] appears to play an important role)

Patient monitoring
The following may be especially important in patient monitoring (other tests may be warranted in some patients, depending on condition; » = major clinical significance):

Alanine aminotransferase (ALT [SGPT]) and
Alkaline phosphatase and
Aspartate aminotransferase (AST [SGOT]) and
Bilirubin and
Gamma-glutamyltransferase (GGT)
(monitoring of serum values is recommended upon initiation of treatment, every 1 to 3 months for the first 3 months of treatment [depending on the indication for use], and then every 6 months during treatment; ursodiol must be discontinued if increased values persist)

Blood glucose
(may be elevated during ursodiol use)

Cholecystogram
(recommended prior to treatment for gallstones to determine whether the gallbladder is functional, and whether gallstones are translucent or radiopaque)

Ultrasonograms
(recommended prior to treatment to confirm the presence of gallstones, and at 6-month intervals during the first year of treatment to monitor stone dissolution; also recommended after gallstone dissolution to monitor for possible recurrence)

Side/Adverse Effects

Note: Hepatotoxicity has not been associated with ursodiol therapy. However, in some individuals with a congenital or acquired reduction in ability to sulfate hepatotoxic lithocholic acid, the theoretical risk of lithocholate-induced liver damage may be increased.

The following side/adverse effects have been selected on the basis of their potential clinical significance (possible signs and symptoms in parentheses where appropriate)—not necessarily inclusive:

Those indicating need for medical attention

Incidence more frequent

Allergy (dizziness, fast heartbeat, shortness of breath, skin rash or itching over the entire body, sweating, weakness, wheezing); ***cholecystitis*** (indigestion, stomach pain, severe nausea, vomiting); ***urinary tract infection [UTI]*** (bladder pain; bloody or cloudy urine; difficult, burning, or painful urination; frequent urge to urinate; lower back or side pain)

Incidence less frequent

Leukopenia (black, tarry stools, chest pain, chills, cough, fever, painful or difficult urination, shortness of breath, sore throat, sores, ulcers, or white spots on lips or in mouth, swollen glands, unusual bleeding or bruising, unusual tiredness or weakness); ***peptic ulcer*** (black, tarry stools, blood in vomit, severe or continuing stomach pain)

Those indicating need for medical attention only if they continue or are bothersome

Incidence more frequent

Alopecia (hair loss); ***arthritis*** (pain, swelling, or redness in joints, muscle pain or stiffness, difficulty in moving); ***back pain; bronchitis*** (cough producing mucus, difficulty breathing, shortness of breath, tightness in chest, wheezing); ***constipation; coughing; diarrhea***—may be dose-related; ***dizziness; dyspepsia*** (heartburn); ***headache; influenza-like symptoms*** (chills, cough, diarrhea, fever, general feeling of discomfort or illness, headache, joint pain, loss of appetite, muscle aches and pains, nausea, runny nose, shivering, sore throat, sweating, trouble sleeping, unusual tiredness or weakness, vomiting); ***musculoskeletal pain*** (muscle or bone pain); ***nausea; pharyngitis*** (body aches or pain, congestion, cough, dryness or soreness of throat, fever, hoarseness, runny nose, tender, swollen glands in neck, trouble in swallowing, voice changes); ***upper respiratory tract infection*** (ear congestion, nasal congestion, chills, cough, fever, sneezing, or sore throat, body aches or pain, headache, loss of voice, runny nose, unusual tiredness or weakness, difficulty in breathing); ***vomiting***

Incidence less frequent or rare

Psoriasis, exacerbation of pre-existing; skin rash; vomiting

Overdose

No cases of ursodiol overdose have been reported.

The most likely manifestation of severe overdose with ursodiol would probably be diarrhea, which should be treated symptomatically.

For information on the management of overdose or unintentional ingestion, **contact a Poison Control Center** (see *Poison Control Center Listing*).

Patient Consultation

As an aid to patient consultation, refer to *Advice for the Patient, Ursodiol (Systemic)*.

In providing consultation, consider emphasizing the following selected information (» = major clinical significance):

Before using this medication

» Conditions affecting use, especially:
  Sensitivity to ursodiol or to other bile acids
  Pregnancy—Not recommended during pregnancy because of possibility that ursodiol can cause fetal harm cannot be ruled out
  Use in the elderly—Dose selection for elderly patients should be cautious reflecting the greater sensitivity and small differences in efficacy of some elderly patients.
  Other medical problems, especially allergy to bile acids or ursodiol, or gallstone complications

Proper use of this medication

Taking with meals for optimal therapeutic effect
» Compliance with full course of therapy
» Proper dosing
Missed dose: Taking as soon as possible or doubling the next dose
» Proper storage

Precautions while using this medication

» Regular visits to physician to check progress; laboratory tests may be required during therapy
Avoiding aluminum-containing antacids; may interfere with absorption of ursodiol
» Notifying physician immediately if symptoms of acute cholecystitis develop

Side/adverse effects

Signs of potential side effects, especially allergy, cholecystitis, leukopenia, peptic ulcer, and urinary tract infection

General Dosing Information

Orally administered ursodiol is indicated for dissolution of cholesterol gallstones in selected patients with uncomplicated radiolucent gallstone disease. However, alternative therapies should be considered since gallstone dissolution with ursodiol may require many months of treatment, complete dissolution does not occur in all patients, and recurrence of stones occurs within 5 years in about 50% of patients who have had stones dissolved by use of bile acid therapy.

Patients with variceal bleeding, hepatic encephalopathy, ascites, or in need of an urgent liver transplant, should receive appropriate specific treatment.

Ursodiol should be taken with meals or a snack since it dissolves more rapidly when bile and pancreatic juice are present in the intestinal chyme.

Gallstone dissolution may require 6 months to 2 years of continuous dosing depending on the size and composition of the stone(s). Response should be monitored by ultrasonograms performed at 6-month intervals during the first year of therapy. After complete dissolution, it is recommended that ursodiol be continued for at least 3 months to promote dissolution of particles that are too small to image.

Ursodiol therapy is unlikely to be effective if partial dissolution has not occurred after 6 to 12 months of treatment.

Gallbladder nonvisualization that develops during therapy is an indication that complete stone dissolution will not occur and therapy should be discontinued.

Oral Dosage Forms

Note: Bracketed uses in the *Dosage Forms* section refer to categories of use and/or indications that are not included in U.S. product labeling.

URSODIOL CAPSULES USP

Usual adult and adolescent dose

Gallstone disease (treatment)—
  Oral, 8 to 10 mg per kg of body weight a day, divided into two or three doses, usually taken with meals.

Gallstone formation (prophylaxis)[1]—
  Oral, 300 mg two times a day. Alternatively, some clinicians continue the dissolution dose of 8 to 10 mg per kg of body weight a day. Bedtime dosing has been reported to enhance dissolution.

Cirrhosis, biliary (treatment)—
  Oral, 13 to 15 mg per kg of body weight per day administered in two to four divided doses with food as follows:

  Note: Each tablet contains 250 mg ursodiol.

  - 40 to 60 kg: 3 tablets per day
  - 61 to 70 kg: 4 tablets per day
  - 71 to 80 kg: 5 tablets per day

[Hepatic disease, cholestatic (treatment)]—
  Oral, 13 to 15 mg per kg of body weight a day, given in two divided doses (morning and bedtime) with food.

Usual pediatric dose

Safety and efficacy have not been established.

Note: In children with cholestatic liver disease and extrahepatic biliary atresia, total daily doses have ranged from 10 to 18 mg per kg of body weight.

Usual geriatric dose

See *Usual adult and adolescent dose*.

Strength(s) usually available

U.S.—
  300 mg (Rx) [*Actigall* (gelatin; iron oxide; magnesium stearate; colloidal silicon dioxide; starch; titanium dioxide)].
  250 mg (Rx) [*URSO 250* (microcrystalline cellulose; povidone; sodium starch glycolate; magnesium stearate; ethylcellulose; dibutyl sebacate; carnauba wax; hydroxypropyl methylcellulose; PEG 3350; PEG 8000; cetyl alcohol; sodium lauryl sulfate; hydrogen peroxide)].

Canada—
  250 mg (Rx) [*URSO* (carnauba wax; dibutyl sebacate; ethylcellulose aqueous; hydroxypropyl methylcellulose; magnesium stearate; microcrystalline cellulose; polyethylene glycol; povidone; sodium starch glycolate)].

250 mg (Rx) [*Ursofalk* (gelatin; Windsor salt; polysorbate; magnesium stearate; colloidal silicon dioxide; corn starch; titanium dioxide)].

Packaging and storage
Store below 40 °C (104 °F), preferably between 15 and 30 °C (59 and 86 °F), in a tight container, unless otherwise specified by manufacturer.

Auxiliary labeling
- Continue medication for full time of treatment.
- Take with food.

[1]Not included in Canadian product labeling.

Selected Bibliography
Rosenbaum CL, Cluxton RJ Jr. Ursodiol: a cholesterol gallstone solubilizing agent. Drug Intell Clin Pharm 1988 Dec; 22: 941-5.

Ward A, Brogden RN, Heel RC, et al. Ursodeoxycholic acid: a review of its pharmacological properties and therapeutic efficacy. Drugs 1984; 27: 95-131.

Revised: 01/08/2004

VACCINIA IMMUNE GLOBULIN INTRAVENOUS (Human) Systemic

VA CLASSIFICATION (Primary): IM402

Commonly used brand name(s): *Vaccinia immune globulin intravenous (human)*.

Note: For a listing of dosage forms and brand names by country availability, see *Dosage Forms* section(s).

Category
Immunizing agent (passive).

Indications

Accepted
Eczema vaccinatum (treatment) or

Vaccinia, progressive (treatment) or

Vaccinia, severe generalized (treatment)—Vaccinia immune globulin intravenous (human) (VIGIV) is indicated for the treatment and/or modification of eczema vaccinatum, progressive vaccinia and severe generalized vaccinia.

Vaccinia infection (treatment)—(VIGIV) is indicated for the treatment and/or modification of vaccinia infections in individuals who have skin conditions such as burns, impetigo, varicella-zoster, or poison ivy; or in individuals who have eczematous skin lesions because of either the activity or extensiveness of such lesions.

Aberrant infections induced by vaccinia virus (treatment)—(VIGIV) is indicated for the treatment and/or modification aberrant infections induced by vaccinia virus that include its accidental implantation in eyes (except in cases of isolated keratitis), mouth, or other areas where vaccinia infection would constitute a special hazard.

Unaccepted
Vaccinia immune globulin intravenous (human) (VIGIV) is not considered to be effective in the treatment of postvaccinial encephalitis.

Pharmacology/Pharmacokinetics

Physicochemical characteristics
Source—Vaccinia immune globulin intravenous (human) is a sterile solution of gamma globulin (IgG) fraction of human plasma from healthy screened donors with high titers of anti-vaccinia antibody. The manufacturing process includes a solvent/detergent treatment step (using tri-n-butyl phosphate and Triton X-100) that is effective in inactivating known enveloped viruses. Vaccinia immune globulin intravenous (human) is filtered using a Planova 35nm Virus Filter designed to remove and/or inactivate lipid-enveloped and non-enveloped viruses.

pH— Between 5 and 6.5.

Distribution
Volume of distribution (Vol_D)—6630 L.

Half-life
30 days.

Time to peak plasma concentration:
2 hours.

Peak plasma concentration
161 Units/mL in healthy volunteers.

Precautions to Consider

Pregnancy/Reproduction
Fertility—Reproduction studies have not been done.

Pregnancy—Studies in humans have not been done.

Studies in animals have not been done.

Immune globulins have been used during pregnancy without negative reproductive effects; however, the risk/benefit should be assessed for each individual case.

FDA Pregnancy Category C

Breast-feeding
It is not known whether vaccinia immune globulin intravenous (human) is distributed into human breast milk. Because many drugs are distributed into human milk, caution should be exercised when vaccinia immune globulin intravenous (human) is administered to a nursing woman.

Pediatrics
Safety and effectiveness in pediatric patients have not been established.

Geriatrics
No information is available on the relationship of age to the effects of vaccinia immune globulin intravenous (human) in geriatric patients.

Drug interactions and/or related problems
The following drug interactions and/or related problems have been selected on the basis of their potential clinical significance (possible mechanism in parentheses where appropriate)—not necessarily inclusive (» = major clinical significance):

Note: Combinations containing any of the following medications, depending on the amount present, may also interact with this medication.

There are no available data on concomitant use of vaccinia immune globulin intravenous (human) (VIGIV) and other medications. It is recommended that VIGIV be administered separately from other drugs or medications.

Nephrotoxic drugs
(administer vaccinia immune globulin intravenous [human] at the minimum concentration available and at the minimum rate of infusion practicable)

» Vaccines, live attenuated such as
Measles or
Rubella or
Mumps or
Varicella
(should be deferred until approximately three months after administration of VIGIV; it may be necessary to revaccinate persons who receive VIGIV shortly after live virus vaccination)

Laboratory value alterations
The following have been selected on the basis of their potential clinical significance (possible effect in parentheses where appropriate)—not necessarily inclusive (» = major clinical significance).

With diagnostic test results
Creatinine, serum or
Urea nitrogen, blood
(increases have been observed 1 to 2 days after treatment with vaccinia immune globulin intravenous [human])

With physiology/laboratory test values
Serological values such as
Anti-HBs
(transitory increase of passively transferred antibodies in patients blood may result)

Medical considerations/Contraindications
The medical considerations/contraindications included have been selected on the basis of their potential clinical significance (reasons given in parentheses where appropriate)—not necessarily inclusive (» = major clinical significance).

Except under special circumstances, this medication should not be used when the following medical problem exists:

» Hypersensitivity to vaccinia immune globulin intravenous (human) or other human immunoglobulin preparations

» Vaccinia keratitis, isolated
(use is contraindicated)

Risk-benefit should be considered when the following medical problems exist:

Atherosclerosis, history of or
Cardiovascular risk factors such as

Advanced age or
Cardiac output, impaired or
Hypercoagulable disorders or
Immobilization, prolonged periods
(increased risk of potential thrombotic events; risk and benefits should be weighed against those of alternative therapies)

Advanced age, (65 years or older) or
Diabetes mellitus or
Paraproteinemia or
Renal insufficiency, pre-existing or at increased risk of developing or
Sepsis or
Thromboembolic events or
Thrombotic events, risk of or
Volume depletion
(administer the minimum concentration available and do not exceed the recommended infusion rate; ensure patients who are predisposed to acute renal failure are not volume depleted before infusion; vaccinia immune globulin intravenous [human] does not contain sucrose as a stabilizer, which has been associated with other IGIV products and reports of renal dysfunction and acute renal failure)

» Hyperviscosity, known or suspected
(increased risk of potential thrombotic events; baseline assessment of blood viscosity should be considered including those with cryoglobulins, fasting chylomicronemia/markedly high triglycerides, or monoclonal gammopathies)

» Immunoglobulin A (IgA) deficiency
(individuals who are deficient in IgA may have the potential to develop IgA antibodies and have an anaphylactoid reaction; if allergic or anaphylactic reaction occur, the infusion should be stopped immediately)

Patient monitoring

The following may be especially important in patient monitoring (other tests may be warranted in some patients, depending on condition; » = major clinical significance):

Hemolysis, sign and symptoms of
(hemolytic anemia can develop subsequent to vaccinia immune globulin intravenous [human] therapy due to enhanced red blood cell sequestration; if signs and symptoms of hemolysis are present confirmatory laboratory testing should be done)

Pulmonary adverse reactions
(if transfusion-related acute lung injury [TRALI] is suspected, appropriate test should be performed for the presence of anti-neutrophil antibodies in both the product and the patients serum)

» Vital sign
(closely monitor throughout the infusion period and immediately following an infusion)

Side/Adverse Effects

The following side/adverse effects have been selected on the basis of their potential clinical significance (possible signs and symptoms in parentheses where appropriate)—not necessarily inclusive:

Note: Vaccinia immune globulin intravenous (human) is prepared using human plasma and therefore carries the possibility for transmission of blood-borne viral agents and theoretically, the Creutzfeldt-Jakob disease agent.

Those indicating need for medical attention

Incidence unknown

Aseptic meningitis syndrome (fever; headache; nausea; stiff neck or back; vomiting)

Observed postmarketing; incidence unknown

Acute respiratory distress syndrome (ARDS) (shortness of breath; tightness in chest; troubled breathing; wheezing); ***apnea*** (bluish lips or skin; not breathing); ***bronchospasm*** (cough; difficulty breathing; noisy breathing; shortness of breath; tightness in chest; wheezing); ***cardiac arrest*** (stopping of heart; no blood pressure or pulse; unconsciousness); ***coma*** (change in consciousness; loss of consciousness); ***Coombs-positive hemolytic anemia*** (back, leg, or stomach pains; bleeding gums; chills; dark urine; difficulty breathing; fatigue; fever; general body swelling; headache; loss of appetite; nausea or vomiting; nosebleeds; pale skin; sore throat; yellowing of the eyes or skin); ***cyanosis*** (bluish color of fingernails, lips, skin, palms, or nail beds); ***dyspnea*** (shortness of breath; difficult or labored breathing; tightness in chest; wheezing); ***epidermolysis*** (blistering, peeling, loosening of skin); ***erythema multiforme*** (blistering, peeling, loosening of skin; chills; cough; diarrhea; fever; itching; joint or muscle pain; red irritated eyes; sore throat; sores, ulcers, or white spots in mouth or on lips; unusual tiredness or weakness); ***hemolysis*** (abdominal pain; back pain; dark urine; decreased urination; fever; tiredness; yellow eyes or skin); ***hepatic dysfunction*** (dark urine light-colored stools; loss of appetite; nausea and vomiting; unusual tiredness; yellow eyes or skin; fever with or without chills; stomach pain); ***hypotension*** (blurred vision; confusion; dizziness, faintness, or lightheadedness when getting up from a lying or sitting position; suddenly sweating; unusual tiredness or weakness); ***hypoxemia*** (bluish lips or skin); ***leukopenia*** (black, tarry stools; chest pain; chills; cough; fever; painful or difficult urination; shortness of breath; sore throat sores, ulcers, or white spots on lips or in mouth; swollen glands; unusual bleeding or bruising; unusual tiredness or weakness); ***loss of consciousness; pancytopenia*** (high fever; chills; unexplained bleeding or bruising; bloody, black, or tarry stools; pale skin; unusual tiredness or weakness; cough; shortness of breath; sores, ulcers, or white spots on lips or in mouth; swollen glands); ***pulmonary edema*** (chest pain; difficult, fast, noisy breathing, sometimes with wheezing; blue lips and fingernails; pale skin; increased sweating; coughing that sometimes produces a pink frothy sputum; shortness of breath; swelling in legs and ankles); ***seizures*** (convulsions; muscle spasm or jerking of all extremities; sudden loss of consciousness; loss of bladder control); ***Stevens-Johnson syndrome*** (blistering, peeling, loosening of skin; chills; cough; diarrhea; itching; joint or muscle pain; red irritated eyes; red skin lesions, often with a purple center; sore throat; sores, ulcers, or white spots in mouth or on lips; unusual tiredness or weakness); ***thromboembolism*** (pain in chest, groin, or legs, especially the calves; difficulty breathing; severe, sudden headache; slurred speech; sudden, unexplained shortness of breath; sudden loss of coordination; sudden; severe weakness or numbness in arm or leg; vision changes); ***transfusion related lung injury*** (shortness of breath; tightness in chest; troubled breathing; wheezing); ***vascular collapse*** (chest pain or discomfort; cold, clammy, pale skin; confusion; dizziness; irregular heartbeats; shortness of breath; slow heart rate; weakness)

Those indicating need for medical attention only if they continue or are bothersome

Incidence more frequent

Appetite decreased; asthenia (lack or loss of strength); ***back pain; dizziness; energy increased; eye disorders; fatigue*** (unusual tiredness or weakness); ***feeling cold; feeling hot; headache; lip dry; muscle pain; nausea; pain; pallor*** (paleness of skin); ***paraesthesia*** (burning, crawling, itching, numbness, prickling, "pins and needles", or tingling feelings); ***pyrexia*** (fever); ***rigors*** (feeling unusually cold; shivering); ***sweating increased; tremor*** (trembling or shaking of hands or feet; shakiness in legs, arms, hands, feet); ***vomiting***

Observed postmarketing; incidence unknown

Abdominal pain (stomach pain); ***bullous dermatitis*** (skin blisters)

Overdose

For more information on the management of overdose or unintentional ingestion, **contact a poison control center** (see *Poison Control Center Listing*).

Treatment of overdose

Consequences of an overdose are not known.

There is no known specific antidote to vaccinia immune globulin intravenous (human). Treatment is generally symptomatic and supportive.

Supportive care—
Patients in whom intentional overdose is confirmed or suspected should be referred for psychiatric consultation.

Patient Consultation

As an aid to patient consultation, refer to *Advice for the Patient, Vaccinia Immune Globulin Intravenous (Human) (Systemic)*.

In providing consultation, consider emphasizing the following selected information (» = major clinical significance):

Before using this medication

» Conditions affecting use, especially:
Hypersensitivity to vaccinia immune globulin intravenous (human) or other human immunoglobulin preparations.
Pregnancy—Risk/benefit assessment for each case.
Breast-feeding—Caution should be exercised when vaccinia immune globulin intravenous (human) is administered to a nursing woman.
Use in children—Safety and effectiveness not established.
Other medical problems, especially hyperviscosity, known or suspected; immunoglobulin A (IgA) deficiency, or vaccinia keratitis

Proper use of this medication

» Discussing the risks and benefits of this medicine with the patient before prescribing or administering it.
» Reporting all infections thought to have been possibly transmitted by this product to Cangene Corporation at 1-877-CANGENE, by the physician or health care provider.
» Proper dosing
» Proper storage

Precautions while using this medication

» Possible transmission of infectious agents, such as viruses, that cause disease.

Side/adverse effects

Signs of potential side effects, especially acute respiratory distress syndrome (ARDS), aseptic meningitis syndrome, apnea, bronchospasm, cardiac arrest, coma, Coombs-positive hemolytic anemia, cyanosis, dyspnea, epidermolysis, multiforme, hemolysis, hepatic dysfunction, hypotension, hypoxemia, leukopenia, loss of consciousness, pancytopenia, pulmonary edema, seizures, Stevens-Johnson syndrome, thromboembolism, transfusion related lung injury, or vascular collapse

General Dosing Information

Vaccinia immune globulin intravenous (human) should only be administered intravenously and the recommended infusion rate should be closely followed.

Vaccinia immune globulin intravenous (human) should be administered in a setting where appropriate equipment and trained personnel in the management of acute anaphylaxis are readily available.

Repeat dosing may be considered, depending upon severity of symptoms and response to treatment.

Slower infusion may be prudent if the patient develops minor adverse reactions or if the patient has risk factors for thrombosis/thromboembolism and/or renal insufficiency. A lower incidence of adverse events occurred when 9000 U/kg was infused at 2 mL/minute compared with 4 mL/minute.

Treatment with vaccinia immune globulin intravenous (human) should be administered with caution in patients with complications that include vaccinia keratitis. Studies in animals have shown increased corneal scarring with intramuscular VIG administration.

Safety considerations for handling this medication

Vaccinia immune globulin intravenous (human) is made from human plasma and may contain infectious agents that can potentially transmit disease.

For treatment of adverse effects

Patients with transfusion-related acute lung injury may be managed using oxygen therapy with adequate ventilatory support.

Patients exhibiting signs and symptoms of aseptic meningitis syndrome should receive a thorough neurological examination to rule out other causes of meningitis.

In the case that hypotension or anaphylaxis occur, the administration of vaccinia immune globulin intravenous (human) should be discontinued immediately and supportive care given.

In case of shock, the current medical standards for treatment of shock should be observed.

Parenteral Dosage Forms

VACCINIA IMMUNE GLOBULIN INTRAVENOUS

Usual adult dose

Eczema vaccinatum and
Vaccinia, progressive and
Vaccinia, severe generalized and
Vaccinia infection and
Aberrant infections induced by vaccinia virus—

Intravenous, 6000 Units/kg dose, as soon as symptoms appear and are judged to due to severe vaccinia-related complications

Note: Vaccinia immune globulin intravenous (human) should be administered through a intravenous line with a rate of injection no higher than 2 mL/min.

• For patients weighing less than 50 kg: infusion rate should be no higher than 0.04 mL/kg/minute.

The maximum assessed rate of infusion has been 4 mL/min.

Usual adult prescribing limits

Up to 9000 Units/kg.

Usual pediatric dose

Safety and effectiveness in pediatric patients have not been established.

Usual geriatric dose

See *Usual adult dose*.

Strength(s) usually available

U.S.—

15 mL single dose vial (greater than 50,000 Units/vial) (Rx) [*Vaccinia immune globulin intravenous (human)* (maltose; polysorbate)].

Packaging and storage

Store between 2 and 8°C (36 and 46 °F).

Preparation of dosage form

If vaccinia immune globulin intravenous (human) is received frozen, use within 60 days of thawing at 2 to 8°C.

Remove the tab portion of the vial cap and clean the rubber stopper with 70% alcohol. Visually inspect for particulate matter and discoloration prior to administration. If the solution is turbid, it should not be used.

Stability

Administration of vaccinia immune globulin intravenous (human) should begin within 4 hours after entering the vial.

Vaccinia immune globulin intravenous (human) contains no preservative. Partially used vials should be discarded and not saved for future use.

Vaccinia immune globulin intravenous (human) should not be used past the expiration date.

Incompatibilities

Compatibility of vaccinia immune globulin intravenous (human) has only been assessed with 0.9% Sodium Chloride USP and not other solutions such as dextrose and water. If a preexisting catheter must be used, the line should be flushed with 0.9% Sodium Chloride USP before use and vaccinia immune globulin intravenous (human) should not be diluted more that 1:2 (v/v).

Auxiliary labeling

• Do not shake.

Developed: 12/07/2005

VALACYCLOVIR Systemic

INN: Valaciclovir

VA CLASSIFICATION (Primary): AM820

Commonly used brand name(s): *Valtrex*.

Note: For a listing of dosage forms and brand names by country availability, see *Dosage Forms* section(s).

Category

Antiviral (systemic).

Indications

Accepted

Herpes genitalis, initial episode (treatment)[1]—Valacyclovir is indicated in the treatment of initial episodes of genital herpes in immunocompetent adults.

Herpes genitalis, recurrent episodes (suppression)[1]—Valacyclovir is indicated in the suppression of recurrent episodes of genital herpes in immunocompetent adults.

Herpes genitalis, recurrent episodes (treatment)—Valacyclovir is indicated in the treatment of recurrent episodes of genital herpes in immunocompetent adults.

Herpes zoster (treatment)—Valacyclovir is indicated in the treatment of herpes zoster (shingles) infections caused by varicella-zoster virus (VZV) in immunocompetent adults. In patients older than 50 years of age, valacyclovir significantly reduced the duration of zoster-associated pain and the duration of postherpetic neuralgia lasting greater than 6 months when compared to acyclovir. Therapy is most effective when started within 48 hours of the onset of rash. There are no data on the safety and effectiveness of valacyclovir in children, immunocompromised patients, or patients with disseminated zoster.

[1]Not included in Canadian product labeling.

Pharmacology/Pharmacokinetics

Physicochemical characteristics

Source—Valacyclovir is the hydrochloride salt of the L-valyl ester of acyclovir.

Molecular weight—
Valacyclovir: 324.34.
Valacyclovir hydrochloride: 360.8.

Mechanism of action/Effect
Valacyclovir is a prodrug that is nearly completely converted to acyclovir and L-valine. Due to its more efficient phosphorylation by viral thymidine kinase, acyclovir's antiviral activity is greatest against herpes simplex virus type 1 (HSV-1), followed by herpes simplex virus type 2 (HSV-2), varicella-zoster virus (VZV), Epstein-Barr virus (EBV), and cytomegalovirus (CMV).

Acyclovir is phosphorylated by thymidine kinase to acyclovir monophosphate, which is then converted into acyclovir diphosphate and triphosphate by cellular enzymes. Acyclovir is selectively converted to the active triphosphate form by cells infected with herpes viruses. Acyclovir triphosphate inhibits herpes viral DNA replication by competitive inhibition of viral DNA polymerase, and by incorporation into and termination of the growing viral DNA chain.

Absorption
Valacyclovir is rapidly absorbed in the gastrointestinal tract; it is then converted to the active compound, acyclovir, by first-pass intestinal and hepatic metabolism. Administration of valacyclovir with food was not found to alter the bioavailability of acyclovir.

The bioavailability of acyclovir following administration of valacyclovir is approximately 54%, which is three to five times greater than its bioavailability following oral administration of acyclovir. After administration of 1 gram of valacyclovir given four times a day, the area under the plasma concentration-time curve (AUC) of acyclovir is approximately that obtained after intravenous administration of 5 mg per kg of body weight of acyclovir every 8 hours.

Distribution
Acyclovir is widely distributed to tissues and body fluids, including brain, kidneys, lungs, liver, aqueous humor, tears, intestines, muscle, spleen, breast milk, uterus, vaginal mucosa, vaginal secretions, semen, amniotic fluid, cerebrospinal fluid (CSF), and herpetic vesicular fluid. Highest concentrations are found in the kidneys, liver, and intestines. Acyclovir concentrations in the CSF are approximately 50% of plasma concentrations. In addition, acyclovir crosses the placenta.

Protein binding
Valacyclovir—Low (13 to 18%).
Acyclovir—Low (9 to 33%).

Biotransformation
Valacyclovir is rapidly and nearly completely (99%) converted to the active compound, acyclovir, and L-valine by first-pass intestinal and hepatic metabolism by enzymatic hydrolysis. Acyclovir is converted to inactive metabolites by alcohol and aldehyde dehydrogenase and, to a small extent, by aldehyde oxidase. The metabolism of valacyclovir and acyclovir is not associated with hepatic microsomal enzyme systems.

Half-life
Valacyclovir—
Less than 30 minutes.
Acyclovir—
After administration of valacyclovir:
Normal renal function—2.5 to 3.3 hours.
End-stage renal disease—Approximately 14 hours.
Geriatric patients (65 to 83 years of age)—3.3 to 3.7 hours.

Time to peak concentration
1.6 to 2.1 hours.

Peak plasma concentrations
Valacyclovir—
Plasma concentrations of unconverted valacyclovir are low, with peak concentrations of less than 0.5 mcg per mL (mcg/mL) after any dose. Plasma concentrations are nonquantifiable within 3 hours after administration.
Acyclovir—
Peak plasma concentrations are not proportional to the dose.
After a single dose of valacyclovir:
500 mg: Approximately 3.3 mcg/mL.
1 gram: 4.8 to 5.6 mcg/mL.
After multiple doses of valacyclovir:
500 mg: Approximately 3.7 mcg/mL.
1 gram: 5 to 5.5 mcg/mL.

Elimination
Valacyclovir—
Less than 1% of valacyclovir is recovered unchanged in the urine over 24 hours.
In dialysis:
It is not known if peritoneal dialysis removes valacyclovir from the blood.
Acyclovir—
Renal; acyclovir accounts for 80 to 89% of the total urinary recovery. There was no accumulation of acyclovir after repeated administration of valacyclovir in patients with normal renal function.
In dialysis:
Hemodialysis—During a 4-hour hemodialysis session, approximately one third of acyclovir in the body is removed. The half-life of acyclovir is approximately 4 hours during hemodialysis.
Peritoneal dialysis—Chronic ambulatory peritoneal dialysis (CAPD) and continuous arteriovenous hemofiltration/dialysis (CAVHD) do not substantially remove acyclovir, with pharmacokinetic parameters resembling those observed in patients with end-stage renal disease not receiving hemodialysis.

Precautions to Consider

Carcinogenicity/Tumorigenicity
Valacyclovir was found to be noncarcinogenic in lifetime carcinogenicity bioassays at single daily doses of up to 120 mg per kg of body weight (mg/kg) per day for mice and 100 mg/kg per day for rats. There was no significant difference in the incidence of tumors between mice and rats treated with valacyclovir and control animals; also, valacyclovir did not shorten the latency of tumors. Plasma concentrations of acyclovir were equivalent to human levels in the mouse bioassay and 1.4 to 2.3 times human levels in the rat bioassay.

Mutagenicity
An *in vitro* cytogenetic study with human lymphocytes, a rat cytogenetic study after a single oral dose of 3000 mg/kg (eight to nine times human plasma concentrations), and Ames tests in the presence or absence of metabolic activation were all negative. Valacyclovir was also negative in the mouse lymphoma assay in the absence of metabolic activation. In the presence of metabolic activation (76 to 88% conversion to acyclovir), valacyclovir was weakly mutagenic. A mouse micronucleus assay was negative at 250 mg/kg, but weakly positive at 500 mg/kg (acyclovir concentrations of 26 and 51 times human plasma concentrations, respectively).

Pregnancy/Reproduction
Fertility—Valacyclovir did not impair fertility in rats given a dose of 200 mg/kg per day (six times human plasma concentrations).

Pregnancy—Acyclovir crosses the placenta. No adequate and well-controlled studies have been done with either valacyclovir or acyclovir in pregnant women. A prospective epidemiologic registry of acyclovir use during pregnancy from 1984 to April 1999 has documented 749 pregnancies that were followed in women with live births who were exposed to systemic acyclovir during the first trimester of pregnancy resulting in 756 outcomes. The rate of birth defects in this group approximates that found in the general population. However, it is thought that the small size of the registry is insufficient to evaluate the risk for less common defects or to make definitive conclusions about the safety of acyclovir in developing fetuses.

FDA Pregnancy Category B.

Breast-feeding
It is not known whether valacyclovir is distributed into breast milk. Acyclovir has been found to pass into breast milk at concentrations ranging from 0.6 to 4.1 times the corresponding plasma concentration. At these concentrations, a nursing infant could potentially be exposed to a dose of acyclovir as high as 0.3 mg/kg per day. However, problems in humans have not been documented.

Pediatrics
No information is available on the relationship of age to the effects of valacyclovir in pediatric patients. Safety and efficacy have not been established.

Geriatrics
Studies performed to date have not demonstrated geriatrics-specific problems that would limit the usefulness of valacyclovir in the elderly. However, elderly patients are more likely to have an age-related decrease in renal function, which may require an adjustment of valacyclovir dosage or dosing interval.In addition, elderly patients are at high risk of dehydration and care should be taken to ensure that these patients have adequate fluid intake.

Drug interactions and/or related problems
The following drug interactions and/or related problems have been selected on the basis of their potential clinical significance (possible mechanism in parentheses where appropriate)—not necessarily inclusive (» = major clinical significance):

Note: Combinations containing any of the following medications, depending on the amount present, may also interact with this medication.

Cimetidine and
Probenecid
(cimetidine and probenecid have been found to decrease the rate, but not the extent, of conversion of valacyclovir to acyclovir; the renal clearance of acyclovir is reduced by approximately 24% and 33% by cimetidine and probenecid, respectively, resulting in an increase in the peak plasma concentration of acyclovir by approximately 8% and 22%, respectively; combined use of cimetidine and probenecid resulted in a reduced renal clearance of acyclovir by approximately 46% and an increase in the peak plasma concentration by approximately 30%)

Medical considerations/Contraindications

The medical considerations/contraindications included have been selected on the basis of their potential clinical significance (reasons given in parentheses where appropriate)—not necessarily inclusive (» = major clinical significance).

Risk-benefit should be considered when the following medical problems exist:

» Bone marrow transplantation or
» Human immunodeficiency virus (HIV) infection, advanced or
» Renal transplantation
(thrombotic thrombocytopenic purpura/hemolytic uremic syndrome [TTP/HUS] has been reported in patients with these conditions who were taking high doses of valacyclovir for prolonged periods of time; in rare cases, death has occurred; therefore, valacyclovir is not indicated in immunocompromised patients; however, TTP/HUS has not been seen in immunocompetent patients treated with valacyclovir)

Hepatic function impairment
(the rate, but not the extent, of conversion of valacyclovir to acyclovir is reduced in patients with moderate or severe liver disease [biopsy-proven cirrhosis]; however, the half-life of acyclovir is not affected and dosage modification is not recommended for patients with cirrhosis)

» Hypersensitivity to valacyclovir or acyclovir

» Renal function impairment
(because valacyclovir is renally excreted, patients with renal function impairment or a history of renal impairment may be at increased risk of toxicity, including enhanced risk of adverse neurological effects; patients with a creatinine clearance of < 50 mL/min [< 0.83 mL/sec] require a reduction in dose)

Side/Adverse Effects

Note: No serious side effects have been noted to date with the administration of valacyclovir in immunocompetent adults.

The following side/adverse effects have been selected on the basis of their potential clinical significance (possible signs and symptoms in parentheses where appropriate)—not necessarily inclusive:

Those indicating need for medical attention

Incidence less frequent
Dysmenorrhea (painful menstruation, including abdominal cramps; diarrhea; nausea)

Incidence rare
Aplastic anemia (chest pain; chills; cough; fever; headache; shortness of breath); ***decreased consciousness*** (reduced mental alertness)—in patients with renal insufficiency; ***hepatitis with liver function test abnormalities*** (flu-like symptoms; unusual tiredness; yellow eyes or skin); ***renal insufficiency*** (lower back/side pain; decreased frequency/amount of urine)—manifested by increased serum creatinine; ***thrombocytopenia*** (black, tarry stools; chest pain; chills; cough; fever)

Incidence not determined—Observed during clinical practice; estimates of frequency cannot be determined
Acute hypersensitivity reactions and anaphylaxis (fast heartbeat; swelling of face; wheezing; difficulty in breathing or swallowing; skin rash; itching); ***aggressive behavior*** (changes in behavior, especially in interactions with other people); ***facial edema*** (swelling or puffiness of face); ***hallucinations*** (seeing, hearing, or feeling things that are not there); ***hemolytic anemia, microangiopathic*** (back, leg, or stomach pains; chills; difficulty breathing; swelling of face, hands, legs, or feet); ***hypertension*** (high blood pressure); ***skin reactions such as erythema multiforme, photosensitivity, or rash*** (redness of the skin); ***tachycardia*** (fast, pounding, or irregular heartbeat; lightheadedness when getting up from a lying or sitting position)

Those indicating need for medical attention only if they continue or are bothersome

Incidence more frequent
Headache; nausea

Incidence less frequent
Arthralgia (joint pain); ***dizziness; fatigue*** (unusual tiredness or weakness); ***gastrointestinal disturbances*** (constipation; diarrhea; loss of appetite; stomach pain; vomiting)

Incidence not determined—Observed during clinical practice; estimates of frequency cannot be determined
Agitation (anxiety; dry mouth; irritability; nervousness; restlessness); ***confusion*** (mood or mental changes)

Overdose

For specific information on the agents used in the management of Valacyclovir overdose, see:
- *Charcoal, Activated (Oral-Local)* monograph.

For more information on the management of overdose or unintentional ingestion, **contact a Poison Control Center** (see *Poison Control Center Listing*).

Clinical effects of overdose

Note: To date, there is limited information on overdosage with valacyclovir. However, precipitation of acyclovir in the renal tubules has occurred with rapid or high intravenous doses of acyclovir. No significant adverse effects have been seen with oral overdoses of acyclovir of up to 20 grams. Confusion headache, nausea, and vomiting have been associated with repeated overdoses of *oral* acyclovir.

The following effects have been selected on the basis of their potential clinical significance (possible signs and symptoms in parentheses where appropriate)—not necessarily inclusive:

Effects of Overdosage with Intravenous Acyclovir
Agitation (anxiety; dry mouth; irritability; nervousness; restlessness); ***coma*** (loss of consciousness); ***elevated serum creatinine with subsequent renal failure*** (lower back/side pain; decreased urine output; decreased frequency of urination); ***hallucinations*** (seeing, hearing, or feeling things that are not there); ***seizures*** (convulsions)

Treatment of overdose

To decrease absorption—Activated charcoal may be used to aid removal of unabsorbed valacyclovir.

Treatment is symptomatic and supportive.

If acute renal failure or anuria occurs, hemodialysis may be helpful until renal function is restored.

Patient Consultation

As an aid to patient consultation, refer to *Advice for the Patient, Valacyclovir (Systemic)*.

In providing consultation, consider emphasizing the following selected information (» = major clinical significance):

Before using this medication

» Conditions affecting use, especially:
Hypersensitivity to valacyclovir or acyclovir
Use in the elderly—Increased risk of dehydration
Other medical problems, especially advanced human immunodeficiency virus infection, bone marrow transplantation, renal function impairment, or renal transplantation

Proper use of this medication

» Initiating use of valacyclovir at the earliest sign or symptom; within 48 hours of the onset of rash, pain, or burning when used to treat shingles or an initial episode of genital herpes, or within 24 hours of onset when used to treat recurrent genital herpes
Valacyclovir may be taken with meals
» Compliance with full course of therapy; not using more often or for longer than prescribed
» Proper dosing
Missed dose: Taking as soon as possible; not taking if almost time for next dose; not doubling doses
» Proper storage

Precautions while using this medication

Checking with physician if no improvement within a few days

Keeping affected areas as clean and dry as possible; wearing loose-fitting clothing to avoid irritating the lesions

Side/adverse effects

Signs of dysmenorrhea, aplastic anemia, decreased consciousness, hepatitis with liver function test abnormalities, renal insufficiency, thrombocytopenia, acute hypersensitivity reactions and anaphylaxis, aggressive behavior, facial edema, hallucinations, microangiopathic hemolytic anemia, hypertension, skin reactions such as erythema multiforme, photosensitivity, rash, or tachycardia

General Dosing Information

For treatment of initial or recurrent episodes of genital herpes, valacyclovir therapy should be initiated as soon as possible following the onset of signs and symptoms. In clinical studies, therapy for an initial episode was most effective when initiated within 48 hours of the onset of signs and symptoms; therapy for recurrent episodes was most effective when initiated within 24 hours.

Therapy should be initiated as soon as possible following the onset of signs and symptoms of varicella-zoster infection. In clinical studies, treatment was started within 72 hours of the onset of rash; however, valacyclovir was found to be more effective if started within 48 hours.

Valacyclovir may be taken with meals since absorption has not been shown to be significantly affected by food.

Adults with impaired renal function may require a change in dosing, as follows:

	Creatinine clearance (mL/min)/(mL/sec)			
Indication	≥ 50/0.83	30–49/ 0.5–0.82	10–29/ 0.16–0.49	< 10/0.16
Genital herpes, treatment of initial episode	1 gram every 12 hours	1 gram every 12 hours	1 gram every 24 hours	500 mg every 24 hours
Genital herpes, treatment of recurrent episodes	500 mg every 12 hours	500 mg every 12 hours	500 mg every 24 hours	500 mg every 24 hours
Genital herpes, suppression	500 mg every 24 hours*	500 mg every 24 hours*	500 mg every 48 hours*	500 mg every 48 hours*
	1 gram every 24 hours	1 gram every 24 hours	500 mg every 24 hours	500 mg every 24 hours
Herpes zoster treatment	1 gram every 8 hours	1 gram every 12 hours	1 gram every 24 hours	500 mg every 24 hours
Hemodialysis patients	Patients requiring hemodialysis should receive the recommended dose after hemodialysis.			
Peritoneal dialysis patients	Supplemental doses should not be required.			

*Recommended for patients with a history of nine or fewer recurrent episodes of herpes genitalis per year.

Patients should maintain adequate fluid intake during valacyclovir therapy, especially elderly patients who are at increased risk of dehydration.

Oral Dosage Forms

Note: Bracketed uses in the *Dosage Forms* section refer to categories of use and/or indications that are not included in U.S. product labeling.

The dosing and strengths of the dosage forms available are expressed in terms of valacyclovir base (not the hydrochloride salt).

VALACYCLOVIR HYDROCHLORIDE TABLETS

Usual adult dose

Herpes genitalis, treatment of initial episode[1]—
Oral, 1 gram (base) two times a day for ten days.

Herpes genitalis, treatment of recurrent episodes[1]—
Oral, 500 mg (base) two times a day for three days.

[Herpes genitalis, treatment of recurrent episodes]—
Oral, 500 mg (base) two times a day for five days.

Herpes genitalis, suppression of recurrent episodes[1]—
Oral, 1 gram (base) once a day.

Note: For patients with a history of nine or fewer recurrent episodes per year, 500 mg once a day may be given.

Herpes zoster, treatment—
Oral, 1 gram (base) three times a day for seven days.

Usual pediatric dose

Safety and efficacy in patients younger than 18 years of age have not been established.

Usual geriatric dose

See *Usual adult dose*.

Strength(s) usually available

U.S.—
500 mg (base) (Rx) [*Valtrex*].
1 gram (base) (Rx) [*Valtrex*].

Canada—
500 mg (base) (Rx) [*Valtrex*].

Packaging and storage

Store between 15 and 25 °C (59 and 77 °F), in a tight container. Protect from light.

Auxiliary labeling

- Continue medicine for full time of treatment.

[1]Not included in Canadian product labeling.

Revised: 08/16/2001
Developed: 05/28/1996

VALGANCICLOVIR Systemic

VA CLASSIFICATION (Primary): AM890

Commonly used brand name(s): *Valcyte*.

Note: For a listing of dosage forms and brand names by country availability, see *Dosage Forms* section(s).

Category

Antiviral (systemic).

Indications

General Considerations

Viral resistance can occur after prolonged treatment with valganciclovir by selection of mutations in the viral protein kinase gene responsible for ganciclovir monophosphorylation and/or in the viral polymerase gene. The mutations may cause resistance to ganciclovir or cross-resistance to other antivirals with similar mechanisms of action. The possibility of viral resistance should be considered in patients who show poor clinical response or who experience persistent viral excretion during therapy.

Accepted

Cytomegalovirus retinitis (treatment)—Valganciclovir is indicated for the treatment of cytomegalovirus (CMV) retinitis in patients with acquired immunodeficiency syndrome (AIDS). Although clinical data on the use of valganciclovir for maintenance of CMV retinitis are not available, this use is supported by the similarity of the plasma concentration-time profile of ganciclovir following administration of valganciclovir and the profiles following oral and parenteral administration of ganciclovir. Both ganciclovir dosage forms are approved for maintenance therapy.

Pharmacology/Pharmacokinetics

Physicochemical characteristics

Molecular weight—Valganciclovir hydrochloride: 390.83.
pKa—Valganciclovir hydrochloride: 7.6.
pH—7.

Mechanism of action/Effect

Valganciclovir is a prodrug of ganciclovir that exists as a mixture of two diastereomers. After administration, these diastereomers are rapidly converted to ganciclovir by hepatic and intestinal esterases.

In cytomegalovirus (CMV)-infected cells, ganciclovir is initially phosphorylated to the monophosphate form by viral protein kinase, then it is further phosphorylated via cellular kinases to produce the triphosphate form. This triphosphate form is slowly metabolized intracellularly. The phosphorylation is dependent upon the viral kinase, and occurs preferentially in virus-infected cells. The virustatic activity of ganciclovir is due to the inhibition of viral DNA synthesis by ganciclovir triphosphate.

Absorption

Valganciclovir is well absorbed from the gastrointestinal tract and the absolute bioavailability from valganciclovir tablets (following administration with food) is approximately 60%.

Distribution

Vol_D (steady state)—Approximately 0.7 L per kg following intravenous administration of ganciclovir.

Protein binding

Due to rapid conversion of valganciclovir to ganciclovir the plasma protein binding was not determined. Plasma protein binding of ganciclovir is 1% to 2% over concentrations of 0.5 and 51 mcg per mL (mcg/mL).

Biotransformation

Valganciclovir is rapidly hydrolyzed in the intestinal wall and liver to ganciclovir. No other metabolites have been detected.

Half-life

Ganciclovir—

Terminal: Oral—Approximately 4.08 hours; increased in patients with renal function impairment.

Time to peak concentration

Ganciclovir—1 to 3 hours.

Peak plasma concentration:

Ganciclovir—Approximately 5.6 mcg/mL.

Elimination

Renal; almost 100% excreted as unchanged ganciclovir in the urine by glomerular filtration and active tubular secretion.

In dialysis—The plasma concentrations of ganciclovir are decreased by approximately 50%. Use of valganciclovir is not recommended in patients who have a creatinine clearance less than 10 mL per minute and who are undergoing hemodialysis because the required daily dose is less than 450 mg.

Precautions to Consider

Cross-sensitivity and/or related problems

Patients hypersensitive to ganciclovir may also be hypersensitive to valganciclovir due to the chemical similarity of the two medications.

Carcinogenicity

No long term carcinogenicity studies have been conducted with valganciclovir. However, ganciclovir is a potential carcinogen and due to the rapid conversion of valganciclovir to ganciclovir, it is also considered a potential carcinogen.

Ganciclovir is carcinogenic in animals and should be considered a potential carcinogen in humans. Ganciclovir was carcinogenic in the mouse at oral doses of 20 and 1000 mg per kg of body weight (mg/kg) per day (approximately 0.1 and 1.4 times, respectively, the mean drug exposure in humans following the recommended intravenous dose of 5 mg/kg, based on the area under the plasma concentration-time curve [AUC]) comparisons. Mice given oral doses of 20 mg/kg per day showed a slightly increased incidence of tumors in the preputial and harderian glands in males, forestomach in males and females, and liver in females. Studies in mice given oral doses of 1000 mg/kg per day showed a significantly increased incidence of tumors of the forestomach in males and females, preputial gland in males, and reproductive tissues and liver in females. No carcinogenic effect occurred at a dose of 1 mg/kg per day (approximately 0.01 time the human dose based on AUC comparison).

Mutagenicity

Valganciclovir causes increased mutations in mouse lymphoma cells. In the mouse micronucleus assay, valganciclovir was clastogenic at a dose of 1500 mg/kg (60 times the mean human exposure of ganciclovir based on AUC). Valganciclovir was not mutagenic in the Ames Salmonella assay. Ganciclovir increased mutations in mouse lymphoma cells and DNA damage in human lymphocytes *in vitro* . In the mouse micronucleus assay, ganciclovir was clastogenic at intravenous doses of 150 and 500 mg/kg (2.8 to 10 times the human exposure based on AUC) but not 50 mg/kg (exposure approximately compared to the human based on AUC). Ganciclovir was not mutagenic in the Ames Salmonella assay.

Pregnancy/Reproduction

Fertility—Valganciclovir is converted to ganciclovir and is expected to have similar reproductive toxicity effects as ganciclovir. Ganciclovir caused decreased mating behavior, decreased fertility, and an increased incidence of embryolethality in female mice following intravenous doses of 90 mg/kg per day (approximately 1.7 times the mean drug exposure in humans following the dose of 5 mg/kg, based on AUC comparisons).

Ganciclovir caused decreased fertility in male mice and hypospermatogenesis in mice and dogs following daily oral or intravenous administration of doses ranging from 0.2 to 10 mg/kg. Systemic drug exposure (AUC) at the lowest dose showing toxicity in each species ranged from 0.03 to 0.1 time the AUC of the recommended human intravenous dose. Valganciclovir caused similar effects on spermatogenesis in mice, rats, and dogs. It is considered likely that ganciclovir and valganciclovir could cause inhibition of human spermatogenesis.

Pregnancy—Valganciclovir is converted to ganciclovir and is expected to have reproductive toxicity effects similar to ganciclovir.

Adequate and well-controlled studies in humans have not been done. However, ganciclovir has been found to cross the placenta. Due to the high toxicity and mutagenic and teratogenic potential of ganciclovir, use during pregnancy should be avoided whenever possible. Women of childbearing age should use effective contraception. Men should use barrier contraception during, and for at least 90 days following, treatment with ganciclovir.

Ganciclovir has been shown to be embryotoxic in rabbits and mice following intravenous administration, and teratogenic in rabbits. Fetal resorptions were present in at least 85% of the rabbits and mice administered 60 and 108 mg/kg per day (2 times the human exposure based on AUC comparisons), respectively. Effects observed in rabbits included fetal growth retardation, embryolethality, teratogenicity and/or maternal toxicity. Teratogenic changes included cleft palate, anophthalmia/microphthalmia, aplastic organs (kidney and pancreas), hydrocephaly and brachygnathia. In mice, effects observed were maternal/fetal toxicity and embryolethality.

Daily intravenous doses of 90 mg/kg administered to female mice prior to mating, during gestation, and during lactation caused hypoplasia of the testes and seminal vesicles in the month-old male offspring, as well as pathologic changes in the nonglandular region of the stomach. The drug exposure in mice as estimated by the AUC was approximately 1.7 times the human AUC.

Valganciclovir may be teratogenic or embryotoxic at dose levels recommended for human use.

FDA Pregnancy Category C.

Breast-feeding

It is not known whether valganciclovir or ganciclovir is distributed into breast milk. The potential of serious adverse events from ganciclovir in nursing infants exists and breast-feeding should be stopped during ganciclovir therapy.

The Centers for Disease Control and Prevention (CDC) recommended that human immunodeficiency virus (HIV)-infected mothers not breast-feed their infants to avoid risking postnatal transmission of HIV.

Pediatrics

No information is available on the relationship of age to the effects of valganciclovir in the pediatric population. Safety and efficacy have not been established.

Geriatrics

No information is available on the relationship of age to the effects of valganciclovir in geriatric patients. However, elderly patients are more likely to have age-related renal function impairment, which may require adjustment of dosage or dosing interval in patients receiving valganciclovir.

Dental

The neutropenic and thrombocytopenic effects of ganciclovir may result in an increased incidence of microbial infection, delayed healing, and gingival bleeding. Patients should be instructed in proper oral hygiene, including caution in the use of regular toothbrushes, dental floss, and toothpicks.

Drug interactions and/or related problems

The following drug interactions and/or related problems have been selected on the basis of their potential clinical significance (possible mechanism in parentheses where appropriate)—not necessarily inclusive (» = major clinical significance):

Note: Combinations containing any of the following medications, depending on the amount present, may also interact with this medication.

No *in vivo* drug-drug interaction studies were done with valganciclovir. Because valganciclovir is rapidly and extensively converted to ganciclovir, interactions associated with ganciclovir will be expected for valganciclovir.

Blood dyscrasia-causing medications (see *Appendix II*) or
» Bone marrow depressants, other (see *Appendix II*) or
Radiation therapy
(concurrent use with valganciclovir may increase the bone marrow–depressant effects of these medications and radiation therapy)

» Didanosine
(concurrent and sequential [2 hours prior] administration of didanosine with valganciclovir results in a significant increase in the steady-state area under the plasma concentration-time curve [AUC] of didanosine [range, 50 to 111%]; patients should be closely monitored for signs of didanosine toxicity)

» Mycophenolate
(patients with impaired renal function should be closely monitored as concentrations of metabolites of both drugs may increase)

» Probenecid
(concurrent use with probenecid increases the AUC of ganciclovir by approximately 53% and decreases its renal clearance by approximately 22%; patients should be monitored for evidence of ganciclovir toxicity)

» Zidovudine
(both valganciclovir and zidovudine have the potential to cause neutropenia and anemia; some patients may not tolerate concomitant therapy at full dosage)

Laboratory value alterations

The following have been selected on the basis of their potential clinical significance (possible effect in parentheses where appropriate)—not necessarily inclusive (» = major clinical significance).

With physiology/laboratory test values
» Absolute neutrophil count and
» Hemoglobin concentration and
» Platelet count
(values may be decreased)
» Creatinine clearance
(value may be decreased)
» Creatinine, serum
(value may be increased)

Medical considerations/Contraindications

The medical considerations/contraindications included have been selected on the basis of their potential clinical significance (reasons given in parentheses where appropriate)—not necessarily inclusive (» = major clinical significance).

Except under special circumstances, this medication should not be used when the following medical problems exist:
» Absolute neutrophil count (ANC) < 500 cells per microliter, hemoglobin concentration < 8 grams per deciliter, or platelet count < 25,000 cells per microliter

Risk-benefit should be considered when the following medical problems exist:
» Hypersensitivity to valganciclovir or ganciclovir
» Renal function impairment
(because ganciclovir is excreted through the kidneys, the dose of valganciclovir should be reduced or the dosing interval increased in patients with renal function impairment; use of valganciclovir is not recommended in patients who have a creatinine clearance less than 10 mL per minute and who are undergoing hemodialysis because the required daily dose is less than 450 mg)

Patient monitoring

The following may be especially important in patient monitoring (other tests may be warranted in some patients, depending on condition; » = major clinical significance):
» Complete blood count (CBC)
(because valganciclovir may cause granulocytopenia and thrombocytopenia, a complete blood count should be performed prior to treatment and frequently during treatment; increased frequency of monitoring may be required in patients with neutrophil counts less than 1000 cells/microliter and those in whom use of valganciclovir or ganciclovir or other nucleoside analogs previously resulted in leukopenia)
» Creatinine clearance or
» Creatinine concentration, serum
(values should be closely monitored in patients with renal function impairment to guide dosing)
» Ophthalmologic examinations
(ophthalmologic examinations should be performed every 4 to 6 weeks during therapy since valganciclovir is not a cure for cytomegalovirus [CMV] retinitis, and progression of retinitis may occur during or following valganciclovir treatment; some patients may require more frequent examinations)

Side/Adverse Effects

The following side/adverse effects have been selected on the basis of their potential clinical significance (possible signs and symptoms in parentheses where appropriate)—not necessarily inclusive:

Those indicating need for medical attention

Incidence more frequent
Anemia (pale skin; troubled breathing, exertional; unusual tiredness or weakness); ***neutropenia*** (chills; cough; fever; hoarseness; lower back or side pain; painful or difficult urination; sore throat; ulcers, sores, or white spots in mouth; unusual tiredness or weakness); ***pyrexia*** (fever); ***retinal detachment*** (veil or curtain appearing across part of vision; seeing flashes or sparks of light; seeing floating spots before eyes); ***thrombocytopenia*** (black, tarry stools; blood in urine or stools; pinpoint red spots on skin; unusual bleeding or bruising)

Incidence less frequent
Bleeding—associated with thrombocytopenia; may be life-threatening; ***bone marrow depression*** (fever; sore throat; unusual bleeding or bruising; unusual tiredness or weakness); ***hallucinations*** (feeling, hearing, or seeing things that are not there); ***hypersensitivity reaction*** (anaphylaxis; angioedema; asthma; dermatitis; rhinitis; urticaria); ***infection, local or systemic, or sepsis*** (chills; fever); ***pancytopenia*** (shortness of breath or troubled breathing; sores, ulcers, or white spots on lips or in mouth; tightness in chest and/or wheezing; unusual bleeding or bruising; unusual tiredness or weakness); ***psychosis*** (confusion; delusions; hallucinations; illogical thinking); ***seizures***

Those indicating need for medical attention only if they continue or are bothersome

Incidence more frequent
Abdominal pain; diarrhea; headache; insomnia (sleeplessness; trouble sleeping); ***nausea and vomiting; paresthesia*** (tingling, burning, or prickly sensations); ***peripheral neuropathy*** (numbness, tingling, pain, or weakness of hands or feet)

Incidence less frequent
Agitation; confusion

Overdose

For more information on the management of overdose or unintentional ingestion, **contact a poison control center** (see *Poison Control Center Listing*).

Clinical effects of overdose

The following effects have been selected on the basis of their potential clinical significance (possible signs and symptoms in parentheses where appropriate)—not necessarily inclusive:
Abdominal pain; acute renal failure (decreased frequency or amount of urine; fast or slow heartbeat; loss of appetite; nausea; shortness of breath; unusual tiredness or weakness); ***bone marrow depression*** (fever; sore throat; unusual bleeding or bruising; unusual tiredness or weakness)—progressed to medullary aplasia in one patient; ***diarrhea; elevated creatinine concentrations; granulocytopenia or leukopenia*** (chills; cough; fever; hoarseness; lower back or side pain; painful or difficult urination; shortness of breath; sore throat; ulcers, sores, or white spots in mouth; unusual tiredness or weakness); ***hematuria*** (blood in the urine)—in patients with existing renal function impairment; ***hepatitis*** (anorexia; diarrhea; nausea; vomiting); ***increased renal toxicity*** (agitation; coma; confusion; decreased urine output; depression; dizziness; headache; hostility; irritability; lethargy; muscle twitching; nausea; rapid weight gain; seizures; stupor; swelling of face, ankles, or hands; unusual tiredness or weakness); ***liver function disorder; pancytopenia*** (shortness of breath or troubled breathing; sores, ulcers, or white spots on lips or in mouth; tightness in chest and/or wheezing; unusual bleeding or bruising; unusual tiredness or weakness); ***seizures; tremor, generalized*** (quivering; trembling); ***vomiting***

Treatment of overdose

To enhance elimination—
Dialysis may be useful in reducing serum concentrations as ganciclovir is dialyzable.

Specific treatment—
The use of hematopoietic growth factors should be considered.

Supportive care—
Adequate hydration should be maintained.
Patients in whom intentional overdose is confirmed or suspected should be referred for psychiatric consultation.

Patient Consultation

As an aid to patient consultation, refer to *Advice for the Patient, Valganciclovir (Systemic)*.

In providing consultation, consider emphasizing the following selected information (» = major clinical significance):

Before using this medication

» Conditions affecting use, especially:
Hypersensitivity to valganciclovir or ganciclovir
Pregnancy—Use of valganciclovir during pregnancy should be avoided whenever possible. Ganciclovir crosses the placenta and has been found to be carcinogenic and teratogenic in animals. Use of effective contraception by men and women who are undergoing treatment and in men for 90 days following treatment is recommended
Breast-feeding—Because of valganciclovir's potential for severe toxicity, breast-feeding should be stopped during therapy
Other medications, especially other bone marrow depressants, didanosine, mycophenolate, probenecid, or zidovudine
Other medical problems, especially an absolute neutrophil count (ANC) < 500 cells per microliter (cells/microliter), platelet count < 25,000 cells/microliter, hemoglobin concentration < 8 grams/deciliter, or renal function impairment

Proper use of this medication

» Taking valganciclovir capsules with food

» Importance of taking medication for full course of therapy and on a regular schedule

» Proper dosing

Proper storage

Precautions while using this medication

» Regular visits to physician to check blood counts

» Regular visits to ophthalmologist to examine eyes since progression of retinitis and visual loss may occur during valganciclovir therapy

Caution if bone marrow depression occurs:

» Avoiding exposure to persons with bacterial infections, especially during periods of low blood counts; checking with physician immediately if fever or chills, cough or hoarseness, lower back or side pain, or painful or difficult urination occur

» Checking with physician immediately if unusual bleeding or bruising, black, tarry stools; blood in urine or stools; or pinpoint red spots on skin occur

Caution in use of regular toothbrush, dental floss, or toothpick; physician, dentist, or nurse may suggest alternatives; checking with physician before having dental work done

Using caution to avoid accidental cuts with use of sharp objects such as safety razor or fingernail or toenail cutters

Not coming into contact with broken or crushed tablets; if contact is made with skin, washing with soap and water; if contact is made with eyes, rinsing with clear water

Side/adverse effects

Signs of potential side effects, especially anemia, neutropenia, pyrexia, retinal detachment, thrombocytopenia, bleeding, bone marrow depression, hallucinations, hypersensitivity reaction, infection or sepsis, pancytopenia, psychosis, and seizures

General Dosing Information

The bioavailability of ganciclovir from valganciclovir tablets is significantly higher than from ganciclovir capsules. Patients switching from ganciclovir capsules to valganciclovir tablets should be advised of the risk of overdosage if they take more than the prescribed number of valganciclovir tablets. Valganciclovir tablets cannot be substituted for ganciclovir capsules on a one-to-one basis.

Diet/Nutrition

Valganciclovir should be taken with food for maximum absorption.

Safety considerations for handling this medication

Caution should be exercised in the handling and preparation of valganciclovir. Because valganciclovir shares some properties of anti-tumor agents (i.e., carcinogenicity and mutagenicity), it should be handled and disposed of according to guidelines issued for cytotoxic drugs. Avoid inhalation, ingestion, or direct contact of broken or crushed valganciclovir tablets with the skin or mucous membranes. If contact does occur, wash area thoroughly with soap and water; rinse eyes thoroughly with plain water.

Oral Dosage Forms

VALGANCICLOVIR HYDROCHLORIDE TABLETS

Note: Strict adherence to dosage recommendations is essential to avoid overdose.

The dosing and strengths of the dosage form are expressed in terms of valganciclovir base (not the hydrochloride salt).

Usual adult dose

Cytomegalovirus retinitis—

Patients with normal renal function—

Induction—Oral, 900 mg (base) two times a day with food for twenty-one days.

Maintenance—Oral, 900 mg once a day with food.

Patients with renal function impairment—

Creatinine clearance ≥ 60 mL per minute:

See *Usual adult dose.*

Creatinine clearance 40 to 59 mL per minute—

Induction: 450 mg two times a day with food for twenty-one days.

Maintenance: 450 mg once a day with food.

Creatinine clearance 25 to 39 mL per minute—

Induction: 450 mg once a day with food for twenty-one days.

Maintenance: 450 mg every two days with food.

Creatinine clearance 10 to 24 mL per minute—

Induction: 450 mg every two days with food for a total of twenty-one days.

Maintenance: 450 mg two times a week with food.

Creatinine clearance < 10 mL per minute—

Use of valganciclovir is not recommended because the required daily dose is less than 450 mg.

Usual pediatric dose

Safety and efficacy have not been established.

Strength(s) usually available

U.S.—

450 mg (base) (Rx) [*Valcyte* (microcrystalline cellulose; povidone K-30; crospovidone; stearic acid)].

Packaging and storage

Store at 25 °C (77 °F), excursions permitted between 15 and 30 °C (59 and 86 °F).

Note

Care should be taken in the handling of valganciclovir as it is a potential carcinogen and teratogen. Avoid direct contact of broken or crushed tablets with skin or mucous membranes. If contact occurs, wash with soap and water and rinse eyes thoroughly with plain water.

Developed: 06/27/2001

VALPROATE SODIUM—See *Valproic Acid (Systemic)*

VALPROIC ACID Systemic

This monograph includes information on the following: 1) Divalproex; 2) Valproate Sodium†; 3) Valproic Acid.

INN: Divalproex Sodium—Valproate Semisodium

BAN: Divalproex Sodium—Semisodium Valproate

JAN: Valproate Sodium—Sodium Valproate

VA CLASSIFICATION (Primary/Secondary):

Divalproex—CN400/CN105; CN900

Valproate Sodium—CN400

Valproic Acid—CN400

Commonly used brand name(s): *Alti-Valproic*[3]; *Depacon*[2]; *Depakene*[3]; *Depakote*[1]; *Depakote Sprinkle*[1]; *Deproic*[3]; *Dom-Valproic*[3]; *Epival*[1]; *Med Valproic*[3]; *Novo-Valproic*[3]; *Nu-Valproic*[3]; *PMS-Valproic Acid*[3]; *Penta-Valproic*[3]; *pms-Valproic Acid*[3]; *pms-Valproic Acid E.C.*[3].

Note: For a listing of dosage forms and brand names by country availability, see *Dosage Forms* section(s).

†Not commercially available in Canada.

Category

Anticonvulsant; antimanic; migraine headache prophylactic.

Indications

Note: Bracketed information in the *Indications* section refers to uses that are not included in U.S. product labeling.

Accepted

Epilepsy, absence seizure pattern (treatment)—Valproic acid, divalproex, and valproate sodium are indicated in the treatment of simple and complex absence (petit mal) seizures. Although these agents may be used alone or with other anticonvulsant medication, monotherapy with valproic acid, divalproex, or valproate sodium is preferred whenever possible because of unpredictable interactions with hepatic enzyme-inducing anticonvulsants and because of the increased risk of hepatotoxicity.

Epilepsy, mixed seizure pattern (treatment adjunct)—Valproic acid, divalproex, and valproate sodium are indicated as adjuncts in conditions of multiple seizures that include absence seizures.

[Epilepsy, myoclonic seizure pattern (treatment)]—Valproic acid, divalproex, and valproate sodium are used as primary agents for myoclonic seizures.

[Epilepsy, simple partial seizure pattern (treatment)] or
Epilepsy, complex partial seizure pattern (treatment)—Valproic acid, divalproex, and valproate sodium may be useful in patients with partial seizures that are refractory to other anticonvulsants.

[Epilepsy, tonic-clonic seizure pattern (treatment)]—Valproic acid, divalproex, and valproate sodium are used as primary agents in the treatment of tonic-clonic (grand mal) seizures.

Bipolar disorder, manic episodes (treatment)—Divalproex is indicated for the treatment of manic episodes associated with bipolar disorder.

[Bipolar disorder (prophylaxis and treatment)]—Valproic acid and divalproex may be useful in the prophylaxis and treatment of manic-depressive illness refractory to treatment with lithium or other agents.

Migraine headaches (prophylaxis)[1]—Divalproex is indicated in the prophylaxis of migraine headaches. There is no evidence that it may be useful in the treatment of acute migraine.

[1]Not included in Canadian product labeling.

Pharmacology/Pharmacokinetics

Note: Divalproex sodium is a stable coordination compound composed of equal parts of valproic acid and sodium valproate. In the gastrointestinal tract, divalproex sodium dissociates into valproate and then produces the bioequivalent pharmacologic activity of valproic acid. Equivalent oral doses of divalproex sodium and valproic acid capsules deliver systemically equivalent quantities of valproate ion. Valproate sodium injection exists as the valproate ion in the blood and yields plasma levels equivalent to those of the oral valproic acid and divalproex products. In this monograph, the term valproate is used to designate the valproate ion in the body, whether administered as valproic acid, divalproex sodium, or valproate sodium.

Physicochemical characteristics

Molecular weight—
- Divalproex sodium: 310.41.
- Valproate sodium: 166.2.
- Valproic acid: 144.21.

pKa—Valproic acid: 4.8.

pH—Valproate sodium injection: 7.6.

Mechanism of action/Effect

The mechanism of action has not been established; however, it is thought to be related to a direct or secondary increase in concentrations of the inhibitory neurotransmitter, gamma-aminobutyric acid (GABA), possibly caused by its decreased metabolism or decreased reuptake in brain tissues. Another hypothesis is that valproate acts on postsynaptic receptor sites to mimic or enhance the inhibitory action of GABA. The effect on the neuronal membrane is not completely understood. Some studies suggest a possible direct effect on membrane activity related to changes in potassium conductance.Also, valproate has been shown in animal studies to block sustained neuronal bursting responses by reducing the amplitude of sodium-dependent action potentials in a voltage- and use-dependent manner.

Other actions/effects

Valproate is a weak inhibitor of some hepatic P450 isoenzymes, as well as epoxide hydrase and glucuronosyl transferase.

Absorption

Divalproex sodium—Enteric coating on the tablet delays absorption for about 1 to 4 hours after ingestion; concomitant administration with food may significantly slow the rate, but not the extent, of absorption.

Valproic acid—Rapid absorption from gastrointestinal tract; slight delay when taken with food.

Distribution

Valproate concentrations in the cerebrospinal fluid approximate unbound concentrations in plasma, which is about 10% of the total concentration. Valproate is distributed into breast milk in concentrations ranging from 1 to 10% of total maternal serum concentrations.

Volume of distribution is increased in children within the first two months of life which decreases the ability to eliminate valproate; in part due to decreased plasma protein binding.

Protein binding

High (90 to 95%) at serum concentrations up to 50 micrograms (mcg) per mL; as the concentration increases from 50 to 100 mcg per mL, the percentage bound decreases to 80 to 85% and the free fraction becomes progressively larger, thus increasing the concentration gradient into the brain. Protein binding of valproate is reduced in the elderly, in patients with hypoalbuminemia, in patients with chronic hepatic diseases, and in patients with renal function impairment.

The plasma protein binding of valproate is concentration dependent and the free fraction increases from approximately 10% at 40 micrograms per milliliter to 18.5% at 130 micrograms per milliliter.

Patients with liver disease have decreased albumin concentrations and larger unbound fractions (2–2.6 fold increase) of valproate.

Biotransformation

Primarily hepatic. Some metabolites may have pharmacologic or toxic activity. Rate of metabolism is faster in children and in patients currently using hepatic enzyme-inducing medications, such as carbamazepine, phenobarbital, phenytoin, and primidone.

Half-life

Variable, from 6 to 16 hours; may be considerably longer in patients with hepatic function impairment, in the elderly, and in children up to 18 months of age; may be considerably shorter in patients receiving hepatic enzyme-inducing anticonvulsants.

Mean terminal half-life for valproate monotherapy following a 60-minute intravenous infusion of 1000 mg was 16 ± 3 hours.

In one study, the half-life in children under 10 days ranged from 10 to 67 hours compared to a range of 7 to 13 hours in children greater than 2 months.

In a study of patients with liver disease, the half-life of valproate was increased from 12 hours in healthy patients to 18 hours in patients with liver disease.

Time to peak serum concentration

Capsules and syrup—1 to 4 hours.

Delayed-release capsules and tablets—3 to 4 hours.

Injection—At the end of a 1-hour intravenous infusion.

Therapeutic plasma concentrations

Variable. The therapeutic range in epilepsy is commonly considered to be 50 to 100 mcg per mL (347 to 693 micromoles per L) of total valproate, although some patients may require higher or lower plasma concentrations.

The relationship between plasma concentration and clinical response is not well documented. One contributing factor is the nonlinear, concentration-dependent protein binding of valproate, which affects the clearance of the medication. Monitoring of total serum valproate cannot provide a reliable index of the bioactive valproate species.

Elimination

Renal, mainly as glucuronide conjugate; small amounts excreted in feces and expired air.

Pediatric patients between 3 months and 10 years have a 50% higher clearance expressed on weight than do adults. Patients over the age of 10 years have pharmacokinetic parameters that approximate adults.

Children within the first two months of life have a markedly decrease ability to eliminate valproate compared to older children and adults; this is a result of reduced clearance, perhaps due to the delay in development of glucuronosyltransferase and other enzyme systems involved in valproate elimination.

The capacity of elderly patients (ages 68 to 89) to eliminate valproate has been shown to be reduced compared to younger adults (ages 22 to 26). Intrinsic clearance is reduced by 39%; the free fraction is increased by 44%.

The capacity to eliminate valproate is impaired in patients with liver disease. In one study, the clearance of free valproate was decreased by 50% in 7 patients with cirrhosis and by 16% in 4 patients with acute hepatitis, compared with healthy subjects.

Precautions to Consider

Carcinogenicity/Tumorigenicity

Studies in rodents given valproic acid doses of 0, 80, and 170 mg per kg of body weight (mg/kg) a day for 2 years showed a variety of neoplasms and an increase in the incidence of subcutaneous fibrosarcomas in male rats receiving high doses, as well as a dose-related trend for benign pulmonary adenomas in male mice. The significance of these findings humans is not known.

Mutagenicity

Valproate was not mutagenic in an *in vitro* bacterial assay (Ames test), did not produce dominant lethal effects in mice, and did not increase chromosome aberration frequency in an *in vivo* cytogenetic study in rats. Increased frequency of sister chromatid exchange (SCE) has been reported in a study of epileptic children taking valproate, but this association was not observed in another study in adults. There is some evidence that increased SCE frequencies may be associated with epilepsy. The biological significance of an increase in SCE frequency is not known.

Pregnancy/Reproduction

Fertility—Long-term toxicity studies in rats given doses greater than 200 mg/kg a day and dogs given doses greater than 90 mg/kg a day have shown reduced spermatogenesis and testicular atrophy. Segment I fertility studies in rats given up to 350 mg/kg a day for 60 days have shown no effect on fertility. However, the effect of valproate on the development of the testes and on sperm production and fertility in humans is unknown.

Pregnancy—First trimester: Valproate crosses the placenta and has been reported to have caused teratogenic effects, including neural tube defects (anencephaly, meningomyelocele, and spina bifida) in the fetus when the mother received valproate during the first trimester of pregnancy. Risk-benefit must be carefully considered when these medications are required to treat epilepsy in pregnant patients for whom other medications are ineffective or cannot be used.

Studies in rodents have shown that skeletal abnormalities, primarily involving ribs and vertebrae, occurred in the offspring when the mother received doses exceeding 65 mg/kg per day during pregnancy.

FDA Pregnancy Category D.

Breast-feeding

Valproate is distributed into breast milk. Concentrations in breast milk have been reported to be l to 10% of the total maternal serum concentration.

Pediatrics

Children are at an increased risk of developing serious or fatal hepatotoxicity. Patients up to 2 years of age, especially those on polytherapy, those with congenital metabolic disorders, those with severe seizure disorders accompanied by mental retardation, and those with organic brain disease, appear to be at greatest risk. Depakote should be used with extreme caution and as a sole agent in patients under 2 years of age. Experience in patients with epilepsy has shown that the risk of fatal hepatotoxicity decreases with advancing age.

Geriatrics

Geriatric patients tend to have increased free, unbound valproate concentrations and lowered intrinsic clearances, indicating a reduction of valproate metabolizing capacity and a fall in serum albumin. These patients may also be more susceptible to certain adverse reactions including somnolence. Therefore, these patients should receive a lower daily dosage, and the serum concentrations should be kept in the lower therapeutic range.

Dental

Valproate inhibits the secondary phase of platelet aggregation, which may be reflected in prolonged bleeding time and/or frank hemorrhaging.

In addition, the leukopenic and thrombocytopenic effects of valproate may result in an increased incidence of microbial infection, delayed healing, and gingival bleeding. If leukopenia or thrombocytopenia occurs, dental work, whenever possible, should be deferred until blood counts have returned to normal. Patients should be instructed in proper oral hygiene, including caution in use of regular toothbrushes, dental floss, and toothpicks.

Surgical

Surgical—Because of the thrombocytopenic effects of valproate, as well as its inhibition of the secondary phase of platelet aggregation and production of abnormal coagulation parameters (e.g., low fibrinogen), monitoring of platelet counts and coagulation tests are recommended in patients prior to scheduled surgery.

Drug interactions and/or related problems

The following drug interactions and/or related problems have been selected on the basis of their potential clinical significance (possible mechanism in parentheses where appropriate)—not necessarily inclusive (» = major clinical significance):

Note: In addition to the interactions listed below, additive or multiple effects leading to impaired blood clotting and/or increased risk of bleeding may occur if valproic acid, divalproex, or valproate sodium is used concurrently with any other medication having a significant potential for inhibiting platelet aggregation or for causing hypoprothrombinemia, thrombocytopenia, or gastrointestinal ulceration or hemorrhage.

Combinations containing any of the following medications, depending on the amount present, may also interact with this medication.

» Alcohol or
» Central nervous system (CNS) depression-producing medications, other (see *Appendix II*)
(concurrent use with valproic acid, divalproex, or valproate sodium may potentiate CNS depressant effects)

» Amitriptyline and nortriptyline
(may decrease plasma clearance of amitriptyline and nortriptyline; consideration should be give to lowering the dose of these medicines)

» Anticoagulants, coumarin- or indandione-derivative or
» Heparin or
» Thrombolytic agents
(valproate-induced hypoprothrombinemia may increase the activity of coumarin- and indandione-derivative anticoagulants and may increase the risk of bleeding in patients receiving heparin or thrombolytic agents)
(inhibition of platelet aggregation and reduction of platelet numbers or thrombocytopenia may increase the risk of hemorrhage in patients receiving anticoagulant or thrombolytic therapy; coagulation tests are recommended)

Antidepressants, tricyclic or
Bupropion or
Clozapine or
Haloperidol or
Loxapine or
Maprotiline or
Molindone or
Monoamine oxidase (MAO) inhibitors or
Phenothiazines or
Pimozide or
Thioxanthenes
(in addition to enhancing CNS depression when used concurrently with valproic acid, divalproex, or valproate sodium, these medications may lower the seizure threshold; dosage adjustments may be necessary to control seizures)

» Aspirin
(may decrease protein binding and inhibit valproate metabolism; caution should be observed)

» Barbiturates or
» Primidone
(concurrent use with valproate causes higher serum concentrations of barbiturates or primidone, leading to increased CNS depression and neurological toxicity because of protein binding displacement of the barbiturate and reduced barbiturate metabolism; half-life of valproate is decreased; dosage adjustment of barbiturates or primidone may be necessary)

» Carbamazepine
(concurrent use may result in decreased serum concentrations and half-life of valproate due to increased metabolism induced by hepatic microsomal enzyme activity; valproate causes an increase in the active 10,11-epoxide metabolite of carbamazepine by inhibiting its breakdown; monitoring of serum concentrations as a guide to dosage is recommended, especially when either medication is added to or withdrawn from an existing regimen)

Clonazepam
(concurrent use with valproic acid, divalproex, or valproate sodium may produce absence status in patients with a history of absence type seizures)

Diazepam
(valproate may displace diazepam from its plasma albumin binding sites and may inhibit its metabolism; coadministration was found to increase the free fraction of diazepam by 90% in healthy volunteers; plasma clearance of free diazepam was reduced by 25% and volume of distribution of free diazepam was reduced by 20% in the presence of valproate; the elimination half-life of diazepam remained unchanged)

Ethosuximide, and possibly other succinimide anticonvulsants
(concurrent use with valproic acid, divalproex, or valproate sodium has been reported to both increase and decrease ethosuximide concentrations; monitoring of serum concentrations as a guide to dosage is recommended)

» Felbamate
(coadministration of felbamate may increase valproate plasma concentrations by 35 to 50%; a decrease in valproic acid, divalproex, or valproate sodium dosage may be needed when felbamate therapy is initiated)

» Hepatotoxic medications, other (see *Appendix II*)
(concurrent use with valproic acid, divalproex, or valproate sodium may increase the risk of hepatotoxicity; patients on prolonged therapy or with a history of liver disease should be carefully monitored)

» Lamotrigine
(elimination half-life of lamotrigine was increased from 26 to 70 hours in a steady-state study in volunteers receiving both lamotrigine and valproate; when coadministered with valproate, the dose of lamotrigine should be reduced; concurrent use of lamotrigine with valproate may increase the risk of dangerous dermatologic reactions)

Levocarnitine
(requirements for carnitine may be increased in patients receiving valproic acid or divalproex)

» Mefloquine
(concurrent use with valproic acid, divalproex, or valproate sodium may result in low valproate serum concentrations and loss of seizure control; monitoring of valproate serum concentrations is rec-

ommended and dosage adjustments may be necessary during and after therapy with mefloquine)

Phenobarbital
(valproate was found to inhibit the metabolism of phenobarbital)

» Phenytoin, and possibly other hydantoin anticonvulsants
(concurrent use with valproic acid, divalproex, or valproate sodium has resulted in breakthrough seizures or phenytoin toxicity because valproate may interfere with phenytoin protein binding, and phenytoin, through enzyme induction, will lower valproate levels; valproate increases unbound phenytoin concentrations and decreases intrinsic clearance by inhibiting metabolism of phenytoin; concurrent use requires close monitoring of the patient since variable serum phenytoin concentrations have resulted; total phenytoin serum concentrations may not reflect unbound phenytoin activity, and unbound phenytoin concentrations may be more reliable; dosage of phenytoin should be adjusted as required by clinical situation)

» Platelet aggregation inhibitors, other (see *Appendix II*)
(concurrent use with valproic acid, divalproex, or valproate sodium may increase the risk of hemorrhage because of additive or multiple actions that may decrease blood-clotting ability)
(the gastrointestinal ulcerative or hemorrhagic potential of aspirin, anti-inflammatory analgesics, or sulfinpyrazone may increase the risk of hemorrhage in patients receiving valproic acid, divalproex, or valproate sodium)
(in addition, aspirin may displace valproic acid, divalproex, or valproate sodium from protein binding sites, as well as altering valproate metabolism and excretion, resulting in increased levels of free [unbound] valproate, which may cause toxic effects)

Rifampin
(unpublished data obtained by the manufacturer suggest that increased clearance of single-dose oral valproate occurs following pretreatment with oral rifampin; dosage adjustments may be necessary if valproate and rifampin are used concurrently)

Sodium benzoate and sodium phenylacetate combination
(valproate-induced hyperammonemia may exacerbate urea cycle enzymopathy deficiency and antagonize the efficacy of sodium benzoate and sodium phenylacetate combination)

Zidovudine
(in six HIV-positive patients, the clearance of zidovudine was decreased by 38% following administration of valproate; the half-life of zidovudine was unaffected)

Laboratory value alterations

The following have been selected on the basis of their potential clinical significance (possible effect in parentheses where appropriate)—not necessarily inclusive (» = major clinical significance).

With diagnostic test results

Metyrapone test
(increased metabolism of metyrapone by a hepatic enzyme inducer such as valproic acid, divalproex, or valproate sodium may decrease the response to metyrapone)

Thyroid function tests
(test results may be altered; decreased T_4, and free T_3 and T_4 concentrations have been reported; clinical significance is unknown)

Urine ketone tests
(use of valproic acid, divalproex, or valproate sodium may produce false-positive results because of a ketone metabolite excreted in urine)

With physiology/laboratory test values

Alanine aminotransferase (ALT [SGPT]) and
Aspartate aminotransferase (AST [SGOT]) and
Lactate dehydrogenase (LDH)
(minor elevations of serum concentrations occur frequently and appear to be dose-related; elevations may indicate asymptomatic hepatotoxicity)

Amino acid screening
(increases in glycine may occur)

Bilirubin
(serum concentrations may be increased; increase may indicate potentially serious hepatotoxicity)

Medical considerations/Contraindications

The medical considerations/contraindications included have been selected on the basis of their potential clinical significance (reasons given in parentheses where appropriate)—not necessarily inclusive (» = major clinical significance).

Except under special circumstances, this medication should not be used when the following medical problems exist:

» Hepatic disease or
» Hepatic function impairment, significant
(symptoms may be exacerbated; hepatic failures resulting in fatalities have been reported; may impair ability to eliminate valproate)

» Pancreatitis
(may be life threatening; valproate should ordinarily be discontinued following diagnosis)

Urea cycle disorders
(may lead to hyperammonemic encephalopathy, sometimes fatal)

Risk-benefit should be considered when the following medical problems exist:

Blood dyscrasias or
Brain disease, organic or
Hepatic disease, history of
(may be exacerbated)

Hypoalbuminemia
(alterations in protein binding may affect serum levels)

Renal function impairment
(metabolites may accumulate; valproate binding to serum albumin is decreased and volume of distribution is increased)

Sensitivity to valproic acid, divalproex, or valproate sodium

Patient monitoring

The following may be especially important in patient monitoring (other tests may be warranted in some patients, depending on condition; » = major clinical significance):

Amitriptyline/ nortriptyline concentrations, serum or
Ethosuximide concentrations, serum
(recommended when these medicines are taken with valproic acid)

Ammonia concentrations, serum
(therapy should be discontinued if hyperammonemia occurs, with or without lethargy or coma)

Bleeding time determinations and
Blood cell counts, including platelets and
Renal function determinations
(recommended prior to therapy and periodically during therapy)

Hepatic function determinations
(should be performed prior to therapy and periodically thereafter, especially during the first 6 months of therapy; valproic acid, divalproex, or valproate sodium should be discontinued immediately if significant hepatic function impairment is apparent or suspected)

Valproate concentrations, serum
(since therapeutic concentrations vary widely, morning trough concentrations with values ranging from 50 to 100 mcg per mL [347 to 693 micromoles per L] may be useful when initiating therapy; doses may be raised gradually until patient achieves a predose serum concentration of at least 50 mcg per mL [347 micromoles per L], the dose then being increased as needed)
(total trough valproate plasma concentrations above 110 mcg/mL in females and 135 mcg/mL in males significantly increase the probability of thrombocytopenia; risk-benefit must be considered)
(since serum valproate concentrations do not always correspond with therapeutic effect, evaluation of dose adjustments must be based on total clinical assessment of the patient)

Side/Adverse Effects

Note: Hepatic failure resulting in death has occurred in patients receiving valproic acid and divalproex. These incidents usually have occurred during the first 6 months of treatment. Patients at greatest risk are children receiving other anticonvulsants along with valproic acid, divalproex, or valproate sodium. Serious or fatal hepatotoxicity may be preceded by nonspecific symptoms such as loss of seizure control, malaise, weakness, lethargy, Reye's-like syndrome, anorexia, vomiting, jaundice, and edema.Hepatic failure, resulting in the death of a newborn and of an infant, have been reported following the use of valproate during pregnancy. In some cases, hepatic function impairment has progressed despite discontinuation of medication.

Valproate can produce teratogenic effects such as neural tube defects in the fetus, such defects may be increased in mothers receiving valproate during the first trimester of pregnancy. There are multiple reports which indicate that the use of antiepileptic drugs during pregnancy resulted in an increase incidence of birth defects in the offspring. The Center for Disease Control (CDC) has estimated the risk of valproic acid exposed to women having children with spina bifida to be approximately 1 to 2%.

Reports of congenital anomalies, compatible and incompatible with life, have been reported (eg, craniofacial defects, cardiovascular malformations and anomalies involving various body systems).

Patients taking valproate may develop clotting abnormalities. Report of a patient with low fibrinogen taking multiple anticonvulsants, including valproate, gave birth to an infant with afibrinogenemia who subsequently died of hemorrhage.

Hyperammonemic encephalopathy, sometimes fatal, have been reported following initiation of valproate therapy in patients with urea cycle disorders, a group of uncommon genetic abnormalities, particularly ornithine transcarbamylase deficiency. Symptoms of hyperammonemic encephalopathy include unexplained lethargy and vomiting or changes in mental status

Cases of life-threatening pancreatitis have been reported in both children and adults receiving valproate. Some of the cases have been described as hemorrhagic with a rapid progression from initial symptoms to death. Cases have been reported shortly after initial use as well as after several years of use. Patients and guardians should be warned that abdominal pain, nausea, vomiting, and/or anorexia can be symptoms of pancreatitis that require prompt medical attention.

The following side/adverse effects have been selected on the basis of their potential clinical significance (possible signs and symptoms in parentheses where appropriate)—not necessarily inclusive:

Those indicating need for medical attention

Incidence more frequent

Infection; pharyngitis (body aches or pain, congestion, cough, dryness or soreness of throat, fever, hoarseness, runny nose, tender, swollen glands in neck, trouble in swallowing, voice changes)

Incidence less frequent or rare

Behavioral, mood, or mental changes; dyspnea (shortness of breath; difficult or labored breathing; tightness in chest; wheezing); ***edema*** (swelling); ***hematemesis*** (vomiting of blood or material that looks like coffee grounds); ***hepatotoxicity or hyperammonemia*** (increase in frequency of seizures; loss of appetite; continuing nausea or vomiting; swelling of face; tiredness and weakness; yellow eyes or skin); ***hypotension*** (blurred vision; confusion; dizziness, faintness, or light-headedness when getting up from a lying or sitting position suddenly; sweating; unusual tiredness or weakness); ***liver dysfunction; nystagmus*** (continuous, uncontrolled back-and-forth and/or rolling eye movements); ***or spots before eyes; ophthalmological effects, specifically diplopia*** (double vision); ***otitis media*** (earache, redness or swelling in ear); ***palpitations*** (fast, irregular, pounding, or racing heartbeat or pulse); ***pancreatitis*** (severe abdominal or stomach cramps; continuing nausea and vomiting); ***periodontal abscess; peripheral edema*** (bloating or swelling of face, arms, hands, lower legs, or feet; rapid weight gain; tingling of hands or feet; unusual weight gain or loss); ***platelet aggregation inhibition or thrombocytopenia*** (unusual bleeding or bruising); ***pneumonia; vaginal hemorrhage*** (heavy, non menstrual vaginal bleeding)

Note: Evidence of hemorrhage, bruising, or a disorder of coagulation or hemostasis is an indication for reduction of dosage or discontinuation of therapy.

Those indicating need for medical attention only if they continue or are bothersome

Incidence more frequent

Abdominal or stomach cramps, mild—may also indicate a risk of pancreatitis; less frequent with divalproex; ***alopecia*** (hair loss, thinning of hair); ***amblyopia*** (blurred vision; change in vision; impaired vision); ***amnesia*** (loss of memory; problems with memory); ***anorexia*** (loss of appetite); ***appetite, increase; asthenia*** (lack or loss of strength); ***ataxia*** (clumsiness or unsteadiness); ***back pain; change in menstrual periods; diarrhea; dizziness; dyspepsia*** (acid or sour stomach; belching; heartburn; indigestion; stomach discomfort, upset or pain); ***emotional lability*** (crying; depersonalization; dysphoria; euphoria; mental depression; paranoia; quick to react or overreact emotionally; rapidly changing moods); ***flu syndrome; hair loss; headache; insomnia*** (sleeplessness; trouble sleeping; unable to sleep); ***indigestion; nausea and vomiting; nervousness; rash; somnolence*** (sleepiness or unusual drowsiness); ***tinnitus*** (continuing ringing or buzzing or other unexplained noise in ears; hearing loss); ***trembling of hands and arms; unusual weight loss or gain***

Incidence less frequent or rare

Abnormal dreams; abnormal gait (change in walking and balance; clumsiness, or unsteadiness); ***agitation*** (anxiety; nervousness; restlessness; irritability; dry mouth; shortness of breath; hyperventilation; trouble sleeping; irregular heartbeats; shaking); ***amenorrhea*** (absent, missed, or irregular menstrual periods; stopping of menstrual bleeding); ***anxiety; arthralgia*** (pain in joints; muscle pain or stiffness; difficulty in moving); ***arthrosis*** (degenerative disease of the joint); ***bronchitis*** (cough producing mucus, difficulty breathing, shortness of breath, tightness in chest, wheezing); ***catatonic reaction*** (decreased awareness or responsiveness; mimicry of speech or movements; mutism; negativism; peculiar postures or movements, mannerisms or grimacing; severe sleepiness); ***chest pain; chills; confusion; conjunctivitis*** (redness, pain, swelling of eye, eyelid, or inner lining of eyelid; burning, dry or itching eyes; discharge; excessive tearing); ***cystitis*** (bloody or cloudy urine; difficult, burning, or painful urination; frequent urge to urinate); ***constipation; deafness; depression*** (discouragement; feeling sad or empty; irritability; lack of appetite; loss of interest or pleasure; tiredness; trouble concentrating; trouble sleeping); ***discoid lupus erythematosis*** (coin-shaped lesions on skin; loss of hair); ***dysarthria*** (trouble in speaking; slurred speech; changes in patterns and rhythms of speech); ***dysmenorrhea*** (pain; cramps; heavy bleeding); ***dysuria*** (difficult or painful urination; burning while urinating); ***drowsiness; dry eyes; dry mouth; dry skin; ear disorder or pain; ecchymosis*** (bruising large, flat, blue or purplish patches in the skin); ***epistaxis*** (bloody nose); ***eye pain; fecal incontinence*** (loss of bowel control); ***fever; flatulence*** (bloated full feeling; excess air or gas in stomach or intestines; passing gas); ***furunculosis*** (multiple swollen and inflamed skin lesions); ***gastroenteritis*** (abdominal or stomach pain; diarrhea; loss of appetite; nausea; weakness); ***glossitis*** (redness, swelling, or soreness of tongue); ***hallucinations*** (seeing, hearing, or feeling things that are not there); ***hypertension*** (blurred vision; dizziness; nervousness; headache; pounding in the ears; slow or fast heartbeat); ***hypertonia*** (excessive muscle tone; muscle tension or tightness; muscle stiffness); ***hypokinesia*** (absence of or decrease in body movement); ***increased cough; leg cramps; malaise*** (general feeling of discomfort or illness; unusual tiredness or weakness); ***metrorrhagia*** (normal menstrual bleeding occurring earlier, possibly lasting longer than expected); ***myalgia*** (joint pain; swollen joints; muscle aching or cramping; muscle pains or stiffness; difficulty in moving); ***myasthenia*** (loss of strength or energy, muscle pain or weakness); ***neck pain; neck rigidity*** (severe muscle stiffness); ***paresthesia*** (burning, crawling, itching, numbness, prickling, "pins and needles", or tingling feelings); ***petechia*** (small red or purple spots on skin); ***postural hypotension*** (chills; cold sweats; confusion; dizziness, faintness, or light-headedness when getting up from lying or sitting position); ***pruritus; reflexes increased; rhinitis*** (stuffy nose; runny nose; sneezing); ***sinusitis*** (pain or tenderness around eyes and cheekbones; fever; stuffy or runny nose; headache; cough; shortness of breath or troubled breathing; tightness of chest or wheezing); ***skin rash; speech disorder*** (difficulty in speaking); ***stomatitis*** (swelling or inflammation of the mouth); ***tachycardia*** (fast, pounding, or irregular heartbeat or pulse); ***tardive dyskinesia*** (lip smacking or puckering; puffing of cheeks; rapid or worm-like movements of tongue; uncontrolled chewing movements; uncontrolled movements of arms and legs); ***taste perversion*** (change in taste; bad, unusual or unpleasant (after)taste); ***thinking abnormalities; twitching; unusual excitement, restlessness, or irritability; urinary incontinence*** (loss of bladder control); ***vaginitis; vasodilation*** (feeling of warmth or heat; flushing or redness of skin, especially on face and neck; headache; feeling faint, dizzy, or light-headedness; sweating); ***vertigo*** (dizziness or light-headedness; feeling of constant movement of self or surroundings, sensation of spinning)

Overdose

For specific information on the agents used in the management of valproic acid overdose, see:

- *Naloxone (Systemic)* monograph.

For more information on the management of overdose or unintentional ingestion, **contact a Poison Control Center** (see *Poison Control Center Listing*).

Treatment of overdose

Treatment of overdose consists primarily of supportive and symptomatic measures.

To decrease absorption—The effectiveness of emesis or gastric lavage will depend upon the time elapsed since ingestion. The enteric-coated tablets will delay absorption about 1 to 4 hours.

To enhance elimination—Hemodialysis, or tandem hemodialysis and hemoperfusion, may result in significant reductions in valproate serum concentrations.

Specific treatment—Maintenance of adequate urinary output must be ensured. Naloxone has been administered to counteract severe CNS depression, but it also theoretically reverses the anticonvulsant effect and should be used with caution.

Supportive care—Patients in whom intentional overdose is confirmed or suspected should be referred for psychiatric consultation.

Patient Consultation

As an aid to patient consultation, refer to *Advice for the Patient, Valproic Acid (Systemic).*

In providing consultation, consider emphasizing the following selected information (» = major clinical significance):

Before using this medication

» Conditions affecting use, especially:

Sensitivity to valproic acid, divalproex, or valproate sodium

Pregnancy—Pregnancy studies in animals have shown skeletal abnormalities involving ribs and vertebrae in offspring of mothers given large doses; in humans, crosses placenta in first trimester and may cause neural tube defects in fetus

Breast-feeding—Distributed into breast milk at concentrations up to 10% of the total maternal serum concentration

Use in children—Children are at an increased risk of serious hepatotoxicity

Use in the elderly—Elderly patients tend to have higher serum concentrations of free (unbound) valproic acid; lower daily dosages recommended

Dental—Prolonged bleeding time and/or hemorrhaging; leukopenia and thrombocytopenia may result in increased incidence of microbial infection, delayed healing, and gingival bleeding

Surgical—Prolonged bleeding time and/or hemorrhaging may occur; leukopenia and thrombocytopenia may cause surgical complications

Other medications, especially alcohol or other CNS depression-producing medications, heparin or thrombolytic agents, barbiturates, primidone, carbamazepine, felbamate, other hepatotoxic medications, lamotrigine, mefloquine, phenytoin, or other platelet aggregation inhibitors

Other medical problems, especially significant hepatic disease or hepatic function impairment

Proper use of this medication

Proper administration

For valproic acid capsules

Swallowing capsules whole with water only; not breaking, chewing, or crushing

For divalproex sodium delayed-release capsules

Swallowing capsules whole, or sprinkling the contents on a small amount of cool, soft food (such as applesauce or pudding) and swallowing, not chewing, immediately after preparation

For divalproex sodium delayed-release tablets

Swallowing tablets whole; not breaking, chewing, or crushing

For valproic acid syrup

Mixing with any liquid or adding to a small amount of food to enhance palatability

For all oral products

Taking with food if necessary to reduce gastrointestinal side effects

» Compliance with therapy; taking exactly as directed by physician

» Proper dosing

Missed dose: If dosing schedule is—

One dose a day: Taking as soon as possible; not taking if not remembered until next day; not doubling doses

Two or more doses a day: Taking if remembered within 6 hours; taking remaining doses for that day at equally spaced intervals; not doubling doses

» Proper storage

Precautions while using this medication

» Regular visits to physician to check progress of therapy

» Checking with physician before discontinuing medication; gradual dosage reduction may be necessary

» Possible prolonged bleeding or hemorrhage: caution if any kind of surgery, dental treatment, or emergency treatment is required

» Avoiding use of alcoholic beverages or other CNS depressants during therapy

Diabetic patients: When testing for urine ketones, possible false-positive test results

Caution if any laboratory tests required; possible interference with results of metyrapone or thyroid function tests

Possible need for carrying medical identification card or bracelet

» Possible drowsiness; caution when driving or doing other things requiring alertness

Side/adverse effects

Signs of potential side effects, especially behavioral, mood, or mental changes; hepatotoxicity; hyperammonemia; ophthalmological effects; pancreatitis; platelet aggregation inhibition; or thrombocytopenia

General Dosing Information

Patients at primary risk for fatal liver failure with valproic acid, divalproex, or valproate sodium treatment include:

- Children up to 2 years of age, especially those on polytherapy, those with congenital metabolic disorders, those with severe epilepsy accompanied by mental retardation, and those with organic brain disease.
- All patients receiving concomitant anticonvulsants, especially those that enhance production of a toxic metabolite through induction of hepatic P450 isoenzymes (e.g., carbamazepine, felbamate, lamotrigine, phenobarbital, phenytoin, primidone)
- Patients with familial liver disease.

Recommendations for reducing the risk of serious hepatotoxicity with valproate include:

- Avoiding the administration of valproate with other anticonvulsants whenever possible, especially in children up to 3 years of age, unless monotherapy has failed or the benefits of polytherapy outweigh the risks.
- Avoiding valproate therapy in patients with pre-existing liver disease or a family history of childhood hepatic disease.
- Administering valproate in as low a dose as possible to achieve seizure control.
- Avoiding concurrent administration with other hepatotoxic medications, especially salicylates.
- Monitoring for prodromal symptoms (e.g., nausea or vomiting, headache, edema, jaundice, or seizure breakthrough, especially after a febrile illness).
- Avoiding administration to patients with congenital metabolic disorders, severe seizure disorders accompanied by mental retardation, or organic brain disease.

When valproic acid, divalproex, or valproate sodium is to be discontinued, dosage should be reduced gradually since abrupt withdrawal may precipitate seizures or status epilepticus.

The serum concentration of valproate does not always correspond with therapeutic effect; therefore, the evaluation of the patient's progress must be based on total clinical assessment.

When valproic acid, divalproex, or valproate sodium is used to replace or supplement other anticonvulsant therapy, the dosage should be increased gradually to achieve therapeutic serum concentrations, while that of the replaced medication is decreased gradually in order to maintain seizure control. The addition of valproic acid, divalproex, or valproate sodium may cause increases in the serum concentrations of hepatic enzyme-inducing anticonvulsants (e.g., carbamazepine, felbamate, lamotrigine, phenobarbital, phenytoin, primidone)

The possible prolongation of bleeding time, in addition to potentiation of depressant effect by CNS depressants, should be considered when surgery, dental treatment, or emergency treatment is required.

Diet/Nutrition

Valproic acid or divalproex may be taken with food to reduce gastrointestinal side effects.

The contents of divalproex sodium delayed-release capsules may be sprinkled on a small amount of cool, soft food (such as applesauce or pudding) and swallowed, not chewed, immediately after preparation.

Valproic acid syrup may be mixed with a small amount of food or liquid to enhance the palatability.

Requirements for carnitine may be increased in patients receiving valproic acid, divalproex, or valproate sodium.

DIVALPROEX

Oral Dosage Forms

DIVALPROEX SODIUM DELAYED-RELEASE CAPSULES

Usual adult and adolescent dose

Anticonvulsant—

Monotherapy: Oral, the equivalent of valproic acid—Initially, 5 to 15 mg per kg of body weight a day, the dosage being increased at one-week intervals by 5 to 10 mg per kg of body weight a day as needed and tolerated.

Polytherapy: Oral, the equivalent of valproic acid—Initially, 10 to 30 mg per kg of body weight a day, the dosage being increased at one-week intervals by 5 to 10 mg per kg of body weight a day as needed and tolerated.

Note: If the total daily dose exceeds 250 mg, it should be divided into two or more doses (usually given every 12 hours) to lessen the possibility of gastrointestinal irritation.

Geriatric patients may need lower doses.

Patients also taking a hepatic enzyme-inducing medication may need higher dosages depending on predose serum concentrations.

Usual adult prescribing limits
60 mg per kg of body weight a day.

Usual pediatric dose
Anticonvulsant: Children 1 to 12 years of age—

Monotherapy: Oral, the equivalent of valproic acid—Initially, 15 to 45 mg per kg of body weight a day, the dosage being increased at one-week intervals by 5 to 10 mg per kg of body weight a day as needed and tolerated.

Polytherapy: Oral, the equivalent of valproic acid—30 to 100 mg per kg of body weight a day.

Note: Dosage adjustments depend on clinical response and serum anticonvulsant concentrations.

Usual geriatric dose
Geriatric patients may need lower doses. See *Usual adult and adolescent dose*.

Strength(s) usually available
U.S.—

The equivalent of valproic acid:

125 mg (Rx) [*Depakote Sprinkle*].

Canada—

Not commercially available.

Packaging and storage
Store below 30 °C (86 °F), preferably between 15 and 30 °C (59 and 86 °F) in a tight, light-resistant container, unless otherwise specified by manufacturer.

Auxiliary labeling
- May cause drowsiness.
- Avoid alcoholic beverages.
- Do not chew contents of capsule.

DIVALPROEX SODIUM DELAYED-RELEASE TABLETS

Usual adult dose
Anticonvulsant—

Monotherapy: Oral, the equivalent of valproic acid—Initially, 5 to 15 mg per kg of body weight a day, the dosage being increased at one-week intervals by 5 to 10 mg per kg of body weight a day as needed and tolerated.

Polytherapy: Oral, the equivalent of valproic acid—Initially, 10 to 30 mg per kg of body weight a day, the dosage being increased at one-week intervals by 5 to 10 mg per kg of body weight a day as needed and tolerated.

Antimanic—

Oral, initially 750 mg a day in divided doses. The dose should be increased as rapidly as possible to achieve the lowest therapeutic dose that produces the desired clinical effect or a desired trough plasma concentration within the range of fifty to one hundred twenty-five micrograms/mL.

Migraine headache prophylactic—

Oral, initially 250 mg two times a day. The dose may be increased as needed and tolerated; some patients may benefit from doses up to 1000 mg a day. However, daily doses above 1000 mg have not demonstrated increased efficacy in clinical trials.

Note: If the total daily dose exceeds 250 mg, it should be divided into two or more doses (usually given every 12 hours) to lessen the possibility of gastrointestinal irritation.

Geriatric patients may need lower doses.

Patients also taking a hepatic enzyme-inducing medication may need higher dosages depending on predose serum concentrations.

Usual adult prescribing limits
See *Divalproex Sodium Delayed-release Capsules*.

Usual pediatric dose
See *Divalproex Sodium Delayed-release Capsules*.

Usual geriatric dose
Geriatric patients may need lower doses. See *Usual adult dose*.

Strength(s) usually available
U.S.—

The equivalent of valproic acid:

125 mg (Rx) [*Depakote*].
250 mg (Rx) [*Depakote*].
500 mg (Rx) [*Depakote*].

Canada—

The equivalent of valproic acid:

125 mg (Rx) [*Epival* (enteric-coated)].
250 mg (Rx) [*Epival* (enteric-coated)].
500 mg (Rx) [*Epival* (enteric-coated)].

Packaging and storage
Store below 40 °C (104 °F), preferably between 15 and 30 °C (59 and 86 °F), in a tight, light-resistant container, unless otherwise specified by manufacturer.

Auxiliary labeling
- May cause drowsiness.
- Avoid alcoholic beverages.
- Swallow tablets whole. Do not break or chew.

VALPROATE SODIUM

Parenteral Dosage Forms

VALPROATE SODIUM INJECTION

Usual adult and adolescent dose
Anticonvulsant—

Initial exposure to valproate—

Monotherapy—Intravenous infusion: Initially, 5 to 15 mg per kg of body weight a day, the dosage being increased at one-week intervals by 5 to 10 mg per kg of body weight a day as needed and tolerated.

Polytherapy—Intravenous infusion: Initially, 10 to 30 mg per kg of body weight a day, the dosage being increased at one-week intervals by 5 to 10 mg per kg of body weight a day as needed and tolerated.

Replacement for oral therapy—

Intravenous infusion—The total daily dose should be equivalent to the total daily dose of the oral valproic acid or divalproex product and should be administered at the same frequency as the oral product. If the total daily dose exceeds 250 mg, it should be given in divided doses.

Note: Valproate sodium injection should be administered as a 60-minute intravenous infusion; the rate of infusion should not exceed 20 mg per minute. Plasma concentration monitoring and dosage adjustments may be necessary. Patients receiving doses approaching the maximum recommended daily dose of 60 mg per kg of body weight per day should be monitored closely, particularly those not receiving hepatic enzyme-inducing medications. Patients should be switched to oral valproate products as soon as clinically feasible.

Geriatric patients may need lower doses.

Patients also taking a hepatic enzyme-inducing medication may need higher dosages, depending on predose serum valproate concentrations.

Usual adult prescribing limits
60 mg per kg of body weight a day.

Usual pediatric dose
Anticonvulsant: Children 1 to 12 years of age—

Monotherapy: Oral, initially, 15 to 45 mg per kg of body weight a day, the dosage being increased at one-week intervals by 5 to 10 mg per kg of body weight a day as needed and tolerated.—Polytherapy: Oral, 30 to 100 mg per kg of body weight a day.

Note: Dosage adjustments depend on clinical response and serum anticonvulsant concentrations.

Usual geriatric dose
Geriatric patients may need lower doses. See *Usual adult and adolescent dose*.

Strength(s) usually available
U.S.—

Equivalent to valproic acid:

100 mg per mL (Rx) [*Depacon* (edetate disodium 0.4 mg per mL)].

Canada—

Not commercially available.

Packaging and storage
Store between 15 and 30 °C (59 and 86 °F), unless otherwise specified by manufacturer.

Preparation of dosage form
Valproate sodium injection should be diluted with at least 50 mL of 5% Dextrose Injection USP, 0.9% Sodium Chloride Injection USP, or Lactated Ringers Injection USP. The product should be inspected visually for particulate matter and discoloration prior to administration.

Stability
Valproate sodium injection is stable in 5% Dextrose Injection USP, 0.9% Sodium Chloride Injection USP, or Lactated Ringers Injection USP for at least 24 hours when stored in glass or polyvinyl chloride (PVC) bags at controlled room temperature. Any valproate sodium remaining in the vial after preparing the intravenous infusion should be discarded.

VALPROIC ACID

Oral Dosage Forms

VALPROIC ACID CAPSULES USP

Usual adult and adolescent dose
Anticonvulsant—
Monotherapy: Oral, initially, 5 to 15 mg per kg of body weight a day, the dosage being increased at one-week intervals by 5 to 10 mg per kg of body weight a day as needed and tolerated.
Polytherapy: Oral, initially, 10 to 30 mg per kg of body weight a day, the dosage being increased at one-week intervals by 5 to 10 mg per kg of body weight a day as needed and tolerated.
Note: If the total daily dose exceeds 250 mg, it should be divided into two or more doses (usually given every 12 hours) to lessen the possibility of gastrointestinal irritation.
Geriatric patients may need lower doses.
Patients also taking a hepatic enzyme-inducing medication may need higher dosages depending on predose serum concentrations.

Usual adult prescribing limits
60 mg per kg of body weight a day.

Usual pediatric dose
Anticonvulsant—Children 1 to 12 years of age—
Monotherapy: Oral, initially, 15 to 45 mg per kg of body weight a day, the dosage being increased at one-week intervals by 5 to 10 mg per kg of body weight a day as needed and tolerated.
Polytherapy: Oral, 30 to 100 mg per kg of body weight a day.
Note: Dosage adjustments depend on clinical response and serum anticonvulsant concentrations.

Usual geriatric dose
Geriatric patients may need lower doses. See *Usual adult and adolescent dose.*

Strength(s) usually available
U.S.—
250 mg (Rx) [*Depakene* (parabens); GENERIC].
Canada—
250 mg (Rx) [*Alti-Valproic; Depakene* (parabens); *Deproic* (parabens); *Dom-Valproic; Med Valproic; Novo-Valproic; Nu-Valproic; Penta-Valproic; pms-Valproic Acid*].
500 mg (Rx) [*Alti-Valproic* (enteric-coated); *Depakene* (enteric-coated; parabens; tartrazine); *Deproic* (enteric-coated); *Dom-Valproic* (enteric-coated); *Novo-Valproic* (enteric-coated); *pms-Valproic Acid E.C.* (enteric-coated)].

Packaging and storage
Store between 15 and 30 °C (59 and 86 °F), in a tight container.

Auxiliary labeling
- May cause drowsiness.
- Avoid alcoholic beverages.
- Swallow capsules whole. Do not break or chew.

VALPROIC ACID SYRUP USP

Usual adult and adolescent dose
See *Valproic Acid Capsules USP.*

Usual adult prescribing limits
See *Valproic Acid Capsules USP.*

Usual pediatric dose
See *Valproic Acid Capsules USP.*

Usual geriatric dose
See *Valproic Acid Capsules USP.*

Strength(s) usually available
U.S.—
250 mg per 5 mL (Rx) [*Depakene* (parabens; sorbitol; sucrose); GENERIC].
Canada—
250 mg per 5 mL (Rx) [*Alti-Valproic; Depakene* (parabens; sucrose); *PMS-Valproic Acid*].

Packaging and storage
Store below 40 °C (104 °F), preferably between 15 and 30 °C (59 and 86 °F), unless otherwise specified by manufacturer. Store in a tight container. Protect from freezing.

Auxiliary labeling
- May cause drowsiness.
- Avoid alcoholic beverages.

Revised: 11/11/2003

VALSARTAN Systemic

VA CLASSIFICATION (Primary/Secondary): CV805/CV409

Commonly used brand name(s): *Diovan.*

Note: For a listing of dosage forms and brand names by country availability, see *Dosage Forms* section(s).

Category

Antihypertensive; vasodilator, congestive heart failure.

Indications

Accepted

Heart failure (treatment)—Valsartan is indicated for the treatment of heart failure (NYHA class II-IV). In a controlled clinical trial, valsartan significantly reduced hospitalizations for heart failure. There is no evidence that valsartan provides added benefits when it is used with an adequate dose of an ACE inhibitor.

Hypertension (treatment)—Valsartan is indicated for the treatment of hypertension. It may be used alone or in combination with other antihypertensive medications. Valsartan is normally used in those patients in whom treatment with a diuretic or beta-blocker was ineffective or associated with unacceptable side effects. Valsartan may be used as an initial agent in those patients in whom the use of diuretics and/or beta-blockers is contraindicated or in patients with medical conditions in which these drugs frequently cause serious side effects.
For additional information on initial therapeutic guidelines related to the treatment of hypertension, see *Appendix III.*

Left ventricular dysfunction, post-myocardial infarction (treatment)—In clinically stable patients with left ventricular failure or left ventricular dysfunction following myocardial infarction, valsartan is indicated to reduce cardiovascular mortality.

Pharmacology/Pharmacokinetics

Physicochemical characteristics
Molecular weight—435.5.

Mechanism of action/Effect
Valsartan is a nonpeptide angiotensin II antagonist that selectively blocks the binding of angiotensin II to the AT_1 receptors in tissues such as vascular smooth muscle and the adrenal gland. In the renin-angiotensin system, angiotensin I is converted by angiotensin-converting enzyme (ACE) to form angiotensin II. Angiotensin II stimulates the adrenal cortex to synthesize and secrete aldosterone, which decreases the excretion of sodium and increases the excretion of potassium. Angiotensin II also acts as a vasoconstrictor in vascular smooth muscle. Valsartan, by blocking the binding of angiotensin II to the AT_1 receptors, promotes vasodilation and decreases the effects of aldosterone. The negative feedback regulation of angiotensin II on renin secretion also is inhibited, resulting in a rise in plasma renin concentrations and a consequent rise in angiotensin II plasma concentrations; however, these effects do not counteract the blood pressure-lowering effect that occurs.

Absorption
Absolute bioavailability for the capsule formulation is approximately 25% (range, 10 to 35%).
Food decreases the area under the plasma concentration-time curve (AUC) and peak plasma concentration (C_{max}) by approximately 40 and 50%, respectively.

Distribution
Vol_D—Steady-state: 17 L.

Protein binding
Very high (95%), mainly to albumin.

Biotransformation
The enzymes responsible for the metabolism of valsartan have not been identified; however, valsartan is not believed to be metabolized by cytochrome P450 isozymes. The primary metabolite, valeryl 4-hydroxy valsartan, is inactive, with an affinity for the AT_1 receptor of about one-two hundredth that of valsartan itself. About 20% of a dose of valsartan is eliminated as metabolites.

Half-life
Elimination—
Approximately 6 hours
6.6 hours in patients with renal failure.

Onset of action
Hypertension, oral: 2 hours.

Time to peak concentration
2 to 4 hours.
3.5 to 4 hours in patients with mild to moderate liver disease.
2 to 3 hours in patients with mild to severe renal disease.

Peak serum concentration
3.3 mg/L following a single 160-mg dose in healthy volunteers.

3.9 to 5.9 mg/L following a single 160-mg dose in patients with mild to moderate liver disease

0.8 to 1.6 mg/L following a single 80-mg dose in 12 patients with mild to severe renal disease.

Duration of action
Hypertension, oral: 24 hours.

Elimination
Renal—13%.
Fecal—83%.
In dialysis—
Valsartan is not removed from the plasma by hemodialysis.

Precautions to Consider

Carcinogenicity
No evidence of carcinogenicity was found in mice or rats given valsartan for up to 2 years in dietary doses of up to 160 and 200 mg per kg of body weight (mg/kg) per day, respectively. These doses represent 2.6 and 6 times the maximum recommended human dose (MRHD), respectively, on a mg per square meter of body surface area (mg/m^2) basis, assuming an oral dose of 320 mg per day and a 60-kg patient.

Mutagenicity
Mutagenicity was not detected at either the gene or chromosome level in bacterial mutagenicity tests with *Salmonella* (Ames test) and *E. coli*, a gene mutation test with Chinese hamster V79 cells, a cytogenetic test with Chinese hamster ovary cells, or a rat micronucleus test.

Pregnancy/Reproduction
Fertility—No impairment of reproductive performance was found in male or female rats given oral doses of up to 200 mg/kg per day. This dose represents six times the MRHD on a mg/m^2 basis, assuming an oral dose of 320 mg per day and a 60-kg patient.

Pregnancy—Medications that act directly on the renin-angiotensin system can cause fetal and neonatal morbidity and mortality when administered to pregnant women during the second and third trimesters. Valsartan should be discontinued as soon as possible when pregnancy is detected, unless no alternative therapy can be used. In the latter instance, serial ultrasound examinations should be performed to assess the intra-amniotic environment. If oligohydramnios is observed, valsartan should be discontinued unless it is considered lifesaving for the mother. Perinatal diagnostic tests, such as contraction-stress testing (CST), a nonstress test (NST), or biophysical profiling (BPP) also may be appropriate during the applicable week of pregnancy. Oligohydramnios may not appear until after the fetus has sustained irreversible damage.

Fetal exposure to drugs that act directly on the renin-angiotensin system during the second and third trimesters can cause hypotension, reversible or irreversible renal failure, anuria, neonatal skull hypoplasia, and death in the fetus or neonate. Maternal oligohydramnios, which may result from decreased fetal renal function, has been reported, and is associated with fetal limb contractures, craniofacial deformation, and hypoplastic lung development. Other adverse effects that have been reported are prematurity, intrauterine growth retardation, and patent ductus arteriosus, although it is not clear how these effects are related to drug exposure. When limited to the first trimester, exposure to this medication does not appear to be associated with these adverse effects.

Infants exposed *in utero* to angiotensin II receptor antagonists should be closely observed for hypotension, oliguria, and hyperkalemia. Oliguria should be treated with support of blood pressure and renal perfusion. Dialysis or exchange transfusion may be necessary to reverse hypotension and/or substitute for disordered renal function.

Teratogenic effects were not observed in pregnant mice or rats given oral doses of up to 600 mg/kg per day or to pregnant rabbits given oral doses of up to 10 mg/kg per day. Studies in rats given oral, maternally toxic (based on a reduction in body weight gain and food consumption) doses of 600 mg/kg per day of valsartan during organogenesis or late gestation and lactation periods resulted in significant decreases in fetal weight, pup birth weight, pup survival rate, and slight delays in developmental milestones. Studies in rabbits given maternally toxic (associated with mortality) doses of 5 and 10 mg/kg per day of valsartan resulted in fetotoxic effects, such as fetal resorptions, litter loss, abortions, and low body weight in pups. No adverse effects were observed in mice, rats, and rabbits given 600, 200, and 2 mg/kg per day, respectively, of valsartan. This represents 9, 6, and 0.1 times, respectively, the MRHD on a mg/m^2 basis, assuming an oral dose of 320 mg/day and a 60-kg patient.

FDA Pregnancy Category C (first trimester).
FDA Pregnancy Category D (second and third trimesters).

Breast-feeding
It is not known whether valsartan is distributed into breast milk. However, valsartan is distributed into the milk of lactating rats. Because of the potential for adverse effects, it is recommended that valsartan not be administered to nursing mothers.

Pediatrics
No information is available on the relationship of age to the effects of valsartan in pediatric patients. Safety and efficacy have not been established in pediatric patients less than 18 years of age.

Geriatrics
Use of valsartan in patients 65 years of age and older (36.2% of patients in clinical studies) has not demonstrated geriatrics-specific problems that would limit the usefulness of valsartan in the elderly. However, the area under the plasma concentration-time curve (AUC) and elimination half-life increased by 70 and 35%, respectively, when compared with those in younger patients. Elderly patients may also experience greater sensitivity to the effects of valsartan.

Drug interactions and/or related problems
The following drug interactions and/or related problems have been selected on the basis of their potential clinical significance (possible mechanism in parentheses where appropriate)—not necessarily inclusive (» = major clinical significance):

Note: Combinations containing any of the following medications, depending on the amount present, may also interact with this medication.

» ACE inhibitors or
» Beta blockers
(in patients with heart failure, concomitant triple use in not recommended; combination of ACE inhibitor, beta blocker and valsartan was associated with an unfavorable heart failure outcome)

» Diuretics
(concurrent use with valsartan may have additive hypotensive effects)

Lithium salts
(concurrent use with valsartan may reduce lithium clearance; monitor serum lithium levels)

» Potassium-sparing drugs, potassium supplements, or potassium-containing salt substitutes
(concurrent use with valsartan may increase serum potassium)

Warfarin
(concurrent use with valsartan may cause an increase (12%) in prothrombin time (PT); activated partial thromboplastin time (APTT) is unaffected)

Laboratory value alterations
The following have been selected on the basis of their potential clinical significance (possible effect in parentheses where appropriate)—not necessarily inclusive (» = major clinical significance).

With physiology/laboratory test values
Blood urea nitrogen (BUN)
(increases observed in heart failure trials)

Creatinine, serum
(minor increases in concentrations may occur)

Hematocrit and

Hemoglobin
(in clinical studies, decreases of greater than 20% occurred in 0.8 and 0.4% of hematocrit and hemoglobin values, respectively, compared with 0.1% and 0.1% in placebo-treated patients. Valsartan therapy was discontinued in one patient because of microcytic anemia)

Liver function tests
(in clinical studies, occasional elevations of greater than 150% have occurred in valsartan-treated patients; three patients (< 0.1%) discontinued valsartan because of elevated liver enzyme values; post-marketing experience reports of elevated liver enzymes)

Leukocyte counts
(in clinical studies, neutropenia occurred in 1.9% of patients who were taking valsartan and in 0.8% of patients treated with placebo)

Potassium, serum
(in clinical studies, increases in concentration of greater than 20% were observed in 4.4% of patients treated with valsartan compared to 2.9% of placebo-treated patients; however, this did not require discontinuation of valsartan therapy)

Medical considerations/Contraindications

The medical considerations/contraindications included have been selected on the basis of their potential clinical significance (reasons given in parentheses where appropriate)—not necessarily inclusive (» = major clinical significance).

Except under special circumstances, this medication should not be used when the following medical problem exists:

» Hypersensitivity to valsartan or any component of the product

Risk-benefit should be considered when the following medical problems exist:

Dehydration (sodium or volume depletion, due to excessive perspiration, vomiting, diarrhea, prolonged diuretic therapy, dialysis, or dietary salt restriction)
(a reduction in salt or fluid volume may increase the risk of symptomatic hypotension)

Heart failure
(caution should be observed; these patients commonly have some blood pressure decrease when given valsartan, but discontinuation usually not necessary due to continuing symptomatic hypotension when dosing instructions are followed)

Hepatic function impairment, mild to moderate, including biliary obstructive disorders or
Hepatic function impairment, severe
(in patients with mild to moderate chronic liver disease, decreased biliary elimination of valsartan may result in an increase in the AUC and peak serum concentration; the AUC in patients with mild to moderate chronic liver disease may be doubled, as compared with healthy volunteers; no information is available on the use of valsartan in patients with severe hepatic function impairment)

Renal artery stenosis, unilateral or bilateral or
Renal function impairment
(increases in serum creatinine or blood urea nitrogen [BUN] and small increases in elimination half-life may occur; long-term effect in patients with unilateral or bilateral renal artery stenosis should be anticipated to be similar to that seen with ACE inhibitors; therapy with angiotensin receptor–antagonists in patients susceptible to changes in the renin-angiotensin-aldosterone system, such as patients with severe congestive heart failure, has been associated with oliguria and/or progressive azotemia, and rarely with acute renal failure and/or death; evaluation of patients with heart failure should always include assessment of renal function)

Patient monitoring

The following may be especially important in patient monitoring (other tests may be warranted in some patients, depending on condition; » = major clinical significance):

» Blood pressure measurements
(periodic monitoring is necessary for titration of dose according to the patient's response)

Renal function
(use of valsartan should include assessment of renal function)

Side/Adverse Effects

The following side/adverse effects have been selected on the basis of their potential clinical significance (possible signs and symptoms in parentheses where appropriate)—not necessarily inclusive:

Those indicating need for medical attention

Incidence less frequent

Hyperkalemia (abdominal pain; confusion; irregular heartbeat; nausea or vomiting; nervousness; numbness or tingling in hands, feet, or lips; shortness of breath; difficult breathing; weakness or heaviness of legs); ***postural hypotension*** (chills; cold sweats; confusion; dizziness, faintness, or lightheadedness when getting up from lying or sitting position); ***renal impairment*** (lower back/side pain; decreased frequency/amount of urine; bloody urine; increased thirst; loss of appetite; nausea; vomiting; unusual tiredness or weakness; swelling of face, fingers, lower legs; weight gain troubled breathing; increased blood pressure); ***syncope*** (fainting)

Incidence rare

Angioedema (sudden trouble in swallowing or breathing; swelling of face, mouth, hands, or feet; hoarseness); ***hypotension*** (dizziness, lightheadedness, or fainting)—usually seen in volume- or salt-depleted patients receiving high doses of a diuretic; ***neutropenia*** (chills; fever; sore throat)—incidence 1.9%

Incidence not determined—Observed during clinical practice; estimates of frequency can not be determined

Hepatitis (dark urine; general tiredness and weakness; light-colored stools; nausea and vomiting; upper right abdominal pain; yellow eyes and skin)—very rare reports; ***impaired renal function*** (lower back/side pain; decreased frequency/amount of urine; bloody urine; increased thirst; loss of appetite; nausea; vomiting; unusual tiredness or weakness; swelling of face, fingers, lower legs; weight gain; troubled breathing, increased blood pressure)

Those indicating need for medical attention only if they continue or are bothersome

Incidence less frequent

Abdominal pain; arthralgia (pain, swelling, or redness in joints; muscle pain or stiffness; difficulty in moving); ***back pain; blurred vision; coughing; diarrhea; dizziness; fatigue; headache; nausea; upper respiratory tract infection*** (cough; fever; sneezing; sore throat); ***viral infection***

Incidence not determined—Observed during clinical practice; estimates of frequency can not be determined

Alopecia (hair loss; thinning of hair)

Note: In clinical trials, the side effects that most often resulted in the discontinuation of therapy were *headache* and *dizziness*, which occurred in 2.3% of patients taking valsartan and in 2% of patients taking placebo.

Overdose

For more information on the management of overdose or unintentional ingestion, **contact a Poison Control Center** (see *Poison Control Center Listing*).

Clinical effects of overdose

The following effects have been selected on the basis of their potential clinical significance (possible signs and symptoms in parentheses where appropriate)—not necessarily inclusive:

Acute and/or chronic

Bradycardia (slow heartbeat)—as a result of parasympathetic (vagal) stimulation; ***hypotension*** (dizziness, lightheadedness, or fainting); ***tachycardia*** (fast heartbeat)

Treatment of overdose

Treatment should be symptomatic and supportive.

Valsartan is not removed from plasma by dialysis.

Supportive care—Patients in whom intentional overdose is confirmed or suspected should be referred for psychiatric consultation.

Patient Consultation

As an aid to patient consultation, refer to *Advice for the Patient, Valsartan (Systemic)*.

In providing consultation, consider emphasizing the following selected information (» = major clinical significance):

Before using this medication

» Conditions affecting use, especially:
Hypersensitivity to valsartan or any component of the product
Pregnancy—Fetal and neonatal hypotension, skull hypoplasia, renal failure, and death have been reported in humans; valsartan should be discontinued as soon as possible when pregnancy is detected
Breast-feeding—Valsartan is distributed into milk of lactating rats; not recommended in nursing mothers
Use in the elderly—Area under the plasma concentration-time curve (AUC) and half-life may be increased; may experience greater sensitivity to the medication's effects
Other medications, especially ACE inhibitors, beta blockers, diuretics, potassium-sparing drugs, potassium supplements, and potassium-containing salt substitutes

Proper use of this medication

» Compliance with therapy; taking medication at the same time each day to maintain the antihypertensive effect

Taking alone or with other antihypertensive agents as directed by the physician

» Proper dosing

Missed dose: Taking as soon as possible; not taking if almost time for next scheduled dose; not doubling doses

» Proper storage

Precautions while using this medication

Regular visits to physician to check progress

Notifying physician immediately if pregnancy is suspected

Not taking other medications without consulting the physician

Caution when driving or doing other things requiring alertness because of possible dizziness

To prevent dehydration and hypotension, checking with physician if severe nausea, vomiting, or diarrhea occurs and continues

Caution when exercising or during exposure to hot weather because of the risk of dehydration and hypotension due to reduced fluid volume

Side/adverse effects

Signs of potential side effects, especially angioedema, hyperkalemia, hypotension, neutropenia, postural hypotension, renal impairment, and syncope

Signs of potential side effects observed during clinical practice, especially hepatitis and impaired renal function

General Dosing Information

Dosage must be adjusted, on the basis of clinical response, to meet the individual requirements of each patient.

Studies using valsartan in patients with severe renal function impairment or in patients undergoing dialysis have not been done. Caution should be used when using valsartan in the treatment of these patients and in patients with hepatic function impairment.

Valsartan may be administered as monotherapy or with other antihypertensive agents.

The antihypertensive effect is considerable after 2 weeks of valsartan therapy. The maximum antihypertensive effect is usually attained after 4 weeks of therapy.

Diet/Nutrition

Valsartan may be taken with or without food.

For treatment of adverse effects

Recommended treatment consists of the following:

- Treatment of symptomatic hypotension involves placing the patient in a supine position and, if needed, administering normal saline intravenously.

Oral Dosage Forms

VALSARTAN TABLETS

Usual adult dose

Antihypertensive—

Oral, initially 80 mg or 160 mg once daily, when used as monotherapy in patients who are not volume-depleted. Patients requiring greater reductions may be started at higher dose. Valsartan may be used over dose range of 80 mg to 320 mg daily, administered once per day.

Note: Antihypertensive effect is substantially present within 2 weeks and maximal reduction is generally attained after 4 weeks. If additional antihypertensive effect is required over the starting dose range, the dose may be increased to a maximum of 320 mg or a diuretic may be added. Addition of a diuretic has a greater effect than dose increases beyond 80 mg.

No initial dosage adjustment is required for patients with mild or moderate renal impairment or for patients with mild or moderate liver insufficiency.

Care should be exercised with dosing of valsartan in patients with hepatic or severe renal impairment.

Heart failure (treatment)—

Oral, recommended starting dose of 40 mg twice daily; uptitration to 80 mg and 160 mg twice daily should be done to the highest dose, as tolerated by the patient.

Note: Consideration should be given to reducing dose of concomitant diuretics.

Concomitant use with an ACE inhibitor and a beta blocker is NOT recommended.

Left ventricular dysfunction, post-myocardial infarction (treatment)—

Oral, 20 mg twice daily initiated as early as 12 hours after a myocardial infarction. Patients may be uptitrated within 7 days to 40 mg twice daily, with subsequent titrations to a target maintenance dose of 160 mg twice daily, as tolerated by the patient.

Note: If symptomatic hypotension or renal dysfunction occurs, consideration should be given to a dosage reduction.

Valsartan may be given with other standard post-myocardial infarction treatment, including thrombolytics, aspirin, beta-blockers, and statins.

Usual adult prescribing limits

320 mg per day (in divided doses for treatment of heart failure).

Usual pediatric dose

Safety and efficacy have not been established.

Usual geriatric dose

See *Usual adult dose*.

Strength(s) usually available

U.S.—

40 mg (Rx) [*Diovan* (colloidal silicon dioxide; crospovidone; hydroxypropyl methylcellulose; iron oxides [yellow, black and/or red]; magnesium stearate; microcrystalline cellulose; polyethylene glycol 8000; titanium dioxide)].

80 mg (Rx) [*Diovan* (colloidal silicon dioxide; crospovidone; hydroxypropyl methylcellulose; iron oxides [yellow, black and/or red]; magnesium stearate; microcrystalline cellulose; polyethylene glycol 8000; titanium dioxide)].

160 mg (Rx) [*Diovan* (colloidal silicon dioxide; crospovidone; hydroxypropyl methylcellulose; iron oxides [yellow, black and/or red]; magnesium stearate; microcrystalline cellulose; polyethylene glycol 8000; titanium dioxide)].

320 mg (Rx) [*Diovan* (colloidal silicon dioxide; crospovidone; hydroxypropyl methylcellulose; iron oxides [yellow, black and/or red]; magnesium stearate; microcrystalline cellulose; polyethylene glycol 8000; titanium dioxide)].

Packaging and storage

Store at 25 °C (77 °F); excursions permitted to 15 to 30 °C (59 to 86 °F). Protect from moisture and store in a tight container.

Auxiliary labeling

- Do not take other medicines without your doctor's advice.
- This medication could be harmful during pregnancy. If you are pregnant or plan to be pregnant, you should consult your doctor about the use of this medication.
- May cause dizziness.
- Please read patient information leaflet enclosed

Revised: 09/08/2005
Developed: 10/31/1997

VALSARTAN AND HYDROCHLOROTHIAZIDE Systemic

VA CLASSIFICATION (Primary): CV401

NOTE: The *Valsartan and Hydrochlorothiazide (Systemic)* monograph is maintained on the *USP DI* electronic data base. A copy of the most recent revision of the complete monograph can be accessed on the *USP DI* Updates Online website. See the front cover of book for details on accessing the site.

For information on the specific components of this combination, see the *USP DI* monographs for *Valsartan (Systemic)*, and *Diuretics, Thiazide (Systemic)*.

The information that follows is selectively abstracted from the complete monograph and is provided to facilitate drug use review and patient counseling.

Note: For a listing of dosage forms and brand names by country availability, see *Dosage Forms* section(s).

Category

Antihypertensive.

Indications

Accepted

Hypertension (treatment)—The combination of valsartan and hydrochlorothiazide is indicated for the treatment of hypertension. However, it is not indicated for initial treatment of hypertension.

For additional information on initial therapeutic guidelines related to the treatment of hypertension, see *Appendix III.*

Patient Consultation

As an aid to patient consultation, refer to *Advice for the Patient, Valsartan and Hydrochlorothiazide (Systemic).*

In providing consultation, consider emphasizing the following selected» information (= major clinical significance):

Before using this medication

» Conditions affecting use, especially:

Hypersensitivity to valsartan, hydrochlorothiazide, or sulfonamide-derived substances

Pregnancy—Fetal and neonatal hypotension, skull hypoplasia, renal failure, and death have been reported in humans with use of drugs similar to valsartan; fetal or neonatal jaundice, thrombocytopenia, and other adverse effects have occurred with use of thiazide diuretics; valsartan and hydrochlorothiazide combination should be discontinued as soon as possible when pregnancy is detected

Breast-feeding—Valsartan is distributed into milk of lactating rats; hydrochlorothiazide is distributed into breast milk; valsartan and hydrochlorothiazide combination is not recommended in nursing mothers

Use in the elderly—Area under the plasma concentration time curve (AUC) and half-life of valsartan may be increased; may experience greater sensitivity to the effects of valsartan and hydrochlorothiazide combination

Surgical—Hypokalemia associated with use of hydrochlorothiazide may increase the responsiveness of muscle tissue to nondepolarizing neuromuscular blocking agents

Other medical problems, especially anuria, severe congestive heart failure, electrolyte and/or fluid imbalance, hepatic function impairment, unilateral or bilateral renal artery stenosis, or renal function impairment

Proper use of this medication

» Compliance with therapy; taking medication at the same time each day to maintain the antihypertensive effect

Possible need for control of weight and diet, especially sodium intake; checking with physician before changing diet

» Patient may not experience symptoms of hypertension; importance of taking medication even if feeling well

» Does not cure, but helps control hypertension; possible need for lifelong therapy; checking with physician before discontinuing medication; serious consequences of untreated hypertension

» Proper dosing

Missed dose: Taking as soon as possible; not taking if almost time for next scheduled dose; not doubling doses

» Proper storage

Precautions while using this medication

Making regular visits to physician to check progress

» Notifying physician as soon as possible if pregnancy is suspected because of possibility of fetal or neonatal injury and/or death

» Notifying physician as soon as possible if lightheadedness or fainting occurs

For diabetic patients: checking with physician if any changes in blood glucose concentrations occur

» Not taking other medications without consulting the physician, including potassium supplements or salt substitutes that contain potassium

Caution when driving or doing other things requiring alertness because of possible dizziness, lightheadedness, and syncope due to symptomatic hypotension

Checking with physician if severe nausea, vomiting, or diarrhea occurs and continues because of risk of dehydration, which may result in hypotension

Caution when exercising or during exposure to hot weather because of risk of dehydration (due to excessive perspiration), which may result in hypotension

Caution if any kind of surgery (including dental surgery) or emergency treatment is required

(Caution when using alcohol because symptomatic hypotension may occur)

(Caution when exposed to sunlight because photosensitivity can occur, which may result in sunburn)

Side/adverse effects

Signs of potential side effects, especially dizziness, fatigue, pharyngitis, viral infection, abdominal pain, allergic reaction, gout, hypotension, jaundice, neutropenia, pancreatitis, rash, confusion, drowsiness, dryness of mouth, gastrointestinal effects such as nausea and vomiting, lethargy, muscle cramps or pain, muscular fatigue, oliguria, restlessness, seizures, tachycardia, thirst, and weakness

Oral Dosage Forms

VALSARTAN AND HYDROCHLOROTHIAZIDE TABLETS

Usual adult dose

Antihypertensive—

Oral, 1 or 2 tablets as determined by individual titration with the component agents.

The usual starting dose of the combination in patients with inadequately controlled hypertension and taking valsartan as single therapy is 80 mg/12.5 mg valsartan/hydrochlorothiazide, once daily. If blood pressure remains uncontrolled after about three or four weeks of therapy, either valsartan or both components may be increased, depending on the clinical response.

The usual starting dose of the combination in patients with inadequately controlled hypertension and taking 25 mg of hydrochlorothiazide as single therapy or in patients with adequately controlled hypertension and experiencing hypokalemia with this regimen is 80 mg/12.5 mg valsartan and hydrochlorothiazide, once daily. If blood pressure remains uncontrolled after three or four weeks of therapy, the dose may be titrated up to 160 mg/25 mg valsartan/hydrochlorothiazide.

Usual adult prescribing limits

160 mg valsartan and 25 mg hydrochlorothiazide in combination.

Usual pediatric dose

Safety and efficacy have not been established.

Strength(s) usually available

U.S.—

80 mg valsartan and 12.5 mg hydrochlorothiazide (Rx) [*Diovan HCT* (colloidal silicon dioxide; crospovidone; hydroxypropyl methylcellulose; iron oxides; magnesium stearate; microcrystalline cellulose; polyethylene glycol; talc; titanium dioxide)].

160 mg valsartan and 12.5 mg hydrochlorothiazide (Rx) [*Diovan HCT* (colloidal silicon dioxide; crospovidone; hydroxypropyl methylcellulose; iron oxides; magnesium stearate; microcrystalline cellulose; polyethylene glycol; talc; titanium dioxide)].

Auxiliary labeling

- Do not take other medications without consulting your physician.

Developed: 09/02/1998

VANCOMYCIN Oral-Local

VA CLASSIFICATION (Primary): AM900

Commonly used brand name(s): *Vancocin.*

Note: For a listing of dosage forms and brand names by country availability, see *Dosage Forms* section(s).

Category

Antibacterial (oral-local).

Indications

Accepted

Colitis, antibiotic-associated (treatment)
Colitis, pseudomembranous (treatment) or
Diarrhea, antibiotic-associated (treatment)—Oral-local vancomycin is indicated in the treatment of antibiotic-associated diarrhea or colitis caused by *Clostridium difficile.* It is also indicated in the treatment of pseudomembranous colitis caused by *C. difficile.*

Oral metronidazole is considered the drug of choice by many clinicians because it has been found to be as effective as vancomycin in the treatment of patients with mild to moderate *C. difficile* colitis, and it is much more cost-effective. Also, the emergence of multidrug-resistant strains of enterococci, including vancomycin-resistant strains, is of concern.

Enterocolitis, staphylococcal (treatment)—Oral-local vancomycin is indicated in the treatment of staphylococcal enterocolitis.

Not all species or strains of a particular organism may be susceptible to vancomycin.

Unaccepted

Oral vancomycin is not effective in the treatment of other intestinal infections or in systemic infections.

Pharmacology/Pharmacokinetics

Physicochemical characteristics

Molecular weight—Vancomycin hydrochloride: 1485.74.

Mechanism of action/Effect

Oral vancomycin inhibits bacterial cell wall synthesis by binding tightly to the D-alanyl-D-alanine portion of cell wall precursors; this leads to destruction of the bacterial cell by lysis; vancomycin may also alter permeability of bacterial cytoplasmic membranes and may selectively inhibit ribonucleic acid (RNA) synthesis.

Absorption

Poorly absorbed from gastrointestinal tract.

Peak serum concentration

<1 mcg per mL; may be somewhat higher in patients with inflammatory disorders of the colonic mucosa or renal function impairment.

Fecal concentration

Approximately 350 mcg per gram following oral doses of 125 mg four times a day.

Approximately 3100 mcg per gram following oral doses of 2 grams daily.

Elimination

Primarily fecal.

Precautions to Consider

Carcinogenicity

No long-term carcinogenicity studies have been performed in animals.

Mutagenicity

No mutagenic potential was found in standard laboratory tests.

Pregnancy/Reproduction

Fertility—No definitive fertility studies have been performed.

Pregnancy—Intravenous vancomycin crosses the placenta. In one small controlled study, infants of mothers treated with vancomycin in their second or third trimester of pregnancy had no sensorineural hearing loss or nephrotoxicity that was attributed to vancomycin.

Teratology studies revealed no evidence of harm to the fetuses of rats given the normal human dose and rabbits given 1.1 times the human dose on a mg per square meter of body surface area basis.

FDA Pregnancy Category B.

Breast-feeding

Orally administered vancomycin is poorly absorbed from the gastrointestinal tracts of the mother and infant, so the small amount of this medication that may be distributed into breast milk will result in only low blood levels in the nursing infant.

Pediatrics

Appropriate studies on the relationship of age to the effects of oral vancomycin have not been performed in the pediatric population. Safety and efficacy have not been established. However, no pediatrics-specific problems have been documented to date.

Geriatrics

Appropriate studies on the relationship of age to the effects of oral vancomycin have not been performed in the geriatric population. However, no geriatrics-specific problems have been documented to date.

Drug interactions and/or related problems

The following drug interactions and/or related problems have been selected on the basis of their potential clinical significance (possible mechanism in parentheses where appropriate)—not necessarily inclusive (» = major clinical significance):

Note: Combinations containing any of the following medications, depending on the amount present, may also interact with this medication.

» Cholestyramine or
» Colestipol
(cholestyramine and colestipol anion-exchange resins have been shown to bind oral vancomycin significantly when used concurrently, resulting in decreased stool concentrations and marked reduction in antibacterial activity; concurrent use is not recommended; patients should be advised to take oral vancomycin and these medications several hours apart)

Nephrotoxic medications, other (see *Appendix II*)
(concurrent use with oral vancomycin may, on rare occasions, increase the potential for nephrotoxicity; this is most likely to occur in patients also receiving aminoglycosides and in patients with severe colitis, which may increase vancomycin absorption; caution is recommended when these medications are used concurrently with oral vancomycin)

Medical considerations/Contraindications

The medical considerations/contraindications included have been selected on the basis of their potential clinical significance (reasons given in parentheses where appropriate)—not necessarily inclusive (» = major clinical significance).

Risk-benefit should be considered when the following medical problems exist:

Hypersensitivity to vancomycin

» Inflammatory intestinal disorders, other
(may result in increased absorption and toxicity)

Renal function impairment, severe
(serum concentrations may be significantly elevated in patients with severe colitis, possibly resulting in increased toxicity)

Patient monitoring

The following may be especially important in patient monitoring (other tests may be warranted in some patients, depending on condition; » = major clinical significance):

Renal function determinations
(may be required periodically during therapy in patients with renal function impairment)

For Clostridium difficile colitis

Colonoscopy and/or
Proctosigmoidoscopy
(proctosigmoidoscopy may be useful to document the presence of pseudomembranes and/or relapse in selected patients who have persistent symptoms of *C. difficile* colitis and do not respond to therapy; however, since proctosigmoidoscopy is not always reliable in the diagnosis of *C. difficile* colitis due to rectal sparing and the presence of colitis in the more distal portions of the colon, colonoscopy may also be required in patients with a negative proctosigmoidoscopy)

» Stool toxin assays
(enzyme immunoassay of stool samples for the presence of *C. difficile* toxins may be required prior to treatment of patients with antibiotic-associated diarrhea or colitis to document the presence of *C. difficile* toxins; however, *C. difficile* and its toxins may persist following treatment with oral vancomycin despite clinical improvement; follow-up cultures and toxin assays are not recommended if clinical improvement is complete)

Side/Adverse Effects

Note: Since vancomycin is poorly absorbed from the gastrointestinal tract and serum concentrations are low, systemic side/adverse effects are unlikely to occur except perhaps during prolonged administration or administration of unusually large oral doses. For systemic side/adverse effects of vancomycin, see *Vancomycin (Systemic)*.

The following side/adverse effects have been selected on the basis of their potential clinical significance (possible signs and symptoms in parentheses where appropriate)—not necessarily inclusive:

Those indicating need for medical attention

Incidence rare

Skin rash, including exfoliative dermatitis (scaling of skin); ***macular rash*** (redness or discoloration of skin); ***urticaria*** (hives); ***or vasculitis*** (welting of skin)

Those indicating need for medical attention only if they continue or are bothersome

Incidence more frequent

Bitter or unpleasant taste; mouth irritation—with oral solution; ***nausea or vomiting***

Overdose

For more information on the management of overdose or unintentional ingestion, **contact a Poison Control Center** (see *Poison Control Center Listing*).

Clinical effects of overdose

Vancomycin overdose may cause acute renal failure and oliguria.

Treatment of overdose

To decrease absorption—Gastric emptying within the first 2 hours of overdose may decrease absorption; multiple doses of activated charcoal may also decrease absorption.

To enhance elimination—Poorly removed by dialysis; hemofiltration and hemoperfusion with polysulfone resin have been used to increase clearance.

Supportive care—Patients in whom intentional overdose is confirmed or suspected should be referred for psychiatric consultation.

Patient Consultation

As an aid to patient consultation, refer to *Advice for the Patient, Vancomycin (Oral)*.

In providing consultation, consider emphasizing the following selected information (» = major clinical significance):

Before using this medication

» Conditions affecting use, especially:
  Hypersensitivity to vancomycin
  Other medications, especially cholestyramine and colestipol
  Other medical problems, especially other inflammatory intestinal disorders

Proper use of this medication

Proper administration technique
  For oral liquids—Using a calibrated liquid-measuring device; not using after expiration date

» Compliance with full course of therapy
» Proper dosing
  Missed dose: Taking as soon as possible; not taking if almost time for next dose; not doubling doses
» Proper storage

Precautions while using this medication

Importance of physician checking progress during and after treatment

Checking with physician if no improvement within a few days

» Avoiding concurrent use of vancomycin and cholestyramine or colestipol; if concurrent use is necessary, taking vancomycin and these medications several hours apart

» Checking with physician or pharmacist before taking any other kind of diarrhea medication

Side/adverse effects

Signs of potential side effects, especially skin rash

General Dosing Information

For *Clostridium difficile* colitis—

• Oral vancomycin is indicated in the treatment of *C. difficile* colitis, which may be caused by various antibiotics (e.g., cephalosporins, lincomycins, penicillins). *C. difficile* colitis may result in severe watery diarrhea, which may occur during therapy or up to several weeks after therapy is discontinued. If diarrhea occurs, administration of antiperistaltic antidiarrheals (e.g., atropine and diphenoxylate combination, loperamide, opiates) is not recommended since they may delay the removal of toxins from the colon, thereby prolonging and/or worsening the condition.

• Mild cases of *C. difficile* colitis may respond to discontinuation of the medication alone. Moderate to severe cases may require fluid, electrolyte, and protein replacement.

• In cases not responding to the above measures or in more severe cases, oral doses of vancomycin, metronidazole, or cholestyramine may be used. Oral vancomycin is usually effective at a dose of 125 mg every six hours for seven to ten days. The dose of metronidazole is 250 to 500 mg every eight hours and the dose of cholestyramine is 4 grams four times a day. Recurrences, which occur in approximately 25% of patients treated with vancomycin or metronidazole, may be treated with a second course of vancomycin, oral metronidazole, or oral bacitracin.

• Cholestyramine resin has been shown to bind *C. difficile* toxin *in vitro* . If cholestyramine resin is administered in conjunction with oral vancomycin, the medications should be administered several hours apart since the cholestyramine resin has been shown to bind oral vancomycin also.

If a patient is too ill for oral therapy, vancomycin may be administered by enema, by passage of a long intestinal tube, or by direct instillation through a colonostomy or ileostomy. In addition, metronidazole may also be administered intravenously since 6 to 15% of metronidazole and its metabolites are excreted into the feces.

Oral Dosage Forms

Note: The dosing and strengths of the dosage forms available are expressed in terms of vancomycin base, not the hydrochloride salt.

VANCOMYCIN HYDROCHLORIDE CAPSULES USP

Usual adult and adolescent dose

Clostridium difficile colitis or diarrhea or
Staphylococcal enterocolitis—
  Oral, 125 to 500 mg (base) every six hours for seven to ten days. May be repeated if necessary.

  Note: Some studies suggest that this dose results in fecal concentrations of vancomycin that far exceed the minimum inhibitory concentration (MIC) for *C. difficile.* Also, studies have shown that 125 mg (base) every six hours is as effective as higher doses.

Usual adult prescribing limits

2 grams (base) per day.

Usual pediatric dose

Clostridium difficile colitis or diarrhea or
Staphylococcal enterocolitis—
  Oral, 10 mg (base) per kg of body weight, up to 125 mg, every six hours for seven to ten days. May be repeated if necessary.

  Note: Some medical experts recommend doses of up to 50 mg (base) per kg of body weight per day.

Usual pediatric prescribing limits

2 grams (base) per day.

Strength(s) usually available

U.S.—
  125 mg (base) (Rx) [*Vancocin*].
  250 mg (base) (Rx) [*Vancocin*].

Canada—
  125 mg (base) (Rx) [*Vancocin*].
  250 mg (base) (Rx) [*Vancocin*].

Packaging and storage

Store below 40 °C (104 °F), preferably between 15 and 30 °C (59 and 86 °F), unless otherwise specified by manufacturer. Store in a tight container.

Auxiliary labeling

• Continue medicine for full time of treatment.

VANCOMYCIN HYDROCHLORIDE FOR ORAL SOLUTION USP

Usual adult and adolescent dose

See *Vancomycin Hydrochloride Capsules USP*.

Usual adult prescribing limits

See *Vancomycin Hydrochloride Capsules USP*.

Usual pediatric dose

See *Vancomycin Hydrochloride Capsules USP*.

Usual pediatric prescribing limits

See *Vancomycin Hydrochloride Capsules USP*.

Strength(s) usually available

U.S.—
  250 mg (base) per 5 mL (when reconstituted according to manufacturer's instructions) (Rx) [*Vancocin*].
  500 mg (base) per 6 mL (when reconstituted according to manufacturer's instructions) (Rx) [*Vancocin* (ethanol up to 40 mg per gram)].

Canada—
  Not commercially available.

Packaging and storage

Prior to reconstitution, store below 40 °C (104 °F), preferably between 15 and 30 °C (59 and 86 °F), unless otherwise specified by manufacturer. Store in a tight container.

Preparation of dosage form

Add 20 mL of distilled or deionized water to each 1-gram bottle to provide a concentration of 250 mg per 5 mL, or 115 mL of diluent to each 10-gram bottle to provide a concentration of 500 mg per 6 mL. Mix thoroughly to dissolve.

For intravenous dosage form used orally—To prepare initial dilution for oral use, the contents of each 500-mg vial may be diluted in distilled water. The resulting solution may be given to the patient to drink or it may be administered through a nasogastric tube to help prevent or minimize the bitter or unpleasant taste and nausea or vomiting.

Stability

After reconstitution, solutions retain their potency for 14 days if refrigerated.

Auxiliary labeling

- Refrigerate.
- Continue medicine for full time of treatment.
- Beyond-use date.

Note

When dispensing, include a calibrated liquid-measuring device.

Revised: 04/15/1998

VANCOMYCIN Systemic

VA CLASSIFICATION (Primary): AM900

Commonly used brand name(s): *Vancocin.*

Note: For a listing of dosage forms and brand names by country availability, see *Dosage Forms* section(s).

Category

Antibacterial (systemic).

Indications

Note: Bracketed information in the *Indications* section refers to uses that are not included in U.S. product labeling.

General Considerations

Vancomycin is a narrow-spectrum antibacterial agent that has excellent antimicrobial activity against gram-positive organisms, including *Clostridium difficile*, diphtheroids, most *Enterococcus* species, staphylococci, and streptococci. Vancomycin is used to treat enterococcal infections in patients with a history of hypersensitivity to beta-lactam antibiotics, and infections due to beta-lactam–resistant microorganisms, including methicillin-resistant *Staphylococcus aureus* (MRSA), methicillin-resistant *Staphylococcus epidermidis* (MRSE), and penicillin-resistant enterococci. The increase in prevalence of disease due to MRSA and MRSE and of antibiotic resistance in general has led to an increase in the use of vancomycin.

One of the consequences of increased vancomycin use has been the emergence of vancomycin-resistant microorganisms. From 1989 through 1993, the Centers for Disease Control and Prevention (CDC) reported an increase in the percentage of nosocomial enterococcal infections caused by vancomycin-resistant enterococci, from 0.3 to 7.9%. Since the determinants of vancomycin resistance in enterococci are located on a conjugative plasmid, vancomycin resistance may be transferred among enterococci and potentially to other gram-positive organisms. *Staphylococcus* species are among the most common causes of community- and hospital-acquired infection; thus, the potential emergence of vancomycin resistance in clinical isolates of *S. aureus* and *S. epidermidis* is a public health concern. Several strains of *S. aureus* with reduced susceptibility to vancomycin have been isolated from patients in Japan. In the U.S., two strains of *S. aureus* and several strains of *Staphylococcus hemolyticus* with intermediate levels of resistance to vancomycin have been reported. The CDC has responded by developing guidelines and recommendations for the detection and prevention of the spread of vancomycin-resistant organisms. The CDC concludes that reduction in the overuse and misuse of vancomycin, as well as of antimicrobials in general, will decrease the risk of emergence of staphylococci with reduced susceptibility to vancomycin.

Accepted

Bone and joint infections (treatment)
Pneumonia (treatment)
Septicemia, bacterial (treatment) or
Skin and soft tissue infections (treatment)—Intravenous vancomycin is indicated in the treatment of bone and joint infections (including osteomyelitis), pneumonia, septicemia, and skin and soft tissue infections caused by susceptible strains of *Staphylococcus* species (including methicillin-resistant strains).

Endocarditis, bacterial (prophylaxis)—Intravenous vancomycin is indicated for prophylaxis of bacterial endocarditis in penicillin-allergic patients with prosthetic heart valves or congenital, rheumatic, or other acquired valvular heart disease who are undergoing dental procedures or surgical procedures of the upper respiratory tract. However, this use is no longer recommended by the American Heart Association or the American Dental Association. Medical experts agree that although vancomycin should not be used routinely in these patients, vancomycin should be available for use in selected patients (including penicillin-allergic patients) based on need for a life-saving medication when microorganisms are resistant to usual antibacterials.

[Vancomycin is indicated as a primary agent for the prophylaxis of bacterial endocarditis in penicillin-allergic patients with prosthetic heart valves or congenital or valvular heart disease who are undergoing gastrointestinal or genitourinary tract procedures; depending on the risk, gentamicin may be administered concurrently (Evidence rating: III).][1]

Endocarditis, bacterial (treatment)—Intravenous vancomycin is indicated in the treatment of endocarditis caused by *Staphylococcus* species (including methicillin-resistant strains).

Vancomycin is also indicated as a primary agent, alone or concurrently with an aminoglycoside or rifampin, in endocarditis caused by *Corynebacterium* species (diphtheroids) (including penicillin-resistant and cephalosporin-resistant strains) in penicillin-allergic patients, and as a secondary agent in endocarditis caused by *Streptococcus viridans* or *Streptococcus bovis*.

[Intravenous vancomycin is indicated as a primary agent, concurrently with gentamicin or streptomycin, in the treatment of endocarditis caused by enterococci (*Enterococcus faecalis*) in penicillin-allergic patients.]

Intravenous vancomycin is indicated in the treatment of severe, potentially life-threatening staphylococcal infections in patients who cannot receive penicillins or cephalosporins or who have failed to respond to them. Vancomycin is also indicated in the treatment of staphylococcal infections that are resistant to other antibacterials, including methicillin.

Note: Not all species or strains of a particular organism may be susceptible to vancomycin.

Acceptance not established

Vancomycin has been used for the treatment of meningitis due to *Streptococcus pneumoniae* or staphylococci. (Evidence rating: III) There is currently not enough medical literature or clinical experience to recommend the use of vancomycin for this indication.

Intravenous vancomycin, administered concurrently with an aminoglycoside (e.g., gentamicin) or rifampin, has been used in the treatment of serious infections caused by *Staphylococcus* species (including methicillin-resistant and multiresistant strains) in penicillin-allergic patients. (Evidence rating: III) The data are insufficient to recommend the use of vancomycin for this indication.

Unaccepted

Vancomycin is not effective against most gram-negative organisms, *Mycobacterium* species, *Bacteroides* species, *Rickettsia* species, *Chlamydia* species, or fungi.

The use of parenteral vancomycin is not recommended in the treatment of antibiotic-associated pseudomembranous colitis.

[1]Not included in Canadian product labeling.

Pharmacology/Pharmacokinetics

Physicochemical characteristics

Chemical Group—Tricyclic glycopeptide.
Molecular weight—Vancomycin hydrochloride: 1485.74.

Mechanism of action/Effect

Bactericidal for most organisms; bacteriostatic for enterococci; inhibits bacterial cell wall synthesis at a site different from that of penicillins and cephalosporins by binding tightly to the D-alanyl-D-alanine portion of cell wall precursors and interfering with bacterial growth; this leads to activation of bacterial autolysins that destroy the cell wall by lysis. Vancomycin also may alter the permeability of bacterial cytoplasmic membranes and may selectively inhibit ribonucleic acid (RNA) synthesis; vancomycin does not compete with penicillins for binding sites.

Absorption

Intraperitoneal—Systemic absorption (up to 60%) may occur.

Distribution

Widely distributed to most tissues and body fluids; adequate therapeutic concentrations in serum and in pleural, pericardial, peritoneal, ascitic, and synovial fluids; high concentrations in urine; inadequate concentrations in bile; does not readily cross normal blood-brain barrier into cerebrospinal fluid (CSF); however, penetrates into CSF when meninges are inflamed and may achieve therapeutic concentrations. Crosses the placenta.

Vol_D—Approximately 0.39 to 0.92 liter per kg.

Protein binding

Healthy adults—Moderate (approximately 37 to 55%).

Adults with infections—Low (approximately 20%).

Half-life

Normal renal function—
- Adults: Approximately 6 hours (range, 4 to 11 hours).
- Newborn infants: Approximately 6 to 10 hours.
- Older infants: Approximately 4 hours.
- Children: Approximately 2 to 3 hours.

Impaired renal function (oliguric or anuric)—
- Adults: 6 to 10 days.

Peak serum concentration

Approximately 49 mcg per mL immediately following a 500-mg intravenous dose infused over a 30-minute period; mean serum concentration is approximately 20 mcg per mL 1 to 2 hours after dosing.

Approximately 63 mcg per mL immediately following a 1-gram intravenous dose infused over a 60-minute period; mean serum concentration is approximately 23 to 30 mcg per mL 1 to 2 hours after dosing.

Elimination

Renal—Approximately 75 to 90% or more excreted by passive glomerular filtration unchanged in urine within 24 hours; slowly eliminated by unknown route and mechanism in anephric patients.

Biliary—Small to moderate amounts may be excreted in bile.

In dialysis—Not appreciably removed from the blood by hemodialysis or peritoneal dialysis.

Precautions to Consider

Carcinogenicity

No long-term carcinogenicity studies have been performed in animals.

Mutagenicity

No mutagenic potential was found in standard laboratory tests.

Pregnancy/Reproduction

Fertility—No definitive fertility studies have been performed.

Pregnancy—Intravenous vancomycin crosses the placenta. In one small controlled study, infants whose mothers were treated with vancomycin in their second or third trimester of pregnancy had no sensorineural hearing loss or nephrotoxicity that was attributed to vancomycin therapy.

FDA Pregnancy Category C.

Breast-feeding

Parenteral vancomycin is distributed into breast milk. Although available data regarding the use of vancomycin while breast-feeding are limited, problems in humans have not been documented.

Pediatrics

Close monitoring of vancomycin serum concentrations is recommended in premature neonates and young infants.

Geriatrics

Elderly patients are more likely to have an age-related decrease in renal function, which may require dosage adjustments to avoid excessive vancomycin serum concentrations. Because of this, geriatric patients are at greater risk of vancomycin-induced ototoxicity (i.e., loss of hearing) and nephrotoxicity.

Drug interactions and/or related problems

The following drug interactions and/or related problems have been selected on the basis of their potential clinical significance (possible mechanism in parentheses where appropriate)—not necessarily inclusive (» = major clinical significance):

Note: Combinations containing any of the following medications, depending on the amount present, may also interact with this medication.

» Aminoglycosides or
» Amphotericin B, parenteral or
Aspirin or other salicylates or
» Bacitracin, parenteral or
» Bumetanide, parenteral or
» Capreomycin or
Carmustine or
» Cisplatin or
» Cyclosporine or
» Ethacrynic acid, parenteral or
» Furosemide, parenteral or
» Paromomycin or
» Polymyxins or
» Streptozocin
(concurrent and/or sequential use of these medications with vancomycin may increase the potential for ototoxicity and/or nephrotoxicity; hearing loss may occur and may progress to deafness, even after discontinuation of the drug; hearing loss may be reversible, but usually is permanent; serial audiometric function determinations may be required with concurrent or sequential use of other ototoxic antibacterials)
(however, vancomycin and aminoglycosides often must be administered concurrently in the prophylaxis of bacterial endocarditis, in the treatment of endocarditis caused by *Streptococcus* species and diphtheroids, in the treatment of resistant staphylococcal infections, or in penicillin-allergic patients; appropriate monitoring will help to reduce the possibility of an interaction between vancomycin and aminoglycosides; renal function determinations, monitoring of serum concentrations, dosage reductions and/or dosage interval adjustments, or alternate antibacterials may be required)

Anesthetic agents or
» Vecuronium
(some clinical studies report that patients experienced vancomycin-dependent hypotension or enhancement of neuromuscular depression with administration of anesthetic agents or vecuronium, respectively; however, other clinicians report no effects or significant differences between patients administered vancomycin before or after induction of anesthesia; it is recommended that vancomycin be administered by infusion over a period of at least 60 minutes, preferably prior to the induction of anesthesia, to minimize potential enhancement of the hypotensive or neuromuscular blockade effects of anesthetic agents or vecuronium)

Antihistamines or
Buclizine or
Cyclizine or
Meclizine or
Phenothiazines or
Thioxanthenes or
Trimethobenzamide
(concurrent use of these medications with vancomycin may mask the symptoms of ototoxicity, such as tinnitus, dizziness, or vertigo)

» Dexamethasone
(studies in animals have demonstrated that concurrent administration of dexamethasone with vancomycin may impair the penetration of vancomycin into cerebrospinal fluid [CSF]; however, the penetration of vancomycin into the CSF of children is better than that demonstrated in the rabbit model; if dexamethasone is to be used as adjunctive therapy in bacterial meningitis, it is recommended that dexamethasone be administered either before or concurrently with the first dose of vancomycin)

Laboratory value alterations

The following have been selected on the basis of their potential clinical significance (possible effect in parentheses where appropriate)—not necessarily inclusive (» = major clinical significance).

With physiology/laboratory test values
Blood urea nitrogen (BUN)
(concentrations may be increased)

Medical considerations/Contraindications

The medical considerations/contraindications included have been selected on the basis of their potential clinical significance (reasons given in parentheses where appropriate)—not necessarily inclusive (» = major clinical significance).

Risk-benefit should be considered when the following medical problems exist:

Hypersensitivity to vancomycin
» Loss of hearing, or deafness, history of
(vancomycin rarely may cause hearing loss or deafness)
» Renal function impairment
(because vancomycin is excreted primarily through the kidneys, patients with renal function impairment may need an adjustment in dosage)

Patient monitoring

The following may be especially important in patient monitoring (other tests may be warranted in some patients, depending on condition; » = major clinical significance):

» Audiograms and
» Renal function determinations
(may be required prior to, periodically during, and following treatment in patients with pre-existing renal or eighth-cranial-nerve impairment, especially in patients older than 60 years of age, and with concurrent or sequential administration of other ototoxic antibacterials; twice-weekly or weekly audiometric testing to detect high-frequency hearing loss in patients old enough to be tested;

daily renal function determinations may also be required in patients on high-dose or prolonged therapy, especially if renal function is changing or borderline)

» Urinalyses
(may be required prior to treatment and periodically during treatment to detect albumin, casts, and cells in the urine, as well as decreased specific gravity)

» Vancomycin serum concentrations
(may be required periodically in patients with renal function impairment, especially if renal function is changing or borderline, and in patients older than 60 years of age; peak concentrations should not be maintained in excess of approximately 40 mcg per mL, and trough concentrations should not exceed approximately 10 mcg per mL; serum concentrations greater than 80 mcg per mL are considered to be in the toxic range)

White blood cell count
(should be monitored periodically to detect possible neutropenia)

Side/Adverse Effects

Note: Side/adverse effects were relatively common with early formulations of vancomycin. Many of these side effects (e.g., chills, fever, hypotension, nephrotoxicity, skin rash, thrombophlebitis, pain at the injection site) were attributed to impurities. Because of subsequent purification, the incidence of these side effects has been substantially reduced.

The following side/adverse effects have been selected on the basis of their potential clinical significance (possible signs and symptoms in parentheses where appropriate)—not necessarily inclusive:

Those indicating need for medical attention

Incidence less frequent

Nephrotoxicity (change in frequency of urination or amount of urine; difficulty in breathing; drowsiness; increased thirst; loss of appetite; nausea or vomiting; weakness); ***neutropenia*** (chills; coughing; difficulty in breathing; fever; sore throat)—usually reversible; ***"red man syndrome"*** (chills or fever; fainting; fast heartbeat; hives; hypotension; itching of skin; nausea or vomiting; rash or redness of the face, base of neck, upper body, back, and arms)—may result from histamine release due to rapid infusion

Incidence rare

Chemical peritonitis (abdominal pain and cramps; abdominal tenderness)—in patients receiving high doses by intraperitoneal administration; ***linear IgA bullous dermatosis*** (large blisters on arms, legs, hands, feet, or upper body); ***ototoxicity*** (loss of hearing; ringing or buzzing or a feeling of fullness in the ears); ***pseudomembranous colitis*** (abdominal or stomach cramps and pain, severe; abdominal tenderness; diarrhea, watery and severe, which may also be bloody; fever); ***thrombocytopenia*** (abnormal bleeding or bruising)

Those indicating possible ototoxicity, nephrotoxicity, or pseudomembranous colitis and the need for medical attention if they occur or progress after medication is discontinued

Abdominal or stomach cramps and pain, severe; abdominal tenderness; change in frequency of urination or amount of urine; diarrhea, watery and severe, which may also be bloody; difficulty in breathing; drowsiness; fever; increased thirst; loss of appetite; loss of hearing; nausea or vomiting; ringing or buzzing or a feeling of fullness in the ears; weakness

Overdose

For more information on the management of overdose or unintentional ingestion, **contact a Poison Control Center** (see *Poison Control Center Listing*).

Clinical effects of overdose

Vancomycin overdose may result in oliguria and acute renal function failure. Two cases of vancomycin overdose have been reported. An adult who received 1 gram of parenteral vancomycin every 4 hours, for a total of 56 grams over a 10-day period, developed acute renal failure. A 47-day-old premature infant inadvertently was given three 12-mg doses and six 240-mg doses of parenteral vancomycin. Both patients survived.

Treatment of overdose

To enhance elimination—Poorly removed by dialysis; hemofiltration and hemoperfusion with polysulfone resin have been used to reduce elevated serum concentrations of vancomycin.

Monitoring—Patients should be monitored for electrolytes, fluid, hearing function, hematologic status (especially platelet and white blood cell counts), renal function, and vestibular function.

Supportive care—Patients in whom intentional overdose is confirmed or suspected should be referred for psychiatric consultation.

Patient Consultation

As an aid to patient consultation, refer to *Advice for the Patient, Vancomycin (Systemic)*.

In providing consultation, consider emphasizing the following selected information (» = major clinical significance):

Before using this medication

» Conditions affecting use, especially:
Hypersensitivity to vancomycin
Pregnancy—Vancomycin crosses the placenta
Breast-feeding—Vancomycin is distributed into breast milk
Use in the elderly—Elderly patients may be at greater risk of nephrotoxicity and ototoxicity
Other medications, especially aminoglycosides, amphotericin B, bacitracin, bumetanide, capreomycin, cisplatin, cyclosporine, dexamethasone, ethacrynic acid, furosemide, paromomycin, polymyxins, streptozocin, or vecuronium
Other medical problems, especially a history of hearing loss or deafness, or renal function impairment

Proper use of this medication

» If medication is being given at home, carefully following physician's instructions

» Importance of receiving medication for full course of therapy and on regular schedule

» Proper dosing
Missed dose: Taking as soon as possible; not taking if almost time for next dose; not doubling doses

Side/adverse effects

Signs of potential side effects, especially nephrotoxicity, neutropenia, "red man syndrome," chemical peritonitis, linear IgA bullous dermatosis, ototoxicity, pseudomembranous colitis, and thrombocytopenia

General Dosing Information

Since vancomycin is highly irritating to tissues and causes necrosis and severe pain on intramuscular administration or extravasation, parenteral vancomycin must be administered by intravenous (or intraperitoneal) infusion only. Avoid extravasation. Sterile vancomycin hydrochloride also may be administered orally for treatment of *Clostridium difficile* colitis, but oral vancomycin is not effective in systemic infections.

Parenteral vancomycin should be administered over a period of at least 60 minutes. To help reduce the incidence of administration rate–related side effects (e.g., cardiac arrest [rarely], hypotension, "red man syndrome"), this medication should not be administered rapidly or as a bolus injection. Vancomycin should be administered intermittently in at least 100 to 200 mL of 5% dextrose injection or 0.9% sodium chloride injection. Veins into which vancomycin is infused should be rotated to help prevent the development of thrombophlebitis, unless vancomycin is being administered via a central venous catheter.

Patients with impaired renal or auditory function may require (1) a reduction in the maintenance dose by administration of the usual dose at prolonged intervals, or (2) discontinuation of vancomycin. Since vancomycin is not metabolized and is excreted primarily in the urine, toxic concentrations may accumulate in patients with impaired renal function. Therapeutic concentrations of vancomycin may persist for 7 to 21 days after dosing, especially in anuric patients.

Serum concentrations should be monitored during therapy, especially during prolonged therapy or in patients with impaired renal function or a history of hearing loss or deafness. Peak concentrations should not be maintained in excess of approximately 40 mcg per mL, and trough concentrations should not exceed approximately 10 mcg per mL. Serum concentrations greater than 80 mcg per mL are considered to be in the toxic range.

Therapy should be continued for at least 4 weeks or longer in the treatment of staphylococcal endocarditis.

Parenteral Dosage Forms

Note: Bracketed information in the *Dosage Forms* section refers to uses that are not included in U.S. product labeling.

Note: The dosing and strengths of the dosage forms available are expressed in terms of vancomycin base (not the hydrochloride salt).

STERILE VANCOMYCIN HYDROCHLORIDE USP

Usual adult and adolescent dose

Antibacterial, treatment—

Intravenous infusion, 7.5 mg (base) per kg of body weight or 500 mg every six hours; or 15 mg per kg of body weight or 1 gram every twelve hours.

Note: After an initial loading dose of 750 mg to 1 gram (base), but not less than 15 mg per kg of body weight, adults with impaired renal function may require a reduction in dose as indicated in the table below. However, the preferred method is to adjust dosage based on serum vancomycin concentrations.

Creatinine clearance (mL/min)/(mL/sec)	Intravenous dose (base)
> 80/1.33	See *Usual adult and adolescent dose*
50–80/0.83–1.33	1 gram every 1 to 3 days
10–50/0.17–0.83	1 gram every 3 to 7 days
< 10/0.17	1 gram every 7 to 14 days

[Endocarditis, prophylaxis, in penicillin-allergic patients with prosthetic heart valves or congenital, rheumatic, or other acquired valvular heart disease who are undergoing gastrointestinal or genitourinary tract procedures][1]—

Intravenous infusion, 1 gram (base) over a period of one to two hours, with or without gentamicin (administered intramuscularly or intravenously at a dose of 1.5 mg per kg of body weight up to 120 mg), depending on risk of bacterial endocarditis; the infusion/injection should be completed within one-half hour of the start of surgery.

Usual adult prescribing limits

3 to 4 grams (base) a day have been used intravenously for short periods of time in very severe infections.

Usual pediatric dose

Antibacterial, treatment—

Neonates up to 1 week of age: Intravenous infusion, 15 mg (base) per kg of body weight initially, followed by 10 mg per kg of body weight every twelve hours.

Infants 1 week to 1 month of age: Intravenous infusion, 15 mg (base) per kg of body weight initially, followed by 10 mg per kg of body weight every eight hours.

Infants and children 1 month to 12 years of age: Intravenous infusion, 10 mg (base) per kg of body weight every six hours; or 20 mg per kg of body weight every twelve hours.

Note: Doses of up to 60 mg (base) per kg of body weight per day have been used in some infections (e.g., staphylococcal infections of the central nervous system [CNS]).

[Endocarditis, prophylaxis, in penicillin-allergic patients with prosthetic heart valves or congenital, rheumatic, or other acquired valvular heart disease who are undergoing gastrointestinal or genitourinary tract procedures][1]—

Intravenous infusion, 20 mg (base) per kg of body weight over a period of one to two hours, with or without gentamicin (administered intramuscularly or intravenously at a dose of 1.5 mg per kg of body weight), depending on degree of risk; the infusion/injection should be completed within one-half hour of the start of surgery.

Strength(s) usually available

U.S.—

500 mg (base) (may be available in ADD-Vantage® vials) (Rx) [*Vancocin;* GENERIC].

1 gram (base) (may be available in ADD-Vantage® vials) (Rx) [*Vancocin;* GENERIC].

5 grams (base) (Rx) [GENERIC].

Canada—

500 mg (base) (may be available in ADD-Vantage® vials) (Rx) [*Vancocin;* GENERIC].

1 gram (base) (may be available in ADD-Vantage® vials) (Rx) [*Vancocin;* GENERIC].

5 grams (base) (Rx) [GENERIC].

Packaging and storage

Prior to reconstitution, store below 40 °C (104 °F), preferably between 15 and 30 °C (59 and 86 °F), unless otherwise specified by manufacturer.

Preparation of dosage form

For intravenous use—

To prepare initial dilution for intravenous use, 10 or 20 mL of sterile water for injection should be added to each 500-mg or 1-gram vial, respectively. For intermittent intravenous infusion (preferred), the 10-mL or 20-mL solution should be further diluted in 100 or 200 mL, respectively, of 5% dextrose injection or 0.9% sodium chloride injection. The resulting solution should be administered over a 60-minute period or longer.

For continuous intravenous infusion (used only when intermittent infusion is not feasible), 1 to 2 grams (20 to 40 mL) may be added to a sufficiently large volume of 5% dextrose injection or 0.9% sodium chloride injection to permit the total daily dose to be administered slowly by intravenous drip over a 24-hour period. Avoid extravasation.

For reconstitution of ADD-Vantage® vials, see manufacturer's labeling for instructions.

For oral use—

See *Vancomycin (Oral-Local)*.

Stability

After reconstitution with 5% dextrose injection or 0.9% sodium chloride injection, solutions retain their potency for 14 days if refrigerated.

Incompatibilities

The admixture of supplementary medication and vancomycin is not recommended. Vancomycin is incompatible with alkaline solutions and may be precipitated by heavy metals. It has also been found to be incompatible with aminophylline, amobarbital sodium, aztreonam, chloramphenicol sodium succinate, chlorothiazide sodium, dexamethasone sodium phosphate, heparin sodium, methicillin sodium, pentobarbital sodium, phenobarbital sodium, secobarbital sodium, and sodium bicarbonate.

Vancomycin should not be added to solutions containing albumin, cefepime, ceftazidime, foscarnet sodium, penicillin G, or piperacillin sodium–tazobactam sodium. If these solutions are administered concurrently, they should be administered at separate sites.

VANCOMYCIN HYDROCHLORIDE FOR INJECTION USP

Usual adult and adolescent dose

See *Sterile Vancomycin Hydrochloride USP*.

Usual adult and adolescent prescribing limits

See *Sterile Vancomycin Hydrochloride USP*.

Usual pediatric dose

See *Sterile Vancomycin Hydrochloride USP*.

Strength(s) usually available

U.S.—

10 grams (base) (Rx) [*Vancocin;* GENERIC].

Canada—

10 grams (base) (Rx) [*Vancocin*].

Packaging and storage

Prior to reconstitution, store below 40 C (104 F), preferably between 15 and 30 C (59 and 86 F), unless otherwise specified by manufacturer.

Preparation of dosage form

For intravenous use—

For reconstitution of pharmacy bulk vials, 95 mL of sterile water for injection should be added to each 10-gram vial to provide a solution of 100 mg per mL. Using aseptic technique, the closure should be penetrated only once after reconstitution using a suitable sterile dispensing set that allows measured dispensing of the contents. Use of a syringe and needle is not recommended as leakage may occur.

Reconstituted solutions of 5 mL containing 500 mg of vancomycin should be diluted with at least 100 mL of suitable diluent (see manufacturers labeling instructions), and reconstituted solutions of 10 mL containing 1 gram of vancomycin should be diluted with at least 200 mL of suitable diluent. The final dose should be administered by intermittent intravenous infusion over a period of at least 60 minutes.

For oral use—

See *Vancomycin (Oral-Local)*.

Stability

After reconstitution, the solution should be dispensed within 4 hours.

Incompatibilities

The admixture of supplementary medication and vancomycin is not recommended. Vancomycin is incompatible with alkaline solutions and may be precipitated by heavy metals. It also has been found to be incompatible with aminophylline, amobarbital sodium, aztreonam, chloramphenicol sodium succinate, chlorothiazide sodium, dexamethasone sodium phosphate, heparin sodium, methicillin sodium, pentobarbital sodium, phenobarbital sodium, secobarbital sodium, and sodium bicarbonate.

Vancomycin should not be added to solutions containing albumin, cefepime, ceftazidime, foscarnet sodium, penicillin G, or piperacillin sodium–tazobactam sodium. If these solutions are administered concurrently, they should be administered at separate sites.

VANCOMYCIN INJECTION USP

Usual adult and adolescent dose
See *Sterile Vancomycin Hydrochloride USP.*

Usual adult and adolescent prescribing limits
See *Sterile Vancomycin Hydrochloride USP.*

Usual pediatric dose
See *Sterile Vancomycin Hydrochloride USP.*

Strength(s) usually available
U.S.—
500 mg per 100 mL (Rx) [*Vancocin*].

Canada—
Not commercially available.

Packaging and storage
Store between −20 and −10 °C (−4 and 14 °F), unless otherwise specified by manufacturer.

Preparation of dosage form
Vancomycin Injection USP should be administered only by the intravenous route. For oral administration of parenteral vancomycin, see *Vancomycin (Oral-Local).*

Frozen containers should be thawed at room temperature (25 C [77 F]) or under refrigeration (5 C [41 F]). Thawing should not be forced by immersion in water baths or by microwave irradiation.

Do not use plastic containers in series connections. Such use may result in an air embolism because of residual air being drawn from the primary container before administration of the fluid from the secondary container is complete.

Stability
Once thawed, solutions remain stable for 72 hours at room temperature, or for 30 days when refrigerated. Thawed solutions should not be refrozen.

Do not use if solution is cloudy or contains a precipitate.

Incompatibilities
The admixture of supplementary medication and vancomycin is not recommended. Vancomycin is incompatible with alkaline solutions and may be precipitated by heavy metals. It has also been found to be incompatible with aminophylline, amobarbital sodium, aztreonam, chloramphenicol sodium succinate, chlorothiazide sodium, dexamethasone sodium phosphate, heparin sodium, methicillin sodium, pentobarbital sodium, phenobarbital sodium, secobarbital sodium, and sodium bicarbonate.

Vancomycin should not be added to solutions containing albumin, cefepime,−ceftazidime, foscarnet sodium, penicillin G, or piperacillin sodiumtazobactam sodium. If these solutions are administered concurrently, they should be administered at separate sites.

[1]Not included in Canadian product labeling.

Selected Bibliography

Centers for Disease Control and Prevention. Recommendations for preventing the spread of vancomycin resistance. MMWR Morb Mortal Wkly Rep 1995; 44(RR−12): [20 screens]. Cited 11/18/97. Available from: URL: http://www.cdc.gov/epo/mmwr/ind95_rr.htm

Centers for Disease Control and Prevention. Interim guidelines for prevention and control of staphylococcal infection associated with reduced susceptibility to vancomycin. MMWR Morb Mortal Wkly Rep 1997; 46(27): [10 screens]. Cited 8/8/97. Available from: URL: http://www.cdc.gov/epo/mmwr/mmwr_wk.html

Revised: 06/15/1999

VARDENAFIL Systemic†

VA CLASSIFICATION (Primary): GU 900

Note: For a listing of dosage forms and brand names by country availability, see *Dosage Forms* section(s).

†Not commercially available in Canada.

Category
Impotence therapy agent (systemic).

Indications

Accepted
Erectile dysfunction (treatment)—Vardenafil is indicated for the treatment of erectile dysfunction.

Pharmacology/Pharmacokinetics

Physicochemical characteristics
Molecular weight—579.1.

Solubility—0.11 mg per mL in water.

Mechanism of action/Effect
Penile erection is a hemodynamic process initiated by the relaxation of smooth muscle in corpus cavernosum and its associated arterioles. During sexual stimulation, nitric oxide is released from nerve endings and endothelial cells in the corpus cavernosum. Nitric oxide activates the enzyme guanylate cyclase resulting in increased synthesis of cyclic guanosine monophosphate (cGMP) in the smooth muscle cells of the corpus cavernosum. The cGMP in turn triggers smooth muscle relaxation, allowing increased blood flow into the penis, resulting in erection. The tissue concentration of cGMP is regulated by both the rates of synthesis and degradation via phosphodiesterases (PDEs). The most abundant PDE in the human corpus cavernosum is the cGMP-specific phosphodiesterase type 5 (PDE5); therefore, the inhibition of PDE5 enhances erectile function by increasing the amount of cGMP. Because sexual stimulation is required to initiate the local release of nitric oxide, the inhibition of PDE5 has no effect in the absence of sexual stimulation.

In vitro studies have shown that vardenafil is a selective inhibitor of PDE5. The inhibitory effect of vardenafil is more selective on PDE5 than for other known phosphodiesterases (>15−fold relative to PDE6, >130−fold relative to PDE1, >300−fold relative to PDE11, and >1,000−fold relative to PDE2, 3, 4, 7, 8, 9, and 10).

Absorption
Rapidly absorbed; absolute bioavailability is approximately 15%. A high-fat meal causes a reduction in C_{max} by 18% to 50%.

Distribution
V_{ss}: 208 L; indicates extensive tissue distribution

A mean of 0.00018% of the dose was obtained in semen 1.5 hours after dosing.

Protein binding
Very high: 95% bound to plasma proteins; reversible and independent of total drug concentrations

Biotransformation
Hepatic metabolism, via CYP3A4, with contribution from CYP3A5 and CYP2C isoforms. Major circulating metabolite, M1, results from desethylation at the piperazine moiety of vardenafil. M1 is subject to further metabolism. The plasma concentration of M1 is approximately 26% of the parent compound and accounts for 7% of total pharmacologic activity. This metabolite shows a phosphodiesterase selectivity profile similar to that of vardenafil and an *in vitro* inhibitory potency for PDE5 28% of that of vardenafil.

Half-life
Terminal: 4 to 5 hours

Time to peak concentration
30 minutes to 2 hours (oral dosing, fasted state)

Elimination
Feces: 91%-95% of administered dose

Urine: 2%-6% of administered dose

Total body clearance: 56 L per hour

Pharmacokinetics in special populations
Geriatrics: Elderly males age 65 years and older have higher vardenafil plasma concentrations than younger males (18-45 years), mean C_{max} and AUC were 34% and 52% higher, respectively.

Renal Insufficiency: CrCl 50−80 mL/min: pharmacokinetics similar to normal renal function; CrCl < 50 mL/min: vardenafil AUC was increased by 20 to 30% compared to normal renal function

Hepatic Insufficiency: Mild hepatic impairment (Child-Pugh Class A): C_{max} and AUC increased by 130% and 160% respectively

Precautions to Consider

Carcinogenicity
Vardenafil was not carcinogenic in rats and mice when administered daily for 24 months. In these studies systemic drug exposures (AUCs) for unbound (free) vardenafil and its major metabolite were approximately 400- and 170-fold for male and female rats, respectively, and 21- and 37-fold for male and female mice, respectively, the exposures observed in human males given the Maximum Recommended Human Dose (MRHD) of 20 mg.

Mutagenicity
Vardenafil was not mutagenic as assessed in either the *in vitro* bacterial Ames assay or the forward mutation assay in Chinese hamster V79

cells. Vardenafil was not clastogenic as assessed in either the *in vitro* chromosomal aberration test or the *in vivo* mouse micronucleus test.

Pregnancy/Reproduction

Fertility—Vardenafil did not impair fertility in male and female rats administered doses up to 100 mg per kg per day for 28 days prior to mating in males, and for 14 days prior to mating and through day 7 of gestation in females. In a corresponding 1-month rat toxicity study, this dose produced an AUC value for unbound vardenafil 200-fold greater than AUC in humans at the MRHD of 20 mg.

There was no effect on sperm motility or morphology after single 20 mg oral doses of vardenafil in healthy male volunteers.

Pregnancy—Adequate and well-controlled studies in humans have not been done. Vardenafil is not indicated for use in females.

No evidence of specific potential for teratogenicity, embryotoxicity or fetotoxicity was observed in rats and rabbits that received vardenafil at up to 18 mg per kg per day during organogenesis. This dose is approximately 100-fold (rat) and 29-fold (rabbit) greater than AUC values for unbound vardenafil and its major metabolite in humans given the MRHD of 20 mg. In the rat pre- and postnatal development study, the NOAEL (no observed adverse effect level) for maternal toxicity was 8 mg per kg per day. Retarded physical development of pups in the absence of maternal effects was observed following maternal exposure to 1 and 8 mg per kg per day possibly due to vasodilation and/or secretion of the drug into milk. The number of living pups born to rats exposed pre- and postnatally was reduced at 60 mg per kg per day. Based on the results of the pre- and postnatal study, the developmental NOAEL is less than 1 mg per kg per day. Based on plasma exposures in the rat developmental toxicity study, 1 mg per kg per day in the pregnant rat is estimated to produce total AUC values comparable to those in humans at the MRHD of 20 mg.

FDA Pregnancy Category B

Breast-feeding

It is not known whether vardenafil is distributed into human breast milk. Vardenafil is not indicated for use in females. However, vardenafil is distributed into the milk of rats at concentrations approximately 10-fold greater than found in plasma. Following a single oral dose of 3 mg per kg, 3.3% of the administered dose was distributed into the milk within 24 hours.

Pediatrics

No information is available on the relationship of age to the effects of vardenafil in the pediatric population. Vardenafil is not indicated for use in pediatric patients.

Geriatrics

Elderly males age 65 years and older have higher vardenafil plasma concentrations than younger males (18-45 years), mean C_{max} and AUC were 34% and 52% higher, respectively. Phase 3 clinical trials included more than 834 elderly patients and no differences in safety and effectiveness of vardenafil 5, 10, or 20 mg were noted when these elderly patients were compared to younger patients. However, due to increased vardenafil concentrations in the elderly, a starting dose of 5 mg should be considered in patients ≥65 years in age.

Drug interactions and/or related problems

The following drug interactions and/or related problems have been selected on the basis of their potential clinical significance (possible mechanism in parentheses where appropriate)—not necessarily inclusive (» = major clinical significance):

Note: Combinations containing any of the following medications, depending on the amount present, may also interact with this medication.

» Class IA antiarrhythmic medications, such as
» Procainamide
» Quinidine
» Class IIIA antiarrhythmic medications, such as
» Amiodarone
» Sotalol
(should not be used together with vardenafil)

Alpha blockers, such as
» Alfuzosin
» Doxazosin
» Prazosin
» Tamsulosin
» Terazosin
(caution is advised; both are vasodilators and when used in combination, an additive effect on blood pressure may be anticipated; in some patients, concomitant use can lower blood pressure significantly; dose adjustments and monitoring may be necessary)

Erectile dysfunction, treatment
(vardenafil has not been studied in combination with other treatments for erectile dysfunction; use of combination erectile dysfunction medication is not recommended)

» Erythromycin
(erythromycin produced a 4–fold increase in vardenafil AUC and a 3–fold increase in C_{max}; dose adjustment is recommended)

» Indinavir
(indinavir produced a 16–fold increase in vardenafil AUC, a 7–fold increased C_{max} and a 2–fold increase in half-life; a dose adjustment is recommended)

» Itraconazole or
» Ketoconazole
(ketoconazole 200 mg once daily or itraconazole produced a 10–fold increase in vardenafil AUC and a 4–fold increase in C_{max} when co-administered with vardenafil in healthy volunteers; dose adjustment is needed)
(higher doses of ketoconazole (400 mg daily) may result in higher increases in AUC and C_{max}, dose adjustment is needed)

» Nitrates, regular or intermittent use, or
» Nitric oxide donors
(use is contraindicated; PDE5 inhibitors potentiates the hypotensive effects of nitrates; a suitable time interval following vardenafil dosing for the safe administration of nitrates or nitrate oxide donors has not been determined)

» Ritonavir
(ritonavir co-administered with vardenafil resulted in a 49–fold increase in vardenafil AUC and a 13–fold increase in vardenafil C_{max}; vardenafil half-life was prolonged to 26 hours; a dose adjustment is recommended)

Laboratory value alterations

The following have been selected on the basis of their potential clinical significance (possible effect in parentheses where appropriate)—not necessarily inclusive (» = major clinical significance).

With physiology/laboratory test values
Creatinine kinase or
Gamma-glutamyl transpeptidase (GGTP)
(values may be increased)
Liver function tests
(values may be abnormal)

Medical considerations/Contraindications

The medical considerations/contraindications included have been selected on the basis of their potential clinical significance (reasons given in parentheses where appropriate)—not necessarily inclusive (» = major clinical significance).

Except under special circumstances, this medication should not be used when the following medical problem exists:

» Hypersensitivity to vardenafil or to any component of the tablet
» Angina, unstable or
» Arrhythmia, life-threatening, or
» Cardiac failure, severe, or
» Hepatic impairment, severe (Child-Pugh C), or
» Hypertension, uncontrolled (< 170/110 mm Hg) or
» Hypotension (resting systolic blood pressure of < 90 mm Hg) or
» Myocardial infarction (within the last 6 months) or
» Renal disease, end-stage, requiring dialysis, or
» Retinal disorders (hereditary and degenerative), including retinitis pigmentosa or
» Stroke, recent history of
(there is no controlled clinical data on the safety or efficacy of vardenafil in patients with these conditions; use is not recommended until further information is available)

QT prolongation, congenital or acquired
(increase in the QT_c interval was seen in a clinical study; avoid using vardenafil in these patients)

Risk-benefit should be considered when the following medical problems exist:

Age >50 years or
Coronary artery disease or
Diabetes or
Hyperlipidemia or
Hypertension or
Low cup to disc ratio ("crowded disc") or
Smoking
(NAION has been reported rarely postmarketing in temporal association with the use of PDE5 inhibitors with most of these patients having one of these underlying anatomic or vascular risk factors for development of NAION; it is not possible to determine

whether these events are related directly to the use of PDE5 inhibitors, to the patient's underlying vascular risk factors or anatomical defects, to a combination of these factors or other factors)

Anatomical deformation of the penis, such as
Angulation or
Cavernosal fibrosis or
Peyronie's disease
(vardenafil should be used with caution in these patients)

Bleeding disorders or
Peptic ulceration, active
(vardenafil has not been administered to patients with these conditions; it should be administered only after careful risk-benefit assessment has been completed)

Cardiovascular disease, underlying
(vardenafil has systemic vasodilatory properties and can result in transient decreases in supine blood pressure; patients with underlying cardiovascular disease could be adversely affected by these vasodilatory effects; caution should be used in these patients)

Cardiovascular status, current
(patients cardiovascular status should be considered when using vardenafil; there is a degree of cardiac risk associated with sexual activity; in men for whom sexual activity is not recommended because of their underlying cardiovascular status, treatment for erectile dysfunction should not be used)

Hepatic insufficiency, moderate
(the C_{max} and AUC following a 10 mg vardenafil dose were increased 130% and 160% respectively; a lower starting dose is recommended and should not exceed the recommended maximum dose)

Left ventricular outflow obstruction, such as
Aortic stenosis
Idiopathic hypertrophic subaortic stenosis
(patients with these conditions can be sensitive to the action of vasodilators including Type 5 phosphodiesterase inhibitors)

NAION in one eye, previous
(may increase risk of NAION recurring; these patients could be adversely affected by use of vasodilators such as PDE5 inhibitors)

Renal insufficiency, moderate to severe
(20 to 30% higher vardenafil AUC observed in patients with moderate to severe renal sufficiency compared with those with normal renal function)

Sickle cell anemia or
Multiple myeloma or
Leukemia
(these conditions may predispose patients to priapism; vardenafil should be used with caution)

Side/Adverse Effects

The following side/adverse effects have been selected on the basis of their potential clinical significance (possible signs and symptoms in parentheses where appropriate)—not necessarily inclusive:

There have been rare reports of prolonged erections (longer than 4 hours) and priapism (painful erections greater than 6 hours in duration) for this class of compounds, including vardenafil. In the event that an erection persists longer than 4 hours, the patient should seek immediate medical assistance. If priapism is not treated immediately penile tissue damage and permanent loss of potency may result.

Those indicating need for medical attention

Incidence less frequent

Anaphylactic reaction (cough; difficulty swallowing; dizziness; fast heartbeat; hives; itching; puffiness or swelling of the eyelids or around the eyes, face, lips or tongue; shortness of breath; skin rash; tightness in chest; unusual tiredness or weakness; wheezing); ***angina pectoris*** (arm, back or jaw pain; chest pain or discomfort; chest tightness or heaviness; fast or irregular heartbeat; shortness of breath; sweating; nausea); ***chest pain; dyspnea*** (shortness of breath; difficult or labored breathing; tightness in chest; wheezing); ***glaucoma*** (blindness; blurred vision; decreased vision; eye pain; headache; nausea or vomiting; tearing); ***hypertension*** (blurred vision; dizziness; nervousness; headache; pounding in the ears; slow or fast heartbeat); ***hypotension*** (blurred vision; confusion; dizziness, faintness, or lightheadedness when getting up from a lying or sitting position suddenly; sweating; unusual tiredness or weakness); ***myocardial ischemia*** (chest pain or discomfort; nausea; pain or discomfort in arms, jaw, back or neck; shortness of breath; sweating; vomiting); ***myocardial infarction*** (chest pain or discomfort; pain or discomfort in arms, jaw, back or neck; shortness of breath; nausea; sweating; vomiting); ***palpitation*** (fast, irregular, pounding, or racing heartbeat or pulse); ***postural hypotension*** (chills; cold sweats; confusion; dizziness, faintness, or lightheadedness when getting up from lying or sitting position); ***priapism*** (painful or prolonged erection of the penis); ***rash; syncope*** (fainting); ***tachycardia*** (fast, pounding, or irregular heartbeat or pulse)

Incidence not determined—Observed during clinical practice; estimates of frequency can not be determined

Non-arteritic anterior ischemic optic neuropathy (NAION) (blindness; blurred vision; decreased vision); ***reduced visual acuity*** (decreased vision); ***retinal vein occlusion*** (blurred vision; change in vision); ***visual field defect*** (blurred vision; decrease or change in vision)

Those indicating need for medical attention only if they continue or are bothersome

Incidence more frequent

Headache; flushing (feeling of warmth; redness of the face, neck, arms and occasionally upper chest); ***rhinitis*** (stuffy nose; runny nose; sneezing)

Incidence less frequent

Abnormal ejaculation; abnormal vision; abdominal pain; arthralgia (muscle or joint pain); ***asthenia*** (lack or loss of strength); ***back pain; blurred vision; changes in color vision; chromatopsia*** (changes in vision); ***conjunctivitis*** (increased redness of the eye); ***diarrhea; dim vision; dizziness; dry mouth; dyspepsia*** (acid or sour stomach; belching; heartburn; indigestion; stomach discomfort, upset, or pain); ***dysphagia*** (difficulty swallowing); ***epistaxis*** (bloody nose); ***esophagitis*** (difficulty in swallowing; pain or burning in throat; chest pain; heartburn; vomiting; sores, ulcers, or white spots on lips or tongue or inside the mouth); ***eye pain; face edema; flu syndrome*** (chills; cough; diarrhea; fever; general feeling of discomfort or illness; headache; joint pain; loss of appetite; muscle aches and pains; nausea; runny nose; shivering; sore throat; sweating; trouble sleeping; unusual tiredness or weakness; vomiting); ***gastritis*** (burning feeling in chest or stomach; tenderness in stomach area; stomach upset; indigestion); ***gastroesophageal reflux*** (heartburn; vomiting); ***hypertonia*** (excessive muscle tone; muscle tension or tightness; muscle stiffness); ***hypesthesia*** (decreased sensitivity to touch and pain); ***insomnia*** (sleeplessness; trouble sleeping; unable to sleep); ***myalgia*** (joint pain; swollen joints; muscle aching or cramping; muscle pains or stiffness; difficulty in moving); ***nausea; neck pain; pain; paresthesia*** (burning, crawling, itching, numbness, prickling, "pins and needles", or tingling feelings); ***pharyngitis*** (body aches or pain; congestion; cough; dryness or soreness of throat; fever; hoarseness; runny nose; tender, swollen glands in neck; trouble in swallowing; voice changes); ***photophobia*** (blurred vision; change in color vision; difficulty seeing at night; increased sensitivity of eyes to sunlight); ***photosensitivity reaction*** (burning reaction similar to those that follow prolonged sun exposure; red skin rash, sometimes with small blisters; dizziness; nausea; vomiting); ***pruritus*** (itching skin); ***sinusitis*** (pain or tenderness around eyes and cheekbones; fever; stuffy or runny nose; headache; cough; shortness of breath or troubled breathing; tightness of chest or wheezing); ***somnolence*** (sleepiness or unusual drowsiness); ***sweating; tinnitus*** (continuing ringing or buzzing or other unexplained noise in ears; hearing loss); ***vertigo*** (dizziness or lightheadedness; feeling of constant movement of self or surroundings; sensation of spinning); ***vomiting; watery eyes***

Overdose

For more information on the management of overdose or unintentional ingestion, **contact a poison control center** (see *Poison Control Center Listing*).

The maximum dose of vardenafil for which human data are available is a single 120 mg dose administered to eight healthy male volunteers. The majority of these subjects experienced reversible back pain/myalgia and/or abnormal vision.

Treatment of overdose

Supportive care—

To enhance elimination—Renal dialysis is not expected to accelerate clearance of vardenafil; vardenafil is highly bound to plasma proteins and is not significantly eliminated in the urine.

Standard supportive measures should be taken as required.

Patients in whom intentional overdose is confirmed or suspected should be referred for psychiatric consultation.

Patient Consultation

As an aid to patient consultation, refer to *Advice for the Patient, Vardenafil (Systemic)*.

In providing consultation, consider emphasizing the following selected information (» = major clinical significance):

Before using this medication

» Conditions affecting use, especially:
Hypersensitivity to vardenafil or any components of the tablet
Use in the elderly—A starting dose 5 mg of vardenafil should be considered in patients 65 years of age and older
Other medications, especially antiarrhythmics, Class IA and III, alpha blockers, erythromycin, indinavir, itraconazole, ketoconazole, nitrates, ritonavir
Other medical problems, especially unstable angina, hypotension (resting systolic < 90 mm Hg), uncontrolled hypertension, recent history of stroke, life-threatening arrhythmia, myocardial infarction (within the last 6 months), severe cardiac failure, severe hepatic failure, end-stage renal disease (requiring dialysis), retinal disorders, retinitis pigmentosa

Proper use of this medication

Importance of knowing the appropriate use and benefits of vardenafil; understanding that medication should be taken 60 minutes before sexual activity and that stimulation is required for an erection
» Reading patient package insert before you start taking vardenafil and each time you get a refill
» Proper dosing
» Proper storage

Precautions while using this medication

» Importance of patient telling physician if using other drugs for impotence; concurrent use of other impotence therapy agents is not presently recommended
» Complying with therapy dose recommendations; importance of not exceeding prescribed dosage and frequency of use
» Checking with physician immediately if a prolonged erection, 4 or more hours in duration, occurs
Advising patients that vardenafil does not provide protection against sexually transmitted diseases; counsel patients about what protective measures are needed to guard against sexually transmitted diseases
Importance of understanding cardiac risk potential in patients with preexisting cardiovascular risk factors
» Advising patient to seek medical attention if sudden loss of vision in one or both eyes occurs

Side/adverse effects

Signs of potential side effects, especially anaphylactic reaction, angina pectoris, chest pain, dyspnea, glaucoma, hypertension, hypotension, myocardial ischemia, myocardial infarction, palpitation, postural hypotension, rash, syncope, tachycardia
Signs of potential side effects observed during clinical practice, especially NAION, reduced visual acuity, retinal vein occlusion, visual field defect

General Dosing Information

For oral dosing forms:

The evaluation of erectile dysfunction should include a determination of potential underlying causes, a medical assessment, and the identification of appropriate treatment.

Sexual stimulation is required for a response to treatment.

Diet/Nutrition

May be taken with or without food.

For treatment of adverse effects

There have been rare reports of prolonged erections (longer than 4 hours) and priapism (painful erections greater than 6 hours in duration) for this class of compounds, including vardenafil. In the event that an erection persists longer than 4 hours, the patient should seek immediate medical assistance. If priapism is not treated immediately penile tissue damage and permanent loss of potency may result.

Oral Dosage Forms

VARDENAFIL HYDROCHLORIDE TABLETS

Usual adult dose

Erectile dysfunction—
Oral, 10 mg taken one hour before sexual activity once a day. As tolerated, subsequent doses may be increased to 20 mg or decreased to 5 mg once a day.

Note: For patients with mild hepatic impairment (Child-Pugh A) no dose adjustment is needed. Vardenafil clearance is reduced in patients with moderate hepatic impairment (Child-Pugh B) and a starting dose of 5 mg is recommended. The maximum dose in patients with moderate hepatic impairment should not exceed 10 mg. Vardenafil has not been evaluated in patients with severe hepatic impairment. No dose adjustment is needed for patients with mild, moderate or severe renal impairment. Vardenafil has not been evaluated in patients on renal dialysis.

Concomitant Medication

Concomitant Medication	Vardenafil Dose Not To Be Exceeded
Erythromycin	5 mg single dose in 24–hour period
Indinavir	2.5 mg single dose in 24–hour period
Itraconazole, 200 mg daily	5 mg single dose in 24–hour period
Itraconazole, 400 mg daily	2.5 mg single dose in 24–hour period
Ketoconazole, 200 mg daily	5 mg single dose in 24–hour period
Ketoconazole, 400 mg daily	2.5 mg single dose in 24–hour period
Ritonavir	2.5 mg single dose in 72–hour period

Concomitant vardenafil and alpha blocker use only when patients are stable on their alpha blocker therapy—Vardenafil should be initiated at a dose of 5 mg (2.5 mg when used concomitantly with certain CYP3A4 inhibitors).

Usual adult prescribing limits

The maximum recommended dosing frequency is once per day.

Usual geriatric dose

Erectile dysfunction—
Oral, a starting dose of 5 mg taken one hour before sexual activity once a day is suggested in patients ≥ 65 years of age. As tolerated, subsequent doses may be increased.

Strength(s) usually available

U.S.—
2.5 mg (Rx) [*Levitra* (microcrystalline cellulose; crospovidone; colloidal silicon dioxide; magnesium stearate; hypromellose; polyethylene glycol; titanium dioxide; yellow ferric oxide; red ferric oxide)].
5 mg (Rx) [*Levitra* (microcrystalline cellulose; crospovidone; colloidal silicon dioxide; magnesium stearate; hypromellose; polyethylene glycol; titanium dioxide; yellow ferric oxide; red ferric oxide)].
10 mg (Rx) [*Levitra* (microcrystalline cellulose; crospovidone; colloidal silicon dioxide; magnesium stearate; hypromellose; polyethylene glycol; titanium dioxide; yellow ferric oxide; red ferric oxide)].
20 mg (Rx) [*Levitra* (microcrystalline cellulose; crospovidone; colloidal silicon dioxide; magnesium stearate; hypromellose; polyethylene glycol; titanium dioxide; yellow ferric oxide; red ferric oxide)].
Canada—
Not commercially available

Packaging and storage

Store at 25 °C (77 °F), excursions permitted to 15 to 30 °C (59 to 86°F), in a tight container. Protect from light.

Auxiliary labeling

- Keep out of the reach of children
- Tell your doctor about all medications you are taking; prescription and nonprescription

Revised: 08/11/2005
Developed: 12/18/2003

VARENICLINE Systemic

VA CLASSIFICATION (Primary): AD600

Commonly used brand name(s): *Chantix*.

Note: For a listing of dosage forms and brand names by country availability, see *Dosage Forms* section(s).

Category

Smoking cessation adjunct.

Indications

Accepted

Nicotine dependence (treatment adjunct)—Varenicline is indicated as an aid to smoking cessation treatment.
Varenicline is more likely to be successful for smoking cessation when the patient is motivated to quit smoking and when the appropriate supportive treatment including educational materials and counseling are provided to the patient.

Pharmacology/Pharmacokinetics

Physicochemical characteristics
Molecular weight—Varenicline tartrate—361.35 Daltons.
Solubility—Highly soluble in water.

Mechanism of action/Effect
Varenicline is highly selective and has a high affinity for binding at alpha 4-beta 2 neuronal nicotinic acetylcholine receptors which produces agonist activity and prevents nicotine binding to the receptor. Varenicline blocks the ability of nicotine to activate alpha 4-beta 2 receptors and, therefore, to stimulate the central nervous mesolimbic dopamine system, thought to be the neuronal mechanism for the reinforcement/reward experienced when smoking.

Absorption
Virtually complete following oral administration
Bioavailability unaffected by food or time of day that dose is given

Protein binding
Low (≤20%)

Biotransformation
Minimal metabolism

Half-life
Elimination—Approximately 24 hours

Time to peak concentration
3 to 4 hours after oral administration

Elimination
Renal, 92% unchanged

Precautions to Consider

Cross-sensitivity and/or related problems

Carcinogenicity
Carcinogenicity studies were performed in CD-1 mice with no evidence of carcinogenic effects in mice given doses by oral gavage of 20 mg per kg of body weight per day (47 times the maximum recommended human daily exposure based on AUC). Sprague Dawley rats were administered 1, 5, and 15 mg per kg of body weight per day doses based on body weight. In male rats, incidences of hibernoma (tumor of the brown fat) were greater at the mid dose and maximum dose. The clinical relevance of this study result to humans has not been established. Carcinogenicity was not observed in the female rats.

Mutagenicity
Varenicline was not genotoxic, regardless of metabolic activation, in the following assays: Ames bacterial mutation assay; mammalian CHO/HGPRT assay; and tests for cytogenetic aberrations *in vivo* in rat bone marrow and *in vitro* in human lymphocytes.

Pregnancy/Reproduction
Fertility—Male and female Sprague-Dawley rats were dosed up to 15 mg per kg of body weight per day (67 and 36 times the maximum recommended human daily exposure). A decrease in fertility was observed in the offspring of pregnant rats dosed 15 mg per kg of body weight per day. The offspring of the pregnant rats also showed decreased fertility and increased auditory startle response at 15 mg per kg of body weight per day. The decreased fertility in the offspring of treated female rats was not present at an oral 3 mg per kg of body weight per day dose.

Pregnancy—There are no adequate and well-controlled studies in pregnant women. Varenicline should be given to pregnant women only if the potential benefit justifies the potential risk to the fetus.

Varenicline was not teratogenic in rats and rabbits given oral dose up to 15 and 30 mg per kg of body weight per day, respectively (36 times and 50 times the maximum recommended human daily [MRHD] exposure based on AUC at 1 mg twice per day, respectively).

Pregnant rabbits administered an oral dose of 30 mg per kg of body weight per day (50 times the MRHD) resulted in decreased fetal weights. This decrease was not evident at 10 mg per kg of body weight per day (23 times the MRHD). At an oral dose of 15 mg per kg of body weight per day (36 times the MRHD) of varenicline, pregnant rats gave birth to offspring with decreased fertility and increased auditory startle response.

FDA Pregnancy Category C

Labor and delivery—The potential effects of varenicline on labor and delivery are not known.

Breast-feeding
It is not known whether varenicline is distributed into human milk. Animal studies have shown that varenicline can be transferred to nursing pups. Because many drugs are distributed into human milk and because of the potential for serious adverse reactions in nursing infants from varenicline, a decision should be made whether to discontinue nursing or to discontinue the drug, taking into account the importance of the drug to the mother.

Pediatrics
Safety and efficacy of varenicline in pediatric patients have not been established. Varenicline is not recommended for use in patients under 18 years of age.

Geriatrics
Appropriate studies performed to date have not demonstrated geriatrics-specific problems that would limit the usefulness of varenicline in the elderly. However, elderly patients are more likely to have age-related renal function impairment which may require care in dose selection and monitoring of renal function.

Drug interactions and/or related problems
The following drug interactions and/or related problems have been selected on the basis of their potential clinical significance (possible mechanism in parentheses where appropriate)—not necessarily inclusive (» = major clinical significance):

Note: Combinations containing any of the following medications, depending on the amount present, may also interact with this medication.

Bupropion or
Other smoking cessation therapies
(safety and efficacy not established)

Medical considerations/Contraindications
The medical considerations/contraindications included have been selected on the basis of their potential clinical significance (reasons given in parentheses where appropriate)—not necessarily inclusive (» = major clinical significance).

Risk-benefit should be considered when the following medical problems exist:

» Renal impairment
(caution warranted with varenicline use; dose adjustment for severe renal impairment and end-stage renal disease undergoing hemodialysis; no dose adjustment for mild or moderate renal impairment)

Patient monitoring
The following may be especially important in patient monitoring (other tests may be warranted in some patients, depending on condition; » = major clinical significance):

Renal function
(should be monitored, especially in elderly patients)

Side/Adverse Effects
The following side/adverse effects have been selected on the basis of their potential clinical significance (possible signs and symptoms in parentheses where appropriate)—not necessarily inclusive:

Those indicating need for medical attention
Incidence less frequent

Dyspnea (shortness of breath; difficult or labored breathing; tightness in chest; wheezing)

Those indicating need for medical attention only if they continue or are bothersome
Incidence more frequent

Abdominal pain (stomach pain); ***abnormal dreams; asthenia*** (lack or loss of strength); ***constipation*** (difficulty having a bowel movement (stool)); ***dry mouth; fatigue*** (unusual tiredness or weakness); ***flatulence*** (bloated full feeling; excess air or gas in stomach or intestines; passing gas); ***headache; insomnia*** (sleeplessness; trouble sleeping; unable to sleep); ***malaise*** (general feeling of discomfort or illness; unusual tiredness or weakness); ***nausea***

Incidence less frequent

Anorexia (loss of appetite; weight loss); ***decreased appetite; dysgeusia*** (loss of taste; change in taste); ***dyspepsia*** (acid or sour stomach; belching; heartburn; indigestion; stomach discomfort, upset, or pain); ***gastroesophageal reflux disease*** (heartburn; vomiting); ***increased appetite; lethargy*** (unusual drowsiness, dullness, tiredness, weakness or feeling of sluggishness); ***nightmares; pruritis*** (itching skin); ***rash; rhinorrhea*** (runny nose); ***sleep disorder*** (difficulty in sleeping); ***somnolence*** (sleepiness or unusual drowsiness); ***upper respiratory tract disorder*** (ear congestion; nasal congestion; chills; cough, fever, sneezing, or sore throat; body aches or pain; headache; loss of voice; runny nose; unusual tiredness or weakness; difficulty in breathing); ***vomiting***

Overdose

For more information on the management of overdose or unintentional ingestion, **contact a poison control center** (see *Poison Control Center Listing*).

Treatment of overdose

There is no experience in dialysis following overdose with varenicline. However, varenicline has been shown to be dialyzed in patients with end stage renal disease.

Supportive care—
Standard supportive measures should be instituted as required.
Patients in whom intentional overdose is confirmed or suspected should be referred for psychiatric consultation.

Patient Consultation

In providing consultation, consider emphasizing the following selected information (» = major clinical significance):

Before using this medication

» Conditions affecting use, especially:
Pregnancy—Risk benefit considerations
Breast-feeding—Risk benefit considerations due to potential for serious adverse effects
Use in children—Safety and efficacy not established; use not recommended in children under 18 years of age
Use in the elderly—May be more likely to have decreased renal function; care should be taken in dose selection and renal function monitoring may be useful
Other medical problems, especially renal impairment

Proper use of this medication

» Importance of setting a date to quit smoking and beginning varenicline a week before the quit date
» Taking varenicline after a meal with a full glass of water
Swallowing whole, not crushing or chewing
» Importance of using educational materials and attending counseling that are provided to aid in smoking cessation
» Proper dosing
» Proper storage

Precautions while using this medication

Telling doctor of all medicines being taken, prescription and nonprescription
Advising patient that quitting smoking may require some medicine doses to need adjusting
Contacting doctor if nausea or insomnia occur that become unbearable
Continuing attempts to quit smoking even if first attempt fails

Side/adverse effects

Signs of potential side effects, especially dyspnea

General Dosing Information

The patient should set a date to stop smoking and varenicline dosing should begin one week prior to this date.

If adverse effects of varenicline cannot be tolerated, the dose may be lowered temporarily or permanently.

Patients who are not successful in smoking cessation during the initial 12 week treatment or who relapse following treatment should be encouraged to start over after identifying and resolving factors that may have contributed to the unsuccessful attempt.

Smoking cessation, regardless of treatment with varenicline, can result in physiological changes. These changes may alter the pharmacokinetics or pharmacodynamics of some drugs (i.e., theophylline, warfarin, and insulin) which may require dose adjustments.

Diet/Nutrition

Varenicline should be taken after eating with a full glass of water.

Adverse effects

For patients with adverse effects, including nausea and insomnia, that they cannot tolerate, dose reduction should be considered.

Parenteral Dosage Forms

VARENICLINE TABLETS

Usual adult dose

Smoking cessation—
Oral, for 12 weeks, as follows:

Days 1 to 3:	0.5 mg once daily
Days 4 to 7:	0.5 mg twice daily
Day 8 to End of treatment:	1 mg twice daily

For patients with success in smoking cessation at the end of 12 weeks, an additional 12 week course of varenicline treatment is recommended to further increase the probability of long-term abstinence.

Note: For patients with severe renal impairment, the recommended starting dose of varenicline is 0.5 mg once daily. The dose may then be titrated, as needed, to a maximum dose of 0.5 mg twice a day.

For patients with end-stage renal disease who are undergoing hemodialysis, a maximum dose of 0.5 mg once daily may be given if tolerated well.

Usual pediatric dose

Safety and efficacy are not established and use is not recommended in children under 18 years of age.

Usual geriatric dose

See *Usual adult dose*.

Strength(s) usually available

U.S.—
0.5 mg varenicline (Rx) [*Chantix* (film-coated; microcrystalline cellulose; anhydrous dibasic calcium phosphate; croscarmellose sodium; colloidal silicon dioxide; magnesium stearate; Opadry® White; Opadry® Clear)].
1 mg varenicline (Rx) [*Chantix* (film-coated; microcrystalline cellulose; anhydrous dibasic calcium phosphate; croscarmellose sodium; colloidal silicon dioxide; magnesium stearate; Opadry® Blue; Opadry® Clear)].

Packaging and storage

Store at 25 °C (77 °F), excursions permitted to 15 to 30 °C (59 to 86 °F).

Auxiliary labeling

- Swallow whole. Do not crush or chew.
- Tell your doctor about all medicines that you are taking; prescription and nonprescription

Developed: 07/20/2006

VARICELLA VIRUS VACCINE LIVE Systemic

VA CLASSIFICATION (Primary): IM100

Commonly used brand name(s): *Varilrix; Varivax; Varivax III; Zostavax.*

Note: For a listing of dosage forms and brand names by country availability, see *Dosage Forms* section(s).

Category

Immunizing agent (active).

Indications

General Considerations

Varicella-zoster virus (VZV) is the cause of two diseases, varicella (chickenpox), which is a primary infection, and zoster (shingles), a secondary infection caused by reactivation of latent VZV. VZV is transmitted person-to-person through direct contact with skin lesions and by airborne respiratory droplets. Skin vesicles in varicella and zoster contain high titers of infectious virus, and patients with zoster can transmit varicella to susceptible contacts. Varicella is one of the most contagious diseases, resembling pertussis and measles. Within households, 80 to 90% of exposed susceptible contacts will develop varicella.

A reliable history of varicella is considered a valid measure of immunity. Because the rash is distinctive and subclinical cases rarely occur, most parents know if their child has had varicella. A negative history of varicella substantiated by a parent may be more accurate than a self-reported negative history given by an adult.

Serologic tests have been used to assess the accuracy of reported histories of varicella. In adults, a positive history of chickenpox is highly predictive of serologic immunity to varicella virus (97 to 99% of persons are seropositive); however, the majority (71 to 93%) of adults who have negative or uncertain history are also seropositive.

Infants, children, adolescents, and adults should be assessed for varicella immune status, and those who are susceptible should be vaccinated. Although usually a benign illness, varicella may have severe complications among both children and adults. These include pneumonia, viral dissemination leading to encephalitis and/or multiple organ involvement, secondary bacterial infections, and hemorrhagic complications. Total burden of disease is greater in children; however, varicella causes a higher risk of hospitalizations and death in adults than in children.

All susceptible health care workers should ensure that they are immune to varicella. In health care institutions, serologic screening of personnel who have a negative or uncertain history of varicella is likely to be cost-effective. However, routine testing for varicella immunity after two doses of vaccine is not necessary for the management of vaccinated health care workers who may be exposed to varicella, because 99% of persons are seropositive after the second dose.

Vaccination should be considered for unvaccinated health care workers who are exposed to varicella and whose immunity is not documented. However, since the protective effects of postexposure vaccination are unknown, persons vaccinated after an exposure should be managed in the manner recommended for unvaccinated persons.

Accepted

Herpes zoster (prophylaxis)—Varicella virus vaccine is indicated for prevention of herpes zoster (shingles) in individuals 60 years of age and older.

Varicella virus (prophylaxis)—Varicella virus vaccine live is indicated for immunization against varicella in individuals 12 months of age and older. The American Academy of Pediatrics (AAP), the American Academy of Family Physicians (AAFP), and the Advisory Committee on Immunization Practices (ACIP) of the Centers for Disease Control and Prevention (CDC) recommend that all individuals 12 months of age and older be immunized against varicella, including:

• Children 12 to 18 months of age. All children should be routinely vaccinated at 12 to 18 months of age. Varicella virus vaccine live may be administered to all children at this age, regardless of whether or not they have a history of varicella. However, vaccination is not necessary for children who have reliable histories of varicella.

• Children 19 months to 13 years of age. Varicella virus vaccine live is recommended for all susceptible children by their 13th birthday. After 12 years of age natural varicella is more severe and complications are more frequent. ACIP recommended establishing a routine immunization visit at 11 to 12 years of age to review immunization status and to administer necessary vaccinations. Varicella virus vaccine live should be administered to all susceptible children during this routine visit.

• Adolescents 13 years of age and older and adults. Natural varicella infection is more severe and complications are more frequent in adolescents 13 years of age and older and adults; therefore, varicella immunity is desirable in these age groups. Adolescents 13 years of age and older and adults who have reliable histories of varicella are considered immune. Those who do not have such histories are considered susceptible and can be tested to determine immune status or can be vaccinated without testing. However, since 71 to 93% of adults who do not have a reliable history of varicella are actually immune, serologic testing before vaccination is likely to be cost-effective for both adolescents and adults. Vaccination should be considered for the following groups of adolescents 13 years of age and older and adults:

—Persons who have close contact with individuals at high risk for serious complications (e.g., health care workers and family contacts of immunocompromised persons).

—Persons who live or work in environments in which transmission of VZV is likely (e.g., teachers of young children, day-care employees, and residents and staff in institutional settings).

—Persons who live or work in environments in which varicella transmission can occur (e.g., college students, inmates and staff of correctional institutions, and military personnel).

—Nonpregnant women of childbearing age. Vaccination of women who are not pregnant, but who may become pregnant in the future, will reduce the risk for VZV transmission to the fetus. Varicella immunity may be ascertained at any routine health care visit or in any setting in which vaccination history may be reviewed (e.g., upon college entry). Women should be asked if they are pregnant and advised to avoid pregnancy for 1 month following each dose of vaccine.

—International travelers. Vaccination should be considered for international travelers who do not have evidence of immunity to VZV (e.g., serologic tests), especially if the traveler expects to have close personal contact with local populations, because varicella is endemic in most countries. However, all susceptible adolescents and adults should be vaccinated prior to international travel.

Unaccepted

Zostavax® is not indicated for the treatment of zoster or postherpetic neuralgia (PHN).

Zostavax® is not a substitute for Varivax® and should not be used in children.

Pharmacology/Pharmacokinetics

Physicochemical characteristics

Source—Varicella virus vaccine live is a preparation of the Oka/Merck strain of live, attenuated varicella virus. The virus was initially obtained from a child with natural varicella, then introduced into human embryonic lung cell cultures, adapted to and propagated in embryonic guinea pig cell cultures, and propagated in human diploid cell cultures (WI-38). The virus for varicella vaccine undergoes further passage in human diploid cell cultures (MRC 5) that are free of adventitious agents. The live attenuated vaccine is a lyophilized preparation.

Mechanism of action/Effect

Vaccination with varicella virus vaccine live induces varicella antibodies and a cell-mediated immune response, which produce active immunity against varicella infection.

Protective effect

In a double-blind, placebo-controlled trial of children 1 to 14 years of age, using a high-titer experimental vaccine, the efficacy was 100% in the first year after vaccination. According to other unpublished studies from the manufacturer, the protection against any disease in vaccinees after household exposure was approximately 70%, and greater than 95% against more severe disease. Rates of protection are similar in adults. All studies demonstrate high rates of protection against severe disease.

Varicella in vaccinees has been much milder than that occurring in unvaccinated children, with fewer skin lesions (range 15 to 32), lower rates of fever (10% of patients with a temperature ≥ 39 °C [102 °F]), and rapid recovery. At times, the disease is so mild that it is not easily recognizable as varicella because the skin lesions may resemble insect bites. Nevertheless, vaccine recipients with mild disease may be potentially infectious to susceptible persons.

Duration of protective effect

Waning immunity in vaccine recipients has not been demonstrated, at least in the context of continued varicella-zoster virus (VZV) circulation. The rate of varicella after immunization during 7 years of study has averaged from less than 1 to 4.4% per year after exposure to wild virus. The rate has not increased with time after immunization.

Duration of protection after vaccination with Zostavax® is unknown. In the Shingles Prevention Study (SPS), protection from zoster was demonstrated through 4 years of follow-up.

Precautions to Consider

Carcinogenicity/Mutagenicity

Varicella virus vaccine live has not been evaluated for its carcinogenic or mutagenic potential.

Pregnancy/Reproduction

Pregnancy—Studies have not been done in humans. However, the effects of varicella virus vaccine live on the fetus are unknown; therefore, pregnant women should not be vaccinated. For susceptible persons, having a pregnant household member is not a contraindication to vaccination.

It is recommended that pregnancy be avoided for 3 months following immunization with the varicella virus vaccine live.

If a pregnant woman is vaccinated or becomes pregnant within 30 days of vaccination, she should be counseled about potential effects on the fetus. Wild-type varicella poses only a very small risk to the fetus. Since the virulence of the attenuated virus used in the vaccine is less than that of the wild-type virus, the risk to the fetus, if any, should be even lower. In most circumstances, the decision to terminate a pregnancy should not be based on whether vaccine was administered during pregnancy.

The manufacturer of varicella virus vaccine live, in collaboration with the Centers for Disease Control and Prevention (CDC), has established the *VARIVAX Pregnancy Registry* to monitor the maternal-fetal outcomes of pregnant women who are inadvertently administered varicella virus vaccine live 3 months before or at any time during pregnancy (telephone: 1-800-986-8999). An annual report will be sent to health care providers participating in the registry.

Studies have not been done in animals.

FDA Pregnancy Category C.

Breast-feeding

It is not known whether varicella vaccine virus is distributed into breast milk or if it is infectious to infants. Because some viruses are distributed into human milk, caution should be exercised if varicella virus vaccine live is administered to a nursing woman. However, varicella virus vaccine live may be considered for a susceptible breast-feeding mother if the risk of exposure to natural VZV is high.

Pediatrics

No information is available about the reactivity, immunogenicity, or the efficacy of the varicella virus vaccine live in infants and children up to 12 months of age. Use is not recommended.

It is not known whether Reye's syndrome results from the administration of salicylates after vaccination for varicella in children. No cases have been reported. However, the manufacturer of the vaccine recommends that salicylates not be administered for 6 weeks after the varicella virus vaccine live has been given because an association between Reye's syndrome, natural varicella, and salicylates is well established. Physicians should weigh the theoretical risks associated with varicella virus vaccine live against the known risks of the wild-type virus in children receiving long-term salicylate therapy.

The potential risks of vaccination with the attenuated virus must always be weighed against the potential risks of becoming infected with wild-type VZV infection in children receiving corticosteroids.

Varicella virus vaccine live should not be administered to children who are receiving high doses of systemic corticosteroids (2 mg per kg of body weight per day or more of prednisone or its equivalent, or 20 mg per day of prednisone if their weight is less than 10 kg) for more than 1 month. After corticosteroid use at this dosage has been discontinued for 3 months, a child may be immunized. However, most experts agree that with varicella virus vaccine live an interval of 1 month or more after discontinuation of corticosteroid use is probably sufficient to administer safely the vaccine.

Children with no history of varicella who are receiving systemic corticosteroids for conditions such as nephrosis and asthma may be immunized if not otherwise immunosuppressed, assuming that they are receiving less than 2 mg per kg of body weight per day of prednisone or its equivalent, or 20 mg per day of prednisone if their weight is less than 10 kg. Some experts, however, suggest discontinuing corticosteroid use for 2 to 3 weeks after immunization, if possible. In studies in Japan, children with nephrosis receiving these doses of systemic corticosteroids were immunized safely when corticosteroid therapy was suspended for 1 to 2 weeks before immunization. Most experts agree that immunization of children receiving only inhaled corticosteroids would not increase the risk of disease from varicella virus vaccine live, although no studies in such children have been performed.

Varicella virus vaccine live is not licensed for routine use in children with malignancies. However, immunization should be considered when a child with acute lymphocytic leukemia (ALL) has been in continuous remission for at least 1 year and has a lymphocyte count over 700/mcL and platelet count over 100,000/mcL 24 hours before vaccination. Immunization has been shown to be safe, immunogenic, and effective in these children.

Note: The vaccine may be obtained free for use in a research protocol. This protocol monitors and evaluates safety and requires approval by the appropriate institutional investigative board. To immunize a child who has ALL, the following organization should be consulted: The Varivax Coordinating Center, Bio-Pharm Clinical Services, Inc., 4 Valley Square, Blue Bell, PA 19422; telephone: (215) 283-0897.

Zostavax® should NOT be used in children.

Geriatrics

No information is available on the relationship of age to the effects of varicella virus vaccine live in geriatric patients. However, geriatrics-specifics problems that would limit the usefulness of this vaccine in the elderly are not expected.

Zostavax® is indicated for use in individuals 60 years of age and older.

Drug interactions and/or related problems

The following drug interactions and/or related problems have been selected on the basis of their potential clinical significance (possible mechanism in parentheses where appropriate)—not necessarily inclusive (» = major clinical significance):

Note: Combinations containing any of the following medications, depending on the amount present, may also interact with this medication.

Blood or plasma products or
Immune globulins or
Varicella zoster immune globulin (VZIG)
(whether immune globulin [IG] can interfere with varicella virus vaccine live–induced immunity is unknown, although IG can interfere with immunity induced by other live virus vaccines; as with other live virus vaccines, varicella virus vaccine live should not be administered within at least 5 months after receipt of any form of IG or other blood products; transplacental antibodies to VZV do not interfere with the immunogenicity of varicella virus vaccine live at 12 months of age or older; following varicella virus vaccine, immune globulins including VZIG should not be given for 2 months after unless its use outweighs the benefits of vaccination)

» Immunosuppressive agents or
» Radiation therapy
(because normal defense mechanisms are suppressed, concurrent use of the varicella virus vaccine live may potentiate the replication of the vaccine virus, may increase the side/adverse effects of the vaccine, and/or may decrease the patient's antibody response to varicella virus vaccine live; individuals who are taking immunosuppressive agents may develop a more extensive vaccine-associated rash or disseminated disease. The interval between discontinuation of the medications that cause immunosuppression and restoration of the patient's ability to respond to varicella virus vaccine live depends on the intensity and type of immunosuppressive medication used, the underlying disease, and other factors)

Corticosteroids
(short-term or alternate-day treatment with low to moderate dosage of corticosteroids is not a contraindication for receiving live virus vaccines; low-to-moderate dosage is considered to be prednisone [or its equivalent] 2 mg per kg of body weight per day; if the patient weighs more than 10 kg, a low-to-moderate dosage is considered to be less than 20 mg a day; patients receiving higher doses of corticosteroids should wait a period of 3 months after completion of corticosteroid therapy before receiving varicella virus vaccine live; topical or inhaled forms of corticosteroids are not considered immunosuppressive and no discontinuation of corticosteroid therapy is necessary before receiving varicella virus vaccine live)

» Salicylates
(it is not known whether Reye's syndrome results from the administration of salicylates after vaccination for varicella in children; no cases have been reported; however, the manufacturer of the vaccine recommends that salicylates not be administered for 6 weeks after the varicella virus vaccine live has been given because an association between Reye's syndrome, natural varicella, and salicylates is well established; physicians should weigh the theoretical risks associated with varicella virus vaccine live against the known risks of the wild-type virus in children receiving long-term salicylate therapy)

Medical considerations/Contraindications

The medical considerations/contraindications included have been selected on the basis of their potential clinical significance (reasons given in parentheses where appropriate)—not necessarily inclusive (» = major clinical significance).

Except under special circumstances, this medication should not be used when the following medical problems exist:

» AIDS or
» Blood dyscrasias or
» Human immunodeficiency viruses, or with other clinical manifestation of infection or
» Leukemia or
» Lymphomas of any type or
» Other malignant neoplasms affecting the bone marrow or lymphatic systems
» Febrile illness
(the decision to administer or delay vaccination because of a current or recent febrile illness depends largely on the cause of illness and the severity of symptoms; minor illnesses, such as upper respiratory infection, do not preclude administration of vaccine; for persons whose compliance with medical care cannot be assured, every opportunity should be taken to provide appropriate vaccinations)
(children with moderate or severe febrile illnesses can be vaccinated as soon as they have recovered from the acute phase of the illness; this wait avoids superimposing adverse effects of vaccination on the underlying illness or mistakenly attributing a manifestation of the underlying illness to the vaccine; performing routine physical examinations and measuring temperatures are not prerequisites for vaccinating infants and children who appear to be in good health; asking the parent or guardian if the child is ill, postponing vaccination for children with moderate or severe febrile illnesses, and vaccinating those without contraindications are appropriate procedures in childhood immunization programs)
» History of anaphylactoid reaction to neomycin
» History of hypersensitivity to any component of the vaccine, including gelatin
» Immunodeficiency conditions, congenital or hereditary, history of or
» Immunodeficiency conditions, primary or acquired
(varicella virus vaccine live should not be given routinely to immunocompromised individuals, such as those with congenital im-

munodeficiency, blood dyscrasias, leukemia, lymphoma, symptomatic human immunodeficiency virus [HIV] infection, and malignancy for which they are receiving immunosuppressive therapy; the exceptions include children with acute lymphocytic leukemia [ALL] under study conditions [see *Pediatrics*])

(asymptomatic HIV infection also is a contraindication for immunization, but since the risk in these persons is so far only theoretical, routine screening for HIV is not indicated; children with a family history of hereditary immunodeficiency and who exhibit immunodeficiency should be excluded from immunization; the presence of an immunodeficient or HIV-positive family member does not contraindicate vaccine use in other family members)

» Tuberculosis, active, untreated

Risk-benefit should be considered when the following medical problems exist:

HIV infection
(safety and efficacy of varicella not established in children and young adults who are known to be infected with HIV with and without evidence of immunosuppression)

Thrombocytopenia or vaccine-associated thrombocytopenia
(persons who experienced thrombocytopenia with the first dose of vaccine may develop thrombocytopenia with additional doses. These persons should have serological testing performed in order to determine the need for additional doses of vaccine. The risk: benefit ratio should be evaluated before vaccination is considered in such cases)

Zoster, previous history of
(use of varicella virus vaccine has not been studied)

Side/Adverse Effects

Note: The spread of vaccine virus from healthy vaccinees to other persons is theoretically possible because varicella vaccine virus has been recovered from vaccine recipients with skin lesions. The spread of vaccine virus to others from vaccinees with leukemia who had a vaccine-associated rash was observed in clinical trials conducted prior to vaccine licensure. Contact cases have been subclinical or have developed extremely mild illness, indicating that the vaccine virus remains attenuated when transmitted. Since licensure, with more than 11 million doses of vaccine distributed, 3 cases of transmission from healthy vaccine recipients to household members have been documented. Transmission has occurred only in the presence of rash in the vaccinee.

A zoster-like illness, marked by rash and minimal or absent systemic symptoms, has been reported in 8 of 9000 healthy children who were immunized with varicella virus vaccine live. No case was severe. This incidence was no higher than that occurring after natural varicella. Zoster is unusual in childhood, and is estimated to occur with a frequency of 77 cases per 100,000 person-years. To date, the frequency in vaccinated children after 7 years of follow-up is 18 cases per 100,000 person-years. Moreover, in children with leukemia, zoster is less common after vaccination than after natural varicella infection. In the U.S., more than 1500 adults have been immunized in clinical trials, with 11 to 13 years of follow-up, and the only case of zoster was caused by the wild virus. Post-marketing surveillance has documented herpes zoster due to the vaccine virus among both children and adults; however, reported rates are lower than seen following natural disease.

The U.S. Department of Health and Human Services has established a Vaccine Adverse Event Reporting System (VAERS) for reports of suspected adverse events following a vaccine administration. To request a vaccine reporting form or for more information, contact VAERS at 1-800-822-7967 or www.vaers.hhs.gov.

The following side/adverse effects have been selected on the basis of their potential clinical significance (possible signs and symptoms in parentheses where appropriate)—not necessarily inclusive:

Those indicating need for medical attention

Incidence more frequent

Fever over 39 °C (102 °F)

Incidence less frequent

Varicella-like skin rash

Incidence rare

Anaphylactic reaction (difficulty in breathing or swallowing; hives; itching, especially of feet or hands; reddening of skin, especially around ears; swelling of eyes, face, or inside of nose; unusual tiredness or weakness, sudden and severe); ***encephalitis*** (confusion; irritability; severe or continuing headache; stiff neck; vomiting); ***lymphadenopathy*** (swelling of glands in neck); ***myalgia or arthralgia*** (muscle or joint pain); ***thrombocytopenia*** (black, tarry stools; blood in urine or stools; pinpoint red spots on skin; unusual bleeding or bruising)

Incidence not determined—Observed during clinical practice; estimates of frequency can not be determine

Ataxia (shakiness and unsteady walk; unsteadiness, trembling, or other problems with muscle control or coordination); ***Bell's palsy*** (weakness of the muscles in your face); ***cerebrovascular accident*** (blurred vision; headache, sudden and severe; inability to speak; seizures; slurred speech; temporary blindness; weakness in arm and/or leg on one side of the body, sudden and severe); ***erythema multiforme*** (blistering, peeling, loosening of skin; chills; cough; diarrhea; fever; itching; joint or muscle pain; red irritated eyes; sore throat; sores, ulcers, or white spots in mouth or on lips unusual tiredness or weakness); ***Guillain-Barre syndrome*** (sudden numbness and weakness in the arms and legs; inability to move arms and legs); ***Henoch-Schonlein purpura*** (blood in urine; bloody or black, tarry stools; fever; large, flat, blue or purplish patches in the skin; painful knees and ankles; raised red swellings on the skin, the buttocks, legs or ankles; stomach pain;); ***herpes zoster*** (painful blisters on trunk of body); ***non-febrile seizures*** (convulsions; muscle spasm or jerking of all extremities; sudden loss of consciousness; loss of bladder control); ***Stevens-Johnson syndrome*** (blistering, peeling, loosening of skin; chills; cough; diarrhea; itching; joint or muscle pain; red irritated eyes; red skin lesions, often with a purple center; sore throat; sores, ulcers, or white spots in mouth or on lips; unusual tiredness or weakness); ***thrombocytopenia*** (black, tarry stools; bleeding gums; blood in urine or stools; pinpoint red spots on skin; unusual bleeding or bruising); ***transverse myelitis*** (back pain, sudden and severe; muscle weakness, sudden and progressing)

Those indicating need for medical attention only if they continue or are bothersome

Incidence more frequent

Fever of 37.7 °C (100 °F) or higher but below 39 °C (102 °F); pain, redness, or soreness at injection site

Incidence less frequent

Gastrointestinal effects (abdominal pain; diarrhea; nausea; vomiting); ***respiratory illness*** (common cold; congestion; cough; sore throat)

Incidence not determined—Observed during clinical practice; estimates of frequency can not be determined

Cellulitis (itching, pain, redness, swelling, tenderness; warmth on skin); ***dizziness; impetigo*** (red rash with watery, yellow-colored, or pus filled blisters; thick yellow to honey-colored crusts); ***paresthesia*** (burning, crawling, itching, numbness, prickling, "pins and needles" or tingling feelings); ***pharyngitis*** (body aches or pain; congestion; cough; dryness or soreness of throat; fever; hoarseness; runny nose; tender, swollen glands in neck; trouble in swallowing; voice changes); ***pneumonia/pneumonitis*** (chest pain; cough; fever or chills; sneezing; shortness of breath; sore throat; troubled breathing; tightness in chest; wheezing); ***secondary bacterial infections of skin and soft tissue***

Patient Consultation

As an aid to patient consultation, refer to *Advice for the Patient, Varicella Virus Vaccine Live (Systemic).*

In providing consultation, consider emphasizing the following selected information (» = major clinical significance):

Before receiving this vaccine

» Conditions affecting use, especially:

Hypersensitivity to varicella virus vaccine live or any of its components, allergy to gelatin, or hypersensitivity to neomycin

Pregnancy—Use of varicella virus vaccine live during pregnancy or becoming pregnant within 30 days of immunization is not recommended. It is recommended that pregnancy be avoided for 3 months following immunization with the varicella virus vaccine live

Breast-feeding—Varicella virus vaccine live may be used with caution in nursing mothers, especially those at high risk for exposure to varicella infection

Use in children—Use is not recommended for infants younger than 12 months of age

Zostavax® should NOT be used in children.

Other medications, especially immunosuppressive agents, radiation therapy, and salicylates

Other medical problems, especially AIDS, blood dyscrasias; febrile illness; human immunodeficiency viruses (other clinical manifestation of infection with), immunodeficiency conditions, congenital or hereditary, history of, or immunodeficiency conditions, primary or acquired; leukemia; lymphomas of any type;

other malignant neoplasms affecting the bone marrow or lymphatic systems; or tuberculosis, active, untreated

Proper use of this medication

» Proper dosing
Proper storage

Precautions after receiving this vaccine

Not becoming pregnant for 3 months after receiving varicella virus vaccine live without first checking with your doctor.

Telling your doctor that you have received this vaccine:

- If you are to receive blood transfusions or other blood products within 5 months of receiving this vaccine.
- If you are to receive varicella-zoster immune globulin (VZIG) or other immune globulins within 2 months after receiving this vaccine.
- If you are to receive any other live virus vaccines within 1 month of receiving this vaccine.

(Not receiving Zostavax® as a substitute for Varivax®)

(Not taking aspirin or aspirin products for 6 weeks after receiving this vaccine.)

(Avoiding contact with individuals who may be at risk for getting chickenpox for up to 6 weeks following vaccination.)

Side/adverse effects

Signs of potential side effects, especially fever over 39 °C (102 °F), varicella-like skin rash, anaphylactic reaction, encephalitis, lymphadenopathy, myalgia or arthralgia, and thrombocytopenia

Signs of potential side effects observed during clinical practice, especially ataxia, Bell's palsy, cerebrovascular accident, erythema multiforme, Guillain-Barre syndrome, Henoch-Schonlein purpura, herpes zoster, non-febrile seizures, Stevens-Johnson syndrome, thrombocytopenia, or transverse myelitis

General Dosing Information

Although systemic reactions to varicella virus vaccine live are rare, anaphylaxis among vaccine recipients has been reported. Therefore, appropriate precautions should be taken prior to varicella virus vaccine live injection to prevent allergic or other unwanted reactions. Precautions should include review of the patient's history regarding possible sensitivity and the ready availability of 1:1000 epinephrine injection and other appropriate agents used for control of immediate allergic reactions.

Varicella virus vaccine live is administered subcutaneously. It should not be injected intravenously.

When sterilizing syringes and skin before vaccination, care should be taken to avoid contact between vaccine and preservatives, antiseptics, detergents, and disinfectants, since the vaccine virus is easily inactivated by these substances.

To prevent inactivation of the vaccine, it is recommended that only the diluent provided by the manufacturer be used for vaccine reconstitution.

Whether administration of immune globulin (IG) can interfere with the immunological response to varicella vaccination is not known. However, IG administration can interfere with the response to other live virus vaccines, such as measles vaccine, and because of the potential inhibition of the response to varicella vaccination by passively transferred antibodies, varicella virus vaccine live should not be given for at least 5 months after the administration of IG preparations, including varicella zoster immune globulin (VZIG), blood products (except washed red blood cells), or plasma transfusion. Infants and children receiving respiratory syncytial virus immune globulin intravenous (RSV-IGIV) should not receive varicella virus vaccine live until at least 9 months after the last dose of RSV-IGIV.

If possible, IG preparations should not be administered for 3 weeks after vaccination. If an IG preparation is given in the interval before vaccination, the recipient either should be revaccinated 5 months later or tested for varicella immunity 6 months later and revaccinated if seronegative.

Healthy persons in whom varicella-like rash develops following vaccination appear to have a minimal risk for transmission of vaccine virus to their close contacts (e.g., family members). Seroconversion has been documented in healthy siblings of healthy vaccinees in whom rash did not develop, although such an occurrence is rare. Vaccinees in whom vaccine-related rash develops, particularly health care workers and household contacts of immunocompromised persons, should avoid contact with susceptible persons who are at high risk for severe complications. Susceptible high risk individuals include: immunocompromised individuals; pregnant women without documented history of chicken pox of laboratory evidence of prior infection, and newborn infants of mothers without documented history of chickenpox or laboratory evidence of prior infection. If a susceptible, immunocompromised person is inadvertently exposed to a person who has a vaccine-related rash, VZIG need not be administered because disease associated with this type of transmission is expected to be mild.

Varicella virus vaccine live may be given simultaneously with measles, mumps, and rubella virus vaccine live, provided different syringes and injection sites are used. If not given simultaneously, the interval between administration of varicella virus vaccine live and measles, mumps, and rubella virus vaccine live should be at least 1 month. Although further immunogenicity studies are needed on the use of varicella virus vaccine live administered simultaneously with diphtheria and tetanus toxoids, and pertussis vaccine adsorbed (DTP or DTaP), poliovirus vaccine live oral (OPV), inactivated poliovirus vaccine (IPV or eIPV), hepatitis B vaccine, and *Haemophilus influenzae* type b vaccine, no reason exists to suspect that varicella virus vaccine live will affect the immune response to these vaccines. When necessary, varicella virus vaccine live may be given simultaneously or at any interval after or before these vaccines.

Zostavax® is NOT a substitute for Varivax® and should not be used in children.

For treatment of adverse effects

Recommended treatment includes:

- For mild hypersensitivity reaction—Administering antihistamines and, if necessary, corticosteroids. In mild anaphylaxis, antihistamines or subcutaneous epinephrine may be all that is necessary if the condition is progressing slowly and is not life-threatening, regardless of the organ or system affected. Under these circumstances, the risks associated with intravenous epinephrine administration outweigh the benefits.
- For severe hypersensitivity or anaphylactic reaction—Administering epinephrine. Antihistamines or corticosteroids may also be administered as required. Epinephrine is the treatment of choice for severe hypersensitivity or anaphylactic reaction. If the patient's condition is not stable, epinephrine should be infused. Norepinephrine may be preferable if there is no bronchospasm. For bronchospasm, epinephrine should be given with corticosteroids. Other bronchodilators, such as intravenous aminophylline or albuterol by nebulization, also should be considered.

Parenteral Dosage Forms

VARICELLA VIRUS VACCINE LIVE FOR INJECTION

Usual adult and adolescent dose

Varicella virus—

Subcutaneous, 0.5 mL, preferably into the outer aspect of the upper arm:

First dose—At initial visit.

Second dose—Four to eight weeks after the first dose.

Herpes zoster—

Subcutaneous, single 0.65 mL dose

Note: Zostavax® is for use only in individuals 60 years of age and older.

Usual pediatric dose

Varicella virus—

Infants up to 12 months of age—Use is not recommended.

Infants and children 12 months to 12 years of age—Subcutaneous, 0.5 mL as a single dose, preferably into the outer aspect of the upper arm. If a second 0.5-mL dose is administered, it should be given a minimum of 3 months later.

Zostavax® for herpes zoster prophylaxis should NOT be used in children.

Usual geriatric dose

See *Usual adult and adolescent dose.*

Strength(s) usually available

U.S.—

Not less than 1350 plaque forming units (PFU) of Oka/Merck varicella virus per 0.5 mL (Rx) [*Varivax* (may contain neomycin and gelatin)].

Minimum of 19,400 plaque forming units (PFU) of Oka/Merck strain of varicella-zoster vaccine (VZV) per 0.65 mL (Rx) [*Zostavax* (preservative-free; 31.16 mg sucrose; 15.58 mg hydrolyzed porcine gelatin; 3.99 mg sodium chloride; 0.62 mg monosodium L-glutamate; 0.57 mg sodium phosphate dibasic; 0.1 mg potassium phosphate monobasic; 0.1 mg potassium chloride; residual components of MRC-5 cells including DNA and protein; trace quantities of neomycin and bovine calf serum)].

Canada—

Minimum of 1350 plaque forming units (PFU) of Oka/Merck varicella virus per 0.5 mL (Rx) [*Varivax III* (18 mg sucrose; 8.9 mg hydrolyzed gelatin; 3.6 mg urea; 2.3 mg sodium chloride; 0.36 mg monosodium L-glutamate; 0.33 mg sodium phosphate dibasic; 57 mcg potassium phosphate monobasic; residual components of MRC-5 cells including DNA and protein; trace quantities of neomycin; fetal bovine serum from MRC-5 culture media)].

Not less than $10^{3.3}$ PFU of the varicella-zoster virus per 0.5 mL (Rx) [*Varilrix* (amino acids; human albumin; lactose; neomycin sulfate; polyalcohols; water for injection)].

Packaging and storage

For *Varivax*—Store the vaccine frozen at an average temperature of −15 °C (+5 °F) or colder until the time of reconstitution. The vaccine may be stored at refrigerator temperature of 2 to 8 °C (36 to 46 °F) for up to 72 continuous hours prior to reconstitution. Vaccine stored at 2 to 8 °C which is not used within 72 hours of removal from -15 °C storage should be discarded. The vaccine should not be refrozen. Before reconstitution, protect from light..

During shipment to ensure that there is no loss of potency, the vaccine must be maintained at a temperature of -20 °C (-4 °F) or colder (for Canadian product *Varivax III*: 2 to 8 °C or colder).

The diluent should be stored separately at room temperature 20 to 25 °C (68 to 77 °F) or in the refrigerator.

For *Varilrix*—Store the lyophilized vaccine in a refrigerator between 2 to 8 °C (36 to 46 °F). The lyophilized vaccine is not affected by freezing. The diluent may be stored in the refrigerator or at ambient temperature (maximum 25 °C).

For *Zostavax*—Store frozen at an average temperature of −15 °C (+5 °F) or colder until it is reconstituted for injection. Protect from light prior to reconstitution.

During shipment, to ensure that there is no potency lost, the vaccine must be maintained at a temperature of −20 °C (−4 °F) or colder.

Store the diluent separately at room temperature between 20 to 25 °C (68 to 77 °F) or in the refrigerator between 2 to 8 °C (36 to 46 °F).

Preparation of dosage form

To reconstitute, only the diluent provided by the manufacturer should be used since it is free of preservatives and other substances that might inactivate the vaccine.

0.7 mL of the diluent should be withdrawn into the syringe. All of the diluent should be injected into the vial of lyophilized vaccine and agitated to mix thoroughly. The entire contents should then be withdrawn into the syringe and the total volume of restored vaccine injected subcutaneously.

Stability

For *Varivax*—Varicella virus vaccine live has a potency level of 1500 PFU or higher per dose for at least 24 months (for Canadian product *Varivax III*: 18 months) in a frost-free freezer with an average temperature of −15 °C (+5 °F) or colder. The vaccine has a minimum potency level of 1350 PFU for 30 minutes after reconstitution at room temperature and should be administered immediately after reconstitution. The vaccine should be discarded if not used within 30 minutes after reconstitution. The reconstituted vaccine should not be frozen.

For information regarding stability under conditions other than those recommended, call 1-800-*VARIVAX*.

For *Varilrix*—The reconstituted vaccine should not be kept for more than 90 minutes at room temperature. Do not use beyond the expiration date printed on the label.

For *Zostavax*—The vaccine should be administered immediately after reconstitution to minimize loss of potency. Discard reconstituted vaccine if it is not used within 30 minutes. Do not freeze the reconstituted vaccine.

For information regarding stability under conditions other than those recommended, call 1-800-MERCK-90.

Incompatibilities

Preservatives or other substances may inactivate the vaccine; therefore, only the diluent supplied by the manufacturer should be used for reconstitution.

A sterile syringe free of preservatives, antiseptics, and detergents should be used for each injection and reconstitution of the vaccine, since these substances may inactivate the live virus vaccine.

Auxiliary labeling

- Keep frozen.
- Discard reconstituted vaccine if not used within 30 minutes.

Note

The date and time of reconstitution should be indicated on the vial if the vaccine is not used immediately.

Selected Bibliography

Centers for Disease Control and Prevention (CDC). Prevention of varicella: recommendations of the Advisory Committee on Immunization Practices (ACIP). MMWR Morb Mortal Wkly Rep 1996; 45(RR-11): 1-37.

American Academy of Pediatrics (AAP). Committee on Infectious Diseases. Recommendations for the use of live attenuated varicella vaccine. Pediatrics 1995; 95(5): 791-6.

American Academy of Pediatrics. Varicella zoster infections. In: Peter G, editor. 1997 Red book: report of the Committee on Infectious Diseases. 24th ed. Elk Grove Village, IL: American Academy of Pediatrics; 1997. p. 573-85.

Revised: 07/31/2006
Developed: 12/01/1998

VASOPRESSIN Systemic

VA CLASSIFICATION (Primary/Secondary): HS702/GA900; DX900

Commonly used brand name(s): *Pitressin; Pressyn.*

Note: For a listing of dosage forms and brand names by country availability, see *Dosage Forms* section(s).

Category

Pituitary (posterior) hormone; antidiuretic (central diabetes insipidus); diagnostic aid (diabetes insipidus).

Indications

Note: Bracketed information in the *Indications* section refers to uses that are not included in U.S. product labeling.

Accepted

Diabetes insipidus, central (treatment)—Vasopressin is indicated in the control or prevention of symptoms of central diabetes insipidus caused by insufficient antidiuretic hormone. It controls the polydipsia, polyuria, and dehydration associated with central diabetes insipidus.

Vasopressin injection may be used initially when diabetes insipidus is transient or due to surgery or head injury, or in unconscious patients receiving intravenous fluids. However, desmopressin is generally preferred for chronic therapy, since it lacks many of the effects on gastrointestinal and vascular smooth muscle vasopressin possesses.

[Diabetes insipidus (diagnosis)][1]—Vasopressin injection is used to differentially diagnose central and nephrogenic diabetes insipidus and psychogenic polydipsia.

Unaccepted

Vasopressin will not control polyuria associated with psychogenic polydipsia, renal disease, nephrogenic diabetes insipidus, hypokalemia, hypercalcemia, or the administration of demeclocycline or lithium.

Vasopressin injection was formerly used for the prevention and treatment of abdominal distention (in intestinal paresis, postoperatively, and complicating pneumonias or toxemias) and in abdominal roentgenography, urography, cholecystography, and kidney biopsy to disperse gas shadows. However, this use of vasopressin is no longer considered to be appropriate, because the risk of significant side effects does not outweigh the possible benefits of its use.

[1]Not included in Canadian product labeling.

Pharmacology/Pharmacokinetics

Physicochemical characteristics

Source—Synthetic vasopressin (8-arginine vasopressin).

Molecular weight—1084.23.

Mechanism of action/Effect

Antidiuretic (central diabetes insipidus) or

Diagnostic aid (diabetes insipidus)—Increases water reabsorption by increasing the cellular permeability of the collecting ducts, resulting in a decrease in urine volume with resultant increase in osmolality.

Other actions/effects

At greater than physiologic doses, vasopressin has a pressor effect due to vasoconstriction and causes contraction of the smooth muscle of the gastrointestinal tract. It also increases secretion of corticotropin, growth hormone, and follicle-stimulating hormone (FSH).

Biotransformation

Hepatic and renal.

Half-life

Approximately 10 to 20 minutes.

Duration of action

Approximately 2 to 8 hours.

Elimination
Renal; approximately 5 to 15% excreted unchanged after intravenous administration.

Precautions to Consider

Pregnancy/Reproduction
Pregnancy—Problems in humans have not been documented; however, caution is recommended because of possible oxytocic effects, although these probably occur only with large doses. Vasopressin is inactivated by the placenta, possibly necessitating use of increased doses.

FDA Pregnancy Category C.

Breast-feeding
Problems in humans have not been documented.

Pediatrics
Caution is recommended in very young children because of the risk of water intoxication and hyponatremia.

Geriatrics
Caution is recommended in the elderly because of the risk of water intoxication and hyponatremia.

Drug interactions and/or related problems
The following drug interactions and/or related problems have been selected on the basis of their potential clinical significance (possible mechanism in parentheses where appropriate)—not necessarily inclusive (» = major clinical significance):

Note: Combinations containing any of the following medications, depending on the amount present, may also interact with this medication.

Carbamazepine or
Chlorpropamide or
Clofibrate
Fludrocortisone or
Tricyclic antidepressants or
Urea
(may potentiate antidiuretic effect of vasopressin when used concurrently)

Alcohol or
Demeclocycline or
Heparin or
Lithium or
Norepinephrine
(may decrease antidiuretic effect of vasopressin when used concurrently)

Ganglionic blocking agents
(may produce a marked increase in sensitivity to the pressor effects of vasopressin)

Medical considerations/Contraindications
The medical considerations/contraindications included have been selected on the basis of their potential clinical significance (reasons given in parentheses where appropriate)—not necessarily inclusive (» = major clinical significance).

Risk-benefit should be considered when the following medical problems exist:
Allergy to vasopressin

Asthma or
Epilepsy or
Heart failure or
Migraine
(rapid addition of extracellular water may be hazardous)

» Coronary artery disease
(vasopressin may precipitate anginal pain; large doses may precipitate a myocardial infarction)

» Hypertensive cardiovascular disease
(vasopressin may increase blood pressure)

» Renal failure, chronic, with nitrogen retention

Patient monitoring
The following may be especially important in patient monitoring (other tests may be warranted in some patients, depending on condition; » = major clinical significance):

Electrocardiograms (ECG) and
Fluid and electrolyte status determinations
(recommended at periodic intervals during therapy)

Side/Adverse Effects
Note: Intra-arterial administration has been reported to cause local gangrene, coronary thrombosis, mesenteric infarction, venous thrombosis, infarction and necrosis of the small bowel, and peripheral emboli.

Large doses may cause increases in blood pressure, cardiac arrhythmias, and myocardial infarction.

The following side/adverse effects have been selected on the basis of their potential clinical significance (possible signs and symptoms in parentheses where appropriate)—not necessarily inclusive:

Those indicating need for medical attention
Incidence rare

Allergic reaction (fever; redness of skin; skin rash, hives, or itching; swelling of face, feet, hands, or mouth; wheezing or troubled breathing); ***angina or myocardial infarction*** (chest pain); ***water intoxication*** (coma; confusion; drowsiness; continuing headache; problems with urination; seizures; weight gain)

Those indicating need for medical attention only if they continue or are bothersome
Incidence less frequent—dose related

Abdominal or stomach cramps; belching; diarrhea; dizziness or lightheadedness; increased sweating; increased urge for bowel movement; nausea or vomiting; pale skin; passage of gas; "pounding" in head; trembling; white-colored area around mouth

Overdose
For specific information on the agents used in the management of vasopressin overdose, see:
- *Furosemide* in *Diuretics, Loop (Systemic)* monograph;
- *Mannitol (Systemic)* monograph; and/or
- *Urea (Parenteral-Local)* monograph.

For more information on the management of overdose or unintentional ingestion, **contact a poison control center** (see *Poison Control Center Listing*).

Treatment of overdose
Specific treatment—Severe water intoxication may require osmotic diuresis with mannitol, hypertonic dextrose, or urea, alone or with furosemide.

Supportive care—Water intoxication may be treated with water restriction and temporary withdrawal of vasopressin until polyuria occurs. Patients in whom intentional overdose is confirmed or suspected should be referred for psychiatric consultation.

Patient Consultation
As an aid to patient consultation, refer to *Advice for the Patient, Vasopressin (Systemic).*

In providing consultation, consider emphasizing the following selected information (» = major clinical significance):

Before using this medication
» Conditions affecting use, especially:
Allergy to vasopressin
Use in children—Very young children may be at greater risk of water intoxication and hyponatremia
Use in the elderly—May be at greater risk of water intoxication and hyponatremia
Other medical problems, especially coronary artery disease, hypertensive cardiovascular disease, or chronic renal failure

Proper use of this medication
» Importance of not using more medication than the amount prescribed
» Proper dosing
Missed dose: Using as soon as possible; not using at all if almost time for next dose; not doubling doses
» Proper storage

Side/adverse effects
Signs of potential side effects, especially allergic reaction, angina, myocardial infarction, and water intoxication

General Dosing Information
Aqueous Vasopressin Injection USP may be administered intramuscularly, subcutaneously, intravenously, or intra-arterially. It may also be administered intranasally for treatment of diabetes insipidus, although this route is now mainly of historical interest.

To achieve optimal control of effect, aqueous Vasopressin Injection USP may be administered intravenously or intra-arterially by means of an infusion pump, a micro-drip regulator, or a similar device to allow precise adjustment of the flow rate.

Caution is recommended to avoid extravasation because of the risk of necrosis and gangrene.

Vasopressin injection is recommended at the onset of the illness in diabetes insipidus, to decrease the risk of water intoxication until the severity of the disease is established, or when close monitoring and a short duration of action are desired (e.g., after skull fracture or surgery).

Parenteral Dosage Forms

Note: Bracketed uses in the *Dosage Forms* section refer to categories of use and/or indications that are not included in U.S. product labeling.

VASOPRESSIN INJECTION USP

Usual adult dose

Antidiuretic (central diabetes insipidus)—
Intramuscular or subcutaneous, 5 to 10 Units two or three times a day as needed.

Note: Ten units will usually elicit full physiologic response in adult patients; 5 units will be adequate in many cases.

[Diagnostic aid (diabetes insipidus [central])][1]—
Subcutaneous, 5 Units.

Usual pediatric dose

Antidiuretic (central diabetes insipidus)—
Intramuscular or subcutaneous, 2.5 to 10 Units three or four times a day.

Strength(s) usually available

U.S.—
20 USP Posterior Pituitary Units per mL (Rx) [*Pitressin;* GENERIC].

Canada—
20 USP Posterior Pituitary Units per mL (Rx) [*Pitressin; Pressyn*].

Packaging and storage

Store below 40 °C (104 °F), preferably between 15 and 30 °C (59 and 86 °F), unless otherwise specified by manufacturer. Protect from freezing.

---

[1]Not included in Canadian product labeling.

Revised: 02/28/2000

VECURONIUM—See *Neuromuscular Blocking Agents (Systemic)*

VENLAFAXINE Systemic

VA CLASSIFICATION (Primary/Secondary): Venlafaxine—CN609/CN304

Commonly used brand name(s): *Effexor; Effexor XR.*

Note: For a listing of dosage forms and brand names by country availability, see *Dosage Forms* section(s).

Category

Antidepressant; antianxiety agent; antipanic agent.

Indications

Accepted

Depressive disorder, major (treatment)—Venlafaxine is indicated for the treatment of major depressive disorder. Treatment of acute depressive episodes typically requires 6 to 12 months of antidepressant therapy. Patients with recurrent or chronic depression may require long-term treatment.

Anxiety (treatment)—The extended-release dosage form of venlafaxine is indicated for the management of generalized anxiety disorder and social anxiety disorder. However, venlafaxine usually is not indicated for the treatment of anxiety or tension associated with the stress of everyday life.

Panic disorder (treatment)—Extended release venlafaxine is indicated for the treatment of panic disorder, with or without agoraphobia, as defined in DSM-IV. Panic disorder is characterized by the occurrence of unexpected panic attacks and associated concern about having additional attacks, worry about the implications or consequences of the attacks, and/or a significant change in behavior related to the attacks.

[Hot flashes (treatment)][1]—Venlafaxine is indicated for the treatment of hot flashes. A double-blind, placebo-controlled trial, conducted in 229 women, demonstrated a 58% reduction in hot flash frequency and 61% reduction in hot flash score. Women included in the study had a history of breast cancer or refused to use hormonal therapy due to fear of developing breast cancer. Additionally, two smaller open-label trials, enrolling women with a history of breast cancer or men with androgen deprivation therapy, also reported reduction in hot flash frequency with venlafaxine.

Unaccepted

Venlafaxine is not approved for use in treating bipolar depression.

---

[1]Not included in Canadian product labeling.

Pharmacology/Pharmacokinetics

Note: A large degree of interpatient variability has been observed in the pharmacokinetic parameters of venlafaxine in patients with hepatic or renal function impairment.

Physicochemical characteristics

Chemically unrelated to tricyclic, tetracyclic, or other currently available antidepressants and to other drugs used to treat anxiety disorders.

Chemical Group—Phenethylamine.

Molecular weight—
Venlafaxine hydrochloride: 313.87.
Venlafaxine: 277.
O-desmethylvenlafaxine (ODV): 263.

pKa—9.4.

Mechanism of action/Effect

The antidepressant action of venlafaxine is believed to be associated with its ability to potentiate neurotransmitter activity in the central nervous system (CNS). Venlafaxine and its active metabolite, *O*-desmethylvenlafaxine (ODV), are potent inhibitors of neuronal serotonin (5-hydroxytryptamine; 5-HT) reuptake, slightly less potent inhibitors of neuronal norepinephrine reuptake, and weak inhibitors of neuronal dopamine reuptake. Venlafaxine inhibits serotonin reuptake less potently than do the selective serotonin reuptake inhibitors. Studies in rats indicate that venlafaxine induces reduced sensitivity of the adenylate-cyclase coupled beta-adrenergic system after single doses. Many other currently available antidepressants induce this change in beta-receptor sensitivity only after repeated dosing. However, not all antidepressants produce beta-adrenergic subsensitivity, and the clinical significance of this effect remains to be determined.

Neither venlafaxine nor ODV has demonstrated specific affinity for adrenergic alpha$_1$ receptors, muscarinic receptors, or histaminergic H$_1$ receptors. Venlafaxine has demonstrated no specific affinity for adrenergic alpha$_2$ or beta receptors, dopaminergic D$_2$ receptors, serotonergic 5HT$_1$ or 5HT$_2$ receptors, benzodiazepine receptors, opiate receptors, phencyclidine (PCP) receptors, or N-methyl-D-aspartic acid (NMDA) receptors *in vitro* . Neither venlafaxine nor ODV inhibits monoamine oxidase.

Other actions/effects

The immediate-release form of venlafaxine induces hypertension in a dose-related manner at an incidence ranging from 3 to 7% (at doses between 100 and 300 mg per day) to 13% (at doses above 300 mg per day). The extended-release form of venlafaxine induces hypertension in 0.4% and 3% of patients treated for generalized anxiety disorder and depression, respectively.

Absorption

Venlafaxine is rapidly and well absorbed. At least 92% of a single dose is absorbed, based on mass balance studies. The bioavailability of venlafaxine is the same with a tablet or with an oral solution and is about 45%. Food delays absorption, but does not impair extent of absorption of venlafaxine.

Venlafaxine release from the extended-release dosage form is membrane-controlled and is not pH-dependent. Although absorption from the extended-release dosage form occurs at a slower rate and results in a lower maximum plasma concentration of venlafaxine, the extent of absorption is the same as with the prompt-release tablet.

Distribution

Venlafaxine Vol$_D$—7.5 ± 3.7 L per kg of body weight (L/kg).

ODV Vol$_D$—5.7 ± 1.8 L/kg.

Venlafaxine is distributed into breast milk.

Protein binding

Low to moderate.
Venlafaxine—25 to 30%.
ODV—18 to 42%.

Biotransformation

Venlafaxine is extensively metabolized in the liver and undergoes significant first-pass metabolism. The primary metabolite is *O*-desmethylvenlafaxine (ODV), which is approximately equivalent in pharmacologic activity and potency to venlafaxine. ODV is formed by *O*-demethylation via the cytochrome P450 2D6 (CYP2D6) isoenzyme. Biotransformation of venlafaxine to ODV is saturable to a modest degree. *In vitro* studies indicate that the CYP3A4 isoenzyme is involved in the metabolism of venlafaxine to a minor, less active metabolite than ODV, *N*-desmethylvenlafaxine.

In nine patients with cirrhosis, hepatic clearance of venlafaxine was decreased by about 50%, and that of ODV was decreased by about 30%. Clearance of venlafaxine in three patients with more severe cirrhosis was decreased by about 90%.

Half-life

Elimination—

Venlafaxine: 5 ± 2 hours.

ODV: 11 ± 2 hours.

In nine patients with cirrhosis, elimination half-lives were increased by about 30% for venlafaxine, and by about 60% for ODV.

In patients with renal function impairment, elimination half-lives were increased by about 50% for venlafaxine, and by about 40% for ODV. In dialysis patients, venlafaxine elimination half-life was increased by up to 1.5 times that of patients with normal renal function.

Onset of action

Although some symptoms of major depression may improve within about 2 weeks, significant overall improvement may take several weeks.

Time to peak concentration

Prompt-release dosage form—

Venlafaxine: Approximately 2 hours.

ODV: 3 to 4 hours.

Extended-release dosage form—

Venlafaxine: Approximately 5.5 hours.

ODV: Approximately 9 hours.

Peak plasma concentration

Mean peak plasma concentrations (C_{max}) following administration of 25, 75, or 150 mg of the prompt-release dosage form of venlafaxine to 18 healthy males every 8 hours for three days were 53, 167, and 393 nanograms/mL (0.19, 0.603, and 1.42 micromoles/L), respectively, for venlafaxine, and 148, 397, and 686 nanograms/mL (0.563, 1.51, and 2.61 micromoles/L), respectively, for ODV. C_{max} is generally lower following administration of the extended-release dosage form. Both venlafaxine and ODV exhibit linear pharmacokinetics over the dose range of 75 to 450 mg of venlafaxine per day.

Steady-state concentrations of venlafaxine and ODV are attained within 3 days with regular oral dosing.

Elimination

Renal—

Approximately 87% of a dose is recovered in the urine within 48 hours, with unchanged venlafaxine comprising about 5%, unconjugated ODV comprising about 29%, conjugated ODV comprising about 26%, and other minor inactive metabolites comprising about 27% of the amount excreted.

In patients with renal function impairment, the clearance of venlafaxine was decreased by about 24%, but the clearance of ODV was unchanged. In patients with end-stage renal disease, total clearance of venlafaxine and ODV was decreased by about 55%.

In dialysis: In one study of six patients on maintenance hemodialysis, a 4-hour dialysis treatment removed only about 5% of a single 50-mg dose of venlafaxine.

Fecal—

Approximately 2% of a dose of venlafaxine is recovered in feces after 35 days.

Precautions to Consider

Carcinogenicity/Tumorigenicity

Studies in rats and mice that received venlafaxine for 24 and 18 months, respectively, have shown no evidence of an increased risk of tumor development.

Mutagenicity

Venlafaxine and its major metabolite, *O*-desmethylvenlafaxine (ODV), were not mutagenic in a battery of *in vivo* and *in vitro* tests. However, there was a clastogenic response in the *in vivo* chromosomal aberration assay in rat bone marrow in male rats receiving 200 times, on a mg per kg of body weight (mg/kg) basis, or 50 times, on a mg per square meter of body surface area (mg/m^2) basis, the maximum recommended human dose (MRHD) of venlafaxine. The no-effect dose was 67 times (mg/kg) or 17 times (mg/m^2) the MRHD.

Pregnancy/Reproduction

Fertility—No effects on male or female fertility were reported in rats administered oral doses of up to eight times the MRHD of venlafaxine on a mg/kg basis, or up to two times the MRHD on a mg/m^2 basis.

Pregnancy—Adequate and well-controlled studies in humans have not been done. Because animal reproduction studies are not always predictive of human response, this drug should be used during pregnancy only if clearly needed.

No teratogenic effects were observed in rats or rabbits given the MRHD of venlafaxine on a mg/kg basis (2.5 or 4 times, respectively, the MRHD on a mg/m^2 basis). However, when dosing in rats began during pregnancy and continued until weaning, a decrease in pup weight, an increase in stillborn pups, and an increase in pup deaths during the first 5 days of lactation occurred. The cause of these deaths is not known.

Non-teratogenic effects—When exposed to venlafaxine and other selective serotonin reuptake inhibitors (SSRIs) or selective norepinephrine reuptake inhibitors (SNRIs) late in the third trimester, neonates have developed complications requiring prolonged hospitalization, respiratory support, and tube feeding and these can arise immediately upon delivery. Features consistent with a direct toxic effect of SSRIs and SNRIs or a drug discontinuation syndrome including respiratory distress, cyanosis, apnea, seizures, temperature instability, feeding difficulty, vomiting, hypoglycemia, hypotonia, hypertonia, hyperreflexia, tremor, jitteriness, irritability, and constant crying have been reported. In some cases, it should be noted that the clinical picture is consistent with serotonin syndrome. When treating a pregnant woman with venlafaxine during the third trimester, the physician should carefully consider the potential risks and benefits of treatment. The physician may consider tapering venlafaxine in the third trimester.

FDA Pregnancy Category C.

Labor and delivery—The effect of venlafaxine on labor and delivery in humans is unknown.

Breast-feeding

Venlafaxine and ODV are distributed into breast milk and may cause unwanted effects in the nursing infant. Because of the potential for serious adverse reactions in nursing infants from venlafaxine, a decision should be made whether to discontinue nursing or to discontinue the drug, taking into account the importance of the drug to the mother.

Pediatrics

Safety and efficacy in children up to 18 years of age have not been established. Venlafaxine is not approved for use in treating any indications in the pediatric population.

Antidepressants increase the risk of suicidal thinking and behavior (suicidality) in children and adolescents with major depressive disorder (MDD) and other psychiatric disorders. Anyone considering the use of venlafaxine or any other antidepressant in a child or adolescent must balance this risk with the clinical need.

Pooled analyses of short-term placebo controlled trials of nine antidepressant drugs in children and adolescents with MDD, obsessive compulsive disorder, or other psychiatric disorders have revealed a greater risk of adverse events representing suicidality during the first few months of treatment in those receiving antidepressants.

Studies suggest that venlafaxine may adversely affect weight and height. Should the decision be made to treat a pediatric patient with venlafaxine, periodic monitoring of weight and height is recommended, particularly for long-term treatment. Safety of treatment has not been assessed for chronic treatment longer than six months.

Geriatrics

Appropriate studies performed to date have not demonstrated geriatrics-specific problems that would limit the usefulness of venlafaxine in the elderly. However, elderly patients are more likely to have age-related renal or hepatic impairment, which may require a dose reduction in patients receiving venlafaxine

Pharmacogenetics

Subjects with low cytochrome P450 2D6 (CYP2D6) activity, known as poor metabolizers, showed decreased ODV and increased venlafaxine concentrations as compared with concentrations in subjects with normal CYP2D6 activity, known as extensive metabolizers. However, since the sums of the concentrations of ODV and venlafaxine in the two groups were similar, this difference in metabolism is not likely to be of clinical significance.

Drug interactions and/or related problems

The following drug interactions and/or related problems have been selected on the basis of their potential clinical significance (possible

mechanism in parentheses where appropriate)—not necessarily inclusive (» = major clinical significance):

Note: Possible interactions with medications that inhibit cytochrome P450 2D6 (CYP2D6) metabolism potentially may result in increased plasma concentrations of venlafaxine and decreased plasma concentrations of *O*-desmethylvenlafaxine (ODV). However, the sum of the venlafaxine and ODV concentrations is not expected to change significantly, and dosage adjustments are not recommended.

CYP3A4 is involved to a lesser extent in the metabolism of venlafaxine and the effects of concomitant use of venlafaxine and a potent inhibitor of both CYP2D6 and CYP3A4 on venlafaxine pharmacokinetics are unknown.

In vivo and *in vitro* studies indicate that venlafaxine weakly inhibits CYP2D6 but does not inhibit CYP1A2, CYP2C9, CYP2C19, or CYP3A4.

Combinations containing any of the following medications, depending on the amount present, may also interact with this medication.

Alcohol or
CNS depression-producing medications (see *Appendix II*)
(although venlafaxine has not been shown to increase impairment of mental and motor skills, concomitant use with alcohol in depressed patients is not recommended)

(similarly, CNS depressants should be administered with caution, since the potential for interactions in clinical practice is not known)

Cimetidine
(in 18 healthy subjects, cimetidine inhibited the first-pass metabolism of venlafaxine, resulting in a decrease in clearance of about 43% and an increase in maximum plasma concentrations of about 60%; however, there was no apparent effect on the pharmacokinetics of ODV, which was present in the circulation in much greater quantities; thus, the overall pharmacologic activity of venlafaxine plus ODV was only slightly increased; dosage adjustments are not needed for most patients)

(this interaction potentially could be more pronounced in the elderly, in patients with pre-existing hypertension, or in patients with hepatic; caution should be exercised when venlafaxine and cimetidine are used concurrently in these patients)

» Clozapine
(post-marketing reports of elevated clozapine levels temporally associated with adverse events, including seizures, following addition of venlafaxine)

Diuretics
(hyponatremia and/or the syndrome of inappropriate antidiuretic hormone secretion [SIADH] may occur with venlafaxine use; this should be taken into consideration when administering venlafaxine to a patient who is taking diuretics)

Haloperidol
(the area under the plasma concentration-time curve [AUC] of haloperidol was increased by 70%, the maximum plasma concentration [C_{max}] was increased by 88%, the oral-dose clearance [Cl/F] was decreased by 42%, and the half-life was unchanged when a single 2-mg dose of haloperidol was administered to 24 healthy subjects who were at steady-state on a venlafaxine dosage of 150 mg per day administered as 75 mg every 12 hours)

» Moclobemide
(because of the potentially fatal consequences of combining nonselective, irreversible monoamine oxidase inhibitors with venlafaxine, and the increased risk of developing the serotonin syndrome with combined use of venlafaxine and the reversible monoamine oxidase-A inhibitor moclobemide, concurrent use is not recommended and a wash-out period of 3 to 7 days is advised between the use of one medication and the other)

» Monoamine oxidase (MAO) inhibitors, including furazolidone, procarbazine, and selegiline
(concurrent use of MAO inhibitors with venlafaxine may result in confusion, agitation, restlessness, and gastrointestinal symptoms, or possibly hyperpyretic episodes, severe convulsions, hypertensive crises, or the serotonin syndrome; concurrent use of an MAO inhibitor with venlafaxine is **contraindicated;** at least 14 days should elapse between discontinuation of an MAO inhibitor and initiation of venlafaxine; at least 7 days should elapse between discontinuation of venlafaxine and initiation of an MAO inhibitor)

Phentermine or
Other weight loss agents
(safety and efficacy not established; concomitant use not recommended; venlafaxine is not indicated for weight loss alone or in combination with other products)

» Serotonergics or other medications or substances with serotonergic activity (see *Appendix II*)
(increased risk of development of the serotonin syndrome, a rare but potentially fatal hyperserotonergic state which may occur in patients receiving serotonergic medications, usually in combination; symptoms typically occur shortly [hours to days] after the addition of a serotonergic agent to a regimen that includes serotonin-enhancing drugs; symptoms include agitation, diaphoresis, diarrhea, fever, hyperreflexia, incoordination, mental status changes [confusion, hypomania], myoclonus, shivering, or tremor; effects including cardiac arrhythmias, coma, disseminated intravascular coagulation, hyper- or hypo-tension, renal failure, respiratory failure, seizures, and severe hyperthermia have been reported also)

» Warfarin
(post-market reports of increases in prothrombin time, partial thromboplastin time, or INR when velafaxine was given to patients receiving warfarin therapy)

Laboratory value alterations

The following have been selected on the basis of their potential clinical significance (possible effect in parentheses where appropriate)—not necessarily inclusive (» = major clinical significance).

With physiology/laboratory test values

Blood pressure
(dose-related sustained hypertension, defined as supine diastolic blood pressure measurements on three consecutive visits that are ≥ 90 mm Hg and that are increased over baseline by ≥ 10 mm Hg, has been reported)

Cholesterol, serum
(mean increases in serum cholesterol concentrations of 3 mg/dL from baseline have been reported; the clinical significance of this finding is not known)

Creatine phosphokinase (CPK) or
Lactic acid dehydrogenase (LDH)
Prolactin
(post-marketing reports of increased levels)

Electrocardiogram (ECG)
(mean change in corrected QT interval [QT_c] in 357 patients receiving the extended-release dosage form of venlafaxine was an increase of 4.7 milliseconds [msec] as opposed to a 1.9 msec decrease in 285 placebo-treated patients)

Gamma-glutamyl transpeptidase (GGT)
(post-marketing reports of elevated levels)

Pulse
(heart rate increases of three to nine beats per minute have been reported, with a mean increase of four beats per minute)

Medical considerations/Contraindications

The medical considerations/contraindications included have been selected on the basis of their potential clinical significance (reasons given in parentheses where appropriate)—not necessarily inclusive (» = major clinical significance).

Except under special circumstances, this medication should not be used when the following medical problem exists:

» Hypersensitivity to venlafaxine hydrochloride or to any excipients in the formulation

Risk-benefit should be considered when the following medical problems exist:

» Bipolar disorder or risk of
(may increase likelihood of precipitation of a mixed/manic episode in these patients; prior to initiating venlafaxine treatment, patient should be adequately screened to determine if they are at risk for bipolar disorder; such screening should include a detailed psychiatric history, including a family history of suicide, bipolar disorder, and depression.)

» Blood pressure problems or
» Cardiac disease
(sustained hypertension or orthostatic hypotension induced by venlafaxine may exacerbate these conditions)

Glaucoma, acute narrow-angle, risk of, or
Intraocular pressure, raised
(mydriasis reported in association with venlafaxine; these patients should be monitored)

Heart failure or
Hyperthyroidism or
Myocardial infarction
(increase in heart rate observed with venlafaxine; caution should be exercised since these conditions might be compromised by increase in heart rate, especially with venlafaxine doses above 200 mg per day)

» Hepatic function impairment
(metabolism of venlafaxine may be altered; large interindividual variation in venlafaxine clearance is seen in these patients; patients with moderate to severe impairment may require dosage reductions of 50% or more)

» Mania, history of
(activation of hypomania or mania has been reported in depressed patients treated with venlafaxine)

Neurological impairment, including mental retardation
(risk of seizures may be increased)

» Renal function impairment or
» Cirrhosis of the liver
(caution should be used; excretion of venlafaxine may be altered; large interindividual variation in venlafaxine clearance is seen in these patients; patients with mild to moderate impairment may require dosage reductions of 25 to 50%; patients undergoing hemodialysis should receive a dosage reduction of 50% and the dose should be administered after the dialysis session is completed)

Seizures, history of
(as with other antidepressants, venlafaxine should be introduced with caution; if seizures develop, venlafaxine should be discontinued)

Volume-depleted
(hyponatremia and/or the syndrome of inappropriate antidiuretic hormone secretion [SIADH] may occur with venlafaxine; this should be considered when giving venlafaxine to volume-depleted patients)

Weight loss
(loss of ≥ 5% of baseline body weight occurred in 6% of patients receiving venlafaxine in clinical trials and in 1% of patients receiving placebo; significant weight loss, if it occurs, may be undesirable in some patients)

Patient monitoring

The following may be especially important in patient monitoring (other tests may be warranted in some patients, depending on condition; » = major clinical significance):

Blood pressure measurements
(recommended at regular intervals because of sustained increases in blood pressure associated with venlafaxine treatment; dosage reduction or discontinuation of venlafaxine treatment should be considered in patients who develop sustained increases in blood pressure)

» Careful supervision of depressed patients including those with:
Abnormal behaviors (i.e., agitation, panic attacks, hostility) or
Clinical worsening of their depression or
Suicidal ideation and behavior (suicidality)
(recommended especially during early treatment phase before peak effectiveness of venlafaxine is achieved or at the time of increases or decreases in dose; prescribing the smallest number of capsules or tablets necessary for good patient management is recommended to decrease the risk of overdose; consideration should be given to changing the therapeutic regimen, including possibly discontinuing the medicine, in patients whose depression is persistently worse or whose emergent suicidality or other symptoms are severe, abrupt in onset, or were not part of the patient's presenting symptoms)

Intraocular pressure determinations
(monitoring recommended because mydriasis has been reported in association with venlafaxine and may increase intraocular pressure)

» Symptoms associated with discontinuation
(patients should be monitored for symptoms upon discontinuation; a gradual reduction in dose rather than abrupt cessation is recommended whenever possible; previously prescribed dose may be considered if intolerable symptoms occur following a decrease in the dose or upon discontinuation of treatment)

Side/Adverse Effects

Note: Venlafaxine is generally well-tolerated, with evidence of dose-dependency for some of the most common adverse effects. In addition, there is evidence of adaptation with continuing therapy to some effects such as nausea, vomiting, somnolence, and dizziness.

The following side/adverse effects have been selected on the basis of their potential clinical significance (possible signs and symptoms in parentheses where appropriate)—not necessarily inclusive:

Those indicating need for medical attention

Incidence more frequent

Headache; hypertension (high blood pressure)—usually asymptomatic; ***vision disturbances, including abnormal accommodation; and blurred vision***

Note: Venlafaxine-induced sustained *hypertension*, defined as supine diastolic blood pressure measurements on three consecutive visits that are ≥ 90 mm Hg and that are increased over baseline by ≥ 10 mm Hg, is reported to be dose-dependent.

Probability of Sustained Hypertension*

Venlafaxine Dose (mg/day)	Incidence (%)
< 100	3
101 to 200	5
201 to 300	7
> 300	13
Placebo	2

*Estimated by the manufacturer from pooled data of premarketing studies of the prompt-release dosage form.

Incidence less frequent

Cardiovascular effects, other, including chest pain; palpitation (fast or irregular heartbeat); ***and tachycardia*** (fast heartbeat); ***CNS effects*** (mood or mental changes); ***including abnormal thinking; agitation; confusion; depersonalization; and emotional lability; tinnitus*** (ringing or buzzing in ears)

Incidence rare

Dyspnea (trouble in breathing); ***edema*** (swelling); ***itching or skin rash; mania or hypomania*** (talking, feeling, and acting with excitement and activity one cannot control); ***menstrual changes; orthostatic hypotension*** (lightheadedness or fainting)—especially when getting up suddenly from a sitting or lying position; ***seizures*** (convulsions); ***trismus*** (lockjaw); ***urinary effects, including impaired urination; urinary frequency; urinary incontinence; or urinary retention*** (problems in urinating or in holding urine)

Incidence not determined—Observed during clinical practice; estimates of frequency can not be observed

Agranulocytosis (cough or hoarseness; fever with or without chills; general feeling of tiredness or weakness; lower back or side pain; painful or difficult urination; sore throat; sores, ulcers, or white spots on lips or in mouth; unusual bleeding or bruising); ***anaphylaxis*** (cough; difficulty swallowing; dizziness; fast heartbeat; hives; itching; puffiness or swelling of the eyelids or around the eyes, face, lips or tongue; shortness of breath; skin rash; tightness in chest; unusual tiredness or weakness; wheezing); ***aplastic anemia*** (chest pain; chills; cough; fever; headache; shortness of breath; sores, ulcers, or white spots on lips or in mouth; swollen or painful glands; tightness in chest; unusual bleeding or bruising; unusual tiredness or weakness; wheezing); ***atrial fibrillation*** (fast or irregular heartbeat; dizziness; fainting); ***cardiac arrhythmias*** (chest pain or discomfort; dizziness; fainting; fast, slow, or irregular heartbeat; lightheadedness; pounding or rapid pulse); ***catatonia*** (decreased awareness or responsiveness; mimicry of speech or movements; mutism; negativism; peculiar postures or movements, mannerisms or grimacing; severe sleepiness); ***congenital anomalies*** (); ***deep vein thrombophlebitis*** (pain, redness, or swelling in arm or leg); ***delirium*** (unusual excitement, nervousness, or restlessness; hallucinations; confusion as to time, place, or person; holding false beliefs that cannot be changed by fact); ***dyskinesia*** (twitching, twisting, uncontrolled repetitive movements of tongue, lips, face, arms, or legs); ***epidermal necrosis*** (blue-green to black skin; discoloration, pain, redness, or sloughing of skin at place of injection); ***erythema multiforme*** (blistering, peeling, loosening of skin; chills; cough; diarrhea; fever; itching; joint or muscle pain; red, irritated eyes; sore throat; sores, ulcers, or white spots in mouth or on lips; unusual tiredness or weakness); ***eye hemorrhage*** (blood in eye; eye pain; redness in whites of eyes); ***fatty liver*** (abdominal pain; bloating of abdomen; dark urine; light-colored stools; nausea and vomiting; yellow eyes or skin); ***gastrointestinal hemmorhage*** (black, tarry stools; bloody stools; vomiting of blood or material that looks like coffee grounds); ***hemorrhage*** (bleeding gums; coughing up blood; difficulty in breathing or swallowing; dizziness; headache; increased menstrual flow or vaginal bleeding; nosebleeds; paralysis; prolonged bleeding from cuts; red or dark brown urine; red or black, tarry stools; shortness of breath); ***involuntary movements; liver damage*** (abdominal pain; bloating of abdomen; dark urine; light-colored stools;

nausea and vomiting; yellow eyes or skin); ***liver failure*** (headache; stomach pain; continuing vomiting; dark-colored urine; general feeling of tiredness or weakness; light-colored stools; yellow eyes or skin); ***liver necrosis*** (abdominal or stomach pain; black, tarry stools; chills; light-colored stools; dark urine; dizziness; fever; headache; itching; loss of appetite; nausea; rash; unpleasant breath odor; unusual tiredness or weakness; vomiting of blood; yellow eyes or skin); ***neuroleptic malignant syndrome-like events*** (convulsions; difficulty in breathing; fast heartbeat; high fever; high or low blood pressure; increased sweating; loss of bladder control; severe muscle stiffness; unusually pale skin; tiredness); ***neutropenia*** (black, tarry stools; chills; cough; fever; lower back or side pain; painful or difficult urination; pale skin; shortness of breath; sore throat; ulcers, sores, or white spots in mouth; unusual bleeding or bruising; unusual tiredness or weakness); ***pancreatitis*** (bloating; chills; constipation; darkened urine; fast heartbeat; fever; indigestion; loss of appetite; nausea; pains in stomach, side, or abdomen, possibly radiating to the back; vomiting; yellow eyes or skin); ***pancytopenia*** (high fever; chills; unexplained bleeding or bruising; bloody, black, or tarry stools; pale skin; unusual tiredness or weakness; cough; shortness of breath; sores, ulcers, or white spots on lips or in mouth; swollen glands); ***panic; pulmonary eosinophilia*** (chest pain; dry cough; fever; general feeling of tiredness or weakness; rapid breathing; shortness of breath; skin rash; wheezing); ***QT prolongation*** (irregular heartbeat; recurrent fainting); ***renal failure*** (lower back/side pain; decreased frequency/amount of urine; bloody urine; increased thirst; loss of appetite; nausea; vomiting; unusual tiredness or weakness; swelling of face, fingers, lower legs; weight gain; troubled breathing; increased blood pressure); ***rhabdomyolysis*** (dark-colored urine; fever; muscle cramps or spasms; muscle pain or stiffness; unusual tiredness or weakness); ***serotonin syndrome*** (agitation; confusion; diarrhea; fever; overactive reflexes; poor coordination; restlessness; shivering; sweating; talking or acting with excitement you cannot control; trembling or shaking; twitching); ***shock-like electrical sensations; Stevens-Johnson syndrome*** (blistering, peeling, loosening of skin; chills; cough; diarrhea; itching; joint or muscle pain; red irritated eyes red skin lesions, often with a purple center sore throat sores, ulcers, or white spots in mouth or on lips unusual tiredness or weakness); ***supraventricular tachycardia*** (fainting; fast, pounding, or irregular heartbeat or pulse; palpitations); ***syndrome of inappropriate antidiuretic hormone secretion*** (agitation; coma; confusion; decreased urine output; depression; dizziness; headache; hostility; irritability; lethargy; muscle twitching; nausea; rapid weight gain; seizures; stupor; swelling of face, ankles, or hands; unusual tiredness or weakness); ***tardive dyskinesia*** (lip smacking or puckering; puffing of cheeks; rapid or worm-like movements of tongue; uncontrolled chewing movements; uncontrolled movements of arms and legs); ***torsade de pointes*** (chest pain or discomfort; irregular or slow heart rate; fainting; shortness of breath); ***ventricular extrasystoles*** (extra heart beats); ***ventricular fibrillation*** (fainting; fast, slow, or irregular heartbeat; shortness of breath; unusual tiredness or weakness); ***ventricular tachycardia*** (fainting; fast, pounding, or irregular heartbeat or pulse; palpitations)

Those indicating need for medical attention only if they continue or are bothersome

Incidence more frequent

Abnormal dreams; anorexia (loss of appetite); ***anxiety or nervousness; asthenia*** (unusual tiredness or weakness); ***chills; constipation; diarrhea; dizziness; dryness of mouth; dyspepsia*** (heartburn); ***increased sweating; insomnia*** (trouble in sleeping); ***nausea; paresthesia*** (tingling, burning, or prickly sensations); ***rhinitis*** (stuffy or runny nose); ***sexual dysfunction, including anorgasmia; decreased libido; delayed ejaculation; or impotence*** (decrease in sexual drive or performance); ***somnolence*** (drowsiness); ***stomach pain or gas; tremor*** (trembling or shaking); ***vomiting; weight loss; yawning***

Note: *Anorexia, chills, dizziness, nausea, somnolence, sweating, tremor, vomiting,* and *weight loss* may be dose-related. Loss of ≥ 5% of baseline body weight occurred in 6% of patients in clinical trials of venlafaxine.

Sexual dysfunction may be dose-related and does not show evidence of adaptation with continuing venlafaxine therapy.

Incidence less frequent

Hypertonia (muscle tension); ***taste perversion*** (change in sense of taste);

Incidence not determined—Observed during clinical practice; estimates of frequency can not be determined

Night sweats

Those indicating the need for medical attention if they occur after medication is discontinued

Agitation (anxiety; nervousness; restlessness; irritability; dry mouth; shortness of breath; hyperventilation; trouble sleeping; irregular heartbeats; shaking); ***anorexia*** (loss of appetite; weight loss); ***anxiety*** (fear; nervousness); ***asthenia*** (unusual tiredness or weakness); ***changes in dreaming; confusion*** (mood or mental changes); ***coordination impaired*** (difficulty with coordination); ***diarrhea; dizziness; dryness of mouth; dysphoric mood*** (feeling unwell or unhappy); ***emotional lability*** (crying; depersonalization; dysphoria; euphoria; mental depression; paranoia; quick to react or overreact emotionally; rapidly changing moods); ***fasciculation*** (twitches of the muscle visible under the skin); ***fatigue*** (unusual tiredness or weakness); ***headache; hypomania*** (actions that are out of control; irritability; nervousness; talking, feeling, and acting with excitement); ***increased sweating; insomnia*** (trouble in sleeping); ***irritability; lethargy*** (unusual drowsiness, dullness, tiredness, weakness or feeling of sluggishness); ***nausea; nightmares; nervousness; seizures*** (convulsions; muscle spasm or jerking of all extremities; sudden loss of consciousness; loss of bladder control); ***sensory disturbances (including shock-like electrical sensations; somnolence*** (sleepiness or unusual drowsiness); ***tinnitus*** (continuing ringing or buzzing or other unexplained noise in ears; hearing loss); ***tremor*** (trembling or shaking of hands or feet; shakiness in legs, arms, hands, feet); ***vertigo*** (dizziness or lightheadedness; feeling of constant movement of self or surroundings, sensation of spinning); ***vomiting***

Note: Dose reduction of venlafaxine at various doses has also been found to be associated with the appearance of new symptoms including: agitation, anorexia, anxiety, confusion, coordination impaired, diarrhea, dizziness, dry mouth, dysphoric mood, fasciculation, fatigue, headaches, hypomania, insomnia, nausea, nervousness, nightmares, sensory disturbances (including shock-like electrical sensations), somnolence, sweating, tremor, vertigo, and vomiting.

Overdose

For specific information on the agents used in the management of venlafaxine overdose, see *Charcoal, Activated (Oral-Local)* monograph.

For more information on the management of overdose or unintentional ingestion, **contact a Poison Control Center** (see *Poison Control Center Listing*).

Clinical effects of overdose

The following effects have been selected on the basis of their potential clinical significance (possible signs and symptoms in parentheses where appropriate)—not necessarily inclusive:

Agitation; electrocardiogram (ECG) changes, specifically QTc prolongation; lethargy (extreme tiredness or weakness); ***paresthesia*** (tingling, burning, or prickling sensations); ***seizures; sinus tachycardia*** (fast heartbeat); ***somnolence*** (drowsiness); ***tremor*** (trembling or shaking)

Note: Only a small number of overdose cases were reported during premarketing studies of venlafaxine. In most of these cases, no symptoms were reported. However, there have been post-marketing reports of fatalities occurring with venlafaxine overdose, predominantly when alcohol or other drugs were co-ingested

Overdosage with venlafaxine may result in development of the serotonin syndrome, a potentially fatal hyperserotonergic state. Symptoms include agitation, diaphoresis, diarrhea, fever, hyperreflexia, incoordination, mental status changes (confusion, hypomania), myoclonus, shivering, and tremor. The non-specific serotonergic receptor antagonists cyproheptadine and methysergide have been reported to be of some use in shortening the duration of the serotonin syndrome.

Treatment of overdose

There is no specific antidote for venlafaxine. Treatment is essentially symptomatic and supportive.

To decrease absorption—

Considering use of activated charcoal or gastric lavage.

Monitoring—

Monitoring cardiac function and vital signs.

Supportive care—

Ensuring adequate airway patency, oxygenation, and ventilation. Patients in whom intentional overdose is known or suspected should be referred for psychiatric consultation.

Note: Due to the large volume of distribution of venlafaxine, forced diuresis, dialysis, hemoperfusion, or exchange transfusion is not likely to be of benefit. In six patients undergoing hemodialysis, less than 5% of an administered dose of venlafaxine was recovered in dialysis fluid as venlafaxine and *O*-desmethylvenlafaxine (ODV).

Patient Consultation

As an aid to patient consultation, refer to *Advice for the Patient, Venlafaxine (Systemic).*

In providing consultation, consider emphasizing the following selected information (» = major clinical significance):

Before using this medication

» Conditions affecting use, especially:

Hypersensitivity to venlafaxine hydrochloride or to any excipients in the formulation

Pregnancy—Should be used during pregnancy only if clearly needed

Complications including prolonged hospitalization, respiratory support and tube feeding in neonates exposed to venlafaxine and other SSRIs late in the third trimester; physician should carefully consider potential risks and benefits when treating a pregnant woman in her third trimester

Breast-feeding—Distributed into breast milk; may cause unwanted effects in nursing infant

Use in children—Because of Food and Drug Administration [FDA] reports of the occurrence of suicidality in clinical trials for various antidepressant drugs in pediatric patients with major depressive disorder [MDD], venlafaxine must be used with caution in treating pediatric patients for MDD.

May affect weight and height in pediatric patients; monitoring recommended; safety not assessed for chronic treatment longer than six months

Contraindicated medications—MAO inhibitors

Other medications, especially clozapine, serotonergics and other medications or substances with serotonergic activity, or warfarin

Other medical problems, especially bipolar disorder or risk of, blood pressure problems, cardiac disease, cirrhosis of the liver, or hepatic or renal function impairment

Proper use of this medication

» Compliance with therapy; not taking more or less medicine than prescribed

» Four weeks or more of therapy may be required before antidepressant effects are achieved

Taking with food to lessen gastrointestinal effects

» For extended-release dosage form: Swallowing capsule whole with fluid; not dividing, crushing, chewing, or placing in liquid

» Proper dosing

Missed dose: For prompt-release dosage form—Taking as soon as possible unless it is within 2 hours of next dose; continuing on regular schedule with next dose; not doubling doses For extended-release dosage form—Taking as soon as possible if remembered the same day; continuing on regular schedule with next dose; not doubling doses

» Proper storage

Precautions while using this medication

Regular visits to physician to check progress of therapy

» Notifying physician immediately if any signs or symptoms of allergic reaction, such as skin rash or hives, occur

Checking with physician before discontinuing medication

» Importance of patient tapering off of the medication as directed by the physician

» Importance of patient or caregiver notifying physician immediately if any signs of abnormal behavior, worsening depression or suicidality occur

Avoiding use of alcoholic beverages; not taking other CNS depressants unless prescribed by physician

» Caution when driving or doing other jobs requiring alertness, judgment, or clear vision until effects of medication are known

» Possible dizziness or lightheadedness; caution when getting up from a lying or sitting position

Side/adverse effects

Signs of potential side effects, especially headache; hypertension; vision disturbances; cardiovascular effects, other; CNS effects; tinnitus; dyspnea; edema; itching or skin rash; mania or hypomania; menstrual changes; orthostatic hypotension; seizures; urinary effects

Signs of potential side effects observed during clinical practice, especially agranulocytosis, anaphylaxis, aplastic anemia, atrial fibrillation, cardiac arrhythmias, catatonia, congenital anomalies, deep vein thrombophlebitis, delirium, dyskinesia, epidermal necrosis, erythema multiforme, eye hemorrhage, fatty liver, gastrointestinal hemorrhage, hemorrhage, involuntary movements, liver damage, liver failure, liver necrosis, neuroleptic malignant syndrome-like events, neutropenia, pancreatitis, pancytopenia, panic, pulmonary eosinophilia, QT prolongation, renal failure, rhabdomyolysis, serotonin syndrome, shock-like electrical sensations, Stevens-Johnson syndrome, supraventricular tachycardia, syndrome of inappropriate antidiuretic hormone secretion, tardive dyskinesia, torsade de pointes, ventricular extrasystoles, ventricular fibrillation, or ventricular tachycardia

Signs of discontinuation symptoms, especially agitation, anorexia, asthenia, confusion, coordination impaired, diarrhea, dysphoric mood, emotional lability, fasciculation, fatigue, headache, hypomania, increased sweating, insomnia, irritability, lethargy, nausea, nightmares, nervousness, seizures, sensory disturbances (including shock-like electrical sensations, somnolence, tinnitus, tremor, vertigo, or vomiting

General Dosing Information

Abrupt discontinuation of venlafaxine may result in symptoms of withdrawal including anorexia, asthenia, changes in dreaming, diarrhea, dizziness, dryness of mouth, headache, increased sweating, insomnia, nausea, nervousness, and somnolence. It is recommended that patients taking venlafaxine for longer than 1 week be tapered off the drug; venlafaxine should be discontinued gradually over 2 weeks or longer in patients receiving therapy for 6 weeks or longer. In clinical trials, the extended-release dosage form was tapered in decrements of 75 mg per day at 1-week intervals.

Potentially suicidal patients should not have access to large quantities of this medication since depressed patients, particularly those who may use alcohol excessively, may continue to exhibit suicidal tendencies until significant improvement occurs. Some clinicians recommend that the patient be supplied with the smallest quantity of medication necessary for satisfactory patient management.

Activation of hypomania or mania has been reported in depressed patients treated with venlafaxine.

The need for continuing medication in patients who improve with venlafaxine treatment should be periodically reassessed.

Patients receiving the prompt-release dosage form of venlafaxine may change to the extended-release dosage form at the most nearly equivalent mg per day dosage available.

Diet/Nutrition

Venlafaxine should be taken with food to lessen gastrointestinal side effects.

Oral Dosage Forms

Note: The available dosage forms contain venlafaxine hydrochloride, but dosage and strength are expressed in terms of the base.

VENLAFAXINE EXTENDED-RELEASE CAPSULES

Usual adult dose

Antidepressant—

Oral, initially 75 mg (base) a day in a single dose, taken with food, in the morning or evening. Some patients may require an initial dosage of 37.5 mg (base) a day for four to seven days in order to adjust to the medication. The dosage may be increased, as needed and tolerated, in increments of 75 mg a day at intervals of at least four days.

Anxiety—

Oral, initially 75 mg (base) a day in a single dose, taken with food, in the morning or evening. Some patients may require an initial dosage of 37.5 mg (base) a day for four to seven days in order to adjust to the medication. The dosage may be increased, as needed and tolerated, in increments of 75 mg a day at intervals of at least four days.

Panic disorder—

Oral, initially 37.5 mg (base) per day in a single dose for 7 days. The dosage may be increased, as needed, in increments up to 75 mg per day at intervals of not less than 7 days.

[Hot flashes][1]—

Oral, initially 37.5 mg a day. The dosage may be increased up to 150 mg a day if no reduction in hot flashes occurs after 1 to 2 weeks.

Note: Patients with moderate hepatic function impairment should receive an initial dosage reduction of 50%. Patients with renal function impairment should receive an initial dosage reduction of 25 to 50%. The total daily dose for patients undergoing hemodialysis should be reduced by 50% and the dose should be administered after completion of the dialysis session.

Usual adult prescribing limits
225 mg per day. The maximum recommended dosage of 225 mg per day reflects experience in moderately depressed outpatients. However, severely depressed inpatients in a study using the prompt-release dosage form responded to dosages up to 375 mg per day. There is little experience with the extended-release dosage form at dosages above 225 mg per day, and whether severely depressed patients will respond to higher dosages has not been established.

Usual pediatric dose
Safety and efficacy have not been established.

Usual geriatric dose
See *Usual adult dose.*

Note: Although no special dosage adjustments based on age are recommended generally, some clinicians recommend a reduced initial dosage and more gradual dosage increases in elderly patients.

Strength(s) usually available
U.S.—
37.5 mg (base) (Rx) [*Effexor XR* (cellulose; ethylcellulose; gelatin; hydroxypropyl methylcellulose; iron oxide; titanium dioxide)].
75 mg (base) (Rx) [*Effexor XR* (cellulose; ethylcellulose; gelatin; hydroxypropyl methylcellulose; iron oxide; titanium dioxide)].
150 mg (base) (Rx) [*Effexor XR* (cellulose; ethylcellulose; gelatin; hydroxypropyl methylcellulose; iron oxide; titanium dioxide)].
Canada—
37.5 mg (base) (Rx) [*Effexor XR*].
75 mg (base) (Rx) [*Effexor XR*].
150 mg (base) (Rx) [*Effexor XR*].

Packaging and storage
Store between 20 and 25 °C (68 and 77 °F) in a well-closed container unless otherwise specified by manufacturer.

Auxiliary labeling
- Avoid alcoholic beverages.
- May cause drowsiness.
- Swallow capsules whole. Do not break or chew.
- Take with food.

Note: Release of venlafaxine from extended-release capsule is membrane-controlled and is not dependent upon pH.

VENLAFAXINE TABLETS

Usual adult dose
Antidepressant—
Oral, initially 75 mg a day, administered in two or three divided doses and taken with food. The dosage may be increased, as needed and tolerated, in increments up to 75 mg a day at intervals of no less than four days, up to 225 mg a day. Although dosages over 225 mg a day have not been shown to be useful in moderately depressed outpatients, more severely depressed patients may respond to dosages of up to 375 mg a day, administered in three divided doses.

Note: Some clinicians recommend an initial dosage of 50 mg a day administered in two divided doses in the treatment of mild depression in order to minimize nausea.
In patients with moderate to severe hepatic function impairment—Dosage reductions of 50% or more are recommended.
In patients with renal function impairment—Mild to moderate: Dosage reductions of 25% are recommended. Moderate to severe ($CL_{cr} < 30$ mL/min): Dosage should be reduced by 50%. The dose may be administered once a day because of the prolonged half-life. In dialysis patients: Total daily dose should be reduced by 50%, and administration withheld until dialysis treatment is completed.

Usual adult prescribing limits
375 mg a day.

Usual pediatric dose
Safety and efficacy in children up to 18 years of age have not been established.

Usual geriatric dose
See *Usual adult dose.*

Note: Although no special dosage adjustments based on age are recommended generally, some clinicians recommend a reduced initial dosage and more gradual dosage increases in elderly patients.

Strength(s) usually available
U.S.—
25 mg (base) (Rx) [*Effexor* (scored; cellulose; iron oxides; lactose; magnesium stearate; sodium starch glycolate)].
37.5 mg (base) (Rx) [*Effexor* (scored; cellulose; iron oxides; lactose; magnesium stearate; sodium starch glycolate)].
50 mg (base) (Rx) [*Effexor* (scored; cellulose; iron oxides; lactose; magnesium stearate; sodium starch glycolate)].
75 mg (base) (Rx) [*Effexor* (scored; cellulose; iron oxides; lactose; magnesium stearate; sodium starch glycolate)].
100 mg (base) (Rx) [*Effexor* (scored; cellulose; iron oxides; lactose; magnesium stearate; sodium starch glycolate)].
Canada—
37.5 mg (base) (Rx) [*Effexor* (scored; cosmetic brown iron oxide; ferric oxide NF yellow; lactose NF hydrous; magnesium stearate NF; microcrystalline cellulose NF; sodium starch glycolate NF)].
75 mg (base) (Rx) [*Effexor* (scored; cosmetic brown iron oxide; ferric oxide NF yellow; lactose NF hydrous; magnesium stearate NF; microcrystalline cellulose NF; sodium starch glycolate NF)].

Packaging and storage
Store in a dry place between 20 and 25 °C (68 and 77 °F) in a well-closed container unless otherwise specified by manufacturer.

Auxiliary labeling
- Avoid alcoholic beverages.
- May cause drowsiness.
- Take with food.

[1]Not included in Canadian product labeling.

Revised: 12/01/2005

VERAPAMIL—See *Calcium Channel Blocking Agents (Systemic)*

VIGABATRIN Systemic*

VA CLASSIFICATION (Primary): CN400
Commonly used brand name(s): *Sabril.*

Note: For a listing of dosage forms and brand names by country availability, see *Dosage Forms* section(s).

*Not commercially available in U.S.

Category
Anticonvulsant.

Indications
Note: Bracketed information in the *Indications* section refers to uses that are not included in U.S. product labeling.

Accepted
[Epilepsy (treatment adjunct)]—Vigabatrin is indicated for the adjunctive management of epilepsy that is not satisfactorily controlled by conventional therapy.
[Infantile spasms (treatment)]—Vigabatrin is indicated as initial monotherapy for the management of infantile spasms (West syndrome).

Pharmacology/Pharmacokinetics

Physicochemical characteristics
Molecular weight—129.16.
pKa—4.02.
Solubility—Freely soluble in water, sparingly soluble in methanol, slightly soluble in ethanol, and in soluble in chloroform, hexane, and toluene.
pH—20% aqueous solution: 6.8

Mechanism of action/Effect
Vigabatrin indirectly increases the levels of gamma-aminobutyric acid (GABA), an inhibitory neurotransmitter, by inhibiting the enzyme responsible for regulating GABA levels, gamma-aminobutyric acid transaminase (GABA-T).

Absorption
Vigabatrin is rapidly absorbed following oral administration. The presence of food may slightly decrease the rate, but not the extent, of absorption.

Distribution
The volume of distribution is slightly greater than that of total body water.

Elimination
Young adults: 5–8 hours
Elderly:12–13 hours
Renal Impairment: Prolonged; rate is directly related to renal clearance of creatinine

Time to peak concentration
2 hours

Elimination
Renal: 70% is excreted as unchanged drug within the first 24 hours post-dose

In dialysis: 40 to 60% reductions in vigabatrin plasma concentrations have been reported in patients with renal failure receiving hemodialysis.

Precautions to Consider

Carcinogenicity
No carcinogenic effects were observed in mice or rats that received doses of vigabatrin as high as 150 mg per kg of body weight per day for up to 24 months.

Mutagenicity
No evidence demonstrating a connection between vigabatrin administration and genotoxicity was found following studies involving *in vitro* and *in vivo* systems, eukaryotic and prokaryotic cells, and tests for both gene mutations and chromosome aberrations.

Pregnancy/Reproduction
Pregnancy—Vigabatrin is not recommended during pregnancy. Risk-benefit must be carefully considered.

Studies in animals have shown that vigabatrin may cause serious neurotoxicity in the fetus.

Breast-feeding
It is not known whether vigabatrin is distributed into breast milk. However, the manufacturer states that vigabatrin therapy is contraindicated during lactation.

Pediatrics
Appropriate studies performed to date have not demonstrated pediatrics-specific problems that would limit the usefulness of vigabatrin in children greater than 2 months of age. However, because of the risks of ophthalmological abnormalities and the difficulty in assessing visual fields in infants and young children, vigabatrin should be used in these patients only if clearly indicated. The need for continued vigabatrin therapy for all infants and young children should be reassessed periodically, and frequent examination by a pediatric ophthalmologist is recommended.

Geriatrics
Although appropriate studies on the relationship of age to the effects of vigabatrin have not been performed in the geriatric population, no geriatrics-specific problems have been documented to date. However, elderly patients are more likely to have age-related renal function impairment, which may require adjustment of dosage in patients receiving vigabatrin.

Drug interactions and/or related problems
The following drug interactions and/or related problems have been selected on the basis of their potential clinical significance (possible mechanism in parentheses where appropriate)—not necessarily inclusive (» = major clinical significance):

Note: Vigabatrin does not appear to induce the hepatic cytochrome P450 system.

Combinations containing any of the following medications, depending on the amount present, may also interact with this medication.

Phenobarbital or
Phenytoin
(mean decreases in phenytoin (16–33%) and phenobarbital (9–21%) levels have been reported following concurrent vigabatrin administration; clinical relevance is unknown)

Laboratory value alterations
The following have been selected on the basis of their potential clinical significance (possible effect in parentheses where appropriate)—not necessarily inclusive (» = major clinical significance).

With physiology/laboratory test values
Alanine aminotransferase (ALT [SGPT])
Aspartate aminotransferase (AST [SGOT]) and
Hemoglobin
(chronic treatment with vigabatrin may lead to slightly decreased levels.)

Medical considerations/Contraindications
The medical considerations/contraindications included have been selected on the basis of their potential clinical significance (reasons given in parentheses where appropriate)—not necessarily inclusive (» = major clinical significance).

Risk-benefit should be considered when the following medical problems exist:

» Aggression or
» Psychotic tendencies
(patients with a history of these behavioral disturbances may be more likely to have an episode following vigabatrin therapy; patients should begin therapy at a lower dose and be monitored closely)

Hypersensitivity to vigabatrin

» Myoclonic seizures
(seizure frequency may increase)

» Renal impairment
(caution is warranted when creatinine clearance is < 60 mL/min; starting dose should be lowered and the patient closely monitored for adverse effects)

Patient monitoring
The following may be especially important in patient monitoring (other tests may be warranted in some patients, depending on condition; » = major clinical significance):

Ophthalmic assessments, including expert mydriatic peripheral fundus examinations and visual field perimetry
(recommended prior to initiation of therapy and at periodic intervals [approximately every 3 months] during vigabatrin treatment)

Side/Adverse Effects
The following side/adverse effects have been selected on the basis of their potential clinical significance (possible signs and symptoms in parentheses where appropriate)—not necessarily inclusive:

Those indicating need for medical attention
Incidence more frequent

Amnesia; ophthalmological abnormalities, including bilateral optic disc pallor (decreased vision); ***diplopia*** (double vision; seeing double); ***nystagmus*** (uncontrolled back-and-forth and/or rolling eye movements); ***optic atrophy*** (blindness; blurred vision; decreased vision; eye pain); ***peripheral retinal atrophy*** (decreased vision); ***and visual field constriction*** (decrease in vision or other change in vision); ***seizures, increased***

Note: *Ophthalmological abnormalities* reportedly occur from six months to more than 6 years following initiation of vigabatrin therapy; however, preliminary data shows that they occur most frequently in the 1st year of treatment with vigabatrin.

Incidence rare

Optic neuritis (blue-yellow color blindness)

Those indicating need for medical attention only if they continue or are bothersome
Incidence more frequent

Abdominal pain; agitation; anxiety; arthralgia (joint pain); ***ataxia*** (shakiness and unsteady walk; clumsiness; unsteadiness; trembling; or other problems with muscle control or coordination); ***confusion; constipation; coordination abnormal; depression; dizziness; drowsiness; diarrhea; fatigue; hyperkinesia*** (hyperactivity; increased movement)—effect seen primarily in pediatric populations; ***paresthesia*** (tingling; burning; prickly sensations); ***somnolence*** (sleepiness or unusual drowsiness); ***tremor***

Incidence less frequent

Aggression—effect seen primarily in pediatric populations; ***concentration impaired; emotional lability; headache; hyporeflexia; hypotonia*** (muscle weakness)—effect seen primarily in pediatric populations; ***increased saliva***—effect seen primarily in pediatric populations; ***insomnia; nausea; speech disorder; thinking abnormal; urinary tract infection; vomiting; weight gain***

Overdose
For more information on the management of overdose or unintentional ingestion, **contact a poison control center** (see *Poison Control Center Listing*).

Clinical effects of overdose
The following effects have been selected on the basis of their potential clinical significance (possible signs and symptoms in parentheses where appropriate)—not necessarily inclusive:

Abnormal behavior; agitation; apnea (bluish lips or skin; difficulty in breathing); ***bradycardia*** (slow or irregular heartbeat (less than 50 beats per minute); light-headedness; dizziness or fainting; unusual tiredness); ***coma; confusion; hypotension*** (low blood pressure); ***irritability; loss of consciousness; psychosis*** (mood or mental changes); ***respiratory depression; speech disorder; vertigo*** (dizziness or light-headedness; feeling of constant movement of self or surroundings; sensation of spinning)

Treatment of overdose

To enhance elimination—

Plasma concentrations have been reduced (40–60%) by hemodialysis within renal failure populations. However, the role of hemodialysis in the treatment of vigabatrin overdose is unknown.

Specific treatment—

There is no specific antidote. Treatment should be symptomatic and supportive.

Supportive care—

Patients in whom intentional overdose is confirmed or suspected should be referred for psychiatric consultation.

Patient Consultation

As an aid to patient consultation, refer to *Advice for the Patient, Vigabatrin (systemic).*

In providing consultation, consider emphasizing the following selected information (» = major clinical significance):

Before using this medication

» Conditions affecting use, especially:
- Hypersensitivity to vigabatrin or any of its components
- Pregnancy—Contraindicated for use during pregnancy
- Breast-feeding—Contraindicated for use during breast feeding
- Use in the elderly—Due to the fact that vigabatrin is eliminated by the kidney, caution should be used when administering the drug to elderly patients
- Other medical problems, especially a history of aggression, myoclonic seizures, psychotic tendencies, or renal impairment

Proper use of this medication

For powder (sachet) dosage form—Mixing contents in 10 mL of water, fruit juice, milk, or infant formula immediately before use, and then administering the appropriate aliquot with an oral syringe

» Proper dosing

Missed dose: Taking as soon as possible; not taking if almost time for next scheduled dose; not doubling doses

» Proper storage

Precautions while using this medication

Regular visits to physician to check progress

» Eye examinations every 3 months to help avoid potential reactions

» Caution when driving, using machines, or doing other jobs requiring alertness

» Checking with physician before discontinuing medication; gradual dosage reduction usually needed to maintain seizure control

Side/adverse effects

Signs of potential side effects, especially amnesia, ophthalmological effects, or increased seizure frequency

General Dosing Information

For oral dosing forms:

Vigabatrin may be taken with or without food

Abrupt discontinuation of vigabatrin treatments may cause an increase in epileptic episodes. The dose should be gradually reduced over a 2 to 4 week period.

Entire contents of packet (sachet) should be dissolved in cold or room temperature water, juice, or milk immediately prior to oral administration.

Oral Dosage Forms

Note: Bracketed information in the *Indications* section refers to uses that are not included in U.S. product labeling.

VIGABATRIN FOR ORAL SOLUTION

Usual adult dose

[Antiepileptic]—

Oral, initially 1 gram per day; increasing by increments of 500 mg to between 2 grams and 4 grams per day depending on clinical response and tolerability.

Note: Lower doses should be used to initiate vigabatrin treatment in elderly patients or in patients with a creatinine clearance < 60 mL per minute. These patients should be observed closely for adverse effects, such as sedation and confusion.

Usual adult prescribing limits

4 grams per day. Doses higher than 4 grams per day do not result in improved efficacy.

Usual pediatric dose

[Antiepileptic]—

Oral, initially 40 mg per kg of body weight (mg/kg) per day; increasing to 80 to 100 mg/kg per day in two divided doses. Therapy may be started at 500 mg per day and increased by increments of 500 mg per day at weekly intervals, depending on response.

For patients weighing 10 to 15 kg: 0.5 to 1 gram per day
For patients weighing 16 to 30 kg: 1 to 1.5 grams per day
For patients weighing 31 to 50 kg: 1.5 to 3 grams per day
For patients weighing over 50 kg: 2 to 4 grams per day

[Infantile spasm treatment]—

Oral, 50 to 100 mg per kg per day in two divided doses, depending on spasm severity Dosage may be titrated upward over 1 week. Daily doses of up to 150 mg/kg/day have been used with good tolerability

Usual pediatric prescribing limits

Usual geriatric dose

See *Usual adult dose.*

Strength(s) usually available

U.S.—

Not commercially available.

Canada—

0.5 grams (500 mg) (Rx) [*Sabril* (film-coated)].

Packaging and storage

Store between 15 and 30 °C (room temperature), in a tight container. Protect from moisture.

Preparation of dosage form

Dissolve contents of the packet (sachet) in 10 mL of cold or room temperature water, juice, or milk, immediately before administration. For an infant, the contents also may be dissolved in 10 mL of infant formula, and the appropriate dose drawn up and administered with an oral syringe.

Auxiliary labeling

- May cause drowsiness.
- May cause dizziness.

Additional information

May be taken with or without food.

VIGABATRIN TABLETS

Usual adult dose

See *Vigabatrin for Oral Solution*

Usual adult prescribing limits

See *Vigabatrin for Oral Solution*

Usual pediatric dose

See *Vigabatrin for Oral Solution*

Usual geriatric prescribing limits

See *Vigabatrin for Oral Solution*

Strength(s) usually available

U.S.—

Not commercially available.

Canada—

500 mg (Rx) [*Sabril*].

Packaging and storage

Store between 15 and 30 °C (59 and 86 °F), in a tight container. Protect from moisture.

Auxiliary labeling

- May cause drowsiness.
- May cause dizziness.

Developed: 03/05/2001

VINBLASTINE Systemic

VA CLASSIFICATION (Primary): AN900

Commonly used brand name(s): *Velban; Velbe.*

Note: For a listing of dosage forms and brand names by country availability, see *Dosage Forms* section(s).

Category

Antineoplastic.

Indications

Note: Bracketed information in the *Indications* section refers to uses that are not included in U.S. product labeling.

Accepted

Carcinoma, breast (treatment)
Tumors, trophoblastic, gestational (treatment)
Carcinoma, testicular (treatment)
[Carcinoma, bladder (treatment)][1]
[Carcinoma, lung, non-small cell (treatment)][1] or
[Carcinoma, renal (treatment)][1]—Vinblastine is indicated for treatment of breast carcinoma unresponsive to appropriate endocrine surgery and hormonal therapy, choriocarcinoma resistant to other chemotherapeutic agents, and advanced testicular germ cell carcinomas (embryonal carcinoma, teratocarcinoma, and choriocarcinoma). Vinblastine also is indicated for treatment of bladder carcinoma, non-small cell lung carcinoma, and renal carcinoma.

Lymphomas, Hodgkin's (treatment) or
Lymphomas, non-Hodgkin's (treatment)—Vinblastine is indicated for treatment of generalized Hodgkin's disease (Stages III and IV, Ann Arbor modification of Rye staging system) and for treatment of lymphocytic lymphoma (nodular and diffuse, poorly and well differentiated) and histiocytic lymphoma.

Sarcoma, Kaposi's (treatment)—Vinblastine is indicated for treatment of Kaposi's sarcoma, including [acquired immunodeficiency syndrome (AIDS)-associated Kaposi's sarcoma][1] by intravenous or intralesional injection.

Histiocytosis X (treatment)—Vinblastine is indicated for treatment of Histiocytosis X (Letterer-Siwe disease; Langerhans cell histiocytoses).

Mycosis fungoides (treatment)—Vinblastine is indicated for treatment of advanced stages of mycosis fungoides.

[Carcinoma, prostatic (treatment)][1]—Vinblastine is indicated as reasonable medical therapy for treatment of prostatic carcinoma (Evidence rating: IIID).

[Melanoma, malignant (treatment)][1]—Vinblastine is indicated for treatment of metastatic malignant melanoma.

[Tumors, germ cell, ovarian (treatment)][1]—Vinblastine is indicated for treatment of germ cell ovarian tumors.

---

[1]Not included in Canadian product labeling.

Pharmacology/Pharmacokinetics

Physicochemical characteristics

Source—Vinblastine is a vinca alkaloid.
Molecular weight—909.07.

Mechanism of action/Effect

Vinblastine blocks mitosis by arresting cells in metaphase, and may also interfere with amino acid metabolism; it is cell cycle–specific for the M phase of cell division.

Distribution

Does not cross the blood-brain barrier in significant amounts.

Biotransformation

Hepatic; metabolism of vinca alkaloids has been shown to be mediated by hepatic cytochrome P450 3A isoenzymes.

Half-life

Following rapid intravenous administration—
Initial phase: 3.7 minutes.
Middle phase: 1.6 hours.
Terminal phase: 24.8 hours.

Elimination

Primary route—Biliary/fecal.
Secondary route—Renal.

Precautions to Consider

Carcinogenicity/Mutagenicity

Secondary malignancies are potential delayed effects of many antineoplastic agents, although it is not clear whether the effect is related to their mutagenic or immunosuppressive action. The effects of dose and duration of therapy are also unknown, although risk seems to increase with long-term use.

In studies in rats and mice, administration of the maximum tolerated dose of vinblastine and half of the maximum tolerated dose for 6 months did not show a clear relationship between vinblastine and tumor development. The test demonstrated that other agents were clearly carcinogenic; however, vinblastine was one of the drugs in the group of drugs that caused slightly increased or the same tumor incidence as controls.

Pregnancy/Reproduction

Fertility—Gonadal suppression, resulting in amenorrhea or azoospermia, has occurred in patients taking vinblastine. In general, these effects appear to be related to dose and length of therapy and may be irreversible. Prediction of the degree of testicular or ovarian function impairment is complicated by the common use of combinations of several antineoplastics, which makes it difficult to assess the effects of individual agents. Vinblastine also has been reported to cause aspermia.

Pregnancy—In general, use of a contraceptive is recommended during cytotoxic drug therapy.

First trimester: It is usually recommended that use of antineoplastics, especially combination chemotherapy, be avoided whenever possible, especially during the first trimester. Although information is limited because of the relatively few instances of antineoplastic administration during pregnancy, the mutagenic, teratogenic, and carcinogenic potential of these medications must be considered.

Administration of vinblastine to animals early in pregnancy results in fetal resorption with surviving fetuses showing gross deformities.

Other hazards to the fetus include adverse reactions seen in adults.

FDA Pregnancy Category D.

Breast-feeding

Although very little information is available regarding distribution of antineoplastic agents into breast milk, breast-feeding is not recommended while vinblastine is being administered because of the risks to the infant (adverse effects, mutagenicity, carcinogenicity). It is not known whether vinblastine is distributed into breast milk.

Pediatrics

Studies performed to date have not demonstrated pediatrics-specific problems that would limit the usefulness of this medication in children.

Geriatrics

Although appropriate studies with vinblastine have not been performed in the geriatric population, the leukopenic response may be increased in elderly patients suffering from malnutrition or skin ulcers.

Dental

The bone marrow depressant effects of vinblastine may result in an increased incidence of microbial infection, delayed healing, and gingival bleeding. Dental work, whenever possible, should be completed prior to initiation of therapy or deferred until blood counts have returned to normal. Patients should be instructed in proper oral hygiene during treatment, including caution in use of regular toothbrushes, dental floss, and toothpicks.

Vinblastine may also cause stomatitis associated with considerable discomfort.

Drug interactions and/or related problems

The following drug interactions and/or related problems have been selected on the basis of their potential clinical significance (possible mechanism in parentheses where appropriate)—not necessarily inclusive (» = major clinical significance):

Note: Combinations containing any of the following medications, depending on the amount present, may also interact with this medication.

Allopurinol or
Colchicine or
» Probenecid or
» Sulfinpyrazone
(vinblastine may raise the concentration of blood uric acid; dosage adjustment of antigout agents may be necessary to control hyperuricemia and gout; allopurinol may be preferred to prevent or reverse vinblastine-induced hyperuricemia because of risk of uric acid nephropathy with uricosuric antigout agents)

Blood dyscrasia-causing medications (see *Appendix II*)
(leukopenic and/or thrombocytopenic effects of vinblastine may be increased with concurrent or recent therapy if these medications cause the same effects; dosage adjustment of vinblastine, if necessary, should be based on blood counts)

» Bone marrow depressants, other (see *Appendix II*) or
Radiation therapy
(additive bone marrow depression may occur; dosage reduction may be required when two or more bone marrow depressants, including radiation, are used concurrently or consecutively)

Vaccines, killed virus
(because normal defense mechanisms may be suppressed by vinblastine therapy, the patient's antibody response to the vaccine may be decreased. The interval between discontinuation of medications that cause immunosuppression and restoration of the patient's ability to respond to the vaccine depends on the intensity and type of immunosuppression-causing medication used, the un-

derlying disease, and other factors; estimates vary from 3 months to 1 year)

» Vaccines, live virus
(because normal defense mechanisms may be suppressed by vinblastine therapy, concurrent use with a live virus vaccine may potentiate the replication of the vaccine virus, may increase the side/adverse effects of the vaccine virus, and/or may decrease the patient's antibody response to the vaccine; immunization of these patients should be undertaken only with extreme caution after careful review of the patient's hematologic status and only with the knowledge and consent of the physician managing the vinblastine therapy. The interval between discontinuation of medications that cause immunosuppression and restoration of the patient's ability to respond to the vaccine depends on the intensity and type of immunosuppression-causing medication used, the underlying disease, and other factors; estimates vary from 3 months to 1 year. Immunization with oral poliovirus vaccine should also be postponed in persons in close contact with the patient, especially family members)

Laboratory value alterations

The following have been selected on the basis of their potential clinical significance (possible effect in parentheses where appropriate)—not necessarily inclusive (» = major clinical significance).

With physiology/laboratory test values
Uric acid concentrations in blood and urine
(may be increased)

Medical considerations/Contraindications

The medical considerations/contraindications included have been selected on the basis of their potential clinical significance (reasons given in parentheses where appropriate)—not necessarily inclusive (» = major clinical significance).

Risk-benefit should be considered when the following medical problems exist:

» Bone marrow depression
» Chickenpox, existing or recent (including recent exposure) or
» Herpes zoster
(risk of severe generalized disease)

Gout, history of or
Urate renal stones, history of
(risk of hyperuricemia)

» Hepatic function impairment
(a 50% dosage reduction is recommended for patients with a direct serum bilirubin concentration greater than 3 mg per 100 mL)

» Infection

Sensitivity to vinblastine

» Tumor cell infiltration of bone marrow
(in patients with malignant-cell infiltration of bone marrow, leukocyte and platelet counts have been reported to fall precipitously following administration of moderate doses of vinblastine; further administration of vinblastine in such patients is not recommended)

» Caution should be used also in patients who have had previous cytotoxic drug therapy or radiation therapy.

Patient monitoring

The following may be especially important in patient monitoring (other tests may be warranted in some patients, depending on condition; » = major clinical significance):

Alanine aminotransferase (ALT [SGPT]), serum and
Aspartate aminotransferase (AST [SGOT]), serum and
Bilirubin, serum and
Lactate dehydrogenase (LDH)
(determinations recommended prior to initiation of therapy and at periodic intervals during therapy; frequency varies according to clinical state, agent, dose, and other agents being used concurrently; toxicity may be enhanced in the presence of hepatic insufficiency)

» Hematocrit or hemoglobin and
» Platelet count and
» Total and, if appropriate, differential leukocyte count
(determinations recommended prior to initiation of therapy and at periodic intervals during therapy; frequency varies according to clinical state, agent, dose, and other agents being used concurrently)

Uric acid concentrations, serum
(determinations recommended prior to initiation of therapy and at periodic intervals during therapy; frequency varies according to clinical state, agent, dose, and other agents being used concurrently)

Side/Adverse Effects

Note: Many "side effects" of antineoplastic therapy are unavoidable and represent the medication's pharmacologic action. Some of these (for example, leukopenia and thrombocytopenia) are actually used as parameters to aid in individual dosage titration.

Incidence of side effects is generally dose-related.

The following side/adverse effects have been selected on the basis of their potential clinical significance (possible signs and symptoms in parentheses where appropriate)—not necessarily inclusive:

Those indicating need for medical attention

Incidence more frequent

Leukopenia (fever or chills; cough or hoarseness; lower back or side pain; painful or difficult urination)—usually asymptomatic

Note: With *leukopenia,* the nadir of the leukocyte count occurs 5 to 10 days after the last day of administration, and recovery is usually complete within another 7 to 14 days.

Incidence less frequent

Cellulitis (pain or redness at site of injection)—caused by extravasation; ***hyperuricemia or uric acid nephropathy*** (joint pain; lower back or side pain; swelling of feet or lower legs); ***stomatitis*** (sores in mouth and on lips); ***thrombocytopenia, transient*** (unusual bleeding or bruising; black, tarry stools; blood in urine or stools; pinpoint red spots on skin)—usually asymptomatic

Note: *Hyperuricemia or uric acid nephropathy* occurs most commonly during initial treatment of patients with lymphoma as a result of rapid cell breakdown that leads to elevated serum uric acid concentrations.

Incidence rare

Rectal bleeding, hemorrhagic colitis, or bleeding from a previously existing peptic ulcer (black, tarry stools); ***neurotoxicity*** (difficulty in walking; dizziness; double vision; drooping eyelids; headache; jaw pain; mental depression; numbness or tingling in fingers and toes; pain in fingers and toes; pain in testicles; weakness)

Those indicating need for medical attention only if they continue or are bothersome

Incidence less frequent

Nausea and vomiting; pain in bone or tumor-containing tissues

Those not indicating need for medical attention

Incidence more frequent

Loss of hair

Note: *Hair growth* should return after treatment has ended and possibly during therapy.

Patient Consultation

As an aid to patient consultation, refer to *Advice for the Patient, Vinblastine (Systemic).*

In providing consultation, consider emphasizing the following selected information (» = major clinical significance):

Before using this medication

» Conditions affecting use, especially:
Sensitivity to vinblastine
Pregnancy—Advisability of using contraception; telling physician immediately if pregnancy is suspected
Breast-feeding—Not recommended because of risk of serious side effects
Other medications, especially other bone marrow depressants, probenecid, or sulfinpyrazone
Other medical problems, especially chickenpox or recent exposure, hepatic function impairment, herpes zoster, other infections, previous cytotoxic medication or radiation therapy, or tumor cell infiltration of bone marrow

Proper use of this medication

Caution in taking combination therapy; taking each medication at the right time

Importance of ample fluid intake and subsequent increase in urine output to aid in excretion of uric acid

Frequency of nausea and vomiting; importance of continuing medication despite stomach upset

» Proper dosing

Precautions while using this medication

» Importance of close monitoring by physician

» Avoiding immunizations unless approved by physician; other persons in patient's household should avoid immunizations with oral poliovirus vaccine; avoiding other persons who have taken oral poliovirus vaccine within the past several months or wearing a protective mask that covers nose and mouth

Caution if bone marrow depression occurs:

» Avoiding exposure to persons with infections, especially during periods of low blood counts; checking with physician immediately if fever or chills, cough or hoarseness, lower back or side pain, or painful or difficult urination occurs

» Checking with physician immediately if unusual bleeding or bruising; black, tarry stools; blood in urine or stools; or pinpoint red spots on skin occur

Caution in use of regular toothbrush, dental floss, or toothpick; physician, dentist, or nurse may suggest alternatives; checking with physician before having dental work done

Not touching eyes or inside of nose unless hands washed immediately before

Using caution to avoid accidental cuts with use of sharp objects such as safety razor or fingernail or toenail cutters

Avoiding contact sports or other situations where bruising or injury could occur

» Possibility of local tissue injury and scarring if infiltration of intravenous solution occurs; telling physician or nurse right away about redness, swelling, or pain at site of injection

Side/adverse effects

May cause adverse effects such as blood problems, loss of hair, and cancer; importance of discussing possible effects with physician

Signs of potential side effects, especially leukopenia, cellulitis caused by extravasation, hyperuricemia, uric acid nephropathy, stomatitis, transient thrombocytopenia, rectal bleeding, hemorrhagic colitis, bleeding from existing peptic ulcer, and neurotoxicity

Physician or nurse can help in dealing with side effects

Possibility of hair loss; growth should return after treatment has ended and possibly during therapy

General Dosing Information

Vinblastine may be administered by intravenous push or injected into the tubing of a running intravenous infusion, over a 1-minute period. *Do not administer vinblastine intrathecally because death of the patient will occur.*

Patients receiving vinblastine should be under supervision of a physician experienced in cancer chemotherapy.

Dosage must be adjusted to meet the individual requirements of each patient, on the basis of clinical response and degree of bone marrow depression.

Development of uric acid nephropathy in patients with lymphoma may be prevented by adequate oral hydration and, in some cases, administration of allopurinol. Alkalinization of urine may be necessary if serum uric acid concentrations are elevated.

It is recommended that vinblastine be administered no more frequently than every 7 days, to allow the full effect of each dose on the leukocyte count to be seen.

Dilution in larger volumes (100 to 250 mL) or administration over longer periods (30 to 60 minutes and longer) is recommended only with great caution because of irritation to the vein and increased risk of extravasation.

To minimize the risk of extravasation, rinsing of the syringe and needle with venous blood before withdrawal of the needle is recommended.

If extravasation of vinblastine occurs during intravenous administration, the injection should be stopped immediately and the remaining dose injected into another vein.

Injection of vinblastine into an extremity in which circulation is compromised by conditions such as compressing or invading neoplasm, phlebitis, or viscosity is not recommended because of the increased risk of thrombosis.

If marked leukopenia (particularly granulocytopenia) or thrombocytopenia occurs, it is recommended that vinblastine therapy be withdrawn until leukocyte counts return to satisfactory levels (at least 4000 per cubic millimeter).

Special precautions are recommended in patients who develop thrombocytopenia as a result of administration of vinblastine. These may include extreme care in performing invasive procedures; regular inspection of intravenous sites, skin (including perirectal area), and mucous membrane surfaces for signs of bleeding or bruising; limiting frequency of venipuncture and avoiding intramuscular injections; testing urine, emesis, stool, and secretions for occult blood; care in use of regular toothbrushes, dental floss, toothpicks, safety razors, and fingernail and toenail cutters; avoiding constipation; and using caution to prevent falls and other injuries. Such patients should avoid alcohol and aspirin intake because of the risk of gastrointestinal bleeding. Platelet transfusions may be required.

Patients who develop leukopenia should be observed carefully for signs of infection. Antibiotic support may be required. In neutropenic patients who develop fever, broad-spectrum antibiotic coverage should be initiated empirically, pending bacterial cultures and appropriate diagnostic tests.

Safety considerations for handling this medication

There is limited but increasing evidence and concern that personnel involved in preparation and administration of parenteral antineoplastics may be at some risk because of the potential mutagenicity, teratogenicity, and/or carcinogenicity of these agents, although the actual risk is unknown. USP advisory panels recommend cautious handling both in preparation and disposal of antineoplastic agents. Precautions that have been suggested include:

- Use of a biological containment cabinet during reconstitution and dilution of parenteral medications and wearing of disposable surgical gloves and masks.
- Use of proper technique to prevent contamination of the medication, work area, and operator during transfer between containers (including proper training of personnel in this technique).
- Cautious and proper disposal of needles, syringes, vials, ampuls, and unused medication.

A number of medical centers have developed detailed guidelines for handling of antineoplastic agents.

Combination chemotherapy

Vinblastine may be used in combination with other agents in various regimens. As a result, incidence and/or severity of side effects may be altered and different dosages (usually reduced) may be used. For example, vinblastine is part of the following chemotherapeutic combinations (some commonly used acronyms are in parentheses):

—doxorubicin, bleomycin, vinblastine, and dacarbazine (ABVD).

—carmustine, cyclophosphamide, vinblastine, procarbazine, and prednisone (BCVPP).

For specific dosages and schedules, consult the literature. For information regarding each agent, consult the individual monograph.

Parenteral Dosage Forms

Note: Bracketed uses in the *Dosage Forms* section refer to categories of use and/or indications that are not included in U.S. product labeling.

VINBLASTINE SULFATE INJECTION

Usual adult dose

Carcinoma, breast or
Tumors, trophoblastic, gestational or
Carcinoma, testicular or
[Carcinoma, renal][1] or
Lymphomas, Hodgkin's or
Lymphomas, non-Hodgkin's or
Sarcoma, Kaposi's or
Histiocytosis X or
Mycosis fungoides or
[Tumors, germ cell, ovarian][1]—

Initial: Intravenous, 100 mcg (0.1 mg) per kg of body weight or 3.7 mg per square meter of body surface area a week, with successive weekly doses increased by increments of 50 mcg (0.05 mg) per kg of body weight or 1.8 to 1.9 mg per square meter of body surface area until the leukocyte count falls to 3000 per cubic millimeter, or a decrease in tumor size occurs, or a maximum dose of 500 mcg (0.5 mg) per kg of body weight or 18.5 mg per square meter of body surface area is reached (usual range 150 to 200 mcg [0.15 to 0.2 mg] per kg of body weight or 5.5 to 7.4 mg per square meter of body surface area).

Maintenance: Intravenous, dosage one increment smaller than the final initial dosage every seven days, or 10 mg one or two times a month.

Note: Each subsequent dose should not be given until the leukocyte count after the preceding dose returns to 4000 per cubic millimeter, even if seven days have passed.

A reduction in dosage of 50% is recommended in patients with a direct serum bilirubin concentration above 3 mg per 100 mL.

A variety of dosage schedules and regimens of vinblastine, alone or in combination with other antitumor agents, are used. The prescriber may consult the medical literature in choosing a specific dosage.

[Carcinoma, bladder][1] or
[Carcinoma, lung, non-small cell][1] or
[Carcinoma, prostatic][1] or

[Melanoma, malignant][1]—
Consult medical literature or manufacturer's literature for appropriate dosage.

Usual pediatric and adolescent dose

Carcinoma, breast or
Tumors, trophoblastic, gestational or
Carcinoma, testicular or
[Carcinoma, renal][1] or
Lymphomas, Hodgkin's or
Lymphomas, non-Hodgkin's or
Sarcoma, Kaposi's or
Histiocytosis X or
Mycosis fungoides or
[Tumors, germ cell, ovarian][1]—

Initial: Intravenous, 2.5 mg per square meter of body surface area a week, with successive weekly doses increased by increments of 1.25 mg per square meter of body surface area until the leukocyte count falls to 3000 per cubic millimeter, or a decrease in tumor size occurs, or a maximum dose of 7.5 mg per square meter of body surface area is reached.

Maintenance: Intravenous, dosage one increment smaller than the final initial dosage every seven days.

Note: Each subsequent dose should not be given until the leukocyte count after the preceding dose returns to 4000 per cubic millimeter, even if seven days have passed.

A reduction in dosage of 50% is recommended in patients with a direct serum bilirubin concentration above 3 mg per 100 mL.

A variety of dosage schedules and regimens of vinblastine, alone or in combination with other antitumor agents, are used. The prescriber may consult the medical literature in choosing a specific dosage.

[Carcinoma, bladder][1] or
[Carcinoma, lung, non-small cell][1] or
[Carcinoma, prostatic][1] or
[Melanoma, malignant][1]—
Consult medical literature or manufacturer's literature for appropriate dosage.

Strength(s) usually available

U.S.—
1 mg per mL (Rx) [GENERIC].

Canada—
Not commercially available.

Packaging and storage

Store between 2 and 8 °C (36 and 46 °F).

Stability

After withdrawal of the first dose, the remainder of the vial may be stored for 30 days between 2 and 8 °C (36 and 46 °F) without significant loss of potency.

Caution

When dispensed, the container or the syringe holding the individual dose prepared for administration to the patient must be enclosed in an overwrap bearing the statement: "DO NOT REMOVE COVERING UNTIL THE MOMENT OF INJECTION. FATAL IF GIVEN INTRATHECALLY. FOR INTRAVENOUS USE ONLY." USP does not specifically define the term "overwrap," but it is believed a ziplock bag or similar wrap utilized in hospitals may suffice to meet this requirement.

Note

If accidental contamination of the eye with vinblastine occurs, the eye should be immediately and thoroughly flushed with water to prevent severe irritation and possible corneal ulceration.

STERILE VINBLASTINE SULFATE USP

Usual adult dose

Carcinoma, breast or
Tumors, trophoblastic, gestational or
Carcinoma, testicular or
[Carcinoma, renal][1] or
Lymphomas, Hodgkin's or
Lymphomas, non-Hodgkin's or
Sarcoma, Kaposi's or
Histiocytosis X or
Mycosis fungoides or
[Tumors, germ cell, ovarian][1]—

Initial: Intravenous, 100 mcg (0.1 mg) per kg of body weight or 3.7 mg per square meter of body surface area a week, with successive weekly doses increased by increments of 50 mcg (0.05 mg) per kg of body weight or 1.8 to 1.9 mg per square meter of body surface area until the leukocyte count falls to 3000 per cubic millimeter, or a decrease in tumor size occurs, or a maximum dose of 500 mcg (0.5 mg) per kg of body weight or 18.5 mg per square meter of body surface area is reached (usual range 150 to 200 mcg [0.15 to 0.2 mg] per kg of body weight or 5.5 to 7.4 mg per square meter of body surface area).

Maintenance: Intravenous, dosage one increment smaller than the final initial dosage every seven days, or 10 mg one or two times a month.

Note: Each subsequent dose should not be given until the leukocyte count after the preceding dose returns to 4000 per cubic millimeter, even if seven days have passed.

A reduction in dosage of 50% is recommended in patients with a direct serum bilirubin concentration above 3 mg per 100 mL.

A variety of dosage schedules and regimens of vinblastine, alone or in combination with other antitumor agents, are used. The prescriber may consult the medical literature in choosing a specific dosage.

[Carcinoma, bladder][1] or
[Carcinoma, lung, non-small cell][1] or
[Carcinoma, prostatic][1] or
[Melanoma, malignant][1]—
Consult medical literature or manufacturer's literature for appropriate dosage.

Usual pediatric and adolescent dose

Carcinoma, breast or
Tumors, trophoblastic, gestational or
Carcinoma, testicular or
[Carcinoma, renal][1] or
Lymphomas, Hodgkin's or
Lymphomas, non-Hodgkin's or
Sarcoma, Kaposi's or
Histiocytosis X or
Mycosis fungoides or
[Tumors, germ cell, ovarian][1]—

Initial: Intravenous, 2.5 mg per square meter of body surface area a week, with successive weekly doses increased by increments of 1.25 mg per square meter of body surface area until the leukocyte count falls to 3000 per cubic millimeter, or a decrease in tumor size occurs, or a maximum dose of 7.5 mg per square meter of body surface area is reached.

Maintenance: Intravenous, dosage one increment smaller than the final initial dosage every seven days.

Note: Each subsequent dose should not be given until the leukocyte count after the preceding dose returns to 4000 per cubic millimeter, even if seven days have passed.

A reduction in dosage of 50% is recommended in patients with a direct serum bilirubin concentration above 3 mg per 100 mL.

A variety of dosage schedules and regimens of vinblastine, alone or in combination with other antitumor agents, are used. The prescriber may consult the medical literature in choosing a specific dosage.

[Carcinoma, bladder][1] or
[Carcinoma, lung, non-small cell][1] or
[Carcinoma, prostatic][1] or
[Melanoma, malignant][1]—
Consult medical literature or manufacturer's literature for appropriate dosage.

Strength(s) usually available

U.S.—
10 mg (Rx) [*Velban*; GENERIC].

Canada—
10 mg (Rx) [*Velbe*].

Packaging and storage

Store between 2 and 8 °C (36 and 46 °F).

Preparation of dosage form

Sterile Vinblastine Sulfate USP is reconstituted for intravenous use by adding 10 mL of 0.9% sodium chloride injection preserved with benzyl alcohol to the vial to produce a solution containing 1 mg of vinblastine sulfate per mL. It is not necessary to use preservative-containing 0.9% sodium chloride injection if unused solution is discarded immediately.

Stability

Solutions of vinblastine that are reconstituted with sodium chloride injection containing a preservative may be stored for 28 days between 2 and 8 °C (36 and 46 °F). Preservative-free solutions should be discarded immediately.

Caution

When dispensed, the container or the syringe holding the individual dose prepared for administration to the patient must be enclosed in an overwrap bearing the statement: "DO NOT REMOVE COVERING UNTIL THE MOMENT OF INJECTION. FATAL IF GIVEN INTRATHECALLY. FOR INTRAVENOUS USE ONLY." USP does not specifically define the term "overwrap," but it is believed a ziplock bag or similar wrap utilized in hospitals may suffice to meet this requirement.

Use of diluents containing benzyl alcohol is not recommended for preparation of medications for use in neonates. A fatal toxic syndrome consisting of metabolic acidosis, central nervous system (CNS) depression, respiratory problems, renal failure, hypotension, and possibly seizures and intracranial hemorrhages has been associated with this use.

Note

If accidental contamination of the eye with vinblastine occurs, the eye should be immediately and thoroughly flushed with water to prevent severe irritation and possible corneal ulceration.

---

[1]Not included in Canadian product labeling.

Revised: 07/19/2000

VINCRISTINE Systemic

VA CLASSIFICATION (Primary): AN900

Commonly used brand name(s): *Oncovin; Vincasar PFS.*

Note: For a listing of dosage forms and brand names by country availability, see *Dosage Forms* section(s).

Category

Antineoplastic.

Indications

Note: Bracketed information in the *Indications* section refers to uses that are not included in U.S. product labeling.

Accepted

Leukemia, acute lymphocytic (treatment)
[Leukemia, chronic lymphocytic (treatment)][1] or
[Leukemia, chronic myelocytic (treatment)][1]—Vincristine is indicated for treatment of acute lymphocytic, chronic lymphocytic, and chronic myelocytic (blastic phase) leukemias.

Neuroblastoma (treatment)
Wilms' tumor (treatment)
[Carcinoma, breast (treatment)]
[Carcinoma, lung, small cell (treatment)]
[Carcinoma, ovarian, epithelial (treatment)][1]
[Carcinoma, cervical (treatment)] or
[Carcinoma, colorectal (treatment)]—Vincristine is indicated for treatment of neuroblastoma, Wilms' tumor, breast carcinoma, small cell lung carcinoma, epithelial carcinoma of the ovaries, cancer of the uterine cervix, and colorectal carcinoma.

Lymphomas, Hodgkin's (treatment) or
Lymphomas, non-Hodgkin's (treatment)—Vincristine is indicated for treatment of Hodgkin's and non-Hodgkin's lymphomas.

Kaposi's sarcoma, acquired immunodeficiency syndrome (AIDS)-associated (treatment)
Rhabdomyosarcoma (treatment)
[Ewing's sarcoma (treatment)] or
[Osteosarcoma (treatment)]—Vincristine is indicated for treatment of AIDS-associated Kaposi's sarcoma, rhabdomyosarcoma, Ewing's sarcoma, and osteogenic sarcoma.

[Hepatoblastoma (treatment)][1]
[Retinoblastoma (treatment)][1]
[Tumors, trophoblastic, gestational (treatment)][1] or
[Tumors, brain, primary (treatment)][1]—Vincristine is used for the treatment of hepatoblastoma, retinoblastoma, gestational trophoblastic tumors, and primary brain tumors.

[Melanoma, malignant (treatment)]—Vincristine is indicated for treatment of malignant melanoma.

[Multiple myeloma (treatment)][1] or
[Waldenström's macroglobulinemia (treatment)][1]—Vincristine is used for treatment of multiple myeloma and Waldenström's macroglobulinemia.

[Tumors, germ cell, ovarian (treatment)][1]—Vincristine is used for treatment of germ cell ovarian tumors.

[Mycosis fungoides (treatment)][1]—Vincristine is used for treatment of mycosis fungoides.

[Thrombocytopenic purpura, idiopathic (treatment)]—Vincristine is used to treat true idiopathic thrombocytopenic purpura (ITP) resistant to the usual treatment of splenectomy and short-term treatment with adrenocorticoids.

[However, although it may raise the platelet count in patients with chronic ITP, vincristine is recommended for use only in severe hematological disorders.][1]

---

[1]Not included in Canadian product labeling.

Pharmacology/Pharmacokinetics

Physicochemical characteristics

Source—Vincristine is a vinca alkaloid.
Molecular weight—Vincristine sulfate: 923.04.

Mechanism of action/Effect

Vincristine blocks mitosis by arresting cells in metaphase, and may also interfere with amino acid metabolism; it is cell cycle–specific for the M phase of cell division.

Distribution

Within 15 to 30 minutes after injection, > 90% distributed from blood into tissue; does not cross the blood-brain barrier in significant amounts.

Protein binding

High (75%); extensive tissue binding.

Biotransformation

Hepatic; metabolism of vinca alkaloids has been shown to be mediated by hepatic cytochrome P450 3A isoenzymes.

Half-life

Following rapid intravenous administration—
Initial phase: 5 minutes.
Middle phase: 2.3 hours.
Terminal phase: 85 hours.

Elimination

Primary route—Biliary/fecal (about 80%).
Secondary route—Renal (about 10 to 20%).

Precautions to Consider

Carcinogenicity/Mutagenicity

Secondary malignancies are potential delayed effects of many antineoplastic agents, although it is not clear whether the effect is related to their mutagenic or immunosuppressive action. The effects of dose and duration of therapy are also unknown, although risk seems to increase with long-term use. Some patients who received chemotherapy with vincristine in combination with other medications known to be carcinogenic have developed second malignancies.

In a limited study in rats and mice, intraperitoneal administration of vincristine showed no evidence of carcinogenicity.

Pregnancy/Reproduction

Fertility—Gonadal suppression, resulting in amenorrhea or azoospermia, may occur in patients taking combination antineoplastic therapy that includes vincristine. In general, these effects appear to be related to dose and length of therapy and may be irreversible. Prediction of the degree of testicular or ovarian function impairment is complicated by the common use of combinations of several antineoplastics, which makes it difficult to assess the effects of individual agents.

Pregnancy—Adequate and well-controlled studies in humans have not been done. However, studies in animals have shown that vincristine causes fetal resorption, fetal malformations, and embryo death, even at doses that are not toxic to the pregnant animal.

First trimester: It is usually recommended that use of antineoplastics, especially combination chemotherapy, be avoided whenever possible, especially during the first trimester. Although information is limited because of the relatively few instances of antineoplastic administration during pregnancy, the mutagenic, teratogenic, and carcinogenic potential of these medications must be considered.

Other hazards to the fetus include adverse reactions seen in adults.

In general, use of a contraceptive is recommended during cytotoxic drug therapy.

FDA Pregnancy Category D.

Breast-feeding

Although very little information is available regarding distribution of antineoplastic agents into breast milk, breast-feeding is not recommended while vincristine is being administered because of the risks to the infant (adverse effects, mutagenicity, carcinogenicity). It is not known whether vincristine is distributed into breast milk.

Pediatrics
Studies performed to date have not demonstrated pediatrics-specific problems that would limit the usefulness of vincristine in children.

Geriatrics
Although appropriate studies with vincristine have not been performed in the geriatric population, elderly patients appear to be more susceptible to the neurotoxic effects.

Dental
Vincristine may cause stomatitis, which is associated with considerable discomfort.

Drug interactions and/or related problems
The following drug interactions and/or related problems have been selected on the basis of their potential clinical significance (possible mechanism in parentheses where appropriate)—not necessarily inclusive (» = major clinical significance):

Note: Combinations containing any of the following medications, depending on the amount present, may also interact with this medication.

Allopurinol or
Colchicine or
» Probenecid or
» Sulfinpyrazone
(vincristine may raise the concentration of blood uric acid; dosage adjustment of antigout agents may be necessary to control hyperuricemia and gout; allopurinol may be preferred to prevent or reverse vincristine-induced hyperuricemia because of risk of uric acid nephropathy with uricosuric antigout agents)

» Asparaginase
(concurrent use may result in additive neurotoxicity; if vincristine and asparaginase are to be used concurrently, toxicity appears to be less pronounced when asparaginase is administered after vincristine rather than before or with it)

Bleomycin
(sequential administration of vincristine prior to bleomycin arrests cells in mitosis so that they are more susceptible to bleomycin; frequently used to therapeutic advantage)

Blood dyscrasia-causing medications (see *Appendix II*)
(leukopenic and/or thrombocytopenic effects of vincristine may be increased with concurrent or recent therapy if these medications cause the same effects; dosage adjustment of vincristine, if necessary, should be based on blood counts)

Bone marrow depressants, other (see *Appendix II*) or
Radiation therapy
(concurrent use may increase the bone marrow depressant effects of these medications and radiation therapy, although myelosuppressive effects of vincristine are mild)

» Doxorubicin
(concurrent use with vincristine and prednisone may produce increased myelosuppression; it is recommended that the combination be avoided)

Neurotoxic medications, other (see *Appendix II*) or
Spinal cord irradiation
(concurrent use with vincristine may produce additive neurotoxicity)

Vaccines, killed virus
(because normal defense mechanisms may be suppressed by vincristine therapy, the patient's antibody response to the vaccine may be decreased. The interval between discontinuation of medications that cause immunosuppression and restoration of the patient's ability to respond to the vaccine depends on the intensity and type of immunosuppression-causing medication used, the underlying disease, and other factors; estimates vary from 3 months to 1 year)

» Vaccines, live virus
(because normal defense mechanisms may be suppressed by vincristine therapy, concurrent use with a live virus vaccine may potentiate the replication of the vaccine virus, may increase the side/adverse effects of the vaccine virus, and/or may decrease the patient's antibody response to the vaccine; immunization of these patients should be undertaken only with extreme caution after careful review of the patient's hematologic status and only with the knowledge and consent of the physician managing the vincristine therapy. The interval between discontinuation of medications that cause immunosuppression and restoration of the patient's ability to respond to the vaccine depends on the intensity and type of immunosuppression-causing medication used, the underlying disease, and other factors; estimates vary from 3 months to 1 year. Patients with leukemia in remission should not receive live virus vaccine until at least 3 months after their last chemotherapy. Immunization with oral poliovirus vaccine should also be postponed in persons in close contact with the patient, especially family members)

Laboratory value alterations
The following have been selected on the basis of their potential clinical significance (possible effect in parentheses where appropriate)—not necessarily inclusive (» = major clinical significance).

With physiology/laboratory test values
Uric acid concentrations in blood and urine
(may be increased)

Medical considerations/Contraindications
The medical considerations/contraindications included have been selected on the basis of their potential clinical significance (reasons given in parentheses where appropriate)—not necessarily inclusive (» = major clinical significance).

Risk-benefit should be considered when the following medical problems exist:

» Chickenpox, existing or recent, including recent exposure or
» Herpes zoster
(risk of severe generalized disease)

Gout, history of or
Urate renal stones, history of
(risk of hyperuricemia)

» Hepatic function impairment
(a 50% dosage reduction is recommended for patients with a direct bilirubin concentration in serum greater than 3 mg per 100 mL)

» Infection

» Leukopenia

» Neuromuscular disease

Sensitivity to vincristine

» Caution should be used also in patients who have had previous cytotoxic drug therapy or radiation therapy, and in those with existing neuromuscular problems who appear to be more susceptible to the neurotoxic effects of vincristine.

Patient monitoring
The following may be especially important in patient monitoring (other tests may be warranted in some patients, depending on condition; » = major clinical significance):

» Hematocrit or hemoglobin and
» Platelet count and
» Total and, if appropriate, differential leukocyte count
(determinations recommended prior to initiation of therapy and at periodic intervals during therapy; frequency varies according to clinical state, agent, dose, and other agents being used concurrently)

Alanine aminotransferase (ALT [SGPT]) and
Aspartate aminotransferase (AST [SGOT]) and
Bilirubin, serum and
Lactate dehydrogenase (LDH)
(determinations recommended prior to initiation of therapy and at periodic intervals during therapy; frequency varies according to clinical state, agent, dose, and other agents being used concurrently)

Uric acid, serum
(determinations recommended prior to initiation of therapy and at periodic intervals during therapy; frequency varies according to clinical state, agent, dose, and other agents being used concurrently)

Side/Adverse Effects
Note: Many "side effects" of antineoplastic therapy are unavoidable and represent the medication's pharmacologic action. Some of these (for example, leukopenia and thrombocytopenia) are actually used as parameters to aid in individual dosage titration.

Incidence of side effects is generally dose-related.

The following side/adverse effects have been selected on the basis of their potential clinical significance (possible signs and symptoms in parentheses where appropriate)—not necessarily inclusive:

Those indicating need for medical attention
Incidence more frequent
Constipation, severe; decrease or increase in or painful or difficult urination; hyperuricemia or uric acid nephropathy (joint pain;

lower back or side pain); ***neurotoxicity, progressive*** (blurred or double vision; difficulty in walking; drooping eyelids; headache; jaw pain; numbness or tingling in fingers and toes; pain in fingers and toes; pain in testicles; weakness)

Note: *Hyperuricemia or uric acid nephropathy* occurs most commonly during initial treatment of patients with leukemia or lymphoma as a result of rapid cell breakdown that leads to elevated serum uric acid concentrations.

Neurotoxicity may become more severe with continued treatment; although most symptoms usually disappear by about 6 weeks following discontinuation of treatment with vincristine, some neuromuscular symptoms may persist for prolonged periods.

Incidence less frequent

Cellulitis (pain or redness at site of injection)—caused by extravasation

Incidence rare

Leukopenia (fever or chills; cough or hoarseness; lower back or side pain; painful or difficult urination)—usually asymptomatic; ***thrombocytopenia*** (unusual bleeding or bruising; black, tarry stools; blood in urine or stools; pinpoint red spots on skin)—usually asymptomatic; ***stomatitis*** (sores in mouth and lips); ***syndrome of inappropriate antidiuretic hormone (SIADH)***

Note: Although *thrombocytopenia* is possible, platelet count changes little and may actually increase in some patients.

Those indicating need for medical attention only if they continue or are bothersome

Incidence less frequent

Bloating; diarrhea; loss of weight; nausea and vomiting; skin rash

Those not indicating need for medical attention

Incidence more frequent

Loss of hair

Note: *Hair growth* should return after treatment has ended and possibly during therapy.

Overdose

For more information on the management of overdose or unintentional ingestion, **contact a Poison Control Center** (see *Poison Control Center Listing*).

Treatment of overdose

Treatment of overdose is symptomatic and supportive; it may include:

Administration of anticonvulsants.

Enemas to prevent ileus.

Cardiovascular function and blood count monitoring.

Patient Consultation

As an aid to patient consultation, refer to *Advice for the Patient, Vincristine (Systemic)*.

In providing consultation, consider emphasizing the following selected information (» = major clinical significance):

Before using this medication

» Conditions affecting use, especially:

Sensitivity to vincristine

Pregnancy—Advisability of using contraception; telling physician immediately if pregnancy is suspected

Breast-feeding—Not recommended because of risk of serious side effects

Use in the elderly—Elderly patients may be more susceptible to the neurotoxic effects

Other medications, especially asparaginase, doxorubicin, previous cytotoxic medication or radiation therapy, probenecid, or sulfinpyrazone

Other medical problems, especially chickenpox or recent exposure, hepatic function impairment, herpes zoster, other infection, leukopenia, or neuromuscular disease

Proper use of this medication

Caution in taking combination therapy; taking each medication at the right time

Importance of ample fluid intake and subsequent increase in urine output to aid in excretion of uric acid

Possible nausea and vomiting; importance of continuing medication despite stomach upset

Checking with physician about using laxative if constipation and stomach pain occur

» Proper dosing

Precautions while using this medication

» Importance of close monitoring by physician

» Avoiding immunizations unless approved by physician; other persons in patient's household should avoid immunizations with oral poliovirus vaccine; avoiding other persons who have taken oral poliovirus vaccine or wearing a protective mask that covers nose and mouth

» Possibility of local tissue injury and scarring if infiltration of intravenous solution occurs; telling physician or nurse right away about redness, swelling, or pain at site of injection

Side/adverse effects

Signs of potential side effects, especially severe constipation, decrease or increase in or painful or difficult urination, hyperuricemia, uric acid nephropathy, neurotoxicity, cellulitis caused by extravasation, leukopenia, thrombocytopenia, stomatitis, and SIADH

Physician or nurse can help in dealing with side effects

Possibility of hair loss; growth should return after treatment has ended and possibly during therapy

General Dosing Information

Vincristine may be administered by intravenous push or injected into the tubing of a running intravenous infusion, over a 1-minute period. *Do not administer vincristine intrathecally, because death of the patient will occur.*

Patients receiving vincristine should be under supervision of a physician experienced in cancer chemotherapy.

A variety of dosage schedules and regimens of vincristine, alone or in combination with other antitumor agents, are used. The prescriber may consult the medical literature as well as the manufacturer's literature in choosing a specific dosage.

Dosage must be adjusted to meet the individual requirements of each patient, on the basis of clinical response and appearance or severity of toxicity.

The needle should be carefully positioned in the vein to avoid extravasation and tissue damage.

If extravasation of vincristine occurs during intravenous administration, the injection should be stopped immediately and the remaining dose injected into another vein. Local discomfort and cellulitis may be minimized by local injection of hyaluronidase and application of moderate heat.

Development of uric acid nephropathy in patients with leukemia or lymphoma may be prevented by adequate oral hydration and, in some cases, administration of allopurinol. Alkalinization of urine may be necessary if serum uric acid concentrations are elevated.

Caution is required in encouraging large fluid intake because of the risk of inappropriate secretion of antidiuretic hormone (ADH), which is treated with fluid deprivation.

If signs of hyponatremia or inappropriate ADH secretion occur, vincristine therapy should be temporarily discontinued and the patient treated with fluid restriction and, if necessary, a diuretic affecting the loop of Henle and distal tubule.

If depression of reflexes, paresthesia, hypotension, and/or motor weakness develops, a reduction in dosage or withdrawal of vincristine is recommended.

Prophylactic administration of a laxative or enema is recommended to prevent upper colon impaction.

Safety considerations for handling this medication

There is limited but increasing evidence and concern that personnel involved in preparation and administration of parenteral antineoplastics may be at some risk because of the potential mutagenicity, teratogenicity, and/or carcinogenicity of these agents, although the actual risk is unknown. USP advisory panels recommend cautious handling both in preparation and disposal of antineoplastic agents. Precautions that have been suggested include:

- Use of a biologic containment cabinet during reconstitution and dilution of parenteral medications and wearing of disposable surgical gloves and masks.
- Use of proper technique to prevent contamination of the medication, work area, and operator during transfer between containers (including proper training of personnel in this technique).
- Cautious and proper disposal of needles, syringes, vials, ampuls, and unused medication.

A number of medical centers have developed detailed guidelines for handling of antineoplastic agents.

Combination chemotherapy

Vincristine may be used in combination with other agents in various regimens. As a result, incidence and/or severity of side effects may be altered and different dosages (usually reduced) may be used. For example, vincristine is part of the following chemotherapeutic combinations (some commonly used acronyms are in parentheses):
—cyclophosphamide, doxorubicin, vincristine, and prednisone (CHOP).
—cyclophosphamide, methotrexate, fluorouracil, vincristine, and prednisone (CMFVP).
—cyclophosphamide, vincristine, and prednisone (COP or CVP).
—cyclophosphamide, vincristine, procarbazine, and prednisone (COPP).
—cyclophosphamide, vincristine, doxorubicin, and dacarbazine (CyVADIC).
—mechlorethamine, vincristine, procarbazine, and prednisone (MOPP).
—vincristine, dactinomycin, and cyclophosphamide (VAC).

For specific dosages and schedules, consult the literature. For information regarding each agent, consult the individual monographs.

Parenteral Dosage Forms

Note: Bracketed uses in the *Dosage Forms* section refer to categories of use and/or indications that are not included in U.S. product labeling.

VINCRISTINE SULFATE INJECTION USP

Usual adult dose

Leukemia, acute lymphocytic or
Neuroblastoma or
Wilms' tumor or
[Carcinoma, breast] or
[Carcinoma, lung, small cell] or
[Carcinoma, ovarian, epithelial] or
[Carcinoma, cervical] or
[Carcinoma, colorectal] or
Lymphomas, Hodgkin's or
Lymphomas, non-Hodgkin's or
Rhabdomyosarcoma or
[Ewing's sarcoma] or
[Osteosarcoma]or
[Melanoma, malignant] or
[Tumors, germ cell, ovarian][1] or
[Mycosis fungoides][1] or
[Thrombocytopenic purpura, idiopathic]—

Intravenous, 10 to 30 mcg (0.01 to 0.03 mg) per kg of body weight or 400 mcg (0.4 mg) to 1.4 mg per square meter of body surface area a week as a single dose.

Note: A 50% reduction in dose is recommended in patients with direct bilirubin concentrations in serum above 3 mg per 100 mL.

Usual pediatric dose

Leukemia, acute lymphocytic or
Neuroblastoma or
Wilms' tumor or
[Carcinoma, breast] or
[Carcinoma, lung, small cell] or
[Carcinoma, ovarian, epithelial] or
[Carcinoma, cervical] or
[Carcinoma, colorectal] or
Lymphomas, Hodgkin's or
Lymphomas, non-Hodgkin's or
Rhabdomyosarcoma or
[Ewing's sarcoma] or
[Osteosarcoma]or
[Melanoma, malignant] or
[Tumors, germ cell, ovarian][1] or
[Mycosis fungoides][1] or
[Thrombocytopenic purpura, idiopathic]—

Intravenous, 1.5 to 2 mg per square meter of body surface area a week as a single dose.

Note: For children weighing 10 kg or less, the initial dose is 50 mcg (0.05 mg) per kg of body weight intravenously once a week.

A 50% reduction in dose is recommended in patients with direct bilirubin concentrations in serum above 3 mg per 100 mL.

Strength(s) usually available

U.S.—

1 mg per mL (Rx) [*Oncovin* (mannitol; methylparaben; propylparaben); *Vincasar PFS;* GENERIC].

Canada—

1 mg per mL (Rx) [*Oncovin* (mannitol; methylparaben; propylparaben)].

Packaging and storage

Store between 2 and 8 °C (36 and 46 °F), in a light-resistant, glass container.

Caution

When dispensed, the container or the syringe holding the individual dose prepared for administration to the patient must be enclosed in an overwrap bearing the statement: "DO NOT REMOVE COVERING UNTIL THE MOMENT OF INJECTION. FATAL IF GIVEN INTRATHECALLY. FOR INTRAVENOUS USE ONLY." USP does not specifically define the term "overwrap," but it is believed a ziplock bag or similar wrap utilized in hospitals may suffice to meet this requirement.

Note

If accidental contamination of the eye with vincristine occurs, the eye should be immediately and thoroughly flushed with water to prevent severe irritation and possible corneal ulceration.

[1]Not included in Canadian product labeling.

Revised: 03/06/2001

VINORELBINE Systemic

VA CLASSIFICATION (Primary): AN900

Commonly used brand name(s): *Navelbine.*

Note: For a listing of dosage forms and brand names by country availability, see *Dosage Forms* section(s).

Category

Antineoplastic.

Indications

Note: Bracketed information in the *Indications* section refers to uses that are not included in U.S. product labeling.

Accepted

Carcinoma, lung, non-small cell (treatment)—Vinorelbine is indicated, as a single agent or in combination with cisplatin, for first-line treatment of ambulatory patients with unresectable, advanced non-small cell lung carcinoma (NSCLC). Vinorelbine is indicated as a single agent in Stage IV NSCLC and in combination with cisplatin in Stage III or IV NSCLC.

[Carcinoma, breast (treatment)]—Vinorelbine is indicated for the treatment of patients with metastatic breast cancer who did not respond to standard first-line chemotherapy for metastatic disease. Vinorelbine is also indicated for the treatment of patients with metastatic breast cancer who have relapsed within 6 months of anthracycline-based adjuvant therapy.

[Carcinoma, cervical (treatment)][1]—Vinorelbine is indicated as reasonable medical therapy at some point in the treatment of cervical carcinoma.

[Carcinoma, ovarian, epithelial (treatment)][1]—Vinorelbine is indicated as reasonable medical therapy at some point in the treatment of epithelial ovarian carcinoma.

Acceptance not established

Use of vinorelbine for the treatment of non-Hodgkin's lymphoma has not been established.

Use of vinorelbine for the treatment of hormone-refractory prostate carcinoma has not been established, due to insufficient data supporting efficacy.

Note: The USP medical experts chose to *not include* recurrent, untreated/unresectable, and/or metastatic squamous cell carcinoma of the head and neck as an indication for vinorelbine. Vinorelbine is appropriate for use in the treatment of this indication only in a clinical trial setting.

[1]Not included in Canadian product labeling.

Pharmacology/Pharmacokinetics

Note: Vinorelbine pharmacokinetics were analyzed in preclinical animal studies and in patients enrolled in disparate clinical trials. Concentrations of vinorelbine and its metabolites in biological fluids have been determined by measuring total radioactivity, by radioimmunoassay, and by high-performance liquid chromatography (HPLC). Most of the early studies involved the total-radioactivity assay, which measures both unchanged vinorelbine and all metabolites that retain the labeled moiety. The total-radioactivity assay is highly sensitive but lacks the specificity needed in pharmacokinetic studies. Radioimmunoassay was primarily used in animal studies and in some early clinical studies. Although radioimmunoassay is more specific than measuring total radioactivity, there is cross-sensitivity with metabolites of the vindoline ring structure. Three HPLC methods were developed for analyzing vinorelbine. HPLC has complete specificity for the parent drug and allows for measurement of its metabolites. Therefore, clinical studies in which HPLC is used are thought to provide the most valid pharmacokinetic estimates for vinorelbine.

Physicochemical characteristics

Source—Vinorelbine is a semisynthetic vinca alkaloid, derived from vinblastine. Vinorelbine differs in structure from other vinca alkaloids in that it contains an eight-member catharanthine ring structure, whereas vincristine and vinblastine contain a nine-member catharanthine ring structure.

Molecular weight—1079.13.

Mechanism of action/Effect

Vinca alkaloids appear to exert their antitumor activity by binding to tubulin with high affinity. Two types of tubulin, alpha and beta, exist as dimers that polymerize to form microtubules, of which many cellular structures, including the mitotic spindle, are constituted. The cellular functions of microtubules include neurotransmission and mitosis. Vinca alkaloids are cell cycle–specific agents that arrest mitosis by interfering with microtubule assembly and inducing depolarization of microtubules. Like other vinca alkaloids, vinorelbine may also interfere with amino acid, cyclic adenosine monophosphate (cAMP), and glutathione metabolism; with calmodulin-dependent calcium-transport–adenosinetriphosphatase activity; with cellular respiration; and with nucleic acid and lipid biosynthesis.

All vinca alkaloids are thought to have slightly different mechanisms of action due in part to differences in their interaction with microtubule-associated proteins, which are believed to modify the interaction of vinca alkaloids with tubulin. At least two sites of vinca alkaloid fixation on tubulin have been reported: one site with high affinity, which is responsible for depolymerization activity, and one site with low affinity, which induces unwinding of microtubules and spiral formation. Researchers found that vinorelbine was as active as vincristine and vinblastine in inducing the assembly of tubulin *in vitro* but was uniquely inefficient in causing spiral formation. This observation led to the hypothesis that vinorelbine may have a mechanism of action differing slightly from that of other vinca alkaloids and may be potentially less toxic.

Vinorelbine appears to have selective activity against mitotic microtubules. Researchers compared the effect of vinorelbine, vinblastine, and vincristine on mitotic and axonal microtubules in postimplantation mouse embryos at the earliest stage of neuronal development. Mitotic microtubule activity appeared to be correlated with antitumor activity, while axonal microtubule activity was thought to be correlated with neurotoxicity. At low concentrations (2 micromolar), vincristine, vinblastine, and vinorelbine inhibited spindle assembly by arresting cell division at metaphase. At higher concentrations (25 micromolar), only vinorelbine arrested mitosis at prophase. Depolymerization of axonal microtubules was concentration-dependent and occurred at markedly higher concentrations of vinorelbine (40 micromolar) than of vincristine (5 micromolar) or vinblastine (30 micromolar); presumably this accounts for the decreased neurotoxicity of vinorelbine. Further research is needed to describe clearly the interaction of vinorelbine with tubulin and to determine the clinical relevance of this activity.

Distribution

Preclinical tissue distribution studies in mice, rats, and monkeys showed that radiolabeled vinorelbine was widely distributed in the body after intravenous administration. High amounts of radioactivity were localized in the spleen, liver, kidneys, lungs, and thymus; moderate amounts in the heart and muscles; and minimal amounts in fat, the brain, and bone marrow.

In human hepatocytes, the degree of cellular accumulation of the vinca alkaloids increases with increasing lipophilicity of the compound. Since vinorelbine is one of the most lipid-soluble vinca alkaloids, there is rapid uptake and extensive distribution in cells. Measurements in human lung tissue show that vinorelbine has up to a 300-fold greater concentration in lung tissue than in serum.

Protein binding

Vinorelbine is highly bound to platelets and lymphocytes, and is also bound to alpha$_1$-acid glycoprotein, albumin, and lipoproteins. In one study in 24 cancer patients, serum binding of vinorelbine ranged from 79.6 to 91.2%. The fraction of unbound vinorelbine averaged 0.135 (range 0.088 to 0.204). Because of high binding to platelets, the fraction bound in blood was 98.3%. Concurrent administration of other anticancer agents is unlikely to cause displacement of vinorelbine from its binding sites in serum. In control serum, vinorelbine binding (85.2%) was not significantly different from binding in the presence of 5-fluorouracil (87.4%), doxorubicin (85%), or cisplatin (85.6%).

Biotransformation

Hepatic. Metabolism of vinorelbine was initially suggested by *in vitro* studies that used human hepatic subcellular fractions and identified two metabolites. Radiochromatography of urine and fecal samples found at least three unidentified vinorelbine metabolites after intravenous and oral administration of the agent to cancer patients. An HPLC method was developed for the measurement of two likely vinorelbine metabolites, vinorelbine *N*-oxide and deacetylvinorelbine. Although vinorelbine *N*-oxide appears to be inactive, evidence indicates that deacetylvinorelbine possesses pharmacologic activity similar to that of vinorelbine. However, this finding may have minimal clinical significance, since a pharmacokinetics study in 20 patients who received intravenous vinorelbine revealed no vinorelbine *N*-oxide in serum or urine and no deacetylvinorelbine in serum. A small amount of deacetylvinorelbine, however, was found in urine.

Half-life

There is a prolonged terminal phase due to relatively slow efflux of vinorelbine from peripheral compartments, which results in a long terminal-phase half-life, with average value ranging from 27.7 to 43.6 hours.

Elimination

Preclinical animal studies indicated that vinorelbine and its metabolites are excreted in the bile. Significant amounts of vinorelbine and metabolites were found in the feces of all species studied and in the bile of cannulated rats after intravenous administration of vinorelbine. Researchers used an HPLC method to study the biliary excretion of vinorelbine in micropigs following administration of doses comparable to those used in humans and found that 25.8% of the vinorelbine dose was excreted unchanged in the bile. Low amounts of deacetylvinorelbine ($< 5\%$) were found, and treatment of urine with beta-glucuronidase did not indicate glucuronidation of vinorelbine. Most likely, biliary excretion also occurs in humans, since, as mentioned above, a large percentage of radiolabeled vinorelbine administered intravenously is eliminated in the feces.

Precautions to Consider

Carcinogenicity

Carcinogenicity studies with vinorelbine have not been done.

Mutagenicity

In vivo studies found that vinorelbine affected chromosome number and possibly structure (polyploidy in bone marrow cells from Chinese hamsters and a positive micronucleus test in mice). Results of the Ames mutagenicity test were negative and results were inconclusive in the mouse lymphoma TK Locus assay.

Pregnancy/Reproduction

Fertility—Studies in rats given either 9 mg per square meter of body surface area (mg/m^2) (approximately one third the human dose) once a week or 4.2 mg/m^2 (approximately one seventh the human dose) every other day, prior to and during mating, found no significant effect on fertility. However, studies in male rats given 2.1 and 7.2 mg/m^2 (approximately one fifteenth and one fourth the human dose, respectively) biweekly for 13 or 26 weeks found decreased spermatogenesis and prostate/seminal vesicle secretion.

Pregnancy—Studies have not been done in humans.

Vinorelbine has been shown to be embryotoxic and/or fetotoxic in animals; nonmaternotoxic doses of vinorelbine caused a reduction in fetal weight and a delay in ossification. However, vinorelbine has not been shown to be teratogenic. Women of childbearing potential should be informed about the potential hazard to the fetus if they become pregnant during vinorelbine therapy. They should also be advised to avoid becoming pregnant during vinorelbine therapy.

FDA Pregnancy Category D.

Breast-feeding

It is not known whether vinorelbine is distributed into breast milk. However, because of vinorelbine's potential for serious adverse reactions in nursing infants, it is recommended that nursing be discontinued in women receiving vinorelbine therapy.

Pediatrics

Appropriate studies on the relationship of age to the effects of vinorelbine have not been performed in the pediatric population. Safety and efficacy in children have not been established.

Geriatrics

Approximately one third of the patients enrolled in the North American clinical trials of vinorelbine were over the age of 65 years. Although this subset of patients did experience a slight increase in grades 3 and 4 leukopenia and granulocytopenia compared with patients under 65 years of age, the overall safety profile and antitumor efficacy were not significantly different for the older people. Furthermore, examination of pharmacokinetic parameters from the clinical trials did not suggest any differences in drug metabolism in older patients. As a result, no specific dosage adjustments are recommended for geriatric patients. The safety profile of vinorelbine suggests that vinorelbine may be particularly well suited to elderly patients, as this patient population is typically intolerant of severe side effects.

Dental

The leukopenic and thrombocytopenic effects of vinorelbine may result in an increased incidence of certain microbial infections of the mouth, delayed healing, and gingival bleeding. If leukopenia or thrombocytopenia occurs, dental work should be deferred until blood counts have returned to normal. Patients should be instructed in proper oral hygiene, including caution in use of regular toothbrushes, dental floss, and toothpicks.

Drug interactions and/or related problems

The following drug interactions and/or related problems have been selected on the basis of their potential clinical significance (possible mechanism in parentheses where appropriate)—not necessarily inclusive (» = major clinical significance):

Note: Combinations containing any of the following medications, depending on the amount present, may also interact with this medication.

Blood dyscrasia-causing medications (see *Appendix II*)
(leukopenic effects of vinorelbine may be increased with concurrent or recent therapy if these medications cause the same effects; dosage adjustment of vinorelbine, if necessary, should be based on blood count)

» Bone marrow depressants, other (see *Appendix II*) or
Radiation therapy
(concurrent use may increase the bone marrow depressant effect of these medications and radiation therapy)

Cisplatin
(although the pharmacokinetics of vinorelbine are not influenced by the concurrent administration of cisplatin, the incidence of toxicities, specifically granulocytopenia, with the combination of vinorelbine and cisplatin is significantly higher than with single-agent vinorelbine)

» Mitomycin
(acute pulmonary reactions have been reported with vinorelbine used in conjunction with mitomycin; vinorelbine should be administered with caution in combination with mitomycin)

» Paclitaxel
(concomitant or sequential use may result in neuropathy; routine monitoring for symptoms of neuropathy is recommended)

Vaccines, killed virus
(because normal defense mechanisms may be suppressed by vinorelbine therapy, the patient's antibody response to the vaccine may be decreased. The interval between discontinuation of medications that cause immunosuppression and restoration of the patient's ability to respond to the vaccine depends on the intensity and type of immunosuppression-causing medication used, the underlying disease, and other factors; estimates vary from 3 months to 1 year)

» Vaccines, live virus
(because normal defense mechanisms may be suppressed by vinorelbine therapy, concurrent use with a live virus vaccine may potentiate the replication of the vaccine virus, may increase the side/adverse effects of the vaccine virus, and/or may decrease the patient's antibody response to the vaccine; immunization of these patients should be undertaken only with extreme caution after careful review of the patient's hematologic status and only with the knowledge and consent of the physician managing the vinorelbine therapy. The interval between discontinuation of medications that cause immunosuppression and restoration of the patient's ability to respond to the vaccine depends on the intensity and type of immunosuppression-causing medication used, the underlying disease, and other factors; estimates vary from 3 months to 1 year. Patients with leukemia in remission should not receive live virus vaccine until at least 3 months after their last chemotherapy. Immunization with oral poliovirus vaccine should also be postponed in persons in close contact with the patient, especially family members)

Laboratory value alterations

The following have been selected on the basis of their potential clinical significance (possible effect in parentheses where appropriate)—not necessarily inclusive (» = major clinical significance).

With physiology/laboratory test values
Alanine aminotransferase (ALT [SGPT]) and
Alkaline phosphatase and
Aspartate aminotransferase (AST [SGOT])
(values may be increased)

Bilirubin, serum
(concentrations may be increased)

Note: Transient increases in alanine aminotransferase and aspartate aminotransferase values were reported in approximately 50% of patients, but patients with elevated liver enzymes values were typically asymptomatic and did not require discontinuation of therapy. A somewhat greater effect was observed on total bilirubin concentrations, with 6% of patients developing concentrations of grade 3 or 4 severity. Although vinorelbine treatment may have contributed to these increases in bilirubin concentrations, these abnormalities also may be related to disease progression in the liver.

Medical considerations/Contraindications

The medical considerations/contraindications included have been selected on the basis of their potential clinical significance (reasons given in parentheses where appropriate)—not necessarily inclusive (» = major clinical significance).

Risk-benefit should be considered when the following medical problems exist:

» Bone marrow depression
(administration of vinorelbine is not recommended if pretreatment granulocyte counts are less than 1000 cells per cubic millimeter; as with other vinca alkaloids, vinorelbine should not be used in patients who have drug-induced severe granulocytopenia or severe thrombocytopenia)

» Chickenpox, existing or recent (including recent exposure) or
» Herpes zoster
(risk of severe generalized disease)

» Infection

» Sensitivity to vinorelbine

» Tumor cell infiltration of the bone marrow

» Caution should be used also in patients with inadequate bone marrow reserves due to previous cytotoxic drug or radiation therapy.

Patient monitoring

The following may be especially important in patient monitoring (other tests may be warranted in some patients, depending on condition; » = major clinical significance):

Alanine aminotransferase (ALT [SGPT]) values, and
Alkaline phosphatase values, serum and
Aspartate aminotransferase (AST [SGOT]) values, and
Bilirubin concentrations, serum
(recommended prior to initiation of therapy and at periodic intervals during therapy)

» Leukocyte count, total and differential
(determinations and review recommended on the day of treatment prior to administering each dose of vinorelbine)

Side/Adverse Effects

Note: Extensive clinical experience has been obtained with the antineoplastic agent vinorelbine in Europe and elsewhere. This experience has been supplemented by more clinical trials of patients with advanced non-small cell lung cancer or breast cancer conducted in North America. Data from these trials indicate that vinorelbine is safe and well tolerated in the outpatient population. Granulocytopenia is the dose-limiting toxicity. Although the incidence of this condition is high among vinorelbine-treated patients, it is uncommonly associated with severe complications. Elevations in alkaline phosphatase values are seen in the majority of patients, but this effect may be due in part to liver and bone metastases. Nonhematologic toxicities are mostly mild or moderate. Injection site reactions have been noted in some patients, but improved administration techniques may help reduce the incidence of the effect. Gastrointestinal and respiratory effects are seldom severe and usually respond to treatment. Drug-associated neurotoxicity occurs less often with vinorelbine than with other commonly used vinca alkaloid compounds. Overall, vinorelbine is associated with few severe toxicities, which, for the most part, are easily managed.

The following side/adverse effects have been selected on the basis of their potential clinical significance (possible signs and symptoms in parentheses where appropriate)—not necessarily inclusive:

Those indicating need for medical attention

Incidence more frequent

Anemia (unusual tiredness or weakness); ***asthenia*** (loss of strength and energy); ***granulocytopenia or leukopenia*** (fever or chills; cough or hoarseness; lower back or side pain; painful or difficult urination; sore throat); ***injection site reactions*** (redness, increased warmth, pain, or discoloration of vein at place of injection)

Note: *Asthenia* is one of the most common adverse effects of vinorelbine, occurring in one third of patients. The fatigue is generally mild or moderate but increases with repeated administration.

Injection site reactions are common with vinorelbine treatment, although, in one study, only approximately 2% of patients experienced severe reactions. Like other vinca alkaloids, vinorelbine is a vesicant that can cause extravasation injuries as well as local effects at the injection site. The occurrence and severity of venous irritation appear to be reduced when vinorelbine is administered as a 6- to 10-minute infusion with a free-flowing intravenous fluid to ensure proper flushing of veins. Phlebitis occurs in approximately 6% of patients; however, the frequency of phlebitis was notably greater in clinical trials in which vinorelbine was administered over a period of 1 hour.

The most notable toxicity associated with vinorelbine treatment is hematologic. *Granulocytopenia* is the dose-limiting toxicity, with grade 3 or 4 granulocytopenia occurring in 64% of treated patients. Nadir of granulocyte counts occurs 7 to 10 days after a dose; recovery usually occurs within the following 7 to 14 days. White blood cell counts are also severely affected; grade 3 or 4 *leukopenia* was reported in 50% of vinorelbine-treated patients. A lesser effect was observed in red blood cells, as indicated by hemoglobin concentrations; only 9% of patients reached grade 3 or 4 toxicity. Although *anemia* was fairly common among vinorelbine-treated patients, it was rarely severe, and transfusions were required rarely. Platelets are relatively unaffected.

Incidence less frequent

Chest pain; neuropathy, peripheral, mild to moderate, including paresthesia and hypesthesia (numbness or tingling in fingers and toes); ***pulmonary reactions*** (shortness of breath); ***stomatitis*** (sores in mouth and on lips)

Note: *Chest pain* has been reported in 5% of patients receiving vinorelbine therapy. The majority of patients reporting chest pain have either a history of cardiovascular disease or a tumor within the chest. One report describes a fatal myocardial infarction in a patient with a previous infarction who received two courses of vinorelbine. It is unclear what role vinorelbine played in the patient's myocardial infarction. Cardiovascular toxicity has been rarely reported with vincristine and vinblastine. The pathogenesis of cardiovascular toxicity is postulated to involve transitory coronary artery spasm.

Shortness of breath has been noted in 5% of patients; 2% of these patients described severe shortness of breath. As with other vinca alkaloids, vinorelbine can produce both acute and subacute *pulmonary reactions.* The acute reaction resembles an allergic reaction and responds to bronchodilators. Subacute pulmonary reactions generally occur within 1 hour after drug administration and are characterized by cough, dyspnea, hypoxemia, and interstitial infiltration. Subacute pulmonary reactions typically respond to corticosteroid therapy.

The neurotoxic effects of vinorelbine, such as *peripheral neuropathy,* seem to be reversible on discontinuation of vinorelbine. The addition of cisplatin does not appear to increase the neurotoxic effects of vinorelbine. However, prior treatment with paclitaxel may result in cumulative neurotoxicity.

Incidence rare

Hemorrhagic cystitis (blood in urine; painful urination)—reported in less than 1% of patients; ***pancreatitis*** (bloating; chills; constipation; darkened urine; fast heartbeat; indigestion; loss of appetite; nausea; pains in stomach; vomiting; yellow eyes or skin); ***skin rash***—reported in 4% of patients; ***thrombocytopenia*** (unusual bleeding or bruising; black, tarry stools; blood in urine or stools; pinpoint red spots on skin)

Note: Grades 3 and 4 *thrombocytopenia* have been reported in less than 1% of patients; however, in one study no grade 3 or 4 thrombocytopenia was observed in vinorelbine recipients.

Those indicating need for medical attention only if they continue or are bothersome

Incidence more frequent

Anorexia (loss of appetite); ***constipation; nausea and vomiting***

Note: Prophylactic antiemetic therapy has not been used routinely in clinical trials of vinorelbine. Nausea and vomiting occur in approximately 40% and 20% of patients, respectively. Vinorelbine-associated *nausea and vomiting* are typically mild to moderate and appear to respond to conventional antiemetic therapy; serotonin-receptor antagonists are not generally required.

Incidence less frequent

Diarrhea; jaw pain; joint or muscle pain

Those not indicating need for medical attention

Incidence more frequent

Alopecia (loss of hair)

Note: Vinorelbine has caused *alopecia* in about 10% of patients, manifested as a gradual thinning of hair. Few patients suffer total hair loss. Alopecia appears to occur with cumulative toxicity of vinorelbine.

Overdose

For specific information on the agents used in the managment of vinorelbine overdose, see:

- *Filgrastim* and/or *Sargramostim* in *Colony Stimulating Factors (Systemic)* monograph.

For more information on the management of overdose, **contact a Poison Control Center** (see *Poison Control Center Listing*)

Clinical effects of overdose

The following effects have been selected on the basis of their potential clinical significance (possible signs and symptoms in parentheses where appropriate)—not necessarily inclusive:

Acute and chronic effects

Bone marrow suppression (fever or chills; cough or hoarseness; lower back or side pain; painful or difficult urination; sore throat; unusual bleeding or bruising; unusual tiredness or weakness); ***esophagitis*** (chest pain; heartburn; vomiting); ***neurotoxicity, peripheral*** (numbness or tingling in fingers and toes); ***paralytic ileus*** (abdominal pain, mild; constipation; nausea; vomiting); ***stomatitis*** (sores in mouth and on lips)

Note: Bone marrow aplasia, sepsis, paresis, and fatalities have been reported following overdose.

Treatment of overdose

There are no known antidotes for the treatment of vinorelbine overdosage. Therefore, treatment of overdose is supportive and may include appropriate blood transfusions, antibiotics, and administration of colony stimulating factors (filgrastim [rG-CSF] or sargramostim [rGM-CSF]).

Patient Consultation

As an aid to patient consultation, refer to *Advice for the Patient, Vinorelbine (Systemic).*

In providing consultation, consider emphasizing the following selected information (» = major clinical significance):

Before using this medication

» Conditions affecting use, especially:

Hypersensitivity to vinorelbine

Pregnancy—Advisability of using contraception; telling physician immediately if pregnancy is suspected

Breast-feeding—Not recommended because of the risk of serious side effects

Other medications, especially bone marrow depressants, mitomycin, or previous cytotoxic or radiation therapy

Other medical problems, especially bone marrow depression; chickenpox; herpes zoster; or tumor cell infiltration of the bone marrow

Proper use of this medication

Caution in taking combination therapy; taking each medication at the right time

Importance of ample fluid intake and subsequent increase in urine output to aid in excretion of uric acid

Possible nausea and vomiting; importance of continuing medication despite stomach upset

» Proper dosing

Precautions while using this medication

» Importance of close monitoring by physician

» Possibility of local tissue injury if infiltration of intravenous solution occurs; telling physician or nurse right away about redness, swelling, or pain at site of injection

» Avoiding immunizations unless approved by physician; other persons in patient's household should avoid immunizations with oral poliovirus vaccine; avoiding other persons who have taken oral poliovirus vaccine or wearing a protective mask that covers nose and mouth

Caution if bone marrow depression occurs:

» Avoiding exposure to persons with infections, especially during periods of low blood counts; checking with physician immediately if fever or chills, cough or hoarseness, lower back or side pain, or painful or difficult urination occurs

» Checking with physician immediately if unusual bleeding or bruising; black, tarry stools; blood in urine or stools; or pinpoint red spots on skin occur

Caution in use of regular toothbrush, dental floss, or toothpick; physician, dentist, or nurse may suggest alternatives; checking with physician before having dental work done

Not touching eyes or inside of nose unless hands washed immediately before

Using caution to avoid accidental cuts with use of sharp objects such as safety razor or fingernail or toenail cutters

Avoiding contact sports or other situations where bruising or injury could occur

Side/adverse effects

Signs of potential side effects, especially anemia, asthenia, granulocytopenia or leukopenia, injection site reaction, chest pain, pancreatitis, peripheral neuropathy, pulmonary reactions, stomatitis, hemorrhagic cystitis, skin rash, and thrombocytopenia

General Dosing Information

Patients receiving vinorelbine should be under the supervision of a physician experienced in cancer chemotherapy. Patients and/or family members should be instructed to report any side/adverse effects immediately.

Clinical trials have demonstrated that vinorelbine is an effective chemotherapeutic agent in the treatment of patients with advanced non-small cell lung cancer (NSCLC). Vinorelbine has also been shown to increase survival without compromising quality of life (QOL) in several randomized, controlled trials. A summary of preliminary QOL findings for two vinorelbine (randomized and single-arm) trials in patients with NSCLC shows that symptoms status was as good or better for patients receiving vinorelbine as for those receiving 5-fluorouracil/leucovorin in the randomized study.

Although vinorelbine is effective as monotherapy, a higher overall response rate and median duration of survival are seen when it is combined with cisplatin. Data from some clinical studies indicate that vinorelbine plus cisplatin is superior to vindesine plus cisplatin and to vinorelbine alone.

Patients with renal insufficiency do not require dosage adjustments. However, in patients with hepatic insufficiency, the dosage of vinorelbine should be adjusted on the basis of degree of hyperbilirubinemia.

Vinorelbine should be administered intravenously. Intrathecal administration of other vinca alkaloids has resulted in death.

It is very important that the intravenous needle or catheter be positioned properly before any vinorelbine is injected. Leakage into surrounding tissue during intravenous administration of vinorelbine may cause considerable irritation, local tissue necrosis, and/or thrombophlebitis. If extravasation occurs, the injection should be discontinued immediately, and any remaining portion of the dose should then be introduced into another vein. Local injection of hyaluronidase and the application of moderate heat to the area of leakage has been reported to help disperse the agent and minimize discomfort associated with the extravasation of other vinca alkaloids.

Although venous irritation is a problem associated with peripherally administered vinorelbine, it does not necessitate central line placement. Incidence of this problem can be reduced with a shorter duration of administration. Vinorelbine should be diluted in either a syringe or intravenous bag and administered by intravenous injection, over a period of 6 to 10 minutes. However, if a central line is to be considered for patients receiving vinorelbine, the following can be used as a guide:

- If the patient has poor venous access, early placement of a central line should be considered.
- If the patient has reasonable venous access, treatment should be started with peripheral administration (especially until therapeutic response is determined). Placement of a central line should be considered only if difficulty in venous access is encountered.

After vinorelbine has been infused, flushing of the vein should be continued with at least 100 mL of normal saline or 5% dextrose in water to prevent injection site reactions. Inadequate flushing may increase the risk of phlebitis; therefore, the catheter should not be removed without flushing the vein.

Vinorelbine has shown reduced neurotoxicity, at both the cellular and clinical levels, compared with other vinca alkaloids. However, physicians should make clinical judgment before initiating vinorelbine treatment in patients with pre-existing neurologic disorders. Patients who previously have received neurologic chemotherapy are at high risk for developing neurologic complications. Patients receiving paclitaxel concomitantly with vinorelbine should be monitored for neurologic symptoms. It is recommended that vinorelbine be discontinued if moderate or severe neurotoxicity occurs during treatment.

Granulocytopenia is the major dose-limiting adverse effect with vinorelbine therapy; however, it is reversible and not cumulative over time. Patients who develop leukopenia (particularly granulocytopenia) should be observed carefully for signs of infection. Prophylactic hematologic growth factors have not been used routinely with vinorelbine; however, if medically necessary, growth factors may be administered at recommended doses no earlier than 24 hours after the administration of cytotoxic chemotherapy.

Safety considerations for handling this medication

Note: As with other toxic compounds, caution should be exercised in handling and preparing the solution of vinorelbine. The use of gloves is recommended since skin reactions are reported with accidental exposure. If the solution of vinorelbine contacts the skin or mucosa, the skin or mucosa should be washed immediately with soap and water. Severe irritation of the eye has been reported with accidental contamination of the eye with another vinca alkaloid. If this happens with vinorelbine, the affected eye should be washed with water immediately and thoroughly.

There is limited but increasing evidence and concern that personnel involved in preparation and administration of parenteral antineoplastics may be at some risk because of the potential mutagenicity, teratogenicity, and/or carcinogenicity of these agents, although the actual risk is unknown. USP advisory panels recommend cautious handling both in preparation and disposal of antineoplastic agents. Precautions that have been suggested include:

- Use of a biologic containment cabinet during reconstitution and dilution of parenteral medications and wearing of disposable surgical gloves and masks.
- Use of proper technique to prevent contamination of the medication, work area, and operator during transfer between containers (including proper training of personnel in this technique).
- Cautious and proper disposal of needles, syringes, vials, ampuls, and unused medication.

A number of medical centers have developed detailed guidelines for handling of antineoplastic agents.

For treatment of adverse effects

If shortness of breath or bronchospasm occurs during concurrent treatment with vinorelbine and mitomycin, treatment with supplemental oxygen, bronchodilators, and/or corticosteroids may be required.

Parenteral Dosage Forms

Note: Bracketed use in the *Dosage Forms* section refers to category of use and/or indication that is not included in U.S. product labeling.

VINORELBINE TARTRATE INJECTION

Note: The dosing and strength of the dosage form available are expressed in terms of vinorelbine base (not the tartrate salt).

Usual adult dose

Carcinoma, lung, non-small cell or
[Carcinoma, breast]—

Intravenous (over six to ten minutes), 30 mg (base) per square meter of body surface area once a week, as a single agent. The same dose is used in combination therapy with cisplatin, which is given in a dose of 120 mg (base) per square meter of body surface area on Days 1 and 29, followed by one dose every six weeks.

Dosage adjustment is recommended according to hematologic toxicity or hepatic insufficiency, as outlined below, whichever results in a lower dose. (If both hematologic and hepatic toxicity occur, the lower of the doses determined from the following is recommended.)

Dosage adjustment for hematologic toxicity is—

Granulocytes 1500 cells per cubic millimeter (cells/mm^3) or more on days of treatment:

Give 30 mg (base) per square meter of body surface area.

Granulocytes 1000 to 1499 cells/mm^3 on days of treatment:

Give 15 mg (base) per square meter of body surface area.

Granulocytes less than 1000 cells/mm^3 on days of treatment:

Do not administer vinorelbine. Repeat granulocyte count in one week. If three consecutive weekly doses have to be held because of low granulocyte counts, it is recommended that vinorelbine be discontinued.

Note: In patients who have experienced fever and/or sepsis while granulocytopenic during vinorelbine therapy or have had two consecutive doses held because of granulocytopenia, subsequent doses should be 22.5 mg (base) per square meter of body surface area (for granulocytes greater than or equal to 1500 cells/mm^3) or 11.25 mg (base) per square meter of body surface area (for granulocytes 1000 to 1499 cells/mm^3).

Dosage adjustment for hepatic insufficiency is—

Total bilirubin 2 mg per deciliter (mg/dL) or less:

Give 30 mg (base) per square meter of body surface area.

Total bilirubin 2.1 to 3 mg/dL:

Give 15 mg (base) per square meter of body surface area.

Total bilirubin 3 mg/dL or more:

Give 7.5 mg (base) per square meter of body surface area.

[Carcinoma, cervical][1]—

Patients have benefited from intravenous doses of 25 to 30 mg per square meter of body surface area, once a week, depending on white blood cell and absolute neutrophil counts.

[Carcinoma, ovarian, epithelial][1]—

Patients have benefited from intravenous doses of 18 to 30 mg per square meter of body surface area, once every 7 to 21 days, depending on white blood cell and absolute neutrophil counts.

Usual pediatric dose

Safety and efficacy have not been established.

Strength(s) usually available

U.S.—

10 mg (base) per mL (1- and 5-mL vials) (Rx) [*Navelbine*].

Canada—

10 mg (base) per mL (1- and 5-mL vials) (Rx) [*Navelbine*].

Packaging and storage

Store between 2 and 8 °C (36 and 46 °F), in the carton. Protect from light. Protect from freezing.

Preparation of dosage form

For intravenous administration via syringe, the calculated dose of vinorelbine tartrate injection is diluted to a concentration of 1.5 to 3 mg per mL (mg/mL) with either 5% dextrose injection or 0.9% sodium chloride injection. For administration via an intravenous bag, the calculated dose of vinorelbine tartrate injection is diluted to a concentration of 0.5 to 2 mg/mL with 5% dextrose injection, 0.9% sodium chloride injection, 0.45% sodium chloride injection, 5% dextrose in 0.45% sodium chloride injection, Ringer's injection, or lactated Ringer's injection.

Stability

Unopened vials of vinorelbine tartrate injection are stable for up to 72 hours at 25 °C (77 °F). Diluted injection is stable for up to 24 hours at 5 to 30 °C (41 to 86 °F) under normal room light when stored in polypropylene syringes or polyvinyl chloride bags.

Incompatibilities

Vinorelbine tartrate is not compatible with acyclovir sodium, aminophylline, amphotericin B, ampicillin sodium, cefoperazone sodium, ceforanide, cefotetan sodium, ceftriaxone sodium, fluorouracil, furosemide, ganciclovir sodium, methylprednisolone sodium succinate, mitomycin, piperacillin sodium, sodium bicarbonate, thiotepa, and sulfamethoxazole and trimethoprim when administered with these medications via Y-site injection. Therefore, vinorelbine should not be administered simultaneously with these medications via a Y-site injection.

Note

If accidental contamination of the eye with vinorelbine occurs, the eye should be immediately and thoroughly washed with water to prevent severe irritation.

[1]Not included in Canadian product labeling.

Revised: 01/07/2002
Developed: 08/29/1997

VITAMIN D AND ANALOGS Systemic

This monograph includes information on the following: 1) Alfacalcidol*; 2) Calcifediol†; 3) Calcitriol; 4) Dihydrotachysterol; 5) Doxercalciferol; 6) Ergocalciferol; 7) Paricalcitol.

VA CLASSIFICATION (Primary):

Alfacalcidol—VT509
Calcifediol—VT501
Calcitriol—VT502
Dihydrotachysterol—VT503
Doxercalciferol—VT509
Ergocalciferol—VT504
Paricalcitol—VT509

Commonly used brand name(s): *Calciferol*[6]; *Calciferol Drops*[6]; *Calcijex*[3]; *Calderol*[2]; *DHT*[4]; *DHT Intensol*[4]; *Drisdol*[6]; *Drisdol Drops*[6]; *Hectorol*[5]; *Hytakerol*[4]; *One-Alpha*[1]; *Ostoforte*[6]; *Radiostol Forte*[6]; *Rocaltrol*[3]; *Zemplar*[7].

Note: For a listing of dosage forms and brand names by country availability, see *Dosage Forms* section(s).

*Not commercially available in U.S.
†Not commercially available in Canada.

Category

Note: Vitamin D is a fat-soluble vitamin.
Antihypocalcemic—Alfacalcidol; Calcifediol; Calcitriol; Dihydrotachysterol; Ergocalciferol.
Nutritional supplement (vitamin)—Calcifediol; Calcitriol; Ergocalciferol.
Antihypoparathyroid—Calcitriol; Dihydrotachysterol; Ergocalciferol.
Antihyperparathyroid—Doxercalciferol; Paricalcitol

Indications

Note: Bracketed information in the *Indications* section refers to uses that are not included in U.S. product labeling.

Accepted

Hypocalcemia, chronic (treatment)
Hypophosphatemia (treatment)
Osteodystrophy (treatment) or
Rickets (prophylaxis and treatment)—Therapeutic doses of specific vitamin D analogs are used in the treatment of chronic hypocalcemia, hypophosphatemia, rickets, and osteodystrophy associated with various medical conditions including chronic renal failure, familial hypophosphatemia, and hypoparathyroidism (postsurgical or idiopathic, or pseudohypoparathyroidism). Some analogs have been found to reduce elevated parathyroid hormone concentrations in patients with renal osteodystrophy associated with hyperparathyroidism.

Theoretically, any of the vitamin D analogs may be used for the above conditions. However, because of their pharmacologic properties, some may be more useful in certain situations than others. Alfacalcidol, calcitriol, and dihydrotachysterol are usually preferred in patients with renal failure since these patients have impaired ability to synthesize calcitriol from cholecalciferol and ergocalciferol; therefore, the response is more predictable. In addition, their shorter half-lives may make toxicity easier to manage (hypercalcemia reverses more quickly). Ergocalciferol may not be the preferred agent in the treatment of familial hypophosphatemia or hypoparathyroidism because the large doses needed are associated with a risk of overdose and hypercalcemia; dihydrotachysterol and calcitriol may be preferred.

Secondary hyperparathyroidism (prophylaxis and treatment)—Paricalcitol is indicated for the prevention and treatment of secondary hyperparathyroidism associated with chronic kidney disease (CKD) Stage 3 and 4.

Doxercalciferol is indicated for the treatment of elevated intact parathyroid hormone (iPTH) levels in the management of secondary hyperparathyroidism in patients undergoing chronic renal dialysis.

Tetany (prophylaxis and treatment)—Dihydrotachysterol is indicated [and ergocalciferol and calcitriol are used] for treatment of chronic and latent forms of postoperative tetany and idiopathic tetany.

Vitamin D deficiency (prophylaxis and treatment)—Ergocalciferol is indicated for prevention and treatment of vitamin D deficiency states. Vitamin D deficiency may occur as a result of inadequate nutrition, intestinal malabsorption, or lack of exposure to sunlight, but does not occur in healthy individuals receiving an adequate balanced diet and exposure to sunlight. Vitamin D therapy, alone, as treatment for osteoporosis is not generally recommended; however, vitamin D supplements in doses of 400 to 800 Units may be used as part of the prevention and treatment of osteoporosis in patients with an inadequate vitamin D and/or calcium intake. For prophylaxis of vitamin D deficiency, dietary improvement, rather than supplementation, is advisable. For treatment of vitamin D deficiency, supplementation is preferred.

Deficiency of vitamin D may lead to rickets and osteomalacia.

Recommended intakes may be increased and/or supplementation may be necessary in the following persons or conditions (based on documented vitamin D deficiency):

- Alcoholism
- Dark-skinned individuals
- Hepatic-biliary tract disease—hepatic function impairment, cirrhosis, obstructive jaundice
- Infants, breast-fed, with inadequate exposure to sunlight
- Intestinal diseases—celiac, tropical sprue, regional enteritis, persistent diarrhea
- Lack of exposure to sunlight combined with reduced vitamin D intake
- Renal function impairment
- In general, vitamin D absorption will be impaired in any condition in which fat malabsorption (steatorrhea) occurs.

Some unusual diets (e.g., strict vegetarian diets with no milk intake such as vegan-vegetarian or macrobiotic, or reducing diets that drastically restrict food selection) may not supply minimum daily requirements of vitamin D. Supplementation may be necessary in patients receiving total parenteral nutrition (TPN) or undergoing rapid weight loss or in those with malnutrition, because of inadequate dietary intake.

Recommended intakes for all vitamins and most minerals are increased during pregnancy. Many physicians recommend that pregnant women receive multivitamin and mineral supplements, especially those pregnant women who do not consume an adequate diet and those in high-risk categories (i.e., women carrying more than one fetus, heavy cigarette smokers, and alcohol and drug abusers). Taking excessive amounts of a multivitamin and mineral supplement may be harmful to the mother and/or fetus and should be avoided.

Pregnant women who are strict vegetarians (vegan-vegetarians) and/or have minimal exposure to sunlight may need vitamin D supplementation.

Congenital rickets have been reported in newborns whose mothers had low serum levels of vitamin D.

Recommended intakes for all vitamins and most minerals are increased during breast-feeding.

Recommended intakes may be increased by the following medications: Barbiturates, cholestyramine, colestipol, hydantoin anticonvulsants, mineral oil, and primidone.

Acceptance not established

There are insufficient data to show that vitamin D supplementation is beneficial in the treatment of *psoriasis*.

Unaccepted

Ergocalciferol has not been proven effective for treatment of lupus vulgaris or rheumatoid arthritis, or prevention of nearsightedness or nervousness.

Table 1. Indications

Note: Bracketed information in the *Category/Indications* section refers to uses that are not included in U.S. product labeling.

Legend:
I=Alfacalcidol
II=Calcifediol
III=Calcitriol
IV=Dihydrotachysterol
V=Doxercalciferol
VI=Ergocalciferol
VII=Paricalcitol

	I	II	III	IV	V	VI	VII
Vitamin D deficiency (prophylaxis and treatment)		[✓]				✓	
Vitamin D–dependent rickets (prophylaxis and treatment)			[✓]				
Familial hypophosphatemia (vitamin D–resistant rickets) (treatment)		[✓]	[✓]	[✓]		✓	
Hypocalcemia associated with hypoparathyroidism (treatment)	✓	[✓]	✓	✓		✓	
Chronic renal failure (treatment adjunct)	✓		✓	[✓]	✓		✓
Chronic, and latent forms of postoperative tetany and idiopathic tetany (treatment)				✓		[✓]	

Pharmacology/Pharmacokinetics

Physicochemical characteristics

Molecular weight—
- Alfacalcidol: 400.64.
- Calcifediol: 418.66.
- Calcitriol: 416.64.
- Dihydrotachysterol: 398.67.
- Doxercalciferol: 412.66.
- Ergocalciferol: 396.65.
- Paricalcitol: 416.65.

Mechanism of action/Effect

Vitamin D is essential for promoting absorption and utilization of calcium and phosphate and for normal calcification of bone. Along with parathyroid hormone and calcitonin, it regulates serum calcium concentrations by increasing serum calcium and phosphate concentrations as needed. Vitamin D stimulates calcium and phosphate absorption from the small intestine and mobilizes calcium from bone.

Exposure of the skin to ultraviolet rays in sunlight results in formation of cholecalciferol (vitamin D_3). Ergocalciferol (calciferol, vitamin D_2) is found in commercial vitamin preparations and is used as a food additive; cholecalciferol is found in vitamin D–fortified milk. Cholecalciferol and ergocalciferol are transferred to the liver where they are converted to calcifediol (25-hydroxycholecalciferol), which is then transferred to the kidneys and converted to calcitriol (1,25-dihydroxycholecalciferol, thought to be the most active form) and 24,25-dihydroxycholecalciferol (physiologic role not determined). Dihydrotachysterol is a synthetic reduction product of ergocalciferol; it has only weak antirachitic activity; it is metabolically activated by 25-hydroxylation in the liver. Alfacalcidol is rapidly converted to 1,25-dihydroxycholecalciferol in the liver. Doxercalciferol is activated by CYP 27 in the liver to form 1α, 25–dihydroxyvitamin D_2 (major metabolite); activation does not require involvement of the kidneys.

Calcitriol appears to act by binding to a specific receptor in the cytoplasm of the intestinal mucosa and subsequently being incorporated into the nucleus, probably leading to formation of the calcium-binding protein that results in increased absorption of calcium from the intestine. Also, calcitriol may regulate the transfer of calcium ion from bone and stimulate reabsorption of calcium in the distal renal tubule, thereby effecting calcium homeostasis in the extracellular fluid.

Vitamin D, doxercalciferol, and paricalcitol have been shown to reduce parathyroid hormone levels.

Absorption

Readily absorbed from small intestine (proximal or distal); cholecalciferol may be absorbed more rapidly and completely than ergocalciferol. Ergocalciferol requires presence of bile salts.

There is evidence that some metabolites of vitamin D are reabsorbed from bile; however, the benefit to overall vitamin D status is thought to be negligible.

Protein binding
Bound to specific alpha globulins for transport.
In vitro plasma protein binding of paricalcitol is extensive (>99.8%).

Storage
Stored mainly in liver and other fat depots.

Biotransformation
Metabolic activation of cholecalciferol and ergocalciferol occurs in 2 steps, the first in the liver and the second in the kidneys. Metabolic activation of calcifediol occurs in the kidneys; dihydrotachysterol, alfacalcidol and doxercalciferol are activated in the liver. Calcitriol does not require metabolic activation. Degradation also occurs partly in the kidney.
Unidentified metabolites of paricalcitol were detected in urine and feces, with no parent drug detected in the urine.

Plasma half-life
Alfacalcidol—3 hours
Calcifediol—Approximately 16 days (10 to 22 days).
Calcitriol—3 to 6 hours.
Doxercalciferol—32 to 37 hours (range up to 96 hours, similar in end-stage renal disease patients on hemodialysis).
Ergocalciferol—19 to 48 hours (however, stored in fat deposits in body for prolonged periods).
Paricalcitol—15 hours.

Onset of action
Hypercalcemic—
Alfacalcidol—6 hours
Calcitriol: Oral—2 to 6 hours.
Dihydrotachysterol: Several hours (maximal after 1 to 2 weeks).
Ergocalciferol: 12 to 24 hours; therapeutic effect may take 10 to 14 days.

Time to peak serum concentration
Alfacalcidol—Approximately 12 hours after a single dose.
Calcifediol—Approximately 4 hours.
Calcitriol—Oral: Approximately 3 to 6 hours.
Doxercalciferol—Oral: Approximately 11 to 12 hours, after repeated oral doses of 5 to 15 mcg.

Duration of action
Following oral administration—
Alfacalcidol: Up to 48 hours.
Calcifediol: 15 to 20 days (increased 2 to 3 times in renal failure).
Calcitriol: 3 to 5 days.
Dihydrotachysterol: Up to 9 weeks.
Ergocalciferol: Up to 6 months; repeated doses have a cumulative action.

Elimination
Biliary/renal.

Precautions to Consider

Mutagenicity
Studies with calcitriol, paricalcitol, or doxercalciferolhave found no evidence of mutagenicity.
Doxercalciferol caused structural chromatid and chromosome aberrations in an *in vitro* human lymphocyte clastogenicity assay with metabolic activation. Doxercalciferol was not clastogenic in an *in vivo* mouse clastogenicity assay.

Pregnancy/Reproduction
Fertility—Paricalcitol had no effect on the fertility of rats at intravenous doses up to 20 micrograms/kg (mcg/kg) per dose (equivalent to 13 times the highest recommended human dose (0.24 mcg/kg) based on body surface area (mg/m^2)).
Doxercalciferol had no effect on the fertility of rats at doses up to 2.5 micrograms/kg/day (mcg/kg/day) (approximately 3 times and less than the maximum recommended human dose of 60 mcg/week based on mg/m^2 body surface area).
Pregnancy—Problems in humans have not been documented with intake of normal daily recommended amounts. There are insufficient data on acute and chronic vitamin D toxicity in pregnant women. Maternal hypercalcemia during pregnancy in humans may be associated with increased sensitivity to effects of vitamin D, suppression of parathyroid function, or a syndrome of peculiar (elfin) facies, mental retardation, and congenital aortic stenosis in infants.
Overdosage of vitamin D has been associated with fetal abnormalities in animals. Animal studies have shown calcitriol to be teratogenic when given in doses 4 and 15 times the dose recommended for human use. Excessive doses of dihydrotachysterol are also teratogenic in animals. Animal studies have also shown calcifediol to be teratogenic when given in doses of 6 to 12 times the human dose.
Adequate and well-controlled studies in pregnant women have not been conducted with paricalcitol or doxercalciferol. Paricalcitol or doxercalciferol should be used during pregnancy only if the potential benefit justifies the potential risk to the fetus. Studies, using paricalcitol, in rabbits and rats have shown decreased fetal viability at doses 0.5 and 2 times the 0.24 mcg/kg human dose based on body surface area (mg/m^2), respectively. A significant increase in the mortality of newborn rats was reported at maternally toxic doses of 20 mcg/kg given 3 times per week (13 times the 0.24 mcg/kg human dose) based on body surface area (mg/m^2). Paricalcitol was not teratogenic at the doses tested. Studies, using doxercalciferol, in rats and rabbits, at doses up 20 micrograms/kg/day (mcg/kg/day) and 0.1 mcg/kg/day (approximately 25 times and less than the maximum recommended human dose of 60 mcg/week based on mg/m^2 body surface area, respectively, revealed no teratogenic or fetotoxic effects due to doxercalciferol.
FDA Pregnancy Category C.
FDA Pregnancy Category B.
Note: Doxercalciferol only

Breast-feeding
Only small amounts of vitamin D metabolites appear in human milk. Infants who are totally breast-fed and have little exposure to the sun may require vitamin D supplementation.
It is not known whether paricalcitol or doxercalciferol is excreted in human milk. Because many drugs are excreted in human milk, caution should be exercised when paricalcitol or doxercalciferol is administered to a nursing woman.

Pediatrics
Some studies have shown that infants who are exclusively breast-fed, especially from dark-skinned mothers, and/or have little exposure to sunlight may be at risk for vitamin D deficiency.
Because of varying sensitivity, some infants may be sensitive to even small doses.
Also, growth may be arrested in children, especially after prolonged administration of 1800 Units of ergocalciferol a day.
Appropriate studies on the relationship of age to the effects of paricalcitol or doxercalciferol have not been performed in the pediatric population. Safety and efficacy have not been established.

Geriatrics
Studies have shown that the elderly may have an increased need for vitamin D due to a possible decrease in the capacity of the skin to produce previtamin D_3 ora decrease in exposure to the sun orimpaired renal function or impaired vitamin D absorption.
Studies performed in 40 chronic renal patients, including 10 patients 65 years of age or older, have not demonstrated geriatrics-specific problems that would limit the usefulness of paricalcitol in the elderly.

Drug interactions and/or related problems
The following drug interactions and/or related problems have been selected on the basis of their potential clinical significance (possible mechanism in parentheses where appropriate)—not necessarily inclusive (» = major clinical significance):
Note: Combinations containing any of the following, depending on the amount present, may also interact with vitamin D.

Antacids, aluminum-containing
(long-term use of aluminum-containing antacids as phosphate binders in hyperphosphatemia in conjunction with vitamin D has been found to increase blood levels for aluminum and may lead to aluminum bone toxicity, especially in patients with chronic renal failure)

» Antacids, magnesium-containing
(concurrent use with vitamin D may result in hypermagnesemia, especially in patients with chronic renal failure)

Anticonvulsants, hydantoin or
Barbiturates or
Primidone
(may reduce effect of vitamin D by accelerating metabolism by hepatic microsomal enzyme induction; patients on long-term anticonvulsant therapy may require vitamin D supplementation to prevent osteomalacia)

Calcitonin or
Etidronate or
Gallium nitrate or
Pamidronate or
Plicamycin
(concurrent use with vitamin D may antagonize these medications in the treatment of hypercalcemia)

» Calcium-containing preparations, in high doses or
» Diuretics, thiazide
(concurrent use with vitamin D may increase the risk of hypercalcemia; however, it may be therapeutically advantageous in elderly and high-risk groups when it is necessary to prescribe vitamin D or its derivatives together with calcium; careful monitoring of serum calcium concentrations is essential during long-term therapy)

Cholestyramine or
Colestipol or
Mineral oil
(concurrent use may impair intestinal absorption of vitamin D since these medications have been reported to reduce intestinal absorption of fat-soluble vitamins; requirements for vitamin D may be increased in patients receiving these medications)

Corticosteroids
(vitamin D supplementation may be recommended by some clinicians for prolonged corticosteroids use, because corticosteroids may interfere with vitamin D action)

Digitalis glycosides
(caution is recommended in patients being treated with these medications since the hypercalcemia that may be caused by vitamin D may potentiate the effects of digitalis glycosides, resulting in cardiac arrhythmias)

Hepatic enzyme inhibitors (see *Appendix II*)
(May affect 25–hydroxylation and necessitate dosage adjustments of doxercalciferol)

Phosphorus-containing preparations, in high doses
(concurrent use with vitamin D may increase the potential for hyperphosphatemia, because of vitamin D enhancement of phosphate absorption)

» Vitamin D and analogs, other
(concurrent use of one analog with another, especially calcifediol, is not recommended because of additive effects and increased potential for toxicity)

Laboratory value alterations

The following have been selected on the basis of their potential clinical significance (possible effect in parentheses where appropriate)—not necessarily inclusive (» = major clinical significance).

With physiology/laboratory test values

Alkaline phosphatase
(serum concentrations may be decreased prior to development of hypercalcemia in patients receiving excessive doses)

Alanine aminotransferase (ALT[SGPT]) or
Aspartate aminotransferase (AST[SGOT]) or
Blood urea nitrogen (BUN)
(serum concentrations may be increased in cases of vitamin D toxicity with hypercalcemia)

Calcium concentrations, serum and
Cholesterol concentrations, serum and
Phosphate concentrations, serum
(may be increased with high doses)

Albumin concentrations, urinary
Calcium concentrations, urinary and
Phosphate concentrations, urinary
(may be increased with therapeutic doses, even when serum concentrations are still low)

Magnesium
(serum concentrations may be increased)

Medical considerations/Contraindications

The medical considerations/contraindications included have been selected on the basis of their potential clinical significance (reasons given in parentheses where appropriate)—not necessarily inclusive (» = major clinical significance).

Except under special circumstances, this medication should not be used when the following medical problems exist:

» Hypercalcemia
» Hypervitaminosis D
» Renal osteodystrophy with hyperphosphatemia
(risk of metastatic calcification; however, vitamin D therapy can begin once serum phosphate levels have stabilized)

Risk-benefit should be considered when the following medical problems exist:

» Arteriosclerosis or
» Cardiac function impairment
(conditions may be exacerbated due to possibility of hypercalcemia and elevated serum cholesterol concentrations)

» Hyperphosphatemia
(risk of metastatic calcification; dietary phosphate restriction or administration of intestinal phosphate binders is recommended to produce normal serum phosphorus concentrations)

» Hypersensitivity to effects of vitamin D
(may be involved in causing idiopathic hypercalcemia in infants)

» Renal function impairment
(toxicity may occur in patients receiving vitamin D for nonrenal problems, although toxicity is also possible during treatment of renal osteodystrophy because of increased requirements and decreased renal function)

Sarcoidosis, and possibly other granulomatous diseases
(increased sensitivity to effects of vitamin D)

Patient monitoring

The following may be especially important in patient monitoring (other tests may be warranted in some patients, depending on condition; » = major clinical significance):

Blood urea nitrogen (BUN) and
Creatinine, serum
(determinations recommended at periodic intervals in patients receiving therapeutic doses)

Alkaline phosphatase concentrations, serum and
Phosphorus concentrations, serum and
Calcium concentrations, urinary, 24-hour and
Calcium/creatinine, urinary ratio
(determinations recommended every 1 to 3 months during therapy, as long as the patient remains stable)
(serum phosphorus concentrations recommended twice weekly until stable, then once a month, while on paricalcitol therapy)
(more frequent monitoring of these parameters should be conducted in patients with impaired hepatic function receiving doxercalciferol)
(for dialysis patients receiving doxercalciferol, serum calcium, and phosphorus should be determined prior to initiation of therapy and then weekly during the early phases of treatment.)

» Calcium concentrations, serum or
Ionized calcium concentration, serum
(determinations recommended at least once weekly in early period of treatment to aid in dosage adjustment because of narrow therapeutic range, then at periodic intervals during therapy in patients receiving therapeutic doses; serum calcium concentrations should be maintained at 8.8 to 10.3 mg per 100 mL, depending on lab variability; serum ionized calcium concentrations are preferable to determine free and bound calcium, but may not be readily available from a reliable lab)
(serum calcium concentrations recommended twice weekly until stable, then once a month, while on paricalcitol therapy)

Ophthalmological examinations
(recommended periodically to promote early detection of ectopic calcifications)

Parathyroid hormone (PTH) concentration, serum or plasma
(recommended every 3 months)
(for dialysis patients receiving doxercalciferol, serum or plasma iPTH should be determined prior to initiation of therapy and then weekly during the early phases of treatment.)

Protein, serum
(for correction of plasma calcium in instances of hypercalcemia)

X-rays of bones
(recommended by some clinicians every 3 to 6 months until patient is stable, then yearly to determine when treatment of familial hypophosphatemia or hypoparathyroidism is sufficient; serum calcium times serum phosphorus (Ca X P) prduct should not exceed 70 with doxercalciferol)

Side/Adverse Effects

Note: Ingestion of excessive doses of vitamin D over prolonged periods (20,000 to 60,000 Units a day or more for several weeks or months in adults and 2,000 to 4,000 Units a day for several months in children) can result in severe toxicity. Acute excessive doses of vitamin D can also result in severe toxicity, but there are insufficient data to determine at what dose.

Chronic vitamin D–induced hypercalcemia may result in generalized vascular calcification, nephrocalcinosis, and other soft tissue calcification that may lead to hypertension and renal failure. These effects are more likely to occur when the hypercalcemia is accompanied by hyperphosphatemia.

Growth may be arrested in children, especially after prolonged administration of 1800 Units of ergocalciferol per day.

Death may occur as a result of renal or cardiovascular failure caused by vitamin D toxicity.

Dosage necessary to cause toxicity varies with individual sensitivity, but in individuals without malabsorption problems, 10,000 Units a day for more than several weeks or months is the maximum dose.

Toxicity may occur with therapeutic doses of calcitriol.

The following side/adverse effects have been selected on the basis of their potential clinical significance (possible signs and symptoms in parentheses where appropriate)—not necessarily inclusive:

Those indicating need for medical attention

Early symptoms of vitamin D toxicity associated with hypercalcemia

Bone pain; constipation—usually more frequent in children and adolescents; ***diarrhea; drowsiness; dryness of mouth; headache, continuing; increased thirst; increase in frequency of urination, especially at night, or in amount of urine; irregular heartbeat; loss of appetite; metallic taste; muscle pain; nausea or vomiting***—usually more frequent in children and adolescents; ***pruritus; unusual tiredness or weakness***

Late symptoms of vitamin D toxicity associated with hypercalcemia

bone pain; cloudy urine; conjunctivitis (redness or discharge of the eye, eyelid, or lining of the eyelid)—calcific; ***decreased libido*** (loss of sex drive); ***ectopic calcification*** (calcium deposits in tissues other than bone); ***high fever; high blood pressure; increased sensitivity of eyes to light or irritation of eyes; irregular heartbeat; itching of skin; lethargy*** (drowsiness); ***loss of appetite; muscle pain; nausea or vomiting and pancreatitis*** (stomach pain, severe); ***psychosis, overt*** (mood or mental changes)—rare; ***rhinorrhea*** (runny nose); ***weight loss***

Patient Consultation

As an aid to patient consultation, refer to *Advice for the Patient, Vitamin D and Related Compounds (Systemic).*

In providing consultation, consider emphasizing the following selected information (» = major clinical significance):

Description of use

For ergocalciferol

Description should include function in the body, signs of deficiency, and unproven uses

For doxercalciferol and paricalcitol

Description should include use in hyperparathyroidism associated with chronic renal failure

Importance of diet

For ergocalciferol

Importance of proper nutrition; supplement may be needed because of inadequate dietary intake

Food sources of vitamin D; importance of sunlight exposure; effects of processing

Recommended daily intake for vitamin D

» Importance of not exceeding recommended daily intake if self-medicating with vitamin supplements

Before using this dietary supplement

» Conditions affecting use, especially:

Sensitivity to vitamin D or any vitamin D analog

Pregnancy—No problems documented with normal intake; overdose associated with increased sensitivity to vitamin D, suppression of parathyroid function, or syndrome of peculiar facies, mental retardation, and congenital aortic stenosis in infants

Studies with doxercalciferol and paricalcitol in pregnant women not done; problems in newborn animals reported

Breast-feeding—Possible vitamin D deficiency in totally breast-fed infants

Use in children—Possible vitamin D deficiency in breast-fed infants especially of dark-skinned mothers; varying sensitivity in infants may make some children sensitive to small doses; children may show slowed growth when receiving high doses of vitamin D for long periods; studies with doxercalciferol and paricalcitol not done in pediatrics

Other medications, especially calcium-containing preparations, magnesium-containing antacids, thiazide diuretics, or other vitamin D analogs

Other medical problems, especially hypercalcemia, hypervitaminosis D, renal or cardiac impairment, arteriosclerosis, or hyperphosphatemia

Proper use of this medication

» Proper storage

For the oral solution dosage form

Proper administration

Taking by mouth even though dietary supplement comes in a dropper bottle

May be dropped directly into the mouth or mixed with cereal, fruit juice, or other food

For use as an antihypocalcemic

» Importance of not taking more medication than the amount prescribed

Carefully following instructions for special diet or calcium supplementation, if prescribed

Making sure physician knows if calcium supplement or any calcium-containing preparation is already being taken

» Proper dosing

For use in hyperparathyroidism

» Proper dosing

Missed dose: If dosing schedule is—

Every other day: Taking as soon as possible if remembered same day; if remembered later, not taking until next day, then skipping a day; not doubling doses

Once a day: Taking as soon as possible; taking next day if not remembered until then; not doubling doses

Several times a day: Taking as soon as possible; not taking if almost time for next dose; not doubling doses

For use as a dietary supplement

» Importance of not taking more dietary supplement than the amount recommended; risk of toxicity with chronic overdose

Missed dose: No cause for concern because of length of time necessary for depletion; remembering to take as directed

Precautions while using this dietary supplement

Avoiding concurrent use of nonprescription medications or dietary supplements containing calcium, phosphorus, or vitamin D, unless otherwise directed by health care professional

» Avoiding concurrent use of magnesium-containing antacids

For use as a dietary supplement:

Risk of toxicity with overdose; upper limits for vitamin D toxicity

For use as an antihypocalcemic:

» Regular visits to physician to check progress during therapy

Side/adverse effects

Signs of potential side effects, especially bone pain, constipation, diarrhea, drowsiness, dry mouth, headache (continuing), increased thirst, increase in frequency of urination (especially at night) or in the amount of urine, loss of appetite, metallic taste, muscle pain, nausea or vomiting, unusual tiredness or weakness, cloudy urine, conjunctivitis (calcific), decreased libido, ectopic calcification, high fever, high blood pressure, increased sensitivity of eyes to light or irritation of eyes, irregular heartbeat, itching of skin, lethargy, loss of appetite, pancreatitis, psychosis (overt), rhinorrhea, and weight loss

General Dosing Information

For use as an antihypocalcemic

Before vitamin D therapy is begun, elevated serum phosphate concentrations must be controlled.

Clinical response to vitamin D depends on adequate dietary calcium.

Because of individual variation in sensitivity to its effects, dosage of vitamin D must be adjusted on the basis of clinical response. Some infants are hyperreactive to even small doses. Careful titration is necessary to avoid overdosage, which induces hypercalcemia and can cause hypercalciuria and hyperphosphatemia.

Dosage of vitamin D from dietary and other sources should be evaluated in determining the therapeutic dosage.

The serum calcium times phosphorus (Ca × P, in mg/dL) product should not exceed 60.

To control elevated serum phosphate concentrations in patients undergoing dialysis, a phosphate binding agent should be used. The dosage of the binding agent may need to be increased during vitamin D therapy since phosphate absorption is enhanced.

For use as a dietary supplement

Because of the infrequency of vitamin D deficiency alone, combinations of several vitamins are commonly administered. Many commercial vitamin complexes are available.

Diet/Nutrition
Recommended dietary intakes for vitamin D are defined differently worldwide:
For U.S.—
The Recommended Dietary Allowances (RDAs) for vitamins and minerals are determined by the Food and Nutrition Board of the National Research Council and are intended to provide adequate nutrition in most healthy persons under usual environmental stresses. In addition, a different designation may be used by the FDA for food and dietary supplement labeling purposes, as with Daily Value (DV). DVs replace the previous labeling terminology United States Recommended Daily Allowances (USRDAs).
For Canada—
Recommended Nutrient Intakes (RNIs) for vitamins, minerals, and protein are determined by Health and Welfare Canada and provide recommended amounts of a specific nutrient while minimizing the risk of chronic diseases.

The expression of vitamin D activity has changed from Units to micrograms (mcg), with 1 Unit of vitamin D equal to the activity of 0.025 mcg of cholecalciferol (vitamin D_3). This change was made to reflect a broader activity for vitamin D_3 compared to vitamin D_2.

Normal daily recommended intakes in mcg and Units are generally defined as follows:

Persons	U.S. (mcg)	U.S. Units	Canada (mcg)	Canada Units
Infants and children				
Birth to 3 years of age	7.5–10	300–400	5–10	200–400
4 to 6 years of age	10	400	5	200
7 to 10 years of age	10	400	2.5–5	100–200
Adolescents and adults	5–10	200–400	2.5–5	100–200
Pregnant and breast-feeding females	10	400	5–7.5	200–300

These are usually provided by adequate diets and adequate exposure to sunlight (1.5 to 2 hours of exposure per week is sufficient for most people).

Best dietary sources of vitamin D (as cholecalciferol) include some fish and fish liver oils and vitamin D–fortified milk. The vitamin D content of foods is not affected by cooking.

For parenteral dosage forms only
Parenteral administration may be indicated in patients with malabsorption problems.

Intravenous administration may be indicated in patients undergoing hemodialysis.

For treatment of adverse effects
Recommended treatment includes the following:
- Hypervitaminosis D is treated by withdrawal of the vitamin, low-calcium diet, and generous fluid intake.
- If hypercalcemia persists, prednisone may be started. Severe hypercalcemia may be treated with calcitonin, etidronate, pamidronate, or gallium nitrate.
- Hypercalcemic crisis requires vigorous hydration with intravenous saline to increase calcium excretion, with or without a loop diuretic.
- Cardiac arrhythmias may be treated with small doses of potassium with continuous cardiac monitoring.
- Therapy may be reinstituted at a lower dose when serum calcium concentrations return to normal. Serum or urinary calcium levels should be obtained twice weekly after dosage changes.

ALFACALCIDOL

Oral Dosage Forms

ALFACALCIDOL CAPSULES

Usual adult and adolescent dose
For pre-dialysis patients—
Initial: Oral, 0.25 mcg a day as a single dose taken with food for two months, the dosage being increased in increments of 0.25 mcg a day every two months as necessary.
Maintenance: Oral, 0.5 to 1 mcg a day.
Note: Serum calcium and phosphate levels should be monitored every month. Calcium supplements should not exceed 500 mg of elemental calcium a day. If hypercalcemia develops, the dosage should be reduced by 50% and all calcium supplements should be stopped until serum calcium levels return to normal.

For dialysis patients—
Initial: Oral, 1 mcg a day for four weeks, the dosage being increased in increments of 0.5 mcg a day every two to four weeks as necessary, up to 1 to 2 mcg a day. In rare cases, a maximum dose of 3 mcg a day may be needed.
Maintenance: Oral, 0.25 to 1 mcg a day.
Note: Serum calcium levels should be monitored on a weekly basis and at least twice a week during the initial dosage adjustment period. If hypercalcemia develops, alfacalcidol should be stopped immediately until serum calcium levels return to normal.

Strength(s) usually available
U.S.—
Not commercially available.
Canada—
0.25 mcg (Rx) [*One-Alpha* (sesame oil; alpha-tocopherol)].
0.5 mcg (Rx) [*One-Alpha* (sesame oil; alpha-tocopherol)].
1 mcg (Rx) [*One-Alpha* (sesame oil; alpha-tocopherol)].

Packaging and storage
Store below 40 °C (104 °F), preferably between 15 and 30 °C (59 and 86 °F), unless otherwise specified by manufacturer. Store in a tight, light-resistant container.

ALFACALCIDOL ORAL SOLUTION

Usual adult and adolescent dose
See *Alfacalcidol Capsules*.

Strength(s) usually available
U.S.—
Not commercially available.
Canada—
0.2 mcg per mL (Rx) [*One-Alpha* (citric acid monohydrate; ethanol; methyl parahydroxybenzoate; polyoxyl 40 hydrogenated castor oil; sodium citrate; sorbitol; alpha tocopherol)].

Packaging and storage
Store below 40 °C (104 °F), preferably between 15 and 30 °C (59 and 86 °F), unless otherwise specified by manufacturer. Store in a tight, light-resistant container.

ALFACALCIDOL ORAL DROPS

Usual adult and adolescent dose
See *Alfacalcidol Capsules*.

Strength(s) usually available
U.S.—
Not commercially available.
Canada—
2 mcg per mL (Rx) [*One-Alpha* (citric acid monohydrate; ethanol; methyl parahydroxybenzoate; polyoxyl 40 hydrogenated castor oil; purified water; sodium citrate; sorbitol; alpha tocopherol)].

Packaging and storage
Store at 2 to 8° C, unless otherwise specified by manufacturer. Store in a tight, light-resistant container.

Parenteral Dosage Forms

ALFACALCIDOL INJECTION

Usual adult and adolescent dose—
Initial: Intravenous, 1 mcg per dialysis two to three times a week, the dosage being increased in increments of 1 mcg per dialysis every week as necessary, up to 12 mcg a week. The total dose titration period should not exceed six weeks.
Maintenance: Intravenous, 6 mcg a week. Doses may range from 1.5 to 12 mcg a week.
Note: Serum calcium and phosphate levels should be monitored every other week. If hypercalcemia develops, alfacalcidol should be stopped immediately until serum calcium levels return to normal.

Strength(s) usually available
U.S.—
Not commercially available
Canada—
2 mcg per mL (Rx) [*One-Alpha* (citric acid monohydrate 0.16 mg per mL; ethanol 80 mg per mL; propylene glycol 415 mg per mL; purified water 1 mL; sodium citrate 6.8 mg per mL)].

Packaging and storage
Store at 2 to 8° C, unless otherwise specified by manufacturer. Store in a tight, light-resistant container.

CALCIFEDIOL

Oral Dosage Forms

CALCIFEDIOL CAPSULES USP

Usual adult and adolescent dose

Oral, initially 300 to 350 mcg (0.3 to 0.35 mg) per week administered on a once-a-day or alternate-day schedule, the dosage being increased, if necessary, at four-week intervals.

Note: Most patients respond to doses of 50 to 100 mcg (0.05 to 0.1 mg) per day or 100 to 200 mcg (0.1 to 0.2 mg) on alternate days; as low as 20 mcg (0.02 mg) every other day may be sufficient in patients with normal serum calcium concentrations.

Usual pediatric dose

Children up to 2 years of age—Oral, 20 to 50 mcg (0.02 to 0.05 mg) per day.

Children 2 to 10 years of age—Oral, 50 mcg (0.05 mg) per day.

Note: For use of calcifediol in hypoparathyroidism, a dose of 3 to 6 mcg per kilogram of body weight a day in children less than 10 years of age may be necessary.

Children 10 years of age and over—See *Usual adult and adolescent dose.*

Strength(s) usually available

U.S.—

20 mcg (0.02 mg) (Rx) [*Calderol*].

50 mcg (0.05 mg) (Rx) [*Calderol*].

Canada—

Not commercially available.

Packaging and storage

Store below 40 °C (104 °F), preferably between 15 and 30 °C (59 and 86 °F), unless otherwise specified by manufacturer. Store in a tight, light-resistant container.

CALCITRIOL

Oral Dosage Forms

Note: Bracketed uses in the *Dosage Forms* section refer to categories of use and/or indications that are not included in U.S. product labeling.

CALCITRIOL CAPSULES

Usual adult and adolescent dose

Initial—Oral, 0.25 mcg per day, the dosage being increased in increments of 0.25 mcg every two to four weeks as necessary, up to the following usual doses:

[Familial hypophosphatemia]—

Oral, 2 mcg per day.

Hypocalcemia in chronic dialysis—

Oral, 0.5 to 3 mcg or more per day.

Hypoparathyroidism—

Oral, 0.25 to 2.7 mcg per day.

Renal osteodystrophy—

Oral, 0.25 mcg every other day to 3 mcg or more per day.

Note: Some clinicians believe that in order for calcitriol to be most effective, it should be given in divided doses, at least two or three times a day.

Usual pediatric dose

Oral, 0.25 mcg per day, the dosage being increased in increments of 0.25 mcg every two to four weeks as necessary up to the following usual doses:

[Vitamin D–dependent rickets]—

Oral, 1 mcg per day.

Hypocalcemia in chronic dialysis—

Oral, 0.25 to 2 mcg per day.

Hypoparathyroidism—

Oral, 0.04 to 0.08 mcg per kg of body weight per day.

Renal osteodystrophy—

Oral, 0.014 to 0.041 mcg per kg of body weight per day.

Note: Pediatric patients with liver disease may need initial doses of up to 0.1 to 0.2 mcg per kilogram of body weight per day.

Strength(s) usually available

U.S.—

0.25 mcg (Rx) [*Rocaltrol*].

0.5 mcg (Rx) [*Rocaltrol*].

Canada—

0.25 mcg (Rx) [*Rocaltrol*].

0.5 mcg (Rx) [*Rocaltrol*].

Packaging and storage

Store below 40 °C (104 °F), preferably between 15 and 30 °C (59 and 86 °F), in a tight container, unless otherwise specified by manufacturer. Protect from light.

CALCITRIOL ORAL SOLUTION

Usual adult and adolescent dose

See *Calcitriol Capsules*.

Usual pediatric dose

See *Calcitriol Capsules*.

Strength(s) usually available

U.S.—

Not commercially available.

Canada—

1 mcg per mL (Rx) [*Rocaltrol*].

Packaging and storage

Store below 40 °C (104 °F), preferably between 15 and 30 °C (59 and 86 °F), unless otherwise specified by manufacturer. Protect from light.

Parenteral Dosage Forms

CALCITRIOL INJECTION

Usual adult and adolescent dose

Antihypocalcemic—

Initial: Intravenous (rapid), 0.5 mcg (or 0.01 mcg per kg of body weight) three times a week, the dosage being increased in increments of 0.25 to 0.5 mcg every two to four weeks as necessary.

Maintenance: Intravenous (rapid), 0.5 to 3.0 mcg (or 0.01 to 0.05 mcg per kg of body weight) three times a week.

Usual pediatric dose

Dosage has not been established.

Strength(s) usually available

U.S.—

1 mcg per mL (Rx) [*Calcijex*].

2 mcg per mL (Rx) [*Calcijex*].

Canada—

1 mcg per mL (Rx) [*Calcijex*].

2 mcg per mL (Rx) [*Calcijex*].

Packaging and storage

Store below 40 °C (104 °F), preferably between 15 and 30 °C (59 and 86 °F), unless otherwise specified by manufacturer. Protect from light.

DIHYDROTACHYSTEROL

Oral Dosage Forms

Note: Bracketed uses in the *Dosage Forms* section refer to categories of use and/or indications that are not included in U.S. product labeling.

DIHYDROTACHYSTEROL CAPSULES USP

Usual adult and adolescent dose

Oral, 125 mcg (0.125 mg) to 2 mg per day.

[Familial hypophosphatemia]—

Initial: Oral, 500 mcg (0.5 mg) to 2 mg per day.

Maintenance: Oral, 200 mcg (0.2 mg) to 1.5 mg per day.

Hypocalcemic tetany—

Initial: Acute—Oral, 750 mcg (0.75 mg) to 2.5 mg per day for three days.

Less acute—Oral, 250 to 500 mcg (0.25 to 0.5 mg) per day for three days.

Maintenance: Oral, 250 mcg (0.25 mg) per week to 1 mg per day, as necessary.

Hypoparathyroidism—

Initial: Oral, 750 mcg (0.75 mg) to 2.5 mg per day for several days.

Maintenance: Oral, 200 mcg (0.2 mg) to 1 mg per day.

[Renal osteodystrophy]—

Initial: Oral, 100 to 250 mcg (0.1 to 0.25 mg) per day.

Maintenance: Oral, 200 mcg (0.2 mg) to 1 mg per day.

Usual pediatric dose

[Familial hypophosphatemia]—

See *Usual adult and adolescent dose.*

Hypoparathyroidism—
Initial: Oral, 1 to 5 mg per day for four days, then continued or decreased to one-fourth the dose.
Maintenance: Oral, 500 mcg (0.5 mg) to 1.5 mg per day.

Strength(s) usually available
U.S.—
125 mcg (0.125 mg) (Rx) [*Hytakerol*].
Canada—
125 mcg (0.125 mg) (Rx) [*Hytakerol*].

Packaging and storage
Store below 40 °C (104 °F), preferably between 15 and 30 °C (59 and 86 °F), unless otherwise specified by manufacturer. Store in a well-closed, light-resistant container.

DIHYDROTACHYSTEROL ORAL SOLUTION USP

Usual adult and adolescent dose
Oral, 125 mcg (0.125 mg) to 2 mg per day.
[Familial hypophosphatemia]—
Initial: Oral, 500 mcg (0.5 mg) to 2 mg per day.
Maintenance: Oral, 200 mcg (0.2 mg) to 1.5 mg per day.
Hypocalcemic tetany—
Initial: Acute—Oral, 750 mcg (0.75 mg) to 2.5 mg per day for three days.
Less acute—Oral, 250 to 500 mcg (0.25 to 0.5 mg) per day for three days.
Maintenance: Oral, 250 mcg (0.25 mg) per week to 1 mg per day, as necessary.
Hypoparathyroidism—
Initial: Oral, 750 mcg (0.75 mg) to 2.5 mg per day for several days.
Maintenance: Oral, 200 mcg (0.2 mg) to 1 mg per day.
[Renal osteodystrophy]—
Initial: Oral, 100 to 250 mcg (0.1 to 0.25 mg) per day.
Maintenance: Oral, 200 mcg (0.2 mg) to 1 mg per day.

Usual pediatric dose
[Familial hypophosphatemia]—
See *Usual adult and adolescent dose.*
Hypoparathyroidism—
Initial: Oral, 1 to 5 mg per day for four days, then continued or decreased to one-fourth the dose.
Maintenance: Oral, 500 mcg (0.5 mg) to 1.5 mg per day.

Strength(s) usually available
U.S.—
200 mcg (0.2 mg) per mL (Rx) [*DHT Intensol* (alcohol 20%)].
Canada—
Not commercially available.

Packaging and storage
Store below 40 °C (104 °F), preferably between 15 and 30 °C (59 and 86 °F), unless otherwise specified by manufacturer. Store in a tight, light-resistant glass container. Protect from freezing.

DIHYDROTACHYSTEROL TABLETS USP

Usual adult and adolescent dose
Oral, 125 mcg (0.125 mg) to 2 mg per day.
[Familial hypophosphatemia]—
Initial: Oral, 500 mcg (0.5 mg) to 2 mg per day.
Maintenance: Oral, 200 mcg (0.2 mg) to 1.5 mg per day.
Hypocalcemic tetany—
Initial: Acute—Oral, 750 mcg (0.75 mg) to 2.5 mg per day for three days.
Less acute—Oral, 250 to 500 mcg (0.25 to 0.5 mg) per day for three days.
Maintenance: Oral, 250 mcg (0.25 mg) per week to 1 mg per day, as necessary.
Hypoparathyroidism—
Initial: Oral, 750 mcg (0.75 mg) to 2.5 mg per day for several days.
Maintenance: Oral, 200 mcg (0.2 mg) to 1 mg per day.
[Renal osteodystrophy]—
Initial: Oral, 100 to 250 mcg (0.1 to 0.25 mg) per day.
Maintenance: Oral, 200 mcg (0.2 mg) to 1 mg per day.

Usual pediatric dose
[Familial hypophosphatemia]—
See *Usual adult and adolescent dose.*
Hypoparathyroidism—
Initial: Oral, 1 to 5 mg per day for four days, then continued or decreased to one-fourth the dose.
Maintenance: Oral, 500 mcg (0.5 mg) to 1.5 mg per day.

Strength(s) usually available
U.S.—
125 mcg (0.125 mg) (Rx) [*DHT*].
200 mcg (0.2 mg) (Rx) [*DHT*].
400 mcg (0.4 mg) (Rx) [*DHT*].
Canada—
Not commercially available.

Packaging and storage
Store below 40 °C (104 °F), preferably between 15 and 30 °C (59 and 86 °F), unless otherwise specified by manufacturer. Store in a well-closed, light-resistant container.

DOXERCALCIFEROL

Oral Dosage Forms

DOXERCALCIFEROL CAPSULES

Usual adult dose
Note: The initial dose should be adjusted in order to lower blood iPTH into the range of 150 to 300 pg/mL.

Antihyperparathyroid—
Initial: Oral, 10 micrograms (mcg) three times weekly at dialysis, approximately every other day.
Maintenance: Oral, if iPTH is not lowered by 50% and fails to meet the target range, the dose may be increased by 2.5 mcg at 8 week intervals. Therapy should be suspended if iPTH falls below 100 pg/mL and restarted one week later at a dose at least 2.5 mcg lower than the last administered dose. If an elevated calcium (Ca) or phosphorus (P) level, or a calcium-phosphorus (Ca × P) product is greater than 70 is noted, drug dosage should be immediately suspended until levels are normalized, and reinitiated at a dose that is at least 2.5 mcg lower.

Note: Doxercalciferol doses may need to be decreased as the iPTH levels decrease in response to therapy. Incremental dosing must be individualized.

Suggested Dosing Guidelines

iPTH Level	Doxercalciferol Dose
decreased by < 50% and above 300 pg/mL	increase by 2.5 mcg at eight week intervals as necessary
150 to 300 pg/mL	maintain
< 100 pg/mL	suspend for one week, then resume at a dose that is at least 2.5 mcg lower

Usual adult prescribing limits
The maximum recommended dose is 20 mcg administered 3 times weekly for a total of 60 mcg per week.

Usual pediatric dose
Safety and efficacy have not been established.

Strength(s) usually available
U.S.—
2.5 mcg capsules (Rx) [*Hectorol*].

Packaging and storage
Store at controlled room temperature 20 to 25 °C (68 to 77 °F).

ERGOCALCIFEROL

Oral Dosage Forms

Note: Bracketed uses in the *Dosage Forms* section refer to categories of use and/or indications that are not included in U.S. product labeling.

ERGOCALCIFEROL CAPSULES USP

Usual adult and adolescent dose
Deficiency (prophylaxis)—
Oral, amount based on normal daily recommended intakes:

Persons	U.S. (mcg)	U.S. Units	Canada (mcg)	Canada Units
Adolescents and adults	5–10	200–400	2.5–5	100–200
Pregnant and breast-feeding females	10	400	5–7.5	200–300

Deficiency (treatment)—
Treatment dose is individualized by prescriber based on severity of deficiency.
Vitamin D–resistant rickets—
Oral, 12,000 to 150,000 Units per day.
Vitamin D–dependent rickets—
Oral, 10,000 to 60,000 Units per day (up to 150,000 Units per day).
Osteomalacia due to prolonged use of anticonvulsants—
Oral, 1000 to 4000 Units per day.
Familial hypophosphatemia—
Oral, 50,000 to 100,000 Units per day.
Hypoparathyroidism—
Oral, 50,000 to 150,000 Units per day.
[Renal function impairment]—
Oral, 40,000 to 100,000 Units per day.
[Renal osteodystrophy]—
Initial: Oral, 20,000 Units per day.
Maintenance: Oral, 10,000 to 300,000 Units per day.

Usual pediatric dose
Deficiency (prophylaxis)—
Oral, amount based on normal daily recommended intakes:

Persons	U.S. (mcg)	U.S. Units	Canada (mcg)	Canada Units
Infants and children				
Birth to 3 years of age	7.5–10	300–400	5–10	200–400
4 to 6 years of age	10	400	5	200
7 to 10 years of age	10	400	2.5–5	100–200

Deficiency (treatment)—
Treatment dose in individualized by prescriber based on severity of deficiency.
Vitamin D–dependent rickets—
Oral, 3000 to 10,000 Units per day (up to 50,000 Units per day).
Osteomalacia due to prolonged use of anticonvulsants—
Oral, 1000 Units per day.
Hypoparathyroidism—
Oral, 50,000 to 200,000 Units per day.
[Renal osteodystrophy]—
Oral, 4000 to 40,000 Units per day.

Strength(s) usually available
U.S.—
50 Units (OTC) [GENERIC].
400 Units (0.01 mg) (OTC) [GENERIC].
25,000 Units (0.625 mg) (Rx) [GENERIC].
50,000 Units (1.25 mg) (Rx) [*Drisdol* (tartrazine); GENERIC].
Canada—
50,000 Units (1.25 mg) (Rx) [*Ostoforte*].

Note: Lower strengths are also available as over-the-counter dietary supplements.

Packaging and storage
Store below 40 °C (104 °F), preferably between 15 and 30 °C (59 and 86 °F), unless otherwise specified by manufacturer. Store in a tight, light-resistant container.

ERGOCALCIFEROL ORAL SOLUTION USP

Usual adult and adolescent dose
Deficiency (prophylaxis or treatment)—
See *Ergocalciferol Capsules USP*.
Vitamin D–resistant rickets—
Oral, 12,000 to 500,000 Units per day.
Vitamin D–dependent rickets—
Oral, 10,000 to 60,000 Units per day (up to 500,000 Units per day).
Osteomalacia due to prolonged use of anticonvulsants—
Oral, 1000 to 4000 Units per day.
Familial hypophosphatemia—
Oral, 50,000 to 100,000 Units per day.
Hypoparathyroidism—
Oral, 50,000 to 150,000 Units per day.
[Renal function impairment]—
Oral, 40,000 to 100,000 Units per day.
[Renal osteodystrophy]—
Initial: Oral, 20,000 Units per day.
Maintenance: Oral, 10,000 to 300,000 Units per day.

Usual pediatric dose
See *Ergocalciferol Capsules USP*.

Strength(s) usually available
U.S.—
8000 Units (0.2 mg) per mL (OTC) [*Calciferol Drops; Drisdol Drops*].
Canada—
8000 Units (0.2 mg) per mL (OTC) [*Drisdol*].
300,000 Units (7.5 mg) per mL (Rx) [*Radiostol Forte* (alcohol)].

Packaging and storage
Store below 40 °C (104 °F), preferably between 15 and 30 °C (59 and 86 °F), unless otherwise specified by manufacturer. Store in a tight, light-resistant container. Protect from freezing.

ERGOCALCIFEROL TABLETS USP

Usual adult and adolescent dose
See *Ergocalciferol Oral Solution USP*.

Usual pediatric dose
See *Ergocalciferol Capsules USP*.

Strength(s) usually available
U.S.—
400 Units (0.01 mg) (OTC) [GENERIC].
50,000 Units (1.25 mg) [GENERIC].
Canada—
1,000 Units (0.025 mg) (OTC) [GENERIC].

Packaging and storage
Store below 40 °C (104 °F), preferably between 15 and 30 °C (59 and 86 °F), unless otherwise specified by manufacturer. Store in a tight, light-resistant container.

Parenteral Dosage Forms

ERGOCALCIFEROL INJECTION

Usual adult and adolescent dose
Deficiency (prophylaxis or treatment)—
Intravenous infusion, as part of total parenteral nutrition solutions, the specific amount determined by individual patient need.
Malabsorption—
Intramuscular, 10,000 Units per day.

Usual pediatric dose
See *Usual adult and adolescent dose*.

Strength(s) usually available
U.S.—
500,000 Units (12.5 mg) per mL (Rx) [*Calciferol*].
Canada—
500,000 Units (12.5 mg) per mL (Rx) [*Calciferol*].

Packaging and storage
Store below 40 °C (104 °F), preferably between 15 and 30 °C (59 and 86 °F), unless otherwise specified by manufacturer. Protect from light. Protect from freezing.

PARICALCITOL

Oral Dosage Forms

PARICALCITOL CAPSULES

Usual adult and adolescent dose
Secondary hyperparathyroidism (prophylaxis and treatment)—
Initial: Oral, administered daily or three times weekly. When dosing three times weekly, the dose should be administered no more frequently than every other day. The average weekly doses for both daily and three times a week dosage regimens are similar based on baseline intact parathyroid hormone (iPTH) levels as follows

Baseline iPTH Level	Daily Dose	Three times a Week Dose
≤500 pg/mL	1 mcg	2 mcg
>500 pg/mL	2 mcg	4 mcg

Maintenance: Oral, individualized and based on serum or plasma iPTH levels with monitoring of serum calcium and serum phosphorus with the following suggested approach to titration:

iPTH Level Relative to Baseline	Paricalcitol Capsule Dose	Dose Adjustment at 2 to 4 Week Intervals: Daily Dosage	Three Times a Week Dosage
The same or increased	Increase	1 mcg	2 mcg
Decreased by < 30%	Increase	1 mcg	2 mcg
Decreased by ≥ 30%, ≤ 60%	Maintain	—	—
Decreased > 60%	Decrease	1 mcg	2 mcg
iPTH < 60 pg/mL	Decrease	1 mcg	2 mcg

If a patient is taking the lowest dose on the daily regimen and a dose reduction is needed, the dose can be decreased to 1 mcg three times a week. If a further dose reduction is required, the drug should be withheld as needed and can be restarted at a lower dose. If a patient is on a calcium-based phosphate binder, the binder dose may be decreased or withheld, or the patient may be switched to a non-calcium-based phosphate binder. If hypercalcemia or an elevated Ca x P is observed, the dose of paricalcitol should be reduced or interrupted until these parameters are normalized.

Serum calcium and phosphorus levels should be closely monitored after initiation of paricalcitol capsule and during dose titration periods and coadministration with strong P450 3A inhibitors.

Note: No dosing adjustment is required in patients with mild and moderate hepatic impairment.

Strength(s) usually available

U.S.—

1 mcg (Rx) [*Zemplar* (medium change triglycerides; alcohol; butylated hydroxytoluene; gelatin; glycerin; titanium dioxide; iron oxide black; water)].

2 mcg (Rx) [*Zemplar* (medium change triglycerides; alcohol; butylated hydroxytoluene; gelatin; glycerin; titanium dioxide; iron oxide red; iron oxide yellow; water)].

4 mcg (Rx) [*Zemplar* (medium change triglycerides; alcohol; butylated hydroxytoluene; gelatin; glycerin; titanium dioxide; iron oxide yellow; water)].

Packaging and storage

Store below 25 °C (77 °F); excursions permitted between 15 and 30 °C (59 and 86 °F).

Parenteral Dosage Forms

PARICALCITOL INJECTION

Usual adult dose

Note: The currently accepted target range for iPTH levels in chronic renal failure patients is no more than 1.5 to 3 times the non-uremic upper limit of normal.

Antihyperparathyroid—

Initial: Intravenous (rapid), 0.04 mcg/kg to 0.1 mcg/kg (2.8 mcg to 7 mcg) administered no more frequently than every other day at anytime during dialysis.

Maintenance: Intravenous (rapid), if a satisfactory response is not observed, the dose may be increased by 2 mcg to 4 mcg at 2 to 4 week intervals. If an elevated calcium (Ca) level, or a calcium-phosphorus (Ca × P) product is greater than 75 is noted, drug dosage should be immediately reduced or interrupted until levels are normalized, and reinitiated at a lower dose.

Note: Paricalcitol doses may need to be decreased as the PTH levels decrease in response to therapy. Incremental dosing must be individualized.

Suggested Dosing Guidelines

PTH Level	Paricalcitol Dose
the same or increasing	increase
decreasing by <30%	increase
decreasing by >30%, <60%	maintain
decreasing by >60%	decrease
1.5 to 3.0 times the upper limit of normal	maintain

Usual adult prescribing limits

Doses as high as 0.24 mcg/kg (16.8 mcg) have been safely administered.

Usual pediatric dose

Safety and efficacy have not been established.

Strength(s) usually available

U.S.—

5 mcg per mL (Rx) [*Zemplar* (propylene glycol, 30%; alcohol, 20%)].

Packaging and storage

Store at 25 °C (77 °F), excursions permitted to 15 °C to 30 °C (59 °F to 86 °F).

Revised: 07/13/2005

VITAMIN K Systemic†

Note: Products containing phytonadione injection were voluntarily withdrawn from the Canadian market by International Medication Systems, Limited

This monograph includes information on the following: 1) Menadiol†; 2) Phytonadione†.

INN: Phytonadione—Phytomenadione

JAN: Phytonadione—Phylloquinone

VA CLASSIFICATION (Primary/Secondary):

Menadiol—VT701/BL116
Phytonadione—VT702/BL116

Commonly used brand name(s): *AquaMEPHYTON*[2]; *Mephyton*[2].

Other commonly used names for [phytonadione] are phylloquinone, phytomenadione, and vitamin K_1.

Another commonly used name for [menadiol] is Vitamin K_4.

Note: For a listing of dosage forms and brand names by country availability, see *Dosage Forms* section(s).

*Not commercially available in U.S.
†Not commercially available in Canada.

Category

Nutritional supplement (vitamin), prothrombogenic—Menadiol sodium diphosphate; Phytonadione.

Antidote (to drug-induced hypoprothrombinemia)—Menadiol sodium diphosphate; Phytonadione.

Antihemorrhagic—Phytonadione

Note: Vitamin K is a fat-soluble vitamin.

Indications

Note: Products containing phytonadione injection have been voluntarily withdrawn from the Canadian market by International Medication Systems, Limited.

Accepted

Hypoprothrombinemia (prophylaxis and treatment)—Vitamin K is indicated for the treatment and prevention of various coagulation disorders involving impaired formation of factors II, VII, IX, and X resulting from vitamin K deficiency or impairment of vitamin K activity, including hypoprothrombinemia due to coumarin- or indanedione-derivative (oral) anticoagulants, salicylates, and some antibiotics. Vitamin K does not return abnormal platelet function to normal. Vitamin K does not counteract the anticoagulant activity of heparin. Vitamin K may not be effective in hepatic function impairment since prothrombin synthesis occurs in the liver.

Hypoprothrombinemia secondary to vitamin K deficiency may occur in the following persons or conditions: Patients with hepatic or biliary tract disease, including obstructive jaundice or biliary fistula; in malabsorption syndromes or diseases affecting the small intestine or pancreas, such as celiac disease, cystic fibrosis, intestinal resection, persistent diarrhea or dysentery, regional enteritis, sprue, or ulcerative colitis; prolonged T-tube drainage; abetalipoproteinemia; patients receiving total parenteral nutrition (TPN); or in infants receiving unfortified milk substitute formulas or those who are exclusively breast-fed. Also, Vitamin K deficiency may occur when vitamin K activity is impaired by sulfonamides, quinine, quinidine, or dactinomycin, or when absorption is decreased by concurrent administration of cholestyramine, colestipol, mineral oil, or sucralfate.

Hemorrhagic disease of the newborn (prophylaxis and treatment)—The American Academy of Pediatrics recommends routine vitamin K_1 administration at birth to prevent hemorrhagic disease of the newborn, since vitamin K from the mother may be inadequate because of poor passage through the placenta and because intestinal bacteria responsible for natural synthesis of vitamin K are not present for 5 to 8 days following birth. In addition, the risk of hemorrhagic disease of the newborn is increased in infants of mothers who received anticonvulsants (e.g., phenobarbital, phenytoin) during pregnancy. Phytonadione is preferred over menadiol in the prophylaxis and treatment of hemorrhagic disease of the newborn, because phytonadione is less likely to cause hyperbilirubinemia and hemolytic anemia, especially in premature infants.

Unaccepted

Menadiol sodium diphosphate may be used as a liver function test, although it has generally been replaced by newer methods.

Pharmacology/Pharmacokinetics

Physicochemical characteristics

Source—Phytonadione (vitamin K_1) occurs naturally in plants as phylloquinone, and also is produced synthetically. Another naturally occurring form of vitamin K is synthesized by human intestinal flora. Menadiol sodium diphosphate (vitamin K_4) is a water-soluble derivative converted in the body to menadione (vitamin K_3).

Chemical Group—All vitamin K compounds are 2-methyl-1,4-naphthoquinones.

Molecular weight—
Menadiol sodium diphosphate: 530.18.
Phytonadione: 450.71.

Solubility—Vitamin K is a fat-soluble vitamin. Phytonadione and menadione are lipid-soluble. Menadiol sodium diphosphate is a water-soluble salt.

Mechanism of action/Effect

Vitamin K promotes the hepatic formation of active prothrombin (factor II), proconvertin (factor VII), plasma thromboplastin component or Christmas factor (factor IX), and Stuart factor (factor X), which are required for normal blood clotting. Vitamin K is an essential cofactor for a hepatic microsomal enzyme that catalyzes the post-translational carboxylation of multiple, specific, peptide-bound glutamic acid residues in inactive hepatic precursor proteins of factors II, VII, IX, and X. The resulting gamma-carboxyglutamic acid residues convert the precursor proteins to active coagulation factors that subsequently are secreted by liver cells into the blood.

In healthy individuals, supplemental vitamin K is virtually devoid of pharmacodynamic activity. However, in the presence of vitamin K deficiency, or in the presence of coumarin- or indanedione-derivative anticoagulants, the pharmacologic activity of vitamin K is related to its normal physiological function, which is to promote the hepatic formation of vitamin K-dependent clotting factors.

Vitamin K does not return abnormal platelet function to normal. Vitamin K does not counteract the anticoagulant activity of heparin.

Absorption

Oral—Vitamin K is readily absorbed from healthy gastrointestinal tract (duodenum); phytonadione requires the presence of bile salts for absorption.

Parenteral—Following subcutaneous administration, phytonadione is readily absorbed.

Distribution

Phytonadione is concentrated in the liver initially, but the concentration declines rapidly. Very little vitamin K accumulates in tissues.

Biotransformation

Hepatic (rapid).

Onset of action

Menadiol sodium diphosphate—
Parenteral: 8 to 24 hours.

Phytonadione—
Oral: 6 to 12 hours.
Parenteral: 1 to 2 hours, with hemorrhage usually controlled in 3 to 6 hours; normal prothrombin concentrations are often obtained in 12 to 14 hours.

Elimination

Renal/biliary. Almost no free, unmetabolized vitamin K appears in bile or urine. Bacterial synthesis of vitamin K in the intestine may result in high fecal concentrations.

Precautions to Consider

Carcinogenicity

Studies have not been done.

Mutagenicity

Phytonadione, at concentrations of up to 2000 mcg per plate with or without metabolic activation, was negative in the Ames microbial mutagen test.

Pregnancy/Reproduction

Pregnancy—Studies have not been done in humans.
Studies have not been done in animals.
FDA Pregnancy Category C.

In general, administration before delivery to prevent hemorrhagic disease of the newborn is not recommended because of possible neonatal toxicity.

Breast-feeding

It is not known whether supplemental vitamin K is distributed into breast milk. However, problems in humans have not been documented. Vitamin K is especially needed in breast-fed infants since there is little vitamin K in breast milk.

Pediatrics

Note: Menadiol sodium diphosphate has been shown to cause hepatotoxicity and hemolytic anemia in children, and hemolytic anemia, hyperbilirubinemia, and kernicterus in neonates; administration to newborns (especially premature infants) is not recommended. Also, hemolysis, hyperbilirubinemia, and jaundice have been associated with the administration of high doses of phytonadione in neonates, especially premature infants; therefore, the recommended dose should not be exceeded.

The parenteral dosage form of phytonadione contains benzyl alcohol, which is not recommended for use in neonates. However, the small amount of benzyl alcohol contained in these preparations, when used as directed, has not been shown to cause toxicity.

Geriatrics

No information is available on the relationship of age to the effects of vitamin K in geriatric patients.

Drug interactions and/or related problems

The following drug interactions and/or related problems have been selected on the basis of their potential clinical significance (possible mechanism in parentheses where appropriate)—not necessarily inclusive (» = major clinical significance):

Note: Combinations containing any of the following medications, depending on the amount present, may also interact with this medication.

Antacids
(large amounts of aluminum hydroxide may precipitate bile acids in the upper small intestine, thereby decreasing absorption of fat-soluble vitamins)

Antibiotics, broad-spectrum, or
Quinidine or
Quinine or
Salicylates, high doses, or
Sulfonamides, antibacterial
(requirements for vitamin K may be increased in patients receiving these medications)

» Anticoagulants, coumarin- or indanedione-derivative
(concurrent use with vitamin K may decrease the effects of these anticoagulants as a result of increased hepatic synthesis of procoagulant factors. When reinstituting oral anticoagulant therapy after the administration of large doses of vitamin K, it may be necessary to temporarily increase the dose of the oral anticoagulant, or to use one such as heparin that acts on a different principle.)

Cholestyramine or
Colestipol or
Mineral oil or
Sucralfate
(concurrent use may decrease absorption of vitamin K; requirements for vitamin K may be increased in patients receiving these medications)

Dactinomycin
(concurrent use may decrease the effects of vitamin K; evidence is inconclusive; observation of patients is recommended and a higher dose of vitamin K may be required)

» Hemolytics, other (see *Appendix II*)
(concurrent use with vitamin K, especially menadiol, may increase the potential for toxic side effects)

Medical considerations/Contraindications

The medical considerations/contraindications included have been selected on the basis of their potential clinical significance (reasons given in parentheses where appropriate)—not necessarily inclusive (» = major clinical significance).

Risk-benefit should be considered when the following medical problems exist:

Glucose-6-phosphate dehydrogenase (G6PD) deficiency
(menadiol sodium diphosphate may induce erythrocyte hemolysis)

» Hepatic function impairment
(vitamin K administration may not be effective in the treatment of hypoprothrombinemia in these patients; large doses of vitamin K may further impair liver function in the presence of severe hepatic disease)

Sensitivity to the vitamin K analog considered for use, or history of

Patient monitoring

The following may be especially important in patient monitoring (other tests may be warranted in some patients, depending on condition; » = major clinical significance):

» Prothrombin time (PT) determinations
(The prothrombin test is sensitive to the levels of three of the vitamin K-dependent clotting factors (II, VII, and X); regular prothrombin level determinations are recommended to determine responsiveness to and need for additional vitamin K therapy.)

Side/Adverse Effects

Note: A rare hypersensitivity-like reaction, which has occasionally resulted in death, has been reported after intravenous and following intramuscular administration of phytonadione, especially when administration was rapid. Typically this severe reaction has resembled hypersensitivity or anaphylaxis, including shock and cardiac and/or respiratory arrest. This reaction has occurred in some patients after receiving phytonadione for the first time, even when precautions have been taken to dilute the drug and to avoid rapid infusion. Therefore, the intravenous and intramuscular routes of administration should be restricted to those situations in which other routes are not feasible, and the potential benefits have been determined to justify the serious risks.

In newborns, especially premature infants, menadiol sodium diphosphate has been associated with hemolytic anemia, hyperbilirubinemia, and kernicterus because of immature hepatic function in these infants. There is less risk with phytonadione, unless high doses are given.

The following side/adverse effects have been selected on the basis of their potential clinical significance (possible signs and symptoms in parentheses where appropriate)—not necessarily inclusive:

Those indicating need for medical attention

Incidence less frequent

Hemolytic anemia (difficulty in breathing; enlarged liver; general body swelling; paleness)—in children or neonates, with menadiol or large doses of phytonadione; ***hyperbilirubinemia*** (yellow eyes or skin)—in children or neonates, with menadiol or large doses of phytonadione; may be clinically asymptomatic; ***jaundice*** (yellow eyes or skin)—in neonates, with menadiol or large doses of phytonadione; ***kernicterus*** (decreased appetite; decreased movement or activity; difficulty in breathing; muscle stiffness)—in neonates, with menadiol

Incidence rare

Anaphylaxis (difficult, fast, or irregular breathing; difficulty in swallowing; flushing or redness of skin; shortness of breath; skin rash, hives and/or itching; sudden, severe decrease in blood pressure; swelling of the eyelids, face or lips; tightness in chest; wheezing)—with injection only; ***cyanosis*** (bluish discoloration of skin); ***dizziness; hypotension***—transient; ***profuse sweating; rapid and weak pulse***

Those indicating need for medical attention only if they continue or are bothersome

Incidence less frequent

Flushing of face; redness, pain, or swelling at injection site—with parenteral administration; ***skin lesions (plaques)***—very rare, with repeated injection at one site; ***unusual taste***

Patient Consultation

Note: Products containing phytonadione injection were voluntarily withdrawn from the Canadian market by International Medication Systems, Limited.

As an aid to patient consultation, refer to *Advice for the Patient, Vitamin K (Systemic).*

In providing consultation, consider emphasizing the following selected information (» = major clinical significance):

Description of use

For use as a nutritional supplement (vitamin)—Description should include function of vitamin K in the body, dietary sources, and signs of deficiency

For use as an antidote to hypoprothrombinemia—Description should include the role of vitamin K in blood clotting, its effect on oral anticoagulants, and the importance of not varying the level of intake of foods rich in vitamin K while taking oral anticoagulants

Before using this medication

» Conditions affecting use, especially:
Sensitivity to vitamin K analog considered for use, or history of
Use in children—Menadiol may cause hepatotoxicity, hemolytic anemia, and kernicterus, and is not recommended for use in newborns, especially premature infants. The risk of side effects is lower with phytonadione
Other medications, especially coumarin- or indanedione-derivative anticoagulants and hemolytics
Other medical problems, especially hepatic function impairment

Proper use of this medication

» Importance of not taking more medication than the amount prescribed
» Proper dosing
Missed dose: Taking as soon as remembered; not taking if almost time for next dose; not doubling doses; telling physician about any missed doses
» Proper storage

Precautions while using this medication

» Need for patient to inform all physicians and dentists that this medication is being used

» Not taking any other medications unless discussed with physician since they may alter the effect

» Regular visits to physician to check progress and to perform regular prothrombin time tests

Side/adverse effects

Signs of potential side effects, especially anaphylaxis, cyanosis, dizziness, hypotension (transient), profuse sweating, rapid and weak pulse, and, in newborns, hemolytic anemia and liver toxicity, which may progress to kernicterus

General Dosing Information

Note: Severe reactions, including fatalities, have occurred with the intravenous and with the intramuscular administration of phytonadione. The intravenous and intramuscularadministration of vitamin K is not recommended and should be restricted to those situations where the subcutaneous route is not feasible and the serious risk involved is considered justified; however, when it is considered necessary, intravenous injection should be conducted *very slowly* at a rate not exceeding 1 mg per minute.

Dosage of vitamin K should be based on laboratory tests of clotting function, specifically, determinations of the prothrombin time (PT). Also, intake of vitamin K from dietary and other sources should be evaluated in determining the therapeutic dosage.

For treatment of hypoprothrombinemia secondary to coumarin- or indanedione-derivative anticoagulants, use of the smallest effective dose of vitamin K is recommended, since excessive dosage may result in temporary refractoriness to subsequent oral anticoagulant therapy. Depending on the severity of the hemorrhagic condition, withdrawal of or reduction in the dose of oral anticoagulant may be sufficient to correct the prothrombin deficiency. The use of vitamin K to correct excessive anticoagulation may restore underlying conditions that originally permitted a hypercoagulable or thromboembolic state. Therefore, dosage should be kept as low as possible and the PT should be monitored regularly.

In the event of severe hemorrhage, administration of fresh whole blood, plasma, or component therapy may be required because of the delay in onset of vitamin K activity.

For treatment of hemorrhagic disease of the newborn, empiric administration of vitamin K_1 should not replace proper laboratory evaluation and clinical assessment. A prompt response to vitamin K_1 therapy consists of shortening of the PT within 2 to 4 hours, and is usually diagnostic of hemorrhagic disease of the newborn. Failure to respond to vitamin K_1 suggests a different condition or a coagulation disorder unrelated to vitamin K status.

Note: In neonates, particularly in premature infants, toxicity has been associated with the administration of menadiol sodium diphosphate, or high doses of phytonadione. When the administration of vitamin K_1 is considered necessary in this age group, the recommended dose of phytonadione should not be exceeded. The use of menadiol in newborns is not recommended.

Hypoprothrombinemia due to hepatocellular damage is not corrected by administration of vitamin K. Repeated large doses of vitamin K should not be used in the presence of liver disease if the initial response is unsatisfactory, as it may further depress liver function. Failure to respond to vitamin K therapy may indicate a coagulation defect or a condition unresponsive to vitamin K.

For oral dosage forms only

The oral route of administration should be avoided when the clinical condition may prevent proper absorption of vitamin K. Bile salts must be given concurrently with the oral dosage form of vitamin K when the endogenous supply of bile to the gastrointestinal tract is deficient.

For parenteral dosage forms only
The subcutaneous route of administration is preferred whenever possible, especially when oral administration is not possible because of malabsorption problems.

Because of the risk of severe hypersensitivity-like or anaphylactic reactions, the intravenous and intramuscular administration of vitamin K is not recommended; however, when intravenous administration is considered necessary, intravenous injection should be conducted very slowly at a rate not exceeding 1 mg per minute.

Diet/Nutrition
Recommended Dietary Allowances (RDAs) for vitamin K usually are met or exceeded by a normal diet and intestinal bacterial synthesis. The minimum daily requirement for vitamin K is estimated to be.03 mcg per kilogram of body weight for adults, and 1 to 5 mcg of vitamin K per kilogram of body weight for infants.

The best dietary sources of vitamin K include green, leafy vegetables, meats, and dairy products. There is little loss of vitamin K from foods with ordinary cooking.

MENADIOL

Oral Dosage Forms

MENADIOL SODIUM DIPHOSPHATE TABLETS USP

Usual adult and adolescent dose
Hypoprothrombinemia secondary to obstructive jaundice and biliary fistulas—
Oral, 5 mg per day.

Hypoprothrombinemia secondary to the administration of antibacterials or salicylates—
Oral, 5 to 10 mg per day.

Usual pediatric dose
Vitamin (prothrombogenic); or
Antidote (to drug-induced hypoprothrombinemia)—
Oral, 5 to 10 mg per day.

Strength(s) usually available
U.S.—
Not commercially available.

Canada—
Not commercially available.

Packaging and storage
Store below 40 °C (104 °F), preferably between 15 and 30 °C (59 and 86 °F), unless otherwise specified by manufacturer. Store in a well-closed, light-resistant container.

Parenteral Dosage Forms

MENADIOL SODIUM DIPHOSPHATE INJECTION USP

Usual adult and adolescent dose
Nutritional supplement (vitamin), prothrombogenic; or
Antidote (to drug-induced hypoprothrombinemia)—
Intramuscular or subcutaneous, 5 to 15 mg one or two times a day.

Usual pediatric dose
Vitamin (prothrombogenic); or
Antidote (to drug-induced hypoprothrombinemia)—
Intramuscular or subcutaneous, 5 to 10 mg one or two times a day.

Strength(s) usually available
U.S.—
Not commercially available.

Canada—
Not commercially available.

Packaging and storage
Store below 40 °C (104 °F), preferably between 15 and 30 °C (59 and 86 °F), unless otherwise specified by manufacturer. Store in a light-resistant container. Protect from freezing.

Incompatibilities
Incompatible with protein hydrolysate.

PHYTONADIONE

Oral Dosage Forms

PHYTONADIONE TABLETS USP

Usual adult and adolescent dose
Hypoprothrombinemia, anticoagulant-induced (coumarin- or indanedione-derivative)—
Oral, 2.5 to 10 mg, or up to 25 mg (rarely up to 50 mg); subsequent doses should be determined by prothrombin time (PT) response and/or clinical condition.

Hypoprothrombinemia due to other causes—
Oral, 2.5 to 25 mg or more (rarely up to 50 mg); the amount administered depends on the severity of the condition and the clinical and/or PT response obtained.

Usual pediatric dose
Safety and efficacy have not been established.

Strength(s) usually available
U.S.—
5 mg (Rx) [*Mephyton* (scored; acacia; calcium phosphate; colloidal silicon dioxide; lactose; magnesium stearate; starch; talc)].

Canada—
Not commercially available.

Packaging and storage
Store below 40 °C (104 °F), preferably between 15 and 30 °C (59 and 86 °F), unless otherwise specified by manufacturer. Store in a well-closed container. Protect from light.

Parenteral Dosage Forms

PHYTONADIONE INJECTION USP
Note: Products containing phytonadione injection were voluntarily withdrawn from the Canadian market by International Medication Systems, Limited

Note: Severe reactions, including fatalities have been reported following intramuscular administration of phytonadione. The intravenous and intramuscular routes should be restricted to those situations where the subcutaneous route is not feasible and the serious risk involved in considered justified.

Note: Some preparations are for intramuscular use only.

Usual adult and adolescent dose
Hypoprothrombinemia, anticoagulant-induced (coumarin- or indanedione-derivative)—
Subcutaneous, 2.5 to 10 mg, or up to 25 mg (rarely up to 50 mg); may be repeated after six to eight hours if necessary; subsequent doses should be determined by prothrombin time (PT) response and/or clinical condition.

Hypoprothrombinemia due to other causes—
Subcutaneous, 2.5 to 25 mg or more (rarely up to 50 mg); the amount administered depends on the severity of the condition and the clinical and/or PT response obtained.

[Prevention of hypoprothrombinemia during prolonged total parenteral nutrition]

Usual pediatric dose
[Infants receiving unfortified milk substitutes or who are exclusively breast-fed]

[Prevention of hypoprothrombinemia during prolonged total parenteral nutrition]

[Treatment of hypoprothrombinemia, anticoagulant-induced (coumarin- or indanedione-derivative]

[Treatment of hypoprothrombinemia due to other causes]

Hemorrhagic disease of the newborn—
Prophylaxis—Intramuscular, 0.5 to 1 mg within one hour of birth;.
Treatment—Subcutaneous, 1 mg; higher doses may be required for infants whose mothers received oral anticoagulants or anticonvulsants during pregnancy.

Note: The parenteral dosage form of phytonadione contains benzyl alcohol, which is not recommended for use in neonates. However, the small amount of benzyl alcohol contained in these preparations, when used as directed, has not been shown to cause toxicity.

Strength(s) usually available
U.S.—
2 mg per mL (1 mg per 0.5-mL ampul) (Rx) [*AquaMEPHYTON* (benzyl alcohol 0.9%; dextrose 18.75 mg; polyoxyethylated fatty acid derivative 35 mg)].

10 mg per mL (Rx) [*AquaMEPHYTON* (benzyl alcohol 0.9%; dextrose 37.5 mg; polyoxyethylated fatty acid derivative 70 mg)].

Canada—

Note: Not commercially available

Packaging and storage

Store below 40 °C (104 °F), preferably between 15 and 30 °C (59 and 86 °F), unless otherwise specified by manufacturer. Protect from light. Protect from freezing.

Preparation of dosage form

Phytonadione injection may be diluted with 0.9% sodium chloride injection, 5% dextrose injection, or 5% dextrose and sodium chloride injection. All diluents should be preservative-free. Other diluents should not be used.

Stability

Solutions should be prepared immediately prior to use and any unused portion discarded.

Incompatibilities

Phytonadione injection is physically incompatible with phenytoin injection.

Additional information

The administration of large amounts of benzyl alcohol in newborns has been associated with a fatal toxic syndrome consisting of metabolic acidosis, central nervous system depression, respiratory problems, renal failure, hypotension, and possibly seizures and intracranial hemorrhage. Therefore, products containing benzyl alcohol should be used with caution in newborns, especially those who are receiving other benzyl alcohol–containing medications. However, the small amount of benzyl alcohol contained in the parenteral dosage form of commercial preparations of vitamin K_1, when used as directed, has not been shown to cause toxicity in neonates.

Revised: 01/17/2002

VORICONAZOLE Systemic†

VA CLASSIFICATION (Primary): AM700

Commonly used brand name(s): *VFEND*.

Note: For a listing of dosage forms and brand names by country availability, see *Dosage Forms* section(s).

†Not commercially available in Canada.

Category

Antifungal (systemic).

Indications

Accepted

Aspergillosis (treatment)—Voriconazole is indicated in the treatment of invasive aspergillosis caused by *Aspergillus fumigatus* and other *Aspergillus* species.

Candidiasis, abdominal (treatment) or
Candidiasis, bladder wall (treatment) or
Candidiasis, disseminated (treatment) or
Candidiasis, esophageal (treatment) or
Candidiasis, kidney (treatment)—Voriconazole is indicated for use in Candidemia in nonneutropenic patients and the following *Candida* infections: disseminated infections in skin and infections in abdomen, kidney, bladder wall, and wounds.

Fungal infections, serious (treatment)—Voriconazole is indicated for the treatment of serious fungal infections caused by *Scedosporium apiospermum* (asexual form of *Pseudallescheria boydii*) and *Fusarium* species including *Fusarium solani* in patients intolerant of, or refractory to, other therapy.

Pharmacology/Pharmacokinetics

Physicochemical characteristics

Chemical Group—Triazole derivative

Molecular weight—349.3.

Absorption

Oral bioavailability: 96%

Multiple doses administered with high fat meals reduces the C_{max} and AUC_{τ} by 34% and 24%, respectively.

Distribution

Extensively distributed into tissues

Volume of distribution (Vol_D)—4.6 L/kg

Protein binding

Moderate (58%)

Biotransformation

The pharmacokinetics of voriconazole are non-linear due to saturation of its metabolism. The interindividual variability of voriconazole pharmacokinetics is high. Greater than proportional increase in exposure is observed with increasing dose.

The major metabolite is N-oxide (72%)

Half-life

As a result of non-linear pharmacokinetics, the terminal half-life of voriconazole is dose dependent and therefore not useful in predicting the accumulation of voriconazole.

Time to peak concentration

Oral or intravenous loading dose regimen: Peak plasma concentrations are close to steady state within 24 hours

Oral or intravenous without loading dose regimen: Peak plasma concentrations are at steady state by day 6

Peak plasma concentration:

Oral C_{max}: 2.08 μg/mL

Intravenous C_{max}: 3.06 μg/mL

Elimination

Hepatic; less than 2% of the dose excreted unchanged in the urine

Voriconazole is hemodialyzed with clearance of 121 mL per min. The intravenous vehicle, SBECD, is hemodialyzed with clearance of 55 mL per min.

Precautions to Consider

Cross-sensitivity and/or related problems

Patients allergic to other azole antifungal agents may be allergic to voriconazole. Caution is advised.

Carcinogenicity

Rats, given voriconazole doses of 6 to 50 mg per kg of body weight (0.2 to 1.6 times the recommended maintenance dose [RMD]), and mice, given oral voriconazole doses of 10 to 100 mg per kg of body weight (0.1 to 1.4 times the RMD), showed signs of hepatocellular adenomas and hepatocellular carcinomas.

Mutagenicity

Voriconazole demonstrated clastogenic activity in human lymphocyte cultures *in vitro*. Voriconazole was not genotoxic in the Ames assay, CHO assay, the mouse micronucleus assay or the DNA repair test.

Pregnancy/Reproduction

Pregnancy—Voriconazole crosses the placenta and has been shown to cause fetal harm. Risk benefit must be carefully considered when this medication is required in life-threatening situations or in serious diseases for which other medications cannot be used or are ineffective.

Women of childbearing potential should use effective contraception during treatment.

Voriconazole was teratogenic in rats from 10 mg per kg of body weight (0.3 times the RMD on a mg per m^2 basis) and embryotoxic in rabbits at 100 mg per kg of body weight (6 times the RMD).

FDA Pregnancy Category D.

Breast-feeding

It is not known if voriconazole is distributed in human milk. However, voriconazole should not be used by nursing mothers unless the benefit clearly outweighs the risk.

Pediatrics

Safety and efficacy have not been established in patients less than 12 years of age.

Geriatrics

Appropriate studies performed to date have not demonstrated geriatrics-specific problems that would limit the usefulness of voriconazole in the elderly.

Pharmacogenetics

In a multiple oral dose study, the mean C_{max} and AUC for healthy young females were 83% and 113% higher, respectively, than in healthy young males (18 to 45 years of age). In the same study no significant differences in the mean C_{max} and AUC were observed between healthy elderly males and healthy elderly females (> 65 years of age). No dosage adjustment based on gender is needed.

Drug interactions and/or related problems

The following drug interactions and/or related problems have been selected on the basis of their potential clinical significance (possible

mechanism in parentheses where appropriate)—not necessarily inclusive (» = major clinical significance):

Note: Combinations containing any of the following medications, depending on the amount present, may also interact with this medication.

» Alprazolam or
» Midazolam or
» Triazolam
(may increase plasma concentrations of these drugs; may prolong the sedative effect; dosage adjustment should be considered.)

» Astemizole or
» Cisapride or
» Pimozide or
» Quinidine or
» Terfenadine
(may result in inhibition of the metabolism of these drugs; increased plasma concentrations of these drugs can lead to QT prolongation and rare occurrences of torsade de pointes; coadministration is **contraindicated**)

» Barbiturates, long acting or
» Carbamazepine
(may significantly decrease plasma voriconazole concentrations; coadministration is **contraindicated**)

» Calcium channel blockers, dihydropyridine, including:
» Felodipine
(plasma concentrations may be increased; dosage adjustment may be necessary)

Cimetidine
(may increase C_{max} and AUC of voriconazole; no dosage adjustment is required)

» Coumarin anticoagulants, oral, such as:
» Warfarin
(plasma concentrations may be increased; prothrombin time or other anti-coagulation tests should be monitored at close intervals and anticoagulant dosage adjusted accordingly)

» Cyclosporine or
» Tacrolimus
(may increase C_{max} and AUC of cyclosporine and tacrolimus; careful monitoring and/or dosage adjustment is needed; when voriconazole is discontinued, cyclosporine levels should be frequently monitored and dose increased as necessary)

» Efavirenz
(concurrent use of efavirenz and voriconazole significantly decreases voriconazole plasma concentrations and voriconazole significantly increases efavirenz plasma concentrations; coadministration is **contraindicated**)

» Ergot alkaloids
(may increase plasma concentrations of ergot alkaloids; coadministration is **contraindicated**)

Glipizide or
Glyburide or
Oral hypoglycemics, sulfonylurea, other, metabolized by CYP2C9 or
Tolbutamide
(plasma concentrations may be increased; may lead to hypoglycemia; dosage adjustment and/or frequent monitoring of blood glucose may be required)

» HMG CoA reductase inhibitors (statins) including:
» Lovastatin or
» Other statins metabolized by CYP3A4
(plasma concentrations may be increased; recommended dose adjustment of the statin during coadministration)

» Methadone
(increased plasma concentrations of methadone with concomitant use have been associated with toxicity including QT prolongation; frequent monitoring for adverse events and toxicity recommended during coadministration; dose reduction of methadone may be needed)

Non-nucleoside reverse transcriptase inhibitors (NNRTIs), other, such as:
Delavirdine
(CYP3A4 inhibition or CYP450 induction may occur; frequent monitoring for adverse events and toxicity related to voriconazole **and** careful assessment of voriconazole effectiveness is recommended when voriconazole is coadministered with other NNRTIs)

Phenytoin
(may decrease the C_{max} and AUC of voriconazole; the maintenance dose of voriconazole may need to be increased)
(voriconazole may increase the C_{max} and AUC of phenytoin; frequent monitoring of plasma phenytoin concentrations and phenytoin-related adverse effects is recommended)

» Protease inhibitors, such as:
Amprenavir or
Nelfinavir or
Saquinavir
(voriconazole may inhibit the metabolism of protease inhibitors and protease inhibitors may inhibit the metabolism of voriconazole; plasma concentrations of voriconazole and protease inhibitors may be increased)

Protease inhibitors, other
(*In vitro* studies demonstrate potential for inhibition of voriconazole metabolism [CYP3A4 inhibition] which may increase voriconazole exposure; frequent monitoring for adverse events and toxicity related to voriconazole is recommended when coadministered with other HIV protease inhibitors)

Proton pump inhibitors including:
Omeprazole or
Other proton pump inhibitors that are CYP2C19 inhibitors
(concomitant administration with voriconazole may increase the C_{max} and AUC of omeprazole; when initiating voriconazole in patients already receiving omeprazole doses of 40 mg or greater, it is recommended that the omeprazole dose be reduced by one half)
(the metabolism of other proton pump inhibitors that are CYP2C19 substrates also may be inhibited by voriconazole and may result in increased plasma concentrations of these drugs)

» Rifabutin
(rifabutin may decrease the C_{max} and AUC of voriconazole and voriconazole increases the C_{max} and AUC of rifabutin; coadministration is **contraindicated**)

» Rifampin
(may decrease C_{max} and AUC of voriconazole; increasing the voriconazole dose will not adequately compensate for this effect; coadministration is **contraindicated**)

» Ritonavir
(concurrent administration of ritonavir 400 mg Q12h and voriconazole significantly decreases plasma voriconazole concentrations; coadministration is **contraindicated**)

» Sirolimus
(may increase C_{max} and AUC of sirolimus; coadministration is **contraindicated**)

Vinca alkaloids, metabolized by CYP3A4, such as:
Vinblastine or
Vincristine
(plasma concentrations may be increased and may lead to neurotoxicity; frequent monitoring for adverse events and toxicity related to vinca alkaloids [e.g., neurotoxicity] and dose adjustment of the vinca alkaloid recommended with concomitant use)

Laboratory value alterations

The following have been selected on the basis of their potential clinical significance (possible effect in parentheses where appropriate)—not necessarily inclusive (» = major clinical significance).

With physiology/laboratory test values
Alanine aminotransferase (ALT [SGPT]) or
Alkaline phosphatase or
Aspartate aminotransferase (AST [SGOT]) or
Bilirubin or
Creatinine or
Hepatic enzymes
(levels may be increased)

Potassium, serum
(values may be decreased)

Note: Electrolyte disturbances such as hypokalemia, hypomagnesemia, and hypocalcemia should be corrected prior to initiation of voriconazole therapy.

Medical considerations/Contraindications

The medical considerations/contraindications included have been selected on the basis of their potential clinical significance (reasons given in parentheses where appropriate)—not necessarily inclusive (» = major clinical significance).

Except under special circumstances, this medication should not be used when the following medical problems exist:

» Hypersensitivity to voriconazole or any of its excipients or other azoles.

Galactose intolerance or
Glucose-galactose malabsorption or

Lapp lactase deficiency
(voriconazole tablets contain lactose and should not be given to patients with these rare hereditary conditions)

Risk-benefit should be considered when the following medical problems exist:

Hepatic insufficiency
(dosage adjustment may be necessary)

Proarrhythmic conditions
(should be used with caution in patients with a history of cardiotoxic chemotherapy, cardiomyopathy, and hypokalemia)

Renal dysfunction, moderate to severe (creatinine clearance less than 50 mL per min)
(accumulation of the intravenous vehicle may occur; oral voriconazole is recommended)

Patient monitoring

The following may be especially important in patient monitoring (other tests may be warranted in some patients, depending on condition; » = major clinical significance):

Blood glucose levels
(may be necessary when coadministered with sulfonylureas)

» Cyclosporine blood levels or
» Tacrolimus blood levels
(frequent monitoring of blood levels during and after treatment with voriconazole is recommended)

» Electrolytes
(rigorous attempts to correct potassium, magnesium and calcium should be made before starting voriconazole)

Liver function
(tests should be performed at the start and during the course of voriconazole therapy; discontinuation of therapy is recommended if signs or symptoms of liver disease develop)

» Phenytoin monitoring
(frequent monitoring of phenytoin levels and adverse effects in patients taking phenytoin is recommended)

Prothrombin time
(may be necessary when coadministered with warfarin or oral coumarin anticoagulants)

» Serum creatinine
(may be especially important in patients whose creatinine clearance is less than 50 mL per min and still use intravenous voriconazole)

Visual function
(if treatment continues beyond 28 days, visual function including visual acuity, visual field, and color perception should be monitored)

Side/Adverse Effects

The following side/adverse effects have been selected on the basis of their potential clinical significance (possible signs and symptoms in parentheses where appropriate)—not necessarily inclusive:

Note: Voriconazole treatment-related visual disturbances, such as blurred vision and seeing bright spots or wavy lines are common. These visual disturbances usually occur within approximately 30 minutes after taking the medication and are generally mild and rarely resulted in discontinuation of therapy. Visual disturbances may be associated with higher plasma concentrations and/or doses.

Dermatological reactions were common in patients treated with voriconazole. The majority of rashes were of mild to moderate severity. If patients develop a rash they should be monitored closely and consideration given to discontinuation of voriconazole. Cases of photosensitivity reactions appear to be more likely to occur with long term treatment. Patients have rarely developed serious cutaneous reactions, including Stevens-Johnson syndrome, toxic epidermal necrolysis and erythema multiforme during treatment with voriconazole.

Those indicating need for medical attention

Incidence more frequent

Rash

Incidence less frequent

Cholestatic jaundice (chills; clay-colored stools; dark urine; dizziness; fever; headache; itching; loss of appetite; nausea, abdominal or stomach pain; area rash; unpleasant breath odor; unusual tiredness or weakness; vomiting of blood; yellow eyes or skin); ***hypertension*** (blurred vision; dizziness; nervousness; headache; pounding in the ears; slow or fast heartbeat); ***hypokalemia*** (convulsions; decreased urine; dry mouth; irregular heartbeat; increased thirst; loss of appetite; mood changes; muscle pain or cramps; nausea or vomiting; numbness or tingling in hands, feet, or lips; shortness of breath; unusual tiredness or weakness); ***hypomagnesemia*** (drowsiness; loss of appetite; mood or mental changes; muscle spasms [tetany] or twitching; seizures; nausea or vomiting; trembling; unusual tiredness or weakness); ***hypotension*** (blurred vision; confusion; dizziness, faintness, or lightheadedness when getting up from a lying or sitting position; suddenly sweating); ***liver function tests, abnormal; maculopapular rash*** (rash with flat lesions or small raised lesions on the skin); ***peripheral edema*** (bloating or swelling of face, arms, hands, lower legs, or feet; rapid weight gain; tingling of hands or feet; unusual weight gain or loss); ***tachycardia*** (fast, pounding, or irregular heartbeat or pulse); ***vasodilation***

Incidence rare

Anemia (pale skin; troubled breathing with exertion; unusual bleeding or bruising; unusual tiredness or weakness); ***bilirubinemia*** (yellow eyes or skin); ***eye hemorrhage*** (blood in eye; eye pain; redness in whites of eyes); ***jaundice*** (chills; clay-colored stools; dark urine; dizziness; fever; headache; itching; loss of appetite; nausea; abdominal or stomach pain; area rash; unpleasant breath odor; unusual tiredness or weakness; vomiting of blood; yellow eyes or skin); ***kidney function, abnormal; kidney failure, acute; leukopenia*** (black, tarry stools; chest pain; chills; cough; fever; painful or difficult urination; shortness of breath; sore throat; sores, ulcers, or white spots on lips or in mouth; swollen glands; unusual bleeding or bruising; unusual tiredness or weakness); ***pancytopenia*** (high fever; chills; unexplained bleeding or bruising; bloody, black, or tarry stools; pale skin; unusual tiredness or weakness; cough; shortness of breath; sores, ulcers, or white spots on lips or in mouth; swollen glands); ***QT prolongation*** (irregular heartbeat; recurrent fainting); ***thrombocytopenia*** (black, tarry stools; bleeding gums; blood in urine or stools; pinpoint red spots on skin; unusual bleeding or bruising); ***torsade de pointes*** (chest pain or discomfort; irregular or slow heart rate; fainting; shortness of breath)

Those indicating need for medical attention only if they continue or are bothersome

Incidence more frequent

Abnormal vision (changes in vision); ***fever; nausea***

Incidence less frequent

Abdominal pain (stomach pain); ***chills*** (feeling unusually cold, shivering); ***chromatopsia*** (disturbance in vision); ***diarrhea; dizziness; dry mouth; headache; hallucinations*** (seeing things that are not there); ***photophobia*** (blurred vision; change in color vision; difficulty seeing at night; increased sensitivity of eyes to sunlight); ***pruritus*** (itching skin); ***vomiting***

Incidence rare

Chest pain

Overdose

For more information on the management of overdose or unintentional ingestion, **contact a poison control center** (see *Poison Control Center Listing*).

Clinical effects of overdose

The following effects have been selected on the basis of their potential clinical significance (possible signs and symptoms in parentheses where appropriate)—not necessarily inclusive:

Photophobia (blurred vision, change in color vision, difficulty seeing at night, increased sensitivity of eyes to sunlight)

Treatment of overdose

There is no antidote for voriconazole overdose.

To enhance elimination—
Hemodialysis may assist in the removal of voriconazole and SBECD from the body. Voriconazole is hemodialyzed with clearance of 121 mL per min. The intravenous vehicle, SBECD, is hemodialyzed with clearance of 55 mL per min.

Supportive care—
Patients in whom intentional overdose is confirmed or suspected should be referred for psychiatric consultation.

Patient Consultation

As an aid to patient consultation, refer to *Advice for the Patient, Voriconazole (Systemic)*.

In providing consultation, consider emphasizing the following selected information (» = major clinical significance):

Before using this medication

» Conditions affecting use, especially:
Hypersensitivity to voriconazole or any of its excipients or other azole antifungals

Pregnancy—Crosses the placenta and has been shown to cause fetal harm; patient should be apprised of potential hazard to the fetus

Breast-feeding—Unknown if distributed into breast milk; should not be used in nursing mothers unless benefit outweighs risk

Other medications, especially alprazolam, astemizole, long acting barbiturates, dihydropyridine calcium channel blockers, carbamazepine, cisapride, coumarin anticoagulants, cyclosporine, efavirenz, ergot alkaloids, HMG CoA reductase inhibitors, methadone, midazolam, pimozide, protease inhibitors, quinidine, rifabutin, rifampin, ritonavir, sirolimus, tacrolimus, terfenadine, triazolam

Proper use of this medication

» Proper dosing

Missed dose: Taking as soon as possible; not taking if almost time for next scheduled dose; not doubling doses

» Proper storage

Precautions while using this medication

Caution if changes in vision occur

Avoid strong direct sunlight while taking this medication

For women of childbearing potential—Using effective contraception during treatment with voriconazole

Side/adverse effects

Signs of potential side effects, especially abnormal kidney function, acute kidney failure, anemia, bilirubinemia, cholestatic jaundice, hypertension, hypokalemia, hypomagnesemia, hypotension, leukopenia, maculopapular rash, pancytopenia, peripheral edema, rash, tachycardia, thrombocytopenia, or vasodilation

General Dosing Information

Prior to therapy with voriconazole, fungal culture specimens and other relevant laboratory studies should be obtained to identify causative organisms. Therapy may be instituted before the laboratory results are known. However, once these results become available, antifungal therapy should be adjusted accordingly.

Duration of therapy should be based on the severity of the patient's underlying disease, recovery from immunosuppression, and clinical response.

Women of childbearing potential should use effective contraception during treatment with voriconazole.

In patients with moderate to severe renal dysfunction (creatinine clearance less than 50 mL/min) accumulation of the intravenous vehicle, SBECD, occurs. Oral voriconazole should be administered unless risk/benefit assessment justifies use of intravenous voriconazole.

For parenteral dosing forms:

Voriconazole is NOT for IV bolus injection.

The reconstituted solution can be diluted with 0.9% Sodium Chloride; Lactated Ringers; 5% Dextrose and Lactated Ringers; 5% Dextrose and 0.45% Sodium Chloride; 5% Dextrose; 5% Dextrose and 20 mEq Potassium Chloride; 0.45% Sodium Chloride; or 5% Dextrose and 0.9% Sodium Chloride. The compatibility of voriconazole with diluents other than those described above is unknown.

Diet/Nutrition

Tablets or oral suspension should be taken at least one hour before, or one hour following, a meal.

Oral Dosage Forms

VORICONAZOLE FOR ORAL SUSPENSION

Usual adult dose

Aspergillosis (treatment) or
Candidiasis, abdominal (treatment) or
Candidiasis, bladder wall (treatment) or
Candidiasis, disseminated (treatment) or
Candidiasis, esophageal (treatment) or
Candidiasis, kidney (treatment)
Fungal infections, serious (treatment)—

Adult patients weighing more than 40 kg—

Oral, 200-mg maintenance dose every 12 hours taken at least one hour before, or one hour following, a meal. If patient response is inadequate, the oral maintenance dose may be increased to 300 mg every 12 hours. If patient is unable to tolerate treatment, reduce the oral maintenance dose by 50-mg increments to a minimum of 200 mg every 12 hours.

Concomitantly with phenytoin in adult patients weighing more than 40 kg—

Oral, 400-mg maintenance dose every 12 hours.

Adult patients weighing less than 40 kg—

Oral, 100-mg maintenance dose every 12 hours taken at least one hour before, or one hour following, a meal. If patient response is inadequate, the oral maintenance dose may be increased to 150 mg every 12 hours. If patient is unable to tolerate treatment, reduce the oral maintenance dose to 100 mg every 12 hours.

Concomitantly with phenytoin in adult patients weighing less than 40 kg—

Oral, 200-mg maintenance dose every 12 hours.

Note: Hepatic insufficiency: No dose adjustment is necessary in patients with baseline liver function tests (ALT, AST) up to 5 times the upper limit of normal. The maintenance dose should be halved in patients with mild to moderate hepatic cirrhosis (Child-Pugh Class A and B).

Renal insufficiency: No adjustment is necessary for **oral** dosing in patients with mild to severe renal impairment.

Usual pediatric dose

Safety and effectiveness have not been established in children less than 12 years of age.

Usual geriatric dose

See *Usual adult dose*.

Strength(s) usually available

U.S.—

40 mg per mL when reconstituted (Rx) [*VFEND* (colloidal silicon dioxide; titanium dioxide; xanthan gum; sodium citrate dihydrate; sodium benzoate; anhydrous citric acid; natural orange flavor; sucrose)].

Canada—

Not commercially available

Packaging and storage

Powder for suspension: Store in a refrigerator at 2 to 8 °C (36 to 46°F) before reconstitution.

Reconstituted suspension: Store at 15 to 30 °C (59 to 86°F) after reconstitution. Do not refrigerate or freeze. Keep in tightly closed container.

Preparation of dosage form

Tap the bottle to release the powder.

Add 46 mL of water to the bottle.

Shake the closed bottle vigorously for about one minute.

Remove child-resistant cap and push bottle adaptor into the neck of the bottle. Replace the cap.

Write the date of expiration of the reconstituted suspension on the bottle label.

Stability

Powder for suspension: The shelf-life of the powder for oral suspension is 18 months.

Reconstituted suspension: The shelf-life of the reconstituted suspension is 14 days. Any remaining suspension should be discarded 14 days after reconstitution.

Auxiliary labeling

- Shake well. Discard after 14 days.
- Take at least one hour before or one hour following a meal.
- May cause changes to vision including blurring and/or photophobia.
- Avoid driving at night while taking this medication.
- Avoid potentially hazardous tasks, such as driving or operating machinery if any change in vision is perceived.
- Avoid strong direct sunlight while taking this medication.

Note

Use oral dispenser supplied to administer reconstituted oral suspension.

Do not mix the reconstituted oral suspension with any other medication or additional flavoring agent.

VORICONAZOLE TABLETS

Usual adult dose

Aspergillosis (treatment) or
Candidiasis, abdominal (treatment) or
Candidiasis, bladder wall (treatment) or
Candidiasis, disseminated (treatment) or
Candidiasis, esophageal (treatment) or
Candidiasis, kidney (treatment)
Fungal infections, serious (treatment)—

Adult patients weighing more than 40 kg—

Oral, 200-mg maintenance dose every 12 hours taken at least one hour before, or one hour following, a meal. If patient response is inadequate, the oral maintenance dose may be increased to 300 mg every 12 hours. If patient is unable to tolerate treatment, reduce the oral maintenance dose by 50-mg increments to a minimum of 200 mg every 12 hours.

Concomitantly with phenytoin in adult patients weighing more than 40 kg—

Oral, 400-mg maintenance dose every 12 hours.

Adult patients weighing less than 40 kg—

Oral, 100-mg maintenance dose every 12 hours taken at least one hour before, or one hour following, a meal. If patient response is inadequate, the oral maintenance dose may be increased to 150 mg every 12 hours. If patient is unable to tolerate treatment, reduce the oral maintenance dose to 100 mg every 12 hours.

Concomitantly with phenytoin in adult patients weighing less than 40 kg—

Oral, 200-mg maintenance dose every 12 hours.

Note: Hepatic insufficiency: No dose adjustment is necessary in patients with baseline liver function tests (ALT, AST) up to 5 times the upper limit of normal. The maintenance dose should be halved in patients with mild to moderate hepatic cirrhosis (Child-Pugh Class A and B).

Renal insufficiency: No adjustment is necessary for **oral** dosing in patients with mild to severe renal impairment.

Usual pediatric dose
Safety and effectiveness have not been established in children less than 12 years of age.

Usual geriatric dose
See *Usual adult dose*.

Strength(s) usually available
U.S.—

50 mg (Rx) [*VFEND* (film-coated; lactose monohydrate; pregelatinized starch; croscarmellose sodium; povidone; magnesium stearate; hypromellose; titanium dioxide; triacetin)].

200 mg (Rx) [*VFEND* (film-coated; lactose monohydrate; pregelatinized starch; croscarmellose sodium; povidone; magnesium stearate; hypromellose; titanium dioxide; triacetin)].

Canada—

Not commercially available

Packaging and storage
Store between 15 and 30 °C (59 and 86 °F).

Auxiliary labeling
• Take at least one hour before or one hour following a meal.
• May cause changes to vision including blurring and/or photophobia. Avoid driving at night while taking this medication.
• Avoid potentially hazardous tasks, such as driving or operating machinery if any change in vision is perceived.
• Avoid strong direct sunlight while taking this medication.

Parenteral Dosage Forms

VORICONAZOLE FOR INJECTION

Usual adult dose
Antifungal—

Intravenous infusion, loading dose of 6 mg per kg of body weight every 12 hours for two doses, followed by a maintenance dose of 4 mg per kg of body weight every 12 hours. Administer at a maximum rate of 3 mg per kg of body weight per hour over 1 to 2 hours. If patient is unable to tolerate treatment, reduce the intravenous maintenance dose to 3 mg per kg of body weight every 12 hours. See *Oral Dosage Forms* when the patient can tolerate medication given by mouth.

Concomitantly with phenytoin—

Intravenous infusion, maintenance dose of 5 mg per kg of body weight every 12 hours.

Candidiasis, abdominal (treatment) or
Candidiasis, bladder wall (treatment) or
Candidiasis, disseminated (treatment) or
Candidiasis, kidney (treatment)—

Intravenous infusion, loading dose of 6 mg per kg of body weight every 12 hours for the first 24 hours, followed by a maintenance dose of 4 mg per kg of body weight every 12 hours. Patients should be treated for at least 14 days following resolution of symptoms or following last positive culture, whichever is longer. If patient is unable to tolerate treatment, reduce the intravenous maintenance dose to 3 mg per kg of body weight every 12 hours. See *Oral Dosage Forms* when the patient can tolerate medication given by mouth.

Note: In clinical trials, patients with candidemia received 3 mg per kg of body weight every 12 hours as primary therapy, while patients with other deep tissue *Candida* infections received 4 mg per kg of body weight as salvage therapy. Appropriate dose should be based on the severity and nature of the infection.

Intravenous infusion treatment has not been evaluated in patients with esophageal candidiasis.

Note: The following dose adjustments are recommended in patients with varying degrees of hepatic insufficiency:
• Baseline liver function tests (ALT, AST) up to 5 times the upper limit of normal—No dose adjustment is necessary
• Mild to moderate hepatic cirrhosis—use standard loading dose regimens but half the standard maintenance dose
• Severe hepatic cirrhosis—should be used only if the benefit outweighs the potential risk

Renal impairment—No dose adjustment needed for patients on hemodialysis

Usual pediatric dose
Safety and effectiveness have not been established in children less than 12 years of age.

Usual geriatric dose
See *Usual adult dose*.

Strength(s) usually available
U.S.—

200 mg of voriconazole lyophilized powder per single-use unpreserved vial (Rx) [*VFEND* (3200 mg sulfobutyl ether beta-cyclodextrin sodium [SBECD])].

Canada—

Not commercially available

Packaging and storage
Store the lyophilized drug between 15 and 30 °C (59 and 86 °F).
The reconstituted solution should be stored between 2 and 8 °C (36 and 46 °F) not longer than 24 hours.

Preparation of dosage form
The voriconazole lyophilized powder is reconstituted by adding 19 mL of Water for Injection to obtain 20 mL of clear concentrate containing 10 mg per mL of voriconazole. Shake the vial until all the powder is dissolved. Do not administer the reconstituted solution without further dilution. The reconstituted solution must be further diluted by calculating the volume of 10 mg per mL of voriconazole required based on the patient's weight. Then, withdraw and discard at least an equal volume of diluent from the infusion bag or bottle to be used to allow for the required volume of voriconazole to be added. The volume of diluent remaining in the bag or bottle should be such that when the 10 mg per mL voriconazole concentrate is added, the final concentration is not less than 0.5 mg per mL nor greater than 5 mg per mL. Using a syringe, withdraw the required volume of voriconazole from the appropriate number of vials and add to the infusion bag or bottle. Discard any partially used vials.

Stability
The reconstituted solution should be used immediately. If not used immediately, in-use storage times and conditions prior to use are the responsibility of the user and should not be longer than 24 hours at 2 and 8 °C (36 and 46 °F).

Incompatibilities
Voriconazole must not be infused into the same line concomitantly with other drug infusions, including parenteral nutrition such as Aminofusin 10% Plus. Aminofusin 10% Plus is physically incompatible, with an increase in subvisible particulate matter after 24 hours storage at 4 °C.

Voriconazole must not be infused simultaneously with other drug infusions, including parenteral nutrition (e.g., Aminofusin 10% Plus) or infusions of blood products.

Voriconazole must not be diluted with 4.2% Sodium Bicarbonate infusion. The mildly alkaline nature of this diluent caused slight degradation of voriconazole after 24 hours storage at room temperature. Although refrigerated storage is recommended following reconstitution, use of this diluent is not recommended as a precautionary measure. Compatibility with other concentrations is unknown.

Auxiliary labeling
• The reconstituted solution should be visually inspected for particulate matter and discoloration prior to administration. Samples containing visible particulates or samples that are discolored should not be used.
• This product is for single use only and any unused solution should be discarded.

Revised: 04/12/2005
Developed: 10/22/2003

WARFARIN—See *Anticoagulants (Systemic)*

ZAFIRLUKAST Systemic†

VA CLASSIFICATION (Primary): RE180

Commonly used brand name(s): *Accolate.*

Note: For a listing of dosage forms and brand names by country availability, see *Dosage Forms* section(s).

†Not commercially available in Canada.

Category

Antiasthmatic (leukotriene receptor antagonist).

Indications

Accepted

Asthma, chronic (prophylaxis and treatment)—Zafirlukast is indicated in patients with chronic asthma to improve daytime asthma symptoms, forced expiratory volume in 1 second (FEV_1), and morning peak expiratory flow rates, and to decrease nighttime awakenings, mornings with asthma symptoms, and use of a rescue $beta_2$ agonist. When used daily with an as-needed, inhaled $beta_2$ agonist in patients with mild-to-moderate asthma, zafirlukast significantly reduces asthma symptoms and use of an as-needed, inhaled $beta_2$ agonist as compared with use of an as-needed, inhaled $beta_2$ agonist alone.

Only patients with mild-to-moderate asthma have been treated with zafirlukast in clinical trials; therefore, its use in the management of patients with more severe asthma and in those receiving antiasthma therapy other than as-needed, inhaled $beta_2$ agonists remains to be studied, as does use of zafirlukast as an oral or inhaled corticosteroid-sparing agent.

Unaccepted

Zafirlukast is not indicated for the treatment of bronchospasm in acute asthma attacks, including status asthmaticus; however, use of zafirlukast can be continued during an acute exacerbation.

Pharmacology/Pharmacokinetics

Physicochemical characteristics

Molecular weight—575.69.

Mechanism of action/Effect

Zafirlukast is a selective and competitive receptor antagonist of the cysteinyl leukotrienes D_4 and E_4. The cysteinyl leukotrienes, originally described as slow-reacting substances of anaphylaxis, produce airway edema, smooth muscle constriction, and altered cellular activity associated with the inflammatory process, all of which are associated with the pathophysiology of asthma. In humans, pretreatment with single oral doses of zafirlukast inhibited bronchoconstriction caused by sulfur dioxide and cold air and reduced the early- and late-phase reaction in patients with asthma caused by inhalation of various antigens, such as grass, cat dander, and ragweed. Zafirlukast reduced the increase in bronchial hyperresponsiveness to inhaled histamine that followed inhaled allergen challenge.

Absorption

Rapid.

Bioavailability is reduced following administration with a high-fat or high-protein meal.

Protein binding

High (more than 99% bound to plasma proteins, predominantly albumin).

Biotransformation

Hepatic; extensively metabolized by the cytochrome P450 2C9 enzyme pathway to metabolites that are 90 times less potent antagonists of leukotriene D_4 receptors than zafirlukast *in vitro* .

Half-life

Elimination—The mean terminal elimination half-life is approximately 10 hours.

Onset of action

In clinical trials, improvement in asthma symptoms was seen within 1 week of starting treatment with zafirlukast.

Time to peak plasma concentration

3 hours after dosing.

Mean peak plasma concentration reached is 2.5 hours in children (between 7 and 11 years of age).

Elimination

Fecal—Approximately 90%.

Renal—Approximately 10%.

Precautions to Consider

Carcinogenicity/Tumorigenicity

A 2-year study in mice given zafirlukast orally in doses of 10, 100, and 300 mg per kg of body weight (mg/kg) per day showed a greater incidence of hepatocellular adenomas in males and whole-body histocytic sarcomas in females given the highest dose, as compared with controls. Plasma concentrations of zafirlukast following the 100- and 300-mg-per-kg-per-day doses were approximately 70 and 220 times, respectively, the plasma concentrations found at the maximum recommended human daily oral dose.

A 2-year study in rats given zafirlukast orally in doses of 40, 400, and 2000 mg/kg per day found a greater incidence of urinary bladder transitional cell papillomas at doses of 2000 mg/kg per day, as compared with controls. Plasma concentrations of zafirlukast following the 400- and 2000-mg-per-kg-per-day doses were approximately 170 and 200 times, respectively, the plasma concentrations found at the maximum recommended human daily oral dose.

Mutagenicity

Zafirlukast was not mutagenic in reverse or forward point mutation assays or in human and rat assays for chromosomal abnormalities.

Pregnancy/Reproduction

Fertility—Reproduction studies in rats given oral zafirlukast in doses approximately 400 times the maximum recommended human daily oral dose on a mcg per square meter of body surface area (mcg/m²) basis showed no effect on fertility.

Pregnancy—Adequate and well-controlled studies have not been done in humans.

No teratogenicity was observed in mice, rats, or monkeys given oral zafirlukast in doses up to approximately 160, 400, and 800 times the maximum recommended human daily oral dose on a mg per square meter of body surface area (mg/m²) basis.

In rats given oral doses of 2000 mg/kg per day, maternal toxicity and deaths were seen, as well as an increased incidence of early fetal resorptions. In monkeys, the same dose resulted in maternal toxicity and an increased incidence of spontaneous abortions.

FDA Pregnancy Category B.

Breast-feeding

Zafirlukast is distributed into human breast milk. Steady-state concentrations of zafirlukast in breast milk and plasma were 50 and 255 nanograms per mL, respectively, after administration of 40 mg two times a day. Because of the potential for tumorigenicity and adverse effects in the neonate shown in animal studies, use of zafirlukast during breast-feeding is not recommended.

Pediatrics

Appropriate studies on the relationship of age to the effects of zafirlukast have not been performed in the pediatric population. Safety and efficacy in children up to 7 years of age have not been established.

Geriatrics

In patients 65 years of age and older, the clearance of zafirlukast is reduced, resulting in peak plasma concentration and area under the plasma concentration-time curve (AUC) values that are approximately two to three times greater than those of younger patients. However, the recommended dose of 20 mg two times a day did not result in increased adverse effects or withdrawal from the study in elderly patients during clinical trials when compared with patients younger than 65 years of age.

In clinical trials, a greater incidence of mild or moderate infections, predominantly affecting the respiratory tract, occurred in patients older than 55 years of age treated with zafirlukast, as compared with other age groups and placebo-treated patients. The number of infections was proportional to the amount, in milligrams, of zafirlukast administered and was associated with concurrent use of inhaled corticosteroids. The clinical significance of this finding is unknown.

Drug interactions and/or related problems

The following drug interactions and/or related problems have been selected on the basis of their potential clinical significance (possible mechanism in parentheses where appropriate)—not necessarily inclusive (» = major clinical significance):

Note: In *in vitro* studies using human liver microsomes, zafirlukast has been shown to inhibit the cytochrome P450 3A4 and 2C9 isoenzymes at concentrations close to those achieved following recommended dosing.

In a 3-week study in females taking oral contraceptives, 40 mg of zafirlukast two times a day had no significant effect on ethinyl estradiol plasma concentrations or contraceptive efficacy.

Aspirin
(concurrent administration of 40 mg a day of zafirlukast with aspirin at a dosage of 650 mg four times a day increased mean plasma concentrations of zafirlukast by approximately 45%)

Astemizole or
Cisapride or
Cyclosporine or
Dihydropyridine calcium channel blocking agents, such as:
Felodipine
Isradipine
Nicardipine
Nifedipine
Nimodipine
(although studies have not been done with zafirlukast and medications known to be metabolized by the cytochrome P450 3A4 isoenzyme, such as astemizole, cisapride, cyclosporine, and the dihydropyridine calcium channel blocking agents, concurrent use of these medications with zafirlukast should be monitored carefully, since zafirlukast is known to inhibit cytochrome P450 3A4 *in vitro*)

Carbamazepine or
Phenytoin or
Tolbutamide
(although studies have not been done with zafirlukast and medications known to be metabolized by the cytochrome P450 2C9 isoenzyme, such as carbamazepine, phenytoin, and tolbutamide, patients in whom these medications are coadministered with zafirlukast should be appropriately monitored clinically, since zafirlukast is known to inhibit cytochrome P450 2C9 *in vitro*)

Erythromycin
(administration of a single 40-mg dose of zafirlukast during steady-state erythromycin therapy resulted in a 40% decrease in the mean plasma concentration of zafirlukast, due to decreased zafirlukast bioavailability)

Terfenadine
(concurrent administration of zafirlukast with terfenadine resulted in a 66% and 54% decrease in the mean peak plasma concentration and area under the plasma concentration-time curve, respectively, of zafirlukast; no effect was observed on terfenadine plasma concentrations or electrocardiogram results)

Theophylline
(concurrent administration of 80 mg a day of zafirlukast with a single 6-mg-per-kg dose of theophylline decreased the mean plasma concentration of zafirlukast by approximately 30%; no effect on theophylline plasma concentration was observed)

» Warfarin
(the concurrent use of a single 25-mg warfarin dose with multiple doses of zafirlukast resulted in an increase of approximately 35% in the mean prothrombin time, due to an inhibition of the cytochrome P450 2C9 isoenzyme; prothrombin times should be monitored closely and warfarin dose adjusted accordingly)

Side/Adverse Effects

Note: In clinical trials, a greater incidence of mild or moderate infections, predominantly affecting the respiratory tract, occurred in patients older than 55 years of age treated with zafirlukast, as compared with other age groups and placebo-treated patients. The number of infections was proportional to the amount, in milligrams, of zafirlukast administered and was associated with concurrent use of inhaled corticosteroids. The clinical significance of this finding is unknown.

Rarely, elevation of one or more hepatic transaminases has occurred in patients receiving zafirlukast at doses four times higher than the recommended dose during controlled clinical trials. Most patients were asymptomatic. Hepatic enzyme values returned to normal after a variable period of time following discontinuation of zafirlukast. Rare cases of symptomatic hepatitis and hyperbilirubinemia have been reported in patients who received the recommended dosage of zafirlukast. In these patients, the hepatic transaminase elevations returned to normal or near-normal after discontinuation of the medication.

Note: In rare cases, patients receiving zafirlukast therapy may present with systemic eosinophilia. Systemic eosinophilia sometimes is characterized by clinical features of vasculitis consistent with Churg-Strauss syndrome, a condition that often is treated with systemic corticosteroid therapy. These events usually, but not always, have been associated with the reduction of oral corticosteroid therapy. Churg-Strauss syndrome is a systemic eosinophilic vasculitis, which may present as generalized, flu-like symptoms (fever, muscle aches or pains, and weight loss), eosinophilia, vasculitic rash, worsening pulmonary symptoms, cardiac complications, or neuropathy. If left untreated, Churg-Strauss syndrome can result in damage to major organs and death. Although a causal relationship between the use of zafirlukast and the development of Churg-Strauss syndrome has not been established, adult asthma patients should be monitored carefully, especially when corticosteroid therapy is being reduced or discontinued.

The following side/adverse effects have been selected on the basis of their potential clinical significance (possible signs and symptoms in parentheses where appropriate)—not necessarily inclusive:

Those indicating need for medical attention only if they continue or are bothersome

Incidence less frequent
Headache; nausea

Patient Consultation

As an aid to patient consultation, refer to *Advice for the Patient, Zafirlukast (Systemic)*.

In providing consultation, consider emphasizing the following selected information (» = major clinical significance):

Before using this medication

» Conditions affecting use, especially:
Breast-feeding—Distributed into breast milk; use not recommended
Use in the elderly—Mild to moderate respiratory infections may be more likely to develop in patients older than 55 years of age; whether this is related to taking zafirlukast or to other factors, such as use of inhaled corticosteroids, is not clear
Other medications, especially warfarin

Proper use of this medication

» Importance of not using this medication to treat acute asthma symptoms
» Taking medication on an empty stomach, 1 hour before or 2 hours after meals
» Proper dosing
Missed dose: Taking as soon as possible; if almost time for next dose, skipping missed dose; not doubling doses
» Proper storage

Precautions while using this medication

» Compliance with therapy by using every day in regularly spaced doses, even during symptom-free periods
» Checking with health care professional before stopping or reducing therapy with any other asthma medications

Side/adverse effects

Signs of potential side effects, especially headache or nausea

General Dosing Information

Diet/Nutrition

In two separate studies, administration of zafirlukast with a high-fat meal and a high-protein meal resulted in a reduction of the mean bioavailability by approximately 40%; therefore, the medication should be taken on an empty stomach at least 1 hour before or 2 hours after meals.

Oral Dosage Forms

ZAFIRLUKAST TABLETS

Usual adult and adolescent dose

Antiasthmatic—
Oral, 20 mg two times a day, one hour before or two hours after a meal.

Usual adult and adolescent prescribing limits

20 mg two times a day.

Usual pediatric dose

Antiasthmatic—
Children 12 years of age and older—See *Usual adult and adolescent dose*
Children 7 to 11 years of age—Oral, 10 mg two times a day, one hour before or two hours after a meal
Children up to 7 years of age—Safety and efficacy have not been established.

Usual geriatric dose
See *Usual adult and adolescent dose.*

Strength(s) usually available
U.S.—
20 mg (Rx) [*Accolate* (film-coated)].
10 mg (Rx) [*Accolate* (film–coated)].

Canada—
Not commercially available.

Packaging and storage
Store between 20 and 25 °C (68 and 77 °F). Protect from light and moisture.

Auxiliary labeling
• Take on empty stomach.

Selected Bibliography
Holgate ST, Bradding P, Sampson AP. Leukotriene antagonists and synthesis inhibitors: new directions in asthma therapy. J Allergy Clin Immunol 1996; 98: 1-13.

Revised: 01/13/2000

ZALCITABINE Systemic

VA CLASSIFICATION (Primary): AM890

Commonly used brand name(s): *HIVID.*

Another commonly used name is ddC.

Note: For a listing of dosage forms and brand names by country availability, see *Dosage Forms* section(s).

Category
Antiviral (systemic).

Indications

Accepted
Human immunodeficiency virus (HIV) infection (treatment)—Zalcitabine is indicated, in combination with zidovudine, for the treatment of HIV infection in patients with limited prior exposure (< 3 months) to zidovudine. Zalcitabine is also indicated, in combination with antiretroviral agents, for the treatment of HIV infection.

[Human immunodeficiency virus (HIV) infection, advanced (treatment)]—Zalcitabine is indicated as a monotherapy for the treatment of advanced HIV infection in adult patients who are intolerant of, or who have demonstrated significant clinical or immunologic deterioration while receiving, zidovudine therapy.

Pharmacology/Pharmacokinetics

Physicochemical characteristics
Molecular weight—211.22.

Mechanism of action/Effect
Zalcitabine is phosphorylated by cellular enzymes to its active moiety, 2,3-dideoxycytidine-5-triphosphate (ddCTP)Incorporation of ddCTP into the growing DNA chain leads to premature chain termination. ddCTP is a competitive inhibitor of the natural substrate dCTP for the active site of viral reverse transcriptase and inhibits viral as well as cellular DNA synthesis. *In vitro*, zalcitabine is approximately 10 times more potent than zidovudine against HIV.

Absorption
Bioavailability in adults is greater than 80%; one small study done in children found a mean bioavailability of approximately 54%.

Administration with food resulted in a decrease in peak plasma concentration (C_{max}) of 39%, a decrease in the mean area under the plasma concentration-time curve (AUC) of 14%, and a twofold increase in time to peak plasma concentration (T_{max}).

Distribution
Crosses the blood-brain barrier and distributes into the cerebrospinal fluid (CSF); the mean CSF plasma concentration ratio is 20 (range, 7 to 37).

Vol_D—
Adults: Approximately 0.54 L per kg (L/kg).
Children: Approximately 9.3 L per square meter of body surface (L/m²).

Plasma protein binding
Low (< 4%)

Biotransformation
Phosphorylated intracellularly to ddCTP, the active substrate for HIV reverse transcriptase. Zalcitabine does not appear to undergo significant metabolism by the liver. The primary metabolite that has been identified is dideoxyuridine (ddU).

Half-life
Normal renal function—
Elimination—Adults: 1 to 3 hours.
Elimination—Children (ages 6 months to 13 years): Approximately 0.8 hour.

Renal function impairment in adults (creatinine clearance < 55 mL/min [0.92 mL/sec])—
Up to 8.5 hours.

Intracellular half-life of ddCTP is 2.6 to 10 hours.

Time to peak concentration
1 to 2 hours.

Peak serum concentration
7.6 nanograms/mL after a single oral dose of 0.5 mg.

25.2 nanograms/mL after a single oral dose of 1.5 mg.

Elimination
Renal; approximately 60 to 80% of zalcitabine is excreted in the urine as the parent drug. Less than 10% (as ddCTP and ddU) is found in the feces.

Total clearance: 285 mL/min

Renal clearance: 235 mL/min (approximately 80% of total clearance) Renal clearance exceeds the glomerular filtration rate, suggesting that renal tubular secretion contributes to elimination of zalcitabine.

In dialysis—It is not known whether zalcitabine is removed by hemodialysis or peritoneal dialysis.

Precautions to Consider

Carcinogenicity
Zalcitabine was administered orally to CLR:CD-1®(ICR) Br mice at dosages of 3, 83, or 250 mg per kg of body weight per day for two years. Plasma exposure (measured by the AUC) at these doses were 6-fold to 704-fold greater than the systemic exposure in humans with the therapeutic dose. When zalcitabine was administered orally to CDF® (F-344)/CrlBR/CdBR rats at the highest dose of 250 mg per kg per day exposure to zalcitabine was 833 times the systemic exposure in humans with the therapeutic dose. A significant increase in thymic lymphoma was observed at all doses, and Harderian gland adenoma in the two highest dose groups in female CD-1 mice after 2 years. No increase in tumors was observed in rats or male mice.

Tumorigenicity
High doses of zalcitabine administered for 3 months to $B_6C_3F_1$ mice (resulting in plasma concentrations of over 1000 times those seen in patients taking the recommended doses of zalcitabine) induced an increased incidence of thymic lymphoma.

Of 13 comparative studies and 7 expanded-access studies of zalcitabine, one study demonstrated a statistically significant increased rate of lymphoma in patients receiving zalcitabine or combination zalcitabine and zidovudine compared with zidovudine alone (rates of 1.3, 2.3 and zero per 100 person years, respectively). Lymphoma has been identified as a consequence of HIV infection; however, an association between lymphoma and antiviral therapy cannot be excluded.

Mutagenicity
Zalcitabine was positive in a cell transformation assay and induced chromosomal aberration *in vitro* in human peripheral blood lymphocytes. Oral doses of zalcitabine at 2500 and 4500 mg per kg of body weight (mg/kg) were clastogenic in the mouse micronucleus assay. No evidence of mutagenicity was found in the Ames test, in the mouse lymphoma assay, or in the Chinese hamster lung cell assay. An unscheduled DNA synthesis assay in rat hepatocytesshowed no effect on DNA repair.

Pregnancy/Reproduction
Fertility—No adverse effects on the rate of conception or general reproductive performance were observed in rats at concentrations of zalcitabine up to 2142 times those achieved with the maximum recommended human dose (MRHD). The fertility of F1 males was significantly reduced at a calculated dose of 2142 (but not 485) times the MRHD (based on area under the plasma concentration-time curve [AUC] measurements) in a teratology study in which rat mothers were dosed on gestation days 7 to 15. No adverse effects were observed on the fertility of parents or F1 generation in the study of fertility and general reproductive performance or in the perinatal and postnatal reproduction study.

Pregnancy—*An Antiretroviral Pregnancy Registry has been established to monitor the maternal-fetal outcomes of pregnant women exposed to zalcitabine. Physicians are encouraged to register patients by calling (800) 258-4263.*

It is not known whether zalcitabine crosses the placenta. Adequate and well-controlled studies have not been done in pregnant women. Unlike zidovudine, it is not known whether zalcitabine reduces perinatal transmission of HIV infection. Zalcitabine should be used in pregnancy only if the potential benefit to the mother outweighs the potential risk to the fetus. Fertile women should not receive zalcitabine unless they are using effective contraception during therapy.

Zalcitabine was teratogenic in mice at calculated exposure levels 1365 and 2730 times the MRHD. It was teratogenic in rats at a calculated exposure level 2142 times the MRHD, but not at 485 times the MRHD. Increased embryolethality was seen in pregnant mice at doses 2730 times the MRHD and in rats at doses above 485 times the MRHD. Average fetal body weight was significantly decreased in mice at doses 1365 times the MRHD and in rats at 2142 times the MRHD. A high incidence of hydrocephalus was observed in F_1 offspring of rats treated with 1071 times the MRHD that was associated with deficiencies in learning and memory, and hyperactivity.

FDA Pregnancy Category C.

Breast-feeding

It is not known whether zalcitabine is distributed into breast milk.

Of 13 comparative studies and 7 expanded-access studies of zalcitabine, one study demonstrated a statistically significant increased rate of lymphoma in patients receiving zalcitabine or combination zalcitabine and zidovudine compared with zidovudine alone (rates of 1.3, 2.3 and zero per 100 person years, respectively). Lymphoma has been identified as a consequence of HIV infection; however, an association between lymphoma and antiviral therapy cannot be excluded.

Pediatrics

Safety and efficacy of zalcitabine have not been fully established in HIV-infected children under 13years of age. However, zalcitabine has been both given as a monotherapy and alternated with zidovudine in children 6 months to 12 years of age. Preliminary data show that zalcitabine appears to be well tolerated, and there was clinical improvement and improvement in immunologic and virologic indicators of disease activity. The side effects profile appears to be similar in children and adults.

Geriatrics

Although appropriate studies on the relationship of age to the effects of zalcitabine have not been performed, no geriatrics-specific problems have been documented to date. However, dose selection for elderly patients should be cautious, reflecting the greater frequency of decreased hepatic, renal, or cardiac function, and of concomitant disease or other drug therapy. Because zalcitabine is excreted by the kidney and elderly patients may be more likely to have decreased renal function, renal function should be monitored and dosage adjustments made accordingly.,

Drug interactions and/or related problems

The following drug interactions and/or related problems have been selected on the basis of their potential clinical significance (possible mechanism in parentheses where appropriate)—not necessarily inclusive (» = major clinical significance):

Note: Combinations containing any of the following medications, depending on the amount present, may also interact with this medication.

» Alcohol or
» Asparaginase or
» Azathioprine or
» Estrogens or
» Furosemide or
» Methyldopa or
» Pentamidine, intravenous or
» Sulfonamides or
» Sulindac or
» Tetracyclines or
» Thiazide diuretics or
» Valproic acid or
Other drugs associated with pancreatitis
(medications associated with the development of pancreatitis should be avoided during zalcitabine therapy or, if concurrent use is necessary, used with caution since zalcitabine may cause pancreatitis, which, on rare occasion, has been fatal)
(treatment with zalcitabine should be interrupted if intravenous pentamidine is required)

» Aminoglycosides, parenteral or
» Amphotericin B or
» Foscarnet
(these medications may increase the risk of peripheral neuropathy or other toxicity of zalcitabine by interfering with its renal clearance; frequent clinical and laboratory monitoring with dose adjustment for any change in renal function is recommended)

» Antacids, aluminum- and/or magnesium-containing
(concurrent administration of antacids and zalcitabine resulted in a 25% reduction in zalcitabine absorption; it is recommended that antacids and zalcitabine not be administered simultaneously)

» Chloramphenicol or
» Cisplatin or
» Dapsone or
» Didanosine or
» Disulfiram or
» Ethionamide or
» Glutethimide or
» Gold or
» Hydralazine or
Iodoquinol
» Isoniazid or
» Lithium or
» Metronidazole or
» Phenytoin or
» Ribavirin or
» Stavudine or
» Vincristine or
Other drugs associated with peripheral neuropathy
(since zalcitabine has been shown to cause peripheral neuropathy, other medications associated with the development of neuropathy should be avoided during zalcitabine therapy or, if concurrent use is necessary, used with caution)

» Cimetidine or
» Probenecid
(these drugs decrease the elimination of zalcitabine, most likely by inhibition of renal tubular secretion of zalcitabine;; patients should be monitored for signs of toxicity and the dose of zalcitabine may need to be reduced)

» Doxorubicin, or
(doxorubicin decreased in zalcitabine phosphorylation *in vitro;* clinical relevance is unknown)

» Lamivudine
(lamivudine and zalcitabine may inhibit the phosphorylation of one another; concurrent administration is not recommended)

Metoclopramide
(zalcitabine bioavailability is reduced by approximately 10% when administered with metoclopramide)

» Nitrofurantoin
(concurrent use of nitrofurantoin with zalcitabine may increase the risk of pancreatitis and peripheral neuropathy; if concurrent use is necessary, patients should be monitored for signs of toxicity and the dose of zalcitabine may need to be reduced)

Trimethoprim
(trimethoprim increased the AUC of zalcitabine by 37% due to inhibition of renal tubular secretion of zalcitabine by trimethoprim)

Laboratory value alterations

The following have been selected on the basis of their potential clinical significance (possible effect in parentheses where appropriate)—not necessarily inclusive (» = major clinical significance).

With physiology/laboratory test values
Absolute eosinophil count or
Total bilirubin
(serum values may be slightly increased; less than 5%)

Absolute neutrophil count or
Hemoglobin or
Platelets or
White blood cell count
(serum values may be decreased)

Alanine aminotransferase (ALT [SGPT]) and
Alkaline phosphatase and
Aspartate aminotransferase (AST [SGOT]) and
Gamma-glutamyl transferase (GGT)
(serum values may be increased; values greater than five times the upper normal limit occurred more frequently in patients with abnormal baseline values; in clinical trials; drug interruption was recommended if liver function tests exceeded 5 times the upper limit of normal)

» Amylase and
Lipase and
Triglycerides
(serum values may be increased)

Creatine phosphokinase (CPK)
(serum values may be increased)

Medical considerations/Contraindications

The medical considerations/contraindications included have been selected on the basis of their potential clinical significance (reasons given in parentheses where appropriate)—not necessarily inclusive (» = major clinical significance).

Except under special circumstances, this medication should not be used when the following medical problem exists:

» Hypersensitivity to zalcitabine or any of the excipients contained in the tablet
(zalcitabine is contraindicated in these patients)

Risk-benefit should be considered when the following medical problems exist:

» Alcoholism, active or
» Amylase, elevated, history of or
» Hypertriglyceridemia, or history of or
» Pancreatitis, history of or
» Pancreatitis, risk of or
» Parenteral nutrition
(zalcitabine has caused pancreatitis, which, on rare occasion, has been fatal; patients who have pancreatitis or a history of pancreatitis, or are at risk for pancreatitis, either should not take zalcitabine or should take it with extreme caution; serum amylase levels should be monitored)

Bone marrow reserve, poor
(particularly in patients with advanced symptomatic HIV disease; frequent monitoring of hematologic indices to detect serious anemia or granulocytopenia; a treatment interruption or dosage reduction may be required)

Cardiomyopathy, or
Congestive heart failure, history of
(nucleoside analogues have been associated with development of these conditions; caution is advised)

CD_4 count decreased or
(patients with decreased CD_4 cell counts appear to have an increased incidence of adverse events)

» Ethanol abuse, history of or
» Hepatic disease or
» Hepatitis or
» Liver enzyme abnormalities or
» Obesity or
» Prolonged nucleoside exposure or
» Risk factors for hepatic disease
(lactic acidosis and severe hepatomegaly with steatosis have been reported with the use of nucleoside analogues alone or in combination; fatal cases have been reported; obesity and prolonged nucleoside exposure may be risk factors; majority of cases have been in women; treatment should be suspended in patients with evidence of lactic acidosis or pronounced hepatotoxicity which may include hepatomegaly with steatosis even in the absence of marked transaminase elevations; in clinical trials, drug interruption was recommended if liver function tests exceeded 5 times the upper limit of normal)

» Peripheral neuropathy or
» Risk factors for developing neuropathy, including
» CD_4 count $\leq$ 50 cells/mm^3 or
» Diabetes or
» Weight loss
(zalcitabine may cause peripheral neuropathy; patients with mild peripheral neuropathy should consider alternative agents; patients with moderate to severe peripheral neuropathy should not take zalcitabine)

» Renal impairment
(patients with renal impairment may be at increased risk of toxicity due to decreased clearance of zalcitabine through the kidneys; dose adjustment is recommended in patients with creatinine clearance $<$ 55 mL/min [0.92 mL/sec])

Patient monitoring

The following may be especially important in patient monitoring (other tests may be warranted in some patients, depending on condition; » = major clinical significance):

» Alanine aminotransferase (ALT [SGPT]) and
» Alkaline phosphatase and
» Aspartate aminotransferase (AST [SGOT])
(serum values may be increased to greater than five times the upper normal limit; the incidence of laboratory abnormalities is higher in patients with preexisting abnormal baseline values or a history of alcohol abuse)

» Amylase, serum and
Calcium, serum and
» Lipase, serum and
Triglycerides, serum
(zalcitabine administration has been associated with pancreatitis; patients should be monitored for laboratory changes consistent with pancreatitis, such as elevated amylase, lipase, and triglyceride concentrations and decreasing serum calcium levels; zalcitabine should be discontinued if amylase concentration is elevated by 1.5 to 2 times normal limits and/or the patient has symptoms consistent with pancreatitis)

Blood count complete and
Chemistry, clinical
(should be performed at baseline and at appropriate intervals thereafter)

» Blood urea nitrogen (BUN) and
» Creatinine, serum
(blood urea nitrogen and serum creatinine concentrations should be monitored in patients with renal function impairment; an adjustment in dosage or dosage interval may be required)

» Pancreatitis, symptoms of
(zalcitabine should be discontinued immediately if clinical signs and symptoms (nausea, vomiting, abdominal pain))

» Peripheral neuropathy
(zalcitabine should be discontinued promptly if signs and symptoms of peripheral neuropathy occur, such as progression of moderate discomfort form numbness, tingling, burning, or pain of the extremities, or any related symptoms accompanied by an objective finding)

Side/Adverse Effects

Note: In general, patients with decreased CD4 cell counts appear to have an increased incidence of adverse events related to zalcitabine.

Some side effects of zalcitabine (ddC), such as peripheral neuropathy, may also be seen with severe HIV disease; therefore, differentiation between the side effects of ddC and the complications of HIV disease may be difficult. Also, toxicities associated with zidovudine monotherapy are likely to occur when zidovudine is administered concurrently with zalcitabine; these side effects should also be monitored.

Dose-related peripheral neuropathy occurred in 17 to 31% of adult patients treated with zalcitabine monotherapy. Sensorimotor neuropathy starts with numbness and a burning sensation in the distal extremities, followed by sharp shooting pain or severe continuous burning pain if the drug is not discontinued. Peripheral neuropathy is usually dose-related and slowly reversible; however, it is potentially irreversible if zalcitabine is not stopped promptly, and may initially progress despite discontinuation of the drug. Patients with a very low CD4 count ($<$ 50 cells/mm^3) are at the greatest risk of developing peripheral neuropathy. Zalcitabine should be discontinued as soon as there is mild progressive discomfort from numbness, tingling, burning, or pain of the extremities.

Fatal pancreatitis has been observed when zalcitabine was given alone and in combination with zidovudine. Pancreatitis is relatively uncommon with zalcitabine monotherapy, occurring in up to 1.1% Of the patients treated in the expanded access trial (n=528) who had a prior history of pancreatitis or an elevated serum amylase, 5.3% developed pancreatitis and 4.4% developed an asymptomatic increase in serum amylase.

Severe hepatotoxicity has occurred rarely. Lactic acidosis, in the absence of hypoxemia, and severe hepatomegaly with steatosis have been reported with the use of nucleoside analogues, including zalcitabine, and are potentially fatal. In addition, rare cases of hepatic failure and death considered possibly related to underlying hepatitis B and zalcitabine monotherapy have been reported.

Other serious toxicities reported with zalcitabine therapy include, oral ulcers, esophageal ulcers, cardiomyopathy/congestive heart failure and anaphylactoid reaction.

For additional information on side effects (less than 1% frequency) please refer to manufacturer's package insert.

The following side/adverse effects have been selected on the basis of their potential clinical significance (possible signs and symptoms in parentheses where appropriate)—not necessarily inclusive:

Those indicating need for medical attention

Incidence more frequent

Abnormal hepatic function (lab results that show problems with liver); ***peripheral neuropathy*** (tingling, burning, numbness, or pain in the hands, arms, feet, or legs)

Incidence less frequent

Abdominal pain (stomach pain); ***arthralgia*** (joint pain); ***convulsions*** (seizures); ***hypersensitivity*** (fever; skin rash); ***myalgia*** (muscle pain); ***pancreatitis*** (abdominal pain, severe; nausea; vomiting); ***ulceration of the mouth and throat***

Incidence rare

Depression (discouragement; feeling sad or empty; irritability; lack of appetite; loss of interest or pleasure; tiredness; trouble concentrating; trouble sleeping); ***hepatotoxicity*** (yellow eyes or skin); ***leukopenia or neutropenia*** (fever and sore throat)

Those indicating need for medical attention only if they continue or are bothersome

Incidence less frequent

Constipation (difficulty having a bowel movement (stool)); ***diarrhea; fatigue*** (unusual tiredness or weakness); ***fever; gastrointestinal disturbances*** (abdominal pain, mild; diarrhea; nausea); ***headache; nausea; pruritus*** (itching skin); ***rash; stomatitis*** (swelling or inflammation of the mouth); ***urticaria*** (hives or welts; itching; redness of skin; skin rash); ***vomiting***

Overdose

For more information on the management of overdose or unintentional ingestion, **contact a Poison Control Center** (see *Poison Control Center Listing*).

Clinical effects of overdose

Doses of up to 1.5 mg per kg of body weight have inadvertently been given to pediatric patients. The children received prompt gastric lavage and treatment with activated charcoal and had no sequelae. Mixed overdoses of zalcitabine with other medications have caused drowsiness and vomiting, increased gamma-glutamyltransferase values, or increased creatine kinase (CK) serum values.

Chronic

Peripheral neuropathy (tingling, burning, numbness, or pain in the hands, arms, feet, or legs)

Treatment of overdose

Supportive care—It is not known if zalcitabine is removed by hemodialysis or peritoneal dialysis.

There is no known antidote for zalcitabine overdosage.

Patients in whom intentional overdose is confirmed or suspected should be referred for psychiatric consultation.

Patient Consultation

As an aid to patient consultation, refer to *Advice for the Patient, Zalcitabine (Systemic)*.

In providing consultation, consider emphasizing the following selected information (» = major clinical significance):

Before using this medication

» Conditions affecting use, especially:

Pregnancy—Zalcitabine should be used during pregnancy only if the benefit to the mother outweighs the potential risk to the fetus; fertile women should not receive zalcitabine unless they are using effective contraception during therapy

Breast-feeding—Not recommended, because of the potential for postnatal transmission of HIV to the nursing infant

Use in children—Preliminary data suggest zalcitabine is well tolerated and produces clinical improvement in some children; the side effect profile is similar to that for adults

Other medications, especially parenteral aminoglycosides, amphotericin B, antacids, cimetidine, doxorubicin, foscarnet, lamivudine, nitrofurantoin, other drugs associated with pancreatitis, other drugs associated with peripheral neuropathy, pentamidine, and probenecid

Other medical problems, especially active alcoholism or a history of alcoholism, cardiomyopathy, congestive heart failure, hepatic impairment, hepatitis, hypertriglyceridemia or a history of hypertriglyceridemia, hypersensitivity, liver function abnormalities, obesity, pancreatitis or a history of pancreatitis or risk for pancreatitis, paternal nutrition, peripheral neuropathy or risk factors for developing peripheral neuropathy including diabetes mellitus, low CD4 count, and weight loss, prolonged nucleoside exposure, renal impairment, or risk factors for hepatic disease

Proper use of this medication

» Importance of not taking more medication than prescribed; importance of not discontinuing medication without checking with physician

» Compliance with full course of therapy

» Importance of not missing doses and of taking at evenly spaced times

Not sharing medication with others

» Proper dosing

Missed dose: Taking as soon as possible; not taking if almost time for next dose; not doubling doses

» Proper storage

Precautions while using this medication

» Regular visits to physician for blood tests

» Importance of not taking other medications concurrently without checking with physician

» Taking steps to avoid spreading HIV infection

Side/adverse effects

Signs of potential side effects, especially, abdominal pain, abnormal hepatic function, arthralgia, convulsions, depression, hepatotoxicity, hypersensitivity, leukopenia, myalgia, neutropenia, and pancreatitis, peripheral neuropathy, or ulceration of the mouth and throat,

General Dosing Information

No adjustment in dose needs to be made for patients who weigh 30 kg or more; this is based on pharmacokinetic weight-ranging data.

According to the US manufacturer, zalcitabine is indicated in combination with antiretroviral agents and not recommended as a monotherapy.

If patients receiving zalcitabine and zidovudine combination therapy develop what are thought to be medication-related side effects, the dose of the medication associated with that particular toxicity profile should be modified. When the toxicity is more likely to be caused by zalcitabine, the dose of that drug should be reduced or the drug should be discontinued; the same is true for zidovudine. For severe toxicity in which the causative drug cannot be identified, or side effects continue despite dose reduction or discontinuation of one medication, the dose of the other medication should also be reduced or the medication discontinued.

Patients with mild, new onset, or progressive symptoms of peripheral neuropathy should discontinue taking zalcitabine, especially if the symptoms last for more than 3 days and are bilateral. Zalcitabine may be reintroduced at 50% of the regular dose (0.375 mg every 8 hours) only if the peripheral neuropathy improves to very mild symptoms.

Oral Dosage Forms

ZALCITABINE TABLETS USP

Usual adult and adolescent dose

Human immunodeficiency virus (HIV) infection—

Oral, 0.75 mg every 8 hours in combination with other antiretroviral agents 200 mg zidovudine, every eight hours.

[Human immunodeficiency virus (HIV) infection, advanced]—

Oral, 0.75 mg every eight hours.

Note: Adults with acute or chronic renal impairment may require a reduction in dose of zalcitabine as follows:

Creatinine clearance (mL/min)/(mL/sec)	Dose (mg)	Dosing interval (hr)
> 40/0.67	0.75	8
10–40/0.17–0.67	0.75	12
0–10/0–0.17	0.75	24

Usual pediatric dose

Safety and effectiveness of zalcitabine given alone or in combination with zidovudine have not been established in children up to 13 years of age. The doses being studied in ongoing clinical trials are 0.005 and 0.01 mg per kg of body weight every eight hours.

Strength(s) usually available

U.S.—

0.375 mg (Rx) [*HIVID* (lactose)].

0.75 mg (Rx) [*HIVID* (lactose)].

Canada—

0.375 mg (Rx) [*HIVID* (lactose)].

0.75 mg (Rx) [*HIVID* (lactose)].

Packaging and storage
Store between 15 and 30 °C (59 and 86 °F), in a tight, light-resistant container.

Auxiliary labeling
- Continue medicine for full time of treatment.

Revised: 01/06/2004

ZALEPLON Systemic

VA CLASSIFICATION (Primary): CN309

Note: Controlled substance classification

U.S.: Schedule IV

Commonly used brand name(s): *Sonata*.

Note: For a listing of dosage forms and brand names by country availability, see *Dosage Forms* section(s).

Category

Sedative-hypnotic.

Indications

Accepted

Insomnia (treatment)—Zaleplon is indicated for the short-term treatment of insomnia. Zaleplon decreases the time to sleep onset but has not been shown to increase total sleep time or decrease number of awakenings. Failure of insomnia to remit after 7 to 10 days of treatment may indicate the presence of a primary psychiatric or medical illness. Worsening of insomnia or the emergence of new abnormalities of thinking or behavior may be a consequence of an unrecognized psychiatric or physical disorder.

Pharmacology/Pharmacokinetics

Physicochemical characteristics

Chemical Group—Pyrazolopyrimidine; structurally unrelated to benzodiazepines, barbiturates, or other drugs with known hypnotic properties.

Molecular weight—305.34.

Solubility—Practically insoluble in water; sparingly soluble in alcohol or propylene glycol.

Partition coefficient—Log partition coefficient is 1.23 in octanol/water over a pH range of 1 to 7.

Mechanism of action/Effect

Zaleplon interacts with the gamma-aminobutyric acid type A-benzodiazepine (GABA-BZ) receptor complex. Modulation of the GABA-BZ receptor chloride channel macromolecular complex appears to be responsible for the pharmacological properties of the benzodiazepines including sedative, anxiolytic, muscle relaxant, and anticonvulsant effects. Zaleplon binds selectively to the brain alpha subunit of the $GABA_A$ omega-1 receptor.

Absorption

Zaleplon absorption is rapid and almost complete. Due to significant presystemic metabolism, its absolute bioavailability is approximately 30%. Food may prolong the absorption.

Distribution

The volume of distribution of zaleplon is approximately 1.4 L/kg following intravenous administration. Substantial distribution into extravascular tissues occurs. The blood to plasma ratio for zaleplon is approximately 1, indicating uniform distribution throughout the blood with no extensive distribution into red blood cells. Small amounts of zaleplon are distributed into breast milk, with the highest concentrations occurring during a feeding approximately 1 hour post-administration.

Protein binding

Moderate (60%).

Biotransformation

Zaleplon is extensively metabolized, primarily by aldehyde oxidase and, to a lesser extent, by CYP3A4 All metabolites are inactive.

Elimination

Approximately 1 hour

Onset of action

Rapid

Time to peak concentration

Peak concentrations are attained within approximately 1 hour. Peaks may be delayed if zaleplon is taken with food.

Elimination

Renal—

71% of a single dose is eliminated in the urine; almost all is recovered as zaleplon metabolites and their glucuronides. Less than 1% is excreted unchanged.

Fecal—

17% of a single dose is eliminated in the feces.

Precautions to Consider

Carcinogenicity

In mice receiving doses of 25, 50, 100, and 200 mg per kg of body weight (mg/kg) a day (6 to 49 times the maximum recommended human dose [MRHD] on a mg per square meter of body surface area [mg/m^2] basis), there was a significant increase in the incidence of hepatocellular adenomas in females receiving the highest dose. No evidence of carcinogenic potential was seen in rats receiving 1, 10, and 20 mg/kg a day (0.5 to 10 times the MRHD on a mg/m^2 basis).

Mutagenicity

When testing for chromosomal aberrations, in the *in vitro* Chinese hamster ovary cell assay, zaleplon was clastogenic in both the presence and absence of metabolic activation, causing structural and numerical aberrations. In the *in vitro* human lymphocyte assay, zaleplon was clastogenic causing numerical but not structural aberrations. In other *in vitro* studies including the Ames bacterial gene mutation assay and the Chinese hamster ovary HGPRT gene mutation assay, zaleplon was not mutagenic. In two *in vivo* assays, the mouse bone marrow micronucleus assay and the rat bone marrow chromosomal aberration assay, zaleplon was not clastogenic. Zaleplon did not cause DNA damage in the rat hepatocyte unscheduled DNA synthesis assay.

Pregnancy/Reproduction

Fertility—In studies in rats, mortality and decreased fertility were associated with administration of zaleplon 100 mg/kg a day (49 times the MRHD on a mg/m^2 basis) to males and females prior to and during mating. The impaired fertility was due to an effect on the female rat.

Pregnancy—Zaleplon has not been studied in pregnant women.

No teratogenicity was seen in rat and rabbit studies. Female rats administered 100 mg of zaleplon per kg a day (49 times the MRHD on a mg/m^2 basis) produced offspring with reduced pre- and postnatal growth. This dose was also maternally toxic (clinical signs and decreased maternal body weight during gestation). Rats treated with doses of 7 mg/kg a day or greater during the latter part of gestation and throughout lactation produced a greater number of stillbirths, and offspring with increased postnatal mortality, and decreased growth and physical development. The no-effect dose on growth reduction and offspring development was five times the MRHD (10 mg/kg) and 0.5 times the MRHD (1 mg/kg), respectively, for rat offspring. No adverse effects on embryofetal development were observed in rabbits.

FDA Pregnancy Category C.

Breast-feeding

A small amount of zaleplon is distributed into breast milk. The effect of zaleplon on the infant is unknown.

Pediatrics

Appropriate studies on the relationship of age to the effects of zaleplon have not been performed in the pediatric population. Safety and efficacy have not been established.

Geriatrics

In studies performed on 628 elderly patients, sleep latency improved with a reduced dose of 5 mg. The incidence of adverse events with a frequency of at least 1% was not significantly different between placebo and zaleplon at doses of either 5 mg or 10 mg during studies of a 14 day duration. The pharmacokinetics of zaleplon in the elderly, age 65 to 85 years, are not significantly different from those in younger patients. However, elderly patients appear to be more sensitive to the effects of hypnotics.

Pharmacogenetics

Pharmacokinetics between men and women are not significantly different. The peak serum concentration of zaleplon was 37% higher in Japanese subjects. The effects of race on pharmacokinetic characteristics among other ethnic groups are not well-defined.

Drug interactions and/or related problems

The following drug interactions and/or related problems have been selected on the basis of their potential clinical significance (possible

mechanism in parentheses where appropriate)—not necessarily inclusive (» = major clinical significance):

Note: Combinations containing any of the following medications, depending on the amount present, may also interact with this medication.

» Alcohol, or
» Central nervous system (CNS) depression-producing medications, other (see *Appendix II*), especially
Diphenhydramine
Imipramine
Thioridazine
(concurrent use may cause additive CNS depressant effects such as decreased alertness and impaired psychomotor performance)

» Cimetidine
(concurrent use with an enzyme inhibitor of both aldehyde oxidase and CYP3A4, such as cimetidine, may increase peak concentrations and area under the time-concentration curve [AUC] of zaleplon; dosage reductions of zaleplon are needed)

» Enzyme inducers, hepatic, cytochrome P450 (see *Appendix II*), especially
Carbamazepine
Phenobarbital
Phenytoin
Rifampin
(concurrent use with CYP3A4 enzyme inducers may greatly decrease concentrations of zaleplon, rendering it ineffective)

Medical considerations/Contraindications

The medical considerations/contraindications included have been selected on the basis of their potential clinical significance (reasons given in parentheses where appropriate)—not necessarily inclusive (» = major clinical significance).

Except under special circumstances, this medications should not be used when the following medical problems exist:

» Severe hepatic function impairment
(zaleplon is metabolized primarily by the liver and undergoes significant presystemic metabolism)

Risk-benefit should be considered when the following medical problems exist:

» Alcohol abuse (or history of) or
» Drug abuse or dependence (or history of)
(dependence on zaleplon may develop)

» Mental depression
(potential for suicidal tendencies in depressed patients; likelihood of intentional overdose is greater in depressed patients)

» Hepatic function impairment, mild to moderate
(reduced metabolism may lead to toxicity; dosage reductions are necessary)

» Respiratory disease
(possibility of depressed respiratory drive)

Sensitivity to zaleplon

Side/Adverse Effects

The following side/adverse effects have been selected on the basis of their potential clinical significance (possible signs and symptoms in parentheses where appropriate)—not necessarily inclusive:

Those indicating need for medical attention

Incidence less frequent

Abnormal vision (blurred or double vision); ***anxiety; depersonalization*** (not feeling like oneself)

Incidence rare

Epistaxis (nosebleed); ***hallucinations*** (seeing, hearing, smelling, or feeling things that are not there)

Those indicating need for medical attention only if they continue or are bothersome

Incidence more frequent

Dizziness; headache; myalgia (muscle pain); ***nausea***

Incidence less frequent

Abdominal pain; amnesia (memory loss); ***arthritis*** (joint stiffness and/or pain); ***asthenia*** (unusual weakness or tiredness); ***bronchitis*** (cough; shortness of breath; tightness in chest; troubled breathing; wheezing); ***conjunctivitis*** (dry, itching, or burning eyes); ***constipation; difficulty concentrating; dryness of mouth; dyspepsia*** (heartburn, indigestion, or acid stomach); ***dysmenorrhea*** (menstrual pain); ***eye pain; fever; hyperacusis*** (sensitive hearing); ***hypertonia*** (excess muscle tone); ***mental depression; migraine*** (severe headache); ***nervousness; paresthesia*** (burning, prickling, or tingling sensation); ***pruritus*** (itching); ***skin rash; somnolence*** (drowsiness); ***tremor*** (trembling or shaking)

Incidence rare

Anorexia (loss of appetite); ***back pain; chest pain; ear pain; hypesthesia*** (numbness); ***malaise*** (general feeling of discomfort or illness); ***parosmia*** (sense of smell difficulty); ***peripheral edema*** (swelling of fingers, hands, arms, legs, ankles, and feet; bloating or swelling of face; rapid weight gain); ***photosensitivity*** (increased sensitivity of skin and eyes to sunlight; blisters; skin rash; redness; burning sensation; severe sunburn)

Those indicating need for medical attention if they occur after medication is discontinued

Incidence rare

Abdominal and muscle cramps; dysphoria (sadness); ***increased sweating; seizures; tremors*** (trembling or shaking); ***vomiting***

Overdose

For specific information on the agents used in the management of zaleplon overdose, see:

- *Flumazenil (Systemic)* monograph

For more information on the management of overdose or unintentional ingestion, **contact a Poison Control Center** (see *Poison Control Center Listing*).

Clinical effects of overdose

The following effects have been selected on the basis of their potential clinical significance (possible signs and symptoms in parentheses where appropriate)—not necessarily inclusive:

Ataxia, severe (clumsiness or unsteadiness); ***coma; drowsiness, severe; hypotension*** (dizziness or fainting); ***hypotonia*** (weak muscle tone); ***lethargy*** (unusual drowsiness, dullness, or feeling sluggish); ***mental confusion; respiratory problems*** (troubled breathing)

Treatment of overdose

To decrease absorption—Perform gastric lavage as appropriate.

Specific treatment—Flumazenil may be useful in reversing zaleplon's sedative and respiratory depressant effects. See the package insert or *Flumazenil (Systemic) monograph* for specific dosing guidelines for the use of this product.

Monitoring—Monitor respiratory, cardiac, and central nervous system status.

Supportive care—Providing general supportive therapy as indicated. Intravenous fluids should be administered as appropriate. Patients in whom intentional overdose is confirmed or suspected should be referred for psychiatric consultation.

Patient Consultation

As an aid to patient consultation, refer to *Advice for the Patient, Zaleplon (Systemic)*.

In providing consultation, consider emphasizing the following selected information (» = major clinical significance):

Before using this medication

» Conditions affecting use, especially:
Hypersensitivity to zaleplon
Breast-feeding—Small amount of zaleplon is distributed into breast milk; effect on infant is unknown
Use in the elderly—Elderly patients are usually more sensitive to central nervous system effects of zaleplon
Other medications, especially alcohol, CNS depressants, cimetidine, and hepatic P450 enzyme inducers
Other medical problems, especially alcohol or drug abuse (or history of), hepatic function impairment, mental depression, and respiratory disease

Proper use of this medication

Not taking more medication than the amount prescribed, because of habit-forming potential

Not increasing dose if medication becomes less effective over time; checking with physician

» Being prepared to go to sleep immediately after taking medicine
» Proper dosing
Missed dose: Skipping missed dose; not doubling doses
» Proper storage

Precautions while using this medication

» Avoid use of alcohol or other central nervous system depressants during therapy

Caution if clumsiness or unsteadiness, drowsiness, dizziness, visual disturbances or changes in behavior or thinking occur, especially in the elderly

Checking with physician before discontinuing medication after more than 1 to 2 weeks of use; gradual dosage reduction may be necessary to avoid withdrawal symptoms

Side/adverse effects

Signs of potential side effects, especially abnormal vision, anxiety, depersonalization, epistaxis, and hallucinations

General Dosing Information

Geriatric and debilitated patients should receive a decreased initial dosage since they may be more sensitive to the central nervous system effects of zaleplon.

Patients with mild to moderate hepatic impairment or low weight individuals should receive a decreased initial dosage since elimination of zaleplon may be prolonged, resulting in increased central nervous system side effects. Individual dosage adjustments should be made.

The minimal effective dose should be used for the shortest period with reevaluation of the patient if taken for more than 2 to 3 weeks.

Worsening of insomnia or the emergence of new thinking or behavior abnormalities may be the consequence of an unrecognized psychiatric or physical disorder.

Because of zaleplon's rapid onset of action, the patients should be ready for sleep when the dose is taken.

To minimize the occurrence of anterograde amnesia and hangover effects, zaleplon should be taken only when the patient's schedule will allow for 4 or more hours of sleep.

For the most rapid effect, zaleplon should be taken on an empty stomach.

Following prolonged administration, zaleplon should be withdrawn gradually to lessen the possibility of precipitating withdrawal symptoms.

Potentially suicidal patients, particularly those who use alcohol excessively, should not have access to large quantities of zaleplon.

Oral Dosage Forms

ZALEPLON CAPSULES

Usual adult dose

Hypnotic—

Oral, 10 milligrams at bedtime.

Note: Debilitated patients, or patients with hepatic function impairment or low body weight—Oral, initially 5 milligrams at bedtime, the dosage being adjusted as needed and tolerated.

Usual adult prescribing limits

20 milligrams a day.

Usual pediatric dose

Children up to 18 years of age—

Safety and efficacy have not been established.

Usual geriatric dose

Hypnotic—

Oral, initially 5 milligrams at bedtime, the dosage being adjusted as needed and tolerated.

Strength(s) usually available

U.S.—

5 mg (Rx) [*Sonata* (microcrystalline cellulose; pregelatinized starch; silicon dioxide; sodium lauryl sulfate; magnesium stearate; lactose; gelatin; titanium dioxide)].

10 mg (Rx) [*Sonata* (microcrystalline cellulose; pregelatinized starch; silicon dioxide; sodium lauryl sulfate; magnesium stearate; lactose; gelatin; titanium dioxide)].

Canada—

Not commercially available in Canada.

Packaging and storage

Store at controlled room temperature between 20 and 25 °C (68 and 77 °F). Store in a light-resistant container.

Auxiliary labeling

- Avoid alcoholic beverages.
- May cause daytime drowsiness.

Note

Controlled substance in the U.S.

Developed: 12/02/1999

ZANAMIVIR Inhalation–Systemic

VA CLASSIFICATION (Primary): AM809

Commonly used brand name(s): *Relenza*.

Note: For a listing of dosage forms and brand names by country availability, see *Dosage Forms* section(s).

Category

Antiviral (systemic).

Indications

Note: Bracketed information in the *Indications* section refers to uses that are not included in U.S. product labeling.

Accepted

Influenza A (treatment)—Zanamivir is indicated for the treatment of uncomplicated acute illness due to influenza A virus in adults and children 7 years and older[1] who have been symptomatic for no more than 2 days. Zanamivir must be started within 48 hours after the onset of influenza symptoms.

Influenza B (treatment)—Zanamivir is indicated for the treatment of uncomplicated acute illness due to influenza B virus in adults and children 7 years and older[1] who have been symptomatic for no more than 2 days. Zanamivir must be started within 48 hours after the onset of influenza symptoms.

Note: Zanamivir showed no difference in efficacy in the treatment of patients with influenza A compared with those with influenza B; however, the trials included small numbers of patients with influenza B. Therefore, less evidence exists to support the efficacy in influenza B.

Safety and efficacy data in patients who initiate zanamivir after 48 hours of symptom onset have not been determined.

Safety and efficacy in patients with underlying chronic medical conditions, including respiratory and cardiovascular disease, have not been demonstrated.

[Influenza A (prophylaxis) and][1]

[Influenza B (prophylaxis)][1]—Zanamivir is indicated for the prophylaxis of influenza A and B. Although not a substitute for influenza virus vaccine, use of zanamivir may be considered if the vaccine is not available, in conjunction with the vaccine late in the influenza season, before the vaccine has induced an immune response, or if there is no immune response to the vaccine.

[1]Not included in Canadian product labeling.

Pharmacology/Pharmacokinetics

Physicochemical characteristics

Molecular weight—Molecular weight 332.3.

Mechanism of action/Effect

Zanamivir is a selective inhibitor of influenza A and B virus neuraminidase, possibly altering particle aggregation and release.

Absorption

Orally inhaled zanamivir is systemically absorbed, approximately 4% to 17%.

Protein binding

Very low (<10%).

Biotransformation

Not metabolized.

Half-life

Elimination—2.5 to 5.1 hours.

Time to peak concentration

1 to 2 hours following a 10-mg dose.

Peak serum concentration

17 to 142 nanograms/milliliter following a 10-mg dose.

Time to peak effect

72 hours.

Elimination

Renal—Excreted unchanged in the urine with excretion of a single dose completed within 24 hours. Total clearance ranges from 2.5 to 10.9 L per hour.

Fecal—Unabsorbed drug is excreted in the feces.

Precautions to Consider

Carcinogenicity
No carcinogenic effects were seen when zanamivir was evaluated in animals given doses up to 25 times the human dose.

Tumorigenicity
An increase in lymphoma incidence over controls was seen in male rats given a high dose (30 to 50 mg per kg per day); there was no dose relationship.

Mutagenicity
No mutagenic effects were seen when zanamivir was evaluated in several mutagenicity assays.

Pregnancy/Reproduction
Fertility—No impairment of fertility or mating in male or female rats and no effect on the male sperm were demonstrated.

Pregnancy—Adequate and well-controlled studies in humans have not been done. No malformations, maternal toxicity, or embryotoxicity were observed in pregnant rats or rabbits and their fetuses. Zanamivir readily crosses the placenta in rats and rabbits. Fetal blood concentrations of zanamivir in rats and rabbits were significantly lower than zanamivir concentrations in the maternal blood.

U.S. FDA Pregnancy Category B

Breast-feeding
Zanamivir is distributed in the breast milk of rats. It is unknown if zanamivir is distributed in human breast milk.

Pediatrics
Safety and efficacy have not been established in pediatric patients under 7 years of age.

Note: The Canadian manufacturer states that safety and efficacy have not been established in pediatric patients under 12 years of age

Adolescents
Appropriate studies performed to date have not demonstrated pediatrics-specific problems that would limit the usefulness of zanamivir in children older than 12 years of age.

Geriatrics
Appropriate studies performed to date have not demonstrated geriatrics-specific problems that would limit the usefulness of zanamivir in the elderly.

Medical considerations/Contraindications
The medical considerations/contraindications included have been selected on the basis of their potential clinical significance (reasons given in parentheses where appropriate)—not necessarily inclusive (» = major clinical significance).

The medication should not be used when the following medical problem exists:

» Hypersensitivity to zanamivir or any component of the formulation

Risk-benefit should be considered when the following medical problems exist:

» Respiratory disease, chronic, such as asthma or chronic obstructive pulmonary disease
(zanamivir may cause bronchospasm or a decrease in lung function)

Cardiovascular disease
(efficacy not established)

Note: Safety and efficacy of zanamivir are not established in patients with high-risk underlying medical conditions.

Side/Adverse Effects
The following side/adverse effects have been selected on the basis of their potential clinical significance (possible signs and symptoms in parentheses where appropriate)—not necessarily inclusive:

Those indicating need for immediate medical attention
Incidence rare

Bronchospasm (wheezing)—mainly exhibited in patients with asthma or chronic obstructive pulmonary disease

Note: An increased susceptibility to bronchospasm and/or a decline in lung function has been reported in patients with chronic obstructive lung disease (COPD) and asthma. Zanamivir should be stopped if a decrease in lung function or bronchospasm is experienced. A fast-acting bronchodilator should be available when zanamivir is administered in patients with respiratory disease.

Incidence not determined—Observed during clinical practice; estimates of frequency can not be determined

Allergic or allergic type reactions, including oropharyngeal edema (itching, pain, redness, swelling or watering of eye or eyelid; troubled breathing or wheezing; severe skin rash or hives; flushing; increased sensitivity to sunlight; joint pain; swollen glands or tightness in throat); ***Arrythmias*** (dizziness; fainting or fast, slow, or irregular heartbeat); ***Bronchospasm*** (difficulty breathing; shortness of breath; tightness in chest or wheezing); ***facial edema*** (swelling or puffiness of face); ***seizures*** (convulsions)

Those indicating need for medical attention only if they continue or are bothersome
Incidence less frequent

Bronchitis (cough producing mucus; difficulty breathing; shortness of breath; tightness in chest; wheezing); ***cough; diarrhea; dizziness; ear, nose and throat infections*** (change in hearing; earache; pain in ear; ear drainage); ***headache; nausea; nasal signs and symptoms; sinusitis*** (pain and pressure over the cheeks); ***vomiting***

Incidence not determined—Observed during clinical practice; estimates of frequency can not be determined

Dyspnea (shortness of breath; difficult or labored breathing; tightness in chest or wheezing); ***rash*** (red, scaly, swollen, or peeling areas of skin)—including severe cutaneous reactions; ***syncope*** (fainting or lightheadedness when getting up from a lying or sitting position; unusually fast heartbeat or palpitations)

Overdose
For more information on the management of overdose or unintentional ingestion, **contact a poison control center** (see *Poison Control Center Listing*).

There is a lack of data on overdose of zanamivir. Adverse effects are similar between patients administered recommended doses and patients administered doses of up to 1200 milligrams per day intravenously for 5 days.

There is no known specific antidote to zanamivir. Treatment is generally symptomatic and supportive.

Patients in whom an intentional overdose is confirmed or suspected should be referred for psychiatric consultation.

Patient Consultation
As an aid to patient consultation, refer to *Advice for the Patient, Zanamivir (Inhalation-Systemic)*.

In providing consultation, consider emphasizing the following selected information (» = major clinical significance):

Before using this medication
» Conditions affecting use, especially:

Use in children—Not recommended in pediatric patients under 7 years of age

Note: Canadian manufacturer states use is not recommended in patients under 12 years of age.

Other medical problems, especially chronic pulmonary disease such as chronic obstructive lung disease and asthma; and hypersensitivity

Proper use of this medication
» Reading patient package insert carefully

Proper administration technique for inhaler:

» Compliance with full 5-day course of therapy

Starting therapy within 2 days after the onset of signs and symptoms of influenza (weakness, headache, fever, cough, and sore throat)

» Proper dosing

Missed dose: Using as soon as possible; not using if almost time for the next dose; not doubling doses

» Proper storage

Precautions while using this medication
The use of zanamivir has not been shown to reduce the risk of transmission of influenza to others

Fast-acting inhaled bronchodilator should be available for patients with asthma or chronic obstructive pulmonary disease

Administer inhaled bronchodilators before zanamivir for patients who take scheduled inhaled bronchodilators

Side/adverse effects
» Signs of potential side effects, especially Allergic reaction, arrythmias, bronchospasm, dyspnea, facial swelling, oropharyngeal edema, seizures

General Dosing Information

Zanamivir must be started within 2 days after the onset of signs and symptoms of influenza (weakness, headache, fever, cough, and sore throat).

Patients should be instructed on the use of the delivery system. Instructions should include a demonstration whenever possible.

If zanamivir is prescribed for children, it should be used only under adult supervision and instruction, and the supervising adult should first be instructed by a healthcare professional.

Patients with underlying respiratory disease should be instructed to have a fast acting inhalation bronchodilator available when treated with zanamivir. Patients scheduled to take bronchodilator at the same time as zanamivir should be advised to use their bronchodilator before using zanamivir.

Serious bacterial infections may begin with influenza-like symptoms, may co-exist with, or occur as complications during the course of this illness. Zanamivir has not been shown to prevent these complications.

Inhalation Dosage Form

Note: Bracketed uses in the *Dosage Forms* section refer to categories of use and/or indications that are not included in U.S. product labeling.

ZANAMIVIR POWDER FOR INHALATION

Usual adult and adolescent dose

Influenza A (treatment) or
Influenza B (treatment)—

Two oral inhalations (5 milligram per inhalation) twice daily (approximately 12 hours apart in the morning and evening) for 5 days. Two doses should be taken on the first day of treatment whenever possible provided there are at least 2 hours between doses. Zanamivir must be initiated within 48 hours after the onset of signs and symptoms of influenza. Administer zanamivir with the DISKHALER.

[Influenza A (prophylaxis)][1] or
Influenza B (prophylaxis)—

Two oral inhalations (5 mg per inhalation) once daily for 10 to 14 days until the vaccine response takes place or for the remainder of the exposure.

Usual pediatric dose

Influenza A (treatment) or
Influenza B (treatment)—

Children under 7 years of age: Safety and efficacy have not been established[1].

Children 7 years of age and older: See *Usual adult and adolescent dose*[1].

[Children under 12 years of age: Safety and efficacy have not been established]

Children 12 years of age and older: See *Usual adult and adolescent dose*.

[Influenza A (prophylaxis)][1] or
[Influenza B (prophylaxis)][1]—

Children under 7 years of age: Safety and efficacy have not been established.

Children 7 years of age and older: See *Usual adult and adolescent dose*.

Strength(s) usually available

U.S.—

Note: The package is supplied with 5 circular double-foil packs in a white polypropylene tube and one DISKHALER inhalation device. Each circular double-foil pack (a ROTADISK) contains 4 blisters of the drug.

5 mg per blister (delivering 4 mg) (Rx) [*Relenza* (lactose)].

Canada—

5 mg per blister (Rx) [*Relenza* (lactose [20 mg])].

Packaging and storage

Store at 25 °C (77 °F); excursions permitted to 15 °C to 30 °C (59 °F to 86 °F).

Auxiliary labeling

• Continue medication for full time of treatment.

Note

Include patient instructions when dispensing.
Demonstrate administration technique.

[1]Not included in Canadian product labeling.

Revised: 12/23/2002

ZICONOTIDE Systemic

VA CLASSIFICATION (Primary): CN103

Commonly used brand name(s): *Prialt*.

Note: For a listing of dosage forms and brand names by country availability, see *Dosage Forms* section(s).

Category

Analgesic.

Indications

Accepted

Pain, chronic (treatment)—Ziconotide is indicated for the management of severe chronic pain in patients for whom intrathecal therapy is warranted, and who are intolerant of or refractory to other treatment, such as systemic analgesics, adjunctive therapies or intrathecal morphine.

Unaccepted

Ziconotide is not an opiate and should not be used to relieve the symptoms associated with the withdrawal of opiates.

Pharmacology/Pharmacokinetics

Physicochemical characteristics

Source—Synthetic equivalent of a naturally occurring conopeptide found in the piscivorous marine snail, *Conus magnus*..

Molecular weight—2369 daltons.

Solubility—Freely soluble in water and practically insoluble in methyl t-butyl ether.

Mechanism of action/Effect

Although the mechanism of action has not been established in humans, results in animals suggest that ziconotide binds to afferent nerves of the spinal cord, which blocks N-type calcium channels and leads to a blockade of excitatory neurotransmitter release in the primary afferent nerve terminals and antinociaption.

Ziconotide does not interact with opioid receptors and does not potentiate opioid induced respiratory depression.

Absorption

AUC: 83.6 to 608 ng h per mL following 1–hour intrathecal administration of 1 to 10 mg of ziconotide

Distribution

Volume of distribution (Vol_D): 155 ± 263 mL

Protein binding

Moderate (50%) to human plasma proteins

Biotransformation

Proteolytic cleavage by peptidases/proteases present in most organs; readily degraded to peptide fragments and their individual constituent free amino acids. *In vitro*, human and animal.

Half-life

Intrathecal: 4.6 ± 0.9 hrs; Intravenous: 1.3 ± 0.3 hrs

Peak serum concentration

Plasma concentration: Using an assay with a lower limit of detection of approximately 0.04 ng per mL, ziconotide plasma levels could not be quantified in 56% of patients following intrathecal administration.

Peak CSF concentration

16.4 to 132 ng per mL following 1–hour intrathecal administration

Elimination

Renal: <1% following IV infusion of 1 to 10 mg ziconotide

Clearance: Intravenous—270 ± 44 mL per min; Intrathecal—0.38 ± 0.56 mL per min; approximate adult human turnover rate (0.3–0.4 mL per min)

Precautions to Consider

Carcinogenicity

No carcinogenicity studies have been conducted in animals.

Mutagenicity

Ziconotide was negative in the *in vitro* bacterial reverse mutation assay, *in vitro* mouse lymphoma assay, *in vivo* mouse micronucleus assay, and the *in vitro* Syrian hamster embryo cell transformation assay.

Pregnancy/Reproduction

Fertility—Ziconotide did not affect male fertility in rats when administered as a continuous intravenous infusion at a dose of up to 10 mg per kg per day for approximately 8 weeks (6500 times the expected exposure from the maximum human daily intrathecal dose). Ziconotide did not effect female fertility in rats at a dose of 3 mg per kg per day for approximately 6 weeks (1700 times the expected exposure from the maximum human daily intrathecal dose). Significant reductions in corpora lutea, implantation sites, and number of live fetuses were observed when female rats were given a continuous intravenous infusion of 10 mg per kg per day.

Pregnancy—Adequate and well controlled studies in humans have not been done. Because animal studies are not always predictive of human response, ziconotide should be used during pregnancy only if the potential benefits justify risk to the fetus.

Studies in animals have shown that ziconotide is embryolethal during organogenesis and may lead to lead to transient, delayed ossification of the pubic bones.

FDA Pregnancy Category C

Breast-feeding

It is not known whether ziconotide is distributed in human breast milk. Because many drugs are distributed in human milk, and because of the potential for serious adverse reactions in nursing infants from ziconotide, a decision should be made whether to discontinue nursing or to discontinue the drug, taking into account the importance of the drug to the mother.

Pediatrics

No information is available on the relationship of age to the effects of ziconotide in the pediatric population. Safety and efficacy have not been established.

Geriatrics

Although appropriate studies on the relationship of age to the effects of ziconotide have not been performed in the geriatric population, elderly patients have been shown to have a higher incidence of confusion. The dose selection for an elderly patient should be cautious, usually starting at the low end of the dosing range.

Drug interactions and/or related problems

The following drug interactions and/or related problems have been selected on the basis of their potential clinical significance (possible mechanism in parentheses where appropriate)—not necessarily inclusive (» = major clinical significance):

Note: Combinations containing any of the following medications, depending on the amount present, may also interact with this medication.

Antidepressants or
Antiepileptics or
Morphine, IT
(concomitant use with these medicines may lead to elevated serum creatine kinase)

Antiepileptics or
CNS depressants or
Diuretics or
Neuroleptics or
Sedatives
(concomitant use may lead to higher risk of depressed levels of consciousness, including dizziness and confusion)

» Opioids, intrathecal
(concomitant use of intrathecal ziconotide and intrathecal opioids is not recommended. Intrathecal opioid infusion should be gradually tapered over a few weeks and replaced with a pharmacologically equivalent dose of oral opioid to avoid opioid withdrawal; ziconotide is NOT an opioid and can not prevent or relieve the symptoms associated with opioid withdrawal.)

Laboratory value alterations

The following have been selected on the basis of their potential clinical significance (possible effect in parentheses where appropriate)—not necessarily inclusive (» = major clinical significance).

With physiology/laboratory test values
Creatine kinase, serum
(may increase levels above the upper limit of normal)

Medical considerations/Contraindications

The medical considerations/contraindications included have been selected on the basis of their potential clinical significance (reasons given in parentheses where appropriate)—not necessarily inclusive (» = major clinical significance).

Except under special circumstances, this medication should not be used when the following medical problem exists:

» Hypersensitivity to ziconotide

» Psychosis, history of
(severe psychiatric symptoms and neurological impairment may occur during treatment with ziconotide; ziconotide can be discontinued abruptly in the event of serious neurologic or psychosis signs or symptoms without evidence of withdrawal effects)

» Presence of infection at the microinfusion site or
» Spinal canal obstruction or
» Uncontrolled bleeding diathesis
(these conditions contraindicate the use of intrathecal analgesia)

Patient monitoring

The following may be especially important in patient monitoring (other tests may be warranted in some patients, depending on condition; » = major clinical significance):

Changes in mood or
Changes in consciousness or
Cognitive impairment or
Hallucinations
(monitor frequently; ziconotide can be discontinued abruptly in the event of serious neurologic or psychiatric signs or symptoms)

Creatine kinase, serum
(monitor every other week for the first month and monthly as appropriate thereafter)

Side/Adverse Effects

The following side/adverse effects have been selected on the basis of their potential clinical significance (possible signs and symptoms in parentheses where appropriate)—not necessarily inclusive:

Note: Patients, caregivers and healthcare providers must be particularly vigilant for the signs and symptoms of meningitis. Serious infection or meningitis can occur within 24 hours of a breach in sterility such as disconnected catheter, the most common cause of meningitis with external microfusion devices.

Those indicating need for medical attention

Incidence more frequent

Confusion; hallucinations (seeing, hearing, or feeling things that are not there)

Incidence less frequent

Acute kidney failure (back or side pain, nausea, vomiting); ***atrial fibrillation*** (fast or irregular heartbeat, dizziness, fainting); ***grand mal convulsion*** (convulsions, muscle spasm or jerking of all extremities sudden loss of consciousness, loss of bladder control); ***meningitis*** (severe headache, drowsiness. confusion. stiff neck and/or back. general feeling of illness or nausea); ***pneumonia*** (chest pain, cough, fever or chills, sneezing, shortness of breath, sore throat, troubled breathing, tightness in chest, wheezing); ***respiratory distress*** (shortness of breath, troubled breathing, tightness in chest, or wheezing); ***rhabdomylosis*** (dark-colored urine, fever, muscle cramps or spasms, muscle pain or stiffness, unusual tiredness or weakness); ***sepsis*** (chills, confusion, dizziness, lightheadedness, fainting, fast heartbeat, fever, rapid, shallow breathing); ***suicidal ideation*** (thoughts of killing oneself, changes in behavior)

Incidence rare

Aspiration pneumonia (infection from breathing foreign substance into the lungs); ***suicide*** (attempts at killing oneself)

Those indicating need for medical attention only if they continue or are bothersome

Incidence more frequent

Abnormal gait (change in walking and balance, clumsiness, or unsteadiness); ***abnormal vision; anorexia*** (loss of appetite, weight loss); ***anxiety*** (fear, nervousness); ***aphasia*** (problems with speech or speaking); ***asthenia*** (lack or loss of strength); ***ataxia*** (shakiness and unsteady walk, unsteadiness. trembling, or other problems with muscle control or coordination); ***diarrhea; dizziness; dysesthesia*** (burning, crawling, itching, numbness, prickling, "pins and needles", or tingling feelings); ***fever; headache; hypertonia*** (excessive muscle tone, muscle tension or tightness, muscle stiffness); ***memory impairment; nausea; nervousness; nystagmus*** (uncontrolled eye movements); ***pain; paresthesia*** (burning, crawling, itching, numbness, prickling, "pins and needles", or tingling feelings); ***somnolence*** (sleepiness or unusual drowsiness); ***speech disorder*** (difficulty in speaking); ***thinking abnormal; urinary retention; vertigo*** (dizziness or lightheadedness, feeling of constant movement of self or surroundings, sensation of spinning); ***vomiting***

Incidence less frequent

Abdominal pain; abnormal dreams; accidental injury; agitation; amnesia (loss of memory, problems with memory); ***anemia*** (pale skin, troubled breathing with exertion, unusual bleeding or bruising, unusual tiredness or weakness); ***arthralgia*** (pain in joints, muscle pain or stiffness, difficulty in moving); ***arthritis*** (pain, swelling, or redness in joints muscle pain or stiffness, difficulty in moving); ***bronchitis*** (cough producing mucus, difficulty breathing, shortness of breath, tightness in chest, wheezing); ***catheter complication*** (redness or pain at the catheter site, fever); ***catheter site pain; cellulitis*** (itching, pain, redness, swelling, tenderness, warmth on skin); ***cerebrospinal fluid abnormal; chest pain; chills; constipation; cough increased; creatinine phosphokinase increased; cutaneous surgical complication*** (red, scaly, swollen, or peeling areas of skin); ***dehydration; depression*** (discouragement, feeling sad or empty, irritability, lack of appetite, loss of interest or pleasure, tiredness, trouble concentrating, trouble sleeping); ***difficulty concentrating; diplopia*** (double vision seeing double); ***dry mouth; dry skin; dyspepsia*** (acid or sour stomach, belching, heartburn, indigestion, stomach discomfort, upset, or pain); ***dyspnea*** (shortness of breath; difficult or labored breathing; tightness in chest; wheezing); ***dysuria*** (difficult or painful urination, burning while urinating); ***ecchymosis*** (bruising; large, flat, blue or purplish patches in the skin); ***edema*** (swelling); ***electrocardiogram abnormal; emotional lability*** (crying; depersonalization; dysphoria; euphoria; mental depression; paranoia; quick to react or overreact emotionally; rapidly changing moods); ***flu syndrome; gastrointestinal disorder; hostility; hyperesthesia*** (increased sensitivity to pain; increased sensitivity to touch; tingling in the hands and feet); ***hypertension*** (blurred vision; dizziness; nervousness; headache; pounding in the ears; slow or fast heartbeat); ***hypertonia*** (excessive muscle tone; muscle tension or tightness; muscle stiffness); ***hypokalemia*** (abdominal pain; confusion; irregular heartbeat; nausea or vomiting; nervousness; numbness or tingling in hands, feet, or lips; shortness of breath; difficult breathing; weakness or heaviness of legs); ***hypotension*** (blurred vision; confusion; dizziness, faintness, or lightheadedness when getting up from a lying or sitting position suddenly; sweating; unusual tiredness or weakness); ***incoordination; insomnia*** (sleeplessness; trouble sleeping; unable to sleep); ***infection; leg cramps; lung disorder; malaise*** (general feeling of discomfort or illness; unusual tiredness or weakness); ***mental slowing; myoclonus*** (muscle twitching or jerking, rhythmic movement of muscles); ***myalgia*** (muscle pain); ***myasthenia*** (loss of strength or energy; muscle pain or weakness); ***neck rigidity*** (severe muscle stiffness); ***neuralgia*** (nerve pain); ***pain, back or neck; paranoid reaction; pharyngitis*** (body aches or pain; congestion; cough; dryness or soreness of throat; fever; hoarseness; runny nose; tender, swollen glands in neck; trouble in swallowing; voice changes); ***photophobia*** (blurred vision; change in color vision; difficulty seeing at night; increased sensitivity of eyes to sunlight); ***postural hypotension*** (chills; cold sweats; confusion; dizziness, faintness, or lightheadedness when getting up from lying or sitting position); ***pruritis*** (itching skin); ***psychosis*** (feeling that others can hear your thoughts; feeling that others are watching you or controlling your behavior; feeling, seeing, or hearing things that are not there; severe mood or mental changes; unusual behavior); ***pump site complication; pump site mass; pump site pain; rash; reflexes decreased; rhinitis*** (stuffy nose; runny nose; sneezing); ***sinusitis*** (pain or tenderness around eyes and cheekbones; fever; stuffy or runny nose; headache; cough; shortness of breath or troubled breathing; tightness of chest or wheezing); ***skin disorder; stupor*** (decreased awareness or responsiveness; severe sleepiness); ***sweating; syncope*** (fainting); ***tachycardia*** (fast, pounding, or irregular heartbeat or pulse); ***taste perversion*** (change in taste; bad unusual or unpleasant (after)taste); ***tinnitus*** (continuing ringing or buzzing or other unexplained noise in ears; hearing loss); ***tremor*** (trembling or shaking of hands or feet; shakiness in legs, arms, hands, feet); ***twitching; urinary incontinence*** (loss of bladder control); ***urinary tract infection*** (bladder pain; bloody or cloudy urine; difficult, burning, or painful urination; frequent urge to urinate; lower back or side pain); ***urination impaired; vasodilation*** (feeling of warmth or heat; flushing or redness of skin, especially on face and neck; headache; feeling faint, dizzy, or light-headedness; sweating); ***viral infection*** (chills; cough or hoarseness; fever; cold flu-like symptoms); ***weight loss***

Overdose

For more information on the management of overdose or unintentional ingestion, **contact a poison control center** (see *Poison Control Center Listing*).

Clinical effects of overdose

The following effects have been selected on the basis of their potential clinical significance (possible signs and symptoms in parentheses where appropriate)—not necessarily inclusive:

Ataxia (shakiness and unsteady walk, unsteadiness, trembling, or other problems with muscle control or coordination); ***confusion; dizziness; garbled speech; hypotension*** (blurred vision; confusion; dizziness, faintness, or lightheadedness when getting up from a lying or sitting position suddenly; sweating; unusual tiredness or weakness); ***nausea; nystagmus*** (uncontrolled eye movements); ***sedation*** (drowsiness, sleepiness, relaxed and calm); ***spinal myoclonus; stupor*** (decreased awareness or responsiveness; severe sleepiness); ***unresponsiveness; word finding difficulties; vomiting***

Treatment of overdose

Specific treatment—

There is no known antidote to ziconotide

See the package insert or *Ziconotide (Systemic)* for specific dosing guidelines for use of this product.

Supportive care—

General medical supportive measures should be administered until the exaggerated effects of ziconotide have been resolved. Ziconotide should be either temporarily discontinued or permanently withdrawn. Most patients recovered within 24 hours after withdrawal of drug when overdose occurred due to pump programming errors or incorrect drug concentration preparations.

Patients in whom intentional overdose is confirmed or suspected should be referred for psychiatric consultation.

Patient Consultation

As an aid to patient consultation, refer to *Advice for the Patient, Ziconotide (Intrathecal)*.

In providing consultation, consider emphasizing the following selected information (» = major clinical significance):

Before using this medication

» Conditions affecting use, especially:

Pregnancy—Studies in animals have shown that ziconotide is embryolethal during organogenesis and may lead to transient, delayed ossification of the pubic bones

Breast-feeding—Should be used in nursing woman only if the potential benefits justify the risks to the fetus

Other medications, especially intrathecal opioids

Other medical problems, especially hypersensitivity to ziconotide and history of psychosis.

Proper use of this medication

» Proper dosing

Proper storage

Precautions while using this medication

» Caution if dizziness or drowsiness occurs; not driving, using machines, or doing anything else that requires alertness while taking ziconotide and for 24 hours after discontinuing it

» Contacting a physician if changes in mood or mental status occur

» Contacting a physician if symptoms of depression or suicidal ideation occur

» Contacting a physician if nausea, vomiting, seizures, fever, headache, or stiff neck occur, as these may be signs of meningitis

Side/adverse effects

Signs of potential side effects, especially acute kidney failure, atrial fibrillation, cerebrovascular accident, confusion, grand mal convulsion, hallucinations, meningitis, pneumonia, respiratory distress, rhabdomylosis, sepsis, suicidal ideation

General Dosing Information

Ziconotide is for use in the Meditronic Synchromed® EL, Meditronic Synchromed ® II Infusion system and Simms Deltec Cadd Micro® External Microfusion Device and Catheter.

Ziconotide is not intended for intravenous administration.

Intrathecal Dosage Forms

ZICONOTIDE INJECTION

Usual adult dose

Analgesic—

Intrathecal, 2.4 mcg per day (0.1 mcg per hr) titrated to patient response. Doses may be titrated up at 2.4 mcg per day at intervals of no more than 2 to 3 times per week

Usual adult prescribing limits

19.2 mcg per day (0.8 mcg per hr) at day 21

Usual pediatric dose

Safety and efficacy have not been established

Usual geriatric dose

See *Usual adult dose*.

Strength(s) usually available

U.S.—

25 mcg per mL (Rx) [*Prialt* (L-methionine; sodium chloride)].

100 mcg per mL (Rx) [*Prialt* (L-methionine; sodium chloride)].

Packaging and storage

Store between 2 and 8 °C (36 and 46 °F). Protect from light. Protect from freezing.

Saline diluted solution may be stored at 2 and 8 °C (36 and 46 °F) for 24 hrs.

Preparation of dosage form

Ziconotide should be administered by or under the direction of a physician experienced in the technique of intrathecal administration and who is familiar with the drug and device labeling. Ziconotide should be delivered using a programmable implanted variable-rate microfusion device or an external microinfusion device and catheter. Diluted ziconotide (100mcg per mL is prepared with 0.9% sodium chloride injection, USP (preservative free) using aseptic procedures. Once an appropriate dose is established, ziconotide 100 mcg per mL may be administered undiluted.

See the manufacturer's package insert for instructions.

Auxiliary labeling

- May cause drowsiness.
- Be careful while driving or operating machinery.
- Use caution until you become familiar with its effects

Developed: 05/18/2005

ZIDOVUDINE Systemic

VA CLASSIFICATION (Primary): AM840

Commonly used brand name(s): *Apo-Zidovudine; Novo-AZT; Retrovir.*

Another commonly used name is AZT.

Note: For a listing of dosage forms and brand names by country availability, see *Dosage Forms* section(s).

Category

Antiviral (systemic).

Indications

Note: Bracketed information in the *Indications* section refers to uses that are not included in U.S. product labeling.

General Considerations

In vitro resistance of human immunodeficiency virus (HIV) isolates to zidovudine has been reported in patients with acquired immunodeficiency syndrome (AIDS) who received zidovudine treatment for 6 months or longer. Deterioration of clinical status has been observed in some patients with resistant virus; evidence of a direct association of viral resistance with lack of drug effect continues to mount. Patients can simultaneously carry several viral strains with different susceptibilities to zidovudine. Reduced *in vitro* sensitivity of HIV to zidovudine develops at a slower rate and to a lesser degree in patients with early stages of infection than in those with advanced disease.

Zidovudine is not a cure for HIV infection. Patients treated with zidovudine may continue to develop complications of AIDS, including opportunistic infections. The treatment or prevention of these infections may require the concurrent administration of other anti-infectives.

Accepted

Human immunodeficiency virus (HIV) infection (treatment)—Zidovudine is indicated in combination with other antiretroviral agents for the treatment of HIV infection. Antiretroviral therapy is recommended in all patients with clinical symptoms associated with HIV infection. In adults, therapy also is recommended in asymptomatic patients with CD4+ T cell counts less than 200 cells per mm³ (cells/mm³) and should be offered to those with cell counts between 200 and 300 cells/mm³ regardless of HIV RNA concentration. However, some experts recommend initiating therapy in asymptomatic patients with CD4+ T cell counts greater than 350 cells/mm³ if the HIV RNA concentration is greater than 30,000 copies per mL using the branched chain DNA assay or greater than 55,000 copies per mL using the Roche polymerase chain reaction assay. Children who should receive antiretroviral therapy include those who are less than 12 months of age, regardless of clinical, immunologic, or virologic status, and those with moderate or severe immune suppression as determined by CD4+ T cell absolute number or percentage. When to initiate antiretroviral therapy in asymptomatic children 1 year of age or older is less well-defined. One approach is to initiate therapy regardless of age or symptom status. Alternatively, therapy may be deferred until there is high or increasing HIV RNA copy number, rapidly declining CD4+ T cell absolute number or percentage to values approaching those indicative of moderate suppression, or development of clinical symptoms. If the latter approach is taken, virologic, immunologic, and clinical status must be monitored regularly.

Mother-to-child transmission of HIV-1 infection (prophylaxis)—Zidovudine is indicated for the prevention of mother-to-child transmission of HIV-1 infection as part of a regimen that includes oral zidovudine beginning between 14 and 34 weeks gestation, continuous intravenous infusion of zidovudine during labor, and administration of zidovudine syrup to the neonate for the first 6 weeks of life. However, transmission to infants may still occur in some cases despite the use of this regimen.

[Human immunodeficiency virus (HIV) infection, occupational exposure (prophylaxis)][1]—Zidovudine has been used prophylactically in health care workers at risk of acquiring HIV infection after occupational exposure to the virus. Risk of transmission from a single needlestick is approximately 0.3%. Efficacy, and optimal dose and duration of prophylactic treatment are unknown at this time; however, HIV infection has occurred in persons who received zidovudine prophylaxis after a needlestick or other parenteral exposure.

Unaccepted

Zidovudine is not effective in the treatment of infections caused by gram-positive organisms, gram-negative organisms, cytomegalovirus, vaccinia, herpes simplex, varicella zoster, anaerobes, mycobacteria, or fungi.

Zidovudine has not been shown to reduce the risk of transmission of HIV to others through sexual contact or blood contamination.

[1]Not included in Canadian product labeling.

Pharmacology/Pharmacokinetics

Physicochemical characteristics

Molecular weight—267.25.

Mechanism of action/Effect

Virustatic; zidovudine, a structural analog of thymidine, is phosphorylated intracellularly by cellular thymidine kinase to zidovudine monophosphate. The monophosphate is converted to the diphosphate by cellular thymidylate kinase and is further converted to the triphosphate by other cellular enzymes. Zidovudine triphosphate competes with the natural substrate, thymidine triphosphate, for incorporation into growing chains of viral RNA-dependent DNA polymerase (reverse transcriptase), thereby inhibiting viral DNA replication. Once incorporated, zidovudine triphosphate also prematurely terminates the growing DNA chain since the 3′-azido group prevents further 5′ to 3′ phosphodiester linkages. Zidovudine has a 100- to 300-fold greater affinity for inhibiting HIV reverse transcriptase than it does for inhibiting human DNA polymerase.

Other actions/effects

Zidovudine has been found to have activity against hepatitis B virus and Epstein-Barr virus *in vitro* ; however, one small study found that zidovudine did not markedly inhibit hepatitis B virus replication when used alone in patients with AIDS. Low concentrations of zidovudine also have been shown to inhibit many strains of Enterobacteriaceae *in vitro* , including strains of *Shigella*, *Salmonella*, *Klebsiella*, *Enterobacter*, and *Citrobacter* species, and *Escherichia coli*. However, bacterial resistance to zidovudine develops rapidly. No activity was seen against *Pseudomonas aeruginosa in vitro* . At very high concentrations (1.9 mcg/mL [7 micromoles per L]), zidovudine also has been shown to inhibit *Giardia lamblia*, although no activity has been observed against other protozoal pathogens.

Absorption

Rapid and nearly complete absorption from the gastrointestinal tract following oral administration; however, because of first-pass metabolism, systemic bioavailability of zidovudine capsules and solution is approximately 65% (range, 52 to 75%). Bioavailability in neonates up to 14 days of age is approximately 89%, and it decreases to approximately 61% and 65% in neonates over 14 days of age and children 3 months to 12 years, respectively. Administration with a high-fat meal may decrease the rate and extent of absorption.

Distribution

Crosses the blood-brain barrier; distribution to cerebrospinal fluid (CSF) averages approximately 68% of the plasma concentration in children (ages three months to twelve years) and 60% of the plasma concentration in adults.

Crosses the placenta. One case report and a study in three pregnant women found that the zidovudine concentrations in the infant cord blood were slightly higher than simultaneous maternal serum concentrations, and that the amniotic fluid concentrations were several times higher than the simultaneous umbilical cord concentrations. The concentration of zidovudine in the central nervous system (CNS) tissue of a gestational 13-week fetus (0.01 micromole per liter) was below effective antiviral concentrations.

Also shown to concentrate in the semen of HIV-infected patients, with concentrations ranging from 1.3 to 20.4 times those found in the serum; zidovudine does not appear to affect the recovery of HIV from the semen, and, therefore, may not prevent sexual transmission of HIV.

Vol_D—Adults and children: 1.4 to 1.7 liters per kg (42 to 52 liters per m^2).

Protein binding
Low (30 to 38%).

Biotransformation
Hepatic; metabolized by glucuronide conjugation to major, inactive metabolite, 3′-azido-3′-deoxy-5′-*O*-beta-*D*-glucopyranuronosylthymidine (GZDV).

In children under 1 year of age—The glucuronide conjugation pathway is underdeveloped at birth; however, a study done in infants older than 30 days of age found that the clearance and half-life of zidovudine were comparable to those in adults.

Half-life
Intracellular zidovudine-triphosphate—
- Approximately 3.3 hours.

Zidovudine (serum)—
- Adults (oral and intravenous):
  - Normal renal function—Approximately 1 hour (range, 0.8 to 1.2 hours).
  - Renal function impairment (creatinine clearance < 30 mL per min)—1.4 to 2.9 hours.
  - Cirrhosis—Variable, depending on the degree of liver function impairment; however, one study found the half-life to be approximately 2.4 hours.
- Children age 2 weeks to 13 years (oral and intravenous):
  - Approximately 1 to 1.8 hours.
- Children up to 14 days of age:
  - Approximately 3 hours.
- Neonates (mother receiving zidovudine):
  - Approximately 13 hours.

GZDV (serum)—
- Adults (oral and intravenous):
  - Normal renal function—
    - Approximately 1 hour.
  - Renal function impairment—
    - Approximately 8 hours.
  - Anuria—
    - 29 to 94 hours.
  - Cirrhosis—
    - Variable, depending on the degree of liver function impairment; however, one study found the half-life to be approximately 2.4 hours.

Time to peak concentration
Serum—0.5 to 1.5 hours.

CSF—1 hour after end of 1-hour infusion.

Peak serum concentration
Linear kinetics—
- Intravenous infusion: 1 mg per kg of body weight (mg/kg) (over 1 hour)—1.5 to 2.5 micromoles per L (0.40 to 0.68 mcg/mL).
- Oral (capsules and solution): 2 mg/kg—1.5 to 2 micromoles per L (0.41 to 0.54 mcg/mL).
- Continuous intravenous infusion in children (age 14 months to 12 years): Steady state concentrations—0.5 mg/kg per hour (360 per square meter of body surface area [mg/m^2] per day): 1.9 micromoles per L (0.51 mcg/mL).

Elimination
Adults—
- Zidovudine: Renal; approximately 14 to 18% excreted by glomerular filtration and active tubular secretion in urine.
- GZDV: Renal; approximately 60 to 74% recovered in urine.
- Total of zidovudine and GZDV: Approximately 63 to 95% recovered in urine.
- In dialysis: Current available data vary; it appears that hemodialysis and peritoneal dialysis have a negligible effect on the removal of zidovudine. Hemodialysis does enhance the elimination of GZDV; however, dialysis clearance of GZDV is minimal compared to the clearance of GZDV in patients with normal renal function.

Children (age 14 months to 12 years)—
- Zidovudine: Renal; approximately 30% excreted by the kidneys.
- GZDV: Renal; approximately 45% recovered in the urine.

Precautions to Consider

Carcinogenicity
Long-term carcinogenicity studies found five malignant and two benign vaginal squamous cell tumors in 60 female mice given zidovudine in doses of 120 mg per kg of body weight (mg/kg) per day, later reduced to 40 mg/kg per day. Two out of 60 rats were found to have vaginal squamous cell carcinoma after receiving doses of 600 mg/kg per day, later reduced to 450, then 300 mg/kg per day. The tumors occurred at the end of the life span of the animals. No treatment-related tumors were seen in the 60 male mice or 60 male rats.

Two transplacental carcinogenicity studies in pregnant mice showed carcinogenic potential. In the first study, zidovudine was administered at doses of 20 mg/kg per day or 40 mg/kg per day from day 10 of gestation through parturition and lactation and continuing in the offspring for 24 months postnatally. After 24 months, an increase in incidence of vaginal tumors was observed in the offspring. In the second study, zidovudine was administered at maximum tolerated doses of 12.5 mg per day or 25 mg per day (approximately 1000 or 450 mg/kg of nonpregnant or term body weight, respectively) from days 12 through 18 of gestation. An increase in incidence of tumors was observed in the lung, liver, and female reproductive tracts in the offspring of the mice receiving the higher dose of zidovudine.

Mutagenicity
Zidovudine was shown to be mutagenic in a 5178Y/TK$^{+/-}$ mouse lymphoma assay and positive in an *in vitro* cell transformation assay. Zidovudine was clastogenic in a cytogenetic assay using cultured human lymphocytes. Zidovudine was negative in one cytogenetic study in rats given a single dose; however, it was positive in mouse and rat micronucleus tests after repeated doses.

Pregnancy/Reproduction
Fertility—The effects of zidovudine on fertility have not been studied in humans.

Studies in rats given oral zidovudine at dosages up to 450 mg/kg per day showed no effect on male or female fertility.

Pregnancy—*An Antiretroviral Pregnancy Registry has been established to monitor the outcomes of pregnant women exposed to zidovudine. Physicians are encouraged by the manufacturer to register patients by calling (800) 258-4263. Canadian health care professionals should call (800) 387–7374 to register their patients.*

Zidovudine crosses the placenta with a cord-to–maternal blood ratio of approximately 0.8. The rate of HIV transmission from pregnant women to their infants has been shown to be decreased in women treated with zidovudine compared with women treated with placebo. A randomized, double-blind, placebo-controlled study was conducted in HIV-positive pregnant women to evaluate the utility of zidovudine in preventing the transmission of HIV from mother to fetus. In this study, oral zidovudine therapy was initiated in pregnant women between weeks 14 and 34 of gestation (median 11 weeks of therapy), and intravenous zidovudine was administered during labor and delivery. Zidovudine therapy was continued orally in the newborn after birth for 6 weeks. The study showed a reduced incidence of HIV infection in the newborns of the zidovudine group; the estimated risk of infection was 7.8% in the group receiving zidovudine and 24.9% in the placebo group, indicating a relative reduction in transmission risk of 68.7%. No differences in pregnancy-related adverse events were noted between the zidovudine-treated and placebo groups. Congenital abnormalities occurred at similar rates among the newborns of zidovudine-treated mothers and the newborns of mothers who received placebo. The abnormalities noted were either problems in embryogenesis (prior to 14 weeks) or were identified on ultrasound before or immediately after the initiation of zidovudine. Neither the efficacy of zidovudine therapy in preventing mother-to-child transmission of HIV-1 infection in women who had received zidovudine for a prolonged period prior to pregnancy nor the safety of zidovudine in the first trimester for the mother or fetus was evaluated in this study. One survey of 43 women who took zidovudine (300 to 1200 mg per day) during various stages of pregnancy found that zidovudine was well tolerated by the mothers and was not associated with teratogenic abnormalities, premature birth, or fetal distress. One early report suggested that zidovudine caused mito chondrial dysfunction with neurologic sequelae in children exposed *in utero* and postnatally. However, review of 20,000 children born to HIV-infected women with or without exposure to zidovudine did not confirm the finding. This review failed to show any evidence of cardiac, immunologic, neurologic, or oncologic complications. Three small studies done in women given zidovudine during their last trimester of pregnancy found that peak plasma concentrations and the elimination half-life were similar to values reported in nonpregnant adults, although volume of distribution and plasma clearance were significantly increased during pregnancy in two of the studies. Therapeutic plasma concentrations have been measured in the newborn infant. Therapeutic levels also have been measured in the amniotic fluid of a gestational 13-week fetus; however, the concentration of zidovudine in this fetus' CNS tissue (0.01 micromole per liter) was below effective antiviral concentrations.

Studies in rats and rabbits given oral doses of up to 500 mg/kg per day have not shown zidovudine to be teratogenic. There was an increased incidence of fetal resorption in rats given 150 or 450 mg/kg per day of zidovudine, rabbits given 500 mg/kg per day, and mice given 0.25 mg/mL in drinking water, producing serum concentrations of 0.12 mcg/mL. In an *in vitro* experiment with fertilized mouse oocytes, exposure to zidovudine resulted in a dose-dependent reduction in blastocyst formation. In rats, 3000 mg/kg per day (resulting in peak plasma concentrations of 350 times the peak human plasma concentration) caused marked maternal toxicity and an increase in the incidence of fetal malformations. Teratogenic effects were not seen in this experiment at doses of 600 mg/kg per day or less.

FDA Pregnancy Category C.

Breast-feeding

Zidovudine is distributed into human breast milk. After administration of a single 200-mg dose, the mean concentration of zidovudine in breast milk is similar to that of serum concentrations. In addition, the Centers for Disease Control and Prevention recommends that HIV-infected mothers refrain from breast-feeding their infants, to avoid risking postnatal transmission of HIV

Pediatrics

Zidovudine is approved for use in children at birth up to 12 years of age. Results of uncontrolled studies showed that children with symptomatic HIV disease and a CD4 lymphocyte count of 500 per mm³ or less had a positive response to zidovudine, including improvement in neuropsychological function, immunological function, p24 antigen concentrations, and weight gain. No studies have been published addressing the efficacy of zidovudine in asymptomatic children with a CD4 lymphocyte count of 500 per mm³ or less. It is also not known whether doses lower than 180 mg per square meter of body surface every 6 hours would maintain adequate CNS concentrations of zidovudine to provide improvement of HIV-related CNS disease in children. The pharmacokinetics of zidovudine in children greater than 3 months of age have been found to be similar to those in adults.The half-life in neonates immediately following birth was found to be 10 times that of the mother (13 vs 1.3 hours, respectively). The side effects seen in children, including the hematologic effects, were also similar to those seen in adults.

Geriatrics

Studies have not been performed to determine the safety and effectiveness of zidovudine in the geriatric population. However, 1 case reports that a 90-year-old patient responded well to zidovudine therapy. Preliminary data indicate that the elimination rate of zidovudine may be decreased in the elderly.

Dental

The bone marrow–depressant effects of zidovudine may result in an increased incidence of certain microbial infections and delayed healing.

Drug interactions and/or related problems

The following drug interactions and/or related problems have been selected on the basis of their potential clinical significance (possible mechanism in parentheses where appropriate)—not necessarily inclusive (» = major clinical significance):

Note: Combinations containing any of the following medications, depending on the amount present, may also interact with this medication.

Atovaquone
(concurrent use decreases zidovudine clearance and increases area under the plasma concentration-time curve [AUC] of zidovudine)

Blood dyscrasia-causing medications (see *Appendix II*) or
» Bone marrow depressants, other (see *Appendix II*) or
Radiation therapy
(concurrent use of these medications and/or radiation therapy with zidovudine may cause an additive or synergistic myelosuppression; dosage reductions may be required)

» Clarithromycin
(initial results of a dose escalation study in HIV-infected patients showed that concurrent use of zidovudine and clarithromycin resulted in a lower peak serum concentration [C_{max}], lower AUC, and delayed time to peak concentration [T_{max}] of zidovudine)

» Combination drugs that contain zidovudine
(should not be administered concomitantly)

» Doxorubicin
(*in vitro* studies detected an antagonistic relationship between doxorubicin and zidovudine; concurrent use is not recommended)

Fluconazole
(concurrent use of fluconazole interferes with zidovudine clearance and metabolism, increasing zidovudine AUC by 74% [range 28 to 173%] and zidovudine half-life by 128% [range −4 to 189%])

» Ganciclovir
(concurrent use with zidovudine has caused severe hematologic toxicity even when the zidovudine dose was reduced to 300 mg per day; this effect is thought to be the result of synergistic myelosuppressive toxicity rather than a pharmacokinetic interaction; concurrent administration should be used with extreme caution; hematologic parameters, such as hemoglobin, hematocrit, and white blood cell count with differential should be monitored frequently in all patients receiving both zidovudine and ganciclovir)

Hepatic glucuronidation–metabolized medications, other
(other medications metabolized by hepatic glucuronidation, such as acetaminophen, aspirin, benzodiazepines, cimetidine, indomethacin, morphine, and sulfonamides, may, in theory, compete with zidovudine for metabolism and decrease the clearance of zidovudine or the other medication; this could potentially increase the risk of toxicity of either zidovudine or the other medication)

» Interferon alfa
(hematologic toxicities may occur with concurrent use; dose reduction or discontinuation of one or both of the medications may be necessary; hematologic parameters, such as hemoglobin, hematocrit, and white blood cell count with differential should be monitored frequently in all patients receiving both zidovudine and interferon alfa)

Lamivudine
(concurrent use may increase zidovudine peak plasma concentration [C_{max}]; however, AUC and total clearance of zidovudine are not significantly altered)

Methadone
(concurrent use may increase zidovudine AUC)

Nelfinavir or
Rifampin or
Ritonavir
(concurrent use may decrease zidovudine AUC)

Phenytoin
(there have been several reports of decreased phenytoin plasma concentrations, and one case of increased phenytoin plasma concentration, with concurrent use; however, a pharmacokinetic interaction study showed no effect on phenytoin kinetics, but a 30% decrease in zidovudine clearance was observed with concurrent use)

» Probenecid
(concurrent use inhibits hepatic glucuronidation and secretion of zidovudine through the renal tubules, resulting in increased serum concentrations and a prolonged elimination half-life; this may increase the risk of toxicity, or possibly permit a reduction in daily zidovudine dosage; however, in one small trial, a very high incidence of rash was observed in patients receiving probenecid concurrently with zidovudine; influenza-like symptoms, such as myalgia, malaise, and/or fever, have also occurred)

» Ribavirin
(*in vitro* studies have shown that, when combined, ribavirin and zidovudine are reproducibly antagonistic and should not be used concurrently; ribavirin inhibits the phosphorylation of zidovudine to its active triphosphate form)

Stavudine (d4T)
(*in vitro* studies detected an antagonistic antiviral effect between stavudine and zidovudine at a molar ratio of 20 to 1, respectively; concurrent use is not recommended until *in vivo* studies demonstrate that these medications are not antagonistic in their anti-HIV activity)

Valproic acid
(valproic acid may increase zidovudine oral bioavailability by interfering with zidovudine's first-pass metabolism; an increase of

zidovudine AUC of 79% ± 61% and a decrease in the plasma GZDV AUC of 22% ± 10% were observed with concurrent use; patients taking both medications should be monitored for a possible increase in zidovudine-related adverse effects; the effect of zidovudine on the pharmacokinetics of valproic acid was not evaluated)

Laboratory value alterations

The following have been selected on the basis of their potential clinical significance (possible effect in parentheses where appropriate)—not necessarily inclusive (» = major clinical significance).

With physiology/laboratory test values

Mean corpuscular volume (MCV)
(usually will be increased)

Medical considerations/Contraindications

The medical considerations/contraindications included have been selected on the basis of their potential clinical significance (reasons given in parentheses where appropriate)—not necessarily inclusive (» = major clinical significance).

Except under special circumstances, this medication should not be used when the following medical problem exists:

» Hypersensitivity to zidovudine or any of the components of the formulation
(zidovudine is contraindicated in these patients)

Risk-benefit should be considered when the following medical problems exist:

» Obesity or
» Prolonged nucleoside exposure or
» Risk factors for hepatic disease
((lactic acidosis and severe hepatomegaly with steatosis have been reported with the use of nucleoside analogues alone or in combination; fatal cases have been reported; obesity and prolonged nucleoside exposure may be risk factors; majority of cases have been in women; treatment should be suspended in patients with evidence of lactic acidosis or pronounced hepatotoxicity which may include hepatomegaly and steatosis even in the absence of marked transaminase elevations)

» Bone marrow depression
(zidovudine may cause bone marrow depression, worsening any pre-existing granulocytopenia and anemia)

Folic acid deficiency or
Vitamin B_{12} deficiency
(patients with folic acid or vitamin B_{12} deficiency may be more prone to anemia since zidovudine can cause impaired erythrocyte maturation, resulting in a macrocytic anemia)

» Hepatic function impairment
(because zidovudine is metabolized in the liver to an inactive metabolite, GZDV, hepatic function impairment may lead to accumulation of zidovudine and increased toxicity)

Patient monitoring

The following may be especially important in patient monitoring (other tests may be warranted in some patients, depending on condition; » = major clinical significance):

» CD4+ T lymphocyte count
(CD4+ T cell counts should be monitored at the time of diagnosis and generally every 3 to 6 months thereafter)

» Complete blood counts (CBCs)
(in patients with HIV disease who are asymptomatic or have early symptoms, CBCs are recommended monthly during the first 3 months, then every 3 months thereafter, unless indicated for other reasons. CBCs are recommended at least every 2 weeks during the first 8 weeks of therapy to detect serious anemia or granulocytopenia in patients with advanced HIV disease taking zidovudine; the frequency of CBCs may be decreased to every 4 weeks after the first 2 months if zidovudine is well tolerated. Decreases in hemoglobin concentrations may occur as early as 2 to 4 weeks after the beginning of therapy, and peak falls in hemoglobin usually occur during the first 4 to 6 weeks. Granulocytopenia usually occurs after 6 to 8 weeks; when significant anemia [hemoglobin of < 7.5 grams/dL] and/or significant granulocytopenia [granulocyte count of < 750 cells/mm³] occurs, dosage adjustments, discontinuation of the drug, blood transfusions, or, in selected patients, treatment with epoetin [recombinant human erythropoietin] or GM-CSF [granulocyte-macrophage colony-stimulating factor] may be necessary. Zidovudine should not be restarted until some evidence of bone marrow recovery is evident; if bone marrow recovery occurs following dosage adjustments, gradual increases in dose may be appropriate, depending on blood counts and patient tolerance; patients should be informed of the importance of having blood counts followed closely during therapy)

» Drug resistance tests
(drug resistance testing [genotyping or phenotyping] is recommended when there is suboptimal viral load suppression after initiation of antiretroviral therapy or during virologic failure on an existing antiretroviral regimen; drug resistance testing also should be considered in acute HIV infection to determine if the virus transmitted was drug-resistant and to guide the change in antiretroviral therapy, if necessary)

» Human immunodeficiency virus (HIV) RNA, plasma
(monitoring of HIV RNA, which is an indicator of viral load, is essential when deciding to initiate or modify antiretroviral therapies; HIV RNA concentrations should be measured immediately prior to and 2 to 8 weeks following initiation of antiretroviral therapy; thereafter, HIV RNA should be measured every 3 to 4 months to evaluate the continuing efficacy of therapy; optimally, plasma concentrations should be undetectable, i.e., less than 50 copies per mL, at 6 months; if after 16 to 20 weeks of therapy HIV RNA remains detectable in plasma and a repeat test confirms the result, a modification in antiretroviral therapy should be considered)

(HIV RNA should not be measured during or within 4 weeks after successful treatment of intercurrent infection, resolution of symptomatic illness, or immunization)

Liver function tests
(liver function tests, including serum ALT [SGPT], alkaline phosphatase, and AST [SGOT] values, and serum bilirubin concentration, should be monitored periodically since elevations, usually reversible, have been reported on rare occasions with zidovudine therapy; however, in two large placebo-controlled studies, the difference in incidence of aminotransferase elevation between the treatment and the placebo groups was not statistically significant; elevations in liver function tests in some cases may be related to reactivation of hepatitis virus or due to HIV infection itself)

Therapeutic drug monitoring
(there is growing evidence that measurement of drug concentrations can be used to individualize therapy, identify abnormal pharmacokinetics or noncompliance, improve response to therapy, and decrease toxicity)

Side/Adverse Effects

Note: Because of the complexity of this disease state, it is often difficult to differentiate between the manifestations of HIV infection and the adverse effects of zidovudine. In addition, very little placebo-controlled data are available to assess this difference, with most of the information coming from uncontrolled studies and case reports. The long-term effects of zidovudine are still not known; however, hematologic side effects are more likely to occur with higher doses and in patients with more advanced disease.

Lactic acidosis, in the absence of hypoxemia, and severe hepatomegaly with steatosis, including fatal cases, have been reported with the use of antiretroviral nucleoside analogs, including zidovudine.

The most frequent side/adverse effects of zidovudine are granulocytopenia and anemia. These have been shown to be inversely related to the CD4 lymphocyte count, hemoglobin concentration, and granulocyte count at the time of therapy initiation and directly related to dosage and duration of therapy. Significant anemia most commonly occurs after 4 to 6 weeks of therapy.

The incidence of adverse reactions from zidovudine therapy appears to increase as the disease progresses.

The following side/adverse effects have been selected on the basis of their potential clinical significance (possible signs and symptoms in parentheses where appropriate)—not necessarily inclusive:

Those indicating need for medical attention

Incidence more frequent

Anemia (pale skin; unusual tiredness or weakness); ***leukopenia or neutropenia*** (fever, chills, or sore throat)

Note: These hematological abnormalities occur more frequently and with greater severity in patients who have more advanced HIV infection when zidovudine therapy is initiated.

Incidence less frequent

Changes in platelet count—often increased with therapy; however, may be decreased infrequently

Incidence rare

Hepatotoxicity (abdominal discomfort; nausea; decreased appetite; general feeling of discomfort); *lactic acidosis* (diarrhea; fast, shallow breathing; muscle pain or cramping; shortness of breath; sleepiness; unusual tiredness or weakness); *myopathy* (muscular atrophy, tenderness, and weakness); *neurotoxicity* (confusion; mood or mental changes; seizures)

Those indicating need for medical attention only if they continue or are bothersome

Incidence more frequent

Anorexia (loss of appetite, weight loss); *asthenia* (lack or loss of strength); *constipation* (difficulty having a bowel movement (stool)); *headache, severe; insomnia* (trouble in sleeping); *malaise* (general feeling of discomfort or illness unusual tiredness or weakness); *myalgia* (muscle soreness); *nausea; vomiting*

Incidence less frequent

Changes in skin pigmentation (changes in skin coloring); *hyperpigmentation of nails* (bluish-brownish bands)

Incidence unknown

Abdominal cramps (stomach cramps); *abdominal pain* (stomach pain); *chills; dyspepsia* (acid or sour stomach; belching; heartburn; indigestion; stomach discomfort upset or pain); *fatigue* (unusual tiredness or weakness); *hyperbilirubinemia* (yellow eyes or skin); *musculoskeletal pain* (muscle or bone pain); *neuropathy* (burning, tingling, numbness or pain in the hands, arms, feet, or legs; sensation of pins and needles stabbing pain)

Those indicating need for medical attention if they occur after medication is discontinued

Bone marrow depression (fever, chills, or sore throat; pale skin; unusual tiredness or weakness)

Overdose

For more information on the management of overdose or unintentional ingestion, **contact a Poison Control Center** (see *Poison Control Center Listing*).

Clinical effects of overdose

The following effects have been selected on the basis of their potential clinical significance (possible signs and symptoms in parentheses where appropriate)—not necessarily inclusive:

Symptoms of overdose

Bone marrow toxicity, specifically anemia, leukopenia, thrombocytopenia (pale skin; unusual tiredness or weakness; fever, chills, or sore throat; increase in bleeding or bruising); *gastrointestinal disturbances* (severe nausea and vomiting); *neurotoxicity, specifically ataxia, fatigue, lethargy, nystagmus, seizures* (lack of coordination; involuntary, rapid, rhythmic movement of the eyes; convulsions)

Note: At this time, the information available on acute zidovudine overdose is limited to several case reports. These patients took between 6 and 50 grams of zidovudine. Severe *nausea and vomiting* are the most common symptoms after an overdose. Other reported symptoms include *ataxia, nystagmus, lethargy, fatigue*, and, in one patient, a single *tonic-clonic seizure*. One patient who took a chronic overdose of zidovudine, 500 mg five times a day for 16 days, had an increase in liver transaminases, which resolved when the dose was reduced. There is also one case report of a patient who ingested 6 grams in a suicide attempt who experienced *hematologic toxicity;* the lowest blood cell count occurred 8 days after the ingestion and returned to previous levels by day 20.

Treatment of overdose

Specific treatment—Zidovudine is not removed from the blood by peritoneal dialysis or hemodialysis in sufficient amounts to warrant the use of dialysis in an overdose situation.

Monitoring—Close observation of the patient for evidence of neurotoxicity and bone marrow suppression.

Supportive care—Supportive therapy. Patients in whom intentional overdose is known or suspected should be referred for psychiatric consultation.

Patient Consultation

As an aid to patient consultation, refer to *Advice for the Patient, Zidovudine (Systemic)*.

In providing consultation, consider emphasizing the following selected information (» = major clinical significance):

Before using this medication

» Conditions affecting use, especially:

Hypersensitivity to zidovudine

Pregnancy—Zidovudine crosses the placenta and reaches concentrations in the fetus similar to those observed in adults; zidovudine has been shown to decrease perinatal transmission of HIV

Breast-feeding—Zidovudine is distributed into breast milk; breast-feeding is not recommended in HIV-infected mothers because of the risk of passing HIV to the infant

Dental—The bone marrow–depressant effects of zidovudine may result in an increased incidence of certain microbial infections and delayed healing

Other medications, especially alfa interferons, other bone marrow depressants, clarithromycin, doxorubicin, ganciclovir, probenecid, ribavirin or combination drugs that contain zidovudine.

Other medical problems, especially bone marrow depression, hepatic function impairment, obesity, prolonged nucleoside exposure or risk factors for hepatic disease

Proper use of this medication

Supplying patient information about zidovudine

» Importance of not taking more medication than prescribed; importance of not discontinuing medication without checking with physician

» Compliance with full course of therapy

Using a specially marked measuring spoon or other device for zidovudine oral solution

» Importance of not missing doses and taking at evenly spaced times

» Proper dosing

Missed dose: Taking as soon as possible; not taking if almost time for next dose; not doubling doses

» Proper storage

Precautions while using this medication

» Regular visits to physician for blood tests

» Importance of not taking other medications concurrently without checking with physician

Using caution in use of regular toothbrushes, dental floss, and toothpicks; checking with physician or dentist concerning proper oral hygiene

» Avoiding sexual intercourse or using a condom to help prevent transmission of the AIDS virus to others; not sharing needles with anyone

Side/adverse effects

Signs of potential side effects, especially anemia, leukopenia or neutropenia, changes in platelet count, hepatotoxicity, lactic acidosis, myopathy, and neurotoxicity

General Dosing Information

Zidovudine monotherapy is not recommended except as prophylaxis against perinatal transmission in pregnant women with low viral loads and high CD4+ T cell counts and in HIV-exposed infants during the first 6 weeks of life. In adults, it is recommended that antiretroviral therapy consist of two nucleoside reverse transcriptase inhibitors (NRTIs) plus a non-nucleoside reverse transcriptase inhibitor (NNRTI) or one or two protease inhibitors (PIs). In children, it is recommended that antiretroviral therapy consist of one highly active PI plus two NRTIs. Children who can swallow capsules may be given efavirenz plus two NRTIs or efavirenz plus nelfinavir plus one NRTI.

Patients should be advised of the importance of taking zidovudine exactly as prescribed. Patients should not exceed the prescribed dose or dosing frequency.

Zidovudine infusion should be administered at a constant rate over a period of 1 hour. It should not be administered intramuscularly or by rapid infusion or direct injection.

Patients with significant anemia (hemoglobin < 7.5 grams/dL) and/or significant granulocytopenia (granulocyte count of < 750 cells/mm^3) may require interruption of zidovudine therapy or reduction of dosage until bone marrow recovery is seen. Additionally, patients with anemia may require blood transfusions or treatment with epoetin (recombinant human erythropoetin). Patients with granulocytopenia may require treatment with filgrastim (granulocyte colony-stimulating factor; G-CSF) or sargramostim (granulocyte-macrophage colony-stimulating factor; GM-CSF).

Granulocytopenia and anemia have been shown to be inversely related to the CD4 lymphocyte count, hemoglobin concentration, and granulocyte count at time of therapy initiation, and directly related to dosage and duration of therapy. Significant anemia most commonly occurs after 4 to 6 weeks of therapy.

If a patient receiving zidovudine develops unexplained dyspnea, tachypnea, or a fall in serum bicarbonate concentration, therapy with zidovudine should be suspended until the diagnosis of lactic acidosis can be ruled out, usually with a venous or arterial lactic acid concentration. Treatment with zidovudine also should be suspended in the case of rapid elevations of serum aminotransferase concentrations or progressive hepatomegaly of unknown etiology.

Diet/Nutrition
Zidovudine may be taken with or without food.

Oral Dosage Forms

Note: Zidovudine, in a dose of 300 mg, is available in combination with 150 mg of lamivudine as *Combivir* and with 300 mg of abacavir and 150 mg of lamivudine as *Trizivir.*

ZIDOVUDINE CAPSULES USP

Usual adult and adolescent dose
Human immunodeficiency virus (HIV) infection (treatment)—
Oral, 600 mg of zidovudine daily in divided doses (300 mg every twelve hours or 200 mg every eight hours).
Note: Patients with end-stage renal disease may require a reduction in dosage to 300 mg per day.

Mother-to-child transmission of HIV-1 infection (prophylaxis)—
Oral, 100 mg five times a day, 200 mg every eight hours, or 300 mg every twelve hours beginning after fourteen weeks of gestation and continuing until the start of labor. At that time, intravenous zidovudine should be administered (see *Zidovudine Injection USP*).

Usual pediatric dose
HIV infection (treatment)—
Children up to 6 weeks of age: Oral, 2 mg per kg of body weight every six hours.
Children 6 weeks to 12 years of age: Oral, 160 mg per square meter of body surface area every eight hours.
Children 12 years of age and older: See *Usual adult and adolescent dose.*

Note: Pediatric patients with granulocytopenia may require a dose reduction to 120 mg per square meter of body surface area every six hours.

Usual pediatric prescribing limits
480 mg per square meter of body surface area per day up to a maximum of 200 mg every eight hours.

Strength(s) usually available
U.S.—
100 mg (Rx) [*Retrovir* (corn starch; magnesium stearate; microcrystalline cellulose; sodium starch glycolate)].
Canada—
100 mg (Rx) [*Apo-Zidovudine; Novo-AZT; Retrovir*].

Packaging and storage
Store between 15 and 25 °C (59 and 77 °F), in a tight container. Protect from light and moisture.

Auxiliary labeling
- Continue medicine for full time of treatment.

ZIDOVUDINE ORAL SOLUTION USP

Usual adult and adolescent dose
See *Zidovudine Capsules USP.*

Usual pediatric dose
HIV infection (treatment)—
See *Zidovudine Capsules USP.*
Mother-to-child transmission of HIV-1 infection (prophylaxis)—
Neonate dosing: Oral, 2 mg per kg of body weight every six hours starting within eight to twelve hours after birth and continuing through six weeks of age. If the infant cannot take zidovudine oral solution, intravenous zidovudine may be administered (see *Zidovudine Injection USP*).

Note: If HIV infection is confirmed in the infant, zidovudine therapy should be changed to a combination antiretroviral regimen.

Strength(s) usually available
U.S.—
50 mg per 5 mL (Rx) [*Retrovir* (sodium benzoate; citric acid; flavors; glycerin; liquid sucrose)].
Canada—
50 mg per 5 mL (Rx) [*Retrovir*].

Packaging and storage
Store between 15 and 25 °C (59 and 77 °F), in a tight container. Protect from light.

Auxiliary labeling
- Continue medicine for full time of treatment.

ZIDOVUDINE TABLETS USP

Usual adult and adolescent dose
HIV infection (treatment)—
600 mg daily in two to three divided doses.

Usual pediatric dose
Children up to 12 years of age—See *Zidovudine Capsules USP.*
Children 12 years of age and older—See *Usual adult and adolescent dose.*

Strength(s) usually available
U.S.—
300 mg (Rx) [*Retrovir* (hypromellose; magnesium stearate; microcrystalline cellulose; polyethylene glycol; sodium starch glycolate; titanium dioxide)].
Canada—
300 mg (Rx) [*Retrovir*].

Packaging and storage
Store between 15 and 25 °C (59 and 77 °F).

Auxiliary labeling
- Continue medicine for full time of treatment.

Parenteral Dosage Forms

ZIDOVUDINE INJECTION USP

Usual adult and adolescent dose
HIV infection (treatment)—
In the U.S.: Intravenous infusion, 1 mg per kg of body weight, infused over one hour, every four hours, five or six times a day (5 to 6 mg per kg of body weight per day) until oral therapy can be administered.
In Canada: Intravenous infusion, 1 to 2 mg per kg of body weight, infused over one hour, every four hours around the clock (six times a day) until oral therapy can be administered.

Note: Intravenous administration of 1 mg per kg of body weight every four hours is equivalent to oral administration of 100 mg every four hours.

Patients with end-stage renal disease require a reduction in dose to 1 mg per kg of body weight, infused over one hour, every six to eight hours.

Mother-to-child transmission of HIV-1 infection (prophylaxis), maternal dose at the start of labor and delivery—
Intravenous, 2 mg per kg of total body weight over one hour, followed by a continuous infusion of 1 mg per kg of total body weight per hour until clamping of the umbilical cord.

Usual pediatric dose
HIV infection (treatment)—
Children up to 6 weeks of age: Intravenous infusion, 1.5 mg per kg of body weight, infused over one hour, every six hours until oral therapy can be administered.
Children 3 months to 12 years of age: [Intravenous infusion, 120 mg per square meter of body surface area, infused over one hour, every six hours]. [Alternatively, continuous infusion of 20 mg per square meter of body surface area per hour.]
Children 12 years of age and older: See *Usual adult and adolescent dose.*

Note: Pediatric patients with granulocytopenia may require a dose reduction to 90 mg per square meter of body surface area every six hours.

Mother-to-child transmission of HIV-1 infection (prophylaxis)—
Intravenous, 1.5 mg per kg of body weight over thirty minutes every six hours.

Usual pediatric prescribing limits
160 mg per individual dose.

Strength(s) usually available
U.S.—
200 mg in 20 mL (Rx) [*Retrovir*].
Canada—
200 mg in 20 mL (Rx) [*Retrovir*].

Packaging and storage
Store between 15 and 25 °C (59 and 77 °F). Protect from light.

Preparation of dosage form
Zidovudine injection must be diluted prior to administration to a concentration of no greater than 4 mg per mL in 5% dextrose injection, 0.9% sodium chloride injection, 5% dextrose and 0.45% sodium chloride injection, lactated Ringer's injection, or 5% dextrose and lactated Ringer's injection.

Stability
After dilution, solutions are physically and chemically stable for 24 hours at room temperature (25 °C [77 °F]) and 48 hours if refrigerated (2 to 8 °C [36 to 46 °F]).

It is recommended that diluted solutions be administered within 8 hours if stored at 25 °C (77 °F) or within 24 hours if refrigerated (2 to 8 °C [36 to 46 °F]) to minimize potential microbial contamination.

The solution should be visually inspected prior to administration for discoloration and particulate matter. If either of these are detected, the solution should be discarded.

Incompatibilities

Zidovudine injection should not be admixed with biological or colloidal solutions (e.g., blood products, protein-containing solutions).

Selected Bibliography

Department of Health and Human Services (DHHS) and the Henry J. Kaiser Family Foundation. Guidelines for the use of antiretroviral agents in HIV-infected adults and adolescents. Available at http://www.hivatis.org/. Accessed March 2002.

The Working Group on Antiretroviral Therapy, Medical Management of HIV-infected Children, the Health Resources and Services Administration (HRSA), and the National Institutes of Health. Guidelines for the use of antiretroviral agents in pediatric HIV infection. Available at http://www.hivatis.org/. Accessed March 2002.

Revised: 04/05/2004

ZILEUTON Systemic†

VA CLASSIFICATION (Primary): RE180

Commonly used brand name(s): *Zyflo*.

Note: For a listing of dosage forms and brand names by country availability, see *Dosage Forms* section(s).

†Not commercially available in Canada.

Category

Antiasthmatic (leukotriene inhibitor).

Indications

Accepted

Asthma, chronic (prophylaxis and treatment)—Zileuton is indicated in patients with chronic asthma to improve asthma symptoms, improve pulmonary function (forced expiratory volume in 1 second [FEV_1], morning and evening peak expiratory flow rates), and to decrease the use of an inhaled $beta_2$-agonist. In clinical trials, zileuton was used to treat patients with mild to moderate persistent asthma.

Unaccepted

Zileuton is not indicated for the treatment of bronchospasm in acute asthma attacks, including status asthmaticus; however, zileuton does not need to be discontinued during an acute exacerbation.

Pharmacology/Pharmacokinetics

Physicochemical characteristics

Molecular weight—236.29.

Mechanism of action/Effect

Zileuton is a selective inhibitor of 5-lipoxygenase, which is the enzyme that catalyzes the formation of leukotrienes from arachidonic acid. Specifically, it inhibits the formation of leukotrienes LTC_4, LTD_4, and LTE_4, which are the active constituents of slow-reacting substances of anaphylaxis, and LTB_4, a substance that attracts neutrophils and eosinophils. Leukotrienes produce numerous biological effects, including augmentation of neutrophil and eosinophil migration, neutrophil and monocyte aggregation, leukocyte adhesion, increased capillary permeability, and smooth muscle contraction. These effects contribute to inflammation, edema, mucus secretion, and bronchoconstriction in the airways of asthmatic patients.

Absorption

Rapidly and almost completely absorbed.

Protein binding

High (93%). Bound primarily to albumin.

Biotransformation

Hepatic. *In vitro* studies using human liver microsomes have shown that zileuton and its *N*-dehydroxylated metabolite are oxidatively metabolized by the cytochrome P450 isoenzymes 1A2, 2C9, and 3A4.

Half-life

Mean terminal half-life is 2.5 hours.

Onset of action

Significant improvement from baseline in FEV_1 occurred 2 hours after initial administration in clinical trials.

Time to peak plasma concentration

1.7 hours.

Precautions to Consider

Carcinogenicity/Tumorigenicity

A 2-year study in female mice given zileuton in doses of approximately four times the systemic exposure achieved at the maximum recommended human daily oral dose showed an increased incidence of liver, kidney, and vascular tumors. The same study in male mice given zileuton in doses of approximately seven times the systemic exposure achieved at the maximum recommended human daily oral dose showed a trend toward an increase in the incidence of liver tumors. Zileuton was not tumorigenic in mice given zileuton in doses of approximately two times the systemic exposure achieved at the maximum recommended human daily oral dose.

In rats, an increased incidence of kidney tumors was shown in females and males given zileuton in doses of approximately 14 and 6 times, respectively, the systemic exposure achieved at the maximum recommended human daily oral dose. Zileuton was not tumorigenic in male and female rats given doses of approximately four and six times, respectively, the systemic exposure achieved at the maximum recommended human daily oral dose.

Mutagenicity

Zileuton was not mutagenic in multiple *in vivo* and *in vitro* assays; however, the livers and kidneys of female mice treated with zileuton showed a dose-related increase in DNA adduct formation. Although some evidence of DNA damage was shown in the hepatocytes of *Aroclor 1254*–treated rats in an unscheduled DNA synthesis assay, the results of a similar study in monkeys were negative.

Pregnancy/Reproduction

Fertility—Zileuton produced no effects on fertility in male and female rats given oral doses of up to approximately 8 and 18 times, respectively, the systemic exposure achieved at the maximum recommended human daily oral dose. However, a reduction in rat fetal implantations was seen with oral doses of approximately nine times the systemic exposure achieved at the maximum recommended human daily oral dose. In addition, reduced rat pup survival and growth were noted following maternal oral doses of approximately 18 times the systemic exposure achieved at the maximum recommended human daily oral dose.

Pregnancy—Adequate and well-controlled studies have not been done in humans.

Zileuton and its metabolites cross the placenta in rats. When zileuton was administered orally to pregnant rats in doses of approximately 18 times the systemic exposure achieved at the maximum recommended human daily oral dose, the fetuses showed reduced body weight and increased skeletal variations.

Administration of zileuton to pregnant rabbits in doses equivalent to the maximum recommended human daily oral dose produced cleft palate in 2.5% of the fetuses.

FDA Pregnancy Category C.

Breast-feeding

It is not known whether zileuton is distributed into the breast milk of humans; however, the drug and its metabolites are distributed into the milk of lactating rats. Because of the potential for tumorigenicity shown in animal studies, use of zileuton during breast-feeding is not recommended.

Pediatrics

Appropriate studies on the relationship of age to the effects of zileuton have not been performed in the pediatric population. Safety and efficacy in children up to 12 years of age have not been established.

Geriatrics

In clinical studies, the pharmacokinetics of zileuton in healthy adults 65 years of age and older were similar to those of adults 18 to 40 years of age.

Drug interactions and/or related problems

The following drug interactions and/or related problems have been selected on the basis of their potential clinical significance (possible mechanism in parentheses where appropriate)—not necessarily inclusive (» = major clinical significance):

Note: Drug interaction studies have been conducted with zileuton and prednisone and with zileuton and ethinyl estradiol, an oral contraceptive; no significant interactions were shown.

Combinations containing any of the following medications, depending on the amount present, may also interact with this medication.

Astemizole or
Cisapride or
Cyclosporine or
Dihydropyridine calcium channel blocking agents, such as:
Felodipine
Isradipine
Nicardipine
Nifedipine
Nimodipine
(these medications are metabolized by the cytochrome P450 isoenzyme 3A4; although studies have not been done with zileuton and these medications, concurrent use should be monitored carefully, since zileuton is known to inhibit CYP3A4 *in vitro*)

» Beta-adrenergic blocking agents (systemic and ophthalmic)
(concurrent administration of zileuton and propranolol doubles the area under the plasma concentration-time curve and increases the pharmacologic effects of propranolol; although studies have not been done with other beta-adrenergic blocking agents, patients using beta-adrenergic blocking agents and zileuton should be monitored carefully)

» Terfenadine
(concurrent administration of recommended doses of terfenadine and zileuton for 7 days increased the mean area under the plasma concentration-time curve and peak serum concentration of terfenadine by approximately 35%; although no cardiac effects were noted, concurrent administration of these medications is not recommended)

» Theophylline
(concurrent administration of zileuton and theophylline approximately doubles the serum theophylline concentration; theophylline dosage should be reduced approximately by half and serum theophylline concentrations monitored closely in patients using these medications concurrently)

» Warfarin
(concurrent administration of zileuton and warfarin results in a clinically significant increase in the prothrombin time; prothrombin times should be monitored closely and warfarin dose adjusted accordingly in patients using these medications concurrently)

Laboratory value alterations

The following have been selected on the basis of their potential clinical significance (possible effect in parentheses where appropriate)—not necessarily inclusive (» = major clinical significance).

With physiology/laboratory test values

Transaminases, hepatic
(elevations of one or more liver function tests may occur during therapy with zileuton; the values may continue to rise, remain unchanged, or return to normal during continued therapy)
(if clinical signs or symptoms of hepatic function impairment or ALT values ≥ five times the upper limit of normal develop, therapy with zileuton should be stopped and ALT monitored until values return to normal)
(in clinical trials involving more than 5000 patients treated with zileuton, there was a 3.2% incidence of serum ALT values at least three times the upper limit of normal. One patient developed symptomatic hepatitis with jaundice that resolved following discontinuation of zileuton. Three patients with transaminase elevations developed hyperbilirubinemia that was less than three times the upper limit of normal. In subset analyses, females older than 65 years of age and patients with pre-existing transaminase elevations appeared to be at increased risk for ALT elevations)

Medical considerations/Contraindications

The medical considerations/contraindications included have been selected on the basis of their potential clinical significance (reasons given in parentheses where appropriate)—not necessarily inclusive (» = major clinical significance).

Except under special circumstances, this medication should not be used when the following medical problems exist:

» Hepatic disease, active
» Hepatic function impairment
(zileuton is not recommended in patients with active hepatic disease or transaminase elevations three times the upper limit of normal or greater)

Risk-benefit should be considered when the following medical problems exist:

» Alcoholism, active
(caution is recommended in patients taking zileuton who consume substantial quantities of alcohol, because of possible hepatic function impairment)

Hypersensitivity to zileuton

Patient monitoring

The following may be especially important in patient monitoring (other tests may be warranted in some patients, depending on condition; » = major clinical significance):

» Alanine aminotransferase, serum (ALT [SGPT])
(serum ALT determinations are recommended before treatment starts, once a month for the first 3 months, every 2 to 3 months for the remainder of the first year, and periodically thereafter during zileuton therapy)
(if clinical signs or symptoms of hepatic function impairment or ALT values ≥ five times the upper limit of normal develop, therapy with zileuton should be stopped and ALT monitored until values return to normal)

Side/Adverse Effects

Note: In clinical trials involving more than 5000 patients treated with zileuton, there was a 3.2% incidence of serum ALT values at least three times the upper limit of normal. One patient developed symptomatic hepatitis with jaundice that resolved following discontinuation of zileuton. Three patients with transaminase elevations developed hyperbilirubinemia that was less than three times the upper limit of normal. In subset analyses, females older than 65 years of age and patients with pre-existing transaminase elevations appeared to be at increased risk for ALT elevations.

The following side/adverse effects have been selected on the basis of their potential clinical significance (possible signs and symptoms in parentheses where appropriate)—not necessarily inclusive:

Those indicating need for medical attention

Incidence rare

Hepatic function impairment (flu-like symptoms; itching; nausea; right upper abdominal pain; unusual tiredness or weakness; yellow eyes or skin)

Those indicating need for medical attention only if they continue or are bothersome

Incidence more frequent

Dyspepsia (upset stomach); ***nausea***

Incidence less frequent

Abdominal pain; asthenia (weakness)

Patient Consultation

As an aid to patient consultation, refer to *Advice for the Patient, Zileuton (Systemic)*.

In providing consultation, consider emphasizing the following selected information (» = major clinical significance):

Before using this medication

» Conditions affecting use, especially:
Hypersensitivity to zileuton
Pregnancy—Risk-benefit should be considered because of the potential for fetal abnormalities shown in animal studies
Breast-feeding—Use is not recommended
Other medications, especially beta-adrenergic blocking agents, terfenadine, theophylline, or warfarin
Other medical problems, especially active alcoholism, hepatic function impairment, or hepatic disease

Proper use of this medication

» Importance of not using this medication to treat acute asthma symptoms
» Proper dosing
Missed dose: Taking as soon as possible; if almost time for next dose, skipping missed dose; not doubling doses
» Proper storage

Precautions while using this medication

» Compliance with therapy by using every day in regularly spaced doses, even during symptom-free periods

» Importance of regular visits to physician to check progress and to test liver enzymes

» Checking with health care professional if more inhalations than usual of an inhaled, short-acting bronchodilator are needed to relieve an acute attack or if more than the maximum number of inhalations of the bronchodilator prescribed for a 24-hour period are needed

» Checking with health care professional before stopping or reducing therapy with any other asthma medications

Side/adverse effects

Signs of potential side effects, especially hepatic function impairment

Oral Dosage Forms

ZILEUTON TABLETS

Usual adult and adolescent dose

Antiasthmatic—

Oral, 600 mg four times a day.

Usual adult and adolescent prescribing limits

2400 mg a day.

Usual pediatric dose

Children up to 12 years of age—Safety and efficacy have not been established.

Usual geriatric dose

See *Usual adult and adolescent dose.*

Strength(s) usually available

U.S.—

600 mg (Rx) [*Zyflo*].

Canada—

Not commercially available.

Packaging and storage

Store at controlled room temperature, between 20 and 25 °C (68 and 77 °F). Protect from light.

Selected Bibliography

Sorkness CA. The use of 5-lipoxygenase inhibitors and leukotriene receptor antagonists in the treatment of chronic asthma. Pharmacotherapy 1997; 17(1 Pt 2): 50S-54S.

Revised: 03/22/1999

ZINC CHLORIDE—See *Zinc Supplements (Systemic)*

ZINC GLUCONATE—See *Zinc Supplements (Systemic)*

ZINC SULFATE—See *Zinc Supplements (Systemic)*

ZIPRASIDONE Systemic†

VA CLASSIFICATION (Primary): CN709

Commonly used brand name(s): *Geodon.*

Note: For a listing of dosage forms and brand names by country availability, see *Dosage Forms* section(s).

†Not commercially available in Canada.

Category

Antipsychotic.

Indications

Accepted

Acute agitation in schizophrenic patients (treatment)—Ziprasidone intramuscular is indicated for the treatment of acute agitation in schizophrenic patients for whom treatment with ziprasidone is appropriate and who need intramuscular antipsychotic medication for rapid control of agitation.

Bipolar mania (treatment)—Ziprasidone is indicated for the treatment of acute manic or mixed episodes associated with bipolar disorder, with or without psychotic features.

Schizophrenia (treatment)—Ziprasidone is indicated for the treatment of schizophrenia.

Unaccepted

Ziprasidone is not approved for the treatment of behavioral symptoms in elderly patients with dementia.

Pharmacology/Pharmacokinetics

Physicochemical characteristics

Molecular weight—467.42.

Mechanism of action/Effect

The exact mechanism of action of ziprasidone is unknown. It is thought that the drug's efficacy in the treatment of schizophrenia is mediated through a combination of dopamine type 2 (D_2) and serotonin type 2 ($5\text{-}HT_2$) antagonism. Antagonism at receptors other than those listed that have similar receptor affinities may explain some of the other therapeutic and side effects of ziprasidone.

Absorption

Ziprasidone is well absorbed after oral administration.Absolute bioavailability of a 20-mg dose under fed conditions is approximately 60%. Absorption is increased up to two-fold in the presence of food.

Distribution

Mean apparent Volume of Distribution (Vol_D)—1.5 L per kilogram of body weight (L/kg).

Protein binding

Very high (> 99%) to plasma proteins. It is primarily bound to albumin and α_1-acid glycoprotein.

The *in vitro* plasma protein binding of ziprasidone was not altered by warfarin or propranolol, nor did ziprasidone alter the binding of these two drugs in human plasma. The potential for drug interactions due to displacement is minimal.

Biotransformation

Ziprasidone is primarily cleared via hepatic metabolism, by three metabolic routes, to yield benzisothiazole (BITP) sulphoxide, BITP-sulphone, ziprasidone sulphoxide and S-methyl-dihydroziprasidone.

Half-life

Elimination—Mean terminal half-life is about 7 hours.

Time to peak concentration

6 to 8 hours

Elimination

Renal—20 %, < 1% as unchanged drug.

Fecal—66 %, < 4% as unchanged drug.

Precautions to Consider

Carcinogenicity

Lifetime carcinogenicity studies were done in Long Evans rats and CD-1 mice. Ziprasidone was administered for 24 months at doses of 2, 6, or 12 mg/kg/day in rats and 50, 100, or 200 mg/kg/day in mice (0.1 to 0.6 times the maximum recommended human dose [MRHD] of 200 mg/day on a mg/m² basis, respectively).

In the rat study there was no evidence of an increased incidence of tumors. In the mice, male mice there was no evidence of an increased incidence of tumors. In female mice there were dose related increases in the incidences of pituitary gland adenoma and carcinomas, and mammary gland adenocarcinoma at all doses tested (50 to 200 mg/kg/day or 1 to 5 times the MRHD on a mg/m² basis). Proliferative changes in the pituitary gland and mammary glands of rodents have been observed following chronic administration of other antipsychotic agents and are considered to be prolactin mediated.

Increases in serum prolactin were observed in a 1–month dietary study in female mice at doses of 100 and 200 mg/kg/day (or 2.5 and 5 times the MRHD on a mg/mg² basis). Ziprasidone had no effect on serum prolactin in rats in a 5 week dietary study at the doses used in the carcinogenicity study. The relevance for human risk of the findings of the prolactin-mediated endocrine tumors in rodents is unknown.

Mutagenicity

Ziprasidone was tested in the Ames bacterial mutation assay, the *in vitro* mammalian cell gene mutation mouse lymphoma assay, the *in vitro* chromosomal aberration assay in human lymphocytes, and the *in vivo* chromosomal aberration in mouse bone marrow. There was a reproducible mutagenic response in the Ames assay in one strain of *S. typhimurium* in the absence of metabolic activation. Positive results were obtained in both the *in vitro* mammalian cell gene mutation assay and the *in vitro* chromosomal aberration assay in human lymphocytes.

Pregnancy/Reproduction

Fertility—Ziprasidone was shown to increase copulation time in Sprague-Dawley rats in two fertility and early embryonic development studies at doses of 10 to 160 mg/kg/day (0.5 to 8 times the MRHD of 200 mg/day on a mg/m² basis). Fertility rate was reduced at doses of 160 mg/kg/day (8 times the MRHD of 200 mg/day on a mg/m² basis). The effect on fertility appeared to be in the female since fertility was not impaired when males given 160 mg/kg/day (8 times the MRHD of 200 mg/day on a mg/m² basis) were mated with untreated females. In a 6 month study in male rats given 200 mg/kg/day (10 times the MRHD on a mg/m² basis) there were no treatment related findings observed in the testes.

Pregnancy—There are no adequate and well controlled studies in humans.

Developmental toxicity was demonstrated in animal studies, including possible teratogenic effects at doses similar to human therapeutic doses. When ziprasidone was administered to pregnant rabbits during organogenesis, an increased incidence of fetal structural abnormalities (ventricular septal defects and other cardiovascular malformations and kidney alterations) were observed at doses of 30 mg/kg/day (3 times the MRHD of 200 mg/day on a mg/m² basis). There was no evidence to suggest that these developmental effects were secondary to maternal toxicity.

The developmental no effect dose was 10 mg/kg/day (equivalent to the MRHD on a mg/m² basis). In rats, embryofetal toxicity (decreased fetal weights, delayed skeletal ossification) was observed following administration of 10 to 160 mg/kg/day (0.5 to 8 times the MRHD of 200 mg/day on a mg/m² basis) during organogenesis or throughout gestation, but there was no evidence of teratogenicity. Doses of 40 and 60 mg/kg/day (2 and 8 times the MRHD on a mg/m² basis) were associated with maternal toxicity. The developmental no-effect dose was 5 mg/kg/day (0.2 times the MRHD of 200 mg/day on a mg/m² basis).

There was an increase in the number of pups born dead and a decrease in postnatal survival throughout the first 4 days of lactation among the offspring of female rats treated during gestation and lactation with doses of 10 mg/kg/day (0.5 times the MRHD of 200 mg/day on a mg/m² basis) or greater. Offspring developmental delays and neurobehavioral functional impairment were observed at doses of 5 mg/kg/day (0.2 times the MRHD of 200 mg/day on a mg/m² basis) or greater. A no-effect level was not established for these effects.

Effect on labor and delivery is unknown.

FDA Pregnancy Category C

Breast-feeding

It is not known whether ziprasidone is distributed into human breast milk. Breast-feeding is not recommended in women receiving ziprasidone.

Pediatrics

No information is available on the relationship of age to the effects of ziprasidone in the pediatric population. Safety and efficacy have not been established.

Geriatrics

Although appropriate studies on the relationship of age to the effects of ziprasidone have not been performed, geriatrics-specific problems are not expected to limit the usefulness of ziprasidone in the elderly. However, elderly patients are more likely to age-related medical problems which may require a lower starting dose, slower titration, and careful monitoring during the initial dosing period.

According to an FDA Public Health Advisory, ziprasidone is not approved for the treatment of behavioral symptoms in elderly patients with dementia. Clinical studies of ziprasidone and other atypical antipsychotic drugs for treatment of behavioral symptoms in the elderly with dementia have shown a higher death rate associated with their use compared to patients receiving a placebo. Causes of death varied, but most seemed to be either heart-related (i.e., heart failure or sudden death) or from infections (i.e., pneumonia).

Drug interactions and/or related problems

The following drug interactions and/or related problems have been selected on the basis of their potential clinical significance (possible mechanism in parentheses where appropriate)—not necessarily inclusive (» = major clinical significance):

Note: Combinations containing any of the following medications, depending on the amount present, may also interact with this medication.

Antihypertensive agents
(ziprasidone has the potential for inducing hypotension, and it may enhance the effects of certain antihypertensive agents; risk of priapism increases with concomitant use of ziprasidone and alpha-adrenergic blocking agents)

Carbamazepine
(may decrease the AUC of ziprasidone, this effect may be greater as doses increase)

CNS stimulation-producing medications (see *Appendix II*) and
CNS depression-producing medications (see *Appendix II*)
(given the primary CNS effects of ziprasidone caution should be used when using other centrally acting drugs)

Ketoconazole and
CYP3A4 hepatic enzyme inhibitors, other
(may increase the AUC and the C_{max} of ziprasidone)

Levodopa and
Dopamine agonists
(ziprasidone may antagonize the effects of these drugs)

» QT Interval prolongation drugs, including:
Arsenic trioxide
Chlorpromazine
Class Ia and III anti-arrhythmics
Dofetilide
Dolasetron mesylate
Droperidol
Gatifloxacin
Halofantrine
Levomethadyl acetate
Mefloquine
Mesoridazine
Moxifloxacin
Pentamidine
Pimozide
Probucol
Quinidine
Sotalol
Sparfloxacin
Tacrolimus
Thioridazine
(concurrent use of these medications with ziprasidone is contraindicated; dose related prolongation of the QT interval with ziprasidone and the known associated fatal arrhythmias with QT prolongation by some other drugs; associated with torsade de pointes-type arrhythmia, a potentially fatal polymorphic ventricular tachycardia, and sudden death.)

Laboratory value alterations

The following have been selected on the basis of their potential clinical significance (possible effect in parentheses where appropriate)—not necessarily inclusive (» = major clinical significance).

With physiology/laboratory test values
Glucose, serum
(values may be increased)
Prolactin
(ziprasidone elevates prolactin levels, clinical significance is unknown; hyperprolactinemia linked to one-third of human breast cancers, *in vitro*, but no studies to date associate ziprasidone and tumorigenesis in humans)

Medical considerations/Contraindications

The medical considerations/contraindications included have been selected on the basis of their potential clinical significance (reasons given in parentheses where appropriate)—not necessarily inclusive (» = major clinical significance).

Except under special circumstances, this medication should not be used when the following medical problem exists:

» Acute myocardial infarction, recent, or
Bradycardia or
Cardiac arrhythmias, history of, or
QT prolongation, history of or congenital, or
Heart failure, uncompensated
(certain cardiovascular circumstances may increase the risk of QT prolongation, arrhythmia, torsade de pointes, and risk of sudden death)

» Hypersensitivity to ziprasidone

» Uncorrected electrolyte disorders, including:
Hypokalemia
Hypomagnesemia
(may increase the risk of QT prolongation, arrhythmia, torsade de pointes, and risk of sudden death)

Risk-benefit should be considered when the following medical problems exist:

Diabetes mellitus or
Hyperglycemia
(use with caution in those that have or are more predisposed to these conditions)

Neuroleptic Malignant Syndrome (NMS)
(potentially fatal symptom complex [e.g., hyperpyrexia, muscle rigidity, altered mental status, evidence of autonomic instability, elevated creatinine phosphokinase, myoglobinuria, acute renal failure] has been reported in association with administration of antipsychotic drugs; management includes immediate discontinuation of the antipsychotic drugs and other non-necessary drugs, intensive symptomatic treatment and medical monitoring and treatment of any comitant serious medical problems for which there is a treatment; after recovery from NMS, if antipsychotic therapy is required, careful monitoring is warranted as antipsychotic therapy is reintroduced)

Tardive Dyskinesia
(potentially irreversible, involuntary, dyskinetic movements may develop in patients undergoing treatment with antipsychotic drugs; more likely to occur in the elderly, especially elderly women; risk of irreversible tardive dyskinesia increases with duration of treatment and total cumulative dose; therapy should be given at the smallest dose and for the shortest duration; if signs and symptoms of tardive dyskinesia appear, consider drug discontinuation; some patients may require treatment with ziprasidone despite the presence of the syndrome)

Seizures, history of, or
Alzheimer's dementia
(use with caution in patients with a history of seizures or with conditions that potentially lower the seizure threshold; use with caution due to increased risk of aspiration pneumonia)

Patient monitoring

The following may be especially important in patient monitoring (other tests may be warranted in some patients, depending on condition; » = major clinical significance):

Careful supervision of patients with suicidal tendencies
(recommended in high-risk patients)

Glucose, serum
(patients with an established diagnosis of diabetes mellitus who are started on atypical antipsychotics should be monitored regular for worsening of glucose control.)

(patients with risk factors for diabetes mellitus [e.g., obesity, family history of diabetes] who are starting treatment with atypical antipsychotics should undergo fasting blood glucose at the beginning of treatment and periodically during treatment)

(patients should be monitored for symptoms of hyperglycemia including polydipsia, polyuria, polyphagia and weakness)

» Magnesium, serum and
» Potassium, serum
(baseline measurements should be taken in patients who are at risk for significant electrolyte disturbances [e.g., diuretic therapy, diarrhea], and patients with low values should be replenished before treatment begins; periodic monitoring of serum electrolytes should be done in patients who are started on diuretics during ziprasidone treatment.)

» QTc interval
(ziprasidone therapy should be discontinued in patients with persistent QTc measurements > 500 msec; occurrence of symptoms of torsade de pointes [e.g., dizziness, palpitations, or syncope] warrant further evaluation with a Holter monitor)

Side/Adverse Effects

The following side/adverse effects have been selected on the basis of their potential clinical significance (possible signs and symptoms in parentheses where appropriate)—not necessarily inclusive:

Those indicating need for medical attention

Incidence less frequent
Chest pain; tachycardia (fast, pounding, or irregular heartbeat or pulse; palpitations); ***QTc prolongation*** (irregular heartbeat recurrent fainting)

Incidence rare
Cardiac arrhythmias (dizziness; feeling faint or fainting; fast or racing heartbeat; pounding or irregular heartbeat); ***convulsions*** (seizures); ***priapism*** (persistent, painful erection)—may require surgical intervention; ***syncope*** (fainting)

Those indicating need for medical attention only if they continue or are bothersome

Note: *Asthenia, orthostatic hypotension, anorexia, dry mouth, increased salivation, arthralgia, anxiety, dizziness, dystonia, hypertonia, somnolence, tremor, rhinitis, rash, and abnormal vision* may be dose-related

Incidence more frequent
Asthenia (lack or loss of strength; weakness); ***akathisia*** (involuntary movements); ***constipation; diarrhea; dizziness; dyspepsia*** (acid or sour stomach; belching; heartburn; indigestion; stomach discomfort upset or pain); ***extrapyramidal syndrome*** (difficulty in speaking; drooling; loss of balance control; muscle trembling, jerking, or stiffness; restlessness; shuffling walk; stiffness of limbs; twisting movements of body; uncontrolled movements, especially of face, neck, and back); ***nausea; rash***—may require antihistamine or steroid therapy or discontinuation of ziprasidone; ***somnolence*** (sleepiness or unusual drowsiness); ***weight gain***

Incidence less frequent
Abnormal vision (change in vision); ***anorexia*** (loss of appetite; weight loss); ***cough increased; depression; dry mouth; dystonia*** (inability to move eyes; increased blinking or spasms of eyelid; sticking out of tongue; trouble in breathing, speaking, or swallowing; uncontrolled twisting movements of neck, trunk, arms, or legs; unusual facial expressions; weakness of arms and legs); ***fungal dermatitis*** (red, itchy skin); ***hypertonia*** (muscle tightness); ***myalgia*** (muscle ache); ***orthostatic hypotension*** (feeling faint upon standing); ***respiratory tract infection*** (coughing, sneezing, sore throat, stuffy or runny nose); ***rhinitis*** (stuffy nose; runny nose; sneezing); ***vomiting***

Overdose

For more information on the management of overdose or unintentional ingestion, **contact a poison control center** (see *Poison Control Center Listing*).

Clinical effects of overdose

The following effects have been selected on the basis of their potential clinical significance (possible signs and symptoms in parentheses where appropriate)—not necessarily inclusive:

Acute effects
Sedation (drowsiness; sleepiness); ***slurring of speech; transitory hypertension***

Treatment of overdose

There is no specific antidote for ziprasidone. Treatment is essentially symptomatic and supportive.

To decrease absorption—
Gastric lavage should be considered. Activated charcoal may be administered with a laxative. The risk of aspiration with induced emesis is increased if the patient is obtunded, seizing, or experiencing dystonic movements of the head and neck.

To enhance elimination—
Ziprasidone is not dialyzable.

Specific treatment—
Maintain an open airway and ensure adequate oxygenation and ventilation.

For treatment of severe extrapyramidal symptoms: Administration of anticholinergic agents may be indicated.

For treatment of arrhythmias caused by ziprasidone toxicity: Selection of an appropriate antiarrhythmic agent—Use of disopyramide, procainamide, or quinidine may add to ziprasidone toxicity by prolonging the QT interval.

For treatment of hypotension or circulatory collapse: Selection of an appropriate sympathomimetic—Beta-adrenergic stimulation properties of epinephrine or dopamine may worsen the hypotension induced by ziprasidone's alpha-adrenergic blockade

Also, the alpha-adrenergic blocking properties of bretylium may add to ziprasidone's effects, producing problematic hypotension.

Monitoring—
Cardiovascular monitoring should begin immediately and should include continuous electrocardiographic monitoring to detect possible arrhythmias.

Supportive care—
Supportive measures such as establishing intravenous lines, hydration, correction of electrolyte imbalance, oxygenation, and support of ventilatory function are essential for maintaining the vital functions of the patient.

Patients in whom intentional overdose is confirmed or suspected should be referred for psychiatric consultation.

Patient Consultation

As an aid to patient consultation, refer to *Advice for the Patient, Ziprasidone (Systemic)*.

In providing consultation, consider emphasizing the following selected information (» = major clinical significance):

Before using this medication

» Conditions affecting use, especially:
Hypersensitivity to ziprasidone.

Use in the elderly—Not approved for the treatment of behavioral disorders in elderly patients with dementia; associated with a higher death rate

Other medications, especially QT interval prolongation drugs.

Other medical problems, especially cardiac disease, including recent acute myocardial infarction, bradycardia, cardiac arrhythmias, QT prolongation, uncompensated heart failure; uncorrected electrolyte disorders, including hypokalemia and hypomagnesemia

Proper use of this medication

» Importance of caregivers contacting doctor and not giving this medicine for treatment of behavioral problems in elderly patients with dementia

» Proper dosing

Swallow capsules whole, do not chew

Missed dose: Taking as soon as possible; not taking if almost time for next scheduled dose; not doubling doses

Proper storage

Precautions while using this medication

» Importance of close monitoring by physician

» Obtaining medical attention if fainting, dizziness, fast, racing, pounding, or irregular heartbeat, or other unusual symptoms occur

» Caution while performing activities requiring mental alertness, driving or operating machinery due to potential to impair judgment, thinking, or motor skills

Avoid situations involving high temperature or humidity, due to potential interference with ability of the body to adjust to heat

Avoid use of alcohol

Side/adverse effects

Signs of potential side effects, especially, tachycardia, cardiac arrhythmias, convulsions, priapism, and syncope

General Dosing Information

Ziprasidone should be administered with food.

Dosage adjustments, if needed, should occur at intervals of not less than 2 days, but more appropriately, patients should be observed for improvement for several weeks before upward dose adjustment to ensure use of the lowest effective dose.

Periodically reassess to determine the need for maintenance treatment.

Dispense/prescribe a small number of doses to reduce the risk of attempted overdose.

Oral Dosage Forms

ZIPRASIDONE CAPSULES

Usual adult dose

Bipolar mania—

Oral, initial dose 40 mg twice a day, taken with food. Dose should be increased to 60 or 80 mg twice a day on the second day of treatment and subsequently adjusted on the basis of toleration and efficacy within the range 40 to 80 mg twice a day

Schizophrenia—

Oral, initial dose 20 mg twice a day, taken with food. Dose may be adjusted, at intervals of not less than 2 days, up to 80 mg twice a day.

Usual adult prescribing limits

The safety and efficacy of doses over 100 mg twice a day has not been evaluated in clinical trials, and an increase to a dose above 80 mg twice a day is not recommended.

Usual pediatric dose

Safety and efficacy have not been established.

Usual geriatric dose

See *Usual adult dose*.

Usual geriatric prescribing limits

See *Usual adult prescribing limits*.

Strength(s) usually available

U.S.—

20 mg (Rx) [*Geodon* (lactose; pregelatinized starch; magnesium stearate)].

40 mg (Rx) [*Geodon* (lactose; pregelatinized starch; magnesium stearate)].

60 mg (Rx) [*Geodon* (lactose; pregelatinized starch; magnesium stearate)].

80 mg (Rx) [*Geodon* (lactose; pregelatinized starch; magnesium stearate)].

Packaging and storage

Store between 15 and 30°C (59 and 86 °F).

Parenteral Dosage Forms

ZIPRASIDONE FOR INJECTION

Usual adult dose

Acute agitation in schizophrenia—

Intramuscular, 10 to 20 mg as required; 10 mg may be administered every 2 hours; 20 mg may be administered every 4 hours

Usual adult prescribing limits

40 mg per day; intramuscular administration of ziprasidone for more than 3 consecutive days have not been studied

Usual pediatric dose

Safety and efficacy have not been established.

Usual geriatric dose

See *Usual adult dose*.

Usual geriatric prescribing limits

See *Usual adult prescribing limits*.

Strength(s) usually available

U.S.—

20 mg (Rx) [*Geodon* (methanesulfonic acid; sulfobutylether β-cyclodextrin sodium (SBECD))].

Packaging and storage

Store between 15 and 30°C (59 and 86 °F) in dry form. Protect from light. Following reconstitution, when protected from light, ziprasidone for injection can be stored for up to 24 hours at 15 to 30°C (59 and 86 °F) or up to 7 days refrigerated at 2 to 8°C (36 to 46°F).

Revised: 05/04/2005
Developed: 05/30/2001

ZOLEDRONIC ACID Systemic

VA CLASSIFICATION (Primary): HS 302

Commonly used brand name(s): *Zometa*.

Note: For a listing of dosage forms and brand names by country availability, see *Dosage Forms* section(s).

Category

Bone resorption inhibitor; antihypercalcemic.

Indications

Note: Bracketed information in the *Indications* section refers to uses that are not included in U.S. product labeling.

Accepted

Hypercalcemia, neoplasm-associated (treatment)—Zoledronic acid is indicated for the treatment of hypercalcemia of malignancy.

Metastases, bone (treatment adjunct)—Zoledronic acid is indicated for the treatment of bone metastases from solid tumors in conjunction with standard antineoplastic therapy,including bone metastases from multiple myeloma,[1] breast carcinoma,[1] prostate carcinoma, and other solid tumors[1].

Note: Prostate cancer should have progressed after treatment with at least one hormonal therapy.

In Canada, this indication is restricted to osteoblastic or mixed osteoblastic/osteolytic bone metastases from prostate cancer.

Multiple myeloma (treatment)[1]—Zoledronic acid is indicated for the treatment of multiple myeloma

[Drug-induced osteopenia, secondary to androgen-deprivation therapy in prostate cancer patients (prophylaxis)][1]—Long-term androgen deprivation therapy (AST) can lead to significant decreases in bone mineral density (BMD). Results of a multicenter, double-blind, placebo-controlled study demonstrated increased BMD in the hip and spine of men with nonmetastatic prostate cancer beginning ADT plus zoledronic acid (4 milligrams intravenously every 3 months) for 1 year. In abstract form, a smaller, open-label controlled trial demonstrated similar preliminary results. Retrospective studies have reported a potential association between chronic bisphosphonate therapy and osteonecrosis of the jaws.

Patients with clinically significant signs of bone loss should be considered for treatment with intravenous zoledronic acid. Baseline BMD and follow-up monitoring are warranted. Further studies are needed to assess the long-term effects of bisphosphonates on fracture risk and disease-related outcomes.

Acceptance not established

The safety and efficacy of zoledronic acid in the treatment of hypercalcemia associated with hyperparathyroidism or with other non-tumor related conditions have not been established.

[1]Not included in Canadian product labeling.

Pharmacology/Pharmacokinetics

Physicochemical characteristics

Molecular weight—Molar mass—290.1 g/Mol.

Solubility—Zoledronic acid is highly soluble in 0.1N sodium hydroxide solution, sparingly soluble in water and 0.1N hydrochloric acid, and practically insoluble in organic solvents.

pH—The pH of a 0.7% solution of zoledronic acid in water is approximately 2.0

Mechanism of action/Effect

Zoledronic acid inhibits bone resorption. The antiresorptive mechanism is not fully understood and several factors are thought to contribute to this action. *In vitro*, zoledronic acid inhibits osteoclastic activity and induces osteoclast apoptosis. Osteoclastic resorption of mineralized bone and cartilage through its binding to bone is blocked by zoledronic acid. Increased osteoclastic activity and skeletal calcium release induced by various stimulatory factors released by tumors are inhibited by zoledronic acid.

Absorption

Area under the plasma concentration versus time curve (AUC) of zoledronic acid was dose proportional from 2 to 16 mg. The accumulation of zoledronic acid measured over three cycles was low, with mean $AUC_{0\text{-}24h}$ ratios for cycles 2 and 3 versus 1 of 1.13 ± 0.30 and 1.16 ± 0.36, respectively.

Protein binding

Approximately 22% and independent of the concentration.

Canadian product information states binding to human plasma protein is approximately 56%

Terminal Elimination—

146 hours

Elimination

Renal—Approximately 44%

Renal clearance was 3.7 ± 2.0 liters per hour. Remainder is drug bound to bone, and is slowly released back into systemic circulation, giving rise to the 146 hour terminal half-life.

Patients with mild, and moderate renal impairment showed an increased AUC of 15% and 43%, respectively. The risk of renal deterioration appears to increase with AUC, which is doubled at creatine clearance of 10 mL per min.

Precautions to Consider

Cross-sensitivity and/or related problems

Patients hypersensitive to any bisphosphonate may also be hypersensitive to zoledronic acid.

Carcinogenicity

Standard lifetime carcinogenicity assays were conducted in mice and rats. Mice were given oral doses of zoledronic acid of 0.1, 0.5, or 2.0 mg/kg/day. There was an increased incidence of Harderian gland adenomas in males and females in all treatment groups (at doses ≥0.002 times a human intravenous dose of 4 mg, based on a comparison of relative body surface areas).

Rats were given oral doses of zoledronic acid of 0.1, 0.5, or 0.2 mg/kg/day. No increased incidence of tumors was observed (at doses ≤ 0.2 times the human intravenous dose of 4 mg, based on a comparison of relative body surface areas).

Mutagenicity

Zoledronic acid was not genotoxic in the Ames bacterial mutagenicity assay, in the Chinese hamster ovary cell assay, or in the Chinese hamster gene mutation assay, with or without metabolic activation. Zoledronic acid was not genotoxic in the *in vivo* rat micronucleus assay.

Pregnancy/Reproduction

Fertility—Female rats were given subcutaneous doses of zoledronic acid of 0.01, 0.03, or 0.1 mg/kg/day beginning 15 days before mating and continuing through gestation. Effects observed in the high dose group (with systemic exposure of 1.2 times the human systemic exposure following an intravenous dose of 4 mg, based on an AUC comparison) included inhibition of ovulation and a decrease in the number of pregnant rats. Effects observed in both the mid-dose group (with systemic exposure of 0.2 times the human systemic exposure following an intravenous dose of 4 mg, based on an AUC comparison) and the high-dose group included an increase in preimplantation losses and a decrease in the number of implantations and live fetuses.

Pregnancy—Adequate and well controlled studies in humans have not been done. Studies in animals have shown that zoledronic acid causes an adverse effect on the fetus. Zoledronic acid should not be used during pregnancy. If the patient becomes pregnant while taking this drug, the patient should be apprised of the potential harm to the fetus. Women of childbearing potential should be advised to avoid becoming pregnant.

In female rats given subcutaneous doses of zoledronic acid of 0.01, 0.03, or 0.1 mg/kg/day beginning 15 days before mating and continuing through gestation, the number of stillbirths was increased and survival of neonates was decreased in the mid- and high-dose groups (≥0.2 times the human systemic exposure following an intravenous dose of 4 mg, based on an AUC comparison). Adverse maternal effects were observed in all dose groups (with a systemic exposure of ≥0.7 times the human systemic exposure following an intravenous dose of 4 mg, based on an AUC comparison) and included dystocia and periparturient mortality in pregnant rats allowed to deliver. Maternal mortality may have been related to drug-induced inhibition of skeletal calcium mobilization, resulting in periparturient hypocalcemia. This appears to be a bisphosphonate class effect.

In pregnant rats given a subcutaneous dose of zoledronic acid of 0.1, 0.2, or 0.4 mg/kg/day during gestation, adverse fetal effects were observed in the mid- and high-dose groups (with systemic exposures of 2.4 and 4.8 times, respectively, the human systemic exposure following an intravenous dose of 4 mg, based on an AUC comparison). These adverse effects included increases in pre- and post-implantation losses, decreases in viable fetuses, and fetal skeletal, visceral, and external malformations. Fetal skeletal effects observed in the high-dose group included unossified or completely ossified bones, thickened, curved or shortened bones, wavy ribs and shortened jaw. Other adverse fetal effects observed in the high-dose group included reduced lens, rudimentary cerebellum, reduction or absence of liver lobes, reduction of lung lobes, vessel dilation, cleft palate and edema. Skeletal variations were also observed in the high-dose group and included reduced body weights and food consumption.

In pregnant rabbits given subcutaneous doses of zoledronic acid of 0.01, 0.03, or 0.1 mg/kg/day during gestation (≤ 0.5 times the human intravenous dose of 4 mg, based on a comparison of body surface areas). Maternal mortality and abortion occurred in all treatment groups (at doses ≥ 0.05 times the human intravenous dose of 4 mg, based on a comparison of body surface areas). Adverse maternal effects were associated with, and may have been caused by drug induced hypocalcemia.

FDA Pregnancy CategoryD

Breast-feeding

Since it is not known whether zoledronic acid is distributed into the breast milk and because zoledronic acid binds to bone long-term, zoledronic acid should not be administered to nursing women.

Pediatrics

No information is available on the relationship of age to the effects of zoledronic acid in the pediatric population. Safety and efficacy have not been established. Because of long-term retention in bone, zoledronic acid should only be used in children if potential benefit outweighs potential risk

Geriatrics

Appropriate studies performed to date have not demonstrated geriatric-specific problems that would limit the usefulness of zoledronic acid in the elderly. However, elderly patients are more likely to have age-related problems such as renal function impairment, which may require caution and renal function monitoring in elderly patients receiving zoledronic acid.

Dental

Osteonecrosis of the jaw (ONJ) has been reported in patients with cancer and with concomitant risk factors including chemotherapy, corticosteroids, and poor oral hygiene receiving treatment regimens including bisphosphonates. A dental examination with appropriate preventive dentistry should be considered prior to treatment in these patients. While on treatment, these patients should avoid invasive dental procedures, if possible. For patients who develop ONJ while on bisphosphonate therapy, dental surgery may exacerbate the condition.

Drug interactions and/or related problems

The following drug interactions and/or related problems have been selected on the basis of their potential clinical significance (possible mechanism in parentheses where appropriate)—not necessarily inclusive (» = major clinical significance):

Note: Combinations containing any of the following medications, depending on the amount present, may also interact with this medication.

Aminoglycosides
(concomitant use with zoledronic acid may have an additive effect to lower serum calcium level for prolonged periods.)

Chemotherapy and/or
Corticosteroids
(cancer patients receiving treatment regimens including bisphosphonates and also receiving chemotherapy and corticosteroids may be at risk for osteonecrosis of the jaw [ONJ]; individual benefit/risk needs to be assessed with appropriate preventive dentistry and examination prior to treatment and avoidance of invasive dental procedures while being treated with zoledronic acid, if possible)

Loop diuretics
(concomitant use with zoledronic acid may cause an increased risk of hypocalcemia.)

Nephrotoxic drugs
(should be used with caution with other nephrotoxic drugs)

Thalidomide
(concomitant use with zoledronic acid may increase the risk of renal dysfunction)

Medical considerations/Contraindications

The medical considerations/contraindications included have been selected on the basis of their potential clinical significance (reasons given in parentheses where appropriate)—not necessarily inclusive (» = major clinical significance).

Except under special circumstances, this medication should not be used when the following medical problem exists:

» Hypersensitivity to zoledronic acid or other bisphosphonates, or any of the excipients in the formulation

» Renal function, severe impairment
(Bone metastases: administration of zoledronic acid to patients with severe renal impairment (serum creatine > 3.0 mg per dL) is not recommended due to the risk of significant deterioration of renal function which may progress to renal failure.)

Risk-benefit should be considered when the following medical problems exist:

Asthma, aspirin–sensitive
(while not observed in zoledronic acid clinical trials, administration of other bisphosphonates has been associated with bronchoconstriction in aspirin–sensitive asthma patients.)

Cardiac disease
(overhydration should be avoided when zoledronic acid is administered in patients with cardiac disease, especially in the elderly, because saline overload may precipitate cardiac failure.)

» Dehydration or
» Other factors predisposing to renal deterioration
(should be identified and managed, if possible)

Hepatic insufficiency
(limited clinical data available for use of zoledronic acid to treat hypercalcemia of malignancy in these patients; these data are not adequate to provide guidance on dosage selection or how to safely use zoledronic acid in these patients)

Osteonecrosis of the jaw [ONJ] risk factors including:
Cancer or
Poor oral hygiene or
Tooth extraction or other dental procedures
(dental examination with appropriate preventive dentistry should be considered; invasive dental procedures should be avoided, if possible; clinical judgment should guide management plan of each patient based on individual benefit/risk assessment)

» Renal function impairment
(Hypercalcemia of malignancy—treatment should be considered only if risks and benefits of treatment are evaluated in patients with serum creatinine > 400 micromole per L or > 4.5 mg per dL. Increased risk of renal adverse reactions due to zoledronic acid being primarily excreted by the kidney)

Patient monitoring

The following may be especially important in patient monitoring (other tests may be warranted in some patients, depending on condition; » = major clinical significance):

Calcium, serum and
Electrolytes, serum and
Magnesium, serum and
Phosphate, serum and
Potassium, serum
(determinations recommended periodically during therapy; either serum ionized calcium or total serum calcium concentrations corrected [adjusted] for albumin should be monitored; if hypocalcemia, hypophosphatemia, or hypomagnesemia occur, short-term supplemental therapy may be necessary)

Complete blood count with differential and
Hematocrit and
Hemoglobin
(determinations recommended periodically during therapy; patients with pre-existing anemia, leukopenia, or thrombocytopenia should be assessed regularly)

» Creatinine, serum and
Renal function
(determinations recommended prior to, during, and periodically after treatment; serum creatinine should be evaluated prior to each dose for patients requiring repeated treatment with zoledronic acid)

Dental examination
(consider dental exam prior to treatment in patients with concomitant risk factors [e.g., cancer chemotherapy, corticosteroids, poor oral hygiene] for osteonecrosis of the jaw)

Side/Adverse Effects

In trials and post-marketing experience, renal deterioration, progression to renal failure and dialysis, have occurred in patients, including those treated with the approved dose of 4 mg infused over 15 minutes. There have been instances of this occurring after the initial zoledronic acid dose.

The following side/adverse effects have been selected on the basis of their potential clinical significance (possible signs and symptoms in parentheses where appropriate)—not necessarily inclusive:

Those indicating need for medical attention

Incidence more frequent

Anemia (pale skin; troubled breathing; unusual bleeding or bruising; unusual tiredness or weakness)—underlying disease or other comorbid risk factors may be contributing factors; ***asthenia*** (lack or loss of strength); ***chest pain; dyspnea*** (shortness of breath, difficult or labored breathing; tightness in chest; wheezing); ***granulocytopenia, pancytopenia, or thrombocytopenia*** (black, sticky stools; lower back or side pain; painful or difficult urination; unusual bleeding or bruising; unusual tiredness or weakness); ***hypocalcemia*** (convulsions; irregular heartbeats; mood or mental changes, confusion; muscle cramps or shaking of hands, arms, feet, legs, or face; numbness and tingling around the mouth, fingertips, or feet); ***hypokalemia*** (convulsions; irregular heartbeat; nausea or vomiting; mood changes; muscle pain or cramps); ***hypomagnesemia*** (muscle trembling or twitching); ***hypophosphatemia*** (unusual tiredness or weakness); ***hypotension*** (blurred vision; confusion; dizziness, faintness, or lightheadedness when getting up from a lying or sitting position; suddenly sweating; unusual tiredness or weakness); ***moniliasis*** (skin rash; cracks in skin at the corners of mouth; soreness or redness around fingernails and toenails); ***neutropenia*** (chills; cough; fever; sore throat; sores, ulcers, or white spots on lips or in mouth; swollen glands; black, tarry, stools; lower back or side pain; painful or difficult urination; pale skin; shortness of breath; unusual bleeding or bruising; unusual tiredness or weakness); ***pleural effusion*** (chest pain; shortness of breath); ***renal toxicity*** (agitation; blood in urine; coma; confusion; decreased urine output; depression; dizziness; headache; irritability; lethargy; muscle twitching; nausea; rapid weight gain; seizures; stupor; swelling of face, ankles, or hands; unusual tiredness or weakness)

Incidence not determined—Observed during clinical practice; estimates of frequency can not be determined

Osteonecrosis of the jaw [ONJ] (heavy jaw feeling; loosening of a tooth; pain, swelling, or numbness in the mouth or jaw)—majority are in cancer patients attendant to a dental procedure or risk factors and co-morbid conditions; ***renal deterioration or failure*** (lower back/side pain; decreased frequency/amount of urine; bloody urine; increased thirst; loss of appetite; nausea; vomiting; unusual tiredness or weakness; swelling of face, fingers, lower legs; weight gain; troubled breathing; increased blood pressure)

Those indicating need for medical attention only if they continue or are bothersome

Incidence more frequent

Abdominal pain; agitation (anxiety; nervousness; restlessness; irritability; dry mouth; shortness of breath; hyperventilation; trouble sleeping; irregular heartbeats; shaking); ***alopecia*** (hair loss; thinning of hair); ***anorexia*** (loss of appetite; weight loss); ***anxiety*** (fear; nervousness); ***arthralgias*** (pain, swelling, or redness in joints; muscle pain or stiffness; difficulty in moving); ***back pain; constipation; confusion; cough; dehydration; depression*** (discouragement; feeling sad or empty; irritability; lack of appetite; loss of interest or pleasure; tiredness; trouble concentrating; trouble sleeping); ***dermatitis*** (blistering, crusting, irritation, itching, or reddening of skin; cracked, dry, scaly skin; swelling); ***diarrhea; dizziness; dysphagia*** (difficulty swallowing); ***fatigue*** (unusual tiredness or weakness); ***fever; headache; hypoesthesia*** (partial loss of feeling); ***insomnia*** (sleeplessness; trouble sleeping; unable to sleep); ***leg edema*** (swelling of leg); ***mucositis*** (cracked lips; diarrhea; difficulty in swallowing; sores, ulcers, or white spots on lips, tongue, or inside mouth); ***myalgia*** (joint pain; swollen joints; muscle aching or cramping; muscle pains or stiffness; difficulty in moving); ***nausea; paresthesia*** (burning, crawling, itching, numbness, prickling, "pins and needles", or tingling feelings); ***pyrexia*** (fever); ***rigors*** (feeling unusually cold, shivering); ***skeletal pain; somnolence*** (sleepiness or unusual drowsiness); ***sore throat; stomatitis*** (swelling or inflammation of the mouth); ***upper respiratory tract infection*** (ear congestion; nasal congestion; chills; cough; fever; sneezing; sore throat; body aches or pain; headache; loss of voice; runny nose; unusual tiredness or weakness; difficulty in breathing); ***urinary tract infection*** (bladder pain; bloody or cloudy urine; difficult, burning, or painful urination; frequent urge to urinate; lower back or side pain); ***vomiting; weakness***

Incidence less frequent

Bradycardia (chest pain or discomfort; lightheadedness, dizziness or fainting; shortness of breath; slow or irregular heartbeat; unusual tiredness); ***hallucination*** (seeing, hearing, or feeling things that are not there); ***pruritus*** (itching skin); ***taste perversion*** (change in taste; bad, unusual or unpleasant (after)taste); ***thirst***

Overdose

For more information on the management of overdose or unintentional ingestion, **contact a poison control center** (see *Poison Control Center Listing).*

Clinical effects of overdose

There has been no experience of acute overdose with zoledronic acid. It has been shown to cause clinically relevant reductions in serum levels of calcium, phosphorus, and magnesium.

In controlled clinical trails zoledronic acid has been shown to cause increased risk of renal toxicity when infused over 5 minutes rather than 15 minutes.

Hypocalcemia (convulsions; irregular heartbeats; mood or mental changes, confusion; muscle cramps or shaking of hands, arms, feet, legs, or face; numbness and tingling around the mouth, fingertips, or feet); ***hypophosphatemia*** (unusual tiredness or weakness); ***hypomagnesemia*** (drowsiness; loss of appetite; muscle twitching or trembling; nausea or vomiting; unusual tiredness or weakness)

Treatment of overdose

There is no known specific antidote to zoledronic acid. Treatment is generally symptomatic and supportive.

Reductions in serum levels of calcium, phosphorus, and magnesium should be corrected by intravenous administration of calcium gluconate, potassium or sodium phosphate, and magnesium sulfate, respectively.

Patient Consultation

As an aid to patient consultation, refer to *Advice for the Patient, Zoledronic Acid (Systemic).*

Before using this medication

» Conditions affecting use, especially:

Hypersensitivity to zoledronic acid or other bisphosphonates or any other component of the product

Pregnancy—Should not be used during pregnancy; if patient becomes pregnant during treatment, patient should be apprised of potential harm to fetus; women of childbearing potential should be advised to avoid becoming pregnant

Breast-feeding—Should not be used by nursing women because it is not known if distributed into human breast milk and because zoledronic acid binds to bones long-term

Dental—Increased risk of osteonecrosis of the jaw (ONJ) in cancer patients at high risk (e.g., chemotherapy, corticosteroids, poor oral hygiene); dental examination with appropriate preventive dentistry should be considered prior to treatment; invasive dental procedures or surgery should be avoided

Other medical problems, especially dehydration, other factors predisposing to renal deterioration, or renal function impairment

Proper use of this medication

» Importance of patient being adequately hydrated prior to administration of this drug

» Administering a single dose intravenous infusion of 4 mg over **no less than 15 minutes**

» Importance of following a reduced dosing schedule for mild or moderate renal impairment as directed by the physician

» Proper dosing

Precautions while using this medication

» Importance of renal function assessment before treatment and during treatment.

» Importance to informing physician immediately of symptoms of renal toxicity

» Avoiding dental surgery or other dental procedures if patient has risk factors for ONJ or co-morbid conditions (e.g., anemia, coagulopathies, infection, pre-existing oral disease)

Follow Up

Periodic renal function monitoring post treatment

Side/adverse effects

Signs of potential side effects, especially anemia, asthenia, chest pain, dyspnea, granulocytopenia, hypocalcemia, hypokalemia, hypomagnesia, hypophosphatemia, hypotension, moniliasis, neutropenia pancytopenia, pleural effusion, renal toxicity, or thrombocytopenia

Signs of potential side effects observed during clinical practice, especially osteonecrosis of the jaw (ONJ) and renal deterioration or failure

General Dosing Information

Patients should be adequately rehydrated prior to administration of zoledronic acid.

Patients should also be administered an oral calcium supplement of 500 mg and a multiple vitamin containing 400 IU of vitamin D daily while being treated with zoledronic acid.

Parenteral drug products should be inspected visually for particulate matter and discoloration prior to administration, whenever solution and container permit.

Strict adherence to the intravenous route is recommended for the parenteral administration of zoledronic acid.

Single doses of zoledronic acid should not exceed 4 mg and the duration of the intravenous infusion should be no less than 15 minutes. In the trials and in post-marketing experience, renal deterioration, progression to renal failure and dialysis, have occurred in patients, including those treated with the approved dose of 4 mg infused over 15 minutes. There have been instances of this occurring after the initial zoledronic acid dose.

No clinical or pharmacokinetic data exists for patients with severe renal impairment and should be used in these patients only if the expected benefits outweighs the risk.

Consideration should be given to the severity of, as well as the symptoms of, tumor-induced hypercalcemia when considering the use of zoledronic acid. Vigorous saline hydration (with or without loop diuretics) alone may be sufficient to treat mild, asymptomatic hypercalcemia.

Vigorous saline hydration, an integral part of hypercalcemia therapy, should be initiated promptly and an attempt should be made to restore the urine output to about 2 L/day throughout treatment. Patients should be hydrated throughout the treatment, but over-hydration, especially in those patients who have cardiac failure, must be avoided. Diuretic therapy should not be employed prior to correction of hypovolemia.

Retreatment criteria—Retreatment with a 4 mg dose of zoledronic acid may be considered if serum calcium does not return to normal or remain normal after initial treatment. It is recommended that a minimum of 7 days elapse before retreatment to allow for full response to the initial dose. Serum creatinine must be evaluated prior to each dose. The potential risk for renal failure with subsequent dosing must be carefully weighed against the potential benefits of treatment and other treatment options. Consideration should be given as to whether the potential benefit of treatment outweighs the possible risk.

The following criteria should be applied in patients requiring retreatment and who experience a decrease in renal function after the initial treatment.

- If patients have a normal serum creatinine prior to treatment but have an increase of 0.5 mg/dL within two weeks of their next dose the next dose should be withheld until the serum creatinine is at least within 10% of their baseline value.
- If patients have an abnormal serum creatinine prior to treatment but have an increase of 1.0 mg/dL within two weeks of their next dose the next dose should be withheld until the serum creatinine is at least within 10% of their baseline value.

Note: Canadian manufacturer states that the recommended dose for retreatment is 8 mg.

Parenteral dosage form

Note: Bracketed uses in the *Dosage Forms* section refer to categories of use and/or indications that are not included in U.S. product labeling.

ZOLEDRONIC ACID FOR INJECTION

Usual adult dose

Hypercalcemia—

Intravenous infusion, 4 mg in 100–mL solution, given as a single dose over no less than 15 minutes.

Metastases, bone from solid tumors or
Multiple myeloma[1]—

Intravenous infusion, 4 mg in 100–mL solution, infused over no less than 15 minutes every 3 to 4 weeks.

Daily administration of an oral calcium supplement of 500 mg and a multiple vitamin containing 400 IU of Vitamin D is recommended.

Note: Canadian product information states bone metastases specifically due to prostate cancer.

Note: Upon treatment initiation, the recommended zoledronic acid doses for patients with reduced renal function (mild and moderate renal impairment) are as follows: • Creatinine clearance >60 mL per minute—4 mg

- Creatinine clearance 50 to 60 mL per minute—3.5 mg
- Creatinine clearance 40 to 49 mL per minute—3.3 mg
- Creatinine clearance 30 to 39 mL per minute—3 mg

These doses are calculated to achieve the same AUC as that achieved in patients with creatinine clearance of 75 mL per minute. Creatine clearance is calculated using the Cockcroft-Gault formula.

Due to the risk of clinically significant deterioration in renal function, which may progress to renal failure, single doses of zoledronic acid should not exceed 4 mg and the duration of infusion should be no less than 15 minutes. *There must be strict adherence to the intravenous administration recommendations for zoledronic acid in order to decrease risk of deterioration in renal function.*

Usual adult prescribing limits

4 mg per dose, and it is recommended that there must be a minimum of 7 days before retreatment.

Usual pediatric dose

Safety and efficacy have not been established.

Usual geriatric dose

Dose selection for elderly patients should be cautious due to the greater frequency of geriatric-specific problems.

Strength(s) usually available

U.S.—

4 mg per vial (Rx) [*Zometa* (mannitol, USP; sodium citrate, USP)].

Canada—

4 mg per vial (Rx) [*Zometa* (mannitol, USP; sodium citrate, USP)].

Packaging and storage

Store at 25 °C (77 °F), excursions permitted between 15 and 30 °C (59 and 86 °F).

Preparation of dosage form

Zoledronic acid is reconstituted by adding 5 mL of Sterile Water for Injection, USP to the vial. The drug must be completely dissolved before the solution is withdrawn.

Vials of zoledronic acid concentrate for infusion contain overfill allowing for the withdrawal of 5 mL of concentrate. Do not store undiluted concentrate in a syringe to avoid inadvertent injection.

Reduced doses for patients with baseline creatinine clearance of less than or equal to 60 mL per minute. Withdraw an appropriate volume of the 5-mL zoledronic acid concentrate as needed:

- 4.4 mL for 3.5 mg dose
- 4.1 mL for 3.3 mg dose
- 3.8 mL for 3 mg dose

The maximum recommended 4 mg dose must be further diluted in 100 mL of sterile 0.9% Sodium Chloride, USP, or 5% Dextrose Injection, USP.

Stability

Zoledronic acid parenteral drug products should be inspected visually for particulate matter and discoloration prior to administration, whenever solution and container permit.

If not used immediately, the solution should be refrigerated between 2 and 8 °C (36 and 46 °F). The total time between reconstitution, dilution, storage in the refrigerator, and end of administration must not exceed 24 hours.

Incompatibilities

Zoledronic acid for injection should not be mixed with calcium-containing infusion solutions, such as Lactated Ringer's solution.

Zoledronic acid should be administered as a single intravenous solution in a separate line from all other drugs.

[1]Not included in Canadian product labeling.

Revised: 08/10/2005
Developed: 10/15/2001

ZOLMITRIPTAN Systemic

VA CLASSIFICATION (Primary): CN105

Note: For a listing of dosage forms and brand names by country availability, see *Dosage Forms* section(s).

Category

Antimigraine agent.

Indications

General Considerations

Zolmitriptan should only be prescribed for patients who have an established clear diagnosis of migraine. Zolmitriptan is not intended for the prophylactic therapy of migraine.

Accepted

Headache, migraine (treatment)—Zolmitriptan is indicated to relieve (abort) acute migraine headaches (with or without aura).

Unaccepted

Zolmitriptan is not recommended for treatment of basilar artery migraine or hemiplegic migraine. Efficacy and safety of zolmitriptan in these conditions have not been established.

Zolmitriptan is not recommended for treatment of cluster headaches. Efficacy and safety of zolmitriptan in this condition have not been established.

Pharmacology/Pharmacokinetics

Physicochemical characteristics

Source—Synthetic. Zolmitriptan is structurally related to serotonin (5-hydroxytryptamine, 5-HT).

Molecular weight—287.36.

Mechanism of action/Effect

Zolmitriptan's mechanism of action has not been established. It is thought that agonist activity at the 5-HT_{1D} and 5-HT_{1B} receptor subtypes provides relief of headaches. Zolmitriptan is a highly selective agonist at these receptor subtypes; it has no significant activity at 5-HT_2, 5-HT_3, or 5-HT_4 receptor subtypes or at adrenergic, dopaminergic, histamine, or muscarinic receptors. However, zolmitriptan has moderate activity at the 5-HT_{1A} receptor subtype. It has been proposed that constriction of cerebral blood vessels resulting from 5-$HT_{1D/1B}$ receptor stimulation reduces the pulsation that may be responsible for the pain of vascular headaches. It has also been proposed that zolmitriptan may relieve migraines by decreasing the release of neuropeptides.

Absorption

Oral—Rapid; bioavailability is moderate (40%). The rate and extent of absorption are not affected by administration with food.

Protein binding

Low (25%).

Biotransformation

Hepatic; three metabolites have been identified: indole acetic acid, *N*-oxide, and *N*-desmethyl metabolites. However, *N*-desmethyl is the only active metabolite.

Half-life

Elimination—

Zolmitriptan: Approximately 3 hours
N-desmethyl metabolite: Approximately 3 hours

Time to peak concentration

Tablet—1.5 hours.

Orally disintegrating tablet—3 hours.

Elimination

Renal—65% (8% of the dose as unchanged zolmitriptan; 31% as the indole acetic acid metabolite; 7% as the *N*-oxide metabolite; 4% as the *N*desmethyl metabolite.

Fecal—30%.

Precautions to Consider

Carcinogenicity/Tumorigenicity

In 85- and 92-week carcinogenicity studies in male and female mice, respectively, given zolmitriptan by oral gavage at doses of 400 mg per kg of body weight (mg/kg) (quantities sufficient to achieve peak concentrations of up to 800 times the maximum recommended human dose [MRHD]), no evidence of tumorigenicity was found. However, in a 104- to 105-week study in rats, the high-dose male and female rats were sacrificed, due to excess mortality, after receiving zolmitriptan

400 mg/kg per day for 101 weeks and 86 weeks, respectively. Although there was no evidence of tumorigenicity in male rats receiving 400 mg/kg per day of zolmitriptan (quantities sufficient to achieve peak concentrations approximately 3000 times the MRHD); an increased incidence of thyroid follicular cell hyperplasia and thyroid follicular cell adenomas occurred in male rats.

Mutagenicity

Zolmitriptan demonstrated mutagenic effects in two of five strains of *Salmonella typhimurium* tested in an Ames test in the presence of metabolic activation. However, no mutagenic activity was found in an *in vitro* mammalian gene cell mutation assay. There was evidence of clastogenic activity in an *in vitro* human lymphocyte assay, with and without metabolic activation, but no evidence of clastogenic activity was observed in the *in vivo* mouse micronucleus assay. Also, there was no genotoxicity observed in an unscheduled DNA synthesis study.

Pregnancy/Reproduction

Fertility—Reproduction studies in male and female rats given zolmitriptan doses of up to 400 mg per kg of body weight (mg/kg) per day (approximately 3000 times the maximum recommended human dose [MRHD]) found no effect on fertility.

Pregnancy—Adequate and well-controlled trials have not been done in pregnant women.

Reproductive toxicity studies in pregnant rats and rabbits found evidence of embryolethality and fetal abnormalities. During the organogenesis period, studies in pregnant rats receiving doses of 100, 400, and 1200 mg/kg per day (approximately 280, 1100, and 5000 times the MRHD, respectively) resulted in a dose-related increase in embryolethality. The higher dose was found to be maternotoxic, which resulted in decreased maternal body weight gain during gestation. In a study in rabbits, embryolethality was increased at maternally toxic doses of 10 and 30 mg/kg per day (equivalent to 11 and 42 times the MRHD, respectively). In addition, at doses of 30 mg/kg per day there was evidence of an increase in fetal malformations, such as fused sternebrae, rib anomalies, major blood vessel variations, and an irregular ossification pattern of ribs. Also, hydronephrosis was observed in the offspring of female rats receiving zolmitriptan 400 mg/kg per day (approximately 1100 times the MRHD).

FDA Pregnancy Category C.

Breast-feeding

It is not known whether zolmitriptan is distributed into breast milk.

Zolmitriptan was found to be distributed into the milk of lactating rats. The concentration of zolmitriptan in the rat milk was equivalent to maternal plasma concentrations at 1 hour and four times higher than maternal plasma concentrations at 4 hours.

Pediatrics

Appropriate studies on the relationship of age to the effects of zolmitriptan have not been performed in children up to 12 years of age.

Adolescents

Appropriate studies performed to date have not demonstrated pediatrics-specific problems that would limit the usefulness of zolmitriptan in adolescents.

Geriatrics

No information is available on the relationship of age to the effects of zolmitriptan in geriatric patients.

Drug interactions and/or related problems

The following drug interactions and/or related problems have been selected on the basis of their potential clinical significance (possible mechanism in parentheses where appropriate)—not necessarily inclusive (» = major clinical significance):

Note: Combinations containing any of the following medications, depending on the amount present, may also interact with this medication.

Cimetidine
(concurrent use of cimetidine and zolmitriptan may cause an increase in half-life and area under the plasma concentration-time curve of zolmitriptan)

Dihydroergotamine or
Ergotamine or
Methysergide or
Other 5-hydroxytryptamine agonists such as:
Sumatriptan
(a delay of 24 hours between administration of dihydroergotamine, ergotamine, methysergide, or other 5-hydroxytryptamine agonists and zolmitriptan is recommended because of the possibility of additive and/or prolonged vasoconstriction)

Selective serotonin reuptake inhibitors, such as:
Fluoxetine
Fluvoxamine
Paroxetine
Sertraline
(concurrent use may result in weakness, hyperreflexia, and incoordination; monitoring is recommended)

» Monoamine oxidase-A (MAO-A) inhibitors, including furazolidone, procarbazine, and selegiline
(concurrent use may increase systemic exposure of zolmitriptan; zolmitriptan should not be taken during or within 14 days following administration of an MAO-A inhibitor)

Laboratory value alterations

The following have been selected on the basis of their potential clinical significance (possible effect in parentheses where appropriate)—not necessarily inclusive (» = major clinical significance).

With physiology/laboratory test values
Blood pressure
(may be increased; in healthy volunteers blood pressure elevations [increase in systolic and diastolic by 1 mm Hg and 5 mm Hg, respectively] occurred in patients receiving a 5-mg dose; however, a small study evaluating patients with moderate to severe liver disease receiving a 10-mg dose, resulted in elevations in systolic and/or diastolic pressure [20 mm Hg to 80 mm Hg]; monitoring is recommended in patients with hepatic impairment and hepatic disease)

Medical considerations/Contraindications

The medical considerations/contraindications included have been selected on the basis of their potential clinical significance (reasons given in parentheses where appropriate)—not necessarily inclusive (» = major clinical significance).

Except under special circumstances, this medication should not be used when the following medical problems exist:

» Cardiac arrythmias or
» Wolff-Parkinson-White syndrome
(may exacerbate condition)

» Coronary artery disease, especially:
Angina pectoris
Myocardial infarction, history of
Myocardial ischemia, silent, documented
Prinzmetal's angina or
» Other conditions in which coronary vasoconstriction would be detrimental
(zolmitriptan may cause coronary vasospasms)

» Hypertension, uncontrolled
(may be exacerbated)

Risk-benefit should be considered when the following medical problems exist:

» Cerebrovascular accident, history of
(zolmitriptan may cause cerebral hemorrhage, subarachnoid hemorrhage, or stroke; caution should be used when administering in patients at risk for cerebrovascular events)

» Coronary artery disease, predisposition to
(zolmitriptan may cause serious coronary adverse effects; patients in whom coronary artery disease is a possibility on the basis of age or the presence of other risk factors, such as diabetes, hypercholesterolemia, obesity, a strong family history of coronary artery disease, or tobacco smoking, should be evaluated for the presence of cardiovascular disease before zolmitriptan is prescribed; even after a satisfactory evaluation, the advisability of administering the patient's first dose under medical supervision should be considered)

» Hepatic disease or
» Hepatic function impairment, severe or
Renal function impairment, severe
(studies have shown a decreased clearance in zolmitriptan in patients with severe renal or hepatic impairment; caution is recommended; a dosage adjustment is recommended in patients with hepatic impairment and hepatic disease)

» Hypertension, controlled
(may precipitate an increase in systolic and diastolic blood pressure)

» Hypersensitivity to zolmitriptan

» Phenylketonuria (PKU)
(Zomig-ZMT brand of oral disintegrating tablets contains aspartame, which is metabolized to phenylalanine, and must be used with caution in patients with PKU)

Patient monitoring

The following may be especially important in patient monitoring (other tests may be warranted in some patients, depending on condition; » = major clinical significance):

Blood pressure determinations
(monitoring is recommended for patients with hepatic impairment)

Electrocardiogram (ECG)
(monitoring is recommended for long-term intermittent users of zolmitriptan)

Side/Adverse Effects

The following side/adverse effects have been selected on the basis of their potential clinical significance (possible signs and symptoms in parentheses where appropriate)—not necessarily inclusive:

Those indicating need for medical attention

Incidence more frequent

Chest pain, severe; heaviness, tightness, or pressure in chest and/or neck; paresthesias (sensation of burning, warmth, heat, numbness, tightness, or tingling)

Note: Although *chest pain and heaviness, tightness, or pressure in the chest and/or neck* are suggestive of angina pectoris, monitoring of the electrocardiogram (ECG) during such symptoms in clinical studies failed to detect evidence of myocardial ischemia or arrythmias. Zolmitriptan-induced coronary artery vasospasm resulting in symptomatic myocardial ischemia and myocardial infarction have not been documented in patients taking zolmitriptan.

Incidence less frequent

Arrythmias (irregular heartbeat); ***gastroenteritis*** (severe abdominal pain; diarrhea; loss of appetite; nausea; weakness)

Incidence rare

Leukopenia (fever or chills; cough or hoarseness; lower back or side pain; painful or difficult urination)

Those indicating need for medical attention only if they continue or are bothersome

Incidence more frequent

Asthenia (unusual tiredness or muscle weakness); ***dizziness; nausea; somnolence*** (sleepiness)

Incidence less frequent

Central nervous system effects, including agitation; anxiety; and depression; discomfort in jaw, mouth, or throat; dry mouth; dyspepsia (heartburn); ***dysphagia*** (difficulty swallowing); ***ecchymosis*** (large, nonelevated blue or purplish patches in the skin); ***edema*** (swelling of face, fingers, feet and/or lower legs); ***hypertension*** (increased blood pressure); ***myalgia*** (muscle aches); ***palpitations*** (pounding heartbeat); ***polyuria*** (sudden, large increase in frequency and quantity of urine); ***pruritus*** (itching of the skin); ***skin rash; sweating; syncope*** (fainting)

Overdose

For more information on the management of overdose or unintentional ingestion, **contact a Poison Control Center** (see *Poison Control Center Listing*).

Treatment of overdose

Monitoring—Patients should be monitored for at least 15 hours after an overdose of zolmitriptan.

Supportive care—Maintaining an open airway and breathing, maintaining proper fluid and electrolyte balance, and/or correcting hypertension. Patients in whom intentional overdose is confirmed or suspected should be referred for psychiatric consultation.

Patient Consultation

As an aid to patient consultation, refer to *Advice for the Patient, Zolmitriptan (Systemic).*

In providing consultation, consider emphasizing the following selected information (» = major clinical significance):

Before using this medication

» Conditions affecting use, especially:
Sensitivity to zolmitriptan
Other medications, especially monamine oxidase inhibitors
Other medical problems, especially cardiac arrythmias, cerebrovascular accident (history of), coronary artery disease, predisposition to coronary artery disease, or other conditions that may be adversely affected by coronary artery constriction, hepatic disease, hepatic function impairment (severe), hypertension, phenylketonuria, Wolf-Parkinson-White syndrome

Proper use of this medication

» Not administering if atypical headache symptoms are present; checking with physician instead
Administering after onset of headache pain
Additional benefit may be obtained if the patient lies down in a quiet, dark room after administering medication
» Not using additional doses if first dose does not provide substantial relief; additional zolmitriptan is not likely to be effective in these circumstances; taking alternate medication as previously advised by physician, then checking with physician as soon as possible
Taking additional doses, if needed, for return of migraine after initial relief was obtained, provided that prescribed limits (quantity used and frequency of administration) are not exceeded
Compliance with prophylactic therapy, if prescribed
Proper handling/administration of oral disintegrating tablets
» Proper dosing
» Proper storage

Precautions while using this medication

Avoiding alcohol, which aggravates headache
» Caution when driving or doing anything else requiring alertness because of possible drowsiness, dizziness, lightheadedness, impairment of physical or mental abilities

Side/adverse effects

Signs of potential side effects, especially chest pain, severe; heaviness, tightness, or pressure in chest and/or neck; paresthesias; arrhythmias; gastroenteritis; leukopenia

General Dosing Information

For oral dosing forms:

The orally disintegrating tablet is packaged in a blister. Patients should be instructed not to remove the tablet from the blister until just prior to dosing. The blister pack should be peeled open and the orally disintegrating tablet placed on the tongue, where it is dissolved and swallowed with the saliva.

Unlike the swallow tablets, the orally disintegrating tablets should not be broken.

Oral disintegrating tablets may contain aspartame, which is metabolized to phenylalanine. This substance must be used with caution in patients with phenylketonuria (PKU).

Oral Dosage Forms

ZOLMITRIPTAN TABLETS

Usual adult

Antimigraine agent—
Oral, initially 2.5 mg or lower (tablet may be broken in half). If necessary, additional doses may be taken at intervals of at least two hours.
A single dose of less than 2.5 mg is recommended for patients with hepatic disease or impairment.

Usual adult limits

10 mg in twenty-four hours.

Usual pediatric dose

Safety and efficacy have not been established in children under 18 years of age.

Usual geriatric dose

See *Usual adult dose*.

Strength(s) usually available

U.S.—
2.5 mg (Rx) [*Zomig* (anhydrous lactose; microcrystalline cellulose; sodium starch glycolate; magnesium stearate; hydroxypropyl methylcellulose; titanium dioxide; polyethylene glycol 400; yellow iron oxide; red iron oxide; polyethylene glycol 8000)].
5 mg (Rx) [*Zomig* (anhydrous lactose; microcrystalline cellulose; sodium starch glycolate; magnesium stearate; hydroxypropyl methylcellulose; titanium dioxide; polyethylene glycol 400; yellow iron oxide; red iron oxide; polyethylene glycol 8000)].

Packaging and storage

Store at room temperature, preferably between 20 and 25 °C (68 and 77 °F).

ZOLMITRIPTAN ORAL DISINTEGRATING TABLETS

Usual adult dose

Antimigraine agent—
Oral, initially 2.5 mg. If necessary, additional doses may be taken at intervals of at least two hours to a maximum of 10 mg in a twenty-four-hour period.

Note: Patients with moderate to severe hepatic function impairment should receive a low dose. Blood pressure monitoring is recommended.

Usual adult limits
See *Zolmitriptan Tablets.*

Usual pediatric dose
Safety and efficacy have not been established in children under 18 years of age.

Usual geriatric dose
See *Usual adult dose.*

Strength(s) usually available
U.S.—

2.5 mg (Rx) [*Zomig-ZMT* (Orally disintegrating tablets; mannitol USP; microcrystalline cellulose NF; crospovidone anhydrous NF; aspartame NF; sodium bicarbonate USP; citric acid anhydrousUSP; colloidal silicon dioxide NF; magnesium stearate NF; orange flavor SN 027512)].

Packaging and storage
Store at controlled room temperature 20 to 25°C (68 to 77°F). Protect from light and moisture.

Note
Each *Zomig-ZMT* tablet contains 2.81 mg of phenylalanine.

Liquid is not necessary for administration. The tablet will dissolve when placed directly on the patients tongue.

Revised: 05/21/2001
Developed: 04/09/1998

ZOLPIDEM Systemic†

VA CLASSIFICATION (Primary): CN309

Note: Controlled substance classification

U.S.: Schedule IV

Commonly used brand name(s): *Ambien; Ambien CR.*

Note: For a listing of dosage forms and brand names by country availability, see *Dosage Forms* section(s).

†Not commercially available in Canada.

Category
Sedative-hypnotic.

Indications
Accepted
Insomnia (treatment)—Zolpidem is indicated for short-term treatment of insomnia. A decrease in sleep latency and increase in the duration of sleep for up to 5 weeks have been demonstrated in controlled clinical studies with zolpidem.Failure of insomnia to remit after 7 to 10 days of treatment may indicate the presence of a primary psychiatric or medical illness. Worsening of insomnia or the emergence of new abnormalities of thinking or behavior may be the consequence of an unrecognized psychiatric or physical disorder.

Extended-release zolpidem tartrate is indicated for the treatment of insomnia, characterized by difficulties with sleep onset and/or sleep maintenance (as measured by wake time after sleep onset).

Pharmacology/Pharmacokinetics
Physicochemical characteristics
Chemical Group—Imidazopyridine sedative hypnotic structurally unrelated to benzodiazepines, barbiturates, or other available sedative-hypnotics.

Molecular weight—764.9.

pKa—6.16.

Mechanism of action/Effect
Zolpidem is a potent agonist with high intrinsic activity at the omega (ω) 1 subtype (also called the benzodiazepine 1 [BZ_1] subtype) of the gamma-aminobutyric acid type A ($GABA_A$) receptor-chloride ionophore complex. The omega 1 $GABA_A$ receptor is thought to be located primarily in the cerebellum, sensory-motor cortex, substantia nigra, inferior colliculus, olfactory bulb, ventral thalamic complex, pons, and globus pallidus in the central nervous system (CNS). The receptor complex resides on neuronal membranes and functions in the gating of the chloride channel. Activation of the $GABA_A$ receptor results in the opening of the chloride channel, allowing the flow of chloride ions through the neuronal membrane and into the neuron. This results in hyperpolarization, which inhibits firing of that neuron.

In contrast to the benzodiazepines, which bind non-selectively to the omega 1, omega 2, and omega 3 $GABA_A$ receptors, zolpidem possesses relative selectivity for the omega 1 $GABA_A$ receptor. This preference for the omega 1 $GABA_A$ receptor may account for zolpidem's relative lack of anticonvulsant, myorelaxant, and anxiolytic effects at therapeutic doses, and for the general preservation of sleep architecture seen with zolpidem use.

Absorption
Rapid and complete, although first-pass metabolism results in 70% bioavailability. Food may decrease the rate and extent of absorption.

The mean AUC of a 12.5 mg zoldipem extended-release dose was 740 nanogram hours/mL (295 to 1359 nanogram hours/mL). With food, the mean AUC was decreased by 23%.

Distribution
The volume of distribution (Vol_D) of zolpidem in healthy volunteers was 0.54 L per kg (L/kg) following an 8 mg intravenous dose. Zolpidem is distributed into breast milk; amounts ranging from 0.004 to 0.019% of a 20-mg oral dose were present in milk samples taken 3 hours following administration.

Protein binding
Very high (92%).

Biotransformation
Hepatic, resulting in 3 major and several minor metabolites, all of which are inactive.

Half-life
Elimination—

Zolpidem—2.6 hours (range, 1.4 to 4.5 hours).
Zolpidem extended-release—2.8 hours (range, 1.62 to 4.05 hours)
Patients with cirrhosis—9.9 hours (range, 4.1 to 25.8 hours)

Onset of action
Rapid.

Time to peak concentration
Zolpidem tablets—30 minutes to 2 hours; may be longer if zolpidem is taken with food

Zolpidem extended-release tablets—1.5 hours

Peak serum concentration
Mean peak plasma concentration (C_{max}) following oral administration of 5 mg of zolpidem to healthy volunteers was 59 nanograms per mL (nanograms/mL) (0.077 micromoles per L [micromoles/L]), with a range of 29 to 113 nanograms/mL (0.038 to 0.148 micromoles/L); C_{max} following administration of 10 mg of zolpidem was 121 nanograms/mL (0.158 micromoles/L) with a range of 58 to 272 nanograms/mL (0.076 to 0.356 micromoles/L); C_{max} following a 12.5-mg extended-release dose of zolpidem was 134 nanograms/mL (68.9 to 197 nanograms/mL). With food, C_{max} was decreased by 30%.

Elimination
Renal—

48 to 67% of a single dose is eliminated in the urine. Unchanged zolpidem is present in trace amounts in urine and feces.

Fecal—

29 to 42% of a single dose is eliminated in the feces. Unchanged zolpidem is present in trace amounts in urine and feces.

In dialysis—

Not hemodialyzable.

Precautions to Consider
Carcinogenicity/Tumorigenicity
No evidence of carcinogenic potential was observed in mice administered zolpidem in doses of 4, 18, and 80 mg per kg of body weight (mg/kg) per day (26 to 520 times the recommended human dose of 10 mg per day on a mg/kg basis) for 2 years. In rats administered zolpidem in doses of 4, 18, and 80 mg/kg per day (43 to 876 times the recommended human dose on a mg/kg basis) for 2 years, the incidences of lipoma and liposarcoma were comparable to those seen in historical controls.

Mutagenicity
Zolpidem showed no evidence of mutagenicity based on unscheduled DNA synthesis in rat hepatocytes *in vitro* , the Ames test, or the micronucleus test in mice. Zolpidem showed no evidence of genotoxicity in mouse lymphoma cells *in vitro;* and caused no chromosomal aberrations in cultured human lymphocytes.

Pregnancy/Reproduction

Fertility—In rats given daily oral doses of 4 to 100 mg/kg of zolpidem base (5 to 130 times the recommended human dose in mg per square meter of body surface area [mg/m²]), neither male nor female fertility was affected. However, female rats receiving 100 mg/kg of zolpidem base per day displayed irregular estrus cycles and prolonged precoital intervals. The significance to humans is not known.

Pregnancy—Zolpidem has not been studied in pregnant women.

No frank teratogenicity was seen in rat and rabbit studies. Rats administered 20 and 100 mg/kg of zolpidem base (25 to 125 times the recommended human dose in mg/m²) showed maternal lethargy and ataxia as well as a dose-related trend toward incomplete ossification of fetal skull bones, which was believed to be secondary to delayed maturation. Rabbits administered 16 mg/kg of zolpidem base (28 times the recommended human dose in mg/m²) showed an increase in postimplantation fetal loss and underossification of fetal sternebrae. These effects were believed to be secondary to decreased maternal weight gain.

FDA Pregnancy Category B.

Postpartum—

Studies of children whose mothers received zolpidem during pregnancy have not been conducted. However, flaccidity and withdrawal symptoms have been reported in neonates born to mothers receiving other sedative-hypnotics during pregnancy.

Breast-feeding

One study in 5 nursing mothers showed <0.02% of a single oral dose of zolpidem was distributed into breast milk. The effect of zolpidem on the infant is not known.

In rats, zolpidem doses greater than 4 mg/kg (6 times the recommended human dose in mg/m²) inhibited milk secretion.

Pediatrics

Appropriate studies on the relationship of age to the effects of zolpidem have not been performed in children up to 18 years of age. Safety and efficacy have not been established.

Geriatrics

Studies have shown zolpidem to have an increased half-life, peak plasma concentration, and area under the plasma concentration time curve in geriatric patients. Elderly patients may be more likely to experience confusion or falls while taking zolpidem. A reduced starting dosage and careful monitoring are recommended. In addition, geriatric patients are more likely to have age-related renal function impairment, which may require dosage reductions.

Drug interactions and/or related problems

The following drug interactions and/or related problems have been selected on the basis of their potential clinical significance (possible mechanism in parentheses where appropriate)—not necessarily inclusive (» = major clinical significance):

Note: Combinations containing any of the following medications, depending on the amount present, may also interact with this medication.

» Alcohol or

» CNS depression-producing medications, other (See *Appendix II*)
(concurrent use may increase the CNS depressant effects of either these medications or zolpidem; caution is recommended, and dosage of one or both agents should be reduced)

Chlorpromazine
(concurrent use may prolong elimination half-life of chlorpromazine)

Imipramine
(concurrent use may increase drowsiness and incidence of anterograde amnesia, and decrease peak concentrations of imipramine)

Medical considerations/Contraindications

The medical considerations/contraindications included have been selected on the basis of their potential clinical significance (reasons given in parentheses where appropriate)—not necessarily inclusive (» = major clinical significance).

Risk-benefit should be considered when the following medical problems exist:

» Alcohol intoxication, acute, with depressed vital signs
(additive CNS depression may occur)

Alcohol or drug abuse or dependence, history of
(predisposition to habituation and dependence may exist)

Hepatic function impairment
(zolpidem elimination may be prolonged due to biphasic elimination with prolonged terminal half-life)

Mental depression
(condition may be exacerbated)

Pulmonary disease, severe chronic obstructive
(ventilatory failure may be exacerbated)

Renal function impairment
(zolpidem elimination may be prolonged)

» Sensitivity to zolpidem

» Sleep apnea, established or suspected
(condition may be exacerbated)

Side/Adverse Effects

The following side/adverse effects have been selected on the basis of their potential clinical significance (possible signs and symptoms in parentheses where appropriate)—not necessarily inclusive:

Those indicating need for medical attention

Incidence less frequent

Ataxia (clumsiness or unsteadiness); ***confusion***—higher incidence in the elderly; ***mental depression***

Incidence rare

Allergic reaction or rash; anaphylaxis (fast heartbeat; swelling of face; wheezing or difficulty in breathing); ***falling***—higher incidence in the elderly; ***hypotension*** (dizziness, lightheadedness, or fainting); ***paradoxical reactions, including agitation*** (unusual excitement or nervousness); ***or irritability; hallucinations*** (seeing, hearing, or feeling things that are not there); ***or insomnia*** (trouble in sleeping)

Those indicating need for medical attention only if they continue or are bothersome

Incidence more frequent

Somnolence (sleepiness or unusual drowsiness)

Incidence less frequent

Abnormal dreams, including nightmares; anterograde amnesia (memory problems); ***anxiety*** (fear; nervousness); ***appetite disorder; asthenia*** (lack or loss of strength); ***balance disorder; binge eating; daytime drowsiness; depersonalization*** (feeling of unreality; sense of detachment from self or body.); ***depression*** (discouragement; feeling sad or empty; irritability; lack of appetite; loss of interest or pleasure; tiredness; trouble concentrating; trouble sleeping); ***disinhibition*** (lack or loss of self-control); ***disorientation*** (confusion about identity, place, and time); ***dizziness; lightheadedness; or vertigo; drugged feelings; dryness of mouth; dysuria*** (difficult or painful urination; burning while urinating); ***euphoria*** (false or unusual sense of well-being); ***eye redness; gastrointestinal effects, including abdominal or gastric pain; constipation; diarrhea; flatulence; frequent bowel movements; heartburn; nausea; or vomiting; headache; hypoaesthesia*** (abnormal or decreased touch sensation); ***labyrinthitis*** (dizziness, loss of balance, hearing loss, ringing in ears, abnormal sensation of movement); ***malaise*** (general feeling of discomfort or illness); ***menorrhagia*** (longer or heavier menstrual periods); ***mood swings; myalgia*** (joint pain; swollen joints; muscle aching or cramping; muscle pains or stiffness; difficulty in moving); ***paresthesia*** (burning, crawling, itching, numbness, prickling, "pins and needles", or tingling feelings); ***psychomotor retardation*** (generalized slowing of mental and physical activity); ***skin wrinkling; stress symptoms; throat irritation*** (redness or soreness of throat); ***tinnitus*** (continuing ringing or buzzing or other unexplained noise in ears; hearing loss); ***urticaria*** (hives or welts; itching; redness of skin; skin rash); ***vision abnormalities, including diplopia*** (double vision); ***vision blurred; visual depth perception altered; vulvovaginal dryness*** (itching or pain of the vagina or genital area)

Those indicating possible withdrawal and/or the need for medical attention if they occur after medication is discontinued, usually within 48 hours

Abdominal or stomach cramps or discomfort; agitation, nervousness, or feelings of panic; flushing; lightheadedness; muscle cramps; nausea; psychotic exacerbation (worsening of mental or emotional problems); ***seizures; sweating; tremors; uncontrolled crying; unusual tiredness or weakness; or vomiting***

Overdose

For specific information on the agents used in the management of zolpidem overdose, see:

- *Charcoal, Activated (Oral-Local)* monograph; and/or
- *Flumazenil (Systemic)* monograph.

For more information on the management of overdose or unintentional ingestion, **contact a Poison Control Center** (see *Poison Control Center Listing*).

Clinical effects of overdose

The following effects have been selected on the basis of their potential clinical significance (possible signs and symptoms in parentheses where appropriate)—not necessarily inclusive:

Ataxia, severe (clumsiness or unsteadiness); ***cardiovascular compromise*** (slow heartbeat); ***diplopia*** (double vision); ***or disturbed vision; dizziness, severe; drowsiness, severe; nausea, severe; respiratory problems*** (troubled breathing); ***unconsciousness; vomiting, severe***

Treatment of overdose

Treatment is essentially symptomatic and supportive, possibly including:

To decrease absorption—
Inducing emesis or performing gastric lavage as appropriate.

To enhance elimination—
Administering activated charcoal to increase clearance and decrease absorption of zolpidem.
Zolpidem is not dialyzable.

Specific treatment—
Withholding sedating drugs even if excitation occurs.
Flumazenil may be useful in reversing zolpidem's sedative and respiratory depressant effects.

Monitoring—
Monitoring respiratory, cardiac, and CNS status.

Supportive care—
Providing general supportive therapy as indicated. Patients in whom intentional overdose is known or suspected should be referred for psychiatric consultation.

Patient Consultation

As an aid to patient consultation, refer to *Advice for the Patient, Zolpidem (Systemic).*

In providing consultation, consider emphasizing the following selected information (» = major clinical significance):

Before using this medication

» Conditions affecting use, especially:
Sensitivity to zolpidem
Breast-feeding—Small amounts of zolpidem are distributed into breast milk; effect on infant is not known
Use in the elderly—Elderly patients are usually more sensitive to CNS effects of zolpidem
Other medications, especially other CNS depression-producing medications
Other medical problems, especially acute alcohol intoxication or sleep apnea

Proper use of this medication

» Not taking more medication than the amount prescribed, because of habit-forming potential

» Not increasing dose if medication becomes less effective over time; checking with physician

» Taking zolpidem on an empty stomach; not taking with food or eating immediately after

» For the extended-release tablet: Swallowing whole; not chewing or crushing

Being prepared to go to sleep immediately after taking medicine

» Proper dosing
Missed dose: Skipping missed dose; not doubling doses

» Proper storage

Precautions while using this medication

» Avoiding use of alcohol or other CNS depressants during therapy

» Avoiding driving, using machines, or anything else that requires alertness while taking zolpidem

» Caution if clumsiness or unsteadiness, drowsiness, dizziness, or visual disturbances occur, especially in the elderly

» Changes in behavior or thinking such as more outgoing or aggressive behavior than normal; loss of personal identity; confusion; strange behavior; agitation; hallucinations; worsening of depression; or suicidal thoughts.

Amnesia; avoid by only taking zolpidem when able to get a full night's sleep (7 to 8 hours) before the need to be active again.

Checking with physician before discontinuing medication after more than 1 to 2 weeks of use; gradual dosage reduction may be necessary to avoid withdrawal symptoms

Side/adverse effects

Signs of potential side effects, especially ataxia, confusion, mental depression, allergic reaction or rash, anaphylaxis, falling, hypotension, or paradoxical reactions

General Dosing Information

Geriatric or debilitated patients, or patients with hepatic or renal function impairment should receive decreased initial dosage since elimination of zolpidem may be prolonged, resulting in increased CNS and gastrointestinal side effects.

Optimal dosage of zolpidem varies with patient response. Individual dosage adjustments should be made. The minimal effective dose should be used for the shortest period, with the need for continuing therapy with zolpidem reviewed regularly.

Because of zolpidem's rapid onset of action, the patient should be ready for sleep when the dose is taken.

To minimize the occurrence of anterograde amnesia and hang-over effects, zolpidem should be taken only when the patient's schedule will allow for a full night's sleep (7 to 8 hours).

Following prolonged administration, zolpidem should be withdrawn gradually to lessen the possibility of precipitating withdrawal symptoms.

Potentially suicidal patients, particularly those who use alcohol excessively, should not have access to large quantities of zolpidem.

Diet/Nutrition

For the most rapid effect, zolpidem should be taken on an empty stomach. The effect of zolpidem may be slowed by ingestion with or immediately after a meal.

Oral Dosage Forms

ZOLPIDEM TARTRATE EXTENDED-RELEASE TABLETS

Usual adult dose

Hypnotic—
Oral, 12.5 mg immediately before bedtime.

Note: Debilitated patients or patients with hepatic insufficiency—Oral, 6.25 mg immediately at bedtime.

Usual pediatric dose

Children up to 18 years of age: Safety and efficacy have not been established.

Usual geriatric dose

Hypnotic—
Oral, 6.25 immediately at bedtime.

Strength(s) usually available

U.S.—
6.25 mg (Rx) [*Ambien CR* (two-layer tablet; colloidal silicon dioxide; hypromellose; lactose monohydrate; magnesium stearate; microcrystalline cellulose; polyethylene glycol; potassium bitartrate; red ferric oxide; sodium starch glycolate; titanium dioxide)].
12.5 mg (Rx) [*Ambien CR* (two-layer tablet; colloidal silicon dioxide; FD&C blue #2; hypromellose; lactose monohydrate; magnesium stearate; microcrystalline cellulose; polyethylene glycol; potassium bitartrate; sodium starch glycolate; titanium dioxide; yellow ferric oxide)].

Canada—
Not commercially available.

Packaging and storage

Store between 15 and 25 °C (59 and 77 °F). Limited excursions permissible up to 30 °C (86 °F).

Auxiliary labeling

- Avoid alcoholic beverages.
- Swallow whole. Do not crush or chew.
- May cause drowsiness.

Note

Controlled substance in the U.S.

ZOLPIDEM TARTRATE TABLETS

Usual adult dose

Hypnotic—
Oral, 10 mg at bedtime.

Note: Debilitated patients or patients with hepatic or renal function impairment—Oral, initially 5 mg at bedtime, the dosage being adjusted as needed and tolerated.

Usual adult prescribing limits

Up to 10 mg a day.

Usual pediatric dose

Children up to 18 years of age—
Safety and efficacy have not been established.

Usual geriatric dose

Hypnotic—
Oral, initially 5 mg at bedtime, the dosage being adjusted as needed and tolerated.

Usual geriatric prescribing limits

Up to 10 mg a day.

Strength(s) usually available

U.S.—

5 mg (Rx) [*Ambien* (hydroxypropyl methylcellulose; lactose; magnesium stearate; microcrystalline cellulose; polyethylene glycol; sodium starch glycolate; titanium dioxide; FD&C Red No. 40; iron oxide colorant; and polysorbate 80)].

10 mg (Rx) [*Ambien* (hydroxypropyl methylcellulose; lactose; magnesium stearate; microcrystalline cellulose; polyethylene glycol; sodium starch glycolate; titanium dioxide)].

Canada—

Not commercially available.

Packaging and storage

Store below 40 °C (104 °F), preferably between 15 and 30 °C (59 and 86 °F), unless otherwise specified by manufacturer. Store in a well-closed container.

Auxiliary labeling

- Avoid alcoholic beverages.
- May cause daytime drowsiness.

Note

Controlled substance in the U.S.

Selected Bibliography

Langtry HD, Benfield P. Zolpidem: A review of its pharmacodynamic and pharmacokinetic properties and therapeutic potential. Drugs 1990; 40(2): 291-313.

Hoehns JD, Perry PJ. Zolpidem: A nonbenzodiazepine hypnotic for treatment of insomnia [published erratum appears in Clin Pharm 1993 Dec; 12: 881]. Clin Pharm 1993 Nov; 12: 814-28.

Revised: 04/26/2006

ZONISAMIDE Systemic†

VA CLASSIFICATION (Primary): CN400

Commonly used brand name(s): *Zonegran*.

Note: For a listing of dosage forms and brand names by country availability, see *Dosage Forms* section(s).

†Not commercially available in Canada.

Category

Anticonvulsant.

Indications

Accepted

Epilepsy, partial (treatment)—Zonisamide is indicated for adjunctive therapeutic use in the treatment of partial seizures in adults with epilepsy.

Pharmacology/Pharmacokinetics

Physicochemical characteristics

Chemical Group—Sulfonamide.

Molecular weight—212.23.

pKa—10.2.

Solubility—Zonisamide is moderately soluble in water and in 0.1N hydrochloric acid.

Mechanism of action/Effect

The exact method by which zonisamide exerts its anticonvulsant effect is unknown. Some *in vitro* studies suggest a blockade of sodium channels, with consequent stabilization of neuronal membranes and suppression of neuronal hypersynchronization, whereas other *in vitro* studies have shown zonisamide to suppress synaptically-driven electrical activity without affecting postsynaptic GABA or glutamate responses. It appears then, that zonisamide does not potentiate the synaptic activity of GABA. Zonisamide also serves as a weak inhibitor of carbonic anhydrase

Absorption

Variable, yet relatively rapid rate of absorption, with delays in time to maximum concentration when administered with food.

Distribution

The apparent volume of distribution (V_d) of zonisamide is 1.45 L/kg.

Zonisamide is distributed to breast milk, cerebrospinal fluid, and erythrocytes. Concentration in erythrocytes is approximately 8 times higher than in plasma and the milk-to-plasma ratio is 0.93.

The concentration of zonisamide in cerebrospinal fluid is approximately 76% of the concentration found in plasma.

Protein binding

Moderate (40%)

Biotransformation

Hepatic, does not induce own metabolism. Zonisamide undergoes acetylation and reduction, forming N-acetyl zonisamide, and the open-ring metabolite 2–sulfamoylacetyl phenol, respectively. Reduction of zonisamide is mediated by cytochrome P450 isoenzyme 3A4 (CYP3A4).

Half-life

Elimination, in plasma—63 hours

Elimination, in erythrocytes—105 hours

Note: Concurrent administration of CYP3A4–inducing or inhibiting medications with zonisamide has altered serum concentrations and half-life values. Zonisamide serum half-life values are decreased to 27 hours in the presence of phenytoin, to 38 hours in the presence of either carbamazepine or phenobarbital, and to 46 hours when administered concomitantly with valproate.

Time to peak concentration

2 to 6 hours

Note: In the presence of food, delayed to between 4 and 6 hours. However, food does not alter the absolute bioavailability of zonisamide.

Peak plasma concentration:

2 to 5 mcg/mL, following a 200 to 400 mg zonisamide oral dose

Note: In patients with significant renal function impairment, where the creatinine clearance is <20 mL/min, the area under the concentration-time curve (AUC) for zonisamide is increased by 35%.

Elimination

Renal—62%

Fecal—3%

Note: Plasma clearance of zonisamide is approximately 0.30 to 0.35 mL/min/kg in patients not receiving concomitant therapy with enzyme-inducing anticonvulsants. Zonisamide clearance is increased to 0.5 mL/min/kg in patients concurrently receiving enzyme-inducing anticonvulsant medications.

Precautions to Consider

Cross-sensitivity and/or related problems

Patients with hypersensitivity reactions to sulfonamide antibiotics may also be allergic to zonisamide.

Carcinogenicity

No evidence of carcinogenicity was found in mice or rats receiving zonisamide in their diet at doses of up to 80 mg per kg of body weight (mg/kg) a day (equivalent to the maximum recommended human dose [MRHD] of 400 mg a day on a mg per square meter of body surface area [mg/m^2] basis in mice and 1 to 2 times the MRHD on a mg/m^2 basis in rats) for two years.

Mutagenicity

Zonisamide increased mutation frequency in Chinese hamster lung cells in the absence of metabolic activation. Zonisamide was neither mutagenic nor clastogenic in the Ames test, the *in vitro* mouse lymphoma assay, sister chromatid exchange test, and human lymphocyte cytogenetics assay, and the *in vivo* rat bone cytogenetics assay.

Pregnancy/Reproduction

Fertility—Studies in female rats receiving zonisamide at doses of 20, 60, and 200 mg per kg of body weight (mg/kg) (the low end of the dosing range corresponds to approximately one half the MRHD on a mg per m^2 basis), before mating and during the initial phase of gestation, exhibited signs of reproductive toxicity as indicated by decreases in corpora lutea, implantations, and live fetuses. These effects were observed at all doses.

The effect of zonisamide on human fertility is unknown.

Pregnancy—Zonisamide crosses the placenta. Adequate and well-controlled studies in humans have not been done. Zonisamide should be used during pregnancy only if the benefit justifies the potential risk to the fetus. Effective contraception should be used in women of child-bearing potential who are taking zonisamide.

Zonisamide has been shown to be embryolethal in pregnant cynomolgus monkeys and teratogenic in pregnant mice, rats, and dogs when administered during the gestational phase of organogenesis. Cardiovascular and skeletal malformations predominated in the offspring of pregnant dogs receiving up to 60 mg/kg/day, while increased frequencies of skeletal and craniofacial defects were observed in the offspring of pregnant mice administered up to 500 mg/kg/day. These fetal abnormalities were observed at zonisamide doses and maternal plasma concentration levels that were similar to or lower than therapeutic levels in humans.

FDA Pregnancy Category C

Labor and delivery—The effect of zonisamide on labor and delivery in humans is not known.

Breast-feeding

Zonisamide is distributed into human breast milk, at a milk-to-plasma ratio of 0.93. Zonisamide should be used by nursing mothers only if the potential benefit outweighs the potential risk to the nursing infant.

Pediatrics

Safety and effectiveness of zonisamide in pediatric patients have not been established. Zonisamide is not approved for use in pediatric patients. However, oligohidrosis, sometimes resulting in heat stroke and hospitalization, and hyperthermia have been reported in pediatric patients after receiving zonisamide.

Geriatrics

Single-dose pharmacokinetic study of zonisamide in healthy elderly adults (mean age 69 years) was similar to that in healthy young adults (mean age 28 years). Although appropriate studies on the relationship of age to the effects of zonisamide have not been performed in the geriatric population, no geriatrics-specific problems have been reported to date. However, elderly patients are more likely to have age-related impairments in cardiac, hepatic, or renal function, which may require adjustments in dosing for patients receiving zonisamide. It is recommended that elderly patients receive dosages at the low end of the normal range.

Drug interactions and/or related problems

The following drug interactions and/or related problems have been selected on the basis of their potential clinical significance (possible mechanism in parentheses where appropriate)—not necessarily inclusive (» = major clinical significance):

Note: Other anticonvulsants that induce cytochrome P450 isoenzymes (particularly CYP3A4) will increase metabolism and plasma clearance of zonisamide, resulting in lower plasma concentrations. Conversely, other medications that inhibit CYP3A4 will likewise inhibit zonisamide metabolism and plasma clearance. Zonisamide neither induces nor inhibits cytochrome P450 isoenzymes and is not expected to interfere with other medications that are metabolized by the P450 isoenzyme group.

Note: Combinations containing any of the following medications, depending on the amount present, may also interact with this medication.

» Anticholinergics or (see *Appendix II*)

» Carbonic anhydrase inhibitors
(these drugs predispose patients to heat-related disorders; caution should be used when administered concurrently with zonisamide)

» CNS depression-producing medications, other (see *Appendix II*)
(additive sedation effects may occur)

Anticonvulsants, including

» Carbamazepine

» Phenobarbital

» Phenytoin

» Valproate
(Antiepileptic agents that are cytochrome P450 inducers have caused decreased serum concentrations of zonisamide)

Laboratory value alterations

The following have been selected on the basis of their potential clinical significance (possible effect in parentheses where appropriate)—not necessarily inclusive (» = major clinical significance).

With physiology/laboratory test values

Alkaline phosphatase, serum
(Mean increases of 7% have been observed in patients receiving zonisamide)

Blood urea nitrogen, serum
(Elevations of approximately 8% over baseline levels were observed in patients receiving zonisamide)

Creatinine, serum
(Elevations of approximately 8% over baseline levels have been observed during administration of zonisamide)

Medical considerations/Contraindications

The medical considerations/contraindications included have been selected on the basis of their potential clinical significance (reasons given in parentheses where appropriate)—not necessarily inclusive (» = major clinical significance).

Except under special circumstances, this medication should not be used when the following medical problem exists:

» Previous hypersensitivity reaction to zonisamide or any other sulfonamide

» Renal failure (glomerular filtration rate < 50 mL/min)

Risk-benefit should be considered when the following medical problems exist:

Hepatic dysfunction
(Zonisamide is metabolized by the liver; plasma clearance may be impaired)

Renal dysfunction
(Zonisamide excretion may be reduced in the presence of impaired renal function)

Patient monitoring

The following may be especially important in patient monitoring (other tests may be warranted in some patients, depending on condition; » = major clinical significance):

» Body temperature elevation and/or

» Decreased sweating
(monitor closely in patients, especially pediatric patients or patients exposed to warm or hot weather; could indicate oligohidrosis or hyperthermia)

Impaired renal function

Creatinine, serum

Blood Urea Nitrogen, serum

Side/Adverse Effects

Oligohidrosis, sometimes resulting in heat stroke and hospitalization, and hyperthermia have been reported in pediatric patients treated with zonisamide.

Many cases of heat stroke with symptoms of decreased sweating and elevated body temperature have occurred in patients when exposed to elevated environmental temperatures.

Fatalities have occurred rarely as a result of severe reactions to sulfonamides including, Stevens-Johnson syndrome, toxic epidermal necrolysis, fulminant hepatic necrosis, agranulocytosis, aplastic anemia, and other blood dyscrasias. These reactions may occur when sulfonamides are readministered irrespective of the route of administration.

The following side/adverse effects have been selected on the basis of their potential clinical significance (possible signs and symptoms in parentheses where appropriate)—not necessarily inclusive:

Those indicating need for medical attention

Incidence more frequent

Ataxia (shakiness and unsteady walk); ***confusion*** (mood or mental changes); ***depression*** (discouragement; feeling sad or empty; irritability; lack of appetite; loss of interest or pleasure; tiredness; trouble concentrating; trouble sleeping)

Incidence less frequent

Ecchymosis (bruising; large, flat, blue or purplish patches on the skin); ***rash; schizophrenic or schizophreniform behavior*** (agitation; delusions; hallucinations)

Those indicating need for medical attention only if they continue or are bothersome

Incidence more frequent

Abdominal pain; anorexia (loss of appetite); ***agitation or irritability*** (anxiety; restlessness); ***difficulty in concentrating; difficulty with memory; diplopia*** (double vision); ***dizziness; fatigue*** (unusual tiredness or weakness); ***headache; insomnia*** (sleeplessness; trouble sleeping); ***nausea; somnolence*** (sleepiness; unusual drowsiness); ***tiredness***

Incidence less frequent

Anxiety; constipation; diarrhea; difficulty in verbal expression (problems with speech or speaking); ***dry mouth; dyspepsia*** (acid or sour stomach; belching; heartburn; indigestion); ***flu syndrome*** (aching muscles and joints; chills; headache; fever; general feeling of discomfort); ***mental slowing; nervousness; nystagmus*** (uncontrolled back and forth and/or rolling eye movements); ***paresthesia*** (tingling, burning, or prickly sensations); ***rhinitis*** (runny nose; sneezing; stuffy nose); ***speech abnormalities*** (difficulty in speaking); ***taste perversion*** (bad, unusual, or unpleasant taste; change in taste); ***weight loss***

Overdose

For more information on the management of overdose or unintentional ingestion, **contact a poison control center** (see *Poison Control Center Listing*).

Clinical effects of overdose

The following effects have been selected on the basis of their potential clinical significance (possible signs and symptoms in parentheses where appropriate)—not necessarily inclusive:

Bradycardia (slow or irregular heartbeat); ***coma*** (loss of consciousness); ***hypotension*** (confusion; dizziness, faintness or light-headedness when getting up from a lying down or sitting position; unusual tiredness or weakness); ***respiratory depression*** (blue fingernails, lips, or skin; difficult or troubled breathing)

Treatment of overdose

To decrease absorption—
Emesis should be induced or gastric lavage applied, employing appropriate airway protection techniques.

To enhance elimination—
Renal dialysis may not be effective, due to the low protein binding profile (40%) of zonisamide

Specific treatment—
There are no specific treatments or antidotes for zonisamide toxicity. Treatment is generally symptomatic and supportive

Monitoring—
Monitoring of electrocardiographic rhythm, blood pressure, and respiratory function

Supportive care—
Maintaining respiratory and cardiac function
Usual and customary measures of managing circulatory collapse
Patients in whom intentional overdose is confirmed or suspected should be referred for psychiatric consultation.

Patient Consultation

As an aid to patient consultation, refer to *Advice for the Patient, Zonisamide (Systemic)*.

In providing consultation, consider emphasizing the following selected information (» = major clinical significance):

Before using this medication

» Conditions affecting use, especially:
Hypersensitivity to zonisamide or other sulfonamides
Pregnancy—Risk-benefit should be considered because of selective developmental toxicity including teratogenicity demonstrated in animal studies.
FDA Pregnancy Category C
Breast-feeding—Distributed into breast milk. Risk-benefit should be considered.
Use in children—Safety and effectiveness of zonisamide in pediatric patients have not been established. Zonisamide is not approved for use in pediatric patients. However, oligohidrosis, sometimes resulting in heat stroke and hospitalization, and hyperthermia have been reported in pediatric patients after receiving zonisamide.
Other medications, especially anticholinergics, carbonic anhydrase inhibitors, CNS depression-producing agents, carbamazepine, phenobarbital, phenytoin, or valproate.
Other medical problems, especially renal failure (glomerular filtration rate < 50 mL/min)

Proper use of this medication

» Swallowing whole, not chewing or breaking capsule
» Proper dosing
Missed dose: Taking as soon as possible; not taking if almost time for next scheduled dose; not doubling doses
» Proper storage

Precautions while using this medication

» Importance of regular visits to physician to check progress of therapy
» Discussing alcohol use or use of other CNS depressants with physician
» Possible blurred or double vision, dizziness, drowsiness, or light-headedness; caution when driving, using machinery, or doing other jobs that require alertness
» Caution during exercise or hot weather; overheating may result in heat stroke
Checking with physician if condition does not improve within a few weeks or if it becomes worse
» Contacting physician immediately if skin rash develops, if experiencing fever, sore throat, oral ulcers, easy bruising, or worsening of seizures
» Checking with physician immediately if a child taking zonisamide is not sweating as usual
» Using effective contraception (in woman of childbearing age)
» Not discontinuing zonisamide abruptly; checking with physician about gradually reducing dosage before stopping completely
» Importance of adequate fluid intake during therapy to help prevent kidney stone formation

Side/adverse effects

Signs of potential side effects, especially ataxia, confusion, depression, ecchymosis, rash, schizophrenic or schizophreniform behavior

General Dosing Information

Abrupt discontinuation in a responsive epileptic patient may result in convulsions and possibly status epilepticus; gradual withdrawal is recommended.

Many of the side effects of zonisamide are dose-related. Side effects may be minimized by initiating therapy with low doses, which should be increased gradually at weekly intervals until an adequate response is obtained.

Patients with renal or hepatic dysfunction may require slower titration and more frequent monitoring.

Diet/Nutrition

Drinking plenty of water (6–8 glasses per day) may be useful to help prevent kidney stones.

Zonisamide may be taken with or without food. Capsules should be swallowed whole.

Oral Dosage Forms

ZONISAMIDE CAPSULES

Usual adult dose

Anticonvulsant—
Patients 16 years of age and olderInitial—Oral, 100 mg a day, the dosage being increased by 100 mg a day increments at intervals of at least two weeks to allow for attainment of steady state plasma levels, up to 400 mg a day. Since many side effects are more frequent at doses of 300 mg and above, it is suggested that treatment may be prolonged at lower dosing levels in order to more accurately assess all effects of zonisamide at steady state.

Note: The long half-life of zonisamide may require a waiting period of up to two weeks after dosing adjustment, for the achievement of steady state plasma concentrations.
Patients with renal or hepatic dysfunction may require slower titration and more frequent monitoring.

Maintenance—Oral, 200 to 400 mg a day, in one single, or two equally-divided doses

Usual adult prescribing limits

Dosage should generally not exceed 400 mg/day; little information is available regarding doses greater than 600 mg/day.

Usual pediatric dose

Anticonvulsant—
Safety and efficacy have not been established for children younger than 16 years of age

Usual geriatric dose

Geriatric patients should start at the low end of the dosing range.See *Usual adult dose.*

Usual geriatric prescribing limit

See *Usual adult prescribing limits.*

Strength(s) usually available

U.S.—
100 mg (Rx) [*Zonegran* (2–piece capsule; microcrystalline cellulose; hydrogenated vegetable oil; sodium laurel sulfate; gelatin)].

Packaging and storage

Store below 25° C (77° F), preferably between 15 and 30° C (59 and 86° F). Protect from light and moisture.

Auxiliary labeling

- May cause dizziness, light-headedness, or drowsiness.
- Swallow capsule whole. Do not break or chew.
- Drink plenty of fluids.
- Protect from light and moisture.

Revised: 06/05/2003
Developed: 06/13/2000

Appendix I

SELECTED LIST OF DRUG-INDUCED EFFECTS

The following list of selected drug-induced side effects has been compiled for use in conjunction with the drug interactions section of *USP DI* monographs. This listing gives examples of certain substances that may contribute to additive effects of the medication being referred to where such an effect has been identified as posing a potentially clinically significant problem with the concurrent use of two or more medications. The listing of drugs is not meant to be inclusive.

Anticholinergics

- Anisotropine
- Atropine
- Belladonna
- Clidinium
- Dicyclomine
- Glycopyrrolate
- Homatropine
- Hyoscyamine
- Ipratropium
- Mepenzolate
- Methantheline
- Methscopolamine
- Pirenzepine
- Propantheline
- Scopolamine

Other medications with anticholinergic activity

- Antidepressants, monoamine oxidase (MAO) inhibitor
- Antidepressants, tricyclic
- Antihistamines, H_1-receptor
- Benztropine
- Biperiden
- Buclizine
- Carbamazepine
- Clozapine
- Cyclizine
- Cyclobenzaprine
- Digoxin
- Disopyramide
- Dronabinol
- Ethopropazine
- Loxapine
- Maprotiline
- Meclizine
- Molindone
- Orphenadrine
- Oxybutynin
- Phenothiazines
- Pimozide
- Procainamide
- Procyclidine
- Quinidine
- Thioxanthenes
- Trihexyphenidyl

Blood dyscrasia–causing medications—Defined as those drugs causing unpredictable myelotoxicity that usually occurs in a minority of patients and is not dose-dependent

- Alemtuzumab
- Aminopyrine
- Amodiaquine
- Amphotericin B lipid complex
- Angiotensin-converting enzyme (ACE) inhibitors
- Anticonvulsants, hydantoin
- Anticonvulsants, succinimide
- Antidepressants, tricyclic
- Antidiabetic agents, sulfonylurea
- Anti-inflammatory drugs, nonsteroidal (NSAIDS), especially phenylbutazone
- Antithyroid agents
- Bexarotene
- Carbamazepine

Blood dyscrasia–causing medications—Defined as those drugs causing unpredictable myelotoxicity that usually occurs in a minority of patients and is not dose-dependent *(continued)*

- Cetirizine and Pseudoephedrine
- Chloramphenicol
- Clozapine
- Dapsone
- Divalproex
- Epirubicin
- Felbamate
- Flecainide
- Foscarnet
- Gemtuzumab Ozogamicin
- Gold compounds
- Levamisole
- Loxapine
- Maprotiline
- Mirtazapine
- Peginterferon Alfa-2B
- Penicillamine
- Pentamidine
- Phenothiazines
- Pimozide
- Primaquine
- Primidone
- Procainamide
- Propafenone
- Pyrimethamine (with high doses)
- Rifapentine
- Rituximab
- Sulfasalazine
- Sulfamethoxazole and Trimethoprim
- Sulfonamides, systemic
- Temozolomide
- Thioxanthenes
- Ticlopidine
- Tiopronin
- Tocainide
- Trastuzumab
- Trimethobenzamide
- Trimethoprim
- Valproic acid

Bone marrow depressants—Defined as those drugs producing a predictable dose-related myelotoxicity

- Abacavir, Lamivudine, and Zidovudine
- Aldesleukin
- Alemtuzumab
- Altretamine
- Amphotericin B, systemic
- Amphotericin B cholesteryl complex
- Amphotericin B lipid complex
- Amphotericin B liposomal complex
- Anastrazole
- Azathioprine
- Bexarotene
- Busulfan
- Capecitabine
- Carboplatin
- Carmustine, systemic
- Chlorambucil
- Chloramphenicol

Bone marrow depressants—Defined as those drugs producing a predictable dose-related myelotoxicity *(continued)*

- Cisplatin
- Cladribine
- Clozapine
- Colchicine
- Cyclophosphamide
- Cytarabine
- Dacarbazine
- Dactinomycin
- Daunorubicin
- Daunorubicin, liposomal
- Didanosine
- Docetaxel
- Doxorubicin
- Doxorubicin, liposomal
- Eflornithine
- Epirubicin
- Etoposide
- Floxuridine
- Flucytosine
- Fludarabine
- Fluorouracil, systemic
- Ganciclovir
- Gemcitabine
- Gemtuzumab Ozogamicin
- Hydroxyurea
- Ibritumomab Tiuxetan
- Idarubicin
- Ifosfamide
- Imatinib
- Interferons, Alpha
- Irinotecan
- Lomustine
- Mechlorethamine, systemic
- Melphalan
- Mercaptopurine
- Methotrexate
- Mitomycin
- Mitoxantrone
- Oxaliplatin
- Paclitaxel
- Pegaspargase
- Pentostatin
- Plicamycin
- Procarbazine
- Sodium iodide I 131
- Sodium phosphate P 32
- Strontium 89 chloride
- Streptozocin
- Temozolomide
- Teniposide
- Thioguanine
- Thiotepa
- Topotecan
- Trimetrexate
- Uracil Mustard
- Valganciclovir
- Valrubicin
- Vidarabine, systemic (with high doses)
- Vinblastine
- Vincristine
- Vinorelbine
- Zidovudine
- Zidovudine and Lamivudine
- Zoledronic Acid

CNS depression–producing medications
- Alcohol
- Aminoglutethimide
- Anesthetics, general
- Anesthetics, parenteral-local
- Anticonvulsants
- Antidepressants, monoamine oxidase (MAO) inhibitor
- Antidepressants, tricyclic
- Antidyskinetics (except amantadine)
- Antihistamines, H_1-receptor (except astemizole, cetirizine, fexofenadine, loratadine, and terfenadine)
- Apomorphine
- Azelastine
- Baclofen
- Barbiturates
- Benzodiazepines
- Beta-Adrenergic Blocking Agents
- Brimonidine
- Buclizine
- Carbamazepine
- Cetirizine (dose-related)
- Cetirizine and Pseudoephedrine (dose-related)
- Chlophedianol
- Chloral hydrate
- Chlorzoxazone
- Clonidine
- Clozapine
- Cyclizine
- Difenoxin and Atropine
- Diphenoxylate and Atropine
- Disulfiram
- Donepezil
- Dronabinol
- Ethchlorvynol
- Ethinamate
- Etomidate
- Glutethimide
- Guanabenz
- Guanfacine
- Haloperidol
- Hydroxyzine
- Ketamine
- Levomethadyl
- Loratadine (dose-related)
- Loxapine
- Magnesium sulfate, parenteral
- Maprotiline
- Meclizine
- Meprobamate
- Methyldopa
- Methyprylon
- Metoclopramide
- Metyrosine
- Mirtazapine
- Mitotane
- Molindone
- Nabilone
- Olanzapine
- Opioid (Narcotic) Analgesics
- Paraldehyde
- Paregoric
- Pargyline
- Peginterferon Alfa-2B
- Phenothiazines
- Pimozide
- Procarbazine
- Promethazine
- Propiomazine
- Propofol
- Quetiapine
- Rauwolfia alkaloids
- Risperidone
- Scopolamine
- Skeletal muscle relaxants (centrally acting)
- Sodium Oxybate
- Thalidomide

CNS depression–producing medications *(continued)*
- Thioxanthenes
- Trazodone
- Tramadol
- Trimeprazine
- Trimethobenzamide
- Zolpidem

CNS stimulation–producing medications
- Amantadine
- Amphetamines
- Anesthetics, local
- Appetite suppressants, sympathomimetic
- Bronchodilators, theophylline
- Bupropion
- Caffeine
- Chlophedianol
- Cocaine
- Dexmethylphenidate
- Doxapram
- Dronabinol
- Dyphylline
- Fluoroquinolones
- Meropenem
- Methylphenidate
- Modafinil
- Nabilone
- Pemoline
- Selegiline
- Sympathomimetics

Enzyme inducers, hepatic, cytochrome P450
- Alcohol (with chronic use)
- Aminoglutethimide
- Barbiturates, especially phenobarbital
- Carbamazepine
- Efavirenz
- Glutethimide
- Griseofulvin
- Modafinil
- Nevirapine
- Oxcarbazepine
- Phenylbutazone (mixed inducing and inhibiting effect)
- Phenytoin (and possibly other hydantoins)
- Primidone
- Rifabutin
- Rifampin
- Rifapentine
- St John's Wort
- Troglitazone

Enzyme inhibitors, hepatic, various
- Note: The following agents may affect single or multiple enzymes.
- Alcohol (with acute, high-dose use)
- Allopurinol
- Antidepressants, monoamine oxidase (MAO) inhibitor
- Antifungals, azole
- Chloramphenicol
- Cimetidine
- Clarithromycin
- Contraceptives, estrogen-containing, oral
- Diltiazem
- Disulfiram
- Divalproex
- Efavirenz
- Erythromycin
- Fluoroquinolones
- Fluoxetine
- Fluvoxamine
- Indinavir
- Isoniazid
- Letrozole
- Lopinavir and Ritonavir
- Mibefradil
- Modafinil
- Nefazodone

Enzyme inhibitors, hepatic, various *(continued)*
- Nelfinavir
- Nilutamide
- Omeprazole
- Paroxetine
- Phenylbutazone (mixed inducing and inhibiting effect)
- Quinidine
- Quinine
- Quinupristin and Dalfopristin
- Ritonavir
- Saquinavir
- Tamoxifen
- Valproic acid
- Verapamil

Extrapyramidal reaction–causing medications
- Amoxapine
- Haloperidol
- Loxapine
- Metoclopramide
- Metyrosine
- Molindone
- Olanzapine
- Phenothiazines
- Pimozide
- Rauwolfia alkaloids
- Risperidone
- Tacrine
- Thioxanthenes

Folate antagonists
- Anticonvulsants, hydantoin
- Anticonvulsants, succinimide
- Divalproex
- Methotrexate
- Phenobarbital (with long-term use)
- Pyrimethamine
- Sulfonamides
- Triamterene
- Trimethoprim
- Trimetrexate
- Valproic acid

Hemolytics
- Acetohydroxamic acid
- Antidiabetic agents, sulfonylurea
- Doxapram
- Furazolidone
- Mefenamic acid
- Menadiol
- Methyldopa
- Nitrofurans
- Primaquine
- Procainamide
- Quinidine
- Quinine
- Sulfonamides, systemic
- Sulfones

Hepatotoxic medications
- Abacavir, Lamivudine, and Zidovudine
- Acetaminophen (with long-term, high-dose use or acute overdose)
- Acitretin
- Alcohol
- Aldesleukin
- Amiodarone
- Anabolic steroids
- Androgens
- Angiotensin-converting enzyme (ACE) inhibitors
- Anti-inflammatory drugs, nonsteroidal (NSAIDS)
- Asparaginase
- Bexarotene
- Carbamazepine
- Carmustine
- Cytarabine

Hepatotoxic medications *(continued)*
Dantrolene
Dapsone
Daunorubicin
Disulfiram
Divalproex
Epirubicin
Erythromycins
Estrogens
Ethionamide
Etretinate
Fat emulsions, intravenous (with prolonged use)
Felbamate
Fluconazole
Flutamide
Gold compounds
Halothane
HMG-CoA Reductase Inhibitors
Imatinib
Iron (overdose)
Isoniazid
Itraconazole
Ketoconazole, oral
Labetalol
Mercaptopurine
Methimazole
Methotrexate
Methyldopa
Naltrexone (with long-term, high-dose use)
Nevirapine
Niacin (with high doses, sustained release, and antihyperlipidemic use)
Nilutamide
Nitrofurans
Pemoline
Phenothiazines
Phenytoin
Plicamycin
Propylthiouracil
Rifampin
Rosiglitazone
Sulfamethoxazole and Trimethoprim
Sulfonamides, systemic
Tacrine
Tenofovir
Tizanidine
Tolcapone
Toremifene
Tretinoin
Troleandomycin
Valproic Acid
Vitamin A (with chronic overdose)
Zidovudine
Zidovudine and Lamivudine

Hyperkalemia-causing medications
Angiotensin-converting enzyme (ACE) inhibitors
Anti-inflammatory drugs, nonsteroidal (NSAIDS), especially indomethacin
Anti-thymocyte globulin (rabbit)
Cyclosporine
Digitalis Glycosides (with acute overdose)
Diuretics, potassium-sparing
Heparin
Penicillins, potassium-containing (with high doses)
Pentamidine
Phosphates, potassium-containing
Potassium citrate-containing medications
Potassium Iodide
Potassium supplements
Succinylcholine chloride
Tacrolimus

Hypokalemia-causing medications
Alcohol
Amphotericin B, systemic
Amphotericin B cholesteryl complex

Hypokalemia-causing medications *(continued)*
Amphotericin B lipid complex
Amphotericin B liposomal complex
Bronchodilators, adrenergic, beta-2 selective
Capreomycin
Carbenicillin, parenteral
Carbonic anhydrase inhibitors
Corticosteroids, systemic
Diuretics, loop
Diuretics, thiazide
Edetate Disodium (with prolonged use)
Fludrocortisone
Foscarnet
Indapamide
Insulin
Insulin Lispro
Laxatives (with acute overdose or chronic misuse)
Mannitol
Mezlocillin
Piperacillin
Piperacillin and Tazobactam
Salicylates
Sodium bicarbonate
Sodium polystyrene sulfonate
Ticarcillin
Ticarcillin and Clavulanate
Urea, systemic

Hypotension-producing medications
Alcohol
Aldesleukin
Alprostadil
Amantadine
Amifostine
Anesthetics, general
Angiotensin-converting enzyme (ACE) inhibitors
Antidepressants, monoamine oxidase (MAO) inhibitor
Antidepressants, tricyclic
Antihypertensives
Benzodiazepines (used as preanesthetics)
Beta-Adrenergic Blocking Agents
Bretylium
Brimonidine
Bromocriptine
Cabergoline
Calcium Channel Blocking Agents
Calcium supplements, parenteral
Carbidopa and Levodopa
Clozapine
Contrast agents, radiopaque, water-soluble organic iodides (with intravascular use)
Contrast agents, paramagnetic
Contrast agents, superparamagnetic
Deferoxamine (when given IV at doses >15 mg/kg/hr)
Diuretics
Droperidol
Edetate Calcium Disodium
Edetate Disodium
Gadopentetate
Haloperidol
Hydralazine
Levodopa
Lidocaine, systemic
Loxapine
Magnesium sulfate, parenteral
Mirtazapine
Molindone
Nabilone (with high doses)
Nefazodone
Nitrates
Nitrites
Olanzapine
Opioid (Narcotic) Analgesics (including alfentanil, fentanyl, and sufentanil)
Paclitaxel

Hypotension-producing medications *(continued)*
Pentamidine
Pentoxifylline
Phenothiazines
Pimozide
Pramipexole
Procainamide
Propofol
Protamine (with too rapid administration)
Quetiapine
Quinidine
Ranitidine bismuth citrate
Risperidone
Rituximab
Ropinirole
Thioxanthenes
Thrombolytic agents
Tizanidine
Tocainide
Tolcapone

Hypothermia-producing medications
Alcohol, ethyl
Alpha-adrenergic blocking agents (dihydroergotamine, ergotamine, labetalol, phenoxybenzamine, phentolamine, prazosin, tolazoline)
Anesthetics, general
Barbiturates (with high doses or acute overdose)
Beta-Adrenergic Blocking Agents
Clonidine
Insulin
Minoxidil, systemic
Opioid Analgesics (with overdose)
Polyethylene Glycol and Electrolytes (with large amounts of refrigerated solution)
Vasodilators

Methemoglobinemia-causing medications
Acetanilid
Aminosalicylic Acid
Articaine
Benzocaine
Castellani solution
Cetrimide
Chloroquine
Coal tar
Dapsone
Flutamide
Lidocaine
Mafenide
Methylene Blue (with high doses)
Nitrates
Nitric oxide
Nitrites
Nitrofurantoin
Nitroglycerin
Nitroprusside
Pamaquine
Phenacetin
Phenobarbital
Prilocaine
Primaquine
Quinine
Silver nitrate
Sulfonamides
Thiopental
Triclocarban

Nephrotoxic medications
Acetaminophen (in acute high doses)
Acyclovir, parenteral
Adefovir
Aldesleukin
Aminoglycosides, parenteral and topical irrigation (only on denuded surfaces or mucous membranes)
Amphotericin B, parenteral

Nephrotoxic medications *(continued)*
- Amphotericin B cholesteryl complex
- Amphotericin B lipid complex
- Amphotericin B liposomal complex
- Analgesic combinations containing acetaminophen and aspirin or other salicylates (with chronic high-dose use)
- Anti-inflammatory drugs, nonsteroidal (NSAIDS)
- Bacitracin, parenteral
- Capreomycin
- Carmustine
- Cholecystographic agents, oral
- Cidofovir
- Ciprofloxacin
- Cisplatin
- Contrast agents, radiopaque, water-soluble organic iodides (with intravascular administration)
- Cyclosporine
- Deferoxamine (with long-term use)
- Demeclocycline (in nephrogenic diabetes insipidus)
- Edetate Calcium Disodium (with high doses)
- Edetate Disodium (with high doses)
- Foscarnet
- Gallium nitrate
- Gold compounds
- Ifosfamide
- Lithium
- Methotrexate (with high-dose therapy)
- Methoxyflurane
- Neomycin, oral
- Oxaliplatin
- Pamidronate
- Penicillamine
- Pentamidine
- Phenacetin
- Plicamycin
- Polymyxins, parenteral
- Rifampin
- Streptozocin
- Sulfamethoxazole and trimethoprim
- Sulfonamides, systemic
- Tacrolimus
- Tetracyclines, other (except doxycycline and minocycline)
- Tiopronin
- Tretinoin
- Vancomycin, parenteral

Neurotoxic medications
- Altretamine
- Aminoglycosides, parenteral and topical irrigation (only on denuded surfaces or mucous membranes)
- Anticonvulsants, hydantoin
- Asparaginase
- Capreomycin
- Carbamazepine
- Carboplatin
- Chloramphenicol, systemic
- Chloroquine
- Cilastatin
- Ciprofloxacin
- Cisplatin
- Cycloserine
- Cyclosporine
- Cytarabine
- Didanosine
- Disulfiram
- Docetaxel
- Ethambutol
- Ethionamide
- Fludarabine
- Hydroxychloroquine
- Imipenem
- Interferons, Alpha
- Isoniazid

Neurotoxic medications *(continued)*
- Lincomycins
- Lindane, topical
- Lithium
- Methotrexate, intrathecal
- Metronidazole
- Mexiletine
- Nitrofurantoin
- Oxaliplatin
- Oxamniquine
- Pemoline
- Penicillins, parenteral
- Polymyxins, parenteral
- Pyridoxine (with long-term, high-dose use)
- Quinacrine
- Quinidine
- Quinine
- Stavudine
- Tacrolimus
- Tetracyclines
- Thalidomide
- Vincristine
- Zalcitabine

Ototoxic medications
- Aminoglycosides, parenteral and topical irrigation (only on denuded surfaces or mucous membranes)
- Anti-inflammatory drugs, nonsteroidal (NSAIDS)
- Bumetanide, parenteral
- Capreomycin
- Carboplatin
- Chloroquine
- Cisplatin
- Deferoxamine (with long-term, high-dose use)
- Erythromycins (with high doses and renal function impairment)
- Ethacrynic acid
- Furosemide
- Hydroxychloroquine
- Oxaliplatin
- Quinidine
- Quinine
- Salicylates (especially with long-term, high-dose use or overdose)
- Vancomycin, parenteral (with high doses and renal function impairment)

Platelet aggregation inhibitors or other medications with platelet aggregation–inhibiting activity
- Abciximab
- Alprostadil, systemic
- Anagrelide
- Anti-inflammatory drugs, nonsteroidal (NSAIDS)
- Aspirin
- Cephalosporins
- Clopidogrel
- Contrast agents, radiopaque, water-soluble organic iodides (with intravascular administration)
- Dextran
- Dipyridamole
- Divalproex
- Epoprostenol
- Eptifibatide
- Mezlocillin
- Pentoxifylline
- Piperacillin
- Plicamycin
- Sulfinpyrazone
- Thrombolytic Agents
- Ticarcillin
- Ticlopidine
- Tirofiban
- Valproic Acid

Prolong QTc Interval
- Amiodarone
- Amitriptyline
- Arsenic Trioxide
- Bepridil
- Chlorpromazine
- Cisapride
- Clarithromycin
- Clomipramine
- Clozapine
- Desipramine
- Disopyramide
- Dofetilide
- Dolasetron
- Droperidol
- Erythromycin
- Gatifloxacin
- Halofantrine
- Haloperidol
- Ibutilide
- Levofloxacin
- Levomethadyl
- Mefloquine
- Mesoridazine
- Moxifloxacin
- N-acetylprocainamide
- Ondansetron
- Pimozide
- Procainamide
- Propafenone
- Quinidine
- Sotalol
- Sumatriptan
- Thioridazine
- Ziprasidone
- Zolmitriptan

Serotonergics
- Citalopram
- Clomipramine
- Fluoxetine
- Fluvoxamine
- Lysergic Acid Diethylamide (LSD)
- Methylenedioxymethamphetamine (MDMA ["ecstacy"])
- Moclobemide
- Monoamine Oxidase Inhibitors, irreversible (furazolidone, phenelzine, procarbazine, selegiline, tranylcypromine)
- Nefazodone
- Paroxetine
- Sertraline
- Sibutramine
- Tryptophan
- Venlafaxine

Other medications or substances with serotonergic activity
- Ademetionine
- Almotriptan
- Amitriptyline
- Bromocriptine
- Buspirone
- Dextromethorphan
- Imipramine
- Levodopa
- Lithium
- Marijuana
- Meperidine
- Naratriptan
- Pentazocine
- Sumatriptan
- Tramadol
- Trazodone
- Zomitriptan

The Medicine Chart

The Medicine Chart presents sample photographs of prescribed medicines in the United States. In general, commonly used brand name products and a representative sampling of generic products have been included. The pictorial listing is not intended to be inclusive and does not represent all products on the market. The inclusion of a product does not mean the authors have any particular knowledge that the product included has properties different from other products, nor should it be interpreted as an endorsement. Similarly, the fact that a particular product has not been included does not indicate that the product has been judged to be unsatisfactory or unacceptable.

The drug products in *The Medicine Chart* are listed alphabetically by generic name of active ingredient(s). In some instances, not all dosage forms and sizes are pictured. If others are available, a † symbol proceeds the products name. Letters or numbers representing the manufacturer's identification code are followed by an asterisk.

The size and color of the products shown are intended to match the actual product as closely as possible; however, there may be some differences due to variations caused by the photographic process. Also, manufacturers may occasionally change the color, imprinting, or shape of their products, and for a period of time both the "old" and the newly changed dosage forms may be on the market. Such changes may not occur uniformly throughout the different dosages of the product. When applicable these types of changes will be incorporated in the subsequent versions of *The Medicine Chart* as they are brought to our attention.

Use of this chart is limited to serving as an initial guide in identifying drug products. The identity of a product should be verified further before any action is taken.

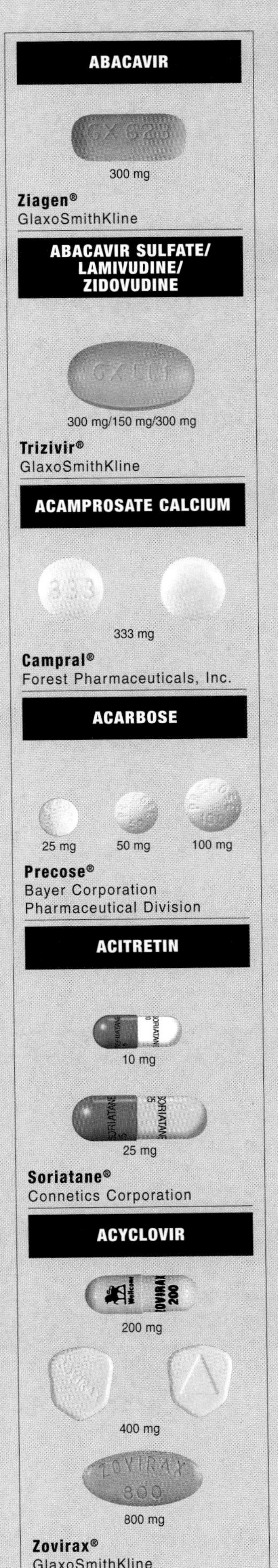

ABACAVIR

300 mg

Ziagen®
GlaxoSmithKline

ABACAVIR SULFATE/ LAMIVUDINE/ ZIDOVUDINE

300 mg/150 mg/300 mg

Trizivir®
GlaxoSmithKline

ACAMPROSATE CALCIUM

333 mg

Campral®
Forest Pharmaceuticals, Inc.

ACARBOSE

25 mg 50 mg 100 mg

Precose®
Bayer Corporation
Pharmaceutical Division

ACITRETIN

10 mg

25 mg

Soriatane®
Connetics Corporation

ACYCLOVIR

200 mg

400 mg

800 mg

Zovirax®
GlaxoSmithKline

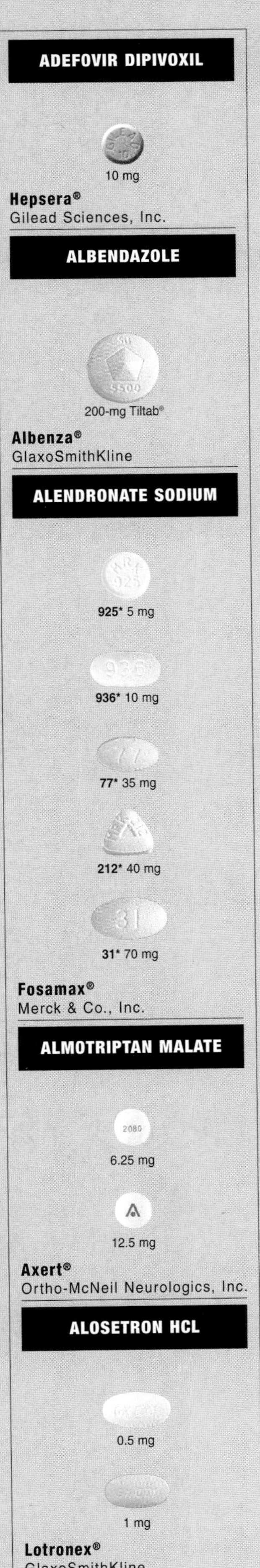

ADEFOVIR DIPIVOXIL

10 mg

Hepsera®
Gilead Sciences, Inc.

ALBENDAZOLE

200-mg Tiltab®

Albenza®
GlaxoSmithKline

ALENDRONATE SODIUM

925* 5 mg

936* 10 mg

77* 35 mg

212* 40 mg

31* 70 mg

Fosamax®
Merck & Co., Inc.

ALMOTRIPTAN MALATE

6.25 mg

12.5 mg

Axert®
Ortho-McNeil Neurologics, Inc.

ALOSETRON HCL

0.5 mg

1 mg

Lotronex®
GlaxoSmithKline

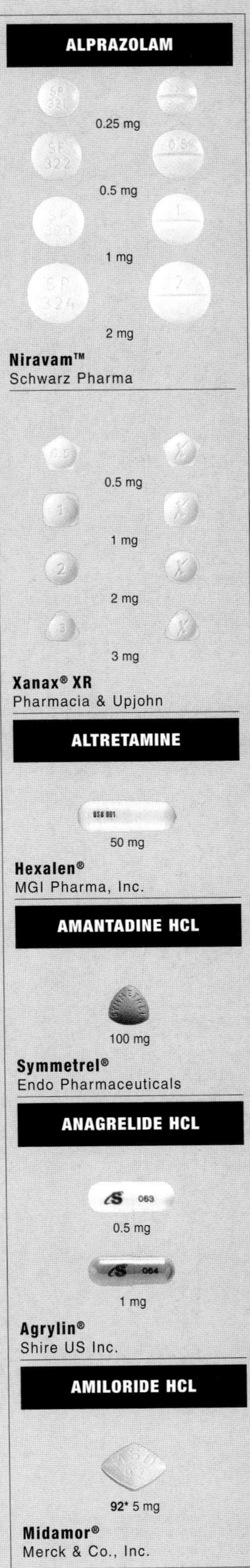

ALPRAZOLAM

0.25 mg

0.5 mg

1 mg

2 mg

Niravam™
Schwarz Pharma

0.5 mg

1 mg

2 mg

3 mg

Xanax® XR
Pharmacia & Upjohn

ALTRETAMINE

50 mg

Hexalen®
MGI Pharma, Inc.

AMANTADINE HCL

100 mg

Symmetrel®
Endo Pharmaceuticals

ANAGRELIDE HCL

0.5 mg

1 mg

Agrylin®
Shire US Inc.

AMILORIDE HCL

92* 5 mg

Midamor®
Merck & Co., Inc.

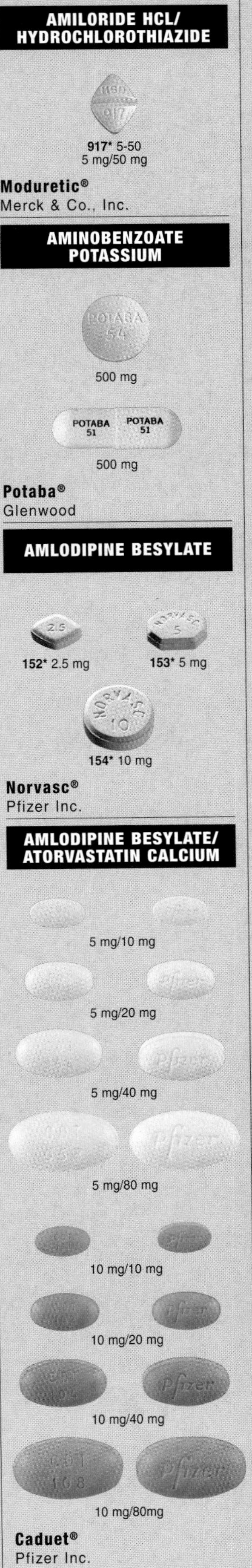

AMILORIDE HCL/ HYDROCHLOROTHIAZIDE

917* 5-50
5 mg/50 mg

Moduretic®
Merck & Co., Inc.

AMINOBENZOATE POTASSIUM

500 mg

500 mg

Potaba®
Glenwood

AMLODIPINE BESYLATE

152* 2.5 mg 153* 5 mg

154* 10 mg

Norvasc®
Pfizer Inc.

AMLODIPINE BESYLATE/ ATORVASTATIN CALCIUM

5 mg/10 mg

5 mg/20 mg

5 mg/40 mg

5 mg/80 mg

10 mg/10 mg

10 mg/20 mg

10 mg/40 mg

10 mg/80mg

Caduet®
Pfizer Inc.

* Manufacturer's Identification Code

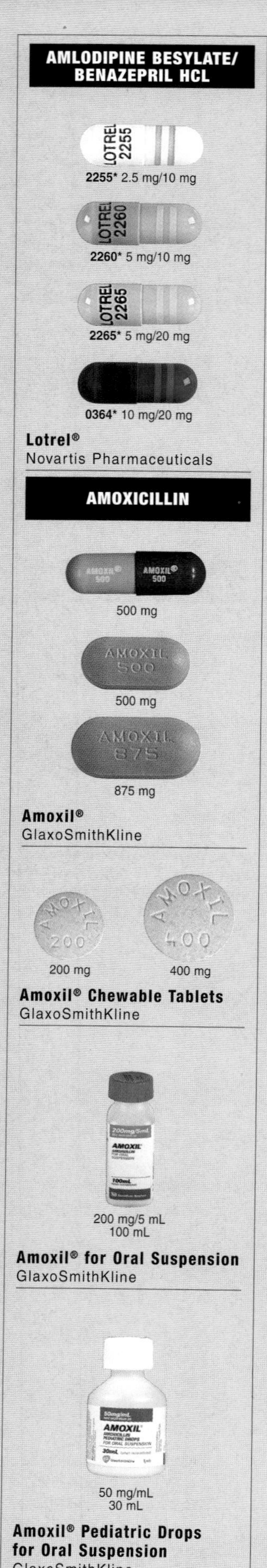

AMLODIPINE BESYLATE/ BENAZEPRIL HCL

2255* 2.5 mg/10 mg

2260* 5 mg/10 mg

2265* 5 mg/20 mg

0364* 10 mg/20 mg

Lotrel®
Novartis Pharmaceuticals

AMOXICILLIN

500 mg

500 mg

875 mg

Amoxil®
GlaxoSmithKline

200 mg

400 mg

Amoxil® Chewable Tablets
GlaxoSmithKline

200 mg/5 mL
100 mL

Amoxil® for Oral Suspension
GlaxoSmithKline

50 mg/mL
30 mL

Amoxil® Pediatric Drops for Oral Suspension
GlaxoSmithKline

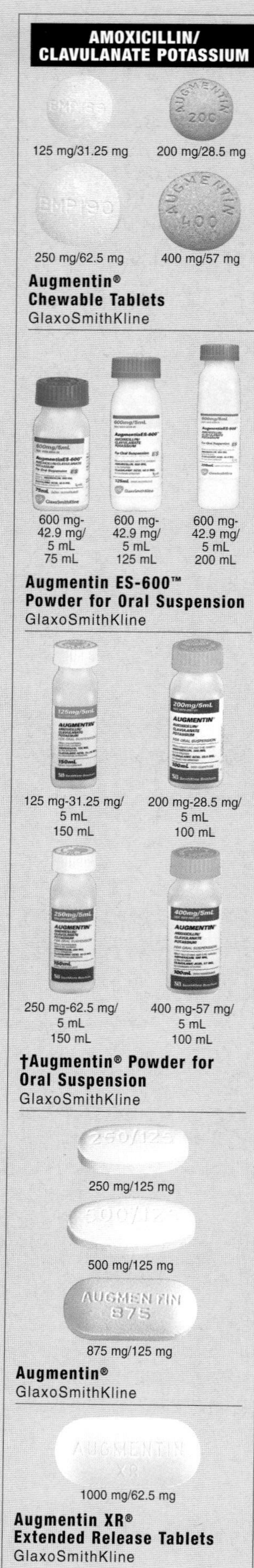

AMOXICILLIN/ CLAVULANATE POTASSIUM

125 mg/31.25 mg

200 mg/28.5 mg

250 mg/62.5 mg

400 mg/57 mg

Augmentin® Chewable Tablets
GlaxoSmithKline

600 mg-42.9 mg/5 mL
75 mL

600 mg-42.9 mg/5 mL
125 mL

600 mg-42.9 mg/5 mL
200 mL

Augmentin ES-600™ Powder for Oral Suspension
GlaxoSmithKline

125 mg-31.25 mg/5 mL
150 mL

200 mg-28.5 mg/5 mL
100 mL

250 mg-62.5 mg/5 mL
150 mL

400 mg-57 mg/5 mL
100 mL

†Augmentin® Powder for Oral Suspension
GlaxoSmithKline

250 mg/125 mg

500 mg/125 mg

875 mg/125 mg

Augmentin®
GlaxoSmithKline

1000 mg/62.5 mg

Augmentin XR® Extended Release Tablets
GlaxoSmithKline

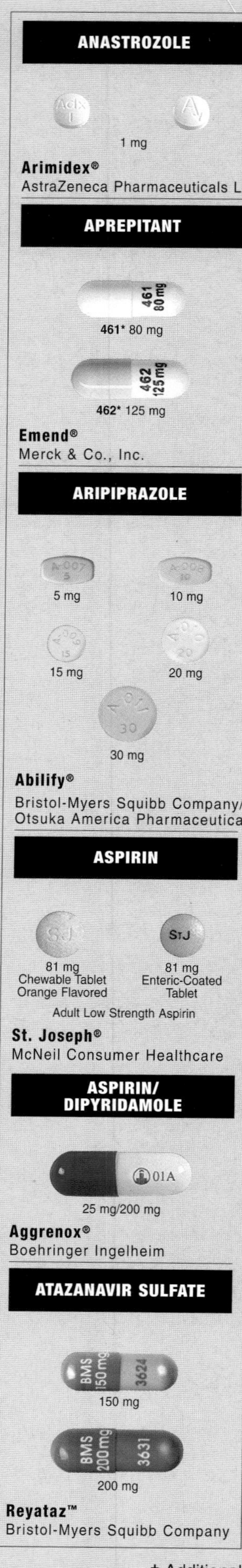

ANASTROZOLE

1 mg

Arimidex®
AstraZeneca Pharmaceuticals LP

APREPITANT

461* 80 mg

462* 125 mg

Emend®
Merck & Co., Inc.

ARIPIPRAZOLE

5 mg

10 mg

15 mg

20 mg

30 mg

Abilify®
Bristol-Myers Squibb Company/ Otsuka America Pharmaceutical

ASPIRIN

81 mg
Chewable Tablet
Orange Flavored

81 mg
Enteric-Coated
Tablet

Adult Low Strength Aspirin

St. Joseph®
McNeil Consumer Healthcare

ASPIRIN/ DIPYRIDAMOLE

25 mg/200 mg

Aggrenox®
Boehringer Ingelheim

ATAZANAVIR SULFATE

150 mg

200 mg

Reyataz™
Bristol-Myers Squibb Company

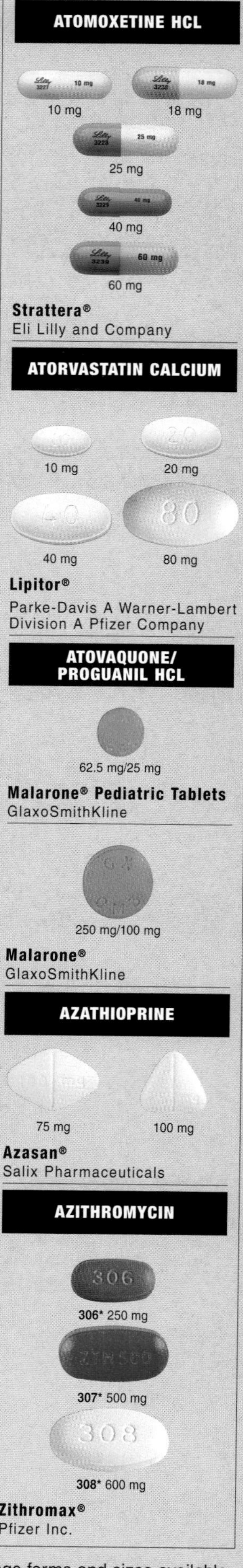

ATOMOXETINE HCL

10 mg

18 mg

25 mg

40 mg

60 mg

Strattera®
Eli Lilly and Company

ATORVASTATIN CALCIUM

10 mg

20 mg

40 mg

80 mg

Lipitor®
Parke-Davis A Warner-Lambert Division A Pfizer Company

ATOVAQUONE/ PROGUANIL HCL

62.5 mg/25 mg

Malarone® Pediatric Tablets
GlaxoSmithKline

250 mg/100 mg

Malarone®
GlaxoSmithKline

AZATHIOPRINE

75 mg

100 mg

Azasan®
Salix Pharmaceuticals

AZITHROMYCIN

306* 250 mg

307* 500 mg

308* 600 mg

Zithromax®
Pfizer Inc.

* Manufacturer's Identification Code

† Additional dosage forms and sizes available.

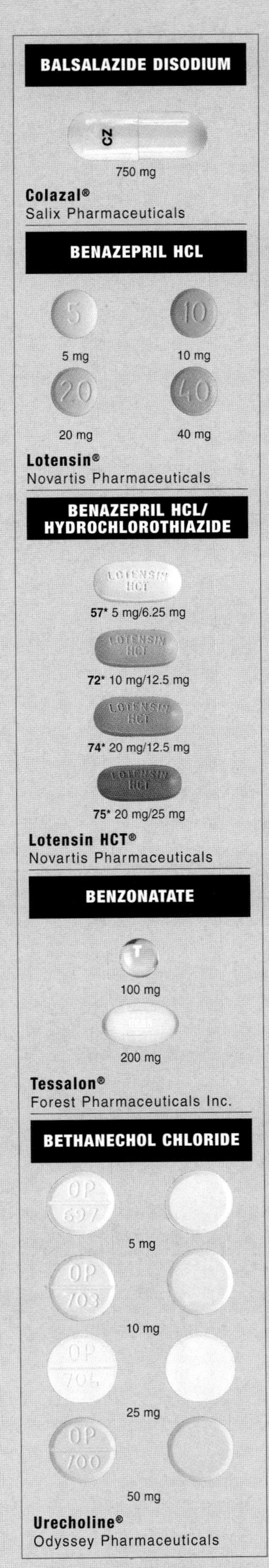

BALSALAZIDE DISODIUM

750 mg

Colazal®
Salix Pharmaceuticals

BENAZEPRIL HCL

5 mg | 10 mg
20 mg | 40 mg

Lotensin®
Novartis Pharmaceuticals

BENAZEPRIL HCL/ HYDROCHLOROTHIAZIDE

57* 5 mg/6.25 mg
72* 10 mg/12.5 mg
74* 20 mg/12.5 mg
75* 20 mg/25 mg

Lotensin HCT®
Novartis Pharmaceuticals

BENZONATATE

100 mg
200 mg

Tessalon®
Forest Pharmaceuticals Inc.

BETHANECHOL CHLORIDE

5 mg
10 mg
25 mg
50 mg

Urecholine®
Odyssey Pharmaceuticals

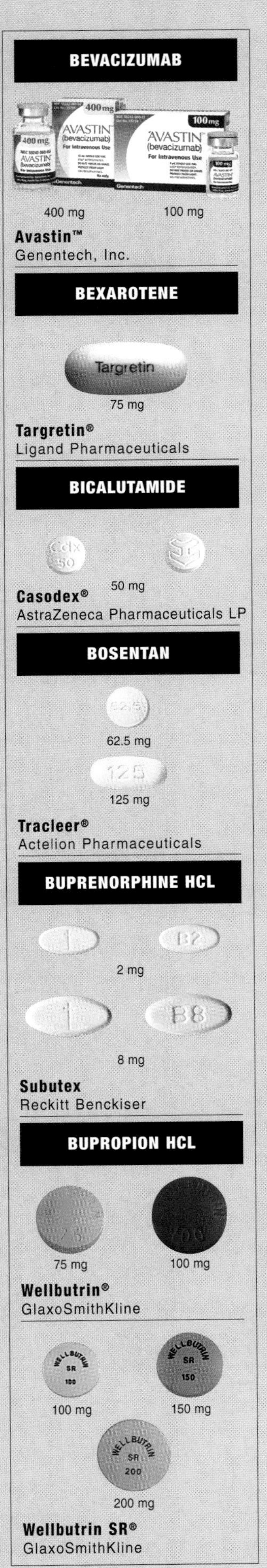

BEVACIZUMAB

400 mg | 100 mg

Avastin™
Genentech, Inc.

BEXAROTENE

75 mg

Targretin®
Ligand Pharmaceuticals

BICALUTAMIDE

50 mg

Casodex®
AstraZeneca Pharmaceuticals LP

BOSENTAN

62.5 mg
125 mg

Tracleer®
Actelion Pharmaceuticals

BUPRENORPHINE HCL

2 mg
8 mg

Subutex
Reckitt Benckiser

BUPROPION HCL

75 mg | 100 mg

Wellbutrin®
GlaxoSmithKline

100 mg | 150 mg
200 mg

Wellbutrin SR®
GlaxoSmithKline

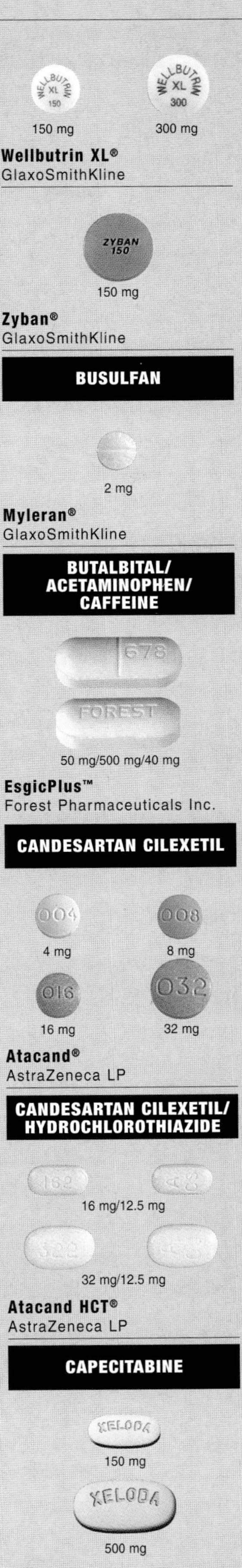

150 mg | 300 mg

Wellbutrin XL®
GlaxoSmithKline

150 mg

Zyban®
GlaxoSmithKline

BUSULFAN

2 mg

Myleran®
GlaxoSmithKline

BUTALBITAL/ ACETAMINOPHEN/ CAFFEINE

50 mg/500 mg/40 mg

EsgicPlus™
Forest Pharmaceuticals Inc.

CANDESARTAN CILEXETIL

4 mg | 8 mg
16 mg | 32 mg

Atacand®
AstraZeneca LP

CANDESARTAN CILEXETIL/ HYDROCHLOROTHIAZIDE

16 mg/12.5 mg
32 mg/12.5 mg

Atacand HCT®
AstraZeneca LP

CAPECITABINE

150 mg
500 mg

Xeloda®
Roche

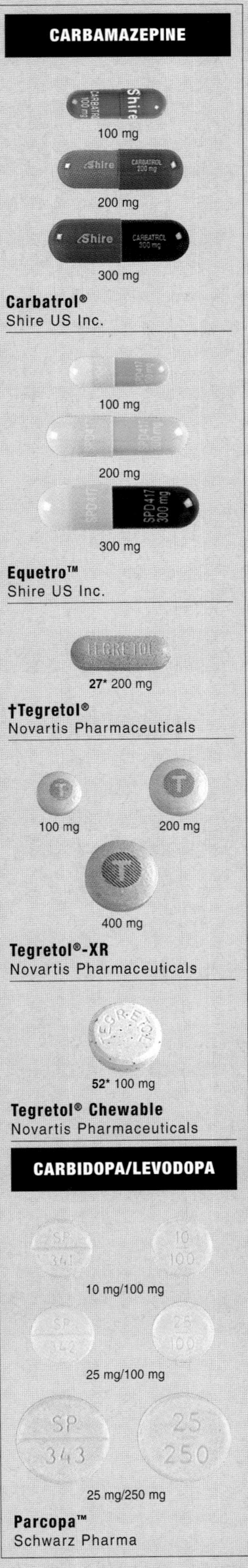

CARBAMAZEPINE

100 mg
200 mg
300 mg

Carbatrol®
Shire US Inc.

100 mg
200 mg
300 mg

Equetro™
Shire US Inc.

27* 200 mg

†Tegretol®
Novartis Pharmaceuticals

100 mg | 200 mg
400 mg

Tegretol®-XR
Novartis Pharmaceuticals

52* 100 mg

Tegretol® Chewable
Novartis Pharmaceuticals

CARBIDOPA/LEVODOPA

10 mg/100 mg
25 mg/100 mg
25 mg/250 mg

Parcopa™
Schwarz Pharma

† Additional dosage forms and sizes available.

* Manufacturer's Identification Code

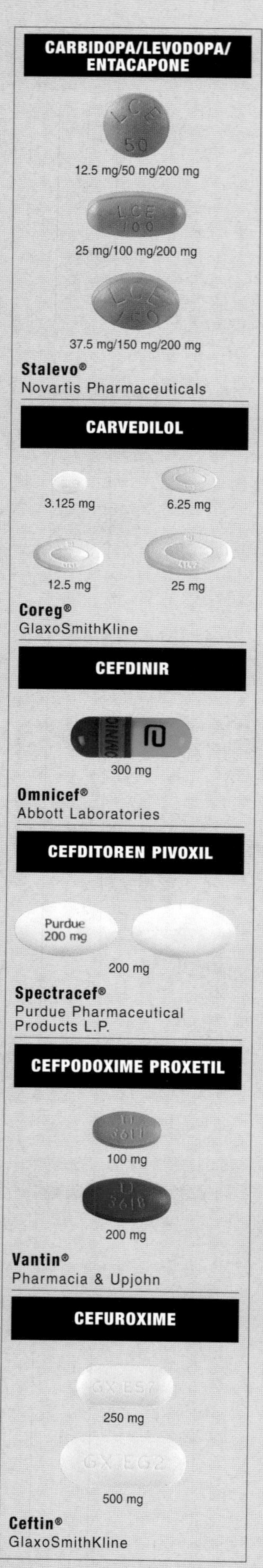

CARBIDOPA/LEVODOPA/ENTACAPONE

12.5 mg/50 mg/200 mg

25 mg/100 mg/200 mg

37.5 mg/150 mg/200 mg

Stalevo®
Novartis Pharmaceuticals

CARVEDILOL

3.125 mg 6.25 mg

12.5 mg 25 mg

Coreg®
GlaxoSmithKline

CEFDINIR

300 mg

Omnicef®
Abbott Laboratories

CEFDITOREN PIVOXIL

200 mg

Spectracef®
Purdue Pharmaceutical Products L.P.

CEFPODOXIME PROXETIL

100 mg

200 mg

Vantin®
Pharmacia & Upjohn

CEFUROXIME

250 mg

500 mg

Ceftin®
GlaxoSmithKline

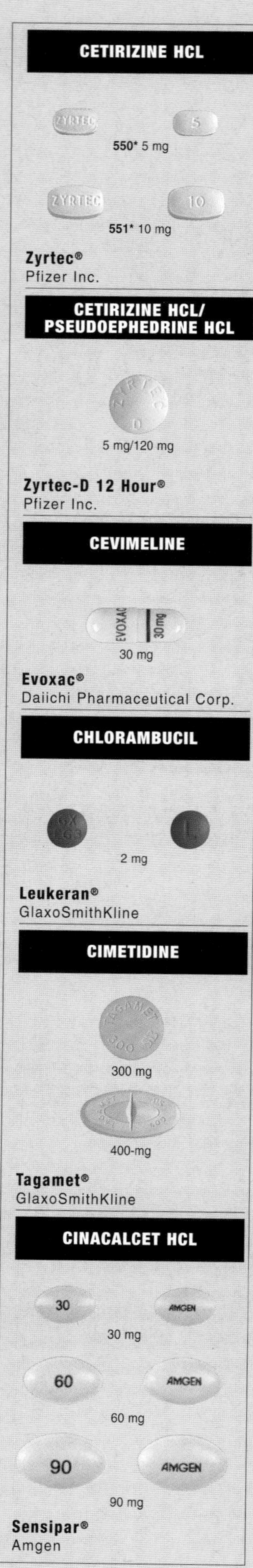

CETIRIZINE HCL

550* 5 mg

551* 10 mg

Zyrtec®
Pfizer Inc.

CETIRIZINE HCL/ PSEUDOEPHEDRINE HCL

5 mg/120 mg

Zyrtec-D 12 Hour®
Pfizer Inc.

CEVIMELINE

30 mg

Evoxac®
Daiichi Pharmaceutical Corp.

CHLORAMBUCIL

2 mg

Leukeran®
GlaxoSmithKline

CIMETIDINE

300 mg

400-mg

Tagamet®
GlaxoSmithKline

CINACALCET HCL

30 mg

60 mg

90 mg

Sensipar®
Amgen

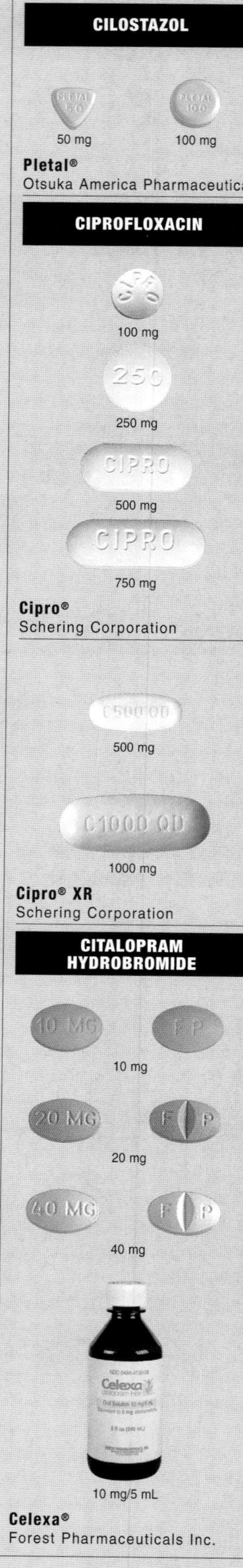

CILOSTAZOL

50 mg 100 mg

Pletal®
Otsuka America Pharmaceutical

CIPROFLOXACIN

100 mg

250 mg

500 mg

750 mg

Cipro®
Schering Corporation

500 mg

1000 mg

Cipro® XR
Schering Corporation

CITALOPRAM HYDROBROMIDE

10 mg

20 mg

40 mg

10 mg/5 mL

Celexa®
Forest Pharmaceuticals Inc.

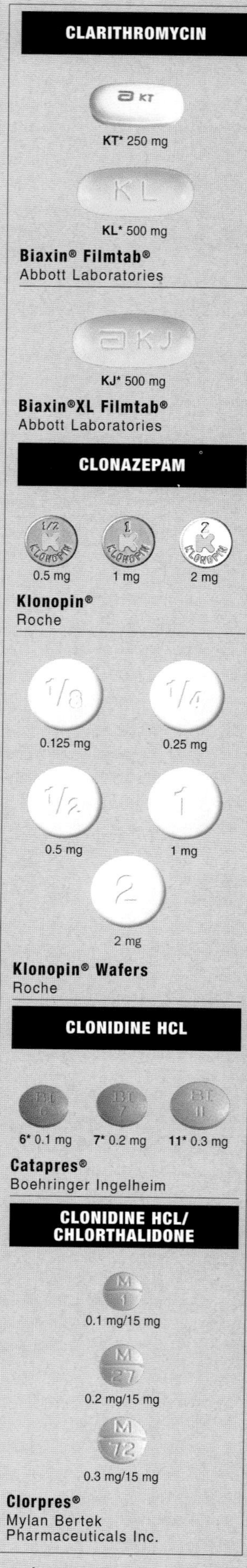

CLARITHROMYCIN

KT* 250 mg

KL* 500 mg

Biaxin® Filmtab®
Abbott Laboratories

KJ* 500 mg

Biaxin®XL Filmtab®
Abbott Laboratories

CLONAZEPAM

0.5 mg 1 mg 2 mg

Klonopin®
Roche

0.125 mg 0.25 mg

0.5 mg 1 mg

2 mg

Klonopin® Wafers
Roche

CLONIDINE HCL

6* 0.1 mg **7*** 0.2 mg **11*** 0.3 mg

Catapres®
Boehringer Ingelheim

CLONIDINE HCL/ CHLORTHALIDONE

0.1 mg/15 mg

0.2 mg/15 mg

0.3 mg/15 mg

Clorpres®
Mylan Bertek Pharmaceuticals Inc.

* Manufacturer's Identification Code

† Additional dosage forms and sizes available.

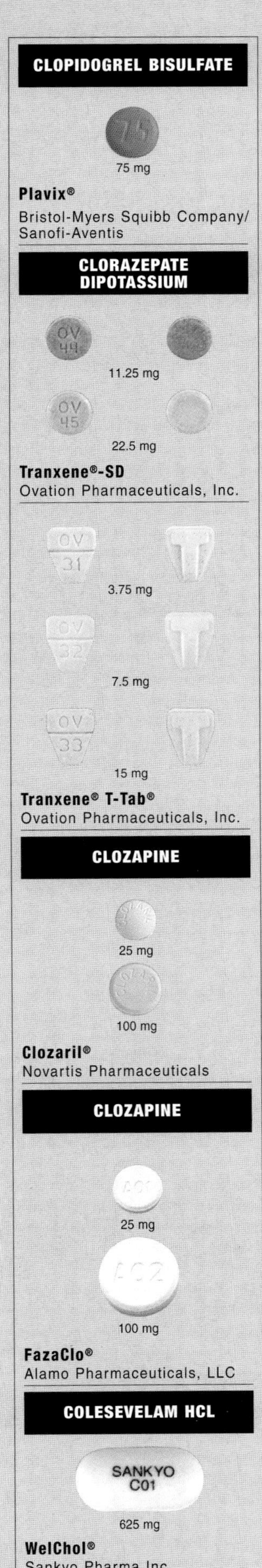

CLOPIDOGREL BISULFATE

75 mg

Plavix®
Bristol-Myers Squibb Company/ Sanofi-Aventis

CLORAZEPATE DIPOTASSIUM

11.25 mg

22.5 mg

Tranxene®-SD
Ovation Pharmaceuticals, Inc.

3.75 mg

7.5 mg

15 mg

Tranxene® T-Tab®
Ovation Pharmaceuticals, Inc.

CLOZAPINE

25 mg

100 mg

Clozaril®
Novartis Pharmaceuticals

CLOZAPINE

25 mg

100 mg

FazaClo®
Alamo Pharmaceuticals, LLC

COLESEVELAM HCL

625 mg

WelChol®
Sankyo Pharma Inc.

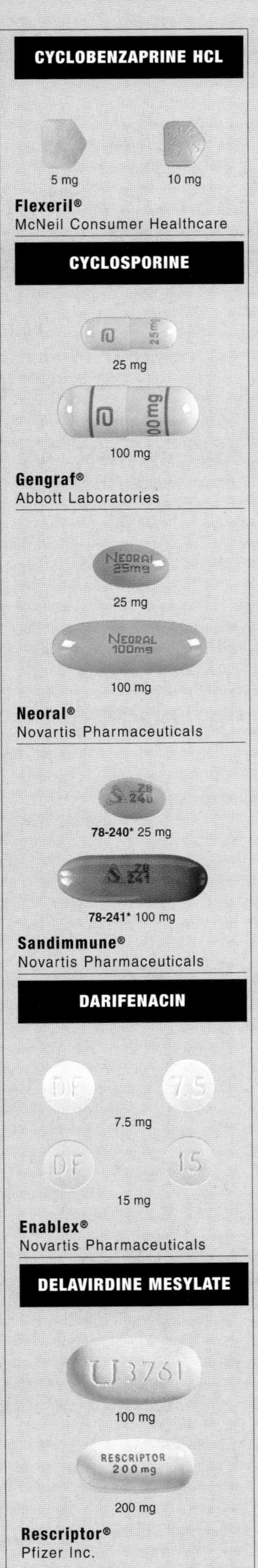

CYCLOBENZAPRINE HCL

5 mg 10 mg

Flexeril®
McNeil Consumer Healthcare

CYCLOSPORINE

25 mg

100 mg

Gengraf®
Abbott Laboratories

25 mg

100 mg

Neoral®
Novartis Pharmaceuticals

78-240* 25 mg

78-241* 100 mg

Sandimmune®
Novartis Pharmaceuticals

DARIFENACIN

7.5 mg

15 mg

Enablex®
Novartis Pharmaceuticals

DELAVIRDINE MESYLATE

100 mg

200 mg

Rescriptor®
Pfizer Inc.

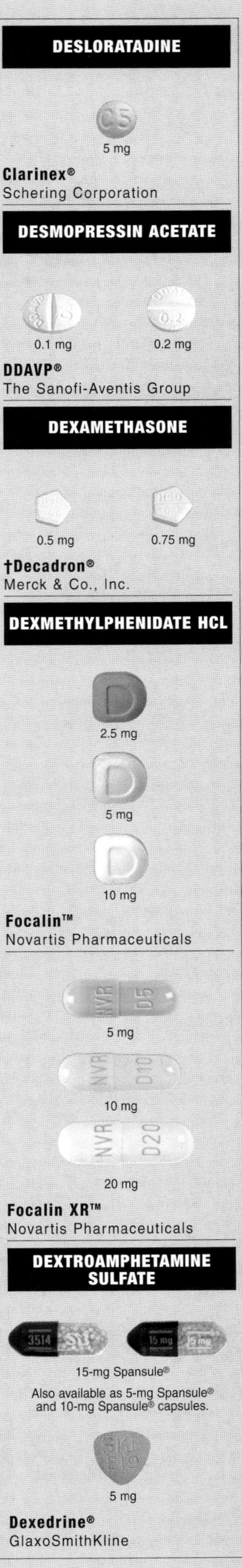

DESLORATADINE

5 mg

Clarinex®
Schering Corporation

DESMOPRESSIN ACETATE

0.1 mg 0.2 mg

DDAVP®
The Sanofi-Aventis Group

DEXAMETHASONE

0.5 mg 0.75 mg

†Decadron®
Merck & Co., Inc.

DEXMETHYLPHENIDATE HCL

2.5 mg

5 mg

10 mg

Focalin™
Novartis Pharmaceuticals

5 mg

10 mg

20 mg

Focalin XR™
Novartis Pharmaceuticals

DEXTROAMPHETAMINE SULFATE

15-mg Spansule®

Also available as 5-mg Spansule® and 10-mg Spansule® capsules.

5 mg

Dexedrine®
GlaxoSmithKline

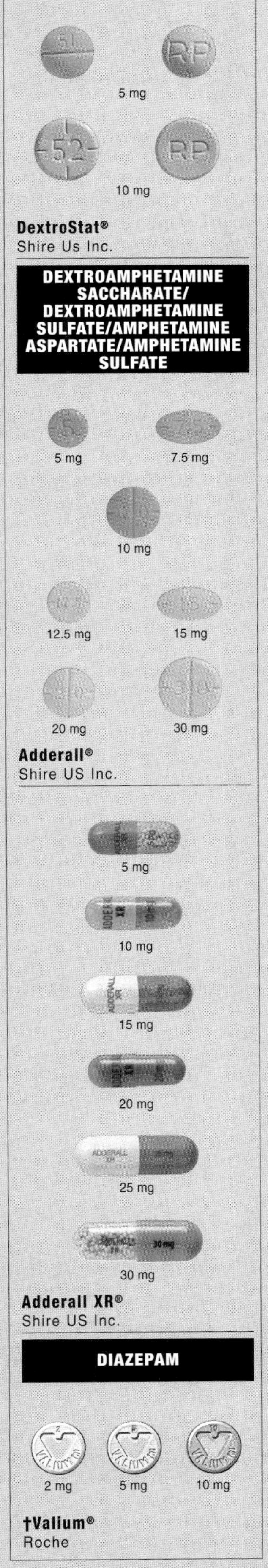

5 mg

10 mg

DextroStat®
Shire Us Inc.

DEXTROAMPHETAMINE SACCHARATE/ DEXTROAMPHETAMINE SULFATE/AMPHETAMINE ASPARTATE/AMPHETAMINE SULFATE

5 mg 7.5 mg

10 mg

12.5 mg 15 mg

20 mg 30 mg

Adderall®
Shire US Inc.

5 mg

10 mg

15 mg

20 mg

25 mg

30 mg

Adderall XR®
Shire US Inc.

DIAZEPAM

2 mg 5 mg 10 mg

†Valium®
Roche

† Additional dosage forms and sizes available.

* Manufacturer's Identification Code

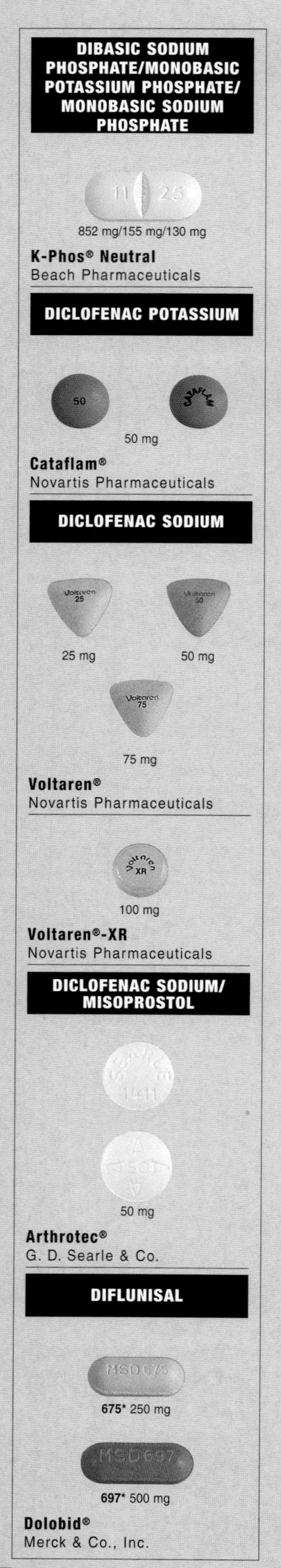
DIBASIC SODIUM PHOSPHATE/MONOBASIC POTASSIUM PHOSPHATE/ MONOBASIC SODIUM PHOSPHATE
852 mg/155 mg/130 mg
K-Phos® Neutral
Beach Pharmaceuticals
DICLOFENAC POTASSIUM
50 mg
Cataflam®
Novartis Pharmaceuticals
DICLOFENAC SODIUM
25 mg
50 mg
75 mg
Voltaren®
Novartis Pharmaceuticals
100 mg
Voltaren®-XR
Novartis Pharmaceuticals
DICLOFENAC SODIUM/ MISOPROSTOL
50 mg
Arthrotec®
G. D. Searle & Co.
DIFLUNISAL
675* 250 mg
697* 500 mg
Dolobid®
Merck & Co., Inc.

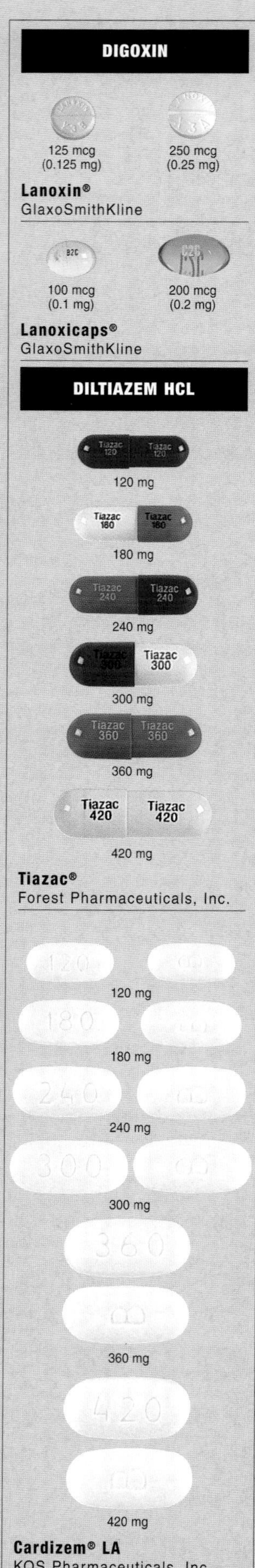
DIGOXIN
125 mcg (0.125 mg)
250 mcg (0.25 mg)
Lanoxin®
GlaxoSmithKline
100 mcg (0.1 mg)
200 mcg (0.2 mg)
Lanoxicaps®
GlaxoSmithKline
DILTIAZEM HCL
120 mg
180 mg
240 mg
300 mg
360 mg
420 mg
Tiazac®
Forest Pharmaceuticals, Inc.
120 mg
180 mg
240 mg
300 mg
360 mg
420 mg
Cardizem® LA
KOS Pharmaceuticals, Inc.

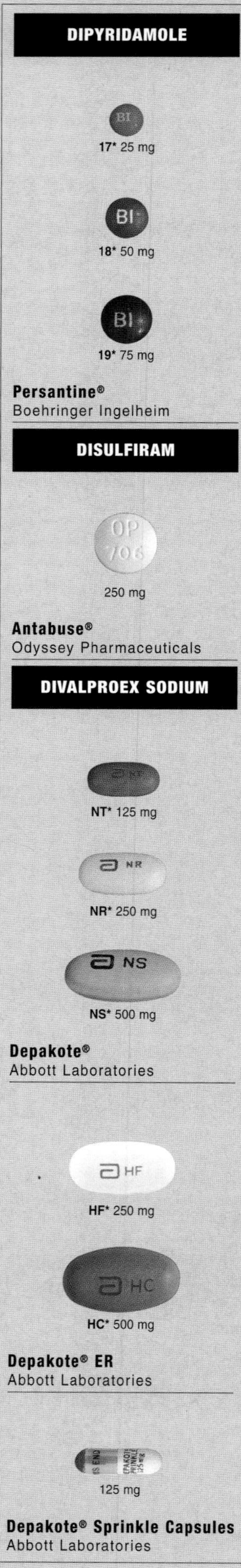
DIPYRIDAMOLE
17* 25 mg
18* 50 mg
19* 75 mg
Persantine®
Boehringer Ingelheim
DISULFIRAM
250 mg
Antabuse®
Odyssey Pharmaceuticals
DIVALPROEX SODIUM
NT* 125 mg
NR* 250 mg
NS* 500 mg
Depakote®
Abbott Laboratories
HF* 250 mg
HC* 500 mg
Depakote® ER
Abbott Laboratories
125 mg
Depakote® Sprinkle Capsules
Abbott Laboratories

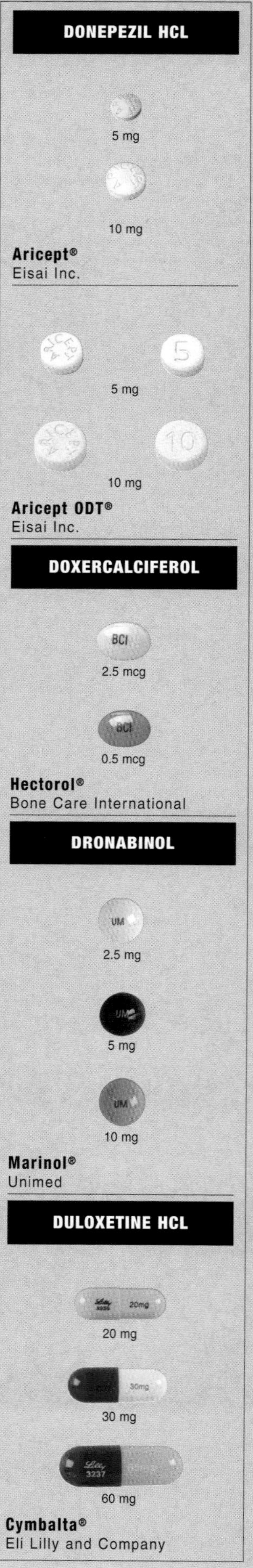
DONEPEZIL HCL
5 mg
10 mg
Aricept®
Eisai Inc.
5 mg
10 mg
Aricept ODT®
Eisai Inc.
DOXERCALCIFEROL
2.5 mcg
0.5 mcg
Hectorol®
Bone Care International
DRONABINOL
2.5 mg
5 mg
10 mg
Marinol®
Unimed
DULOXETINE HCL
20 mg
30 mg
60 mg
Cymbalta®
Eli Lilly and Company

* Manufacturer's Identification Code

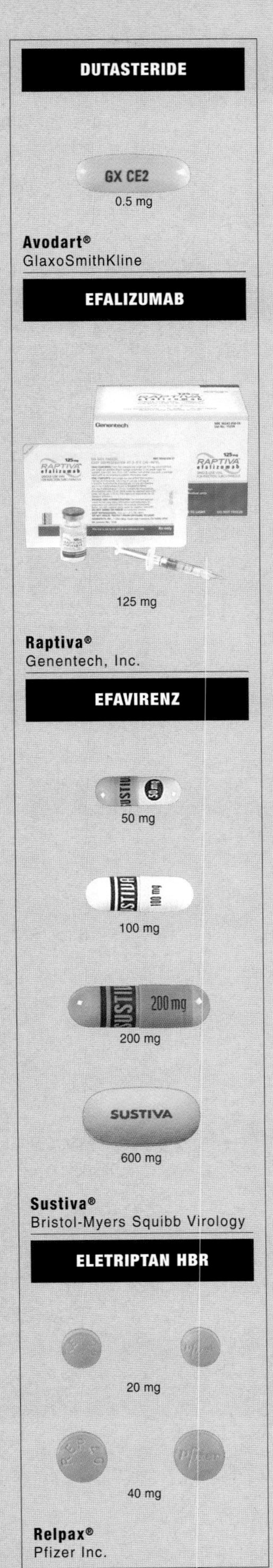

DUTASTERIDE

0.5 mg

Avodart®
GlaxoSmithKline

EFALIZUMAB

125 mg

Raptiva®
Genentech, Inc.

EFAVIRENZ

50 mg

100 mg

200 mg

600 mg

Sustiva®
Bristol-Myers Squibb Virology

ELETRIPTAN HBR

20 mg

40 mg

Relpax®
Pfizer Inc.

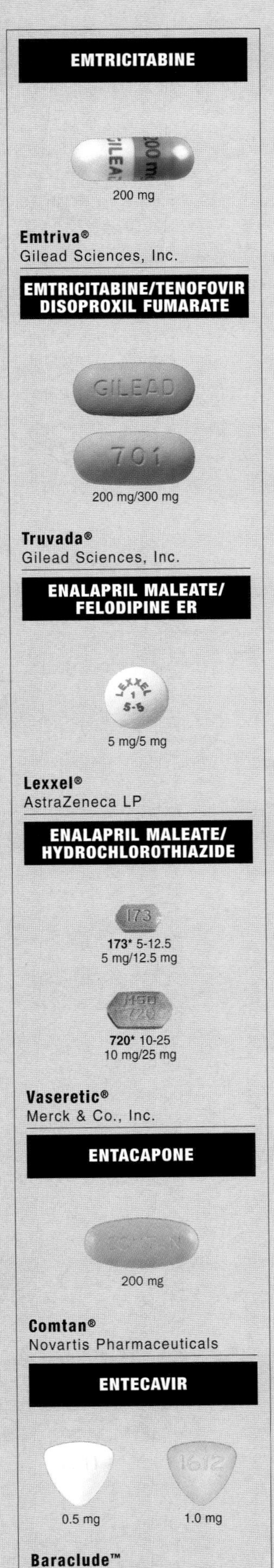

EMTRICITABINE

200 mg

Emtriva®
Gilead Sciences, Inc.

EMTRICITABINE/TENOFOVIR DISOPROXIL FUMARATE

200 mg/300 mg

Truvada®
Gilead Sciences, Inc.

ENALAPRIL MALEATE/ FELODIPINE ER

5 mg/5 mg

Lexxel®
AstraZeneca LP

ENALAPRIL MALEATE/ HYDROCHLOROTHIAZIDE

173* 5-12.5
5 mg/12.5 mg

720* 10-25
10 mg/25 mg

Vaseretic®
Merck & Co., Inc.

ENTACAPONE

200 mg

Comtan®
Novartis Pharmaceuticals

ENTECAVIR

0.5 mg

1.0 mg

Baraclude™
Bristol-Myers Squibb Company

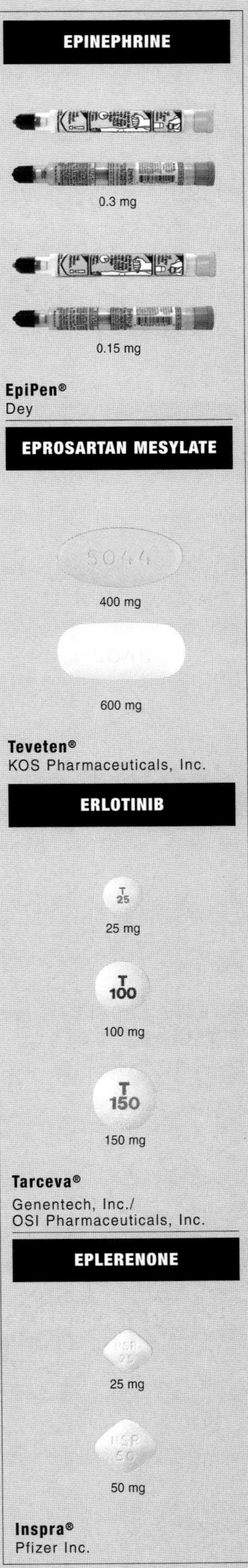

EPINEPHRINE

0.3 mg

0.15 mg

EpiPen®
Dey

EPROSARTAN MESYLATE

400 mg

600 mg

Teveten®
KOS Pharmaceuticals, Inc.

ERLOTINIB

25 mg

100 mg

150 mg

Tarceva®
Genentech, Inc./
OSI Pharmaceuticals, Inc.

EPLERENONE

25 mg

50 mg

Inspra®
Pfizer Inc.

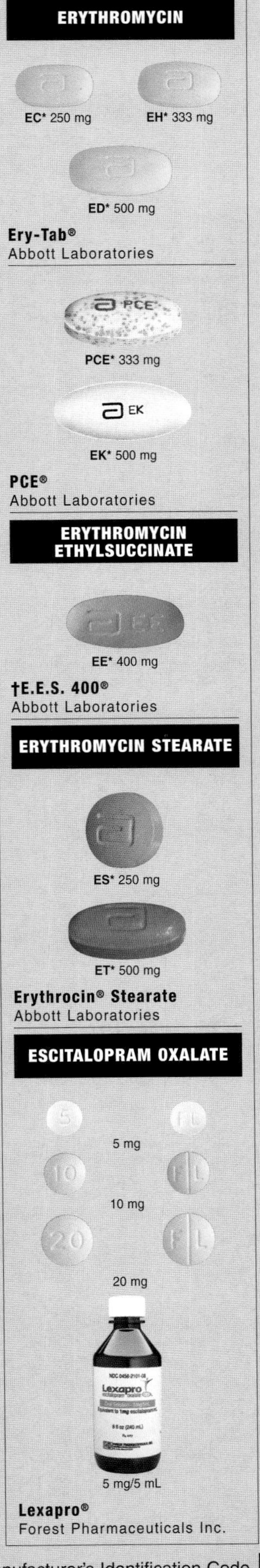

ERYTHROMYCIN

EC* 250 mg

EH* 333 mg

ED* 500 mg

Ery-Tab®
Abbott Laboratories

PCE* 333 mg

EK* 500 mg

PCE®
Abbott Laboratories

ERYTHROMYCIN ETHYLSUCCINATE

EE* 400 mg

†E.E.S. 400®
Abbott Laboratories

ERYTHROMYCIN STEARATE

ES* 250 mg

ET* 500 mg

Erythrocin® Stearate
Abbott Laboratories

ESCITALOPRAM OXALATE

5 mg

10 mg

20 mg

5 mg/5 mL

Lexapro®
Forest Pharmaceuticals Inc.

† Additional dosage forms and sizes available.

* Manufacturer's Identification Code

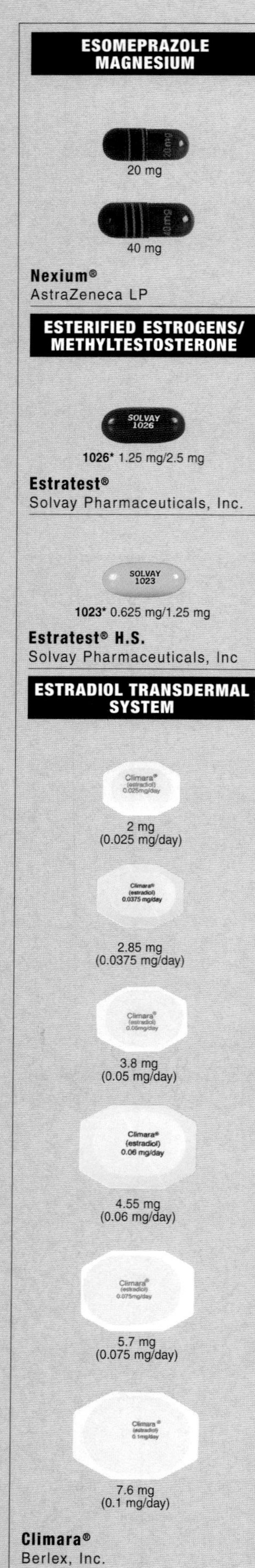

ESOMEPRAZOLE MAGNESIUM

20 mg

40 mg

Nexium®
AstraZeneca LP

ESTERIFIED ESTROGENS/ METHYLTESTOSTERONE

1026* 1.25 mg/2.5 mg

Estratest®
Solvay Pharmaceuticals, Inc.

1023* 0.625 mg/1.25 mg

Estratest® H.S.
Solvay Pharmaceuticals, Inc

ESTRADIOL TRANSDERMAL SYSTEM

2 mg (0.025 mg/day)

2.85 mg (0.0375 mg/day)

3.8 mg (0.05 mg/day)

4.55 mg (0.06 mg/day)

5.7 mg (0.075 mg/day)

7.6 mg (0.1 mg/day)

Climara®
Berlex, Inc.

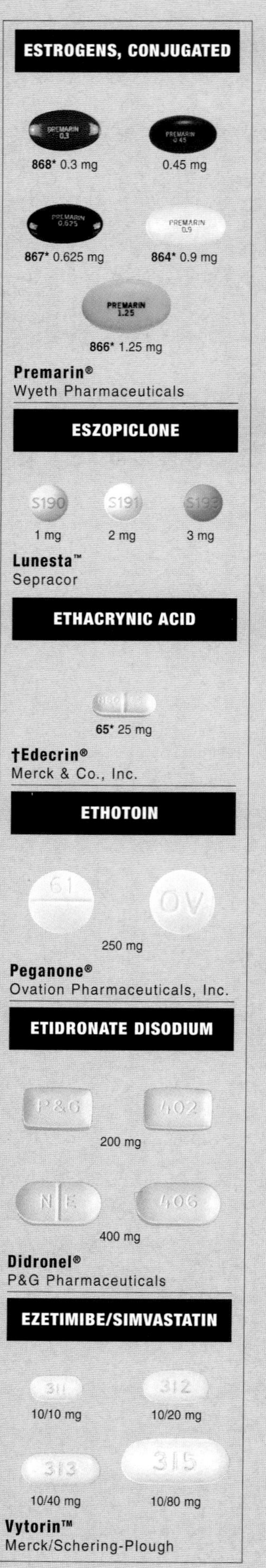

ESTROGENS, CONJUGATED

868* 0.3 mg

0.45 mg

867* 0.625 mg

864* 0.9 mg

866* 1.25 mg

Premarin®
Wyeth Pharmaceuticals

ESZOPICLONE

1 mg

2 mg

3 mg

Lunesta™
Sepracor

ETHACRYNIC ACID

65* 25 mg

†Edecrin®
Merck & Co., Inc.

ETHOTOIN

250 mg

Peganone®
Ovation Pharmaceuticals, Inc.

ETIDRONATE DISODIUM

200 mg

400 mg

Didronel®
P&G Pharmaceuticals

EZETIMIBE/SIMVASTATIN

10/10 mg

10/20 mg

10/40 mg

10/80 mg

Vytorin™
Merck/Schering-Plough

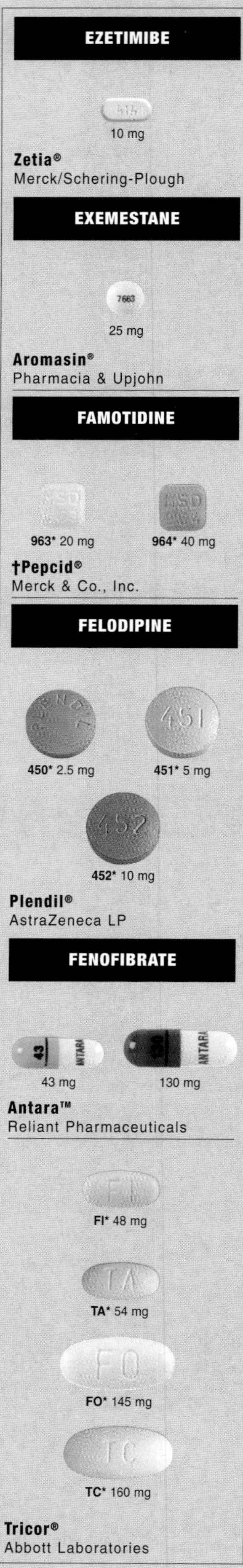

EZETIMIBE

10 mg

Zetia®
Merck/Schering-Plough

EXEMESTANE

25 mg

Aromasin®
Pharmacia & Upjohn

FAMOTIDINE

963* 20 mg

964* 40 mg

†Pepcid®
Merck & Co., Inc.

FELODIPINE

450* 2.5 mg

451* 5 mg

452* 10 mg

Plendil®
AstraZeneca LP

FENOFIBRATE

43 mg

130 mg

Antara™
Reliant Pharmaceuticals

FI* 48 mg

TA* 54 mg

FO* 145 mg

TC* 160 mg

Tricor®
Abbott Laboratories

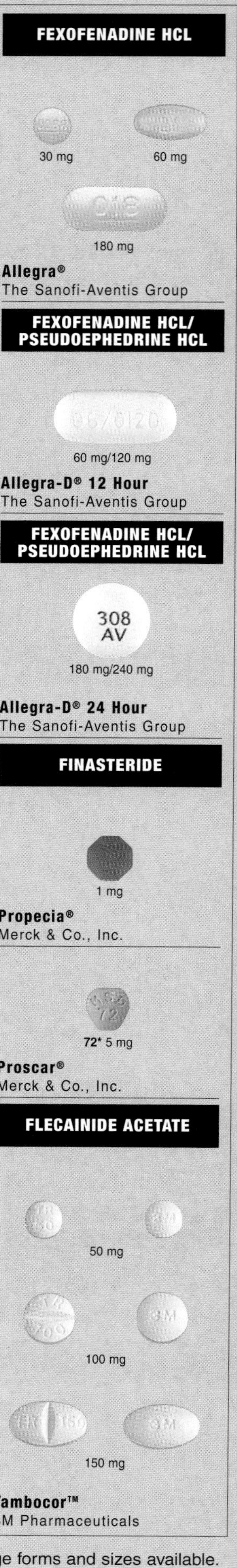

FEXOFENADINE HCL

30 mg

60 mg

180 mg

Allegra®
The Sanofi-Aventis Group

FEXOFENADINE HCL/ PSEUDOEPHEDRINE HCL

60 mg/120 mg

Allegra-D® 12 Hour
The Sanofi-Aventis Group

FEXOFENADINE HCL/ PSEUDOEPHEDRINE HCL

180 mg/240 mg

Allegra-D® 24 Hour
The Sanofi-Aventis Group

FINASTERIDE

1 mg

Propecia®
Merck & Co., Inc.

72* 5 mg

Proscar®
Merck & Co., Inc.

FLECAINIDE ACETATE

50 mg

100 mg

150 mg

Tambocor™
3M Pharmaceuticals

* Manufacturer's Identification Code

† Additional dosage forms and sizes available.

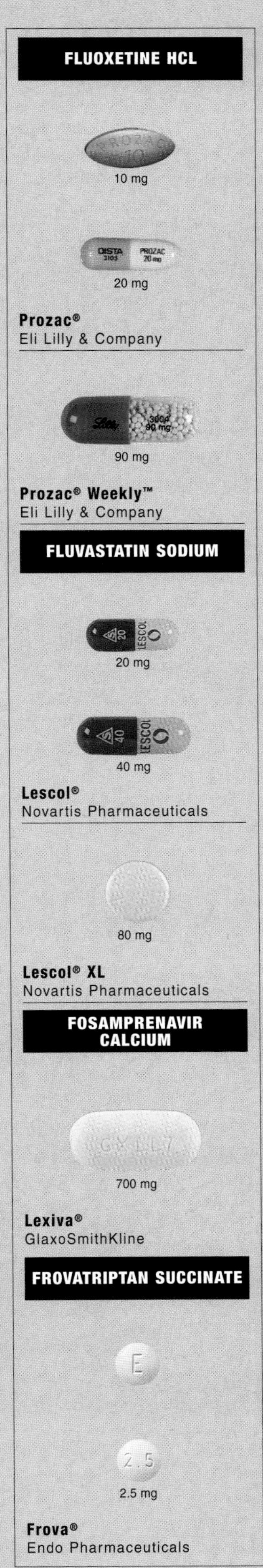

FLUOXETINE HCL

10 mg

20 mg

Prozac®
Eli Lilly & Company

90 mg

Prozac® Weekly™
Eli Lilly & Company

FLUVASTATIN SODIUM

20 mg

40 mg

Lescol®
Novartis Pharmaceuticals

80 mg

Lescol® XL
Novartis Pharmaceuticals

FOSAMPRENAVIR CALCIUM

700 mg

Lexiva®
GlaxoSmithKline

FROVATRIPTAN SUCCINATE

2.5 mg

Frova®
Endo Pharmaceuticals

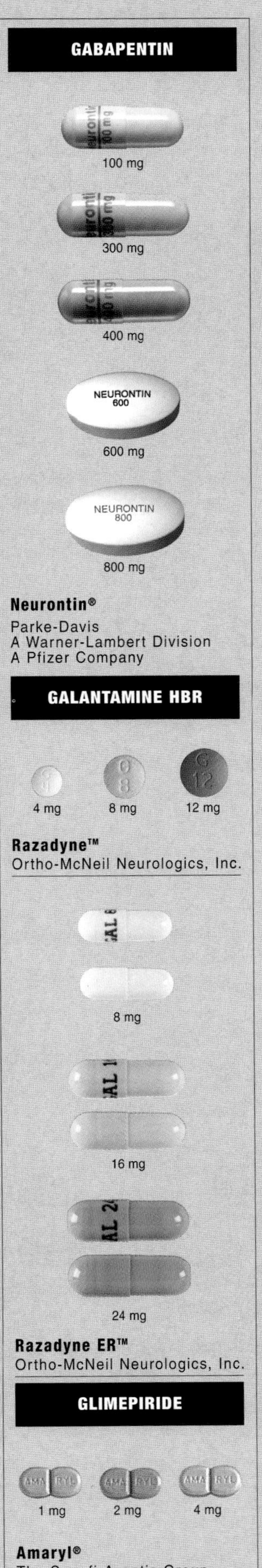

GABAPENTIN

100 mg

300 mg

400 mg

600 mg

800 mg

Neurontin®
Parke-Davis
A Warner-Lambert Division
A Pfizer Company

GALANTAMINE HBR

4 mg 8 mg 12 mg

Razadyne™
Ortho-McNeil Neurologics, Inc.

8 mg

16 mg

24 mg

Razadyne ER™
Ortho-McNeil Neurologics, Inc.

GLIMEPIRIDE

1 mg 2 mg 4 mg

Amaryl®
The Sanofi-Aventis Group

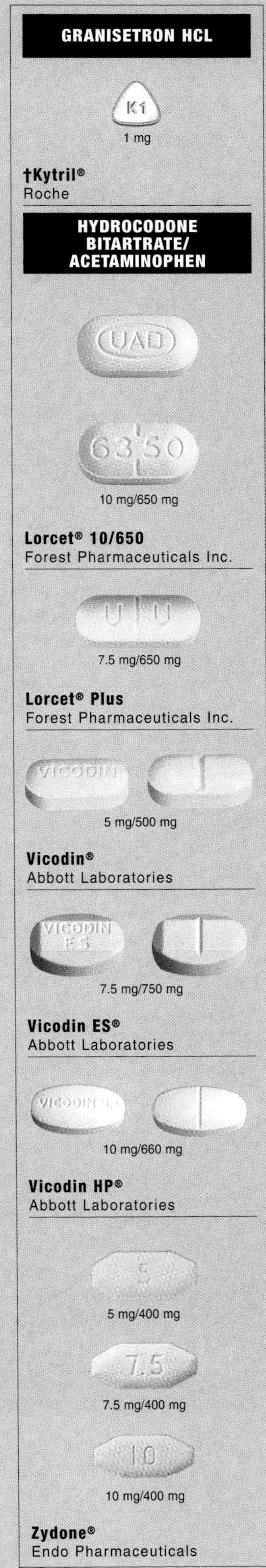

GRANISETRON HCL

1 mg

†Kytril®
Roche

HYDROCODONE BITARTRATE/ ACETAMINOPHEN

10 mg/650 mg

Lorcet® 10/650
Forest Pharmaceuticals Inc.

7.5 mg/650 mg

Lorcet® Plus
Forest Pharmaceuticals Inc.

5 mg/500 mg

Vicodin®
Abbott Laboratories

7.5 mg/750 mg

Vicodin ES®
Abbott Laboratories

10 mg/660 mg

Vicodin HP®
Abbott Laboratories

5 mg/400 mg

7.5 mg/400 mg

10 mg/400 mg

Zydone®
Endo Pharmaceuticals

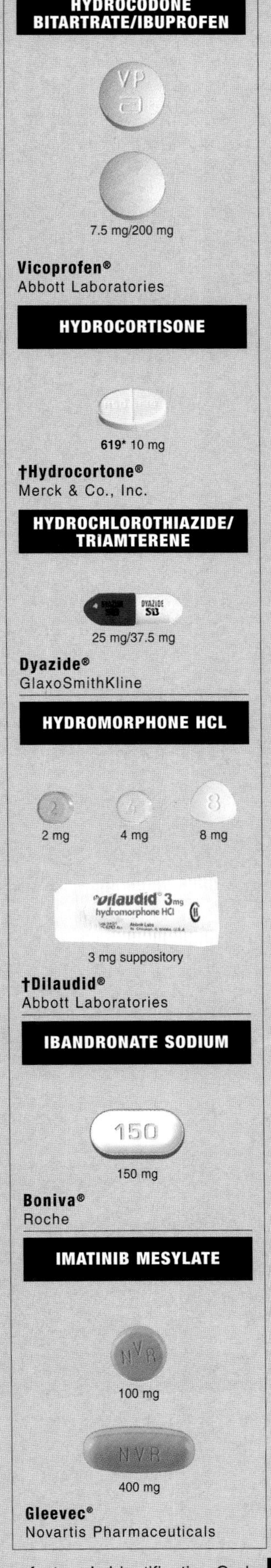

HYDROCODONE BITARTRATE/IBUPROFEN

7.5 mg/200 mg

Vicoprofen®
Abbott Laboratories

HYDROCORTISONE

619* 10 mg

†Hydrocortone®
Merck & Co., Inc.

HYDROCHLOROTHIAZIDE/ TRIAMTERENE

25 mg/37.5 mg

Dyazide®
GlaxoSmithKline

HYDROMORPHONE HCL

2 mg 4 mg 8 mg

3 mg suppository

†Dilaudid®
Abbott Laboratories

IBANDRONATE SODIUM

150 mg

Boniva®
Roche

IMATINIB MESYLATE

100 mg

400 mg

Gleevec®
Novartis Pharmaceuticals

† Additional dosage forms and sizes available.

* Manufacturer's Identification Code

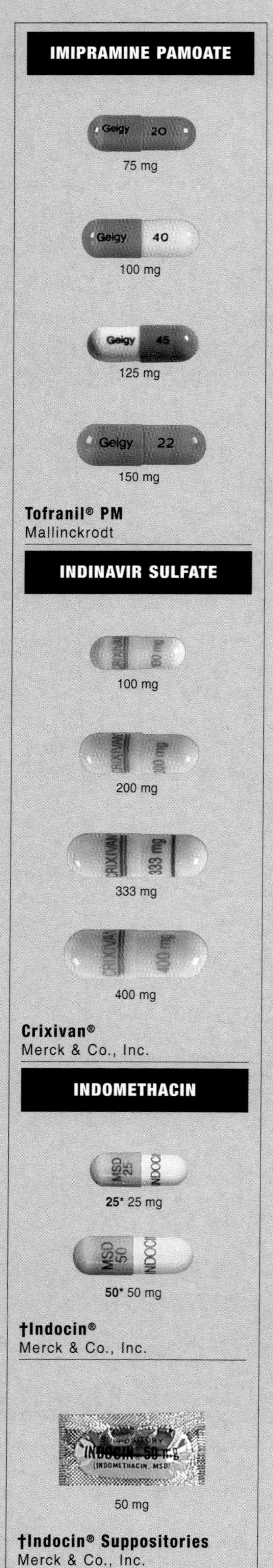

IMIPRAMINE PAMOATE

75 mg

100 mg

125 mg

150 mg

Tofranil® PM
Mallinckrodt

INDINAVIR SULFATE

100 mg

200 mg

333 mg

400 mg

Crixivan®
Merck & Co., Inc.

INDOMETHACIN

25* 25 mg

50* 50 mg

†Indocin®
Merck & Co., Inc.

50 mg

†Indocin® Suppositories
Merck & Co., Inc.

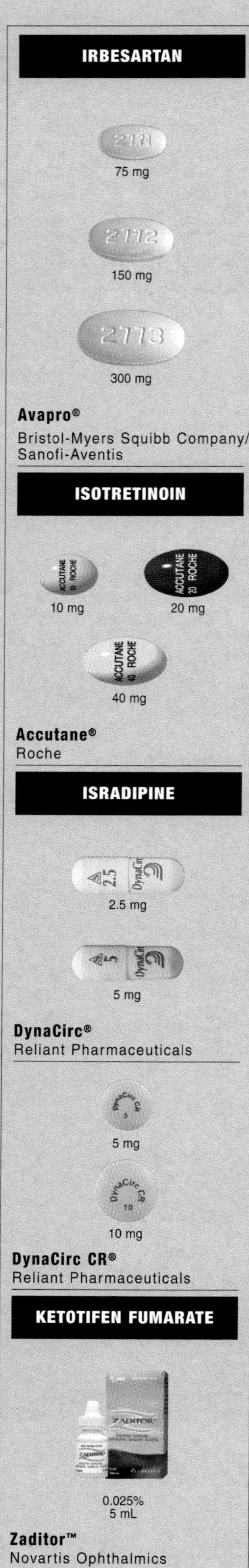

IRBESARTAN

75 mg

150 mg

300 mg

Avapro®
Bristol-Myers Squibb Company/
Sanofi-Aventis

ISOTRETINOIN

10 mg

20 mg

40 mg

Accutane®
Roche

ISRADIPINE

2.5 mg

5 mg

DynaCirc®
Reliant Pharmaceuticals

5 mg

10 mg

DynaCirc CR®
Reliant Pharmaceuticals

KETOTIFEN FUMARATE

0.025%
5 mL

Zaditor™
Novartis Ophthalmics

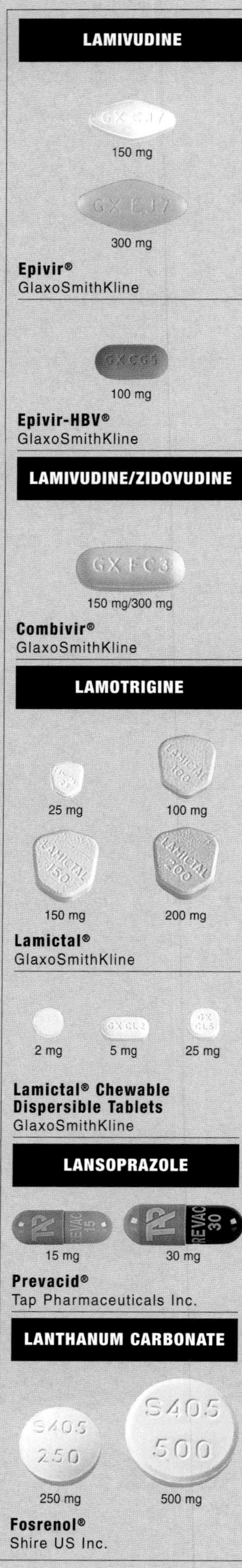

LAMIVUDINE

150 mg

300 mg

Epivir®
GlaxoSmithKline

100 mg

Epivir-HBV®
GlaxoSmithKline

LAMIVUDINE/ZIDOVUDINE

150 mg/300 mg

Combivir®
GlaxoSmithKline

LAMOTRIGINE

25 mg

100 mg

150 mg

200 mg

Lamictal®
GlaxoSmithKline

2 mg

5 mg

25 mg

Lamictal® Chewable Dispersible Tablets
GlaxoSmithKline

LANSOPRAZOLE

15 mg

30 mg

Prevacid®
Tap Pharmaceuticals Inc.

LANTHANUM CARBONATE

250 mg

500 mg

Fosrenol®
Shire US Inc.

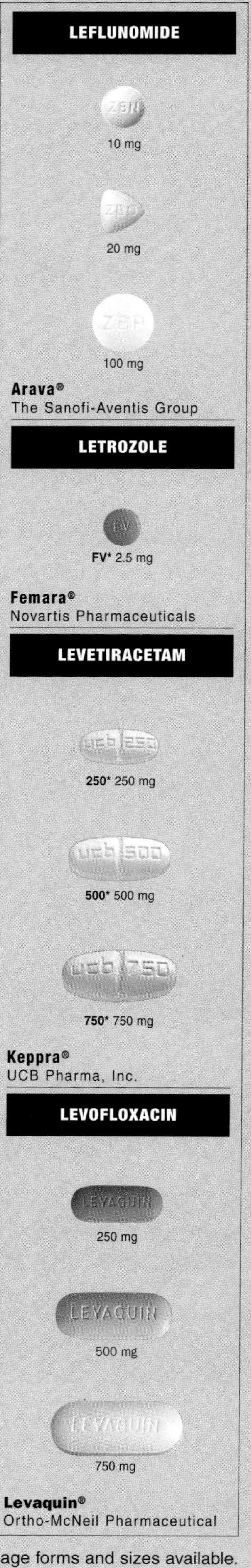

LEFLUNOMIDE

10 mg

20 mg

100 mg

Arava®
The Sanofi-Aventis Group

LETROZOLE

FV* 2.5 mg

Femara®
Novartis Pharmaceuticals

LEVETIRACETAM

250* 250 mg

500* 500 mg

750* 750 mg

Keppra®
UCB Pharma, Inc.

LEVOFLOXACIN

250 mg

500 mg

750 mg

Levaquin®
Ortho-McNeil Pharmaceutical

* Manufacturer's Identification Code

† Additional dosage forms and sizes available.

LEVOTHYROXINE SODIUM

25 mcg 50 mcg
75 mcg 88 mcg
100 mcg 125 mcg
137 mcg 150 mcg
175 mcg 200 mcg
300 mcg

Levothroid®
Forest Pharmaceuticals Inc.

25 mcg (0.025 mg) 50 mcg (0.05 mg) 75 mcg (0.075 mg)
88 mcg (0.088 mg) 100 mcg (0.1 mg) 112 mcg (0.112 mg)
125 mcg (0.125 mg) 137 mcg (0.137 mg) 150 mcg (0.15 mg)
175 mcg (0.175 mg) 200 mcg (0.2 mg) 300 mcg (0.3 mg)

Levoxyl®
King Pharmaceuticals

25 mcg 50 mcg 75 mcg
88 mcg 100 mcg 112 mcg
125 mcg 137 mcg 150 mcg
175 mcg 200 mcg 300 mcg

Synthroid®
Abbott Laboratories

LINEZOLID

600 mg

Zyvox®
Pharmacia & Upjohn

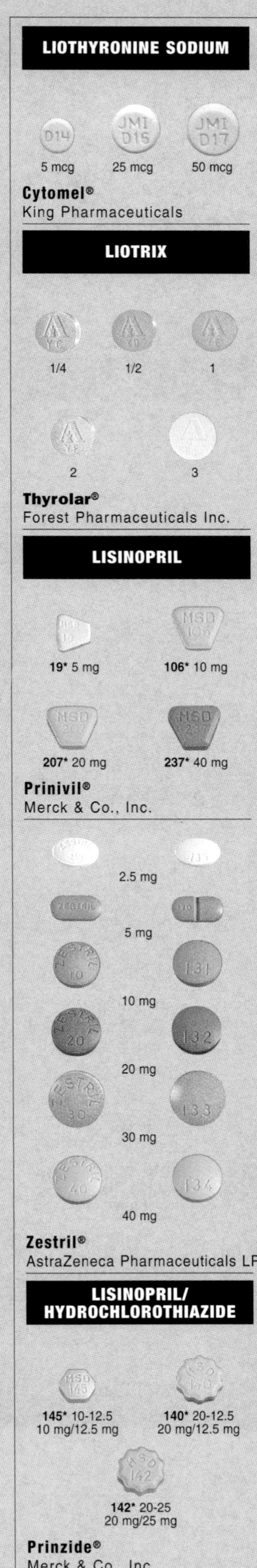

LIOTHYRONINE SODIUM

5 mcg 25 mcg 50 mcg

Cytomel®
King Pharmaceuticals

LIOTRIX

1/4 1/2 1
2 3

Thyrolar®
Forest Pharmaceuticals Inc.

LISINOPRIL

19* 5 mg **106*** 10 mg
207* 20 mg **237*** 40 mg

Prinivil®
Merck & Co., Inc.

2.5 mg
5 mg
10 mg
20 mg
30 mg
40 mg

Zestril®
AstraZeneca Pharmaceuticals LP

LISINOPRIL/ HYDROCHLOROTHIAZIDE

145* 10-12.5 10 mg/12.5 mg
140* 20-12.5 20 mg/12.5 mg
142* 20-25 20 mg/25 mg

Prinzide®
Merck & Co., Inc.

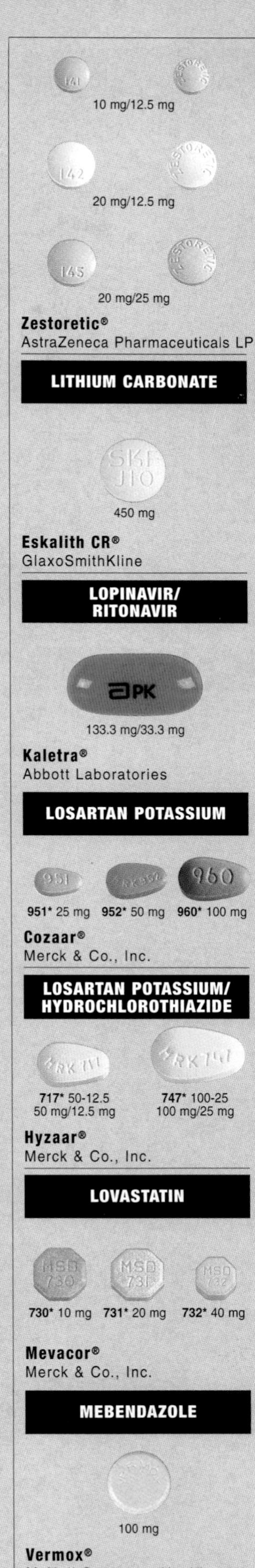

10 mg/12.5 mg
20 mg/12.5 mg
20 mg/25 mg

Zestoretic®
AstraZeneca Pharmaceuticals LP

LITHIUM CARBONATE

450 mg

Eskalith CR®
GlaxoSmithKline

LOPINAVIR/ RITONAVIR

133.3 mg/33.3 mg

Kaletra®
Abbott Laboratories

LOSARTAN POTASSIUM

951* 25 mg **952*** 50 mg **960*** 100 mg

Cozaar®
Merck & Co., Inc.

LOSARTAN POTASSIUM/ HYDROCHLOROTHIAZIDE

717* 50-12.5 50 mg/12.5 mg
747* 100-25 100 mg/25 mg

Hyzaar®
Merck & Co., Inc.

LOVASTATIN

730* 10 mg **731*** 20 mg **732*** 40 mg

Mevacor®
Merck & Co., Inc.

MEBENDAZOLE

100 mg

Vermox®
McNeil Consumer Healthcare

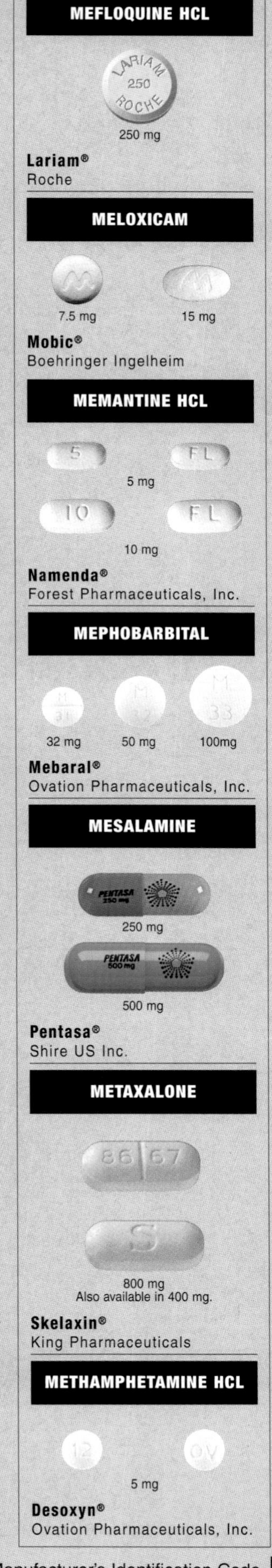

MEFLOQUINE HCL

250 mg

Lariam®
Roche

MELOXICAM

7.5 mg 15 mg

Mobic®
Boehringer Ingelheim

MEMANTINE HCL

5 mg
10 mg

Namenda®
Forest Pharmaceuticals, Inc.

MEPHOBARBITAL

32 mg 50 mg 100mg

Mebaral®
Ovation Pharmaceuticals, Inc.

MESALAMINE

250 mg
500 mg

Pentasa®
Shire US Inc.

METAXALONE

800 mg
Also available in 400 mg.

Skelaxin®
King Pharmaceuticals

METHAMPHETAMINE HCL

5 mg

Desoxyn®
Ovation Pharmaceuticals, Inc.

* Manufacturer's Identification Code

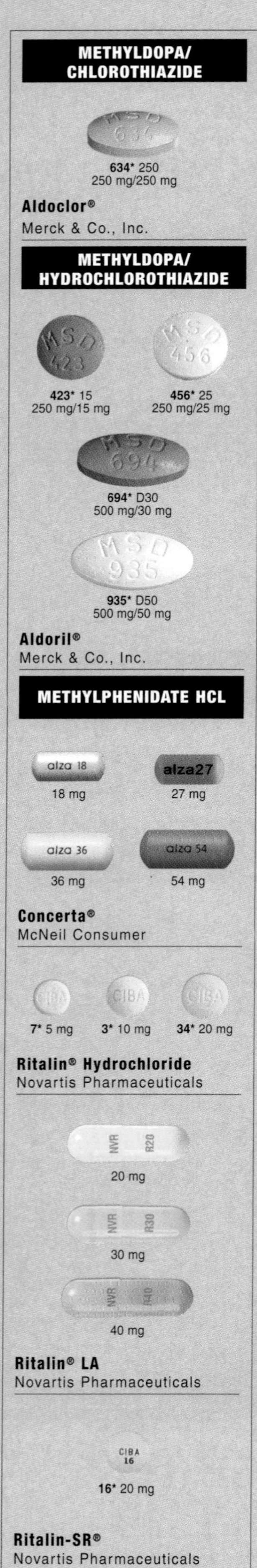

METHYLDOPA/ CHLOROTHIAZIDE

634* 250
250 mg/250 mg

Aldoclor®
Merck & Co., Inc.

METHYLDOPA/ HYDROCHLOROTHIAZIDE

423* 15
250 mg/15 mg

456* 25
250 mg/25 mg

694* D30
500 mg/30 mg

935* D50
500 mg/50 mg

Aldoril®
Merck & Co., Inc.

METHYLPHENIDATE HCL

18 mg

27 mg

36 mg

54 mg

Concerta®
McNeil Consumer

7* 5 mg

3* 10 mg

34* 20 mg

Ritalin® Hydrochloride
Novartis Pharmaceuticals

20 mg

30 mg

40 mg

Ritalin® LA
Novartis Pharmaceuticals

16* 20 mg

Ritalin-SR®
Novartis Pharmaceuticals

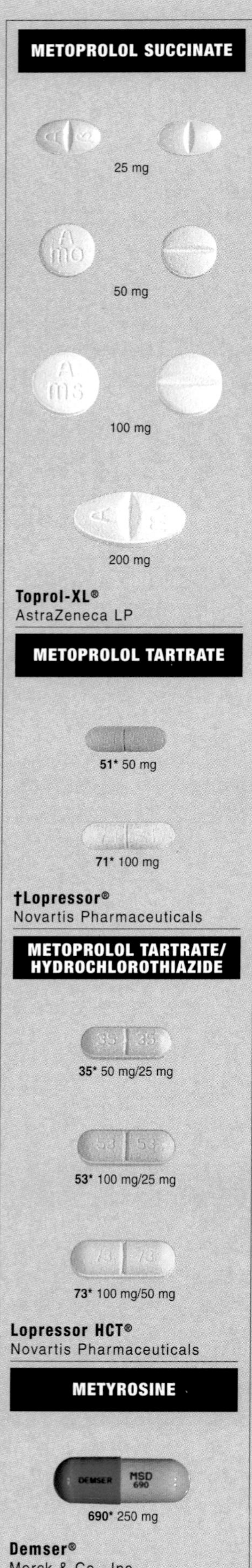

METOPROLOL SUCCINATE

25 mg

50 mg

100 mg

200 mg

Toprol-XL®
AstraZeneca LP

METOPROLOL TARTRATE

51* 50 mg

71* 100 mg

†Lopressor®
Novartis Pharmaceuticals

METOPROLOL TARTRATE/ HYDROCHLOROTHIAZIDE

35* 50 mg/25 mg

53* 100 mg/25 mg

73* 100 mg/50 mg

Lopressor HCT®
Novartis Pharmaceuticals

METYROSINE

690* 250 mg

Demser®
Merck & Co., Inc.

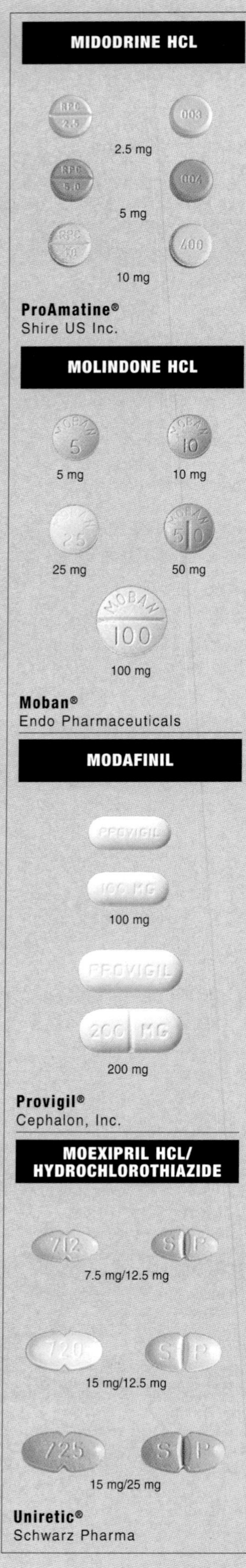

MIDODRINE HCL

2.5 mg

5 mg

10 mg

ProAmatine®
Shire US Inc.

MOLINDONE HCL

5 mg

10 mg

25 mg

50 mg

100 mg

Moban®
Endo Pharmaceuticals

MODAFINIL

100 mg

200 mg

Provigil®
Cephalon, Inc.

MOEXIPRIL HCL/ HYDROCHLOROTHIAZIDE

7.5 mg/12.5 mg

15 mg/12.5 mg

15 mg/25 mg

Uniretic®
Schwarz Pharma

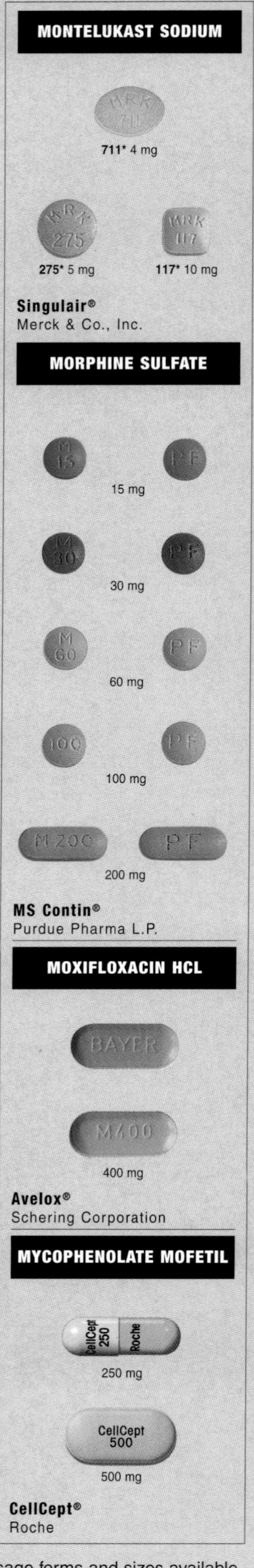

MONTELUKAST SODIUM

711* 4 mg

275* 5 mg

117* 10 mg

Singulair®
Merck & Co., Inc.

MORPHINE SULFATE

15 mg

30 mg

60 mg

100 mg

200 mg

MS Contin®
Purdue Pharma L.P.

MOXIFLOXACIN HCL

400 mg

Avelox®
Schering Corporation

MYCOPHENOLATE MOFETIL

250 mg

500 mg

CellCept®
Roche

* Manufacturer's Identification Code

† Additional dosage forms and sizes available.

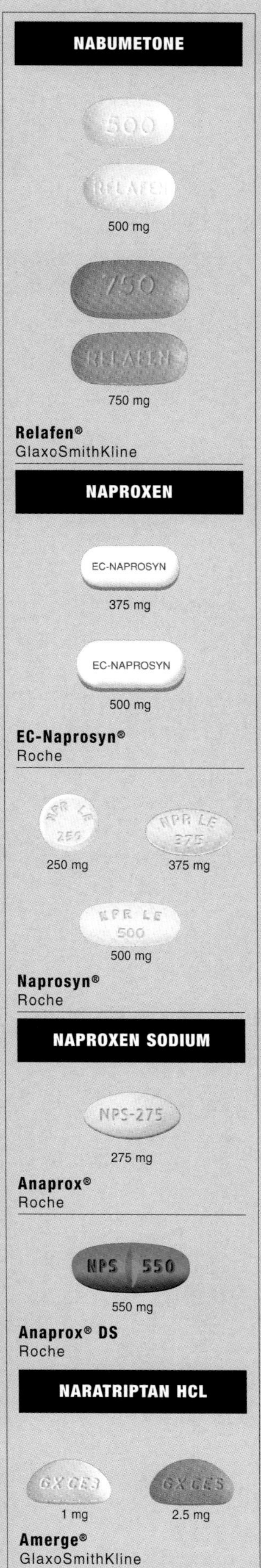

NABUMETONE

500 mg

750 mg

Relafen®
GlaxoSmithKline

NAPROXEN

375 mg

500 mg

EC-Naprosyn®
Roche

250 mg

375 mg

500 mg

Naprosyn®
Roche

NAPROXEN SODIUM

275 mg

Anaprox®
Roche

550 mg

Anaprox® DS
Roche

NARATRIPTAN HCL

1 mg

2.5 mg

Amerge®
GlaxoSmithKline

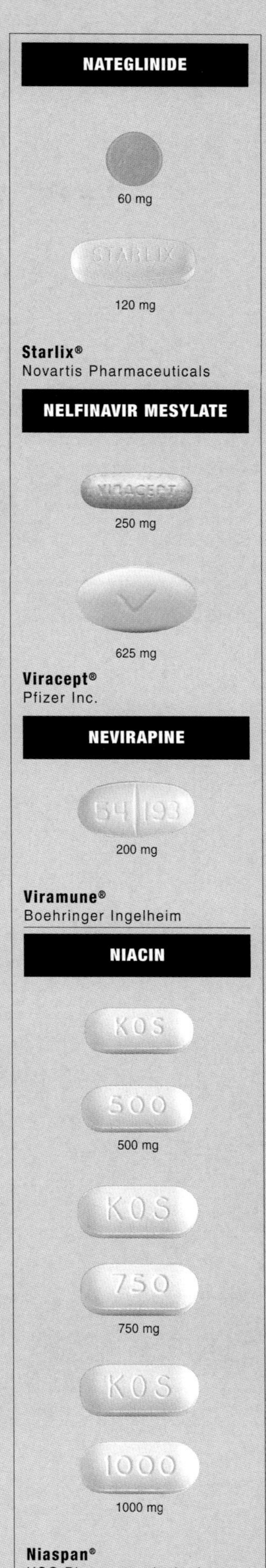

NATEGLINIDE

60 mg

120 mg

Starlix®
Novartis Pharmaceuticals

NELFINAVIR MESYLATE

250 mg

625 mg

Viracept®
Pfizer Inc.

NEVIRAPINE

200 mg

Viramune®
Boehringer Ingelheim

NIACIN

500 mg

750 mg

1000 mg

Niaspan®
KOS Pharmaceuticals, Inc

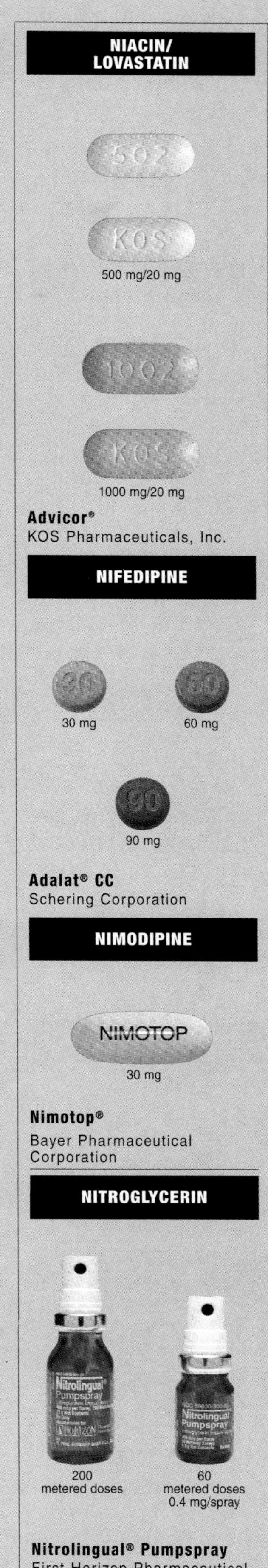

NIACIN/ LOVASTATIN

500 mg/20 mg

1000 mg/20 mg

Advicor®
KOS Pharmaceuticals, Inc.

NIFEDIPINE

30 mg

60 mg

90 mg

Adalat® CC
Schering Corporation

NIMODIPINE

30 mg

Nimotop®
Bayer Pharmaceutical Corporation

NITROGLYCERIN

200 metered doses

60 metered doses 0.4 mg/spray

Nitrolingual® Pumpspray
First Horizon Pharmaceutical

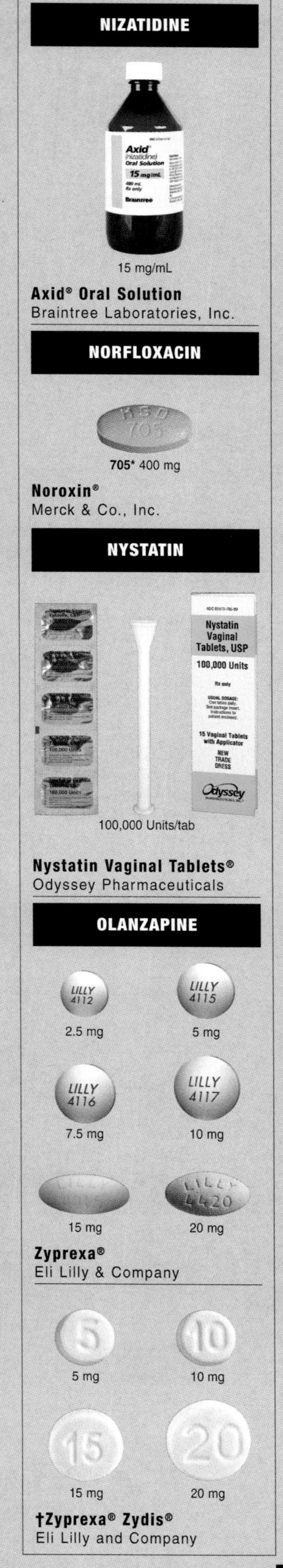

NIZATIDINE

15 mg/mL

Axid® Oral Solution
Braintree Laboratories, Inc.

NORFLOXACIN

705* 400 mg

Noroxin®
Merck & Co., Inc.

NYSTATIN

100,000 Units/tab

Nystatin Vaginal Tablets®
Odyssey Pharmaceuticals

OLANZAPINE

2.5 mg

5 mg

7.5 mg

10 mg

15 mg

20 mg

Zyprexa®
Eli Lilly & Company

5 mg

10 mg

15 mg

20 mg

†Zyprexa® Zydis®
Eli Lilly and Company

† Additional dosage forms and sizes available.

* Manufacturer's Identification Code

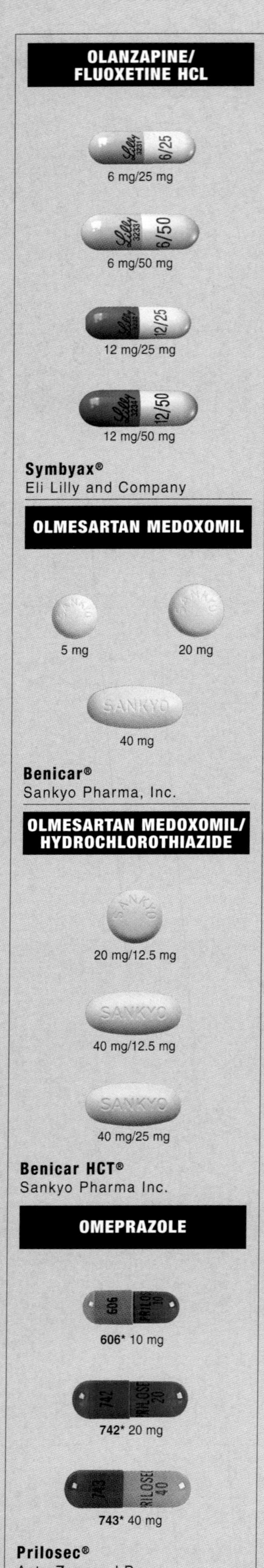

OLANZAPINE/ FLUOXETINE HCL

6 mg/25 mg

6 mg/50 mg

12 mg/25 mg

12 mg/50 mg

Symbyax®
Eli Lilly and Company

OLMESARTAN MEDOXOMIL

5 mg 20 mg

40 mg

Benicar®
Sankyo Pharma, Inc.

OLMESARTAN MEDOXOMIL/ HYDROCHLOROTHIAZIDE

20 mg/12.5 mg

40 mg/12.5 mg

40 mg/25 mg

Benicar HCT®
Sankyo Pharma Inc.

OMEPRAZOLE

606* 10 mg

742* 20 mg

743* 40 mg

Prilosec®
AstraZeneca LP

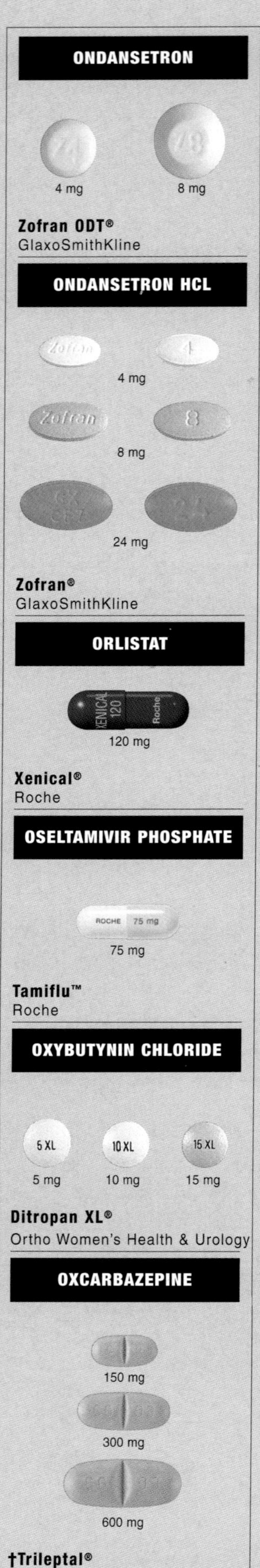

ONDANSETRON

4 mg 8 mg

Zofran ODT®
GlaxoSmithKline

ONDANSETRON HCL

4 mg

8 mg

24 mg

Zofran®
GlaxoSmithKline

ORLISTAT

120 mg

Xenical®
Roche

OSELTAMIVIR PHOSPHATE

75 mg

Tamiflu™
Roche

OXYBUTYNIN CHLORIDE

5 mg 10 mg 15 mg

Ditropan XL®
Ortho Women's Health & Urology

OXCARBAZEPINE

150 mg

300 mg

600 mg

†Trileptal®
Novartis Pharmaceuticals

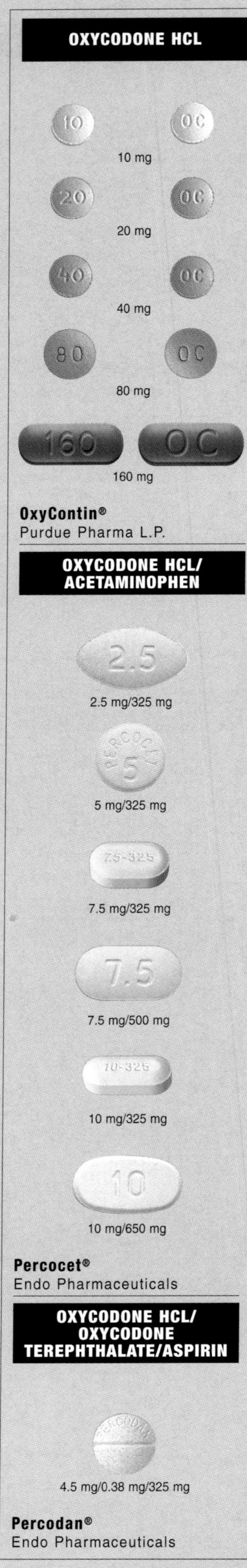

OXYCODONE HCL

10 mg

20 mg

40 mg

80 mg

160 mg

OxyContin®
Purdue Pharma L.P.

OXYCODONE HCL/ ACETAMINOPHEN

2.5 mg/325 mg

5 mg/325 mg

7.5 mg/325 mg

7.5 mg/500 mg

10 mg/325 mg

10 mg/650 mg

Percocet®
Endo Pharmaceuticals

OXYCODONE HCL/ OXYCODONE TEREPHTHALATE/ASPIRIN

4.5 mg/0.38 mg/325 mg

Percodan®
Endo Pharmaceuticals

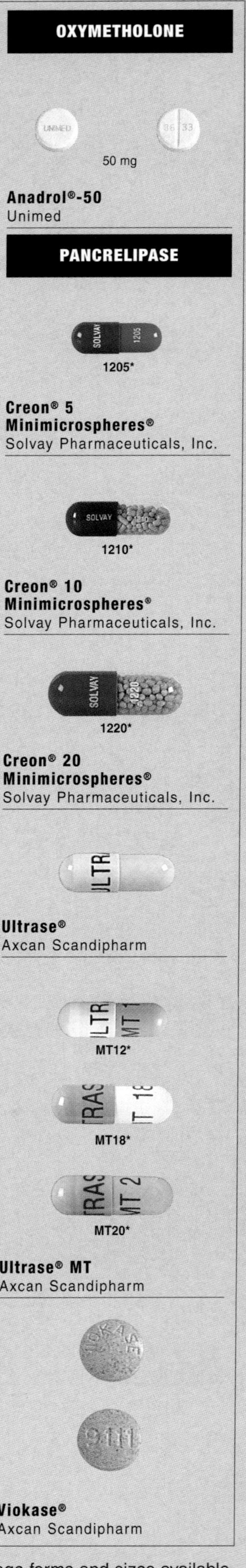

OXYMETHOLONE

50 mg

Anadrol®-50
Unimed

PANCRELIPASE

1205*

Creon® 5 Minimicrospheres®
Solvay Pharmaceuticals, Inc.

1210*

Creon® 10 Minimicrospheres®
Solvay Pharmaceuticals, Inc.

1220*

Creon® 20 Minimicrospheres®
Solvay Pharmaceuticals, Inc.

Ultrase®
Axcan Scandipharm

MT12*

MT18*

MT20*

Ultrase® MT
Axcan Scandipharm

Viokase®
Axcan Scandipharm

* Manufacturer's Identification Code

† Additional dosage forms and sizes available.

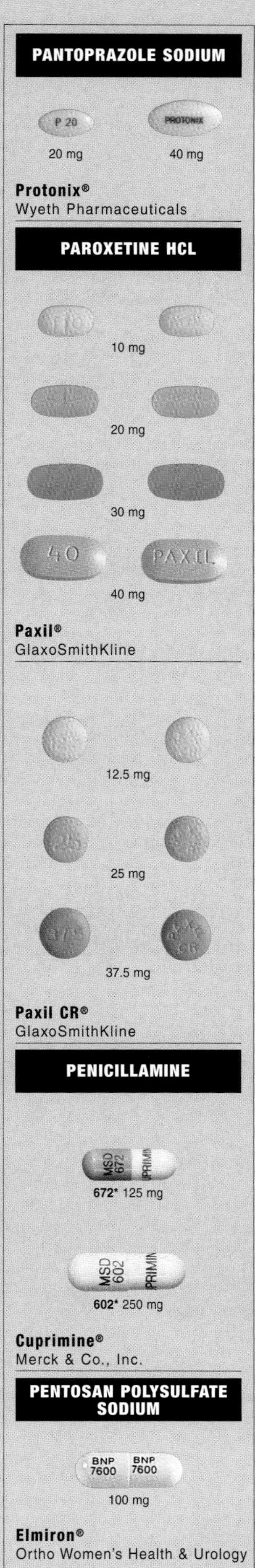

PANTOPRAZOLE SODIUM

20 mg 40 mg

Protonix®
Wyeth Pharmaceuticals

PAROXETINE HCL

10 mg

20 mg

30 mg

40 mg

Paxil®
GlaxoSmithKline

12.5 mg

25 mg

37.5 mg

Paxil CR®
GlaxoSmithKline

PENICILLAMINE

672* 125 mg

602* 250 mg

Cuprimine®
Merck & Co., Inc.

PENTOSAN POLYSULFATE SODIUM

100 mg

Elmiron®
Ortho Women's Health & Urology

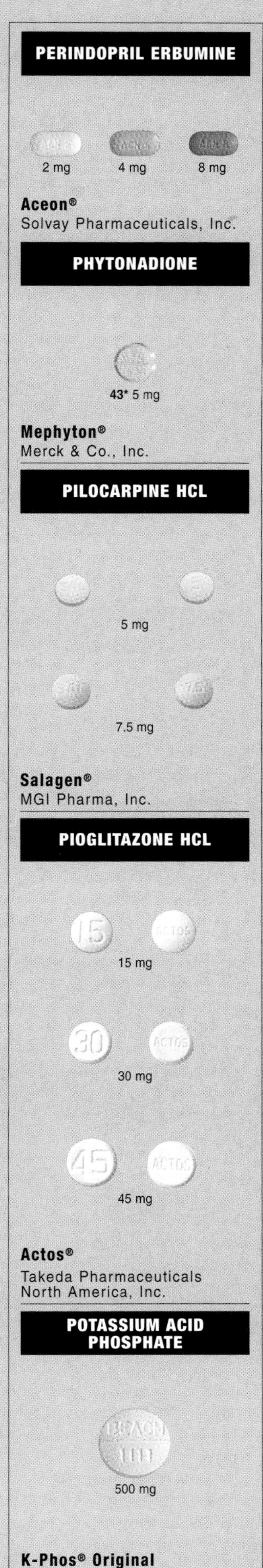

PERINDOPRIL ERBUMINE

2 mg 4 mg 8 mg

Aceon®
Solvay Pharmaceuticals, Inc.

PHYTONADIONE

43* 5 mg

Mephyton®
Merck & Co., Inc.

PILOCARPINE HCL

5 mg

7.5 mg

Salagen®
MGI Pharma, Inc.

PIOGLITAZONE HCL

15 mg

30 mg

45 mg

Actos®
Takeda Pharmaceuticals North America, Inc.

POTASSIUM ACID PHOSPHATE

500 mg

K-Phos® Original
Beach Pharmaceuticals

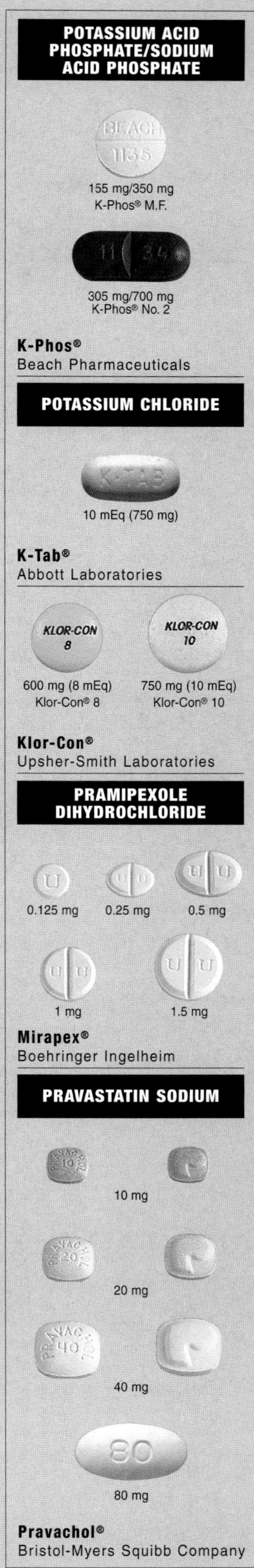

POTASSIUM ACID PHOSPHATE/SODIUM ACID PHOSPHATE

155 mg/350 mg
K-Phos® M.F.

305 mg/700 mg
K-Phos® No. 2

K-Phos®
Beach Pharmaceuticals

POTASSIUM CHLORIDE

10 mEq (750 mg)

K-Tab®
Abbott Laboratories

600 mg (8 mEq)
Klor-Con® 8

750 mg (10 mEq)
Klor-Con® 10

Klor-Con®
Upsher-Smith Laboratories

PRAMIPEXOLE DIHYDROCHLORIDE

0.125 mg 0.25 mg 0.5 mg

1 mg 1.5 mg

Mirapex®
Boehringer Ingelheim

PRAVASTATIN SODIUM

10 mg

20 mg

40 mg

80 mg

Pravachol®
Bristol-Myers Squibb Company

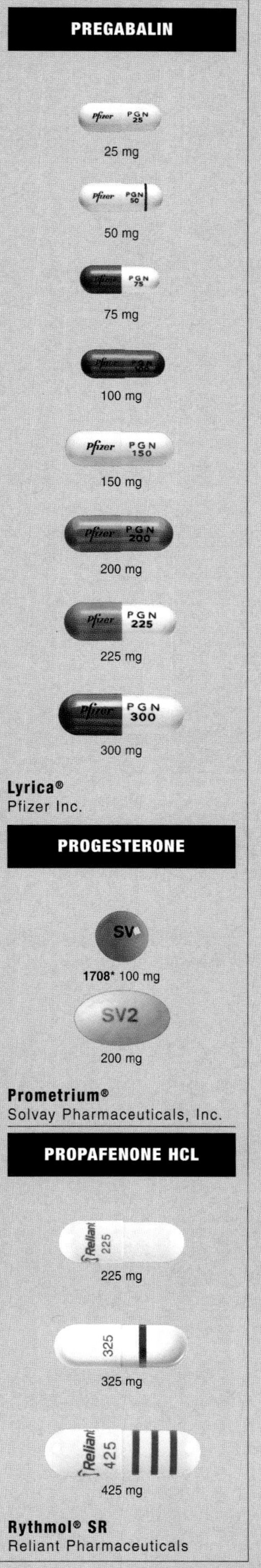

PREGABALIN

25 mg

50 mg

75 mg

100 mg

150 mg

200 mg

225 mg

300 mg

Lyrica®
Pfizer Inc.

PROGESTERONE

1708* 100 mg

200 mg

Prometrium®
Solvay Pharmaceuticals, Inc.

PROPAFENONE HCL

225 mg

325 mg

425 mg

Rythmol® SR
Reliant Pharmaceuticals

* Manufacturer's Identification Code

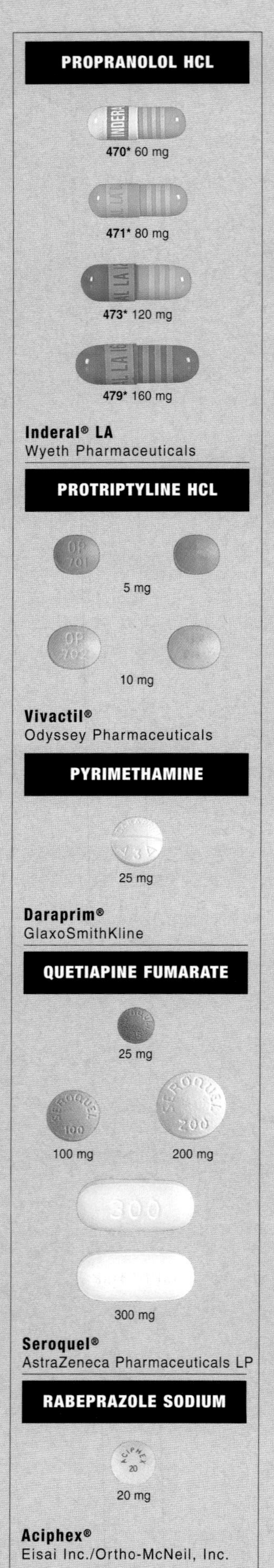

PROPRANOLOL HCL

470* 60 mg

471* 80 mg

473* 120 mg

479* 160 mg

Inderal® LA
Wyeth Pharmaceuticals

PROTRIPTYLINE HCL

5 mg

10 mg

Vivactil®
Odyssey Pharmaceuticals

PYRIMETHAMINE

25 mg

Daraprim®
GlaxoSmithKline

QUETIAPINE FUMARATE

25 mg

100 mg

200 mg

300 mg

Seroquel®
AstraZeneca Pharmaceuticals LP

RABEPRAZOLE SODIUM

20 mg

Aciphex®
Eisai Inc./Ortho-McNeil, Inc.

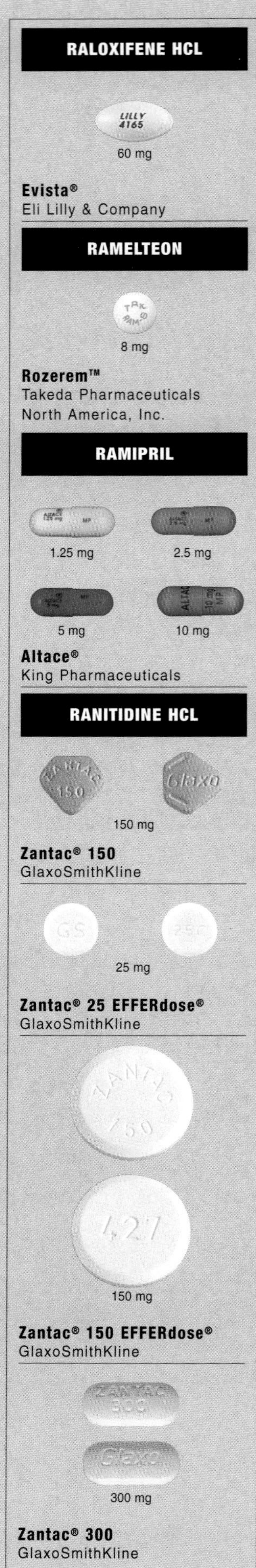

RALOXIFENE HCL

60 mg

Evista®
Eli Lilly & Company

RAMELTEON

8 mg

Rozerem™
Takeda Pharmaceuticals North America, Inc.

RAMIPRIL

1.25 mg

2.5 mg

5 mg

10 mg

Altace®
King Pharmaceuticals

RANITIDINE HCL

150 mg

Zantac® 150
GlaxoSmithKline

25 mg

Zantac® 25 EFFERdose®
GlaxoSmithKline

150 mg

Zantac® 150 EFFERdose®
GlaxoSmithKline

300 mg

Zantac® 300
GlaxoSmithKline

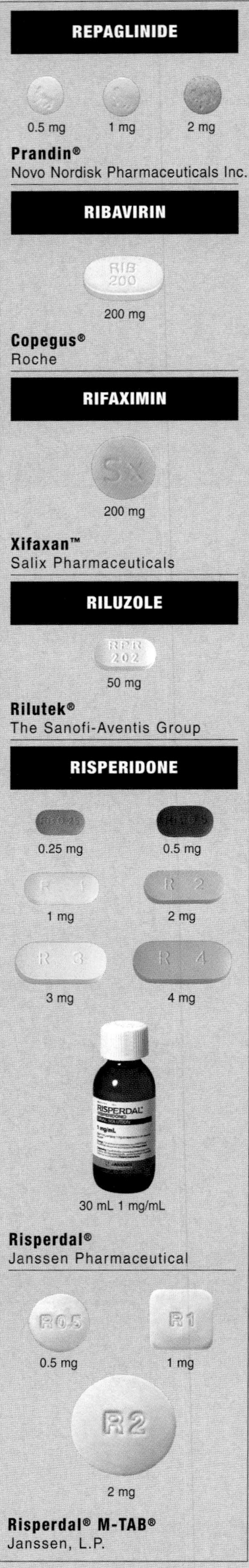

REPAGLINIDE

0.5 mg

1 mg

2 mg

Prandin®
Novo Nordisk Pharmaceuticals Inc.

RIBAVIRIN

200 mg

Copegus®
Roche

RIFAXIMIN

200 mg

Xifaxan™
Salix Pharmaceuticals

RILUZOLE

50 mg

Rilutek®
The Sanofi-Aventis Group

RISPERIDONE

0.25 mg

0.5 mg

1 mg

2 mg

3 mg

4 mg

30 mL 1 mg/mL

Risperdal®
Janssen Pharmaceutical

0.5 mg

1 mg

2 mg

Risperdal® M-TAB®
Janssen, L.P.

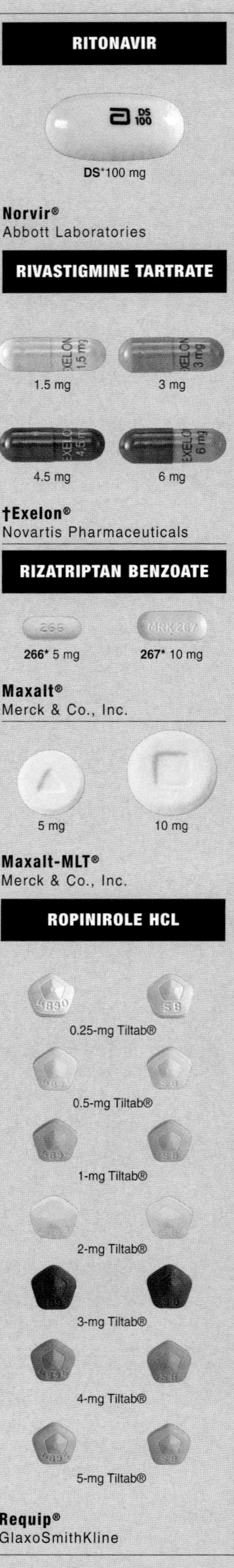

RITONAVIR

DS*100 mg

Norvir®
Abbott Laboratories

RIVASTIGMINE TARTRATE

1.5 mg

3 mg

4.5 mg

6 mg

†Exelon®
Novartis Pharmaceuticals

RIZATRIPTAN BENZOATE

266* 5 mg

267* 10 mg

Maxalt®
Merck & Co., Inc.

5 mg

10 mg

Maxalt-MLT®
Merck & Co., Inc.

ROPINIROLE HCL

0.25-mg Tiltab®

0.5-mg Tiltab®

1-mg Tiltab®

2-mg Tiltab®

3-mg Tiltab®

4-mg Tiltab®

5-mg Tiltab®

Requip®
GlaxoSmithKline

* Manufacturer's Identification Code

† Additional dosage forms and sizes available.

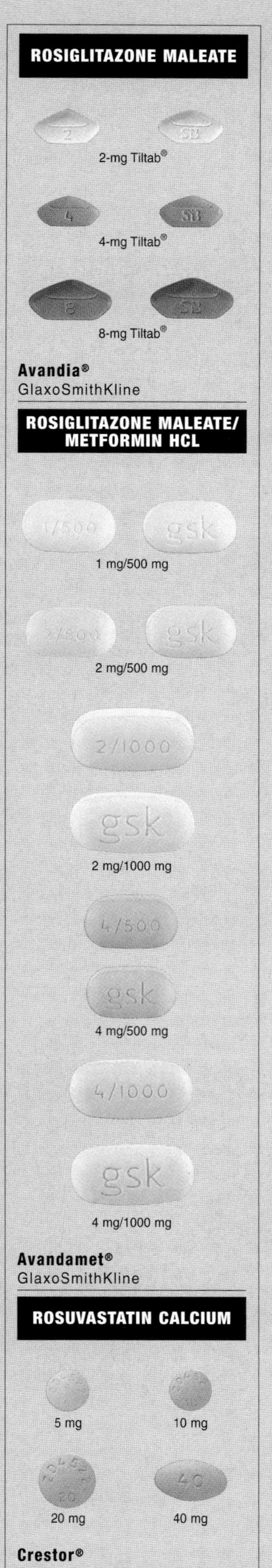

ROSIGLITAZONE MALEATE

2-mg Tiltab®

4-mg Tiltab®

8-mg Tiltab®

Avandia®
GlaxoSmithKline

ROSIGLITAZONE MALEATE/ METFORMIN HCL

1 mg/500 mg

2 mg/500 mg

2 mg/1000 mg

4 mg/500 mg

4 mg/1000 mg

Avandamet®
GlaxoSmithKline

ROSUVASTATIN CALCIUM

5 mg

10 mg

20 mg

40 mg

Crestor®
Astrazeneca Pharmaceuticals LP

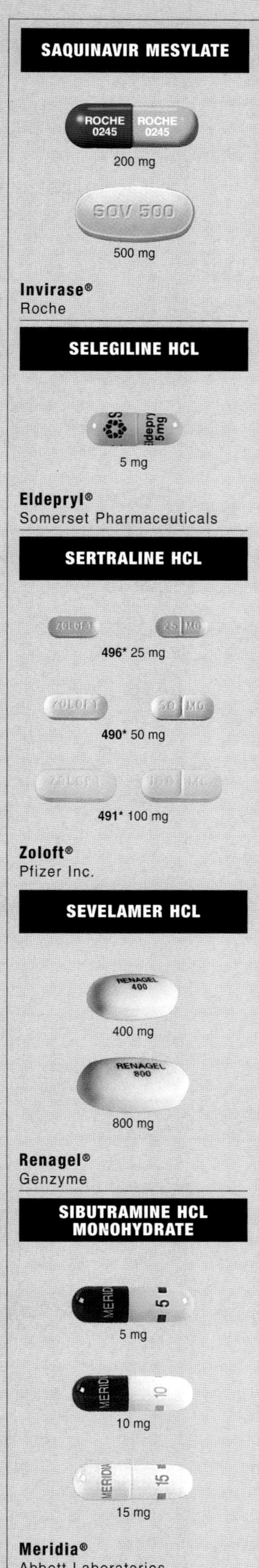

SAQUINAVIR MESYLATE

200 mg

500 mg

Invirase®
Roche

SELEGILINE HCL

5 mg

Eldepryl®
Somerset Pharmaceuticals

SERTRALINE HCL

496* 25 mg

490* 50 mg

491* 100 mg

Zoloft®
Pfizer Inc.

SEVELAMER HCL

400 mg

800 mg

Renagel®
Genzyme

SIBUTRAMINE HCL MONOHYDRATE

5 mg

10 mg

15 mg

Meridia®
Abbott Laboratories

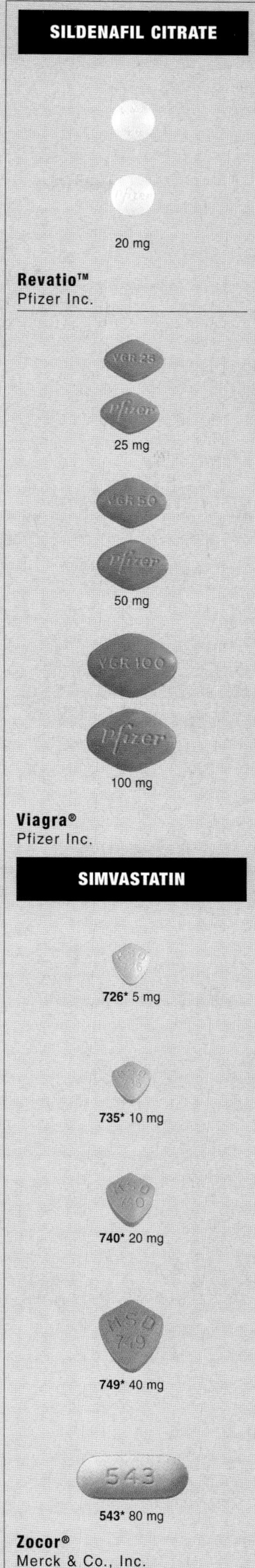

SILDENAFIL CITRATE

20 mg

Revatio™
Pfizer Inc.

25 mg

50 mg

100 mg

Viagra®
Pfizer Inc.

SIMVASTATIN

726* 5 mg

735* 10 mg

740* 20 mg

749* 40 mg

543* 80 mg

Zocor®
Merck & Co., Inc.

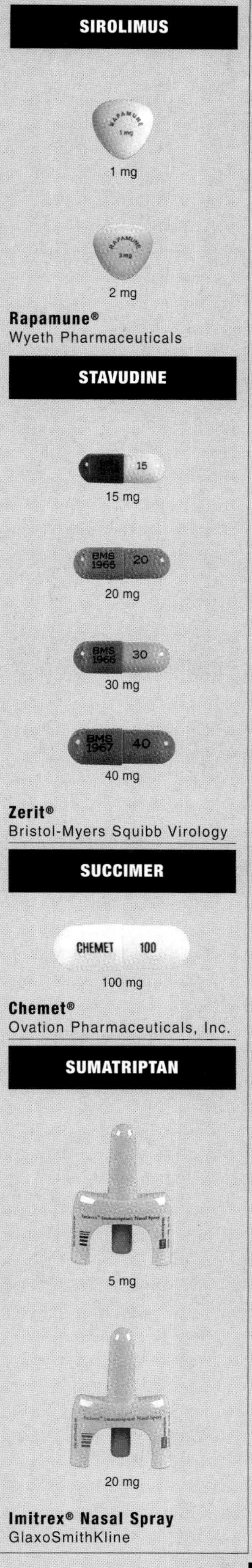

SIROLIMUS

1 mg

2 mg

Rapamune®
Wyeth Pharmaceuticals

STAVUDINE

15 mg

20 mg

30 mg

40 mg

Zerit®
Bristol-Myers Squibb Virology

SUCCIMER

100 mg

Chemet®
Ovation Pharmaceuticals, Inc.

SUMATRIPTAN

5 mg

20 mg

Imitrex® Nasal Spray
GlaxoSmithKline

* Manufacturer's Identification Code

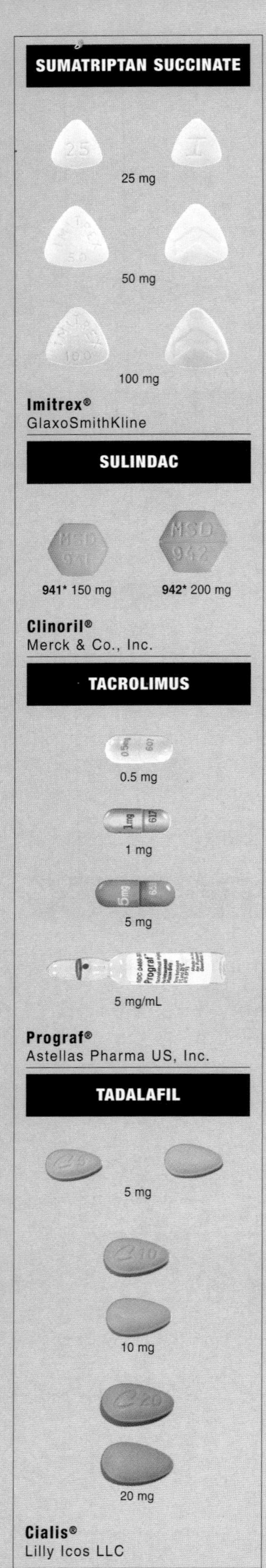

SUMATRIPTAN SUCCINATE

25 mg

50 mg

100 mg

Imitrex®
GlaxoSmithKline

SULINDAC

941* 150 mg **942*** 200 mg

Clinoril®
Merck & Co., Inc.

TACROLIMUS

0.5 mg

1 mg

5 mg

5 mg/mL

Prograf®
Astellas Pharma US, Inc.

TADALAFIL

5 mg

10 mg

20 mg

Cialis®
Lilly Icos LLC

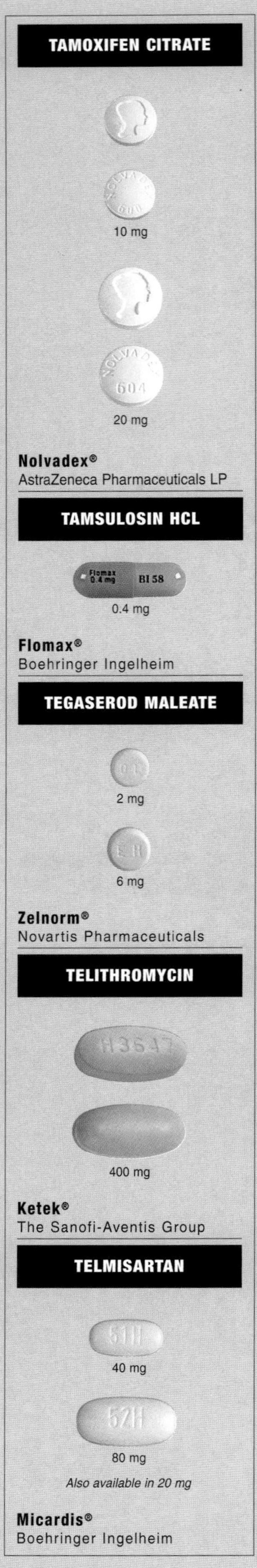

TAMOXIFEN CITRATE

10 mg

20 mg

Nolvadex®
AstraZeneca Pharmaceuticals LP

TAMSULOSIN HCL

0.4 mg

Flomax®
Boehringer Ingelheim

TEGASEROD MALEATE

2 mg

6 mg

Zelnorm®
Novartis Pharmaceuticals

TELITHROMYCIN

400 mg

Ketek®
The Sanofi-Aventis Group

TELMISARTAN

40 mg

80 mg

Also available in 20 mg

Micardis®
Boehringer Ingelheim

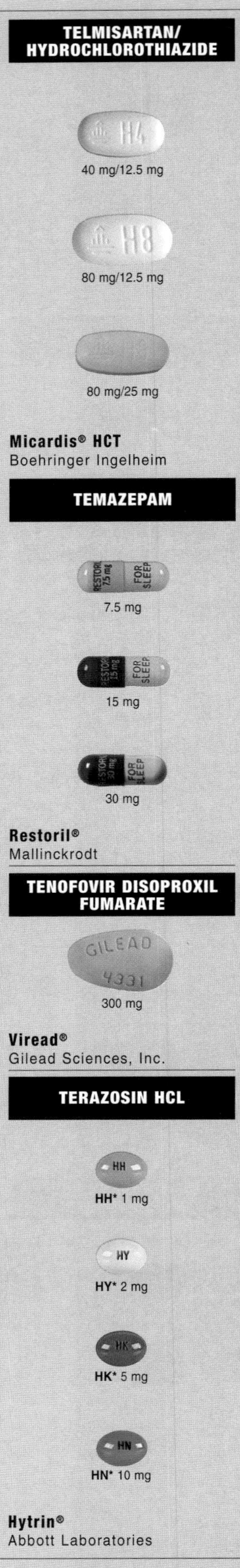

TELMISARTAN/ HYDROCHLOROTHIAZIDE

40 mg/12.5 mg

80 mg/12.5 mg

80 mg/25 mg

Micardis® HCT
Boehringer Ingelheim

TEMAZEPAM

7.5 mg

15 mg

30 mg

Restoril®
Mallinckrodt

TENOFOVIR DISOPROXIL FUMARATE

300 mg

Viread®
Gilead Sciences, Inc.

TERAZOSIN HCL

HH* 1 mg

HY* 2 mg

HK* 5 mg

HN* 10 mg

Hytrin®
Abbott Laboratories

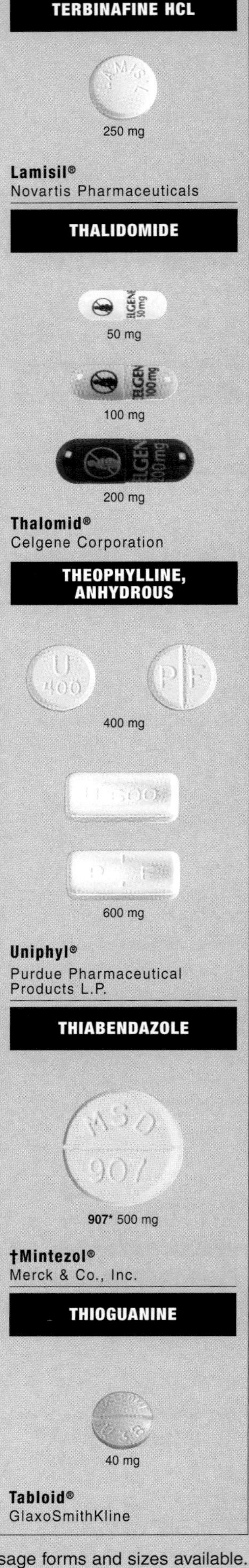

TERBINAFINE HCL

250 mg

Lamisil®
Novartis Pharmaceuticals

THALIDOMIDE

50 mg

100 mg

200 mg

Thalomid®
Celgene Corporation

THEOPHYLLINE, ANHYDROUS

400 mg

600 mg

Uniphyl®
Purdue Pharmaceutical Products L.P.

THIABENDAZOLE

907* 500 mg

†Mintezol®
Merck & Co., Inc.

THIOGUANINE

40 mg

Tabloid®
GlaxoSmithKline

* Manufacturer's Identification Code

† Additional dosage forms and sizes available.

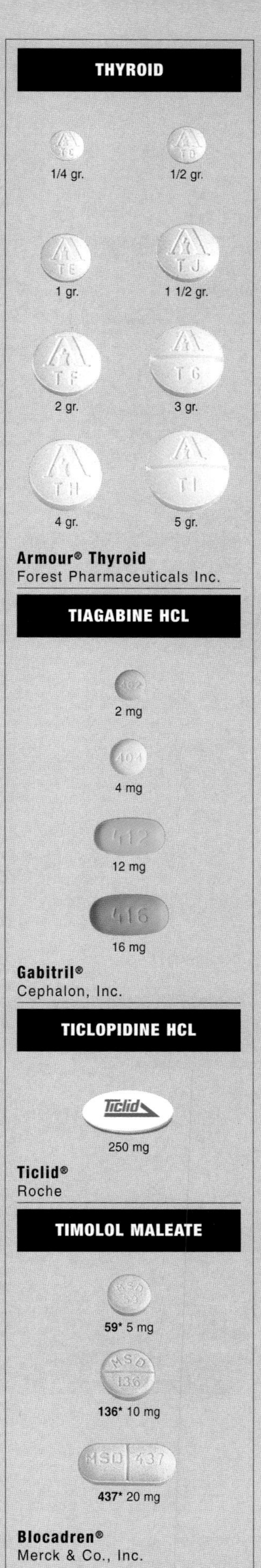

THYROID

1/4 gr. 1/2 gr.

1 gr. 1 1/2 gr.

2 gr. 3 gr.

4 gr. 5 gr.

Armour® Thyroid
Forest Pharmaceuticals Inc.

TIAGABINE HCL

2 mg

4 mg

12 mg

16 mg

Gabitril®
Cephalon, Inc.

TICLOPIDINE HCL

250 mg

Ticlid®
Roche

TIMOLOL MALEATE

59* 5 mg

136* 10 mg

437* 20 mg

Blocadren®
Merck & Co., Inc.

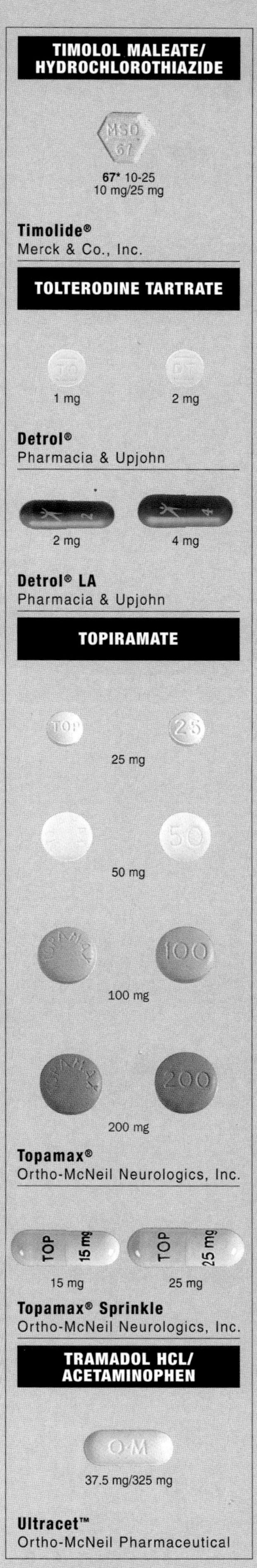

TIMOLOL MALEATE/ HYDROCHLOROTHIAZIDE

67* 10-25
10 mg/25 mg

Timolide®
Merck & Co., Inc.

TOLTERODINE TARTRATE

1 mg 2 mg

Detrol®
Pharmacia & Upjohn

2 mg 4 mg

Detrol® LA
Pharmacia & Upjohn

TOPIRAMATE

25 mg

50 mg

100 mg

200 mg

Topamax®
Ortho-McNeil Neurologics, Inc.

15 mg 25 mg

Topamax® Sprinkle
Ortho-McNeil Neurologics, Inc.

TRAMADOL HCL/ ACETAMINOPHEN

37.5 mg/325 mg

Ultracet™
Ortho-McNeil Pharmaceutical

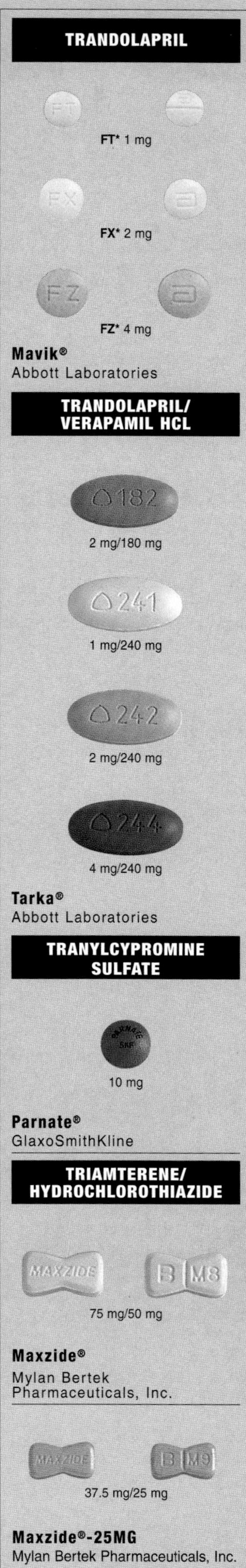

TRANDOLAPRIL

FT* 1 mg

FX* 2 mg

FZ* 4 mg

Mavik®
Abbott Laboratories

TRANDOLAPRIL/ VERAPAMIL HCL

2 mg/180 mg

1 mg/240 mg

2 mg/240 mg

4 mg/240 mg

Tarka®
Abbott Laboratories

TRANYLCYPROMINE SULFATE

10 mg

Parnate®
GlaxoSmithKline

TRIAMTERENE/ HYDROCHLOROTHIAZIDE

75 mg/50 mg

Maxzide®
Mylan Bertek Pharmaceuticals, Inc.

37.5 mg/25 mg

Maxzide®-25MG
Mylan Bertek Pharmaceuticals, Inc.

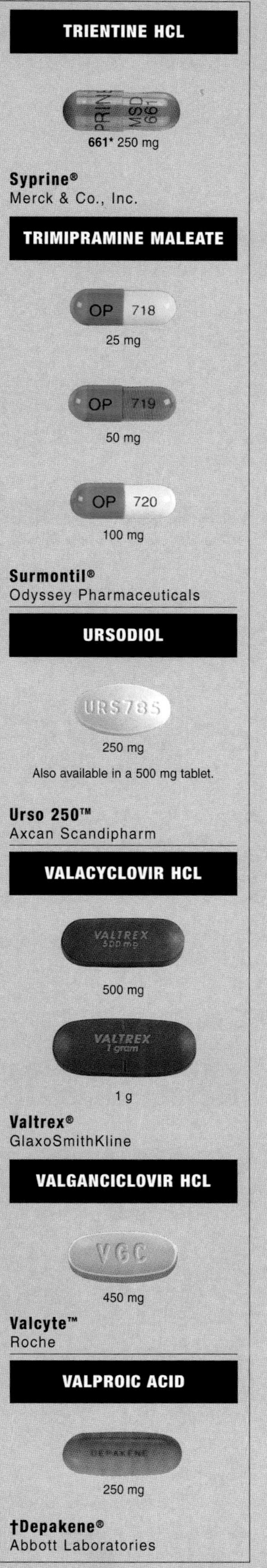

TRIENTINE HCL

661* 250 mg

Syprine®
Merck & Co., Inc.

TRIMIPRAMINE MALEATE

25 mg

50 mg

100 mg

Surmontil®
Odyssey Pharmaceuticals

URSODIOL

250 mg

Also available in a 500 mg tablet.

Urso 250™
Axcan Scandipharm

VALACYCLOVIR HCL

500 mg

1 g

Valtrex®
GlaxoSmithKline

VALGANCICLOVIR HCL

450 mg

Valcyte™
Roche

VALPROIC ACID

250 mg

†Depakene®
Abbott Laboratories

† Additional dosage forms and sizes available.

* Manufacturer's Identification Code

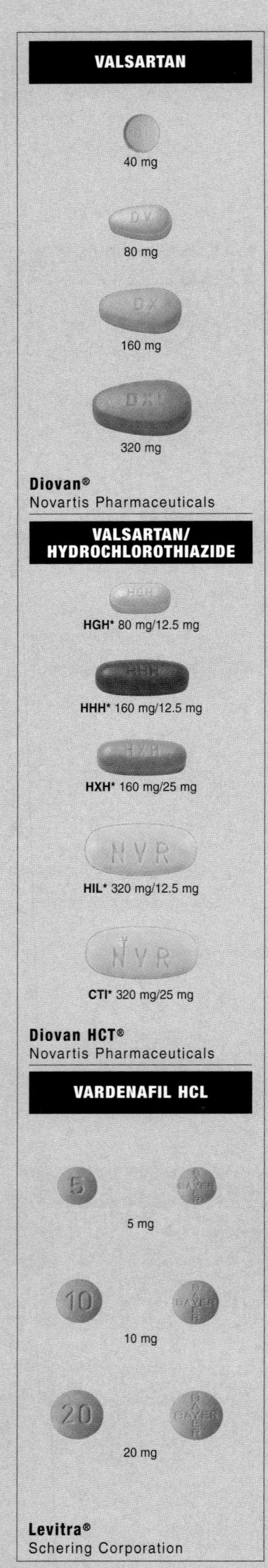

VALSARTAN

40 mg

80 mg

160 mg

320 mg

Diovan®
Novartis Pharmaceuticals

VALSARTAN/ HYDROCHLOROTHIAZIDE

HGH* 80 mg/12.5 mg

HHH* 160 mg/12.5 mg

HXH* 160 mg/25 mg

HIL* 320 mg/12.5 mg

CTI* 320 mg/25 mg

Diovan HCT®
Novartis Pharmaceuticals

VARDENAFIL HCL

5 mg

10 mg

20 mg

Levitra®
Schering Corporation

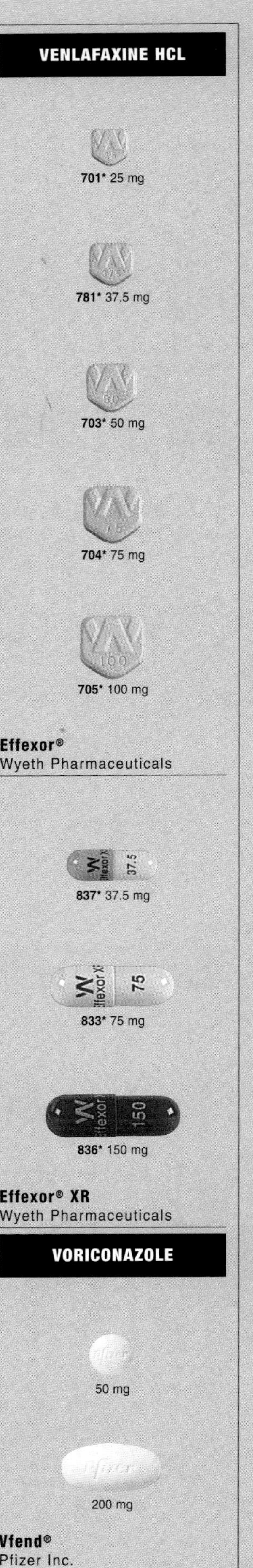

VENLAFAXINE HCL

701* 25 mg

781* 37.5 mg

703* 50 mg

704* 75 mg

705* 100 mg

Effexor®
Wyeth Pharmaceuticals

837* 37.5 mg

833* 75 mg

836* 150 mg

Effexor® XR
Wyeth Pharmaceuticals

VORICONAZOLE

50 mg

200 mg

Vfend®
Pfizer Inc.

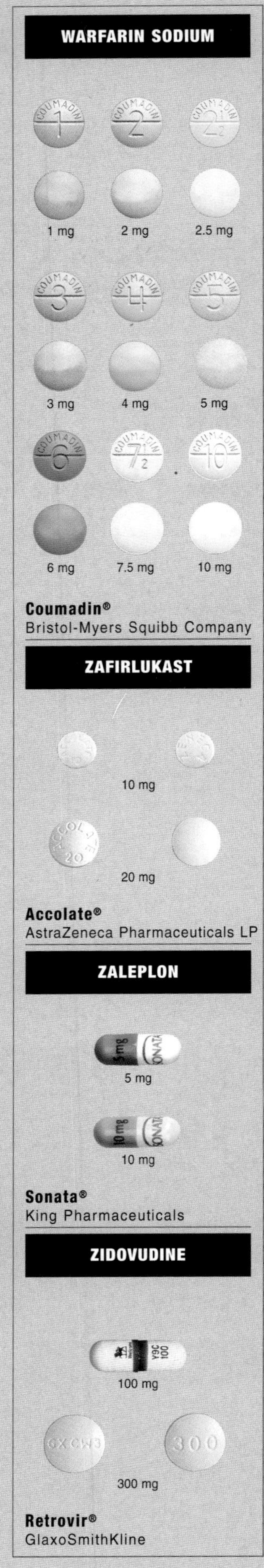

WARFARIN SODIUM

1 mg　2 mg　2.5 mg

3 mg　4 mg　5 mg

6 mg　7.5 mg　10 mg

Coumadin®
Bristol-Myers Squibb Company

ZAFIRLUKAST

10 mg

20 mg

Accolate®
AstraZeneca Pharmaceuticals LP

ZALEPLON

5 mg

10 mg

Sonata®
King Pharmaceuticals

ZIDOVUDINE

100 mg

300 mg

Retrovir®
GlaxoSmithKline

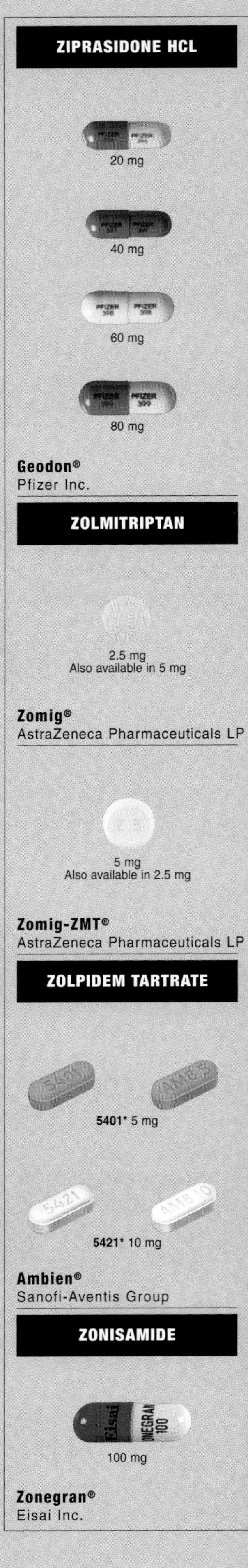

ZIPRASIDONE HCL

20 mg

40 mg

60 mg

80 mg

Geodon®
Pfizer Inc.

ZOLMITRIPTAN

2.5 mg
Also available in 5 mg

Zomig®
AstraZeneca Pharmaceuticals LP

5 mg
Also available in 2.5 mg

Zomig-ZMT®
AstraZeneca Pharmaceuticals LP

ZOLPIDEM TARTRATE

5401* 5 mg

5421* 10 mg

Ambien®
Sanofi-Aventis Group

ZONISAMIDE

100 mg

Zonegran®
Eisai Inc.

* Manufacturer's Identification Code

Appendix III

THERAPEUTIC GUIDELINES

Hyperlipidemia

Since the publication of the third report of the National Cholesterol Education Program Expert Panel on Detection, Evaluation, and Treatment of High Blood Cholesterol in Adults (Adult Treatment Panel III) in 2001, five major clinical trials of statin therapy have been published. The following guidelines for the treatment of high blood cholesterol are recommended:

Therapeutic lifestyle changes (TLC), especially reduction in dietary intake of saturated fat and cholesterol, use of plant stanols/sterols and viscous (soluble) fiber, smoking cessation, control of hypertension, weight reduction, increase in physical activity, and improved nutrition, remain essential in clinical management for all patients and as an adjunct to all pharmacologic therapy.

The trials confirm the benefit of cholesterol-lowering therapy in high-risk patients and support the ATP-III treatment goal of low-density lipoprotein cholesterol (LDL-C) $<$ 100 milligrams per deciliter (mg/dL). The trials support the inclusion of patients with diabetes in the high-risk category and confirm the benefits of LDL-lowering therapy in these patients. Furthermore, the trials confirm that older persons (aged 65 years and older) benefit from therapeutic lowering of LDL-C.

The major classes of medications available for pharmacologic therapy are HMG-CoA reductase inhibitors (atorvastatin, fluvastatin, lovastatin, pravastatin, simvastatin), bile acid sequestrants (cholestyramine, colesevelam, colestipol), nicotinic acid, and fibric acid derivatives (clofibrate, fenofibrate, gemfibrozil).

The HMG-CoA reductase inhibitors should be considered as first-line medication when LDL-lowering medications are indicated to achieve LDL treatment goals.

Bile acid sequestrants should be considered as LDL-lowering therapy for:

- persons with moderate elevations in LDL cholesterol
- younger persons with elevated LDL cholesterol
- women with elevated LDL cholesterol who are considering pregnancy
- persons needing only modest reductions of LDL cholesterol to achieve target goals
- combination therapy with HMG-CoA reductase inhibitors in persons with very high LDL-cholesterol concentrations

Nicotinic acid is useful for patients with moderately elevated LDL cholesterol concentrations combined with an increase in triglycerides and low high-density lipoprotein (HDL) cholesterol concentrations.

The fibric acid derivatives are primarily effective in lowering very high triglyceride concentrations to reduce the risk of pancreatitis and, to a lesser extent, increasing HDL cholesterol concentrations.

If patient response to initial medication therapy is not adequate after 6 weeks, treatment should be intensified or the patient may be switched to another class of medication or to a combination of two medications. Most antihyperlipidemic agents may be used in combination. The combination of a bile acid sequestrant with either nicotinic acid or an HMG-CoA reductase inhibitor may be particularly effective. The use of an HMG-CoA reductase inhibitor plus a fibric acid derivative increases the risk of myopathy.

In postmenopausal women, hormone replacement therapy cannot be recommended for the express purpose of preventing CHD.

Consultation with a lipid specialist may be necessary in cases of unusually severe, complex, or refractory lipid disorders.

Reference: National Cholesterol Education Program: Third Report on the National Cholesterol Education Program (NCEP) Expert Panel on Detection, Evaluation, and Treatment of High Blood Cholesterol in Adults (Adult Treatment Panel III), Final Report. NIH Publication No. 02-5215 (September) 2002.

Grundy SM, Cleeman JI, Merz CN et al: Implications of recent clinical trials for the national cholesterol education program adult treatment panel III guidelines. Circulation 2004; 110:227-239.

Hypertension

In the seventh report of the Joint National Committee on the Detection, Evaluation, and Treatment of High Blood Pressure (JNC 7), management of blood pressure in adults includes life-style modifications for all patients. Initial drug therapy should be considered for patients classified with prehypertension (120-139/80-89 mm Hg) with compelling indications (heart failure, post-myocardial infarction, high coronary disease risk, dia betes, chronic kidney disease, or recurrent stroke prevention), stage 1 hypertension (140-159/90-99 mm Hg), or stage 2 hypertension ($\geq$160/$\geq$100 mm Hg).

Life-style modifications decrease blood pressure, decrease cardiovascular risk, and enhance antihypertensive drug efficacy. Life-style modifications include weight reduction, adoption of Dietary Approaches to Stop Hypertension (DASH) eating plan, increased physical activity, smoking cessation, and moderation of dietary sodium and alcohol intake.

Thiazide diuretics should be used for initial drug treatment for most patients with uncomplicated hypertension. Certain high-risk conditions may require the initial use of other antihypertensive drug classes. Most patients with hypertension will require two or more antihypertensive medications to achieve their blood pressure goals. Consideration should be given to initiating therapy with two drugs when blood pressure is more than 20/10 mm Hg above goal. Caution is advised in patients at risk for orthostatic hypotension (diabetes, autonomic dysfunction) and some older persons.

In JNC 7, classes of agents with clinical outcome data that demonstrates blood pressure lowering efficacy and reduction of complications of hypertension include angiotensin-converting enzyme (ACE) inhibitors, angiotensin-receptor blockers (ARBs), beta-adrenergic blocking agents, calcium channel blockers (CCBs), and thiazide-type diuretics. Classes of other commonly used agents include loop diuretics, potassium-sparing diuretics, aldosteron e-receptor blockers, alpha1-blockers, central alpha2-agonists and other centrally acting drugs, or direct vasodilators.

Factors such as the cost of medication, side effects, drug interactions, concomitant diseases, additional risk factors, and other prescribed medications should be considered in choosing an initial antihypertensive agent. In addition, special population groups and situations such as ethnic, demographic, and other clinical situations should be considered in that choice.

Antihypertensives preferred for the treatment of hypertension during pregnancy include methyldopa, beta-blockers, or vasodilators.

The patient with hypertension and certain comorbidities require certain antihypertensive drug classes based on favorable outcome data from clinical trials.

- Hypertension + stable angina pectoris: beta-blockers or long-acting CCBs
- Hypertension + acute coronary syndromes (unstable angina or myocardial infarction): beta-blockers + ACE inhibitors + other drugs as needed for blood pressure control
- Hypertension + post-myocardial infarction: ACE inhibitors + beta-blockers + aldosterone antagonists
- Heart Failure (asymptomatic with demonstrable ventricular dysfunction): ACE inhibitors + beta-blockers
- Heart Failure (symptomatic ventricular dysfunction or end-stage heart disease): ACE inhibitors + beta-blockers + ARBs + aldosterone antagonists + loop diuretics
- Diabetic Hypertension: thiazide diuretics + beta-blockers + ACE inhibitors + ARBs + CCBs
- Chronic Kidney Disease: ACE inhibitors + ARBs
- Advanced Kidney Disease: loop diuretics + other drug classes
- Cerebrovascular Disease: ACE inhibitors + thiazide diuretics

Reference: The Seventh Report of the Joint National Committee on Prevention, Detection, Evaluation, and Treatment of High Blood Pressure (The JNC 7 Report). JAMA 2003; 289:2560-2572.

Appendix IV

COMBINATION CROSS-REFERENCE LISTING

The following alphabetic listing identifies the therapeutically active ingredients found in combination products included in the *USP DI*, along with a cross-reference to the title of the monograph where the specific combination product can be found.

Abacavir-containing Combinations
Abacavir, Lamivudine, and Zidovudine (Systemic), 7

Acetaminophen-containing Combinations
Acetaminophen, Aspirin, Salicylamide, and Caffeine (Systemic)—See *Acetaminophen and Salicylates (Systemic), #*
Acetaminophen, Aspirin, and Caffeine, Buffered (Systemic)—See *Acetaminophen and Salicylates (Systemic), #*
Acetaminophen, Aspirin, and Caffeine (Systemic)—See *Acetaminophen and Salicylates (Systemic), #*
Acetaminophen, Codeine, and Caffeine (Systemic)—See *Opioid (Narcotic) Analgesics and Acetaminophen (Systemic), 2215*
Acetaminophen, Salicylamide, and Caffeine (Systemic)—See *Acetaminophen and Salicylates (Systemic), #*
Acetaminophen, Sodium Bicarbonate, and Citric Acid (Systemic), #
Acetaminophen and Caffeine (Systemic)—See *Acetaminophen (Systemic), 15*
Acetaminophen and Codeine (Systemic)—See *Opioid (Narcotic) Analgesics and Acetaminophen (Systemic), 2215*
Brompheniramine, Pseudoephedrine, and Acetaminophen (Systemic)—See *Antihistamines, Decongestants, and Analgesics (Systemic), 358*
Butalbital, Acetaminophen, Caffeine, and Codeine (Systemic)—See *Barbiturates and Analgesics (Systemic), #*
Butalbital, Acetaminophen, and Caffeine (Systemic)—See *Barbiturates and Analgesics (Systemic), #*
Butalbital and Acetaminophen (Systemic)—See *Barbiturates and Analgesics (Systemic), #*
Chlorpheniramine, Phenindamine, Phenylephrine, Dextromethorphan, Acetaminophen, Salicylamide, Caffeine, and Ascorbic Acid (Systemic)—See *Cough/Cold Combinations (Systemic), #*
Chlorpheniramine, Phenylephrine, Acetaminophen, Salicylamide, and Caffeine (Systemic)—See *Antihistamines, Decongestants, and Analgesics (Systemic), 358*
Chlorpheniramine, Phenylephrine, Acetaminophen, and Salicylamide (Systemic)—See *Antihistamines, Decongestants, and Analgesics (Systemic), 358*
Chlorpheniramine, Phenylephrine, Dextromethorphan, Acetaminophen, and Salicylamide (Systemic)—See *Cough/Cold Combinations (Systemic), #*
Chlorpheniramine, Phenylephrine, Hydrocodone, Acetaminophen, and Caffeine (Systemic)—See *Cough/Cold Combinations (Systemic), #*
Chlorpheniramine, Phenylephrine, and Acetaminophen (Systemic)—See *Antihistamines, Decongestants, and Analgesics (Systemic), 358*
Chlorpheniramine, Pseudoephedrine, Codeine, and Acetaminophen (Systemic)—See *Cough/Cold Combinations (Systemic), #*
Chlorpheniramine, Pseudoephedrine, Dextromethorphan, and Acetaminophen (Systemic)—See *Cough/Cold Combinations (Systemic), #*
Chlorpheniramine, Pseudoephedrine, and Acetaminophen (Systemic)—See *Antihistamines, Decongestants, and Analgesics (Systemic), 358*
Dexbrompheniramine, Pseudoephedrine, and Acetaminophen (Systemic)—See *Antihistamines, Decongestants, and Analgesics (Systemic), 358*
Dextromethorphan and Acetaminophen (Systemic)—See *Cough/Cold Combinations (Systemic), #*
Dihydrocodeine, Acetaminophen, and Caffeine (Systemic)—See *Opioid (Narcotic) Analgesics and Acetaminophen (Systemic), 2215*
Diphenhydramine, Pseudoephedrine, and Acetaminophen (Systemic)—See *Antihistamines, Decongestants, and Analgesics (Systemic), 358*
Doxylamine, Codeine, and Acetaminophen (Systemic)—See *Cough/Cold Combinations (Systemic), #*
Doxylamine, Pseudoephedrine, Dextromethorphan, and Acetaminophen (Systemic)—See *Cough/Cold Combinations (Systemic), #*
Hydrocodone and Acetaminophen (Systemic)—See *Opioid (Narcotic) Analgesics and Acetaminophen (Systemic), 2215*
Isometheptene, Dichloralphenazone, and Acetaminophen (Systemic), 1739
Oxycodone and Acetaminophen (Systemic)—See *Opioid (Narcotic) Analgesics and Acetaminophen (Systemic), 2215*
Pentazocine and Acetaminophen (Systemic)—See *Opioid (Narcotic) Analgesics and Acetaminophen (Systemic), 2215*
Pheniramine, Phenylephrine, and Acetaminophen (Systemic)—See *Antihistamines, Decongestants, and Analgesics (Systemic), 358*
Phenylephrine, Guaifenesin, Acetaminophen, Salicylamide, and Caffeine (Systemic)—See *Cough/Cold Combinations (Systemic), #*
Phenylephrine and Acetaminophen (Systemic)—See *Decongestants and Analgesics (Systemic), 1035*
Propoxyphene and Acetaminophen (Systemic)—See *Opioid (Narcotic) Analgesics and Acetaminophen (Systemic), 2215*
Pseudoephedrine, Dextromethorphan, Guaifenesin, and Acetaminophen (Systemic)—See *Cough/Cold Combinations (Systemic), #*
Pseudoephedrine, Dextromethorphan, and Acetaminophen (Systemic)—See *Cough/Cold Combinations (Systemic), #*
Pseudoephedrine and Acetaminophen (Systemic)—See *Decongestants and Analgesics (Systemic), 1035*
Pyrilamine, Pseudoephedrine, Dextromethorphan, and Acetaminophen (Systemic)—See *Cough/Cold Combinations (Systemic), #*
Tramadol and Acetaminophen (Systemic), 2806
Triprolidine, Pseudoephedrine, and Acetaminophen (Systemic)—See *Antihistamines, Decongestants, and Analgesics (Systemic), 358*

Acetic Acid–containing Combinations
Desonide and Acetic Acid (Otic)—See *Corticosteroids and Acetic Acid (Otic), 937*
Hydrocortisone and Acetic Acid (Otic)—See *Corticosteroids and Acetic Acid (Otic), 937*

Acrivastine-containing Combinations
Acrivastine and Pseudoephedrine (Systemic)—See *Antihistamines and Decongestants (Systemic), 350*

Albuterol-containing Combinations
Ipratropium and Albuterol (Inhalation-Local), 1728
Ipratropium and Albuterol (Systemic), 1728

Alumina-containing Combinations
Alumina, Magnesia, Calcium Carbonate, and Simethicone (Oral-Local)—See *Antacids (Oral-Local), #*
Alumina, Magnesia, and Calcium Carbonate (Oral-Local)—See *Antacids (Oral-Local), #*
Alumina, Magnesia, and Simethicone (Oral-Local)—See *Antacids (Oral-Local), #*
Alumina, Magnesium Trisilicate, and Sodium Bicarbonate (Oral-Local)—See *Antacids (Oral-Local), #*
Alumina and Magnesia (Oral-Local)—See *Antacids (Oral-Local), #*
Alumina and Magnesium Carbonate (Oral-Local)—See *Antacids (Oral-Local), #*
Alumina and Magnesium Trisilicate (Oral-Local)—See *Antacids (Oral-Local), #*
Aspirin, Buffered (Systemic)—See *Salicylates (Systemic), 2574*
Aspirin and Codeine, Buffered (Systemic)—See *Opioid (Narcotic) Analgesics and Aspirin (Systemic), 2220*
Simethicone, Alumina, Magnesium Carbonate, and Magnesia (Oral-Local)—See *Antacids (Oral-Local), #*

Amiloride-containing Combinations
Amiloride and Hydrochlorothiazide (Systemic)—See *Diuretics, Potassium-sparing, and Hydrochlorothiazide (Systemic), 1125*

Aminobenzoic Acid-containing Combinations
Aminobenzoic Acid, Padimate O,and Oxybenzone (Topical)—See *Sunscreen Agents (Topical), #*
Aminobenzoic Acid and Titanium Dioxide (Topical)—See *Sunscreen Agents (Topical), #*

Amitriptyline-containing Combinations
Chlordiazepoxide and Amitriptyline (Systemic), #
Perphenazine and Amitriptyline (Systemic), #

Ammonium Chloride–containing Combinations
Bromodiphenhydramine, Diphenhydramine, Codeine, Ammonium Chloride, and Potassium Guaiacolsulfonate (Systemic)—See *Cough/Cold Combinations (Systemic), #*
Chlorpheniramine, Ephedrine, Phenylephrine, Dextromethorphan, Ammonium Chloride, and Ipecac (Systemic)—See *Cough/Cold Combinations (Systemic), #*
Chlorpheniramine, Phenylephrine, Codeine, and Ammonium Chloride (Systemic)—See *Cough/Cold Combinations (Systemic), #*
Chlorpheniramine, Phenylephrine, Dextromethorphan, Guaifenesin, and Ammonium Chloride (Systemic)—See *Cough/Cold Combinations (Systemic), #*
Codeine, Ammonium Chloride, and Guaifenesin (Systemic)—See *Cough/Cold Combinations (Systemic), #*
Diphenhydramine, Codeine, and Ammonium Chloride (Systemic)—See *Cough/Cold Combinations (Systemic), #*
Diphenhydramine, Dextromethorphan, and Ammonium Chloride (Systemic)—See *Cough/Cold Combinations (Systemic), #*
Pyrilamine, Phenylephrine, Hydrocodone, and Ammonium Chloride (Systemic)—See *Cough/Cold Combinations (Systemic), #*

Amobarbital-containing Combinations
Secobarbital and Amobarbital (Systemic)—See *Barbiturates (Systemic), 496*

Amoxicillin-containing Combinations
Amoxicillin and Clavulanate (Systemic)—See *Penicillins and Beta-Lactamase Inhibitors (Systemic), 2327*

Glucono-delta-lactone-containing Combinations
Citric Acid, Glucono-delta-lactone, and Magnesium (Mucosal-Local), #

Glyburide-containing Combinations
Glyburide and Metformin (Systemic), 1527

Glycerin-containing Combinations
Mineral Oil, Glycerin, and Phenolphthalein (Oral-Local)—See *Laxatives (Local), #*
Mineral Oil and Glycerin (Oral-Local)—See *Laxatives (Local), #*

Gramicidin-containing Combinations
Neomycin, Polymyxin B, and Gramicidin (Ophthalmic), 2069

Guaifenesin-containing Combinations
Chlorpheniramine, Ephedrine, and Guaifenesin (Systemic)—See *Cough/Cold Combinations (Systemic), #*
Chlorpheniramine, Phenylephrine, Dextromethorphan, Guaifenesin, and Ammonium Chloride (Systemic)—See *Cough/Cold Combinations (Systemic), #*
Chlorpheniramine, Phenylephrine, Dextromethorphan, and Guaifenesin (Systemic)—See *Cough/Cold Combinations (Systemic), #*
Chlorpheniramine, Phenylephrine, and Guaifenesin (Systemic)—See *Cough/Cold Combinations (Systemic), #*
Chlorpheniramine, Pseudoephedrine, Dextromethorphan, and Guaifenesin (Systemic)—See *Cough/Cold Combinations (Systemic), #*
Chlorpheniramine, Pseudoephedrine, and Guaifenesin (Systemic)—See *Cough/Cold Combinations (Systemic), #*
Codeine, Ammonium Chloride, and Guaifenesin (Systemic)—See *Cough/Cold Combinations (Systemic), #*
Codeine and Guaifenesin (Systemic)—See *Cough/Cold Combinations (Systemic), #*
Dexchlorpheniramine, Pseudoephedrine, and Guaifenesin (Systemic)—See *Cough/Cold Combinations (Systemic), #*
Dextromethorphan and Guaifenesin (Systemic)—See *Cough/Cold Combinations (Systemic), #*
Ephedrine, Carbetapentane, and Guaifenesin (Systemic)—See *Cough/Cold Combinations (Systemic), #*
Ephedrine and Guaifenesin (Systemic)—See *Cough/Cold Combinations (Systemic), #*
Hydrocodone and Guaifenesin (Systemic)—See *Cough/Cold Combinations (Systemic), #*
Hydromorphone and Guaifenesin (Systemic)—See *Cough/Cold Combinations (Systemic), #*
Oxtriphylline and Guaifenesin (Systemic), #
Pheniramine, Codeine, and Guaifenesin (Systemic)—See *Cough/Cold Combinations (Systemic), #*
Phenylephrine, Dextromethorphan, and Guaifenesin (Systemic)—See *Cough/Cold Combinations (Systemic), #*
Phenylephrine, Guaifenesin, Acetaminophen, Salicylamide, and Caffeine (Systemic)—See *Cough/Cold Combinations (Systemic), #*
Phenylephrine, Hydrocodone, and Guaifenesin (Systemic)—See *Cough/Cold Combinations (Systemic), #*
Phenylephrine and Guaifenesin (Systemic)—See *Cough/Cold Combinations (Systemic), #*
Pseudoephedrine, Codeine, and Guaifenesin (Systemic)—See *Cough/Cold Combinations (Systemic), #*
Pseudoephedrine, Dextromethorphan, Guaifenesin, and Acetaminophen (Systemic)—See *Cough/Cold Combinations (Systemic), #*
Pseudoephedrine, Dextromethorphan, and Guaifenesin (Systemic)—See *Cough/Cold Combinations (Systemic), #*
Pseudoephedrine, Hydrocodone, and Guaifenesin (Systemic)—See *Cough/Cold Combinations (Systemic), #*
Pseudoephedrine and Guaifenesin (Systemic)—See *Cough/Cold Combinations (Systemic), #*
Theophylline and Guaifenesin (Systemic), #
Triprolidine, Pseudoephedrine, Codeine, and Guaifenesin (Systemic)—See *Cough/Cold Combinations (Systemic), #*

Hepatitis A Virus Vaccine Inactived-containing
Hepatitis A Virus Vaccine Inactivated and Hepatitis B Virus Vaccine Recombinant (Systemic), 1563

Hepatitis B Virus Vaccine Recombinant-containing
Hepatitis A Virus Vaccine Inactivated and Hepatitis B Virus Vaccine Recombinant (Systemic), 1563

Homatropine-containing Combinations
Hydrocodone and Homatropine (Systemic)—See *Cough/Cold Combinations (Systemic), #*

Homosalate-containing Combinations
Homosalate, Menthyl Anthranilate, Octyl Methoxycinnamate, Octyl Salicylate, and Oxybenzone (Topical)—See *Sunscreen Agents (Topical), #*
Homosalate, Menthyl Anthranilate, and Octyl Methoxycinnamate (Topical)—See *Sunscreen Agents (Topical), #*
Homosalate, Octocrylene, Octyl Methoxycinnamate, and Oxybenzone (Topical)—See *Sunscreen Agents (Topical), #*
Homosalate, Octyl Methoxycinnamate, Octyl Salicylate, and Oxybenzone (Topical)—See *Sunscreen Agents (Topical), #*
Homosalate, Octyl Methoxycinnamate, and Oxybenzone (Topical)—See *Sunscreen Agents (Topical), #*
Homosalate and Oxybenzone (Topical)—See *Sunscreen Agents (Topical), #*

Hydralazine-containing Combinations
Hydralazine and Hydrochlorothiazide (Systemic), 1604
Reserpine, Hydralazine, and Hydrochlorothiazide (Systemic), #

Hydrochlorothiazide-containing Combinations
Benazepril and Hydrochlorothiazide (Systemic)—See *Angiotensin-converting Enzyme (ACE) Inhibitors and Hydrochlorothiazide (Systemic), 212*
Bisoprolol and Hydrochlorothiazide (Systemic)—See *Beta-adrenergic Blocking Agents and Thiazide Diuretics (Systemic), 563*
Candesartan and Hydrochlorothiazide (Systemic), 694
Captopril and Hydrochlorothiazide (Systemic)—See *Angiotensin-converting Enzyme (ACE) Inhibitors and Hydrochlorothiazide (Systemic), 212*
Deserpidine and Hydrochlorothiazide (Systemic)—See *Rauwolfia Alkaloids and Thiazide Diuretics (Systemic), #*
Enalapril and Hydrochlorothiazide (Systemic)—See *Angiotensin-converting Enzyme (ACE) Inhibitors and Hydrochlorothiazide (Systemic), 212*
Hydralazine and Hydrochlorothiazide (Systemic), 1604
Lisinopril and Hydrochlorothiazide (Systemic)—See *Angiotensin-converting Enzyme (ACE) Inhibitors and Hydrochlorothiazide (Systemic), 212*
Losartan and Hydrochlorothiazide (Systemic), 1865
Methyldopa and Hydrochlorothiazide (Systemic)—See *Methyldopa and Thiazide Diuretics (Systemic), #*
Metoprolol and Hydrochlorothiazide (Systemic)—See *Beta-adrenergic Blocking Agents and Thiazide Diuretics (Systemic), 563*
Moexipril and Hydrochlorothiazide (Systemic), #
Moexipril and Hydrochlorothiazide (Systemic)—See *Angiotensin-converting Enzyme (ACE) Inhibitors and Hydrochlorothiazide (Systemic), 212*
Olmesartan and Hydrochlorothiazide (Systemic), 2167
Pindolol and Hydrochlorothiazide (Systemic)—See *Beta-adrenergic Blocking Agents and Thiazide Diuretics (Systemic), 563*
Propranolol and Hydrochlorothiazide (Systemic)—See *Beta-adrenergic Blocking Agents and Thiazide Diuretics (Systemic), 563*
Quinapril and Hydrochlorothiazide (Systemic)—See *Angiotensin-converting Enzyme (ACE) Inhibitors and Hydrochlorothiazide (Systemic), 212*
Reserpine, Hydralazine, and Hydrochlorothiazide (Systemic), #
Reserpine and Hydrochlorothiazide (Systemic)—See *Rauwolfia Alkaloids and Thiazide Diuretics (Systemic), #*
Spironolactone and Hydrochlorothiazide (Systemic)—See *Diuretics, Potassium-sparing, and Hydrochlorothiazide (Systemic), 1125*
Telmisartan and Hydrochlorothiazide (Systemic), 2701
Timolol and Hydrochlorothiazide (Systemic)—See *Beta-adrenergic Blocking Agents and Thiazide Diuretics (Systemic), 563*
Triamterene and Hydrochlorothiazide (Systemic)—See *Diuretics, Potassium-sparing, and Hydrochlorothiazide (Systemic), 1125*
Valsartan and Hydrochlorothiazide (Systemic), 2863

Hydrocodone-containing Combinations
Chlorpheniramine, Pheniramine, Pyrilamine, Phenylephrine, Hydrocodone, Salicylamide, Caffeine, and Ascorbic Acid (Systemic)—See *Cough/Cold Combinations (Systemic), #*
Chlorpheniramine, Phenylephrine, Hydrocodone, Acetaminophen, and Caffeine (Systemic)—See *Cough/Cold Combinations (Systemic), #*
Chlorpheniramine, Phenylephrine, and Hydrocodone (Systemic)—See *Cough/Cold Combinations (Systemic), #*
Chlorpheniramine, Pseudoephedrine, and Hydrocodone (Systemic)—See *Cough/Cold Combinations (Systemic), #*
Chlorpheniramine and Hydrocodone (Systemic)—See *Cough/Cold Combinations (Systemic), #*
Doxylamine, Etafedrine, and Hydrocodone (Systemic)—See *Cough/Cold Combinations (Systemic), #*
Hydrocodone and Acetaminophen (Systemic)—See *Opioid (Narcotic) Analgesics and Acetaminophen (Systemic), 2215*
Hydrocodone and Aspirin (Systemic)—See *Opioid (Narcotic) Analgesics and Aspirin (Systemic), 2220*
Hydrocodone and Homatropine (Systemic)—See *Cough/Cold Combinations (Systemic), #*
Hydrocodone and Potassium Guaiacolsulfonate (Systemic)—See *Cough/Cold Combinations (Systemic), #*
Pheniramine, Pyrilamine, Hydrocodone, Potassium Citrate, and Ascorbic Acid (Systemic)—See *Cough/Cold Combinations (Systemic), #*
Phenylephrine, Hydrocodone, and Guaifenesin (Systemic)—See *Cough/Cold Combinations (Systemic), #*
Phenylephrine and Hydrocodone (Systemic)—See *Cough/Cold Combinations (Systemic), #*
Phenyltoloxamine and Hydrocodone (Systemic)—See *Cough/Cold Combinations (Systemic), #*
Pseudoephedrine, Hydrocodone, and Guaifenesin (Systemic)—See *Cough/Cold Combinations (Systemic), #*
Pseudoephedrine, Hydrocodone, and Potassium Guaiacolsulfonate (Systemic)—See *Cough/Cold Combinations (Systemic), #*
Pseudoephedrine and Hydrocodone (Systemic)—See *Cough/Cold Combinations (Systemic), #*
Pyrilamine, Phenylephrine, Hydrocodone, and Ammonium Chloride (Systemic)—See *Cough/Cold Combinations (Systemic), #*
Pyrilamine, Phenylephrine, and Hydrocodone (Systemic)—See *Cough/Cold Combinations (Systemic), #*

Hydrocortisone-containing Combinations
Clioquinol and Hydrocortisone (Topical), #
Colistin, Neomycin, and Hydrocortisone (Otic), #
Hydrocortisone and Acetic Acid (Otic)—See *Corticosteroids and Acetic Acid (Otic), 937*
Neomycin, Polymyxin B, and Hydrocortisone (Ophthalmic), 2070
Neomycin, Polymyxin B, and Hydrocortisone (Otic), 2072

Hydromorphone-containing Combinations
Hydromorphone and Guaifenesin (Systemic)—See *Cough/Cold Combinations (Systemic), #*

Hydroxyamphetamine-containing combinations
Hydroxyamphetamine and Tropicamide (Ophthalmic), #

Hyoscyamine-containing Combinations
Atropine, Hyoscyamine, Methenamine, Methylene Blue, Phenyl Salicylate, and Benzoic Acid (Systemic), #
Atropine, Hyoscyamine, Scopolamine, and Phenobarbital (Systemic)—See *Belladonna Alkaloids and Barbiturates (Systemic), 509*

Ibuprofen-containing Combinations
Pseudoephedrine and Ibuprofen (Systemic)—See *Decongestants and Analgesics (Systemic), 1035*

Imipenem-containing Combinations
Imipenem and Cilastatin (Systemic), 1638

Iodine-containing Combinations
Chlorpheniramine, Phenylephrine, Codeine, and Potassium Iodide (Systemic)—See *Cough/Cold Combinations (Systemic), #*
Codeine and Calcium Iodide (Systemic)—See *Cough/Cold Combinations (Systemic), #*
Codeine and Iodinated Glycerol (Systemic)—See *Cough/Cold Combinations (Systemic), #*
Dextromethorphan and Iodinated Glycerol (Systemic)—See *Cough/Cold Combinations (Systemic), #*
Ephedrine and Potassium Iodide (Systemic)—See *Cough/Cold Combinations (Systemic), #*

Iodipamide-containing Combinations
Diatrizoate and Iodipamide (Local), #

Ipecac-containing Combinations
Chlorpheniramine, Ephedrine, Phenylephrine, Dextromethorphan, Ammonium Chloride, and Ipecac (Systemic)—See *Cough/Cold Combinations (Systemic), #*

Ipratropium-containing Combinations
Ipratropium and Albuterol (Inhalation-Local), 1728
Ipratropium and Albuterol (Systemic), 1728

Isometheptene-containing Combinations
Isometheptene, Dichloralphenazone, and Acetaminophen (Systemic), 1739

Isoniazid-containing Combinations
Rifampin, Isoniazid, and Pyrazinamide (Systemic), 2528
Rifampin and Isoniazid (Systemic), 2526

Kaolin-containing Combinations
Kaolin and Pectin (Oral-Local), #

Lamivudine-containing Combinations
Abacavir, Lamivudine, and Zidovudine (Systemic), 7
Lamivudine and Zidovudine (Systemic), 1775

Levodopa-containing Combinations
Carbidopa and Levodopa (Systemic), 712

Levonordefrin-containing Combinations
Mepivacaine and Levonordefrin (Parenteral-Local)—See *Anesthetics (Parenteral-Local), 174*

Lidocaine-containing Combinations
Lidocaine and Dextrose (Parenteral-Local)—See *Anesthetics (Parenteral-Local), 174*
Lidocaine and Epinephrine (Parenteral-Local)—See *Anesthetics (Parenteral-Local), 174*
Lidocaine and Prilocaine (Topical), 1834

Lisadimate-containing Combinations
Lisadimate, Oxybenzone, and Padimate O (Topical)—See *Sunscreen Agents (Topical), #*
Lisadimate and Padimate O (Topical)—See *Sunscreen Agents (Topical), #*

Lisinopril-containing Combinations
Lisinopril and Hydrochlorothiazide (Systemic)—See *Angiotensin-converting Enzyme (ACE) Inhibitors and Hydrochlorothiazide (Systemic), 212*

Lopinavir-containing Combinations
Lopinavir and Ritonavir (Systemic), 1855

Loratadine-containing Combinations
Loratadine and Pseudoephedrine (Systemic)—See *Antihistamines and Decongestants (Systemic), 350*

Losartan-containing Combinations
Losartan and Hydrochlorothiazide (Systemic), 1865

Lovastatin-containing combinations
Niacin and Lovastatin (Systemic), 2106

Magaldrate-containing Combinations
Magaldrate and Simethicone (Oral-Local)—See *Antacids (Oral-Local), #*

Magnesia-containing Combinations
Alumina, Magnesia, Calcium Carbonate, and Simethicone (Oral-Local)—See *Antacids (Oral-Local), #*
Alumina, Magnesia, and Simethicone (Oral-Local)—See *Antacids (Oral-Local), #*
Alumina and Magnesia (Oral-Local)—See *Antacids (Oral-Local), #*
Aspirin, Buffered (Systemic)—See *Salicylates (Systemic), 2574*
Aspirin and Codeine, Buffered (Systemic)—See *Opioid (Narcotic) Analgesics and Aspirin (Systemic), 2220*
Calcium Carbonate, Magnesia, and Simethicone (Oral-Local)—See *Antacids (Oral-Local), #*
Calcium Carbonate and Magnesia (Oral-Local)—See *Antacids (Oral-Local), #*
Magnesium Hydroxide and Cascara Sagrada (Oral-Local)—See *Laxatives (Local), #*
Magnesium Hydroxide and Mineral Oil (Oral-Local)—See *Laxatives (Local), #*
Simethicone, Alumina, Magnesium Carbonate, and Magnesia (Oral-Local)—See *Antacids (Oral-Local), #*

Magnesium Carbonate–containing Combinations
Alumina and Magnesium Carbonate (Oral-Local)—See *Antacids (Oral-Local), #*
Calcium and Magnesium Carbonates (Oral-Local)—See *Antacids (Oral-Local), #*
Magnesium Carbonate and Sodium Bicarbonate (Oral-Local)—See *Antacids (Oral-Local), #*
Simethicone, Alumina, Magnesium Carbonate, and Magnesia (Oral-Local)—See *Antacids (Oral-Local), #*

Magnesium-containing Combinations
Citric Acid, Glucono-delta-lactone, and Magnesium (Mucosal-Local), #

Magnesium Oxide–containing Combinations
Aspirin, Buffered (Systemic)—See *Salicylates (Systemic), 2574*

Magnesium Salicylate–containing Combinations
Choline and Magnesium Salicylates (Systemic)—See *Salicylates (Systemic), 2574*

Magnesium Trisilicate–containing Combinations
Alumina, Magnesium Trisilicate, and Sodium Bicarbonate (Oral-Local)—See *Antacids (Oral-Local), #*
Alumina and Magnesium Trisilicate (Oral-Local)—See *Antacids (Oral-Local), #*

Malt Soup Extract–containing Combinations
Malt Soup Extract and Psyllium (Oral-Local)—See *Laxatives (Local), #*

Medroxyprogesterone–containing Combinations
Conjugated Estrogens and Medroxyprogesterone (Systemic)—See *Conjugated Estrogens and Medroxyprogesterone for Ovarian Hormone Therapy (OHT) (Systemic), 883*
Conjugated Estrogens (Systemic), and Conjugated Estrogens and Medroxyprogesterone (Systemic)—See *Conjugated Estrogens and Medroxyprogesterone for Ovarian Hormone Therapy (OHT) (Systemic), 883*
Medroxyprogesterone and Estradiol (Systemic), 1900

Menthyl Anthranilate-containing Combinations
Homosalate, Menthyl Anthranilate, Octyl Methoxycinnamate, Octyl Salicylate, and Oxybenzone (Topical)—See *Sunscreen Agents (Topical), #*
Homosalate, Menthyl Anthranilate, Octyl Methoxycinnamate, and Octyl Salicylate (Topical)—See *Sunscreen Agents (Topical), #*

Menthyl Anthranilate-containing Combinations *(continued)*
Homosalate, Menthyl Anthranilate, Octyl Methoxycinnamate, and Oxybenzone (Topical)—See *Sunscreen Agents (Topical), #*
Homosalate, Menthyl Anthranilate, and Octyl Methoxycinnamate (Topical)—See *Sunscreen Agents (Topical), #*
Menthyl Anthranilate, Octocrylene, Octyl Methoxycinnamate, and Oxybenzone (Topical)—See *Sunscreen Agents (Topical), #*
Menthyl Anthranilate, Octocrylene, and Octyl Methoxycinnamate (Topical)—See *Sunscreen Agents (Topical), #*
Menthyl Anthranilate, Octyl Methoxycinnamate, Octyl Salicylate, and Oxybenzone (Topical)—See *Sunscreen Agents (Topical), #*
Menthyl Anthranilate, Octyl Methoxycinnamate, and Octyl Salicylate (Topical)—See *Sunscreen Agents (Topical), #*
Menthyl Anthranilate, Octyl Methoxycinnamate, and Oxybenzone (Topical)—See *Sunscreen Agents (Topical), #*
Menthyl Anthranilate and Octyl Methoxycinnamate (Topical)—See *Sunscreen Agents (Topical), #*
Menthyl Anthranilate and Padimate O (Topical)—See *Sunscreen Agents (Topical), #*
Menthyl Anthranilate and Titanium Dioxide (Topical)—See *Sunscreen Agents (Topical), #*

Mepivacaine-containing Combinations
Mepivacaine and Levonordefrin (Parenteral-Local)—See *Anesthetics (Parenteral-Local), 174*

Meprobamate-containing Combinations
Meprobamate and Aspirin (Systemic), #

Mequinol-containing Combinations
Mequinol and Tretinoin (Topical), 1923

Mestranol–containing Combinations
Norethindrone and Mestranol (Systemic)—See *Estrogens and Progestins (Systemic), 1310*

Metformin-containing Combinations
Glyburide and Metformin (Systemic), 1527
Metformin and Pioglitazone (Systemic), 1943

Methenamine-containing Combinations
Atropine, Hyoscyamine, Methenamine, Methylene Blue, Phenyl Salicylate, and Benzoic Acid (Systemic), #

Methscopolamine-containing Combinations
Chlorpheniramine, Phenylephrine, and Methscopolamine (Systemic)—See *Antihistamines, Decongestants, and Anticholinergics (Systemic), 361*
Chlorpheniramine, Pseudoephedrine, and Methscopolamine (Systemic)—See *Antihistamines, Decongestants, and Anticholinergics (Systemic), 361*

Methyclothiazide-containing Combinations
Deserpidine and Methyclothiazide (Systemic)—See *Rauwolfia Alkaloids and Thiazide Diuretics (Systemic), #*
Reserpine and Methyclothiazide (Systemic)—See *Rauwolfia Alkaloids and Thiazide Diuretics (Systemic), #*

Methyldopa-containing Combinations
Methyldopa and Chlorothiazide (Systemic)—See *Methyldopa and Thiazide Diuretics (Systemic), #*
Methyldopa and Hydrochlorothiazide (Systemic)—See *Methyldopa and Thiazide Diuretics (Systemic), #*

Methylene Blue–containing Combinations
Atropine, Hyoscyamine, Methenamine, Methylene Blue, Phenyl Salicylate, and Benzoic Acid (Systemic), #

Methyltestosterone-containing Combinations
Conjugated Estrogens and Methyltestosterone (Systemic)—See *Androgens and Estrogens (Systemic), 163*
Diethylstilbestrol and Methyltestosterone (Systemic)—See *Androgens and Estrogens (Systemic), 163*

Methyltestosterone-containing Combinations *(continued)*
Esterified Estrogens and Methyltestosterone (Systemic)—See *Androgens and Estrogens (Systemic), 163*

Metoprolol-containing Combinations
Metoprolol and Hydrochlorothiazide (Systemic)—See *Beta-adrenergic Blocking Agents and Thiazide Diuretics (Systemic), 563*

Mineral Oil–containing Combinations
Magnesium Hydroxide and Mineral Oil (Oral-Local)—See *Laxatives (Local), #*
Mineral Oil, Glycerin, and Phenolphthalein (Oral-Local)—See *Laxatives (Local), #*
Mineral Oil and Cascara Sagrada (Oral-Local)—See *Laxatives (Local), #*
Mineral Oil and Glycerin (Oral-Local)—See *Laxatives (Local), #*
Mineral Oil and Phenolphthalein (Oral-Local)—See *Laxatives (Local), #*

Misoprostol-containing Combinations
Diclofenac and Misoprostol (Systemic), 1062

Moexipril-containing Combinations
Moexipril and Hydrochlorothiazide (Systemic), #
Moexipril and Hydrochlorothiazide (Systemic)—See *Angiotensin-converting Enzyme (ACE) Inhibitors and Hydrochlorothiazide (Systemic), 212*

Nadolol-containing Combinations
Nadolol and Bendroflumethiazide (Systemic)—See *Beta-adrenergic Blocking Agents and Thiazide Diuretics (Systemic), 563*

Naloxone-containing Combinations
Pentazocine and Naloxone (Systemic)—See *Opioid (Narcotic) Analgesics (Systemic), 2184*

Neomycin-containing Combinations
Colistin, Neomycin, and Hydrocortisone (Otic), #
Neomycin, Polymyxin B, and Bacitracin (Ophthalmic), 2067
Neomycin, Polymyxin B, and Bacitracin (Topical), 2068
Neomycin, Polymyxin B, and Gramicidin (Ophthalmic), 2069
Neomycin, Polymyxin B, and Hydrocortisone (Ophthalmic), 2070
Neomycin, Polymyxin B, and Hydrocortisone (Otic), 2072
Neomycin and Polymyxin B (Topical), 2066

Niacin-containing combinations
Niacin and Lovastatin (Systemic), 2106

Norelgestromin-containing combinations
Norelgestromin and Ethinyl Estradiol (Systemic), 2140

Norethindrone-containing Combinations
Norethindrone and Estradiol (Systemic)—See *Estrogens and Progestins (Ovarian Hormone Therapy) (Systemic), 1306*
Norethindrone and Ethinyl Estradiol (Systemic)—See *Estrogens and Progestins (Ovarian Hormone Therapy) (Systemic), 1306*

Norgestimate–containing Combinations
Norgestimate and 17 Beta-Estradiol (Systemic)—See *Estrogens and Progestins (Ovarian Hormone Therapy) (Systemic), 1306*

Nystatin-containing Combinations
Nystatin and Triamcinolone (Topical), 2150

Octocrylene-containing Combinations
Avobenzone, Octocrylene, Octyl Salicylate, and Oxybenzone (Topical)—See *Sunscreen Agents (Topical), #*
Homosalate, Octocrylene, Octyl Methoxycinnamate, and Oxybenzone (Topical)—See *Sunscreen Agents (Topical), #*
Menthyl Anthranilate, Octocrylene, Octyl Methoxycinnamate, and Oxybenzone (Topical)—See *Sunscreen Agents (Topical), #*
Menthyl Anthranilate, Octocrylene, and Octyl Methoxycinnamate (Topical)—See *Sunscreen Agents (Topical), #*
Octocrylene, Octyl Methoxycinnamate, Octyl Salicylate, Oxybenzone, and Titanium Dioxide (Topical)—See *Sunscreen Agents (Topical), #*

Octocrylene-containing Combinations *(continued)*
Octocrylene, Octyl Methoxycinnamate, Octyl Salicylate, and Oxybenzone (Topical)—See *Sunscreen Agents (Topical), #*
Octocrylene, Octyl Methoxycinnamate, Oxybenzone, and Titanium Dioxide (Topical)—See *Sunscreen Agents (Topical), #*
Octocrylene, Octyl Methoxycinnamate, and Oxybenzone (Topical)—See *Sunscreen Agents (Topical), #*
Octocrylene, Octyl Methoxycinnamate, and Titanium Dioxide (Topical)—See *Sunscreen Agents (Topical), #*
Octocrylene and Octyl Methoxycinnamate (Topical)—See *Sunscreen Agents (Topical), #*

Octyl Methoxycinnamate-containing Combinations
Avobenzone, Octyl Methoxycinnamate, Octyl Salicylate, and Oxybenzone (Topical)—See *Sunscreen Agents (Topical), #*
Avobenzone, Octyl Methoxycinnamate, and Oxybenzone (Topical)—See *Sunscreen Agents (Topical), #*
Avobenzone and Octyl Methoxycinnamate (Topical)—See *Sunscreen Agents (Topical), #*
Homosalate, Menthyl Anthranilate, Octyl Methoxycinnamate, Octyl Salicylate, and Oxybenzone (Topical)—See *Sunscreen Agents (Topical), #*
Homosalate, Menthyl Anthranilate, and Octyl Methoxycinnamate (Topical)—See *Sunscreen Agents (Topical), #*
Homosalate, Octocrylene, Octyl Methoxycinnamate, and Oxybenzone (Topical)—See *Sunscreen Agents (Topical), #*
Homosalate, Octyl Methoxycinnamate, Octyl Salicylate, and Oxybenzone (Topical)—See *Sunscreen Agents (Topical), #*
Homosalate, Octyl Methoxycinnamate, and Oxybenzone (Topical)—See *Sunscreen Agents (Topical), #*
Menthyl Anthranilate, Octocrylene, Octyl Methoxycinnamate, and Oxybenzone (Topical)—See *Sunscreen Agents (Topical), #*
Menthyl Anthranilate, Octocrylene, and Octyl Methoxycinnamate (Topical)—See *Sunscreen Agents (Topical), #*
Menthyl Anthranilate, Octyl Methoxycinnamate, Octyl Salicylate, and Oxybenzone (Topical)—See *Sunscreen Agents (Topical), #*
Menthyl Anthranilate, Octyl Methoxycinnamate, and Octyl Salicylate (Topical)—See *Sunscreen Agents (Topical), #*
Menthyl Anthranilate, Octyl Methoxycinnamate, and Oxybenzone (Topical)—See *Sunscreen Agents (Topical), #*
Menthyl Anthranilate and Octyl Methoxycinnamate (Topical)—See *Sunscreen Agents (Topical), #*
Octocrylene, Octyl Methoxycinnamate, Octyl Salicylate, Oxybenzone, and Titanium Dioxide (Topical)—See *Sunscreen Agents (Topical), #*
Octocrylene, Octyl Methoxycinnamate, Octyl Salicylate, and Oxybenzone (Topical)—See *Sunscreen Agents (Topical), #*
Octocrylene, Octyl Methoxycinnamate, Oxybenzone, and Titanium Dioxide (Topical)—See *Sunscreen Agents (Topical), #*
Octocrylene, Octyl Methoxycinnamate, and Oxybenzone (Topical)—See *Sunscreen Agents (Topical), #*
Octocrylene, Octyl Methoxycinnamate, and Titanium Dioxide (Topical)—See *Sunscreen Agents (Topical), #*
Octocrylene and Octyl Methoxycinnamate (Topical)—See *Sunscreen Agents (Topical), #*
Octyl Methoxycinnamate, Octyl Salicylate, Oxybenzone, Padimate O, and Titanium Dioxide (Topical)—See *Sunscreen Agents (Topical), #*
Octyl Methoxycinnamate, Octyl Salicylate, Oxybenzone, Phenylbenzimidazole, and Titanium Dioxide (Topical)—See *Sunscreen Agents (Topical), #*
Octyl Methoxycinnamate, Octyl Salicylate, Oxybenzone, and Padimate O (Topical)—See *Sunscreen Agents (Topical), #*

Octyl Methoxycinnamate-containing Combinations *(continued)*
Octyl Methoxycinnamate, Octyl Salicylate, Oxybenzone, and Titanium Dioxide (Topical)—See *Sunscreen Agents (Topical), #*
Octyl Methoxycinnamate, Octyl Salicylate, Phenylbenzimidazole, and Titanium Dioxide (Topical)—See *Sunscreen Agents (Topical), #*
Octyl Methoxycinnamate, Octyl Salicylate, and Oxybenzone (Topical)—See *Sunscreen Agents (Topical), #*
Octyl Methoxycinnamate, Octyl Salicylate, and Titanium Dioxide (Topical)—See *Sunscreen Agents (Topical), #*
Octyl Methoxycinnamate, Oxybenzone, Padimate O, and Titanium Dioxide (Topical)—See *Sunscreen Agents (Topical), #*
Octyl Methoxycinnamate, Oxybenzone, and Padimate O (Topical)—See *Sunscreen Agents (Topical), #*
Octyl Methoxycinnamate, Oxybenzone, and Titanium Dioxide (Topical)—See *Sunscreen Agents (Topical), #*
Octyl Methoxycinnamate and Octyl Salicylate (Topical)—See *Sunscreen Agents (Topical), #*
Octyl Methoxycinnamate and Oxybenzone (Topical)—See *Sunscreen Agents (Topical), #*
Octyl Methoxycinnamate and Padimate O (Topical)—See *Sunscreen Agents (Topical), #*
Octyl Methoxycinnamate and Phenylbenzimidazole (Topical)—See *Sunscreen Agents (Topical), #*

Octyl Salicylate-containing Combinations
Avobenzone, Octocrylene, Octyl Salicylate, and Oxybenzone (Topical)—See *Sunscreen Agents (Topical), #*
Avobenzone, Octyl Methoxycinnamate, Octyl Salicylate, and Oxybenzone (Topical)—See *Sunscreen Agents (Topical), #*
Homosalate, Menthyl Anthranilate, Octyl Methoxycinnamate, Octyl Salicylate, and Oxybenzone (Topical)—See *Sunscreen Agents (Topical), #*
Homosalate, Octyl Methoxycinnamate, Octyl Salicylate, and Oxybenzone (Topical)—See *Sunscreen Agents (Topical), #*
Menthyl Anthranilate, Octyl Methoxycinnamate, Octyl Salicylate, and Oxybenzone (Topical)—See *Sunscreen Agents (Topical), #*
Menthyl Anthranilate, Octyl Methoxycinnamate, and Octyl Salicylate (Topical)—See *Sunscreen Agents (Topical), #*
Octocrylene, Octyl Methoxycinnamate, Octyl Salicylate, Oxybenzone, and Titanium Dioxide (Topical)—See *Sunscreen Agents (Topical), #*
Octocrylene, Octyl Methoxycinnamate, Octyl Salicylate, and Oxybenzone (Topical)—See *Sunscreen Agents (Topical), #*
Octyl Methoxycinnamate, Octyl Salicylate, Oxybenzone, Padimate O, and Titanium Dioxide (Topical)—See *Sunscreen Agents (Topical), #*
Octyl Methoxycinnamate, Octyl Salicylate, Oxybenzone, Phenylbenzimidazole, and Titanium Dioxide (Topical)—See *Sunscreen Agents (Topical), #*
Octyl Methoxycinnamate, Octyl Salicylate, Oxybenzone, and Padimate O (Topical)—See *Sunscreen Agents (Topical), #*
Octyl Methoxycinnamate, Octyl Salicylate, Oxybenzone, and Titanium Dioxide (Topical)—See *Sunscreen Agents (Topical), #*
Octyl Methoxycinnamate, Octyl Salicylate, Phenylbenzimidazole, and Titanium Dioxide (Topical)—See *Sunscreen Agents (Topical), #*
Octyl Methoxycinnamate, Octyl Salicylate, and Oxybenzone (Topical)—See *Sunscreen Agents (Topical), #*
Octyl Methoxycinnamate, Octyl Salicylate, and Titanium Dioxide (Topical)—See *Sunscreen Agents (Topical), #*
Octyl Methoxycinnamate and Octyl Salicylate (Topical)—See *Sunscreen Agents (Topical), #*
Octyl Salicylate and Padimate O (Topical)—See *Sunscreen Agents (Topical), #*

Olmesartan-containing Combinations
Olmesartan and Hydrochlorothiazide (Systemic), 2167

Orphenadrine-containing Combinations
Orphenadrine, Aspirin, and Caffeine (Systemic)—See *Orphenadrine and Aspirin (Systemic), #*

Oxtriphylline-containing Combinations
Oxtriphylline and Guaifenesin (Systemic), #

Oxybenzone-containing Combinations
Aminobenzoic Acid, Padimate O,and Oxybenzone (Topical)—See *Sunscreen Agents (Topical), #*
Avobenzone, Octocrylene, Octyl Salicylate, and Oxybenzone—See *Sunscreen Agents (Topical), #*
Avobenzone, Octyl Methoxycinnamate, Octyl Salicylate, and Oxybenzone (Topical)—See *Sunscreen Agents (Topical), #*
Avobenzone, Octyl Methoxycinnamate, and Oxybenzone—See *Sunscreen Agents (Topical), #*
Dioxybenzone, Oxybenzone,and Padimate O (Topical)—See *Sunscreen Agents (Topical), #*
Homosalate, Menthyl Anthranilate, Octyl Methoxycinnamate, Octyl Salicylate, and Oxybenzone (Topical)—See *Sunscreen Agents (Topical), #*
Homosalate, Octocrylene, Octyl Methoxycinnamate, and Oxybenzone (Topical)—See *Sunscreen Agents (Topical), #*
Homosalate, Octyl Methoxycinnamate, Octyl Salicylate, and Oxybenzone (Topical)—See *Sunscreen Agents (Topical), #*
Homosalate, Octyl Methoxycinnamate, and Oxybenzone (Topical)—See *Sunscreen Agents (Topical), #*
Homosalate and Oxybenzone (Topical)—See *Sunscreen Agents (Topical), #*
Lisadimate, Oxybenzone, and Padimate O (Topical)—See *Sunscreen Agents (Topical), #*
Menthyl Anthranilate, Octocrylene, Octyl Methoxycinnamate, and Oxybenzone (Topical)—See *Sunscreen Agents (Topical), #*
Menthyl Anthranilate, Octyl Methoxycinnamate, Octyl Salicylate, and Oxybenzone (Topical)—See *Sunscreen Agents (Topical), #*
Menthyl Anthranilate, Octyl Methoxycinnamate, and Oxybenzone (Topical)—See *Sunscreen Agents (Topical), #*
Octocrylene, Octyl Methoxycinnamate, Octyl Salicylate, Oxybenzone, and Titanium Dioxide (Topical)—See *Sunscreen Agents (Topical), #*
Octocrylene, Octyl Methoxycinnamate, Octyl Salicylate, and Oxybenzone (Topical)—See *Sunscreen Agents (Topical), #*
Octocrylene, Octyl Methoxycinnamate, Oxybenzone, and Titanium Dioxide (Topical)—See *Sunscreen Agents (Topical), #*
Octocrylene, Octyl Methoxycinnamate, and Oxybenzone (Topical)—See *Sunscreen Agents (Topical), #*
Octyl Methoxycinnamate, Octyl Salicylate, Oxybenzone, Padimate O, and Titanium Dioxide (Topical)—See *Sunscreen Agents (Topical), #*
Octyl Methoxycinnamate, Octyl Salicylate, Oxybenzone, Phenylbenzimidazole, and Titanium Dioxide (Topical)—See *Sunscreen Agents (Topical), #*
Octyl Methoxycinnamate, Octyl Salicylate, Oxybenzone, and Padimate O (Topical)—See *Sunscreen Agents (Topical), #*
Octyl Methoxycinnamate, Octyl Salicylate, Oxybenzone, and Titanium Dioxide (Topical)—See *Sunscreen Agents (Topical), #*
Octyl Methoxycinnamate, Octyl Salicylate, and Oxybenzone (Topical)—See *Sunscreen Agents (Topical), #*
Octyl Methoxycinnamate, Oxybenzone, Padimate O, and Titanium Dioxide (Topical)—See *Sunscreen Agents (Topical), #*
Octyl Methoxycinnamate, Oxybenzone, and Padimate O (Topical)—See *Sunscreen Agents (Topical), #*
Octyl Methoxycinnamate, Oxybenzone, and Titanium Dioxide (Topical)—See *Sunscreen Agents (Topical), #*
Octyl Methoxycinnamate and Oxybenzone (Topical)—See *Sunscreen Agents (Topical), #*
Oxybenzone and Padimate O (Topical)—See *Sunscreen Agents (Topical), #*
Oxybenzone and Roxadimate (Topical)—See *Sunscreen Agents (Topical), #*

Oxycodone-containing Combinations
Oxycodone and Acetaminophen (Systemic)—See *Opioid (Narcotic) Analgesics and Acetaminophen (Systemic), 2215*
Oxycodone and Aspirin (Systemic)—See *Opioid (Narcotic) Analgesics and Aspirin (Systemic), 2220*

Padimate O-containing Combinations
Aminobenzoic Acid, Padimate O,and Oxybenzone (Topical)—See *Sunscreen Agents (Topical), #*
Dioxybenzone, Oxybenzone,and Padimate O (Topical)—See *Sunscreen Agents (Topical), #*
Lisadimate, Oxybenzone, and Padimate O (Topical)—See *Sunscreen Agents (Topical), #*
Lisadimate and Padimate O (Topical)—See *Sunscreen Agents (Topical), #*
Menthyl Anthranilate and Padimate O (Topical)—See *Sunscreen Agents (Topical), #*
Octyl Methoxycinnamate, Octyl Salicylate, Oxybenzone, Padimate O, and Titanium Dioxide (Topical)—See *Sunscreen Agents (Topical), #*
Octyl Methoxycinnamate, Octyl Salicylate, Oxybenzone, and Padimate O (Topical)—See *Sunscreen Agents (Topical), #*
Octyl Methoxycinnamate, Oxybenzone, Padimate O, and Titanium Dioxide (Topical)—See *Sunscreen Agents (Topical), #*
Octyl Methoxycinnamate, Oxybenzone, and Padimate O (Topical)—See *Sunscreen Agents (Topical), #*
Octyl Methoxycinnamate and Padimate O (Topical)—See *Sunscreen Agents (Topical), #*
Octyl Salicylate and Padimate O (Topical)—See *Sunscreen Agents (Topical), #*
Oxybenzone and Padimate O (Topical)—See *Sunscreen Agents (Topical), #*

Pectin-containing Combinations
Kaolin and Pectin (Oral-Local), #

Pentazocine-containing Combinations
Pentazocine and Acetaminophen (Systemic)—See *Opioid (Narcotic) Analgesics and Acetaminophen (Systemic), 2215*
Pentazocine and Aspirin (Systemic)—See *Opioid (Narcotic) Analgesics and Aspirin (Systemic), 2220*
Pentazocine and Naloxone (Systemic)—See *Opioid (Narcotic) Analgesics (Systemic), 2184*

Pentobarbital-containing Combinations
Ergotamine, Caffeine, Belladonna Alkaloids, and Pentobarbital (Systemic)—See *Vascular Headache Suppressants, Ergot Derivative–containing (Systemic), #*

Perphenazine-containing Combinations
Perphenazine and Amitriptyline (Systemic), #

Phenazopyridine-containing Combinations
Sulfamethoxazole and Phenazopyridine (Systemic)—See *Sulfonamides and Phenazopyridine (Systemic), #*
Sulfisoxazole and Phenazopyridine (Systemic)—See *Sulfonamides and Phenazopyridine (Systemic), #*

Phenindamine-containing Combinations
Chlorpheniramine, Phenindamine, Phenylephrine, Dextromethorphan, Acetaminophen, Salicylamide, Caffeine, and Ascorbic Acid (Systemic)—See *Cough/Cold Combinations (Systemic), #*

Pheniramine-containing Combinations
Chlorpheniramine, Pheniramine, Pyrilamine, Phenylephrine, Hydrocodone, Salicylamide, Caffeine, and Ascorbic Acid (Systemic)—See *Cough/Cold Combinations (Systemic), #*
Pheniramine, Codeine, and Guaifenesin (Systemic)—See *Cough/Cold Combinations (Systemic), #*
Pheniramine, Phenylephrine, Codeine, Sodium Citrate, Sodium Salicylate, and Caffeine (Systemic)—See *Cough/Cold Combinations (Systemic), #*
Pheniramine, Phenylephrine, Sodium Salicylate, and Caffeine (Systemic)—See *Antihistamines, Decongestants, and Analgesics (Systemic), 358*

Pheniramine-containing Combinations *(continued)*
Pheniramine, Phenylephrine, and Acetaminophen (Systemic)—See *Antihistamines, Decongestants, and Analgesics (Systemic), 358*
Pheniramine, Phenylephrine, and Dextromethorphan (Systemic)—See *Cough/Cold Combinations (Systemic), #*
Pheniramine, Pyrilamine, Hydrocodone, Potassium Citrate, and Ascorbic Acid (Systemic)—See *Cough/Cold Combinations (Systemic), #*
Pheniramine and Phenylephrine (Systemic)—See *Antihistamines and Decongestants (Systemic), 350*

Phenobarbital-containing Combinations
Atropine, Hyoscyamine, Scopolamine, and Phenobarbital (Systemic)—See *Belladonna Alkaloids and Barbiturates (Systemic), 509*
Atropine and Phenobarbital (Systemic)—See *Belladonna Alkaloids and Barbiturates (Systemic), 509*
Phenobarbital, ASA, and Codeine (Systemic)—See *Barbiturates and Analgesics (Systemic), #*
Theophylline, Ephedrine, and Phenobarbital (Systemic), #

Phenolphthalein-containing Combinations
Cascara Sagrada and Phenolphthalein (Oral-Local)—See *Laxatives (Local), #*
Dehydrocholic Acid, Docusate, and Phenolphthalein (Oral-Local)—See *Laxatives (Local), #*
Docusate and Phenolphthalein (Oral-Local)—See *Laxatives (Local), #*
Mineral Oil, Glycerin, and Phenolphthalein (Oral-Local)—See *Laxatives (Local), #*
Mineral Oil and Phenolphthalein (Oral-Local)—See *Laxatives (Local), #*
Phenolphthalein and Senna (Oral-Local)—See *Laxatives (Local), #*

Phenylbenzimidazole-containing Combinations
Octyl Methoxycinnamate, Octyl Salicylate, Oxybenzone, Phenylbenzimidazole, and Titanium Dioxide (Topical)—See *Sunscreen Agents (Topical), #*
Octyl Methoxycinnamate, Octyl Salicylate, Phenylbenzimidazole, and Titanium Dioxide (Topical)—See *Sunscreen Agents (Topical), #*
Octyl Methoxycinnamate and Phenylbenzimidazole (Topical)—See *Sunscreen Agents (Topical), #*
Phenylbenzimidazole and Sulisobenzone (Topical)—See *Sunscreen Agents (Topical), #*

Phenylephrine-containing Combinations
Brompheniramine and Phenylephrine (Systemic)—See *Antihistamines and Decongestants (Systemic), 350*
Chlorpheniramine, Ephedrine, Phenylephrine, Dextromethorphan, Ammonium Chloride, and Ipecac (Systemic)—See *Cough/Cold Combinations (Systemic), #*
Chlorpheniramine, Ephedrine, Phenylephrine, and Carbetapentane (Systemic)—See *Cough/Cold Combinations (Systemic), #*
Chlorpheniramine, Phenindamine, Phenylephrine, Dextromethorphan, Acetaminophen, Salicylamide, Caffeine, and Ascorbic Acid (Systemic)—See *Cough/Cold Combinations (Systemic), #*
Chlorpheniramine, Pheniramine, Pyrilamine, Phenylephrine, Hydrocodone, Salicylamide, Caffeine, and Ascorbic Acid (Systemic)—See *Cough/Cold Combinations (Systemic), #*
Chlorpheniramine, Phenylephrine, Acetaminophen, Salicylamide, and Caffeine (Systemic)—See *Antihistamines, Decongestants, and Analgesics (Systemic), 358*
Chlorpheniramine, Phenylephrine, Acetaminophen, and Salicylamide (Systemic)—See *Antihistamines, Decongestants, and Analgesics (Systemic), 358*
Chlorpheniramine, Phenylephrine, Codeine, and Ammonium Chloride (Systemic)—See *Cough/Cold Combinations (Systemic), #*
Chlorpheniramine, Phenylephrine, Codeine, and Potassium Iodide (Systemic)—See *Cough/Cold Combinations (Systemic), #*

Phenylephrine-containing Combinations *(continued)*

Chlorpheniramine, Phenylephrine, Dextromethorphan, Acetaminophen, and Salicylamide (Systemic)—See *Cough/Cold Combinations (Systemic), #*

Chlorpheniramine, Phenylephrine, Dextromethorphan, Guaifenesin, and Ammonium Chloride (Systemic)—See *Cough/Cold Combinations (Systemic), #*

Chlorpheniramine, Phenylephrine, Dextromethorphan, and Guaifenesin (Systemic)—See *Cough/Cold Combinations (Systemic), #*

Chlorpheniramine, Phenylephrine, Hydrocodone, Acetaminophen, and Caffeine (Systemic)—See *Cough/Cold Combinations (Systemic), #*

Chlorpheniramine, Phenylephrine, and Acetaminophen (Systemic)—See *Antihistamines, Decongestants, and Analgesics (Systemic), 358*

Chlorpheniramine, Phenylephrine, and Dextromethorphan (Systemic)—See *Cough/Cold Combinations (Systemic), #*

Chlorpheniramine, Phenylephrine, and Guaifenesin (Systemic)—See *Cough/Cold Combinations (Systemic), #*

Chlorpheniramine, Phenylephrine, and Hydrocodone (Systemic)—See *Cough/Cold Combinations (Systemic), #*

Chlorpheniramine, Phenylephrine, and Methscopolamine (Systemic)—See *Antihistamines, Decongestants, and Anticholinergics (Systemic), 361*

Chlorpheniramine, Phenyltoloxamine, and Phenylephrine (Systemic)—See *Antihistamines and Decongestants (Systemic), 350*

Chlorpheniramine, Pyrilamine, Phenylephrine, and Acetaminophen (Systemic)—See *Antihistamines, Decongestants, and Analgesics (Systemic), 358*

Chlorpheniramine, Pyrilamine, and Phenylephrine (Systemic)—See *Antihistamines and Decongestants (Systemic), 350*

Chlorpheniramine and Phenylephrine (Systemic)—See *Antihistamines and Decongestants (Systemic), 350*

Diphenhydramine, Phenylephrine, and Dextromethorphan (Systemic)—See *Cough/Cold Combinations (Systemic), #*

Diphenylpyraline, Phenylephrine, and Dextromethorphan (Systemic)—See *Cough/Cold Combinations (Systemic), #*

Pheniramine, Phenylephrine, Codeine, Sodium Citrate, Sodium Salicylate, and Caffeine (Systemic)—See *Cough/Cold Combinations (Systemic), #*

Pheniramine, Phenylephrine, Sodium Salicylate, and Caffeine (Systemic)—See *Antihistamines, Decongestants, and Analgesics (Systemic), 358*

Pheniramine, Phenylephrine, and Acetaminophen (Systemic)—See *Antihistamines, Decongestants, and Analgesics (Systemic), 358*

Pheniramine, Phenylephrine, and Dextromethorphan (Systemic)—See *Cough/Cold Combinations (Systemic), #*

Pheniramine and Phenylephrine (Systemic)—See *Antihistamines and Decongestants (Systemic), 350*

Phenylephrine, Hydrocodone, and Guaifenesin (Systemic)—See *Cough/Cold Combinations (Systemic), #*

Phenylephrine and Acetaminophen (Systemic)—See *Decongestants and Analgesics (Systemic), 1035*

Phenylephrine and Guaifenesin (Systemic)—See *Cough/Cold Combinations (Systemic), #*

Phenylephrine and Hydrocodone (Systemic)—See *Cough/Cold Combinations (Systemic), #*

Promethazine, Phenylephrine, and Codeine (Systemic)—See *Cough/Cold Combinations (Systemic), #*

Promethazine, Phenylephrine, and Potassium Guaiacolsulfonate (Systemic)—See *Cough/Cold Combinations (Systemic), #*

Promethazine and Phenylephrine (Systemic)—See *Antihistamines and Decongestants (Systemic), 350*

Phenylephrine-containing Combinations *(continued)*

Pyrilamine, Phenylephrine, Hydrocodone, and Ammonium Chloride (Systemic)—See *Cough/Cold Combinations (Systemic), #*

Pyrilamine, Phenylephrine, and Codeine (Systemic)—See *Cough/Cold Combinations (Systemic), #*

Pyrilamine, Phenylephrine, and Dextromethorphan (Systemic)—See *Cough/Cold Combinations (Systemic), #*

Pyrilamine, Phenylephrine, and Hydrocodone (Systemic)—See *Cough/Cold Combinations (Systemic), #*

Phenyl Salicylate–containing Combinations

Atropine, Hyoscyamine, Methenamine, Methylene Blue, Phenyl Salicylate, and Benzoic Acid (Systemic), #

Phenyltoloxamine-containing Combinations

Chlorpheniramine, Phenyltoloxamine, Ephedrine, Codeine, and Guaiacol Carbonate (Systemic)—See *Cough/Cold Combinations (Systemic), #*

Chlorpheniramine, Phenyltoloxamine, and Phenylephrine (Systemic)—See *Antihistamines and Decongestants (Systemic), 350*

Phenyltoloxamine and Hydrocodone (Systemic)—See *Cough/Cold Combinations (Systemic), #*

Pindolol-containing Combinations

Pindolol and Hydrochlorothiazide (Systemic)—See *Beta-adrenergic Blocking Agents and Thiazide Diuretics (Systemic), 563*

Piperacillin-containing Combinations

Piperacillin and Tazobactam (Systemic)—See *Penicillins and Beta-lactamase Inhibitors (Systemic), 2327*

Polymyxin B–containing Combinations

Neomycin, Polymyxin B, and Bacitracin (Ophthalmic), 2067

Neomycin, Polymyxin B, and Bacitracin (Topical), 2068

Neomycin, Polymyxin B, and Gramicidin (Ophthalmic), 2069

Neomycin, Polymyxin B, and Hydrocortisone (Ophthalmic), 2070

Neomycin, Polymyxin B, and Hydrocortisone (Otic), 2072

Neomycin and Polymyxin B (Topical), 2066

Polythiazide-containing Combinations

Prazosin and Polythiazide (Systemic), #

Potassium Guaiacolsulfonate–containing Combinations

Bromodiphenhydramine, Diphenhydramine, Codeine, Ammonium Chloride, and Potassium Guaiacolsulfonate (Systemic)—See *Cough/Cold Combinations (Systemic), #*

Hydrocodone and Potassium Guaiacolsulfonate (Systemic)—See *Cough/Cold Combinations (Systemic), #*

Promethazine, Codeine, and Potassium Guaiacolsulfonate (Systemic)—See *Cough/Cold Combinations (Systemic), #*

Promethazine, Phenylephrine, Codeine, and Potassium Guaiacolsulfonate (Systemic)—See *Cough/Cold Combinations (Systemic), #*

Promethazine, Phenylephrine, and Potassium Guaiacolsulfonate (Systemic)—See *Cough/Cold Combinations (Systemic), #*

Promethazine and Potassium Guaiacolsulfonate (Systemic)—See *Cough/Cold Combinations (Systemic), #*

Pseudoephedrine, Hydrocodone, and Potassium Guaiacolsulfonate (Systemic)—See *Cough/Cold Combinations (Systemic), #*

Prazosin-containing Combinations

Prazosin and Polythiazide (Systemic), #

Prilocaine-containing Combinations

Lidocaine and Prilocaine (Topical), 1834

Prilocaine and Epinephrine (Parenteral-Local)—See *Anesthetics (Parenteral-Local), 174*

Probenecid-containing Combinations

Probenecid and Colchicine (Systemic), 2419

Proguantil-containing Combinations

Atovaquone and Proguanil (Systemic), 463

Promethazine-containing Combinations

Promethazine, Codeine, and Potassium Guaiacolsulfonate (Systemic)—See *Cough/Cold Combinations (Systemic), #*

Promethazine, Phenylephrine, Codeine, and Potassium Guaiacolsulfonate (Systemic)—See *Cough/Cold Combinations (Systemic), #*

Promethazine, Phenylephrine, and Codeine (Systemic)—See *Cough/Cold Combinations (Systemic), #*

Promethazine, Phenylephrine, and Potassium Guaiacolsulfonate (Systemic)—See *Cough/Cold Combinations (Systemic), #*

Promethazine and Codeine (Systemic)—See *Cough/Cold Combinations (Systemic), #*

Promethazine and Dextromethorphan (Systemic)—See *Cough/Cold Combinations (Systemic), #*

Promethazine and Phenylephrine (Systemic)—See *Antihistamines and Decongestants (Systemic), 350*

Promethazine and Potassium Guaiacolsulfonate (Systemic)—See *Cough/Cold Combinations (Systemic), #*

Propoxyphene-containing Combinations

Propoxyphene, Aspirin, and Caffeine (Systemic)—See *Opioid (Narcotic) Analgesics and Aspirin (Systemic), 2220*

Propoxyphene and Acetaminophen (Systemic)—See *Opioid (Narcotic) Analgesics and Acetaminophen (Systemic), 2215*

Propoxyphene and Aspirin (Systemic)—See *Opioid (Narcotic) Analgesics and Aspirin (Systemic), 2220*

Propranolol-containing Combinations

Propranolol and Hydrochlorothiazide (Systemic)—See *Beta-adrenergic Blocking Agents and Thiazide Diuretics (Systemic), 563*

Pseudoephedrine-containing Combinations

Acrivastine and Pseudoephedrine (Systemic)—See *Antihistamines and Decongestants (Systemic), 350*

Azatadine and Pseudoephedrine (Systemic)—See *Antihistamines and Decongestants (Systemic), 350*

Brompheniramine, Pseudoephedrine, and Acetaminophen (Systemic)—See *Antihistamines, Decongestants, and Analgesics (Systemic), 358*

Brompheniramine, Pseudoephedrine, and Dextromethorphan (Systemic)—See *Cough/Cold Combinations (Systemic), #*

Brompheniramine and Pseudoephedrine (Systemic)—See *Antihistamines and Decongestants (Systemic), 350*

Carbinoxamine, Pseudoephedrine, and Dextromethorphan (Systemic)—See *Cough/Cold Combinations (Systemic), #*

Carbinoxamine and Pseudoephedrine (Systemic)—See *Antihistamines and Decongestants (Systemic), 350*

Cetirizine and Pseudoephedrine (Systemic)—*See Antihistamines and Decongestants (Systemic), 350*

Cetirizine and Pseudoephedrine (Systemic), 793

Chlorpheniramine, Pseudoephedrine, Codeine, and Acetaminophen (Systemic)—See *Cough/Cold Combinations (Systemic), #*

Chlorpheniramine, Pseudoephedrine, Dextromethorphan, and Acetaminophen (Systemic)—See *Cough/Cold Combinations (Systemic), #*

Chlorpheniramine, Pseudoephedrine, Dextromethorphan, and Guaifenesin (Systemic)—See *Cough/Cold Combinations (Systemic), #*

Chlorpheniramine, Pseudoephedrine, and Acetaminophen (Systemic)—See *Antihistamines, Decongestants, and Analgesics (Systemic), 358*

Chlorpheniramine, Pseudoephedrine, and Codeine (Systemic)—See *Cough/Cold Combinations (Systemic), #*

Chlorpheniramine, Pseudoephedrine, and Dextromethorphan (Systemic)—See *Cough/Cold Combinations (Systemic), #*

Chlorpheniramine, Pseudoephedrine, and Guaifenesin (Systemic)—See *Cough/Cold Combinations (Systemic), #*

Pseudoephedrine-containing Combinations *(continued)*

Chlorpheniramine, Pseudoephedrine, and Hydrocodone (Systemic)—See *Cough/Cold Combinations (Systemic), #*

Chlorpheniramine, Pseudoephedrine, and Methscopolamine (Systemic)—See *Antihistamines, Decongestants, and Anticholinergics (Systemic), 361*

Chlorpheniramine and Pseudoephedrine (Systemic)—See *Antihistamines and Decongestants (Systemic), 350*

Dexbrompheniramine, Pseudoephedrine, and Acetaminophen (Systemic)—See *Antihistamines, Decongestants, and Analgesics (Systemic), 358*

Dexbrompheniramine and Pseudoephedrine (Systemic)—See *Antihistamines and Decongestants (Systemic), 350*

Dexchlorpheniramine, Pseudoephedrine, and Guaifenesin (Systemic)—See *Cough/Cold Combinations (Systemic), #*

Diphenhydramine, Pseudoephedrine, and Acetaminophen (Systemic)—See *Antihistamines, Decongestants, and Analgesics (Systemic), 358*

Diphenhydramine and Pseudoephedrine (Systemic)—See *Antihistamines and Decongestants (Systemic), 350*

Doxylamine, Pseudoephedrine, Dextromethorphan, and Acetaminophen (Systemic)—See *Cough/Cold Combinations (Systemic), #*

Loratadine and Pseudoephedrine (Systemic)—See *Antihistamines and Decongestants (Systemic), 350*

Promethazine, Pseudoephedrine, and Dextromethorphan (Systemic)—See *Cough/Cold Combinations (Systemic), #*

Pseudoephedrine, Dextromethorphan, Guaifenesin, and Acetaminophen (Systemic)—See *Cough/Cold Combinations (Systemic), #*

Pseudoephedrine, Dextromethorphan, and Acetaminophen (Systemic)—See *Cough/Cold Combinations (Systemic), #*

Pseudoephedrine, Dextromethorphan, and Guaifenesin (Systemic)—See *Cough/Cold Combinations (Systemic), #*

Pseudoephedrine, Hydrocodone, and Guaifenesin (Systemic)—See *Cough/Cold Combinations (Systemic), #*

Pseudoephedrine, Hydrocodone, and Potassium Guaiacolsulfonate (Systemic)—See *Cough/Cold Combinations (Systemic), #*

Pseudoephedrine and Acetaminophen (Systemic)—See *Decongestants and Analgesics (Systemic), 1035*

Pseudoephedrine and Dextromethorphan (Systemic)—See *Cough/Cold Combinations (Systemic), #*

Pseudoephedrine and Guaifenesin (Systemic)—See *Cough/Cold Combinations (Systemic), #*

Pseudoephedrine and Ibuprofen (Systemic)—See *Decongestants and Analgesics (Systemic), 1035*

Pyrilamine, Pseudoephedrine, Dextromethorphan, and Acetaminophen (Systemic)—See *Cough/Cold Combinations (Systemic), #*

Terfenadine and Pseudoephedrine (Systemic)—See *Antihistamines and Decongestants (Systemic), 350*

Triprolidine, Pseudoephedrine, Codeine, and Guaifenesin (Systemic)—See *Cough/Cold Combinations (Systemic), #*

Triprolidine, Pseudoephedrine, and Acetaminophen (Systemic)—See *Antihistamines, Decongestants, and Analgesics (Systemic), 358*

Triprolidine, Pseudoephedrine, and Codeine (Systemic)—See *Cough/Cold Combinations (Systemic), #*

Triprolidine, Pseudoephedrine, and Dextromethorphan (Systemic)—See *Cough/Cold Combinations (Systemic), #*

Triprolidine and Pseudoephedrine (Systemic)—See *Antihistamines and Decongestants (Systemic), 350*

Psyllium-containing Combinations

Malt Soup Extract and Psyllium (Oral-Local)—See *Laxatives (Local), #*

Psyllium-containing Combinations *(continued)*

Psyllium Hydrophilic Mucilloid and Carboxymethylcellulose (Oral-Local)—See *Laxatives (Local), #*

Psyllium Hydrophilic Mucilloid and Senna (Oral-Local)—See *Laxatives (Local), #*

Psyllium Hydrophilic Mucilloid and Sennosides (Oral-Local)—See *Laxatives (Local), #*

Psyllium and Senna (Oral-Local)—See *Laxatives (Local), #*

Pyrazinamide-containing Combinations

Rifampin, Isoniazid, and Pyrazinamide (Systemic), 2528

Pyrilamine-containing Combinations

Chlorpheniramine, Pheniramine, Pyrilamine, Phenylephrine, Hydrocodone, Salicylamide, Caffeine, and Ascorbic Acid (Systemic)—See *Cough/Cold Combinations (Systemic), #*

Chlorpheniramine, Pyrilamine, Phenylephrine, and Acetaminophen (Systemic)—See *Antihistamines, Decongestants, and Analgesics (Systemic), 358*

Chlorpheniramine, Pyrilamine, and Phenylephrine (Systemic)—See *Antihistamines and Decongestants (Systemic), 350*

Pheniramine, Pyrilamine, Hydrocodone, Potassium Citrate, and Ascorbic Acid (Systemic)—See *Cough/Cold Combinations (Systemic), #*

Pyrilamine, Phenylephrine, Hydrocodone, and Ammonium Chloride (Systemic)—See *Cough/Cold Combinations (Systemic), #*

Pyrilamine, Pseudoephedrine, Dextromethorphan, and Acetaminophen (Systemic)—See *Cough/Cold Combinations (Systemic), #*

Pyrilamine and Codeine (Systemic)—See *Cough/Cold Combinations (Systemic), #*

Pyrimethamine-containing Combinations

Sulfadoxine and Pyrimethamine (Systemic), #

Quinapril-containing Combinations

Quinapril and Hydrochlorothiazide (Systemic)—See *Angiotensin-converting Enzyme (ACE) Inhibitors and Hydrochlorothiazide (Systemic), 212*

Quinupristin-containing Combinations

Quinupristin and Dalfopristin (Systemic), 2477

Rauwolfia Serpentina–containing Combinations

Rauwolfia Serpentina and Bendroflumethiazide (Systemic)—See *Rauwolfia Alkaloids and Thiazide Diuretics (Systemic), #*

Reserpine-containing Combinations

Reserpine, Hydralazine, and Hydrochlorothiazide (Systemic), #

Reserpine and Chlorothiazide (Systemic)—See *Rauwolfia Alkaloids and Thiazide Diuretics (Systemic), #*

Reserpine and Chlorthalidone (Systemic)—See *Rauwolfia Alkaloids and Thiazide Diuretics (Systemic), #*

Reserpine and Hydrochlorothiazide (Systemic)—See *Rauwolfia Alkaloids and Thiazide Diuretics (Systemic), #*

Reserpine and Methyclothiazide (Systemic)—See *Rauwolfia Alkaloids and Thiazide Diuretics (Systemic), #*

Resorcinol-containing Combinations

Resorcinol and Sulfur (Topical), #

Rifampin-containing Combinations

Rifampin, Isoniazid, and Pyrazinamide (Systemic), 2528

Rifampin and Isoniazid (Systemic), 2526

Ritonavir-containing Combinations

Lopinavir and Ritonavir (Systemic), 1855

Roxadimate-containing Combinations

Oxybenzone and Roxadimate (Topical)—See *Sunscreen Agents (Topical), #*

Salicylamide-containing Combinations

Acetaminophen, Aspirin, Salicylamide, and Caffeine (Systemic)—See *Acetaminophen and Salicylates (Systemic), #*

Acetaminophen, Salicylamide, and Caffeine (Systemic)—See *Acetaminophen and Salicylates (Systemic), #*

Chlorpheniramine, Phenindamine, Phenylephrine, Dextromethorphan, Acetaminophen, Salicylamide, Caffeine, and Ascorbic Acid (Systemic)—See *Cough/Cold Combinations (Systemic), #*

Salicylamide-containing Combinations *(continued)*

Chlorpheniramine, Pheniramine, Pyrilamine, Phenylephrine, Hydrocodone, Salicylamide, Caffeine, and Ascorbic Acid (Systemic)—See *Cough/Cold Combinations (Systemic), #*

Chlorpheniramine, Phenylephrine, Acetaminophen, Salicylamide, and Caffeine (Systemic)—See *Antihistamines, Decongestants, and Analgesics (Systemic), 358*

Chlorpheniramine, Phenylephrine, Acetaminophen, and Salicylamide (Systemic)—See *Antihistamines, Decongestants, and Analgesics (Systemic), 358*

Chlorpheniramine, Phenylephrine, Dextromethorphan, Acetaminophen, and Salicylamide (Systemic)—See *Cough/Cold Combinations (Systemic), #*

Phenylephrine, Guaifenesin, Acetaminophen, Salicylamide, and Caffeine (Systemic)—See *Cough/Cold Combinations (Systemic), #*

Salicylic Acid–containing Combinations

Salicylic Acid, Sulfur, and Coal Tar (Topical), #

Salicylic Acid and Sulfur (Topical), #

Salmeterol-containing combinations

Fluticasone and Salmeterol (Inhalation-Local), 1447

Scopolamine-containing Combinations

Atropine, Hyoscyamine, Scopolamine, and Phenobarbital (Systemic)—See *Belladonna Alkaloids and Barbiturates (Systemic), 509*

Secobarbital-containing Combinations

Secobarbital and Amobarbital (Systemic)—See *Barbiturates (Systemic), 496*

Senna-containing Combinations

Phenolphthalein and Senna (Oral-Local)—See *Laxatives (Local), #*

Psyllium Hydrophilic Mucilloid and Senna (Oral-Local)—See *Laxatives (Local), #*

Psyllium and Senna (Oral-Local)—See *Laxatives (Local), #*

Sennosides-containing Combinations

Psyllium Hydrophilic Mucilloid and Sennosides (Oral-Local)—See *Laxatives (Local), #*

Sennosides and Docusate (Oral-Local)—See *Laxatives (Local), #*

Simethicone-containing Combinations

Alumina, Magnesia, Calcium Carbonate,, and Simethicone (Oral-Local)—See *Antacids (Oral-Local), #*

Alumina, Magnesia, and Simethicone (Oral-Local)—See *Antacids (Oral-Local), #*

Calcium Carbonate, Magnesia, and Simethicone (Oral-Local)—See *Antacids (Oral-Local), #*

Calcium Carbonate and Simethicone (Oral-Local)—See *Antacids (Oral-Local), #*

Magaldrate and Simethicone (Oral-Local)—See *Antacids (Oral-Local), #*

Simethicone, Alumina, Magnesium Carbonate, and Magnesia (Oral-Local)—See *Antacids (Oral-Local), #*

Sodium Benzoate–containing Combinations

Caffeine and Sodium Benzoate (Systemic)—See *Caffeine (Systemic), #*

Sodium Benzoate and Sodium Phenylacetate (Systemic), #

Sodium Bicarbonate–containing Combinations

Acetaminophen, Sodium Bicarbonate, and Citric Acid (Systemic), #

Alumina, Magnesium Carbonate, and Sodium Bicarbonate (Oral-Local)—See *Antacids (Oral-Local), #*

Alumina, Magnesium Trisilicate, and Sodium Bicarbonate (Oral-Local)—See *Antacids (Oral-Local), #*

Aspirin, Sodium Bicarbonate, and Citric Acid (Systemic), #

Magnesium Carbonate and Sodium Bicarbonate (Oral-Local)—See *Antacids (Oral-Local), #*

Potassium Bitartrate and Sodium Bicarbonate (Rectal-Local)—See *Laxatives (Local), #*

Appendix V

VA MEDICATION CLASSIFICATION SYSTEM

Note to Users: The Veterans Administration Medication Classification system printed below may differ from the list found on the VA's website, *www.vapbm.org/PBM/natform.htm.* The list below includes updates from the VA that could not be included (as of May 2002) on the VA's website, due to technical considerations. The VA's website should be used as the primary source if the information sought differs between the two sources.

INTRODUCTION

The Veterans Administration Medication Classification system was developed to provide a systematic and management approach to the classification of medications, including investigational and over-the-counter drugs, prosthetic items, and expendable supplies for hospital patients. The system was designed to:

1. Support the inpatient and outpatient pharmacy activities;
2. Facilitate the identification of drug-drug, drug-allergy, drug-lab, and drug-food interactions;
3. Uphold the requirements for inventory accountability;
4. Substantiate and improve all patient medication-related activity;
5. Provide an improved database to assist the physician;
6. Provide a coordinated method of database communication for VA management;
7. Facilitate the monitoring of investigational drugs; and Facilitate the control of prosthetic and supply items.

Each 5-character alpha-numeric code specifies a broad classification and a specific type of product. The first two characters are letters and form the mnemonic for the major classification (e.g., AM for antimicrobials). Characters 3 through 5 are numbers and form the basis for product. For example, the classification system for the penicillins is as follows:

AM000 ANTIMICROBIALS
- AM100 Beta-Lactam Antimicrobials
  - AM111 Penicillin G-related Penicillins
  - AM112 Penicillins, Amino Derivatives
  - AM113 Penicillinase-resistant Penicillins
  - AM114 Extended Spectrum Penicillins

Descriptive comments are included in the following listing only when the classification system itself is not considered to be self-explanatory. The VA Drug Classification system classifies drug products, not generic ingredients. Drug products with local effects are classified by route of administration (e.g., dermatological, ophthalmic, otic, nasal and throat, rectal-local). If a product is not classified by route of administration, in most instances it is classified under a specific chemical or pharmacological classification (e.g., beta-blockers, cephalosporins). If a product is not classified by route of administration or chemical or pharmacological subclassification, it may be classified under a therapeutic category (e.g., antilipemic agents, antiparkinson agents).

Most combination products are found in the "other" subclassification under each major classification unless a specific subcategory for combination products has been added or a descriptive comment indicates inclusion elsewhere. In addition, products which are not adequately described by a minor category or subcategory within the major classification are classified as "other" (e.g., metronidazole, vancomycin).

The "notes" included in the following master classification list define assignment of codes for *primary* classifications only. These notes may or may not be applicable to any *secondary* classifications.

AD000 ANTIDOTES, DETERRENTS, AND POISON CONTROL

Note: Includes nicotine polacrilex and other deterrents (AD900).

Excludes anticoagulant antagonists (VT700); antifolate antagonists (VT120); antivenins (IM300); dialysis solutions (IR200); emetics (GA600); opioid antagonists (CN102).

- AD100 Alcohol Deterrents
- AD200 Cyanide Antidotes
- AD300 Heavy Metal Antagonists
- AD400 Exchange Resins
- AD500 Antivenins
- AD600 Smoking Deterrents
- AD700 Benzodiazepine Antagonists
- AD800 Opioid Antagonists
- AD900 Antidotes/Deterrents, Other

AH000 ANTIHISTAMINES

Note: Excludes H_2-antagonists (GA301); combination cold products (RE500).

- AH101 Antihistamines, Phenothiazine
- AH102 Antihistamines, Non-Sedating
- AH109 Antihistamines, Other

AM000 ANTIMICROBIALS

Note: Combination products containing two or more active ingredients from the same product are classified in that product (e.g., triple sulfas in AM650). Products containing two or more active ingredients from different products are classified under "anti-infectives, other" (e.g., tetracycline and amphotericin B in AM900). Products containing probenecid or clavulanic acid are classified under the product of the antimicrobial agent. Beta-lactam antibiotics not classified under penicillins or cephalosporins are classified under AM119.

Excludes topical anti-infectives (DE100); topical anti-infective/anti-inflammatory combinations (DE250); ophthalmic anti-infectives (OP200); ophthalmic anti-infective/anti-inflammatory combinations (OP350); otic anti-infectives (OT100); otic anti-infective/anti-inflammatory combinations (OT250); vaginal anti-infectives (GU300).

- AM100 Beta-Lactam Antimicrobials
  - AM111 Penicillin G-related Penicillins
  - AM112 Penicillins, Amino Derivatives
  - AM113 Penicillinase-resistant Penicillins
  - AM114 Extended Spectrum Penicillins
  - AM115 Cephalosporins, 1st Generation
  - AM116 Cephalosporins, 2nd Generation
  - AM117 Cephalosporins, 3rd Generation
  - AM118 Cephalosporins, 4th Generation
  - AM119 Beta-lactam Antimicrobials, Other
- AM200 Macrolides
- AM250 Tetracyclines
- AM300 Aminoglycosides
- AM400 Quinolones
  - AM401 Quinolones
  - AM402 Quinolones, Extended Spectrum
- AM500 Antituberculars
- AM550 Methenamine Salt Antimicrobials
- AM600 Nitrofuran Antimicrobials
- AM650 Sulfonamide/Related Antimicrobials
- AM700 Antifungals
- AM800 Antivirals
  - AM810 Antivirals, Antihepatitis Agents
  - AM820 Antivirals, Antiherpetic Agents
  - AM830 Antivirals, Protease Inhibitors
  - AM840 Antivirals, Reverse Transcriptase Inhibitors
  - AM890 Antivirals, Other
- AM900 Anti-infectives, Other

AN000 ANTINEOPLASTICS

Note: Includes antineoplastic hormones (AN500) which are only used as antineoplastics (e.g., tamoxifen).

Excludes other hormones (HS000).

- AN100 Alkylating Agents
- AN200 Antineoplastic Antibiotics
- AN300 Antimetabolites
- AN400 Antineoplastic Adjuvants
- AN500 Antineoplastic Hormones
- AN600 Antineoplastic Radiopharmaceuticals
- AN700 Protective Agents
- AN900 Antineoplastics, Other

AP000 ANTIPARASITICS

Note: Includes topical pediculicides (AP300).

- AP100 Antiprotozoals
  - AP101 Antimalarials
  - AP109 Antiprotozoals, Other
- AP200 Anthelmintics
- AP300 Pediculicides

AP900 Antiparasitics, Other

AS000 ANTISEPTICS/DISINFECTANTS

Note: Includes products used only for the disinfection of inanimate objects and surfaces (e.g., benzalkonium chloride).

Excludes products used for the cleansing or disinfection of animate objects (e.g., hexachlorophene [DE400]) and products used for the cleansing or disinfection of both animate and inanimate objects (e.g., povidone iodine [DE101]).

AU000 AUTONOMIC MEDICATIONS

Note: Includes single ingredient anticholinergic products used as antiparkinson agents (e.g., benztropine, trihexyphenidyl) and single ingredient anticholinergic products used as antispasmodics in the gastrointestinal tract (e.g., glycopyrrolate).

Excludes those products classified under selected cardiovascular (beta-blockers [CV100], alpha-blockers [CV150], antihypertensives [CV400]), respiratory (sympathomimetic bronchodilators [RE125], anticholinergic bronchodilators [RE150]), or ophthalmic (beta-blockers [OP110, OP111]) products; gastrointestinal tract antispasmodic combinations (GA802); and urinary tract antispasmodics (GU200).

AU100 Sympathomimetics (Adrenergics)
AU105 Antiadrenergics
AU300 Parasympathomimetics (Cholinergics)
AU305 Anticholinergics
AU900 Autonomic Agents, Other

BL000 BLOOD PRODUCTS/MODIFIERS/VOLUME EXPANDERS

BL100 Blood Coagulation Modifiers
BL110 Heparin, Unfractionated
BL111 Low Molecular Weight Heparin
BL112 Heparinoid Fragments
BL113 Hiruidin Anticoagulants
BL114 Anticoagulants, Oral
BL115 Thrombolytics
BL116 Antihemorrhagics
BL117 Platelet Aggregation Inhibitors
BL118 Heparin Antagonists
BL119 Blood Coagulation Modifiers, Other
BL400 Blood Formation Products
BL500 Blood Derivatives
BL800 Volume Expanders
BL900 Blood Products, Other

CN000 CENTRAL NERVOUS SYSTEM MEDICATIONS

Note: Includes all single-entity and combination analgesic products containing an opioid agonist or partial agonist (CN101); non-opioid single-entity and combination analgesic products containing acetaminophen and/or salicylates (CN103); single-entity monocyclic, bicyclic, or tetracyclic antidepressants (CN609); and single-entity products containing a phenothiazine or thioxanthene (CN701).

Excludes antitussive products containing an agonist or partial agonist opioid (RE301); antidiarrheal products containing tincture of opium or paregoric (GA208); single-entity anticholinergic products and dopamine agonists (AU305); pargyline (CV409); procarbazine (AN900); "anesthetics, local topical" (DE700).

CN100 Analgesics
CN101 Opioid Analgesics
CN102 Opioid Antagonists
CN103 Non-opioid Analgesics
CN104 Nonsteroidal Anti-inflammatories
CN105 Antimigraine Agents
CN200 Anesthetics
CN201 Gaseous Anesthetics
CN202 Barbituric Acid Derivatives, Anesthetic
CN203 General Anesthetics, Other
CN204 Local Anesthetics
CN205 Peripheral Nerve Blocking Agents
CN206 Anesthetic Adjuncts
CN300 Sedatives/Hypnotics/Anxiolytics
CN301 Barbituric Acid Derivatives, Sedatives/Anxiolytics
CN302 Benzodiazepine Derivatives, Sedatives/Anxiolytics
CN303 Benzodiazepine Antagonists
CN304 Anxiolytics, Other
CN309 Sedatives/Hypnotics, Other
CN400 Anticonvulsants
CN500 Antiparkinson Agents
CN550 Antivertigo Agents
CN600 Antidepressants
CN601 Tricyclic Antidepressants
CN602 Monoamine Oxidase Inhibitors
CN603 Selective Serotonin Reuptake Inhibitors
CN609 Antidepressants, Other
CN700 Antipsychotics
CN701 Phenothiazine Antipsychotics
CN709 Antipsychotics, Other
CN750 Lithium Salts
CN800 CNS Stimulants
CN801 Amphetamines
CN802 Amphetamine-like Stimulants
CN809 CNS Stimulants, Other
CN850 Antipyretics
CN900 CNS Medications, Other

CV000 CARDIOVASCULAR MEDICATIONS

Note: The beta-blockers/related product (CV100) includes all single-entity beta-blockers and alpha-beta-blockers. Combinations containing a beta-blocker are included with the combination antihypertensives (CV400). The alpha-blockers/related product (CV150) includes both peripheral and central single-entity products. All antihypertensive combinations, with the exception of potassium-sparing diuretics in combination with other diuretics (CV704), are included in the CV400 product.

CV050 Cardiac Inotropic Agents
CV051 Digitalis Glycosides
CV052 Cardiac Inotropic Agents, Phosphodiasterase Inhibitors
CV053 Cardiac Inotropic Agents, Adrenergics
CV059 Cardiac Inotropic Agents, Other
CV100 Beta-blockers/Related
CV150 Alpha-blockers/Related
CV200 Calcium Channel Blockers
CV250 Antianginals
CV300 Antiarrhythmics
CV350 Antilipemic Agents
CV351 Antilipemic Agents, HMG CoA Reductase Inhibitors
CV359 Antilipemic Agents, Other
CV400 Antihypertensives
CV401 Antihypertensives, Centrally Acting
CV402 Antihypetensives, Direct Acting Vasodilators
CV408 Antihypertensives, Combinations
CV409 Antihypertensives, Other
CV500 Peripheral Vasodilators
CV600 Sclerosing Agents
CV700 Diuretics
CV701 Thiazides/Related
CV702 Loop Diuretics
CV703 Carbonic Anhydrase Inhibitors
CV704 Potassium-sparing/Combinations
CV709 Diuretics, Other
CV800 ACE Inhibitors
CV805 Angiotensin II Inhibitors
CV900 Cardiovascular Agents, Other

DE000 DERMATOLOGICAL AGENTS

Note: The topical anti-inflammatory product (DE200) includes all single-entity anti-inflammatory agents and all combinations containing an adrenocorticoid except those which also contain an anti-infective agent (DE250) or an antipsoriatic agent (DE802). The topical antipsoriatic product (DE802) includes products containing adrenocorticoids in combination with coal tar or salicylic acid and products containing coal tar. The "anti-infective, topical, other" product (DE109) includes products containing combinations of agents from any one or more products of "anti-infectives, topical" (DE101, DE102, DE103). Topical pediculicides are included under AP300.

DE100 Anti-infective, Topical
DE101 Antibacterial, Topical
DE102 Antifungal, Topical
DE103 Antiviral, Topical
DE109 Anti-infective, Topical, Other
DE200 Anti-inflammatories, Topical
DE250 Anti-infective/Anti-inflammatory Combinations, Topical
DE300 Sun Protectants/Screens
DE350 Emollients
DE400 Soaps/Shampoos
DE450 Deodorants/Antiperspirants
DE500 Keratolytics/Caustics
DE600 Antineoplastics, Topical
DE650 Analgesics, Topical
DE700 Local Anesthetics, Topical
DE750 Antiacne Agents
DE751 Antiacne Agents, Systemic
DE752 Antiacne Agents, Topical
DE800 Antipsoriatics
DE801 Antipsoriatics, Systemic
DE802 Antipsoriatics, Topical
DE890 Dermatologicals, Systemic, Other
DE900 Dermatologicals, Topical, Other

DX000 DIAGNOSTIC AGENTS

Note: DX401 includes control solutions. DX409 includes combination blook test strips. DX509 includes combination urine test strips.

DX100 Radiological/Contrast Media
DX101 Non-ionic Contrast Media
DX102 Ionic Contrast Media
DX200 Radiopharmaceuticals, Diagnostic
DX201 Imaging Agents (in vivo), Radiopharmaceutical
DX202 Non-imaging Agents, Radiopharmaceutical
DX300 Diagnostic Antigens
DX400 Blood Test Strips/Reagents
DX401 Blood Glucose Test Strips/Reagents
DX409 Blood Test Strips/Reagents, Other
DX500 Urine Test Strips/Reagents
DX501 Urine Glucose Test Strips/Reagents
DX509 Urine Test Strips/Reagents, Other
DX900 Diagnostics, Other

GA000 GASTRIC MEDICATIONS

Note: The "laxatives, other" product (GA209) includes combination products. The digestant product (GA500) includes any single-entity or combination product containing a digestive enzyme. Antacid and simethicone combinations are included in product "antacids, other" (GA199).GA303 includes combination products.

GA100 Antacids
GA101 Aluminum-containing Antacids
GA102 Aluminum/Calcium/Magnesium-containing Antacids
GA103 Aluminum/Magnesium-containing Antacids
GA104 Aluminum/Magnesium/Sodium Bicarbonate-containing Antacids
GA105 Calcium-containing Antacids
GA106 Calcium/Magnesium-containing Antacids
GA107 Magaldrate-containing Antacids
GA108 Magnesium-containing Antacids
GA109 Magnesium/Sodium Bicarbonate-containing Antacids
GA110 Sodium Bicarbonate-containing Antacids
GA199 Antacids, Other
GA200 Laxatives/Antidiarrheal Agents
GA201 Bulk-forming Laxatives
GA202 Hyperosmotic Laxatives
GA203 Lubricant Laxatives
GA204 Stimulant Laxatives
GA205 Stool Softeners
GA208 Antidiarrheal Agents

GA209 Laxatives/Antidiarrheal Agents, Other
GA300 Antiulcer Agents
GA301 Histamine Antagonists
GA302 Protectants, Ulcer
GA303 Anti-*H. pylori* Antiulcer Agents
GA304 Antiulcer Agents, Proton Pumping Inhibitors
GA309 Antiulcer Agents, Other
GA400 Inflammatory Bowel Disease Agents
GA500 Digestants
GA600 Emetics/Antiemetics
GA601 Emetics
GA605 Antiemetics, 5-HT3 Antagonists
GA609 Emetics/Antiemetics, Other
GA750 Appetite Suppressants/Stimulants
GA751 Centrally-acting Appetite Suppressants
GA752 Bulking Agent Appetite Suppressants
GA753 Appetite Stimulants
GA759 Appetite Suppressants/Stimulants, Other
GA800 Antimuscarinics/Antispasmodics
GA801 Antimuscarinics/Antispasmodics
GA802 Antimuscarinic/Antispasmodic Combinations
GA900 Gastric Medications, Other

GU000 GENITOURINARY MEDICATIONS

Note: The oxytocic product (GU600) includes 20% sodium chloride, 40 to 60% urea solutions, ergonovine, and methylergonovine but does not include oxytocin (HS702) or prostaglandins (HS200). The "antispasmodics, urinary" product (GU201) includes single-entity products. The "antispasmodics, urinary, other" product (GU209) includes any combination containing an anticholinergic ingredient that is intended for genitourinary use.

GU100 Analgesics, Urinary
GU200 Antispasmodics, Urinary
GU201 Antispasmodics, Urinary
GU209 Antispasmodics, Urinary, Other
GU300 Anti-infectives, Vaginal
GU301 Antimicrobials, Vaginal
GU302 Antifungals, Vaginal
GU309 Anti-Infectives, Vaginal, Other
GU400 Contraceptives, Non-Hormonal
GU500 Estrogens, Vaginal
GU600 Oxytocics
GU650 Labor Suppressants
GU700 Benign Prostatic Hypertrophy Agents
GU900 Genitourinary Agents, Other

HS000 HORMONES/SYNTHETICS/MODIFIERS

HS050 Adrenal Corticosteroids
HS051 Glucocorticoids
HS052 Mineralocorticoids
HS100 Sex Hormones/Modifiers
HS101 Androgens/Anabolics
HS102 Estrogens
HS103 Progestins
HS104 Contraceptives, Hormonal
HS105 Estrogen/Progestin Replacement Combinations
HS106 Gonadotropins
HS109 Sex Hormones, Modifiers, Other
HS200 Prostaglandins
HS300 Calcium Regulating Agents
HS301 Biphosphonates, Osteoporosis Agent
HS302 Biphosphanates, Hypercalcemia Agent
HS303 Biphosphanates, Pagets Disease
HS304 Calcium Regulating Hormones
HS305 Calcium Regulating Antineoplastics
HS309 Calcium Regulating Agents, Other
HS450 Enzyme Replacements/Modifiers
HS451 Enzyme Replacement Agents
HS452 Enzyme Modifiers/Inhibitors
HS459 Enzyme Replacements/Modifiers, Other
HS500 Blood Glucose Regulation Agents
HS501 Insulin
HS502 Oral Antidiabetic Agents, Sulfonylureas
HS503 Oral Antidiabetic Agents, Biguanides
HS504 Oral Antidiabetic Agents, Alpha Glucosidase Inhibitors
HS505 Oral Antidiabetic Agents, Insulin Sensitizing
HS508 Antihypoglycemics
HS509 Blood Glucose Regulation Agents, Other
HS600 Parathyroid
HS700 Pituitary
HS701 Anterior Pituitary
HS702 Posterior Pituitary
HS850 Thyroid Modifiers
HS851 Thyroid Supplements
HS852 Antithyroid Agents
HS900 Hormones/Synthetics/Modifiers, Other

IM000 IMMUNOLOGICAL AGENTS

IM100 Vaccines
IM200 Toxoids
IM300 Antitoxins
IM400 Immunomodulators
IM401 Immune Serums
IM402 Immunoglobulins
IM403 Immune Suppressants
IM404 Immune Stimulants
IM409 Immunomodulators, Other
IM900 Immunological Agents, Other

IN000 INVESTIGATIONAL AGENTS

Note: Drugs/devices used for investigational purposes are included in this classification.

IP000 INTRAPLEURAL MEDICATIONS

Note: Includes all medications introduced into the intrapleural space.

IP100 Intrapleural Sclerosing Agents
IP900 Intrapleural Agents, Other

IR000 IRRIGATION/DIALYSIS SOLUTIONS

Note: Excludes 50% dimethyl sulfoxide (GU900).

IR100 Irrigation Solutions
IR200 Peritoneal Dialysis Solutions
IR300 Hemodialysis Solutions
IR900 Irrigation/Dialysis Solutions, Other

MS000 MUSCULOSKELETAL MEDICATIONS

Note: The antigout product (MS400) includes colchicine, uricosuric agents, and xanthine-oxidase inhibitors. The skeletal muscle relaxant product includes all combinations, except those containing an opioid ingredient (CN101).

MS100 Antirheumatics
MS101 Salicylates, Antirheumatic
MS102 Nonsalicylate NSAIs, Antirheumatic
MS103 Cytotoxics, Antirheumatic
MS109 Antirheumatics, Other
MS200 Skeletal Muscle Relaxants
MS300 Neuromuscular Blockers
MS400 Antigout Agents
MS900 Musculoskeletal Agents, Other

NT000 NASAL AND THROAT AGENTS, TOPICAL

NT100 Decongestants, Nasal
NT200 Anti-inflammatories, Nasal
NT201 Anti-inflammatories, Steroid-containing, Nasal, Topical
NT209 Anti-inflammatories, Nasal, Topical, Other
NT300 Anesthetics, Mucosal
NT400 Antihistamines, Nasal
NT900 Nasal and Throat, Topical, Other

OP000 OPHTHALMIC AGENTS

Note: The "anti-infectives, other" product (OP209) includes products containing combinations from any one or more products (OP201, OP202, OP203) of anti-infectives, topical. The "ophthalmic, other" product (OP900) includes all combination ophthalmics except those classified under antiglaucoma combinations (OP117), anti-infective/anti-inflammatory combinations (OP350), or "anti-infectives, other" (OP209).

OP100 Intraocular Pressure Modifiers
OP110 Intraocular Hypotensive Beta-blockers, Topical
OP111 Intraocular Hypotensive Beta-blockers, Systemic
OP112 Intraocular Hypotensive Carbonic Anhydrase Inhibitors, Topical
OP113 Intraocular Hypotensive Carbonic Anhydrase Inhibitors, Systemic
OP114 Intraocular Hypotensive Adrenergics
OP115 Intraocular Hypotensive Osmotic Agents, Systemic
OP116 Intraocular Hypotensive Prostaglandins, Topical
OP117 Intraocular Hypotensive Combinations, Topical
OP118 Miotics, Topical
OP119 Intraocular Pressure Modifiers, Other
OP200 Anti-infective, Topical Ophthalmic
OP201 Antibacterials, Topical Ophthalmic
OP202 Antifungal, Topical Ophthalmic
OP203 Antivirals, Topical Ophthalmic
OP209 Anti-infective, Topical Ophthalmic, Other
OP300 Anti-inflammatory, Topical Ophthalmic
OP301 Anti-inflammatory, Steroidal, Topical Ophthalmic
OP302 Anti-inflammatory, Non-Steroidal, Topical Ophthalmic
OP350 Anti-infective/Anti-inflammatory Combinations, Topical Ophthalmic
OP400 Contact Lens Solutions
OP500 Eye Washes/Lubricants
OP600 Mydriatics/Cycloplegics, Topical Ophthalmic
OP700 Anesthetics, Topical Ophthalmic
OP800 Antihistamine/Decongestants, Topical Ophthalmic
OP801 Antihistamine, Topical Ophthalmic
OP802 Decongestant, Topical Ophthalmic
OP809 Antihistamine/Decongestant Combinations, Topical Ophthalmic
OP900 Ophthalmics, Other

OR000 DENTAL AND ORAL AGENTS, TOPICAL

Note: The cariostatic product (OR100) includes topical fluoride products only. Sodium fluoride tablets are included under TN407. Dental and oral anesthetics, topical OR600 includes combinations.

OR100 Cariostatics
OR200 Dental Protectants
OR300 Dentifrices
OR400 Denture Adhesives
OR500 Mouthwashes
OR600 Dental/Oral Anesthetics, Topical
OR900 Dental and Oral Agents, Topical, Other

OT000 OTIC AGENTS

Note: The "anti-infectives, other" product (OT109) includes products containing combinations from any one or more products (OT101, OT102) of "anti-infectives, otic." The "otic, other" product (OT900) includes all combination otic products except those classified under anti-infective/anti-inflammatory combinations (OT250), otic analgesics (OT400), or "anti-infectives, otic, other" (OT109).

OT100 Anti-infective, Topical Otic
OT101 Antibacterials, Topical Otic
OT102 Antifungals, Topical Otic
OT109 Anti-infective, Topical Otic, Other
OT200 Anti-inflammatories, Topical Otic
OT250 Anti-infective/Anti-inflammatory Combinations, Topical Otic
OT300 Ceruminolytics
OT400 Analgesics, Topical Otic
OT900 Otic Agents, Other

PH000 PHARMACEUTICAL AIDS/REAGENTS

Note: Includes agents used in the preparation or reconstitution of pharmaceutical products. All diluents with separate NDC codes are included.

RE000 RESPIRATORY TRACT MEDICATIONS

Note: The xanthine bronchodilator product (RE140) includes single-entity dyphylline-containing products. Antiasthma combination products containing two or more active ingredients from different products are included in the "antiasthma, other" product (RE190). Both single-entity and combinations of antitussives and expectorants will be included in products RE301 or RE302. Any of these products with at least one opioid is included in product RE301. The "cold remedies, other" product (RE599) contains all cold/cough preparations which are not included in product RE200, RE301, RE302, or RE501 through RE516.

RE100 Antiasthma/Bronchodilators
- RE110 Anti-inflammatories, Inhalation
- RE120 Bronchodilators, Sympathomimetic, Inhalation
- RE125 Bronchodilators, Sympathomimetic, Systemic
- RE140 Bronchodilators, Xanthine-derivative
- RE150 Bronchodilators, Anticholinergic
- RE160 Mast Cell Stabilizers, Inhalation
- RE180 Antiasthma, Antileukotrienes
- RE190 Antiasthma, Other

RE200 Decongestants, Systemic
RE300 Antitussives/Expectorants
- RE301 Antitussives/Expectorants, Opioid-containing
- RE302 Antitussives/Expectorants, Non-opioid-containing

RE400 Mucolytics
RE500 Cold Remedies, Combinations
- RE501 Antihistamine/Decongestant
- RE502 Antihistamine/Decongestant/Antitussive
- RE503 Antihistamine/Decongestant/Expectorant
- RE504 Antihistamine/Decongestant/Antitussive/Expectorant
- RE505 Antihistamine/Decongestant/Antitussive/Expectorant/Analgesic
- RE506 Antihistamine/Decongestant/Antitussive/Analgesic
- RE507 Antihistamine/Antitussive
- RE508 Antihistamine/Antitussive/Expectorant
- RE509 Antihistamine/Antitussive/Analgesic
- RE510 Antitussive/Antimuscarinic
- RE511 Antitussive/Bronchodilator
- RE512 Decongestant/Antitussive
- RE513 Decongestant/Antitussive/Expectorant
- RE514 Decongestant/Antitussive/Expectorant/Analgesic
- RE515 Decongestant/Antitussive/Analgesic
- RE516 Decongestant/Expectorant
- RE599 Cold Remedies, Other

RE600 Non-anesthetic Gases
RE700 Respiratory Surfactants
RE900 Respiratory Agents, Other

RS000 RECTAL, TOPICAL

Note: Includes only those products administered rectally with local activity. Products administered rectally for their systemic effect are classified under the appropriate pharmacological or therapeutic category (e.g., acetaminophen suppositories [CN103]).

RS100 Anti-inflammatories, Rectal
RS200 Hemorrhoidal Preparations, Rectal
- RS201 Hemorrhoidal Preparations without Steroid
- RS202 Hemorrhoidal Preparations with Steroid

RS300 Laxatives, Rectal
RS900 Rectal, Topical, Other

TN000 THERAPEUTIC NUTRIENTS/MINERALS/ELECTROLYTES

Note: Products TN501 and TN502 include kits and products containing dextrose.

TN100 IV Solutions
- TN101 IV Solutions without Electrolytes
- TN102 IV Solutions with Electrolytes

TN200 Enteral Nutrition
TN300 Lipid Supplements
TN400 Electrolytes/Minerals
- TN401 Iron
- TN402 Calcium
- TN403 Potassium
- TN404 Sodium
- TN405 Zinc
- TN406 Magnesium
- TN407 Fluoride
- TN408 Phosphorus
- TN409 Bicarbonates
- TN410 Citrates

TN490 Electrolytes/Minerals, Combinations
- TN499 Electrolytes/Minerals, Other

TN500 Amino Acids/Proteins
- TN501 Amino Acids/Proteins, Parenteral, without added electrolytes
- TN502 Amino Acids/Proteins, Parenteral, with added electrolytes
- TN503 Amino Acids/Proteins, Oral
- TN509 Amino Acids/Proteins, Other

TN900 Therapeutic Nutrients/Minerals/Electrolytes, Other

VT000 VITAMINS

Note: The "vitamin B, other" product (VT190) includes combinations containing only vitamin B complex. Combinations containing only vitamin D are included in product (VT509) and product (VT709) includes combinations of vitamin K only. The "vitamins, other" product (VT809) includes any product in which a vitamin is found in combination with an ingredient which is neither a vitamin nor a mineral.

VT050 Vitamin A
VT100 Vitamin B
- VT110 Cyanocobalamin
- VT120 Folic Acid/Leucovorin
- VT130 Nicotinic Acid
- VT140 Pyridoxine
- VT150 Thiamine
- VT160 Riboflavin
- VT170 Pantothenic Acid
- VT190 Vitamin B, Other

VT400 Vitamin C
VT500 Vitamin D
- VT501 Calcifediol
- VT502 Calcitriol
- VT503 Dihydrotachysterol
- VT504 Ergocalciferol
- VT509 Vitamin D, Other

VT600 Vitamin E
VT700 Vitamin K
- VT701 Menadiol
- VT702 Phytonadione
- VT709 Vitamin K, Other

VT800 Vitamins, Combinations
- VT801 Multivitamins
- VT802 Multivitamins with Minerals
- VT809 Vitamin Combinations, Other

VT900 Vitamins, Other

XA000 PROSTHETICS/SUPPLIES/DEVICES

XA100 Bandages/Dressings
- XA101 Pads, Gauze, Sterile
- XA102 Pads, Gauze, Non-Sterile
- XA103 Pads, Non-Adhering
- XA104 Pads, Gauze with Adhesive
- XA105 Pads, Gauze with Medication Added
- XA106 Gauze, Fine Mesh
- XA107 Bandage, Film
- XA108 Bandage, Elastic
- XA109 Bandage, Stretch
- XA110 Foam with Adhesive
- XA111 Packing, Gauze, Plain
- XA112 Packing, Gauze, Medicated
- XA199 Bandages/Dressing, Other

XA200 Tape
- XA201 Tape, Paper
- XA202 Tape, Cloth
- XA203 Tape, Plastic
- XA204 Tape, Foam
- XA205 Straps, Montgomery
- XA206 Tape, Trach
- XA299 Tape, Other

XA300 Pads/Diapers
- XA301 Pads, Bed
- XA302 Pads, Combination
- XA303 Pants, Rubber
- XA304 Liner, Rubber Pants
- XA305 Diapers
- XA306 Pads, Mattress
- XA399 Pads/Diapers, Other

XA400 Colostomy/Ileostomy Collection Devices
- XA401 Bag, Drainable with Adhesive, Colostomy/Ileostomy
- XA402 Bag, Drainable without Adhesive, Colostomy/Ileostomy
- XA403 Bags, Closed, with Adhesive, Colostomy/Ileostomy
- XA404 Bags, Closed without Adhesive, Colostomy/Ileostomy
- XA405 Bags, Disposable with Adhesive, Colostomy/Ileostomy
- XA406 Bags, Disposable without Adhesive, Colostomy/Ileostomy
- XA407 Sets, Appliances, Colostomy/Ileostomy
- XA499 Colostomy/Ileostomy Collection Devices, Other

XA500 Urostomy/Urinary Collection Devices

Note: Includes urinary catheters and irrigation syringes. Excludes suction catheters.

- XA501 Bag, Bedside Urinary Collection Device
- XA502 Bottles/Other Bedside Urinary Collection Devices
- XA503 Sets, Appliance, Urostomy
- XA504 Bag, Drainable with Adhesive, Urostomy
- XA505 Bag, Drainable without Adhesive, Urostomy
- XA506 Bag, Closed with Adhesive, Urostomy
- XA507 Bag, Closed without Adhesive, Urostomy
- XA508 Bag, Urinary Collection Device
- XA509 Catheter, Foley
- XA510 Catheter, Coude-tip
- XA511 Catheter, Balloon
- XA512 Catheter, Red Rubber
- XA513 Catheter, External Urinary
- XA514 Plug, Catheter
- XA515 Kit, Catheter Care
- XA516 Set, Irrigation
- XA599 Urostomy/Urinary Collection Devices, Other

XA600 Ostomy Supplies, Other
- XA601 Rings, Ostomy
- XA602 Discs, Ostomy
- XA603 Adhesive, Ostomy
- XA604 Protectants, Skin, Ostomy
- XA605 Belts, Ostomy
- XA606 Odor Control Products, Ostomy
- XA607 Irrigators/Sets, Ostomy
- XA608 Caps, Ostomy
- XA699 Ostomy Supplies, Other

XA700 Bags/Tubes/Supplies for Oral Nutrition, Other
- XA701 Bags, Feeding
- XA702 Pumps, Feeding
- XA703 Tubes, Feeding
- XA799 Bags/Tubes/Supplies for Oral Nutrition, Other

XA800 Intravenous Sets
- XA801 Sets, Volumetric, Intravenous
- XA802 Sets, Maxi Drip, Intravenous
- XA803 Sets, Mini Drip, Intravenous
- XA804 Sets, Filter, Intravenous
- XA805 Sets, Butterfly, Intravenous
- XA809 Intravenous Sets, Other

XA850 Syringes/Needles

Note: Includes only syringes for injectable use.

- XA851 Syringes, Slip Tip, Injection
- XA852 Syringes, Luer Lock, Injection
- XA853 Syringes with Needle, Injection
- XA854 Syringe, Insulin, Injection
- XA855 Caps, Syringe
- XA856 Needles, Injection
- XA859 Syringes/Needles, Other

XA900 Supplies, Other

XX000 MISCELLANEOUS AGENTS

Note: Includes all products not elsewhere classified.

The following list identifies all drugs in the USP DI database by their primary and secondary VA code assignments. This list groups all drugs by their VA code; an asterisk identifies primary assignments.

DRUG LISTING BY VA CODE
(* = primary)

AD100 *Acamprosate (Systemic)
Naltrexone (Systemic)
AD200 Amyl Nitrite (Systemic)
*Sodium Nitrite (Systemic)
*Sodium Thiosulfate (Systemic)
AD300 *Deferoxamine (Systemic)
*Dimercaprol (Systemic)
*Edetate Calcium Disodium (Systemic)
*Edetate Disodium (Systemic)
Penicillamine (Systemic)
*Pentetate Calcium Trisodium (Systemic)
*Pentetate Zinc Trisodium (Systemic)
*Prussian Blue (Oral-Local)
*Succimer (Systemic)
*Trientine (Systemic)
Zinc Chloride (Systemic)
Zinc Gluconate (Systemic)
Zinc Sulfate (Systemic)
AD400 Cholestyramine (Oral-Local)
*Sodium Polystyrene Sulfonate (Local)
AD500 *Antivenin (Crotalidae) Polyvalent Immune Fab (Ovine) (Systemic)
*Antivenin (Crotalidae) Polyvalent (Systemic)
*Antivenin (Latrodectus Mactans) (Systemic)
*Antivenin (Micrurus Fulvius) (Systemic)
AD600 Bupropion (Systemic)
*Charcoal, Activated, and Sorbitol (Oral-Local)
*Charcoal, Activated (Oral-Local)
*Varenicline (Systemic)
AD700 *Flumazenil (Systemic)
AD800 *Nalmefene (Systemic)
*Naloxone (Systemic)
*Naltrexone (Systemic)
AD900 Acetylcysteine, Oral (Systemic)
*Acetylcysteine, Parenteral (Systemic)
Ascorbic Acid (Systemic)
Atropine (Systemic)
*Digoxin Immune Fab (Ovine) (Systemic)
Edrophonium and Atropine (Systemic)
Edrophonium (Systemic)
Epinephrine (Systemic)
*Fomepizole (Systemic)
Glucagon (Systemic)
Glycopyrrolate, Parenteral (Systemic)
Hyoscyamine, Parenteral (Systemic)
Iodine, Strong (Systemic)
*Lanthanum (Oral-Local)
Leucovorin (Systemic)
*Mesna (Systemic)
Methadone (Systemic)
*Methylene Blue (Systemic)
*Nicotine (Inhalation-Systemic)
*Nicotine (Nasal)
*Nicotine (Systemic)
Nitroprusside (Systemic)
Potassium Iodide (Systemic)
*Pralidoxime (Systemic)
Prazosin (Systemic)
*Pyridostigmine For Military Combat Medical Use (Systemic)
Racemethionine (Systemic)
*Sevelamer (Oral-Local)
Sodium Ascorbate (Systemic)
*Sodium Benzoate and Sodium Phenylacetate (Systemic)
*Sodium Phenylbutyrate (Systemic)
Sodium Thiosulfate (Systemic)
AH101 *Methdilazine (Systemic)
*Promethazine (Systemic)
*Trimeprazine (Systemic)
AH102 *Astemizole (Systemic)
Desloratadine (Systemic)
*Fexofenadine (Systemic)
*Loratadine (Systemic)
*Terfenadine (Systemic)
AH109 *Azatadine (Systemic)
*Brompheniramine (Systemic)
*Cetirizine (Systemic)
*Chlorpheniramine (Systemic)
*Clemastine (Systemic)
*Cyproheptadine (Systemic)
*Dexchlorpheniramine (Systemic)
*Dimenhydrinate (Systemic)
*Diphenhydramine, Oral (Systemic)
*Doxylamine (Systemic)
*Hydroxyzine (Systemic)
*Phenindamine (Systemic)
AM111 *Penicillin G (Systemic)
*Penicillin V (Systemic)
AM112 *Amoxicillin and Clavulanate (Systemic)
*Amoxicillin (Systemic)
*Ampicillin and Sulbactam (Systemic)
*Ampicillin (Systemic)
*Bacampicillin (Systemic)
*Pivampicillin (Systemic)
*Pivmecillinam (Systemic)
AM113 *Cloxacillin (Systemic)
*Dicloxacillin (Systemic)
*Flucloxacillin (Systemic)
*Methicillin (Systemic)
*Nafcillin (Systemic)
*Oxacillin (Systemic)
AM114 *Carbenicillin (Systemic)
*Mezlocillin (Systemic)
*Piperacillin and Tazobactam (Systemic)
*Piperacillin (Systemic)
*Ticarcillin and Clavulanate (Systemic)
*Ticarcillin (Systemic)
AM115 *Cefadroxil (Systemic)
*Cefazolin (Systemic)
*Cephalexin (Systemic)
*Cephalothin (Systemic)
*Cephapirin (Systemic)
*Cephradine (Systemic)
AM116 *Cefaclor (Systemic)
*Cefamandole (Systemic)
*Cefonicid (Systemic)
*Cefotetan (Systemic)
*Cefoxitin (Systemic)
*Cefprozil (Systemic)
*Cefuroxime (Systemic)
AM117 *Cefditoren (Systemic)
*Cefixime (Systemic)
*Cefoperazone (Systemic)
*Cefotaxime (Systemic)
*Cefpodoxime (Systemic)
*Ceftazidime (Systemic)
*Ceftibuten (Systemic)
*Ceftizoxime (Systemic)
*Ceftriaxone (Systemic)
Cefuroxime (Systemic)
AM118 *Cefepime (Systemic)
AM119 *Aztreonam (Systemic)
Ertapenem (Systemic)
*Imipenem and Cilastatin (Systemic)
*Loracarbef (Systemic)
*Meropenem (Systemic)
AM200 *Azithromycin (Systemic)
*Clarithromycin (Systemic)
*Dirithromycin (Systemic)
*Erythromycin (Systemic)
*Erythromycin Estolate (Systemic)
*Erythromycin Ethylsuccinate (Systemic)
*Erythromycin Gluceptate (Systemic)
*Erythromycin Lactobionate (Systemic)
*Erythromycin Stearate (Systemic)
*Spiramycin (Systemic)
AM250 *Demeclocycline (Systemic)
*Doxycycline (Systemic)
*Minocycline (Systemic)
*Oxytetracycline (Systemic)
*Tetracycline (Systemic)
AM300 *Amikacin (Systemic)
*Clindamycin (Systemic)
*Gentamicin (Systemic)
*Kanamycin (Oral-Local)
*Kanamycin (Systemic)
*Lincomycin (Systemic)
*Neomycin (Oral-Local)
*Neomycin (Systemic)
*Netilmicin (Systemic)
*Streptomycin (Systemic)
*Tobramycin (Systemic)
AM401 *Cinoxacin (Systemic)
*Nalidixic Acid (Systemic)
AM402 *Ciprofloxacin (Systemic)
*Enoxacin (Systemic)
*Gatifloxacin (Systemic)
*Gemifloxacin (Systemic)
*Levofloxacin (Systemic)
*Lomefloxacin (Systemic)
*Moxifloxacin (Systemic)
*Norfloxacin (Systemic)
*Ofloxacin (Systemic)
*Sparfloxacin (Systemic)
AM500 *Aminosalicylate Sodium (Systemic)
*Capreomycin (Systemic)
*Cycloserine (Systemic)
*Ethambutol (Systemic)
*Ethionamide (Systemic)
*Isoniazid (Systemic)
*Pyrazinamide (Systemic)
*Rifampin, Isoniazid, and Pyrazinamide (Systemic)
*Rifampin and Isoniazid (Systemic)
*Rifampin (Systemic)
*Rifapentine (Systemic)
Streptomycin (Systemic)
AM550 *Methenamine (Systemic)
AM600 *Furazolidone (Oral-Local)
*Nitrofurantoin (Systemic)
AM650 *Sulfadiazine and Trimethoprim (Systemic)
*Sulfadiazine (Systemic)
*Sulfamethizole (Systemic)
*Sulfamethoxazole and Phenazopyridine (Systemic)
*Sulfamethoxazole and Trimethoprim (Systemic)
*Sulfamethoxazole (Systemic)
*Sulfisoxazole and Phenazopyridine (Systemic)
*Sulfisoxazole (Systemic)
AM700 *Amphotericin B Cholesteryl Complex (Systemic)
*Amphotericin B Lipid Complex (Systemic)
*Amphotericin B Liposomal Complex (Systemic)
*Amphotericin B (Systemic)
*Anidulafungin (Systemic)
*Caspofungin (Systemic)
*Clotrimazole (Oral-Local)
Dapsone (Systemic)
*Fluconazole (Systemic)
*Flucytosine (Systemic)
*Griseofulvin (Systemic)
*Itraconazole (Systemic)
*Ketoconazole (Systemic)
*Micafungin (Systemic)
*Nystatin (Oral-Local)
Potassium Iodide (Systemic)
*Terbinafine (Systemic)
*Voriconazole (Systemic)
AM810 Adefovir (Systemic)
*Entecavir (Systemic)
*Ribavirin and Interferon Alfa-2b, Recombinant (Systemic)
AM820 *Acyclovir (Systemic)
*Famciclovir (Systemic)
*Foscarnet (Systemic)
*Valacyclovir (Systemic)
AM830 *Amprenavir (Systemic)
*Atazanavir (Systemic)
*Fosamprenavir (Systemic)
*Indinavir (Systemic)
*Lopinavir and Ritonavir (Systemic)
*Nelfinavir (Systemic)
*Ritonavir (Systemic)
*Saquinavir (Systemic)
AM840 *Abacavir, Lamivudine, and Zidovudine (Systemic)
*Abacavir and Lamivudine (Systemic)
*Abacavir (Systemic)
*Delavirdine (Systemic)
*Didanosine (Systemic)
*Efavirenz (Systemic)

*Emtricitabine and Tenofovir (Systemic)
* Emtricitabine (Systemic)
*Lamivudine and Zidovudine (Systemic)
*Lamivudine (Systemic)
*Nevirapine (Systemic)
*Tenofovir (Systemic)
*Zidovudine (Systemic)

AM890 *Amantadine (Systemic)
*Cidofovir (Systemic)
*Enfuvirtide (Systemic)
*Ganciclovir (Systemic)
*Oseltamivir (Systemic)
*Ribavirin (Systemic)
*Rimantadine (Systemic)
*Stavudine (Systemic)
*Valganciclovir (Systemic)
*Zalcitabine (Systemic)
*Zanamivir (Inhalation-Systemic)

AM900 *Chloramphenicol (Systemic)
Clarithromycin (Systemic)
*Clofazimine (Systemic)
*Dapsone (Systemic)
*Daptomycin (Systemic)
*Erythromycin and Sulfisoxazole (Systemic)
*Fosfomycin (Systemic)
*Fusidic Acid (Systemic)
Immune Globulin Intravenous (Human) (Systemic)
*Linezolid (Systemic)
*Metronidazole (Systemic)
*Quinupristin and Dalfopristin (Systemic)
*Rifabutin (Systemic)
Rifampin (Systemic)
*Rifaximin (Oral-Local)
*Spectinomycin (Systemic)
*Telithromycin (Systemic)
*Tinidazole (Systemic)
*Trimethoprim (Systemic)
*Trovafloxacin (Systemic)
*Vancomycin (Oral-Local)
*Vancomycin (Systemic)

AN100 *Busulfan (Systemic)
*Carmustine (Implantation-Local)
*Carmustine (Systemic)
*Chlorambucil (Systemic)
*Cyclophosphamide (Systemic)
*Ifosfamide (Systemic)
*Lomustine (Systemic)
*Mechlorethamine (Systemic)
*Melphalan (Systemic)
*Temozolomide (Systemic)
*Thiotepa (Systemic)

AN200 *Bleomycin (Systemic)
*Dactinomycin (Systemic)
*Daunorubicin, Liposomal (Systemic)
*Daunorubicin (Systemic)
*Doxorubicin, Liposomal (Systemic)
*Doxorubicin (Systemic)
*Epirubicin (Systemic)
*Idarubicin (Systemic)
*Mitomycin (Systemic)
*Plicamycin (Systemic)
*Streptozocin (Systemic)
Trimetrexate (Systemic)
*Valrubicin (Mucosal-Local)

AN300 Azacitidine (Systemic)
*Bortezomib (Systemic)
*Capecitabine (Systemic)
*Cladribine (Systemic)
*Clofarabine (Systemic)
*Cytarabine, Liposomal (Intrathecal)
*Cytarabine (Systemic)
*Denileukin (Systemic)
*Erlotinib (Systemic)
*Floxuridine (Systemic)
*Fludarabine (Systemic)
*Fluorouracil (Systemic)
*Gefitinib (Systemic)
*Gemcitabine (Systemic)
*Hydroxyurea (Systemic)
*Imatinib (Systemic)
*Mercaptopurine (Systemic)
*Methotrexate—For Cancer (Systemic)
*Pemetrexed (Systemic)
*Raltitrexed (Systemic)
*Thioguanine (Systemic)

AN400 Leucovorin (Systemic)
Levamisole (Systemic)

AN500 *Abarelix (Parenteral)
*Abarelix (Systemic)
Aminoglutethimide (Systemic)
*Anastrozole (Systemic)
*Buserelin (Systemic)
*Cyproterone (Systemic)
Diethylstilbestrol (Systemic)
Estradiol (Systemic)
Estrogens, Conjugated (Systemic)
Estrogens, Esterified (Systemic)
Estrone (Systemic)
Ethinyl Estradiol (Systemic)
*Exemestane (Systemic)
*Fulvestrant (Systemic)
Goserelin (Systemic)
*Histrelin (Systemic)
*Letrozole (Systemic)
Leuprolide (Systemic)
Levothyroxine (Systemic)
Liothyronine (Systemic)
Liotrix (Systemic)
Medroxyprogesterone (Systemic)
Megestrol (Systemic)
*Tamoxifen (Systemic)
*Testolactone (Systemic)
Thyroglobulin (Systemic)
Thyroid (Systemic)
*Toremifene (Systemic)
*Triptorelin (Systemic)

AN600 *Chromic Phosphate P 32 (Parenteral-Local)
*Iobenguane I 131 Sulfate (Systemic—Therapeutic)
*Samarium Sm 153 Lexidronam (Systemic)
*Sodium Iodide I 131 (Systemic—Therapeutic)
*Sodium Phosphate P 32 (Systemic)
*Strontium Chloride Sr 89 (Systemic)

AN700 *Amifostine (Systemic)
*Dexrazoxane (Systemic)
*Lenalidomide (Systemic)
*Palifermin (Systemic)
Rasburicase (Systemic)

AN900 *Aldesleukin (Systemic)
*Alemtuzumab (Systemic)
*Altretamine (Systemic)
*Amsacrine (Systemic)
*Arsenic Trioxide (Systemic)
*Asparaginase (Systemic)
*Bacillus Calmette-Guerin (BCG) Live (Mucosal-Local)
*Bevacizumab (Systemic)
*Bexarotene (Systemic)
*Bicalutamide (Systemic)
*Carboplatin (Systemic)
*Cetuximab (Systemic)
*Cisplatin (Systemic)
*Dacarbazine (Systemic)
*Docetaxel (Systemic)
*Estramustine (Systemic)
*Etoposide (Systemic)
Fluoxymesterone (Systemic)
*Flutamide (Systemic)
*Gemtuzumab Ozogamicin (Systemic)
*Ibritumomab (Systemic)
Interferon Alfa-2a, Recombinant (Systemic)
Interferon Alfa-2b, Recombinant (Systemic)
Interferon Alfa-n1 (Ins) (Systemic)
Interferon Alfa-n3 (Systemic)
*Irinotecan (Systemic)
Ketoconazole (Systemic)
*Methoxsalen (Extracorporeal-Systemic)
Methoxsalen (Systemic)
Methyltestosterone (Systemic)
*Mitotane (Systemic)
*Mitoxantrone (Systemic)
Nandrolone (Systemic)
*Nilutamide (Systemic)
*Oxaliplatin (Systemic)
*Paclitaxel Protein-Bound (Systemic)
*Paclitaxel (Systemic)
*Pegaspargase (Systemic)
*Pentostatin (Systemic)
*Porfimer (Systemic)
*Procarbazine (Systemic)
*Rituximab (Systemic)
*Sorafenib (Systemic)
*Teniposide (Systemic)
Testosterone Cypionate (Systemic)
Testosterone Enanthate (Systemic)
Testosterone Propionate (Systemic)
Testosterone (Systemic)
Thyrotropin (Systemic)
*Topotecan (Systemic)
*Tositumomab and Iodine I 131 Tositumomab (Systemic)
*Trastuzumab (Systemic)
*Tretinoin (Systemic)
*Vinblastine (Systemic)
*Vincristine (Systemic)
*Vindesine (Systemic)
*Vinorelbine (Systemic)

AP101 *Atovaquone and Proguanil (Systemic)
*Chloroquine (Systemic)
Clindamycin (Systemic)
Dapsone (Systemic)
Doxycycline (Systemic)
*Hydroxychloroquine (Systemic)
*Mefloquine (Systemic)
*Primaquine (Systemic)
*Proguanil (Systemic)
*Pyrimethamine (Systemic)
Quinidine (Systemic)
*Quinine (Systemic)
*Sulfadoxine and Pyrimethamine (Systemic)
Tetracycline (Systemic)

AP109 Amphotericin B Liposomal Complex (Systemic)
Amphotericin B (Systemic)
*Atovaqone (Systemic)
Dapsone (Systemic)
Demeclocycline (Systemic)
Doxycycline (Systemic)
*Eflornithine (Systemic)
Furazolidone (Oral-Local)
*Iodoquinol (Oral-Local)
*Meglumine Antimoniate (Systemic)
Metronidazole (Systemic)
Minocycline (Systemic)
*Nitazoxanide (Systemic)
Oxytetracycline (Systemic)
*Pentamidine (Inhalation)
*Pentamidine (Systemic)
Pyrimethamine (Systemic)
*Suramin (Systemic)
Tetracycline (Systemic)
*Trimetrexate (Systemic)

AP200 *Albendazole (Systemic)
*Diethylcarbamazine (Systemic)
*Ivermectin (Systemic)
*Mebendazole (Systemic)
Metronidazole (Systemic)
*Niclosamide (Oral-Local)
*Piperazine (Systemic)
*Praziquantel (Systemic)
*Pyrantel (Oral-Local)
*Pyrvinium (Oral-Local)
*Thiabendazole (Systemic)
*Thiabendazole (Topical)

AP300 *Benzyl Benzoate (Topical)
*Lindane (Topical)
*Malathion (Topical)
*Permethrin (Topical)
*Pyrethrins and Piperonyl Butoxide (Topical)

AP900 Benzyl Benzoate (Topical)
*Crotamiton (Topical)
Lindane (Topical)
Permethrin (Topical)
Spiramycin (Systemic)
Sulfur Ointment (Topical)

AU100 *Arbutamine (Systemic)
*Dobutamine (Parenteral-Systemic)
*Dopamine (Parenteral-Systemic)
*Ephedrine (Parenteral-Systemic)
*Epinephrine (Parenteral-Systemic)
*Isoproterenol (Parenteral-Systemic)
*Mephentermine (Parenteral-Systemic)
*Metaraminol (Parenteral-Systemic)
*Methoxamine (Parenteral-Systemic)
*Norepinephrine (Parenteral-Systemic)
*Phenylephrine (Parenteral-Systemic)

*Ritodrine (Systemic)
AU105 *Phentolamine (Intracavernosal)
*Phentolamine (Systemic)
AU300 *Ambenonium (Systemic)
*Bethanechol (Systemic)
*Cevimeline (Systemic)
*Domperidone (Systemic)
*Edrophonium and Atropine (Systemic)
*Edrophonium (Systemic)
*Metoclopramide (Systemic)
*Neostigmine (Systemic)
*Physostigmine (Systemic)
*Pilocarpine (Systemic)
Pyridostigmine For Military Combat Medical Use (Systemic)
*Pyridostigmine (Systemic)
AU305 Amantadine (Systemic)
*Anisotropine (Systemic)
*Atropine (Systemic)
*Belladonna (Systemic)
*Benztropine (Systemic)
*Biperiden (Systemic)
Chlorpromazine (Systemic)
*Clidinium (Systemic)
Darifenacin (Systemic)
*Dicyclomine (Systemic)
Diphenhydramine, Oral (Systemic)
*Ethopropazine (Systemic)
*Glycopyrrolate (Systemic)
*Homatropine (Systemic)
*Hyoscyamine (Systemic)
*Mepenzolate (Systemic)
*Methantheline (Systemic)
*Methscopolamine (Systemic)
*Orphenadrine Hydrochloride (Systemic)
*Pirenzepine (Systemic)
*Procyclidine (Systemic)
*Propantheline (Systemic)
*Scopolamine, Oral (Systemic)
*Scopolamine, Parenteral (Systemic)
*Scopolamine, Rectal (Systemic)
Thioridazine (Systemic)
*Tolterodine (Systemic)
*Trihexyphenidyl (Systemic)
*Trospium (Systemic)
AU900 *Bromocriptine (Systemic)
*Cabergoline (Systemic)
BL110 *Heparin (Systemic)
BL111 *Ardeparin (Systemic)
*Dalteparin (Systemic)
*Enoxaparin (Systemic)
*Nadroparin (Systemic)
*Tinzaparin (Systemic)
BL112 *Danaparoid (Systemic)
BL113 *Lepirudin (Systemic)
BL114 *Acenocoumarol (Systemic)
*Anisindione (Systemic)
*Dicumarol (Systemic)
*Warfarin (Systemic)
BL115 *Alteplase, Recombinant (Systemic)
*Anistreplase (Systemic)
*Reteplase, Recombinant (Systemic)
*Streptokinase (Systemic)
*Tenecteplase (Systemic)
*Urokinase (Systemic)
BL116 *Aminocaproic Acid (Systemic)
*Antihemophilic Factor (Systemic)
*Anti-inhibitor Coagulant Complex (Systemic)
*Aprotinin (Systemic)
Desmopressin (Systemic)
Epinephrine (Systemic)
*Factor IX (Systemic)
*Factor VIIa (Systemic)
Menadiol (Systemic)
Octreotide (Systemic)
Phytonadione (Systemic)
*Tranexamic Acid (Systemic)
BL117 *Abciximab (Systemic)
Aspirin, Buffered (Systemic)
Aspirin, Sodium Bicarbonate, and Citric Acid (Systemic)
Aspirin Delayed-release Tablets USP (Systemic)
Aspirin Tablets USP (Chewable) (Systemic)
Aspirin Tablets USP (Systemic)
*Clopidogrel (Systemic)
*Dipyridamole and Aspirin (Systemic)
*Dipyridamole (Systemic)
*Eptifibatide (Systemic)
*Ticlopidine (Systemic)
Tirofiban (Systemic)
BL118 *Protamine (Systemic)
BL119 *Antithrombin III (Systemic)
*Argatroban (Systemic)
*Bivalirudin (Systemic)
Drotecogin Alfa (Systemic)
Fondaparinux (Systemic)
BL400 *Anagrelide (Systemic)
*Darbepoetin Alfa (Systemic)
*Epoetin (Systemic)
*Filgrastim (Systemic)
Fluoxymesterone (Systemic)
Hydroxyurea (Systemic)
Leucovorin (Systemic)
Lithium (Systemic)
Nandrolone (Systemic)
*Oprelvekin (Systemic)
Oxymetholone (Systemic)
Pegfilgrastim (Systemic)
*Sargramostim (Systemic)
Stanozolol (Systemic)
Testosterone Cypionate (Systemic)
Testosterone Enanthate (Systemic)
BL700 *Cilostazol (Systemic)
BL800 *Albumin Human (Systemic)
BL900 Immune Globulin Intravenous (Human) (Systemic)
CN101 *Acetaminophen and Codeine (Systemic)
*Alfentanil (Systemic)
*Anileridine (Systemic)
*Aspirin and Codeine, Buffered (Systemic)
*Aspirin and Codeine (Systemic)
*Aspirin and Dihydrocodeine (Systemic)
*Buprenorphine (Systemic)
*Butalbital, Acetaminophen, Caffeine, and Codeine (Systemic)
*Butalbital, Aspirin, Caffeine, and Codeine (Systemic)
*Butorphanol (Nasal-Systemic)
*Butorphanol (Systemic)
*Codeine (Systemic)
*Dihydrocodeine and Acetaminophen (Systemic)
*Fentanyl Citrate (Systemic)
*Fentanyl (Systemic)
*Fentanyl (Transdermal-Systemic)
*Hydrocodone and Acetaminophen (Systemic)
*Hydrocodone and Aspirin (Systemic)
*Hydrocodone (Systemic)
*Hydromorphone (Systemic)
*Ibuprofen and Oxycodone (Systemic)
*Levomethadyl (Systemic)
*Levorphanol (Systemic)
*Meperidine (Systemic)
*Methadone (Systemic)
*Morphine (Systemic)
*Nalbuphine (Systemic)
Opium, Oral (Systemic)
*Opium, Parenteral (Systemic)
*Oxycodone and Acetaminophen (Systemic)
*Oxycodone and Aspirin (Systemic)
*Oxycodone (Systemic)
*Oxymorphone (Systemic)
Paregoric (Systemic)
*Pentazocine and Acetaminophen (Systemic)
*Pentazocine and Aspirin (Systemic)
*Pentazocine (Systemic)
*Phenobarbital, ASA, and Codeine (Systemic)
*Propoxyphene and Acetaminophen (Systemic)
*Propoxyphene and Aspirin (Systemic)
*Propoxyphene (Systemic)
Remifentanil (Systemic)
*Sufentanil (Systemic)
*Tramadol (Systemic)
CN103 *Aspirin (Systemic)
*Acetaminophen, Aspirin, Salicylamide, and Caffeine (Systemic)
*Acetaminophen, Aspirin and Caffeine, Buffered (Systemic)
*Acetaminophen, Aspirin and Caffeine (Systemic)
*Acetaminophen, Salicylamide, and Caffeine (Systemic)
*Acetaminophen, Sodium Bicarbonate, and Citric Acid (Systemic)
*Acetaminophen (Systemic)
Amitriptyline (Systemic)
*Aspirin, Buffered (Systemic)
*Aspirin, Sodium Bicarbonate, and Citric Acid (Systemic)
Baclofen (Systemic)
*Butalbital and Acetaminophen (Systemic)
*Butalbital and Aspirin (Systemic)
Carbamazepine (Systemic)
*Choline and Magnesium Salicylates (Systemic)
*Choline Salicylate (Systemic)
Clomipramine (Systemic)
*Clonidine (Parenteral-Local)
Desipramine (Systemic)
Doxepin (Systemic)
Fluphenazine (Systemic)
Imipramine (Systemic)
*Isometheptene, Dichloralphenazone, and Acetaminophen (Systemic)
*Ketorolac (Systemic)
*Magnesium Salicylate (Systemic)
Maprotiline (Systemic)
*Meprobamate and Aspirin (Systemic)
Methotrimeprazine (Systemic)
Nortriptyline (Systemic)
Salsalate (Systemic)
*Sodium Salicylate (Systemic)
*Tramadol (Systemic)
Trazodone (Systemic)
*Trimipramine (Systemic)
*Ziconotide (Intrathecal)
CN104 Aspirin, Buffered (Systemic)
Aspirin and Caffeine Capsules (Systemic)
Aspirin and Caffeine Tablets (Systemic)
Aspirin Delayed-release Tablets USP (Systemic)
Aspirin Extended-release Tablets USP (Systemic)
Aspirin Suppositories USP (Systemic)
Aspirin Tablets USP (Chewable) (Systemic)
Aspirin Tablets USP (Systemic)
Choline Salicylate (Systemic)
Celecoxib (Systemic)
Choline and Magnesium Salicylates (Systemic)
Diclofenac (Systemic)
Diflunisal (Systemic)
Etodolac (Systemic)
Fenoprofen (Systemic)
*Floctafenine (Systemic)
Ibuprofen (Systemic)
Ketoprofen (Systemic)
Magnesium Salicylate (Systemic)
Meclofenamate (Systemic)
*Mefenamic Acid (Systemic)
Naproxen (Systemic)
Salsalate (Systemic)
Sodium Salicylate (Systemic)
CN105 Acetaminophen, Aspirin, and Caffeine, Buffered (Systemic)
Acetaminophen, Aspirin, and Caffeine (Systemic)
Acetaminophen, Aspirin, Salicylamide, and Caffeine (Systemic)
Acetaminophen, Salicylamide, and Caffeine (Systemic)
*Almotriptan (Systemic)
Atenolol (Systemic)
Clonidine, Oral (Systemic)
Diclofenac (Systemic)
Diflunisal (Systemic)
*Dihydroergotamine (Nasal-Systemic)
*Dihydroergotamine (Systemic)
Divalproex (Systemic)
*Eletriptan (Systemic)

*Ergotamine, Caffeine, and Belladonna Alkaloids (Systemic)
*Ergotamine, Caffeine, and Cyclizine (Systemic)
*Ergotamine, Caffeine, and Diphenhydramine (Systemic)
*Ergotamine, Caffeine, Belladonna Alkaloids, and Pentobarbital (Systemic)
*Ergotamine, Caffeine. and Dimenhydrinate (Systemic)
*Ergotamine and Caffeine (Systemic)
*Ergotamine (Systemic)
Etodolac (Systemic)
Fenoprofen (Systemic)
Floctafenine (Systemic)
Flunarizine (Systemic)
Frovatriptan (Systemic)
Ibuprofen (Systemic)
Indomethacin—For Patent Ductus Arteriosus, Oral (Systemic)
Indomethacin (Systemic)
Isometheptene, Dichloralphenazone, and Acetaminophen (Systemic)
Ketoprofen (Systemic)
Meclofenamate (Systemic)
Mefenamic Acid (Systemic)
*Methysergide (Systemic)
Metoprolol (Systemic)
Nadolol (Systemic)
Naproxen (Systemic)
Naratriptan (Systemic)
Propranolol (Systemic)
*Rizatriptan (Systemic)
*Sumatriptan (Systemic)
Timolol (Systemic)
Verapamil (Systemic)
*Zolmitriptan (Systemic)

CN201 *Desflurane (Inhalation-Systemic)
*Enflurane (Systemic)
*Halothane (Systemic)
*Isoflurane (Systemic)
*Methoxyflurane (Systemic)
*Nitrous Oxide (Systemic)
*Sevoflurane (Inhalation-Systemic)

CN202 *Methohexital (Systemic)
*Thiopental (Systemic)

CN203 *Etomidate (Systemic)
*Ketamine (Systemic)
*Propofol (Systemic)

CN204 *Articaine (Parenteral-Local)
*Bupivacaine (Parenteral-Local)
*Chloroprocaine (Parenteral-Local)
*Diphenhydramine, Parenteral (Systemic)
*Etidocaine (Parenteral-Local)
*Levobupivacaine (Parenteral-Local)
*Lidocaine (Parenteral-Local)
*Mepivacaine (Parenteral-Local)
*Prilocaine (Parenteral-Local)
*Procaine (Parenteral-Local)
*Ropivacaine (Parenteral-Local)
*Tetracaine (Parenteral-Local)

CN205 Epinephrine (Systemic)
*Methoxsalen (Topical)

CN206 Alfentanil (Systemic)
Anileridine (Systemic)
Buprenorphine (Systemic)
Butorphanol (Systemic)
Chlorpromazine (Systemic)
*Droperidol (Systemic)
Etomidate (Systemic)
Fentanyl (Systemic)
Hydromorphone, Parenteral (Systemic)
Ketamine (Systemic)
Levorphanol, Parenteral (Systemic)
Meperidine, Parenteral (Systemic)
Methotrimeprazine (Systemic)
Midazolam (Systemic)
Morphine, Parenteral (Systemic)
Nalbuphine (Systemic)
Oxymorphone, Parenteral (Systemic)
Pentazocine, Parenteral (Systemic)
Propofol (Systemic)
*Remifentanil (Systemic)
Scopolamine, Parenteral (Systemic)
Sufentanil (Systemic)

CN301 *Amobarbital (Systemic)
*Aprobarbital (Systemic)
*Butabarbital (Systemic)
*Pentobarbital (Systemic)
*Phenobarbital (Systemic)
*Secobarbital (Systemic)

CN302 *Alprazolam (Systemic)
*Bromazepam (Systemic)
*Chlordiazepoxide (Systemic)
*Clonazepam (Systemic)
*Clorazepate (Systemic)
*Diazepam, Oral (Systemic)
*Diazepam, Parenteral (Systemic)
*Estazolam (Systemic)
*Flurazepam (Systemic)
*Halazepam (Systemic)
*Ketazolam (Systemic)
*Lorazepam (Systemic)
*Midazolam (Systemic)
*Nitrazepam (Systemic)
*Oxazepam (Systemic)
*Prazepam (Systemic)
*Quazepam (Systemic)
*Temazepam (Systemic)
*Triazolam (Systemic)

CN303 Flumazenil (Systemic)

CN304 *Buspirone (Systemic)
*Escitalopram (Systemic)
*Meprobamate (Systemic)
Venlafaxine (Systemic)

CN309 *Chloral Hydrate (Systemic)
Chlorpromazine (Systemic)
*Dexmedetomidine (Systemic)
Diphenhydramine, Oral (Systemic)
Doxylamine (Systemic)
*Eszopiclone (Systemic)
*Ethchlorvynol (Systemic)
Hydroxyzine (Systemic)
Methotrimeprazine (Systemic)
Promethazine (Systemic)
Propofol (Systemic)
*Ramelteon (Systemic)
Thioridazine (Systemic)
*Zaleplon (Systemic)
*Zolpidem (Systemic)
*Zopiclone (Systemic)

CN400 Acetazolamide (Systemic)
Amobarbital, Parenteral (Systemic)
*Carbamazepine (Systemic)
*Clobazam (Systemic)
Clonazepam (Systemic)
Clorazepate (Systemic)
*Corticotropin, Repository, Injection (Systemic)
Diazepam, Oral (Systemic)
Diazepam, Parenteral (Systemic)
*Diazepam, Rectal (Systemic)
*Divalproex (Systemic)
*Ethosuximide (Systemic)
*Ethotoin (Systemic)
*Felbamate (Systemic)
*Fosphenytoin (Systemic)
*Gabapentin (Systemic)
*Lamotrigine (Systemic)
*Levetiracetam (Systemic)
Lorazepam, Parenteral (Systemic)
Magnesium Sulfate (Systemic)
*Mephenytoin (Systemic)
*Mephobarbital (Systemic)
*Metharbital (Systemic)
*Methsuximide (Systemic)
Midazolam (Systemic)
Nitrazepam (Systemic)
*Oxcarbazepine (Systemic)
*Paraldehyde (Systemic)
*Paramethadione (Systemic)
Pentobarbital, Parenteral (Systemic)
Phenobarbital (Systemic)
*Phenytoin (Systemic)
Pregabalin (Systemic)
*Primidone (Systemic)
Secobarbital, Parenteral (Systemic)
*Tiagabine (Systemic)
*Topiramate (Systemic)
*Trimethadione (Systemic)
*Valproate Sodium (Systemic)
*Valproic Acid (Systemic)
*Vigabatrin (Systemic)
*Zonisamide (Systemic)

CN500 *Apomorphine (Systemic)
*Carbidopa, Entacapone and Levodopa (Systemic)
*Carbidopa and Levodopa (Systemic)
*Entocapone (Systemic)
*Levodopa (Systemic)
*Pergolide (Systemic)
*Pramipexole (Systemic)
*Rasagiline (Systemic)
*Ropinirole (Systemic)
*Selegiline (Systemic)
*Tolcapone (Systemic)

CN550 Dimenhydrinate (Systemic)
Diphenhydramine, Oral (Systemic)
*Diphenidol (Systemic)
Meclizine (Systemic)
Scopolamine, Oral (Systemic)
Scopolamine, Parenteral (Systemic)
*Scopolamine, Transdermal (Systemic)

CN601 *Amitriptyline (Systemic)
*Amoxapine (Systemic)
*Clomipramine (Systemic)
*Desipramine (Systemic)
*Doxepin (Systemic)
*Nortriptyline (Systemic)
*Protriptyline (Systemic)

CN602 *Isocarboxazid (Systemic)
*Moclobemide (Systemic)
*Phenelzine (Systemic)
*Tranylcypromine (Systemic)

CN603 *Citalopram (Systemic)
*Duloxetine (Systemic)
*Escitalopram (Systemic)
*Fluoxetine (Systemic)
Fluvoxamine (Systemic)
*Paroxetine (Systemic)
*Sertraline (Systemic)

CN609 *Bupropion (Systemic)
*Maprotiline (Systemic)
*Mirtazapine (Systemic)
*Nefazodone (Systemic)
*Trazodone (Systemic)
*Venlafaxine (Systemic)

CN701 *Chlorpromazine (Systemic)
*Fluphenazine (Systemic)
*Mesoridazine (Systemic)
*Methotrimeprazine (Systemic)
*Pericyazine (Systemic)
*Perphenazine (Systemic)
*Pipotiazine (Systemic)
*Prochlorperazine (Systemic)
*Promazine (Systemic)
*Thioproperazine (Systemic)
*Thioridazine (Systemic)
*Trifluoperazine (Systemic)
*Triflupromazine (Systemic)

CN709 Aripiprazole (Systemic)
*Chlorprothixene (Systemic)
*Clozapine (Systemic)
Droperidol (Systemic)
*Flupenthixol (Systemic)
*Haloperidol (Systemic)
*Loxapine (Systemic)
*Molindone (Systemic)
*Olanzapine (Systemic)
Pimozide (Systemic)
*Quetiapine (Systemic)
*Risperidone (Systemic)
*Thiothixene (Systemic)
*Ziprasidone (Systemic)

CN750 *Lithium (Systemic)

CN801 *Amphetamine and Dextroamphetamine (Systemic)
*Amphetamine (Systemic)
*Dextroamphetamine (Systemic)
*Methamphetamine (Systemic)

CN802 Dexmethylphenidate (Systemic)
*Methylphenidate (Systemic)

CN809 *Caffeine, Citrated (Systemic)
*Caffeine and Sodium Benzoate (Systemic)
*Caffeine (Systemic)
*Modafinil (Systemic)
*Pemoline (Systemic)

CN850 Acetaminophen, Aspirin, and Caffeine, Buffered (Systemic)
Acetaminophen, Aspirin, and Caffeine (Systemic)
Acetaminophen, Aspirin, Salicylamide, and Caffeine (Systemic)

Acetaminophen, Salicylamide, and Caffeine (Systemic)
Acetaminophen (Systemic)
Aspirin, Buffered (Systemic)
Aspirin and Caffeine Capsules (Systemic)
Aspirin and Caffeine Tablets (Systemic)
Aspirin Delayed-release Tablets USP (Systemic)
Aspirin Extended-release Tablets USP (Systemic)
Aspirin Suppositories USP (Systemic)
Aspirin Tablets USP (Chewable) (Systemic)
Aspirin Tablets USP (Systemic)
Choline Salicylate (Systemic)
Choline and Magnesium Salicylates (Systemic)
Ibuprofen (Systemic)
Indomethacin—For Patent Ductus Arteriosus, Oral (Systemic)
Indomethacin (Systemic)
Magnesium Salicylate (Systemic)
Naproxen (Systemic)
Salsalate (Systemic)
Sodium Salicylate (Systemic)

CN900 Acebutolol (Systemic)
Amantadine (Systemic)
Amitriptyline (Systemic)
Atenolol (Systemic)
Atomoxetine (Systemic)
Carbamazepine (Systemic)
*Chlordiazepoxide and Amitriptyline (Systemic)
Clomipramine (Systemic)
Clonidine, Oral (Systemic)
Desipramine (Systemic)
Divalproex (Systemic)
*Donepezil (Systemic)
Doxepin (Systemic)
*Ergoloid Mesylates (Systemic)
Fluoxetine (Systemic)
*Fluvoxamine (Systemic)
*Gabapentin (Systemic)
*Galantamine (Systemic)
*Glatiramer Acetate (Systemic)
Haloperidol (Systemic)
*Hydrocodone and Ibuprofen (Systemic)
*Imipramine (Systemic)
*Interferon, Beta-1b (Systemic)
*Interferon Beta-1a (Systemic)
Isocarboxazid (Systemic)
Lamotrigine (Systemic)
Lithium (Systemic)
Loxapine (Systemic)
L-Tryptophan (Systemic)
*Memantine (Systemic)
Metoprolol (Systemic)
Nadolol (Systemic)
*Natalizumab (Systemic)
Nortriptyline (Systemic)
Oxprenolol (Systemic)
Paroxetine (Systemic)
*Perphenazine and Amitriptyline (Systemic)
Phenelzine (Systemic)
*Pimozide (Systemic)
Pindolol (Systemic)
*Pregabalin (Systemic)
Propranolol (Systemic)
Protriptyline (Systemic)
*Riluzole (Systemic)
*Rivastigmine (Systemic)
*Sertraline (Systemic)
*Sodium Oxybate (Systemic)
Sotalol (Systemic)
*Tacrine (Systemic)
Timolol (Systemic)
Tranylcypromine (Systemic)
*Tretinoin (Topical)

CV051 *Digitoxin (Systemic)
*Digoxin (Systemic)

CV052 *Milrinone (Systemic)

CV100 *Acebutolol (Systemic)
*Atenolol (Systemic)
*Betaxolol (Systemic)
*Bisoprolol (Systemic)
*Carteolol (Systemic)
*Carvedilol (Systemic)
*Esmolol (Systemic)
*Labetalol (Systemic)
*Metoprolol (Systemic)
*Nadolol (Systemic)
*Oxprenolol (Systemic)
*Penbutolol (Systemic)
*Pindolol (Systemic)
*Propranolol (Systemic)
*Sotalol (Systemic)
*Timolol (Systemic)

CV150 *Doxazosin (Systemic)
*Phenoxybenzamine (Systemic)
Phentolamine (Systemic)
*Prazosin (Systemic)
*Terazosin (Systemic)
*Yohimbine (Systemic)

CV200 Amlodipine and Atorvastatin (Systemic)
*Amlodipine (Systemic)
*Bepridil (Systemic)
*Diltiazem (Systemic)
Enalapril and Felodipine (Systemic)
*Felodipine (Systemic)
*Flunarizine (Systemic)
*Isradipine (Systemic)
*Nicardipine (Systemic)
*Nifedipine (Systemic)
*Nimodipine (Systemic)
*Nisoldipine (Systemic)
*Verapamil (Systemic)

CV250 Acebutolol (Systemic)
Amlodipine and Atorvastatin (Systemic)
Amlodipine (Systemic)
*Amyl Nitrite (Systemic)
Atenolol (Systemic)
Bepridil (Systemic)
Diltiazem (Systemic)
*Isosorbide Dinitrate (Systemic)
*Isosorbide Mononitrate (Systemic)
Labetalol (Systemic)
Metoprolol (Systemic)
Nadolol (Systemic)
Nicardipine (Systemic)
Nifedipine (Systemic)
*Nitroglycerin (Systemic)
Oxprenolol (Systemic)
Pindolol (Systemic)
Propranolol (Systemic)
Sotalol (Systemic)
Timolol (Systemic)
Verapamil (Systemic)

CV300 Acebutolol (Systemic)
*Adenosine (Systemic)
*Amiodarone (Systemic)
Atenolol (Systemic)
Atropine, Parenteral (Systemic)
*Bretylium (Systemic)
Digitoxin (Systemic)
Digoxin (Systemic)
Diltiazem (Systemic)
*Disopyramide (Systemic)
*Dofetilide (Systemic)
Esmolol (Systemic)
*Flecainide (Systemic)
Glycopyrrolate, Parenteral (Systemic)
Hyoscyamine, Parenteral (Systemic)
*Ibutilide (Systemic)
Isoproterenol (Parenteral-Systemic)
*Lidocaine (Systemic)
Magnesium Sulfate (Systemic)
Metoprolol (Systemic)
*Mexiletine (Systemic)
*Moricizine (Systemic)
Nadolol (Systemic)
Oxprenolol (Systemic)
Phenylephrine (Parenteral-Systemic)
Phenytoin (Systemic)
*Procainamide (Systemic)
*Propafenone (Systemic)
Propranolol (Systemic)
*Quinidine (Systemic)
Scopolamine, Parenteral (Systemic)
Sotalol (Systemic)
Timolol (Systemic)
*Tocainide (Systemic)
Verapamil (Systemic)

CV351 Amlodipine and Atorvastatin (Systemic)
*Atorvastatin (Systemic)
*Cerivastatin (Systemic)
*Fluvastatin (Systemic)
*Lovastatin (Systemic)
*Pravastatin (Systemic)
*Rosuvastatin (Systemic)
*Simvastatin (Systemic)

CV359 *Cholestyramine (Oral-Local)
*Clofibrate (Systemic)
*Colesevelam (Oral-Local)
*Colestipol (Oral-Local)
*Ezetimibe and Simvastatin (Systemic)
Ezetimibe (Systemic)
*Fenofibrate (Systemic)
*Gemfibrozil (Systemic)
Niacinamide (Systemic)
Niacin and Lovastatin (Systemic)
Niacin (Systemic)
*Omega-3-Acid Ethyl Esters (Systemic)
*Probucol (Systemic)

CV401 *Hydralazine and Hydrochlorothiazide (Systemic)
*Trandolapril and Verapamil (Systemic)
*Valsartan and Hydrochlorothiazide (Systemic)

CV402 *Epoprostenol (Systemic)
*Fenoldopam (Systemic)
*Hydralazine (Systemic)
*Nitric Oxide (Inhalation-Local)
Nitroglycerin (Systemic)
*Nitroprusside (Systemic)
Treprostinil (Systemic)

CV408 Amiloride and Hydrochlorothiazide (Systemic)
*Amlodipine and Benazepril (Systemic)
*Atenolol and Chlorthalidone (Systemic)
*Benazepril and Hydrochlorothiazide (Systemic)
*Bisoprolol and Hydrochlorothiazide (Systemic)
*Candesartan and Hydrochlorothiazide (Systemic)
*Captopril and Hydrochlorothiazide (Systemic)
*Deserpidine and Hydrochlorothiazide (Systemic)
*Deserpidine and Methyclothiazide (Systemic)
*Enalapril and Felodipine (Systemic)
*Enalapril and Hydrochlorothiazide (Systemic)
*Lisinopril and Hydrochlorothiazide (Systemic)
*Losartan and Hydrochlorothiazide (Systemic)
*Methyldopa and Chlorothiazide (Systemic)
*Methyldopa and Hydrochlorothiazide (Systemic)
*Metoprolol and Hydrochlorothiazide (Systemic)
*Moexipril and Hydrochlorothiazide (Systemic)
*Nadolol and Bendroflumethiazide (Systemic)
*Olmesartan and Hydrochlorothiazide (Systemic)
*Pindolol and Hydrochlorothiazide (Systemic)
*Prazosin and Polythiazide (Systemic)
*Propranolol and Hydrochlorothiazide (Systemic)
*Quinapril and Hydrochlorothiazide (Systemic)
*Rauwolfia Serpentina and Bendroflumethiazide (Systemic)
*Reserpine, Hydralazine, and Hydrochlorothiazide (Systemic)
*Reserpine and Chlorothiazide (Systemic)
*Reserpine and Chlorthalidone (Systemic)
*Reserpine and Hydrochlorothiazide (Systemic)

*Reserpine and Methyclothiazide (Systemic)
Spironolactone and Hydrochlorothiazide (Systemic)
Telmisartan and Hydrochlorothiazide (Systemic)
*Timolol and Hydrochlorothiazide (Systemic)
Triamterene and Hydrochlorothiazide (Systemic)

CV409 Acebutolol (Systemic)
Amiloride (Systemic)
Amlodipine and Atorvastatin (Systemic)
Amlodipine (Systemic)
Atenolol (Systemic)
Benazepril (Systemic)
Bendroflumethiazide (Systemic)
Betaxolol (Systemic)
Bisoprolol (Systemic)
Bumetanide (Systemic)
Candesartan (Systemic)
Captopril (Systemic)
Carteolol (Systemic)
Carvedilol (Systemic)
Chlorothiazide (Systemic)
Chlorthalidone (Systemic)
Cilazapril (Systemic)
*Clonidine, Transdermal (Systemic)
*Clonidine and Chlorthalidone (Systemic)
*Deserpidine (Systemic)
*Diazoxide (Parenteral-Systemic)
Diltiazem (Systemic)
Doxazosin (Systemic)
Enalaprilat (Systemic)
Enalapril (Systemic)
*Eplerenone (Systemic)
Eprosartan (Systemic)
Ethacrynic Acid (Systemic)
Felodipine (Systemic)
Fosinopril (Systemic)
Furosemide (Systemic)
*Guanabenz (Systemic)
*Guanadrel (Systemic)
*Guanethidine (Systemic)
*Guanfacine (Systemic)
Hydrochlorothiazide (Systemic)
Hydroflumethiazide (Systemic)
Indapamide (Systemic)
Irbesartan (Systemic)
Isradipine (Systemic)
Labetalol (Systemic)
Lisinopril (Systemic)
Losartan (Systemic)
*Mecamylamine (Systemic)
Methyclothiazide (Systemic)
*Methyldopa (Systemic)
Metolazone (Systemic)
Metoprolol (Systemic)
*Metyrosine (Systemic)
*Minoxidil (Systemic)
Moexipril (Systemic)
Nadolol (Systemic)
Nicardipine (Systemic)
Nifedipine (Systemic)
Nisoldipine (Systemic)
Oxprenolol (Systemic)
Penbutolol (Systemic)
Perindopril (Systemic)
Phenoxybenzamine (Systemic)
Phentolamine (Systemic)
Pindolol (Systemic)
Polythiazide (Systemic)
Prazosin (Systemic)
Propranolol (Systemic)
Quinapril (Systemic)
Quinethazone (Systemic)
Ramipril (Systemic)
*Rauwolfia Serpentina (Systemic)
*Reserpine (Systemic)
Sotalol (Systemic)
Spironolactone (Systemic)
Telmisartan (Systemic)
Terazosin (Systemic)
Timolol (Systemic)
*Torsemide (Systemic)
Trandolapril (Systemic)
Triamterene (Systemic)
Trichlormethiazide (Systemic)
*Trimethaphan (Systemic)
Valsartan (Systemic)
Verapamil (Systemic)

CV500 Alprostadil (Local)
*Cyclandelate (Systemic)
Fenoldopam (Systemic)
*Isoxsuprine (Systemic)
Nitroprusside (Systemic)
*Nylidrin (Systemic)
*Papaverine (Intracavernosal)
*Papaverine (Systemic)
*Tolazoline (Parenteral-Systemic)

CV600 *Sodium Tetradecyl Sulfate (Systemic)

CV609 Psyllium Hydrophilic Mucilloid (Local)

CV701 Benazepril and Hydrochlorothiazide (Systemic)
*Bendroflumethiazide (Systemic)
Candesartan and Hydrochlorothiazide (Systemic)
Captopril and Hydrochlorothiazide (Systemic)
*Chlorothiazide (Systemic)
*Chlorthalidone (Systemic)
Enalapril and Hydrochlorothiazide (Systemic)
*Hydrochlorothiazide (Systemic)
*Hydroflumethiazide (Systemic)
*Indapamide (Systemic)
Lisinopril and Hydrochlorothiazide (Systemic)
*Methyclothiazide (Systemic)
*Metolazone (Systemic)
Moexipril and Hydrochlorothiazide (Systemic)
*Polythiazide (Systemic)
Quinapril and Hydrochlorothiazide (Systemic)
*Quinethazone (Systemic)
*Trichlormethiazide (Systemic)

CV702 *Bumetanide (Systemic)
*Ethacrynic Acid (Systemic)
*Furosemide (Systemic)
Torsemide (Systemic)

CV703 *Acetazolamide (Systemic)
*Dichlorphenamide (Systemic)
*Methazolamide (Systemic)

CV704 *Amiloride and Hydrochlorothiazide (Systemic)
*Amiloride (Systemic)
*Spironolactone and Hydrochlorothiazide (Systemic)
*Spironolactone (Systemic)
*Triamterene and Hydrochlorothiazide (Systemic)
*Triamterene (Systemic)

CV709 Demeclocycline (Systemic)
*Glycerin (Systemic)
*Mannitol (Systemic)
*Urea (Systemic)

CV800 Benazepril and Hydrochlorothiazide (Systemic)
*Benazepril (Systemic)
Captopril and Hydrochlorothiazide (Systemic)
*Captopril (Systemic)
*Cilzapril (Systemic)
Enalapril and Felodipine (Systemic)
Enalapril and Hydrochlorothiazide (Systemic)
*Enalaprilat (Systemic)
*Enalapril (Systemic)
*Fosinopril (Systemic)
Lisinopril and Hydrochlorothiazide (Systemic)
*Lisinopril (Systemic)
Moexipril and Hydrochlorothiazide (Systemic)
*Moexipril (Systemic)
*Perindopril (Systemic)
Quinapril and Hydrochlorothiazide (Systemic)
*Quinapril (Systemic)
*Ramipril (Systemic)
*Trandolapril (Systemic)

CV805 Candesartan and Hydrochlorothiazide (Systemic)
*Candesartan (Systemic)
*Eprosartan (Systemic)
*Irbesartan (Systemic)
*Losartan (Systemic)
Olmesartan (Systemic)
*Telmisartan (Systemic)
*Valsartan (Systemic)

CV900 Abciximab (Systemic)
Acebutolol (Systemic)
*Amlodipine and Atorvastatin (Systemic)
Atenolol (Systemic)
Atorvastatin (Systemic)
Benazepril (Systemic)
*Bosentan (Systemic)
Calcium Chloride (Systemic)
Calcium Gluconate, Parenteral (Systemic)
Captopril (Systemic)
Cerivastatin (Systemic)
Chlorpropamide (Systemic)
Cilazepril (Systemic)
Cilostazol (Systemic)
Desmopressin (Systemic)
Digitoxin (Systemic)
Digoxin (Systemic)
Dihydroergotamine (Systemic)
Dobutamine (Parenteral-Systemic)
Dopamine (Parenteral-Systemic)
Enalaprilat (Systemic)
Enalapril (Systemic)
Ephedrine (Parenteral-Systemic)
Epinephrine (Parenteral-Systemic)
*Ethanolamine Oleate (Parenteral-Local)
Fludrocortisone (Systemic)
Fluvastatin (Systemic)
Fosinopril (Systemic)
Hydralazine (Systemic)
*Iloprost (Inhalation)
Immune Globulin Intravenous (Human) (Systemic)
*Inamrinone (Systemic)
*Indomethacin—For Patent Ductus Arteriosus, Parenteral (Systemic)
Indomethacin—For Patent Ductus Arteriosus, Oral (Systemic)
Indomethacin (Systemic)
Isosorbide Dinitrate (Systemic)
Lisinopril (Systemic)
Lovastatin (Systemic)
Mephentermine (Parenteral-Systemic)
Metaraminol (Parenteral-Systemic)
Methoxamine (Parenteral-Systemic)
Metoprolol (Systemic)
*Midodrine (Systemic)
Moexipril (Systemic)
Nadolol (Systemic)
*Nesiritide (Systemic)
Nitroglycerin (Systemic)
Nitroprusside (Systemic)
Norepinephrine (Parenteral-Systemic)
Octreotide (Systemic)
Oxprenolol (Systemic)
*Pentoxifylline (Systemic)
Perindopril (Systemic)
Phentolamine (Systemic)
Phenylephrine (Parenteral-Systemic)
Pravastatin (Systemic)
Prazosin (Systemic)
Propranolol (Systemic)
Quinapril (Systemic)
Ramipril (Systemic)
Sildenafil (Systemic)
Simvastatin (Systemic)
Sotalol (Systemic)
Timolol (Systemic)
Trandolapril (Systemic)
Verapamil (Systemic)

DE101 *Ammoniated Mercury (Systemic)
Chlorhexidine (Mucosal-Local)
*Chlortetracycline (Topical)
Clindamycin (Topical)
*Clioquinol (Topical)
Erythromycin (Topical)
*Gentamicin (Topical)
*Iodine (Topical)
*Mafenide (Topical)
*Mupirocin (Topical)
*Neomycin, Polymyxin B, and Bacitracin (Topical)

*Neomycin and Polymyxin B (Topical)
*Neomycin (Topical)
*Nitrofurazone (Topical)
*Silver Sulfadiazine (Topical)
Tetracycline Periodontal Fibers (Mucosal-Local)
Tetracycline (Topical)

DE102 *Amphotericin B (Topical)
*Butenafine (Topical)
*Carbol-Fuchsin (Topical)
*Ciclopirox (Topical)
Clioquinol (Topical)
*Clotrimazole (Topical)
*Econazole (Topical)
*Gentian Violet (Topical)
*Ketoconazole (Topical)
Mafenide (Topical)
*Miconazole (Topical)
*Naftifine (Topical)
*Nystatin (Topical)
*Oxiconazole (Topical)
*Sertaconazole (Topical)
Silver Sulfadiazine (Topical)
*Sulconazole (Topical)
*Terbinafine (Topical)
*Tioconazole (Topical)
*Tolnaftate (Topical)
*Undecylenic Acid, Compound (Topical)

DE103 *Acyclovir (Topical)
*Docosanol (Topical)
*Penciclovir (Topical)

DE200 *Alclometasone (Topical)
*Amcinonide (Topical)
*Beclomethasone (Topical)
*Betamethasone (Topical)
*Clobetasol (Topical)
*Clobetasone (Topical)
*Clocortolone (Topical)
*Desonide (Topical)
*Desoximetasone (Topical)
*Dexamethasone (Topical)
*Diflorasone (Topical)
*Diflucortolone (Topical)
*Flumethasone (Topical)
*Fluocinolone (Topical)
*Fluocinonide (Topical)
*Flurandrenolide (Topical)
*Fluticasone (Topical)
*Halcinonide (Topical)
*Halobetasol (Topical)
*Hydrocortisone (Topical)
*Mometasone (Topical)
*Triamcinolone (Topical)

DE250 *Clioquinol and Hydrocortisone (Topical)
*Clotrimazole and Betamethasone (Topical)
*Nystatin and Triamcinolone (Topical)

DE300 *Aminobenzoic Acid, Padimate O, and Oxybenzone (Topical)
*Aminobenzoic Acid and Titanium Dioxide (Topical)
*Avobenzone, Octocrylene, Octyl Salicylate, and Oxybenzone (Topical)
*Avobenzone, Octyl Methoxycinnamate, and Oxybenzone (Topical)
*Avobenzone, Octyl Methoxycinnamate, Octyl Salicylate, and Oxybenzone (Topical)
*Avobenzone and Octyl Methoxycinnamate (Topical)
*Dioxybenzone, Oxybenzone, and Padimate O (Topical)
*Homosalate, Menthyl Anthranilate, and Octyl Methoxycinnamate (Topical)
*Homosalate, Menthyl Anthranilate, Octyl Methoxycinnamate, Octyl Salicylate, and Oxybenzone (Topical)
*Homosalate, Octocrylene, Octyl Methoxycinnamate, and Oxybenzone (Topical)
*Homosalate, Octyl Methoxycinnamate, and Oxybenzone (Topical)
*Homosalate, Octyl Methoxycinnamate, Octyl Salicylate, and Oxybenzone (Topical)
*Homosalate and Oxybenzone (Topical)
*Homosalate (Topical)
*Lisadimate, Oxybenzone, and Padimate O (Topical)
*Lisadimate and Padimate O (Topical)
*Menthyl Anthranilate, Octocrylene, and Octyl Methoxycinnamate (Topical)
*Menthyl Anthranilate, Octocrylene, Octyl Methoxycinnamate, and Oxybenzone (Topical)
*Menthyl Anthranilate, Octyl Methoxycinnamate, Octyl Salicylate, and Oxybenzone (Topical)
*Menthyl Anthranilate, Octyl Methoxycinnamate and Octyl Salicylate (Topical)
*Menthyl Anthranilate, Octyl Methoxycinnamate and Oxybenzone (Topical)
*Menthyl Anthranilate and Octyl Methoxycinnamate (Topical)
*Menthyl Anthranilate and Padimate O(Topical)
*Menthyl Anthranilate and Titanium Dioxide (Topical)
*Menthyl Anthranilate (Topical)
*Octocrylene, Octyl Methoxycinnamate, Octyl Salicylate, and Oxybenzone (Topical)
*Octocrylene, Octyl Methoxycinnamate, Octyl Salicylate, Oxybenzone, and Titanium Dioxide (Topical)
*Octocrylene, Octyl Methoxycinnamate, Oxybenzone, and Titanium Dioxide (Topical)
*Octocrylene, Octyl Methoxycinnamate and Oxybenzone (Topical)
*Octocrylene, Octyl Methoxycinnamate and Titanium Dioxide (Topical)
*Octocrylene and Octyl Methoxycinnamate (Topical)
*Octyl Methoxycinnamate, Octyl Salicylate, and Titanium Dioxide (Topical)
*Octyl Methoxycinnamate, Octyl Salicylate, Oxybenzone, and Padimate O (Topical)
*Octyl Methoxycinnamate, Octyl Salicylate, Oxybenzone, and Titanium Dioxide (Topical)
*Octyl Methoxycinnamate, Octyl Salicylate, Oxybenzone, Padimate O, and Titanium Dioxide (Topical)
*Octyl Methoxycinnamate, Octyl Salicylate, Oxybenzone, Phenylbenzimidazole, and Titanium Dioxide (Topical)
*Octyl Methoxycinnamate, Octyl Salicylate, Phenylbenzimidazole, and Titanium Dioxide (Topical)
*Octyl Methoxycinnamate, Octyl Salicylate and Oxybenzone (Topical)
*Octyl Methoxycinnamate, Oxybenzone, and Padimate O (Topical)
*Octyl Methoxycinnamate, Oxybenzone, and Titanium Dioxide (Topical)
*Octyl Methoxycinnamate, Oxybenzone, Padimate O, and Titanium Dioxide (Topical)
*Octyl Methoxycinnamate and Octyl Salicylate (Topical)
*Octyl Methoxycinnamate and Oxybenzone (Topical)
*Octyl Methoxycinnamate and Padimate O (Topical)
*Octyl Methoxycinnamate and Phenylbenzimidazole (Topical)
*Octyl Methoxycinnamate (Topical)
*Octyl Salicylate and Padimate O (Topical)
*Octyl Salicylate (Topical)
*Oxybenzone and Roxadimate (Topical)
*Padimate O (Topical)
*Phenylbenzimidazole and Sulisobenzone (Topical)
*Phenylbenzimidazole (Topical)
*Titanium Dioxide and Zinc Oxide (Topical)
*Titanium Dioxide (Topical)
*Trolamine Salicylate (Topical)

DE400 *Chloroxine (Topical)
*Pyrithione (Topical)
*Selenium Sulfide (Topical)

DE500 Alcohol and Sulfur (Topical)
Benzoyl Peroxide (Topical)
Coal Tar (Topical)
Podofilox (Topical)
*Podophyllum (Topical)
Resorcinol and Sulfur (Topical)
Resorcinol (Topical)
*Salicylic Acid, Sulfur, and Coal Tar (Topical)
*Salicylic Acid and Sulfur (Topical)
*Salicylic Acid Cream (Topical)
*Salicylic Acid Gel (Topical)
*Salicylic Acid Lotion (Topical)
*Salicylic Acid Ointment (Topical)
*Salicylic Acid Pads (Topical)
*Salicylic Acid Plaster (Topical)
*Salicylic Acid Shampoo (Topical)
*Salicylic Acid Soap (Topical)
*Salicylic Acid Topical Solution (Topical)
*Sulfur Bar Soap (Topical)
*Sulfur Cream (Topical)
*Sulfur Lotion (Topical)
*Sulfur Ointment (Topical)
Tretinoin Cream USP (Oil-in-water) (Topical)
Tretinoin Gel USP (Topical)
Tretinoin Topical Solution USP (Topical)

DE600 *Alitretinoin (Topical)
Bleomycin (Systemic)
Carmustine (Systemic)
*Diclofenac (Topical)
*Fluorouracil (Topical)
Imiquimod (Topical)
*Mechlorethamine (Topical)
Mitomycin (Systemic)

DE700 *Benzocaine and Menthol (Topical)
*Benzocaine Cream USP (Topical)
Benzocaine Ointment (Mucosal-Local)
Benzocaine Ointment USP (Topical)
*Benzocaine Topical Aerosol (Mucosal-Local)
*Benzocaine Topical Aerosol USP (Topical)
*Benzocaine Topical Spray Solution (Topical)
*Butamben (Topical)
*Dibucaine Cream USP (Topical)
Dibucaine Ointment (Mucosal-Local)
Dibucaine Ointment USP (Topical)
*Lidocaine and Prilocaine (Topical)
*Lidocaine Hydrochloride Film-forming Gel (Topical)
Lidocaine Hydrochloride Jelly USP (Topical)
*Lidocaine Hydrochloride Ointment (Topical)
*Lidocaine Hydrochloride Topical Aerosol (Topical)
Lidocaine Ointment (Mucosal-Local)
Lidocaine 5% Ointment USP (Topical)
*Lidocaine 2.5% Ointment USP (Topical)
*Lidocaine (Topical)
*Lidocaine Topical Spray Solution (Topical)
*Pramoxine and Menthol (Topical)
Pramoxine Cream (Mucosal-Local)
Pramoxine Hydrochloride Cream USP (Topical)
*Pramoxine Hydrochloride Lotion USP (Topical)
Tetracaine and Menthol Ointment (Mucosal-Local)

Tetracaine and Menthol (Topical)
Tetracaine Cream (Mucosal-Local)
Tetracaine (Topical)

DE751 Doxycycline (Systemic)
Erythromycin (Systemic)
Erythromycin Estolate (Systemic)
Erythromycin Ethylsuccinate (Systemic)
Erythromycin Stearate (Systemic)
*Isotretinoin (Systemic)
Minocycline (Systemic)
Tetracycline (Systemic)

DE752 *Adapalene (Topical)
*Alcohol and Acetone (Topical)
*Alcohol and Sulfur (Topical)
*Azelaic Acid (Topical)
*Benzoyl Peroxide (Topical)
*Clindamycin (Topical)
*Dapsone (Topical)
*Erythromycin and Benzoyl Peroxide (Topical)
*Erythromycin (Topical)
*Meclocycline (Topical)
*Metronidazole (Topical)
*Resorcinol and Sulfur (Topical)
*Resorcinol (Topical)
Salicylic Acid and Sulfur Bar Soap (Topical)
Salicylic Acid and Sulfur Cleansing Lotion (Topical)
Salicylic Acid Gel (Topical)
Salicylic Acid Lotion (Topical)
Salicylic Acid Ointment (Topical)
Salicylic Acid Pads (Topical)
Salicylic Acid Soap (Topical)
Salicylic Acid Topical Solution (Topical)
Sulfur Bar Soap (Topical)
Sulfur Cream (Topical)
Sulfur Lotion (Topical)
Sulfur Ointment (Topical)
Tazarotene (Topical)
*Tetracycline (Topical)
*Tretinoin Cream USP (Oil-in-water) (Topical)
*Tretinoin Gel USP (Topical)
*Tretinoin Topical Solution, USP (Topical)

DE801 *Acitretin (Systemic)
*Alefacept (Systemic)
Cyclophosphamide (Systemic)
Cyclosporine (Systemic)
*Efalizumab (Systemic)
*Methotrexate—For Noncancerous Conditions (Systemic)
*Methoxsalen (Systemic)
Trioxsalen (Systemic)

DE802 *Anthralin (Topical)
*Calcipotriene (Topical)
*Coal Tar (Topical)
Salicylic Acid, Sulfur, and Coal Tar (Topical)
Salicylic Acid Gel (Topical)
Salicylic Acid Ointment (Topical)
*Tazarotene (Topical)

DE890 *Aminobenzoate Potassium (Systemic)
Beta-carotene (Systemic)
Cholestyramine (Oral-Local)
Cimetidine (Systemic)
Colestipol (Oral-Local)
Doxepin (Systemic)
Finasteride (Systemic)
Isotretinoin (Systemic)
Methoxsalen (Systemic)
*Sulfapyridine (Systemic)
*Trioxsalen (Systemic)

DE900 *Aminolevulinic Acid (Topical)
Anthralin (Topical)
Azelaic Acid (Topical)
*Becaplermin (Topical)
*Bentoquatam (Topical)
*Bexarotene (Topical)
*Calamine (Topical)
*Capsaicin (Topical)
Carbol-Fuchsin (Topical)
Coal Tar (Topical)
*Diethyltoluamide (Topical)
*Doxepin (Topical)
*Eflornithine (Topical)
*Mequinol and Tretinoin (Topical)
Methoxsalen (Topical)
*Minoxidil (Topical)
Pimecrolimus (Topical)
Salicylic Acid, Sulfur, and Coal Tar (Topical)
Salicylic Acid and Sulfur Shampoo (Topical)
Salicylic Acid Lotion (Topical)
Salicylic Acid Ointment (Topical)
Salicylic Acid Shampoo (Topical)
Sulfur Ointment (Topical)
*Tacrolimus (Topical)

DX101 *Barium Sulfate (Local)
*Iodixanol (Systemic)
*Iohexol (Local)
*Iohexol (Systemic)
*Iopamidol (Systemic)
*Iopromide (Systemic)
*Ioversol (Systemic)
*Ioxilan (Systemic)

DX102 *Diatrizoate and Iodipamide (Local)
*Diatrizoate Meglumine and Diatrizoate Sodium (Systemic)
*Diatrizoate Meglumine (Local)
*Diatrizoate Meglumine (Systemic)
*Diatrizoate Sodium (Local)
*Diatrizoate Sodium (Systemic)
*Iocetamic Acid (Systemic)
*Iodipamide (Systemic)
*Iopanoic Acid (Systemic)
*Iothalamate (Local)
*Iothalamate (Systemic)
*Ioxaglate (Local)
*Ioxaglate (Systemic)
*Ipodate (Systemic)
*Tyropanoate (Systemic)

DX201 *Ferrous Citrate Fe 59 (Systemic)
*Gallium Citrate Ga 67 (Systemic)
*Indium In 111 Capromab Pendetide (Systemic)
*Indium In 111 Oxyquinoline (Systemic)
*Indium In 111 Pentetate (Systemic)
*Indium In 111 Pentetreotide (Systemic)
*Indium In 111 Satumomab Pendetide (Systemic)
*Iobenguane I 123 (Systemic—Diagnostic)
*Iobenguane I 131 (Systemic—Diagnostic)
*Iodohippurate Sodium I 123 (Systemic)
*Iodohippurate Sodium I 131 (Systemic)
*Iofetamine I 123 (Systemic)
*Krypton Kr 81m (Systemic)
*Rubidium Rb 82 (Systemic)
*Sodium Chromate Cr 51 (Systemic)
*Sodium Iodide I 123 (Systemic)
*Sodium Iodide I 131 (Systemic—Diagnostic)
*Technetium Tc 99m Albumin Aggregated (Systemic)
*Technetium Tc 99m Albumin (Systemic)
*Technetium Tc 99m Apcitide (Systemic)
*Technetium Tc 99m Arcitumomab (Systemic)
*Technetium Tc 99m Bicisate (Systemic)
*Technetium Tc 99m Disofenin (Systemic)
*Technetium Tc 99m Exametazime (Systemic)
*Technetium Tc 99m Gluceptate (Systemic)
*Technetium Tc 99m Mebrofenin (Systemic)
*Technetium Tc 99m Medronate (Systemic)
*Technetium Tc 99m Mertiatide (Systemic)
*Technetium Tc 99m Oxidronate (Systemic)
*Technetium Tc 99m Pentetate (Systemic)
*Technetium Tc 99m (Pyro- and Trimeta-) Phosphates (Systemic)
*Technetium Tc 99m Pyrophosphate (Systemic)
*Technetium Tc 99m Sestamibi (Systemic)
*Technetium Tc 99m Succimer (Systemic)
*Technetium Tc 99m Sulfur Colloid (Systemic)
*Technetium Tc 99m Teboroxime (Systemic)
*Technetium Tc 99m Tetrofosmin (Systemic)
*Thallous Chloride Tl 201 (Systemic)
*Xenon Xe 127 (Systemic)
*Xenon Xe 133 (Systemic)

DX202 *Iodinated I 125 Albumin (Systemic)
*Iodinated I 131 Albumin (Systemic)
*Urea C 14 (Systemic)

DX300 *Tuberculin, Purified Protein Derivative (Parenteral-Local)

DX900 Acetylcysteine (Inhalation)
Adenosine (Systemic)
*Albumin Microspheres Sonicated (Systemic)
Alprostadil (Local)
Amyl Nitrite (Systemic)
Ascorbic Acid (Systemic)
*Bentiromide (Systemic)
Cholecystokinin (Systemic)
Chorionic Gonadotropin (Systemic)
Clomiphene (Systemic)
Clonidine, Oral (Systemic)
*Corticorelin Ovine (Systemic-Diagnostic)
*Corticotropin for Injection USP (Systemic)
*Cosyntropin (Systemic)
Cyanocobalamin (Systemic)
Demecarium (Ophthalmic)
Desmopressin (Systemic)
Dexamethasone (Systemic)
Dinoprost (Parenteral-Local)
Dipyridamole (Systemic)
Echothiophate (Ophthalmic)
Edetate Calcium Disodium (Systemic)
Edrophonium (Systemic)
Ergonovine (Systemic)
*Ferumoxides (Systemic)
Fludrocortisone (Systemic)
*Gadobenate (Systemic)
*Gadodiamide (Systemic)
*Gadopentetate (Systemic)
*Gadoteridol (Systemic)
*Gadoversetamide (Systemic)
Glucagon (Systemic)
Gonadorelin (Systemic)
*Histamine (Systemic)
Hydroxocobalamin (Systemic)
Insulin, Isophane, Human, and Insulin Human (Systemic)
Insulin, Isophane, Human (Systemic)
Insulin, Isophane (Systemic)
Insulin Human, Buffered (Systemic)
Insulin Human (Systemic)
Insulin (Systemic)
Insulin Zinc, Extended, Human (Systemic)
Insulin Zinc, Extended (Systemic)
Insulin Zinc, Human (Systemic)
Insulin Zinc (Systemic)
*Inulin (Systemic)
Isoflurophate (Ophthalmic)
Levothyroxine (Systemic)
Liothyronine (Systemic)
*Mangafodipir (Systemic)
Methylene Blue (Systemic)
*Metyrapone (Systemic)
Oxytocin (Systemic)
*Phenolsulfonphthalein (Systemic)
Phenylephrine (Ophthalmic)
*Protirelin (Systemic)
Simethicone (Oral-Local)
Sincalide (Systemic)
*Teriparatide (Systemic)
*Thyrotropin Alfa (Systemic)
*Thyrotropin (Systemic)
Tropicamide (Ophthalmic)

Tubocurarine (Systemic)
Vasopressin (Systemic)

GA101 *Alumina, Calcium Carbonate, and Sodium Bicarbonate (Oral-Local)
*Alumina and Sodium Bicarbonate (Oral-Local)
*Aluminum Carbonate, Basic (Oral-Local)
*Aluminum Hydroxide (Oral-Local)

GA103 *Alumina, Magnesia, and Magnesium Carbonate (Oral-Local)
*Alumina, Magnesium Alginate, and Magnesium Carbonate (Oral-Local)
*Alumina and Magnesia (Oral-Local)
*Alumina and Magnesium Carbonate (Oral-Local)
*Alumina and Magnesium Trisilicate (Oral-Local)

GA104 *Alumina, Magnesium Carbonate, and Sodium Bicarbonate (Oral-Local)
*Alumina, Magnesium Trisilicate, and Sodium Bicarbonate (Oral-Local)

GA105 *Calcium Carbonate (Oral-Local)
Calcium Carbonate (Systemic)

GA106 *Calcium Carbonate and Magnesia (Oral-Local)
*Calcium and Magnesium Carbonates (Oral-Local)

GA107 *Magaldrate (Oral-Local)

GA108 Magnesium Hydroxide (Local)
*Magnesium Hydroxide (Oral-Local)
Magnesium Oxide (Local)
*Magnesium Oxide (Oral-Local)

GA109 *Magnesium Carbonate and Sodium Bicarbonate (Oral-Local)

GA110 Alumina, Calcium Carbonate, and Sodium Bicarbonate (Oral-Local)
Alumina and Sodium Bicarbonate (Oral-Local)
Aspirin, Sodium Bicarbonate, and Citric Acid (Systemic)
*Sodium Bicarbonate (Systemic)

GA199 *Alumina, Magnesia, and Simethicone (Oral-Local)
*Alumina, Magnesia, Calcium Carbonate, and Simethicone (Oral-Local)
*Alumina, Magnesia, Magnesium Carbonate, and Simethicone (Oral-Local)
*Alumina, Magnesium Carbonate, and Simethicone (Oral-Local)
*Alumina and Simethicone (Oral-Local)
*Aluminum Carbonate, Basic and Simethicone (Oral-Local)
*Calcium Carbonate, Magnesia, and Simethicone (Oral-Local)
*Calcium Carbonate and Simethicone (Oral-Local)
*Magaldrate and Simethicone (Oral-Local)

GA201 *Malt Soup Extract and Psyllium (Local)
*Malt Soup Extract (Local)
*Methylcellulose (Local)
*Polycarbophil (Local)
*Psyllium Hydrophilic Mucilloid and Carboxymethylcellulose (Local)
*Psyllium Hydrophilic Mucilloid (Local)
*Psyllium (Local)

GA202 *Lactulose (Local)
*Magnesium Citrate (Local)
*Magnesium Hydroxide (Local)
Magnesium Hydroxide (Oral-Local)
*Magnesium Oxide (Local)
*Magnesium Oxide (Oral-Local)
*Magnesium Sulfate (Local)
*Polyethylene Glycol 3550 (Systemic)
*Sodium Phosphate, Oral (Local)

GA203 *Mineral Oil, Oral (Local)

GA204 *Bisacodyl, Oral (Local)
*Casanthranol (Local)
*Cascara Sagrada and Aloe (Local)
*Cascara Sagrada and Phenolphthalein (Local)
*Cascara Sagrada (Local)
*Castor Oil (Local)
*Dehydrocholic Acid (Local)
*Phenolphthalein and Senna (Local)
*Phenolphthalein (Local)
*Senna, Oral (Local)
*Sennosides (Local)

GA205 *Docusate, Oral (Local)
*Poloxamer 188 (Local)

GA208 Aluminum Hydroxide (Oral-Local)
*Attapulgite (Oral-Local)
*Bismuth Subsalicylate (Oral-Local)
Cholestyramine (Oral-Local)
Colestipol (Oral-Local)
Dehydrocholic Acid (Local)
Desipramine (Systemic)
*Difenoxin and Atropine (Systemic)
*Diphenoxylate and Atropine (Systemic)
Glycopyrrolate (Systemic)
Imipramine (Systemic)
*Kaolin and Pectin (Oral-Local)
Lactulose (Local)
*Loperamide (Oral-Local)
*Octreotide (Systemic)
Polycarbophil (Local)
*Rifaximin (Oral-Local)

GA209 *Bisacodyl and Docusate (Local)
*Casanthranol and Docusate (Local)
*Danthron and Docusate (Local)
*Dehydrocholic Acid, Docusate, and Phenolphthalein (Local)
*Dehydrocholic Acid and Docusate (Local)
*Dehydrocholic Acid (Local)
*Magnesium Hydroxide and Cascara Sagrada (Local)
*Magnesium Hydroxide and Mineral Oil (Local)
*Mineral Oil, Glycerin, and Phenolphthalein (Local)
*Mineral Oil and Glycerin (Local)
*Mineral Oil and Phenolphthalein (Local)
*Phenolphthalein and Docusate (Local)
*Polyethylene Glycol and Electrolytes (Local)
*Psyllium and Senna (Local)
*Psyllium Hydrophilic Mucilloid and Senna (Local)
*Psyllium Hydrophilic Mucilloid and Sennosides (Local)
*Sennosides and Docusate (Local)

GA250 Psyllium Hydrophilic Mucilloid (Local)

GA301 *Cimetidine (Systemic)
*Famotidine (Systemic)
*Nizatidine (Systemic)
*Ranitidine (Systemic)

GA302 *Sucralfate (Oral-Local)

GA303 *Bismuth Subsalicylate, Metronidazole, and Tetracycline—For *H. pylori* (Systemic)

GA304 *Esomeprazole (Systemic)
*Lansoprazole (Systemic)
*Omeprazole (Systemic)
*Pantoprazole (Systemic)
*Rabeprazole (Systemic)

GA309 Amitriptyline (Systemic)
Doxepin (Systemic)
Trimipramine (Systemic)

GA400 Azathioprine (Systemic)
*Balsalazide (Systemic)
Codeine (Systemic)
*Infliximab (Systemic)
*Mesalamine (Oral-Local)
Morphine, Parenteral (Systemic)
Morphine (Systemic)
*Olsalazine (Oral-Local)
*Opium, Oral (Systemic)
*Paregoric (Systemic)
*Sulfasalazine (Systemic)

GA500 Pancrelipase (Systemic)

GA601 *Ipecac (Oral-Local)

GA605 *Dolasetron (Systemic)
*Granisetron (Systemic)
*Ondansetron (Systemic)
*Palonosetron (Systemic)

GA609 *Aprepitant (Systemic)
*Buclizine (Systemic)
Chlorpromazine (Systemic)
*Cyclizine (Systemic)
Dexamethasone (Systemic)
Diphenidol (Systemic)
Domperidone (Systemic)
*Dronabinol (Systemic)
Droperidol (Systemic)
*Fructose, Dextrose, and Phosphoric Acid (Oral-Local)
Haloperidol (Systemic)
Hydrocortisone (Systemic)
Lorazepam, Parenteral (Systemic)
*Meclizine (Systemic)
Methotrimeprazine (Systemic)
Metoclopramide (Systemic)
*Nabilone (Systemic)
Perphenazine (Systemic)
Prednisone (Systemic)
Prochlorperazine (Systemic)
Scopolamine, Oral (Systemic)
Scopolamine, Parenteral (Systemic)
*Thiethylperazine (Systemic)
Trifluoperazine (Systemic)
Triflupromazine (Systemic)
*Trimethobenzamide (Systemic)

GA751 *Benzphetamine (Systemic)
*Diethylpropion (Systemic)
*Mazindol (Systemic)
*Phendimetrazine (Systemic)
*Phentermine (Systemic)
*Sibutramine (Systemic)

GA753 Dronabinol (Systemic)
Promethazine (Systemic)

GA801 Anisotropine (Systemic)
Atropine (Systemic)
Belladonna (Systemic)
Clidinium (Systemic)
Dicyclomine (Systemic)
Glucagon (Systemic)
Glycopyrrolate (Systemic)
Homatropine (Systemic)
Hyoscyamine (Systemic)
Mepenzolate (Systemic)
Methantheline (Systemic)
Methscopolamine (Systemic)
Pirenzepine (Systemic)
Scopolamine, Oral (Systemic)
Scopolamine, Parenteral (Systemic)

GA802 *Atropine, Hyoscyamine, Scopolamine, and Phenobarbital (Systemic)
*Atropine and Phenobarbital (Systemic)

GA900 *Alosetron (Systemic)
*Cisapride (Systemic)
Diazoxide (Oral-Systemic)
*Glutamine (Systemic)
Insulin, Isophane, Human, and Insulin Human (Systemic)
Insulin, Isophane, Human (Systemic)
Insulin, Isophane (Systemic)
Insulin Human, Buffered (Systemic)
Insulin Human (Systemic)
Insulin (Systemic)
Insulin Zinc, Extended, Human (Systemic)
Insulin Zinc, Extended (Systemic)
Insulin Zinc, Human (Systemic)
Insulin Zinc, Prompt (Systemic)
Insulin Zinc (Systemic)
Kanamycin (Oral-Local)
Mercaptopurine (Systemic)
Metronidazole (Systemic)
*Monoctanoin (Local)
Neomycin (Oral-Local)
Phenobarbital (Systemic)
*Simethicone (Oral-Local)
Tegaserod (Systemic)
*Ursodiol (Systemic)
Vasopressin (Systemic)

GU100 *Phenazopyridine (Systemic)

GU201 *Atropine, Hyoscyamine, Methenamine, Methylene Blue, Phenyl Salicylate, and Benzoic Acid (Systemic)
Atropine (Systemic)
*Darifenacin (Systemic)
*Flavoxate (Systemic)
Hyoscyamine (Systemic)
Methantheline (Systemic)
*Oxybutynin (Systemic)
Scopolamine, Oral (Systemic)
*Solifenacin (Systemic)

GU301 *Metronidazole (Vaginal)
*Sulfanilamide (Vaginal)
*Triple Sulfa (Vaginal)

GU302 *Butoconazole (Vaginal)

*Clindamycin (Vaginal)
*Clotrimazole (Vaginal)
*Econazole (Vaginal)
*Gentian Violet (Vaginal)
*Miconazole (Vaginal)
*Nystatin (Vaginal)
*Terconazole (Vaginal)
*Tioconazole (Vaginal)
GU309 *Clindamycin (Vaginal)
GU400 *Benzalkonium Chloride (Vaginal)
*Cellulose Sodium Phosphate (Systemic)
*Nonoxynol 9 (Vaginal)
*Octoxynol 9 (Vaginal)
GU500 *Dienestrol (Vaginal)
*Estradiol (Vaginal)
*Estrogens, Conjugated (Vaginal)
*Estrone (Vaginal)
*Estropipate (Vaginal)
GU600 *Carbetocin (Systemic)
Carboprost (Systemic)
Dinoprostone (Cervical/Vaginal)
Dinoprost (Parenteral-Local)
*Ergonovine (Systemic)
*Methylergonovine (Systemic)
*Oxytocin (Systemic)
*Sodium Chloride (Parenteral-Local)
*Urea (Parenteral-Local)
GU650 Terbutaline, Parenteral (Systemic)
GU700 *Dutasteride (Systemic)
*Finasteride (Systemic)
*Tamsulosin (Systemic)
GU900 Acetazolamide (Systemic)
*Alfuzosin (Systemic)
Allopurinol (Systemic)
Alprostadil (Local)
Aluminum Hydroxide (Oral-Local)
Amitriptyline (Systemic)
Bendroflumethiazide (Systemic)
Benzocaine, Butamben, and Tetracaine Gel (Mucosal-Local)
Benzocaine Gel (Mucosal-Local)
Chlorothiazide (Systemic)
Chlorthalidone (Systemic)
Cholestyramine (Oral-Local)
Citric Acid, Glucono-delta-lactone, and Magnesium (Mucosal-Local)
Diethylstilbestrol and Methyltestosterone (Systemic)
*Dimethyl Sulfoxide (Mucosal-Local)
Dinoprostone (Cervical/Vaginal)
Doxazosin (Systemic)
Dyclonine Topical Solution (Mucosal-Local)
Epinephrine (Systemic)
Ergonovine (Systemic)
Estrogens, Conjugated, and Methyltestosterone (Systemic)
Estrogens, Esterified, and Methyltestosterone (Systemic)
Fluoxymesterone and Ethinyl Estradiol (Systemic)
Hydrochlorothiazide (Systemic)
Hydroflumethiazide (Systemic)
Imipramine (Systemic)
Isoxsuprine (Systemic)
Lidocaine Hydrochloride Jelly (Mucosal-Local)
Lidocaine Hydrochloride Jelly USP (Topical)
Magnesium Hydroxide (Oral-Local)
Magnesium Sulfate (Systemic)
Methyclothiazide (Systemic)
Metolazone (Systemic)
Papaverine (Intracavernosal)
Penicillamine (Systemic)
*Pentosan (Systemic)
Phenoxybenzamine (Systemic)
Phentolamine (Intracavernosal)
Polythiazide (Systemic)
Potassium Citrate and Citric Acid (Systemic)
Potassium Citrate and Sodium Citrate (Systemic)
Potassium Citrate (Systemic)
Potassium and Sodium Phosphates (Systemic)
Potassium Phosphates (Systemic)
Prazosin (Systemic)
Quinethazone (Systemic)
*Racemethionine (Systemic)
Ritodrine (Systemic)
*Sildenafil (Systemic)
Sodium Citrate and Citric Acid (Systemic)
Sodium Phosphates (Systemic)
*Tadalafil (Systemic)
Terazosin (Systemic)
Testosterone and Estradiol (Systemic)
*Tiopronin (Systemic)
Trichlormethiazide (Systemic)
Tricitrates (Systemic)
*Vardenafil (Systemic)
Yohimbine (Systemic)
HS051 *Betamethasone (Systemic)
*Budesonide (Systemic)
*Cortisone (Systemic)
*Dexamethasone (Systemic)
*Hydrocortisone (Systemic)
*Methylprednisolone (Systemic)
*Prednisolone (Systemic)
*Prednisone (Systemic)
*Triamcinolone (Systemic)
HS052 *Fludrocortisone (Systemic)
HS101 *Fluoxymesterone (Systemic)
*Methyltestosterone (Systemic)
*Nandrolone (Systemic)
*Oxandrolone (Systemic)
*Oxymetholone (Systemic)
*Stanozolol (Systemic)
*Testosterone Cypionate (Systemic)
*Testosterone Enanthate (Systemic)
*Testosterone Propionate (Systemic)
*Testosterone (Systemic)
*Testosterone Undecanoate (Systemic)
HS102 *Conjugated Estrogens (Systemic)
Dienestrol (Vaginal)
*Diethylstilbestrol (Systemic)
*Estradiol (Systemic)
Estradiol (Vaginal)
Estrogens, Conjugated (Vaginal)
*Estrogens, Conjugated (Systemic)
*Estrogens, Esterified (Systemic)
*Estrone (Systemic)
Estrone (Vaginal)
*Estropipate (Systemic)
Estropipate (Vaginal)
*Ethinyl Estradiol (Systemic)
HS103 *Hydroxyprogesterone (Systemic)
*Levonorgestrel (Systemic)
*Medrogestone (Systemic)
*Medroxyprogesterone (Systemic)
*Megestrol (Systemic)
*Norethindrone (Systemic)
*Norgestrel (Systemic)
*Progesterone (Systemic)
HS104 *Desogestrel and Ethinyl Estradiol (Systemic)
Diethylstilbestrol (Systemic)
Estrogens, Conjugated (Systemic)
Ethinyl Estradiol (Systemic)
*Ethynodiol Diacetate and Ethinyl Estradiol (Systemic)
*Etonogestrel and Ethinyl Estradiol (Vaginal)
*Levonorgestrel and Ethinyl Estradiol (Systemic)
Levonorgestrel (Systemic)
*Medroxyprogesterone and Estradiol (Systemic)
Medroxyprogesterone (Systemic)
Norelgestromin and Ethinyl Estradiol (Systemic)
*Norethindrone and Ethinyl Estradiol (Systemic)
*Norethindrone and Mestranol (Systemic)
Norethindrone (Systemic)
*Norgestimate and Ethinyl Estradiol (Systemic)
*Norgestrel and Ethinyl Estradiol (Systemic)
Norgestrel (Systemic)
HS105 *Conjugated Estrogens and Medroxyprogesterone Acetate (Systemic)
*Drospirenone and Estradiol (Systemic)
*Norethindrone Acetate and Ethinyl Estradiol (Systemic)
*Norgestimate and 17 Beta-Estradiol (Systemic)
HS106 *Choriogonadotropin Alfa (Systemic)
*Chorionic Gonadotropin (Systemic)
*Clomiphene (Systemic)
*Follitropin Alfa (Systemic)
*Follitropin Beta (Systemic)
*Lutropin Alfa (Systemic)
*Menotropins (Systemic)
*Urofollitropin (Systemic)
HS109 *Cetrorelix (Systemic)
*Danazol (Systemic)
*Desogestrel and Ethinyl Estradiol (Systemic)
Ethynodiol Diacetate and Ethinyl Estradiol (Systemic)
*Mifepristone (Systemic)
Norethindrone Acetate and Ethinyl Estradiol (Systemic)
Norethindrone and Ethinyl Estradiol (Systemic)
Norethindrone and Mestranol (Systemic)
Norgestrel and Ethinyl Estradiol (Systemic)
*Testosterone Undecanoate (Systemic)
HS200 *Alprostadil (Local)
*Alprostadil (Systemic)
*Carboprost (Systemic)
*Dinoprostone (Cervical/Vaginal)
*Dinoprost (Parenteral-Local)
*Misoprostol (Systemic)
HS301 *Alendronate (Systemic)
*Ibandronate (Systemic)
HS302 Clodronate (Systemic)
Etidronate (Systemic)
*Pamidronate (Systemic)
*Zoledronic Acid (Systemic)
HS303 Alendronate (Systemic)
*Etidronate (Systemic)
*Pamidronate (Systemic)
*Risedronate (Systemic)
Tiludronate (Systemic)
HS304 Bromocriptine (Systemic)
*Calcitonin-Human (Systemic)
*Calcitonin (Nasal-Systemic)
*Calcitonin-Salmon (Systemic)
HS305 Plicamycin (Systemic)
HS309 *Gallium Nitrate (Systemic)
HS451 *Agalsidase Beta (Systemic)
*Alglucerase (Systemic)
*Galsulfase (Systemic)
*Imiglucerase (Systemic)
*Laronidase (Systemic)
*Pancrelipase (Systemic)
*Sacrosidase (Systemic)
HS452 *Betaine (Systemic)
*Miglustat (Systemic)
Nitisinone (Systemic)
*Orlistat (Oral-Local)
HS501 *Insulin, Isophane, Human, and Insulin Human (Systemic)
*Insulin, Isophane, Human (Systemic)
*Insulin, Isophane (Systemic)
*Insulin Aspart (Systemic)
*Insulin Detemir (Systemic)
*Insulin Glargine (Systemic)
*Insulin Glulisine (Systemic)
*Insulin Human, Buffered (Systemic)
*Insulin Human (Systemic)
*Insulin Lispro (Systemic)
*Insulin (Systemic)
*Insulin Zinc, Extended, Human (Systemic)
*Insulin Zinc, Extended (Systemic)
*Insulin Zinc, Human (Systemic)
*Insulin Zinc, Prompt (Systemic)
*Insulin Zinc (Systemic)
HS502 *Acetohexamide (Systemic)
*Chlorpropamide (Systemic)
*Gliclazide (Systemic)
*Glimepiride (Systemic)
*Glipizide (Systemic)
*Glyburide (Systemic)
*Tolazamide (Systemic)
*Tolbutamide, Oral (Systemic)
HS503 *Metformin (Systemic)

HS504 *Acarbose (Systemic)
*Miglitol (Systemic)
HS505 *Pioglitazone (Systemic)
*Rosiglitazone (Systemic)
*Troglitazone (Systemic)
HS508 *Diazoxide (Oral-Systemic)
*Glucagon (Systemic)
HS509 *Exenatide (Systemic)
*Glipizide and Metformin (Systemic)
*Glyburide and Metformin (Systemic)
*Metformin and Pioglitazone (Systemic)
*Nateglinide (Systemic)
*Pramlintide (Systemic)
*Repaglinide (Systemic)
*Rosiglitazone and Metformin (Systemic)
HS600 *Cinacalcet (Systemic)
Teriparatide (Systemic)
HS701 Cosyntropin (Systemic)
*Somatrem (Systemic)
*Somatropin, Recombinant (Systemic)
HS702 *Desmopressin (Systemic)
*Vasopressin (Systemic)
HS851 *Levothyroxine (Systemic)
*Liothyronine (Systemic)
*Liotrix (Systemic)
*Thyroglobulin (Systemic)
*Thyroid (Systemic)
HS852 *Iodine, Strong (Systemic)
Iopodate (Systemic)
*Methimazole (Systemic)
*Potassium Iodide (Systemic)
*Propylthiouracil (Systemic)
Sodium Iodide (Systemic)
HS900 *Aminoglutethimide (Systemic)
*Cabergoline (Systemic)
Carbamazepine (Systemic)
*Cholecystokinin (Systemic)
Chorionic Gonadotropin (Systemic)
Clomiphene (Systemic)
*Diethylstilbestrol and Methyltestosterone (Systemic)
*Estrogens, Conjugated, and Methyltestosterone (Systemic)
*Estrogens, Esterified, and Methyltestosterone (Systemic)
*Fluoxymesterone and Ethinyl Estradiol (Systemic)
*Ganirelix (Systemic)
*Gonadorelin (Systemic)
*Goserelin (Systemic)
Ketoconazole (Systemic)
*Leuprolide (Systemic)
*Mecasermin (Systemic)
Metyrapone (Systemic)
Mitotane (Systemic)
*Nafarelin (Systemic)
Octreotide (Systemic)
Oxytocin (Systemic)
*Pegvisomant (Systemic)
*Raloxifene (Systemic)
*Sermorelin (Systemic)
*Sincalide (Systemic)
Spironolactone (Systemic)
*Testosterone and Estradiol (Systemic)
IM100 *Bacillus Calmette-Guerin (BCG) Live (Systemic)
*Cholera Vaccine (Systemic)
*Haemophilus B Conjugate Vaccine (HbOC—Diphtheria CRM_{197} Protein Conjugate) (Systemic)
*Haemophilus B Conjugate Vaccine (PRP-D—Diphtheria Toxoid Conjugate) (Systemic)
*Haemophilus B Conjugate Vaccine (PRP-OMP—Meningococcal Protein Conjugate) (Systemic)
*Haemophilus B Conjugate Vaccine (PRP-T—Tetanus Protein Conjugate) (Systemic)
*Haemophilus B Polysaccharide Vaccine (Systemic)
*Hepatitis A Vaccine Inactivated (Systemic)
*Hepatitis A Virus Vaccine Inactivated and Hepatitis B Virus Vaccine Recombinant (Systemic)
*Hepatitis B Vaccine Recombinant (Systemic)
*Influenza Virus Vaccine (Systemic)
*Japanese Encephalitis Virus Vaccine (Systemic)
*Lyme Disease Vaccine (Systemic)
*Measles, Mumps, and Rubella Virus Vaccine Live (Systemic)
*Measles and Rubella Virus Vaccine Live (Systemic)
*Measles Virus Vaccine Live (Systemic)
*Meningococcal Polysaccharide Vaccine (Systemic)
*Meningococcal Vaccine, Diphtheria Conjugate (Systemic)
*Mumps Virus Vaccine Live (Systemic)
*Pneumococcal Conjugate Vaccine (Systemic)
*Pneumococcal Vaccine Polyvalent (Systemic)
*Poliovirus Vaccine Inactivated Enhanced Potency (Systemic)
*Poliovirus Vaccine Inactivated (Systemic)
*Poliovirus Vaccine Live Oral (Systemic)
*Rabies Vaccine, Human Diploid Cell (Systemic)
*Rabies Vaccine Adsorbed (Systemic)
*Rubella and Mumps Virus Vaccine Live (Systemic)
*Rubella Virus Vaccine Live (Systemic)
*Typhoid Vaccine Inactivated (Parenteral-Systemic)
*Typhoid Vaccine Live Oral (Systemic)
*Typhoid Vi Polysaccharide Vaccine (Systemic)
*Varicella Virus Vaccine (Systemic)
*Yellow Fever Vaccine (Systemic)
IM200 *Diphtheria and Tetanus Toxoids (Systemic)
*Tetanus and Diphtheria Toxoids (Systemic)
*Tetanus Toxoid (Systemic)
IM300 *Diphtheria Antitoxin (Systemic)
IM402 *Anti-thymocyte Globulin (Rabbit) (Systemic)
* Hepatitis B Immune Globulin (Human) (Systemic)
*Immune Globulin Intravenous (Human) (Systemic)
*Palivizumab (Systemic)
*Rabies Immune Globulin (Systemic)
*Respiratory Syncytial Virus Immune Globulin Intravenous (Systemic)
*Rho(D) Immune Globulin (Systemic)
*Tetanus Immune Globulin (Systemic)
*Vaccinia Immune Globulin Intravenous (Human) (Systemic)
IM403 Anti-thymocyte Globulin (Rabbit) (Systemic)
*Azathioprine (Systemic)
*Basilixumab (Systemic)
Betamethasone (Systemic)
Chlorambucil (Systemic)
Cortisone (Systemic)
Cyclophosphamide (Systemic)
*Cyclosporine (Systemic)
*Daclizumab (Systemic)
Dexamethasone (Systemic)
Efalizumab (Systemic)
Hydrocortisone (Systemic)
Mercaptopurine (Systemic)
Methylprednisolone (Systemic)
*Muromonab-CD3 (Systemic)
*Mycophenolate (Systemic)
Prednisolone (Systemic)
Prednisone (Systemic)
*Sirolimus (Systemic)
*Tacrolimus (Systemic)
Triamcinolone (Systemic)
IM404 *Imiquimod (Topical)
*Interferon, Alfacon-1 (Systemic)
*Interferon, Gamma (Systemic)
*Interferon Alfa-2a, Recombinant (Systemic)
*Interferon Alfa-2b, Recombinant (Systemic)
*Interferon Alfa-n1 (Ins) (Systemic)
*Interferon Alfa-n3 (Systemic)
*Levamisole (Systemic)
*Peginterferon Alfa-2a (Systemic)
*Peginterferon Alfa-2b (Parenteral)
IM409 *Glatiramer Acetate (Systemic)
*Interferon, Beta-1b (Systemic)
*Interferon Beta-1a (Systemic)
Natalizumab (Systemic)
IM900 *Cromolyn (Systemic/Oral-Local)
Danazol (Systemic)
*Diphtheria, Tetanus, Pertussis, Hepatitis B, Poliovirus Vaccine (Systemic)
*Diphtheria and Tetanus Toxoids and Pertussis Vaccine Adsorbed and Haemophilus b Conjugate Vaccine (Systemic)
*Diphtheria and Tetanus Toxoids and Pertussis Vaccine Adsorbed (Systemic)
Oxymetholone (Systemic)
*Pegademase (Systemic)
Stanozolol (Systemic)
*Thalidomide (Systemic)
Tranexamic Acid (Systemic)
IP100 *Talc (Intrapleural-Local)
Tetracycline (Systemic)
MS101 Aspirin, Buffered (Systemic)
Aspirin and Caffeine Capsules (Systemic)
Aspirin and Caffeine Tablets (Systemic)
Aspirin Delayed-release Tablets USP (Systemic)
Aspirin Extended-release Tablets USP (Systemic)
Aspirin Suppositories USP (Systemic)
Aspirin Tablets USP (Chewable) (Systemic)
Aspirin Tablets USP (Systemic)
Choline Salicylate (Systemic)
Choline and Magnesium Salicylates (Systemic)
Magnesium Salicylate (Systemic)
*Salsalate (Systemic)
Sodium Salicylate (Systemic)
MS102 *Celecoxib (Systemic)
*Diclofenac (Systemic)
*Diflunisal (Systemic)
*Etodolac (Systemic)
*Fenoprofen (Systemic)
*Flurbiprofen (Systemic)
*Ibuprofen (Systemic)
*Indomethacin—For Patent Ductus Arteriosus, Oral (Systemic)
*Indomethacin (Systemic)
*Ketoprofen (Systemic)
*Meclofenamate (Systemic)
*Meloxicam (Systemic)
*Nabumetone (Systemic)
*Naproxen (Systemic)
*Oxaprozin (Systemic)
*Phenylbutazone (Systemic)
*Piroxicam (Systemic)
*Rofecoxib (Systemic)
*Sulindac (Systemic)
*Tenoxicam (Systemic)
Thalidomide (Systemic)
*Tiaprofenic Acid (Systemic)
*Tolmetin (Systemic)
*Valdecoxib (Systemic)
MS103 Cyclophosphamide (Systemic)
Mercaptopurine (Systemic)
Methotrexate—For Noncancerous Conditions (Systemic)
MS109 *Adalimumab (Systemic)
Anakinra (Systemic)
*Auranofin (Systemic)
*Aurothioglucose (Systemic)
Azathioprine (Systemic)
Chloroquine (Systemic)
Cyclosporine (Systemic)
*Diclofenac and Misoprostol (Systemic)
*Etanercept (Systemic)
*Gold Sodium Thiomalate (Systemic)
Hydroxychloroquine (Systemic)
Infliximab (Systemic)
*Leflunomide (Systemic)
Minocycline (Systemic)
*Penicillamine (Systemic)

Sulfasalazine (Systemic)
MS200 *Baclofen (Intrathecal-Systemic)
*Baclofen (Systemic)
*Carisoprodol (Systemic)
*Chlorphenesin (Systemic)
*Chlorzoxazone (Systemic)
*Cyclobenzaprine (Systemic)
*Dantrolene (Systemic)
Diazepam, Oral (Systemic)
Diazepam, Parenteral (Systemic)
Lorazepam (Systemic)
*Metaxalone (Systemic)
*Methocarbamol (Systemic)
*Orphenadrine, Aspirin, and Caffeine (Systemic)
*Orphenadrine Citrate (Systemic)
Phenytoin (Systemic)
MS300 *Atracurium (Systemic)
Botulinum Toxin Type A (Parenteral-Local)
*Botulinum Toxin Type B (Parenteral-Local)
*Cisatracurium (Systemic)
*Doxacurium (Systemic)
*Gallamine (Systemic)
*Mivacurium (Systemic)
*Pancuronium (Systemic)
*Rocuronium (Systemic)
*Succinylcholine (Systemic)
*Tubocurarine (Systemic)
*Vecuronium (Systemic)
MS400 *Allopurinol (Systemic)
*Colchicine (Systemic)
Diclofenac (Systemic)
Diflunisal (Systemic)
Etodolac (Systemic)
Fenoprofen (Systemic)
Floctafenine (Systemic)
Ibuprofen (Systemic)
Indomethacin—For Patent Ductus Arteriosus, Oral (Systemic)
Indomethacin (Systemic)
Ketoprofen (Systemic)
Naproxen (Systemic)
Phenylbutazone (Systemic)
Piroxicam (Systemic)
*Probenecid and Colchicine (Systemic)
*Probenecid (Systemic)
*Sulfinpyrazone (Systemic)
Sulindac (Systemic)
MS900 Acetazolamide (Systemic)
*Chondrocytes, Autologous Cultured (Systemic)
*Chymopapain (Parenteral-Local)
Conjugated Estrogens and Medroxyprogesterone Acetate (Systemic)
Conjugated Estrogens (Systemic)
Diethylstilbestrol (Systemic)
Estradiol (Systemic)
Estrogens, Conjugated (Systemic)
Estrogens, Esterified (Systemic)
Estropipate (Systemic)
Ethinyl Estradiol (Systemic)
*Hyaluronate Sodium Derivative (Systemic)
*Hyaluronate Sodium (Systemic)
Quinine (Systemic)
*Tizanidine (Systemic)
MS1029 *Flavocoxid (Systemic)
NT100 *Oxymetazoline (Nasal)
*Phenylephrine (Nasal)
*Xylometazoline (Nasal)
NT201 *Beclomethasone (Nasal)
*Budesonide (Nasal)
*Dexamethasone (Nasal)
*Flunisolide (Nasal)
*Fluticasone (Nasal)
*Mometasone (Nasal)
*Triamcinolone (Nasal)
NT300 *Benzocaine, Butamben, and Tetracaine Gel (Mucosal-Local)
*Benzocaine, Butamben, and Tetracaine Ointment (Mucosal-Local)
*Benzocaine, Butamben, and Tetracaine Topical Aerosol (Mucosal-Local)
*Benzocaine, Butamben, and Tetracaine Topical Solution (Mucosal-Local)
*Benzocaine Gel (Mucosal-Local)
Benzocaine Topical Aerosol (Mucosal-Local)
Benzocaine Topical Aerosol USP (Topical)
*Benzocaine Topical Solution (Mucosal-Local)
*Cocaine (Mucosal-Local)
*Dyclonine Topical Solution (Mucosal-Local)
*Lidocaine Hydrochloride Jelly (Mucosal-Local)
*Lidocaine Hydrochloride Jelly USP (Topical)
*Lidocaine Hydrochloride Topical Solution (Mucosal-Local)
*Lidocaine Hydrochloride Topical Spray Solution (Mucosal-Local)
*Lidocaine Ointment (Mucosal-Local)
*Lidocaine 5% Ointment USP (Topical)
*Lidocaine Topical Aerosol (Mucosal-Local)
*Tetracaine Hydrochloride Topical Solution (Mucosal-Local)
NT400 *Azelastine (Nasal)
NT900 *Cromolyn (Nasal)
*Ipratropium (Nasal)
*Mupirocin (Nasal)
OP109 Fluorouracil (Systemic)
OP110 *Betaxolol (Ophthalmic)
*Carteolol (Ophthalmic)
*Levobetaxolol (Ophthalmic)
*Levobunolol (Ophthalmic)
*Metipranolol (Ophthalmic)
*Timolol (Ophthalmic)
OP111 Timolol (Systemic)
OP112 *Brinzolamide (Ophthalmic)
*Dorzolamide (Ophthalmic)
OP113 Acetazolamide (Systemic)
Dichlorphenamide (Systemic)
Methazolamide (Systemic)
OP114 *Apraclonidine (Ophthalmic)
*Brimonidine (Ophthalmic)
*Dipivefrin (Ophthalmic)
*Epinephrine (Ophthalmic)
OP115 Glycerin (Systemic)
Mannitol (Systemic)
Urea (Systemic)
OP116 *Bimatoprost (Ophthalmic)
*Latanoprost (Ophthalmic)
*Travoprost (Ophthalmic)
OP117 *Dorzolamide and Timolol (Ophthalmic)
OP118 *Carbachol (Ophthalmic)
*Demecarium (Ophthalmic)
*Echothiophate (Ophthalmic)
*Isoflurophate (Ophthalmic)
*Physostigmine (Ophthalmic)
*Pilocarpine (Ophthalmic)
OP119 *Unoprostone (Ophthalmic)
OP201 *Chloramphenicol (Ophthalmic)
*Chlortetracycline (Ophthalmic)
*Ciprofloxacin (Ophthalmic)
*Erythromycin (Ophthalmic)
*Framycetin (Ophthalmic)
*Gatifloxacin (Ophthalmic)
*Gentamicin (Ophthalmic)
*Levofloxacin (Ophthalmic)
*Moxifloxacin (Ophthalmic)
*Neomycin, Polymyxin B, and Bacitracin (Ophthalmic)
*Neomycin, Polymyxin B, and Gramicidin (Ophthalmic)
*Neomycin (Ophthalmic)
*Norfloxacin (Ophthalmic)
*Ofloxacin (Ophthalmic)
*Sulfacetamide (Ophthalmic)
*Sulfisoxazole (Ophthalmic)
*Tetracycline (Ophthalmic)
Tobramycin and Dexamethasone (Ophthalmic)
*Tobramycin (Ophthalmic)
OP202 *Natamycin (Ophthalmic)
OP203 *Idoxuridine (Ophthalmic)
*Trifluridine (Ophthalmic)
*Vidarabine (Ophthalmic)
OP301 *Betamethasone (Ophthalmic)
*Dexamethasone (Ophthalmic)
*Fluorometholone (Ophthalmic)
*Hydrocortisone (Ophthalmic)
*Loteprednol (Ophthalmic)
*Medrysone (Ophthalmic)
*Prednisolone (Ophthalmic)
*Rimexolone (Ophthalmic)
*Tobramycin and Dexamethasone (Ophthalmic)
OP302 *Bromfenac (Ophthalmic)
*Diclofenac (Ophthalmic)
Flurbiprofen (Ophthalmic)
Indomethacin (Ophthalmic)
*Ketorolac (Ophthalmic)
*Nepafenac (Ophthalmic)
OP350 *Loteprednol and Tobramycin (Ophthalmic)
*Neomycin, Polymyxin B, and Hydrocortisone (Ophthalmic)
OP500 *Hydroxypropyl Cellulose (Ophthalmic)
*Hydroxypropyl Methylcellulose (Ophthalmic)
OP600 *Atropine (Ophthalmic)
*Cyclopentolate (Ophthalmic)
*Homatropine (Ophthalmic)
Hydroxyamphetamine and Tropicamide (Ophthalmic)
*Phenylephrine (Ophthalmic)
*Scopolamine (Ophthalmic)
*Tropicamide (Ophthalmic)
OP700 *Proparacaine (Ophthalmic)
*Tetracaine (Ophthalmic)
OP801 *Azelastine (Ophthalmic)
*Cromolyn (Ophthalmic)
*Emadastine (Ophthalmic)
*Epinastine (Ophthalmic)
*Ketotifen (Ophthalmic)
*Levocabastine (Ophthalmic)
*Lodoxamide (Ophthalmic)
*Nedocromil (Ophthalmic)
*Olopatadine (Ophthalmic)
*Pemirolast (Ophthalmic)
OP802 *Naphazoline (Ophthalmic)
*Oxymetazoline (Ophthalmic)
Phenylephrine (Ophthalmic)
OP900 *Botulinum Toxin Type A (Parenteral-Local)
*Cyclosporine (Ophthalmic)
*Dapiprazole (Ophthalmic)
Demecarium (Ophthalmic)
Diclofenac (Ophthalmic)
Echothiophate (Ophthalmic)
*Edetate Disodium (Ophthalmic)
*Flurbiprofen (Ophthalmic)
*Fomiversen (Parenteral-Local)
*Ganciclovir (Implantation-Ophthalmic)
*Hydroxypropyl Methylcellulose (Parenteral-Local)
*Indomethacin (Ophthalmic)
Isoflurophate (Ophthalmic)
Ketorolac (Ophthalmic)
*Sodium Chloride (Ophthalmic)
*Suprofen (Ophthalmic)
*Verteporfin (Parenteral-Local)
Yohimbine (Systemic)
OR500 *Chlorhexidine (Mucosal-Local)
OR600 Benzocaine, Butamben, and Tetracaine Gel (Mucosal-Local)
Benzocaine, Butamben, and Tetracaine Ointment (Mucosal-Local)
Benzocaine, Butamben, and Tetracaine Topical Aerosol (Mucosal-Local)
Benzocaine, Butamben, and Tetracaine Topical Solution (Mucosal-Local)
*Benzocaine and Menthol Lozenges (Mucosal-Local)
*Benzocaine and Phenol Gel (Mucosal-Local)
*Benzocaine and Phenol Topical solution (Mucosal-Local)
*Benzocaine Dental Paste (Mucosal-Local)
Benzocaine Gel (Mucosal-Local)
*Benzocaine Lozenges (Mucosal-Local)
Benzocaine Ointment (Mucosal-Local)

Benzocaine Topical Aerosol (Mucosal-Local)
Benzocaine Topical Aerosol USP (Topical)
Benzocaine Topical Solution (Mucosal-Local)
Cocaine (Mucosal-Local)
*Dyclonine Lozenges (Mucosal-Local)
Dyclonine Topical Solution (Mucosal-Local)
Lidocaine Hydrochloride Oral Topical Solution (Mucosal-Local)
Lidocaine Hydrochloride Topical Solution (Mucosal-Local)
Lidocaine Ointment (Mucosal-Local)
Lidocaine 5% Ointment USP (Topical)
*Lidocaine Oral Topical Solution (Mucosal-Local)
Lidocaine Topical Aerosol (Mucosal-Local)
OR900 *Amlexanox (Mucosal-Local)
*Chlorhexidine (Implantation-Local)
*Doxycycline (Mucosal-Local)
*Hydrocortisone (Dental)
*Minocycline (Mucosal-Local)
*Tetracycline Periodontal Fibers (Mucosal-Local)
*Triamcinolone (Dental)
OT101 *Chloramphenicol (Otic)
*Gentamicin (Otic)
*Ofloxacin (Otic)
OT200 *Betamethasone (Otic)
*Dexamethasone (Otic)
OT250 *Ciprofloxacin and Dexamethasone (Otic)
*Colistin, Neomycin, and Hydrocortisone (Otic)
*Hydrocortisone and Acetic Acid (Otic)
*Neomycin, Polymyxin B, and Hydrocortisone (Otic)
OT300 Antipyrine and Benzocaine (Otic)
OT400 *Antipyrine and Benzocaine (Otic)
PH000 *Hyaluronidase (Parenteral-Local)
RE110 *Beclomethasone (Inhalation-Local)
*Budesonide (Inhalation-Local)
*Cromolyn (Inhalation-Local)
*Dexamethasone (Inhalation-Local)
*Flunisolide (Inhalation-Local)
*Fluticasone and Salmeterol (Inhalation-Local)
*Fluticasone (Inhalation-Local)
*Mometasone (Inhalation-Local)
*Nedocromil (Inhalation-Local)
*Triamcinolone (Inhalation-Local)
RE120 *Albuterol (Inhalation-Local)
*Bitolterol (Inhalation-Local)
*Epinephrine (Inhalation-Local)
*Fenoterol (Inhalation-Local)
*Fluticasone and Salmeterol (Inhalation-Local)
*Formoterol (Inhalation-Local)
*Isoetharine (Inhalation-Local)
*Isoproterenol (Inhalation-Local)
*Levalbuterol (Inhalation-Local)
*Metaproterenol (Inhalation-Local)
*Pirbuterol (Inhalation-Local)
*Procaterol (Inhalation-Local)
*Racepinephrine (Inhalation-Local)
*Salmeterol (Inhalation-Local)
*Terbutaline (Inhalation-Local)
RE125 *Terbutaline, Oral (Systemic)
RE140 *Aminophylline, Parenteral (Systemic)
*Aminophylline Extended-release Tablets (Systemic)
*Aminophylline Oral Solution USP (Systemic)
*Aminophylline Tablets USP (Systemic)
*Dyphylline (Systemic)
*Oxtriphylline (Systemic)
*Theophylline, Parenteral (Systemic)
*Theophylline Capsules USP (Systemic)
*Theophylline Elixir (Systemic)
*Theophylline Extended-release Capsules USP (Systemic)
*Theophylline Oral Solution (Systemic)
*Theophylline Tablets (Systemic)
RE150 *Ipratropium (Inhalation-Local)
*Tiotropium (Inhalation-Local)
RE160 Cromolyn (Inhalation-Local)
RE180 *Montelukast (Systemic)
*Zafirlukast (Systemic)
*Zileuton (Systemic)
RE190 *Aminophylline Extended-release Tablets (Systemic)
Aminophylline Oral Solution USP (Systemic)
Beclomethasone (Inhalation-Local)
Budesonide (Inhalation-Local)
Dexamethasone (Inhalation-Local)
*Epinephrine (Systemic)
Flunisolide (Inhalation-Local)
*Fluticasone and Salmeterol (Inhalation-Local)
Fluticasone (Inhalation-Local)
*Ipratropium and Albuterol (Inhalation-Local)
*Isoproterenol (Systemic)
*Ketotifen (Systemic)
Mometasone (Inhalation-Local)
Nedocromil (Inhalation-Local)
*Omalizumab (Systemic)
*Oxtriphylline and Guaifenesin (Systemic)
Oxtriphylline (Systemic)
*Terbutaline, Parenteral (Systemic)
*Theophylline, Ephedrine, and Phenobarbital (Systemic)
*Theophylline and Guaifenesin (Systemic)
Theophylline Capsules USP (Systemic)
Theophylline Elixir (Systemic)
Theophylline Extended-release Capsules USP (Systemic)
Theophylline Extended-release Tablets (Systemic)
Theophylline Oral Solution (Systemic)
Theophylline Tablets (Systemic)
Triamcinolone (Inhalation-Local)
RE200 *Pseudoephedrine (Systemic)
RE301 *Chlorpheniramine, Pheniramine, Pyrilamine, Phenylephrine, Hydrocodone, Salicylamide, Caffeine, and Ascorbic Acid (Systemic)
*Chlorpheniramine, Phenylephrine, and Hydrocodone (Systemic)
*Chlorpheniramine, Phenylephrine, Codeine and Ammonium Chloride (Systemic)
*Chlorpheniramine, Phenylephrine, Codeine and Potassium Iodide (Systemic)
*Chlorpheniramine, Phenylephrine, Hydrocodone, Acetaminophen, and Caffeine (Systemic)
*Chlorpheniramine, Pseudoephedrine and Codeine (Systemic)
*Chlorpheniramine, Pseudoephedrine and Hydrocodone (Systemic)
*Chlorpheniramine and Hydrocodone (Systemic)
*Codeine, Ammonium Chloride, and Guaifenesin (Systemic)
*Codeine and Guaifenesin (Systemic)
Codeine (Systemic)
*Diphenhydramine, Codeine, and Ammonium Chloride (Systemic)
*Hydrocodone and Homatropine (Systemic)
*Hydrocodone and Potassium Guaiacolsulfonate (Systemic)
Hydrocodone (Systemic)
Hydromorphone, Parenteral (Systemic)
*Hydromorphone and Guaifenesin (Systemic)
Hydromorphone (Systemic)
Methadone (Systemic)
Morphine (Systemic)
*Pheniramine, Codeine, and Guaifenesin (Systemic)
*Pheniramine, Phenylephrine, Codeine, Sodium Citrate, Sodium Salicylate, and Caffeine (Systemic)
*Pheniramine, Pyrilamine, Hydrocodone, Potassium Citrate, and Ascorbic Acid (Systemic)
*Phenylephrine, Hydrocodone, and Guaifenesin (Systemic)
*Phenyltoloxamine and Hydrocodone (Systemic)
*Promethazine, Codeine, and Potassium Guaiacolsulfonate (Systemic)
*Promethazine, Phenylephrine, and Codeine (Systemic)
*Promethazine and Codeine (Systemic)
*Pseudoephedrine, Codeine, and Guaifenesin (Systemic)
*Pseudoephedrine, Hydrocodone and Guaifenesin (Systemic)
*Pseudoephedrine, Hydrocodone and Potassium Guaiacolsulfonate (Systemic)
*Pyrilamine, Phenylephrine, Hydrocodone, and Ammonium Chloride (Systemic)
*Pyrilamine and Codeine (Systemic)
*Triprolidine, Pseudoephedrine, and Codeine (Systemic)
*Triprolidine, Pseudoephedrine, Codeine, and Guaifenesin (Systemic)
RE302 *Benzonatate (Systemic)
*Chlophedianol (Systemic)
*Dextromethorphan and Acetaminophen (Systemic)
*Dextromethorphan and Guaifenesin (Systemic)
*Dextromethorphan and Iodinated Glycerol (Systemic)
*Dextromethorphan (Systemic)
Diphenhydramine, Oral (Systemic)
*Guaifenesin (Systemic)
RE400 *Acetylcysteine, Oral (Systemic)
*Acetylcysteine (Inhalation)
RE501 *Acrivastine and Pseudoephedrine (Systemic)
*Azatadine and Pseudoephedrine (Systemic)
*Brompheniramine and Phenylephrine (Systemic)
*Brompheniramine and Pseudoephedrine (Systemic)
*Carbinoxamine and Pseudoephedrine (Systemic)
*Cetirizine and Pseudoephedrine (Systemic)
*Chlorpheniramine, Phenyltoloxamine, and Phenylephrine (Systemic)
*Chlorpheniramine, Pyrilamine, and Phenylephrine (Systemic)
*Chlorpheniramine and Phenylephrine (Systemic)
*Chlorpheniramine and Pseudoephedrine (Systemic)
*Desloratadine and Pseudoephedrine (Systemic)
*Dexbrompheniramine and Pseudoephedrine (Systemic)
*Diphenhydramine and Pseudoephedrine (Systemic)
*Fexofenadine and Pseudoephedrine (Systemic)
*Loratadine and Pseudoephedrine (Systemic)
*Pheniramine and Phenylephrine (Systemic)
*Promethazine and Phenylephrine (Systemic)
*Terfenadine and Pseudoephedrine (Systemic)
*Triprolidine and Pseudoephedrine (Systemic)
RE502 *Brompheniramine, Pseudoephedrine, and Dextromethorphan (Systemic)
*Carbinoxamine, Pseudoephedrine, and Dextromethorphan (Systemic)
*Chlorpheniramine, Ephedrine, Phenylephrine, and Carbetapentane (Systemic)
*Chlorpheniramine, Phenylephrine, and Dextromethorphan (Systemic)

*Chlorpheniramine, Pseudoephedrine, and Dextromethorphan (Systemic)
*Diphenhydramine, Dextromethorphan, and Ammonium Chloride (Systemic)
*Doxylamine, Etafedrine, and Hydrocodone (Systemic)
*Pheniramine, Phenylephrine, and Dextromethorphan (Systemic)
RE503 *Chlorpheniramine, Ephedrine, and Guaifenesin (Systemic)
*Chlorpheniramine, Pseudoephedrine, and Guaifenesin (Systemic)
*Promethazine, Phenylephrine, and Potassium Guaiacolsulfonate (Systemic)
RE504 *Chlorpheniramine, Ephedrine, Phenylephrine, Dextromethorphan, Ammonium Chloride, and Ipecac (Systemic)
*Chlorpheniramine, Phenylephrine, Dextromethorphan, and Guaifenesin (Systemic)
*Chlorpheniramine, Phenylephrine, Dextromethorphan, Guaifenesin, and Ammonium Chloride (Systemic)
*Chlorpheniramine, Pseudoephedrine, Dextromethorphan, and Guaifenesin (Systemic)
RE506 *Chlorpheniramine, Pseudoephedrine, Codeine, and Acetaminophen (Systemic)
*Chlorpheniramine, Pseudoephedrine, Dextromethorphan, and Acetaminophen (Systemic)
*Doxylamine, Pseudoephedrine, Dextromethorphan, and Acetaminophen (Systemic)
*Pyrilamine, Pseudoephedrine, Dextromethorphan, and Acetaminophen (Systemic)
RE507 *Chlorpheniramine and Codeine (Systemic)
*Chlorpheniramine and Dextromethorphan (Systemic)
*Promethazine and Dextromethorphan (Systemic)
RE509 *Doxylamine, Codeine, and Acetaminophen (Systemic)
RE512 *Phenylephrine and Hydrocodone (Systemic)
*Pseudoephedrine and Dextromethorphan (Systemic)
RE513 *Pseudoephedrine, Dextromethorphan, and Guaifenesin (Systemic)
RE514 *Pseudoephedrine, Dextromethorphan, Guaifenesin, and Acetaminophen (Systemic)
RE515 *Pseudoephedrine, Dextromethorphan, and Acetaminophen (Systemic)
RE516 *Ephedrine and Guaifenesin (Systemic)
*Phenylephrine and Guaifenesin (Systemic)
*Pseudoephedrine and Guaifenesin (Systemic)
RE599 *Chlorpheniramine, Phenylephrine, and Acetaminophen (Systemic)
*Chlorpheniramine, Phenylephrine, and Methscopolamine (Systemic)
*Chlorpheniramine, Pseudoephedrine, and Acetaminophen (Systemic)
*Chlorpheniramine, Pseudoephedrine, and Methscopolamine (Systemic)
*Chlorpheniramine, Pyrilamine, Phenylephrine, and Acetaminophen (Systemic)
*Dexbrompheniramine, Pseudoephedrine, and Acetaminophen (Systemic)
*Diphenhydramine, Pseudoephedrine, and Acetaminophen (Systemic)
*Pheniramine, Phenylephrine, and Acetaminophen
*Pheniramine, Phenylephrine, Sodium Salicylate, and Caffeine (Systemic)
*Phenylephrine and Acetaminophen (Systemic)
*Promethazine and Potassium Guaiacolsulfonate (Systemic)
*Pseudoephdrine and Acetaminophen (Systemic)
*Pseudoephdrine and Ibuprofen (Systemic)
*Triprolidine, Pseudoephedrine, and Acetaminophen (Systemic)
RE700 *Beractant (Intratracheal-Local)
*Calfactant (Intratracheal-Local)
*Colfosceril, Cetyl Alcohol, and Tyloxapol (Intratracheal-Local)
*Poractant Alfa (Intratracheal-Local)
RE900 *Alpha$_1$-proteinase Inhibitor, Human (Systemic)
*Aminophylline, Parenteral (Systemic)
Aminophylline Oral Solution (Systemic)
Aminophylline Tablets (Systemic)
Ammonia Spirit, Aromatic (Systemic)
Caffeine, Citrated (Systemic)
Caffeine (Systemic)
*Dornase Alfa (Inhalation-Local)
*Doxapram (Systemic)
Epinephrine (Inhalation-Local)
Tetracaine and Menthol (Topical)
Tetracaine (Topical)
Theophylline, Parenteral (Systemic)
Theophylline Elixir (Systemic)
Theophylline Oral Solution (Systemic)
Theophylline Syrup (Systemic)
Theophylline Tablets (Systemic)
RS100 *Betamethasone (Rectal)
*Budesonide (Rectal)
*Hydrocortisone (Rectal)
*Mesalamine (Rectal-Local)
*Tixocortol (Rectal)
RS201 *Benzocaine Ointment (Mucosal-Local)
*Benzocaine Ointment USP (Topical)
*Dibucaine Ointment (Mucosal-Local)
*Dibucaine Ointment USP (Topical)
*Pramoxine Aerosol Foam (Mucosal-Local)
*Pramoxine Cream (Mucosal-Local)
*Pramoxine Hydrochloride Cream USP (Topical)
*Pramoxine Ointment (Mucosal-Local)
*Tetracaine and Menthol Ointment (Mucosal-Local)
*Tetracaine and Menthol (Topical)
*Tetracaine (Topical)
RS300 *Bisacodyl, Rectal (Local)
*Docusate, Rectal (Local)
*Glycerin (Local)
*Mineral Oil, Rectal (Local)
*Potassium Bitartrate and Sodium Bicarbonate (Local)
*Senna, Rectal (Local)
*Sodium Phosphate, Rectal (Local)
RS900 Benzocaine, Butamben, and Tetracaine Gel (Mucosal-Local)
Benzocaine Gel (Mucosal-Local)
Benzocaine Ointment (Mucosal-Local)
Benzocaine Ointment USP (Topical)
Dibucaine Ointment (Mucosal-Local)
Dibucaine Ointment USP (Topical)
Dyclonine Topical Solution (Mucosal-Local)
Pramoxine Aerosol Foam (Mucosal-Local)
Pramoxine Cream (Mucosal-Local)
Pramoxine Hydrochloride Cream USP (Topical)
Tetracaine and Menthol Ointment (Mucosal-Local)
TN200 *Enteral Nutrition Formulas, Blenderized (Systemic)
*Enteral Nutrition Formulas, Disease-specific (Systemic)
*Enteral Nutrition Formulas, Fiber-containing (Systemic)
*Enteral Nutrition Formulas, Milk-based (Systemic)
*Enteral Nutrition Formulas, Modular (Systemic)
*Enteral Nutrition Formulas, Monomeric (Elemental) (Systemic)
*Enteral Nutrition Formulas, Polymeric (Systemic)
*Infant Formulas, Hypoallergenic (Systemic)
*Infant Formulas, Milk-based (Systemic)
*Infant Formulas, Soy-based (Systemic)
TN300 *Fat Emulsions (Systemic)
TN401 *Ferrous Fumarate (Systemic)
*Ferrous Gluconate (Systemic)
*Ferrous Sulfate (Systemic)
*Iron Dextran (Systemic)
*Iron-Polysaccharide (Systemic)
*Iron Sorbitol (Systemic)
*Sodium Ferric Gluconate (Systemic)
TN402 *Calcium Acetate (Systemic)
*Calcium Carbonate (Oral-Local)
*Calcium Carbonate (Systemic)
*Calcium Chloride (Systemic)
*Calcium Citrate (Systemic)
*Calcium Glubionate (Systemic)
*Calcium Gluceptate and Calcium Gluconate (Systemic)
*Calcium Gluceptate (Systemic)
*Calcium Gluconate (Systemic)
*Calcium Glycerophosphate and Calcium Lactate (Systemic)
*Calcium Lactate-Gluconate and Calcium Carbonate (Systemic)
*Calcium Lactate (Systemic)
*Calcium Phosphate, Dibasic (Systemic)
*Calcium Phosphate, Tribasic (Systemic)
TN403 *Potassium Bicarbonate (Systemic)
*Potassium Bicarbonate and Potassium Chloride (Systemic)
*Potassium Bicarbonate and Potassium Citrate (Systemic)
*Potassium Chloride (Systemic)
*Potassium Gluconate (Systemic)
*Potassium Gluconate and Potassium Chloride (Systemic)
*Potassium Gluconate and Potassium Citrate (Systemic)
*Trikates (Systemic)
TN405 *Zinc Chloride (Systemic)
*Zinc Gluconate (Systemic)
*Zinc Sulfate (Systemic)
TN406 *Magnesium Chloride (Systemic)
*Magnesium Citrate (Systemic)
*Magnesium Gluceptate (Systemic)
*Magnesium Gluconate (Systemic)
*Magnesium Hydroxide (Systemic)
*Magnesium Lactate (Systemic)
*Magnesium Oxide (Systemic)
*Magnesium Pidolate (Systemic)
*Magnesium Sulfate (Systemic)
TN407 *Sodium Fluoride (Systemic)
TN408 *Potassium and Sodium Phosphates (Systemic)
*Potassium Phosphates (Systemic)
*Sodium Phosphates (Systemic)
TN409 Sodium Bicarbonate (Systemic)
TN410 *Potassium Citrate and Citric Acid (Systemic)
*Potassium Citrate and Sodium Citrate (Systemic)
*Potassium Citrate (Systemic)
*Sodium Citrate and Citric Acid (Systemic)
*Tricitrates (Systemic)
TN490 *Chromic Chloride (Systemic)
*Chromium (Systemic)
*Dextrose and Electrolytes (Systemic)
*Oral Rehydration Salts (Systemic)
*Rice Syrup Solids and Electrolytes (Systemic)
TN499 *Ammonium Molybdate (Systemic)
*Copper Gluconate (Systemic)
*Cupric Sulfate (Systemic)
Iodine, Strong (Systemic)
*Manganese Chloride (Systemic)
*Manganese Sulfate (Systemic)
Potassium Iodide (Systemic)
*Selenious Acid (Systemic)
*Selenium (Systemic)
*Sodium Iodide (Systemic)
TN503 *Glutamine (Systemic)

TN900 Amiloride and Hydrochlorothiazide (Systemic)
Amiloride (Systemic)
Bumetanide (Systemic)
Chloroquine (Systemic)
Ethacrynic Acid (Systemic)
Furosemide (Systemic)
Hydroxychloroquine (Systemic)
*Levocarnitine (Systemic)
Potassium Citrate and Citric Acid (Systemic)
Sodium Citrate and Citric Acid (Systemic)
Spironolactone and Hydrochlorothiazide (Systemic)
Spironolactone (Systemic)
Triamterene and Hydrochlorothiazide (Systemic)
Triamterene (Systemic)
Tricitrates (Systemic)

VT050 *Beta-carotene (Systemic)
*Vitamin A (Systemic)

VT110 *Cyanocobalamin (Systemic)
*Hydroxocobalamin (Systemic)

VT120 *Folic Acid (Systemic)
*Leucovorin (Systemic)

VT130 *Niacinamide (Systemic)
*Niacin (Systemic)

VT140 *Pyridoxine (Systemic)

VT150 *Thiamine (Systemic)

VT160 *Riboflavin (Systemic)

VT170 *Calcium Pantothenate (Systemic)
*Pantothenic Acid (Systemic)

VT190 *Biotin (Systemic)

VT400 *Ascorbic Acid (Systemic)
*Sodium Ascorbate (Systemic)

VT501 *Calcifediol (Systemic)

VT502 *Calcitriol (Systemic)

VT503 *Dihydrotachysterol (Systemic)

VT504 *Ergocalciferol (Systemic)

VT509 *Alfacalcidol (Systemic)
*Doxercalciferol (Systemic)
*Paricalcitol (Systemic)

VT600 *Vitamin E (Systemic)

VT701 *Menadiol (Systemic)

VT702 *Phytonadione (Systemic)

VT802 *Vitamins, Multiple, and Fluoride (Systemic)
*Vitamins A, D, and C and Fluoride (Systemic)

XX000 *Cysteamine (Systemic)
*Doxycycline—For Dental Use (Systemic)
Immune Globulin Intravenous (Human) (Systemic)

Appendix VI

POISON CONTROL CENTER LISTING

The following is a list of emergency telephone numbers for United States and Canadian poison control centers.

UNITED STATES
American Association of Poison Control Centers
U.S. Poison Control Center Members
Updated May 2003

ALABAMA
Alabama Poison Center
2503 Phoenix Drive
Tuscaloosa, AL 35405
Emergency Phone: (800) 222-1222

Regional Poison Control Center
Children's Hospital
1600 7th Avenue South
Birmingham, AL 35233
Emergency Phone: (800) 222-1222

ALASKA
Oregon Poison Center
Oregon Health and Science University
3181 SW Sam Jackson Park Road
CB550
Portland, OR 97201
Emergency Phone: (800) 222-1222
(Voice and TTY/TDD)

ARIZONA
Arizona Poison & Drug Info Center
Arizona Health Sciences Center
Room 1156
1501 North Campbell Avenue
Tucson, AZ 85724
Emergency Phone: (800) 222-1222

Banner Poison Control Center
901 Willetta St.
Room 2701
Phoenix, AZ 85006
Emergency Phone: (800) 222-1222

ARKANSAS
Arkansas Poison & Drug Information Center
College of Pharmacy
University of Arkansas for Medical Sciences
4301 W. Markham
Mail Slot 522-2
Little Rock, AR 72205
Emergency Phone: (800) 222-1222
TDD/TTY: (800) 641-3805

CALIFORNIA
California Poison Control System - Fresno/Madera Division
Children's Hospital Central California
9300 Valley Children's Place, MB 15
Madera, CA 93638-8762
Emergency Phone: (800) 222-1222
TDD/TTY: (800) 972-3323

California Poison Control System - Sacramento Division
UC Davis Medical Center
2315 Stockton Boulevard
Sacramento, CA 95817
Emergency Phone: (800) 222-1222
TDD/TTY: (800) 972-3323

California Poison Control System - San Diego Division
University of California, San Diego, Medical Center
200 West Arbor Drive
San Diego, CA 92103-8925
Emergency Phone: (800) 222-1222
TDD/TTY: (800) 972-3323

California Poison Control System - San Francisco Division
UCSF Box 1369
San Francisco, CA 94143-1369
Emergency Phone: (800) 222-1222
TDD/TTY: (800) 972-3323

COLORADO
Rocky Mountain Poison & Drug Ctr
777 Bannock Street
Mail Code 0180
Denver, CO 80204-4507
Emergency Phone: (800) 222-1222
TDD/TTY: (303) 739-1127
Emergency Phone: (800) 332-3073
(CO only/outside metro area)

CONNECTICUT
Connecticut Poison Control Center
University of Connecticut Health Center
263 Farmington Avenue
Farmington, CT 06030-5365
Emergency Phone: (800) 222-1222
TTY/TDD: (866) 218-5372

DELAWARE
The Poison Control Center
Children's Hospital of Philadelphia
3400 Civic Center Blvd
Philadelphia, PA 19104-4303
Emergency Phone: (800) 222-1222
TDD/TTY: (215) 590-8789

DISTRICT OF COLUMBIA
National Capital Poison Center
3201 New Mexico Avenue, NW
Suite 310
Washington, DC 20016
Emergency Phone: (800) 222-1222
(Voice and TTY)

FLORIDA
Florida Poison Information Center - Jacksonville
655 West Eighth Street
Jacksonville, FL 32209
Emergency Phone: (800) 222-1222
(Voice and TTY/TDD)

Florida Poison Information Center - Miami
University of Miami, Department of Pediatrics
P.O. Box 110626 (R-131)
Miami, FL 33101
Emergency Phone: (800) 222-1222

Florida Poison Information Center - Tampa
Tampa General Hospital
P.O. Box 1289
Tampa, FL 33601
Emergency Phone: (800) 222-1222

GEORGIA
Georgia Poison Center
Hughes Spalding Children's Hospital
Grady Health System
80 Butler Street, SE
P.O. Box 26066
Atlanta, GA 30335-3801
Emergency Phone: (800) 222-1222
TDD/TTY: (404) 616-9287

HAWAII
Rocky Mountain Poison & Drug Ctr
777 Bannock Street
Mail Code 0180
Denver, CO 80204-4507
Emergency Phone: (800) 222-1222
TDD/TYY: (303) 739-1127

IDAHO
Rocky Mountain Poison & Drug Center
777 Bannock Street
Mail Code 0180
Denver, CO 80204-4507
Emergency Phone: (800) 222-1222
(800) 860-0620 (ID only)

ILLINOIS
Illinois Poison Center
222 S. Riverside Plaza, Suite 1900
Chicago, IL 60606
Emergency Phone: (800) 222-1222
TDD/TTY: (312) 906-6185

INDIANA
Indiana Poison Center
Methodist Hospital
Clarian Health Partners
I-65 at 21st Street
Indianapolis, IN 46206-1367
Emergency Phone: (800) 222-1222
TDD/TTY: (317) 962-2336 (TTY)

IOWA
Iowa Statewide Poison Control Center
St. Luke's Regional Medical Center
2720 Stone Park Boulevard
Sioux City, IA 51104
Emergency Phone: (800) 222-1222

KANSAS
Mid-America Poison Control Center
University of Kansas Medical Center
3901 Rainbow Blvd., Room B-400
Kansas City, KS 66160-7231
Emergency Phone: (800) 222-1222
TDD/TTY: (913) 588-6639 (TDD)

KENTUCKY
Kentucky Regional Poison Center
Medical Towers South, Suite 572
234 East Gray Street
Louisville, KY 40202
Emergency Phone: (800) 222-1222

LOUISIANA
Louisiana Drug and Poison Information Center
University of Louisiana at Monroe
College of Pharmacy
Sugar Hall
Monroe, LA 71209-6430
Emergency Phone: (800) 222-1222

MAINE
Northern New England Poison
22 Bramhall Street
Portland, ME 04102
Emergency Phone: (800) 222-1222
TDD/TTY: (877) 299-4447 (ME only)
(207) 871-2879

MARYLAND
Maryland Poison Center
University of MD at Baltimore
School of Pharmacy
20 North Pine Street, PH 772
Baltimore, MD 21201
Emergency Phone: (800) 222-1222
TDD/TTY: (410) 706-1858 (TDD)

National Capital Poison Center
Montgomery and Prince Georges Counties only
3201 New Mexico Avenue, NW
Suite 310
Washington, DC 20016
Emergency Phone & TDD/TTY: (800) 222-1222

MASSACHUSETTS
Regional Center for Poison Control and Prevention Serving Massachusetts & Rhode Island
300 Longwood Avenue
Boston, MA 02115
Emergency Phone: (800) 222-1222
TDD/TTY: (888) 244-5313

MICHIGAN
Children's Hospital of Michigan
Regional Poison Control Center
4160 John R Harper Professional Office Building
Suite 616
Detroit, MI 48201
Emergency Phone: (800) 222-1222
TDD/TTY: (800) 356-3232 (TDD)

DeVos Children's Hospital Regional Poison Center
1300 Michigan, NE
Suite 203
Grand Rapids, MI 49506-2968
Emergency Phone: (800) 222-1222
(Voice and TTY)

MINNESOTA
Hennepin Regional Poison Center
Hennepin County Medical Center
701 Park Avenue
Minneapolis, MN 55415
Emergency Phone: (800) 222-1222
TDD/TTY: (800) 222-1222 (Voice and TTY)

MISSISSIPPI
Mississippi Regional Poison Control Center
University of Mississippi Medical Center
2500 N. State Street
Jackson, MS 39216
Emergency Phone: (800) 222-1222

MISSOURI
Missouri Regional Poison Center
7980 Clayton Rd
Suite 200
St. Louis, MO 63117
Emergency Phone: (800) 222-1222
TDD/TTY: (314) 612-5705

MONTANA
Rocky Mountain Poison & Drug Ctr
777 Bannock Street
Mail Code 0180
Denver, CO 80204-4028
Emergency Phone: (800) 222-1222
(800) 525-5042 (MT only)
TDD/TTY: (303) 739-1127

NEBRASKA
Nebraska Regional Poison Center
8401 W. Dodge Rd, Ste 115
Omaha, NE 68114
Emergency Phone: (800) 222-1222

NEVADA
Northern Nevada
Oregon Poison Center
Oregon Health Sciences University
3181 SW Sam Jackson Park Road
CB550
Portland, OR 97201
Emergency Phone: (800) 222-1222
(Voice and TTY/TDD)

Southern Nevada
Rocky Mountain Poison & Drug Ctr
777 Bannock Street
Mail Code 0180
Denver, CO 80204-4028
Emergency Phone: (800) 222-1222
(800) 446-6179 (NV only)
TDD/TTY: (303) 739-1127

NEW HAMPSHIRE
New Hampshire Poison Information Center
Dartmouth-Hitchcock Medical Center
One Medical Center Drive
Lebanon, NH 03756
Emergency Phone: (800) 222-1222
TTY/TDD (877) 299-4447 (ME only)
(207) 871-2879

NEW JERSEY
New Jersey Poison Information and Education System
located at Univ of Medicine and Dentistry of New Jersey
65 Bergen Street
Newark, NJ 07107-3001
Emergency Phone: (800) 222-1222
TDD/TTY: (973) 926-8008

NEW MEXICO
New Mexico Poison & Drug Information Center
MSC09 5080
University of New Mexico
Albuquerque, NM 87131-0001
Emergency Phone: (800) 222-1222

NEW YORK
Central New York Poison Center
750 East Adams Street
Syracuse, NY 13210
Emergency Phone: (800) 222-1222

Finger Lakes Regional Poison & Drug Info Center
University of Rochester Medical Center
601 Elmwood Avenue
Box 321
Rochester, NY 14642
Emergency Phone: (800) 222-1222
TDD/TTY: (585) 273-3854

Long Island Regional Poison and Drug Information Center
Winthrop University Hospital
259 First Street
Mineola, NY 11501
Emergency Phone: (800) 222-1222
TDD/TTY: (516) 924-8811 (TDD Suffolk)
(516) 747-3323 (TDD Nassau)

New York City Poison Control Center
NYC Bureau of Labs
455 First Avenue
Room 123, Box 81
New York, NY 10016
Emergency Phone: (800) 222-1222
TDD/TTY: (212) 689-9014

Western New York Regional Poison Control Center
Children's Hospital of Buffalo
219 Bryant Street
Buffalo, NY 14222
Emergency Phone: (800) 222-1222

NORTH CAROLINA
Carolinas Poison Center
Carolinas Medical Center
5000 Airport Center Parkway, Suite B
Charlotte, NC 28208
Emergency Phone: (800) 222-1222

NORTH DAKOTA
Hennepin Regional Poison Center
Hennepin County Medical Center
701 Park Avenue
Minneapolis, MN 55415
Emergency Phone: (800) 222-1222
TDD/TTY: (800) 222-1222
(612) 904-4691 (TTY)

OHIO
Central Ohio Poison Center
700 Children's Drive, Room L032
Columbus, OH 43205
Emergency Phone: (800) 222-1222
TDD/TTY: (614) 228-2272 (TTY)

Cincinnati Drug & Poison Information Center
Regional Poison Control System
3333 Burnet Avenue
Vernon Place - 3rd Floor
Cincinnati, OH 45229
Emergency Phone: (800) 222-1222
TDD/TTY: (800) 253-7955

Greater Cleveland Poison Control Center
11100 Euclid Avenue
Cleveland, OH 44106-6010
Emergency Phone: (800) 222-1222

OKLAHOMA

Oklahoma Poison Control Center
Children's Hospital at OU Medical Center
940 N.E. 13th Street
Room 3510
Oklahoma City, OK 73104
Emergency Phone: (800) 222-1222
(Voice and TDD/TTY)

OREGON

Oregon Poison Center
Oregon Health Sciences University
3181 SW Sam Jackson Park Road
CB550
Portland, OR 97201
Emergency Phone: (800) 222-1222
(Voice and TTY/TDD)

PENNSYLVANIA

Pittsburgh Poison Center
Children's Hospital of Pittsburgh
3705 Fifth Avenue
Pittsburgh, PA 15213
Emergency Phone: (800) 222-1222

The Poison Control Center
Children's Hospital of Philadelphia
3400 Civic Center Blvd
Philadelphia, PA 19104-4303
Emergency Phone: (800) 222-1222
TDD/TTY: (215) 590-8789

PUERTO RICO

Puerto Rico Poison Center
Calle San Jorge #252
Santurce, Puerto Rico 00912
Emergency Phone: (800) 222-1222

RHODE ISLAND

Regional Center for Poison Control and Prevention Serving Massachusetts and Rhode Island
300 Longwood Avenue
Boston, MA 02115
Emergency Phone: (800) 222-1222
TDD/TTY: (888) 244-5313

SOUTH CAROLINA

Palmetto Poison Center
College of Pharmacy
University of South Carolina
Columbia, SC 29208
Emergency Phone: (800) 222-1222

SOUTH DAKOTA

Hennepin Regional Poison Center
Hennepin County Medical Center
701 Park Avenue
Minneapolis, MN 55415
Emergency Phone: (800) 222-1222
(Voice and TDD/TTY)

TENNESSEE

Middle Tennessee Poison Center
501 Oxford House
1161 21st Avenue South
Nashville, TN 37232-4632
Emergency Phone: (800) 222-1222
TDD/TTY: (615) 936-2047

TEXAS

Central Texas Poison Center
Scott and White Memorial Hospital
2401 South 31st Street
Temple, TX 76508
Emergency Phone: (800) 222-1222

North Texas Poison Center
Parkland Memorial Hospital
5201 Harry Hines Blvd.
Dallas, TX 75235
Emergency Phone: (800) 222-1222

South Texas Poison Center
The Univ of Texas Health Science Ctr - San Antonio
Department of Surgery
Mail Code 7849
7703 Floyd Curl Drive
San Antonio, TX 78229-3900
Emergency Phone: (800) 222-1222
(Voice and TTY/TDD)

Southeast Texas Poison Center
The University of Texas Medical Branch
3.112 Trauma Building
Galveston, TX 77555-1175
Emergency Phone: (800) 222-1222

Texas Panhandle Poison Center
1501 S. Coulter
Amarillo, TX 79106
Emergency Phone: (800) 222-1222

West Texas Regional Poison Center
Thomason Hospital
4815 Alameda Avenue
El Paso, TX 79905
Emergency Phone: (800) 222-1222

UTAH

Utah Poison Control Center
585 Komas Drive, Suite 200
Salt Lake City, UT 84108
Emergency Phone: (800) 222-1222

VERMONT

Northern New England Poison Center
22 Bramhall Street
Portland, ME 04102
Emergency Phone: (800) 222-1222
TDD/TTY: (877) 299-4474 (ME only)
(207) 871-2879

VIRGINIA

Blue Ridge Poison Center
Jefferson Park Place
1222 Jefferson Park Avenue
Charlottesville, VA 22903
Emergency Phone: (800) 222-1222

National Capital Poison Center
3201 New Mexico Avenue, NW
Suite 310
Washington, DC 20016
Emergency Phone: (800) 222-1222
(Voice and TTY/TDD)

Virginia Poison Center
Medical College of Virginia Hospitals
Virginia Commonwealth University
P.O. Box 980522
Richmond, VA 23298-0522
Emergency Phone: (800) 222-1222

WASHINGTON

Washington Poison Center
155 NE 100th Street, Suite 400
Seattle, WA 98125-8012
Emergency Phone: (800) 222-1222
TDD/TTY: (206) 517-2394 (TDD)
(800) 572-0638 (TDD WA only)

WEST VIRGINIA

West Virginia Poison Center
3110 MacCorkle Ave, S.E.
Charleston, WV 25304
Emergency Phone: (800) 222-1222

WISCONSIN

Children's Hospital of Wisconsin Poison Center
PO Box 1997, Mail Station 677A
Milwaukee, WI 53201-1997
Emergency Phone: (800) 222-1222
TDD/TTY: (414) 266-2542

WYOMING

Nebraska Regional Poison Center
Children's Hospital
8200 Dodge Street
Omaha, NE 68114
Emergency Phone: (800) 222-1222

ANIMAL POISON CONTROL

ASPCA Animal Poison Control Center
Animal Poison Control Center
1717 South Philo Road, Suite 36
Urbana, IL 61802
Emergency Phone: (888) 426-4435

CANADA

Source: Canadian Poison Control Centres.

ALBERTA
Foothills Medical Center
1403 29th Street N.W.
Calgary, AB T2N 2T9
1-800-332-1414 toll-free
(403) 944-1414 local
(403) 944-1472 fax

BRITISH COLUMBIA
British Columbia Drug and Poison Information Centre
St. Paul's Hospital
1081 Burrard Street
Vancouver, B.C. V6Z 1Y6
1-800-567-8911 toll-free
(604) 682-5050 Greater Vancouver & lower mainland
(604) 631-5262 fax

MANITOBA
Provincial Poison Information Centre
Children's Hospital Health Science Centre
840 Sherbrook Street
Winnipeg. MB R3A 1S1
(204) 787-2591 local
(204) 787-1775 fax

NEW BRUNSWICK
Poison Information Centre
Clinidata
774 Main St. 6th floor
Moncton, NB E1C 9Y3
(506) 857-5555
(506) 867-3259 fax

NEWFOUNDLAND
Poison Control Centre
The Janeway Child Health Centre
710 Janeway Place
St. John's, NF A1A 1R8
(709) 722-1110
(709) 726-0830 fax

NOVA SCOTIA / PEI
Poison Control Centre
The IWK/Grace Health Care Centre
P.O. Box 3070
Halifax, NS B3J 3G9
1-800-565-8161
(902) 470-8161
(902) 470-7213 fax

ONTARIO
Ontario Regional Poison Information Centre
Children's Hospital of Eastern Ontario
401 Smyth Road
Ottawa, ON K1V 8L1
1-800-267-1373 toll-free
(613) 737-1100 local
(613) 738-4862 fax

Ontario Regional Poison Information Centre
The Hospital for Sick Children
555 University Avenue
Toronto, ON M5G 1X8
1-800-268-9017 toll-free
(416) 598-5900 local
(416) 813-7489 fax

QUEBEC
Centre Anti-Poison du Québec
1050 Chemin Ste-Foy, 1er étage
Quebec, QC G1S 4L8
1-800-463-5060 Toll-free
(418) 656-8090 local
(418) 654-2747 fax

SASKATCHEWAN
Saskatchewan Poison Centre
(866) 454-1212

Appendix VII

Additional Drug Information Now Available Online

The following monographs are not included in the published version of this book but are available on line. Copies of the monographs are available on the Micromedex *USP DI* Updates Online Website. See the front inside cover of this book for details on how to access the site.

Abciximab (Systemic)
Acetaminophen And Salicylates (Systemic)
Acetaminophen, Sodium Bicarbonate, And Citric Acid (Systemic)
Acetylcysteine (Systemic)
Albendazole (Systemic)
Albumin Microspheres Sonicated (Systemic)
Alcohol And Acetone (Topical)
Alglucerase (Systemic)
Alpha1-Proteinase Inhibitor, Human (Systemic)
Alprostadil (Systemic)
Altretamine (Systemic)
Aminobenzoate Potassium (Systemic)
Aminoglutethimide (Systemic)
Aminolevulinic Acid (Topical)
Aminosalicylate Sodium (Systemic)
Amlexanox (Mucosal-Local)
Ammonia Spirit, Aromatic (Systemic)
Ammoniated Mercury (Topical)
Amprenavir (Systemic)
Amsacrine (Systemic)
Amyl Nitrite (Systemic)
Anesthetics (Ophthalmic)
Anesthetics, Barbiturate (Systemic)
Anesthetics, Inhalation (Systemic)
Anthralin (Topical)
Anticonvulsants, Dione (Systemic)
Antihemophilic Factor (Systemic)
Anti-Inhibitor Coagulant Complex (Systemic)
Antipyrine And Benzocaine (Otic)
Antithrombin III (Systemic)
Anti-thymocyte Globulin (Rabbit) (Systemic)
Antivenin (Crotalidae) Polyvalent (Systemic)
Antivenin (Latrodectus Mactans) (Systemic)
Antivenin (Micrurus Fulvius) (Systemic)
Apraclonidine (Ophthalmic)
Aprotinin (Systemic)
Arbutamine (Systemic)
Ardeparin (Systemic)
Ascorbic Acid (Systemic)
Aspirin, Sodium Bicarbonate, And Citric Acid (Systemic)
Atovaquone (Systemic)
Atropine, Hyoscyamine, Methenamine, Methylene Blue, Phenyl Salicylate, And Benzoic Acid (Systemic)
Attapulgite (Oral-Local)
Bacillus Calmette-Gurin (BCG) Live (Systemic)
Barium Sulfate (Local)
Basiliximab (Systemic)
Becaplermin (Topical)
Bentiromide (Systemic)
Bentoquatam (Topical)
Benzoyl Peroxide (Topical)
Benzyl Benzoate (Topical)
Beractant (Intratracheal-Local)
Beta-Carotene (Systemic)
Betaine (Systemic)
Biotin (Systemic)
Bivalirudin (Systemic)
Bretylium (Systemic)
Buclizine (Systemic)
Buprenorphine (Systemic)
Buserelin (Systemic)
Butenafine (Topical)
Calamine (Topical)
Calfactant (Intratracheal-Local)
Capreomycin (Systemic)
Carbetocin (Systemic)
Carbohydrates And Electrolytes (Systemic)
Carbol-Fuchsin (Topical)
Carboprost (Systemic)
Carmustine (Implantation-Local)
Cellulose Sodium Phosphate (Systemic)
Cetrorelix (Systemic)
Chlophedianol (Systemic)
Chloral Hydrate (Systemic)
Chloramphenicol (Ophthalmic)
Chloramphenicol (Otic)
Chloramphenicol (Systemic)
Chlordiazepoxide And Amitriptyline (Systemic)
Chlorhexidine (Implantation-Local)
Chloroquine (Systemic)
Chloroxine (Topical)
Cholecystographic Agents, Oral (Systemic)
Cholecystokinin (Systemic)
Cholera Vaccine (Systemic)
Chondrocytes, Autologous Cultured (Implantation-Local)
Chromic Phosphate P 32 (Parenteral-Local)
Chromium Supplements (Systemic)
Chymopapain (Parenteral-Local)
Cinoxacin (Systemic)
Cisapride (Systemic)
Cisatracurium (Systemic)
Citrates (Systemic)
Citric Acid, Glucono-delta-lactone, and Magnesium (Mucosal-Local)
Cladribine (Systemic)
Clioquinol (Topical)
Clioquinol And Hydrocortisone (Topical)
Clodronate (Systemic)
Clofazimine (Systemic)
Clofibrate (Systemic)
Coal Tar (Topical)
Cocaine (Mucosal-Local)
Colesevelam (Oral-Local)
Colfosceril, Cetyl Alcohol, And Tyloxapol (Intratracheal-Local)
Colistin, Neomycin, And Hydrocortisone (Otic)
Copper Supplements (Systemic)
Corticorelin Ovine (Systemic-Diagnostic)
Cromolyn (Systemic/Oral-Local)
Crotamiton (Topical)
Cyclandelate (Systemic)
Cyclizine (Systemic)
Cycloserine (Systemic)
Cyproterone (Systemic)
Cysteamine (Systemic)
Dactinomycin (Systemic)
Dantrolene (Systemic)
Dapiprazole (Ophthalmic)
Deferoxamine (Systemic)
Denileukin Dioftitox (Systemic)
Desflurane (Inhalation-Systemic)
Dexmedetomidine (Systemic)
Diatrizoate And Iodipamide (Local)
Diatrizoates (Local)
Diatrizoates (Systemic)
Diazoxide (Oral-Systemic)
Diazoxide (Parenteral-Systemic)
Diethylcarbamazine (Systemic)
Diethyltoluamide (Topical)
Difenoxin And Atropine (Systemic)
Dimercaprol (Systemic)
Dimethyl Sulfoxide (Mucosal-Local)
Dinoprost (Parenteral-Local)
Diphenidol (Systemic)
Diphtheria And Tetanus Toxoids And Pertussis Vaccine Adsorbed (Systemic)
Diphtheria Antitoxin (Systemic)
Dipivefrin (Ophthalmic)
Dirithromycin (Systemic)
Domperidone (Systemic)
Doxacurium (Systemic)
Doxapram (Systemic)
Doxepin (Topical)
Doxycycline For Dental Use (Systemic)
Doxycycline (Mucosal-Local)
Dyphylline (Systemic)
Edetate Calcium Disodium (Systemic)
Edetate Disodium (Ophthalmic)
Edetate Disodium (Systemic)
Edrophonium (Systemic)
Edrophonium And Atropine (Systemic)
Eflornithine (Topical)
Epinephrine (Ophthalmic)
Epoprostenol (Systemic)
Eptifibatide (Systemic)
Ergoloid Mesylates (Systemic)
Ergonovine (Systemic)
Ethanolamine Oleate (Parenteral-Local)
Ethchlorvynol (Systemic)
Ethionamide (Systemic)
Etomidate (Systemic)
Factor IX (Systemic)
Factor VIIa (Systemic)
Fat Emulsions (Systemic)
Felbamate (Systemic)
Fenoldopam (Systemic)
Ferrous Citrate Fe 59 (Systemic)
Ferumoxides (Systemic)
Flecainide (Systemic)
Flumazenil (Systemic)
Fluticasone (Nasal)
Fomepizole (Systemic)
Fomivirsen (Parenteral-Local)
Foscarnet (Systemic)
Fosfomycin (Systemic)
Framycetin (Ophthalmic)
Furazolidone (Oral-Local)
Fusidic Acid (Systemic)
Gadodiamide (Systemic)
Gadopentetate (Systemic)
Gadoteridol (Systemic)
Gadoversetamide (Systemic)
Gallium Citrate Ga 67 (Systemic)
Ganciclovir (Implantation-Ophthalmic)
Ganirelix (Systemic)
Gentamicin (Otic)
Gentamicin (Topical)
Gentian Violet (Topical)
Gentian Violet (Vaginal)
Glimepiride (Systemic)
Glycerin (Systemic)
Gold Compounds (Systemic)
Gonadorelin (Systemic)
Goserelin (Systemic)
Griseofulvin (Systemic)
Guanabenz (Systemic)
Guanadrel (Systemic)
Guanethidine (Systemic)
Haemophilus b Polysaccharide Vaccine (Systemic)
Histamine (Systemic)
Hyaluronate Sodium (Systemic)

Hyaluronate Sodium Derivative (Systemic)
Hydroxyamphetamine and Tropicamide (Ophthalmic)
Hydroxypropyl Cellulose (Ophthalmic)
Hydroxypropyl Methylcellulose (Parenteral-Local)
Hydroxypropyl Methylcellulose (Ophthalmic)
Ibutilide (Systemic)
Idarubicin (Systemic)
Idoxuridine (Ophthalmic)
Imiglucerase (Systemic)
Indium In 111 Capromab Pendetide (Systemic)
Indium In 111 Oxyquinoline (Systemic)
Indium In 111 Pentetate (Systemic)
Indium In 111 Pentetreotide (Systemic)
Indium In 111 Satumomab Pendetide (Systemic)
Inulin (Systemic)
Iobenguane, Radioiodinated (Systemic-Diagnostic)
Iobenguane, Radioiodinated (Systemic-Therapeutic)
Iodine (Topical)
Iodine, Strong (Systemic)
Iodipamide (Systemic)
Iodixanol (Systemic)
Iodohippurate Sodium I 123 (Systemic)
Iodohippurate Sodium I 131 (Systemic)
Iodoquinol (Oral-Local)
Iofetamine I 123 (Systemic)
Iohexol (Local)
Iohexol (Systemic)
Iopamidol (Systemic)
Iopromide (Systemic)
Iothalamate (Local)
Iothalamate (Systemic)
Ioversol (Systemic)
Ioxaglate (Local)
Ioxaglate (Systemic)
Ioxilan (Systemic)
Ipecac (Oral-Local)
Isoxsuprine (Systemic)
Ivermectin (Systemic)
Japanese Encephalitis Virus Vaccine (Systemic)
Kanamycin (Oral-Local)
Kaolin And Pectin (Oral-Local)
Ketamine (Systemic)
Krypton Kr 81m (Systemic)
Levamisole (Systemic)
Levodopa (Systemic)
Levomethadyl (Systemic)
Lincomycin (Systemic)
Lodoxamide (Ophthalmic)
L-Tryptophan (Systemic)
Lyme Disease Vaccine (Systemic)
Mafenide (Topical)
Magnesium Supplements (Systemic)
Malathion (Topical)
Mangafodipir (Systemic)
Manganese Supplements (Systemic)
Mannitol (Systemic)
Maprotiline (Systemic)
Measles And Rubella Virus Vaccine Live (Systemic)
Mecamylamine (Systemic)
Mechlorethamine (Topical)
Meglumine Antimoniate (Systemic)
Menotropins (Systemic)
Meprobamate (Systemic)
Meprobamate And Aspirin (Systemic)
Methenamine (Systemic)
Methoxsalen (Extracorporeal-Systemic)
Methoxsalen (Topical)
Methyldopa (Systemic)
Methyldopa And Thiazide Diuretics (Systemic)
Methylene Blue (Systemic)
Methysergide (Systemic)
Metyrapone (Systemic)
Metyrosine (Systemic)
Mexiletine (Systemic)
Miconazole (Topical)
Milrinone (Systemic)
Minocycline (Mucosal-Local)
Mivacurium (Systemic)
Moclobemide (Systemic)
Moexipril and Hydrochlorothiazide (Systemic)
Molindone (Systemic)
Molybdenum Supplements (Systemic)
Mometasone (Nasal)
Monoctanoin (Local)
Moricizine (Systemic)
Nabilone (Systemic)
Nadroparin (Systemic)
Nafarelin (Systemic)
Naftifine (Topical)
Nalidixic Acid (Systemic)
Nalmefene (Systemic)
Naloxone (Systemic)
Naphazoline (Ophthalmic)
Natamycin (Ophthalmic)
Nefazodone (Systemic)
Neomycin (Ophthalmic)
Neomycin (Oral-Local)
Neomycin (Topical)
Niclosamide (Oral-Local)
Nitric Oxide (Inhalation-Local)
Nitrofurazone (Topical)
Norfloxacin (Ophthalmic)
Nylidrin (Systemic)
Olsalazine (Oral-Local)
Oprelvekin (Systemic)
Orphenadrine And Aspirin (Systemic)
Oxtriphylline And Guaifenesin (Systemic)
Oxymetazoline (Nasal)
Pantothenic Acid (Systemic)
Papaverine (Intracavernosal)
Papaverine (Systemic)
Paraldehyde (Systemic)
Paregoric (Systemic)
Pegademase (Systemic)
Pemoline (Systemic)
Pentamidine (Systemic)
Pentetate Calcium Trisodium (Systemic)
Pentetate Zinc Trisodium (Systemic)
Perflubron (Oral-Local)
Perphenazine And Amitriptyline (Systemic)
Phenolsulfonphthalein (Systemic)
Phenoxybenzamine (Systemic)
Phentolamine (Intracavernosal)
Phentolamine (Systemic)
Physostigmine (Ophthalmic)
Physostigmine (Systemic)
Pilocarpine (Systemic)
Piperazine (Systemic)
Plicamycin (Systemic)
Poliovirus Vaccine (Systemic)
Poliovirus Vaccine Live Oral (Systemic)
Poractant Alfa (Intratracheal-Local)
Porfimer (Systemic)
Potassium Iodide (Systemic)
Pralidoxime (Systemic)
Praziquantel (Systemic)
Prazosin And Polythiazide (Systemic)
Primaquine (Systemic)
Probenecid (Systemic)
Probucol (Systemic)
Proguanil (Systemic)
Protamine (Systemic)
Protirelin (Systemic)
Prussian Blue (Oral-Local)
Pyrantel (Oral-Local)
Pyridostigmine For Military Combat Medical Use (Systemic) (Systemic)
Pyridoxine (Systemic)
Pyrimethamine (Systemic)
Pyrithione (Topical)
Pyrvinium (Oral-Local)
Rabies Vaccine (Systemic)
Racemethionine (Systemic)
Radioiodinated Albumin (Systemic)
Rauwolfia Alkaloids (Systemic)
Rauwolfia Alkaloids And Thiazide Diuretics (Systemic)
Remifentanil (Systemic)
Reserpine, Hydralazine, And Hydrochlorothiazide (Systemic)
Resorcinol (Topical)
Resorcinol And Sulfur (Topical)
Reteplase, Recombinant (Systemic)
Rho (D) Immune Globulin (Systemic)
Riboflavin (Systemic)
Rifapentine (Systemic)
Riluzole (Systemic)
Rimexolone (Ophthalmic)
Ritodrine (Systemic)
Rocuronium (Systemic)
Rofecoxib (Systemic)
Ropivicaine (Parenteral-Local)
Rubella And Mumps Virus Vaccine Live (Systemic)
Rubella Virus Vaccine Live (Systemic)
Rubidium Rb 82 (Systemic)
Sacrosidase (Systemic)
Salicylic Acid (Topical)
Salicylic Acid And Sulfur (Topical)
Salicylic Acid, Sulfur, And Coal Tar (Topical)
Samarium Sm 153 Lexidronam (Systemic)
Scopolamine (Ophthalmic)
Selenium Sulfide (Topical)
Selenium Supplements (Systemic)
Sermorelin (Systemic)
Sevelamer (Oral-Local)
Sevoflurane (Inhalation-Systemic)
Sincalide (Systemic)
Sodium Benzoate And Sodium Phenylacetate (Systemic)
Sodium Bicarbonate (Systemic)
Sodium Chloride (Parenteral-Local)
Sodium Chromate Cr 51 (Systemic)
Sodium Iodide (Systemic)
Sodium Iodide I 123 (Systemic)
Sodium Iodide I 131 (Systemic-Diagnostic)
Sodium Iodide I 131 (Systemic-Therapeutic)
Sodium Nitrite (Systemic)
Sodium Phenylbutyrate (Systemic)
Sodium Phosphate P 32 (Systemic)
Sodium Polystyrene Sulfonate (Local)
Sodium Thiosulfate (Systemic)
Sparfloxacin
Spectinomycin (Systemic)
Spermicides (Vaginal)
Spiramycin (Systemic)
Streptozocin (Systemic)
Strontium Chloride Sr 89 (Systemic)
Succimer (Systemic)
Sulconazole (Topical)
Sulfadoxine And Pyrimethamine (Systemic)
Sulfapyridine (Systemic)
Sulfinpyrazone (Systemic)
Sulfonamides (Vaginal)
Sulfonamides And Phenazopyridine (Systemic)
Sulfur (Topical)
Sunscreen Agents (Topical)
Suramin (Systemic)
Sympathomimetic Agents-Cardiovascular Use (Parenteral-Systemic)
Tacrine (Systemic)
Talc, Sterile (Intrapleural-Local)
Tazarotene (Topical)
Technetium Tc 99m (Pyro- And Trimeta-) Phosphates (Systemic)
Technetium Tc 99m Albumin (Systemic)
Technetium Tc 99m Albumin Aggregated (Systemic)
Technetium Tc 99m Apicitide
Technetium Tc 99m Arcitumomab (Systemic)
Technetium Tc 99m Bicisate (Systemic)
Technetium Tc 99m Disofenin (Systemic)
Technetium Tc 99m Exametazime (Systemic)
Technetium Tc 99m Fanolesomab (Systemic)
Technetium Tc 99m Mebrofenin (Systemic)
Technetium Tc 99m Medronate (Systemic)

Technetium Tc 99m Mertiatide (Systemic)
Technetium Tc 99m Oxidronate (Systemic)
Technetium Tc 99m Pentetate (Systemic)
Technetium Tc 99m Pyrophosphate (Systemic)
Technetium Tc 99m Sestamibi (Systemic)
Technetium Tc 99m Succimer (Systemic)
Technetium Tc 99m Sulfur Colloid (Systemic)
Technetium Tc 99m Teboroxime (Systemic)
Technetium Tc 99m Tetrofosmin (Systemic)
Tenecteplase (Systemic)
Teniposide (Systemic)
Teriparatide (Systemic)
Testolactone (Systemic)
Tetanus Toxoid (Systemic)
Tetracycline Periodontal Fibers (Musocal-Local)
Tetracyclines (Topical)
Thallous Chloride Tl 201 (Systemic)
Theophylline And Guaifenesin (Systemic)
Theophylline, Ephedrine, And Phenobarbital (Systemic)
Thiabendazole (Systemic)
Thiabendazole (Topical)
Thiamine (Systemic)
Thiethylperazine (Systemic)
Thioguanine (Systemic)
Thiotepa (Systemic)
Thioxanthenes (Systemic)
Thyrotropin (Systemic)
Thyrotropin Alfa (Systemic)
Tiludronate (Systemic)
Tiopronin (Systemic)
Tocainide (Systemic)
Tolazoline (Parenteral-Systemic)
Tolcapone (Systemic)
Tolnaftate (Topical)
Trandolapril (Systemic)
Trientine (Systemic)
Trimethaphan (Systemic)
Trimetrexate (Systemic)
Trioxsalen (Systemic)
Tropicamide (Ophthalmic)
Trovafloxacin (Systemic)
Typhoid Vaccine Inactivated (Parenteral-Systemic)
Typhoid Vaccine Live Oral (Systemic)
Typhoid VI Polysaccharide Vaccine (Systemic)
Undecylenic Acid, Coumpound (Topical)
Urea (Paarental-Local)
Urea (Systemic)
Urea C14 (Systemic)
Urofollitropin (Systemic)
Valdecoxib (Systemic)
Valrubicin (Mucosal-Local)
Vascular Headache Suppressants, Ergot Derivative-Containing (Systemic)
Verteporfin (Parenteral-Local)
Vidarabine (Ophthalmic)
Vindesine (Systemic)
Vitamin A (Systemic)
Vitamin B12 (Systemic)
Vitamin E (Systemic)
Vitamins, Multiple, And Fluoride (Systemic)
Xenon Xe 127 (Systemic)
Xenon Xe 133 (Systemic)
Xylometazoline (Nasal)
Yellow Fever Vaccine (Systemic)
Yohimbine (Systemic)
Zinc Supplements (Systemic)
Zopiclone (Systemic)

Index Guide

Indications Index / Off-Label Uses Indices

The following excerpts are examples of the information included in the indicies:

Brackets – Identifies an indication not included in U.S. FDA-approved product labeling (off-label use).

Menopause, vasomotor symptoms of (treatment)
[Clonidine, Oral (systemic)] 943

Definition – Further defines indication by prophylaxis, diagnosis, or treatment.

Inflammation, nonrheumatic (treatment)
Aspirin, Buffered (Systemic), 2732
Aspirin (Systemic), 2732

Drug Name – Identifies drug used for an indication.

Insomnia (treatment)
[Alprazolam (Systemic)][1], 568
Bromazepam (Systemic)*[1], 568
[Diazepam(Systemic)][1], 568
Diphenhydramine(Systemic), 343

Indication – Lists indication identified in a drug monograph or in the Orphan Drug and Biological Listing appendix.

Diabetes, type 2 (treatment)
Acarbose (Systemic), 5
Acetohexamide (Systemic), 300
Chlorpropamide (Systemic), 300
Gliclazide (Systemic)*, 300
Glimepride (Systemic)†, 300
Glipizide (Systemic)†, 300
Glyburide (Systemic), 300

Pound sign – Identifies a drug not published in the printed version of the *USP DI.* Exclusions can be accessed on the *USP DI* Updates Online website. See the front cover of book for details on accessing the site.

Diarrhea (treatment)
Attapulgite (Oral-Local), #

Superscript 1 – Identifies an indication not included in Canadian product labeling.

Meningitis (prophylaxis)
Sulfadiazine (Systemic) [1], 2851
Sulfamethoxazole (Systemic)[1], 2851
Sulfisoxasole (Systemic)[1], 2851

Indications Index

The indications listed have been extracted from the monographs included in *USP DI*. Since the *USP DI* database does not yet include monographs on every therapeutic agent available, users should not assume that all medications appropriate for a given indication are listed or that those not listed are inappropriate. In addition, since any indication listed may encompass varying degrees of severity and since different medications may not be appropriate for differing degrees of severity or because of other patient-related factors, it can not be assumed that the agents listed for any specific indication are interchangeable. *This indications index can not be used by itself to determine the appropriateness of therapy;* rather, it should be used as a tool in searching out more information about the therapies available.

Drugs are listed alphabetically. Symbols denote the following:

[ ] Used to identify a medication available in the U.S. whose FDA-approved labeling does not include the stated indication but which is included in the *USP DI* monograph

[1] Indications not included in Canadian product labeling.

Drugs for which monographs are not included in this published version of the *USP DI* database due to space constraints. Copies of the monographs are available on the Micromedex *USP DI* Updates Online website. See the front cover of this book for details on how to access the site.

A

B

E

F

G

H

J

K

L

M

N

P

Q

R

S

T

U

V

W

X

Y

Z

Off Label Uses Index by Drug

The off-label indications have been extracted from the monographs included in the *USP DI*®. An off-label indication is the use of a drug for a disease or condition other than the indication it was licensed for by U.S. Food and Drug Administration (FDA). Prior to 2004 the USP Advisory Panels selected as appropriate the off-label indications to be included in the *USP DI*. Thereafter, the Thomson Micromedex Off-Label Advisory Boards review off-label indications to be included in *USP DI*. Since the *USP DI* database does not yet include all possible off-label indications for every therapeutic agent available, users should not assume that all off-label indications appropriate for a given medication are listed or that those not listed are inappropriate. *The off-label indication index can not be used by itself to determine the appropriateness of therapy;* rather, it should be used as a tool in searching out more information about the therapies available.

Drugs are listed alphabetically. Symbols denote the following:

[ ] Used to identify a medication available in the U.S. whose FDA-approved labeling does not include the stated indication but which is included in the *USP DI* monograph

\# Drugs for which monographs are not included in this published version of the *USP DI* database due to space constraints. Copies of the monographs are available on the Thomson Micromedex *USP DI* Updates Online website. See the front cover of this book for details on how to access the site.

[1]Indications not included in Canadian product labeling.

A

C

[Chlorpromazine (Systemic)][1], 2351
Huntington's disease, choreiform movement of (treatment)
Migraine headaches (treatment)
Chlorpromazine (Systemic)[1], 2351
Porphyria, acute, intermittent (treatment)
Tetanus (treatment adjunct)
[Chlorpromazine] (Systemic)], 2351
Anesthesia, general, adjunct
[Chlorpropamide (Systemic)][1], 293
Diabetes insipidus, central, partial (treatment)
[Chlortetracycline (Ophthalmic)][1], 2721
Blepharitis, bacterial (treatment)
Blepharoconjunctivitis (treatment)
Conjunctivitis, bacterial (treatment)
Keratitis, bacterial (treatment)
Keratoconjunctivitis, bacterial (treatment)
Meibomianitis (treatment)
Ocular infections (treatment)
Ophthalmia neonatorum (prophylaxis)
Trachoma (treatment)
[Chlortetracycline (Topical)], #
Skin infections, bacterial, minor (prophylaxis)
Ulcer, dermal (treatment)
[Chlorthalidone (Systemic)][1], 1127
Diabetes insipidus, central (treatment)
Diabetes insipidus, nephrogenic (treatment)
Renal calculi, calcium (prophylaxis)
[Cholestyramine (Oral-Local)], 802
Diarrhea, due to bile acids (treatment)
[Cholestyramine (Oral-Local)][1], 802
Hyperoxaluria (treatment)
[Chorionic Gonadotropin (Systemic)][1], 805
Corpus luteum insufficiency (treatment)
Cryptorchidism (diagnosis)
Hypogonadism, male (diagnosis)
[Cilazapril (Systemic)], 198
Heart failure, congestive (treatment)
[Cilazapril (Systemic)][1], 198
Scleroderma, hypertension in (treatment)
Scleroderma, renal crisis in (treatment)
[Cimetidine (Systemic)], 1573
Arthritis, rheumatoid (treatment adjunct)
Pneumonitis, aspiration (prophylaxis)
[Cimetidine (Systemic)][1], 1573
Pancreatic insufficiency (treatment adjunct)
Urticaria, acute (treatment adjunct)
[Ciprofloxacin (Systemic)], 1409
Meningococcal carriers (treatment)
[Ciprofloxacin (Systemic)][1], 1409
Chancroid (treatment)
Ciprofloxacin (Systemic), 1409
Anthrax, inhalational (treatment)[1]
Ciprofloxacin (Systemic)[1], 1409
Cystic fibrosis, pulmonary complications of (treatment)
Sinusitis (treatment)
[Ciprofloxacin, Parenteral (Systemic)], 1409
Septicemia, bacterial (treatment)
[Cisapride (Systemic)][1], #
Gastroparesis (treatment)
Intestinal pseudo-obstruction (treatment)
Reflux, gastroesophageal (prophylaxis)
Reflux, gastroesophageal (treatment)
[Cisplatin (Systemic)][1], 823
Carcinoma, adrenocortical (treatment)
Carcinoma, anal (treatment)
Carcinoma, biliary tract (treatment)
Carcinoma, breast (treatment)
Carcinoma, cervical (treatment)
Carcinoma, endometrial (treatment)
Carcinoma, esophageal (treatment)
Carcinoma, gastric (treatment)
Carcinoma, head and neck (treatment)
Carcinoma, hepatocellular, primary (treatment)
Carcinoma, lung, non-small cell (treatment)
Carcinoma, lung, small cell (treatment)
Carcinoma, prostatic (treatment)
Carcinoma, skin (treatment)
Carcinoma, thyroid (treatment)
Carcinoma, unknown primary site (treatment)
Carcinoma, vulvar (treatment)
[Cisplatin (Systemic)][1] 823 *(continued)*
Hepatoblastoma (treatment)
Kaposi's sarcoma, AIDS-associated (treatment)
Lymphomas, Hodgkin's (treatment)
Lymphomas, non-Hodgkin's (treatment)
Melanoma, malignant (treatment)
Neuroblastoma (treatment)
Osteosarcoma (treatment)
Retinoblastoma (treatment)
Sarcoma, soft tissue (treatment)
Thymoma (treatment)
Tumors, germ cell (treatment)
Tumors, germ cell, ovarian (treatment)
Tumors, trophoblastic, gestational (treatment)
Wilms' tumor (treatment)
[Cladribine (Systemic)][1], #
Leukemia, chronic lymphocytic (treatment)
Lymphomas, non-Hodgkin's (treatment)
Waldenstrom's macroglobulinemia (treatment)
[Clarithromycin (Systemic)][1], 832
Legionnaires' disease (treatment)
Clarithromycin (Systemic)[1], 832
Mycobacterium avium complex (MAC) disease, disseminated (prophylaxis)
[Clemastine (Systemic)][1], 333
Pruritus, associated with pityriasis rosea (treatment)
[Clidinium (Systemic)], 230
Bowel syndrome, irritable (treatment)
[Clindamycin (Systemic)][1], 837
Actinomycosis (treatment)
Babesiosis (treatment)
Erysipelas (treatment)
Malaria (treatment)
Otitis media, chronic suppurative (treatment)
Pneumonia, *Pneumocystis carinii* (treatment)
Sinusitis (treatment)
Toxoplasmosis, central nervous system (CNS) (treatment)
[Clindamycin (Topical)][1], 841
Skin infections, bacterial, minor (treatment)
Ulcer, dermal (treatment)
[Clioquinol (Topical)], #
Burns, mild, infected (treatment)
Dermatomycoses, superficial (treatment)
Eczema, infected (treatment)
Pyoderma, infected (treatment)
Skin infections, bacterial, minor (prophylaxis)
Skin infections, bacterial, minor (treatment)
Tinea barbae (treatment)
Tinea capitis (treatment)
Ulcer, dermal (treatment)
[Clofazimine (Systemic)], #
Mycobacterial infections, atypical (treatment)
[Clomiphene (Systemic)][1], 848
Corpus luteum insufficiency (treatment)
Hypothalamic-pituitary-gonadal axis function, in males (diagnosis)
Infertility, male (treatment)
Ovarian function studies
[Clomipramine (Systemic)], 280
Depression, mental (treatment)
[Clomipramine (Systemic)][1], 280
Bulimia nervosa (treatment)
Headache (prophylaxis)
Narcolepsy/cataplexy syndrome (treatment)
Pain, neurogenic (treatment)
Panic disorder (treatment)
[Clonazepam (Systemic)]‡, 512
Convulsive disorders (treatment adjunct)
[Clonazepam (Systemic)][1], 512
Epilepsy, complex partial seizure pattern (treatment)
Epilepsy, simple partial seizure pattern (treatment)
Epilepsy, tonic-clonic seizure pattern (treatment)
Clonazepam (Systemic)[1], 512
Panic disorder (treatment)
[Clonidine (Parenteral-Local)][1], 850
Shivering, post-operative (prophylaxis and treatment)
[Clonidine, Oral (Systemic)], 853
Menopause, vasomotor symptoms of (treatment)
[Clonidine, Oral (Systemic)][1], 853
Dysmenorrhea (treatment)
Gilles de la Tourette's syndrome (treatment)
Headache, vascular (prophylaxis)
Nicotine dependence (treatment adjunct)
Opioid (narcotic) abstinence syndrome (treatment)
Pheochromocytoma (diagnosis)
[Clopramine (Systemic)][1], 280
Narcolepsy/cataplexy syndrome (treatment adjunct)
Clorazepate (Systemic)[1], 512
Epilepsy, complex partial seizure pattern (treatment adjunct)
Epilepsy, simple partial seizure pattern (treatment adjunct)
[Clotrimazole (Topical)][1], 861
Paronychia (treatment)
Tinea barbae (treatment)
Tinea capitis (treatment)
[Clotrimazole and Betamethasone (Topical)][1], 863
Candidiasis, cutaneous (treatment)
Cocaine (Mucosal-Local)[1], #
Anesthesia, local
[Codeine (Systemic)][1], 2184
Diarrhea (treatment)
[Colchicine (Systemic)], 868
Mediterranean fever, familial (prophylaxis)
Mediterranean fever, familial (treatment)
[Colchicine (Systemic)][1], 868
Amyloidosis (treatment)
Arthritis, sarcoid (treatment)
Behçet's syndrome (treatment)
Calcium pyrophosphate deposition disease, acute (prophylaxis)
Calcium pyrophosphate deposition disease, acute (treatment)
Cirrhosis, biliary (treatment)
Pericarditis, recurrent (treatment)
[Colestipol (Oral-Local)][1], 874
Diarrhea, due to bile acids (treatment)
Pruritus, associated with partial biliary obstruction (treatment)
[Colistin, Neomycin, and Hydrocortisone (Otic)][1], #
Otitis media, chronic suppurative (treatment)
Colistin, Neomycin, and Hydrocortisone (Otic)[1], #
Mastoidectomy cavity infections (treatment)
[Corticosteroids (Inhalation-Local)][1], 889
Croup (treatment)
[Corticosteroids (Topical)][1], 917
Gingival disorders (treatment)
Phimosis
[Corticotropin for Injection (Systemic)][1], 964
Adrenocortical insufficiency (diagnosis)
[Corticotropin, Repository, Injection (Systemic)][1], 964
Seizures, myoclonic, infantile (treatment)
[Cortisone (Systemic)][1], 938
Bronchitis, asthmatic, acute or chronic (treatment)
Calcium pyrophosphate deposition disease, acute (treatment)
Carcinoma, breast (treatment)
Carcinoma, prostatic (treatment)
Carditis, nonrheumatic, acute (treatment)
Connective tissue disease, mixed (treatment)
Eczema, severe (treatment)
Edema, pulmonary, noncardiogenic (treatment)
Fever, due to malignancy (treatment adjunct)
Gingivitis, desquamative (treatment)
Hemangioma, airway-obstructing, in infants (treatment)
Hemolysis (treatment)

[Cortisone (Systemic)][1] 938 *(continued)*
Hypercalcemia, sarcoidosis-associated (treatment)
Lesions, oral, corticosteroid-responsive disorders-associated (treatment)
Multiple myeloma (treatment)
Myasthenia gravis (treatment)
Pemphigoid (treatment)
Pericarditis (treatment)
Polyarteritis nodosa (treatment)
Polychondritis, relapsing (treatment)
Pulmonary disease, chronic obstructive (treatment)
Reiter's disease (treatment)
Rheumatic fever (treatment)
Status asthmaticus (treatment)
Stomatitis, aphthous, recurrent (treatment)
Transplant rejection (prophylaxis)
Transplant rejection (treatment)
Tumors, brain, primary (treatment adjunct)
Vasculitis (treatment)
Cromolyn (Systemic/Oral-Local)[1], #
Mastocytosis, systemic (treatment)
[Cromolyn (Ophthalmic)], 972
Conjunctivitis, seasonal allergic (treatment)
Cromolyn (Ophthalmic)[1], 972
Conjunctivitis, vernal (treatment)
Keratitis, vernal (treatment)
[Cyanocobalamin (Systemic)], #
Vitamin B_{12} deficiency (diagnosis)
[Cyclobenzaprine (Systemic)][1], 973
Fibromyalgia syndrome
[Cyclopentolate (Ophthalmic)][1], 976
Synechiae, posterior (prophylaxis)
Uveitis (treatment)
[Cyclophosphamide (Systemic)], 978
Carcinoma, lung, non-small cell (treatment)
[Cyclophosphamide (Systemic)][1], 978
Arthritis, rheumatoid (treatment)
Carcinoma, adrenocortical (treatment)
Carcinoma, bladder (treatment)
Carcinoma, cervical (treatment)
Carcinoma, endometrial (treatment)
Carcinoma, lung, small cell (treatment)
Carcinoma, prostatic (treatment)
Carcinoma, testicular (treatment)
Dermatomyositis, systemic (treatment)
Ewing's sarcoma (treatment)
Histiocytosis X
Lupus erythematosus, systemic (treatment)
Multiple sclerosis (treatment)
Osteosarcoma (treatment)
Sarcoma, soft tissue (treatment)
Thymoma (treatment)
Transplant rejection, organ (prophylaxis)
Tumors, brain, primary (treatment)
Tumors, germ cell, ovarian (treatment)
Tumors, trophoblastic, gestational (treatment)
Waldenstrom's macroglobulinemia (treatment)
Wegener's granuloma (treatment)
Wilms' tumor (treatment)
Cyclophosphamide (Systemic)[1], 978
Nephrotic syndrome (treatment)
[Cyclophosphamide (Systemic)][1], 978
Lymphomas, non-Hodgkin's (treatment)
[Cycloserine (Systemic)], #
Mycobacterial infections, atypical (treatment)
[Cyclosporine (Systemic)], 985
Graft-*versus*-host disease (prophylaxis)
Graft-*versus*-host disease (treatment)
Nephrotic syndrome (treatment)
[Cyproheptadine (Systemic)], 333
Appetite, lack of (treatment)
Headache, vascular (treatment)
[Cyproheptadine (Systemic)][1], 333
Pruritus, associated with pityriasis rosea (treatment)
[Cytarabine (Systemic)], 993
Lymphomas, Hodgkin's (treatment)
Lymphomas, non-Hodgkin's (treatment)
[Cytarabine (Systemic)][1], 993
Meningitis, carcinomatous (treatment)
Myelodysplastic syndrome (treatment)

D

[Dacarbazine (Systemic)][1], 999
Carcinoma, islet cell (treatment)
Sarcoma, soft tissue (treatment)
Dacarbazine (Systemic)[1], 999
Lymphomas, Hodgkin's (treatment)
[Dactinomycin (Systemic)][1], #
Carcinoma, ovarian (treatment)
Kaposi's sarcoma (treatment)
Osteosarcoma (treatment)
[Dalteparin (Systemic)], 1004
Thrombosis, deep venous (treatment)
Thrombosis, of the extracorporeal system during hemodialysis (prophylaxis)
[Danazol (Systemic)][1], 1010
Gynecomastia (treatment)
Menorrhagia, primary (treatment)
Puberty, precocious (treatment)
Danazol (Systemic)[1], 1010
Angioedema, hereditary (prophylaxis)
[Dantrolene (Systemic)][1], #
Neuroleptic malignant syndrome (treatment)
[Dantrolene, Oral (Systemic)][1], #
Pain, exercise-induced, in Duchenne muscular dystrophy (treatment)
Pain, exercise-induced, in muscle phosphorylase deficiency (treatment)
Spasm, flexor (treatment)
[Dapsone (Systemic)], 1013
Actinomycotic mycetoma (treatment)
[Dapsone (Systemic)][1], 1013
Cicatricial pemphigoid (treatment)
Dermatosis, subcorneal pustular (treatment)
Granuloma annulare (treatment)
Lupus erythematosus, systemic (treatment)
Malaria (prophylaxis)
Pemphigoid (treatment)
Pneumonia, *Pneumocystis carinii* (prophylaxis)
Pneumonia, *Pneumocystis carinii* (treatment)
Polychondritis, relapsing (treatment)
Pyoderma gangrenosum (treatment)
[Darbepoetin Alfa (Systemic)][1], 1021
Anemia, malignancy-associated (treatment)
[Daunorubicin (Systemic)], 1028
Ewing's sarcoma (treatment)
Leukemia, chronic myelocytic (treatment)
Lymphomas, non-Hodgkin's (treatment)
Wilms' tumor (treatment)
[Daunorubicin (Systemic)][1], 1028
Neuroblastoma (treatment)
Daunorubicin (Systemic)[1], 1028
Erythroleukemia (treatment)
Leukemia, acute monocytic (treatment)
[Deferoxamine (Systemic)], #
Toxicity, aluminum (diagnosis)
Toxicity, aluminum (treatment)
[Demeclocycline (Systemic)], 2722
Traveler's diarrhea (treatment)
[Demeclocycline (Systemic)][1], 2722
Arthritis, gonococcal (treatment)
Bartonellosis (treatment)
Syndrome of inappropriate diuretic hormone (treatment)
[Desipramine (Systemic)][1], 280
Attention-deficit hyperactivity disorder (treatment)
Bulimia nervosa (treatment)
Cocaine withdrawal (treatment)
Headache (prophylaxis)
Narcolepsy/cataplexy syndrome (treatment adjunct)
Narcolepsy/cataplexy syndrome (treatment)
Pain, neurogenic (treatment)
Panic disorder (treatment)
[Desmopressin (Systemic)], 1048
Uremia (treatment adjunct)
[Desmopressin (Systemic)][1], 1048
Cushing's syndrome, adrenocorticotropic hormone-dependent (diagnosis)
[Desogestrel and Ethinyl Estradiol (Systemic)][1], 1310
Amenorrhea (treatment)
Bleeding, uterine, dysfunctional (treatment)
Dysmenorrhea (treatment)
Endometriosis (prophylaxis)
Endometriosis (treatment)
Hirsutism, female (treatment adjunct)
Hirsutism, female (treatment)
Hyperandrogenism, ovarian (treatment adjunct)
Hyperandrogenism, ovarian (treatment)
Hypermenorrhea (treatment)
Polycystic ovary syndrome (treatment)
[Dexamethasone (Nasal)], 897
Polyps, nasal, postsurgical recurrence of (prophylaxis)
Rhinitis, seasonal (prophylaxis)
Rhinitis, vasomotor nonallergic (treatment)
[Dexamethasone (Otic)], 911
Lichen simplex chronicus, localized (treatment)
Otitis externa, eczematoid, chronic (treatment)
Otitis externa, seborrheic (treatment)
[Dexamethasone (Systemic)][1], 938
Bronchitis, asthmatic, acute or chronic (treatment)
Calcium pyrophosphate deposition disease, acute (treatment)
Carcinoma, breast (treatment)
Carcinoma, prostatic (treatment)
Connective tissue disease, mixed (treatment)
Depression, mental, endogenous (diagnosis)
Eczema, severe (treatment)
Edema, pulmonary, noncardiogenic (treatment)
Fever, due to malignancy (treatment adjunct)
Gingivitis, desquamative (treatment)
Hemangioma, airway-obstructing, in infants (treatment)
Hemolysis (treatment)
Ischemia, cerebral (treatment)
Lesions, oral, corticosteroid-responsive disorders-associated (treatment)
Multiple myeloma (treatment)
Myasthenia gravis (treatment)
Pemphigoid (treatment)
Pericarditis (treatment)
Polyarteritis nodosa (treatment)
Polychondritis, relapsing (treatment)
Polyps, nasal (treatment)
Pseudotumor cerebri (treatment)
Pulmonary disease, chronic obstructive (treatment)
Reiter's disease (treatment)
Respiratory distress syndrome, adult (treatment)
Rheumatic fever (treatment)
Sarcoid, localized cutaneous (treatment)
Stomatitis, aphthous, recurrent (treatment)
Transplant rejection (prophylaxis)
Transplant rejection (treatment)
Tumors, brain, primary (treatment adjunct)
Vasculitis (treatment)
[Dexamethasone Acetate, Parenteral (Systemic)][1], 938
Carditis, nonrheumatic, acute (treatment)
Hypercalcemia, sarcoidosis-associated (treatment)
[Dexamethasone Sodium Phosphate, Parenteral (Systemic)], 938
Fibrositis (treatment)
Myositis (treatment)
Nausea and vomiting, cancer chemotherapy-induced (prophylaxis)
Neuritis, retrobulbar (treatment)
Respiratory distress syndrome, neonatal (prophylaxis)
Status asthmaticus (treatment)

[Dexamethasone Sodium Phosphate, Parenteral (Systemic)][1], 938
Carditis, nonrheumatic, acute (treatment)
Edema, cerebral, especially when associated with primary or metastatic brain tumor, craniotomy, or head injury (prophylaxis)
Hypercalcemia, sarcoidosis-associated (treatment)
[Dexamethasone Tablets (Systemic)], 938
Nausea and vomiting, cancer chemotherapy-induced (prophylaxis)
[Dexamethasone, Oral (Systemic)][1], 938
Carditis, nonrheumatic, acute (treatment)
Croup (treatment)
Edema, cerebral, especially when associated with primary or metastatic brain tumor, craniotomy, or head injury (prophylaxis)
Hypercalcemia, sarcoidosis-associated (treatment)
[Dexchlorpheniramine (Systemic)][1], 333
Pruritus, associated with pityriasis rosea (treatment)
Diatrizoate Meglumine and Diatrizoate Sodium, Parenteral (Systemic)[1], #
Cholangiography, direct
Cholangiography, direct, postoperative T-tube
Cholangiography, percutaneous transhepatic
[Diatrizoate Meglumine and Diatrizoate Sodium, Rectal (Systemic)][1], #
Meconium ileus (treatment)
[Diatrizoate Meglumine and Iodipamide Meglumine (Local)][1], #
Sexual anomalies, congenital (diagnosis)
[Diatrizoate Meglumine, Parenteral (Systemic)][1], #
Amniography
Diatrizoate Meglumine, Parenteral (Systemic)[1], #
Cholangiography, percutaneous transhepatic
Urography, retrograde
Diatrizoate Sodium, Parenteral (Systemic)[1], #
Cholangiography, percutaneous transhepatic
Splenoportography
Urography, retrograde
[Diatrizoate Sodium, Rectal (Systemic)][1], #
Meconium ileus (treatment)
[Diazepam (Systemic)][1], 512
Headache, tension (treatment)
Insomnia (treatment)
Panic disorder (treatment)
[Diazepam for Rectal Solution (Systemic)], 512
Seizures (treatment)
Status epilepticus (treatment)
Diazepam For Rectal Solution (Systemic)[1], 512
Convulsions (treatment adjunct)
[Diazepam, Oral (Systemic)][1], 512
Epilepsy, myoclonic seizure pattern (treatment adjunct)
Tremors (treatment)
Diazepam, Oral (Systemic)[1], 512
Convulsive disorders (treatment adjunct)
[Diazepam, Parenteral (Systemic)][1], 512
Sedation, conscious
[Diclofenac (Ophthalmic)], 371
Edema, cystoid macular, following cataract surgery (prophylaxis)
Edema, cystoid macular, following cataract surgery (treatment)
Miosis, during ophthalmic surgery (prophylaxis)
[Diclofenac (Systemic)][1], 375
Calcium pyrophosphate deposition disease, acute (treatment)
Gouty arthritis, acute (treatment)
Headache, vascular (treatment)
Hypermenorrhea (treatment)
Inflammation, nonrheumatic (treatment)
[Diflunisal (Systemic)][1], 375
Ankylosing spondylitis (treatment)
Arthritis, psoriatic (treatment)
Calcium pyrophosphate deposition disease, acute (treatment)
[Diflunisal (Systemic)][1] 375 *(continued)*
Dysmenorrhea (treatment)
Gouty arthritis, acute (treatment)
Headache, vascular (treatment)
Inflammation, nonrheumatic (treatment)
[Dihydroergotamine (Systemic)][1], #
Hypotension, orthostatic (prophylaxis)
Hypotension, orthostatic (treatment)
Thromboembolism, pulmonary (prophylaxis adjunct)
Thrombosis, deep venous (prophylaxis adjunct)
[Dihydrotachysterol (Systemic)], 2904
Hypophosphatemia, familial (treatment)
Renal failure, chronic (treatment adjunct)
[Dimenhydrinate (Systemic)][1], 333
Pruritus, associated with pityriasis rosea (treatment)
Dinoprost (Parenteral-Local)[1], #
Abortion, incomplete (treatment)
Abortion, therapeutic
Angiography adjunct
Labor, induction of
[Dinoprostone Vaginal Gel (Cervical/Vaginal)], 1081
Labor, induction of
[Dinoprostone Vaginal Suppositories (Cervical/Vaginal)], 1081
Hemorrhage, postabortion (treatment)
Hemorrhage, postpartum (treatment)
[Diphenhydramine (Systemic)][1], 333
Pruritus, associated with pityriasis rosea (treatment)
Diphenhydramine (Systemic)[1], 333
Extrapyramidal reactions, drug-induced (treatment)
Parkinsonism (treatment)
[Diphenidol (Systemic)][1], #
Nausea and vomiting (prophylaxis)
Nausea and vomiting, cancer chemotherapy-induced (prophylaxis)
Nausea and vomiting, cancer chemotherapy-induced (treatment)
Vertigo (prophylaxis)
Vertigo (treatment)
[Dipivefrin (Ophthalmic)][1], #
Glaucoma, secondary (treatment)
[Dipyridamole (Systemic)], 1100
Myocardial reinfarction (prophylaxis adjunct)
[Dipyridamole (Systemic)][1], 1100
Ischemic attacks, transient, in females (treatment)
Ischemic attacks, transient, in males (treatment)
Stress echocardiography adjunct
[Disopyramide (Systemic)][1], 1105
Tachycardia, supraventricular (prophylaxis)
Tachycardia, supraventricular (treatment)
[Divalproex (Systemic)], 2853
Bipolar disorder (prophylaxis)
Bipolar disorder (treatment)
Epilepsy, myoclonic seizure pattern (treatment)
Epilepsy, simple partial seizure pattern (treatment)
Epilepsy, tonic-clonic seizure pattern (treatment)
[Docetaxel (Systemic)], 1136
Carcinoma, lung, non-small cell (treatment)
[Docetaxel (Systemic)][1], 1136
Carcinoma, bladder (treatment)
Carcinoma, esophageal (treatment)
Carcinoma, head and neck (treatment)
Carcinoma, lung, small cell (treatment)
Carcinoma, ovarian (treatment)
[Doxepin (Systemic)][1], 280
Headache (prophylaxis)
Pain, neurogenic (treatment)
Panic disorder (treatment)
Pruritus (treatment)
Ulcer, peptic (treatment)
[Doxorubicin (Systemic)], 1165
Carcinoma, cervical (treatment)
Carcinoma, endometrial (treatment)
[Doxorubicin (Systemic)] 1165 *(continued)*
Carcinoma, head and neck (treatment)
Carcinoma, lung, non-small cell (treatment)
Tumors, germ cell, ovarian (treatment)
[Doxorubicin (Systemic)][1], 1165
Carcinoid tumors (treatment)
Carcinoma, adrenocortical (treatment)
Carcinoma, bladder (prophylaxis)
Carcinoma, esophageal (treatment)
Carcinoma, hepatocellular, primary (treatment)
Carcinoma, pancreatic (treatment)
Carcinoma, prostatic (treatment)
Ewing's sarcoma (treatment)
Hepatoblastoma (treatment)
Kaposi's sarcoma, AIDS-associated (treatment)
Leukemia, chronic lymphocytic (treatment)
Multiple myeloma (treatment)
Retinoblastoma (treatment)
Thymoma (treatment)
Tumors, trophoblastic, gestational (treatment)
[Doxorubicin, Liposomal (Systemic)][1], 1170
Carcinoma, breast (treatment)
Multiple myeloma
[Doxycycline (Systemic)], 2722
Traveler's diarrhea (treatment)
[Doxycycline (Systemic)][1], 2722
Arthritis, gonococcal (treatment)
Enterocolitis, *Shigella* species (prophylaxis)
Enterocolitis, *Shigella* species (treatment)
Lyme disease (treatment)
Malignant effusions, pleural (treatment)
Nocardiosis (treatment)
Doxycycline (Systemic)[1], 2722
Acne vulgaris (treatment adjunct)
Malaria (prophylaxis)
[Doxycycline, Oral (Systemic)][1], 2722
Malaria (treatment)
Rosacea, ocular (treatment)
Doxycycline[1] (Systemic), 2722
Bartonellosis (treatment)
[Doxylamine (Systemic)], 333
Pruritus, associated with pityriasis rosea (treatment)
[Droperidol (Systemic)], 1182
Sedation, conscious
[Droperidol (Systemic)][1], 1182
Psychotic disorders (treatment)

E

[Econazole (Topical)][1], 1202
Paronychia (treatment)
Tinea barbae (treatment)
Tinea capitis (treatment)
[Edetate Calcium Disodium (Systemic)][1], #
Lead mobilization determination
[Edetate Disodium (Ophthalmic)][1], #
Calcium deposits, corneal (treatment)
Calcium hydroxide burns, in eye (treatment)
Zinc chloride injury, in eye (treatment)
[Enalapril (Systemic)][1], 198
Scleroderma, hypertension in (treatment)
Scleroderma, renal crisis in (treatment)
Enalapril (Systemic)[1], 198
Ventricular dysfunction, left, asymptomatic (treatment)
[Enalapril and Hydrochlorothiazide (Systemic)], 212
Heart failure, congestive (treatment)
[Enalaprilat (Systemic)][1], 198
Scleroderma, hypertension in (treatment)
Scleroderma, renal crisis in (treatment)
Enoxaparin (Systemic)[1], 1228
Thrombosis, coronary arterial, acute (prophylaxis)
[Epinephrine (Inhalation-Local)][1], 605
Croup (treatment)
[Epinephrine (Ophthalmic)][1], #
Congestion, conjunctival, during surgery (treatment)

[Epinephrine (Ophthalmic)][1] # *(continued)*
Glaucoma, secondary (treatment)
[Epinephrine (Systemic) used topically][1], 618
Hemorrhage, gingival (treatment)
Hemorrhage, pulpal (treatment)
[Epinephrine (Systemic)][1], 618
Priapism (treatment)
[Epirubicin (Systemic)], 1240
Carcinoma, gastric (treatment)
Carcinoma, lung, non-small cell (treatment)
Carcinoma, lung, small cell (treatment)
Carcinoma, ovarian (treatment)
Lymphomas, Hodgkin's (treatment)
Lymphomas, non-Hodgkin's (treatment)
[Epirubicin (Systemic)][1], 1240
Carcinoma, esophageal (treatment adjunct)
Sarcoma, soft tissue (treatment)
[Epoetin (Systemic)][1], 1248
Anemia associated with the management of hepatitis C (treatment)
Anemia, in critically ill patients (treatment)
[Epoetin Alfa (Systemic)], 1248
Anemia, frequent blood donation-associated (prophylaxis)
Anemia, malignancy-associated (treatment)
[Epoetin Alfa (Systemic)][1], 1248
Anemia, myelodysplastic syndromes-associated (treatment)
[Epoprostenol (Systemic)], #
Hypertension, pulmonary, secondary to scleroderma spectrum of diseases (treatment)
[Epoprostenol (Systemic)][1], #
Hypertension, pulmonary, secondary to congenital diaphragmatic hernia (treatment)
Hypertension, pulmonary, secondary to congenital heart disease (treatment)
Eptifibatide (Systemic)[1], #
Thrombosis, percutaneous coronary intervention-related (prophylaxis)
[Ergocalciferol (Systemic)], 2904
Tetany, idiopathic (treatment)
Tetany, postoperative (treatment)
[Ergonovine (Systemic)][1], #
Abortion, incomplete (treatment)
Angina pectoris (diagnosis)
[Erythromycin (Ophthalmic)][1], 1262
Blepharitis, bacterial (treatment)
Blepharoconjunctivitis (treatment)
Chlamydial infections (treatment)
Conjunctivitis, bacterial (treatment)
Keratitis, bacterial (treatment)
Keratoconjunctivitis, bacterial (treatment)
Meibomianitis (treatment)
Trachoma (treatment)
[Erythromycin (Systemic)][1], 1268
Actinomycosis (treatment)
Anthrax (treatment)
Chancroid (treatment)
Enteritis, *Campylobacter* (treatment)
Gastroparesis (treatment)
Lyme disease (treatment)
Lymphogranuloma venereum (treatment)
Relapsing fever (treatment)
Respiratory tract infections (treatment)
[Erythromycin and Sulfisoxazole (Systemic)][1], 1266
Sinusitis (treatment)
[Erythromycin Ointment (Topical)][1], 1264
Skin infections, bacterial, minor (prophylaxis)
Skin infections, bacterial, minor (treatment)
[Erythromycin, Oral (Systemic)], 1268
Acne vulgaris (treatment)
Estradiol (Systemic)[1], 1289
Estrogen deficiency due to ovariectomy (treatment)
Osteoporosis, premenopausal, estrogen deficiency-induced (prophylaxis)
Estradiol, Oral (Systemic)[1], 1289
Carcinoma, prostatic (treatment)
[Estrogens (Systemic)], 1289
Gender identity disorder, male-to-female transsexualism
[Estrogens, Conjugated, Oral (Systemic)][1], 1289
Osteoporosis, premenopausal, estrogen deficiency-induced (prophylaxis)
[Estrogens, Esterified (Systemic)][1], 1289
Osteoporosis, premenopausal, estrogen deficiency-induced (prophylaxis)
Estrogens, Esterified (Systemic)[1], 1289
Carcinoma, breast (treatment)
Carcinoma, prostatic (treatment)
[Estropipate (Systemic)][1], 1289
Osteoporosis, premenopausal, estrogen deficiency-induced (prophylaxis)
Estropipate (Systemic)[1], 1289
Estrogen deficiency due to ovariectomy (treatment)
[Etanercept (Systemic)][1], 1329
Inflammatory bowel disease arthritis (treatment)
Reactive arthritis (treatment)
[Ethacrynic Acid (Systemic)][1], 1112
Hypercalcemia (treatment)
Hypertension (treatment)
[Ethambutol (Systemic)], 1333
Mycobacterial infections, atypical (treatment)
[Ethinyl Estradiol (Systemic)][1], 1289
Turner's syndrome (treatment)
Ethinyl Estradiol (Systemic)[1], 1289
Estrogen deficiency due to ovariectomy (treatment)
Menopause, vasomotor symptoms of (treatment)
[Ethionamide (Systemic)], #
Leprosy (treatment)
Mycobacterial infections, atypical (treatment)
[Ethopropazine (Systemic)][1], 307
Athetosis, congenital (treatment)
Degeneration, hepatolenticular (treatment)
[Ethynodiol Diacetate and Ethinyl Estradiol (Systemic)][1], 1310
Amenorrhea (treatment)
Bleeding, uterine, dysfunctional (treatment)
Dysmenorrhea (treatment)
Endometriosis (prophylaxis)
Endometriosis (treatment)
Hirsutism, female (treatment adjunct)
Hirsutism, female (treatment)
Hyperandrogenism, ovarian (treatment adjunct)
Hyperandrogenism, ovarian (treatment)
Hypermenorrhea (treatment)
Polycystic ovary syndrome (treatment)
[Etodolac (Systemic)], 375
Calcium pyrophosphate deposition disease, acute (treatment)
Dysmenorrhea (treatment)
Gouty arthritis, acute (treatment)
Headache, vascular (treatment)
Hypermenorrhea (treatment)
Inflammation, nonrheumatic (treatment)
[Etoposide (Systemic)], 1346
Carcinoma, lung, non-small cell (treatment)
Lymphomas, non-Hodgkin's (treatment)
[Etoposide (Systemic)][1], 1346
Carcinoma, adrenocortical (treatment)
Carcinoma, endometrial (treatment)
Carcinoma, gastric (treatment)
Carcinoma, unknown primary site (treatment adjunct)
Ewing's sarcoma (treatment)
Hepatoblastoma (treatment)
Kaposi's sarcoma, AIDS-associated (treatment)
Leukemia, acute lymphocytic (treatment)
Leukemia, acute nonlymphocytic (treatment)
Lymphomas, cutaneous T-cell (treatment)
Lymphomas, Hodgkin's (treatment)
Multiple myeloma (treatment)
Myelodysplastic syndromes (treatment)
Neuroblastoma (treatment)
Osteosarcoma (treatment)
Retinoblastoma (treatment)
Sarcoma, soft tissue (treatment)
Thymoma (treatment)
Tumors, brain, primary (treatment)
[Etoposide (Systemic)][1] 1346 *(continued)*
Tumors, germ cell, ovarian (treatment)
Tumors, trophoblastic, gestational (treatment)
Wilms' tumor (treatment)

F

Famciclovir (Systemic)[1], 1361
Herpes genitalis, recurrent episodes (suppression)
[Famotidine (Systemic)], 1573
Pneumonitis, aspiration (prophylaxis)
[Famotidine (Systemic)][1], 1573
Bleeding, upper gastrointestinal (treatment)
[Felodipine (Systemic)], 673
Angina pectoris, chronic (treatment)
Raynaud's phenomenon (treatment)
[Fenoprofen (Systemic)][1], 375
Ankylosing spondylitis (treatment)
Arthritis, psoriatic (treatment)
Calcium pyrophosphate deposition disease, acute (treatment)
Dysmenorrhea (treatment)
Gouty arthritis, acute (treatment)
Headache, vascular (prophylaxis)
Headache, vascular (treatment)
Inflammation, nonrheumatic (treatment)
Fenoprofen (Systemic)[1], 375
Pain (treatment)
[Fentanyl (Systemic)][1], 1379
Sedation and analgesia
[Filgrastim (Systemic)], 876
Myeloid engraftment following hematopoietic stem cell transplantation, promotion of (treatment adjunct)
[Filgrastim (Systemic)][1], 876
Myelodysplastic syndrome (treatment)
Myeloid engraftment following bone marrow transplantation, delay of (treatment)
Myeloid engraftment following bone marrow transplantation, failure of (treatment)
Neutropenia, AIDS-associated (treatment)
Neutropenia, drug-induced (treatment)
Flecainide (Systemic)[1], #
Arrhythmias, supraventricular (prophylaxis)
Floctafenine (Systemic)[1], 375
Calcium pyrophosphate deposition disease, acute (treatment)
Dysmenorrhea (treatment)
Gouty arthritis, acute (treatment)
Headache, vascular (treatment)
Hypermenorrhea (treatment)
Inflammation, nonrheumatic (treatment)
[Floxuridine (Systemic)], 1396
Carcinoma, hepatic (treatment)
Carcinoma, ovarian, epithelial (treatment)
Carcinoma, renal (treatment)
[Fluconazole (Systemic)], 312
Onychomycosis (treatment)
[Fluconazole (Systemic)][1], 312
Candidiasis, mucocutaneous, chronic (treatment)
Coccidioidomycosis (treatment)
Cryptococcosis (treatment)
Neutropenia, febrile (prophylaxis)
Neutropenia, febrile (treatment)
Pneumonia, fungal (treatment)
Septicemia, fungal (treatment)
Tinea corporis (treatment)
Tinea cruris (treatment)
Tinea manuum (treatment)
Tinea pedis (treatment)
[Flucytosine (Systemic)][1], 1399
Chromomycosis (treatment)
[Fludarabine (Systemic)], 1401
Lymphomas, non-Hodgkin's (treatment)
[Fludarabine (Systemic)][1], 1401
Leukemia, chronic lymphocytic (first-line treatment)
[Fludrocortisone (Systemic)][1], 1406
Acidosis, in renal tubular disorders (diagnosis)
Acidosis, in renal tubular disorders (treatment)

[Fludrocortisone (Systemic)][1] 1406 *(continued)*
Hypotension, idiopathic orthostatic (treatment)
[Flunisolide (Nasal)], 897
Polyps, nasal, postsurgical recurrence of (prophylaxis)
Rhinitis, seasonal (prophylaxis)
Rhinitis, vasomotor nonallergic (treatment)
[Fluocinonide Gel (Topical)], 917
Lichen planus, oral (treatment)
[Fluorouracil (Systemic)], 1430
Carcinoma, anal (treatment)
Carcinoma, bladder (treatment)
Carcinoma, esophageal (treatment)
Carcinoma, head and neck (treatment)
Carcinoma, ovarian, epithelial (treatment)
Carcinoma, prostatic (treatment)
Carcinoma, skin (treatment)
Hepatoblastoma (treatment)
[Fluorouracil (Systemic)][1], 1430
Carcinoma, adrenocortical (treatment)
Carcinoma, cervical (treatment)
Carcinoma, endometrial (treatment)
Carcinoma, hepatocellular, primary (treatment)
Carcinoma, penile (treatment)
Carcinoma, vulvar (treatment)
Tumors, carcinoid (treatment)
[Fluorouracil (Topical)][1], 1434
Actinic cheilitis (treatment)
Bowen's disease (treatment)
Erythroplasia of Queyrat (treatment)
Leukoplakia, mucosal (treatment)
Radiodermatitis (treatment)
[Fluoruracil (Systemic)][1], 1430
Glaucoma, open-angle (treatment)
[Fluoxetine (Systemic)][1], 1436
Premature ejaculation (treatment)
Premenstrual dysphoric disorder (treatment)
[Fluoxymesterone (Systemic)][1], 153
Anemia (treatment)
Growth, constitutional delay in (treatment)
[Fluphenazine (Systemic)], 2351
Behavior problems, severe (treatment)
[Fluphenazine (Systemic)][1], 2351
Pain, neurogenic (treatment adjunct)
[Flurbiprofen (Ophthalmic)], 371
Inflammation, ocular (treatment)
[Flurbiprofen (Systemic)], 375
Ankylosing spondylitis (treatment)
Dysmenorrhea (treatment)
Inflammation, nonrheumatic (treatment)
[Flurbiprofen (Systemic)][1], 375
Hypermenorrhea (treatment)
[Fluticasone (Inhalation-Local)][1], 1443
Pulmonary disease, chronic obstructive (treatment)
[Fluticasone (Nasal)], 897
Rhinitis, seasonal (prophylaxis)
Rhinitis, vasomotor nonallergic (treatment)
[Fluticasone (Nasal)], #
Rhinitis, nonallergic (treatment)
[Fluticasone and Salmeterol (Inhalation-Local)], 1447
Pulmonary disease, obstructive, reversible (treatment)
[Fluvoxamine (Systemic)], 1452
Depression, mental (treatment)
[Folic Acid (Systemic)][1], 1457
Folate deficiency (diagnosis)
Formoterol (Inhalation-Local), 605
Chronic obstructive pulmonary disease [COPD] (treatment) , 1468
[Formoterol (Systemic)], 1468
Asthma (treatment)
[Foscarnet (Systemic)], #
Cytomegalovirus disease (treatment)
Varicella-zoster (treatment)
[Fosinopril (Systemic)][1], 198
Scleroderma, hypertension in (treatment)
Scleroderma, renal crisis in (treatment)
[Furosemide (Systemic)][1], 1112
Hypercalcemia (treatment)
Renal imaging, radionuclide, adjunct
[Furosemide (Systemic)][1] 1112 *(continued)*
Renography, adjunct
[Fusidic Acid (Systemic)], #
Bone and joint infections (treatment)
Skin and soft tissue infections (treatment)

G

[Gabapentin (Systemic)][1], 1482
Pain, peripheral neuropathic, diabetic (treatment)
Gabapentin (Systemic)[1], 1482
Epilepsy, simple partial seizure pattern (treatment adjunct)
Postherpetic Neuralgial
[Gadopentetate (Systemic)], #
Cardiac imaging, magnetic resonance
Gadopentetate (Systemic)[1], #
Body imaging, magnetic resonance
[Gallamine (Systemic)], 2077
Convulsions (treatment)
[Gallium Citrate Ga 67 (Systemic)][1], #
Fever, unknown origin, source of (diagnosis)
Immunodeficiency syndrome, acquired, related disorders (diagnosis)
Ganciclovir (Systemic)[1], 1495
Cytomegalovirus disease (prophylaxis)
[Ganciclovir, Parenteral (Systemic)][1], 1495
Cytomegalovirus disease (treatment)
Polyradiculopathy (treatment)
[Gemcitabine (Systemic)][1], 1503
Carcinoma, biliary tract (treatment)
Carcinoma, bladder (treatment)
Carcinoma, gallbladder (treatment)
Carcinoma, ovarian, epithelial (treatment)
Lymphomas, Hodgkin's (treatment)
Lymphomas, non-Hodgkin's (treatment)
Tumors, germ cell (treatment)
Tumors, germ cell, ovarian (treatment)
Tumors, germ cell, testicular (treatment)
Gemcitabine (Systemic)[1], 1503
Carcinoma, breast (treatment)
[Gentamicin (Ophthalmic)], 1517
Episcleritis (treatment)
[Gentamicin (Topical)], #
Ulcer, dermal (treatment)
[Gentamicin (Topical)][1], #
Skin infections, bacterial, minor (prophylaxis)
[Glucagon (Systemic)][1], 1522
Abdominal imaging, computed tomographic, adjunct
Abdominal imaging, digital angiographic, adjunct
Abdominal imaging, magnetic resonance, adjunct
Bleeding, gastrointestinal (diagnosis adjunct)
Esophageal obstruction, foreign body (treatment)
Hysterosalpingography, adjunct
Pelvic imaging, magnetic resonance, adjunct
Toxicity, beta-adrenergic blocking agent (treatment)
Toxicity, calcium channel blocking agent (treatment)
Glutamine (Systemic)[1], 1525
Bowel syndrome, short (treatment)
[Glycerin (Systemic)], #
Edema, cerebral (treatment)
[Glycopyrrolate (Systemic)], 230
Bowel syndrome, irritable (treatment)
[Glycopyrrolate (Systemic)][1], 230
Diarrhea (treatment)
[Glycopyrrolate, Oral (Systemic)][1], 230
Salivation, excessive, in dental procedures (prophylaxis)
[Gold Sodium Thiomalate (Systemic)][1], #
Arthritis, psoriatic (treatment)
Felty's syndrome (treatment)
[Gonadorelin (Systemic)][1], #
Infertility, male, due to primary hypothalamic hypogonadism (treatment)
Puberty, delayed (treatment)
[Granisetron (Systemic)][1], 1528
Nausea and vomiting, cancer radiotherapy-induced (prophylaxis)
Granisetron (Systemic)[1], 1528
Nausea and vomiting, cancer radiotherapy-induced ,in bone-marrow transplantation (prophylaxis)

H

[Halazepam (Systemic)], 512
Insomnia (treatment)
[Haloperidol (Systemic)][1], 1546
Autism, infantile (treatment)
Chorea, Huntington's (treatment)
Nausea and vomiting, cancer chemotherapy-induced (prophylaxis)
Nausea and vomiting, cancer chemotherapy-induced (treatment)
[Heparin (Systemic)][1], 1552
Thromboembolism, cerebral, recurrence (prophylaxis)
[Histamine (Systemic)][1], #
Asthma (diagnosis)
[Hydralazine (Systemic)][1], 1599
Heart failure, congestive (treatment)
[Hydrochlorothiazide (Systemic)][1], 1127
Diabetes insipidus, central (treatment)
Diabetes insipidus, nephrogenic (treatment)
Renal calculi, calcium (prophylaxis)
[Hydrocortisone (Systemic)][1], 938
Bronchitis, asthmatic, acute or chronic (treatment)
Calcium pyrophosphate deposition disease, acute (treatment)
Carcinoma, breast (treatment)
Carcinoma, prostatic (treatment)
Connective tissue disease, mixed (treatment)
Eczema, severe (treatment)
Edema, pulmonary, noncardiogenic (treatment)
Fever, due to malignancy (treatment adjunct)
Gingivitis, desquamative (treatment)
Hemangioma, airway-obstructing, in infants (treatment)
Hemolysis (treatment)
Lesions, oral, corticosteroid-responsive disorders-associated (treatment)
Multiple myeloma (treatment)
Myasthenia gravis (treatment)
Nausea and vomiting, cancer chemotherapy-induced (prophylaxis)
Pemphigoid (treatment)
Pericarditis (treatment)
Polyarteritis nodosa (treatment)
Polychondritis, relapsing (treatment)
Pulmonary disease, chronic obstructive (treatment)
Reiter's disease (treatment)
Respiratory distress syndrome, neonatal (prophylaxis)
Rheumatic fever (treatment)
Sarcoid, localized cutaneous (treatment)
Stomatitis, aphthous, recurrent (treatment)
Transplant rejection (prophylaxis)
Transplant rejection (treatment)
Tumors, brain, primary (treatment adjunct)
Vasculitis (treatment)
[Hydrocortisone Acetate Dental Paste (Topical)], 917
Lichen planus, oral (treatment)
[Hydrocortisone Acetate Dental Paste (Topical)][1], 917
Gingivitis, desquamative (treatment)
[Hydrocortisone and Acetic Acid (Otic)], 937
Ear canal infections, external (prophylaxis)
Otitis externa, eczematoid, chronic (prophylaxis)
Otitis externa, eczematoid, chronic (treatment)
Otitis externa, seborrheic (prophylaxis)
Otitis externa, seborrheic (treatment)

[Hydrocortisone Cypionate, Oral (Systemic)][1], 938
Carditis, nonrheumatic, acute (treatment)
Hypercalcemia, sarcoidosis-associated (treatment)
[Hydrocortisone Sodium Phosphate, Parenteral (Systemic)][1], 938
Carditis, nonrheumatic, acute (treatment)
Hypercalcemia, sarcoidosis-associated (treatment)
[Hydrocortisone Sodium Succinate, Parenteral (Systemic)], 938
Status asthmaticus (treatment)
[Hydrocortisone Sodium Succinate, Parenteral (Systemic)][1], 938
Carditis, nonrheumatic, acute (treatment)
Hypercalcemia, sarcoidosis-associated (treatment)
[Hydrocortisone, Enema (Rectal)], 912
Crohn's disease (treatment)
[Hydrocortisone, Oral (Systemic)][1], 938
Carditis, nonrheumatic, acute (treatment)
Hypercalcemia, sarcoidosis-associated (treatment)
[Hydroflumethiazide (Systemic)], 1127
Diabetes insipidus, central (treatment)
Diabetes insipidus, nephrogenic (treatment)
Renal calculi, calcium (prophylaxis)
[Hydromorphone, Parenteral (Systemic)], 2184
Anesthesia, general, adjunct
Anesthesia, local, adjunct
[Hydroxocobalamin (Systemic)], #
Vitamin B_{12} deficiency (diagnosis)
Hydroxyamphetamine and Tropicamide (Ophthalmic) [1], #
Mydriasis, in diagnostic procedures
[Hydroxychloroquine (Systemic)][1], 1605
Arthritis, juvenile (treatment)
Hypercalcemia, sarcoid-associated (treatment)
Polymorphous light eruption (treatment)
Porphyria cutanea tarda (treatment)
Urticaria, solar (treatment)
Vasculitis, chronic cutaneous (treatment)
[Hydroxypropyl Cellulose (Ophthalmic)][1], #
Keratitis, neuroparalytic (treatment)
Ocular lubrication
Hydroxypropyl Cellulose (Ophthalmic)[1], #
Corneal erosions, recurrent (treatment)
[Hydroxypropyl Methylcellulose (Ophthalmic)][1], #
Corneal erosions, recurrent (treatment)
Corneal sensitivity, decreased (treatment)
Hydroxypropyl Methylcellulose (Ophthalmic)[1], #
Ocular lubrication
[Hydroxyurea (Systemic)][1], 1609
Carcinoma, cervical (treatment)
Polycythemia vera (treatment)
Thrombocytosis, essential (treatment)
Hydroxyurea (Systemic)[1], 1609
Sickle cell disease crisis (treatment)
[Hydroxyzine (Systemic)][1], 333
Pruritus, associated with pityriasis rosea (treatment)
[Hyoscyamine and Scopolamine (Systemic)][1], 230
Parkinsonism (treatment)
[Hyoscyamine, Oral (Systemic)][1], 230
Parkinsonism (treatment)

I

[I 123 Iobenguane (Systemic—Diagnostic)], #
Pheochromocytoma (diagnosis)
[Ibuprofen (Systemic)][1], 375
Ankylosing spondylitis (treatment)
Arthritis, psoriatic (treatment)
Calcium pyrophosphate deposition disease, acute (treatment)
Gouty arthritis, acute (treatment)
Headache, vascular (prophylaxis)
[Ibuprofen (Systemic)][1] 375 *(continued)*
Headache, vascular (treatment)
Hypermenorrhea (treatment)
Inflammation, nonrheumatic (treatment)
[Idarubicin (Systemic)], #
Leukemia, acute lymphocytic (treatment)
[Idoxuridine (Ophthalmic)][1], #
Keratitis, vaccinia virus (treatment)
Keratoconjunctivitis, herpes simplex virus (treatment)
[Ifosfamide (Systemic)], 1627
Carcinoma, cervical (treatment)
Sarcoma, soft tissue (treatment)
[Ifosfamide (Systemic)][1], 1627
Carcinoma, bladder (treatment)
Carcinoma, breast (treatment)
Carcinoma, endometrial (treatment)
Carcinoma, head and neck (treatment)
Carcinoma, lung, non-small cell (treatment)
Carcinoma, lung, small cell (treatment)
Carcinoma, ovarian, epithelial (treatment)
Carcinoma, thymic (treatment)
Ewing's sarcoma (treatment)
Leukemia, acute lymphocytic (treatment)
Lymphomas, Hodgkin's (treatment)
Lymphomas, non-Hodgkin's (treatment)
Neuroblastoma (treatment)
Osteosarcoma (treatment)
Thymoma (treatment)
Wilms' tumor (treatment)
Ifosfamide (Systemic)[1], 1627
Tumors, germ cell, testicular (treatment)
[Imatinib (Systemic)], 1633
Acute lymphoblastic leukemia, Philadelphia chromosome-positive, newly diagnosed, as part of combination chemotherapy
[Imatinib (Systemic)][1], 1633
Tumors, gastrointestinal stromal treatment)
[Imipenem and Cilastatin (Systemic)][1], 1638
Melioidosis (treatment)
[Imipenem and Cilastatin (Systemic)][1], 1638
Neutropenia, febrile (treatment)
[Imipramine (Systemic)][1], 280
Attention-deficit hyperactivity disorder (treatment)
Bulimia nervosa (treatment)
Cocaine withdrawal (treatment)
Headache (prophylaxis)
Narcolepsy/cataplexy syndrome (treatment adjunct)
Narcolepsy/cataplexy syndrome (treatment)
Pain, neurogenic (treatment)
Panic disorder (treatment)
Urinary incontinence (treatment)
[Immune Globulin Intravenous (Human) (Systemic)][1], 1645
Dermatomyositis, systemic (treatment)
Guillain-Barré syndrome (treatment)
Hyperimmunoglobulinemia E syndrome (treatment)
Kawasaki disease (treatment adjunct)
Lambert-Eaton myasthenic syndrome (treatment)
Multiple sclerosis, relapsing-remitting (treatment)
Neonates, high-risk, preterm, low-birthweight, infections in (prophylaxis)
Neonates, high-risk, preterm, low-birthweight, infections in (treatment adjunct)
Neuropathy, motor, multifocal (treatment)
Parovirus B19 infection, chronic (treatment)
Polyneuropathies, chronic inflammatory demyelinating (treatment)
Inamrinone (Systemic)[1], 1651
Heart failure, congestive (treatment)
[Indium In 111 Oxyquinoline (Systemic)][1], #
Platelet survival studies (diagnosis)
Thrombosis, arterial (diagnosis)
Thrombosis, cardiac (diagnosis)
[Indium In 111 Oxyquinoline (Systemic)][1] # *(continued)*
Thrombosis, deep venous (diagnosis)
Indomethacin (Ophthalmic)[1], 371
Inflammation, ocular (treatment)
[Indomethacin (Systemic)][1], 375
Arthritis, psoriatic (treatment)
Bartter's syndrome (treatment)
Calcium pyrophosphate deposition disease, acute (treatment)
Dysmenorrhea (treatment)
Fever, due to malignancy (treatment)
Headache, vascular (prophylaxis)
Headache, vascular (treatment)
Hypermenorrhea (treatment)
Paget's disease of bone, rheumatologic complications associated with (treatment)
Pericarditis, inflammation, pain, and fever associated with (treatment)
Reiter's disease (treatment)
Indomethacin (Systemic)[1], 375
Inflammation, nonrheumatic (treatment)
[Indomethacin—For Patent Ductus Arteriosus, Oral (Systemic)][1], 1659
Ductus arteriosus, patent (treatment)
[Infliximab (Systemic)][1], 1662
Inflammatory bowel disease arthritis (treatment)
Psoriasis (treatment)
Reactive arthritis (treatment)
Infliximab (Systemic)[1], 1662
Arthritis, psoriatic (treatment)
Colitis, ulcerative
[Insulin (Systemic)][1], 1675
Growth hormone deficiency (diagnosis)
Hyperglycemia during intravenous nutrition in low birth weight infants (treatment)
Nephropathy, diabetic (prophylaxis)
Neuropathy, diabetic (prophylaxis)
Retinopathy, diabetic (prophylaxis)
[Insulin Human (Systemic)][1], 1675
Growth hormone deficiency (diagnosis)
Nephropathy, diabetic (prophylaxis)
Neuropathy, diabetic (prophylaxis)
Retinopathy, diabetic (prophylaxis)
[Insulin Human, Buffered (Systemic)][1], 1675
Nephropathy, diabetic (prophylaxis)
Neuropathy, diabetic (prophylaxis)
Retinopathy, diabetic (prophylaxis)
[Insulin Isophane (Systemic)][1], 1675
Nephropathy, diabetic (prophylaxis)
Neuropathy, diabetic (prophylaxis)
Retinopathy, diabetic (prophylaxis)
[Insulin Isophane, Human (Systemic)][1], 1675
Nephropathy, diabetic (prophylaxis)
Neuropathy, diabetic (prophylaxis)
Retinopathy, diabetic (prophylaxis)
[Insulin Zinc (Systemic)][1], 1675
Nephropathy, diabetic (prophylaxis)
Neuropathy, diabetic (prophylaxis)
Retinopathy, diabetic (prophylaxis)
[Insulin Zinc, Extended (Systemic)][1], 1675
Nephropathy, diabetic (prophylaxis)
Neuropathy, diabetic (prophylaxis)
Retinopathy, diabetic (prophylaxis)
[Insulin Zinc, Extended, Human (Systemic)][1], 1675
Nephropathy, diabetic (prophylaxis)
Neuropathy, diabetic (prophylaxis)
Retinopathy, diabetic (prophylaxis)
[Insulin Zinc, Human (Systemic)][1], 1675
Nephropathy, diabetic (prophylaxis)
Neuropathy, diabetic (prophylaxis)
Retinopathy, diabetic (prophylaxis)
[Insulin Zinc, Prompt (Systemic)][1], 1675
Nephropathy, diabetic (prophylaxis)
Neuropathy, diabetic (prophylaxis)
Retinopathy, diabetic (prophylaxis)
[Insulin, Isophane, Human, and Insulin Human (Systemic)][1], 1675
Nephropathy, diabetic (prophylaxis)
Neuropathy, diabetic (prophylaxis)
Retinopathy, diabetic (prophylaxis)

[Interferon Alfa-2a, Recombinant (Systemic)], 1715
Carcinoma, renal (treatment)
Carcinoma, skin (treatment)
Leukemia, chronic myelocytic (treatment)
[Interferon Alfa-2a, Recombinant (Systemic)][1], 1715
Carcinoma, ovarian, epithelial (treatment)
Hepatitis, chronic, active (treatment)
Lymphomas, non-Hodgkin's (treatment)
Melanoma, malignant (treatment)
Multiple myeloma (treatment)
Mycosis fungoides (treatment)
Polycythemia vera (treatment)
Thrombocytosis, essential (treatment)
Tumors, carcinoid (treatment)
[Interferon Alfa-2b, Recombinant (Systemic)], 1715
Carcinoma, skin (treatment)
[Interferon Alfa-2b, Recombinant (Systemic)][1], 1715
Carcinoma, ovarian, epithelial (treatment)
Carcinoma, renal (treatment)
Leukemia, chronic myelocytic (treatment)
Lymphomas, non-Hodgkin's (treatment)
Papillomatosis, laryngeal (treatment)
Polycythemia vera (treatment)
Thrombocytosis, essential (treatment)
Tumors, carcinoid (treatment)
Interferon Alfa-2b, Recombinant (Systemic)[1], 1715
Condyloma acuminata (treatment)
Hepatitis B, chronic (treatment)
Melanoma, malignant (treatment)
Multiple myeloma (treatment)
Mycosis fungoides (treatment)
[Interferon Alfa-n1 (Ins) (Systemic)], 1715
Carcinoma, skin (treatment)
[Interferon Alfa-n1 (Ins) (Systemic)][1], 1715
Carcinoma, ovarian, epithelial (treatment)
Thrombocytosis, essential (treatment)
Tumors, carcinoid (treatment)
Interferon Alfa-n1 (Ins) (Systemic)[1], 1715
Hepatitis, chronic, active (treatment)
Kaposi's sarcoma, AIDS-associated (treatment)
Leukemia, chronic myelocytic (treatment)
Lymphomas, non-Hodgkin's (treatment)
Melanoma, malignant (treatment)
Multiple myeloma (treatment)
Mycosis fungoides (treatment)
[Interferon Alfa-n3 (Systemic)], 1715
Carcinoma, bladder (treatment)
Carcinoma, ovarian, epithelial (treatment)
Carcinoma, renal (treatment)
Carcinoma, skin (treatment)
Hepatitis, chronic, active (treatment)
Kaposi's sarcoma, AIDS-associated (treatment)
Leukemia, chronic myelocytic (treatment)
Leukemia, hairy cell (treatment)
Lymphomas, non-Hodgkin's (treatment)
Melanoma, malignant (treatment)
Multiple myeloma (treatment)
Mycosis fungoides (treatment)
Papillomatosis, laryngeal (treatment)
Thrombocytosis, essential (treatment)
[Interferon Alfa-n3 (Systemic)][1], 1715
Tumors, carcinoid (treatment)
[Interferon Beta-1a (Systemic)], 1706
Condyloma acuminata (treatment)
[Iobenguane I 123 (Systemic—Diagnostic)], #
Carcinoma, thyroid (diagnosis)
Hyperplasia, adrenal medulla (diagnosis)
Tumors, adrenal medulla (diagnosis)
Tumors, carcinoid (diagnosis)
[Iobenguane I 131 (Systemic—Diagnostic)], #
Carcinoma, thyroid (diagnosis)
Hyperplasia, adrenal medulla (diagnosis)
Tumors, carcinoid (diagnosis)
[Iobenguane I 131 Sulfate (Systemic—Therapeutic)][1], #
Carcinoid syndrome (treatment)
Neuroblastoma (treatment)
Pheochromocytoma (treatment)
[Iodine, Strong (Systemic)], #
Iodine deficiency (treatment)
[Iodine, Strong (Systemic)][1], #
Hyperthyroidism (treatment adjunct)
Radiation protectant, thyroid gland
Thyroid involution, preoperative (treatment adjunct)
Thyrotoxic crisis (treatment adjunct)
[Iodoquinol (Oral-Local)][1], #
Amebiasis, extraintestinal (treatment)
Balantidiasis (treatment)
[Iofetamine I 123 (Systemic)][1], #
Dementia, Alzheimer-type (diagnosis)
Seizures (diagnosis)
Iohexol (Local)[1], #
Cystourethrography, retrograde
Hysterosalpingography
Iohexol (Systemic)[1], #
Abdominal imaging, computed tomographic, adjunct
Cholangiopancreatography, endoscopic retrograde
Herniography
Pancreatography, endoscopic retrograde
Radiography, gastrointestinal
[Iopamidol (Systemic)][1], #
Arthrography
Cholangiopancreatography, endoscopic retrograde
Herniography
Pancreatography, endoscopic retrograde
Iopamidol (Systemic)[1], #
Aortography
Body imaging, computed tomographic
Brain imaging, computed tomographic
Cisternography, computed tomographic
Myelography, cervical
Myelography, thoracic
Myelography, total columnar
[Iopanoic Acid (Systemic)], #
Hyperthyroidism, in Graves' disease (treatment)
[Iothalamate Meglumine (Systemic)][1], #
Splenoportography
Iothalamate Meglumine (Systemic)[1], #
Angiography
[Iothalamate Meglumine and Iothalamate Sodium (Systemic)], #
Splenoportography
[Iothalamate Sodium (Systemic)][1], #
Splenoportography
[Ioversol (Systemic)][1], #
Arthrography
Cholangiopancreatography, endoscopic retrograde
Herniography
Pancreatography, endoscopic retrograde
[Iphenidol (Systemic)][1], #
Nausea and vomiting (treatment)
[Ipodate (Systemic)], #
Hyperthyroidism, in Graves' disease (treatment)
[Ipratropium (Inhalation-Local)], 1723
Asthma (treatment adjunct)
[Irinotecan (Systemic)], 1733
Extensive-stage small-cell lung cancer, first-line treatment, in combination with cisplatin
[Irinotecan (Systemic)][1], 1733
Carcinoma, lung, non-small cell (treatment)
[Isocarboxazid (Systemic)], 274
Headache, tension (prophylaxis)
Headache, vascular (prophylaxis)
[Isoflurophate (Ophthalmic)][1], 328
Esotropia, accommodative (diagnosis)
Esotropia, accommodative (treatment)
Glaucoma (treatment)
[Isosorbide Dinitrate Capsules (Systemic)][1], 2124
Heart failure, congestive (treatment)
Myocardial infarction (treatment adjunct)
[Isosorbide Dinitrate Chewable Tablets (Systemic)], 2124
Heart failure, congestive (treatment)
Myocardial infarction (treatment adjunct)
[Isosorbide Dinitrate Tablets (Systemic)][1], 2124
Heart failure, congestive (treatment)
Myocardial infarction (treatment adjunct)
[Isosorbide Dinitrate, Sublingual (Systemic)][1], 2124
Heart failure, congestive (treatment)
Myocardial infarction (treatment adjunct)
Isosorbide Dinitrate, Sublingual (Systemic)[1], 2124
Angina pectoris, acute (treatment)
[Isotretinoin (Systemic)][1], 1750
Erythroderma, congenital ichthyosiform (treatment)
Folliculitis, gram-negative (treatment)
Hidradenitis suppurativa (treatment)
Ichthyosis, lamellar (treatment)
Keratosis follicularis (treatment)
Keratosis palmaris et plantaris (treatment)
Pityriasis rubra pilaris (treatment)
Rosacea, severe (treatment)
[Isoxsuprine (Systemic)], #
Labor, premature (prophylaxis)
Labor, premature (treatment)
[Isoxsuprine (Systemic)][1], #
Dysmenorrhea (treatment)
Isoxsuprine (Systemic)[1], #
Vascular disease, peripheral (treatment)
[Isradipine (Systemic)], 673
Angina pectoris, chronic (treatment)
Raynaud's phenomenon (treatment)
[Itraconazole (Systemic)], 312
Chromomycosis (treatment)
Paracoccidioidomycosis (treatment)
Sporotrichosis, disseminated (treatment)
Tinea corporis (treatment)
Tinea cruris (treatment)
Tinea pedis (treatment)
[Itraconazole (Systemic)][1], 312
Penicillium marneffei infection (treatment)
Candidiasis, mucocutaneous, chronic (treatment)
Candidiasis, vulvovaginal (treatment)
Coccidioidomycosis (treatment)
Cryptococcosis (treatment)
Histoplasmosis (suppression)
Leishmaniasis, cutaneous (treatment)
Meningitis, cryptococcal (suppression)
Meningitis, cryptococcal (treatment)
Neutropenia, febrile (prophylaxis)
Paronychia (treatment)
Pneumonia, fungal (treatment)
Septicemia, fungal (treatment)
Tinea manuum (treatment)
Itraconazole (Systemic)[1], 312
Onychomycosis (treatment)
[Ivermectin (Systemic)][1], #
Filariasis, Bancroft's (treatment)
Scabies (treatment)

K

[Ketamine (Systemic)][1], #
Anesthesia, local, adjunct
Sedation and analgesia
[Ketazolam (Systemic)][1], 512
Insomnia (treatment)
[Ketoconazole (Systemic)], 312
Onychomycosis (treatment)
Tinea barbae (treatment)
[Ketoconazole (Systemic)][1], 312
Penicillium marneffei infection (treatment)
Candidiasis, vulvovaginal (treatment)
Carcinoma, prostatic (treatment)

[Ketoconazole (Systemic)][1] 312 *(continued)*
Cushing's syndrome (treatment)
Hirsutism (treatment)
Leishmaniasis, cutaneous (treatment)
Paronychia (treatment)
Pneumonia, fungal (treatment)
Septicemia, fungal (treatment)
Sporotrichosis, disseminated (treatment)
Tinea capitis (treatment)
Ketoconazole (Systemic)[1], 312
Blastomycosis (treatment)
[Ketoconazole (Topical)][1], 1757
Paronychia (treatment)
Tinea barbae (treatment)
Tinea capitis (treatment)
Ketoconazole (Topical)[1], 1757
Candidiasis, cutaneous (treatment)
[Ketoprofen (Systemic)], 375
Ankylosing spondylitis (treatment)
[Ketoprofen (Systemic)][1], 375
Arthritis, psoriatic (treatment)
Calcium pyrophosphate deposition disease, acute (treatment)
Gouty arthritis, acute (treatment)
Headache, vascular (treatment)
Hypermenorrhea (treatment)
Inflammation, nonrheumatic (treatment)
[Ketorolac (Ophthalmic)], 1759
Inflammation, ocular (prophylaxis)
Inflammation, ocular (treatment)
Ketorolac (Ophthalmic)[1], 1759
Conjunctivitis, allergic (treatment)
[Krypton Kr 81m (Systemic)], #
Embolism, pulmonary (diagnosis)

L

[Labetalol (Systemic)][1], 546
Angina pectoris, chronic (treatment)
Pheochromocytoma (treatment adjunct)
[Labetalol, Parenteral (Systemic)][1], 546
Hypotension, controlled (induction)
Hypotension, controlled (maintenance)
[Lamivudine (Systemic)][1], 1771
Human immunodeficiency virus (HIV) infection, occupation exposure (prophylaxis)
[Lamotrigine (Systemic)], 1776
Epilepsy (treatment)
Lamotrigine (Systemic)[1], 1776
Epilepsy, Lennox-Gastaut syndrome (treatment adjunct)
[Leucovorin (Systemic)][1], 1804
Carcinoma, head and neck (treatment adjunct)
Ewing's sarcoma (treatment adjunct)
Lymphomas, non-Hodgkin's (treatment adjunct)
Tumors, trophoblastic (treatment adjunct)
[Leuprolide (Systemic)][1], 1807
Carcinoma, breast (treatment)
Leuprolide (Systemic)[1], 1807
Anemia, uterine leiomyomata-associated (treatment)
[Levobetaxolol (Ophthalmic)], 537
Glaucoma, angle-closure (treatment adjunct)
[Levobunolol (Ophthalmic)][1], 537
Glaucoma, angle-closure (treatment adjunct)
Glaucoma, angle-closure, *during* or *after* iridectomy (treatment)
Glaucoma, malignant (treatment)
[Levocarnitine Oral Solution (Systemic)][1], 1819
Carnitine deficiency, secondary to valproic acid toxicity (prophylaxis)
Carnitine deficiency, secondary to valproic acid toxicity (treatment)
[Levonorgestrel and Ethinyl Estradiol (Systemic)][1], 1310
Amenorrhea (treatment)
Bleeding, uterine, dysfunctional (treatment)
Contraception, emergency postcoital
Dysmenorrhea (treatment)
Endometriosis (prophylaxis)
Endometriosis (treatment)
[Levonorgestrel and Ethinyl Estradiol (Systemic)][1] 1310 *(continued)*
Hirsutism, female (treatment adjunct)
Hirsutism, female (treatment)
Hyperandrogenism, ovarian (treatment adjunct)
Hyperandrogenism, ovarian (treatment)
Hypermenorrhea (treatment)
Polycystic ovary syndrome (treatment)
Levothyroxine (Systemic)[1], 2747
Carcinoma, thyroid (prophylaxis)
Carcinoma, thyroid (treatment)
Goiter (prophylaxis)
Thyroid function studies
Lidocaine (Parenteral-Local)[1], 174
Intravenous regional anesthesia
[Lidocaine Hydrochloride Oral Topical Solution (Mucosal-Local)], 164
Pain, esophageal (treatment)
[Lidocaine Topical Aerosol (Mucosal-Local)], 164
Gag reflex suppression
[Lindane Cream (Topical)], #
Pediculosis capitis (treatment, secondary)
Pediculosis pubis (treatment, secondary)
[Lindane Lotion (Topical)], #
Pediculosis capitis (treatment, secondary)
Pediculosis pubis (treatment, secondary)
Liothyronine (Systemic)[1], 2747
Goiter (prophylaxis)
[Lisinopril (Systemic)][1], 198
Scleroderma, hypertension in (treatment)
Scleroderma, renal crisis in (treatment)
[Lisinopril and Hydrochlorothiazide (Systemic)], 212
Heart failure, congestive (treatment)
[Lithium (Systemic)][1], 1843
Depression, mental (treatment)
Headache, vascular (prophylaxis)
Neutropenia (treatment)
[Lodoxamide (Ophthalmic)], #
Conjunctivitis, allergic (treatment)
Conjunctivitis, atopic (treatment)
Conjunctivitis, vernal (treatment)
Keratoconjunctivitis, vernal (treatment)
[Lomustine (Systemic)], 1849
Carcinoma, breast (treatment)
Carcinoma, lung, non-small cell (treatment)
Melanoma, malignant (treatment)
[Lomustine (Systemic)][1], 1849
Carcinoma, colorectal (treatment)
Multiple myeloma (treatment)
[Loratadine (Systemic)][1], 333
Asthma, bronchial (treatment adjunct)
Pruritus, associated with pityriasis rosea (treatment)
[Lorazepam (Systemic)][1], 512
Alcohol withdrawal (treatment)
Headache, tension (treatment)
Panic disorder (treatment)
Spasm, skeletal muscle (treatment adjunct)
Lorazepam (Systemic)[1], 512
Insomnia (treatment)
[Lorazepam, Oral (Systemic)][1], 512
Tremors (treatment)
Lorazepam, Oral (Systemic)[1], 512
Anxiety, mental-depression-associated (treatment adjunct)
[Lorazepam, Parenteral (Systemic)], 512
Status epilepticus (treatment)
[Lorazepam, Parenteral (Systemic)][1], 512
Amnesia, in endoscopic procedures
Anxiety, in endoscopic procedures (treatment adjunct)
Nausea and vomiting, cancer chemotherapy-induced (prophylaxis)
Losartan and Hydrochlorothiazide (Systemic)[1], 1865
Hypertensive patients with left ventricular hypertrophy
Lovastatin (Systemic)[1], 1587
Heart disease, coronary (prophylaxis)
[Loxapine (Systemic)][1], 1870
Anxiety, mental-depression associated (treatment)

M

[Magnesium Sulfate (Systemic)][1], 1877
Labor, premature (treatment)
Tachycardia, ventricular, polymorphous (treatment)
[Malt Soup Extract (Local)], #
Bowel syndrome, irritable (treatment adjunct)
[Malt Soup Extract and Psyllium (Local)], #
Bowel syndrome, irritable (treatment adjunct)
[Maprotiline (Systemic)][1], #
Pain, neurogenic (treatment)
[Mebendazole (Systemic)][1], 1889
Capillariasis (treatment)
Gnathostomiasis (treatment)
Hydatid disease, alveolar (treatment)
Hydatid disease, unilocular (treatment)
Trichinosis (treatment)
[Mechlorethamine (Systemic)][1], 1894
Lymphomas, cutaneous T-cell (treatment)
[Mechlorethamine (Topical)][1], #
Mycosis fungoides (treatment)
[Meclizine (Systemic)], 1897
Nausea and vomiting, radiotherapy-induced (prophylaxis)
Nausea and vomiting, radiotherapy-induced (treatment)
[Meclofenamate (Systemic)], 375
Arthritis, psoriatic (treatment)
Calcium pyrophosphate deposition disease, acute (treatment)
Gouty arthritis, acute (treatment)
Headache, vascular (treatment)
Inflammation, nonrheumatic (treatment)
[Medrogesterone, Oral (Systemic)], 2429
Hyperplasia, endometrial, estrogen-induced (prophylaxis)
[Medroxyprogesterone (Oral) (Systemic)][1], 2429
Endometriosis (treatment)
Hyperplasia, endometrial, estrogen-induced (prophylaxis)
[Medroxyprogesterone (Parenteral) (Systemic)], 2429
Endometriosis (treatment)
[Medroxyprogesterone (Systemic)], 2429
Carcinoma, breast (treatment)
[Medroxyprogesterone (Systemic)][1], 2429
Polycystic ovary syndrome (treatment)
[Medroxyprogesterone, Oral (Systemic)], 2429
Carcinoma, endometrial (treatment)
Estrogen production, endogenous (diagnosis)
[Medroxyprogesterone, Oral (Systemic)][1], 2429
Hyperplasia, endometrial (treatment)
[Medroxyprogesterone, Parenteral (Systemic)][1], 2429
Puberty, precocious (treatment)
[Medrysone (Ophthalmic)][1], 906
Iridocyclitis (treatment)
Keratitis, herpes zoster (treatment)
Keratitis, not associated with herpes simplex or fungal infection (treatment)
Keratitis, punctate, superficial (treatment)
Keratitis, vernal (treatment)
Keratoconjunctivitis, allergic (treatment)
Ocular infections, superficial (treatment adjunct)
Ophthalmia, sympathetic (treatment)
Rosacea, ocular (treatment)
[Mefenamic Acid (Systemic)][1], 375
Calcium pyrophosphate deposition disease, acute (treatment)
Gouty arthritis, acute (treatment)
Headache, vascular (prophylaxis)
Headache, vascular (treatment)
Hypermenorrhea (treatment)
Inflammation, nonrheumatic (treatment)
[Megestrol (Systemic)], 2429
Carcinoma, prostatic (treatment)

[Megestrol (Systemic)][1], 2429
Hyperplasia, endometrial (treatment)
[Megestrol Tablets (Systemic)][1], 2429
Weight loss, significant, carcinoma-associated (treatment)
[Meglumine Antimoniate (Systemic)][1], #
Leishmaniasis, cutaneous (treatment)
Leishmaniasis, diffuse cutaneous (treatment)
Leishmaniasis, mucosal (treatment)
Leishmaniasis, visceral (treatment)
[Melphalan (Systemic)], 1911
Melanoma, malignant (treatment)
[Melphalan (Systemic)][1], 1911
Carcinoma, breast (treatment)
Carcinoma, endometrial (treatment)
Leukemia, chronic myelocytic (treatment)
Lymphomas, Hodgkin's (treatment)
Waldenstrom's macroglobulinemia (treatment)
Menotropins (Systemic)[1], #
Reproductive technologies, assisted
[Mepivacaine (Parenteral-Local)][1], 174
Anesthesia, transtracheal
Intravenous regional anesthesia
[Mercaptopurine (Systemic)], 1925
Leukemia, acute myelocytic (treatment)
[Mercaptopurine (Systemic)][1], 1925
Arthritis, psoriatic (treatment)
Bowel disease, inflammatory (treatment)
Lymphomas, non-Hodgkin's (treatment)
[Meropenem (Systemic)][1], 1928
Neutropenia, febrile (treatment)
[Mesalamine (Rectal-Local)], 1934
Bowel disease, inflammatory (prophylaxis)
[Metformin (Systemic)][1], 1937
Polycystic ovary syndrome (treatment)
[Methadone (Systemic)], 2184
Cough (treatment)
[Methantheline (Systemic)][1], 230
Salivation, excessive, in dental procedures (prophylaxis)
[Metharbital (Systemic)][1], 496
Epilepsy, simple partial seizure pattern (treatment)
Epilepsy, tonic-clonic seizure pattern (treatment)
[Methenamine (Systemic)], #
Urinary tract infections, bacterial (prophylaxis)
[Methicillin (Systemic)], 2304
Bone and joint infections (treatment)
[Methicillin (Systemic)][1], 2304
Endocarditis, bacterial (treatment)
[Methotrexate—For Cancer (Systemic)], 1947
Carcinoma, bladder (treatment)
Carcinoma, gastric (treatment)
[Methotrexate—For Cancer (Systemic)][1], 1947
Carcinoma, cervical (treatment)
Carcinoma, colorectal (treatment)
Carcinoma, esophageal (treatment)
Carcinoma, ovarian, epithelial (treatment)
Carcinoma, pancreatic (treatment)
Carcinoma, penile (treatment)
Leukemia, acute nonlymphocytic (treatment)
Lymphomas, Hodgkin's (treatment)
Meningitis, carcinomatous (treatment)
Sarcoma, soft tissue (treatment)
Methotrexate—For Cancer (Systemic)[1], 1947
Carcinoma, lung, non-small cell (treatment)
Carcinoma, lung, small cell (treatment)
[Methoxsalen (Systemic)], 1954
Dermatitis, atopic (treatment)
Skin, intolerance to sunlight
[Methoxsalen (Systemic)][1], 1954
Alopecia areata (treatment)
Dermatoses, inflammatory (treatment)
Eczema (treatment)
Lichen planus (treatment)
[Methoxsalen (Topical)], #
Psoriasis (treatment)
[Methoxsalen (Topical)][1], #
Alopecia areata (treatment)
Dermatoses, inflammatory (treatment)
Eczema (treatment)
[Methoxsalen (Topical)][1] # *(continued)*
Lichen planus (treatment)
Mycosis fungoides (treatment)
Skin, increased tolerance to sunlight
Methoxsalen Capsules (XXI) (Hard Gelatin) (Systemic)[1], 1954
Mycosis fungoides (treatment)
[Methoxsalen Capsules (XXII) (Soft Gelatin) (Systemic)], 1954
Vitiligo (treatment)
[Methoxsalen Capsules (XXII) (Soft Gelatin) (Systemic)][1], 1954
Mycosis fungoides (treatment)
[Methsuximide (Systemic)][1], 271
Epilepsy, complex partial seizure pattern (treatment)
[Methyclothiazide (Systemic)][1], 1127
Diabetes insipidus, central (treatment)
Diabetes insipidus, nephrogenic (treatment)
Renal calculi, calcium (prophylaxis)
[Methylcellulose (Local)], #
Bowel syndrome, irritable (treatment adjunct)
[Methylergonovine (Systemic)], 1958
Abortion, incomplete (treatment)
[Methylphenidate (Systemic)][1], 1961
Depressive disorder, secondary to medical illness (treatment)
[Methylprednisole (Systemic)][1], 938
Myasthenia gravis (treatment)
[Methylprednisolone (Systemic)][1], 938
Bronchitis, asthmatic, acute or chronic (treatment)
Calcium pyrophosphate deposition disease, acute (treatment)
Carcinoma, breast (treatment)
Carcinoma, prostatic (treatment)
Carditis, nonrheumatic, acute (treatment)
Connective tissue disease, mixed (treatment)
Eczema, severe (treatment)
Edema, pulmonary, noncardiogenic (treatment)
Fever, due to malignancy (treatment adjunct)
Gingivitis, desquamative (treatment)
Hemangioma, airway-obstructing, in infants (treatment)
Hemolysis (treatment)
Hepatitis, alcoholic with encepalopathy (treatment)
Hepatitis, chronic, active (treatment)
Hepatitis, nonalcoholic in women (treatment)
Lesions, oral, corticosteroid-responsive disorders-associated (treatment)
Multiple myeloma (treatment)
Necrosis, hepatic, subacute (treatment)
Pemphigoid (treatment)
Pericarditis (treatment)
Polyarteritis nodosa (treatment)
Polychondritis, relapsing (treatment)
Polyps, nasal (treatment)
Pulmonary disease, chronic obstructive (treatment)
Reiter's disease (treatment)
Sarcoid, localized cutaneous (treatment)
Stomatitis, aphthous, recurrent (treatment)
Tumors, brain, primary (treatment adjunct)
Vasculitis (treatment)
[Methylprednisolone Sodium Succinate for Injection (Systemic)][1], 938
Hypercalcemia, sarcoidosis-associated (treatment)
[Methylprednisolone Sodium Succinate, Parenteral (Systemic)], 938
Rheumatic fever (treatment)
Spinal cord injury, acute (treatment)
Status asthmaticus (treatment)
Transplant rejection (prophylaxis)
Transplant rejection (treatment)
[Methylprednisolone Sodium Succinate, Parenteral (Systemic)][1], 938
Edema, cerebral, especially when associated with primary or metastatic brain tumor, craniotomy, or head injury (prophylaxis)
[Methylprednisolone Tablets (Systemic)][1], 938
Hypercalcemia, sarcoidosis-associated (treatment)
[Methylprednisolone, Oral (Systemic)], 938
Transplant rejection (prophylaxis)
Transplant rejection (treatment)
[Methylprednisolone, Parenteral (Systemic)][1], 938
Pneumonia, *Pneumocystis carinii*, AIDS-associated (treatment adjunct)
[Methyltestosterone (Systemic)][1], 153
Growth, constitutional delay in (treatment)
[Metipranolol (Ophthalmic)], 537
Glaucoma, angle-closure (treatment adjunct)
Glaucoma, angle-closure, *during* or *after* iridectomy (treatment)
Glaucoma, malignant (treatment)
[Metoclopramide (Systemic)], 1967
Gastric emptying, slow (treatment)
Gastric stasis, in preterm infants (treatment)
Nausea and vomiting, postoperative, drug-related (treatment)
[Metoclopramide (Systemic)][1], 1967
Headache, vascular (treatment adjunct)
Hiccups, intractable (treatment)
Pneumonitis, aspiration (prophylaxis)
Metoclopramide (Systemic)[1], 1967
Gastroparesis (treatment)
Metoclopramide, Oral (Systemic)[1], 1967
Reflux, gastroesophageal (treatment)
[Metolazone (Systemic)][1], 1127
Diabetes insipidus, central (treatment)
Diabetes insipidus, nephrogenic (treatment)
Renal calculi, calcium (prophylaxis)
[Metoprolol (Systemic)][1], 546
Akathisia, neuroleptic-induced (treatment)
Anxiety (treatment adjunct)
Arrhythmias, cardiac (prophylaxis)
Arrhythmias, cardiac (treatment)
Arrhythmias, supraventricular (prophylaxis)
Arrhythmias, supraventricular (treatment)
Cardiomyopathy, hypertrophic (treatment)
Headache, vascular (prophylaxis)
Mitral valve prolapse syndrome (treatment)
Pheochromocytoma (treatment adjunct)
Tachycardia, ventricular (prophylaxis)
Tachycardia, ventricular (treatment)
Thyrotoxicosis (treatment adjunct)
Tremors (treatment)
[Metronidazole (Systemic)][1], 1971
Balantidiasis (treatment)
Bowel disease, inflammatory (treatment)
Colitis, antibiotic-associated (treatment)
Dracunculiasis (treatment)
Gastritis, *Helicobacter pylori*-associated (treatment adjunct)
Periodontal infections (treatment)
Ulcer, duodenal, *Helicobacter pylori*-associated (treatment adjunct)
[Metronidazole Vaginal Cream (Vaginal)], 1977
Trichomoniasis (treatment)
[Metronidazole Vaginal Tablets (Vaginal)], 1977
Trichomoniasis (treatment)
[Metronidazole, Oral (Systemic)][1], 1971
Giardiasis (treatment)
Vaginosis, bacterial (treatment)
[Metyrapone (Systemic)][1], #
Cushing's syndrome (diagnosis)
Cushing's syndrome (treatment)
[Miconazole (Topical)], #
Paronychia (treatment)
Tinea barbae (treatment)
Tinea capitis (treatment)
[Midazolam (Systemic)][1], 1983
Anesthesia, local, adjunct
Status epilepticus (treatment)
[Midodrine (Systemic)][1], 1990
Hypotension, intradialytic (treatment)
Hypotension, secondary, infection-related (treatment)

[Midodrine (Systemic)][1] 1990 *(continued)*
Hypotension, secondary, psychotropic agent-induced (treatment)
[Minocycline (Systemic)], 2722
Gallbladder infections (treatment)
Traveler's diarrhea (treatment)
[Minocycline (Systemic)][1], 2722
Arthritis, gonococcal (treatment)
Leprosy (treatment)
Nocardiosis (treatment)
Minocycline (Systemic)[1], 2722
Bartonellosis (treatment)
Mycobacterial infections, atypical (treatment)
[Minocycline, Oral (Systemic)][1], 2722
Arthritis, rheumatoid (treatment)
Minocycline, Oral (Systemic)[1], 2722
Acne vulgaris (treatment adjunct)
[Misoprostol (Systemic)][1], 2008
Abortion, second trimester (treatment)
Abortion, therapeutic (treatment)
Cervical ripening
Labor, induction of
Ulcer, duodenal (treatment)
Ulcer, gastric, nonsteroidal anti-inflammatory drug-induced (treatment)
[Mitomycin (Systemic)], 2011
Carcinoma, bladder (treatment)
Carcinoma, colorectal (treatment)
[Mitomycin (Systemic)][1], 2011
Carcinoma, anal (treatment)
Carcinoma, biliary (treatment)
Carcinoma, breast (treatment)
Carcinoma, cervical (treatment)
Carcinoma, esophageal (treatment)
Carcinoma, head and neck (treatment)
Carcinoma, lung, non-small cell (treatment)
Leukemia, chronic myelocytic (treatment)
[Mitotane (Systemic)][1], 2014
Cushing's syndrome (treatment)
[Mitoxantrone (Systemic)], 2016
Carcinoma, breast (treatment)
Hepatoma (treatment)
Leukemia, acute lymphocytic (treatment)
Lymphomas, non-Hodgkin's (treatment)
Mitoxantrone (Systemic)[1], 2016
Carcinoma, prostatic, advanced hormone-refractory (treatment)
Multiple sclerosis (treatment)
[Moexipril (Systemic)][1], 198
Scleroderma, hypertension in (treatment) , 2022
Scleroderma, renal crisis in (treatment) , 2022
[Mometasone (Nasal)], 897
Rhinitis, seasonal (prophylaxis)
Rhinitis, vasomotor nonallergic (treatment)
[Mometasone (Nasal)], #
Sinusitis (treatment adjunct)
[Morphine (Systemic)], 2184
Cough (treatment)
Diarrhea (treatment)
Pain, during mechanical ventilation, neonatal (treatment)
Pain, postoperative, neonatal (treatment)
[Mupirocin (Topical)], 2039
Eczema, infected (treatment)
Skin infections, bacterial, minor (prophylaxis)
[Mupirocin (Topical)][1], 2039
Folliculitis (treatment)
Mycophenolate (Systemic), 2043
[Lupus nephritis (treatment)][1]

N

[Nabumetone (Systemic)][1], 375
Inflammation, nonrheumatic (treatment)
[Nadolol (Systemic)][1], 546
Akathisia, neuroleptic-induced (treatment)
Arrhythmias, cardiac (prophylaxis)
Arrhythmias, cardiac (treatment)
Arrhythmias, supraventricular (prophylaxis)
Arrhythmias, supraventricular (treatment)
Cardiomyopathy, hypertrophic (treatment)
[Nadolol (Systemic)][1] 546 *(continued)*
Headache, vascular (prophylaxis)
Mitral valve prolapse syndrome (treatment)
Myocardial infarction (prophylaxis)
Myocardial infarction (treatment)
Pheochromocytoma (treatment adjunct)
Tachycardia, ventricular (prophylaxis)
Tachycardia, ventricular (treatment)
Thyrotoxicosis (treatment adjunct)
Tremors (treatment)
[Nafcillin, Parenteral (Systemic)][1], 2304
Bone and joint infections (treatment)
Endocarditis, bacterial (treatment)
Meningitis, bacterial (treatment)
[Nafcillin, Parenteral][1], 2304
Pericarditis, bacterial (treatment)
[Naftifine (Topical)], #
Tinea barbae (treatment)
Tinea capitis (treatment)
Tinea versicolor (treatment)
[Naloxone (Systemic)][1], #
Opioid (narcotic) drug use, illicit (diagnosis)
Naloxone (Systemic)[1], #
Shock, septic (treatment adjunct)
[Nandrolone (Systemic)], 142
Growth failure (treatment adjunct)
[Nandrolone Decanoate (Systemic)], 142
Catabolic or tissue-depleting processes (treatment)
[Nandrolone Decanoate (Systemic)][1], 142
Carcinoma, breast (treatment)
Nandrolone Decanoate (Systemic)[1], 142
Anemia (treatment)
[Nandrolone Phenpropionate (Systemic)], 142
Anemia (treatment)
[Naproxen (Systemic)][1], 375
Calcium pyrophosphate deposition disease, acute (treatment)
Headache, vascular (prophylaxis)
Headache, vascular (treatment)
Hypermenorrhea (treatment)
Naproxen (Systemic)[1], 375
Fever (treatment)
Gouty arthritis, acute (treatment)
[Nedocromil (Inhalation-Local)], 2060
Bronchospasm (prophylaxis)
[Neomycin (Ophthalmic)][1], #
Blepharitis, bacterial (treatment)
Blepharoconjunctivitis (treatment)
Conjunctivitis, bacterial (treatment)
Keratitis, bacterial (treatment)
Keratoconjunctivitis, bacterial (treatment)
Ocular infections (treatment)
[Neomycin (Topical)], #
Skin infections, bacterial, minor (treatment)
Ulcer, dermal (treatment)
[Neomycin and Polymyxin B (Topical)][1], 2066
Skin infections, bacterial, minor (prophylaxis)
Ulcer, dermal (treatment)
[Neomycin, Polymyxin B, and Bacitracin (Ophthalmic)], 2067
Blepharitis, bacterial (treatment)
Blepharoconjunctivitis (treatment)
Conjunctivitis, bacterial (treatment)
Keratitis, bacterial (treatment)
Keratoconjunctivitis, bacterial (treatment)
[Neomycin, Polymyxin B, and Bacitracin (Topical)], 2068
Skin infections, bacterial, minor (treatment)
Ulcer, dermal (treatment)
[Neomycin, Polymyxin B, and Gramicidin (Ophthalmic)], 2069
Blepharitis, bacterial (treatment)
Blepharoconjunctivitis (treatment)
Conjunctivitis, bacterial (treatment)
[Neomycin, Polymyxin B, and Hydrocortisone (Otic)][1], 2072
Otitis media, chronic suppurative (treatment)
[Neostigmine, Parenteral (Systemic)][1], 420
Myasthenia gravis (diagnosis)
[Nevirapine (Systemic)][1], 2093
Human immunodeficiency virus (HIV) infection, type 1, mother-to-child transmission of (treatment)
[Nicardipine (Systemic)], 673
Raynaud's phenomenon (treatment)
Subarachnoid hemorrhage-associated neurologic deficits (treatment)
[Niclosamide (Oral-Local)], #
Dipylidiasis (treatment)
[Nifedipine (Systemic)][1], 673
Raynaud's phenomenon (treatment)
Nitisinone (Systemic)[1], 2121
Hereditary tyrosinemia type 1 [HT-1] (treatment adjunct)
[Nitrates (Systemic)][1], 2124
Anal fissures, chronic (treatment)
Nitroglycerin, Buccal (Systemic)[1], 2124
Angina pectoris, acute (treatment)
[Nitroglycerin, Lingual (Systemic)][1], 2124
Heart failure, congestive (treatment)
Myocardial infarction (treatment adjunct)
Nitroglycerin, Lingual (Systemic)[1], 2124
Angina pectoris, acute (prophylaxis)
[Nitroglycerin, Sublingual (Systemic)][1], 2124
Heart failure, congestive (treatment)
Myocardial infarction (treatment adjunct)
[Nitroglycerin, Topical (Systemic)][1], 2124
Heart failure, congestive (treatment)
Myocardial infarction (treatment adjunct)
[Nitroprusside (Systemic)][1], 2136
Hypertension, paroxysmal, in surgery for pheochromocytoma (treatment)
Myocardial infarction (treatment adjunct)
Toxicity, ergot alkaloid (treatment)
Valvular regurgitation (treatment adjunct)
Nitroprusside (Systemic)[1], 2136
Heart failure, congestive (treatment)
[Nizatidine (Systemic)][1], 1573
Adenoma, multiple endocrine (treatment)
Hypersecretory conditions, gastric (treatment)
Mastocytosis, systemic (treatment)
Zollinger-Ellison syndrome (treatment)
Nizatidine (Systemic)[1], 1573
Reflux, gastroesophageal (treatment)
[Nonoxynol 9 (Systemic)][1], #
Pelvic inflammatory disease (prophylaxis)
Sexually transmitted diseases (prophylaxis)
Norelgestromin and Ethinyl Estradiol (Systemic) [1], 2140
Pregnancy prevention
[Norethindrone (Systemic)][1], 2429
Hyperplasia, endometrial, estrogen-induced (prophylaxis)
[Norethindrone Acetate and Ethinyl Estradiol (Systemic)][1], 1310
Amenorrhea (treatment)
Bleeding, uterine, dysfunctional (treatment)
Dysmenorrhea (treatment)
Endometriosis (prophylaxis)
Endometriosis (treatment)
Hirsutism, female (treatment adjunct)
Hirsutism, female (treatment)
Hyperandrogenism, ovarian (treatment adjunct)
Hyperandrogenism, ovarian (treatment)
Hypermenorrhea (treatment)
Polycystic ovary syndrome (treatment)
[Norethindrone and Ethinyl Estradiol (Systemic)][1], 1310
Amenorrhea (treatment)
Bleeding, uterine, dysfunctional (treatment)
Dysmenorrhea (treatment)
Endometriosis (prophylaxis)
Endometriosis (treatment)
Hirsutism, female (treatment adjunct)
Hirsutism, female (treatment)
Hyperandrogenism, ovarian (treatment adjunct)
Hyperandrogenism, ovarian (treatment)
Hypermenorrhea (treatment)
Polycystic ovary syndrome (treatment)

Norethindrone and Ethinyl Estradiol, Triphasic (Systemic)[1], 1310
Acne vulgaris (treatment)
[Norethindrone and Mestranol (Systemic)], 1310
Amenorrhea (treatment)
Bleeding, uterine, dysfunctional (treatment)
Dysmenorrhea (treatment)
Endometriosis (prophylaxis)
Hypermenorrhea (treatment)
[Norethindrone and Mestranol (Systemic)][1], 1310
Endometriosis (treatment)
Hirsutism, female (treatment adjunct)
Hirsutism, female (treatment)
Hyperandrogenism, ovarian (treatment adjunct)
Hyperandrogenism, ovarian (treatment)
Polycystic ovary syndrome (treatment)
Norfloxacin (Systemic)[1], 1409
Diarrhea, infectious (treatment)
Prostatitis, bacterial (treatment)
[Norgestimate and Ethinyl Estradiol (Systemic)][1], 1310
Amenorrhea (treatment)
Bleeding, uterine, dysfunctional (treatment)
Dysmenorrhea (treatment)
Endometriosis (prophylaxis)
Endometriosis (treatment)
Hirsutism, female (treatment adjunct)
Hirsutism, female (treatment)
Hyperandrogenism, ovarian (treatment adjunct)
Hyperandrogenism, ovarian (treatment)
Hypermenorrhea (treatment)
Polycystic ovary syndrome (treatment)
Norgestimate and Ethinyl Estradiol, Triphasic (Systemic)[1], 1310
Acne vulgaris (treatment)
[Norgestrel and Ethinyl Estradiol (Systemic)][1], 1310
Amenorrhea (treatment)
Bleeding, uterine, dysfunctional (treatment)
Contraception, emergency postcoital
Dysmenorrhea (treatment)
Endometriosis (prophylaxis)
Endometriosis (treatment)
Hirsutism, female (treatment adjunct)
Hirsutism, female (treatment)
Hyperandrogenism, ovarian (treatment adjunct)
Hyperandrogenism, ovarian (treatment)
Hypermenorrhea (treatment)
Polycystic ovary syndrome (treatment)
[Nortriptyline (Systemic)][1], 280
Headache (prophylaxis)
Nicotine dependence (treatment adjunct)
Pain, neurogenic (treatment)
Panic disorder (treatment)
[Nystatin (Topical)], 2147
Tinea barbae (treatment)
Tinea capitis (treatment)
[Nystatin for Oral Suspension (Oral-Local)], 2145
Candidiasis, oropharyngeal (prophylaxis)
[Nystatin Lozenges (Pastilles) (Oral-Local)], 2145
Candidiasis, oropharyngeal (prophylaxis)
[Nystatin Oral Suspension (Oral-Local)], 2145
Candidiasis, oropharyngeal (prophylaxis)
[Nystatin Tablets (Vaginal)], 2148
Candidiasis, oropharyngeal (treatment)

O

[Octoxynol 9 (Systemic)][1], #
Pelvic inflammatory disease (prophylaxis)
Sexually transmitted diseases (prophylaxis)
[Octreotide (Systemic)], 2151
Pancreatic surgery, complications of (prophylaxis)
Varices, gastroesophageal, bleeding (treatment)
[Octreotide (Systemic)][1], 2151
Diarrhea, AIDS-associated (treatment)
Diarrhea, chemotherapy-induced (treatment)
[Octreotide (Systemic)][1] 2151 *(continued)*
Hypotension (treatment)
Tumors, pancreatic (treatment adjunct)
Octreotide (Systemic)[1], 2151
Acromegaly (treatment)
Ofloxacin (Ophthalmic)[1], 2155
Corneal ulcers, bacterial (treatment)
[Olsalazine (Oral-Local)], #
Bowel disease, inflammatory (treatment)
[Omeprazole (Systemic)], 2176
Dyspepsia (treatment)
Ulcer, peptic, nonsteroidal anti-inflammatory drug-induced (treatment)
[Opium Tincture (Systemic)], 2184
Opioid (narcotic) dependence, neonatal (treatment)
[Oxacillin, Parenteral (Systemic)], 2304
Bone and joint infections (treatment)
Endocarditis, bacterial (treatment)
Meningitis, bacterial (treatment)
[Oxaliplatin (Systemic)], 2230
Colon cancer, stage II, adjuvant treatment in combination with 5-fluorouracil/leucovorin
Gastric carcinoma, advanced/metastatic
[Oxaliplatin (Systemic)][1], 2230
Carcinoma, metastatic colon (first-line treatment)
Carcinoma, metastatic rectal (first-line treatment)
[Oxandrolone (Systemic)], 142
Growth failure (treatment adjunct)
Turner's syndrome (treatment)
[Oxaprozin (Systemic)], 375
Inflammation, nonrheumatic (treatment)
Oxazepam (Systemic)[1], 512
Anxiety, mental-depression-associated (treatment adjunct)
Oxprenolol (Systemic)[1], 546
Anxiety (treatment adjunct)
Arrhythmias, cardiac (prophylaxis)
Arrhythmias, cardiac (treatment)
Arrhythmias, supraventricular (prophylaxis)
Arrhythmias, supraventricular (treatment)
Cardiomyopathy, hypertrophic (treatment)
Mitral valve prolapse syndrome (treatment)
Myocardial infarction (prophylaxis)
Myocardial infarction (treatment)
Pheochromocytoma (treatment adjunct)
Tachycardia, ventricular (prophylaxis)
Tachycardia, ventricular (treatment)
Thyrotoxicosis (treatment adjunct)
Tremors (treatment)
[Oxymetazoline (Nasal)], #
Congestion, sinus (treatment)
[Oxymetholone (Systemic)], 142
Growth failure (treatment adjunct)
Oxymetholone (Systemic)[1], 142
Angioedema, hereditary (prophylaxis)
Angioedema, hereditary (treatment)
[Oxytetracycline (Systemic)], 2722
Arthritis, gonococcal (treatment)
Traveler's diarrhea (treatment)
[Oxytocin, Parenteral (Systemic)][1], 2244
Fetal distress (diagnosis)
Utero-placental insufficiency (diagnosis)

P

[Paclitaxel (Systemic)][1], 2247
Carcinoma, bladder (treatment)
Carcinoma, breast (treatment, first-line)
Carcinoma, cervical (treatment)
Carcinoma, endometrial (treatment)
Carcinoma, esophageal (treatment)
Carcinoma, gastric (treatment)
Carcinoma, head and neck (treatment)
Carcinoma, lung, small cell (treatment)
Carcinoma, prostate (treatment)
Carcinoma, unknown primary site (treatment adjunct)
Tumors, germ cell, testicular (treatment)
Paclitaxel (Systemic)[1], 2247
Carcinoma, breast, node-positive (treatment adjunct)
Kaposi's sarcoma, AIDS-associated (treatment)
[Pamidronate (Systemic)][1], 2260
Osteogenesis imperfecta (treatment)
[Pancrelipase (Systemic)][1], 2264
Pancreatic insufficiency (diagnosis)
[Pancuronium (Systemic)][1], 2077
Convulsions (treatment)
[Pantoprazole (Systemic)], 2266
Gastroesophageal reflux disease (prophylaxis)
Ulcer, duodenal (treatment)
Ulcer, duodenal, *Helicobacter pylori*-associated (treatment)
Ulcer, gastic (treatment)
[Papaverine (Intracavernosal)][1], #
Erectile dysfunction (diagnosis)
Erectile dysfunction (treatment)
[Paramethadione (Systemic)][1], #
Epilepsy, absence seizure pattern (treatment)
[Penbutolol (Systemic)], 546
Angina pectoris, chronic (treatment)
[Penicillamine (Systemic)], 2300
Toxicity, heavy metal (treatment)
[Penicillamine (Systemic)][1], 2300
Felty's syndrome (treatment)
Vasculitis, rheumatoid (treatment)
[Penicillin G Benzathine (Systemic)][1], 2304
Diphtheria (prophylaxis)
Erysipeloid (treatment)
[Penicillin G Procaine (Systemic)][1], 2304
Erysipeloid (treatment)
[Penicillin G, Parenteral (Systemic)], 2304
Yaws (treatment)
[Penicillin G, Parenteral (Systemic)][1], 2304
Bone and joint infections (treatment)
Endocarditis, bacterial (treatment)
Gas gangrene infections (treatment)
Gonorrhea, endocervical, uncomplicated (treatment)
Gonorrhea, urethral, uncomplicated (treatment)
Intra-abdominal infections (treatment)
Leptospirosis (treatment)
Lyme disease (treatment)
Scarlet fever (treatment)
Skin and soft tissue infections (treatment)
[Penicillin V (Systemic)][1], 2304
Pasteurella multocida infections (treatment)
Actinomycosis (treatment)
Anthrax (treatment)
Erysipeloid (treatment)
Lyme disease (treatment)
Rat-bite fever (treatment)
Relapsing fever (treatment)
[Pentamidine (Inhalation)][1], 2337
Pneumonia, *Pneumocystis carinii* (treatment)
[Pentamidine (Systemic)][1], #
Leishmaniasis, cutaneous (treatment)
Leishmaniasis, visceral (treatment)
Trypanosomiasis, African (treatment)
[Pentobarbital, Parenteral (Systemic)][1], 496
Hypertension, cerebral (treatment)
Ischemia, cerebral (treatment)
[Pentostatin (Systemic)][1], 2341
Leukemia, chronic lymphocytic (treatment)
Leukemia, prolymphocytic (treatment)
Lymphoma, cutaneous T-cell (treatment)
[Perindopril (Systemic)][1], 198
Scleroderma, hypertension in (treatment)
Scleroderma, renal crisis in (treatment)
[Phenelzine (Systemic)][1], 274
Headache, tension (prophylaxis)
Headache, vascular (prophylaxis)
Panic disorder (treatment)
[Phenindamine (Systemic)], 333
Pruritus, associated with pityriasis rosea (treatment)
[Phenobarbital (Systemic)][1], 496
Hyperbilirubinemia (prophylaxis)
Hyperbilirubinemia (treatment)

Phenobarbital (Systemic)[1], 496
Seizures (prophylaxis)
Seizures (treatment)
Phenobarbital, ASA, and Codeine (Systemic)[1], #
Headache, migraine (treatment)
[Phenoxybenzamine (Systemic)], #
Benign prostatic hyperplasia (treatment)
[Phentolamine (Intracavernosal)][1], #
Impotence (diagnosis)
Impotence (treatment adjunct)
[Phenylbutazone (Systemic)][1], 375
Arthritis, psoriatic (treatment)
Calcium pyrophosphate deposition disease, acute (treatment)
Inflammation, nonrheumatic (treatment)
Phenylbutazone (Systemic)[1], 375
Osteoarthritis (treatment)
Wegener's granuloma (treatment)
[Phenylephrine (Nasal)], 2374
Congestion, sinus (treatment)
[Phenytoin (Systemic)][1], 259
Arrhythmias, digitalis-induced (treatment)
Choreoathetosis, paroxysmal (treatment)
Myotonia congenita (treatment)
Myotonic muscular dystrophy (treatment)
Neuralgia, trigeminal (treatment)
Neuromyotonia (treatment)
[Phenytoin, Parenteral (Systemic)][1], 259
Toxicity, tricyclic antidepressant (treatment adjunct)
[Physostigmine (Ophthalmic)], #
Glaucoma, angle-closure, *during* or *after* iridectomy (treatment)
Glaucoma, secondary (treatment)
[Pilocarpine (Systemic)], #
Xerophthalmia (treatment)
[Pimozide (Systemic)], 2383
Psychotic disorders (treatment adjunct)
Pimozide (Systemic)[1], 2383
Gilles de la Tourette's syndrome (treatment)
[Pindolol (Systemic)], 546
Angina pectoris, chronic (treatment)
[Pindolol (Systemic)][1], 546
Cardiomyopathy, hypertrophic (treatment)
Mitral valve prolapse syndrome (treatment)
Tremors (treatment)
[Piperacillin (Systemic)][1], 2304
Meningitis, bacterial (treatment)
[Piperacillin and Tazobactam (Systemic)][1], 2327
Septicemia, bacterial (treatment)
[Pirbuterol (Inhalation-Local)], 605
Bronchospasm, exercise-induced (prophylaxis)
[Piroxicam (Systemic)], 375
Ankylosing spondylitis (treatment)
Dysmenorrhea (treatment)
[Piroxicam (Systemic)][1], 375
Calcium pyrophosphate deposition disease, acute (treatment)
Gouty arthritis, acute (treatment)
Hypermenorrhea (treatment)
Inflammation, nonrheumatic (treatment)
[Plicamycin (Systemic)], #
Paget's disease of bone (treatment)
[Poliovirus Vaccine Inactivated (Systemic)][1], #
Poliomyelitis (prophylaxis)
[Polyethylene Glycol 3550 (Local)], #
Constipation (prophylaxis)
[Polythiazide (Systemic)], 1127
Diabetes insipidus, central (treatment)
Diabetes insipidus, nephrogenic (treatment)
Renal calculi, calcium (prophylaxis)
[Potassium Iodide (Systemic)][1], #
Erythema nodosum (treatment)
Iodine deficiency (treatment)
Sporotrichosis, cutaneous lymphatic (treatment)
Thyroid involution, preoperative
Potassium Iodide (Systemic)[1], #
Hyperthyroidism (treatment)
[Prazepam (Systemic)][1], 512
Anxiety (treatment)
Insomnia (treatment)
[Praziquantel (Systemic)], #
Cysticercosis (treatment)
Diphyllobothriasis (treatment)
Dipylidiasis (treatment)
Hymenolepiasis (treatment)
Metagonimiasis (treatment)
Neurocysticercosis (treatment)
Paragonimiasis (treatment)
Taeniasis (treatment)
[Prazosin (Systemic)][1], 2409
Benign prostatic hyperplasia (treatment)
Heart failure, congestive (treatment)
Pheochromocytoma (treatment)
Raynaud's phenomenon (treatment)
Toxicity, ergot alkaloid (treatment)
[Prednisolone (Systemic)][1], 938
Bronchitis, asthmatic, acute or chronic (treatment)
Calcium pyrophosphate deposition disease, acute (treatment)
Carcinoma, breast (treatment)
Carcinoma, prostatic (treatment)
Connective tissue disease, mixed (treatment)
Eczema, severe (treatment)
Edema, pulmonary, noncardiogenic (treatment)
Fever, due to malignancy (treatment adjunct)
Gingivitis, desquamative (treatment)
Hemangioma, airway-obstructing, in infants (treatment)
Hemolysis (treatment)
Hepatitis, alcoholic with encepalopathy (treatment)
Hepatitis, chronic, active (treatment)
Hepatitis, nonalcoholic in women (treatment)
Lesions, oral, corticosteroid-responsive disorders-associated (treatment)
Multiple myeloma (treatment)
Myasthenia gravis (treatment)
Necrosis, hepatic, subacute (treatment)
Pemphigoid (treatment)
Pericarditis (treatment)
Polyarteritis nodosa (treatment)
Polychondritis, relapsing (treatment)
Polyps, nasal (treatment)
Pulmonary disease, chronic obstructive (treatment)
Reiter's disease (treatment)
Rheumatic fever (treatment)
Sarcoid, localized cutaneous (treatment)
Status asthmaticus (treatment)
Stomatitis, aphthous, recurrent (treatment)
Transplant rejection (prophylaxis)
Transplant rejection (treatment)
Tumors, brain, primary (treatment adjunct)
Vasculitis (treatment)
[Prednisolone Sodium Phosphate Oral Solution (Systemic)][1], 938
Carditis, nonrheumatic, acute (treatment)
[Prednisolone Sodium Phosphate, Oral (Systemic)][1], 938
Hypercalcemia, sarcoidosis-associated (treatment)
[Prednisolone Syrup (Systemic)][1], 938
Carditis, nonrheumatic, acute (treatment)
Hypercalcemia, sarcoidosis-associated (treatment)
[Prednisone (Systemic)][1], 938
Bronchitis, asthmatic, acute or chronic (treatment)
Calcium pyrophosphate deposition disease, acute (treatment)
Carcinoma, breast (treatment)
Carcinoma, prostatic (treatment)
Carditis, nonrheumatic, acute (treatment)
Connective tissue disease, mixed (treatment)
Eczema, severe (treatment)
[Prednisone (Systemic)][1] 938 *(continued)*
Edema, cerebral, especially when associated with primary or metastatic brain tumor, craniotomy, or head injury (prophylaxis)
Edema, cerebral, especially when associated with primary or metastatic brain tumor, craniotomy, or head injury (treatment)
Edema, pulmonary, noncardiogenic (treatment)
Fever, due to malignancy (treatment adjunct)
Gingivitis, desquamative (treatment)
Hemangioma, airway-obstructing, in infants (treatment)
Hemolysis (treatment)
Hepatitis, alcoholic with encepalopathy (treatment)
Hepatitis, chronic, active (treatment)
Hepatitis, nonalcoholic in women (treatment)
Lesions, oral, corticosteroid-responsive disorders-associated (treatment)
Multiple myeloma (treatment)
Myasthenia gravis (treatment)
Nausea and vomiting, cancer chemotherapy-induced (prophylaxis)
Necrosis, hepatic, subacute (treatment)
Pemphigoid (treatment)
Pericarditis (treatment)
Pneumonia, *Pneumocystis carinii*, AIDS-associated (treatment adjunct)
Polyarteritis nodosa (treatment)
Polychondritis, relapsing (treatment)
Pulmonary disease, chronic obstructive (treatment)
Reiter's disease (treatment)
Rheumatic fever (treatment)
Stomatitis, aphthous, recurrent (treatment)
Transplant rejection (prophylaxis)
Transplant rejection (treatment)
Tumors, brain, primary (treatment adjunct)
Vasculitis (treatment)
[Prednisone Tablets (Systemic)][1], 938
Hypercalcemia, sarcoidosis-associated (treatment)
Pregabalin (Systemic)[1], 2412
Seizures, partial (treatment adjunctive)
[Primaquine (Systemic)][1], #
Pneumonia, *Pneumocystis carinii* (treatment)
[Primidone (Systemic)][1], 2415
Essential tremor (treatment)
[Procainamide (Systemic)], 2420
Arrhythmias, supraventricular (treatment)
Fibrillation, atrial (treatment)
Tachycardia, atrial, paroxysmal (treatment)
[Procaine (Parenteral-Local)][1], 174
Retrobulbar block
Procaine (Parenteral-Local)[1], 174
Central neural blocks
[Procarbazine (Systemic)][1], 2424
Lymphomas, non-Hodgkin's (treatment)
Multiple myeloma (treatment)
Tumors, brain, primary (treatment)
[Progesterone Gel (Systemic)][1], 2429
Assisted reproductive technologies, female (treatment)
Corpus luteum insufficiency (treatment)
[Progesterone Suppositories (Systemic)][1], 2429
Assisted reproductive technologies, female (treatment)
[Progesterone, Oral (Systemic)], 2429
Hyperplasia, endometrial, estrogen-induced (prophylaxis)
Progesterone, Oral (Systemic)[1], 2429
Amenorrhea, secondary (treatment)
[Progesterone, Parenteral (Systemic)], 2429
Estrogen production, endogenous (diagnosis)
[Progesterone, Parenteral (Systemic)][1], 2429
Corpus luteum insufficiency (treatment)
[Progestins (Systemic)][1], 2429
Hot flashes
[Propafenone (Systemic)][1], 2443
Arrhythmias, supraventricular, other (treatment)

[Propantheline (Systemic)], 230
Bowel syndrome, irritable (treatment)
[Propantheline (Systemic)][1], 230
Salivation, excessive, in dental procedures (prophylaxis)
Urinary incontinence (treatment)
[Propranolol (Systemic)][1], 546
Akathisia, neuroleptic-induced (treatment)
Anxiety (treatment adjunct)
Mitral valve prolapse syndrome (treatment)
Thyrotoxicosis (treatment adjunct)
[Protamine (Systemic)][1], #
Toxicity, enoxaparin (treatment)
[Protriptyline (Systemic)][1], 280
Attention-deficit hyperactivity disorder (treatment)
Headache (prophylaxis)
Narcolepsy/cataplexy syndrome (treatment)
[Prussian Blue (Oral-Local)][1], #
Toxicity, radiocesium (treatment)
Toxicity, thallium (treatment)
[Psyllium (Local)], #
Bowel syndrome, irritable (treatment adjunct)
[Psyllium Hydrophilic Mucilloid (Local)], #
Bowel syndrome, irritable (treatment adjunct)
Diarrhea (treatment)
Hyperlipidemia (treatment)
[Psyllium Hydrophilic Mucilloid and Carboxymethylcellulose (Local)], #
Bowel syndrome, irritable (treatment adjunct)
[Pyrantel (Oral-Local)], #
Ascariasis (treatment)
Helminth infections, multiple (treatment)
Hookworm infection (treatment)
Trichostrongyliasis (treatment)
[Pyridoxine (Systemic)], #
Toxicity, cycloserine (treatment)
Toxicity, isoniazid (treatment)
[Pyrimethamine (Systemic)][1], #
Isosporiasis (prophylaxis)
Isosporiasis (treatment)
Pneumonia, *Pneumocystis carinii* (treatment)

Q

[Quinapril (Systemic)], 198
Scleroderma, hypertension in (treatment)
[Quinapril (Systemic)][1], 198
Scleroderma, renal crisis in (treatment)
[Quinethazone (Systemic)], 1127
Diabetes insipidus, central (treatment)
Diabetes insipidus, nephrogenic (treatment)
Renal calculi, calcium (prophylaxis)
[Quinine (Systemic)], 2474
Leg cramps (prophylaxis)
Leg cramps (treatment)
[Quinine (Systemic)][1], 2474
Babesiosis (treatment)

R

[Racemethionine (Systemic)], #
Toxicity, acetaminophen (treatment)
[Ramipril (Systemic)][1], 198
Heart failure, congestive (treatment)
Scleroderma, hypertension in (treatment)
Scleroderma, renal crisis in (treatment)
[Ranitidine (Systemic)], 1573
Bleeding, upper gastrointestinal (treatment)
Pneumonitis, aspiration (prophylaxis)
[Ranitidine (Systemic)][1], 1573
Arthritis, rheumatoid (treatment adjunct)
[Ranitidine, Parenteral (Systemic)], 1573
Stress-related mucosal damage (prophylaxis)
Stress-related mucosal damage (treatment)
[Reserpine (Systemic)][1], #
Raynaud's phenomenon (treatment)
[Ribavirin (Systemic)][1], 2505
Influenza A (treatment)
Influenza B (treatment)
Lassa fever (prophylaxis)
Lassa fever (treatment)
[Ribavirin (Systemic)][1] 2505 *(continued)*
Viral hemorrhagic fever (prophylaxis)
Viral hemorrhagic fever (treatment)
[Rifabutin (Systemic)][1], 2513
Tuberculosis, in HIV-infected patients on antiretroviral therapy (treatment)
[Rifampin (Systemic)][1], 2518
Haemophilus influenzae type b infection (prophylaxis)
Staphylococcus infection (treatment)
Leprosy (treatment)
Meningitis, tuberculous (treatment)
Mycobacterial infections, atypical (treatment)
[Rituximab (Systemic)][1], 2547
Chronic lymphocytic leukemia, in combination for first line treatment
Leukemia, chronic lymphocytic (treatment)
Thrombocytopenic purpura, immune or idiopathic (treatment)
Waldenstrom's macroglobulinemia (treatment)
[Rubidium Rb 82 (Systemic)], #
Coronary artery disease (diagnosis)
Ischemia, myocardial (diagnosis)

S

Salmeterol (Inhalation-Local)[1], 605
Bronchospasm, exercise-induced (prophylaxis)
[Sargramostim (Systemic)], 876
Myelodysplastic syndrome (treatment)
Neutropenia, AIDS-associated (treatment)
Neutropenia, chemotherapy-related (treatment)
Neutropenia, chronic, severe (treatment)
Neutropenia, drug-induced (treatment)
[Scopolamine (Ophthalmic)], #
Iridocyclitis (treatment)
Synechiae, posterior (prophylaxis)
[Scopolamine (Systemic)], 230
Bowel syndrome, irritable (treatment)
[Scopolamine, Oral (Systemic)][1], 230
Parkinsonism (treatment)
Scopolamine, Parenteral (Systemic)[1], 230
Anesthesia, general, adjunct
Respiratory tract secretions, excessive, in anesthesia (prophylaxis)
Salivation, excessive, in anesthesia (prophylaxis)
[Scopolamine, Transdermal (Systemic)][1], 230
Salivation, excessive, medical condition-associated (prophylaxis)
Salivation, excessive, medical condition-related (prophylaxis)
Salivation, excessive, post-surgical (prophylaxis)
Scopolamine, Transdermal (Systemic)[1], 230
Nausea and vomiting, postoperative (prophylaxis)
[Sertraline (Systemic)], 2600
Post-traumatic stress disorder (treatment)
[Sertraline (Systemic)][1], 2600
Premature ejaculation (treatment)
Sertraline (Systemic)[1], 2600
Premenstrual dysphoric disorder (treatment)
Social anxiety disorder (treatment)
[Silver Sulfadiazine (Topical)], 2615
Skin infections, bacterial, minor (treatment)
Ulcer, dermal (treatment)
[Simethicone (Oral-Local)][1], 2617
Gastroscopy adjunct
Radiography, bowel, adjunct
Simvastatin (Systemic)[1], 1587
Hypercholesterolemia, familial (treatment adjunct)
Ischemic attack, transient (prophylaxis)
Stroke (prophylaxis)
[Sincalide (Systemic)], #
Ileus, gastrointestinal, postoperative (treatment)
[Sodium Ascorbate (Systemic)], #
Toxicity, iron, chronic (treatment adjunct)
[Sodium Chloride (Parenteral-Local)][1], #
Abortion, elective
[Sodium Chromate Cr 51 (Systemic)], #
Platelet survival studies
Platelets, labeling of
[Sodium Iodide (Systemic)], #
Thyrotoxicosis crisis (treatment adjunct)
[Sodium Phosphate P 32 (Systemic)][1], #
Thrombocythemia, essential (treatment)
Sodium Thiosulfate (Systemic)[1], #
Nephrotoxicity, cisplatin-induced (prophylaxis)
[Somatrem (Systemic)], 1530
Growth failure, Prader-Willi syndrome-associated (treatment)
[Somatropin, Recombinant (Systemic)], 1530
Growth failure, Turner's syndrome-associated (treatment)
[Sotalol (Systemic)], 546
Angina pectoris, chronic (treatment)
Hypertension (treatment)
[Sotalol (Systemic)][1], 546
Anxiety (treatment adjunct)
Cardiomyopathy, hypertrophic (treatment)
Mitral valve prolapse syndrome (treatment)
Myocardial infarction (prophylaxis)
Myocardial infarction (treatment)
Pheochromocytoma (treatment adjunct)
Thyrotoxicosis (treatment adjunct)
Tremors (treatment)
Sotalol (Systemic)[1], 546
Arrhythmias, cardiac (prophylaxis)
Arrhythmias, cardiac (treatment)
Arrhythmias, supraventricular (prophylaxis)
Arrhythmias, supraventricular (treatment)
Tachycardia, ventricular (prophylaxis)
Tachycardia, ventricular (treatment)
[Spectinomycin (Systemic)][1], #
Gonorrhea, disseminated (treatment)
[Spiramycin (Systemic)][1], #
Toxoplasmosis (treatment)
[Spironolactone (Systemic)][1], 1120
Hirsutism, female (treatment)
Polycystic ovary syndrome (treatment)
Spironolactone and Hydrochlorothiazide (Systemic)[1], 1125
Hypokalemia (treatment)
[Stanozolol (Systemic)], 142
Anemia (treatment)
Angioedema, hereditary (treatment)
Antithrombin III deficiency (treatment)
Catabolic or tissue-depleting processes (treatment)
Fibrinogen excess (treatment)
Growth failure (treatment adjunct)
[Streptokinase (Systemic)][1], 2737
Cortical necrosis, renal, impending (treatment)
Hemolytic uremic syndrome (treatment)
Occlusions, retinal blood vesse (treatment)
Thrombosis, arterial, renal (treatment)
[Streptozocin (Systemic)][1], #
Tumors, gastrointestinal carcinoid (treatment)
[Succinylcholine (Systemic)], 2077
Convulsions (treatment)
[Sucralfate (Oral-Local)], 2652
Reflux, gastroesophageal (treatment)
Stress-related mucosal damage (prophylaxis)
Stress-related mucosal damage (treatment)
Ulcer, gastric (treatment)
[Sucralfate (Oral-Local)][1], 2652
Arthritis, rheumatoid (treatment adjunct)
[Sufentanil (Systemic)], 1379
Pain, postoperative (treatment)
[Sufentanil (Systemic)][1], 1379
Anesthesia, local, adjunct
[Sulconazole (Topical)], #
Candidiasis, cutaneous (treatment)
[Sulfacetamide (Ophthalmic)], 2658
Blepharitis, bacterial (treatment)
Blepharoconjunctivitis (treatment)
Keratitis, bacterial (treatment)
Keratoconjunctivitis, bacterial (treatment)
[Sulfadiazine (Systemic)][1], 2660
Lymphogranuloma venereum (treatment)
Meningitis, carcinomatous (treatment)
Paracoccidioidomycosis (treatment)

U

Off Label Uses Index by Indication

The off-label indications have been extracted from the monographs included in the *USP DI*®. An off-label indication is the use of a drug for a disease or condition other than the indication it was licensed for by U.S. Food and Drug Administration (FDA). Prior to 2004 the USP Advisory Panels selected as appropriate the off-label indications to be included in the *USP DI*. Thereafter, the Thomson Micromedex Off-Label Advisory Boards review off-label indications to be included in *USP DI*. Since the *USP DI* database does not yet include all possible off-label indications for every therapeutic agent available, users should not assume that all off-label indications appropriate for a given medication are listed or that those not listed are inappropriate. *The off-label indication index can not be used by itself to determine the appropriateness of therapy;* rather, it should be used as a tool in searching out more information about the therapies available.

Indications are listed alphabetically. Symbols denote the following:

[ ] Used to identify a medication available in the U.S. whose FDA-approved labeling does not include the stated indication but which is included in the *USP DI* monograph

\# Drugs for which monographs are not included in this published version of the *USP DI* database due to space constraints. Copies of the monographs are available on the Thomson Micromedex *USP DI* Updates Online website. See the front cover of this book for details on how to access the site.

[1]Indications not included in Canadian product labeling.

A

U

V

W

X

Y

Z

Index Guide

General Index

The following excerpts are examples of the information included in the General Index:

Asterisk – Identifies a product not available in the United States.

Bisacodyl and Docusate* (local), 1901

Brand name – Identified by *italics*.

Lanoxin—See Digitalis Glycosides (Systemic), 1248

Combination Listing – Includes a series of ingredients. For further reference, see Combination Cross-reference Listing.

Pseudoephedrine Hydrochloride and Codeine Phosphate
See Cough/Cold Combinations (Systemic),1066

Common name – Identified by plain text followed by a reference to the monograph title.

AZT—See Zidovudine (Systemic), 3176

Dagger – Identifies a product not available in Canada

Amlodipine† (Systemic), 95

Drug Effect – Example (e.g., topical, otic, nasal, systemic) identified by parenthesis.

Losartan Potassium (Systemic), 2001

Family Monograph Title – Groups multiple drugs into a common grouping.

Calcium Channel Blocking Agents (Systemic), 736

Capoten–See Angiotensin-converting Enzyme (ACE) Inhibitors (Systemic), 192

Generic name – Identified by plain text.

Fexofenadine Hydrochloride (Systemic), 1531

Page number – Identifies the location of the drug entry on the first page of a monograph.

Pound sign – Identifies a drug not published in the printed version of the *USP DI*. Exclusions can be accessed on the *USP DI* Updates Online website. See the front cover of book for details on accessing the site.

Ancobon—See Flucytosine (Systemic), #

Single Monograph Title – Includes one drug; each drug may have multiple brand names and common names but only one generic name.

Celecoxib (Systemic), 817

General Index

This index references drug products included within the *USP DI* monographs; however, the index is not inclusive of all marketed products. The inclusion of a brand name does not mean Micromedex has any particular knowledge that the brand listed has properties different from other brands of the same drug, nor should it be interpreted as an endorsement. Similarly, the fact that a particular brand has not been included does not indicate that the product has been judged to be unsatisfactory or unacceptable.

- * Products not available in the U.S.
- † Products not available in Canada
- # Drugs for which monographs are not included in this published version of the *USP DI* database due to space constraints. Copies of the monographs are available on the Micromedex *USP DI* Updates Online website. See the front cover of this book for details on how to access the site.

A

B

C

D

E

F

G

H

J

K

L

M

N

O

P

Q

R

S

T

U

V

W

X

Y

Z

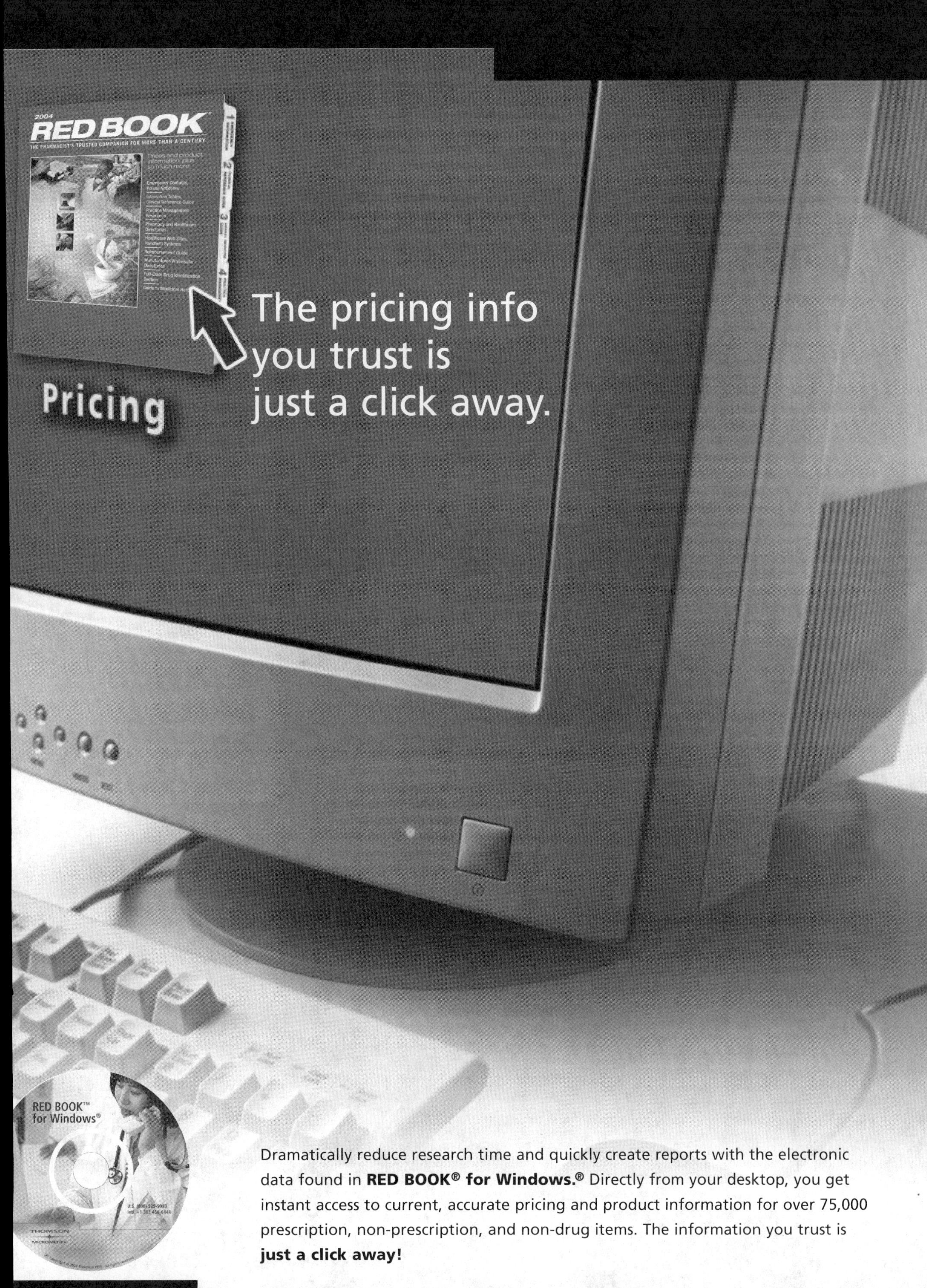
2004
RED BOOK
THE PHARMACIST'S TRUSTED COMPANION FOR MORE THAN A CENTURY
Pricing
The pricing info
you trust is
just a click away.
RED BOOK™
for Windows®
THOMSON
MICROMEDEX
Dramatically reduce research time and quickly create reports with the electronic data found in **RED BOOK® for Windows.®** Directly from your desktop, you get instant access to current, accurate pricing and product information for over 75,000 prescription, non-prescription, and non-drug items. The information you trust is **just a click away!**

Dramatically reduce research time and quickly create reports with the electronic data found in **RED BOOK® for Windows.®** Directly from your desktop, you get instant access to current, accurate pricing and product information for over 75,000 prescription, non-prescription, and non-drug items. The information you trust is **just a click away!**

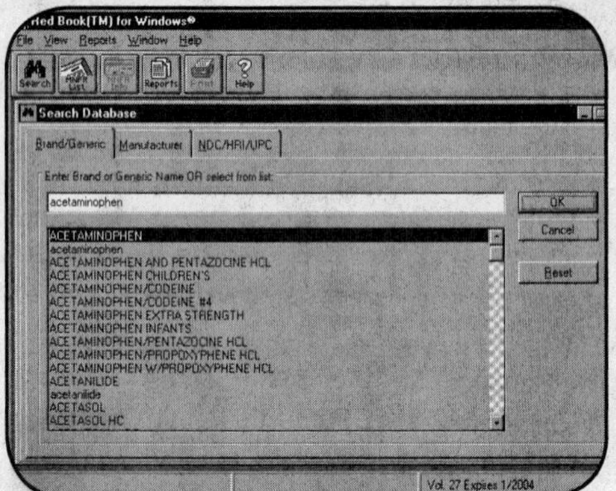

Search by Brand or Generic Name

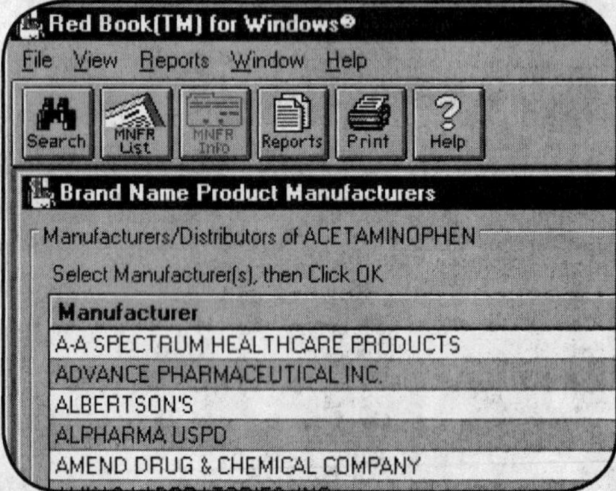

Specific Drug Manufacturer Listings

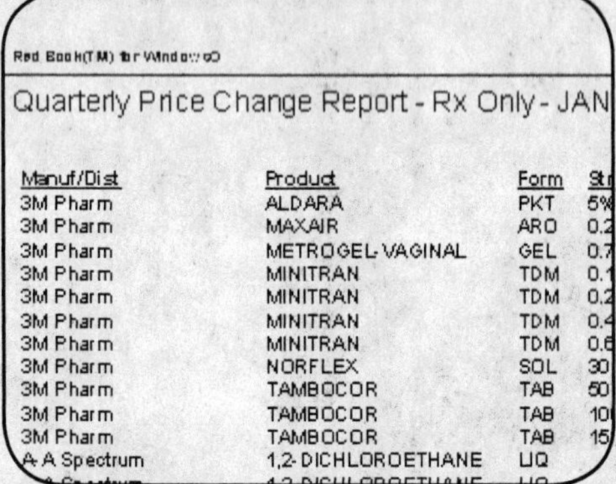

Report View

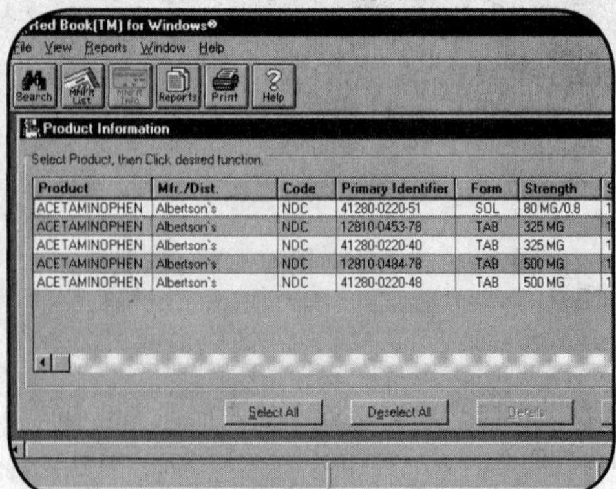

Product Information per Manufacturer

RED BOOK for Windows®...

- Instantly searches by brand or generic name, manufacturer, or NDC number
- Conveniently lists manufacturer names, address, phone, etc...
- Reports on the latest price changes, new products, and deactivated products
- Easily enables the export of data into spreadsheets for further analysis and manipulation
- Also includes non-drug items such as medical devices and supplies

Don't miss this special offer for 2007...

FREE shipping on all first-time orders.

RED BOOK for Windows is available as an annual or quarterly subscription.

Call **(800) 737-2577** for more information or to place an order.

Also available...

ReadyPrice®

This easy-to-use, Windows-based application provides the same comprehensive product information as RED BOOK for Windows, but also gives you access to advanced features such as:

- User-created custom product groups
- Historical pricing information
- Therapeutic category search function

RED BOOK Database Services

Compatible with virtually any computer system!

RED BOOK Database Services presents pricing and descriptive information for over 180,000 healthcare items and can be integrated directly into your computer system to help facilitate utilization review, market analysis and research, claims adjudication and processing, and much more!

(800) 525-9083
www.micromedex.com

Ordering Information

Mail Order: Thomson Micromedex USP DI Customer Service
P.O. Box 187
Montvale, NJ 07645-0187 USA

Phone Order: (800) 877-6209
Fax Order: (201) 722-2680

International Phone Order: For international orders, please call +1 201 358-2233 for a distributor near you.
Order On-line: www.pdrbookstore.com

Payment Required in advance in U.S. dollars drawn on a U.S. bank. Any bank fees, customs duties, tariffs, and taxes are the customer's responsibility. Errors in fax transmissions are the responsibility of the sender. Prices subject to change without notice.

Sales Tax: Add appropriate sales tax to product costs for orders according to the sales tax schedule below the order form.

Drug Information Publications

2007 USP DI® Volume I
Drug Information for the Health Care Professional
Organized in a concise, outline format, *Drug Information for the Health Care Professional* contains medically accepted uses—labeled and off-label—of more than 11,000 generic and brand-name drug products throughout the United States and Canada.
Item Number: U20061 **ISBN:** 1-56363-574-7 **Price:** $174.00 plus S&H ($9.95)

2007 USP DI® Volume II
Advice for the Patient® Drug Information in Lay Language
Written in patient-friendly terms, *Advice for the Patient* is specifically designed to make important drug information easy to grasp. Simplified monographs provide detailed information on proper drug use, available dosage forms, precautions, side effects, and special consideration.
Item Number: U20062 **ISBN:** 1-56363-575-5 **Price:** $93.00 plus S&H ($9.95)

2007 USP DI® Volume III
Approved Drug Products and Legal Requirements
Contains important therapeutic equivalence information and selected federal requirements that affect the prescribing and dispensing of prescription drugs and controlled substances.
Item Number: U20063 **ISBN:** 1-56363-576-3 **Price:** $145.00 plus S&H ($9.95)

FREE USP DI On-Line

With your purchase of any USP DI print book, you have FREE access to the USP DI On-line site, containing over 400 additional monographs.

To visit USP DI On-line, log on to the Micromedex Web site at http://uspdi.micromedex.com.
Then enter the USER NAME
and PASSWORD listed below.

USERNAME: **usp2007** PASSWORD: **moredrugs**

If you have questions regarding USP DI On-line, please contact Thomson Micromedex at (800) 877-6209, (303) 486-6400, or http://www.micromedex.com/support/request

Change of Address Notification
If your address has changed, please send your new address with your latest mailing label to:
Thomson Micromedex USP DI P.O. Box 187 Montvale, NJ 07645-0187

To order, remove this form, fill out completely, and mail to Thomson Micromedex Customer Service Department with payment or credit card information. For faster service, order by phone or fax.

Mail Order
Thomson Micromedex USP DI Customer Service Department
P.O. Box 187
Montvale, NJ 07645-0187

Phone Order (800) 877-6209
Fax Order (201) 722-2680
International Phone Order For international orders, please call +1 201 358-2233 for a distributor near you.

Ordered By:

Name ______________________
Title ______________________
Company ______________________
E-mail ______________________
Street Address ______________________
City ________ State ______ ZIP ________ Country ______
Phone (______) ____________ Fax (______) ____________

Ship To **(Only complete if different):**

Name ______________________
Title ______________________
Company ______________________
Street Address ______________________
City ________ State ______ ZIP ________ Country ______
Phone (______) ____________ Fax (______) ____________

Payment is required in advance in U.S. dollars drawn on a U.S. bank. Any bank fees, customs duties, tariffs, and taxes are the customer's responsibility. Errors in fax transmissions are the responsibility of the sender. Prices subject to change without notice. Please allow 2-4 weeks for normal delivery. Inquire for faster delivery (additional charge).

Valid for 2007 editions only; prices and shipping and handling higher outside U.S.

Payment Method

❑ Enclosed is my check payable to Thomson Micromedex.

❑ VISA ❑ MasterCard ❑ AmFex ❑ Discover

Card No. ______________________ Exp. Date________

Signature ______________________

Item #	Description	Price	Quantity	Total Price	Domestic Shipping	Shipping Quantity	Total Shipping
160101	2007 USP DI® Volume I, *Drug Information for the Health Care Professional* ISBN 1-56363-574-7	$174.00			$9.95		
160119	2007 USP DI® Volume II, Advice for the Patient® *Drug Information in Lay Language* ISBN 1-56363-575-5	$ 93.00			$9.95		
160127	2007 USP DI® Volume III, *Approved Drug Products and Legal Requirements* ISBN 1-56363-576-3	$145.00			$9.95		

Total Price	
Add Sales Tax in FL, IA, NJ	
Subtotal	
Shipping	← Shipping Total
GRAND TOTAL	

THOMSON
MICROMEDEX™